CONCORDANCE TO SHAKESPEARE

A COMPLETE CONCORDANCE

OR VERBAL INDEX TO WORDS, PHRASES
AND PASSAGES IN THE DRAMATIC WORKS
OF

SHAKESPEARE

WITH A SUPPLEMENTARY CONCORDANCE
TO THE POEMS

JOHN BARTLETT, A.M.
SOMETIME FELLOW OF THE AMERICAN ACADEMY
OF ARTS AND SCIENCES

MACMILLAN
ST. MARTIN'S PRESS

First Edition 1894
Reprinted 1896, 1906, 1913, 1922, 1927, 1937, 1953, 1956, 1960, 1962, 1963, 1965, 1966, 1967, 1972, 1979

Published by
THE MACMILLAN PRESS LTD
London and Basingstoke
Associated companies in Delhi Dublin Hong Kong Johannesburg Lagos Melbourne New York Singapore Tokyo

ISBN 0 333 04275 1

Printed in Hong Kong

AFFECTIONATELY INSCRIBED

TO MY WIFE

WHOSE EVER-READY ASSISTANCE IN THE PREPARATION OF THIS BOOK
HAS MADE MY LABOUR A PASTIME

NOTE

THIS Concordance, begun in 1876, was prepared from the text of the *Globe* edition of Shakespeare (1875); but as new readings have since been introduced into the text of the later issues, the manuscript has been revised and collated with the latest edition (1891).

Apart from the merit of presenting the latest and most approved text, now the standard with scholars and critics, the plan of this Concordance to the Dramatic Works of Shakespeare is more comprehensive than that of any which has preceded it, in that it aims to give passages of some length for the most part independent of the context; and it is made more nearly complete by the inclusion of select examples of the verbs *to be, to do, to have, may,* and their tenses, and the auxiliary verb *to let;* of the adjectives, *much, many, more, most,* and many adverbs; and of pronouns, prepositions, interjections, and conjunctions.

Two or more words are sometimes given together as Index-words in connection with those to which they are immediately joined in the text, to show more directly the particular use of a word. Phrases of frequent occurrence, not related necessarily to the context, are grouped in paragraphs, with only the Act and Scene where they are found.

The definite and indefinite articles, *the, a, an;* the words, *a', ah, an* [*if*], *and;* some repetitions of words used interjectionally, which are merely the prefix and terminal of a sentence; and titles when joined to proper names,—are not included among the Index-words.

The work has been prepared chiefly in the leisure taken from active duties, and from time to time has been delayed by other avocations.

CAMBRIDGE, MASS., U.S.A.
January 1894.

COMPLETE CONCORDANCE

TO

SHAKESPEARE'S DRAMATIC WORKS

A

Aaron. Then, Aaron, arm thy heart, and fit thy thoughts, To mount aloft with thy imperial mistress . . . . *T. Andron.* ii 1 12
Fetter'd in amorous chains And faster bound to Aaron's charming eyes Than is Prometheus tied to Caucasus . . . ii 1 17
Aaron, a thousand deaths Would I propose to achieve her whom I love ii 1 79
Aaron, thou hast hit it.—Would you had hit it too! . . . . ii 1 97
My lovely Aaron, wherefore look'st thou sad? . . . . ii 3 10
Under their sweet shade, Aaron, let us sit . . . . ii 3 16
Bring thou her husband: This is the hole where Aaron bid us hide him ii 3 186
Aaron and thou look down into this den . . . . ii 3 215
Aaron is gone; and my compassionate heart Will not permit mine eyes once to behold The thing whereat it trembles by surmise . . ii 3 217
O gentle Aaron! Did ever raven sing so like a lark? . . . iii 1 157
My hand: Good Aaron, wilt thou help to chop it off? . . . iii 1 162
Good Aaron, give his majesty my hand . . . . iii 1 194
Aaron will have his soul black like his face . . . . iii 1 206
O, tell me, did you see Aaron the Moor? . . . . iv 2 52
Here Aaron is; and what with Aaron now? . . . . iv 2 54
O gentle Aaron, we are all undone! Now help, or woe betide thee! . iv 2 55
It shall not die.—Aaron, it must; the mother wills it so . . iv 2 81
Aaron, what shall I say unto the empress?—Advise thee, Aaron . iv 2 128
The mountain lioness, The ocean swells not so as Aaron storms . iv 2 139
What mean'st thou, Aaron? wherefore didst thou this? . . . iv 2 147
Aaron, I see thou wilt not trust the air With secrets . . . iv 2 169
If Aaron now be wise, Then is all safe, the anchor's in the port . iv 4 37
See justice done on Aaron, that damn'd Moor . . . . v 3 201

Abaissiez. Je ne veux point que vous abaissiez votre grandeur en baisant la main d'une de votre seigneurie indigne serviteur *Hen. V.* v 2 274

Abandon,—which is in the vulgar leave . . . . *As Y. Like It* v 1 52
Abandon the society of this female, or, clown, thou perishest . v 1 55
If thou wouldst not reside But where one villain is, then him abandon *T. of Athens* v 1 114
Never pray more; abandon all remorse . . . . *Othello* iii 3 369

Abandoned. Left and abandon'd of his velvet friends . *As Y. Like It* ii 1 50
What you would have I'll stay to know at your abandon'd cave . v 4 202
Being all this time abandon'd from your bed . . *T. of Shrew*, Ind. 2 117
He hath abandoned his physicians . . . . *All's Well* i 1 15
If she be so abandon'd to her sorrow As it is spoke . . *T. Night* i 4 19
Live in peace abandon'd and despised! . . . . *3 Hen. VI.* i 1 188
Through the sight I bear in things to love, I have abandon'd Troy *Tr. and Cr.* iii 3 5
Is it Dian, habited like her, Who hath abandoned her holy groves? *T. A.* ii 3 58

Abase. We'll both together lift our heads to heaven, And never more abase our sight so low As to vouchsafe one glance unto the ground *2 Hen. VI.* i 2 15

Abashed. Do you with cheeks abash'd behold our works? *Troi. and Cres.* i 3 18

Abate. The white cold virgin snow upon my heart Abates the ardour of my liver . . . . *Tempest* iv 1 55
Abate throw at novum, and the whole world again Cannot pick out five such . . . . *L. L. Lost* v 2 547
O long and tedious night, Abate thy hours! . . *M. N. Dream* iii 2 432
Abate the strength of your displeasure . . . *Mer. of Venice* v 1 198
My presence May well abate the over-merry spleen . *T. of Shrew*, Ind. 1 137
An oath of mickle might; and fury shall abate . . . *Hen. V.* ii 1 70
Abate thy rage, abate thy manly rage, Abate thy rage! . . . ii 2 24
Tell him my fury shall abate, and I The crowns will take . . iv 4 50
Abate the edge of traitors, gracious Lord! . . . *Richard III.* v 5 35
Withdraw you and abate your strength; Dismiss your followers *T. Andron.* i 1 43
This shall free thee from this present shame; If no inconstant toy, nor womanish fear, Abate thy valour in the acting it . *Rom. and Jul.* iv 1 120
There lives within the very flame of love A kind of wick or snuff that will abate it; And nothing is at a like goodness still . *Hamlet* iv 7 116
I would abate her nothing, though I profess myself her adorer *Cymbeline* i 4 73

Abated. She hath abated me of half my train . . . *Lear* ii 4 161
Which once in him abated, all the rest Turn'd on themselves *2 Hen. IV.* i 1 117
Deliver you as most Abated captives to some nation . *Coriolanus* iii 3 132

Abatement. Falls into abatement and low price . . . *T. Night* i 1 13
This 'would' changes And hath abatements and delays . *Hamlet* iv 7 121
There's a great abatement of kindness . . . . *Lear* i 4 64
Who of their broken debtors take a third, A sixth, a tenth, letting them thrive again On their abatement . . . . *Cymbeline* v 4 21

Abbess. Take perforce my husband from the abbess . *Com. of Errors* v 1 117
Justice, most sacred duke, against the abbess! . . . . v 1 133
Here the abbess shuts the gates on us . . . . v 1 155
Knock at the abbey-gate And bid the lady abbess come to me . . v 1 166
Go call the abbess hither. I think you are all mated or stark mad . v 1 280

Abbey. Behind the ditches of the abbey here . . . . v 1 122
Kneel to the duke before he pass the abbey . . . . v 1 129
They fled Into this abbey, whither we pursued them . . . v 1 155
Even now we housed him in the abbey here . . *Com. of Errors* v 1 188
You fled into this abbey here, From whence, I think, you are come . v 1 263
Saw'st thou him enter at the abbey here? . . . . v 1 278
Into the abbey here And hear at large discoursed all our fortunes . v 1 394
Our abbeys and our priories shall pay This expedition's charge *K. John* i 1 48
Toward Swinstead, to the abbey there . . . . v 3 8
Where have you been broiling?—Among the crowd i' the Abbey *Hen. VIII.* iv 1 57
At last, with easy roads, he came to Leicester, Lodged in the abbey . iv 2 18

Abbey-gate. Go, some of you, knock at the abbey-gate . *Com. of Errors* v 1 165

Abbey-wall. Out at the postern by the abbey-wall . . *T. G. of Ver.* v 1 9
I never came within these abbey-walls . . . *Com. of Errors* v 1 265
And stay, good nurse, behind the abbey-wall . . *Rom. and Jul.* ii 4 199

Abbot. See thou shake the bags Of hoarding abbots; imprisoned angels Set at liberty . . . . *K. John* iii 3 8
The abbot, With all the rest of that consorted crew, Destruction straight shall dog them . . . . *Richard II.* v 3 137
He came to Leicester, Lodged in the abbey; where the reverend abbot, With all his covent, honourably received him . . *Hen. VIII.* iv 2 18
O, father abbot, An old man, broken with the storms of state, Is come to lay his weary bones among ye; Give him a little earth for charity! iv 2 20

Abbreviated. Neighbour vocatur nebour; neigh abbreviated ne *L. L. Lost* v 1 26

A-bed. Her attendants of her chamber Saw her a-bed . *As Y. Like It* ii 2 6
And this was it I gave him, being a-bed . . . *All's Well* v 3 228
Not to be a-bed after midnight is to be up betimes . . *T. Night* ii 3 1
Gentlemen in England now a-bed Shall think themselves accursed they were not here . . . . *Hen. V.* iv 3 64
I would they were a-bed!—I would they were in Tiber! . *Coriolanus* iii 1 261
She is deliver'd.—To whom?—I mean, she is brought a-bed *T. Andron.* iv. 2 62
But for your company, I would have been a-bed an hour ago *Rom. and Jul.* iii 4 7
You have not been a-bed, then?—Why, no; the day had broke Before we parted . . . . *Othello* iii 1 33
Unto us it is A cell of ignorance; travelling a-bed . . *Cymbeline* iii 3 33

Abel. Which blood, like sacrificing Abel's, cries . . *Richard II.* i 1 104
Be thou cursed Cain, To slay thy brother Abel, if thou wilt *1 Hen. VI.* i 3 40

Abergavenny. O my Lord Abergavenny, fare you well! . *Hen. VIII.* i 1 211
These very words I've heard him utter to his son-in-law, Lord Abergavenny i 2 137

Abet. You that do abet him in this kind Cherish rebellion *Richard II.* ii 3 146

Abetting. To counterfeit thus grossly with your slave, Abetting him to thwart me in my mood . . . . *Com. of Errors* ii 2 172

Abhominable,—which he would call abbominable . . *L. L. Lost* v 1 26

Abhor. Whom my very soul abhors . . . . *T. G. of Ver.* iv 3 17
I had been drowned, but that the shore was shelvy and shallow,—a death that I abhor . . . . *Mer. Wives* iii 5 16
There is a vice that most I do abhor, And most desire should meet the blow of justice . . . . *Meas. for Meas.* ii 2 29
This night's the time That I should do what I abhor to name . iii 1 102
She that doth call me husband, even my soul Doth for a wife abhor *Com. of Errors* iii 2 164
Whom she hath in all outward behaviours seemed ever to abhor *M. Ado* ii 3 101
I abhor such fanatical phantasimes, such insociable and point-devise companions; such rackers of orthography . . . *L. L. Lost* v 1 20
This house is but a butchery: Abhor it, fear it, do not enter it *As Y. Like It* ii 3 28
He will come to her in yellow stockings, and 't is a colour she abhors *T. N.* ii 5 220
Thou perhaps mayst move That heart, which now abhors, to like his love iii 1 176
Away with me, all you whose souls abhor The uncleanly savours of a slaughter-house; For I am stifled with this smell of sin . *K. John* iv 3 111
Therefore I say again, I utterly abhor, yea, from my soul Refuse you for my judge . . . . *Hen. VIII.* ii 4 81
I abhor This dilatory sloth and tricks of Rome . . . . ii 4 236
Not Afric owns a serpent I abhor More than thy fame and envy *Coriolanus* i 8 3
O, how my heart abhors To hear him named, and cannot come to him! *Rom. and Jul.* iii 5 100
From the glass-faced flatterer To Apemantus, that few things loves better Than to abhor himself . . . . *T. of Athens* i 1 60
Moe things like men! Eat, Timon, and abhor them . . . iv 3 398
If ever I did dream of such a matter, Abhor me . . . *Othello* i 1 6
Her delicate tenderness will find itself abused, begin to heave the gorge, disrelish, and abhor . . . . ii 1 236
I cannot say say 'whore;' It doth abhor me now I speak the word . iv 2 162
Nature doth abhor to make his bed With the defunct, or sleep upon the dead . . . . *Cymbeline* iv 2 357

Abhorred. Thou wast a spirit too delicate To act her earthy and abhorr'd commands . . . . *Tempest* i 2 273
Abhorred slave, Which any print of goodness wilt not take! . . i 2 351
Before his sister should her body stoop To such abhorr'd pollution . . . . *Meas. for Meas.* ii 4 183
Till they attain to their abhorred ends . . . *All's Well* iv 3 28

Abhorred. But if one present The abhorr'd ingredient to his eye, make known How he hath drunk, he cracks his gorge . . . *W. Tale* ii 1 43
Taking note of thy abhorr'd aspect, Finding thee fit for bloody villany, Apt, liable to be employ'd in danger . . . . . *K. John* iv 2 224
Peevish vows: They are polluted offerings, more abhorr'd Than spotted livers in the sacrifice . . . . . . *Troi. and Cres.* v 3 17
Boils and plagues Plaster you o'er, that you may be abhorr'd! *Coriolanus* i 4 32
Destroy'd his country, and his name remains To the ensuing age abhorr'd v 3 148
They show'd me this abhorred pit . . . . . *T. Andron.* ii 3 98
Shall I believe That unsubstantial death is amorous, And that the lean abhorred monster keeps Thee here in dark to be his paramour *R. and J.* v 3 104
Therefore, be abhorr'd All feasts, societies, and throngs of men! *T. of Athens* iv 3 20
With all the abhorred births below crisp heaven . . . . iv 3 183
O abhorred spirits! Not all the whips of heaven are large enough . v 1 63
Abhorred tyrant; with my sword I'll prove the lie thou speak'st . *Macb.* v 7 10
And now, how abhorred in my imagination it is! my gorge rises at it *Ham.* v 1 206
Abhorred villain! Unnatural, detested, brutish villain! worse than brutish! Go, sirrah, seek him; I'll apprehend him . . *Lear* i 2 81
Whilst I was big in clamour came there in a man, Who, having seen me in my worst estate, Shunn'd my abhorr'd society . . . v 3 210
Married your royalty, was wife to your place; Abhorr'd your person *Cymb.* v 5 40
It is I That all the abhorred things o' the earth amend By being worse than they . . . . v 5 216
Abhorredst. Though thou abhorr'dst in us our human griefs *T. of Athens* v 4 75
Abhorring. He that will give good words to thee will flatter Beneath abhorring . . . . *Coriolanus* i 1 172
Rather on Nilus' mud Lay me stark naked, and let the water-flies Blow me into abhorring! . . . . . . *Ant. and Cleo.* v 2 60
Abhorson. What, ho! Abhorson! Where's Abhorson, there? *M. for M.* iv 2 20
How now, Abhorson? what's the news with you? . . . . iv 3 41
Abide. Had that in't which good natures Could not abide to be with *Temp.* i 2 360
The king, His brother and yours, abide all three distracted . . . v 1 12
By my troth, I cannot abide the smell of hot meat since . *Mer. Wives* i 1 297
But women, indeed, cannot abide 'em; they are very ill-favoured rough things . . . . i 1 311
He cannot abide the old woman of Brentford . . . . . iv 2 87
The deputy cannot abide a whoremaster . . . *Meas. for Meas.* iii 2 36
Compound with him by the year, and let him abide here with you . iv 2 26
Your provost knows the place where he abides . . . . v 1 252
We shall entreat you to abide here till he come . . . . v 1 266
When you depart from me, sorrow abides and happiness takes his leave *Much Ado* i 1 102
Pyramus must draw a sword to kill himself; which the ladies cannot abide . . . . *M. N. Dream* iii 1 12
Abide me, if thou darest; for well I wot Thou runn'st before me . iii 2 422
There is a monastery two miles off; And there will we abide *Mer. of Venice* iii 4 32
There is no firm reason to be render'd, Why he cannot abide a gaping pig iv 1 54
There's no virtue whipped out of the court: they cherish it to make it stay there; and yet it will no more but abide . . . *W. Tale* iv 3 99
Living, to abide Thy kingly doom and sentence of his pride *Richard II.* v 6 22
To abide a field Where nothing but the sound of Hotspur's name Did seem defensible . . . . *2 Hen. IV.* ii 3 36
I cannot abide swaggerers . . . . ii 4 117
She would always say she could not abide Master Shallow . . . iii 2 215
A rotten case abides no handling . . . . iv 1 161
A' could never abide carnation; 'twas a colour he never liked *Hen. V.* ii 3 35
Then they will endure handling, which before would not abide looking on v 2 338
All comfort go with thee! For none abides with me: my joy is death *2 Hen. VI.* ii 4 88
I dare your quenchless fury to more rage: I am your butt, and I abide your shot . . . . *3 Hen. VI.* i 4 29
Whiles lions war and battle for their dens, Poor harmless lambs abide their enmity . . . . ii 5 75
What fates impose, that men must needs abide . . . . iv 3 58
Dorset's fled To Richmond, in those parts beyond the sea Where he abides . . . . *Richard III.* iv 2 48
Though far more cause, yet much less spirit to curse Abides in me iv 4 197
Wilt thou not, beast, abide? Why, then fly on, I'll hunt thee for thy hide . . . . *Troi. and Cres.* v 6 30
As I took note of the place, it cannot be far where he abides *T. of Athens* v 1 2
Let no man abide this deed, But we the doers . . . *J. Cæsar* iii 1 94
'Tis certain he was not ambitious.—If it be found so, some will dear abide it iii 2 119
I'll call upon you straight: abide within. It is concluded *Macbeth* iii 1 140
Heaven preserve you! I dare abide no longer . . . . . iv 2 73
Our separation so abides, and flies, That thou, residing here, go'st yet with me, And I, hence fleeting, here remain with thee *Ant. and Cleo.* i 3 102
Make yourself my guest Whilst you abide here.—Humbly, sir, I thank you ii 2 250
Shall I abide In this dull world, which in thy absence is No better than a sty? . . . . iv 15 60
I shall here abide the hourly shot Of angry eyes, not comforted to live, But that there is this jewel in the world That I may see again *Cymb.* i 1 89
Not any, but abide the change of time, Quake in the present winter's state and wish That warmer days would come . . . . ii 4 4
This attempt I am soldier to, and will abide it with A prince's courage iii 4 186
I am very sick.—Go you to hunting; I'll abide with him . . iv 2 6
Ability. Alas! what poor ability's in me To do him good? *Meas. for Meas.* i 4 75
Policy of mind, Ability in means and choice of friends . . *Much Ado* iv 1 201
Have ability enough to make such knaveries yours. . . *All's Well* i 3 12
Out of my lean and low ability I'll lend you something . . *T. Night* iii 4 378
Any thing, my lord, That my ability may undergo . . . *W. Tale* ii 3 164
Infirmity Which waits upon worn times hath something seized His wish'd ability . . . . v 1 143
Which if we find outweighs ability, What do we then but draw anew the model In fewer offices? . . . . *2 Hen. IV.* i 3 45
My endeavours Have ever come too short of my desires, Yet filed with my abilities . . . . *Hen. VIII.* iii 2 171
All our abilities, gifts, natures, shapes, Severals and generals of grace exact, Achievements, plots, . . . serves As stuff . *Troi. and Cres.* i 3 179
All lovers swear more performance than they are able and yet reserve an ability that they never perform . . . . iii 2 92
Your abilities are too infant-like for doing much alone . . *Coriolanus* ii 1 40
Where should we have our thanks?—Not from his mouth, Had it the ability of life to thank you . . . . *Hamlet* v 2 384
But altogether lacks the abilities That Rhodes is dress'd in . . *Othello* i 3 25
Be thou assured, good Cassio, I will do All my abilities in thy behalf . iii 3 2
Though it be fit that Cassio have his place, For, sure, he fills it up with great ability . . . . iii 3 247
A-birding. We'll a-birding together; I have a fine hawk. *Mer. Wives* iii 3 247
Her husband goes this morning a-birding . . . . . . iii 5 46

Abject. To make a loathsome abject scorn of me . . *Com. of Errors* iv 4 106
You have among you many a purchased slave, Which, like your asses and your dogs and mules, You use in abject and in slavish parts *M. of Ven.* iv. 1 92
Banish hence these abject lowly dreams . . . . *T. of Shrew*, Ind. 2 34
Base and abject routs, Led on by bloody youth, guarded with rags *2 Hen. IV.* iv 1 33
Disgrace not so your king, That he should be so abject, base, and poor, To choose for wealth and not for perfect love . . . *1 Hen. VI.* v 5 49
Ill can thy noble mind abrook The abject people gazing on thy face *2 Hen. VI.* ii 4 11
O that I were a god, to shoot forth thunder Upon these paltry, servile, abject drudges! . . . . iv 1 105
Scarce can I speak, my choler is so great: O, I could hew up rocks and fight with flint, I am so angry at these abject terms . . . v 1 25
We are the queen's abjects, and must obey . . . *Richard III.* i 1 106
I read in 's looks Matter against me; and his eye reviled Me, as his abject object: at this instant He bores me with some trick . *Hen. VIII.* i 1 127
Nature, what things there are Most abject in regard and dear in use! What things again most dear in the esteem And poor in worth! *Troi. and Cres.* iii 3 128
Like a gallant horse fall'n in first rank, Lie there for pavement to the abject rear, O'er-run and trampled on . . . . . . iii 3 162
A barren-spirited fellow; one that feeds On abjects, orts . *J. Cæsar* iv 1 37
Abjectly. Let him that thinks of me so abjectly Know that this gold must coin a stratagem . . . . *T. Andron.* ii 3 4
Abjure. But this rough magic I here abjure . . . . *Tempest* v 1 51
Either to die the death or to abjure For ever the society of men *M. N. Dream* i 1 65
Here abjure The taints and blames I laid upon myself For strangers to my nature . . . . *Macbeth* iv 3 123
I abjure all roofs, and choose To wage against the enmity o' the air *Lear* ii 4 211
Abjured. Or so devote to Aristotle's checks As Ovid be an outcast quite abjured . . . . *T. of Shrew* i 1 33
They say, she hath abjured the company And sight of men . *T. Night* i 2 40
Able. If the river were dry, I am able to fill it with my tears *T. G. of Ver.* ii 3 58
Got deliver to a joyful resurrections!—give, when she is able to overtake seventeen years old . . . . *Mer. Wives* i 1 54
More than the villanous inconstancy of man's disposition is able to bear iv 5 111
I will never mistrust my wife again, till thou art able to woo her in good English . . . . v 5 142
I am not able to answer the Welsh flannel . . . . . v 5 171
Then no more remains, But that to your sufficiency . . . as your worth is able, And let them work . . . . . *Meas. for Meas.* i 1 9
And not being able to buy out his life According to the statute of the town Dies ere the weary sun set in the west . . *Com. of Errors* i 2 5
Man's hand is not able to taste, his tongue to conceive, nor his heart to report, what my dream was . . . . . *M. N. Dream* iv 1 218
You have not a man in all Athens able to discharge Pyramus but he . iv 2 8
He borrowed a box of the ear of the Englishman and swore he would pay him again when he was able . . . . *Mer. of Venice* i 2 88
Is he not able to discharge the money?—Yes, here I tender it for him . iv 1 208
I pity her And wish, for her sake more than for mine own, My fortunes were more able to relieve her . . . . . *As Y. Like It* ii 4 77
What 'cerns it you if I wear pearl and gold? I thank my good father, I am able to maintain it . . . . *T. of Shrew* v 1 78
Be able for thine enemy Rather in power than use . . . *All's Well* i 1 74
I have seen a medicine That's able to breathe life into a stone . . ii 1 76
Why, he's able to lead her a coranto . . . . . . ii 3 49
Not able to produce more accusation Than your own weak-hinged fancy *W. T.* ii 3 118
Ballad-makers cannot be able to express it . . . . . v 2 27
His treasons will sit blushing in his face, Not able to endure the sight of day . . . . *Richard II.* iii 2 52
Thou hast damnable iteration and art indeed able to corrupt a saint *1 Hen. IV.* i 2 102
This foolish-compounded clay, man, is not able to invent any thing that tends to laughter, more than I invent or is invented on me *2 Hen. IV.* i 2 9
How able such a work to undergo, To weigh against his opposite . . i 3 54
An honest man, sir, is able to speak for himself, when a knave is not . v 1 50
Would I were able to load him with his desert! . . . *Hen. V.* iii 7 85
Or am not able Verbatim to rehearse the method of my pen *1 Hen. VI.* iii 1 12
But your discretions better can persuade Than I am able to instruct or teach . . . . iv 1 159
Would make a volume of enticing lines, Able to ravish any dull conceit v 5 15
Henry is able to enrich his queen And not to seek a queen to make him rich . . . . v 5 51
O Lord, have mercy upon me! I shall never be able to fight a blow *2 Hen. VI.* i 3 220
I am not able to stand alone: You go about to torture me in vain . ii 1 145
I am never able to deal with my master, he hath learnt so much fence ii 3 78
Now of late, not able to travel with her furred pack . . . iv 2 50
I am able to endure much.—No question of that . . . . iv 2 60
Thou hast appointed justices of peace, to call poor men before them about matters they were not able to answer . . . . . iv 7 47
Whose smile and frown, like to Achilles' spear, Is able with the change to kill and cure . . . . v 1 101
You have a father able to maintain you . . . . *3 Hen. VI.* iii 3 154
The power that Edward hath in field Should not be able to encounter mine iv 8 36
He is equal ravenous As he is subtle, and as prone to mischief As able to perform 't . . . . *Hen. VIII.* i 1 161
The clothiers all, not able to maintain The many to them longing. . i 2 31
I am able now, methinks, Out of a fortitude of soul I feel, To endure more miseries and greater far Than my weak-hearted enemies dare offer . iii 2 387
Good sir, speak it to us.—As well as I am able . . . . iv 1 62
No audience, but the tribulation of Tower-hill, or the limbs of Limehouse, their dear brothers, are able to endure . . . . . v 4 66
They say all lovers swear more performance than they are able and yet reserve an ability that they never perform . *Troi. and Cres.* iii 2 92
None of you but is Able to bear against the great Aufidius A shield as hard as his . . . . *Coriolanus* i 6 79
He is able to pierce a corslet with his eye; talks like a knell. . . v 4 20
I am as able and as fit as thou To serve, and to deserve my mistress' grace; And that my sword upon thee shall approve . *T. Andron.* ii 1 33
Me they shall feel while I am able to stand . . . *Rom. and Jul.* i 1 33
I am the greatest, able to do least, Yet most suspected . . . v 3 223
Before the gods, I am not able to do,—the more beast, I say *T. of Athens* iii 2 54
Now or whensoever, provided I be so able as now . . . *Hamlet* v 2 211
None does offend, none, I say, none; I'll able 'em . . . *Lear* iv 6 172
Both what by sea and land I can be able To front this present time *A. and C.* i 4 78
She's able to freeze the god Priapus, and undo a whole generation *Pericles* iv 6 3

Able body. Of as able body as when he numbered thirty . *All's Well* iv 5 86
Breeds no bate with telling of discreet stories; and such other gambol faculties a' has, that show a weak mind and an able body 2 *Hen. IV.* ii 4 274
Able horses. Give my horse to Timon, Ask nothing, give it him, it foals me, straight, And able horses . *T. of Athens* ii 1 10
Able man. Would it not grieve an able man to leave So sweet a bed-fellow? . . . *Hen. VIII.* ii 2 142
Able means. If heaven had pleased to have given me longer life And able means, we had not parted thus . . . iv 2 153
A-bleeding. My nose fell a-bleeding on Black-Monday last *Mer. of Ven.* ii 5 25
My blood for your rude brawls doth lie a-bleeding *Rom. and Jul.* iii 1 194
Abler. I am a soldier, I, Older in practice, abler than yourself To make conditions . . . *J. Cæsar* iv 3 31
Aboard. Good, yet remember whom thou hast aboard . . *Tempest* i 1 21
They hurried us aboard a bark, Bore us some leagues to sea . . i 2 144
Go, go, be gone, to save your ship from wreck, Which cannot perish having thee aboard . . . *T. G. of Ver.* i 1 157
Away, away, aboard! thy master is shipped and thou art to post after ii 3 36
Unwilling I agreed; alas! too soon We came aboard . *Com. of Errors* i 1 62
There is a bark of Epidamnum That stays but till her owner comes aboard . . . iv 1 86
Our fraughtage, sir, I have convey'd aboard and I have bought The oil iv 1 88
Fetch our stuff from thence: I long that we were safe and sound aboard iv 4 154
I will not stay to-night for all the town; Therefore away, to get our stuff aboard . . . iv 4 162
The wind is come about; Bassanio presently will go aboard *Mer. of Venice* ii 6 65
As if he had been aboard, carousing to his mates After a storm *T. of Shrew* iii 2 173
Go, get aboard; Look to thy bark: I'll not be long before I call upon thee . . . *W. Tale* iii 3 7
I never saw The heavens so dim by day. A savage clamour! Well may I get aboard! . . . iii 3 57
He is gone aboard a new ship to purge melancholy and air himself iv 4 790
I'll bring you where he is aboard, tender your persons to his presence . iv 4 826
I will bring these two moles, these blind ones, aboard him . . . v 4 868
I brought the old man and his son aboard the prince . . . v 2 124
Now sits the wind fair, and we will aboard . . . *Hen. V.* ii 2 12
My Lord of Westmoreland, and uncle Exeter, We will aboard to-night ii 2 71
I lost mine eye in laying the prize aboard, And therefore to revenge it, shalt thou die . . . 2 *Hen. VI.* iv 1 25
There is a nobleman in town, one Paris, that would fain lay knife aboard; but she, good soul, had as lief see a toad . *Rom. and Jul.* ii 4 214
Aboard, aboard, for shame! The wind sits in the shoulder of your sail, And you are stay'd for . . . *Hamlet* i 3 55
Follow him at foot; tempt him with speed aboard; Delay it not . iv 3 56
Myself will straight aboard; and to the state This heavy act with heavy heart relate . . . *Othello* v 2 370
Aboard my galley I invite you all: Will you lead, lords? *Ant. and Cleo.* ii 6 82
Come, sir, will you aboard? I have a health for you . . . ii 6 142
You shall at least Go see my lord aboard . . . *Cymbeline* i 1 178
I must aboard to-morrow.—O, no, no . . . i 6 199
Convey thy deity Aboard our dancing boat . . . *Pericles* iii 1 13
Half-part, mates, half-part. Come, let's have her aboard suddenly . iv 1 96
Perhaps they will but please themselves upon her, Not carry her aboard iv 1 102
In it is Lysimachus the governor, Who craves to come aboard . . v 1 5
Gentlemen, there's some of worth would come aboard . . . v 1 9
'Gainst whose shore Riding, her fortunes brought the maid aboard . v 3 11
Abode. To Mantua, where I hear he makes abode . . *T. G. of Ver.* iv 3 23
Sweet friends, your patience for my long abode . *Mer. of Venice* ii 6 21
Fair and fresh and sweet, Whither away, or where is thy abode? *T. of Shrew* iv 5 38
I leave my curse: May never glorious sun reflex his beams Upon the country where you make abode! . . . 1 *Hen. VI.* v 4 88
I do find more pain in banishment Than death can yield me here by my abode . . . *Richard III.* i 3 169
With reservation of an hundred knights, By you to be sustain'd, shall our abode Make with you . . . *Lear* i 1 136
Unless his abode be lingered here by some accident . . *Othello* iv 2 231
Which wholly depends on your abode . . . *Ant. and Cleo.* i 2 182
Desire My man's abode where I did leave him . . . *Cymbeline* i 6 53
Aboded. This tempest, Dashing the garment of this peace, aboded The sudden breach on 't . . . *Henry VIII.* i 1 93
Abodement. Tush, man, abodements must not now affright us 3 *Hen. VI.* iv 7 13
Aboding. The night-crow cried, aboding luckless time; Dogs howl'd, and hideous tempest shook down trees . . . v 6 45
Abominable. The poor monster's in drink: an abominable monster! *Temp.* ii 2 163
I shall not only receive this villanous wrong, but stand under the adoption of abominable terms . . . *Mer. Wives* ii 2 309
From their abominable and beastly touches I drink, I eat. *M. for Meas.* iii 2 25
This is abhominable,—which he would call abbominable . *L. L. Lost* v 1 26
Abominable fellows and betray themselves to every modern censure worse than drunkards . . . *As Y. Like It* iv 1 6
That villanous abominable misleader of youth, Falstaff . . 1 *Hen. IV.* ii 4 508
Thou abominable damned cheater, art thou not ashamed to be called captain? . . . 2 *Hen. IV.* ii 4 151
Abominable Gloucester, guard thy head; For I intend to have it 1 *Hen. VI.* i 3 87
Such abominable words as no Christian ear can endure to hear 2 *Hen. VI.* iv 7 44
'Tis government that makes them seem divine; The want thereof makes thee abominable . . . 3 *Hen. VI.* i 4 133
That dissembling abominable varlet, Diomed . . *Troi. and Cres.* v 4 3
You vile abominable tents, Thus proudly pight upon our Phrygian plains . . . v 10 23
His body's hue, Spotted, detested, and abominable . *T. Andron.* ii 3 74
Acts of black night, abominable deeds, Complots of mischief, treason v 1 64
I'll apprehend him: abominable villain! Where is he? . . *Lear* i 2 83
O abominable!—She makes our profession as it were to stink *Pericles* iv 6 143
Abominably. They imitated humanity so abominably . . *Hamlet* iii 2 39
Abomination. The adulterous Antony, most large In his abominations, turns you off . . . *Ant. and Cleo.* iii 6 94
Abortive. Why should I joy in any abortive birth? . . *L. L. Lost* i 1 104
Call them meteors, prodigies and signs, Abortives, presages . *K. John* iii 4 158
Remember it and let it make thee crest-fall'n, Ay, and allay this thy abortive pride . . . 2 *Hen. VI.* iv 1 60
If ever he have child, abortive be it, Prodigious! . . *Richard III.* i 2 21
Thou elvish-mark'd, abortive, rooting hog! . . . i 3 228
Abound. The moon, the governess of floods, Pale in her anger, washes all the air, That rheumatic diseases do abound . . *M. N. Dream* ii 1 105
When you shall know your mistress Has deserved prison, then abound in tears . . . *W. Tale* ii 1 120
The plain-song is most just; for humours do abound . *Hen. V.* iii 2 7
So cares and joys abound, as seasons fleet . . . 2 *Hen. VI.* ii 4 4
Abound. So sicken'd their estates, that never They shall abound as formerly . . . *Hen. VIII.* i 1 83
Though perils did Abound, as thick as thought could make 'em . . iii 2 195
I have no relish of them, but abound In the division of each several crime, Acting it many ways . . . *Macbeth* iv 3 95
Aboundest. Which, like a usurer, abound'st in all, And usest none in that true use indeed Which should bedeck thy shape *Rom. and Jul.* iii 3 123
Abounding. Mark then abounding valour in our English *Hen. V.* iv 3 104
About. Do not turn me about; my stomach is not constant . *Tempest* ii 2 118
I will tell you what I am about.—Two yards, and more . *Mer. Wives* i 3 43
Indeed, I am in the waist two yards about; but I am now about no waste; I am about thrift . . . i 3 46
At a word, hang no more about me, I am no gibbet for you . . . ii 2 17
I will about it; better three hours too soon than a minute too late . ii 2 327
See how he goes about to abuse me! . . *Meas. for Meas.* ii 2 215
I was about to protest I loved you.—And do it with all thy heart *M. Ado* iv 1 286
The wind is come about; Bassanio presently will go aboard *Mer. of Venice* ii 6 64
Who shall go about To cozen fortune and be honourable Without the stamp of merit? . . . ii 9 37
Go not about; my love hath in 't a bond, Whereof the world takes note: come, come, disclose The state of your affection . *All's Well* i 3 194
Shall we set about some revels?—What shall we do else? . *T. Night* i 3 145
Something about, a little from the right, In at the window, or else o'er the hatch . . . *K. John* i 1 170
She has nobody to do any thing about her when I am gone; and she is old, and cannot help herself . . . 2 *Hen. IV.* iii 2 246
And a' would about and about, and come you in and come you in . . iii 2 302
And those about her From her shall read the perfect ways of honour, And by those claim their greatness, not by blood . *Hen. VIII.* v 5 37
Stay, hold, peace!—What is about to be? I am out of breath *Coriolanus* iii 1 189
He must, and will. Prithee now, say you will, and go about it . . iii 2 98
To see, now, how a jest shall come about! . . . *Rom. and Jul.* i 3 45
He is about it: The doors are open; and the surfeited grooms Do mock their charge with snores . . . *Macbeth* ii 2 4
His horses go about.—Almost a mile: but he does usually, So all men do, from hence to the palace gate Make it their walk . . . iii 3 11
About some act That has no relish of salvation in 't . . *Hamlet* iii 3 91
Let me speak to the yet unknowing world How these things came about v 2 391
Who sometime, in his better tune, remembers What we are come about *Lear* iv 3 42
How wouldst thou praise me?—I am about it; but indeed my invention Comes from my pate as birdlime does from frize . . *Othello* ii 1 126
Above. The wills above be done! but I would fain die a dry death *Temp.* i 1 70
Shall I not lose my suit?—Troth, sir, all is in his hands above *Mer. Wives* i 4 154
Over and above that you have suffered, I think to repay that money will be a biting affliction . . . v 5 177
O you blessed ministers above, Keep me in patience! . *Meas. for Meas.* v 1 115
The god of love, That sits above, And knows me, and knows me *Much Ado* v 2 27
Stand indebted, over and above, In love and service to you evermore *M. of V.* iv 1 413
Thrice-crowned queen of night, survey With thy chaste eye, from thy pale sphere above, Thy huntress' name . . *As Y. Like It* iii 2 3
Whom I serve above is my master.—Who? God?—Ay, sir . *All's Well* ii 3 261
In my stars I am above thee; but be not afraid of greatness . *T. Night* ii 5 156
You witnesses above Punish my life for tainting of my love! . . v 1 140
I must not yield to any rites of love, For my profession's sacred from above . . . 1 *Hen. VI.* i 2 114
I'll stay above the hill, so both may shoot . . 3 *Hen. VI.* iii 1 5
What can happen To me above this wretchedness? . . *Hen. VIII.* iii 1 123
Well, the gods are above; time must friend or end . *Troi. and Cres.* i 2 83
She praised his complexion above Paris.—Why, Paris hath colour enough i 2 107
If she praised him above, his complexion is higher than his . . i 2 111
Whom thy upward face Hath to be marbled mansion all above Never presented . . . *T. of Athens* iv 3 191
Where liest o' nights, Timon?—Under that's above me . . iv 3 292
But God above Deal between thee and me! . . . *Macbeth* iv 3 120
This, in obedience, hath my daughter shown me, And more above *Hamlet* ii 2 126
'Tis not so above; There is no shuffling, there the action lies In his true nature . . . iii 3 60
This shows you are above, You justicers, that these our nether crimes So speedily can venge! . . . *Lear* iv 2 78
Above all. One that, above all other strifes, contended especially to know himself . . . *Meas. for Meas.* iii 2 246
This above all: to thine own self be true, And it must follow, as the night the day, Thou canst not then be false to any man . *Hamlet* i 3 78
God's above all; and there be souls must be saved, and there be souls must not be saved . . . *Othello* ii 3 106
Above compare. With that same tongue Which she hath praised him with above compare So many thousand times . . *Rom. and Jul.* iii 5 238
Above conscience. For policy sits above conscience . *T. of Athens* iii 2 94
Above deck. I'll be sure to keep him above deck . . *M. Wives* i 1 94
Above heat. One draught above heat makes him a fool; the second mads him; and a third drowns him . . . *T. Night* i 5 140
Above her degree. She'll not match above her degree . . i 3 116
Above human thought Enacted wonders with his sword . 1 *Hen. VI.* i 1 121
Above measure false!—Have patience, sir. . . *Cymbeline* ii 4 113
Above once. It was never acted; or, if it was, not above once *Hamlet* ii 2 455
Above our power. Tempt us not to bear above our power! . *K. John* v 6 38
Above the clouds. He would be above the clouds . 2 *Hen. VI.* ii 1 15
Above the earth. This foul deed shall smell above the earth. *J. Cæsar* iii 1 274
Above the reach or compass of thy thought . . 2 *Hen. VI.* i 2 46
Above the rest, we parley to you: Are you content? . *T. G. of Ver.* iv 1 60
And what a pitch she flew above the rest! . . 2 *Hen. VI.* ii 1 6
Do as I bid thee, or rather do thy pleasure; Above the rest, be gone *Lear* iv 1 50
Above this world. And did value me Above this world . . *L. L. Lost* v 2 446
Above thy life. But life itself, my wife, and all the world, Are not with me esteem'd above thy life . . *Mer. of Venice* iv 1 285
Above water. Forty thousand fathom above water . . *W. Tale* iv 4 281
Abraham. Leave our pribbles and prabbles, and desire a marriage between Master Abraham and Mistress Anne Page . *Mer. Wives* i 1 57
Sweet peace conduct his sweet soul to the bosom Of good old Abraham! *Richard II.* iv 1 104
The sons of Edward sleep in Abraham's bosom . . *Richard III.* iv. 3 38
Abram. This Jacob from our holy Abram was, As his wise mother wrought in his behalf, The third possessor . . *Mer. of Venice* i 3 73
O father Abram, what these Christians are! . . . i 3 162
Abreast. Tarry, sweet soul, for mine, then fly abreast . *Hen. V.* iv 6 17
All abreast, Charged our main battle's front . . 3 *Hen. VI.* i 1 7
Take the instant way; For honour travels in a strait so narrow, Where one but goes abreast . . . *Troi. and Cres.* iii. 3 155
A-brewing. There is some ill a-brewing towards my rest *Mer. of Venice* ii 5 17
Abridge. Thy staying will abridge thy life . . *T. G. of Ver.* iii 1 245

Abridge. Then death rock me asleep, abridge my doleful days! *2 Hen. IV.* ii. 4 211
Abridged. Nor do I now make moan to be abridged From such a noble rate . . . . *Mer. of Venice* i 1 126
So are we Cæsar's friends, that have abridged His time of fearing death *J. Cæsar* iii 1 104
Abridgement. For look, where my abridgement comes . . *Hamlet* ii 2 439
Say, what abridgement have you for this evening? . . *M. N. Dream* v 1 39
Then brook abridgement, and your eyes advance, After your thoughts, straight back again to France . . . . . *Hen. V.* v Prol. 44
This fierce abridgement Hath to it circumstantial branches . *Cymbeline* v 5 382
Abroach. Who set this ancient quarrel new abroach? *Rom. and Jul.* i 1 111
Alack, what mischiefs might he set abroach In shadow of such greatness! *2 Hen. IV.* iv 2 14
The secret mischiefs that I set abroach I lay unto the grievous charge of others . . . . . . *Richard III.* i 3 325
Abroad. How features are abroad, I am skilless of . . . *Tempest* iii 1 52
Here have I few attendants And subjects none abroad . . . v 1 167
I rather would entreat thy company To see the wonders of the world abroad Than, living dully sluggardized at home . *T. G. of Ver.* i 1 6
What news abroad i' the world?—None . . . *Meas. for Meas.* iii 2 234
There 's villany abroad: this letter will tell you more . *L. L. Lost* i 1 189
All-telling fame Doth noise abroad . . . . . ii 1 22
Had I such venture forth, The better part of my affections would Be with my hopes abroad . . . . *Mer. of Venice* i 1 17
Other ventures he hath, squandered abroad . . . . i 3 22
I do wonder, Thou naughty gaoler, that thou art so fond To come abroad with him at his request . . . . iii 3 10
And so am come abroad to see the world . . *T. of Shrew* i 2 58
I have for the most part been aired abroad . . *W. Tale* iv 2 6
Indeed, sir, there are cozeners abroad; therefore it behoves men to be wary iv 4 257
Why should I carry lies abroad? . . . . . . iv 4 275
There's toys abroad: anon I'll tell thee more . . *K. John* i 1 232
Hear'st thou the news abroad, who are arrived? . . . iv 2 160
Come, come; sans compliment, what news abroad? . . . v 6 16
Thieves and robbers range abroad unseen In murders . *Richard II.* iii 2 39
There's villanous news abroad . . . . *1 Hen. IV.* ii 4 367
My office is To noise abroad that Harry Monmouth fell . *2 Hen. IV.* Ind. 29
I am glad to see your lordship abroad: I heard say your lordship was sick . . . . i 2 108
I hope your lordship goes abroad by advice . . . . i 2 109
How now! rain within doors, and none abroad! . . . iv 5 9
While that the armed hand doth fight abroad, The advised head defends itself at home . . . . *Hen. V.* i 2 178
Some, like magistrates, correct at home, Others, like merchants, venture trade abroad . . . . i 2 192
Is this the scourge of France? Is this the Talbot, so much fear'd abroad That with his name the mothers still their babes? . *1 Hen. VI.* ii 3 16
His hands abroad display'd, as one that grasp'd And tugg'd for life and was by strength subdued . . . . . *2 Hen. VI.* iii 2 172
How now, fair lords! What fare? what news abroad? . *3 Hen. VI.* ii 1 95
For how can tyrants safely govern home, Unless abroad they purchase great alliance? . . . . iii 3 70
I here proclaim myself thy mortal foe, With resolution, wheresoe'er I meet thee—As I will meet thee, if thou stir abroad . . . v 1 96
I will buz abroad such prophecies That Edward shall be fearful of his life v 6 86
What news abroad?—No news so bad abroad as this at home *Richard III.* i 1 134
Hear you the news abroad?—Ay, that the king is dead.—Bad news . ii 3 3
Rumour it abroad That Anne, my wife, is sick and like to die . iv 2 51
None here, he hopes, In all this noble bevy, has brought with her One care abroad . . . . *Hen. VIII.* i 4 5
Is he ready To come abroad?—I think, by this he is . . . iii 2 83
What news abroad?— . . The worst Is your displeasure with the king iii 2 391
But to the sport abroad: are you bound thither? . *Troi. and Cres.* i 1 118
And set abroad new business for you all . . . *T. Andron.* i 1 192
The angry northern wind Will blow these sands, like Sibyl's leaves, abroad iv 1 105
A troubled mind drave me to walk abroad . . *Rom. and Jul.* i 1 127
Let's retire: The day is hot, the Capulets abroad . . . iii 1 2
What should it be, that they so shriek abroad? . . . v 3 190
If there be Such valour in the bearing, what make we abroad? *T. of A.* iii 5 47
Common pleasures, To walk abroad, and recreate yourselves . *J. Cæsar* iii 2 256
Thy spirit walks abroad, and turns our swords In our own proper entrails v 3 95
Foul whisperings are abroad: unnatural deeds Do breed unnatural troubles: infected minds To their deaf pillows will discharge their secrets . . . . *Macb.* v 1 79
What 's more to do, Which would be planted newly with the time, As calling home our exiled friends abroad That fled the snares of watchful tyranny . . . . v 8 66
And then, they say, no spirit dare stir abroad; The nights are wholesome; then no planets strike, No fairy takes, nor witch hath power *Hamlet* i 1 161
If you do stir abroad, go armed . . . . . . *Lear* i 2 186
You have heard of the news abroad; I mean the whispered ones? . . ii 1 8
It is thought abroad, that 'twixt my sheets He has done my office *Othello* i 3 393
Thy biddings have been done; and every hour, Most noble Cæsar, shalt thou have report How 'tis abroad . . . . *Ant. and Cleo.* i 4 36
What you shall know meantime Of stirs abroad, I shall beseech you, sir, To let me be partaker . . . . i 4 82
Where air comes out, air comes in: there's none abroad so wholesome as that you vent . . . . *Cymbeline* i 2 4
Your means abroad, You have me, rich; and I will never fail . iii 4 180
No companies abroad?—None in the world . . . . iv 2 101
What company Discover you abroad?—No single soul Can we set eye on iv 2 130
Abrogate. Perge; so it shall please you to abrogate scurrility *L. L. L.* iv 2 55
Abrook. Ill can thy noble mind abrook The abject people gazing on thy face, With envious looks, laughing at thy shame . *2 Hen. VI.* ii 4 10
Abrupt. My lady craves To know the cause of your abrupt departure.—Marry, for that she's in a wrong belief . . . *1 Hen. VI.* ii 3 30
Abruption. What makes this pretty abruption? . *Troi. and Cres.* iii 2 70
Abruptly. Or if thou hast not broke from company Abruptly, as my passion now makes me, Thou hast not loved . . *As Y. Like It* ii 4 41
Absence. Let me hear from thee by letters Of thy success in love and what news else Betideth here in absence of thy friend *T. G. of Ver.* i 1 59
I will not be absence at the grace . . . . . *Mer. Wives* i 1 273
Her husband will be absence from his house between ten and eleven . ii 2 86
To take an ill advantage of his absence . . . . . iii 3 117
We have with special soul Elected him our absence to supply *M. for Meas.* i 1 19
Lord Angelo dukes it well in his absence; he puts transgression to 't . iii 2 101
I met you at the prison, in the absence of the duke.—O, did you so? . v 1 331
From whom my absence was not six months old . *Com. of Errors* i 1 45
What buys your company?—Your absence only . . *L. L. Lost* v 2 225
Absence. My own fault; Which death or absence soon shall remedy *M. N. Dream* iii 2 244
There is not one among them but I dote on his very absence . *M. of V.* i 2 121
Which appears most strongly In bearing thus the absence of your lord iii 4 4
We should hold day with the Antipodes, If you would walk in absence of the sun . . . . v 1 128
By reason of his absence, there is nothing That you will feed on *As Y. L.* ii 4 85
My lady will hang thee for thy absence . . . *T. Night* i 5 4
I am question'd by my fears, of what may chance Or breed upon our absence . . . . *W. Tale* i 2 12
Holds his wife by the arm, That little thinks she has been sluiced in 's absence And his pond fish'd by his next neighbour . . . i 2 194
You knew of his departure, as you know What you have underta'en to do in 's absence . . . . iii 2 79
Marry her, And, with my best endeavours in your absence, Your discontenting father strive to qualify And bring him up to liking . iv 4 542
Our absence makes us unthrifty to our knowledge . . . . v 2 120
The advantage of his absence took the king And in the meantime sojourn'd at my father's . . . . *K. John* i 1 102
Thy grief is but thy absence for a time . . . *Richard II.* i 3 258
We create, in absence of ourself, Our uncle York lord governor of England . . . . ii 1 219
This absence of your father's draws a curtain, That shows the ignorant a kind of fear Before not dreamt of . . . . *1 Hen. IV.* iv 1 73
I rather of his absence make this use: It lends a lustre and more great opinion, A larger dare to our great enterprise . . . . iv 1 76
What with Owen Glendower's absence thence, . . . I fear the power of Percy is too weak To wage an instant trial with the king . iv 4 16
Our navy is address'd, our power collected, Our substitutes in absence well invested, And every thing lies level to our wish *2 Hen. IV.* iv 4 6
Playing the mouse in absence of the cat, To tear and havoc more than she can eat . . . . *Hen. V.* i 2 172
Your nobles, jealous of your absence, Seek through your camp to find you . . . . iv 1 302
I hope, My absence doth neglect no great designs *Richard III.* iii 4 25
The queen is comfortless, and we forgetful In our long absence *Hen. VIII.* ii 3 106
Had she no lover there That wails her absence? . *Troi. and Cres.* iv 5 289
I should freelier rejoice in that absence wherein he won honour . *Coriol.* i 3 4
All the yarn she spun in Ulysses' absence did but fill Ithaca full of moths . . . . i 3 93
Defend yourself By calmness or by absence . . . . . iii 2 95
And lose advantage, which doth ever cool I' the absence of the needer iv 1 44
All thy safety were remotion and thy defence absence . *T. of Athens* iv 3 346
Upon what sickness?—Impatient of my absence . . *J. Cæsar* iv 3 152
Whose absence is no less material to me Than is his father's *Macbeth* iii 1 136
His absence, sir, Lays blame upon his promise . . . . iii 4 43
I a heavy interim shall support By his dear absence . . . *Othello* i 3 260
I shall, in a more continuate time, Strike off this score of absence . iii 4 179
To the felt absence now I feel a cause: Is 't come to this? . . iii 4 182
The business she hath broached in the state Cannot endure my absence *Ant. and Cleo.* i 2 179
Shall I abide In this dull world, which in thy absence is No better than a sty? . . . . iv 15 61
He hath a drug of mine; I pray his absence Proceed by swallowing that *Cymbeline* iii 5 57
Such a welcome as I'ld give to him After long absence, such is yours iii 6 74
A fever with the absence of her son, A madness, of which her life's in danger . . . . iv 3 2
Failing of her end by his strange absence, Grew shameless-desperate . v 5 57
But should he wrong my liberties in my absence? . . . *Pericles* i 2 112
Let me entreat you to Forbear the absence of your king . . . ii 4 46
Absent. Would the duke that is absent have done this? *Meas. for Meas.* iii 2 123
For my poor self, I am combined by a sacred vow And shall be absent iv 3 150
I will so fashion the matter that Hero shall be absent . *Much Ado* ii 2 48
Take No note at all of our being absent hence . *Mer. of Venice* v 1 120
You shall be my bedfellow: When I am absent, then lie with my wife v 1 285
Fetch that gallant hither; If he be absent, bring his brother to me *As Y. Like It* ii 2 18
Your physicians have expressly charged, In peril to incur your former malady, That I should yet absent me from your bed *T. of Shrew* Ind. 2 125
Paris and the medicine and the king Had from the conversation of my thoughts Haply been absent . . . . *All's Well* i 3 241
In fine, delivers me to fill the time, Herself most chastely absent . iii 7 34
Yet you will be hanged for being so long absent; or, to be turned away *T. Night* i 5 18
They have seemed to be together, though absent . . *W. Tale* i 1 32
Twenty-three days They have been absent: 'tis good speed . . ii 3 199
Joy absent, grief is present for that time . . . *Richard II.* i 3 259
The queen hath best success when you are absent . *3 Hen. VI.* iv 1 7
The queen being absent, 'tis a needful fitness That we adjourn *Hen. VIII.* ii 4 231
She fell distract, And, her attendants absent, swallow'd fire *J. Cæsar* iv 3 156
Both more and less have given him the revolt, And none serve with him but constrained things Whose hearts are absent too . . *Macbeth* v 4 14
If thou didst ever hold me in thy heart, Absent thee from felicity awhile, And in this harsh world draw thy breath in pain, To tell my story . . . . *Hamlet* v 2 358
I being absent and my place supplied, My general will forget my love and service . . . . *Othello* iii 3 17
The perturb'd court, For my being absent? whereunto I never Purpose return . . . . *Cymbeline* iii 4 109
Absent argument. I should not seek an absent argument Of my revenge, thou present . . . . *As Y. Like It* iii 1 3
Absent child. Grief fills the room up of my absent child, Lies in his bed, walks up and down with me, Puts on his pretty looks *K. John* iii 4 93
Absent duke. And much please the absent duke . . *Meas. for Meas.* i 1 209
I never heard the absent duke much detected for women . . . iii 2 129
How came it that the absent duke had not either delivered him to his liberty or executed him? . . . . iv 2 136
Absent friends. The solemn feast Shall more attend upon the coming space, Expecting absent friends . . . . *All's Well* ii 3 189
Absent hours. And lovers' absent hours, More tedious than the dial eight score times . . . . *Othello* iii 4 174
Absent king. All the favourites that the absent king In deputation left behind . . . . *1 Hen. IV.* iv 3 86
What with the absent king, What with the injuries of a wanton time v 1 49
Absent time. To take advantage of the absent time . . *Richard II.* ii 3 79
Absey. Then comes answer like an Absey book . . . *K. John* i 1 196
Like a schoolboy that had lost his A B C. . . . . *T. G. of Ver.* ii 1 23
Absolute. Be absolute for death; either death or life Shall thereby be the sweeter . . . . *Meas. for Meas.* iii 1 5

Absolute. The wicked'st caitiff on the ground May seem as shy, as grave, as just, as absolute As Angelo . . . . . *Meas. for Meas.* v 1 54
You shall have your desires with interest And pardon absolute 1 *Hen. IV.* iv 3 50
Upon such large terms and so absolute As our conditions shall consist upon, Our peace shall stand as firm as rocky mountains 2 *Hen. IV.* iv 1 186
It is a most absolute and excellent horse . . . . . *Hen. V.* iii 7 27
You are too absolute; Though therein you can never be too noble *Coriol.* iii 2 39
With an absolute 'Sir, not I,' The cloudy messenger turns me his back, And hums . . . . . *Macbeth* iii 6 40
How absolute the knave is! we must speak by the card, or equivocation will undo us . . . . . *Hamlet* v 1 148
My soul hath her content so absolute That not another comfort like to this Succeeds in unknown fate . . . . . *Othello* ii 1 193
The snatches in his voice, And burst of speaking, were as his: I am absolute 'Twas very Cloten . . . . . *Cymbeline* iv 2 106
How absolute she 's in 't, Not minding whether I dislike or no! *Pericles* ii 5 19
Absolute Alexas. Sweet Alexas, most any thing Alexas, almost most absolute Alexas . . . . . *Ant. and Cleo.* i 2 2
Absolute commission. For this immediate levy, he commends His absolute commission . . . . . *Cymbeline* iii 7 10
Absolute courtier. Thou wouldst make an absolute courtier *M. Wives* iii 3 66
Absolute fear. I speak not as in absolute fear of you . . *Macbeth* iv 3 38
Absolute gentleman. An absolute gentleman, full of most excellent differences, of very soft society . . . . . *Hamlet* v 2 111
Absolute hope. If to-morrow Our navy thrive, I have an absolute hope Our landmen will stand up. . . . . *Ant. and Cleo.* iv 3 10
Absolute lord. Most absolute lord, My mistress Cleopatra sent me . iv 14 117
Absolute lust. Not out of absolute lust, though peradventure I stand accountant for as great a sin . . . . . *Othello* ii 1 301
Absolute madness. Not Absolute madness could so far have raved To bring him here alone . . . . . *Cymbeline* iv 2 135
Absolute master. By sea He is an absolute master . . *Ant. and Cleo.* ii 2 166
Absolute Milan. He needs will be Absolute Milan . . . *Tempest* i 2 109
Absolute power and place here in Vienna . . . *Meas. for Meas.* i 3 13
Though there the people had more absolute power, I say *Coriolanus* iii 1 116
Thou shalt be met with thanks, Allow'd with absolute power *T. of Athens* v 1 165
We will resign, During the life of this old majesty, To him our absolute power . . . . . *Lear* v 3 300
Absolute queen. Made her Of lower Syria, Cyprus, Lydia, Absolute queen . . . . . *Ant. and Cleo.* iii 6 11
Absolute 'shall.' Hear you this Triton of the minnows? mark you His absolute 'shall'? . . . . . *Coriolanus* iii 1 89
Absolute sir. Most absolute sir, if thou wilt have The leading of thine own revenges . . . . . iv 5 142
Absolute soldiership. Most worthy sir, you therein throw away The absolute soldiership you have . . . *Ant. and Cleo.* iii 7 43
Absolute trust. A gentleman on whom I built An absolute trust *Macb.* i 4 14
Absolutely. This shall absolutely resolve you . . *Meas. for Meas.* iv 2 225
To hear and absolutely to determine Of what conditions 2 *Hen. IV.* iv 1 164
Absolved. The willing'st sin I ever yet committed May be absolved in English . . . . . *Hen. VIII.* iii 1 50
Out of holy pity, Absolved him with an axe . . . . . iii 2 264
To make confession and to be absolved . . . *Rom. and Jul.* iii 5 233
Abstain. And who abstains from meat that is not gaunt? *Richard II.* ii 1 76
Abstemious. Be more abstemious, Or else, good night your vow! *Temp.* iv 1 53
Abstinence. A man of stricture and firm abstinence *Meas. for Meas.* i 3 12
He doth with holy abstinence subdue That in himself which he spurs on his power To qualify in others . . . . . iv 2 84
Your stomachs are too young; And abstinence engenders maladies *L. L. L.* iv 3 295
Refrain to-night, And that shall lend a kind of easiness To the next abstinence: the next more easy . . . . . *Hamlet* iii 4 167
Abstract. They are the abstract and brief chronicles of the time . ii 2 548
He hath an abstract for the remembrance of such places *Mer. Wives* iv 2 63
Dispatched sixteen businesses, a month's length a-piece, by an abstract of success . . . . . *All's Well* iv 3 99
This little abstract doth contain that large Which died in Geffrey *K. John* ii 1 101
Brief abstract and record of tedious days, Rest thy unrest! *Richard III.* iv 4 28
A man who is the abstract of all faults That all men follow *Ant. and Cleo.* i 4 9
Absurd. This proffer is absurd and reasonless . . . 1 *Hen. VI.* v 4 137
'Tis a fault to heaven, A fault against the dead, a fault to nature, To reason most absurd . . . . . *Hamlet* i 2 103
Let the candied tongue lick absurd pomp, And crook the pregnant hinges of the knee . . . . . iii 2 65
That's the way To fool their preparation, and to conquer Their most absurd intents . . . . . *Ant. and Cleo.* v 2 226
Absyrtus. Into as many gobbets will I cut it As wild Medea young Absyrtus did . . . . . 2 *Hen. VI.* v 2 59
Abundance. Nature should bring forth, Of it own kind, all foison, all abundance . . . . . *Tempest* ii 1 163
You would be, sweet madam, if your miseries were in the same abundance as your good fortunes are . . . *Mer. of Ven.* i 2 4
Rather than lack it where there is such abundance. . . *All's Well* i 1 12
What cracker is this same that deafs our ears With this abundance of superfluous breath? . . . . . *K. John* ii 1 148
One that hath abundance of charge too, God knows what . 1 *Hen. IV.* ii 1 63
He may sleep in security; for he hath the horn of abundance 2 *Hen. IV.* i 2 52
Such are the rich, That have abundance and enjoy it not . . iv 4 108
An inventory to particularize their abundance . . . *Coriolanus* i 1 22
In what enormity is Marcius poor in, that you two have not in abundance? ii 1 19
Who but of late, earth, sea, and air, Were all too little to content and please, Although they gave their creatures in abundance *Pericles* i 4 36
Abundant. When the tongue's office should be prodigal To breathe the abundant dolour of the heart . . . . . *Richard II.* i 3 257
Thy abundant goodness shall excuse This deadly blot in thy digressing son v 3 65
Which short-armed ignorance itself knows is so abundant scarce *Troi. and Cres.* ii 3 16
Abundantly. Though abundantly they lack discretion . . *Coriolanus* i 1 206
Abuse. Whether thou be'st he or no, Or some enchanted trifle to abuse me, As late I have been, I not know . . . . . *Tempest* v 1 112
If he were twenty Sir John Falstaffs, he shall not abuse Robert Shallow, esquire . . . . . *Mer. Wives* i 1 3
My husband will not rejoice so much at the abuse of Falstaff . v 3 8
If these be good people in a commonweal that do nothing but use their abuses in common houses, I know no law . . *Meas. for Meas.* ii 1 43
See how he goes about to abuse me! . . . . . iii 2 215
This is a strange abuse . . . . . v 1 205
Lend him your kind pains To find out this abuse . . . . v 1 247
How the villain would close now, after his treasonable abuses! . . v 1 347
There is a man haunts the forest, that abuses our young plants *As Y. Like It* iii 2 378
That blind rascally boy that abuses every one's eyes . . . iv 1 219
She does abuse our ears: to prison with her . . . *All's Well* v 3 295
So did I abuse Myself, my servant, and, I fear me, you . . *T. Night* iii 1 124
If your lass Interpretation should abuse and call this Your lack of love or bounty, you were straited For a reply . . . . . *W. Tale* iv 4 364
The poor abuses of the time want countenance . . . 1 *Hen. IV.* i 2 174
Cries out upon abuses, seems to weep Over his country's wrongs . . iv 3 81
Would turn their own perfection to abuse, To seem like him 2 *Hen. IV.* ii 3 27
I shall drive you then to confess the wilful abuse . . . . ii 4 339
No abuse, Hal, o' mine honour; no abuse . . . . . ii 4 340
Would he abuse the countenance of the king, Alack, what mischiefs might he set abroach In shadow of such greatness! . . . . . iv 2 13
Linger your patience on; and we'll digest The abuse of distance *Hen. V.* ii Prol. 32
It was ourself thou didst abuse.—Your majesty came not like yourself iv 8 52
Pardon my abuse: I find thou art no less than fame hath bruited 1 *Hen. VI.* ii 3 67
Talk with him And give him chastisement for this abuse . . . iv 1 69
Your renowned name: shall flight abuse it? . . . . . iv 5 41
In thine own person answer thy abuse . . . . 2 *Hen. VI.* ii 1 41
Hast thou broken faith with me, Knowing how hardly I can brook abuse? v 1 92
Why art thou old, and want'st experience? Or wherefore dost abuse it? v 1 172
Did I let pass the abuse done to my niece? . . . 3 *Hen. VI.* iii 3 188
So weak of courage and in judgement That they'll take no offence at our abuse . . . . . iv 1 13
Nor aught so good but strain'd from that fair use Revolts from true birth, stumbling on abuse . . . . . *Rom. and Jul.* ii 3 20
Nor tears nor prayers shall purchase out abuses: Therefore use none iii 1 198
Let's ha' some sport with 'em.—Hang him, he'll abuse us *T. of Athens* ii 2 49
The abuse of greatness is, when it disjoins Remorse from power *J. Cæsar* ii 1 18
The sufferance of our souls, the time's abuse . . . . . ii 1 115
Nature seems dead, and wicked dreams abuse The curtain'd sleep *Macb.* ii 1 50
As he is very potent with such spirts, Abuses me to damn me *Hamlet* ii 2 632
Or is it some abuse, and no such thing? . . . . . iv 7 51
Am I in France?—In your own kingdom, sir.—Do not abuse me . *Lear* iv 7 77
That thought abuses you . . . . . v 1 11
How, how?—Let's see.—After some time, to abuse Othello's ear That he is too familiar with his wife . . . . . *Othello* i 3 401
I'll have our Michael Cassio on the hip, Abuse him to the Moor in the rank garb—For I fear Cassio with my night-cap too. . . ii 1 315
I confess, it is my nature's plague To spy into abuses . . . iii 3 147
If you think other, Remove your thought; it doth abuse your bosom . iv 2 14
Dost thou in conscience think,—tell me, Emilia,—That there be women do abuse their husbands In such gross kind? . . . . iv 3 62
I am no strumpet; but of life as honest As you that thus abuse me . v 1 123
Do not abuse my master's bounty by The undoing of yourself *A. and C.* v 2 43
I have such a heart that both mine ears Must not in haste abuse *Cymbeline* i 6 131
Which portends—Unless my sins abuse my divination—Success . iv 2 351
With foul incest to abuse your soul . . . . . *Pericles* i 1 126
They do abuse the king that flatter him . . . . . i 2 38
Abused. My bed shall be abused, my coffers ransacked . *Mer. Wives* ii 2 306
My wife, that hath abused and dishonour'd me . *Com. of Errors* v 1 199
Hero hath been falsely accused, the prince and Claudio mightily abused *Much Ado* v 2 100
O, that a lady, of one man refused, Should of another therefore be abused! *M. N. Dream* ii 2 134
This civil war of wits were much better used On Navarre and his bookmen; for here 'tis abused . . . . . *L. L. Lost* ii 1 227
Though all the world could see, None could be so abused in sight as he *As Y. Like It* iii 5 80
Thus strangers may be haled and abused: O monstrous villain! *T. of Shr.* v 1 111
This lord, Who hath abused me, as he knows himself . *All's Well* v 3 299
I say, there was never man thus abused . . . *T. Night* iv 2 51
There was never man so notoriously abused . . . . iv 2 95
By my foes, sir, I profit in the knowledge of myself, and by my friends I am abused . . . . . v 1 22
He hath been most notoriously abused . . . . . v 1 388
You are abused and by some putter-on That will be damn'd for't *W. Tale* ii 1 141
The noble duke hath been too much abused . . . *Richard II.* ii 3 137
None of the French upbraided or abused in disdainful language *Hen. V.* iii 6 117
Cannot a plain man live and think no harm, But thus his simple truth must be abused? . . . . . *Richard III.* i 3 52
To hear the city Abused extremely, and to cry, 'That's witty!' *Hen. VIII.* Epil. 6
Let's be calm.—The people are abused; set on . . *Coriolanus* iii 1 58
Tell the traitor, in the high'st degree He hath abused your powers . v 6 86
Good king, to be so mightily abused! . . . . . *T. Andron.* ii 3 87
Poor soul, thy face is much abused with tears. . . *Rom. and Jul.* iv 1 29
The whole ear of Denmark Is by a forged process of my death Rankly abused . . . . . *Hamlet* i 5 38
Old fools are babes again; and must be used With checks as flatteries,—when they are seen abused . . . . . *Lear* i 3 20
Much more worse, To have her gentleman abused, assaulted . . ii 2 156
What they may incense him to, being apt To have his ear abused . . ii 4 310
O my follies! then Edgar was abused. Kind gods, forgive me that! . iii 7 91
O dear son Edgar, The food of thy abused father's wrath! . . iv 1 24
O you kind gods, Cure this great breach in his abused nature! . . iv 7 15
I am mightily abused. I should e'en die with pity, To see another thus iv 7 53
Is there not charms By which the property of youth and maidhood May be abused? . . . . . *Othello* i 1 174
Abused her delicate youth with drugs or minerals That weaken motion i 2 74
She is abused, stol'n from me, and corrupted By spells and medicines . i 3 60
Her delicate tenderness will find itself abused . . . . ii 1 235
I would not have your free and noble nature, Out of self-bounty, be abused iii 3 200
I am abused; and my relief Must be to loathe her . . . iii 3 267
'Tis better to be much abused Than but to know't a little . . iii 3 336
The Moor's abused by some most villanous knave . . . iv 2 139
He his high authority abused, And did deserve his change *Ant. and Cleo.* iii 6 33
You are abused Beyond the mark of thought . . . . iii 6 86
And by a gem of women, to be abused By One that looks on feeders iii 13 108
You are a great deal abused in too bold a persuasion . *Cymbeline* i 4 124
Why hast thou abused So many miles with a pretence? . . . iii 4 105
It cannot be But that my master is abused . . . . iii 4 123
Abuser. I therefore apprehend and do attach thee For an abuser of the world . . . . . *Othello* i 2 78
Abusing. An old abusing of God's patience and the king's English *M. W.* i 4 5
To draw forth your noble ancestry From the corruption of abusing times, Unto a lineal true-derived course . . . *Richard III.* iii 7 199
Abusing better men than they can be, Out of a foreign wisdom *Hen. VIII.* i 3 28
Abut. Now upon The leafy shelter that abuts against The island's side *Per.* v 1 51
Abutting. Whose high upreared and abutting fronts The perilous narrow ocean parts asunder . . . . . *Hen. V.* Prol. 21

Aby. Lest, to thy peril, thou aby it dear . . . . *M. N. Dream* iii 2 175
If thou dost intend Never so little show of love to her, Thou shalt aby it iii 2 335
Abysm. In the dark backward and abysm of time . . . *Tempest* i 2 50
And shot their fires Into the abysm of hell . . . *Ant. and Cleo.* iii 13 147
Academe. A little Academe, Still and contemplative in living art *L. L. L.* i 1 13
The academes From whence doth spring the true Promethean fire . iv 3 303
The arts, the academes, That show, contain and nourish all the world . iv 3 352
Accent. You find not the apostraphas, and so miss the accent . iv 2 123
Action and accent did they teach him there . . . . v 2 99
Throttle their practised accent in their fears . . . *M. N. Dream* v 1 97
Your accent is something finer than you could purchase in so removed a dwelling . . . . . . *As Y. Like It* iii 2 359
A terrible oath, with a swaggering accent sharply twanged off *T. Night* iii 4 197
The accent of his tongue affecteth him . . . . *K. John* i 1 86
Pardon me, That any accent breaking from thy tongue Should 'scape the true acquaintance of mine ear . . . . v 6 14
The heavy accent of thy moving tongue . . . *Richard II.* v 1 47
To pant, And breathe short-winded accents of new broils . 1 *Hen. IV.* i 1 3
Speaking thick, which nature made his blemish, Became the accents of the valiant . . . . 2 *Hen. IV.* ii 3 25
And return your mock In second accent of his ordnance . *Hen. V.* ii 4 126
I have a touch of your condition, Which cannot brook the accent of reproof . . . . *Richard III.* iv 4 158
Do not take His rougher accents for malicious sounds . *Coriolanus* iii 3 55
With an accent tuned in selfsame key Retorts to chiding fortune *Tr. and Cr.* i 3 53
The pox of such antic, lisping, affecting fantasticoes ; these new tuners of accents ! . . . . *Rom. and Jul.* ii 4 30
How many ages hence Shall this our lofty scene be acted over In states unborn and accents yet unknown . . . . *J. Cæsar* iii 1 113
Prophesying with accents terrible Of dire combustion . . *Macbeth* ii 3 62
Well spoken, with good accent and good discretion . . *Hamlet* ii 2 489
Neither having the accent of Christians, nor the gait of Christian . . iii 2 35
If but as well I other accents borrow, That can my speech defuse . *Lear* i 4 1
I am no flatterer : he that beguiled you in a plain accent was a plain knave ii 2 117
I'll call aloud.—Do, with like timorous accent and dire yell . *Othello* i 1 75
Accept. You should refuse to perform your father's will, if you should refuse to accept him . . . . . . *Mer. of Venice* i 2 101
His ring I do accept most thankfully : And so, I pray you, tell him . iv 2 9
So please your lordship to accept our duty.—With all my heart *T. of Shr.* Ind. 1 82
Accept of him, or else you do me wrong . . . . . ii 1 59
Pray, accept his service.—A thousand thanks . . . . ii 1 83
If you accept them, then their worth is great . . . . ii 1 102
If this be courtesy, sir, accept of it.—O sir, I do . . . iv 2 111
I dare my life lay down and will do't, sir, Please you to accept it *W. Tale* ii 3 131
Repose you for this night.—An offer, uncle, that we will accept *Rich. II.* ii 3 162
I would you would accept of grace and love . . 1 *Hen. IV.* iv 3 112
We will suddenly Pass our accept and peremptory answer . *Hen. V.* v 2 82
Accept this scroll, most gracious sovereign . . 1 *Hen. VI.* iii 1 149
And, lords, accept this hearty kind embrace . . . . iii 3 82
There is my pledge ; accept it, Somerset.—Nay, let it rest where it began iv 1 120
Wilt thou accept of ransom? yea, or no . . . . . v 3 79
Accept the title thou usurp'st, Of benefit proceeding from our king . v 4 151
I accept the combat willingly . . . . . 2 *Hen. VI.* i 3 216
I accept thy greeting. Art thou a messenger, or come of pleasure? . v 1 15
I accept her, for she well deserves it . . . . 3 *Hen. VI.* iii 3 249
Whether you accept our suit or no, Your brother's son shall never reign our king . . . . *Richard III.* iii 7 214
Call them again, my lord, and accept their suit . . . . iii 7 221
I cannot make you what amends I would, Therefore accept such kindness as I can . . . . iv 4 310
I'll bring you to the gates.—Accept distracted thanks . *Troi. and Cres.* v 2 189
The first conditions, which they did refuse And cannot now accept *Cor.* v 3 15
The gods bless you for your tidings ; next, Accept my thankfulness . v 4 62
The people will accept whom he admits . . . *T. Andron.* i 1 222
Love you the maid?—Ay, my good lord, and she accepts of it *T. of A.* i 1 135
A piece of painting, which I do beseech Your lordship to accept . i 1 156
Honour me so much As to advance this jewel ; accept it and wear it . i 2 176
I shall accept them fairly ; let the presents Be worthily entertain'd . i 2 190
I beg of you to know me, good my lord, To accept my grief . . iv 3 495
If you, born in these latter times, When wit's more ripe, accept my rhymes . . . . *Pericles* i Gower 12
Your grace is welcome to our town and us.—Which welcome we'll accept i 4 107
Acceptance. I leave him to your gracious acceptance *Mer. of Venice* iv 1 165
I would have ransack'd The pedlar's silken treasury and have pour'd it To her acceptance . . . . *W. Tale* iv 4 362
How did this offer seem received, my lord?—With good acceptance of his majesty . . . . *Hen. V.* i 1 83
In your fair minds let this acceptance take . . . . . Epil. 14
If he tell us his noble deeds, we must also tell him our noble acceptance of them . . . . *Coriolanus* ii 3 9
I greet thy love, Not with vain thanks, but with acceptance bounteous *Oth.* iii 3 470
Accepted. Unwillingly I left the ring, When nought would be accepted but the ring . . . . *Mer. of Venice* v 1 197
Take it advisedly.—It will not be accepted, on my life . 1 *Hen. IV.* v 1 115
Her presence Shall quite strike off all service I have done, In most accepted pain . . . . *Troi. and Cres.* iii 3 30
Access. Kept severely from resort of men, That no man hath access by day to her . . . . *T. G. of Ver.* iii 1 109
Upon this warrant shall you have access . . . . . iii 2 60
Under the colour of commending him, I have access my own love to prefer iv 2 4
Here is the sister of the man condemn'd Desires access to you *M. for M.* ii 2 19
One Isabel, a sister, desires access to you.—Teach her the way . ii 4 18
So please you, he is here at the door and importunes access to you *As Y. L.* i 1 97
We may yet again have access to our fair mistress . . *T. of Shrew* i 1 119
That none shall have access unto Bianca Till Katharine the curst have got a husband . . . . i 2 127
The youngest daughter whom you hearken for Her father keeps from all access of suitors . . . . i 2 261
Achieve the elder, set the younger free For our access . . . . i 2 269
I may have welcome 'mongst the rest that woo And free access . ii 1 98
Be not denied access, stand at her doors . . . *T. Night* i 4 16
To lock up honesty and honour from The access of gentle visitors *W. Tale* ii 2 11
She, The fairest I have yet beheld, desires access . . . . v 1 87
Who would be thence that has the benefit of access? . . . v 2 119
We are denied access unto his person . . . 2 *Hen. IV.* iv 1 78
If you cannot Bar his access to the king, never attempt Any thing on him *Hen. VIII.* iii 2 17
This varlet here,—this, who, like a block, hath denied my access *Coriol.* v 2 85
Being held a foe, he may not have access To breathe such vows as lovers use to swear . . . . *Rom. and Jul.* ii Prol. 9
Access. Make thick my blood ; Stop up the access and passage to remorse, That no compunctious visitings of nature Shake my fell purpose ! *Macbeth* i 5 45
I did repel his letters and denied His access to me . . . *Hamlet* ii 1 110
My suit to her Is, that she will to virtuous Desdemona Procure me some access . . . . *Othello* iii 1 38
May we not get access to her, my lord?—Faith, by no means *Pericles* ii 5 7
Accessary. I am your accessary ; and so, farewell . *All's Well* ii 1 35
To both their deaths thou shalt be accessary . . . *Richard III.* i 2 192
Accessible is none but Milford way . . . *Cymbeline* iii 2 84
Accidence. Ask him some questions in his accidence *Mer. Wives* iv 1 16
Accident. By accident most strange, bountiful Fortune, Now my dear lady, hath mine enemies Brought to this shore . . . *Tempest* i 2 178
Which to you shall seem probable, of every These happen'd accidents . v 1 250
The story of my life And the particular accidents gone by . . v 1 305
'Tis an accident that heaven provides ! Dispatch it presently *M. for Meas.* iv 3 81
This is an accident of hourly proof, Which I mistrusted not . *Much Ado* ii 1 188
Think no more of this night's accidents . . . . *M. N. Dream* iv 1 73
Yet doth this accident and flood of fortune So far exceed all instance *T. N.* iv 3 11
I tremble To think your father, by some accident, Should pass this way *W. T.* iv 4 19
But as the unthought-on accident is guilty To what we wildly do. . iv 4 549
'Tis not a visitation framed, but forced By need and accident . . v 1 92
And nothing pleaseth but rare accidents . . . 1 *Hen. IV.* i 2 231
Dismay not, princes, at this accident . . . 1 *Hen. VI.* iii 3 1
Spirits that admonish me And give me signs of future accidents . v 3 4
That none of you may live your natural age, But by some unlook'd accident cut off ! . . . . *Richard III.* i 3 214
As place, riches, favour, Prizes of accident as oft as merit *Troi. and Cres.* iii 3 83
Let these threats alone, Till accident or purpose bring you to't . iv 5 262
Romeo Hath had no notice of these accidents . . *Rom. and Jul.* v 2 26
Friar John Was stay'd by accident, and yesternight Return'd my letter back v 3 251
That he, as 'twere by accident, may here Affront Ophelia . *Hamlet* iii 1 30
Grief joys, joy grieves, on slender accident . . . . iii 2 209
Even his mother shall uncharge the practice And call it accident . iv 7 69
Delays as many As there are tongues, are hands, are accidents . iv 7 122
This accident is not unlike my dream : Belief of it oppresses me already *Oth.* i 1 143
Of moving accidents by flood and field, Of hair-breadth scapes i' the imminent deadly breach . . . . i 3 135
Whose solid virtue The shot of accident, nor dart of chance, Could neither graze nor pierce . . . . iv 1 278
Unless his abode be lingered here by some accident . . . iv 2 231
These bloody accidents must excuse my manners . . . . v 1 94
Thy precedent services are all But accidents unpurposed *Ant. and Cleo.* iv 14 84
It is great To do that thing that ends all other deeds ; Which shackles accidents and bolts up change . . . . v 2 6
All solemn things Should answer solemn accidents . . *Cymbeline* iv 2 192
Be not with mortal accidents opprest ; No care of yours it is . . v 4 99
Consider, sir, the chance of war : the day Was yours by accident . v 5 76
By accident, I had a feigned letter of my master's Then in my pocket . v 5 278
Accidental. Thy sin's not accidental, but a trade . *Meas. for Meas.* iii 1 149
Of your philosophy you make no use, If you give place to accidental evils *J. Cæsar* iv 3 146
Accidental judgements, casual slaughters, Of deaths put on by cunning *Hamlet* v 2 393
Accidentally. Which accidentally are met together *Com. of Errors* v 1 361
Which accidentally, or by the way of progression, hath miscarried *L. L. L.* iv 2 143
I am most fortunate, thus accidentally to encounter you *Coriolanus* iv 3 40
Accite. What accites your most worshipful thought to think so? 2 *Hen. IV.* ii 2 64
We will accite, As I before remember'd, all our state . . . v 2 141
Accited. He by the senate is accited home From weary wars *T. Andron.* i 1 27
Acclamation. You shout me forth In acclamations hyperbolical *Coriol.* i 9 51
Accommodate. The safer sense will ne'er accommodate His master *Lear* iv 6 81
Accommodated. A soldier is better accommodated than with a wife. . . . Better accommodated ! it is good ; yea, indeed, is it 2 *Hen. IV.* iii 2 72
Accommodated ! it comes of 'accommodo' ; very good ; a good phrase . iii 2 77
Accommodated ; that is, when a man is, as they say, accommodated ; or when a man is, being, whereby a' may be thought to be accommodated iii 2 84
Accommodated by the place, more charming With their own nobleness *Cymbeline* v 3 32
Accommodation. All the accommodations that thou bear'st Are nursed by baseness . . . . *Meas. for Meas.* iii 1 14
Such accommodation and besort As levels with her breeding *Othello* i 3 239
Accommodo. Accommodated ! it comes of 'accommodo' 2 *Hen. IV.* iii 2 78
Accompanied. I do not only marvel where thou spendest thy time, but also how thou art accompanied . . . . . . 1 *Hen. IV.* ii 4 440
And how accompanied?—I do not know . . . 2 *Hen. IV.* iv 4 15
He dines in London.—And how accompanied? canst thou tell that? . iv 4 52
You shall find me well accompanied With reverend fathers *Richard III.* iii 5 99
Accompanied with other Learned and reverend fathers . *Hen. VIII.* iii 1 25
He's coming.—How accompanied?—With old Menenius *Coriolanus* iii 3 6
And wander'd hither to an obscure plot, Accompanied but with a barbarous Moor . . . . *T. Andron.* ii 3 78
Accompany. Fresh days of love Accompany your hearts ! *M. N. Dream* v 1 30
Let me be thus bold with you To give you over at this first encounter, Unless you will accompany me thither . . . *T. of Shrew* i 2 106
I fear, the angle that plucks our son thither. Thou shalt accompany us to the place . . . . *W. Tale* iv 2 53
Such barren pleasures, rude society, As thou art match'd withal and grafted to, Accompany the greatness of thy blood . 1 *Hen. IV.* iii 2 16
You have ended my business, and I will merrily accompany you home *Cor.* iv 3 41
Lords, accompany Your noble emperor and his lovely bride *T. Andron.* i 1 333
He must be buried with his brethren.—And shall, or him we will accompany . . . . i 1 358
That which should accompany old age, As honour, love, obedience, troops of friends, I must not look to have . . . *Macbeth* v 3 24
Accompanying. Not one accompanying his declining foot *T. of Athens* i 1 88
Accomplice. Success unto our valiant general, And happiness to his accomplices ! . . . . 1 *Hen. VI.* v 2 9
Accomplish. More unlikely Than to accomplish twenty golden crowns ! 3 *Hen. VI.* iii 2 152
Let him choose Out of my files, his projects to accomplish, My best and freshest men . . . . *Coriolanus* v 6 34
So must you resolve, That what you cannot as you would achieve, You must perforce accomplish as you may . . . *T. Andron.* ii 1 107
Accomplished. Valiant, wise, remorseful, well accomplish'd *T. G. of V.* iv 3 13
That they shall think we are accomplished With that we lack *M. of V.* iii 4 61
Such as he hath observed in noble ladies Unto their lords, by them accomplished . . . . *T. of Shrew* Ind. 1 112
Which holy undertaking with most austere sanctimony she accomplished *All's Well* iv 3 60

Accomplished. Most excellent accomplished lady, the heavens rain odours on you! *T. Night* iii 1 95
Even so look'd he, Accomplish'd with the number of thy hours *Rich. II.* ii 1 177
All the number of his fair demands Shall be accomplish'd iii 3 124
A cunning thief, or a that way accomplished courtier *Cymbeline* i 4 101
Italy contains none so accomplished a courtier i 4 103
The vision . . at this instant Is full accomplish'd v 5 470
Accomplishing. The armourers, accomplishing the knights *Hen. V.* iv Prol. 12
Accomplishment. Turning the accomplishment of many years Into an hour-glass i Prol. 30
Accompt. Our compell'd sins Stand more for number than for accompt *Meas. for Meas.* ii 4 58
Our duty is so rich, so infinite, That we may do it still without accompt *L. L. Lost* v 2 200
Let us, ciphers to this great accompt, On your imaginary forces work *Hen. V.* Prol. 17
He can write and read and cast accompt.—O monstrous! *2 Hen. VI.* iv 2 93
Accord. Then let your will attend on their accords *Com. of Errors* ii 1 25
My heart accords thereto, And yet a thousand times it answers 'no' *T. G. of V.* i 3 90
For your father's remembrance, be at accord *As Y. Like It* i 1 67
You to his love must accord, Or have a woman to your lord v 4 139
'Gamut' I am, the ground of all accord *T. of Shrew* iii 1 73
On mine own accord I'll off; But first I'll do my errand *W. Tale* ii 3 63
How apt our love was to accord To furnish him with all appertinents *Hen. V.* ii 2 86
You must buy that peace With full accord to all our just demands v 2 71
Plant neighbourhood and Christian-like accord In their sweet bosoms v 2 381
This merry inclination Accords not with the sadness of my suit *3 Hen. VI.* iii 2 77
Good arms, strong joints, true swords; and, Jove's accord *Troi. and Cres.* i 3 238
This gentle and unforced accord of Hamlet Sits smiling to my heart *Hamlet* i 2 123
Accordant. If he found her accordant, he meant to take the present time by the top *Much Ado* i 2 14
Accordeth. My heart accordeth with my tongue *2 Hen. VI.* iii 1 269
According. The ort is, according to our meaning, 'resolutely' *M. Wives* i 1 262
I'll show my mind According to my shallow simple skill *T. G. of Ver.* i 2 8
Welcome him then according to his worth ii 4 83
Is your countryman According to our proclamation gone? iii 2 12
According to your ladyship's impose, I am thus early come iv 3 8
See this be done, And sent according to command *Meas. for Meas.* iv 3 84
That apprehends no further than this world, And squarest thy life according v 1 487
'Faith, my lord, I spoke it but according to the trick v 1 509
Not being able to buy out his life According to the statute *Com. of Errors* i 2 6
According to our law Immediately provided in that case *M. N. Dream* i 1 44
Call them generally, man by man, according to the scrip i 2 3
So every one according to his cue iii 1 78
According to my description, level at my affection *Mer. of Venice* i 2 41
According to Fates and Destinies and such odd sayings ii 2 65
Bid me tear the bond.—When it is paid according to the tenour iv 1 235
According as marriage binds and blood breaks *As Y. Like It* v 4 59
According to the fool's bolt, sir, and such dulcet diseases v 4 67
According to the measure of their states v 4 181
Make it orderly and well, According to the fashion and the time *T. of Shrew* iv 3 95
Since fate, against thy better disposition, Hath made thy person for the thrower-out Of my poor babe, according to thine oath *W. Tale* iii 3 30
According to the fair play of the world, Let me have audience *K. John* v 2 118
Hast thou, according to thy oath and band, Brought hither Henry Hereford? *Richard II* i 1 2
According to our law, Depose him in the justice of his cause i 3 29
Shall we divide our right According to our threefold order ta'en? *1 Hen. IV.* iii 1 71
As we hear you do reform yourselves, We will, according to your strengths and qualities, Give you advancement *2 Hen. IV.* v 5 73
Desert and merit According to the weight and worthiness *Hen. V.* ii 2 35
The mines is not according to the disciplines of the war iii 2 63
In sequel all, According to their firm proposed natures v 2 362
According as your ladyship desired, By message craved *1 Hen. VI.* ii 3 12
To be used according to your state.—That's bad enough *2 Hen. VI.* ii 4 95
Is all things well, According as I gave directions? iii 2 12
Had he match'd according to his state, He might have kept that glory to this day *3 Hen. VI.* ii 2 152
Not according to the prayer of the people *Coriolanus* ii 1 4
Within her scope of choice Lies my consent and fair according voice *Rom. and Jul.* i 2 19
Clap him and hiss him, according as he pleased and displeased them *J. Cæsar* i 2 261
According to the which, thou shalt discourse To young Octavius iii 1 295
According to his virtue let us use him, With all respect v 5 76
According to the gift which bounteous nature Hath in him closed *Macbeth* iii 1 98
Shall take upon's what else remains to do, According to our order v 6 6
According to the phrase or the addition Of man and country *Hamlet* ii 1 47
I will use them according to their desert ii 2 552
I love your majesty According to my bond; nor more nor less *Lear* i 1 95
We must receive him According to the honour of his sender *Cymbeline* ii 3 63
Accordingly. That I may minister To them accordingly *Meas. for Meas.* ii 3 8
When you have seen more and heard more, proceed accordingly *M. Ado* iii 2 125
He is very great in knowledge and accordingly valiant *All's Well* ii 5 9
To make a faithless error in your ears: Which trust accordingly *K. John* ii 1 231
Accordingly You tread upon my patience *1 Hen. IV.* i 3 3
You perceive my mind?—I do, my lord, and mean accordingly *1 Hen. VI.* ii 2 60
Keep decorum, and fortune him accordingly! *Ant. and Cleo.* i 2 78
We may the number of the ships behold, And so proceed accordingly iii 9 4
Reflect upon him accordingly, as you value your trust *Cymbeline* i 6 24
Accost, Sir Andrew, accost.—What's that?—My niece's chambermaid *T. N.* i 3 52
Good Mistress Accost, I desire better acquaintance.—My name is Mary, sir.—Good Mistress Mary Accost i 3 55
'Accost' is front her, board her, woo her, assail her i 3 59
Is that the meaning of 'accost'? i 3 63
Accosted. You should then have accosted her; and with some excellent jests, fire-new from the mint iii 2 23
Accosting. O, these encounterers, so glib of tongue, That give accosting welcome ere it comes! *Troi. and Cres.* iv 5 59
Account. How esteemest thou me? I account of her beauty *T. G. of Ver.* ii 1 66
To make an account of her life to a clod of wayward marl *Much Ado* ii 1 65
By this hand, Claudio shall render me a dear account iv 1 338
That only to stand high in your account, I might in virtues, beauties, livings, friends, Exceed account *Mer. of Venice* iii 2 157
Am satisfied And therein do account myself well paid iv 1 417
If from me he have wholesome beverage, Account me not your servant *W. Tale* i 2 347
Their speed Hath been beyond account ii 3 198
My account I well may give, And in the stocks avouch it iv 3 21

Account. 'Tis strange to think how much King John hath lost In this which he accounts so clearly won *K. John* iii 4 122
O, when the last account 'twixt heaven and earth Is to be made! iv 2 216
Was in my debt Upon remainder of a dear account *Richard II.* i 1 130
Call him to so strict account, That he shall render every glory up *1 Hen. IV.* iii 2 149
By which account, Our business valued, some twelve days hence Our general forces at Bridgenorth shall meet iii 2 176
You were in place and in account Nothing so strong and fortunate as I v 1 37
I have a truant been to chivalry; And so I hear he doth account me too v 1 95
And summ'd the account of chance, before you said, 'Let us make head' *2 Hen. IV.* i 1 167
Great is the rumour of this dreadful knight, And his achievements of no less account *1 Hen. VI.* ii 3 8
By this account then Margaret may win him; For she's a woman to be pitied much *3 Hen. VI.* iii 1 35
I'll make my heaven to dream upon the crown, And, whiles I live, to account this world but hell iii 2 169
The princes both make high account of you; For they account his head upon the bridge *Richard III.* iii 2 71
Our battalion trebles that account: Besides, the king's name is a tower of strength v 3 11
O Thou, whose captain I account myself, Look on my forces with a gracious eye! v 3 108
The account Of all that world of wealth I have drawn together *Hen. VIII.* iii 2 210
What he cannot help in his nature, you account a vice in him *Coriolanus* i 1 43
Account me the more virtuous that I have not been common in my love ii 3 100
'Tis a condition they account gentle ii 3 104
When he shall come to his account, he knows not What I can urge iv 7 18
That which shall break his neck or hazard mine, Whene'er we come to our account iv 7 26
Say I account of them As jewels purchased at an easy price *T. Andron.* iii 1 198
O dear account! my life is my foe's debt *Rom. and Jul.* i 5 120
About his shelves A beggarly account of empty boxes v 1 45
Takes no account How things go from him, nor resumes no care *T. of A.* ii 2 3
Do it then, that we may account thee a whore-master and a knave ii 2 110
At many times I brought in my accounts, Laid them before you ii 2 142
In some sort, these wants of mine are crown'd, That I account them blessings ii 2 191
From this time Such I account thy love *Macbeth* i 7 39
What need we fear who knows it, when none can call our power to account? v 1 43
Sent to my account With all my imperfections on my head *Hamlet* i 5 78
Who yet is no dearer in my account *Lear* i 1 21
They jump not on a just account *Othello* i 3 5
In himself, 'tis much; In you, which I account his beyond all talents, Whilst I am bound to wonder, I am bound To pity too *Cymbeline* i 6 80
But custom what they did begin Was with long use account no sin *Per.* i Gower 30
He that otherwise accounts of me, This sword shall prove he's honour's enemy ii 5 63
Accountant. Peradventure I stand accountant for as great a sin *Othello* ii 1 302
His offence is so, as it appears, Accountant to the law *Meas. for Meas.* ii 4 86
Accounted. Your honour is accounted a merciful man ii 2 203
Now mercy goes to kill, And shooting well is then accounted ill *L. L. Lost* iv 1 25
Was yet of many accounted beautiful *T. Night* ii 1 27
And if thou be not then created York, I will not live to be accounted Warwick *1 Hen. VI.* ii 4 120
We are accounted poor citizens, the patricians good *Coriolanus* i 1 15
To do harm Is often laudable, to do good sometime Accounted dangerous folly *Macbeth* iv 2 77
And was accounted a good actor.—What did you enact? *Hamlet* iii 2 105
Accountest. If thou account'st it shame, lay it on me *T. of Shrew* iv 3 183
Accoutred. When we are both accoutred like young men, I'll prove the prettier fellow *Mer. of Venice* iii 4 63
Accoutred as I was, I plunged in And bade him follow *J. Cæsar* i 2 105
Accoutrement. In all the accoutrement, complement, and ceremony of it *Mer. Wives* iv 2 5
You are rather point-device in your accoutrements *As Y. Like It* iii 2 402
Could I repair what she will wear in me, As I can change these poor accoutrements *T. of Shrew* iii 2 121
Not alone in habit and device, Exterior form, outward accoutrement *K. John* i 1 211
Accrue. I shall sutler be Unto the camp, and profits will accrue *Hen. V.* ii 1 117
Accumulate. On horror's head horrors accumulate *Othello* iii 3 370
Accumulated. What piles of wealth hath he accumulated! *Hen. VIII.* iii 2 107
Accumulation. For quick accumulation of renown, Which he achieved by the minute, lost his favour *Ant. and Cleo.* iii 1 19
Accursed. I am accursed to rob in that thief's company *1 Hen. IV.* ii 2 10
Alack, for lesser knowledge! how accursed In being so blest! *W. Tale* ii 1 38
Most accursed am I To be by oath enjoin'd to this iii 3 52
O thoughts of men accursed! Past and to come seems best *2 Hen. IV.* i 3 107
Gentlemen in England now a-bed Shall think themselves accursed they were not here *Hen. V.* iv 3 65
Accursed tower! accursed fatal hand That hath contrived this woful tragedy! *1 Hen. VI.* i 4 76
Of all base passions, fear is most accursed v 2 18
Consume to ashes, Thou foul accursed minister of hell! v 4 93
Accursed be he that seeks to make them foes! *3 Hen. VI.* i 1 205
As for the brat of this accursed duke, Whose father slew my father, he shall die i 3 4
And till I root out their accursed line And leave not one alive, I live in hell i 3 32
Thou art the cause, and most accursed effect *Richard III.* i 2 120
Accursed and unquiet wrangling days, How many of you have mine eyes beheld! ii 4 55
O ill-dispersing wind of misery! O my accursed womb, the bed of death! iv 1 54
'Be thou,' quoth I, 'accursed, For making me, so young, so old a widow!' iv 1 72
O, she that might have intercepted thee, By strangling thee in her accursed womb iv 4 138
This fell fault of my accursed sons, Accursed, if the fault be proved *T. A.* ii 3 290
What accursed hand Hath made thee handless in thy father's sight? iii 1 66
Accursed the offspring of so foul a fiend! v 2 79
This barbarous Moor, This ravenous tiger, this accursed devil v 3 5
Die, frantic wretch, for this accursed deed! v 3 64
Accursed, unhappy, wretched, hateful day! *Rom. and Jul.* iv 5 43
That time serves still.—The more accursed thou, that still omitt'st it *T. of A.* i 1 268
Bless'd, to be most accursed, Rich, only to be wretched iv 2 42
Bless the accursed, Make the hoar leprosy adored iv 3 34
That a swift blessing May soon return to this our suffering country Under a hand accursed! *Macbeth* iii 6 49
Let this pernicious hour Stand aye accursed in the calendar! iv 1 134
By his own interdiction stands accursed, And does blaspheme his breed iv 3 107
Accursed be that tongue that tells me so, For it hath cow'd my better part of man! v 8 17

Accursed. It was in Rome,—accursed The mansion where!—'twas at a feast . . . . . *Cymbeline* v 5 154
Accurst. O time most accurst, 'Mongst all foes that a friend should be the worst! . . . . . *T. G. of Ver.* v 4 71
There is scarce truth enough alive to make societies secure; but security enough to make fellowships accurst *Meas. for Meas.* iii 2 242
In second husband let me be accurst! None wed the second but who kill'd the first . . . . . *Hamlet* iii 2 189
Accusation. My place i' the state Will so your accusation overweigh, That you shall stifle in your own report *Meas. for Meas.* ii 4 157
As the matter now stands, he will avoid your accusation . . . iii 1 201
Be you constant in the accusation, and my cunning shall not shame me *Much Ado* ii 2 55
Then shall he mourn, If ever love had interest in his liver, And wish he had not so accused her, No, though he thought his accusation true iv 1 235
With public accusation, uncovered slander, unmitigated rancour . iv 1 307
The lady is dead upon mine and my master's false accusation . v 1 249
Not able to produce more accusation Than your own weak-hinged fancy *W. Tale* ii 3 118
What I am to say must be but that Which contradicts my accusation iii 2 24
Innocence shall make False accusation blush and tyranny Tremble . iii 2 32
Read These accusations and these grievous crimes Committed by your person . . . . . *Richard II.* iv 1 223
Let not his report Come current for an accusation . . 1 *Hen. IV.* i 3 68
Engenders thunder in his breast And makes him roar these accusations forth . . . . . 1 *Hen. VI.* iii 1 40
Do not cast away an honest man for a villain's accusation . 2 *Hen. VI.* i 3 206
Came to the bar; where to his accusations He pleaded still not guilty *Hen. VIII.* ii 1 12
We come not by the way of accusation, to taint that honour . iii 1 54
I need not be barren of accusations; he hath faults, with surplus *Coriol.* i 1 46
The accusation Which they have often made . . . . ii 1 127
Prepared With accusations, as I hear, more strong Than are upon you yet . . . . . iii 2 140
The people know it; and have now received His accusations *Ant. and Cleo.* iii 6 23
Accusative. What is your accusative case?—Accusativo, hinc *M. Wives* iv 1 45
Accusativo, hinc.—I pray you, have your remembrance . . iv 1 47
Accusativo, hung, hang, hog . . . . . . iv 1 49
Accuse. These that accuse him in his intent towards our wives are a yoke of his discarded men . . . . . ii 1 180
And to the head of Angelo Accuse him home and home *Meas. for Meas.* iv 3 148
I would say the truth; but to accuse him so, That is your part . iv 6 2
Accuses him of fornication, In self-same manner doth accuse my husband v 1 196
Put your trial in the villain's mouth Which here you come to accuse v 1 305
Thou hast suborn'd these women To accuse this worthy man . . v 1 309
What man is he you are accused of?—They know that do accuse me *Much Ado* iv 1 179
I charge you, in the prince's name, accuse these men . . iv 2 40
To speak on the part of virginity, is to accuse your mothers *All's Well* i 1 149
May, though they cannot praise us, as little accuse us . *W. Tale* i 1 17
The queen is spotless I' the eyes of heaven and to you; I mean, In this which you accuse her . . . . . ii 1 133
Let not my cold words here accuse my zeal . . *Richard II.* i 1 47
Get before him to the king, And beg thy pardon ere he do accuse thee v 2 113
If thou canst accuse, Or aught intend'st to lay unto my charge 1 *Hen. VI.* iii 1 3
Doth any one accuse York for a traitor? . . 2 *Hen. VI.* i 3 182
This is the man that doth accuse his master . . . i 3 185
Who can accuse me? wherein am I guilty? . . . . iii 1 103
By false accuse doth level at my life . . . . iii 1 160
By such despair, I should accuse myself . . *Richard III.* i 2 85
What is my offence? Where are the evidence that do accuse me? . i 4 188
The queen is obstinate, Stubborn to justice, apt to accuse it, and Disdainful to be tried by 't . . . *Hen. VIII.* ii 4 122
You are a counsellor, And, by that virtue, no man dare accuse you v 3 50
Many dare accuse you boldly, More than, I fear, you are provided for v 3 56
Let them accuse me by invention, I Will answer in mine honour *Coriol.* iii 2 143
Him I accuse The city ports by this hath enter'd and Intends to appear v 6 5
Plot the way to do it, Accuse some innocent and forswear myself *T. A.* v 1 130
I could accuse me of such things that it were better my mother had not borne me . . . . . *Hamlet* iii 1 124
These hairs, which thou dost ravish from my chin, Will quicken, and accuse thee . . . . . *Lear* iii 7 39
Accuses him of letters he had formerly wrote to Pompey *Ant. and Cleo.* iii 5 10
Who does he accuse?—Cæsar . . . . . iii 6 23
I do accuse myself so sorely, That I will joy no more . . iv 6 19
I care not for you, And am so near the lack of charity—To accuse myself—I hate you . . . . *Cymbeline* ii 3 115
Iachimo, Thou didst accuse him of incontinency . . . iii 4 49
How dare you ghosts Accuse the thunderer, whose bolt, you know, Sky-planted batters all rebelling coasts? . . . . v 4 95
The gods have done their part in you.—I accuse them not *Pericles* iv 2 76
Accused. Who, if she had been a woman cardinally given, might have been accused in fornication . . *Meas. for Meas.* ii 1 82
First, hath this woman Most wrongfully accused your substitute . v 1 140
To justify this worthy nobleman, So vulgarly and personally accused v 1 160
What man is he you are accused of?—They know that do accuse me *Much Ado* iv 1 178
Dying, as it must be so maintain'd, Upon the instant that she was accused . . . . . . iv 1 217
Then shall he mourn, If ever love had interest in his liver, And wish he had not so accused her, No, though he thought his accusation true iv 1 234
Was in this manner accused, in this very manner refused . v 2 64
It is proved my Lady Hero hath been falsely accused . . v 2 99
Did I not tell you she was innocent?—So are the prince and Claudio, who accused her . . . . . . v 4 2
Be thou damn'd, inexecrable dog! And for thy life let justice be accused *Mer. of Venice* iv 1 129
Wherefore hast thou accused him all this while?—Because he's guilty, and he is not guilty . . . . *All's Well* v 3 289
As she hath Been publicly accused, so shall she have A just and open trial . . . . . *W. Tale* ii 3 204
Thou art here accused and arraigned of high treason . . iii 2 13
For Polixenes, With whom I am accused, I do confess I loved him iii 2 63
Ourselves will hear The accuser and the accused freely speak *Richard II.* i 1 17
Here is a man accused of treason: Pray God the Duke of York excuse himself! . . . . . 2 *Hen. VI.* i 3 180
God is my witness, I am falsely accused by the villain . i 3 192
Who being accused a crafty murderer, His guilt should be but idly posted . . . . . . iii 1 254
If she be accused in true report, Bear with her weakness *Richard III.* i 3 27
Accused. Might better wear their heads Than some that have accused them wear their hats . . . . . *Richard III.* iii 2 95
All these accused him strongly; which he fain Would have flung from him . . . . . . *Hen. VIII.* ii 1 24
Confess yourselves wondrous malicious, Or be accused of folly *Coriolanus* i 1 92
All the body's members Rebell'd against the belly, thus accused it i 1 100
Peradventure thou wert accused by the ass . *T. of Athens* iv 3 334
Accuser. You must call forth the watch that are their accusers *M. Ado* iv 2 37
Ourselves will hear The accuser and the accused freely speak *Richard II.* i 1 17
Hang me, if ever I spake the words. My accuser is my 'prentice 2 *Hen. VI.* i 3 201
The envious slanders of her false accusers . . *Richard III.* i 3 26
I am richer than my base accusers, That never knew what truth meant *Hen. VIII.* ii 1 104
I should have ta'en some pains to bring together Yourself and your accusers . . . . . . v 1 120
In this case of justice, my accusers, Be what they will, may stand forth v 3 46
Was deliberate, Not rash like his accusers . . *Coriolanus* i 1 133
Take that of me, . . who have the power To seal the accuser's lips *Lear* iv 6 174
Adultery? Wherefore write you not What monster 's her accuser? *Cymb.* iii 2 2
Accuseth. A man cannot steal, but it [conscience] accuseth him *Rich. III.* i 4 139
Accusing. He had received a thousand ducats of Don John for accusing the Lady Hero wrongfully . . . *Much Ado* iv 2 50
Accusing it, I put it on my head, To try with it, as with an enemy 2 *Hen. IV.* iv 5 166
Accustomed. Rather than she will bate one breath of her accustomed crossness . . . . . *Much Ado* ii 3 184
Whose heart the accustom'd sight of death makes hard . *As Y. Like It* iii 5 4
Quick appearance argues proof Of your accustom'd diligence 1 *Hen. VI.* v 3 9
His majesty Will soon recover his accustom'd health *Richard III.* i 3 2
I hold an old accustom'd feast, Whereto I have invited many a guest *Rom. and Jul.* i 2 20
It is an accustomed action with her, to seem thus washing her hands *Macb.* v 1 32
Ace. But an ace, for him; for he is but one.—Less than an ace *M. N. D.* v 1 312
The most patient man in loss, the most coldest that ever turned up ace *Cymbeline* ii 3 3
Ache. Rack thee with old cramps, Fill all thy bones with aches *Tempest* i 2 370
I can go no further, sir; My old bones ache . . . iii 3 2
That age, ache, penury, and imprisonment Can lay on nature *M. for Meas.* iii 1 130
Knock the door hard.—Let him knock till it ache . *Com of Errors* iii 1 58
Charm ache with air and agony with words . . *Much Ado* v 1 26
When your head did but ache, I knit my handkercher about your brows, The best I had, a princess wrought it me . . *K. John* iv 1 41
A fellow that never had the ache in his shoulders . 2 *Hen. IV.* iv 1 93
You great fellow, Stand close up, or I'll make your head ache *Hen. VIII.* v 4 92
I have a rheum in mine eyes too, and such an ache in my bones *Troi. and Cres.* v 3 105
My soul aches To know, when two authorities are up, Neither supreme, how soon confusion May enter 'twixt the gap of both *Coriolanus* iii 1 108
Fie, how my bones ache! what a jaunt have I had! *Rom. and Jul.* ii 5 26
Lord, how my head aches! what a head have I! It beats as it would fall in twenty pieces . . . . . ii 5 49
Aches contract and starve your supple joints! . . *T. of Athens* i 1 257
My wounds ache at you.—Do you dare our anger? . . . iii 5 96
Their aches, losses, Their pangs of love . . . . v 1 202
Did these bones cost no more the breeding, but to play at loggats with 'em? mine ache to think on 't . . . . *Hamlet* v 1 101
For let our finger ache, and it indues Our other healthful members even to that sense Of pain . . . . *Othello* iii 4 146
Who art so lovely fair and smell'st so sweet That the sense aches at thee . . . . . . iv 2 69
Acheron. With drooping fog as black as Acheron . . *M. N. Dream* iii 2 357
I'll dive into the burning lake below, And pull her out of Acheron *T. A.* iv 3 44
Get you gone, And at the pit of Acheron Meet me i' the morning *Macbeth* iii 5 15
Achieve. I perish, Tranio, If I achieve not this young modest girl *T. of Shr.* i 1 161
If you love the maid, Bend thoughts and wits to achieve her . i 1 184
Let me be a slave, to achieve that maid . . . i 1 224
Achieve the elder, set the younger free For our access . . i 2 268
She derives her honesty and achieves her goodness . *All's Well* i 1 52
Some achieve greatness and some have greatness thrust upon 'em *T. Night* ii 5 157
Bid them achieve me and then sell my bones . . *Hen. V.* iv 3 91
To achieve The silver livery of advised age . . 2 *Hen. VI.* v 2 46
Fights dragon-like, and does achieve as soon As draw his sword *Coriolanus* iv 7 23
A thousand deaths Would I propose to achieve her whom I love *T. Andron.* ii 1 80
That what you cannot as you would achieve, You must perforce accomplish as you may . . . . . ii 1 106
Achieved. Experience is by industry achieved . . *T. G. of Ver.* i 3 22
To have her love, provided that your fortune Achieved her mistress *Mer. of Ven.* iii 2 210
By virtue specially to be achieved . . . *T. of Shrew* i 1 20
There is no sure foundation set on blood, No certain life achieved by others' death . . . . . *K. John* iv 2 105
Basely yielded upon compromise That which his noble ancestors achieved with blows . . . . . *Richard II.* ii 1 254
And thou with all pleased, that hast all achieved! . . . iv 1 217
Which they shall have no sooner achieved, but we'll set upon them 1 *Hen. IV.* i 2 193
His sword; By which the world's best garden he achieved *Hen. V.* Epil. 7
Of all The treasure in this field achieved and city, We render you the tenth . . . . . . *Coriolanus* i 9 33
He hath achieved a maid That paragons description and wild fame *Othello* ii 1 61
For quick accumulation of renown, Which he achieved by the minute, lost his favour . . . . *Ant. and Cleo.* iii 1 20
Where were you bred? And how achieved you these endowments? *Pericles* v 1 117
Achievement. All the soil of the achievement goes With me into the earth . . . . . . 2 *Hen. IV.* iv 5 190
He'll drop his heart into the sink of fear And for achievement offer us his ransom . . . . . *Hen. V.* iii 5 60
Great is the rumour of this dreadful knight, And his achievements of no less account . . . . 1 *Hen. VI.* ii 3 8
Achievement is command; ungain'd, beseech . *Troi. and Cres.* i 2 319
Achievements, plots, orders, preventions, Excitements to the field . i 3 181
How my achievements mock me! . . . . . iv 2 71
It takes From our achievements, though perform'd at height, the pith and marrow of our attribute . . . . *Hamlet* i 4 21
Achiever. A victory is twice itself when the achiever brings home full numbers . . . . . . *Much Ado* i 1 8
Achilles. Hide thy head, Achilles: here comes Hector in arms *L. L. Lost* v 2 635
Like to Achilles' spear, Is able with the change to kill and cure 2 *Hen. VI.* v 1 100

Achilles. There is among the Greeks Achilles, a better man than Troilus.—Achilles! a drayman, a porter, a very camel . . *Troi. and Cres.* i 2 268
The great Achilles, . . . The sinew and the forehand of our host . . i 3 142
The large Achilles, on his press'd bed lolling, from his deep chest laughs out a loud applause . . . . i 3 162
Yet God Achilles still cries, 'Excellent!' . . . . i 3 169
Bears his head In such a rein, in full as proud a place As broad Achilles i 3 190
Achilles' horse Makes many Thetis' sons . . . . . . i 3 211
With surety stronger than Achilles' arm 'Fore all the Greekish heads . i 3 220
Achilles shall have word of this intent . . . . . . i 3 306
The seeded pride That hath to this maturity blown up In rank Achilles . i 3 318
However it is spread in general name, Relates in purpose only to Achilles i 3 323
But that Achilles, were his brain as barren As banks of Libya,—though, Apollo knows, 'Tis dry enough,—will . . . find Hector's purpose . i 3 327
Whom may you else oppose, That can from Hector bring his honour off, If not Achilles? . . . . i 3 335
Therefore 'tis meet Achilles meet not Hector . . . . . i 3 358
Do not consent That ever Hector and Achilles meet . . . . i 3 363
What glory our Achilles shares from Hector, Were he not proud, we all should share with him. . . . . i 3 367
Our project's life this shape of sense assumes: Ajax employ'd plucks down Achilles' plumes. . . . . i 3 386
Thou grumblest and railest every hour on Achilles . . . . ii 1 36
This lord, Achilles, Ajax, who wears his wit in his belly and his guts in his head . . . . ii 1 79
I will hold my peace when Achilles' brach bids me, shall I? . . . ii 1 125
Then there's Achilles, a rare enginer! . . . . ii 3 8
Where's Achilles?—What, art thou devout? wast thou in prayer? . . ii 3 37
Come, what's Agamemnon?—Thy commander, Achilles. Then tell me, Patroclus, what's Achilles? . . . . ii 3 47
Agamemnon commands Achilles; Achilles is my lord . . . . ii 3 56
Achilles is a fool; Thersites is a fool, and, as aforesaid, Patroclus is a fool . . . . ii 3 63
Agamemnon is a fool to offer to command Achilles; Achilles is a fool to be commanded of Agamemnon . . . . ii 3 68
Where is Achilles?—Within his tent; but ill disposed . . . . ii 3 83
Achilles hath inveigled his fool from him. . . . . . . ii 3 99
Here comes Patroclus.—No Achilles with him. . . . . . ii 3 112
Achilles bids me say, he is much sorry . . . . ii 3 116
Achilles will not to the field to-morrow.—What's his excuse? . . . ii 3 172
'Twixt his mental and his active parts Kingdom'd Achilles in commotion rages. . . . . ii 3 185
We'll consecrate the steps that Ajax makes When they go from Achilles ii 3 194
Nor, by my will, assubjugate his merit, As amply titled as Achilles is, By going to Achilles . . . . ii 3 203
Jupiter forbid, And say in thunder, 'Achilles go to him' . . . ii 3 209
You must prepare to fight without Achilles . . . . . . ii 3 238
He is not emulous, as Achilles is.—Know the whole world, he is as valiant ii 3 242
There is no tarrying here; the hart Achilles Keeps thicket . . . ii 3 269
Let Achilles sleep: Light boats sail swift, though greater hulks draw deep ii 3 276
Achilles stands i' the entrance of his tent . . . . . . iii 3 38
What says Achilles? would he aught with us? . . . . . iii 3 57
What mean these fellows? Know they not Achilles? . . . . . iii 3 70
They were used to bend, To send their smiles before them to Achilles iii 3 72
'Tis known, Achilles, that you are in love With one of Priam's daughters iii 3 193
And better would it fit Achilles much To throw down Hector than Polyxena iii 3 207
Greekish girls shall tripping sing, 'Great Hector's sister did Achilles win' iii 3 212
To this effect, Achilles, have I moved you . . . . . . iii 3 216
Though the great bulk Achilles be thy guard, I'll cut thy throat . . iv 4 130
I'll take that winter from your lips, fair lady: Achilles bids you welcome iv 5 25
If not Achilles, sir, What is your name?—If not Achilles, nothing . iv 5 75
But for Achilles, mine own searching eyes Shall find him by his large and portly size . . . . iv 5 161
Is this Achilles?—I am Achilles.—Stand fair, I pray thee . . . iv 5 233
Achilles, let these threats alone, Till accident or purpose bring you to't iv 5 261
Thou art thought to be Achilles' male varlet . . . . . . v 1 17
That mongrel cur, Ajax, against that dog of as bad a kind, Achilles . v 4 15
And now is the cur Ajax prouder than the cur Achilles . . . . v 4 16
Go, bear Patroclus' body to Achilles . . . . v 5 17
Great Achilles Is arming, weeping, cursing, vowing vengeance . . . v 5 30
Thou boy-queller, show thy face; Know what it is to meet Achilles angry v 5 46
Cry you all amain, 'Achilles hath the mighty Hector slain' . . . v 8 14
Achilles! Achilles! Hector's slain! Achilles! . . . . . . v 9 3
Let one be sent To pray Achilles see us at our tent. . . . . v 9 8

Aching. A goodly medicine for my aching bones! O world! world! world! v 10 35
Yet give some groans, Though not for me, yet for your aching bones . v 10 51
Is this the poultice for my aching bones? . . . *Rom. and Jul.* ii 5 65

Achitophel. A whoreson Achitophel! a rascally yea-forsooth knave! *2 Hen. IV.* i 2 41

Acknowledge. This thing of darkness I Acknowledge mine . *Tempest* v 1 276
If the encounter acknowledge itself hereafter, it may compel him to her recompense . . . . *Meas. for Meas.* iii 1 262
Thou shamest to acknowledge me in misery . . *Com. of Errors* v 1 322
He loved my niece your daughter and meant to acknowledge it *Much Ado* i 2 13
My people do already know my mind, And will acknowledge you *M. of Ven.* iii 4 38
He's of a most facinerious spirit that will not acknowledge it *All's Well* ii 3 35
He does acknowledge; But puts it off to a compell'd restraint . . ii 4 43
By all the parts of man Which honour does acknowledge . *W. Tale* iv 4 401
Which comes to me in name of fault, I must not At all acknowledge . iii 2 62
Acknowledge then the king, and let me in . . . . *K. John* ii 1 269
Through all the kingdoms that acknowledge Christ . 1 *Hen. IV.* iii 2 111
It discolours the complexion of my greatness to acknowledge it 2 *Hen. IV.* ii 2 6
If ever thou darest acknowledge it, I will make it my quarrel *Hen. V.* iv 1 225
I'll ne'er acknowledge thee, Nor what is mine shall never do thee good *Rom. and Jul.* iii 5 195
The five best senses Acknowledge thee their patron . *T. of Athens* i 2 130
I have so often blushed to acknowledge him, that now I am brazed to it *Lear* i 1 10
A wretch whom nature is ashamed Almost to acknowledge hers . . i 1 216
The greatest tributaries That do acknowledge Cæsar . *Ant. and Cleo.* iii 13 97

Acknowledged. Thou art too base To be acknowledged . . *W. Tale* iv 4 430
Good sport at his making, and the whoreson must be acknowledged *Lear* i 1 24
To be acknowledged, madam, is o'erpaid . . . . . . iv 7 4
Not what you have reserved, nor what acknowledged . *Ant. and Cleo.* v 2 180

Acknowledgement. With this acknowledgement, That God fought for us . . . . *Hen. V.* iv 8 124

Acknown. Be not acknown on't . . . . . . *Othello* iii 3 319

A-cold. Tom's a-cold,—O, do de, do de, do de . . . . *Lear* iii 4 59

A-coming. There are Worthies a-coming will speak their mind *L. L. L.* v 2 589

Aconitum. Though it do work as strong As aconitum . 2 *Hen. IV.* iv 4 48

Acordo linta. Come on . . . . *All's Well* iv 1 97

Acorn. Wither'd roots and husks Wherein the acorn cradled . *Tempest* i 2 464
You minimus, of hindering knot-grass made; You bead, you acorn *M. N. Dream* iii 2 330
I found him under a tree, like a dropped acorn . . *As Y. Like It* iii 2 248

Acorn-cup. All their elves for fear Creep into acorn-cups *M. N. Dream* ii 1 31

Acquaint. Misery acquaints a man with strange bed-fellows . *Tempest* ii 2 41
Acquaint her with the danger of my state . . *Meas. for Meas.* i 2 184
Acquaint my daughter withal, that she may be the better prepared *M. Ado* i 2 22
They did entreat me to acquaint her of it . . . . . . iii 1 40
I came to acquaint you with a matter . . . *As Y. Like It* i 1 128
Out of my love to you, I came hither to acquaint you withal. . . i 1 138
Acquaint my mother with my hate to her, And wherefore I am fled *A. W.* ii 3 304
May I be bold to acquaint his grace you are gone about it? . . iii 6 84
I'll presently Acquaint the queen of your most noble offer . *W. Tale* ii 2 48
I not acquaint My father of this business . . . . . . iv 4 423
If I thought it were a piece of honesty to acquaint the king withal . iv 4 696
I left him almost speechless; and broke out To acquaint you *K. John* v 6 25
I must acquaint you that I have received New-dated letters . 2 *Hen. IV.* iv 1 7
I will acquaint his majesty With those gross taunts . . *Richard III.* i 3 105
I'll acquaint our duteous citizens With all your just proceedings . iii 5 65
Acquaint the princess With the sweet silent hours of marriage joys . iv 4 329
Our empress . . . Will we acquaint with all that we intend *T. Andron.* ii 1 122
Ere you go to bed; Acquaint her here of my son Paris' love *Rom. and Jul.* iii 4 16
Acquaint you with the perfect spy o' the time, The moment on't *Macb.* iii 1 130
Do you consent we shall acquaint him with it, As needful in our loves, fitting our duty? . . . . *Hamlet* i 1 172
Convey the business as I shall find means, and acquaint you withal *Lear* i 2 110
Acquaint my daughter no further with any thing you know . . . i 5 2

Acquaintance. Your eld'st acquaintance cannot be three hours *Temp.* v 1 186
Yet heaven may decrease it upon better acquaintance . *Mer. Wives* i 1 255
It is a 'oman that altogether's acquaintance with Mistress Anne Page . i 2 8
Good Master Brook, I desire more acquaintance of you . . . ii 2 168
I am blest in your acquaintance . . . . ii 2 279
We'll talk with Margaret, How her acquaintance grew with this lewd fellow . . . . *Much Ado* v 1 341
I shall desire you of more acquaintance . . . *M. N. Dream* iii 1 185
I do feast to-night My best-esteem'd acquaintance . *Mer. of Venice* ii 2 181
Or have acquaintance with mine own desires . . *As Y. Like It* i 3 50
Is't possible that on so little acquaintance you should like her? . . v 2 1
The small acquaintance, my sudden wooing . . . . . . v 2 7
Balk logic with acquaintance that you have And practise rhetoric in your common talk . . . . *T. of Shrew* i 1 34
I have a desire to hold my acquaintance with thee . . *All's Well* ii 3 240
I saw him hold acquaintance with the waves So long as I could see *T. Night* i 2 16
Good Mistress Accost, I desire better acquaintance . . . . i 3 56
I will wash off gross acquaintance, I will be point-devise the very man ii 5 177
Taught him to face me out of his acquaintance . . . . . v 1 91
Should 'scape the true acquaintance of mine ear . . *K. John* v 6 15
Be no more opposed Against acquaintance, kindred, and allies 1 *Hen. IV.* i 1 16
What, old acquaintance! could not all this flesh Keep in a little life? . v 4 102
To see how many of my old acquaintance are dead! 2 *Hen. IV.* iii 2 38
At your return visit our house; let our old acquaintance be renewed . iii 2 314
Not know them, and yet must Perforce be their acquaintance *Hen. VIII.* i 2 47
Ay, utterly Grow from the king's acquaintance, by this carriage . iii 1 161
All That time, acquaintance, custom and condition Made tame *T. and C.* iii 3 9
I urged our old acquaintance, and the drops That we have bled together *Coriolanus* v 1 10
What sorrow craves acquaintance at my hand, That I yet know not? *Rom. and Jul.* iii 3 5
You shall not grieve Lending me this acquaintance . . . *Lear* iv 3 56
How does my old acquaintance of this isle? . . . . *Othello* ii 1 205
Expectations and comforts of sudden respect and acquaintance . . iv 2 192
How comes it he is to sojourn with you? How creeps acquaintance? *Cymb.* i 4 25
My acquaintance lies little amongst them . . . . *Pericles* iv 6 206

Acquainted. Having been acquainted with the smell before *T. G. of V.* iv 4 25
I'll entertain myself like one that I am not acquainted withal *Mer. Wives* i 1 90
Has Ford's wife and Page's wife acquainted each other how they love me? ii 2 114
Master Brook below would fain speak with you, and be acquainted with you ii 2 151
I had never so good means, as desire, to make myself acquainted with you ii 2 189
A cowardly knave as you would desires to be acquainted withal . . iii 1 68
From time to time I have acquainted you With the dear love I bear . iv 6 8
I would not have you acquainted with tapsters: they will draw you *Meas. for Meas.* ii 1 214
I pray you, be acquainted with this maid; She comes to do you good . iv 1 51
I am as well acquainted here as I was in our house of profession . iv 3 1
What need she be acquainted? What simple thief brags of his own attaint? . . . . *Com. of Errors* iii 2 15
Belike his wife, acquainted with his fits, On purpose shut the doors . iv 3 91
I have acquainted you withal, to the end to crave your assistance *L. L. L.* v 1 122
They have acquainted me with their determinations . *Mer. of Venice* i 2 110
I acquainted him with the cause in controversy . . . . . iv 1 154
Are you acquainted with the difference That holds this present question? iv 1 171
Have you not been acquainted with goldsmiths' wives? . *As Y. Like It* iii 2 288
Let me be better acquainted with thee . . . . iv 1 2
One, Kate, that you must kiss, and be acquainted with . *T. of Shrew* iv 1 155
Made me acquainted with a weighty cause Of love . . . . iv 4 26
I was well born, Nothing acquainted with these businesses *All's Well* iii 7 5
Art not acquainted with him? knows he not thy voice? . . . . iv 1 10
If you know That you are well acquainted with yourself . . . v 3 106
You taught me how to know the face of right, Acquainted me with interest to this land . . . . *K. John* v 2 89
I am well acquainted with your manner of wrenching the true cause the false way . . . . 2 *Hen. IV.* ii 1 120
I'll be acquainted with him, if I return . . . . iii 2 353
May be As things acquainted and familiar to us . . . . . v 2 139
As one that are best acquainted with her humour . . *Richard III.* iv 4 269
The queen shall be acquainted Forthwith for what you come *Hen. VIII.* ii 2 108
Be Acquainted with this stranger: 'tis as like you As cherry is to cherry v 1 168
We are too well acquainted with these answers . . *Troi. and Cres.* ii 3 122
Doors, that were ne'er acquainted with their wards Many a bounteous year, must be employ'd Now to guard sure their master *T. of Athens* iii 3 38
Make me acquainted with your cause of grief . . . *J. Cæsar* ii 1 256
I did not think he had been acquainted with her . . . *Othello* iii 3 99
Mark Antony, Hearing that you prepared for war, acquainted My grieved ear withal . . . . *Ant. and Cleo.* ii 6 58
Let it die as it was born, and, I pray you, be better acquainted *Cymbeline* i 4 132
The king my father shall be made acquainted Of thy assault . . . i 6 149
I will make them acquainted with your purpose . . . *Pericles* iv 6 209

Acquire. The which To leave a thousand-fold more bitter than 'Tis sweet at first to acquire . . . . *Hen. VIII.* ii 3 9

Acquire. You must acquire and beget a temperance that may give it smoothness . . . *Hamlet* iii 2 8
Better to leave undone, than by our deed Acquire too high a fame when him we serve's away . . . *Ant. and Cleo.* iii 1 15
Octavia, with her modest eyes And still conclusion, shall acquire no honour Demuring upon me . . . iv 15 28
Acquired. The great dignity that his valour hath here acquired *A. W.* iv 3 80
This thrice worthy and right valiant lord Must not so stale his palm, nobly acquired . . . *Troi. and Cres.* ii 3 201
Acquisition. As my gift and thine own acquisition Worthily purchased, take my daughter . . . *Tempest* iv 1 13
Acquit. I am glad I am so acquit of this tinder-box . *Mer. Wives* i 3 27
He that escapes me without some broken limb shall acquit him well *As Y. Like It* i 1 134
I will acquit you.—Well; come again to-morrow . *T. Night* iii 4 235
If my tongue cannot entreat you to acquit me, will you command me to use my legs? . . . 2 *Hen. IV.* Epil. 18
Arrest them to the answer of the law; And God acquit them! *Hen. V.* ii 2 144
Pray God he may acquit him of suspicion! . 2 *Hen. VI.* iii 2 25
Give me leave, By circumstance, but to acquit myself *Richard III.* i 2 77
Courageous Richmond, well hast thou acquit thee . v 5 3
Acquittance. You can produce acquittances For such a sum *L. L. Lost* ii 1 161
Your mere enforcement shall acquittance me . *Richard III.* iii 7 233
Now must your conscience my acquittance seal *Hamlet* iv 7 1
Your neck, sir, is pen, book, and counters; so the acquittance follows *Cymbeline* v 4 174
Acquitted. I and my friend Have by your wisdom been this day acquitted . . . *Mer. of Venice* iv 1 409
He was much bound for you.—No more than I am well acquitted of . v 1 138
Acquitted by a true substantial form And present execution of our wills 2 *Hen. IV.* iv 1 173
Acre. Now would I give a thousand furlongs of sea for an acre of barren ground . . . *Tempest* i 1 69
My bosky acres and my unshrubb'd down, Rich scarf to my proud earth iv 1 81
Between the acres of the rye, With a hey, and a ho, and a hey *As Y. Like It* v 3 23
You may ride's With one soft kiss a thousand furlongs ere With spur we heat an acre . . . *W. Tale* i 2 96
In those holy fields Over whose acres walk'd those blessed feet 1 *Hen. IV.* i 1 25
If thou prate of mountains, let them throw Millions of acres on us! *Ham.* v 1 304
Search every acre in the high-grown field, And bring him to our eye *Lear* iv 4 7
Across. I will break thy pate across . *Com. of Errors* ii 1 78
So I had broke thy pate, And ask'd thee mercy for't.—Good faith, across *All's Well* ii 1 70
He has broke my head across and has given Sir Toby a bloody coxcomb *T. Night* v 1 178
When my good falcon made her flight across Thy father's ground *W. Tale* iv 4 15
Walk'd about, Musing and sighing, with your arms across . *J. Cæsar* ii 1 240
Act. Too delicate To act her earthy and abhorr'd commands . *Tempest* i 2 273
To perform an act Whereof what's past is prologue . ii 1 252
Thy brother was a furtherer in the act . v 1 73
I will consent to act any villany against him *Mer. Wives* ii 1 101
Remember you your cue.—I warrant thee; if I do not act it, hiss me . iii 3 40
We do not act that often jest and laugh . iv 2 108
Now puts the drowsy and neglected act Freshly on me *Meas. for Meas.* i 2 174
As mice by lions—hath pick'd out an act, Under whose heavy sense your brother's life Falls into forfeit . . i 4 64
And do him right that, answering one foul wrong, Lives not to act another . . . ii 2 104
Condemn'd upon the act of fornication To lose his head . . . v 1 70
His act did not o'ertake his bad intent, And must be buried but as an intent . . . v 1 456
In the act, The skilful shepherd peel'd me certain wands *Mer. of Venice* i 3 84
Thou but lead'st this fashion of thy malice To the last hour of act iv 1 19
Is that the law?—Thyself shalt see the act iv 1 314
One man in his time plays many parts, His acts being seven ages *As Y. Like It* ii 7 143
On us both did haggish age steal on And wore us out of act *All's Well* i 2 30
It is presumption in us when The help of heaven we count the act of men ii 1 155
Honours thrive, When rather from our acts we them derive ii 3 143
And would not put my reputation now In any staining act . iii 7 7
Is wicked meaning in a lawful deed And lawful meaning in a lawful act iii 7 46
Let it be forbid, sir; so should I be a great deal of his act . iv 3 55
It shall become thee well to act my woes . . *T. Night* i 4 26
And heavens so shine, That they may fairly note this act of mine! iv 3 35
He finished indeed his mortal act That day that made my sister thirteen years . . . v 1 254
In an act of this importance 'twere Most piteous to be wild . *W. Tale* ii 1 181
If one jot beyond The bound of honour, or in act or will That way inclining . . . iii 2 52
Each your doing, So singular in each particular, Crowns what you are doing in the present deed, That all your acts are queens . iv 4 146
The dignity of this act was worth the audience of kings and princes v 2 86
They gape and point At your industrious scenes and acts of death *K. John* ii 1 376
The better act of purposes mistook Is to mistake again . iii 1 274
Though that my death were adjunct to my act, By heaven, I would do it iii 3 57
This act so evilly born shall cool the hearts Of all his people . iii 4 149
This act is as an ancient tale new told, And in the last repeating troublesome . . . iv 2 18
Without stop, didst let thy heart consent, And consequently thy rude hand to act The deed, which both our tongues held vile to name . iv 2 240
If thou didst but consent To this most cruel act, do but despair . iv 3 126
If I in act, consent, or sin of thought, Be guilty . . iv 3 135
Why look you sad? Be great in act, as you have been in thought v 1 45
The blood of English shall manure the ground, And future ages groan for this foul act . . *Richard II.* iv 1 138
My manors, rents, revenues, I forego; My acts, decrees, and statutes I deny . . . iv 1 213
Still unfold The acts commenced on this ball of earth . 2 *Hen. IV.* Ind. 5
Let this world no longer be a stage To feed contention in a lingering act i 1 156
By his light Did all the chivalry of England move To do brave acts ii 3 21
Look to taste the due Meet for rebellion and such acts as yours . iv 2 117
Sack commences it and sets it in act and use . iv 3 126
Princes to act And monarchs to behold the swelling scene! . *Hen. V.* Prol. 3
Creatures that by a rule in nature teach The act of order . i 2 189
Our history shall with full mouth Speak freely of our acts, or else our grave . . . i 2 231
Doing the execution and the act For which we have in head assembled them . . . ii 2 17
For his acts So much applauded through the realm of France 1 *Hen. VI.* ii 2 35
Thy acts in Ireland, In bringing them to civil discipline . 2 *Hen. VI.* i 1 194
As Ascanius did When he to madding Dido would unfold His father's acts . . . 2 *Hen. VI.* iii 2 118
A hand to hold a sceptre up And with the same to act controlling laws v 1 103
Thrice I led him off, Persuaded him from any further act . v 3 10
The soldiers should have toss'd me on their pikes Before I would have granted to that act . . 3 *Hen. VI.* i 1 245
Until that act of parliament be repeal'd Whereby my son is disinherited i 1 249
Have caused him, by new act of parliament, To blot out me . ii 2 91
What scene of death hath Roscius now to act? . v 6 10
What means this scene of rude impatience?—To make an act of tragic violence . . . *Richard III.* ii 2 39
The most arch act of piteous massacre That ever yet this land was guilty of iv 3 2
If this inducement force her not to love, Send her a story of thy noble acts iv 4 280
What worst, as oft, Hitting a grosser quality, is cried up For our best act *Hen. VIII.* i 2 85
I would have play'd The part my father meant to act upon The usurper i 2 195
The honour of it Does pay the act of it . . iii 2 182
Some come to take their ease, And sleep an act or two . . Epil. 3
Such to-be-pitied and o'er-wrested seeming He acts thy greatness in *Troi. and Cres.* i 3 158
Count wisdom as no member of the war, Forestall prescience and esteem no act But that of hand . . . i 3 199
Choice, being mutual act of all our souls, Makes merit her election . i 3 348
We may not think the justness of each act Such and no other than event doth form it . . . ii 2 119
The desire is boundless and the act a slave to limit . iii 2 90
They that have the voice of lions and the act of hares . iii 2 96
An act that very chance doth throw upon him . . iii 3 131
Repeal daily any wholesome act established against the rich *Coriolanus* i 1 85
What ever have been thought on in this state, That could be brought to bodily act ere Rome Had circumvention? . . i 2 5
He that has but effected his good will Hath overta'en mine act . i 9 19
When he might act the woman in the scene, He proved best man . ii 2 100
The book of his good acts, whence men have read His fame unparallel'd v 2 15
Acts of black night, abominable deeds, Complots of mischief *T. Andron.* v 1 64
So smile the heavens upon this holy act! . *Rom. and Jul.* ii 6 1
Thy wild acts denote The unreasonable fury of a beast . iii 3 110
My dismal scene I needs must act alone . . iv 3 19
Performance is ever the duller for his act . *T. of Athens* v 1 26
Stir up their servants to an act of rage, And after seem to chide 'em *J. Cæsar* ii 1 176
As, by our hands and this our present act, You see we do . iii 1 166
Two truths are told, As happy prologues to the swelling act . *Macbeth* i 3 128
Art thou afeard To be the same in thine own act and valour As thou art in desire? . . . i 7 40
The heavens, as troubled with man's act, Threaten his bloody stage . ii 4 5
He hath a wisdom that doth guide his valour To act in safety . iii 1 54
Even now, To crown my thoughts with acts, be it thought and done . iv 1 149
Whilst they, distill'd Almost to jelly with the act of fear, Stand dumb *Hamlet* i 2 205
As he in his particular act and place May give his saying deed . i 3 26
Give thy thoughts no tongue, Nor any unproportion'd thought his act . i 3 60
Howsoever thou pursuest this act, Taint not thy mind . . i 5 84
With more offences at my beck than I have thoughts to put them in, imagination to give them shape, or time to act them in . iii 1 129
When thou seest that act afoot, Even with the very comment of thy soul Observe mine uncle . . . iii 2 83
About some act That has no relish of salvation in't . iii 3 91
Such an act That blurs the grace and blush of modesty . iii 4 40
With tristful visage, as against the doom, Is thought-sick at the act . iii 4 51
Ay me, what act, That roars so loud, and thunders in the index? . iii 4 51
That treason can but peep to what it would, Acts little of his will . iv 5 125
It argues an act: and an act hath three branches; it is, to act, to do, and to perform . . . v 1 11
You that look pale and tremble at this chance, That are but mutes or audience to this act . . . v 2 346
So shall you hear Of carnal, bloody, and unnatural acts . v 2 392
I have one thing, of a queasy question, Which I must act *Lear* ii 1 20
This act persuades me That this remotion of the duke and her Is practice only . . . ii 4 114
Served the lust of my mistress' heart, and did the act of darkness with her iii 4 90
Enkindle all the sparks of nature, To quit this horrid act . iii 7 87
A servant that he bred, thrill'd with remorse, Opposed against the act . iv 2 74
My outward action doth demonstrate The native act and figure of my heart In compliment extern . . *Othello* i 1 62
Trust not your daughters' minds By what you see them act . . i 1 172
When the blood is made dull with the act of sport . . ii 1 230
Though I am bound to every act of duty, I am not bound to that all slaves are free to . . . iii 3 134
Which at the first are scarce found to distaste, But with a little act upon the blood, Burn like the mines of sulphur . . iii 3 328
To do the act that might the addition earn Not the world's mass of vanity could make me . . . iv 2 163
It is true, indeed.—'Tis a strange truth.—O monstrous act! . v 2 190
I know this act shows horrible and grim . . v 2 203
The act of shame A thousand times committed . v 2 211
And to the state This heavy act with heavy heart relate . v 2 371
I do think there is mettle in death, which commits some loving act upon her, she hath such a celerity in dying *Ant. and Cleo.* i 2 148
My brother never Did urge me in his act . . ii 2 46
We shall remain in friendship, our conditions So differing in their acts . ii 2 116
Let me have thy hand: Further this act of grace . ii 2 149
Repent that e'er thy tongue Hath so betray'd thine act . . ii 7 84
A lower place, note well, May make too great an act . iii 1 13
To this great fairy I'll commend thy acts, Make her thanks bless thee . iv 8 12
That self hand, Which writ his honour in the acts it did . v 1 22
I see him rouse himself To praise my noble act . v 2 288
Thyself art coming To see perform'd the dreaded act . v 2 335
To try the vigour of them and apply Allayments to their act . *Cymbeline* i 5 22
That horrid act Of the divorce he'ld make . . ii 1 66
Senseless bauble, Art thou a feodary for this act? . . iii 2 21
Hath as oft a slanderous epitaph As record of fair act . iii 3 53
Strains his young nerves and puts himself in posture That acts my words . . . iii 3 95
It is no act of common passage, but A strain of rareness . iii 4 94
These three, Three thousand confident, in act as many . v 3 29
What, makest thou me a dullard in this act? . . v 5 265
O you powers That give heaven countless eyes to view men's acts! *Pericles* i 1 73
Few love to hear the sins they love to act . . i 1 92
I am too little to contend, Since he's so great can make his will his act i 2 18
Smiling Extremity out of act . . . v 1 140

Actæon. Prevent, or go thou, Like Sir Actæon he . . . *Mer. Wives* ii 1 122
Divulge Page himself for a secure and wilful Actæon . . . iii 2 44
Had I the power that some say Dian had, Thy temples should be planted presently With horns, as was Actæon's? . . . *T. Andron.* ii 3 63

Acted. Which I so lively acted with my tears . . . *T. G. of Ver.* iv 4 174
Worth the audience of kings and princes; for by such was it acted *W. T.* v 2 88
Till strange love, grown bold, Think true love acted simple modesty *Rom. and Jul.* iii 2 16
How many ages hence Shall this our lofty scene be acted over! *J. Cæsar* iii 1 112
Strange things I have in head, that will to hand; Which must be acted ere they may be scann'd *Macbeth* iii 4 140
I heard thee speak me a speech once, but it was never acted . *Hamlet* ii 2 455
Let the world see His nobleness well acted . . . *Ant. and Cleo.* v 2 45

Acting. It is a part That I shall blush in acting . . . *Coriolanus* ii 2 149
The resolute acting of your blood Could have attain'd the effect *M. for M.* ii 1 12
Acting this in an obedient hope . . . *T. Night* v 1 348
All my reign hath been but as a scene Acting that argument 2 *Hen. IV.* iv 5 199
If no inconstant toy, nor womanish fear, Abate thy valour in the acting it *Rom. and Jul.* iv 1 120
Between the acting of a dreadful thing And the first motion, all the interim is Like a phantasma, or a hideous dream . *J. Cæsar* ii 1 63
Abound In the division of each several crime, Acting it many ways *Macb.* iv 3 97
Lets go by The important acting of your dread command *Hamlet* iii 4 108

Action. The rarer action is In virtue than in vengeance . . *Tempest* v 1 27
What dangerous action, stood it next to death, Would I not undergo for one calm look! . . . *T. G. of Ver.* v 4 41
I can construe the action of her familiar style . . . *Mer. Wives* i 3 50
My counterfeiting the action of an old woman, delivered me . . iv 5 121
Moe reasons for this action At our more leisure shall I render you *M. for M.* i 3 48
Bore many gentlemen, myself being one, In hand and hope of action i 4 52
In action all of precept, he did show me The way twice o'er . . iv 1 40
His actions show much like to madness . . . iv 4 4
How many gentlemen have you lost in this action? . . *Much Ado* i 1 6
When you went onward on this ended action . . . i 1 299
Long-during action tires The sinewy vigour of the traveller . *L. L. Lost* iv 3 307
Action and accent did they teach him there . . . v 2 99
We will do it in action as we will do it before the duke . *M. N. Dream* iii 1 5
Do not fret yourself too much in the action . . . iv 1 14
How many actions most ridiculous Hast thou been drawn to? *As Y. Like It* ii 4 30
Certainly a woman's thought runs before her actions . . iv 1 141
As I guess By the stern brow and waspish action . . iv 3 9
Tell him from me, as he will win my love, He bear himself with honourable action . . . *T. of Shrew* Ind. 1 110
I know the boy will well usurp the grace, Voice, gait and action . Ind. 1 132
I'll bring mine action on the proudest he That stops my way . . iii 2 236
I would I knew in what particular action to try him *All's Well* iii 6 18
So he that in this action contrives against his own nobility, in his proper stream o'erflows himself . . . iv 3 28
'I am a gentleman.' I'll be sworn thou art; Thy tongue, thy face, thy limbs, actions, and spirit, Do give thee five-fold blazon *T. Night* i 5 311
He upon some action Is now in durance . . . v 1 282
This action I now go on Is for my better grace . . *W. Tale* ii 1 121
If powers divine Behold our human actions, as they do . . iii 2 30
Your actions are my dreams . . . iii 2 83
Her actions shall be holy as You hear my spell is lawful . v 3 104
Labour'd spirits, Forwearied in this action of swift speed . *K. John* ii 1 233
Who hath read or heard Of any kindred action like to this? . iii 4 14
Strong reasons make strong actions . . . iii 4 182
Whilst he that hears makes fearful action, With wrinkled brows . iv 2 191
The graceless action of a heavy hand, If that it be the work of any hand iv 3 58
And on our actions set the name of right With holy breath . v 2 67
What men provided, what munition sent, To underprop this action? . v 2 99
York commends the plot and the general course of the action 1 *Hen. IV.* ii 3 23
I could divide myself and go to buffets, for moving such a dish of skim milk with so honourable an action! . . . ii 3 36
Thou hast lost much honour, that thou wert not with me in this action ii 4 23
Am I not fallen away vilely since this last action? do I not bate? . iii 3 2
None of this, Though strongly apprehended, could restrain The stiff-borne action . . . 2 *Hen. IV.* i 1 177
That same word, rebellion, did divide The action of their bodies from their souls . . . i 1 195
You may thank the unquiet time for your quiet o'er-posting that action i 2 171
Not a dangerous action can peep out his head but I am thrust upon it . i 2 238
The instant action: a cause on foot Lives so in hope . . i 3 37
Have you entered the action?—It is entered . . . ii 1 2
Go, wash thy face, and draw the action . . . ii 1 162
The undeserver may sleep, when the man of action is called on . ii 4 406
All members of our cause, both here and hence, That are insinew'd to this action . . . iv 1 172
Every idle, nice and wanton reason Shall to the king taste of this action iv 1 192
The manner how this action hath been borne Here at more leisure may your highness read . . . iv 4 88
That action, hence borne out, May waste the memory of the former days iv 5 215
The wearing out of six fashions, which is four terms, or two actions v 1 90
Stand laughing by, All out of work and cold for action! . . *Hen. V.* i 2 114
So may a thousand actions, once afoot, End in one purpose . . i 2 211
Let every man now task his thought, That this fair action may on foot be brought . . . i 2 310
When the blast of war blows in our ears, Then imitate the action of the tiger . . . iii 1 6
I cannot give due action to my words, Except a sword or sceptre balance it . . . 2 *Hen. VI.* v 1 8
My soul and body on the action both!—A dreadful lay! . . v 2 26
Your interior hatred, Which in your outward actions shows itself *Rich. III.* i 3 66
The tract of every thing Would by a good discourser lose some life, Which action's self was tongue to . . . *Hen. VIII.* i 1 42
We must not stint Our necessary actions, in the fear To cope malicious censurers . . . i 2 77
It was a gentle business, and becoming The action of good women . ii 3 55
So much I am happy Above a number, if my actions Were tried by every tongue . . . iii 1 34
After my death I wish no other herald, No other speaker of my living actions, To keep mine honour from corruption . . . iv 2 70
Checks and disasters Grow in the veins of actions highest rear'd *Tr. and Cr.* i 3 6
Sith every action that hath gone before, Whereof we have record, trial did draw Bias and thwart . . . i 3 13
With ridiculous and awkward action, Which, slanderer, he imitation calls i 3 149
Our imputation shall be oddly poised In this wild action . . i 3 340
Would not lose So rich advantage of a promised glory As smiles upon the forehead of this action . . . ii 2 205

Action. As if The passage and whole carriage of this action Rode on his tide . . . *Troi. and Cres.* ii 3 140
Bring action hither, this cannot go to war . . . ii 3 145
A woman impudent and mannish grown Is not more loathed than an effeminate man In time of action . . . iii 3 219
He in heat of action Is more vindicative than jealous love . . iv 5 106
They are in action.—Now, Ajax, hold thine own! . . . iv 5 113
And in what fashion . . . he goes Upon this present action . *Coriolanus* i 1 283
I had rather had eleven die nobly for their country than one voluptuously surfeit out of action . . . i 3 28
Take your choice of those That best can aid your action . . . i 6 66
Your helps are many, or else your actions would grow wondrous single ii 1 39
He hath in this action outdone his former deeds doubly . . ii 1 150
In human action and capacity, Of no more soul nor fitness for the world Than camels in the war . . . ii 1 265
He hath so planted his honours in their eyes, and his actions in their hearts . . . ii 2 33
For in such business Action is eloquence . . . iii 2 76
By my body's action teach my mind A most inherent baseness . . iii 2 122
And am the man, I think, that shall set them in present action . iv 3 53
You are darken'd in this action, sir . . . iv 7 5
But either Had borne the action of yourself, or else To him had left it solely . . . iv 7 15
My partner in this action, You must report . . . v 3 2
He sold the blood and labour Of our great action . . . v 6 48
More than counterpoise a full third part The charges of the action . v 6 79
In thy dumb action will I be as perfect As begging hermits in their holy prayers . . . *T. Andron.* iii 2 40
How can I grace my talk, Wanting a hand to give it action? . . v 2 18
Virtue itself turns vice, being misapplied; And vice sometimes by action dignified . . . *Rom. and Jul.* ii 3 22
A man no mightier than thyself or me In personal action . *J. Cæsar* i 3 77
I have neither wit, nor words, nor worth, Action, nor utterance . iii 2 226
When our actions do not, Our fears do make us traitors . *Macbeth* iv 2 3
It is an accustomed action with her, to seem thus washing her hands . v 1 32
These indeed seem, For they are actions that a man might play *Hamlet* i 2 84
Look, with what courteous action It waves you to a more removed ground i 4 60
In action how like an angel! in apprehension how like a god! . ii 2 318
With devotion's visage And pious action we do sugar o'er The devil himself iii 1 48
With this regard their currents turn awry, And lose the name of action iii 1 88
Suit the action to the word, the word to the action . . iii 2 19
'Tis not so above; There is no shuffling, there the action lies In his true nature . . . iii 3 61
Do not look upon me; Lest with this piteous action you convert My stern effects . . . iii 4 128
To the use of actions fair and good He likewise gives a frock or livery . iii 4 163
It is no vicious blot, murder, or foulness, No unchaste action . *Lear* i 1 231
When my outward action doth demonstrate The native act and figure of my heart In compliment extern . . . *Othello* i 1 61
If such actions may have passage free, Bond-slaves and pagans shall our statesmen be . . . i 2 98
Yea, though our proper son Stood in your action . . . i 3 70
They have used Their dearest action in the tented field . . i 3 85
'Mongst this flock of drunkards, Am I to put our Cassio in some action That may offend the isle . . . ii 3 62
It were an honest action to say So to the Moor . . . ii 3 146
I cannot speak Any beginning to this peevish odds; And would in action glorious I had lost Those legs that brought me to a part of it! . ii 3 186
Pleasure and action make the hours seem short . . . ii 3 385
That which combined us was most great, and let not A leaner action rend us . . . *Ant. and Cleo.* ii 2 19
Would not let him partake in the glory of the action . . . iii 5 10
But his whole action grows Not in the power on 't . . . iii 7 69
I never saw an action of such shame . . . iii 10 22
And what thou think'st his very action speaks In every power that moves . . . iii 12 35
The violence of action hath made you reek as a sacrifice . *Cymbeline* i 2 2
Than in my every action to be guided by others' experiences . . i 4 48
If you will make 't an action, call witness to 't . . . ii 3 156
Her pretty action did outsell her gift, And yet enrich'd it too . ii 4 102
Though his actions were not visible, yet Report should render him hourly to your ear . . . iii 4 152
The common men are now in action 'Gainst the Pannonians and Dalmatians . . . iii 7 2
What pleasure, sir, find we in life, to lock it From action and adventure? iv 4 3
Be what it is, The action of my life is like it, which I'll keep . . v 4 150
Wisdom sees, those men Blush not in actions blacker than the night *Pericles* i 1 135
Our mind partakes Her private actions to your secrecy . . i 1 153
Never did my actions yet commence A deed might gain her love . ii 5 53
My actions are as noble as my thoughts, That never relish'd of a base descent . . . ii 5 59
I nill relate, action may Conveniently the rest convey . . iii. Gower 55
They with continual action are even as good as rotten . . iv 2 9
Where what is done in action, more, if might, Shall be discover'd . v. Gower 23

Action of battery. I'll have mine action of battery on thee *M. for M.* ii 1 187
I'll have an action of battery against him, if there be any law in Illyria . . . *T. Night* iv 1 36
And will not tell him of his action of battery . . *Hamlet* v 1 111

Action of slander. You might have your action of slander too *M. for M.* v 1 190

Action-taking. A lily-livered, action-taking knave . . *Lear* ii 2 18

Actium. From the head of Actium Beat the approaching Cæsar *A. and C.* iii 7 52

Active. Simply the most active fellow in Europe . . 2 *Hen. IV.* iv 3 24
Despite his nice fence and his active practice, His May of youth *M. Ado* v 1 75
He is simply the most active gentleman of France . . *Hen. V.* iii 7 105
Sweet is the country, because full of riches; The people liberal, valiant, active, wealthy . . . 2 *Hen. VI.* iv 7 68
'Twixt his mental and his active parts Kingdom'd Achilles in commotion rages . . . *Troi. and Cres.* ii 3 184

Actively. Since frost itself as actively doth burn And reason pandars will . . . *Hamlet* iii 4 87

Active-valiant. More active-valiant or more valiant-young . 1 *Hen. IV.* v 1 90

Activity. Doing is activity; and he will still be doing . *Hen. V.* iii 7 107
She'll bereave you o' the deeds too, if she call your activity in question *Troi. and Cres.* ii 2 60
That your activity may defeat and quell The source of all erection *T. of Athens* iv 3 163

Actor. These our actors, As I foretold you, were all spirits . *Tempest* iv 1 148
Condemn the fault, and not the actor of it? . . *Meas. for Meas.* ii 2 37
To fine the faults whose fine stands in record, And let go by the actor ii 2 41

Actor. The actors, sir, will show whereuntil it doth amount . *L. L. Lost* v 2 501
Read the names of the actors, and so grow to a point . *M. N. Dream* i 2 9
Call forth your actors by the scroll. Masters, spread yourselves . i 2 16
I'll be an auditor; An actor too perhaps, if I see cause . iii 1 82
Most dear actors, eat no onions nor garlic, for we are to utter sweet
breath . . . . iv 2 43
The actors are at hand and by their show You shall know all . v 1 116
And you shall say I'll prove a busy actor in their play . *As Y. Like It* iii 4 62
A showing of a heavenly effect in an earthly actor . *All's Well* ii 3 28
As in a theatre, the eyes of men, After a well-graced actor leaves the
stage, Are idly bent on him that enters next . *Richard II.* v 2 24
As if the tragedy Were play'd in jest by counterfeiting actors 3 *Hen. VI.* ii 3 28
A prologue arm'd, but not in confidence Of author's pen or actor's voice
Troi. and Cres. Prol. 24
Like a dull actor now, I have forgot my part, and I am out . *Coriolanus* v 3 40
Bear it as our Roman actors do, With untired spirits . *J. Cæsar* ii 1 226
When Roscius was an actor in Rome;—The actors are come hither *Ham.* ii 2 410
Then came each actor on his ass,—The best actors in the world . ii 2 414
And was accounted a good actor.—What did you enact? . iii 2 106
When good will is show'd, though 't come too short, The actor may
plead pardon . . . . *Ant. and Cleo.* ii 5 9
Actual. Besides her walking and other actual performances . *Macbeth* v 1 13
Either in discourse of thought or actual deed . . . *Othello* iv 2 153
A-cursing. And fall a-cursing, like a very drab . *Hamlet* ii 2 615
Acute. A most acute juvenal; volable and free of grace! . *L. L. Lost* iii 1 67
The gift is good in those in whom it is acute, and I am thankful for it iv 2 73
Acutely. I am so full of businesses, I cannot answer thee acutely . *A. W.* i 1 221
Adage. Unless the adage must be verified, That beggars mounted run
their horse to death . . . . . 3 *Hen. VI.* i 4 126
Letting 'I dare not' wait upon 'I would,' Like the poor cat i' the adage
Macbeth i 7 45
Adallas. The Thracian king, Adallas; King Malchus of Arabia *A. and C.* iii 6 71
Adam. As I remember, Adam, it was upon this fashion *As Y. Like It* i 1 1
This is it, Adam, that grieves me; and the spirit of my father, which I
think is within me, begins to mutiny . . . . . i 1 22
Go apart, Adam, and thou shalt hear how he will shake me up . i 1 29
Here feel we but the penalty of Adam, The seasons' difference . ii 1 5
Whither, Adam, wouldst thou have me go?—No matter whither . ii 3 29
Why, how now, Adam! no greater heart in thee? Live a little . ii 6 4
What, have you got the picture of old Adam new-apparelled? *Com. of Err.* iv 3 13
Not that Adam that kept the Paradise, but that Adam that keeps the
prison . . . . iv 3 17
He that hits me, let him be clapped on the shoulder, and called Adam
Much Ado i 1 261
Adam's sons are my brethren; and, truly, I hold it a sin to match in
my kindred . . . . ii 1 66
Though she were endowed with all that Adam had left him before he
transgressed . . . . ii 1 259
The moon was a month old when Adam was no more . *L. L. Lost* iv 2 40
Had he been Adam, he had tempted Eve; A' can carve too, and lisp . v 2 322
There were none fine but Adam, Ralph, and Gregory . *T. of Shrew* iv 1 139
Thou, old Adam's likeness, set to dress this garden . *Richard II.* iii 4 73
Since the old days of goodman Adam to the pupil age of this present
twelve o'clock . . . . 1 *Hen. IV.* ii 4 106
Thou knowest in the state of innocency Adam fell . . . iii 3 186
Consideration, like an angel, came And whipp'd the offending Adam out
of him . . . . *Hen. V.* i 1 29
Adam was a gardener.—And what of that? . . 2 *Hen. VI.* iv 2 142
Young Adam Cupid, he that shot so trim, When King Cophetua loved
the beggar-maid . . . . . . *Rom. and Jul.* ii 1 13
Gardeners, ditchers, and grave-makers: they hold up Adam's profession
Hamlet v 1 35
The Scripture says, 'Adam digged': could he dig without arms? . v 1 42
Adamant. You draw me, you hard-hearted adamant . *M. N. Dream* ii 1 195
Rend bars of steel And spurn in pieces posts of adamant . 1 *Hen. VI.* i 4 52
As true as steel, as plantage to the moon, As sun to day, as turtle to
her mate, As iron to adamant, as earth to the centre *Troi. and Cres.* iii 2 186
A-day. Which cannot go but thirty mile a-day . . 2 *Hen. IV.* ii 4 179
Who twice a-day their wither'd hands hold up Toward heaven *Hen. V.* iv 1 316
Add. O, death 's a great disguiser; and you may add to it *M. for Meas.* iv 2 187
All the grace that she hath left Is that she will not add to her damna-
tion A sin of perjury . . . . *Much Ado* iv 1 174
It adds a precious seeing to the eye . . . *L. L. Lost* iv 3 333
To our perjury to add more terror, We are again forsworn, in will and
error . . . . v 2 470
If I could add a lie unto a fault, I would deny it . *Mer. of Venice* v 1 186
But to her love concerneth us to add Her father's liking . *T. of Shrew* iii 2 130
I will add Unto their losses twenty thousand crowns . . . v 2 112
I'll add three thousand crowns To what is past already . *All's Well* iii 7 35
Who are they?—They that add, moreover, he's drunk nightly *T. Night* i 3 38
She adds, moreover, that you should put your lord into a desperate
assurance . . . . ii 2 7
His life I gave him and did thereto add My love, without retention . v 1 83
The justice of your hearts will thereto add, ''Tis pity she's not honest,
honourable' . . . . *W. Tale* ii 1 67
Over that art Which you say adds to nature, is an art That nature makes iv 4 91
We'll put thee down, 'gainst whom these arms we bear, Or add a royal
number to the dead . . . . *K. John* ii 1 347
Add thus much more, that no Italian priest Shall tithe or toll in our
dominions . . . . iii 1 153
To smooth the ice, or add another hue Unto the rainbow . . iv 2 13
Until the heavens, envying earth's good hap, Add an immortal title to
your crown! . . . . *Richard II.* i 1 24
Add proof unto mine armour with thy prayers . . . . i 3 73
It adds more sorrow to my want of joy . . . . . iii 4 16
And to thy worth will add right worthy gains . . . . v 6 12
These unseason'd hours perforce must add Unto your sickness 2 *Hen. IV.* iii 1 105
That may with reasonable swiftness add More feathers to our wings
Hen. V. i 2 306
To this add defiance: and tell him, for conclusion, he hath betrayed
his followers . . . . iii 6 142
To add to your laments, Wherewith you now bedew King Henry's
hearse, I must inform you of a dismal fight . 1 *Hen. VI.* i 1 103
Thou wilt but add increase unto my wrath . . 2 *Hen. VI.* i 2 292
The words would add more anguish than the wounds . 3 *Hen. VI.* i 1 99
To add more measure to your woes, I come to tell you things . ii 1 105
I can add colours to the chameleon, Change shapes with Proteus . iii 2 191
Add water to the sea And give more strength to that which hath too
much . . . . v 4 8
I need not add more fuel to your fire, For well I wot ye blaze . v 4 70

Add. A thousand pound a year, annual support, Out of his grace he adds
Hen. VIII. ii 3 65
Yet will I add an honour, a great patience . . . . iii 1 137
And, to add greater honours to his age Than man could give him, he
died fearing God . . . . iv 2 67
Soft infancy, that nothing canst but cry, Add to my clamours! *Tr. and Cr.* ii 2 106
And add, That if he overhold his price so much, We'll none of him . ii 3 141
That were to enlard his fat already pride And add more coals to Cancer ii 3 206
This love that thou hast shown Doth add more grief . *Rom. and Jul.* i 1 195
May these add to the number that may scald thee! . *T. of Athens* iii 1 54
And tempt the rheumy and unpurged air To add unto his sickness *J. C.* ii 1 267
Add thereto a tiger's chaudron, For the ingredients of our cauldron
Macbeth iv 1 33
To relate the manner, Were, on the quarry of these murder'd deer, To
add the death of you . . . . iv 3 207
And thereto add such reasons of your own As may compact it more *Lear* i 4 361
Nothing canst thou to damnation add Greater than that . *Othello* iii 3 372
Promise, And in our name, what she requires; add more, From thine
invention, offers . . . . . . *Ant. and Cleo.* iii 12 28
Which I will add To you, the liver, heart and brain of Britain *Cymbeline* v 5 13
Further to boast were neither true nor modest, Unless I add, we are
honest . . . . v 5 19
Nor come we to add sorrow to your tears, But to relieve them. *Pericles* i 4 90
Then honour be but a goal to my will, This day I'll rise, or else add ill
to ill . . . . ii 1 172
Added. If that be sin, I'll make it my morn prayer To have it added to
the faults of mine . . . . . . *Meas. for Meas.* ii 4 72
Ba, pueritia, with a horn added . . . . . *L. L. Lost* v 1 52
Camillo's flight, Added to their familiarity . . *W. Tale* ii 1 175
The word 'farewell' have lengthen'd hours And added years . *Richard II.* i 4 17
A thought of added honour torn from Hector . . *Troi. and Cres.* iv 5 145
What fool hath added water to the sea, Or brought a faggot to bright-
burning Troy? . . . . *T. Andron.* iii 1 68
You have added worth unto 't and lustre . . . *T. of Athens* i 2 154
Till another Cæsar Have added slaughter to the sword of traitors *J. Cæsar* v 1 55
It weeps, it bleeds; and each new day a gash Is added to her wounds
Macbeth iv 3 41
Drew from my heart all love, And added to the gall . . *Lear* i 4 292
I rather added A lustre to it . . . . . *Cymbeline* i 1 142
You have land enough of your own: but he added to your having . i 2 19
To such proceeding Who ever but his approbation added, Though not his
prime consent . . . . *Pericles* iv 3 26
Adder. Sometime am I All wound with adders . . . . *Tempest* ii 2 13
Could not a worm, an adder, do so much? An adder did it . *M. N. Dr.* iii 2 71
With doubler tongue Than thine, thou serpent, never adder stung . iii 2 73
Is the adder better than the eel, Because his painted skin contents the
eye? . . . . *T. of Shrew* iv 3 179
How she longed to eat adders' heads and toads carbonadoed . *W. Tale* iv 4 268
A lurking adder Whose double tongue may with a mortal touch Throw
death . . . . *Richard II.* iii 2 20
Art thou, like the adder, waxen deaf? Be poisonous too 2 *Hen. VI.* iii 2 76
Whose tongue more poisons than the adder's tooth! . 3 *Hen. VI.* i 4 112
Adders, spiders, toads, Or any creeping venom'd thing that lives
Richard III. i 2 19
Pleasure and revenge Have ears more deaf than adders . *Troi. and Cres.* ii 2 172
Even as an adder when she doth unroll To do some fatal execution *T. A.* ii 3 35
The black toad and adder blue, The gilded newt . *T. of Athens* iv 3 181
It is the bright day that brings forth the adder . . *J. Cæsar* ii 1 14
Adder's fork and blind-worm's sting, Lizard's leg and howlet's wing *Macb.* iv 1 16
My two schoolfellows, Whom I will trust as I will adders fang'd *Ham.* iii 4 203
Each jealous of the other, as the stung Are of the adder . . *Lear* v 1 57
Were it Toad, or Adder, Spider, 'Twould move me sooner . *Cymbeline* iv 2 90
Addict. To forswear thin potations and to addict themselves to sack
2 *Hen. IV.* iv 3 135
Addicted. Being addicted to a melancholy as she is . . *T. Night* ii 5 223
If 't be he I mean, he's very wild; Addicted so and so . *Hamlet* ii 1 19
Addiction. Each man to what sport and revels his addiction leads him
Othello ii 2 7
Since his addiction was to courses vain, His companies unletter'd *Hen. V.* i 1 54
Adding. I only have made a mouth of his eye, By adding a tongue which
I know will not lie . . . . *L. L. Lost* ii 1 252
Until the goose came out of door, And stay'd the odds by adding four . iii 1 93
Of one sore I an hundred make by adding but one more L . . iv 2 63
Adding thereto moreover That he would wed me . . . . v 2 446
Adding to clouds more clouds with his deep sighs . *Rom. and Jul.* i 1 139
Addition. Yet they are devils' additions, the names of fiends *Mer. Wives* ii 2 312
Take unmingled thence that drop again, Without addition *Com. of Errors* ii 2 130
It is no addition to her wit, nor no great argument of her folly *Much Ado* ii 3 242
Where great additions swell 's, and virtue none, It is a dropsied honour
All's Well ii 3 134
Titled goddess; and worth it, with addition! . . . . iv 2 3
This addition more, Full thirty thousand marks of English coin *K. John* ii 1 529
Bear The addition nobly ever! . . . . . *Coriolanus* i 9 66
To undercrest your good addition To the fairness of my power . i 9 72
'You are welcome,' with this shrill addition, 'Anon, anon, sir!' 1 *Hen. IV.* ii 4 29
This man, lady, hath robbed many beasts of their particular additions
Troi. and Cres. i 2 20
And, for thy vigour, Bull-bearing Milo his addition yield To sinewy Ajax ii 3 258
We will not name desert before his birth, and, being born, his addition
shall be humble . . . . iii 2 102
I came to kill thee, cousin, and bear hence A great addition . . iv 5 141
Myself have letters of the selfsame tenour.—With what addition?
J. Cæsar iv 3 172
He bade me, from him, call thee thane of Cawdor: In which addition,
hail, most worthy thane! . . . . *Macbeth* i 3 106
Whereby he does receive Particular addition, from the bill That writes
them all alike . . . . iii 1 100
They clepe us drunkards, and with swinish phrase Soil our addition *Ham.* i 4 20
According to the phrase or the addition Of man and country . . ii 1 48
Truly to speak, and with no addition, We go to gain a little patch of
ground . . . . iv 4 17
Only we still retain The name, and all the additions to a king . *Lear* i 1 138
One whom I will beat into clamorous whining, if thou deniest the least
syllable of thy addition . . . . ii 2 26
I will piece out the comfort with what addition I can . . . iii 6 3
In his own grace he doth exalt himself, More than in your addition . v 3 68
Such addition as your honours Have more than merited. . . v 3 301
And think it no addition, nor my wish, To have him see me woman'd
Othello iii 4 194
You give me the addition Whose want even kills me . . . iv 1 105

Addition. To do the act that might the addition earn Not the world's mass of vanity could make me . . . . . . *Othello* iv 2 163
Parcel the sum of my disgraces by Addition of his envy! *Ant. and Cleo.* v 2 164
Addle. He esteems her no more than I esteem an addle egg *Tr. and Cr.* i 2 145
If you love an addle egg as well as you love an idle head . . i 2 146
Thy head hath been beaten as addle as an egg for quarrelling *R. and J.* iii 1 26
Address. I will then address me to my appointment *Mer. Wives* iii 5 135
He will make no deed at all of this that so seriously he does address himself unto . . . . . . *All's Well* iii 6 103
Good youth, address thy gait unto her; Be not denied access *T. Night* i 4 15
Address yourself to entertain them sprightly . . . *W. Tale* iv 4 53
Unto your grace do I in chief address The substance of my speech *2 Hen. IV.* iv 1 31
A dreadful lav! Address thee instantly . . . . . *2 Hen. VI.* v 2 27
Let us address to tend on Hector's heels . . *Troi. and Cres.* iv 4 148
But dare all imminence that gods and men Address their dangers in . . v 10 14
Once methought It lifted up its head and did address Itself to motion *Hamlet* i 2 216
We first address towards you, who with this king Hath rivall'd for our daughter . . . . *Lear* i 1 193
Addressed. So please your grace, the Prologue is address'd . *M. N. Dr.* v 1 106
He and his competitors in oath Were all address'd to meet you *L. L. L.* ii 1 83
And so have I address'd me. Fortune now To my heart's hope! *M. of V.* ii 9 19
Address'd a mighty power; which were on foot . *As Y. Like It* v 4 162
Our navy is address'd, our power collected, Our substitutes in absence well invested . . . . . . *2 Hen. IV.* iv 4 5
He is address'd: press near and second him . . *J. Cæsar* iii 1 29
But they did say their prayers, and address'd them Again to sleep *Macb.* ii 2 25
Even in your armours, as you are address'd, Will very well become a soldier's dance . . . . . . *Pericles* ii 3 94
Addrest. I might behold addrest The king and his companions *L. L. L.* v 2 92
To-morrow for the march are we addrest . . . . *Hen. V.* iii 3 58
Ad dunghill. Thou hast it ad dunghill, at the fingers' ends . *L. L. Lost* v 1 81
Adhere. They do no more adhere and keep place together *Mer. Wives* ii 1 62
Why, every thing adheres together . . . . *T. Night* iii 4 86
What to her adheres, which follows after, Is the argument of Time *W. T.* iv 1 28
Nor time nor place Did then adhere, and yet you would make both *Macb.* i 7 52
And sure I am two men there are not living To whom he more adheres *Hamlet* ii 2 21
Adieu, valour! rust, rapier! be still, drum! . . . *L. L. Lost* i 2 187
Please it you, As much in private, and I'll bid adieu . . . v 2 241
Twenty adieus, my frozen Muscovits . . . . . v 2 265
And so adieu, sweet Jude! nay, why dost thou stay? . . . v 2 629
If sight and shape be true, Why then, my love adieu! . *As Y. Like It* v 4 127
You have restrained yourself within the list of too cold an adieu *All's Well* ii 1 53
Adieu, till then; then, fail not . . . . . . v 2 64
Congied with the duke, done my adieu with his nearest; buried a wife . iv 3 101
Then, England's ground, farewell; sweet soil, adieu! . *Richard II.* i 3 306
We make woe wanton with this fond delay: Once more, adieu . . v 1 102
Adieu, and take thy praise with thee to heaven! . . *1 Hen. IV.* v 4 99
And thus I seal my truth, and bid adieu . . . *3 Hen. VI.* iv 8 29
Poor heart, adieu! I pity thy complaining . . *Richard III.* iv 1 88
Adieu, poor soul, that takest thy leave of it! . . . . . v 1 91
Once more, adieu: be valiant, and speed well! . . . . v 3 102
He fumbles up into a loose adieu, And scants us with a single famish'd kiss . . . . *Troi. and Cres.* iv 4 48
I hear some noise within; dear love, adieu! Anon, good nurse! *R. and J.* ii 2 136
Hie you to horse: adieu, Till you return at night . . *Macbeth* iii 1 35
Adieu, adieu! Hamlet, remember me . . . . *Hamlet* i 5 91
Now to my word; It is 'Adieu, adieu! remember me.' I have sworn't . i 5 111
Adieu, brave Moor; use Desdemona well . . . . *Othello* i 3 292
Then bid adieu to me, and say the tears Belong to Egypt *Ant. and Cleo.* i 3 77
Write to him—I will subscribe—gentle adieus and greetings . . iv 5 14
Adjacent. And the demesnes that there adjacent lie . *Rom. and Jul.* ii 1 20
A strange invisible perfume hits the sense Of the adjacent wharfs *A. and C.* ii 2 218
Adjoined. To whose huge spokes ten thousand lesser things Are mortised and adjoin'd . . . . *Hamlet* iii 3 20
Adjoining. Our foot Upon the hills adjoining to the city *Ant. and Cleo.* iv 10 5
Adjourn. 'Tis a needful fitness That we adjourn this court *Hen. VIII.* ii 4 232
Adjourned. Why hast thou thus adjourn'd The graces for his merits due, Being all to dolours turn'd? . . . . . *Cymbeline* v 4 78
Adjudged. He adjudged your brother,—Being criminal *Meas. for Meas.* v 1 408
Thou art adjudged to the death And passed sentence may not be recall'd *Com. of Errors* i 1 147
For sins Such as by God's book are adjudged to death . *2 Hen. VI.* ii 3 4
To whom the heavens in thy nativity Adjudged an olive branch *3 Hen. VI.* iv 6 34
To be adjudged some direful slaughtering death, As punishment *T. Andron.* v 3 144
Adjunct. Learning is but an adjunct to ourself . . *L. L. Lost* iv 3 314
Though that my death were adjunct to my act, By heaven, I would do it *K. John* iii 3 57
Administer. To keep the oath that we administer . . . *Richard II.* i 3 182
Administration. In the administration of his law . . *2 Hen. IV.* v 2 75
Admirable. A gentleman of excellent breeding, admirable discourse *M. W.* ii 2 234
It is admirable pleasures and fery honest knaveries . . . . iv 4 80
My admirable dexterity of wit . . . delivered me . . . . iv 5 120
Of great constancy; But, howsoever, strange and admirable *M. N. Dream* v 1 27
O, 'tis brave wars!—Most admirable: I have seen those wars *All's Well* ii 1 26
Beshrew me, the knight's in admirable fooling . . . *T. Night* ii 3 85
O, 'twill be admirable!—Sport royal, I warrant you . . . ii 3 186
Believe me, thou talkest of an admirable conceited fellow *W. Tale* iv 4 203
O admirable youth! he ne'er saw three and twenty. *Troi. and Cres.* i 2 255
O admirable man! Paris? Paris is dirt to him . . . . i 2 258
Admirable: how this grace Speaks his own standing *T. of Athens* i 1 30
In form and moving how express and admirable! . . . *Hamlet* ii 2 318
An admirable evasion of whoremaster man, to lay his goatish disposition to the charge of a star! . . . . *Lear* i 2 137
An admirable musician: O! she will sing the savageness out of a bear *Oth.* iv 1 199
A wonderful sweet air, with admirable rich words to it . . *Cymbeline* ii 3 19
Admiral. Jacques of Chatillon, admiral of France . . *Hen. V.* iv 8 98
Thou art our admiral, thou bearest the lantern in the poop *1 Hen. IV.* iii 3 28
Our high admiral, Shalt waft them over with our royal fleet *3 Hen. VI.* iii 3 252
'Tis thought that Richmond is their admiral . . *Richard III.* iv 4 437
The Antoniad, the Egyptian admiral, With all their sixty, fly *A. and C.* iii 10 2
Admiration. Indeed the top of admiration! . . . *Tempest* iii 1 38
Bring in the admiration; that we with thee May spend our wonder *A. W.* ii 1 91
The changes I perceived . . . were very notes of admiration . *W. Tale* v 2 12
Working so grossly in a natural cause, That admiration did not hoop at them . . . . *Hen. V.* ii 2 108
It is the greatest admiration in the universal world. . . . iv 1 66
Her ashes new create another heir, As great in admiration *Hen. VIII.* v 5 43

Admiration. Season your admiration for a while With an attent ear *Hamlet* i 2 192
Your behaviour hath struck her into amazement and admiration . iii 2 339
But is there no sequel at the heels of this mother's admiration? . . iii 2 342
This admiration, sir, is much o' the savour Of other your new pranks *Lear* i 4 258
I could then have looked on him without the help of admiration *Cymbeline* i 4 5
What makes your admiration?—It cannot be i' the eye . . . i 6 38
Let us bury him, And not protract with admiration what Is now due debt iv 2 232
Admire. These lords At this encounter do so much admire That they devour their reason . . . . *Tempest* v 1 154
Which is to me some praise that I thy parts admire . . *L. L. Lost* iv 2 118
We do admire This virtue and this moral discipline . . *T. of Shrew* i 1 29
Wonder not, nor admire not in thy mind, why I do call thee so *T. Night* iii 4 165
Repent his folly, see his weakness, and admire our sufferance. *Hen. V.* iii 6 132
Where great patricians shall attend and shrug, I' the end admire *Coriol.* i 9 5
Admired Miranda! Indeed the top of admiration! . . *Tempest* iii 1 37
The heaven such grace did lend her That she might admired be *T. G. of V.* iv 2 43
This article is made in vain, Or vainly comes the admired princess *L. L. L.* i 1 141
Hangs the verses on the trees, wherein Rosalind is so admired *As Y. L.* iii 2 412
He came sighing on After the admired heels of Bolingbroke *2 Hen. IV.* i 3 105
All the court admired him for submission . . . . *2 Hen. VI.* iii 1 12
'Tis virtue that doth make them most admired . . . *3 Hen. VI.* i 4 130
With all the admired beauties of Verona . . . *Rom. and Jul.* i 2 89
'Tis thou that rigg'st the bark and plough'st the foam, Settlest admired reverence in a slave . . . . *T. of Athens* v 1 54
You have displaced the mirth, broke the good meeting, With most admired disorder . . . . *Macbeth* iii 4 110
Passion fully strives To make itself, in thee, fair and admired! *A. and C.* i 1 51
Thou hast a sister by the mother's side, Admired Octavia . . . ii 2 121
Celerity is never more admired Than by the negligent . . . iii 7 25
He served with glory and admired success . . . *Cymbeline* i 1 32
She dances As goddess-like to her admired lays . . *Pericles* v Gower 4
Admirer. And ever since a fresh admirer Of what I saw there *Hen. VIII.* i 1 3
Admiring. And as he errs, doting on Hermia's eyes, So I, admiring of his qualities . . . . *M. N. Dream* i 1 231
No feeling, but my sir's song, and admiring the nothing of it. *W. Tale* iv 4 625
And From thy admiring daughter took the spirits, Standing like stone with thee . . . . v 3 41
No extraordinary gaze, Such as is bent on sun-like majesty When it shines seldom in admiring eyes . . . . *1 Hen. IV.* iii 2 80
With modesty admiring thy renown . . . . . *1 Hen. VI.* ii 2 39
Admiringly. The king very lately spoke of him admiringly *All's Well* i 1 33
Admiringly, my liege, at first I stuck my choice upon her . . . v 3 44
Admit. No kind of traffic Would I admit; no name of magistrate *Temp.* ii 1 149
Though Love use Reason for his physician, he admits him not for his counsellor . . . . *Mer. Wives* ii 1 5
We may bring you something on the way.—My haste may not admit it *Meas. for Meas.* i 1 63
Admit no other way to save his life,—As I subscribe not that, nor any other . . . . ii 4 88
To admit no traffic to our adverse towns . . . *Com. of Errors* i 1 15
They will not admit any good part to intermingle with them . *M. Ado* v 2 63
Hard by, To know your answer, whether you'll admit him *Mer. of Venice* iv 1 146
She will admit no kind of suit, No, not the duke's . . *T. Night* i 2 45
If she be so abandon'd to her sorrow As it is spoke, she never will admit me i 4 20
Let us hear them speak Whose title they admit, Arthur's or John's *K. John* ii 1 200
Whose party do the townsmen yet admit?—Speak, citizens, for England ii 1 361
Other gambol faculties a' has, that show a weak mind and an able body, for the which the prince admits him . . . *2 Hen. IV.* ii 4 274
By my will we shall admit no parley. . . . . . . iv 1 159
Our argument Is all too heavy to admit much talk . . . . v 2 24
For the which supply, Admit me Chorus to this history. . *Hen. V.* Prol. 32
Therefore we must needs admit the means How things are perfected . i 1 68
Although I did admit it as a motive The sooner to effect what I intended ii 2 156
This is the latest parle we will admit . . . . . . iii 3 2
Admit the excuse Of time, of numbers and due course of things . v Prol. 3
If sorrow can admit society, Tell o'er your woes again . *Richard III.* iv 4 38
Admit him entrance, Griffith: but this fellow Let me ne'er see *Hen. VIII.* iv 2 107
My love admits no qualifying dross; No more my grief . *Troi. and Cres.* iv 4 9
Admits no orifex for a point as subtle As Ariachne's broken woof . . v 2 151
The people do admit you, and are summon'd To meet anon . *Coriolanus* ii 3 151
My pretext to strike at him admits A good construction . . . v 6 20
Making a treaty where There was a yielding,—this admits no excuse . v 6 69
The people will accept whom he admits . . . . *T. Andron.* i 1 222
She should lock herself from his resort, Admit no messengers . *Hamlet* ii 2 144
If you be honest and fair, your honesty should admit no discourse to your beauty . . . . iii 1 108
Admittance. Now, what admittance, lord? . . . *L. L. Lost* ii 1 80
Of excellent breeding, admirable discourse, of great admittance *M. W.* ii 2 235
The brow that becomes the ship-tire, the tire-valiant, or any tire of Venetian admittance . . . . iii 3 61
Too confident To give admittance to a thought of fear . *2 Hen. IV.* iv 1 153
There are certain ladies most desirous of admittance.—Ladies! *T. of A.* i 2 122
Let 'em have kind admittance: Music, make their welcome! . . i 2 134
Give first admittance to the ambassadors . . . . *Hamlet* ii 2 51
Had I admittance and opportunity to friend . . . *Cymbeline* i 4 115
What If I do line one of their hands? 'Tis gold Which buys admittance ii 3 73
Admitted. Well, let her be admitted . . . . *Meas. for Meas.* ii 2 22
Pluck out his eyes!—You shall not be admitted to his sight . . iv 3 125
I was thinking with what manners I might safely be admitted *All's Well* iv 5 94
I might not be admitted; But from her handmaid do return this answer *T. Night* i 1 24
Surmise Of aids incertain should not be admitted . . *2 Hen. IV.* i 3 24
Excuses shall not be admitted; there is no excuse shall serve . . v 1 6
Or be admitted to your highness' council. . . . *2 Hen. VI.* iii 1 27
To have the warrant, That we may be admitted where he is *Richard III.* i 3 343
Never admitted A private whisper, no, not with such friends *Coriolanus* v 3 6
I pray, let them be admitted . . . . . . *T. of Athens* i 2 127
He fell upon me ere admitted . . . . . *Ant. and Cleo.* ii 2 75
'Tis exactly valued; Not petty things admitted . . . . . v 2 140
Admitting. Never admitting Counsel o' the war . . . *Coriolanus* v 6 96
Admonish. Choice spirits that admonish me . . . *1 Hen. VI.* v 3 3
Admonishing That we should dress us fairly for our end . *Hen. V.* iv 1 9
Admonishment. Thy grave admonishments prevail with me . *1 Hen. VI.* ii 5 98
Ungently temper'd, To stop his ears against admonishment *Tr. and Cr.* v 3 2
Admonition. Double and treble admonition, and still forfeit! *M. for M.* iii 2 205
Darest with thy frozen admonition Make pale our cheek . *Richard II.* ii 1 117
Ado. Good hearts, what ado here is to bring you together! *Mer. Wives* iv 5 128
He makes me no more ado, but whips me out of the chamber *T. G. of V.* iv 4 31
I have much ado to know myself . . . . . *Mer. of Venice* i 1 7
Let's follow, to see the end of this ado . . . . *T. of Shrew* v 1 147

Ado. You had much ado to make his anchor hold . . . *W. Tale* i 2 213
Here's ado, To lock up honesty and honour . . . ii 2 9
Here's such ado to make no stain a stain As passes colouring . . ii 2 19
Show the inside of your purse to the outside of his hand, and no more ado iv 4 834
With much ado at length have gotten leave . . . *Richard II.* v 5 74
I made them no more ado but took all their seven points . 1 *Hen. IV.* ii 4 223
Come then, away; let's ha' no more ado . . . 3 *Hen. VI.* iv 5 27
Make me no more ado, but all embrace him: Be friends . *Hen. VIII.* v 3 159
Would you had hit it too! Then should not we be tired with this ado *T. Andron.* ii 1 98
Make no more ado, But give your pigeons to the emperor . . iv 3 102
We'll keep no great ado,—a friend or two . . *Rom. and Jul.* iii 4 23
No more ado With that harsh, noble, simple nothing . *Cymbeline* iii 4 134
A-doing. The precedent was full as long a-doing . . *Richard III.* iii 6 7
Now we have shown our power, Let us seem humbler after it is done Than when it was a-doing . . . *Coriolanus* iv 2 5
Adonis painted by a running brook, And Cytherea all in sedges hid *T. of Shrew* Ind. 2 52
Thy promises are like Adonis' gardens, That one day bloom'd and fruitful were the next . . . . . 1 *Hen. VI.* i 6 6
Adopt. Who with willing soul Adopts thee heir . . *Richard II.* i 1 109
My title's weak.—Tell me, may not a king adopt an heir? 3 *Hen. VI.* i 1 135
Which, for your best ends, You adopt your policy . . *Coriolanus* iii 2 48
I had rather to adopt a child than get it . . . . *Othello* i 3 191
Adopted. And would not change that calling, To be adopted heir *As Y. L. It* i 2 247
An adopted name of privilege . . . . . 1 *Hen. IV.* v 2 18
And this is he was his adopted heir . . . . 3 *Hen. VI.* ii 4 98
I was adopted heir by his consent: Since when, his oath is broke . ii 2 88
I am incorporate in Rome, A Roman now adopted happily . *T. Andron.* i 1 463
Adoptedly; as school-maids change their names . *Meas. for Meas.* i 4 47
Adoption. Stand under the adoption of abominable terms *Mer. Wives* ii 2 309
'Tis often seen Adoption strives with nature . . . *All's Well* i 3 151
Those friends thou hast, and their adoption tried, Grapple them to thy soul with hoops of steel . . . . . . *Hamlet* i 3 62
To work Her son into the adoption of the crown . . *Cymbeline* v 5 56
Adoptious. With a world Of pretty, fond, adoptious christendoms *All's Well* i 1 188
Adoration. All adoration, duty, and observance, All humbleness *As Y. L. It* v 2 102
With adorations, fertile tears, With groans that thunder love *T. Night* i 5 274
Show me but thy worth! What is thy soul of adoration? *Hen. V.* iv 1 262
Adore. I have seen thee in her and I do adore thee . . *Tempest* ii 2 143
I did adore a twinkling star, But now I worship a celestial sun *T. G. of V.* ii 6 9
To worship shadows and adore false shapes . . . . iv 2 131
I do adore thy sweet grace's slipper.—Loves her by the foot *L. L. Lost* iv 2 672
I adore The sun, that looks upon his worshipper . . *All's Well* i 3 211
Come what may, I do adore thee so, That danger shall seem sport *T. N.* ii 1 48
She's a beagle, true-bred, and one that adores me: what o' that? . . ii 3 196
I may command where I adore . . . . ii 5 115
In the Capitol and senate's right, Whom you pretend to honour and adore *T. Andron.* i 1 42
By the gods that warlike Goths adore, This petty brabble will undo us all ii 1 61
Now, gods that we adore, whereof comes this? . . . *Lear* i 4 312
Loves Cæsar!—Nay, but how dearly he adores Mark Antony! *A. and C.* iii 2 8
In our own filth drop our clear judgements; make us Adore our errors iii 13 114
This gate Instructs you how to adore the heavens . . *Cymbeline* iii 3 3
Adored. Thou shalt be worshipp'd, kiss'd, loved, and adored! *T. G. of V.* iv 4 204
One that adores me: what o' that?—I was adored once too *T. Night* ii 3 197
Bless the accursed, Make the hoar leprosy adored . . *T. of Athens* iv 3 35
That all those eyes adored them ere their fall Scorn now their hand should give them burial . . . . . . *Pericles* ii 4 11
Adorer. I profess myself her adorer, not her friend . . . *Cymbeline* i 4 74
Adorest. By that same god, what god soe'er it be, That thou adorest *T. Andron.* v 1 83
Adoreth. Let the soul forth that adoreth thee . . . *Richard III.* i 2 177
Adorn. Clerk-like experienced, which no less adorns Our gentry than our parents' noble names . . . . . . *W. Tale* i 2 392
Adorn his temples with a coronet . . . . 1 *Hen. VI.* v 4 134
Some score or two of tailors, To study fashions to adorn my body *Richard III.* i 2 258
Till we with trophies do adorn thy tomb . . . *T. Andron.* i 1 388
Adorned. She came adorned hither like sweet May . . *Richard II.* v 1 79
Men and dames so jetted and adorn'd, Like one another's glass *Pericles* i 4 26
Adorning. And made their bends adornings . . *Ant. and Cleo.* ii 2 213
Adornment. The adornment of her bed; the arras; figures *Cymbeline* ii 2 26
Together with the adornment of my qualities . . . . iii 5 140
A-down-a. And down, down, adown-a,—Vat is you sing? . *Mer. Wives* i 4 44
You must sing a-down a-down, An you call him a-down-a *Hamlet* iv 5 170
Adramadio. Where hadst thou it?—Of Dun Adramadio . *L. L. Lost* iv 3 199
Adrian. You know me: your name, I think, is Adrian . *Coriolanus* iv 3 2
Which, of he or Adrian, for a good wager, first begins to crow? *Tempest* ii 1 28
Adriana. I am not Adriana nor thy wife . . . . *Com. of Errors* ii 2 114
To Adriana, villain, hie thee straight: Give her this key . . iv 1 102
Adriano. Don Adriano de Armado . . . . . . *L. L. Lost* i 1 280
In the dearest design of industry, Don Adriano de Armado . . iv 1 89
Who is intituled, nominated, or called, Don Adriano de Armado . . v 1 9
Adriatic. Were she as rough As are the swelling Adriatic seas *T. of Shrew* i 2 74
Adsum.—Asmath, . . . answer that I shall ask . 2 *Hen. VI.* i 4 26
A-ducking. The Egyptians And the Phœnicians go a-ducking *A. and C.* iii 7 65
Adulation. Think'st thou the fiery fever will go out With titles blown from adulation? . . . . *Hen. V.* iv 1 271
Adulterate. I am possess'd with an adulterate blot . *Com. of Errors* ii 2 142
She adulterates hourly with thine uncle John, And with her golden hand hath pluck'd on France . . . . . . *K. John* iii 1 56
The adulterate Hastings, Rivers, Vaughan, Grey, Untimely smother'd in their dusky graves . . . . . . *Richard III.* iv 4 69
That incestuous, that adulterate beast, With witchcraft of his wit *Hamlet* i 5 42
Adulterers, by an enforced obedience of planetary influence . *Lear* i 2 135
Adulteress. Be't known, From him that has most cause to grieve it should be, She's an adulteress . . . . . *W. Tale* ii 1 78
I have said She's an adulteress; I have said with whom . . ii 1 88
If The cause were not in being,—part o' the cause, She the adulteress iii 3 4
And then they call'd me foul adulteress, Lascivious Goth *T. Andron.* ii 3 109
I would divorce me from thy mother's tomb, Sepulchring an adultress *Lear* ii 4 134
Adulteries. With Juno chide, That thy adulteries Rates . . *Cymbeline* v 4 33
Adulterous thief, An hypocrite, a virgin-violator . . *Meas. for Meas.* v 1 40
Adulterous Antony, most large In his abominations, turns you off *Ant. and Cleo.* iii 6 93
Adultery. In fornication, adultery, and all uncleanliness *Meas. for Meas.* ii 1 82
Committing adultery with Polixenes, king of Bohemia . *W. Tale* iii 2 15
We shall see wilful adultery and murder committed . . *Hen. V.* ii 1 40

Adultery. What was thy cause? Adultery? Thou shalt not die: die for adultery! . . . . *Lear* iv 6 112
Of adultery? Wherefore write you not What monster's her accuser? *Cymbeline* iii 2 1
And win this ring By hers and mine adultery . . . . v 5 186
Advance. Who to advance and who To trash for over-topping *Tempest* i 2 80
The fringed curtains of thine eye advance And say what thou seest yond i 2 408
I must advance the colours of my love And not retire *Mer. Wives* iii 4 85
Like favourites, Made proud by princes, that advance their pride *M. Ado* iii 1 10
To the field!—Advance your standards, and upon them . *L. L. Lost* iv 3 367
Every one his love-feat will advance Unto his several mistress . v 2 123
You do advance your cunning more and more . . *M. N. Dream* iii 2 128
Better satisfied How in our means we should advance ourselves 2 *Hen. IV.* i 3 7
Signs of war advance: No king of England, if not king of France *Hen. V.* ii 2 192
Your eyes advance, After your thoughts, straight back again . v Prol. 44
That never war advance His bleeding sword 'twixt England and fair France v 2 382
Advance our waving colours on the walls; Rescued is Orleans 1 *Hen. VI.* i 6 1
Bring forth the body of old Salisbury, And here advance it in the market-place, The middle centre of this cursed town . . . . ii 2 5
How haps it I seek not to advance Or raise myself . . . iii 1 31
Whose hopeful colours Advance our half-faced sun, striving to shine 2 *Hen. VI.* iv 1 98
Advance thy halberd higher than my breast, Or, by Saint Paul, I'll strike thee to my foot . . . . *Richard III.* i 2 40
In the name of God and all these rights, Advance your standards . v 3 264
Advance our standards, set upon our foes; Our ancient word of courage, fair Saint George, Inspire us . . . . v 3 348
He will advance thee; Some little memory of me will stir him *Hen. VIII.* iii 2 416
Advance, brave Titus: They do disdain us much beyond our thoughts *Coriolanus* i 4 25
Have hearts Inclinable to honour and advance The theme of our assembly ii 2 60
To advance Thy name and honourable family, Lavinia will I make my empress . . . . *T. Andron.* i 1 238
If Saturnine advance the Queen of Goths, She will a handmaid be to his desires . . . . i 1 330
That will not suffer you to square yourselves, But to your wishes' height advance you both . . . . ii 1 125
Ere the sun advance his burning eye, The day to cheer and night's dank dew to dry . . . . *Rom. and Jul.* ii 3 5
I must entreat you, honour me so much As to advance this jewel; accept it and wear it . . . . *T. of Athens* i 2 176
Certain issue strokes must arbitrate: Towards which advance the war *Macbeth* v 4 21
For your faithfulness we will advance you . . . *Pericles* i 1 154
Advanced. Like unback'd colts, they prick'd their ears, Advanced their eyelids, lifted up their noses As they smelt music . . *Tempest* iv 1 177
Your son here at home, more advanced by the king . . *All's Well* iv 5 6
You are like to be much advanced: he hath known you but three days, and already you are no stranger . . . . . *T. Night* i 4 2
How he jets under his advanced plumes! . . . . . . ii 5 36
These flags of France, that are advanced here Before the eye *K. John* ii 1 207
By whose fell working I was first advanced . . 2 *Hen. IV.* iv 5 207
When thou hast hung thy advanced sword i' the air, Not letting it decline on the declined . . . . . . *Troi. and Cres.* iv 5 188
Filling the air with swords advanced and darts . . . *Coriolanus* i 6 61
Death, that dark spirit, in's nervy arm doth lie; Which, being advanced, declines, and then men die . . . . ii 1 178
The subtle Queen of Goths Is of a sudden thus advanced in Rome *T. Andron.* i 1 393
Secure of thunder's crack or lightning flash; Advanced above pale envy's threatening reach . . . . ii 1 4
Was't not a happy star Led us to Rome, strangers, and more than so, Captives, to be advanced to this height? . . . . . . iv 2 34
Tell them both the circumstance of all; And how by this their child shall be advanced . . . . iv 2 157
The most you sought was her promotion; For 'twas your heaven she should be advanced . . . . *Rom. and Jul.* iv 5 72
And weep ye now, seeing she is advanced Above the clouds, as high as heaven itself? . . . . iv 5 73
Death's pale flag is not advanced there . . . . . . v 3 96
The poor advanced makes friends of enemies . . . *Hamlet* iii 2 215
One step I have advanced thee . . . . *Lear* v 3 28
Late Advanced in time to great and high estate . . . *Pericles* iv 4 14
Advancement. What a sleep were this For your advancement! *Tempest* ii 1 268
Who knows how that may turn back to my advancement? . *W. Tale* iv 4 867
We will, according to your strengths and qualities, Give you advancement 2 *Hen. IV.* v 5 74
Fear not your advancements; I will be the man yet that shall make you v 5 84
Finding his usurpation most unjust, Endeavour'd my advancement to the throne . . . . 1 *Hen. VI.* ii 5 69
You envy my advancement and my friends' . . . *Richard III.* i 3 75
The advancement of your children, gentle lady.—Up to some scaffold iv 4 241
Do not think I flatter; For what advancement may I hope? . *Hamlet* iii 2 62
Sir, I lack advancement.—How can that be? . . . . iii 2 354
His own disorders Deserved much less advancement . . . *Lear* ii 4 203
Advantage. Make the rope of his destiny our cable, for our own doth little advantage . . . . *Tempest* i 1 34
The next advantage Will we take throughly . . . . . iii 3 13
Made use and fair advantage of his days . . . *T. G. of Ver.* ii 4 68
Where your good word cannot advantage him, Your slander never can endamage him . . . . iii 2 42
He gives her folly motion and advantage . . . *Mer. Wives* iii 2 36
To take an ill advantage of his absence . . . . . . iii 3 116
I something do excuse the thing I hate, For his advantage that I dearly love . . . . *Meas. for Meas.* ii 4 120
Only refer yourself to this advantage, first, that your stay with him may not be long . . . . iii 1 255
I will call upon you anon, for some advantage to yourself . . . iv 1 24
When I did him at this advantage take, An ass's nole I fixed on his head *M. N. Dream* iii 2 16
Methought you said you neither lend nor borrow Upon advantage *M. of V.* i 3 71
Men that hazard all Do it in hope of fair advantages . . . ii 7 19
No other advantage in the process but only the losing of hope *All's Well* i 1 17
That's for advantage.—So is running away, when fear proposes the safety i 1 215
She herself, without other advantage, may lawfully make title to as much love as she finds . . . . i 3 106
It shall advantage thee more than ever . . . . . *T. Night* iv 2 119
The advantage of his absence took the king And in the mean time sojourn'd at my father's . . . . *K. John* i 1 102

Advantage. Call for our chiefest men of discipline, To cull the plots of best advantages . . . . *K. John* ii 1 40
Our trumpet call'd you to this gentle parle—For our advantage . . ii 1 206
Speed then, to take advantage of the field.—It shall be so . . ii 1 297
Till this advantage, this vile-drawing bias, This sway of motion, this Commodity, Makes it take head . . . . ii 1 577
A soul counts thee her creditor And with advantage means to pay thy love . . . . iii 3 22
Freeze up their zeal, That none so small advantage shall step forth iii 4 151
Choke his days With barbarous ignorance and deny his youth The rich advantage of good exercise . . . . iv 2 60
The best part of my power, As I upon advantage did remove . . v 7 62
Ere furthur leisure yield them further means For their advantage *Rich. II.* i 4 41
To know what pricks you on To take advantage of the absent time . ii 3 79
I'll use the advantage of my power And lay the summer's dust with showers of blood . . . . iii 3 42
In those holy fields Over whose acres walk'd those blessed feet Which fourteen hundred years ago were nail'd For our advantage on the bitter cross . . . . *1 Hen. IV.* i 1 27
What there is else, keep close; we'll read it at more advantage . i 3 294
The money shall be paid back again with advantage . . . ii 4 599
Bears his course, and runs me up With like advantage on the other side iii 1 109
Let's away; Advantage feeds him fat, while men delay . . iii 2 180
You give him then advantage.—Not a whit.—Why say you so? . iv 3 2
From this swarm of fair advantages You took occasion to be quickly woo'd v 1 55
Blunt not his love, Nor lose the good advantage of his grace *2 Hen. IV.* iv 4 28
By which his grace must mete the lives of others, Turning past evils to advantages . . . . iv 4 78
Who will make road upon us With all advantages . . . *Hen. V.* i 2 139
Advantage is a better soldier than rashness . . . . iii 6 127
Dying so, death is to him advantage . . . . . . iv 1 190
What watch the king keeps to maintain the peace, Whose hours the peasant best advantages . . . . iv 1 301
But he'll remember with advantages What feats he did that day . iv 3 50
Thence discover how with most advantage They may vex us . *1 Hen. VI.* i 4 12
Or make my ill the advantage of my good . . . . . ii 5 129
Drops bloody sweat from his war-wearied limbs, And, in advantage lingering, looks for rescue . . . . iv 4 19
On that advantage, bought with such a shame . . . . iv 6 44
And, when I spy advantage, claim the crown, For that's the golden mark I seek to hit . . . . *2 Hen. VI.* i 1 242
His advantage following your decease, That he should come about your royal person . . . . iii 1 25
I can add colours to the chameleon, Change shapes with Proteus for advantages . . . . *3 Hen. VI.* iii 2 192
Take all the swift advantage of the hours . . . *Richard III.* iv 1 49
With best advantage will deceive the time, And aid thee . . v 3 92
Does buy and sell his honour as he pleases, And for his own advantage *Hen. VIII.* i 1 193
Hector would not lose So rich advantage of a promised glory *Tr. and Cr.* ii 2 204
The advantage of the time prompts me aloud To call for recompense . iii 3 2
Do not give advantage To stubborn critics, apt, without a theme . v 2 130
So putting him to rage, You should have ta'en the advantage of his choler *Coriolanus* ii 3 206
And lose advantage, which doth ever cool I' the absence of the needer . iv 1 43
Wondrous things, That highly may advantage thee to hear *T. Andron.* v 1 56
It shall advantage more than do us wrong . . . *J. Cæsar* iii 1 242
From which advantage shall we cut him off, If at Philippi we do face him iv 3 210
Who, having some advantage on Octavius, Took it too eagerly . v 3 6
Where there is advantage to be given, Both more and less have given him the revolt . . . . *Macbeth* v 4 11
Colleagued with the dream of his advantage, He hath not fail'd to pester us with message . . . . *Hamlet* i 2 21
You have now the good advantage of the night . . . *Lear* ii 1 24
This is the letter he spoke of, which approves him an intelligent party to the advantages of France . . . . iii 5 13
Let thy wife attend on her; And bring them after in the best advantage *Othello* i 3 298
A finder of occasions, that has an eye can stamp and counterfeit advantages, though true advantage never present itself . . . ii 1 248
Give me advantage of some brief discourse . . . . . iii 3 55
She let it drop by negligence, And, to the advantage, I, being here, took 't up . . . . iii 3 312
Keepest from me all conveniency than suppliest me with the least advantage of hope . . . . iv 2 179
Our advantage serves For a fair victory . . . *Ant. and Cleo.* iv 7 11
To the vales, And hold our best advantage . . . . iv 11 4
With no more advantage than the opportunity of a second conference *Cymbeline* i 4 140
Beyond him in the advantage of the time, above him in birth . . iv 1 12
Stand, stand! We have the advantage of the ground . . . v 2 11
Which gave advantage to an ancient soldier, An honest one, I warrant . v 3 15
Some neighbouring nation, Taking advantage of our misery *Pericles* i 4 66
Advantageable. As your wisdoms best Shall see advantageable *Hen. V.* v 2 88
Advantaged. Your honour untainted, the poor Mariana advantaged, and the corrupt deputy scaled . . . . . . *Meas. for Meas.* iii 1 265
Advantageous. Here is every thing advantageous to life . *Tempest* ii 1 49
Advantageous care Withdrew me from the odds of multitude *Tr. and Cr.* v 4 22
Advantaging their loan with interest Of ten times double gain *Rich. III.* iv 4 323
Adventure. I will not adventure my discretion so weakly . *Tempest* ii 1 187
Would serve to scale another Hero's tower, So bold Leander would adventure it . . . . *T. G. of Ver.* iii 1 120
Say and persever so And in this mist at all adventures go *Com. of Errors* ii 2 218
The fear of your adventure would counsel you to a more equal enterprise *As Y. Like It* i 2 187
Searching of thy wound, I have by hard adventure found mine own . ii 4 45
Of your royal presence I'll adventure The borrow of a week . *W. Tale* i 2 38
What will you adventure To save this brat's life?—Any thing, my lord . . . . ii 3 162
Wouldst adventure To mingle faith with him! . . . . iv 4 470
A man not worth her pains, much less The adventure of her person . v 1 156
The day shall not be up so soon as I, To try the fair adventure of tomorrow . . . . *K. John* v 5 22
The prisoners, Which he in this adventure hath surprised, To his own use he keeps . . . . *1 Hen. IV.* i 1 93
I will lay him down such reasons for this adventure that he shall go . i 2 169
Then will they adventure upon the exploit themselves . . . i 2 192
In the adventure of this perilous day . . . . . . v 2 96
I would he were, and I by him, at all adventures, so we were quit here *Hen. V.* iv 1 121

Adventure. Sullied all his gloss of former honour By this unheedful, desperate, wild adventure . . . . . . *1 Hen. VI.* iv 4 7
I will repeal thee, or, be well assured, Adventure to be banished myself *2 Hen. VI.* iii 2 350
Our scouts have found the adventure very easy . . *3 Hen. VI.* iv 2 18
I dare adventure to be sent to the Tower . . . *Richard III.* i 3 116
I would adventure for such merchandise . . . *Rom. and Jul.* ii 2 84
Almost afraid to stand alone Here in the churchyard; yet I will adventure v 3 11
If you fall in the adventure, our crows shall fare the better for you *Cymb.* iii 1 82
Though peril to my modesty, not death on 't, I would adventure . iii 4 156
What pleasure, sir, find we in life, to lock it From action and adventure? iv 4 3
To taste the fruit of yon celestial tree, Or die in the adventure *Pericles* i 1 22
Who, looking for adventures in the world, Was by the rough seas reft ii 3 83
Adventured. I have adventured To try your taking of a false report *Cymb.* i 6 172
Adventuring. By adventuring both I oft found both . *Mer. of Ven.* i 1 143
Adventurous. As full of peril and adventurous spirit As to o'er-walk a current roaring loud . . . . *1 Hen. IV.* i 3 191
Took the enemy's point, Sheathing the steel in my adventurous body *T. A.* v 3 112
The adventurous knight shall use his foil and target . *Hamlet* ii 2 333
Like thyself, Drawn by report, adventurous by desire . *Pericles* i 1 35
And in your search spend your adventurous worth . . . ii 4 51
Adventurously. If he durst steal any thing adventurously . *Hen. V.* iv 4 79
Adversary. I will be thy adversary toward Anne Page . *Mer. Wives* ii 3 98
Thou art come to answer A stony adversary, an inhuman wretch *M. of V.* iv 1 4
Do as adversaries do in law, Strive mightily, but eat and drink as friends *T. of Shrew* i 2 278
Carried into the leaguer of the adversaries . . . *All's Well* iii 6 28
Think us some band of strangers i' the adversary's entertainment . iv 1 17
His soon-believing adversaries . . . . . *Richard II.* i 1 101
My dancing soul doth celebrate This feast of battle with mine adversary i 3 92
Render'd such aspect As cloudy men use to their adversaries *1 Hen. IV.* iii 2 83
His valour shown upon our crests to-day Hath taught us how to cherish such high deeds Even in the bosom of our adversaries . . . v 5 31
Forsaketh yet the lists By reason of his adversary's odds . *1 Hen. VI.* v 5 33
Instead of mounting barbed steeds To fright the souls of fearful adversaries . . . . *Richard III.* i 1 11
A weeder-out of his proud adversaries, A liberal rewarder of his friends i 3 123
His ancient knot of dangerous adversaries . . . . iii 1 182
Slily have I lurk'd, To watch the waning of mine adversaries . . iv 4 4
Crush down with a heavy fall The usurping helmets of our adversaries! v 3 112
Thy adversary's wife doth pray for thee . . . . . v 3 166
All tending to the good of their adversaries . . . *Coriolanus* iv 3 45
Here were the servants of your adversary, And yours . *Rom. and Jul.* i 1 113
Yet am I noble as the adversary I come to cope . . . *Lear* v 3 123
Adverse. If peradventure He speak against me on the adverse side, I should not think it strange . . . . . *Meas. for Meas.* iv 6 6
It hath in solemn synods been decreed, Both by the Syracusians and ourselves, To admit no traffic to our adverse towns . *Com. of Errors* i 1 15
Grow this to what adverse issue it can, I will put it in practice *Much Ado* ii 2 52
Though time seem so adverse and means unfit . . *All's Well* v 1 26
For his sake Did I expose myself, pure for his love, Into the danger of this adverse town . . . . *T. Night* v 1 87
The adverse winds, Whose leisure I have stay'd, have given him time *K. John* ii 1 57
O, let me have no subject enemies, When adverse foreigners affright my towns! . . . . iv 2 172
Let thy blows, doubly redoubled, Fall like amazing thunder on the casque Of thy adverse pernicious enemy . . . *Richard II* i 3 82
Prosper this realm, keep it from civil broils, Combat with adverse planets in the heavens! . . . . *1 Hen. VI.* i 1 54
My prayers on the adverse party fight . . . *Richard III.* iv 4 190
The king's name is a tower of strength, Which they upon the adverse party want . . . . v 3 13
Adversely. If the drink you give me touch my palate adversely, I make a crooked face at it . . . . *Coriolanus* ii 1 61
Adversity. A man I am cross'd with adversity . *T. G. of Ver.* iv 1 12
A wretched soul, bruised with adversity, We bid be quiet when we hear it cry . . . . *Com. of Errors* ii 1 34
Be patient.—Nay, 'tis for me to be patient; I am in adversity . iv 4 21
Sweet are the uses of adversity, Which, like the toad, ugly and venomous, Wears yet a precious jewel in his head . . *As Y. Like It* ii 1 12
Ring'd about with bold adversity . . . . . *1 Hen. VI.* iv 4 14
Let me embrace thee, sour adversity, For wise men say it is the wisest course . . . . *3 Hen. VI.* iii 1 24
Well said, adversity! and what need these tricks? . *Troi. and Cres.* v 1 14
Adversity's sweet milk, philosophy . . . *Rom. and Jul.* iii 3 55
All indign and base adversities Make head! . . . . *Othello* i 3 274
Advertise. But I do bend my speech To one that can my part in him advertise . . . . *Meas. for Meas.* i 1 42
Wherein he might the king his lord advertise Whether our daughter were legitimate . . . . *Hen. VIII.* ii 4 178
Advertised. Be advertised The Duke of York is newly come *2 Hen. VI.* iv 9 23
By my scouts I was advertised That she was coming . *3 Hen. VI.* ii 1 116
I have advertised him by secret means . . . . . iv 5 9
We are advertised by our loving friends That they do hold their course v 3 18
As I by friends am well advertised . . . . *Richard III.* iv 4 501
I was advertised their great general slept, Whilst emulation in the army crept . . . . *Troi. and Cres.* ii 2 211
Advertisement. My griefs cry louder than advertisement . *Much Ado* v 1 32
That is an advertisement to a proper maid in Florence . *All's Well* iv 3 240
This advertisement is five days old . . . . *1 Hen. IV.* iii 2 172
Yet doth he give us bold advertisement . . . . . iv 1 36
Advertising. As I was then Advertising and holy to your business *Meas. for Meas.* v 1 388
Advice. I chose her when I could not ask my father For his advice, nor thought I had one . . . . *Tempest* v 1 191
How shall I dote on her with more advice, That thus without advice begin to love her! . . . . *T. G. of Ver.* ii 4 208
This pride of hers, Upon advice, hath drawn my love from her . iii 1 73
Thy advice this night I'll put in practice . . . . iii 2 89
A sonnet that will serve the turn To give the onset to thy good advice . iii 2 94
Your own science Exceeds, in that, the lists of all advice *Meas. for Meas.* i 1 6
A man of comfort, whose advice Hath often still'd my brawling discontent iv 1 8
He wants advice.—He will hear none . . . . . iv 2 154
Confess the truth, and say by whose advice Thou camest here to complain v 1 113
I thought it was a fault, but knew it not; Yet did repent me, after more advice . . . . v 1 469
Bassanio upon more advice Hath sent you here this ring *Mer. of Venice* iv 2 6
Know now, upon advice, it toucheth us both . . *T. of Shrew* i 1 117
And understand what advice shall thrust upon thee . *All's Well* i 1 224

Advice. Share the advice betwixt you; if both gain, all The gift doth stretch itself as 'tis received, And is enough for both *All's Well* ii 1 3
You did never lack advice so much . . . iii 4 19
Inform yourselves We need no more of your advice . . *W. Tale* ii 1 168
I would your spirit were easier for advice, Or stronger for your need iv 4 516
So hot a speed with such advice disposed . . . *K. John* iii 4 11
Upon good advice, Whereto thy tongue a party-verdict gave . *Richard II.* i 3 233
I hope your lordship goes abroad by advice . . *2 Hen. IV.* i 2 109
His former strength may be restored With good advice and little medicine . . . . iii 1 43
It was excess of wine that set him on; And on his more advice we pardon him . . . . . . *Hen. V.* ii 2 43
By the grace of God, and Hume's advice . . . . *2 Hen. VI.* i 2 72
That's not suddenly to be perform'd, But with advice and silent secrecy . . . . ii 2 68
By thy advice And thy assistance is King Richard seated *Richard III.* iv 2 3
Now I begin to relish thy advice; And I will give a taste of it *Tr. and Cr.* i 3 388
If you will elect by my advice, Crown him . . *T. Andron.* i 1 228
The Greeks upon advice did bury Ajax that slew himself . . i 1 379
By my advice, all humbled on your knees, You shall ask pardon . . i 1 472
And she shall file our engines with advice, That will not suffer you to square yourselves . . . . ii 1 123
We will prosecute by good advice Mortal revenge . . . iv 1 92
Advise thee, Aaron, what is to be done, And we will all subscribe to thy advice . . . . iv 2 130
We should have else desired your good advice, Which still hath been both grave and prosperous . . . . . *Macbeth* iii 1 21
If you will take a homely man's advice, Be not found here . . iv 2 68
By my advice, Let us impart what we have seen to-night *Hamlet* i 1 168
So by my former lecture and advice, Shall you my son . . ii 1 67
Which done, she took the fruits of my advice . . . . ii 2 145
Some poise, Wherein we must have use of your advice . . *Lear* ii 1 123
This advice is free I give and honest, Probal to thinking . *Othello* ii 3 343
Be prepared to know The purposes I bear; which are, or cease, As you shall give the advice . . . . . *Ant. and Cleo.* i 3 68
Make yourself some comfort Out of your best advice . . *Cymbeline* i 1 156
Scorning advice, read the conclusion, then . . . *Pericles* i 1 56
Nor ask advice of any other thought But faithfulness and courage . i 1 62
Advise. As thou art a gentleman of blood, Advise me . *T. G. of Ver.* iii 1 122
I advise you, let me not find you before me again . . *Meas. for Meas.* ii 1 259
We shall advise this wronged maid to stead up your appointment . . iii 1 260
She'll take the enterprise upon her, father, If you advise it . . iv 1 67
I will give him a present shrift and advise him for a better place . . iv 2 223
I am come to advise you, comfort you, and pray with you . . iv 3 55
Friar, advise him; I leave him to your hand . . . . v 1 490
Let the friar advise you . . . . *Much Ado* iv 1 246
Gramercies, Tranio, well dost thou advise . . . *T. of Shrew* i 1 41
I advise You use your manners discreetly in all kind of companies . i 1 246
Be gone, or talk not, I advise you . . . . i 2 44
To do you courtesy, This will I do, and this I will advise you . . iv 2 92
Now do your duty throughly, I advise you . . . . . iv 4 11
'Tis an unseason'd courtier; good my lord, Advise him . *All's Well* i 1 81
Go with me to my chamber, and advise me . . . . . iii 3 311
I hope I need not to advise you further . . . . . . iii 5 27
She thus advises thee that sighs for thee . . . *T. Night* ii 5 165
Advise you what you say; the minister is here . . . . iv 2 102
Thou dost advise me Even so as I mine own course have set down *W. Tale* i 2 339
Go, bid thy master well advise himself . . . . *Hen. V.* iii 6 168
I advise you—And take it from a heart that wishes towards you Honour and plenteous safety . . . . *Hen. VIII.* i 1 102
Lo, where comes that rock That I advise your shunning . . . i 1 114
Not a man in England Can advise me like you . . . . . i 1 135
I shall anon advise you Further in the proceeding . . . i 2 107
But, good sir, What peace you'll make, advise me . . *Coriolanus* v 3 197
A Roman now adopted happily, And must advise the emperor *T. Andron.* i 1 464
Advise thee, Aaron, what is to be done, And we will all subscribe to thy advice . . . . iv 2 129
Lay hand on heart, advise: An you be mine, I'll give you to my friend *Rom. and Jul.* iii 5 192
'Tis in the malice of mankind that he thus advises us . *T. of Athens* iv 3 457
Within this hour at most I will advise you where to plant yourselves *Macbeth* iii 1 129
That well might Advise him to a caution, to hold what distance His wisdom can provide . . . . iii 6 44
Can you advise me?—I'm lost in it, my lord . . . *Hamlet* iv 7 54
Brother, I advise you to the best; go armed . . . *Lear* i 2 188
What grows of it, no matter; advise your fellows so . . . i 3 23
Advise yourself.—I am sure on 't, not a word . . . . ii 1 29
Advise the duke, where you are going, to a most festinate preparation . iii 7 9
Therefore I do advise you, take this note . . . . . iv 5 29
You advise me well.—I protest, in the sincerity of love . . *Othello* ii 3 332
You shall advise me in all for Cleopatra . . *Ant. and Cleo.* v 2 137
I would advise you to shift a shirt; the violence of action hath made you reek . . . . *Cymbeline* i 2 1
What your own love will out of this advise you, follow . . . iii 2 46
With dead cheeks advise thee to desist For going on death's net *Pericles* i 1 39
But yet I know you'll do as I advise . . . . . . iv 3 51
Advised. I like thy counsel; well hast thou advised . *T. G. of Ver.* i 3 34
And advised him for the entertainment of death . *Meas. for Meas.* iii 2 225
Yet I am advised to do it; He says, to veil full purpose . . iv 6 3
I am advised what I say, Neither disturbed with the effect of wine, Nor heady-rash . . . . *Com. of Errors* v 1 214
Be first advised, In conflict that you get the sun of them . *L. L. Lost* iv 3 368
If by me you'll be advised, Let's mock them still . . . v 2 300
And were you well advised?—I was, fair madam . . . . v 2 434
Be advised, fair maid: To you your father should be as a god *M. N. Dream* i 1 46
Never to speak to lady afterward In way of marriage: therefore be advised . . . . *Mer. of Venice* ii 1 42
Be well advised How you do leave me to mine own protection . . v 1 234
Art thou not advised, he took some care To get her cunning schoolmasters? . . . . *T. of Shrew* i 1 191
I will seem friendly, as thou hast advised me . . . *W. Tale* i 2 350
Be advised.—I am, and by my fancy: if my reason Will thereto be obedient, I have reason . . . . iv 4 492
Be well advised, tell o'er thy tale again . . . . *K. John* iii 1 5
Be advised; stir not to-night.—Do not, my lord . . *1 Hen. IV.* iv 3 5
You were advised his flesh was capable Of wounds and scars *2 Hen. IV.* i 1 172
As I was then advised by my learned counsel in the laws . . . i 2 153
Be advised there's nought in France That can be with a nimble galliard won . . . . *Hen. V.* i 2 251

Advised. Advised by good intelligence Of this most dreadful preparation *Hen. V.* ii Prol. 12
Are ye advised? the east side of the grove? . . . . . *2 Hen. VI.* ii 1 48
The envious people laugh And bid me be advised how I tread . . . ii 4 36
Kneeled at my feet, and bade me be advised . . . *Richard III.* ii 1 107
Be advised; Heat not a furnace for your foe so hot That it do singe yourself . . . . *Hen. VIII.* i 1 139
Spare me, till I may Be by my friends in Spain advised . . . ii 4 55
Or whether since he is advised by aught To change the course . *Lear* v 1 2
Be advised; He comes to bad intent . . . . . *Othello* i 2 55
I am advised to give her music o' mornings . . . *Cymbeline* ii 3 13
Advised age. To achieve The silver livery of advised age . *2 Hen. VI.* v 2 47
Advised head. While that the armed hand doth fight abroad, The advised head defends itself at home . . . . . *Hen. V.* i 2 179
Advised purpose. Nor never by advised purpose meet To plot *Richard II.* i 3 188
Advised respect. More upon humour than advised respect . *K. John* iv 2 214
Advised watch. In my school-days, when I had lost one shaft, I shot his fellow of the self-same flight The self-same way with more advised watch, To find the other forth . . . . . *Mer. of Venice* i 1 142
Advisedly. Your lord Will never more break faith advisedly . . v 1 253
We will not now be troubled with reply: We offer fair; take it advisedly *1 Hen. IV.* v 1 114
Advising. Therefore fasten your ear on my advisings . *Meas. for Meas.* iii 1 203
Advocate. What! An advocate for an impostor! . . . *Tempest* i 2 477
My soul should sue as advocate for thee . . . *Com. of Errors* iv 2 146
And undertake to be Her advocate to the loud'st . . . *W. Tale* ii 2 39
What advocate hast thou to him?—I know not . . . . iv 4 766
Advocate's the court-word for a pheasant . . . . . iv 4 768
Step forth mine advocate; at your request My father will grant precious things as trifles . . . . v 1 221
Have been An earnest advocate to plead for him . . *Richard III.* i 3 87
So soon as I can win the offended king, I will be known your advocate *Cymbeline* i 1 76
Advocation. My advocation is not now in tune . . . *Othello* iii 4 123
A-dying. Thou, now a-dying, say'st thou flatterest me . *Richard II.* ii 1 90
Æacida. Aio te, Æacida, Romanos vincere posse . . *2 Hen. VI.* i 4 65
Æacides Was Ajax, call'd so from his grandfather . *T. of Shrew* iii 1 52
Ædile. Seize him, ædiles!—Down with him! . . . *Coriolanus* iii 1 183
Have we not had a taste of his obedience? Our ædiles smote? . . iii 1 319
Ægeon. Hapless Ægeon, whom the fates have mark'd . *Com. of Errors* i 1 141
Helpless doth Ægeon wend, But to procrastinate his lifeless end . . i 1 158
Ægeon art thou not? or else his ghost? . . . . . . v 1 337
Speak, old Ægeon, if thou be'st the man That hadst a wife once call'd Æmilia . . . . v 1 341
O, if thou be'st the same Ægeon, speak, And speak unto the same Æmilia! . . . . v 1 344
Ægle. And make him with fair Ægle break his faith, With Ariadne and Antiopa . . . . *M. N. Dream* ii 1 79
Æmilia. The man that hadst a wife once call'd Æmilia . *Com. of Errors* v 1 342
If thou be'st the same Ægeon, speak, And speak unto the same Æmilia! v 1 345
Æmilius, do this message honourably . . . . *T. Andron.* iv 4 104
Æneas. Widow Dido!—What if he had said 'widower Æneas' too? *Temp.* ii 1 79
As did Æneas old Anchises bear, So bear I thee . . . *2 Hen. VI.* v 2 62
Æneas bare a living load, Nothing so heavy as these woes of mine . . v 2 64
What news, Æneas, from the field to-day? . . . *Troi. and Cres.* i 1 111
That's Æneas: is not that a brave man? he's one of the flowers of Troy i 2 202
Jove, let Æneas live, If to my sword his fate be not the glory! . . iv 1 25
As you and Lord Æneas Consent upon the order of their fight, So be it iv 5 89
Thus says Æneas; one that knows the youth Even to his inches . . iv 5 110
Æneas is a-field; And I do stand engaged to many Greeks . . . v 3 67
Ajax hath ta'en Æneas: shall it be? . . . . v 6 22
Bid Æneas tell the tale twice o'er, How Troy was burnt . *T. Andron.* iii 2 27
As Æneas, our great ancestor, Did from the flames of Troy upon his shoulder The old Anchises bear . . . . . . *J. Cæsar* i 2 112
One speech in it I chiefly loved: 'twas Æneas' tale to Dido . *Hamlet* ii 2 468
Dido and her Æneas shall want troops, And all the haunt be ours *Ant. and Cleo.* iv 14 53
Like false Æneas, Were in his time thought false . . *Cymbeline* iii 4 60
Æolus would not be a murderer, But left that hateful office unto thee *2 Hen. VI.* iii 2 92
Aerial. Till we make the main and the aerial blue An indistinct regard *Othello* ii 1 39
Aery. Like an eagle o'er his aery towers, To souse annoyance . *K. John* v 2 149
I was born so high, Our aery buildeth in the cedar's top *Richard III.* i 3 264
Your aery buildeth in our aery's nest . . . . . . i 3 270
An aery of children, little eyases, that cry out on the top of question *Ham.* ii 2 354
Æsculapius. What says my Æsculapius? my Galen? . *Mer. Wives* ii 3 29
Her relapse is mortal. Come, come; And Æsculapius guide us! *Pericles* iii 2 111
Æson. In such a night Medea gather'd the enchanted herbs, That did renew old Æson . . . . *Mer. of Venice* v 1 14
Æsop. Let Æsop fable in a winter's night; His currish riddles sort not with this place . . . . *3 Hen. VI.* v 5 25
Ætna. Now let hot Ætna cool in Sicily, And be my heart an ever-burning hell! . . . . *T. Andron.* iii 1 242
Afar. There is, as 'twere, a tender, a kind of tender, made afar off *M. W.* i 1 216
Saw afar off in the orchard this amiable encounter . . *Much Ado* iii 3 160
He who shall speak for her is afar off guilty But that he speaks *W. Tale* ii 1 104
New broils To be commenced in strands afar remote . *1 Hen. IV.* i 1 4
Afeard. I have not 'scaped drowning to be afeard now . *Tempest* ii 2 62
I am Trinculo—be not afeard—thy good friend Trinculo . . . ii 2 106
I afeard of him! A very weak monster! . . . . . . ii 2 148
Art thou afeard?—No, monster, not I.—Be not afeard . . . iii 2 142
I care not for that, but that I am afeard . . . *Mer. Wives* iii 4 28
A conqueror, and afeard to speak! run away for shame . *L. L. Lost* v 2 582
Will not the ladies be afeard of the lion? . . . *M. N. Dream* iii 1 28
This is a knavery of them to make me afeard . . . . . iii 1 116
To be afeard of my deserving Were but a weak disabling of myself *Mer. of Venice* ii 7 29
I am half afeard Thou wilt say anon he is some kin to thee . . ii 9 96
Then never trust me, if I be afeard . . . . *T. of Shrew* v 2 17
Hortensio is afeard of you . . . . v 2 19
I am afeard the life of Helen, lady, Was foully snatch'd . *All's Well* v 3 153
I was not much afeard; for once or twice I was about to speak *W. Tale* iv 4 453
I am but sorry, not afeard; delay'd, But nothing alter'd . . . iv 4 474
If you be afeard to hear the worst, Then let the worst unheard fall on your head . . . . *K. John* iv 2 135
But tell me, Hal, art not thou horrible afeard? . . *1 Hen. IV.* ii 4 402
I am afeard there are few die well that die in a battle . . *Hen. V.* iv 1 148
From their ashes shall be rear'd A phœnix that shall make all France afeard . . . . *1 Hen. VI.* iv 7 93

Afeard. Death, at whose name I oft have been afear'd . 2 *Hen. VI.* ii 4 89
Jealousy—Which, I beseech you, call a virtuous sin—Makes me afeard *Troi. and Cres.* iv 4 84
Blessed night! I am afeard, Being in night, all this is but a dream *R. and J.* ii 2 139
Have I in conquest stretch'd mine arm so far, To be afeard to tell graybeards the truth? . *J. Cæsar* ii 2 67
Nothing afeard of what thyself didst make, Strange images of death *Macb.* i 3 96
Art thou afeard To be the same in thine own act and valour As thou art in desire? . . . . i 7 39
Fie, my lord, fie! a soldier, and afeard? . . . . v 1 41
Pass with your best violence; I am afeard you make a wanton of me *Ham.* v 2 310
He is afeard to come.—I will not hurt him . . . *Ant. and Cleo.* ii 5 81
Where is the fellow?—Half afeard to come . . . iii 3 1
Art not afeard?—Those that I reverence those I fear, the wise: At fools I laugh, not fear them . . . *Cymbeline* iv 2 94
Affability. Her wit, Her affability and bashful modesty . *T. of Shrew* ii 1 49
You do not use me with that affability as in discretion you ought *Hen. V.* iii 2 139
Seek none, conspiracy; Hide it in smiles and affability . *J. Cæsar* ii 1 82
Affable. An affable and courteous gentleman . *T. of Shrew* i 2 98
With gentle conference, soft and affable . . . ii 1 253
Wondrous affable and as bountiful As mines of India . 1 *Hen. IV.* iii 1 168
We know the time since he was mild and affable . 2 *Hen. VI.* iii 1 9
Courteous destroyers, affable wolves, meek bears! . . *T. of Athens* iii 6 105
Affair. I'll leave you to confer of home affairs . . *T. G. of Ver.* ii 4 119
Go with me to my chamber, In these affairs to aid me with thy counsel ii 4 185
I am to break with thee of some affairs That touch me near . . iii 1 59
Hope is a curtal dog in some affairs . . . *Mer. Wives* ii 1 114
No longer staying but to give the mother Notice of my affair *M. for Meas.* i 4 87
Lord Angelo, having affairs to heaven, Intends you for his swift ambassador . . . . iii 1 57
My stay must be stolen out of other affairs . . . . iii 1 159
Whiles I in this affair do thee employ, I'll to my queen . *M. N. Dream* iii 2 374
Not I, but my affairs, have made you wait . *Mer. of Venice* ii 6 22
He dies that touches any of this fruit Till I and my affairs are answered *As Y. Like It* ii 7 99
We serve you, madam, In that and all your worthiest affairs *All's Well* iii 2 99
You have made the days and nights as one, To wear your gentle limbs in my affairs . . . . v 1 4
I know thy constellation is right apt For this affair . *T. Night* i 4 36
One thing more, that you be never so hardy to come again in his affairs ii 2 10
She could not sway her house, command her followers, Take and give back affairs and their dispatch . . . . . iv 3 18
My affairs Do even drag me homeward . . . . *W. Tale* i 2 23
In your affairs, my lord, If ever I were wilful-negligent, It was my folly i 2 254
What his happier affairs may be, are to me unknown . . iv 2 34
And, for the ordering your affairs, To sing them too . . iv 4 139
Is not your father grown incapable Of reasonable affairs? . . iv 4 409
Whereupon I command thee to open thy affair . . . iv 4 764
To treat of high affairs touching that time . . *K. John* i 1 101
Why may not I demand Of thine affairs, as well as thou of mine? . v 6 5
And for these great affairs do ask some charge, Towards our assistance we do seize to us The plate, coin, revenues, and moveables *Richard II.* ii 1 159
If I know how or which way to order these affairs Thus thrust disorderly into my hands, Never believe me . . . ii 2 109
The devil and mischance look big Upon the maidenhead of our affairs 1 *Hen. IV.* iv 1 59
Being upon hasty employment in the king's affairs . . 2 *Hen. IV.* ii 1 140
Loving wife, and gentle daughter, Give even way unto my rough affairs ii 3 2
Like a brother toil'd in my affairs And laid his love and life under my foot iii 1 62
A cough, sir, which I caught with ringing in the king's affairs . iii 2 194
The Lord bless you! God prosper your affairs! God send us peace! iii 2 313
In these great affairs, I must acquaint you that I have received New-dated letters . . . . iv 1 6
Putting all affairs else in oblivion, as if there were nothing else to be done v 5 27
Hear him debate of commonwealth affairs, You would say it hath been all in all his study . . . . . *Hen. V.* i 1 41
Let it rest; Other affairs must now be managed . 1 *Hen. VI.* iv 1 181
I come to talk of commonwealth affairs . . . 2 *Hen. VI.* i 3 157
My lord is cold in great affairs, Too full of foolish pity . . iii 1 224
Provide me soldiers, lords, Whiles I take order for mine own affairs iii 1 320
First of all your chief affairs, Let me entreat . . 3 *Hen. VI.* iv 6 58
I was a pack-horse in his great affairs . . . *Richard III.* i 3 122
All that dare Look into these affairs see this main end . *Hen. VIII.* ii 2 41
Know your times of business: Is this an hour for temporal affairs? . ii 2 73
They should be good men; their affairs as righteous . . . iii 1 22
Affairs that walk, As they say spirits do, at midnight, have In them a wilder nature than the business That seeks dispatch by day . . v 1 13
From your affairs I hinder you too long . . . . v 1 53
What's your affair, I pray you? . . . . *Troi. and Cres.* i 3 247
Should not our father Bear the great sway of his affairs with reasons? . ii 2 35
Antenor, I know, is such a wrest in their affairs That their negotiations all must slack, Wanting his manage . . . . . iii 3 23
Wife, mother, child, I know not. My affairs Are servanted to others *Cor.* v 2 88
Will follow The fortunes and affairs of noble Brutus . *J. Cæsar* iii 1 135
We have lost Best half of our affair . . . . *Macbeth* iii 3 21
Nor have we herein barr'd Your better wisdoms, which have freely gone With this affair along . . . . . . *Hamlet* i 2 16
I know you are no truant. But what is your affair in Elsinore? . i 2 174
Put your discourse into some frame and start not so wildly from my affair iii 2 321
Every thing is seal'd and done That else leans on the affair . iv 3 59
The sight is dismal; And our affairs from England come too late . v 2 379
Her gentleman abused, assaulted, For following her affairs . *Lear* ii 2 157
The affair cries haste, And speed must answer it . . *Othello* i 3 278
Let's have no more of this; let's to our affairs.—Forgive us our sins! . ii 3 115
There are a kind of men so loose of soul, That in their sleeps will mutter their affairs . . . . iii 3 417
I protest, I have dealt most directly in thy affair . . . iv 2 212
I have eyes upon him, And his affairs come to me on the wind *A. and C.* iii 6 63
Alexas did revolt; and went to Jewry on Affairs of Antony . . iv 6 13
If one of mean affairs May plod it in a week, why may not I Glide thither in a day? . . . . *Cymbeline* iii 2 52
Affaire. Je m'en vais a la cour—la grande affaire . . *Mer. Wives* i 4 54
Affairs in hand. The revenue whereof shall furnish us For our affairs in hand . . . . *Richard II.* i 4 47
Affairs of death. How did you dare To trade and traffic with Macbeth In riddles and affairs of death? . . . . *Macbeth* iii 5 5
Affairs of love. Friendship is constant in all other things Save in the office and affairs of love . . . . . *Much Ado* ii 1 183
Break but a part of the thousandth part of a minute in the affairs of love *As Y. Like It* iv 1 47

Affairs of men. There is a tide in the affairs of men, Which, taken at the flood, leads on to fortune . . . . *J. Cæsar* iv 3 218
Since the affairs of men rest still incertain, Let's reason with the worst that may befall . . . . v 1 96
Affairs of state. Beseech you, proceed to the affairs of state . *Othello* i 3 220
Affect. There is a lady in Verona here Whom I affect . *T. G. of Ver.* iii 1 82
Sir John affects thy wife.—Why, sir, my wife is not young *Mer. Wives* ii 1 115
That Slender, though well landed, is an idiot; And he my husband best of all affects . . . . iv 4 87
Of government the properties to unfold, Would seem in me to affect speech and discourse . . . . . *Meas. for Meas.* i 1 4
Nor do I think the man of safe discretion That does affect it . . i 1 73
No child but Hero; she's his only heir. Dost thou affect her? *Much Ado* i 1 298
Every man with his affects is born, Not by might master'd but by special grace . . . . *L. L. Lost* i 1 152
I do affect the very ground, which is base, where her shoe, which is baser, guided by her foot, which is basest, doth tread . . . i 2 172
I will something affect the letter, for it argues facility . . iv 2 56
In brief, sir, study what you most affect . . *T. of Shrew* i 1 40
If you affect him, sister, here I swear I'll plead for you myself . ii 1 14
Lest it be rather thought you affect a sorrow than have it *All's Well* i 1 60
I do affect a sorrow indeed, but I have it too . . . i 1 62
Maria once told me she did affect me . . . *T. Night* ii 5 28
Wooing poor craftsmen with the craft of smiles And patient underbearing of his fortune, As 'twere to banish their affects with him *Rich. II.* i 4 30
If I affect it more Than as your honour and as your renown, Let me no more from this obedience rise . . . 2 *Hen. IV.* iv 5 145
How doth your grace affect their motion? . . 1 *Hen. VI.* v 1 7
Not whom we will, but whom his grace affects, Must be companion . v 5 57
By this I shall perceive the commons' mind, How they affect the house and claim of York . . . . . . 2 *Hen. VI.* iii 1 375
As I belong to worship and affect In honour honesty . *Hen. VIII.* i 1 39
The will dotes that is attributive To what infectiously itself affects *Troi. and Cres.* ii 2 59
Mock not, that I affect the untraded oath . . . iv 5 178
To seem to affect the malice and displeasure of the people . *Coriolanus* ii 2 23
In this point charge him home, that he affects Tyrannical power . . iii 3 1
'Tis policy and stratagem must do That you affect . . *T. Andron.* ii 1 105
He does neither affect company, nor is he fit for't . . *T. of Athens* i 2 30
I know, no man Can justly praise but what he does affect . . i 2 221
Thou dost affect my manners, and dost use them . . . iv 3 199
This is some fellow, Who, having been praised for bluntness, doth affect A saucy roughness . . . . *Lear* ii 2 102
Not To please the palate of my appetite, Nor to comply with heat—the young affects In me defunct—and proper satisfaction . *Othello* i 3 264
Not to affect many proposed matches Of her own clime, complexion, and degree, Whereto we see in all things nature tends . . iii 3 229
Affectation. 'He hears with ear'? why, it is affectations *Mer. Wives* i 1 152
Three-piled hyperboles, spruce affectation, Figures pedantical *L. L. Lost* v 2 407
No matter in the phrase that might indict the author of affectation *Ham.* ii 2 464
Affected. And how stand you affected to his wish? . *T. G. of Ver.* i 3 60
In conclusion, I stand affected to her . . . . ii 1 90
My daughter will I question how she loves you, And as I find her, so am I affected . . . . *Mer. Wives* iii 4 95
He surely affected her for her wit.—It was so, sir; for she had a green wit *L. L. Lost* i 2 92
With what?—With that which we lovers entitle affected . . ii 1 232
Men of note—do you note me?—that most are affected to these . iii 1 26
Too spruce, too affected, too odd, as it were, too peregrinate . v 1 15
Gentle master mine, I am in all affected as yourself . *T. of Shrew* i 1 26
Have I affected wealth or honour? speak . . 2 *Hen. VI.* iv 7 104
Sound thou Lord Hastings, How he doth stand affected. *Richard III.* iii 1 171
A woman's heart; which ever yet Affected eminence . *Hen. VIII.* ii 3 29
And the will dotes that is attributive To what infectiously itself affects, Without some image of the affected merit . . *Troi. and Cres.* ii 2 60
Were it not glory that we more affected Than the performance of our heaving spleens . . . . ii 2 195
Thou hast affected the fine strains of honour, To imitate the graces of the gods . . . . *Coriolanus* v 3 149
And may, for aught thou know'st, affected be . . *T. Andron.* ii 1 28
I thought the king had more affected the Duke of Albany . . *Lear* i 1 1
He was of that consort.—No marvel, then, though he were ill affected . ii 1 100
She never loved you, only Affected greatness got by you, not you *Cymb.* v 5 38
Affectest. Thou a sceptre's heir, That thus affect'st a sheep-hook! *W. T.* iv 4 431
I go from hence Thy soldier, servant; making peace or war As thou affect'st . . . . *Ant. and Cleo.* i 3 71
Affecteth. He hath a trick of Cœur-de-lion's face; The accent of his tongue affecteth him . . . . *K. John* i 1 86
Affecting. I never heard such a drawling, affecting rogue *Mer. Wives* ii 1 145
Self-loving,—And affecting one sole throne, Without assistance *Coriol.* iv 6 32
Such antic, lisping, affecting fantasticoes . . *Rom. and Jul.* ii 4 29
Affection. Were't not affection chains thy tender days *T. G. of Ver.* i 1 3
I stand affected to her.—I would you were set, so your affection would cease . . . . ii 1 91
And your affection not gone forth, I'll make you The queen of Naples *Tempest* i 2 448
My affections Are then most humble; I have no ambition to see a goodlier man . . . . i 2 481
Fair encounter Of two most rare affections! . . . . iii 1 75
If you now beheld them, your affections Would become tender . v 1 18
But can you affection the 'oman? . . . . *Mer. Wives* i 1 234
Would it apply well to the vehemency of your affection? . . ii 2 248
Anne Page; Who mutually hath answer'd my affection . . iv 6 10
As school-maids change their names By vain though apt affection *M. for M.* i 4 48
In the working of your own affections, Had time cohered with place or place with wishing . . . . ii 1 10
By the affection that now guides me most, I'll prove a tyrant to him . ii 4 168
Thou hast neither heat, affection, limb, nor beauty, To make thy riches pleasant . . . . iii 1 37
Has he affections in him, That thus can make him bite the law by the nose? . . . . iii 1 108
This forenamed maid hath yet in her the continuance of her first affection iii 1 249
Do their gay vestments his affections bait? . *Com. of Errors* ii 1 94
Hath not else his eye Stray'd his affection in unlawful love? . . v 1 51
How know you he loves her?—I heard him swear his affection *M. Ado* ii 1 175
Into a mountain of affection . . . . . . ii 1 382
Whatsoever comes athwart his affection ranges evenly with mine . ii 2 7
She loves him with an enraged affection; it is past the infinite of thought ii 3 106
I would have thought her spirit had been invincible against all assaults of affection . . . . ii 3 120

Affection. Hath she made her affection known? . *Much Ado* ii 3 127

It seems her affections have their full bent . ii 3 231

She will rather die than give any sign of affection . ii 3 236

To wish him wrestle with affection . . . . iii 1 42

She cannot love, Nor take no shape nor project of affection . iii 1 55

Writ in my cousin's hand, stolen from her pocket, Containing her affection unto Benedick . . . . v 4 90

Brave conquerors,—for so you are, That war against your own affections *L. L. Lost* i 1 9

If drawing my sword against the humour of affection would deliver me from the reprobate thought of it . . . . i 2 63

Pleasant without scurrility, witty without affection . v 1 4

It is the king's most sweet pleasure and affection . v 1 93

O that my prayers could such affection move! . *M. N. Dream* i 1 197

Tender me, forsooth, affection, But by your setting on, by your consent iii 2 230

The better part of my affections would Be with my hopes *Mer. of Venice* i 1 16

But what warmth is there in your affection towards any of these? i 2 37

According to my description, level at my affection . i 2 41

Stood as fair As any comer I have look'd on yet For my affection . ii 1 22

With affection wondrous sensible He wrung Bassanio's hand . ii 8 48

Hath not a Jew hands, organs, dimensions, senses, affections, passions? iii 1 62

Affection, Mistress of passion, sways it to the mood Of what it likes iv 1 50

The motions of his spirit are dull as night And his affections dark as Erebus . . . . v 1 87

I will render thee again in affection; by mine honour *As You Like It* i 2 22

Come, come, wrestle with thy affections . . i 3 21

My affection hath an unknown bottom, like the bay of Portugal.—Or rather, bottomless, that as fast as you pour affection in, it runs out iv 1 212

Affection is not rated from the heart . *T. of Shrew* i 1 165

'B mi,' Bianca, take him for thy lord, 'C fa ut,' that loves with all affection . . . . iii 1 76

I have often heard Of your entire affection to Bianca . iv 2 23

Lucentio here Doth love my daughter and she loveth him, Or both dissemble deeply their affections . . . . . . iv 4 42

Come, come, disclose The state of your affection . *All's Well* i 3 196

How will she love, when the rich golden shaft Hath kill'd the flock of all affections else That live in her! . . . *T. Night* i 1 36

Let thy love be younger than thyself, Or thy affection cannot hold the bent . . . . ii 4 38

There rooted betwixt them then such an affection, which cannot choose but branch now . . . . . *W. Tale* i 1 26

Affection! thy intention stabs the centre . . i 2 138

This shows a sound affection . . . . iv 4 390

I Am heir to my affection . . . . . iv 4 492

With thought of such affections, Step forth mine advocate . v 1 220

The affection of nobleness which nature shows above her breeding v 2 40

Thither with all greediness of affection are they gone . v 2 111

Great affections wrestling in thy bosom Doth make an earthquake of nobility . . . . *K. John* v 2 41

Yet let me wonder, Harry, At thy affections . 1 *Hen. IV.* iii 2 30

In speech, in gait, In diet, in affections of delight . . 2 *Hen. IV.* ii 3 29

Thou hast a better place in his affection Than all thy brothers . iv 4 22

O, with what wings shall his affections fly Towards fronting peril! iv 4 65

Did with the least affection of a welcome Give entertainment . iv 5 173

My father is gone wild into his grave, For in his tomb lie my affections v 2 124

It shows my earnestness of affection,—It doth so . . v 5 17

His affections are higher mounted than ours . *Hen. V.* iv 1 110

Your affections and your appetites and your digestions doo's not agree with it . . . . v 1 26

Bear her this jewel, pledge of my affection . 1 *Hen. VI.* v 1 47

Have I with all my full affections Still met the king? *Hen. VIII.* iii 1 129

My king is tangled in affection to A creature of the queen's . iii 2 35

If this law Of nature be corrupted through affection . *Troi. and Cres.* ii 2 177

If I could temporise with my affection, Or brew it to a weak and colder palate . . . . iv 4 6

Unto the appetite and affection common Of the whole body *Coriolanus* i 1 107

Your affections are A sick man's appetite . . i 1 181

More after our commandment than as guided By your own true affections ii 3 239

Out, affection! All bond and privilege of nature, break! . v 3 24

Measuring his affections by my own, That most are busied when they're most alone . . . . . *Rom. and Jul.* i 1 133

Old desire doth in his death-bed lie, And young affection gapes to be his heir . . . . ii Prol. 2

Had she affections and warm youthful blood, She would be as swift in motion as a ball . . . . ii 5 12

Affection makes him false; he speaks not true . . iii 1 182

I weigh my friend's affection with mine own; I'll tell you true *T. of Athens* i 2 222

I have not known when his affections sway'd More than his reason *J. C.* ii 1 20

The people 'twixt Philippi and this ground Do stand but in a forced affection . . . . iv 3 205

There grows In my most ill-composed affection such A stanchless avarice that, were I king, I should cut off the nobles for their lands *Macbeth* iv 3 77

Keep you in the rear of your affection, Out of the shot and danger of desire . . . . *Hamlet* i 3 34

He hath, my lord, of late made many tenders Of his affection to me . i 3 100

Affection! pooh! you speak like a green girl . . i 3 101

Love! his affections do not that way tend . . . iii 1 170

Dipping all his faults in their affection . . . iv 7 19

Or your fore-vouch'd affection Fall'n into taint . *Lear* i 1 223

He hath wrote this to feel my affection to your honour . i 2 94

Not entertained with that ceremonious affection as you were wont . i 4 63

Preferment goes by letter and affection, And not by old gradation *Othello* i 1 36

Did you by indirect and forced courses Subdue and poison this young maid's affections? . . . . i 3 112

For the better compassing of his salt and most hidden loose affection . ii 1 245

Is it sport? I think it is: and doth affection breed it? I think it doth iv 3 99

Have not we affections, Desires for sport, and frailty, as men have? iv 3 101

Hast thou affections?—Yes, gracious madam.—Indeed! *Ant. and Cleo.* i 5 12

Yet have I fierce affections, and think What Venus did with Mars i 5 17

Antony will use his affection where it is: he married but his occasion here ii 6 139

My sword, made weak by my affection, would Obey it on all cause . iii 11 67

The itch of his affection should not then Have nick'd his captainship . iii 13 7

Pitying The pangs of barr'd affections . . *Cymbeline* i 1 82

And will continue fast to your affection, Still close as sure . i 6 138

Will you, not having my consent, Bestow your love and your affections Upon a stranger? . . . . *Pericles* ii 5 77

Affections' counsellor. He, his own affections' counsellor, Is to himself —I will not say how true . . . . *Rom. and Jul.* i 1 153

Affection's edge. She moves me not, or not removes, at least, Affection's edge in me . . . . . *T. of Shrew* i 2 73

Affection's men at arms. Have at you, then, affection's men at arms *L. L. Lost* iv 3 290

Affectionate. Your—wife, so I would say—Affectionate servant *Lear* iv 6 277

Affectionately. Commends himself most affectionately to you *Tr. and Cr.* iii 1 74

Affectioned. An affectioned ass, that cons state without book *T. Night* ii 3 160

Affeered. Wear thou thy wrongs; The title is affeer'd! . *Macbeth* iv 3 34

Affiance. How hast thou with jealousy infected The sweetness of affiance! *Hen. V.* ii 2 127

What's more dangerous than this fond affiance! Seems he a dove? 2 *Hen. VI.* iii 1 74

I have spoke this, to know if your affiance Were deeply rooted *Cymbeline* i 6 163

Affianced. Was affianced to her by oath . . *Meas. for Meas.* iii 1 222

I am affianced this man's wife as strongly As words could make up vows v 1 227

Affied. Where then do you know best We be affied? . *T. of Shrew* iv 4 49

Affined. The hard and soft, seem all affined and kin *Troi. and Cres.* i 3 25

Be judge youself, Whether I in any just term am affined To love the Moor . . . . *Othello* i 1 39

If partially affined, or leagued in office, Thou dost deliver more or less than truth . . . . ii 3 218

Affinity. He you hurt is of great fame in Cyprus And great affinity iii 1 49

Affirm. Their own authors faithfully affirm That the land Salique is in Germany . . . . *Hen. V.* i 2 43

I said so, dear Katharine; and I must not blush to affirm it . v 2 117

Renege, affirm, and turn their halcyon beaks With every gale . *Lear* ii 2 84

There's no motion That tends to vice in man, but I affirm It is the woman's part . . . . . . *Cymbeline* ii 5 21

Affirmation. At that time vouching—and upon warrant of bloody affirmation . . . . i 4 63

Affirmative. If your four negatives make your two affirmatives, why then, the worse for my friends . . . *T. Night* v 1 24

Afflict. A breath thou art, Servile to all the skyey influences, That dost this habitation, where thou keep'st, Hourly afflict *Meas. for Meas.* iii 1 11

When that time comes, Afflict me with thy mocks, pity me not *As Y. L. It* iii 5 33

I have thus far stirr'd you: but I could afflict you farther *W. Tale* v 3 75

O, how this discord doth afflict my soul! . 1 *Hen. VI.* iii 1 106

Ambitious churchman, leave to afflict my heart . 2 *Hen. VI.* ii 1 182

Scorning whate'er you can afflict me with . 3 *Hen. VI.* i 4 38

O coward conscience, how dost thou afflict me *Richard III.* v 3 179

The leanness that afflicts us, the object of our misery . *Coriolanus* i 1 20

Lose not so noble a friend on vain suppose, Nor with sour looks afflict his gentle heart . . . . . . *T. Andron.* i 1 441

Shoot all your shafts into the court: We will afflict the emperor in his pride . . . . iv 3 62

If thou wert the wolf, thy greediness would afflict thee . *T. of Athens* iv 3 337

As oft as any passion under heaven That does afflict our natures *Hamlet* ii 1 106

You may glean, Whether aught, to us unknown, afflicts him thus . ii 2 17

Never afflict yourself to know the cause . . *Lear* i 4 313

My heart parted betwixt two friends That do afflict each other! *A. and C.* iii 6 78

Afflicted. If they can find in their hearts the poor unvirtuous fat knight shall be any further afflicted, we two will still be the ministers *Mer. Wives* iv 2 233

I come to visit the afflicted spirits . . *Meas. for Meas.* ii 3 4

Holding the eternal spirit, against her will, In the vile prison of afflicted breath . . . . *K. John* iii 4 19

How sad he looks! sure, he is much afflicted . *Hen. VIII.* ii 2 63

Shall we be thus afflicted in his wreaks, His fits, his frenzy? *T. Andron.* iv 4 11

Is not this a lamentable thing, grandsire, that we should be thus afflicted with these strange flies? . . . . *Rom. and Jul.* ii 4 34

He was gentle, but unfortunate; Dishonestly afflicted, but yet honest *Cymbeline* iv 2 40

Affliction. Hast thou, which art but air, a touch, a feeling Of their afflictions? . . . . *Tempest* v 1 22

Since I saw thee, The affliction of my mind amends . v 1 115

I think to repay that money will be a biting affliction *Mer. Wives* v 5 178

Welcome the sour cup of prosperity! Affliction may one day smile again; and till then, sit thee down, sorrow! . *L. L. Lost* i 1 316

Do not receive affliction At my petition . *W. Tale* iii 2 224

Whose fresh complexion and whose heart together Affliction alters . iv 4 586

I think affliction may subdue the cheek, But not take in the mind . iv 4 587

This affliction has a taste as sweet As any cordial comfort . v 3 76

O fair affliction, peace!—No, no, I will not, having breath to cry *K. John* iii 4 36

Heart's discontent and sour affliction Be playfellows to keep you company 2 *Hen. VI.* iii 2 301

My friends, They that must weigh out my afflictions *Hen. VIII.* iii 1 88

Affliction is enamour'd of thy parts, And thou art wedded to calamity *Rom. and Jul.* iii 3 2

I count it one of my greatest afflictions, say, that I cannot pleasure such an honourable gentleman . . . . *T. of Athens* iii 2 62

Thy great fortunes Are made thy chief afflictions . . iv 3 44

Whoso please To stop affliction, let him take his haste . v 1 213

In the affliction of these terrible dreams That shake us nightly *Macbeth* iii 2 18

If't be the affliction of his love or no That thus he suffers for *Hamlet* iii 1 36

Your mother, in most great affliction of spirit, hath sent me to you . iii 2 324

Thought and affliction, passion, hell itself, She turns to favour . iv 5 188

Man's nature cannot carry The affliction nor the fear . *Lear* iii 2 49

This world I do renounce, and in your sights, Shake patiently my great affliction off . . . . iv 6 36

Henceforth I'll bear Affliction till it do cry out itself 'Enough, enough' iv 6 76

Had it pleased heaven To try me with affliction . . *Othello* iv 2 48

Will poor folks lie, That have afflictions on them? . *Cymbeline* iii 6 10

And happier much by his affliction made . . . v 4 108

Afford. Good meat, sir, is common; that every churl affords *C. of Err.* iii 1 24

Only this commendation I can afford her, that were she other than she is, she were unhandsome . . . . . *Much Ado* i 1 176

We can afford no more at such a price.—Prize you yourselves *L. L. Lost* v 2 223

You have a double tongue within your mask, And would afford my speechless vizard half . . . . . . v 2 246

Let them want nothing that my house affords . *T. of Shrew*, Ind. 1 104

Sit and eat and eat!—Padua affords this kindness, son Petruchio.—Padua affords nothing but what is kind . . . v 2 14

We cannot afford you so . . . . *All's Well* iv 1 53

Now Jove afford you cause! To me the difference forges dread *W. Tale* iv 4 16

The purest treasure mortal times afford Is spotless reputation *Richard II.* i 1 177

Such eyes As, sick and blunted with community, Afford no extraordinary gaze . . . . 1 *Hen. IV.* iii 2 78

I will see what physic the tavern affords . . . 1 *Hen. VI.* iii 1 148

With ruder terms, such as my wit affords And over-joy of heart doth minister . . . . 2 *Hen. VI.* i 1 30

Afford. Pity me!—Such pity as my rapier's point affords . 3 *Hen. VI.* i 3 37
What other pleasure can the world afford? . . . . iii 2 147
Since this earth affords no joy to me, But to command, to check, to o'erbear. . . . . iii 2 165
A lovelier gentleman . . . The spacious world cannot again afford *Richard III.* i 2 246
What scourge for perjury Can this dark monarchy afford false Clarence? i 4 51
Towards three or four o'clock Look for the news that the Guildhall affords . . . . iii 5 102
O, that thou wouldst as well afford a grave As thou canst yield a melancholy seat! . . . . iv 4 31
All comfort that the dark night can afford Be to thy person! v 3 80
How easy?—As easy as a down-bed would afford it . . *Hen. VIII.* i 4 18
Rome could afford no tribune like to these . . *T. Andron.* iii 1 44
Tigers must prey, and Rome affords no prey But me and mine . iii 1 55
Could not all hell afford you such a devil? . . . . . . v 2 86
The hate I bear thee can afford No better term than this,—thou art a villain . . . . *Rom. and Jul.* iii 1 63
These times of woe afford no time to woo . . . . . . iii 4 8
Love give me strength! and strength shall help afford . . . iv 1 125
The world affords no law to make thee rich; Then be not poor v 1 73
What charitable men afford to beggars . . *T. of Athens* iii 2 82
The sweet degrees that this brief world affords . . . . iv 3 253
Affordeth. Came it by request and such fair question As soul to soul affordeth? . . . . *Othello* i 3 114
Affray. Since arm from arm that voice doth us affray . *Rom. and Jul.* iii 5 33
Affright. Which Lion hight by name, The trusty Thisby, coming first by night, Did scare away, or rather did affright *M. N. Dream* v 1 142
When adverse foreigners affright my towns With dreadful pomp *K. John* iv 2 172
The very casques That did affright the air at Agincourt . *Hen. V.* Prol. 14
Terror of the French, The scarecrow that affrights our children 1 *Hen. VI.* i 4 43
Lay not thy hands on me; forbear, I say; Their touch affrights me as a serpent's sting . . . . 2 *Hen. VI.* iii 2 47
What, doth death affright?—Thy name affrights me . . . iv 1 32
Even to affright thee with the view thereof . . . . . v 1 207
Tush, man, abodements must not now affright us . . 3 *Hen. VI.* iv 7 13
Some tormenting dream Affrights thee with a hell of ugly devils *Rich. III.* i 3 227
Let not our babbling dreams affright our souls . . . . . v 3 308
You curs, That like nor peace nor war? the one affrights you, The other makes you proud . . . . . . *Coriolanus* i 1 173
Leave me: think upon these gone; Let them affright thee *Rom. and Jul.* v 3 61
As one would beat his offenceless dog to affright an imperious lion *Othello* ii 3 276
Death-like dragons here affright thee hard . . . . *Pericles* i 1 29
Affrighted much, I did in time collect myself . . *W. Tale* iii 3 37
Who then, affrighted with their bloody looks, Ran fearfully 1 *Hen. IV.* i 3 104
No marvel, my lord, though it affrighted you; I promise you, I am afraid to hear you tell it . . . . . . *Richard III.* i 4 64
Be not affrighted; Fly not; stand still: ambition's debt is paid *J. Cæsar* iii 1 82
O, my lord, my lord, I have been so affrighted! . . . *Hamlet* ii 1 75
And that the affrighted globe Should yawn at alteration . *Othello* v 2 100
Affront. Unless another, As like Hermione as is her picture, Affront his eye . . . . *W. Tale* v 1 75
That he, as 'twere by accident, may here Affront Ophelia . *Hamlet* iii 1 31
Your preparation can affront no less Than what you hear of . *Cymbeline* iv 3 29
There was a fourth man, in a silly habit, That gave the affront with them v 3 87
Affronted. That my integrity and truth to you Might be affronted with the match and weight Of such a winnow'd purity in love *Tr. and Cr.* iii 2 173
Affy. For daring to affy a mighty lord Unto the daughter of a worthless king . . . . 2 *Hen. VI.* iv 1 80
So I do affy In thy uprightness and integrity . . . *T. Andron.* i 1 47
A-field. When thou didst keep my lambs a-field, I wish some ravenous wolf had eaten thee! . . . . . . 1 *Hen. VI.* v 4 30
Wherefore not afield?—Because not there: this woman's answer sorts *Troi. and Cres.* i 1 108
Sweet lord, who's a-field to-day? . . . . iii 1 140
Æneas is a-field; And I do stand engaged to many Greeks . . v 3 67
Afire. All but mariners Plunged in the foaming brine and quit the vessel, Then all afire with me . . . . *Tempest* i 2 212
I am hush'd until our city be afire, And then I'll speak a little *Coriolanus* v 3 181
Like powder in a skilless soldier's flask, Is set a-fire by thine own ignorance . . . . *Rom. and Jul.* iii 3 133
Afloat. On such a full sea are we now afloat . . *J. Cæsar* iv 3 222
Afoot. He would have walked ten mile a-foot to see a good armour *Much Ado* ii 3 17
Demand of him, of what strength they are a-foot . . *All's Well* iv 3 181
Were I tied to run afoot Even to the frozen ridges of the Alps *Richard II.* i 3 63
Before the game is afoot, thou still let'st slip . . . 1 *Hen. IV.* i 3 278
If I travel but four foot by the squier further afoot, I shall break my wind . . . . ii 2 13
Eight yards of uneven ground is threescore and ten miles afoot with me ii 2 27
I'll not bear mine own flesh so far afoot again . . . . ii 2 38
When a jest is so forward, and afoot too! I hate it . . . . ii 2 50
We'll walk afoot awhile, and ease our legs . . . . . . ii 2 83
But if you go,—So far afoot, I shall be weary, love . . . . ii 3 87
O' horseback, ye cuckoo; but afoot he will not budge a foot . . ii 4 387
And pause us, till these rebels, now afoot, Come underneath the yoke of government . . . . 2 *Hen. IV.* iv 4 9
So may a thousand actions, once afoot, End in one purpose . *Hen. V.* i 2 211
The game's afoot: Follow your spirit . . . . iii 1 32
How now, my noble lord! what, all afoot? . . . 2 *Hen. VI.* v 2 8
Went all afoot in summer's scalding heat . . . 3 *Hen. VI.* v 7 18
Anon he's there afoot, And there they fly or die . *Troi. and Cres.* v 5 21
To take in many towns ere almost Rome Should know we were afoot *Coriolanus* i 2 25
But were our witty empress well afoot, She would applaud *T. Andron.* iv 2 29
Mischief, thou art afoot, Take thou what course thou wilt! . *J. Cæsar* iii 2 265
When thou seest that act afoot, Even with the very comment of thy soul Observe mine uncle . . . . *Hamlet* iii 2 83
And, squire-like, pension beg To keep base life afoot . . . *Lear* ii 4 218
Of Albany's and Cornwall's powers you heard not?—'Tis so, they are afoot . . . . iv 3 51
Afore. He shall taste of my bottle: if he have never drunk wine afore, it will go near to remove his fit . . . . . *Tempest* ii 2 78
Here, afore Heaven, I ratify this my rich gift . . . . . iv 1 7
Now, afore God—God forbid I say true! . . . *Richard II.* ii 1 200
And drive all thy subjects afore thee like a flock of wild-geese 1 *Hen. IV.* ii 4 152
Fortune is painted blind, with a muffler afore her eyes . . *Hen. V.* iii 6 33
Now, afore God, I am so vexed, that every part about me quivers *Rom. and Jul.* ii 4 170
Afore me! it is so very very late, That we may call it early by and by . iii 4 34

Afore. If your diligence be not speedy, I shall be there afore you . *Lear* i 5 5
Come, here's my heart. Something's afore't. Soft, soft! . *Cymbeline* iii 4 81
Now, afore me, a handsome fellow! . . . . . . *Pericles* ii 1 84
She makes our profession as it were to stink afore the face of the gods . iv 6 145
Aforehand. Knowing aforehand of our merriment . *L. L. Lost* v 2 461
Aforesaid. Which I apprehended with the aforesaid swain . . i 1 277
'Honest Gobbo,' or, as aforesaid, 'honest Launcelot Gobbo' *M. of Ven.* ii 2 8
Thersites is a fool, and, as aforesaid, Patroclus is a fool . *Troi. and Cres.* ii 3 64
Afraid. We are less afraid to be drowned than thou art . . *Tempest* i 1 47
Of her society Be not afraid . . . . iv 1 92
How fine my master is! I am afraid He will chastise me . . v 1 262
You are afraid, if you see the bear loose, are you not? . *Mer. Wives* i 1 304
I am half afraid he will have need of washing . . . . . iii 3 193
Hold up your head; answer your master, be not afraid . . . iv 1 20
I see these witches are afraid of swords . . *Com. of Errors* iv 4 151
I will sing, that they shall hear I am not afraid . . *M. N. Dream* iii 1 127
Be not afraid; she shall not harm thee . . . . . . iii 2 321
I am afraid, sir, Do what you can, yours will not be entreated *T. of Shrew* v 2 88
Be not afraid that I your hand should take . . . *All's Well* ii 3 95
My life, sir, in any case: not that I am afraid to die . . . iv 3 271
Be not afraid of greatness: some are born great, some achieve greatness, and some have greatness thrust upon 'em . . *T. Night* ii 5 156; iii 4 42
Be not afraid, good youth, I will not have you . . . . iii 1 142
I am afraid this great lubber, the world, will prove a cockney iv 1 14
My uncle practises more harm to me: He is afraid of me . *K. John* iv 1 21
I am afraid; and yet I'll venture it . . . . iv 3 5
I am afraid my daughter will run mad . . . . 1 *Hen. IV.* iii 1 145
I am afraid of this gunpowder Percy, though he be dead . . . v 4 123
By my faith, I am afraid he would prove the better counterfeit . v 4 126
Shall we think the subtle-witted French Conjurers and sorcerers, that afraid of him By magic verses have contrived his end? 1 *Hen. VI.* i 1 26
I never saw a fellow worse bested, Or more afraid to fight . 2 *Hen. VI.* ii 3 57
Here, Peter, I drink to thee: and be not afraid . . . . ii 3 69
What, do you tremble? are you all afraid? Alas, I blame you not *Rich. III.* i 2 43
I promise you, I am afraid to hear you tell it . . . . . i 4 65
Art thou afraid?—Not to kill him, having a warrant for it; but to be damned for killing him, from which no warrant can defend us . i 4 111
I fear, I fear,—Nay, good my lord, be not afraid of shadows . v 3 215
I am afraid His thinkings are below the moon . . . *Hen. VIII.* iii 2 133
I am almost afraid to stand alone Here in the churchyard *Rom. and Jul.* v 3 10
If Cæsar hide himself, shall they not whisper, 'Lo, Cæsar is afraid'? *J. C.* ii 2 101
I am afraid they have awaked, And 'tis not done . . *Macbeth* ii 2 10
I am afraid to think what I have done; Look on't again I dare not . ii 2 51
Alas, poor country! Almost afraid to know itself . . . . iv 3 165
I will not be afraid of death and bane, Till Birnam forest come to Dunsinane . . . . v 3 59
What is thy name?—Thou'lt be afraid to hear it.—No; though thou call'st thyself a hotter name Than any is in hell . . . . v 7 5
Many wearing rapiers are afraid of goose-quills . . *Hamlet* ii 2 359
Be not afraid, though you do see me weapon'd; Here is my journey's end *Othello* v 2 266
Thy spirit Is all afraid to govern thee near him; But, he away, 'tis noble *Ant. and Cleo.* ii 3 29
You are afraid, and therein the wiser . . . . *Cymbeline* i 4 146
Afresh. We set his youngest free for a husband, and then have to't afresh . . . . *T. of Shrew* i 1 143
Whose loss of his most precious queen and children are even now to be afresh lamented . . . . *W. Tale* iv 2 28
The wrongs I have done thee stir Afresh within me . . . . v 1 149
Dead Henry's wounds Open their congeal'd mouths and bleed afresh! *Richard III.* i 2 56
Afric. Methinks our garments are now as fresh as when we put them on first in Afric . . . . *Tempest* ii 1 69
We were better parch in Afric sun . . . *Troi. and Cres.* i 3 370
Not Afric owns a serpent I abhor More than thy fame and envy *Coriolanus* i 8 3
I would they were in Afric both together . . . *Cymbeline* i 1 167
Africa. I speak of Africa and golden joys . . . . 2 *Hen. IV.* v 3 104
African. But rather lose her to an African . . . *Tempest* ii 1 125
A-front. These four came all a-front, and mainly thrust at me 1 *Hen. IV.* ii 4 222
After. Whose influence If now I court not but omit, my fortunes Will ever after droop . . . . *Tempest* i 2 184
He's in his fit now and does not talk after the wisest . . . ii 2 76
Their great guilt, Like poison given to work a great time after, Now 'gins to bite the spirits . . . . iii 3 105
He after honour hunts, I after love: He leaves his friends to dignify them more . . . . *T. G. of Ver.* i 1 63
But, after all this fooling, I would not have it so . *Meas. for Meas.* i 2 71
I'll rent the fairest house in it after three-pence a bay . . . ii 1 255
Do as I bid you; shut doors after you: Fast bind, fast find *M. of Venice* ii 5 53
An you mean to mock me after, you should not have mocked me before *As Y. Like It* i 2 220
He's in the third degree of drink, he's drowned: go, look after him *T. N.* i 5 144
Shall we after them?—After them! nay, before them, if we can 2 *Hen. VI.* v 3 27
O churl! drunk all, and left no friendly drop To help me after? *R. and J.* v 3 164
He that made us with such large discourse, Looking before and after *Ham.* iv 4 37
Frame the business after your own wisdom . . . . *Lear* i 2 107
Pray you, hasten Your generals after . . . . *Ant. and Cleo.* ii 4 2
You shall not find me, daughter, After the slander of most stepmothers *Cymbeline* i 1 71
After-dinner. As it were, an after-dinner's sleep . *Meas. for Meas.* iii 1 33
For your health and your digestion sake, An after-dinner's breath *Troi. and Cres.* ii 3 121
After-eye. Thou shouldst have made him As little as a crow, or less, ere left To after-eye him . . . . *Cymbeline* i 3 16
After hours. Men shall deal unadvisedly sometimes, Which after hours give leisure to repent . . . . *Richard III.* iv 4 293
So smile the heavens upon this holy act, That after hours with sorrow chide us not! . . . . *Rom. and Jul.* ii 6 2
After inquiry. Or jump the after inquiry on your own peril *Cymbeline* v 4 189
After-love. Scorn at first makes after-love the more . *T. G. of Ver.* iii 1 95
How heinous e'er it be, To win thy after-love I pardon thee *Richard II.* v 3 35
After-meeting. As the main point of this our after-meeting *Coriolanus* ii 2 43
Afternoon. 'Tis a custom with him, I' th' afternoon to sleep *Tempest* iii 2 96
What is that Barnardine who is to be executed in the afternoon? *M. for M.* iv 2 133
Barnardine must die this afternoon . . . . iv 3 87
Till this afternoon his passion Ne'er brake into extremity of rage *C. of Err.* v 1 47
When would you have it done, sir?—This afternoon . . *L. L. Lost* iii 1 156
To-morrow morning.—It must be done this afternoon . . . . iii 1 163
In the afternoon We will with some strange pastime solace them . iv 3 376
In the posteriors of this day, which the rude multitude call the afternoon v 1 95

Afternoon. Liable, congruent, and measurable for the afternoon *L. L. Lost* v 1 98
Very vilely in the morning, when he is sober, and most vilely in the afternoon, when he is drunk . . . . . *Mer. of Ven.* i 2 93
Falling out that year on Ash-Wednesday was four year, in the afternoon ii 5 27
We may contrive this afternoon, And quaff carouses . . *T. of Shrew* i 2 276
I knew a wench married in an afternoon as she went to the garden for parsley to stuff a rabbit . . . . . . iv 4 100
While shame full late sleeps out the afternoon . . *All's Well* v 3 66
This afternoon will post To consummate this business happily *K. John* v 7 94
To-morrow in the temple hall at two o'clock in the afternoon *1 Hen. IV.* iii 3 224
I was born about three of the clock in the afternoon . . *2 Hen. IV.* i 2 211
I take my leave of thee, fair son, Born to eclipse thy life this afternoon *1 Hen. VI.* iv 5 53
Even in the afternoon of her best days . . . *Richard III.* iii 7 186
I must have you play the idle huswife with me this afternoon *Coriolanus* i 3 76
You shall have the drum struck up this afternoon . . . . iv 5 230
Come you this afternoon, To know our further pleasure in this case *R. and J.* i 1 107
Bid her devise Some means to come to shrift this afternoon . . ii 4 192
This afternoon, sir? well, she shall be there . . . . ii 4 197
Ride you this afternoon?—Ay, my good lord . . . *Macbeth* iii 1 19
Sleeping within my orchard, My custom always of the afternoon *Hamlet* i 5 60
After-nourishment. The passions of the mind, That have their first conception by mis-dread, Have after-nourishment and life by care *Per.* i 2 13
After-supper. Between our after-supper and bed-time . *M. N. Dream* v 1 34
After the flesh. Such is the simplicity of man to hearken after the flesh . . . . *L. L. Lost* i 1 220
After-times. Much too shallow, To sound the bottom of the after-times *2 Hen. IV.* iv 2 51
Afterward. Awake till you are executed, and sleep afterwards *M. for M.* iv 3 35
And afterward consort you till bed-time . . . *Com. of Errors* i 2 28
You must hang it first, and draw it afterwards . . . *Much Ado* iii 2 25
You shall recount their particular duties afterwards . . . iv 1 3
We'll have dancing afterward . . . . v 4 122
Never to speak to lady afterward In way of marriage . *Mer. of Venice* ii 1 41
Without rescue in the first assault or ransom afterward . . *All's Well* iii 3 121
Say 'pardon' first, and afterwards 'stand up' . . *Richard II.* v 3 112
Afterwards We may digest our complots in some form . *Richard III.* iii 1 199
And afterward by substitute betroth'd To Bona . . . . iii 7 181
I shall cut out your tongue.—'Tis no matter; I shall speak as much as thou afterwards . . . . *Troi. and Cres.* ii 1 123
Afterwards, As Hector's leisure and your bounties shall Concur . . iv 5 272
Then, afterwards, to order well the state . . . *T. Andron.* v 3 203
Hack the limbs, Like wrath in death and envy afterwards . *J. Cæsar* ii 1 164
I have seen her . . . take forth paper, fold it, write upon't, read it, afterwards seal it, and again return to bed . . . *Macbeth* v 1 7
Being done unknown, I should have found it afterwards well done *A. and C.* ii 7 85
She'll prove on cats and dogs, Then afterward up higher . *Cymbeline* i 5 39
If you seek us afterwards in other terms, you shall find us . . iii 1 80
After wrath. I hear him mock The luck of Cæsar, which the gods give men To excuse their after wrath . . . *Ant. and Cleo.* v 2 290
Again. Yet again! what do you here? Shall we give o'er and drown? *Temp.* i 1 41
Lay her a-hold, a-hold! set her two courses off to sea again; lay her off i 1 53
I, not remembering how I cried out then, Will cry it o'er again . i 2 134
They all have met again And are upon the Mediterranean flote . . i 2 233
A torment To lay upon the damn'd, which Sycorax Could not again undo i 2 291
Sitting on a bank, Weeping again the king my father's wreck . i 2 390
It hath drawn me rather. But 'tis gone. No, it begins again . . i 2 395
Thy nerves are in their infancy again And have no vigour in them . i 2 484
She too, Who is so far from Italy removed I ne'er again shall see her . ii 1 111
We all were sea-swallow'd, though some cast again . . . ii 1 251
Lately suffered by a thunderbolt. Alas, the storm is come again! . ii 2 39
You cannot tell who's your friend: open your chaps again . . ii 2 89
Bear my bottle: fellow Trinculo, we'll fill him by and by again . ii 2 181
Lo, lo, again! bite him to death, I prithee . . . . . iii 2 38
Wilt thou be pleased to hearken once again to the suit I made to thee? iii 2 45
Voices That, if I then had waked after long sleep, Will make me sleep again . . . . iii 2 149
When I waked, I cried to dream again . . . . . . iii 2 152
Who once again I tender to thy hand: all thy vexations Were but my trials of thy love . . . . iv 1 4
Mars's hot minion is return'd again; Her waspish-headed son has broke his arrows, Swears he will shoot no more . . . . . iv 1 98
My dukedom since you have given me again, I will requite you with as good a thing . . . . v 1 168
It were a shame to call her back again . . . . *T. G. of Ver.* i 2 51
And yet I will not name it; and yet I care not; And yet take this again ii 1 124
The lines are very quaintly writ; But since unwillingly, take them again ii 1 129
In modesty, Or else for want of idle time, could not again reply . ii 1 172
Here have I brought him back again.—What, didst thou offer her this? iv 4 57
Get thee hence, and find my dog again, Or ne'er return again into my sight . . . . iv 4 64
This is the letter to your ladyship.—I pray thee, let me look on that again iv 4 130
Then I am paid; And once again I do receive thee honest . . v 4 78
I here forget all former griefs, Cancel all grudge, repeal thee home again v 4 143
O' my life, if I were young again, the sword should end it . *Mer. Wives* i 1 40
Would I might never come in mine own great chamber again else . . i 1 158
I'll ne'er be drunk whilst I live again, but in honest, civil, godly company i 1 187
If he come under my hatches, I'll never to sea again . . . . ii 1 96
Why, woman, your husband is in his old lunes again . . . . iv 2 22
Shall I put him into the basket again?—No, I'll come no more i' the basket iv 2 49
I'll appoint my men to carry the basket again, to meet him at the door iv 2 97
Take the basket again on your shoulders: your master is hard at door iv 2 110
Pray heaven it be not full of knight again.—I hope not . . . iv 2 116
Have you any way then to unfool me again? . . . . . . iv 2 120
There was one conveyed out of my house yesterday in this basket: why may not he be there again? . . . . iv 2 153
If I cry out thus upon no trail, never trust me when I open again . iv 2 209
He will never, I think, in the way of waste, attempt us again . . iv 2 227
I'll to him again in name of Brook: He'll tell me all his purpose . iv 4 76
Never take you for my love again; but I will always count you my deer v 5 122
I will never mistrust my wife again, till thou art able to woo her in good English . . . . v 5 141
What's thy offence, Claudio?—What but to speak of would offend again. —What, is't murder? . . . . *Meas. for Meas.* i 2 140
He calls again; I pray you, answer him.—Peace and prosperity! . . i 4 14
I could not give you three-pence again.—No, indeed . . . . ii 1 107
Let me not find you before me again upon any complaint whatsoever . ii 1 260
Why dost thou ask again?—Lest I might be too rash . . . . ii 2 9
Give't not o'er so: to him again, entreat him; Kneel down before him ii 2 43
I, that do speak a word, May call it back again . . . . . ii 2 58

Again. Do I love her, That I desire to hear her speak again? *M. for M.* ii 2 178
Dear sir, ere long I'll visit you again.—Most holy sir, I thank you . iii 1 46
But indeed I can do you little harm; you'll forswear this again . . iii 2 177
I would the duke we talk of were returned again . . . . . iii 2 184
But my kisses bring again, bring again; Seals of love, but sealed in vain iv 1 5
The phrase is to the matter.—Mended again. The matter; proceed . v 1 91
Back again, thou slave, and fetch him home.—Go back again *Com. of Err.* ii 1 75
Till he come home again, I would forbear.—Patience unmoved! . . ii 1 31
Is your merry humour alter'd? As you love strokes, so jest with me again . . . . ii 2 8
Get you in again; Comfort my sister, cheer her, call her wife . . iii 2 25
Establish him in his true sense again, And I will please you what you will demand . . . . iv 4 51
God, for thy mercy! they are loose again.—And come with naked swords iv 4 147
He took this place for sanctuary, And it shall privilege him from your hands Till I have brought him to his wits again . . . . . v 1 96
Shall I never see a bachelor of threescore again? . . . . *Much Ado* i 1 202
Prove that ever I lose more blood with love than I will get again with drinking, pick out mine eyes with a ballad-maker's pen . . . . i 1 253
I would have thee hence, and here again . . . . ii 3 7
We'll hear that song again.—O, good my lord, tax not so bad a voice . ii 3 46
And send her home again without a husband . . . . . . iii 3 174
Take her back again: Give not this rotten orange to your friend . . iv 1 32
The wide sea Hath drops too few to wash her clean again . . . iv 1 143
Welcome the sour cup of prosperity! Affliction may one day smile again; and till then, sit thee down, sorrow! . . . *L. L. Lost* i 1 316
Fair princess, welcome to the court of Navarre.—'Fair' I give you back again; and 'welcome' I have not yet . . . . ii 1 91
Excuse me, and farewell: To-morrow shall we visit you again . . ii 1 177
What? first praise me and again say no? O short-lived pride! . . iv 1 14
I will look again on the intellect of the letter . . . . . iv 2 137
Immediately they will again be here In their own shapes . . . v 2 287
Pecks up wit as pigeons pease, And utters it again when God doth please . . . . v 2 316
Will you have me, or your pearl again?—Neither of either . . . v 2 458
Now, to our perjury to add more terror, We are again forsworn . . v 2 471
The whole world again Cannot pick out five such, take each one in his vein . . . . v 2 547
I'll do it by the sword. I bepray you, let me borrow my arms again . v 2 702
Yet swear not, lest ye be forsworn again . . . . v 2 842
Call you me fair? that fair again unsay . . . *M. N. Dream* i 1 181
Herein mean I to enrich my pain, To have his sight thither and back again . . . . i 1 251
I will make the duke say, 'Let him roar again, let him roar again' . i 2 75
Return again, As from a voyage, rich with merchandise . . . ii 1 133
And be thou here again Ere the leviathan can swim a league . . . ii 1 173
He goes but to see a noise that he heard, and is to come again . . iii 1 94
Gentle mortal, sing again: Mine ear is much enamour'd of thy note . iii 1 140
Though she be but little, she is fierce.—'Little' again! nothing but 'low' and 'little'! Why will you suffer her to flout me thus? . . . iii 2 326
Speak again: Thou runaway, thou coward, art thou fled? . . . iii 2 404
The man shall have his mare again, and all shall be well . . . iii 2 463
All to Athens back again repair And think no more of this night's accidents iv 1 72
The wall, methinks, being sensible, should curse again . . . . v 1 184
Bring your latter hazard back again And thankfully rest *Mer. of Venice* i 1 151
And swore he would pay him again when he was able . . . . i 2 87
I am as like to call thee so again, To spit on thee again, to spurn thee too i 3 131
Where is the horse that doth untread again His tedious measures with the unbated fire That he did pace them first? . . . . . ii 6 10
Let me see; I will survey the inscriptions back again . . . . ii 7 14
I shall never see my gold again: fourscore ducats at a sitting! . . iii 1 116
Wooing here until I sweat again, And swearing till my very roof was dry iii 2 205
Till I come again, No bed shall e'er be guilty of my stay . . . iii 2 327
And so farewell, till we shall meet again . . . . iii 4 40
Know me when we meet again: I wish you well, and so I take my leave iv 1 419
I dare be bound again, My soul upon the forfeit . . . . . v 1 251
If ever he go alone again, I'll never wrestle for prize more *As Y. Like It* i 1 167
What he hath taken away from thy father perforce, I will render thee again in affection . . . . i 2 22
Love no man in good earnest; nor no further in sport neither than with safety of a pure blush thou mayst in honour come off again . . i 2 32
Let not search and inquisition quail To bring again these foolish runaways ii 2 21
His big manly voice, Turning again toward childish treble . . . ii 7 162
Most wonderful wonderful! and yet again wonderful, and after that, out of all hooping! . . . . iii 2 202
How parted he with thee? and when shalt thou see him again? . . iii 2 237
I marvel why I answer'd not again: But that's all one . . . . iii 5 132
By two o'clock I will be with thee again.—Ay, go your ways . . iv 1 185
He left a promise to return again Within an hour . . . . . iv 3 100
If I sent him word again 'it was not well cut,' he would send me word, he cut it to please himself . . . . v 4 77
And all their lands restored to them again That were with him exiled . v 4 170
Bring our lady hither to our sight; And once again, a pot o' the smallest ale . . . . *T. of Shrew* Ind. 2 77
But I would be loath to fall into my dreams again . . . . Ind. 2 129
I swear I'll cuff you, if you strike again . . . . ii 1 221
The treble jars.—Spit in the hole, man, and tune again . . . . iii 1 40
What said the wench when he rose again?—Trembled and shook . . iii 2 168
I commanded the sleeves should be cut out and sewed up again . . iv 3 148
What, pale again? My fear hath catch'd your fondness . . *All's Well* i 3 175
I am there before my legs.—Haste you again . . . . . . ii 2 74
Let the white death sit on thy cheek for ever; We'll ne'er come there again . . . . ii 3 78
I have now found thee; when I lose thee again, I care not . . . ii 3 217
I'll beat him, an if I could but meet him again . . . . . . ii 3 256
And, after some dispatch in hand at court, Thither we bend again . . iii 2 57
And hope I may that she, Hearing so much, will speed her foot again . iii 4 37
Let me buy your friendly help thus far, Which I will over-pay and pay again . . . . iii 7 16
But what linsey-woolsey hast thou to speak to us again? . . . . iv 1 14
My reasons are most strong; and you shall know them When back again this ring shall be deliver'd . . . . iv 2 60
I will never trust a man again for keeping his sword clean . . . iv 3 165
I pray you, sir, put it up again.—Nay, I'll read it first, by your favour iv 3 243
She ceased In heavy satisfaction and would never Receive the ring again v 3 101
Send for your ring, I will return it home, And give me mine again . v 3 224
That strain again! it had a dying fall . . . . . . *T. Night* i 1 4
Sir Andrew, would thou mightst never draw sword again . . . . i 3 66
An you part so, mistress, I would I might never draw sword again . i 3 68
The lady bade take away the fool; therefore, I say again, take her away i 5 58

Again. Let him send no more; Unless, perchance, you come to me again *T. Night* i 5 300
She is drowned already, sir, with salt water, though I seem to drown her remembrance again with more ii 1 33
And one thing more, that you be never so hardy to come again in his affairs ii 2 10
O, by your leave, I pray you, I bade you never speak again of him iii 1 118
Why, then, methinks 'tis time to smile again iii 1 137
Yet come again; for thou perhaps mayst move That heart, which now abhors, to like his love iii 1 175
Well, come again to-morrow: fare thee well iii 4 236
I will return again into the house and desire some conduct of the lady iii 4 264
'Slid, I'll after him again and beat him.—Do; cuff him soundly iii 4 426
This is, to give a dog, and in recompense desire my dog again v 1 8
Time as long again Would be fill'd up, my brother, with our thanks *W. Tale* i 2 3
Take again your queen as yours at first, Even for your son's sake i 2 336
Come, sir, now I am for you again: pray you, sit by us, And tell's a tale ii 1 22
A moiety of my rest Might come to me again ii 3 9
The love I bore your queen—lo, fool again!—I'll speak of her no more iii 2 229
I have heard, but not believed, the spirits o' the dead May walk again iii 3 17
If you did but hear the pedlar at the door, you would never dance again after a tabor and pipe iv 4 182
He has paid you more, which will shame you to give him again iv 4 243
And again does nothing But what he did being childish iv 4 412
Then recovered again with aqua-vitæ or some other hot infusion iv 4 815
You are one of those Would have him wed again v 1 24
To bless the bed of majesty again With a sweet fellow to't v 1 33
Would make her sainted spirit Again possess her corpse v 1 58
We shall not marry till thou bid'st us.—That Shall be when your first queen's again in breath v 1 83
Cease; thou know'st He dies to me again when talk'd of v 1 120
Then again worries he his daughter with clipping her v 2 58
Do not shun her Until you see her die again v 3 106
Were I to get again, Madam, I would not wish a better father *K. John* i 1 259
We will bear home that lusty blood again Which here we came to spout ii 1 255
Dissever your united strengths, And part your mingled colours once again ii 1 389
Again wants nothing, to name want, If want it be not that she is not he ii 1 435
Thou hast misspoke, misheard; Be well advised, tell o'er thy tale again iii 1 5
Then speak again; not all thy former tale, But this one word, whether thy tale be true iii 1 25
That faith would live again by death of need iii 1 214
The better act of purposes mistook Is to mistake again iii 1 275
But now I envy at their liberty, And will again commit them to their bonds iii 4 74
If that be true, I shall see my boy again iii 4 78
And so he'll die; and, rising so again, When I shall meet him in the court of heaven I shall not know him iii 4 86
A princess wrought it me, And I did never ask it you again iv 1 44
Here once again we sit, once again crown'd, And looked upon, I hope, with cheerful eyes.—This 'once again' . . . Was once superfluous iv 2 1
Now I breathe again Aloft the flood, and can give audience To any tongue iv 2 138
Set feathers to thy heels, And fly like thought from them to me again iv 2 175
But thou didst understand me by my signs And didst in signs again parley with sin iv 2 238
Your sword is bright, sir; put it up again.—Not till I sheathe it in a murderer's skin iv 3 79
Take again From this my hand, as holding of the pope Your sovereign greatness and authority v 1 2
My tongue shall hush again this storm of war And make fair weather in your blustering land v 1 20
Would not my lords return to me again, After they heard young Arthur was alive? v 1 37
Up once again; put spirit in the French: If they miscarry, we miscarry too v 4 2
Unthread the rude eye of rebellion And welcome home again discarded faith v 4 12
The English lords By his persuasion are again fall'n off v 5 11
And instantly return with me again, To push destruction v 7 76
Now these her princes are come home again, Come the three corners of the world in arms v 7 115
When, Harry, when? Obedience bids I should not bid again *Richard II.* i 1 163
Let them lay by their helmets and their spears, And both return back to their chairs again i 3 120
Return again, and take an oath with thee. Lay on our royal sword your banish'd hands i 3 178
Let him ne'er speak more That speaks thy words again to do thee harm! ii 1 231
We three here part that ne'er shall meet again ii 2 143
Farewell at once, for once, for all, and ever.—Well, we may meet again ii 2 149
I weep for joy To stand upon my kingdom once again iii 2 5
Till so much blood thither come again, Have I not reason to look pale? iii 2 78
Again uncurse their souls; their peace is made With heads iii 2 137
Let no man speak again To alter this, for counsel is but vain iii 2 213
Provided that my banishment repeal'd And lands restored again iii 3 41
He shall be, And, though mine enemy, restored again To all his lands iv 1 88
Look up, behold, That you in pity may dissolve to dew, And wash him fresh again with true-love tears v 1 10
Wilt know again, Being ne'er so little urged, another way v 1 63
Thus take I thy heart.—Give me mine own again; 'twere no good part To take on me to keep and kill thy heart. So, now I have mine own again, be gone, That I may strive to kill it with a groan v 1 97
Speak it again; Twice saying 'pardon' doth not pardon twain v 3 133
As thus, 'Come, little ones,' and then again, 'It is as hard to come as for a camel To thread the postern of a small needle's eye' v 5 15
Then am I king'd again: and by and by Think that I am unking'd v 5 36
So inform the lords: But come yourself with speed to us again *1 Hen. IV.* i 1 105
That, when he please again to be himself, Being wanted, he may be more wonder'd at i 2 224
'Twixt his finger and his thumb he held A pouncet-box, which ever and anon He gave his nose and took't away again i 3 39
When I urged the ransom once again Of my wife's brother, then his cheek look'd pale i 3 141
Restore yourselves Into the good thoughts of the world again i 3 182
Tell your tale; I have done.—Nay, if you have not, to it again i 3 257
Have you any levers to lift me up again, being down? ii 2 36
I'll not bear mine own flesh so far afoot again for all the coin in thy father's exchequer ii 2 38
I say unto you again, you are a shallow cowardly hind, and you lie ii 3 16

Again. Well, breathe awhile, and then to it again *1 Hen. IV.* ii 4 276
Could the world pick thee out three such enemies again? ii 4 404
The money shall be paid back again with advantage ii 4 599
The money is paid back again.—O, I do not like that paying back iii 3 200
Let there be impawn'd Some surety for a safe return again iv 3 109
I must go write again To other friends; and so farewell iv 4 40
Will you again unknit This churlish knot of all-abhorred war? v 1 15
Hold up thy head, vile Scot, or thou art like Never to hold it up again! v 4 40
And since we are o'erset, venture again *2 Hen. IV.* i 1 185
And I brandish any thing but a bottle, I would I might never spit white again i 2 237
I will have some of it out again, or I will ride thee o' nights like the mare ii 1 83
Whether I shall ever see thee again or no, there is nobody cares ii 4 73
If I be not sent away post, I will see you again ere I go ii 4 408
A likely fellow! Come, prick me Bullcalf till he roar again iii 2 187
And away again would a' go, and again would a' come iii 2 304
I never thought to hear you speak again.—Thy wish was father, Harry, to that thought iv 5 92
Thou wilt be a wilderness again, Peopled with wolves iv 5 137
And, again, sir, shall we sow the headland with wheat? v 1 15
'Couple a gorge!' That is the word. I thee defy again *Hen. V.* ii 1 76
I saw him down; thrice up again, and fighting iv 6 5
I will be so bold as to wear it in my cap till I see him once again v 1 13
Again return'd! How wert thou handled being prisoner? *1 Hen. VI.* i 4 23
And once again we'll sleep secure in Rouen iii 2 19
The Duke of Burgundy will fast Before he'll buy again at such a rate iii 2 43
I'll have a bout with you again, Or else let Talbot perish with this shame iii 2 56
Lost, and recover'd in a day again! This is a double honour iii 2 115
Done like a Frenchman: turn, and turn again! iii 3 85
Fly, to revenge my death, if I be slain.—He that flies so will ne'er return again iv 5 19
The stout Parisians do revolt And turn again unto the warlike French v 2 3
If this servile usage once offend, Go and be free again as Suffolk's friend v 3 59
I must trouble you again; No loving token to his majesty? v 3 180
Were there hope to conquer them again, My sword should shed hot blood *2 Hen. VI.* i 1 117
Are the cities, that I got with wounds, Deliver'd up again? i 1 122
From hence to prison back again; From thence unto the place of execution ii 3 5
The world may laugh again; And I may live to do you kindness ii 4 82
O Henry, ope thine eyes!—He doth revive again: madam, be patient iii 2 36
From England's bank Drove back again unto my native clime iii 2 84
Alive again? then show me where he is: I'll give a thousand pound to look upon him iii 3 12
Who in contempt shall hiss at thee again iv 1 78
Thus will I reward thee, the Lent shall be as long again as it is iv 3 7
Clifford, kneel again; For thy mistaking so, we pardon thee v 1 127
You were best to go to bed and dream again v 1 196
With this, we charged again: but, out, alas! We bodged again *3 Hen. VI.* i 4 18
But bethink thee once again, And in thy thought o'er-run my former time i 4 44
Never henceforth shall I joy again, Never, O never, shall I see more joy! ii 1 77
Making another head to fight again ii 1 141
And once again bestride our foaming steeds, And once again cry 'Charge upon our foes!' But never once again turn back and fly ii 1 183
Here on my knee I vow to God above, I'll never pause again ii 3 30
Take leave until we meet again, Where'er it be, in heaven or in earth ii 3 42
Thou shalt not dread The scatter'd foe that hopes to rise again ii 6 93
The air blows it to me again, Obeying with my wind when I do blow iii 1 85
Subjects to the king, King Edward.—So would you be again to Henry iii 1 95
I was the chief that raised him to the crown, And I'll be chief to bring him down again iii 3 263
I will hence again: I came to serve a king and not a duke iv 7 48
Let's levy men, and beat him back again iv 8 6
Seize on the shame-faced Henry, bear him hence; And once again proclaim us king of England iv 8 53
And, weakling, Warwick takes his gift again; And Henry is my king v 1 37
They no doubt Will issue out again and bid us battle v 1 63
Wert thou as we are, We might recover all our loss again v 2 30
Take up the sword again, or take up me *Richard III.* i 2 184
Tush, that was in thy rage: Speak it again i 2 189
A lovelier gentleman . . . The spacious world cannot again afford i 2 246
There's few or none will entertain it.—How if it come to thee again? i 4 136
I shall be reconciled to him again.—Never, my lord i 4 184
If you be hired for meed, go back again i 4 234
If I live until I be a man, I'll win our ancient right in France again iii 1 92
Murder thy breath in middle of a word, And then begin again, and stop again iii 5 3
Then he was urged to tell my tale again iii 7 31
Would you enforce me to a world of care? Well, call them again iii 7 224
Come, let us to our holy task again iii 7 246
Lo, ere I can repeat this curse again iv 1 78
I say again, give out That Anne my wife is sick and like to die iv 2 57
If sorrow can admit society, Tell o'er your woes again by viewing mine iv 4 39
Hear me a word; For I shall never speak to thee again iv 4 181
And never look upon thy face again iv 4 186
The liquid drops of tears that you have shed Shall come again, transform'd to orient pearl iv 4 322
Let's whip these stragglers o'er the seas again v 3 327
Peace lives again: That she may long live here, God say amen! v 5 40
Point by point the treasons of his master He shall again relate *Hen. VIII.* i 2 8
And understand again like honest men i 3 32
I have half a dozen healths To drink to these fair ladies, and a measure To lead 'em once again i 4 107
He was brought again to the bar, to hear His knell rung out ii 1 31
But he fell to himself again, and sweetly In all the rest show'd a most noble patience ii 1 35
Never found again But where they mean to sink ye ii 1 130
That slander, sir, Is found a truth now: for it grows again ii 1 154
Alas, poor lady! She's a stranger now again ii 3 17
I swear again, I would not be a queen For all the world ii 3 45
I say again, I utterly abhor, yea, from my soul Refuse you for my judge ii 4 80
I must tell you, . . . that again I do refuse you for my judge ii 4 117
Again, there is sprung up An heretic, an arch one, Cranmer iii 2 101
Springs out into fast gait; then stops again, Strikes his breast hard iii 2 116
'Tis well said again; And 'tis a kind of good deed to say well iii 2 152
I know A way, if it take right, in spite of fortune Will bring me off again iii 2 220
And when he falls, he falls like Lucifer, Never to hope again iii 2 372
No sun shall ever usher forth mine honours, Or gild again the noble troops that waited Upon my smiles iii 2 411

Again. You're well met once again.—So are you *Hen VIII.* iv 1 1
So she parted, And with the same full state paced back again iv 1 93
He gave his honours to the world again, His blessed part to heaven iv 2 29
But this fellow Let me ne'er see again iv 2 108
Being but a private man again, You shall know many dare accuse you v 3 55
Win straying souls with modesty again, Cast none away v 3 64
Let me ne'er hope to see a chine again v 4 26
I'll unarm again: Why should I war without the walls of Troy? *Tr. and Cr.* i 1 1
And such again As venerable Nestor, hatch'd in silver i 3 64
After so many hours, lives, speeches spent, Thus once again says Nestor ii 2 2
You have broke it, cousin: and, by my life, you shall make it whole again iii 1 54
Are you gone again? you must be watched ere you be made tame iii 2 45
Heat them and they retort that heat again To the first giver iii 3 101
Who, like an arch, reverberates The voice again iii 3 121
What things again most dear in the esteem And poor in worth! iii 3 129
The cry went once on thee, And still it might, and yet it may again iii 3 185
Would the fountain of your mind were clear again! iii 3 314
When shall we see again?—Hear me, my love: be thou but true of heart iv 4 59
But yet be true.—O heavens! 'be true' again! iv 4 76
Princes, enough, so please you.—I am not warm yet; let us fight again iv 5 118
You palter.—In faith, I do not: come hither once again v 2 49
Give't me again.—Whose was't?—It is no matter, now I have't again v 2 70
Farewell! Thou never shalt mock Diomed again v 2 99
But thou anon shalt hear of me again; Till when, go seek thy fortune v 6 18
When he caught it, he let it go again; and after it again; and over and over he comes, and up again; catched it again *Coriolanus* i 3 67
If e'er again I meet him beard to beard, He's mine, or I am his i 10 11
I had rather have my wounds to heal again Than hear say how I got them ii 2 73
I have your alms: adieu.—But this is something odd.—An 'twere to give again ii 3 89
And, knowing myself again, Repair to the senate-house ii 3 155
And now again Of him that did not ask, but mock, bestow Your sued-for tongues ii 3 214
Ready, when time shall prompt them, to make road Upon's again iii 1 6
We shall hardly in our ages see Their banners wave again iii 1 8
Tell me of corn! This was my speech, and I will speak't again iii 1 62
Being once chafed, he cannot Be rein'd again to temperance iii 3 28
The main blaze of it is past, but a small thing would make it flame again iv 3 21
But when they shall see, sir, his crest up again, and the man in blood, they will out of their burrows iv 5 225
Why, then we shall have a stirring world again iv 5 234
Who, hearing of our Marcius' banishment, Thrusts forth his horns again iv 6 44
The weaker sort may wish Good Marcius home again iv 6 70
Thy hand once more; I will not loose again, Till thou art here aloft, or I below *T. Andron.* ii 3 243
I shall never come to bliss Till all these mischiefs be return'd again iii 1 274
Be blithe again, And bury all thy fear in my devices iv 4 111
Stay with me; Or else I'll call my brother back again v 2 135
Smooth and speak him fair, And tarry with him till I turn again v 2 141
Let me teach you how to knit again This scatter'd corn into one mutual sheaf v 3 70
Even with all my heart Would I were dead, so you did live again! v 3 173
If ever you disturb our streets again, Your lives shall pay the forfeit of the peace *Rom. and Jul.* i 1 103
Nurse, give leave awhile, We must talk in secret:—nurse, come back again i 3 8
And being thus frighted swears a prayer or two And sleeps again i 4 88
She speaks: O, speak again, bright angel! ii 2 26
I gave thee mine before thou didst request it: And yet I would it were to give again ii 2 129
Sweet Montague, be true. Stay but a little, I will come again ii 2 138
O, for a falconer's voice, To lure this tassel-gentle back again! ii 2 160
But where hast thou been, then?—I'll tell thee, ere thou ask it me again ii 3 48
Now, Tybalt, take the villain back again, That late thou gavest me iii 1 130
Hear me but speak a word.—O, thou wilt speak again of banishment iii 3 53
Tybalt calls; and then on Romeo cries, And then down falls again iii 3 102
I shall be much in years Ere I again behold my Romeo iii 5 47
O, think'st thou we shall ever meet again?—I doubt it not iii 5 51
Farewell! God knows when we shall meet again iv 3 14
What, dress'd! and in your clothes! and down again! iv 5 12
How fares my Juliet? that I ask again; For nothing can be ill, if she be well v 1 15
I could not send it,—here it is again v 2 14
Will stay with thee; And never from this palace of dim night Depart again v 3 108
So soon as dinner's done, we'll forth again *T. of Athens* ii 2 14
And nature, as it grows again toward earth, Is fashion'd for the journey ii 2 227
Often I ha' dined with him, and told him on't, and come again to supper iii 1 26
Who, then, dares to be half so kind again? For bounty, that makes gods, does still mar men iv 2 40
This is it That makes the wappen'd widow wed again iv 3 38
This embalms and spices To the April day again iv 3 41
If I thrive well, I'll visit thee again.—If I hope well, I'll never see thee more iv 3 170
Turn rascal; hadst thou wealth again, Rascals should have't iv 3 217
Thou'ldst courtier be again, Wert thou not beggar iv 3 241
When I know not what else to do, I'll see thee again iv 3 359
Bid every noise be still: peace yet again! *J. Cæsar* i 2 14
What say'st thou to me now? speak once again.—Beware the ides of March i 2 22
Then he offered it to him again; then he put it by again i 2 241
An I tell you that, I'll ne'er look you i' the face again i 2 285
To bed again; it is not day. Is not to-morrow, boy, the ides of March? ii 1 39
I would have had thee there, and here again, Ere I can tell thee what thou shouldst do there ii 4 4
Say I am merry: come to me again, And bring me word what he doth say ii 4 45
Now mark him, he begins again to speak iii 2 122
Who, much enforced, shows a hasty spark, And straight is cold again iv 3 113
I have slept, my lord, already.—It was well done; and thou shalt sleep again iv 3 264
Thou shalt see me at Philippi.—Well; then I shall see thee again? iv 3 285
When think you that the sword goes up again? v 1 52
And whether we shall meet again I know not v 1 115
If we do meet again, why, we shall smile; If not, why then, this parting was well made v 1 118
I will be here again, even with a thought v 3 19
When shall we three meet again In thunder, lightning, or in rain? *Macb.* i 1 1
Thrice to thine and thrice to mine And thrice again, to make up nine i 3 36

Again. But they did say their prayers, and address'd them Again to sleep *Macbeth* ii 2 26
I am afraid to think what I have done; Look on't again I dare not ii 2 52
Is Banquo gone from court?—Ay, madam, but returns again to-night iii 2 2
Then comes my fit again: I had else been perfect, Whole as the marble iii 4 21
Get thee gone: to-morrow We'll hear, ourselves, again iii 4 32
Keep seat; The fit is momentary; upon a thought He will again be well iii 4 56
But now they rise again, With twenty mortal murders on their crowns iii 4 80
Be alive again, And dare me to the desert with thy sword iii 4 103
Unreal mockery, hence! Why, so: being gone, I am a man again iii 4 108
Come, let's make haste; she'll soon be back again iii 5 37
We may again Give to our tables meat, sleep to our nights iii 6 33
I take my leave of you: Shall not be long but I'll be here again iv 2 23
When shalt thou see thy wholesome days again? iv 3 105
I have seen her . . . take forth paper, fold it, write upon't, read it, afterwards seal it, and again return to bed v 1 8
I would applaud thee to the very echo, That should applaud again v 3 54
Profit again should hardly draw me here v 3 62
My sword with an unbatter'd edge I sheathe again undeeded v 7 20
What, has this thing appear'd again to-night?—I have seen nothing *Hamlet* i 1 21
That if again this apparition come, He may approve our eyes and speak to it i 1 28
Sit down awhile; And let us once again assail your ears i 1 31
Peace, break thee off; look, where it comes again! i 1 40
But soft, behold! lo, where it comes again! i 1 126
He was a man, take him for all in all, I shall not look upon his like again i 2 188
I will watch to-night; Perchance 'twill walk again.—I warrant it will i 2 243
I'll speak to him again. What do you read, my lord? ii 2 193
So many journeys may the sun and moon Make us again count o'er ere love be done! iii 2 172
And will he not come again? No, no, he is dead: Go to thy death-bed: He never will come again iv 5 190
My arrows, Too slightly timber'd for so loud a wind, Would have reverted to my bow again iv 7 23
Whose worth, if praises may go back again, Stood challenger on mount of all the age iv 7 27
How much I had to do to calm his rage! Now fear I this will give it start again iv 7 194
'Tis a quick lie, sir; 'twill away again, from me to you v 1 140
A hit, a very palpable hit.—Well; again.—Stay; give me drink v 2 292
The foul practice Hath turn'd itself on me; lo, here I lie, Never to rise again v 2 330
He hath been out nine years, and away he shall again *Lear* i 1 34
Nothing will come of nothing: speak again i 1 92
We Have no such daughter, nor shall ever see That face of hers again i 1 267
Now, by my life, Old fools are babes again; and must be used With checks i 3 19
If you will measure your lubber's length again, tarry: but away! i 4 101
Old fond eyes, Beweep this cause again, I'll pluck ye out i 4 324
Keep peace, upon your lives: He dies that strikes again ii 2 53
There could I have him now,—and there,—and there again, and there iii 4 63
Might I but live to see thee in my touch, I'ld say I had eyes again iv 1 26
Let not my worser spirit tempt me again To die before you please! iv 6 222
If ever I return to you again, I'll bring you comfort v 2 3
A man may rot even here.—What, in ill thoughts again? v 2 9
I have told thee often, and I re-tell thee again and again *Othello* i 3 372
Which now again you are most apt to play the sir in ii 1 175
Even as again they were When you yourself did part them ii 3 238
Sue to him again, and he's yours.—I will rather sue to be despised ii 3 277
I will ask him for my place again; he shall tell me I am a drunkard! ii 3 306
If you have any music that may not be heard, to't again iii 1 17
I will have my lord and you again As friendly as you were iii 3 6
But I do love thee! and when I love thee not, Chaos is come again iii 3 92
'Twill away again: Let me but bind it hard, within this hour It will be well iii 3 285
Give't me again: poor lady, she'll run mad When she shall lack it iii 3 317
A trick to put me from my suit: Pray you, let Cassio be received again iii 4 88
By your virtuous means I may again Exist, and be a member of his love iii 4 111
O good Iago, What shall I do to win my lord again? iv 2 149
If I quench thee, thou flaming minister, I can again thy former light restore v 2 9
When I have pluck'd the rose, I cannot give it vital growth again v 2 14
Shall she come in? were't good?—I think she stirs again: no v 2 95
What our contempt doth often hurl from us, We wish it ours again *Ant. and Cleo.* i 2 128
I will give thee bloody teeth, If thou with Cæsar paragon again My man of men i 5 71
I see it in My motion, have it not in my tongue: but yet Hie you to Egypt again ii 3 15
I say again, thy spirit Is all afraid to govern thee near him ii 3 28
Pompey doth this day laugh away his fortune.—If he do, sure, he cannot weep't back again ii 6 112
He will to his Egyptian dish again: then shall the sighs of Octavia blow the fire up in Cæsar ii 6 135
Thou must not take my former sharpness ill: I will employ thee back again iii 3 39
To him again: tell him he wears the rose Of youth upon him iii 13 20
But, since my lord is Antony again, I will be Cleopatra iii 13 187
I will live, Or bathe my dying honour in the blood Shall make it live again iv 2 7
Hie thee again: I have spoke already, and it is provided v 2 194
Go fetch My best attires: I am again for Cydnus, To meet Mark Antony v 2 228
Downy windows, close; And golden Phœbus never be beheld Of eyes again so royal! v 2 321
But that there is this jewel in the world That I may see again *Cymbeline* i 1 92
O the gods! When shall we see again? i 1 124
They were again together: you have done Not after our command i 1 151
I have enough: To the trunk again, and shut the spring of it i 2 47
I beg but leave to air this jewel; see! And now 'tis up again: it must be married To that your diamond ii 4 97
Have patience, sir, And take your ring again; 'tis not yet won ii 4 114
That opportunity Which then they had to take from's, to resume We have again iii 1 16
Of him I gather'd honour; Which he to seek of me again, perforce, Behoves me keep at utterance iii 1 72
I thought you would not back again.—Most like; Bringing me here to kill me iii 4 119
Where is thy lady? or, by Jupiter,—I will not ask again iii 5 86
O Imogen, Safe mayst thou wander, safe return again! iii 5 105

Again. To the court I'll knock her back, foot her home again *Cymbeline* iii 5 149
The ground that gave them first has them again . . . iv 2 289
No more a Briton, I have resumed again The part I came in . . v 3 75
I come to spend my breath; Which neither here I'll keep nor bear again v 3 82
Who of their broken debtors take a third, A sixth, a tenth, letting them thrive again On their abatement . . . . v 4 20
Think that you are upon a rock; and now Throw me again . . v 5 263
Prithee, valiant youth, Deny't again.—I have spoke it, and I did it . v 5 290
I am down again: But now my heavy conscience sinks my knee . v 5 412
Death may usurp on nature many hours, And yet the fire of life kindle again The o'erpress'd spirits . . . . . *Pericles* iii 2 83
See how she 'gins to blow Into life's flower again! . . . . iii 2 96
But since King Pericles, My wedded lord, I ne'er shall see again . iii 4 9
To her father turn our thoughts again, Where we left him . . v Gower 12
Against. She is too bright to be looked against . . . *Mer. Wives* ii 2 254
I can speak Against the thing I say . . . . *Meas. for Meas.* ii 4 60
I'll charm his eyes against she do appear . . . *M. N. Dream* iii 2 99
I will chide no breather in the world but myself, against whom I know most faults . . . . *As Y. Like It* iii 2 298
Bid the priest be ready to come against you come with your appendix *T. of Shrew* iv 4 104
But we must do good against evil . . . . . . *All's Well* ii 5 53
I was promised them against the feast; but they come not too late now *W. Tale* iv 4 237
Every one doth so Against a change . . . . . . *Richard II.* iii 4 28
Albeit considerations infinite Do make against it . . *1 Hen. IV.* v 1 103
I am his kinsman and his subject, Strong both against the deed *Macbeth* i 7 14
Little is the wisdom, where the flight So runs against all reason . iv 2 14
Against the grain. Made you against the grain To voice him consul *Coriolanus* ii 3 241
Agamemnon. Worth five of Agamemnon, and ten times better than the Nine Worthies . . . . *2 Hen. IV.* ii 4 237
As magnanimous as Agamemnon; and a man that I love and honour *Hen. V.* iii 6 7
And ne'er was Agamemnon's brother wrong'd By that false woman, as this king by thee . . . . *3 Hen. VI.* ii 2 148
I had rather be such a man as Troilus than Agamemnon . *Troi. and Cres.* i 2 267
Great Agamemnon, Nestor shall apply Thy latest words . . . i 3 32
Agamemnon, Thou great commander, nerve and bone of Greece . . i 3 54
Such As Agamemnon and the hand of Greece Should hold up high in brass . . . . i 3 63
Agamemnon, This chaos, when degree is suffocate, Follows the choking i 3 124
Sometime, great Agamemnon, Thy topless deputation he puts on . . i 3 151
Excellent! 'tis Agamemnon just. Now play me Nestor . . . i 3 164
Is this great Agamemnon's tent, I pray you?—Even this . . . i 3 216
All the Greekish heads, which with one voice call Agamemnon head . i 3 222
Which is that god in office, guiding men? Which is the high and mighty Agamemnon? . . . . i 3 232
What's your affair, I pray you?—Sir, pardon; 'tis for Agamemnon's ears i 3 248
Speak frankly as the wind; It is not Agamemnon's sleeping hour . i 3 254
We have, great Agamemnon, here in Troy A prince call'd Hector . i 3 260
I begin to relish thy advice; And I will give a taste of it forthwith To Agamemnon . . . . i 3 390
Agamemnon, how if he had boils? full, all over, generally? . . ii 1 2
Come, what's Agamemnon?—Thy commander, Achilles . . . ii 3 46
Agamemnon commands Achilles; Achilles is my lord . . . . ii 3 55
Agamemnon is a fool; Achilles is a fool; Thersites is a fool . . ii 3 63
Agamemnon is a fool to offer to command Achilles; Achilles is a fool to be commanded of Agamemnon . . . . ii 3 67
O Agamemnon, let it not be so! We'll consecrate the steps that Ajax makes When they go from Achilles . . . . ii 3 192
I said, 'Good morrow, Ajax;' and he replies, 'Thanks, Agamemnon' iii 3 262
The magnanimous and most illustrious six-or-seven-times-honoured captain-general of the Grecian army, Agamemnon, et cetera . . iii 3 280
Procure safe-conduct from Agamemnon.—Agamemnon! . . . iii 3 289
'Tis Agamemnon's wish, and great Achilles Doth long to see unarm'd the valiant Hector . . . . iv 5 152
Great Agamemnon comes to meet us here . . . . . . iv 5 159
Great Hector, welcome.—I thank thee, most imperious Agamemnon . iv 5 172
Shall I, sweet lord, be bound to you so much, After we part from Agamemnon's tent, To bring me thither? . . . . . . iv 5 285
Here's Agamemnon, an honest fellow enough, and one that loves quails v 1 56
Agate. An agate very vilely cut . . . . . *Much Ado* iii 1 65
His heart, like an agate, with your print impress'd . *L. L. Lost* ii 1 236
I was never manned with an agate till now . . *2 Hen. IV.* i 2 19
Agate-ring, puke-stocking, caddis-garter, smooth-tongue . *1 Hen IV.* ii 4 78
Agate-stone. In shape no bigger than an agate-stone . *Rom. and Jul.* i 4 55
Agazed. All the whole army stood agazed on him . . *1 Hen. VI.* i 1 126
Age. Who with age and envy Was grown into a hoop . . *Tempest* i 2 258
I would with such perfection govern, sir, To excel the golden age . ii 1 168
And as with age his body uglier grows, So his mind cankers . . iv 1 191
Let me embrace thine age, whose honour cannot Be measured or confined v 1 121
Which would be great impeachment to his age . . *T. G. of Ver.* i 3 15
Omitting the sweet benefit of time To clothe mine age with angel-like perfection . . . . ii 4 66
It would be much vexation to your age . . . . . . iii 1 16
Mine age Should have been cherish'd by her child-like duty . . iii 1 74
Falstaff will learn the humour of the age, French thrift, you rogues *M. W.* i 3 92
One that is well-nigh worn to pieces with age . . . . . ii 1 22
The superstitious idle-headed eld Received and did deliver to our age This tale . . . . iv 4 37
All sects, all ages smack of this vice . . . *Meas. for Meas.* ii 2 5
Thou hast nor youth nor age, But, as it were, an after-dinner's sleep . iii 1 32
That age, ache, penury, and imprisonment Can lay on nature . . iii 1 130
Hath homely age the alluring beauty took From my poor cheek? *Comedy of Err.* ii 1 89
I see thy age and dangers make thee dote . . . . . . v 1 329
He hath borne himself beyond the promise of his age . . *Much Ado* i 1 14
A man loves the meat in his youth that he cannot endure in his age . ii 3 248
As they say, When the age is in, the wit is out . . . . iii 5 37
Trust not my age, My reverence, calling, nor divinity . . . iv 1 169
Time hath not yet so dried this blood of mine, Nor age so eat up my invention . . . . iv 1 196
Beshrew my hand, If it should give your age such cause of fear . v 1 56
I speak not like a dotard nor a fool, As under privilege of age to brag . v 1 60
If a man do not erect in this age his own tomb ere he dies, he shall live no longer in monument than the bell rings and the widow weeps . v 2 80
The world was very guilty of such a ballad some three ages since *L. L. Lost* i 2 117
Beauty doth varnish age, as if new-born, And gives the crutch the cradle's infancy . . . . iv 3 244

Age. This long age of three hours Between our after-supper and bed-time *M. N. Dream* v 1 33
The boy was the very staff of my age, my very prop . *Mer. of Venice* ii 2 70
To view with hollow eye and wrinkled brow An age of poverty . . iv 1 271
And unregarded age in corners thrown . . . . *As Y. Like It* ii 3 42
Be comfort to my age! . . . . ii 3 45
Therefore my age is as a lusty winter, Frosty, but kindly . . ii 3 52
Oppress'd with two weak evils, age and hunger . . . . ii 7 132
One man in his time plays many parts, His acts being seven ages . ii 7 143
The sixth age shifts Into the lean and slipper'd pantaloon . . ii 7 157
The stretching of a span Buckles in his sum of age . . . . iii 2 140
'Tis a word too great for any mouth of this age's size . . . iii 2 240
The foolish coroners of that age found it was 'Hero of Sestos' . iv 1 106
Under an oak, whose boughs were moss'd with age And high top bald . iv 3 105
How old are you, friend?—Five and twenty, sir.—A ripe age . . v 1 22
A lady far more beautiful Than any woman in this waning age *T. of Shr.* Ind. 2 65
Skipper, stand back: 'tis age that nourisheth . . . . . ii 1 341
Your father were a fool To give thee all, and in his waning age Set foot under thy table . . . . ii 1 403
By law, as well as reverend age, I may entitle thee my loving father . iv 5 60
On us both did haggish age steal on And wore us out of act . *All's Well* i 2 29
I write man; to which title age cannot bring thee . . . . ii 3 209
For doing I am past; as I will by thee, in what motion age will give me leave . . . . ii 3 247
I'll have no more pity of his age than I would have of— I'll beat him ii 3 255
My heart is heavy and mine age is weak; Grief would have tears . iii 4 41
Whose age and honour Both suffer under this complaint . . . v 3 162
And dallies with the innocence of love, Like the old age . . *T. Night* ii 4 49
To see this age! A sentence is but a cheveril glove to a good wit . iii 1 12
Either thou art most ignorant by age, Or thou wert born a fool *W. Tale* ii 1 173
I would there were no age between sixteen and three-and-twenty . iii 3 59
A fair one are you—well you fit our ages With flowers of winter . iv 4 78
These are flowers Of middle summer, and I think they are given To men of middle age . . . . iv 4 108
Is he not stupid With age and altering rheums? can he speak? hear? . iv 4 410
He has his health and ampler strength indeed Than most have of his age iv 4 415
The place of your dwelling, your names, your ages, of what having, breeding . . . . iv 4 740
Age, thou hast lost thy labour . . . . iv 4 787
When she was young you woo'd her; now in age Is she become the suitor? . . . . v 3 108
Sweet, sweet, sweet poison for the age's tooth . . . *K. John* i 1 213
None but in this iron age would do it! . . . . . . iv 1 60
To be a make-peace shall become my age . . . . . *Richard II.* i 1 160
My oil-dried lamp and time-bewasted light Shall be extinct with age . i 3 222
Thou canst help time to furrow me with age, But stop no wrinkle . i 3 229
Like crooked age, To crop at once a too long wither'd flower . . ii 1 133
Let them die that age and sullens have; For both hast thou . . ii 1 139
Impute his words To wayward sickliness and age in him . . . ii 1 142
Who, weak with age, cannot support myself . . . . . . ii 2 83
The blood of English shall manure the ground, And future ages groan for this foul act . . . . iv 1 138
Let them tell thee tales Of woeful ages long ago betid . . . v 1 42
The time shall not be many hours of age More than it is . . . v 1 57
Wilt thou pluck my fair son from mine age, And rob me of a happy mother's name? . . . . v 2 92
Look, 'when his infant fortune came to age,' And 'gentle Harry Percy,' and 'kind cousin' . . . . *1 Hen. IV.* i 3 253
To the pupil age of this present twelve o'clock at midnight . . ii 4 106
As I think, his age some fifty, or, by'r lady, inclining to three score . ii 4 466
O for a fine thief, of the age of two and twenty or thereabouts! . iii 3 212
If speaking truth In this fine age were not thought flattery . . iv 1 2
Is now alive To grace this latter age with noble deeds . . . v 2 92
Though not clean past your youth, hath yet some smack of age in you *2 Hen. IV.* i 2 111
All the other gifts appertinent to man, as the malice of this age shapes them, are not worth a gooseberry . . . . i 2 195
That are written down old with all the characters of age . . . i 2 203
A man can no more separate age and covetousness than a' can part young limbs and lechery . . . . i 2 256
Mingled with venom of suggestion—As, force perforce, the age will pour it in . . . . iv 4 46
To relief of lazars and weak age, Of indigent faint souls past corporal toil *Hen. V.* i 1 15
You must learn to know such slanders of the age . . . . iii 6 84
He that shall live this day, and see old age, Will yearly on the vigil feast his neighbours . . . . iv 3 44
Old age, that ill layer up of beauty, can do no more spoil upon my face v 2 248
That hereafter ages may behold What ruin happen'd in revenge of him *1 Hen. VI.* ii 2 10
Kind keepers of my weak decaying age . . . . . . ii 5 1
Grey locks, the pursuivants of death, Nestor-like aged in an age of care ii 5 6
Would some part of my young years Might but redeem the passage of your age! . . . . ii 5 108
Becomes it thee to taunt his valiant age And twit with cowardice a man half dead? . . . . iii 2 54
In some better place, Fitter for sickness and for crazy age . . iii 2 89
When sapless age and weak unable limbs Should bring thy father to his drooping chair . . . . iv 5 4
My age was never tainted with such shame . . . . . iv 5 46
Leaden age, Quicken'd with youthful spleen and warlike rage . . iv 6 12
If I to-day die not with Frenchmen's rage, To-morrow I shall die with mickle age . . . . iv 6 35
For what is wedlock forced but a hell, An age of discord and continual strife? . . . . v 5 63
He being of age to govern of himself . . . . . *2 Hen. VI.* i 1 166
My son, the comfort of my age . . . . i 1 190
This dishonour in thine age Will bring thy head with sorrow to the ground! . . . . ii 3 18
Give me leave to go; Sorrow would solace and mine age would ease . ii 3 21
O miserable age! virtue is not regarded in handicrafts-men . . iv 2 11
Ignorant of his birth and parentage, Became a bricklayer when he came to age . . . . iv 2 153
Wilt thou go dig a grave to find out war, And shame thine honourable age with blood? . . . . v 1 170
In duty bend thy knee to me That bows unto the grave with mickle age v 1 174
To lose thy youth in peace, and to achieve The silver livery of advised age . . . . v 2 47
Shall be eternized in all age to come . . . . v 3 31
Had slipp'd our claim until another age . . . . *3 Hen. VI.* ii 2 162

Age. O, pity, God, this miserable age! . . . 3 *Hen. VI.* ii 5 88
God, I pray him, That none of you may live your natural age! *Rich. III.* i 3 213
Weigh it but with the grossness of this age . . . iii 1 46
Which, since, succeeding ages have re-edified . . . iii 1 71
I prophesy the fearfull'st time to thee That ever wretched age hath look'd upon . . . . iii 4 107
Thy age confirm'd, proud, subtle, bloody, treacherous . . iv 4 171
I with grief and extreme age shall perish And never look upon thy face again . . . . iv 4 185
Your children were vexation to your youth, But mine shall be a comfort to your age . . . . iv 4 306
The children live, whose parents thou hast slaughter'd, Ungovern'd youth, to wail it in their age; The parents live, whose children thou hast butcher'd, Old wither'd plants, to wail it with their age . . iv 4 392
If you do free your children from the sword, Your children's children quit it in your age . . . . v 3 262
He would not in mine age Have left me naked to mine enemies *Hen. VIII* iii 2 456
To add greater honours to his age Than man could give him, he died fearing God . . . . iv 2 67
The primogenitive and due of birth, Prerogative of age . *Troi. and Cres.* i 3 107
And then, forsooth, the faint defects of age Must be the scene of mirth i 3 172
His pupil age Man-enter'd thus, he waxed like a sea *Coriolanus* ii 2 102
We shall hardly in our ages see Their banners wave again . . iii 1 7
Three examples of the like have been Within my age . . . iv 6 51
For you, be that you are, long; and your misery increase with your age! v 2 114
His name remains To the ensuing age abhorr'd . . . v 3 148
Let my father's honours live in me, Nor wrong mine age with this indignity *T. Andron.* i 1 8
That hast thus lovingly reserved The cordial of mine age to glad my heart! . . . . i 1 166
A better head her glorious body fits Than his that shakes for age and feebleness . . . . i 1 188
Give me a staff of honour for mine age, But not a sceptre to control the world . . . . i 1 198
For pity of mine age, whose youth was spent In dangerous wars . iii 1 2
I bring consuming sorrow to thine age . . . . iii 1 61
I am of age To keep mine own . . . . . . iv 2 104
Nor age nor honour shall shape privilege . . . . iv 4 57
My frosty signs and chaps of age, Grave witnesses of true experience . v 3 77
My daughter's of a pretty age.—Faith, I can tell her age *Rom. and Jul.* i 3 10
Susan and she—God rest all Christian souls!—Were of an age . i 3 19
Thou wilt fall backward when thou comest to age . . . i 3 56
This sight of death is as a bell, That warns my old age to a sepulchre v 3 207
What further woe conspires against mine age? . . . v 3 212
It hath pleased the gods to remember my father's age, And call him to long peace . . . . *T. of Athens* i 2 2
Upon whose age we void it up again, With poisonous spite and envy . i 2 143
I know your reverend ages love Security . . . . iii 5 80
I cannot think but your age has forgot me . . . . iii 5 93
Pity not honour'd age for his white beard; He is an usurer . . iv 3 111
Groaning underneath this age's yoke . . . . *J. Cæsar* i 2 61
Age, thou art shamed! Rome, thou hast lost the breed of noble bloods! i 2 150
When went there by an age, since the great flood, But it was famed with more than with one man? . . . . i 2 152
Lest that the people, Rushing on us, should do your age some mischief iii 1 93
How many ages hence Shall this our lofty scene be acted over! . iii 1 111
The choice and master spirits of this age . . . . iii 1 163
The gods to-day stand friendly, that we may, Lovers in peace, lead on our days to age! . . . . v 1 95
What's the newest grief?—That of an hour's age doth hiss the speaker *Macbeth* iv 3 175
And that which should accompany old age, As honour, love, obedience, troops of friends, I must not look to have . . . . . v 3 24
It is as proper to our age To cast beyond ourselves in our opinions As it is common for the younger sort To lack discretion *Hamlet* ii 1 114
That so his sickness, age, and impotence Was falsely borne in hand . ii 2 66
The very age and body of the time his form and pressure . . iii 2 26
At your age The heyday in the blood is tame, it's humble . . iii 4 68
Stood challenger on mount of all the age For her perfections . . iv 7 28
Youth no less becomes The light and careless livery that it wears Than settled age his sables and his weeds . . . . . . iv 7 81
Age, with his stealing steps, Hath clawed me in his clutch . . v 1 79
The age is grown so picked that the toe of the peasant comes so near the heel of the courtier, he galls his kibe . . . . . v 1 151
And many more of the same breed that I know the drossy age dotes on v 2 197
'Tis our fast intent To shake all cares and business from our age *Lear* i 1 40
The argument of your praise, balm of your age, Most best, most dearest i 1 218
You see how full of changes his age is . . . . . i 1 291
'Tis the infirmity of his age: yet he hath ever but slenderly known himself i 1 296
Then must we look to receive from his age, not alone the imperfections of long-engraffed condition . . . . i 1 300
This policy and reverence of age makes the world bitter to the best of our times . . . . i 2 49
That, sons at perfect age, and fathers declining, the father should be as ward to the son . . . . i 2 77
Such men as may besort your age, And know themselves and you. . i 4 272
Dear daughter, I confess that I am old; Age is unnecessary . . ii 4 157
A poor old man, As full of grief as age; wretched in both! . . ii 4 276
O world! But that thy strange mutations make us hate thee, Life would not yield to age . . . . iv 1 12
Whose age has charms in it, whose title more, To pluck the common bosom on his side. . . . . v 3 48
It yet hath felt no age nor known no sorrow *Othello* iii 4 37
Though age from folly could not give me freedom, It does from childishness *Ant. and Cleo.* i 3 57
Age cannot wither her, nor custom stale Her infinite variety. . ii 2 240
Thou heap'st A year's age on me . . . . *Cymbeline* i 1 133
Well corresponding With your stiff age . . . . iii 3 32
I had rather Have skipp'd from sixteen years of age to sixty . . iv 2 199
He it is that hath Assumed this age . . . . . v 5 319
The colour of her hair, complexion, height, age . *Pericles* iv 2 62
The gods preserve you!—And you, sir, to outlive the age I am . v 1 15
Age to age. Is it upon record, or else reported Successively from age to age? . . . . *Richard III.* iii 1 73
Truth should live from age to age, As 'twere retail'd to all posterity . iii 1 76
Aged. Shorten up their sinews With aged cramps . . *Tempest* iv 1 261
She is nice and coy And nought esteems my aged eloquence *T. G. of Ver.* iii 1 83
All thy blessed youth Becomes as aged, and doth beg the alms Of palsied eld. . . . . *Meas. for Meas.* iii 1 35
Aged. It is as dangerous to be aged in any kind of course, as it is virtuous to be constant in any undertaking . . *Meas. for Meas.* iii 2 238
Aged ears play truant at his tales And younger hearings are quite ravished; So sweet and voluble is his discourse . . *L. L. Lost* ii 1 74
Whose aged honour cites a virtuous youth . . . *All's Well* i 3 216
Not so much wrinkled, nothing So aged as this seems . . *W. Tale* v 3 29
What comfort, man? how is't with aged Gaunt? *Richard II.* ii 1 72
Here comes the Duke of York.—With signs of war about his aged neck ii 2 74
These grey locks, the pursuivants of death, Nestor-like aged in an age of care . . . . 1 *Hen. VI.* ii 5 6
Lean thine aged back against mine arm; And, in that ease, I'll tell thee ii 5 43
Who in rage forgets Aged contusions and all brush of time . 2 *Hen. VI.* v 3 3
Right for right Hath dimm'd your infant morn to aged night *Rich. III.* iv 4 16
She shall be, to the happiness of England, An aged princess . *Hen. VIII.* v 5 58
Aged custom, But by your voices, will not so permit me . *Coriolanus* ii 3 176
Aged sir, hands off.—Hence, rotten thing! or I shall shake thy bones . iii 1 178
Tears, which now you see Filling the aged wrinkles in my cheeks *T. A.* iii 1 7
O reverend tribunes! O gentle, aged men! Unbind my sons . . iii 1 23
Prepare thy aged eyes to weep; Or, if not so, thy noble heart to break iii 1 59
For I can smooth and fill his aged ear With golden promises . . iv 4 96
This do thou for my love; and so let him, As he regards his aged father's life. . . . . v 2 130
Sack fair Athens, And take our goodly aged men by the beards *T. of Athens* v 1 175
In pity of our aged and our youth, I cannot choose but tell him, that I care not . . . . v 1 179
An aged interpreter, though young in days . . . v 3 8
I begin to find an idle and fond bondage in the oppression of aged tyranny *Lear* i 2 52
A gracious aged man, Whose reverence even the head-lugg'd bear would lick . . . . iv 2 41
But love, dear love, and our aged father's right . . . iv 4 28
Let her languish A drop of blood a day; and, being aged, Die! *Cymbeline* i 1 157
He not return, I shall with aged patience bear your yoke . *Pericles* ii 4 48
Agenor. Beauty in her face, Such as the daughter of Agenor had *T. of Shr.* i 1 173
Agent. Here is her hand, the agent of her heart . *T. G. of Ver.* i 3 46
This ungenitured agent will unpeople the province with continency *Meas. for Meas.* iii 2 184
Let every eye negotiate for itself And trust no agent . . *Much Ado* ii 1 186
This entertainment May a free face put on, derive a liberty From heartiness, from bounty, fertile bosom, And well become the agent *W. Tale* i 2 114
Whiles we, God's wrathful agent, do correct Their proud contempt *K. John* ii 1 87
Being the agents, or base second means . . . 1 *Hen. IV.* i 3 165
Suffolk's tongue, The agent of thy foul inconstancy . 2 *Hen. VI.* iii 2 115
Is posted, as the agent of our cardinal, To second all his plot *Hen. VIII.* iii 2 59
O world! world! world! thus is the poor agent despised! *Troi. and Cres.* v 10 36
The former agents, if they did complain, What could the belly answer? *Coriolanus* i 1 127
I am settled, and bend up Each corporal agent to this terrible feat *Macb.* i 7 80
Whiles night's black agents to their preys do rouse. . . iii 2 53
The agent for his master And the remembrancer of her to hold The handfast to her lord . . . . *Cymbeline* i 5 76
Aggravate. I will aggravate his style . . . . *Mer. Wives* ii 2 296
I will aggravate my voice so that I will roar you as gently as any sucking dove . . . . *M. N. Dream* i 2 84
The more to aggravate the note, With a foul traitor's name stuff I thy throat . . . . *Richard II.* i 1 43
I beseek you now, aggravate your choler . . . 2 *Hen. IV.* ii 4 175
Aggriefed. I would fain see the man, that has but two legs, that shall find himself aggriefed . . . . *Hen. V.* iv 7 170
Agile. His agile arm beats down their fatal points . *Rom. and Jul.* iii 1 171
Agincourt. The very casques That did affright the air at Agincourt *Hen. V.* Prol. 14
Then call we this the field of Agincourt, Fought on the day of Crispin . iv 7 93
Agitation. So now I speak my agitation of the matter *Mer. of Venice* iii 5 5
In this slumbery agitation, besides her walking and other actual performances . . . . *Macbeth* v 1 12
Aglet-baby. Marry him to a puppet or an aglet-baby . *T. of Shrew* i 2 79
Agnize. I do agnize A natural and prompt alacrity I find in hardness *Oth.* i 3 232
Ago. Hath this been proclaimed?—Four days ago . . *L. L. Lost* i 1 122
'Tis but an hour ago since it was nine, And after one hour more 'twill be eleven . . . . *As Y. Like It* ii 7 24
I am past my gamut long ago.—Yet read the gamut of Hortensio *T. of Shrew* iii 1 71
Near twenty years ago, in Genoa, Where we were lodgers at the Pegasus iv 4 4
But a month ago I went from hence, And then 'twas fresh in murmur *T. Night* i 2 31
But yet I cannot love him; He might have took his answer long ago . i 5 282
Pardon me, sweet one, even for the vows We made each other but so late ago . . . . v 1 222
A great while ago the world begun, With hey, ho . . . v 1 414
My people did expect my hence departure Two days ago . . *W. Tale* i 2 451
'Tis in three parts.—We had the tune on't a month ago . . iv 4 300
Wreck'd three nights ago on Goodwin Sands . . . *K. John* v 3 11
And let them tell thee tales Of woeful ages long ago betid *Richard II.* v 1 42
Over whose acres walk'd those blessed feet Which fourteen hundred years ago were nail'd For our advantage on the bitter cross 1 *Hen. IV.* i 1 26
Is Gilliams with the packet gone?—He is, my lord, an hour ago . ii 3 69
O villain, thou stolest a cup of sack eighteen years ago . . ii 4 346
How long is't ago, Jack, since thou sawest thine own knee? . . ii 4 360
And, as he said to me, 'Twas no longer ago than Wednesday last 2 *Hen. IV.* ii 4 93
Before I came to Clement's Inn.—That's fifty five year ago . . iii 2 224
Ten days ago I drown'd these news in tears . . 3 *Hen. VI.* ii 1 104
Who saw the sun to-day? . . . By the book He should have braved the east an hour ago . . . . *Richard III.* v 3 279
Alas, has banish'd me his bed already, His love, too long ago! *Hen. VIII.* iii 1 120
'Tis a verse in Horace; I know it well: I read it in the grammar long ago *T. Andron.* iv 2 23
Will you tell me that? His son was but a ward two years ago *R. and J.* i 5 42
But for your company, I would have been a-bed an hour ago . . iii 4 7
Not long ago, one of his men was with the Lord Lucullus *T. of Athens* iii 2 12
O heavens! die two months ago, and not forgotten yet? . . *Hamlet* iii 2 139
Is it two days ago since I tripped up thy heels? . . . . *Lear* ii 2 31
I will make him tell the tale anew, Where, how, how oft, how long ago, and when He hath, and is again to cope your wife . *Othello* iv 1 86
How long is this ago?—Some twenty years . . . *Cymbeline* i 1 61
Are you ready for death?—Over-roasted rather; ready long ago . v 4 154
A-going. Whither were you a-going?—To the cardinal's . *Hen. VIII.* i 3 50
Agone. Long agone I have forgot to court. . . *T. G. of Ver.* iii 1 85
O, he's drunk, Sir Toby, an hour agone . . . . . *T. Night* v 1 204

Agony. Charm ache with air and agony with words . . . *Much Ado* v 1 26
It cannot be; it is impossible: Mirth cannot move a soul in agony *L. L. Lost* v 2 867
Take that, to end thy agony *3 Hen. VI.* v 5 39
Awaked you not with this sore agony? *Richard III.* i 4 42
I have stay'd for thee, God knows, in anguish, pain, and agony iv 4 163
He was stirr'd With such an agony, he sweat extremely *Hen. VIII.* ii 1 33
Agood. At that time I made her weep agood *T. G. of Ver.* iv 4 170
Agree. The dozen white louses do become an old coat well; it agrees well, passant *Mer. Wives* i 1 20
With a plausible obedience; agree with his demands *Meas. for Meas.* iii 1 254
How ill agrees it with your gravity To counterfeit thus grossly! *Com. of Errors* ii 2 170
Good wits will be jangling; but, gentles, agree *L. L. Lost* ii 1 225
How dost thou and thy master agree? *Mer. of Venice* ii 2 107
At last, though long, our jarring notes agree: And time it is *T. of Shrew* v 2 1
Our soft conditions and our hearts Should well agree with our external parts v 2 168
I very well agree with you in the hopes of him: it is a gallant child *W. T.* i 1 41
How agrees the devil and thee about thy soul? *1 Hen. IV.* i 2 126
Then the gentlemen do not agree with the gentlewomen. *2 Hen. IV.* Epil. 24
Your appetites and your digestions doo's not agree with it *Hen. V.* v 1 28
He will be here, and yet he is not here: How can these contrarieties agree? *1 Hen. VI.* ii 3 59
Post, my lord, to France; Agree to any covenants v 5 88
Whose large style Agrees not with the leanness of his purse *2 Hen. VI.* i 1 112
I will apparel them all in one livery, that they may agree like brothers iv 2 81
If our queen and this young prince agree, I'll join mine eldest daughter and my joy To him forthwith in holy wedlock bands *3 Hen. VI.* iii 3 241
Yes, I agree, and thank you for your motion iii 3 244
Those that come to see Only a show or two, and so agree The play may pass *Hen. VIII.* Prol. 10
Full well, Andronicus, Agree these deeds with that proud brag *T. Andron.* i 1 306
Nay, come, agree whose hand shall go along iii 1 175
Agree between you; I will spare my hand iii 1 184
An she agree, within her scope of choice Lies my consent *Rom. and Jul.* i 2 18
If love be blind, It best agrees with night. Come, civil night iii 2 10
Make not a city feast of it, to let the meat cool ere we can agree upon the first place *T. of Athens* iii 6 76
Therein our letters do not well agree; Mine speak of seventy senators *J. Cæsar* iv 3 176
Your choice agrees with mine; I like that well *Pericles* ii 5 18
Agreed. How agreed?—She'll take the enterprise upon her *M. for M.* iv 1 65
Are you agreed?—Sir, I will serve him iv 2 51
Unwilling I agreed; alas! too soon We came aboard *Com. of Errors* i 1 61
And there heard it agreed upon that the prince should woo Hero *M. Ado* i 3 64
I am agreed; and would I had given him the best horse in Padua! *T. of Shrew* i 1 147
Forget, forgive; conclude and be agreed *Richard II.* i 1 156
The traitors are agreed; The king is set from London *Hen. V.* ii Prol. 33
Agreed: I'll to yond corner.—And I to this *1 Hen. VI.* ii 1 33
It is thus agreed That peaceful truce shall be proclaim'd in France v 4 116
It is further agreed between them *2 Hen. VI.* i 1 57
The peers agreed, and Henry was well pleased. i 1 218
It stands agreed, I take it, by all voices *Hen. VIII.* v 3 87
Are you all agreed, lords?—We are v 3 91
My horse to yours, no.—'Tis done.—Agreed *Coriolanus* i 4 2
Thus we are agreed: I crave our composition may be written *A. and C.* ii 6 58
Are you both agreed?—Yes, if it please your majesty *Pericles* ii 5 90
Agreeing. Most of all, agreeing with the proclamation . *Meas. for Meas.* i 2 80
All agreeing In earnestness to see him *Coriolanus* ii 1 228
Many a matter hath he told to thee, Meet and agreeing with thine infancy *T. Andron.* v 3 165
Thoughts black, hands apt, drugs fit, and time agreeing . *Hamlet* iii 2 266
Agreement. Whom by chance I met, Upon agreement *T. of Shrew* i 2 183
Upon some agreement Me shall you find ready. iv 4 33
And such assurance ta'en As shall with either part's agreement stand iv 4 50
Three times did they drink, Upon agreement *1 Hen. IV.* i 3 103
Agrippa. Who comes here?—Worthy Menenius Agrippa *Coriolanus* i 1 52
I do not know, Mecænas; ask Agrippa *Ant. and Cleo.* ii 2 17
Speak, Agrippa.—Thou hast a sister by the mother's side ii 2 119
I am not married, Cæsar: let me hear Agrippa further speak. ii 2 126
What power is in Agrippa, If I would say, 'Agrippa, be it so'? ii 2 143
Go forth, Agrippa, and begin the fight: Our will is Antony be took alive iv 6 1
Go charge Agrippa Plant those that have revolted in the van iv 6 8
Aground. Fall to't, yarely, or we run ourselves aground . *Tempest* i 1 4
A-growing. He was the wretched'st thing when he was young, So long a-growing *Richard III.* ii 4 19
Ague. Who hath got, as I take it, an ague *Tempest* ii 2 68
If all the wine in my bottle will recover him, I will help his ague . ii 2 97
How now, moon-calf! how does thine ague? ii 2 139
My wind cooling my broth Would blow me to an ague *Mer. of Venice* i 1 23
He will look as hollow as a ghost, As dim and meagre as an ague's fit *K. John* iii 4 85
A lunatic lean-witted fool, Presuming on an ague's privilege *Richard II.* ii 1 116
This ague fit of fear is over-blown iii 2 190
Without boots, and in foul weather too! How 'scapes he agues? *1 Hen. IV.* iii 1 69
Worse than the sun in March, This praise doth nourish agues iv 1 112
An untimely ague Stay'd me a prisoner in my chamber . *Hen. VIII.* i 1 4
Danger, like an ague, subtly taints Even then when we sit idly in the sun *Troi. and Cres.* iii 3 232
You'll swear, terribly swear Into strong shudders and to heavenly agues The immortal gods *T. of Athens* iv 3 137
Cæsar was ne'er so much your enemy As that same ague *J. Cæsar* ii 2 113
Here let them lie Till famine and the ague eat them up *Macbeth* v 5 4
Aguecheek. Her wooer.—Who, Sir Andrew Aguecheek? . *T. Night* i 3 18
And thy sworn enemy, ANDREW AGUECHEEK iii 4 187
Set upon Aguecheek a notable report of valour iii 4 210
Agued. Backs red, and faces pale With flight and agued fear! *Coriolanus* i 4 38
Agueface. Here comes Sir Andrew Agueface *T. Night* i 3 46
Ague-proof. They told me I was every thing; 'tis a lie, I am not ague-proof *Lear* iv 6 107
A-hanging. I kill'd the slave that was a-hanging thee v 3 274
A-height. Look up a-height; the shrill-gorged lark so far Cannot be seen or heard iv 6 58
A-high. One heaved a-high, to be hurl'd down below *Richard III.* iv 4 86
A-hold. Lay her a-hold, a-hold! set her two courses off . *Tempest* i 1 52
A-hungry. Dinner attends you, sir.—I am not a-hungry . *Mer. Wives* i 1 280
'Twere as good a deed as to drink when a man's a-hungry *T. Night* ii 3 136

Aid. By whose aid, Weak masters though ye be, I have bedimm'd The noontide sun *Tempest* v 1 40
I have her sovereign aid And rest myself content v 1 143
Go with me to my chamber, In these affairs to aid me *T. G. of Ver.* ii 4 185
Lest the devil that guides him should aid him, I will search impossible places *Mer. Wives* iii 5 150
Chased us away, till raising of more aid We came again . *Com. of Errors* v 1 153
The Florentine will move us For speedy aid *All's Well* i 2 7
If you should tender your supposed aid, He would receive it . i 3 242
Cannot, By the good aid that I of you shall borrow, Err in bestowing it iii 7 11
Aid me with that store of power you have v 1 20
I can guess that by thy honest aid Thou kept'st a wife herself v 3 329
Be my aid For such disguise as haply shall become The form of my intent *T. Night* i 2 53
Didst counsel and aid them, for their better safety, to fly away *W. Tale* iii 2 21
We'll make an instrument of this, omit Nothing may give us aid . iv 4 638
Hath drawn him from his own determined aid *K. John* ii 1 584
We all have strongly sworn to give him aid *Richard II.* ii 3 150
We swore our aid. But in short space It rain'd down fortune *1 Hen. IV.* v 1 46
Expectation and surmise Of aids incertain should not be admitted *2 Hen. IV.* i 3 24
In aid whereof we of the spiritualty Will raise your highness such a mighty sum As never did the clergy at one time Bring in *Hen. V.* i 2 132
A worthy leader, wanting aid, Unto his dastard foemen is betray'd *1 Hen. VI.* i 1 143
Her aid she promised and assured success i 2 82
Renowned Talbot doth expect my aid, And I am lowted by a traitor villain iv 3 12
No more my fortune can, But curse the cause I cannot aid the man iv 3 44
Who with me Set from our o'ermatch'd forces forth for aid iv 4 11
Let not your private discord keep away The levied succours that should lend him aid iv 4 23
York set him on; York should have sent him aid iv 4 29
Within six hours they will be at his aid.—Too late comes rescue iv 4 41
You speedy helpers, that are substitutes Under the lordly monarch of the north, Appear and aid me in this enterprise v 3 7
The lord mayor craves aid of your honour from the Tower *2 Hen. VI.* iv 5 4
Such aid as I can spare you shall command iv 5 7
He was lately sent . . . With aid of soldiers to this needful war *3 Hen. VI.* ii 1 147
Weep, wretched man, I'll aid thee tear for tear ii 5 76
My queen and son are gone to France for aid iii 1 28
She, on his left side, craving aid for Henry, He, on his right. iii 1 43
I poor Margaret, . . . Am come to crave thy just and lawful aid . iii 3 32
Then 'tis but reason that I be released From giving aid iii 3 148
At last I firmly am resolved You shall have aid iii 3 220
How can we aid you with our kindred tears? *Richard III.* ii 2 63
There they hull, expecting but the aid Of Buckingham iv 4 438
More competitors Flock to their aid, and still their power increaseth . iv 4 507
The fear of that withholds my present aid iv 5 5
With best advantage will deceive the time, And aid thee v 3 93
I died for hope ere I could lend thee aid: But cheer thy heart v 3 173
He may furnish and instruct great teachers, And never seek for aid out of himself *Hen. VIII.* i 2 114
Take your choice of those That best can aid your action. . *Coriolanus* i 6 66
If I do send, dispatch Those centuries to our aid i 7 3
If you refuse your aid In this so never-needed help, yet do not Upbraid 's v 1 33
Deliver him this petition; Tell him, it is for justice and for aid *T. Andron.* iv 3 15
Feeling in itself A lack of Timon's aid, hath sense withal Of it own fail, restraining aid to Timon *T. of Athens* v 1 150
New honours come upon him, Like our strange garments, cleave not to their mould But with the aid of use *Macbeth* i 3 146
Which fate and metaphysical aid doth seem To have thee crown'd withal i 5 30
Macduff Is gone to pray the holy king, upon his aid iii 6 30
Friends both, go join you with some further aid *Hamlet* iv 1 33
To lend me arms and aid when I required them *Ant. and Cleo.* ii 2 88
That will pray in aid for kindness, Where he for grace is kneel'd to v 2 27
Lucina lent not me her aid, But took me in my throes *Cymbeline* v 4 43
Made familiar To me and to my aid the blest infusions That dwell in vegetives, in metals, stones *Pericles* iii 2 35
Aidance. Who, in the conflict that it holds with death, Attracts the same for aidance *2 Hen. VI.* iii 2 165
Aidant. Be aidant and remediate In the good man's distress! *Lear* iv 4 17
Aided. All the instruments which aided to expose the child were even then lost when it was found *W. Ta'* - 77
Aiding. Heaven aiding, And by the leave of my good lord . *All's Well* iv 4 12
She may help you to many fair preferments, And then deny her aiding hand therein *Richard III.* i 3 96
Aidless came off, And with a sudden re-inforcement struck Corioli *Coriol.* ii 2 116
Ail. What does she ail, that she's not very well? *All's Well* ii 4 6
Ailest. What ailest thou, man?—I have seen two such sights! *W. Tale* iii 3 83
Aim. Fearing lest my jealous aim might err *T. G. of Ver.* iii 1 28
Behold her that gave aim to all thy oaths, And entertain'd 'em deeply . v 4 101
To these violent proceedings all my neighbours shall cry aim *Mer. Wives* iii 2 45
'Tis the very riches of thyself That now I aim at iii 4 18
More grave and wrinkled than the aims and ends Of burning youth *Meas. for Meas.* i 3 5
My sweet hope's aim, My sole earth's heaven *Com. of Errors* iii 2 63
Let that appear hereafter, and aim better at me *Much Ado* iii 2 99
If all aim but this be levell'd false iv 1 239
A certain aim he took At a fair vestal throned by the west *M. N. Dream* ii 1 157
I do not doubt, As I will watch the aim *Mer. of Venice* i 1 150
A poor sequester'd stag, That from the hunter's aim had ta'en a hurt *As Y. Like It* ii 1 34
I am not an impostor that proclaim Myself against the level of mine aim *All's Well* ii 1 159
Fly with false aim; move the still-peering air, That sings with piercing iii 2 113
It ill beseems this presence to cry aim To these ill-tuned repetitions *K. John* ii 1 196
Arrows fled not swifter toward their aim Than did our soldiers *2 Hen. IV.* i 1 123
A man may prophesy, With a near aim, of the main chance of things iii 1 83
The foeman may with as great aim level at the edge of a penknife . iii 2 285
To which is fixed, as an aim or butt, Obedience *Hen. V.* i 2 186
Oft have shot at them, Howe'er unfortunate I miss'd my aim *1 Hen. VI.* i 4 4
Here stand we both, and aim we at the best *3 Hen. VI.* iii 1 8
My mind will never grant what I perceive Your highness aims at . iii 2 68
My thoughts aim at a further matter iv 1 125
But canst thou guess that he doth aim at it? *Richard III.* iii 2 45
A sign of dignity, a garish flag, To be the aim of every dangerous shot . iv 4 90
Madam, you wander from the good we aim at . *Hen. VIII.* iii 1 138

Aim. One that, in all obedience, makes the church The chief aim of his honour . . . *Hen. VIII.* v 3 118
Trial did draw Bias and thwart, not answering the aim . *Troi. and Cres.* i 3 15
In fellest manner execute your aims . . . v 7 6
Fame, at the which he aims, In whom already he's well graced *Coriolanus* i 1 267
By the discovery We shall be shorten'd in our aim . . . i 2 23
I aim a mile beyond the moon; Your letter is with Jupiter by this *T. Andron.* iv 3 65
Gentle people, give me aim awhile, For nature puts me to a heavy task v 3 149
What you would work me to, I have some aim . . . *J. Cæsar* i 2 163
I did present myself Even in the aim and very flash of it . . . i 3 52
Our safest way Is to avoid the aim . . . *Macbeth* ii 3 149
They aim at it, And botch the words up fit to their own thoughts *Hamlet* iv 5 9
In these cases, where the aim reports, 'Tis oft with difference . *Othello* i 3 6
My speech should fall into such vile success As my thoughts aim not at iii 3 223
Shall I do that which all the Parthian darts, Though enemy, lost aim, and could not? . . . *Ant. and Cleo.* iv 14 71
Aimed. Do it so cunningly That my discovery be not aimed at *T. G. of Ver.* iii 1 45
Well aim'd of such a young one . . . *T. of Shrew* ii 1 236
This bird you aim'd at, though you hit her not . . . v 2 50
Some apparent danger seen in him Aim'd at your highness . *Richard II.* i 1 14
In faith, it is exceedingly well aim'd . . . 1 *Hen. IV.* i 3 282
I aim'd so near, when I supposed you loved . . *Rom. and Jul.* i 1 211
My arrows, Too slightly timber'd for so loud a wind, Would have reverted to my bow again, And not where I had aim'd them *Hamlet* iv 7 24
That never aim'd so high to love your daughter . . . *Pericles* ii 5 47
Aimest. Thou aimest all awry; I must offend before I be attainted 2 *Hen. VI.* ii 4 58
Let all the ends thou aim'st at be thy country's, Thy God's *Hen. VIII.* iii 2 447
Aiming at Silvia as a sweeter friend . . . *T. G. of Ver.* ii 6 30
Arrows fled not swifter toward their aim Than did our soldiers, aiming at their safety . . . 2 *Hen. IV.* i 1 124
Aiming, belike, at your interior hatred, Which in your outward actions shows itself . . . *Richard III.* i 3 65
Air. Whom I left cooling of the air with sighs . . . *Tempest* i 2 222
Where should this music be? i' the air or the earth? It sounds no more i 2 387
This music crept by me upon the waters, Allaying both their fury and my passion With its sweet air . . . i 2 393
The goddess On whom these airs attend . . . i 2 422
The air breathes upon us here most sweetly . . . ii 1 46
Sounds and sweet airs, that give delight and hurt not . . . iii 2 145
And thy sea-marge, sterile and rocky-hard, Where thou thyself dost air iv 1 70
Were all spirits and Are melted into air, into thin air . . . iv 1 150
So full of valour that they smote the air For breathing in their faces iv 1 172
Shortly shall all my labours end, and thou Shalt have the air at freedom iv 1 266
Hast thou, which art but air, a touch, a feeling Of their afflictions? . v 1 21
A solemn air and the best comforter To an unsettled fancy . . v 1 58
I drink the air before me, and return Or ere your pulse twice beat . v 1 102
The chameleon Love can feed on the air . . *T. G. of Ver.* ii 1 179
He is a kind of chameleon.—That hath more mind to feed on your blood than live in your air . . . ii 4 28
The air hath starved the roses in her cheeks . . . iv 4 159
My gravity, Wherein—let no man hear me—I take pride, Could I with boot change for an idle plume, Which the air beats for vain *M. for M.* ii 4 12
Come all to help him, and so stop the air By which he should revive . iv 4 25
Now, divine air! now is his soul ravished! . . . *Much Ado* ii 3 60
Who dare tell her so? If I should speak, She would mock me into air . iii 1 75
Charm ache with air and agony with words . . . v 1 26
I did commend the black-oppressing humour to the most wholesome physic of thy health-giving air . . . *L. L. Lost* i 1 236
Concolinel.—Sweet air! Go, tenderness of years . . . iii 1 4
Spied a blossom passing fair Playing in the wanton air . . . iv 3 104
Air, quoth he, thy cheeks may blow; Air, would I might triumph so! . iv 3 109
Blow like sweet roses in this summer air . . . v 2 293
Your tongue's sweet air More tuneable than lark to shepherd's ear *M. N. Dream* i 1 183
The moon, the governess of floods, Pale in her anger, washes all the air, That rheumatic diseases do abound . . . ii 1 104
In the spiced Indian air, by night, Full often hath she gossip'd . . ii 1 124
How all the other passions fleet to air, As doubtful thoughts! *Mer. of Ven.* iii 2 108
Bring your music forth into the air . . . v 1 53
If they but hear perchance a trumpet sound, Or any air of music . . v 1 76
Thou liest in the bleak air: come, I will bear thee to some shelter *As Y. Like It* ii 6 16
And with her breath she did perfume the air . . . *T. of Shrew* i 1 180
Fly with false aim; move the still-peering air, That sings with piercing *All's Well* iii 2 113
Although The air of paradise did fan the house And angels officed all . iii 2 128
Methought she purged the air of pestilence! . . . *T. Night* i 1 20
And make the babbling gossip of the air Cry out . . . i 5 292
O, you should not rest Between the elements of air and earth . . i 5 294
Methought it did relieve my passion much, More than light airs . . ii 4 5
Pursue him now, lest the device take air and taint . . . iii 4 145
This is the air; that is the glorious sun; This pearl she gave me . . iv 3 1
The climate's delicate, the air most sweet, Fertile the isle . *W. Tale* iii 1 1
I' the open air, before I have got strength of limit . . . iii 2 106
And so, with shrieks, She melted into air . . . iii 3 37
Seest thou not the air of the court in these enfoldings? . . . iv 4 755
Your father's image is so hit in you, His very air . . . v 1 128
Gods Purge all infection from our air whilst you Do climate here! . v 1 169
Still, methinks, There is an air comes from her . . . v 3 78
Even till unfenced desolation Leave them as naked as the vulgar air *K. John* ii 1 387
Mocking the air with colours idly spread, And find no check . . . v 1 72
And holds belief That, being brought into the open air, It would allay the burning quality Of that fell poison . . . v 7 7
Pestilence hangs in our air And thou art flying to a fresher clime *Richard II.* i 3 284
Not so deep a maim As to be cast forth in the common air . . . i 3 157
Had the king permitted us, One of our souls had wander'd in the air . i 3 195
How brooks your grace the air, After your late tossing on the breaking seas? . . . iii 2 2
Two buckets, filling one another, The emptier ever dancing in the air . iv 1 186
I will lift the down-trod Mortimer As high in the air as this unthankful king . . . 1 *Hen. IV.* i 3 136
Those musicians that shall play to you Hang in the air a thousand leagues from hence . . . iii 1 227
What is in that word honour? what is that honour? air. . . . v 1 137
Who lined himself with hope, Eating the air on promise of supply 2 *Hen. IV.* i 3 28
Stand from him, give him air; he'll straight be well . . . iv 4 116

Air. Marry, good air. Spread, Davy; spread . . . 2 *Hen. IV.* v 3 9
The very casques That did affright the air at Agincourt . . *Hen. V.* Prol. 14
When he speaks, The air, a charter'd libertine, is still . . . i 1 48
Now sits Expectation in the air, And hides a sword . . . ii Prol. 8
On mountain standing, Up in the air, crown'd with the golden sun . ii 4 58
This your air of France Hath blown that vice in me . . . iii 6 160
He trots the air; the earth sings when he touches it . . . iii 7 16
It is a beast for Perseus: he is pure air and fire . . . iii 7 22
Les eaux et la terre.—Rien puis? l'air et le feu . . . iv 2 5
Our air shakes them passing scornfully . . . iv 2 42
To keep them here, They would but stink, and putrefy the air 1 *Hen. VI.* iv 7 90
The milk-white rose, With whose sweet smell the air shall be perfumed 2 *Hen. VI.* i 1 255
He shall not breathe infection in this air But three days longer . . iii 2 287
Sickness took him, That makes him gasp and stare and catch the air . iii 2 371
I breathe my soul into the air, As mild and gentle as the cradle-babe . iii 2 391
From their misty jaws Breathe foul contagious darkness in the air . iv 1 7
And if mine arm be heaved in the air, Thy grave is digg'd already iv 10 54
The angry trumpet sounds alarum And dead men's cries do fill the empty air . . . v 2 4
For what doth cherish weeds but gentle air? . . 3 *Hen. VI.* ii 6 21
The air hath got into my deadly wounds, And much effuse of blood doth make me faint . . . ii 6 27
Look, as I blow this feather from my face, And as the air blows it to me iii 1 85
Not knowing how to find the open air, But toiling desperately to find it out . . . iii 2 177
Well are you welcome to the open air . . . *Richard III.* i 1 124
Curses never pass The lips of those that breathe them in the air . i 3 286
Would not let it forth To seek the empty, vast and wandering air . i 4 39
Who builds his hopes in air of your good looks, Lives like a drunken sailor on a mast . . . iii 4 100
If yet your gentle souls fly in the air And be not fix'd in doom perpetual iv 4 11
In to our tent; the air is raw and cold . . . v 3 46
Leave it with a root, thus hack'd, The air will drink the sap *Hen. VIII.* i 2 98
There's fresher air, my lord, In the next chamber.—Lead in your ladies i 4 101
A bond of air, strong as the axletree On which heaven rides *Tr. and Cr.* i 3 66
Will he not upon our fair request Untent his person and share the air with us? . . . ii 3 178
Build there, carpenter; the air is sweet . . . iii 2 54
As false As air, as water, wind, or sandy earth, As fox to lamb . . iii 2 199
Like a dew-drop from the lion's mane, Be shook to air . . . iii 3 225
That the appalled air May pierce the head of the great combatant . iv 5 4
When thou hast hung thy advanced sword i' the air, Not letting it decline iv 5 188
Filling the air with swords advanced and darts . . *Coriolanus* i 6 61
I prize As the dead carcasses of unburied men That do corrupt my air . iii 3 123
You are they That made the air unwholesome . . . iv 6 130
To tear with thunder the wide cheeks o' the air . . . v 3 151
He returns, Splitting the air with noise . . . v 6 52
And buzz lamenting doings in the air! Poor harmless fly! *T. Andron.* iii 2 62
I see thou wilt not trust the air With secrets . . . iv 2 169
Ere he can spread his sweet leaves to the air, Or dedicate his beauty to the sun . . . *Rom. and Jul.* i 1 158
As thin of substance as the air And more inconstant than the wind . i 4 99
Bestrides the lazy-pacing clouds And sails upon the bosom of the air . ii 2 32
A lover may bestride the gossamer That idles in the wanton summer air ii 6 19
Then sweeten with thy breath This neighbour air . . . ii 6 27
When the sun sets, the air doth drizzle dew . . . iii 5 127
To whose foul mouth no healthsome air breathes in . . . iv 3 34
Make sacred even his stirrup, and through him Drink the free air *T. of A.* i 1 83
His poor self, A dedicated beggar to the air . . . iv 2 13
We must all part Into this sea of air . . . iv 2 22
Rotten humidity; below thy sister's orb Infect the air! . . . iv 3 3
When Jove Will o'er some high-viced city hang his poison In the sick air iv 3 110
Think'st That the bleak air, thy boisterous chamberlain, Will put thy shirt on warm? . . . iv 3 222
Promising is the very air o' the time: it opens the eyes of expectation . v 1 25
Fearful scouring Doth choke the air with dust . . . v 2 16
I durst not laugh, for fear of opening my lips and receiving the bad air *J. C.* i 2 252
Exhalations whizzing in the air Give so much light that I may read by them . . . ii 1 44
And tempt the rheumy and unpurged air To add unto his sickness . ii 1 266
Noise of battle hurtled in the air, Horses did neigh, and dying men did groan . . . ii 2 22
Fair is foul, and foul is fair: Hover through the fog and filthy air *Macbeth* i 1 12
Whither are they vanish'd?—Into the air; and what seem'd corporal melted As breath into the wind . . . i 3 81
They made themselves air, into which they vanished . . . i 5 5
The air Nimbly and sweetly recommends itself Unto our gentle senses . i 6 1
Where they most breed and haunt, I have observed, The air is delicate . i 6 10
Heaven's cherubim, horsed Upon the sightless couriers of the air . . i 7 23
Lamentings heard i' the air; strange screams of death . . . ii 3 61
Founded as the rock, As broad and general as the casing air . . iii 4 23
I am for the air; this night I'll spend Unto a dismal and a fatal end . iii 5 20
I'll charm the air to give a sound, While you perform your antic round iv 1 129
Infected be the air whereon they ride! . . . iv 1 138
Where sighs and groans and shrieks that rend the air Are made, not mark'd . . . iv 3 168
I have words That would be howl'd out in the desert air . . . iv 3 194
As easy mayst thou the intrenchant air With thy keen sword impress . v 8 9
It is, as the air, invulnerable, And our vain blows malicious mockery *Ham.* i 1 145
In earth or air, The extravagant and erring spirit hies To his confine . i 1 153
The air bites shrewdly; it is very cold.—It is a nipping and an eager air i 4 2
Bring with thee airs from heaven or blasts from hell . . . i 4 41
But, soft! methinks I scent the morning air; Brief let me be . . i 5 58
Will you walk out of the air, my lord?—Into my grave.—Indeed, that is out o' the air . . . ii 2 209
This most excellent canopy, the air, look you, this brave o'erhanging firmament, this majestical roof fretted with golden fire . . . ii 2 311
His sword, Which was declining on the milky head Of reverend Priam, seem'd i' the air to stick . . . ii 2 501
Do not saw the air too much with your hand, thus, but use all gently . iii 2 5
I eat the air, promise-crammed: you cannot feed capons so . . iii 2 99
You do bend your eye on vacancy And with the incorporal air do hold discourse . . . iii 4 118
His poison'd shot may miss our name, And hit the woundless air . . iv 1 44
Strike her young bones, You taking airs, with lameness! . . . *Lear* ii 4 166
I abjure all roofs, and choose To wage against the enmity o' the air . ii 4 212
All the plagues that in the pendulous air Hang fated o'er men's faults . iii 4 69
Here is better than the open air; take it thankfully . . . iii 6 1
Welcome, then, Thou unsubstantial air that I embrace! . . . iv 1 7

Air. This kiss, if it durst speak, Would stretch thy spirits up into the air . . . . *Lear* iv 2 23
Choughs that wing the midway air Show scarce so gross as beetles . iv 6 13
Hadst thou been aught but gossamer, feathers, air, So many fathom down precipitating, Thou'dst shiver'd like an egg . . . . . iv 6 49
Thou know'st, the first time that we smell the air, We wawl and cry . iv 6 183
I'll away: go; vanish into air; away! . . . . . *Othello* iii 1 21
Trifles light as air Are to the jealous confirmations strong As proofs of holy writ . . . . iii 3 322
I have seen the cannon, When it hath blown his ranks into the air . iii 4 135
Look you pale? O, bear him out o' the air . . . . . v 1 104
Antony . . . did sit alone, Whistling to the air . . *Ant. and Cleo.* ii 2 221
Hark!—Music i' the air.—Under the earth.—It signs well, does it not? iv 3 13
I would they'ld fight i' the fire or i' the air; We'ld fight there too . iv 10 3
Blue promontory With trees upon't, that nod unto the world, And mock our eyes with air . . . . iv 14 7
I am fire and air; my other elements I give to baser life . . . v 2 292
As sweet as balm, as soft as air, as gentle,—O Antony! . . . v 2 314
Which he took, As we do air, fast as 't was minister'd . . *Cymbeline* i 1 45
Were you but riding forth to air yourself, Such parting were too petty . i 1 110
You reek as a sacrifice: where air comes out, air comes in . . i 2 3
Follow'd him, till he had melted from The smallness of a gnat to air . i 3 21
A wonderful sweet air, with admirable rich words to it . . . ii 3 19
Then, if you can, Be pale: I beg but leave to air this jewel . . ii 4 96
Never wing'd from view o' the nest, nor know not What air's from home iii 3 29
The air on't Revengingly enfeebles me . . . . . . v 2 3
And be embraced by a piece of tender air . . . . v 4 140; v 5 437
The piece of tender air, thy virtuous daughter, Which we call 'mollis aer' v 5 446
Unknown to you, unsought, were clipp'd about With this most tender air v 5 452
The sore eyes see clear To stop the air would hurt them . . *Pericles* i 1 100
That I should open to the listening air How many worthy princes' bloods were shed . . . . i 2 87
Our tongues and sorrows do sound deep Our woes into the air . . i 4 14
These mouths, who but of late, earth, sea, and air, Were all too little . i 4 34
Thou hast as chiding a nativity As fire, air, water, earth, and heaven can make . . . . iii 1 33
Music there!—I pray you, give her air. Gentlemen, This queen will live iii 2 91
The air is quick there, And it pierces and sharpens the stomach . . iv 1 28
Though they did change me to the meanest bird That flies i' the purer air . . . . iv 6 109

Air-braving. Even with the earth Shall lay your stately and air-braving towers . . . . *1 Hen. VI.* iv 2 13

Air-drawn. This is the air-drawn dagger which, you said, Led you to Duncan . . . . *Macbeth* iii 4 62

Aired. Though I have for the most part been aired abroad . *W. Tale* iv 2 6
Died where they were made, or shortly after This world had air'd them *Hen. VIII.* ii 4 193

Airless. Nor airless dungeon, nor strong links of iron, Can be retentive to the strength of spirit . . . . *J. Cæsar* i 3 94

Airy. To work mine end upon their senses that This airy charm is for *Temp.* v 1 54
Elves, list your names; silence, you airy toys . . *Mer. Wives* v 5 46
I will purge thy mortal grossness so That thou shalt like an airy spirit go *M. N. Dream* iii 1 164
Gives to airy nothing A local habitation and a name . . . v 1 16
Some airy devil hovers in the sky And pours down mischief . *K. John* iii 2 2
Hover about me with your airy wings And hear your mother's lamentation! . . . . *Richard III.* iv 4 13
Airy succeeders of intestate joys, Poor breathing orators of miseries! . iv 4 128
Having his ear full of his airy fame, Grows dainty of his worth *Troi. and Cres.* i 3 144
Three civil brawls, bred of an airy word . . . *Rom. and Jul.* i 1 96
Her eyes in heaven Would through the airy region stream so bright . ii 2 21
Else would I tear the cave where Echo lies, And make her airy tongue more hoarse than mine . . . . ii 2 163
Of so airy and light a quality that it is but a shadow's shadow *Hamlet* ii 2 267

Ajax. By the Lord, this love is as mad as Ajax . . . *L. L. Lost* iv 3 7
Your lion, that holds his poll-axe sitting on a close-stool, will be given to Ajax . . . . v 2 581
Æacides Was Ajax, call'd so from his grandfather . . *T. of Shrew* iii 1 53
Like Ajax Telamonius, On sheep or oxen could I spend my fury *2 Hen. VI.* v 1 26
A lord of Trojan blood, nephew to Hector; They call him Ajax *Troi. and Cres.* i 2 14
Ajax is grown self-will'd, and bears his head In such a rein . . . i 3 188
By device, let blockish Ajax draw The sort to fight with Hector . . i 3 375
If the dull brainless Ajax come safe off, We'll dress him up in voices . i 3 381
Ajax employ'd plucks down Achilles' plumes . . . . . . i 3 386
For, whosoever you take him to be, he is Ajax . . . . . ii 1 70
Ajax, who wears his wit in his belly and his guts in his head . . ii 1 79
No man is beaten voluntary: Ajax was here the voluntary . . . ii 1 105
To, Achilles! to, Ajax! to!—I shall cut out your tongue . . . ii 1 120
Shall the elephant Ajax carry it thus? he beats me, and I rail at him . ii 3 2
What moves Ajax thus to bay at him? . . . . ii 3 98
Then will Ajax lack matter, if he have lost his argument . . . ii 3 103
Noble Ajax; you are as strong, as valiant, as wise, no less noble . . ii 3 158
Your mind is the clearer, Ajax, and your virtues the fairer . . . ii 3 163
Let Ajax go to him. Dear lord, go you and greet him in his tent . . ii 3 188
We'll consecrate the steps that Ajax makes When they go from Achilles ii 3 193
What a vice were it in Ajax now,—If he were proud,—Or covetous of praise,—Ay, or surly borne,—Or strange, or self-affected! . . . ii 3 246
And, for thy vigour, Bull-bearing Milo his addition yield To sinewy Ajax ii 3 259
Were your days As green as Ajax' and your brain so temper'd, You should not have the eminence of him, But be as Ajax . . . . . ii 3 265
Come knights from east to west, And cull their flower, Ajax shall cope the best . . . . ii 3 275
Hector will to-morrow Be answer'd in his challenge: Ajax is ready . iii 3 35
Good morrow, Ajax.—Ha?—Good morrow.—Ay, and good next day too iii 3 66
And apprehended here immediately The unknown Ajax . . . . iii 3 125
An act that very chance did throw upon him—Ajax renown'd . . iii 3 132
Already They clap the lubber Ajax on the shoulder . . . . iii 3 139
Marvel not, thou great and complete man, That all the Greeks begin to worship Ajax . . . . iii 3 182
Hector's sister did Achilles win, But our great Ajax bravely beat down him . . . . iii 3 213
Shall Ajax fight with Hector?—Ay, and perhaps receive much honour . iii 3 225
I'll send the fool to Ajax and desire him To invite the Trojan lords . iii 3 235
Ajax goes up and down the field, asking for himself . . . . iii 3 244
He knows not me: I said 'Good morrow, Ajax;' and he replies 'Thanks, Agamemnon' . . . . iii 3 261
Let Patroclus make demands to me, you shall see the pageant of Ajax . iii 3 273
Ajax. I humbly desire the valiant Ajax to invite the most valorous Hector *Troi. and Cres.* iii 3 275
Jove bless great Ajax!—Hum! . . . . iii 3 281
Give with thy trumpet a loud note to Troy, Thou dreadful Ajax . . iv 5 4
This Ajax is half made of Hector's blood . . . . . . iv 5 83
Stand by our Ajax: as you and Lord Æneas Consent upon the order of their fight, So be it . . . . iv 5 89
Now, Ajax, hold thine own!—Hector, thou sleep'st; Awake thee! . iv 5 114
Let me embrace thee, Ajax: By him that thunders, thou hast lusty arms iv 5 135
I bid good night. Ajax commands the guard to tend on you . . . v 1 79
That mongrel cur, Ajax, against that dog of as bad a kind, Achilles . v 4 14
And now is the cur Ajax prouder than the cur Achilles . . . v 4 16
Bid the snail-paced Ajax arm for shame . . . . v 5 18
Ajax hath lost a friend And foams at mouth . . . . . . v 5 35
Ajax hath ta'en Æneas: shall it be? No, by the flame of yonder glorious heaven, He shall not carry him . . . . v 6 22
The Greeks upon advice did bury Ajax That slew himself . *T. Andron.* i 1 379
None of these rogues and cowards But Ajax is their fool . . *Lear* ii 2 132
The seven-fold shield of Ajax cannot keep The battery from my heart. O, cleave, my sides! . . . . *Ant. and Cleo.* iv 14 38
Thersites' body is as good as Ajax', When neither are alive . *Cymbeline* iv 2 252

Alabaster. Sit like his grandsire cut in alabaster . *Mer. of Venice* i 1 84
Girdling one another Within their innocent alabaster arms *Richard III.* iv 3 11
Yet I'll not shed her blood; Nor scar that whiter skin of hers than snow, And smooth as monumental alabaster . . . . *Othello* v 2 5

Alack, for pity! I, not remembering how I cried out then, Will cry it o'er . . . . *Tempest* i 2 132
Alack, what trouble Was I then to you! . . . . i 2 151
Alack, where are you? speak, an if you hear . . *M. N. Dream* ii 2 153
O night, which ever art when day is not! O night, O night! alack, alack! . . . . v 1 172
Alack, why am I sent for to a king? . . . . . *Richard II.* iv 1 162
Alack the heavy day, That I have worn so many winters out! . . iv 1 257
What, myself upon myself? Alack, I love myself. Wherefore? *Richard III.* v 3 187
Alack, that heaven should practise stratagems! . . *Rom. and Jul.* iii 5 211
Alack, our terrene moon Is now eclipsed! . . . *Ant. and Cleo.* iii 13 153

Alacrity. I have a kind of alacrity in sinking . . . *Mer. Wives* iii 5 13
I have not that alacrity of spirit, Nor cheer of mind . *Richard III.* v 3 73
Make ready straight.—Yea, with a bridegroom's fresh alacrity *Tr. and Cr.* iv 4 147
I do agnize A natural and prompt alacrity I find in hardness . . *Othello* i 3 233

A-land. I marvel how the fishes live in the sea.—Why, as men do a-land *Pericles* ii 1 31
Here I give to understand, If e'er this coffin drive a-land . . . iii 2 69

Alarbus goes to rest; and we survive . . . . . *T. Andron.* i 1 133
Alarbus' limbs are lopp'd, And entrails feed the sacrificing fire . . i 1 143

Alarm. Be ready to direct these home alarms . . . *Richard II.* i 1 205
Now play him me, Patroclus, Arming to answer in a night alarm *Tr. and Cr.* i 3 171
Their dear causes Would to the bleeding and the grim alarm Excite the mortified man . . . . *Macbeth* v 2 4
About her lank and all o'er-teemed loins, A blanket, in the alarm of fear caught up . . . . *Hamlet* ii 2 532
As the sleeping soldiers in the alarm, Your bedded hair, like life in excrements, Start up . . . . iii 4 120

Alarum. But, hark! what new alarum is this same? . . . *Hen. V.* iv 6 35
It pass your patience and mine to endure her loud alarums . *T. of Shrew* i 1 131
Sound, sound alarum! we will rush on them . . . *1 Hen. VI.* i 2 18
What tumult's in the heavens? Whence cometh this alarum and the noise? . . . . i 4 99
To wake and leave our beds, Hearing alarums at our chamber-doors . ii 1 42
Sharp dissension in my breast, Such fierce alarums both of hope and fear v 5 85
Sound, trumpets, alarum to the combatants! . . . *2 Hen. VI.* ii 3 95
When the angry trumpet sounds alarum . . . . v 2 3
Our stern alarums changed to merry meetings . . . *Richard III.* i 1 7
A flourish, trumpets! strike alarum, drums! . . . . . iv 4 148
I had rather have one scratch my head i' the sun When the alarum were struck than idly sit To hear my nothings monster'd . *Coriolanus* ii 2 80
And when she speaks, is it not an alarum to love? . . *Othello* ii 3 27

Alarum-bell. Awake, awake! Ring the alarum-bell . . *Macbeth* ii 3 79
Ring the alarum-bell! Blow, wind! come, wrack! . . . . v 5 51

Alarumed. Wither'd murder, Alarum'd by his sentinel, the wolf . ii 1 53
When he saw my best alarum'd spirits, Bold in the quarrel's right *Lear* ii 1 55

Alas. The dukedom yet unbow'd—alas, poor Milan! . . *Tempest* i 2 115
I come, I come. Alas! this parting strikes poor lovers dumb *T. G. of Ver.* ii 2 21
Why dost thou cry 'alas'?—I cannot choose but pity her . . iv 4 82
Out, alas! here comes my master.—We shall all be shent . *Mer. Wives* i 4 37
Alas! the sweet woman leads an ill life with him: he's a very jealous man . . . . ii 2 92
May be he will relent. Alas, He hath but as offended in a dream! *Meas. for Meas.* ii 2 3

Alas the day! good heart, that was not her fault . *Mer. Wives* iii 5 39
How might we disguise him!—Alas the day, I know not . . . iv 2 71
Alas the day! what shall I do with my doublet and hose? *As Y. Like It* iii 2 231
Alas the day, how loath you are to offend daylight . . *Troi. and Cres.* iii 2 50
Alas the day! *2 Hen. IV.* ii 1; *Rom. and Jul.* iii 2; *Macbeth* ii 4; *Othello* iv 2
Alas the day! I never gave him cause . . . . . *Othello* iii 4 158

Alas the heavy day! Why do you weep? . . . . . . iv 2 42

Alas the while! . . . . *Mer. of Venice* ii 1 31

Alban. To say the truth, stolen from my host at Saint Alban's *1 Hen. IV.* iv 2 50
As common as the way between Saint Alban's and London *2 Hen. IV.* ii 2 185
His highness' pleasure You do prepare to ride unto Saint Alban's *2 Hen. VI.* i 2 57
When from Saint Alban's we do make return, We'll see these things . i 2 83
The king is now in progress towards Saint Alban's . . . . i 4 76
A blind man at Saint Alban's shrine, Within this half-hour, hath received his sight . . . . ii 1 63
Call'd A hundred times and oftener, in my sleep, By good Saint Alban . ii 1 91
Thou see'st not well.—Yes, master, clear as day, I thank God and Saint Alban . . . . ii 1 108
My lords, Saint Alban here hath done a miracle . . . . . ii 1 131
My masters of Saint Alban's, have you not beadles in your town? . . ii 1 135
Underneath an alehouse' paltry sign, The Castle in Saint Alban's . . v 2 68
Saint Alban's battle won by famous York Shall be eternized in all age . v 3 30
March'd toward Saint Alban's to intercept the queen . . *3 Hen. VI.* ii 1 114
Short tale to make, we at Saint Alban's met, Our battles join'd . . ii 1 120
When you and I met at Saint Alban's last, Your legs did better service ii 2 103
At Saint Alban's field This lady's husband, Sir Richard Grey, was slain iii 2 1
Was not your husband In Margaret's battle at Saint Alban's slain? *Richard III.* i 3 130

Albany. I thought the king had more affected the Duke of Albany *Lear* i 1 2
And you, our no less loving son of Albany . . . . . . i 1 43
To thine and Albany's issue Be this perpetual . . . . . . i 1 67

Albany. Cornwall and Albany, With my two daughters' dowers digest this third . . . . *Lear* i 1 129
Have you heard of no likely wars toward, 'twixt the Dukes of Cornwall and Albany? . . . . ii 1 12
Have you nothing said Upon his party 'gainst the Duke of Albany? ii 1 28
There is division, Although as yet the face of it be cover'd With mutual cunning, 'twixt Albany and Cornwall . . . iii 1 21
Of Albany's and Cornwall's powers you heard not?—'Tis so, they are afoot . . . . iv 3 50
Albeit I will confess thy father's wealth Was the first motive *Mer. Wives* iii 4 13
Albeit my wrongs might make one wiser mad . *Com. of Errors* v 1 217
Albeit I'll swear that I do know your tongue . *Mer. of Venice* ii 6 27
Albeit, I confess, your coming before me is nearer to his reverence *As Y. L.* i 1 53
Albeit you have deserved High commendation, true applause and love i 2 274
Albeit the quality of the time and quarrel Might well have given us bloody argument . . . . . . *T. Night* iii 3 31
Albeit we swear A voluntary zeal and an unurged faith . *K. John* v 2 9
I will ease my heart, Albeit I make a hazard of my head 1 *Hen. IV.* i 3 128
We venture thee, Albeit considerations infinite Do make against it . v 1 102
Albeit I could tell to thee, as to one it pleases me, for fault of a better, to call my friend . . . . . 2 *Hen. IV.* ii 2 43
Albeit against my conscience and my soul . . *Richard III.* iii 7 226
Stop my mouth.—And shall, albeit sweet music issues thence *Tr. and Cr.* iii 2 142
Albeit unused to the melting mood . . . . *Othello* v 2 349
A worthy fellow, Albeit he comes on angry purpose now . *Cymbeline* ii 3 61
Albion. A dirty farm In that nook-shotten isle of Albion . *Hen. V.* iii 5 14
And this the royalty of Albion's king? . . . . 2 *Hen. VI.* i 3 48
For losing ken of Albion's wished coast . . . . iii 2 113
Great Albion's queen in former golden days . . . 3 *Hen. VI.* iii 3 7
Worthy Edward, King of Albion, My lord and sovereign . . iii 3 49
Then shall the realm of Albion Come to great confusion . . . *Lear* iii 2 91
Alchemist. This day the glorious sun Stays in his course and plays the alchemist . . . . *K. John* iii 1 78
You are an alchemist; make gold of that . . . *T. of Athens* v 1 117
Alchemy. That which would appear offence in us, His countenance, like richest alchemy, Will change to virtue . . *J. Cæsar* i 3 159
Alcibiades. 'Tis Alcibiades, and some twenty horse . *T. of Athens* i 1 250
Alcibiades, your heart's in the field now.—My heart is ever at your service . . . . i 2 74
Alcibiades, Thou art a soldier, therefore seldom rich . . . . i 2 227
So soon as dinner's done, we'll forth again, My Alcibiades . . ii 2 15
Alcibiades is banished: hear you of it?—Alcibiades banished! . . iii 6 60
So soon we shall drive back Of Alcibiades the approaches wild . v 1 167
If Alcibiades kill my countrymen, Let Alcibiades know this of Timon, That Timon cares not . . . . v 1 172
Go, live still; Be Alcibiades your plague, you his, And last so long enough! . . . . v 1 192
I'll teach them to prevent wild Alcibiades' wrath . . . . v 1 206
This man was riding From Alcibiades to Timon's cave . . . v 2 10
Alcides. So is Alcides beaten by his page . . *Mer. of Venice* ii 1 35
With no less presence, but with much more love, Than young Alcides . iii 2 55
Leave that labour to great Hercules: and let it be more than Alcides' twelve . . . . *T. of Shrew* i 2 258
That lion's robe, . . . It lies as sightly on the back of him As great Alcides' shows upon an ass . . . . . *K. John* ii 1 144
Where's the great Alcides of the field? . . . 1 *Hen. VI.* iv 7 60
Nor great Alcides, nor the god of war, Shall seize this prey *T. Andron.* iv 2 95
Teach me, Alcides, thou mine ancestor, thy rage . *Ant. and Cleo.* iv 12 44
Alder-liefest. With you, mine alder-liefest sovereign . 2 *Hen. VI.* i 1 28
Alderman. I could have crept into any alderman's thumb-ring 1 *Hen. IV.* ii 4 364
No bigger than an agate-stone On the fore-finger of an alderman *R. and J.* i 4 56
Ale. Thou hast not so much charity in thee as to go to the ale with a Christian . . . . *T. G. of Ver.* ii 5 61
She brews good ale.—And thereof comes the proverb: 'Blessing of your heart, you brew good ale' . . . . iii 1 304
Against her lips I bob And on her withered dewlap pour the ale *M. N. Dr.* ii 1 50
Were he not warmed with ale, This were a bed but cold to sleep so soundly . . . . *T. of Shrew* Ind. 1 32
For God's sake, a pot of small ale . . . . . . Ind. 2 1
If she say I am not fourteen pence on the score for sheer ale, score me up for the lyingest knave . . . . Ind. 2 25
And once again, a pot o' the smallest ale . . . . . Ind. 2 77
Dost thou think, because thou art virtuous, there shall be no more cakes and ale? . . . . *T. Night* ii 3 125
For a quart of ale is a dish for a king . . . . *W. Tale* iv 3 8
I would have him poison'd with a pot of ale . . 1 *Hen. IV.* i 3 233
I would give all my fame for a pot of ale and safety . *Hen. V.* iii 2 13
Did, in his ales and his angers, look you, kill his best friend, Cleitus . iv 7 40
Alexander killed his friend Cleitus, being in his ales and his cups . . iv 7 48
Do you look for ale and cakes here, you rude rascals? . *Hen. VIII.* v 4 11
Alecto. Rouse up revenge from ebon den with fell Alecto's snake 2 *Hen. IV.* v 5 39
Alehouse. I'll to the alehouse with you presently . *T. G. of Ver.* ii 5 9
If thou wilt, go with me to the alehouse . . . . . ii 5 57
Call at all the ale-houses, and bid those that are drunk get them to bed *Much Ado* iii 3 45
Do ye make an alehouse of my lady's house? . . *T. Night* ii 3 96
When triumph is become an alehouse guest . . . *Richard II.* v 1 15
Would I were in an alehouse in London! . . . *Hen. V.* iii 2 12
Erect his statua and worship it, And make my image but an alehouse sign 2 *Hen. VI.* iii 2 81
Underneath an alehouse' paltry sign, The Castle in Saint Alban's . v 2 67
Ye white-limed walls! ye alehouse painted signs! . *T. Andron.* iv 2 98
These are old fond paradoxes to make fools laugh i' the alehouse *Othello* ii 1 140
Alençon. I saw him at the Duke Alençon's once . . *L. L. Lost* ii 1 61
What lady is that same?—The heir of Alençon, Katharine her name . ii 1 195
When Alençon and myself were down together, I plucked this glove from his helm: if any man challenge this, he is a friend to Alençon *Hen. V.* iv 7 161
Apprehend him: he's a friend of the Duke Alençon's . . . . iv 8 19
The glove which your majesty is take out of the helmet of Alençon . iv 8 28
This is the glove of Alençon, that your majesty is give me . . iv 8 39
Anjou doth take his part; The Duke of Alençon flieth to his side 1 *Hen. VI.* i 1 95
Duke of Alençon, this was your default . . . . . ii 1 60
I speak not to that railing Hecate, But unto thee, Alençon, and the rest iii 2 65
From thence to England; where I hope ere long To be presented, by your victories, With Charles, Alençon, and that traitorous rout . iv 1 173
Quicken'd with youthful spleen and warlike rage, Beat down Alençon . iv 6 14
It was Alençon that enjoy'd my love.—Alençon, that notorious Machiavel! v 4 73
Alençon, Seven earls, twelve barons and twenty reverend bishops 2 *Hen. VI.* i 1 7
Alençon. It shall be to the Duchess of Alençon, The French king's sister *Hen. VIII.* iii 2 85
Aleppo. Her husband's to Aleppo gone, master o' the Tiger . *Macbeth* i 3 7
In Aleppo once, Where a malignant and a turban'd Turk Beat a Venetian and traduced the state . . . . *Othello* v 2 352
Ale-washed. Among foaming bottles and ale-washed wits . *Hen. V.* iii 6 82
Ale-wife. Marian Hacket, the fat ale-wife of Wincot . *T. of Shrew,* Ind. 2 23
Methought he had made two holes in the ale-wife's new petticoat 2 *Hen. IV.* ii 2 89
Alexander. He presents Hector of Troy; . . . the parish curate, Alexander . . . . *L. L. Lost* v 2 539
The conqueror is dismay'd. Proceed, good Alexander . . . v 2 570
The crown will find an heir: great Alexander Left his to the worthiest *W. Tale* v 1 47
Like so many Alexanders, Have in these parts from morn till even fought *Hen. V.* iii 1 19
What call you the town's name where Alexander the Pig was born? . iv 7 14
I think Alexander the Great was born in Macedon . . . . iv 7 20
If you mark Alexander's life well, Harry of Monmouth's life is come after it indifferent well . . . . iv 7 33
As Alexander killed his friend Cleitus, being in his ales and his cups . iv 7 47
He sits in his state, as a thing made for Alexander . . *Coriolanus* v 4 23
Dost thou think Alexander looked o' this fashion i' the earth? *Hamlet* v 1 218
Why may not imagination trace the noble dust of Alexander, till he find it stopping a bung-hole? . . . . v 1 225
Alexander died, Alexander was buried, Alexander returneth into dust v 1 231
Great Media, Parthia, and Armenia, He gave to Alexander *Ant. and Cleo.* iii 6 15
Alexander Iden, an esquire of Kent . . . 2 *Hen. VI.* iv 10 46
Alexander Iden, that's my name; A poor esquire of Kent . . . v 1 74
Alexandria. From Alexandria This is the news: he fishes, drinks, and wastes The lamps of night in revel . . . *Ant. and Cleo.* i 4 3
I wrote to you When rioting in Alexandria; you Did pocket up my letters ii 2 72
Contemning Rome, he has done all this, and more, In Alexandria . . iii 6 2
Cæsar sits down in Alexandria; where I will oppose his fate . iii 13 168
Through Alexandria make a jolly march; Bear our hack'd targets like the men that owe them . . . . iv 8 30
Alexandrian. This is not yet an Alexandrian feast . . . ii 7 102
The quick comedians Extemporally will stage us, and present our Alexandrian revels . . . . v 2 218
Alexas, most any thing Alexas, almost most absolute Alexas . . . i 2 1
Alexas,—come, his fortune, his fortune! O, let him marry a woman that cannot go! . . . . i 2 65
Go to the fellow, good Alexas; bid him Report the feature of Octavia . ii 5 111
Alexas did revolt; and went to Jewry on Affairs of Antony . . iv 6 12
Alias. The black prince, sir; alias, the prince of darkness; alias, the devil *All's Well* iv 5 44
A brace of unmeriting, proud, violent, testy magistrates, alias fools *Coriol.* ii 1 48
Al'ce. What must I call her?—Madam.—Al'ce madam, or Joan madam? *T. of Shrew,* Ind. 2 112
Alice, tu as été en Angleterre, et tu parles bien le langage . *Hen. V.* iii 4 1
Excusez-moi, Alice; écoutez: de hand, de fingres, de nails, de arma . iii 4 30
Alice Ford. What? thou liest! Sir Alice Ford! . . *Mer. Wives* ii 1 51
Alice Shortcake. Why, did you not lend it to Alice Shortcake? . . i 1 211
Alien. It is enacted in the laws of Venice, If it be proved against an alien *Mer. of Venice* iv 1 349
Almost an alien to the hearts Of all the court . . 1 *Hen. IV.* iii 2 34
Aliena. What will you be call'd?—No longer Celia, but Aliena *As Y. L.* i 3 130
Doublet and hose ought to show itself courageous to petticoat: therefore courage, good Aliena! . . . . ii 4 8
I'll tell thee, Aliena, I cannot be out of the sight of Orlando . . iv 1 221
Say with me, I love Aliena; say with her that she loves me . . v 2 9
Go you and prepare Aliena; for look you, here comes my Rosalind . v 2 18
If you do love Rosalind so near the heart as your gesture cries it out, when your brother marries Aliena, shall you marry her . . . v 2 70
Alight. Bid her alight, And her troth plight . . . *Lear* iii 4 127
Alighted. There is alighted at your gate A young Venetian *Mer. of Ven.* ii 9 86
How near is our master?—E'en at hand, alighted by this *T. of Shrew* iv 1 120
There are certain nobles of the senate Newly alighted . *T. of Athens* i 2 181
Alike. If our virtues Did not go forth of us, 'twere all alike As if we had them not . . . . *Meas. for Meas.* i 1 35
Male twins, both alike . . . . *Com. of Errors* i 1 56
Fortune had left to both of us alike What to delight in, what to sorrow for . . . . i 1 106
All men are not alike; alas, good neighbour! . . . *Much Ado* iii 5 43
For none offend where all alike do dote . . . *L. L. Lost* iv 3 126
If I Had servants true about me, that bare eyes To see alike mine honour as their profits . . . . *W. Tale* i 2 310
The selfsame sun that shines upon his court Hides not his visage from our cottage but Looks on alike . . . . iv 4 457
The odds for high and low's alike . . . . v 1 207
Both are alike; and both alike we like. One must prove greatest *K. John* ii 1 331
The situations, look you, is both alike . . . . *Hen. V.* iv 7 27
'Tis all one, 'tis alike as my fingers is to my fingers . . . iv 7 31
At all times will you have my power alike? . . 1 *Hen. VI.* i 1 38
'Good Gloucester' and 'good devil' were alike . . 3 *Hen. VI.* v 6 4
You that are blamed for it alike with us, Know you of this? *Hen. VIII.* i 2 39
You know no more than others; but you frame Things that are known alike . . . . i 2 45
His curses and his blessings Touch me alike, they're breath I not believe in . . . . ii 2 54
Each in my love alike and none less dear . . . . *Coriolanus* i 3 25
Let's fetch him off, or make remain alike . . . . . . i 4 63
I do hate thee Worse than a promise-breaker.—We hate alike . . i 8 2
When the sea was calm all boats alike Show'd mastership in floating . iv 1 6
Your fortunes are alike in all, That in your country's service drew your swords . . . . *T. Andron.* i 1 174
Yet every mother breeds not sons alike . . . . . . ii 3 146
Two households, both alike in dignity, In fair Verona *Rom. and Jul.* Prol. 1
Montague is bound as well as I, In penalty alike . . . . i 2 2
Is beloved and loves again, Alike bewitched by the charm of looks ii Prol. 6
Your diet shall be in all places alike . . . *T. of Athens* iii 6 75
We are fellows still, Serving alike in sorrow . . . . iv 2 19
At all times alike Men are not still the same . . . . v 1 124
Whereby he does receive Particular addition, from the bill That writes them all alike . . . . *Macbeth* iii 1 101
Our dungy earth alike Feeds beast as man . . *Ant. and Cleo.* i 1 35
Your fortunes are alike.—But how, but how? give me particulars . i 2 56
And make the wars alike against my stomach, Having alike your cause ii 2 50
Things outward Do draw the inward quality after them, To suffer all alike . . . . iii 13 34

Alike. A lady that disdains Thee and the devil alike . . . *Cymbeline* i 6 148
Lovers And men in dangerous bonds pray not alike . . . iii 2 37
Above him in birth, alike conversant in general services . . . iv 1 13
But clay and clay differs in dignity, Whose dust is both alike . . . iv 2 5
Creatures may be alike: were't he, I am sure He would have spoke to us v 5 125
Alisander. My scutcheon plain declares that I am Alisander *L. L. Lost* v 2 567
Most true, 'tis right; you were so, Alisander . . . v 2 572
Take away the conqueror, take away Alisander . . . v 2 576
O, sir, you have overthrown Alisander the conqueror! . . . v 2 578
Afeard to speak! run away for shame, Alisander . . . v 2 583
But, for Alisander,—alas, you see how 'tis, a little o'erparted . . . v 2 587
Alit. Quod me alit, me extinguit . . . *Pericles* ii 2 33
Alive. I not doubt He came alive to land.—No, no, he's gone. *Tempest* ii 1 122
Only Professes to persuade,—the king his son's alive . . . ii 1 236
A man or a fish? dead or alive? A fish: he smells like a fish . . . ii 2 26
I will forget that Julia is alive . . . *T. G. of Ver.* ii 6 27
By her fair influence Foster'd, illumined, cherish'd, kept alive . . . iii 1 184
I dare not say I have one friend alive . . . v 4 66
There is scarce truth enough alive to make societies secure *M. for Meas.* iii 2 240
The danger that might come If he were known alive . . . iv 3 90
One in the prison, That should by private order else have died, I have reserved alive . . . v 1 472
If I know more of any man alive . . . *Much Ado* iv 1 180
I pray you, tell me, is my boy, God rest his soul, alive or dead? *Mer. of Ven.* ii 2 75
There be fools alive, I wis, Silver'd o'er . . . ii 9 68
Of all the men alive I never yet beheld that special face *T. of Shrew* ii 1 10
There's place and means for every man alive . . . *All's Well* iv 3 375
You are the cruell'st she alive . . . *T. Night* i 5 259
Tell me what blessings I have here alive, That I should fear to die? *W. Tale* iii 2 108
O that he were alive, and here beholding His daughter's trial! . . . iii 2 121
I had not left a purse alive in the whole army . . . iv 4 631
He has a son, who shall be flayed alive . . . iv 4 812
Remember 'stoned,' and 'flayed alive' . . . iv 4 835
Young Arthur is alive . . . *K. John* iv 2 251
And when I mount, alive may I not light, If I be traitor! *Richard II.* i 1 82
Methinks in you I see old Gaunt alive . . . ii 3 118
That man is not alive Might so have tempted him . . . 1 *Hen. IV.* iii 1 173
Is now alive To grace this latter age with noble deeds . . . v 1 91
There's not three of my hundred and fifty left alive . . . v 3 38
If Percy be alive, thou get'st not my sword; but take my pistol . . . v 3 52
If Percy be alive, I'll pierce him. If he do come in my way . . . v 3 59
This earth that bears thee dead Bears not alive so stout a gentleman . . . v 4 93
Art thou alive? Or is it fantasy that plays upon our eyesight? . . . v 4 137
If the man were alive and would deny it . . . v 4 156
A noble earl and many a creature else Had been alive this hour . . . v 5 8
He doth sin that doth belie the dead, Not he which says the dead is not alive . . . 2 *Hen. IV.* i 1 99
If it be a sin to covet honour, I am the most offending soul alive *Hen. V.* iv 3 29
'Tis certain there's not a boy left alive . . . iv 7 5
'Tis the gage of one that I should fight withal, if he be alive . . . iv 7 128
Heaven, be thou gracious to none alive, If Salisbury wants mercy at thy hands! . . . 1 *Hen. VI.* i 4 85
You would not have him die.—Ah, York, no man alive so fain as I! 2 *Hen. VI.* iii 1 244
And all to have the noble duke alive . . . iii 2 64
Alive again? then show me where he is . . . iii 3 12
The bricks are alive at this day to testify it; therefore deny it not . . . iv 2 157
Were the Duke of Suffolk now alive, These Kentish rebels would be soon appeased! . . . iv 4 41
They loved well when they were alive . . . iv 7 140
May that ground gape and swallow me alive, Where I shall kneel to him that slew my father! . . . 3 *Hen. VI.* i 1 161
Till I root out their accursed line And leave not one alive, I live in hell . . . i 3 33
I did not kill your husband.—Why, then he is alive . . . *Richard III.* i 2 91
I do not know that Englishman alive With whom my soul is any jot at odds . . . ii 1 69
Call us wretches, orphans, castaways, If that our noble father be alive? . . . ii 2 7
Save that, for reverence to some alive, I give a sparing limit to my tongue . . . iii 7 193
What heir of York is there alive but we? . . . iv 4 472
The greatest monarch now alive may glory In such an honour *Hen. VIII.* v 3 164
If thou wouldst not entomb thyself alive And case thy reputation in thy tent . . . *Troi. and Cres.* iii 3 186
No man alive can love in such a sort The thing he means to kill . . . iv 1 23
Behold the poor remains, alive and dead! . . . *T. Andron.* i 1 81
These are their brethren, whom you Goths beheld Alive and dead . . . i 1 123
We know not where you left him all alive . . . ii 3 257
The villain is alive in Titus' house, And as he is, to witness this is true . . . v 3 123
Here comes the furious Tybalt back again.—Alive, in triumph! *R. and J.* iii 1 127
Thy Juliet is alive, For whose dear sake thou wast but lately dead . . . iii 3 135
Is't possible the world should so much differ, And we alive? *T. of Athens* iii 1 50
Thou art the cap of all the fools alive . . . iv 3 363
Away, thou issue of a mangy dog! Choler does kill me that thou art alive . . . iv 3 372
Here lie I, Timon; who, alive, all living men did hate . . . v 4 72
Will you dine with me to-morrow?—Ay, if I be alive and your mind hold . . . *J. Cæsar* i 2 295
Well, to our work alive. What do you think Of marching to Philippi? iv 3 196
I dare assure thee that no enemy Shall ever take alive the noble Brutus v 4 22
When you do find him, or alive or dead, He will be found like Brutus v 4 24
Or be alive again, And dare me to the desert with thy sword *Macbeth* iii 4 103
'Twould have anger'd any heart alive To hear the men deny't . . . iii 6 15
If thou speak'st false, Upon the next tree shalt thou hang alive . . . v 5 39
As the cockney did to the eels when she put 'em i' the paste alive *Lear* ii 4 124
Had he been where he thought, By this, had thought been past. Alive or dead? . . . iv 6 45
Both? one? or neither? Neither can be enjoy'd, If both remain alive . . . v 1 59
Hardly shall I carry out my side, Her husband being alive . . . v 1 62
Produce their bodies, be they alive or dead . . . v 3 230
Within these three days let me hear thee say That Cassio 's not alive . . . *Othello* iii 3 473
There's millions now alive That nightly lie in those unproper beds . . . iv 1 68
Begin the fight: Our will is Antony be took alive . . . *Ant. and Cleo.* iv 6 2
These boys know little they are sons to the king; Nor Cymbeline dreams that they are alive . . . *Cymbeline* iii 3 81
Thersites' body is as good as Ajax', When neither are alive . . . iv 2 253
The same dead thing alive . . . v 5 123

Alive. For though he strive To killen bad, keep good alive *Pericles* ii Gower 20
She is alive; behold, Her eyelids, cases to those heavenly jewels Which Pericles hath lost . . . iii 2 98
All. We split! Let's all sink with the king . . . *Tempest* i 1 67
But by being so retired, O'er-prized all popular rate . . . i 2 92
All but mariners Plunged in the foaming brine and quit the vessel . . . i 2 210
I'll rack thee with old cramps, Fill all thy bones with aches . . . i 2 370
It is foul weather in us all, good sir, When you are cloudy . . . ii 1 141
We all were sea-swallow'd, though some cast again . . . ii 1 251
All thy vexations Were but my trials of thy love . . . iv 1 5
This must crave, An if this be at all, a most strange story . . . v 1 117
All this service Have I done since I went . . . v 1 225
We were dead of sleep, And—how we know not—all clapp'd under hatches v 1 231
Let no man take care for himself; for all is but fortune . . . v 1 257
So eating love Inhabits in the finest wits of all . . . *T. G. of Ver.* i 1 44
I leave myself, my friends and all, for love . . . i 1 65
Sir, I could perceive nothing at all from her . . . i 1 141
For all you are my man, go wait upon my cousin Shallow *Mer. Wives* i 1 28
Troth, sir, all is in his hands above . . . i 4 154
Say what she will, take all, pay all, go to bed when she list . . . ii 2 123
Talk not to me; my mind is heavy: I will give over all . . . iv 6 2
For all he was in woman's apparel, I would not have had him . . . v 5 204
I'll take it as a peril to my soul, It is no sin at all, but charity *Meas. for Meas.* ii 4 66
They stay for nought at all But for their owner . . . *Com. of Errors* iv 1 91
For the man, as you know all, hath a contemptible spirit *Much Ado* ii 3 187
Would you not swear, All you that see her, that she were a maid? iv 1 40
Else none at all in aught proves excellent . . . *L. L. Lost* iv 3 354
I thank you, gracious lords, For all your fair endeavours . . . v 2 740
Some of your French crowns have no hair at all . . . *M. N. Dream* i 2 100
You speak all your part at once, cues and all . . . iii 1 102
I see you all are bent To set against me for your merriment . . . iii 2 145
Extort A poor soul's patience, all to make you sport . . . iii 2 161
O, is it all forgot? All school-days' friendship, childhood innocence? . . . iii 2 201
The man shall have his mare again, and all shall be well . . . iii 2 463
Whilst the heavy ploughman snores, All with weary task fordone . . . v 1 381
All that glisters is not gold; Often have you heard that told *M. of Ven.* ii 7 65
I would lose all, ay, sacrifice them all Here to this devil, to deliver you iv 1 286
And the offender's life lies in the mercy Of the duke only, 'gainst all other voice . . . iv 1 356
They take No note at all of our being absent hence . . . v 1 120
Either too much at once, or none at all . . . *As Y. Like It* iii 2 212
Yes, faith, will I, Fridays and Saturdays and all . . . iv 1 117
Amid this hurly I intend That all is done in reverend care of her *T. of S.* iv 1 207
And this is all I have done . . . *All's Well* iii 6 124
'Tis but fortune; all is fortune . . . *T. Night* ii 5 27
To whom should this be?—This wins him, liver and all . . . ii 5 106
I had a pass with him, rapier, scabbard, and all . . . iii 4 303
This is all: Do't and thou hast the one half of my heart . . . *W. Tale* i 2 347
Now, good now, Say so but seldom.—Not at all, good lady . . . v 1 20
Make all the claim that Arthur did.—And lose it, life and all, as Arthur did . . . *K. John* iii 4 144
Words, life and all, old Lancaster hath spent . . . *Richard II.* ii 1 150
Farewell at once, for once, for all, and ever . . . ii 2 148
For the right of that We all have strongly sworn to give him aid . . . ii 3 150
And all goes worse than I have power to tell . . . iii 2 120
The weeds . . . Are pluck'd up root and all by Bolingbroke . . . iii 4 52
There is order ta'en for you; With all swift speed you must away . . . v 1 54
Fought you with them all?—All! I know not what you call all . . . 1 *Hen. IV.* ii 4 203
I have entered him and all.—It may chance cost some of us our lives . . . 2 *Hen. IV.* ii 1 11
'Tis one o'clock, and past.—Why, then, good morrow to you all . . . iii 1 35
My wife has all; For women are shrews, both short and tall . . . v 3 35
Not to us, but to thy arm alone, Ascribe we all! . . . *Hen. V.* iv 8 113
I pray you, mock at 'em; that is all . . . v 1 59
When but in all I was six thousand strong. . . . 1 *Hen. VI.* iv 1 20
Undoing all, as all had never been! . . . 2 *Hen. VI.* i 1 103
Sort how it will, I shall have gold for all . . . i 2 107
That threatest where's no cause.—True, madam, none at all . . . i 4 52
To Pomfret; where, as all you know, Harmless Richard was murder'd . ii 2 26
There shall be no money; all shall eat and drink on my score. . . . iv 2 79
Swearing both They prosper best of all when I am thence 3 *Hen. VI.* ii 5 18
And I nothing to back my suit at all, But the plain devil and dissembling looks . . . *Richard III.* i 2 236
On me, whose all not equals Edward's moiety? . . . i 2 250
Henry's death, my lovely Edward's death, Their kingdom's loss, my woful banishment, Could all but answer for that peevish brat? . i 3 194
Better it were they all came by the father, Or by the father there were none at all . . . ii 3 24
Good lords, make all the speedy haste you may . . . iii 1 60
I do not know What kind of my obedience I should tender; More than my all is nothing . . . *Hen. VIII.* ii 3 67
My most malicious foe, and think not At all a friend to truth. . . . ii 4 84
The one almost as infinite as all, The other blank as nothing *Troi. and Cres.* iv 5 80
A certain number, Though thanks to all, must I select from all *Coriol.* i 6 81
This no more dishonours you at all Than to take in a town with gentle words . . . iii 2 58
He'ld make an end of thy posterity.—Bastards and all . . . iv 2 27
But, out, affection! All bond and privilege of nature, break! . . . v 3 25
This way, or not at all, stand you in hope . . . *T. Andron.* ii 1 119
Hear all, all see, And like her most whose merit most shall be *Rom. and Jul.* i 2 30
Do not swear at all; Or, if thou wilt, swear by thy gracious self . . . ii 2 112
What if this mixture do not work at all? . . . iv 3 21
I will choose Mine heir from forth the beggars of the world, And dispossess her all . . . *T. of Athens* i 1 139
Rather one that smiles and still invites All that pass by . . . ii 1 12
Were it all yours to give it in a breath, How quickly were it gone! ii 2 162
All these Owe their estates unto him . . . iii 3 4
They have all been touch'd and found base metal, for They have all denied him . . . iii 3 6
Now all are fled, Save only the gods . . . iii 3 36
And this is all a liberal course allows . . . iii 3 41
Go, bid all my friends again . . . All, sirrah, all . . . iii 4 111
Thou shalt build from men; Hate all, curse all, show charity to none . iv 3 534
We were not all unkind, nor all deserve The common stroke of war . v 4 21
Till the lowest stream Do kiss the most exalted shores of all . *J. Cæsar* i 1 65
Else shall you not have any hand at all About his funeral . . . iii 1 248

All. I dare do all that may become a man; Who dares do more is none *Macbeth* i 7 46
Nought's had, all's spent, Where our desire is got without content . iii 2 4
All is the fear and nothing is the love; As little is the wisdom, where the flight So runs against all reason . iv 2 12
All my pretty ones? Did you say all? O hell-kite! All? . iv 3 216
What, all my pretty chickens and their dam At one fell swoop? . iv 3 218
Last night of all, When yond same star that's westward from the pole Had made his course . *Hamlet* i 1 35
This above all: to thine own self be true . i 3 78
This is for all . i 3 131
Deep grief; it springs All from her father's death . iv 5 77
We will our kingdom give, Our crown, our life, and all that we call ours iv 5 208
All with me's meet that I can fashion fit . *Lear* i 2 200
All's not offence that indiscretion finds And dotage terms so . ii 4 199
'Tis wonder that thy life and wits at once Had not concluded all iv 7 42
Let them all, All, all, cry shame against me, yet I'll speak *Othello* v 2 221
Believe not all; or, if you must believe, Stomach not all *Ant. and Cleo.* iii 4 11
No midway 'Twixt these extremes at all . iii 4 20
Leap thou, attire and all, Through proof of harness to my heart . iv 8 14
Carry me now, good friends, And have my thanks for all . iv 14 140
All's but naught; Patience is sottish, and impatience does Become a dog that's mad . iv 15 78
And learn now, for all, . . . I care not for you . *Cymbeline* ii 3 111
Take No stricter render of me than my all . v 4 17
Best of all Amongst the rarest of good ones . v 5 159
All-abhorred. Unknit This churlish knot of all-abhorred war 1 *Hen. IV.* v 1 16
All about. She could have run and waddled all about . *Rom. and Jul.* i 3 37
All above. Whom thy upward face Hath to the marbled mansion all above Never presented! *T. of Athens* iv 3 191
Down from the waist they are Centaurs, Though women all above *Lear* iv 6 127
All-admiring. And all-admiring with an inward wish . *Hen. V.* i 1 39
All adoration, duty, and observance, All humbleness *As Y. Like It* v 2 102
All afire. And quit the vessel, Then all afire . *Tempest* i 2 212
All afoot. Went all afoot in summer's scalding heat . 3 *Hen. VI.* v 7 18
All alike. If our virtues Did not go forth of us, 'twere all alike As if we had them not *Meas. for Meas.* i 1 35
For none offend where all alike do dote . *L. L. Lost* iv 3 126
Receive Particular addition, from the bill That writes them all alike *Macbeth* iii 1 101
And things outward Do draw the inward quality after them, To suffer all alike . *Ant. and Cleo.* iii 13 34
All alive. We know not where you left him all alive *T. Andron.* ii 3 257
All alone. Thou seest we are not all alone unhappy . *As Y. Like It* ii 7 136
All alone At the prefixed hour of her waking, Came I . *Rom. and Jul.* v 3 252
And thy commandment all alone shall live . *Hamlet* i 5 102
All alone To-night we'll wander through the streets *Ant. and Cleo.* i 1 52
All along. Under yond yew-trees lay thee all along . *Rom. and Jul.* v 3 3
All aloof. The rest stand all aloof, and bark at him . 3 *Hen. VI.* ii 1 17
Stand all aloof: but, uncle, draw you near . *T. Andron.* v 3 151
Whate'er thou hear'st or seest, stand all aloof . *Rom. and Jul.* v 3 26
All aloud. When all aloud the wind doth blow . *L. L. Lost* v 2 931
All-amazed, the priest let fall the book . *T. of Shrew* iii 2 163
All amiss. And these and all are all amiss employ'd *Richard II.* ii 3 132
This dream is all amiss interpreted . *J. Cæsar* ii 2 83
All armed. Cupid all arm'd: a certain aim he took At a fair vestal *M. N. Dream* ii 1 157
All as loud. A drum is ready braced That shall reverberate all as loud as thine . *K. John* v 2 170
All as mad. With him his bondman, all as mad as he *Com. of Errors* v 1 141
All as soon. Have given him time To land his legions all as soon as I *K. John* ii 1 59
All Athens. Every man's name, which is thought fit, through all Athens, to play . *M. N. Dream* i 2 5
All at once. Who might be your mother, That you insult, exult, and all at once? *As Y. Like It* iii 5 36
Never Hydra-headed wilfulness So soon did lose his seat and all at once *Hen. V.* i 1 36
All at one cast. Were it good To set the exact wealth of all our states All at one cast? 1 *Hen. IV.* iv 1 47
All at one side. I have much to do, But to go hang my head all at one side . *Othello* iv 3 32
All away. And by and by a cloud takes all away *T. G. of Ver.* i 3 87
All bound up. My spirits, as in a dream, are all bound up *Tempest* i 2 486
All-building. Manacles Of the all-building law. *Meas. for Meas.* ii 4 94
All but now. Friends all but now, even now *Othello* ii 3 179
All cause. The extreme parts of time extremely forms All causes to the purpose of his speed *L. L. Lost* v 2 751
All cause unborn, could never be the motive Of our so frank donation *Coriolanus* iii 1 129
My sword, made weak by my affection, would Obey it on all cause *Ant. and Cleo.* iii 11 68
All-changing. This broker, this all-changing word . *K. John* ii 1 582
All-cheering. So soon as the all-cheering sun Should in the furthest east begin to draw The shady curtains from Aurora's bed *Rom. and Jul.* i 1 140
All corners else o' the earth Let liberty make use of . *Tempest* i 2 491
All day. Not been inquired after: I have sat here all day *M. for Meas.* iv 1 20
And in the shape of Corin sat all day, Playing on pipes of corn *M. N. Dr.* ii 1 66
You shall seek all day ere you find them . *Mer. of Ven.* i 1 116
Nay, I'll fit you, And not be all day neither . *All's Well* ii 1 94
The Frenchmen are secure, Having all day caroused . 1 *Hen. VI.* ii 1 12
He'll wrest the sense and hold us here all day . 2 *Hen. VI.* iii 1 186
All day long. Trot, like a servile footman, all day long *T. Andron.* v 2 55
All dedicated To closeness and the bettering of my mind *Tempest* i 2 89
All design. My brother, my competitor In top of all design *Ant. and Cleo.* v 1 43
All-disgraced. From Egypt drive her all-disgraced friend . iii 12 22
All distrained. My father's goods are all distrain'd and sold *Richard II.* ii 3 131
All doubt. He will deserve more.—Yes, without all doubt *Hen. VIII.* iv 1 113
All-dreaded. Fear no more the lightning-flash,—Nor the all-dreaded thunder-stone . *Cymbeline* iv 2 271
All-ending. As 'twere retail'd to all posterity, Even to the general all-ending day *Richard III.* iii 1 78
All Europe. Whose bloody deeds shall make all Europe quake 1 *Hen. VI.* i 1 156
All eyes. Appear, and pertly! No tongue! all eyes! be silent *Tempest* iv 1 59
Or purblind Argus, all eyes and no sight . *Troi. and Cres.* i 2 31
All fancy-sick she is and pale of cheer *M. N. Dream* iii 2 96
All faults. It [prayer] assaults Mercy itself and frees all faults *Temp.* Epil. 18
Laws for all faults, But faults so countenanced . *Meas. for Meas.* v 1 321
Would take her with all faults, and money enough . *T. of Shrew* i 1 134
A man who is the abstract of all faults That all men follow *Ant. and Cleo.* i 4 9

All faults. All faults that may be named, nay, that hell knows . *Cymb.* ii 5 27
All foison. Nature should bring forth, Of it own kind, all foison, all abundance *Tempest* ii 1 163
All France with their chief assembled strength . 1 *Hen. VI.* i 1 139
All France will be replete with mirth and joy, When they shall hear i 6 15
All gaze. Gives all gaze and bent of amorous view . *Troi. and Cres.* iv 5 282
When youth with comeliness plucked all gaze his way . *Coriolanus* i 3 8
All goes well. Yet all goes well, yet all our joints are whole 1 *Hen. IV.* iv 1 83
All good. Time is the nurse and breeder of all good . *T. G. of Ver.* iii 1 243
But speak all good you can devise of Cæsar . *J. Cæsar* iii 1 246
All grease. She's the kitchen wench and all grease . *Com. of Errors* iii 2 97
All hail, great master! grave sir, hail! *Tempest* i 2 189
All hail, the richest beauties on the earth! *L. L. Lost* v 2 158
All hail, sweet madam, and fair time of day! . v 2 339
'Fair' in 'all hail' is foul, as I conceive . v 2 340
Did they not sometime cry 'all hail!' to me? *Richard II.* iv 1 169
So Judas kiss'd his master, And cried 'all hail!' when as he meant all harm . 3 *Hen. VI.* v 7 34
Each in either side Give the all-hail to thee, and cry, 'Be blest!' *Coriol.* v 3 139
All hail, Macbeth! hail to thee, thane of Glamis!—All hail, Macbeth! hail to thee, thane of Cawdor!—All hail, Macbeth, that shalt be king hereafter! *Macbeth* i 3 48
Great Glamis! worthy Cawdor! Greater than both, by the all-hail hereafter! . i 5 56
All-hailed. Who all-hailed me 'Thane of Cawdor' . i 5 7
All-hallond. Was't not at Hallowmas, Master Froth?—All-hallond eve *Meas. for Meas.* ii 1 130
All-hallowmas last, a fortnight afore Michaelmas . *Mer. Wives* i 1 211
All-hallown. Farewell, All-hallown summer! . 1 *Hen. IV.* i 2 178
All happiness bechance to thee in Milan! *T. G. of Ver.* i 1 61
All happy. She is all happy as the fairest of all . *Pericles* v 1 49
All haste. That done, trudge with it in all haste *Mer. Wives* iii 3 14
All-hating. Love to Richard Is a strange brooch in this all-hating world *Richard II.* v 5 66
All headlong. Will, hand in hand, all headlong cast us down *T. Andron.* v 3 132
All hearts. Set all hearts i' the state To what tune pleased his ear *Tempest* i 2 84
All her trim. Where we, in all her trim, freshly beheld Our royal, good, and gallant ship . v 1 236
All hid, all hid; an old infant play . *L. L. Lost* iv 3 78
All his ancestors. And all his ancestors that come after him *Mer. Wives* i 1 15
All his arm. Then goes he to the length of all his arm . *Hamlet* ii 1 88
All his bulk. It did seem to shatter all his bulk . ii 1 95
All his quality. To thy strong bidding task Ariel and all his quality *Temp.* i 2 193
All-honoured. The all-honour'd, honest Roman, Brutus *Ant. and Cleo.* ii 6 16
All humbled. Like a testy babe, will scratch the nurse And presently all humbled kiss the rod . *T. G. of Ver.* i 2 59
All humbleness, all patience and impatience, All purity *As Y. Like It* v 2 103
All I had. My husband, Whom I made lord of me and all I had *C. of Err.* v 1 137
All ill. Which any print of goodness wilt not take, Being capable of all ill *Tempest* i 2 353
All in all. That is, her love; for that is all in all . *T. of Shrew* i 1 130
You would say it hath been all in all his study . *Hen. V.* i 1 42
He that can do all in all With her that hateth thee and hates us all 2 *Hen. VI.* ii 4 51
He will do all in all as Hastings doth . *Richard III.* iii 1 168
Take him for all in all, I shall not look upon his like again . *Hamlet* i 2 187
Patience; Or I shall say you are all in all in spleen, And nothing of a man . *Othello* iv 1 89
Is this the noble Moor whom our full senate Call all in all sufficient? . iv 1 276
All in buff. A wolf, nay, worse, a fellow all in buff . *Com. of Errors* iv 2 36
All in post. Where's Richard gone?—To London, all in post 3 *Hen. VI.* v 5 84
All in white. Her father means she shall be all in white *Mer. Wives* iv 6 35
All is done. Why, this is the best fooling, when all is done . *T. Night* ii 3 31
The match is made, and all is done . *T. of Shrew* iv 4 46
What's to say? A very little little let us do, And all is done. *Hen. V.* iv 2 34
Why do you make such faces? When all's done, You look but on a stool *Macbeth* iii 4 67
All's for the best. I hope all's for the best . 3 *Hen. VI.* iii 3 170
All's not well. Approach, ho! All's not well . *Ant. and Cleo.* v 2 326
All is one *Mer. Wives* ii 2; *Much Ado* v 1; *All's Well* iv 3; *Othello* iv 3
All's one for that 1 *Hen. IV.* ii 4 172; *Richard III.* v 3 8
All's one to me. But 'tis all one to me . *W. Tale* v 2 131
Or Somerset or York, all's one to me . 2 *Hen. VI.* i 3 105
I care not an she were a black-a-moor; 'tis all one to me *Troi. and Cres.* i 1 80
All's too weak: For brave Macbeth—well he deserves that name *Macbeth* i 2 15
All's well that ends well yet, Though time seem so adverse and means unfit *All's Well* v 1 25
All joy. Madam, all joy befal your grace!—And you! *Cymbeline* iii 5 9
All labour. Now all labour Mars what it does; yea, very force entangles Itself with strength *Ant. and Cleo.* iv 14 47
All-licensed. Not only, sir, this your all-licensed fool, But other of your insolent retinue *Lear* i 4 220
All limit. I Beyond all limit of what else i' the world Do love, prize, honour you *Tempest* iii 1 72
All lost! to prayers, to prayers! all lost! . i 1 54
On whom my pains, Humanely taken, all, all lost, quite lost . iv 1 190
All love. My desire, More sharp than filed steel, did spur me forth; And not all love to see you *T. Night* iii 3 6
All made of fantasy, All made of passion and all made of wishes *As Y. Like It* v 2 100
All mated. I think you are all mated or stark mad . *Com. of Errors* v 1 281
All matter. Her wit Values itself so highly that to her All matter else seems weak . *Much Ado* iii 1 54
All means. Shall we tell our husbands how we have served him?—Yes, by all means *Mer. Wives* iv 2 230
By all means stir on the youth to an answer *T. Night* iii 2 62
All men idle, all; And women too, but innocent and pure *Tempest* ii 1 154
All men are not alike; alas, good neighbour! . *Much Ado* iii 5 43
All men's office. 'Tis all men's office to speak patience . v 1 27
All mirth. I was born to speak all mirth and no matter . ii 1 343
From the crown of his head to the sole of his foot, he is all mirth . iii 2 10
All my best. As I have spoken for you all my best . *Othello* iii 4 127
All my child. Thou art all my child . *All's Well* iii 2 71
All my days. Ah, let me live in prison all my days . 3 *Hen. VI.* iv 6 ...
All my flowering youth. Hath detain'd me all my flowering youth Within a loathsome dungeon . 1 *Hen. VI.* ii 5 56
All my heart. With all good will, with all my heart *M. N. Dream* iii 2 164
Admit him.—With all my heart . *Mer. of Venice* iv 1 147
Give me this dagger.—My dagger, little cousin? with all my heart *Richard III.* iii 1 111

All my heart. I here do give thee that with all my heart Which, but thou hast already, with all my heart I would keep from thee . *Othello* i 3 193
You must away to-night.—With all my heart . . . . . i 3 279
Please To give me hearing.—Ay, with all my heart . . . *Cymbeline* v 5 116
I am glad on't with all my heart . . . . . . *Pericles* ii 5 74
Shall we refresh us, sir, upon your shore . . . ?—Sir, with all my heart v 1 261
All my labours. Shortly shall all my labours end . . . *Tempest* iv 1 265
All myself. You shall have any thing.—No seconds? all myself? *Lear* iv 6 198
All my study. And for the liberal arts Without a parallel; those being all my study . . . . *Tempest* i 2 74
All night. He that drinks all night, and is hanged betimes in the morning, may sleep the sounder all the next day . *Meas. for Meas.* iv 3 48
When I was wont to think no harm all night . . . *L. L. Lost* i 1 44
She shall watch all night: And if she chance to nod I'll rail *T. of Shrew* iv 1 208
I would you were a little sick, That I might sit all night and watch *K. John* iv 1 30
The king, I can tell you, looks for us all: we must away all night *1 Hen. IV.* iv 2 63
I have watch'd ere now All night for lesser cause . *Rom. and Jul.* iv 4 10
I have been up this hour, awake all night . . . *J. Cæsar* ii 1 88
All night long. The bird of dawning singeth all night long . *Hamlet* i 1 160
All-obeying. From his all-obeying breath I hear The doom *A. and C.* iii 13 77
All of all. The very all of all is,—but, sweet heart, I do implore secrecy *L. L. Lost* v 1 115
All of her. Tell her, . . . our whole discourse Is all of her . *Much Ado* iii 1 6
All of her that is out of door most rich! . . . *Cymbeline* i 6 15
All of luxury. A coward, One all of luxury, an ass . . *Meas. for Meas.* v 1 506
All of them. I do forgive Thy rankest fault; all of them . *Tempest* v 1 132
That shall Claudio know; so shall the prince And all of them *Much Ado* v 1 44
All of us. You were kneel'd to and importuned otherwise By all of us *Temp.* ii 1 129
And all of us ourselves When no man was his own . . . v 1 212
Well, heaven forgive you and all of us, I pray! . . *Mer. Wives* ii 2 58
All of us have cause To wail the dimming of our shining star *Richard III.* ii 2 101
We will all of us be there to fetch him.—By the eighth hour *J. Cæsar* ii 1 212
All of you have laid your heads together . . *2 Hen. VI.* iii 1 165
A husband and a son thou owest to me; And thou a kingdom; all of you allegiance . . . . *Richard III.* i 3 171
All of yours. So betide to me As well I tender you and all of yours! . ii 4 72
All office. Infirmity doth still neglect all office . . *Lear* ii 4 107
All on a heap, like to a slaughter'd lamb . . *T. Andron.* ii 3 223
All on foot. Methinks I see this hurly all on foot . . *K. John* iii 4 169
His horse is slain, and all on foot he fights . . *Richard III.* v 4 4
All one. That is all one. *T. G. of Ver.* iii 1; *Mer. Wives* i 1; *L. L. Lost* v 2; *M. N. Dream* i 2; *As Y. Like It* iii 5; *T. of Shrew* iii 2; *1 Hen. IV.* iv 2
'Twere all one That I should love a bright particular star . *All's Well* i 1 96
An he will, I care not: give me faith, say I. Well, it's all one *T. Night* i 5 137
How is't with you?—That's all one: has hurt me, and there's the end on't . . . . v 1 201
'Tis all one, 'tis alike as my fingers is to my fingers . . *Hen. V.* iv 7 31
Were't not all one, an empty eagle were set To guard the chicken from a hungry kite? . . . . *2 Hen. VI.* iii 1 248
He cares not; an the devil come to him, it's all one . *Troi. and Cres.* i 2 228
'Tis all one, I will show myself a tyrant . . *Rom. and Jul.* i 1 25
All one pain. Of all one pain, save for a night of groans Endured of her. . . . . *Richard III.* iv 4 303
All other. Do you speak in the sick tune?—I am out of all other tune *Much Ado* iii 4 43
Must he needs trouble me in't,—hum!—'bove all others? *T. of Athens* iii 3 1
It is great To do that thing that ends all other deeds . *Ant. and Cleo.* v 2 5
All our lamentation. We should by this, to all our lamentation, If he had gone forth consul, found it so . . . . *Coriolanus* iv 6 34
All our reasons. Encourage him, and show him all our reasons *Richard III.* iii 1 175
All our sorrows. This will break out To all our sorrows . . *K. John* iv 2 102
All over. A south-west blow on ye And blister you all o'er! . *Tempest* i 2 324
All patience and impatience, All purity, all trial, all observance *As Y. Like It* v 2 103
All points. But then exactly do All points of my command . *Tempest* i 2 500
Is Harry Hereford arm'd?—Yea, at all points . . *Richard II.* i 3 2
All praise. Our then dictator, Whom with all praise I point at *Coriol.* ii 2 94
All-praised. This gallant Hotspur, this all-praised knight . *1 Hen. IV.* iii 2 140
All prerogative. Executing the outward face of royalty, With all prerogative . . . . *Tempest* i 2 105
All reason. Where one part does disdain with cause, the other Insult without all reason . . . . *Coriolanus* iii 1 144
Little is the wisdom, where the flight So runs against all reason *Macbeth* iv 2 14
All remedy. Things without all remedy Should be without regard . iii 2 11
All rites. And do all rites That appertain unto a burial . . *Much Ado* iv 1 209
All rules. Against all rules of nature . . . . *Othello* i 3 101
All safe. Then is all safe, the anchor's in the port . *T. Andron.* iv 4 38
All saws of books, all forms, all pressures past . . . *Hamlet* i 5 100
All-seeing heaven, what a world is this! . . . *Richard III.* ii 1 82
The all-seeing sun Ne'er saw her match since first the world begun *R. and J.* i 2 97
All-Seer. That high All-Seer that I dallied with Hath turn'd my feigned prayer on my head . . . . *Richard III.* v 1 20
All-shaking. Thou, all-shaking thunder, Smite flat the thick rotundity o' the world! . . . . *Lear* iii 2 6
All-shunned. His poor self, A dedicated beggar to the air, With his disease of all-shunn'd poverty . . . . . *T. of Athens* iv 2 14
All sides. On all sides the authority allow'd . . . *Hen. VIII.* ii 4 4
All single and alone, Yet an arch-villain keeps him company *T. of Athens* v 1 110
All sleep. How stand I then, . . . And let all sleep? . . *Hamlet* iv 4 59
All so long. What occasion of import Hath all so long detain'd you! *T. of Shrew* iii 2 105
All so much. Not all so much for love As for another secret close intent *Richard III.* i 1 157
All-Souls' day. This is All-Souls' day, fellows, is it not? . . v 1 10
Why, then All-Souls' day is my body's doomsday . . . . v 1 12
This All-Souls' day to my fearful soul Is the determined respite of my wrongs . . . . v 1 18
All suspicion. And, out of all suspicion, she is virtuous . . *Much Ado* ii 3 166
All tears. Like Niobe, all tears . . . . . . *Hamlet* i 2 149
All-telling fame Doth noise abroad . . . . *L. L. Lost* ii 1 21
All temperance. A gentleman of all temperance . . *Meas. for Meas.* iii 2 251
All terms. In the name of justice, Without all terms of pity . *All's Well* ii 3 173
All the age. Stood challenger on mount of all the age . . *Hamlet* iv 7 28
All the blessings Of a glad father compass thee about! . . *Tempest* v 1 179
All the charms Of Sycorax, toads, beetles, bats, light on you! . . i 2 339
All the creatures. Incensed the seas and shores, yea, all the creatures, Against your peace . . . . iii 3 74
All the day. And not be seen to wink of all the day . . *L. L. Lost* i 1 43
A merry heart goes all the day, Your sad tires in a mile-a . *W. Tale* iv 3 134
All the devils. Hell is empty, And all the devils are here . *Tempest* i 2 215
All the difference. If that be all the difference in his love, I'll get me such a colour'd periwig . . . . . . *T. G. of Ver.* iv 4 194
All the draff. 'Tis old, but true, Still swine eats all the draff *Mer. Wives* iv 2 109
All the fool. I am yours, and all that I possess!—All the fool mine? *L. L. Lost* v 2 384
All the grace that she hath left Is that she will not add to her damnation *Much Ado* iv 1 173
All the honours. And confer fair Milan With all the honours on my brother . . . . *Tempest* i 2 127
All the infections that the sun sucks up From bogs, fens, flats . ii 2 1
All the kind of the Launces have this very fault . . *T. G. of Ver.* ii 3 2
All the mother's. He is all the mother's, from the top to toe *Rich. III.* iii 1 156
All the night. They have travell'd all the night? Mere fetches . *Lear* ii 4 90
All the ocean. Put but a little water in a spoon, And it shall be as all the ocean . . . . *K. John* iv 3 132
All the pack. God keep the prince from all the pack of you! A knot you are of damned blood-suckers . . . . *Richard III.* iii 3 5
All the qualities o' the isle, The fresh springs, brine-pits, barren place and fertile . . . . *Tempest* i 2 337
All the question. In the true course of all the question . . *Much Ado* v 4 6
All the rest. The mariners say how thou hast disposed And all the rest o' the fleet . . . . *Tempest* i 2 226
For all the rest, They'll take suggestion as a cat laps milk . ii 1 287
Why he, of all the rest, hath never moved me.—Yet he, of all the rest, I think, best loves ye . . . . *T. G. of Ver.* i 2 28
You twain, of all the rest, Are near to Warwick by blood *3 Hen. VI.* iv 1 135
All the subjects. I am all the subjects that you have . . *Tempest* i 2 341
All the wine. If all the wine in my bottle will recover him, I will help his ague . . . . ii 2 96
All the world. He whom next thyself Of all the world I loved . . i 2 69
For all the orld, as just as you will desire . . . *Mer. Wives* i 1 50
The academes, That show, contain, and nourish all the world *L. L. Lost* iv 3 353
For you in my respect are all the world . . . . *M. N. Dream* ii 1 224
Can it be said I am alone, When all the world is here to look on me? ii 1 226
Whose posy was For all the world like cutler's poetry Upon a knife *Mer. of Venice* v 1 149
Let all the world say no, I'll keep mine own, despite of all the world *T. of Shrew* iii 2 143
If, one by one, you wedded all the world, Or from the all that are took something good . . . . *W. Tale* v 1 13
My life, my joy, my food, my all the world! . . . *K. John* iii 4 104
For all the world As thou art to this hour was Richard . *1 Hen. IV.* iii 2 93
He was, for all the world, like a forked radish, with a head fantastically carved upon it . . . . *2 Hen. IV.* iii 2 333
Charles, it shall be thine, Let Henry fret and all the world repine *1 Hen. VI.* v 2 20
As all the world is cheered by the sun . . . *Richard III.* i 2 129
I would not be a queen For all the world . . . . *Hen. VIII.* ii 3 46
I care not, I, knew she and all the world: I love Lavinia more than all the world . . . . *T. Andron.* ii 1 71
All-thing. As a gap in our great feast, And all-thing unbecoming *Macb.* iii 1 13
All things. Some hats, from yielders all things catch . . *M. N. Dream* iii 2 30
All things that are, Are with more spirit chased than enjoy'd *M. of Ven.* ii 6 12
All this is so: but what of this, my lord? . . . *Much Ado* iv 1 73
All this isle. That blood which owed the breadth of all this isle *K. John* iv 2 99
All three. I'll be thy second.—All three of them are desperate *Temp.* iii 3 104
All times. At all times alike Men are not still the same *T. of Athens* v 1 124
All-to. The very principals did seem to rend, And all-to topple *Pericles* iii 2 17
All to all. To all, and him, we thirst, And all to all . . *Macbeth* iii 4 92
All together. Then all together They fell upon me . . *Com. of Errors* v 1 245
We are not to stay all together . . . . *Coriolanus* ii 3 45
All too base To stain the temper of my knightly sword *Richard II.* iv 1 28
All too dear. He held them sixpence all too dear . . . *Othello* ii 3 94
All too heavy. Our argument Is all too heavy to admit much talk *2 Hen. IV.* v 2 24
All too little. Who but of late, earth, sea, and air, Were all too little to content and please . . . . *Pericles* i 4 34
All too much. For all the favours Which all too much I have bestow'd on thee . . . . *T. G. of Ver.* iii 1 162
All too soon. Come to the matter.—All too soon I shall . . *Cymbeline* v 5 169
All too wanton. Is all too wanton and too full of gawds . *K. John* iii 3 36
All to pieces. A brave vessel, Who had, no doubt, some noble creature in her, Dash'd all to pieces . . . . *Tempest* i 2 8
We'll bend it to our awe, Or break it all to pieces . . . *Hen. V.* i 2 225
I'll tear her all to pieces.—Nay, but be wise . . . . *Othello* iii 3 431
All under hatches. The mariners all under hatches . . *Tempest* i 2 230
All unknown. Is all unknown to me. . . . . *Richard III.* ii 4 48
All unwarily Devoured by the unexpected flood . . . *K. John* v 7 63
All wanton as a child, skipping and vain . . . . *L. L. Lost* v 2 771
All-watched. Unto the weary and all-watched night . . *Hen. V.* iv Prol. 38
All-worthy lord!—All-worthy villain! . . . . . *Cymbeline* iii 5 94
All wound. Sometime am I all wound with adders . . . *Tempest* ii 2 13
All yourself. Which by the interpretation of full time May show like all yourself. . . . . *Coriolanus* v 3 70
Alla stoccata. Vile submission! Alla stoccata carries it away *R. and J.* iii 1 77
Allay. You have Put the wild waters in this roar, allay them . *Tempest* i 2 2
Allay with some cold drops of modesty Thy skipping spirit *Mer. of Venice* ii 2 195
Be moderate; allay thy ecstasy; In measure rein thy joy . . . iii 2 112
He hath the gift of a coward to allay the gust he hath in quarrelling *T. Night* i 3 32
To whose feeling sorrows I might be some allay . . *W. Tale* iv 2 9
A rage whose heat hath this condition, That nothing can allay *K. John* iii 1 342
It would allay the burning quality Of that fell poison which assaileth him . . . . v 7 8
Let it make thee crest-fall'n, Ay, and allay this thy abortive pride *2 Hen. VI.* iv 1 60
Raging wind blows up incessant showers, And when the rage allays, the rain begins . . . . *3 Hen. VI.* i 4 146
If with the sap of reason you would quench, Or but allay, the fire of passion . . . . *Hen. VIII.* i 1 149
Stop the rumour, and allay those tongues That durst disperse it . . ii 1 152
Desire not To allay my rages and revenges with Your colder reasons *Cor.* v 3 85
With the mischief of your person it would scarcely allay . . *Lear* i 2 179
I do not like 'But yet,' it does allay The good precedence *Ant. and Cleo.* ii 5 50
Allayed. My mildness hath allay'd their swelling griefs . *3 Hen. VI.* iv 8 42
Allaying. This music crept by me upon the waters, Allaying both their fury and my passion With its sweet air . . . . . *Tempest* i 2 392
A cup of hot wine with not a drop of allaying Tiber in't. . *Coriolanus* ii 1 53

Allayment. The like allayment could I give my grief . *Troi. and Cres.* iv 4 8
Try the vigour of them and apply Allayments to their act . *Cymbeline* i 5 22
Allegation. Reprove my allegation, if you can . . 2 *Hen. VI.* iii 1 40
As if she had suborned some to swear False allegations . . . . iii 1 181
Allege. The reasons you allege do more conduce To the hot passion of distemper'd blood *Troi. and Cres.* ii 2 168
Alleged. He pleaded still not guilty and alleged Many sharp reasons to defeat the law . . . *Hen. VIII.* ii 1 13
The sharp thorny points Of my alleged reasons drive this forward . ii 4 225
Allegiance. I charge thee on thy allegiance . . . *Much Ado* i 1 210
On my allegiance, mark you this, on my allegiance . . . i 1 213
Too good for them, if they should have any allegiance in them . iii 3 5
On your allegiance, Out of the chamber with her! *W. Tale* ii 3 121
Contrary to the faith and allegiance of a true subject . . iii 2 20
Blessed shall he be that doth revolt From his allegiance to an heretic *K. John* iii 1 175
Swearing allegiance and the love of soul . . v 1 10
Those thoughts Which honour and allegiance cannot think *Richard II.* ii 1 208
And sends allegiance and true faith of heart . iii 3 37
In such humility That I did pluck allegiance from men's hearts 1 *Hen. IV.* iii 2 52
As if allegiance in their bosoms sat, Crowned with faith . *Hen. V.* ii 2 4
We charge you, on allegiance to ourself . 1 *Hen. VI.* iii 1 86
Then swear allegiance to his majesty, As thou art knight . v 4 169
Confirm our peace And keep the Frenchmen in allegiance . v 5 43
Against thy oath and true allegiance sworn . 2 *Hen. VI.* v 1 20
Hast thou not sworn allegiance unto me?—I have . . v 1 179
We his subjects sworn in all allegiance Will apprehend you 3 *Hen. VI.* iii 1 70
Shut the gates for safety of ourselves; For now we owe allegiance unto Henry . . . iv 7 19
A husband and a son thou owest to me; And thou a kingdom; all of you allegiance . . *Richard III.* i 3 171
This makes bold mouths: Tongues spit their duties out, and cold hearts freeze Allegiance in them . *Hen. VIII.* i 2 62
Pray heaven, the king may never find a heart With less allegiance in it! v 3 43
Still keep My bosom franchised and allegiance clear *Macbeth* ii 1 28
To hell, allegiance! vows, to the blackest devil! . *Hamlet* iv 5 131
Hear me, recreant! On thine allegiance, hear me! . *Lear* i 1 170
He that can endure To follow with allegiance a fall'n lord *Ant. and Cleo.* iii 13 44
Allegiant. I Can nothing render but allegiant thanks . *Hen. VIII.* iii 2 176
Alley. One that countermands The passages of alleys . *Com. of Errors* iv 2 38
Walking in a thick-pleached alley in mine orchard *Much Ado* i 2 10
As we do trace this alley up and down, Our talk must only be of Benedick iii 1 16
Swift as quicksilver it courses through The natural gates and alleys of the body *Hamlet* i 5 67
Alliance. For alliance! Thus goes every one to the world but I *M. Ado* ii 1 330
One day shall crown the alliance on't, so please you . *T. Night* v 1 326
In himself too mighty, And in his parties, his alliance *W. Tale* ii 3 21
In love and dear alliance, Let that one article rank with the rest *Hen. V.* v 2 373
And for alliance sake, declare the cause . 1 *Hen. VI.* ii 5 53
Can this be so, That in alliance, amity, and oaths, There should be found such false dissembling guile? iv 1 62
His alliance will confirm our peace And keep the Frenchmen in allegiance v 5 42
How can tyrants safely govern home, Unless abroad they purchase great alliance? 3 *Hen. VI.* iii 3 70
It was thy device By this alliance to make void my suit . iii 3 142
Is this the alliance that he seeks with France? . iii 3 177
Such alliance Would more have strengthen'd this our commonwealth . iv 1 36
You twain, of all the rest, Are near to Warwick by blood and by alliance iv 1 136
This fair alliance quickly shall call home To high promotions *Rich. III.* iv 4 313
Infer fair England's peace by this alliance.—Which she shall purchase with still lasting war . iv 4 343
This alliance may so happy prove, To turn your households' rancour to pure love . *Rom. and Jul.* ii 3 91
We must straight make head: Therefore let our alliance be combined *J. C.* iv 1 43
Allicholy. Methinks you're allicholy: I pray you, why is it? *T. G. of V.* iv 2 27
But indeed she is given too much to allicholy and musing . *Mer. Wives* i 4 164
Allied. A lady, An heir, and near allied unto the duke . *T. G. of Ver.* iv 1 49
The vice is of a great kindred; it is well allied: but it is impossible to extirp it quite . *Meas. for Meas.* iii 2 109
She's nothing allied to your disorders . *T. Night* ii 3 104
Thereby for sealing The injury of tongues in courts and kingdoms Known and allied to yours . *W. Tale* i 2 339
Neither allied To eminent assistants . *Hen. VIII.* i 1 61
Allies. You to your land and love and great allies *As Y. Like It* v 4 195
Be no more opposed Against acquaintance, kindred and allies 1 *Hen. IV.* i 1 16
Say it is the queen and her allies That stir the king against the duke *Richard III.* i 3 330
Seal thou this league With thy embracements to my wife's allies . ii 1 30
Going prisoner to the Tower, By the suggestion of the queen's allies iii 2 103
When I was found False to his children or his wife's allies . v 1 15
Alligant. In silk and gold; and in such alligant terms *Mer. Wives* ii 2 69
Alligator. An alligator stuff'd, and other skins Of ill-shaped fishes *R. and J.* v 1 43
Allons! allons! Sow'd cockle reap'd no corn . *L. L. Lost* iv 3 383
Allons! we will employ thee . . v 1 159
Allons-nous. C'est assez pour une fois: allons-nous à diner *Hen. V.* iii 4 65
Allot. Happier the man, whom favourable stars Allot thee for his lovely bed-fellow! *T. of Shrew* iv 5 41
Five days we do allot thee, for provision To shield thee from diseases of the world *Lear* i 1 176
Allotted. Thou art allotted to be ta'en by me . 1 *Hen. VI.* v 3 55
Allottery. The poor allottery my father left me by testament *As Y. Like* i 1 76
Allow. The law allows it, and the court awards it . *Mer. of Venice* iv 1 303
If the law would allow it, sir.—But the law will not allow it *M. for Meas.* ii 1 239
The courtesy of nations allows you my better, in that you are the first-born *As Y. Like It* i 1 49
Therefore allow me such exercises as may become a gentleman i 1 75
Allow the wind.—Nay, you need not to stop your nose . *All's Well* v 2 10
I can sing And speak to him in many sorts of music That will allow me very worth his service . *T. Night* i 2 59
Thou shalt hold the opinion of Pythagoras ere I will allow of thy wits, and fear to kill a woodcock . iv 2 63
An your ladyship will have it as it ought to be, you must allow Vox v 1 304
Of this allow, If ever you have spent time worse ere now *W. Tale* iv 1 29
You know your father's temper: at this time He will allow no speech . iv 4 479
Which to maintain I would allow him odds, And meet him . *Richard II.* i 1 62
Free speech and fearless I to thee allow . i 1 123
Whose state and honour I for aye allow . v 2 40
They will allow us ne'er a jordan, and then we leak in your chimney 1 *Hen. IV.* ii 1 21
Allow. I well allow the occasion of our arms . . 2 *Hen. IV.* i 3 5
I do allow this wen to be as familiar with me as my dog . ii 2 115
I like them all, and do allow them well . iv 2 54
For competence of life I will allow you, That lack of means enforce you not to evil . v 5 70
Praise us as we are tasted, allow us as we prove . *Troi. and Cres.* iii 2 98
If you submit you to the people's voices, Allow their officers *Coriolanus* iii 3 45
Doth grace for grace and love for love allow . *Rom. and Jul.* ii 3 86
This is all a liberal course allows; Who cannot keep his wealth must keep his house . *T. of Athens* iii 3 41
More than the scope Of these delated articles allow . *Hamlet* i 2 38
If your sweet sway Allow obedience, if yourselves are old, Make it your cause . *Lear* ii 4 194
Allow not nature more than nature needs, Man's life's as cheap as beast's ii 4 269
Which, if convenience will not allow, Stand in hard cure . iii 6 106
His roguish madness Allows itself to any thing . iii 7 105
The time will not allow the compliment Which very manners urges . v 3 233
Allowance. Without the king's will or the state's allowance *Hen. VIII.* iii 2 322
Among ourselves Give him allowance for the better man *Troi. and Cres.* i 3 377
A stirring dwarf we do allowance give Before a sleeping giant ii 3 146
Syllables Of no allowance to your bosom's truth *Coriolanus* iii 2 57
Such regards of safety and allowance As therein are set down *Hamlet* ii 2 79
The censure of the which one must in your allowance o'erweigh a whole theatre of others . iii 2 31
You protect this course, and put it on By your allowance *Lear* i 4 228
In sincere verity, Under the allowance of your great aspect ii 2 112
If this be known to you and your allowance, We then have done you bold and saucy wrongs . *Othello* i 1 128
His bark is stoutly timber'd, and his pilot Of very expert and approved allowance . ii 1 49
Allowed. Authentic in your place and person, generally allowed for your many war-like, court-like, and learned preparations *Mer. Wives* ii 2 236
The law will not allow it, Pompey; nor it shall not be allowed *Meas. for Meas.* ii 1 241
Allowed by order of law a furred gown to keep him warm . iii 2 8
She is allowed for the day-woman . *L. L. Lost* i 2 136
You are allow'd; Die when you will, a smock shall be your shroud v 2 478
There is no slander in an allowed fool, though he do nothing but rail *T. N.* i 5 101
Allowed your approach rather to wonder at you than to hear you . i 5 210
Such allow'd infirmities that honesty Is never free of *W. Tale* i 2 263
Why not Ned and I For once allow'd the skilful pilot's charge? 3 *Hen. VI.* v 4 20
Anger is like A full-hot horse, who being allow'd his way, Self-mettle tires him *Hen. VIII.* i 1 133
What we oft do best, By sick interpreters, once weak ones, is Not ours, or not allow'd . i 2 83
Scholars allow'd freely to argue for her . ii 2 113
It hath already publicly been read, And on all sides the authority allow'd . ii 4 4
No friends, no hope; no kindred weep for me; Almost no grave allow'd me . iii 1 151
Thou shalt be met with thanks, Allow'd with absolute power and thy good name Live with authority *T. of Athens* v 1 165
Which Mark Antony, By our permission, is allow'd to make . *J. Cæsar* iii 2 64
She is allow'd her virgin crants, Her maiden strewments *Hamlet* v 1 255
Put to sudden death, Not shriving-time allow'd . v 2 47
We have there a substitute of most allowed sufficiency . *Othello* i 3 224
He was then of a crescent note, expected to prove so worthy as since he hath been allowed the name of *Cymbeline* i 4 3
Though it be allow'd in meaner parties—Yet who than he more mean? ii 3 121
This service is not service, so being done, But being so allow'd iii 3 17
Allowing. Arms her with the boldness of a wife To her allowing husband! *W. Tale* i 2 185
Your patience this allowing, I turn my glass and give my scene such growing As you had slept between . iv 1 15
Scoffing his state and grinning at his pomp, Allowing him a breath *Richard II.* iii 2 164
Allure him, burn him up; Let your close fire predominate his smoke *T. of Athens* iv 3 141
Let her beauty Look through a casement to allure false hearts *Cymbeline* ii 4 34
Would allure, And make a battery through his deafen'd parts *Pericles* v 1 46
Allured. Sluttery to such neat excellence opposed Should make desire vomit emptiness, Not so allured to feed . *Cymbeline* i 6 46
Allurement. Take heed of the allurement of one Count Rousillon *A. W.* iv 3 241
Alluring. Hath homely age the alluring beauty took From my poor cheek? *Com. of Errors* ii 1 89
Allusion. I say, the allusion holds in the exchange . *L. L. Lost* iv 2 45
Ally. The prince's near ally, My very friend, hath got his mortal hurt *Rom. and Jul.* iii 1 114
Almain. He sweats not to overthrow your Almain; he gives your Hollander a vomit . *Othello* ii 3 86
Almanac. Here comes the almanac of my true date *Com. of Errors* i 2 41
A calendar! look in the almanac; find out moonshine . *M. N. Dream* iii 1 54
Saturn and Venus this year in conjunction! what says the almanac to that? 2 *Hen IV.* ii 4 287
They are greater storms and tempests than almanacs can report *A. and C.* i 2 154
Almighty. Of his almighty dreadful little might . *L. L. Lost* iii 1 205
The armipotent Mars, of lances the almighty, Gave Hector a gift . v 2 650
He wills you, in the name of God Almighty, That you divest yourself *Hen. V.* ii 4 77
God Almighty! There is some soul of goodness in things evil . iv 1 3
Ay, God Almighty help me! . 2 *Hen. VI.* ii 1 95
Which shipmen do the hurricano call, Constringed in mass by the almighty sun *Troi. and Cres.* v 2 173
Almond. The parrot will not do more for an almond . v 2 194
Almost. Come away; it is almost clear dawn . *Meas. for Meas.* iv 2 226
As like almost to Claudio as himself . v 1 494
Of such enchanting presence and discourse, Hath almost made me traitor to myself *Com. of Errors* iii 2 167
I have not breathed almost since I did see it . v 1 181
I have almost matter enough in me for such an embassage . *Much Ado* i 1 281
'Tis almost five o'clock, cousin; 'tis time you were ready . iii 4 52
My brother hath a daughter, Almost the copy of my child . v 1 298
Have you forgot your love?—Almost I had.—Negligent student! *L. L. Lost* iii 1 35
Speak, of all loves! I swoon almost with fear . *M. N. Dream* ii 2 154
Thou almost makest me waver in my faith . *M. of Ven.* iv 1 130
I assure thee, and almost with tears I speak it *As Y. Like It* i 1 160
From seventeen years till now almost fourscore Here lived I . ii 3 71
The poor world is almost six thousand years old . iv 1 95
On the reading it he changed almost into another man . *All's Well* iv 3 5

Almost. Time was, I did him a desired office, Dear almost as his life *All's Well* iv 4 6
They seemed almost, with staring on one another, to tear the cases of their eyes; there was speech in their dumbness *W. Tale* v 2 13
My lord's almost so far transported that He'll think anon it lives . v 3 69
Last in the field, and almost lords of it! . . . *K. John* v 5 8
Which is almost to pluck a kingdom down And set another up 2 *Hen. IV.* i 3 49
Coming to look on you, thinking you dead, And dead almost, my liege, to think you were . . . . iv 5 157
That knew'st the very bottom of my soul, That almost mightst have coin'd me into gold . . . . . . *Hen. V.* ii 2 98
Those few I have Almost no better than so many French . . iii 6 156
The French were almost ten to one, Before we met . 1 *Hen. VI.* iv 1 21
Ye cannot reason almost with a man That looks not heavily and full of fear . . . . *Richard III.* ii 3 39
My son of York Hath almost overta'en him in his growth . . ii 4 7
When we, Almost with ravish'd listening, could not find His hour of speech a minute . . . . . . *Hen. VIII.* i 2 120
No kindred weep for me; Almost no grave allow'd me . . . iii 1 151
Together with all famous colleges Almost in Christendom . . iii 2 67
Her sufferance made Almost each pang a death . . . . v 1 69
And almost, like the gods, Does thoughts unveil . . *Troi. and Cres.* iii 3 199
Nay, these are almost thoroughly persuaded . . . *Coriolanus* i 1 205
Ere almost Rome Should know we were afoot . . . . . i 2 24
They are near the city?—Almost at point to enter . . . . v 4 64
She swooned almost at my pleasing tale . . . *T. Andron.* v 1 119
Even when their sorrows almost were forgot . . . . . v 1 137
Painting is welcome. The painting is almost the natural man *T. of Athens* i 1 157
Yet he spurs on. Now they are almost on him . . . *J. Cæsar* v 3 30
What is the night?—Almost at odds with morning, which is which *Macb.* iii 4 127
The day almost itself professes yours, And little is to do . . . v 7 27
Do you see yonder cloud that's almost in shape of a camel? . *Hamlet* iii 2 393
For use almost can change the stamp of nature . . . . . iii 4 168
The queen his mother Lives almost by his looks . . . . . iv 7 12
And yet 'tis almost 'gainst my conscience . . . . . v 2 307
A wretch whom nature is ashamed Almost to acknowledge hers . *Lear* i 1 216
Nothing almost sees miracles But misery . . . . . . ii 2 172
Her cock, a buoy Almost too small for sight . . . . . iv 6 20
Whom love hath turn'd almost the wrong side out . . *Othello* ii 3 54
I have rubb'd this young quat almost to the sense . . . . v 1 11
Sweet Alexas, most any thing Alexas, almost most absolute Alexas *Ant. and Cleo.* i 2 2
Overbuys me Almost the sum he pays . . . . . *Cymbeline* i 1 147
I have cried her almost to the number of her hairs . . *Pericles* iv 2 100
Almost a fault. Is not almost a fault To incur a private check *Othello* iii 3 66
Almost a fray. You are almost come to part almost a fray . *M. Ado* v 1 114
Almost a man. I see into thy end, and am almost A man already *Cymb.* iii 4 169
Almost a mile. His horses go about.—Almost a mile . . *Macbeth* iii 3 12
Almost a miracle. May this, almost a miracle, be done? . *W. Tale* v 4 545
Almost afraid. I am almost afraid to stand alone . . *Rom. and Jul.* v 3 10
Alas, poor country! Almost afraid to know itself . . . *Macbeth* iv 3 165
Almost all Repent in their election . . . . . *Coriolanus* ii 3 262
With almost all the holy vows of heaven . . . . . *Hamlet* i 3 114
Almost an alien to the hearts Of all the court and princes 1 *Hen. IV.* iii 2 34
Almost an apple. Or a codling when 'tis almost an apple . *T. Night* i 5 167
Almost anticked. The wild disguise hath almost Antick'd us all *Ant. and Cleo.* ii 7 131
Almost any. You shall find Many, nay, almost any . . *Tempest* iii 3 34
Almost appears In loud rebellion.—Not almost appears, It doth appear *Hen. VIII.* i 2 28
Almost as bad, good mother, As kill a king . . . . *Hamlet* iii 4 28
Almost as great. Whose skill was almost as great as his honesty *A. W.* i 1 21
Almost as infinite. The one almost as infinite as all . *Troi. and Cres.* iv 5 80
Almost as like. They say we are Almost as like as eggs . *W. Tale* i 2 130
Almost as well. Dost thou know her?—Almost as well as I do know myself . . . . *T. G. of Ver.* iv 4 148
Almost ashamed. I am almost ashamed To say what good respect I have of thee . . . . *K. John* iii 3 27
Almost believe. Would you imagine, or almost believe? . *Richard III.* iii 5 35
Almost beyond credit. Indeed almost beyond credit . . . *Tempest* ii 1 59
Almost blunted. To whet thy almost blunted purpose . . *Hamlet* iii 4 111
Almost burst. Which almost burst to belch it in the sea *Richard III.* i 4 41
Endured a sea That almost burst the deck . . . . *Pericles* iv 1 57
Almost changed my mind . . . . *Richard III.* iv 3 15
Almost charmed me from my profession . . . . *T. of Athens* iv 3 454
Almost chide God for making you that countenance you are *As Y. L. It* iv 1 36
Almost choked. It had almost choked Cæsar . . . *J. Cæsar* i 2 249
Almost come. The minute of their plot Is almost come . *Tempest* iv 1 142
You are almost come to part almost a fray . . . . *M. Ado* v 1 113
My hour is almost come, When I to sulphurous and tormenting flames Must render up myself . . . . *Hamlet* i 5 2
Almost damn. Would almost damn those ears . . *Mer. of Venice* i 1 98
Almost damned. A fellow almost damn'd in a fair wife . . *Othello* i 1 21
Almost day. Trust me, I think 'tis almost day . . *T. G. of Ver.* iv 2 139
Good morrow; for, as I take it, it is almost day . . *Meas. for Meas.* iv 2 109
Almost dead for breath . . . . *Macbeth* i 5 37
Almost die. I almost die for food; and let me have it . *As Y. Like It* ii 7 104
Almost done. His eyes do show his days are almost done . *T. Night* ii 3 112
Almost embossed. We have almost embossed him . . . *All's Well* iii 6 107
Almost ended. Brutus' tongue Hath almost ended his life's history *J. Cæsar* v 5 40
Almost fairy time. To bed; 'tis almost fairy time . . *M. N. Dream* v 1 371
Almost finished. Her monument Is almost finish'd . . *Pericles* iv 3 43
Almost forgot. Pardon, madam: The one I have almost forgot *W. Tale* v 1 104
Almost forgot my prayers to content him . . . . *Hen. VIII.* iii 1 132
I have almost forgot the taste of fears . . . . . *Macbeth* v 5 9
That truth should be silent I had almost forgot . . *Ant. and Cleo.* ii 2 109
I had almost forgot To entreat your grace but in a small request *Cymb.* i 6 180
Almost forspent with speed . . . . 2 *Hen. IV.* i 1 37
Almost freezes up the heat of life . . . . *Rom. and Jul.* iv 3 16
Almost here. Come, come, they are almost here . . . *Coriolanus* ii 2 1
Almost impossible. 'Tis hard; almost impossible . . . . *Lear* ii 4 245
Almost impregnable. His heart Almost impregnable . . *T. Andron.* iv 4 98
Almost inaccessible. Uninhabitable and almost inaccessible . *Tempest* ii 1 37
Almost kingly. O'er France and all her almost kingly dukedoms *Hen. V.* i 2 227
Almost like. Were almost like a sharp-quill'd porpentine 2 *Hen. VI.* iii 1 363
Almost mad. I'll tell thee, friend, I am almost mad myself . *Lear* iii 4 171
Almost mature for the violent breaking out . . . *Coriolanus* iv 3 26
Almost midnight. What hour is it?—Almost midnight . . *Cymbeline* ii 2 2
Almost morning. 'Tis almost morning; I would have thee gone *R. and J.* ii 2 177
Almost morning. It is almost morning, And yet I am sure you are not satisfied . . . . *Mer. of Venice* v 1 295
It's almost morning, is't not?—Day, my lord . . . *Cymbeline* ii 3 10
Almost natural. The good gifts of nature.—He hath indeed, almost natural . . . . *T. Night* i 3 30
Almost night. 'Tis almost night: you shall have better cheer *Cymb.* iii 6 67
Almost out. I am almost out at heels . . . . *Mer. Wives* i 3 34
You that have worn your eyes almost out . . . *Meas. for Meas.* i 2 113
He may keep his own grace, but he's almost out of mine . 2 *Hen IV.* i 2 32
Almost past. His hour is almost past . . . *Mer. of Venice* ii 6 2
Almost persuade. Ah, balmy breath, that dost almost persuade Justice to break her sword! . . . . *Othello* v 2 16
Almost persuaded,—For he's a spirit of persuasion . . *Tempest* ii 1 234
Almost read. Could almost read The thoughts of people . *Othello* iii 4 57
Almost ready to wrangle with mine own honesty . . *Mer. Wives* iii 1 88
I am almost ready to dissolve, Hearing of this . . . . *Lear* v 3 203
Almost receive. The fix'd sentinels almost receive The secret whispers of each other's watch . . . . . . *Hen. V.* iv Prol. 6
Almost run. Now our sands are almost run . . . *Pericles* v 2 266
Almost set. Thy eyes are almost set in thy head . . *Tempest* iii 2 10
Almost shoulder'd in the swallowing gulf Of blind forgetfulness and dark oblivion . . . . *Richard III.* iii 7 128
Almost sick. They swore that you were almost sick for me *Much Ado* v 4 80
A beard!—By my troth, I'll tell thee, I am almost sick for one *T. Night* iii 1 52
Almost slain. Then is my sovereign slain?—Ay, almost slain 3 *Hen. VI.* iv 4 7
Almost slipped. I have almost slipp'd the hour . . . *Macbeth* iii 3 52
Almost speechless. I left him almost speechless . . . *K. John* v 6 24
Almost spent. The day is almost spent . . . 2 *Hen. VI.* iii 1 325
My money is almost spent . . . . *Othello* ii 3 371
Almost spent with hunger, I am fall'n in this offence *Cymbeline* iii 6 63
Almost stops. Away! vexation almost stops my breath . 1 *Hen. VI.* iv 3 41
Almost supped. He has almost supp'd . . . . . *Macbeth* i 7 29
Almost sweat. Did almost sweat to bear The pride upon them *Hen. VIII.* i 1 24
Almost think. Could you think? Or do you almost think? *K. John* iv 3 43
Almost to bursting. Did stretch his leathern coat Almost to bursting *As Y. Like It* ii 1 38
Almost to death. I faint almost to death . . . . . ii 4 66
When we both lay in the field Frozen almost to death . *Richard III.* ii 1 115
Will crowd a feeble man almost to death . . . . *J. Cæsar* ii 4 36
Almost to doomsday. Was sick almost to doomsday with eclipse *Ham.* i 1 120
Almost to jelly. Distill'd Almost to jelly with the act of fear . . i 2 205
Almost to roaring. He cried almost to roaring . . *Ant. and Cleo.* iii 2 55
Almost wither'd. A gather'd lily almost wither'd . *T. Andron.* iii 1 113
Almost yield. Made me almost yield upon my knees . 1 *Hen. VI.* iii 3 80
Alms. And doth beg the alms Of palsied eld . . *Meas. for Meas.* iii 1 35
It were an alms to hang him . . . . *Much Ado* ii 3 164
Beggars, that come unto my father's door, Upon entreaty have a present alms . . . . *T. of Shrew* iv 3 5
I'ld have you buy and sell so, so give alms, Pray so . . *W. Tale* iv 4 138
Time hath, my lord, a wallet at his back, Wherein he puts alms for oblivion . . . . *Troi. and Cres.* iii 3 146
There's in all two worthy voices begged. I have your alms *Coriolanus* ii 3 87
My arm'd knees, Who bow'd but in my stirrup, bend like his That hath received an alms! . . . . iii 2 120
As with a man by his own alms empoison'd, And with his charity slain v 6 11
That have their alms out of the empress' chest . . *T. Andron.* ii 3 9
Let your study Be to content your lord, who hath received you At fortune's alms . . . . *Lear* i 1 281
And shut myself up in some other course, To fortune's alms . *Othello* iii 4 122
One bred of alms and foster'd with cold dishes . . . *Cymbeline* ii 3 119
Alms-basket. They have lived long on the alms-basket of words *L. L. L.* v 1 41
Alms-deed. Murder is thy alms-deed; Petitioners for blood thou ne'er put'st back . . . . 3 *Hen. VI.* v 5 79
Alms-drink. They have made him drink alms-drink . *Ant. and Cleo.* ii 7 5
Almshouse. A hundred almshouses right well supplied . . *Hen. V.* i 1 17
Almsman. My gay apparel for an almsman's gown . *Richard II.* iii 3 149
Aloft. Her chamber is aloft, far from the ground . *T. G. of Ver.* iii 1 114
Now I breathe again Aloft the flood . . . . . *K. John* iv 2 139
Then will I raise aloft the milk-white rose . . . 2 *Hen. VI.* i 1 254
Be by her aloft, while we be busy below . . . . i 4 11
They know their master loves to be aloft . . . . . . ii 1 11
This day I'll wear aloft my burgonet . . . . v 1 204
Sits aloft, Secure of thunder's crack or lightning flash . *T. Andron.* ii 1 2
Fit thy thoughts, To mount aloft with thy imperial mistress . . ii 1 13
I will not loose again, Till thou art here aloft, or I below . . ii 3 244
And rear'd aloft the bloody battle-axe . . . . . . iii 1 169
The Roman eagle, From south to west on wing soaring aloft *Cymbeline* v 5 471
Alone. Let it alone, thou fool; it is but trash . . *Tempest* iv 1 223
Let's alone And do the murder first . . . . . . iv 1 231
Now we are alone, Wouldst thou then counsel me to fall in love? *T. G. of Ver.* i 2 1
To walk alone, like one that had the pestilence . . . ii 1 21
She is alone.—Then let her alone . . . . ii 4 167
'Tis not to have you gone; For why, the fools are mad, if left alone iii 1 99
But, hark thee; I will go to her alone . . . . . iii 1 127
That I may venture to depart alone . . . . . . iv 3 36
Here can I sit alone, unseen of any . . . . . . v 4 4
Go tell thy master I am alone . . . . . . *Mer. Wives* iii 3 38
Are you not ashamed? let the clothes alone . . . . . iv 2 145
And some condemned for a fault alone . . . *Meas. for Meas.* ii 1 40
He promised me a chain; Would that alone, alone he would detain! *Com. of Errors* ii 1 107
About evening come yourself alone To know the reason . . . iv 1 96
Alone, it was the subject of my theme; In company I often glanced it v 1 65
This is thy office; Bear thee well in it and leave us alone *Much Ado* iii 1 13
How if they will not?—Why, then, let them alone till they are sober . iii 3 48
Thou . . hast kill'd Mine innocent child?—Yea, even I alone . v 1 274
The copy of my child that's dead, And she alone is heir to both of us . v 1 299
As I for praise alone now seek to spill The poor deer's blood *L. L. Lost* iv 1 34
But love, first learned in a lady's eyes, Lives not alone immured in the brain . . . . iv 3 328
How can it be said I am alone, When all the world is here? *M. N. Dream* ii 1 225
O, wilt thou darkling leave me? do not so.—Stay, on thy peril: I alone will go . . . . ii 2 87
Then will two at once woo one; That must needs be sport alone . iii 2 119
Let her alone: speak not of Helena; Take not her part . . . iii 2 332
Though for myself alone I would not be ambitious . *Mer. of Ven.* iii 2 151
Let him alone: I'll follow him no more with bootless prayers . iii 3 19
If I be left alone, Now, by mine honour, which is yet mine own, I'll have that doctor for my bedfellow . . . . v 1 231

Alone. If ever he go alone again, I'll never wrestle for prize more *As Y. Like It* i 1 167
He'll go along o'er the wide world with me; Leave me alone to woo him i 3 135
Being there alone, Left and abandon'd of his velvet friends . . . ii 1 49
Thou seest we are not all alone unhappy . . . . . . ii 7 136
But, good faith, I had as lief have been myself alone . . . iii 2 270
Leave me and her alone . . . . *T. of Shrew* Ind. 2 118
When I am alone, why, then I am Tranio . . . . . . i 1 248
'Tis bargain'd 'twixt us twain, being alone, That she shall still be curst in company . . . . ii 1 306
'Tis a world to see, How tame, when men and women are alone, A meacock wretch can make the curstest shrew . . . . ii 1 314
Take in your love, and then let me alone . . . . . iv 2 71
Sirs, let't alone: I will not go to-day . . . . . iv 3 195
And show what we alone must think, which never Returns us thanks *All's Well* i 1 199
Alone she was, and did communicate to herself her own words to her own ears . . . . i 3 111
Good alone Is good without a name. Vileness is so . . . ii 3 135
Let thy courtesies alone, they are scurvy ones . . . . v 3 324
So full of shapes is fancy That it alone is high fantastical *T. Night* i 1 15
Speak your office.—It alone concerns your ear . . . . i 5 224
Give us the place alone: we will hear this divinity . . . i 5 235
I shall crave of you your leave that I may bear my evils alone . ii 1 6
Let me alone with him; if I do not gull him into a nayword . . ii 3 145
Peace, peace; we must deal gently with him: let me alone . . iii 4 106
Nay, let him alone: I'll go another way to work with him . . iv 1 35
Not he alone shall suffer what wit can make heavy and vengeance bitter *W. Tale* iv 4 800
And not alone in habit and device, Exterior form *K. John* i 1 210
One that will play the devil, sir, with you, And a' may catch your hide and you alone . . . . ii 1 136
Leave those woes alone which I alone Am bound to under-bear . iii 1 64
We will alone uphold, Without the assistance of a mortal hand . iii 1 157
Yet I alone, alone do me oppose Against the pope . . . iii 1 170
Let me alone with him.—I am best pleased to be from such a deed . iv 1 85
This fester'd joint cut off, the rest rest sound; This let alone will all the rest confound *Richard II.* v 3 86
I prithee, leave the prince and me alone . . . *1 Hen. IV.* i 2 168
I have a jest to execute that I cannot manage alone . . . i 2 181
I tell thee, He durst as well have met the devil alone . . . i 3 116
O, my good lord, why are you thus alone? . . . . . ii 3 40
Why dost thou bend thine eyes upon the earth, And start so often when thou sit'st alone? . . . . ii 3 46
Let them alone awhile, and then open the door . . . . ii 4 95
Prithee, let him alone; we shall have more anon . . . ii 4 231
Good my lord, hear me.—Prithee, let her alone, and list to me . iii 3 110
I might have let alone The insulting hand of Douglas over you . v 4 53
I am loath to pawn my plate, so God save me, la!—Let it alone *2 Hen. IV.* ii 1 169
Let them alone: The marshal and the archbishop are strong . . iii 3 41
I was pricked well enough before, an you could have let me alone . iii 2 123
How fares your grace?—Why did you leave me here alone? . . iv 5 51
Come hither to me, Harry. Depart the chamber, leave us here alone iv 5 91
He would not wish himself any where but where he is.—Then I would he were here alone *Hen. V.* iv 1 126
Would you and I alone, Without more help, could fight this royal battle! iv 3 74
O God, thy arm was here; And not to us, but to thy arm alone, Ascribe we all! . . . . iv 8 112
By my consent, we'll even let them alone.—Be it so . *1 Hen. VI.* i 2 44
Well then, alone, since there's no remedy . . . . . ii 2 57
Not that alone But all the whole inheritance I give . . . iii 1 163
The quarrel toucheth none but us alone . . . . . . iv 1 118
Fear not, man, We are alone; here's none but thee and I *2 Hen. VI.* i 2 69
I am not able to stand alone: You go about to torture me in vain . ii 1 145
'Twill go hard with you.—Let me alone . . . . . . iv 2 109
In this city will I stay And live alone as secret as I may . . iv 4 48
I have singled thee alone . . . . *3 Hen. VI.* ii 4 1
I am with thee here alone: This is the hand that stabb'd thy father ii 4 5
I challenge nothing but my dukedom, As being well content with that alone . . . . iv 7 24
I am myself alone. Clarence, beware; thou keep'st me from the light v 6 83
He that doth naught with her, excepting one, Were best he do it secretly, alone *Richard III.* i 1 100
Execute thy wrath in me alone, O, spare my guiltless wife and my poor children! . . . . i 4 71
He himself wander'd away alone, No man knows whither . . iv 4 514
Let it alone; my state now will but mock me . . *Hen. VIII.* ii 1 101
Have not alone Employ'd you where high profits might come home . iii 2 157
Let 'em alone, and draw the curtain close . . . . . . v 2 34
They say he is a very man per se, And stands alone *Troi. and Cres.* i 2 16
Were I alone to pass the difficulties And had as ample power . ii 2 139
Let these threats alone, Till accident or purpose bring you to't . iv 5 261
I'll fight with him alone: stand, Diomed.—He is my prize . . v 6 9
Hie you to your bands: Let us alone to guard Corioli . *Coriolanus* i 2 27
He is himself alone, To answer all the city . . . . . i 4 51
O, me alone! make you a sword of me? . . . . . . i 6 76
Alone I fought in your Corioli walls, And made what work I pleased i 8 8
We do it not alone, sir.—I know you can do very little alone . ii 1 37
Your abilities are too infant-like for doing much alone . . ii 1 41
Alone he enter'd The mortal gate of the city . . . . . ii 2 114
Though I go alone, Like to a lonely dragon . . . . . iv 1 29
I Flutter'd your Volscians in Corioli: Alone I did it . . . v 6 117
When wert thou wont to walk alone, Dishonour'd thus? *T. Andron.* i 1 339
Let me alone: I'll find a day to massacre them all . . . . i 1 449
I'll be at hand, sir; see you do it bravely.—I warrant you, sir, let me alone . . . . iv 3 114
I, measuring his affections by my own, That most are busied when they're most alone *Rom. and Jul.* i 1 134
And since that time it is eleven years; For then she could stand alone i 3 36
Gentle coz, let him alone; He bears him like a portly gentleman . i 5 67
That kind of fruit As maids call medlars, when they laugh alone . ii 1 36
You shall not stay alone Till holy church incorporate two in one . ii 6 36
Day, night, hour, tide, time, work, play, Alone, in company . . iii 5 179
Her tears; Which, too much minded by herself alone, May be put from her by society . . . . iv 1 13
My lord, we must entreat the time alone . . . . . . iv 1 40
To-morrow night look that thou lie alone; Let not thy nurse lie with thee . . . . iv 1 91
I'll not to bed to-night; let me alone; I'll play the housewife . . iv 2 42
Let me now be left alone, And let the nurse this night sit up with you iv 3 9

Alone. My dismal scene I needs must act alone. Come, vial *Rom. and Jul.* iv 3 19
Now must I to the monument alone . . . . v 2 23
I am almost afraid to stand alone Here in the churchyard . . v 3 10
I'll go alone. Fear comes upon me: O, much I fear some ill . v 3 135
Then all alone At the prefixed hour of her waking, Came I . . v 3 252
With his disease of all-shunn'd poverty, Walks, like contempt, alone *T. of Athens* iv 2 15
How dost thou pity him whom thou dost trouble? I had rather be alone . . . . iv 3 99
Thy saints for aye Be crown'd with plagues that thee alone obey! . v 1 56
All single and alone, Yet an arch-villain keeps him company . . v 1 110
So get the start of the majestic world And bear the palm alone *J. Cæsar* i 2 131
Is he alone?—No, sir, there are moe with him . . . . . ii 1 71
Good countrymen, let me depart alone, And, for my sake, stay here . iii 2 60
I do entreat you, not a man depart, Save I alone, till Antony have spoke . . . . iii 2 66
Revenge yourselves alone on Cassius, For Cassius is aweary of the world iv 3 94
There is some grudge between 'em, 'tis not meet They be alone . iv 3 126
To make society The sweeter welcome, we will keep ourself Till supper-time alone *Macbeth* iii 1 44
Why do you keep alone, Of sorriest fancies your companions making? . iii 2 8
The main part Pertains to you alone . . . . iv 3 199
'Tis not alone my inky cloak, good mother *Hamlet* i 2 77
For nature, crescent, does not grow alone In thews and bulk . . i 3 11
As if it some impartment did desire To you alone . . . . i 4 60
And thy commandment all alone shall live Within the book and volume of my brain . . . . i 5 102
Now I am alone. O, what a rogue and peasant slave am I! . . ii 2 575
Let his queen mother all alone entreat him To show his grief . . iii 1 190
The cease of majesty Dies not alone . . . . iii 3 16
Never alone Did the king sigh, but with a general groan . . . iii 3 22
I alone became their prisoner . . . . iv 6 19
And in a postscript here, he says, 'alone' . . . . . . iv 7 53
And find I am alone felicitate In your dear highness' love *Lear* i 1 77
The tyranny of the open night's too rough For nature to endure.—Let me alone . . . . iii 4 3
Who alone suffers suffers most i' the mind . . . . . . iii 6 111
Then away she started To deal with grief alone . . . . . iv 3 34
He's scarce awake: let him alone awhile . . . . iv 7 51
We two alone will sing like birds i' the cage . . . . . v 3 9
Give me advantage of some brief discourse With Desdemona alone *Oth.* iii 1 56
Your napkin is too little: Let it alone. Come, I'll go in with you . iii 3 288
How now! what do you here alone?—Do not you chide . . . iii 3 300
Leave procreants alone and shut the door; Cough, or cry 'hem,' if any body come . . . . iv 2 28
All alone To-night we'll wander through the streets *Ant. and Cleo.* i 1 52
And Antony . . . did sit alone, Whistling to the air . . . ii 2 220
The music, ho!—Let it alone; let's to billiards . . . . ii 5 3
The senators alone of this great world, Chief factors for the gods . ii 6 9
He alone Dealt on lieutenantry, and no practice had In the brave squares iii 11 38
Answer me declined, sword against sword, Ourselves alone . . iii 13 28
Our terrene moon Is now eclipsed; and it portends alone The fall of Antony! . . . . iii 13 154
I am alone the villain of the earth, And feel I am so most . . iv 6 30
Let him alone, for I remember now How he's employ'd . . . v 1 71
If she be furnish'd with a mind so rare, She is alone the Arabian bird *Cymbeline* i 6 17
Search What companies are near: pray you, away; Let me alone with him iv 2 70
Not Absolute madness could so far have raved To bring him here alone iv 2 136
Would I had done't, So the revenge alone pursued me! . . . iv 2 157
She alone knew this; And, but she spoke it dying, I would not Believe her lips in opening it . . . . v 5 40
He spake of her, as Dian had hot dreams, And she alone were cold . v 5 181
Let his arms alone; They were not born for bondage . . . . v 5 305
Why do you keep alone? How chance my daughter is not with you? *Pericles* iv 1 22
Care not for me; I can go home alone . . . . iv 1 43

Along. This is the gentleman I told your ladyship Had come along with me . . . . *T. G. of Ver.* ii 4 88
My foolish rival . . . Is gone with her along, and I must after . ii 4 176
In what habit will you go along?—Not like a woman . . . ii 7 39
Though not for thyself, Regard thy danger, and along with me! . iii 1 256
I give consent to go along with you, Recking as little what betideth me iv 3 39
As we walk along, I dare be bold With our discourse to make your grace to smile . . . . v 4 162
I'll tell you as we pass along, That you will wonder what hath fortuned v 4 168
Boy, go along with this woman . . . . *Mer. Wives* ii 2 139
Which means she to deceive, father or mother?—Both, my good host, to go along with me . . . . iv 6 47
I am in haste; go along with me: I'll tell you all . . . . v 1 25
I have made him know I have a servant comes with me along *M. for Meas.* iv 1 46
Tarry; I'll go along with thee: I can tell thee pretty tales . . iv 3 174
Come, go along; my wife is coming yonder . . *Com. of Errors* iv 4 43
Along with them They brought one Pinch, a hungry lean-faced villain . v 1 237
Did point you to buy them, along as you pass'd . . *L. L. Lost* ii 1 245
Came nothing else along with that?—Nothing but this! . . . v 2 5
Travelling along this coast, I here am come by chance . . . v 2 557
Go along: I must employ you in some business . . *M. N. Dream* i 1 123
With him is Gratiano gone along . . . . . . *Mer. of Venice* ii 8 2
He did intreat me, past all saying nay, To come with him along . iii 2 233
Bring your true friend along . . . . iii 2 310
We stay'd her for your sake, Else had she with her father ranged along *As Y. Like It* i 3 70
Say what thou canst, I'll go along with thee . . . . . . i 3 107
So shall we pass along And never stir assailants . . . . . i 3 115
He'll go along o'er the wide world with me; Leave me alone to woo him i 3 134
As he lay along Under an oak whose antique root peeps out Upon the brook . . . . ii 1 30
Anon a careless herd, Full of the pasture, jumps along by him . ii 1 53
But come thy ways; we'll go along together . . . . . . ii 3 66
There lay he, stretched along, like a wounded knight . . . iii 2 253
And bring along these rascal knaves with thee . . . *T. of Shrew* iv 1 134
If along with us, We shall be joyful of thy company . . . . iv 5 51
Come, go along, and see the truth hereof . . . . iv 5 75
All as I would have had it, save that he comes not along with her *A. W.* iii 2 2
More I'll entreat you Written to bear along . . . . . . iii 2 98
Bring her along with you, it may awake my bounty further *T. Night* v 1 46
Enclosed in this trunk which you Shall bear along impawn'd *W. Tale* i 2 436
Our absence makes us unthrifty to our knowledge. Let's along . v 2 121
With him along is come the mother-queen . . . . . *K. John* ii 1 62

Along. Bear not along The clogging burthen of a guilty soul *Richard II.* i 3 199
Will you go along with us?—No; I will to Ireland to his majesty ii 2 140
And thus still doing, thus he pass'd along v 2 21
They will along with company, for they have great charge 1 *Hen. IV.* ii 1 50
Falstaff sweats to death, And lards the lean earth as he walks along ii 2 116
Who leads his power? Under whose government come they along? iv 1 19
I learn'd in Worcester, as I rode along, He cannot draw his power iv 1 125
Sirrah, with a new wound in your thigh, come you along with me v 4 131
Go along with me 2 *Hen. IV.* ii 1 191; *Lear* iv 3 57
As I came along, I met and overtook a dozen captains 2 *Hen. IV.* ii 4 386
Please your grace to go along with us?—No; I will sit and watch iv 5 19
Carry Sir John Falstaff to the Fleet: Take all his company along with him v 5 98
If they march along Unfought withal, but I will sell my dukedom *Hen. V.* iii 5 11
And like a peacock sweep along his tail 1 *Hen. VI.* iii 3 6
Methinks I should not thus be led along, Mail'd up in shame 2 *Hen. VI.* ii 4 30
Mischance and sorrow go along with you! iii 2 300
And still proclaimeth, as he comes along, His arms are only to remove from thee The Duke of Somerset iv 9 28
To intercept the queen, Bearing the king in my behalf along 3 *Hen. VI.* ii 1 115
King of England shalt thou be proclaim'd In every borough as we pass along ii 1 195
Therefore hence amain.—Away! for vengeance comes along with them ii 5 134
Your crown content and you must be contented To go along with us iii 1 68
Widow, go you along. Lords, use her honourably iii 2 123
Wilt thou go along?—Better do so than tarry and be hang'd iv 5 25
And lo, where George of Clarence sweeps along v 1 76
Our strength will be augmented In every county as we go along v 3 23
My lord, will't please you pass along? *Richard III.* iii 1 136
And, see, he brings the mayor along iii 5 13
I am thankful to you; and I'll go along By your prescription *Hen. VIII.* i 1 150
My barge stays; Your lordship shall along ii 1 64
With thy approach, I know, My comfort comes along ii 4 241
As he pass'd along, How earnestly he cast his eyes upon me! v 2 11
Put on A form of strangeness as we pass along *Troi. and Cres.* iii 3 51
Tie his body to my horse's tail; Along the field I will the Trojan trail v 8 22
He goes Upon this present action.—Let's along *Coriolanus* i 1 283
Turn thy solemness out o' door, and go along with us i 3 121
Will you along?—We stay here for the people ii 3 157
Be gone, beseech you.—Come, sir, along with us iii 1 237
Yet, for I loved thee, Take this along; I writ it for thy sake v 2 96
When he lies along, After your way his tale pronounced shall bury His reasons with his body v 6 57
Till from forth this place I lead espoused my bride along with me *T. A.* i 1 328
Along with me: I'll see what hole is here ii 3 246
Nay, come, agree whose hand shall go along, For fear they die iii 1 175
I'll come and be thy waggoner, And whirl along with thee about the globe v 2 49
Now will I hence about thy business, And take my ministers along v 2 133
All the rest depart away: You, Capulet, shall go along with me *R. and J.* i 1 106
Soft! I will go along; An if you leave me so, you do me wrong i 1 201
I'll go along, no such sight to be shown, But to rejoice in splendour of mine own i 2 105
Under yond yew-trees lay thee all along v 3 3
Take the bonds along with you, And have the dates in compt *T. of A.* ii 1 34
Not One friend to take his fortune by the arm, And go along with him! iv 2 8
Know I these men that come along with you? *J. Cæsar* ii 1 89
Go along by him: He loves me well, and I have given him reasons ii 1 218
Here will I stand till Cæsar pass along, And as a suitor will I give him this ii 3 11
And there Speak to great Cæsar as he comes along ii 4 38
How many times shall Cæsar bleed in sport, That now on Pompey's basis lies along No worthier than the dust! iii 1 115
Stand, ho! Speak the word along.—Stand! iv 2 33
The enemy, marching along by them, By them shall make a fuller number up iv 3 207
Go on; We'll along ourselves, and meet them v 3 225
I have entreated him along With us to watch *Hamlet* i 1 26
Nor have we herein barr'd Your better wisdoms, which have freely gone With this affair along i 2 16
He to England shall along with you iii 3 4
Get good guard and go along with me.—Pray you, l· l on *Othello* i 1 180
Come, stand not amazed at it, but go along with me iv 2 246
Makes her desire—Which who shall cross?—along to go *Per.* iii Gower 41
Alonso. Thee of thy son, Alonso, They have bereft *Tempest* iii 3 75
Most cruelly Didst thou, Alonso, use me and my daughter v 1 72
Aloof. Hence, away! now all is well: One aloof stand sentinel *M. N. Dr.* ii 2 26
Nerissa and the rest, stand all aloof. Let music sound *Mer. of Venice* iii 2 42
The rest aloof are the Dardanian wives, With bleared visages iii 2 58
Stand you a while aloof *T. Night* i 4 12
We of the offering side Must keep aloof from strict arbitrement 1 *Hen. IV.* iv 1 70
Turn on the bloody hounds with heads of steel And make the cowards stand aloof at bay 1 *Hen. VI.* iv 2 52
Keep off aloof with worthless emulation iv 4 21
Now the matter grows to compromise, Stand'st thou aloof upon comparison? v 4 150
Shakes his head and trembling stands aloof, While all is shared and all is borne away 2 *Hen. VI.* i 1 227
The rest stand all aloof, and bark at him 3 *Hen. VI.* ii 1 17
Stand all aloof: but, uncle, draw you near *T. Andron.* v 3 151
Give me thy torch, boy: hence, and stand aloof *Rom. and Jul.* v 3 1
Whate'er thou hear'st or seest, stand all aloof, And do not interrupt me v 3 26
He came with flowers to strew his lady's grave; And bid me stand aloof v 3 282
With a crafty madness, keeps aloof, When we would bring him on to some confession Of his true state *Hamlet* iii 1 8
But in my terms of honour I stand aloof v 2 258
Love's not love When it is mingled with regards that stand Aloof from the entire point *Lear* i 1 243
You have heard something of my power, and so stand aloof *Pericles* iv 6 95
Aloud. I'll tell the world aloud What man thou art *Meas. for Meas.* ii 4 153
I say my prayers aloud.—I love you the better *Much Ado* ii 1 108
When all aloud the wind doth blow *L. L. Lost* v 2 931
The spirit of humours intimate reading aloud to him! *T. Night* ii 5 94
I tore them from their bonds and cried aloud *K. John* iii 4 70
I will tell thee aloud, 'England is thine, Ireland is thine' *Hen. V.* v 2 258
Why ring not out the bells aloud throughout the town? 1 *Hen. VI.* i 6 11
I am sent to tell his majesty That even now he cries aloud for him 2 *Hen. VI.* iii 2 378
Ring, bells, aloud; burn, bonfires, clear and bright v 1 3
Aloud. He squeak'd out aloud, 'Clarence is come' *Richard III.* i 4 54
Let him know, What Troy means fairly shall be spoke aloud *Tr. and Cr.* i 3 259
These moral laws Of nature and of nations speak aloud To have her back ii 2 185
The advantage of the time prompts me aloud To call for recompense iii 3 2
Bondage is hoarse, and may not speak aloud *Rom. and Jul.* ii 2 161
Romeo he cries aloud, 'Hold, friends! friends, part!' iii 1 169
Whose voices I desire aloud with mine *Macbeth* v 8 58
He was met even now As mad as the vex'd sea; singing aloud *Lear* iv 4 2
Here is her father's house; I'll call aloud *Othello* i 1 74
Methinks the wind hath spoke aloud at land ii 1 5
Like a boy, you see him cringe his face, And whine aloud *Ant. and Cleo.* iii 13 101
So far I read aloud: But even the very middle of my heart Is warm'd by the rest *Cymbeline* i 6 26
Come, stand thou by our side; Make thy demand aloud v 5 130
Alphabet. Nor make a sign, But I of these will wrest an alphabet *T. A.* iii 2 44
Alphabetical. What should that alphabetical position portend? *T. Night* ii 5 130
Alphonso. Don Alphonso With other gentlemen of good esteem *T. G. of Ver.* i 3 39
Alps. Talking of the Alps and Apennines, The Pyrenean *K. John* i 1 202
Were I tied to run afoot Even to the frozen ridges of the Alps *Richard II.* i 1 64
Whose low vassal seat The Alps doth spit and void his rheum upon *Hen. V.* iii 5 52
On the Alps It is reported thou didst eat strange flesh *Ant. and Cleo.* i 4 66
Already. Twenty to one then he is shipp'd already *T. G. of Ver.* i 1 72
My ears are stopt and cannot hear good news, So much of bad already hath possess'd them iii 1 206
I have fed upon this woe already, And now excess of it will make me surfeit iii 1 219
You are already Love's firm votary And cannot soon revolt iii 2 58
Already have I been false to Valentine iv 2 1
He is dead already, if he be come *Mer. Wives* ii 3 9
'Tis past eight already, sir ii 5 134
Is he at Master Ford's already, think'st thou? iv 1 1
Has censured him Already *Meas. for Meas.* i 4 73
To be shortly of a sisterhood, If not already ii 2 22
That hath from nature stolen A man already made ii 4 44
The image of it gives me content already iii 1 270
Already he hath carried Notice to Escalus and Angelo iv 3 134
You have told me too many of him already, sir iv 3 177
I have already delivered him letters *Much Ado* i 1 20
I am here already, sir.—I know that; but I would have thee hence ii 3 5
The old ornament of his cheek hath already stuffed tennis-balls iii 2 47
It is proved already that you are little better than false knaves iv 2 23
I have already sworn, That is, to live and study here three years *L. L. L.* i 1 34
She hath one o' my sonnets already: the clown bore it, the fool sent it iv 3 16
Already to their wormy beds are gone *M. N. Dream* iii 2 384
He dares not come there for the candle; for, you see, it is already in snuff v 1 254
She hath spied him already with those sweet eyes v 1 328
My people do already know my mind *Mer. of Venice* iii 4 37
A quarrel, ho, already! what's the matter?—About a hoop of gold v 1 146
They say he is already in the forest of Arden *As Y. Like It* i 1 120
I have done already: The blushes in my cheeks thus whisper me *A. W.* ii 3 74
I am a youth of fourteen; I have known thee already ii 3 108
There's four or five, to great Saint Jaques bound, Already at my house iii 5 99
I'll add three thousand crowns To what is past already iii 7 36
I have told your lordship already, the stocks carry him iv 3 121
Thou hast spoken all already, unless thou canst say they are married iv 3 268
He hath known you but three days, and already you are no stranger *T. N.* i 4 4
Look you now, he's out of his guard already i 5 93
She is drowned already, sir, with salt water ii 1 31
My niece is already in the belief that he's mad iii 4 149
Gone already! Inch-thick, knee-deep! *W. Tale* i 2 185
They're here with me already, whispering, rounding 'Sicilia is a so-forth' i 2 217
We'll none on't: here has been too much homely foolery already iv 4 341
Which I have given already, But not deliver'd iv 4 370
Dispatch: the gentleman is half flayed already iv 4 655
Already appearing in the blossoms of their fortune v 2 135
Would I were dead, but that, methinks, already—What was he? v 3 62
If that young Arthur be not gone already, Even at that news he dies *K. John* iii 4 163
It is in a manner done already v 7 89
That blood already, like the pelican, Hast thou tapp'd out *Richard II.* ii 1 126
Depress'd he is already, and deposed 'Tis doubt he will be iii 4 68
I'll be · brave judge.—Thou judgest false already 1 *Hen. IV.* i 2 74
See already how he doth begin To make us strangers to his looks of love i 3 289
They are up already, and call for eggs and butter ii 1 65
Are they not some of them set forward already? ii 2 31
They take it already upon their salvation ii 4 9
I thought your honour had already been at Shrewsbury iv 2 58
'Tis more than time that I were there, and you too; but my powers are there already iv 2 62
To steal cream indeed, for thy theft hath already made thee butter iv 2 67
Make haste; Percy is already in the field iv 2 81
She is in hell already, and burns poor souls 2 *Hen. IV.* ii 4 365
The powers that you already have sent forth Shall bring this prize in iii 1 100
We have sent forth already.—'Tis well done iv 1 5
Our army is dispersed already: Like youthful steers unyoked iv 2 102
I have him already tempering between my finger and my thumb iv 3 140
Falstaff shall die of a sweat, unless already a' be killed with your hard opinions Epil. 32
He is footed in this land already *Hen. V.* ii 4 143
Your ships already are in readiness 1 *Hen. VI.* i 1 186
'Tis known already that I am possess'd With more than half the Gallian territories, And therein reverenced v 4 138
He hath learnt so much fence already 2 *Hen. VI.* ii 3 79
Methinks already in this civil broil I see them lording it in London streets iv 8 46
If mine arm be heaved in the air, Thy grave is digg'd already in the earth iv 10 55
Hear me speak.—Thou hast spoke too much already 3 *Hen. VI.* i 1 258
Is he dead already? or is it fear That makes him close his eyes? i 3 10
We, the sons of brave Plantagenet, Each one already blazing by our meeds ii 1 36
They are already, or quickly will be landed iv 1 132
Bid me kill myself, and I will do it.—I have already *Richard III.* i 2 188
Imagine I have said farewell already i 2 225
Hath she forgot already that brave prince, Edward, her lord? i 2 240
My life is spann'd already: I am the shadow of poor Buckingham *Hen. VIII.* i 1 223

Already. It hath already publicly been read, And on all sides the authority allow'd *Hen. VIII.* ii 4 3
Alas, has banish'd me his bed already, His love, too long ago! iii 1 119
You shall sustain moe new disgraces, With these you bear already iii 2 6
The king already Hath married the fair lady iii 2 41
Master O' the jewel house, And one, already, of the privy council iv 1 112
The trumpets sound; They're come already from the christening v 4 87
But he already is too insolent *Troi. and Cres.* i 3 369
That were to enlard his fat already pride And add more coals to Cancer ii 3 205
Behold thy fill.—Nay, I have done already.—Thou art too brief iv 5 236
Will you undo yourselves?—We cannot, sir, we are undone already *Cor.* i 1 66
Fame, at the which he aims, In whom already he's well graced i 1 268
Some parcels of their power are forth already, And only hitherward i 2 32
Distinctly billeted, already in the entertainment iv 3 48
We have nothing else to ask, but that Which you deny already v 3 89
How now! has sorrow made thee dote already? *T. Andron.* iii 2 23
Younger than you . . . Are made already mothers *Rom. and Jul.* i 3 71
The envious moon, Who is already sick and pale with grief ii 2 5
He is already dead; stabbed with a white wench's black eye ii 4 13
I already know thy grief; It strains me past the compass of my wits iv 1 46
Make haste; the bridegroom he is come already: Make haste, I say iv 4 26
I am so far already in your gifts,—So are we all *T. of Athens* i 2 178
There's the fool hangs on your back already ii 2 57
I have moved already Some certain of the noblest-minded Romans *J. C.* i 3 121
Three parts of him Is ours already i 3 155
I have slept, my lord, already.—It was well done iv 3 263
He is already named, and gone to Scone To be invested *Macbeth* ii 4 31
The rest That are within the note of expectation Already are i' the court iii 3 11
My soul is too much charged With blood of thine already v 8 6
We have sworn, my lord, already.—Indeed, upon my sword, indeed *Ham.* i 5 147
They have already order This night to play before him iii 1 20
Those that are married already, all but one, shall live iii 1 155
What to this was sequent Thou know'st already v 2 55
His purse is empty already; all's golden words are spent v 2 136
Who already, Wise in our negligence, have secret feet In some of our best ports *Lear* iii 1 31
There's part of a power already footed iii 3 14
'Certes,' says he, 'I have already chose my officer' *Othello* i 1 17
This accident is not unlike my dream: Belief of it oppresses me already i 1 144
Which, but thou hast already, with all my heart I would keep from thee i 3 194
A pestilent complete knave; and the woman hath found him already ii 1 253
If I can fasten but one cup upon him, With that which he hath drunk to-night already ii 3 51
'Fore God, they have given me a rouse already.—Good faith, a little one ii 3 67
The Moor already changes with my poison iii 3 325
Look, how he laughs already!—I never knew woman love man so iv 1 110
To put up in peace what already I have foolishly suffered iv 2 181
Will Cæsar speak?—Not till he hears how Antony is touch'd With what is spoke already *Ant. and Cleo.* ii 2 143
Some o' their plants are ill-rooted already ii 7 2
Queasy with his insolence Already, will their good thoughts call from him iii 6 21
This should be answer'd.—'Tis done already, and the messenger gone iii 6 31
He is already Traduced for levity iii 7 13
Six kings already Show me the way of yielding iii 10 34
I have spoke already, and it is provided; Go put it to the haste v 2 195
The paper Hath cut her throat already *Cymbeline* iii 4 35
I see into thy end, and am almost A man already iii 4 170
Fore-thinking this, I have already fit . . . doublet, hat, hose iii 4 171
Lucius hath wrote already to the emperor How it goes here iii 5 21
To beat us down, the which are down already *Pericles* i 4 68

Also. And also, I think, thou art not ignorant *T. G. of Ver.* iii 2 25
And there is also another device in my prain *Mer. Wives* i 1 43
I most fehemently desire you you will also look that way iii 1 9
I will be like a jack-an-apes also, to burn the knight with my taber iv 4 67
Because I know also life is a shuttle v 1 24
You were also, Jupiter, a swan for the love of Leda v 5 7
You shall also make no noise in the streets *Much Ado* iii 3 35
And also, the watch heard them talk of one Deformed v 1 316
The roynish clown, at whom so oft Your grace was wont to laugh, is also missing *As Y. Like It* ii 2 9
Her brother, Who shortly also died *T. Night* i 2 39
It will also be the bondage of certain ribbons and gloves *W. Tale* iv 4 235
I do not only marvel where thou spendest thy time, but also how thou art accompanied 1 *Hen. IV.* ii 4 440
Not in words only, but in woes also ii 4 459
To the infernal deep, with Erebus and tortures vile also 2 *Hen. IV.* ii 4 171
Let vultures vile seize on his lungs also! v 3 146
Also King Lewis the Tenth, Who was sole heir to the usurper Capet *Hen. V.* i 2 77
By his bloody side . . . The noble Earl of Suffolk also lies iv 6 10
There is a river in Macedon; and there is also moreover a river at Monmouth iv 7 28
And also being a little intoxicates in his prains iv 7 39
So also Harry Monmouth, being in his right wits and his good judgements iv 7 48
The good time of day to you, sir.—I also wish it to you *T. of Athens* iii 6 2
But are not some whole that we must make sick?—That must we also *J. Cæsar* ii 1 329
Of that I shall have also cause to speak *Hamlet* v 2 402
The duke himself also and your daughter *Lear* i 4 66

Altar. I'll have the cudgel hallowed and hung o'er the altar *Mer. Wives* iv 2 217
Say that upon the altar of her beauty You sacrifice your tears *T. G. of Ver.* iii 2 73
On Diana's altar to protest For aye austerity and single life *M. N. Dream* i 1 89
Now, Dian, from thy altar do I fly *All's Well* ii 3 80
To whose ingrate and unauspicious altars My soul the faithfull'st offerings hath breathed out *T. Night* v 1 116
On that altar where we swore to you Dear amity and everlasting love *K. John* v 4 19
The mailed Mars shall on his altar sit Up to the ears in blood 1 *Hen. IV.* iv 1 116
Rest your minds in peace: Let's to the altar 1 *Hen. VI.* i 1 45
With modest paces Came to the altar *Hen. VIII.* iv 1 83
To come as humbly as they used to creep To holy altars *Troi. and Cres.* iii 3 74
To his hand when I deliver her, Think it an altar, and thy brother Troilus A priest there offering to it his own heart iv 3 8
Laud we the gods; And let our crooked smokes climb to their nostrils From our blest altars *Cymbeline* v 5 478
Hie thee thither, And do upon mine altar sacrifice *Pericles* v 1 242
If you have told Diana's altar true, This is your wife v 3 17

Alter. So thou shouldst not alter the article of thy gentry *Mer. Wives* ii 1 53
In the meantime let me be that I am and seek not to alter me *Much Ado* i 3 39
Doth not the appetite alter? a man loves the meat in his youth that he cannot endure in his age *Much Ado* ii 3 247
And thorough this distemperature we see The seasons alter *M. N. Dream* ii 1 107
Good night, sweet friend: Thy love ne'er alter till thy sweet life end! ii 2 61
There is no power in Venice Can alter a decree established *Mer. of Venice* iv 1 219
There is no power in the tongue of man To alter me iv 1 242
She that would alter services with thee *T. Night* ii 5 172
There is not in the world either malice or matter to alter it *W. Tale* i 1 37
Whose fresh complexion and whose heart together Affliction alters iv 4 586
Alter not the doom Forethought by heaven! *K. John* iii 1 311
Let no man speak again To alter this, for counsel is but vain *Richard II.* iii 2 214
Augment, or alter, as your wisdoms best Shall see advantageable *Hen. V.* v 2 87
The emperor thus desired, That he would please to alter the king's course *Hen. VIII.* i 1 189
Is't possible that so short a time can alter the condition of a man? *Coriol.* v 4 9
Look up clear; To alter favour ever is to fear *Macbeth* i 5 73
Thither, gentle mariner, Alter thy course *Pericles* iii 1 76

Alteration. For I must be A party in this alteration *W. Tale* i 2 383
Your more ponderous and settled project May suffer alteration iv 4 536
And changes fill the cup of alteration With divers liquors 2 *Hen. IV.* iii 1 52
Doth this churlish superscription Pretend some alteration? 1 *Hen. VI.* iv 1 54
Here's a strange alteration! *Coriolanus* iv 5 154
What an alteration of honour Has desperate want made! *T. of Athens* iv 3 468
He's full of alteration And self-reproving *Lear* v 1 3
That the affrighted globe Should yawn at alteration *Othello* v 2 101

Altered. Life is alter'd now: I have done penance for contemning Love *T. G. of Ver.* ii 4 128
My brother Angelo will not be altered; Claudio must die *Meas. for Meas.* iii 2 220
How now, sir! is your merry humour alter'd? *Com. of Errors* ii 2 7
Would we had so ended! but you, sir, altered that *T. Night* ii 1 22
'No man must know.' What follows? the numbers altered! ii 5 112
I must be A party in this alteration, finding Myself thus alter'd with 't *W. Tale* i 2 384
I am but sorry, not afeard; delay'd, But nothing alter'd iv 4 475
Our scene is alter'd from a serious thing *Richard II.* v 3 79
I'll not have it alter'd.—Will not you?—No, nor you shall not 1 *Hen. IV.* iii 1 116
Tell it him.—He alter'd much upon the hearing it 2 *Hen. IV.* iv 5 13
Observe The strangeness of his alter'd countenance 2 *Hen. VI.* iii 1 5
Thou call'dst me king.—Ay, but the case is alter'd 3 *Hen. VI.* iv 3 31
'Tis so lately alter'd, that the old name Is fresh about me *Hen. VIII.* iv 1 98
Do you note How much her grace is alter'd on the sudden? iv 2 96
The times and titles now are alter'd strangely With me iv 2 112
Methinks thy voice is alter'd *Lear* iv 6 7
Nor should I know him, Were he in favour as in humour alter'd *Othello* iii 4 125
Who was he That, otherwise than noble nature did, Hath alter'd that good picture? *Cymbeline* iv 2 365
Had I brought hither a corrupted mind, Thy speech had alter'd it *Pericles* iv 6 112

Altering. Is he not stupid With age and altering rheums? *W. Tale* iv 4 410

Althæa. Away, you rascally Althæa's dream, away! 2 *Hen. IV.* ii 2 93
Althæa dreamed she was delivered of a fire-brand ii 2 96
The fatal brand Althæa burn'd Unto the prince's heart of Calydon 2 *Hen. VI.* i 1 234

Although. Doth very foolishly, although he smart, Not to seem senseless of the bob *As Y. Like It* ii 7 54
Although the sheet were big enough for the bed of Ware *T. Night* iii 2 50
Although the print be little, the whole matter And copy of the father *W. Tale* ii 3 98
Although my will to give is living, The suit which you demand is gone and dead *K. John* iv 2 83
Speak sweetly, man, although thy looks be sour *Richard II.* iii 2 193
No better than an earl, Although in glorious titles he excel 1 *Hen. VI.* v 5 38
Although by his sight his sin be multiplied 2 *Hen. VI.* ii 1 71
Better than I fare, Although thou hast been conduct of my shame ii 4 101
Although the duke was enemy to him, Yet he most Christian-like laments his death iii 2 57
Although the kite soar with unbloodied beak iii 2 193
Although my head still wear the crown, I here resign 3 *Hen. VI.* iv 6 23
I stay dinner there.—And supper too, although thou know'st it not *Richard III.* iii 2 123

Altitude. Which he is, even to the altitude of his virtue *Coriolanus* i 1 40
Your ladyship is nearer to heaven than when I saw you last, by the altitude of a chopine *Hamlet* ii 2 446
Ten masts at each make not the altitude Which thou hast perpendicularly fell *Lear* iv 6 53

Altogether. Yet I am not altogether an ass *Mer. Wives* i 1 175
A 'oman that altogether's acquaintance with Mistress Anne Page i 2 8
My wife, master doctor, is for you altogether iii 2 64
A thing of his own search and altogether against my will *As Y. Like It* i 1 142
I am altogether misprised: but it shall not be so long i 1 177
I perceive, by this demand, you are not altogether of his council *All's Well* iv 3 53
Not altogether so great as the first in goodness, but greater a great deal in evil iv 3 319
I delight in masques and revels sometimes altogether *T. Night* i 3 121
Apollo be my judge!—This your request Is altogether just *W. Tale* iii 2 118
If of joy, being altogether wanting, It doth remember me the more of sorrow; Or if of grief, being altogether had, It adds more sorrow to my want of joy *Richard II.* iii 4 13
You are altogether governed by humours 1 *Hen. IV.* iii 1 237
But thou art altogether given over iii 3 40
Is altogether directed by an Irishman, a very valiant gentleman *Hen. V.* iii 2 70
I am she, and altogether joyless. I can no longer hold me patient *Richard III.* i 3 156
Much more gentle, and altogether more tractable *Troi. and Cres.* ii 3 160
Thou are not altogether a fool.—Nor thou altogether a wise man *T. of Athens* ii 2 122
We have reformed that indifferently with us, sir.—O, reform it altogether *Hamlet* iii 2 42
This is not altogether fool, my lord *Lear* i 4 165
Not altogether so: I look'd not for you yet, nor am provided ii 4 234
It was not altogether your brother's evil disposition made him seek his death iii 5 6
Altogether lacks the abilities That Rhodes is dress'd in *Othello* i 3 25
My quarrel was not altogether slight *Cymbeline* i 4 51

Always. They always use to laugh at nothing *Tempest* ii 1 175
Yet always bending Towards their project iv 1 174
You always end ere you begin *T. G. of Ver.* ii 4 31
I reckon this always, that a man is never undone till he be hanged ii 5 4
You would have them always play but one thing?—I would always have one play but one thing iv 2 70

Always. I thank you always with my heart . . . *Mer. Wives* i 1 85
There they always use to discharge their birding-pieces . . . . iv 2 58
I will never take you for my love again; but I will always count you my deer . . . . v 5 122
Always obedient to your grace's will, I come to know your pleasure *Meas. for Meas.* i 1 26
Thou art always figuring diseases in me . . . . . . i 2 53
Which sorrow is always toward ourselves, not heaven . . . ii 3 32
I am always bound to you . . . . iv 1 25
Before the always wind-obeying deep . . . *Com. of Errors* i 1 64
One that thinks a man always going to bed and says, 'God give you good rest!' . . . . iv 3 32
You always end with a jade's trick: I know you of old . *Much Ado* i 1 145
You have been always called a merciful man . . . . iii 3 64
Always hath been just and virtuous In any thing that I do know by her v 1 311
Why, shall I always keep below stairs? . . . . . v 2 10
Justice always whirls in equal measure . . . . *L. L. Lost* iv 3 384
By Jove, I always took three threes for nine . . . . v 2 495
I was always plain with you, and so now I speak . *Mer. of Venice* iii 5 4
For always the dulness of the fool is the whetstone of the wits *As Y. L. It* i 2 57
He would always say—Methinks I hear him now . . *All's Well* i 2 52
I am a woodland fellow, sir, that always loved a great fire . iv 5 49
For that's it that always makes a good voyage of nothing . *T. Night* ii 4 80
Give us better credit: We have always truly served you . *W. Tale* ii 3 148
To whose venom sound The open ear of youth doth always listen *Richard II.* ii 1 20
He is just and always loved us well . . . . . . ii 1 221
The king will always think him in our debt . . . *1 Hen. IV.* i 3 286
She would always say she could not abide Master Shallow *2 Hen. IV.* iii 2 214
O, give me always a little, lean, old, chapt, bald shot . . iii 2 294
They do always reason themselves out again . . . *Hen. V.* v 2 165
For soldiers' stomachs always serve them well . . *1 Hen. VI.* ii 3 80
But always resolute in most extremes . . . . . iv 1 38
I always thought It was both impious and unnatural . . . v 1 11
Justice with favour have I always done . . . *2 Hen. VI.* iv 7 72
Happy always was it for that son Whose father for his hoarding went to hell? . . . . *3 Hen. VI.* ii 2 47
Commanded always by the greater gust . . . . . iii 1 88
Edward will always bear himself as king . . . . . iv 3 45
Suspicion always haunts the guilty mind . . . . . v 6 11
O, may such purple tears be alway shed! . . . . . v 6 64
The benefit thereof is always granted . . . . *Richard III.* iii 1 48
I know your majesty has always loved her So dear in heart *Hen. VIII.* ii 2 110
I thank you; You are always my good friend . . . . v 3 59
One that hath always loved the people . . . . *Coriolanus* i 1 53
Those senators That always favour'd him . . . . . iii 3 8
But he was always good enough for him . . . . . iv 5 193
Always factionary on the party of your general . . . . v 2 30
We always have confess'd it.—Ho, ho, confess'd it! . *T. of Athens* i 2 21
I do not always follow lover, elder brother, and woman . . ii 2 130
I have noted thee always wise . . . . iii 1 33
I have observed thee always for a towardly prompt spirit . . iii 1 36
To vex thee.—Always a villain's office or a fool's . . . iv 3 237
I rather tell thee what is to be fear'd Than what I fear; for always I am Cæsar . . . . *J. Cæsar* i 2 212
Always thought That I require a clearness . . . *Macbeth* iii 1 132
Sleeping within my orchard, My custom always of the afternoon *Hamlet* i 5 60
It did always seem so to us . . . . *Lear* i 1 3
He always loved our sister most . . . . i 1 293
Always reserved my holy duty . . . . . *Cymbeline* i 1 87
I told you always, her beauty and her brain go not together . i 2 31
Always excepted. The only man of Italy, Always excepted my dear Claudio . . . . *Much Ado* iii 1 93
Amaimon sounds well; Lucifer, well; Barbason, well *Mer. Wives* ii 2 311
He of Wales, that gave Amamon the bastinado . *1 Hen. IV.* ii 4 370
Amain. Come and sport: her peacocks fly amain . . *Tempest* iv 1 74
We discovered Two ships from far making amain to us . *Com. of Errors* i 1 93
The ship is under sail, and here she comes amain . *L. L. Lost* v 2 549
Cried out amain And rush'd into the bowels of the battle *1 Hen. VI.* i 1 128
Great lords, from Ireland am I come amain . . *2 Hen. VI.* iii 1 282
Call hither Clifford; bid him come amain . . . . v 1 114
To London will we march amain . . . . *3 Hen. VI.* ii 1 182
Forslow no longer, make we hence amain . . . . . ii 3 56
Mount you, my lord; towards Berwick post amain . . . ii 5 128
And therefore hence amain.—Away! for vengeance comes along . ii 5 133
Doth march amain to London; And many giddy people flock to him iv 8 4
Brave warriors, march amain towards Coventry . . . . iv 8 64
Cry you all amain, 'Achilles hath the mighty Hector slain' *Tr. and Cr.* v 8 13
They hither march amain, under conduct Of Lucius . *T. Andron.* iv 4 65
A-making. The feast is sold That is not often vouch'd, while 'tis a-making, 'Tis given with welcome . . . . *Macbeth* iii 4 34
Extinct in both, Even in their promise, as it is a-making *Hamlet* i 3 119
A many. In the forest of Arden, and a many merry men with him *As Y. Like It* i 1 121
Jet did he never see.—But cloaks and gowns, before this day, a many *2 Hen. VI.* ii 1 115
Amaze. That cannot choose but amaze him . . . *Mer. Wives* v 3 18
You do amaze her: hear the truth of it . . . . . v 5 233
You amaze me: I would have thought her spirit had been invincible *Much Ado* ii 3 118
His face's own margent did quote such amazes . . *L. L. Lost* ii 1 246
You amaze me, ladies . . . . *As Y. Like It* i 2 115
Make up, Lest your retirement do amaze your friends . *1 Hen. IV.* v 4 6
It would amaze the proudest of you all . . . *1 Hen. VI.* iv 7 84
Amaze the welkin with your broken staves! . . *Richard III.* v 3 341
Ye gods, it doth amaze me A man of such a feeble temper should So get the start of the majestic world . . . . *J. Cæsar* i 2 128
And amaze indeed The very faculties of eyes and ears . *Hamlet* ii 2 591
Be like a beacon fired to amaze your eyes . . . . *Pericles* i 4 87
Amazed. Be not amazed; call all your senses to you . *Mer. Wives* iii 3 125
If he be not amazed, he will be mocked; if he be amazed, he will every way be mocked . . . . v 3 19
Stand not amazed; here is no remedy . . . . . . v 5 244
Yet you are amazed; but this shall absolutely resolve you *Meas. for Meas.* iv 2 224
I am more amazed at his dishonour Than at the strangeness of it . v 1 385
That I amazed ran from her as a witch . . . *Com. of Errors* iii 2 149
Amazed, my lord? why looks your highness sad? . *L. L. Lost* v 2 391
I am amazed at your passionate words. I scorn you not *M. N. Dream* iii 2 220
I am amazed, and know not what to say . . . . . iii 2 344
You are all amazed: Here is a letter; read it . . *Mer. of Venice* v 1 266

Amazed. There I stood amazed for a while, As on a pillory *T. of Shrew* iii 1 156
And swore so loud, That, all-amazed, the priest let fall the book . iii 2 163
That with your strange encounter much amazed me . . . iv 5 54
Hath amazed me more Than I dare blame my weakness . *All's Well* ii 1 87
You stand amazed; But be of comfort . . . . . *T. Night* iii 4 371
Be not amazed; right noble is his blood . . . . . v 1 271
Behold, the French amazed vouchsafe a parle . . . *K. John* ii 1 226
Why stand these royal fronts amazed thus? . . . . . ii 1 356
I was amazed Under the tide: but now I breathe again Aloft the flood iv 2 137
I am amazed, methinks, and lose my way Among the thorns and dangers of this world . . . . iv 3 140
Makes me more amazed Than had I seen the vaulty top of heaven . v 2 51
We are amazed; and thus long have we stood . . *Richard II.* iii 3 72
Strike him, Aumerle. Poor boy, thou art amazed . . . v 2 85
Be not amazed, there's nothing hid from me . . . *1 Hen. VI.* i 2 6
No power to speak, sir.—What, amazed At my misfortunes? *Hen. VIII.* iii 2 373
You are amazed, my liege, at her exclaim . . *Troi. and Cres.* v 3 91
Stand not amazed: the prince will doom thee death . *Rom. and Jul.* iii 1 139
Thou hast amazed me: by my holy order, I thought thy disposition better temper'd . . . . iii 3 114
Where is Antony?—Fled to his house amazed . . . *J. Cæsar* iii 1 96
Who can be wise, amazed, temperate and furious, Loyal and neutral, in a moment? No man . . . . *Macbeth* ii 3 114
My mind she has mated, and amazed my sight. I think, but dare not speak . . . . v 1 86
It would have much amazed you.—Very like, very like . *Hamlet* i 2 236
How do you, sir? Stand you not so amazed . . . *Lear* iv 6 35
Do deeds to make heaven weep, all earth amazed . . *Othello* iii 3 371
Stand not amazed at it, but go along with me . . . . iv 2 246
I am amazed with matter . . . . *Cymbeline* iv 3 28
Amazedly. I shall reply amazedly, Half sleep, half waking *M. N. Dr.* iv 1 151
I speak amazedly; and it becomes My marvel and my message *W. Tale* v 1 187
All this is so: but why Stands Macbeth thus amazedly? *Macbeth* iv 1 126
Amazedness. We too in great amazedness will fly *Mer. Wives* iv 4 55
After a little amazedness, we were all commanded out of the chamber *W. Tale* v 2 5
Amazement. Be collected: No more amazement . . *Tempest* i 2 14
In every cabin I flamed amazement . . . . i 2 198
All torment, trouble, wonder, and amazement Inhabits here . . v 1 104
Put not yourself into amazement how these things should be *M. for Meas.* iv 2 220
All this amazement can I qualify . . . . . *Much Ado* v 4 67
Resolve you For more amazement . . . . . . *W. Tale* v 3 87
Wild amazement hurries up and down The little number of your doubtful friends . . . . *K. John* v 1 35
Will strike amazement to their drowsy spirits . *Troi. and Cres.* ii 2 210
Distraction, frenzy and amazement, Like witless antics, one another meet . . . . v 3 85
To the amazement of mine eyes That look'd upon't . . . *Macbeth* ii 4 19
Your behaviour hath struck her into amazement and admiration *Hamlet* iii 2 339
Amazement on thy mother sits: O, step between her and her fighting soul . . . . iii 4 112
Amazement shall drive courage from the state . . . *Pericles* i 2 26
Amazing. Let thy blows, doubly redoubled, Fall like amazing thunder on the casque Of thy adverse pernicious enemy . . *Richard II.* i 3 81
Amazon. The bouncing Amazon, Your buskin'd mistress *M. N. Dream* ii 1 70
Pale-visaged maids Like Amazons come tripping after drums *K. John* v 2 155
Thou art an Amazon And fightest with the sword of Deborah *1 Hen. VI.* i 2 104
Belike she minds to play the Amazon . . . *3 Hen. VI.* iv 1 106
Amazonian. How ill-beseeming is it in thy sex To triumph, like an Amazonian trull, Upon their woes! . . . . i 4 114
When with his Amazonian chin he drove The bristled lips before him *Cor.* ii 2 95
Ambassador. Lord Angelo, having affairs to heaven, Intends you for his swift ambassador . . . . *Meas. for Meas.* iii 1 57
A horse to be ambassador for an ass . . . . *L. L. Lost* iii 1 53
We have received your letters full of love; Your favours, the ambassadors of love . . . . v 2 788
I have not seen So likely an ambassador of love *Mer. of Venice* ii 9 92
The French ambassador upon that instant Craved audience . *Hen. V.* i 1 91
Shall we call in the ambassador, my liege?—Not yet, my cousin . i 2 3
Question your grace the late ambassadors, With what great state he heard their embassy . . . . ii 4 31
Ambassadors from Harry King of England Do crave admittance . . ii 4 65
Suppose the ambassador from the French comes back . . . iii Prol. 28
Call the ambassadors; and, as you please, So let them have their answers every one . . . . *1 Hen. VI.* v 1 24
My lords ambassadors, your several suits Have been consider'd . . v 1 34
He was the lord ambassador Sent from a sort of tinkers . *2 Hen. VI.* iii 2 276
Cade, we come ambassadors from the king Unto the commons whom thou hast misled . . . . iv 8 7
My lord ambassador, these letters are for you . . *3 Hen. VI.* iii 3 163
I came from Edward as ambassador, But I return his sworn and mortal foe . . . . iii 3 256
How should you govern any kingdom, That know not how to use ambassadors? . . . . iv 3 36
Is it therefore The ambassador is silenced? . . . *Hen. VIII.* i 1 97
And hither make, as great ambassadors From foreign princes . . i 4 55
Speeches utter'd By the Bishop of Bayonne, then French ambassador . ii 4 172
When you went Ambassador to the emperor, you made bold To carry into Flanders the great seal . . . . iii 2 318
If my sight fail not, You should be lord ambassador . . . . iv 2 109
Thou must be my ambassador to him . . . *Troi. and Cres.* iii 3 267
Go thou before, be our ambassador . . . . *T. Andron.* iv 4 100
The ambassadors from Norway, my good lord, Are joyfully returned *Ham.* ii 2 40
Give first admittance to the ambassadors . . . . . . ii 2 51
There's a letter for you, sir; it comes from the ambassador . . iv 6 10
To the ambassadors of England gives This warlike volley . . . v 2 362
What sport to-night?—Hear the ambassadors . . *Ant. and Cleo.* i 1 48
So like you, sir, ambassadors from Rome . . . *Cymbeline* iii 3 59
The ambassador, Lucius the Roman, comes to Milford-Haven To-morrow iii 4 144
Amber. Her amber hair for foul hath amber quoted . *L. L. Lost* iv 3 87
With amber bracelets, beads, and all this knavery . *T. of Shrew* iv 3 58
Their eyes purging thick amber and plum-tree gum . *Hamlet* ii 2 201
Amber-coloured. An amber-colour'd raven was well noted *L. L. Lost* iv 3 88
Ambiguities. Out of doubt and out of question too, and ambiguities *Hen. V.* v 1 48
Seal up the mouth of outrage for a while, Till we can clear these ambiguities, And know their spring . . . . *Rom. and Jul.* v 3 217
Ambiguous. Or such ambiguous giving out . . . . *Hamlet* i 5 178
Ambition. Hence his ambition growing—Dost thou hear? . *Tempest* i 2 105
I have no ambition To see a goodlier man . . . . . . i 2 482

Ambition. So high a hope that even Ambition cannot pierce a wink beyond *Tempest* ii 1 242
You, brother mine, that entertain'd ambition, Expell'd remorse and nature v 1 75
This is the period of my ambition: O this blessed hour! *Mer. Wives* iii 3 47
Full of ambition, an envious emulator of every man's good parts *As Y. L.* i 1 149
Who doth ambition shun And loves to live i' the sun ii 5 40
The ambition in my love thus plagues itself *All's Well* i 1 101
His humble ambition, proud humility, His jarring concord i 1 185
Urge them while their souls Are capable of this ambition *K. John* ii 1 476
Thoughts tending to ambition, they do plot Unlikely wonders *Richard II.* v 5 18
Ill-weaved ambition, how much art thou shrunk! *1 Hen. IV.* v 4 88
Now, beshrew my father's ambition! he was thinking of civil wars when he got me *Hen. V.* v 2 242
Go forward and be choked with thy ambition! *1 Hen. VI.* ii 4 112
Choked with ambition of the meaner sort ii 5 123
Pride went before, ambition follows him *2 Hen. VI.* i 1 180
Suffolk, England knows thine insolence.—And thy ambition, Gloucester ii 1 32
Wink at the Duke of Suffolk's insolence, At Beaufort's pride, at Somerset's ambition ii 2 71
Virtue is choked with foul ambition iii 1 143
Fie on ambition! fie on myself, that have a sword, and yet am ready to famish! iv 10 1
Might haply think Tongue-tied ambition, not replying, yielded *Richard III.* iii 7 145
Thy ambition, Thou scarlet sin, robb'd this bewailing land *Hen. VIII.* iii 2 254
Out of mere ambition, you have caused Your holy hat to be stamp'd on the king's coin iii 2 324
Cromwell, I charge thee, fling away ambition: By that sin fell the angels iii 2 440
Love and meekness, lord, Become a churchman better than ambition v 3 63
Force him with praises: pour in, pour in; his ambition is dry *T. and C.* ii 3 233
A beastly ambition, which the gods grant thee t' attain to! *T. of Athens* iv 3 329
Whose fall the mark of his ambition is v 3 10
Wherein obscurely Cæsar's ambition shall be glanced at *J. Cæsar* i 2 324
'Tis a common proof, That lowliness is young ambition's ladder ii 1 22
Stand still: ambition's debt is paid iii 1 83
Joy for his fortune; honour for his valour; and death for his ambition iii 2 31
Ambition should be made of sterner stuff iii 2 97
On the Lupercal I thrice presented him a kingly crown, Which he did thrice refuse: was this ambition? iii 2 102
Thou wouldst be great; Art not without ambition *Macbeth* i 5 20
Vaulting ambition, which o'erleaps itself And falls on the other i 7 27
Thriftless ambition, that wilt ravin up Thine own life's means! ii 4 28
To me it is a prison.—Why then, your ambition makes it one *Hamlet* ii 2 258
I have bad dreams.—Which dreams indeed are ambition ii 2 263
I hold ambition of so airy and light a quality that it is but a shadow's shadow ii 2 267
Villanous, and shows a most pitiful ambition in the fool that uses it iii 2 49
Those effects for which I did the murder, My crown, mine own ambition iii 3 55
Whose spirit with divine ambition puff'd Makes mouths at the invisible event iv 4 49
No blown ambition doth our arms incite, But love, dear love *Lear* iv 4 27
Farewell content! Farewell the plumed troop, and the big wars, That make ambition virtue! *Othello* iii 3 350
Ambition, The soldier's virtue, rather makes choice of loss *Ant. and Cleo.* iii 1 22
Ambitions, covetings, change of prides, disdain, Nice longing *Cymbeline* ii 5 25
Cæsar's ambition, Which swell'd so much that it did almost stretch The sides o' the world iii 1 49

Ambitious. His eye ambitious, his gait majestical *L. L. Lost* v 1 12
Whose ambitious head Spits in the face of heaven *Mer. of Venice* ii 7 44
I would not be ambitious in my wish, To wish myself much better iii 2 152
O that I were a fool! I am ambitious for a motley coat *As Y. Like It* ii 7 43
The soldier's, which is ambitious, nor the lawyer's, which is politic iv 1 13
Ambitious love hath so in me offended *All's Well* iii 4 5
Have I not ever said How that ambitious Constance would not cease? *K. John* i 1 32
If love ambitious sought a match of birth, Whose veins bound richer blood ii 1 430
The eagle-winged pride Of sky-aspiring and ambitious thoughts *Richard II.* i 3 130
How now, ambitious Humphry! what means this? *1 Hen. VI.* i 3 29
Farewell, ambitious Richard.—How I am braved! ii 4 114
If I were covetous, ambitious, or perverse, As he will have me, how am I so poor? iii 1 29
Banish the canker of ambitious thoughts *2 Hen. VI.* i 2 18
Ambitious Warwick, let thy betters speak i 3 112
Ambitious churchman, leave to afflict my heart ii 1 182
Like ambitious Sylla, overgorged With gobbets of thy mother's bleeding heart iv 1 84
Ambitious humour Makes him oppose himself against his king v 1 132
Ambitious York did level at thy crown *3 Hen. VI.* ii 2 19
Proud ambitious Edward Duke of York Usurps the regal title iii 3 27
Speak like a subject, proud ambitious York! v 5 17
No man's pie is freed From his ambitious finger *Hen. VIII.* i 1 53
You are ambitious for poor knaves' caps and legs *Coriolanus* ii 1 76
As ever in ambitious strength I did Contend against thy valour iv 5 118
O'ercome with pride, ambitious past all thinking, Self-loving iv 6 31
Oppose not Scythia to ambitious Rome *T. Andron.* i 1 132
Proud and ambitious tribune, canst thou tell? i 1 202
I have seen The ambitious ocean swell and rage and foam *J. Cæsar* i 3 7
As he was valiant, I honour him: but, as he was ambitious, I slew him iii 2 28
The noble Brutus Hath told you Cæsar was ambitious iii 2 83
But Brutus says he was ambitious; And Brutus is an honourable man iii 2 91
Did this in Cæsar seem ambitious? iii 2 95
He was not ambitious.—If it be found so, some will dear abide it iii 2 118
When he the ambitious Norway combated *Hamlet* i 1 61
The very substance of the ambitious is merely the shadow of a dream ii 2 264
I am very proud, revengeful, ambitious iii 1 126

Ambitiously. I leave it As others would ambitiously receive it *2 Hen. VI.* ii 3 36
Ambitiously for rule and empery *T. Andron.* i 1 19

Amble. Sir, your wit ambles well; it goes easily *Much Ado* v 1 159
I'll tell you who Time ambles withal, who Time trots withal *As Y. Like It* iii 2 328
Who ambles Time withal?—With a priest that lacks Latin iii 2 336
These Time ambles withal.—Who doth he gallop withal? iii 2 343
You jig, you amble, and you lisp, and nick-name God's creatures *Hamlet* iii 1 151

Ambled. He ambled up and down With shallow jesters *1 Hen. IV.* iii 2 60

Ambling. Or a thief to walk my ambling gelding *M. Wives* ii 2 319
And want love's majesty To strut before a wanton ambling nymph *Richard III.* i 1 17
Give me a torch: I am not for this ambling *Rom. and Jul.* i 4 11

Ambuscadoes. Of cutting foreign throats, Of breaches, ambuscadoes i 4 84

Ambush. Who may, in the ambush of my name, strike home *Meas. for Meas.* i 3 41
Who would have suspected an ambush where I was taken? *All's Well* iv 3 335
Once did I lay an ambush for your life *Richard II.* i 1 137
In secret ambush on the forest side *3 Hen. VI.* iv 6 83
See the ambush of our friends be strong *T. Andron.* v 2 9
I fear some ambush. I saw him not these many years *Cymbeline* iv 2 65

Amen. I will help his ague. Come. Amen! *Tempest* ii 2 98
Lady, a happy evening!—Amen, amen! *T. G. of Ver.* v 1 8
Heaven make you better than your thoughts!—Amen! *Mer. Wives* iii 3 220
Heaven keep your honour safe!—Amen *Meas. for Meas.* ii 2 157
Amen, if you love her; for the lady is very well worthy *Much Ado* i 1 223
I say my prayers aloud.—I love you the better: the hearers may cry, Amen ii 1 110
His grace hath made the match, and all grace say Amen to it ii 1 315
And send you many lovers!—Amen, so you be none *L. L. Lost* ii 1 127
O that I had my wish!—And I had mine!—And I mine too, good Lord!—Amen, so I had mine iv 3 51
Amen, amen, to that fair prayer, say I *M. N. Dream* ii 2 62
Hood mine eyes Thus with my hat, and sigh, and say 'amen' *Mer. of Ven.* ii 2 203
Let me say 'amen' betimes, lest the devil cross my prayer iii 1 22
Well, the gods give us joy!—Amen *As Y. Like It* iii 3 48
'Tis a match.—Amen, say we: we will be witnesses *T. of Shrew* ii 1 322
God be wi' you, good Sir Topas. Marry, amen *T. Night* iv 2 109
Amen, amen! Mount, chevaliers! to arms! *K. John* ii 1 287
Cry thou amen To my keen curses iii 1 181
Strong as a tower in hope, I cry amen *Richard II.* i 3 102
Will no man say amen? Am I both priest and clerk? well then, amen iv 1 172
And a vengeance too! marry, and amen! *1 Hen. IV.* ii 4 128
To cry amen to that, thus we appear *Hen. V.* v 2 21
God speak this Amen!—Amen! v 2 396
To your good prayers will scarcely say amen *Richard III.* i 3 21
More cause, yet much less spirit to curse Abides in me; I say amen to all iv 4 197
Great God of heaven, say Amen to all! v 5 8
What traitor hears me, and says not amen? v 5 22
That she may long live here, God say amen! v 5 41
There is hope All will be well.—Now, I pray God, amen! *Hen. VIII.* iii 2 56
Now, all my joy Trace the conjunction!—My amen to't! iii 2 45
Methinks I could Cry the amen v 1 24
I have said my prayers and devil Envy say Amen *Troi. and Cres.* ii 3 23
Here lacks but your mother for to say amen *T. Andron.* iv 2 44
Marry, and amen, how sound is she asleep! *Rom. and Jul.* iv 5 8
Or my friends, if I should need 'em. Amen. So fall to't *T. of Athens* i 2 71
One cried 'God bless us!' and 'Amen' the other *Macbeth* ii 2 27
I could not say 'Amen,' When they did say 'God bless us!' ii 2 29
But wherefore could not I pronounce 'Amen'? I had most need of blessing, and 'Amen' Stuck in my throat ii 2 31
Good God, betimes remove The means that makes us strangers!—Sir, amen iv 3 163
Amen to that, sweet powers! I cannot speak enough of this content *Oth.* ii 1 197

Amend. Your compensation makes amends *Tempest* iv 1 2
The affliction of my mind amends, with which, I fear, a madness held me v 1 115
I'll kiss each several paper for amends *T. G. of Ver.* i 2 108
She hath a sweet mouth.—That makes amends for her sour breath iii 1 331
Return, return, and make thy love amends iv 2 99
That is, he will make thee amends *Mer. Wives* ii 3 70
I desire you in friendship, and I will one way or other make you amends iii 1 90
Let him be sent for to-morrow, eight o'clock, to have amends iii 3 210
I must carry her word quickly: she'll make you amends iii 5 49
I'll make you amends next, to give you nothing for something *C. of Err.* ii 2 54
God amend us, God amend! We are much out o' the way *L. L. Lost* iv 3 76
Do you amend it then; it lies in you *M. N. Dream* ii 1 118
The worst are no worse, if imagination amend them v 1 214
We will make amends ere long; Else the Puck a liar call v 1 441
Give me your hands, if we be friends, And Robin shall restore amends v 1 445
Now Lord be thanked for my good amends!—Amen *T. of Shrew* Ind. 2 99
Two faults, madonna, that drink and good counsel will amend *T. Night* i 5 48
Sin that amends is but patched with virtue i 5 54
You must amend your drunkenness ii 5 81
Thou wilt amend thy life?—Ay, an it like your good worship *W. Tale* v 2 166
For amends to his posterity, At our importance hither is he come *K. John* ii 1 6
You must needs learn, lord, to amend this fault *1 Hen. IV.* iii 1 180
Do thou amend thy face, and I'll amend my life iii 3 27
To punish you by the heels would amend the attention of your ears *2 Hen. IV.* i 2 142
Yet thus far fortune maketh us amends *3 Hen. VI.* iv 7 2
Pardon me, Edward, I will make amends v 1 100
The readiest way to make the wench amends Is to become her husband and her father *Richard III.* i 1 155
Would it might please your grace, At our entreaties, to amend that fault! iii 7 115
If I did take the kingdom from your sons, To make amends, I'll give it to your daughter iv 4 295
I cannot make you what amends I would iv 4 309
Make amends now: get you gone *Macbeth* iii 5 14
Such sanctity hath heaven given his hand—They presently amend iv 3 145
It is my shame to be so fond; but it is not in my virtue to amend it *Othello* i 3 321
Make her amends; she weeps.—O devil, devil! iv 1 255
Half all men's hearts are his.—You make amends *Cymbeline* i 6 168
Which horse-hairs and calves'-guts, nor the voice of unpaved eunuch to boot, can never amend ii 3 35
I am ill, but your being by me Cannot amend me iv 2 12
It is I That all the abhorred things o' the earth amend By being worse v 5 216

Amended. With sainted vow my faults to have amended *All's Well* iii 4 7
Look, what is done cannot be now amended *Richard III.* iv 4 291
I must excuse What cannot be amended *Coriolanus* iv 7 12
Ay, by my troth, the case may be amended *Rom. and Jul.* iv 5 101

Amendment. What hope is there of his majesty's amendment? *All's Well* i 1 14
Players, hearing your amendment, Are come to play *T. of Shrew* Ind. 2 131
I see a good amendment of life in thee *1 Hen. IV.* i 2 114
What likelihood of his amendment, lords? *Richard III.* i 3 33

Amerce. I'll amerce you with so strong a fine That you shall all repent the loss of mine *Rom. and Jul.* iii 1 195

America. Where America, the Indies?—Oh, sir, upon her nose *C. of Err.* iii 2 136

Ames-ace. Rather be in this choice than throw ames-ace for my life *All's Well* ii 3 85

Amiable. To lay an amiable siege to the honesty of this Ford's wife *Mer. Wives* ii 2 243
Don John saw afar off in the orchard this amiable encounter *Much Ado* iii 3 161
Bull Jove, sir, had an amiable low v 4 48

Amiable. Sit thee down upon this flowery bed, While I thy amiable cheeks do coy *M. N. Dream* iv 1 2
In no sense is meet or amiable *T. of Shrew* v 2 141
Amiable lovely death! Thou odoriferous stench! sound rottenness! *K. John* iii 4 25
She told her, while she kept it, 'Twould make her amiable *Othello* iii 4 59
Amid this hurly I intend That all is done in reverend care *T. of Shrew* iv 1 206
Amidst. Enthroned and sphered Amidst the other *Troi. and Cres.* i 3 91
Amiens. My Lord of Amiens and myself Did steal behind him *As Y. L.* ii 1 29
Amiss. That shall not be much amiss *Meas. for Meas.* iii 1 200
What error drives our eyes and ears amiss? *Com. of Errors* ii 2 186
It had not been amiss the rod had been made *Much Ado* ii 1 234
Never any thing can be amiss, When simpleness and duty tender it *M. N. Dream* v 1 82
Seven times tried that judgement is, That did never choose amiss *Mer. of Venice* ii 9 65
Why, nothing comes amiss, so money comes withal *T. of Shrew* i 2 82
How but well? It were impossible I should speed amiss ii 1 285
All the world, That talk'd of her, have talk'd amiss of her ii 1 293
I like him well; 'tis not amiss *All's Well* iv 5 72
If thou thou'st him some thrice, it shall not be amiss *T. Night* iii 2 49
That which thou hast sworn to do amiss Is not amiss when it is truly done *K. John* iii 1 270
These and all are all amiss employ'd *Richard II.* ii 3 132
God may finish it when he will, 'tis not a hair amiss yet *2 Hen. IV.* i 2 27
Then judge, great lords, if I have done amiss *1 Hen. VI.* iv 1 27
Gold cannot come amiss, were she a devil *2 Hen. VI.* i 2 92
Which is not amiss to cool a man's stomach this hot weather iv 10 10
'Twere not amiss He were created knight for his good service v 1 76
Take it not amiss; I cannot nor I will not yield to you *Richard III.* iii 7 206
Have we done aught amiss,—show us wherein *T. Andron.* v 3 129
Something hath been amiss—a noble nature May catch a wrench *T. of A.* ii 2 217
What is amiss in them, you gods, make suitable for destruction iii 6 91
'Tis not amiss we tender our loves to him, in this supposed distress v 1 14
What is amiss plague and infection mend! v 1 224
If he had done or said any thing amiss *J. Cæsar* i 2 273
This dream is all amiss interpreted; It was a vision fair and fortunate ii 2 83
What is now amiss That Cæsar and his senate must redress? iii 1 31
What is amiss?—You are, and do not know't *Macbeth* ii 3 102
Each toy seems prologue to some great amiss *Hamlet* iv 5 18
Such a sight as this Becomes the field, but here shows much amiss v 2 413
Nor know I aught By me that's said or done amiss *Othello* ii 3 201
That's not amiss; But yet keep time in all iv 1 92
It is not Amiss to tumble on the bed of Ptolemy *Ant. and Cleo.* i 4 17
What's amiss, May it be gently heard ii 2 19
'Twere not amiss to keep our door hatched *Pericles* iv 2 36
Amities. And stand a comma 'tween their amities *Hamlet* v 2 42
Death, dearth, dissolutions of ancient amities *Lear* i 2 159
Amity. Now thou and I are new in amity *M. N. Dream* iv 1 92
As well be amity and life 'Tween snow and fire *Mer. of Venice* iii 2 30
You have a noble and a true conceit Of god-like amity iii 4 3
I pray you, make us friends; I will pursue the amity *All's Well* ii 5 15
I lost—All mine own folly—the society, Amity too, of your brave father *W. Tale* v 1 136
Let in that amity which you have made *K. John* ii 1 537
Rough frown of war Is cold in amity and painted peace iii 1 105
Deep-sworn faith, peace, amity, true love iii 1 231
On that altar where we swore to you Dear amity and everlasting love v 4 20
Foretelling this same time's condition And the division of our amity *2 Hen. IV.* iii 1 79
Bear those tokens home Of our restored love and amity iv 2 65
To join your hearts in love and amity *1 Hen. VI.* iii 1 68
Can this be so, That in alliance, amity and oaths, There should be found such false dissembling guile? iv 1 62
The sooner to effect And surer bind this knot of amity v 1 16
To crave a league of amity; And lastly, to confirm that amity *3 Hen. VI.* iii 3 53
I'll kiss thy hand, In sign of league and amity with thee *Richard III.* i 3 281
Might, through their amity, Breed him some prejudice *Hen. VIII.* i 1 181
The amity that wisdom knits not, folly may easily untie *Troi. and Cres.* ii 3 110
How, in one house, Should many people, under two commands, Hold amity? *Lear* ii 4 245
To hold you in perpetual amity, To make you brothers *Ant. and Cleo.* ii 2 127
The band that seems to tie their friendship together will be the very strangler of their amity ii 6 130
That which is the strength of their amity shall prove the immediate author of their variance ii 6 137
Among. Slow in words.—O villain, that set this down among her vices! *T. G. of Ver.* iii 1 337
As honest a'omans as I will desires among five thousand *Mer. Wives* iii 3 236
You have among you killed a sweet and innocent lady *Much Ado* v 1 194
There's not one wise man among twenty that will praise himself v 2 76
And, among three, to love the worst of all *L. L. Lost* iii 1 197
Among other important and most serious designs v 1 104
Dost thou infamonize me among potentates? v 2 684
A lion among ladies is a most dreadful thing *M. N. Dream* iii 1 32
Henceforth be never number'd among men! iii 2 67
Not one among them but I dote on his very absence *Mer. of Venice* i 2 120
What news among the merchants? iii 1 25
Among the buzzing pleased multitude iii 2 182
Howsoe'er thou speak'st, 'mong other things I shall digest it iii 5 94
You have among you many a purchased slave iv 1 90
Among nine bad if one be good, There's yet one good in ten *All's Well* i 3 81
Among the infinite doings of the world *W. Tale* i 2 253
It would not have relished among my other discredits v 2 132
Ran fearfully among the trembling reeds *1 Hen. IV.* i 3 105
An you do not make him hanged among you, the gallows shall have wrong *2 Hen. IV.* ii 2 105
I must live among my neighbours; I'll no swaggerers ii 4 80
So merrily, And ever among so merrily v 3 23
And bloody strife Should reign among professors of one faith *1 Hen. VI.* v 1 14
Among the people gather up a tenth v 5 93
A woman lost among ye, laugh'd at, scorn'd *Hen. VIII.* iii 1 107
Let his knights have colder looks among you *Lear* i 3 22
That such a king should play bo-peep, And go the fools among i 4 194
Amongst. The most unnatural That lived amongst men *As Y. Like It* iv 3 124
To make a stale of me amongst these mates *T. of Shrew* i 1 58
You are the man Must stead us all and me amongst the rest i 2 266
Amongst the rest There is a remedy, approved, set down *All's Well* i 3 233
What wisdom stirs amongst you? *W. Tale* ii 1 21
Amongst much other talk, that very time *Richard II.* iv 1 14
Amongst a grove, the very straightest plant *1 Hen. IV.* i 1 82
The man is dead that you and Pistol beat amongst you *2 Hen. IV.* v 4 19
Amongst the soldiers this is muttered *1 Hen. VI.* i 1 70
The presence of a king engenders love Amongst his subjects iii 1 182
Remember where we are; In France, amongst a fickle wavering nation iv 1 138
Were but his picture left amongst you here, It would amaze the proudest iv 7 83
Peace be amongst them, if they turn to us! v 2 6
All the friends that thou, brave Earl of March, Amongst the loving Welshmen canst procure *3 Hen. VI.* ii 1 180
For this, amongst the rest, was I ordain'd v 6 58
Amongst this princely heap, if any here . . . Hold me a foe *Richard III.* ii 1 53
With burial amongst their ancestors *T. Andron.* i 1 84
As loathsome as a toad Amongst the fairest breeders of our clime iv 2 68
Good fellows all, The latest of my wealth I'll share amongst you *T. of A.* iv 2 23
Flew on him, and amongst them fell'd him dead *Lear* iv 2 76
Amorous. Take her hearing prisoner with the force And strong encounter of my amorous tale *Much Ado* i 1 327
My brother is amorous on Hero ii 1 161
Playing on pipes of corn and versing love To amorous Phillida *M. N. Dr.* ii 1 68
In a gondola were seen together Lorenzo and his amorous Jessica *Mer. of Ven.* ii 8 9
A proper stripling and an amorous! *T. of Shrew* i 2 144
But I be deceived, Our fine musician groweth amorous iii 1 63
The quaint musician, amorous Licio iii 2 149
May be the amorous count solicits her In the unlawful purpose *All's Well* iii 5 72
Send forth your amorous token for fair Maudlin v 3 68
I, that am not shaped for sportive tricks, Nor made to court an amorous looking-glass *Richard III.* i 1 15
Rouse yourself; and the weak wanton Cupid Shall from your neck unloose his amorous fold *Troi. and Cres.* iii 3 223
But gives all gaze and bent of amorous view On the fair Cressid iv 5 282
Tell her I have chastised the amorous Trojan v 5 4
Long Hast prisoner held, fetter'd in amorous chains *T. Andron.* ii 1 15
Lovers can see to do their amorous rites By their own beauties *R. and J.* iii 2 8
Shall I believe That unsubstantial death is amorous? v 3 103
Long in our court have made their amorous sojourn *Lear* i 1 48
She did gratify his amorous works With that recognizance and pledge of love Which I first gave her *Othello* v 2 213
Me, That am with Phœbus' amorous pinches black *Ant. and Cleo.* i 5 28
I did not think This amorous surfeiter would have donn'd his helm ii 1 33
Made The water which they beat to follow faster, As amorous of their strokes ii 2 202
The wide difference 'Twixt amorous and villanous *Cymbeline* v 5 195
Amort. How fares my Kate? What, sweeting, all amort? *T. of Shrew* iv 3 36
Now where's the Bastard's braves, and Charles his gleeks? What, all amort? *1 Hen. VI.* iii 2 124
Amount. Thy substance, valued at the highest rate, Cannot amount unto a hundred marks *Com. of Errors* i 1 25
Which doth amount to three odd ducats more Than I stand debted iv 1 30
You know how much the gross sum of deuce-ace amounts to *L. L. Lost* i 2 49
It doth amount to one more than two.—Which the base vulgar do call three i 2 50
Under correction, sir, we know whereuntil it doth amount v 2 494
The actors, sir, will show whereuntil it doth amount v 2 501
My land amounts not to so much in all *T. of Shrew* ii 1 375
Upon my life, amounts not to fifteen thousand poll *All's Well* iv 3 190
For indeed three such antics do not amount to a man *Hen. V.* iii 2 33
Will but amount to five and twenty thousand *3 Hen. VI.* ii 1 181
Amour. Pour l'amour de Dieu, me pardonner! *Hen. V.* iv 4 42
Amphimachus and Thoas deadly hurt *Troi. and Cres.* v 5 12
Ample. Of worth To undergo such ample grace and honour *M. for Meas.* i 1 24
Whom I beseech To give me ample satisfaction *Com. of Errors* v 1 252
I think I know your hostess As ample as myself *All's Well* iii 5 46
Shall at home be encountered with a shame as ample iv 3 82
The element itself, till seven years' heat, Shall not behold her face at ample view *T. Night* i 1 27
I will not return Till my attempt so much be glorified As to my ample hope was promised *K. John* v 2 112
In very ample virtue of his father *2 Hen. IV.* iv 1 163
Like the tide into a breach, With ample and brim fulness of his force *Hen. V.* i 2 150
There we'll sit, Ruling in large and ample empery i 2 226
Vows of love And ample interchange of sweet discourse *Richard III.* v 3 99
The ample proposition that hope makes In all designs *Troi. and Cres.* i 3 3
Were I alone to pass the difficulties And had as ample power as I have will ii 2 140
I do enjoy At ample point all that I did possess, Save these men's looks iii 3 89
You see, my lord, how ample you're beloved *T. of Athens* i 2 136
To thee and thine hereditary ever Remain this ample third *Lear* i 1 82
Now and then an ample tear trill'd down Her delicate cheek iv 3 14
Ampler strength indeed Than most have of his age *W. Tale* iv 4 414
Amplest. May plead For amplest credence *All's Well* i 2 11
Embrace and hug With amplest entertainment *T. of Athens* i 1 45
Amplified. Have read His fame unparallel'd, haply amplified *Coriolanus* v 2 16
Amplify. But another, To amplify too much, would make much more, And top extremity *Lear* v 3 206
Is't not meet That I did amplify my judgement in Other conclusions? *Cymbeline* i 5 17
Amply. Lords that can prate As amply and unnecessarily *Tempest* ii 1 264
Amply to imbar their crooked titles *Hen. V.* i 2 94
As amply titled as Achilles is *Troi. and Cres.* ii 3 203
Ampthill. At Dunstable, six miles off From Ampthill *Hen. VIII.* iv 1 28
Amurath. Not Amurath an Amurath succeeds, But Harry Harry *2 Hen. IV.* v 2 48
Amyntas. Polemon and Amyntas, The kings of Mede and Lycaonia *Ant. and Cleo.* iii 6 74
Anatomize. Should I anatomize him to thee as he is, I must blush *As Y. Like It* i 1 162
But what need I thus My well-known body to anatomize? *2 Hen. IV.* Ind. 21
Then let them anatomize Regan; see what breeds about her heart *Lear* iii 6 80
Anatomized. The wise man's folly is anatomized Even by the squandering glances of the fool *As Y. Like It* ii 7 56
I would gladly have him see his company anatomized *All's Well* iv 3 37
Anatomy. A mere anatomy, a mountebank *Com. of Errors* v 1 238
If he were opened, and you find so much blood in his liver as will clog the foot of a flea, I'll eat the rest of the anatomy *T. Night* iii 2 67
That fell anatomy Which cannot hear a lady's feeble voice *K. John* iii 4 40
In what vile part of this anatomy Doth my name lodge? *Rom. and Jul.* iii 3 106
Ancestor. All his ancestors that come after him may *Mer. Wives* i 1 15

Ancestor. She lies buried with her ancestors . . . *Much Ado* v 1 69
An honour 'longing to our house, Bequeathed down from many ancestors *All's Well* iv 2 43
My chastity 's the jewel of our house, Bequeathed down from many ancestors . . . iv 2 47
Of six preceding ancestors, that gem, Conferr'd by testament to the sequent issue, Hath it been owed and worn . . . v 3 196
Basely yielded upon compromise That which his noble ancestors achieved with blows . . . *Richard II.* ii 1 254
Which do hold a wing Quite from the flight of all thy ancestors *1 Hen. IV.* iii 2 31
Will have a wild trick of his ancestors . . . v 2 11
When I am sleeping with my ancestors . . . *2 Hen. IV.* iv 4 61
Look back into your mighty ancestors . . . *Hen. V.* i 2 102
Derived From his most famed of famous ancestors . . . ii 4 92
The scepter'd office of your ancestors, Your state of fortune *Richard III.* iii 7 119
[Censorinus,] nobly named so, Twice being [by the people chosen] censor, Was his great ancestor . . . *Coriolanus* ii 3 253
I bring unto their latest home, With burial amongst their ancestors *T. A.* i 1 84
As erst our ancestor, When with his solemn tongue he did discourse . . . v 3 80
An ancient receptacle, Where, for these many hundred years, the bones Of all my buried ancestors are pack'd . . . *Rom. and Jul.* iv 3 41
As Æneas, our great ancestor, Did from the flames of Troy . *J. Cæsar* i 2 112
For Romans now Have thews and limbs like to their ancestors . . . i 3 81
My ancestors did from the streets of Rome The Tarquin drive . . . ii 1 53
Give him a statue with his ancestors . . . iii 2 55
Teach me, Alcides, thou mine ancestor, thy rage . *Ant. and Cleo.* iv 12 44
Remember, sir, my liege, The kings your ancestors . . . *Cymbeline* iii 1 17
Our ancestor was that Mulmutius which Ordain'd our laws . . . iii 1 55
This youth, howe'er distress'd, appears he hath had Good ancestors . . . iv 2 48
From ancestors Who stood equivalent with mighty kings . . . *Pericles* v 1 91
Ancestry. Now, by the honour of my ancestry . . . *T. G. of Ver.* v 4 139
To draw forth your noble ancestry From the corruption of abusing times, Unto a lineal true-derived course . . . *Richard III.* iii 7 198
Not propp'd by ancestry, whose grace Chalks successors their way *Hen. VIII.* i 1 59
Great nature, like his ancestry, Moulded the stuff so fair . *Cymbeline* v 4 48
Anchises. As did Æneas old Anchises bear, So bear I thee . *2 Hen. VI.* v 2 62
Welcome to Troy! now, by Anchises' life, Welcome, indeed! *Tr. and Cr.* iv 1 21
As Æneas, our great ancestor, Did from the flames of Troy upon his shoulder The old Anchises bear . . . *J. Cæsar* i 2 114
Anchor. The anchor is deep: will that humour pass? . *Mer. Wives* i 3 56
Whilst my invention, hearing not my tongue, Anchors on Isabel *M. for M.* ii 4 4
You had much ado to make his anchor hold . . . *W. Tale* i 2 213
Nothing so certain as your anchors, who Do their best office, if they can but stay you Where you'll be loath to be . . . iv 4 581
Whilst our pinnace anchors in the Downs . . . *2 Hen. VI.* iv 1 9
The cable broke, the holding-anchor lost . . . *3 Hen. VI.* v 4 4
Say Warwick was our anchor; what of that? . . . v 4 13
Is not Oxford here another anchor? And Somerset another goodly mast? v 4 16
Wedges of gold, great anchors, heaps of pearl . . . *Richard III.* i 4 26
Then is all safe, the anchor's in the port . . . *T. Andron.* iv 4 38
An anchor's cheer in prison be my scope! . . . *Hamlet* iii 2 229
There would he anchor his aspect and die With looking on his life *Ant. and Cleo.* i 5 33
Posthumus anchors upon Imogen . . . *Cymbeline* v 5 393
On this coast Suppose him now at anchor . . . *Pericles* v Gower 16
Anchorage. From whence at first she weigh'd her anchorage *T. Andron.* i 1 73
Anchored. Till that my nails were anchor'd in thine eyes *Richard III.* iv 4 231
Anchoring. To cast up, with a pair of anchoring hooks *T. G. of Ver.* iii 1 118
Yond tall anchoring bark, Diminish'd to her cock . . . *Lear* iv 6 18
Anchovies and sack after supper . . . *1 Hen. IV.* ii 4 588
Ancient. If I read it not truly, my ancient skill beguiles me *M. for M.* iv 2 164
To the perpetual wink for aye might put This ancient morsel *Tempest* ii 1 286
He smells like a fish; a very ancient and fish-like smell . . . ii 2 27
You speak like an ancient and most quiet watchman . *Much Ado* iii 3 41
I beg the ancient privilege of Athens . . . *M. N. Dream* i 1 41
And will you rent our ancient love asunder? . . . iii 2 215
I will feed fat the ancient grudge I bear him . *Mer. of Venice* i 3 48
The ancient saying is no heresy, Hanging and wiving goes by destiny ii 9 82
One in whom The ancient Roman honour more appears Than any that draws breath . . . iii 2 297
Call home thy ancient thoughts from banishment *T. of Shrew* Ind. 2 33
Your ancient, trusty, pleasant servant Grumio . . . i 2 47
I spied An ancient angel coming down the hill . . . iv 2 61
Sir, you seem a sober ancient gentleman by your habit . . . v 1 75
A wretched Florentine, Derived from the ancient Capilet . *All's Well* v 3 159
The year growing ancient, Not yet on summer's death . *W. Tale* iv 4 79
O, hear me breathe my life Before this ancient sir! . . . iv 4 372
As an ancient tale new told, And in the last repeating troublesome *K. John* iv 2 18
Hast thou sounded him, If he appeal the duke on ancient malice? *Rich. II.* i 1 9
The nobles hath he fined For ancient quarrels, and quite lost their hearts ii 1 248
Go to the rude ribs of that ancient castle . . . iii 3 32
This pitch, as ancient writers do report, doth defile . *1 Hen. IV.* ii 4 455
Leads ancient lords and reverend bishops on To bloody battles . iii 2 104
My whole charge consists of ancients, corporals, lieutenants . . . iv 2 26
Ten times more dishonourable ragged than an old faced ancient . iv 2 34
You do draw my spirits from me With new lamenting ancient oversights *2 Hen. IV.* ii 3 47
Sir, Ancient Pistol's below, and would speak with you . . . ii 4 74
Dost thou hear? it is mine ancient.—Tilly-fally . . . ii 4 89
Your ancient swaggerer comes not in my doors . . . ii 4 91
Pray thee, go down, good ancient . . . ii 4 164
Be gone, good ancient: this will grow to a brawl anon . . . ii 4 186
Will you mock at an ancient tradition? . . . *Hen. V.* v 1 74
Attainted, Corrupted, and exempt from ancient gentry . *1 Hen. VI.* ii 4 93
My ancient incantations are too weak, And hell too strong for me . v 3 27
In the famous ancient city Tours, In presence of the Kings of France and Sicil . . . *2 Hen. VI.* i 1 5
If I longer stay, We shall begin our ancient bickerings . . . i 1 144
The ancient proverb will be well effected . . . iii 1 170
Till you had recovered your ancient freedom . . . iv 8 27
I'll win our ancient right in France again, Or die a soldier *Richard III.* iii 1 92
His ancient knot of dangerous adversaries . . . iii 1 182
Pity, you ancient stones, those tender babes Whom envy hath immured within your walls! . . . iv 1 99
If ancient sorrow be most reverend, Give mine the benefit of seniory . iv 4 35
Our ancient word of courage, fair Saint George . . . v 3 349
They Upon their ancient malice will forget With the least cause *Coriolanus* ii 1 244
Nay, mother, Where is your ancient courage? . . . iv 1 3

Ancient. Say their great enemy is gone, and they Stand in their ancient strength . . . *Coriolanus* iv 2 7
And present My throat to thee and to thy ancient malice . . . iv 5 102
Each word thou hast spoke hath weeded from my heart A root of ancient envy . . . iv 5 109
From ancient grudge break to new mutiny . *Rom. and Jul.* Prol. 3
Made Verona's ancient citizens Cast by their grave beseeming ornaments i 1 99
Who set this ancient quarrel new abroach? . . . i 1 111
At this same ancient feast of Capulet's Sups the fair Rosaline . . . i 2 87
Thy old groans ring yet in my ancient ears . . . ii 3 74
Farewell, ancient lady; farewell, 'lady, lady, lady' . . . ii 4 150
Ancient damnation! O most wicked fiend! . . . iii 5 235
That same ancient vault Where all the kindred of the Capulets lie . iv 1 111
In a vault, an ancient receptacle . . . iv 3 39
I met a courier, one mine ancient friend . . . *T. of Athens* v 2 6
There is no ancient gentlemen but gardeners, ditchers, and grave-makers: they hold up Adam's profession . . . *Hamlet* v 1 33
Death, dearth, dissolutions of ancient amities; divisions in state . *Lear* i 2 159
This ancient ruffian, sir, whose life I have spared at suit of his gray beard . . . ii 2 67
You stubborn ancient knave, you reverend braggart, We'll teach you . ii 2 133
Do it for ancient love; And bring some covering for this naked soul iv 1 45
Let's then determine With the ancient of war on our proceedings . . . v 1 32
And I—God bless the mark!—his Moorship's ancient . . . *Othello* i 1 33
Ancient, what makes he here? . . . i 2 49
My ancient; A man he is of honesty and trust . . . i 3 284
How now! who has put in?—'Tis one Iago, ancient to the general . ii 1 66
Not before me; the lieutenant is to be saved before the ancient . ii 3 114
This is my ancient; this is my right hand, and this is my left . ii 3 118
This is Othello's ancient, as I take it.—The same indeed . . . v 1 51
Which gave advantage to an ancient soldier, An honest one, I warrant *Cymbeline* v 3 15
From ashes ancient Gower is come . . . *Pericles* i Gower 2
I left behind an ancient substitute: Can you remember? . . . v 3 51
Ancientest. The same I am, ere ancient'st order was . *W. Tale* iv 1 10
Ancientry. A measure, full of state and ancientry . . . *Much Ado* ii 1 80
Wronging the ancientry, stealing, fighting . . . *W. Tale* iii 3 63
Ancle. His stockings foul'd, Ungarter'd, and down-gyved to his ancle *Hamlet* ii 1 80
Ancus Marcius, Numa's daughter's son . . . *Coriolanus* ii 3 247
Andiron. Her andirons—I had forgot them—were two winking Cupids Of silver . . . *Cymbeline* ii 4 88
Andren. Those two lights of men Met in the vale of Andren *Hen. VIII.* i 1 7
Andrew. And see my wealthy Andrew dock'd in sand . *Mer. of Venice* i 1 27
Andrew Aguecheek. Thy friend, and thou usest him, and thy sworn enemy, ANDREW AGUECHEEK . . . *T. Night* iii 4 187
Andrew Agueface. Here comes Sir Andrew Agueface . . . ii 3 46
Andromache. He chid Andromache and struck his armourer *Tr. and Cr.* i 2 6
Andromache, I am offended with you . . . v 3 77
How poor Andromache shrills her dolours forth! . . . v 3 84
Andronici. Ne'er let my heart know merry cheer indeed, Till all the Andronici be made away . . . *T. Andron.* ii 3 189
The poor remainder of Andronici Will, hand in hand, all headlong cast us down . . . v 3 131
You sad Andronici, have done with woes . . . v 3 176
Andronicus, surnamed Pius For many good and great deserts to Rome . i 1 23
At last, laden with honour's spoils, Returns the good Andronicus to Rome . . . i 1 37
Marcus Andronicus, so I do affy In thy uprightness and integrity . . . i 1 47
Andronicus, Patron of virtue, Rome's best champion . . . i 1 64
Cometh Andronicus, bound with laurel boughs, To re-salute his country i 1 74
Andronicus, stain not thy tomb with blood . . . i 1 116
And let Andronicus Make this his latest farewell to their souls . i 1 148
Andronicus, would thou wert shipp'd to hell! . . . i 1 206
Andronicus, I do not flatter thee, But honour thee, and will do till I die i 1 212
To gratify the good Andronicus, And gratulate his safe return to Rome i 1 220
Titus Andronicus, for thy favours done To us in our election this day, I give thee thanks . . . i 1 234
Tell me, Andronicus, doth this motion please thee? . . . i 1 243
Full well, Andronicus, Agree these deeds with that proud brag of thine i 1 305
Come, come, sweet emperor; come, Andronicus . . . i 1 456
But fierce Andronicus would not relent: Therefore, away with her . ii 3 165
The unhappy son of old Andronicus; Brought hither in a most unlucky hour . . . ii 3 250
Who found this letter? Tamora, was it you?—Andronicus himself . ii 3 294
Andronicus, I will entreat the king: Fear not thy sons . . . ii 3 304
I go, Andronicus: and for thy hand Look by and by to have thy sons . iii 1 201
Andronicus, ill art thou repaid For that good hand thou sent'st the emperor . . . iii 1 235
Now, farewell, flattery: die, Andronicus; Thou dost not slumber . iii 1 254
Farewell, Andronicus, my noble father, The woful'st man that ever lived iii 1 289
Revenge, ye heavens, for old Andronicus! . . . iv 1 129
With all the humbleness I may, I greet your honours from Andronicus iv 2 5
Were our witty empress well afoot, She would applaud Andronicus' conceit . . . iv 2 30
Old Andronicus, Shaken with sorrows in ungrateful Rome . . . iv 3 16
Nought hath pass'd, But even with law, against the wilful sons Of old Andronicus . . . iv 4 9
I will enchant the old Andronicus With words more sweet . . . iv 4 89
Now will I to that old Andronicus, And temper him with all the art I have . . . iv 4 108
Brave slip, sprung from the great Andronicus, Whose name was once our terror . . . v 1 9
This is the incarnate devil That robb'd Andronicus of his good hand v 1 41
I will encounter with Andronicus, And say I am Revenge . . . v 2 2
What wouldst thou have us do, Andronicus?—Show me a murderer . v 2 92
Farewell, Andronicus: Revenge now goes To lay a complot to betray thy foes.—I know thou dost . . . v 2 146
Why art thou thus attired, Andronicus?—Because I would be sure to have all well . . . v 3 30
We are beholding to you, good Andronicus . . . v 3 33
Anew. I in going, madam, weep o'er my father's death anew *All's Well* i 1 4
What do we then but draw anew the model In fewer offices? *2 Hen. IV.* i 3 46
Under the wings of our protector's grace, Begin your suits anew *2 Hen. VI.* i 3 42
Of the hue That I would choose, were I to choose anew . . . *T. Andron.* i 1 262
I will make him tell the tale anew . . . *Othello* iv 1 85
Ange. Que dit-il? que je suis semblable à les anges? . . . *Hen. V.* v 2 113
Angel. What angel wakes me from my flowery bed? . *M. N. Dream* iii 1 132
To the most of men this is a Caliban And they to him are angels *Tempest* i 2 481
Now, good angels Preserve the king . . . ii 1 307

Angel. She has all the rule of her husband's purse: he hath a legion of angels . . . *Mer. Wives* i 3 60
The humour rises; it is good: humour me the angels . . . i 3 64
I had myself twenty angels given me this morning; but I defy all angels, in any such sort, as they say, but in the way of honesty . . . ii 2 73
Like an angry ape, Plays such fantastic tricks before high heaven As make the angels weep . . . *Meas. for Meas.* ii 2 122
Let's write good angel on the devil's horn; 'Tis not the devil's crest . ii 4 16
O, what may man within him hide, Though angel on the outward side! iii 2 286
He that came behind you, sir, like an evil angel *Com. of Errors* iv 3 20
Here are the angels that you sent for . . . iv 3 41
Mild, or come not near me; noble, or not I for an angel . *Much Ado* ii 3 35
Love is a devil: there is no evil angel but Love . *L. L. Lost* i 2 178
An angel shalt thou see; Yet fear not thou, but speak audaciously . v 2 103
An angel is not evil; I should have fear'd her had she been a devil . v 2 105
Their damask sweet commixture shown, Are angels vailing clouds . v 2 297
A coin that bears the figure of an angel Stamped in gold *Mer. of Venice* ii 7 56
Here an angel in a golden bed Lies all within . . . ii 7 58
In his motion like an angel sings, Still quiring to the young-eyed cherubins . . . v 1 61
At last I spied An ancient angel coming down the hill . *T. of Shrew* iv 2 61
Although The air of paradise did fan the house And angels officed all *All's Well* iii 2 129
What angel shall Bless this unworthy husband? . . . iii 4 25
When his fair angels would salute my palm . . . *K. John* ii 1 590
Shake the bags Of hoarding abbots; imprisoned angels Set at liberty . iii 3 8
An if an angel should have come to me And told me . . iv 1 68
Even there, methinks, an angel spake . . . v 2 64
God for his Richard hath in heavenly pay A glorious angel *Richard II.* iii 2 61
If angels fight, Weak men must fall, for heaven still guards the right iii 2 61
By this fire, that's God's angel . . . *1 Hen. IV.* iii 3 40
O, my sweet beef, I must still be good angel to thee . . . iii 3 200
As if an angel dropp'd down from the clouds . . . iv 1 108
This bottle makes an angel.—An if it do, take it for thy labour . iv 2 6
You follow the young prince up and down, like his ill angel . *2 Hen. IV.* i 2 186
Your ill angel is light; but I hope he that looks upon me will take me without weighing . . . i 2 187
There is a good angel about him; but the devil outbids him too . ii 4 362
Consideration, like an angel, came . . . *Hen. V.* i 1 28
God and his angels guard your sacred throne! . . . i 2 7
An angel is like you, Kate, and you are like an angel . . . v 2 110
More wonderful, when angels are so angry . . . *Richard III.* i 2 74
Then came wandering by A shadow like an angel, with bright hair . i 4 53
Go thou to Richard, and good angels guard thee! . . . iv 1 93
Good angels guard thy battle! live, and flourish! . . . v 3 138
Good angels guard thee from the boar's annoy! . . . v 3 156
God and good angels fight on Richmond's side . . . v 3 175
Go with me, like good angels, to my end . . . *Hen. VIII.* ii 1 75
Good angels keep it from us! What may it be? . . . iii 1 142
Loves him with that excellence That angels love good men with . ii 2 35
I charge thee, fling away ambition: By that sin fell the angels . . iii 2 441
Sir, as I have a soul, she is an angel . . . iv 1 44
Now, good angels Fly o'er thy royal head, and shade thy person! . . v 1 159
We all are men, In our own natures frail, and capable Of our flesh; few are angels . . . v 3 12
Women are angels, wooing: Things won are done *Troi. and Cres.* i 2 312
Courtiers as free, as debonair, unarm'd, As bending angels . i 3 236
She speaks: O, speak again, bright angel! . . . *Rom. and Jul.* ii 2 26
And her immortal part with angels lives . . . v 1 19
Brutus, as you know, was Cæsar's angel . . . *J. Cæsar* iii 2 185
Art thou any thing? Art thou some god, some angel, or some devil? . iv 3 279
His virtues Will plead like angels, trumpet-tongued . . . *Macbeth* i 7 19
Some holy angel Fly to the court of England and unfold His message! . iii 6 45
Angels are bright still, though the brightest fell . . . iv 3 22
Let the angel whom thou still hast served Tell thee . . . v 8 14
Angels and ministers of grace defend us! . . . *Hamlet* i 4 39
Lust, though to a radiant angel link'd, Will sate itself in a celestial bed i 5 55
In action how like an angel! in apprehension how like a god! . . ii 2 318
Help, angels! Make assay! Bow, stubborn knees! . . . iii 3 69
That monster, custom, who all sense doth eat, Of habits devil, is angel yet in this . . . iii 4 162
A ministering angel shall my sister be, When thou liest howling . v 1 264
Good night, sweet prince; And flights of angels sing thee to thy rest! . v 2 371
Croak not, black angel; I have no food for thee . . . *Lear* iii 6 34
O, the more angel she, And you the blacker devil! . . . *Othello* v 2 130
Curse his better angel from his side, And fall to reprobation . . v 2 208
Near him, thy angel Becomes a fear, as being o'erpower'd *Ant. and Cleo.* ii 3 21
I lodge in fear; Though this a heavenly angel, hell is here . *Cymbeline* ii 2 50
By Jupiter, an angel! or, if not, An earthly paragon! . . . iii 6 43
Reverence, That angel of the world, doth make distinction Of place 'tween high and low . . . iv 2 248
'Tis thought the old man and his sons were angels . . . v 3 85
Angel husband. When scarce the blood was well wash'd from his hands Which issued from my other angel husband . *Richard III.* iv 1 69
Angel knowledge. Though I have for barbarism spoke more Than for that angel knowledge you can say . . . *L. L. Lost* i 1 113
Angel-like. To clothe mine age with angel-like perfection *T. G. of Ver.* i 4 66
How angel-like he sings! . . . *Cymbeline* iv 2 48
Angel's face. Though ne'er so black, say they have angels' faces *T. G. of Ver.* iii 1 103
Ye have angels' faces, but heaven knows your hearts . *Hen. VIII.* iii 1 145
Thou art like the harpy, Which, to betray, dost, with thine angel's face, Seize with thine eagle's talons . . . *Pericles* iv 3 47
Angels of light. They appear to men like angels of light *Com. of Err.* iv 3 56
Angel whiteness. A thousand innocent shames In angel whiteness beat away those blushes . . . *Much Ado* iv 1 163
Angelica. Look to the baked meats, good Angelica . . *Rom. and Jul.* iv 4 5
Angelical. Beautiful tyrant! fiend angelical! . . . iii 2 75
Angelo. Call hither, I say, bid come before us Angelo . *Meas. for Meas.* i 1 16
If any in Vienna be of worth To undergo such ample grace and honour, It is Lord Angelo . . . i 1 25
Angelo, There is a kind of character in thy life . . . i 1 27
Hold therefore, Angelo:—In our remove be thou at full ourself . i 1 43
I do it not in evil disposition, But from Lord Angelo by special charge i 2 123
Lord Angelo, A man of stricture and firm abstinence . . i 3 11
It in you more dreadful would have seem'd Than in Lord Angelo . i 3 34
I have on Angelo imposed the office . . . i 3 40
Lord Angelo is precise; Stands at a guard with envy . . i 3 50
Upon his place, And with full line of his authority, Governs Lord Angelo i 4 57
Unless you have the grace by your fair prayer To soften Angelo . i 4 70

Angelo. Go to Lord Angelo, And let him learn to know, when maidens sue, Men give like gods . . . *Meas. for Meas.* i 4 79
What dost thou, or what art thou, Angelo? Dost thou desire her foully for those things That make her good? . . . ii 2 173
I'll tell him yet of Angelo's request, And fit his mind to death . ii 4 186
Lord Angelo, having affairs to heaven, Intends you for his swift ambassador . . . iii 1 56
Angelo had never the purpose to corrupt her . . . iii 1 162
I am confessor to Angelo, and I know this to be true . . iii 1 168
The assault that Angelo hath made to you, fortune hath conveyed to my understanding . . . iii 1 189
But that frailty hath examples for his falling, I should wonder at Angelo iii 1 192
O, how much is the good duke deceived in Angelo! . . . iii 1 197
She should this Angelo have married . . . iii 1 221
Her combinate husband, this well-seeming Angelo . . . iii 1 232
Go you to Angelo; answer his requiring with a plausible obedience . iii 1 253
Dispatch with Angelo, that it may be quickly . . . iii 1 279
Lord Angelo dukes it well in his absence; he puts transgression to't . iii 2 100
They say this Angelo was not made by man and woman after this downright way of creation . . . iii 2 111
My brother Angelo will not be altered; Claudio must die to-morrow . iii 2 219
Twice treble shame on Angelo, To weed my vice and let his grow! . iii 2 283
With Angelo to-night shall lie His old betrothed but despised . . iii 2 292
Lord Angelo hath to the public ear Profess'd the contrary . . iv 2 102
Lord Angelo, belike thinking me remiss in mine office, awakens me . iv 2 118
His fact, till now in the government of Lord Angelo, came not to an undoubtful proof . . . iv 2 142
Is no greater forfeit to the law than Angelo who hath sentenced him . iv 2 168
Let this Barnardine be this morning executed, and his head borne to Angelo.—Angelo hath seen them both, and will discover the favour iv 2 183
This is a thing that Angelo knows not . . . iv 2 214
The hour draws on Prefix'd by Angelo . . . iv 3 83
Quick, dispatch, and send the head to Angelo . . . iv 3 96
Now will I write letters to Angelo,—The provost, he shall bear them . iv 3 97
By cold gradation and well-balanced form, We shall proceed with Angelo iv 3 105
Wretched Isabel! Injurious world! most damned Angelo! . . iv 3 127
To the head of Angelo Accuse him home and home . . . iv 3 147
Relate your wrongs; in what? by whom? be brief. Here is Lord Angelo v 1 27
That Angelo's forsworn; is it not strange? That Angelo's a murderer; is't not strange? That Angelo is an adulterous thief, An hypocrite v 1 38
It is not truer he is Angelo Than this is all as true as it is strange . v 1 43
As shy, as grave, as just, as absolute As Angelo . . . v 1 55
So may Angelo, In all his dressings, characts, titles, forms, Be an arch-villain . . . v 1 55
I am the sister of one Claudio, Condemn'd upon the act of fornication To lose his head; condemn'd by Angelo . . . v 1 71
And desired her To try her gracious fortune with Lord Angelo . . v 1 76
Knowledge that there was complaint Intended 'gainst Lord Angelo . v 1 154
Do you not smile at this, Lord Angelo? . . . v 1 163
Cousin Angelo; In this I'll be impartial; be you judge Of your own cause . . . v 1 165
This is no witness for Lord Angelo . . . v 1 193
You say your husband.—Why, just, my lord, and that is Angelo . v 1 202
This is that face, thou cruel Angelo, Which once thou sworest was worth the looking on . . . v 1 207
Did you set these women on to slander Lord Angelo? . . . v 1 290
The very mercy of the law cries out Most audible, even from his proper tongue, 'An Angelo for Claudio, death for death!' . . . v 1 414
Then, Angelo, thy fault's thus manifested . . . v 1 417
For Angelo, His act did not o'ertake his bad intent, And must be buried but as an intent That perish'd by the way . . . v 1 455
I am sorry, one so learned and so wise As you, Lord Angelo, have still appear'd, Should slip so grossly . . . v 1 476
By this Lord Angelo perceives he's safe; Methinks I see a quickening in his eye. Well, Angelo, your evil quits you well . . . v 1 499
Love her, Angelo: I have confess'd her and I know her virtue . v 1 532
Good Signior Angelo, you must excuse us all; My wife is shrewish *Com. of Errors* iii 1 1
Whose suit is he arrested at?—One Angelo, a goldsmith . . iv 4 135
So was I bid report here to the state By Signior Angelo . *Othello* i 3 17
Anger. Which, not to anger bent, is music and sweet fire . *L. L. Lost* iv 2 120
Never till this day Saw I him touch'd with anger so distemper'd *Tempest* iv 1 145
I thought to have told thee of it, but I fear'd Lest I might anger thee . iv 1 169
Let the papers lie: You would be fingering them, to anger me *T. G. of Ver.* i 2 101
Urge not my father's anger, Eglamour, But think upon my grief . iv 3 27
With anger, with sickness, or with hunger, my lord, not with love *Much Ado* i 1 251
He both pleases men and angers them, and then they laugh at him . ii 1 146
The moon, the governess of floods, Pale in her anger, washes all the air, That rheumatic diseases do abound . . . *M. N. Dream* ii 1 104
Here comes the duke.—With his eyes full of anger . . *As Y. Like It* i 3 42
He's fallen in love with your foulness and she'll fall in love with my anger . . . iii 5 67
It engenders choler, planteth anger . . . *T. of Shrew* iv 1 175
My tongue will tell the anger of my heart, Or else my heart concealing it will break . . . iv 3 77
Do not plunge thyself too far in anger . . . *All's Well* ii 3 222
To anger him we'll have the bear again . . . *T. Night* ii 5 11
O, what a deal of scorn looks beautiful In the contempt and anger of his lip! . . . iii 1 158
If I prove honey-mouth'd, let my tongue blister And never to my red-look'd anger be The trumpet any more . . . *W. Tale* ii 2 34
Not a party to The anger of the king . . . ii 2 62
More is to be said and to be done Than out of anger can be uttered *1 Hen. IV.* i 1 107
Give it him, To keep his anger still in motion . . . i 3 226
Sometime he angers me With telling me of the moldwarp and the ant . iii 1 148
This is the deadly spite that angers me . . . iii 1 192
By the mass, I could anger her to the heart . . . *2 Hen. IV.* ii 2 216
Free from gross passion or of mirth or anger . . . *Hen. V.* ii 2 132
Did, in his ales and his angers, look you, kill his best friend . . iv 7 40
'Tis not for fear but anger that thy cheeks Blush . . *1 Hen. VI.* ii 4 65
My heart for anger burns; I cannot brook it . . *3 Hen. VI.* i 1 60
Here comes the queen, whose looks bewray her anger . . . i 1 211
Anger is like A full-hot horse, who being allow'd his way, Self-mettle tires him . . . *Hen. VIII.* i 1 132
Out of anger He sent command to the lord mayor straight . . ii 1 150
What friend of mine That had to him derived your anger, did I Continue? ii 4 32
By some of these The queen is put in anger . . . ii 4 161

Anger. He's discontented.—May be, he hears the king Does whet his anger to him *Hen. VIII.* iii 2 92
What should this mean? What sudden anger's this? iii 2 204
I must read this paper; I fear, the story of his anger iii 2 209
What it foresaw In Hector's wrath.—What was his cause of anger? *Troi. and Cres.* i 2 11
Hector was stirring early.—That were we talking of, and of his anger i 2 54
You part in anger.—Doth that grieve thee? O wither'd truth! v 2 45
Both observe and answer The vantage of his anger *Coriolanus* ii 3 268
A brain that leads my use of anger To better vantage iii 2 30
Defend yourself By calmness or by absence; all's in anger iii 2 95
Anger's my meat; I sup upon myself, And so shall starve with feeding iv 2 50
Leave this faint puling and lament as I do, In anger, Juno-like iv 2 53
If he hear thee, thou wilt anger him.—This cannot anger him *R. and J.* ii 1 22
'Twould anger him To raise a spirit in his mistress' circle ii 1 23
I anger her sometimes and tell her that Paris is the properer man ii 4 216
I eat not lords.—An thou shouldst, thou 'ldst anger ladies *T. of Athens* i 1 208
He did behave his anger, ere 't was spent, As if he had but proved an argument iii 5 22
To be in anger is impiety; But who is man that is not angry? iii 5 56
Do you dare our anger? 'Tis in few words, but spacious in effect iii 5 96
You are yoked with a lamb That carries anger as the flint bears fire *J. C.* iv 3 111
Let grief Convert to anger; blunt not the heart, enrage it *Macbeth* iv 3 229
A countenance more in sorrow than in anger *Hamlet* i 2 232
Know you no reverence?—Yes, sir; but anger hath a privilege *Lear* ii 2 76
Fool me not so much To bear it tamely; touch me with noble anger ii 4 279
Nay, then, come on, and take the chance of anger iii 7 79
Find some occasion to anger Cassio *Othello* ii 1 274
Never anger Made good guard for itself *Ant. and Cleo.* iv 1 9
My master rather play'd than fought And had no help of anger *Cymbeline* i 1 163
How durst thy tongue move anger to our face? *Pericles* i 2 54
Go travel for a while, Till that his rage and anger be forgot i 2 107

Angered. And, being anger'd, puffs away from thence *Rom. and Jul.* i 4 102
She would be best pleased To be so anger'd with another letter *T. G. of Ver.* i 2 103
Would I were so anger'd with the same! i 2 104
It angered him to the heart: but he hath forgot that *2 Hen. IV.* ii 4 9
'Twould have anger'd any heart alive To hear the men deny 't *Macbeth* iii 6 15
She that being anger'd, her revenge being nigh, Bade her wrong stay *Othello* ii 1 153
My navy; at whose burthen The anger'd ocean foams *Ant. and Cleo.* ii 6 21
I am sprited with a fool, Frighted, and anger'd worse *Cymbeline* ii 3 145

Angering. Bad is the trade that must play fool to sorrow, Angering itself and others *Lear* iv 1 41

Angerly. How angerly I taught my brow to frown! *T. G. of Ver.* i 2 62
I will sit as quiet as a lamb; I will not stir, nor wince, nor speak a word, Nor look upon the iron angerly *K. John* iv 1 82
Why, how now, Hecate! you look angerly.—Have I not reason? *Macbeth* iii 5 1

Angiers. Before Angiers well met, brave Austria *K. John* ii 1 1
Welcome before the gates of Angiers, duke ii 1 17
Till Angiers and the right thou hast in France, Together with that pale, that white-faced shore, . . . Salute thee for her king ii 1 22
Some trumpet summon hither to the walls These men of Angiers ii 1 199
You men of Angiers, and my loving subjects,—You loving men of Angiers, Arthur's subjects, Our trumpet call'd you to this gentle parle ii 1 203
You men of Angiers, open wide your gates, And let young Arthur, Duke of Bretagne, in ii 1 300
Rejoice, you men of Angiers, ring your bells ii 1 312
Lord of our presence, Angiers, and of you ii 1 367
By heaven, these scroyles of Angiers flout you, kings ii 1 373
Shall we knit our powers And lay this Angiers even with the ground? ii 1 399
Citizens of Angiers, ope your gates, Let in that amity which you have made ii 1 536
Are we not beaten? Is not Angiers lost? Arthur ta'en prisoner? iii 4 6

Angle. In an odd angle of the isle *Tempest* i 2 223
The pleasant'st angling is to see the fish Cut with her golden oars the silver stream, And greedily devour the treacherous bait: So angle we for Beatrice *Much Ado* iii 1 29
She knew her distance and did angle for me, Madding my eagerness *A. W.* v 3 212
I fear, the angle that plucks our son thither *W. Tale* iv 2 52
Did he win The hearts of all that he did angle for *1 Hen. IV.* iv 3 84
I show more craft than love; And fell so roundly to a large confession, To angle for your thoughts *Troi. and Cres.* iii 2 162
Thrown out his angle for my proper life *Hamlet* v 2 66
Give me mine angle; we'll to the river *Ant. and Cleo.* ii 5 10

Angled. One of the prettiest touches of all and that which angled for mine eyes, caught the water though not the fish *W. Tale* v 2 90

Angler. Nero is an angler in the lake of darkness *Lear* iii 6 8

Angleterre. Tu as été en Angleterre, et tu parles bien le langage *Hen. V.* iii 4 1
Vous prononcez les mots aussi droit que les natifs d'Angleterre iii 4 42
Le plus brave, vaillant, et très distingué seigneur d'Angleterre iv 4 61
Notre très-cher fils Henri, Roi d'Angleterre v 2 368

Angliæ. Præclarissimus filius noster Henricus, Rex Angliæ v 2 370

Angling. The pleasant'st angling is to see the fish Cut with her golden oars the silver stream, And greedily devour the treacherous bait *Much Ado* iii 1 26
I am angling now, Though you perceive me not how I give line *W. Tale* i 2 180
'Twas merry when You wager'd on your angling *Ant. and Cleo.* ii 5 16

Anglois. Comment appelez-vous la main en Anglois? *Hen. V.* iii 4 6
J'ai gagné deux mots d'Anglois vitement iii 4 14
Il est fort bon Anglois.—Dites-moi l'Anglois pour le bras iii 4 21
Le François que vous parlez, il est meilleur que l'Anglois lequel je parle v 2 200

Angry. Be not angry.—No, I warrant you; I will not adventure *Tempest* ii 1 186
What, angry, Sir Thurio! do you change colour? *T. G. of Ver.* ii 4 23
She must needs go in; Her father will be angry *Mer. Wives* iii 4 97
Be not angry: I knew of your purpose v 5 213
I pray you, be not angry with me, madam, Speaking my fancy *Much Ado* iii 1 94
As I am an honest man, he looks pale. Art thou sick, or angry? v 1 131
He changes more and more: I think he be angry indeed v 1 141
O, when she's angry, she is keen and shrewd! *M. N. Dream* iii 2 323
Come, come, you wasp; i' faith, you are too angry *T. of Shrew* ii 1 210
Prithee, be not angry.—I will be angry: what hast thou to do? iii 2 217
Apollo's angry; and the heavens themselves Do strike *W. Tale* iii 2 147
The heavens with that we have in hand are angry And frown upon 's iii 3 5
Who therewith angry, when it next came there, Took it in snuff *1 Hen. IV.* i 3 40
I should be angry with you, if the time were convenient *Hen. V.* iv 1 217
I was not angry since I came to France Until this instant iv 7 58
Nay, be not angry; I am pleased again *2 Hen. VI.* ii 1 55
Angry, wrathful, and inclined to blood, If you go forward iv 2 134
I could hew up rocks and fight with flint, I am so angry v 1 25
More wonderful, when angels are so angry *Richard III.* i 2 74
Good madam, be not angry with the child.—Pitchers have ears ii 4 36
The king is angry: see, he bites the lip iv 2 27
Who's there, ha?—Pray God he be not angry.—Who's there? *Hen. VIII.* ii 2 64
Who can be angry now? what envy reach you? ii 2 89
What, art thou angry, Pandarus? what, with me? *Troi. and Cres.* i 1 74
How should this man, that makes me smile, make Hector angry? i 2 33
Was he angry?—So he says here.—True, he was so: I know the cause i 2 55
Take heed of Troilus, I can tell them that too.—What, is he angry? i 2 62
That the bless'd gods, as angry with my fancy, . . . take thee from me iv 4 27
Thou boy-queller, show thy face; Know what it is to meet Achilles angry v 5 46
Because you talk of pride now,—will you not be angry? *Coriolanus* ii 1 29
Give your dispositions the reins, and be angry at your pleasures ii 1 34
And, being angry, does forget that ever He heard the name of death iii 1 259
The commonwealth doth stand, and so would do, Were he more angry at it iv 6 15
'Ira furor brevis est'; but yond man is ever angry *T. of Athens* i 2 29
I'm angry at him, That might have known my place iii 3 13
To be in anger is impiety; But who is man that is not angry? iii 5 57
Be angry when you will, it shall have scope *J. Cæsar* iv 3 108
I did not think you could have been so angry iv 3 143
Why art thou angry?—That such a slave as this should wear a sword *Lear* ii 2 77
Is my lord angry?—He went hence but now, And certainly in strange unquietness.—Can he be angry? *Othello* iii 4 132
Can he be angry? Something of moment then: I will go meet him iii 4 137
There's matter in 't indeed, if he be angry iii 4 139
What, is he angry?—May be the letter moved him iv 1 246
I have rubb'd this young quat almost to the sense, And he grows angry v 1 12
Nay, hear them, Antony: Fulvia perchance is angry *Ant. and Cleo.* i 1 20
He makes me angry with him; for he seems Proud and disdainful iii 13 141
He makes me angry; And at this time most easy 'tis to do't iii 13 143
Poor venomous fool, Be angry, and dispatch v 2 309
Be not angry, Most mighty princess, that I have adventured To try your taking of a false report *Cymbeline* i 6 171
Be our good deed, Though Rome be therefore angry iii 1 59
Your labourasome and dainty trims, wherein You made great Juno angry iii 4 168
I see you're angry: Know, if you kill me for my fault, I should Have died had I not made it iii 6 56
May haply be a little angry for my so rough usage iv 1 21
Be not angry, sir.—'Lack, to what end? iv 3 59
Farewell; you 're angry.—Still going? This is a lord! O noble misery! v 3 63

Angry ape. Like an angry ape, Plays such fantastic tricks before high heaven As make the angels weep *Meas. for Meas.* ii 2 120

Angry arm. Let heaven revenge; for I may never lift An angry arm against His minister *Richard II.* i 2 41

Angry bears. And penetrate the breasts Of ever angry bears *Tempest* i 2 289

Angry boar. Have I not heard the sea puff'd up with winds Rage like an angry boar chafed with sweat? *T. of Shrew* i 2 203

Angry brow. Thou smiling while he knit his angry brows *3 Hen. VI.* ii 2 20
Thou Hast moved us: what seest thou in our looks?—An angry brow *Pericles* i 2 52

Angry choler. Digest Your angry choler on your enemies *1 Hen. VI.* iv 1 168

Angry crest. Now for the bare-pick'd bone of majesty Doth dogged war bristle his angry crest *K. John* iv 3 149

Angry eye. He knits his brow and shows an angry eye *2 Hen. VI.* iii 1 15
I shall here abide the hourly shot Of angry eyes *Cymbeline* i 1 90

Angry father. Resolve your angry father, if my tongue Did e'er solicit, or my hand subscribe *Pericles* ii 5 68

Angry flood. Darest thou, Cassius, now Leap in with me into this angry flood, And swim to yonder point? *J. Cæsar* i 2 103

Angry frown. Cheer the heart That dies in tempest of thy angry frown *T. Andron.* i 1 458

Angry ghost. What should you fear?—Marry, my uncle Clarence' angry ghost *Richard III.* iii 1 144

Angry god. To offer up a weak poor innocent lamb To appease an angry god *Macbeth* iv 3 17

Angry guardant. When my angry guardant stood alone *1 Hen. VI.* iv 7 9

Angry heart. On them shalt thou ease thy angry heart *T. Andron.* v 2 119

Angry heavens. O war, thou son of hell, Whom angry heavens do make their minister! *2 Hen. VI.* v 2 34

Angry hive of bees. The commons, like an angry hive of bees That want their leader, scatter up and down iii 2 125

Angry law. Redeem your brother from the angry law *Meas. for Meas.* iii 1 207

Angry look. Nay, do not fright us with an angry look *2 Hen. VI.* iv 1 126

Angry lords. To my closet bring The angry lords *K. John* iv 2 268

Angry Mab. Which oft the angry Mab with blisters plagues *Rom. and Jul.* i 4 75

Angry mood. Stabb'd in my angry mood at Tewksbury *Richard III.* i 2 242

Angry northern wind. The angry northern wind Will blow *T. Andron.* iv 1 104

Angry note. I have done sin: For which the heavens, taking angry note, Have left me issueless *W. Tale* v 1 173

Angry parle. So frown'd he once, when, in an angry parle, He smote the sledded Polacks on the ice *Hamlet* i 1 62

Angry purpose. He comes on angry purpose now *Cymbeline* ii 3 61

Angry rose. This pale and angry rose, As cognizance of my blood-drinking hate, Will I for ever and my faction wear *1 Hen. VI.* ii 4 107

Angry soul. So in the Lethe of thy angry soul Thou drown the sad remembrance of those wrongs *Richard III.* iv 4 250

Angry spot. The angry spot doth glow on Cæsar's brow *J. Cæsar* i 2 183

Angry stars. Yet cease your ire, you angry stars of heaven! *Pericles* ii 1 1

Angry tenour. It bears an angry tenour: pardon me *As Y. Like It* iv 3 11

Angry trumpet. When the angry trumpet sounds alarum *2 Hen. VI.* v 2 3

Angry wafture. With an angry wafture of your hand *J. Cæsar* ii 1 246

Angry wenches. Nor bite the lip, as angry wenches will *T. of Shrew* ii 1 250

Angry winter. The childing autumn, angry winter *M. N. Dream* ii 1 112

Angry wit. Wherefore?—That I had no angry wit to be a lord *T. of Athens* i 1 241

Angry word. She gave me none, except an angry word *T. G. of Ver.* ii 1 164

Anguish. The words would add more anguish than the wounds *3 Hen. VI.* ii 1 99
Is there no play, To ease the anguish of a torturing hour? *M. N. Dream* v 1 37
One pain is lessen'd by another's anguish *Rom. and Jul.* i 2 47
Many simples operative, whose power Will close the eye of anguish *Lear* iv 4 15
Your other senses grow imperfect By your eyes' anguish iv 6 6
O Spartan dog, More fell than anguish, hunger, or the sea! *Othello* v 2 362

Angus. Earl of Athol, Of Murray, Angus, and Menteith *1 Hen. IV.* i 1 73

An-heires. It is a merry knight. Will you go, An-heires? *Mer. Wives* ii 1 228

An-hungry. They said they were an-hungry *Coriolanus* i 1 209

A-night. Bid him take that for coming a-night to Jane Smile *As Y. Like It* ii 4 48

Animal. Those pamper'd animals That rage in savage sensuality *Much Ado* iv 1 61
He is only an animal, only sensible in the duller parts *L. L. Lost* iv 2 28
That souls of animals infuse themselves Into the trunks of men *Mer. of Venice* iv 1 132

Animal. His animals on his dunghills are as much bound to him as I *As Y. Like It* i 1 16
The wretched animal heaved forth such groans . . . . ii 1 36
To fright the animals and to kill them up In their assign'd and native dwelling-place . . . . ii 1 62
The beauty of the world! the paragon of animals! . . *Hamlet* ii 2 320
Unaccommodated man is no more but such a poor, bare, forked animal *Lear* iii 4 113

Animis. Tantæne animis cœlestibus iræ? . . . *2 Hen. VI.* ii 1 24

Anjou. To Ireland, Poictiers, Anjou, Touraine, Maine . *K. John* i 1 11
Anjou, Touraine, Maine, In right of Arthur do I claim of thee ii 1 152
Reignier, Duke of Anjou, doth take his part . . . *1 Hen. VI.* i 1 94
Though her father be the King of Naples, Duke of Anjou and Maine v 3 95
Command in Anjou what your honour pleases . . . . v 3 147
I may quietly Enjoy mine own, the country Maine and Anjou . v 3 154
The duchy of Anjou and the county of Maine shall be released *2 Hen. VI.* i 1 50
Anjou and Maine! myself did win them both . . . . . i 1 119
Anjou and Maine are given to the French; Paris is lost . . . i 1 214
By thee Anjou and Maine were sold to France . . . . iv 1 86

Anna. As dear As Anna to the queen of Carthage was . *T. of Shrew* i 1 159

Annals. If you have writ your annals true, 'tis there . *Coriolanus* v 6 114

Anne. You do not mind the play.—Yes, by Saint Anne, do I . *T. of Shrew* i 1 255
Yes, by Saint Anne, and ginger shall be hot i' the mouth too . *T. Night* ii 3 126
Roger Earl of March; Roger had issue, Edmund, Anne . *2 Hen. VI.* ii 2 38
Anne, My mother, being heir unto the crown, Married Richard . . ii 2 43
I invocate thy ghost, To hear the lamentations of poor Anne *Richard III.* i 2 9
Rumour it abroad That Anne, my wife, is sick and like to die . iv 2 52
And Anne my wife hath bid the world good night . . . iv 3 39
And, for her sake, Madest quick conveyance with her good aunt Anne . iv 4 283
That wretched Anne thy wife, That never slept a quiet hour with thee . v 3 159
A creature of the queen's, Lady Anne Bullen . . . *Hen. VIII.* iii 2 36
Anne Bullen! No; I'll no Anne Bullens for him: There's more in't than fair visage. Bullen! No, we'll no Bullens . . . . . iii 2 87
Lady Anne, Whom the king hath in secrecy long married . . . iii 2 402
Stand here, and behold The Lady Anne pass from her coronation . iv 1 3

Anne intelligis, domine? to make frantic, lunatic . *L. L. Lost* v 1 28

Anne Page, which is daughter to Master Thomas Page . *Mer. Wives* i 1 45
Desire a marriage between Master Abraham and Mistress Anne Page . i 1 58
Fair Mistress Anne. Would I were young for your sake, Mistress Anne! i 1 267
My father desires your worships' company.—I will wait on him, fair Mistress Anne . . . . i 1 272
Come on, sir.—Mistress Anne, yourself shall go first.—Not I, sir . . i 1 320
It is a 'oman that altogether's acquaintance with Mistress Anne Page . i 2 9
Well, heaven send Anne Page no worse fortune! . . . . i 4 33
Speak a good word to Mistress Anne Page for my master . . . i 4 88
My master himself is in love with Mistress Anne Page: but notwithstanding that, I know Anne's mind . . . . i 4 111
Do not you tell-a me dat I shall have Anne Page for myself? . . . i 4 122
By gar, if I have not Anne Page, I shall turn your head out of my door i 4 131
I know Anne's mind for that: never a woman in Windsor knows more of Anne's mind than I do . . . . i 4 135
How does pretty Mistress Anne?—In truth, sir, and she is pretty . . i 4 147
But Anne loves him not; for I know Anne's mind . . . . i 4 177
You are come to see my daughter Anne?—Ay, forsooth; and, I pray, how does good Mistress Anne? . . . . ii 1 168
By gar, me vill kill de priest; for he speak for a jack-an-ape to Anne Page . . . . ii 3 87
I will bring thee where Mistress Anne Page is, at a farm-house . . ii 3 91
For the which I will be thy adversary toward Anne Page . . . ii 3 99
O sweet Anne Page! . . . . iii 1 72, 117
He promise to bring me where is Anne Page; by gar, he deceive me too . . . . iii 1 126
We have appointed to dine with Mistress Anne . . . . iii 2 56
We have lingered about a match between Anne Page and my cousin Slender . . . . iii 2 59
Thy father's wealth Was the first motive that I woo'd thee, Anne . . iii 4 14
O boy, thou hadst a father!—I had a father, Mistress Anne . . iii 4 38
Tell Mistress Anne the jest, how my father stole two geese out of a pen iii 4 40
Mistress Anne, my cousin loves you.—Ay, that I do . . . iii 4 42
I would my master had Mistress Anne; or I would Master Slender had her . . . . iii 4 109
They were nothing but about Mistress Anne Page . . . . iv 5 48
I have acquainted you With the dear love I bear to fair Anne Page . iv 6 9
If Anne Page be my daughter, she is, by this, Doctor Caius' wife . v 5 185
I came yonder at Eton to marry Mistress Anne Page . . . v 5 195
If I did not think it had been Anne Page, would I might never stir! . v 5 198
I went to her in white, and cried 'mum,' and she cried 'budget,' as Anne and I had appointed; and yet it was not Anne . . . . v 5 210
Un garçon, a boy; un paysan, by gar, a boy; it is not Anne Page . v 5 219
This is strange. Who hath got the right Anne?—My heart misgives me v 5 225

Annexed. Whose heart I thought I had, for she had mine; Which whilst it was mine had annex'd unto't A million more. . *Ant. and Cleo.* iv 14 17

Annexment. Each small annexment, petty consequence, Attends the boisterous ruin *Hamlet* iii 3 21

Annothanize. Veni, vidi, vici; which to annothanize in the vulgar,—O base and obscure vulgar!—videlicet, He came, saw, and overcame *L. L. Lost* iv 1 69

Annoy. One spark of evil That might annoy my finger . *Hen. V.* ii 2 102
To mow down thorns that would annoy our foot, Is worthy praise *2 Hen. VI.* iii 1 67
Farewell sour annoy! For here, I hope, begins our lasting joy *3 Hen. VI.* v 7 45
Good angels guard thee from the boar's annoy! . . *Richard III.* v 3 156
And rape, I fear, was root of thine annoy . . . *T. Andron.* iv 1 49
You know, his means, If he improve them, may well stretch so far As to annoy us all . . . . *J. Cæsar* ii 1 160
We fear not What can from Italy annoy us . . . *Cymbeline* iv 3 34

Annoyance. A dust, a gnat, a wandering hair, Any annoyance *K. John* iv 1 94
O'er his aery towers, To souse annoyance that comes near his nest . v 2 150
Heavy-gaited toads lie in their way, Doing annoyance . *Richard II.* iii 2 16
The herd hath more annoyance by the breese Than by the tiger *Troi. and Cres.* i 3 48
Remove from her the means of all annoyance . . . . *Macbeth* v 1 84

Annoyed. She will not be annoy'd with suitors . . . *T. of Shrew* i 1 189

Annoying. And went surly by, Without annoying me . *J. Cæsar* i 3 22

Annual. To give him annual tribute, do him homage . *Tempest* i 2 113
There stay until the twelve celestial signs Have brought about the annual reckoning . . . . *L. L. Lost* v 2 808
A thousand pound a year, annual support . . . . *Hen. VIII.* ii 3 64
Gives him three thousand crowns in annual fee . . . *Hamlet* ii 2 73
The city strived God Neptune's annual feast to keep . *Pericles* v Gower 17

Anoint his eyes; But do it when the next thing he espies May be the lady *M. N. Dream* ii 1 261
For that purpose, I'll anoint my sword . . . . *Hamlet* iv 7 141

Anointed. The anointed sovereign of sighs and groans . *L. L. Lost* iii 1 184
Anointed, I implore so much expense of thy royal sweet breath . v 2 523
If I could find example Of thousands that had struck anointed kings And flourish'd after, I'ld not do't . . . . *W. Tale* i 2 358
Hail, you anointed deputies of heaven! . . . . *K. John* iii 1 136
God's substitute, His deputy anointed in His sight. . . *Richard II.* i 2 38
Too careless patient as thou art, Commit'st thy anointed body to the cure Of those physicians that first wounded thee . . . . . ii 1 98
Comest thou because the anointed king is hence? . . . . ii 3 96
Not all the water in the rough rude sea Can wash the balm off from an anointed king . . . . iii 2 55
His captain, steward, deputy-elect, Anointed, crowned, planted many years . . . . iv 1 127
You stand against anointed majesty . . . . *1 Hen. IV.* iv 3 40
Before the Douglas' rage Stoop'd his anointed head as low as death *2 Hen. IV.* Ind. 32
And be crown'd King Henry's faithful and anointed queen . *1 Hen. VI.* v 5 91
Thy balm wash'd off wherewith thou wast anointed . . *3 Hen. VI.* iii 1 17
I was anointed king at nine months old . . . . . . iii 1 76
Anointed let me be with deadly venom . . . . *Richard III.* iv 1 62
Let not the heavens hear these tell-tale women Rail on the Lord's anointed iv 4 150
My anointed body By thee was punched full of deadly holes . . . v 3 124
Most sacrilegious murder hath broke ope The Lord's anointed temple! *Macbeth* ii 3 73
In his anointed flesh stick boarish fangs . . . . *Lear* iii 7 58

Anon. Thou dost me yet but little hurt; thou wilt anon . *Tempest* ii 2 83
Kiss the book: I will furnish it anon with new contents . . . ii 2 146
Up, gentlemen; you shall see sport anon . . . *Mer. Wives* iii 3 180
Hard by; at street end; he will be here anon . . . . iv 2 41
May be I will call upon you anon, for some advantage to yourself *Meas. for Meas.* iv 1 23
There's other of our friends Will greet us here anon . . . iv 5 13
Sneak not away, sir; for the friar and you Must have a word anon . v 1 364
Ever and anon . . . *L. L. Lost* v 2 101; *1 Hen. IV.* i 3 38
I'll be gone: Our queen and all her elves come here anon *M. N. Dream* ii 1 17
Of this discourse we more will hear anon . . . . . iv 1 183
Desire Gratiano to come anon to my lodging . . *Mer. of Venice* ii 2 125
I am half afeard Thou wilt say anon he is some kin to thee . . ii 9 97
But ask my opinion too of that.—I will anon . . . . iii 5 91
Anon a careless herd, Full of the pasture, jumps along by him *As Y. L. It* ii 1 52
Anon I'll give thee more instructions . . . . *T. of Shrew* Ind. 1 130
Get you gone, sir; I'll talk with you more anon . . . *All's Well* i 3 69
I thank you for your honest care: I will speak with you further anon . i 3 133
I'll be with you anon . . . . . *T. Night* iii 4 353; *2 Hen. IV.* v 3 28
I am gone, sir, And anon, sir, I'll be with you again . . *T. Night* iv 2 131
Let your bounty take a nap, I will awake it anon . . . . . v 1 52
Three months this youth hath tended upon me; But more of that anon v 1 103
Now the ship boring the moon with her main-mast, and anon swallowed with yest and froth . . . . *W. Tale* iii 3 94
Let's first see moe ballads; we'll buy the other things anon . . iv 4 278
We'll have this song out anon by ourselves . . . . . iv 4 315
My lord's almost so far transported that He'll think anon it lives. . v 3 70
There's toys abroad: anon I'll tell thee more . . . . *K. John* i 1 232
As a little snow, tumbled about, Anon becomes a mountain . . . iii 4 177
Still and anon cheer'd up the heavy time . . . . . . iv 1 47
And do thou never leave calling 'Francis,' that his tale to me may be nothing but 'Anon' . . . . *1 Hen. IV.* ii 4 36
Anon, anon.—Anon, Francis? No, Francis; but to-morrow, Francis . ii 4 72
What's o'clock, Francis?—Anon, anon, sir.—That ever this fellow should have fewer words than a parrot! . . . . ii 4 109
Prithee, let him alone; we shall have more anon . . . . ii 4 232
Some sack, Francis.—Anon, anon, sir . . . . *2 Hen. IV.* ii 4 306
This Sir John, cousin, that comes hither anon about soldiers . . iii 2 31
I'll give you a health for that anon . . . . v 3 25
We shall heat you thoroughly anon . . . . . *2 Hen. VI.* v 1 159
Shroud ourselves; For through this laund anon the deer will come *3 Hen. VI.* iii 1 2
A cup of wine.—You shall have wine enough, my lord, anon *Richard III.* i 4 168
If my weak oratory Can from his mother win the Duke of York, Anon expect him here . . . . iii 1 39
I shall anon advise you Further in the proceeding . . . *Hen. VIII.* i 2 107
Strikes his breast hard, and anon he casts His eye against the moon . iii 2 117
Let 'em alone, and draw the curtain close: We shall hear more anon . v 2 35
You'll leave your noise anon, ye rascals . . . . . . v 4 1
Anon behold The strong-ribb'd bark through liquid mountains cut, Bounding between the two moist elements . . . *Troi. and Cres.* i 3 39
Anon he's there afoot, And there they fly or die . . . . . v 5 21
But thou anon shalt hear of me again . . . . v 6 18
That, in the official marks invested, you Anon do meet the senate *Coriol.* ii 3 149
The people do admit you, and are summon'd To meet anon . . . ii 3 152
Are you so brave? I'll have you talked with anon . . . . . iv 5 19
But a deed of charity To that which thou shalt hear of me anon *T. Andron.* v 1 90
And then anon Drums in his ear, at which he starts and wakes *R. and J.* i 4 85
Dear love, adieu! Anon, good nurse! . . . . ii 2 137
Madam!—I come, anon.—But if thou mean'st not well, I do beseech thee—Madam!—By and by, I come . . . . ii 2 150
Anon comes one with light to ope the tomb . . . . . . v 3 283
You shall hear from me anon: Go not away . . . *T. of Athens* i 1 153
Pray you, walk near: I'll speak with you anon . . . . . ii 2 132
I come, Graymalkin!—Paddock calls.—Anon . . . . *Macbeth* i 1 10
Anon, anon! I pray you, remember the porter . . . . . ii 3 22
Resolve yourselves apart: I'll come to you anon . . . . . iii 1 139
Be large in mirth; anon we'll drink a measure The table round . . iii 4 11
'Tis hard to reconcile.—Well; more anon . . . . . . iv 3 140
I look'd toward Birnam, and anon, methought, The wood began to move v 5 34
Anon he finds him Striking too short at Greeks . . . *Hamlet* ii 2 490
Anon the dreadful thunder Doth rend the region . . . . . ii 2 508
You shall see anon how the murderer gets the love of Gonzago's wife . iii 2 274
Anon, as patient as the female dove . . . . v 1 309
Shall I hear from you anon?—I do serve you in this business . *Lear* i 2 193
Laid good 'scuse upon your ecstasy, Bade him anon return *Othello* iv 1 81
Get you away; I'll send for you anon . . . . v 1 270
Hear me speak a word.—Forbear me till anon . . . *Ant. and Cleo.* ii 7 44
I forgot to ask him one thing; I'll remember't anon . . *Cymbeline* iii 5 134
Then began A stop i' the chaser, a retire, anon A rout, confusion thick v 3 40

Another. It shall go hard but I'll prove it by another . *T. G. of Ver.* i 1 86
Thus will I fold them one upon another . . . . i 2 128

Another. Please you, I'll write your ladyship another . *T. G. of Ver.* ii 1 135
Or as one nail by strength drives out another . . . . . ii 4 193
Send her another; never give her o'er . . . . . iii 1 94
'Out with the dog!' says one: 'What cur is that?' says another . iv 4 23
When we are married and have more occasion to know one another
Mer. Wives i 1 257
I know Anne's mind as well as another does . . . . i 4 179
He wooes both high and low, both rich and poor, Both young and old, one with another . . . . . ii 1 118
As you have one eye upon my follies, as you hear them unfolded, turn another into the register of your own . . . . . ii 2 193
Let the court of France show me such another . . . . iii 3 58
We have a nay-word how to know one another: I come to her in white, and cry 'mum;' she cries 'budget;' and by that we know one another . . . . v 2 5
That, answering one foul wrong, Lives not to act another *Meas. for Meas.* ii 2 104
What pleasure was he given to?—Rather rejoicing to see another merry iii 2 249
Have at you with a proverb—. . . Have at you with another *C. of Err.* iii 1 53
Now let's go hand in hand, not one before another . . . . v 1 425
Will you have me, lady?—No, my lord, unless I might have another for working-days . . . . . . *Much Ado* ii 1 340
One woman is fair, yet I am well; another is wise, yet I am well; another virtuous, yet I am well . . . . . ii 3 29
Then the two bears will not bite one another when they meet . . iii 2 80
My cousin's a fool, and thou art another . . . . . iii 4 11
Yet Benedick was such another, and now is he become a man . iii 4 87
Here's a paper written in his hand, . . . —And here's another . . v 4 88
Another of these students at that time Was there with him . *L. L. Lost* ii 1 64
An I cannot, cannot, cannot, An I cannot, another can . . . iv 1 130
Sweet fellowship in shame!—One drunkard loves another of the name . iv 3 50
Another, with his finger and his thumb, Cried, 'Via!' . . . . v 2 111
O, that a lady, of one man refused, Should of another therefore be abused!
M. N. Dream ii 2 134
Became his surety and sealed under for another . . *Mer. of Venice* i 2 89
Whiles we shut the gates upon one wooer, another knocks at the door . i 2 147
Here comes another of the tribe: a third cannot be matched . . iii 1 80
Christians enow before; e'en as many as could well live, one by another iii 5 25
Is there yet another dotes upon rib-breaking? . . . *As Y. Like It* i 2 150
The big round tears Coursed one another down his innocent nose . . ii 1 39
They were all like one another as half-pence are . . . . iii 2 372
I were better to be married of him than of another . . . . iii 3 92
No sooner sighed but they asked one another the reason . . . v 2 39
Another bear the ewer, the third a diaper . . . *T. of Shrew* Ind. 1 57
Another tell him of his hounds and horse . . . . . Ind. 1 61
I have met a gentleman Hath promised me to help me to another . . i 2 173
A pair of boots that have been candle-cases, one buckled, another laced iii 2 46
I know she will lie at my house; thither they send one another *All's Well* iii 5 34
I would have that drum or another, or 'hic jacet' . . . . iii 6 66
Be a man of his own fancy, not to know what we speak one to another . iv 1 20
Tongue, I must put you into a butter-woman's mouth and buy myself another of Bajazet's mule . . . . iv 1 46
Pleasure will be paid, one time or another . . . . *T. Night* ii 4 73
They will kill one another by the look, like cockatrices . . . iii 4 214
But that it would be double-dealing, sir, I would you could make it another . . . . v 1 33
Sometimes her head on one side, some another . . . *W. Tale* iii 3 20
If I make not this cheat bring out another and the shearers prove sheep iv 3 129
There is not half a kiss to choose Who loves another best . . . iv 4 176
No hope to help you, But as you shake off one to take another . . iv 4 580
Unless another, As like Hermione as is her picture, Affront his eye . v 1 73
They seemed almost, with staring on one another, to tear the cases of their eyes . . . . v 2 13
There might you have beheld one joy crown another . . . . v 2 48
One eye declined for the loss of her husband, another elevated . . v 2 82
From one sign of dolour to another . . . . v 2 95
They shake their heads And whisper one another in the ear . *K. John* iv 2 189
Another lean unwash'd artificer Cuts off his tale and talks of Arthur's death . . . . iv 2 201
Could thought, without this object, Form such another? . . . iv 3 45
Sound but another, and another shall As loud as thine rattle . . v 2 171
Like a deep well That owes two buckets, filling one another *Richard II.* iv 1 185
A plague upon it when thieves cannot be true one to another! *1 Hen. IV.* ii 2 30
I hope I shall as soon be strangled with a halter as another . . ii 4 548
Which is almost to pluck a kingdom down And set another up *2 Hen. IV.* i 3 50
The prince admits him: for the prince himself is such another . . ii 4 275
Ignorant carriage is caught, as men take diseases, one of another . . v 1 86
Here's my glove: give me another of thine . . . *Hen. V.* iv 1 226
One would have lingering wars . . .; Another would fly swift *1 Hen. VI.* i 1 75
Let them kiss one another, for they loved well . . *2 Hen. VI.* iv 7 139
Now one the better, then another best; Both tugging to be victors
3 Hen. VI. ii 5 10
The air blows it to me again, Obeying with my wind when I do blow, And yielding to another when it blows . . . . . . iii 1 87
Is not Oxford here another anchor? And Somerset another goodly mast? . . . . v 4 16
He might infect another And make him of like spirit to himself . . v 4 46
Be resident in men like one another And not in me: I am myself alone v 6 82
Not all so much for love As for another secret close intent *Richard III.* i 1 158
And see another, as I see thee now, Deck'd in thy rights, as thou art stall'd in mine! . . . . i 3 205
Girdling one another Within their innocent alabaster arms . . . iv 3 10
His mind and place Infecting one another, yea, reciprocally . *Hen. VIII.* i 1 162
With one hand on his dagger, Another spread on's breast . . . i 2 205
I'll venture one have-at-him.—I another . . . . . . ii 2 85
Is this the honour they do one another? 'Tis well there's one above 'em yet . . . . v 2 26
You are such another! . . . . *Troi. and Cres.* i 2 296
When thou art forth in the incursions, thou strikest as slow as another ii 1 33
What is he more than another?—No more than what he thinks he is . ii 3 151
We understand not one another: I am too courtly and thou art too cunning . . . . iii 1 29
If ever you prove false one to another . . . . . . iii 2 206
Do one pluck down another and together Die in the fall . . . iii 3 86
Let me bear another to his horse; for that's the more capable creature iii 3 309
One another meet, And all cry, Hector! Hector's dead! . . . . v 3 86
What one thing, what another, that I shall leave you one o' these days v 3 103
My love with words and errors still she feeds; But edifies another with her deeds . . . . v 3 112
Now they are clapper-clawing one another; I'll go look on . . . v 4 2
The wenching rogues? I think they have swallowed one another . . v 4 36

Another. One bear will not bite another, and wherefore should one bastard? . . . . *Troi. and Cres.* v 7 19
Keep you in awe, which else Would feed on one another . . *Coriolanus* i 1 192
That you may be abhorr'd Further than seen and one infect another! . . i 4 33
Here's a letter from him: the state hath another, his wife another . ii 1 119
Put not your worthy rage into your tongue; One time will owe another iii 1 242
Men hate one another.—Reason; because they then less need one another iv 5 248
He that hath a will to die by himself fears it not from another . . v 2 111
Not to be his wife, That is another's lawful promised love *T. Andron.* i 1 298
When it is thy hap To find another that is like to thee . . . v 2 102
Examine every married lineament And see how one another lends content
Rom. and Jul. i 3 84
Bad'st me bury love.—Not in a grave, To lay one in, another out to have it ii 3 84
Or my true heart with treacherous revolt Turn to another . . . iv 1 59
I dreamt my master and another fought, And that my master slew him v 3 138
Friend or brother, He forfeits his own blood that spills another
T. of Athens iii 5 88
Lend to each man enough, that one need not lend to another . . iii 6 83
Love not yourselves: away, Rob one another . . . . . iv 3 448
Another general shout! . . . . *J. Cæsar* i 2 132
Those that understood him smiled at one another and shook their heads i 2 286
Here was a Cæsar! when comes such another?—Never, never . . iii 2 257
When your vile daggers Hack'd one another in the sides of Cæsar . v 1 40
I'll give thee a wind.—Thou'rt kind.—And I another . . *Macbeth* i 3 13
And I another So weary with disasters, tugg'd with fortune . . . iii 1 111
One word more,—He will not be commanded: here's another, More potent than the first . . . . iv 1 75
God has given you one face, and you make yourselves another *Hamlet* iii 1 150
There's another: why may not that be the skull of a lawyer? . . v 1 106
A tanner will last you nine year.—Why he more than another? . . v 1 185
This is too heavy, let me see another.—This likes me well . . . v 2 275
Farewell: We'll no more meet, no more see one another . . *Lear* ii 4 223
Another, whose warp'd looks proclaim What store her heart is made on iii 6 56
One side will mock another; the other too . . . . . . iii 7 71
I should e'en die with pity, To see another thus. I know not what to say iv 7 54
But another, To amplify too much, would make much more . . . v 3 205
Another of his fathom they have none, To lead their business . *Othello* i 1 153
Some one way, some another. Do you know Where we may apprehend her? . . . . i 1 177
One scale of reason to poise another of sensuality . . . . . i 3 331
One unperfectness shows me another, to make me frankly despise myself ii 3 299
As for my wife, I would you had her spirit in such another *Ant. and Cleo.* ii 2 62
As they pinch one another by the disposition, he cries out, 'No more' . ii 7 7
To shift his being Is to exchange one misery with another . *Cymbeline* i 5 55
Leonatus! a banished rascal; and he's another, whatsoever he be . ii 1 43
One sand another Not more resembles that sweet rosy lad Who died . v 5 120
One sin, I know, another doth provoke . . . . . *Pericles* i 1 137
Another age. Had slipp'd our claim until another age . . *3 Hen. VI.* ii 2 162
Another anchor. Is not Oxford here another anchor? . . . . v 4 16
Another Antony. She looks like sleep, As she would catch another Antony In her strong toil of grace . . . *Ant. and Cleo.* v 2 350
Another arrow. If you please To shoot another arrow that self way Which you did shoot the first . . . *Mer. of Venice* i 1 148
Another bad match. There I have another bad match . . . . iii 1 46
Another ballad. Here's another ballad of a fish . . . *W. Tale* iv 4 279
Another benefice. Then dreams he of another benefice . *Rom. and Jul.* i 4 81
Another Cæsar. Or till another Cæsar Have added slaughter to the sword of traitors . . . . *J. Cæsar* v 1 54
Another coast. Yet have I gold flies from another coast . *2 Hen. VI.* i 2 93
Another comfort. I conjure thee, as thou believest There is another comfort than this world, That thou neglect me not *Meas. for Meas.* v 1 49
Not another comfort like to this Succeeds in unknown fate . . *Othello* ii 1 194
Another counterfeit. I fear thou art another counterfeit *1 Hen. IV.* v 4 35
Another course. Not so; I'll teach thee another course . *T. Andron.* iv 1 119
We must take another course with you . . . . . *Pericles* iv 6 129
Another curtsy. Make another curtsy and say, 'Father, as it please me' . . . . *Much Ado* ii 1 58
Another daughter. Another dowry to another daughter . *T. of Shrew* v 2 114
Another day. Put up this: 'twill be thine another day . *L. L. Lost* iv 1 109
If e'er those eyes of yours Behold another day break in the east *K. John* v 4 32
We will disperse ourselves: farewell.—Stay yet another day *Richard II.* ii 4 5
Shall lose his sway, Meeting the check of such another day . *1 Hen. IV.* v 5 42
I dare say This quarrel will drink blood another day . *1 Hen. VI.* ii 4 134
If I fail not in my deep intent, Clarence hath not another day to live: Which done, God take King Edward! . . . . . *Richard III.* i 1 150
Remember this another day, When he shall split thy very heart with sorrow . . . . i 3 299
Another deed. Ere this hand, by thee to Romeo seal'd, Shall be the label to another deed . . . . *Rom. and Jul.* iv 1 57
Another device. There is also another device in my prain *Mer. Wives* i 1 43
Another dowry to another daughter . . . . . *T. of Shrew* v 2 114
Another drop. I to the world am like a drop of water That in the ocean seeks another drop . . . . *Com. of Errors* i 2 36
Another dry basting. And purchase me another dry basting . . ii 2 64
Another embassy of meeting; 'twixt eight and nine . *Mer. Wives* iii 5 131
Another emphasis. Be choked with such another emphasis! *A. and C.* i 5 68
Another encounter. I never heard of such another encounter *W. Tale* v 2 61
Another errand. I must of another errand to Sir John . *Mer. Wives* iii 4 114
Another experiment. To make another experiment of his suspicion . iv 2 35
Another fall. Methinks, is like Another fall of man . . *Hen. V.* ii 2 142
Another father. I would thou hadst told me of another father *As Y. L.* i 2 243
Another fault. And then another fault in the semblance of a fowl *M. W.* v 5 11
I have bethought me of another fault . . . . *Meas. for Meas.* v 1 461
Another fitchew. Such another fitchew! marry, a perfumed one *Oth.* iv 1 150
Another flood. There is, sure, another flood toward, and these couples are coming to the ark . . . . *As Y. Like It* v 4 35
Another friar. There is another friar that set them on *Meas. for Meas.* v 1 248
Another garment. There's another garment for't . . . *Tempest* iv 1 244
Another Golgotha. Or memorize another Golgotha . . . *Macbeth* i 2 40
Another half stand laughing by, All out of work and cold . *Hen. V.* i 2 113
Another head. Making another head to fight again . . *3 Hen. VI.* ii 1 141
Another heat. Even as one heat another heat expels . *T. G. of Ver.* ii 4 192
Another heir. Let my father seek another heir . . *As Y. Like It* i 3 101
The maiden phœnix, Her ashes new create another heir . . *Hen. VIII.* v 5 42
Another herb. We may pick a thousand salads ere we light on such another herb . . . . *All's Well* iv 5 16
Another Hero. Would serve to scale another Hero's tower *T. G. of Ver.* iii 1 119
Another Hero!—Nothing certainer: One Hero died defiled . *Much Ado* v 4 62
Another hit; what say you?—A touch, a touch, I do confess . *Hamlet* v 2 296
Another hold. The law hath yet another hold on you . *Mer. of Venice* iv 1 347

Another hope. Give him another hope, to betray him to another punishment . . . . *Mer. Wives* iii 3 207
Another horse. Give me another horse : bind up my wounds *Rich. III.* v 3 177
Another house. Thou shouldst have better pleased me with this deed, Hadst thou descended from another house *As Y. Like It* i 2 241
Another hue. To throw a perfume on the violet, To smooth the ice, or add another hue Unto the rainbow . . . *K. John* iv 2 13
Coal-black is better than another hue, In that it scorns to bear another hue . . . . *T. Andron.* iv 2 100
Another indictment. There is another indictment upon thee 2 *Hen. IV.* ii 4 371
Another island. Enough to purchase such another island 2 *Hen. VI.* iii 3 3
Another jest. Ask no other dowry with her but such another jest *T. N.* ii 5 202
Another Julius. There be many Cæsars, Ere such another Julius *Cymb.* iii 1 12
Another Juno. In pace another Juno . . . . . *Pericles* v 1 112
Another key. But I will wed thee in another key . . *M. N. Dream* i 1 18
Another king! they grow like Hydra's heads . . . 1 *Hen. IV.* v 4 25
Another knot. With another knot, five-finger-tied . . *Troi. and Cres.* v 2 157
Another lady. Your highness is betroth'd Unto another lady 1 *Hen VI.* v 5 27
His conscience Has crept too near another lady . . *Hen. VIII.* ii 2 19
Another leek. I have another leek in my pocket . . . *Hen. V.* v 1 65
Another leer. Here's a young lad framed of another leer *T. Andron.* iv 2 119
Another length. I'll get me one of such another length *T. G. of Ver.* iii 1 133
Another letter. She would be best pleased To be so anger'd with another letter . . . . i 2 103
Here's another letter to her : she bears the purse too . *Mer. Wives* i 3 75
Another man. Like a fair house built on another man's ground . . ii 2 224
To pay a fine for a periwig and recover the lost hair of another man *Com. of Errors* ii 2 77
I do much wonder that one man, seeing how much another man is a fool when he dedicates his behaviours to love . . . *Much Ado* ii 3 8
Let me see his eyes, That, when I note another man like him, I may avoid him . . . . v 1 270
I thank God I have as little patience as another man . *L. L. Lost* i 2 171
I am shepherd to another man . . . . *As Y. Like It* ii 4 78
How bitter a thing it is to look into happiness through another man's eyes ! . . . . v 2 49
This is flat knavery, to take upon you another man's name *T. of Shrew* v 1 38
On the reading it he changed almost into another man . *All's Well* iv 3 5
If I become not a cart as well as another man . . . 1 *Hen. IV.* ii 4 546
I have more flesh than another man, and therefore more frailty . . iii 3 188
It will endure cold as another man's sword will : and there's an end *Hen. V.* ii 1 10
Nay, your wit will not so soon out as another man's will . *Coriolanus* ii 3 30
I dare draw as soon as another man, if I see occasion . *Rom. and Jul.* ii 4 167
O, such another sleep, that I might see But such another man ! *Ant. and Cleo.* v 2 78
Let there be no honour Where there is beauty ; truth, where semblance ; love, Where there's another man . . . *Cymbeline* ii 4 110
Another master. To-morrow You'll serve another master *A. and C.* iv 2 28
Try many, all good, serve truly, never Find such another master *Cymb.* v 5 374
Another messenger. I have another messenger to your worship *M. W.* ii 2 98
Another moon. Four happy days bring in Another moon *M. N. Dream* i 1 3
Another Nan. Good faith, it is such another Nan . *Mer. Wives* i 4 160
Another nature. The cutter Was as another nature, dumb . *Cymb.* ii 4 84
Another neighbour. Though France himself and such another neighbour Stand in our way . . . . *Hen. V.* i 2 166
Another one. Should I your true love know From another one ? *Ham.* iv 5 24
Another Penelope. You would be another Penelope . . *Coriolanus* i 3 92
Another place. Who were below him He used as creatures of another place . . . . *All's Well* i 2 42
I must go and meet with danger there, Or it will seek me in another place And find me worse provided . . . 2 *Hen. IV.* ii 3 49
Another prisoner. This is another prisoner that I saved *M. for Meas.* v 1 492
Another prologue must tell he is not a lion . . . *M. N. Dream* iii 1 35
Another proof. Such another proof will make me cry 'baa' *T. G. of V.* i 1 97
Another punishment. Give him another hope, to betray him to another punishment . . . . *Mer. Wives* iii 3 208
Another purse. Here, friend, 's another purse ; in it a jewel . . *Lear* iv 6 28
Another question. I'll put another question to thee . . . *Hamlet* v 1 43
Another request. Grant me another request.—Any thing . *T. Night* v 1 3
Another ring. On your finger in the night I'll put Another ring *A. W.* iv 2 62
Another room. Go thou, and fill another room in hell . *Richard II.* v 5 108
I'll throw thy body in another room . . . . 3 *Hen. VI.* v 6 92
Another scandal. You must not put another scandal on him . *Hamlet* ii 1 29
Another sense. Although I think 'twas in another sense . . *T. of Shrew* i 1 220
Ay, but, I fear me, in another sense . . . . 3 *Hen. VI.* iii 2 60
Another service. Mightst have sooner got another service *T. of Athens* iv 3 511
Another ship. At length, another ship had seized on us . *Com. of Errors* i 1 113
Another simple sin. That is another simple sin in you . *As Y. Like It* iii 2 82
Another sin. Put not another sin upon my head . . *Rom. and Jul.* v 3 62
Another sleep. O, such another sleep ! . . . . . *Ant. and Cleo.* v 2 77
Another sort. But we are spirits of another sort . . *M. N. Dream* iii 2 388
I'll deceive you in another sort, And that you'll say . *T. Andron.* iii 1 191
Another spur. Which is another spur to my departure . . *W. Tale* iv 2 10
Another staff. Give him another staff : this last was broke cross *M. Ado* v 1 138
Another stain, as big as hell can hold . . . . *Cymbeline* ii 4 140
Another stanzo: call you 'em stanzos ?—What you will *As Y. Like It* ii 5 18
Another storm brewing ; I hear it sing i' the wind . . . *Tempest* ii 2 19
Another style. Count's man : count's master is of another style *A. W.* ii 3 205
Another subject. I pray you choose another subject . . *Much Ado* v 1 137
Another such. I would not spend another such a night . *Richard III.* i 4 5
A young man More fit to do another such offence Than die for this *Meas. for Meas.* ii 3 14
There shall not at your father's house these seven years Be born another such . . . . *W. Tale* iv 4 590
Another suit. Would you undertake another suit . . . *T. Night* iii 1 119
When you come ashore, I have another suit.—You shall prevail *Pericles* v 1 262
Another tale. That peradventures shall tell you another tale *Mer. Wives* i 1 79
You shall tell me another tale, when th'other's come to't *Troi. and Cres.* i 2 91
Come, mistress, you must tell's another tale . . . . *Othello* v 1 125
Another tear. Why, I have not another tear to shed . . *T. Andron.* iii 1 267
Another thing. Now, of another thing she may, and that cannot I help *T. G. of Ver.* iii 1 358
'Tis one thing to be tempted, Escalus, Another thing to fall *M. for Meas.* ii 1 18
There is another thing : we must have a wall in the great chamber *M. N. Dream.* iii 1 63
Another time. As you like this, give me the lie another time *Tempest* iii 2 85
I'll tell thee more of this another time . . . *Mer. of Venice* i 1 108
You spurn'd me such a day ; another time You call'd me dog . . . i 3 128
It does concern you near.—Near ! why then, another time *T. of Athens* i 2 184
Break up the senate till another time . . . . *J. Cæsar* ii 2 98

Another tongue. Is't not possible to understand in another tongue? *Hamlet* v 2 131
Another trick. I must use you In such another trick . . . *Tempest* iv 1 37
If I be served such another trick, I'll have my brains ta'en out *Mer. Wives* iii 5 7
An you serve me such another trick, never come in my sight more *As Y. Like It* iv 1 40
Another troop. Here comes another troop to seek for you . . *Othello* i 2 54
Another Troy. And, like a Sinon, take another Troy . 3 *Hen. VI.* iii 2 190
Another way. No hope that way is Another way so high a hope *Tempest* ii 1 241
Another way I have to man my haggard, To make her come *T. of Shrew* iv 1 196
And what impossibility would slay In common sense, sense saves another way . . . . *All's Well* ii 1 181
Let him alone : I'll go another way to work with him . . *T. Night* iv 1 35
Which we, God knows, have turn'd another way, To our own vantage *K. John* ii 1 549
Wilt know again, Being ne'er so little urged, another way To pluck him headlong . . . . *Richard II.* v 1 64
O, turn thy edged sword another way ; Strike those that hurt 1 *Hen. VI.* iii 3 52
The effect doth operate another way . . . . . *Troi. and Cres.* v 3 109
Hie you to church ; I must another way, To fetch a ladder *Rom. and Jul.* ii 5 74
Another way, The news is not so tart.—I'll read, and answer . . *Lear* iv 2 87
Another weapon. I have another weapon in this chamber . . *Othello* v 2 252
Another while. I climbed into this garden, to see if I can eat grass, or pick a sallet another while . . . . . . 2 *Hen. VI.* iv 10 9
Another wife. Keep it till you woo another wife . . . *Cymbeline* i 1 113
Another word. You are not worth another word . . . *All's Well* ii 3 280
Another word, Menenius, I will not hear thee speak . . *Coriolanus* v 2 97
Another world. If heaven would make me such another world Of one entire and perfect chrysolite, I'ld not have sold her for it . *Othello* v 2 144
Another yet. And yet you will ; and yet another 'yet' . *T. G. of Ver.* ii 1 126
Another yet ! A seventh ! I'll see no more . . . *Macbeth* iv 1 118
Another's anguish. One fire burns out another's burning, One pain is lessen'd by another's anguish . . . . . *Rom. and Jul.* i 2 47
Another's confirmities. As rheumatic as two dry toasts ; you cannot one bear with another's confirmities . . . 2 *Hen. IV.* ii 4 63
Another's dotage. They hold one an opinion of another's dotage *M. Ado* ii 3 224
Another's enterprise. Words, vows, gifts, tears, and love's full sacrifice, He offers in another's enterprise . . . *Troi. and Cres.* i 2 309
Another's eyes. O hell ! to choose love by another's eyes *M. N. Dream* i 1 140
Another's fool. But an unkind self, that itself will leave, To be another's fool . . . . *Troi. and Cres.* iii 2 157
Another's fortunes. Like brothers, commanding one another's fortunes *T. of Athens* i 2 109
Another's gain. Not as protector, steward, substitute, Or lowly factor for another's gain . . . . *Richard III.* iii 7 134
Another's glass. Like one another's glass to trim them by . . *Pericles* i 4 27
Another's heel. One woe doth tread upon another's heel . . *Hamlet* iv 7 164
Sent a dozen sequent messengers This very night at one another's heels *Othello* i 2 42
Another's issue. No, I'll not rear Another's issue . . . *W. Tale* ii 3 193
Another's love. Borrow one another's love for the instant . *A. and C.* ii 2 103
Another's mind. That you may know one another's mind *Mer. Wives* ii 2 132
Another's pate. Do pelt so fast at one another's pate . . 1 *Hen. VI.* iii 1 82
Another's pocket. Which makes much against my manhood, if I should take from another's pocket to put into mine . . . *Hen. V.* iii 2 53
Another's pride. How one man eats into another's pride ! *Tr. and Cr.* iii 3 136
Another's throats. Why the devil should we keep knives to cut one another's throats? . . . . *Hen V.* ii 1 96
Another's throne. What are you, I pray, But one imperious in another's throne? . . . . 1 *Hen. VI.* iii 1 44
Another's way. Lead these testy rivals so astray As one come not within another's way . . . . . . *M. N. Dream* iii 2 359
Anselme. County Anselme and his beauteous sisters . *Rom. and Jul.* i 2 68
Answer. I come To answer thy best pleasure . . . . *Tempest* i 2 190
We'll visit Caliban my slave, who never Yields us kind answer . . . i 2 309
Be quick, thou 'rt best, To answer other business . . . . . i 2 367
Leave your crisp channels and on this green land Answer your summons iv 1 131
A silly answer and fitting well a sheep . . . *T. G. of Verona* i 1 81
My heart accords thereto, And yet a thousand times it answers 'no' . i 3 91
My father stays my coming ; answer not ; The tide is now . . . ii 2 13
Come, answer not, but to it presently ! I am impatient of my tarriance ii 7 89
I will answer it straight ; I have done all this . . . *Mer. Wives* i 1 118
I am freely dissolved, and dissolutely.—It is a fery discretion answer . i 1 261
And this day we shall have our answer . . . . iii 2 60
Hold up your head ; answer your master, be not afraid . . . . iv 1 20
I am dejected ; I am not able to answer the Welsh flannel . . . v 5 172
He calls again ; I pray you, answer him . . . *Meas. for Meas.* i 4 14
Some by virtue fall : Some run from brakes of ice, and answer none . ii 1 39
Answer to this : I, now the voice of the recorded law, Pronounce a sentence . . . . ii 4 60
I'll make it my morn prayer To have it added to the faults of mine, And nothing of your answer . . . . ii 4 73
Answer me to-morrow, Or, by the affection that now guides me most, I'll prove a tyrant to him . . . . ii 4 167
Answer his requiring with a plausible obedience . . . . . iii 1 253
And the place answer to convenience . . . . iii 1 258
Let me desire you to make your answer before him . . . . iii 2 165
If his own life answer the straitness of his proceeding, it shall become him well . . . . iii 2 269
Leave me your snatches, and yield me a direct answer . . . . iv 2 7
Thus fail not to do your office, as you will answer it at your peril . iv 2 129
Well, you'll answer this one day. Fare ye well . . . . iv 3 172
Haste still pays haste, and leisure answers leisure . . . . v 1 415
Answer me In what safe place you have bestow'd my money *Com. of Errors* i 2 77
Wast thou mad, That thus so madly thou didst answer me ? . . . ii 2 12
Pray God our cheer May answer my good will and your good welcome . iii 1 20
My business cannot brook this dalliance. Good sir, say whether you'll answer me or no . . . . iv 1 60
I answer you ! what should I answer you? . . . . . . iv 1 62
You shall buy this sport as dear As all the metal in your shop will answer . . . . iv 1 82
He that brings any man to answer it that breaks his band . . . iv 3 31
Why bear you these rebukes and answer not ? . . . . . . v 1 89
Mark how short his answer is . . . . *Much Ado* i 1 215
I will acquaint my daughter withal, that she may be the better prepared for an answer . . . . i 2 24
If the prince do solicit you in that kind, you know your answer . . ii 1 71
Tell him there is measure in every thing and so dance out the answer . ii 1 75
Answer, clerk.—No more words : the clerk is answered . . . . ii 1 114

Answer. Thus answer I in name of Benedick *Much Ado* ii 1 179
If their singing answer your saying, by my faith, you say honestly ii 1 241
A time too brief, too, to have all things answer my mind ii 1 376
I knew it would be your answer iii 3 19
If they make you not then the better answer, you may say they are not the men you took them for iii 3 50
Will never answer a calf when he bleats iii 3 75
I will owe thee an answer for that: and now forward with thy tale iii 3 108
Know you any, count?—I dare make his answer, none iv 1 18
Bid her answer truly.—I charge thee do so, as thou art my child iv 1 76
To make you answer truly to your name iv 1 80
Now, if you are a maid, answer to this iv 1 86
How answer you for yourselves? iv 2 25
Measure his woe the length and breadth of mine And let it answer every strain for strain v 1 12
Let him answer me. Come, follow me, boy v 1 82
Dare as well answer a man indeed As I dare take a serpent by the tongue v 1 89
Who have you offended, masters, that you are thus bound to your answer? v 1 233
Let me go no farther to mine answer v 1 237
What's your will?—Your answer, sir, is enigmatical v 4 27
Which is Beatrice?—I answer to that name. What is your will? v 4 73
I do say thou art quick in answers: thou heatest my blood *L. L. Lost* i 2 31
Your sun-beamed eyes—They will not answer to that epithet v 2 170
Behold the window of my heart, mine eye, What humble suit attends thy answer there v 2 849
Masters, spread yourselves.—Answer as I call you *M. N. Dream* i 2 18
How answer you that?—By'r lakin, a parlous fear iii 1 12
You must not speak that yet; that you answer to Pyramus iii 1 101
Whose note full many a man doth mark, And dares not answer nay iii 1 136
What, will you tear Impatient answers from my gentle tongue? iii 2 287
Is not this the day That Hermia should give answer of her choice? iv 1 141
When my cue comes, call me, and I will answer iv 1 206
May you stead me? will you pleasure me? shall I know your answer? *Mer. of Venice* i 3 8
Your answer to that.—Antonio is a good man i 3 11
Had you been as wise as bold, Young in limbs, in judgement old, Your answer had not been inscroll'd ii 7 72
O happy torment, when my torturer Doth teach me answers for deliverance! iii 2 38
I shall answer that better to the commonwealth iii 5 40
Thou art come to answer A stony adversary, an inhuman wretch iv 1 3
We all expect a gentle answer, Jew iv 1 34
I'll not answer that: But, say, it is my humour: is it answer'd? iv 1 42
Now, for your answer iv 1 52
This is no answer, thou unfeeling man, To excuse the current of thy cruelty iv 1 63
I am not bound to please thee with my answers iv 1 65
You will answer, 'The slaves are ours'; so do I answer you iv 1 97
I stand for judgement: answer; shall I have it? iv 1 103
He attendeth here hard by, To know your answer iv 1 146
Charge us there upon inter'gatories, And we will answer all things faithfully v 1 299
How shall I answer you?—As wit and fortune will *As You Like It* i 2 109
When shalt thou see him again? Answer me in one word iii 2 237
To say ay and no to these particulars is more than to answer in a catechism iii 2 241
You are full of pretty answers iii 2 287
Not so; but I answer you right painted cloth iii 2 290
As she answers thee with frowning looks, I'll sauce her with bitter words iii 5 68
Never take her without her answer, unless you take her without her tongue iv 1 176
Go with us.—That will I, for I must bear answer back iv 3 180
Ay, sir, I thank God.—'Thank God;' a good answer v 1 27
He would answer, I spake not true: this is called the Reproof Valiant v 4 82
I'll answer him by law: I'll not budge an inch, boy *T. of Shrew*, Ind. 1 14
Thy hounds shall make the welkin answer them Ind. 2 47
Is that an answer?—Ay, and a kind one too v 2 83
Say, I command her come to me.—I know her answer.—What? v 2 97
Off with't while 'tis vendible; answer the time of request *All's Well* i 1 168
I am so full of businesses, I cannot answer thee acutely i 1 221
He hath arm'd our answer, And Florence is denied before he comes i 2 11
But for me, I have an answer will serve all men ii 2 14
Marry, that's a bountiful answer that fits all questions ii 2 15
Will your answer serve fit to all questions? ii 2 20
Have you, I say, an answer of such fitness for all questions? ii 2 30
It must be an answer of most monstrous size that must fit all demands ii 2 34
I will be a fool in question, hoping to be the wiser by your answer ii 2 42
You would answer very well to a whipping, if you were but bound to't ii 2 57
Give Helen this, And urge her to a present answer back ii 2 67
But follows it, my lord, to bring me down Must answer for your raising? ii 3 120
But to answer you as you would be understood; he weeps like a wench that had shed her milk iv 3 122
Our general bids you answer to what I shall ask you out of a note iv 3 145
Shall I set down your answer so?—Do: I'll take the sacrament on't iv 3 155
I beseech you, let me answer to the particular of the inter'gatories iv 3 206
Which gratitude Through flinty Tartar's bosom would peep forth, And answer, thanks iv 4 8
I could not answer in that course of honour As she had made the overture v 3 98
But from her handmaid do return this answer *T. Night* i 1 25
A good lenten answer i 5 9
Good my mouse of virtue, answer me i 5 69
Speak to me; I shall answer for her. Your will? i 5 179
In his bosom! In what chapter of his bosom?—To answer by the method, in the first of his heart i 5 244
I cannot love him; He might have took his answer long ago i 5 282
I will answer you with gait and entrance iii 1 93
By all means stir on the youth to an answer iii 2 63
I can no other answer make but thanks, And thanks iii 3 14
Nightingales answer daws iii 4 39
Unless you undertake that with me which with as much safety you might answer him iii 4 273
On the answer, he pays you as surely as your feet hit the ground iii 4 305
There's no remedy; I shall answer it iii 4 367
The offences we have made you do we'll answer *W. Tale* i 2 83
Imprison't not In ignorant concealment.—I may not answer i 2 397
This is not, no, Laid to thy answer iii 2 200
That they say one would speak to her and stand in hope of answer v 2 111
It is a surplus of your grace, which never My life may last to answer v 3 8

Answer. Where we may leisurely Each one demand and answer to his part *W. Tale* v 3 153
Then comes answer like an Absey book *K. John* i 1 196
And so, ere answer knows what question would i 1 200
Stay for an answer to your embassy, Lest unadvised you stain your swords ii 1 44
From whom hast thou this great commission, France, To draw my answer from thy articles? ii 1 111
Who is it thou dost call usurper, France?—Let me make answer ii 1 121
When I have said, make answer to us both ii 1 235
Why answer not the double majesties This friendly treaty? ii 1 480
Thou canst not, cardinal, devise a name So slight, unworthy and ridiculous, To charge me to an answer, as the pope iii 1 151
The king is moved, and answers not to this iii 1 217
O, be removed from him, and answer well! iii 1 218
O, answer not, but to my closet bring The angry lords iv 2 267
As you answer, I do know the scope And warrant limited unto my tongue v 2 122
Where heaven He knows how we shall answer him v 7 60
Or my divine soul answer it in heaven *Richard II.* i 1 38
I'll answer thee in any fair degree, Or chivalrous design of knightly trial i 1 80
Be ready, as your lives shall answer it, At Coventry i 1 198
My message is to you.—My lord, my answer is—to Lancaster ii 3 70
What answer shall I make to this base man? iv 1 20
I have a thousand spirits in one breast, To answer twenty thousand such iv 1 59
Procure your sureties for your days of answer iv 1 159
It is no more Than my poor life must answer.—Thy life answer! v 2 83
What said the gallant?—His answer was, he would unto the stews v 3 16
I have sent for him to answer this *1 Hen. IV.* i 1 100
Who studies day and night To answer all the debt he owes to you i 3 185
You paraquito, answer me Directly unto this question that I ask ii 3 88
And answers, 'Some fourteen,' an hour after; 'a trifle, a trifle' ii 4 120
Are not you a coward? answer me to that ii 4 157
Shall I give him his answer?—Prithee, do, Jack ii 4 326
If thou love me, practise an answer ii 4 412
By to-morrow dinner-time, Send him to answer thee, or any man ii 4 565
And, but for shame, In such a parley should I answer thee iii 1 204
And if it make twenty, take them all; I'll answer the coinage iv 2 8
Shall I return this answer to the king?—Not so iv 3 106
On their answer, will we set on them: And God befriend us! v 1 119
Knock but at the gate, And he himself will answer *2 Hen. IV.* i 1 6
Let him be brought in to his answer i 2 34
Answer in the effect of your reputation, and satisfy the poor woman ii 1 142
The answer is as ready as a borrower's cap ii 2 124
Answer, thou dead elm, answer ii 4 358
Answer them directly How far forth you do like their articles iv 2 52
In answer of which claim, the prince our master Says *Hen. V.* i 2 249
Their faults are open: Arrest them to the answer of the law ii 2 143
And more than carefully it us concerns To answer royally in our defences ii 4 3
He'll call you to so hot an answer of it ii 4 123
A night is but small breath and little pause To answer matters of this consequence ii 4 146
The sum of all our answer is but this: We would not seek a battle iii 6 172
Fire answers fire, and through their paly flames Each battle sees the other's umber'd face iv Prol. 8
The king is not bound to answer the particular endings of his soldiers iv 1 163
Every man that dies ill, the ill upon his own head, the king is not to answer it.—I do not desire he should answer for me iv 1 200
Bear my former answer back: Bid them achieve me and then sell my bones iv 3 90
A gentleman of great sort, quite from the answer of his degree iv 7 142
Let his neck answer for it, if there is any martial law in the world iv 8 46
The king hath heard them; to the which as yet There is no answer made v 2 75
Well then the peace, Which you before so urged, lies in his answer v 2 76
We will suddenly Pass our accept and peremptory answer v 2 82
Give me your answer; i' faith, do: and so clap hands and a bargain v 2 133
How answer you, la plus belle Katharine du monde? v 2 230
Come, your answer in broken music; for thy voice is music v 2 262
Pardon the frankness of my mirth, if I answer you for that v 2 319
Ask me what question thou canst possible, And I will answer *1 Hen. VI.* i 2 88
Answer you so the lord protector?—The Lord protect him! so we answer him i 3 8
Gloucester, thou wilt answer this before the pope i 3 52
I will not answer thee with words, but blows i 3 69
What means this silence? Dare no man answer in a case of truth? ii 4 2
And answer was return'd that he will come ii 5 20
As I with sudden and extemporal speech Purpose to answer iii 1 7
What is that wrong whereof you both complain? First let me know, and then I'll answer you iv 1 88
As you please, So let them have their answers every one v 1 25
And yet I would that you would answer me v 3 86
I descend To give thee answer of thy just demand v 3 144
What answer makes your grace? *1 Hen. VI.* v 3 150; *2 Hen. VI.* iv 4 7
Her valiant courage and undaunted spirit, More than in women commonly is seen, Will answer our hope in issue of a king *1 Hen. VI.* v 5 72
A spirit raised from depth of under-ground, That shall make answer *2 Hen. VI.* i 2 80
By the eternal God, whose name and power Thou tremblest at, answer i 4 29
In thine own person answer thy abuse ii 1 41
Call these foul offenders to their answers ii 1 203
An answer from the king, or we will all break in! iii 2 278
O gross and miserable ignorance!—Nay, answer, if you can iv 2 179
What canst thou answer to my majesty for giving up of Normandy? iv 7 29
To call poor men before them about matters they were not able to answer iv 7 47
As for words, whose greatness answers words iv 10 56
Pardon me, That I have given no answer all this while v 1 33
Why whisper you, my lords, and answer not? *3 Hen. VI.* i 1 149
Here I stand to answer thee, Or any he the proudest of thy sort ii 2 96
Answer no more, for thou shalt be my queen iii 2 106
Hear me speak, Before you answer Warwick iii 3 66
But answer me one doubt, What pledge have we of thy firm loyalty? iii 3 238
Matter of marriage was the charge he gave me, But dreadful war shall answer his demand iii 3 259
What answer makes King Lewis unto our letters? iv 1 91
What answers Clarence to his sovereign's will?—That he consents iv 6 45
Do but answer this: What is the body when the head is off? v 1 40

Answer. I propose the selfsame words to thee, Which, traitor, thou wouldst have me answer to . . . . 3 *Hen. VI.* v 5 21
Since the heavens have shaped my body so, Let hell make crook'd my mind to answer it . . . . v 6 79
Could all but answer for that peevish brat? . . . *Richard III.* i 3 194
His answer was, the people were not wont To be spoke to but by the recorder . . . . iii 7 29
Play the maid's part, still answer nay, and take it . . . iii 7 51
If not to answer, you might haply think Tongue-tied ambition, not replying, yielded . . . . iii 7 144
Definitively thus I answer you. Your love deserves my thanks . iii 7 153
Look to your wife: if she convey Letters to Richmond, you shall answer it . . . . iv 2 96
But how to make ye suddenly an answer, In such a point of weight . . . In truth, I know not . . . . . . *Hen. VIII.* iii 1 70
I am a woman, lacking wit To make a seemly answer to such persons . iii 1 178
All else This talking lord can lay upon my credit, I answer is most false iii 2 266
For your stubborn answer About the giving back the great seal to us, The king shall know it . . . . iii 2 346
And brought him forward, As a man sorely tainted, to his answer . iv 2 14
Till further trial in those charges Which will require your answer . v 1 104
You must be godfather, and answer for her . . . . . v 3 163
Because not there: this woman's answer sorts . . *Troi. and Cres.* i 1 109
They laughed not so much at the hair as at his pretty answer . . i 2 169
Now play him me, Patroclus, Arming to answer in a night alarm . . i 3 171
One noble man that hath one spark of fire, To answer for his love . . i 3 295
And wake him to the answer, think you? . . . . . . i 3 332
Who shall answer him?—I know not: 'tis put to lottery . . . ii 1 139
We are too well acquainted with these answers . . . . . ii 3 122
He'll answer nobody; he professes not answering: speaking is for beggars . . . . iii 3 269
Your answer, sir.—Fare you well, with all my heart . . . iii 3 299
When I am hence, I'll answer to my lust . . . . . iv 4 134
Thou blow'st for Hector.—No trumpet answers.—'Tis but early days iv 5 12
We'll answer it; The issue is embracement . . . . . iv 5 147
Welcome hither.—Who must we answer?—The noble Menelaus . iv 5 176
Answer me, heavens!—It would discredit the blest gods, proud man, To answer such a question . . . . iv 5 246
The belly answer'd— Well, sir, what answer made the belly? *Coriolanus* i 1 109
The former agents, if they did complain, What could the belly answer? i 1 128
Patience awhile, you'll hear the belly's answer . . . . i 1 130
What say you to't?—It was an answer: how apply you this? . . i 1 150
We never yet made doubt but Rome was ready To answer us . . . i 2 19
He is himself alone, To answer all the city . . . . . i 4 52
Both observe and answer The vantage of his anger . . . . ii 3 267
Has spoken like a traitor, and shall answer As traitors do . . iii 1 162
Obey, I charge thee, And follow to thine answer . . . . iii 1 177
Where he shall answer, by a lawful form, In peace, to his utmost peril . iii 1 325
Arm yourself To answer mildly; for they are prepared With accusations iii 2 139
Let them accuse me by invention, I Will answer in mine honour . iii 2 144
Answer to us.—Say, then: 'tis true, I ought so . . . . iii 3 61
Coriolanus He would not answer to: forbad all names . . . v 1 12
His answer to me was, He could not stay to pick them in a pile . v 1 24
What I have done, as best I may, Answer I must and shall do with my life . . . . *T. Andron.* i 1 412
Ready at your highness' will To answer their suspicion with their lives ii 3 298
I tell my sorrows to the stones; Who, though they cannot answer my distress, Yet in some sort they are better than the tribunes . . iii 1 38
Her eye discourses; I will answer it . . . . *Rom. and Jul.* ii 2 13
A challenge, on my life.—Romeo will answer it . . . . ii 4 9
Any man that can write may answer a letter.—Nay, he will answer the letter's master, how he dares, being dared . . . . . ii 4 10
Is thy news good, or bad? answer to that; Say either . . . ii 5 35
I am not I, if there be such an I; Or those eyes shut, that make thee answer 'I' . . . . iii 2 49
Speak not, reply not, do not answer me; My fingers itch . . iii 5 164
A whining mammet, in her fortune's tender, To answer, 'I'll not wed' iii 5 187
Come you to make confession to this father?—To answer that, I should confess to you . . . . iv 1 23
Answer me like men . . . . iv 5 127
Would I had a rod in my mouth, that I might answer thee profitably *T. of Athens* i 2 80
That answer might have become Apemantus . . . . . ii 2 125
They answer, in a joint and corporate voice . . . . . ii 2 213
This answer join: Who bates mine honour shall not know my coin . iii 3 25
But this answer will not serve.—If 'twill not serve, 'tis not so base as you iii 4 57
Now we shall know some answer . . . . iii 4 67
We cannot take this for answer, sir . . . . . . iii 4 78
To the conflicting elements exposed, Answer mere nature . . . iv 3 231
For their knives care not, While you have throats to answer . . v 1 182
Shall be render'd to your public laws At heaviest answer . . . v 4 63
But what trade art thou? answer me directly . . . . *J. Cæsar* i 1 12
And find a time Both meet to hear and answer such high things . i 2 170
I perhaps speak this Before a willing bondman; then I know My answer must be made. But I am arm'd . . . . i 3 114
Run to the senate-house; Stay not to answer me, but get thee gone . ii 4 2
If then that friend demand why Brutus rose against Cæsar, this is my answer . . . . iii 2 22
They are wise and honourable, And will, no doubt, with reasons answer you . . . . iii 2 219
Answer every man directly.—Ay, and briefly.—Ay, and wisely . iii 3 10
Then, to answer every man directly and briefly, wisely and truly . iii 3 16
He was but a fool that brought My answer back . . . . iv 3 85
We will answer on their charge. Make forth . . . . . v 1 24
Stand not to answer: here, take thou the hilts . . . . v 3 43
You'll rue the time That clogs me with this answer . . *Macbeth* iii 6 43
I conjure you, by that which you profess, Howe'er you come to know it, answer me . . . . iv 1 51
Answer me To what I ask you.—Speak.—Demand.—We'll answer . iv 1 60
Would I could answer This comfort with the like! . . . . iv 3 192
Who's there?—Nay, answer me: stand, and unfold yourself . *Hamlet* i 1 2
Speak! I charge thee, speak!—'Tis gone, and will not answer . . i 1 52
But answer made it none: yet once methought It lifted up it head . i 2 215
O, answer me! Let me not burst in ignorance . . . . . i 4 45
We'll read, Answer, and think upon this business . . . . ii 2 82
I have nothing with this answer, Hamlet; these words are not mine . iii 2 101
If it shall please you to make me a wholesome answer . . . iii 2 328
Make you a wholesome answer; my wit's diseased: but, sir, such answer as I can make, you shall command . . . . iii 2 333
Come, come, you answer with an idle tongue . . . . . iii 4 11

Answer. I will bestow him, and will answer well The death I gave him *Hamlet* iii 4 176
It would come to immediate trial, if your lordship would vouchsafe the answer.—How if I answer 'no'? . . . . v 2 176
Give the first or second hit, Or quit in answer of the third exchange . v 2 280
Answer my life my judgement . . . . *Lear* i 1 153
She's there, and she is yours.—I know no answer . . . . i 1 204
The fault of it I'll answer . . . . i 3 10
Differences, which I least thought it fit To answer from our home . . ii 1 126
Commanded me to follow, and attend The leisure of their answer . . ii 4 37
Mere fetches; The images of revolt and flying off. Fetch me a better answer . . . . ii 4 92
To answer with thy uncovered body this extremity of the skies . . iii 4 106
Wherefore to Dover? Let him first answer that . . . . iii 7 53
I told him you were coming; His answer was, 'The worse' . . iv 2 6
He'll not feel wrongs Which tie him to an answer . . . . iv 2 14
This letter, madam, craves a speedy answer; 'Tis from your sister . iv 2 82
Another way, The news is not so tart.—I'll read, and answer . . iv 2 88
I am not well; else I should answer From a full-flowing stomach . v 3 73
Your name, your quality? and why you answer This present summons? v 3 120
By the law of arms thou wast not bound to answer An unknown opposite v 3 152
This thou shalt answer; . . .—Sir, I will answer any thing . *Othello* i 1 121
Where will you that I go To answer this your charge?—To prison, till fit time Of law and course of direct session Call thee to answer . . i 2 87
The affair cries haste, And speed must answer it . . . . i 3 278
Had I as many mouths as Hydra, such an answer would stop them all . ii 3 308
Better have been born a dog Than answer my waked wrath! . . iii 3 363
Make questions, and by them answer . . . . . . iii 4 17
I cannot weep; nor answer have I none, But what should go by water iv 2 103
No more light answers. Let our officers Have notice . *Ant. and Cleo.* i 2 183
I shall entreat him To answer like himself . . . . . . ii 2 4
Possess it, I'll make answer: But I had rather fast from all four days Than drink so much in one . . . . ii 7 107
Make thine own edict for thy pains, which we Will answer as a law . iii 12 33
And answer me declined, sword against sword . . . . . iii 13 27
That he should dream, Knowing all measures, the full Cæsar will Answer his emptiness! . . . . iii 13 36
Where's Antony?—There, Diomed, there.—Lives he? Wilt thou not answer? . . . . iv 14 115
And, when we fall, We answer others' merits in our name . . . v 2 178
Let us have articles betwixt us. Only, thus far you shall answer *Cymb.* i 4 170
You shall answer me with your sword . . . . i 4 176
Deliver with more openness your answers To my demands . . . i 6 88
This is no answer.—But that you shall not say I yield being silent, I would not speak . . . . ii 3 98
I hope the briefness of your answer made The speediness of your return iii 4 30
Doublet, hat, hose, all That answer to them . . . . . iii 4 173
There's no answer That will be given to the loudest noise we make . iii 5 43
Who's here? If any thing that's civil, speak; if savage, Take or lend. Ho! No answer? Then I'll enter . . . . iii 6 24
Thus did he answer me: yet said, hereafter I might know more . . iv 2 41
Would seek us through And put us to our answer . . . . iv 2 161
All solemn things Should answer solemn accidents . . . . iv 2 192
Whose answer would be death Drawn on with torture . . . . iv 4 13
Great the slaughter is Here made by the Roman; great the answer be Britons must take . . . . v 3 79
Step you forth; Give answer to this boy, and do it freely . . . v 5 131
If that thy prosperous and artificial feat Can draw him but to answer *Per.* v 1 73
If this but answer to my just belief, I'll well remember you . . v 1 239
Answer for. We that have good wits have much to answer for *As Y. Like It* v 1 13
Answerable. And all things answerable to this portion . *T. of Shrew* ii 1 361
If he have robb'd these men, He shall be answerable . . 1 *Hen. IV.* ii 4 571
Thou shalt see an answerable sequestration . . . . *Othello* i 3 351
Answered. This shall be answered.—I will answer it straight; I have done all this. That is now answered . . . . *Mer. Wives* i 1 117
Who mutually hath answer'd my affection . . . . . . iv 6 10
Those many had not dared to do that evil, If the first that did the edict infringe Had answer'd for his deed . . *Meas. for Meas.* ii 2 93
The duke yet would have dark deeds darkly answered . . . iii 2 188
If thy name be call'd Luce,—Luce, thou hast answer'd him well *Com. of Err.* iii 1 54
Answer, clerk.—No more words: the clerk is answered . *Much Ado* ii 1 115
An oak but with one green leaf on it would have answered her . . ii 1 248
Thou heatest my blood.—I am answered, sir . . . . *L. L. Lost* i 2 33
Anon his Thisbe must be answered, And forth my mimic comes *M. N. Dream* iii 2 18
I'll not answer that: But, say, it is my humour: is it answer'd *M. of V.* iv 1 43
What, are you answer'd yet? . . . . iv 1 46
Are you answer'd?—This is no answer, thou unfeeling man . . iv 1 62
You taught me first to beg; and now methinks You teach me how a beggar should be answer'd . . . . iv 1 440
Forbear, I say: He dies that touches any of this fruit Till I and my affairs are answered . . . . *As Y. Like It* ii 7 99
An you will not be answered with reason, I must die . . . . ii 7 100
I marvel why I answer'd not again: But that's all one . . . iii 5 132
You have answered to his reputation with the duke . . *All's Well* iv 3 277
I cannot be so answer'd.—Sooth, but you must . . . *T. Night* ii 4 91
You cannot love her; You tell her so; must she not then be answer'd? ii 4 95
I did some service; of such note indeed, That were I ta'en here it would scarce be answer'd . . . . iii 3 28
It might have since been answer'd in repaying What we took from them iii 3 33
We should have answer'd heaven Boldly 'not guilty' . . *W. Tale* i 2 73
I may not answer.—A sickness caught of me, and yet I well! I must be answer'd. Dost thou hear? . . . . i 2 399
Blows have answer'd blows; Strength match'd with strength . *K. John* ii 1 329
This must be answer'd either here or hence . . . . . iv 2 89
Out of my grief and my impatience, Answer'd neglectingly . 1 *Hen. IV.* i 3 52
This bald unjointed chat of his, my lord, I answer'd indirectly, as I said i 3 66
Now, Hal, to the news at court: for the robbery, lad, how is that answered? . . . . iii 3 198
All these bold fears Thou see'st with peril I have answered 2 *Hen. IV.* iv 5 197
These faults are easy, quickly answer'd . . . 2 *Hen. VI.* iii 1 133
Measure for measure must be answered . . . . 3 *Hen. VI.* ii 6 55
He answer'd, 'Tush, It can do me no damage' . . . *Hen. VIII.* i 2 182
Fairly answer'd; A loyal and obedient subject is Therein illustrated . iii 2 179
Bring word if Hector will to-morrow Be answer'd in his challenge *Troi. and Cres.* iii 3 35
The belly answer'd—Well, sir, what answer made the belly? *Coriolanus* i 1 108
Being answer'd, And a petition granted them . . . . . i 1 213
Yet I insisted, yet you answer'd not . . . . . *J. Cæsar* ii 1 245

Answered. It was a grievous fault, And grievously hath Cæsar answer'd it . . . . *J. Cæsar* iii 2 85
That matter is answered directly . . . . iii 3 25
How covert matters may be best disclosed, And open perils surest answered . . . . iv 1 47
Was that done like Cassius? Should I have answer'd Caius Cassius so? iv 3 78
Now, Antony, our hopes are answered . . . . . . v 1 1
Alas, how shall this bloody deed be answer'd? It will be laid to us *Hamlet* iv 1 16
Great rivals in our youngest daughter's love, Long in our court have made their amorous sojourn, And here are to be answer'd . *Lear* i 1 49
He answered me in the roundest manner, he would not . . . i 4 58
But jealous souls will not be answer'd so . . . . *Othello* iii 4 159
Sir, this should be answer'd.—'Tis done already . *Ant. and Cleo.* iii 6 30
Where is she, sir? How Can her contempt be answer'd? . *Cymbeline* iii 5 42
I thought he slept, and put My clouted brogues from off my feet, whose rudeness Answer'd my steps too loud . . . . . . iv 2 215
Who had not now been drooping here, if seconds Had answer'd him v 3 91
Answerer. Be simple answerer, for we know the truth . . *Lear* iii 7 43
Answerest. Why pratest thou to thyself and answer'st not? *Com. of Err.* ii 2 195
I tell thee I am mad In Cressid's love: thou answer'st, 'she is fair' *Troi. and Cres.* i 1 52
If thou answerest me not to the purpose, confess thyself . *Hamlet* v 1 43
Answering. And do him right that, answering one foul wrong, Lives not to act another . . . *Meas. for Meas.* ii 2 103
Trial did draw Bias and thwart, not answering the aim . *Troi. and Cres.* i 3 15
Why, he'll answer nobody; he professes not answering . . . iii 3 270
Answering us With our own charge . . . . . *Coriolanus* v 6 67
Answering before we do demand of them . . . . *J. Cæsar* v 1 6
Your loss is as yourself, great; and you bear it As answering to the weight . . . . *Ant. and Cleo.* v 2 102
What slave art thou?—A thing More slavish did I ne'er than answering A slave without a knock . . . . . . *Cymbeline* iv 2 73
Answering the letter of the oracle, Unknown to you . . . v 5 450
Fame answering the most strange inquire . . . *Pericles* iii Gower 22
Ant. He angers me With telling me of the moldwarp and the ant 1 *Hen. IV.* iii 1 149
We'll set thee to school to an ant, to teach thee there's no labouring i' the winter . . . . *Lear* ii 4 68
Antenor. That's Antenor: he has a shrewd wit, I can tell you *Tr. and Cr.* i 2 206
You have a Trojan prisoner, call'd Antenor, Yesterday took . . iii 3 18
This Antenor, I know, is such a wrest in their affairs That their negotiations all must slack, Wanting his manage . . . . . . iii 3 22
And there to render him, For the enfreed Antenor, the fair Cressid iv 1 38
The devil take Antenor! the young prince will go mad: a plague upon Antenor! . . . . iv 2 77
Wench, thou must be gone; thou art changed for Antenor . . iv 2 96
Welcome, Sir Diomed! here is the lady Which for Antenor we deliver you . . . . iv 4 112
Antenorides. Priam's six-gated city, Dardan, and Tymbria, Helias, Chetas, Troien, And Antenorides . . . . Prol. 17
Anthem. As ending anthem of my endless dolour . . *T. G. of Ver.* iii 1 240
For my voice, I have lost it with halloing and singing of anthems 2 *Hen. IV.* i 2 213
Anthony Dull; a man of good repute, carriage, bearing . *L. L. Lost* i 1 271
Anthropophagi and men whose heads Do grow beneath their shoulders *Othello* i 3 144
Anthropophaginian. He'll speak like an Anthropophaginian . *M. Wives* iv 5 10
Antiates. Their bands i' the vaward are the Antiates, Of their best trust; o'er them Aufidius . . . . *Coriolanus* i 6 53
Directly Set me against Aufidius and his Antiates . . . . i 6 59
The spoil got on the Antiates Was ne'er distributed . . . . iii 3 4
Made peace With no less honour to the Antiates Than shame to the Romans . . . . v 6 80
Antic. Were he the veriest antic in the world . . . *T. of Shrew* Ind. 1 101
There the antic sits, Scoffing his state and grinning at his pomp *Rich. II.* iii 2 162
Fobbed as it is with the rusty curb of old father antic the law 1 *Hen. IV.* i 2 69
For indeed three such antics do not amount to a man . *Hen. V.* iii 2 32
Thou antic death, which laugh'st us here to scorn . 1 *Hen. VI.* iv 7 18
Behold, distraction, frenzy, and amazement, Like witless antics *T. and C.* v 3 86
What dares the slave Come hither, cover'd with an antic face? *R. and J.* i 5 58
The pox of such antic, lisping, affecting fantasticoes! . . . ii 4 29
I'll charm the air to give a sound, While you perform your antic round *Macbeth* iv 1 130
I perchance hereafter shall think meet To put an antic disposition on *Hamlet* i 5 172
Anticipates our thoughts A se'nnight's speed . . . . . *Othello* ii 1 76
Anticipatest. Time, thou anticipatest my dread exploits . *Macbeth* iv 1 144
Anticipating time with starting courage . . . *Troi. and Cres.* iv 5 2
Anticipation. So shall my anticipation prevent your discovery *Hamlet* ii 2 304
Anticked. The wild disguise hath almost Antick'd us all . *Ant. and Cleo.* ii 7 132
Anticly. Go anticly, show outward hideousness . . . *Much Ado* v 1 96
Antidote. Trust not the physician; His antidotes are poison *T. of Athens* iv 3 435
And with some sweet oblivious antidote Cleanse the stuff'd bosom *Macbeth* v 3 43
Antigonus, I charged thee that she should not come about me: I knew she would . . . . *W. Tale* ii 3 42
He cried to me for help and said his name was Antigonus . . . iii 3 98
All as monstrous to our human reason As my Antigonus to break his grave . . . . v 1 42
The letters of Antigonus found with it which they know to be his character . . . . v 2 37
What, pray you, became of Antigonus, that carried hence the child? v 2 64
Antioch. This Antioch, then, Antiochus the Great Built up *Pericles* i Gower 17
Antioch, farewell! for wisdom sees, those men Blush not in actions blacker than the night, Will shun no course . . . . . . i 1 134
And danger, which I fear'd, is at Antioch . . . . . . i 2 7
I went to Antioch, Where, as thou know'st, against the face of death, I sought the purchase of a glorious beauty . . . . i 2 70
I'll give some light unto you. Being at Antioch—What from Antioch? i 3 19
This we desire, As friends to Antioch, we may feast in Tyre . . i 3 40
The third of Antioch; And his device, a wreath of chivalry . . ii 2 28
Antiochus. This Antioch, then, Antiochus the Great Built up . i Gower 17
Prince Pericles,—That would be son to great Antiochus . . . i 1 26
Antiochus, I thank thee, who hath taught My frail mortality to know itself . . . . i 1 41
Ready for the way of life or death, I wait the sharpest blow, Antiochus i 1 55
To trumpet forth my infamy, Nor tell the world Antiochus doth sin . i 1 146
The great Antiochus, 'Gainst whom I am too little to contend . . i 2 16
Antiochus you fear, And justly too, I think, you fear the tyrant . i 2 102
Antiochus—on what cause I know not—Took some displeasure at him . i 3 20

Antiochus. Lord Thaliard from Antiochus is welcome.—From him I come *Pericles* i 3 31
Know this of me, Antiochus from incest lived not free . . ii 4 2
The tenour these: Antiochus and his daughter dead . . . iii Gower 25
Antiopa. Break his faith With Ariadne and Antiopa . . *M. N. Dream* ii 1 80
Antipathy. No contraries hold more antipathy Than I and such a knave *Lear* ii 2 93
Antipholus, look strange and frown: Some other mistress hath thy sweet aspects . . . . *Com. of Errors* ii 2 112
Come, come, Antipholus, we dine too late . . . . . ii 2 221
Shall, Antipholus, Even in the spring of love, thy love-springs rot? . iii 2 2
Master Antipholus,—Ay, that's my name.—I know it well, sir . . iii 2 170
Even just the sum that I do owe to you Is growing to me by Antipholus iv 1 8
Out of doubt Antipholus is mad, Else would he never so demean himself iv 3 82
Antipholus, I wonder much That you would put me to this shame . v 1 13
Antipholus my husband, Whom I made lord of me and all I had . . v 1 136
Is not your name, sir, call'd Antipholus? And is not that your bondman? . . . . v 1 286
These old witnesses—I cannot err—Tell me thou art my son Antipholus v 1 318
I tell thee, Syracusian, twenty years Have I been patron to Antipholus v 1 327
These two Antipholuses, these two so like . . . . . . v 1 357
Antipholus, thou camest from Corinth first?—No, sir, not I . . v 1 362
Antipodes. I will go on the slightest errand now to the Antipodes *Much Ado* ii 1 273
The moon May through the centre creep and so displease Her brother's noontide with the Antipodes . . . . . . *M. N. Dream* iii 2 55
We should hold day with the Antipodes, If you would walk in absence of the sun . . . . *Mer. of Venice* v 1 127
Whilst we were wandering with the antipodes . . . *Richard II.* iii 2 49
Thou art as opposite to every good As the Antipodes are unto us 3 *Hen. VI.* i 4 135
Antiquary. Instructed by the antiquary times, He must, he is, he cannot but be wise . . . . *Troi. and Cres.* ii 3 262
Antique. Nature, drawing of an antique, Made a foul blot *Much Ado* iii 1 63
Some delightful ostentation, or show, or pageant, or antique *L. L. Lost* v 1 119
We will have, if this fadge not, an antique . . . . . v 1 154
I never may believe These antique fables, nor these fairy toys *M. N. Dream* v 1 3
Under an oak whose antique root peeps out Upon the brook *As Y. Like It* ii 1 31
How well in thee appears The constant service of the antique world! . ii 3 57
That old and antique song we heard last night . . . *T. Night* ii 4 3
The antique and well noted face Of plain old form is much disfigured *K. John* iv 2 21
In best sort, Like to the senators of the antique Rome . *Hen. V.* v Prol. 26
The dust on antique time would lie unswept . . . . *Coriolanus* ii 3 126
His antique sword, Rebellious to his arm, lies where it falls . *Hamlet* ii 2 491
Never believe it: I am more an antique Roman than a Dane . . v 2 352
A handkerchief, an antique token My father gave my mother *Othello* v 2 216
Antiquity. Bawd is he doubtless, and of antiquity too . *Meas. for Meas.* iii 2 71
Moss'd with age And high top bald with dry antiquity . *As Y. Like It* iv 3 106
Hadst thou not the privilege of antiquity upon thee . . *All's Well* ii 3 220
And every part about you blasted with antiquity . . . 2 *Hen. IV.* i 2 208
As the world were now but to begin, Antiquity forgot . . *Hamlet* iv 5 104
Antiquius. Et bonum quo antiquius, eo melius . . *Pericles* i Gower 10
Antium. He is retired to Antium.—Spoke he of me? . *Coriolanus* iii 1 11
At Antium lives he?—At Antium.—I wish I had a cause to seek him . iii 1 17
A goodly city is this Antium. City, 'Tis I that made thy widows . . iv 4 1
Is he in Antium?—He is, and feasts the nobles of the state . . iv 4 8
Antoniad. The Antoniad, the Egyptian admiral, With all their sixty, fly and turn the rudder . . . . *Ant. and Cleo.* iii 10 2
Antonio. My brother and thy uncle, call'd Antonio . . . . *Tempest* i 2 66
One midnight Fated to the purpose did Antonio open The gates of Milan i 2 129
What things are these, my lord Antonio? Will money buy 'em? . . v 1 264
Know ye Don Antonio, your countryman?—Ay, my good lord *T. G. of Ver.* ii 4 54
I know you well enough; you are Signior Antonio . . . *Much Ado* ii 1 117
I know, Antonio Is sad to think upon his merchandise . *Mer. of Venice* i 1 39
Since you have found Antonio, We two will leave you . . . . i 1 69
Signior Antonio; You have too much respect upon the world . . i 1 73
Antonio—I love thee, and it is my love that speaks . . . . i 1 86
'Tis not unknown to you, Antonio, How much I have disabled mine estate . . . . i 1 122
To you, Antonio, I owe the most, in money and in love . . . i 1 130
O my Antonio, had I but the means To hold a rival place with one of them! . . . . i 1 173
Antonio shall be bound.—Antonio shall become bound; well . . i 3 4
Three thousand ducats for three months and Antonio bound . . i 3 10
Antonio is a good man.—Have you heard any imputation to the contrary? i 3 12
May I speak with Antonio?—If it please you to dine with us . . i 3 32
This is Signior Antonio.—How like a fawning publican he looks! . . i 3 41
Signior Antonio, many a time and oft In the Rialto you have rated me . i 3 107
Antonio certified the duke They were not with Bassanio in his ship . ii 8 10
Let good Antonio look he keep his day, Or he shall pay for this . . ii 8 25
I thought upon Antonio when he told me; And wish'd in silence that it were not his . . . . ii 8 31
Tell Antonio what you hear; Yet do not suddenly, for it may grieve him . . . . ii 8 33
It lives there unchecked that Antonio hath a ship of rich lading wrecked iii 1 3
The good Antonio, the honest Antonio,—O that I had a title good enough to keep his name company! . . . . iii 1 14
Do you hear whether Antonio have had any loss at sea or no? . . iii 1 45
My master Antonio is at his house and desires to speak with you both . iii 1 77
Yes, other men have ill luck too: Antonio, as I heard in Genoa . iii 1 102
There came divers of Antonio's creditors in my company to Venice . iii 1 118
But Antonio is certainly undone.—Nay, that's true, that's very true . iii 1 129
Signior Antonio Commends him to you . . . . iii 2 234
News from Venice? How doth that royal merchant, good Antonio? . iii 2 242
He would rather have Antonio's flesh Than twenty times the value of the sum That he did owe him . . . . iii 2 288
If law, authority, and power deny not, It will go hard with poor Antonio . . . . iii 2 292
Antonio, Being the bosom lover of my lord, Must needs be like my lord iii 4 16
What, is Antonio here?—Ready, so please your grace . . . . iv 1 1
A lodged hate and a certain loathing I bear Antonio . . . . iv 1 61
Good cheer, Antonio! What, man, courage yet! . . . . . iv 1 111
The cause in controversy between the Jew and Antonio the merchant . iv 1 156
Antonio and old Shylock, both stand forth.—Is your name Shylock? . iv 1 175
Your honourable wife: Tell her the process of Antonio's end . . iv 1 274
Antonio, I am married to a wife Which is as dear to me as life itself iv 1 282
Half thy wealth, it is Antonio's; The other half comes to the general state . . . . iv 1 370
What mercy can you render him, Antonio?—A halter gratis . . iv 1 378
Antonio, gratify this gentleman, For, in my mind, you are much bound iv 1 406

Antonio. Give him the ring, and bring him, if thou canst, Unto Antonio's house . . . *Mer. of Venice* iv 1 454
This is the man, this is Antonio, To whom I am so infinitely bound . v 1 134
Thus it stands with me: Antonio, my father, is deceased *T. of Shrew* i 2 54
Antonio's son, A man well known throughout all Italy . . ii 1 68
That is Antonio, the duke's eldest son . . . . *All's Well* iii 5 79
You must know of me then, Antonio, my name is Sebastian . *T. Night* ii 1 16
O good Antonio, forgive me your trouble . . . . . ii 1 35
My kind Antonio, I can no other answer make but thanks, And thanks iii 3 13
Antonio, I arrest thee at the suit of Count Orsino . . . iii 4 360
Where's Antonio, then? I could not find him at the Elephant . . iv 3 4
Antonio never yet was thief or pirate . . . . . v 1 77
Antonio, O my dear Antonio! How have the hours rack'd and tortured me! . . . . v 1 225
Antonius. Stand you directly in Antonius' way . . *J. Cæsar* i 2 3
Forget not, in your speed, Antonius, To touch Calpurnia . . i 2 6
He did bid Antonius Send word to you he would be there to-morrow . i 3 37
Is Cæsar with Antonius prized so slight? . . . *Ant. and Cleo.* i 1 56
Were I the wearer of Antonius' beard, I would not shave't to-day . ii 2 7
Antonius dead!—If thou say so, villain, Thou kill'st thy mistress . ii 5 26
But she is now the wife of Marcus Antonius . . . . ii 6 119
I could do more to do Antonius good, But 'twould offend him . . iii 1 25
Antony. Brother Antony,—Come, 'tis no matter . . . *Much Ado* v 1 100
In my very conscience he is as valiant a man as Mark Antony *Hen. V.* iii 6 15
Antony, and Potpan!—Ay, boy, ready.—You are looked for *Rom. and Jul.* i 5 11
I do lack some part Of that quick spirit that is in Antony . *J. Cæsar* i 2 29
He loves no plays, As thou dost, Antony; he hears no music . i 2 204
Who offered him the crown?—Why, Antony.—Tell us the manner of it i 2 233
I saw Mark Antony offer him a crown;—yet 'twas not a crown neither i 2 237
Not meet, Mark Antony, so well beloved of Cæsar, Should outlive Cæsar . . . . ii 1 156
Let Antony and Cæsar fall together.—Our course will seem too bloody ii 1 161
Antony is but a limb of Cæsar: Let us be sacrificers, but not butchers . ii 1 165
For Mark Antony, think not of him; For he can do no more than Cæsar's arm When Cæsar's head is off . . . . . ii 1 181
Send Mark Antony to the senate-house; And he shall say you are not well . . . . ii 2 52
Antony shall say I am not well; And, for thy humour, I will stay at home . . . . ii 2 55
See! Antony, that revels long o' nights, Is notwithstanding up . . ii 2 116
Good morrow, Antony.—So to most noble Cæsar . . . . ii 2 117
Look you, Brutus, He draws Mark Antony out of the way . . iii 1 26
Where is Antony?—Fled to his house amazed . . . . iii 1 95
Thus did Mark Antony bid me fall down . . . . . iii 1 124
If Brutus will vouchsafe that Antony May safely come to him . . iii 1 130
Mark Antony shall not love Cæsar dead So well as Brutus living . iii 1 133
So says my master Antony.—Thy master is a wise and valiant Roman . iii 1 137
Here comes Antony. Welcome, Mark Antony . . . . . iii 1 147
O Antony, beg not your death of us . . . . . . iii 1 164
To you our swords have leaden points, Mark Antony . . . iii 1 173
To see thy Antony making his peace, Shaking the bloody fingers of thy foes . . . . iii 1 197
Were you, Antony, the son of Cæsar, You should be satisfied . . iii 1 225
Do not consent That Antony speak in his funeral . . . . iii 1 233
What Antony shall speak, I will protest He speaks by leave . . iii 1 238
Mark Antony, here, take you Cæsar's body . . . . . iii 1 244
Here comes his body, mourned by Mark Antony . . . . iii 2 45
Stay here with Antony: Do grace to Cæsar's corpse, and grace his speech Tending to Cæsar's glories; which Mark Antony, By our permission, is allow'd to make . . . . iii 2 61
I do entreat you, not a man depart, Save I alone, till Antony have spoke . . . . iii 2 66
Let us hear Mark Antony.—Let him go up into the public chair . . iii 2 67
Noble Antony, go up.—For Brutus' sake, I am beholding to you . . iii 2 69
Peace! let us hear what Antony can say.—You gentle Romans . . iii 2 76
There's not a nobler man in Rome than Antony . . . . iii 2 121
We'll hear the will: read it, Mark Antony.—The will, the will! . . iii 2 143
We'll hear it, Antony; You shall read us the will, Cæsar's will . . iii 2 152
Stand from the body.—Room for Antony, most noble Antony . . iii 2 170
Hear the noble Antony.—We'll hear him, we'll follow him . . iii 2 211
Were I Brutus, And Brutus Antony, there were an Antony Would ruffle up your spirits . . . . iii 2 231
Yet hear me speak.—Peace, ho! Hear Antony. Most noble Antony! iii 2 239
Prick him down, Antony.—Upon condition Publius shall not live, Who is your sister's son, Mark Antony . . . . . . iv 1 3
Antony, and young Octavius, come, Revenge yourselves alone on Cassius . . . . iv 3 93
Impatient of my absence, And grief that young Octavius with Mark Antony Have made themselves so strong . . . . . iv 3 153
Young Octavius and Mark Antony Come down upon us with a mighty power . . . . iv 3 168
Now, Antony, our hopes are answered . . . . . . v 1 1
We must out and talk.—Mark Antony, shall we give sign of battle? . v 1 23
Antony, The posture of your blows are yet unknown; But for your words, they rob the Hybla bees . . . . v 1 32
You have stol'n their buzzing, Antony, And very wisely threat before you sting . . . . v 1 37
His soldiers fell to spoil, Whilst we by Antony are all enclosed . . v 3 8
Mark Antony is in your tents, my lord: Fly, therefore, noble Cassius . v 3 10
Octavius Is overthrown by noble Brutus' power, As Cassius' legions are by Antony . . . . v 3 53
Tell Antony, Brutus is ta'en.—I'll tell the news . . . . v 4 16
Brutus is ta'en, my lord.—Where is he?—Safe, Antony; Brutus is safe v 4 20
I shall have glory by this losing day More than Octavius and Mark Antony . . . . v 5 37
My Genius is rebuked; as, it is said, Mark Antony's was by Cæsar *Macbeth* iii 1 57
Nay, hear them, Antony: Fulvia perchance is angry *Ant. and Cleo.* i 1 19
Hear it, Antony. Where's Fulvia's process? Cæsar's I would say? both? . . . . i 1 27
As I am Egypt's queen, Thou blushest, Antony . . . . i 1 30
I'll seem the fool I am not; Antony Will be himself . . . i 1 42
Sometimes, when he is not Antony, He comes too short of that great property Which still should go with Antony . . . . . i 1 57
But here comes Antony.—I am sick and sullen . . . . i 3 13
But let it be: I am quickly ill, and well, So Antony loves . . i 3 73
O, my oblivion is a very Antony, And I am all forgotten . . i 3 90
Yet must Antony No way excuse his soils, when we do bear So great weight in his lightness . . . . i 4 23
Antony. Antony, Leave thy lascivious wassails . . *Ant. and Cleo.* i 4 55
That I might sleep out this great gap of time My Antony is away . i 5 6
Is he on his horse? O happy horse, to bear the weight of Antony! . i 5 21
How much unlike art thou Mark Antony! . . . . . i 5 35
How goes it with my brave Mark Antony? . . . . . i 5 38
Who's born that day When I forget to send to Antony, Shall die a beggar . . . . i 5 64
O that brave Cæsar!—Be choked with such another emphasis! Say, the brave Antony . . . . i 5 69
Mark Antony In Egypt sits at dinner, and will make No wars . ii 1 11
Mark Antony is every hour in Rome Expected . . . . . ii 1 29
Can from the lap of Egypt's widow pluck The ne'er-lust-wearied Antony ii 1 38
I cannot hope Cæsar and Antony shall well greet together . . ii 1 39
His brother warr'd upon him; although, I think, Not moved by Antony ii 1 42
Let Antony look over Cæsar's head And speak as loud as Mars . ii 2 5
Here comes The noble Antony.—And yonder, Cæsar . . . ii 2 14
Great Mark Antony Is now a widower . . . . . . ii 2 121
Will Cæsar speak?—Not till he hears how Antony is touch'd . . ii 2 142
Noble Antony, Not sickness should detain me . . . . . ii 2 172
When she first met Mark Antony, she pursed up his heart, upon the river of Cydnus . . . . ii 2 191
O, rare for Antony! . . . . ii 2 210
Antony, Enthroned i' the market-place, did sit alone, Whistling to the air . . . . ii 2 219
Upon her landing, Antony sent to her, Invited her to supper . . ii 2 224
Our courteous Antony, Whom ne'er the word of 'No' woman heard speak . . . . ii 2 227
Now Antony must leave her utterly.—Never; he will not . . ii 2 238
If beauty, wisdom, modesty, can settle The heart of Antony, Octavia is A blessed lottery to him . . . . ii 2 247
Therefore, O Antony, stay not by his side . . . . . ii 3 18
Sir, Mark Antony Will e'en but kiss Octavia, and we'll follow . ii 4 2
I'll think them every one an Antony, And say, 'Ah, ha! you're caught' ii 5 14
There's no goodness in thy face: if Antony Be free and healthful,—so tart a favour To trumpet such good tidings! . . . . . ii 5 37
If thou say Antony lives, is well, Or friends with Cæsar . . ii 5 43
In praising Antony, I have dispraised Cæsar.—Many times, madam . ii 5 107
But Mark Antony Put me to some impatience . . . . . ii 6 42
Draw lots who shall begin.—That will I, Pompey.—No, Antony . ii 6 63
Who would not have his wife so?—Not he that himself is not so; which is Mark Antony . . . . ii 6 134
Antony will use his affection where it is: he married but his occasion here . . . . ii 6 138
Good Antony, your hand.—I'll try you on the shore.—And shall, sir . ii 7 133
O Antony, You have my father's house,—But, what? we are friends . ii 7 134
Thy grand captain Antony Shall set thee on triumphant chariots . iii 1 9
Cæsar and Antony have ever won More in their officer than person . iii 1 16
O, how he loves Cæsar!—Nay, but how dearly he adores Mark Antony! iii 2 8
Why, he's the Jupiter of men.—What's Antony? The god of Jupiter . iii 2 10
Spake you of Cæsar? How! the nonpareil!—O Antony! O thou Arabian bird! . . . . iii 2 12
But he loves Cæsar best; yet he loves Antony . . . . iii 2 15
Scribes, bards, poets, cannot Think, speak, cast, write, sing, number, ho! His love to Antony . . . . iii 2 18
When Antony found Julius Cæsar dead, He cried almost to roaring . iii 2 54
That Herod's head I'll have: but how, when Antony is gone? . . iii 3 5
And saw her led Between her brother and Mark Antony . . . iii 3 13
Where's Antony?—He's walking in the garden—thus . . . iii 5 16
'Twill be naught: But let it be. Bring me to Antony . . . iii 5 24
The wife of Antony Should have an army for an usher . . . iii 6 43
Antony, Hearing that you prepared for war, acquainted My grieved ear iii 6 57
Only the adulterous Antony, most large In his abominations, turns you off . . . . iii 6 93
What is't you say?—Your presence needs must puzzle Antony . . iii 7 11
The noble ruin of her magic, Antony, Claps on his sea-wing, and, like a doting mallard, Leaving the fight in height, flies after her . . iii 10 19
I'll yet follow The wounded chance of Antony . . . . iii 10 36
Let him appear that's come from Antony. Know you him? . . iii 12 1
Approach, and speak.—Such as I am, I come from Antony . . iii 12 7
For Antony, I have no ears to his request . . . . . iii 12 19
Now 'tis time: dispatch; From Antony win Cleopatra . . . iii 12 27
Observe how Antony becomes his flaw . . . . . . iii 12 34
Is Antony or we in fault for this?—Antony only . . . . iii 13 2
So, haply, are they friends to Antony.—He needs as many, sir, as Cæsar . . . . iii 13 48
You embrace not Antony As you did love, but as you fear'd him . . iii 13 56
Mine honour was not yielded, But conquer'd merely.—To be sure of that, I will ask Antony . . . . iii 13 63
It would warm his spirits, To hear from me you had left Antony . iii 13 70
Have you no ears? I am Antony yet . . . . . . iii 13 93
Our terrene moon Is now eclipsed; and it portends alone The fall of Antony! . . . . iii 13 155
But, since my lord Is Antony again, I will be Cleopatra . . . . iii 13 187
Dares me to personal combat, Cæsar to Antony . . . . iv 1 4
Within our files there are, Of those that served Mark Antony but late, Enough to fetch him in . . . . iv 1 13
We have store to do't, And they have earn'd the waste. Poor Antony! iv 1 16
I wish I could be made so many men, And all of you clapp'd up together in An Antony, that I might do you service . . . . . iv 2 18
'Tis the god Hercules, whom Antony loved, Now leaves him . . iv 3 16
That he and Cæsar might Determine this great war in single fight! Then, Antony,—but now—Well, on . . . . . . iv 4 38
The gods make this a happy day to Antony! . . . . . iv 5 1
Begin the fight: Our will is Antony be took alive; Make it so known . iv 6 2
Antony Is come into the field.—Go charge Agrippa Plant those that have revolted in the van, That Antony may seem to spend his fury Upon himself . . . . iv 6 7
Alexas did revolt; and went to Jewry on Affairs of Antony; there did persuade Great Herod to incline himself to Cæsar, And leave his master Antony . . . . iv 6 13
Antony Hath after thee sent all thy treasure, with His bounty overplus . . . . iv 6 20
O Antony, Thou mine of bounty, how wouldst thou have paid My better service! . . . . iv 6 31
O Antony, Nobler than my revolt is infamous, Forgive me . . iv 9 18
A master-leaver and a fugitive: O Antony! O Antony! . . . iv 9 23
Antony Is valiant, and dejected; and, by starts, His fretted fortunes give him hope, and fear, Of what he has, and has not . . . iv 12 6
Fortune and Antony part here; even here Do we shake hands . . iv 12 19
Say, that the last I spoke was 'Antony,' And word it, prithee, piteously iv 13 8

Antony. Here I am Antony; Yet cannot hold this visible shape, my knave . . . *Ant. and Cleo.* iv 14 13
The last she spake Was 'Antony! most noble Antony!' . . . iv 14 30
Then in the midst a tearing groan did break The name of Antony . iv 14 32
There then: thus I do escape the sorrow Of Antony's death . . iv 14 95
O Antony, Antony, Antony! Help, Charmian, help, Iras, help . . iv 15 11
Not Cæsar's valour hath o'erthrown Antony, But Antony's hath triumph'd on itself . . . . iv 15 14
So it should be, that none but Antony Should conquer Antony . . iv 15 16
But come, come, Antony,—Help me, my women,—we must draw thee up . . . . iv 15 29
Mark Antony I served, who best was worthy Best to be served . v 1 6
What is't thou say'st?—I say, O Cæsar, Antony is dead . . v 1 13
The death of Antony Is not a single doom; in the name lay A moiety of the world . . . . v 1 17
O Antony! I have follow'd thee to this . . . . v 1 35
Antony Did tell me of you, bade me trust you. . . . v 2 12
I dream'd there was an Emperor Antony: O, such another sleep! . v 2 76
Yet, to imagine An Antony, were nature's piece 'gainst fancy . v 2 99
By taking Antony's course, you shall bereave yourself Of my good purposes . . . . v 2 130
Antony Shall be brought drunken forth, and I shall see Some squeaking Cleopatra boy my greatness . . . . . . v 2 218
I am again for Cydnus, To meet Mark Antony . . . . v 2 229
Methinks I hear Antony call; I see him rouse himself . . . v 2 287
If she first meet the curled Antony, He'll make demand of her . v 2 304
As sweet as balm, as soft as air, as gentle,—O Antony! . . . v 2 315
As she would catch another Antony In her strong toil of grace . v 2 350
She shall be buried by her Antony: No grave upon the earth shall clip in it A pair so famous . . . . v 2 361
Antres vast and deserts idle, Rough quarries, rocks and hills . *Othello* i 3 140
Anvil. I saw a smith stand with his hammer, thus, The whilst his iron did on the anvil cool . . . . . . *K. John* iv 2 194
Here I clip The anvil of my sword . . . . *Coriolanus* iv 5 116
Any. Their manners are more gentle-kind than Of our human generation you shall find Many, nay, almost any . . . *Tempest* iii 3 34
Sweet, except not any; Except thou wilt except against my love *T. G. of Ver.* ii 4 154
Here can I sit alone, unseen of any . . . . . v 4 4
As art and practice hath enriched any That we remember *Meas. for Meas.* i 1 13
If any ask you for your master, Say he dines forth . *Com. of Errors* ii 2 211
If there be any of him left, I'll bury it.—That's a good deed . *W. Tale* iii 3 136
And hold their manhoods cheap whiles any speaks That fought with us *Hen. V.* iv 3 66
Have you a precedent Of this commission? I believe, not any *Hen. VIII.* i 2 92
Is as common As any the most vulgar thing to sense . . *Hamlet* i 2 99
And less attemptable than any the rarest of our ladies in France *Cymbeline* i 4 65
Any body. If he do, i' faith, and find any body in the house . *Mer. Wives* i 4 4
Tell me, hath any body inquired for me here to-day? . *Meas. for Meas.* iv 1 16
Any business. They'll tell the clock to any business that We say *Tempest* ii 1 289
Any companion. Not wish Any companion in the world but you . iii 1 55
Any else. Is there any else longs to see this broken music? *As Y. Like It* i 2 149
Any emperor. He's a present for any emperor that ever trod *Tempest* ii 2 72
Any engine. Knife, gun, or need of any engine, Would I not have . ii 1 161
Any further. Before we proceed any further, hear me speak *Coriolanus* i 1 1
Nor construe any further my neglect . . . *J. Cæsar* i 2 45
I would not, so with love I might entreat you, Be any further moved . i 2 167
Any god. Had I been any god of power, I would Have sunk the sea *Tempest* i 2 10
Any longer. You'll lose the tide, if you tarry any longer *T. G. of Ver.* ii 3 39
You are not to go loose any longer; you must be pinioned *Mer. Wives* iv 2 128
I am a Jew, if I serve the Jew any longer. . *Mer. of Venice* ii 2 120
Any man. That I will do any man's heart good to hear me *M. N. Dream* i 2 73
It [conscience] beggars any man that keeps it . . . *Richard III.* i 4 145
Any means. If I can by any means light on a fit man to teach her *T. of Shrew* i 1 112
By any means prove a tall fellow . . . . *W. Tale* v 2 183
Have you importuned him by any means? . . *Rom. and Jul.* i 1 151
Any more. Hast any more of this?—The whole butt, man *Tempest* ii 2 136
Go with me?—I prithee now, lead the way without any more talking . ii 2 177
If you trouble him any more in's tale, by this hand, I will supplant some of your teeth . . . . iii 2 55
As, in faith, I mean not To see him any more . . *W. Tale* iv 4 506
I'll hate him everlastingly That bids me be of comfort any more *Richard II.* iii 2 208
Any print. Which any print of goodness wilt not take . . *Tempest* i 2 352
Any reason. At thy request, monster, I will do reason, any reason . iii 2 129
Any such. If you . . . know any such, Prefer them hither . *T. of Shrew* i 1 96
Any thing. Of any thing the image tell me that Hath kept with thy remembrance . . . . *Tempest* i 2 43
Have you any thing to take to?—Nothing but my fortune *T. G. of Ver.* iv 1 42
I have a fine hawk for the bush. Shall it be so?—Any thing *Mer. Wives* iii 3 249
You speak upon the rack, Where men enforced do speak anything *Mer. of Venice* iii 2 33
I was called any thing; and I would have done any thing 2 *Hen. IV.* iii 2 19
For any thing I know, Falstaff shall die of a sweat . . . Epil. 31
You may partake of any thing we say: We speak no treason *Richard III.* i 1 89
Sweet Alexas, most any thing Alexas, almost most absolute Alexas *Ant. and Cleo.* i 2 1
Any time this two and twenty years . . 1 *Hen. IV.* ii 2 16
Any weather. Neither bush nor shrub, to bear off any weather *Tempest* ii 2 19
Any where. If any where I have them, 'tis by the seaside *W. Tale* iii 3 68
Her means much less To meet her new-beloved any where *Rom. and Jul.* ii Prol. 12
Murder'd!—Woe, alas! What, in our house?—Too cruel any where *Macbeth* ii 3 93
Where Lieutenant Cassio lies?—I dare not say he lies any where *Othello* iii 4 3
Apace. The charm dissolves apace . . . . . *Tempest* v 1 64
You are pleasant, sir, and speak apace . . *Meas. for Meas.* iii 2 120
Here they stay'd an hour, And talk'd apace . . *L. L. Lost* v 2 369
Our nuptial hour Draws on apace . . . . *M. N. Dream* i 1 2
I prithee, tell me who is it quickly, and speak apace . *As Y. Like It* iii 2 208
Come apace, good Audrey: I will fetch up your goats . . . iii 3 1
Sunday comes apace: We will have rings and things and fine array *T. of Shrew* ii 1 324
He is dieted to his hour.—That approaches apace . . *All's Well* iv 3 36
Hark ye; The queen your mother rounds apace . . *W. Tale* ii 1 16
Look, where the holy legate comes apace . . . *K. John* v 2 65
The king comes on apace.—I thank him, that he cuts me from my tale 1 *Hen. IV.* v 2 90
Come apace to the king: there is more good toward you. . *Hen. V.* iv 8 2

Apace. Small herbs have grace, great weeds do grow apace *Richard III.* ii 4 13
Gallop apace, you fiery-footed steeds, Towards Phœbus' lodging *Rom. and Jul.* iii 2 1
The future comes apace: What shall defend the interim? *T. of Athens* ii 2 157
Brutus, come apace, And see how I regarded Caius Cassius *J. Cæsar* v 3 87
Now spurs the lated traveller apace To gain the timely inn . *Macbeth* iii 3 6
I bleed apace: Untimely comes this hurt . . . . *Lear* iii 7 97
'Tis time to look about; the powers of the kingdom approach apace . iv 7 94
Creeps apace Into the hearts of such as have not thrived *Ant. and Cleo.* i 3 50
Thou bleed'st apace.—I had a wound here that was like a T . iv 7 6
Apace, Eros, apace. No more a soldier: bruised pieces, go . . iv 14 41
Too slow a messenger. O, come apace, dispatch! I partly feel thee . v 2 325
Apart. Stay, stand apart; I know not which is which *Com. of Errors* v 1 364
Go apart, Adam, and thou shalt hear how he will shake me up *As Y. Like It* i 1 29
Why, thy godhead laid apart, Warr'st thou with a woman's heart? . iv 3 44
So please you, madam, To put apart these your attendants *W. Tale* ii 2 14
Therefore I keep it Lonely, apart. But here it is . . . v 3 18
So tell the pope, all reverence set apart To him . . *K. John* iii 1 159
Stand all apart, And show fair duty to his majesty. . *Richard II.* iii 3 187
Divest yourself, and lay apart The borrow'd glories . . *Hen. V.* ii 4 78
To lay apart their particular functions and wonder at him . . iii 7 41
In private will I talk with thee apart . . . 1 *Hen. VI.* i 2 69
And Henry put apart, the next for me . . . 2 *Hen. VI.* iii 1 383
Stand apart; the king shall know your mind . . . iii 2 242
Drew myself apart And almost broke my heart with extreme laughter *T. Andron.* v 1 112
Each man apart, all single and alone, Yet an arch-villain keeps him company . . . . *T. of Athens* v 1 110
Thy heart is big, get thee apart and weep . . . *J. Cæsar* iii 1 282
Resolve yourselves apart: I'll come to you anon . . *Macbeth* iii 1 138
Where is he gone?—To draw apart the body he hath kill'd *Hamlet* iv 1 24
Go but apart, Make choice of whom your wisest friends you will . . iv 5 203
I'll set her on; Myself the while to draw the Moor apart *Othello* ii 3 391
Come, go with me apart; I will withdraw, To furnish me . . iii 3 476
Stand you awhile apart; Confine yourself but in a patient list . iv 1 75
I dare him therefore To lay his gay comparisons apart *Ant. and Cleo.* iii 13 26
Cæsar's will?—Hear it apart.—None but friends: say boldly . . iii 13 47
Some nobler token I have kept apart For Livia and Octavia . . v 2 168
Come on, away: apart upon our knees . . . *Cymbeline* iv 2 288
Ape. Sometime like apes that mow and chatter at me . . *Tempest* ii 2 9
Be turn'd to barnacles, or to apes With foreheads villanous low . iv 1 249
By gar, you are de coward, de Jack dog, John ape . *Mer. Wives* iii 1 86
His glassy essence, like an angry ape, Plays such fantastic tricks before high heaven As make the angels weep . . *Meas. for Meas.* ii 2 120
Thou hast thine own form.—No, I am an ape . . *Com. of Errors* ii 2 200
I will even take sixpence in earnest of the bear-ward, and lead his apes into hell . . . . *Much Ado* ii 1 43
So deliver I up my apes, and away to Saint Peter for the heavens . ii 1 49
Boys, apes, braggarts, Jacks, milksops! . . . . v 1 91
He is then a giant to an ape; but then is an ape a doctor to such a man v 1 205
The fox, the ape, and the humble-bee, Were still at odds . *L. L. Lost* iii 1 85
Imitari is nothing: so doth the hound his master, the ape his keeper . iv 2 131
This is the ape of form, monsieur the nice . . . . v 2 325
On meddling monkey, or on busy ape . . . *M. N. Dream* ii 1 181
More new-fangled than an ape, more giddy in my desires than a monkey *As Y. Like It* iv 1 153
And for your love to her lead apes in hell . . *T. of Shrew* ii 1 34
Would beguile Nature of her custom, so perfectly he is her ape *W. Tale* v 2 108
You mad-headed ape! A weasel hath not such a deal of spleen 1 *Hen. IV.* ii 3 80
Look, if the fat villain have not transformed him ape . 2 *Hen. IV.* ii 2 77
Ah, you sweet little rogue, you! Alas, poor ape, how thou sweatest! ii 4 234
To the English court assemble now, From every region, apes of idleness! iv 5 123
Because that I am little, like an ape, He thinks that you should bear me on your shoulders . . . . . . *Richard III.* iii 1 130
How have you run From slaves that apes would beat! . . *Coriolanus* i 4 36
He moveth not; The ape is dead, and I must conjure him *Rom. and Jul.* ii 1 16
You show'd your teeth like apes, and fawn'd like hounds . *J. Cæsar* v 1 41
Like the famous ape, To try conclusions, in the basket creep *Hamlet* iii 4 194
He keeps them, like an ape, in the corner of his jaw . . iv 2 19
Apes and monkeys 'Twixt two such shes would chatter this way *Cymb.* i 6 39
O sleep, thou ape of death, lie dull upon her! . . . ii 2 31
Triumphs for nothing and lamenting toys Is jollity for apes . . iv 2 194
Ape-bearer. He hath been since an ape-bearer . . *W. Tale* iv 3 101
Apemantus. From the glass-faced flatterer To Apemantus *T. of Athens* i 1 59
Good morrow to thee, gentle Apemantus!—Till I be gentle, stay thou . i 1 178
You know me, Apemantus?—Thou know'st I do . . . i 1 185
Thou art proud, Apemantus.—Of nothing so much as that I am not like Timon . . . . i 1 188
How likest thou this picture, Apemantus?—The best, for the innocence i 1 197
Wilt dine with me, Apemantus?—No; I eat not lords . . i 1 206
How dost thou like this jewel, Apemantus?—Not so well as plain-dealing . . . . i 1 214
What wouldst do then, Apemantus?—E'en as Apemantus does now . i 1 235
What time o' day is't, Apemantus?—Time to be honest . . i 1 265
O, Apemantus, you are welcome.—No; You shall not make me welcome i 2 23
Much good dich thy good heart, Apemantus! . . . . i 2 73
Apemantus, if thou wert not sullen, I would be good to thee. . i 2 242
Here comes the fool with Apemantus: let's ha' some sport with 'em ii 2 48
What are we, Apemantus?—Asses . . . . . ii 2 63
Apemantus, read me the superscription of these letters . . ii 2 81
That answer might have become Apemantus . . . ii 2 125
Where feed'st thou o' days, Apemantus?—Where my stomach finds meat . . . . iv 3 293
What wouldst thou do with the world, Apemantus, if it lay in thy power? iv 3 322
I had rather be a beggar's dog than Apemantus . . . iv 3 362
Apennines. Talking of the Alps and Apennines . . . *K. John* i 1 202
Apex. Me pompæ provexit apex. . . . . . *Pericles* ii 2 30
A-piece. Cost me two shilling and two pence a-piece . *Mer. Wives* i 1 160
Dispatched sixteen businesses, a month's length a-piece. . *All's Well* iv 3 99
Three or four bonds of forty pound a-piece . . . 1 *Hen. IV.* iii 3 117
Forty, fifty, an hundred ducats a-piece for his picture in little *Hamlet* ii 2 383
A-pieces. What so many may do, Not being torn a-pieces, we have done *Hen. VIII.* v 4 80
Apish, shallow, inconstant, full of tears, full of smiles *As Y. Like It* iii 2 432
This apish and unmannerly approach . . . . *K. John* v 2 131
Whose manners still our tardy apish nation Limps after *Richard II.* ii 1 22
Duck with French nods and apish courtesy . . *Richard III.* i 3 49
They know not how their wits to wear, Their manners are so apish *Lear* i 4 184
Apollinem. 'Ad Jovem,' that's for you: here, 'Ad Apollinem' *T. And.* iv 3 53

Apollo. As sweet and musical As bright Apollo's lute *L. L. Lost* iv 3 343
The words of Mercury are harsh after the songs of Apollo v 2 941
Apollo flies, and Daphne holds the chase *M. N. Dream* ii 1 231
Apollo plays And twenty caged nightingales do sing *T. of Shrew* Ind. 2 37
At that sight shall sad Apollo weep Ind. 2 61
I have dispatch'd in post To sacred Delphos, to Apollo's temple *W. Tale* ii 1 183
The great Apollo suddenly will have The truth of this appear ii 3 200
Great Apollo Turn all to the best! iii 1 14
When the oracle, Thus by Apollo's great divine seal'd up, Shall the contents discover, something rare iii 1 19
I do refer me to the oracle: Apollo be my judge! iii 2 117
Bring forth, And in Apollo's name, his oracle iii 2 119
This seal'd-up oracle, by the hand deliver'd Of great Apollo's priest iii 2 129
Apollo's angry; and the heavens themselves Do strike iii 2 147
The fire-robed god, Golden Apollo iv 4 30
For has not the divine Apollo said, Is't not the tenour of his oracle? v 1 37
Tell me, Apollo, for thy Daphne's love, What Cressid is? *Troi. and Cres.* i 1 101
Though, Apollo knows, 'Tis dry enough i 3 328
Whose youth and freshness Wrinkles Apollo's ii 2 79
Unless the fiddler Apollo gets his sinews to make catlings on iii 3 305
Apollo, Pallas, Jove, or Mercury, Inspire me! *T. Andron.* iv 1 66
This to Mercury; This to Apollo; this to the god of war iv 4 15
Now, by Apollo,—Now, by Apollo, king, Thou swear'st thy gods in vain *Lear* i 1 162
A passport too! Apollo, perfect me in the characters! *Pericles* iii 2 67
Apollodorus. I have heard, Apollodorus carried—No more *Ant. and Cleo.* ii 6 69
Apology. I will have an apology for that purpose *L. L. Lost* v 1 142
Quoniam he seemeth in minority, Ergo I come with this apology v 2 597
Strengthen'd with what apology you think *All's Well* ii 4 51
No such apology: I rather do beseech you pardon me *Richard III.* iii 7 104
Spoke for our excuse? Or shall we on without apology? *Rom. and Jul.* i 4 2
Apoplexed. But sure, that sense Is apoplex'd *Hamlet* iii 4 73
Apoplexy. Fallen into this same whoreson apoplexy 2 *Hen. IV.* i 2 123
This apoplexy is, as I take it, a kind of lethargy i 2 126
This apoplexy will certain be his end iv 4 130
Peace is a very apoplexy, lethargy; mulled, deaf, sleepy *Coriolanus* iv 5 239
Apostle. His champions are the prophets and apostles 2 *Hen. VI.* i 3 60
By the apostle Paul, shadows to-night Have struck more terror to the soul of Richard *Richard III.* v 3 216
Apostrapha. You find not the apostraphas, and so miss the accent *L. L. Lost* iv 2 123
Apothecary. Bid the apothecary Bring the strong poison 2 *Hen. VI.* iii 3 17
I do remember an apothecary,—And hereabouts he dwells *Rom. and Jul.* v 1 37
Being holiday, the beggar's shop is shut. What, ho! apothecary! v 1 57
O true apothecary! Thy drugs are quick. Thus with a kiss I die v 3 119
He writes that he did buy a poison Of a poor 'pothecary v 3 289
An ounce of civet, good apothecary, to sweeten my imagination *Lear* iv 6 133
Give this to the 'pothecary, And tell me how it works *Pericles* iii 2 9
Appal. The dreadful Sagittary Appals our numbers *Troi. and Cres.* v 5 15
How is't with me, when every noise appals me? *Macbeth* ii 2 58
A bold one, that dare look on that Which might appal the devil iii 4 60
Make mad the guilty and appal the free, Confound the ignorant *Hamlet* ii 2 590
Appalled. Methinks your looks are sad, your cheer appall'd 1 *Hen. VI.* i 2 48
That the appalled air May pierce the head of the great combatant *Troi. and Cres.* iv 5 4
Apparel. That come like women in men's apparel *Mer. Wives* iii 3 78
For all he was in woman's apparel, I would not have had him v 5 204
Every true man's apparel fits your thief *Meas. for Meas.* iv 2 46
Apparel vice like virtue's harbinger; Bear a fair presence *Com. of Errors* iii 2 12
What should I do with him? dress him in my apparel? *Much Ado* ii 1 37
You shall find her the infernal Ate in good apparel ii 1 263
Thou knowest that the fashion of a doublet, or a hat, or a cloak, is nothing to a man.—Yes, it is apparel iii 3 127
The fashion wears out more apparel than the man iii 3 149
Remember thy courtesy; I beseech thee, apparel thy head *L. L. Lost* v 1 104
For briers and thorns at their apparel snatch *M. N. Dream* iii 2 29
Get your apparel together, good strings to your beards iv 2 36
And sleep and snore, and rend apparel out *Mer. of Venice* ii 5 5
I could find in my heart to disgrace my man's apparel *As Y. Like It* ii 4 5
Doth he know that I am in this forest and in man's apparel? iii 2 243
Not out of your apparel, and yet out of your suit iv 1 88
Ask him what apparel he will wear *T. of Shrew* Ind. 1 60
To save my life, Puts my apparel and my countenance on i 1 234
I will unto Venice, To buy apparel 'gainst the wedding-day ii 1 317
Costly apparel, tents, and canopies, Fine linen, Turkey cushions ii 1 354
A very monster in apparel, and not like a Christian footboy iii 2 71
Formal in apparel, In gait and countenance surely like a father iv 2 64
Nor believe he can have every thing in him by wearing his apparel neatly *All's Well* iv 3 167
I am robbed, sir, and beaten; my money and apparel ta'en from me *W. Tale* iv 3 65
That's the rogue that put me into this apparel iv 3 111
My gay apparel for an almsman's gown *Richard II.* iii 3 149
Nothing but some bond, that he is enter'd into For gay apparel v 2 66
Neither in gold nor silver, but in vile apparel 2 *Hen. IV.* i 2 20
His apparel is built upon his back and the whole frame stands upon pins iii 2 154
You might have thrust him and all his apparel into an eel-skin iii 2 350
I will apparel them all in one livery, that they may agree 2 *Hen. VI.* iv 2 80
Are my chests fill'd up with extorted gold? Is my apparel sumptuous? iv 7 106
What dost thou with thy best apparel on? *J. Cæsar* i 1 8
Rich, not gaudy; For the apparel oft proclaims the man *Hamlet* i 3 72
I'll bring him the best 'parel that I have, Come on't what will *Lear* iv 1 51
Bring this apparel to my chamber; that is the second thing *Cymbeline* iii 5 156
Apparelled. Every lovely organ of her life Shall come apparell'd in more precious habit *Much Ado* iv 1 229
Apparell'd thus, Like Muscovites or Russians *L. L. Lost* v 2 120
Not so well apparell'd As I wish you were *T. of Shrew* iii 2 91
On my side it is so well apparell'd, So clear, so shining 1 *Hen. VI.* ii 4 22
See where she comes, apparell'd like the spring *Pericles* i 1 12
Apparent. One cannot climb it Without apparent hazard *T. G. of Ver.* iii 1 116
It is now apparent?—Most manifest, and not denied *Meas. for Meas.* iv 2 144
Remorse more strange Than is thy strange apparent cruelty *Mer. of Venice* iv 1 21
Next to thyself and my young rover, he's Apparent to my heart *W. Tale* i 2 177
For to a vision so apparent rumour Cannot be mute i 2 270
It is apparent foul play; and 'tis shame *K. John* iv 2 93
On some apparent danger seen in him *Richard II.* i 1 13
Thieves are not judged but they are by to hear, Although apparent guilt be seen in them iv 1 124
Were it not here apparent that thou art heir apparent 1 *Hen. IV.* i 2 65
Apparent. What starting-hole canst thou now find out to hide thee from this open and apparent shame? 1 *Hen. IV.* ii 4 292
By some apparent sign Let us have knowledge 1 *Hen. VI.* ii 1 3
Death doth front thee with apparent spoil And pale destruction meets thee iv 2 26
If death be so apparent, then both fly.—And leave my followers? iv 5 44
He is the next of blood, And heir apparent to the English crown 2 *Hen. VI.* i 1 152
By your kingly leave, I'll draw it as apparent to the crown 3 *Hen. VI.* ii 2 64
As well the fear of harm, as harm apparent, In my opinion, ought to be prevented *Richard III.* ii 2 130
It should be put To no apparent likelihood of breach ii 2 136
His apparent open guilt omitted, . . . He lived from all attainder of suspect iii 5 30
So he thinks, and is no less apparent To the vulgar eye *Coriolanus* iv 7 20
If it be proved! you see it is apparent *T. Andron.* ii 3 292
These apparent prodigies, The unaccustom'd terror of this night *J. Cæsar* ii 1 198
If you can make't apparent That you have tasted her in bed *Cymbeline* ii 4 56
Apparently. I would not spare my brother in this case, If he should scorn me so apparently *Com. of Errors* iv 1 78
Apparition. Fine apparition! My quaint Ariel, Hark *Tempest* i 2 317
I have mark'd A thousand blushing apparitions To start into her face *Much Ado* iv 1 161
I think it is the weakness of mine eyes That shapes this monstrous apparition *J. Cæsar* iv 3 277
That if again this apparition come, He may approve our eyes *Hamlet* i 1 28
Each word made true and good, The apparition comes i 2 211
Appeach. By my troth, I will appeach the villain *Richard II.* v 2 79
Were he twenty times my son, I would appeach him v 2 102
Appeached. Your passions Have to the full appeach'd *All's Well* i 3 197
Appeal. Send after the duke and appeal to him *Meas. for Meas.* i 2 179
The duke's unjust, Thus to retort your manifest appeal v 1 303
I appeal To your own conscience, sir *W. Tale* iii 2 46
Here to make good the boisterous late appeal *Richard II.* i 1 4
Hast thou sounded him, If he appeal the duke on ancient malice? i 1 9
To appeal each other of high treason i 1 27
Against the Duke of Hereford that appeals me i 3 21
His honour is as true In this appeal as thou art all unjust iv 1 45
Aumerle is guilty of my true appeal iv 1 79
When ever yet was your appeal denied? 2 *Hen. IV.* iv 1 88
This lies all within the will of God, To whom I do appeal *Hen. V.* i 2 290
And do submit me to your highness' mercy.—To which we all appeal ii 2 78
For myself, to heaven I do appeal, How I have loved my king 2 *Hen. VI.* ii 1 190
Appeal unto the pope, To bring my whole cause 'fore his holiness *Hen. VIII.* ii 4 119
Call back her appeal She intends unto his holiness ii 4 234
Your appeal to us There make before them v 1 151
Upon his own appeal, seizes him: so the poor third is up *Ant. and Cleo.* iii 5 12
Help, Jupiter; or we appeal, And from thy justice fly *Cymbeline* v 4 91
Appealed. As for the rest appeal'd, It issues from the rancour of a villain *Richard II.* i 1 142
Appear. My father's of a better nature, sir, Than he appears *Tempest* i 2 497
Appear, and pertly! No tongue! all eyes! be silent iv 1 58
It appears, by their bare liveries, that they live by your bare words *T. G. of Ver.* ii 4 45
That my love may appear plain and free v 4 82
Though she appear honest to me, yet in other places she enlargeth her mirth so far that there is shrewd construction made of her *Mer. Wives* ii 2 230
Where their untaught love Must needs appear offence *Meas. for Meas.* ii 4 30
Thus wisdom wishes to appear most bright When it doth tax itself ii 4 78
His offence is so, as it appears, Accountant to the law upon that pain ii 4 85
His filth within being cast, he would appear A pond as deep as hell iii 1 93
I have spirit to do any thing that appears not foul iii 1 213
He shall appear to the envious a scholar, a statesman and a soldier iii 2 154
Let your reason serve To make the truth appear where it seems hid v 1 66
Let her appear, And he shall marry her v 1 517
Thou art an ass.—Marry, so it doth appear By the wrongs I suffer *Com. of Errors* iii 1 15
It is written, they appear to men like angels of light iv 3 56
There appears much joy in him *Much Ado* i 1 21
We will hold it as a dream till it appear itself i 2 22
You are he: graces will appear, and there's an end ii 1 129
So covertly that no dishonesty shall appear in me ii 2 10
There shall appear such seeming truth of Hero's disloyalty ii 2 48
Unless he have a fancy to this foolery, as it appears he hath, he is no fool for fancy, as you would have it appear he is iii 2 39
You may think I love you not: let that appear hereafter iii 2 99
Let that appear when there is no need of such vanity iii 3 21
I am now in great haste, as it may appear unto you iii 5 55
To cover with excuse That which appears in proper nakedness iv 1 177
Now thy image doth appear In the rare semblance that I loved it first v 1 259
Against her will, as it appears In the true course of all the question v 4 5
Now, in thy likeness, one more fool appear! *L. L. Lost* iv 3 46
In your tears There is no certain princess that appears iv 3 156
Ridiculous appears, To check their folly, passion's solemn tears v 2 117
When wheat is green, when hawthorn buds appear *M. N. Dream* i 1 185
In thy eye that shall appear When thou wakest, it is thy dear ii 2 32
Stay thou but here awhile, And by and by I will to thee appear iii 1 89
I'll charm his eyes against she do appear iii 2 99
When I vow, I weep; and vows so born, In their nativity all truth appears iii 2 125
It appears, by his small light of discretion, that he is in the wane v 1 257
You have but slumber'd here While these visions did appear v 1 433
Well then, it now appears you need my help *Mer. of Venice* i 3 115
In such eyes as ours appear not faults ii 2 192
Still more fool I shall appear By the time I linger here ii 9 73
As . . . there doth appear Among the buzzing pleased multitude iii 2 181
One in whom The ancient Roman honour more appears Than any that draws breath iii 2 297
You have a noble and a true conceit Of god-like amity; which appears most strongly iii 4 3
If this will not suffice, it must appear That malice bears down truth iv 1 213
It doth appear you are a worthy judge; You know the law iv 1 236
For it appears, by manifest proceeding iv 1 358
It must appear in other ways than words v 1 140
In thee appears The constant service of the antique world *As Y. Like It* ii 3 56
The more my wrong, the more his spite appears *T. of Shrew* iv 3 2
If it appear not plain and prove untrue *All's Well* v 3 318
Cast thy humble slough and appear fresh *T. Night* ii 5 162
If thou entertainest my love, let it appear in thy smiling ii 5 190
Why appear you with this ridiculous boldness? iii 4 40

Appear. She sends him on purpose, that I may appear stubborn to him *T. Night* iii 4 74
His dishonesty appears in leaving his friend here in necessity . iii 4 421
Your most obedient counsellor, yet that dare Less appear so . *W. Tale* ii 3 56
The great Apollo suddenly will have The truth of this appear . iii 3 201
With what encounter so uncurrent I Have strain'd to appear thus . iii 2 51
We are not furnish'd like Bohemia's son, Nor shall appear in Sicilia iv 4 600
And on this stage, Where we're offenders now, appear soul-vex'd . v 1 59
But it appears she lives, Though yet she speak not . . v 3 117
See, see, King Richard doth himself appear, As doth the blushing discontented sun . . . . . *Richard II.* iii 3 62
The manner of their taking may appear At large discoursed in this paper v 6 9
You picked my pocket?—It appears so by the story . 1 *Hen. IV.* iii 3 191
You have, as it appears to me, practised . . 2 *Hen. IV.* ii 1 125
Let them appear as I call; let them do so . . . . iii 2 109
It not appears to me Either from the king or in the present time . iv 1 107
Wherein It shall appear that your demands are just, You shall enjoy them . . . . iv 1 144
Sorrow so royally in you appears That I will deeply put the fashion on v 2 51
All are banish'd till their conversations Appear more wise and modest . v 5 107
Then doth it well appear the Salique law Was not devised for the realm of France . . . . *Hen. V.* i 2 54
All appear To hold in right and title of the female . . . i 2 88
When capital crimes, chew'd, swallow'd, and digested, Appear before us ii 2 57
Let housewifery appear: keep close, I thee command . . ii 3 65
A city on the inconstant billows dancing; For so appears this fleet iii Prol. 16
The dull elements of earth and water never appear in him . . iii 7 23
A hooded valour; and when it appears, it will bate . . . iii 7 122
Though it appear a little out of fashion . . . . . iv 1 85
His ceremonies laid by, in his nakedness he appears but a man . iv 1 110
To cry amen to that, thus we appear . . . . . . v 2 21
The elder I wax, the better I shall appear . . . . . v 2 247
I cannot so conjure up the spirit of love in her, that he will appear in his true likeness . . . . v 2 317
In his true likeness, he must appear naked and blind . . v 2 321
God's mother deigned to appear to me . . . 1 *Hen. VI.* i 2 78
Shall this night appear How much in duty I am bound to both . ii 1 36
The truth appears so naked on my side That any purblind eye may find it out . . . . ii 4 20
As by his smoothed brows it doth appear . . . . . iii 1 124
You speedy helpers, that are substitutes Under the lordly monarch of the north, Appear and aid me in this enterprise . . . . v 3 7
If your title to the crown be weak, As may appear . 3 *Hen. VI.* iii 3 146
I do pronounce him in that very shape He shall appear in proof *Hen. VIII.* i 1 197
Almost appears In loud rebellion.—Not almost appears, It doth appear i 2 28
Wherein he appears As I would wish mine enemy . . . iii 2 27
Though perils did Abound, as thick as thought could make 'em, and Appear in forms more horrid . . . . iii 2 196
How sleek and wanton Ye appear in every thing may bring my ruin! . iii 2 242
This morning see You do appear before them . . . . v 1 145
Nothing of that shall from mine eyes appear . . *Troi. and Cres.* i 2 321
Appear it to your mind That, through the sight I bear in things to love, I have abandon'd Troy . . . . iii 3 3
Even in the faith of valour, to appear This morning to them . . v 3 69
Cracking ten thousand curbs Of more strong link asunder than can ever Appear in your impediment . . . . . *Coriolanus* i 1 74
To Aufidius thus I will appear, and fight . . . . . i 5 21
Who's yonder, That does appear as he were flay'd? . . . . i 6 22
Never would he Appear i' the market-place . . . . . ii 1 249
To beg of Hob and Dick, that do appear, Their needless vouches . ii 3 123
Your noble Tullus Aufidius will appear well in these wars . . iv 3 35
A goodly house: the feast smells well; but I Appear not like a guest . iv 5 6
Intends to appear before the people, hoping To purge himself with words v 6 7
Madman! passion! lover! Appear thou in the likeness of a sigh *Rom. and Jul.* ii 1 8
Shall, stiff and stark and cold, appear like death . . . iv 1 103
Sometime 't appears like a lord; sometime like a lawyer . *T. of Athens* ii 2 115
How fairly this lord strives to appear foul! . . . . iii 3 32
He hath conjured me beyond them, and I must needs appear . . iii 6 13
And when you saw his chariot but appear, Have you not made an universal shout? . . . . *J. Cæsar* i 1 48
That which would appear offence in us, His countenance, like richest alchemy, Will change to virtue . . . . i 3 158
Our youths and wildness shall no whit appear . . . . ii 1 148
Beg not your death of us. Though now we must appear bloody and cruel . . . . iii 1 165
Will appear Such as he is, full of regard and honour . . . iv 2 11
That you have wrong'd me doth appear in this . . . . iv 3 1
You say you are a better soldier: Let it appear so . . . . iv 3 52
Though they do appear As huge as high Olympus . . . . iv 3 91
A seventh! I'll see no more: And yet the eighth appears *Macbeth* iv 1 119
If this which he avouches does appear, There is nor flying hence nor tarrying here . . . . v 5 47
Tush, tush, 'twill not appear.—Sit down awhile . . *Hamlet* i 1 30
As it doth well appear unto our state . . . . . . i 1 101
Armed at point exactly, cap-a-pe, Appears before them . . . i 2 201
It appears no other thing to me than a foul and pestilent congregation of vapours . . . . ii 2 314
It well appears: but tell me Why you proceeded not against these feats iv 7 5
It appears not which of the dukes he values most . . *Lear* i 1 4
Sith thus thou wilt appear, Freedom lives hence, and banishment is here i 1 183
With what poor judgement he hath now cast her off appears too grossly i 1 295
The sweet and bitter fool Will presently appear . . . . i 4 159
The fishermen, that walk upon the beach, Appear like mice . . iv 6 18
Through tatter'd clothes small vices do appear . . . . iv 6 168
When time shall serve, let but the herald cry, And I'll appear again . v 1 49
They are ready To-morrow, or at further space, to appear . . v 3 53
If none appear to prove upon thy head Thy heinous, manifest, and many treasons, There is my pledge . . . . v 3 91
Let him appear by the third sound of the trumpet . . . . v 3 113
Ask him his purposes, why he appears Upon this call o' the trumpet . v 3 118
It appears he is beloved of those That only have fear'd Cæsar *A. and C.* i 4 37
Hadst thou Narcissus in thy face, to me Thou wouldst appear most ugly ii 5 97
With what haste The weight we must convey with's will permit, We shall appear before him . . . . iii 1 37
When it appears to you where this begins, Turn your displeasure that way . . . . iii 4 33
The neighs of horse to tell of her approach Long ere she did appear . iii 6 46
And, as the president of my kingdom, will Appear there for a man . iii 7 19

Appear. How appears the fight?—On our side like the token'd pestilence *Ant. and Cleo.* iii 10 8
Let him appear that's come from Antony. Know you him? . iii 12 1
If from the field I shall return once more To kiss these lips, I will appear in blood . . . . iii 13 174
What art thou that darest Appear thus to us? . . . . . v 1 5
If they had swallow'd poison, 'twould appear By external swelling . v 2 348
How worthy he is I will leave to appear hereafter . *Cymbeline* i 4 34
Disguise That which, to appear itself, must not yet be But by self-danger iii 4 148
To show less sovereignty than they, must needs Appear unkinglike . iii 5 7
This youth, howe'er distress'd, appears he hath had Good ancestors . iv 2 47
With it I may appear a gentleman . . . . . *Pericles* ii 1 147
He appears To have practised more the whipstock than the lance . ii 2 50
The diamonds of a most praised water Do appear, to make the world twice rich . . . . iii 2 103
I was mortally brought forth, and am No other than I appear . . v 1 106
Appearance. There is no appearance of fancy in him . *Much Ado* iii 2 31
Had three times slain the appearance of the king . . 2 *Hen. IV.* i 1 128
You see what a ragged appearance it is . . . . . iii 2 279
That hath so cowarded and chased your blood Out of appearance *Hen. V.* ii 2 76
In reason, no man should possess him with any appearance of fear . iv 1 116
If she deny the appearance of a naked blind boy in her naked seeing self v 2 324
This speedy and quick appearance argues proof Of your accustom'd diligence to me . . . . 1 *Hen. VI.* v 3 8
Nor ever more Upon this business my appearance make . *Hen. VIII.* ii 4 132
For not appearance and The king's late scruple, by the main assent Of all these learned men she was divorced . . . . iv 1 30
Thou hast a grim appearance, and thy face Bears a command in 't *Coriol.* iv 5 66
He requires your haste-post-haste appearance, Even on the instant *Othello* i 2 37
Bearing with frank appearance Their purposes toward Cyprus . . i 3 38
Appeared. I am sorry, one so learned and so wise As you, Lord Angelo, have still appear'd, Should slip so grossly . *Meas. for Meas.* v 1 476
In her eye there hath appear'd a fire . . . . *Much Ado* iv 1 164
Is our whole dissembly appeared? . . . . iv 2 1
The rudeness that hath appeared in me have I learned from my entertainment . . . . *T. Night* i 5 230
If such thing be, thy mother Appear'd to me last night . *W. Tale* iii 3 18
Is less frequent to his princely exercises than formerly he hath appeared iv 2 38
In thy face strange motions have appear'd . . . 1 *Hen. IV.* ii 3 63
If damn'd commotion so appear'd . . . . 2 *Hen. IV.* iv 1 36
You appeared to me but as a common man . . . *Hen. V.* iv 8 54
The issue was not his begot; Which well appeared in his lineaments *Richard III.* iii 5 91
To which She was often cited by them, but appear'd not *Hen. VIII.* iv 1 29
Which in the hatching, It seem'd, appear'd to Rome . . *Coriolanus* i 2 22
The ghost of Cæsar hath appear'd to me Two several times by night *J. C.* v 5 17
What, has this thing appear'd again to-night?—I have seen nothing *Ham.* i 1 21
Our last king, Whose image even but now appear'd to us . . . i 1 81
Which to him appear'd To be a preparation 'gainst the Polack . . ii 2 62
It hath not appeared.—I grant indeed it hath not appeared *Othello* iv 2 213
There she appeared indeed; or my reporter devised well for her *A. and C.* ii 2 193
She In the habiliments of the goddess Isis That day appear'd . . iii 6 18
When vantage like a pair of twins appear'd, Both as the same . iii 10 12
Methought Great Jupiter, upon his eagle back'd, Appear'd to me *Cymb.* v 5 428
Appearer. This is your wife.—Reverend appearer, no . . *Pericles* v 3 18
Appeareth. The law Hath full relation to the penalty, Which here appeareth due upon the bond . . . . . *Mer. of Venice* iv 1 249
Yet one but flatters us, As well appeareth by the cause you come *Rich. II.* i 1 26
Appearing. We will, not appearing what we are, have some question *W. Tale* iv 2 54
Already appearing in the blossoms of their fortune . . . . v 2 135
Lives so in hope as in an early spring We see the appearing buds 2 *Hen. IV.* i 3 39
Whose memory is written on the earth With yet appearing blood . . i 1 82
Whose chin is but enrich'd With one appearing hair *Hen. V.* iii Prol. 23
Which so appearing to the common eyes, We shall be call'd purgers *J. C.* ii 1 179
Appease. O God! if my deep prayers cannot appease thee *Richard III.* i 4 69
Die he must, To appease their groaning shadows that are gone *T. Andron.* i 1 126
To offer up a weak poor innocent lamb To appease an angry god *Macbeth* iv 3 17
Is't enough I am sorry? So children temporal fathers do appease *Cymb.* v 4 12
Appeased. By penitence the Eternal's wrath's appeased . *T. G. of Ver.* v 4 81
Were the Duke of Suffolk now alive, These Kentish rebels would be soon appeased! . . . . 2 *Hen. VI.* iv 4 42
Appeased By such invention as I can devise . . 3 *Hen. VI.* iv 1 34
Only be patient till we have appeased The multitude . *J. Cæsar* iii 1 179
That their good souls may be appeased with slaughter . *Cymbeline* v 5 72
Appelés. Les doigts? je pense qu'ils sont appelés de fingres . *Hen. V.* iii 4 11
Appelez-vous. Comment appelez-vous la main en Anglois?—La main? elle est appelée de hand . . . . iii 4 5
Comment appelez-vous les ongles?—Les ongles? . . . . iii 4 15
Comment appelez-vous le col?—De neck, madame . . . . iii 4 34
Comment appelez-vous le pied et la robe?—De foot, madame; et de coun iii 4 53
Appellant. Come I appellant to this princely presence . *Richard II.* i 1 34
Sprightfully and bold, Stays but the summons of the appellant's trumpet i 3 4
The appellant in all duty greets your highness . . . . i 3 52
Lords appellants, Your differences shall all rest under gage . . iv 1 104
And ready are the appellant and defendant . . . 2 *Hen. VI.* ii 3 49
I never saw a fellow worse bested, Or more afraid to fight, than is the appellant . . . . ii 3 57
Appelons. Les ongles? nous les appelons de nails . . *Hen. V.* iii 4 16
Appendix. Bid the priest be ready to come against you come with your appendix . . . . *T. of Shrew* iv 4 104
Apperil. Let me stay at thine apperil, Timon . . *T. of Athens* i 2 32
Appertain. Do all rites That appertain unto a burial . . *Much Ado* iv 1 210
Is it excepted I should know no secrets That appertain to you? *J. Cæsar* ii 1 282
Not a little I have to say of what most nearly appertains to us both *Lear* i 1 287
Appertaining. For yet ere supper-time must I perform Much business appertaining . . . . *Tempest* iii 1 96
Appertaining to thy young days, which we may nominate tender *L. L. Lost* i 2 15
Doth much excuse the appertaining rage To such a greeting *R. and J.* iii 1 66
Appertainment. We lay by Our appertainments, visiting of him *Troi. and Cres.* ii 3 87
Appertinent. Tough senior, as an appertinent title to your old time *L. L. Lost* i 2 17
All the other gifts appertinent to man . . . 2 *Hen. IV.* i 2 194
Furnish him with all appertinents Belonging to his honour . *Hen. V.* ii 2 87
Appetite. The appetite of her eye did seem to scorch me . . *Mer. Wives* i 3 73
Or that his appetite Is more to bread than stone . *Meas. for Meas.* i 3 52
Fit thy consent to my sharp appetite . . . . ii 4 161

Appetite. Hooking both right and wrong to the appetite, To follow as it draws! *Meas. for Meas.* ii 4 176
But doth not the appetite alter? a man loves the meat in his youth that he cannot endure in his age. *Much Ado* ii 3 247
Who riseth from a feast With that keen appetite that he sits down? *Mer. of Venice* ii 6 9
That, surfeiting, The appetite may sicken, and so die *T. Night* i 1 3
You are sick of self-love, Malvolio, and taste with a distempered appetite i 5 98
Their love may be call'd appetite, No motion of the liver, but the palate ii 4 100
Threw off his spirit, his appetite, his sleep, And downright languish'd *W. Tale* ii 3 16
Or cloy the hungry edge of appetite By bare imagination of a feast *Richard II.* i 3 296
Belike then my appetite was not princely got *2 Hen. IV.* ii 2 11
Your appetites and your digestions doo's not agree with it *Hen. V.* v 1 27
Urge his hateful luxury, And bestial appetite in change of lust *Rich. III.* iii 5 81
Then to breakfast with What appetite you have *Hen. VIII.* iii 2 203
Then every thing includes itself in power, Power into will, will into appetite *Troi. and Cres.* i 3 120
Appetite, an universal wolf, So doubly seconded with will and power i 3 121
Curb those raging appetites that are Most disobedient and refractory ii 2 181
I have a woman's longing, An appetite that I am sick withal iii 3 238
Dexterity so obeying appetite That what he will he does v 5 27
Unto the appetite and affection common Of the whole body *Coriolanus* i 1 107
Your affections are A sick man's appetite i 1 182
Let my tears stanch the earth's dry appetite *T. Andron.* iii 1 14
The sweetest honey Is loathsome in his own deliciousness And in the taste confounds the appetite *Rom. and Jul.* ii 6 13
Which gives men stomach to digest his words With better appetite *J. C.* i 2 306
Now, good digestion wait on appetite, And health on both! *Macbeth* iii 4 38
As if increase of appetite had grown By what it fed on *Hamlet* i 2 144
He that makes his generation messes To gorge his appetite *Lear* i 1 120
The fitchew, nor the soiled horse, goes to't With a more riotous appetite iv 6 125
I therefore beg it not, To please the palate of my appetite *Othello* i 3 263
To give satiety a fresh appetite ii 1 231
Make, unmake, do what she list, Even as her appetite shall play the god ii 3 353
O curse of marriage, That we can call these delicate creatures ours, And not their appetites! iii 3 270
Epicurean cooks Sharpen with cloyless sauce his appetite *Ant. and Cleo.* ii 1 25
Other women cloy The appetites they feed; but she makes hungry ii 2 242
I am weak with toil, yet strong in appetite *Cymbeline* iii 6 37
Applaud. O, that our fathers would applaud our loves! *T. G. of Ver.* i 3 48
Now, by the honour of my ancestry, I do applaud thy spirit v 4 140
O, let the hours be short Till fields and blows and groans applaud our sport! *1 Hen. IV.* i 3 302
Follow me to this attempt, Applaud the name of Henry *3 Hen. VI.* iv 2 27
Whose fortunes Rome's best citizens applaud *T. Andron.* i 1 164
Speak, Queen of Goths, dost thou applaud my choice? i 1 321
Were our witty empress well afoot, She would applaud Andronicus' conceit iv 2 30
Be innocent of the knowledge, dearest chuck, Till thou applaud the deed *Macbeth* iii 2 46
I would applaud thee to the very echo, That should applaud again v 3 53
Caps, hands, and tongues, applaud it to the clouds *Hamlet* iv 5 107
Now, by the gods, I do applaud his courage *Pericles* ii 5 58
Applauded. For his acts So much applauded through the realm *1 Hen. VI.* ii 2 36
Applauding. And enter in our ears like great triumphers In their applauding gates *T. of Athens* v 1 200
That heaven and earth may strike their sounds together, Applauding our approach *Ant. and Cleo.* iv 8 39
Applause. I do not relish well Their loud applause *Meas. for Meas.* i 1 71
Hearing applause and universal shout, Giddy in spirit *Mer. of Venice* iii 2 144
You have deserved High commendation, true applause, and love *As Y. L.* i 2 275
O thou fond many, with what loud applause Didst thou beat heaven! *2 Hen. IV.* i 3 91
This general applause and loving shout Argues your wisdoms *Rich. III.* iii 7 39
Besides the applause and approbation The which, most mighty for thy place and sway, I give to both *Troi. and Cres.* i 3 59
From his deep chest laughs out a loud applause i 3 163
That will physic the great Myrmidon Who broils in loud applause i 3 379
How his silence drinks up this applause! ii 3 211
Nor doth he of himself know them for aught Till he behold them form'd in the applause Where they're extended iii 3 119
Call him, With all the applause and clamour of the host *Coriolanus* i 9 64
With voices and applause of every sort, Patricians and plebeians *T. Andron.* i 1 230
I do believe that these applauses are For some new honours *J. Cæsar* i 2 133
That we should, with joy, pleasance, revel and applause, transform ourselves into beasts! *Othello* ii 3 293
Apple. He will carry this island home in his pocket and give it his son for an apple *Tempest* ii 1 91
And laugh upon the apple of her eye *L. L. Lost* v 2 475
Hit with Cupid's archery, Sink in apple of his eye *M. N. Dream* iii 2 104
Like a villain with a smiling cheek, A goodly apple rotten at the heart *Mer. of Venice* i 3 102
Faith, as you say, there's small choice in rotten apples *T. of Shrew* i 1 139
Somewhat doth resemble you.—As much as an apple doth an oyster iv 2 101
Or a codling when 'tis almost an apple *T. Night* i 5 167
An apple, cleft in two, is not more twin Than these two creatures v 1 230
Have their heads crushed like rotten apples *Hen. V.* iii 7 155
Youths that thunder at a playhouse, and fight for bitten apples *Hen. VIII.* v 4 64
Though she's as like this as a crab's like an apple, yet I can tell *Lear* i 5 16
Apple-john. I am withered like an old apple-john *1 Hen. IV.* iii 3 5
Apple-johns? thou knowest Sir John cannot endure an apple-john *2 Hen. IV.* ii 4 2
The prince once set a dish of apple-johns before him, and told him there were five more Sir Johns ii 4 5
Apple-tart. What, up and down, carved like an apple-tart? *T. of Shrew* iv 3 89
Appliance. Too noble to conserve a life In base appliances *Meas. for Meas.* iii 1 89
I come to tender it and my appliance With all bound humbleness *A. W.* ii 1 116
With all appliances and means to boot *2 Hen. IV.* iii 1 29
Ask God for temperance; that's the appliance only Which your disease requires *Hen. VIII.* i 1 124
Diseases desperate grown By desperate appliance are relieved *Hamlet* iv 3 10
Had nine hours lien dead, Who was by good appliance recovered *Pericles* iii 2 86
Application. The rest have worn me out With several applications *A. W.* i 2 74
Applied. Though parting be a fretful corrosive, It is applied to a deathful wound *2 Hen. VI.* iii 2 404
Applied. Conducted to a gentle bath And balms applied to you *Coriol.* i 6 64
What comfort to this great decay may come Shall be applied *Lear* v 3 298
Applies. He has heard that word of some great man and now applies it to a fool *T. Night* iv 1 13
Apply. Would it apply well to the vehemency of your affection? *M. W.* ii 2 247
Craft against vice I must apply *Meas. for Meas.* iii 2 291
To apply a moral medicine to a mortifying mischief *Much Ado* i 3 13
I'll apply To your eye, Gentle lover, remedy *M. N. Dream* iii 2 450
I never did apply Hot and rebellious liquors in my blood *As Y. Like It* ii 3 48
That part of philosophy Will I apply that treats of happiness *T. of Shrew* i 1 19
Tenderly apply to her Some remedies for life *W. Tale* iii 2 153
Great Agamemnon, Nestor shall apply Thy latest words *Troi. and Cres.* i 3 32
It was an answer: how apply you this? *Coriolanus* i 1 151
These does she apply for warnings, and portents *J. Cæsar* ii 2 80
Let your remembrance apply to Banquo; Present him eminence *Macbeth* iii 2 30
Some flax and whites of eggs To apply to his bleeding face *Lear* iii 7 107
If you apply yourself to our intents *Ant. and Cleo.* v 2 126
To try the vigour of them and apply Allayments to their act *Cymbeline* i 5 21
Appoint. Let's appoint him a meeting *Mer. Wives* ii 1 97
I'll appoint my men to carry the basket again iv 2 96
To make us public sport, Appoint a meeting with this old fat fellow iv 4 15
At any unseasonable instant of the night, appoint her to look out *Much Ado* ii 2 17
Ere she seems as won, Desires this ring; appoints him an encounter *All's Well* iii 7 32
Dost think I am so muddy, so unsettled, To appoint myself in this vexation? *W. Tale* i 2 326
Appoint them a place of meeting, wherein it is at our pleasure to fail *1 Hen. IV.* i 2 190
Pleaseth your grace To appoint some of your council presently *Hen. V.* v 2 79
Took he upon him, Without the privity o' the king, to appoint Who should attend on him? *Hen. VIII.* i 1 74
Appoint the meeting Even at his father's house *T. Andron.* iv 4 102
And for that I do appoint him store of provender *J. Cæsar* iv 1 30
Goes the king hence to-day?—He does: he did appoint so *Macbeth* ii 3 58
Appointed. Being then appointed Master of this design *Tempest* i 2 162
I have appointed mine host of de Jarteer to measure our weapon *M. W.* i 4 124
And, I think, hath appointed them contrary places ii 1 216
As I am a Christians soul now, look you, this is the place appointed iii 1 97
We have appointed to dine with Mistress Anne iii 2 55
I will not lie to you: I was at her house the hour she appointed me iii 5 66
For Doctor Caius, hath appointed That he shall likewise shuffle her away iv 6 28
Went you not to her yesterday, sir, as you told me you had appointed? v 1 15
She cried 'budget,' as Anne and I had appointed v 5 210
Was affianced to her by oath, and the nuptial appointed *Meas. for Meas.* iii 1 223
Swore he would meet her, as he was appointed, next morning *Much Ado* iii 3 171
In that same place thou hast appointed me, To-morrow truly will I meet with thee.—Keep promise, love. *M. N. Dream* i 1 177
Here is the place appointed for the wrestling *As Y. Like It* i 2 154
Shall I be appointed hours; as though, belike, I knew not what to take, and what to leave? *T. of Shrew* i 1 103
My master hath appointed me to go to Saint Luke's iv 4 102
I am appointed him to murder you *W. Tale* i 2 412
It shall be so my care To have you royally appointed iv 4 603
And such officers Appointed to direct these fair designs *Richard II.* i 3 45
To meet your father and the Scottish power, As is appointed us *1 Hen. IV.* iii 1 86
Well appointed, Stands with the snares of war to tangle thee *1 Hen. VI.* iv 2 21
If I be appointed for the place, My Lord of Somerset will keep me here, Without discharge, money, or furniture *2 Hen. VI.* i 3 170
Let these have a day appointed them For single combat i 3 211
Please it your majesty, This is the day appointed for the combat ii 3 48
Ten is the hour that was appointed me To watch iii 4 6
Sir John Stanley is appointed now To take her with him to the Isle of Man ii 4 77
Thou hast appointed justices of peace, to call poor men before them iv 7 45
Whenever you have need, You may be armed and appointed well *T. Andron.* iv 2 16
To some retention and appointed guard *Lear* v 3 47
You are appointed for that office *Cymbeline* iii 5 10
Appointment. With her, I may tell you, by her own appointment *Mer. Wives* ii 2 272
I will knog your urinals about your knave's cogscomb for missing your meetings and appointments iii 1 92
I will then address me to my appointment iii 5 135
Therefore your best appointment make with speed *Meas. for Meas.* iii 1 60
We shall advise this wronged maid to stead up your appointment iii 1 261
My appointments have in them a need Greater than shows itself *All's Well* ii 5 72
We'll set forth In best appointment all our regiments *K. John* ii 1 296
Our fair appointments may be well perused *Richard II.* iii 3 53
'Tis like that they will know us by our horses, by our habits and by every other appointment *1 Hen. IV.* i 2 197
That good fellow, If I command him, follows my appointment *Hen. VIII.* ii 2 134
Here art thou in appointment fresh and fair, Anticipating time *Troi. and Cres.* iv 5 1
A pirate of very warlike appointment gave us chase *Hamlet* iv 6 16
Where their appointment we may best discover *Ant. and Cleo.* iv 10 8
Apprehends death no more dreadfully but as a drunken sleep *Meas. for Meas.* iv 2 149
A stubborn soul, That apprehends no further than this world v 1 486
You apprehend passing shrewdly *Much Ado* ii 1 84
That apprehend More than cool reason ever comprehends *M. N. Dream* v 1 5
If it would but apprehend some joy, It comprehends some bringer of that joy v 1 19
In private brabble did we apprehend him *T. Night* v 1 68
Apprehend Nothing but jollity *W. Tale* iv 4 24
He apprehends a world of figures here *1 Hen. IV.* i 3 209
If thou encounter any such, apprehend him *Hen. V.* iv 7 165
I charge you in his majesty's name, apprehend him iv 8 18
We his subjects sworn in all allegiance Will apprehend you *3 Hen. VI.* iii 1 71
O, let my lady apprehend no fear *Troi. and Cres.* iii 2 80
Condemned villain, I do apprehend thee: Obey, and go with me *Rom. and Jul.* v 3 56
I do defy thy conjurations, And apprehend thee for a felon here v 3 69
Go, sirrah, seek him; I'll apprehend him: abominable villain! *Lear* i 2 83
Received This hurt you see, striving to apprehend him ii 1 110
Do you know Where we may apprehend her? *Othello* i 1 178
I therefore apprehend and do attach thee For an abuser of the world i 2 77
To apprehend thus, Draws us a profit from all things we see *Cymbeline* iii 3 17

Apprehended for the witch of Brentford . *Mer. Wives* iv 5 119
A Syracusian merchant Is apprehended for arrival here . *Com. of Errors* i 2 4
Which I apprehended with the aforesaid swain *L. L. Lost* i 1 276
Where being apprehended, his false cunning . . . Taught him *T. Night* v 1 89
None of this, Though strongly apprehended, could restrain The stiff-borne action . . . . 2 *Hen. IV.* i 1 176
His grace is bold, to trust these traitors.—They shall be apprehended *Hen. V.* ii 2 2
Whom we have apprehended in the fact . 2 *Hen. VI.* ii 1 173
And apprehended here immediately The unknown Ajax *Troi. and Cres.* iii 3 124
The ædiles, ho! Let him be apprehended . *Coriolanus* iii 1 173
Apprehendest. That's a lascivious apprehension.—So thou apprehendest it: take it for thy labour . *T. of Athens* i 1 212
Apprehension. The sense of death is most in apprehension *Meas. for Meas.* iii 1 78
God help me! how long have you professed apprehension? *Much Ado* iii 4 68
Full of forms, figures, shapes, objects, ideas, apprehensions . *L. L. Lost* iv 2 69
Dark night, that from the eye his function takes, The ear more quick of apprehension makes . . . *M. N. Dream* iii 2 178
The apprehension of the good Gives but the greater feeling to the worse *Richard II.* i 3 300
Such an apprehension May turn the tide of fearful faction . 1 *Hen. IV.* iv 1 66
If the English had any apprehension, they would run away . *Hen. V.* iii 7 145
To scourge you for this apprehension . . . . . 1 *Hen. VI.* ii 4 102
To the man that took him, To question of his apprehension 3 *Hen. VI.* iii 2 122
But his evasion, wing'd thus swift with scorn, Cannot outfly our apprehensions . *Troi. and Cres.* ii 3 124
Took from you The apprehension of his present portance . *Coriolanus* ii 3 232
That's a lascivious apprehension.—So thou apprehendest it *T. of Athens* i 1 211
In action how like an angel! in apprehension how like a god! *Hamlet* ii 2 319
In this brainish apprehension, kills The unseen good old man . iv 1 11
Seek out where thy father is, that he may be ready for our apprehension *Lear* iii 5 20
Who has a breast so pure, But some uncleanly apprehensions Keep leets and law-days? . . . *Othello* iii 3 139
He had not apprehension Of roaring terrors . *Cymbeline* iv 2 110
Apprehensive. Younger spirits, whose apprehensive senses All but new things disdain . *All's Well* i 2 60
Makes it apprehensive, quick, forgetive . 2 *Hen. IV.* iv 3 107
Men are flesh and blood, and apprehensive . *J. Cæsar* iii 1 67
Apprendre. Je ne doute point d'apprendre, par la grace de Dieu *Hen. V.* iii 4 43
Apprenne. Il faut que j'apprenne à parler . . iii 4 5
Apprenticehood. Must I not serve a long apprenticehood To foreign passages? . . . . *Richard II.* i 3 271
Appris. Je m'en fais la répétition de tous les mots que vous m'avez appris dès à présent *Hen. V.* iii 4 26
Approach. I am ready now. Approach, my Ariel, come. *Tempest* i 2 188
Do not approach Till thou dost hear me call . iv 1 49
Her peacocks fly amain: Approach, rich Ceres, her to entertain . . iv 1 75
By thy approach thou makest me most unhappy . *T. G. of Ver.* v 4 31
Here's a woman would speak with you.—Let her approach *Mer. Wives* ii 2 33
Comes in one Mistress Page; gives intelligence of Ford's approach . iii 5 86
No woman may approach his silent court. . . . *L. L. Lost* ii 1 24
Navarre had notice of your fair approach . . ii 1 81
Love doth approach disguised, Armed in arguments . v 2 83
They will shame us: let them not approach.—We are shame-proof . v 2 512
Beetles black, approach not near . *M. N. Dream* ii 2 22
At whose approach, ghosts, wandering here and there, Troop home . iii 2 381
By day's approach look to be visited . iii 2 430
The Prologue is address'd.—Let him approach . . . v 1 107
Approach, ye Furies fell! O Fates, come, come, Cut thread and thrum v 1 289
I should be glad of his approach . *Mer. of Venice* i 2 142
He saves my labour by his own approach . *As Y. Like It* ii 7 8
Orlando did approach the man And found it was his brother . . iv 3 120
The remembrance of her father never approaches her heart . *All's Well* i 1 57
If they do approach the city, we shall lose all the sight . . iii 5 1
He is dieted to his hour.—That approaches apace . . . iv 3 36
Let him approach, A stranger, no offender . . . v 3 25
Allowed your approach rather to wonder at you than to hear you *T. Night* i 5 210
Mark his first approach before my lady . . ii 5 218
A savour that may strike the dullest nostril Where I arrive, and my approach be shunn'd . *W. Tale* i 2 422
Like very sanctity, she did approach My cabin where I lay . iii 3 23
Your guests approach: Address yourself to entertain them sprightly . iv 4 52
Bring him in; and let him approach singing . . iv 4 213
His approach, So out of circumstance and sudden . . v 1 89
Approach; Strike all that look upon with marvel . . v 3 99
Shall I produce the men?—Let them approach *K. John* i 1 47
When he shall hear of your approach, If that young Arthur be not gone already, Even at that news he dies . iii 4 162
This apish and unmannerly approach, This harness'd masque . v 2 131
Are prepared, and stay For nothing but his majesty's approach *Richard II.* i 3 6
Approach The ragged'st hour that time and spite dare bring! 2 *Hen. IV.* i 1 150
When thou dost hear I am as I have been, Approach me . v 5 65
For England his approaches makes as fierce As waters to the sucking of a gulf . *Hen. V.* ii 4 9
We have no great cause to desire the approach of day . . iv 1 90
Our approach shall so much dare the field That England shall couch down in fear and yield . iv 2 36
And death approach not ere my tale be done . 1 *Hen. VI.* ii 5 62
What a sign it is of evil life, Where death's approach is seen so terrible! 2 *Hen. VI.* iii 3 6
With thy approach, I know, My comfort comes along . *Hen. VIII.* ii 4 239
Should the approach of this wild river break, And stand unshaken yours iii 2 198
Rouse him and give him note of our approach . *Troi. and Cres.* iv 1 43
My boy Marcius approaches; for the love of Juno, let's go . *Coriolanus* ii 1 111
Suffer not dishonour to approach The imperial seat . *T. Andron.* i 1 13
At the first approach you must kneel, then kiss his foot . . iv 3 110
Ay, now begin our sorrows to approach . . . iv 4 72
Close fighting ere I did approach . *Rom. and Jul.* i 1 114
Whistle then to me, As signal that thou hear'st something approach . v 3 8
They approach sadly, and go away merry . *T. of Athens* ii 2 106
So soon we shall drive back Of Alcibiades the approaches wild . v 1 167
His expedition promises Present approach . . v 2 4
Sound to this coward and lascivious town Our terrible approach . v 4 2
Like a shepherd, Approach the fold and cull the infected forth . v 4 43
And make joyful The hearing of my wife with your approach *Macbeth* i 4 46
Approach the chamber, and destroy your sight With a new Gorgon . ii 3 76
Near approaches The subject of our watch . . iii 3 7
Approach thou like the rugged Russian bear, The arm'd rhinoceros . iii 4 100
I doubt some danger does approach you nearly . . iv 2 67
Approach. The time approaches That will with due decision make us know . . . . . . *Macbeth* v 4 16
The warm sun! Approach, thou beacon to this under globe! . *Lear* ii 2 170
'Tis time to look about; the powers of the kingdom approach apace . iv 7 93
He that dares approach, On him, on you, who not? I will maintain My truth and honour firmly . . . . v 3 99
You have seen and proved a fairer former fortune Than that which is to approach . *Ant. and Cleo.* i 2 34
My lord approaches.—We will not look upon him . i 2 90
Sextus Pompeius Makes his approaches to the port of Rome . i 3 46
An army for an usher, and The neighs of horse to tell of her appproach iii 6 45
The queen approaches: Her head's declined, and death will seize her . iii 11 46
Approach, and speak.—Such as I am, I come from Antony . iii 12 6
Approach, there! Ah, you kite! Now, gods and devils! . iii 13 89
That heaven and earth may strike their sounds together, Applauding our approach . . . . iv 8 39
Approach, ho! All's not well: Cæsar's beguiled . v 2 326
Approached. Return'd so soon! rather approach'd too late *Com. of Errors* i 2 43
Don Pedro is approached . . *Much Ado* i 1 95
Nimble in threats approach'd The opening of his mouth . *As Y. Like It* iv 3 110
He was expected then, But not approach'd *Cymbeline* ii 4 39
Approacher. Thou gavest thine ears like tapsters that bid welcome To knaves and all approachers . *T. of Athens* iv 3 216
Approacheth. By thy approach thou makest me most unhappy.—And me, when he approacheth to your presence *T. G. of Ver.* v 4 32
The period of thy tyranny approacheth . 1 *Hen. VI.* iv 2 17
The Dauphin and his train Approacheth, to confer about some matter . v 4 101
What's he approacheth boldly to our presence? 3 *Hen. VI.* iii 3 44
Approaching. The approaching tide Will shortly fill the reasonable shore *Tempest* v 1 80
One that comes before To signify the approaching of his lord *Mer. of Venice* ii 9 88
The iron of itself, though heat red-hot, Approaching near these eyes, would drink my tears . *K. John* iv 1 62
From the head of Actium Beat the approaching Cæsar . *Ant. and Cleo.* iii 7 53
Approbation. This day my sister should the cloister enter And there receive her approbation . . . *Meas. for Meas.* i 2 183
Testimonies against his worth and credit That's seal'd in approbation . v 1 245
Gives manhood more approbation than ever proof itself would have earned him . . . *T. Night* iii 4 198
That lack'd sight only, nought for approbation But only seeing *W. Tale* ii 1 177
How many now in health Shall drop their blood in approbation *Hen. V.* i 2 19
And that not pass'd me but By learned approbation of the judges *Hen. VIII.* i 2 71
Besides the applause and approbation The which, most mighty for thy place and sway, . . . I give to both . . *Troi. and Cres.* ii 3 59
With most prosperous approbation . *Coriolanus* ii 1 114
Are summon'd To meet anon, upon your approbation . ii 3 152
Revoke Your sudden approbation . ii 3 259
And give them title, knee and approbation With senators *T. of Athens* iv 3 36
The approbation of those that weep this lamentable divorce . *Cymbeline* i 4 19
Would I had put my estate and my neighbour's on the approbation of what I have spoke! . . . . . i 4 134
To such proceeding Who ever but his approbation added, Though not his prime consent, he did not flow From honourable sources *Pericles* iv 3 26
Approof. O perilous mouths, That bear in them one and the self-same tongue, Either of condemnation or approof! *Meas. for Meas.* ii 4 174
So in approof lives not his epitaph As in your royal speech . *A. W.* i 2 50
And of very valiant approof.—You have it from his own deliverance ii 5 3
As my farthest band Shall pass on thy approof . *Ant. and Cleo.* iii 2 27
Appropriation. He makes it a great appropriation to his own good parts *Mer. of Venice* i 2 46
Approve. On whose eyes I might approve This flower's force *M. N. Dr.* ii 2 68
Some sober brow Will bless it and approve it with a text *Mer. of Venice* iii 2 79
You have show'd me that which well approves You're great *All's Well* iii 7 13
I think nobly of the soul, and no way approve his opinion *T. Night* iv 2 60
To defend himself and to approve Henry of Hereford . . . disloyal *Richard II.* i 3 112
Nay, task me to my word; approve me, lord . 1 *Hen. IV.* iv 1 9
If I did say of wax, my growth would approve the truth 2 *Hen. IV.* i 2 180
To approve my youth further, I will not . i 2 214
Approves her fit for none but for a king . 1 *Hen. VI.* v 5 69
I shall not fail to approve the fair conceit The king hath of you *Hen. VIII.* ii 3 74
True swains in love shall in the world to come Approve their truths by Troilus . . *Troi. and Cres.* iii 2 181
I muse my mother Does not approve me further *Coriolanus* iii 2 8
And that my sword upon thee shall approve . *T. Andron.* ii 1 35
The temple-haunting martlet does approve, By his loved mansionry, that the heaven's breath Smells wooingly here . *Macbeth* i 6 4
That if again this apparition come, He may approve our eyes *Hamlet* i 1 29
Yet, in faith, if you did, it would not much approve me . v 2 141
And your large speeches may your deeds approve . . *Lear* i 1 187
Good king, that must approve the common saw . ii 2 167
This approves her letter, That she would soon be here . ii 4 186
This is the letter he spoke of, which approves him an intelligent party iii 5 12
I do not so secure me in the error, But the main article I do approve *Oth.* i 3 11
Thanks, you the valiant of this warlike isle, That so approve the Moor! ii 1 44
If consequence do but approve my dream, My boat sails freely . ii 3 64
My love doth so approve him . . iv 3 19
Let nobody blame him; his scorn I approve,—Nay, that's not next . iv 3 52
I am full sorry That he approves the common liar . *Ant. and Cleo.* i 1 60
Nay, blush not, Cleopatra; I approve Your wisdom in the deed . v 2 149
Thy name?—Fidele, sir.—Thou dost approve thyself the very same *Cymbeline* iv 2 380
One thing which the queen confess'd, Which must approve thee honest v 5 245
All that may men approve or men detect . *Pericles* ii 1 55
Approved. O, 'tis the curse in love, and still approved! . *T. G. of Ver.* v 4 43
Till I have used the approved means I have . *Com. of Errors* v 1 103
Of a noble strain, of approved valour and confirmed honesty *Much Ado* ii 1 394
Not to knit my soul to an approved wanton . iv 1 45
Is he not approved in the height a villain? . iv 1 303
My trusty servant, well approved in all . *T of Shrew* i 1 7
My best beloved and approved friend . i 2 3
His love and wisdom, Approved so to your majesty. *All's Well* i 2 10
A remedy, approved, set down, To cure the desperate languishings . i 3 234
Which elder days shall ripen and confirm To more approved service *Richard II.* ii 3 44
Brave Archibald, That ever-valiant and approved Scot . 1 *Hen. IV.* i 1 54
Proceed no straiter 'gainst our uncle Gloucester Than from true evidence of good esteem He be approved in practice culpable . 2 *Hen VI.* iii 2 22

Approved. Your favour is well approved by your tongue . *Coriolanus* iv 3 9
Approved warriors, and my faithful friends . . *T. Andron.* v 1 1
My very noble and approved good masters . . *Othello* i 3 77
His pilot Of very expert and approved allowance . . . ii 1 49
He that is approved in this offence, Though he had twinn'd with me, both at a birth, Shall lose me . . . . . . ii 3 211
I think you think I love you.—I have well approved it, sir . . iii 3 317
Approver. Will make known To their approvers . . *Cymbeline* ii 4 25
Appurtenance of welcome is fashion and ceremony . . *Hamlet* ii 2 388
Apricock. Feed him with apricocks and dewberries . . *M. N. Dream* iii 1 169
Go, bind thou up yon dangling apricocks . . . *Richard II.* iii 4 29
April. Which spongy April at thy hest betrims . *Tempest* iv 1 65
The uncertain glory of an April day . . . *T. G. of Ver.* i 3 85
He writes verses, he speaks holiday, he smells April and May *Mer. Wives* iii 2 69
A day in April never came so sweet . . . *Mer. of Venice* ii 9 93
Men are April when they woo, December when they wed *As Y. Like It* iv 1 147
No shepherdess, but Flora Peering in April's front . *W. Tale* iv 4 3
On Wednesday the four-score of April, forty thousand fathom above water . . . . iv 4 281
He will weep you, an 'twere a man born in April . *Troi. and Cres.* i 2 189
Than youthful April shall with all his showers . *T. Andron.* iii 1 18
Well-apparell'd April on the heel Of limping winter treads *Rom. and Jul.* i 2 27
This embalms and spices To the April day again . *T. of Athens* iv 3 41
The April's in her eyes: it is love's spring . *Ant. and Cleo.* iii 2 43
Apron. Put on two leathern jerkins and aprons . . *2 Hen. IV.* ii 2 190
They will put on two of our jerkins and aprons . . . ii 4 18
Here, Robin, an if I die, I give thee my apron . . *2 Hen. VI.* ii 3 75
The nobility think scorn to go in leather aprons . . . iv 2 14
Hold up, you sluts, Your aprons mountant . . *T. of Athens* iv 3 135
A carpenter.—Where is thy leather apron and thy rule? . *J. Cæsar* i 1 7
Mechanic slaves With greasy aprons, rules, and hammers *Ant. and Cleo.* v 2 210
He will line your apron with gold . . . . *Pericles* iv 6 64
Apron-men. You have made good work, You and your apron-men! *Coriolanus* iv 6 96
Apt. By vain though apt affection . . . *Meas. for Meas.* i 4 48
I find an apt remission in myself . . . . . . v 1 503
Thou shalt see how apt it is to learn Any hard lesson . *Much Ado* ii 1 294
Yea, but so I am apt to do myself wrong . . . . ii 1 213
Pretty and apt.—How mean you, sir? I pretty, and my saying apt? or I apt, and my saying pretty? . . . . *L. L. Lost* i 2 19
Wherefore apt?—And therefore apt, because quick . . . . i 2 24
In such apt and gracious words That aged ears play truant at his tales ii 1 73
Vow, alack, for youth unmeet, Youth so apt to pluck a sweet! . iv 3 114
In all the play There is not one word apt, one player fitted *M. N. Dream* v 1 65
She's apt to learn and thankful for good turns . *T. of Shrew* ii 1 166
I know thy constellation is right apt For this affair . *T. Night* i 4 35
Apt, in good faith; very apt . . . . i 5 28
O world, how apt the poor are to be proud! . . . . iii 1 138
I, most jocund, apt and willingly, To do you rest, a thousand deaths would die . . . . v 1 135
Madam, I am most apt to embrace your offer . . . . v 1 328
Fit for bloody villany, Apt, liable to be employ'd in danger . *K. John* iv 2 226
You know how apt our love was to accord To furnish him . *Hen. V.* ii 2 86
Is she not apt?—Our tongue is rough, coz . . . . v 2 312
Stubborn to justice, apt to accuse it . . . . *Hen. VIII.* ii 4 122
Stubborn critics, apt, without a theme, For depravation *Troi. and Cres.* v 2 131
I have a heart as little apt as yours . . . *Coriolanus* iii 2 29
An I were so apt to quarrel as thou art . . *Rom. and Jul.* iii 1 34
You shall find me apt enough to that, sir, an you will give me occasion iii 1 44
Hasten all the house to bed, Which heavy sorrow makes them apt unto iii 3 157
Does she love him?—She is young and apt . *T. of Athens* i 1 132
Besides, it were a mock Apt to be render'd . . *J. Cæsar* ii 2 97
Live a thousand years, I shall not find myself so apt to die . . iii 1 160
Why dost thou show to the apt thoughts of men The things that are not? v 3 68
I find thee apt . . . . *Hamlet* i 5 31
Thoughts black, hands apt, drugs fit, and time agreeing . . iii 2 266
What they may incense him to, being apt To have his ear abused, wisdom bids fear . . . . *Lear* ii 4 309
Apt enough to dislocate and tear Thy flesh and bones . . iv 2 65
Which now again you are most apt to play the sir in . *Othello* ii 1 175
That she loves him, 'tis apt and of great credit . . . ii 1 296
She is of so free, so kind, so apt, so blessed a disposition . . ii 3 326
And told no more Than what he found himself was apt and true . v 2 177
The fit and apt construction of thy name . . . *Cymbeline* v 5 444
Apter. I warrant, she is apter to do than to confess she does *As Y. L. It* iii 2 408
Thy cheek Is apter than thy tongue to tell thy errand . *2 Hen. IV.* i 1 69
Aptest. Counsel every man The aptest way for safety . . . i 1 213
Aptly. That part Was aptly fitted and naturally perform'd *T. of Shrew* Ind. 1 87
As I know his youth will aptly receive it . . . *T. Night* iii 4 212
He prettily and aptly taunts himself . . . *Richard III.* iii 1 134
It stains the glory in that happy verse Which aptly sings the good *T. of A.* i 1 17
A frock or livery, That aptly is put on . . . *Hamlet* iii 4 165
You aptly will suppose What pageantry, what feats, what shows *Pericles* v 2 270
Aptness. They are in a ripe aptness to take all power . *Coriolanus* iv 3 23
And be friended With aptness of the season . . *Cymbeline* ii 3 53
Aqua-vitæ. I will rather trust a Fleming with my butter, . . . an Irishman with my aqua-vitæ bottle . . . . *Mer. Wives* ii 2 318
I have bought The oil, the balsamum and aqua-vitæ . *Com. of Errors* iv 1 89
Does it work upon him?—Like aqua-vitæ with a midwife . *T. Night* ii 5 216
Recovered again with aqua-vitæ or some other hot infusion . *W. Tale* iv 4 816
Ah, where's my man? give me some aqua vitæ . *Rom. and Jul.* iii 2 88
My lady's dead! O, well-a-day, that ever I was born! Some aqua vitæ, ho! . . . . iv 5 16
Aquilon. Outswell the colic of puff'd Aquilon . . . *Troi. and Cres.* iv 5 9
Aquitaine. About surrender up of Aquitaine . . . *L. L. Lost* i 1 138
The plea of no less weight Than Aquitaine, a dowry for a queen . ii 1 8
In surety of the which, One part of Aquitaine is bound to us . . ii 1 136
We will give up our right in Aquitaine, And hold fair friendship . ii 1 140
On payment of a hundred thousand crowns, To have his title live in Aquitaine . . . . ii 1 146
And have the money by our father lent Than Aquitaine so gelded as it is ii 1 149
If you prove it, I'll repay it back Or yield up Aquitaine . . ii 1 160
I'll give you Aquitaine and all that is his, An you give him for my sake but one loving kiss . . . . ii 1 248
Arabia. In Arabia There is one tree, the phœnix' throne . . *Tempest* iii 3 22
The vasty wilds Of wide Arabia are as throughfares now *Mer. of Venice* ii 7 42
I would my son Were in Arabia, and thy tribe before him *Coriolanus* iv 2 24
All the perfumes of Arabia will not sweeten this little hand . *Macbeth* v 1 57
King Malchus of Arabia; King of Pont; Herod of Jewry *Ant. and Cleo.* iii 6 72
Arabian. Drop tears as fast as the Arabian trees Their medicinal gum *Oth.* v 2 350
O Antony! O thou Arabian bird! . . . . . *Ant. and Cleo.* iii 2 12
If she be furnish'd with a mind so rare, She is alone the Arabian bird *Cymbeline* i 6 17
Araise. Whose simple touch Is powerful to araise King Pepin *All's Well* ii 1 79
Arbitrate. And often at his very loose decides That which long process could not arbitrate . . . . *L. L. Lost* v 2 753
With fearful bloody issue arbitrate . . . . *K. John* i 1 38
'Tis not the trial of a woman's war, The bitter clamour of two eager tongues, Can arbitrate this cause betwixt us twain . . *Richard II.* i 1 50
There shall your swords and lances arbitrate The swelling difference . i 1 200
But certain issue strokes must arbitrate . . . . *Macbeth* v 4 20
Arbitrating that Which the commission of thy years and art Could to no issue of true honour bring . . . . . *Rom. and Jul.* iv 1 63
Arbitrator. The arbitrator of despairs, Just death . . *1 Hen. VI.* ii 5 28
That old common arbitrator, Time, Will one day end it . *Troi. and Cres.* iv 5 225
Arbitrement. Even to a mortal arbitrement . . . *T. Night* iii 4 286
We of the offering side Must keep aloof from strict arbitrement *1 Hen. IV.* iv 1 70
If it come to the arbitrement of swords . . . *Hen. V.* iv 1 168
And put thy fortune to the arbitrement Of bloody strokes *Richard III.* v 3 89
The arbitrement is like to be bloody . . . . . *Lear* iv 7 95
To be put to the arbitrement of swords . . . . *Cymbeline* i 4 52
Arbour. I will hide me in the arbour . . . . . *Much Ado* ii 3 38
Where, in an arbour, we will eat a last year's pippin . *2 Hen. IV.* v 3 2
His walks, His private arbours and new-planted orchards . *J. Cæsar* iii 2 253
Arc. His new-come champion, virtuous Joan of Arc . . *1 Hen. VI.* ii 2 20
Joan of Arc hath been A virgin from her tender infancy . . . v 4 49
Arch. The most arch act of piteous massacre . . . *Richard III.* iv 3 2
The queen o' the sky, Whose watery arch and messenger am I *Tempest* iv 1 71
There is sprung up An heretic, an arch one, Cranmer . . *Hen. VIII.* iii 2 102
Who, like an arch, reverberates The voice again . . *Troi. and Cres.* iii 3 120
Ne'er through an arch so hurried the blown tide . . *Coriolanus* v 4 50
The noble duke my master, My worthy arch and patron, comes to-night *Lear* ii 1 61
And the wide arch Of the ranged empire fall! . . *Ant. and Cleo.* i 1 33
Hath nature given them eyes To see this vaulted arch? . . *Cymbeline* i 6 33
Archbishop. Keep Stephen Langton, chosen archbishop Of Canterbury, from that holy see? . . . . *K. John* iii 1 143
His brother, Archbishop late of Canterbury . . . *Richard II.* ii 1 282
That same noble prelate, well beloved, The archbishop . . *1 Hen. IV.* i 3 268
The gentle Archbishop of York is up With well-appointed powers *2 Hen. IV.* i 1 189
Let them alone: The marshal and the archbishop are strong . . ii 3 42
Fain would I go to meet the archbishop, But many thousand reasons hold me back . . . . ii 3 65
You, lord archbishop, Whose see is by a civil peace maintain'd . iv 1 41
Good day to you, gentle lord archbishop . . . . . iv 2 2
I do arrest thee, traitor, of high treason: And you, lord archbishop . iv 2 108
We shall see him For it an archbishop.—So I hear . . *Hen. VIII.* iii 2 74
He of Winchester Is held no great good lover of the archbishop's . iv 1 104
The archbishop Is the king's hand and tongue . . . . v 1 37
I have brought my lord the archbishop, As you commanded me . . v 1 80
O lord archbishop, Thou hast made me now a man! . . . v 5 64
Archbishopric. For not bestowing on him, at his asking, The archbishopric of Toledo . . . . ii 1 164
Archdeacon. The archdeacon hath divided it Into three limits *1 Hen. IV.* iii 1 72
Arched. Thou hast the right arched beauty of the brow . *Mer. Wives* iii 3 59
To sit and draw His arched brows, his hawking eye, his curls *All's Well* i 1 105
The gates of monarchs Are arch'd so high that giants may jet through *Cymbeline* iii 3 5
Archelaus, Of Cappadocia; Philadelphos, king Of Paphlagonia *A. and C.* iii 6 69
Arch-enemy. Yonder's the head of that arch-enemy . . *3 Hen. VI.* ii 2 2
Archer. If we can do this, Cupid is no longer an archer . *Much Ado* ii 1 401
He wanted pikes to set before his archers . . . *1 Hen. VI.* i 1 116
Our archers shall be placed in the midst . . . *Richard III.* v 3 295
Draw, archers, draw your arrows to the head! . . . . v 3 339
You are a good archer, Marcus . . . . . *T. Andron.* iv 3 52
A well-experienced archer hits the mark His eye doth level at *Pericles* i 1 164
Archery. Flower of this purple dye, Hit with Cupid's archery *M. N. Dr.* iii 2 103
Now let me see your archery; Look ye draw home enough *T. Andron.* iv 3 2
Arch-heretic. Let go the hand of that arch-heretic . . *K. John* iii 1 192
A most arch heretic, a pestilence That does infect the land *Hen. VIII.* v 1 45
Archibald. Brave Archibald, That ever-valiant and approved Scot *1 Hen. IV.* i 1 53
Architect. Chief architect and plotter of these woes . *T. Andron.* v 3 122
Arch-mock. O, 'tis the spite of hell, the fiend's arch-mock! . *Othello* iv 1 71
Arch-villain. Even so may Angelo, In all his dressings, characts, titles, forms, Be an arch-villain . . . . . . *Meas. for Meas.* v 1 57
All single and alone, Yet an arch-villain keeps him company *T. of Athens* v 1 111
Arcu. Integer vitæ, scelerisque purus, Non eget Mauri jaculis, nec arcu.— O, 'tis a verse in Horace . . . . *T. Andron.* iv 2 21
Arde. In the vale of Andren.—'Twixt Guynes and Arde . . *Hen. VIII.* i 1 7
Arden. In the forest of Arden, and a many merry men with him *As Y. Like It* i 1 121
To seek my uncle in the forest of Arden . . . . . i 3 109
This is the forest of Arden.—Ay, now am I in Arden . . . ii 4 15
Ardent. Like those that under hot ardent zeal would set whole realms on fire . . . . *T. of Athens* iii 3 33
Ardour. The white cold virgin snow upon my heart Abates the ardour of my liver . . . . *Tempest* iv 1 56
Proclaim no shame When the compulsive ardour gives the charge *Ham.* iii 4 86
A-repairing. Like a German clock, Still a-repairing . . *L. L. Lost* iii 1 193
Argal, she drowned herself wittingly . . . . . *Hamlet* v 1 13
Argal, he that is not guilty of his own death shortens not his own life . v 1 21
Argal, the gallows may do well to thee . . . . . . v 1 55
Argentine. Celestial Dian, goddess argentine, I will obey thee *Pericles* v 1 251
Argier. Where was she born? speak; tell me.—Sir, in Argier . *Tempest* i 2 261
From Argier, Thou know'st, was banish'd . . . . . i 2 265
Argo, their thread of life is spun . . . . . . *2 Hen. VI.* iv 2 31
Argosies with portly sail, Like signiors and rich burghers *Mer. of Venice* i 1 9
Three of your argosies Are richly come to harbour suddenly . . v 1 276
My father hath no less Than three great argosies . . *T. of Shrew* ii 1 380
Argosy. He hath an argosy bound to Tripolis . . *Mer. of Venice* i 3 18
Ill luck?—Hath an argosy cast away, coming from Tripolis . . iii 1 105
Besides an argosy That now is lying in Marseilles' road . *T. of Shrew* ii 1 376
What, have I choked you with an argosy? . . . . . ii 1 378
As doth a sail, fill'd with a fretting gust, Command an argosy to stem the waves . . . . *3 Hen. VI.* ii 6 36
Argue. I will something affect the letter, for it argues facility *L. L. Lost* iv 2 57
I had rather You would have bid me argue like a father . *Richard II.* i 3 238

Argue. Admit no parley.—That argues but the shame of your offence . 2 *Hen. IV.* iv 1 160
This speedy and quick appearance argues proof Of your accustom'd diligence to me . . . . 1 *Hen. VI.* v 3 8
This argues what her kind of life hath been, Wicked and vile . . v 4 15
So bad a death argues a monstrous life . . . . 2 *Hen. VI.* iii 3 30
Her looks do argue her replete with modesty . . 3 *Hen. VI.* iii 2 84
This general applause and loving shout Argues your wisdoms *Rich. III.* iii 7 40
My lord, this argues conscience in your grace . . . . . iii 7 174
We are too open here to argue this; Let's think in private more *Hen. VIII.* ii 1 168
Scholars allow'd freely to argue for her.—Ay, and the best . . . ii 2 113
It argues a distemper'd head So soon to bid good morrow to thy bed *Rom. and Jul.* ii 3 33
Which argues a great sickness in his judgement that makes it *T. of Athens* v 1 30
If I drown myself wittingly, it argues an act . . . . *Hamlet* v 1 11
This argues fruitfulness and liberal heart . . . . *Othello* iii 4 38
Argued. Well have you argued, sir . . . . . *Richard II.* iv 1 150
Stubbornly he did repugn the truth About a certain question in the law Argued betwixt the Duke of York and him . . 1 *Hen. VI.* iv 1 96
Which argued thee a most unloving father . . 3 *Hen. VI.* ii 2 25
Arguing. I should be arguing still upon that doubt . . *T. of Shrew* iii 1 55
And throw forth greater themes For insurrection's arguing . *Coriolanus* i 1 225
If arguing make us sweat, The proof of it will turn to redder drops *J. C.* v 1 48
Argument. My desires had instance and argument to commend themselves . . . . *Mer. Wives* ii 2 256
If ever thou dost fall from this faith, thou wilt prove a notable argument *Much Ado* i 1 258
Become the argument of his own scorn by falling in love . . . ii 3 11
If thou wilt hold longer argument, Do it in notes . . . ii 3 55
It is no addition to her wit, nor no great argument of her folly . ii 3 243
For shape, for bearing, argument and valour, Goes foremost in report . iii 1 96
I shall be forsworn, which is a great argument of falsehood, if I love *L. L. Lost* i 2 175
How did this argument begin? . . . . iii 1 106
Thus came your argument in . . . . iii 1 109
Rhetoric of thine eye, 'Gainst whom the world cannot hold argument . iv 3 61
He draweth out the thread of his verbosity finer than the staple of his argument . . . . v 1 19
Therefore I'll darkly end the argument . . . . . . v 2 23
Love doth approach disguised, Armed in arguments . . . . v 2 84
Since love's argument was first on foot, Let not the cloud of sorrow justle it. . . . . v 2 757
If you have any pity, grace, or manners, You would not make me such an argument . . . . *M. N. Dream* iii 2 242
Hath not Fortune sent in this fool to cut off the argument? *As Y. Like It* i 2 50
Grounded upon no other argument But that the people praise her . i 2 291
I should not seek an absent argument Of my revenge, thou present . iii 1 3
'Tis the rarest argument of wonder that hath shot out . . *All's Well* ii 3 7
In argument of praise, or to the worth Of the great count himself . iii 5 62
Let thy tongue tang arguments of state . . . *T. Night* ii 5 163
This was a great argument of love in her toward you . . . . iii 2 12
The rather by these arguments of fear, Set forth in your pursuit . . iii 3 12
Might well have given us bloody argument . . . . . iii 3 32
Let thy tongue tang with arguments of state . . . . . iii 4 78
What to her adheres, which follows after, Is the argument of Time *W. T.* iv 1 29
Prevented and made whole With very easy arguments of love *K. John* i 1 36
Doth move the murmuring lips of discontent To break into this dangerous argument . . . . iv 2 54
As near as I could sift him on that argument . . . . *Richard II.* i 1 12
It would be argument for a week, laughter for a month . 1 *Hen. IV.* ii 2 100
Have a play extempore?—Content; and the argument shall be thy running away . . . . ii 4 310
All my reign hath been but as a scene Acting that argument 2 *Hen. IV.* iv 5 199
Our argument Is all too heavy to admit much talk . . . . v 2 23
And sheathed their swords for lack of argument . . *Hen. V.* iii 1 21
He will maintain his argument as well as any military man in the world iii 2 85
In the way of argument, look you, and friendly communication . iii 2 104
Turn the sands into eloquent tongues, and my horse is argument for them all . . . . iii 7 37
How can they charitably dispose of any thing, when blood is their argument? . . . . iv 1 150
Not a piece of feather in our host—Good argument, I hope, we will not fly . . . . iv 3 113
Unless my study and my books be false, The argument you held was wrong in you . . . . 1 *Hen. VI.* ii 4 57
Now, Somerset, where is your argument? . . . . . ii 4 59
In argument upon a case, Some words there grew . . . . ii 5 45
In argument and proof of which contract, Bear her this jewel . . v 1 46
Nothing but an argument That he that breaks a stick of Gloucester's grove Shall lose his head . . . . . . 2 *Hen. VI.* i 2 32
And yet we have but trivial argument, More than mistrust . . . iii 1 241
Play'd the orator, Inferring arguments of mighty force . . 3 *Hen. VI.* ii 2 44
Smooths the wrong, Inferreth arguments of mighty strength . . . iii 1 49
With lies well steel'd with weighty arguments . . . *Richard III.* i 1 148
And that, without delay, their arguments Be now produced *Hen. VIII.* ii 4 67
But suited In like conditions as our argument . *Troi. and Cres.* Prol. 25
I cannot fight upon this argument . . . . i 1 95
All the argument is a cuckold and a whore . . . . . ii 3 78
Then will Ajax lack matter, if he have lost his argument . . . ii 3 104
No, you see, he is his argument that has his argument . . . ii 3 105
I had good argument for kissing once.—But that's no argument for kissing now . . . . iv 5 26
Thus popp'd Paris in his hardiment, And parted thus you and your argument . . . . iv 5 29
And meant, indeed, to occupy the argument no longer . *Rom. and Jul.* ii 4 105
Try the argument of hearts by borrowing . . . *T. of Athens* ii 2 187
So it may prove an argument of laughter To the rest . . . iii 3 20
He did behave his anger, ere 'twas spent, As if he had but proved an argument . . . . iii 5 23
Why do we hold our tongues, That most may claim this argument? *Macbeth* ii 3 126
There was, for a while, no money bid for argument . . . *Hamlet* ii 2 372
Belike this show imports the argument of the play . . . . iii 2 149
Have you heard the argument? Is there no offence in't? . . iii 2 242
Rightly to be great Is not to stir without great argument . . iv 4 54
The argument of your praise, balm of your age . . . *Lear* i 1 218
I mean the whispered ones, for they are yet but ear-kissing arguments ii 1 9
'Tis his schoolmaster: An argument that he is pluck'd *Ant. and Cleo.* iii 12 3
It was much like an argument that fell out last night . . *Cymbeline* i 4 60

Argus. Though Argus were her eunuch and her guard . . *L. L. Lost* iii 1 201
Lie not a night from home; watch me like Argus . *Mer. of Venice* v 1 230
Purblind Argus, all eyes and no sight . . *Troi. and Cres.* i 2 31
Ariachne. Admits no orifex for a point as subtle As Ariachne's broken woof to enter . . . . v 2 152
Ariadne. 'Twas Ariadne passioning For Theseus' perjury *T. G. of Ver.* iv 4 172
And make him with fair Ægle break his faith, With Ariadne *M. N. Dr.* ii 1 80
Ariel. Approach, my Ariel, come.—All hail, great master! . *Tempest* i 2 188
To thy strong bidding task Ariel and all his quality . . . . i 2 193
Ariel, thy charge Exactly is perform'd: but there's more work . . i 2 237
Fine apparition! My quaint Ariel, Hark in thine ear . . . i 2 317
Delicate Ariel, I'll set thee free for this . . . . . . i 2 441
It works. Come on. Thou hast done well, fine Ariel! . . . i 2 494
Bravely the figure of this harpy hast thou Perform'd, my Ariel . . iii 3 84
Ariel! my industrious servant, Ariel!—What would my potent master? iv 1 33
Do you love me, master? no?—Dearly, my delicate Ariel . . . iv 1 49
Now come, my Ariel! bring a corollary, Rather than want a spirit . iv 1 57
Come with a thought. I thank thee, Ariel: come . . . . iv 1 164
That's my dainty Ariel! I shall miss thee; But yet thou shalt have freedom . . . . v 1 95
My Ariel, chick, That is thy charge: then to the elements Be free . v 1 316
Aries. The Bull, being gall'd, gave Aries such a knock That down fell both the Ram's horns . . . . *T. Andron.* iv 3 71
Aright. Ever out of frame, And never going aright . . *L. L. Lost* iii 1 194
Are not you he?—Thou speak'st aright . . . *M. N. Dream* ii 1 42
My mind will never grant what I perceive Your highness aims at, if I aim aright . . . . 3 *Hen. VI.* iii 2 68
Would you represent our queen aright . . . . *T. Andron.* v 2 89
For thy good caution, thanks; Thou hast harp'd my fear aright *Macbeth* iv 1 74
Report me and my cause aright To the unsatisfied . . . *Hamlet* v 2 350
I do beseech you To understand my purposes aright . . . *Lear* i 4 260
When I am known aright, you shall not grieve Lending me this acquaintance. . . . . iv 3 55
Arion. Like Arion on the dolphin's back . . . . *T. Night* i 2 15
A-ripening. And, when he thinks, good easy man, full surely His greatness is a-ripening, nips his root . . . . *Hen. VIII.* iii 2 357
Arise. Now I arise: Sit still, and hear the last . . . *Tempest* i 2 169
There he must stay until the officer Arise to let him in *Meas. for Meas.* iv 2 94
To have my love to bed and to arise . . . . *M. N. Dream* iii 1 174
But rise more great, Arise sir Richard and Plantagenet . . *K. John* i 1 162
Arise forth from the couch of lasting night, Thou hate and terror to prosperity . . . . iii 4 27
Some sudden mischief may arise of it . . . . . *Hen. V.* iv 7 186
Such factious emulations shall arise . . . . 1 *Hen. VI.* iv 1 113
Beside, what infamy will there arise! . . . . iv 1 143
What showers arise, Blown with the windy tempest of my heart! 3 *Hen. VI.* ii 5 85
And like the owl by day, If he arise, be mock'd and wonder'd at . . v 4 57
Take up the sword again, or take up me.—Arise, dissembler *Richard III.* i 2 185
I am a suitor.—Arise, and take place by us . . . *Hen. VIII.* i 2 10
So much fairer And spotless shall mine innocence arise . . . iii 2 301
Pray you, arise, My good and gracious Lord of Canterbury . . . v 1 91
Faint-hearted boy, arise, and look upon her . . *T. Andron.* iii 1 65
Arise, fair sun, and kill the envious moon . . *Rom. and Jul.* ii 2 4
Come, sir, arise, away! I'll teach you differences . . . *Lear* i 4 99
Arise, arise; Awake the snorting citizens with the bell . . *Othello* i 1 89
Arise, black vengeance, from thy hollow cell! . . . . . iii 3 447
Arise; the queen approaches: Her head's declined *Ant. and Cleo.* iii 11 46
Arise, you shall not kneel: I pray you, rise; rise, Egypt . . v 2 114
The lark at heaven's gate sings, And Phœbus 'gins arise . *Cymbeline* ii 3 23
With every thing that pretty is, My lady sweet, arise: Arise, arise . ii 3 29
Some falls are means the happier to arise . . . . . . iv 2 403
Bow your knees. Arise my knights o' the battle . . . . v 5 20
Here's my knee: Ere I arise, I will prefer my sons . . . . v 5 326
Ariseth. Why, how now, ho! from whence ariseth this? . . *Othello* ii 3 169
Aristotle. So devote to Aristotle's checks As Ovid be an outcast *T. of Shrew* i 1 32
Whom Aristotle thought Unfit to hear moral philosophy *Troi. and Cres.* ii 2 166
Arithmetic. A tapster's arithmetic may soon bring his particulars therein to a total . . . . i 2 123
Ruminates like an hostess that hath no arithmetic but her brain to set down her reckoning . . . . iii 3 253
But now 'tis odds beyond arithmetic . . . . *Coriolanus* iii 1 245
A rogue, a villain, that fights by the book of arithmetic! *Rom. and Jul.* iii 1 106
To divide him inventorially would dizzy the arithmetic of memory *Hamlet* v 2 119
Spare your arithmetic: never count the turns . . . *Cymbeline* i 4 142
Arithmetician. What was he? Forsooth, a great arithmetician *Othello* i 1 19
Ark. There is, sure, another flood toward, and these couples are coming to the ark . . . . *As Y. Like It* v 4 36
Arm. Sitting, His arms in this sad knot . . . . . *Tempest* i 2 224
And oar'd Himself with his good arms in lusty stroke To the shore . ii 1 119
Legged like a man! and his fins like arms! . . . . . . ii 2 35
To wreathe your arms, like a malecontent . . . *T. G. of Ver.* ii 1 20
Give me my gown; or else keep it in your arms . . *Mer. Wives* iii 1 35
Pinch them, arms, legs, backs, shoulders, sides and shins . . . v 5 58
I will encounter darkness as a bride, And hug it in mine arms *M. for M.* iii 1 85
I'll depose I had him in mine arms With all the effect of love . . v 1 198
Though others have the arm, show us the sleeve . *Com. of Errors* iii 2 23
The mole in my neck, the great wart on my left arm . . . . iii 2 148
Under your arm, like a lieutenant's scarf . . . . *Much Ado* ii 1 197
Well fitted in arts, glorious in arms . . . . . *L. L. Lost* ii 1 45
With your arms crossed on your thin-belly doublet like a rabbit on a spit iii 1 18
Dan Cupid; Regent of love-rhymes, lord of folded arms . . . iii 1 183
Lay his wreathed arms athwart His loving bosom to keep down his heart . . . . iv 3 135
Have at you, then, affection's men at arms . . . . . . iv 3 290
Arm, wenches, arm! encounters mounted are Against your peace . . v 2 82
And lay my arms before the legs of this sweet lass of France . . v 2 558
Hide thy head, Achilles: here comes Hector in arms . . . . v 2 636
I bepray you, let me borrow my arms again . . . . . v 2 702
Look you arm yourself To fit your fancies to your father's will *M. N. Dr.* i 1 117
Sleep thou, and I will wind thee in my arms . . . . . iv 1 45
At first the infant, Mewling and puking in the nurse's arms *As Y. L. It* ii 7 144
Thou art right welcome as thy master is. Support him by the arm . ii 7 199
Here upon his arm The lioness had torn some flesh away . . iv 3 147
We'll lead you thither. I pray you, will you take him by the arm? . iv 3 163
It grieves me to see thee wear thy heart in a scarf!—It is my arm . v 2 24
I'll cuff you, if you strike again.—So may you lose your arms *T. of Shr.* ii 1 222
If you strike me, you are no gentleman; And if no gentleman, why then no arms . . . . ii 1 224

Arm. Lend me an arm; the rest have worn me out — *All's Well* i 2 73
Why dost thou garter up thy arms o' this fashion? — ii 3 265
Hugs his kicky-wicky here at home, Spending his manly marrow in her arms — ii 3 298
Arms her with the boldness of a wife To her allowing husband! — *W. Tale* i 2 184
Holds his wife by the arm, That little thinks she has been sluiced! — i 2 193
Quite beyond mine arm, out of the blank And level of my brain, plot-proof — ii 3 5
Not to be buried, But quick and in mine arms — iv 4 132
I see Leontes opening his free arms and weeping His welcomes forth — iv 4 559
It should take joy To see her in your arms — v 1 81
If my legs were two such riding-rods, My arms such eel-skins stuff'd — *K. John* i 1 141
Till then, fair boy, Will I not think of home, but follow arms — ii 1 31
England, impatient of your just demands, Hath put himself in arms — ii 1 57
Wilt thou resign them and lay down thy arms?—My life as soon — ii 1 154
Our arms, like to a muzzled bear, Save in aspect, hath all offence seal'd up — ii 1 249
Mount, chevaliers! to arms! — ii 1 287
Before we will lay down our just-borne arms, We'll put thee down, 'gainst whom these arms we bear — ii 1 345
You came in arms to spill mine enemies' blood, But now in arms you strengthen it with yours — iii 1 102
Arm, arm, you heavens, against these perjured kings! — iii 1 107
Therefore to arms! be champion of our church — iii 1 255
Arm thy constant and thy nobler parts Against these giddy loose suggestions — iii 1 291
Father, to arms!—Upon thy wedding-day? — iii 1 300
Upon my knee I beg, go not to arms Against mine uncle — iii 1 308
If but a dozen French Were there in arms, they would be as a call — iii 4 174
Arm you against your other enemies — iv 2 249
The very top, The height, the crest, or crest unto the crest, Of murder's arms — iv 3 47
Go, bear him in thine arms. I am amazed, methinks, and lose my way — iv 3 139
Go I to make the French lay down their arms — v 1 24
Make compromise, Insinuation, parley and base truce To arms invasive? — v 1 69
Let us, my liege, to arms: Perchance the cardinal cannot make your peace — v 1 73
Neptune's arms, who clippeth thee about — v 2 34
He flatly says he'll not lay down his arms — v 2 126
And is well prepared To whip this dwarfish war, these pigmy arms — v 2 135
The gallant monarch is in arms And like an eagle o'er his aery towers — v 2 148
My arm shall give thee help to bear thee hence — v 4 58
That you might The better arm you to the sudden time — v 6 26
Come the three corners of the world in arms, And we shall shock them — v 7 116
This arm shall do it, or this life be spent — *Richard II.* i 1 106
Command our officers at arms Be ready to direct these home alarms — i 1 204
Let heaven revenge; for I may never lift An angry arm against His minister — i 2 41
Demand of yonder champion The cause of his arrival here in arms — i 3 8
Say who thou art And why thou comest thus knightly clad in arms — i 3 12
By the grace of God and this mine arm — i 3 22
Ask yonder knight in arms, Both who he is and why he cometh hither — i 3 26
Here do stand in arms, To prove, by God's grace and my body's valour — i 3 36
We will descend and fold him in our arms — i 3 54
Trumpets' dreadful bray, And grating shock of wrathful iron arms — i 3 136
Bolingbroke repeals himself, And with uplifted arms is safe arrived — ii 2 50
And fright our native peace with self-born arms — ii 3 80
Frighting her pale-faced villages with war And ostentation of despised arms — ii 3 95
Quickly should this arm of mine, Now prisoner to the palsy, chastise thee — ii 3 103
And here art come Before the expiration of thy time, In braving arms — ii 3 112
My rights and royalties Pluck'd from my arms perforce and given away — ii 3 121
I see the issue of these arms: I cannot mend it — ii 3 152
Ere her native king Shall falter under foul rebellion's arms — iii 2 26
Nor near nor farther off, my gracious lord, Than this weak arm — iii 2 65
Arm, arm, my name! a puny subject strikes At thy great glory — iii 2 86
Strive to speak big and clap their female joints In stiff unwieldy arms — iii 2 115
Your northern castles yielded up, And all your southern gentlemen in arms — iii 2 202
Hither come Even at his feet to lay my arms and power — iii 3 39
Should so with civil and uncivil arms Be rush'd upon — iii 3 102
His glittering arms he will commend to rust, His barbed steeds to stables — iii 3 116
I heard you say, 'Is not my arm of length?' — iv 1 11
Tell us how near is danger, That we may arm us to encounter it — v 3 48
Whose arms were moulded in their mothers' womb To chase these pagans in those holy fields — *1 Hen. IV.* i 1 23
If he fight longer than he sees reason, I'll forswear arms — i 2 208
To bear our fortunes in our own strong arms — i 3 188
Have I not all their letters to meet me in arms? — ii 3 29
To bloody battles and to bruising arms — iii 2 105
And great name in arms Holds from all soldiers chief majority — iii 2 108
All furnish'd, all in arms; All plumed like estridges — iv 1 97
Dear men Of estimation and command in arms — iv 4 32
Both together Are confident against the world in arms — v 1 117
Can honour set to a leg? no: or an arm? no — v 1 134
And will scourge With haughty arms this hateful name in us — v 2 41
Unless a brother should a brother dare To gentle exercise and proof of arms — v 2 55
I will embrace him with a soldier's arm, That he shall shrink — v 2 74
Arm, arm with speed: and, fellows, soldiers, friends, Better consider what you have to do — v 2 76
The arms are fair, When the intent of bearing them is just — v 2 88
Turk Gregory never did such deeds in arms as I have done this day — v 3 47
Stain'd nobility lies trodden on, And rebels' arms triumph in massacres — v 4 14
The spirits Of valiant Shirley, Stafford, Blunt, are in my arms — v 4 41
Would to God Thy name in arms were now as great as mine! — v 4 70
Northumberland and the prelate Scroop, Who, as we hear, are busily in arms — v 5 38
Breaks like a fire Out of his keeper's arms — *2 Hen. IV.* i 1 143
What say you to it?—I well allow the occasion of our arms — i 3 5
I have in equal balance justly weigh'd What wrongs our arms may do, what wrongs we suffer — iv 1 68
Hath put us in these ill-beseeming arms, Not to break peace — iv 1 84
Our men more perfect in the use of arms, Our armour all as strong — iv 1 155
And knit our powers to the arm of peace — iv 1 177
Hangs resolved correction in the arm That was uprear'd to execution — iv 1 213
Most shallowly did you these arms commence — iv 2 118

Arm. Gives warning to all the rest of this little kingdom, man, to arm — *2 Hen. IV.* iv 3 118
And put the world's whole strength Into one giant arm — iv 5 45
Do arm myself To welcome the condition of the time — v 2 10
With your puissant arm renew their feats — *Hen. V.* i 2 116
We must not only arm to invade the French — i 2 136
Yoke-fellows in arms, Let us to France; like horse-leeches, my boys — ii 3 56
It is most meet we arm us 'gainst the foe — ii 4 15
And, princes, look you strongly arm to meet him — ii 4 49
Dites-moi l'Anglois pour le bras.—De arm, madame — iii 4 22
'Tis midnight; I'll go arm myself — iii 7 97
Now is it time to arm: come, shall we about it? — iii 7 167
All those legs and arms and heads, chopped off in a battle, shall join together at the latter day — iv 1 142
God's arm strike with us! 'tis a fearful odds — iv 3 5
And over Suffolk's neck He threw his wounded arm and kiss'd his lips — iv 6 25
Kill the poys and the luggage! 'tis expressly against the law of arms — iv 7 2
O God, thy arm was here; And not to us, but to thy arm alone, Ascribe we all! — iv 8 111
His arms spread wider than a dragon's wings — *1 Hen. VI.* i 1 11
Instead of gold, we'll offer up our arms; Since arms avail not now — i 1 46
Cropp'd are the flower-de-luces in your arms — i 1 80
The French exclaim'd, the devil was in arms — i 1 125
By some odd gimmors or device Their arms are set like clocks — i 2 42
All manner of men assembled here in arms this day against God's peace — i 3 75
With a baser man of arms by far Once in contempt they would have barter'd me — i 4 30
From my shoulders crack my arms asunder — i 5 11
How much he wrongs his fame, Despairing of his own arm's fortitude! — ii 1 17
Arm! arm! the enemy doth make assault! — ii 1 38
Of all exploits since first I follow'd arms — ii 1 43
And I will chain these legs and arms of thine — ii 3 39
These are his substance, sinews, arms and strength — ii 3 63
Pithless arms, like to a wither'd vine That droops his sapless branches — ii 5 11
Before whose glory I was great in arms — ii 5 24
Direct mine arms I may embrace his neck — ii 5 37
Lean thine aged back against mine arm — ii 5 43
And dare not take up arms like gentlemen — iii 2 70
Thou wandering lord Charles and the rest will take thee in their arms — iii 3 77
This arm, that hath reclaim'd To your obedience fifty fortresses — iii 4 5
The law of arms is such That whoso draws a sword, 'tis present death — iii 4 38
In defence of my lord's worthiness, I crave the benefit of law of arms — iv 1 100
Servant in arms to Harry King of England — iv 2 4
Come, come and lay him in his father's arms — iv 7 29
He lies inhearsed in the arms Of the most bloody nurser of his harms! — iv 7 45
Created, for his rare success in arms, Great Earl of Washford — iv 7 62
Those provinces these arms of mine did conquer — *2 Hen. VI.* i 1 120
Whose overweening arm I have pluck'd back — iii 1 159
The uncivil kerns of Ireland are in arms — iii 1 310
I know no pain they can inflict upon him Will make him say I moved him to those arms — iii 1 378
Broke be my sword, my arms torn and defaced, And I proclaim'd a coward! — iv 1 42
The Nevils all, . . . As hating thee, are rising up in arms — iv 1 93
The commons here in Kent are up in arms — iv 1 100
I thought ye would never have given out these arms till you had recovered your ancient freedom — iv 8 27
His arms are only to remove from thee The Duke of Somerset — iv 9 29
And now is York in arms to second him — iv 9 35
Go and meet him, And ask him what's the reason of these arms — iv 9 37
If mine arm be heaved in the air, Thy grave is digg'd already in the earth — iv 10 54
To know the reason of these arms in peace — v 1 18
If thy arms be to no other end, The king hath yielded unto thy demand — v 1 39
Call Buckingham, and bid him arm himself — v 1 192
And so to arms, victorious father, To quell the rebels and their complices — v 1 211
Clifford of Cumberland, Warwick is hoarse with calling thee to arms — v 2 7
As thou lovest and honourest arms, Let's fight it out — *3 Hen. VI.* i 1 116
To arms! And, father, do but think How sweet a thing it is to wear a crown — i 2 28
Such mercy as his ruthless arm, With downright payment, show'd unto my father — i 4 31
That raught at mountains with outstretched arms — i 4 68
Slaughter'd by the ireful arm Of unrelenting Clifford and the queen — ii 1 57
Shall we on the helmets of our foes Tell our devotion with revengeful arms? — ii 1 164
Let me embrace thee in my weary arms — ii 3 45
Suppose this arm is for the Duke of York, And this for Rutland — ii 4 2
These arms of mine shall be thy winding-sheet — ii 5 114
She did corrupt frail nature with some bribe, To shrink mine arm up — iii 2 156
While life upholds this arm, This arm upholds the house of Lancaster — iii 3 106
Well, I will arm me, being thus forewarn'd — iv 1 113
But why come you in arms?—To help King Edward — iv 7 42
Away with scrupulous wit! now arms must rule — iv 7 61
The cedar, . . . Whose arms gave shelter to the princely eagle — v 2 12
And make him, naked, foil a man at arms — v 4 42
What satisfaction canst thou make For bearing arms? — v 5 15
Our bruised arms hung up for monuments — *Richard III.* i 1 6
This good king's blood, Which his hell-govern'd arm hath butchered! — i 2 67
Take not the quarrel from his powerful arm — i 4 223
He hugg'd me in his arms, and swore, with sobs — i 4 252
Go with him, And from her jealous arms pluck him perforce — iii 1 36
I am bewitch'd; behold mine arm Is, like a blasted sapling, wither'd up — iii 4 70
Girdling one another Within their innocent alabaster arms — iv 3 11
When this arm of mine hath chastised The petty rebel — iv 4 331
So thrive I in my dangerous attempt Of hostile arms! — iv 4 399
Exeter, his brother there, With many moe confederates, are in arms — iv 4 504
My liege, in Kent the Guildfords are in arms — iv 4 505
Fellows in arms, and my most loving friends — v 2 1
Send out a pursuivant at arms To Stanley's regiment — v 3 59
About the mid of night come to my tent And help to arm me — v 3 78
And aid thee in this doubtful shock of arms — v 3 93
Awake, awake! Arm, fight, and conquer, for fair England's sake! — v 3 150
Why, then 'tis time to arm and give direction — v 3 236
That he was never trained up in arms — v 3 272
Arm, arm, my lord; the foe vaunts in the field.—Come, bustle, bustle — v 3 288
Our strong arms be our conscience, swords our law — v 3 311
God and your arms be praised, victorious friends; The day is ours — v 5 1
Their heralds challenged The noble spirits to arms — *Hen. VIII.* i 1 35

Arm. Once more in mine arms I bid him welcome . *Hen. VIII.* ii 2 99
When the brown wench Lay kissing in your arms, lord cardinal . iii 2 296
Our king has all the Indies in his arms, And more and richer, when he strains that lady . . . iv 1 45
With surety stronger than Achilles' arm . *Troi. and Cres.* i 3 220
And dare avow her beauty and her worth In other arms than hers . i 3 272
A lady, wiser, fairer, truer, Than ever Greek did compass in his arms . i 3 276
To-morrow morning call some knight to arms That hath a stomach . ii 1 136
For what, alas, can these my single arms? . . . ii 2 135
But he that disciplined thy arms to fight, Let Mars divide eternity in twain, And give him half . . . ii 3 255
And with his arms outstretch'd, as he would fly, Grasps in the comer . iii 3 167
Speaking is for beggars; he wears his tongue in's arms . iii 3 271
By him that thunders, thou hast lusty arms . . iv 5 136
Worthy of arms! as welcome as to one That would be rid of such an enemy . . . iv 5 163
I would my arms could match thee in contention, As they contend with thee in courtesy . . . iv 5 205
Believe, I come to lose my arm, or win my sleeve . . v 3 96
Now is the cur Ajax prouder than the cur Achilles, and will not arm to-day . . . v 4 17
Bid the snail-paced Ajax arm for shame . . . v 5 18
Be happy that my arms are out of use . . . v 6 16
They say poor suitors have strong breaths: they shall know we have strong arms too . *Coriolanus* i 1 62
For the dearth, The gods, not the patricians, make it, and Your knees to them, not arms, must help . . . i 1 76
The vigilant eye, The counsellor heart, the arm our soldier . i 1 120
The Volsces are in arms.—I am glad on 't . . . i 1 228
O, let me clip ye In arms as sound as when I woo'd! . i 6 30
Where is he wounded?—I' the shoulder and i' the left arm . ii 1 163
Death, that dark spirit, in's nervy arm doth lie . . ii 1 177
Arm yourself To answer mildly . . . . iii 2 138
If I could shake off but one seven years From these old arms and legs . iv 1 56
Let me twine Mine arms about that body . . . iv 5 113
To hew thy target from thy brawn, Or lose mine arm for't . iv 5 127
What an arm he has! he turned me about with his finger and his thumb iv 5 159
All the swords In Italy, and her confederate arms, Could not have made this peace . . . . v 3 208
Defend the justice of my cause with arms . *T. Andron.* i 1 2
Hath yoked a nation strong, train'd up in arms . . i 1 30
Chastised with arms Our enemies' pride . . . i 1 32
Renowned Titus, flourishing in arms . . . i 1 38
One and twenty valiant sons, Knighted in field, slain manfully in arms i 1 196
Arm thy heart, and fit thy thoughts, To mount aloft . ii 1 12
Each wreathed in the other's arms . . . ii 3 25
And cannot passionate our tenfold grief With folded arms . iii 2 7
Why lifts she up her arms in sequence thus? . . iv 1 37
And arm the minds of infants to exclaims . . . iv 1 86
What dost thou wrap and fumble in thine arms? . . iv 2 58
There to dispose this treasure in mine arms . . . iv 2 173
Arm, arm, my lord;—Rome never had more cause . . iv 4 62
For he understands you are in arms, He craves a parley . v 1 158
If one arm's embracement will content thee, I will embrace thee in it . v 2 68
Drown'd their enmity in my true tears, And oped their arms to embrace me . . . . . v 3 108
What's Montague? it is nor hand, nor foot, Nor arm, nor face *R. and J.* ii 2 41
Why the devil came you between us? I was hurt under your arm . iii 1 108
Swifter than his tongue, His agile arm beats down their fatal points . iii 1 171
Underneath whose arm An envious thrust from Tybalt hit the life Of stout Mercutio . . . . iii 1 172
And Romeo Leap to these arms, untalk'd of and unseen . . iii 2 7
Since arm from arm that voice doth us affray . . iii 5 33
Eyes, look your last! Arms, take your last embrace! . v 3 113
His right arm might purchase his own time *T. of Athens* iii 5 77
All gone! and not One friend to take his fortune by the arm! . iv 2 7
A slave, whom Fortune's tender arm With favour never clasp'd . iv 3 250
Wander'd with our traversed arms and breathed Our sufferance vainly . v 4 7
Yea, to chimney-tops, Your infants in your arms . *J. Cæsar* i 1 45
For he can do no more than Cæsar's arm When Cæsar's head is off . ii 1 182
Walk'd about, Musing and sighing, with your arms across . ii 1 240
Have I in conquest stretch'd mine arm so far, To be afeard? . ii 2 66
Our arms, in strength of malice, and our hearts Of brothers' temper, do receive you in With all kind love . . . iii 1 174
Ingratitude, more strong than traitors' arms, Quite vanquish'd him . iii 2 189
With furbish'd arms and new supplies of men Began a fresh assault *Macb.* i 2 32
Point against point rebellious, arm 'gainst arm, Curbing his lavish spirit i 2 56
Arm, arm, and out! If this which he avouches does appear, There is nor flying hence nor tarrying here . . . v 5 46
I cannot strike at wretched kerns, whose arms Are hired . v 7 17
My father's spirit in arms! all is not well *Hamlet* i 2 255
With arms encumber'd thus, or this head-shake . . i 5 174
Then goes he to the length of all his arm . . . ii 1 88
A little shaking of mine arm . . . . ii 1 92
Makes vow before his uncle never more To give the assay of arms . ii 2 71
He whose sable arms, Black as his purpose, did the night resemble . ii 2 474
His antique sword, Rebellious to his arm, lies where it falls . ii 2 492
To take arms against a sea of troubles, And by opposing end them . iii 1 59
Arm you, I pray you, to this speedy voyage . . . iii 3 24
To his good friends thus wide I'll ope my arms . . iv 5 145
Was he a gentleman?—A' was the first that ever bore arms . v 1 38
The Scripture says 'Adam digged:' could he dig without arms? . v 1 42
Hold off the earth awhile, Till I have caught her once more in mine arms . . . . . v 1 273
Is't not perfect conscience, To quit him with this arm? . . v 2 68
He charges home My unprovided body, lanced mine arm . *Lear* ii 1 54
Weapons! arms! What's the matter here? . . . ii 2 50
Strike in their numb'd and mortified bare arms Pins, wooden pricks, nails . . . . . . ii 3 15
Stop her there! Arms, arms, sword, fire! Corruption in the place! . iii 6 58
I prithee, take him in thy arms; I have o'erheard a plot of death upon him . . . . . iii 6 95
Ingrateful fox! 'tis he.—Bind fast his corky arms . . iii 7 29
I bleed apace: Untimely comes this hurt: give me your arm . iii 7 98
Give me thy arm: Poor Tom shall lead thee . . . iv 1 81
I must change arms at home, and give the distaff Into my husband's hands . . . . . iv 2 17
No blown ambition doth our arms incite, But love, dear love . iv 4 27
Arm it in rags, a pigmy's straw does pierce it . . iv 6 171
If my speech offend a noble heart, Thy arm may do thee justice . v 3 128
Arm. This sword, this arm, and my best spirits, are bent To prove upon thy heart . . . . . *Lear* v 3 139
By the law of arms thou wast not bound to answer An unknown opposite v 3 152
With his strong arms He fasten'd on my neck, and bellow'd out . v 3 211
Since these arms of mine had seven years' pith . *Othello* i 3 83
Make love's quick pants in Desdemona's arms . . ii 1 80
If I once stir, Or do but lift this arm, the best of you Shall sink in my rebuke . . . . . ii 3 208
And, like the devil, from his very arm Puff'd his own brother . iii 4 136
With this little arm and this good sword, I have made my way through more impediments . . . . . v 2 262
The demi-Atlas of this earth, the arm And burgonet of men *Ant. and Cleo.* i 5 23
To lend me arms and aid when I required them; The which you both denied . . . . . ii 2 88
Ere we put ourselves in arms, dispatch we The business we have talk'd of ii 2 168
Let's to billiards: come, Charmian.—My arm is sore . ii 5 4
See Thy master thus with pleach'd arms, bending down His corrigible neck . . . . . iv 14 73
The arm of mine own body, and the heart Where mine his thoughts did kindle . . . . . v 1 45
His legs bestrid the ocean: his rear'd arm Crested the world . v 2 82
There is a vent of blood and something blown: The like is on her arm . v 2 353
Arm me, audacity, from head to foot! . . *Cymbeline* i 6 19
Search for a jewel that too casually Hath left mine arm . ii 3 147
Confident I am Last night 'twas on mine arm . . ii 3 151
She stripp'd it from her arm; I see her yet . . ii 4 101
By Jupiter, I had it from her arm.—Hark you, he swears . ii 4 121
There is no moe such Cæsars: other of them may have crook'd noses, but to owe such straight arms, none . . . iii 1 38
The Pannonians and Dalmatians for Their liberties are now in arms . iii 1 75
Have not I An arm as big as thine? a heart as big? . . iv 2 77
And brings the dire occasion in his arms Of what we blame him for . iv 2 196
His arms thus leagued: I thought he slept . . . iv 2 213
Make him with our pikes and partisans A grave: come, arm him . iv 2 400
The poor soldier that so richly fought, Whose rags shamed gilded arms v 5 4
Let his arms alone; They were not born for bondage . . v 5 305
Whose arm seems far too short to hit me here . . *Pericles* i 2 8
From whence an issue I might propagate, Are arms to princes . i 2 74
He'll fill this land with arms, And make pretence of wrong that I have done . . . . . . i 2 90
I'll show the virtue I have borne in arms . . . ii 1 151
Spite of all the rapture of the sea, This jewel holds his building on my arm . . . . . . ii 1 162
To place upon the volume of your deeds, As in a title-page, your worth in arms . . . . . . ii 3 4
My name, Pericles; My education been in arts and arms . ii 3 82
Since they love men in arms as well as beds . . . ii 3 98
Take in your arms this piece Of your dead queen . . iii 1 17
Take her by the arm, walk with her . . . . iv 1 30
I threw her overboard with these very arms . . . v 3 19
O, come, be buried A second time within these arms . . v 3 44
Arm in arm they both came swiftly running . . 1 *Hen. VI.* ii 2 29
No harm to us, That thus he marcheth with thee arm in arm? 2 *Hen. VI.* v 1 57
Arms' end. I'll woo you like a soldier, at arms' end *T. G. of Ver.* v 4 57
Be comfortable; hold death awhile at the arm's end *As Y. Like It* ii 6 10
Arms of York. In my standard bear the arms of York . 2 *Hen. VI.* i 1 256
Arm to arm. Will I make good against thee, arm to arm . *Richard II.* i 1 76
Arma. Ecoutez: de hand, de fingres, de nails, de arma, de bilbow *Hen. V.* iii 4 31
Armado. This child of fancy that Armado hight . . *L. L. Lost* i 1 171
Armado is a most illustrious wight, A man of fire-new words . . i 1 178
This Armado is a Spaniard, that keeps here in court . . iv 1 100
Who is intituled, nominated, or called, Don Adriano de Armado . v 1 9
Armado, a soldier, a man of travel, that hath seen the world . . v 1 113
A blister on his sweet tongue, with my heart, That put Armado's page out of his part . . . . . . v 2 336
Sent whole armadoes of caracks to be ballast at her nose *Com. of Errors* iii 2 140
A whole armado of convicted sail Is scatter'd . . *K. John* iii 4 2
Armagnac. Have you perused the letters from the pope, The emperor and the Earl of Armagnac? . . . 1 *Hen. VI.* v 1 2
Earl of Armagnac, near knit to Charles, A man of great authority in France . . . . v 1 17
So the Earl of Armagnac may do, Because he is near kinsman unto Charles v 5 44
Arme. Signior Arme—Arme—commends you . *L. L. Lost* i 1 188
Armed and reverted, making war against her heir *Com. of Errors* iii 2 126
Is ta'en in flight, And brought with armed men back . *Much Ado* v 4 128
If you are arm'd to do as sworn to do, Subscribe to your deep oaths *L. L. Lost* i 1 22
Love doth approach disguised, Armed in arguments . . v 2 84
Flying between the cold moon and the earth, Cupid all arm'd *M. N. Dr.* ii 1 157
And am arm'd To suffer, with a quietness of spirit . *Mer. of Venice* iv 1 11
Any thing to say?—But little: I am arm'd and well prepared . iv 1 264
He comes armed in his fortune . . . *As Y. Like It* iv 1 61
Arm'd With his good will and thy good company . *T. of Shrew* i 1 5
But be thou arm'd for some unhappy words . . . ii 1 140
That I'll prove upon thee, though thy little finger be armed in a thimble iv 3 149
He hath arm'd our answer, And Florence is denied before he comes *A. W.* i 2 11
She is arm'd for him and keeps her guard In honestest defence . iii 5 76
Ere sunset, Set armed discord 'twixt these perjured kings! . *K. John* iii 1 111
Thinking his voice an armed Englishman . . . v 2 145
Their thimbles into armed gauntlets change, Their needles to lances . v 2 156
Their is Harry Hereford arm'd?—Yea, at all points . . *Richard II.* i 3 1
This earth shall have a feeling and these stones Prove armed soldiers . iii 2 25
Glad am I that your highness is so arm'd To bear the tidings . . iii 2 104
White-beards have arm'd their thin and hairless scalps . . iii 2 112
Nor bruise her flowerets with the armed hoofs Of hostile paces 1 *Hen. IV.* i 1 8
Turns head against the lion's armed jaws . . . iii 2 102
With his beaver on, His cuisses on his thighs, gallantly arm'd . iv 1 105
Struck his armed heels Against the panting sides of his poor jade 2 *Hen. IV.* i 1 44
Their armed staves in charge, their beavers down . . iv 1 120
While that the armed hand doth fight abroad, The advised head defends itself at home . . . . . . *Hen. V.* i 2 178
Armed in their stings, Make boot upon the summer's velvet buds . i 2 193
And with wild rage Yerk out their armed heels at their dead masters . iv 7 83
They did amongst the troops of armed men Leap o'er the walls 1 *Hen. VI.* ii 2 24
Thrice is he armed that hath his quarrel just . 2 *Hen. VI.* iii 2 233
Arm'd as we are, let's stay within this house . 3 *Hen. VI.* i 1 38
I will fill the house with armed men . . . . i 1 167
Yet am I arm'd against the worst can happen . . . iv 1 128
What means this armed guard That waits upon your grace? *Richard III.* i 1 42
Than can the substance of ten thousand soldiers Armed in proof . . v 3 219

Armed. A prologue arm'd, but not in confidence Of author's pen *Troi. and Cres.* Prol. 23
Was Hector armed and gone ere ye came to Ilium? . . i 2 49
If I go to him, with my armed fist I'll pash him o'er the face . ii 3 212
I would fain have armed to-day, but my Nell would not have it so . iii 1 150
But when I meet you arm'd, as black defiance As heart can think . iv 1 12
Arm'd, and bloody in intent. Consort with me in loud and dear petition v 3 8
He is arm'd and at it, Roaring for Troilus . . . . v 5 36
Once subdued in armed tail, Sweet honey and sweet notes together fail v 10 44
My arm'd knees, Who bow'd but in my stirrup . . *Coriolanus* iii 2 118
The self-same gods that arm'd the Queen of Troy . *T. Andron.* i 1 136
That, whenever you have need, You may be armed and appointed well . iv 2 16
In strong proof of chastity well arm'd . . *Rom. and Jul.* i 1 216
I love thee better than myself; For I come hither arm'd against myself v 3 65
I am arm'd, And dangers are to me indifferent . . *J. Cæsar* i 3 114
I am arm'd so strong in honesty That they pass by me as the idle wind iv 3 67
No sooner justice had with valour arm'd Compell'd these skipping kerns to trust their heels . . . . *Macbeth* i 2 29
Approach thou like the rugged Russian bear, The arm'd rhinoceros iii 4 101
That this portentous figure Comes armed through our watch . *Hamlet* i 1 110
A figure like your father, Armed at point exactly, cap-a-pe . i 2 200
Arm'd, say you?—Arm'd, my lord.—From top to toe?—My lord, from head to foot . . . . i 2 226
If you do stir abroad, go armed.—Armed, brother!—Brother, I advise you to the best; go armed . . . . . . *Lear* i 2 186
Thou art arm'd, Gloucester: let the trumpet sound . . v 3 90
Never,—O fault!—reveal'd myself unto him, Until some half-hour past, when I was arm'd . . . . v 3 193
The all-honour'd, honest Roman, Brutus, With the arm'd rest *Ant. and Cleo.* ii 6 17
O thou day o' the world, Chain mine arm'd neck! . . iv 8 14
The device he bears upon his shield Is an arm'd knight . *Pericles* ii 2 26
Armenia. Media, Parthia, and Armenia, He gave to Alexander *Ant. and Cleo.* iii 6 14
In his Armenia, And other of his conquer'd kingdoms . . iii 6 35
Arm-gaunt. He nodded, And soberly did mount an arm-gaunt steed i 5 48
Armies. From off our towers we might behold, From first to last, the onset and retire Of both your armies . . . *K. John* ii 1 327
Unto a pagan shore; Where these two Christian armies might combine v 2 37
God omnipotent Is mustering in his clouds on our behalf Armies of pestilence . . . . *Richard II.* iii 3 87
In both your armies there is many a soul Shall pay full dearly for this encounter, If once they join . . . . *1 Hen. IV.* v 1 83
Had been alive this hour, If like a Christian thou hadst truly borne Betwixt our armies true intelligence . . . . . v 5 10
Pray, all you that kiss my lady Peace at home, that our armies join not in a hot day . . . . *2 Hen. IV.* i 2 233
Pleaseth your lordship To meet his grace just distance 'tween our armies iv 1 226
Here between the armies Let's drink together friendly and embrace iv 2 62
The dragon wing of night o'erspreads the earth, And, stickler-like, the armies separates . . . . . . *Troi. and Cres.* v 8 18
How far off lie these armies?—Within this mile and half *Coriolanus* i 4 8
Before the eyes of both our armies here . . *J. Cæsar* iv 2 43
Were we before our armies, and to fight, I should do thus *Ant. and Cleo.* ii 2 26
Armigero. Who writes himself 'Armigero,' in any bill, warrant, quittance, or obligation, 'Armigero' . . . *Mer. Wives* i 1 10
Arming. Confirmations, point from point, to the full arming of the verity *All's Well* iv 3 72
Now play him me, Patroclus, Arming to answer in a night alarm *Troi. and Cres.* i 3 171
Hector, by this, is arming him in Troy . . . . v 2 183
Great Achilles Is arming, weeping, cursing, vowing vengeance v 5 31
Arming myself with patience . . . . *J. Cæsar* v 1 106
Armipotent Mars, of lances the almighty . *L. L. Lost* v 2 650
The manifold linguist and the armipotent soldier . *All's Well* iv 3 265
Armour. Like unscour'd armour, hung by the wall . *Meas. for Meas.* i 2 171
He would have walked ten mile a-foot to see a good armour *Much Ado* ii 3 17
For that England's sake With burden of our armour here we sweat *K. John* ii 1 92
Their armours, that march'd hence so silver-bright, Hither return all gilt with Frenchmen's blood . . . . . . ii 1 315
Whose armour conscience buckled on . . . . ii 1 564
Add proof unto mine armour with thy prayers . *Richard II.* i 3 73
Provide some carts And bring away the armour that is there . ii 2 107
Our armour all as strong, our cause the best *2 Hen. IV.* iv 1 156
Like a rich armour worn in heat of day, That scalds with safety . iv 5 30
Tut! I have the best armour of the world . . *Hen. V.* iii 7 1
You have an excellent armour; but let my horse have his due . iii 7 3
My lord high constable, you talk of horse and armour? . . iii 7 8
The armour that I saw in your tent to-night, are those stars or suns upon it? . . . . iii 7 73
If their heads had any intellectual armour, they could never wear such heavy head-pieces . . . . iii 7 148
The sun doth gild our armour; up, my lords! . . . iv 2 1
Or by vaulting into my saddle with my armour on my back . v 2 143
Would have armour here out of the Tower, To crown himself king *1 Hen. VI.* i 3 67
I cannot stay them; A woman clad in armour chaseth them . i 5 3
Pray God she prove not masculine ere long, If underneath the standard of the French She carry armour as she hath begun . . . ii 1 24
One night, as we were scouring my Lord of York's armour . *2 Hen. VI.* i 3 195
Lands, goods, horse, armour, any thing I have, Is his to use . v 1 52
For York in justice puts his armour on . . *3 Hen. VI.* ii 2 130
I am ready to put armour on . . . . . iii 3 230; iv 1 105
Thine uncles and myself Have in our armours watch'd the winter's night . . . . v 7 17
Take with thee my most heavy curse; Which, in the day of battle, tire thee more Than all the complete armour that thou wear'st! *Richard III.* iv 4 189
Is my beaver easier than it was? And all my armour laid into my tent? v 3 51
Your friends are up, and buckle on their armour . . . v 3 211
When we have our armours buckled on . . *Troi. and Cres.* v 3 46
I like thy armour well; I'll frush it and unlock the rivets all, But I'll be master of it . . . . v 6 28
Thy goodly armour thus hath cost thy life . . . . v 8 2
I would put mine armour on, Which I can scarcely bear *Coriolanus* iii 2 34
I'll give thee armour to keep off that word . *Rom. and Jul.* iii 3 54
Put armour on thine ears and on thine eyes . *T. of Athens* iv 3 123
Give me my armour.—'Tis not needed yet.—I'll put it on . *Macbeth* v 3 33
Hang those that talk of fear. Give me mine armour . . v 3 36
Armour. The very armour he had on When he the ambitious Norway combated . . . . *Hamlet* i 1 60
Never did the Cyclops' hammers fall On Mars's armour forged for proof eterne With less remorse . . . . ii 2 512
With all the strength and armour of the mind . . . iii 3 12
Sleep a little.—No, my chuck. Eros, come; mine armour *Ant. and Cleo.* iv 4 2
I'll give thee, friend, An armour all of gold; it was a king's . iv 8 27
'Tis come at last, and 'tis turned to a rusty armour . *Pericles* ii 1 125
On set purpose let his armour rust Until this day, to scour it in the dust ii 2 54
Even in your armours, as you are address'd . . . ii 3 94
Armourer. Now thrive the armourers . . . *Hen. V.* ii Prol. 3
The armourers, accomplishing the knights, With busy hammers . iv Prol. 12
Ready are the appellant and defendant, The armourer and his man *2 Hen. VI.* ii 3 50
The appellant, The servant of this armourer . . . ii 3 58
He chid Andromache and struck his armorer . *Troi. and Cres.* i 2 6
Thou art The armourer of my heart . . *Ant. and Cleo.* iv 4 7
Armoury. Come, go with me into mine armoury . *T. Andron.* iv 1 113
Well advised, hath sent by me The goodliest weapons of his armoury . iv 2 11
Army. A treacherous army levied, one midnight . *Tempest* i 2 128
There was none such in the army of any sort . . *Much Ado* i 1 33
I stood like a man at a mark, with a whole army shooting at me . ii 1 254
The huge army of the world's desires . . *L. L. Lost* i 1 10
The fool hath planted in his memory An army of good words *Mer. of Ven.* iii 5 72
Whipped through the army with this rhyme in's forehead *All's Well* iv 3 262
The army breaking, My husband hies him home . . iv 4 11
I had not left a purse alive in the whole army . *W. Tale* iv 4 631
I am with both: each army hath a hand . . *K. John* iii 1 328
Where is my mother's care, That such an army could be drawn in France? . . . . iv 2 118
For, lo! within a ken our army lies . . . *2 Hen. IV.* iv 1 151
Deliver to the army This news of peace: let them have pay, and part . iv 2 69
Go, my lord, And let our army be discharged too . . iv 2 92
Our army is dispersed already: Like youthful steers unyoked . iv 2 102
The army is discharged all and gone.—Let them go . . iv 3 137
When he shall see our army, He'll drop his heart into the sink of fear *Hen. V.* iii 5 58
My army but a weak and sickly guard . . . . iii 6 164
Through the foul womb of night The hum of either army stilly sounds . . . . iv Prol. 5
Upon his royal face there is no note How dread an army hath enrounded him . . . . iv Prol. 36
No man should possess him with any appearance of fear, lest he, by showing it, should dishearten his army . . . . iv 1 117
An army have I muster'd in my thoughts . . *1 Hen. VI.* i 1 101
All the whole army stood agazed on him . . . . i 1 126
Orleans is besieged; The English army is grown weak and faint . i 1 158
In pity of my hard distress Levied an army . . . ii 5 88
Are not the speedy scouts return'd again, That dogg'd the mighty army? iv 3 2
The English army, that divided was Into two parties, is now conjoin'd v 2 11
So, now dismiss your army when ye please . . . . v 4 173
Seeing gentle words will not prevail, Assail them with the army *2 Hen. VI.* iv 2 185
His army is a ragged multitude Of hinds and peasants, rude and merciless iv 4 32
There's an army gathered together in Smithfield.—Come, then, let's go iv 6 13
We will commit thee thither, Until his army be dismiss'd from him . iv 9 40
Why I have brought this army hither Is to remove proud Somerset . v 1 35
Northumberland . . . Cheer'd up the drooping army . *3 Hen. VI.* i 1 6
Come, son, let's away; Our army is ready; come, we'll after them . i 1 256
The army of the queen mean to besiege us.—She shall not need . i 2 64
The army of the queen hath got the field: My uncles both are slain . i 4 1
Buckingham's army is dispersed and scatter'd . *Richard III.* iv 4 513
From troop to troop Went through the army, cheering up the soldiers . v 3 71
The sky doth frown and lour upon our army . . . v 3 283
An army cannot rule 'em . . . . . *Hen. VIII.* v 4 81
Their great general slept, Whilst emulation in the army crept *Tr. and Cr.* ii 2 212
Six-or-seven-times-honoured captain-general of the Grecian army . iii 3 279
Our army's in the field: We never yet made doubt but Rome was ready To answer us . . . . *Coriolanus* i 2 17
If they set down before's, for the remove Bring up your army . i 2 29
The Volsces have an army forth; against whom Cominius the general is gone . . . . i 3 107
List, what work he makes Amongst your cloven army . . i 4 21
Not to reward What you have done—before our army hear me . i 9 27
Have you an army ready, say you?—A most royal one . . iv 3 46
A fearful army, led by Caius Marcius Associated with Aufidius . . iv 6 75
Your good tongue, More than the instant army we can make, Might stop our countryman . . . . v 1 37
The army marvell'd at it . . . . v 6 42
Comes his army on?—They mean this night in Sardis to be quarter'd *J. Cæsar* iv 2 27
A canopy most fatal, under which Our army lies, ready to give up the ghost . . . . v 1 89
Witness this army of such mass and charge . . . *Hamlet* iv 4 47
Show him this letter: the army of France is landed . . *Lear* iii 7 2
I told him of the army that was landed; He smiled at it . . iv 2 4
How near's the other army?—Near and on speedy foot . . iv 6 216
Though that the queen on special cause is here, Her army is moved on iv 6 220
Bear the king's son's body Before our army . . *Ant. and Cleo.* iii 1 4
The wife of Antony Should have an army for an usher . . iii 6 44
Distract your army, which doth most consist Of war-mark'd footmen . iii 7 44
Feast the army; we have store to do't, And they have earn'd the waste iv 1 15
'Tis a brave army, And full of purpose . . . . iv 3 11
Our army shall In solemn show attend this funeral; And then to Rome v 2 366
O, I am known Of many in the army . . . *Cymbeline* iv 4 22
Than be so Better to cease to be. Pray, sir, to the army . . iv 4 31
The army broken, And but the backs of Britons seen, all flying . v 3 5
'Aroint thee, witch!' the rump-fed ronyon cries . . *Macbeth* i 3 6
Bid her alight, And her troth plight, And, aroint thee, witch, aroint thee! . . . . *Lear* iii 4 129
A-rolling. I told ye all, When we first put this dangerous stone a-rolling, 'Twould fall upon ourselves . . . . *Hen. VIII.* v 3 104
Arose. And thereupon these ERRORS are arose . *Com. of Errors* v 1 389
Such a noise arose As the shrouds make at sea in a stiff tempest *Hen. VIII.* iv 1 71
Yesternight, at supper, You suddenly arose, and walk'd about *J. Cæsar* ii 1 239
Arouse. And now loud-howling wolves arouse the jades That drag the tragic melancholy night . . . . . . *2 Hen. VI.* iv 1 3
Aroused vengeance sets him new a-work . . . *Hamlet* ii 2 510
A-row. Beaten the maids a-row and bound the doctor . *Com. of Errors* v 1 170

Arragon. Don Peter of Arragon comes this night to Messina *Much Ado* i 1 2
And then go I toward Arragon.—I'll bring you thither iii 2 2
The Prince of Arragon hath ta'en his oath *Mer. of Venice* ii 9 2
Arraign. I'll teach you how you shall arraign your conscience *M. for M.* ii 3 21
Summon a session, that we may arraign Our most disloyal lady *W. Tale* ii 3 202
Will nothing stick our person to arraign In ear and ear *Hamlet* iv 5 93
It shall be done; I will arraign them straight *Lear* iii 6 22
Pur! the cat is gray.—Arraign her first; 'tis Goneril iii 6 48
The laws are mine, not thine: Who can arraign me for't? v 3 159
Arraigned. Thou art here accused and arraigned of high treason *W. Tale* iii 2 14
Arraigning. I was, unhandsome warrior as I am, Arraigning his unkindness with my soul *Othello* iii 4 152
Arrant. A couple of as arrant knaves as any in Messina *Much Ado* iii 5 35
I leave an arrant knave with your worship v 1 330
An the Prince and Poins be not two arrant cowards *1 Hen. IV.* ii 2 106
That arrant malmsey-nose knave, Bardolph *2 Hen. IV.* ii 1 42
They are arrant knaves, and will backbite v 1 35
That Visor is an arrant knave, on my knowledge v 1 45
Thou arrant knave; I would to God that I might die v 4 1
This is an arrant counterfeit rascal; I remember him now *Hen. V.* iii 6 64
'Tis as arrant a piece of knavery, mark you now, as can be offer't iv 7 2
His reputation is as arrant a villain and a Jacksauce iv 7 148
An arrant traitor as any is in the universal world iv 8 10
What an arrant, rascally, beggarly, lousy knave it is iv 8 36
The moon's an arrant thief *T. of Athens* iv 3 440
Ne'er a villain dwelling in all Denmark But he's an arrant knave *Hamlet* i 5 124
We are arrant knaves, all; believe none of us. Go thy ways to a nunnery iii 1 131
Fortune, that arrant whore, Ne'er turns the key to the poor *Lear* ii 4 52
Arras. I will ensconce me behind the arras *Mer. Wives* iii 3 97
I whipt me behind the arras; and there heard it agreed upon *Much Ado* i 3 63
In cypress chests my arras counterpoints *T. of Shrew* ii 1 353
Heat me these irons hot; and look thou stand Within the arras *K. John* iv 1 2
Go, hide thee behind the arras: the rest walk up above *1 Hen. IV.* ii 4 549
Falstaff!—Fast asleep behind the arras, and snorting like a horse ii 4 577
I fell asleep here behind the arras and had my pocket picked iii 3 113
Be you and I behind an arras then; Mark the encounter *Hamlet* ii 2 163
Behind the arras I'll convey myself, To hear the process iii 3 28
Behind the arras hearing something stir, Whips out his rapier, cries, 'A rat, a rat!' iv 1 9
The arras; figures, Why, such and such *Cymbeline* ii 2 26
Array. I drink, I eat, array myself, and live *Meas. for Meas.* iii 2 26
Gave me fresh array and entertainment *As Y. Like It* iv 3 144
Put you in your best array; bid your friends v 2 79
We will have rings and things and fine array *T. of Shrew* ii 1 325
Neither art thou the worse For this poor furniture and mean array iv 3 182
In which array, brave soldier, doth he lie, Larding the plain *Hen. V.* iv 6 7
Thee I'll chase hence, thou wolf in sheep's array *1 Hen. VI.* i 3 55
Is marching hitherward in proud array *2 Hen. VI.* iv 9 27
Stand we in good array; for they no doubt Will issue out again *3 Hen. VI.* v 1 62
Happiness courts thee in her best array *Rom. and Jul.* iii 3 142
As the custom is, In all her best array bear her to church iv 5 81
Set not thy sweet heart on proud array *Lear* iii 4 85
Arrayed. War, Array'd in flames like to the prince of fiends *Hen. V.* iii 3 16
Is he array'd?—Ay, madam; in the heaviness of his sleep We put fresh garments on him *Lear* iv 7 20
Arrearages. I think He'll grant the tribute, send the arrearages *Cymb.* ii 4 13
Arrest. If I could speak so wisely under an arrest *Meas. for Meas.* i 2 136
He arrests him on it; And follows close the rigour of the statute i 4 66
Let me be bold; I do arrest your words ii 4 134
Well, officer, arrest him at my suit *Com. of Errors* iv 1 69
Pay thee that I never had! Arrest me, foolish fellow, if thou darest iv 1 75
Arrest him, officer. I would not spare my brother in this case iv 1 76
I do arrest you, sir: you hear the suit.—I do obey thee iv 1 79
Thou hast suborn'd the goldsmith to arrest me iv 4 85
For the which He did arrest me with an officer v 1 230
We arrest your word *L. L. Lost* ii 1 160
I arrest thee at the suit of Count Orsino.—You do mistake me *T. Night* iii 4 360
And, for your pains, Of capital treason we arrest you here *Richard II.* iv 1 151
You that here are under our arrest, Procure your sureties iv 1 158
Snare, we must arrest Sir John Falstaff.—Yea *2 Hen. IV.* ii 1 9
Sir John, I arrest you at the suit of Mistress Quickly ii 1 48
Their faults are open: Arrest them to the answer of the law *Hen. V.* ii 2 143
Thou shalt not see me blush Nor change my countenance for this arrest *2 Hen. VI.* iii 1 99
I do arrest you in his highness' name iii 1 136
Sends out arrests On Fortinbras; which he, in brief, obeys *Hamlet* ii 2 67
This fell sergeant, death, Is strict in his arrest v 2 348
I arrest thee On capital treason; and, in thine attaint, This gilded serpent *Lear* v 3 82
I arrest thee of high treason *2 Hen. IV.* iv 2; *Hen. V.* ii 2; *2 Hen. VI.* iii 1; *Hen. VIII.* i 1
Arrested. His horses are arrested for it, Master Brook *Mer. Wives* v 5 119
There's one yonder arrested and carried to prison *Meas. for Meas.* i 2 60
I saw him arrested, saw him carried away i 2 68
Tell her I am arrested in the street And that shall bail me *C. of Err.* iv 1 106
He is 'rested on the case.—What, is he arrested? Tell me at whose suit iv 2 43
I know not at whose suit he is arrested well; But he's in a suit of buff which 'rested him, that can I tell iv 2 44
Was he arrested on a band?—Not on a band, but on a stronger thing iv 2 49
He is arrested at my suit.—For what sum? *2 Hen. IV.* ii 1 77
He is arrested, but will not obey *2 Hen. VI.* v 1 134
After the stout Earl Northumberland Arrested him at York *Hen. VIII.* iv 2 13
Arrival. A Syracusian merchant Is apprehended for arrival here *C. of Err.* i 2 4
To signify . . . my arrival and my wife's in safety *W. Tale* v 1 167
Demand of yonder champion The cause of his arrival *Richard II.* i 3 8
If life did ride upon a dial's point, Still ending at the arrival of an hour *1 Hen. IV.* v 2 85
Hearing of your arrival in this realm *1 Hen. VI.* iii 4 2
Arrivance. Every minute is expectancy Of more arrivance *Othello* ii 1 42
Arrive. A savour that may strike the dullest nostril Where I arrive *W. T.* i 2 422
My letters, by this means being there So soon as you arrive iv 4 633
To suffer shipwreck or arrive Where I may have fruition of her love *1 Hen. VI.* v 5 8
Too swift arrives as tardy as too slow *Rom. and Jul.* ii 6 15
Many so arrive at second masters, Upon their first lord's neck *T. of A.* iv 3 512
But ere we could arrive the point proposed, Cæsar cried 'Help me!' *J. C.* i 2 110
Where he arrives he moves All hearts against us *Lear* iv 5 10
Arrived. It was mine art, When I arrived and heard thee *Tempest* i 2 292
Arrived. And soon and safe arrived where I was *Com. of Errors* i 1 49
I am arrived for fruitful Lombardy *T. of Shrew* i 1 3
This gentleman is happily arrived, My mind presumes i 2 213
Happily I have arrived at the last Unto the wished haven of my bliss v 1 130
There's one arrived, If you will see her *All's Well* ii 1 82
On a moderate pace I have since arrived but hither *T. Night* ii 2 4
Cleomenes and Dion, Being well arrived from Delphos *W. Tale* ii 3 196
Lo, upon thy wish, Our messenger Chatillon is arrived! *K. John* ii 1 51
When you should be told they do prepare, The tidings comes that they are all arrived iv 2 115
Hear'st thou the news abroad, who are arrived?—The French, my lord iv 2 160
Bolingbroke repeals himself, And with uplifted arms is safe arrived *Richard II.* ii 2 50
Either past or not arrived to pith and puissance *Hen. V.* iii Prol. 21
To England then; Where ne'er from France arrived more happy men iv 8 131
What then remains, we being thus arrived? *3 Hen. VI.* iv 7 7
Those powers that the queen Hath raised in Gallia have arrived our coast v 3 8
To confirm this too, Cardinal Campeius is arrived, and lately *Hen. VIII.* ii 1 160
Hark! he is arrived. March gently on to meet him *J. Cæsar* iv 2 30
I would the friends we miss were safe arrived *Macbeth* v 8 35
And you from England, Are here arrived *Hamlet* v 2 388
Sir, go forth, And give us truth who 'tis that is arrived *Othello* ii 1 58
He is not yet arrived: nor know I aught But that he's well ii 1 89
That, upon certain tidings now arrived ii 2 3
He is arrived Here where his daughter dwells *Pericles* v Gower 14
Arriving A place of potency and sway o' the state *Coriolanus* ii 3 189
Arrogance. O monstrous arrogance! Thou liest *T. of Shrew* iv 3 107
Exempted be from me the arrogance To choose from forth the royal blood of France *All's Well* ii 1 198
I hate not you for her proud arrogance *Richard III.* i 3 24
Can ye endure to hear this arrogance? And from this fellow? *Hen. VIII.* iii 2 278
The proud lord That bastes his arrogance with his own seam *Tr. and Cr.* ii 3 195
Supple knees Feed arrogance and are the proud man's fees iii 3 49
Arrogancy. Your heart Is cramm'd with arrogancy *Hen. VIII.* ii 4 110
Arrogant Winchester, that haughty prelate *1 Hen. VI.* i 3 23
Nor cease to be an arrogant controller *2 Hen VI.* iii 2 205
Whose self-same mettle, Whereof thy proud child, arrogant man, is puff'd, Engenders the black toad *T. of Athens* iv 3 180
Why should we be tender To let an arrogant piece of flesh threat us? *Cymbeline* iv 2 127
Arrow. Her waspish-headed son has broke his arrows *Tempest* iv 1 99
I am glad, though you have ta'en a special stand to strike at me, that your arrow hath glanced *Mer. Wives* v 5 248
Of this matter Is little Cupid's crafty arrow made *Much Ado* iii 1 22
Then loving goes by haps: Some Cupid kills with arrows, some with traps iii 1 106
Their conceits have wings Fleeter than arrows, bullets, wind *L. L. Lost* v 2 261
By Cupid's strongest bow, By his best arrow with the golden head *M. N. Dream* i 1 170
Look how I go, Swifter than arrow from the Tartar's bow iii 2 101
If you please To shoot another arrow that self way *Mer. of Venice* i 1 148
The wounds invisible That love's keen arrows make *As Y. Like It* iii 5 31
He hath ta'en his bow and arrows and is gone forth to sleep iv 3 4
Arrows fled not swifter toward their aim Than did our soldiers *2 Hen. IV.* i 1 123
Do you think me a swallow, an arrow, or a bullet? iv 3 36
As many arrows, loosed several ways, Come to one mark *Hen. V.* i 2 207
Draw, archers, draw your arrows to the head! *Richard III.* v 3 339
She'll not be hit With Cupid's arrow; she hath Dian's wit *Rom. and Jul.* i 1 215
Whether 'tis nobler in the mind to suffer The slings and arrows of outrageous fortune *Hamlet* iii 1 58
So that my arrows, Too slightly timber'd for so loud a wind, Would have reverted to my bow again iv 7 21
I have shot mine arrow o'er the house, And hurt my brother v 2 254
Like an arrow shot From a well-experienced archer hits the mark *Pericles* i 1 163
Art. If by your art, my dearest father, you have Put the wild waters in this roar, allay them *Tempest* i 2 1
Lie there, my art. Wipe thou thine eyes; have comfort i 2 25
I have with such provision in mine art So safely ordered i 2 28
So reputed In dignity, and for the liberal arts Without a parallel i 2 73
It was mine art, When I arrived and heard thee, that made gape The pine i 2 291
His art is of such power, It would control my dam's god, Setebos, i 2 372
My master through his art foresees the danger That you, his friend, are in ii 1 297
I must Bestow upon the eyes of this young couple Some vanity of mine art iv 1 41
Spirits, which by mine art I have from their confines call'd iv 1 120
Graves at my command Have waked their sleepers, oped, and let 'em forth By my so potent art v 1 50
Now I want Spirits to enforce, art to enchant Epil. 14
Use your art of wooing; win her to consent to you *Mer. Wives* ii 2 244
Boys of art, I have deceived you both iii 1 109
You're as pregnant in As art and practice hath enriched any That we remember *Meas. for Meas.* i 1 13
She hath prosperous art When she will play with reason and discourse i 2 189
The strumpet, With all her double vigour, art and nature i 2 184
A little Academe, Still and contemplative in living art *L. L. Lost* i 1 14
Well fitted in arts, glorious in arms ii 1 45
Thine eyes, Where all those pleasures live that art would comprehend iv 2 114
Other slow arts entirely keep the brain iv 3 324
They are the books, the arts, the academes, That show, contain and nourish all the world iv 3 352
With what art You sway the motion of Demetrius' heart *M. N. Dream* i 1 192
Nature shows art, That through thy bosom makes me see thy heart ii 2 104
He that hath learned no wit by nature nor art may complain *As Y. L. It* iii 2 31
A magician, most profound in his art and yet not damnable v 2 67
Fair Padua, nursery of arts *T. of Shrew* i 1 2
I must begin with rudiments of art; To teach you gamut iii 1 66
I read that I profess, the Art to Love.—And may you prove, sir, master of your art! iv 2 8
Labouring art can never ransom nature From her inaidible estate *A. W.* ii 1 121
What at full I know, thou know'st no part, I knowing all my peril, thou no art ii 1 136
I know most sure My art is not past power nor you past cure ii 1 161
O, had I but followed the arts! *T. Night* i 3 99
This is a practice As full of labour as a wise man's art iii 1 73
Be that thou know'st thou art, and then thou art As great as that thou fear'st v 1 152

Art. An art which in their piedness shares With great creating nature *W. Tale* iv 4 87
Over that art Which you say adds to nature, is an art That nature makes iv 4 90
This is an art Which does mend nature, change it rather, but The art itself is nature.—So it is . . . iv 4 95
The fixure of her eye has motion in't, As we are mock'd with art . . v 3 68
If this be magic, let it be an art Lawful as eating . . . . v 3 110
Can trace me in the tedious ways of art . . . *1 Hen. IV.* iii 1 48
Thoughtful to invest Their sons with arts and martial exercises *2 Hen. IV.* iv 5 74
The art and practic part of life Must be the mistress to this theoric *Hen. V.* i 1 51
Poor and mangled Peace, Dear nurse of arts, plenties and joyful births v 2 35
My wit untrain'd in any kind of art . . . . . . *1 Hen. VI.* i 2 73
Contrived by art and baleful sorcery . . . . . . ii 1 15
Her virtues that surmount, And natural graces that extinguish art . v 3 192
In sweet music is such art, Killing care and grief of heart *Hen. VIII.* iii 1 12
So famous, So excellent in art, and still so rising . . . iv 2 62
Flowing and swelling o'er with arts and exercise . *Troi. and Cres.* iv 4 80
And temper him with all the art I have . . . *T. Andron.* iv 4 109
Now art thou what thou art, by art as well as by nature *Rom. and Jul.* ii 4 94
Arbitrating that Which the commission of thy years and art Could to no issue of true honour bring . . . . iv 1 64
Then gave I her, so tutor'd by my art, A sleeping potion . . v 3 243
Thou art even natural in thine art . . . . *T. of Athens* v 1 88
I have as much of this in art as you . . . . *J. Cæsar* iv 3 194
Art thou any thing? Art thou some god, some angel, or some devil? . iv 3 278
Speak to me what thou art.—Thy evil spirit, Brutus . . . iv 3 281
Two spent swimmers, that do cling together And choke their art *Macbeth* i 2 9
There's no art To find the mind's construction in the face . . i 4 11
Art thou afeard To be the same in thine own act and valour As thou art in desire? . . . . i 7 39
Was never call'd to bear my part, Or show the glory of our art . iii 5 9
My heart Throbs to know one thing: tell me, if your art Can tell so much . . . . iv 1 101
Their malady convinces The great assay of art . . . . iv 3 143
More matter, with less art.—Madam, I swear I use no art at all *Hamlet* ii 2 95
A foolish figure; But farewell it, for I will use no art . . . ii 2 99
I am ill at these numbers; I have not art to reckon my groans . . ii 2 121
The harlot's cheek, beautied with plastering art, Is not more ugly . iii 1 51
Gave you such a masterly report For art and exercise . . . iv 7 98
I want that glib and oily art, To speak and purpose not . . . *Lear* i 1 227
The art of our necessities is strange, That can make vile things precious iii 2 70
Nature's above art in that respect . . . . iv 6 86
By the art of known and feeling sorrows, Am pregnant to good pity . iv 6 226
A practiser Of arts inhibited and out of warrant . . . *Othello* i 2 79
I think that thou art just and think thou art not. I'll have some proof iii 3 385
Be it art or hap, He hath spoken true . . . *Ant. and Cleo.* ii 3 32
The art o' the court, As hard to leave as keep . . . *Cymbeline* iii 3 46
Some villain, ay, and singular in his art . . . . . iii 4 124
Those arts they have as I Could put into them . . . . v 5 338
Yet neither pleasure's art can joy my spirits . . . *Pericles* i 2 9
In framing an artist, art hath thus decreed, To make some good, but others to exceed . . . . ii 3 15
My name, Pericles; My education been in arts and arms . . . ii 3 82
Through which secret art, By turning o'er authorities, I have, Together with my practice, made familiar . . . . iii 2 32
That even her art sisters the natural roses . . . . . v Gower 7
Artemidorus. The mighty gods defend thee! Thy lover, ARTEMIDORUS *J. Cæsar* ii 3 10
Arteries. Universal plodding poisons up The nimble spirits in the arteries . . . . *L. L. Lost* iv 3 306
Artery. Makes each petty artery in this body As hardy as the Nemean lion's nerve . . . . *Hamlet* i 4 82
Arthur Plantagenet, lays most lawful claim To this fair island . *K. John* i 1 9
Into young Arthur's hand, Thy nephew and right royal sovereign . . i 1 14
Arthur, that great forerunner of thy blood, Richard . . . . ii 1 2
Ireland, Anjou, Touraine, Maine, In right of Arthur do I claim . ii 1 153
Arthur of Bretagne, yield thee to my hand . . . . . ii 1 156
Let us hear them speak Whose title they admit, Arthur's or John's . ii 1 200
You loving men of Angiers, Arthur's subjects . . . . . ii 1 204
Open wide your gates, And let young Arthur, Duke of Bretagne, in . ii 1 301
Proclaim Arthur of Bretagne England's king and yours . . . ii 1 311
We'll create young Arthur Duke of Bretagne And Earl of Richmond . ii 1 551
John, to stop Arthur's title in the whole, Hath willingly departed with a part . . . . ii 1 562
Is not Angiers lost? Arthur ta'en prisoner? divers dear friends slain? . iii 4 7
Therefore never, never Must I behold my pretty Arthur more . . iii 4 89
My Arthur, my fair son! My life, my joy, my food, my all the world! iii 4 103
Are not you grieved that Arthur is his prisoner?—As heartily as he is glad . . . . iii 4 123
And therefore mark. John hath seized Arthur . . . . iii 4 131
That John may stand, then Arthur needs must fall . . . . iii 4 139
But what shall I gain by young Arthur's fall? . . . . . iii 4 141
Your wife May then make all the claim that Arthur did.—And lose it, life and all, as Arthur did . . . . iii 4 143
May be he will not touch young Arthur's life . . . . . iii 4 160
If that young Arthur be not gone already, Even at that news he dies . iii 4 163
Read here, young Arthur. How now, foolish rheum! . . . . iv 1 33
Heartily request The enfranchisement of Arthur . . . . iv 2 52
Arthur is deceased to-night.—Indeed we fear'd his sickness was past cure . . . . iv 2 85
Going to seek the grave Of Arthur, whom they say is kill'd to-night iv 2 165
Young Arthur's death is common in their mouths . . . . iv 2 187
Another lean unwash'd artificer Cuts off his tale and talks of Arthur's death . . . . iv 2 202
Why urgest thou so oft young Arthur's death? . . . . . iv 2 204
I faintly broke with thee of Arthur's death . . . . . iv 2 227
Arthur is alive: this hand of mine Is yet a maiden and an innocent hand iv 2 251
Doth Arthur live? O, haste thee to the peers! . . . . . iv 2 260
I am hot with haste in seeking you: Arthur doth live . . . iv 3 75
Would not my lords return to me again, After they heard young Arthur was alive?—They found him dead . . . . v 1 38
I, by the honour of my marriage-bed, After young Arthur, claim this land . . . . v 2 94
'When Arthur first in court'—Empty the jordan . *2 Hen. IV.* ii 4 36
I was then Sir Dagonet in Arthur's show . . . . . . iii 2 300
He's in Arthur's bosom, if ever man went to Arthur's bosom *Hen. V.* ii 3 10
Princess dowager And widow to Prince Arthur . . *Hen. VIII.* iii 2 71

Article. Hast thou, spirit, Perform'd to point the tempest that I bade thee?—To every article . . . . . . *Tempest* i 2 195
She was mine, and not mine, twice or thrice in that last article *T. G. of Ver.* iii 1 366
Thou shouldst not alter the article of thy gentry . *Mer. Wives* ii 1 53
What is he, William, that does lend articles?—Articles are borrowed of the pronoun . . . . iv 1 40
Swerve not from the smallest article of it . . *Meas. for Meas.* iv 2 107
This article, my liege, yourself must break . . . *L. L. Lost* i 1 134
This article is made in vain, Or vainly comes the admired princess hither . . . . i 1 140
From whom hast thou this great commission, France, To draw my answer from thy articles? . . . . *K. John* ii 1 111
If thou wouldst, There shouldst thou find one heinous article *Richard II.* iv 1 233
Read o'er these articles.—Mine eyes are full of tears, I cannot see . . iv 1 243
And have the summary of all our griefs, When time shall serve, to show in articles . . . . *2 Hen. IV.* iv 1 74
This contains our general grievances: Each several article herein redress'd . . . . iv 1 170
Answer them directly How far forth you do like their articles . . iv 2 53
I have but with a cursorary eye O'erglanced the articles . . *Hen. V.* v 2 78
A woman's voice may do some good, When articles too nicely urged be stood on . . . . v 2 94
She is our capital demand, comprised Within the fore-rank of our articles v 2 97
The king hath granted every article: His daughter first . . . v 2 360
In love and dear alliance, Let that one article rank with the rest . v 2 374
Here are the articles of contracted peace . . . *2 Hen. VI.* i 1 40
Suffolk concluded on the articles, The peers agreed . . . . i 1 217
I cannot stay to hear these articles . . . . *3 Hen. VI.* i 1 180
And now forthwith shall articles be drawn Touching the jointure . . iii 3 135
The articles o' the combination drew As himself pleased . . *Hen. VIII.* i 1 169
Produce the grand sum of his sins, the articles Collected from his life . iii 2 293
Those articles, my lord, are in the king's hand . . . . . iii 2 299
I thank my memory, I yet remember Some of these articles . . . iii 2 304
His surly nature, Which easily endures not article Tying him to aught *Coriolanus* ii 3 204
By the same covenant, And carriage of the article design'd . *Hamlet* i 1 94
More than the scope Of these delated articles allow . . . . i 2 38
In the verity of extolment, I take him to be a soul of great article . . v 2 122
The main article I do approve In fearful sense . . . . *Othello* i 3 11
If I do vow a friendship, I'll perform it To the last article . . . iii 3 22
To deny each article with oath Cannot remove nor choke the strong conception That I do groan withal . . . . v 2 54
You have broken The article of your oath . . . *Ant. and Cleo.* ii 2 82
I embrace these conditions; let us have articles betwixt us . *Cymbeline* i 4 169
That's an article within our law, As dangerous as the rest . . *Pericles* i 1 88
Articulate. These things indeed you have articulate . . *1 Hen. IV.* v 1 72
Send us to Rome The best, with whom we may articulate . *Coriolanus* i 9 77
Artificer. Another lean unwash'd artificer Cuts off his tale . *K. John* iv 2 201
Artificial. We, Hermia, like two artificial gods, Have with our needles created both one flower . . . . *M. N. Dream* iii 2 203
Wet my cheeks with artificial tears . . . . . *3 Hen. VI.* iii 2 184
Locks fair daylight out And makes himself an artificial night *R. and J.* i 1 146
Artificial strife Lives in these touches, livelier than life . *T. of Athens* i 1 37
Sometime like a philosopher, with two stones moe than's artificial one . ii 2 117
And that distill'd by magic sleights Shall raise such artificial sprites *Macbeth* iii 5 27
If that thy prosperous and artificial feat Can draw him but to answer *Per.* v 1 72
Artillery. Heaven's artillery thunder in the skies . . *T. of Shrew* i 2 205
Turn thou the mouth of thy artillery, As we will ours, against these saucy walls . . . . *K. John* ii 1 403
By discharge of their artillery . . the news was told . *1 Hen. IV.* i 1 57
I'll to the Tower with all the haste I can, To view the artillery *1 Hen. VI.* i 1 168
To rive their dangerous artillery Upon no Christian soul but English Talbot . . . . iv 2 29
Artist. To be relinquished of the artists . . . . *All's Well* ii 3 10
The artist and unread, The hard and soft, seem all affined and kin *Troi. and Cres.* i 3 24
In framing an artist, art hath thus decreed, To make some good, but others to exceed . . . . *Pericles* ii 3 15
Artless. So full of artless jealousy is guilt, It spills itself in fearing to be spilt . . . . *Hamlet* iv 5 19
Artois, Wallon and Picardy are friends to us . . . *1 Hen. VI.* ii 1 9
Arts-man, preambulate, we will be singuled from the barbarous *L. L. Lost* v 1 85
Artus. Gelidus timor occupat artus, it is thee I fear *2 Hen. VI.* iv 1 117
Arviragus. The younger brother, Cadwal, Once Arviragus *Cymbeline* iii 3 96
This gentleman, my Cadwal, Arviragus, Your younger princely son . v 5 359
As. You know him well?—I know him as myself *T. G. of Ver.* ii 4 62
Those as sleep and think not on their sins, Pinch them *Mer. Wives* v 5 57
If he had been as you and you as he, You would have slipt like him *Meas. for Meas.* ii 2 64
Was sent to by my brother; one Lucio As then the messenger . . v 1 74
So befall my soul As this is false he burdens me withal! *Com. of Errors* v 1 209
So heinous is As it makes harmful all that speak of it . . *K. John* iii 1 41
Such fierce alarums both of hope and fear, As I am sick . *1 Hen. VI.* v 5 86
How now, my as fair as noble ladies? . . . . *Coriolanus* ii 1 107
I writ to Romeo, That he should hither come as this dire night *Rom. and Jul.* v 3 247
As love between them like the palm might flourish, As peace should still her wheaten garland wear . . . , And many such-like 'As'es of great charge . . . . *Hamlet* v 2 40
I'll set down the pegs that make this music, As honest as I am *Othello* ii 1 203
Whose love-suit hath been to me As fearful as a siege . *Cymbeline* iii 4 137
Report should render him hourly to your ear As truly as he moves . iii 4 154
As I am a Christian *M. Wives* iii 1; *C. of Err.* i 2; *Rich. III.* i 4; *Othello* iv 2
As I am a gentleman *Mer. Wives* ii 2; iv 6; *Much Ado* v 1; *L. L. Lost* i 1; *T. Night* iv 2; *Richard II.* iii 3; *2 Hen. IV.* ii 1
As I am an honest man . . . . . *Much Ado* v 1 130; *Othello* ii 3 266
As I am a man *Tempest* i 2; *Mer. Wives* iv 2; *T. Night* ii 2; *Lear* iv 7
As I am a soldier . . . . . *Hen. V.* ii 1; iii 3; *Othello* ii 3
As I live . . *Hen. V.* iv 7; *Hen. VIII.* iii 2; v 4; *Coriolanus* iii 1
As I take it . . . . *Hen. V.* iv 7 22; *Othello* v 1 51
As it were *C. of Err.* v 1; *L. L. Lost* v 1; *M. of V.* ii 1; *W. T.* iv 4; *2 Hen. IV.* v 5; *2 Hen. VI.* ii 3; *Rich. III.* iii 1; iii 5; *Cor.* iv 5; *Ham.* i 2; *Per.* i 3; iv 6
As merry as the day is long . . . . *Much Ado* ii 1 51; *K. John* iv 1 18
As much as to say *T. G. of Ver.* iii 1; *C. of Err.* iv 3; *Much Ado* ii 3; *T. Night* i 5; *2 Hen. IV.* ii 2; *Rom. and Jul.* ii 4
As a book. Your face, my thane, is as a book . . . . *Macbeth* i 5 63

As for you, Say what you can . . . . . . *Meas. for Meas.* ii 4 169
As for you, interpreter, you must seem very politic . *All's Well* iv 1 23
As for you, . . . Begin your suits anew . . *2 Hen. VI.* i 3 40
As for Pericles, What should he say? . . . . *Pericles* iv 3 40
As like. I am as like to call thee so again . . *Mer. of Venice* i 3 131
As long again. The Lent shall be as long again as it is . *2 Hen. VI.* iv 3 7
Time as long again Would be fill'd up, my brother, with our thanks *W.T.* i 2 3
As much. My friends told me as much, and I thought no less *As Y. Like It* iv 1 188
As 'tis, We cannot miss him . . . . . *Tempest* i 2 310
Ascanius. And witch me, as Ascanius did When he to madding Dido would unfold His father's acts . . . *2 Hen. VI.* iii 2 116
Ascend. He her chamber-window will ascend . . *T. G. of Ver.* iii 1 39
Ascend my chambers; search, seek, find out . . *Mer. Wives* iii 3 173
Bleed France, and peace ascend to heaven . . *K. John* ii 1 86
Ascend his throne, descending now from him . . *Richard II.* iv 1 111
In God's name, I'll ascend the regal throne . . . iv 1 113
Northumberland, thou ladder wherewithal The mounting Bolingbroke ascends my throne . . . *Richard II.* v 1 56; *2 Hen. IV.* iii 1 71
It [sherris] ascends me into the brain . . *2 Hen. IV.* iv 3 105
A Muse of fire, that would ascend The brightest heaven of invention
Hen. V. Prol. 1
Ascend, brave Talbot; we will follow thee . . . *1 Hen. VI.* ii 1 28
Ascend the sky, And there awake God's gentle-sleeping peace *Richard III.* i 3 287
Ascend, fair queen, Pantheon . . . . *T. Andron.* i 1 333
Ascend her chamber, hence and comfort her . . *Rom. and Jul.* iii 3 147
Scorning the base degrees By which he did ascend . . *J. Cæsar* ii 1 27
Ascended. The noble Brutus is ascended: silence! . . iii 2 11
The dust Should have ascended to the roof of heaven *Ant. and Cleo.* iii 6 49
Ascension. His ascension is More sweet than our blest fields *Cymbeline* v 4 116
Ascension-day. Ere the next Ascension-day at noon . *K. John* iv 2 151
On this Ascension-day, remember well, Upon your oath of service . v 1 22
Before Ascension-day at noon My crown I should give off . . v 1 26
Ascent. His ascent is not by such easy degrees . . *Coriolanus* ii 2 28
Ascribe. Our remedies oft in ourselves do lie, Which we ascribe to heaven
All's Well i 1 232
Not to us, but to thy arm alone, Ascribe we all! . . . *Hen. V.* iv 8 113
Ascribes the glory of his conquest got First to my God . *1 Hen. VI.* ii 4 11
Much attribute he hath, and much the reason Why we ascribe it to him
Troi. and Cres. ii 3 126
Ash. That body, where against My grained ash an hundred times hath broke, And scarr'd the moon with splinters . . *Coriolanus* iv 5 114
Ashamed. Art thou not ashamed To wrong him with thy importunacy?
T. G. of Ver. iv 2 111
Be thou ashamed that I have took upon me Such an immodest raiment v 4 105
Are you not ashamed? What spirit, what devil suggests this imagination?
Mer. Wives iii 3 230
Are you not ashamed? let the clothes alone . . . . iv 2 144
Are you not ashamed? I think you have killed the poor woman . iv 2 197
Perchance, publicly, she'll be ashamed . . *Meas. for Meas.* v 1 278
Fie upon thee! art not ashamed?—Of what, lady? . *Much Ado* iii 4 28
Are you not ashamed? nay, are you not, All three of you? *L. L. Lost* iv 3 159
What heinous sin is it in me To be ashamed to be my father's child!
Mer. of Venice ii 3 17
I am much ashamed of my exchange . . . . . ii 6 35
Ashamed of me?—No, sir, God forbid; but ashamed to kiss *T. of Shrew* v 1 150
I am ashamed that women are so simple To offer war . . v 2 161
Invention is ashamed, Against the proclamation of thy passion *All's Well* i 3 179
I am ashamed: does not the stone rebuke me? . . *W. Tale* v 3 37
I am almost ashamed To say what good respect I have of thee *K. John* iii 3 27
Art thou not ashamed? But, sirrah, henceforth Let me not hear you speak . . . . *1 Hen. IV.* iii 3 118
You will not pocket up wrong: art thou not ashamed? . . . iii 3 184
If I be not ashamed of my soldiers, I am a soused gurnet . . iv 2 12
Are you not ashamed to enforce a poor widow to so rough a course to come by her own? . . . . . . *2 Hen. IV.* ii 1 88
Art thou not ashamed to be called captain? . . . . ii 4 152
I need not to be ashamed of your majesty, praised be God, so long as your majesty is an honest man.—God keep me so! . *Hen. V.* iv 7 118
Presumptuous vassals, are you not ashamed? . . *1 Hen. VI.* iv 1 125
'Twas not my purpose, thus to beg a kiss: I am ashamed *Troi. and Cres.* iii 2 146
Upon his brow shame is ashamed to sit . . *Rom. and Jul.* iii 2 92
Now, before the gods, I am ashamed on't. . . *T. of Athens* iii 2 19
How foolish do your fears seem now, Calpurnia! I am ashamed I did yield to them . . . . *J. Cæsar* ii 2 106
Be not you ashamed to show, he'll not shame to tell you what it means
Hamlet iii 2 155
A wretch whom nature is ashamed Almost to acknowledge hers . *Lear* i 1 215
I am ashamed That thou hast power to shake my manhood thus . i 4 318
Art not ashamed to look upon this beard? . . . . ii 4 196
The land bids me tread no more upon't; It is ashamed to bear me!
Ant. and Cleo. iii 11 2
I am ashamed To look upon the holy sun . . . *Cymbeline* iv 4 40
Asher House. Confine yourself To Asher House . . *Hen. VIII.* iii 2 231
Ashes. Thy rage shall burn thee up, and thou shalt turn To ashes *K. John* iii 1 345
Hath blown his spirit out And strew'd repentant ashes on his head . iv 1 111
Some will mourn in ashes, some coal-black . . *Richard II.* v 1 49
Not in ashes and sackcloth, but in new silk and old sack *2 Hen. IV.* i 2 221
If I begin the battery once again, I will not leave the half-achieved Harfleur Till in her ashes she lie buried . . . *Hen. V.* iii 3 9
Her ashes, in an urn more precious Than the rich-jewel'd coffer of Darius, Transported shall be at high festivals . . *1 Hen. VI.* i 6 24
Burns under feigned ashes of forged love And will at last break out iii 1 190
From their ashes shall be rear'd A phœnix that shall make all France afeard . . . . iv 7 92
Break thou in pieces and consume to ashes! . . . . v 4 92
The witch in Smithfield shall be burn'd to ashes . *2 Hen. VI.* ii 3 7
My ashes, as the phœnix, may bring forth A bird that will revenge upon you all . . . . *3 Hen. VI.* i 4 35
Pale ashes of the house of Lancaster! . . . *Richard III.* i 2 6
Whom I most hated living, thou hast made me, With thy religious truth and modesty, Now in his ashes honour . . . *Hen. VIII.* iv 2 75
Her ashes new create another heir, As great in admiration as herself . v 5 41
Who from the sacred ashes of her honour Shall star-like rise . . v 5 46
A bloody piteous corse; Pale, pale as ashes . *Rom. and Jul.* iii 2 55
The roses in thy lips and cheeks shall fade To paly ashes . iv 1 100
Prithee, go hence; Or I shall show the cinders of my spirits Through the ashes of my chance . . . . *Ant. and Cleo.* v 2 174
From ashes ancient Gower is come . . . *Pericles* i Gower 2
Ashford. A headstrong Kentishman, John Cade of Ashford *2 Hen. VI.* iii 1 357
Where's Dick, the butcher of Ashford? . . . . . iv 3 1

Ashore. How came we ashore?—By Providence divine . . *Tempest* i 2 158
I shall no more to sea, to sea, Here shall I die ashore . . ii 2 45
I made of the bark of a tree with mine own hands since I was cast ashore ii 2 129
Swum ashore, man, like a duck: I can swim like a duck . . ii 2 133
What tempest, I trow, threw this whale, with so many tuns of oil in his belly, ashore at Windsor? . . . . . . *Mer. Wives* ii 1 66
If, Biondello, thou wert come ashore . . . *T. of Shrew* i 1 42
Since I came ashore I kill'd a man and fear I was descried . . i 1 236
Send precepts to the leviathan To come ashore . . *Hen. V.* iii 3 27
Expecting but the aid Of Buckingham to welcome them ashore *Rich. III.* iv 4 439
I must fetch his necessaries ashore . . . . *Othello* ii 1 292
This health to Lepidus!—Bear him ashore. I'll pledge it *Ant. and Cleo.* ii 7 91
Till fortune, tired with doing bad, Threw him ashore *Pericles* ii Gower 38
When you come ashore, I have another suit . . . . v 1 261
Ash-Wednesday. Falling out that year on Ash-Wednesday *M. of Venice* ii 5 26
Ashy. Oft have I seen a timely-parted ghost, Of ashy semblance
2 Hen. VI. iii 2 162
Asia. Roaming clean through the bounds of Asia . *Com. of Errors* i 1 134
Fetch you a toothpicker now from the furthest inch of Asia . *Much Ado* ii 1 275
Hollow pamper'd jades of Asia . . . . *2 Hen. IV.* ii 4 178
Labienus—This is stiff news—hath, with his Parthian force, Extended Asia from Euphrates . . . . . *Ant. and Cleo.* i 2 105
Aside. He trod the water, Whose enmity he flung aside . *Tempest* ii 1 116
Setting the attraction of my good parts aside . . *Mer. Wives* ii 2 110
Will't please you walk aside? . . . . *Meas. for Meas.* iv 1 59
Walk aside with me: I have studied eight or nine wise words *Much Ado* iii 2 73
Walk aside the true folk, and let the traitors stay . *L. L. Lost* iv 3 213
Our purposed hunting shall be set aside . . . *M. N. Dream* iv 1 188
Draw aside the curtains and discover The several caskets *Mer. of Venice* ii 7 1
He threw his eye aside, And mark what object did present itself
As Y. Like It iv 3 103
Setting all this chat aside, Thus in plain terms . . *T. of Shrew* ii 1 270
Prithee, Kate, let's stand aside and see the end of this controversy . v 1 63
Thou art too fine in thy evidence; therefore stand aside . *All's Well* v 3 270
But more of that anon. Take him aside . . . *T. Night* v 1 103
Wolves and bears, they say, Casting their savageness aside have done Like offices of pity . . . . *W. Tale* ii 3 188
Be my present partner in this business, and lay aside the thoughts of Sicilia . . . . iv 2 58
Lay aside the sword Which sways usurpingly these several titles *K. John* ii 1 12
Setting aside his high blood's royalty, . . . I do defy him . *Richard II.* i 1 58
Lay aside life-harming heaviness And entertain a cheerful disposition . ii 2 3
Step aside, and I'll show thee a precedent . . . *1 Hen. IV.* ii 4 36
Here is my leg.—And here is my speech. Stand aside, nobility . ii 4 428
That daff'd the world aside, And bid it pass . . . . iv 1 96
Setting my knighthood and my soldiership aside . . *2 Hen. IV.* v 2 94
I lay aside that which grows to me! . . . . . . i 2 100
Set this unaccustom'd fight aside . . . . *1 Hen. VI.* iii 1 93
This too much lenity And harmful pity must be laid aside . *3 Hen. VI.* ii 2 10
Stand aside, While I use further conference with Warwick . . iii 3 110
All dissembling set aside, Tell me for truth the measure of his love . iii 3 119
Tell him, my mourning weeds are laid aside . . . . iii 3 229
Setting your scorns and your mislike aside, Tell me some reason why iv 1 24
But that thy brothers beat aside the point . . . *Richard III.* iv 2 96
If you give way, Or hedge aside from the direct forthright *Troi. and Cres.* iii 3 158
Lay aside your stitchery; I must have you play the idle huswife
Coriolanus i 3 75
So please you, step aside; I'll know his grievance . *Rom. and Jul.* i 1 162
With one hand beats Cold death aside . . . . . iii 1 167
But the kind prince, Taking thy part, hath rush'd aside the law . iii 3 26
Aside, aside; here comes Lord Timon . . . *T. of Athens* ii 2 127
He is a man, setting his fate aside, Of comely virtues . . . iii 5 14
We did buffet it With lusty sinews, throwing it aside . . *J. Cæsar* i 2 108
Would be worn now in their newest gloss, Not cast aside so soon *Macbeth* i 7 35
But soft! but soft! aside: here comes the king . . . *Hamlet* v 1 240
I prithee, turn aside and weep for her . . . *Ant. and Cleo.* iii 3 76
Stand aside *T. G. of V.* iv 2; *M. Ado* iv 2; *L. L. Lost* iv 1; *M. N. Dr.* iii 2; *T. of Shr.* ii 1; *2 Hen. IV.* iii 2; *J. Cæsar* ii 1
Ask. I chose her when I could not ask my father For his advice *Tempest* v 1 190
How oddly will it sound that I Must ask my child forgiveness! . . v 1 198
I say, she did nod: and you ask me if she did nod . *T. G. of Ver.* i 1 121
Ask my dog: if he say ay, it will; if he say, no, it will . . ii 5 36
Grant one boon that I shall ask of you.—I grant it . . . v 4 150
How dost thou?—The better that it pleases your good worship to ask
Mer. Wives. i 4 145
Ask me no reason why I love you . . . . . . ii 1 4
You may ask your father; here he comes . . . . . iii 4 69
I pray you, ask him some questions in his accidence . . . iv 1 16
Why 'her unhappy brother'? let me ask . . *Meas. for Meas.* i 4 21
Ask him what this man did to my wife.—I beseech your honour, ask me ii 1 148
Hadst thou not order? Why dost thou ask again? . . . . ii 2 9
Go to your bosom; Knock there, and ask your heart what it doth know ii 2 137
Let me ask my sister pardon . . . . iii 1 173
He doth oftener ask forgiveness . . . . iv 2 54
If any ask you for your master, Say he dines forth . *Com. of Errors* ii 2 211
Some devils ask but the parings of one's nail, A rush, a hair . . iv 3 72
What is he that you ask for, niece? . . . . . *Much Ado* i 1 34
Rather ask if it were possible any villany should be so rich . . iii 3 119
First, I ask thee what they have done; thirdly, I ask thee what's their offence . . . . v 1 225
How needless was it then to ask the question! . . . *L. L. Lost* ii 1 117
What time o' day?—The hour that fools should ask. . . . ii 1 123
Ask them how many inches Is in one mile . . . . . v 2 188
I know the reason, lady, why you ask.—O for your reason! quickly, sir v 2 243
That will ask some tears in the true performing of it . *M. N. Dream* i 2 27
I then did ask of her her changeling child; Which straight she gave me iv 1 64
Ask me not what; for if I tell you, I am no true Athenian . . iv 2 30
Nay, but ask my opinion too of that.—I will anon . *Mer. of Venice* iii 5 90
You'll ask me, why I rather choose to have A weight of carrion flesh . iv 1 40
I pardon thee thy life before thou ask it . . . . . iv 1 369
I'll ask him what he would. Did you call, sir? . *As Y. Like It* i 2 265
What makes he here? Did he ask for me? Where remains he? . . iii 2 235
What is't o'clock?—You should ask me what time o' day . . iii 2 318
Think not I love him, though I ask for him; 'Tis but a peevish boy . iii 5 109
Ask me what you will, I will grant it.—Then love me . . . iv 1 113
I take thee, Rosalind, for wife.—I might ask you for your commission . iv 1 138
Ask him what apparel he will wear . . . . *T. of Shrew* Ind. 1 60
Ne'er ask me what raiment I'll wear . . . . . Ind. 2 8
If thou ask me why, sufficeth, my reasons are both good and weighty . i 1 252
Let me be so bold as ask you, Did you yet ever see Baptista's daughter? i 2 251

Ask. If she deny to wed, I'll crave the day When I shall ask the banns *T. of Shrew* ii 1 181
His beard grew thin and hungerly And seem'd to ask him sops . iii 2 178
You have some stain of soldier in you : let me ask you a question *All's Well* i 1 123
I would you had kneel'd, my lord, to ask me mercy . . . ii 1 66
Whom I know Is free for me to ask, thee to bestow . . . ii 1 203
Rather muse than ask why I entreat you . . . . ii 5 70
Ask questions and sing ; pick his teeth and sing . . . iii 2 7
Our general bids you answer to what I shall ask you out of a note iv 3 145
I need not to ask you if gold will corrupt him to revolt . . iv 3 309
Why does he ask him of me ?—What's he ? . . . iv 3 317
Let him not ask our pardon ; The nature of his great offence is dead v 3 22
Good my lord, Ask him upon his oath . . . . v 3 185
Ask no other dowry with her but such another jest . *T. Night* ii 5 202
What shall you ask of me that I'll deny ? . . . iii 4 231
What will you do, now my necessity Makes me to ask you for my purse ? iii 4 369
Can you love this lady ?—Nay, ask me if I can refrain *K. John* ii 1 525
A princess wrought it me, And I did never ask it you again . iv 1 44
Meantime but ask What you would have reform'd that is not well . iv 2 43
Let it be our suit That you have bid us ask his liberty ; Which for our goods we do no further ask . . . . . iv 2 63
I do not ask you much, I beg cold comfort . . . v 7 41
Ask him his name and orderly proceed To swear him . *Richard II.* i 3 9
Ask yonder knight in arms, Both who he is and why he cometh hither . i 3 26
For these great affairs do ask some charge . . . ii 1 159
Being so great, I have no need to beg.—Yet ask.—And shall I have ? iv 1 310
I shall never hold that man my friend Whose tongue shall ask me for one penny cost . . . . . . *1 Hen. IV.* i 3 91
Come, you paraquito, answer me Directly unto this question that I ask ii 3 89
Ask me when thou wilt, and thou shalt have it . . . ii 4 69
May I ask how my lady his wife doth ? . . *2 Hen. IV.* iii 2 71
Your highness bade me ask for it to-day . . . *Hen. V.* ii 2 63
Ask me this slave in French What is his name . . . iv 4 24
Ask me what question thou canst possible, And I will answer unpremeditated . . . . . . *1 Hen. VI.* i 2 87
What means he now ? Go ask him whither he goes . . ii 3 28
Answer that I shall ask ; For, till thou speak, thou shalt not pass *2 Hen. VI.* i 4 29
Ask what thou wilt. That I had said and done . . . i 4 31
Go and meet him, And ask him what's the reason of these arms . iv 9 37
Let me ask of these, If they can brook I bow a knee to man . v 1 109
Clifford, ask mercy and obtain no grace . . *3 Hen. VI.* ii 6 69
Ay, but thou canst do what I mean to ask . . . iii 2 48
Why ask I that ? my mangled body shows . . . v 2 7
How goes the world with thee ?—The better that your lordship please to ask . . . . . . *Richard III.* iii 2 99
Ask those on the banks If they were his assistants . . iv 4 525
What, are you chafed ? Ask God for temperance . *Hen. VIII.* i 1 124
You have half our power : The other moiety, ere you ask, is given . i 2 12
Not to deny her that A woman of less place might ask by law . ii 2 112
That seal, You ask with such a violence, the king . . gave me . iii 2 246
May I be bold to ask what that contains, That paper in your hand ? iv 1 13
I ask, that I might waken reverence . . *Troi. and Cres.* i 3 227
Ask me not what I would be, if I were not Thersites . . v 1 70
You two are old men : tell me one thing that I shall ask you *Coriolanus* ii 1 16
The price is to ask it kindly.—Kindly ! Sir, I pray, let me ha't . ii 3 81
Of him that did not ask, but mock, bestow Your sued-for tongues ? ii 3 215
Who shall ask it ? The tribunes cannot do't for shame . . iv 6 108
I beseech you, peace : Or, if you'ld ask, remember this before . v 3 79
We have nothing else to ask, but that Which you deny already . v 3 88
Yet we will ask ; That, if you fail in our request, the blame May hang upon your hardness . . . . v 3 89
For their brethren slain Religiously they ask a sacrifice . *T. Andron.* i 1 124
Titus, thou shalt obtain and ask the empery . . . i 1 201
I ask your voices and your suffrages : Will you bestow them friendly ? i 1 218
All humbled on your knees, You shall ask pardon of his majesty . i 1 473
But 'tis no wit to go.—Why, may one ask ? . *Rom. and Jul.* i 4 49
Go, ask his name : if he be married, My grave is like to be my wedding bed . . . . i 5 136
Where hast thou been, then ?—I'll tell thee, ere thou ask it me again ii 3 48
Ask for me to-morrow, and you shall find me a grave man . . iii 1 101
How fares my Juliet ? that I ask again . . . . v 1 15
Give my horse to Timon, Ask nothing, give it him, it foals me, straight, And able horses . . . . . *T. of Athens* ii 1 9
That you ask me what you are, and do not know yourselves . . ii 2 66
What do ye ask of me, my friend ?—We wait for certain money here, sir iii 4 45
Have you forgot me, sir.—Why dost ask that ? I have forgot all men iv 3 480
Answer me To what I ask you.—Speak.—Demand . *Macbeth* iv 1 61
But when they ask you what it means, say you this *Hamlet* iv 5 47
Why ask you this ?—Not that I think you did not love your father iv 7 110
Ask her forgiveness ? Do you but mark how this becomes the house *Lear* ii 4 154
Good nuncle, in, and ask thy daughters' blessing . . . iii 2 12
If he ask for me, I am ill, and gone to bed . . . iii 3 17
Let me ask you one word in private.—Importune him once more to go iii 4 165
When thou dost ask me blessing, I'll kneel down, And ask of thee forgiveness . . . . v 3 10
Ask him his purposes, why he appears Upon this call o' the trumpet v 3 118
In wisdom I should ask thy name . . . . . v 3 142
Know'st thou this paper ?—Ask me not what I know . . v 3 160
Are your doors lock'd ?—Why, wherefore ask you this ? . *Othello* i 1 85
I will ask him for my place again ; he shall tell me I am a drunkard ! ii 3 306
I wonder in my soul, What you would ask me, that I should deny . iii 3 69
Why dost thou ask ?—But for a satisfaction of my thought . . iii 3 96
No, by my life and soul ! Send for the man, and ask him . . v 2 50
I never gave you cause.—I do believe it, and I ask you pardon . v 2 300
Do So far ask pardon as befits mine honour To stoop *Ant. and Cleo.* ii 2 97
I have one thing more to ask him yet, good Charmian : But 'tis no matter iii 3 48
Cried he ? and begg'd a' pardon ?—He did ask favour . . iii 13 133
Tend me to-night two hours, I ask no more, And the gods yield you for't iv 2 32
Can we, with manners, ask what was the difference ?—Safely *Cymbeline* i 4 56
I beseech, your grace, without offence,—My conscience bids me ask i 5 7
Where is thy lady ? or, by Jupiter,—I will not ask again . . iii 5 85
O noble misery, To be i' the field, and ask 'what news ?' of me ! . v 3 65
'Tis now the time To ask of whence you are. Report it . . v 5 16
Ask of Cymbeline what boon thou wilt, Fitting my bounty and thy state . . . . v 5 97
I love thee more and more : think more and more What's best to ask . v 5 110
Nor ask advice of any other thought But faithfulness and courage *Pericles* i 1 62
It fits thee not to ask the reason why, Because we bid it . . i 1 157

Ask. Being bid to ask what he would of the king, desired he might know none of his secrets . . . . *Pericles* i 3 5
Pity him ; He asks of you, that never used to beg . . . ii 1 66
Have no more of life than may suffice To give my tongue that heat to ask your help . . . . ii 1 79
Let me ask you one thing : What do you think of my daughter, sir ? . ii 5 32
Askance. Thou canst not frown, thou canst not look askance *T. of Shrew* ii 1 249
Asked. And see the gentleman that you asked for *T. G. of Ver.* iv 2 32
What a taking was he in when your husband asked who was in the basket ! *Mer. Wives* iii 3 192
He ask'd me for a thousand marks in gold *Com. of Errors* ii 1 61
I thought to have ask'd you.—And you said no . . . iii 1 55
Were you in doubt, sir, that you asked her ? . . *Much Ado* i 1 106
It is no boast, being ask'd, to say we are . . *As Y. Like It* iv 3 91
No sooner sighed but they asked one another the reason . . v 2 38
So I had broke thy pate, And ask'd thee mercy for't *All's Well* ii 1 69
Shall the blessed sun of heaven prove a micher and eat blackberries ? a question not to be asked . . . . . *1 Hen. IV.* ii 4 451
Shall the son of England prove a thief and take purses ? a question to be asked . . . . ii 4 453
Contracted bachelors, such as had been asked twice on the banns . iv 2 18
My consent ne'er ask'd herein before ! This is close dealing . *2 Hen. VI.* ii 4 72
And never ask'd for restitution . . . . . . iii 1 118
His suit was granted Ere it was ask'd . . . *Hen. VIII.* i 1 187
They have pardons, being ask'd, as free As words to little purpose *Coriol.* iii 2 88
No question asked him by any of the senators, but they stand bald before him . . . . iv 5 205
Indeed, I should have ask'd you that before . *Rom. and Jul.* i 2 81
Supper served up, you called, my young lady asked for . . i 3 101
You are looked for and called for, asked for and sought for . . i 5 14
Where's the fool now ?—He last asked the question *T. of Athens* ii 2 60
When I ask'd you what the matter was, You stared upon me . *J. Cæsar* ii 1 241
Hath he ask'd for me ?—Know you not he has ? . *Macbeth* i 7 30
The dead man's knell Is there scarce ask'd for who . . iv 3 171
Whoso ask'd her for his wife, His riddle told not, lost his life *Pericles* i Gower 37
So, this was well ask'd, 'twas so well perform'd . . . ii 3 99
Asker. Have you Ere now denied the asker ? and now again Of him that did not ask, but mock, bestow Your sued-for tongues ? *Coriolanus* ii 3 214
Askest. For prisoners ask'st thou ? hell our prison is . *1 Hen. IV.* iv 7 58
I wonder, doctor, Thou ask'st me such a question . *Cymbeline* i 5 11
Asketh. My business asketh haste . . . *T. of Shrew* ii 1 115
The business asketh silent secrecy . . . *2 Hen. VI.* i 2 90
Asking. Married my daughter without asking my good will ? *T. of Shrew* v 1 137
What shall you ask of me that I'll deny, That honour saved may upon asking give ? . . . . . . *T. Night* iii 4 232
Knocking at the taverns, And asking every one for Sir John *2 Hen. IV.* ii 4 389
He, on his right, asking a wife for Edward . . *3 Hen. VI.* iii 1 44
Not bestowing on him, at his asking, The archbishopric . *Hen. VIII.* i 1 163
It values not your asking . . . . . . ii 3 52
Ajax goes up and down the field, asking for himself *Troi. and Cres.* iii 3 244
Yet dare I never Deny your asking : take your choice . *Coriolanus* i 6 65
Were fit for thee to use as they to claim, In asking their good loves . iii 2 84
Now I'll tell you without asking . . . *Rom. and Jul.* i 2 83
What wouldst thou beg, Laertes, That shall not be my offer, not thy asking ? . . . . *Hamlet* i 2 46
I shall, first asking your pardon thereunto, recount the occasion . iv 7 46
Aslant. There is a willow grows aslant a brook . . . iv 7 167
Asleep. Who, with a charm join'd to their suffer'd labour, I have left asleep . . . . *Tempest* i 2 232
Will you laugh me asleep, for I am very heavy ? . . . ii 1 189
What, all so soon asleep ! I wish mine eyes Would, with themselves, shut up my thoughts . . . . ii 1 191
This is a strange repose, to be asleep With eyes wide open . . ii 1 213
Standing, speaking, moving, And yet so fast asleep . . . ii 1 215
I'll yield him thee asleep, Where thou mayst knock a nail into his head iii 2 68
Within this half hour will he be asleep : Wilt thou destroy him then ? iii 2 122
There shalt thou find the mariners asleep Under the hatches . . v 1 98
This love of theirs myself have often seen, Haply when they have judged me fast asleep . . . . . . *T. G. of Ver.* iii 1 25
By my halidom, I was fast asleep . . . . . iv 2 136
How if the nurse be asleep and will not hear us ? . *Much Ado* iii 3 71
Having once this juice, I'll watch Titania when she is asleep *M. N. Dream* ii 1 177
Sing me now asleep ; Then to your offices and let me rest . . ii 2 7
On the ground ! Dead ? or asleep ? I see no blood, no wound . ii 2 101
My lord, this is my daughter here asleep . . . . iv 1 133
God's my life, stolen hence, and left me asleep ! . . . iv 1 209
Asleep, my love ? What, dead, my dove ? . . . . v 1 331
I told him you were asleep ; he seems to have a foreknowledge of that *T. Night* i 5 151
Though credit be asleep and not an ear open . . *W. Tale* v 2 67
I will find him when he lies asleep . . . *1 Hen. IV.* i 3 221
Fast asleep behind the arras, and snorting like a horse . . ii 4 577
I fell asleep here behind the arras and had my pocket picked . iii 3 112
Now their pride and mettle is asleep, Their courage with hard labour tame . . . . iv 3 22
Then death rock me asleep, abridge my doleful days ! . *2 Hen. IV.* ii 4 211
How many thousand of my poorest subjects Are at this hour asleep ! . iii 1 5
Whose dangerous eyes may well be charm'd asleep . . . iv 2 39
As the year Had found some months asleep and leap'd them over . iv 4 124
Where is Pucelle now ? I think her old familiar is asleep *1 Hen. VI.* iii 2 122
Watch thou and wake when others be asleep . . *2 Hen. VI.* i 1 249
There sits the duke asleep : I'll to the king . *Richard III.* i 4 96
Killing care and grief of heart Fall asleep, or hearing, die *Hen. VIII.* iii 1 14
She is asleep : good wench, let's sit down quiet, For fear we wake her . iv 2 81
Small as an eunuch, or the virgin voice That babies lulls asleep *Coriol.* iii 2 115
What service is here ! I think our fellows are asleep . . iv 5 2
As is a nurse's song Of lullaby to bring her babe asleep *T. Andron.* ii 3 29
And fell asleep As Cerberus at the Thracian poet's feet . . ii 4 50
Many a time he danced thee on his knee, Sung thee asleep . . v 3 163
Dreamers often lie.—In bed asleep . . . *Rom. and Jul.* i 4 52
Drawn with a team of little atomies Athwart men's noses as they lie asleep . . . . i 4 58
With a tithe-pig's tail Tickling a parson's nose as a' lies asleep . i 4 80
Because he hath wakened thy dog that hath lain asleep in the sun . iii 1 29
Marry, and amen, how sound is she asleep ! I must needs wake her . iv 5 8
Boy ! Lucius ! Fast asleep ? It is no matter . . *J. Cæsar* ii 1 229
Thou hast been all this while asleep . . . . . v 5 32
When Duncan is asleep—Whereto the rather shall his day's hard journey Soundly invite him . . . . *Macbeth* i 7 61
Here she comes ! This is her very guise ; and, upon my life, fast asleep v 1 23

Asleep. When he is drunk asleep, or in his rage *Hamlet* iii 3 89
A whole tribe of fops, Got 'tween asleep and wake *Lear* i 2 15
Where's my fool, ho? I think the world's asleep? i 4 52
How do you, my good lady?—'Faith, half asleep *Othello* iv 2 97
Dost thou not see my baby at my breast, That sucks the nurse asleep? *Ant. and Cleo.* v 2 313
Asmath. By the eternal God, whose name and power Thou tremblest at, answer that I shall ask 2 *Hen. VI.* i 4 27
Aspect. If you will jest with me, know my aspect And fashion your demeanour to my looks *Com. of Errors* ii 2 32
Some other mistress hath thy sweet aspects ii 2 113
Sapphires, declining their rich aspect to the hot breath of Spain iii 2 139
Should ravish doters with a false aspect *L. L. Lost* iv 3 260
Of such vinegar aspect That they'll not show their teeth in way of smile, Though Nestor swear the jest be laughable *Mer. of Venice* i 1 54
I tell thee, lady, this aspect of mine Hath fear'd the valiant ii 1 8
In me what strange effect Would they work in mild aspect! *As Y. Like It* iv 3 53
Better in thy youth Than in a nuncio's of more grave aspect *T. Night* i 4 28
Be patient till the heavens look With an aspect more favourable *W. Tale* ii 1 107
Like to a muzzled bear, Save in aspect, hath all offence seal'd up *K. John* ii 1 250
That close aspect of his Does show the mood of a much troubled breast iv 2 72
Taking note of thy abhorr'd aspect, Finding thee fit for bloody villany iv 2 224
For our eyes do hate the dire aspect Of civil wounds *Richard II.* i 3 127
Thy sad aspect Hath from the number of his banish'd years Pluck'd four away i 3 209
Malevolent to you in all aspects 1 *Hen. IV.* i 1 97
Render'd such aspect As cloudy men use to their adversaries iii 2 82
Lend the eye a terrible aspect *Hen. V.* iii 1 9
Therefore was I created with a stubborn outside, with an aspect of iron v 2 244
His grim aspect, And large proportion of his strong-knit limbs 1 *Hen. VI.* ii 3 20
Whose ugly and unnatural aspect May fright the hopeful mother *Rich. III.* i 2 23
Those eyes of thine from mine have drawn salt tears, Shamed their aspect i 2 155
That smile we would aspire to, That sweet aspect of princes *Hen. VIII.* iii 2 369
Wherefore frowns he thus? 'Tis his aspect of terror. All's not well v 1 88
Whose medicinable eye Corrects the ill aspects of planets evil *Tr. and Cr.* i 3 92
An aspect of intercession, which Great nature cries 'Deny not' *Coriol.* v 3 32
Put on a most importunate aspect, A visage of demand *T. of Athens* ii 1 28
Tears in his eyes, distraction in's aspect, A broken voice *Hamlet* ii 2 581
In sincere verity, Under the allowance of your great aspect *Lear* ii 2 112
There would he anchor his aspect and die With looking on his life *Ant. and Cleo.* i 5 33
Aspen. Do I? yea, in very truth, do I, an 'twere an aspen leaf 2 *Hen. IV.* ii 4 117
Seen those lily hands Tremble, like aspen-leaves, upon a lute *T. Andron.* ii 4 45
Aspersion. No sweet aspersion shall the heavens let fall To make this contract grow *Tempest* iv 1 18
Aspic. Swell, bosom, with thy fraught, For 'tis of aspics' tongues! *Othello* iii 3 450
Have I the aspic in my lips? *Ant. and Cleo.* v 2 296
This is an aspic's trail: and these fig-leaves Have slime upon them, such as the aspic leaves v 2 354
Aspicious. Comprehended two aspicious persons *Much Ado* iii 5 50
Aspiration. He rises on the toe: that spirit of his In aspiration lifts him from the earth *Troi. and Cres.* iv 5 16
Aspire. Wilt thou aspire to guide the heavenly car? *T. G. of Ver.* iii 1 154
Whose flames aspire As thoughts do blow them, higher and higher *M. W.* v 5 101
He means . . . To aspire unto the crown and reign as king 3 *Hen. VI.* i 1 53
That smile we would aspire to, That sweet aspect of princes *Hen. VIII.* iii 2 368
Who digs hills because they do aspire Throws down one mountain to cast up a higher *Pericles* i 4 5
Aspired. That hath aspired to Solon's happiness *T. Andron.* i 1 177
That gallant spirit hath aspired the clouds *Rom. and Jul.* iii 1 122
Aspiring. Show boldness and aspiring confidence *K. John* v 1 56
Upon a hot and fiery steed Which his aspiring rider seem'd to know *Richard II.* v 2 9
Knowing Dame Eleanor's aspiring humour 2 *Hen. VI.* i 2 97
What, will the aspiring blood of Lancaster Sink in the ground? I thought it would have mounted 3 *Hen. VI.* v 6 61
Put in her tender heart the aspiring flame Of golden sovereignty *Richard III* iv 4 328
A-squint. That eye that told you so look'd but a-squint *Lear* v 3 72
Ass. What a thrice-double ass Was I! *Tempest* v 1 295
Away, ass! you'll lose the tide, if you tarry any longer *T. G. of Ver.* ii 3 39
What an ass art thou! I understand thee not.—What a block art thou, that thou canst not! ii 5 25
Why, thou whoreson ass, thou mistakest me ii 5 49
And pities them.—Wherefore?—That such an ass should owe them v 2 28
Yet I am not altogether an ass *Mer. Wives* i 1 176
Page is an ass, a secure ass: he will trust his wife ii 2 315
I do begin to perceive that I am made an ass v 5 125
Like an ass whose back with ingots bows *Meas. for Meas.* iii 1 26
A fool, a coward, One all of luxury, an ass, a madman v 1 506
There's none but asses will be bridled so *Com. of Errors* ii 1 14
If thou art changed to aught, 'tis to an ass ii 2 201
'Tis true; she rides me and I long for grass. 'Tis so, I am an ass ii 2 203
I think thou art an ass.—Marry, so it doth appear By the wrongs I suffer iii 1 15
Being at that pass, You would keep from my heels and beware of an ass iii 1 18
Thou wouldst have changed thy face for a name or thy name for an ass iii 1 47
I am an ass, I am a woman's man and besides myself iii 2 77
Thou art sensible in nothing but blows, and so is an ass iv 4 29
I am an ass, indeed; you may prove it by my long ears iv 4 30
Away! you are an ass, you are an ass *Much Ado* iv 2 75
O that he were here to write me down an ass! iv 2 78
Remember that I am an ass; though it be not written down, yet forget not that I am an ass iv 2 79
O that I had been writ down an ass! iv 2 90
Do not forget to specify, when time and place shall serve, that I am an ass v 1 265
This plaintiff here, the offender, did call me ass v 1 315
A horse to be ambassador for an ass *L. L. Lost* iii 1 53
You must send the ass upon the horse, for he is very slow-gaited iii 1 55
Therefore, as he is an ass, let him go v 2 628
For the ass to the Jude; give it him:—Jud-as, away! v 2 631
This is to make an ass of me; to fright me, if they could *M. N. Dream* iii 1 124
When I did him at this advantage take, An ass's nole I fixed on his head iii 2 17
So it came to pass, Titania waked and straightway loved an ass iii 2 34
I am such a tender ass, if my hair do but tickle me, I must scratch iv 1 27
What visions have I seen! Methought I was enamour'd of an ass iv 1 82
Man is but an ass, if he go about to expound this dream iv 1 212
Ass. I wonder if the lion be to speak.—No wonder, my lord: one lion may, when many asses do *M. N. Dream* v 1 155
With the help of a surgeon he might yet recover, and prove an ass v 1 317
Many a purchased slave, Which, like your asses and your dogs and mules, You use in abject and in slavish parts *Mer. of Venice* iv 1 91
If it do come to pass That any man turn ass *As Y. Like It* ii 5 53
O this woodcock, what an ass it is! *T. of Shrew* i 2 161
Come, sit on me.—Asses are made to bear, and so are you ii 1 200
Preposterous ass, that never read so far To know the cause why music was ordain'd! iii 1 9
My household stuff, my field, my barn, My horse, my ox, my ass iii 2 234
Away, away, mad ass! his name is Lucentio v 1 87
If thou be'st not an ass, I am a youth of fourteen *All's Well* ii 3 106
For it will come to pass That every braggart shall be found an ass iv 3 372
I am not such an ass but I can keep my hand dry *T. Night* i 3 79
Welcome, ass. Now let's have a catch ii 3 18
An affectioned ass, that cons state without book ii 3 161
Your horse now would make him an ass.—Ass, I doubt not ii 3 184
'Slight, will you make an ass o' me? iii 2 14
Keep me in darkness, send ministers to me, asses iv 2 100
They praise me and make an ass of me; now my foes tell me plainly I am an ass v 1 20
It lies as sightly on the back of him As great Alcides' shows upon an ass: But, ass, I'll take that burthen from your back *K. John* ii 1 144
I was not made a horse; And yet I bear a burthen like an ass *Richard II.* v 5 93
Unless a woman should be made an ass and a beast, to bear every knave's wrong 2 *Hen. IV* ii 1 40
Come, you virtuous ass, you bashful fool, must you be blushing? ii 2 80
He is an ass, as in the world: I will verify as much in his beard *Hen. V.* iii 2 74
Asses, fools, dolts! chaff and bran, chaff and bran! *Troi. and Cres.* i 2 262
An assinego may tutor thee: thou scurvy-valiant ass! ii 1 50
Would the fountain of your mind were clear again, that I might water an ass at it! iii 3 314
To an ass, were nothing; he is both ass and ox: to an ox, were nothing; he is both ox and ass v 1 65
That same young Trojan ass, that loves the whore there v 4 6
I find the ass in compound with the major part of your syllables *Coriol.* ii 1 64
To stuff a botcher's cushion, or to be entombed in an ass's pack-saddle ii 1 99
What an ass it is! Then thou dwellest with daws too? iv 5 47
Now, what a thing it is to be an ass! *T. Andron.* iv 2 25
I will fly, like a dog, the heels o' the ass *T. of Athens* i 1 283
What are we, Apemantus?—Asses ii 2 64
The ass more captain than the lion ii 5 49
If thou wert the fox, the lion would suspect thee, when peradventure thou wert accused by the ass iv 3 334
If thou wert the ass, thy dulness would torment thee iv 3 334
How has the ass broke the wall, that thou art out of the city? iv 3 354
Bear them as the ass bears gold, To groan and sweat *J. Cæsar* iv 1 21
Turn him off, Like to the empty ass, to shake his ears, And graze in commons iv 1 26
Upon mine honour,— Then came each actor on his ass *Hamlet* ii 2 414
O, vengeance! Why, what an ass am I! ii 2 611
Cudgel thy brains no more about it, for your dull ass will not mend his pace with beating v 1 64
It might be the pate of a politician, which this ass now o'er-reaches v 1 87
Thou borest thy ass on thy back o'er the dirt *Lear* i 4 177
May not an ass know when the cart draws the horse? i 4 244
Be my horses ready?—Thy asses are gone about 'em i 5 37
Wears out his time, much like his master's ass, For nought but provender, and when he's old, cashier'd *Othello* i 1 47
Will as tenderly be led by the nose As asses are i 3 408
Love me and reward me, For making him egregiously an ass ii 1 318
Look, they weep, And I, an ass, am onion-eyed *Ant. and Cleo.* iv 2 36
That I might hear thee call great Cæsar ass Unpolicied! v 2 310
Unless it had been the fall of an ass, which is no great hurt *Cymbeline* i 2 39
That such a crafty devil as is his mother Should yield the world this ass! ii 1 58
Assail. But he assails; and our virginity, though valiant, in the defence yet is weak *All's Well* i 1 126
'Accost' is front her, board her, woo her, assail her *T. Night* i 3 60
Seeing gentle words will not prevail, Assail them with the army 2 *Hen. VI.* iv 2 185
Here in the parliament Let us assail the family of York 3 *Hen. VI.* i 1 65
Let us once again assail your ears *Hamlet* i 1 31
And to defend ourselves it be a sin When violence assails us *Othello* ii 3 204
What lady would you choose to assail?—Yours *Cymbeline* i 4 136
Assailable. There's comfort yet; they are assailable *Macbeth* iii 2 39
Assailant. So shall we pass along And never stir assailants *As Y. Like It* i 3 116
Thy assailant is quick, skilful and deadly *T. Night* iii 4 245
Assailed. My mother is assailed in our tent, And ta'en, I fear *K. John* iii 2 6
Assailed by robbers and die in many irreconciled iniquities *Hen. V.* iv 1 159
Stood alone, Tendering my ruin and assail'd of none 1 *Hen. VI.* iv 7 10
I have assailed her with music, but she vouchsafes no notice *Cymbeline* ii 3 44
Although assail'd with fortune fierce and keen. *Pericles* v 3 Gower 88
Assaileth. Of that fell poison which assaileth him *K. John* v 7 9
Assailing. To beat assailing death from his weak legions. 1 *Hen. VI.* iv 4 16
Nor bide the encounter of assailing eyes *Rom. and Jul.* i 1 219
Assassination. If the assassination Could trammel up the consequence, and catch With his surcease success *Macbeth* i 7 2
Assault. Which pierces so that it assaults Mercy itself *Tempest*, Epil. 17
The assault that Angelo hath made to you, fortune hath conveyed to my understanding *Meas. for Meas.* iii 1 188
Invincible against all assaults of affection *Much Ado* ii 3 120
Without rescue in the first assault or ransom afterward *All's Well* i 3 121
Brings in the champion Honour on my part, Against your vain assault iv 2 51
Let it be so. Say, where will you assault? *K. John* ii 1 408
What means death in this rude assault? *Richard II.* v 5 106
Discover how with most advantage They may vex us with shot or with assault 1 *Hen. VI.* i 4 13
Arm! arm! the enemy doth make assault! ii 1 38
In which assault we lost twelve hundred men ii 1 24
I will make a complimental assault upon him *Troi. and Cres.* iii 1 42
For the defence of a town, our general is excellent.—Ay, and for an assault too *Coriolanus* iv 5 180
Thou shalt no sooner March to assault thy country than to tread—Trust to't, thou shalt not—on thy mother's womb v 3 123
With furbish'd arms and new supplies of men Began a fresh assault *Macb.* i 2 33
A savageness in unreclaimed blood, Of general assault *Hamlet* ii 1 35
Speak with me, Or, naked as I am, I will assault thee *Othello* v 2 258
The assault you have made to her chastity you shall answer me *Cymbeline* i 4 175
The king my father shall be made acquainted Of thy assault i 6 150

Assault. Such assaults As would take in some virtue . . *Cymbeline* iii 2 8
Assaulted. Worse, To have her gentleman abused, assaulted . *Lear* ii 2 156
Assay. That he dares in this manner assay me . . . *Mer. Wives* ii 1 26
Bid herself assay him: I have great hope in that . *Meas. for Meas.* i 2 186
Assay the power you have.—My power? Alas, I doubt . . . i 4 76
He hath made an assay of her virtue to practise his judgement . iii 1 164
Why then to-night Let us assay our plot . . . *All's Well* iii 7 44
Seeing thou fall'st on me so luckily, I will assay thee . . 1 *Hen. IV.* v 4 34
Galling the gleaned land with hot assays . . . *Hen. V.* i 2 151
I would assay, proud queen, to make thee blush . . 3 *Hen. VI.* i 4 118
Let us make the assay upon him . . . *T. of Athens* iv 3 406
Their malady convinces The great assay of art . . *Macbeth* iv 3 143
With windlasses and with assays of bias . . . *Hamlet* ii 1 65
Makes vow before his uncle never more To give the assay of arms . ii 2 71
Did you assay him To any pastime? . . . iii 1 14
Help, angels! Make assay! Bow, stubborn knees! . . iii 3 69
This cannot be, By no assay of reason . . . *Othello* i 3 18
Do not put me to't; For I am nothing, if not critical.—Come on, assay ii 1 121
And passion, having my best judgement collied, Assays to lead the way ii 3 207
Assayed. What if we assay'd to steal The clownish fool? . *As Y. Like It* i 3 131
The rebels have assay'd to win the Tower . . 2 *Hen. VI.* iv 5 9
If this should fail, And that our drift look through our bad performance, 'Twere better not assay'd . . . *Hamlet* iv 7 153
Assaying. Till I have brought him to his wits again, Or lose my labour in assaying it . . . *Com. of Errors* v 1 97
Assemblance. Care I for the limb, the thewes, the stature, bulk, and big assemblance of a man! . . . 2 *Hen. IV.* iii 2 277
Assemble. To the state of my great grief Let kings assemble . *K. John* iii 1 71
To the English court assemble now, From every region, apes of idleness! 2 *Hen. IV.* iv 5 122
Let them assemble, And on a safer judgement all revoke Your ignorant election . . . *Coriolanns* ii 3 225
Assemble presently the people hither . . . iii 3 12
Assemble all the poor men of your sort . . . *J. Cæsar* i 1 62
And to that end Assemble we immediate council . *Ant. and Cleo.* i 4 75
Assembled. And all that are assembled in this place *Com. of Errors* v 1 396
When that your flock, assembled by the bell, Encircled you 2 *Hen. IV.* iv 2 5
For which we have in head assembled them . . *Hen. V.* ii 2 18
Defences, musters, preparations, Should be maintain'd, assembled . ii 4 19
Which to reduce into our former favour You are assembled . . v 2 64
Whom all France with their chief assembled strength Durst not presume to look once in the face . . . 1 *Hen. VI.* i 1 139
All manner of men assembled here in arms this day against God's peace i 3 74
He wonders to what end you have assembled Such troops of citizens *Richard III.* iii 7 84
The elect o' the land, who are assembled To plead your cause *Hen. VIII.* ii 4 60
He hath assembled Bocchus, the king of Libya; Archelaus *Ant. and Cleo.* iii 6 68
Assemblies. Held in idle price to haunt assemblies . . *Meas. for Meas.* i 3 9
Haply, in private.—And in assemblies too . . *Com. of Errors* v 1 60
Assembly. To disgrace Hero before the whole assembly . *Much Ado* iv 2 57
Good morrow to this fair assembly.—Good morrow . . . v 4 34
We have no temple but the wood, no assembly but horn-beasts *As Y. Like It* iii 3 50
That bring these tidings to this fair assembly . . . v 4 159
Is this proceeding just and honourable?—Is your assembly so? 2 *Hen. IV.* iv 2 111
Which was never seen before in such an assembly . . . Epil. 26
By whom this great assembly is contrived . . *Hen. V.* v 2 6
Having heard by fame Of this so noble and so fair assembly . *Hen. VIII.* i 4 67
You hold a fair assembly; you do well, lord . . . i 4 87
What do you think, You, the great toe of this assembly? . *Coriolanus* i 1 159
Have hearts Inclinable to honour and advance The theme of our assembly ii 2 61
A fair assembly: whither should they come? . . *Rom. and Jul.* i 2 75
Let no assembly of twenty be without a score of villains *T. of Athens* iii 6 86
If there be any in this assembly, any dear friend of Cæsar's . *J. Cæsar* iii 2 19
I here take my oath before this honourable assembly . . *Lear* iii 6 49
Assent. Without the king's assent or knowledge . *Hen. VIII.* iii 2 310
By the main assent Of all these learned men . . . iv 1 31
Assez. C'est assez pour une fois: allons-nous à dîner . *Hen. V.* iii 4 65
Ass-head. What do I see on thee?—What do you see? you see an ass-head of your own . . . *M. N. Dream* iii 1 119
An ass-head and a coxcomb and a knave, a thin-faced knave . *T. Night* v 1 212
Assign. I pray Your highness to assign our trial day . *Richard II.* i 1 151
Till we assign you to your days of trial . . . iv 1 106
Six French rapiers and poniards, with their assigns . . *Hamlet* v 2 157
Six Barbary horses against six French swords, their assigns . . v 2 169
To his conveyance I assign my wife . . . *Othello* i 3 286
Assigned. In their assign'd and native dwelling-place . *As Y. Like It* ii 1 63
England, from Trent and Severn hitherto, By south and east is to my part assign'd . . . 1 *Hen. IV.* iii 1 75
Assign'd am I to be the English scourge . . 1 *Hen. VI.* i 2 129
To Ptolemy he assign'd Syria, Cilicia, and Phœnicia . *Ant. and Cleo.* iii 6 15
Assinego. An assinego may tutor thee . . *Troi. and Cres.* ii 1 49
Assist. Keep your cabins: you do assist the storm . . *Tempest* i 1 15
Let's assist them, For our case is as theirs . . . i 1 57
Gentle girl, assist me; And even in kind love I do conjure thee *T. G. of Ver.* ii 7 1
Villain, go! Assist me, knight. I am undone! Fly, run! *Mer. Wives* iv 5 92
Assist me in my purpose, And, as I am a gentleman, I'll give thee A hundred pound in gold more than your loss . . . iv 6 3
Now, the hot-blooded gods assist me! . . . v 5 3
If you will take it on you to assist him, it shall redeem you from your gyves . . . *Meas. for Meas.* iv 2 11
You are both sure, and will assist me?—To the death . . *Much Ado* i 3 71
Midnight, assist our moan; Help us to sigh and groan . . . v 3 16
My father's wit and my mother's tongue, assist me! . . *L. L. Lost* i 2 101
Assist me, some extemporal god of rhyme . . . i 2 189
Wherein your cunning can assist me much . . *T. of Shrew* Ind. 1 92
Assist me, Tranio, for I know thou wilt . . . i 1 163
Assist me, then, sweet Warwick, and I will . . 3 *Hen. VI.* i 1 28
We'll all assist you; he that flies shall die . . . i 1 30
The gods assist you!—And keep your honours safe! . . *Coriolanus* i 2 36
Let me find a charter in your voice, To assist my simpleness . . *Othello* i 3 247
If the great gods be just, they shall assist The deeds of justest men *Ant. and Cleo.* ii 1 1
Help me, my women,—we must draw thee up: Assist, good friends . iv 15 31
Patience, good sir; do not assist the storm . . *Pericles* iii 1 19
Assistance. Minister such assistance as I shall give you direction *M. Ado* ii 1 385
I have acquainted you withal, to the end to crave your assistance *L. L. Lost* v 1 123

Assistance. We will alone uphold, Without the assistance of a mortal hand . . . *K. John* iii 1 158
With a treacherous fine of all your lives, If Lewis by your assistance win v 4 39
Towards our assistance we do seize to us The plate, coin *Richard II.* ii 1 160
Swore him assistance and perform'd it too . . 1 *Hen. IV.* iv 3 65
We should not step too far Till we had his assistance by the hand 2 *Hen. IV.* i 3 21
I had many living to upbraid My gain of it by their assistances . . iv 5 194
By the heavens' assistance and your strength . . 3 *Hen. VI.* v 4 68
By thy advice And thy assistance is King Richard seated *Richard III.* iv 2 4
Affecting one sole throne, Without assistance . . . *Coriolanus* iv 6 33
Nothing doubting your present assistance therein . . *T. of Athens* iii 1 21
Thence it is, That I to your assistance do make love . . *Macbeth* iii 1 124
Assistant. Even as you came in to me, her assistant or go-between parted from me . . . *Mer. Wives* ii 2 273
To be rendered by our assistants, at the king's command . *L. L. Lost* v 1 127
Ask those on the banks If they were his assistants, yea or no *Rich. III.* iv 4 526
Neither allied To eminent assistants . . . *Hen. VIII.* i 1 62
Come, go with me, In one respect I'll thy assistant be . *Rom. and Jul.* ii 3 90
As the winds give benefit And convoy is assistant . . *Hamlet* i 3 3
Let me be no assistant for a state, But keep a farm and carters . . ii 2 166
Assisted with your honour'd friends, Bring them to our embracement *W. Tale* v 1 113
You'll think—Which I protest against—I am assisted By wicked powers v 3 90
Assisted by that most disloyal traitor, The thane of Cawdor . *Macbeth* i 2 52
Assisting. You shall have me assisting you in all . . *T. of Shrew* i 2 196
Associate. Friends should associate friends in grief and woe *T. Andron.* v 3 169
Going to find a bare-foot brother out, One of our order, to associate me, Here in this city visiting the sick . . *Rom. and Jul.* v 2 6
The bark is ready, and the wind at help, The associates tend . *Hamlet* iv 3 47
Associated. Led by Caius Marcius Associated with Aufidius *Coriolanus* iv 6 76
Assuage. The good gods assuage thy wrath . . . v 2 83
Assubjugate. Nor, by my will, assubjugate his merit . *Troi. and Cres.* ii 3 202
Assume. I will assume thy part in some disguise . . *Much Ado* i 1 323
My very visor began to assume life and scold with her . . ii 1 249
'As much as he deserves.' I will assume desert . *Mer. of Venice* ii 9 51
There is no vice so simple but assumes Some mark of virtue . . iii 2 81
And these assume but valour's excrement To render them redoubted! . iii 2 87
If spirits can assume both form and suit You come to fright us *T. Night* v 1 242
Assume the port of Mars . . . *Hen. V.* Prol. 6
Hit or miss, Our project's life this shape of sense assumes *Troi. and Cres.* i 3 385
And loss assume all reason Without revolt . . . v 2 145
Do not assume my likeness . . . *T. of Athens* iv 3 218
If it assume my noble father's person, I'll speak to it . *Hamlet* i 2 244
And there assume some other horrible form . . . i 4 72
The devil hath power To assume a pleasing shape . . . ii 2 629
Assume a virtue, if you have it not . . . iii 4 160
To assume a semblance That very dogs disdain'd . . *Lear* v 3 187
Like a bold champion, I assume the lists . . *Pericles* i 1 61
Assumed. He it is that hath Assumed this age . . *Cymbeline* v 5 319
Assuming man's infirmities, To glad your ear . *Pericles* i Gower 3
Assurance. 'Tis far off And rather like a dream than an assurance *Temp.* i 2 45
For more assurance that a living prince Does now speak to thee . v 1 108
My assurance bids me search . . . *Mer. Wives* iii 2 47
That jealousy shall be called assurance . . . *Much Ado* ii 2 50
And, for the more better assurance, tell them that I Pyramus am not Pyramus, but Bottom . . . *M. N. Dream* iii 1 21
Let your father make her the assurance, She is your own *T. of Shrew* ii 1 389
The Sunday following, shall Bianca Be bride to you, if you make this assurance . . . ii 1 398
And make assurance here in Padua Of greater sums than I have promised . . . iii 2 136
And give assurance to Baptista Minola, As if he were the right Vincentio . . . iv 2 69
To pass assurance of a dower in marriage . . . iv 2 117
Such assurance ta'en As shall with either part's agreement stand . . iv 4 49
They are busied about a counterfeit assurance . . . iv 4 92
Take you assurance of her, 'cum privilegio ad imprimendum solum' iv 4 92
Therefore for assurance Let's each one send unto his wife . . v 2 65
Give me modest assurance if you be the lady of the house . *T. Night* i 5 192
Put your lord into a desperate assurance she will none of him . ii 2 8
Underneath that consecrated roof, Plight me the full assurance of your faith . . . iv 3 26
For by this knot thou shalt so surely tie Thy now unsured assurance to the crown . . . *K. John* ii 1 471
You should procure him better assurance than Bardolph . 2 *Hen. IV.* i 2 36
Give me assurance with some friendly vow . 3 *Hen. VI.* iv 1 141
Look your faith be firm, Or else his head's assurance is but frail *Richard III.* iv 4 498
No judge indifferent, nor no more assurance Of equal friendship *Hen. VIII.* ii 4 17
Assurance bless your thoughts! . . . *T. of Athens* ii 2 189
But yet I'll make assurance double sure, And take a bond of fate *Macbeth* iv 1 83
A combination and a form indeed, Where every god did seem to set his seal, To give the world assurance of a man . . *Hamlet* iii 4 62
They are sheep and calves which seek out assurance in that . . v 1 126
By an auricular assurance have your satisfaction . . *Lear* i 2 99
And, from some knowledge and assurance, offer This office to you . . iii 1 41
Quite forego The way which promises assurance . . *Ant. and Cleo.* iii 7 47
Assure. In his grave Assure thyself my love is buried . *T. G. of Ver.* iv 2 115
You have charms, la; yes, in truth.—Not I, I assure thee *Mer. Wives* ii 2 109
A marvellous witty fellow, I assure you . . . *Much Ado* iv 2 27
Sir, I assure ye, it was a buck of the first head . . *L. L. Lost* iv 2 10
You cannot beg us, sir, I can assure you, sir . . . v 2 490
A very good piece of work, I assure you, and a merry . *M. N. Dream* i 2 14
I assure thee, and almost with tears I speak it . . *As Y Like It* i 1 159
And, for that dowry, I'll assure her of Her widowhood . *T. of Shrew* ii 1 124
He of both That can assure my daughter greatest dower Shall have my Bianca's love . . . ii 1 345
Say, Signior Gremio, what can you assure her? . . . ii 1 347
These I will assure her, And twice as much, whate'er thou offer'st next ii 1 381
'Tis now some seven o'clock . . .—I dare assure you, sir, 'tis almost two iv 3 191
I know not how I shall assure you further . . . *All's Well* iii 7 2
I hear there is an overture of peace.—Nay, I assure you, a peace concluded . . . iv 3 47
And, to comfort you with chance, Assure yourself . *T. Night* i 2 9
Assure thyself, there is no love-broker in the world can more prevail . iii 2 38
I do assure you, 'tis against my will . . . iii 4 342
I look to be either earl or duke, I can assure you . . . 1 *Hen. IV.* v 4 146

Assure. He may keep his own grace, but he's almost out of mine, I can assure him . . . *2 Hen. IV.* i 2 33
The knave will stick by thee, I can assure thee that . . . v 3 70
I'll assure you, a' uttered as prave words at the pridge . *Hen. V.* iii 6 66
My heart assures me that the Earl of Warwick Shall one day make the Duke of York a king.—And, Nevil, this I do assure myself *2 Hen. VI.* ii 2 78
Henry, though he be infortunate, Assure yourselves, will never be unkind . . . iv 9 19
This shall assure my constant loyalty . . . *3 Hen. VI.* iii 3 240
There will be The beauty of this kingdom, I'll assure you . *Hen. VIII.* i 3 54
Never greater, Nor, I'll assure you, better taken, sir . . iv 1 12
I fear We shall be much unwelcome.—That I assure you *Troi. and Cres.* iv 1 45
Assure thee, Lucius, 'Twill vex thy soul to hear what I shall speak *T. Andron.* v 1 61
Therefore thy earliness doth me assure Thou art up-roused by some distemperature . . . *Rom. and Jul.* ii 3 39
Brutus is safe enough: I dare assure thee that no enemy Shall ever take alive the noble Brutus . . . *J. Cæsar* v 4 21
I assure my good liege, I hold my duty, as I hold my soul *Hamlet* ii 2 43
I'll not be there.—Nor I, assure thee . . . *Lear* ii 1 106
Assure thee, if I do vow a friendship, I'll perform it . *Othello* iii 3 20
Assure yourself I will seek satisfaction of you . . . iv 2 202
Never plucked yet, I can assure you . . . *Pericles* iv 6 46
I assure you *Tempest* ii 1; *M. Ado* ii 3; *M. N. Dream* v 1; *As Y. L. It* iv 3; *T. Night* iii 4; *Hen. V.* iii 6; *J. Cæsar* v 4
I do assure thee [you] *Tempest* ii 2; *L. L. Lost* v 1; *T. of Shrew* iv 5; *All's Well* ii 5; *1 Hen. IV.* ii 4; *Hen. VIII.* ii 2
Assured. Most ignorant of what he's most assured . *Meas. for Meas.* ii 2 119
Called me Dromio; swore I was assured to her *Com. of Errors* iii 2 145
Be assured, My purse, my person, my extremest means, Lie all unlock'd to your occasions . . . *Mer. of Venice* i 1 137
Be assured you may.—I will be assured I may; and, that I may be assured, I will bethink me . . . i 3 29
As thou urgest justice, be assured Thou shalt have justice . . iv 1 315
I'll plead for you As for my patron, stand you so assured *T. of Shrew* i 2 156
As 'twere, a man assured of a— Uncertain life, and sure death *All's Well* ii 3 19
I am well assured That I did so when I was first assured . *K. John* ii 1 534
Assured loss before the match be play'd . . . iii 1 336
Are gone and fled, As well assured Richard their king is dead *Richard II.* ii 4 17
Which, for divers reasons . . . , be assured, Will easily be granted *1 Hen. IV.* i 3 263
'Tis very true: And therefore be assured . *2 Hen. IV.* iv 1 220
Thou lovedst me not, And thou wilt have me die assured of it . iv 5 106
Though no man be assured what grace to find, You stand in coldest expectation . . . v 2 30
I bid you be assured, I'll be your father and your brother too . v 2 56
You are, I think, assured I love you not.—I am assured . . v 2 64
Be assured, you'll find a difference . . . *Hen. V.* ii 4 134
I come to know of thee, King Harry, If for thy ransom thou wilt now compound, Before thy most assured overthrow . . iv 3 81
Her aid she promised and assured success . . *1 Hen. VI.* i 2 82
But this I am assured, I feel such sharp dissension in my breast . v 5 83
Yet be well assured You put sharp weapons in a madman's hands *2 Hen. VI.* iii 1 346
I will repeal thee, or, be well assured, Adventure to be banished myself iii 2 349
Be well assured Her faction will be full as strong as ours . *3 Hen. VI.* iv 3 16
Be you, good lord, assured I hate not you for her proud arrogance *Richard III.* i 3 23
Be assured We come to use our hands and not our tongues . . i 3 352
When I have most need to employ a friend, And most assured that he is a friend . . . ii 1 37
Unless I have mista'en his colours much, Which well I am assured I have not done . . . v 3 36
To desperate ventures and assured destruction . . . v 3 319
Resting well assured They ne'er did service for't . *Coriolanus* iii 1 121
Being assured none but myself could move thee . . . v 2 79
Yet remain assured That he's a made-up villain . *T. of Athens* v 1 100
That I may rest assured Whether yond troops are friend or enemy *J. Cæsar* v 3 17
Be assured He closes with you in this consequence . *Hamlet* ii 1 44
Be thou assured, if words be made of breath, And breath of life, I have no life to breathe What thou hast said to me . . . iii 4 197
If thou shouldst dally half an hour, his life, With thine, and all that offer to defend him, Stand in assured loss . . . *Lear* iii 6 102
Would I were assured Of my condition! . . . iv 7 56
Be assured of this, That the magnifico is much beloved . *Othello* i 2 11
Be thou assured, good Cassio, I will do All my abilities in thy behalf iii 3 1
Be you well assured He shall in strangeness stand no further off . iii 3 11
But be you well assured, No more than he'll unswear . . iv 1 30
Be assured you shall not find me, daughter, After the slander of most stepmothers, Evil-eyed unto you . . . *Cymbeline* i 1 70
When shall we hear from him?—Be assured, madam, With his next vantage . . . i 3 23
Which she after, Except she bend her humour, shall be assured To taste of . . . i 5 81
Will his free hours languish for Assured bondage . . . i 6 73
The credit that thy lady hath of thee Deserves thy trust, and thy most perfect goodness Her assured credit . . . i 6 159
Were I well assured Came of a gentle kind and noble stock . *Pericles* v 1 67
Assuredly the thing is to be sold . . *As Y. Like It* ii 4 96
This night the siege assuredly I'll raise . . *1 Hen. VI.* i 2 130
Which I feel I am not worthy yet to wear: I shall, assuredly *Hen. VIII.* iv 2 92
Assuredly you know me.—No matter, sir . . *Ant. and Cleo.* v 2 72
Assyrian. O base Assyrian knight, what is thy news? . *2 Hen. IV.* v 3 105
As swift as stones Enforced from the old Assyrian slings . *Hen. V.* iv 7 65
Astonish. Whose beauty did astonish the survey Of richest eyes *All's Well* v 3 16
That with the very shaking of their chains They may astonish these fell-lurking curs . . . *2 Hen. VI.* v 1 146
It is the part of men to fear and tremble, When the most mighty gods by tokens send Such dreadful heralds to astonish us . *J. Cæsar* i 3 56
O wonderful son, that can so astonish a mother! . . *Hamlet* iii 2 340
Astonished. Enough, captain: you have astonished him . *Hen. V.* v 1 40
Thou hast astonish'd me with thy high terms . . *1 Hen. VI.* i 2 93
Your wondrous rare description, noble earl, Of beauteous Margaret hath astonish'd me . . . v 5 2
Astræa. Divinest creature, Astræa's daughter, How shall I honour thee for this success? . . . i 6 4
Terras Astræa reliquit: Be you remember'd, Marcus, she's gone *T. And.* iv 3 4
Astray. Nay: in that you are astray, 'twere best pound you *T. G. of Ver.* i 1 109
Lead these testy rivals so astray As one come not within another's way *M. N. Dream* iii 2 358

Astronomer. When he performs, astronomers foretell it *Troi. and Cres.* v 1 100
Learn'd indeed were that astronomer That knew the stars as I his characters: He'ld lay the future open . . . *Cymbeline* iii 2 27
Astronomical. How long have you been a sectary astronomical? *Lear* i 2 164
Asunder. It appears so by his weapons. Keep them asunder *M. Wives* iii 1 74
And will you rent our ancient love asunder? . . *M. N. Dream* iii 2 215
Having hold of both, They whirl asunder and dismember me *K. John* iii 1 330
Two mighty monarchies, Whose high upreared and abutting fronts The perilous narrow ocean parts asunder . . . *Hen. V.* Prol. 22
And from my shoulders crack my arms asunder . . *1 Hen. VI.* i 5 11
A pair of loving turtle-doves That could not live asunder day or night . ii 2 31
Hew them to pieces, hack their bones asunder . . . iv 7 47
Let them be clapp'd up close, And kept asunder . . *2 Hen. VI.* i 4 54
And so he comes, to rend his limbs asunder . . . *3 Hen. VI.* i 3 15
To be winnow'd, where my chaff And corn shall fly asunder *Hen. VIII.* v 1 111
Cracking ten thousand curbs Of more strong link asunder . *Coriolanus* i 1 73
Villain and he be many miles asunder . . . *Rom. and Jul.* iii 5 82
Hold off thy hand.—Pluck them asunder . . . *Hamlet* v 1 287
Let what is here contain'd relish of love, Of my lord's health, of his content, yet not That we two are asunder . . . *Cymbeline* iii 2 32
At all. Here's neither bush nor shrub, to bear off any weather at all *Tempest* ii 2 19
This must crave, An if this be at all, a most strange story . . v 1 117
Sir, I could perceive nothing at all from her . . *T. G. of Ver.* i 1 144
They say that Love hath not an eye at all . . . ii 4 96
It is no sin at all, but charity . . . *Meas. for Meas.* ii 4 66
Gentle daughter, fear you not at all. He is your husband on a precontract . . . iv 1 71
Else none at all in aught proves excellent . . *L. L. Lost* iv 3 354
I was never curst; I have no gift at all in shrewishness *M. N. Dream* iii 2 301
Do you think he will make no deed at all of this? . *All's Well* iii 6 103
Which comes to me in name of fault, I must not At all acknowledge *W. Tale* iii 2 62
What do we then but draw anew the model In fewer offices, or at last desist To build at all? . . . *2 Hen. IV.* i 3 48
A third thinks, without expense at all, By guileful fair words peace may be obtain'd . . . *1 Hen. VI.* i 1 76
Better it were they all came by the father, Or by the father there were none at all . . . *Richard III.* ii 3 24
This no more dishonours you at all . . . *Coriolanus* iii 2 58
Come, vial. What if this mixture do not work at all? . *Rom. and Jul.* iv 3 21
Without more circumstance at all, I hold it fit that we shake hands *Ham.* i 5 127
At hand. Captain of our fairy band, Helena is here at hand *M. N. Dr.* iii 2 111
Signify, I pray you, Within the house, your mistress is at hand *M. of V.* v 1 52
Like a lion foster'd up at hand . . . *K. John* v 2 75
Like horses hot at hand, Make gallant show . . *J. Cæsar* iv 2 23
At it. They are at it, hark! . . . *Troi. and Cres.* v 3 95
Ajax hath lost a friend And foams at mouth, and he is arm'd and at it . v 5 36
O, they are at it!—Their noise be our instruction . *Coriolanus* i 4 21
At length the sun, gazing upon the earth, Dispersed those vapours *Com. of Errors* i 1 89
With much ado at length have gotten leave . . *Richard II.* v 5 74
My high-blown pride At length broke under me . . *Hen. VIII.* iii 2 362
At length her grace rose, and with modest paces Came to the altar . iv 1 82
And at length How goes our reckoning? . . *T. of Athens* ii 2 158
Our griefs are risen to the top, And now at length they overflow *Pericles* ii 4 24
At once. We could at once put us in readiness . . *T. of Shrew* i 1 43
With thy sharp teeth this knot intrinsicate Of life at once untie *A. and C.* v 2 308
Atalanta's better part, Sad Lucretia's modesty . . *As Y. Like It* iii 2 155
You have a nimble wit: I think 'twas made of Atalanta's heels . iii 2 294
Ate. You shall find her the infernal Ate in good apparel . *Much Ado* ii 1 263
More Ates, more Ates! stir them on! stir them on! . *L. L. Lost* v 2 694
An Ate, stirring him to blood and strife . . . *K. John* ii 1 63
Cæsar's spirit, ranging for revenge, With Ate by his side . *J. Cæsar* iii 1 271
Athenian. Stir up the Athenian youth to merriments *M. N. Dream* i 1 12
To that place the sharp Athenian law Cannot pursue us . . i 1 162
A sweet Athenian lady is in love With a disdainful youth . . ii 1 260
Thou shalt know the man By the Athenian garments he hath on . ii 1 264
Through the forest have I gone, But Athenian found I none . ii 2 67
This is he, my master said, Despised the Athenian maid . . ii 2 73
Rude mechanicals, That work for bread upon Athenian stalls . iii 2 10
But hast thou yet latch'd the Athenian's eyes With the love-juice? . iii 2 36
I took him sleeping, . . . And the Athenian woman by his side . iii 2 39
This is the same Athenian.—This is the woman, but not this the man . iii 2 41
I should know the man By the Athenian garments he had on . iii 2 349
Blameless proves my enterprise, That I have 'nointed an Athenian's eyes iii 2 351
Take this transformed scalp From off the head of this Athenian swain . iv 1 70
Without the peril of the Athenian law . . . iv 1 158
Ask me not what; for if I tell you, I am no true Athenian . iv 2 31
To be sung By an Athenian eunuch to the harp . . . v 1 45
From the Athenian bay Put forth toward Phrygia . *Troi. and Cres.* Prol. 6
Are they not Athenians? . . . *T. of Athens* i 1 182
Whither art going?—To knock out an honest Athenian's brains . i 1 192
Thou'rt an Athenian, therefore welcome . . . i 2 35
Itches, blains, Sow all the Athenian bosoms! . . . iv 1 29
The gods confound—hear me, you good gods all—The Athenians! . iv 1 38
Is this the Athenian minion, whom the world Voiced so regardfully? . iv 3 80
It is our part and promise to the Athenians To speak with Timon . v 1 123
The Athenians, By two of their most reverend senate, greet thee . v 1 131
Spare thy Athenian cradle . . . v 4 40
Come, good Athenian.—No words, no words: hush . . *Lear* iii 4 185
Athens. I beg the ancient privilege of Athens . *M. N. Dream* i 1 41
Fit your fancies to your father's will; Or else the law of Athens yields you up—Which by no means we may extenuate . . i 1 119
From Athens is her house remote seven leagues . . . i 1 159
Before the time I did Lysander see, Seem'd Athens as a paradise to me i 1 205
Through Athens' gates have we devised to steal . . . i 1 213
And thence from Athens turn away our eyes, To seek new friends . i 1 218
Through Athens I am thought as fair as she. But what of that? . i 1 227
Here is the scroll of every man's name, which is thought fit, through all Athens, to play . . . i 2 5
Who is here? Weeds of Athens he doth wear . . . ii 2 71
He murder cries and help from Athens calls . . . iii 2 26
Go swifter than the wind, And Helena of Athens look thou find . iii 2 95
To Athens will I bear my folly back And follow you no further . iii 2 315
Back to Athens shall the lovers wend . . . iii 2 372
Shine comforts from the east, That I may back to Athens by daylight . iii 2 433
May all to Athens back again repair . . . iv 1 72
Our intent Was to be gone from Athens . . . iv 1 157
Our purposed hunting shall be set aside. Away with us to Athens . iv 1 189

Athens. You have not a man in all Athens able to discharge Pyramus but he . . . *M. N. Dream* iv 2 8
He hath simply the best wit of any handicraft man in Athens . . iv 2 10
Hard-handed men that work in Athens here . . v 1 72
The princes orgulous, their high blood chafed, Have to the port of Athens sent their ships . . *Troi. and Cres.* Prol. 3
How this lord is follow'd!—The senators of Athens: happy man! *T. of A.* i 1 40
Whence are you?—Of Athens here, my lord . . ii 2 17
How does that honourable, complete, free-hearted gentleman of Athens? iii 1 10
I would not, for the wealth of Athens, I had done't now . . iii 2 57
If, after two days' shine, Athens contain thee, Attend our weightier judgement . . iii 5 101
It is a cause worthy my spleen and fury, That I may strike at Athens . iii 5 114
The senators of Athens, together with the common lag of people . . iii 6 90
Sink, Athens! henceforth hated be Of Timon man and all humanity! . iii 6 114
O thou wall, That girdlest in those wolves, dive in the earth, And fence not Athens! . . iv 1 3
Plagues, incident to men, Your potent and infectious fevers heap On Athens! . . iv 1 23
Cursed Athens, mindless of thy worth, Forgetting thy great deeds . iv 3 93
When I have laid proud Athens on a heap,— Warr'st thou 'gainst Athens? iv 3 101
Strike up the drum towards Athens! Farewell, Timon . . iv 3 169
That the whole life of Athens were in this! Thus would I eat it . iv 3 281
What wouldst thou have to Athens?—Thee thither in a whirlwind . iv 3 287
The commonwealth of Athens is become a forest of beasts . . iv 3 352
To Athens go, Break open shops . . iv 3 449
Let us first see peace in Athens . . iv 3 461
You shall see him a palm in Athens again, and flourish with the highest v 1 13
Thou draw'st a counterfeit Best in all Athens . . v 1 84
The senators of Athens greet thee, Timon.—I thank them . v 1 139
The senators with one consent of love Entreat thee back to Athens . v 1 144
And of our Athens, thine and ours, to take The captainship . . v 1 163
Shakes his threatening sword Against the walls of Athens . . v 1 170
Sack fair Athens, And take our goodly aged men by the beards . . v 1 174
I do prize it at my love before The reverend'st throat in Athens . v 1 185
Tell Athens, in the sequence of degree From high to low throughout . v 1 211
Before proud Athens he's set down by this . . v 3 9
He lessens his requests; and to thee sues To let him breathe between the heavens and earth, A private man in Athens *Ant. and Cleo.* iii 12 15
Athol. The Earl of Athol, Of Murray, Angus, and Menteith . *1 Hen. IV.* i 1 72
Athversary. Th' athversary, you may discuss unto the duke *Hen. V.* iii 2 65
Th' athversary was have possession of the pridge . . iii 6 98
The perdition of th' athversary hath been very great, reasonable great iii 6 103
Athwart. And quite athwart Goes all decorum . . *Meas. for Meas.* i 3 30
Whatsoever comes athwart his affection ranges evenly with mine *Much Ado* ii 2 6
Nor never lay his wreathed arms athwart His loving bosom to keep down his heart . . *L. L. Lost* iv 3 135
Swears brave oaths and breaks them bravely, quite traverse, athwart the heart of his lover . . *As Y. Like It* iii 4 45
When all athwart there came A post . . *1 Hen. IV.* i 1 36
Heave him away upon your winged thoughts Athwart the sea *Hen. V.* v Prol. 9
Drawn with a team of little atomies Athwart men's noses *Rom. and Jul.* i 4 58
Atlas. Thou art no Atlas for so great a weight . . *3 Hen. VI.* v 1 36
Atomies. It is as easy to count atomies as to resolve the propositions of a lover . . *As Y. Like It* iii 2 245
The frail'st and softest things, Who shut their coward gates on atomies iii 5 13
Drawn with a team of little atomies Athwart men's noses *Rom. and Jul.* i 4 57
Atomy. Thou atomy, thou!—Come, you thin thing . *2 Hen. IV.* v 4 33
Atone. Then is there mirth in heaven, When earthly things made even Atone together . . *As Y. Like It* v 4 116
Since we can not atone you, we shall see Justice design the victor's chivalry . . *Richard II.* i 1 202
He and Aufidius can no more atone Than violentest contrariety *Coriolanus* iv 6 72
To atone your fears With my more noble meaning . *T. of Athens* v 4 58
A most unhappy one: I would do much To atone them . *Othello* iv 1 244
Remember that the present need Speaks to atone you . *Ant. and Cleo.* ii 2 102
I was glad I did atone my countryman and you . . *Cymbeline* i 4 42
Atonement. Will be glad to do my benevolence to make atonements *Mer. Wives* i 1 33
If we do now make our atonement well, Our peace will, like a broken limb united, Grow stronger for the breaking . *2 Hen. IV.* iv 1 221
Make atonement Betwixt the Duke of Gloucester and your brothers *Rich. III.* i 3 36
Atropos. The Sisters Three! Come, Atropos, I say! . *2 Hen. IV.* ii 4 213
Attach. Make present satisfaction, Or I'll attach you . *Com. of Errors* iv 1 6
Either consent to pay this sum for me Or I attach you by this officer . iv 1 73
Then homeward every man attach the hand Of his fair mistress *L. L. Lost* iv 3 375
Desires you to attach his son, who has . . . Fled from his father *W. Tale* v 1 182
If I could, by Him that gave me life, I would attach you all *Richard II.* ii 3 156
Of capital treason I attach you both . . *2 Hen. IV.* iv 2 109
Here is a warrant from The king to attach Lord Montacute . *Hen. VIII.* i 1 217
In whose name myself Attach thee as a traitorous innovator *Coriolanus* iii 1 175
Go, some of you, whoe'er you find attach . . *Rom. and Jul.* v 3 173
I therefore apprehend and do attach thee For an abuser of the world *Othello* i 2 77
Attached. Who am myself attach'd with weariness . . *Tempest* iii 3 5
That I should be attach'd in Ephesus, I tell you, 'twill sound harshly in her ears . . *Com. of Errors* iv 4 6
I had thought weariness durst not have attached one of so high blood *2 Hen. IV.* ii 2 3
My father was attached, not attainted . . *1 Hen. VI.* ii 4 96
Hath attach'd Our merchants' goods at Bourdeaux . . *Hen. VIII.* i 1 95
He is attach'd; Call him to present trial . . i 2 210
May worthy Troilus be half attach'd With that which here his passion doth express? . . *Troi. and Cres.* v 2 161
Attachment. Sleep kill those pretty eyes, And give as soft attachment to thy senses As infants' empty of all thought! . . iv 2 5
Attain. If opportunity and humblest suit Cannot attain it *Mer. Wives* iii 4 21
And so may I, blind fortune leading me, Miss that which one unworthier may attain . . *Mer. of Venice* ii 1 37
In the common course of all treasons, we still see them reveal themselves, till they attain to their abhorred ends . . *All's Well* iv 3 27
Your presence makes us rich, most noble lord.—And far surmounts our labour to attain it . . *Richard II.* ii 3 64
A . . . threatening cloud, That will encounter with our glorious sun, Ere he attain his easeful western bed . . *3 Hen. VI.* v 3 6
A beastly ambition, which the gods grant thee t' attain to! *T. of Athens* iv 3 330
But when he once attains the upmost round, He then unto the ladder turns his back . . *J. Cæsar* ii 1 24
Attain. I shall have glory by this losing day More than Octavius and Mark Antony By this vile conquest shall attain unto . *J. Cæsar* v 5 38
My bones would rest, That have but labour'd to attain this hour . v 5 42
To attain In suit the place of's bed and win this ring . *Cymbeline* v 5 184
Attainder. Stands in attainder of eternal shame . . *L. L. Lost* i 1 158
Mine honour soil'd With the attainder of his slanderous lips *Richard II.* iv 1 24
He lived from all attainder of suspect . . *Richard III.* iii 5 32
Attained. Or that the resolute acting of your blood Could have attain'd the effect of your own purpose . . *Meas. for Meas.* ii 1 13
The green corn Hath rotted ere his youth attain'd a beard *M. N. Dream* ii 1 95
Which once attain'd, Your highness knows, comes to no further use But to be known and hated . . *2 Hen. IV.* iv 4 71
These oracles are hardly attain'd, And hardly understood . *2 Hen. VI.* i 4 74
Fame, at the which he aims, In whom already he's well graced, can not Better be held nor more attain'd than by A place below the first *Coriolanus* i 1 269
Attaint. What simple thief brags of his own attaint? . *Com. of Errors* iii 2 16
Your sins are rack'd, You are attaint with faults and perjury *L. L. Lost* v 2 829
Freshly looks and over-bears attaint With cheerful semblance *Hen. V.* iv Prol. 39
Never yet attaint With any passion of inflaming love . *1 Hen. VI.* v 5 81
Nor any man an attaint but he carries some stain of it . *Troi. and Cres.* i 2 26
I arrest thee On capital treason; and, in thine attaint, This gilded serpent . . *Lear* v 3 83
Attainted, Corrupted, and exempt from ancient gentry . *1 Hen. VI.* ii 4 92
My father was attached, not attainted . . ii 4 96
Thou aimest all awry; I must offend before I be attainted . *2 Hen. VI.* ii 4 59
Attainture. Her attainture will be Humphrey's fall . . i 2 106
Attasked. You are much more attask'd for want of wisdom Than praised for harmful mildness . . *Lear* i 4 366
Attempt. He will never, I think, in the way of waste, attempt us again *Mer. Wives* iv 2 226
Our doubts are traitors And make us lose the good we oft might win By fearing to attempt . . *Meas. for Meas.* i 4 79
The maid will I frame and make fit for his attempt . . iii 1 267
Neither my coat, integrity, nor persuasion can with ease attempt you . iv 2 205
Either not attempt to choose at all Or swear before you choose *M. of Ven.* ii 1 39
That by direct or indirect attempts He seek the life of any citizen . iv 1 350
Of force I must attempt you further: Take some remembrance of us . iv 1 421
Embrace your own safety and give over this attempt . *As Y. Like It* i 2 190
A man may, if he were of a fearful heart, stagger in this attempt . iii 3 49
Impossible be strange attempts to those That weigh their pains in sense and do suppose What hath been cannot be . . *All's Well* i 1 239
I'll stay at home And pray God's blessing into thy attempt . i 3 260
I will grace the attempt for a worthy exploit . . iii 6 71
I know not what the success will be, my lord; but the attempt I vow . iii 6 87
Redeem it by some laudable attempt either of valour or policy *T. Night* iii 2 31
I will not return Till my attempt so much be glorified As to my ample hope was promised . . *K. John* v 2 111
Such poor, such bare, such lewd, such mean attempts . *1 Hen. IV.* iii 2 13
The quality and hair of our attempt Brooks no division . . iv 1 61
In hearty prayers That your attempts may overlive the hazard *2 Hen. IV.* iv 1 15
Though we here fall down, We have supplies to second our attempt . iv 2 45
In this haughty great attempt They laboured . . *1 Hen. VI.* ii 5 79
You that will follow me to this attempt, Applaud the name of Henry with your leader . . *3 Hen. VI.* iv 2 26
To warn false traitors from the like attempts . *Richard III.* iii 5 49
As I intend to prosper and repent, So thrive I in my dangerous attempt! iv 4 398
For me, the ransom of my bold attempt Shall be this cold corpse on the earth's cold face . . v 3 265
If I thrive, the gain of my attempt The least of you shall share . v 3 267
Never attempt Any thing on him; for he hath a witchcraft *Hen. VIII.* iii 2 17
The man was noble, But with his last attempt he wiped it out *Coriolanus* v 3 146
For which attempt the judges have pronounced My everlasting doom of banishment . . *T. Andron.* iii 1 50
And what love can do that dares love attempt . *Rom. and Jul.* ii 2 68
This man of thine Attempts her love . . *T. of Athens* i 1 126
One incorporate To our attempts . . *J. Cæsar* i 3 136
That whatsoever I did bid thee do, Thou shouldst attempt it . v 3 40
The attempt and not the deed Confounds us . . *Macbeth* ii 2 11
Hath so exasperate the king that he Prepares for some attempt of war iii 6 39
Neglecting an attempt of ease and gain . . *Othello* i 3 29
To do this is within the compass of man's wit; and therefore I will attempt the doing it . . iii 4 22
I will be near to second your attempt, and he shall fall between us . iv 2 245
If thou attempt it, it will cost thee dear . . v 2 255
I durst attempt it against any lady in the world . *Cymbeline* i 4 123
I doubt not you sustain what you're worthy of by your attempt . i 4 126
A repulse: though your attempt, as you call it, deserve more . i 4 128
This attempt I am soldier to, and will abide it with A prince's courage . iii 4 185
Attemptable. Chaste, constant-qualified and less attemptable . i 4 65
Attempted. How can that be true love which is falsely attempted? *L. L. Lost* i 2 177
I have attempted and With bloody passage led your wars . *Coriolanus* v 6 75
Attempting. I'll venge thy death, Or die renowned by attempting it *3 Hen. VI.* ii 1 88
Got praises of the king For him attempting who was self-subdued. *Lear* ii 2 129
Attend. Dost thou attend me?—Sir, most heedfully . *Tempest* i 2 78
Most sure, the goddess On whom these airs attend! . . i 2 422
One word more; I charge thee That thou attend me . . i 2 453
Shall step by step attend You and your ways . . iii 3 78
If Venus or her son, as thou dost know, Do now attend the queen . iv 1 88
Youthful Valentine, Attends the emperor in his royal court *T. G. of Ver.* i 3 27
We'll both attend upon your ladyship . . ii 4 121
I'll presently attend you.—Will you make haste? . . ii 4 189
Tarry I here, I but attend on death: But, fly I hence, I fly away from life . . iii 1 186
Your servant and your friend; One that attends your ladyship's command iv 3 5
The dinner attends you, sir.—I am not a-hungry, I thank you *Mer. Wives* i 1 279
At the deanery, where a priest attends, Straight marry her . iv 6 31
You orphan heirs of fixed destiny, Attend your office and your quality. v 5 44
At what hour to-morrow Shall I attend your lordship? *Meas. for Meas.* ii 2 160
My stay must be stolen out of other affairs; but I will attend you awhile iii 1 160
I shall attend your leisure: but make haste . . iv 1 57
Those, for their parents were exceeding poor, I bought and brought up to attend my sons . . *Com. of Errors* i 1 58
Then let your will attend on their accords . . ii 1 25
I will attend my husband, be his nurse, Diet his sickness . . v 1 98

Attend. We here attend you. Are you yet determined? . . *Much Ado* v 4 36
While we attend, Like humble-visaged suitors, his high will . *L. L. Lost* ii 1 33
Shall I tell you a thing?—We attend . . . v 1 153
Behold . . . mine eye, What humble suit attends thy answer there . v 2 849
Go with me; I'll give thee fairies to attend on thee. . *M. N. Dream* iii 1 160
Fairy king, attend, and mark: I do hear the morning lark . iv 1 98
We'll make our leisures to attend on yours . . *Mer. of Venice* i 1 68
Fair thoughts and happy hours attend on you! . . iii 4 41
The princesses call for you.—I attend them . *As Y. Like It* i 2 177
He attends here in the forest on the duke your father . . iii 4 36
I must attend the duke at dinner: by two o'clock I will be with thee . iv 1 184
Let one attend him with a silver basin Full of rose-water *T. of Shrew* Ind. 1 55
Thy servants do attend on thee, Each in his office ready at thy beck Ind. 2 35
I will attend her here, And woo her with some spirit when she comes . ii 1 169
What mockery will it be, To want the bridegroom when the priest attends! . . . iii 2 5
Obey the bride, you that attend on her . . . iii 2 225
I must attend his majesty's command . . . *All's Well* i 1 4
He cannot want the best That shall attend his love. . . i 1 82
Receive The confirmation of my promised gift, Which but attends thy naming . . . ii 3 57
The solemn feast Shall more attend upon the coming space . ii 3 188
That, having this obtain'd, you presently Attend his further pleasure . ii 4 54
She will attend it better in thy youth Than in a nuncio's of more grave aspect . . . *T. Night* i 4 27
Some four or five attend him; All, if you will . . . i 4 36
Grace and good disposition Attend your ladyship! . . . iii 1 147
He attends your ladyship's pleasure.—I'll come to him . . iii 4 64
Full of despite, bloody as the hunter, attends thee at the orchard-end iii 4 243
We are yours i' the garden: shall's attend you there? . *W. Tale* i 2 178
Hubert shall be your man, attend on you With all true duty . *K. John* iii 3 72
Your fears, which, as they say, attend The steps of wrong . . iv 2 56
Nor attend the foot That leaves the print of blood where'er it walks . iv 3 25
Give me leave to speak.—No, I will speak.—We will attend to neither . v 2 163
Dull unfeeling barren ignorance Is made my gaoler to attend on me *Richard II.* i 3 169
In the base court he doth attend To speak with you . . iii 3 176
He apprehends a world of figures here, But not the form of what he should attend . . . *1 Hen. IV.* i 3 210
I'll talk to you When you are better temper'd to attend . . i 3 235
Straight they shall be here: sit, and attend . . . iii 1 228
Tell thou the earl That the Lord Bardolph doth attend him here *2 Hen. IV.* i 1 3
Nor leave not one behind that doth not wish Success and conquest to attend on us . . . *Hen. V.* ii 2 24
That fear attends her not . . . ii 4 29
Shall I attend your grace?—No, my good knight . . iv 1 29
Upon a wooden coffin we attend . . . *1 Hen. VI.* i 1 19
Each hath his place and function to attend: I am left out . i 1 173
Tell her I return great thanks, And in submission will attend on her . ii 2 52
I will attend upon your lordship's leisure. . . v 1 55
May honourable peace attend thy throne! . *2 Hen. VI.* ii 3 38
And will that thou henceforth attend on us . . v 1 80
To White-Friars; there attend my coming . *Richard III.* i 2 227
Sin, death, and hell have set their marks on him, And all their ministers attend on him . . . i 3 294
Lords, will you go with us?—Madam, we will attend your grace . i 3 323
If black scandal or foul-faced reproach Attend the sequel . . iii 7 232
To-morrow, then, we will attend your grace . . iii 7 244
Shame serves thy life and doth thy death attend . . iv 4 195
Took he upon him, Without the privity o' the king, to appoint Who should attend on him? . . . *Hen. VIII.* i 1 75
I'll say't; and make my vouch as strong As shore of rock. Attend . i 1 158
You he bade Attend him here this morning . . . iii 2 82
He attends your highness' pleasure.—Bring him to us . . v 1 83
It is my duty To attend your highness' pleasure . . v 1 91
Their pleasures Must be fulfill'd, and I attend with patience . . v 2 19
All the virtues that attend the good, Shall still be doubled on her . v 5 28
Attend me where I wheel: Strike not a stroke. *Troi. and Cres.* v 7 2
You are transported by calamity Thither where more attends you *Coriolanus* i 1 78
Worthy Marcius, Attend upon Cominius to these wars . . i 1 241
Where, I know, Our greatest friends attend us.—Lead you on . i 1 249
Where great patricians shall attend and shrug, I' the end admire . i 9 4
On the market-place, I know, they do attend us . . ii 2 164
Let a guard Attend us through the city . . . iii 3 141
Attend the emperor's person carefully . . *T. Andron.* ii 2 8
I will most willingly attend your ladyship . . . iv 1 28
Marcus, attend him in his ecstasy . . . iv 1 125
Attend him carefully, And feed his humour kindly as we may . iv 3 28
If my frosty signs and chaps of age . . . Cannot induce you to attend . v 3 79
Even in the time When it should move you to attend me most . v 3 92
If you with patient ears attend . . *Rom. and Jul.* Prol. 13
Bear hence this body and attend our will . . . iii 1 201
'Banished'? O friar, the damned use that word in hell; Howlings attend it . . . iii 3 48
What said my man, when my betossed soul Did not attend him? . . v 3 77
All these spirits thy power Hath conjured to attend . *T. of Athens* i 1 7
Call the man before thee.—Attends he here, or no? . . i 1 114
Ladies, there is an idle banquet attends you . . . i 2 160
We attend his lordship; pray, signify so much.—I need not tell him that iii 4 37
Attend our weightier judgement . . . iii 5 102
Not without ambition, but without The illness should attend it *Macbeth* i 5 21
Sirrah, a word with you: attend those men Our pleasure? . . iii 1 45
Say to the king, I would attend his leisure For a few words . . iii 2 3
Good night; and better health Attend his majesty! . . iii 4 121
Let our just censures Attend the true event . . . v 4 15
When it falls, Each small annexment, petty consequence, Attends the boisterous ruin . . . *Hamlet* iii 3 22
Who brings back to him, that you attend him in the hall . . v 2 205
Attend the lords of France and Burgundy, Gloucester . . *Lear* i 1 35
The several messengers From hence attend dispatch . . ii 1 127
No port is free; no place, That guard, and most unusual vigilance, Does not attend my taking . . . ii 3 5
Commanded me to follow, and attend The leisure of their answer . ii 4 36
I'll bring you to our master Lear, And leave you to attend him . iv 3 53
I shall attend you presently at your tent . . . v 1 33
Let thy wife attend on her; And bring them after . . *Othello* i 3 297
If the gentlewoman that attends the general's wife be stirring, tell her . iii 1 27
The generous islanders By you invited do attend your presence . iii 3 281

Attend. Leave you! wherefore?—I do attend here on the general *Othello* iii 4 193
'Tis but a little way that I can bring you; For I attend here . . iii 4 200
Could not with graceful eyes attend those wars . *Ant. and Cleo.* ii 2 60
There I will attend What further comes . . . iii 10 32
I must attend mine office, Or would have done't myself . . iv 6 27
Adieu, good queen; I must attend on Cæsar . . . v 2 206
Our army shall In solemn show attend this funeral . . . v 2 367
Attend you here the door of our stern daughter? . *Cymbeline* ii 3 42
When you have given good morning to your mistress, Attend the queen ii 3 67
We will fear no poison, which attends In place of greater state . iii 3 77
That had a court no bigger than this cave, That did attend themselves . iii 6 84
Who attends us there?—Doth your highness call? . . *Pericles* i 1 150
Attend me, then: I went to Antioch . . . i 2 70
We attend him here, To know for what he comes, and whence he comes i 4 79
If you please, a niece of mine Shall there attend you . . iii 4 16
Attendance. What, no attendance? no regard? no duty? *T. of Shrew* iv 1 129
Who saw Cesario, ho?—On your attendance, my lord; here . *T. Night* i 4 11
Last time, I danced attendance on his will . *2 Hen. VI.* i 3 174
Welcome, my lord: I dance attendance here . *Richard III.* iii 7 56
To dance attendance on their lordships' pleasures . . *Hen. VIII.* v 2 31
Wait attendance Till you hear further from me . *T. of Athens* i 1 161
Why might not you, my lord, receive attendance From those that she calls servants? . . . *Lear* ii 4 246
Attendant. Here have I few attendants . . . *Tempest* v 1 166
His mad attendant and himself, Each one with ireful passion *C. of Err.* v 1 150
She as her attendant hath A lovely boy . . *M. N. Dream* ii 1 21
The ladies, her attendants of her chamber, Saw her a-bed *As Y. Like It* ii 2 5
And brave attendants near him when he wakes *T. of Shrew* Ind. 1 40
Thou shalt have my leave and love, Means and attendants *All's Well* i 3 258
So please you, madam, To put apart these your attendants . *W. Tale* ii 2 14
My three attendants, Lean famine, quartering steel, and climbing fire *1 Hen. VI.* iv 2 10
A riotous gentleman Lately attendant on the Duke of Norfolk *Rich. III.* ii 1 101
She fell distract, And, her attendants absent, swallow'd fire . *J. Cæsar* iv 3 156
Dismiss your attendant there: look it be done . . *Othello* iv 3 8
Her attendants are All sworn and honourable . . *Cymbeline* ii 4 124
In all safe reason He must have some attendants . . iv 2 132
Attended. I fear I am attended by some spies . . *T. G. of Ver.* v 1 10
Attended by Nerissa here, Until her husband and my lord's return *Mer. of Venice* iii 4 29
The crow doth sing as sweetly as the lark When neither is attended . v 1 103
A fair young man, and well attended . . . *T. Night* i 5 111
The proud day, Attended with the pleasures of the world . *K. John* iii 3 35
It is the curse of kings to be attended By slaves that take their humours for a warrant . . . iv 2 208
Attended him on bridges, stood in lanes, Laid gifts before him *1 Hen. IV.* iv 3 70
Attended by a simple guard, We may surprise and take him *3 Hen. VI.* iv 2 16
Often but attended with weak guard, Comes hunting this way . iv 5 7
Your grace attended to their sugar'd words . . *Richard III.* iii 1 13
Will not you go?—I am attended at the cypress grove . . *Coriolanus* i 10 30
In the emperor's court There is a queen, attended by a Moor *T. Andron.* v 2 105
To speak to you like an honest man, I am most dreadfully attended *Ham.* ii 2 276
Shut up your doors: He is attended with a desperate train . *Lear* ii 4 308
I do condemn mine ears that have So long attended thee . *Cymbeline* i 6 142
They are in a trunk, Attended by my men . . . i 6 197
Attended on by many a lord and knight, To see his daughter *Pericles* iv 4 11
Attendest. Thou attend'st not.—O, good sir, I do . . *Tempest* i 2 87
Attendeth. Where is he?—He attendeth here hard by . *Mer. of Venice* iv 1 145
Attending. She an attending star, scarce seen a light . *L. L. Lost* iv 3 231
The poor suppliant, who by this I know Is here attending . *All's Well* v 3 135
With a free desire Attending but the signal to begin . *Richard II.* i 3 116
Cut off All fears attending on so dire a project. . *Troi. and Cres.* ii 2 134
He did discourse To love-sick Dido's sad attending ear . *T. Andron.* v 3 82
Like softest music to attending ears . . *Rom. and Jul.* ii 2 167
Who, trimm'd in forms and visages of duty, Keep yet their hearts attending on themselves . . . *Othello* i 1 51
O, this life Is nobler than attending for a check . *Cymbeline* iii 3 22
Attending You here at Milford-Haven with your ships . . iv 2 334
I died whilst in the womb he stay'd Attending nature's law . . v 4 38
So, on your patience evermore attending . . *Pericles* v 3 Gower 100
Attent. Season your admiration for a while With an attent ear *Hamlet* i 2 193
Be attent, And time that is so briefly spent With your fine fancies quaintly eche . . . *Pericles* iii Gower 11
Attention. Will you hear this letter with attention? . *L. L. Lost* i 1 217
The tongues of dying men Enforce attention like deep harmony *Rich. II.* ii 1 6
To punish you by the heels would amend the attention of your ears *2 Hen. IV.* i 2 142
I will be bold with time and your attention . . *Hen. VIII.* ii 4 168
Give me hearing.—Ay, with all my heart, And lend my best attention *Cymbeline* v 5 117
Attentive. The very minute bids thee ope thine ear; Obey and be attentive . . . *Tempest* i 2 38
I am never merry when I hear sweet music.—The reason is, your spirits are attentive . . . *Mer. of Venice* v 1 70
Hear him, lords; And be you silent and attentive too, For he that interrupts him shall not live . . *3 Hen. VI.* i 1 122
To awake his ear, To set his sense on the attentive bent . *Troi. and Cres.* i 3 252
Vex not his prescience; be attentive.—Hush! . *Ant. and Cleo.* i 2 20
Attentiveness. How attentiveness wounded his daughter . *W. Tale* v 2 94
Attest. A crooked figure may Attest in little place a million *Henry V.* Prol. 16
Now attest That those whom you call'd fathers did beget you . . iii 1 22
I attest the gods, your full consent Gave wings to my propension *Troi. and Cres.* ii 2 132
So obstinately strong, That doth invert the attest of eyes and ears . v 2 122
Attested by the holy close of lips . . . *T. Night* v 1 161
Attire. Come, go in: I'll show thee some attires . . *Much Ado* iii 1 102
I'll put myself in poor and mean attire . . *As Y. Like It* i 3 113
He hath some meaning in his mad attire . . *T. of Shrew* iii 2 126
If nothing lets to make us happy both But this my masculine usurp'd attire . . . *T. Night* v 1 257
Stern looks, defused attire And every thing that seems unnatural *Hen. V.* v 2 61
Thy sumptuous buildings and thy wife's attire Have cost a mass of public treasury . . . *2 Hen. VI.* i 3 133
Throw off this sheet, And go we to attire you for our journey . ii 4 106
It will hang upon my richest robes And show itself, attire me how I can ii 4 109
Ay, those attires are best: but, gentle nurse, I pray thee, leave me to myself to-night . . . *Rom. and Jul.* iv 3 1
And do you now put on your best attire? And do you now cull out a holiday? . . . *J. Cæsar* i 1 53

Attire. What are these So wither'd and so wild in their attire? *Macbeth* i 3 40
I do not like the fashion of your garments: you will say they are Persian attire; but let them be changed . . . . *Lear* iii 6 85
Leap thou, attire and all, Through proof of harness to my heart! *Ant. and Cleo.* iv 8 14
Show me, my women, like a queen: go fetch My best attires . v 2 228
Attired. Finely attired in a robe of white . *Mer. Wives* iv 4 72
I am so attired in wonder, I know not what to say . *Much Ado* iv 1 146
I should blush To see you so attired . . *W. Tale* iv 4 13
Were they but attired in grave weeds, Rome could afford no tribune like to these . . . *T. Andron.* iii 1 43
Why art thou thus attired, Andronicus?—Because I would be sure to have all well . . . . . v 3 30
Attorney. And will have no attorney but myself . *Com. of Errors* v 1 100
Then in mine own person I die.—No, faith, die by attorney *As Y. L. It* iv 1 94
As fit as ten groats is for the hand of an attorney . *All's Well* ii 2 23
I am a subject, And I challenge law: attorneys are denied me *Richard II.* ii 3 134
I could be well content To be mine own attorney in this case 1 *Hen. VI.* v 3 166
Full of words?—Windy attorneys to their client woes *Richard III.* iv 4 127
Good mother,—I must call you so—Be the attorney of my love to her . iv 4 413
I, by attorney, bless thee from thy mother . . v 3 83
The king's attorney on the contrary Urged on the examinations *Hen. VIII.* ii 1 15
Attorneyed. I am still Attorney'd at your service . *Meas. for Meas.* v 1 390
Have been royally attorneyed with interchange of gifts, letters *W. Tale* i 1 30
Attorney-general. By his attorneys-general to sue His livery *Rich. II.* ii 1 203
Attorneyship. Marriage is a matter of more worth Than to be dealt in by attorneyship . . . 1 *Hen. VI.* v 5 56
Attract. 'Tis that miracle and queen of gems That nature pranks her in attracts my soul . . *T. Night* ii 4 89
My reformation, glittering o'er my fault, Shall show more goodly and attract more eyes . . . 1 *Hen. IV.* i 2 238
Who, in the conflict that it holds with death, Attracts the same for aidance 'gainst the enemy . . 2 *Hen. VI.* iii 2 165
Attraction. Setting the attraction of my good parts aside *Mer. Wives* ii 2 109
The sun's a thief, and with his great attraction Robs the vast sea *T. of A.* iv 3 439
With her sweet harmony And other chosen attractions . . *Pericles* v 1 46
Attractive. She hath blessed and attractive eyes *M. N. Dream* ii 2 91
Sit by me.—No, good mother, here's metal more attractive . *Hamlet* iii 2 117
Attribute. The attribute to awe and majesty . *Mer. of Venice* iv 1 191
It is enthroned in the hearts of kings, It is an attribute to God himself iv 1 195
If I should swear by God's great attributes, I loved you dearly *All's Well* iv 2 25
Much attribute he hath, and much the reason Why we ascribe it to him *Troi. and Cres.* ii 3 125
Could you not find out that by her attributes? . . . iii 1 38
The pith and marrow of our attribute . . . *Hamlet* i 4 22
And for an honest attribute cry out 'She died by foul play' *Pericles* iv 3 18
Attributed. The merit of service is seldom attributed to the true and exact performer . . . . . *All's Well* iii 6 64
Attribution. Such attribution should the Douglas have . 1 *Hen. IV.* iv 1 3
Attributive. The will dotes that is attributive To what infectiously itself affects . . . . *Troi. and Cres.* ii 2 58
A-twain. Like rats, oft bite the holy cords a-twain Which are too intrinse t' unloose . . . . . *Lear* ii 2 80
Aubrey. The Lord Aubrey Vere, Was done to death 3 *Hen. VI.* iii 3 102
Auburn. Her hair is auburn, mine is perfect yellow . *T. G. of Ver.* iv 4 194
Our heads are some brown, some black, some auburn . *Coriolanus* ii 3 21
Audacious without impudency, learned without opinion *L. L. Lost* v 1 5
The rattling tongue Of saucy and audacious eloquence *M. N. Dream* v 1 103
Away with that audacious lady! . . . . *W. Tale* ii 3 42
Teaching his duteous land Audacious cruelty . 1 *Hen. IV.* iv 3 45
Such is thy audacious wickedness . . . 1 *Hen. VI.* iii 1 14
Confounded be your strife! And perish ye, with your audacious prate! iv 1 124
Obey, audacious traitor; kneel for grace . . . 2 *Hen. VI.* v 1 108
Audaciously. Yet fear not thou, but speak audaciously *L. L. Lost* v 2 104
Audacity. Lean raw-boned rascals! who would e'er suppose They had such courage and audacity? . . . 1 *Hen. VI.* i 2 36
Boldness be my friend! Arm me, audacity, from head to foot! *Cymbeline* i 6 19
Audible. The very mercy of the law cries out Most audible *M. for M.* v 1 413
It's [war] spritely, waking, audible, and full of vent *Coriolanus* iv 5 238
Audience. O, dismiss this audience, and I shall tell you more *L. L. Lost* iv 3 210
Shall I have audience? he shall present Hercules in minority . v 1 140
If any of the audience hiss, you may cry 'Well done!' . v 1 145
Vouchsafe me audience for one word . . . . v 2 313
If I do it, let the audience look to their eyes *M. N. Dream* i 2 28
Give me audience, good madam.—Proceed *As Y. Like It* iii 2 251
Let me have audience for a word or two . . . v 4 157
There thy fixed foot shall grow Till thou have audience *T. Night* i 4 18
The dignity of this act was worth the audience of kings and princes *W. Tale* v 2 87
All too wanton and too full of gawds To give me audience *K. John* iii 3 37
And can give audience To any tongue, speak it of what it will . v 2 139
According to the fair play of the world, Let me have audience . v 2 119
Good cousin, give me audience for a while . 1 *Hen. IV.* i 3 211
And might by no suit gain our audience . 2 *Hen. IV.* iv 1 76
To tell you from his grace That he will give you audience . iv 1 143
The French ambassador upon that instant Craved audience . *Hen. V.* i 1 92
We'll give them present audience. Go, and bring them . . ii 4 67
No audience, but the tribulation of Tower-hill . *Hen. VIII.* v 4 65
Rejourn the controversy of three pence to a second day of audience *Coriolanus* ii 1 81
Draw near, ye people.—List to your tribunes. Audience! peace, I say! iii 3 40
Let us be satisfied.—Then follow me, and give me audience . *J. Cæsar* iii 2 2
In my tent, Cassius, enlarge your griefs, And I will give you audience . iv 2 47
Have of your audience been most free and bounteous *Hamlet* i 3 93
'Tis meet that some more audience than a mother, Since nature makes them partial, should o'erhear The speech . . . iii 3 31
In this audience, Let my disclaiming from a purposed evil Free me so far v 2 251
That are but mutes or audience to this act . . . v 2 346
Let us haste to hear it, And call the noblest to the audience . . v 2 398
Hardly gave audience, or Vouchsafed to think he had partners *Ant. and Cleo.* i 4 7
With taunts Did gibe my missive out of audience . . ii 2 74
And oft before gave audience, As 'tis reported, so . . iii 6 18
The queen Of audience nor desire shall fail . . . iii 12 21
Audis. Magni Dominator poli, Tam lentus audis scelera? *T. Andron.* iv 1 82
Audit. You have scarce time To steal from spiritual leisure a brief span To keep your earthly audit . . . *Hen. VIII.* iii 2 141
Yet I can make my audit up, that all From me do back receive the flour of all, And leave me but the bran . *Coriolanus* i 1 148
Audit. Your servants ever Have theirs, themselves and what is theirs, in compt, To make their audit at your highness' pleasure *Macbeth* i 6 27
And how his audit stands who knows save heaven? . . *Hamlet* iii 3 82
If you will take this audit, take this life . . *Cymbeline* v 4 27
Auditor. I'll be an auditor; An actor too perhaps *M. N. Dream* iii 1 81
A kind of auditor; one that hath abundance of charge too 1 *Hen. IV.* ii 1 63
Call me before the exactest auditors And set me on the proof *T. of Athens* ii 2 165
Auditory. Then, noble auditory, be it known to you *T. Andron.* v 3 96
Audrey. Come apace, good Audrey: I will fetch up your goats, Audrey. And how, Audrey? am I the man yet? . . *As Y. Like It* iii 3 1
Come, sweet Audrey: We must be married, or we must live in bawdry . iii 3 98
We shall find a time, Audrey; patience, gentle Audrey . . v 1 1
But, Audrey, there is a youth here in the forest lays claim to you . v 1 6
Good even, Audrey.—God ye good even, William . . v 1 15
Come, away, away!—Trip, Audrey! trip, Audrey! I attend . v 1 68
To-morrow is the joyful day, Audrey; to-morrow will we be married . v 3 1
Bear your body more seeming, Audrey . . . . . v 4 72
Aufidius. The Volsces are in arms.—They have a leader, Tullus Aufidius, that will put you to't . . . . *Coriolanus* i 1 233
So, your opinion is, Aufidius, That they of Rome are enter'd in our counsels . . . . i 2 1
Noble Aufidius, Take your commission; hie you to your bands . i 2 25
See him pluck Aufidius down by the hair, As children from a bear . i 3 33
He'll beat Aufidius' head below his knee And tread upon his neck . i 3 49
Tullus Aufidius, is he within your walls?—No, nor a man that fears you less than he . . . . i 4 13
There is Aufidius; list, what work he makes Amongst your cloven army . . . . i 4 20
There is the man of my soul's hate, Aufidius, Piercing our Romans . i 5 11
To Aufidius thus I will appear, and fight . . . . i 5 20
Aufidius, Their very heart of hope . . . . . i 6 54
Directly Set me against Aufidius and his Antiates . . . i 6 59
None of you but is Able to bear against the great Aufidius A shield as hard as his . . . . i 6 79
But then Aufidius was within my view, And wrath o'erwhelm'd my pity i 9 85
Has he disciplined Aufidius soundly? . . . . . ii 1 139
Titus Lartius writes, they fought together, but Aufidius got off . ii 1 141
Aufidius then had made new head?—He had, my lord . . iii 1 1
Saw you Aufidius?—On safe-guard he came to me . . . iii 1 8
Your noble Tullus Aufidius will appear well in these wars . iv 3 35
Direct me, if it be your will, Where great Aufidius lies: is he in Antium? iv 4 8
'Tis Aufidius, Who, hearing of our Marcius' banishment, Thrusts forth his horns again into the world . . . . iv 6 42
Marcius, Join'd with Aufidius, leads a power 'gainst Rome . iv 6 66
He and Aufidius can no more atone Than violentest contrariety . iv 6 72
A fearful army, led by Caius Marcius Associated with Aufidius, rages Upon our territories . . . . iv 6 76
Aufidius, The second name of men, obeys his points As if he were his officer . . . . iv 6 124
Here comes the clusters. And is Aufidius with him? . . iv 6 129
This man, Aufidius, Was my beloved in Rome: yet thou behold'st! . v 2 98
Aufidius, and you Volsces, mark; for we'll Hear nought from Rome in private . . . . v 3 92
Aufidius, though I cannot make true wars, I'll frame convenient peace v 3 190
Now, good Aufidius, Were you in my stead, would you have heard A mother less? or granted less, Aufidius? . . . . v 3 191
Stand, Aufidius, And trouble not the peace . . . . v 6 128
His own impatience Takes from Aufidius a great part of blame . v 6 147
Aufidiuses. O that I had him, With six Aufidiuses, or more, his tribe, To use my lawful sword! . . . . v 6 130
Auger's bore. And Your franchises, whereon you stood, confined Into an auger's bore . . . . iv 6 87
Auger-hole. Where our fate, Hid in an auger-hole, may rush, and seize us . . . . *Macbeth* ii 3 128
Aught. If thou remember'st aught ere thou camest here . . *Tempest* i 2 51
If I can do it By aught that I can speak in his dispraise . *T. G. of Ver.* iii 2 47
Though you respect not aught your servant doth . . . v 4 20
If aught possess thee from me, it is dross, Usurping ivy *Com. of Errors* ii 2 179
If thou art changed to aught, 'tis to an ass . . . iii 2 201
If your love Can labour aught in sad invention . . *Much Ado* v 1 292
Else none at all in aught proves excellent . . *L. L. Lost* iv 3 354
If for my love . . . You will do aught, this shall you do for me . v 2 803
For aught that I could ever read, Could ever hear . *M. N. Dream* i 1 132
Nor is he dead, for aught that I can tell . . . . iii 2 76
For aught I see, they are as sick that surfeit with too much as they that starve with nothing . . . . . *Mer. of Venice* i 2 5
Gramercy! wouldst thou aught with me? . . . . ii 2 128
I'll then nor give nor hazard aught for lead . . . ii 7 21
Thou meagre lead, Which rather threatenest than dost promise aught . iii 2 105
Neither man nor master would take aught But the two rings . v 1 183
Being perhaps, for aught I see, two and thirty, a pip out *T. of Shrew* i 2 33
It might be yours or hers, for aught I know . *All's Well* v 3 281
If it be aught to the old tune, my lord . . . *T. Night* v 1 111
If you know aught which does behove my knowledge Thereof to be inform'd, imprison't not . . . . . . *W. Tale* i 2 395
If he see aught in you that makes him like . . . *K. John* ii 1 511
Hubert told me he did live.—So, on my soul, he did, for aught he knew v 1 43
I must find that title in your tongue, Before I make reply to aught you say . . . . *Richard II.* ii 3 73
If aught but beasts, I had been still a happy king of men . v 1 35
Hold those justs and triumphs?—For aught I know, my lord, they do v 2 53
Art thou aught else but place, degree and form? . . *Hen. V.* iv 1 263
For aught I see, this city must be famish'd . . . 1 *Hen. VI.* i 4 68
In spite of us or aught that we could do . . . . i 5 37
If thou canst accuse, Or aught intend'st to lay unto my charge, Do it . iii 1 4
When have I aught exacted at your hands? . . . 2 *Hen. VI.* iv 7 74
Thy bloody mind, Which never dreamt on aught but butcheries *Richard III.* i 2 100
If I unwittingly, or in my rage, Have aught committed . . ii 1 57
So loves the prince, That he will not be won to aught against him . iii 1 166
I know but of a single part, in aught Pertains to the state . *Hen. VIII.* i 2 41
To this point hast thou heard him At any time speak aught? . . i 2 146
If . . you can report, And prove it too, against mine honour aught . ii 4 39
What is aught, but as 'tis valued? . . . *Troi. and Cres.* ii 2 52
What says Achilles? would he aught with us?—Would you, my lord, aught with the general?—No . . . . iii 3 57
Nor doth he of himself know them for aught Till he behold them form'd in the applause Where they're extended . . . . . . iii 3 118
Though indeed In aught he merit not . . . *Coriolanus* i 1 280
His surly nature, Which easily endures not article Tying him to aught . ii 3 205
Hear from me still, and never of me aught But what is like me formerly iv 1 52

Aught. And may, for aught thou know'st, affected be . *T. Andron.* ii 1 28
Have we done aught amiss,—show us wherein . . . . v 3 129
Nor aught so good but strain'd from that fair use Revolts from true birth, stumbling on abuse . . . . *Rom. and Jul.* ii 3 19
If aught in this Miscarried by my fault, let my old life Be sacrificed . v 3 266
If it be aught toward the general good . . . *J. Cæsar* i 2 85
Live you? or are you aught That man may question? *Macbeth* i 3 42
Nor let thy soul contrive Against thy mother aught *Hamlet* i 5 86
Or such ambiguous giving out, to note That you know aught of me . i 5 179
Whether aught, to us unknown, afflicts him . . . ii 2 17
I never gave you aught.—My honour'd lord, you know right well you did iii 1 96
If he steal aught the whilst this play is playing, And 'scape detecting, I will pay the theft . . . . iii 2 93
Women's fear and love holds quantity; In neither aught, or in extremity iii 2 178
If my love thou hold'st at aught . . . . . . iv 3 60
If that his majesty would aught with us, We shall express our duty in his eye . . . . iv 4 5
Since no man has aught of what he leaves, what is't to leave betimes? . v 2 234
What is it ye would see? If aught of woe or wonder, cease your search v 2 374
If aught within that little seeming substance, Or all of it, with our displeasure pieced, And nothing more, may fitly like your grace, She's there, and she is yours . . . . *Lear* i 1 201
Hadst thou been aught but gossamer, feathers, air . . iv 6 49
Do you hear aught, sir, of a battle toward?—Most sure and vulgar . iv 6 213
Or whether since he is advised by aught To change the course . v 1 2
Neither my place nor aught I heard of business Hath raised me . *Othello* i 3 53
He is not yet arrived: nor know I aught But that he's well . . ii 1 89
Nor know I aught By me that's said or done amiss . . . ii 3 200
Indeed! ay, indeed: discern'st thou aught in that? Is he not honest? iii 3 102
Honest, my lord!—Honest! ay, honest.—My lord, for aught I know iii 3 104
Speak of me as I am; nothing extenuate, Nor set down aught in malice v 2 343
I take no pleasure In aught an eunuch has . . *Ant. and Cleo.* i 5 10
I hope it be not gone to tell my lord That I kiss aught but he *Cymbeline* ii 3 153
Hath my poor boy done aught but well, Whose face I never saw? . v 4 35
All perishen of man, of pelf, Ne aught escapen but himself *Pericles* ii Gower 36
For aught I know, May be, nor can I think the contrary . . ii 5 78
This is the man that can, in aught you would, Resolve you . . v 1 12
Can draw him but to answer thee in aught . . . . v 1 73
Augment, or alter, as your wisdoms best Shall see advantageable *Hen. V.* v 2 87
I shall not want false witness to condemn me, Nor store of treasons to augment my guilt . . . . . . *2 Hen. VI.* iii 1 169
The fire that mounts the liquor till't run o'er, In seeming to augment it wastes it . . . . *Hen. VIII.* i 1 145
It shall make honour for you.—So I lose none In seeking to augment it, but still keep My bosom franchised . . . *Macbeth* ii 1 27
Augmentation. More lines than is in the new map with the augmentation of the Indies . . . . *T. Night* iii 2 85
Augmented. As we march, our strength will be augmented *3 Hen. VI.* v 3 22
What he is, augmented, Would run to these and these extremities *J. Cæsar* ii 1 30
Supplying every stage With an augmented greeting . *Ant. and Cleo.* iii 6 55
Augmenting. With tears augmenting the fresh morning's dew *Rom. and Jul.* i 1 138
Stood on the extremest verge of the swift brook, Augmenting it with tears . . . . *As Y. Like It* ii 1 43
Augurer. The augurer tells me we shall have news to-night *Coriolanus* ii 1 1
The persuasion of his augurers, May hold him . . *J. Cæsar* ii 1 200
What say the augurers?—They would not have you to stir forth to-day ii 2 37
The augurers Say they know not, they cannot tell; look grimly *Ant. and Cleo.* iv 12 4
O sir, you are too sure an augurer; That you did fear is done . v 2 337
Auguring. My auguring hope Says it will come to the full . ii 1 10
Augurs and understood relations have By magot-pies and choughs and rooks brought forth The secret'st man of blood. . *Macbeth* iii 4 124
Augury. If my augury deceive me not . . *T. G. of Ver.* iv 4 73
We defy augury: there's a special providence in the fall of a sparrow *Hamlet* v 2 230
August. You sunburnt sicklemen, of August weary . . *Tempest* iv 1 134
The tenth of August last this dreadful lord, Retiring from the siege of Orleans, . . . Was round encompassed . . *1 Hen. VI.* i 1 110
Augustus. By this, your king Hath heard of great Augustus . *Cymbeline* ii 4 11
Now say, what would Augustus Cæsar with us? . . . iii 1 1
Augustus Cæsar—Cæsar, that hath more kings his servants than Thyself domestic officers . . . . iii 1 63
I will pursue her Even to Augustus' throne . . . iii 5 101
A Roman with a Roman's heart can suffer: Augustus lives to think on't v 5 82
Auld. Then take thine auld cloak about thee . . *Othello* ii 3 99
Aumerle. My Lord Aumerle, is Harry Hereford arm'd? . *Richard II.* i 3 1
I take my leave of you; Of you, my noble cousin, Lord Aumerle . . i 3 64
Cousin Aumerle, How far brought you high Hereford on his way? . i 4 1
You have a son, Aumerle, my noble cousin . . . . iii 3 125
Aumerle, thou weep'st, my tender-hearted cousin! . . . iii 3 160
Then set before my face the Lord Aumerle . . . . iv 1 6
My Lord Aumerle, I know your daring tongue Scorns to unsay what once it hath deliver'd . . . . iv 1 8
There is my gage, Aumerle, in gage to thine . . . . iv 1 34
Fitzwater, thou art damn'd to hell for this.—Aumerle, thou liest . iv 1 44
I task the earth to the like, forsworn Aumerle . . . . iv 1 52
I do remember well The very time Aumerle and you did talk . . iv 1 61
Aumerle is guilty of my true appeal . . . . . . iv 1 79
Thou, Aumerle, didst send two of thy men To execute the noble duke . iv 1 81
Here comes my son Aumerle.—Aumerle that was . . . v 2 41
Strike him, Aumerle. Poor boy, thou art amazed . . . v 2 85
After, Aumerle! mount thee upon his horse; Spur post, and get before him . . . . v 2 111
Aunchient. Of great expedition and knowledge in th' aunchient wars *Hen. V.* iii 2 83
The true and aunchient prerogatifes and laws of the wars . . iv 1 67
Aunt. Why, it is my maid's aunt of Brentford . . *Mer. Wives* iv 2 178
I have a widow aunt, a dowager Of great revenue . *M. N. Dream* i 1 157
The wisest aunt, telling the saddest tale . . . . ii 1 51
The thrush and the jay, Are summer songs for me and my aunts *W. Tale* iv 3 11
A woman, and thy aunt, great king; 'tis I. Speak with me *Richard II.* v 3 76
Rise up, good aunt.—Not yet, I thee beseech . . . v 3 92
Good aunt, stand up.—Nay, do not say, 'stand up;' Say 'pardon' first v 3 111
She and my aunt Percy Shall follow in your conduct speedily *1 Hen. IV.* iii 1 196
Sweet aunt, be quiet; 'twas against her will.—Against her will! *2 Hen. VI.* i 3 146
For your brother, he was lately sent From your kind aunt . *3 Hen. VI.* ii 1 146
Good aunt, you wept not for our father's death . *Richard III.* ii 2 62
My niece Plantagenet Led in the hand of her kind aunt . . iv 1 2
Their aunt I am in law, in love their mother . . . iv 1 24
Charles the emperor, Under pretence to see the queen his aunt *Hen. VIII.* i 1 177
Aunt. For an old aunt whom the Greeks held captive, He brought a Grecian queen . . . . *Troi. and Cres.* ii 2 77
Why keep we her? the Grecians keep our aunt: Is she worth keeping? ii 2 80
That any drop thou borrow'dst from thy mother, My sacred aunt, should by my mortal sword Be drain'd . . . . iv 5 134
Make my aunt merry with some pleasing tale . . *T. Andron.* iii 2 47
My aunt Lavinia Follows me every where, I know not why . iv 1 1
Alas, sweet aunt, I know not what you mean . . . iv 1 4
Do not fear thine aunt.—She loves thee, boy, too well to do thee harm . iv 1 5
I know my noble aunt Loves me as dear as e'er my mother did . iv 1 22
Aunt-mother. My uncle-father and aunt-mother are deceived *Hamlet* ii 2 394
Auricular. By an auricular assurance have your satisfaction . *Lear* i 2 99
Aurora. Yonder shines Aurora's harbinger . . . *M. N. Dream* iii 2 380
Soon as the all-cheering sun Should in the furthest east begin to draw The shady curtains from Aurora's bed . . . *Rom. and Jul.* i 1 142
Auspicious. My zenith doth depend upon A most auspicious star *Tempest* i 2 182
And promise you calm seas, auspicious gales . . . v 1 314
Then go thou forth; And fortune play upon thy prosperous helm, As thy auspicious mistress! . . . . . . *All's Well* iii 3 8
O lady Fortune, Stand you auspicious! . . . *W. Tale* iv 4 52
With a defeated joy,—With an auspicious and a dropping eye *Hamlet* i 2 11
Conjuring the moon To stand auspicious mistress . . *Lear* ii 1 42
Aussi. Dieu vous garde, monsieur.—Et vous aussi . *T. Night* iii 1 79
Austere. If this austere insociable life Change not your offer made in heat of blood . . . . *L. L. Lost* v 2 809
With most austere sanctimony . . . . . *All's Well* iv 3 59
Quenching my familiar smile with an austere regard of control *T. Night* ii 5 73
Of glib and slippery creatures as Of grave and austere quality *T. of Athens* i 1 54
Austerely. If I have too austerely punish'd you . . *Tempest* iv 1 1
Did he tempt thee so? Mightst thou perceive austerely in his eye That he did plead in earnest? . . . . . *Com. of Errors* iv 2 2
Austereness. My unsoil'd name, the austereness of my life *Meas. for Meas.* ii 4 155
Austerity. On Diana's altar to protest For aye austerity . *M. N. Dream* i 1 90
With such austerity as 'longeth to a father . . . *T. of Shrew* iv 4 7
Commanding peace Even with the same austerity and garb As he controll'd the war . . . . *Coriolanus* iv 7 44
Austria. A certainty, vouch'd from our cousin Austria . *All's Well* i 2 5
Before Angiers well met, brave Austria . . . *K. John* ii 1 1
Austria and France shoot in each other's mouth . . . ii 1 414
O Lymoges! O Austria! thou dost shame That bloody spoil . . iii 1 114
Austria's head lie there, While Philip breathes . . . iii 2 3
Authentic in your place and person . . . *Mer. Wives* ii 2 235
All the learned and authentic fellows . . . . *All's Well* ii 3 14
Crowns, sceptres, laurels, But by degree, stand in authentic place *Troi. and Cres.* i 3 108
After all comparisons of truth, As truth's authentic author to be cited iii 2 188
Author. Don John is the author of all, who is fled and gone *Much Ado* v 2 101
Where is any author in the world Teaches such beauty as a woman's eye! *L. L. Lost* iv 3 312
For men's sake, the authors of these women, Or women's sake, by whom we men are men . . . . iv 3 359
I will be proud, I will read politic authors . . . *T. Night* ii 5 176
When we know the grounds and authors of it . . . . v 1 361
O thou, the earthly author of my blood . . . *Richard II.* i 3 69
If you be not too much cloyed with fat meat, our humble author will continue the story . . . . *2 Hen. IV.* Epil. 28
Yet their own authors faithfully affirm That the land Salique is in Germany, Between the floods of Sala and of Elbe . . *Hen. V.* i 2 43
You may call the business of the master the author of the servant's damnation . . . . iv 1 162
With rough and all-unable pen, Our bending author hath pursued the story . . . . Epil. 2
I thank God and thee; He was the author, thou the instrument *3 Hen. VI.* iv 6 18
It calls, I fear, too many curses on their heads That were the authors *Hen. VIII.* ii 1 139
Not in confidence Of author's pen or actor's voice *Troi. and Cres.* Prol. 24
After all comparisons of truth, As truth's authentic author to be cited . iii 2 188
I do not strain at the position,—It is familiar,—but at the author's drift iii 3 113
As if a man were author of himself And knew no other kin . *Coriolanus* v 3 36
The gods of Rome forfend I should be author to dishonour you! *T. Andron.* i 1 435
No matter in the phrase that might indict the author of affectation *Hamlet* ii 2 464
And he most violent author Of his own just remove . . . iv 5 80
That which is the strength of their amity shall prove the immediate author of their variance . . . . . *Ant. and Cleo.* ii 6 138
The fairest in all Syria, I tell you what mine authors say *Pericles* i Gower 20
Authorities. Why meet him at the gates, and redeliver our authorities there? . . . . *Meas. for Meas.* iv 4 6
So it must fall out To him or our authorities . . . *Coriolanus* i 1 260
My soul aches To know, when two authorities are up, Neither supreme, how soon confusion May enter 'twixt the gap of both and take The one by the other . . . . iii 1 109
Soaks up the king's countenance, his rewards, his authorities *Hamlet* iv 2 17
That still would manage those authorities That he hath given away! *Lear* i 3 17
Which secret art, By turning o'er authorities, I have, Together with my practice, made familiar . . . . . . *Pericles* iii 2 33
Authority. Use your authority: if you cannot, give thanks *Tempest* i 1 26
Thus can the demigod Authority Make us pay down . *Meas. for Meas.* i 2 124
With full line of his authority . . . . . . i 4 56
But man, proud man, Drest in a little brief authority . . . ii 2 118
Authority, though it err like others, Hath yet a kind of medicine in itself . . . . ii 2 134
Thieves for their robbery have authority When judges steal themselves ii 2 176
Hence hath offence his quick celerity, When it is borne in high authority iv 2 114
For my authority bears of a credent bulk . . . . . iv 4 29
O, what authority and show of truth Can cunning sin cover itself withal! *Much Ado* iv 1 36
Small have continual plodders ever won Save base authority from others' books . . . . *L. L. Lost* i 1 87
Most sweet Hercules! More authority, dear boy, name more . i 2 70
O, some authority how to proceed; Some tricks, some quillets . iv 3 287
If law, authority and power deny not, It will go hard . *Mer. of Venice* iii 2 291
Wrest once the law to your authority: To do a great right, do a little wrong . . . . iv 1 215
I must be patient; there is no fettering of authority . *All's Well* ii 3 252
By his authority he remains here . . . . . . iv 5 68
Whereto thy speech serves for authority . . . *T. Night* ii 2 20
It is in mine authority to command The keys . . . *W. Tale* i 2 463
By his great authority; Which often hath no less prevail'd . . ii 1 53

Authority. He seems to be of great authority : close with him *W. Tale* iv 4 830
Though authority be a stubborn bear, yet he is oft led by the nose with gold . . . iv 4 831
That stirs good thoughts In any breast of strong authority . *K. John* ii 1 113
Thou dost usurp authority.—Excuse ; it is to beat usurping down . ii 1 118
So tell the pope, all reverence set apart To him and his usurp'd authority iii 1 160
On the winking of authority To understand a law . . . iv 2 211
As holding of the pope Your sovereign greatness and authority . v 1 4
Have too lavishly Wrested his meaning and authority *2 Hen. IV.* iv 2 58
I gave bold way to my authority And did commit you . . . v 2 82
I am, sir, under the king, in some authority.—Under which king? . v 3 117
A man of great authority in France . . . *1 Hen. VI.* v 1 18
Neither in birth or for authority, The bishop will be overborne by thee v 1 59
In substance and authority, Retain but privilege of a private man v 4 135
Of such great authority in France As his alliance will confirm our peace v 5 41
Our authority is his consent . . . . . *2 Hen. VI.* iii 1 316
Lawful magistrate, That hath authority over him that swears *3 Hen. VI.* i 2 24
Publicly been read, And on all sides the authority allow'd *Hen. VIII.* ii 4 4
Words cannot carry Authority so weighty . . . . iii 2 234
That my teaching And the strong course of my authority Might go one way . . . . v 3 35
Bi-fold authority ! where reason can revolt Without perdition *Tr. and Cr.* v 2 144
What authority surfeits on would relieve us . . . *Coriolanus* i 1 16
They do prank them in authority, Against all noble sufferance . iii 1 23
Let us stand to our authority, Or let us lose it . . . iii 1 208
Yea, 'gainst the authority of manners, pray'd you *T. of Athens* ii 2 147
And thy good name Live with authority . . . . v 1 166
If our father carry authority with such dispositions as he bears *Lear* i 1 308
You have that in your countenance which I would fain call master.—What's that?—Authority . . . . i 4 32
By his authority I will proclaim it . . . . . ii 1 62
Behold the great image of authority : a dog's obeyed in office . iv 6 163
The power and corrigible authority of this lies in our wills *Othello* i 3 329
One that, in the authority of her merit, did justly put on the vouch of very malice itself . . . . ii 1 147
Did he not rather Discredit my authority with yours? *Ant. and Cleo.* ii 2 49
If our eyes had authority, here they might take two thieves kissing . ii 6 100
He his high authority abused, And did deserve his change . . iii 6 33
Now, gods and devils ! Authority melts from me . . . iii 13 90
My authority shall not see thee, or else look friendly upon thee *Pericles* iv 6 96
Authorized. A woman's story at a winter's fire, Authorized by her grandam . . . . *Macbeth* iii 4 66
Autolycus. My father named me Autolycus . . *W. Tale* iv 3 24
He settled only in rogue : some call him Autolycus . . . iv 3 107
Autumn. The childing autumn, angry winter . . *M. N. Dream* ii 1 112
The ewes, being rank, In the end of autumn turned to the rams *Mer. of Venice* i 3 82
Chide as loud As thunder when the clouds in autumn crack *T. of Shrew* i 2 96
What valiant foemen, like to autumn's corn, Have we mow'd down in tops of all their pride ! . . . . . . *3 Hen. VI.* v 7 3
He smiles valiantly.—Does he not?—O yes, an 'twere a cloud in autumn *Troi. and Cres.* i 2 139
Use his eyes for garden water-pots, Ay, and laying autumn's dust *Lear* iv 6 201
An autumn 'twas That grew the more by reaping . . *Ant. and Cleo.* v 2 87
Auvergne. The virtuous lady, Countess of Auvergne . *1 Hen. VI.* ii 2 38
Avail. But how out of this can she avail? . . *Meas. for Meas.* iii 1 243
I charge thee, As heaven shall work in me for thine avail . *All's Well* i 3 190
You know your places well ; When better fall, for your avails they fell iii 1 22
Which to deny concerns more than avails . . . *W. Tale* iii 2 87
Instead of gold, we'll offer up our arms ; Since arms avail not now *1 Hen. VI.* i 1 47
Now will it best avail your majesty To cross the seas . . iii 1 179
Avarice. There grows In my most ill-composed affection such A stanchless avarice that, were I king, I should cut off the nobles *Macbeth* iv 3 78
This avarice Sticks deeper, grows with more pernicious root Than summer-seeming lust . . . . iv 3 84
Avaricious. Bloody, Luxurious, avaricious, false, deceitful . . iv 3 58
Avaunt ! vanish like hailstones, go ; Trudge, plod away o' the hoof *M. W.* i 3 90
Avaunt, thou witch ! Come, Dromio, let us go *Com. of Errors* iv 3 80
Avaunt, perplexity ! What shall we do? . . . *L. L. Lost* v 2 298
Avaunt, thou hateful villain, get thee gone !—I am no villain *K. John* iv 3 77
You hunt counter : hence ! avaunt ! . . . . *2 Hen. IV.* i 2 103
Up to the breach, you dogs ! avaunt, you cullions ! . . *Hen. V.* iii 2 21
Peasant, avaunt ! You have suborn'd this man . . . *1 Hen. VI.* v 4 21
Avaunt, thou dreadful minister of hell ! . . . *Richard III.* i 2 46
After this process, To give her the avaunt ! it is a pity . *Hen. VIII.* ii 3 10
Traitors, avaunt ! Where is the emperor's guard? . . *T. Andron.* i 1 283
Avaunt ! and quit my sight ! let the earth hide thee ! . . *Macbeth* iii 4 93
Tom will throw his head at them. Avaunt, you curs ! . . *Lear* iii 6 68
Avaunt ! be gone ! thou hast set me on the rack . . *Othello* iii 3 335
I obey the mandate, And will return to Venice. Hence, avaunt ! . iv 1 271
Ah, thou spell ! Avaunt !—Why is my lord enraged? *Ant. and Cleo.* iv 12 30
Avaunt, thou damned door-keeper ! . . . . . *Pericles* iv 6 126
Ave. I do not relish well Their loud applause and Aves vehement *Meas. for Meas.* i 1 71
Ave-Maries. All his mind is bent to holiness, To number Ave-Maries on his beads . . . . *2 Hen. VI.* i 3 59
In black mourning gowns, Numbering our Ave-Maries . *3 Hen. VI.* ii 1 162
Avenge. When I am dead and gone, Remember to avenge me *1 Hen. VI.* i 4 94
Avenged. Shall I not live to be avenged on her? . . *2 Hen. VI.* i 3 85
O God ! if my deep prayers cannot appease thee, But thou wilt be avenged on my misdeeds, Yet execute thy wrath in me alone *Richard III.* i 4 70
Be avenged on cursed Tamora.—And as he saith, so say we all *T. Andron.* v 1 16
Never, till Cæsar's three and thirty wounds Be well avenged *J. Cæsar* v 1 54
Averring notes Of chamber-hanging, pictures, this her bracelet *Cymbeline* v 5 203
Avert your liking a more worthier way . . . . *Lear* i 1 214
Avised. Be avised, sir, and pass good humours . . *Mer. Wives* i 1 169
Are you avised o' that? you shall find it a great charge . . i 4 106
Art avised o' that? more on't . . . . *Meas. for Meas.* ii 2 132
Avoid. Well done ! avoid ; no more ! . . . . *Tempest* iv 1 142
What I am I cannot avoid . . . . . . *Mer. Wives* iii 5 152
As the matter now stands, he will avoid your accusation *Meas. for Meas.* iii 1 201
Satan, avoid ! I charge thee, tempt me not . . *Com. of Errors* iv 3 48
Avoid then, fiend ! what tell'st thou me of supping? . . iv 3 66
The fashion of the world is to avoid cost, and you encounter it *Much Ado* i 1 98
Either he avoids them with great discretion, or undertakes them with a most Christian-like fear . . . . ii 3 198
Let me see his eyes, That, when I note another man like him, I may avoid him . . . . v 1 271

Avoid. Therefore red, that would avoid dispraise, Paints itself black *L. L. Lost* iv 3 264
Though yet I know no wise remedy how to avoid it . *As Y. Like It* i 1 27
I have been all this day to avoid him . . . . . ii 5 35
All these you may avoid but the Lie Direct ; and you may avoid that too v 4 102
He cannot by the duello avoid it . . . . *T. Night* iii 4 338
'Tis safer to Avoid what's grown than question how 'tis born *W. Tale* i 2 433
Let us avoid.—It is in mine authority to command The keys . . i 2 462
I will not practise to deceive, Yet, to avoid deceit, I mean to learn *K. John* i 1 215
A partial slander sought I to avoid, And in the sentence my own life destroy'd . . . . *Richard II.* i 3 241
We hear this fearful tempest sing, Yet seek no shelter to avoid the storm . . . . ii 1 264
A fear To be again displaced : which to avoid, I cut them off *2 Hen. IV.* iv 5 209
What say you? will you yield, and this avoid? . . *Hen. V.* iii 3 42
Descend to darkness and the burning lake ! False fiend, avoid ! *2 Hen. VI.* i 4 43
So perhaps he doth : 'Tis but his policy to counterfeit, Because he would avoid such bitter taunts . . . . . *3 Hen. VI.* ii 6 66
To avoid the carping censures of the world . . *Richard III.* iii 5 68
To speak, and to avoid the first, And then, in speaking, not to incur the last . . . . iii 7 151
Avoid the gallery. Ha ! I have said. Be gone . . *Hen. VIII.* v 1 86
How may I avoid, Although my will distaste what it elected, The wife I chose? there can be no evasion . . *Troi. and Cres.* ii 2 65
Pray you, avoid the house.—Let me but stand . . *Coriolanus* iv 5 25
Take up some other station ; here's no place for you ; pray you, avoid iv 5 34
I do not know the man I should avoid So soon as that spare Cassius *J. Cæsar* i 2 200
Our safest way Is to avoid the aim . . . . . *Macbeth* ii 3 149
Which, happily, foreknowing may avoid . . . . *Hamlet* i 1 134
It out-herods Herod : pray you, avoid it . . . . iii 2 16
Confess yourself to heaven ; Repent what's past ; avoid what is to come iii 4 150
Hence, and avoid my sight ! . . . . . . *Lear* i 1 126
This is the man.—Avoid, and leave him . . *Ant. and Cleo.* v 2 242
Thou basest thing, avoid ! hence, from my sight ! . *Cymbeline* i 1 125
I chose an eagle, And did avoid a puttock . . . . i 1 140
Avoided. I embrace this fortune patiently, Since not to be avoided it falls on me . . . . *1 Hen. IV.* v 5 13
Mark'd by the destinies to be avoided . . . *3 Hen. VI.* ii 2 137
What cannot be avoided 'Twere childish weakness to lament or fear . v 4 37
All unavoided is the doom of destiny.—True, when avoided grace makes destiny . . . . *Richard III.* iv 4 218
It cannot be avoided but by this ; It will not be avoided but by this . iv 4 410
What can be avoided Whose end is purposed by the mighty gods? *J. Cæsar* ii 2 26
Of all men else I have avoided thee : But get thee back . *Macbeth* v 8 4
Avoiding. By spying and avoiding fortune's malice . *3 Hen. VI.* iv 6 28
Avoirdupois. The weight of a hair will turn the scales between their avoirdupois . . . . *2 Hen. IV.* ii 4 277
Avouch. I speak and I avouch ; 'tis true . . . *Mer. Wives* ii 1 138
No offence, if the duke avouch the justice of your dealing *Meas. for Meas.* iv 2 200
I'll avouch it to his head . . . . . *M. N. Dream* i 1 106
Then my account I well may give, And in the stocks avouch it *W. Tale* iv 3 22
This avouches the shepherd's son . . . . . . v 2 69
And dare not avouch in your deeds any of your words *Hen. V.* v 1 77
Put off your maiden blushes ; avouch the thoughts of your heart . v 2 253
What I have said I will avouch in presence of the king . *Richard III.* i 3 115
If you'll avouch 'twas wisdom Paris went—As you must needs *Tr. and Cr.* ii 2 84
I could With barefaced power sweep him from my sight And bid my will avouch it, yet I must not . . . . . . *Macbeth* iii 1 120
If this which he avouches does appear, There is nor flying hence nor tarrying here . . . . v 5 47
Without the sensible and true avouch Of mine own eyes . *Hamlet* i 1 57
Is this well spoken?—I dare avouch it . . . . *Lear* ii 4 240
Avouched. Produce a champion that will prove What is avouched there v 1 44
Avouchment. I hope your majesty is pear me testimony and witness, and will avouchment . . . . *Hen. V.* iv 8 38
Avow. There is not one, I dare avow, And now I should not lie *Hen. VIII.* iv 2 142
Dare avow her beauty and her worth In other arms than hers *Tr. and Cr.* i 3 271
Await. Posterity, await for wretched years . . *1 Hen. VI.* ii 1 48
What fates await the Duke of Suffolk?—By water shall he die *2 Hen. VI.* i 4 35
Awake, dear heart, awake ! thou hast slept well ; Awake ! *Tempest* i 2 305
If of life you keep a care, Shake off slumber, and beware : Awake, awake ! . . . . ii 1 305
Why, how now? ho, awake ! Why are you drawn? . . . ii 1 308
I heard a humming, And that a strange one too, which did awake me . ii 1 318
If he awake, From toe to crown he'll fill our skins with pinches . iv 1 232
The master and the boatswain Being awake, enforce them to this place v 1 100
How came you hither?—If I did think, sir, I were well awake, I'ld strive to tell you . . . . v 1 229
Is this a dream? do I sleep? Master Ford, awake ! awake ! *Mer. Wives* iii 5 142
This new governor Awakes me all the enrolled penalties *Meas. for Meas.* i 2 170
Tell him he must awake, and that quickly too . . . iv 3 32
Master Barnardine, awake till you are executed, and sleep afterwards . iv 3 34
Lie ten nights awake, carving the fashion of a new doublet *Much Ado* ii 3 18
Awake the pert and nimble spirit of mirth . . *M. N. Dream* i 1 13
Let love forbid Sleep his seat on thy eyelid : So awake when I am gone ii 2 82
Good sir, awake.—And run through fire I will for thy sweet sake . ii 2 102
Durst thou have look'd upon him being awake, And hast thou kill'd him sleeping? . . . . iii 2 69
The noise they make Will cause Demetrius to awake . . . iii 2 117
Are you sure That we are awake? It seems to me That yet we sleep . iv 1 198
Why, then, we are awake : let's follow him . . . . iv 1 203
'Tis time to stir him from his trance. I pray, awake, sir . *T. of Shrew* i 1 183
And if she chance to nod I'll rail and brawl And with the clamour keep her still awake . . . . iv 1 210
To awake your dormouse valour, to put fire in your heart . *T. Night* iii 2 20
It may awake my bounty further.—Marry, sir, lullaby to your bounty . v 1 47
Let your bounty take a nap, I will awake it anon . . . v 1 52
All proofs sleeping else But what your jealousies awake . *W. Tale* iii 2 114
Being now awake, I'll queen it no inch farther, But milk my ewes and weep . . . . iv 4 460
It is required You do awake your faith . . . . . v 3 95
No foot shall stir.—Music, awake her ; strike ! . . . v 3 98
We must awake endeavour for defence . . . *K. John* ii 1 81
With his innocent prate He will awake my mercy which lies dead . iv 1 26
Awakes my conscience to confess all this . . . . v 4 43
Am I not king? Awake, thou coward majesty ! thou sleepest *Rich. II.* iii 2 84
That, with the hurly, death itself awakes . . *2 Hen. IV.* iii 1 25
Take heed . . . How you awake our sleeping sword of war . *Hen. V.* i 2 22
Awake remembrance of these valiant dead . . . . i 2 115

Awake, awake, English nobility! Let not sloth dim your honours 1 *Hen. VI.* i 1 78
Ascend the sky, And there awake God's gentle-sleeping peace *Richard III.* i 3 288
Awake, and think our wrongs in Richard's bosom Will conquer him! awake, and win the day! v 3 144
Bloody and guilty, guiltily awake, And in a bloody battle end thy days! v 3 146
Quiet untroubled soul, awake, awake! Arm, fight, and conquer! v 3 149
I bring a trumpet to awake his ear *Troi. and Cres.* i 3 251
Trojan, he is awake, He tells thee so himself i 3 255
Hector, thou sleep'st; Awake thee! iv 5 115
Awake Your dangerous lenity *Coriolanus* iii 1 98
I have been broad awake two hours and more *T. Andron.* ii 2 17
Justice lives In Saturninus' health, whom, if she sleep, He'll so awake iv 4 25
And then awake as from a pleasant sleep *Rom. and Jul.* iv 1 106
Against thou shalt awake, Shall Romeo by my letters know our drift iv 1 113
Ere day We will awake him and be sure of him *J. Cæsar* i 3 164
Brutus, thou sleep'st: awake, and see thyself ii 1 46
I have been up this hour, awake all night ii 1 88
Awake your senses, that you may the better judge iii 2 17
Boy, Lucius! Varro! Claudius! Sirs, awake! Claudius! iv 3 290
He thinks he still is at his instrument. Lucius, awake! iv 3 294
Sleep again, Lucius. Sirrah Claudius! Fellow thou, awake! iv 3 301
Awake, awake! Ring the alarum-bell. Murder and treason! *Macbeth* ii 3 78
Awake! Shake off this downy sleep, death's counterfeit! ii 3 80
Doth with his lofty and shrill-sounding throat Awake the god of day *Hamlet* i 1 152
What I have done, That might your nature, honour and exception Roughly awake, I here proclaim was madness v 2 243
Be by, good madam, when we do awake him; I doubt not of his temperance.—Very well *Lear* iv 7 23
He's scarce awake: let him alone awhile iv 7 51
Arise, arise; Awake the snorting citizens with the bell *Othello* i 1 90
Awake, sir, awake; speak to us.—Hear you, sir?—The hand of death hath raught him *Ant. and Cleo.* iv 9 29
If thou canst awake by four o' the clock, I prithee, call me *Cymbeline* ii 2 6
Break it with a fearful dream of him And cry myself awake iii 4 46
They went hence so soon as they were born: And so I am awake v 4 127
They may awake their helps to comfort them *Pericles* i 4 17
I pity his misfortune, And will awake him from his melancholy ii 3 91
Nature awakes; a warmth Breathes out of her iii 2 93
Thunder shall not so awake the beds of eels iv 2 155
By my silver bow! Awake, and tell thy dream v 1 250
Awaked. In my false brother Awaked an evil nature *Tempest* i 2 93
We were awaked; straightway, at liberty v 1 235
We have very oft awaked him, as if to carry him to execution *M. for M.* iv 2 159
They shall find, awaked in such a kind, Both strength of limb and policy of mind *Much Ado* iv 1 199
I wonder if Titania be awaked *M. N. Dream* iii 2 1
The moon sleeps with Endymion And would not be awaked *Mer. of Venice* v 1 110
In which hurtling From miserable slumber I awaked *As Y. Like It* iv 3 133
Contempt nor bitterness Were in his pride or sharpness; if they were, His equal had awaked them *All's Well* i 2 38
The north-east wind ... Awaked the sleeping rheum *Richard II.* i 4 8
Think our former state a happy dream; From which awaked v 1 19
But, being awaked, I do despise my dream 2 *Hen. IV.* v 5 55
Awaked you not with this sore agony? *Richard III.* i 4 42
My master is awaked by great occasion To call upon his own *T. of Athens* ii 2 21
I am afraid they have awaked, And 'tis not done *Macbeth* ii 2 10
Is thy master stirring? Our knocking has awaked him; here he comes ii 3 48
At thy sovereign leisure read The garboils she awaked *Ant. and Cleo.* i 3 61
Awakens me with this unwonted putting-on *Meas. for Meas.* iv 2 119
I offer'd to awaken his regard For's private friends *Coriolanus* v 1 23
Awakened. Hath that awaken'd you?—Ay, but that frighted me *T. of Shr.* v 2 42
Awaking when the other do, May all to Athens back again repair *M. N. Dream* iv 1 71
Such as you Nourish the cause of his awaking *W. Tale* ii 3 36
I came, some minute ere the time Of her awaking *Rom. and Jul.* v 3 258
Award. The court awards it, and the law doth give it *Mer. of Venice* iv 1 300
The law allows it, and the court awards it iv 1 303
And award Either of you to be the other's end *Richard III.* ii 1 14
Away. Put some lime upon your fingers, and away with the rest *Tempest* iv 1 247
A sheep doth very often stray, An if the shepherd be a while away *T. G. of Ver.* i 1 75
Some to discover islands far away; Some to the studious universities i 3 9
For 'get you gone,' she doth not mean 'away!' iii 1 101
Trudge, plod away o' the hoof; seek shelter, pack! *Mer. Wives* i 3 91
I'll weep what's left away, and weeping die *Com. of Errors* ii 1 115
Do not tear away thyself from me! ii 2 126
Far from her nest the lapwing cries away *Much Ado* iv 2 27
I give away myself for you and dote upon the exchange iii 1 319
Whither away so fast? A true man or a thief that gallops so? *L. L. Lost* iv 3 186
Why, this is he That kiss'd his hand away in courtesy v 2 324
Four nights will quickly dream away the time *M. N. Dream* i 1 8
God speed fair Helena! whither away?—Call you me fair? i 1 180
Fairies, be gone, and be all ways away iv 1 46
You must come away to your father *As Y. Like It* i 2 60
Is't possible you will away to-night?—I must away to-day *T. of Shrew* iii 2 191
I thank you all, That have beheld me give away myself iii 2 196
If you shall marry, You give away this hand, and that is mine; You give away heaven's vows, and those are mine; You give away myself, which is known mine *All's Well* v 3 170
Take her away; I do not like her now; To prison with her: and away with him v 3 282
The king, I can tell you, looks for us all: we must away all night 1 *Hen. IV.* iv 2 63
She never could away with me.—Never, never 2 *Hen. IV.* iii 2 213
Thou, like a kind fellow, gavest thyself away gratis iv 3 75
By cock and pie, sir, you shall not away to-night v 1 2
Heave him away upon your winged thoughts Athwart the sea *Hen. V.* v Prol. 8
Away from me, and let me hear no more! 2 *Hen. VI.* i 2 50
Well could I curse away a winter's night iii 2 335
May see away their shilling Richly in two short hours *Hen. VIII.* Prol. 12
Away, my disposition, and possess me Some harlot's spirit! *Coriolanus* iii 2 111
I say to you, as I was said to, Away! v 2 114
Away with slavish weeds and servile thoughts! *T. Andron.* ii 1 18
Where's Potpan, that he helps not to take away? *Rom. and Jul.* i 5 2
Away with the joint-stools, remove the court-cupboard, look to the plate i 5 7
Away to heaven, respective lenity, And fire-eyed fury be my conduct now! iii 1 128
I fear me thou wilt give away thyself in paper shortly *T. of Athens* i 2 247

Away. Were I like thee, I'ld throw away myself.—Thou hast cast away thyself *T. of Athens* iv 3 219
I will mend thy feast.—First mend my company, take away thyself iv 3 283
Companion, hence!—Away, away, be gone! *J. Cæsar* iv 3 138
For thy solicitor shall rather die Than give thy cause away *Othello* iii 3 28
I cannot think it, That he would steal away so guilty-like iii 3 39
Awe. I will awe him with my cudgel *Mer. Wives* ii 2 291
O place, O form, How often dost thou with thy case, thy habit, Wrench awe from fools! *Meas. for Meas.* ii 4 14
Shall quips and sentences and these paper bullets of the brain awe a man from the career of his humour? *Much Ado* ii 3 250
The attribute to awe and majesty *Mer. of Venice* iv 1 191
Now, by my sceptre's awe, I make a vow *Richard II.* i 1 118
That doth with awe and terror kneel to it 2 *Hen. IV.* iv 5 177
We'll bend it to our awe, Or break it all to pieces *Hen. V.* i 2 224
Art thou aught else but place, degree and form, Creating awe and fear in other men? iv 1 264
Thy wife is proud; she holdeth thee in awe 1 *Hen. VI.* i 1 39
How France and Frenchmen might be kept in awe 2 *Hen. VI.* i 1 92
Conscience is but a word that cowards use, Devised at first to keep the strong in awe *Richard III.* v 3 310
The noble senate, who, Under the gods, keep you in awe *Coriolanus* i 1 191
Domestic awe, night-rest, and neighbourhood *T. of Athens* iv 1 17
I had as lief not be as live to be In awe of such a thing as I myself *J. Cæsar* i 2 96
That same eye whose bend doth awe the world Did lose his lustre i 2 123
Shall Rome stand under one man's awe? What, Rome? ii 1 52
Thy free awe Pays homage to us *Hamlet* iv 3 63
O, that that earth, which kept the world in awe, Should patch a wall to expel the winter's flaw! v 1 238
He made a law, To keep her still, and men in awe *Pericles* i Gower 36
Aweary. I am aweary of this moon: would he would change! *M. N. Dream* v 1 255
My little body is aweary of this great world *Mer. of Venice* i 2 2
Do that for me which I am aweary of *All's Well* i 3 47
I begin to be aweary of thee; and I tell thee so before, because I would not fall out with thee iv 5 59
Not an eye But is a-weary of thy common sight, Save mine 1 *Hen. IV.* iii 2 88
I prithee now, to bed.—Are you a-weary of me? *Troi. and Cres.* iv 2 7
I am a-weary, give me leave awhile *Rom. and Jul.* ii 5 25
Cassius is aweary of the world; Hated by one he loves *J. Cæsar* iv 3 95
I gin to be aweary of the sun *Macbeth* v 5 49
Awed. Thou, created to be awed by man, Wast born to bear *Richard II.* v 5 91
A-weeping. Thou'lt set me a-weeping, an thou sayest so 2 *Hen. IV.* ii 4 301
Aweless. Against whose fury and unmatched force The aweless lion could not wage the fight *K. John* i 1 266
The tiger now hath seized the gentle hind; Insulting tyranny begins to jet Upon the innocent and aweless throne *Richard III.* ii 4 52
Awful. Thrust from the company of awful men *T. G. of Ver.* iv 1 46
Love and quiet life And awful rule and right supremacy *T. of Shrew* v 2 109
How dare thy joints forget To pay their awful duty? *Richard II.* iii 3 76
We come within our awful banks again 2 *Hen. IV.* iv 1 176
To pluck down justice from your awful bench, To trip the course of law v 2 86
Thy hand is made to grasp a palmer's staff, And not to grace an awful princely sceptre 2 *Hen. VI.* v 1 98
And wring the awful sceptre from his fist 3 *Hen. VI.* ii 1 154
That will prove awful both in deed and word *Pericles* ii Gower 4
Awhile. Here he means to spend his time awhile *T. G. of Ver.* ii 4 80
Give us leave, I pray, awhile; We have some secrets to confer about iii 1 1
Now, gentlemen, Let's tune, and to it lustily awhile iv 2 25
Love, lend me patience to forbear awhile v 4 27
Yet may he live awhile; and, it may be, As long as you or I *M. for Meas.* ii 4 35
Pause awhile, And let my counsel sway you in this case *Much Ado* iv 1 202
Let her awhile be secretly kept in, And publish it that she is dead iv 1 205
Very good; let it be concealed awhile *All's Well* ii 3 283
Vouchsafe awhile to stay, And I shall show you peace *K. John* ii 1 416
And spite of spite needs must I rest awhile 3 *Hen. VI.* ii 3 5
Let us lay hands upon him.—Forbear awhile; we'll hear a little more iii 1 27
Stay awhile, And teach me how to curse mine enemies! *Richard III.* iv 4 116
Sat down To rest awhile, some half an hour or so *Hen. VIII.* iv 1 66
Give leave awhile, We must talk in secret *Rom. and Jul.* i 3 7
Awkward. 'Tis no sinister nor no awkward claim, Pick'd from the worm-holes of long-vanish'd days *Hen. V.* ii 4 85
Twice by awkward wind from England's bank Drove back again 2 *Hen. VI.* iii 2 83
With ridiculous and awkward action, Which, slanderer, he imitation calls, He pageants us *Troi. and Cres.* i 3 149
To the world and awkward casualties Bound me in servitude *Pericles* v 1 94
Awl. Truly, sir, all that I live by is with the awl *J. Cæsar* i 1 25
I meddle with no tradesman's matters, nor women's matters, but with awl i 1 26
A-wooing. Lucentio that comes a-wooing *T. of Shrew* iii 1 35
What! Michael Cassio, That came a-wooing with you! *Othello* iii 3 71
A-work. Skill in the weapon is nothing without sack, for that sets it a-work 2 *Hen. IV.* iv 3 124
Aroused vengeance sets him new a-work *Hamlet* ii 2 510
A provoking merit, set a-work by a reproveable badness in himself *Lear* iii 5 8
Awry. You pluck my foot awry: Take that *T. of Shrew* iv 1 150
Like perspectives, which rightly gazed upon Show nothing but confusion, eyed awry Distinguish form *Richard II.* ii 2 19
Looking awry upon your lord's departure, Find shapes of grief ii 2 21
Thou aimest all awry; I must offend before I be attainted 2 *Hen. VI.* ii 4 58
This is clean kam.—Merely awry *Coriolanus* iii 1 305
With this regard their currents turn awry *Hamlet* iii 1 87
Your crown's awry; I'll mend it, and then play *Ant. and Cleo.* v 2 321
Axe. Provide your block and your axe to-morrow *Meas. for Meas.* iv 2 56
Is the axe upon the block, sirrah?—Very ready, sir iv 3 39
No metal can, No, not the hangman's axe, bear half the keenness Of thy sharp envy *Mer. of Venice* iv 1 125
The common executioner, Whose heart the accustom'd sight of death makes hard, Falls not the axe upon the humbled neck But first begs pardon *As Y. Like It* iii 5 5
By envy's hand and murder's bloody axe *Richard II.* i 2 21
Nor stir at nothing till the axe of death Hang over thee 2 *Hen. VI.* ii 4 49
Who finds the heifer dead and bleeding fresh And sees fast by a butcher with an axe, But will suspect 'twas he that made the slaughter? iii 2 189
Many strokes, though with a little axe, Hew down and fell the hardest-timber'd oak 3 *Hen. VI.* ii 1 54
We set the axe to thy usurping root ii 2 165
From that torment I will free myself, Or hew my way out with a bloody axe iii 2 181

Axe. Thus yields the cedar to the axe's edge . 3 *Hen. VI.* v 2 11
Heaven bear witness, And if I have a conscience, let it sink me, Even as the axe falls, if I be not faithful! . *Hen VIII.* ii 1 61
Whilst your great goodness, out of holy pity, Absolved him with an axe. . . . . iii 2 264
I'll go fetch an axe.—But I will use the axe *T. Andron.* iii 1 185
Thou cutt'st my head off with a golden axe . *Rom. and Jul.* iii 3 22
Come hither, ere my tree hath felt the axe . *T. of Athens* v 1 214
Where the offence is let the great axe fall . . . *Hamlet* iv 5 218
No leisure bated, No, not to stay the grinding of the axe . v 2 24
I have ground the axe myself; Do you but strike the blow . *Pericles* i 2 58
Axletree. I had rather hear a brazen canstick turn'd, Or a dry wheel grate on the axle-tree . . 1 *Hen. IV.* iii 1 132
Strong as the axletree On which heaven rides . *Troi. and Cres.* i 3 66
Ay. Wilt thou destroy him then?—Ay, on mine honour . *Tempest* iii 2 123
Since maids, in modesty, say 'no' to that Which they would have the profferer construe 'ay' . . . *T. G. of Ver.* i 2 56
Ask my dog: if he say ay, it will; if he say, no, it will . . . ii 5 36
Ay, but she'll think that it is spoke in hate . . . iii 2 34
O husband, hear me! ay, alack, how new Is husband in my mouth! *K. John* iii 1 305
Please you dismiss me, either with 'ay' or 'no.'—Ay, if thou wilt say 'ay' to my request; No, if thou dost say 'no' to my demand 3 *Hen. VI.* iii 2 78
The pretty wretch left crying and said 'Ay' . *Rom. and Jul.* i 3 44
Ay me, what act, That roars so loud, and thunders in the index? *Ham.* iii 4 51
Ay. To say 'ay' and 'no' to every thing that I said!—'Ay' and 'no' too was no good divinity . . . . *Lear* iv 6 100
Ay me, most wretched, That have my heart parted betwixt two friends *Ant. and Cleo.* iii 6 76
Ay, are you thereabouts? Why, then, good night . . . iii 10 29
Aye. To the perpetual wink for aye might put This ancient morsel *Tempest* ii 1 285
I, thy Caliban, For aye thy foot-licker . . . . iv 1 218
Endure the livery of a nun, For aye to be in shady cloister *M. N. Dream* i 1 71
On Diana's altar to protest For aye austerity and single life . i 1 90
And must for aye consort with black-brow'd night . . . iii 2 387
Whose state and honour I for aye allow . . *Richard II.* v 2 40
To feed for aye her lamp and flames of love . . *Troi. and Cres.* iii 2 167
Let him that will a screech-owl aye be call'd . . . v 10 16
Ignomy and shame Pursue thy life, and live aye with thy name! . v 10 34
Thy saints for aye Be crown'd with plagues . . *T. of Athens* v 1 55
Taught thee to make vast Neptune weep for aye On thy low grave . iv 4 78
Let this pernicious hour stand aye accursed in the calendar! . *Macbeth* iv 1 134
This world is not for aye . . . . . . *Hamlet* iii 2 210
I am come To bid my king and master aye good night . . *Lear* v 3 235
Aye hopeless to have the courtesy your cradle promised . *Cymbeline* iv 4 27
The worth that learned charity aye wears . . . . *Pericles* v 3 Gower 94
Azure. White and azure laced With blue of heaven's own tinct *Cymbeline* ii 2 22
Azured. 'Twixt the green sea and the azured vault Set roaring war *Temp.* v 1 43
Thou shalt not lack The flower that's like thy face, pale primrose, nor The azured harebell, like thy veins . . . *Cymbeline* iv 2 222

B

B. Fair as a text B in a copy-book . . *L. L. Lost* v 2 42
Ba. What is a, b, spelt backward, with the horn on his head?—Ba, pueritia, with a horn added . . . . . . v 1 52
Baa. Thou art a sheep.—Such another proof will make me cry 'baa' *T. G. of Ver.* i 1 98
Babble. This babble shall not henceforth trouble me . . . i 2 98
For the watch to babble and to talk is most tolerable and not to be endured . . . . *Much Ado* iii 3 36
Endeavour thyself to sleep, and leave thy vain bibble babble *T. Night* iv 2 105
Babbled. And a' babbled of green fields . . . *Hen. V.* ii 3 17
Babbling. For 'scorn,' 'horn,' a hard rhyme; for 'school,' 'fool,' a babbling rhyme . . . . . . *Much Ado* v 2 39
Make the babbling gossip of the air Cry out 'Olivia!' *T. Night* i 5 292
I hate ingratitude more in a man Than lying, vainness, babbling . iii 4 389
Let not our babbling dreams affright our souls *Richard III.* v 3 308
The babbling echo mocks the hounds, Replying shrilly to the well-tuned horns . . . . *T. Andron.* ii 3 17
A long-tongued babbling gossip . . . . . iv 2 150
Babe. Like a testy babe, will scratch the nurse . *T. G. of Ver.* i 2 58
Piteous plainings of the pretty babes . . *Com. of Errors* i 1 73
When he was a babe, a child, a shrimp, Thus did he strangle serpents *L. L. Lost* v 2 594
For I am rough and woo not like a babe . . *T. of Shrew* ii 1 138
I may have leave to speak; And speak I will; I am no child, no babe . iv 3 74
So holy writ in babes hath judgement shown, When judges have been babes . . . . *All's Well* ii 1 141
A daughter, and a goodly babe, Lusty and like to live . *W. Tale* ii 2 26
If she dares trust me with her little babe, I'll show't the king . . ii 2 37
If't please the queen to send the babe, I know not what I shall incur . ii 2 56
The sacred honour of himself, his queen's, His hopeful son's, his babe's ii 3 85
Look to your babe, my lord; 'tis yours . . . . . ii 3 126
Come on, poor babe: Some powerful spirit instruct the kites and ravens To be thy nurses! . . . . ii 3 185
Leontes a jealous tyrant; his innocent babe truly begotten . . iii 2 135
Come, poor babe . . . . iii 3 15
The thrower-out Of my poor babe, according to thine oath . . iii 3 30
And, for the babe Is counted lost for ever, Perdita, I prithee, call't . iii 3 32
If I were mad, I should forget my son, Or madly think a babe of clouts were he . . . . *K. John* iii 4 58
When at their mothers' moist eyes babes shall suck . . 1 *Hen. VI.* i 1 49
So much fear'd abroad That with his name the mothers still their babes ii 3 17
Was in the mouth of every sucking babe . . . . . iii 1 197
As looks the mother on her lowly babe When death doth close his tender dying eyes . . . . iii 3 47
York not our old men spares; No more will I their babes . 2 *Hen. VI.* v 2 52
Tears then for babes; blows and revenge for me! . 3 *Hen. VI.* ii 1 86
The duty that I owe unto your majesty I seal upon the lips of this sweet babe . . . . v 7 29
'Twas the foulest deed to slay that babe . . *Richard III.* i 3 183
These babes for Clarence weep, and so do I . . . . ii 2 84
Pity, you ancient stones, those tender babes . . . . iv 1 99
'Thus,' quoth Dighton, 'lay those tender babes:' 'Thus, thus,' quoth Forrest . . . . iv 3 9
Ah, my tender babes! My unblown flowers, new-appearing sweets! . iv 4 9
A mother only mock'd with two sweet babes . . . . iv 4 87
Think that thy babes were fairer than they were . . . iv 4 120
My babes were destined to a fairer death . . . . . iv 4 219
As is a nurse's song Of lullaby to bring her babe asleep *T. Andron.* ii 3 29
Here is the babe, as loathsome as a toad Amongst the fairest breeders . iv 2 67
Soon I heard The crying babe controll'd with this discourse . . v 1 26
'Peace, villain, peace!'—even thus he rates the babe . . . v 1 33
Who, when he knows thou art the empress' babe, Will hold thee dearly v 1 35
Thou wast the prettiest babe that e'er I nursed . *Rom. and Jul.* i 3 60
Joy had the like conception in our eyes And at that instant like a babe sprung up . . . . *T. of Athens* i 2 116
Ho, ho! I laugh to think that babe a bastard . . . . i 2 117
Spare not the babe, Whose dimpled smiles from fools exhaust their mercy . . . . iv 3 118
Nor yells of mothers, maids, nor babes, Nor sight of priests . . iv 3 124
Pity, like a naked new-born babe, Striding the blast . . *Macbeth* i 7 21
I have given suck, and know How tender 'tis to love the babe that milks me . . . . i 7 55
Babe. Nose of Turk and Tartar's lips, Finger of birth-strangled babe *Macb.* iv 1 30
Give to the edge o' the sword His wife, his babes . . . iv 1 152
Wisdom! to leave his wife, to leave his babes, His mansion and his titles in a place From whence himself does fly? . . . iv 2 6
Your castle is surprised; your wife and babes Savagely slaughter'd . iv 3 204
And, heart with strings of steel, Be soft as sinews of the new-born babe! . . . . *Hamlet* iii 3 71
Old fools are babes again; and must be used With checks . *Lear* i 3 19
And from her derogate body never spring A babe to honour her! . . i 4 303
Those that do teach young babes Do it with gentle means *Othello* iv 2 111
Come, and take a queen Worth many babes and beggars! *Ant. and Cleo.* v 2 48
The king he takes the babe To his protection, calls him Posthumus *Cymb.* i 1 40
I stole these babes; Thinking to bar thee of succession . . . iii 3 101
Those mothers who, to nousle up their babes, Thought nought too curious, are ready now To eat those little darlings whom they loved . . . . *Pericles* i 4 42
Where, by the loss of maidenhead, A babe is moulded . . . iii Gower 11
Mild may be thy life! For a more blusterous birth had never babe . . iii 1 28
Bring me the satin coffer: lay the babe Upon the pillow . . iii 1 68
O, make for Tarsus! There will I visit Cleon, for the babe Cannot hold out to Tyrus . . . . iii 1 79
My gentle babe Marina, whom, For she was born at sea, I have named so iii 3 12
Baboon. Like a geminy of baboons . . . . *Mer. Wives* ii 2 9
Hang him, baboon! his wit's as thick as Tewksbury mustard 2 *Hen. IV.* ii 4 261
The strain of man's bred out Into baboon and monkey *T. of Athens* i 1 260
Cool it with a baboon's blood, Then the charm is firm and good *Macbeth* iv 1 37
I would change my humanity with a baboon . . . *Othello* i 3 318
A baboon, could he speak, Would own a name too dear . *Pericles* iv 6 189
Baby. The baby beats the nurse, and quite athwart Goes all decorum *Meas. for Meas.* i 3 30
I can find out no rhyme to 'lady' but 'baby,' an innocent rhyme *Much Ado* v 2 37
A cockle or a walnut-shell, A knack, a toy, a trick, a baby's cap *T. of Shrew* iv 3 67
You'll kiss me hard and speak to me as if I were a baby still *W. Tale* ii 1 6
Commend these waters to those baby eyes . . . *K. John* v 2 56
Guarded with grandsires, babies, and old women *Hen. V.* iii Prol. 20
She'll hamper thee, and dandle thee like a baby . 2 *Hen. VI.* i 3 148
Old sullen playfellow For tender princes, use my babies well! *Richard III.* iv 1 103
The baby figure of the giant mass Of things to come at large *Tr. and Cr.* i 3 345
Come, what need you blush? shame's a baby . . . . iii 2 43
Into a rapture lets her baby cry While she chats him . *Coriolanus* ii 1 223
Or the virgin voice That babies lulls asleep . . . . iii 2 115
I am no baby, I, that with base prayers I should repent the evils *T. Andron.* v 3 185
If trembling I inhabit then, protest me The baby of a girl *Macbeth* iii 4 106
Think yourself a baby; That you have ta'en these tenders for true pay *Hamlet* i 3 105
That great baby you see there is not yet out of his swaddling-clouts . ii 2 400
Dost thou not see my baby at my breast? . *Ant. and Cleo.* v 2 312
Baby-brow. Wears upon his baby-brow the round And top of sovereignty *Macbeth* iv 1 88
Baby-daughter. Casting forth to crows thy baby-daughter . *W. Tale* iii 2 192
Babylon. There dwelt a man in Babylon, lady, lady! *T. Night* ii 3 84
He was rheumatic, and talked of the whore of Babylon . *Hen. V.* ii 3 41
Baccare! you are marvellous forward . . . *T. of Shrew* ii 1 73
Bacchanal. The tipsy Bacchanals, Tearing the Thracian singer *M. N. Dream* v 1 48
Shall we dance now the Egyptian Bacchanals? *Ant. and Cleo.* ii 7 110
Bacchus. Love's tongue proves dainty Bacchus gross in taste *L. L. Lost* iv 3 339
Come, thou monarch of the vine, Plumpy Bacchus with pink eyne! *Ant. and Cleo.* ii 7 121
Bachelor. Broom-groves, Whose shadow the dismissed bachelor loves *Tempest* iv 1 67
Can you cut off a man's head?—If the man be a bachelor, sir, I can *Meas. for Meas.* iv 2 3
Shall I never see a bachelor of threescore again? . *Much Ado* i 1 201
And the fine is, for the which I may go the finer, I will live a bacheler . i 1 248
He shows me where the bachelors sit, and there live we . . ii 1 51
When I said I would die a bachelor, I did not think I should live till I were married . . . . ii 3 252

Bachelor. As may well be said Becomes a virtuous bachelor and a maid *M. N. Dream* ii 2 59
My turquoise; I had it of Leah when I was a bachelor *Mer. of Venice* iii 1 127
So is the forehead of a married man more honourable than the bare brow of a bachelor *As Y. Like It* iii 3 62
This youthful parcel Of noble bachelors stand at my bestowing *All's Well* ii 3 59
He was a bachelor then.—And so is now, or was so very late *T. Night* i 2 29
Contracted bachelors, such as had been asked twice on the banns *1 Hen. IV.* iv 2 17
As if he had writ man ever since his father was a bachelor *2 Hen. IV.* i 2 31
Take the word of a king and a bachelor *Hen. V.* v 2 230
I, being but a bachelor, Have other some *3 Hen. VI.* iii 2 103
A bachelor, a handsome stripling too *Richard III.* i 3 101
I swore I would not part a bachelor from the priest *T. Andron.* i 1 488
Marry, bachelor, Her mother is the lady of the house *Rom. and Jul.* i 5 114
Are you a married man or a bachelor?—Answer every man *J. Cæsar* iii 3 9
Wisely and truly: wisely I say, I am a bachelor . . . iii 3 18
Bachelorship. She was the first fruit of my bachelorship *1 Hen. VI.* v 4 13
Back. I saw him beat the surges under him, And ride upon their backs *Tempest* ii 1 115
How shall that Claribel Measure us back to Naples? . ii 1 259
I had rather crack my sinews, break my back, Than you should such dishonour undergo . iii 1 26
With printless foot Do chase the ebbing Neptune and do fly him When he comes back . v 1 36
On the bat's back I do fly After summer merrily . v 1 91
My penance is to call Lucetta back *T. G. of Ver.* i 2 64
Give back, or else embrace thy death . v 4 126
When gods have hot backs, what shall poor men do? *Mer. Wives* v 5 13
Pinch them, arms, legs, backs, shoulders, sides and shins . v 5 58
If he be chaste, the flame will back descend And turn him to no pain . v 5 89
Lead forth and bring you back in happiness! . *Meas. for Meas.* i 1 75
Gentle my lord, turn back.—I will bethink me: come again to-morrow ii 2 143
Hark how I'll bribe you: good my lord, turn back.—How! bribe me? ii 2 145
Like an ass whose back with ingots bows . iii 1 26
Think What 'tis to cram a maw or clothe a back From such a filthy vice iii 2 23
The hours come back! that did I never hear . *Com. of Errors* iv 2 55
If any hour meet a sergeant, a' turns back for very fear . iv 2 56
If Time be in debt and theft, and a sergeant in the way, Hath he not reason to turn back an hour in a day? . iv 2 62
Maiden pride, adieu! No glory lives behind the back of such *Much Ado* iii 1 110
And what have I to give you back? . iv 1 28
He carried the town-gates on his back like a porter . *L. L. Lost* i 2 75
I'll repay it back Or yield up Aquitaine . ii 1 159
The fairest dames, That ever turn'd their—backs—to mortal views! . v 2 161
And stand between her back, sir, and the fire . v 2 476
And heard a mermaid on a dolphin's back . *M. N. Dream* ii 1 150
Counterfeit sad looks, Make mouths upon me when I turn my back iii 2 238
To Athens will I bear my folly back And follow you no further . iii 2 315
Nay, go not back.—I will not trust you . iii 2 340
Shine comforts from the east, That I may back to Athens by daylight . iii 2 433
How chance Moonshine is gone before Thisbe comes back and finds her lover? . v 1 319
I thank you for your wish, and am well pleased To wish it back on you *Mer. of Venice* iii 4 44
Glancing an eye of pity on his losses, That have of late so huddled on his back . iv 1 28
Offer it behind her back; The wish would make else an unquiet house . iv 1 293
I'll take this ring from you: Do not draw back your hand . iv 1 428
He calls us back: my pride fell with my fortunes *As Y. Like It* i 2 264
How now! back, friends! Shepherd, go off a little . iii 2 167
A wretched ragged man, o'ergrown with hair, Lay sleeping on his back iv 3 108
Twice did he turn his back and purposed so . iv 3 128
I must bear answer back How you excuse my brother . iv 3 180
I have no more doublets than backs, no more stockings than legs *T. of Shrew* Ind. 2 9
Skipper, stand back: 'tis age that nourisheth . ii 1 341
Swayed in the back and shoulder-shotten . iii 2 56
His horse comes, with him on his back . iii 2 82
I'll see the church o' your back; and then come back . v 1 6
Urge her to a present answer back . *All's Well* ii 2 67
Like Arion on the dolphin's back, I saw him . *T. Night* i 2 15
I could hardly entreat him back . iii 4 64
Back you shall not to the house . iii 4 271
Sway her house, command her followers, Take and give back affairs iv 3 18
More straining on for plucking back, not following . *W. Tale* iv 4 476
One that will either push on or pluck back thy business . iv 4 762
Will break the back of man, the heart of monster . iv 4 797
Which who knows how that may turn back to my advancement? . iv 4 867
Whose foot spurns back the ocean's roaring tides . *K. John* ii 1 24
Bearing their birthrights proudly on their backs . ii 1 70
As sightly on the back of him As great Alcides' shows upon an ass ii 1 143
But, ass, I'll take that burthen from your back, Or lay on that shall make your shoulders crack . ii 1 145
Bell, book, and candle shall not drive me back . iii 3 12
Let him come back, that his compassion may Give life to yours . iv 1 89
Stand back, I say; By heaven, I think my sword's as sharp as yours iv 3 81
Your grace shall pardon me, I will not back . v 2 78
Must I back Because that John hath made his peace with Rome? . v 2 95
Why, know you not? the lords are all come back, And brought Prince Henry . v 6 33
That they may break his foaming courser's back *Richard II.* i 2 51
Let them lay by their helmets and their spears, And both return back . i 3 120
No way can I stray; Save back to England, all the world's my way . i 3 207
Whose rocky shore beats back the envious siege Of watery Neptune . ii 1 62
He is a flatterer, A parasite, a keeper back of death . ii 2 70
The cloak of night being pluck'd from off their backs, Stand bare and naked . iii 2 45
O, call back yesterday, bid time return! . iii 2 69
Shall we call back Northumberland, and send Defiance to the traitor? . iii 3 129
Northumberland comes back from Bolingbroke . iii 3 142
Sent back like Hallowmas or short'st of day . v 1 80
Bearing their own misfortunes on the back Of such as have before endured the like . v 5 29
So proud that Bolingbroke was on his back! . v 5 84
And break the neck Of that proud man that did usurp his back . v 5 89
I know them to be as true-bred cowards as ever turned back *1 Hen. IV.* i 2 206
When you and he came back from Ravenspurgh . i 3 248
Well, I will back him straight: O esperance! . ii 3 74

Back. You are straight enough in the shoulders, you care not who sees your back . *1 Hen. IV.* ii 4 165
Three misbegotten knaves in Kendal green came at my back . ii 4 247
I sent him Bootless home and weather-beaten back . iii 1 67
I bought you a dozen of shirts to your back . iii 3 78
The money is paid back again.—O, I do not like that paying back . iii 3 201
You foresee not what impediments Drag back our expedition . iv 3 19
Come, bring your luggage nobly on your back . v 4 160
Turn'd me back With joyful tidings . *2 Hen. IV.* i 1 34
And did grace the shame Of those that turn'd their backs . i 1 130
He leaves his back unarm'd, the French and Welsh Baying him at the heels . i 3 79
Comes the king back from Wales, my noble lord? . ii 1 189
Many thousand reasons hold me back . ii 3 66
He'll not swagger with a Barbary hen, if her feathers turn back . ii 4 108
You knew I was at your back, and spoke it on purpose . ii 4 334
His apparel is built upon his back and the whole frame stands upon pins . iii 2 155
These tardy tricks of yours will, on my life, One time or other break some gallows' back . iv 3 32
Look back into your mighty ancestors . *Hen. V.* i 2 102
Convey you safe, and bring you back . ii Prol. 38
To-morrow shall you bear our full intent Back to our brother . ii 4 115
Turn thee back, And tell thy king I do not seek him now . iii 6 148
Methought yesterday your mistress shrewdly shook your back . iii 7 52
Vaulting into my saddle with my armour on my back . v 2 143
A straight back will stoop; a black beard will turn white . v 2 168
His sparkling eyes, replete with wrathful fire, More dazzled and drove back his enemies . *1 Hen. VI.* i 1 13
Thrust Talbot with a spear into the back . i 1 138
Him I forgive my death that killeth me When he sees me go back one foot or fly . i 2 21
Stand back, you lords, and give us leave awhile . i 2 70
Stand back, thou manifest conspirator . i 3 33
Nay, stand thou back; I will not budge a foot . i 3 38
I will not slay thee, but I'll drive thee back . i 3 41
Lean thine aged back against mine arm . ii 5 43
Keep not back your powers in dalliance . v 2 5
I'll be the first, sure.—Come back, fool . *2 Hen. VI.* i 3 9
She bears a duke's revenues on her back . i 3 83
Led along, Mail'd up in shame, with papers on my back . ii 4 31
Whose overweening arm I have pluck'd back . iii 1 159
When from thy shore the tempest beat us back . iii 2 102
Let them break your backs with burthens, take your houses over your heads . iv 8 30
Oft have I seen a hot o'erweening cur Run back and bite . v 1 152
Turn back and fly, like ships before the wind . *3 Hen. VI.* i 4 4
Where are your mess of sons to back you now? . i 4 73
'Charge upon our foes!' But never once again turn back and fly . ii 1 185
Who 'scapes the lurking serpent's mortal sting? Not he that sets his foot upon her back . ii 2 16
And bloody steel grasp'd in their ireful hands, Are at our backs . ii 5 133
An envious mountain on my back, Where sits deformity to mock my body . iii 2 157
Be gone To keep them back that come to succour you . iv 7 56
Let us enter too.—So other foes may set upon our backs . v 1 61
And heave it shall some weight, or break my back: Work thou the way v 7 24
My lord, stand back, and let the coffin pass . *Richard III.* i 2 38
Nothing to back my suit at all, But the plain devil and dissembling looks i 2 236
I can counterfeit the deep tragedian; Speak and look back . iii 5 6
Since you will buckle fortune on my back, To bear her burthen . iii 7 228
Where is thy power, then, to beat him back? Where are thy tenants? iv 4 480
Many Have broke their backs with laying manors on 'em . *Hen. VIII.* i 1 84
Most pestilent to the hearing; and, to bear 'em, The back is sacrifice to the load . i 2 50
If your back Cannot vouchsafe this burthen, 'tis too weak . ii 3 42
I know your back will bear a duchess: say, Are you not stronger than you were? . ii 3 99
Madam, you are call'd back.—What need you note it? . ii 4 127
To call back her appeal She intends unto his holiness . ii 4 234
For your stubborn answer About the giving back the great seal to us, The king shall know it . iii 2 347
Come back: what mean you?—I'll not come back . v 1 157
Upon my back, to defend my belly . *Troi. and Cres.* i 2 284
We turn not back the silks upon the merchant, When we have soil'd them . ii 2 69
These moral laws Of nature and of nations speak aloud To have her back return'd . ii 2 186
Like a gate of steel Fronting the sun, receives and renders back His figure and his heat . iii 3 122
Time hath, my lord, a wallet at his back, Wherein he puts alms for oblivion . iii 3 145
Where injury of chance Puts back leave-taking . iv 4 36
Loads o' gravel i' the back, lethargies, cold palsies . v 1 22
Go back: Thy wife hath dream'd; thy mother hath had visions . v 3 62
This day is ominous: Therefore, come back . v 3 67
Backs red, and faces pale With flight and agued fear! . *Coriolanus* i 4 37
The town is ta'en!—'Twill be deliver'd back on good condition . i 10 2
Thus I turn my back: There is a world elsewhere . iii 3 134
Stay: whence are you?—Stand, and go back.—You guard like men v 2 1
Go back: the virtue of your name Is not here passable . v 2 12
Therefore, back to Rome, and prepare for your execution . v 2 51
Back, I say, go; lest I let forth your half-pint of blood; back . v 2 60
Do you hear how we are shent for keeping your greatness back? . v 2 105
Say my request's unjust, And spurn me back . v 3 165
I'll back with you; and pray you, Stand to me in this cause . v 3 198
You shall bear A better witness back than words . v 3 204
Follow, my lord, and I'll soon bring her back . *T. Andron.* i 1 289
I will not be denied: sweet heart, look back . i 1 481
I'll go fetch thy sons To back thy quarrels, whatsoe'er they be . ii 3 54
Do not draw back, for we will mourn with thee . iii 1 56
And here's thy hand, in scorn to thee sent back . iii 1 238
She's with the lion deeply still in league, And lulls him whilst she playeth on her back . iv 1 99
Steel to the very back, Yet wrung with wrongs more than our backs can bear . iv 3 47
My naked weapon is out: quarrel, I will back thee.—How! turn thy back? . *Rom. and Jul.* i 1 40
This is the hag, when maids lie on their backs, That presses them . i 4 92
Can I go forward when my heart is here? Turn back, dull earth . ii 1 2

Back. Mortals that fall back to gaze on him When he bestrides the lazy-pacing clouds *Rom. and Jul.* ii 2 30
The sun's beams, Driving back shadows over louring hills ii 5 6
My back o' t' other side,—O, my back, my back! ii 5 51
With one hand beats Cold death aside, and with the other sends It back iii 1 168
Then Tybalt fled; But by and by comes back to Romeo iii 1 175
Whiter than new snow on a raven's back iii 2 19
Back, foolish tears, back to your native spring iii 2 102
A pack of blessings lights upon thy back; Happiness courts thee iii 3 141
And call thee back With twenty hundred thousand times more joy iii 3 152
Be fickle, fortune; For then, I hope, thou wilt not keep him long, But send him back iii 5 64
All the world to nothing, That he dares ne'er come back iii 5 216
Of more price, Being spoke behind your back, than to your face iv 1 28
Contempt and beggary hangs upon thy back v 1 71
This dagger hath mista'en,—for, lo, his house Is empty on the back of Montague! v 3 204
I love and honour him, But must not break my back to heal his finger *T. of Athens* ii 1 24
There's the fool hangs on your back already ii 2 57
Some single vantages you took, When my indisposition put you back ii 2 139
I have kept back their foes, While they have told their money iii 5 106
Let me look back upon thee. O thou wall, That girdlest in those wolves! iv 1 1
Bankrupts, hold fast; Rather than render back, out with your knives! iv 1 9
As we do turn our backs From our companion thrown into his grave iv 2 8
I thank them; and would send them back the plague v 1 140
The senators with one consent of love Entreat thee back to Athens v 1 144
So soon we shall drive back Of Alcibiades the approaches wild v 1 166
Being offered him, he put it by with the back of his hand *J. Cæsar* i 2 221
But when he once attains the upmost round, He then unto the ladder turns his back ii 1 25
The things that threaten'd me Ne'er look'd but on my back ii 2 11
Cassius or Cæsar never shall turn back, For I will slay myself iii 1 21
Post back with speed, and tell him what hath chanced iii 1 287
Thou shalt not back till I have borne this corse Into the market-place iii 1 291
My heart is in the coffin there with Cæsar, And I must pause till it come back to me iii 2 112
Press not so upon me; stand far off.—Stand back; room; bear back iii 2 172
He was but a fool that brought My answer back iv 3 85
If at Philippi we do face him there, These people at our back iv 3 212
But, my lord, He came not back: he is or ta'en or slain v 3 5
My liege, They are not yet come back *Macbeth* i 4 3
I wish your horses swift and sure of foot; And so I do commend you to their backs iii 1 39
If charnel-houses and our graves must send Those that we bury back iii 4 72
The cloudy messenger turns me his back, And hums iii 6 41
Blow, wind! come, wrack! At least we'll die with harness on our back v 5 52
Get thee back; my soul is too much charged With blood of thine already v 8 5
Are all the rest come back? Or is it some abuse? *Hamlet* iv 7 50
Therefore this project Should have a back or second, that might hold iv 7 154
He hath borne me on his back a thousand times v 1 205
Your lordship is right welcome back to Denmark.—I humbly thank you v 2 81
Young Osric, who brings back to him, that you attend him in the hall v 2 204
I Return those duties back as are right fit, Obey you, love you *Lear* i 1 99
Turn thy hated back Upon our kingdom i 1 178
I have years on my back forty eight i 4 42
What says the fellow there? Call the clotpoll back i 4 51
Why came not the slave back to me when I called him? i 4 56
Thou borest thy ass on thy back o'er the dirt i 4 177
'Tis strange that they should so depart from home, And not send back my messenger ii 4 2
Three suits to his back, six shirts to his body, horse to ride iii 4 141
The foul fiend bites my back iii 6 18
Why the King of France is so suddenly gone back know you the reason? iv 3 2
Why dost thou lash that whore? Strip thine own back iv 6 165
Back do I toss these treasons to thy head v 3 146
Your daughter and the Moor are now making the beast with two backs *Othello* i 1 118
I prithee, call him back.—Went he hence now?—Ay, sooth iii 3 51
Truly, an obedient lady: I do beseech your lordship, call her back iv 1 260
If haply you my father do suspect An instrument of this your calling back, Lay not your blame on me iv 2 45
Do you go back dismay'd? 'tis a lost fear; Man but a rush against Othello's breast, And he retires v 2 269
The hand could pluck her back that shoved her on *Ant. and Cleo.* i 2 131
This common body, Like to a vagabond flag upon the stream, Goes to and back i 4 46
See, How I convey my shame out of thine eyes By looking back what I have left behind 'Stroy'd in dishonour iii 11 53
We sent our schoolmaster; Is he come back? Love, I am full of lead iii 11 72
Let us score their backs, And snatch 'em up, as we take hares, behind iv 7 12
And o'er green Neptune's back With ships made cities iv 14 58
His delights Were dolphin-like; they show'd his back above The element they lived in v 2 89
What have I kept back?—Enough to purchase what you have made known v 2 147
What, goest thou back? thou shalt Go back, I warrant thee v 2 155
Make her go back, even to the yielding *Cymbeline* i 4 115
Back my ring: Render to me some corporal sign about her ii 4 118
If you'll back to the court— No court, no father iii 4 133
With that suit upon my back, will I ravish her iii 5 141
I'll knock her back, foot her home again iii 5 148
The army broken, And but the backs of Britons seen, all flying v 3 6
But to look back in frown v 3 28
Didst thou not say, when I did push thee back—Which was when I perceived thee—that thou camest From good descending? *Pericles* v 1 127
Back again. Whose pity, sighing back again, Did us but loving wrong *Tempest* i 2 150
It were a shame to call her back again *T. G. of Ver.* i 1 51
Here have I brought him back again iv 4 57
I, that do speak a word, May call it back again *Meas. for Meas.* i 1 58
Go back again, thou slave, and fetch him home.—Go back again, and be new beaten home? *Com. of Errors* ii 1 75
Take her back again: Give not this rotten orange to your friend *Much Ado* iv 1 32
'Fair' I give you back again; and 'welcome' I have not yet *L. L. Lost* ii 1 91
To enrich my pain, To have his sight thither and back again *M. N. Dream* i 1 251
May all to Athens back again repair And think no more of this iv 1 72
Back again. Or bring your latter hazard back again *Mer. of Ven.* i 1 151
I will survey the inscriptions back again ii 7 14
Go on, and fetch our horses back again *T. of Shrew* iv 5 9
Entreating from your royal thoughts A modest one, to bear me back again.—I cannot give thee less *All's Well* ii 1 131
When back again this ring shall be deliver'd iv 2 60
The money shall be paid back again with advantage *1 Hen. IV.* ii 4 599
The money is paid back again.—O, I do not like that paying back iii 3 200
And send you back again to your master, for a jewel *2 Hen. IV.* i 2 21
Call him back again i 2 74
Let us die in honour: once more back again *Hen. V.* iv 5 11
Your eyes advance, After your thoughts, straight back again to France v Prol. 45
To-morrow toward London back again *2 Hen. VI.* ii 1 201
You four, from hence to prison back again ii 3 5
Drove back again unto my native clime iii 2 84
Let's levy men, and beat him back again *3 Hen. VI.* iv 8 6
If you be hired for meed, go back again *Richard III.* i 4 234
And with the same full state paced back again *Hen. VIII.* iv 1 93
Nurse, come back again *Rom. and Jul.* i 3 8
O, for a falconer's voice, To lure this tassel-gentle back again! ii 2 160
And with a silk thread plucks it back again ii 2 181
Here comes the furious Tybalt back again iii 1 126
Take the villain back again, That late thou gavest me iii 1 130
I'll call them back again to comfort me: Nurse! What should she do here? iv 3 17
Let's make haste; she'll soon be back again *Macbeth* iii 5 36
If praises may go back again, Stood challenger on mount of all the age *Hamlet* iv 7 27
He is not here.—No, my good lord; I met him back again *Lear* iv 2 91
If he do, sure, he cannot weep't back again *Ant. and Cleo.* iii 6 111
Thou must not take my former sharpness ill: I will employ thee back again iii 3 39
Madam, I thought you would not back again *Cymbeline* iii 4 119
Backbite. They are arrant knaves, and will backbite *2 Hen. IV.* v 1 36
Back-door. Sir John, is come in at your back-door *Mer. Wives* iii 3 25
Having found the back-door open Of the unguarded hearts *Cymbeline* v 3 45
Backed. Whose western side is with a vineyard back'd *Meas. for Meas.* iv 1 29
Back'd by the power of Warwick, that false peer *3 Hen. VI.* i 1 52
England is safe, if true within itself.—But the safer when 'tis back'd with France iv 1 41
Let us be back'd with God and with the seas iv 1 43
Buckingham, back'd with the hardy Welshmen, Is in the field *Richard III.* iv 3 47
Methinks it is like a weasel.—It is backed like a weasel *Hamlet* iii 2 397
Great Jupiter, upon his eagle back'd, Appear'd to me *Cymbeline* v 5 427
Back-friend. A back-friend, a shoulder-clapper *Com. of Errors* iv 2 37
Backing. Call you that backing of your friends? A plague upon such backing! give me them that will face me *1 Hen. IV.* ii 4 166
With a band of thirty thousand men Comes Warwick, backing of the Duke *3 Hen. VI.* ii 2 69
Back-return. Whatever chanced, Till Harry's back-return again to France *Hen. V.* v Prol. 41
Backside. His steel was in debt; it went o' the backside the town *Cymbeline* i 2 14
Backsword man. I knew him a good backsword man *2 Hen. IV.* iii 2 70
Back to school. For your intent In going back to school in Wittenberg, It is most retrograde to our desire *Hamlet* i 2 113
Back-trick. I have the back-trick simply as strong as any man *T. Night* i 3 131
Backward. In the dark backward and abysm of time *Tempest* i 2 50
His backward voice is to utter foul speeches and to detract ii 2 95
She would spell him backward *Much Ado* iii 1 61
What is a, b, spelt backward, with the horn on his head? *L. L. Lost* v 1 50
It should seem, then, that Dobbin's tail grows backward *Mer. of Venice* ii 2 103
You go so much backward when you fight.—That's for advantage *All's Well* i 1 214
Only doth backward pull Our slow designs when we ourselves are dull i 1 233
Which, follow'd well, would demonstrate them now But goers backward i 2 48
When English measure backward their own ground In faint retire *K. John* v 5 3
Perish the man whose mind is backward now! *Hen. V.* iv 3 72
This neglection of degree it is That by a pace goes backward *Troi. and Cres.* i 3 128
Come your ways; an you draw backward, we'll put you i' the fills iii 2 47
Thou shalt hunt a lion, that will fly With his face backward iv 1 20
Turn giddy, and be holp by backward turning *Rom. and Jul.* i 2 48
Dost thou fall upon thy face? Thou wilt fall backward when thou hast more wit i 3 42
We might have met them dareful, beard to beard, And beat them backward home *Macbeth* v 5 7
Yourself, sir, should be old as I am, if like a crab you could go backward *Hamlet* ii 2 206
Now they do re-stem Their backward course *Othello* i 3 38
To darkness fleet souls that fly backwards *Cymbeline* v 3 25
Backwardly. Does he think so backwardly of me now? *T. of Athens* iii 3 18
Back-wounding calumny The whitest virtue strikes *Meas. for Meas.* iii 2 197
Bacon. 'Hang-hog' is Latin for bacon, I warrant you *Mer. Wives* iv 1 50
A gammon of bacon and two razes of ginger *1 Hen. IV.* ii 1 26
On, bacons, on! What, ye knaves! young men must live ii 2 95
Bacon-fed knaves! they hate us youth: down with them ii 2 88
Bad. He wants wit that wants resolved will To learn his wit to exchange the bad for better *T. G. of Ver.* ii 6 13
Fie, fie, unreverend tongue! to call her bad ii 6 14
My ears are stopt and cannot hear good news, So much of bad already hath possess'd them iii 1 206
In dumb silence will I bury mine, For they are harsh, untuneable and bad iii 1 208
Music oft hath such a charm To make bad good *Meas. for Meas.* iv 1 15
For the most, become much more the better For being a little bad v 1 446
Happy but for me, And by me, had not our hap been bad *Com. of Errors* i 1 39
Still did I tell him it was vile and bad v 1 67
A better death than die with mocks, Which is as bad as die with tickling *Much Ado* iii 1 80
I am much deceived but I remember the style.—Else your memory is bad *L. L. Lost* iv 1 99
Among nine bad if one be good, There's yet one good in ten *All's Well* i 3 82
Even as bad as those That vulgars give bold'st titles *W. Tale* ii 1 93
I, that please some, try all, both joy and terror Of good and bad iv 1 2
A miscreant, Too good to be so and too bad to live *Richard II.* i 1 40
Thy overflow of good converts to bad v 3 64
To wake a wolf is as bad as to smell a fox *2 Hen. IV.* i 2 175
Our corns shall seem as light as chaff And good from bad find no partition iv 1 196

Bad. Scourge the bad revolting stars That have consented unto Henry's death! . . . *1 Hen. VI.* i 1 4
Not half so bad as thine to England's king, Injurious duke . *2 Hen. VI.* i 4 50
Counting myself but bad till I be best . . *3 Hen. VI.* v 6 91
No news so bad abroad as this at home . . *Richard III.* i 1 135
Now, by Saint Paul, this news is bad indeed . . . i 1 138
You know no rules of charity, Which renders good for bad, blessings for curses . . . . . . i 2 69
Bad is the world; and all will come to nought . . iii 6 13
Good news or bad, that thou comest in so bluntly? . iv 3 45
None so bad, but it may well be told.—Hoyday, a riddle! neither good nor bad! . . . . . . iv 4 459
Now good or bad, 'tis but the chance of war . *Troi. and Cres.* Prol. 31
And posts, like the commandment of a king, Sans check to good and bad . . . . i 3 94
Although particular, shall give a scantling Of good or bad unto the general . . . . i 3 342
The augurer tells me we shall have news to-night.—Good or bad? *Coriol.* ii 1 3
To affect the malice and displeasure of the people is as bad as that which he dislikes, to flatter them for their love . . . ii 2 25
Good, or bad? answer to that; Say either, and I'll stay the circumstance *Rom. and Jul.* ii 5 35
A plague on thee! thou art too bad to curse . *T. of Athens* iv 3 365
Excellent workman! thou canst not paint a man so bad as is thyself v 1 33
Those That would make good of bad, and friends of foes . *Macbeth* ii 4 41
There is nothing either good or bad, but thinking makes it so *Hamlet* ii 2 256
Almost as bad, good mother, As kill a king, and marry with his brother iii 4 28
I must be cruel, only to be kind: Thus bad begins and worse remains behind . . . . . . iii 4 179
I know not, madam: 'tis too bad, too bad . . *Lear* ii 1 98
Bad is the trade that must play fool to sorrow, Angering itself and others iv 1 40
Heaven me such uses send, Not to pick bad from bad, but by bad mend! *Othello* iv 3 106
Prithee, friend, Pour out the pack of matter to mine ear, The good and bad together . . . *Ant. and Cleo.* ii 5 55
Is a thing Too bad for bad report . . . *Cymbeline* i 1 17
So slippery that The fear's as bad as falling . . . iii 3 49
Since she is living, let the time run on To good or bad . . v 5 129
If it be true that I interpret false, Then were it certain you were not so bad . . . . . . *Pericles* i 1 125
For though he strive To killen bad, keep good alive . . ii Gower 20
Till fortune, tired with doing bad, Threw him ashore, to give him glad ii Gower 37
Neither of these are so bad as thou art . . . . iv 6 171

Bad a death. So bad a death argues a monstrous life.—Forbear to judge *2 Hen. VI.* iii 3 30

Bad a kind. That mongrel cur, Ajax, against that dog of as bad a kind, Achilles . . . . *Troi. and Cres.* v 4 15

Bad a peer. No malice, sir; no more than well becomes So good a quarrel and so bad a peer . . . . *2 Hen. VI.* ii 1 28

Bad a prayer. So bad a prayer as his Was never yet for sleep *Ant. and Cleo.* iv 9 27

Bad a voice. Tax not so bad a voice To slander music any more than once . . . . *Much Ado* ii 3 46

Bad air. I durst not laugh, for fear of opening my lips and receiving the bad air . . . . *J. Cæsar* i 2 252

Bad an instrument. But loath am to produce So bad an instrument *All's Well* v 3 202

Bad begun. Things bad begun make strong themselves by ill. *Macbeth* iii 2 55

Bad blame. Destruction on my head, if my bad blame Light on the man! *Othello* i 3 177

Bad bondmen. Their mother's bed-chamber should not be safe For these bad bondmen . . . . . *T. Andron.* iv 1 109

Bad cause. No discourse of reason, Nor fear of bad success in a bad cause, Can qualify the same . . . *Troi. and Cres.* ii 2 117
Unto bad causes swear Such creatures as men doubt . *J. Cæsar* ii 1 131

Bad causer. Bettering thy loss makes the bad causer worse . *Rich. III.* iv 4 122

Bad child; worse father! to entice his own To evil . . *Pericles* i Gower 27

Bad courses. But by bad courses may be understood That their events can never fall out good . . . *Richard II.* ii 1 213

Bad dealing. All will come to nought, When such bad dealing must be seen in thought . . . . *Richard III.* iii 6 14

Bad dreams. I have bad dreams.—Which dreams indeed are ambition *Hamlet* ii 2 262

Bad employment. But to win time To lose so bad employment *Cymbeline* iii 4 113

Bad enough. That's bad enough, for I am but reproach . *2 Hen. VI.* ii 4 96
It was bad enough before their spite.—Thou wrong'st it . *Rom. and Jul.* iv 1 31

Bad entertainment. Pardon me, sir, your bad entertainment *T. Night* ii 1 34

Bad epitaph. After your death you were better have a bad epitaph than their ill report while you live . . . . *Hamlet* ii 2 550

Bad friends. At their births good stars were opposite.—No, to their lives bad friends were contrary . . . *Richard III.* iv 4 216

Bad fruit. Truly, the tree yields bad fruit . . *As Y. Like It* iii 2 123

Bad habit. A better bad habit of frowning . *Mer. of Venice* i 2 63

Bad humours. The king hath run bad humours on the knight *Hen. V.* ii 1 127
These be good humours! your honour wins bad humours . . . iii 2 28

Bad intent. His act did not o'ertake his bad intent . *Meas. for Meas.* v 1 456
Be advised; He comes to bad intent . . . *Othello* i 2 56

Bad legs. With his bad legs, falls into the cinque pace . *Much Ado* ii 1 81

Bad life. Now my bad life reft me so much of friends . . iv 1 198
Further I say and further will maintain Upon his bad life to make all this good . . . . . . *Richard II.* i 1 99
Brave death outweighs bad life . . . *Coriolanus* i 6 71

Bad luck. He told me that rebellion had bad luck . . *2 Hen. IV.* i 1 41

Bad man. Bad men, you violate A two-fold marriage . *Richard II.* v 1 71
Eyes, that so long have slept upon This bold bad man . *Hen. VIII.* ii 2 44

Bad marriage. Many a good hanging prevents a bad marriage *T. Night* i 5 20

Bad match. There I have another bad match . *Mer. of Venice* iii 1 46

Bad mischance. View these letters full of bad mischance *1 Hen. VI.* i 1 89

Bad neighbour. Our bad neighbour makes us early stirrers . *Hen. V.* iv 1 6

Bad news. The king is dead.—Bad news, by'r lady! . *Richard III.* ii 3 4
The nature of bad news infects the teller . . *Ant. and Cleo.* i 2 99
Though it be honest, it is never good To bring bad news . . . ii 5 86

Bad parts. Tell me for which of my bad parts didst thou first fall in love with me? . . . . *Much Ado* v 2 60

Bad performance. If this should fail, And that our drift look through our bad performance, 'Twere better not assay'd *Hamlet* iv 7 152

Bad quarrel. In a bad quarrel slain a virtuous son . *T. Andron.* i 1 342

Bad recompense. It were a bad recompense for your love . *T. Night* ii 1 7

Bad report. Is a thing Too bad for bad report . . . *Cymbeline* i 1 17

Bad soles. Indeed, sir, a mender of bad soles . . . *J. Cæsar* i 1 15

Bad sons. Good wombs have borne bad sons . . . *Tempest* i 2 120

Bad strokes. Good words are better than bad strokes . *J. Cæsar* v 1 29

Bad success. Things ill-got had ever bad success . . *3 Hen. VI.* ii 2 46
Nor fear of bad success in a bad cause, Can qualify the same *Troi. and Cres.* ii 2 117

Bad thing. Ay, and that From one bad thing to worse . *Cymbeline* iv 2 134

Bad thinking. An bad thinking do not wrest true speaking, I'll offend nobody . . . . *Much Ado* iii 4 33

Bad verses. Tear him for his bad verses . . . *J. Cæsar* iii 3 34

Bad voice. I pray God his bad voice bode no mischief *Much Ado* ii 3 83
He knows me as the blind man knows the cuckoo, By the bad voice *Mer. of Venice* v 1 113
Without hawking or spitting or saying we are hoarse, which are the only prologues to a bad voice . . . *As Y. Like It* v 3 13

Bad ways. One of two bad ways you must conceit me . *J. Cæsar* iii 1 192

Bad woman. One that serves a bad woman . *Meas. for Meas.* ii 1 64

Bad word. His few bad words are matched with as few good deeds *Hen. V.* iii 2 41
I never spake bad word, nor did ill turn To any living creature *Pericles* iv 1 76

Bad world the while! This must not be thus borne . *K. John* iv 2 100

Bade. Hast thou, spirit, Perform'd to point the tempest that I bade thee? . . . . *Tempest* i 2 194
Who bade you call her?—Your worship, sir; or else I mistook *T. G. of Ver.* ii 1 9
Love bade me swear and Love bids me forswear . . . ii 6 6
I carried Mistress Silvia the dog you bade me . . . . iv 4 50
She bade me tell your worship that her husband is seldom from home *Mer. Wives* ii 2 104
He bade me store up, as a triple eye . . . *All's Well* ii 1 111
I bade her, if her fortunes ever stood Necessitied to help, that by this token I would relieve her . . . . . . v 3 84
The lady bade take away the fool . . . *T. Night* i 5 57
Take her away.—Sir, I bade them take away you . . . i 5 60
My lady bade me tell you, that, though she harbours you as her kinsman ii 3 103
By your leave, I pray you, I bade you never speak again of him . iii 1 118
Bade me come smiling and cross-garter'd to you, To put on yellow stockings . . . . v 1 345
Whom he loves—He bade me say so . . . *W. Tale* v 1 146
Your highness bade me ask for it to-day.—So did you me *Hen. V.* ii 2 63
He that temper'd thee bade thee stand up, Gave thee no instance . ii 2 118
So a' bade me lay more clothes on his feet . . . . ii 3 23
You bade me ban, and will you bid me leave? . *2 Hen. VI.* iii 2 333
Kneel'd at my feet, and bade me be advised . *Richard III.* ii 1 107
Kiss'd my cheek; Bade me rely on him as on my father . . ii 2 25
You he bade Attend him here this morning . . *Hen. VIII.* iii 2 81
Bade me enjoy it, with the place and honours, During my life . iii 2 248
He bade me take a trumpet, And to this purpose speak . *Troi. and Cres.* i 3 263
I bade the vile owl go learn me the tenour of the proclamation . ii 1 99
Hector bade ask.—Which way would Hector have it?—He cares not iv 5 71
She's well, but bade me not commend her to you . . . iv 5 180
As if that luck, in very spite of cunning, Bade him win all . v 5 42
For so he bade me say; And so I do . . . *T. Andron.* iv 2 13
At twelve year old, I bade her come. What, lamb! *Rom. and Jul.* i 3 3
As I told you, my young lady bade me inquire you out; what she bade me say, I will keep to myself . . . . . . ii 4 173
Romeo that spoke him fair, bade him bethink How nice the quarrel was iii 1 158
Hereafter say, A madman's mercy bade thee run away . . v 3 67
Accoutred as I was, I plunged in And bade him follow . *J. Cæsar* i 2 106
That tongue of his that bade the Romans Mark him . . . i 2 125
I will hie, And so bestow these papers as you bade me . . . i 3 151
Bid me fall down; And, being prostrate, thus he bade me say . iii 1 125
Which ne'er shook hands, nor bade farewell to him . *Macbeth* i 2 21
He bade me, from him, call thee thane of Cawdor . . . i 3 105
He chid the sisters When first they put the name of king upon me, And bade them speak to him . . . . iii 1 59
His majesty bade me signify to you that he has laid a great wager *Hamlet* v 2 105
I ran it through, even from my boyish days, To the very moment that he bade me tell it . . . . *Othello* i 3 133
She thank'd me, And bade me, if I had a friend that loved her, I should but teach him how to tell my story . . . . . i 3 164
She that being anger'd, her revenge being nigh, Bade her wrong stay ii 1 154
Bade him anon return and here speak with me . . . . iii 1 81
He hath commanded me to go to bed, And bade me to dismiss you . iv 3 14
I have laid those sheets you bade me on the bed . . . iv 3 22
Sworest thou not then To do this when I bade thee? . *Ant. and Cleo.* iv 14 82
Antony Did tell me of you, bade me trust you . . . . v 2 13
But in no wise Till he had done his sacrifice, As Dian bade . *Pericles* v 2 278

Badest. As thou badest me, In troops I have dispersed them . *Tempest* i 2 219
And bad'st me bury love.—Not in a grave . *Rom. and Jul.* ii 3 83

Badge. Mark but the badges of these men, my lords, Then say if they be true . . . . *Tempest* v 1 267
Joy could not show itself modest enough without a badge of bitterness *Much Ado* i 1 23
Black is the badge of hell, The hue of dungeons . *L. L. Lost* iv 3 254
By these badges understand the king . . . . . v 2 764
Bearing the badge of faith, to prove them true . *M. N. Dream* iii 2 127
Sufferance is the badge of all our tribe . . *Mer. of Venice* i 3 111
With tears and smiles, The badges of his grief and patience *Richard II.* v 2 33
Left the liver white and pale, which is the badge of pusillanimity and cowardice . . . . *2 Hen. IV.* iv 3 113
To this hour is an honourable badge of the service . . *Hen. V.* iv 7 106
And he first took exceptions at this badge . . . *1 Hen. VI.* iv 1 105
I like it not, In that he wears the badge of Somerset . . . iv 1 177
Slanders me with murder's crimson badge . . . *2 Hen. VI.* iii 2 200
That I'll write upon thy burgonet, Might I but know thee by thy household badge . . . . v 1 201
My father's badge, old Nevil's crest, The rampant bear chain'd to the ragged staff . . . . v 1 202
Sweet mercy is nobility's true badge . . . . *T. Andron.* i 1 119
Better than he have worn Vulcan's badge . . . . . ii 1 89

Badged. Their hands and faces were all badged with blood . *Macbeth* ii 3 107

Badly. How goes the day with us? O, tell me, Hubert.—Badly, I fear *K. John* v 3 2

Badness. But he's more, Had I more name for badness . *Meas. for Meas.* v 1 59
A provoking merit, set a-work by a reproveable badness in himself *Lear* iii 5 9
As duteous to the vices of thy mistress As badness would desire . iv 6 259

Bae. The ewe that will not hear her lamb when it baes will never answer a calf when he bleats . . . . *Much Ado* iii 3 75
He's a lamb indeed, that baes like a bear . . . *Coriolanus* ii 1 12

Baffle. I will baffle Sir Toby, I will wash off gross acquaintance *T. Night* ii 5 176
An I do not, call me villain and baffle me . . . *1 Hen. IV.* i 2 113

Baffled. Alas, poor fool, how have they baffled thee! . *T. Night* v 1 377

Baffled. I am disgraced, impeach'd and baffled here, Pierced to the soul *Richard II.* i 1 170
Shall dunghill curs confront the Helicons? And shall good news be baffled? . . . . 2 *Hen. IV.* v 3 109
Bag. I have a bag of money here troubles me: if you will help to bear it *Mer. Wives* ii 2 177
Of more value Than stamps in gold or sums in sealed bags . . . iii 4 16
What, a hodge-pudding? a bag of flax?—A puffed man? . . . v 5 159
And why dost thou deny the bag of gold? . . . . *Com. of Errors* iv 4 99
A sealed bag, two sealed bags of ducats, Of double ducats *Mer. of Venice* ii 8 18
Not with bag and baggage, yet with scrip and scrippage *As Y. Like It* iii 2 170
That my deeds shall prove.—And that his bags shall prove *T. of Shrew* i 2 178
It will let in and out the enemy With bag and baggage . . *W. Tale* i 2 206
See thou shake the bags Of hoarding abbots . . . . *K. John* iii 3 7
The clergy's bags Are lank and lean . . . . . 2 *Hen. VI.* i 3 131
My gracious lord, here is the bag of gold . . . . *T. Andron.* iii 3 280
Fathers that bear bags Shall see their children kind . . . *Lear* ii 4 50
Thieves! Look to your house, your daughter and your bags! *Othello* i 1 80
Put up your pipes in your bag, for I'll away: go; vanish into air . iii 1 20
Tie my treasure up in silken bags, To please the fool and death *Pericles* iii 2 41
Shrouded in cloth of state; balm'd and entreasured With full bags of spices! . . . . iii 2 66
Baggage. Out of my door, you witch, you hag, you baggage! *Mer. Wives* iv 2 194
Thou baggage, let me in.—Can you tell for whose sake? *Com. of Errors* iii 1 57
Not with bag and baggage, yet with scrip and scrippage *As Y. Like It* iii 2 170
Ye are a baggage: the Slys are no rogues; look in the chronicles *T. of Shrew* Ind. 1 3
It will let in and out the enemy With bag and baggage *W. Tale* i 2 206
Out, you green-sickness carrion! out, you baggage! You tallow-face! *Rom. and Jul.* iii 5 157
Hang thee, young baggage! disobedient wretch! . . . . iii 5 161
The poor Transylvanian is dead, that lay with the little baggage *Pericles* iv 2 24
If the peevish baggage would but give way to customers . . iv 6 20
Bagot here and Green Observed his courtship . . . *Richard II.* i 4 23
Bushy, Bagot and their complices, The caterpillars of the commonwealth . . . . ii 3 165
Where is Bagot? What is become of Bushy? where is Green? . . iii 2 122
Call forth Bagot. Now, Bagot, freely speak thy mind . . . iv 1 1
Bagpipe. When the bagpipe sings i' the nose . . . *Mer. of Venice* iv 1 49
Why he cannot abide . . . a woollen bag-pipe . . . . iv 1 56
You would never dance again after a tabor and pipe; no, the bagpipe could not move you . . . . *W. Tale* iv 4 183
Or the drone of a Lincolnshire bagpipe . . . . 1 *Hen. IV.* i 2 86
Bag-piper. And laugh like parrots at a bag-piper . . *Mer. of Venice* i 1 53
Bail. I cry bail. Here's a gentleman and a friend of mine *Meas. for Meas.* iii 2 43
I hope, sir, your good worship will be my bail . . . . iii 2 76
You will not bail me, then, sir?—Then, Pompey, nor now . . iii 2 85
First, provost, let me bail these gentle three . . . . v 1 362
I do obey thee till I give thee bail . . . . . *Com. of Errors* iv 1 80
Tell her I am arrested in the street And that shall bail me . . iv 1 107
I sent you money, sir, to be your bail . . . . . v 1 382
Take her away.—I'll put in bail, my liege . . . *All's Well* v 3 286
To prison with her.—Good mother, fetch my bail . . . v 3 296
Call in my sons to be my bail: I know, ere they will have me go to ward, They'll pawn their swords . . . . 2 *Hen. VI.* v 1 111
The sons of York, thy betters in their birth, Shall be their father's bail v 1 120
Let me be their bail . . . . *T. Andron.* ii 3 295
Thou shalt not bail them . . . . ii 3 299
Bailiff. An ape-bearer; then a process-server, a bailiff . . *W. Tale* iv 3 102
Baille me some paper . . . . *Mer. Wives* i 4 92
Baisant la main d'une de votre seigneurie indigne serviteur *Hen. V.* v 2 275
Baisées. Demoiselles pour être baisées devant leur noces, il n'est pas la coutume de France . . . . v 2 280
Baiser. I cannot tell vat is baiser en Anglish . . . . v 2 285
Bait. O cunning enemy, that, to catch a saint, With saints dost bait thy hook! . . . . *Meas. for Meas.* ii 2 181
Do their gay vestments his affections bait? . . . *Com. of Errors* ii 1 94
Bait the hook well; this fish will bite . . . . *Much Ado* ii 3 114
And greedily devour the treacherous bait . . . . . iii 1 28
That her ear lose nothing Of the false sweet bait that we lay for it . iii 1 33
Have you with these contrived To bait me with this foul derision? *M. N. Dream* iii 2 197
Fish not, with this melancholy bait, For this fool gudgeon *Mer. of Venice* i 1 101
What's that good for?—To bait fish withal . . . . iii 1 55
Of boundless tongue, who late hath beat her husband And now baits me! *W. Tale* ii 3 92
Whilst that my wretchedness doth bait myself . . *Richard II.* iv 1 238
If the young dace be a bait for the old pike . . 2 *Hen. IV.* iii 2 356
Are these thy bears? we'll bait thy bears to death . 2 *Hen. VI.* v 1 148
My half-supp'd sword, that frankly would have fed, Pleased with this dainty bait, thus goes to bed . . . . *Troi. and Cres.* v 8 20
Be caught With cautelous baits and practice . . . *Coriolanus* iv 1 33
Words more sweet, and yet more dangerous, Than baits to fish *T. Andron.* iv 4 91
The one is wounded with the bait, The other rotted with delicious feed iv 4 92
And she steal love's sweet bait from fearful hooks *Rom. and Jul.* ii Prol. 8
See you now; Your bait of falsehood takes this carp of truth *Hamlet* ii 1 63
Not born where't grows, But worn a bait for ladies . . *Cymbeline* iii 4 59
Baited. Alas, poor Maccabæus, how hath he been baited! *L. L. Lost* v 2 634
Set mine honour at the stake And baited it with all the unmuzzled thoughts That tyrannous heart can think . . . . *T. Night* iii 1 130
Baited like eagles having lately bathed . . . 1 *Hen. IV.* iv 1 99
To be thus taunted, scorn'd, and baited at . . . *Richard III.* i 3 109
Why stay we to be baited With one that wants her wits? *Coriolanus* iv 2 43
To be baited with the rabble's curse . . . . . *Macbeth* v 8 29
Baiting. And manacle the bear-ward in their chains, If thou darest bring them to the baiting place . . . . . 2 *Hen. VI.* v 1 150
Here ye lie baiting of bombards, when Ye should do service *Hen. VIII.* v 4 85
Bajazet. Tongue, I must put you into a butter-woman's mouth and buy myself another of Bajazet's mule . . . . . . *All's Well* iv 1 46
Bake. I wash, wring, brew, bake, scour, dress meat and drink, make the beds . . . . *Mer. Wives* i 4 101
Bakes the elf-locks in foul sluttish hairs . . . *Rom. and Jul.* i 4 90
Fillet of a fenny snake, In the cauldron boil and bake . . *Macbeth* iv 1 13
Baked. To do me business in the veins o' the earth When it is baked with frost . . . . *Tempest* i 2 256
If that surly spirit, melancholy, Had baked thy blood . . *K. John* iii 3 43
A minced man: and then to be baked with no date in the pie *Troi. and Cres.* i 2 280
In that paste let their vile heads be baked . . . *T. Andron.* v 2 201
Why, there they are both, baked in that pie . . . . v 3 60
Baked. Look to the baked meats, good Angelica: Spare not for cost *Rom. and Jul.* iv 4 5
The funeral baked meats Did coldly furnish forth the marriage tables *Hamlet* i 2 180
Baked and impasted with the parching streets . . . . ii 2 481
Baker. I have given them away to bakers' wives . . . 1 *Hen. IV.* iii 3 80
They say the owl was a baker's daughter . . . . *Hamlet* iv 5 42
Baking. The making of the cake, the heating of the oven and the baking *Troi. and Cres.* i 1 24
Balance. She shall ne'er weigh more reasons in her balance *Much Ado* v 1 212
A mote will turn the balance . . . . . . *M. N. Dream* v 1 324
Are there balance here to weigh The flesh? . . . *Mer. of Venice* iv 1 255
Many likelihoods informed me of this before, which hung so tottering in the balance that I could neither believe nor misdoubt *All's Well* i 3 130
To whom I promise A counterpoise, if not to thy estate A balance more replete . . . . ii 3 183
Vanities that make him light; But in the balance of great Bolingbroke, Besides himself, are all the English peers . . *Richard II.* iii 4 87
I have in equal balance justly weigh'd What wrongs our arms may do, what wrongs we suffer . . . . . . 2 *Hen. IV.* iv 1 67
You weigh this well; Therefore still bear the balance . . . v 2 103
I cannot give due action to my words, Except a sword or sceptre balance it: A sceptre shall it have . . . . 2 *Hen. VI.* v 1 9
Commit my cause in balance to be weigh'd . . . *T. Andron.* i 1 55
If the balance of our lives had not one scale of reason to poise another of sensuality . . . . *Othello* i 3 330
Bald. You are like to lose your hair and prove a bald jerkin *Tempest* iv 1 238
A rule as plain as the plain bald pate of father Time himself *Com. of Errors* ii 2 71
There's no time for a man to recover his hair that grows bald by nature ii 2 74
Time himself is bald and therefore to the world's end will have bald followers.—I knew 'twould be a bald conclusion . . . ii 2 108
Moss'd with age And high top bald with dry antiquity *As Y. Like It* iv 3 106
Old Time the clock-setter, that bald sexton Time . . *K. John* iii 1 324
This bald unjointed chat of his, my lord, I answer'd indirectly 1 *Hen. IV.* i 3 65
Thy precious rich crown for a pitiful bald crown . . . . ii 4 420
O, give me always a little, lean, old, chapt, bald shot 2 *Hen. IV.* iii 2 294
A curled pate will grow bald; a fair face will wither . . *Hen. V.* v 2 169
Our heads are some brown, some black, some auburn, some bald *Coriol.* ii 3 21
What should the people do with these bald tribunes? . . . iii 1 165
No question asked him by any of the senators, but they stand bald before him . . . . iv 5 206
Make curl'd-pate ruffians bald . . . . . *T. of Athens* iv 3 160
Thou hadst little wit in thy bald crown, when thou gavest thy golden one away . . . . *Lear* i 4 178
Baldpate. Come hither, goodman baldpate: do you know me? *Meas. for Meas.* v 1 329
Bald-pated. You bald-pated, lying rascal, you must be hooded . v 1 357
Baldrick. Or hang my bugle in an invisible baldrick . . *Much Ado* i 1 244
Bale. The one side must have bale . . . . . *Coriolanus* i 1 167
Baleful. Contrived by art and baleful sorcery . . . 1 *Hen. VI.* ii 1 15
Boiling choler chokes The hollow passage of my poison'd voice, By sight of these our baleful enemies . . . . v 4 122
Thou baleful messenger, out of my sight! . . . 2 *Hen. VI.* iii 2 48
If we should recount Our baleful news . . . . . 3 *Hen. VI.* ii 1 97
O'ercome with moss and baleful mistletoe . . . *T. Andron.* ii 3 95
That baleful burning night When subtle Greeks surprised King Priam's Troy . . . . v 3 83
I must up-fill this osier cage of ours With baleful weeds *Rom. and Jul.* ii 3 8
Balk logic with acquaintance that you have And practise rhetoric *T. of Shrew* i 1 34
Balked. This was looked for at your hand, and this was balked *T. Night* iii 2 26
Ten thousand bold Scots, two and twenty knights, Balk'd in their own blood did Sir Walter see . . . . . . 1 *Hen. IV.* i 1 69
Ball. Move these eyes? Or whether, riding on the balls of mine, Seem they in motion? . . . . *Mer. of Venice* iii 2 118
Why, these balls bound; there's noise in it . . . *All's Well* ii 3 314
When from under this terrestrial ball He fires the proud tops of the eastern pines And darts his light . . . . *Richard II.* iii 2 41
If I did not think thou hadst been an ignis fatuus or a ball of wildfire, there's no purchase in money . . . . . 1 *Hen. IV.* iii 3 45
Still unfold The acts commenced on this ball of earth . 2 *Hen. IV.* Ind. 5
When we have match'd our rackets to these balls . . *Hen. V.* i 2 261
This mock of his Hath turn'd his balls to gun-stones . . . i 2 282
As matching to his youth and vanity, I did present him with the Paris balls . . . . ii 4 131
'Tis not the balm, the sceptre and the ball, The sword, the mace . iv 1 277
The fatal balls of murdering basilisks . . . . . . v 2 17
Had she affections and warm youthful blood, She would be as swift in motion as a ball . . . . *Rom. and Jul.* ii 5 13
Some I see That two-fold balls and treble sceptres carry . *Macbeth* iv 1 121
I'll spurn thine eyes Like balls before me . . . *Ant. and Cleo.* ii 5 64
A man whom both the waters and the wind, In that vast tennis-court, have made the ball For them to play upon . . . . *Pericles* ii 1 64
Ballad. Is there not a ballad, boy, of the King and the Beggar? *L. L. Lost* i 2 114
The world was very guilty of such a ballad some three ages since . i 2 117
I will get Peter Quince to write a ballad of this dream . *M. N. Dream* iv 1 221
With a woeful ballad Made to his mistress' eyebrow . *As Y. Like It* ii 7 148
For I the ballad will repeat, Which men full true shall find . *All's Well* i 3 64
A divulged shame Traduced by odious ballads . . . . . ii 1 175
He utters them as he had eaten ballads . . . . . *W. Tale* iv 4 186
I love a ballad but even too well, if it be doleful matter merrily set down . . . . iv 4 188
What hast here? ballads?—Pray now, buy some . . . . iv 4 262
I love a ballad in print o' life, for then we are sure they are true . iv 4 263
Let's first see moe ballads; we'll buy the other things anon . . iv 4 278
Here's another ballad of a fish, that appeared upon the coast . . iv 4 279
And sung this ballad against the hard hearts of maids . . . iv 4 282
The ballad is very pitiful and as true.—Is it true too, think you? . iv 4 285
This is a merry ballad, but a very pretty one . . . . . iv 4 291
Not a ribbon, glass, pomander, brooch, table-book, ballad, knife, tape, glove, shoe-tie, bracelet . . . . iv 4 610
An I have not ballads made on you all and sung to filthy tunes 1 *Hen. IV.* ii 2 48
I will have it in a particular ballad else, with mine own picture 2 *Hen. IV.* iv 3 52
A speaker is but a prater; a rhyme is but a ballad . . . *Hen. V.* v 2 167
And scald rhymers Ballad us out o' tune . . . . *Ant. and Cleo.* v 2 216
Ballad-maker. Pick out mine eyes with a ballad-maker's pen *Much Ado* i 1 254
That ballad-makers cannot be able to express it . . . *W. Tale* v 2 27
This peace is nothing, but to rust iron, increase tailors, and breed ballad-makers.—Let me have war . . . . . *Coriolanus* iv 5 235
Ballad-monger. One of these same metre ballad-mongers 1 *Hen. IV.* iii 1 130

Ballast. Sent whole armadoes of caracks to be ballast at her nose *Com. of Errors* iii 2 141
Ballasting. Then had my prize Been less, and so more equal ballasting To thee . . . . *Cymbeline* iii 6 78
Ballow. Try whether your costard or my ballow be the harder *Lear* iv 6 247
Balm. The several chairs of order look you scour With juice of balm and every precious flower . . . . . *Mer. Wives* v 5 66
Balm his foul head in warm distilled waters . . *T. of Shrew* Ind. 1 48
The which no balm can cure but his heart-blood Which breathed this poison . . . . *Richard II.* i 1 172
Not all the water in the rough rude sea Can wash the balm off from an anointed king . . . . iii 2 55
With mine own tears I wash away my balm . . . . iv 1 207
Let all the tears that should bedew my hearse Be drops of balm 2 *Hen. IV.* iv 5 115
'Tis not the balm, the sceptre and the ball, The sword, the mace *Hen. V.* iv 1 277
Thy balm wash'd off wherewith thou wast anointed . 3 *Hen. VI.* iii 1 17
My pity hath been balm to heal their wounds . . . . iv 8 41
In these windows that let forth thy life, I pour the helpless balm of my poor eyes . . . . *Richard III.* i 2 13
Instead of oil and balm, Thou lay'st in every gash that love hath given me The knife that made it . . . . *Troi. and Cres.* i 1 61
I could wish You were conducted to a gentle bath And balms applied to you . . . . *Coriolanus* i 6 64
To give thy rages balm, To wipe out our ingratitude with loves *T. of Athens* v 4 16
Balm of hurt minds, great nature's second course . *Macbeth* ii 2 39
The argument of your praise, balm of your age, Most best . *Lear* i 1 218
As sweet as balm, as soft as air, as gentle,—O Antony! *Ant. and Cleo.* v 2 314
Balmed. This rest might yet have balm'd thy broken sinews . *Lear* iii 6 105
Balm'd and entreasured With full bags of spices! . . *Pericles* iii 2 65
Balmy. 'Tis the soldiers' life To have their balmy slumbers waked with strife . . . . *Othello* ii 3 258
Ah, balmy breath, that dost almost persuade Justice to break her sword! . . . . v 2 16
Balsam. All those for this? Is this the balsam that the usuring senate Pours into captains' wounds? . . *T. of Athens* iii 5 110
Balsamum. I have bought The oil, the balsamum and aqua-vitæ *Com. of Errors* iv 1 89
Balthazar. Signior Balthazar, either at flesh or fish, A table full of welcome makes scarce one dainty dish . . . . iii 1 22
To the Porpentine, Where Balthazar and I did dine together . v 1 223
A young doctor of Rome; his name is Balthasar . *Mer. of Venice* iv 1 154
How now, Balthasar! Dost thou not bring me letters from the friar? *Rom. and Jul.* v 1 12
'Ban. 'Ban, 'Ban, Cacaliban Has a new master . . . *Tempest* ii 2 188
And ban thine enemies, both mine and thine . 2 *Hen. VI.* ii 4 25
Ay, every joint should seem to curse and ban . . . iii 2 319
You bade me ban, and will you bid me leave? . . . iii 2 333
Take thou that too, with multiplying bans! . . *T. of Athens* iv 1 34
Of midnight weeds collected, With Hecate's ban thrice blasted *Hamlet* iii 2 269
Sometime with lunatic bans, sometime with prayers, Enforce their charity . . . . *Lear* ii 3 19
Banbury. You Banbury cheese! . . . . . *Mer. Wives* i 1 130
Band. Release me from my bands With the help of your good hands *Tempest* Epil. 9
Was he arrested on a band?—Not on a band, but on a stronger thing *Com. of Errors* iv 2 49
The sergeant of the band; he that brings any man to answer it that breaks his band . . . . iv 3 30
My kindness shall incite thee To bind our loves up in a holy band *Much Ado* iii 1 114
Captain of our fairy band, Helena is here at hand . . *M. N. Dream* iii 2 110
Chosen out of the gross band of the unfaithful . . *As Y. Like It* iv 1 199
Here's eight that must take hands To join in Hymen's bands . . v 4 135
Some band of strangers i' the adversary's entertainment . *All's Well* iv 1 16
Now will I charge you in the band of truth . . . . iv 2 56
Writ to me this other day to turn him out o' the band . . iv 3 227
According to thy oath and band . . . . . *Richard II.* i 1 2
Who gently would dissolve the bands of life . . . . ii 2 71
The end of life cancels all bands . . . . 1 *Hen. IV.* iii 2 157
Behold The royal captain of this ruin'd band! . . . *Hen. V.* iv Prol. 29
Do but behold yon poor and starved band . . . . iv 2 16
We few, we happy few, we band of brothers . . . . iv 3 60
Henry the Sixth, in infant bands crown'd King Of France and England Epil. 9
Unite Your troops of horsemen with his bands of foot . 1 *Hen. VI.* iv 1 165
To Ireland will you lead a band of men? . . . 2 *Hen. VI.* iii 1 312
Whiles I in Ireland nourish a mighty band . . . . iii 1 348
And die in bands for this unmanly deed! . . . 3 *Hen. VI.* i 1 186
With a band of thirty thousand men . . . . . . ii 6 68
Vouchsafe to furnish us With some few bands of chosen soldiers . iii 3 204
I'll join mine eldest daughter and my joy To him forthwith in holy wedlock bands . . . . iii 3 243
Hie you to your bands: Let us alone to guard Corioli . *Coriolanus* i 2 26
Their bands i' the vaward are the Antiates, Of their best trust . i 6 53
With all his threatening band of Typhon's brood . . *T. Andron.* iv 2 94
Who leads towards Rome a band of warlike Goths . . . v 2 113
The want whereof doth daily make revolt In my penurious band *T. of Athens* iv 3 92
Hymen did our hands Unite commutual in most sacred bands *Hamlet* iii 2 170
The band that seems to tie their friendship together will be the very strangler of their amity . . . . . *Ant. and Cleo.* ii 6 129
And as my farthest band Shall pass on thy approof . . iii 2 26
Bring him through the bands. To try thy eloquence, now 'tis time iii 12 25
We being not known, not muster'd Among the bands . *Cymbeline* iv 4 11
Hath More of thee merited than a band of Clotens Had ever scar for v 5 304
Bandied. Well bandied both; a set of wit well play'd . *L. L. Lost* v 2 29
Banding themselves in contrary parts . . . . 1 *Hen. VI.* iii 1 81
Banditto. Great men oft die by vile bezonians: A Roman sworder and banditto slave Murder'd sweet Tully . . 2 *Hen. VI.* iv 1 135
Ban-dog. The time when screech-owls cry and ban-dogs howl . i 4 21
Bandy. I will bandy with thee in faction . . . *As Y. Like It* v 1 61
To bandy word for word and frown for frown . . *T. of Shrew* v 2 172
I will not bandy with thee word for word, But buckle with thee blows, twice two for one . . . . 3 *Hen. VI.* i 4 49
One fit to bandy with thy lawless sons . . . *T. Andron.* i 1 312
My words would bandy her to my sweet love, And his to me *Rom. and Jul.* ii 5 14
Do you bandy looks with me, you rascal? . . . . *Lear* i 4 92
'Tis not in thee To grudge my pleasures, to cut off my train, To bandy hasty words . . . . ii 4 178
Bandying. This shouldering of each other in the court, This factious bandying . . . . 1 *Hen. VI.* iv 1 190
Bandying. The prince expressly hath Forbidden bandying in Verona streets . . . . *Rom. and Jul.* iii 1 92
Bane. Our natures do pursue, Like rats that ravin down their proper bane, A thirsty evil . . . . . . *Meas. for Meas.* i 2 133
Bane to those That for my surety will refuse the boys! . 2 *Hen. VI.* v 1 120
'Twill be his death; 'twill be his bane; he cannot bear it *Troi. and Cres.* iv 2 98
Lest Rome herself be bane unto herself . . . . *T. Andron.* v 3 73
I will not be afraid of death and bane, Till Birnam forest come to Dunsinane . . . . *Macbeth* v 3 59
Two boys, an old man twice a boy, a lane, Preserved the Britons, was the Romans' bane . . . . *Cymbeline* v 3 58
Baned. What if my house be troubled with a rat And I be pleased to give ten thousand ducats To have it baned? . . *Mer. of Venice* iv 1 46
Bang. You'll bear me a bang for that, I fear . . *J. Cæsar* iii 3 20
Banged. You should have banged the youth into dumbness . *T. Night* iii 2 24
The desperate tempest hath so bang'd the Turks . . *Othello* ii 1 21
Banish. Her father . . . ; Who, all enraged, will banish Valentine *T. G. of Ver.* ii 6 38
Prolixious blushes, That banish what they sue for . *Meas. for Meas.* ii 4 163
Do not banish reason For inequality . . . . . . v 1 64
Banish hence these abject lowly dreams . . . *T. of Shrew* Ind. 2 34
Therefore, we banish you our territories . . . . *Richard II.* i 3 139
Swear by the duty that you owe to God—Our part therein we banish with yourselves . . . . i 3 181
Six years we banish him, and he shall go . . . . . i 3 248
Think not the king did banish thee, But thou the king . . i 3 279
As 'twere to banish their affects with him . . . . i 4 30
Banish us both and send the king with me . . . . v 1 83
Banish Peto, banish Bardolph, banish Poins . . . 1 *Hen. IV.* ii 4 521
Banish not him thy Harry's company: banish plump Jack, and banish all the world . . . . ii 4 526
As the state stood then, Was force perforce compell'd to banish him 2 *Hen. IV.* iv 1 116
I banish thee, on pain of death, As I have done the rest of my misleaders v 5 67
And you, good uncle, banish all offence . . . 1 *Hen. VI.* v 5 96
If thou dost love thy lord, Banish the canker of ambitious thoughts 2 *Hen. VI.* i 2 18
I banish her my bed and company And give her as a prey to law . ii 1 197
Even from this instant, banish him our city . . *Coriolanus* iii 3 101
As the dead carcasses of unburied men That do corrupt my air, I banish you . . . . iii 3 123
Have the power still To banish your defenders . . . iii 3 128
Hadst thou foxship To banish him that struck more blows for Rome Than thou hast spoken words? . . . . iv 2 19
For mine own part, When I said, banish him, I said, 'twas pity.—And so did I . . . . iv 6 140
We banish thee for ever.—Banish me! Banish your dotage; banish usury . . . . *T. of Athens* iii 5 98
O, banish me, my lord, but kill me not! . . . . *Othello* v 2 78
Heaven and my conscience knows Thou didst unjustly banish me *Cymb.* iii 3 100
Banished. Sycorax . . . From Argier, Thou know'st, was banish'd *Tempest* i 2 266
She at least is banish'd from your eye, Who hath cause to wet the grief on't . . . . ii 1 126
To die is to be banish'd from myself; And Silvia is myself *T. G. of Ver.* iii 1 171
Banish'd from her Is self from self: a deadly banishment! . . iii 1 172
Doth Silvia know that I am banished? . . . . . iii 1 221
She will love you, Now Valentine is banish'd from her sight . . iii 2 2
What, were you banish'd thence?—I was.—For what offence? . iv 1 23
Were you banish'd for so small a fault?—I was, and held me glad . iv 1 31
From Verona banished For practising to steal away a lady . . iv 1 47
You are a banish'd man, Therefore, above the rest, we parley to you iv 1 59
Thou art not ignorant what dear good will I bear unto the banish'd Valentine . . . . iv 3 15
Your grace is welcome to a man disgraced, Banish'd Valentine . v 4 124
These banish'd men that I have kept withal Are men endued with worthy qualities . . . . v 4 152
The old duke is banished by his younger brother the new duke *As Y. Like It* i 1 104
Can you tell if Rosalind, the duke's daughter, be banished with her father? . . . . i 1 111
Teach me to forget a banished father . . . . . . i 2 6
If my uncle, thy banished father, had banished thy uncle . . i 2 10
Daughter to the banish'd duke, And here detain'd by her usurping uncle i 2 285
So was I when your highness banish'd him . . . . i 3 62
She is banish'd.—Pronounce that sentence then on me . . i 3 86
Know'st thou not, the duke Hath banish'd me, his daughter? . . i 3 97
You do more usurp Than doth your brother that hath banish'd you . ii 1 28
This healthful hand, whose banish'd sense Thou hast repeal'd *All's Well* ii 3 54
Frenzy of mine own From my remembrance clearly banish'd his *T. Night* v 1 289
O fair return of banish'd majesty! . . . . . . *K. John* iii 1 321
Lay on our royal sword your banish'd hands . . . *Richard II.* i 3 179
Banish'd this frail sepulchre of our flesh, As now our flesh is banish'd from this land . . . . i 3 196
My name be blotted from the book of life, And I from heaven banish'd! i 3 203
Thy sad aspect Hath from the number of his banish'd years Pluck'd four . . . . i 3 210
Thy son is banish'd upon good advice, Whereto thy tongue a party-verdict gave . . . . i 3 233
Boast of this I can, Though banish'd, yet a trueborn Englishman . i 3 309
I wot your love pursues A banish'd traitor . . . . ii 3 60
Why have those banish'd and forbidden legs Dared once to touch a dust of England's ground? . . . . ii 3 90
Thou art a banish'd man, and here art come Before the expiration of thy time . . . . ii 3 110
As I was banish'd, I was banish'd Hereford; But as I come, I come for Lancaster . . . . ii 3 113
Many a time hath banish'd Norfolk fought For Jesu Christ . . iv 1 92
Yet time serves wherein you may redeem Your banish'd honours 1 *Hen. IV.* i 3 181
For what offence have I this fortnight been A banish'd woman? . ii 3 42
All are banish'd till their conversations Appear more wise 2 *Hen. IV.* v 5 106
The duke Hath banish'd moody discontented fury . 1 *Hen. VI.* iii 1 123
Two pulls at once; His lady banish'd, and a limb lopp'd off 2 *Hen. VI.* ii 3 42
Be done to death, Or banished fair England's territories . . iii 2 245
By the ground that I am banish'd from, Well could I curse away a winter's night . . . . iii 2 334
I will repeal thee, or, be well assured, Adventure to be banished myself: And banished I am, if but from thee . . . . . . iii 2 350
Thus is poor Suffolk ten times banished; Once by the king, and three times thrice by thee . . . . iii 2 357
O, where is loyalty? If it be banish'd from the frosty head . . v 1 167

Banished. Is of a king become a banish'd man . . . 3 *Hen. VI.* iii 3 25
Wert thou not banished on pain of death? . . . . *Richard III.* i 3 167
Alas, has banish'd me his bed already, His love, too long ago! *Hen. VIII.* iii 1 119
When I shall dwell with worms, and my poor name Banish'd the kingdom! . . . . iv 2 127
Let him away: He's banish'd, and it shall be so *Coriolanus* iii 3 107
There's no more to be said, but he is banish'd, As enemy to the people iii 3 117
Our enemy is banish'd! he is gone! Hoo! hoo! . . . iii 3 137
This lady's husband here, this, do you see—Whom you have banish'd, does exceed you all . . . . iv 2 42
Coriolanus banished!—Banished, sir . . . . iv 3 28
Had we no quarrel else to Rome, but that Thou art thence banish'd . iv 5 134
I ever said we were i' the wrong when we banished him . . . . iv 6 156
Made him fear'd, So hated, and so banish'd . . . . . iv 7 48
Go, you that banish'd him; A mile before his tent fall down . v 1 4
The gods will not be good unto us. When we banished him, we respected not them . . . . v 4 35
Unshout the noise that banish'd Marcius, Repeal him . . . v 5 4
Being banish'd for't, he came unto my hearth . . . . . v 6 30
How happy art thou, then, From these devourers to be banished! *T. A.* iii 1 57
Here stands my other son, a banish'd man, And here my brother . iii 1 99
Thy other banish'd son, with this dear sight Struck pale and bloodless iii 1 257
Myself unkindly banished, The gates shut on me . . . . v 3 104
'Romeo—banished;' That 'banished,' that one word 'banished,' Hath slain ten thousand Tybalts . . . . . *Rom. and Jul.* iii 2 112
'Romeo is banished,' to speak that word, Is father, mother, Tybalt, Romeo, Juliet, All slain, all dead. 'Romeo is banished!' . . iii 2 122
Hence from Verona art thou banished: Be patient, for the world is broad . . . . iii 3 15
Hence-banished is banish'd from the world, And world's exile is death: then banished, Is death mis-termed . . . . . . iii 3 19
But Romeo may not; he is banished: Flies may do this, . . . I am banished. And say'st thou yet that exile is not death? . . . iii 3 40
But 'banished' to kill me?—'banished'? O friar, the damned use that word in hell . . . . iii 3 46
My friend profess'd, To mangle me with that word 'banished'? . . iii 3 51
I'll give thee armour to keep off that word; Adversity's sweet milk, philosophy, To comfort thee, though thou art banished . . . iii 3 56
Yet 'banished'? Hang up philosophy! Unless philosophy can make a Juliet . . . . iii 3 57
Tybalt murdered, Doting like me, and like me banished . . . iii 3 67
Romeo is banish'd; and all the world to nothing, That he dares ne'er come back . . . . iii 5 215
Whose untimely death Banish'd the new-made bridegroom from this city . . . . v 3 235
I hate not to be banish'd; It is a cause worthy my spleen and fury, That I may strike at Athens . . . . . *T. of Athens* iii 5 112
Alcibiades is banished: hear you of it?—Alcibiades banished! . iii 6 60
These evils thou repeat'st upon thyself Have banish'd me . *Macbeth* iv 3 113
If, on the tenth day following, Thy banish'd trunk be found in our dominions, The moment is thy death . . . . . *Lear* i 1 180
Kent banish'd thus! and France in choler parted! And the king gone! i 2 23
Banish'd Kent, If thou canst serve where thou dost stand condemn'd . i 4 4
This fellow has banished two on's daughters, and did the third a blessing . . . . i 4 114
Ah, that good Kent! He said it would be thus, poor banish'd man! . iii 4 169
She's wedded; Her husband banish'd; she imprison'd . *Cymbeline* i 1 8
He that hath her—I mean, that married her, alack, good man! And therefore banish'd . . . . i 1 19
To his mistress, For whom he now is banish'd, her own price Proclaims how she esteem'd him . . . . i 1 51
A foolish suitor to a wedded lady, That hath her husband banish'd . i 6 3
A banished rascal; and he's another, whatsoever he be . . . ii 1 42
That thou mayst stand, To enjoy thy banish'd lord and this great land! ii 1 70
What of him? he is A banish'd traitor . . . . . . v 5 318
Indeed a banish'd man; I know not how a traitor . . . . v 5 319
I, old Morgan, Am that Belarius whom you sometime banish'd . . v 5 333

Banisher. To be full quit of those my banishers, Stand I before thee *Coriolanus* iv 5 89

Banishment. Banish'd from her Is self from self: a deadly banishment! *T. G. of Ver.* iii 1 173
Now go we in content To liberty and not to banishment *As Y. Like It* i 3 140
Call home thy ancient thoughts from banishment . . *T. of Shrew* Ind. 2 33
But tread the stranger paths of banishment . . . *Richard II.* i 3 143
His golden beams to you here lent Shall point on me and gild my banishment . . . . i 3 147
You never shall, so help you truth and God! Embrace each other's love in banishment; Nor never look upon each other's face . . . i 3 184
Six frozen winters spent, Return with welcome home from banishment . i 3 212
Would the word 'farewell' have lengthen'd hours And added years to his short banishment, He should have had a volume . . . . i 4 17
But 'tis doubt, When time shall call him home from banishment . . i 4 21
Eating the bitter bread of banishment . . . . . . iii 1 21
Provided that my banishment repeal'd And lands restored again . . iii 3 40
That e'er this tongue of mine, That laid the sentence of dread banishment on yon proud man, should take it off again! . . . . iii 3 134
Left me in reputeless banishment, A fellow of no mark nor likelihood 1 *Hen. IV.* iii 2 44
Welcome is banishment; welcome were my death . . 2 *Hen. VI.* iii 3 14
I do find more pain in banishment Than death can yield me here *Richard III.* i 3 168
My woful banishment, Could all but answer for that peevish brat? . i 3 193
Be it either For death, for fine, or banishment . *Coriolanus* iii 3 15
The nobles receive so to heart the banishment of that worthy Coriolanus iv 3 22
We willingly consented to his banishment, yet it was against our will . iv 6 145
The judges have pronounced My everlasting doom of banishment *T. Andron.* iii 1 51
Hath often over-heard them say, . . . That Lucius' banishment was wrongfully . . . . iv 4 76
Wash they his wounds with tears: mine shall be spent, When theirs are dry, for Romeo's banishment . . . . *Rom. and Jul.* iii 2 131
Not body's death, but body's banishment . . . . . . iii 3 11
Ha, banishment! be merciful, say 'death;' For exile hath more terror in his look, Much more than death: do not say 'banishment' . . iii 3 12
Calling death banishment, Thou cutt'st my head off with a golden axe . iii 3 21
Hath rush'd aside the law, And turn'd that black word death to banishment . . . . iii 3 27
Hear me but speak a word.—O, thou wilt speak again of banishment . iii 3 53
Banishment! It comes not ill; I hate not to be banish'd *T. of Athens* iii 5 111
Freedom lives hence, and banishment is here . . . . *Lear* i 1 184
Such unconstant starts are we like to have from him as this of Kent's banishment . . . . *Lear* i 1 305
Needless diffidences, banishment of friends . . . . . i 2 161
I was confederate with the Romans: so Follow'd my banishment *Cymb.* iii 3 69
Euriphile, Whom for the theft I wedded, stole these children Upon my banishment . . . . v 5 342

Banister. Flying for succour to his servant Banister, Being distress'd, was by that wretch betray'd . . . . . . *Hen. VIII.* ii 1 109

Bank. Sitting on a bank, Weeping again the king my father's wreck *Temp.* i 2 389
Banks with pioned and twilled brims, Which spongy April at thy hest betrims . . . . iv 1 64
I know a bank where the wild thyme blows . . *M. N. Dream* ii 1 249
Find you out a bed; For I upon this bank will rest my head . . ii 2 40
How sweet the moonlight sleeps upon this bank! . . *Mer. of Venice* v 1 54
Like the sweet sound, That breathes upon a bank of violets *T. Night* i 1 6
Like a bank for love to lie and play on . . . *W. Tale* iv 4 130
O, two such silver currents, when they join, Do glorify the banks that bound them in . . . . *K. John* ii 1 442
In this place I'll set a bank of rue, sour herb of grace *Richard II.* iii 4 105
When on the gentle Severn's sedgy bank . . . . 1 *Hen. IV.* i 3 98
And hid his crisp head in the hollow bank . . . . . i 3 106
Clipp'd in with the sea That chides the banks of England, Scotland, Wales . . . . iii 1 45
Thrice from the banks of Wye and sandy-bottom'd Severn have I sent him . . . . iii 1 65
We come within our awful banks again, And knit our powers 2 *Hen. IV.* iv 1 176
The snake roll'd in a flowering bank, With shining checker'd slough 2 *Hen. VI.* iii 1 228
Twice by awkward wind from England's bank Drove back again . . iii 2 83
Ask those on the banks If they were his assistants . . *Richard III.* iv 4 525
Were his brain as barren As banks of Libya . . . *Troi. and Cres.* i 3 328
Like a strange soul upon the Stygian banks Staying for waftage . . iii 2 10
An universal shout, That Tiber trembled underneath her banks *J. Cæsar* i 1 50
Draw them to Tiber banks, and weep your tears Into the channel . . i 1 63
Upon this bank and shoal of time, We'ld jump the life to come *Macbeth* i 7 6
Proud Cleopatra, when she met her Roman, And Cydnus swell'd above the banks . . . . *Cymbeline* ii 4 71
Poor shadows of Elysium, hence, and rest Upon your never-withering banks of flowers . . . . v 4 98
Know that our griefs are risen to the top, And now at length they overflow their banks . . . . *Pericles* ii 4 24

Banked. Have I not heard these islanders shout out 'Vive le roi!' as I have bank'd their towns? . . . . *K. John* v 2 104

Bankrupt. If you spend word for word with me, I shall make your wit bankrupt.—I know it well, sir . . . . . *T. G. of Ver.* ii 4 42
Time is a very bankrupt and owes more than he's worth *Com. of Errors* iv 2 58
Dainty bits Make rich the ribs, but bankrupt quite the wits . *L. L. Lost* i 1 27
For debt that bankrupt sleep doth sorrow owe . . *M. N. Dream* iii 2 85
A bankrupt, a prodigal, who dare scarce show his head on the Rialto *Mer. of Venice* iii 1 47
Why dost thou whet thy knife so earnestly?—To cut the forfeiture from that bankrupt there . . . . iv 1 122
Wherefore do you look Upon that poor and broken bankrupt? *As Y. Like It* ii 1 57
Be York the next that must be bankrupt so! . . . *Richard II.* ii 1 151
The king's grown bankrupt, like a broken man . . . . . ii 1 257
Show me what a face I have, Since it is bankrupt of his majesty . iv 1 267
Big Mars seems bankrupt in their beggar'd host . . . *Hen. V.* iv 2 43
O, break, my heart! poor bankrupt, break at once! . *Rom. and Jul.* iii 2 57
Bankrupts, hold fast; Rather than render back, out with your knives! *T. of Athens* iv 1 8

Banner. Victory, with little loss, doth play Upon the dancing banners of the French . . . . *K. John* ii 1 308
I will the banner from a trumpet take, And use it for my haste *Hen. V.* iv 2 61
And nobles bearing banners, there lie dead One hundred twenty six . iv 8 87
We shall hardly in our ages see Their banners wave again *Coriolanus* iii 1 8
March, noble lord, Into our city with thy banners spread *T. of Athens* v 4 30
The Norweyan banners flout the sky And fan our people cold *Macbeth* i 2 49
Hang out our banners on the outward walls; The cry is still, 'They come' . . . . v 5 1
Are at point To show their open banner . . . . . *Lear* iii 1 34
France spreads his banners in our noiseless land . . . . iv 2 56
The spirit-stirring drum, the ear-piercing fife, The royal banner *Othello* iii 3 353
His conquering banner shook from Syria To Lydia and to Ionia *Ant. and Cleo.* i 2 106
With his banners and his well-paid ranks, The ne'er-yet-beaten horse of Parthia We have jaded out o' the field . . . . . . iii 1 32
His banners sable, trimm'd with rich expense . . . *Pericles* v Gower 19

Banneret. The bannerets about thee did manifoldly dissuade me *All's Well* ii 3 214

Banning. Fell banning hag, enchantress, hold thy tongue! 1 *Hen. VI.* v 3 42

Banns. I'll crave the day When I shall ask the banns . *T. of Shrew* ii 1 181
'Point the day of marriage, Make feasts, invite friends, and proclaim the banns . . . . iii 2 16
Contracted bachelors, such as had been asked twice on the banns 1 *Hen. IV.* iv 2 18
And I, her husband, contradict your bans . . . . . *Lear* v 3 87

Banquet. Come, let us to the banquet . . . . . *Much Ado* ii 1 178
His words are a very fantastical banquet, just so many strange dishes . ii 3 22
The mind shall banquet, though the body pine . . . *L. L. Lost* i 1 25
And I'll go seek the duke: his banquet is prepared . . *As Y. Like It* ii 5 64
Rings put upon his fingers, A most delicious banquet by his bed *T. of Shrew* Ind. 1 39
Welcome his friends, Visit his countrymen and banquet them . . i 1 202
My banquet is to close our stomachs up, After our great good cheer . v 2 9
His hours fill'd up with riots, banquets, sports . . . *Hen. V.* i 1 56
Make bonfires And feast and banquet in the open streets . 1 *Hen. VI.* i 6 13
Come in, and let us banquet royally, After this golden day of victory . i 6 30
Some of these Should find a running banquet ere they rested . *Hen. VIII.* i 4 12
You have now a broken banquet; but we'll mend it. A good digestion to you all . . . . i 4 61
Is the banquet ready I' the privy chamber? . . . . . i 4 98
Saw you not, even now, a blessed troop Invite me to a banquet? . iv 2 88
Besides the running banquet of two beadles that is to come . . v 4 69
Whilst I at a banquet hold him sure, I'll find some cunning practice out of hand . . . . *T. Andron.* v 2 76
Bid him come and banquet at thy house . . . . . . v 2 114
This is the feast . . . , And this the banquet she shall surfeit on . v 2 194
Come, come, be every one officious To make this banquet . . v 2 203
We have a trifling foolish banquet towards . . . *Rom. and Jul.* i 5 124
An idle banquet attends you: Please you to dispose yourselves *T. of Athens* i 2 160

Banquet. In his commendations I am fed; It is a banquet to me *Macbeth* i 4 56
Free from our feasts and banquets bloody knives, Do faithful homage . iii 6 35
Bring in the banquet quickly; wine enough Cleopatra's health to drink *Ant. and Cleo.* i 2 11

Banqueted. This happy night the Frenchmen are secure, Having all day caroused and banqueted . . . . 1 *Hen. VI.* ii 1 12

Banqueting. This night in banqueting must all be spent *Troi. and Cres.* v 1 51
If you know That I profess myself in banqueting To all the rout, then hold me dangerous . . . . . . *J. Cæsar* i 2 77

Banquo. Dismay'd not this Our captains, Macbeth and Banquo? *Macbeth* i 2 34
So all hail, Macbeth and Banquo!—Banquo and Macbeth, all hail! i 3 68
Noble Banquo, That hast no less deserved, nor must be known No less i 4 29
True, worthy Banquo; he is full so valiant, And in his commendations I am fed . . . . i 4 54
Murder and treason! Banquo and Donalbain! Malcolm! awake! ii 3 80
Malcolm! Banquo! As from your graves rise up, and walk like sprites! ii 3 83
O Banquo, Banquo, Our royal master's murder'd! . . . ii 3 91
Our fears in Banquo Stick deep; and in his royalty of nature Reigns that which would be fear'd . . . . iii 1 49
If't be so, For Banquo's issue have I filed my mind . . . iii 1 65
And mine eternal jewel Given to the common enemy of man, To make them kings, the seed of Banquo kings! . . . . . iii 1 70
That might To half a soul and to a notion crazed Say 'Thus did Banquo' iii 1 84
Both of you Know Banquo was your enemy . . . . . iii 1 115
Banquo, thy soul's flight, If it find heaven, must find it out to-night . iii 1 141
Is Banquo gone from court?—Ay, madam, but returns again to-night . iii 2 1
Let your remembrance apply to Banquo; Present him eminence . iii 2 30
O, full of scorpions is my mind, dear wife! Thou know'st that Banquo, and his Fleance, lives . . . . iii 2 37
There's blood upon thy face.—'Tis Banquo's then.—'Tis better thee without than he within . . . . iii 4 13
But Banquo's safe?—Ay, my good lord: safe in a ditch he bides . iii 4 25
Here had we now our country's honour roof'd, Were the graced person of our Banquo present . . . . iii 4 41
I drink to the general joy o' the whole table, And to our dear friend Banquo . . . . iii 4 90
The right-valiant Banquo walk'd too late; Whom, you may say, if't please you, Fleance kill'd . . . . iii 6 5
Shall Banquo's issue ever Reign in this kingdom? . . . . iv 1 102
Thou art too like the spirit of Banquo; down! . . . . iv 1 112
The blood-bolter'd Banquo smiles upon me, And points at them for his iv 1 123
I tell you yet again, Banquo's buried; he cannot come out on's grave . v 1 70

Baptism. In your conscience wash'd As pure as sin with baptism *Hen. V.* i 2 32
A fair young maid that yet wants baptism, You must be godfather *Hen. VIII.* v 3 162
Were't to renounce his baptism, All seals and symbols of redeemed sin *Othello* ii 3 349

Baptista. Signior Baptista, will you be so strange? . *T. of Shrew* i 1 85
Why will you mew her up, Signior Baptista, for this fiend of hell? . i 1 88
By helping Baptista's eldest daughter to a husband we set his youngest free for a husband . . . . i 1 141
Baptista Minola, An affable and courteous gentleman . . . i 2 97
I must go with thee, For in Baptista's keep my treasure is . . i 2 118
Therefore this order hath Baptista ta'en . . . . . i 2 126
And offer me disguised in sober robes To old Baptista as a schoolmaster i 2 133
Beside Signior Baptista's liberality, I'll mend it with a largess . i 2 150
Baptista is a noble gentleman, To whom my father is not all unknown . i 2 240
Let me be so bold as ask you, Did you yet ever see Baptista's daughter? i 2 252
Now, Baptista, to your younger daughter: Now is the day we long have looked for . . . . ii 1 334
Patience, good Katharine, and Baptista too . . . . . iii 2 21
To pass assurance of a dower in marriage 'Twixt me and one Baptista's daughter . . . . iv 2 118
And but I be deceived Signior Baptista may remember me . . iv 4 3
Hast thou done thy errand to Baptista? . . . . . . iv 4 14
Here comes Baptista: set your countenance, sir . . . . iv 4 18
For curious I cannot be with you, Signior Baptista, of whom I hear so well . . . . iv 4 37
Signior Baptista, shall I lead the way? . . . . . . iv 4 69
Baptista is safe, talking with the deceiving father of a deceitful son iv 4 82
Take heed, Signior Baptista, lest you be cony-catched in this business . v 1 101
Fear not, Baptista; we will content you, go to . . . . v 1 138
Gonzago is the duke's name; his wife, Baptista . . *Hamlet* iii 2 250

Baptized. Call me but love, and I'll be new baptized *Rom. and Jul.* ii 2 50

Bar. Other bars he lays before me, My riots past *Mer. Wives* iii 4 7
Any bar, any cross, any impediment will be medicinable to me *Much Ado* ii 2 4
The lottery of my destiny Bars me the right of voluntary choosing *Mer. of Venice* ii 1 16
I bar to-night: you shall not gauge me By what we do to-night . . ii 2 208
The watery kingdom, whose ambitious head Spits in the face of heaven, is no bar To stop the foreign spirits . . . . ii 7 45
O, these naughty times Put bars between the owners and their rights! . iii 2 19
So sweet a bar Should sunder such sweet friends . . . . iii 2 120
He lets me feed with his hinds, bars me the place of a brother *As Y. Like It* i 1 20
I bar confusion: 'Tis I must make conclusion Of these most strange events . . . . v 4 131
Merriment, Which bars a thousand harms and lengthens life *T. of Shrew* Ind. 2 138
Since this bar in law makes us friends, it shall be so far forth friendly maintained . . . . i 1 139
We will bring the device to the bar and crown thee for a finder of madmen *T. Night* iii 4 154
We'll bar thee from succession; Not hold thee of our blood . *W. Tale* iv 4 440
I can produce A will that bars the title of thy son . . *K. John* ii 1 192
When law can do no right, Let it be lawful that law bar no wrong . iii 1 186
I will bar no honest man my house, nor no cheater . . . 2 *Hen. IV.* ii 4 110
Should, or should not, bar us in our claim . . . *Hen. V.* i 2 12
There is no bar To make against your highness' claim to France . i 2 35
Pharamond The founder of this law and female bar . . . . i 2 42
Hold up this Salique law To bar your highness claiming from the female i 2 92
Dukes of Orleans, Bourbon, and of Berri, Alençon, Brabant, Bar . iii 5 42
Bar Harry England, that sweeps through our land With pennons . . iii 5 48
The brother to the Duke of Burgundy, And Edward Duke of Bar . . iv 8 103
To bring your most imperial majesties Unto this bar and royal interview v 2 27
Through a secret grate of iron bars In yonder tower . . 1 *Hen. VI.* i 4 10
I could rend bars of steel And spurn in pieces posts of adamant . . i 4 51
Which obloquy set bars before my tongue . . . . . . ii 5 49
Having God, her conscience, and these bars against me, And I nothing to back my suit at all . . . . *Richard III.* i 2 235

Bar. I'll give my voice on Richard's side, To bar my master's heirs in true descent . . . . *Richard III.* iii 2 54
Heaven and fortune bar me happy hours! Day, yield me not thy light! iv 4 400
All several sins, all used in each degree, Throng to the bar, crying all, Guilty! . . . . v 3 199
I'll tell you in a little. The great duke Came to the bar . *Hen. VIII.* ii 1 12
He was brought again to the bar, to hear His knell rung out . . ii 1 31
If you cannot Bar his access to the king, never attempt Any thing on him . . . . iii 2 17
But life, being weary of these worldly bars, Never lacks power to dismiss itself . . . . *J. Cæsar* i 3 96
You do, surely, bar the door upon your own liberty, if you deny your griefs to your friend . . . . *Hamlet* iii 2 351
All ports I'll bar; the villain shall not 'scape . . . *Lear* ii 1 82
Their injunction be to bar my doors, And let this tyrannous night take hold upon you . . . . iii 4 155
To bar your offence herein too, I durst attempt it against any lady *Cymb.* i 4 122
Thinking to bar thee of succession, As Thou reft'st me of my lands . iii 3 102
His greatness was no guard To bar heaven's shaft . . . *Pericles* ii 4 15

Barbara. My mother had a maid call'd Barbara: She was in love *Othello* iv 3 26
But to go hang my head all at one side, And sing it like poor Barbara . iv 3 33

Barbarian. Bought and sold among those of any wit, like a barbarian slave . . . . *Troi. and Cres.* ii 1 52
I would they were barbarians—as they are, Though in Rome litter'd—not Romans—as they are not . . . . . *Coriolanus* iii 1 238
If sanctimony and a frail vow betwixt an erring barbarian and a supersubtle Venetian be not too hard for my wits . . . *Othello* i 3 363

Barbarism. I have for barbarism spoke more Than for that angel knowledge you can say . . . . *L. L. Lost* i 1 112
Lest barbarism, making me the precedent, Should a like language use to all degrees . . . . *W. Tale* ii 1 84
They must perforce have melted And barbarism itself have pitied him *Richard II.* v 2 36
Whereupon the Grecians begin to proclaim barbarism . *Troi. and Cres.* v 4 18

Barbarous. Most barbarous intimation! yet a kind of insinuation *L. L. Lost* iv 2 13
Arts-man, preambulate, we will be singuled from the barbarous . . v 1 86
Because I will not jump with common spirits And rank me with the barbarous multitudes . . . . *Mer. of Venice* ii 9 33
Ungracious wretch, Fit for the mountains and the barbarous caves! *T. Night* iv 1 52
To choke his days With barbarous ignorance . . . . *K. John* iv 2 59
And therefore, living hence, did give ourself To barbarous license *Hen. V.* i 2 271
Let us quit all And give our vineyards to a barbarous people . . iii 5 4
O barbarous and bloody spectacle! . . . . . 2 *Hen. VI.* iv 1 144
Barbarous villains! hath this lovely face Ruled, like a wandering planet? iv 4 15
O cruel, irreligious piety!—Was ever Scythia half so barbarous? *T. Andron.* i 1 131
Thou art a Roman; be not barbarous . . . . i 1 378
To an obscure plot, Accompanied but with a barbarous Moor . . ii 3 78
Barbarous Tamora, For no name fits thy nature but thy own! . . ii 3 118
O barbarous, beastly villains, like thyself! . . . . . v 1 97
Take you in this barbarous Moor, This ravenous tiger . . . v 3 4
The barbarous Scythian, Or he that makes his generation messes . *Lear* i 1 118
A gracious aged man, . . . Most barbarous, most degenerate! have you madded . . . . iv 2 43
For Christian shame, put by this barbarous brawl! . . . *Othello* ii 3 172
Or receive us For barbarous and unnatural revolts . . *Cymbeline* iv 4 6
That these pirates, Not enough barbarous, had not o'erboard thrown me! *Pericles* iv 2 70

Barbary. From Lisbon, Barbary and India? . . . *Mer. of Venice* iii 2 272
I will be more jealous of thee than a Barbary cock-pigeon over his hen *As Y. Like It* iv 1 151
Roan Barbary, That horse that thou so often hast bestrid *Richard II.* v 5 78
Rode he on Barbary? Tell me, gentle friend, How went he under him? v 5 81
In Barbary, sir, it cannot come to so much . . . 1 *Hen. IV.* ii 4 84
He'll not swagger with a Barbary hen, if her feathers turn back *2 Hen. IV.* ii 4 108
The king, sir, hath wagered with him six Barbary horses . *Hamlet* v 2 155
Six Barbary horses against six French swords, their assigns . . v 2 168
You'll have your daughter covered with a Barbary horse . . *Othello* i 1 112

Barbason. Amaimon sounds well; Lucifer, well; Barbason, well *Mer. Wives* ii 2 311
I am not Barbason; you cannot conjure me . . . *Hen. V.* ii 1 57

Barbed. His glittering arms he will commend to rust, His barbed steeds to stables, and his heart To faithful service . . *Richard II.* iii 3 117
Mounting barbed steeds To fright the souls of fearful adversaries *Richard III.* i 1 10

Barber. Hath any man seen him at the barber's?—No, but the barber's man hath been seen with him . . . . *Much Ado* iii 2 44
I must to the barber's, mounsieur; for methinks I am marvellous hairy *M. N. Dream* iv 1 25
A barber shall never earn sixpence out of it . . . 2 *Hen. IV.* i 2 29
This is too long.—It shall to the barber's, with your beard . *Hamlet* ii 2 521

Barber's chair. A barber's chair that fits all buttocks *All's Well* ii 2 17

Barber's shop. Stand like the forfeits in a barber's shop . *Meas. for Meas.* v 1 323
And cut and slish and slash, Like to a censer in a barber's shop *T. of Shrew* iv 3 91

Barbered. Being barber'd ten times o'er, goes to the feast *Ant. and Cleo.* ii 2 229

Barber-monger. Draw, you whoreson cullionly barber-monger, draw *Lear* ii 2 36

Bard. A bard of Ireland told me once, I should not live long after I saw Richmond . . . . *Richard III.* iv 2 109
Scribes, bards, poets, cannot Think, speak, cast, write, sing, number *Ant. and Cleo.* iii 2 16

Bardolph. Your cony-catching rascals, Bardolph, Nym, and Pistol *Mer. Wives* i 1 129
I will entertain Bardolph; he shall draw, he shall tap . . . i 3 10
Falstaff, Bardolph, Peto and Gadshill shall rob those men . 1 *Hen. IV.* i 2 181
Bardolph! Peto! I'll starve ere I'll rob a foot further . . . ii 2 22
You fought fair; so did you, Peto; so did you, Bardolph . . ii 4 330
Banish Peto, banish Bardolph, banish Poins . . . . . ii 4 521
Bardolph, am I not fallen away vilely since this last action? . . iii 3 1
Bardolph was shaved and lost many a hair . . . . . iii 3 68
Bardolph, get thee before to Coventry; fill me a bottle of sack . iv 2 1
Tell thou the earl That the Lord Bardolph doth attend him . 2 *Hen. IV.* i 1 3
He said, sir, you should procure him better assurance than Bardolph . i 2 36
The nobleman that committed the prince for striking him about Bardolph i 2 64
That arrant malmsey-nose knave, Bardolph . . . . . . ii 1 43
Draw, Bardolph: cut me off the villain's head . . . . . ii 1 50
By the mass, here comes Bardolph . . . . ii 2 74

Bardolph. God save your grace!—And yours, most noble Bardolph! *2 Hen. IV.* ii 2 79
I tell thee what, Corporal Bardolph, I could tear her . . . ii 4 166
Quoit him down, Bardolph, like a shove-groat shilling . . . ii 4 206
Honest Bardolph, whose zeal burns in his nose . . . ii 4 356
The fiend hath pricked down Bardolph irrecoverable . . . ii 4 359
Good Master Corporate Bardolph, stand my friend . . . iii 2 235
Lord Bardolph, With a great power of English and of Scots . iv 4 97
Give Master Bardolph some wine, Davy . . . v 3 26
Be merry, Master Bardolph; and, my little soldier there, be merry . v 3 33
Bardolph, welcome: if thou wantest any thing, and wilt not call, beshrew thy heart . . . v 3 58
I'll drink to Master Bardolph, and to all the cavaleros about London . v 3 62
You'll crack a quart together, ha! will you not, Master Bardolph? v 3 67
Bardolph, put thy face between his sheets, and do the office of a warming-pan *Hen. V.* ii 1 87
Bardolph, be blithe: Nym, rouse thy vaunting veins . . ii 3 4
A' saw a flea stick upon Bardolph's nose, and a' said it was a black soul burning in hell-fire . . . ii 3 43
For Bardolph, he is white-livered and red-faced . . . iii 2 33
Bardolph stole a lute-case, bore it twelve leagues, and sold it . iii 2 45
Nym and Bardolph are sworn brothers in filching . . . iii 2 47
Bardolph, a soldier, firm and sound of heart, And of buxom valour . iii 6 26
Fortune is Bardolph's foe, and frowns on him . . . iii 6 41
Let not Bardolph's vital thread be cut With edge of penny cord . iii 6 49
Bardolph and Nym had ten times more valour than this roaring devil . iv 4 74

Bare. Let me not . . . dwell In this bare island *Tempest* Epil. 8
It appears, by their bare liveries, that they live by your bare words *T. G. of Ver.* ii 4 45
More qualities than a water-spaniel; which is much in a bare Christian iii 1 272
By the bare scalp of Robin Hood's fat friar! . . . iv 1 36
From the seedness the bare fallow brings To teeming foison *M. for Meas.* i 4 42
So that my errand, due unto my tongue, I thank him, I bare home upon my shoulders *Com. of Errors* ii 1 73
How many then should cover that stand bare! . . *Mer. of Venice* ii 9 44
Therefore lay bare your bosom . . . iv 1 252
The thorny point Of bare distress *As Y. Like It* ii 7 95
So is the forehead of a married man more honourable than the bare brow of a bachelor . . . iii 3 61
His left cheek is a cheek of two pile and a half, but his right cheek is worn bare *All's Well* iv 5 104
If I Had servants true about me, that bare eyes To see alike mine honour as their profits *W. Tale* i 2 309
Cloy the hungry edge of appetite By bare imagination of a feast *Richard II.* i 3 297
The cloak of night being pluck'd from off their backs, Stand bare and naked . . . iii 2 46
Such poor, such bare, such lewd, such mean attempts . *1 Hen. IV.* iii 2 13
Methinks they are exceeding poor and bare, too beggarly . iv 2 75
No, I'll be sworn; unless you call three fingers on the ribs bare . iv 2 80
Like the south Borne with black vapour, doth begin to melt And drop upon our bare unarmed heads . *2 Hen. IV.* ii 4 394
Like lean, sterile and bare land, manured, husbanded and tilled . iv 3 129
Health, alack, with youthful wings is flown From this bare wither'd trunk . . . iv 5 230
Like that proud insulting ship Which Cæsar and his fortune bare at once *1 Hen. VI.* i 2 139
Whom with my bare fists I would execute . . . i 4 36
Die, damned wretch, the curse of her that bare thee . *2 Hen. VI.* iv 10 83
But then Æneas bare a living load, Nothing so heavy as these woes . v 2 64
They are too thin and bare to hide offences . . *Hen. VIII.* v 3 125
Our head shall go bare till merit crown it. . *Troi. and Cres.* iii 2 99
Whilst some with cunning gild their copper crowns, With truth and plainness I do wear mine bare . . . iv 4 108
To show bare heads In congregations, to yawn, be still and wonder *Coriolanus* iii 2 10
It was a bare petition of a state To one whom they had punish'd . v 1 20
Lopp'd and hew'd and made thy body bare Of her two branches *T. Andron.* ii 4 17
Say thou but 'I,' And that bare vowel 'I' shall poison more *R. and J.* iii 2 46
Art thou so bare and full of wretchedness, And fear'st to die? . v 1 68
Who bare my letter, then, to Romeo?—I could not send it . v 2 13
This is no time to lend money, especially upon bare friendship *T. of Athens* iii 1 45
Whose bare unhoused trunks, To the conflicting elements exposed . iv 3 229
Left me open, bare For every storm that blows . . iv 3 265
The sauce to meat is ceremony; Meeting were bare without it *Macbeth* iii 4 37
When he himself might his quietus make With a bare bodkin *Hamlet* iii 1 76
Strike in their numb'd and mortified bare arms Pins, wooden pricks *Lear* ii 3 15
Unaccommodated man is no more but such a poor, bare, forked animal as thou art . . . iii 4 112
With such a storm as his bare head In hell-black night endured . iii 7 59
Men do their broken weapons rather use Than their bare hands . *Othello* i 3 175
They rain'd All kinds of sores and shames on my bare head . iv 2 49
Wear thy good rapier bare, and put it home: Quick, quick; fear nothing v 1 2
Swift, you dragons of the night, that dawning May bare the raven's eye! *Cymbeline* ii 2 49
Shook down my mellow hangings, nay, my leaves, And left me bare to weather . . . iii 3 64
Patiently and constantly thou hast stuck to the bare fortune of that beggar . . . iii 5 119

Bare-bone. Here comes lean Jack, here comes bare-bone. *1 Hen. IV.* ii 4 358

Bared. Shave the head, and tie the beard; and say it was the desire of the penitent to be so bared . *Meas. for Meas.* iv 2 189
As you see, Have bared my bosom to the thunder-stone . . *J. Cæsar* i 3 49

Barefaced. And then you will play barefaced . . *M. N. Dream* i 2 100
I could With barefaced power sweep him from my sight. *Macbeth* iii 1 119
They bore him barefaced on the bier; Hey non nonny, nonny *Hamlet* iv 5 164

Barefoot. Like hedgehogs which Lie tumbling in my barefoot way *Tempest* ii 2 11
I must dance bare-foot on her wedding day . *T. of Shrew* ii 1 33
Barefoot plod I the cold ground upon, With sainted vow . *All's Well* iii 4 6
Condition, I had gone barefoot to India . *Troi. and Cres.* i 2 80
Going to find a bare-foot brother out, One of our order . *Rom. and Jul.* v 2 4
Run barefoot up and down, threatening the flames With bisson rheum *Hamlet* ii 2 528
Would have walked barefoot to Palestine for a touch of his nether lip *Othello* iv 3 39

Bare-gnawn. My name is lost; By treason's tooth bare-gnawn and canker-bit . . . *Lear* v 3 122

Bareheaded, lower than his proud steed's neck . . *Richard II.* v 2 19
A dozen captains, Bare-headed, sweating, knocking at the taverns *2 Hen. IV.* ii 4 388
Bare-headed plodded by my foot-cloth mule . . *2 Hen. VI.* iv 1 54
Bare-headed! Gracious my lord, hard by here is a hovel . *Lear* iii 2 60

Barely. Shall I not have barely my principal? . . *Mer. of Venice* iv 1 342
You barely leave our thorns to prick ourselves . . *All's Well* iv 2 19
Barely in title, not in revenue . . . *Richard II.* iii 1 226
In these sear'd hopes, I barely gratify your love . . *Cymbeline* ii 4 7

Bareness. You barely leave our thorns to prick ourselves And mock us with our bareness . . . *All's Well* iv 2 20
For their bareness, I am sure they never learned that of me *1 Hen. IV.* iv 2 77

Bare-picked. Now for the bare-pick'd bone of majesty Doth dogged war bristle his angry crest . . . *K. John* iv 3 148

Bare-ribbed. In his forehead sits A bare-ribb'd death . . v 2 177

Barful. I'll do my best To woo your lady: yet, a barful strife! *T. Night* i 4 41

Bargain. And seal the bargain with a holy kiss . . *T. G. of Ver.* ii 2 7
Upon what bargain do you give it me? . . *Com. of Errors* ii 2 25
The boy hath sold him a bargain, a goose, that's flat . *L. L. Lost* iii 1 102
To sell a bargain well is as cunning as fast and loose . . iii 1 104
A time, methinks, too short To make a world-without-end bargain in . v 2 799
My bargains and my well-won thrift, Which he calls interest *Mer. of Venice* i 3 51
Scorned my nation, thwarted my bargains, cooled my friends . iii 1 59
When your honours mean to solemnize The bargain of your faith . iii 2 195
You'll give yourself to this most faithful shepherd?—So is the bargain *As Y. Like It* v 4 15
A bargain! And, friends unknown, you shall bear witness to't *W. Tale* iv 4 394
No bargains break that are not this day made! . . *K. John* iii 1 93
No longer than we well could wash our hands To clap this royal bargain up . . . iii 1 235
The devil shall have his bargain . . . *1 Hen. IV.* i 2 131
But in the way of bargain, mark ye me, I'll cavil on the ninth part of a hair . . . iii 1 139
It is the soldier's; I by bargain should Wear it myself . *Hen. V.* iv 7 182
Give me your answer; i' faith, do: and so clap hands and a bargain . v 2 134
So worthless peasants bargain for their wives, As market-men for oxen, sheep, or horse . . . *1 Hen. VI.* v 5 53
Go to, a bargain made: seal it, seal it; I'll be the witness *Troi. and Cres.* iii 2 204
Seal with a righteous kiss A dateless bargain to engrossing death! *Rom. and Jul.* v 3 115
There's a bargain made . . . *J. Cæsar* i 3 120
She was too fond of her most filthy bargain . . *Othello* v 2 157
Lest the bargain should catch cold and starve. . *Cymbeline* i 4 179

Bargained. 'Tis bargain'd 'twixt us twain, being alone *T. of Shrew* ii 1 306
While his own lands are bargain'd for and sold . . *2 Hen. VI.* i 1 231
I have bargained for the joint . . . *Pericles* iv 2 141

Barge. My barge stays; Your lordship shall along . *Hen. VIII.* i 3 63
They've left their barge and landed . . . i 4 54
See the barge be ready; And fit it with such furniture as suits . ii 1 98
The barge she sat in, like a burnish'd throne *Ant. and Cleo.* ii 2 196
From the barge A strange invisible perfume hits the sense . ii 2 216
And to him in his barge with fervour hies *Pericles* v Gower 20
Sir, there's a barge put off from Mytilene . . . v 1 3

Bargulus the strong Illyrian pirate . . *2 Hen. VI.* iv 1 108

Baring. Or the baring of my beard; and to say it was in stratagem *All's Well* iv 1 54

Bark. They hurried us aboard a bark, Bore us some leagues to sea *Tempest* i 2 144
Hark, hark! Bow-wow. The watch-dogs bark: Bow-wow . . i 2 383
This bottle; which I made of the bark of a tree . . ii 2 127
Why do your dogs bark so? be there bears i' the town? . *Mer. Wives* i 1 298
Would bark your honour from that trunk you bear . *Meas. for Meas.* iii 1 72
Had not their bark been very slow of sail . *Com. of Errors* i 1 117
If any bark put forth, come to the mart . . . iii 2 155
There is a bark of Epidamnum That stays but till her owner comes aboard . . . iv 1 85
You sent me to the bay, sir, for a bark . . . iv 1 99
I brought you word an hour since that the bark Expedition put forth to-night . . . iv 3 38
I had rather hear my dog bark at a crow than a man swear he loves me *Much Ado* i 1 132
Mine, as sure as bark on tree . . . *L. L. Lost* v 2 285
And neigh, and bark, and grunt, and roar, and burn *M. N. Dream* iii 1 113
I am Sir Oracle, And when I ope my lips let no dog bark! *Mer. of Ven.* i 1 94
Like a younker or a prodigal The scarfed bark puts from her native bay . . . ii 6 15
O Rosalind! these trees shall be my books And in their barks my thoughts I'll character *As Y. Like It* iii 2 6
Mar no more trees with writing love-songs in their barks . . iii 2 277
Abuses our young plants with carving 'Rosalind' on their barks . iii 2 379
Go, get aboard; Look to thy bark . . . *W. Tale* iii 3 8
And make conceive a bark of baser kind By bud of nobler race . iv 4 94
What became of his bark and his followers?—Wrecked . . v 2 73
We at time of year Do wound the bark, the skin of our fruit-trees *Richard II.* iii 4 58
The fox barks not when he would steal the lamb . *2 Hen VI.* iii 1 55
Even as a splitted bark, so sunder we: This way fall I to death . iii 2 411
The rest stand all aloof, and bark at him . . *3 Hen. VI.* ii 1 17
All these the enemies to our poor bark . . . v 4 28
That dogs bark at me as I halt by them . . . *Richard III.* i 1 23
Rather hide me from my greatness, Being a bark to brook no mighty sea iii 7 162
Like a poor bark, of sails and tackling reft, Rush all to pieces . iv 4 233
We take From every tree lop, bark, and part o' the timber . *Hen. VIII.* i 2 96
Like to village-curs, Bark when their fellows do . . . ii 4 160
Deep-drawing barks do there disgorge Their warlike fraughtage *Troi. and Cres.* Prol. 12
Our doubtful hope, our convoy and our bark . . . i 1 107
Anon behold The strong-ribb'd bark through liquid mountains cut . i 3 40
As the bark, that hath discharged her fraught, Returns . . *T. Andron.* i 1 71
On their skins, as on the bark of trees, Have with my knife carved . v 1 138
In one little body Thou counterfeit'st a bark, a sea, a wind *Rom. and Jul.* iii 5 132
The bark thy body is, Sailing in this salt flood; the winds, thy sighs . iii 5 134
Now at once run on The dashing rocks thy sea-sick weary bark! . v 3 118
Leak'd is our bark, And we, poor mates, stand on the dying deck *T. of Athens* iv 2 19
'Tis thou that rigg'st the bark and plough'st the foam . . v 1 53
Blow wind, swell billow and swim bark! The storm is up . *J. Cæsar* v 1 67
Though his bark cannot be lost, Yet it shall be tempest-tost . *Macbeth* i 3 24
Prepare thyself; The bark is ready, and the wind at help . *Hamlet* iv 3 46

Bark. Tray, Blanch, and Sweet-heart, see, they bark at me . . *Lear* iii 6 66
Yond tall anchoring bark, Diminish'd to her cock; her cock, a buoy . iv 6 18
Thou hast seen a farmer's dog bark at a beggar? . . . . iv 6 158
Is he well shipp'd?—His bark is stoutly timber'd . *Othello* ii 1 48
Let the labouring bark climb hills of seas Olympus-high! . . ii 1 189
Yea, like the stag, when snow the pasture sheets, The barks of trees thou browsed'st . . . . *Ant. and Cleo.* i 4 66
Barked. A most instant tetter bark'd about, Most lazar-like . *Hamlet* i 5 71
This pine is bark'd, That overtopp'd them all . *Ant. and Cleo.* iv 12 23
Barkest. Thou art as full of envy at his greatness . that thou barkest at him . . . . *Troi. and Cres.* ii 1 38
Barking. The envious barking of your saucy tongue . . 1 *Hen. VI.* iii 4 33
Dogs that are as often beat for barking As therefore kept to do so *Coriolanus* ii 3 224
Barkloughly castle call they this at hand? . . . *Richard II.* iii 2 1
Barky. The female ivy so Enrings the barky fingers of the elm *M. N. Dream* iv 1 49
Barley. Rich leas Of wheat, rye, barley, vetches, oats and pease *Tempest* iv 1 61
Barley-broth. A drench for sur-rein'd jades, their barley-broth *Hen. V.* iii 5 19
Barm. And sometime make the drink to bear no barm . *M. N. Dream* ii 1 38
Barn. Foison plenty, Barns and garners never empty . . *Tempest* iv 1 111
If your husband have stables enough, you'll see he shall lack no barns *Much Ado* iii 4 49
She is my house, My household stuff, my field, my barn *T. of Shrew* iii 2 233
He loves his own barn better than he loves our house . 1 *Hen. IV.* ii 3 6
Set fire on barns and hay-stacks in the night . . *T. Andron.* v 1 133
Barnacles. And all be turn'd to barnacles, or to apes . *Tempest* iv 1 249
Barnardine. To-morrow morning are to die Claudio and Barnardine *Meas. for Meas.* iv 2 8
Barnardine and Claudio: The one has my pity; not a jot the other . iv 2 63
Where's Barnardine?—As fast lock'd up in sleep as guiltless labour . iv 2 68
Let Claudio be executed by four of the clock; and in the afternoon Barnardine . . . . iv 2 125
What is that Barnardine who is to be executed in the afternoon?—A Bohemian born . . . . iv 2 132
Call your executioner, and off with Barnardine's head . . iv 2 222
Master Barnardine! you must rise and be hanged, Master Barnardine! iv 3 23
Pray, Master Barnardine, awake till you are executed, and sleep afterwards . . . . iv 3 34
Put them in secret holds, both Barnardine and Claudio . . iv 3 91
One . . . I have reserved alive.—What's he?—His name is Barnardine v 1 472
Which is that Barnardine?—This, my lord . . . . v 1 483
Barne. They say barnes are blessings . . . *All's Well* i 3 28
Mercy on's, a barne; a very pretty barne! A boy or a child? *W. Tale* iii 3 70
Barnet. I will away towards Barnet presently, And bid thee battle 3 *Hen. VI.* v 1 110
We, having now the best at Barnet field, Will thither straight . v 3 20
Baron. What say you, then, to Falconbridge, the young baron? *Mer. of Ven.* i 2 72
The lords and barons of the realm . . . . . 1 *Hen. IV.* iv 3 66
High dukes, great princes, barons, lords and knights . *Hen. V.* iii 5 46
Barons, knights and squires, Full fifteen hundred, besides common men iv 8 83
Seven earls, twelve barons and twenty reverend bishops . 2 *Hen. VI.* i 1 8
They that bear The cloth of honour over her, are four barons *Hen. VIII.* iv 1 48
Barony. For a silken point I'll give my barony . . 2 *Hen. IV.* i 1 54
Barrabas. Would any of the stock of Barrabas Had been her husband rather than a Christian! . . . . . *Mer. of Venice* iv 1 296
Barred. Sweet recreation barr'd, what doth ensue But moody and dull melancholy? . . . . . . *Com. of Errors* v 1 78
That is stronger made Which was before barr'd up with ribs of iron *Much Ado* iv 1 153
Things hid and barr'd, you mean, from common sense? . *L. L. Lost* i 1 57
Inspired merit so by breath is barr'd . . . *All's Well* ii 1 151
From his presence I am barr'd, like one infectious . *W. Tale* iii 2 99
Purpose so barr'd, it follows, Nothing is done to purpose *Coriolanus* iii 1 148
Let not young Mutius . . . Be barr'd his entrance here . *T. Andron.* i 1 383
Nor have we herein barr'd Your better wisdoms . . *Hamlet* i 2 14
Pitying The pangs of barr'd affections . . . *Cymbeline* i 1 82
Barrel. Place barrels of pitch upon the fatal stake . 1 *Hen. VI.* v 4 57
Barren. A thousand furlongs of sea for an acre of barren ground *Tempest* i 1 69
The fresh springs, brine-pits, barren place and fertile . . i 2 338
But barren hate, Sour-eyed disdain and discord shall bestrew The union iv 1 19
Are my discourses dull? barren my wit? . . . *Com. of Errors* ii 1 91
O, these are barren tasks, too hard to keep, Not to see ladies, study, fast, not sleep! . . . . *L. L. Lost* i 1 47
Such barren plants are set before us, that we thankful should be . iv 2 29
Finding barren practisers, Scarce show a harvest of their heavy toil . v 3 325
To live a barren sister all your life, Chanting faint hymns *M. N. Dream* i 1 72
The shallowest thick-skin of that barren sort . . . iii 2 13
When did friendship take A breed for barren metal of his friend? *Mer. of Venice* i 3 135
At my fingers' ends: marry, now I let go your hand, I am barren *T. Night* i 3 84
I marvel your ladyship takes delight in such a barren rascal . . i 5 90
Why laugh you at such a barren rascal? an you smile not, he's gagged v 1 383
Naked, fasting, Upon a barren mountain . . *W. Tale* iii 2 213
Of that kind Our rustic garden's barren . . . . iv 4 84
And dull unfeeling barren ignorance Is made my gaoler . *Richard II.* i 3 168
That small model of the barren earth Which serves as paste and cover to our bones . . . . iii 2 153
And we are barren and bereft of friends . . . . iii 3 84
On the barren mountains let him starve . . 1 *Hen. IV.* i 3 89
Such barren pleasures, rude society, As thou art match'd withal . iii 2 14
Barren, barren, barren; beggars all, beggars all . 2 *Hen. IV.* v 3 8
Barren winter, with his wrathful nipping cold . . 2 *Hen. VI.* ii 4 3
I am not barren to bring forth complaints . . *Richard III.* ii 2 67
Were his brain as barren As banks of Libya . . *Troi and Cres.* i 3 327
I need not be barren of accusations; he hath faults, with surplus *Coriol.* i 1 45
A barren detested vale, you see it is . . . . *T. Andron.* ii 3 93
The barren, touched in this holy chase, Shake off their sterile curse *J. Cæsar* i 2 8
Upon my head they placed a fruitless crown, And put a barren sceptre in my gripe . . . . *Macbeth* iii 1 62
Laugh, to set on some quantity of barren spectators to laugh too *Hamlet* iii 2 46
O, from Italy! Ram thou thy fruitful tidings in mine ears, That long time have been barren . . . . . *Ant. and Cleo.* ii 5 25
That made barren the swell'd boast Of him that best could speak *Cymbeline* v 5 162
Barrenness. Where Scotland?—I found it by the barrenness; hard in the palm of the hand . . . . . . *Com. of Errors* iii 2 123
Barren-spirited. A barren-spirited fellow . . . . *J. Cæsar* iv 1 36
Barrest. Thou barr'st us Our prayers to the gods . . *Coriolanus* v 3 104
What, villain boy! Barr'st me my way in Rome? . . *T. Andron.* i 1 291

Barricado. Man is enemy to virginity: how may we barricado it? *All's Well* i 1 124
It hath bay windows transparent as barricadoes . . . *T. Night* iv 2 41
Be it concluded, No barricado for a belly . . . . *W. Tale* i 2 204
Barrow. Had I lived to be carried in a basket, like a barrow of butcher's offal? . . . . *Mer. Wives* iii 5 5
Barson. I think a' be, but goodman Puff of Barson 2 *Hen. IV.* v 3 94
Bartered. With a baser man of arms by far Once in contempt they would have barter'd me . . . . . . 1 *Hen. VI.* i 4 31
Bartholomew. To Barthol'mew my page, And see him dress'd *T. of Shrew* Ind. 1 105
Thou whoreson little tidy Bartholomew boar-pig 2 *Hen. IV.* ii 4 250
Bartholomew-tide. Like flies at Bartholomew-tide . . *Hen. V.* v 2 336
Basan. O, that I were Upon the hill of Basan! . . *Ant. and Cleo.* iii 13 127
Base. The mean is drown'd with your unruly bass.—Indeed, I bid the base for Proteus . . . . *T. G. of Ver.* i 2 97
The more degenerate and base art thou, To make such means . v 4 136
O base Hungarian wight! wilt thou the spigot wield? . *Mer. Wives* i 3 23
Tester I'll have in pouch when thou shalt lack, Base Phrygian Turk! . i 3 97
It is the base, though bitter, disposition of Beatrice . *Much Ado* ii 1 214
As it is base for a soldier to love, so am I in love with a base wench *L. L. Lost* i 2 61
I do affect the very ground, which is base, where her shoe, which is baser, guided by her foot, which is basest, doth tread . . i 2 173
Welcome to the wide fields too base to be mine . . . ii 1 94
Which to annothanize in the vulgar,—O base and obscure vulgar! . iv 1 69
Things base and vile, holding no quantity, Love can transpose *M. N. Dream* i 1 232
Madam, 'tis now in time.—All but the base . . *T. of Shrew* iii 1 46
The base is right; 'tis the base knave that jars . . iii 1 47
She, which late Was in my nobler thoughts most base, is now The praised of the king . . . . *All's Well* ii 3 178
Though I confess, on base and ground enough . . *T. Night* v 1 78
They are most of them means and bases . . . *W. Tale* iv 3 46
Thou art too base To be acknowledged . . . . iv 4 429
To a most base and vile-concluded peace . . . *K. John* ii 1 586
Being all too base To stain the temper of my knightly sword *Richard II.* iv 1 28
Made glory base and sovereignty a slave, Proud majesty a subject . iv 1 251
Herein will I imitate the sun, Who doth permit the base contagious clouds To smother up his beauty . . . 1 *Hen. IV.* i 2 222
Never did base and rotten policy Colour her working with such deadly wounds . . . . i 3 108
You poor, base, rascally, cheating, lack-linen mate! . 2 *Hen. IV.* ii 4 133
In base and abject routs, Led on by bloody youth, guarded with rags . iv 1 33
To dress the ugly form Of base and bloody insurrection . . iv 1 40
Puff! Puff in thy teeth, most recreant coward base! . . v 3 96
A foutre for the world and worldlings base! I speak of Africa . v 3 103
O base Assyrian knight, what is thy news? . . . . v 3 105
Base is the slave that pays . . . . *Hen. V.* ii 1 100
As fearfully as doth a galled rock O'erhang and jutty his confounded base . . . . iii 1 13
None of you so mean and base, That hath not noble lustre in your eyes iii 1 29
Art thou officer? Or art thou base, common and popular? . . iv 1 38
Without all colour Of base insinuating flattery . 1 *Hen. VI.* ii 4 35
So will this base and envious discord breed . . . iii 1 194
Contaminated, base And misbegotten blood . . . iv 6 21
Base ignoble wretch! I am descended of a gentler blood . . iv 4 7
That he should be so abject, base and poor, To choose for wealth . v 5 49
While Gloucester bears this base and humble mind . 2 *Hen. VI.* i 2 62
Base dunghill villain and mechanical, I'll have thy head for this . i 3 196
'Tis but a base ignoble mind That mounts no higher than a bird can soar . . . . ii 1 13
Base and ignominious treasons, makes me betake me to my heels . iv 8 66
Base, fearful and despairing Henry! . . 3 *Hen. VI.* i 1 178
A base foul stone, made precious by the foil Of England's chair *Richard III.* v 3 250
A scum of Bretons, and base lackey peasants . . . v 3 317
O, theft most base, That we have stol'n what we do fear to keep! *Troi. and Cres.* ii 2 92
The strong base and building of my love Is as the very centre of the earth . . . . iv 2 109
I wonder now how yonder city stands When we have here her base . iv 5 212
By Jove himself! It makes the consuls base . . *Coriolanus* iii 1 108
The base o' the mount Is rank'd with all deserts . *T. of Athens* i 1 64
This answer will not serve.—If 'twill not serve, 'tis not so base as you . iii 4 58
I should prove so base, To sue, and be denied such common grace . iii 5 94
Thus much of this [gold] will make black white, foul fair, Wrong right, base noble . . . . iv 3 29
Who is here so base that would be a bondman? If any, speak *J. Cæsar* iii 2 31
Even at the base of Pompey's statua, Which all the while ran blood . iii 2 192
To the dreadful summit of the cliff That beetles o'er his base . *Hamlet* i 4 71
Senseless Ilium, Seeming to feel this blow, with flaming top Stoops to his base . . . . ii 2 498
His very madness, like some ore Among a mineral of metals base, Shows itself pure . . . . iv 1 26
Lag of a brother? Why bastard? wherefore base? . . . *Lear* i 2 6
Why brand they us With base? with baseness? bastardy? base, base? . i 2 10
Edmund the base Shall top the legitimate . . . . i 2 20
Base, proud, shallow, beggarly, three-suited, hundred-pound . ii 2 16
The plague of great ones; Prerogatived are they less than the base *Othello* iii 3 274
Some base notorious knave, some scurvy fellow . . . iv 2 140
Slave, soulless villain, dog! O rarely base! . . *Ant. and Cleo.* v 2 158
This proves me base . . . . v 2 303
By-peeping in an eye Base and unlustrous as the smoky light That's fed with stinking tallow . . . . *Cymbeline* i 6 109
Thou wouldst have told this tale for virtue, not For such an end thou seek'st,—as base as strange . . . . i 6 144
Thou wert too base To be his groom . . . . . ii 3 131
Thou villain base, Know'st me not by my clothes? . . . iv 2 80
Lads more like to run The country base than to commit such slaughter v 3 20
Only, my friend, I yet am unprovided Of a pair of bases . *Pericles* ii 1 167
Base a hue. Is black so base a hue? . . . . . *T. Andron.* iv 2 71
Base a parle. Ere my tongue Shall wound my honour with such feeble wrong, Or sound so base a parle . . . . . *Richard II.* i 1 192
Base a thought. 'Twere damnation To think so base a thought *Mer. of Venice* ii 7 50
Base accusers. Yet I am richer than my base accusers . *Hen. VIII.* ii 1 104
Base adversities. All indign and base adversities Make head! *Othello* i 3 274
Base appliances. Too noble to conserve a life In base appliances *Meas. for Meas.* iii 1 89
Base authority. Small have continual plodders ever won Save base authority from others' books . . . . . *L. L. Lost* i 1 87

Base-born. Contemptuous base-born callet as she is . . . *2 Hen. VI.* i 3 86
Better ten thousand base-born Cades miscarry Than you should stoop . iv 8 49
Shamest thou not, knowing whence thou art extraught, To let thy tongue detect thy base-born heart? . . . . . . *3 Hen. VI.* ii 2 143
Base bribes. Shall we now Contaminate our fingers with base bribes? *J. Cæsar* iv 3 24
Base comparisons. When thou hast tired thyself in base comparisons, hear me speak . . . . *1 Hen. IV.* ii 4 276
Base compulsion. On terms of base compulsion . *Troi. and Cres.* ii 2 153
Base court. In the base court? Base court, where kings grow base *Richard II.* iii 3 180
In the base court? Come down? Down, court! down, king! . . . iii 3 182
Base declension. Seduced the pitch and height of all his thoughts To base declension . . . . *Richard III.* iii 7 189
Base degrees. Looks in the clouds, scorning the base degrees By which he did ascend . . . . *J. Cæsar* ii 1 26
Base descent. My actions are as noble as my thoughts, That never relish'd of a base descent . . . . . . *Pericles* ii 5 60
Base dishonour. Never yet did base dishonour blur our name *2 Hen. VI.* iv 1 39
Base drudge. Will you credit this base drudge's words? . . iv 2 159
Base durance. Is in base durance and contagious prison *2 Hen. IV.* v 5 36
Base earth. Lest the base earth Should from her vesture chance to steal a kiss . . . . *T. G. of Ver.* ii 4 159
I see thy glory like a shooting star Fall to the base earth *Richard II.* ii 4 20
You debase your princely knee To make the base earth proud with kissing it . . . . iii 3 191
Base effect. Base men, that use them to so base effect! . *T. G. of Ver.* ii 7 73
Base fear. In the highest compulsion of base fear . . *All's Well* iii 6 31
Base foot-ball player. Nor tripped neither, you base foot-ball player *Lear* i 4 95
Base fruit. Here's the base fruit of his burning lust. . *T. Andron.* v 1 43
Base ground. Kisses the base ground with obedient breast . *L. L. Lost* iv 3 225
Base humility. And fawn on rage with base humility . *Richard II.* v 1 33
Base humour. I will run no base humour . . . *Mer. Wives* i 3 85
Base imitation. Limps after in base imitation . . . *Richard II.* ii 1 23
Base inclination and the start of spleen . . *1 Hen. IV.* iii 2 125
Base Indian. Like the base Indian, threw a pearl away Richer than all his tribe . . . . *Othello* v 2 347
Base intruder. Go, base intruder! overweening slave! . *T. G. of Ver.* iii 1 157
Base knave. The base is right; 'tis the base knave that jars *T. of Shrew* iii 1 47
Base knight. I vow'd, base knight, when I did meet thee next, To tear the garter from thy craven's leg . . . . . *1 Hen. VI.* iv 1 14
Base lead. Gold; silver; and base lead . . . *Mer. of Venice* ii 9 20
Base life. Squire-like, pension beg To keep base life afoot . . *Lear* ii 4 218
Base man. Base men, that use them to so base effect . *T. G. of Ver.* ii 7 73
Base men by his endowments are made great . . . *Richard II.* ii 3 139
What answer shall I make to this base man? . . . . iv 1 20
Small things make base men proud . . . . . *2 Hen. VI.* iv 1 106
Base men being in love have then a nobility in their natures . *Othello* ii 1 217
Base matter. When it serves For the base matter to illuminate So vile a thing as Cæsar! . . . . *J. Cæsar* i 3 110
Base metal. They have all been touch'd and found base metal *T. of Athens* iii 3 6
Base mind. I'll ne'er bear a base mind: an't be my destiny, so *2 Hen. IV.* iii 2 252
Thou'rt a good fellow.—Faith, I'll bear no base mind . . . . iii 2 257
Base minnow. That low-spirited swain, that base minnow of thy mirth *L. L. Lost* i 1 251
Base muleters of France! Like peasant foot-boys . . *1 Hen. VI.* iii 2 68
Base newsmongers. Pick-thanks and base newsmongers . *1 Hen. IV.* iii 2 25
Base opinion. Envy and base opinion set against 'em *Hen. VIII.* iii 1 36
Base pandar. With his cap in hand, Like a base pandar . *Hen. V.* iv 5 14
Base passions. Of all base passions, fear is most accursed . *1 Hen. VI.* v 2 18
Base peasants. And you, base peasants, do ye believe him? *2 Hen. VI.* iv 8 21
Base practices. We detest such vile base practices . . *T. G. of Ver.* iv 1 73
Base prayers. I am no baby, I, that with base prayers I should repent the evils I have done . . . . . . *T. Andron.* v 3 185
Base prince. Perish, base prince, ignoble Duke of York! *1 Hen. VI.* iii 1 178
Base respects. The instances that second marriage move Are base respects of thrift, but none of love . . . . *Hamlet* iii 2 193
Base sale. Not utter'd by base sale of chapmen's tongues . *L. L. Lost* ii 1 16
Base second means. The agents, or base second means . *1 Hen. IV.* i 3 165
Base servility. To be a queen in bondage is more vile Than is a slave in base servility . . . . *1 Hen. VI.* v 3 113
Base slave, thy words are blunt and so art thou . *2 Hen. VI.* iv 1 67
These base slaves, Ere yet the fight be done, pack up . *Coriolanus* i 5 8
And must not soil The precious note of it with a base slave . *Cymbeline* ii 3 127
Base-string. I have sounded the very base-string of humility *1 Hen. IV.* ii 4 6
Base things. Cowards father cowards and base things sire base *Cymbeline* iv 2 26
Base throats. Patient fools, Whose children he hath slain, their base throats tear With giving him glory . . *Coriolanus* v 6 53
Base tike, call'st thou me host? . . . . . *Hen. V.* ii 1 31
Base tongue. Must I with base tongue give my noble heart A lie? *Coriolanus* iii 2 100
Base treachery. I slew him manfully in fight, Without false vantage or base treachery . . . . *T. G. of Ver.* iv 1 29
Base Trojan. Art thou bedlam? dost thou thirst, base Trojan? *Hen. V.* v 1 20
Base truce. Make compromise, Insinuation, parley and base truce *K. John* v 1 68
Base uses. To what base uses we may return, Horatio! . *Hamlet* v 1 223
Base vocation. Will'd me to leave my base vocation . *1 Hen. VI.* i 2 80
Base vulgar. One more than two.—Which the base vulgar do call three *L. L. Lost* i 2 51
Base Walloon. A base Walloon, to win the Dauphin's grace, Thrust Talbot with a spear . . . . *1 Hen. VI.* i 1 137
Base wench. As it is base for a soldier to love, so am I in love with a base wench . . . . *L. L. Lost* i 2 62
Base wretch, One bred of alms and foster'd with cold dishes . *Cymbeline* ii 3 118
Baseless. Like the baseless fabric of this vision . . *Tempest* iv 1 151
Basely. The king is not himself, but basely led By flatterers *Richard II.* ii 1 241
Basely yielded upon compromise That which his noble ancestors achieved with blows . . . . ii 1 253
The time of life is short! To spend that shortness basely were too long *1 Hen. IV.* v 2 83
He is not Talbot's blood, That basely fled when noble Talbot stood *1 Hen. VI.* iv 5 17
Here none but soldiers and Rome's servitors Repose in fame; none basely slain in brawls . . . . *T. Andron.* i 1 353
What, madam! be dishonour'd openly, And basely put it up without revenge? . . . . i 1 433
Basely. To see so great a lord Basely insinuate and send us gifts *T. Andron.* iv 2 38
Our father's tears despised, and basely cozen'd Of that true hand . . v 3 101
Do now not basely die, Not cowardly put off my helmet *Ant. and Cleo.* iv 15 55
Baseness. Some kinds of baseness Are nobly undergone . . *Tempest* iii 1 2
Such baseness Had never like executor . . . . . . iii 1 12
Thou unconfinable baseness . . . . . . *Mer. Wives* ii 2 21
All the accommodations that thou bear'st Are nursed by baseness *Meas. for Meas.* iii 1 15
It is the baseness of thy fear That makes thee strangle thy propriety *T. Night* v 1 149
For ever Unvenerable be thy hands, if thou Takest up the princess by that forced baseness! . . . . *W. Tale* ii 3 78
Reflect I not on thy baseness court-contempt? . . . . iv 4 758
By my body's action teach my mind A most inherent baseness *Coriolanus* iii 2 123
Fly, damned baseness, To him that worships thee!. . *T. of Athens* iii 1 50
I once did hold it, as our statists do, A baseness to write fair *Hamlet* v 2 34
Why brand they us With base? with baseness? bastardy? base, base? *Lear* i 2 10
The blood and baseness of our natures would conduct us to most preposterous conclusions . . . . *Othello* i 3 332
Is true of mind and made of no such baseness As jealous creatures are . iii 4 27
I have lived in such dishonour, that the gods Detest my baseness *Ant. and Cleo.* iv 14 57
The wheel'd seat Of fortunate Cæsar, drawn before him, branded His baseness that ensued . . . . iv 14 77
Wouldst have made my throne A seat for baseness . . *Cymbeline* i 1 142
From whose so many weights of baseness cannot A dram of worth be drawn . . . . iii 5 88
Baser. The grosser manner of these world's delights He throws upon the gross world's baser slaves . . . . *L. L. Lost* i 1 30
Her shoe, which is baser, guided by her foot, which is basest . . i 2 173
Civet is of a baser birth than tar . . . . *As Y. Like It* iii 2 69
We, the poorer born, Whose baser stars do shut us up in wishes *All's Well* i 1 197
And make conceive a bark of baser kind By bud of nobler race *W. Tale* iv 4 94
And wholesome berries thrive and ripen best Neighbour'd by fruit of baser quality . . . . *Hen. V.* i 1 62
With a baser man of arms by far Once in contempt they would have barter'd me: Which I disdaining scorn'd . . *1 Hen. VI.* i 4 30
What a god's gold, That he is worshipp'd in a baser temple Than where swine feed! . . . . *T. of Athens* v 1 51
Within the book and volume of my brain, Unmix'd with baser matter *Hamlet* i 5 104
'Tis dangerous when the baser nature comes Between the pass and fell incensed points Of mighty opposites . . . . . v 2 60
I am fire and air; my other elements I give to baser life *Ant. and Cleo.* v 2 293
Basest. Her shoe, which is baser, guided by her foot, which is basest *L. L. Lost* i 2 174
What is he of basest function That says his bravery is not on my cost? *As Y. Like It* ii 7 79
The basest horn of his hoof is more musical than the pipe of Hermes *Hen. V.* iii 7 17
For that, being one o' the lowest, basest, poorest, Of this most wise rebellion, thou go'st foremost . . . . . . *Coriolanus* i 1 161
What viler thing upon the earth than friends Who can bring noblest minds to basest ends! . . . . . . *T. of Athens* iv 3 471
See, whether their basest metal be not moved . . . *J. Cæsar* i 1 66
Such as basest and contemned'st wretches For pilferings and most common trespasses Are punish'd with . . . . *Lear* ii 2 150
The basest and most poorest shape That ever penury, in contempt of man, Brought near to beast . . . . ii 3 7
O, reason not the need: our basest beggars Are in the poorest thing superfluous . . . . ii 4 267
Thou basest thing, avoid! hence, from my sight! . . *Cymbeline* i 1 125
Prostitute me to the basest groom That doth frequent your house *Pericles* iv 6 201
Bashful. Hence, bashful cunning! And prompt me, plain and holy innocence! . . . . *Tempest* iii 1 81
As a brother to his sister, show'd Bashful sincerity and comely love *Much Ado* iv 1 55
Her beauty and her wit, Her affability and bashful modesty *T. of Shrew* ii 1 49
Come, you virtuous ass, you bashful fool, must you be blushing? *2 Hen. IV.* ii 2 80
And bashful Henry deposed, whose cowardice Hath made us by-words *3 Hen. VI.* i 1 41
Make bold her bashful years with your experience . *Richard III.* iv 4 326
Bashfulness. Have you no modesty, no maiden shame, No touch of bashfulness? . . . . *M. N. Dream* iii 2 286
Basilisco-like. Knight, knight, good mother, Basilisco-like . *K. John* i 1 244
Basilisk. Make me not sighted like the basilisk . . *W. Tale* i 2 388
Thou hast talk'd . . . Of basilisks, of cannon, culverin . *1 Hen. IV.* ii 3 56
The fatal balls of murdering basilisks . . . . *Hen. V.* v 2 17
Come, basilisk, And kill the innocent gazer with thy sight *2 Hen. VI.* iii 2 52
Their chiefest prospect murdering basilisks! . . . . . iii 2 324
I'll slay more gazers than the basilisk . . . . *3 Hen VI.* iii 2 187
Would they were basilisks, to strike thee dead! . . *Richard III.* i 2 151
It is a basilisk unto mine eye, Kills me to look on't . *Cymbeline* ii 4 107
Basimecu. Giving up of Normandy unto Mounsieur Basimecu *2 Hen. VI.* iv 7 31
Basin. Attend him with a silver basin Full of rose-water *T. of Shrew* Ind. 1 55
Basins and ewers to lave her dainty hands . . . . . ii 1 350
Whilst that Lavinia 'tween her stumps doth hold The basin *T. Andron.* v 2 184
This hits right; I dreamt of a silver basin and ewer to-night *T. of Athens* iii 1 6
Basingstoke. Where lay the king last night?—At Basingstoke *2 Hen. IV.* ii 1 182
Basis. The shore, that o'er his wave-worn basis bow'd *Tempest* ii 1 120
Build me thy fortunes upon the basis of valour . . *T. Night* iii 2 36
We upon this mountain's basis by Took stand for idle speculation *Hen. V.* iv 2 30
Troy, yet upon his basis, had been down . *Troi. and Cres.* i 3 75
How many times shall Cæsar bleed in sport, That now on Pompey's basis lies along No worthier than the dust! . . . *J. Cæsar* iii 1 115
Tyranny! lay thou thy basis sure, For goodness dare not check thee *Macbeth* iv 3 32
Basked. Who laid him down and bask'd him in the sun . *As Y. Like It* ii 7 15
Basket. Take this basket on your shoulders . . *Mer. Wives* iii 3 13
Here is a basket: if he be of any reasonable stature, he may creep in here . . . . iii 3 137
What a taking was he in when your husband asked who was in the basket! . . . . iii 3 192
Have I lived to be carried in a basket, like a barrow of butcher's offal? iii 5 5
Being thus crammed in the basket . . . . iii 5 99
Who asked them once or twice what they had in their basket . . iii 5 104

Basket. Swears he was carried out, the last time he searched for him, in a basket . . . *Mer. Wives* iv 2 33
Shall I put him into the basket again?—No, I'll come no more i' the basket . . . iv 2 49
Is my husband coming?—Ay, in good sadness, is he; and talks of the basket too . . . iv 2 94
I'll appoint my men to carry the basket again, to meet him at the door iv 2 97
I'll first direct my men what they shall do with the basket . . iv 2 102
Take the basket again on your shoulders: your master is hard at door iv 2 110
Set down the basket, villain! Somebody call my wife. Youth in a basket! . . . iv 2 121
Empty the basket, I say?—Why, man, why? . . . iv 2 149
As I am a man, there was one conveyed out of my house yesterday in this basket . . . iv 2 153
Unpeg the basket on the house's top, Let the birds fly . . *Hamlet* iii 4 193
And, like the famous ape, To try conclusions, in the basket creep . iii 4 195
A simple countryman, that brought her figs: This was his basket *Ant. and Cleo.* v 2 343
Basket-hilt. You bottle-ale rascal! you basket-hilt stale juggler! *2 Hen. IV.* ii 4 141
Bass. It did bass my trespass . . . *Tempest* iii 3 99
The mean is drown'd with your unruly bass . . . *T. G. of Ver.* i 2 96
Bassanio. Here comes Bassanio, your most noble kinsman *Mer. of Venice* i 1 57
Lord Bassanio, since you have found Antonio, We two will leave you . i 1 69
I pray you, good Bassanio, let me know it . . . i 1 135
Yes, it was Bassanio; as I think, he was so called . . . i 2 127
Mark you this, Bassanio, The devil can cite Scripture for his purpose . i 3 98
One Master Bassanio, who, indeed, gives rare new liveries . . ii 2 116
Thy eyes shall be thy judge, The difference of old Shylock and Bassanio ii 5 2
The close night doth play the runaway, And we are stay'd for at Bassanio's feast . . . ii 6 48
The wind is come about; Bassanio presently will go aboard . . ii 6 65
I saw Bassanio under sail: With him is Gratiano gone along . . ii 8 1
With outcries raised the duke, Who went with him to search Bassanio's ship . . . ii 8 5
They were not with Bassanio in his ship . . . ii 8 11
I saw Bassanio and Antonio part: Bassanio told him he would make some speed Of his return . . . ii 8 36
Slubber not business for my sake, Bassanio, But stay the very riping of the time . . . ii 8 39
With affection wondrous sensible He wrung Bassanio's hand . . . ii 8 49
Bassanio, lord Love, if thy will it be! . . . ii 9 101
For as I am, I live upon the rack.—Upon the rack, Bassanio! . iii 2 26
You see me, Lord Bassanio, where I stand, Such as I am . . iii 2 150
When this ring Parts from this finger, then parts life from hence: O, then be bold to say Bassanio's dead! . . . iii 2 187
My lord Bassanio and my gentle lady, I wish you all the joy that you can wish . . . iii 2 191
There are some shrewd contents in yon same paper, That steals the colour from Bassanio's cheek . . . iii 2 247
With leave, Bassanio; I am half yourself, And I must freely have the half of anything That this same paper brings you . . iii 2 251
Before a friend of this description Shall lose a hair through Bassanio's fault . . . iii 2 305
Sweet Bassanio, my ships have all miscarried, my creditors grow cruel iii 2 318
Pray God, Bassanio come To see me pay his debt, and then I care not! iii 3 35
Will acknowledge you and Jessica In place of Lord Bassanio and myself . . . iii 4 39
Sweet, say thy opinion, How dost thou like the Lord Bassanio's wife? . iii 5 77
It is very meet The Lord Bassanio live an upright life . . iii 5 79
You cannot better be employ'd, Bassanio, Than to live still and write mine epitaph . . . iv 1 117
Bassanio: fare you well! Grieve not that I am fallen to this for you . iv 1 265
Bid her be judge Whether Bassanio had not once a love . . iv 1 277
My Lord Bassanio, let him have the ring . . . iv 1 449
My Lord Bassanio upon more advice Hath sent you here this ring . iv 2 6
A light wife doth make a heavy husband, And never be Bassanio so for me . . . v 1 131
My Lord Bassanio gave his ring away Unto the judge that begg'd it v 1 179
Here, Lord Bassanio; swear to keep this ring . . . v 1 256
Pardon me, Bassanio; For, by this ring, the doctor lay with me . v 1 258
Bassianus. If ever Bassianus, Cæsar's son, Were gracious in the eyes of royal Rome . . . *T. Andron.* i 1 10
So, Bassianus, you have play'd your prize: God give you joy! . i 1 399
Prince Bassianus, leave to plead my deeds . . . i 1 424
Prince Bassianus, I have pass'd My word and promise to the emperor . i 1 468
What, is Lavinia then become so loose, Or Bassianus so degenerate? ii 1 66
Though Bassianus be the emperor's brother, Better than he have worn Vulcan's badge . . . ii 1 88
Lucrece was not more chaste Than this Lavinia, Bassianus' love . ii 1 109
This is the day of doom for Bassianus . . . ii 3 42
Thy sons make pillage of her chastity And wash their hands in Bassianus' blood . . . ii 3 45
Bassianus comes: Be cross with him . . . ii 3 52
'Tis not life that I have begg'd so long; Poor I was slain when Bassianus died . . . ii 3 171
Lord Bassianus lies embrewed here, All on a heap . . . ii 3 222
This deep pit, poor Bassianus' grave . . . ii 3 240
Brought hither in a most unlucky hour, To find thy brother Bassianus dead . . . ii 3 252
Where is thy brother Bassianus?—Now to the bottom dost thou search my wound: Poor Bassianus here lies murdered . . ii 3 261
Bassianus 'tis we mean—Do thou so much as dig the grave for him ii 3 269
That same pit Where we decreed to bury Bassianus . . ii 3 274
Find the huntsman out That should have murder'd Bassianus . ii 3 279
'Twas her two sons that murder'd Bassianus; They cut thy sister's tongue . . . v 1 91
I train'd thy brethren to that guileful hole Where the dead corpse of Bassianus lay . . . v 1 105
Bass-viol. He that went, like a bass-viol, in a case of leather *Com. of Err.* iv 3 23
Basta; content thee, for I have it full . . *T. of Shrew* i 1 203
Bastard. This demi-devil—For he's a bastard one . . . *Tempest* v 1 273
That's as much as to say, bastard virtues . . *T. G. of Ver.* iii 1 321
We shall have all the world drink brown and white bastard *Meas. for Meas.* iii 2 4
Ere he would have hanged a man for the getting a hundred bastards, he would have paid for the nursing a thousand . . . iii 2 125
Shame hath a bastard fame, well managed . . *Com. of Errors* iii 2 19
The practice of it lives in John the bastard . . . *Much Ado* iv 1 190
Your brother the bastard is fled from Messina . . . v 1 193
O, an the heavens were so pleased that thou wert but my bastard! *L. L. Lost* v 1 79

Bastard. And that is but a kind of bastard hope neither *Mer. of Venice* iii 5 8
That same wicked bastard of Venus that was begot of thought *As Y. Like It* iv 1 216
Sure, they are bastards to the English; the French ne'er got 'em *All's Well* ii 3 100
Give her the bastard. Thou dotard! thou art woman-tired . *W. Tale* ii 3 73
Take up the bastard; Take't up, I say; give't to thy crone . . ii 3 75
The bastard brains with these my proper hands Shall I dash out . ii 3 139
Shall I live on to see this bastard kneel And call me father? . . ii 3 155
To save this bastard's life,—for 'tis a bastard, So sure as this beard's grey . . . ii 3 161
Carry This female bastard hence . . . ii 3 175
Streak'd gillyvors, Which some call nature's bastards . . iv 4 83
Make your garden rich in gillyvors, And do not call them bastards . iv 4 99
He is but a bastard to the time That doth not smack of observation *K. John* i 1 207
With them a bastard of the king's deceased . . . ii 1 65
Out, insolent! thy bastard shall be king, That thou mayst be a queen! ii 1 122
Twice fifteen thousand hearts of England's breed,— Bastards, and else ii 1 276
The bastard Faulconbridge Is now in England . . . iii 4 171
Thou dost suspect That I have been disloyal to thy bed, And that he is a bastard, not thy son . . . *Richard II.* v 2 106
'Anon, anon, sir! Score a pint of bastard in the Half-moon,' or so *1 Hen. IV.* ii 4 30
Why, then, your brown bastard is your only drink . . . ii 4 82
A bastard son of the king's? And art not thou Poins his brother? *2 Hen. IV.* ii 4 307
Ish a villain, and a bastard, and a knave, and a rascal . *Hen. V.* iii 2 133
Normans, but bastard Normans, Norman bastards! . . . iii 5 10
They will give Their bodies to the lust of English youth To new-store France with bastard warriors . . . iii 5 31
The Dauphin Charles is crowned king in Rheims; The Bastard of Orleans with him is join'd . . . *1 Hen. VI.* i 1 93
Bastard of Orleans, thrice welcome to us . . . i 2 47
As good! Thou bastard of my grandfather! . . . iii 1 42
Now where's the Bastard's braves, and Charles his gleeks? . . iii 2 123
Orleans the Bastard, Charles, Burgundy, Alençon, Reignier, compass him about . . . iv 4 26
Dishonour not her honourable name, To make a bastard and a slave of me! . . . iv 5 15
And interchanging blows I quickly shed Some of his bastard blood . iv 6 20
Here, purposing the Bastard to destroy, Came in strong rescue . iv 6 25
We'll have no bastards live; Especially since Charles must father it . v 4 70
Brutus bastard hand Stabb'd Julius Cæsar . . *2 Hen. VI.* iv 1 136
The bastard boys of York Shall be the surety for their traitor father . v 1 115
I wish the bastards dead; And I would have it suddenly perform'd *Richard III.* iv 2 18
Tyrrel, I mean those bastards in the Tower . . . iv 2 76
If we be conquer'd, let men conquer us, And not these bastard Bretons v 3 333
Bastard Margarelon Hath Doreus prisoner . . *Troi. and Cres.* v 5 7
What art thou?—A bastard son of Priam's.—I am a bastard too; I love bastards . . . v 7 15
I am a bastard begot, bastard instructed, bastard in mind, bastard in valour . . . v 7 17
One bear will not bite another, and wherefore should one bastard? . v 7 20
Farewell, bastard.—The devil take thee, coward! . . . v 7 23
Bastards and syllables Of no allowance to your bosom's truth *Coriolanus* iii 2 56
He'ld make an end of thy posterity.—Bastards and all . . iv 2 27
Peace is . . . a getter of more bastard children than war's a destroyer of men . . . iv 5 240
What, wouldst thou have me prove myself a bastard? . *T. Andron.* ii 3 148
Ho, ho! I laugh to think that babe a bastard . . *T. of Athens* i 2 117
Go; thou wast born a bastard, and thou'dt die a bawd . . ii 2 88
A bastard, whom the oracle Hath doubtfully pronounced thy throat shall cut . . . iv 3 120
O, yet hold up your heads!—What bastard doth not? . . *J. Cæsar* iv 4 2
That drop of blood that's calm proclaims me bastard . . *Hamlet* iv 5 117
Why bastard? wherefore base? When my dimensions are as well compact? *Lear* i 2 6
Our father's love is to the bastard Edmund As to the legitimate . i 2 17
I grow; I prosper: Now, gods, stand up for bastards! . . i 2 22
Degenerate bastard! I'll not trouble thee . . . i 4 275
He replied, 'Thou unpossessing bastard!' . . . ii 1 69
Gloucester's bastard son Was kinder to his father than my daughters Got 'tween the lawful sheets . . . iv 6 116
Who is conductor of his people?—As 'tis said, the bastard son of Gloucester . . . iv 7 89
Is there no way for men to be but women Must be half-workers? We are all bastards . . . *Cymbeline* ii 5 2
'Tis not our bringing up of poor bastards,—as, I think, I have brought up some eleven— Ay, to eleven . . . *Pericles* iv 2 15
Bastardizing. I should have been that I am, had the maidenliest star in the firmament twinkled on my bastardizing . . . *Lear* i 2 144
Bastardly. Wilt thou? thou bastardly rogue! . . *2 Hen. IV.* ii 1 55
Bastardy. Once he slander'd me with bastardy . . . *K. John* i 1 74
That thou thyself wast born in bastardy . . *2 Hen. VI.* iii 2 223
Infer the bastardy of Edward's children . . *Richard III.* iii 5 75
Touch'd you the bastardy of Edward's children? . . . iii 7 4
His own bastardy, As being got, your father then in France . . iii 7 9
Hang him on this tree, And by his side his fruit of bastardy *T. Andron.* v 1 48
When every drop of blood That every Roman bears, and nobly bears, Is guilty of a several bastardy . . . *J. Cæsar* ii 1 138
Why brand they us With base? with baseness? bastardy? base, base? *Lear* i 2 10
Baste. The proud lord That bastes his arrogance with his own seam *Troi. and Cres.* ii 3 195
Basted. The body of your discourse is sometime guarded with fragments, and the guards are but slightly basted on neither . *Much Ado* i 1 289
Bastinado. I will deal in poison with thee, or in bastinado *As Y. Like It* v 1 60
He gives the bastinado with his tongue: Our ears are cudgell'd *K. John* ii 1 463
Percy, and he of Wales, that gave Amamon the bastinado . *1 Hen. IV.* ii 4 370
Basting. I think the meat wants that I have.—In good time, sir; what's that?—Basting . . . *Com. of Errors* ii 2 59
Lest it make you choleric and purchase me another dry basting . ii 2 64
Bat. All the charms Of Sycorax, toads, beetles, bats, light on you! *Tempest* i 2 340
On the bat's back I do fly After summer merrily . . . v 1 91
Where go you With bats and clubs? . . . *Coriolanus* i 1 57
But make you ready your stiff bats and clubs . . . i 1 165
Be thou jocund: ere the bat hath flown His cloister'd flight . *Macbeth* iii 2 40
Eye of newt and toe of frog, Wool of bat and tongue of dog . . iv 1 15
From a paddock, from a bat, a gib, Such dear concernings hide *Hamlet* iii 4 190

Bataille. Dieu de batailles! where have they this mettle? . *Hen. V.* iii 5 15
Batch. Thou crusty batch of nature . . . . . *Troi. and Cres.* v 1 5
Bate. Thou didst promise To bate me a full year . . . *Tempest* i 2 250
Bate, I beseech you, widow Dido . . . . . ii 1 100
Rather than she will bate one breath of her accustomed crossness *Much Ado* ii 3 183
May buy That honour which shall bate his scythe's keen edge *L. L. Lost* i 1 6
Stand upon the beach And bid the main flood bate his usual height *Mer. of Venice* iv 1 72
These kites That bate and beat and will not be obedient . *T. of Shrew* iv 1 199
I will not bate thee a scruple . . . . . *All's Well* ii 3 234
Am I not fallen away vilely since this last action? do I not bate? 1 *Hen. IV.* iii 3 2
And breeds no bate with telling of discreet stories . . 2 *Hen. IV.* ii 4 271
Bate me some and I will pay you some and, as most debtors do, promise you infinitely . . . . Epil. 15
Good bawcock, bate thy rage; use lenity, sweet chuck! . . *Hen. V.* iii 2 26
'Tis a hooded valour; and when it appears, it will bate . . iii 7 122
Neither will they bate One jot of ceremony . . . *Coriolanus* ii 2 144
You bate too much of your own merits . . . . *T. of Athens* i 2 212
Who bates mine honour shall not know my coin . . . iii 3 26
Who long'st,—O let me bate,—but not like me—yet long'st . *Cymbeline* iii 2 56
Bated. Of my instruction hast thou nothing bated . . . *Tempest* iii 3 85
Were the world mine, Demetrius being bated, The rest I'ld give to be to you translated . . . . *M. N. Dream* i 1 190
With bated breath and whispering humbleness . . *Mer. of Venice* i 3 125
These griefs and losses have so bated me, That I shall hardly spare a pound of flesh To-morrow . . . . . . iii 3 32
Those bated that inherit but the fall Of the last monarchy . *All's Well* ii 1 13
Like a bated and retired flood, Leaving our rankness . . *K. John* v 4 53
No leisure bated, No, not to stay the grinding of the axe . *Hamlet* v 2 23
I cannot be bated one doit of a thousand pieces . . *Pericles* iv 2 55
Bates. Brother John Bates, is not that the morning which breaks yonder? *Hen. V.* iv 1 87
Bat-fowling. We would so, and then go a bat-fowling . . *Tempest* ii 1 185
Bath. In the height of this bath, when I was more than half stewed in grease, like a Dutch dish . . . . . *Mer. Wives* iii 5 120
I could wish You were conducted to a gentle bath . . *Coriolanus* i 6 63
Season the slaves For tubs and baths . . . . *T. of Athens* iv 3 86
Sore labour's bath, Balm of hurt minds . . . *Macbeth* ii 2 38
Bathe. And the delighted spirit To bathe in fiery floods *Meas. for Meas.* iii 1 122
Many lusty Romans Came smiling, and did bathe their hands *J. Cæsar* i 2 79
Romans, stoop, And let us bathe our hands in Cæsar's blood Up to the elbows . . . . iii 1 106
Except they meant to bathe in reeking wounds . . *Macbeth* i 2 39
Or bathe my dying honour in the blood Shall make it live again *A. and C.* iv 2 6
Had I this cheek To bathe my lips upon . . . *Cymbeline* i 6 100
Bathed. Tears our recountments had most kindly bathed *As Y. Like It* iv 3 141
Baited like eagles having lately bathed . . . 1 *Hen. IV.* iv 1 99
Or bathed thy growing with our heated bloods . 3 *Hen. VI.* ii 2 169
On Pyramus When he by night lay bathed in maiden blood *T. Andron.* ii 3 232
Your statue spouting blood in many pipes, In which so many smiling Romans bathed . . . . *J. Cæsar* ii 2 86
Bathing. And the chimney-piece Chaste Dian bathing . *Cymbeline* ii 4 82
Bating. Hood my unmann'd blood, bating in my cheeks . *Rom. and Jul.* iii 2 14
Batlet. And I remember the kissing of her batlet . *As Y. Like It* ii 4 49
Battalion. Our battalion trebles that account . . *Richard III.* v 3 11
When sorrows come, they come not single spies, But in battalions *Hamlet* iv 5 79
Batten. Follow your function, go, and batten on cold bits *Coriolanus* iv 5 35
Could you on this fair mountain leave to feed, And batten on this moor? *Hamlet* iii 4 67
Batter. With a log Batter his skull, or paunch him with a stake *Tempest* iii 2 98
So that the ram that batters down the wall, For the great swing and rudeness of his poise, They place before his hand that made the engine . . . . *Troi. and Cres.* i 3 206
In commotion rages And batters down himself . . . . ii 3 186
Let not the piece of virtue, which is set Betwixt us as the cement of our love, To keep it builded, be the ram to batter The fortress of it *Ant. and Cleo.* iii 2 30
Whose bolt, you know, Sky-planted batters all rebelling coasts *Cymbeline* v 4 96
Battered. These haughty words of hers Have batter'd me like roaring cannon-shot . . . . 1 *Hen. VI.* iii 3 79
That hath more scars of sorrow in his heart Than foemen's marks upon his batter'd shield . . . . . . *T. Andron.* iv 1 127
The tyrant has not batter'd at their peace? . . . *Macbeth* iv 3 178
Battering. Sconce call you it? so you would leave battering, I had rather have it a head . . . . . . *Com. of Errors* ii 2 36
Their battering cannon charged to the mouths . . *K. John* ii 1 382
Battery. I'll have mine action of battery on thee . *Meas. for Meas.* ii 1 188
I'll have an action of battery against him, if there be any law *T. Night* iv 1 36
This union shall do more than battery can . . . *K. John* ii 1 446
If I begin the battery once again, I will not leave . . *Hen. V.* iii 3 7
Express opinions Where is best place to make our battery next 1 *Hen. VI.* i 4 65
Her sighs will make a battery in his breast . . 3 *Hen. VI.* iii 1 37
Talks like a knell, and his hum is a battery . . . *Coriolanus* v 4 22
And will not tell him of his action of battery . . . *Hamlet* v 1 111
Make battery to our ears with the loud music . . *Ant. and Cleo.* ii 7 115
The seven-fold shield of Ajax cannot keep The battery from my heart . iv 14 39
To fortify her judgement, which else an easy battery might lay flat *Cymb.* i 4 22
She'll never stint, Make raging battery upon shores of flint . *Pericles* iv 4 43
Make a battery through his deafen'd parts, Which now are midway stopp'd . . . . v 1 47
Battle. The battle with the Centaurs, to be sung By an Athenian eunuch to the harp . . . . *M. N. Dream* v 1 44
And nature, stronger than his just occasion, Made him give battle to the lioness, Who quickly fell . . . . . *As Y. Like It* iv 3 131
Have I not in a pitched battle heard Loud 'larums? . . *T. of Shrew* i 2 206
Like heralds 'twixt two dreadful battles set . . . *K. John* iv 2 78
Besides I say and will in battle prove, Or here or elsewhere *Richard II.* i 1 92
My dancing soul doth celebrate This feast of battle with mine adversary i 3 92
To bloody battles and to bruising arms . . . 1 *Hen. IV.* iii 2 105
What may the king's whole battle reach unto? . . . . iv 1 129
Let it be seen to-morrow in the battle Which of us fears . . iv 3 13
Hal, if thou see me down in the battle and bestride me, so . . v 1 121
Uncle, what news?—The king will bid you battle presently . . v 2 31
What is thy name, that in the battle thus Thou crossest me? . . v 3 1
I do haunt thee in the battle thus Because some tell me that thou art a king . . . . v 3 4
Wilt thou make as many holes in an enemy's battle as thou hast done in a woman's petticoat? . . . . . . 2 *Hen. IV.* iii 2 165

Battle. Our battle is more full of names than yours, Our men more perfect . . . . 2 *Hen. IV.* iv 1 154
Please you, lords, In sight of both our battles we may meet . . iv 1 179
You shall hear A fearful battle render'd you in music . *Hen. V.* i 1 44
Witness our too much memorable shame When Cressy battle fatally was struck . . . . ii 4 54
We would not seek a battle, as we are; Nor, as we are, we say we will not shun it . . . . iii 6 173
Through their paly flames Each battle sees the other's umber'd face iv Prol. 9
And so our scene must to the battle fly . . . . . iv Prol. 48
All those legs and arms and heads, chopped off in a battle, shall join together at the latter day . . . . iv 1 143
I am afeard there are few die well that die in a battle . . iv 1 148
O God of battles! steel my soldiers' hearts; Possess them not with fear iv 1 306
Peasants, Who in unnecessary action swarm About our squares of battle iv 2 28
To demonstrate the life of such a battle In life so lifeless . . iv 2 54
The king himself is rode to view their battle . . . . iv 3 2
The French are bravely in their battles set, And will with all expedience charge . . . . iv 3 69
Would you and I alone, Without more help, could fight this royal battle! iv 3 75
The cowardly rascals that ran from the battle ha' done this slaughter iv 7 6
In plain shock and even play of battle, Was ever known so great and little loss? . . . . iv 8 114
The battles of the Lord of hosts he fought . . 1 *Hen. VI.* i 1 31
Cried out amain And rush'd into the bowels of the battle . . i 1 129
In thirteen battles Salisbury o'ercame . . . . . i 4 78
At the battle of Patay, When but in all I was six thousand strong . iv 1 19
Wilt thou yet leave the battle, boy, and fly, Now thou art seal'd the son of chivalry? . . . . iv 6 28
Suddenly made him from my side to start Into the clustering battle . iv 7 13
And means to give you battle presently . . . . . v 2 13
That those which fly before the battle ends May, even in their wives' and children's sight, Be hang'd up for example. . 2 *Hen. VI.* iv 2 188
In thy reverence and thy chair-days, thus To die in ruffian battle . v 2 49
Saint Alban's battle won by famous York Shall be eternized . . v 3 30
All abreast, Charged our main battle's front . . 3 *Hen. VI.* i 1 8
Here's the Earl of Wiltshire's blood, Whom I encounter'd as the battles join'd . . . . i 1 15
Let's set our men in order, And issue forth and bid them battle straight i 2 71
Many a battle have I won in France, When as the enemy hath been ten to one . . . . i 2 74
I saw him in the battle range about . . . . . . ii 1 11
Our battles join'd, and both sides fiercely fought . . . ii 1 121
Darraign your battle, for they are at hand . . . . ii 2 72
This battle fares like to the morning's war, When dying clouds contend with growing light . . . . ii 5 1
Chid me from the battle; swearing both They prosper best of all when I am thence . . . . ii 5 17
Whiles lions war and battle for their dens, Poor harmless lambs abide . ii 5 74
Now the battle's ended, If friend or foe, let him be gently used . ii 6 44
With five thousand men, Shall cross the seas, and bid false Edward battle . . . . iii 3 235
Loss of some pitch'd battle against Warwick . . . . iv 4 4
They no doubt Will issue out again and bid us battle . . . v 1 63
Clarence sweeps along, Of force enough to bid his brother battle . v 1 77
I will away towards Barnet presently, And bid thee battle, Edward . v 1 111
Here pitch our battle; hence we will not budge . . . v 4 66
Was not your husband In Margaret's battle at Saint Alban's slain? *Richard III.* i 3 130
Take with thee my most heavy curse; Which, in the day of battle, tire thee more Than all the complete armour that thou wear'st! . . iv 4 188
While we reason here, A royal battle might be won and lost . . iv 4 538
I'll draw the form and model of our battle, Limit each leader . v 3 24
Prepare thy battle early in the morning . . . . . v 3 88
To-morrow in the battle think on me, And fall thy edgeless sword! . v 3 134
Good angels guard thy battle! live, and flourish! . . . v 3 138
Bloody and guilty, guiltily awake, And in a bloody battle end thy days! . . . . v 3 147
In the battle think on Buckingham, And die in terror of thy guiltiness! v 3 169
And thus my battle shall be ordered . . . . . v 3 292
They thus directed, we will follow In the main battle . . . v 3 299
After the battle let George Stanley die . . . . . v 3 346
I'll unarm again: Why should I war without the walls of Troy, That find such cruel battle here within? . . . . *Troi. and Cres.* i 1 3
Up to the eastern tower, Whose height commands as subject all the vale, To see the battle . . . . i 2 4
He yesterday coped Hector in the battle and struck him down . i 2 35
As doth a battle, when they charge on heaps The enemy flying . iii 2 29
A maiden battle, then? O, I perceive you . . . . . iv 5 87
I am thwarted quite From my great purpose in to-morrow's battle . v 1 43
Rome and her rats are at the point of battle . . . *Coriolanus* i 1 166
How lies their battle? know you on which side They have placed their men of trust? . . . . i 6 51
I do beseech you, By all the battles wherein we have fought . . i 6 56
In the brunt of seventeen battles since He lurch'd all swords of the garland . . . . ii 2 104
His doubled spirit Re-quicken'd what in flesh was fatigate, And to the battle came he . . . . ii 2 122
Of wounds two dozen odd; battles thrice six I have seen and heard of . ii 3 135
Lest that thy wives with spits and boys with stones In puny battle slay me . . . . iv 4 6
Rome's best champion, Successful in the battles that he fights *T. Andron.* i 1 66
Why do fond men expose themselves to battle, And not endure all threats? . . . . *T. of Athens* iii 5 42
The noise of battle hurtled in the air, Horses did neigh . *J. Cæsar* ii 2 22
Their battles are at hand; They mean to warn us at Philippi here . v 1 4
Their bloody sign of battle is hung out, And something to be done immediately . . . . v 1 14
Lead your battle softly on, Upon the left hand of the even field . v 1 16
Shall we give sign of battle?—No, Cæsar, we will answer on their charge v 1 23
As Pompey was, am I compell'd to set Upon one battle all our liberties v 1 76
If we do lose this battle, then is this The very last time we shall speak together . . . . v 1 98
Then, if we lose this battle, You are contented to be led in triumph? . v 1 108
Labeo and Flavius, set our battles on . . . . . v 3 108
When the hurlyburly's done, When the battle's lost and won *Macbeth* i 1 4
You, worthy uncle, Shall, with my cousin, . . . Lead our first battle . v 6 4
Servile ministers, That have with two pernicious daughters join'd Your high engender'd battles 'gainst a head So old and white as this *Lear* iii 2 23
Do you hear aught, sir, of a battle toward?—Most sure and vulgar . iv 6 213

Battle. My point and period will be throughly wrought, Or well or ill, as this day's battle's fought . . . . *Lear* iv 7 98
I had rather lose the battle than that sister Should loosen him and me v 1 18
Now then we'll use His countenance for the battle . . . v 1 63
The battle done, and they within our power, Shall never see his pardon v 1 67
Nor the division of a battle knows More than a spinster . . . *Othello* i 1 23
And little of this great world can I speak, More than pertains to feats of broil and battle . . . . i 3 87
From year to year, the battles, sieges, fortunes, That I have pass'd . i 3 130
His cocks do win the battle still of mine, When it is all to nought *Ant. and Cleo.* ii 3 36
To wage this battle at Pharsalia, Where Cæsar fought with Pompey . iii 7 32
Keep whole : provoke not battle, Till we have done at sea . . iii 8 3
Set we our squadrons on yond side o' the hill, In eye of Cæsar's battle . iii 9 2
Know, that to-morrow the last of many battles We mean to fight . iv 1 11
Close by the battle, ditch'd, and wall'd with turf . *Cymbeline* v 3 14
Arise my knights o' the battle : I create you Companions to our person v 5 20
Your three motives to the battle, with I know not how much more . v 5 388
Ere the stroke Of this yet scarce-cold battle . . . . v 5 469
Battle-axe. And rear'd aloft the bloody battle-axe *T. Andron.* iii 1 169
Battlement. Stand securely on their battlements, As in a theatre *K. John* ii 1 374
From this castle's tatter'd battlements Our fair appointments may be well perused . . . . *Richard II.* iii 3 52
Bid me leap, rather than marry Paris, From off the battlements *Rom. and Jul.* iv 1 78
Many a time and oft Have you climb'd up to walls and battlements *J. Cæsar* i 1 43
And fix'd his head upon our battlements . . . *Macbeth* i 2 23
The raven himself is hoarse That croaks the fatal entrance of Duncan Under my battlements . . . . i 5 41
Let all the battlements their ordnance fire . . . *Hamlet* v 2 281
A fuller blast ne'er shook our battlements . . . *Othello* ii 1 6
Batty. With leaden legs and batty wings doth creep *M. N. Dream* iii 2 365
Bauble. It is a paltry cap, A custard-coffin, a bauble *T. of Shrew* iv 3 82
That cap of yours becomes you not : Off with that bauble . . v 2 122
And I would give his wife my bauble, sir, to do her service . *All's Well* iv 5 32
The sea being smooth, How many shallow bauble boats dare sail! *Troi. and Cres.* i 3 35
For that I know An idiot holds his bauble for a god . *T. Andron.* v 1 79
That runs lolling up and down to hide his bauble in a hole *Rom. and Jul.* ii 4 97
Thither comes the bauble, and, by this hand, she falls me thus about my neck . . . . *Othello* iv 1 139
His shipping—Poor ignorant baubles ! . . . *Cymbeline* iii 1 27
Senseless bauble, Art thou a feodary for this act? . . . iii 2 20
This life Is nobler than attending for a check, Richer than doing nothing for a bauble . . . . iii 3 23
Bavin. Shallow jesters and rash bavin wits, Soon kindled 1 *Hen. IV.* iii 2 61
Bawbling. A bawbling vessel was he captain of . . *T. Night* v 1 57
Bawcock. Why, how now, my bawcock ! how dost thou, chuck? . . iii 4 125
Why, that's my bawcock. What, hast smutch'd thy nose? . *W. Tale* i 2 121
Abate thy rage, great duke ! Good bawcock, bate thy rage ! *Hen. V.* iii 2 26
The king's a bawcock, and a heart of gold, A lad of life . . . iv 1 44
Bawd. If it be not a bawd's house, it is pity of her life . *Meas. for Meas.* ii 1 76
You are partly a bawd, Pompey, howsoever you colour it in being a tapster . . . . ii 1 231
How would you live, Pompey? by being a bawd? . . . ii 1 237
Take order for the drabs and the knaves, you need not to fear the bawds ii 1 248
Mercy to thee would prove itself a bawd . . . . . iii 1 150
Fie, sirrah ! a bawd, a wicked bawd ! . . . . . iii 2 20
Your powdered bawd : an unshunned consequence . . . iii 2 62
Say I sent thee thither. For debt, Pompey? or how?—For being a bawd . . . . iii 2 68
If imprisonment be the due of a bawd, why, 'tis his right: bawd is he doubtless . . . . iii 2 70
A bawd of eleven years' continuance . . . . . iii 2 208
I have been an unlawful bawd time out of mind . . . iv 2 16
A bawd, sir? fie upon him ! he will discredit our mystery . . iv 2 29
Your hangman is a more penitent trade than your bawd . . iv 2 54
Come on, bawd ; I will instruct thee in my trade . . . iv 2 57
To be bawd to a bell-wether . . . . *As Y. Like It* iii 2 85
A most intelligencing bawd ! . . . . . *W. Tale* ii 3 68
This Commodity, This bawd, this broker . . . *K. John* ii 1 582
To tread down fair respect of sovereignty, And made his majesty the bawd to theirs . . . . iii 1 59
France is a bawd to Fortune and King John, That strumpet Fortune ! iii 1 60
So shall my virtue be his vice's bawd . . . *Richard II.* v 3 67
And minutes capons and clocks the tongues of bawds 1 *Hen. IV.* i 2 9
I remember him now ; a bawd, a cutpurse . . . *Hen. V.* iii 6 65
Well, bawd I'll turn, And something lean to cutpurse of quick hand . v 1 90
By the same token, you are a bawd . . . *Troi. and Cres.* i 2 307
O traitors and bawds, how earnestly are you set a-work, and how ill requited ! . . . . v 10 37
She will indite him to some supper.—A bawd, a bawd ! . *Rom. and Jul.* ii 4 136
Poor rogues, and usurers' men ! bawds between gold and want ! *T. of Athens* ii 2 61
Go ; thou wast born a bastard, and thou't die a bawd . . . ii 2 89
It is her habit only that is honest, Herself's a bawd . . . iv 3 114
Breathing like sanctified and pious bawds, The better to beguile *Hamlet* i 3 130
The power of beauty will sooner transform honesty from what it is to a bawd than the force of honesty can translate beauty into his likeness iii 1 113
One that wouldst be a bawd, in way of good service . . . *Lear* ii 2 21
And bawds and whores do churches build . . . . . iii 2 90
She's a simple bawd That cannot say as much . . . *Othello* iv 2 20
I can be modest.—That dignifies the renown of a bawd . . *Pericles* iv 6 42
And her gain She gives the cursed bawd . . . . v Gower 11
Bawd-born. Bawd is he doubtless, and of antiquity too ; bawd-born *Meas. for Meas.* iii 2 71
Bawdry. We must be married, or we must live in bawdry *As Y. Like It* iii 3 99
He has the prettiest love-songs for maids ; so without bawdry *W. Tale* iv 4 194
Prithee, say on : he's for a jig or a tale of bawdry, or he sleeps *Hamlet* ii 2 522
Bawdy. If bawdy talk offend you, we'll have very little of it *M. for M.* iv 3 188
It is a bawdy planet, that will strike Where 'tis predominant *W. Tale* i 2 201
Come sing me a bawdy song ; make me merry . . . 1 *Hen. IV.* iii 3 15
Only they That come to hear a merry bawdy play . *Hen. VIII.* Prol. 14
For every false drop in her bawdy veins A Grecian's life hath sunk *Troi. and Cres.* iv 1 69
The bawdy hand of the dial is now upon the prick of noon *R. and J.* ii 4 118
Bloody, bawdy villain ! Remorseless, treacherous, lecherous, kindless villain ! . . . . *Hamlet* ii 2 609
The bawdy wind that kisses all it meets . . . *Othello* iv 2 77

Bawdy-house. Went to a bawdy-house not above once in a quarter—of an hour . . . . 1 *Hen. IV.* iii 3 19
This house is turned bawdy-house ; they pick pockets . . . iii 3 114
Tavern-reckonings, memorandums of bawdy-houses . . . iii 3 179
For tearing a poor whore's ruff in a bawdy-house . 2 *Hen. IV.* ii 4 157
It will be thought we keep a bawdy house straight . . . *Hen. V.* ii 1 37
I am for no more bawdy-houses . . . . . *Pericles* iv 5 7
Bawl. God knows, whether those that bawl out the ruins of thy linen shall inherit his kingdom . . . . . . 2 *Hen. IV.* ii 2 27
Bawling. You bawling, blasphemous, incharitable dog ! . . *Tempest* i 1 43
Bay. I'll rent the fairest house in it after three-pence a bay *M. for M.* ii 1 255
If any Syracusian born Come to the bay of Ephesus, he dies *Com. of Err.* i 1 20
You sent me to the bay, sir, for a bark . . . . . iv 1 99
A reverend Syracusian merchant, Who put unluckily into this bay . v 1 125
The scarfed bark puts from her native bay . *Mer. of Venice* ii 6 15
My affection hath an unknown bottom, like the bay of Portugal *As Y. Like It* iv 1 212
'Tis thought your deer does hold you at a bay . . *T. of Shrew* v 2 56
From Port le Blanc, a bay In Brittany . . . *Richard II.* ii 1 277
To rouse his wrongs and chase them to the bay . . . ii 3 128
Make the cowards stand aloof at bay : Sell every man his life 1 *Hen. VI.* iv 2 52
And I, in such a desperate bay of death, Like a poor bark *Richard III.* iv 4 232
From the Athenian bay Put forth toward Phrygia *Troi. and Cres.* Prol. 6
What moves Ajax thus to bay at him? . . . . . ii 3 98
As the bark, that hath discharged her fraught, Returns with precious lading to the bay . . . . *T. Andron.* i 1 72
Uncouple here and let us make a bay . . . . . ii 2 3
I would we had a thousand Roman dames At such a bay . . . iv 2 42
You gave Good words the other day of a bay courser I rode on *T. of Athens* i 2 217
I had rather be a dog, and bay the moon, Than such a Roman *J. Cæsar* iv 3 27
Brutus, bay not me ; I'll not endure it . . . . . iv 3 28
To ride on a bay trotting-horse over four-inched bridges . . *Lear* iii 4 57
That he may bless this bay with his tall ship . . . *Othello* ii 1 79
To the bay and disembark my coffers : Bring thou the master to the citadel . . . . ii 1 210
Cast mire upon me, set The dogs o' the street to bay me . *Cymbeline* v 5 223
Marry, come up, my dish of chastity with rosemary and bays ! *Pericles* iv 6 160
Bay Curtal. I'ld give bay Curtal and his furniture, My mouth no more were broken than these boys' . . . . . . *All's Well* ii 3 65
Bayed. They bay'd the bear With hounds of Sparta . *M. N. Dream* iv 1 118
Here wast thou bay'd, brave hart ; Here didst thou fall . *J. Cæsar* iii 1 204
We are at the stake, And bay'd about with many enemies . . iv 1 49
Baying. The French and Welsh Baying him at the heels . 2 *Hen. IV.* i 3 80
Baynard. If you thrive well, bring them to Baynard's Castle *Richard III.* iii 5 98
Bid them both Meet me within this hour at Baynard's Castle. . iii 5 105
Bayonne. Bishop of Bayonne, then French ambassador *Hen. VIII.* ii 4 172
Bay-tree. The bay-trees in our country are all wither'd . *Richard II.* ii 4 8
Bay windows transparent as barricadoes . . . *T. Night* iv 2 40
Be. There be that can rule Naples As well as he . . *Tempest* ii 1 262
If any be Trinculo's legs, these are they . . . . ii 2 108
I took him to be kill'd with a thunder-stroke . . . . ii 2 112
These be fine things, an if they be not sprites . . . . ii 2 120
There be some sports are painful, and their labour Delight in them sets off . . . . iii 1 1
This must crave, An if this be at all, a most strange story . . v 1 117
Whether this be Or be not, I'll not swear . . . . v 1 122
These be brave spirits indeed ! How fine my master is ! . . v 1 261
Mark but the badges of these men, my lords, Then say if they be true . v 1 268
Be they of much import? . . . . . . *T. G. of Ver.* iii 1 55
Why do your dogs bark so? be there bears i' the town? . *Mer. Wives* i 1 298
Well, I hope it be not so.—Hope is a curtal dog in some affairs . ii 1 113
Very rogues, now they be out of service . . . . . ii 1 182
Here be my keys : ascend my chambers ; search, seek, find out . iii 3 172
Hence shall we see, If power change purpose, what our seemers be *Meas. for Meas.* i 3 54
How would you be, If He, which is the top of judgement, should But judge you as you are? . . . . ii 2 75
Be that you are, That is, a woman ; if you be more, you're none . ii 4 134
Here be many of her old customers . . . . . iv 3 3
If this be not a dream I see and hear . . . *Com. of Errors* v 1 376
That is the chain, sir, which you had of me.—I think it be . . v 1 379
If Hero would be my wife.—Is't come to this? . . *Much Ado* i 1 198
If it will not be, I'll leave you . . . . . . ii 1 208
Why, then, some be of laughing, as, ah, ha, he ! . . . iv 1 23
I think he be angry indeed.—If he be, he knows how to turn his girdle v 1 141
Let me be : pluck up, my heart, and be sad . . . . v 1 207
These be the stops that hinder study quite . . *L. L. Lost* i 1 70
The cowslips tall her pensioners be . . . . *M. N. Dream* ii 1 10
Those be rubies, fairy favours, In those freckles live their savours . ii 1 12
Be thou here again Ere the leviathan can swim a league . . ii 1 173
When thou wakest, if she be by, Beg of her for remedy . . iii 2 108
Lord, what fools these mortals be ! . . . . . . iii 2 115
Be as thou wast wont to be ; See as thou wast wont to see . . iv 1 76
Take hands with me, And rock the ground whereon these sleepers be . iv 1 91
There shall the pairs of faithful lovers be Wedded, with Theseus . iv 1 96
There be land-rats and water-rats, water-thieves and land-thieves *Mer. of Venice* i 3 23
There be fools alive, I wis, Silver'd o'er . . . . ii 9 68
These be the Christian husbands . . . . . . iv 1 295
I think he be transform'd into a beast . . . *As Y. Like It* ii 7 1
There be some women, Silvius, had they mark'd him In parcels as I did, would have gone near To fall in love with him . . . . . iii 5 124
I'll have no father, if you be not he : I'll have no husband, if you be not he : Nor ne'er wed woman, if you be not she . . . . v 4 128
I'll assure her of Her widowhood, be it that she survive me *T. of Shrew* ii 1 125
Impossible be strange attempts to those That weigh their pains in sense and do suppose What hath been cannot be . . . . *All's Well* i 1 239
Welcome shall they be . . . . i 2 19
And to be a soldier?—Such is his noble purpose . . . . iii 2 72
I do not know if it be it or no . . . . iv 3 235
Not we ! For such as we are made of, such we be . . *T. Night* ii 2 33
Be that thou know'st thou art, and then thou art As great as that thou fear'st . . . . v 1 152
Let be, let be. Would I were dead . . . . . *W. Tale* v 3 61
Be these sad signs confirmers of thy words? . . . *K. John* iii 1 24
Will't not be? Will not a calf's-skin stop that mouth of thine? . . iii 1 298
So be it, for it cannot be but so . . . . . . iii 4 140
Where be your powers? show now your mended faiths . . . v 7 75
Minding true things by what their mockeries be . . *Hen. V.* iv Prol. 53

Be. His fears, out of doubt, be of the same relish as ours are . *Hen. V.* iv 1 114
Be these the wretches that we play'd at dice for? . . . . iv 5 8
Where be these warders, that they wait not here? . *1 Hen. VI.* i 3 3
I think this Talbot be a fiend of hell . . . . . ii 1 46
Watch thou and wake when others be asleep . *2 Hen. VI.* i 1 249
Be that thou hopest to be, or what thou art Resign to death . iii 1 333
Ay, here they be that dare and will disturb thee . . iv 8 6
Where be thy brothers? Where are thy children? . . *Richard III.* iv 4 92
And they were ratified As he cried 'Thus let be' . *Hen. VIII.* i 1 171
Though he be grown so desperate to be honest . . . iii 1 86
There be moe wasps that buzz about his nose . . . iii 2 55
Every function of your power, Should . . . be more To me, your friend, than any . . . . iii 2 189
Help, You that be noble; help him, young and old! . *Coriolanus* iii 1 228
Be that you are, long; and your misery increase with your age! . v 2 112
That, I think, be young Petrucio . . . . . *Rom. and Jul.* i 5 133
Though they be not to be talked on, yet they are past compare . ii 5 42
See, whether their basest metal be not moved . *J. Cæsar* i 1 66
Such men as he be never at heart's ease . . . . i 2 208
Is it not, Cassius?—Let it be who it is . . . . i 3 80
To be thus is nothing; But to be safely thus . *Macbeth* iii 1 48
I think it be no other but e'en so . . . . *Hamlet* i 1 108
Or 'If we list to speak,' or 'There be, an if they might' . . i 5 177
To be, or not to be: that is the question . . . . iii 1 56
If it be now, 'tis not to come; if it be not to come, it will be now; if it be not now, yet it will come: the readiness is all . . . . v 2 232
To thine and Albany's issue Be this perpetual . . . *Lear* i 1 68
If thou be as poor for a subject as he is for a king, thou art poor enough i 4 22
Where be the sacred vials thou shouldst fill With sorrowful water? *Ant. and Cleo.* i 3 63
'Twill be naught: But let it be . . . . . . iii 5 23
Ah, let be, let be! thou art The armourer of my heart . . iv 4 6
I think the king Be touch'd at very heart . . . *Cymbeline* i 1 10
Which I will be ever to pay and yet pay still . . . . i 4 39
Disguise That which, to appear itself, must not yet be But by self-danger . . . . iii 4 148
I am nothing: or if not, Nothing to be were better . . . iv 2 368
Than be so Better to cease to be . . . . . . iv 4 30
Be-all. That but this blow Might be the be-all and the end-all here *Macb.* i 7 5
Be all day. I'll fit you, And not be all day neither . *All's Well* ii 1 94
Be gone. Wilt thou be gone? Sweet Valentine, adieu! . *T. G. of Ver.* i 1 11
Go, go, be gone, to save your ship from wreck . . . . i 1 156
Will ye be gone?—That you may ruminate . . . . i 2 49
Be gone! I will not hear thy vain excuse . . . . iii 1 168
What's your will, father?—That now you are come, you will be gone *Meas. for Meas.* iii 1 179
If it prove so, I will be gone the sooner . *Com. of Errors* ii 2 103
'Tis time, I think, to trudge, pack and be gone . . . iii 2 158
I'll be gone, sir, and not trouble you . . . . iv 3 71
I'll be gone: Our queen and all our elves come here anon *M. N. Dream* ii 1 16
Fairies, be gone, and be all ways away . . . . iv 1 46
Our intent Was to be gone from Athens . . . . . iv 1 157
I'll be gone about it straight.—And so will I . *Mer. of Venice* ii 4 25
Without more speech, my lord, You must be gone from hence immediately . . . . ii 9 8
Wind away, Begone, I say, I will not to wedding with thee *As Y. Like It* iii 3 106
Sirrah, be gone, or talk not, I advise you . . *T. of Shrew* i 2 44
You'll be gone, sir knave, and do as I command you . *All's Well* i 3 94
So, now I have mine own again, be gone . . *Richard II.* v 1 99
Be gone, good ancient: this will grow to a brawl anon . *2 Hen. IV.* ii 4 186
Let us now persuade you.—Not to be gone from hence . *1 Hen. VI.* iii 2 94
Be gone, I say; for, till you do return, I rest perplexed . . v 5 94
I'll leave you to your fortune and be gone To keep them back *3 Hen. VI.* iv 7 55
Avoid the gallery. Ha! I have said. Be gone . *Hen. VIII.* v 1 86
Thou must be gone, wench, thou must be gone . *Troi. and Cres.* iv 2 95
Thou must to thy father, and be gone from Troilus . . . iv 2 97
Will you be gone?—You shall stay too . . *Coriolanus* iv 2 14
Away, be gone; the sport is at the best . . *Rom. and Jul.* i 5 121
Nay, gentlemen, prepare not to be gone . . . . i 5 123
Wilt thou be gone? it is not yet near day . . . . iii 5 1
It is not day.—It is, it is: hie hence, be gone, away! . . iii 5 26
O, now be gone; more light and light it grows . . . iii 5 35
Therefore be gone Without our grace, our love, our benison . *Lear* i 1 267
Do as I bid thee, or rather do thy pleasure; Above the rest, be gone iv 1 50
Friends, be gone; I have myself resolved upon a course *Ant. and Cleo.* iii 11 8
Be gone: My treasure's in the harbour, take it . . . iii 11 10
Friends, be gone: you shall Have letters from me to some friends . iii 11 15
Hence with thy stripes, begone! . . . . . . iii 13 152
I have done all. Bid them all fly; begone . . . . iv 12 17
Be it possible. We will persuade him, be it possible *T. of Shrew* iii 2 127
Be it so she will not here before your grace Consent to marry *M. N. Dream* i 1 39
It is Menenius.—Be it so; go back . . . *Coriolanus* v 2 12
Be't so: declare thine office . . . . *Ant. and Cleo.* iii 12 10
Be it so, then: Yet none does know, but you, how she came dead *Pericles* iv 3 28
Be so. We'll a-birding together; I have a fine hawk for the bush. Shall it be so? . . . . *Mer. Wives* iii 3 248
If't be so, For Banquo's issue have I filed my mind . *Macbeth* iii 1 64
If it be so, Laertes—As how should it be so? how otherwise? *Hamlet* iv 7 58
Let it be so; thy truth, then, be thy dower . . . *Lear* i 1 110
Yea, is it come to this? Let it be so . . . . . i 4 327
Beach. As well go stand upon the beach And bid the main flood bate his usual height . . . . *Mer. of Venice* iv 1 71
Behold, the English beach Pales in the flood with men . *Hen. V.* v Prol. 9
Then let the pebbles on the hungry beach Fillip the stars . *Coriolanus* v 3 58
The fishermen, that walk upon the beach, Appear like mice . *Lear* iv 6 17
The twinn'd stones Upon the number'd beach . . *Cymbeline* i 6 36
Beached. By rushy brook, Or in the beached margent of the sea *M. N. Dream* ii 1 85
Upon the beached verge of the salt flood . . *T. of Athens* v 1 219
Beachy. Other times, to see The beachy girdle of the ocean Too wide for Neptune's hips . . . . *2 Hen. IV.* iii 1 50
Beacon. It [sherris] illumineth the face, which as a beacon gives warning . . . . iv 3 117
See, noble Charles, the beacon of our friend . . *1 Hen. VI.* iii 2 29
Modest doubt is call'd The beacon of the wise . *Troi. and Cres.* ii 2 16
The warm sun! Approach, thou beacon to this under globe! . *Lear* ii 2 170
Let not our ships and number of our men Be like a beacon fired to amaze your eyes . . . . *Pericles* i 4 87

Bead. O, for my beads! I cross me for a sinner . *Com. of Errors* ii 2 190
You minimus, of hindering knot-grass made; You bead, you acorn *M. N. Dream* iii 2 330
With amber bracelets, beads and all this knavery . *T. of Shrew* iv 3 58
With these crystal beads heaven shall be bribed . *K. John* ii 1 171
I'll give my jewels for a set of beads . . *Richard II.* iii 3 147
Beads of sweat have stood upon thy brow, Like bubbles . *1 Hen. IV.* ii 3 61
Waking and in my dreams, In courtly company or at my beads *2 Hen. VI.* i 1 27
All his mind is bent to holiness, To number Ave-Maries on his beads i 3 59
Numbering our Ave-Maries with our beads . . . *3 Hen. VI.* ii 1 162
When holy and devout religious men Are at their beads, 'tis hard to draw them thence . . . . *Richard III.* iii 7 93
Passion, I see, is catching; for mine eyes, Seeing those beads of sorrow stand in thine, Began to water . . . *J. Cæsar* iii 1 284
Beadle. A very beadle to a humorous sigh . . *L. L. Lost* iii 1 177
Her sin his injury, Her injury the beadle to her sin . *K. John* ii 1 188
Have you not beadles in your town, and things called whips? *2 Hen. VI.* ii 1 136
Sirrah, go fetch the beadle hither straight . . . . ii 1 140
Sirrah beadle, whip him till he leap over that same stool . ii 1 148
Besides the running banquet of two beadles that is to come *Hen. VIII.* v 4 69
Thou rascal beadle, hold thy bloody hand! . . . *Lear* iv 6 164
If all your beggars were whipped, I would wish no better office than to be beadle . . . . *Pericles* ii 1 97
Beadsman. Commend thy grievance to my holy prayers, For I will be thy beadsman . . . . *T. G. of Ver.* i 1 18
Beadsmen. Thy very beadsmen learn to bend their bows Of double-fatal yew against thy state . . . . . *Richard II.* iii 2 116
Beagle. She's a beagle, true-bred, and one that adores me . *T. Night* ii 3 195
Get thee away, and take Thy beagles with thee . *T. of Athens* iv 3 175
Beak. Now on the beak, Now in the waist, the deck . *Tempest* i 2 196
Although the kite soar with unbloodied beak . *2 Hen. VI.* iii 2 193
Renege, affirm, and turn their halcyon beaks With every gale . *Lear* ii 2 84
His royal bird Prunes the immortal wing and cloys his beak . *Cymbeline* v 4 118
Beam. The fair soul herself Weigh'd between loathness and obedience, at Which end o' the beam should bow . . . . *Tempest* ii 1 131
Sometimes the beam of her view gilded my foot . *Mer. Wives* i 3 68
I fear not Goliath with a weaver's beam . . . . v 1 24
When the sun shines let foolish gnats make sport, But creep in crannies when he hides his beams . . . *Com. of Errors* ii 2 31
It is a fault that springeth from your eye.—For gazing on your beams . iii 2 56
The king your mote did see; But I a beam do find in each of three *L. L. Lost* iv 3 162
Cupid's fiery shaft Quench'd in the chaste beams of the watery moon *M. N. Dream* ii 1 162
Opening on Neptune with fair blessed beams . . . iii 2 392
Sweet Moon, I thank thee for thy sunny beams . . . v 1 277
How far that little candle throws his beams! . . *Mer. of Venice* v 1 90
We, poising us in her defective scale, Shall weigh thee to the beam *All's Well* ii 3 162
But to the brightest beams Distracted clouds give way . . v 3 34
A rush will be a beam To hang thee on . . . *K. John* iv 3 129
That sun that warms you here shall shine on me; And those his golden beams to you here lent Shall point on me and gild my banishment *Richard II.* i 3 146
His brandish'd sword did blind men with his beams . *1 Hen. VI.* i 1 10
As plays the sun upon the glassy streams, Twinkling another counter-feited beam . . . . v 3 63
May never glorious sun reflex his beams Upon the country where you make abode! . . . . v 4 87
Poise the cause in justice' equal scales, Whose beam stands sure *2 Hen. VI.* ii 1 205
Cold snow melts with the sun's hot beams . . . . iii 1 223
The golden circuit on my head, Like to the glorious sun's transparent beams . . . . iii 1 353
Dark cloudy death o'ershades his beams of life . . *3 Hen. VI.* ii 6 62
The very beams will dry those vapours up . . . . v 3 12
My son, . . . Whose bright out-shining beams thy cloudy wrath Hath in eternal darkness folded up . . . . . *Richard III.* i 3 268
Whose bright faces Cast thousand beams upon me, like the sun *Hen. VIII.* iv 2 89
Stands colossus-wise, waving his beam . . *Troi. and Cres.* v 5 9
The precipitation might down stretch Below the beam of sight *Coriolanus* iii 2 6
And, having gilt the ocean with his beams, Gallops the zodiac *T. Andron.* ii 1 6
The collars of the moonshine's watery beams . . *Rom. and Jul.* i 4 62
Love's heralds should be thoughts, Which ten times faster glide than the sun's beams . . . . ii 5 5
Sun, hide thy beams! Timon hath done his reign . *T. of Athens* v 1 226
Thy madness shall be paid with weight, Till our scale turn the beam *Hamlet* iv 5 157
That by thy comfortable beams I may Peruse this letter! . . *Lear.* ii 2 171
I am ashamed To look upon the holy sun, to have The benefit of his blest beams . . . . *Cymbeline* iv 4 42
Lessen'd herself, and in the beams o' the sun So vanish'd . . v 5 472
Bean. Peas and beans are as dank here as a dog . . *1 Hen. IV.* ii 1 9
Bean-fed. When I a fat and bean-fed horse beguile . *M. N. Dream* ii 1 45
Bear. Thy groans Did make wolves howl and penetrate the breasts Of ever angry bears . . . . *Tempest* i 2 289
Foot it featly here and there; And, sweet sprites, the burthen bear . i 2 381
Some good instruction give How I may bear me here . . . i 2 425
That's a brave god and bears celestial liquor . . . . ii 2 121
A plague upon the tyrant that I serve! I'll bear him no more sticks . ii 2 167
Bear my bottle: fellow Trinculo, we'll fill him by and by again . ii 2 180
If you'll sit down, I'll bear your logs the while . . . iii 1 24
I am vex'd; Bear with my weakness; my old brain is troubled . iv 1 159
Help to bear this away where my hogshead of wine is . . . iv 1 251
That some whirlwind bear Unto a ragged fearful-hanging rock! *T. G. of Ver.* i 2 120
Which, like a waxen image 'gainst a fire, Bears no impression of the thing it was . . . . ii 4 202
Do him not that wrong To bear a hard opinion of his truth . . ii 7 81
There is a messenger That stays to bear my letters . . . iii 1 53
Fear not; he bears an honourable mind . . . . . v 3 13
Why do your dogs bark so? be there bears i' the town? . *Mer. Wives* i 1 298
You are afraid, if you see the bear loose, are you not? . . i 1 304
She bears the purse too; she is a region in Guiana, all gold and bounty i 3 75
Hold, sirrah, bear you these letters tightly . . . . i 3 88
You'll not bear a letter for me, you rogue! . . . . i 3 90
If you will help to bear it, Sir John, take all, or half . . ii 2 178
Whither bear you this?—To the laundress, forsooth.—Why, what have you to do whither they bear it? . . . . iii 3 162
I had as lief bear so much lead . . . . iv 2 117

Bear. More than the villanous inconstancy of man's disposition is able to bear *Mer. Wives* iv 5 112
From time to time I have acquainted you With the dear love I bear . iv 6 9
The expressure that it bears, green let it be . v 5 71
What figure of us think you he will bear? *Meas. for Meas.* i 1 17
Bear me to prison, where I am committed . i 2 121
Instruct me How I may formally in person bear me Like a true friar . i 3 47
And bear the shame most patiently . ii 3 20
If it be sin, Heaven let me bear it! . ii 4 70
O perilous mouths, That bear in them one and the self-same tongue! . ii 4 173
Would bark your honour from that trunk you bear, And leave you naked iii 1 72
He who the sword of heaven will bear Should be as holy as severe . iii 2 275
Now will I write letters to Angelo,—The provost, he shall bear them . iv 3 98
My authority bears of a credent bulk, That no particular scandal once can touch . iv 4 29
Fainting under The pleasing punishment that women bear *Com. of Errors* i 1 47
Whom the fates have mark'd To bear the extremity of dire mishap . i 1 142
Go bear it to the Centaur, where we host . i 2 9
If I should pay your worship those again, Perchance you will not bear them . i 2 86
Were you wedded, you would bear some sway . ii 1 28
Bear a fair presence, though your heart be tainted . iii 2 13
She bears some breadth?—No longer from head to foot than from hip to hip . iii 2 114
As from a bear a man would run for life, So fly I from her that would be my wife . iii 2 159
Bear it with you, lest I come not time enough . iv 1 41
Bear me forthwith unto his creditor . iv 4 123
Go bear him hence. Sister, go you with me . iv 4 133
His word might bear my wealth at any time . v 1 8
Bind Dromio too, and bear them to my house . v 1 35
That we may bind him fast And bear him home for his recovery . v 1 41
Why bear you these rebukes and answer not? . v 1 89
Will not suffer us to fetch him out, Nor send him forth that we may bear him hence . v 1 158
Let him bear it for a difference between himself and his horse *Much Ado* i 1 69
In time the savage bull doth bear the yoke . i 1 263
Offer them instances; which shall bear no less likelihood . ii 2 42
They say I will bear myself proudly, if I perceive the love come from her . ii 3 233
They say the lady is fair; 'tis a truth, I can bear them witness . ii 3 240
This is thy office; Bear thee well in it and leave us alone . iii 1 13
The two bears will not bite one another when they meet . iii 2 80
Bear it coldly but till midnight, and let the issue show itself . iii 2 132
Therefore bear you the lantern . iii 3 24
O that I were a man! What, bear her in hand until they come to take hands! . iv 1 305
To see him walk before a lady and to bear her fan! *L. L. Lost* iv 1 147
Thy eye Jove's lightning bears, thy voice his dreadful thunder . iv 2 119
Folly in fools bears not so strong a note As foolery in the wise . v 2 75
Did they teach him there; 'Thus must thou speak,' and 'thus thy body bear' . v 2 100
A heavy heart bears not a nimble tongue . v 2 747
Nip not the gaudy blossoms of your love, But that it bear this trial . v 2 813
Cat, or bear, Pard, or boar with bristled hair *M. N. Dream* ii 2 30
I am as ugly as a bear; For beasts that meet me run away for fear . ii 2 94
Sometime a horse I'll be, sometime a hound, A hog, a headless bear . iii 1 112
The hate I bear thee made me leave thee so . iii 2 190
So you will let me quiet go, To Athens will I bear my folly back . iii 2 315
I was with Hercules and Cadmus once, When in a wood of Crete they bay'd the bear With hounds . iv 1 118
In the night, imagining some fear, How easy is a bush supposed a bear! v 1 22
I will feed fat the ancient grudge I bear him *Mer. of Venice* i 3 48
A coin that bears the figure of an angel Stamped in gold . ii 7 56
Tell me once more what title thou dost bear . ii 9 35
I'll keep my oath, Patiently to bear my wroth . ii 9 78
Never did I know A creature, that did bear the shape of man, So keen and greedy . iii 2 278
Whose souls do bear an equal yoke of love . iii 4 13
More than a lodged hate and a certain loathing I bear Antonio . iv 1 61
No, not the hangman's axe, bear half the keenness Of thy sharp envy . iv 1 125
He cannot speak, my lord.—Bear him away *As Y. Like It* i 2 233
Let me the knowledge of my fault bear with me . i 3 48
Devise with me how we may fly, Whither to go, and what to bear with us . i 3 103
Do not seek to take your change upon you, To bear your griefs yourself i 3 105
O, what a world is this, when what is comely Envenoms him that bears it! . ii 3 15
For my part, I had rather bear with you than bear you . ii 4 11
I should bear no cross if I did bear you, for I think you have no money ii 4 12
Come, I will bear thee to some shelter . ii 6 16
The city-woman bears The cost of princes on unworthy shoulders . ii 7 75
Some of them had in them more feet than the verses would bear . iii 2 175
The feet might bear the verses.—Ay, but the feet were lame and could not bear themselves . iii 2 176
Why look you so upon me?—For no ill will I bear you . iii 5 71
The time was that I hated thee, And yet it is not that I bear thee love iii 5 93
I'll write to him a very taunting letter, And thou shalt bear it . iii 5 135
It bears an angry tenour: pardon me; I am but as a guiltless messenger iv 3 11
Bear this, bear all: She says I am not fair, that I lack manners . iv 3 14
I speak not this that you should bear a good opinion of my knowledge . v 2 60
Bear your body more seeming . v 4 72
I charge you, O women, for the love you bear to men . Epil. 13
Tell him from me, as he will win my love, He bear himself with honourable action *T. of Shrew* Ind. 1 110
Make her bear the penance of her tongue . i 1 89
Asses are made to bear, and so are you.—Women are made to bear . ii 1 200
Sirrah, I will not bear these braves of thine . iii 1 15
I tell you, sir, she bears me fair in hand . iv 2 3
While he did bear my countenance in the town . v 1 129
I'll have no halves; I'll bear it all myself . v 2 78
His plausive words He scatter'd not in ears, but grafted them, To grow there and to bear . *All's Well* i 2 55
Entreating from your royal thoughts A modest one, to bear me back again . ii 1 131
More I'll entreat you Written to bear along . iii 2 98
We'll strive to bear it for your worthy sake To the extreme edge of hazard . iii 3 5
Let her in fine consent, As we'll direct her how 'tis best to bear it . iii 7 20
I shall crave of you your leave that I may bear my evils alone *T. Night* ii 1 6

Bear. Make no compare Between that love a woman can bear me And that I owe . *T. Night* ii 4 105
To anger him we'll have the bear again; and we will fool him black and blue . ii 5 11
Will either of you bear me a challenge to him? . iii 2 43
The youth, bears in his visage no great presage of cruelty . iii 2 68
With the same 'haviour that your passion bears Goes on my master's grief . iii 4 226
Fare thee well: A fiend like thee might bear my soul to hell . iii 4 237
Pants and looks pale, as if a bear were at his heels . iii 4 323
He will bear you easily and reins well . iii 4 358
Nor brass nor stone nor parchment bears not one [example] . *W. Tale* i 2 360
Which way to b^ prevented, if to be; If not, how best to bear it . i 2 406
Enclosed in this trunk which you Shall bear along impawn'd . i 2 436
Though he does bear some signs of me, yet you Have too much blood in him . ii 1 57
Bear the boy hence; he shall not come about her; Away with him . ii 1 59
The centre is not big enough to bear A school-boy's top . ii 1 102
Nor night nor day no rest: it is but weakness To bear the matter thus . ii 3 2
Wolves and bears, they say, Casting their savageness aside have done Like offices of pity . ii 3 187
Much surpassing The common praise it bears . iii 1 3
How the poor gentleman roared and the bear mocked him . iii 3 102
The men are not yet cold under water, nor the bear half dined on the gentleman . iii 3 108
I'll go see if the bear be gone from the gentleman and how much he hath eaten . iii 3 133
Will they wear their plackets where they should bear their faces? . iv 4 246
We can both sing it: if thou'lt bear a part, thou shalt hear . iv 4 298
I can bear my part; you must know 'tis my occupation; have at it with you . iv 4 301
I see the play so lies That I must bear a part . iv 4 670
Though authority be a stubborn bear, yet he is oft led by the nose with gold . iv 4 832
More than all the sceptres And those that bear them living . v 1 147
That which I shall report will bear no credit, Were not the proof so nigh . v 1 179
He was torn to pieces with a bear . v 2 69
Would you not deem it breathed? and that those veins Did verily bear blood? . v 3 65
Your brother is legitimate; Your father's wife did after wedlock bear him *K. John* i 1 117
Some sins do bear their privilege on earth, And so doth yours . i 1 261
Our arms, like to a muzzled bear, Save in aspect, hath all offence seal'd up . ii 1 249
We'll put thee down, 'gainst whom these arms we bear . ii 1 346
Well could I bear that England had this praise . iii 4 15
Think you I bear the shears of destiny? . iv 2 91
Would bear thee from the knowledge of thyself . v 2 35
My arm shall give thee help to bear thee hence . v 4 58
Withhold thine indignation, mighty heaven, And tempt us not to bear above our power! . v 6 38
Bear not along The clogging burthen of a guilty soul . *Richard II.* i 3 199
Sweet soil, adieu; My mother, and my nurse, that bears me yet! . i 3 307
Glad am I that your highness is so arm'd To bear the tidings of calamity iii 2 105
They might have lived to bear and he to taste Their fruits of duty . iii 4 62
Bear you well in this new spring of time, Lest you be cropp'd . v 2 50
Thou, created to be awed by man, Wast born to bear . v 5 92
I was not made a horse; And yet I bear a burthen like an ass . v 5 93
I am as melancholy as a gib cat or a lugged bear . *1 Hen. IV.* i 2 83
Who bears hard His brother's death . i 3 270
Bear ourselves as even as we can . i 3 285
To bear our fortunes in our own strong arms . i 3 298
I'll not bear mine own flesh so far afoot again . ii 2 37
In respect of the love I bear your house . ii 3 3
Of many men I do not bear these crossings . iii 1 36
But Mark how he bears his course, and runs me up . iii 1 108
Go bear this letter to Lord John of Lancaster . iii 3 218
His letters bear his mind, not I, my lord . iv 1 20
Let me taste my horse, Who is to bear me like a thunderbolt . iv 1 120
By my faith, that bears a frosty sound . iv 1 128
This earth that bears thee dead Bears not alive so stout a gentleman . v 4 92
If not, let them that should reward valour bear the sin upon their own heads . v 4 153
Bear Worcester to the death and Vernon too . v 5 14
To bear a gentleman in hand, and then stand upon security! *2 Hen. IV.* i 2 42
You are too impatient to bear crosses . i 2 253
Go bear this letter to my Lord of Lancaster; this to the prince . i 2 267
A hundred mark is a long one for a poor lone woman to bear . ii 1 35
To bear the inventory of thy shirts, as, one for superfluity, and another for use! . ii 2 19
You cannot one bear with another's confirmities . ii 4 63
You like well and bear your years very well . iii 2 92
I'll ne'er bear a base mind: an't be my destiny, so; an't be not, so . iii 2 251
Thou'rt a good fellow.—Faith, I'll bear no base mind . iii 2 257
Translate yourself Out of the speech of peace that bears such grace . iv 1 48
That all their eyes may bear those tokens home . iv 2 64
Take me up, and bear me hence Into some other chamber . iv 4 131
They, by observing of him, do bear themselves like foolish justices . v 1 74
Let me but bear your love, I'll bear your cares . v 2 58
You weigh this well; Therefore still bear the balance . v 2 103
I do commit into your hand The unstained sword that you have used to bear . v 2 114
But you must bear; the heart's all . v 3 31
How smooth and even they do bear themselves! . *Hen. V.* ii 2 3
The powers we bear with us Will cut their passage through the force of France . ii 2 15
Inhuman creature! Thou that didst bear the key of all my counsels . ii 2 96
To-morrow shall you bear our full intent Back to our brother England . ii 4 114
My horse is my mistress.—Your mistress bears well.—Me well . iii 7 48
My sky shall not want.—That may be, for you bear a many superfluously iii 7 79
Even as your horse bears your praises . iii 7 82
Foolish curs, that run winking into the mouth of a Russian bear! . iii 7 154
Our children and our sins lay on the king! We must bear all . iv 1 250
Bear my former answer back: Bid them achieve me and then sell my bones . iv 3 90
Now we bear the king Toward Calais: grant him there . v Prol. 6
Good God, these nobles should such stomachs bear! . *1 Hen. VI.* i 3 90
Between two blades, which bears the better temper: Between two horses, which doth bear him best . ii 4 13
He bears him on the place's privilege . ii 4 86

Bear. Methinks you do not well To bear with their perverse objections *1 Hen. VI.* iv 1 129
Never to England shall he bear his life iv 4 38
Before young Talbot from old Talbot fly, The coward horse that bears me fall and die! iv 6 47
My spirit can no longer bear these harms iv 7 30
Give me their bodies, that I may bear them hence And give them burial iv 7 85
Proof of which contract, Bear her this jewel, pledge of my affection v 1 47
Duke of Gloucester Did bear him like a noble gentleman *2 Hen. VI.* i 1 184
And in my standard bear the arms of York i 1 256
I cannot go before, While Gloucester bears this base and humble mind i 2 62
She bears a duke's revenues on her back i 3 83
Their master loves to be aloft And bears his thoughts above his falcon's pitch ii 1 12
Duke of Gloucester scarce himself, That bears so shrewd a maim ii 3 41
Can I bear this shameful yoke? Trow'st thou that e'er I'll look upon the world? ii 4 37
With what a majesty he bears himself! iii 1 6
It is no policy, Respecting what a rancorous mind he bears iii 1 24
The reverent care I bear unto my lord Made me collect these dangers iii 1 34
Throws away his crutch Before his legs be firm to bear his body iii 1 190
More can I bear than you dare execute iv 1 130
His body will I bear unto the king iv 1 145
This monument of the victory will I bear iv 3 12
Hear me but speak, and bear me where you will iv 7 64
Thy most ungracious head; Which I will bear in triumph to the king iv 10 89
Call hither to the stake my two brave bears v 1 144
Are these thy bears? we'll bait thy bears to death v 1 148
Who, being suffer'd with the bear's fell paw, Hath clapp'd his tail between his legs and cried v 1 153
I am resolved to bear a greater storm Than any thou canst conjure up v 1 198
Old Nevil's crest, The rampant bear chain'd to the ragged staff v 1 203
From thy burgonet I'll rend thy bear And tread it under foot v 1 208
Despite the bear-ward that protects the bear v 1 210
If thou dost not hide thee from the bear v 2 2
As did Æneas old Anchises bear, So bear I thee upon my manly shoulders v 2 62
Thy father bears the type of King of Naples *3 Hen. VI.* i 4 121
Bid the father wipe his eyes withal, And yet be seen to bear a woman's face? i 4 140
As a bear, encompass'd round with dogs ii 1 15
Henceforward will I bear Upon my target three fair-shining suns ii 1 39
Blows and revenge for me! Richard, I bear thy name ii 1 87
Blame me not: 'Tis love I bear thy glories makes me speak ii 1 158
Whose hand is that the forest bear doth lick? Not his that spoils her young ii 2 13
Whose father bears the title of a king ii 2 140
I'll bear thee hence, where I may weep my fill ii 5 113
Until my mis-shaped trunk that bears this head Be round impaled iii 2 170
Edward will always bear himself as king iv 3 45
Madam, bear it as you may: Warwick may lose, that now hath won the day iv 4 14
That makes me bridle passion And bear with mildness my misfortune's cross iv 4 20
Bear him hence; And once again proclaim us king of England iv 8 52
I had rather chop this hand off at a blow, And with the other fling it at thy face, Than bear so low a sail, to strike to thee v 1 52
Both shall buy this treason Even with the dearest blood your bodies bear v 1 69
Long mayst thou live To bear his image and renew his glories! v 4 54
Go, bear them hence; I will not hear them speak v 5 4
Go, bear her hence perforce.—Nay, never bear me hence, dispatch me here v 5 68
The two brave bears, Warwick and Montague, That in their chains fetter'd the kingly lion v 7 10
Stay, you that bear the corse, and set it down *Richard III.* i 2 33
Bear with her weakness, which, I think, proceeds From wayward sickness, and no grounded malice i 3 28
Heart-sorrowing peers, That bear this mutual heavy load of moan ii 2 113
Where every horse bears his commanding rein ii 2 128
Go; And thither bear your treasure and your goods ii 4 69
You mean, to bear me, not to bear with me iii 1 128
Because that I am little, like an ape, He thinks that you should bear me on your shoulders iii 1 131
The tender love I bear your grace, my lord, Makes me most forward iii 4 65
Come, lead me to the block; bear him my head iii 4 108
Not replying, yielded To bear the golden yoke of sovereignty iii 7 146
Since you will buckle fortune on my back, To bear her burthen iii 7 229
I'll bear thy blame And take thy office from thee, on my peril iv 1 25
Now thy proud neck bears half my burthen'd yoke iv 4 111
Bear her my true love's kiss; and so, farewell iv 4 430
Sir William Brandon, you shall bear my standard v 3 22
Good Captain Blunt, bear my good-night to him v 3 30
Things now, That bear a weighty and a serious brow *Hen. VIII.* Prol. 2
The madams too, Not used to toil, did almost sweat to bear The pride upon them i 1 24
Pestilent to the hearing; and, to bear 'em, The back is sacrifice to the load i 2 49
That churchman bears a bounteous mind indeed i 3 55
They could do no less, Out of the great respect they bear to beauty i 4 69
After all this, how did he bear himself? ii 1 30
The law I bear no malice for my death ii 1 62
Have you limbs To bear that load of title? ii 3 39
You bear a gentle mind, and heavenly blessings Follow such creatures ii 3 57
By this time I know your back will bear a duchess ii 3 99
That you shall sustain moe new disgraces, With these you bear already iii 2 6
And bear the inventory Of your best graces in your mind iii 2 137
A time To think upon the part of business which I bear i' the state iii 2 146
So farewell to the little good you bear me iii 2 350
To-morrow blossoms, And bears his blushing honours thick upon him iii 2 354
Your enemies are many, and not small; their practices Must bear the same proportion v 1 129
Valiant as the lion, churlish as the bear, slow as the elephant *Troi. and Cres.* i 2 21
Ajax is grown self-will'd, and bears his head In such a rein i 3 188
Should not our father Bear the great sway of his affairs with reasons? ii 2 35
A' should not bear it so, a' should eat swords first ii 3 227
That, through the sight I bear in things to love, I have abandon'd Troy iii 3 4
This shall I undertake; and 'tis a burden Which I am proud to bear iii 3 37
'Twill be his death; 'twill be his bane; he cannot bear it iv 2 99
Thou shouldst not bear from me a Greekish member iv 5 130

Bear. And bear hence A great addition earned in thy death *Troi. and Cres.* iv 5 140
That sleeve is mine that he'll bear on his helm v 2 169
I am offended with you: Upon the love you bear me, get you in v 3 78
One bear will not bite another, and wherefore should one bastard? v 7 19
And there's all the love they bear us *Coriolanus* i 1 89
See him pluck Aufidius down by the hair, As children from a bear i 3 34
You souls of geese, That bear the shapes of men! i 4 35
None of you but is Able to bear against the great Aufidius A shield as hard as his i 6 79
The rest Shall bear the business in some other fight i 6 82
Bear The addition nobly ever! i 9 65
He's a lamb indeed, that baes like a bear.—He's a bear indeed, that lives like a lamb ii 1 13
I must be content to bear with those that say you are reverend grave men ii 1 65
For your voices bear Of wounds two dozen odd ii 3 134
Ever spake against Your liberties and the charters that you bear ii 3 188
Gibingly, ungravely, he did fashion After the inveterate hate he bears you ii 3 234
Bear him to the rock Tarpeian, and from thence Into destruction cast him iii 1 213
Bear him to the rock.—No, I'll die here iii 1 223
Doth rend Like interrupted waters and o'erbear What they are used to bear iii 1 250
For the whole state, I would put mine armour on, Which I can scarcely bear iii 2 35
Must I with base tongue give my noble heart A lie that it must bear? iii 2 101
As an ostler, that for the poorest piece Will bear the knave by the volume iii 3 33
Think Upon the wounds his body bears, which show Like graves iii 3 50
That common chances common men could bear iv 1 5
Good man, the wounds that he does bear for Rome! iv 2 28
Thou hast a grim appearance, and thy face Bears a command in't iv 5 67
And witness of the malice and displeasure Which thou shouldst bear me iv 5 79
He bears himself more proudlier, Even to my person, than I thought he would iv 7 8
He bears all things fairly, And shows good husbandry iv 7 21
You shall bear A better witness back than words v 3 203
Bear from hence his body; And mourn you for him v 6 143
By him that justly may Bear his betroth'd from all the world away *T. Andron.* i 1 286
Thou dost over-ween in all; And so in this, to bear me down with braves ii 1 30
That ever death should let life bear his name! iii 1 249
Take a head; And in this hand the other will I bear iii 1 281
Bear thou my hand, sweet wench, between thy teeth iii 1 283
Coal-black is better than another hue, In that it scorns to bear another hue iv 2 100
There's the privilege your beauty bears iv 2 116
I'll bear you hence; For it is you that puts us to our shifts iv 2 175
Wrung with wrongs more than our backs can bear iv 3 48
Commander of my thoughts, Calm thee, and bear the faults of Titus' age iv 4 29
Letters from great Rome, Which signify what hate they bear their emperor v 1 3
Unspeakable, past patience, Or more than any living man could bear v 3 127
Nay, as they dare. I will bite my thumb at them; which is a disgrace to them, if they bear it *Rom. and Jul.* i 1 50
Nay, I do bear a brain i 3 29
I am not for this ambling; Being but heavy, I will bear the light i 4 12
Presses them and learns them first to bear, Making them women of good carriage i 4 93
He bears him like a portly gentleman i 5 68
I bear no hatred, blessed man ii 3 53
I am the drudge and toil in your delight, But you shall bear the burden soon at night ii 5 78
The hate I bear thee can afford No better term than this,—thou art a villain iii 1 63
Bear hence this body and attend our will iii 1 201
If you could find out but a man To bear a poison, I would temper it iii 5 98
Bid me lurk Where serpents are; chain me with roaring bears iv 1 80
That very night Shall Romeo bear thee hence to Mantua iv 1 117
As the custom is, In all her best array bear her to church iv 5 81
I entreated her come forth, And bear this work of heaven with patience v 3 261
His honesty rewards him in itself; It must not bear my daughter *T. of Athens* i 1 131
Will you be chid?—We'll bear, with your lordship i 1 177
A forerunner, my lord, which bears that office, to signify their pleasures i 2 125
Who dies, that bears not one spurn to their graves Of their friends' gifts? i 2 146
To revenge is no valour, but to bear iii 5 39
How full of valour did he bear himself! iii 5 65
Detested parasites, Courteous destroyers, affable wolves, meek bears! iii 6 105
Nothing I'll bear from thee, But nakedness, thou detestable town! iv 1 32
Not nature, To whom all sores lay siege, can bear great fortune, But by contempt of nature iv 3 7
The senator shall bear contempt hereditary, The beggar native honour iv 3 10
Go great with tigers, dragons, wolves, and bears iv 3 189
I, to bear this, That never knew but better, is some burden iv 3 266
Wert thou a bear, thou wouldst be killed by the horse iv 3 341
You bear too stubborn and too strange a hand Over your friend *J. Cæsar* i 2 35
Cæsar doth bear me hard; but he loves Brutus i 2 317
That part of tyranny that I do bear I can shake off at pleasure i 3 99
Every bondman in his own hand bears The power to cancel his captivity i 3 101
Since the quarrel Will bear no colour for the thing he is, Fashion it thus ii 1 29
Every one doth wish You had but that opinion of yourself Which every noble Roman bears of you ii 1 93
Bear fire enough To kindle cowards ii 1 120
Every drop of blood That every Roman bears, and nobly bears, Is guilty ii 1 137
He loves to hear That unicorns may be betray'd with trees, And bears with glasses ii 1 205
Caius Ligarius doth bear Cæsar hard, Who rated him for speaking ii 1 215
Bear it as our Roman actors do, With untired spirits ii 1 226
Can I bear that with patience, And not my husband's secrets? ii 1 301
Bear my greeting to the senators And tell them that I will not come to-day ii 2 61
Be not fond, To think that Cæsar bears such rebel blood iii 1 40
If you bear me hard, Now, whilst your purpled hands do reek and smoke, Fulfil your pleasure iii 1 157
You'll bear me a bang for that, I fear iii 3 20
He shall but bear them as the ass bears gold, To groan and sweat under the business iv 1 21
It is not meet That every nice offence should bear his comment iv 3 8
A friend should bear his friend's infirmities iv 3 86

Bear. You are yoked with a lamb That carries anger as the flint bears fire *J. Cæsar* iv 3 111
No man bears sorrow better . . . . iv 3 147
Then like a Roman bear the truth I tell . . . . iv 3 188
I have as much of this in art as you, But yet my nature could not bear it so . . . . iv 3 195
He bears too great a mind . . . . v 1 113
Thick as hail Came post with post; and every one did bear Thy praises *Macbeth* i 3 98
Under heavy judgement bears that life Which he deserves to lose . . i 3 110
Bear welcome in your eye, Your hand, your tongue . . . . . i 5 65
Who should against his murderer shut the door, Not bear the knife myself . . . . i 7 16
Put upon His spongy officers, who shall bear the guilt Of our great quell? i 7 71
Approach thou like the rugged Russian bear, The arm'd rhinoceros . iii 4 100
Was never call'd to bear my part, Or show the glory of our art . . iii 5 8
He shall spurn fate, scorn death, and bear His hopes 'bove wisdom . iii 5 30
And yet the eighth appears, who bears a glass Which shows me many more . . . . iv 1 119
The mind I sway by and the heart I bear Shall never sag with doubt . v 3 9
Let every soldier hew him down a bough And bear't before him . . v 4 5
I cannot strike at wretched kerns, whose arms Are hired to bear their staves . . . . v 7 18
I bear a charmed life, which must not yield To one of woman born . v 8 12
It us befitted To bear our hearts in grief . . . . . *Hamlet* i 2 3
With no less nobility of love Than that which dearest father bears his son . . . . i 2 111
Beware Of entrance to a quarrel, but being in, Bear't that the opposed may beware of thee . . . . i 3 67
O, horrible! most horrible! If thou hast nature in thee, bear it not . i 5 81
And you, my sinews, grow not instant old, But bear me stiffly up . . i 5 95
Never, so help you mercy, How strange or odd soe'er I bear myself . i 5 170
Who would bear the whips and scorns of time, The oppressor's wrong? iii 1 70
Who would fardels bear, To grunt and sweat under a weary life? . iii 1 76
Makes us rather bear those ills we have Than fly to others that we know not of . . . . iii 1 81
They bear the mandate; they must sweep my way . . . . iii 4 204
Tell us where 'tis, that we may take it thence And bear it to the chapel iv 2 8
To bear all smooth and even . . . . iv 3 7
The other motive . . . Is the great love the general gender bear him . iv 7 18
What is he whose grief Bears such an emphasis? . . . . . v 1 278
Come, begin: And you, the judges, bear a wary eye . . . . v 2 290
Which nor our nature nor our place can bear . . . . *Lear* i 1 174
If our father carry authority with such dispositions as he bears . . i 1 309
I cannot be so partial, Goneril, To the great love I bear you . . i 4 335
Horses are tied by the heads, dogs and bears by the neck . . . ii 4 8
Fathers that bear bags Shall see their children kind . . . . ii 4 50
Fool me not so much To bear it tamely; touch me with noble anger . ii 4 279
This night, wherein the cub-drawn bear would couch . . . . iii 1 12
Come, help to bear thy master; Thou must not stay behind . . . iii 6 107
I'll repair the misery thou dost bear With something rich about me . iv 1 79
A gracious aged man, Whose reverence even the head-lugg'd bear would lick . . . . iv 2 42
If I could bear it longer, and not fall To quarrel . . . . . iv 6 37
Henceforth I'll bear Affliction till it do cry out itself 'Enough, enough' iv 6 75
Bear free and patient thoughts . . . . iv 6 80
Bear them from hence. Our present business Is general woe . . v 3 318
So may he with more facile question bear it . . . . *Othello* i 3 23
He bears the sentence well that nothing bears But the free comfort which from thence he hears, But he bears both the sentence and the sorrow That, to pay grief, must of poor patience borrow . . . i 3 212
The wind-shaked surge . . . Seems to cast water on the burning bear . ii 1 14
Now I shall have reason To show the love and duty that I bear you . iii 3 194
So prove it, That the probation bear no hinge nor loop To hang a doubt on iii 3 365
Would you would bear your fortune like a man! . . . . . iv 1 62
Bear some charity to my wit; do not think it so unwholesome . . iv 1 123
An admirable musician: O! she will sing the savageness out of a bear . iv 1 200
I would do much To atone them, for the love I bear to Cassio . . iv 1 244
Yet could I bear that too; well, very well . . . . . . iv 2 56
Where I have garner'd up my heart, Where either I must live, or bear no life . . . . iv 2 58
Thrown such despite and heavy terms upon her, As true hearts cannot bear . . . . iv 2 117
O, for a chair, To bear him easily hence! . . . . v 1 83
Some good man bear him carefully from hence . . . . . . v 1 99
What, look you pale? O, bear him out o' the air . . . . . v 1 104
Think on thy sins.—They are loves I bear to you . . . . . v 2 40
What else more serious Importeth thee to know, this bears *Ant. and Cleo.* i 2 125
Quarrel no more, but be prepared to know The purposes I bear . . i 3 67
'Tis sweating labour To bear such idleness so near the heart . . . i 3 94
No way excuse his soils, when we do bear So great weight in his lightness i 4 24
O happy horse, to bear the weight of Antony! . . . . . . i 5 21
This health to Lepidus!—Bear him ashore. I'll pledge it for him . . ii 7 91
A' bears the third part of the world, man; see'st not? . . . . ii 7 96
The holding every man shall bear as loud As his strong sides can volley ii 7 117
A charge we bear i' the war, And, as the president of my kingdom, will Appear . . . . iii 7 17
Hark! the land bids me tread no more upon't; It is ashamed to bear me! . . . . iii 11 2
This Jack of Cæsar's shall Bear us an errand to him . . . . iii 13 104
Prove this a prosperous day, the three-nook'd world Shall bear the olive freely . . . . iv 6 7
Make a jolly march; Bear our hack'd targets like the men that owe them iv 8 31
When men revolted shall upon record Bear hateful memory . . . iv 9 9
A cloud that's dragonish; A vapour sometime like a bear or lion . iv 14 3
Bear me, good friends, where Cleopatra bides; 'Tis the last service . iv 14 131
Bid that welcome Which comes to punish us, and we punish it Seeming to bear it lighty . . . . iv 14 138
Your loss is as yourself, great; and you bear it As answering to the weight . . . . v 2 101
You bear a graver purpose, I hope . . . . . . *Cymbeline* i 4 151
The love I bear him Made me to fan you thus . . . . . . i 6 176
A woman that Bears all down with her brain . . . . . . ii 1 59
With sands that will not bear your enemies' boats . . . . . iii 1 21
I come to spend my breath; Which neither here I'll keep nor bear again v 3 82
Bear with patience Such griefs as you yourself do lay upon yourself *Pericles* i 2 65
The care I had . . . On thee I lay, whose wisdom's strength can bear it i 2 119
The device he bears upon his shield Is a black Ethiope reaching at the sun . . . . ii 2 19
I shall with aged patience bear your yoke . . . . ii 4 48
Bear. To the next chamber bear her. Get linen . . . . *Pericles* iii 2 108
Bear you it in mind, Old Helicanus goes along behind . . . . iv 4 15
He bears A tempest, which his mortal vessel tears . . . . . iv 4 29
And bear his courses to be ordered By Lady Fortune . . . . iv 4 47
Sure, all's effectless; yet nothing we'll omit That bears recovery's name v 1 54
Bear away. That stays but till her owner comes aboard And then, sir, she bears away . . . . *Com. of Errors* iv 1 87
Bear away that child And follow me with speed . . . *K. John* iv 3 156
Bear back. Press not so upon me; stand far off.—Stand back; room; bear back . . . . *J. Cæsar* iii 2 172
And bear back Our targes undinted . . . . *Ant. and Cleo.* ii 6 38
Bear-baiting. I would I had bestowed that time in the tongues that I have in fencing, dancing and bear-baiting . . . . *T. Night* i 3 98
He brought me out o' favour with my lady about a bear-baiting . . ii 5 9
He haunts wakes, fairs and bear-baitings . . . . . *W. Tale* iv 3 109
Bear (him, me, us, you) company. Bear me company and go with me *T. G. of Ver.* iv 3 34
Importuned me That his attendant . . . Might bear him company *Com. of Errors* i 1 130
Come, Mistress Kate, I'll bear you company . . . *T. of Shrew* iv 3 49
Will not your honours bear me company? . . . . *1 Hen. VI.* ii 2 53
He shall die.—And I, my lord, will bear him company . . *3 Hen. VI.* i 3 6
We were sent for to the justices.—And so was I: I'll bear you company *Richard III.* ii 3 47
Fare you well!—Nay, he must bear you company . . . *Hen. VIII.* i 1 212
My lord, you'll bear us company?—Excuse me . . . . . . ii 2 59
Bear down. It must appear That malice bears down truth *Mer. of Venice* iv 1 214
Broke loose And bears down all before him . . . . *2 Hen. IV.* i 1 11
Bear it out. Let summer bear it out . . . . . . *T. Night* i 5 21
They are drown'd; It is impossible they bear it out . . . *Othello* ii 1 19
Bear me witness. God and the rope-maker bear me witness! *Com. of Err.* iv 4 93
Bear me witness all, That here I kiss her as my sovereign queen *Hen. V.* v 2 385
O, bear me witness, night,— What man is this? . . *Ant. and Cleo.* iv 9 5
Bears more toward. My father's bears more toward the market-place *T. of Shrew* v 1 10
Bear off. Neither bush nor shrub, to bear off any weather at all *Tempest* ii 2 18
Bear out. I hope your warrant will bear out the deed . . . *K. John* iv 1 6
If I cannot once or twice in a quarter bear out a knave against an honest man, I have but a very little credit . . . . . . *2 Hen. IV.* v 1 53
Bear question. Thy great employment Will not bear question . . *Lear* v 3 33
Bear the name. What's yet in this That bears the name of life? *Meas. for Meas.* iii 1 39
That, Talbot dead, great York might bear the name . . *1 Hen. VI.* iv 4 9
And bear the name and port of gentlemen . . . . *2 Hen. VI.* iv 1 19
Bear the palm for having bravely shed Thy wife and children's blood *Coriolanus* v 3 117
So get the start of the majestic world And bear the palm alone *J. Cæsar* i 2 131
Bear up. To bear up Against what should ensue . . . . *Tempest* i 2 157
Therefore bear up, and board 'em . . . . iii 2 3
So long as nature Will bear up with this . . . . . *W. Tale* iii 2 242
Bear with. I perceive I must be fain to bear with you.—Why, sir, how do you bear with me? . . . . *T. G. of Ver.* i 1 127
I have a trick Of the old rage: bear with me, I am sick . . *L. L. Lost* v 2 417
Bear with me; I cannot go no further.—For my part, I had rather bear with you than bear you . . . . *As Y. Like It* ii 4 9
Bear with me, cousin; for I was amazed Under the tide . . *K. John* iv 2 137
Your grace knows how to bear with him.—You mean, to bear me, not to bear with me . . . . *Richard III.* iii 1 127
Bear with me; I am hungry for revenge . . . . iv 4 61
Bear with me; My heart is in the coffin there . . . *J. Cæsar* iii 2 110
Have not you love enough to bear with me? . . . . . . iv 3 119
Bear with him, Brutus; 'tis his fashion . . . . iv 3 135
Bear with me, good boy, I am much forgetful . . . . . . iv 3 255
Tell him his pranks have been too broad to bear with . . *Hamlet* iii 4 2
You must bear with me: Pray you now, forget and forgive . . *Lear* iv 7 83
Bear witness. O heaven, O earth, bear witness to this sound! *Tempest* iii 1 68
Bear witness, Heaven, I have my wish for ever . . *T. G. of Ver.* v 4 119
Bear vitness that me have stay six or seven, two, tree hours *Mer. Wives* ii 3 36
My bones bear witness, That since have felt the vigour of his rage *Com. of Errors* iv 4 80
So much for praising myself, who, I myself will bear witness, is praise-worthy . . . . *Much Ado* v 2 89
A bargain! And, friends unknown, you shall bear witness to't *W. Tale* iv 4 395
Bear witness to his oath.—You tempt him over-much . . . . v 1 72
Heaven bear witness, And if I have a conscience, let it sink me! *Hen. VIII.* ii 1 59
Beard. His tears run down his beard, like winter's drops From eaves of reeds . . . . *Tempest* v 1 16
We'll hear him.—Ay, by my beard, will we . . . *T. G. of Ver.* iv 1 10
Does he not wear a great round beard, like a glover's paring-knife? *M. Wives* i 4 20
A little wee face, with a little yellow beard, a Cain-coloured beard . i 4 23
Shave the head, and tie the beard . . . . *Meas. for Meas.* iv 2 188
His beard and head Just of his colour . . . . iv 3 76
Whose beard they have singed off with brands of fire . *Com. of Errors* v 1 171
I could not endure a husband with a beard on his face . . *Much Ado* ii 1 32
You may light on a husband that hath no beard . . . . . ii 1 35
He that hath a beard is more than a youth, and he that hath no beard is less than a man . . . . ii 1 38
Fetch you a hair off the great Cham's beard, do you any embassage . ii 1 277
Indeed, he looks younger than he did, by the loss of a beard . . . iii 2 49
Will smile and stroke his beard, Bid sorrow wag, cry 'hem!' when he should groan . . . . v 1 15
God's blessing on your beard!—Good sir, be not offended . . *L. L. Lost* ii 1 203
A beard, fair health, and honesty; With three-fold love I wish you all these . . . . v 2 834
Let not me play a woman; I have a beard coming . . *M. N. Dream* i 2 50
What beard were I best to play it in? . . . . i 2 92
Either your straw-colour beard, your orange-tawny beard, your purple-in-grain beard, or your French-crown-colour beard, your perfect yellow . . . . i 2 96
The green corn Hath rotted ere his youth attain'd a beard . . . ii 1 95
Get your apparel together, good strings to your beards . . . . iv 2 36
You, that did void your rheum upon my beard And foot me *Mer. of Venice* i 3 118
What a beard hast thou got! . . . . ii 2 99
Wear yet upon their chins The beards of Hercules and frowning Mars . iii 2 85
Stroke your chins, and swear by your beards that I am a knave *As Y. L.* i 2 76
With eyes severe and beard of formal cut, Full of wise saws . . . ii 7 155
Is his head worth a hat, or his chin worth a beard?—Nay, he hath but a little beard.—Why, God will send more . . . . iii 2 218
Let me stay the growth of his beard, if thou delay me not the knowledge of his chin . . . . iii 2 222

Beard. A beard neglected, which you have not; but I pardon you for that . . . *As Y. Like It* iii 2 394
For simply your having in beard is a younger brother's revenue . iii 2 396
I did dislike the cut of a certain courtier's beard: he sent me word, if I said his beard was not cut well, he was in the mind it was . . v 4 74
If I were a woman I would kiss as many of you as had beards that pleased me . . . . Epil. 19
As many as have good beards or good faces or sweet breaths . . Epil. 22
Having no other reason But that his beard grew thin . *T. of Shrew* iii 2 177
I'ld give bay Curtal and his furniture, My mouth no more were broken than these boys', And writ as little beard . . . *All's Well* ii 3 67
The baring of my beard; and to say it was in stratagem . . iv 1 54
By my old beard, And every hair that's on't . . . . . v 3 76
By the colour of his beard, the shape of his leg, the manner of his gait *T. Night* ii 3 170
Now Jove, in his next commodity of hair, send thee a beard! . iii 1 51
Where you will hang like an icicle on a Dutchman's beard . . iii 2 30
Nay, I prithee, put on this gown and this beard . . . . iv 2 2
Thou mightst have done this without thy beard and gown . . iv 2 70
So sure as this beard's grey . . . . . . *W. Tale* ii 3 162
By my white beard, You offer him, if this be so, a wrong Something unfilial . . . . iv 4 415
There is that in this fardel will make him scratch his beard . . iv 4 728
Whose valour plucks dead lions by the beard . . *K. John* ii 1 138
Thy father's beard is turned white with the news . . *1 Hen. IV.* ii 4 393
No man so potent breathes upon the ground But I will beard him . iv 1 12
I will sooner have a beard grow in the palm of my hand than he shall get one on his cheek . . . . . *2 Hen. IV.* i 2 24
Have you not a moist eye? a dry hand? a yellow cheek? a white beard? i 2 205
Whose beard the silver hand of peace hath touch'd . . . iv 1 43
'Tis merry in hall when beards wag all, And welcome merry Shrove-tide v 3 37
He is an ass, as in the world: I will verify as much in his beard *Hen. V.* iii 2 75
Your fathers taken by the silver beards, And their most reverend heads dash'd to the walls . . . . iii 3 36
And what a beard of the general's cut . . . will do . . . . iii 6 80
Takes him by the beard; kisses the gashes That bloodily did yawn upon his face . . . . iv 6 13
A black beard will turn white; a curled pate will grow bald . . v 2 168
Go to Constantinople and take the Turk by the beard . . . v 2 223
Do what thou darest; I beard thee to thy face . . *1 Hen. VI.* i 3 44
Beware your beard; I mean to tug it and to cuff you soundly . i 3 47
His well-proportion'd beard made rough and rugged . *2 Hen. VI.* iii 2 175
Brave thee! ay, by the best blood that ever was broached, and beard thee too . . . . iv 10 40
Now play me Nestor; hem, and stroke thy beard . *Troi. and Cres.* i 3 165
Tell him from me I'll hide my silver beard in a gold beaver . . i 3 296
By this white beard, I'ld fight with thee to-morrow . . . iv 5 209
If e'er again I meet him beard to beard, He's mine, or I am his *Coriol.* i 10 11
When you speak best unto the purpose, it is not worth the wagging of your beards . . . . ii 1 96
Your beards deserve not so honourable a grave as to stuff a botcher's cushion . . . . ii 1 97
You had more beard when I last saw you; but your favour is well approved by your tongue . . . . iv 3 8
Thou wilt quarrel with a man that hath a hair more, or a hair less, in his beard, than thou hast . . . *Rom. and Jul.* iii 1 19
Pity not honour'd age for his white beard; He is an usurer *T. of Athens* iv 3 111
Sack fair Athens, And take our goodly aged men by the beards . v 1 175
You should be women, And yet your beards forbid . . *Macbeth* i 3 46
We might have met them dareful, beard to beard, And beat them . v 5 6
His beard was grizzled,—no?—It was, as I have seen it in his life *Hamlet* i 2 240
The satirical rogue says here that old men have grey beards . . ii 2 199
Comest thou to beard me in Denmark? . . . . . . ii 2 443
This is too long.—It shall to the barber's, with your beard . . ii 2 521
Breaks my pate across? Plucks off my beard, and blows it in my face? ii 2 600
His beard was as white as snow, All flaxen was his poll . . . iv 5 195
We can let our beard be shook with danger And think it pastime . iv 7 32
Whose life I have spared at suit of his gray beard . . . *Lear* ii 2 68
Spare my gray beard, you wagtail? . . . . ii 2 73
Art not ashamed to look upon this beard? . . . . . . ii 4 196
By the kind gods, 'tis most ignobly done To pluck me by the beard . iii 7 36
If you did wear a beard upon your chin, I'ld shake it on this quarrel . iii 7 76
Ha! Goneril, with a white beard! They flattered me like a dog; and told me I had white hairs in my beard ere the black ones were there . . . . iv 6 97
Follow thou the wars; defeat thy favour with an usurped beard *Othello* i 3 346
Such a handkerchief . . . did I to-day See Cassio wipe his beard with iii 3 439
Were I the wearer of Antonius' beard, I would not shave't to-day *Ant. and Cleo.* ii 2 7
Who deserved So long a breeding as his white beard came to *Cymbeline* v 3 17
Bearded. Full of strange oaths and bearded like the pard *As Y. Like It* ii 7 150
If I were sawed into quantities, I should make four dozen of such bearded hermits' staves . . . . . *2 Hen. IV.* v 1 71
What! am I dared and bearded to my face? . . *1 Hen. VI.* i 3 45
Think every bearded fellow that's but yoked May draw with you *Othello* iv 1 67
Beardless. A beardless boy, A cocker'd silken wanton . . *K. John* v 1 69
And stand the push Of every beardless vain comparative *1 Hen. IV.* iii 2 67
Bearer. Stand aside, good bearer . . . . . *L. L. Lost.* iv 1 55
O majesty! When thou dost pinch thy bearer . . *2 Hen. IV.* iv 5 29
But thou, most fine, most honour'd, most renown'd, Hast eat thy bearer up . . . . iv 5 165
If that quarrel, fortune, do divorce It from the bearer . *Hen. VIII.* ii 3 15
The beauty that is borne here in the face The bearer knows not *Troi. and Cres.* iii 3 104
When crouching marrow in the bearer strong Cries of itself 'No more' *T. of Athens* v 4 9
Bearers of this greeting to old Norway . . . . *Hamlet* i 2 35
He should the bearers put to sudden death, Not shriving-time allow'd . . . . v 2 46
Bearest. All the accommodations that thou bear'st Are nursed by baseness *Meas. for Meas.* iii 1 14
Thou bear'st thy heavy riches but a journey, And death unloads thee . iii 1 27
Youth, thou bear'st thy father's face . . . . *All's Well* i 2 19
I will respect thee as a father if Thou bear'st my life off hence *W. Tale* i 2 462
From henceforth bear his name whose form thou bear'st . *K. John* i 1 160
Thou art our admiral, thou bearest the lantern in the poop *1 Hen. IV.* iii 3 28
I fear thou art another counterfeit; And yet, in faith, thou bear'st thee like a king . . . . v 4 36
O God, seest Thou this, and bearest so long? . . . *2 Hen. VI.* ii 1 154
O Tamora! thou bear'st a woman's face . . . *T. Andron.* ii 3 136

Bearest. Milk-liver'd man! That bear'st a cheek for blows . *Lear* iv 2 51
She's thirsty.—Bear'st thou her face in mind? is't long or round? *Ant. and Cleo.* iii 3 32
Beareth. For the love he beareth to your daughter . . *T. of Shrew* iv 4 29
Bear-herd. A bear-herd, and now by present profession a tinker Ind. 2 21
That true valour is turned bear-herd . . . . *2 Hen. IV.* i 2 192
Bearing. You shall have it for bearing the letter . . *T. G. of Ver.* i 1 125
Rushing in their houses, bearing thence Rings, jewels, any thing *C. of Err.* v 1 143
I know him by his bearing . . . . . . *Much Ado* ii 1 166
For bearing, argument and valour, Goes foremost in report . . iii 1 96
A man of good repute, carriage, bearing, and estimation . *L. L. Lost* i 1 272
Bearing the badge of faith, to prove them true . *M. N. Dream* iii 2 127
We shall see your bearing.—Nay, but I bar to-night . *Mer. of Venice* ii 2 207
Which appears most strongly In bearing thus the absence of your lord iii 4 4
'Regia,' bearing my port, 'celsa senis,' that we might beguile the old pantaloon . . . . *T. of Shrew* iii 1 36
It shall advantage thee more than ever the bearing of letter did *T. Night* iv 2 120
With such a smooth, discreet and stable bearing . . . . iv 3 19
The manner of your bearing towards him . . . . *W. Tale* iv 4 569
Though bearing misery, I desire my life Once more to look on him . v 1 137
Bearing their birthrights proudly on their backs . . *K. John* ii 1 70
Superfluous branches We lop away, that bearing boughs may live *Richard II.* iii 4 64
They find a kind of ease, Bearing their own misfortunes on the back Of such as have before endured the like . . . . . . v 5 29
The arms are fair, When the intent of bearing them is just *1 Hen. IV.* v 2 89
Wise bearing or ignorant carriage is caught, as men take diseases *2 Hen. IV.* v 1 84
I judge By his blunt bearing he will keep his word . . *Hen. V.* iv 7 185
And nobles bearing banners, there lie dead One hundred twenty six . iv 8 87
Bearing it to the bloody slaughter-house . . . *2 Hen. VI.* iii 1 212
With thy brave bearing should I be in love, But that thou art so fast mine enemy . . . . v 2 20
Bearing the king in my behalf along . . . . *3 Hen. VI.* ii 1 115
Supply his place; I mean, in bearing weight of government . . iv 6 51
What satisfaction canst thou make For bearing arms? . . . v 5 15
The question . . . , Bearing a state of mighty moment in't *Hen. VIII.* ii 4 213
Who dare cross 'em, Bearing the king's will from his mouth expressly? iii 2 235
Cupboarding the viand, never bearing Like labour with the rest *Coriol.* i 1 103
Of no more soul nor fitness for the world Than camels in the war, who have their provand Only for bearing burdens . . . . ii 1 268
Scaling his present bearing with his past . . . . . . ii 3 257
Bearing his valiant sons In coffins from the field . . *T. Andron.* i 1 34
Bearing a Tartar's painted bow of lath . . . *Rom. and Jul.* i 4 5
If there be Such valour in the bearing, what make we Abroad? *T. of Athens* iii 5 46
Women are more valiant That stay at home, if bearing carry it . iii 5 48
When we our betters see bearing our woes, We scarcely think our miseries our foes . . . . *Lear* iii 6 109
The mind much sufferance doth o'erskip, When grief hath mates, and bearing fellowship . . . . iii 6 114
They all confirm A Turkish fleet, and bearing up to Cyprus . *Othello* i 3 8
Bearing with frank appearance Their purposes toward Cyprus . . i 3 38
Bearing-cloth. Look thee, a bearing-cloth for a squire's child! *W. Tale* iii 3 119
Thy scarlet robes as a child's bearing-cloth I'll use to carry thee out of this place . . . . *1 Hen. VI.* i 3 42
Bear-like. I cannot fly, But, bear-like, I must fight the course *Macbeth* v 7 2
Bear-ward. I will even take sixpence in earnest of the bear-ward *M. Ado* ii 1 43
Are these thy bears? we'll bait thy bears to death, And manacle the bear-ward in their chains . . . . . *2 Hen. VI.* v 1 149
Despite the bear-ward that protects the bear . . . . . v 1 210
Bear-whelp. Like to a chaos, or an unlick'd bear-whelp That carries no impression like the dam . . . . . *3 Hen. VI.* iii 2 161
If you hunt these bear-whelps, then beware: The dam will wake *T. And.* iv 1 96
Beast. Make thee roar That beasts shall tremble at thy din . *Tempest* i 2 371
My poor son.—Heavens keep him from these beasts! . . . ii 1 324
There would this monster make a man; any strange beast there makes a man . . . . ii 2 32
I had forgot that foul conspiracy Of the beast Caliban . . . iv 1 140
I would have been a breakfast to the beast . . *T. G. of Ver.* v 4 34
It is a familiar beast to man, and signifies love . . *Mer. Wives* i 1 21
What a beast am I to slack it! . . . . iii 4 115
O powerful love! that, in some respects, makes a beast a man, in some other, a man a beast . . . . v 5 5
A fault done first in the form of a beast. O Jove, a beastly fault! . v 5 10
O you beast! O faithless coward! O dishonest wretch! *Meas. for Meas.* iii 1 136
If there be no remedy for it, but that you will needs buy and sell men and women like beasts . . . . iii 2 3
Correction and instruction must both work Ere this rude beast will profit . . . . iii 2 34
The beasts, the fishes and the winged fowls Are their males' subjects *Com. of Errors* ii 1 18
Because it is a blessing that he bestows on beasts . . . . ii 2 81
She would have me as a beast: not that, I being a beast, she would have me . . . . iii 2 87
In sport and life-preserving rest To be disturb'd, would mad or man or beast . . . . v 1 84
A bird of my tongue is better than a beast of yours . . *Much Ado* i 1 141
As once Europa did at lusty Jove, When he would play the noble beast in love . . . . v 4 47
About the sixth hour; when beasts most graze, birds best peck *L. L. Lost* i 1 238
Grant pasture for me.—Not so, gentle beast: My lips are no common . ii 1 222
And leave thee to the mercy of wild beasts . . . *M. N. Dream* ii 1 228
I am as ugly as a bear; For beasts that meet me run away for fear . ii 2 95
This grisly beast, which Lion hight by name . . . . . v 1 140
Here come two noble beasts in, a man and a lion . . . . v 1 220
A very gentle beast, and of a good conscience.—The very best at a beast, my lord, that e'er I saw . . . . v 1 230
When he is worst, he is little better than a beast . . *Mer. of Venice* i 2 96
I think he be transform'd into a beast; For I can no where find him like a man . . . . *As Y. Like It* ii 7 1
Meaning me a beast . . . . iv 3 49
'Tis The royal disposition of that beast To prey on nothing that doth seem as dead . . . . iv 3 118
A pair of very strange beasts, which in all tongues are called fools . v 4 37
O monstrous beast! how like a swine he lies! . . . *T. of Shrew* Ind. 1 34
Thou knowest, winter tames man, woman and beast . . . . iv 1 25
Away, you three-inch fool! I am no beast . . . . . . iv 1 28
The gods themselves, Humbling their deities to love, have taken The shapes of beasts upon them . . . . *W. Tale* iv 4 27
Vast confusion waits, As doth a raven on a sick-fall'n beast . *K. John* iv 3 153

Beast. A lion and a king of beasts.—A king of beasts, indeed *Richard II.* v 1 34
Setting thy womanhood aside, thou art a beast to say otherwise.—Say, what beast, thou knave, thou?—What beast! why, an otter *1 Hen. IV.* iii 3 140
There is no honesty in such dealing; unless a woman should be made an ass and a beast, to bear every knave's wrong . *2 Hen. IV.* ii 1 41
It is a beast for Perseus: he is pure air and fire . *Hen. V.* iii 7 22
He is indeed a horse; and all other jades you may call beasts . iii 7 26
The man that once did sell the lion's skin While the beast lived, was killed with hunting him . iv 3 94
I have encounter'd him And made a prey for carrion kites and crows Even of the bonny beast he loved so well . *2 Hen. VI.* v 2 12
To whom do lions cast their gentle looks? Not to the beast that would usurp their den . *3 Hen. VI.* ii 2 12
No beast so fierce but knows some touch of pity *Richard III.* i 2 71
This man, lady, hath robbed many beasts of their particular additions *Troi. and Cres.* i 2 20
Wilt thou not, beast, abide? Why, then fly on . v 6 30
Nature teaches beasts to know their friends . *Coriolanus* ii 1 6
The beast With many heads butts me away . iv 1 1
We loved him; but, like beasts And cowardly nobles, gave way . iv 6 121
That I knew thy heart; and knew the beast, That I might rail at him! *T. Andron.* ii 4 34
Throw her forth to beasts and birds of prey . v 3 198
Will they not hear? What, ho! you men, you beasts *Rom. and Jul.* i 1 90
O, what a beast was I to chide at him! . iii 2 95
Thy wild acts denote The unreasonable fury of a beast . iii 3 111
Unseemly woman in a seeming man! Or ill-beseeming beast in seeming both! . iii 3 113
What a wicked beast was I to disfurnish myself against such a good time! *T. of Athens* iii 2 49
Before the gods, I am not able to do,—the more beast, I say . iii 2 55
Of man and beast the infinite malady Crust you quite o'er! . iii 6 108
He shall find The unkindest beast more kinder than mankind iv 1 36
What art thou there? speak.—A beast, as thou art . iv 3 49
What wouldst thou do with the world, Apemantus, if it lay in thy power?—Give it the beasts, to be rid of the men . iv 3 323
Wouldst thou have thyself fall in the confusion of men, and remain a beast with the beasts? . iv 3 326
What beast couldst thou be, that were not subject to a beast? . iv 3 346
What a beast art thou already, that seest not thy loss in transformation! iv 3 348
The commonwealth of Athens is become a forest of beasts . iv 3 353
Set them into confounding odds, that beasts May have the world in empire! . iv 3 392
We cannot live on grass, on berries, water, As beasts and birds and fishes.—Nor on the beasts themselves . iv 3 426
Timon is dead, who hath outstretch'd his span: Some beast rear'd this v 3 4
Why birds and beasts from quality and kind, Why old men fool *J. Cæsar* i 3 64
They could not find a heart within the beast . ii 2 40
Cæsar should be a beast without a heart, If he should stay at home to-day . ii 2 42
O judgement! thou art fled to brutish beasts, And men have lost their reason . iii 2 109
What beast was't, then, That made you break this enterprise to me? *Macbeth* i 7 47
A beast, that wants discourse of reason, Would have mourn'd longer *Ham.* i 2 150
That adulterate beast, With witchcraft of his wit, with traitorous gifts i 5 42
The rugged Pyrrhus, like the Hyrcanian beast . ii 2 472
What is a man, If his chief good and market of his time Be but to sleep and feed? a beast, no more . iv 4 35
Fair judgement, Without the which we are pictures, or mere beasts . iv 5 86
As had he been incorpsed and demi-natured With the brave beast . iv 7 89
Let a beast be lord of beasts, and his crib shall stand at the king's mess v 2 88
The basest and most poorest shape That ever penury, in contempt of man, Brought near to beast . *Lear* ii 3 9
Allow not nature more than nature needs, Man's life's as cheap as beast's . ii 4 270
Thou owest the worm no silk, the beast no hide, the sheep no wool iii 4 109
Making the beast with two backs . *Othello* i 1 117
With joy, pleasance, revel and applause, transform ourselves into beasts! . ii 3 294
To be now a sensible man, by and by a fool, and presently a beast! . ii 3 310
A horned man's a monster and a beast . iv 1 63
There's many a beast then in a populous city, And many a civil monster iv 1 64
Our dungy earth alike Feeds beast as man *Ant. and Cleo.* i 1 36
The gilded puddle Which beasts would cough at . i 4 63
Will give you that Like beasts which you shun beastly . *Cymbeline* v 3 27
Beastliest. In the beastliest sense you are Pompey the Great *M. for M.* ii 1 229
Beast-like. Her life was beast-like, and devoid of pity . *T. Andron.* v 3 199
Beastliness. That bolting-hutch of beastliness . *1 Hen. IV.* ii 4 496
Beastly. A fault done first in the form of a beast. O Jove, a beastly fault! *Mer. Wives* v 5 10
From their abominable and beastly touches I drink, I eat *Meas. for Meas.* iii 2 25
She, being a very beastly creature, lays claim to me *Com. of Errors* iii 2 88
Fie on her! see, how beastly she doth court him! . *T. of Shrew* iv 2 34
There was such misuse, Such beastly shameless transformation *1 Hen. IV.* i 1 44
Thou, beastly feeder, art so full of him, That thou provokest thyself to cast him up. So, so, thou common dog . *2 Hen. IV.* i 3 95
He stabbed me in mine own house, and that most beastly . ii 1 16
Not to relent is beastly, savage, devilish . *Richard III.* i 4 265
And at the murderer's horse's tail, In beastly sort, dragg'd *T. and Cres.* v 10 5
Being the herdsmen of the beastly plebeians . *Coriolanus* ii 1 105
Ah, beastly creature! The blot and enemy to our general name! *T. Andron.* ii 3 182
O barbarous, beastly villains, like thyself! . v 1 97
In that beastly fury He has been known to commit outrages *T. of Athens* iii 5 71
A beastly ambition, which the gods grant thee t' attain to! . iv 3 329
Giving our holy virgins to the stain Of contumelious, beastly, mad-brain'd war . v 1 177
Peace, sirrah! You beastly knave, know you no reverence? . *Lear* ii 2 75
Who neigh'd so high, that what I would have spoke Was beastly dumb'd by him . *Ant. and Cleo.* i 5 50
To expound His beastly mind to us . *Cymbeline* i 6 153
We are beastly, subtle as the fox for prey, Like warlike as the wolf iii 3 40
We are Romans and will give you that Like beasts which you shun beastly . v 3 27
Beat. I saw him beat the surges under him *Tempest* ii 1 114
A most scurvy monster! I could find in my heart to beat him . ii 2 160
Beat him enough: after a little time I'll beat him too . iii 2 93
Give me thy hand: I am sorry I beat thee . iii 2 119
Beat the ground For kissing of their feet . iv 1 173
Beat. Then I beat my tabor; At which, like unback'd colts, they prick'd their ears . *Tempest* iv 1 175
I drink the air before me, and return Or ere your pulse twice beat v 1 103
Thy pulse Beats as of flesh and blood . v 1 114
Forbade her my house and hath threatened to beat her . *Mer. Wives* iv 2 89
Trust me, he beat him most pitifully.—Nay, by the mass, that he did not; he beat him most unpitifully, methought . iv 2 212
He beat me grievously, in the shape of a woman . v 1 21
The baby beats the nurse, and quite athwart Goes all decorum *M. for M.* i 3 30
I shall beat you to your tent, and prove a shrewd Cæsar to you . ii 1 262
Could I with boot change for an idle plume, Which the air beats for vain ii 4 12
I will have more time to prepare me, or they shall beat out my brains with billets . iv 3 58
In conclusion, he did beat me there . *Com. of Errors* ii 1 74
Self-harming jealousy! fie, beat it hence! . ii 1 102
Fashion your demeanour to my looks, Or I will beat this method in your sconce . ii 2 34
A villain that would face me down He met me on the mart and that I beat him . iii 1 7
That you beat me at the mart, I have your hand to show . iii 1 12
You'll cry for this, minion, if I beat the door down . iii 1 59
For he both pleases men and angers them, and then they laugh at him and beat him *Much Ado* ii 1 147
'Twas the boy that stole your meat, and you'll beat the post . ii 1 207
Then down upon her knees she falls, weeps, sobs, beats her heart, tears her hair . ii 3 153
A thousand innocent shames In angel whiteness beat away those blushes iv 1 163
Beat not the bones of the buried: when he breathed, he was a man *L. L. Lost* v 2 667
The more you beat me, I will fawn on you: Use me but as your spaniel *M. N. Dream* ii 1 204
How he beat me because her horse stumbled . *T. of Shrew* iv 1 79
Watch her, as we watch these kites That bate and beat and will not be obedient . iv 1 199
Beat me to death with a bottom of brown thread . iv 3 137
What's he that knocks as he would beat down the gate? . v 1 17
What are you that offer to beat my servant? . v 1 65
I'll beat him, by my life, if I can meet him with any convenience *A. Well* ii 3 252
By mine honour, if I were but two hours younger, I'ld beat thee . ii 3 269
Methinks, thou art a general offence, and every man should beat thee . ii 3 270
A kind of puritan.—O, if I thought that, I'ld beat him like a dog! *T. Night* ii 3 153
'Slight, I could so beat the rogue! . ii 5 38
'Slid, I'll after him again and beat him . iii 4 426
Say this to him, He's beat from his best ward . *W. Tale* i 2 33
A callat Of boundless tongue, who late hath beat her husband! . ii 3 91
Do correct Their proud contempt that beats His peace to heaven *K. John* ii 1 88
How comes it then that thou art call'd a king, When living blood doth in these temples beat? . ii 1 108
Thou dost usurp authority.—Excuse; it is to beat usurping down . ii 1 119
Whose rocky shore beats back the envious siege Of watery Neptune *Richard II.* ii 1 62
I'll give thee scope to beat, Since foes have scope to beat both thee and me . iii 3 140
Stand in narrow lanes, And beat our watch, and rob our passengers . v 3 9
Beat Cut's saddle, put a few flocks in the point . *1 Hen. IV.* ii 1 6
If I do not beat thee out of thy kingdom with a dagger of lath . ii 4 150
Whose swift wrath beat down The never-daunted Percy . *2 Hen. IV.* i 1 109
With what loud applause Didst thou beat heaven with blessing Bolingbroke! . i 3 92
Your pulsidge beats as extraordinarily as heart would desire . ii 4 26
I saw it, and told John a Gaunt he beat his own name . iii 2 349
The man is dead that you and Pistol beat amongst you . v 4 19
The French may lay twenty French crowns to one, they will beat us *Hen. V.* iv 1 243
Nor the tide of pomp That beats upon the high shore of this world . iv 1 282
A rope! a rope! Now beat them hence . *1 Hen. VI.* i 3 54
To beat assailing death from his weak legions . iv 4 16
Leaden age, Quicken'd with youthful spleen and warlike rage, Beat down Alençon . iv 6 14
Thine eyes and thoughts Beat on a crown, the treasure of thy heart *2 Hen. VI.* ii 1 20
A staff is quickly found to beat a dog . iii 1 171
As the butcher takes away the calf And binds the wretch and beats it . iii 1 211
When from thy shore the tempest beat us back . iii 2 102
O, beat away the busy meddling fiend That lays strong siege unto this wretch's soul! . iii 3 21
At unawares may beat down Edward's guard . *3 Hen. VI.* iv 2 23
Leave the town and fight? Or shall we beat the stones about thine ears? v 1 108
Why do you wring your hands, and beat your breast? *Richard III.* ii 2 3
O, cut my lace in sunder, that my pent heart May have some scope to beat! . iv 1 35
Hollow-hearted friends, Unarm'd, and unresolved to beat them back . iv 4 436
If not to fight with foreign enemies, Yet to beat down these rebels here iv 4 532
No way to cure this? No new device to beat this from his brains? *Hen. VIII.* iii 2 217
Vinewedst leaven, speak: I will beat thee into handsomeness *Troi. and Cres.* ii 1 16
If thou use to beat me, I will begin at thy heel, and tell what thou art by inches . ii 1 52
I have bobbed his brain more than he has beat my bones . ii 1 76
Whose present courage may beat down our foes . ii 2 201
He beats me, and I rail at him: O, worthy satisfaction! would it were otherwise; that I could beat him, whilst he railed at me . ii 3 3
My heart beats thicker than a feverous pulse . iii 2 38
But our great Ajax bravely beat down him . iii 3 213
What's the matter? will you beat down the door? . iv 2 44
Beat loud the tabourines, let the trumpets blow . iv 5 275
The fierce Polydamas Hath beat down Menon . v 5 7
He'll beat Aufidius' head below his knee . *Coriolanus* i 3 49
How have you run From slaves that apes would beat! . i 4 36
Come on; If you'll stand fast, we'll beat them to their wives . i 4 41
Where is that slave Which told me they had beat you to your trenches? i 6 40
So often hast thou beat me, And wouldst do so, I think, should we encounter As often as we eat . i 10 8
Dogs that are as often beat for barking As therefore kept to do so . ii 3 224
On fair ground I could beat forty of them . iii 1 243
Thou hast beat me out Twelve several times . iv 5 127
Lest you shall chance to whip your information And beat the messenger iv 6 54
Beat thou the drum, that it speak mournfully . v 6 151

Beat. When thy poor heart beats with outrageous beating *T. Andron.* iii 2 13
I hang the head As flowers with frost or grass beat down with storms . iv 4 71
Cast us down, And on the ragged stones beat forth our brains v 3 133
Beat them down! Down with the Capulets! down with the Montagues!
Rom. and Jul. i 1 80
Be rough with love; Prick love for pricking, and you beat love down . i 4 28
What a head have I! It beats as it would fall in twenty pieces ii 5 50
And, with a martial scorn, with one hand beats Cold death aside . iii 1 166
Swifter than his tongue, His agile arm beats down their fatal points . iii 1 171
That is not the lark, whose notes do beat The vaulty heaven . iii 5 21
He gave me a jewel th' other day, and now he has beat it out of my hat
T. of Athens iii 6 123
Pluck the lined crutch from thy old limping sire, With it beat out his brains! iv 1 15
I prithee, beat thy drum, and get thee gone iv 3 96
I'll beat thee, but I should infect my hands iv 3 369
Lie where the light foam of the sea may beat Thy grave-stone daily iv 3 379
Our enemies have beat us to the pit *J. Cæsar* v 5 23
There are liars and swearers enow to beat the honest men . *Macbeth* iv 2 57
We might have met them dareful, beard to beard, And beat them backward home v 5 7
Hems, and beats her heart; Spurns enviously at straws . *Hamlet* iv 5 5
Beat at this gate, that let thy folly in, And thy dear judgement out! *Lear* i 4 293
One whom I will beat into clamorous whining. ii 2 24
Is it two days ago since I tripp'd up thy heels, and beat thee before the king? ii 2 32
At their chamber-door I'll beat the drum Till it cry sleep to death . ii 4 119
The tempest in my mind Doth from my senses take all feeling else Save what beats there iii 4 14
A knave teach me my duty! I'll beat the knave into a twiggen bottle
Othello ii 3 152
Even so as one would beat his offenceless dog to affright an imperious lion ii 3 275
In Aleppo once, Where a malignant and a turban'd Turk Beat a Venetian v 2 354
Made The water which they beat to follow faster, As amorous
Ant. and Cleo. ii 2 201
Of that natural luck, He beats thee 'gainst the odds ii 3 27
His quails ever Beat mine, inhoop'd, at odds . ii 3 38
From the head of Actium Beat the approaching Cæsar . iii 7 53
And chides, as he had power To beat me out of Egypt . iv 1 2
We'll beat 'em into bench-holes iv 7 9
We have beat him to his camp iv 8 1
My nightingale, We have beat them to their beds iv 8 19
In our salt-water girdle: if you beat us out of it, it is yours . *Cymbeline* iii 1 81
When we shall hear The rain and wind beat dark December iii 3 37
Thou art some fool; I am loath to beat thee iv 2 86
To beat us down, the which are down already *Pericles* i 4 68
Beaten. You have beaten my men, killed my deer . *Mer. Wives* i 1 114
I have been cozened and beaten too iv 5 96
Is beaten black and blue, that you cannot see a white spot about her . iv 5 115
Black and blue? I was beaten myself into all the colours of the rainbow . iv 5 118
I knew not what 'twas to be beaten till lately v 1 28
Why am I beaten?—Dost thou not know?—Nothing, sir, but that I am beaten *Com. of Errors* ii 2 40
Was there ever any man thus beaten out of season? ii 2 48
Beaten the maids a-row and bound the doctor, Whose beard they have singed off v 1 170
We are high-proof melancholy and would fain have it beaten away *M. Ado* v 1 124
If a man will be beaten with brains, a' shall wear nothing handsome . v 4 104
I did think to have beaten thee v 4 111
So is Alcides beaten by his page *Mer. of Venice* ii 1 35
Yet would you say ye were beaten out of door . *T. of Shrew* Ind. 2 87
Was ever man so beaten? was ever man so rayed? was ever man so weary? iv 1 3
Beaten in Italy for picking a kernel out of a pomegranate . *All's Well* ii 3 275
Should be once heard and thrice beaten ii 5 34
I am robbed, sir, and beaten; my money and apparel ta'en *W. Tale* iv 3 64
Are we not beaten? Is not Angiers lost? *K. John* iii 4 6
Indeed, your drums, being beaten, will cry out; And so shall you, being beaten v 2 166
Hath beaten down young Hotspur and his troops 2 *Hen. IV.* Ind. 25
Thus is the shepherd beaten from thy side 2 *Hen. VI.* iii 1 191
Mine eyes should sparkle like the beaten flint . iii 2 317
Whom our fathers Have in their own land beaten, bobb'd, and thump'd
Richard III. v 3 334
An honest country lord, as I am, beaten A long time out of play
Hen. VIII. i 3 44
Her foes shake like a field of beaten corn, And hang their heads . v 5 32
'Twas not voluntary: no man is beaten voluntary . *Troi. and Cres.* ii 1 105
I'ld have beaten him like a dog, but for disturbing the lords within
Coriolanus iv 5 56
Nor stony tower, nor walls of beaten brass, Nor airless dungeon *J. Cæsar* i 3 93
Let us be beaten, if we cannot fight *Macbeth* v 6 8
But, in the beaten way of friendship, what make you at Elsinore? *Hamlet* ii 2 277
I'ld have thee beaten for being old before thy time . *Lear* i 5 46
Far off, methinks, I hear the beaten drum iv 6 292
When thou once Wast beaten from Modena *Ant. and Cleo.* i 4 57
The poop was beaten gold; Purple the sails ii 2 197
They are beaten, sir; and our advantage serves For a fair victory . iv 7 11
He was carried From off our coast, twice beaten *Cymbeline* iii 1 26
Beaten for loyalty Excited me to treason v 5 344
Beating. For still 'tis beating in my mind, your reason *Tempest* i 2 176
A turn or two I'll walk, To still my beating mind iv 1 163
Do not infest your mind with beating on The strangeness of this business v 1 246
Back, slave, or I will break thy pate across.—And he will bless that cross with other beating *Com. of Errors* ii 1 79
When I am cold, he heats me with beating; when I am warm, he cools me with beating iv 4 34
No woman's sides Can bide the beating of so strong a passion *T. Night* ii 4 97
Beating and hanging are terrors to me *W. Tale* iv 3 29
Alas, poor man! a million of beating may come to a great matter . iv 3 62
Beating your officers, cursing yourselves, Opposing laws with strokes
Coriolanus iii 3 78
That Must bear my beating to his grave v 6 109
When thy poor heart beats with outrageous beating *T. Andron.* iii 2 13
The bell then beating one,— Peace, break thee off; look, where it comes again! *Hamlet* i 1 39
Whereon his brains still beating puts him thus From fashion of himself iii 1 182
Your dull ass will not mend his pace with beating . v 1 65

Beatrice. Get you to heaven, Beatrice, get you to heaven; here's no place for you maids *Much Ado* ii 1 48
But that my Lady Beatrice should know me, and not know me! . ii 1 210
It is the base, though bitter, disposition of Beatrice that puts the world into her person ii 1 215
The Lady Beatrice hath a quarrel to you ii 1 243
Heigh-ho for a husband!—Lady Beatrice, I will get you one ii 1 334
To bring Signior Benedick and the Lady Beatrice into a mountain of affection ii 1 382
In despite of his quick wit and his queasy stomach, he shall fall in love with Beatrice ii 1 400
What was it you told me of to-day, that your niece Beatrice was in love with Signior Benedick? ii 3 93
She found Benedick and Beatrice between the sheet ii 3 143
Here comes Beatrice. By this day! she's a fair lady ii 3 253
I am sent to bid you come in to dinner.—Fair Beatrice, I thank you ii 3 258
There shalt thou find my cousin Beatrice Proposing with the prince . iii 1 2
My talk to thee must be how Benedick Is sick in love with Beatrice . iii 1 21
Beatrice, like a lapwing, runs Close by the ground, to hear our conference iii 1 24
So angle we for Beatrice; who even now Is couched in the woodbine coverture iii 1 29
But are you sure That Benedick loves Beatrice so entirely? iii 1 37
Wish him wrestle with affection, And never to let Beatrice know of it . iii 1 43
Doth not the gentleman Deserve as full as fortunate a bed As ever Beatrice shall couch upon? iii 1 46
Nature never framed a woman's heart Of prouder stuff than that of Beatrice iii 1 50
Not to be so odd and from all fashions As Beatrice is, cannot be commendable iii 1 73
For my life, to break with him about Beatrice.—'Tis even so iii 2 77
Hero and Margaret have by this played their parts with Beatrice . iii 2 79
Lady Beatrice, have you wept all this while?—Yea, and I will weep a while longer iv 1 257
By my sword, Beatrice, thou lovest me.—Do not swear, and eat it iv 1 276
Why, then, God forgive me!—What offence, sweet Beatrice? . iv 1 284
Tarry, sweet Beatrice.—I am gone, though I am here iv 1 294
Beatrice,— In faith, I will go.—We'll be friends first iv 1 297
I'll tell thee how Beatrice praised thy wit the other day v 1 160
In most profound earnest; and, I'll warrant you, for the love of Beatrice v 1 199
Deserve well at my hands by helping me to the speech of Beatrice v 2 3
I will call Beatrice to you, who I think hath legs.—And therefore will come v 2 23
Sweet Beatrice, wouldst thou come when I called thee!—Yea, signior, and depart when you bid me v 2 42
An old instance, Beatrice, that lived in the time of good neighbours v 2 78
Which is Beatrice?—I answer to that name. What is your will? . v 4 72
A halting sonnet of his own pure brain, Fashion'd to Beatrice v 4 88
I had well hoped thou wouldst have denied Beatrice v 4 115
Beau. Here comes Monsieur Le Beau.—With his mouth full of news
As Y. Like It i 2 97
Beaufort. Here's Beaufort, that regards nor God nor king . 1 *Hen. VI.* i 3 60
Fie, uncle Beaufort! I have heard you preach iii 1 127
Beaufort and myself, With all the learned council . 2 *Hen. VI.* i 1 88
Beaufort The imperious churchman i 3 71
Wink at the Duke of Suffolk's insolence, At Beaufort's pride . ii 2 71
York and impious Beaufort, that false priest, Have all limed bushes ii 4 53
Beaufort's red sparkling eyes blab his heart's malice iii 1 154
Traitorously is murder'd By Suffolk and the Cardinal Beaufort's means . iii 2 124
Myself and Beaufort had him in protection iii 2 180
Is Beaufort term'd a kite? Where are his talons? iii 2 196
Cardinal Beaufort is at point of death iii 2 369
How fares my lord? speak, Beaufort, to thy sovereign iii 3 1
Beaumond, and Willoughby, With all their powerful friends *Richard II.* ii 2 54
Beaumont, Grandpré, Roussi, and Fauconberg *Hen. V.* iii 5 44; iv 8 105
Beauteous. How beauteous mankind is! O brave new world . *Tempest* v 1 183
Black men are pearls in beauteous ladies' eyes . *T. G. of Ver.* v 2 12
The beauteous heir Of Jaques Falconbridge *L. L. Lost* ii 1 41
True, that thou art beauteous; truth itself, that thou art lovely iv 1 61
More fairer than fair, beautiful than beauteous, truer than truth itself . iv 1 63
The superscript: 'To the snow-white hand of the most beauteous Lady Rosaline' iv 2 136
Beauteous as ink; a good conclusion.—Fair as a text B in a copy-book . v 2 41
I am beloved of beauteous Hermia *M. N. Dream* i 1 104
This beauteous lady Thisby is certain v 1 131
The beauteous scarf Veiling an Indian beauty . *Mer. of Venice* iii 2 98
A wife With wealth enough and young and beauteous . *T. of Shrew* i 2 86
The one as famous for a scolding tongue As is the other for beauteous modesty i 2 255
Kindness in women, not their beauteous looks, Shall win my love . iv 2 41
Nature with a beauteous wall Doth oft close in pollution *T. Night* i 2 48
The beauteous evil Are empty trunks o'erflourish'd by the devil iii 4 403
With taper-light To seek the beauteous eye of heaven to garnish *K. John* iv 2 15
That sweet breath Which was embounded in this beauteous clay . iv 3 137
Most beauteous inn, Why should hard-favour'd grief be lodged in thee?
Richard II. v 1 13
Your wondrous rare description, noble earl, Of beauteous Margaret hath astonish'd me 1 *Hen. VI.* v 5 2
Given me in this beauteous face A world of earthly blessings . 2 *Hen. VI.* i 1 21
The king, that calls your beauteous daughter wife . *Richard III.* iv 4 315
I tender not thy beauteous princely daughter iv 4 405
You having lands, and blest with beauteous wives v 3 321
Sweet blowse, you are a beauteous blossom, sure *T. Andron.* iv 2 72
County Anselme and his beauteous sisters *Rom. and Jul* i 2 68
This bud of love, by summer's ripening breath, May prove a beauteous flower ii 2 122
Beauteous and swift, the minions of their race *Macbeth* ii 4 15
Where is the beauteous majesty of Denmark? *Hamlet* iv 5 21
Brutus, With the arm'd rest, courtiers of beauteous freedom *Ant. and Cleo.* ii 6 17
Beautied. The harlot's cheek, beautied with plastering art *Hamlet* iii 1 51
Beauties. All hail, the richest beauties on the earth!—Beauties no richer than rich taffeta *L. L. Lost* v 2 158
To you your father should be as a god; One that composed your beauties
M. N. Dream i 1 48
I might in virtues, beauties, livings, friends, Exceed account *Mer. of Ven.* iii 2 158
Good beauties, let me sustain no scorn; I am very comptible *T. Night.* i 5 186
By giving liberty unto thine eyes; Examine other beauties *Rom. and Jul.* i 1 234
With all the admired beauties of Verona i 2 89
Lovers can see to do their amorous rites By their own beauties iii 2 9
That your good beauties be the happy cause Of Hamlet's wildness *Ham.* iii 1 39
Loveliness in favour, sympathy in years, manners and beauties *Othello* ii 1 233

Beautified. Seeing you are beautified With goodly shape *T. G. of Ver.* iv 1 55
'To the celestial and my soul's idol, the most beautified Ophelia,'—That's an ill phrase, a vile phrase; 'beautified' is a vile phrase *Hamlet* ii 2 110
Beautiful. I have loved her ever since I saw her; and still I see her beautiful *T. G. of Ver.* ii 1 73
A virtuous gentlewoman, mild and beautiful! iv 4 185
More fairer than fair, beautiful than beauteous *L. L. Lost* iv 1 63
Thou art as wise as thou art beautiful *M. N. Dream* iii 1 151
Most beautiful pagan, most sweet Jew! *Mer. of Venice* ii 3 11
Far more beautiful Than any woman in this waning age *T. of Shrew* Ind. 2 64
His youngest daughter, beautiful Bianca i 2 120
Is the jay more precious than the lark, Because his feathers are more beautiful? iv 3 178
She much resembled me, was yet of many accounted beautiful *T. Night* ii 1 27
What a deal of scorn looks beautiful In the contempt and anger of his lip! iii 1 157
She's beautiful and therefore to be woo'd; She is a woman, therefore to be won *1 Hen. VI.* v 3 77
Beautiful tyrant! fiend angelical! Dove-feather'd raven! *Rom. and Jul.* iii 2 75
You have . . . fair ladies, Set a fair fashion on our entertainment, Which was not half so beautiful and kind *T. of Athens* i 2 153
Mine eyes Were not in fault, for she was beautiful *Cymbeline* v 5 63
Beautify. Ne'er returneth To blush and beautify the cheek again *2 Hen. VI.* iii 2 167
We are brought to Rome, To beautify thy triumphs and return *T. Andron.* i 1 110
This unbound lover, To beautify him, only lacks a cover *Rom. and Jul.* i 3 88
To grace thy marriage-day, I'll beautify *Pericles* v 3 76
Beauty. He's something stain'd With grief, that's beauty's canker *Tempest* i 2 415
That most deeply to consider is The beauty of his daughter iii 2 107
An April day, Which now shows all the beauty of the sun *T. G. of Ver.* i 3 86
I mean that her beauty is exquisite, but her favour infinite ii 1 59
So painted, to make her fair, that no man counts of her beauty.—How esteemest thou me? I account of her beauty ii 1 65
Let her beauty be her wedding-dower iii 1 78
Say that upon the altar of her beauty You sacrifice your tears, your sighs iii 2 73
When to her beauty I commend my vows, She bids me think how I have been forsworn iv 2 9
Is she kind as she is fair? For beauty lives with kindness iv 2 45
What, have I scaped love-letters in the holiday-time of my beauty? *Mer. Wives* ii 1 2
Thou hast the right arched beauty of the brow that becomes the ship-tire iii 3 59
These black masks Proclaim an enshield beauty *Meas. for Meas.* ii 4 80
Hast neither heat, affection, limb, nor beauty, To make thy riches pleasant iii 1 37
The goodness that is cheap in beauty makes beauty brief in goodness iii 1 186
Hath homely age the alluring beauty took From my poor cheek? *Com. of Errors* ii 1 89
I see the jewel best enamelled Will lose his beauty ii 1 110
Since that my beauty cannot please his eye, I'll weep what's left away ii 1 114
First he did praise my beauty, then my speech iv 2 15
There's her cousin . . . exceeds her as much in beauty as the first of May doth the last of December *M. Ado* i 1 194
Thou wast ever an obstinate heretic in the despite of beauty i 1 237
Beauty is a witch Against whose charms faith melteth into blood ii 1 186
On my eyelids shall conjecture hang, To turn all beauty into thoughts of harm iv 1 108
Will you then write me a sonnet in praise of my beauty? v 2 5
My beauty, though but mean, Needs not the painted flourish of your praise: Beauty is bought by judgement of the eye *L. L Lost* ii 1 13
I thank my beauty, I am fair that shoot iv 1 11
My beauty will be saved by merit! O heresy in fair! iv 1 21
Shall I teach you to know?—Ay, my continent of beauty iv 1 111
Never faith could hold, if not to beauty vow'd! iv 2 110
Beauty doth varnish age, as if new-born iv 3 244
Where is a book? That I may swear beauty doth beauty lack iv 3 251
And beauty's crest becomes the heavens well iv 3 256
When would you . . . Have found the ground of study's excellence Without the beauty of a woman's face? iv 3 301
Where is any author in the world Teaches such beauty as a woman's eye? iv 3 313
As the prompting eyes Of beauty's tutors have enrich'd you with iv 3 323
A light condition in a beauty dark v 2 20
Your beauty, ladies, Hath much deform'd us v 2 766
No fault of mine.—None, but your beauty: would that fault were mine! *M. N. Dream* i 1 201
The lover, all as frantic, Sees Helen's beauty in a brow of Egypt v 1 11
Look on beauty, And you shall see 'tis purchased by the weight *Mer. of Venice* iii 2 88
The beauteous scarf Veiling an Indian beauty iii 2 99
Beauty provoketh thieves sooner than gold *As Y. Like It* i 3 112
Honesty coupled to beauty is to have honey a sauce to sugar iii 3 30
What though you have no beauty iii 5 37
Sweet beauty in her face, Such as the daughter of Agenor had *T. of Shrew* i 1 172
Her beauty and her wit, Her affability and bashful modesty ii 1 48
Praised in every town, Thy virtues spoke of, and thy beauty sounded ii 1 193
I see thy beauty, Thy beauty, that doth make me like thee well ii 1 275
What stars do spangle heaven with such beauty, As those two eyes become that heavenly face? iv 5 31
Sweet Kate, embrace her for her beauty's sake iv 5 34
It blots thy beauty as frosts do bite the meads v 2 139
Like a fountain troubled, Muddy, ill-seeming, thick, bereft of beauty v 2 143
In thee hath estimate, Youth, beauty, wisdom, courage, all That happiness and prime can happy call *All's Well* ii 1 184
He wooes your daughter, Lays down his wanton siege before her beauty iii 7 18
Whose beauty did astonish the survey Of richest eyes v 3 16
As there is no true cuckold but calamity, so beauty's a flower *T. Night* i 5 57
Most radiant, exquisite and unmatchable beauty! i 5 182
'Tis beauty truly blent, whose red and white Nature's own sweet and cunning hand laid on i 5 257
I will give out divers schedules of my beauty i 5 263
Though you were crown'd The nonpareil of beauty i 5 273
Virtue is beauty, but the beauteous evil Are empty trunks o'erflourish'd by the devil iii 4 403
Their transformations Were never for a piece of beauty rarer *W. Tale* iv 4 32
Daffodils, That come before the swallow dares, and take The winds of March with beauty iv 4 120
I'll have thy beauty scratch'd with briers, and made More homely iv 4 436
Your verse Flow'd with her beauty once: 'tis shrewdly ebb'd v 1 102
Sorry Your choice is not so rich in worth as beauty v 1 214
If lusty love should go in quest of beauty, Where should he find it fairer than in Blanch? *K. John* ii 1 426
Such as she is, in beauty, virtue, birth, Is the young Dauphin ii 1 432

Beauty. If that the Dauphin there, thy princely son, Can in this book of beauty read 'I love' *K. John* ii 1 485
She in beauty, education, blood, Holds hand with any princess of the world ii 1 493
Now will canker sorrow eat my bud And chase the native beauty from his cheek iii 4 83
O death, made proud with pure and princely beauty! iv 3 35
When he doom'd this beauty to a grave, Found it too precious-princely for a grave iv 3 39
And stain'd the beauty of a fair queen's cheeks With tears *Richard II.* iii 1 14
Let not us that are squires of the night's body be called thieves of the day's beauty *1 Hen. IV.* i 2 28
Imitate the sun, Who doth permit the base contagious clouds To smother up his beauty from the world i 2 222
Leaves behind a stain Upon the beauty of all parts besides iii 1 188
Rough thistles, kecksies, burs, Losing both beauty and utility *Hen. V.* v 2 53
Old age, that ill layer up of beauty, can do no more spoil upon my face v 2 248
That beauty am I bless'd with which you see *1 Hen. VI.* i 2 86
Liking of the lady's virtuous gifts, Her beauty and the value of her dower v 1 44
O fairest beauty, do not fear nor fly! For I will touch thee but with reverent hands; I kiss these fingers v 3 46
So seems this gorgeous beauty to mine eyes. Fain would I woo her v 3 64
Beauty's princely majesty is such, Confounds the tongue v 3 70
Could I come near your beauty with my nails *2 Hen. VI.* i 3 144
Or as the snake roll'd in a flowering bank, With shining checker'd slough, doth sting a child That for the beauty thinks it excellent iii 1 230
Beauty that the tyrant oft reclaims Shall to my flaming wrath be oil and flax v 2 54
'Tis beauty that doth oft make women proud *3 Hen. VI.* i 4 128
Fame, late entering at his heedful ears, Hath placed thy beauty's image iii 3 64
The leaves and fruit maintain'd with beauty's sun iii 3 126
Your beauty, which did haunt me in my sleep *Richard III.* i 2 122
If I thought that, I tell thee, homicide, These nails should rend that beauty from my cheeks i 2 126
These eyes could never endure sweet beauty's wreck i 2 127
And what these sorrows could not thence exhale, Thy beauty hath i 2 167
Now thy beauty is proposed my fee, My proud heart sues i 2 170
I did kill King Henry, But 'twas thy beauty that provoked me i 2 181
Their lips were four red roses on a stalk, Which in their summer beauty kiss'd each other iv 3 13
O, let her live, And I'll corrupt her manners, stain her beauty iv 4 206
There will be The beauty of this kingdom, I'll assure you *Hen. VIII.* i 3 54
Where this heaven of beauty Shall shine at full upon them i 4 59
They could do no less, Out of the great respect they bear to beauty i 4 69
The fairest hand I ever touch'd! O beauty, Till now I never knew thee! i 4 75
Beauty and honour in her are so mingled That they have caught the king ii 3 76
Opposing freely The beauty of her person to the people iv 1 68
For virtue and true beauty of the soul, For honesty and decent carriage iv 2 144
Nor his beauty.—'Twould not become him; his own's better *Troi. and Cres.* i 2 96
Birth, beauty, good shape, discourse, manhood, learning, gentleness i 2 275
My mask, to defend my beauty i 2 287
And dare avow her beauty and her worth In other arms than hers i 3 271
Thou art as full of envy at his greatness as Cerberus is at Proserpina's beauty ii 1 37
I propose not merely to myself The pleasures such a beauty brings with it ii 2 147
The mortal Venus, the heart-blood of beauty, love's invisible soul iii 1 35
What he shall receive of us in duty Gives us more palm in beauty iii 1 170
Outliving beauty's outward, with a mind That doth renew iii 2 169
The beauty that is borne here in the face The bearer knows not iii 3 103
O beauty! where is thy faith? v 2 67
If beauty have a soul, this is not she v 2 138
Commend my service to her beauty v 5 3
There's the privilege your beauty bears: Fie, treacherous hue! *T. Andron.* iv 2 116
Bit with an envious worm, Ere he can spread his sweet leaves to the air, Or dedicate his beauty to the sun *Rom. and Jul.* i 1 159
Rich in beauty, only poor, That when she dies with beauty dies her store i 1 221
For beauty starved with her severity Cuts beauty off from all posterity i 1 225
What doth her beauty serve, but as a note Where I may read who pass'd that passing fair? i 1 241
Read o'er the volume of young Paris' face, And find delight writ there with beauty's pen i 3 82
Beauty too rich for use, for earth too dear! i 5 49
Did my heart love till now? forswear it, sight! For I ne'er saw true beauty till this night i 5 55
Thy beauty hath made me effeminate iii 1 119
Her beauty makes This vault a feasting presence full of light v 3 85
Death, that hath suck'd the honey of thy breath, Hath had no power yet upon thy beauty v 3 93
Beauty's ensign yet Is crimson in thy lips and in thy cheeks v 3 94
Upon my knees, I charm you, by my once-commended beauty *J. Cæsar* ii 1 271
The chariest maid is prodigal enough, If she unmask her beauty to the moon *Hamlet* i 3 37
The beauty of the world! the paragon of animals! ii 2 319
If you be honest and fair, your honesty should admit no discourse to your beauty iii 1 108
Could beauty, my lord, have better commerce than with honesty? iii 1 109
The power of beauty will sooner transform honesty from what it is to a bawd than the force of honesty can translate beauty into his likeness iii 1 111
No less than life, with grace, health, beauty, honour *Lear* i 1 59
Infect her beauty, You fen-suck'd fogs, drawn by the powerful sun! ii 4 168
Tying her duty, beauty, wit and fortunes In an extravagant and wheeling stranger Of here and every where *Othello* i 1 136
If virtue no delighted beauty lack, Your son-in-law is far more fair than black i 3 290
As having sense of beauty, do omit Their mortal natures ii 1 71
I'll not expostulate with her, lest her body and beauty unprovide my mind again iv 1 218
He hath a daily beauty in his life That makes me ugly v 1 19
Let witchcraft join with beauty, lust with both! *Ant. and Cleo.* ii 1 22
Whose beauty claims No worse a husband than the best of men ii 2 130
If beauty, wisdom, modesty, can settle The heart of Antony ii 2 246
As I told you always, her beauty and her brain go not together *Cymbeline* i 2 32
Let her beauty Look through a casement to allure false hearts ii 4 33
Let there be no honour Where there is beauty; truth, where semblance ii 4 109
For beauty that made barren the swell'd boast Of him that best could speak v 5 162
The beauty of this sinful dame Made many princes thither frame *Per.* i Gower 31

Beauty. Against the face of death, I sought the purchase of a glorious beauty . . . . *Pericles* i 2 72
Beauty's child, whom nature gat For men to see, and seeing wonder at. ii 2 6
Beauty hath his power and will, Which can as well inflame as it can kill ii 2 34
My giving out her beauty stir up the lewdly-inclined . . . iv 2 156
Beauty-waning. A beauty-waning and distressed widow, Even in the afternoon of her best days . . . . *Richard III.* iii 7 185
Beaver. I saw young Harry, with his beaver on . . . 1 *Hen. IV.* iv 1 104
Their armed staves in charge, their beavers down . . . 2 *Hen. IV.* iv 1 120
Big Mars seems bankrupt in their beggar'd host And faintly through a rusty beaver peeps . . . . . . *Hen. V.* iv 2 44
I cleft his beaver with a downright blow . . . . . 3 *Hen. VI.* i 1 12
What, is my beaver easier than it was? . . . . *Richard III.* v 3 50
Tell him from me I'll hide my silver beard in a gold beaver *Troi. and Cres.* i 3 296
Saw you not his face?—O, yes, my lord; he wore his beaver up *Hamlet* i 2 230
Became. Wringing her hands, whose whiteness so became them *T. G. of Ver.* iii 1 227
She became A joyful mother of two goodly sons . *Com. of Errors* i 1 50
At eighteen years became inquisitive After his brother . . . i 1 126
What then became of them I cannot tell . . . . . v 1 354
The Frenchman became his surety and sealed under for another *Mer. of Venice* i 2 88
The tenderness of her nature became as a prey to her grief . *All's Well* iv 3 61
Gasping to begin some speech, her eyes Became two spouts . *W. Tale* iii 3 26
Jupiter Became a bull, and bellow'd; the green Neptune A ram . iv 4 28
What, pray you, became of Antigonus? . . . . . . v 2 64
Which became him like a prince indeed . . . 1 *Hen. IV.* v 2 61
And speaking thick, which nature made his blemish, Became the accents of the valiant . . . . 2 *Hen. IV.* ii 3 25
Became a bricklayer when he came to age . . . 2 *Hen. VI.* iv 2 153
Since every Jack became a gentleman . . . . *Richard III.* i 3 72
Each following day Became the next day's master . . . *Hen. VIII.* i 1 17
Nothing in his life Became him like the leaving it . . . *Macbeth* i 4 8
Being unprepared, Our will became the servant to defect . . ii 1 18
So I alone became their prisoner . . . . . *Hamlet* iv 6 19
Became his guide, Led him, begg'd for him, saved him from despair *Lear* v 3 190
She replied, It should be better he became her guest . *Ant. and Cleo.* ii 2 226
And in's spring became a harvest, lived in court . *Cymbeline* i 1 46
Like fragments in hard voyages, became The life o' the need . . v 3 44
What became of him I further know not . . . . . v 5 285
Because. A woman's reason; I think him so because I think him so *T. G. of Ver.* i 2 24
Forgive me that I do not dream on thee, Because thou see'st me dote . ii 4 173
Wilt thou reach stars, because they shine on thee? . . . iii 1 156
We dare trust you in this kind, Because we know . . . . iii 2 57
Because you are a banish'd man, Therefore, above the rest, we parley to you . . . . iv 1 59
Because he loves her, he despiseth me; Because I love him, I must pity him . . . . iv 4 100
I give thee this for thy sweet mistress' sake, because thou lovest her . iv 4 182
Because that I familiarly sometimes Do use you for my fool *Com. of Errors* ii 2 26
This swain, because of his great limb or joint, shall pass Pompey *L. L. Lost* v 1 135
Because that she as her attendant hath A lovely boy . . *M. N. Dream* ii 1 21
Were it not better, Because that I am more than common tall? *As Y. Like It* i 3 117
Not for because Your brows are blacker . . . . *W. Tale* ii 1 7
And why rail I on this Commodity? But for because he hath not woo'd me yet . . . . *K. John* ii 1 588
Must I back Because that John hath made his peace with Rome? . . v 2 96
And for because the world is populous And here is not a creature but myself, I cannot do it . . . . *Richard II.* v 5 3
Because that I am little, like an ape, He thinks that you should bear me on your shoulders . . . . *Richard III.* iii 1 130
Wherefore not afield?—Because not there: this woman's answer sorts, For womanish it is to be from thence . . *Troi. and Cres.* i 1 109
Why force you this?—Because that now it lies you on to speak *Coriolanus* iii 2 52
They dare not fight with me, because of the queen my mother *Cymbeline* ii 1 21
Bechance. All happiness bechance to thee in Milan! . *T. G. of Ver.* i 1 61
Bechanced. Shall I lack the thought That such a thing bechanced would make me sad? . . . . *Mer. of Venice* i 1 38
My sons, God knows what hath bechanced them . . . 3 *Hen. VI.* i 4 6
Beck. Each in his office ready at thy beck . . . *T. of Shrew* Ind. 2 36
Bell, book, and candle shall not drive me back, When gold and silver becks me to come on . . . . *K. John* iii 3 13
And they have troops of soldiers at their beck . . . 3 *Hen. VI.* i 1 68
What a coil's here! Serving of becks! . . . . . *T. of Athens* i 2 237
With more offences at my beck than I have thoughts to put them in *Hamlet* iii 1 127
Thy beck might from the bidding of the gods Command me *Ant. and Cleo.* iii 11 60
Becked. Whose eye beck'd forth my wars, and call'd them home . iv 12 26
Beckon. He beckons with his hand and smiles on me . . . 1 *Hen. VI.* i 4 92
It beckons you to go away with it, As if it some impartment did desire To you alone . . . . *Hamlet* i 4 58
Iago beckons me; now he begins the story . . . *Othello* iv 1 134
Beckoned. One man beckon'd from the rest below . . *T. of Athens* i 1 74
Beckoning. Not fate, obedience, nor the hand of Mars Beckoning with fiery truncheon my retire . . . . . *Troi. and Cres.* v 3 53
Become. It would become me As well as it does you . . . *Tempest* iii 1 28
She will become thy bed, I warrant . . . . iii 2 112
If you now beheld them, your affections Would become tender . . v 1 19
She hath taught her suitor, He being her pupil, to become her tutor *T. G. of Ver.* ii 1 144
How sayest thou, that my master is become a notable lover? . . ii 5 43
I tell thee, my master is become a hot lover . . . . . ii 5 53
May become a youth Of greater time than I shall show to be . . ii 7 47
The night's dead silence Will well become such sweet-complaining grievance . . . . iii 2 86
Since your falsehood shall become you well To worship shadows . . iv 2 130
That now she is become as black as I . . . . . . iv 4 161
The dozen white louses do become an old coat well . . . *Mer. Wives* i 1 19
I will do as it shall become one that would do reason . . . . i 1 241
Shall I Sir Pandarus of Troy become, And by my side wear steel? . i 3 83
A plain kerchief, Sir John: my brows become nothing else . . . iii 3 63
The night is dark; light and spirits will become it well . . . v 2 14
Do not these fair yokes Become the forest better than the town? . v 5 112
And what shall become of those in the city? . *Meas. for Meas.* i 2 100
What shall become of me?—Come; fear not you . . . . i 2 108
In time the rod Becomes more mock'd than fear'd . . . . i 3 27
Nor the judge's robe, Become them with one half so good a grace As mercy does . . . . ii 2 62
Thy blessed youth Becomes as aged, and doth beg the alms Of palsied eld iii 1 35
Become. This sensible warm motion to become A kneaded clod *Meas. for Meas.* iii 1 120
Nature dispenses with the deed so far That it becomes a virtue . . iii 1 136
If his own life answer the straitness of his proceeding, it shall become him well . . . . iii 2 270
For the most, become much more the better For being a little bad . v 1 445
Look sweet, speak fair, become disloyalty . . *Com. of Errors* iii 2 11
Your silence most offends me, and to be merry best becomes you *M. Ado* ii 1 346
Become the argument of his own scorn by falling in love . . . ii 3 11
Doth not my wit become me rarely?—It is not seen enough . . iii 4 70
Yet Benedick was such another, and now is he become a man . . iii 4 88
What shall become of this? what will this do? . . . . iv 1 211
Nothing becomes him ill that he would well . . . *L. L. Lost* ii 1 46
As it would ill become me to be vain, indiscreet, or a fool . . iv 2 31
And beauty's crest becomes the heavens well . . . . . iv 3 256
Such separation as may well be said Becomes a virtuous bachelor and a maid, So far be distant . . . . *M. N. Dream* ii 2 59
Reason becomes the marshal to my will . . . . . . ii 2 120
Antonio shall become bound; well.—May you stead me? *Mer. of Venice* i 3 6
If it be preferment To leave a rich Jew's service, to become The follower of so poor a gentleman . . . . ii 2 156
Parts that become thee happily enough . . . . . . ii 2 191
I shall end this strife, Become a Christian and thy loving wife . ii 3 21
Such fair ostents of love As shall conveniently become you there . ii 8 45
It [mercy] becomes The throned monarch better than his crown . iv 1 188
That, for this favour, He presently become a Christian . . . iv 1 387
Soft stillness and the night Become the touches of sweet harmony . v 1 57
I will become as liberal as you; I'll not deny him any thing I have . v 1 226
I will no further offend you than becomes me for my good *As Y. Like It* i 1 83
Though it be pity to see such a sight, it well becomes the ground . iii 2 256
Have the grace to consider that tears do not become a man . . iii 4 3
He's proud, and yet his pride becomes him: He'll make a proper man. iii 5 114
I am not furnished like a beggar, therefore to beg will not become me . Epil. 11
Wait you on him, I charge you, as becomes, While I make way *T. of Shrew* i 1 238
Young and beauteous, Brought up as best becomes a gentlewoman . i 2 87
Did ever Dian so become a grove As Kate this chamber? . . . ii 1 260
Go with me to clothe you as becomes you . . . . . iv 2 120
What stars do spangle heaven with such beauty, As those two eyes become that heavenly face? . . . . iv 5 32
That cap of yours becomes you not: Off with that bauble . . . v 2 121
'Tis a hard bondage to become the wife Of a detesting lord . *All's Well* iii 5 67
And extend to you what further becomes his greatness . . . iii 6 74
Such disguise as haply shall become The form of my intent . *T. Night* i 2 54
It becomes me well enough, does't not?—Excellent; it hangs like flax on a distaff . . . . i 3 106
It shall become thee well to act my woes . . . . . . i 4 26
What will become of this? As I am man, My state is desperate . . ii 2 37
Thy smiles become thee well; therefore in my presence still smile . ii 5 191
Shall I play my freedom at tray-trip, and become thy bond-slave? . ii 5 209
I am not tall enough to become the function well . . . . iv 2 8
Even what it please my lord, that shall become him . . . . v 1 119
Derive a liberty From heartiness . . . And well become the agent *W. Tale* i 2 114
You never spoke what did become you less Than this . . . . i 2 282
Your brows are blacker; yet black brows, they say, Become some women best . . . . ii 1 9
The office Becomes a woman best; I'll take't upon me . . . ii 2 32
With such a kind of love as might become A lady like me . . iii 2 65
Sir, my gracious lord, To chide at your extremes it not becomes me . iv 4 6
I would I had some flowers o' the spring that might Become your time of day . . . . iv 4 114
It becomes thy oath full well, Thou to me thy secrets tell . . iv 4 306
A father Is at the nuptial of his son a guest That best becomes the table iv 4 407
Where you shall have such receiving As shall become your highness . iv 4 538
She shall be habited as it becomes The partner of your bed . . iv 4 557
Let me have no lying: it becomes none but tradesmen . . . iv 4 745
I speak amazedly; and it becomes My marvel and my message . . v 1 187
When she was young you woo'd her; now in age Is she become the suitor? v 3 109
O, well did he become that lion's robe That did disrobe the lion! *K. John* ii 1 141
Being but the shadow of your son, Becomes a sun and makes your son a shadow . . . . ii 1 500
France friend with England, what becomes of me? . . . . iii 1 35
Then I should not love thee, no, nor thou Become thy great birth. . iii 1 50
Or as a little snow, tumbled about, Anon becomes a mountain . . iii 4 177
Glister like the god of war, When he intendeth to become the field . v 1 55
To be a make-peace shall become my age . . . . . *Richard II.* i 1 160
Let them die that age and sullens have; For both hast thou, and both become the grave . . . . ii 1 140
But what, o' God's name, doth become of this? . . . . . ii 1 251
What is become of Bushy? where is Green? . . . . . . iii 2 123
Ten thousand bloody crowns of mothers' sons Shall ill become the flower of England's face . . . . iii 3 97
When triumph is become an alehouse guest . . . . . . v 1 15
Have the hanging of the thieves and so become a rare hangman 1 *Hen. IV.* i 2 76
If I become not a cart as well as another man, a plague on my bringing up! . . . . ii 4 545
I care not if I do become your physician . . . . . 2 *Hen. IV.* i 2 143
Are now become enamour'd on his grave . . . . . . i 3 102
What are you brawling here? Doth this become your place? . . ii 1 72
If they become me not, he was a fool that taught them me . . ii 1 204
What a maidenly man-at-arms are you become! . . . . . ii 2 83
Such things become the hatch and brood of time . . . . . iii 1 86
I dare say my cousin William is become a good scholar . . . iii 2 11
And now is this Vice's dagger become a squire. . . . . . iii 2 343
Delivered o'er to the voice, the tongue, which is the birth, becomes excellent wit . . . . iv 3 110
He is become very hot and valiant . . . . iv 3 132
How quickly nature falls into revolt When gold becomes her object! . iv 5 67
Yet be sad, good brothers, For, by my faith, it very well becomes you . v 2 50
How ill white hairs become a fool and jester! . . . . . v 5 52
God and his angels guard your sacred throne And make you long become it!—Sure, we thank you . . . . *Hen. V.* i 2 8
In peace there's nothing so becomes a man As modest stillness and humility . . . . iii 1 3
As I am a soldier, A name that in my thoughts becomes me best . . iii 3 6
This becomes the great. Sorry am I his numbers are so few . . iii 5 55
Yon island carrions, desperate of their bones, Ill-favouredly become the morning field . . . . iv 2 40
Or do not learn for want of time, The sciences that should become our country . . . . v 2 58
Becomes it thee to taunt his valiant age? . . . . 1 *Hen. VI.* iii 2 54

Become. Doth my uncle Burgundy revolt?—He doth, my lord, and is become your foe *1 Hen. VI.* iv 1 65
O thou, whose wounds become hard-favour'd death, Speak to thy father! iv 7 23
Set this diamond safe In golden palaces, as it becomes v 3 170
Such commendations as becomes a maid v 3 177
You shall become true liegemen to his crown v 4 128
First of the king: what shall of him become? *2 Hen. VI.* i 4 32
No malice, sir; no more than well becomes So good a quarrel ii 1 27
How insolent of late he is become, How proud, how peremptory! iii 1 7
That head of thine doth not become a crown v 1 96
I cannot joy, until I be resolved Where our right valiant father is become. I saw him in the battle *3 Hen. VI.* ii 1 10
Now my soul's palace is become a prison ii 1 74
Proud insulting boy! Becomes it thee to be thus bold in terms? ii 2 85
Henry, sole possessor of my love, Is of a king become a banish'd man iii 3 25
Tell me some reason why the Lady Grey Should not become my wife iv 1 26
King Lewis Becomes your enemy, for mocking him iv 1 30
But, madam, where is Warwick then become? iv 4 25
The readiest way to make the wench amends Is to become her husband *Richard III.* i 1 156
Much it joys me too, To see you are become so penitent i 2 221
I'll join with black despair against my soul, And to myself become an enemy ii 2 37
Inter their bodies as becomes their births v 5 15
And is become as black As if besmear'd in hell *Hen. VIII.* i 2 123
To the hall, to hear what shall become Of the great Duke of Buckingham ii 1 2
What will become of me now, wretched lady! iii 1 146
What's become of Katharine, The princess dowager? iv 1 22
Love and meekness, lord, Become a churchman better than ambition v 3 63
He had better starve Than but once think this place becomes thee not. v 3 133
'Twould not become him; his own's better *Troi. and Cres.* i 2 97
I think his smiling becomes him better than any man in all Phrygia i 2 135
And here, to do you service, am become As new into the world iii 3 11
What's become of the wenching rogues? I think they have swallowed one another v 4 35
Let us revenge this with our pikes, ere we become rakes *Coriolanus* i 1 24
Considering how honour would become such a person i 3 11
Away, you fool! it [blood] more becomes a man Than gilt his trophy i 3 42
Our very priests must become mockers, if they shall encounter such ridiculous subjects as you are ii 1 93
The wounds become him ii 1 135
This paltering Becomes not Rome iii 1 59
And bereaves the state Of that integrity which should become't iii 1 159
Do not take His rougher accents for malicious sounds, But, as I say, such as become a soldier iii 3 56
But let us give him burial, as becomes *T. Andron.* i 1 347
Is Lavinia then become so loose, Or Bassianus so degenerate? ii 1 65
Then must my earth with her continual tears Become a deluge iii 1 230
A deed of death done on the innocent Becomes not Titus' brother iii 2 57
The law that threaten'd death becomes thy friend *Rom. and Jul.* iii 3 139
Thou'rt a churl; ye've got a humour there Does not become a man *T. of Athens* i 2 27
That answer might have become Apemantus ii 2 125
The commonwealth of Athens is become a forest of beasts iv 3 352
These words become your lips as they pass through them v 1 198
And this man Is now become a god *J. Cæsar* i 2 116
Sound them, it doth become the mouth as well; Weigh them, it is as heavy i 2 145
It would become me better than to close In terms of friendship with thine enemies iii 1 202
And in the pulpit, as becomes a friend, Speak in the order of his funeral iii 1 229
So well thy words become thee as thy wounds; They smack of honour *Macbeth* i 2 43
I dare do all that may become a man; Who dares do more is none i 7 46
I must become a borrower of the night For a dark hour or twain iii 1 27
Would well become A woman's story at a winter's fire iii 4 64
O, how the wheel becomes it! It is the false steward *Hamlet* iv 5 172
Youth no less becomes The light and careless livery that it wears Than settled age his sables iv 7 79
Such a sight as this Becomes the field, but here shows much amiss v 2 413
Ask her forgiveness? Do you but mark how this becomes the house *Lear* ii 4 155
Sorrow would be a rarity most beloved, If all could so become it iv 3 26
Men Are as the time is: to be tender-minded Does not become a sword v 3 32
Whatever shall become of Michael Cassio, He's never any thing but your true servant *Othello* iii 3 8
And is become the bellows and the fan To cool a gipsy's lust *A. and C.* i 1 9
Whom every thing becomes, to chide, to laugh, To weep i 1 49
Present pleasure, By revolution lowering, does become The opposite of itself i 2 129
How this Herculean Roman does become The carriage of his chafe i 3 84
This becomes him,—As his composure must be rare indeed Whom these things cannot blemish i 4 21
Be'st thou sad or merry, The violence of either thee becomes i 5 60
'Tis a worthy deed, And shall become you well ii 2 2
For vilest things Become themselves in her; that the holy priests Bless her ii 2 244
Near him, thy angel Becomes a fear, as being o'erpower'd ii 3 22
I shall see you in your soldier's dress, Which will become you ii 4 5
Enjoy thy plainness, It nothing ill becomes thee ii 6 81
Who does i' the wars more than his captain can Becomes his captain's captain iii 1 22
Observe how Antony becomes his flaw iii 12 34
Fare thee well, dame, whate'er becomes of me: This is a soldier's kiss iv 4 29
Patience is sottish, and impatience does Become a dog that's mad iv 15 80
Weep no more, lest I give cause To be suspected of more tenderness Than doth become a man *Cymbeline* i 1 95
No further halting: satisfy me home What is become of her iii 5 93
Though valour Becomes thee well enough iv 2 156
And to become the geck and scorn O' th' other's villany v 4 67
Who worse than a physician Would this report become? v 5 28
How well this honest mirth becomes their labour! *Pericles* ii 1 99
Prepare for mirth, for mirth becomes a feast ii 3 7
In your armours, as you are address'd, Will very well become a soldier's dance ii 3 95
No visor does become black villany So well as soft and tender flattery iv 4 44
Becomed. Gave him what becomed love I might *Rom. and Jul.* iv 2 26
A good rebuke, Which might have well becomed the best of men *Ant. and Cleo.* ii 7 27
He would have well becomed this place *Cymbeline* v 5 406
Becomest. And joy that thou becomest King Henry's friend *3 Hen. VI.* iii 3 201
Becomest. Bravely thou becomest thy bed, fresh lily, And whiter than the sheets! *Cymbeline* ii 2 15
Becoming. But a merrier man, Within the limit of becoming mirth, I never spent an hour's talk withal *L. L. Lost* ii 1 67
I never saw a vessel of like sorrow, So fill'd and so becoming *W. Tale* iii 3 22
A gentle business, and becoming The action of good women *Hen. VIII.* ii 3 54
My becomings kill me, when they do not Eye well to you *Ant. and Cleo.* i 3 96
A doubt In such a time nothing becoming you, Nor satisfying us *Cymb.* iv 4 15
And will fit you With dignities becoming your estates v 5 22
If thou hadst drunk to him, 't had been a kindness Becoming well thy fact: what canst thou say? *Pericles* iv 3 12
Bed. Whom I, with this obedient steel, three inches of it, Can lay to bed for ever *Tempest* ii 1 284
She will become thy bed, I warrant. And bring thee forth brave brood iii 2 112
Sour-eyed disdain and discord shall bestrew The union of your bed with weeds iv 1 21
I wish Myself were mudded in that oozy bed Where my son lies v 1 151
My bosom as a bed Shall lodge thee *T. G. of Ver.* i 2 114
I was in love with my bed: I thank you, you swinged me for my love ii 1 87
My will is even this: That presently you hie you home to bed iv 2 94
I wash, wring, brew, bake, scour, dress meat and drink, make the beds *Mer. Wives* i 4 102
Go to bed when she list, rise when she list, all is as she will ii 2 124
My bed shall be abused, my coffers ransacked ii 2 306
Upon a true contract I got possession of Julietta's bed *Meas. for Meas.* i 2 150
And strip myself to death, as to a bed That longing have been sick for. ii 4 102
If for this night he entreat you to his bed, give him promise of satisfaction iii 1 275
Should she kneel down in mercy of this fact, Her brother's ghost his paved bed would break v 1 440
Would that alone, alone he would detain, So he would keep fair quarter with his bed! *Com. of Errors* ii 1 108
Keep then fair league and truce with thy true bed ii 2 147
'Tis double wrong, to truant with your bed And let her read it in thy looks iii 2 17
Your weeping sister is no wife of mine, Nor to her bed no homage do I owe iii 2 43
Spread o'er the silver waves thy golden hairs, And as a bed I'll take them iii 2 49
One that thinks a man always going to bed and says 'God give you good rest!' iv 3 32
In bed he slept not for my urging it v 1 63
Doth not the gentleman Deserve as full as fortunate a bed As ever Beatrice shall couch upon? *Much Ado* iii 1 45
Call at all the ale-houses, and bid those that are drunk get them to bed iii 3 46
Let us go sit here upon the church-bench till two, and then all to bed iii 3 96
She knows the heat of a luxurious bed iv 1 42
Never rest, But seek the weary beds of people sick *L. L. Lost* v 2 832
I have forsworn his bed and company *M. N. Dream* ii 1 62
You come To give their bed joy and prosperity ii 1 73
Find you out a bed; For I upon this bank will rest my head ii 2 39
One heart, one bed, two bosoms and one troth ii 2 42
Here is my bed: sleep give thee all his rest! ii 2 64
What angel wakes me from my flowery bed? iii 1 132
To have my love to bed and to arise iii 1 174
Damned spirits all, That in crossways and floods have burial, Already to their wormy beds are gone iii 2 384
Faintness constraineth me To measure out my length on this cold bed iii 2 429
Sit thee down upon this flowery bed, While I thy amiable cheeks do coy iv 1 1
More than to us Wait in your royal walks, your board, your bed! v 1 31
The iron tongue of midnight hath told twelve: Lovers, to bed v 1 371
Sweet friends, to bed v 1 375
But here an angel in a golden bed Lies all within *Mer. of Venice* ii 7 58
Take what wife you will to bed, I will ever be your head ii 9 70
Till I come again, No bed shall e'er be guilty of my stay iii 2 329
Shall I say to you, . . . let their beds Be made as soft as yours? iv 1 95
I will ne'er come in your bed Until I see the ring v 1 190
I'll not deny him any thing I have, No, not my body nor my husband's bed v 1 228
Whether till the next night she had rather stay, Or go to bed now v 1 303
I see no more in you Than without candle may go dark to bed *As Y. L. It* iii 5 39
Till you met your wife's wit going to your neighbour's bed iv 1 171
Wedding is great Juno's crown: O blessed bond of board and bed! v 4 148
You to your land and love and great allies: You to a long and well-deserved bed v 4 196
Go to thy cold bed, and warm thee *T. of Shrew* Ind. 1 10; *Lear* iii 4 48
Were he not warm'd with ale, This were a bed but cold to sleep so soundly *T. of Shrew* Ind. 1 33
What think you, if he were convey'd to bed, Wrapp'd in sweet clothes? Ind. 1 37
Rings put upon his fingers, A most delicious banquet by his bed Ind. 1 39
Take him up gently and to bed with him Ind. 1 72
Sweeter than the lustful bed On purpose trimm'd up for Semiramis Ind. 2 40
Being all this time abandon'd from your bed Ind. 2 117
Madam, undress you and come now to bed Ind. 2 119
Have expressly charged, In peril to incur your former malady, That I should yet absent me from your bed Ind. 2 125
Woo her, wed her and bed her and rid the house of her! i 1 149
Keep you warm.—Marry, so I mean, sweet Katharine, in thy bed ii 1 269
Some undeserved fault I'll find about the making of the bed iv 1 203
Come, Kate, we'll to bed. We three are married, but you two are sped v 2 184
On's bed of death Many receipts he gave me *All's Well* i 1 107
And in your bed Find fairer fortune, if you ever wed! ii 3 97
Thou know'st she has raised me from my sickly bed ii 3 118
Although before the solemn priest I have sworn, I will not bed her ii 3 287
I'll to the Tuscan wars, and never bed her ii 3 290
When you have conquer'd my yet maiden bed, Remain there but an hour iv 2 57
She would never put it from her finger, Unless she gave it to yourself in bed v 3 110
You shall as easy Prove that I husbanded her bed v 3 126
I was in that credit with them at that time that I knew of their going to bed v 3 264
Here I quit him: He knows himself my bed he hath defiled v 3 301
Away before me to sweet beds of flowers *T. Night* i 1 40
To be up after midnight and to go to bed then, is early ii 3 8
To go to bed after midnight is to go to bed betimes ii 3 8
Do not think I have wit enough to lie straight in my bed: I know I can ii 3 148
For this night, to bed, and dream on the event ii 3 191
I'll go burn some sack; 'tis too late to go to bed now ii 3 207
Big enough for the bed of Ware in England iii 2 51
To bed! ay, sweet-heart, and I'll come to thee iii 4 33

Bed. Behold me A fellow of the royal bed . . . *W. Tale* iii 2 39
The marigold, that goes to bed wi' the sun And with him rises weeping iv 4 105
Is there not milking-time, when you are going to bed? . . . iv 4 247
A usurer's wife was brought to bed of twenty money-bags . . . iv 4 266
To die upon the bed my father died . . . iv 4 466
She shall be habited as it becomes The partner of your bed . . . iv 4 558
To bless the bed of majesty again With a sweet fellow to't . . . v 1 33
I was seduced To make room for him in my husband's bed . *K. John* i 1 255
My bed was ever to thy son as true As thine was to thy husband . . ii 1 124
From their fixed beds of lime Had been dishabited . . . ii 1 219
Rescue those breathing lives to die in beds, That here come sacrifices for the field . . . ii 1 419
Shall gild her bridal bed and make her rich In titles, honours . . ii 1 491
Lies in his bed, walks up and down with me, Puts on his pretty looks . iii 4 94
That bed, that womb, . . . that fashion'd thee Made him a man *Rich. II.* i 2 22
Convey me to my bed, then to my grave . . . ii 1 137
Made a divorce betwixt his queen and him, Broke the possession of a royal bed . . . iii 1 13
And send the hearers weeping to their beds . . . v 1 45
Thou dost suspect That I have been disloyal to thy bed . . . v 2 105
Time enough to go to bed with a candle, I warrant thee . 1 *Hen. IV.* ii 1 48
This fortnight been A banish'd woman from my Harry's bed . . . ii 3 42
What doth gravity out of his bed at midnight? . . . ii 4 325
Doth he keep his bed?—He did, my lord, four days ere I set forth . iv 1 21
A merry song, come: it grows late; we'll to bed . 2 *Hen. IV.* ii 4 300
O thou dull god, why liest thou with the vile In loathsome beds? . . iii 1 16
Please it your grace To go to bed . . . iii 1 99
The block of death, Treason's true bed and yielder up of breath . . iv 2 123
Come hither, Harry, sit thou by my bed . . . iv 5 182
He is very sick, and would to bed . . . *Hen. V.* ii 1 87
I put my hand into the bed and felt them, and they were as cold as any stone . . . ii 3 25
Do as every sick man in his bed, wash every mote out of his conscience iv 1 189
Laid in bed majestical, Can sleep so soundly as the wretched slave . iv 1 284
Fell jealousy, Which troubles oft the bed of blessed marriage . . v 2 392
If I did but stir out of my bed, Ready they were to shoot me 1 *Hen. VI.* i 4 55
Thus are poor servitors, When others sleep upon their quiet beds, Constrain'd to watch . . . ii 1 6
'Twas time, I trow, to wake and leave our beds, Hearing alarums at our chamber-doors . . . ii 1 41
Roused on the sudden from their drowsy beds . . . ii 2 23
And may ye both be suddenly surprised By bloody hands, in sleeping on your beds! . . . v 3 41
Whom his grace affects, Must be companion of his nuptial bed . . v 5 58
I banish her my bed and company . . . 2 *Hen. VI.* ii 1 197
Have you laid fair the bed? Is all things well? . . . iii 2 11
Dead in his bed, my lord; Gloucester is dead . . . iii 2 29
Thy mother took into her blameful bed Some stern untutor'd churl . . iii 2 212
Died he not in his bed? where should he die? Can I make men live? . iii 3 9
If dreams prove true.—You were best to go to bed and dream again . v 1 196
I here divorce myself Both from thy table, Henry, and thy bed 3 *Hen. VI.* i 1 248
He took a beggar to his bed, And graced thy poor sire with his bridal-day . . . ii 2 154
His viands sparkling in a golden cup, His body couched in a curious bed . . . ii 5 53
The king by this is set him down to sleep.—What, will he not to bed? . iv 3 3
Will encounter with our glorious sun, Ere he attain his easeful western bed . . . v 3 6
He that will not fight for such a hope, Go home to bed . . . v 4 56
What, is he in his bed?—He is . . . *Richard III.* i 1 142
And made her widow to a woful bed . . . i 2 249
By her, in his unlawful bed, he got This Edward . . . iii 7 190
O ill-dispersing wind of misery! O my accursed womb, the bed of death! . . . iv 1 54
And, when thou wed'st, let sorrow haunt thy bed! . . . iv 1 74
Never yet one hour in his bed Have I enjoy'd the golden dew of sleep . iv 1 83
Slander myself as false to Edward's bed; Throw over her the veil of infamy . . . iv 4 207
And lead thy daughter to a conqueror's bed . . . iv 4 334
Alas, has banish'd me his bed already, His love, too long ago! *Hen. VIII.* iii 1 119
So went to bed; where eagerly his sickness Pursued him still . . iv 2 24
Nay, Patience, You must not leave me yet: I must to bed . . . iv 2 166
I must to him too, Before he go to bed. I'll take my leave . . . v 1 9
Prithee, to bed; and in thy prayers remember The estate of my poor queen . . . v 1 73
Her bed is India; there she lies, a pearl . . *Troi. and Cres.* i 1 103
Upon a lazy bed the livelong day Breaks scurril jests . . . i 3 147
On his press'd bed lolling, From his deep chest laughs out a loud applause . . . i 3 162
Whereupon I will show you a chamber with a bed . . . iii 2 216
Cupid grant all tongue-tied maidens here Bed, chamber, Pandar! . . iii 2 220
Trouble him not; To bed, to bed: sleep kill those pretty eyes! . . iv 2 4
I prithee now, to bed.—Are you a-weary of me? . . . iv 2 7
Thy master now lies thinking in his bed Of thee and me . . . v 2 78
My half-supp'd sword, that frankly would have fed, Pleased with this dainty bait, thus goes to bed . . . v 8 20
I should freelier rejoice in that absence wherein he won honour than in the embracements of his bed . . . *Coriolanus* i 3 5
Whose hours, whose bed, whose meal, and exercise, Are still together . iv 4 14
And triumphs over chance in honour's bed . . . *T. Andron.* i 1 178
I never wept, Because they died in honour's lofty bed . . . iii 1 11
As Tarquin erst, That left the camp to sin in Lucrece' bed . . . iv 1 64
His wife but yesternight was brought to bed . . . iv 2 153
To draw The shady curtains from Aurora's bed . . . *Rom. and Jul.* i 1 142
Dreamers often lie.—In bed asleep, while they do dream things true . i 4 52
Come on then, let's to bed. Ah, sirrah, by my fay, it waxes late . . i 5 127
If he be married, My grave is like to be my wedding bed . . . i 5 137
He is wise; And, on my life, hath stol'n him home to bed . . . ii 1 4
It argues a distemper'd head So soon to bid good-morrow to thy bed . ii 3 34
Here I hit it right, Our Romeo hath not been in bed to-night . . ii 3 42
He made you for a highway to my bed; But I, a maid, die maiden-widowed . . . iii 2 134
O, she says nothing, sir, but weeps and weeps; And now falls on her bed iii 3 100
Commend me to thy lady; And bid her hasten all the house to bed . . iii 3 156
Go you to Juliet ere you go to bed, Prepare her, wife . . . iii 4 31
Make the bridal bed In that dim monument where Tybalt lies . . . iii 5 202
Take thou this vial, being then in bed, And this distilled liquor drink thou . . . iv 1 93
When the bridegroom in the morning comes To rouse thee from thy bed, there art thou dead . . . iv 1 108

Bed. I'll not to bed to-night; let me alone; I'll play the housewife for this once . . . *Rom. and Jul.* iv 2 42
Good night: Get thee to bed, and rest; for thou hast need . . . iv 3 13
Get you to bed; faith, you'll be sick to-morrow For this night's watching . . . iv 4 7
Let the county take you in your bed; He'll fright you up, i' faith . . iv 5 10
Sweet flower, with flowers thy bridal bed I strew . . . v 3 12
Why I descend into this bed of death, Is partly to behold my lady's face v 3 28
Maid, to thy master's bed; Thy mistress is o' the brothel! *T. of Athens* iv 1 12
Melted down thy youth In different beds of lust . . . iv 3 257
Thou bright defiler [gold] Of Hymen's purest bed! thou valiant Mars! iv 3 384
Get you to bed again; it is not day . . . *J. Cæsar* ii 1 39
Break off betimes, And every man hence to his idle bed . . . ii 1 117
You've ungently, Brutus, Stole from my bed . . . ii 1 238
What, is Brutus sick, And will he steal out of his wholesome bed? . . ii 1 264
To keep with you at meals, comfort your bed, And talk to you sometimes ii 1 284
But this bird Hath made his pendent bed and procreant cradle *Macbeth* i 6 8
Go bid thy mistress, when my drink is ready, She strike upon the bell. Get thee to bed . . . ii 1 32
Was it so late, friend, ere you went to bed, That you do lie so late? . ii 3 24
I have seen her rise from her bed, throw her nightgown upon her, unlock her closet, take forth paper, fold it, write upon't, read it, afterwards seal it, and again return to bed . . . v 1 5
I have known those which have walked in their sleep who have died holily in their beds . . . v 1 67
To bed, to bed! there's knocking at the gate: come, come, come, come v 1 73
What's done cannot be undone.—To bed, to bed, to bed! . . . v 1 76
'Tis now struck twelve; get thee to bed, Francisco. . . *Hamlet* i 1 7
Lust, though to a radiant angel link'd, Will sate itself in a celestial bed i 5 56
Let not the royal bed of Denmark be A couch for luxury . . . i 5 82
A second time I kill my husband dead, When second husband kisses me in bed . . . iii 2 195
She desires to speak with you in her closet, ere you go to bed . . iii 2 344
I'll call upon you ere you go to bed, And tell you what I know . . iii 3 34
Or in his rage, Or in the incestuous pleasure of his bed . . . iii 3 90
Nay, but to live In the rank sweat of an enseamed bed . . . iii 4 92
Go not to mine uncle's bed; Assume a virtue, if you have it not . . iii 4 159
Let the bloat king tempt you again to bed; Pinch wanton on your cheek . . . iii 4 182
That, for a fantasy and trick of fame, Go to their graves like beds . iv 4 62
So would I ha' done, by yonder sun, An thou hadst not come to my bed iv 5 66
A son for her cradle ere she had a husband for her bed . . *Lear* i 1 16
Within a dull, stale, tired bed . . . i 2 13
On my knees I beg That you'll vouchsafe me raiment, bed, and food . ii 4 158
If he ask for me, I am ill, and gone to bed . . . iii 3 18
We'll go to supper i' the morning. So, so, so.—And I'll go to bed at noon . . . iii 6 92
Nor aught I heard of business Hath raised me from my bed . . *Othello* i 3 54
Hath made the flinty and steel couch of war My thrice-driven bed of down . . . i 3 232
What will I do, thinkest thou?—Why, go to bed, and sleep . . . i 3 305
Players in your housewifery, and housewives in your beds . . . ii 1 113
You rise to play and go to bed to work . . . ii 1 116
In quarter, and in terms like bride and groom Devesting them for bed . ii 3 181
What's the matter?—All's well now, sweeting; come away to bed . . ii 3 252
His bed shall seem a school, his board a shrift . . . iii 3 24
There's millions now alive That nightly lie in those unproper beds Which they dare swear peculiar . . . iv 1 69
Strangle her in her bed, even the bed she hath contaminated . . . iv 1 221
Prithee, to-night Lay on my bed my wedding sheets: remember . . iv 2 105
Get you to bed on the instant; I will be returned forthwith . . . iv 3 7
He hath commanded me to go to bed, And bade me to dismiss you . . iv 3 13
I have laid those sheets you bade me on the bed . . . iv 3 22
Thy bed, lust-stain'd, shall with lust's blood be spotted . . . v 1 36
Will you come to bed, my lord?—Have you pray'd to-night, Desdemona? v 2 24
I am bound to speak: My mistress here lies murder'd in her bed . . v 2 185
Look on the tragic loading of this bed; This is thy work . . . v 2 363
Mine, and most of our fortunes, to-night, shall be—drunk to bed *Ant. and Cleo.* i 2 46
Let us grant, it is not Amiss to tumble on the bed of Ptolemy . . i 4 17
She made great Cæsar lay his sword to bed . . . ii 2 232
And next morn, Ere the ninth hour, I drunk him to his bed . . . ii 5 21
For what good turn?—For the best turn i' the bed . . . ii 5 59
The beds i' the east are soft; and thanks to you, That call'd me timelier . ii 6 51
My nightingale, We have beat them to their beds . . . iv 8 19
I will be A bridegroom in my death, and run into't As to a lover's bed . iv 14 101
Take up her bed; And bear her women from the monument . . v 2 359
More noble than that runagate to your bed . . . *Cymbeline* i 6 137
To bed: Take not away the taper, leave it burning . . . ii 2 4
How bravely thou becomest thy bed, fresh lily, And whiter than the sheets! . . . ii 2 15
Such and such pictures; there the window; such The adornment of her bed . . . ii 2 26
If you can make't apparent That you have tasted her in bed . . . ii 4 57
Thy mistress, Pisanio, hath played the strumpet in my bed . . . iii 4 22
False to his bed! What is it to be false? To lie in watch there and to think on him? . . . iii 4 42
Do't, and to bed then.—I'll wake mine eye-balls blind first . . . iii 4 103
For two nights together Have made the ground my bed . . . iii 6 3
Why, he but sleeps: If he be gone, he'll make his grave a bed . . iv 2 216
Nature doth abhor to make his bed With the defunct . . . iv 2 357
My queen Upon a desperate bed, and in a time When fearful wars point at me . . . iv 3 6
If in your country wars you chance to die, That is my bed too, lads . iv 4 52
Being an ugly monster, 'Tis strange he hides him in fresh cups, soft beds v 3 71
But a man that were to sleep your sleep, and a hangman to help him to bed, I think he would change places with his officer . . . v 4 179
She an eater of her mother's flesh, By the defiling of her parent's bed *Pericles* i 1 131
Many worthy princes' bloods were shed, To keep his bed of blackness unlaid ope . . . i 2 89
Since they love men in arms as well as beds . . . ii 3 98
And then with what haste you can get you to bed . . . ii 5 93
Hymen hath brought the bride to bed . . . iii Gower 9
He went to bed to her very description . . . iv 2 109
Thunder shall not so awake the beds of eels . . . iv 2 155

Bedabbled with the dew and torn with briers . . *M. N. Dream* iii 2 443

Bedashed. All the standers-by had wet their cheeks, Like trees bedash'd with rain . . . *Richard III.* i 2 164

Bedaubed. Pale, pale as ashes, all bedaub'd in blood . *Rom. and Jul.* iii 2 55

Bedazzled. My mistaking eyes, That have been so bedazzled *T. of Shrew* iv 5 46
Bed-chamber. Your bed-chamber.—I'll rest betide the chamber where thou liest! *Richard III.* i 2 111
Gave't you the king?—To his own hand, in's bedchamber *Hen. VIII.* iii 2 77
If I were a man, Their mother's bed-chamber should not be safe *T. And.* iv 1 108
Breeds him and makes him of his bed-chamber. *Cymbeline* i 1 42
Since My lord hath interest in them, I will keep them In my bedchamber i 6 196
First, her bedchamber,—Where, I confess, I slept not ii 4 66
Bed-clothes. In his sleep he does little harm, save to his bed-clothes *All's Well* iv 3 287
Bedded. Therefore my son i' the ooze is bedded *Tempest* iii 3 100
I have wedded her, not bedded her *All's Well* iii 2 23
Your bedded hair, like life in excrements, Start up *Hamlet* iii 4 121
Bede. Where's Bede? *Mer. Wives* v 5 53
Bedeck. Abound'st in all, And usest none in that true use indeed Which should bedeck thy shape *Rom. and Jul.* iii 3 125
Bedecking. Garnished With such bedecking ornaments of praise *L. L. Lost* ii 1 79
Bedew Her pastures' grass with faithful English blood *Richard II.* iii 3 99
Let all the tears that should bedew my hearse Be drops of balm *2 Hen. IV.* iv 5 114
To add to your laments, Wherewith you now bedew King Henry's hearse *1 Hen. VI.* i 1 104
Bedfellow. Misery acquaints a man with strange bed-fellows *Tempest* ii 2 42
Were you her bedfellow last night?—No, truly not; although, until last night, I have this twelvemonth been her bedfellow *Much Ado* iv 1 149
I'll have that doctor for my bedfellow *Mer. of Venice* v 1 233
Sweet doctor, you shall be my bedfellow v 1 284
Happy the parents of so fair a child; Happier the man, whom favourable stars Allot thee for his lovely bed-fellow! *T. of Shrew* iv 5 41
And how doth my cousin, your bedfellow? and your fairest daughter? *2 Hen. IV.* iii 2 6
Why doth the crown lie there upon his pillow, Being so troublesome a bedfellow? iv 5 22
Nay, but the man that was his bedfellow *Hen. V.* ii 2 8
Would it not grieve an able man to leave So sweet a bedfellow? *Hen. VIII.* ii 2 143
He loves your people; But tie him not to be their bedfellow *Coriolanus* ii 2 69
Go, you wild bedfellow, you cannot soothsay *Ant. and Cleo.* i 2 51
'Faith, I'll lie down and sleep. But, soft! no bedfellow! *Cymbeline* iv 2 295
To seek her as a bed-fellow, In marriage-pleasures play-fellow *Pericles* i Gower 33
Bedford. Harry the king, Bedford and Exeter *Hen. V.* iv 3 53
Bedford, if thou be slack, I'll fight it out *1 Hen. VI.* i 1 99
The Duke of Bedford had a prisoner Call'd the brave Lord Ponton i 4 27
Ere we go, regard this dying prince, The valiant Duke of Bedford iii 2 87
Courageous Bedford, let us now persuade you.—Not to be gone from hence iii 2 93
Heavens keep old Bedford safe! And now no more ado iii 2 100
Before we go, let's not forget The noble Duke of Bedford late deceased iii 2 132
Did my brother Bedford toil his wits, To keep by policy what Henry got? *2 Hen. VI.* i 1 83
Shall Henry's conquest, Bedford's vigilance, Your deeds of war and all our counsel die? i 1 96
Bed-hangings. These bed-hangings and these fly-bitten tapestries *2 Hen. IV.* ii 1 158
Bedimmed. I have bedimm'd The noontide sun *Tempest* v 1 41
Bedlam, have done.—I have but this to say *K. John* ii 1 183
Art thou bedlam? dost thou thirst, base Trojan, To have me fold up Parca's fatal web? *Hen. V.* v 1 20
And such high vaunts of his nobility Did instigate the bedlam *2 Hen. VI.* iii 1 51
To Bedlam with him! is the man grown mad? v 1 131
A bedlam and ambitious humour Makes him oppose himself v 1 132
Villanous melancholy, with a sigh like Tom o' Bedlam *Lear* i 2 148
The country gives me proof and precedent Of Bedlam beggars ii 3 14
Let's follow the old earl, and get the Bedlam To lead him where he would iii 7 103
Bed-mate. Nothing but heavenly business Should rob my bed-mate of my company *Troi. and Cres.* iv 1 5
Bed-presser. This bed-presser, this horse-back-breaker *1 Hen. IV.* ii 4 268
Bedrench. Such crimson tempest should bedrench The fresh green lap of fair King Richard's land *Richard II.* iii 3 46
Bed-rid. Her decrepit, sick and bedrid father *L. L. Lost* i 1 139
Lies he not bed-rid? and again does nothing But what he did being childish? *W. Tale* iv 4 412
Impotent and bed-rid, scarcely hears Of this his nephew's purpose *Hamlet* i 2 29
Bed-right. No bed-right shall be paid Till Hymen's torch be lighted *Tempest* iv 1 96
Bed-room. Then by your side no bed-room me deny *M. N. Dream* ii 2 51
Bed-swerver. She's A bed-swerver *W. Tale* ii 1 93
Bed-time. And afterward consort you till bed-time *Com. of Errors* i 2 28
Three hours Between our after-supper and bed-time *M. N. Dream* v 1 34
I would 'twere bed-time, Hal, and all well *1 Hen. IV.* v 1 125
Bedward. As merry as when our nuptial day was done, And tapers burn'd to bedward *Coriolanus* i 6 32
Bed-work. They call this bed-work, mappery, closet-war *Troi. and Cres.* i 3 205
Bee. Each pinch more stinging Than bees that made 'em *Tempest* i 2 330
Where the bee sucks, there suck I: In a cowslip's bell I lie v 1 88
Injurious wasps, to feed on such sweet honey And kill the bees that yield it with your stings! *T. G. of Ver.* i 2 107
Seldom when the bee doth leave her comb In the dead carrion *2 Hen. IV.* iv 4 79
Like the bee, culling from every flower The virtuous sweets iv 5 75
We bring it to the hive, and, like the bees, Are murdered for our pains iv 5 78
So bees with smoke and doves with noisome stench Are from their hives and houses driven away *1 Hen. VI.* i 5 23
Like an angry hive of bees That want their leader *2 Hen. VI.* iii 2 125
Some say the bee stings: but I say, 'tis the bee's wax iv 2 89
We'll follow where thou lead'st, Like stinging bees in hottest summer's day Led by their master *T. Andron.* v 1 14
For your words, they rob the Hybla bees, And leave them honeyless *J. Cæsar* v 1 34
Good wax, thy leave. Blest be You bees that make these locks of counsel! *Cymbeline* iii 2 36
We would purge the land of these drones, that rob the bee of her honey *Pericles* ii 1 51
Beef. She hath eaten up all her beef, and she is herself in the tub *Meas. for Meas.* iii 2 58
Flesh taken from a man Is not so estimable, profitable neither, As flesh of muttons, beefs, or goats *Mer. of Venice* i 3 168
If you give me any conserves, give me conserves of beef *T. of Shrew* Ind. 2 8
What say you to a piece of beef and mustard?—A dish that I do love iv 3 23
The mustard is too hot a little.—Why then, the beef, and let the mustard rest iv 3 26
You shall have the mustard, Or else you get no beef iv 3 28
Any thing thou wilt.—Why then, the mustard without the beef iv 3 30
I am a great eater of beef and I believe that does harm to my wit *T. Night* i 3 90
Beef. O, my sweet beef, I must still be good angel to thee *1 Hen. IV.* iii 3 199
And now has he land and beefs *2 Hen. IV.* iii 2 353
Give them great meals of beef and iron and steel *Hen. V.* iii 7 161
Ay, but these English are shrewdly out of beef iii 7 164
Or cut not out the burly-boned clown in chines of beef *2 Hen. VI.* iv 10 61
Beef-witted. Thou mongrel beef-witted lord! *Troi. and Cres.* ii 1 14
Bee-hives. Drones suck not eagles' blood but rob bee-hives *2 Hen. VI.* iv 1 109
Beelzebub. Knock, knock, knock! Who's there, i' the name of Beelzebub? *Macbeth* ii 3 4
Been. He hath been all this day to look you *As Y. Like It* ii 5 34
Or that I could forget what I have been, Or not remember what I must be now! *Richard II.* iii 3 138
Undoing all, as all had never been! *2 Hen. VI.* i 1 103
It had been so with us, had we been there *Hamlet* iv 1 13
I am sorry to find you thus: I have been to seek you *Othello* v 1 81
Put forth to seas, Where when men been, there's seldom ease *Pericles* ii Gower 28
My name, Pericles; My education been in arts and arms ii 3 82
Beer. Doth it not show vilely in me to desire small beer? *2 Hen. IV.* ii 2 8
By my troth, I do now remember the poor creature, small beer ii 2 13
A pot of good double beer, neighbour: drink, and fear not *2 Hen. VI.* ii 3 65
I will make it felony to drink small beer: all the realm shall be in common iv 2 73
To suckle fools and chronicle small beer *Othello* ii 1 161
Beer-barrel. Why of that loam, whereto he was converted, might they not stop a beer-barrel? *Hamlet* v 1 235
Beest. If thou beest Stephano, touch me and speak to me . . . If thou beest Trinculo, come forth *Tempest* ii 2 104
Speak once in thy life, if thou beest a good moon-calf iii 2 25
If thou beest a man, show thyself in thy likeness: if thou beest a devil, take't as thou list iii 2 137
Whether thou be'st he or no, Or some enchanted trifle to abuse me, As late I have been, I not know v 1 111
If thou be'st Prospero, Give us particulars of thy preservation v 1 134
If thou be'st the man That hadst a wife once call'd Æmilia *Com. of Errors* v 1 341
If thou be'st rated by thy estimation, Thou dost deserve enough *Mer. of Venice* ii 7 26
If that thou be'st found So near our public court as twenty miles, Thou diest for it *As Y. Like It* i 3 45
If thou beest not damned for this, the devil himself will have no shepherds iii 2 88
If thou be'st not an ass, I am a youth of fourteen *All's Well* ii 3 106
If thou beest yet a fresh uncropped flower, Choose thou thy husband v 3 327
If thou beest capable of things serious, thou must know the king is full of grief *W. Tale* iv 4 791
If ever thou beest mine, Kate, as I have a saving faith within me *Hen. V.* v 2 216
If, after three days' space, thou here be'st found On any ground that I am ruler of, The world shall not be ransom for thy life *2 Hen. VI.* iii 2 295
If thou be'st death, I'll give thee England's treasure ii 3 2
If thou beest not immortal, look about you *J. Cæsar* ii 3 7
If that thou be'st a Roman, take it forth iv 3 103
Come hither. If thou be'st valiant, . . . list me *Othello* ii 1 216
Disprove this villain, if thou be'st a man v 2 172
Be'st thou sad or merry, The violence of either thee becomes *Ant. and Cleo.* i 5 59
Bee's-wax. Some say the bee stings: but I say, 'tis the bee's wax *2 Hen. VI.* iv 2 89
Beetle. All the charms Of Sycorax, toads, beetles, bats, light on you! *Tempest* i 2 340
The poor beetle, that we tread upon, In corporal sufferance finds a pang as great As when a giant dies *Meas. for Meas.* iii 1 79
Beetles black, approach not near *M. N. Dream* ii 2 22
If I do, fillip me with a three-man beetle *2 Hen. IV.* i 2 255
The shard-borne beetle with his drowsy hums Hath rung night's yawning peal *Macbeth* iii 2 42
The dreadful summit of the cliff That beetles o'er his base *Hamlet* i 4 71
Choughs that wing the midway air Show scarce so gross as beetles *Lear* iv 6 14
They are his shards, and he their beetle *Ant. and Cleo.* iii 2 20
And often, to our comfort, shall we find The sharded beetle in a safer hold Than is the full-wing'd eagle *Cymbeline* iii 3 20
Beetle brows. Here are the beetle brows shall blush for me *Rom. and Jul.* i 4 32
Beetle-headed, flap-ear'd knave! *T. of Shrew* iv 1 160
Befall. Do look to know What doth befall you here *Meas. for Meas.* i 1 59
So befall my soul As this is false he burdens me withal! *Com. of Errors* v 1 208
Now fair befall your mask!—Fair fall the face it covers! *L. L. Lost* ii 1 124
Befall what will befall, I'll jest a twelvemonth in an hospital v 2 880
I beseech your grace that I may know The worst that may befall me *M. N. Dream* i 1 63
Those things do best please me That befal preposterously iii 2 121
It doth befall That I, one Snout by name, present a wall v 1 156
Now, fair befal thee, good Petruchio! The wager thou hast won *T. of Shrew* v 2 111
But jealousy what might befall your travel *T. Night* iii 3 8
It grieves me Much more for what I cannot do for you Than what befalls myself iii 4 371
Many years of happy days befal My gracious sovereign! *Richard II.* i 1 20
Plain well-meaning soul, Whom fair befal in heaven! ii 1 129
More blessed hap did ne'er befall our state *1 Hen. VI.* i 6 10
And peace, no war, befall thy parting soul! ii 5 115
O, let me stay, befall what may befall! *2 Hen. VI.* iii 2 402
And more such days as these to us befall! v 3 33
What danger or what sorrow can befall thee? *3 Hen. VI.* iv 1 76
So doth my heart misgive me, in these conflicts What may befall him iv 6 95
Now fair befall thee and thy noble house *Richard III.* i 3 282
Now, fair befall you! he deserved his death iii 5 47
Befall what may befall, I'll speak no more *T. Andron.* v 1 57
Since the affairs of men rest still incertain, Let's reason with the worst that may befall *J. Cæsar* v 1 97
Catch at mine intent By what did here befal me *Ant. and Cleo.* ii 2 42
Madam, all joy befal your grace! *Cymbeline* iii 5 9
Befallen. Dilate at full What hath befall'n of them and thee *Com. of Errors* i 1 124
What hath then befallen, Or what hath this bold enterprise brought forth? *2 Hen. IV.* i 1 177
I come to tell you things sith then befall'n *3 Hen. VI.* ii 1 106
Learn What late misfortune is befall'n King Edward iv 4 3
And cited up a thousand fearful times, During the wars of York and Lancaster That had befall'n us *Richard III.* i 4 16
How now! what hath befall'n? *Hamlet* iv 3 11
I could heartily wish this had not befallen; but, since it is as it is, mend it for your own good *Othello* ii 3 304
You shall understand what hath befall'n, Which, as I think, you know not v 2 307

Befell. Mark how heavily this befell to the poor gentlewoman *M. for Meas.* iii 1 227
Lo, what befel! he threw his eye aside, And mark what object did present itself *As Y. Like It* iv 3 103
I'll tell thee what befel me on a day In this self-place 3 *Hen. VI.* iii 1 10
Befit. They'll tell the clock to any business that We say befits the hour *Tempest* ii 1 290
You may conceal her, As best befits her wounded reputation *Much Ado* iv 1 243
How is't with aged Gaunt?—O, how that name befits my composition! *Richard II.* ii 1 73
Good Master Silence, it well befits you should be of the peace 2 *Hen. IV.* iii 2 98
It ill befits thy state And birth, that thou shouldst stand 3 *Hen. VI.* iii 3 2
Mirthful comic shows, Such as befits the pleasure of the court v 7 44
Blind is his love and best befits the dark *Rom. and Jul.* ii 1 32
So far ask pardon as befits mine honour To stoop in such a case *A. and C.* ii 2 97
Your entertain shall be As doth befit our honour and your worth *Pericles* i 1 120
My father, it befits not me Unto a stranger knight to be so bold ii 3 66
Befitted. It us befitted To bear our hearts in grief *Hamlet* i 2 2
Befitting. A chronicle of day by day, Not a relation for a breakfast nor Befitting this first meeting *Tempest* v 1 165
Before. Not a blemish, But fresher than before i 2 219
If it should thunder as it did before, I know not where to hide my head ii 2 23
When the butt is out, we will drink water; not a drop before iii 2 2
As I told thee before, I am subject to a tyrant iii 2 48
Before you can say 'come' and 'go,' And breathe twice iv 1 44
I drink the air before me v 1 102
Of whom so often I have heard renown, But never saw before v 1 194
Lovers break not hours, Unless it be to come before their time *T. G. of Ver.* v 1 5
If thou seest her before me, commend me *Mer. Wives* i 4 168
They say, if money go before, all ways do lie open ii 2 175
I had rather, forsooth, go before you like a man than follow him like a dwarf iii 2 5
As I told you before, John and Robert, be ready here iii 3 9
I'll speak it before the best lord iii 3 53
Besides these, other bars he lays before me iii 4 7
Hath taught me more wit than ever I learned before in my life iv 5 62
Call hither, I say, bid come before us Angelo *Meas. for Meas.* i 1 16
My wife, sir, whom I detest before heaven and your honour ii 1 69
Let me not find you before me again upon any complaint ii 1 260
Plays such fantastic tricks before high heaven As make the angels weep ii 2 121
Shall I attend your lordship?—At any time 'fore noon ii 2 160
He'ld yield them up, Before his sister should her body stoop ii 4 182
He must before the deputy, sir; he has given him warning iii 2 35
My absence was not six months old Before herself . . . Had made provision for her following me *Com. of Errors* i 1 46
Weeping before for what she saw must come i 1 72
O, let me say no more! Gather the sequel by that went before i 1 96
Was carried with more speed before the wind i 1 110
Are you there, wife? you might have come before iii 1 63
And now let's go hand in hand, not one before another v 1 425
Once before he won it of me with false dice *Much Ado* ii 1 289
O, that is stronger made Which was before barr'd up with ribs of iron! iv 1 153
Submissive fall his princely feet before *L. L. Lost* iv 1 92
A little western flower, Before milk-white, now purple with love's wound *M. N. Dream* ii 1 167
Well I wot Thou runn'st before me, shifting every place iii 2 423
I am sent with broom before, To sweep the dust behind the door v 1 396
One that comes before To signify the approaching of his lord *M. of Ven.* ii 9 87
Then treble that, Before a friend of this description Shall lose a hair iii 2 304
We were Christians enow before; e'en as many as could well live iii 5 24
Know you before whom, sir?—Ay, better than him I am before knows me *As Y. Like It* i 1 45
Swayed in the back and shoulder-shotten; near-legged before *T. of Shrew* iii 2 57
You will away to-night?—I must away to-day, before night come iii 2 192
I confess, Here on my knee, before high heaven and you, That before you, and next unto high heaven, I love your son *All's Well* i 3 198
'Fore whose throne 'tis needful, Ere I can perfect mine intents, to kneel iv 4 3
I tell thee so before, because I would not fall out with thee iv 5 60
How much the better To fall before the lion than the wolf! *T. Night* iii 1 140
They have been grand-jurymen since before Noah was a sailor iii 2 18
To prate and talk for life and honour 'fore Who please to come *W. Tale* iii 2 42
I'll not be long before I call upon thee iii 3 8
But, come on, Contract us 'fore these witnesses iv 4 401
Not a month 'Fore your queen died, she was more worth such gazes v 1 226
Even before this truce, but new before *K. John* iii 1 233
Assured loss before the match be play'd iii 1 336
The better foot before iv 2 170; *T. Andron.* ii 3 192
Use all your power To stop their marches 'fore we are inflamed *K. John* v 1 7
Get thee before to Coventry; fill me a bottle of sack 1 *Hen. IV.* iv 2 1
I was before Master Tisick, the debuty, t'other day 2 *Hen. IV.* ii 4 92
And to us all That feel the bruises of the days before iv 1 100
Then, set forward.—Before, and greet his grace: my lord, we come iv 1 228
A little time before That our great-grandsire, Edward, sick'd and died iv 4 127
For, God before, We'll chide this Dauphin at his father's door *Hen. V.* i 2 307
Yet, God before, tell him we will come on iii 6 165
The farced title running 'fore the king iv 1 280
Let it not disgrace me, If I demand, before this royal view v 2 32
I know thee well, though never seen before 1 *Hen. VI.* i 2 67
Before we met or that a stroke was given, Like to a trusty squire did run away iv 1 22
Then take my soul, my body, soul and all, Before that England give the French the foil v 3 23
How canst thou tell she will deny thy suit, Before thou make a trial? v 3 76
France should have torn and rent my very heart, Before I would have yielded to this league 2 *Hen. VI.* i 1 127
I must offend before I be attainted ii 4 59
And my consent ne'er ask'd herein before! This is close dealing ii 4 72
Shall we after them?—After them! nay, before them, if we can v 3 28
Make speed; Or else come after: I'll away before 3 *Hen. VI.* ii 5 136
We shall have more wars before't be long iv 6 91
We are contented To wear our mortal state to come with her, Katharine our queen, before the primest creature That's paragon'd o' the world *Hen. VIII.* ii 4 229
I am not Samson, nor Sir Guy, nor Colbrand, To mow 'em down before me v 4 23
You follow the young Lord Paris?—Ay, sir, when he goes before me *Troi. and Cres.* iii 1 3
Before him he carries noise, and behind him he leaves tears *Coriolanus* ii 1 174
That prefer A noble life before a long iii 1 153
'Tis this slave;—Go whip him 'fore the people's eyes iv 6 60
Your soldiers use him as the grace 'fore meat, Their talk at table iv 7 3
Before. He moves like an engine, and the ground shrinks before his treading *Coriolanus* v 4 20
This before all the world do I prefer *T. Andron.* iv 2 109
Marry, go before to field, he'll be your follower *Rom. and Jul.* iii 1 61
That I should purchase the day before for a little part *T. of Athens* iii 2 52
By all the gods that Romans bow before! *J. Cæsar* ii 1 320
Thou art so far before That swiftest wing of recompense is slow To overtake thee *Macbeth* i 4 16
Had he his hurts before?—Ay, on the front v 8 46
Before my God, I might not this believe *Hamlet* i 1 56
He that made us with such large discourse, Looking before and after iv 4 37
The grace of heaven, Before, behind thee and on every hand, Enwheel thee round! *Othello* ii 1 86
To-morrow, Before the sun shall see's *Ant. and Cleo.* iv 8 3
You must not so far prefer her 'fore ours of Italy *Cymbeline* i 4 70
Madam, you're best consider.—I see before me, man iii 2 80
Whose false oaths prevail'd Before my perfect honour iii 3 67
Yet who this should be, Doth miracle itself, loved before me iv 2 29
Since death of my dear'st mother It did not speak before iv 2 191
If that thy gentry, Britain, go before This lout as he exceeds our lords v 2 8
Some slain before; some dying; some their friends O'er-borne v 3 47
Before thee stands this fair Hesperides, With golden fruit *Pericles* i 1 27
I am thinking of the poor men that were cast away before us even now ii 1 19
Before God! *Much Ado* ii 3; iv 2; *All's Well* ii 3; 1 *Hen. IV.* v 3; 2 *Hen. IV.* ii 2; iii 2; v 3; *Hen. V.* ii 2; v 2; *Hamlet* ii 2; *Othello* ii 3
Before me! *All's Well* ii 3; *T. Night* ii 3; *Coriolanus* i 1; *Othello* iv 1
Before the gods *T. of Athens* iii 2 19; iii 2 54
Before-breach. Punished for before-breach of the king's laws *Hen. V.* iv 1 179
Beforehand. O, let us pay the time but needful woe, Since it hath been beforehand with our griefs *K. John* v 7 111
Before-time. I have Before-time seen him thus *Coriolanus* i 6 24
Befortune. Recking as little what betideth me As much I wish all good befortune you *T. G. of Ver.* iv 3 41
Befriend. And if thou please, Thou mayst befriend me *K. John* v 6 10
And God befriend us, as our cause is just! 1 *Hen. IV.* v 1 120
My rest and negligence befriends thee now *Troi. and Cres.* v 6 17
O earth, I will befriend thee more with rain *T. Andron.* iii 1 16
Will you befriend me so far, as to use mine own words? *T. of Athens* iii 2 64
I shall beseech him to befriend himself *J. Cæsar* ii 4 30
Befriended. If in his death the gods have us befriended, Great Troy is ours *Troi. and Cres.* v 9 9
O happy man! they have befriended thee *T. Andron.* iii 1 52
Beg. A smaller boon than this I cannot beg *T. G. of Ver.* v 4 24
That I do beg his life, if it be sin, Heaven let me bear it! *Meas. for Meas.* ii 4 69
Thy blessed youth Becomes as aged, and doth beg the alms Of palsied eld iii 1 35
Immediate sentence then and sequent death Is all the grace I beg v 1 379
Beg thou, or borrow, To make up the sum, And live *Com. of Errors* i 1 154
I shall beg with it from door to door iv 4 41
How I would make him fawn and beg and seek And wait the season! *L. L. Lost* v 2 62
O vain petitioner! beg a greater matter v 2 207
Thou bid'st me beg: this begging is not strange v 2 210
You cannot beg us, sir, I can assure you, sir; we know what we know v 2 490
I beg the ancient privilege of Athens, As she is mine *M. N. Dream* i 1 41
I do but beg a little changeling boy, To be my henchman ii 1 120
What worser place can I beg in your love? ii 1 208
When thou wakest, if she be by, Beg of her for remedy iii 2 109
I'll to my queen and beg her Indian boy iii 2 375
I beg the law, the law, upon his head iv 1 160
Down therefore and beg mercy of the duke *Mer. of Venice* iv 1 363
Beg that thou mayst have leave to hang thyself iv 1 364
You are liberal in offers: You taught me first to beg iv 1 439
And what wilt thou do? beg, when that is spent? *As Y. Like It* i 1 79
What, wouldst thou have me go and beg my food? ii 3 31
I am not furnished like a beggar, therefore to beg will not become me Epil. 11
Wilt thou needs be a beggar?—I do beg your good will in this case *All's Well* i 3 23
You beg a single penny more: come, you shall ha't; save your word v 2 39
You beg more than 'word,' then v 2 42
And on our knees we beg, As recompense of our dear services *W. Tale* ii 3 149
A race or two of ginger, but that I may beg iv 3 51
I'ld beg your precious mistress, Which he counts but a trifle v 1 223
Upon my knee I beg, go not to arms *K. John* iii 1 308
I do not ask you much, I beg cold comfort v 7 42
I'll beg one boon, And then be gone and trouble you no more *Richard II.* iv 1 302
Being so great, I have no need to beg.—Yet ask.—And shall I have? iv 1 309
Pity me, open the door: A beggar begs that never begg'd before v 3 78
Yet such extenuation let me beg 1 *Hen. IV.* iii 2 22
He came but to be Duke of Lancaster, To sue his livery and beg his peace iv 3 62
There is no seeming mercy in the king.—Did you beg any? God forbid! v 2 36
And they are for the town's end, to beg during life v 3 39
It is worse shame to beg than to be on the worst side 2 *Hen. IV.* i 2 88
Never shall you see that I will beg A ragged and forestall'd remission v 2 37
My lord, most humbly on my knee I beg The leading of the vaward *Hen. V.* iv 3 129
I beg mortality, Rather than life preserved with infamy 1 *Hen. VI.* iv 5 32
Take me hence; I care not whither, for I beg no favour 2 *Hen. VI.* ii 4 92
But she's come to beg, Warwick, to give 3 *Hen. VI.* iii 1 42
That love which virtue begs and virtue grants iii 2 63
At his hands beg mercy? And he shall pardon thee v 1 23
And humbly beg the death upon my knee *Richard III.* i 2 179
If thy poor devoted suppliant may But beg one favour at thy gracious hand i 2 208
Entreat for me, As you would beg, were you in my distress i 4 273
This do I beg of God, When I am cold in zeal to you or yours ii 1 39
She now begs, That little thought, when she set footing here, She should have bought her dignities so dear *Hen. VIII.* iii 1 182
Pardon me; 'Twas not my purpose, thus to beg a kiss *Troi. and Cres.* iii 2 145
May I, sweet lady, beg a kiss of you?—You may.—I do desire it.—Why, beg, then iv 5 47
I, that now Refused most princely gifts, am bound to beg *Coriolanus* i 9 80
Nor, showing, as the manner is, his wounds To the people, beg their stinking breaths ii 1 252
Why in this woolvish toge should I stand here, To beg of Hob and Dick? ii 3 123
To beg of thee, it is my more dishonour Than thou of them iii 2 124
Make them know what 'tis to let a queen Kneel in the streets and beg for grace in vain *T. Andron.* i 1 455
'Tis present death I beg; and one thing more ii 3 173
Upon my feeble knee I beg this boon, with tears not lightly shed iii 3 289
Beg at the gates, like Tarquin and his queen iii 1 299

Beg. Villains, for shame you could not beg for grace *T. Andron.* v 2 180
Turn'd weeping out, To beg relief among Rome's enemies v 3 106
I beg for justice, which thou, prince, must give *Rom. and Jul.* iii 1 185
Beg, starve, die in the streets, For, by my soul, I'll ne'er acknowledge thee iii 5 194
I beg of you to know me, good my lord, To accept my grief *T. of Athens* iv 3 494
To beg enfranchisement for Publius Cimber *J. Cæsar* iii 1 57
O Antony, beg not your death of us iii 1 164
To beg the voice and utterance of my tongue iii 1 261
Yea, beg a hair of him for memory iii 2 139
Speak then to me, who neither beg nor fear Your favours nor your hate *Macbeth* i 3 60
Let me find him, fortune! And more I beg not v 7 23
What wouldst thou beg, Laertes, That shall not be my offer? *Hamlet* i 2 45
Here stooping to your clemency, We beg your hearing patiently iii 2 161
In the fatness of these pursy times Virtue itself of vice must pardon beg iii 4 154
And when you are desirous to be bless'd, I'll blessing beg of you iii 4 172
To-morrow shall I beg leave to see your kingly eyes iv 7 45
He could nothing do but wish and beg Your sudden coming o'er, to play with him iv 7 105
Such-a-one, that praised my lord such-a-one's horse, when he meant to beg it v 1 94
Be then desired By her, that else will take the thing she begs *Lear* i 4 269
On my knees I beg That you'll vouchsafe me raiment, bed, and food ii 4 157
Squire-like, pension beg To keep base life afoot ii 4 217
Madman and beggar too.—He has some reason, else he could not beg iv 1 33
I therefore beg it not, To please the palate of my appetite *Othello* i 3 262
We, ignorant of ourselves, Beg often our own harms *Ant. and Cleo.* ii 1 6
And I will boot thee with what gift beside Thy modesty can beg ii 5 72
He partly begs To be desired to give iii 13 66
Majesty, to keep decorum, must No less beg than a kingdom v 2 18
Then, if you can, Be pale: I beg but leave to air this jewel *Cymbeline* ii 4 96
I do not bid thee beg my life, good lad; And yet I know thou wilt v 5 101
Would now be glad of bread, and beg for it *Pericles* i 4 41
He asks of you, that never used to beg ii 1 66
Hark you, my friend; you said you could not beg.—I did but crave ii 1 90
What mean you, sir?—To beg of you, kind friends, this coat of worth ii 1 142
Beg pardon . *As Y. Like It* iii 5; *All's Well* v 3; *Richard II.* v 2; *2 Hen. IV.* Epil.; *2 Hen. VI.* iii 2; *Rom. and Jul.* iii 3; iv 2

Began. My very visor began to assume life and scold with her *Much Ado* ii 1 248
My lungs began to crow like chanticleer *As Y. Like It* ii 7 30
This carol they began that hour, With a hey, and a ho v 3 27
Mark'd you not how her sister Began to scold? *T. of Shrew* i 1 177
This his good melancholy oft began *All's Well* i 2 56
My words are as full of peace as matter.—Yet you began rudely *T. Night* i 5 228
Who began to be much sea-sick *W. Tale* v 2 128
That ended when I but began v 3 45
Began to give me ground: but I followed me close *1 Hen. IV.* ii 4 240
Nay, let it rest where it began at first *1 Hen. VI.* iv 1 121
When the dusky sky began to rob My earnest-gaping sight *2 Hen. VI.* iii 2 104
O, then began the tempest to my soul *Richard III.* i 4 44
First I began in private With you *Hen. VIII.* ii 4 206
How youngly he began to serve his country, How long continued *Coriolanus* ii 3 244
I would he had continued to his country As he began iv 2 31
I look'd toward Birnam, and anon, methought, The wood began to move *Macbeth* v 5 35
His grief grew puissant, and the strings of life Began to crack *Lear* v 3 217
Speak, who began this? on thy love, I charge thee *Othello* ii 3 178
Give me to know How this foul rout began, who set it on ii 3 210
'Tis monstrous. Iago, who began't? ii 3 217
Then began A stop i' the chaser, a retire, anon A rout *Cymbeline* v 3 39
Therein He was as calm as virtue—he began His mistress' picture v 5 174
Thaisa was my mother, who did end The minute I began *Pericles* v 1 214

Beganest. Was't not to this end That thou began'st to twist so fine a story? *Much Ado* i 1 313

Beget. Did beget of him A falsehood in its contrary as great As my trust was *Tempest* i 2 94
'Tis not in hate of you, But rather to beget more love *T. G. of Ver.* iii 1 97
His eye begets occasion for his wit *L. L. Lost* ii 1 69
Such friends as time in Padua shall beget *T. of Shrew* i 1 45
Fear, and not love, begets his penitence *Richard II.* v 3 56
And these two beget A generation of still-breeding thoughts v 5 7
These lies are like their father that begets them *1 Hen. IV.* ii 4 250
Now attest That those whom you call'd fathers did beget you *Hen. V.* iii 1 23
Thy friendship makes us fresh.—And doth beget new courage in our breasts *1 Hen. VI.* iii 3 87
I did beget her, all the parish knows v 4 11
Henry, son unto a conqueror, Is likely to beget more conquerors v 5 74
What stratagems . . . This deadly quarrel daily doth beget! *3 Hen. VI.* ii 5 91
If to have done the thing you gave in charge Beget your happiness, be happy then *Richard III.* iv 3 26
I will beget Mine issue of your blood upon your daughter iv 4 297
Live, and beget a happy race of kings! v 3 157
On my Christian conscience, this one christening will beget a thousand *Hen. VIII.* v 4 38
And hot blood begets hot thoughts, and hot thoughts beget hot deeds *Troi. and Cres.* iii 1 141
Cunningly effected, will beget A very excellent piece of villany *T. Andron.* ii 3 6
Till time beget some careful remedy iv 3 30
Where the bull and cow are both milk-white, They never do beget a coal-black calf v 1 32
You must acquire and beget a temperance that may give it smoothness *Hamlet* iii 2 8
Some blood drawn on me would beget opinion Of my more fierce endeavour *Lear* ii 1 35
One self mate and mate could not beget Such different issues iv 3 36
Unless a man would marry a gallows and beget young gibbets *Cymbeline* v 4 207
Seldom but that pity begets you a good opinion *Pericles* iv 2 131
O, come hither, Thou that beget'st him that did thee beget! v 1 197

Begettest. O, come hither, Thou that beget'st him that did thee beget! v 1 197

Begetting. I lost a couple, that 'twixt heaven and earth Might thus have stood begetting wonder *W. Tale* v 1 133
O heavy times, begetting such events! *3 Hen. VI.* ii 5 63
They are the issue of your loins, my liege, And blood of your begetting *Cymbeline* v 5 331

Beggar. They will not give a doit to relieve a lame beggar *Tempest* ii 2 34
To speak puling, like a beggar at Hallowmas *T. G. of Ver.* ii 1 26
I say to thee, he would mouth with a beggar, though she smelt brown bread and garlic *Meas. for Meas.* iii 2 194

Beggar. Four suits of peach-coloured satin, which now peaches him a beggar *Meas. for Meas.* iv 3 13
I bear it on my shoulders, as a beggar wont her brat *Com. of Errors* iv 4 40
Is not marriage honourable in a beggar? *Much Ado* iii 4 30
Why had I not with charitable hand Took up a beggar's issue at my gates? iv 1 134
Is there not a ballad, boy, of the King and the Beggar? *L. L. Lost* i 2 115
Pernicious and indubitate beggar Zenelophon iv 1 67
To whom came he? to the beggar: what saw he? the beggar: who overcame he? the beggar iv 1 74
The captive is enriched: on whose side? the beggar's iv 1 77
Thou the beggar; for so witnesseth thy lowliness iv 1 81
A beggar, that was used to come so smug upon the mart *Mer. of Venice* iii 1 48
Now methinks You teach me how a beggar should be answer'd iv 1 440
Be married under a bush like a beggar *As Y. Like It* iii 3 85
I am not furnished like a beggar, therefore to beg will not become me Epil. 10
When he wakes, Would not the beggar then forget himself? *T. of Shrew* Ind. 1 41
Who for this seven years hath esteemed him No better than a poor and loathsome beggar Ind. 1 123
Beggars, that come unto my father's door, Upon entreaty have a present alms iv 3 4
Wilt thou needs be a beggar?—I do beg your good will *All's Well* i 3 22
The king's a beggar, now the play is done Epil. 335
The king lies by a beggar, if a beggar dwell near him *T. Night* iii 1 9
The matter, I hope, is not great, sir, begging but a beggar: Cressida was a beggar iii 1 62
Mannerly distinguishment leave out Betwixt the prince and beggar *W. Tale* ii 1 87
He that wins of all, Of kings, of beggars, old men, young men, maids *K. John* ii 1 570
Like a poor beggar, raileth on the rich ii 1 592
Whiles I am a beggar, I will rail And say there is no sin but to be rich ii 1 593
Pity me, open the door: A beggar begs that never begg'd before *Rich. II.* v 3 78
Our scene is alter'd from a serious thing, And now changed to 'The Beggar and the King' v 3 80
Like silly beggars Who sitting in the stocks refuge their shame, That many have and others must sit there v 5 25
Sometimes am I king; Then treasons make me wish myself a beggar v 5 33
Moody beggars, starving for a time Of pellmell havoc and confusion *1 Hen. IV.* v 1 81
Barren, barren, barren; beggars all, beggars all! *2 Hen. IV.* v 3 8
Canst thou, when thou command'st the beggar's knee, Command the health of it? *Hen. V.* iv 1 273
Beggars mounted run their horse to death *3 Hen. VI.* i 4 127
He took a beggar to his bed, And graced thy poor sire with his bridal-day ii 2 154
I'll strike thee to my foot, And spurn upon thee, beggar *Richard III.* i 2 42
It [conscience] beggars any man that keeps it i 4 145
A begging prince what beggar pities not? i 4 274
A beggar, brother?—Of my kind uncle, that I know will give iii 1 112
You will part but with light gifts; In weightier things you'll say a beggar nay iii 1 119
Lash hence these overweening rags of France, These famish'd beggars v 3 329
This masque Was cried incomparable; and the ensuing night Made it a fool and beggar *Hen. VIII.* i 1 28
A beggar's book Outworths a noble's blood i 1 122
Beggar the estimation which you prized Richer than sea and land *Troi. and Cres.* ii 2 91
They pass'd by me As misers do by beggars iii 3 143
Speaking is for beggars; he wears his tongue in's arms iii 3 271
The honour'd number, Who lack not virtue, no, nor power, but that Which they have given to beggars *Coriolanus* iii 1 74
A beggar's tongue Make motion through my lips! iii 2 117
They are but beggars that can count their worth *Rom. and Jul.* ii 6 32
Being holiday, the beggar's shop is shut. What, ho! apothecary! v 1 56
I will choose Mine heir from forth the beggars of the world *T. of Athens* i 1 138
What a beggar his heart is, Being of no power to make his wishes good i 2 201
If I want gold, steal but a beggar's dog, And give it Timon ii 1 5
He does deny him, in respect of his, What charitable men afford to beggars iii 2 82
I was so unfortunate a beggar iii 6 48
His poor self, A dedicated beggar to the air iv 2 13
Raise me this beggar, and deny't that lord iv 3 9
The senator shall bear contempt hereditary, The beggar native honour iv 3 11
Thou 'ldst courtier be again, Wert thou not beggar iv 3 242
Who in spite put stuff To some she beggar and compounded thee Poor rogue hereditary iv 3 273
I had rather be a beggar's dog than Apemantus iv 3 361
Let the famish'd flesh slide from the bone, Ere thou relieve the beggar iv 3 536
When beggars die, there are no comets seen *J. Cæsar* ii 2 30
Then are our beggars bodies, and our monarchs and outstretched heroes the beggars' shadows *Hamlet* ii 2 269
Beggar that I am, I am even poor in thanks; but I thank you ii 2 280
Your fat king and your lean beggar is but variable service, two dishes, but to one table iv 3 25
To show you how a king may go a progress through the guts of a beggar iv 3 33
Art nothing but the composition of a knave, beggar, coward, pandar *Lear* ii 2 23
The country gives me proof and precedent Of Bedlam beggars ii 3 14
Our basest beggars Are in the poorest thing superfluous ii 4 267
So beggars marry many iii 2 30
Fellow, where goest?—Is it a beggar-man?—Madman and beggar too iv 1 32
What thing was that Which parted from you?—A poor unfortunate beggar iv 6 68
Thou hast seen a farmer's dog bark at a beggar? iv 6 159
A beggar in his drink Could not have laid such terms upon his callat *Othello* iv 2 120
Who's born that day When I forget to send to Antony, Shall die a beggar *Ant. and Cleo.* i 5 65
Never palates more the dug, The beggar's nurse and Cæsar's v 2 8
If your master Would have a queen his beggar, you must tell him, That majesty, to keep decorum, must No less beg than a kingdom v 2 16
Come, come, and take a queen Worth many babes and beggars! v 2 48
I chose an eagle, And did avoid a puttock.—Thou took'st a beggar *Cymbeline* i 1 141
An easy battery might lay flat, for taking a beggar without less quality i 4 23
Patiently and constantly thou hast stuck to the bare fortune of that beggar iii 5 120
Two beggars told me I could not miss my way iii 6 8
Falsehood Is worse in kings than beggars iii 6 14
Are all your beggars whipped, then?—O, not all, my friend, not all *Per.* ii 1 94
If all your beggars were whipped, I would wish no better office than to be beadle ii 1 96

Beggared. Lean, rent and beggar'd by the strumpet wind *Mer. of Venice* ii 6 19
Big Mars seems bankrupt in their beggar'd host . *Hen. V.* iv 2 43
Hath bow'd you to the grave And beggar'd yours for ever . . *Macbeth* iii 1 91
Wherein necessity, of matter beggar'd, Will nothing stick our person to arraign In ear and ear . . . . *Hamlet* iv 5 92
For her own person, It beggar'd all description . . *Ant. and Cleo.* ii 2 203
Beggar-fear. With pale beggar-fear impeach my height . . *Richard II.* i 1 189
Beggarly. Methinks I have given him a penny and he renders me the beggarly thanks . . . . *As Y. Like It* ii 5 29
The rest were ragged, old, and beggarly . . . *T. of Shrew* iv 1 140
Methinks they are exceeding poor and bare, too beggarly 1 *Hen. IV.* iv 2 75
What an arrant, rascally, beggarly, lousy knave it is . . *Hen. V.* iv 8 36
The rascally, scauld, beggarly, lousy, pragging knave . . . . v 1 5
My dukedom to a beggarly denier, I do mistake my person all this while *Richard III.* i 2 252
I have been begging sixteen years in court, Am yet a courtier beggarly, nor could Come pat . . . . *Hen. VIII.* ii 3 83
About his shelves A beggarly account of empty boxes . *Rom. and Jul.* v 1 45
Beggarly, three-suited, hundred-pound, filthy, worsted-stocking knave *Lear* ii 2 16
Though he do shake me off To beggarly divorcement—love him dearly *Othello* iv 2 158
Beggar-maid. When King Cophetua loved the beggar-maid *Rom. and Jul.* ii 1 14
Beggar-man. Is it a beggar-man?—Madman and beggar too . . *Lear* iv 1 31
Beggar-woman. Was by a beggar-woman stolen away . 2 *Hen. VI.* iv 2 151
Beggary. Usurp the beggary he was never born to . *Meas. for Meas.* iii 2 99
Mourning for the death Of Learning, late deceased in beggary *M. N. Dr.* v 1 53
Being rich, my virtue then shall be To say there is no vice but beggary *K. John* ii 1 596
Guarded with rags, And countenanced by boys and beggary 2 *Hen. IV.* iv 1 35
Reproach and beggary Is crept into the palace of our king 2 *Hen. VI.* iv 1 101
Valiant I am.—A' must needs; for beggary is valiant . . . iv 2 58
Delay leads impotent and snail-paced beggary. . . *Richard III.* iv 3 53
Contempt and beggary hangs upon thy back . . *Rom. and Jul.* v 1 71
There's beggary in the love that can be reckon'd . *Ant. and Cleo.* i 1 15
Not I, Inclined to this intelligence, pronounce The beggary of his change; but 'tis your graces . . . . . . *Cymbeline* i 6 115
On whom there is no more dependency But brats and beggary . . ii 3 124
Such precious deeds in one that promised nought But beggary . . v 5 10
Begged. What said he?—That love I begg'd for you he begg'd of me *Com. of Errors* iv 2 12
And she in mild terms begg'd my patience . . *M. N. Dream* iv 1 63
A prating boy, that begg'd it as a fee . . . *Mer. of Venice* v 1 164
My Lord Bassanio gave his ring away Unto the judge that begg'd it . v 1 180
Then the boy, his clerk, That took some pains in writing, he begg'd mine v 1 182
Did refuse three thousand ducats of me And begg'd the ring . . v 1 212
I think you would have begg'd The ring of me to give the worthy doctor v 1 221
I understand you, sir; 'tis well begged . . . . *T. Night* iii 1 60
Youth is bought more oft than begg'd or borrow'd . . . . iii 4 3
I did confess it, and exactly begg'd Your grace's pardon . . *Richard II.* i 1 140
Pity me, open the door: A beggar begs that never begg'd before . v 3 78
But that I am prevented, I should have begg'd I might have been employ'd . . . . 1 *Hen. VI.* iv 1 72
And given in earnest what I begg'd in jest . . *Richard III.* v 1 22
I request you To give my poor host freedom.—O, well begg'd! *Coriolanus* i 9 87
There's in all two worthy voices begged. I have your alms . . ii 3 87
To my poor unworthy notice, He mock'd us when he begg'd our voices ii 3 167
That proud brag of thine, That said'st I begg'd the empire at thy hands *T. Andron.* i 1 307
Kill me in this place! For 'tis not life that I have begg'd so long. . ii 3 170
On her knee Hath begg'd that I will stay at home to-day *J. Cæsar* ii 2 82
Became his guide, Led him, begg'd for him, saved him from despair *Lear* v 3 191
With a solemn earnestness, More than indeed belong'd to such a trifle, He begg'd of me to steal it . . . . . . *Othello* v 2 229
I begg'd His pardon for return.—Which soon he granted *Ant. and Cleo.* iii 6 59
Cried he? and begg'd a' pardon?—He did ask favour . . iii 13 132
And thought To have begg'd or bought what I have took *Cymbeline* iii 6 48
Beggest. What begg'st thou, then? fond woman, let me go *T. Andron.* ii 3 172
Begging. Thou bid'st me beg: this begging is not strange *L. L. Lost* v 2 210
The matter, I hope, is not great, sir, begging but a beggar . *T. Night* iii 1 62
What! a young knave, and begging! Is there not wars? . 2 *Hen. IV.* i 2 84
A begging prince what beggar pities not? . . . *Richard III* i 4 274
Like a Jack, thou keep'st the stroke Betwixt thy begging and my meditation . . . . iv 2 118
I have been begging sixteen years in court . . *Hen. VIII.* ii 3 82
'Twas never my desire yet to trouble the poor with begging . *Coriolanus* ii 3 76
In thy dumb action will I be as perfect As begging hermits *T. Andron.* iii 2 41
Here's them in our country of Greece gets more with begging than we can do with working . . . . *Pericles* ii 1 69
Begin. But 'tis gone. No, it begins again. . . . *Tempest* i 2 395
For a good wager, first begins to crow . . . . . . ii 1 28
Give me thy hand. I do begin to have bloody thoughts . . . iv 1 220
Their rising senses Begin to chase the ignorant fumes . . . v 1 67
Their understanding Begins to swell, and the approaching tide Will shortly fill the reasonable shore . . . . v 1 80
Thrive therein, Even as I would when I to love begin . *T. G. of Ver.* i 1 10
You always end ere you begin . . . . ii 4 32
How shall I dote on her with more advice, That thus without advice begin to love her! . . . . ii 4 208
The sun begins to gild the western sky . . . . . v 1 1
Inconstancy falls off ere it begins . . . . . . v 4 113
I do begin to perceive that I am made an ass . *Mer. Wives* v 5 124
I will, out of thine own confession, learn to begin thy health *M. for Meas.* i 2 39
The vile conclusion I now begin with grief and shame to utter . v 1 96
But, like a shrew, you first begin to brawl . *Com. of Errors* iv 1 51
Why, here begins his morning story right . . . . . v 1 356
Now will I begin your moral, and do you follow . . *L. L. Lost* iii 1 94
How did this argument begin? . . . . iii 1 106
Begin, sir; you are my elder.—Well followed . . . . v 2 609
Made senseless things begin to do them wrong . . *M. N. Dream* iii 2 28
Her dotage now I do begin to pity . . . . . . iv 1 52
Saint Valentine is past: Begin these wood-birds but to couple now? . iv 1 145
Let us all ring fancy's knell: I'll begin it. . . *Mer. of Venice* iii 2 71
And there begins my sadness . . . . . *As Y. Like It* i 1 5
Is it even so? begin you to grow upon me? . . . . . i 1 90
Then she puts you to entreaty, and there begins new matter . . iv 1 81
We will begin these rites, As we do trust they'll end, in true delights . v 4 203
An he begin once, he'll rail in his rope-tricks . . . *T. of Shrew* i 2 112
Ay, marry, sir, now it begins to work . . . . . iii 2 220
A match! 'tis done.—Who shall begin?—That will I . . . v 2 75

Begin. When I should take possession of the bride, End ere I do begin *All's Well* ii 5 29
I begin to love, as an old man loves money, with no stomach. . iii 2 17
They begin to smoke me . . . . iv 1 30
Say thou art mine, and ever My love as it begins shall so persever . iv 2 37
I begin to love him for this . . . . iv 3 293
You might begin an impudent nation . . . . . . iv 3 363
Go thy ways, I begin to be aweary of thee; and I tell thee so before . iv 5 59
Begin, fool: it begins 'Hold thy peace.'—I shall never begin if I hold my peace.—Good, i' faith. Come, begin . . . *T. Night* ii 3 72
M,—why, that begins my name . . . . ii 5 137
Methinks My favour here begins to warp . . . . *W. Tale* i 2 365
Gasping to begin some speech, her eyes Became two spouts . . iii 3 25
The storm begins: poor wretch! . . . . iii 3 49
When daffodils begin to peer, With heigh! the doxy over the dale . iv 3 1
Would make her sainted spirit . . . appear soul-vex'd, And begin, 'Why to me?' . . . . v 1 60
Would she begin a sect, might quench the zeal Of all professors else . v 1 107
Thus, leaning on mine elbow, I begin . . . . *K. John* i 1 194
With a free desire Attending but the signal to begin . *Richard II.* i 3 116
Thine eye begins to speak; set thy tongue there . . . . v 3 125
He doth begin To make us strangers to his looks of love . 1 *Hen. IV.* i 3 289
How bloodily the sun begins to peer Above yon busky hill! . . v 1 1
Like the south Borne with black vapour, doth begin to melt 2 *Hen. IV.* ii 4 393
And purge the obstructions which begin to stop Our very veins of life . iv 1 65
If that you will France win, Then with Scotland first begin . *Hen. V.* i 2 168
If I begin the battery once again, I will not leave . . . . iii 3 7
I have heard a sonnet begin so to one's mistress . . . . iii 7 44
Yet my blood begins to flatter me that thou dost . . . . v 2 239
The day begins to break, and night is fled. . . . 1 *Hen. VI.* ii 2 1
There comes the ruin, there begins confusion . . . . . iv 1 194
Ere the glass, that now begins to run . . . . . . iv 2 35
If I longer stay, We shall begin our ancient bickerings . 2 *Hen. VI.* i 1 144
Dispatch: this knave's tongue begins to double . . . . ii 3 94
And when the rage allays, the rain begins . . . 3 *Hen. VI.* i 4 146
Ay, now begins a second storm to rise . . . . . . iii 3 47
What! can so young a thorn begin to prick? . . . . . v 5 13
Here, I hope, begins our lasting joy . . . . v 7 46
And, for my name of George begins with G, It follows in his thought that I am he . . . . *Richard III.* i 1 58
I do the wrong, and first begin to brawl . . . . . . i 3 324
Insulting tyranny begins to jet Upon the innocent and aweless throne . ii 4 51
He did, my gracious lord, begin that place; Which, since, succeeding ages have re-edified . . . . iii 1 70
Murder thy breath in middle of a word, And then begin again . . iii 5 3
Prosperity begins to mellow And drop into the rotten mouth of death . iv 4 1
He begins A new hell in himself . . . . . *Hen. VIII.* ii 1 71
Now I begin to relish thy advice . . . . *Troi. and Cres.* i 3 388
I will begin at thy heel, and tell what thou art by inches . . . ii 1 53
All his virtues . . . Do in our eyes begin to lose their gloss . . ii 3 128
The combatants being kin Half stints their strife before their strokes begin . . . . iv 5 93
How the sun begins to set; How ugly night comes breathing at his heels v 8 5
The gods begin to mock me . . . . *Coriolanus* i 9 79
A curse begin at very root on's heart, That is not glad to see thee! . ii 1 202
He cannot temperately transport his honours From where he should begin and end . . . . ii 1 241
But there to end Where he was to begin . . . . . . v 6 66
Thy sight is young, And thou shalt read when mine begin to dazzle *T. Andron.* iii 2 85
Ay, now begin our sorrows to approach . . . . . . iv 4 72
Thy child shall live.—Swear that he shall, and then I will begin . . v 1 70
Bind them sure, And stop their mouths, if they begin to cry . . v 2 162
Let us take the law of our sides; let them begin . *Rom. and Jul.* i 1 45
Begin to draw The shady curtains from Aurora's bed . . . . i 1 141
Some consequence yet hanging in the stars Shall bitterly begin his fearful date With this night's revels . . . . i 4 108
Doth not rosemary and Romeo begin both with a letter? . . . ii 4 220
I know it begins with some other letter . . . . . . ii 4 224
This day's black fate on more days doth depend; This but begins the woe iii 1 125
An you begin to rail on society once, I am sworn not to give regard to you *T. of Athens* i 2 250
My long sickness Of health and living now begins to mend . . . v 1 190
Those that with haste will make a mighty fire Begin it with weak straws: what trash is Rome! . . . . *J. Cæsar* i 3 108
He will never follow any thing That other men begin . . . . ii 1 152
Now mark him, he begins again to speak . . . . . . iii 2 122
Which, out of use and staled by other men, Begin his fashion. . . iv 1 39
When love begins to sicken and decay, It useth an enforced ceremony . iv 2 20
Time is come round, And where I did begin, there shall I end . . v 3 24
Good things of day begin to droop and drowse . . . *Macbeth* iii 2 52
I pull in resolution, and begin To doubt the equivocation of the fiend . v 5 42
If it live in your memory, begin at this line . . . . *Hamlet* ii 2 470
It is not so:—it begins with Pyrrhus . . . . ii 2 473
Begin, murderer; pox, leave thy damnable faces, and begin . . . iii 2 262
I stand in pause where I shall first begin, And both neglect . . iii 3 42
Thus bad begins and worse remains behind . . . . . . iii 4 179
As the world were now but to begin, Antiquity forgot, custom not known iv 5 103
Come, begin: And you, the judges, bear a wary eye. . . . . v 2 289
I begin to find an idle and fond bondage in the oppression of aged tyranny . . . . *Lear* i 2 51
Will pack when it begins to rain, And leave thee in the storm . . ii 4 81
My wits begin to turn . . . . iii 2 67
He begins at curfew, and walks till the first cock . . . . iii 4 121
His wits begin to unsettle . . . . iii 4 167
My tears begin to take his part so much, They'll mar my counterfeiting iii 6 63
With plumed helm thy state begins to threat . . . . . iv 2 57
Begin to heave the gorge, disrelish and abhor . . . . *Othello* ii 1 236
My blood begins my safer guides to rule . . . . . . ii 3 205
Iago beckons me; now he begins the story . . . . . . iv 1 134
I think it is scurvy, and begin to find myself fopped in it . . . iv 2 197
Begin to throw . . . all his dignities Upon his son . *Ant. and Cleo.* i 2 194
We'll feast each other ere we part; and let's Draw lots who shall begin ii 6 62
When it appears to you where this begins, Turn your displeasure that way iii 4 33
Mine honesty and I begin to square . . . . iii 13 41
When one so great begins to rage, he's hunted Even to falling . . iv 1 7
This morning, like the spirit of a youth That means to be of note, begins betimes . . . . iv 4 27
Begin the fight: Our will is Antony be took alive . . . . iv 6 1
My desolation does begin to make A better life . . . . . v 2 1

Begin. And winking Mary-buds begin To ope their golden eyes *Cymbeline* ii 3 26
We'll say our song the whilst. Brother, begin . . . . . iv 2 254
I will begin The fashion, less without and more within . . v 1 32
To the purpose.—Your daughter's chastity—there it begins . . v 5 179
But custom what they did begin Was with long use account no sin *Pericles* i Gower 29
For now the wind begins to blow . . . . . . ii Gower 29
Are the knights ready to begin the triumph? . . . . ii 2 1
Her eyelids . . . Begin to part their fringes of bright gold . iii 2 101
Beginner. Where are the vile beginners of this fray? . *Rom. and Jul.* iii 1 146
Some, turn'd coward But by example—O, a sin in war, Damn'd in the first beginners! . . . . *Cymbeline* v 3 37
Beginning. The latter end of his commonwealth forgets the beginning *Tempest* ii 1 158
If there be no great love in the beginning, yet heaven may decrease it *Mer. Wives* i 1 254
There are pretty orders beginning, I can tell you . *Meas. for Meas.* ii 1 249
This says she now when she is beginning to write to him . *Much Ado* ii 3 135
To show our simple skill, That is the true beginning of our end *M. N. Dr.* v 1 111
I will tell you the beginning; and, if it please your ladyships, you may see the end . . . . *As Y. Like It* i 2 119
Well, the beginning, that is dead and buried . . . . i 2 123
I could match this beginning with an old tale . . . . i 2 127
A strange beginning: 'borrow'd majesty!' . . . . *K. John* i 1 5
To the latter end of a fray and the beginning of a feast Fits a dull fighter and a keen guest . . . . . . *1 Hen. IV.* iv 2 85
Which in their seeds And weak beginnings lie intreasured *2 Hen. IV.* iii 1 85
Dangerous treason lurking in our way To hinder our beginnings *Hen. V.* ii 2 187
We see yonder the beginning of the day, but I think we shall never see the end of it . . . . iv 1 91
Beginning in the middle, starting thence away . *Troi. and Cres.* Prol. 28
The other course Will prove too bloody, and the end of it Unknown to the beginning . . . . *Coriolanus* iii 1 329
By whom our heavy haps had their beginning . . *T. Andron.* v 3 202
This was an ill beginning of the night . . . . *J. Cæsar* iv 3 234
I cannot speak Any beginning to this peevish odds . . *Othello* ii 3 185
You have me, rich; and I will never fail Beginning nor supplyment *Cymbeline* iii 4 182
Begnaw. The worm of conscience still begnaw thy soul! *Richard III.* i 3 222
Begnawn. Stark spoiled with the staggers, begnawn with the bots *T. of Shrew* iii 2 55
Begot. Tell me this: who begot thee? . . . . *T. G. of Ver.* iii 1 294
He was begot between two stock-fishes . . *Meas. for Meas.* iii 2 116
There's one Whom he begot with child . . . . . v 1 517
Begot in the ventricle of memory, nourished in the womb of pia mater *L. L. Lost* iv 2 70
Whose influence is begot of that loose grace Which shallow laughing hearers give to fools . . . . v 2 869
How begot, how nourished? Reply, reply. It is engender'd in the eyes *Mer. of Venice* iii 2 65
He is thrice a villain that says such a father begot villains *As Y. Like It* i 1 61
Begot of thought, conceived of spleen and born of madness . . iv 1 217
Let us do those ends That here were well begun and well begot . v 4 177
Whether I be as true begot or no, That still I lay upon my mother's head, But that . . . . *K. John* i 1 75
I am as well begot, my liege,—Fair fall the bones that took the pains for me! . . . . i 1 77
Near or far off, well won is still well shot, And I am I, howe'er I was begot . . . . i 1 175
When Richard me begot, If thou hadst said him nay, it had been sin . i 1 274
I think His father never was so true begot . . . . . ii 1 130
What cannoneer begot this lusty blood? . . . . . ii 1 461
For nothing hath begot my something grief . . *Richard II.* ii 2 36
And, by just computation of the time, Found that the issue was not his begot . . . . *Richard III.* iii 5 90
I am a bastard begot, bastard instructed, bastard in mind *Troi. and Cres.* v 7 17
Know thou, I begot him on the empress . . . *T. Andron.* v 1 87
Children of an idle brain, Begot of nothing but vain fantasy *Rom. and Jul.* i 4 98
You have begot me, bred me, loved me: I Return those duties back *Lear* i 1 98
'Twas this flesh begot Those pelican daughters . . . . iii 4 76
'Tis a monster Begot upon itself, born on itself . . *Othello* iii 4 162
Why should excuse be born or e'er begot? We'll talk of that hereafter *Cymbeline* iii 2 67
Sleep, thou hast been a grandsire, and begot A father to me . . v 4 123
Begotten. Show me a child begotten of thy body that I am father to, then call me husband . . . . *All's Well* iii 2 61
His innocent babe truly begotten . . . . . *W. Tale* iii 2 135
Leaving no heir begotten of his body . . . *1 Hen. VI.* ii 5 72
Not me begotten of a shepherd swain . . . . . . v 4 37
Begrimed. Is now begrimed and black As mine own face . *Othello* iii 3 387
Beguile. And high and low beguiles the rich and poor . *Mer. Wives* i 3 95
If I read it not truly, my ancient skill beguiles me . *Meas. for Meas.* iv 2 164
Light seeking light doth light of light beguile . . . *L. L. Lost* i 1 77
Make him smile When I a fat and bean-fed horse beguile *M. N. Dream* ii 1 45
How shall we beguile The lazy time, if not with some delight? . . v 1 40
See, to beguile the old folks, how the young folks lay their heads together! . . . . *T. of Shrew* ii 2 138
'Celsa senis,' that we might beguile the old pantaloon . . . iii 1 37
Here he comes, to beguile two hours in a sleep . . . *All's Well* iv 1 25
To beguile the supposition of that lascivious young boy . . . iv 3 333
Is there no exorcist Beguiles the truer office of mine eyes? . . v 3 306
I will bespeak our diet, Whiles you beguile the time . . *T. Night* iii 3 41
Ay me, detested! how am I beguiled!—Who does beguile you? . v 1 143
Would beguile Nature of her custom, so perfectly he is her ape *W. Tale* v 2 107
O flattering glass, Like to my followers in prosperity, Thou dost beguile me! . . . . *Richard II.* iv 1 281
I know you, Sir John: you owe me money, Sir John; and now you pick a quarrel to beguile me of it . . . . . . *1 Hen. IV.* iii 3 77
Is't thou that thinkest to beguile me? . . . *1 Hen. VI.* i 2 65
Beguiles him as the mournful crocodile With sorrow snares relenting passengers . . . . *2 Hen. VI.* iii 1 226
Rudely beguiles our lips Of all rejoindure . . *Troi. and Cres.* iv 4 37
Take choice of all my library, And so beguile thy sorrow *T. Andron.* iv 1 35
If thou wert the lion, the fox would beguile thee . *T. of Athens* iv 3 331
To beguile the time, Look like the time; bear welcome in your eye *Macb.* i 5 64
Breathing like sanctified and pious bawds, The better to beguile *Hamlet* i 3 131
My spirits grow dull, and fain I would beguile The tedious day with sleep . . . . iii 2 236
'Twas yet some comfort, When misery could beguile the tyrant's rage *Lear* iv 6 63

Beguile. I did consent, And often did beguile her of her tears *Othello* i 3 156
So let the Turk of Cyprus us beguile; We lose it not . . . ii 3 210
I am not merry; but I do beguile The thing I am, by seeming otherwise ii 1 123
'Tis the strumpet's plague To beguile many and be beguiled by one . iv 1 98
Beguiled. Treacherous man! Thou hast beguiled my hopes *T. G. of Ver.* v 4 64
One Nym, sir, that beguiled him of a chain . . *Mer. Wives* iv 5 33
The very same man that beguiled Master Slender of his chain cozened him of it . . . . iv 5 38
And therefore is Love said to be a child, Because in choice he is so oft beguiled . . . . *M. N. Dream* i 1 239
This palpable-gross play hath well beguiled The heavy gait of night . v 1 374
We'll show thee Io as she was a maid, And how she was beguiled *T. of Shrew* Ind. 2 57
Ay me, detested! how am I beguiled!—Who does beguile you? *T. Night* v 1 142
You have beguiled me with a counterfeit Resembling majesty *K. John* iii 1 99
Hath very much beguiled The tediousness and process of my travel *Richard II.* ii 3 11
Take up those cords: poor ropes, you are beguiled, Both you and I *Rom. and Jul.* iii 2 132
Beguiled, divorced, wronged, spited, slain! . . . . . . iv 5 55
Most detestable death, by thee beguiled! . . . . . . iv 5 56
He that beguiled you in a plain accent was a plain knave . *Lear* ii 2 117
Thou art not vanquish'd, But cozen'd and beguiled . . . . v 3 154
Whoe'er he be that in this foul proceeding Hath thus beguiled your daughter of herself And you of her . . . . *Othello* i 3 66
'Tis the strumpet's plague To beguile many and be beguiled by one . iv 1 98
His power went out in such distractions as Beguiled all spies *A. and C.* iii 7 78
Like a right gipsy, hath, at fast and loose, Beguiled me to the very heart of loss . . . . iv 12 29
All's not well; Cæsar's beguiled . . . . v 2 326
Beguiling them of commendation . . . . . *1 Hen. IV.* iii 1 189
Beguiling virgins with the broken seals of perjury . . . *Hen. V.* iv 1 171
Begun. You have often Begun to tell me what I am . . *Tempest* i 2 34
I have begun, And now I give my sensual race the rein *Meas. for Meas.* ii 4 159
Let us do those ends That here were well begun and well begot *As Y. L.* v 4 177
Comes there any more of it?—My lord, 'tis but begun . *T. of Shrew* i 1 257
Thus have I politicly begun my reign, And 'tis my hope to end successfully . . . . iv 1 191
Since you have begun, Have at you for a bitter jest or two! . . v 2 44
A great while ago the world begun, With hey, ho, the wind and the rain *T. Night* v 1 414
What is thy name?—Philip, my liege, so is my name begun . *K. John* i 1 158
This day, all things begun come to ill end! . . . . . . iii 1 94
Let this end where it begun . . . . . . *Richard II.* i 1 158
I take my leave before I have begun, For sorrow ends not when it seemeth done . . . . i 2 60
Will you mock at an ancient tradition, begun upon an honourable respect? . . . . *Hen. V.* v 1 75
An uproar, I dare warrant, Begun through malice . . . *1 Hen. VI.* iii 1 75
Since we have begun to strike, We'll never leave . . *3 Hen. VI.* ii 2 167
The ample proposition that hope makes In all designs begun on earth below Fails in the promised largeness . . . . *Troi. and Cres.* i 3 4
And when such time they have begun to cry, Let them not cease *Coriol.* iii 3 19
The all-seeing sun Ne'er saw her match since first the world begun *Rom. and Jul.* i 2 98
This same day Must end that work the ides of March begun . *J. Cæsar* v 1 114
I have begun to plant thee, and will labour To make thee full of growing . . . . *Macbeth* i 4 28
Things bad begun make strong themselves by ill . . . . . iii 2 55
But, orderly to end where I begun . . . . *Hamlet* iii 2 220
Till I know 'tis done, Howe'er my haps, my joys were ne'er begun . iv 3 70
Love is begun by time; And that I see, in passages of proof, Time qualifies the spark and fire of it . . . . iv 7 112
Ere I could make a prologue to my brains, They had begun the play . v 2 31
O, make an end Of what I have begun . . . . *Ant. and Cleo.* iv 14 106
Behalf. Let me have thy voice in my behalf . . . *Mer. Wives* i 4 168
This well carried shall on her behalf Change slander to remorse *Much Ado* iv 1 212
In that behalf, Bold of your worthiness, we single you . *L. L. Lost* ii 1 27
You are too officious In her behalf that scorns your services *M. N. Dream* iii 2 331
As his wise mother wrought in his behalf . . . *Mer. of Venice* i 3 74
Nor cannot insinuate with you in the behalf of a good play *As Y. Like It* Epil. 9
Was very honest in the behalf of the maid . . . . . *All's Well* iv 3 247
Yet must suffer Something in my behalf . . . . . . iv 4 28
I moved the king my master to speak in the behalf of my daughter . iv 5 76
I come to whet your gentle thoughts On his behalf . . . *T. Night* iii 1 117
Tender your persons to his presence, whisper him in your behalfs *W. Tale* iv 4 827
A true gentleman may swear it in the behalf of his friend . . . v 2 176
In right and true behalf Of thy deceased brother . . . *K. John* ii 1 7
Hither is he come, To spread his colours, boy, in thy behalf . . ii 1 8
Shall your city call us lord, In that behalf which we have challenged it? ii 1 264
God omnipotent, Is mustering in his clouds on our behalf *Richard II.* iii 3 86
Demanded My prisoners in your majesty's behalf . . . *1 Hen. IV.* i 3 48
Men of your nobility and power Did gage them both in an unjust behalf i 3 173
Play out the play: I have much to say in the behalf of that Falstaff . ii 4 532
But my factor, good my lord, To engross up glorious deeds on my behalf iii 2 148
Even in thy behalf, I'll thank myself For doing these fair rites . . v 4 97
The emperor's coming in behalf of France . . . . *Hen. V.* v Prol. 38
That you on my behalf would pluck a flower.—In your behalf still will I wear the same . . . . *1 Hen. VI.* ii 4 129
Every word you speak in his behalf Is slander . . . *2 Hen. VI.* iii 2 208
This hand of mine hath writ in thy behalf . . . . . . iv 1 63
To intercept the queen, Bearing the king in my behalf along *3 Hen. VI.* i 1 115
In our king's behalf, I am commanded, with your leave and favour . iii 3 59
You shall give me leave To play the broker in mine own behalf . . iv 1 63
You in our behalf Go levy men, and make prepare for war . . . iv 1 130
In the duke's behalf I'll give my voice . . . . *Richard III.* iii 4 20
Be eloquent in my behalf to her . . . . iv 4 357
The wronged souls Of butcher'd princes fight in thy behalf . . v 3 122
Which, you say, live to come in my behalf . . *Troi. and Cres.* iii 3 16
Use violent thefts, And rob in the behalf of charity . . . . v 3 22
The nobility are vex'd, whom we see have sided In his behalf *Coriolanus* iv 2 3
Told as many lies in his behalf as you have uttered words in your own . v 2 25
My very friend, hath got his mortal hurt In my behalf . *Rom. and Jul.* iii 1 116
I have told more of you to myself than you can with modesty speak in your own behalf . . . . *T. of Athens* i 2 97
Which, in my lord's behalf, I come to entreat your honour . . . iii 1 17
To hear, If you dare venture in your own behalf, A mistress's command *Lear* iv 2 20
Good Cassio, I will do All my abilities in thy behalf . . *Othello* iii 3 2
Tell him I have moved my lord on his behalf, and hope all will be well iii 4 19

Behalf. Horses have been nimbler than the sands That run i' the clock's behalf . . . . *Cymbeline* iii 2 75
Behave. He did behave his anger, ere 'twas spent . . . *T. of Athens* iii 5 22
Behaved. Gather by him, as he is behaved, If 't be the affliction of his love or no That thus he suffers for . . . . . *Hamlet* iii 1 35
How have I been behaved, that he might stick The small'st opinion on my least misuse? . . . . *Othello* iv 2 108
Behavedst. Thou behavedst thyself as if thou hadst been in thine own slaughter-house . . . . 2 *Hen. VI.* iv 3 5
Behaviour. But chiefly for thy face and thy behaviour . *T. G. of Ver.* iv 4 72
The hardest voice of her behaviour, to be Englished rightly, is, 'I am Sir John Falstaff's' . . . . *Mer. Wives* i 3 52
What an unweighed behaviour hath this Flemish drunkard picked? . ii 1 23
I will teach the children their behaviours . . . . . . iv 4 66
Man is a fool when he dedicates his behaviours to love . . *Much Ado* ii 3 9
Whom she hath in all outward behaviours seemed ever to abhor . . ii 3 100
All his behaviours did make their retire To the court of his eye *L. L. Lost* ii 1 234
His gait majestical, and his general behaviour vain, ridiculous . . v 1 13
Behaviour, what wert thou Till this madman show'd thee? and what art thou now? . . . . v 2 337
I think he bought his doublet in Italy, his round hose in France, his bonnet in Germany and his behaviour every where . *Mer. of Venice* i 2 81
Lest through thy wild behaviour I be misconstrued . . . . ii 2 196
The behaviour of the country is most mockable at the court *As Y. Like It* iii 2 48
Lest over-eyeing of his odd behaviour . . . *T. of Shrew* Ind. 1 95
In the other's silence do I see Maid's mild behaviour and sobriety . . i 1 71
This young man, for learning and behaviour Fit for her turn . . . i 2 169
Affability and bashful modesty, Her wondrous qualities and mild behaviour . . . . ii 1 50
He was a frantic fool, Hiding his bitter jests in blunt behaviour . . iii 2 13
Thine eyes See it so grossly shown in thy behaviours . . *All's Well* i 3 184
There is a fair behaviour in thee, captain . . . . . *T. Night* i 2 47
He has been yonder i' the sun practising behaviour to his own shadow . ii 5 20
The behaviour of the young gentleman gives him out to be of good capacity and breeding . . . . iii 4 203
Thus, after greeting, speaks the King of France In my behaviour to the majesty, The borrow'd majesty, of England here . . *K. John* i 1 3
So shall inferior eyes, That borrow their behaviours from the great . v 1 51
This loose behaviour I throw off And pay the debt . . . 1 *Hen. IV.* i 2 232
What cause Hath my behaviour given to your displeasure? *Hen. VIII.* i 4 20
You are to blame, Knowing she will not lose her wonted greatness, To use so rude behaviour . . . . iv 2 103
Here he comes, and in the gown of humility: mark his behaviour *Coriol.* ii 3 45
It were a very gross kind of behaviour, as they say . *Rom. and Jul.* ii 4 177
Which give some soil perhaps to my behaviours . . . *J. Cæsar* i 2 42
Make inquire Of his behaviour . . . . *Hamlet* ii 1 5
Your behaviour hath struck her into amazement and admiration . . iii 2 338
When we are sick in fortune,—often the surfeit of our own behaviour *Lear* i 2 130
His unbookish jealousy must construe Poor Cassio's smiles, gestures and light behaviour, Quite in the wrong . . . . . *Othello* iv 1 103
I have seen thee fight, When I have envied thy behaviour *Ant. and Cleo.* ii 6 77
Behead. Take him away, and behead him . . . . . 2 *Hen. VI.* iv 7 102
Beheaded. How came it Claudio was beheaded At an unusual hour? *Meas. for Meas.* v 1 462
Beheaded publicly for his offence . . . . . *Com. of Errors* v 1 127
But, as the rest, so fell that noble earl And was beheaded . 1 *Hen. VI.* ii 5 91
He shall be beheaded for it ten times . . . . 2 *Hen. VI.* iv 7 26
To-day the lords you talk of are beheaded . . . *Richard III.* iii 2 93
For their fell faults our brothers were beheaded . . *T. Andron.* v 3 100
Beheld. Who with mine eyes, never since at ebb, beheld The king my father wreck'd . . . . *Tempest* i 2 435
If you now beheld them, your affections Would become tender . . v 1 18
We, in all her trim, freshly beheld Our royal, good and gallant ship . v 1 236
'Tis but her picture I have yet beheld, And that hath dazzled my reason's light . . . . *T. G. of Ver.* ii 4 209
Any madness I ever yet beheld seemed but tameness, civility and patience, to this his distemper . . . . . . *Mer. Wives* iv 2 27
You saw the mistress, I beheld the maid . . . *Mer. of Venice* iii 2 200
Of all the men alive I never yet beheld that special face Which I could fancy more than any other . . . . *T. of Shrew* ii 1 11
I thank you all, That have beheld me give away myself . . . . iii 2 196
Tell me truly too, Hast thou beheld a fresher gentlewoman? . . . iv 5 29
With his princess, she The fairest I have yet beheld . . . *W. Tale* v 1 87
There might you have beheld one joy crown another . . . . v 2 48
Infixed I beheld myself Drawn in the flattering table of her eye *K. John* ii 1 502
Have you beheld, Or have you read or heard? or could you think? . iv 3 41
A woeful pageant have we here beheld . . . . *Richard II.* iv 1 321
How it yearn'd my heart when I beheld In London streets, that coronation-day! . . . . v 5 76
That she may boast she hath beheld the man Whose glory fills the world with loud report . . . . 1 *Hen. VI.* ii 2 42
Accursed and unquiet wrangling days, How many of you have mine eyes beheld! . . . . *Richard III.* ii 4 56
Beheld them, when they lighted, how they clung In their embracement *Hen. VIII.* i 1 9
Stand upon my common part with those That have beheld the doing *Coriolanus* i 9 40
There's some among you have beheld me fighting: Come, try upon yourselves . . . . iii 1 224
I have seen thee stern, and thou hast oft beheld Heart-hardening spectacles iv 1 24
Beheld his tears, and laugh'd so heartily, That both mine eyes were rainy like to his . . . . *T. Andron.* v 1 116
That I beheld: Mine eyes did sicken at the sight . *Ant. and Cleo.* iii 10 16
And golden Phœbus never be beheld Of eyes again so royal! . . . v 2 320
She went before others I have seen, as that diamond of yours outlustres many I have beheld . . . . *Cymbeline* i 4 79
And strangers ne'er beheld but wonder'd at . . . . *Pericles* i 4 25
None that beheld him, but, like lesser lights, Did vail their crowns . ii 3 41
Behest. Where I have learn'd me to repent the sin Of disobedient opposition To you and your behests . . . . . *Rom. and Jul.* iv 2 19
Away! and, to be blest, Let us with care perform his great behest *Cymbeline* v 4 122
Behind. No matter, since They have left their viands behind . *Tempest* iii 3 41
She will outstrip all praise And make it halt behind her. . . . iv 1 11
Like this insubstantial pageant faded, Leave not a rack behind . . iv 1 156
Far behind his worth Comes all the praises that I now bestow *T. G. of Ver.* ii 4 71
I will ensconce me behind the arras . . . . . *Mer. Wives* iii 3 97
They threw me off from behind one of them . . . . . . iv 5 69
There's more behind that is more gratulate . . . *Meas. for Meas.* v 1 535
Where we'll show What's yet behind, that's meet you all should know . v 1 545
Ay, and break it in your face, so he break it not behind . *Com. of Errors* iii 1 76
Behind. He that came behind you, sir, like an evil angel *Com. of Errors* iv 3 19
Behind the ditches of the abbey here . . . . v 1 122
I whipt me behind the arras . . . . *Much Ado* i 3 63
No glory lives behind the back of such . . . . iii 1 110
An two men ride of a horse, one must ride behind . . . . . iii 5 41
A foolish heart, that I leave here behind . . . *M. N. Dream* iii 2 319
Meeting her of late behind the wood . . . . iv 1 53
I am sent with broom before, To sweep the dust behind the door . . v 1 397
Turning his face, he put his hand behind him . . *Mer. of Venice* ii 8 47
So far this shadow Doth limp behind the substance . . . . iii 2 130
'Tis well you offer it behind her back . . . . iv 1 293
She would have followed her exile, or have died to stay behind her *As Y. Like It* i 1 115
Amiens and myself Did steal behind him as he lay along . . . ii 1 30
If you break one jot of your promise or come one minute behind your hour . . . . iv 1 195
So shall I no whit be behind in duty. . . . . . *T. of Shrew* i 2 175
I'll give him my commission To let him there a month behind the gest *W. Tale* i 2 41
Thought there was no more behind But such a day to-morrow as to-day i 2 63
Thou art a coward, Which hoxes honesty behind . . . . . i 2 244
Art thou gone so? I do but stay behind . . . . . *K. John* v 7 70
The king is left behind, And in my loyal bosom lies his power *Richard II.* ii 3 97
I fell asleep here behind the arras and had my pocket picked 1 *Hen. IV.* iii 3 112
He, being in the vaward, placed behind With purpose to relieve and follow them, Cowardly fled . . . . 1 *Hen. VI.* i 1 132
Come from behind; I know thee well, though never seen before . . i 2 66
Fortune in favour makes him lag behind . . . . iii 3 34
The Black Prince died before his father And left behind him Richard 2 *Hen. VI.* ii 2 19
O monstrous coward! what, to come behind folks? . . . . . iv 7 89
I'll leave my son my virtuous deeds behind . . . 3 *Hen. VI.* ii 2 49
Look behind you, my lord.—Take that, and that . . *Richard III.* i 4 275
For God's sake, let not us two be behind . . . . . . ii 2 147
But, hear you, leave behind Your son, George Stanley . . . . iv 4 496
Are ye all gone, And leave me here in wretchedness behind ye? *Hen. VIII.* iv 2 84
She's a fool to stay behind her father . . . . *Troi. and Cres.* i 1 83
I'll lean upon one crutch and fight with t'other, Ere stay behind *Coriolanus* i 1 247
All hurt behind; backs red, and faces pale With flight and agued fear! . i 4 37
Before him he carries noise, and behind him he leaves tears . . . ii 1 175
It will be of more price, Being spoke behind your back *Rom. and Jul.* iv 1 28
'Tis pity bounty had not eyes behind . . . . . *T. of Athens* i 2 169
Damned Casca, like a cur, behind Struck Cæsar on the neck . *J. Cæsar* v 1 43
Glamis, and thane of Cawdor! The greatest is behind . . *Macbeth* i 3 117
Thou shalt live in this fair world behind, Honour'd, beloved . *Hamlet* iii 2 185
I must be cruel, only to be kind: Thus bad begins and worse remains behind . . . . iii 4 179
What a wounded name, Things standing thus unknown, shall live behind me! . . . . v 2 356
He, conjunct, and flattering his displeasure, Tripp'd me behind . *Lear* ii 2 126
If I be left behind, A moth of peace, and he go to the war . . *Othello* i 3 256
The grace of heaven, Before, behind thee and on every hand, Enwheel thee round! . . . . ii 1 86
See suitors following and not look behind . . . . . . ii 1 158
Speak not against it; I will not stay behind.—Nay, I have done *Ant. and Cleo.* iii 7 20
Snatch 'em up, as we take hares, behind . . . . iv 7 13
The strait pass was damm'd With dead men hurt behind . *Cymbeline* v 3 12
Behind-door-work. Some stair-work, some trunk-work, some behind-door-work . . . . *W. Tale* iii 3 76
Behind-hand. Are as interpreters Of my behind-hand slackness . . v 1 151
Behold. Might I but through my prison once a day Behold this maid *Tempest* i 2 491
Behold her that gave aim to all thy oaths . . . *T. G. of Ver.* v 4 101
Will you go with us to behold it? . . . . . . *Mer. Wives* ii 1 214
With these nails I'll pluck out these false eyes That would behold in me this shameful sport . . . . *Com. of Errors* iv 4 108
Most mighty duke, behold a man much wrong'd . . . . . . v 1 330
Do but behold the tears that swell in me . . . . . *L. L. Lost* iv 3 36
Once to behold with your sun-beamed eyes . . . . v 2 168
Behold the window of my heart, mine eye . . . . v 2 848
The moon, like to a silver bow New-bent in heaven, shall behold the night Of our solemnities . . . . *M. N. Dream* i 1 10
Ere a man hath power to say 'Behold!' The jaws of darkness do devour it up . . . . i 1 147
When Phœbe doth behold Her silver visage in the watery glass . . i 1 209
Many a man his life hath sold But my outside to behold *Mer. of Venice* ii 7 68
Some, that are mad if they behold a cat . . . . iv 1 48
Do not believe him. O, behold this ring . . . . *All's Well* v 3 191
And now behold the meaning . . . . v 3 305
The element itself, till seven years' heat, Shall not behold her face *T. Night* i 1 27
If powers divine Behold our human actions, as they do . . *W. Tale* iii 2 30
Behold me A fellow of the royal bed . . . . iii 2 38
Strangle such thoughts as these with any thing That you behold the while . . . . iv 4 48
Pale primroses, That die unmarried, ere they can behold Bright Phœbus iv 4 123
Behold him with flies blown to death . . . . iv 4 820
Behold, and say 'tis well. I like your silence . . . . . . v 3 20
If you can behold it, I'll make the statue move indeed, descend . . v 3 87
Therefore never, never Must I behold my pretty Arthur more *K. John* iii 4 89
He is forsworn, if e'er those eyes of yours Behold another day break . v 4 32
Yet look up, behold, That you in pity may dissolve to dew *Richard II.* v 1 8
To behold the face Of that occasion that shall bring it on 1 *Hen. IV.* i 3 275
My lord, do you see these meteors? do you behold these exhalations? . ii 4 352
Behold yourself so by a son disdain'd . . . . . 2 *Hen. IV.* v 2 95
A kingdom for a stage, princes to act And monarchs to behold *Hen. V.* Prol. 4
Stood smiling to behold his lion's whelp . . . . i 2 109
That it is most lamentable to behold . . . . ii 1 125
Behold Upon the hempen tackle ship-boys climbing . . . . iii Prol. 7
Behold the threaden sails, Borne with the invisible and creeping wind iii Prol. 10
Behold A city on the inconstant billows dancing . . . . . iii Prol. 14
Behold the ordnance on their carriages, With fatal mouths gaping iii Prol. 26
O now, who will behold The royal captain of this ruin'd band! . iv Prol. 28
Mean and gentle all Behold, as may unworthiness define . . . iv Prol. 46
Will you have them weep our horses' blood? How shall we, then, behold their natural tears? . . . . iv 2 13
Do but behold yon poor and starved band, And your fair show shall suck away their souls . . . . iv 2 16
Right joyous are we to behold your face . . . . v 2 9
As we are now glad to behold your eyes . . . . v 2 14

Behold. Hereafter ages may behold What ruin happen'd in revenge of him *1 Hen. VI.* ii 2 10
Behold My sighs and tears and will not once relent? iii 1 107
Behold the wounds, the most unnatural wounds iii 3 50
Desiring still You may behold confusion of your foes iv 1 77
Now it is my chance to find thee out, Must I behold thy timeless cruel death? v 4 5
Will her ladyship behold and hear our exorcisms? *2 Hen. VI.* i 4 4
Is my apparel sumptuous to behold? iv 7 106
That this is true, father, behold his blood *3 Hen. VI.* i 1 13
Full of truth, I make King Lewis behold Thy sly conveyance iii 3 159
Behold this pattern of thy butcheries. *Richard III.* i 2 54
To-day shalt thou behold a subject die For truth, for duty, and for loyalty iii 3 3
If that your moody discontented souls Do through the clouds behold v 1 8
Let's stand close, and behold him *Hen. VIII.* ii 1 55
I'm very sorry To sit here at this present, and behold That chair stand empty v 3 9
Few now living can behold that goodness—A pattern to all princes living v 5 22
Do you with cheeks abash'd behold our works? *Troi. and Cres.* i 3 18
And anon behold The strong-ribb'd back through liquid mountains cut i 3 39
Who marvels then, when Helenus beholds A Grecian . . . , if he . . . fly? ii 2 42
Nor doth the eye itself . . . behold itself, Not going from itself iii 3 106
Till he behold them form'd in the applause Where they're extended iii 3 119
To talk with him and to behold his visage, Even to my full of view iii 3 240
Stand fair, I pray thee: let me look on thee.—Behold thy fill iv 5 236
You look upon that sleeve; behold it well v 2 69
Behold, distraction, frenzy and amazement, Like witless antics v 3 85
Let them Regard me as I do not flatter, and Therein behold themselves *Coriolanus* iii 1 68
Behold Dissentious numbers pestering streets iv 6 6
Behold now presently, and swoon for what's to come upon thee v 2 72
Behold the poor remains, alive and dead! *T. Andron.* i 1 81
Into some loathsome pit, Where never man's eye may behold my body ii 3 177
My compassionate heart Will not permit mine eyes once to behold ii 3 218
What shall I do Now I behold thy lively body so? iii 1 105
Behold our cheeks How they are stain'd, as meadows iii 1 124
Can the son's eye behold his father bleed? v 3 65
From the place where you behold us now, The poor remainder of Andronici Will, hand in hand, all headlong cast us down v 3 130
Look to behold this night Earth-treading stars *Rom. and Jul.* i 2 24
Can you love the gentleman? This night you shall behold him at our feast i 3 80
O, by this count I shall be much in years Ere I again behold my Romeo! iii 5 47
Indeed, I never shall be satisfied With Romeo, till I behold him—dead iii 5 95
Most lamentable day, most woful day, That ever, ever, I did yet behold! iv 5 51
Why I descend into this bed of death, Is partly to behold my lady's face v 3 29
May you a better feast never behold, You knot of mouth-friends! *T. of Athens* iii 6 98
Let me behold thy face. Surely, this man Was born of woman iv 3 500
Such men as he be never at heart's ease Whiles they behold a greater than themselves *J. Cæsar* i 2 209
Mothers shall but smile when they behold Their infants quarter'd with the hands of war iii 1 267
Weep you when you but behold Our Cæsar's vesture wounded? iii 2 199
Come down, behold no more. O, coward that I am! v 3 33
Prithee, see there! behold! look! lo! how say you? Why, what care I? *Macbeth* iii 4 69
You can behold such sights, And keep the natural ruby of your cheeks iii 4 114
Seyton!—I am sick at heart, When I behold—Seyton, I say! v 3 19
Hail, king! for so thou art: behold, where stands The usurper's cursed head v 8 54
But soft, behold! lo, where it comes again! *Hamlet* i 1 126
Take vantage, heavy eyes, not to behold This shameful lodging *Lear* ii 2 178
Behold yond simpering dame, Whose face between her forks presages snow iv 6 120
If fortune brag of two she loved and hated, One of them we behold v 3 281
Behold her well; I pray you, look upon her *Othello* v 1 108
The triple pillar of the world transform'd Into a strumpet's fool: behold and see *Ant. and Cleo.* i 1 13
It is a deadly sorrow to behold a foul knave uncuckolded i 2 76
Didst thou behold Octavia?—Ay, dread queen iii 3 8
From which place We may the number of the ships behold iii 9 3
Naught, naught, all naught! I can behold no longer iii 10 1
Behold this man; Commend unto his lips thy favouring hand iv 8 22
I robb'd his wound of it; behold it stain'd With his most noble blood v 1 25
O, behold, How pomp is follow'd! mine will now be yours v 2 150
Where is the queen?—Behold, sir v 2 197
Many there could behold the sun with as firm eyes as he *Cymbeline* i 4 12
Once more let me behold it: is it that Which I left with her? ii 4 99
An earthly paragon! Behold divineness No elder than a boy! iii 6 44
When they hear the Roman horses neigh, Behold their quarter'd fires iv 4 18
She is alive; behold, Her eyelids . . . Begin to part *Pericles* iii 2 98
Yet let me obtain my wish.—Behold him v 1 36
Behold (prefix) *repeated often.*
Beholder. All the beholders take his part with weeping *As Y. Like It* i 2 139
The wisest beholder, that knew no more but seeing, could not say *W. Tale* v 2 18
Was this the face That, like the sun, did make beholders wink? *Richard II.* iv 1 284
Digg'd stones out of the ground, To hurl at the beholders of my shame *1 Hen. VI.* i 4 46
And the beholders of this tragic play *Richard III.* iv 4 68
To tell you, fair beholders, that our play Leaps o'er the vaunt and first-lings of those broils *Troi. and Cres.* Prol. 26
Beholdest. Thou viewest, beholdest, surveyest, or seest *L. L. Lost* i 1 247
There's not the smallest orb which thou behold'st But in his motion like an angel sings *Mer. of Venice* v 1 60
This man, Aufidius, Was my beloved in Rome: yet thou behold'st! *Coriol.* v 2 99
Eros, thou yet behold'st me?—Ay, noble lord *Ant. and Cleo.* iv 14 1
Beholding. She is beholding to thee, gentle youth *T. G. of Ver.* iv 4 178
A justice of peace sometime may be beholding to his friend for a man *Mer. Wives* i 1 283
Marvellous little beholding to your reports *Meas. for Meas.* iv 3 166
Well, Shylock, shall we be beholding to you? *Mer. of Venice* i 3 106
Horns, which such as you are fain to be beholding to your wives for *As Y. Like It* iv 1 60
Gratify this gentleman, To whom we all rest generally beholding *T. of Shrew* i 2 274
Myself, that have been more kindly beholding to you than any ii 1 78
To whom am I beholding for these limbs? *K. John* i 1 239
Little are we beholding to your love *Richard II.* iv 1 160
I think you are more beholding to the night than to fern-seed for your walking invisible *1 Hen. IV.* ii 1 98

Beholding. Would, by beholding him, have wash'd his knife With gentle eye-drops *2 Hen. IV.* iv 5 87
Beholding him, plucks comfort from his looks *Hen. V.* iv Prol. 42
Like thee, Nero, Play on the lute, beholding the towns burn *1 Hen. VI.* i 4 96
The proudest of you all Have been beholding to him *Richard III.* ii 1 129
Then is he more beholding to you than I iii 1 107
I am hungry for revenge, And now I cloy me with beholding it iv 4 62
My Lord Sands, I am beholding to you *Hen. VIII.* i 4 41
Had I not known those customs, I should have been beholding to your paper iv 1 21
I will say thus much for him, if a prince May be beholding to a subject v 3 157
To you, my good lord mayor, And your good brethren, I am much beholding v 5 71
Find out Something not worth in me such rich beholding *Troi. and Cres.* iii 3 91
When for a day of kings' entreaties a mother should not sell him an hour from her beholding *Coriolanus* i 3 10
Is she not then beholding to the man That brought her for this high good turn so far? *T. Andron.* i 1 396
We are beholding to you, good Andronicus v 3 33
For Brutus' sake, I am beholding to you *J. Cæsar* iii 2 70
He says, for Brutus' sake, He finds himself beholding to us all iii 2 72
The revenges we are bound to take upon your traitorous father are not fit for your beholding *Lear* iii 7 9
I am beholding to you For your sweet music this last night *Pericles* ii 5 25
I am wild in my beholding v 1 224
Behoof. This tongue hath parley'd unto foreign kings For your behoof *2 Hen. VI.* iv 7 83
Behove. If you know aught which does behove my knowledge *W. Tale* i 2 395
Therefore it behoves men to be wary iv 4 257
Behoves it us to labour for the realm *2 Hen. VI.* i 1 182
You do not understand yourself so clearly As it behoves my daughter *Hamlet* i 3 97
To contract, O, the time, for, ah, my behove, O, methought, there was nothing meet v 1 71
Which he to seek of me again, perforce, Behoves me keep at utterance *Cymbeline* iii 1 73
Behoveful. Such necessaries As are behoveful for our state *Rom. and Jul.* iv 3 8
Behowl. And the wolf behowls the moon *M. N. Dream* v 1 379
Being so reputed In dignity, and for the liberal arts Without a parallel; those being all my study *Tempest* i 2 72
Being transported And rapt in secret studies i 2 76
Being once perfected how to grant suits, How to deny them, who to advance i 2 79
Being so retired, O'er-prized all popular rate i 2 91
He being thus lorded, Not only with what my revenue yielded i 2 97
This King of Naples, being an enemy To me inveterate i 2 121
Which any print of goodness wilt not take, Being capable of all ill! i 2 353
The Duke of Milan And his brave son being twain i 2 438
You 'mongst men Being most unfit to live iii 3 58
Whose shadow the dismissed bachelor loves, Being lass-lorn iv 1 68
They being penitent, The sole drift of my purpose doth extend Not a frown further v 1 28
Being destined to a drier death on shore *T. G. of Ver.* i 1 158
And yet I was last chidden for being too slow ii 1 12
Being blind, How could he see his way to seek out you? ii 4 93
The current that with gentle murmur glides, Thou know'st, being stopp'd, impatiently doth rage ii 7 26
The tenour of them doth but signify My health and happy being iii 1 57
Which, being writ to me, shall be deliver'd iii 1 249
Being nimble-footed, he hath outrun us v 3 7
You are partly a bawd, Pompey, howsoever you colour it in being a tapster *Meas. for Meas.* ii 1 232
How would you live, Pompey? by being a bawd? ii 1 237
Being that I flow in grief, The smallest twine may lead me *Much Ado* iv 1 251
Pisa renown'd for grave citizens Gave me my being *T. of Shrew* i 1 11
If The cause were not in being *W. Tale* ii 3 3
She being none of your flesh and blood iv 4 710
Being altogether wanting, It doth remember me the more of sorrow *Richard II.* iii 4 13
Being altogether had, It adds more sorrow to my want of joy iii 4 15
Being now a subject, I have a king here to my flatterer iv 1 307
You loiter here too long, being you are to take soldiers up in counties as you go *2 Hen. IV.* ii 1 199
Would I had no being, If this salute my blood a jot: it faints me, To think what follows *Hen. VIII.* ii 3 102
Best state, contentless, Hath a distracted and most wretched being, Worse than the worst, content *T. of Athens* iv 3 246
Thou shouldst desire to die, being miserable.—Not by his breath that is more miserable iv 3 248
Whose star-like nobleness gave life and influence To their whole being v 1 67
There is none but he Whose being I do fear *Macbeth* iii 1 55
Every minute of his being thrusts Against my near'st of life iii 1 117
Beware Of entrance to a quarrel, but being in, Bear't that the opposed may beware of thee *Hamlet* i 3 66
Being nature's livery, or fortune's star i 4 32
It did seem to shatter all his bulk And end his being ii 1 96
I fetch my life and being From men of royal siege *Othello* i 2 21
She that being anger'd, her revenge being nigh, Bade her wrong stay ii 1 153
My being in Egypt, Cæsar, What was't to you? *Ant. and Cleo.* ii 2 35
If you there Did practise on my state, your being in Egypt Might be my question ii 2 39
He frets That Lepidus of the triumvirate Should be deposed; and, being, that we detain All his revenue iii 6 29
Thou hast forspoke my being in these wars, And say'st it is not fit iii 7 3
Took such sorrow That he quit being *Cymbeline* i 1 38
Return he cannot, nor Continue where he is: to shift his being Is to exchange one misery with another i 5 54
This service is not service, so being done, But being so allow'd iii 3 16
Thief, any thing That's due to all the villains past, in being, To come! v 5 212
It is fit, What being more known grows worse, to smother it *Pericles* i 1 106
All love the womb that their first being bred i 1 107
We'll mingle our bloods together in the earth, From whence we had our being i 2 114
Bel. Like god Bel's priests in the old church-window *Much Ado* iii 3 144
Belarius. Myself, Belarius, that am Morgan call'd, They take for natural father *Cymbeline* iii 3 106
Thou hadst, great king, a subject who Was call'd Belarius v 5 317
I, old Morgan, Am that Belarius whom you sometime banish'd v 5 333
Belch. The never-surfeited sea Hath caused to belch up you *Tempest* iii 3 56
Sir Toby Belch! how now, Sir Toby Belch! *T. Night* i 3 47

Belch. Smother'd it within my panting bulk, Which almost burst to belch it . . . . *Richard III.* i 4 41
They eat us hungerly, and when they are full, They belch us *Othello* iii 4 106
The bitterness of it I now belch from my heart . *Cymbeline* iii 5 137
If the sea's stomach be o'ercharged with gold, 'Tis a good constraint of fortune it belches upon us . . . . *Pericles* iii 2 55
Belched. Thy food is such As hath been belch'd on by infected lungs . iv 6 179
Belching. Like scaled sculls Before the belching whale . *Troi. and Cres.* v 5 23
The belching whale And humming water must o'erwhelm thy corpse *Pericles* iii 1 63
Beldam. Old men and beldams in the streets Do prophesy upon it dangerously . . . . *K. John* iv 2 185
Shakes the old beldam earth and topples down Steeples . 1 *Hen. IV.* iii 1 32
Beldam, I think we watch'd you at an inch . . . 2 *Hen. VI.* i 4 45
You look angerly.—Have I not reason, beldams as you are? . *Macbeth* iii 5 2
Be-lee'd. Must be be-lee'd and calm'd By debitor and creditor . *Othello* i 1 30
Belfry. If I had been the sexton, I would have been that day in the belfry . . . . *Pericles* ii 1 41
Belgia. Where stood Belgia, the Netherlands? . . . *Com. of Errors* iii 2 142
Edward from Belgia, With hasty Germans . . 3 *Hen. VI.* iv 8 1
Belie. To belie him, I will not, and more of his soldiership I know not *All's Well* iv 3 299
They shall yet belie thy happy years, That say thou art a man *T. Night* i 4 30
Thou art not holy to belie me so; I am not mad . *K. John* iii 4 44
Speak comfortable words.—Should I do so, I should belie my thoughts *Richard II.* ii 2 77
Thou dost belie him, Percy, thou dost belie him . . . 1 *Hen. IV.* i 3 113
He doth sin that doth belie the dead. . . . 2 *Hen. IV.* i 1 98
We say lie on her, when they belie her . . . . *Othello* iv 1 36
Thou dost belie her, and thou art a devil . . . . . v 2 133
'Tis slander, . . . whose breath Rides on the posting winds and doth belie All corners of the world . . . . . *Cymbeline* iii 4 38
Belied. O, on my soul, my cousin is belied! . . . . *Much Ado* iv 1 148
My soul doth tell me Hero is belied; And that shall Claudio know . v 1 42
I say thou has belied mine innocent child . . . . . v 1 67
Sixth and lastly, they have belied a lady . . . . . v 1 222
I have belied a lady, The princess of this country, and the air on't Revengingly enfeebles me . . . . *Cymbeline* v 2 2
Belief. Drove the grossness of the foppery into a received belief *Mer. Wives* v 5 132
May in some little measure draw a belief from you . . *As Y. Like It* v 2 63
My niece is already in the belief that he's mad . . . *T. Night* iii 4 149
Let belief and life encounter so As doth the fury of two desperate men *K. John* iii 1 31
His highness yet doth speak, and holds belief That, being brought into the open air, It would allay the burning quality Of that fell poison v 7 6
That she's in a wrong belief, I go to certify her . 1 *Hen. VI.* ii 3 31
To be king Stands not within the prospect of belief. . . *Macbeth* i 3 74
Which was to my belief witness'd the rather . . . . iv 3 184
Will not let belief take hold of him Touching this dreaded sight *Hamlet* i 1 24
This accident is not unlike my dream: Belief of it oppresses me already *Othello* i 1 144
This speed of Cæsar's Carries beyond belief . . *Ant. and Cleo.* iii 7 76
Wounding his belief in her renown . . . . . *Cymbeline* v 5 202
See how belief may suffer by foul show! . . . . *Pericles* iv 4 23
If this but answer to my just belief, I'll well remember you . . v 1 239
Beliest. No, not so, villain; thou beliest thyself . . *Much Ado* v 1 275
Believe. To credit his own lie, he did believe He was indeed the duke *Tempest* i 2 102
Now I will believe That there are unicorns . . . . . iii 3 21
If in Naples I should report this now, would they believe me? . iii 3 28
Who would believe that there were mountaineers Dew-lapp'd like bulls? iii 3 44
I do believe it Against an oracle . . . . iv 1 11
Some subtilties o' the isle, that will not let you Believe things certain . v 1 125
So I believe; but Thurio thinks not so . . *T. G. of Ver.* iii 2 16
You look very ill.—Nay, I'll ne'er believe that . . *Mer. Wives* ii 1 37
I will not believe such a Cataian, though the priest o' the town commended him . . . . ii 1 148
I'll be sworn, . . .—I do believe the swearer . . . . ii 2 40
Believe not that the dribbling dart of love Can pierce a complete bosom *Meas. for Meas.* i 3 2
Whom I believe to be most strait in virtue . . . . . ii 1 9
Did I tell this, Who would believe me? . . . . . . ii 4 172
I do make myself believe that you may . . . . . . iii 1 205
Canst thou believe thy living is a life, So stinkingly depending? . . iii 2 27
I believe I know the cause of his withdrawing . . . . iii 2 139
I know what I know.—I can hardly believe that, since you know not what you speak . . . . iii 2 162
Let me excuse me, and believe me so . . . . . . iv 1 12
I have sat here all day.—I do constantly believe you . . . iv 1 21
If she be mad,—as I believe no other . . . . . . v 1 60
Who is as free from touch or soil with her As she from one ungot.—We did believe no less . . . . v 1 142
Make us but believe, Being compact of credit, that you love us *Com. of Err.* iii 2 21
Whatsoever a man denies, you are now bound to believe him. . . v 1 306
They will scarcely believe this without trial . . . *Much Ado* ii 2 41
For others say thou dost deserve, and I Believe it better than reportingly iii 1 116
Surely I do believe your fair cousin is wronged . . . . iv 1 261
Believe me not; and yet I lie not; I confess nothing, nor I deny nothing iv 1 273
He hath the tongues: 'That I believe,' said she . . . . v 1 168
Who I believe was pack'd in all this wrong, Hired to it by your brother v 1 308
But I believe, although I seem so loath, I am the last that will last keep his oath . . . . *L. L. Lost* i 1 160
Do not believe But I shall do thee mischief . . *M. N. Dream* ii 1 236
I believe we must leave the killing out, when all is done. . . . iii 1 15
I'll believe as soon This whole earth may be bored . . . . iii 2 52
I never may believe These antique fables, nor these fairy toys . . v 1 2
Made her neighbours believe she wept for the death of a third husband *Mer. of Venice* iii 1 11
Nerissa teaches me what to believe . . . . v 1 207
And she believes, wherever they are gone, That youth is surely in their company . . . . *As Y. Like It* ii 2 15
Fair youth, I would I could make thee believe I love.—Me believe it! you may as soon make her that you love believe it . . . . iii 2 405
Believe then, if you please, that I can do strange things . . . v 2 64
I sometimes do believe, and sometimes do not . . . . . v 4 3
I tell you, 'tis incredible to believe How much she loves me . *T. of Shrew* ii 1 308
In time I may believe, yet I mistrust . . . . iii 1 51
I must believe my master; else, I promise you, I should be arguing still iii 1 54
So his mother says, if I may believe her . . . . . . v 1 35
I believe a' means to cozen somebody in this city . . . . v 1 39
Believe. The complaints I have heard of you I do not all believe *All's Well* i 3 10
Which hung so tottering in the balance that I could neither believe nor misdoubt . . . . i 3 130
Dost thou believe't?—Ay, madam, knowingly . . . . . . i 3 255
Believe not thy disdain, but presently Do thine own fortunes that obedient right . . . . ii 3 166
O, I believe with him, In argument of praise . . . . . . iii 5 61
Would you believe my oaths, When I did love you ill? . . . . iv 2 26
If your lordship be in't, as I believe you are . . . . . iv 3 132
Nor believe he can have every thing in him by wearing his apparel neatly iv 3 166
Which nothing, but to close Her eyes myself, could win me to believe . v 3 119
Yet of thee I will believe thou hast a mind that suits With this *T. Night* i 2 50
I am a great eater of beef and I believe that does harm to my wit . . i 3 91
I could not with such estimable wonder overfar believe that . . ii 1 29
No Christian, that means to be saved by believing rightly, can ever believe such impossible passages of grossness . . . . . . iii 2 76
His words do from such passion fly, That he believes himself. . . iii 4 408
Will you make me believe that I am not sent for you? . . . . iv 1 1
I'll ne'er believe a madman till I see his brains . . . . . iv 2 125
I cannot Believe this crack to be in my dread mistress . *W. Tale* i 2 322
Would I do this? Could man so blench?—I must believe you, sir. . i 2 333
I'll be sworn you would believe my saying, Howe'er you lean to the nayward . . . . ii 1 63
I do believe Hermione hath suffer'd death . . . . . . iii 3 41
I have it Upon his own report and I believe it. . . . . . iv 4 170
Believe me, I do not believe thee, man . . . . *K. John* iii 1 9
Whether thy tale be true.—As true as I believe you think them false . iii 1 27
If thou teach me to believe this sorrow, Teach thou this sorrow how to make me die . . . . iii 1 29
I do fearfully believe 'tis done, What we so fear'd . . . . iv 2 74
I will upon all hazards well believe Thou art my friend . . . v 6 7
If I know how or which way to order these affairs Thus thrust disorderly into my hands, Never believe me . . . . . *Richard II.* ii 2 111
Believe not this hard-hearted man! Love loving not itself none other can . . . . v 3 87
I well believe Thou wilt not utter what thou dost not know . 1 *Hen. IV.* ii 3 113
He would swear truth out of England but he would make you believe it ii 4 338
Make me believe that thou art only mark'd For the hot vengeance and the rod of heaven To punish my mistreadings . . . . . . iii 2 9
What didst thou lose, Jack?—Wilt thou believe me, Hal? . . . iii 3 116
Your son is dead.—I am sorry I should force you to believe That which I would to God I had not seen . . . . . 2 *Hen. IV.* i 1 105
O, who shall believe But you misuse the reverence of your place? . . iv 2 22
Believe not the word of the noble: therefore let me have right . . iv 3 59
We will hear, note and believe in heart That what you speak *Hen. V.* i 2 30
I do believe your majesty takes no scorn to wear the leek upon Saint Tavy's day . . . . iv 7 106
Believe my words, For they are certain and unfallible . 1 *Hen. VI.* i 2 58
I do believe that violent hands were laid Upon the life . 2 *Hen. VI.* iii 2 156
And you, base peasants, do ye believe him? . . . . . . iv 8 22
Either not believe The envious slanders of her false accusers *Richard III.* i 3 25
I'll not believe but they [curses] ascend the sky . . . . . i 3 287
For a season after Could not believe but that I was in hell . . . i 4 62
Take the devil in thy mind, and believe him not . . . . . i 4 152
A reeling world, indeed, my lord; And I believe 'twill never stand upright . . . . iii 2 39
Would you imagine, or almost believe? . . . . iii 5 35
Such as give Their money out of hope they may believe . *Hen. VIII.* Prol. 8
Have you a precedent Of this commission? I believe, not any . . i 2 92
His curses and his blessings Touch me alike, they're breath I not believe in . . . . ii 2 54
Shortly, I believe, His second marriage shall be publish'd . . . iii 2 67
I must not believe you: There they stand yet . . *Troi. and Cres.* iv 5 221
Wert thou an oracle to tell me so, I'ld not believe thee . . . iv 5 253
I am a rascal; a scurvy railing knave; a very filthy rogue.—I do believe thee . . . . v 4 32
God-a-mercy, that thou wilt believe me! . . . . v 4 33
If I should tell thee o'er this thy day's work, Thou'ldst not believe thy deeds: but I'll report it . . . . *Coriolanus* i 9 2
And believe't not lightly—though I go alone . . . . . . iv 1 29
If Jupiter Should from yond cloud speak divine things, And say 'Tis true,' I'ld not believe them more Than thee . . . . . iv 5 111
Thou believest no god: That granted, how canst thou believe an oath? *T. Andron.* v 1 72
Or, if thou wilt, swear by thy gracious self, Which is the god of my idolatry, And I'll believe thee . . . . . *Rom. and Jul.* ii 2 115
Believe me, love, it was the nightingale . . . . . . iii 5 5
Shall I believe That unsubstantial death is amorous? . . . . v 3 102
Scolds against the quality of flesh, And not believes himself *T. of Athens* iv 3 157
I'll believe him as an enemy, and give over my trade . . . . iv 3 459
I do believe that these applauses are For some new honours . *J. Cæsar* i 2 133
I believe, they are portentous things Unto the climate that they point upon . . . . i 3 31
Believe me for mine honour, and have respect to mine honour . . iii 2 14
Believe not so—but believe it partly . . . . v 1 90
I believe drink gave thee the lie last night.—That it did, sir . *Macbeth* ii 3 41
What I believe I'll wail, What know believe . . . . . . iv 3 8
Before my God, I might not this believe Without the sensible and true avouch Of mine own eyes . . . . *Hamlet* i 1 56
So have I heard and do in part believe it . . . . i 1 165
If he says he loves you, It fits your wisdom so far to believe it . . i 3 25
Do you believe his tenders, as you call them? . . . . . . i 3 103
Believe so much in him, that he is young . . . . i 3 124
In few, Ophelia, Do not believe his vows . . . . i 3 127
Marry, sir, here's my drift; And, I believe, it is a fetch of wit . . ii 1 38
I most powerfully and potently believe, yet I hold it not honesty to have it thus set down . . . . ii 2 204
I did love you once.—Indeed, my lord, you made me believe so . . iii 1 117
We are arrant knaves, all; believe none of us. Go thy ways to a nunnery iii 1 131
I believe The origin and commencement of his grief Sprung from neglected love . . . . iii 1 184
I do believe you think what now you speak; But what we do determine oft we break . . . . iii 2 196
Do not believe it.—Believe what?—That I can keep your counsel and not mine own . . . . iv 2 9
Report me and my cause aright To the unsatisfied.—Never believe it . v 2 351
Which to believe of her, Must be a faith that reason without miracle Could never plant in me . . . . *Lear* i 1 224
He will not believe a fool.—A bitter fool! . . . . i 4 148

Believe. I can scarce speak to thee; thou'lt not believe With how depraved a quality—O Regan! . . . . *Lear* ii 4 138
Do not believe That, from the sense of all civility, I thus would play and trifle . . . . *Othello* i 1 131
With his free duty recommends you thus, And prays you to believe him i 3 42
I cannot believe that in her; she's full of most blessed condition . ii 1 254
Cassio, I believe, received From him that fled some strange indignity . ii 3 244
If she be false, O, then heaven mocks itself! I'll not believe't . . iii 3 279
Which I have greater reason to believe now than ever . . . iv 2 217
Believe not all; or, if you must believe, Stomach not all *Ant. and Cleo.* iii 4 11
And believe, Cæsar's no merchant, to make prize with you Of things that merchants sold . . . . v 2 182
He that will believe all that they say, shall never be saved by half that they do . . . . v 2 256
I could not but believe she excelled many . . . *Cymbeline* i 4 80
I do believe, Statist though I am none, nor like to be . . . ii 4 15
My circumstances, Being so near the truth as I will make them, Must first induce you to believe . . . . ii 4 63
Thus may poor fools Believe false teachers . . . . . iii 4 87
He believes It is a thing most precious . . . . . iii 5 58
And, but she spoke it dying, I would not Believe her lips . . v 5 42
I believe you; Your honour and your goodness teach me to't *Pericles* iii 3 25
I will believe thee, And make my senses credit thy relation . . v 1 123
You said you would believe me; But, not to be a troubler of your peace, I will end here . . . . v 1 152
I will believe you by the syllable Of what you shall deliver . . v 1 169
Believe it *Mer. Wives* ii 1; ii 2; *Meas. for Meas.* v 1; *All's Well* iii 2; iii 6; *T. Night* i 4; *Hen. VIII.* iii 2; *Coriolanus* v 3; *T. of Athens* i 1; iii 4; iv 3; *Hamlet* ii 2; *Ant. and Cleo.* iii 2; *Cymbeline* i 4; *Pericles* ii 1
Believe me *Tempest* i 2; *T. G. of Ver.* ii 1; *Mer. Wives* i 1; ii 1; iii 3; *Meas. for Meas.* i 2; ii 4; *Much Ado* ii 1; *M. N. Dream* iii 2; *Mer. of Venice* i 1; *T. of Shrew* Ind. 1; ii 1; iii 2; v 2; *T. Night* i 4; iv 2; *W. Tale* i 1; iv 4; *K. John* iii 1; v 2; *Richard II.* ii 3; *2 Hen. IV.* iv 2; v 2; 1 *Hen. VI.* iii 1; 2 *Hen. VI.* ii 1; iii 1; 3 *Hen. VI.* iv 5; *Hen. VIII.* ii 2; iii 1; iv 1; *Coriolanus* i 6; *T. Andron.* ii 3; *Rom. and Jul.* i 4; iii 5; *Hamlet* ii 2; v 2; *Othello* iii 4; *Pericles* iv 1
Believe this *Meas. for Meas.* ii 2; ii 4; *All's Well* ii 5
Do not believe it *Meas. for Meas.* i 4; *T. of Athens* iii 2; *Hamlet* iv 2
I do believe it *W. Tale* ii 2; *Troi. and Cres.* iii 3; *Othello* v 2
I do well believe *Tempest* ii 1; *W. Tale* v 3; *Othello* ii 1; *Cymbeline* i 1

Believed. On mine honour, My words express my purpose.—Ha! little honour to be much believed! . . . . *Meas. for Meas.* ii 4 149
That which I must speak Must either punish me, not being believed, Or wring redress from you . . . . v 1 31
Three great oaths would scarce make that be believed . *All's Well* iv 1 65
I have too much believed mine own suspicion . . . *W. Tale* iii 2 152
I have heard, but not believed, the spirits o' the dead May walk again . iii 3 16
If an angel should have come to me And told me Hubert should put out mine eyes, I would not have believed him . . . *K. John* iv 1 70
What thou speakest may move and what he hears may be believed 1 *Hen. IV.* i 2 173
If I may be believed, so; if not, let them that should reward valour bear the sin upon their own heads . . . . v 4 152
If something thou wilt swear to be believed, Swear then by something that thou hast not wrong'd . . . . *Richard III.* iv 4 372
That former fabulous story, Being now seen possible enough, got credit, That Bevis was believed . . . . *Hen. VIII.* i 1 38
Some design, which, being believed, It was much like to do . . i 2 181
Let it not be believed for womanhood! . . . *Troi. and Cres.* v 2 129
And be these juggling fiends no more believed, That palter with us in a double sense . . . . *Macbeth* v 8 19
You made me believe so.—You should not have believed me . *Hamlet* iii 1 118
What, i' the storm? i' the night? Let pity not be believed! . . *Lear* iv 3 31
This would not be believed in Venice, Though I should swear I saw't *Othello* iv 1 253
This is not strong enough to be believed Of one persuaded well of *Cymb.* ii 4 131

Believest. I conjure thee, as thou believest There is another comfort than this world . . . . *Meas. for Meas.* v 1 48
Thou believest no god: That granted, how canst thou believe an oath? *T. Andron.* v 1 71

Believing. No, believe me.—No believing you, indeed, sir *T. G. of Ver.* ii 1 162
If he be not in love with some woman, there is no believing old signs *Much Ado* iii 2 41
Believing thee a vessel of too great a burthen . . . *All's Well* ii 3 215
No Christian, that means to be saved by believing rightly, can ever believe such impossible passages of grossness . . *T. Night* iii 2 76
God be praised, that to believing souls Gives light in darkness! 2 *Hen. VI.* ii 1 66

Belike. Heavy! belike it hath some burden then? . *T. G. of Ver.* i 2 85
Belike, boy, then, you are in love . . . . . . ii 1 85
Belike that now she hath enfranchised them . . . . . ii 4 90
She is dead, belike?—Not so; I think she lives . . . . iv 4 80
Belike she thinks that Proteus hath forsook her.—I think she doth . iv 4 151
Who, belike having received wrong by some person *Mer. Wives* iii 1 53
Belike thinking me remiss in mine office . . . *Meas. for Meas.* iv 2 118
Friar Lodowick.—A ghostly father, belike . . . . . v 1 126
Words against me! this is a good friar, belike! . . . . v 1 131
Belike you thought our love would last too long . *Com. of Errors* iv 1 25
Belike his wife, acquainted with his fits, On purpose shut the doors . iv 3 91
Some merry mocking lord, belike; is't so? . . . *L. L. Lost* v 1 52
An if my hand be out, then belike your hand is in . . . . iv 1 137
How chance the roses there do fade so fast?—Belike for want of rain *M. N. Dream* i 1 130
See what trumpet 'tis that sounds: Belike, some noble gentleman *T. of Shrew* Ind. 1 75
As though, belike, I knew not what to take, and what to leave . i 1 104
O then, belike, you fancy riches more . . . . . . ii 1 16
Belike you mean to make a puppet of me.—Why, true . . . iv 3 103
A noble scar, is a good livery of honour; so belike is that . *All's Well* iv 5 106
Belike you slew great number of his people . . . *T. Night* iii 3 29
Belike this is a man of that quirk . . . . . . iii 4 268
Who, I cannot learn.—O, belike it is the Bishop of Carlisle *Richard II* iii 3 30
Belike then my appetite was not princely got . . . 2 *Hen. IV.* ii 2 11
Mine was not bridled.—O then belike she was old and gentle. *Hen. V.* iii 7 55
Belike your lordship takes us then for fools . . . 1 *Hen. VI.* iii 2 62
Then you, belike, suspect these noblemen . . . 2 *Hen. VI.* iii 2 186
Belike he means . . . To aspire unto the crown . . 3 *Hen. VI.* i 1 51
'Twas odds, belike, when valiant Warwick fled . . . . ii 1 148
Is Lewis so brave? belike he thinks me Henry . . . . . iv 1 96
Belike she minds to play the Amazon . . . . . . iv 1 106
Prince Edward marries Warwick's daughter.—Belike the elder . . iv 1 118
Belike. To-morrow then belike shall be the day . . 3 *Hen. VI.* iv 3 7
Who should that be? belike, unlook'd-for friends . . . . v 1 14
O, belike his majesty hath some intent . . . *Richard III.* i 1 49
Aiming, belike, at your interior hatred . . . . . . i 3 65
Belike they had some notice of the people, How I had moved them *J. Cæsar* iii 2 275
Belike this show imports the argument of the play . . *Hamlet* iii 2 149
For if the king like not the comedy, Why then, belike, he likes it not, perdy . . . . iii 2 305
Belike, Something—I know not what . . . . . . *Lear* iv 5 20
But that belike Iago in the interim Came in and satisfied him *Othello* v 2 317
Then belike my children shall have no names . . *Ant. and Cleo.* i 2 35
What news?—Belike 'tis but a rumour . . . . . iv 3 5

Bell. Ding-dong.—Hark! now I hear them,—Ding-dong, bell . *Tempest* i 2 404
Where the bee sucks, there suck I: In a cowslip's bell I lie . . v 1 89
The Windsor bell hath struck twelve; the minute draws on *Mer. Wives* v 5 1
The clock hath strucken twelve upon the bell . . *Com. of Errors* i 2 45
Do you not hear it ring?—What, the chain?—No, no, the bell . . iv 2 53
He hath a heart as sound as a bell and his tongue is the clapper *Much Ado* iii 2 13
He shall live no longer in monument than the bell rings . . . v 2 81
Slow in pursuit, but match'd in mouth like bells, Each under each *M. N. Dream* iv 1 128
Let us all ring fancy's knell: I'll begin it,—Ding, dong, bell *Mer. of Ven.* iii 2 71
If ever been where bells have knoll'd to church . . *As Y. Like It* ii 7 114
We have seen better days, And have with holy bell been knoll'd to church . . . . ii 7 121
As the ox hath his bow, sir, the horse his curb and the falcon her bells iii 3 81
Or the bells of Saint Bennet, sir, may put you in mind; one, two, three *T. Night* v 1 42
Rejoice, you men of Angiers, ring your bells . . . *K. John* ii 1 312
Bell, book, and candle shall not drive me back . . . . iii 3 12
The midnight bell Did, with his iron tongue and brazen mouth, Sound on . . . . iii 3 37
The sound that tells what hour it is Are clamorous groans, which strike upon my heart, Which is the bell . . . . *Richard II.* v 5 57
His tongue Sounds ever after as a sullen bell . . . 2 *Hen IV.* i 1 102
Assembled by the bell, Encircled you to hear with reverence Your exposition . . . . iv 2 5
Bid the merry bells ring to thine ear That thou art crowned . . iv 5 112
Why ring not out the bells aloud throughout the town? . 1 *Hen. VI.* i 6 11
A warning bell, Sings heavy music to thy timorous soul . . . iv 2 39
I have seen Him caper upright like a wild Morisco, Shaking the bloody darts as he his bells . . . . . . 2 *Hen. VI.* iii 1 366
Ring, bells, aloud; burn, bonfires, clear and bright . . . v 1 3
Nor he that loves him best, The proudest he that holds up Lancaster, Dares stir a wing, if Warwick shake his bells . 3 *Hen. VI.* i 1 47
My sighing breast shall be thy funeral bell . . . . . ii 5 117
I'll startle you Worse than the sacring bell . . . *Hen. VIII.* iii 2 295
No mournful bell shall ring her burial . . . . *T. Andron.* v 3 197
Our instruments to melancholy bells . . . . *Rom. and Jul.* iv 5 86
This sight of death is as a bell, That warns my old age to a sepulchre . v 3 206
Bid thy mistress, when my drink is ready, She strike upon the bell *Macbeth* ii 1 32
I go, and it is done; the bell invites me. Hear it not, Duncan . ii 1 62
Ring the bell.—What's the business, That such a hideous trumpet calls to parley? . . . . ii 3 85
The bell then beating one,— Peace, break thee off; look, where it comes again! . . . . *Hamlet* i 1 39
Like sweet bells jangled, out of tune and harsh . . . . iii 1 166
She is allow'd her virgin crants, Her maiden strewments and the bringing home Of bell and burial . . . . v 1 257
Arise, arise; Awake the snorting citizens with the bell . . . *Othello* i 1 90
You are pictures out of doors, Bells in your parlours . . . ii 1 111
From this present hour of five till the bell have told eleven . . ii 2 11
Who's that which rings the bell?—Diablo, ho! The town will rise . ii 3 161
Silence that dreadful bell: it frights the isle From her propriety . ii 3 175
Fill our bowls once more; Let's mock the midnight bell *Ant. and Cleo.* iii 13 185
Never leave gaping till they've swallowed the whole parish, church, steeple, bells, and all . . . . *Pericles* ii 1 38
I would have kept such a jangling of the bells, that he should never have left, till he cast bells, steeple, church, and parish, up again . ii 1 45

Bellario. Render this Into my cousin's hand, Doctor Bellario *Mer. of Ven.* iii 4 50
Bellario, a learned doctor, Whom I have sent for to determine this . iv 1 105
Came you from Padua, from Bellario?—From both, my lord. Bellario greets your grace . . . . iv 1 119
You hear the learn'd Bellario, what he writes: And here, I take it, is the doctor come . . . . iv 1 167
Come you from old Bellario?—I did, my lord . . . . . iv 1 169
Read it at your leisure; It comes from Padua, from Bellario . . v 1 268

Belle. How answer you, la plus belle Katharine du monde? *Hen. V.* v 2 231

Bellied. Your breath of full consent bellied his sails . *Troi. and Cres.* ii 2 74

Bellies. With hearts in their bellies no bigger than pins' heads 1 *Hen. IV.* iv 2 23
O, they eat lords; so they come by great bellies . *T. of Athens* i 1 210

Bellman. The fatal bellman, Which gives the stern'st good-night *Macbeth* ii 2 3

Bellona's bridegroom, lapp'd in proof, Confronted him . . . i 2 54

Bellow. The croaking raven doth bellow for revenge . . *Hamlet* iii 2 265

Bellowed. Jupiter Became a bull, and bellow'd . . . *W. Tale* iv 4 28
So strutted and bellowed . . . . *Hamlet* iii 2 36
He fasten'd on my neck, and bellow'd out As he'ld burst heaven *Lear* v 3 212

Bellowing. A hollow burst of bellowing Like bulls, or rather lions *Temp.* ii 1 311
Unhandled colts, Fetching mad bounds, bellowing and neighing *Mer. of Venice* v 1 73

Bellows. And is become the bellows and the fan To cool a gipsy's lust *Ant. and Cleo.* i 1 9
Flattery is the bellows blows up sin . . . . . *Pericles* i 2 39

Bellows-mender. Francis Flute, the bellows-mender . *M. N. Dream* i 2 44
Peter Quince! Flute, the bellows-mender! Snout, the tinker! . . iv 1 207

Bell-wether. To be detected with a jealous rotten bell-wether *Mer. Wives* iii 5 111
To be bawd to a bell-wether, and to betray a she-lamb . *As Y. Like It* iii 2 85

Belly. The beam of her view gilded my foot, sometimes my portly belly *Mer. Wives* i 3 69
This whale, with so many tuns of oil in his belly . . . . ii 1 66
My belly's as cold as if I had swallowed snowballs for pills . . iii 5 23
I was thrown into the ford; I have my belly full of ford . . . iii 5 37
I dare not for my head fill my belly . . . *Meas. for Meas.* iv 3 160
She's quick; the child brags in her belly already . . *L. L. Lost* v 2 683
No more man's blood in's belly than will sup a flea . . . v 2 698
The getting up of the negro's belly . . . . *Mer. of Venice* iii 5 42
Then the justice, In fair round belly with good capon lined *As Y. Like It* ii 7 154
So you may put a man in your belly . . . . iii 2 215

Belly. My very lips might freeze to my teeth, my tongue to the roof of my mouth, my heart in my belly . . . *T. of Shrew* iv 1 8
Be it concluded, No barricado for a belly . . . . *W. Tale* i 2 204
That roasted Manningtree ox with the pudding in his belly 1 *Hen. IV.* ii 4 499
'Sblood, I would my face were in your belly ! . . . . iii 3 57
I am the fellow with the great belly, and he my dog . 2 *Hen. IV.* i 2 165
A white beard ? a decreasing leg ? an increasing belly ? . . . . i 2 205
With a white head and something a round belly . . . . i 2 212
He hath put all my substance into that fat belly of his . . ii 1 82
A' made a shrewd thrust at your belly . . . . . ii 4 228
I have a whole school of tongues in this belly of mine . . . iv 3 21
An I had but a belly of any indifferency, I were simply the most active fellow in Europe . . . . iv 3 23
Underneath the belly of their steeds . . . . . 3 *Hen. VI.* ii 3 20
Upon my back, to defend my belly . . . *Troi. and Cres.* i 2 284
Who wears his wit in his belly and his guts in his head . . ii 1 80
A time when all the body's members Rebell'd against the belly *Coriolanus* i 1 100
The belly answer'd— Well, sir, what answer made the belly ? . . i 1 109
For, look you, I may make the belly smile As well as speak . . i 1 113
Should by the cormorant belly be restrain'd, Who is the sink o' the body i 1 125
What could the belly answer ?—I will tell you . . . . i 1 128
Patience awhile, you 'll hear the belly's answer . . . . i 1 130
Your most grave belly was deliberate, Not rash like his accusers . i 1 132
The senators of Rome are this good belly, And you the mutinous members . . . . i 1 152
Hopdance cries in Tom's belly for two white herring . . *Lear* iii 6 33
When I had been in his belly, I would have kept such a jangling *Pericles* ii 1 44
Bellyful. Rumble thy bellyful ! Spit, fire ! spout, rain ! . . *Lear* iii 2 14
Every Jack-slave hath his bellyful of fighting . . . *Cymbeline* ii 1 23
Belly-pinched. The lion and the belly-pinched wolf Keep their fur dry *Lear* iii 1 13
Belman. I would not lose the dog for twenty pound.—Why, Belman is as good as he . . . . *T. of Shrew* Ind. 1 22
Belmont. In Belmont is a lady richly left . . . *Mer. of Venice* i 1 161
Which makes her seat of Belmont Colchos' strand, And many Jasons come in quest of her . . . . i 1 171
Shall be rack'd, even to the uttermost, To furnish thee to Belmont . i 1 182
I must go with you to Belmont.—Why, then you must . . . ii 2 188
In the morning early will we both Fly toward Belmont . . . iv 1 457
With an unthrift love did run from Venice As far as Belmont . . v 1 17
My mistress will before the break of day Be here at Belmont . . v 1 30
Belocked. This is the hand which, with a vow'd contract, Was fast belock'd in thine . . . . *Meas. for Meas.* v 1 210
Belong. We know what belongs to a frippery . . . *Tempest* iv 1 224
We will rather sleep than talk : we know what belongs to a watch *Much Ado* iii 3 40
To things of sale a seller's praise belongs . . . *L. L. Lost* iv 3 240
But that you take what doth to you belong, It were a fault to snatch words from my tongue . . . . v 2 381
Thy beauty sounded, Yet not so deeply as to thee belongs *T. of Shrew* ii 1 194
Pewter and brass and all things that belong To house or housekeeping . ii 1 357
This thorn Doth to our rose of youth rightly belong . *All's Well* i 3 136
Here it is, and all that belongs to 't . . . . . . ii 2 38
Belong you to the Lady Olivia, friends ? . . . . *T. Night* v 1 9
I am proof against that title and what shame else belongs to't *W. Tale* iv 4 873
Doth not thy embassage belong to me, And am I last that knows it? *Richard II.* iii 4 93
To you This honourable bounty shall belong . . 1 *Hen. IV.* v 5 26
There is no need of any such redress ; Or if there were, it not belongs to you.—Why not to him? . . . . . 2 *Hen. IV.* iv 1 98
Doth any name particular belong Unto the lodging where I first did swoon ? . . . . iv 5 233
My lord should be religious And know the office that belongs to such 1 *Hen. VI.* iii 1 55
Disdaining duty that to us belongs . . . . 2 *Hen. VI.* iii 1 17
Forgive me, God, For judgement only doth belong to thee . . v 2 140
As I belong to worship and affect In honour honesty . *Hen. VIII.* i 1 39
An if there be No great offence belongs to 't . . . . . v 1 12
I belong to the larder.—Belong to the gallows, and be hanged ! . v 4 4
The duty which To a mother's part belongs . . . *Coriolanus* v 3 168
Stay, madam ; here is more belongs to her . . . *T. Andron.* ii 3 122
Your tributary drops belong to woe . . . . *Rom. and Jul.* iii 2 103
Did not you chiefly belong to my heart ? . . . *T. of Athens* i 2 95
No blame belongs to thee . . . . ii 2 231
One that knows what belongs to reason . . . . . . iii 1 38
Bid adieu to me, and say the tears Belong to Egypt . *Ant. and Cleo.* i 3 78
Wilt thou hear more, my lord ?—All that belongs to this . *Cymbeline* v 5 147
Belonged. And showed what necessity belonged to 't . *T. of Athens* iii 2 15
With a solemn earnestness, More than indeed belong'd to such a trifle *Othello* v 2 228
Belonging. Thyself and thy belongings Are not thine own so proper as to waste Thyself upon thy virtues, they on thee . *Meas. for Meas.* i 1 30
Belonging to whom ?—To my fortunes and me . . . *L. L. Lost* ii 1 224
Furnish him with all appertinents Belonging to his honour . *Hen. V.* ii 2 88
In token of the which, My noble steed, known to the camp, I give him, With all his trim belonging . . . . . . *Coriolanus* i 9 62
Nor arm, nor face, nor any other part Belonging to a man *Rom. and Jul.* ii 2 42
Beloved. He writes How happily he lives, how well beloved *T. G. of Ver.* i 3 57
'Tis the curse in love, and still approved, When women cannot love where they're beloved !—When Proteus cannot love where he's beloved . . . . v 4 44
Of credit infinite, highly beloved, Second to none . *Com. of Errors* v 1 6
I am beloved of beauteous Hermia . . . . *M. N. Dream* i 1 104
As, after some oration fairly spoke By a beloved prince . *Mer. of Venice* iii 2 181
And no less beloved of her uncle than his own daughter . *As Y. Like It* i 1 116
Full of noble device, of all sorts enchantingly beloved . . . i 1 174
Who could be out, being before his beloved mistress ? . . . iv 1 82
My best beloved and approved friend . . . . *T. of Shrew* i 2 3
So shall I no whit be behind in duty To fair Bianca, so beloved of me . i 2 176
Nay, I told you your son was well beloved . . . . . v 1 26
Unstaid and skittish in all motions else, Save in the constant image of the creature That is beloved . . . . *T. Night* ii 4 20
To the unknown beloved, this, and my good wishes . . . ii 5 101
Our wife, and one Of us too much beloved . . . *W. Tale* iii 2 4
Not for Bohemia . . . will I break my oath To this my fair beloved . iv 4 503
Into the bosom creep Of that same noble prelate, well beloved 1 *Hen. IV.* i 3 267
And the protector's wife, beloved of him . . . 2 *Hen. VI.* i 2 44
No less beloved Than when thou wert protector . . . . ii 3 26
And am I then a man to be beloved ? O monstrous fault, to harbour such a thought ! . . . . 3 *Hen. VI.* iii 2 163
Beloved. And thou, brave Oxford, wondrous well beloved 3 *Hen. VI.* iv 8 17
Ten times more beloved Than if thou never hadst deserved our hate . v 1 103
Ever beloved and loving may his rule be ! . . . *Hen. VIII.* ii 1 92
That she beloved knows nought that knows not this . *Troi. and Cres.* i 2 314
She was beloved, she loved ; she is, and doth . . . . . iv 5 292
Lest parties, as he is beloved, break out, And sack great Rome *Coriol.* iii 1 315
And come home beloved Of all the trades in Rome . . . . iii 2 133
This man, Aufidius, Was my beloved in Rome . . . . . v 2 99
Long live Lord Titus, my beloved brother ! . . . *T. Andron.* i 1 169
Let us go ; and pray to all the gods For our beloved mother . . iv 2 47
Now Romeo is beloved and loves again . . . *Rom. and Jul.* ii Prol. 5
When Fortune in her shift and change of mood Spurns down her late beloved, all his dependants . . . let him slip down *T. of Athens* i 1 85
You see, my lord, how ample you 're beloved . . . . . i 2 136
Make the meat be beloved more than the man that gives it . . iii 6 85
What man didst thou ever know unthrift that was beloved after his means ?—Who, without those means thou talkest of, didst thou ever know beloved ? . . . . iv 3 312
It is not meet, Mark Antony, so well beloved of Cæsar, Should outlive Cæsar . . . . *J. Cæsar* ii 1 156
Thou shalt live in this fair world behind, Honour'd, beloved . *Hamlet* iii 2 186
The sway, revenue, execution of the rest, Beloved sons, be yours . *Lear* i 1 140
And live the beloved of your brother . . . . i 2 57
Beloved Regan, Thy sister 's naught . . . . ii 4 135
Sorrow would be a rarity most beloved, If all could so become . . iv 3 25
The magnifico is much beloved, And hath in his effect a voice potential *Othello* i 2 12
I'll set a bourn how far to be beloved . . . . *Ant. and Cleo.* i 1 16
You shall be more beloving than beloved . . . . . . i 2 22
It appears he is beloved of those That only have fear'd Cæsar . . i 4 37
Wilt take thy chance with me? I will not say Thou shalt be so well master'd, but, be sure, No less beloved . . . . . *Cymbeline* iv 2 384
The main grief springs from the loss Of a beloved daughter and a wife *Pericles* v 1 30
Beloving. You shall be more beloving than beloved . *Ant. and Cleo.* i 2 22
Below. I pray now, keep below . . . . *Tempest* i 1 12
Or Phœbus steeds are founder'd, Or Night kept chain'd below . . iv 1 31
One Master Brook below would fain speak with you . *Mer. Wives* ii 2 151
Meet me at the consecrated fount A league below the city *Meas. for Meas.* iv 3 103
Why, shall I always keep below stairs ? . . . . *Much Ado* v 2 10
And place your hands below your husband's foot . . *T. of Shrew* v 2 177
Who were below him He used as creatures of another place . . *All's Well* i 2 41
From below your duke to beneath your constable . . . . ii 3 32
Ancient Pistol's below, and would speak with you . . 2 *Hen. IV.* ii 4 74
You be by her aloft, while we be busy below . . . . 2 *Hen. VI.* i 4 11
One heaved a-high, to be hurl'd down below . . . *Richard III.* iv 4 86
They are as children but one step below . . . . . . iv 4 301
His thinkings are below the moon, not worth His serious considering *Hen. VIII.* iii 2 134
That hope makes In all designs begun on earth below . *Troi. and Cres.* i 3 4
The general's disdain'd By him one step below, he by the next . . i 3 130
Feebling such as stand not in their liking Below their cobbled shoes *Cor.* i 1 200
Can not Better be held nor more attain'd than by A place below the first i 1 270
So men obey'd And fell below his stem . . . . . . ii 2 111
That the precipitation might down stretch Below the beam of sight . iii 2 5
I will not loose again, Till thou art here aloft, or I below *T. Andron.* ii 3 244
I'll dive into the burning lake below . . . . . . iv 3 43
Say I am Revenge, sent from below To join with him . . . . v 2 3
O God, I have an ill-divining soul ! Methinks I see thee, now thou art below, As one dead in the bottom of a tomb . *Rom. and Jul.* iii 5 55
One man beckon'd from the rest below . . . . *T. of Athens* i 1 74
Below thy sister's orb Infect the air ! . . . . iv 3 2
For every grise of fortune Is smooth'd by that below . . . . iv 3 17
Pluck stout men's pillows from below their heads . . . . . iv 3 32
With all the abhorred births below crisp heaven . . . . . iv 3 183
To stay the providence of some high powers That govern us below *J. C.* v 1 108
The bold winds speechless and the orb below As hush as death *Hamlet* ii 2 507
My words fly up, my thoughts remain below . . . . . . iii 3 97
I will delve one yard below their mines, And blow them at the moon . iii 4 208
Down, thou climbing sorrow, Thy element's below ! . . . *Lear* ii 4 58
As I stood here below, methought his eyes Were two full moons . . iv 6 69
From the extremest upward of thy head To the descent and dust below thy foot . . . . v 3 137
Help, friends below ; let's draw him hither . . *Ant. and Cleo.* iv 15 13
They are as gentle As zephyrs blowing below the violet . *Cymbeline* iv 2 172
We here below Recall not what we give . . . . . *Pericles* iii 1 24
Belt. He that buckles him in my belt cannot live in less . 2 *Hen. IV.* i 2 157
He cannot buckle his distemper'd cause Within the belt of rule *Macbeth* v 2 16
Belzebub. He holds Belzebub at the staves's end . . . *T. Night* v 1 291
Bemadding. Unnatural and bemadding sorrow . . . . *Lear* iii 1 38
Be-mete. I shall so be-mete thee with thy yard . . *T. of Shrew* iv 3 113
Bemoaned. Was ever father so bemoan'd his son ? . . 3 *Hen. VI.* ii 5 110
Be-mock the modest moon . . . . *Coriolanus* i 1 261
Bemocked-at. Or with bemock'd-at stabs Kill the still-closing waters *Tempest* iii 3 63
Bemoiled. In how miry a place, how she was bemoiled . *T. of Shrew* iv 1 77
Be-monster. For shame, Be-monster not thy feature . . . *Lear* iv 2 63
Bench. He'll stand at your door like a sheriff's post, and be the supporter to a bench . . . . *T. Night* i 5 158
And sleeping upon benches after noon . . . . . 1 *Hen. IV.* i 2 4
To pluck down justice from your awful bench . . . 2 *Hen. IV.* v 2 86
Who puts his 'shall,' His popular 'shall,' against a graver bench Than ever frown'd in Greece . . . . *Coriolanus* iii 1 106
Their obedience fails To the greater bench . . . . . . iii 1 167
Who stand so much on the new form, that they cannot sit at ease on the old bench . . . . *Rom. and Jul.* ii 4 37
Pluck the grave wrinkled senate from the bench, And minister in their steads . . . . *T. of Athens* iv 1 5
Place thieves And give them title, knee and approbation With senators on the bench . . . . iv 3 37
Pluck down benches.—Pluck down forms, windows, any thing *J. Cæsar* iii 2 263
Take thy place ; And thou, his yoke-fellow of equity, Bench by his side *Lear* iii 6 40
Benched. From meaner form Have bench'd and rear'd to worship *W. Tale* i 2 314
Bencher. You are well understood to be a perfecter giber for the table than a necessary bencher in the Capitol . . . . *Coriolanus* ii 1 92
Bench-hole. We'll beat 'em into bench-holes . . . *Ant. and Cleo.* iv 7 9
Bend. And bend The dukedom yet unbow'd . . . . *Tempest* i 2 114
I do bend my speech To one that can my part in him advertise *M. for M.* i 1 41
Homeward did they bend their course . . . . *Com. of Errors* i 1 118

Bend. Bend not all the harm upon yourself . . . *Much Ado* v 1 39
I would bend under any heavy weight That he'll enjoin me to . . . v 1 287
For praise, an outward part, We bend to that the working of the heart *L. L. Lost* iv 1 33
Shall I bend low and in a bondman's key, With bated breath? *Mer. of Ven.* i 3 124
If you love the maid, Bend thoughts and wits to achieve her *T. of Shrew* i 1 184
After some dispatch in hand at court, Thither we bend again *All's Well* iii 2 57
Be friends awhile and both conjointly bend Your sharpest deeds of malice on this town . . . *K. John* ii 1 379
For the which myself and them Bend their best studies . . . iv 2 51
Why do you bend such solemn brows on me? . . . iv 2 90
Have ever made me sour my patient cheek, Or bend one wrinkle *Rich. II.* ii 1 170
Thy very beadsmen learn to bend their bows Of double-fatal yew against thy state . . . iii 2 116
I hardly yet have learn'd To insinuate, flatter, bow, and bend my limbs iv 1 165
Unto my mother's prayers I bend my knee . . . v 3 97
Why dost thou bend thine eyes upon the earth, And start so often? *1 Hen. IV.* ii 3 45
Westmoreland Towards York shall bend you with your dearest speed . v 5 36
We'll bend it to our awe, Or break it all to pieces . . . *Hen. V.* i 2 224
Hold hard the breath and bend up every spirit To his full height . iii 1 16
I'll either make thee stoop and bend thy knee, Or sack this country *1 Hen. VI.* v 1 61
See, how the ugly witch doth bend her brows! . . . v 3 34
In duty bend thy knee to me That bows unto the grave with mickle age *2 Hen. VI.* v 1 173
O Warwick, I do bend my knee with thine; And in this vow do chain my soul to thine! . . . *3 Hen. VI.* ii 3 33
Lords, towards Coventry bend we our course . . . iv 8 58
Speak gentle words and humbly bend thy knee . . . v 1 22
So blunt, unnatural, To bend the fatal instruments of war Against his brother? . . . v 1 87
The which thou once didst bend against her breast. . *Richard III.* i 2 95
Towards London they do bend their course . . . iv 5 14
And make him fall His crest that prouder than blue Iris bends *T. and C.* i 3 380
They were used to bend, To send their smiles before them to Achilles . iii 3 71
As we walk, To our own selves bend we our needful talk . . iv 4 141
My arm'd knees, Who bow'd but in my stirrup, bend like his That hath received an alms! . . . *Coriolanus* iii 2 119
Cassius is A wretched creature and must bend his body, If Cæsar carelessly but nod on him . . . *J. Cæsar* i 2 117
That same eye whose bend doth awe the world Did lose his lustre . i 2 123
If thou dost bend and pray and fawn for him, I spurn thee . . iii 1 45
I am settled, and bend up Each corporal agent to this terrible feat *Macb.* i 7 79
My thoughts and wishes bend again toward France . . *Hamlet* i 2 55
Bend you to remain Here, in the cheer and comfort of our eye . . i 2 115
How is't with you, That you do bend your eye on vacancy? . . iii 4 117
The revenging gods 'Gainst parricides did all their thunders bend *Lear* ii 1 48
How light and portable my pain seems now, When that which makes me bend makes the king bow! . . . iii 6 116
Those his goodly eyes . . now bend, now turn, The office and devotion of their view Upon a tawny front . . . *Ant. and Cleo.* i 1 4
Tended her i' the eyes, And made their bends adornings . . ii 2 213
Except she bend her humour, shall be assured To taste of too *Cymbeline* i 5 81
Then was I as a tree Whose boughs did bend with fruit . . . iii 3 61
Now to Marina bend your mind . . . *Pericles* iv Gower 5
If he be none of mine, my sanctity Will to my sense bend no licentious ear . . . v 3 30

Bended. Neither bended knees, pure hands held up . . *T. G. of Ver.* iii 1 229
Against them both my true joints bended be . . . *Richard II.* v 3 98
His bruised helmet and his bended sword . . . *Hen. V.* v Prol. 18
Humbly now upon my bended knee, In sight of England . *2 Hen. VI.* i 1 10
The nobles bended, As to Jove's statue . . . *Coriolanus* ii 1 281
And, to the last, bended their light on me . . . *Hamlet* ii 1 100
My bended hook shall pierce Their slimy jaws. . *Ant. and Cleo.* ii 5 12

Bending. Yet always bending Towards their project . . *Tempest* iv 1 174
Rich embroidery, Buckled below fair knighthood's bending knee *M. Wives* v 5 76
Die, perish! Might but my bending down Reprieve thee from thy fate, it should proceed . . . *Meas. for Meas.* iii 1 144
Thus long have we stood To watch the fearful bending of thy knee *Richard II.* iii 3 73
Give some supportance to the bending twigs . . . iii 4 32
And bending forward struck his armed heels Against the panting sides of his poor jade . . . *2 Hen. IV.* i 1 44
This prostrate and exterior bending . . . iv 5 149
Will it give place to flexure and low bending? . . *Hen. V.* iv 1 272
With rough and all-unable pen, Our bending author hath pursued the story . . . Epil. 2
No bending knee will call thee Cæsar now . . *3 Hen. VI.* iii 1 18
Where be the bending peers that flatter'd thee? *Richard III.* iv 4 95
Courtiers as free, as debonair, unarm'd, As bending angels *Tr. and Cr.* i 3 236
A mighty power, Bending their expedition toward Philippi *J. Cæsar* iv 3 170
There is a cliff, whose high and bending head Looks fearfully . *Lear* iv 1 76
Bending his sword To his great master . . . iv 2 74
Most humbly therefore bending to your state . . . *Othello* i 3 236
Thus with pleach'd arms, bending down His corrigible neck *A. and C.* iv 14 73

Bene. But omne bene, say I; being of an old father's mind . *L. L. Lost* iv 2 33
Laus Deo, bene intelligo . . . v 1 30

Beneath. It [mercy] droppeth as the gentle rain from heaven Upon the place beneath . . . *Mer. of Venice* iv 1 186
From below your duke to beneath your constable . . *All's Well* ii 2 32
So far beneath your soft and tender breeding . . *T. Night* v 1 331
You'll be found, Be you beneath the sky . . . *W. Tale* i 2 180
The general's disdain'd By him one step below, he by the next, That next by him beneath . . . *Troi. and Cres.* i 3 131
He that will give good words to thee will flatter Beneath abhorring *Coriol.* i 1 172
I think our country sinks beneath the yoke . . . *Macbeth* iv 3 39
For all beneath the moon Would I not leap upright . . *Lear* iv 6 26
Beneath is all the fiends'; There's hell, there's darkness . . iv 6 129
Men whose heads Do grow beneath their shoulders . . *Othello* i 3 145
O, I were damn'd beneath all depth in hell . . . v 2 137
It smites me Beneath the fall I have . . . *Ant. and Cleo.* v 2 172
Not beneath him in fortunes, beyond him in the advantage of the time, above him in birth . . . *Cymbeline* iv 1 11
Of all the faults beneath the heavens, the gods Do like this worst *Pericles* iv 3 20

Beneath world. A man, Whom this beneath world doth embrace and hug With amplest entertainment . . . *T. of Athens* i 1 44

Benedicite. Grace go with you, Benedicite! . . *Meas. for Meas.* ii 3 39
Good morrow, father.—Benedicite! What early tongue so sweet saluteth me! . . . *Rom. and Jul.* ii 3 31

Benedick. My cousin means Signior Benedick of Padua . . *Much Ado* i 1 35
You tax Signior Benedick too much; but he'll be meet with you . . i 1 46
There is a kind of merry war betwixt Signior Benedick and her . . i 1 63
If he have caught the Benedick, it will cost him a thousand pound ere a' be cured . . . i 1 89
You have it full, Benedick: we may guess by this what you are . i 1 110
I wonder that you will still be talking, Signior Benedick: nobody marks you . . . i 1 118
Is it possible disdain should die while she hath such meet food to feed it as Signior Benedick? . . . i 1 122
If ever the sensible Benedick bear it, pluck off the bull's horns and set them in my forehead . . . i 1 265
Here you may see Benedick the married man . . . i 1 269
In the meantime, good Signior Benedick, repair to Leonato's . . i 1 277
He were an excellent man that were made just in the midway between him and Benedick . . . ii 1 8
Then half Signior Benedick's tongue in Count John's mouth, and half Count John's melancholy in Signior Benedick's face . . . ii 1 12
Well, this was Signior Benedick that said so.—What's he? . . ii 1 136
Are not you Signior Benedick?—You know me well; I am he . . ii 1 167
Thus answer I in name of Benedick, But hear these ill news with the ears of Claudio . . . ii 1 179
You have lost the heart of Signior Benedick.—Indeed, my lord, he lent it me awhile . . . ii 1 286
She were an excellent wife for Benedick . . . ii 1 367
To bring Signior Benedick and the Lady Beatrice into a mountain of affection . . . ii 1 381
Benedick is not the unhopefullest husband that I know . . ii 1 392
I will teach you how to humour your cousin, that she shall fall in love with Benedick . . . ii 1 397
See you where Benedick hath hid himself? . . . ii 3 42
What was it you told me of to-day, that your niece Beatrice was in love with Signior Benedick? . . . ii 3 94
Most wonderful that she should so dote on Signior Benedick . . ii 3 99
Invincible against all assaults of affection.—I would have sworn it had, my lord; especially against Benedick . . . ii 3 122
Hath she made her affection known to Benedick?—No; and swears she never will . . . ii 3 128
Reading it over, she found Benedick and Beatrice between the sheet . ii 3 143
Prays, curses; 'O sweet Benedick! God give me patience!' . . ii 3 154
It were good that Benedick knew of it by some other . . . ii 3 160
She is exceeding wise.—In every thing but in loving Benedick . . ii 3 168
I pray you, tell Benedick of it, and hear what a' will say . . ii 3 177
Shall we go seek Benedick, and tell him of her love? . . . ii 3 207
I love Benedick well; and I could wish he would modestly examine himself . . . ii 3 213
As we do trace this alley up and down, Our talk must only be of Benedick . . . iii 1 17
My talk to thee must be how Benedick Is sick in love with Beatrice . iii 1 20
But are you sure That Benedick loves Beatrice so entirely? . . iii 1 37
I persuaded them, if they loved Benedick, To wish him wrestle with affection . . . iii 1 41
Therefore let Benedick, like cover'd fire, Consume away in sighs . iii 1 77
I will go to Benedick And counsel him to fight against his passion . iii 1 82
To refuse So rare a gentleman as Signior Benedick . . . iii 1 91
Benedick, For shape, for bearing, argument and valour, Goes foremost in report . . . iii 1 95
And, Benedick, love on; I will requite thee, Taming my wild heart . iii 1 111
I will only be bold with Benedick for his company . . . iii 2 8
Yet Benedick was such another, and now is he become a man . . iii 4 87
When shall we set the savage bull's horns on the sensible Benedick's head? . . . v 1 184
Here dwells Benedick the married man . . . v 1 186
Good morrow, Benedick. Why, what's the matter? . . . v 4 40
Stolen from her pocket, Containing her affection unto Benedick . . v 4 90
How dost thou, Benedick, the married man? . . . v 4 99

Benediction. As if my trinkets had been hallowed and brought a benediction to the buyer . . . *W. Tale* iv 4 614
To the succeeding royalty he leaves The healing benediction . *Macbeth* iv 3 156
Thou out of heaven's benediction comest To the warm sun! . . *Lear* ii 2 168
His own unkindness, That stripp'd her from his benediction . . iv 3 45
O, look upon me, sir, And hold your hands in benediction o'er me . iv 7 58
The benediction of these covering heavens Fall on their heads like dew! *Cymbeline* v 5 350

Benedictus. Get you some of this distilled Carduus Benedictus *Much Ado* iii 4 74
Benedictus! why Benedictus? you have some moral in this Benedictus iii 4 77

Benefactor. Two notorious benefactors.—Benefactors? Well; what benefactors are they? are they not malefactors? . . *Meas. for Meas.* ii 1 50
You great benefactors, sprinkle our society with thankfulness *T. of Athens* iii 6 79

Benefice. Tickling a parson's nose as a' lies asleep, Then dreams he of another benefice . . . *Rom. and Jul.* i 4 81

Beneficial. I'll limit thee this day To seek thy life by beneficial help: Try all the friends thou hast . . . *Com. of Errors* i 1 152
Can with his very bulk Take up the rays o' the beneficial sun *Hen. VIII.* i 1 56
Besides these beneficial news, it is the celebration of his nuptial *Othello* ii 2 7

Benefit. Omitting the sweet benefit of time . . . *T. G. of Ver.* ii 4 65
Throwing him into the water will do him a benefit . . *Mer. Wives* iii 3 195
The satisfaction I would require is likewise your own benefit *M. for M.* iii 1 157
You may most uprighteously do a poor wronged lady a merited benfit . iii 1 207
The doubleness of the benefit defends the deceit from reproof . . iii 1 268
He was drunk then my lord: it can be no better.—For the benefit of silence, would thou wert so too! . . . v 1 190
By the benefit of his wished light, The seas wax'd calm . *Com. of Errors* i 1 91
Certain merchants, Of whom I hope to make much benefit . . . i 2 25
Her benefits are mightily misplaced . . . *As Y. Like It* i 2 37
Freeze, freeze, thou bitter sky, That dost not bite so nigh As benefits forgot . . . ii 7 186
Disable all the benefits of your own country, be out of love with your nativity . . . iv 1 34
Yet have I the benefit of my senses . . . *T. Night* v 1 313
What course I mean to hold Shall nothing benefit your knowledge *W. Tale* iv 4 514
A thousand things that would Have done the time more benefit . . v 1 22
Who would be thence that has the benefit of access? . . . v 2 119
Sweetened with the hope to have The present benefit . *Richard II.* ii 3 14
In defence of my lord's worthiness, I crave the benefit of law of arms *1 Hen. VI.* iv 1 100
And give it you In earnest of a further benefit . . . v 3 16
Sold their bodies for their country's benefit . . . v 4 106
Of benefit proceeding from our king And not of any challenge of desert v 4 152
This late complaint Will make but little for his benefit . *2 Hen. VI.* i 3 101

Benefit. The benefit thereof is always granted . . . *Richard III.* iii 1 48
Take to your royal self This proffer'd benefit of dignity . . . iii 7 196
If ancient sorrow be most reverend, Give mine the benefit of seniory . iv 4 36
But benefit no further Than vainly longing . . . *Hen. VIII.* i 2 80
Yet see, When these so noble benefits shall prove Not well disposed . i 2 115
Beseech you, as in way of taste, To give me now a little benefit *Troi. and Cres.* iii 3 14
No public benefit which you receive But it proceeds or comes from them to you And no way from yourselves . . . . . *Coriolanus* i 1 156
My revengeful services may prove As benefits to thee . . . . iv 5 96
The benefit Which thou shalt thereby reap is such a name . . . v 3 142
There to end Where he was to begin and give away The benefit of our levies . . . . v 6 67
We are born to do benefits . . . . *T. of Athens* i 2 106
For any benefit that points to me, Either in hope or present, I'ld exchange . . . . iv 3 526
Grant that, and then is death a benefit . . . . . . *J. Cæsar* iii 1 103
Antony: who, though he had no hand in his death, shall receive the benefit of his dying . . . . iii 2 47
To receive at once the benefit of sleep, and do the effects of watching! *Macbeth* v 1 11
As the winds give benefit And convoy is assistant . . . *Hamlet* i 3 2
Turn all her mother's pains and benefits To laughter and contempt *Lear* i 4 308
Is wretchedness deprived that benefit, To end itself by death? . . iv 6 61
Since I could distinguish betwixt a benefit and an injury . . *Othello* i 3 314
But to know so must be my benefit; So shall I clothe me in a forced content . . . . iii 4 119
You shall find A benefit in this change . . . . *Ant. and Cleo.* v 2 128
When expect you them?—With the next benefit o' the wind . *Cymbeline* iv 2 342
I am ashamed To look upon the holy sun, to have The benefit of his blest beams . . . . iv 4 42
Benefited. Could my good brother suffer you to do it? A man, a prince, by him so benefited! . . . . *Lear* iv 2 45
Be-netted. Being thus be-netted round with villanies . . *Hamlet* v 2 29
Benevolence. Will be glad to do my benevolence to make atonements and compremises . . . . *Mer. Wives* i 1 33
Daily new exactions are devised, As blanks, benevolences *Richard II.* ii 1 250
Benign. A better prince and benign lord, That will prove awful *Per.* ii Gower 3
Benison. God's benison go with you! . . . . . *Macbeth* ii 4 40
Therefore be gone Without our grace, our love, our benison . . *Lear* i 1 268
The bounty and the benison of heaven To boot, and boot! . . . iv 6 229
The good in conversation, To whom I give my benison . *Pericles* ii Gower 10
Bennet. The bells of Saint Bennet, sir, may put you in mind . *T. Night* v 1 42
Sent to London The heads of Brocas and Sir Bennet Seely *Richard II.* v 6 14
Bent. Met us again and madly bent on us Chased us away *Com. of Errors* v 1 152
It seems her affections have their full bent . . . . *Much Ado* ii 3 232
Two of them have the very bent of honour . . . . . . iv 1 188
Which, not to anger bent, is music and sweet fire . . . *L. L. Lost* iv 2 120
I see you all are bent To set against me for your merriment *M. N. Dream* iii 2 145
And forgotten all; Though my revenges were high bent upon him *All's Well* v 3 10
Then let thy love be younger than thyself, Or thy affection cannot hold the bent . . . . *T. Night* ii 4 38
To your own bents dispose you: you'll be found . . . *W. Tale* i 2 179
Our cannon shall be bent Against the brows of this resisting town *K. John* ii 1 37
Speak on with favour; we are bent to hear . . . . . . ii 1 422
When he perceives the envious clouds are bent To dim his glory *Richard II.* iii 3 65
As in a theatre, the eyes of men, After a well-graced actor leaves the stage, Are idly bent on him that enters next . . . . . . v 2 25
No extraordinary gaze, Such as is bent on sun-like majesty . 1 *Hen. IV.* iii 2 79
To come off the breach with his pike bent bravely . . 2 *Hen. IV.* ii 4 55
Your eyes, . . . Against the French, that met them in their bent *Hen. V.* v 2 16
More dazzled . . . Than mid-day sun fierce bent against their faces 1 *Hen. VI.* i 1 14
All his mind is bent to holiness, To number Ave-Maries . . 2 *Hen. VI.* i 3 58
A sort of naughty persons, lewdly bent . . . . . . ii 1 167
And who durst smile when Warwick bent his brow? . . 3 *Hen. VI.* v 2 22
With two right reverend fathers, Divinely bent to meditation *Richard III.* iii 7 62
To set his sense on the attentive bent, And then to speak *Troi. and Cres.* i 3 252
'Tis like he'll question me Why such unplausive eyes are bent on him . iii 3 43
Gives all gaze and bent of amorous view On the fair Cressid . . . iv 5 282
These three lead on this preparation Whither 'tis bent . . *Coriolanus* i 2 16
With a power Of high-resolved men, bent to the spoil . . *T. Andron.* iv 4 64
If that thy bent of love be honourable, Thy purpose marriage *Rom. and Jul.* ii 2 143
Let me work; For I can give his humour the true bent . . *J. Cæsar* ii 1 210
There is but one mind in all these men, and it is bent against Cæsar . ii 3 6
Now I am bent to know, By the worst means, the worst. . *Macbeth* iii 4 134
In the full bent To lay our service freely at your feet . . . *Hamlet* ii 2 30
They fool me to the top of my bent . . . . iii 2 401
The associates tend, and every thing is bent For England . . . iv 3 47
The bow is bent and drawn, make from the shaft . . . . *Lear* i 1 145
This arm, and my best spirits, are bent To prove upon thy heart . . v 3 139
Eternity was in our lips and eyes, Bliss in our brows' bent *Ant. and Cleo.* i 3 36
Although they wear their faces to the bent Of the king's looks *Cymbeline* i 1 13
How Thaliard came full bent with sin . . . . *Pericles* ii Gower 23
Never aim'd so high to love your daughter, But bent all offices to honour her. . . . . ii 5 48
Bentii. Mine own company, Chitopher, Vaumond, Bentii . *All's Well* iv 3 188
Bentivolii. A merchant of great traffic through the world, Vincentio, come of the Bentivolii . . . . *T. of Shrew* i 1 13
Ben trovato. Con tutto il cuore, ben trovato . . . . i 2 24
Benumbed. Great minds, of partial indulgence To their benumbed wills, resist the same . . . . *Troi. and Cres.* ii 2 179
Ben venuto. Undertake your ben venuto . . . . . *L. L. Lost* iv 2 164
Alla nostra casa ben venuto, molto honorato signor mio Petruchio *T. of Shrew* i 2 25
Petruchio, I shall be your ben venuto . . . . i 2 282
Benvolio. Turn thee, Benvolio, look upon thy death . *Rom. and Jul.* i 1 74
Come between us, good Benvolio; my wits faint . . . . ii 4 71
Help me into some house, Benvolio, Or I shall faint . . . . iii 1 110
As he fell, did Romeo turn and fly. This is the truth, or let Benvolio die. . . . . iii 1 180
Bepaint. The mask of night is on my face, Else would a maiden blush bepaint my cheek. . . . . ii 2 86
Bepray. I bepray you, let me borrow my arms again . . *L. L. Lost* v 2 702
Bequeath. My horns I bequeath your husbands . . . *Mer. Wives* v 5 30
I yield you up my part; And yours of Helena to me bequeath *M. N. Dream* iii 2 166
You to your former honour I bequeath . . . . *As Y. Like It* v 4 192
Stir, nay, come away, Bequeath to death your numbness . *W. Tale* v 3 102

Bequeath. Wilt thou forsake thy fortune, Bequeath thy land to him and follow me? . . . . *K. John* i 1 149
I do bequeath my faithful services And true subjection everlastingly . v 7 104
What can we bequeath Save our deposed bodies to the ground? *Rich. II.* iii 2 149
Till then I'll sweat and seek about for eases, And at that time bequeathe you my diseases . . . . *Troi. and Cres.* v 10 57
A sister I bequeath you, whom no brother Did ever love so dearly *Ant. and Cleo.* ii 2 152
So I bequeath a happy peace to you And all good men . . *Pericles* i 1 50
Part of my heritage, Which my dead father did bequeath to me . . ii 1 130
Bequeathed me by will but poor a thousand crowns . . *As Y. Like It* i 1 2
His sole child, my lord, and bequeathed to my overlooking . *All's Well* i 1 44
Her father bequeathed her to me . . . . i 3 105
It is an honour 'longing to our house, Bequeathed down from many ancestors . . . . iv 2 43
My chastity's the jewel of our house, Bequeathed down from many ancestors . . . . iv 2 47
He by will bequeath'd His lands to me . . . . . . *K. John* i 1 109
Bequeathing. His crown bequeathing to his banish'd brother *As Y. Like It* v 4 169
Bequeathing it as a rich legacy Unto their issue . . . *J. Cæsar* iii 2 141
Berattle. And so berattle the common stages . . . . *Hamlet* ii 2 357
Bereave. Thou mayst bereave him of his wits with wonder . 1 *Hen. VI.* v 3 195
She'll bereave you o' the deeds too, if she call your activity in question *Troi. and Cres.* iii 2 59
And bereaves the state Of that integrity which should become't *Coriol.* iii 1 158
You shall bereave yourself Of my good purposes . . *Ant. and Cleo.* v 2 130
I'll not bereave you of your servant . . . . . . *Pericles* iv 1 32
Bereaved. And I, who at his hands received my life, Have by my hands of life bereaved him . . . . 3 *Hen. VI.* ii 5 68
What can man's wisdom In the restoring his bereaved sense? . *Lear* iv 4 9
Bereft. Thee of thy son, Alonso, They have bereft . . *Tempest* iii 3 76
But, if thou live to see like right bereft, This fool-begg'd patience in thee will be left . . . . *Com. of Errors* ii 1 40
You have bereft me of all words, Only my blood speaks . *Mer. of Venice* iii 2 177
Like a fountain troubled, Muddy, ill-seeming, thick, bereft of beauty *T. of Shrew* v 2 143
Bereft and gelded of his patrimony . . . . . *Richard II.* ii 1 237
And we are barren and bereft of friends . . . . ii 3 84
That all your interest in those territories Is utterly bereft you 2 *Hen. VI.* iii 1 85
A raven's note, Whose dismal tune bereft my vital powers . . . iii 2 41
Your loving uncle, twenty times his worth, They say, is shamefully bereft of life . . . . iii 2 269
O boy, thy father gave thee life too soon, And hath bereft thee of thy life too late! . . . . 3 *Hen. VI.* ii 5 93
I think his understanding is bereft . . . . ii 6 60
He that bereft thee, lady, of thy husband, Did it to help thee to a better husband.—His better doth not breathe . . . . *Richard III.* i 2 138
You have bereft me of all words, lady . . . . *Troi. and Cres.* iii 2 57
Fell curs of bloody kind, Have here bereft my brother of his life *T. And.* ii 3 282
Here lies a wretched corse, of wretched soul bereft . . *T. of Athens* v 4 70
The rites for which I love him are bereft me . . . . *Othello* i 3 258
Let it suffice the greatness of your powers To have bereft a prince of all his fortunes . . . . *Pericles* ii 1 9
Bergamo. Thy father! O villain! he is a sail-maker in Bergamo *T. of Shrew* v 1 81
Bergomask. Will it please you to see the epilogue, or to hear a Bergomask dance between two of our company? . . . *M. N. Dream* v 1 360
But, come, your Bergomask: let your epilogue alone . . . . v 1 368
Be-rhyme. She had a better love to be-rhyme her . *Rom. and Jul.* ii 4 43
Be-rhymed. I was never so be-rhymed since Pythagoras' time *As Y. L. It* iii 2 186
Berkeley. Meet me presently at Berkeley . . . . *Richard II.* ii 2 119
How far is it, my lord, to Berkeley now? . . . . ii 3 1
But who comes here?—It is my Lord of Berkeley, as I guess . . ii 3 68
Bermoothes. To fetch dew From the still-vex'd Bermoothes . *Tempest* i 2 229
Bernardo has my place. Give you good night.—Holla! Bernardo! *Hamlet* i 1 17
Well, sit we down, And let us hear Bernardo speak of this . . . i 1 34
Two nights together had these gentlemen, Marcellus and Bernardo, on their watch, In the dead vast and middle of the night, Been thus encounter'd . . . . i 2 197
Berri. Dukes of Berri and of Bretagne, Of Brabant and of Orleans *Hen. V.* ii 4 4
Berries. Madest much of me, wouldst give me Water with berries in't *Tempest* i 2 334
I'll show thee the best springs; I'll pluck thee berries . . . . ii 2 164
Two lovely berries moulded on one stem . . . . *M. N. Dream* iii 2 211
And wholesome berries thrive and ripen best Neighbour'd by fruit of baser quality. . . . . *Hen. V.* i 1 61
I'll make you feed on berries and on roots . . . *T. Andron.* iv 2 177
Want! why want?—We cannot live on grass, on berries, water *T. of Athens* iv 3 425
Berry. Thy palate then did deign The roughest berry . *Ant. and Cleo.* i 4 64
Deep clerks she dumbs; and with her neeld composes Nature's own shape, of bud, bird, branch, or berry . . . . . *Pericles* v Gower 6
Bertram. Be thou blest, Bertram, and succeed thy father In manners, as in shape! . . . . *All's Well* i 1 70
Heaven bless him! Farewell, Bertram . . . . i 1 83
My imagination Carries no favour in't but Bertram's . . . . . i 1 94
There is no living, none, If Bertram be away . . . . . . i 1 96
It is the Count Rousillon, my good lord, Young Bertram . . . . i 2 19
This is the man.—Why, then, young Bertram, take her; she's thy wife ii 3 112
Know'st thou not, Bertram, What she has done for me? . . . . ii 3 115
Berwick. Where wert thou born?—At Berwick in the north . 2 *Hen. VI.* ii 1 83
Let them be whipped through every market-town, till they come to Berwick . . . . ii 1 159
Mount you, my lord; towards Berwick post amain . . . 3 *Hen. VI.* ii 5 128
Bescreened. What man art thou that thus bescreen'd in night So stumblest on my counsel? . . . . *Rom. and Jul.* ii 2 52
Beseech you, father.—Hence! hang not on my garments . . *Tempest* i 2 473
Beseech you, sir, be merry; you have cause . . . . ii 1 1
I do beseech you—Chiefly that I might set it in my prayers—What is your name? . . . . iii 1 34
Whom I beseech To give me ample satisfaction . . . *Com. of Errors* v 1 251
Fare you well.—I beseech you a word . . . . . *L. L. Lost* ii 1 197
I beseech your society.—And thank you too . . . . iv 2 166
Most heartily I do beseech the court To give the judgement *Mer. of Ven.* iv 1 243
This cuff was but to knock at your ear, and beseech listening *T. of Shrew* iv 1 68
I most unfeignedly beseech your lordship . . . . . *All's Well* ii 3 259
I shall beseech your lordship to remain with me . . . . . . iv 5 91
Press me not, beseech you, so . . . . *W. Tale* i 2 19
I humbly beseech you, sir, to pardon me all the faults I have committed v 2 160
Rise up, good aunt.—Not yet, I thee beseech . . . *Richard II.* v 3 92
Beseech your lordship to have a reverent care of your health 2 *Hen. IV.* i 2 112

Beseech. Which I beseech you to let me have home with me . 2 *Hen. IV.* v 5 79
Captain, I thee beseech to do me favours . . . . . *Hen. V.* iii 6 22
I will speak lower.—I pray you and beseech you that you will . iv 1 83
I beseech God on my knees thou mayst be turned to hobnails 2 *Hen. VI.* iv 10 62
I beseech your graces both to pardon me . . . *Richard III.* i 1 84
There needs no such apology: I rather do beseech you pardon me . iii 7 105
I say, take heed; Yes, heartily beseech you . . . *Hen. VIII.* i 2 176
Achievement is command; ungain'd, beseech . . . *Troi. and Cres.* i 2 319
I do beseech you, as in way of taste, To give me now a little benefit . iii 3 13
I beseech you, on my knees I beseech you, what's the matter? . iv 2 93
A kind of godly jealousy—Which, I beseech you, call a virtuous sin . iv 4 83
I beseech you next To feast with me . . . . . . iv 5 228
I beseech you—In sign of what you are, not to reward What you have done—before our army hear me . . . . *Coriolanus* i 9 25
I have not the face To say 'Beseech you, cease' . . . . iv 6 117
Good father, I beseech you on my knees, Hear me *Rom. and Jul.* iii 5 159
If I might beseech you, gentlemen, to repair some other hour *T. of Athens* iii 4 68
I shall beseech him to befriend himself . . . . *J. Cæsar* iii 4 30
I beseech you instantly to visit My too much changed son *Hamlet* ii 2 35
Therefore beseech you To avert your liking a more worthier way *Lear* i 1 213
I yet beseech your majesty,—If for I want that glib and oily art, To speak and purpose not . . . . i 1 226
I do beseech you To understand my purposes aright . . . i 4 259
Let me beseech your grace not to do so . . . . . ii 2 147
I humbly beseech you, proceed to the affairs of state . . *Othello* i 3 220
In the morning I will beseech the virtuous Desdemona . . . ii 3 336
I humbly do beseech you of your pardon For too much loving you . iii 3 212
Then, noble partners, The rather, for I earnestly beseech *Ant. and Cleo.* ii 2 23
Beseech your patience. Peace, Dear lady daughter, peace! *Cymbeline* i 1 153
Continues well my lord? His health, beseech you? . . . i 6 56
To your protection I commend me, gods. . . . Guard me, beseech ye . ii 2 10
Let us beseech you That for our gold we may provision have *Pericles* v 1 55
I beseech you / I do beseech you } *repeated often.*

Beseeched. The town is beseeched, and the trumpet call us . *Hen. V.* iii 2 115
He beseech'd me to entreat your majesties To hear and see the matter *Hamlet* iii 1 22

Beseeching God and you to pardon me . . . . . *Hen. V.* ii 2 160
Beseeching thee, if with thy will it stands . . . . 3 *Hen. VI.* ii 3 38
Beseeching him to give her virtuous breeding . . . *Hen. VIII.* iv 2 134
Beseeching you To give her princely training . . . *Pericles* iii 3 15

Beseek. I beseek you now, aggravate your choler . . 2 *Hen. IV.* ii 4 175

Beseem. Such weeds As may beseem some well-reputed page *T. G. of Ver.* ii 7 43
Ill it doth beseem your holiness To separate the husband and the wife *Com. of Errors* v 1 110
So qualified as may beseem The spouse of any noble gentleman *T. of Shrew* iv 5 66
It ill beseems this presence to cry aim To these ill-tuned repetitions *K. John* ii 1 196
It would beseem the Lord Northumberland To say 'King Richard' *Richard II.* iii 3 7
More than well beseems A man of thy profession and degree 1 *Hen. VI.* iii 1 19
And give them burial as beseems their worth . . . . . iv 7 86
Such it seems As may beseem a monarch like himself 3 *Hen. VI.* iii 3 122
How evil it beseems thee, To flatter Henry and forsake thy brother! . iv 7 84

Beseemeth. To teach a teacher ill beseemeth me . . *L. L. Lost* ii 1 108

Beseeming. Qualities Beseeming such a wife as your fair daughter *T. G. of Ver.* iii 1 66
Yet best beseeming me to speak the truth . . . *Richard II.* iv 1 116
This fact was infamous And ill beseeming any common man 1 *Hen. VI.* iv 1 31
Ancient citizens Cast by their grave beseeming ornaments *Rom. and Jul.* i 1 100
I am, sir, The soldier that did company these three In poor beseeming *Cymbeline* v 5 409

Beset. Daughter Silvia, you are hard beset . . *T. G. of Ver.* ii 4 49
We'll follow him that's fled; The thicket is beset; he cannot 'scape v 3 11
How am I beset! What kind of catechising call you this? *Much Ado* iv 1 78
I was beset with shame and courtesy . . . *Mer. of Venice* v 1 217
Draw forth thy weapon, we are beset with thieves . . *T. of Shrew* iii 2 238
Drew to defend him when he was beset . . . . *T. Night* v 1 88

Beshrew. He told his mind upon mine ear: Beshrew his hand *C. of Err.* ii 1 49
Beshrew my hand, If it should give your age such cause of fear *Much Ado* v 1 55
A pox of that jest! and I beshrew all shrows . . *L. L. Lost* v 2 46
Much beshrew my manners and my pride . . . *M. N. Dream* ii 2 54
Beshrew my heart, but I pity the man . . . . . v 1 295
Beshrew your eyes, They have o'erlook'd me and divided me *Mer. of Ven.* iii 2 14
Beshrew his soul for me, He started one poor heart of mine in thee *T. Night* iv 1 62
These dangerous unsafe lunes i' the king, beshrew them! He must be told on't . . . . *W. Tale* ii 2 30
Beshrew my soul But I do love the favour and the form Of this most fair occasion . . . . *K. John* v 4 49
Beshrew thy very heart! I did not think to be so sad to-night . v 5 14
Beshrew thee, cousin, which didst lead me forth Of that sweet way I was in to despair! . . . . *Richard II.* iii 2 204
Now, beshrew my father's ambition! . . . . . *Hen. V.* v 2 241
I lose, indeed; Beshrew the winners, for they play'd me false! 2 *Hen. VI.* iii 1 184
Beshrew the witch! with venomous wights she stays *Troi. and Cres.* iv 2 12
Beshrew my very heart, I think you are happy . . *Rom. and Jul.* iii 5 223
From thy heart?—And from my soul too; Or else beshrew them both . iii 5 229
She will beshrew me much that Romeo Hath had no notice . . v 2 25
But, beshrew my jealousy! . . . . *Hamlet* ii 1 113
Beshrew me much, Emilia, I was, unhandsome warrior as I am *Othello* iii 4 150
Beshrew him for't! How comes this trick upon him? . . . iv 2 128

Beshrew me *T. G. of Ver.* i 1; ii 4; *Mer. of Venice* ii 6; *T. Night* ii 3; 3 *Hen. VI.* i 4; *Hen. VIII.* ii 3; *Othello* iv 3

Beshrew thy (your) **heart** 2 *Hen. IV.* ii 3; v 3; *Troi. and Cres.* iv 2; *Rom. and Jul.* ii 5

Besides, the gentleman Is full of virtue . . . . *T. G. of Ver.* iii 1 64
Besides, the fashion of the time is changed . . . . . iii 1 86
Thou canst not see thy love; Besides, thy staying will abridge thy life iii 1 245
He is a knave besides; a cowardly knave . . . . *Mer. Wives* iii 1 67
Besides your cheer, you shall have sport . . . . . iii 2 81
Besides these, other bars he lays before me . . . . . iii 4 7
So shall I evermore be bound to thee; Besides, I'll make a present recompense . . . . iv 6 55
Beside, she hath prosperous art When she will play with reason *M. for M.* i 2 189
I confess besides I am no maid . . . . v 1 185
I am an ass, I am a woman's man and besides myself.—What woman's man? and how besides thyself?—Marry, sir, besides myself, I am due to a woman . . . . *Com. of Errors* iii 2 78
Besides, I have some business in the town . . . . . iv 1 35
Besides. Besides this present instance of his rage, Is a mad tale he told to-day . . . . *Com. of Errors* iv 3 88
Beside the charge, the shame, imprisonment, You have done wrong . v 1 18
Besides her urging of her wreck at sea . . . . . . v 1 359
Very many have been beside their wit . . . . *Much Ado* v 1 128
And one day in a week to touch no food And but one meal on every day beside . . . . *L. L. Lost* i 1 40
She did starve the general world beside And prodigally gave them all to you . . . . ii 1 11
Besides the groves, The skies, the fountains, every region near Seem'd all one mutual cry . . . . *M. N. Dream* iv 1 120
Besides commends and courteous breath, Gifts of rich value *Mer. of Ven.* ii 9 90
Besides this nothing that he so plentifully gives me . *As Y. Like It* i 1 17
Besides, the oath of a lover is no stronger than the word of a tapster . iii 4 33
I am falser than vows made in wine: Besides, I like you not . . iii 5 74
Over and beside Signior Baptista's liberality, I'll mend it . *T. of Shrew* i 2 149
Beside, so qualified as may beseem The spouse of any noble gentleman . iv 5 66
At the Saint Francis here beside the port . . . *All's Well* iii 5 39
I'll no more of you: besides, you grow dishonest . . *T. Night* i 5 46
Alas, sir, how fell you besides your five wits? . . . . iv 2 92
If it be in man besides the king to effect your suits . . *W. Tale* iv 4 828
Lord of thy presence and no land beside . . . . *K. John* i 1 137
And this respect besides, For that my grandsire was an Englishman . v 4 41
But in the balance of great Bolingbroke, Besides himself, are all the English peers . . . . *Richard II.* iii 4 88
We pray with heart and soul and all beside . . . . . v 3 104
And leaves behind a stain Upon the beauty of all parts besides 1 *Hen. IV.* iii 1 188
Beside, I fear me, if thy thoughts were sifted . . 1 *Hen. VI.* iii 1 24
Seven walled towns of strength, Beside five hundred prisoners . . iii 4 8
Myself and divers gentlemen beside . . . . iv 1 25
Beside, what infamy will there arise! . . . . . . iv 1 143
Beside, his wealth doth warrant a liberal dower . . . . v 5 46
More intolerable Than all the princes in the land beside . 2 *Hen. VI.* i 1 176
Beside the haughty protector, have we Beaufort The imperious churchman . . . . i 3 71
To frustrate both his oath and what beside May make against 3 *Hen. VI.* ii 1 175
Besides, the king's name is a tower of strength *Richard III.* v 3 12
Beside forfeiting Our own brains . . . . . *Hen. VIII.* Prol. 19
One thus descended, That hath beside well in his person wrought *Coriol.* ii 3 254
He owes nine thousand; besides my former sum . . *T. of Athens* ii 1 2
Note beside, That we have tried the utmost of our friends . *J. Cæsar* iv 3 213
Might yet enkindle you unto the crown, Besides the thane of Cawdor *Macbeth* i 3 122
Your vessels and your spells provide, Your charms and every thing beside . . . . iii 5 19
We have met with foes That strike beside us . . . . . v 7 29
Who's there, besides foul weather? . . . . . *Lear* iii 1 1
I will boot thee with what gift beside Thy modesty can beg *Ant. and Cleo.* ii 5 71
Besides what hotter hours, Unregister'd in vulgar fame . . . iii 13 118
Besides, the seeing these effects will be Both noisome and infectious *Cymbeline* i 5 25
Wert thou the son of Jupiter and no more But what thou art besides, thou wert too base To be his groom . . . . ii 3 131
Quite besides The government of patience! . . . . . ii 4 149
Save him, sir, And spare no blood beside . . . . . . v 5 92
Besides that hook of wiving, Fairness which strikes the eye . . . v 5 167

Beside his patience. Enough To put him quite beside his patience 1 *Hen. IV.* iii 1 179

Beside that, 'twas a pricket that the princess killed . . *L. L. Lost* iv 2 48
His horses are bred better; for, besides that they are fair with their feeding, they are taught their manage . . . *As Y. Like It* i 1 12
Besides that he's a fool, he's a great quarreller . . . *T. Night* i 3 31
Besides that it is excellently well penned, I have taken great pains to con it . . . . i 5 184

Beside themselves. Only be patient till we have appeased The multitude, beside themselves with fear . . . . *J. Cæsar* iii 1 180

Besides yourself. Nor can imagination form a shape, Besides yourself, to like of . . . . *Tempest* iii 1 57
Who's at home besides yourself? . . . . . *Mer. Wives* iv 2 13

Besiege. The fire and cracks Of sulphurous roaring the most mighty Neptune Seem to besiege . . . . . . *Tempest* i 2 205
Like one that comes here to besiege his court . . *L. L. Lost* ii 1 86
And yet my heart Will not confess he owes the malady That doth my life besiege . . . . *All's Well* ii 1 10
Otherwhiles the famish'd English, like pale ghosts, Faintly besiege us one hour in a month . . . . 1 *Hen. VI.* i 2 8
The northern earls and lords Intend here to besiege you in your castle 3 *Hen. VI.* i 2 50
The women so besiege us . . . . . . *Hen. VIII.* v 4 35

Besieged with sable-coloured melancholy . . . *L. L. Lost* i 1 233
Except this city now by us besieged . . . . . *K. John* ii 1 489
Orleans is besieged; The English army is grown weak and faint 1 *Hen. VI.* i 1 157
Thou know'st how Orleans is besieged, And how the English have the suburbs won . . . . i 4 1
I danced attendance on his will Till Paris was besieged . . 2 *Hen. VI.* i 3 175

Beslubber. And then to beslubber our garments with it . 1 *Hen. IV.* ii 4 341

Besmear. I was beset with shame and courtesy; My honour would not let ingratitude So much besmear it . . . . . *Mer. of Venice* v 1 219
Let us bathe our hands in Cæsar's blood Up to the elbows, and besmear our swords . . . . *J. Cæsar* iii 1 107

Besmear'd As black as Vulcan in the smoke of war . . *T. Night* v 1 55
They were besmear'd and overstain'd With slaughter's pencil *K. John* iii 1 236
And is become as black As if besmear'd in hell . . *Hen. VIII.* i 2 124

Besmirch. No soil nor cautel doth besmirch The virtue of his will *Hamlet* i 3 15

Besmirched. Our gayness and our gilt are all besmirch'd With rainy marching in the painful field . . . . . . *Hen. V.* iv 3 110

Besom. I am the besom that must sweep the court clean . 2 *Hen. VI.* iv 7 34

Besort. Such men as may besort your age . . . . . *Lear* i 4 272
With such accommodation and besort As levels with her breeding *Othello* i 3 239

Besotted. You speak Like one besotted on your sweet delights *Tr. and Cr.* ii 2 143

Bespake. But I bespake you fair, and hurt you not . . *T. Night* v 1 192
Bespake them thus: 'I thank you, countrymen' . . *Richard II.* v 2 20

Bespeak. Expect spoon-meat; or bespeak a long spoon . *Com. of Errors* iv 3 62
He did bespeak a chain for me, but had it not . . . . iv 4 139
Fee me an officer; bespeak him a fortnight before . *Mer. of Venice* iii 1 131
Here is the cap your worship did bespeak . . . *T. of Shrew* iv 3 63
I will bespeak our diet, Whiles you beguile the time . *T. Night* iii 3 40
I went round to work, And my young mistress thus I did bespeak *Hamlet* ii 2 140

Bespice a cup, To give mine enemy a lasting wink . . . *W. Tale* i 2 316
Bespoke. Made it for me, sir! I bespoke it not . . *Com. of Errors* iii 2 176
Then fairly I bespoke the officer . . . . . . v 1 233
I have bespoke supper to-morrow night in Eastcheap . . *1 Hen. IV.* i 2 144
And in disgrace Bespoke him thus . . . . *1 Hen. VI.* iv 6 21
If you will marry, make your loves to me, My lady is bespoke . *Lear* v 3 89
Bess. Come hither, Bess, and let me kiss my boy . . *3 Hen. VI.* v 7 15
Bessy. Come o'er the bourn, Bessy, to me . . . . *Lear* iii 6 27
Best. Be quick, thou 'rt best, To answer other business . . *Tempest* i 2 366
'Tis best we stand upon our guard, Or that we quit this place . . ii 1 321
O you, So perfect and so peerless, are created Of every creature's best! iii 1 48
Invert What best is boded me to mischief! . . . . . iii 1 71
Although my last: no matter, since I feel The best is past . . iii 3 51
If the ground be overcharged, you were best stick her . *T. G. of Ver.* i 1 108
In that you are astray, 'twere best pound you . . . . i 1 109
Of many good I think him best . . . . . . i 2 21
Best sing it to the tune of 'Light o' love' . . . . i 2 83
If you respect them, best to take them up . . . . i 2 134
Then tell me, whither were I best to send him? . . . . i 3 24
In such wine and sugar of the best and the fairest . *Mer. Wives* ii 2 70
You were best meddle with buck-washing . . . . . iii 3 165
I'll make the best in Gloucestershire know on't . . . . v 1 190
He that might the vantage best have took Found out the remedy
Meas. for Meas. ii 2 74
'Tis best that thou diest quickly . . . . . . iii 1 151
The best and wholesomest spirits of the night Envelope you! . iv 2 76
Do with your injuries as seems you best, In any chastisement . . v 1 256
In debating which was best, we shall part with neither . *Com. of Errors* iii 1 67
Get us some excellent music . . .—The best I can, my lord . *Much Ado* ii 3 90
Have thy counsel Which is the best to furnish me to-morrow . . iii 1 103
This is not so well as I looked for, but the best that ever I heard.—Ay,
the best for the worst . . . . *L. L. Lost* i 1 283
You were best call it 'daughter-beamed eyes' . . . . v 2 171
You were best to call them generally, man by man . *M. N. Dream* i 2 2
What beard were I best to play it in? . . . . . . i 2 93
Do thy best To pluck this crawling serpent from my breast! . . ii 2 145
The best in this kind are but shadows; and the worst are no worse . v 1 213
The very best at a beast, my lord, that e'er I saw . . . . v 1 232
When he is best, he is a little worse than a man . *Mer. of Venice* i 2 94
You were best to tell Antonio what you hear . . . . ii 8 33
I were best to cut my left hand off And swear I lost the ring defending it v 1 177
And thou wert best look to't . . . . . *As Y. Like It* i 1 154
You may see the end; for the best is yet to do . . . . i 2 121
A pretty peat! it is best Put finger in the eye, an she knew why *T. of Shr.* i 1 78
I have thrust myself into this maze, Haply to wive and thrive as best I
may . . . . i 2 56
Of all thy suitors, here I charge thee, tell Whom thou lovest best . ii 1 9
If I be waspish, best beware my sting . . . . . ii 1 211
I must confess your offer is the best . . . . . . ii 1 388
Old fashions please me best; I am not so nice, To change . . iii 1 80
Revel it as bravely as the best, With silken coats and caps and golden
rings . . . . iv 3 54
Your betters have endured me say my mind, And if you cannot, best
you stop your ears . . . . iv 3 76
Where then do you know best We be affied? . . . . . iv 4 48
They're busy within; you were best knock louder . . . . v 1 15
Thou wert best say that I am not Lucentio . . . . . v 1 106
Feast with the best, and welcome to my house . . . . v 2 8
Thou wert best set thy lower part where thy nose stands . *All's Well* ii 3 267
We'll direct her how 'tis best to bear it . . . . . iii 7 20
Myself am best When least in company . . . . *T. Night* i 4 37
I'll do my best To woo your lady: yet, a barful strife! . . . i 4 40
Here comes my lady: make your excuse wisely, you were best . i 5 34
Best first go see your lodging . . . . iii 3 20
In the south suburbs, at the Elephant, Is best to lodge . . . iii 3 40
Your ladyship were best to have some guard about you . . . iii 4 12
Which way to be prevented, if to be; If not, how best to bear it *W. Tale* i 2 406
And my name Be yoked with his that did betray the Best! . . . i 2 419
Black brows, they say, Become some women best . . . . ii 1 9
A sad tale's best for winter: I have one Of sprites and goblins . ii 1 25
Come on, and do your best To fright me with your sprites . . ii 1 27
The office Becomes a woman best; I'll take't upon me . . . ii 2 32
Great Apollo Turn all to the best! . . . . . . iii 1 15
I think there is not half a kiss to choose Who loves another best . iv 4 176
By which means I saw whose purse was best in picture . . . iv 4 615
So his successor Was like to be the best . . . . . v 1 49
You were best say these robes are not gentlemen born . . . v 2 143
Well, ruffian, I must pocket up these wrongs, Because— Your breeches
best may carry them . . . . *K. John* iii 1 201
I knit my handkercher about your brows, The best I had . . . iv 1 43
Whate'er you think, good words, I think, were best . . . iv 3 28
With other princes that may best be spared . . . . . v 7 97
I would he were the best In all this presence that hath moved me so
Richard II. iv 1 31
See how this river comes me cranking in, And cuts me from the best of
all my land . . . . *1 Hen. IV.* iii 1 99
Only this—Let each man do his best . . . . . . v 2 93
Past and to come seems best; things present worst . . *2 Hen. IV.* i 3 108
I am in good name and fame with the very best . . . . ii 4 82
They are your likeliest men, and I would have you served with the best iii 2 274
Our armour all as strong, our cause the best . . . . iv 1 156
And wholesome berries thrive and ripen best Neighbour'd by fruit of
baser quality . . . . *Hen. V.* i 1 61
No doubt, my liege, if each man do his best . . . . ii 2 19
In cases of defence 'tis best to weigh The enemy more mighty than he
seems . . . . ii 4 43
I am a soldier, A name that in my thoughts becomes me best . . iii 3 6
Your mightiness on both parts best can witness . . . . v 2 28
Augment, or alter, as your wisdoms best Shall see advantageable . v 2 87
As fitting best to quittance their deceit . . . *1 Hen. VI.* ii 1 14
Between two horses, which doth bear him best . . . . ii 4 14
How will she specify Where is the best and safest passage in? . . iii 2 22
I were best to leave him, for he will not hear . . . . v 3 82
And look thyself be faultless, thou wert best . . *2 Hen. VI.* ii 1 189
What to your wisdoms seemeth best, Do or undo, as if ourself were here iii 1 195
You were best to go to bed and dream again . . . . . v 1 196
Now one the better, then another best; Both tugging to be victors
3 Hen. VI. ii 5 10
As ourself, Shall do and undo as him pleaseth best . . . . ii 6 105
Here stand we both, and aim we at the best . . . . . iii 1 8

Best. Stamps, as he were nettled: I hope all's for the best *3 Hen. VI.* iii 3 170
We, having now the best at Barnet field, Will thither straight . . v 3 20
Counting myself but bad till I be best . . . . . . v 6 91
Excepting one, Were best he do it secretly, alone . . *Richard III.* i 1 100
Where it seems best unto your royal self . . . . . . iii 1 63
An honest tale speeds best being plainly told . . . . . iv 4 358
The two kings, Equal in lustre, were now best, now worst . *Hen. VIII.* i 1 29
Best Not wake him in his slumber . . . . i 1 121
What we oft do best, By sick interpreters, once weak ones, is Not ours,
or not allow'd . . . . i 2 81
And then let's dream Who's best in favour . . . . . i 4 108
Ay, and the best she shall have; and my favour To him that does best ii 2 114
You, that best should teach us, Have misdemean'd yourself . . v 3 13
Men that make Envy and crooked malice nourishment Dare bite the
best . . . . v 3 45
Shall make it good, or do his best to do it . . . *Troi. and Cres.* i 3 274
Cull their flower, Ajax shall cope the best . . . . . ii 3 275
But that that likes not you pleases me best . . . . . v 2 103
Take your choice of those That best can aid your action . *Coriolanus* i 6 66
Send us to Rome The best, with whom we may articulate . . . i 9 77
When you speak best unto the purpose, it is not worth the wagging of
your beards . . . . ii 1 95
And set down—As best thou art experienced . . .—thine own ways . iv 5 145
That we did, we did for the best . . . . iv 6 144
Nay, let him choose Out of my files . . . My best and freshest men . v 6 35
What I have done, as best I may, Answer I must and shall do *T. Andron.* i 1 411
Rather comfort his distressed plight Than prosecute the meanest or the
best . . . . iv 4 33
Bid him demand what pledge will please him best . . . . iv 4 106
Away, be gone; the sport is at the best . . . *Rom. and Jul.* i 5 121
I thought all for the best . . . . iii 1 109
I think it best you married with the county . . . . . iii 5 219
Those attires are best: but, gentle nurse, I pray thee, leave me . iv 3 1
I have bred her at my dearest cost In qualities of the best *T. of Athens* i 1 125
How likest thou this picture, Apemantus?—The best, for the innocence i 1 199
My lord, you take us even at the best . . . . . . i 2 157
How fare you?—Ever at the best, hearing well of your lordship . iii 6 29
Here is no use for gold.—The best and truest . . . . iv 3 290
Good as the best . . . . v 1 24
Thou draw'st a counterfeit Best in all Athens: thou'rt, indeed, the best v 1 84
'Twere best he speak no harm of Brutus here . . . . *J. Cæsar* iii 2 73
And wisely.—Ay, and truly, you were best . . . . . iii 3 13
To know my deed, 'twere best not know myself . . . *Macbeth* ii 2 73
His throat is cut; that I did for him.—Thou art the best o' the cut-
throats . . . . iii 4 17
To feed were best at home; From thence the sauce to meat is ceremony iii 4 35
Cheer we up his sprites, And show the best of our delights . . iv 1 128
I shall in all my best obey you, madam . . . . . *Hamlet* i 2 120
Murder most foul, as in the best it is . . . . . . i 5 27
But that I love thee best, O most best, believe it . . . . ii 2 122
Confine him where Your wisdom best shall think . . . . iii 1 195
The argument of your praise, balm of your age, Most best, most dearest *Lear* i 1 219
The best and soundest of his time hath been but rash . . . . i 1 298
I advise you to the best; go armed . . . . i 2 188
Sirrah, you were best take my coxcomb . . . . . . i 4 109
The better! best! This weaves itself perforce into my business . ii 1 16
'Tis best to give him way; he leads himself . . . . . ii 4 301
The lamentable change is from the best; The worst returns to laughter iv 1 5
In my rights, By me invested, he compeers the best . . . . v 3 69
Who are you? Mine eyes are not o' the best: I'll tell you straight . v 3 279
You were best go in.—Not I; I must be found . . . *Othello* i 2 30
Take up this mangled matter at the best . . . . . . i 3 173
O heavy ignorance! thou praisest the worst best . . . . ii 1 145
But men are men; the best sometimes forget . . . . . ii 3 241
As men in rage strike those that wish them best . . . . ii 3 243
They say, the wars must make examples Out of their best . . . iii 3 66
I have spoken for you all my best . . . . iii 4 127
Shall she come in? were't good?—I think she stirs again:—no. What's
best to do? . . . . v 2 95
Peace, you were best . . . . v 2 161
Torments will ope your lips.—Well, thou dost best . . . . v 2 306
Read The garboils she awaked; at the last, best . . *Ant. and Cleo.* i 3 61
Still he mends; But this is not the best . . . . . . i 3 83
My arm is sore; best play with Mardian . . . . . . ii 5 4
Best you safed the bringer Out of the host . . . . . iv 6 26
Mark Antony I served, who best was worthy Best to be served . . v 1 6
It shall content me best: be gentle to her . . . . . v 2 68
One of the fairest that I have look'd upon.—And therewithal the best
Cymbeline ii 4 33
Madam, you're best consider . . . . iii 2 79
Haply this life is best, If quiet life be best . . . . . iii 3 29
May the gods Direct you to the best! . . . . . . iii 4 196
From every one The best she hath, and she, of all compounded, Outsells
them all . . . . iii 5 73
'Tis some savage hold: I were best not call; I dare not call . . iii 6 19
Then I'll enter. Best draw my sword . . . . . . iii 6 25
That best Could deem his dignity . . . . v 4 56
Whom best I love I cross; to make my gift, The more delay'd, delighted v 4 101
I love thee more and more: think more and more What's best to ask . v 5 110
For beauty that made barren the swell'd boast Of him that best could
speak . . . . v 5 163
What now ensues, to the judgement of your eye I give, my cause who
best can justify . . . . *Pericles* i Gower 42
And wanting breath to speak help me with tears.—I'll do my best, sir. i 4 20
And that in Tarsus was not best Longer for him to make his rest ii Gower 25
All have done well, But you the best . . . . . . ii 3 109
Each one betake him to his rest; To-morrow all for speeding do their
best . . . . ii 3 116
The fairest, sweet'st, and best lies here, Who wither'd in her spring of
year . . . . iv 4 34
Believe me, 'twere best I did give o'er . . . . . . v 1 168
Best acquainted. That would I learn of you, As one that are best
acquainted with her humour . . . . . . *Richard III.* iv 4 269
Best act. What worst, as oft, Hitting a grosser quality, is cried up For
our best act . . . . *Hen. VIII.* i 2 85
Best actors. The best actors in the world . . . . *Hamlet* ii 2 415
Best advice. Make yourself some comfort Out of your best advice *Cymb.* i 1 156
Best agrees. If love be blind, It best agrees with night *Rom. and Jul.* iii 2 10
Best alarumed. He saw my best alarum'd spirits, Bold in the quarrel's
right . . . . *Lear* ii 1 55

Best apparel. What dost thou with thy best apparel on? . *J. Cæsar* i 1 8
I'll bring him the best 'parel that I have . . . . . *Lear* iv 1 51
Best appointment. Your best appointment make with speed *M. for M.* iii 1 60
We 'll set forth In best appointment all our regiments . . *K. John* ii 1 296
Best armour. I have the best armour of the world . . *Hen. V.* iii 7 1
Best array. Therefore, put you in your best array . . *As Y. Like It* v 2 79
Happiness courts thee in her best array . . . *Rom. and Jul.* iii 3 142
And, as the custom is, In all her best array bear her to church . iv 5 81
Best arrow. By Cupid's strongest bow, By his best arrow *M. N. Dream* i 1 170
Best attention. And lend my best attention . . . *Cymbeline* v 5 117
Best attire. And do you now put on your best attire? . *J. Cæsar* i 1 53
Show me, my women, like a queen : go fetch My best attires *A. and C.* v 2 228
Best avail. Now will it best avail your majesty To cross the seas
1 Hen. VI. iii 1 179
Best becomes. To be merry best becomes you . . . . *Much Ado* ii 1 346
Brought up as best becomes a gentlewoman . . *T. of Shrew* i 2 87
A father Is at the nuptial of his son a guest That best becomes the table . . . . *W. Tale* iv 4 407
Best befits. Conceal her, As best befits her wounded reputation *M. Ado* iv 1 243
Blind is his love and best befits the dark . . . *Rom. and Jul.* ii 1 32
Best beloved. My best beloved and approved friend . *T. of Shrew* i 2 3
Best beseeming. Yet best beseeming me to speak the truth *Richard II.* iv 1 116
Best blood. O, then my best blood turn To an infected jelly! *W. Tale* i 2 417
Even in the best blood chamber'd in his bosom . . *Richard II.* i 1 149
I intend to stain With the best blood that I can meet withal *1 Hen. IV.* v 2 95
Ay, by the best blood that ever was broached . . . *2 Hen. VI.* iv 10 39
Best breed. Of the best breed in the north . . . *Hen. VIII.* ii 2 4
Best bride-bed. To the best bride-bed will we . . *M. N. Dream* v 1 410
Best brine. 'Tis the best brine a maiden can season her praise in *A. W.* i 1 55
Best brother. What cheer? how is't with you, best brother? *W. Tale* i 2 148
Best Camillo. My best Camillo! We must disguise ourselves . iv 2 61
Best cards. Have I not here the best cards for the game? . *K. John* v 2 105
Best champion. Patron of virtue, Rome's best champion . *T. Andron.* i 1 65
Best citizens. Whose fortunes Rome's best citizens applaud . . i 1 164
Best coat. There's a hole made in your best coat . . *Mer. Wives* iii 5 143
Best comforter. The best comforter To an unsettled fancy . *Tempest* v 1 58
Best command. At your best command ; At your employment *K. John* i 1 197
Best-conditioned. The best-condition'd and unwearied spirit In doing courtesies . . . . *Mer. of Venice* iii 2 295
Best conscience. Their best conscience Is not to leave't undone, but keep't unknown . . . . *Othello* iii 3 203
Best contents. A woman sometimes scorns what best contents her
T. G. of Ver. iii 1 93
Best courses. We have taken No care to your best courses . *Pericles* iv 1 39
Best courtier. The best courtier of them all, when the court lay at Windsor, could never have brought her to such a canary *Mer. Wives* ii 2 62
Best days. Even in the afternoon of her best days . . *Richard III.* iii 7 186
Best deserved. Richard hath best deserved of all my sons . *3 Hen. VI.* i 1 17
Best deserving. Was the best deserving a fair lady . . *Mer. of Venice* i 2 130
Best devise. And for his safety there I'll best devise . . *1 Hen. VI.* i 1 172
Best disclosed. Go sit in council, How covert matters may be best disclosed . . . . *J. Cæsar* iv 1 46
Best discover. They have put forth the haven . . . Where their appointment we may best discover . . . *Ant. and Cleo.* iv 10 8
Best elders. See, our best elders . . . . . *Coriolanus* i 1 230
Best enamelled. I see the jewel best enamelled Will lose his beauty
Com. of Errors ii 1 109
Best endeavour. My best endeavours shall be done herein *Mer. of Venice* ii 2 182
With my best endeavours in your absence . . . *W. Tale* iv 4 542
With your best endeavour have stirr'd up My liefest liege *2 Hen. VI.* iii 1 163
Best ends. Which, for your best ends, You adopt your policy *Coriolanus* iii 2 47
Best-esteemed. I do feast to-night My best-esteem'd acquaintance
Mer. of Venice ii 2 181
Best express. As the fits and stirs of's mind Could best express *Cymb.* i 3 13
Best eyes. Whose equality By our best eyes cannot be censured *K. John* ii 1 328
Now, the good gods Throw their best eyes upon't . . . *Pericles* iii 1 37
Best feather. Your lord—The best feather of our wing . *Cymbeline* i 6 186
Best fits. That time best fits the work we have in hand . *2 Hen. VI.* i 4 23
There let it stand Where it best fits to be. . . . . . ii 3 44
The foul'st best fits My latter part of life . . . *Ant. and Cleo.* iv 6 38
Best fitteth my degree or your condition . . *Richard III.* iii 7 143
Best fooling. This is the best fooling, when all is done . *T. Night* ii 3 30
Best force. His best force Is forth to man his galleys *Ant. and Cleo.* iv 11 2
Best fortunes. Women are not In their best fortunes strong . . iii 12 30
Best friend. Would thy best friends did know How it doth grieve me!
3 Hen. VI. ii 2 54
For his best friends, if they Should say 'Be good to Rome,' they charged him even As those should do that had deserved his hate
Coriolanus iv 6 111
O Tybalt, Tybalt, the best friend I had! . . . *Rom. and Jul.* iii 2 61
I could wish my best friend at such a feast . . *T. of Athens* i 2 81
So near will I be, That your best friends shall wish I had been further
J. Cæsar ii 2 125
Our best friends made, our means stretch'd . . . . . iv 1 44
O, coward that I am, to live so long, To see my best friend ta'en before my face! . . . . v 3 35
Best garden. This best garden of the world, Our fertile France *Hen. V.* v 2 36
Fortune made his sword ; By which the world's best garden he achieved Epil. 7
Best governed. In equal rank with the best govern'd nation . *2 Hen. IV.* v 2 137
Best grace. The best grace of wit will shortly turn into silence
Mer. of Venice iii 5 49
And bear the inventory Of your best graces in your mind *Hen. VIII.* iii 2 138
Time be thine, And thy best graces spend it at thy will! . *Hamlet* i 2 63
Best half. The best half should have return'd to him . *T. of Athens* iii 2 91
We have lost Best half of our affair . . . . . *Macbeth* iii 3 21
Best haste. Make your best haste, and go not Too far . *W. Tale* iii 3 10
Best having. Our content Is our best having . . . *Hen. VIII.* ii 3 23
Best heads. Let our best heads Know, that to-morrow the last of many battles We mean to fight . . . . . *Ant. and Cleo.* iv 1 10
Best health. Most fit For your best health and recreation *Richard III.* iii 1 67
Even to the state's best health, I have Deserved this hearing *T. of Athens* iii 5 206
Best heart. My life itself, and the best heart of it, Thanks you *Hen. VIII.* i 2 1
We will grace his heels With the most boldest and best hearts of Rome
J. Cæsar iii 1 121
Best heir. My kingdom, Well worthy the best heir o' the world *Hen. VIII.* ii 4 195
Best hint. When the best hint was given him, he not took't *Ant. and Cleo.* iii 4 9
Best hope. For the best hope I have . . . . . *Hen. V.* iv 3 33
This was my lord's best hope . . . . . *T. of Athens* iii 3 36
Best horse. Would I had given him the best horse in Padua! *T. of Shrew* i 1 148
It is the best horse of Europe . . . . . . *Hen. V.* iii 7 5

Best inclined. Four shall quickly draw out my command, Which men are best inclined . . . . *Coriolanus* i 6 85
Best indued. He is best indued in the small . . . . *L. L. Lost* v 2 646
To mark the full-fraught man and best indued. . . *Hen. V.* ii 2 139
Best instruct. As your charities Shall best instruct you, measure me
W. Tale ii 1 114
Best is. She is curst.—Well, the best is, she hath no teeth to bite
T. G. of Ver. iii 1 348
The duke is marvellous little beholding to your reports ; but the best is, he lives not in them. . . . . . . *Meas. for Meas.* iv 3 167
Best judgement. Passion, having my best judgement collied. *Othello* ii 3 206
Best kindness. I shall unfold equal discourtesy To your best kindness
Cymbeline ii 3 102
Best king. If he be not fellow with the best king, thou shalt find the best king of good fellows . . . . *Hen. V.* v 2 261
Best know. My own people, who best know him . . *As Y. Like It* i 1 176
You, my lord, best know, Who least will seem to do so . *W. Tale* iii 2 33
He is noble, wise, judicious, and best knows The fits o' the season *Macbeth* iv 2 16
How he solicits heaven, Himself best knows . . . . . iv 3 150
Conduct them : you best know the place . . . . *Othello* i 3 121
Hers you are.—The gods best know . . . . *Ant. and Cleo.* i 3 24
That best know how to rule and how to reign . . . *Pericles* ii 4 38
Best known. The fortitude of the place is best known to you . . *Othello* i 3 223
Best knowest. Thou best know'st What torment I did find thee in
Tempest i 2 286
Best leisure. O'er-read, At your best leisure, this . . *Jul. Cæsar* iii 1 5
Best lies. Grant it me, O king! in you it best lies . . *All's Well* v 3 145
Best likest. Even what fashion thou best likest . . *T. G. of Ver.* ii 7 52
Best lord. I'll speak it before the best lord . . . *Mer. Wives* iii 3 53
Best love. He, of all the rest, I think, best loves ye . *T. G. of Ver.* i 2 28
Thy first best love, For whose dear sake thou didst then rend thy faith v 4 46
Lay our best love and credence Upon thy promising fortune *All's Well* iii 3 2
Gentle Octavia, Let your best love draw to that point, which seeks Best to preserve it . . . . *Ant. and Cleo.* iii 4 21
Best lover. As I slew my best lover for the good of Rome . *J. Cæsar* iii 2 49
Best maker. God, the best maker of all marriages . . . *Hen. V.* v 2 387
Best man. They say, best men are moulded out of faults *Meas. for Meas.* v 1 444
He hath heard that men of few words are the best men . . *Hen. V.* iii 2 39
Tell Kent from me, she hath lost her best man . . *2 Hen. VI.* iv 10 79
Within a while All the best men are ours . . . . *Hen. VIII.* Epil. 13
Then, we did our main opinion crush In taint of our best man *Tr. and Cr.* i 3 374
He proved best man i' the field . . . . . . *Coriolanus* ii 2 101
Best married. She's best married that dies married young *Rom. and Jul.* iv 5 78
Best meaning. We are not the first Who, with best meaning, have incurr'd the worst . . . . *Lear* v 3 4
Best mercy. Therefore to our best mercy give yourselves . . *Hen. V.* iii 3 3
Best-moving. We single you As our best-moving fair solicitor *L. L. Lost* ii 1 29
Best news. The best news is, that we have safely found Our king *Tempest* v 1 221
The Duke of Buckingham is taken ; That is the best news *Richard III.* iv 4 534
Best obedience. Commend my best obedience to the queen . *W. Tale* ii 2 36
Best object. She, that even but now was your best object . . *Lear* i 1 217
Best of all. An idiot ; And he my husband best of all affects *Mer. Wives* iv 4 87
Warwick may live to be the best of all . . . *2 Hen. VI.* i 3 115
Swearing both They prosper best of all when I am thence . *3 Hen. VI.* ii 5 18
Best of all Amongst the rarest of good ones . . . . *Cymbeline* v 5 159
Best of comfort ; And ever welcome to us . . . . *Ant. and Cleo.* iii 6 89
Best of gold. Therefore, thou best of gold art worst of gold *2 Hen. IV.* iv 5 161
Best of happiness. The best of happiness, Honour and fortunes, keep with you! . . . . *T. of Athens* i 2 234
Best of it. I'll none of it : hence! make your best of it . *T. of Shrew* iv 3 100
Let's make the best of it . . . . *Coriolanus* v 6 148
Best of me. The best of me is diligence . . . . . *Lear* i 4 37
Best of men. Whose beauty claims No worse a husband than the best of men . . . . *Ant. and Cleo.* ii 2 131
A good rebuke, Which might have well becomed the best of men . iii 7 27
Best of my flesh, Forgive my tyranny . . . . . *Coriolanus* v 3 42
Best of note. My report was once First with the best of note *Cymbeline* iii 3 58
Best of our time. This policy and reverence of age makes the world bitter to the best of our times . . . . *Lear* i 2 49
We have seen the best of our time . . . . i 2 122
Best of rest. Thy best of rest is sleep . . . . *Meas. for Meas.* iii 1 17
Best of them. I am the best of them that speak this speech . *Tempest* i 2 429
As I have read, sir ; and the best of them too . . *L. L. Lost* i 2 88
And had the best of them all at commandment . . *2 Hen. IV.* iii 2 27
Some of the best of 'em were hereditary hangmen . . *Coriolanus* ii 1 102
I could myself Take up a brace o' the best of them . . . . iii 1 244
Best of you. If I once stir, Or do but lift this arm, the best of you Shall sink in my rebuke . . . . *Othello* ii 3 208
Best office. Your anchors, who Do their best office . . *W. Tale* iv 4 582
Best part. The best part of my power, As I upon advantage did remove, Were in the Washes . . . . *K. John* v 7 61
He did confound the best part of an hour . . . *1 Hen. IV.* i 3 100
Thee and all thy best parts bound together, Weigh'd not a hair of his
Hen. VIII. iii 2 258
Best peck. The sixth hour ; when beasts most graze, birds best peck
L. L. Lost i 1 239
Best person. The best wit of any handicraft man in Athens.—Yea, and the best person too . . . . *M. N. Dream* iv 2 11
Best persuaded. The best persuaded of himself . . . *T. Night* ii 3 162
Best persuasions. The best persuasions to the contrary . *Hen. VIII.* v 1 147
Best pierce. Honest plain words best pierce the ear of grief *L. L. Lost* v 2 763
Best place. Opinions Where is best place to make our battery next
1 Hen. VI. i 4 65
Best please. That sport best pleases that doth least know how *L. L. Lost* v 2 517
Those things do best please me That befal preposterously *M. N. Dream* iii 2 120
Best pleased. In private, then.—I am best pleased with that. *L. L. Lost* v 2 229
She would be best pleased To be so anger'd with another letter *T. G. of Ver.* i 2 102
I am best pleased to be from such a deed . . . . *K. John* iv 1 86
Best pleasure. I come To answer thy best pleasure . . . *Tempest* i 2 190
Best ports. Have secret feet In some of our best ports . . . *Lear* iii 1 33
Best quarrels. And the best quarrels, in the heat, are cursed By those that feel their sharpness . . . . v 3 56
Best rank. The best rank and station Are of a most select and generous chief in that . . . . *Hamlet* i 3 73
Best regard. Full many a lady I have eyed with best regard . *Tempest* iii 1 40
Best-regarded. By my love, I swear The best-regarded virgins of our clime Have loved it too . . . . *Mer. of Venice* ii 1 10
Best respect. Many of the best respect in Rome, Except immortal Cæsar, speaking of Brutus . . . . *J. Cæsar* i 2 59
Best robes. In thy best robes uncover'd on the bier . *Rom. and Jul.* iv 1 110

Best ruff. We shall have him here to-morrow with his best ruff on Pericles iv 2 111
Best safety. Be wary then; best safety lies in fear . Hamlet i 3 43
Best seeing. When we greet, With eyes best seeing, heaven's fiery eye, By light we lose light . L. L. Lost v 2 375
Best seen. You that are honest, by being what you are, Make them best seen and known . T. of Athens v 1 72
Best senses. The five best senses Acknowledge thee their patron . i 2 129
Best service. Such officers do the king best service in the end Hamlet iv 2 18
Best sheep. They have scared away two of my best sheep . W. Tale iii 3 66
Best sort. The mayor and all his brethren in best sort Hen. V. v Prol. 25
Best spirits. This sword, this arm, and my best spirits, are bent To prove upon thy heart, whereto I speak . Lear v 3 139
Best springs. I'll show thee the best springs . Tempest ii 2 164
Best state, contentless, Hath a distracted and most wretched being T. of Athens iv 3 245
Best studies. Myself and them Bend their best studies . K. John iv 2 51
Best success. The queen hath best success when you are absent 3 Hen. VI. ii 2 74
Best-tempered. Took fire and heat away From the best-temper'd courage in his troops . 2 Hen. IV. i 1 115
Best that is. His brother is reputed one of the best that is . All's Well iv 3 322
Best thing. The best thing in him Is his complexion . As Y. Like It iii 5 115
Best time. In best time We will require her welcome . Macbeth iii 4 5
Best train. My best train I have from your Sicilian shores dismiss'd W. Tale v 1 163
Best trust. I' the vaward are the Antiates, Of their best trust Coriolanus i 6 54
Best turn. For what good turn?—For the best turn i' the bed A. and C. ii 5 59
Best use. Dignities, which vacant lie For thy best use . T. of Athens v 1 146
Make your best use of this . Ant. and Cleo. v 2 203
Have the best use of eyes to see the way of blindness! . Cymbeline v 4 196
Best violence. I pray you, pass with your best violence . Hamlet v 2 309
Best virtue. A fault I will not change for your best virtue As Y. Like It iii 2 302
Drunkenness is his best virtue, for he will be swine-drunk . All's Well iv 3 285
Best ward. The best ward of mine honour is rewarding my dependents L. L. Lost iii 1 133
Say this to him, He's beat from his best ward . W. Tale i 2 33
Best water. Our best water brought by conduits hither . Coriolanus ii 3 250
Best way. My best way is to creep under his gaberdine . Tempest ii 2 39
The best way is to slander Valentine With falsehood T. G. of Ver. iii 2 31
The best way were to entertain him with hope. Mer. Wives ii 1 67
The best way is to venge my Gloucester's death . Richard II. i 2 36
Best will. I'll ever serve his mind with my best will T. of Athens iv 2 49
Do your best wills, And make me blest to obey! . Cymbeline v 1 16
Best wishes. The best wishes that can be forged in your thoughts be servants to you! . All's Well i 1 84
Best wit. He hath simply the best wit of any handicraft man in Athens M. N. Dream iv 2 9
Best woodman. You, Polydore, have proved best woodman . Cymbeline iii 6 28
Best worthy. Pompey proves the best Worthy . L. L. Lost v 2 564
Best's son. There's Best's son, the tanner of Wingham . 2 Hen. VI. iv 2 23
Bestained. We will not line his thin bestained cloak With our pure honours . K. John iv 3 24
Bested. I never saw a fellow worse bested, Or more afraid to fight 2 Hen. VI. ii 3 56
Bestial. Urge his hateful luxury, And bestial appetite Richard III. iii 5 81
Whether it be Bestial oblivion, or some craven scruple Hamlet iv 4 40
I have lost the immortal part of myself, and what remains is bestial Othello ii 3 264
Bestir. We run ourselves aground: bestir, bestir Tempest i 1 4
Bestirred. And thus hath so bestirr'd thee in thy sleep . 1 Hen. IV. ii 3 60
I am scarce in breath, my lord.—No marvel, you have so bestirred your valour . Lear ii 2 58
Bestow. I must Bestow upon the eyes of this young couple Some vanity of mine art . Tempest iv 1 40
Hence, and bestow your luggage where you found it . v 1 299
Far behind his worth Comes all the praises that I now bestow T. G. of Ver. ii 4 72
Which way I may bestow myself To be regarded in her sun-bright eye . iii 1 87
Overweening slave! Bestow thy fawning smiles on equal mates . iii 1 158
Which way should he go? how should I bestow him? Mer. Wives iv 2 48
It is a blessing that he bestows on beasts . Com. of Errors ii 2 80
That chain will I bestow—Be it for nothing but to spite my wife . iii 1 117
Buy a rope's end: that will I bestow Among my wife and her confederates iv 1 16
If I were as tedious as a king, I could find it in my heart to bestow it all of your worship . Much Ado iii 5 24
They'll know By favours several which they did bestow L. L. Lost v 2 125
Sweet royalty, bestow on me the sense of hearing . v 2 670
Silence bestows that virtue on it, madam . Mer. of Venice v 1 101
Of female favour, and bestows himself Like a ripe sister As Y. Like It iv 3 87
If I bring in your Rosalind, You will bestow her on Orlando here? v 4 7
That is, not to bestow my youngest daughter . T. of Shrew i 1 50
Toward the education of your daughters, I here bestow a simple instrument . ii 1 100
He will'd me In heedfull'st reservation to bestow them . All's Well i 3 231
Whom I know Is free for me to ask, thee to bestow . ii 1 203
To requite you further, I will bestow some precepts . iii 5 103
For what is yours to bestow is not yours to reserve T. Night i 5 200
He says he'll come; How shall I feast him? what bestow of him? . iii 4 2
Tell me how you would bestow yourself K. John iii 1 225
How might we see Falstaff bestow himself to-night in his true colours? 2 Hen. IV. ii 2 186
I will bestow a breakfast to make you friends . Hen. V. ii 1 12
Bestow yourself with speed: The French are bravely in their battles set iv 3 68
We will bestow you in some better place, Fitter for sickness 1 Hen. VI. iii 2 88
Bestow your pity on me: for I am a most poor woman . Hen. VIII. ii 4 14
Come, reverend fathers, Bestow your counsels on me . iii 1 182
Pared my present havings, to bestow My bounties upon you . iii 2 159
What did you swear you would bestow on me? . Troi. and Cres. v 2 25
If you'll bestow a small—of what you have little—Patience awhile Coriol. i 1 129
Of him that did not ask, but mock, bestow Your sued-for tongues . ii 3 215
I ask your voices and your suffrages: Will you bestow them? T. Andron. i 1 219
And you must needs bestow her funeral . iv 2 163
Give him thy daughter: What you bestow, in him I'll counterpoise T. of Athens i 1 145
I will hie, And so bestow these papers as you bade me . J. Cæsar i 3 151
Wilt thou bestow thy time with me? . v 5 61
Can you tell Where he bestows himself? Macbeth iii 6 24
Lawful espials, Will so bestow ourselves that, seeing, unseen, We may of their encounter frankly judge . Hamlet iii 1 33
So please you, We will bestow ourselves . iii 1 44
I will bestow him, and will answer well The death I gave him . iii 4 176
Bestow this place on us a little while . iv 1 4
Kill thy physician, and the fee bestow Upon thy foul disease . Lear i 1 166
Bestow. Bestow Your needful counsel to our business . Lear ii 1 128
Come, father, I'll bestow you with a friend . ii 6 293
Would she give you so much of her lips As of her tongue she oft bestows on me, You'ld have enough . Othello ii 1 102
But what praise couldst thou bestow on a deserving woman indeed? ii 1 145
I will bestow you where you shall have time To speak your bosom freely iii 1 57
'Tis hers, my lord; and, being hers, She may, I think, bestow't on any man . iv 1 13
Still be't yours, Bestow it at your pleasure . Ant. and Cleo. v 2 182
Will you, not having my consent, Bestow your love and your affections Upon a stranger? . Pericles ii 5 77
Bestowed. More than for all the favours Which all too much I have bestow'd on thee . T. G. of Ver. iii 1 162
If she be otherwise, 'tis labour well bestowed . Mer. Wives ii 1 248
I have long loved her, and, I protest to you, bestowed much on her . ii 2 202
The devil take one party and his dam the other! and so they shall be both bestowed . iv 5 109
In few, bestowed her on her own lamentation . Meas. for Meas. iii 1 237
Answer me In what safe place you have bestow'd my money Com. of Err. i 2 78
Don Peter hath bestowed much honour on a young Florentine Much Ado i 1 10
The rod he might have bestowed on you . ii 1 237
I would she had bestowed this dotage on me . ii 3 175
Surely suit ill spent and labour ill bestowed . iii 2 103
These things being bought and orderly bestow'd, Return in haste Mer. of Venice ii 2 179
Little is the cost I have bestow'd In purchasing the semblance of my soul . iii 4 19
That her gifts may henceforth be bestowed equally. As Y. Like It i 2 36
Ready and willing With one consent to have her so bestow'd T. of Shrew iv 4 35
I would I had bestowed that time in the tongues that I have in fencing T. Night i 3 97
The parts that fortune hath bestow'd upon her, Tell her, I hold as giddily as fortune . ii 4 86
I saw your niece do more favours to the count's serving-man than ever she bestowed upon me . iii 2 8
If you knew what pains I have bestow'd to breed this present peace 2 Hen. IV. iv 2 74
I would have bestowed the thousand pound I borrowed of you . v 5 12
And on it have bestow'd more contrite tears . Hen. V. iv 1 313
Large gifts have I bestow'd on learned clerks . 2 Hen. VI. iv 7 76
Else you would not have bestow'd the heir Of the Lord Bonville on your new wife's son . 3 Hen. VI. iv 1 56
Nor none so noble Whose life were ill bestow'd or death unfamed Troi. and Cres. ii 2 159
O monument And wonder of good deeds evilly bestow'd! T. of Athens iv 3 467
We hear, our bloody cousins are bestow'd In England and in Ireland Macb. iii 1 30
Will you see the players well bestowed? Hamlet ii 2 547
Where the dead body is bestow'd, my lord, We cannot get from him . iv 3 12
This house is little: the old man and his people Cannot be well bestow'd Lear ii 4 292
Bestow'd his lips on that unworthy place, As it rain'd kisses A. and C. iii 13 84
Hath Thetis' birth-child on the heavens bestow'd . Pericles iv 4 41
Bestowing. Send forth thine eye: this youthful parcel Of noble bachelors stand at my bestowing . All's Well ii 3 59
You cannot, By the good aid that I of you shall borrow, Err in bestowing it . iii 7 12
For not bestowing on him, at his asking, The archbishopric Hen. VIII. ii 1 163
In bestowing, madam, He was most princely . iv 2 56
And all my powers do their bestowing lose . Troi. and Cres. iii 2 39
Bestraught. What! I am not bestraught . T. of Shrew Ind. 2 26
Bestrew. Sour-eyed disdain and discord shall bestrew The union of your bed with weeds . Tempest iv 1 20
Say thou wilt walk; we will bestrew the ground . T. of Shrew Ind. 2 42
Bestrewed. A silver basin Full of rose-water and bestrew'd with flowers Ind. 1 56
Bestrid. When I bestrid thee in the wars and took Deep scars to save thy life . Com. of Errors v 1 192
Roan Barbary, That horse that thou so often hast bestrid Richard II. v 5 79
Three times to-day I holp him to his horse, Three times bestrid him 2 Hen. VI. v 3 9
He bestrid An o'er-press'd Roman and i' the consul's view Slew three Coriolanus ii 2 96
His legs bestrid the ocean: his rear'd arm Crested the world A. and C. v 2 82
Never bestrid a horse, save one that had A rider like myself Cymbeline iv 4 38
Bestride. Hal, if thou see me down in the battle and bestride me, so; 'tis a point of friendship . 1 Hen. IV. v 1 122
He doth bestride a bleeding land, Gasping for life . 2 Hen. IV. i 1 207
When I bestride him, I soar, I am a hawk: he trots the air . Hen. V. iii 7 15
Once again bestride our foaming steeds, And once again cry 'Charge!' 3 Hen. VI. ii 1 183
Bestride the rock; the tide will wash you off, Or else you famish . v 4 31
More dances my rapt heart Than when I first my wedded mistress saw Bestride my threshold . Coriolanus iv 5 124
Bestrides the lazy-pacing clouds And sails upon the bosom of the air Rom. and Jul. ii 2 31
A lover may bestride the gossamer That idles in the wanton summer air . ii 6 18
Why, man, he doth bestride the narrow world Like a Colossus J. Cæsar i 2 135
And like good men Bestride our down-fall'n birthdom Macbeth iv 3 4
Bet. That's the French bet against the Danish . Hamlet v 2 170
Betake thee to thy faith, for seventeen poniards are at thy bosom All's Well iv 1 83
That defence thou hast, betake thee to't . T. Night iii 4 240
If you hold your life at any price, betake you to your guard . iii 4 252
Therefore betake thee To nothing but despair . W. Tale iii 2 210
Base and ignominious treasons, makes me betake me to my heels 2 Hen. VI. iv 8 67
And no sooner in, But every man betake him to his legs Rom. and Jul. i 4 34
Each one betake him to his rest; To-morrow all for speeding do their best . Pericles ii 3 115
Beteem. I could well Beteem them from the tempest of my eyes M. N. Dr. i 1 131
He might not beteem the winds of heaven Visit her face too roughly Ham. i 2 141
Bethink you of some conveyance . Mer. Wives iii 3 135
Bethink you; Who is it that hath died for this offence? Meas. for Meas. ii 2 87
I will bethink me: come again to-morrow . ii 2 144
'Twas bravely done, if you bethink you of it . Much Ado v 1 280
For truly would I speak, And now I do bethink me, so it is M. N. Dr. iv 1 155
Should I go to church And see the holy edifice of stone, And not bethink me straight of dangerous rocks? Mer. of Venice i 1 31
I will be assured I may; and, that I may be assured, I will bethink me i 3 31
Bethink thee of thy birth, Call home thy ancient thoughts T. of Shrew Ind. 2 32
And now I do bethink me, it was she First told me . T. Night v 1 356

Bethink. But I bethink me what a weary way *Richard II.* ii 3 8
Bethink thee on her virtues that surmount, And natural graces 1 *Hen. VI.* v 3 191
Bethink thee once again, And in thy thought o'er-run my former time 3 *Hen. VI.* i 4 44
As I bethink me, you should not be king Till our King Henry had shook hands with death . i 4 101
With patience calm the storm, While we bethink a means to break it off iii 3 39
Madam, bethink you, like a careful mother *Richard III.* ii 2 96
Bade him bethink How nice the quarrel was . . . *Rom. and Jul.* iii 1 158
Nor what is mine shall never do thee good : Trust to't, bethink you . iii 5 197
It may be I shall otherwise bethink me . . . . *J. Cæsar* iv 3 251
Bethink yourself wherein you may have offended him . . . *Lear* i 2 174
If you bethink yourself of any crime Unreconciled as yet to heaven and grace, Solicit for it straight *Othello* v 2 26
Bethought. I have bethought me of another fault . *Meas. for Meas.* v 1 461
He hath better bethought him of his quarrel . . *T. Night* iii 4 327
Marry, well bethought : 'Tis told me, he hath very oft of late Given private time to you . . . *Hamlet* i 3 90
And am bethought To take the basest and most poorest shape . *Lear* ii 3 6
Being here, Bethought me what was past, what might succeed . *Pericles* i 2 83
'Tis well bethought . . . . v 1 44
Bethumped. I was never so bethump'd with words . . *K. John* ii 1 466
Betid. Not so much perdition as an hair Betid to any creature *Tempest* i 2 31
Let them tell thee tales Of woeful ages long ago betid . *Richard II.* v 1 42
Neither know I What is betid to Cloten . . . . *Cymbeline* iv 3 40
Betide. More health and happiness betide my liege! . *Richard II.* iii 2 91
What shall betide the Duke of Somerset? . . . . 2 *Hen. VI.* i 4 69
To provide A salve for any sore that may betide 3 *Hen. VI.* iv 6 88
More direful hap betide that hated wretch! . . *Richard III.* i 2 17
Ill rest betide the chamber where thou liest! . . . i 2 112
If he were dead, what would betide of me? . . . . i 3 6
And so betide to me As well I tender you and all of yours! . ii 4 71
We are all undone! Now help, or woe betide thee evermore! *T. Andron.* iv 2 56
Betideth. And what news else Betideth here . . *T. G. of Ver.* i 1 59
Recking as little what betideth me As much I wish all good befortune you . . . . iv 3 40
Betime. He that drinks all night, and is hanged betimes in the morning, may sleep the sounder all the next day . . *Meas. for Meas.* iv 3 49
Let it be proclaimed betimes i' the morn . . . . iv 4 18
The next morn betimes, His purpose surfeiting . . . v 1 101
No time shall be omitted That will betime, and may by us be fitted *L. L. Lost* iv 3 382
Let me say 'amen' betimes, lest the devil cross my prayer *Mer. of Ven.* iii 1 22
Not to be a-bed after midnight is to be up betimes . . *T. Night* ii 3 2
To go to bed after midnight is to go to bed betimes . . . ii 3 9
Be cured Of this diseased opinion, and betimes . . *W. Tale* i 2 297
Put up thy sword betime ; Or I'll so maul you and your toasting-iron *K. John* iv 3 98
He tires betimes that spurs too fast betimes . . *Richard II.* ii 1 36
Be with me betimes in the morning ; and so, good morrow 1 *Hen. IV.* ii 4 600
Stop the rage betime, Before the wound do grow uncurable 2 *Hen. VI.* iii 1 285
I rather would have lost my life betimes Than bring a burthen of dishonour home . . . . iii 1 297
Away betimes, before his forces join . . . . 3 *Hen. VI.* iv 8 62
He should have leave to go away betimes . . . . v 4 45
Let us sup betimes, that afterwards We may digest our complots *Richard III.* iii 1 199
Let us pay betimes A moiety of that mass of moan to come *Tr. and Cr.* ii 2 106
If these be motives weak, break off betimes, And every man hence *J. C.* ii 1 116
Bid him set on his powers betimes before, And we will follow . iv 3 308
I will to-morrow, And betimes I will, to the weird sisters *Macbeth* iii 4 133
Good God, betimes remove The means that makes us strangers! . iv 3 162
To-morrow is Saint Valentine's day, All in the morning betime *Hamlet* iv 5 49
Since no man has aught of what he leaves, what is't to leave betimes? v 2 235
We meet i' the morning?—At my lodging.—I'll be with thee betimes *Oth.* i 3 383
Betimes in the morning I will beseech the virtuous Desdemona . ii 3 335
To business that we love we rise betime . . *Ant. and Cleo.* iv 4 20
Like the spirit of a youth That means to be of note, begins betimes . iv 4 27
It is a day turn'd strangely : or betimes Let's re-inforce, or fly *Cymbeline* v 2 17
Betoken. This doth betoken The corse they follow did with desperate hand Fordo it own life . . . . . . *Hamlet* v 1 242
Betook. And, as I am a gentleman, betook myself to walk *L. L. Lost* i 1 237
Your lord has betook himself to unknown travels . . *Pericles* i 3 35
Betossed. What said my man, when my betossed soul Did not attend him as we rode? . . . . . . *Rom. and Jul.* v 3 76
Betray. Do not betray me, sir. I fear you love Mistress Page *Mer. Wives* iii 3 82
Give him another hope, to betray him to another punishment . iii 3 208
We'll betray him finely . . . . v 3 22
Those that betray them do no treachery . . . . v 3 24
She did betray me to my own reproof . . *Com. of Errors* v 1 90
I do betray myself with blushing . . . *L. L. Lost* i 2 138
These betray nice wenches, that would be betrayed without these . iii 1 23
To betray a she-lamb of a twelvemonth . . *As Y. Like It* iii 2 85
And betray themselves to every modern censure worse than drunkards iv 1 6
In the highest compulsion of base fear, offer to betray you *All's Well* iii 6 32
A' will betray us all unto ourselves . . . . . iv 1 102
Will you undertake to betray the Florentine? . . . . iv 3 326
He does obey every point of the letter that I dropped to betray him *T. Night* iii 2 83
How sometimes nature will betray its folly! . . *W. Tale* i 2 151
My name Be yoked with his that did betray the Best! . . i 2 419
The sacred honour of himself, his queen's, His hopeful son's, his babe's, betrays to slander . . . . ii 3 85
Sleeping neglection doth betray to loss The conquest . 1 *Hen. VI.* iv 3 49
Have all limed bushes to betray thy wings . . . 2 *Hen. VI.* ii 4 54
Villain, thou wilt betray me, and get a thousand crowns of the king . iv 10 28
I know thee not ; why, then, should I betray thee? . . . iv 10 34
Her husband, knave : wouldst thou betray me? . . *Richard III.* i 1 102
Nor to betray you any way to sorrow, You have too much, good lady *Hen. VIII.* iii 1 56
Wilt thou betray thy noble mistress thus? . . *T. Andron.* iv 2 106
Betray with blushing The close enacts and counsels of the heart . iv 2 117
Shall she live to betray this guilt of ours, A long-tongued babbling gossip? . . . . iv 2 149
Revenge now goes To lay a complot to betray thy foes . . v 2 147
Win us with honest trifles, to betray's In deepest consequence *Macbeth* i 3 125
Would not betray The devil to his fellow . . . . iv 3 128
Let not the creaking of shoes nor the rustling of silks betray thy poor heart to woman . . . . *Lear* iii 4 98
Yet she must die, else she'll betray more men . . . *Othello* v 2 6
Betray. My music playing far off, I will betray Tawny-finn'd fishes *Ant. and Cleo.* ii 5 11
Make him swear The shes of Italy should not betray Mine interest *Cymb.* i 3 29
Like the harpy, Which, to betray, dost, with thine angel's face, Seize with thine eagle's talons . . . . . *Pericles* iv 3 47
Betrayed. These betray nice wenches, that would be betrayed without these . . . . *L. L. Lost* iii 1 24
Too bitter is thy jest. Are we betray'd thus to thy over-view? . iv 3 175
Not you to me, but I betray'd by you : I, that am honest . . iv 3 176
I am betray'd, by keeping company With men like men of inconstancy iv 3 179
Camillo has betray'd me ; Whose honour and whose honesty till now Endured all weathers . . . . *W. Tale* v 1 193
Wilfully betray'd The lives of those that he did lead to fight 1 *Hen. IV.* i 3 81
He hath betrayed his followers, whose condemnation is pronounced *Hen. V.* iii 6 143
Unto his dastard foemen is betray'd . . . . 1 *Hen. VI.* i 1 144
But dies, betray'd to fortune by your strife . . . . iv 4 39
Trust nobody, for fear you be betray'd . . . 2 *Hen. VI.* iv 4 58
Either betray'd by falsehood of his guard Or by his foe surprised 3 *Hen. VI.* iv 4 8
Poor Clarence, by thy guile betrayed to death! . . *Richard III.* v 3 133
Was by that wretch betray'd, And without trial fell . *Hen. VIII.* i 1 110
Perfidiously He has betray'd your business . . . *Coriolanus* v 6 92
Unicorns may be betray'd with trees, And bears with glasses *J. Cæsar* ii 1 204
Alas! he is betray'd and I undone . . . . . *Othello* v 2 76
O, never was there queen So mightily betray'd! . *Ant. and Cleo.* i 3 25
Repent that e'er thy tongue Hath so betray'd thine act . . iii 7 84
This foul Egyptian hath betrayed me : My fleet hath yielded to the foe iv 12 10
Betray'd I am : O this false soul of Egypt! . . . . iv 12 24
Peace! She hath betray'd me and shall die the death . . iv 14 26
Do not yourself such wrong, who are in this Relieved, but not betray'd v 2 41
Some jay of Italy, Whose mother was her painting, hath betray'd him *Cymbeline* iii 4 52
Those that are betray'd Do feel the treason sharply . . . iii 4 87
Betrayedst. That thou betray'dst Polixenes, 'twas nothing . *W. Tale* iii 2 186
Betraying. For, by oppressing and betraying me, Thou mightst have sooner got another service . . . . . *T. of Athens* iv 3 510
Betrim. Which spongy April at thy hest betrims . . . *Tempest* iv 1 65
Betroth. What is he for a fool that betroths himself to unquietness? *Much Ado* i 3 49
Betrothed. But she loves you?—Ay, and we are betroth'd *T. G. of Ver.* ii 4 179
To whom, thyself art witness, I am betroth'd . . . . iv 2 111
With Angelo to-night shall lie His old betrothed but despised *Meas. for Meas.* iii 2 293
To her, my lord, Was I betroth'd ere I saw Hermia . *M. N. Dream* iv 1 177
You are betroth'd both to a maid and man . . . . *T. Night* v 1 270
Pining maidens' groans, For husbands, fathers and betrothed lovers *Hen. V.* ii 4 108
You know, my lord, your highness is betroth'd Unto another lady 1 *Hen. VI.* v 5 26
By substitute betroth'd To Bona, sister to the King of France *Richard III.* iii 7 181
Him that justly may Bear his betroth'd from all the world away *T. Andron.* i 1 286
Betroth'd and would have married her perforce . . *Rom. and Jul.* v 3 238
Betted. Loved him well, and betted much money on his head 2 *Hen. IV.* iii 2 50
Better. Nought knowing Of whence I am, nor that I am more better *Tempest* i 2 19
Here lies your brother, No better than the earth he lies upon . ii 1 281
Has done little better than played the Jack with us . . iv 1 197
O excellent device! was there ever heard a better? . *T. G. of Ver.* ii 1 145
He wants wit that wants resolved will To learn his wit to exchange the bad for better . . . . ii 6 13
Better forbear till Proteus make return . . . . ii 7 14
Therefore is she better than a jade . . . . . iii 1 276
For thou hast shown some sign of good desert—Makes me the better to confer with thee . . . . iii 2 19
Better, indeed, when you hold your peace . . . . v 2 18
Better have none Than plural faith which is too much by one . v 4 51
I wished your venison better ; it was ill killed . *Mer. Wives* i 1 84
The council shall know this.—'Twere better for you if it were known in counsel . . . . i 1 121
Simple, you say your name is?—Ay, for fault of a better . i 4 17
How dost thou?—The better that it pleases your good worship to ask . i 4 144
I like it never the better for that . . . . . ii 1 186
Better three hours too soon than a minute too late . . . ii 2 327
I know not which pleases me better, that my husband is deceived, or Sir John . . . . iii 3 189
Heaven make you better than your thoughts! . . . . iii 3 218
They can tell you how things go better than I can . . . iii 4 69
Away with him! better shame than murder . . . . iv 2 45
Better a little chiding than a great deal of heart-break . . v 3 10
Do not these fair yokes Become the forest better than the town? . v 5 112
Come, tell me true : it shall be the better for you *Meas. for Meas.* ii 1 233
Let me be ignorant, and in nothing good, But graciously to know I am no better . . . . ii 4 77
Better it were a brother died at once, Than that a sister, by redeeming him, Should die for ever . . . . ii 4 106
He shall know you better, sir, if I may live to report you . . iii 2 171
I have been drinking all night ; I am not fitted for't.—O, the better, sir iv 3 48
Good morning to you, fair and gracious daughter.—The better, given me by so holy a man . . . . iv 3 117
He was drunk then, my lord : it can be no better . . . v 1 189
Not better than he, by her own report . . . . . v 1 274
For the most, become much more the better For being a little bad . v 1 445
Ah, but I think him better than I say . . *Com. of Errors* iv 2 25
How much better is it to weep at joy than to joy at weeping! *Much Ado* i 1 28
A bird of my tongue is better than a beast of yours . . . i 1 140
I say my prayers aloud.—I love you the better . . . ii 1 109
Others say thou dost deserve, and I Believe it better than reportingly iii 1 116
Let that appear hereafter, and aim better at me . . . iii 2 99
Troth, I think your other rabato were better . . . . iii 4 7
It is proved already that you are little better than false knaves . iv 2 23
Did you ever hear better?—I am much deceived but I remember the style *L. L. Lost* iv 1 97
Construe my speeches better, if you may.—Then wish me better . v 2 341
This falls out better than I could devise . . *M. N. Dream* iii 2 35
Would you desire lime and hair to speak better? . . . v 1 167
A mote will turn the balance, which Pyramus, which Thisbe, is the better . . . . v 1 325
Good sentences and well pronounced.—They would be better, if well followed . . . . *Mer. of Venice* i 2 12
He hath a horse better than the Neapolitan's . . . . i 2 62

Better. When he is worst, he is little better than a beast *Mer. of Venice* i 2 96
'Tis vile, unless it may be quaintly order'd, And better in my mind not undertook ii 4 7
Is that my prize? are my deserts no better? ii 9 60
The villany you teach me, I will execute, and it shall go hard but I will better the instruction iii 1 76
I would not be ambitious in my wish, To wish myself much better iii 2 153
I shall answer that better to the commonwealth iii 5 40
You cannot better be employ'd, Bassanio, Than to live still and write mine epitaph iv 1 117
It [mercy] becomes The throned monarch better than his crown iv 1 189
Our husbands' healths, Which speed, we hope, the better for our words v 1 115
Give him this And bid him keep it better than the other v 1 255
His horses are bred better *As Y. Like It* i 1 11
Know you before whom, sir?—Ay, better than him I am before knows me i 1 46
The courtesy of nations allows you my better, in that you are the first-born i 1 50
Then shall we be news-crammed.—All the better; we shall be the more marketable i 2 102
Were it not better, Because that I am more than common tall, That I did suit me all points like a man? i 3 116
Fortune cannot recompense me better Than to die well ii 3 75
Who calls?—Your betters, sir.—Else are they very wretched ii 4 68
By how much defence is better than no skill iii 3 63
I am not in the mind but I were better to be married of him than of another iii 3 92
Look on him better, And be not proud iii 5 79
You are a melancholy fellow.—I am so; I do love it better than laughing iv 1 4
I would kiss before I spoke.—Nay, you were better speak first iv 1 73
Good plays prove the better by the help of good epilogues Epil. 6
Esteemed him No better than a poor and loathsome beggar *T. of Shrew* Ind. 1 123
The better for him: would I were so too! i 1 243
Pedascule, I'll watch you better yet iii 1 50
Not so well apparell'd As I wish you were.—Were it better, I should rush in thus iii 2 93
'Twere well for Kate and better for myself iii 2 122
We will persuade him, be it possible, To put on better ere he go to church iii 2 128
Better 'twere that both of us did fast, Since, of ourselves, ourselves are choleric iv 1 176
He that knows better how to tame a shrew, Now let him speak iv 1 213
I am no child, no babe: Your betters have endured me say my mind iv 3 75
Is the adder better than the eel, Because his painted skin contents the eye? iv 3 179
Better once than never, for never too late v 1 155
I will win my wager better yet v 2 116
In her they are the better for their simpleness *All's Well* i 1 51
Your date is better in your pie and your porridge than in your cheek i 1 172
'Tis a withered pear; it was formerly better i 1 177
I'll like a maid the better, whilst I have a tooth in my head ii 3 48
No better, if you please ii 3 90
I have spoken better of you than you have or will to deserve at my hand ii 5 51
You know your places well; When better fall, for your avails they fell iii 1 22
Better 'twere I met the ravin lion when he roar'd iii 2 119
Better 'twere That all the miseries which nature owes Were mine at once iii 2 121
Damns himself to do and dares better be damned than to do't iii 6 96
Which better than the first, O dear heaven, bless! v 3 71
Under the degree of my betters *T. Night* i 3 125
She will attend it better in thy youth Than in a nuncio's of more grave aspect i 4 27
What says Quinapalus? 'Better a witty fool than a foolish wit' i 5 39
No better than the fools' zanies i 5 96
If it be so, as 'tis, Poor lady, she were better love a dream ii 2 27
How much the better To fall before the lion than the wolf! iii 1 139
I would you were as I would have you be!—Would it be better, madam, than I am? iii 1 155
Love sought is good, but given unsought is better iii 1 168
My hope is better, and so look to thyself iii 4 185
You are mad indeed, if you be no better in your wits than a fool iv 2 98
The better for my foes and the worse for my friends v 1 13
Why then, the worse for my friends and the better for my foes v 1 25
I have look'd on thousands, who have sped the better By my regard *W. Tale* i 2 389
You'll kiss me hard and speak to me as if I were a baby still. I love you better ii 1 6
Better burn it now Than curse it then ii 3 156
Which I receive much better Than to be pitied of thee iii 2 234
Better not to have had thee than thus to want thee iv 2 14
How do you now?—Sweet sir, much better than I was iv 3 119
Yet nature is made better by no mean But nature makes that mean iv 4 89
What you do Still betters what is done iv 4 136
He could never come better; he shall come in iv 4 187
I cannot speak So well, nothing so well; no, nor mean better iv 4 392
The swifter speed the better iv 4 683
Things that would Have done the time more benefit and graced Your kindness better v 1 23
As every present time doth boast itself Above a better gone v 1 97
Your verse Flow'd with her beauty once: 'tis shrewdly ebb'd, To say you have seen a better v 1 103
Who began to be much sea-sick, and himself little better v 2 129
Our country manners give our betters way *K. John* i 1 156
A foot of honour better than I was; But many a many foot of land the worse i 1 182
Not a word of his But buffets better than a fist of France ii 1 465
When workmen strive to do better than well, They do confound their skill iv 2 28
Thou wert better gall the devil iv 3 95
That you might The better arm you to the sudden time v 6 26
Each day still better other's happiness! *Richard II.* i 1 22
Why hopest thou so? 'tis better hope he is; For his designs crave haste ii 2 43
But thou shouldst please me better, wouldst thou weep iii 4 20
Better far off than near, be ne'er the near v 1 88
Then crushing penury Persuades me I was better when a king v 5 35
Now am I, if a man should speak truly, little better than one of the wicked. I must give over this life *1 Hen. IV.* i 2 106
By how much better than my word I am, By so much shall I falsify men's hopes i 2 234
He loves his own barn better than he loves our house ii 3 6
I never dealt better since I was a man ii 4 188
I shall think the better of myself and thee during my life ii 4 302
Better. Food for powder; they'll fill a pit as well as better *1 Hen IV.* iv 2 73
Making you ever better than his praise By still dispraising praise valued with you v 2 59
Fellows, soldiers, friends, Better consider what you have to do v 2 77
If thou takest leave, thou wert better be hanged *2 Hen. IV.* i 2 102
I were better to be eaten to death with a rust i 2 245
The tennis-court-keeper knows better than I ii 2 22
As to one it pleases me, for fault of a better, to call my friend ii 2 45
Never a man's thought in the world keeps the road-way better than thine ii 2 63
How do you now?—Better than I was: hem! ii 4 33
Ten times better than the Nine Worthies ii 4 238
I love thee better than I love e'er a scurvy young boy of them all ii 4 295
A better than thou: I am a gentleman; thou art a drawer ii 4 311
I am, my lord, but as my betters are That led me hither iv 3 71
I would you had but the wit: 'twere better than your dukedom iv 3 93
A friend i' the court is better than a penny in purse v 1 34
Thou wert better thou hadst struck thy mother, thou paper-faced villain v 4 11
This poor show doth better: this doth infer the zeal I had v 5 14
And those few I have Almost no better than so many French *Hen. V.* iii 6 156
I was told that by one that knows him better than you iii 7 114
You are the better at proverbs, by how much 'A fool's bolt is soon shot' iii 7 131
A good soft pillow for that good white head Were better than a churlish turf iv 1 15
This lodging likes me better iv 1 16
Then you are a better than the king iv 1 43
Now thou hast unwish'd five thousand men; Which likes me better than to wish us one iv 3 77
The elder I wax, the better I shall appear v 2 247
Better far, I guess, That we do make our entrance several ways *1 Hen. VI.* ii 1 29
Did look no better to that weighty charge ii 1 62
I myself Will see his burial better than his life ii 5 121
Your discretions better can persuade Than I am able to instruct or teach iv 1 158
No better than an earl, Although in glorious titles he excel v 5 37
Find the like event in love, But prosper better than the Trojan did v 5 106
Let thy betters speak.—The cardinal's not my better in the field *2 Hen. VI.* i 3 112
To this gear the sooner the better i 4 17
Farewell, and better than I fare ii 4 100
Better ten thousand base-born Cades miscarry Than you should stoop iv 8 49
Let's in, and learn to govern better iv 9 48
The sons of York, thy betters in their birth, Shall be their father's bail v 1 119
My title's good, and better far than his *3 Hen. VI.* i 1 130
I can better play the orator.—But I have reasons strong i 2 2
You love the breeder better than the male ii 1 42
Sometime the flood prevails, and then the wind; Now one the better, then another best ii 5 10
Methinks it were a happy life, To be no better than a homely swain ii 5 22
You have a father able to maintain you; And better 'twere you troubled him iii 3 155
'Tis better using France than trusting France iv 1 42
She better would have fitted me iv 1 54
Give me worship and quietness; I like it better than a dangerous honour iv 3 17
Wilt thou go along?—Better do so than tarry and be hang'd iv 5 26
I am your better, traitors as ye are v 5 36
My good lord:—my lord, I should say rather; 'Tis sin to flatter; 'good' was little better v 6 3
His better doth not breathe upon the earth *Richard III.* i 2 140
Whom God preserve better than you would wish! i 3 59
Are you so brief?—O sir, it is better to be brief than tedious i 4 89
Gloucester, Who shall reward you better for my life Than Edward will for tidings of my death i 4 236
Bad news, by'r lady; seldom comes the better ii 3 4
Better it were they all came by the father ii 3 23
Might better wear their heads Than some that have accused them wear their hats iii 2 94
How goes the world with thee?—The better that your lordship please to ask iii 2 99
'Tis better with me now Than when I met thee last where now we meet iii 2 100
I never look'd for better at his hands iii 5 50
He smiled and said 'The better for our purpose' v 3 274
'Tis better to be lowly born, And range with humble livers *Hen. VIII.* ii 3 19
'Twill be much Both for your honour better and your cause iii 1 95
Better Have burnt that tongue than said so iii 2 253
We'll leave you to your meditations How to live better iii 2 346
I swear he is true-hearted; and a soul None better in my kingdom v 1 155
He had better starve Than but once think this place becomes thee not v 3 132
Let her be as she is: if she be fair, 'tis the better for her *Troi. and Cres.* i 1 67
What good sport is out of town to-day!—Better at home i 1 117
'Twould not become him; his own's better i 2 98
I think his smiling becomes him better than any man i 2 135
The lustre of the better yet to show, Shall show the better i 3 361
Better parch in Afric sun Than in the pride and salt scorn of his eyes i 3 370
All the better; their fraction is more our wish than their faction ii 3 107
Friend, know me better; I am the Lord Pandarus.—I hope I shall know your honour better iii 1 11
Aught with the general?—No.—Nothing, my lord.—The better iii 3 61
Better would it fit Achilles much To throw down Hector than Polyxena iii 3 207
Yet is the kindness but particular; 'Twere better she were kiss'd in general iv 5 21
I'll make my match to live, The kiss you take is better than you give iv 5 38
I'll be your fool no more.—Thy better must v 2 33
Tell me whose it was.—'Twas one's that loved me better than you will v 2 89
Can not Better be held nor more attain'd than by A place below the first *Coriolanus* i 1 269
It was no better than picture-like to hang by the wall i 3 12
I wish no better Than have him hold that purpose and to put it In execution ii 1 255
Better it is to die, better to starve, Than crave the hire which first we do deserve ii 3 120
This mutiny were better put in hazard, Than stay, past doubt, for greater ii 3 264
You are like to do such business.—Not unlike, Each way, to better yours iii 1 49
All's well; and might have been much better, if He could have temporized iv 6 16
Made by some other deity than nature, That shapes man better iv 6 92
Go to; have your lath glued within your sheath Till you know better how to handle it *T. Andron.* ii 1 42
Better than he have worn Vulcan's badge ii 1 89
Coal-black is better than another hue, In that it scorns to bear another hue iv 2 99

Better. I serve as good a man as you.—No better.—Well, sir.—Say 'better' *Rom. and Jul.* i 1 63
Is not this better now than groaning for love? . . . . . . ii 4 92
Though his face be better than any man's, yet his leg excels all men's . ii 5 40
I never injured thee, But love thee better than thou canst devise . iii 1 72
Now heaven hath all, And all the better is it for the maid . . . iv 5 68
I love thee better than myself; For I come hither arm'd against myself v 3 64
Few things loves better Than to abhor himself *T. of Athens* i 1 59
Some better than his value, on the moment Follow his strides . i 1 79
Wrought he not well that painted it?—He wrought better that made the painter . . . . i 1 201
If our betters play at that game, we must not dare To imitate them . i 2 12
What better or properer can we call our own than the riches of our friends? . . . . i 2 106
If I would sell my horse, and buy twenty more Better than he . ii 1 8
Who seeks for better of thee, sauce his palate With thy most operant poison! . . . . iv 3 24
I love thee better now than e'er I did.—I hate thee worse . iv 3 233
I, to bear this, That never knew but better, is some burden . iv 3 267
An thou hadst hated meddlers sooner, thou shouldst have loved thyself better now . . . . iv 3 310
Let it [ingratitude] go naked, men may see't the better . . v 1 70
I will strive with things impossible; Yea, get the better of them *J. Cæsar* ii 1 326
It would become me better than to close In terms of friendship with thine enemies . . . . iii 1 202
I said, an elder soldier, not a better: Did I say 'better'? . iv 3 56
When thou didst hate him worst, thou lovedst him better Than ever thou lovedst Cassius . . . . iv 3 106
No man bears sorrow better . . . . iv 3 147
'Tis better that the enemy seek us: So shall he waste his means . iv 3 199
Good reasons must, of force, give place to better . . . iv 3 203
Not that we love words better, as you do.—Good words are better than bad strokes . . . . v 1 28
Go not my horse the better, I must become a borrower of the night *Macbeth* iii 1 26
Better be with the dead, Whom we, to gain our peace, have sent to peace iii 2 19
'Tis better thee without than he within . . . . . iii 4 14
Better Macbeth Than such an one to reign . . . . iv 3 65
Whiles I see lives, the gashes Do better upon them . . . v 8 3
Breathing like sanctified and pious bawds, The better to beguile *Hamlet* i 3 131
Their residence, both in reputation and profit, was better both ways . ii 2 344
It is most like, if their means are no better . . . . ii 2 366
You were better have a bad epitaph than their ill report while you live . ii 2 550
I will use them according to their desert.—God's bodykins, man, much better . . . . ii 2 554
That it were better my mother had not borne me . . . iii 1 125
It would cost you a groaning to take off my edge.—Still better, and worse . . . . iii 2 261
Thou wretched, rash, intruding fool, farewell! I took thee for thy better . . . . iii 4 32
If this should fail, And that our drift look through our bad performance, 'Twere better not assay'd . . . . iv 7 153
I must love you, and sue to know you better . . . *Lear* i 1 31
See better, Lear; and let me still remain The true blank of thine eye . i 1 160
Better thou Hadst not been born than not to have pleased me better . i 1 236
I am better than thou art now; I am a fool, thou art nothing . i 4 212
Your disorder'd rabble Make servants of their betters . . i 4 278
Striving to better, oft we mar what's well . . . . i 4 369
Be here to-night? The better! best! . . . . . ii 1 16
By some discretion, that discerns your state Better than you yourself . ii 4 152
Mend when thou canst; be better at thy leisure: I can be patient . ii 4 232
Court holy-water in a dry house is better than this rain-water out o' door iii 2 11
Why, thou wert better in thy grave . . . . . . iii 4 105
Here is better than the open air; take it thankfully . . iii 6 1
When we our betters see bearing our woes, We scarcely think our miseries our foes . . . . iii 6 109
Yet better thus, and known to be contemn'd, Than still contemn'd and flatter'd . . . . iv 1 1
Better I were distract: So should my thoughts be sever'd from my griefs iv 6 288
'Tis better as it is.—Nay, but he prated . . . *Othello* i 2 6
He holds me well; The better shall my purpose work on him . i 3 397
It had been better you had not kissed your three fingers so oft . ii 1 174
'Tis better to be much abused Than but to know't a little . iii 3 336
Thou hadst been better have been born a dog Than answer my waked wrath! . . . . iii 3 362
Your case is better. O, 'tis the spite of hell! . . . iv 1 70
That thrust had been mine enemy indeed, But that my coat is better than thou know'st . . . . v 1 25
I have a weapon; A better never did itself sustain Upon a soldier's thigh v 2 260
I love long life better than figs . . . *Ant. and Cleo.* i 2 32
Am I not an inch of fortune better than she? . . . i 2 59
If you were but an inch of fortune better than I, where would you choose it? . . . . i 2 62
You can do better yet; but this is meetly . . . . i 3 81
She replied, It should be better he became her guest . . ii 2 226
Better to leave undone, than by our deed Acquire too high a fame when him we serve's away . . . . iii 1 14
For better might we Have loved without this mean . . . iii 2 31
Better I were not yours Than yours so branchless . . . iii 4 23
I have sixty sails, Cæsar none better . . . . . iii 7 50
'Tis better playing with a lion's whelp Than with an old one dying . iii 13 94
Better 'twere Thou fell'st into my fury, for one death Might have prevented many . . . . iv 12 40
Shall I abide In this dull world, which in thy absence is No better than a sty? . . . . iv 15 62
If this penetrate, I will consider your music the better . *Cymbeline* ii 3 32
The very devils cannot plague them better . . . . . ii 5 35
If you fall in the adventure, our crows shall fare the better for you . iii 1 83
'Tis all the better; Your valiant Britons have their wishes in it . iii 1 85
He rages; none Dare come about him.—All the better . . iii 5 68
I am nothing: or if not, Nothing to be were better . . . iv 2 368
Than be so Better to cease to be . . . . . . iv 4 31
How many Must murder wives much better than themselves! . v 1 4
Yet am I better Than one that's sick o' the gout . . . v 4 4
Must I repent? I cannot do it better than in gyves . . v 4 14
This man is better than the man he slew, As well descended as thyself . v 5 302
Live, And deal with others better.—Nobly doom'd! . . . v 5 420
If that ever my low fortune's better, I'll pay your bounties *Pericles* ii 1 148
He had need mean better than his outward show Can any way speak . ii 2 48
Now, by the gods, he could not please me better . . . . ii 3 72

Better. Other sorts offend as well as we.—As well as we! ay, and better too . . . . *Pericles* iv 2 41
'Tis the better for you that your resorters stand upon sound legs . . iv 6 26
Neither of these are so bad as thou art, Since they do better thee in their command . . . . iv 6 172
Any of these ways are yet better than this . . . . . iv 6 188
Now I know you better . . . . v 3 37
Better a ground. If they love they know not why, they hate upon no better a ground . . . . *Coriolanus* ii 2 13
Better a musician. No better a musician than the wren *Mer. of Venice* v 1 106
Better accommodated. A soldier is better accommodated than with a wife . . . . *2 Hen. IV.* iii 2 72
Better accommodated! it is good; yea, indeed, is it . . . iii 2 75
Better acquaintance. If there be no great love in the beginning, yet heaven may decrease it upon better acquaintance . *Mer. Wives* i 1 255
Good Mistress Accost, I desire better acquaintance . . *T. Night* i 3 55
Better acquainted. Let me be better acquainted with thee *As Y. Like It* iv 1 1
Let it die as it was born, and, I pray you, be better acquainted *Cymbeline* i 4 132
Better act. The better act of purposes mistook Is to mistake again *K. John* iii 1 274
Better and better. Thou shalt wear me, if thou wear me, better and better . . . . *Hen. V.* v 2 251
Better angel. Yea, curse his better angel from his side . . *Othello* v 2 208
Better answer. If they make you not then the better answer, you may say they are not the men you took them for . . *Much Ado* iii 3 49
Fetch me a better answer . . . . *Lear* ii 4 92
Better appetite. Digest his words With better appetite . . *J. Cæsar* i 2 306
Better assurance. For the more better assurance . . *M. N. Dream* iii 1 21
He said, sir, you should procure him better assurance . . *2 Hen. IV.* i 2 36
Better bad habit of frowning . . . . . . *Mer. of Venice* i 2 63
Better bethought. He hath better bethought him . . *T. Night* iii 4 327
Better bettered. He hath indeed better bettered expectation *Much Ado* i 1 16
Better bit. Ne'er a king christen could be better bit . . *1 Hen. IV.* ii 1 19
Better blood. Yea, and much better blood than his or thine *Richard III.* i 3 126
Better born. I am far better born than is the king . . . *2 Hen. VI.* v 1 28
Better breath. The king shall drink to Hamlet's better breath *Hamlet* v 2 282
Better brook. Unfrequented woods, I better brook than flourishing peopled towns . . . . *T. G. of Ver.* v 4 3
I better brook the loss of brittle life Than those proud titles *1 Hen. IV.* v 4 78
My breast can better brook thy dagger's point . . . *3 Hen. VI.* v 6 27
Better care. Give me leave, I'll take the better care . . *Cymbeline* iv 4 45
Better cause. Thou mayst be valiant in a better cause . . . iii 4 74
Better cheer may you have, but not with better heart . *Com. of Errors* iii 1 29
I prithee, lady, have a better cheer . . . . . *All's Well* iii 2 67
You shall have better cheer Ere you depart . . . *Cymbeline* iii 6 67
Better cherished. We shall feed like oxen at a stall, The better cherish'd, still the nearer death . . . . . . *1 Hen. IV.* v 2 15
Better choice. I'ld wish no better choice . . . . . *Pericles* v 1 69
Better comfort. Had you such a loss as I, I could give better comfort than you do . . . . *K. John* iii 4 100
Better command. No man could better command his servants *2 Hen. IV.* v 1 83
Better commerce. Could beauty, my lord, have better commerce than with honesty? . . . . *Hamlet* iii 1 109
Better companion. God send the prince a better companion!—God send the companion a better prince! . . . . *2 Hen. IV.* i 2 223
Better company. We leave you now with better company *Mer. of Venice* i 1 59
Hath your grace no better company? . . . . . . *Lear* iii 4 147
Better compassing. For the better compassing of his salt and most hidden loose affection . . . . *Othello* ii 1 244
Better confirmation. To thee it shall descend with better quiet, Better opinion, better confirmation . . . . . . *2 Hen. IV.* iv 5 189
Better conquest never canst thou make . . . . *K. John* iii 1 290
Better counsel. When a wise man gives thee better counsel, give me mine again . . . . *Lear* ii 4 76
Better counterfeit. He would prove the better counterfeit . *1 Hen. IV.* v 4 126
Better course. Let me persuade you take a better course . *1 Hen. VI.* iv 1 132
Better credit. Give us better credit . . . . . . *W. Tale* ii 3 146
Better cunning. My better cunning faints Under his chance *Ant. and Cleo.* ii 3 34
Better days. If ever you have look'd on better days . . *As Y. Like It* ii 7 113
We have seen better days *As Y. Like It* ii 7 120; *T. of Athens* iv 2 27
Better dealing. Were my worth as is my conscience firm, You should find better dealing . . . . *T. Night* iii 3 18
Better death. It were a better death than die with mocks . *Much Ado* iii 1 79
Better deeds. Truth hath better deeds than words to grace it *T. G. of Ver.* ii 2 18
I will hope Of better deeds to-morrow . . . . *Ant. and Cleo.* i 1 62
Better determine. I shall follow it as the flesh and fortune shall better determine . . . . *Meas. for Meas.* ii 1 268
Better directions. I think a' will plow up all, if there is not better directions . . . . *Hen. V.* iii 2 68
Better disposition. Against thy better disposition . . . *W. Tale* iii 3 28
Better dog. I take him for the better dog . . . . *T. of Shrew* Ind. 1 25
Better dreams. When Cæsar's wife shall meet with better dreams *J. C.* ii 2 99
Better ear. I could have given less matter A better ear . *Ant. and Cleo.* ii 1 32
Better employed. Be better employed, and be naught awhile *As Y. Like It* i 1 38
Better ended. My life were better ended by their hate . *Rom. and Jul.* ii 2 77
Better English. I am glad thou canst speak no better English *Hen. V.* v 2 127
Better Englishwoman. The princess is the better Englishwoman . . v 2 124
Better entertainment. I have deserved no better entertainment *Coriol.* iv 5 10
Better face. That superfluous case That hid the worse and show'd the better face . . . . *L. L. Lost* v 2 388
If he break, thou mayst with better face Exact the penalty *Mer. of Ven.* i 3 137
I have seen better faces in my time Than stands on any shoulder that I see . . . . *Lear* ii 2 99
Better-fashioned. I never saw a better-fashion'd gown *T. of Shrew* iv 3 101
Better father. I would not wish a better father . . . *K. John* i 1 260
Better feared. Never was monarch better fear'd and loved . *Hen. V.* ii 2 25
Better feast. May you a better feast never behold! . . *T. of Athens* iii 6 98
Better fed. My ears were never better fed . . . . *Pericles* ii 5 27
Better fit. One Julia, that his changing thoughts forget, Would better fit his chamber . . . . *T. G. of Ver.* iv 4 125
It better fits my blood to be disdained of all than to fashion a carriage to rob love from any . . . . *Much Ado* i 3 29
It would better fit your honour to change your mind . . . iii 2 119
You have a vice of mercy in you, Which better fits a lion than a man *Troi. and Cres.* v 3 38
Better fool. Infirmity, that decays the wise, doth ever make the better fool . . . . *T. Night* i 5 83
Better foot. The better foot before . . *K. John* iv 2 170; *T. Andron.* ii 3 192
Better fortune. He thinks, being twenty times of better fortune, He is twenty men to one . . . . *Ant. and Cleo.* iv 2 3

Better friends. It is A way to make us better friends . . *W. Tale* iv 4 66
Better grace. This action I now go on Is for my better grace . *W. Tale* ii 1 122
He does it with a better grace, but I do it more natural . . *T. Night* ii 3 88
Better guard. With no worse nor better guard But with a knave of common hire, a gondolier . . . . *Othello* i 1 125
Better guiding. Jove send her A better guiding spirit! . . *W. Tale* ii 3 127
Better half. We lose the better half of our possession . . *Hen. V.* i 1 8
Better head. A better head her glorious body fits Than his that shakes for age and feebleness . . . . . . *T. Andron.* i 1 187
Better health. Good night; and better health Attend his majesty! *Macb.* iii 4 120
Better heart. Better cheer may you have, but not with better heart *Com. of Errors* iii 1 29
Better heed. Sit with us once more, with better heed . . *Hen. V.* v 2 80
Sorry that with better heed and judgement I had not quoted him *Hamlet* ii 1 111
Better hope. I see some sparks of better hope, which elder years May happily bring forth . . . . *Richard II.* v 3 21
Better horsed. Being better horsed, Out-rode me . . . *2 Hen. IV.* i 1 35
Better hour. In a better hour, Let what is meet be said . *Coriolanus* iii 1 169
Better husband. I seek you a better husband . . . *Mer. Wives* iii 4 88
We do instate and widow you withal, To buy you a better husband *Meas. for Meas.* v 1 430
Better increasing. God send you, sir, a speedy infirmity, for the better increasing your folly! . . . . *T. Night* i 5 85
Better instance. Shallow, shallow. A better instance . *As Y. Like It* iii 2 59
Better issue. Whose better issue in the war, from Italy, Upon the first encounter, drave them. . . . . . . *Ant. and Cleo.* i 2 97
Better jointure. He carries his house on his head; a better jointure, I think, than you make a woman . . . . . *As Y. Like It* iv 1 55
Better judge. Awake your senses, that you may the better judge *J. Cæsar* iii 2 18
Better judgement. Weed your better judgements Of all opinion that grows rank in them . . . . *As Y. Like It* ii 7 45
Her will, recoiling to her better judgement . . . . *Othello* iii 3 236
Better knowest. Thou better know'st The offices of nature . *Lear* ii 4 180
Better knowledge. Love talks with better knowledge *Meas. for Meas.* iii 2 159
Better known. I have ere now, sir, been better known to you *All's Well* v 2 2
I beseech you all, be better known to this gentleman . . *Cymbeline* i 4 31
Better knows. None better knows than you . . . *Meas. for Meas.* i 3 7
Better leer. He hath a Rosalind of a better leer than you *As Y. Like It* iv 1 67
Better life. Never a wife in Windsor leads a better life . *Mer. Wives* ii 2 122
Peace be with him! That life is better life, past fearing death, Than that which lives to fear . . . . . . *Meas. for Meas.* v 1 402
My desolation does begin to make A better life . . *Ant. and Cleo.* v 2 2
Better looked into. Appear'd To be a preparation 'gainst the Polack; But, better look'd into, he truly found It was against your highness *Hamlet* ii 2 64
Better love. She had a better love to be-rhyme her . . *Rom. and Jul.* ii 4 43
Better loved. Away with her, and use her as you will, The worse to her, the better loved of me . . . . . . *T. Andron.* ii 3 167
Better luck. Ween you of better luck? . . . . . *Hen. VIII.* v 1 135
Better man. He hath stayed for a better man than thee . *T. G. of Ver.* iii 1 385
I crave no other, nor no better man . . . . *Meas. for Meas.* v 1 431
Which is the better man, the greater throw May turn by fortune from the weaker hand . . . . *Mer. of Venice* ii 1 33
I could have better spared a better man . . . . *1 Hen. IV.* v 4 104
That I'll prove on better men than Somerset . . . *1 Hen. VI.* ii 4 98
Abusing better men than they can be . . . . . *Hen. VIII.* i 3 28
Troilus is the better man of the two . . . . *Troi. and Cres.* i 2 63
No, Hector is not a better man than Troilus . . . . . . i 2 86
There is among the Greeks Achilles, a better man than Troilus . . i 2 269
Among ourselves Give him allowance for the better man . . . i 3 377
Yet go we under our opinion still That we have better men . . i 3 384
Do you not think he thinks himself a better man than I am? . . . ii 3 154
Better matter. O, what better matter breeds for you! . *K. John* iii 4 170
Better messenger. I must go send some better messenger *T. G. of Ver.* i 1 159
Better mirth. As she is now, she will but disease our better mirth *Coriol.* i 3 117
Better music. Farewell; and come with better music . *T. of Athens* i 2 252
Better nature. My father's of a better nature . . . *Tempest* i 2 496
The selfsame name, but one of better nature . . . *Richard III.* i 2 143
Better news in store for you Than you expect . . *M. of Venice* v 1 274
I have heard better news.—What's the news? . . . *2 Hen. IV.* i 1 179
Take that, until thou bring me better news . . . *Richard III.* iv 4 510
Better note. Three in Egypt Cannot make better note . *Ant. and Cleo.* iii 3 26
Better office. I would wish no better office than to be beadle . *Pericles* ii 1 97
Better opinion. With better quiet, Better opinion . . *2 Hen. IV.* iv 5 189
Even from this instant do build on thee a better opinion than ever before *Othello* iv 2 208
Better opportunity. When there is more better opportunity to be required, look you, I will be so bold as to tell you . . *Hen. V.* iii 2 151
Better part. Am better than thy dear self's better part . *Com. of Errors* ii 2 125
It is thyself, mine own self's better part, Mine eye's clear eye . . iii 2 61
The better part of my affections would Be with my hopes abroad *Mer. of Venice* i 1 16
My better parts Are all thrown down . . . . *As Y. Like It* i 2 261
Were I not the better part made mercy . . . . iii 1 2
Atalanta's better part, Sad Lucretia's modesty . . . . . iii 2 155
Upon which better part our prayers come in . . . . *K. John* ii 1 293
The better part of ours are full of rest . . . . *1 Hen. IV.* iv 3 27
The better part of valour is discretion; in the which better part I have saved my life . . . . v 4 122
You are as a candle, the better part burnt out . . . *2 Hen. IV.* i 2 178
Cæsar's better parts Shall be crown'd in Brutus . . *J. Cæsar* iii 2 56
It hath cow'd my better part of man! . . . . . *Macbeth* v 8 18
Better person. To o'erbear such As are of better person than myself *3 Hen. VI.* iii 2 167
Better phrase. Thou speak'st In better phrase . . . . *Lear* iv 6 8
Better place. I will give him a present shrift and advise him for a better place . . . . *Meas. for Meas.* iv 2 224
I do know A many fools, that stand in better place . *Mer. of Venice* iii 5 73
When I was at home, I was in a better place: but travellers must be content . . . . *As Y. Like It* ii 4 17
Thou hast a better place in his affection Than all thy brothers *2 Hen. IV.* iv 4 22
We will bestow you in some better place . . . . *1 Hen. VI.* iii 2 88
I would prefer him to a better place . . . . . . *Lear* i 1 277
Better please. That you might know it, would much better please me Than to demand what 'tis . . . . . . *Meas. for Meas.* ii 4 32
A running banquet . . ., I think would better please 'em . *Hen. VIII.* i 4 13
Better pleased. Thou shouldst have better pleased me with this deed Hadst thou descended from another house . . *As Y. Like It* i 2 240
My senses, better pleased with madness, Do bid it welcome . *W. Tale* iv 4 495
Better plight. I think myself in better plight for a lender *Mer. Wives* ii 2 172
Better prepared. I will acquaint my daughter withal, that she may be the better prepared for an answer . . . . . . *Much Ado* i 2 23
Better prince. God send the companion a better prince! . *2 Hen. IV.* i 2 225
A better prince and benign lord, That will prove awful . *Pericles* ii Gower 3
Better proclamation. The business he hath helmed must upon a warranted need give him a better proclamation *Meas. for Meas.* iii 2 152
Better proposer. And by what more dear a better proposer could charge you withal . . . . *Hamlet* ii 2 297
Better publish. Whose trial shall better publish his commendation *Mer. of Venice* iv 1 165
Better purpose. My dearest, thou never spokest To better purpose *W. Tale* i 2 89
Better quiet. With better quiet, Better opinion . . *2 Hen. IV.* iv 5 188
Better reasons. If better reasons can supplant, I will subscribe *2 Hen. VI.* iii 1 37
Better reckoned. All gold and silver rather turn to dirt! As 'tis no better reckon'd, but of those Who worship dirty gods . *Cymbeline* iii 6 55
Better remembrance. Let it not cumber your better remembrance *T. of Athens* iii 6 52
Better report. Of no better report than a horse-drench . . *Coriolanus* ii 1 129
Better safety. For their better safety, to fly away by night . *W. Tale* iii 2 21
Better said. 'Tis better said than done . . . . *3 Hen. VI.* iii 2 90
Better satisfaction. For my better satisfaction . . *Meas. for Meas.* iv 2 125
Better satisfied. But gladly would be better satisfied . . *2 Hen. IV.* i 3 6
Better scholar. He is a better scholar than I thought . *Mer. Wives* iv 1 82
Better service. I must leave them, and seek some better service *Hen. V.* iii 2 56
Your legs did better service than your hands . . . *3 Hen. VI.* ii 2 104
Better service have I never done you Than now to bid you hold . *Lear* iii 7 74
How wouldst thou have paid My better service! . . *Ant. and Cleo.* iv 6 33
Better sewed. That could have better sew'd than Philomel *T. Andron.* ii 4 43
Better shape. Doubt not but success Will fashion the event in better shape . . . . *Much Ado* iv 1 237
Better showed. My Lord of York, it better show'd with you *2 Hen. IV.* iv 2 4
Better sign. There's no better sign of a brave mind than a hard hand *2 Hen. VI.* iv 2 21
Better skilled. Thou art deeper read, and better skill'd . *T. Andron.* iv 1 33
Better soldier. Advantage is a better soldier than rashness . *Hen. V.* iii 6 127
You say you are a better soldier: Let it appear so . . *J. Cæsar* iv 3 51
An older and a better soldier none That Christendom gives out *Macbeth* iv 3 191
Better sort. The better sort, As thoughts of things divine, are intermix'd With scruples . . . . *Richard II.* v 5 11
Better spare. My youth can better spare my blood than you *T. Andron.* iii 1 166
Better spared. I could have better spared a better man . . *1 Hen. IV.* v 4 104
Better speak. Shall better speak of you than you deserve . *2 Hen. IV.* iv 3 91
Better speech. A better speech was never spoke before . . *L. L. Lost* v 2 110
Better spoken. Methinks you're better spoken . . . . *Lear* iv 6 10
Better sport. I saw not better sport these seven years' day . *2 Hen. VI.* ii 1 2
Better stars. Her better stars Brought her to Mytilene . . *Pericles* v 3 9
Better state. Fresh expectation troubled not the land With any long'd-for change or better state . . . . . . *K. John* iv 2 8
In better state than e'er I was . . . . . *Richard III.* iii 2 106
Better stead. I could never better stead thee than now . . *Othello* i 3 344
Better strangers. I do desire we may be better strangers *As Y. Like It* iii 2 275
Better stuffed. You have not seen a hulk better stuffed . . *2 Hen. IV.* ii 4 70
Better suited. Be better suited: These weeds are memories of those worser hours . . . . *Lear* iv 7 6
Better supplied. I fill up a place, which may be better supplied when I have made it empty . . . . . . *As Y. Like It* i 2 205
Better sympathy. Would you desire better sympathy? . . *Mer. Wives* ii 1 10
Better taken. Never greater, Nor, I'll assure you, better taken *Hen. VIII.* iv 1 12
Better temper. Between two blades, which bears the better temper *1 Hen. VI.* ii 4 13
Better tempered. I'll talk to you When you are better temper'd to attend . . . . *1 Hen. IV.* i 3 235
I thought thy disposition better temper'd . . . *Rom. and Jul.* iii 3 115
Better testimony. Suspend your indignation against my brother till you can derive from him better testimony of his intent . . . *Lear* i 2 88
Better thing. Darest thou, thou little better thing than earth, Divine his downfal? . . . . *Richard II.* iii 4 78
Better thought of. To make us no better thought of, a little help will serve . . . . *Coriolanus* ii 3 15
Better time. Take this mercy to provide For better times *Meas. for Meas.* v 1 490
I had a thing to say, But I will fit it with some better time . *K. John* iii 3 26
Better told. His wife, an't like your worship.—Hadst thou been his mother, thou couldst have better told . . . . *2 Hen. VI.* ii 1 81
Better treasure. Our copper buys no better treasure . . *L. L. Lost* iv 3 386
Better trial. And our consent, for better trial of you . . *Hen. VIII.* v 3 53
Better tune. Who sometime, in his better tune, remembers . . *Lear* iv 3 41
Better understand. My legs do better understand me, sir, than I understand what you mean . . . . *T. Night* iii 1 89
Better understanding. Thou perishest; or, to thy better understanding, diest . . . . *As Y. Like It* v 1 57
Better used. This civil war of wits were much better used . *L. L. Lost* ii 1 226
Therefore, no wife: one worse, And better used, would make her sainted spirit Again possess her corpse . . . . . . *W. Tale* v 1 57
Better vantage. A brain that leads my use of anger To better vantage *Coriolanus* iii 2 31
Better way. There is no better way than that . . . *Mer. Wives* iv 4 17
Her smiles and tears Were like a better way . . . . *Lear* iv 3 21
Better Welsh. There's no man speaks better Welsh . . *1 Hen. IV.* iii 1 50
Better wench. There's not a better wench in England . . *2 Hen. IV.* ii 1 161
Better where. Thou losest here, a better where to find . . . *Lear* i 1 264
Better wife. Who shall report he has A better wife, let him in nought be trusted . . . . *Hen. VIII.* ii 4 135
Better wisdoms. Nor have we herein barr'd Your better wisdoms *Hamlet* i 2 15
Better wishes. And, sweet lady, does Deserve our better wishes *Hen. VIII.* v 1 26
Better witness. You shall bear A better witness back than words *Coriol.* v 3 204
Better wits have worn plain statute-caps . . . . *L. L. Lost* v 2 281
Better woodman. He's a better woodman than thou takest him for *Meas. for Meas.* iv 3 170
Better world. In a better world than this, I shall desire more love and knowledge of you . . . . *As Y. Like It* i 2 296
Better worth. His health was never better worth than now *1 Hen. IV.* iv 1 27
Her worst wearing gown Was better worth than all my father's lands *2 Hen. VI.* i 3 89
Better wrestler. Wrestle with thy affections.—O, they take the part of a better wrestler than myself! . . . . . . *As Y. Like It* i 3 22
Bettered. He hath indeed better bettered expectation . . *Much Ado* i 1 16
Bettered with his own learning . . . . . . *Mer. of Venice* iv 1 158
Which I have better'd rather than decreased . . *T. of Shrew* ii 1 119
Since he is better'd, we have therefore odds . . . . *Hamlet* v 2 274

Bettering. Dedicated To closeness and the bettering of my mind *Tempest* i 2 90
Bettering thy loss makes the bad causer worse . *Richard III.* iv 4 122
Betting. I shall have my eight shillings I won of you at betting? *Hen. V.* ii 1 111
Bettre. Your majesty entendre bettre que moi . . . . v 2 288
Between. To have no screen between this part he play'd And him he play'd it for . . . . *Tempest* i 2 107
The fair soul herself Weigh'd between loathness and obedience . ii 1 130
Heavens rain grace On that which breeds between 'em ! . . iii 1 76
I would I could do a good office between you . *Mer. Wives* i 1 102
He is as tall a man of his hands as any is between this and his head . i 4 27
And, look you, he may come and go between you both . . ii 2 130
There is such a league between my good man and he ! . . iii 2 25
Well, there went but a pair of shears between us . *Meas. for Meas.* i 2 29
I have overheard what hath passed between you and your sister . iii 1 162
Between which time of the contract and limit of the solemnity . iii 1 223
He was begot between two stock-fishes . . . . . . iii 2 116
But not a thousand marks between you both . . . *Com. of Errors* i 2 84
Between you I shall have a holy head . . . . . . ii 1 80
Between them they will kill the conjuror . . . . . . v 1 177
They never meet but there's a skirmish of wit between them *Much Ado* i 1 64
For what is inward between us, let it pass . . *L. L. Lost* v 1 102
Flying between the cold moon and the earth . . *M. N. Dream* ii 1 156
Now I perceive that she hath made compare Between our statures . iii 2 291
This long age of three hours Between our after-supper and bed-time . v 1 34
O lovely wall, That stand'st between her father's ground and mine ! . v 1 176
Now is the mural down between the two neighbours . . . v 1 208
When the work of generation was Between these woolly breeders *Mer. of Venice* i 3 84
The old proverb is very well parted between my master Shylock and you . . . . ii 2 159
There may as well be amity and life 'Tween snow and fire . . . iii 2 31
Thou pale and common drudge 'Tween man and man . . . iii 2 104
All debts are cleared between you and I . . . . . . iii 2 321
And speak between the change of man and boy . . . . . iii 4 66
Heavy news within between two soldiers and my young lady ! *All's Well* iii 2 36
I did go between them, as I said . . . . v 3 259
When you have said 'she's goodly,' come between Ere you can say 'she's honest' . . . . *W. Tale* ii 1 75
There is nothing in the between but getting wenches with child . iii 3 62
I turn my glass and give my scene such growing As you had slept between . . . . iv 1 17
Is too far gone with grief, Or else he never would compare between *Richard II.* ii 1 185
Pleaseth your lordship To meet his grace just distance 'tween our armies . . . . *2 Hen. IV.* iv 1 226
The river hath thrice flow'd, no ebb between . . . . . iv 4 125
Between two hawks, which flies the higher pitch ; Between two dogs, which hath the deeper mouth ; Between two blades, which bears the better temper : Between two horses, which doth bear him best ; Between two girls, which hath the merriest eye . *1 Hen. VI.* ii 4 11
Between my soul's desire and me . . . Is Clarence, Henry *3 Hen. VI.* iii 2 128
Gone between and between, but small thanks for my labour *Tr. and Cr.* i 1 72
Bounding between the two moist elements . . . . . . i 3 41
That we labour'd, No impediment between, but that you must Cast your election on him . . . . *Coriolanus* ii 3 236
And vows revenge as spacious as between The young'st and oldest thing iv 6 67
We are not brought so low, But that between us we can kill a fly *T. Andron.* iii 2 77
Whilst that Lavinia 'tween her stumps doth hold The basin . . v 2 183
Come between us, good Benvolio ; my wits faint . *Rom. and Jul.* ii 4 71
Why the devil came you between us? . . . . iii 1 107
Between the acting of a dreadful thing And the first motion, all the interim is Like a phantasma, or a hideous dream . . *J. Cæsar* ii 1 63
Set a huge mountain 'tween my heart and tongue ! . . . . ii 4 7
There is some grudge between 'em, 'tis not meet They be alone . iv 3 125
Never come such division 'tween our souls ! . . . . . iv 3 235
What is between you? give me up the truth . . . . *Hamlet* i 3 98
For your desire to know what is between us, O'ermaster't as you may . i 5 139
What is the matter, my lord?—Between who? . . . . . ii 2 196
Your grace hath screen'd and stood between Much heat and him . iii 4 3
O, step between her and her fighting soul . . . . . iii 4 113
And stand a comma 'tween their amities . . . . . . v 2 42
Come not between the dragon and his wrath . . . . *Lear* i 1 124
And with strain'd pride To come between our sentence and our power . i 1 173
Go to the creating a whole tribe of fops, Got 'tween asleep and wake . i 2 15
Gloucester's bastard son Was kinder to his father than my daughters Got 'tween the lawful sheets . . . . iv 6 118
That profit's yet to come 'tween me and you . . . . *Othello* ii 3 10
O, yes ; and went between us very oft . . . . . . iii 3 100
I will be near to second your attempt, and he shall fall between us . iv 2 245
Between them [women] and a great cause, they should be esteemed nothing . . . . *Ant. and Cleo.* i 2 143
Like to the time o' the year between the extremes Of hot and cold . i 5 51
He was not sad, . . . he was not merry, . . . but between both . i 5 58
I crave our composition may be written, And seal'd between us . . ii 6 60
A more unhappy lady, If this division chance, ne'er stood between, Praying for both . . . . iii 4 13
But, as you requested, Yourself shall go between's . . . . iii 4 25
Throw between them all the food thou hast, They'll grind the one the other . . . . iii 5 15
Being an obstruct 'tween his lust and him . . . . . . iii 6 61
Reverence, That angel of the world, doth make distinction Of place 'tween high and low . . . . *Cymbeline* iv 2 249
'Tween man and man they weigh not every stamp . . . . v 4 24
Come you between, And save poor me, the weaker . . *Pericles* iv 1 90
Betwixt. The time 'twixt six and now Must by us both be spent most preciously . . . . *Tempest* i 2 240
'Twixt which regions There is some space . . . . . . ii 1 256
Twenty consciences, That stand 'twixt me and Milan . . . ii 1 279
And 'twixt the green sea and the azured vault Set roaring war . v 1 43
Just 'twixt twelve and one, Must my sweet Nan present the Fairy Queen *Mer. Wives* iv 6 19
That's my pith of business 'Twixt you and your poor brother *M. for M.* i 4 71
For which I must now plead, but that I am At war 'twixt will and will not . . . . ii 2 33
Five years since there was some speech of marriage Betwixt myself and her . . . . v 1 218
There is a kind of merry war betwixt Signior Benedick and her *M. Ado* i 1 62
Out at your window betwixt twelve and one . . . . . iv 1 85
The sealing-day betwixt my love and me . . . . *M. N. Dream* i 1 84
Betwixt. No rest be interposer 'twixt us twain . . . *Mer. of Venice* iii 2 329
Takes not away my blood, were there twenty brothers betwixt us *As Y. Like It* i 1 52
Of violated vows 'Twixt the souls of friend and friend . . . iii 2 142
Just the difference Betwixt the constant red and mingled damask . iii 5 123
From the first to last betwixt us two . . . . . . iv 3 140
Why, this's a heavy chance 'twixt him and you . . *T. of Shrew* i 2 46
'Twixt such friends as we Few words suffice . . . . . i 2 65
What's that to you? 'Tis bargain'd 'twixt us twain . . . ii 1 306
My lords, farewell : Share the advice betwixt you . . *All's Well* ii 1 3
There rooted betwixt them then such an affection . . *W. Tale* i 1 25
False As dice are to be wish'd by one that fixes No bourn 'twixt his and mine . . . . i 2 134
Upon mine honour, I Will stand betwixt you and danger . . ii 2 66
O'er and o'er divides him 'Twixt his unkindness and his kindness . iv 4 563
Things known betwixt us three, I'll write you down . . . iv 4 571
I lost a couple, that 'twixt heaven and earth Might thus have stood . v 1 132
But O, the noble combat that 'twixt joy and sorrow was fought in Paulina ! . . . . v 2 79
Ere sunset, Set armed discord 'twixt these perjured kings ! . *K. John* iii 1 111
Like heralds 'twixt two dreadful battles set . . . . . . iv 2 78
O, when the last account 'twixt heaven and earth Is to be made ! . iv 2 216
Can arbitrate this cause betwixt us twain . . . *Richard II.* i 1 50
You violate A twofold marriage, 'twixt my crown and me, And then betwixt me and my married wife . . . . v 1 72
'Twixt his finger and his thumb he held A pouncet-box . *1 Hen. IV.* i 3 37
To bring a slovenly unhandsome corse Betwixt the wind and his nobility i 3 45
Making such difference 'twixt wake and sleep As is the difference betwixt day and night . . . . iii 1 219
Walking with thee in the night betwixt tavern and tavern . . iii 3 49
The villains march wide betwixt the legs, as if they had gyves on . iv 2 44
That never war advance His bleeding sword 'twixt England and fair France . . . . *Hen. V.* v 2 383
Some words there grew 'twixt Somerset and me . . *1 Hen. VI.* ii 5 46
Betwixt ourselves let us decide it then . . . . . . iv 1 119
To take occasion from their mouths To raise a mutiny betwixt yourselves . . . . iv 1 131
His fortunes I will weep and 'twixt each groan Say Who's a traitor?' *2 Hen. VI.* iii 1 221
Betwixt their titles and low names, There's nothing differs *Richard III.* i 4 82
Hath he set bounds betwixt their love and me? . . . . . iv 1 21
Thou keep'st the stroke Betwixt thy begging and my meditation . iv 2 118
Nor could Come pat betwixt too early and too late . *Hen. VIII.* ii 3 84
'Twixt his mental and his active parts Kingdom'd Achilles in commotion rages And batters down himself . . . . . *Troi. and Cres.* ii 3 184
The obligation of our blood forbids A gory emulation 'twixt us twain . iv 5 123
He waved indifferently 'twixt doing them neither good nor harm *Coriol.* ii 2 19
His agile arm beats down their fatal points, And 'twixt them rushes *Rom. and Jul.* iii 1 172
'Twixt my extremes and me this bloody knife Shall play the umpire . iv 1 62
Sweet king-killer [gold], and dear divorce 'Twixt natural son and sire ! *T. of Athens* iv 3 383
As far, my lord, as will fill up the time 'Twixt this and supper *Macbeth* iii 1 26
Upon the platform, 'twixt eleven and twelve, I'll visit you . *Hamlet* i 2 252
No midway 'Twixt these extremes at all . . . *Ant. and Cleo.* iii 4 20
Which can distinguish 'twixt The fiery orbs above and the twinn'd stones Upon the number'd beach . . . . . . *Cymbeline* i 6 34
How many score of miles may we well ride 'Twixt hour and hour?—One score 'twixt sun and sun . . . . iii 2 70
Beverage. If from me he have wholesome beverage, Account me not your servant . . . . *W. Tale* i 2 346
Bevis. That former fabulous story, Being now seen possible enough, got credit, That Bevis was believed . . . . . . *Hen. VIII.* i 1 38
Bevy. None here, he hopes, In all this noble bevy, has brought with her One care abroad . . . . i 4 4
Bewail. Like tears that did their own disgrace bewail *M. N. Dream* iv 1 61
Even so myself bewails good Gloucester's case . *2 Hen. VI.* iii 1 217
Unchilded many a one, Which to this hour bewail the injury *Coriolanus* v 6 154
Bewailing. Thou scarlet sin, robb'd this bewailing land *Hen. VIII.* iii 2 255
Beware. If of life you keep a care, Shake off slumber, and beware *Temp.* ii 1 304
Keep from my heels and beware of an ass. . . *Com. of Errors* iii 1 18
The prophecy like the parrot, 'beware the rope's-end' . . . iv 4 46
Since I am a dog, beware my fangs . . . . *Mer. of Venice* iii 3 7
Therefore beware my censure and keep your promise . *As Y. Like It* iv 1 200
You are too angry.—If I be waspish, best beware my sting *T. of Shrew* ii 1 211
Beware of being captives, Before you serve . . . . *All's Well* ii 1 21
My liege, beware : look to thyself . . . . . *Richard II.* v 3 39
Beware instinct ; the lion will not touch the true prince . *1 Hen. IV.* ii 4 299
Beware your beard ; I mean to tug it . . . . *1 Hen. VI.* i 3 47
Clarence, beware ; thou keep'st me from the light . *3 Hen. VI.* v 6 84
Have not to do with him, beware of him . . . . *Richard III.* i 3 292
The king loves you ; Beware you lose it not . . . *Hen. VIII.* iii 1 172
O, then, beware ; Those wounds heal ill that men do give themselves *Troi. and Cres.* iii 3 228
And beat the messenger who bids beware Of what is to be dreaded *Cor.* iv 6 54
Speak ; Cæsar is turn'd to hear.—Beware the ides of March . *J. Cæsar* i 2 18
A soothsayer bids you beware the ides of March . . . . . i 2 19
Cæsar, beware of Brutus ; take heed of Cassius ; come not near Casca . ii 3 1
Macbeth ! Macbeth ! beware Macduff ; Beware the thane of Fife *Macbeth* iv 1 71
Beware of entrance to a quarrel, but being in, Bear't that the opposed may beware of thee . . . . *Hamlet* i 3 65
Pray, innocent, and beware the foul fiend . . . . . *Lear* iii 6 9
O, beware, my lord, of jealousy ; It is the green-eyed monster *Othello* iii 3 165
Beweep. I do beweep to many simple gulls . . . *Richard III.* i 3 328
Lend me a fool's heart and a woman's eyes, And I'll beweep these comforts . . . . *T. of Athens* v 1 161
Old fond eyes, Beweep this cause again, I'll pluck ye out . . *Lear* i 4 324
Bewept. I have bewept a worthy husband's death . *Richard III.* ii 2 49
Which bewept to the grave did go With true-love showers . *Hamlet* iv 5 38
Bewet. His napkin, with his true tears all bewet . . *T. Andron.* iii 1 146
Bewhored. Alas, Iago, my lord hath so bewhored her . . *Othello* iv 2 115
Bewitch. Let not his smoothing words Bewitch your hearts *2 Hen. VI.* i 1 157
Heavens grant that Warwick's words bewitch him not ! *3 Hen. VI.* iii 3 112
Bewitched. This man hath bewitch'd the bosom of my child *M. N. Dr.* i 1 27
Pray God, he be not bewitched ! . . . . . . *T. Night* iii 4 113
I am bewitched with the rogue's company . . . *1 Hen. IV.* ii 2 18
Either she hath bewitch'd me with her words, Or nature makes me suddenly relent . . . . *1 Hen. VI.* iii 3 58
See how I am bewitch'd ; behold mine arm Is, like a blasted sapling *Richard III.* iii 4 70

Bewitched. Tell us what Sinon hath bewitch'd our ears . *T. Andron.* v 3 85
Is beloved and loves again, Alike bewitched by the charm of looks *Rom. and Jul.* ii Prol. 6
Thou hast bewitch'd my daughter, and thou art A villain *Pericles* ii 5 49
Bewitchment. I will counterfeit the bewitchment of some popular man and give it bountiful . . . *Coriolanus* ii 3 108
Bewray. Here comes the queen, whose looks bewray her anger 3 *Hen. VI.* i 1 211
And not bewray thy treason with a blush . . . . . iii 3 97
Our raiment And state of bodies would bewray what life We have led *Coriolanus* v 3 95
Write down thy mind, bewray thy meaning so . *T. Andron.* ii 4 3
Did not thy hue bewray whose brat thou art . . . v 1 28
He did bewray his practice ; and received This hurt you see *Lear* ii 1 109
Thyself bewray, When false opinion, whose wrong thought defiles thee iii 6 118
Bewrayed. Pronouncing that the paleness of this flower Bewray'd the faintness of my master's heart . . . 1 *Hen. VI.* iv 1 107
Beyond. Our escape Is much beyond our loss . . *Tempest* ii 1 3
Which is indeed almost beyond credit . . . . . ii 1 59
That even Ambition cannot pierce a wink beyond . . . ii 1 242
She that dwells Ten leagues beyond man's life . . . ii 1 247
I Beyond all limit of what else i' the world Do love, prize, honour you iii 1 72
At last I left them I' the filthy-mantled pool beyond your cell . iv 1 182
O, rejoice Beyond a common joy . . . . . v 1 207
She works by charms, by spells, by the figure, and such daubery as this is, beyond our element . . . . *Mer. Wives* iv 2 186
Soon as I came beyond Eton, they threw me off . . . v 5 68
Beyond imagination is the wrong . . *Com. of Errors* v 1 201
He hath borne himself beyond the promise of his age . *Much Ado* i 1 14
Shrewd and froward, so beyond all measure . . *T. of Shrew* i 2 90
Thou dost, And that beyond commission . . *W. Tale* i 2 144
Quite beyond mine arm, out of the blank And level of my brain . ii 3 5
Their speed Hath been beyond account . . . . . ii 3 198
From very nothing, and beyond the imagination of his neighbours . iv 2 45
Beyond the infinite and boundless reach Of mercy . *K. John* iv 3 117
Drives him beyond the bounds of patience . . . 1 *Hen. IV.* i 3 200
All westward, Wales beyond the Severn shore . . . iii 1 76
Like one that draws the model of a house Beyond his power to build it 2 *Hen. IV.* i 3 59
My grief Stretches itself beyond the hour of death . . . iv 4 57
My gracious lord, you look beyond him quite . . . iv 4 67
Beyond the river we'll encamp ourselves . . . *Hen. V.* iii 6 180
The Dauphin hath prevail'd beyond the seas . . 2 *Hen. VI.* i 3 128
Is far beyond a prince's delicates . . . . 3 *Hen. VI.* ii 5 51
In those parts beyond the sea Where he abides . *Richard III.* iv 2 47
One that ne'er dream'd a joy beyond his pleasure . *Hen. VIII.* iii 1 135
Which went Beyond all man's endeavours . . . . . iii 2 169
In a sea of glory, But far beyond my depth . . . . iii 2 361
The king has gone beyond me : all my glories In that one woman I have lost for ever . . . . iii 2 408
He fought Beyond the mark of others . . . *Coriolanus* ii 2 93
But now 'tis odds beyond arithmetic . . . . . iii 1 245
Weapons wrapp'd about with lines, That wound, beyond their feeling *T. Andron.* iv 2 28
I aim a mile beyond the moon ; Your letter is with Jupiter by this . iv 3 65
His promises fly so beyond his state . . . *T. of Athens* i 2 203
If it be so far beyond his health, Methinks he should the sooner pay his debts . . . . iii 4 75
He hath conjured me beyond them, and I must needs appear . . iv 6 13
These things are beyond all use, And I do fear them . . *J. Cæsar* ii 2 25
This disease is beyond my practice . . . . *Macbeth* v 1 65
With thoughts beyond the reaches of our souls . . . *Hamlet* i 4 56
It is as proper to our age To cast beyond ourselves in our opinions . ii 1 115
Beyond what can be valued, rich or rare . . . . *Lear* i 1 58
You are abused Beyond the mark of thought . . . *Ant. and Cleo.* iii 6 87
This speed of Cæsar's Carries beyond belief . . . . iii 7 76
But in a fainter kind :—O, not like me ; For mine's beyond beyond *Cymbeline* iii 2 58
In simple and low things to prince it much Beyond the trick of others iii 3 86
Would be interpreted a thing perplex'd Beyond self-explication . iv 4 8
Not beneath him in fortunes, beyond him in the advantage of the time iv 1 12
Venus, or straight-pight Minerva, Postures beyond brief nature . v 5 165
Bezonian. Under which king, Bezonian? speak, or die . 2 *Hen. IV.* v 3 119
Great men oft die by vile bezonians . . . . 2 *Hen. VI.* iv 1 134
Bianca, get you in : And let it not displease thee, good Bianca *T. of Shrew* i 1 75
Sorry am I that our good will effects Bianca's grief . . . . i 1 87
Katharina, you may stay ; For I have more to commune with Bianca . i 1 101
And be happy rivals in Bianca's love . . . . . . i 1 120
Sweet Bianca ! Happy man be his dole ! . . . . . i 1 144
His youngest daughter, beautiful Bianca . . . . . i 2 120
None shall have access unto Bianca Till Katharine the curst have got a husband . . . . i 2 127
A schoolmaster Well seen in music, to instruct Bianca . . . i 2 134
I promised to inquire carefully About a schoolmaster for the fair Bianca i 2 167
So shall I no whit be behind in duty To fair Bianca, so beloved of me . i 2 176
Fair Leda's daughter had a thousand wooers ; Then well one more may fair Bianca have . . . . i 2 245
Bianca, stand aside. Poor girl ! she weeps. Go ply thy needle . . ii 1 24
I'll be revenged.—What, in my sight? Bianca, get thee in . . . ii 1 30
A suitor to your daughter, Unto Bianca, fair and virtuous . . . ii 1 92
And I am one that love Bianca more than words can witness . . . ii 1 337
And he of both That can assure my daughter greatest dower Shall have my Bianca's love . . . . ii 1 346
On the Sunday following, shall Bianca Be bride to you . . . . ii 1 397
'B mi,' Bianca, take him for thy lord, 'C fa ut,' that loves with all affection . . . . iii 1 75
So shall you quietly enjoy your hope, And marry sweet Bianca . . iii 2 139
Let Bianca take her sister's room.—Shall sweet Bianca practise how to bride it? . . . . iii 2 252
Is't possible, friend Licio, that Mistress Bianca Doth fancy any other? iv 2 1
You that durst swear that your mistress Bianca Loved none in the world so well as Lucentio . . . . iv 2 12
I have often heard Of your entire affection to Bianca . . . . iv 2 23
I will with you, if you be so contented, Forswear Bianca . . . iv 2 26
Bianca, bless you with such grace As 'longeth to a lover's blessed case ! iv 2 44
Stand good father to me now, Give me Bianca for my patrimony . . iv 4 22
Hie you home, And bid Bianca make her ready straight . . . . iv 4 63
I have no more to say, But bid Bianca farewell for ever and a day . . iv 4 97
Look not pale, Bianca ; thy father will not frown . . . . . v 1 143
Bianca, bid my father welcome, While I with self-same kindness welcome thine . . . . v 2 4
Bianca. Son, I'll be your half, Bianca comes.—I'll have no halves *T. of Shrew* v 2 78
The wisdom of your duty, fair Bianca, Hath cost me an hundred crowns v 2 127
How is it with you, my most fair Bianca? I' faith, sweet love, I was coming to your house . . . . *Othello* iii 4 170
Sweet Bianca, Take me this work out . . . . . . iii 4 179
Now will I question Cassio of Bianca . . . . . . iv 1 94
Now, if this suit lay in Bianca's power, How quickly should you speed ! iv 1 108
I'll take out no work on't.—How now, my sweet Bianca ! . . . iv 1 162
Bias. Study his bias leaves and makes his book thine eyes . *L. L. Lost* iv 2 113
Thus the bowl should run, And not unluckily against the bias *T. of Shrew* iv 5 25
Lady, you have been mistook : But nature to her bias drew in that *T. Night* v 1 267
Commodity, the bias of the world . . . . . *K. John* ii 1 574
This advantage, this vile-drawing bias, This sway of motion, this Commodity . . . . ii 1 577
This same bias, this Commodity, This bawd, this broker . . . ii 1 581
'Twill make me think the world is full of rubs, And that my fortune runs against the bias . . . . *Richard II.* iii 4 5
Trial did draw Bias and thwart, not answering the aim . *Troi. and Cres.* i 3 15
Blow, villain, till thy sphered bias cheek Outswell the colic of puff'd Aquilon . . . . iv 5 8
And with assays of bias, By indirections find directions out . *Hamlet* ii 1 65
The king falls from bias of nature . . . . . *Lear* i 2 120
Bias-drawing. Faith and troth, Strain'd purely from all hollow bias-drawing . . . . *Troi. and Cres.* iv 5 169
Bibble babble. Leave thy vain bibble babble . . . *T. Night* iv 2 105
Bickering. In thy face I see thy fury : if I longer stay, We shall begin our ancient bickerings . . . . . . 2 *Hen. VI.* i 1 144
Bid. The very minute bids thee ope thine ear . . . . *Tempest* i 2 37
Drink, servant-monster, when I bid thee . . . . . . iii 2 9
To thee and thy company I bid A hearty welcome . . . . v 1 110
Indeed, I bid the base for Proteus . . . . *T. G. of Ver.* i 2 97
Love bade me swear and Love bids me forswear . . . . ii 6 6
That which I would discover The law of friendship bids me to conceal . iii 1 5
If thou seest my boy, Bid him make haste and meet me . . . iii 1 258
She bids me think how I have been forsworn In breaking faith . iv 2 10
Did not I bid thee still mark me and do as I do? . . . . iv 4 39
Wife, bid these gentlemen welcome . . . . . *Mer. Wives* i 1 201
The clock gives me my cue, and my assurance bids me search . . iii 2 47
Defend your reputation, or bid farewell to your good life for ever . . iii 3 127
Bid her think what a man is : let her consider his frailty . . . iii 5 51
If he bid you set it down, obey him : quickly, dispatch . . . iv 2 112
Take her by the hand and bid her go . . . . . . iv 6 37
Call hither, I say, bid come before us Angelo . . *Meas. for Meas.* i 1 16
'Twould be my tyranny to strike and gall them For what I bid them do : for we bid this be done, When evil deeds have their permissive pass i 3 37
Bid them bring the trumpets to the gate . . . . . . iv 5 9
You bid me seek redemption of the devil : Hear me yourself . . v 1 29
You were not bid to speak.—No, my good lord . . . . v 1 78
I will not show my face Until my husband bid me . . . . v 1 170
Let's see thy face.—My husband bids me ; now I will unmask . . v 1 206
A wretched soul, bruised with adversity, We bid be quiet *Com. of Errors* ii 1 35
Dromio, go bid the servants spread for dinner . . . . . ii 2 189
But, soft ! my door is lock'd. Go bid them let us in . . . iii 1 30
They stand at the door, master ; bid them welcome hither . . iii 1 68
Take the chain and bid my wife Disburse the sum on the receipt thereof iv 1 37
Came behind you, sir, like an evil angel, and bid you forsake your liberty iv 3 20
To what end did I bid thee hie thee home? . . . . . iv 4 15
Let me bid you welcome, my lord . . . . . *Much Ado* i 1 155
Against my will I am sent to bid you come in to dinner . . . ii 3 256
Bid her steal into the pleached bower . . . . . . iii 1 7
Did they bid you tell her of it? . . . . iii 1 39
You are to bid any man stand, in the prince's name . . . . iii 3 26
Call at all the ale-houses, and bid those that are drunk get them to bed iii 3 45
If you hear a child cry in the night, you must call to the nurse and bid her still it . . . . iii 3 70
Bids me a thousand times good night . . . . iii 3 156
Desire her to rise.—I will, lady.—And bid her come hither . . . iii 4 4
Bid him bring his pen and inkhorn to the gaol . . . . . iii 5 63
By that fatherly and kindly power That you have in her, bid her answer truly . . . . iv 1 76
Bid me do any thing for thee.—Kill Claudio.—Ha ! not for the wide world . . . . iv 1 290
And bid him speak of patience . . . . v 1 10
I will bid thee draw, as we do the minstrels ; draw, to pleasure us . v 1 128
He hath bid me to a calf's head and a capon . . . . . v 1 155
I cannot bid you bid my daughter live ; That were impossible . . v 1 288
Wouldst thou come when I called thee?—Yea, signior, and depart when you bid me . . . . v 2 44
And bid them so be gone . . . . *L. L. Lost* v 2 182
The princess bids you tell How many inches doth fill up one mile . . v 2 192
Please it you, As much in private, and I'll bid adieu . . . . v 2 241
Hast thou yet latch'd the Athenian's eyes With the love-juice, as I did bid thee do? . . . . *M. N. Dream* iii 2 37
Go, bid the huntsmen wake them with their horns . . . . iv 1 143
Do not you think The duke was here, and bid us follow him? . . iv 1 200
If I could bid the fifth welcome with so good a heart as I can bid the other four farewell, I should be glad of his approach *Mer. of Venice* i 2 140
The most courageous fiend bids me pack . . . . . . ii 2 10
To bid my old master the Jew to sup to-night with my new master . ii 4 17
Who bids thee call? I do not bid thee call . . . . . ii 5 7
I am bid forth to supper, Jessica : There are my keys . . . ii 5 11
But wherefore should I go? I am not bid for love ; they flatter me . ii 5 13
Perhaps I will return immediately : Do as I bid you ; shut doors after you . . . . ii 5 53
Welcome hither ; If that the youth of my new interest here Have power to bid you welcome . . . . iii 2 225
Bid your friends welcome, show a merry cheer . . . . . iii 2 314
Bid them prepare for dinner.—That is done, sir . . . . iii 5 51
Then bid them prepare dinner.—That is done too, sir . . . iii 5 56
Go to thy fellows ; bid them cover the table, serve in the meat . . iii 5 63
You may as well go stand upon the beach And bid the main flood bate . iv 1 72
Be merciful : Take thrice thy money ; bid me tear the bond . . iv 1 234
And, when the tale is told, bid her be judge . . . . . iv 1 276
Give him this And bid him keep it better than the other . . . v 1 255
By mine honour, but I was bid to come for you . . . *As Y. Like It* i 2 63
My gentle Phebe bid me give you this : I know not the contents . . iv 3 7
Therefore, put you in your best array ; bid your friends . . . . v 2 79
When I make curtsy, bid me farewell . . . . Epil. 23
Bid them come near. Now, fellows, you are welcome . *T. of Shrew* Ind. 1 79

Bid. Bid him shed tears, as being overjoy'd To see her noble lord *T. of Shrew* Ind. 1 120
Now, knock when I bid you, sirrah villain! i 2 19
Look you, sir, he bid me knock him and rap him soundly i 2 30
Tell them both, These are their tutors: bid them use them well ii 1 111
If she do bid me pack, I'll give her thanks, As though she bid me stay ii 1 178
Provide the feast, father, and bid the guests ii 1 318
A fool am I to chat with you, When I should bid good morrow to my bride iii 2 124
Did I not bid thee meet me in the park? iv 1 133
You bid me make it orderly and well, According to the fashion iv 3 94
If you be remember'd, I did not bid you mar it iv 3 97
I bid thy master cut out the gown; but I did not bid him cut it to pieces iv 3 127
I have no more to say, But bid Bianca farewell for ever and a day iv 4 97
To bid the priest be ready to come against you come with your appendix iv 4 103
Bid my father welcome, While I with self-same kindness welcome thine v 2 4
She will not come; she bids you come to her v 2 92
Knew the true minute when Exception bid him speak *All's Well* i 2 40
When I consider What great creation and what dole of honour Flies where you bid it ii 3 177
His taken labours bid him me forgive iii 4 12
Grief would have tears, and sorrow bids me speak iii 4 42
My house, mine honour, yea, my life, be thine, And I'll be bid by thee iv 2 53
When he swears oaths, bid him drop gold, and take it iv 3 252
Bid the dishonest man mend himself *T. Night* i 5 49
And bid him turn you out of doors ii 3 78
Take leave of her, she is very willing to bid you farewell ii 3 108
Shall I bid him go?—What an if you do?—Shall I bid him go, and spare not? ii 3 118
I am not sent to you by my lady, to bid you come iv 1 7
Pray you, bid These unknown friends to's welcome *W. Tale* iv 4 64
Come on, And bid us welcome to your sheep-shearing iv 4 69
My senses, better pleased with madness, Do bid it welcome iv 4 496
The one He chides to hell and bids the other grow iv 4 564
Let's before as he bids us: he was provided to do us good iv 4 860
Were I the ghost that walk'd, I'ld bid you mark Her eye v 1 63
Make proselytes Of who she but bid follow v 1 109
Some speedy messenger bid her repair To our solemnity *K. John* ii 1 554
Here I and sorrows sit; Here is my throne, bid kings come bow to it iii 1 74
What you bid me undertake, Though that my death were adjunct to my act By heaven, I would do it iii 3 56
Do as I bid you do.—O, save me, Hubert, save me! iv 1 72
Let it be our suit That you have bid us ask his liberty iv 2 63
Or turn'd an eye of doubt upon my face, As bid me tell my tale in express words iv 2 234
After such bloody toil, we bid good night v 5 6
And none of you will bid the winter come v 7 36
Bid his ears a little while be deaf, Till I have told this slander *Richard II.* i 1 112
Obedience bids I should not bid again i 1 163
Bid him—ah, what?—With all good speed at Plashy visit me i 2 65
I had rather You would have bid me argue like a father i 3 238
Cousin, farewell; and, uncle, bid him so i 3 247
Bid her send me presently a thousand pound ii 2 91
Whom both my oath And duty bids defend ii 2 113
Discomfort guides my tongue And bids me speak of nothing but despair iii 2 66
O, call back yesterday, bid time return! iii 2 69
I'll hate him everlastingly That bids me be of comfort any more iii 2 208
Until thou bid me joy, By pardoning Rutland v 3 95
'Tis no little reason bids us speed *1 Hen. IV.* i 3 283
When you breathe in your watering, they cry 'hem!' and bid you play it off ii 4 18
That daff'd the world aside, And bid it pass iv 1 97
If well-respected honour bid me on, I hold as little counsel with weak fear iv 3 10
The king will bid you battle presently v 2 31
We are time's subjects, and time bids be gone *2 Hen. IV.* i 3 110
Do not speak like a death's-head; do not bid me remember mine end ii 4 255
Bid them o'er-read these letters, And well consider of them iii 1 2
I bid you be assured, I'll be your father and your brother too v 2 56
My tongue is weary; when my legs are too, I will bid you good night Epil. 35
And bids you be advised there's nought in France That can be with a nimble galliard won *Hen. V.* i 2 251
Now I, to comfort him, bid him a' should not think of God ii 3 21
He bids you then resign Your crown and kingdom ii 4 93
If requiring fail, he will compel; And bids you ii 4 102
They bid us to the English dancing-schools, And teach lavoltas high iii 5 32
Bid him therefore consider of his ransom iii 6 133
Go, bid thy master well advise himself iii 6 168
We'll encamp ourselves, And on to-morrow bid them march away iii 6 181
Bids them good morrow with a modest smile And calls them brothers iv Prol. 33
O, be sick, great greatness, And bid thy ceremony give thee cure! iv 1 269
Bid them achieve me and then sell my bones iv 3 91
Bid him prepare; for I will cut his throat iv 4 34
If they will fight with us, bid them come down iv 7 61
And prings me pread and salt yesterday, look you, and bid me eat my leek v 1 10
To bid his young son welcome to his grave *1 Hen. VI.* iv 3 40
The envious people laugh And bid me be advised how I tread *2 Hen. VI.* ii 4 36
What, gone, my lord, and bid me not farewell! ii 4 85
Bid them blow towards England's blessed shore iii 2 90
You bade me ban, and will you bid me leave? iii 2 333
Go, bid her hide him quickly from the duke v 1 84
Call Buckingham, and bid him arm himself v 1 192
I would speak blasphemy ere bid you fly v 2 85
Issue forth and bid them battle straight *3 Hen. VI.* i 2 71
To bid the father wipe his eyes withal i 4 139
Ne'er may he live to see a sunshine day, That cries 'Retire,' if Warwick bid him stay ii 1 188
Now breathe we, lords: good fortune bids us pause ii 6 31
With five thousand men, Shall cross the seas, and bid false Edward battle iii 3 235
I take my leave.—And thus I seal my truth, and bid adieu iv 8 29
They no doubt Will issue out again and bid us battle v 1 63
Clarence sweeps along, Of force enough to bid his brother battle v 1 77
I will away towards Barnet presently, And bid thee battle v 1 111
Fly, lords, and save yourselves; For Warwick bids you all farewell v 2 49
Then bid me kill myself, and I will do it.—I have already *Richard III.* i 2 187
Bid me farewell.—'Tis more than you deserve i 2 223
And, with a piece of scripture, Tell them that God bids us do good for evil i 3 335
Bid my friend, for joy of this good news, Give Mistress Shore one gentle kiss iii 1 184

Bid. Bid him not fear the separated councils *Richard III.* iii 2 20
Go, bid thy master rise and come to me iii 2 31
There's some conceit or other likes him well, When he doth bid good morrow with such a spirit iii 4 52
And so, my good lord mayor, we bid farewell iii 5 71
Bid them both Meet me within this hour iii 5 104
So foolish sorrow bids your stones farewell iv 1 104
And Anne my wife hath bid the world good night iv 3 39
And bid her dry her weeping eyes therewith iv 4 278
Save for a night of groans Endured of her, for whom you bid like sorrow iv 4 304
Bid him levy straight The greatest strength and power he can make iv 4 448
Bid him bring his power Before sunrising v 3 60
In brief,—for so the season bids us be,—Prepare thy battle early v 3 87
Despair, and die! Harry the Sixth bids thee despair and die! v 3 127
Thy nephews' souls bid thee despair and die! v 3 154
Edward's unhappy sons do bid thee flourish v 3 158
Call up Lord Stanley, bid him bring his power v 3 290
Bid him recount The fore-recited practices *Hen. VIII.* i 2 126
Bid him strive To gain the love o' the commonalty i 2 169
Bid the music leave, They are harsh and heavy to me iv 2 94
Did my commission Bid ye so far forget yourselves? v 3 142
Let me speak, sir, For heaven now bids me v 5 16
For 'tis ill hap, If they hold when their ladies bid 'em clap. Epil. 14
And bid the cheek be ready with a blush *Troi. and Cres.* i 3 228
I will hold my peace when Achilles' brach bids me, shall I? ii 1 126
Achilles bids me say, he is much sorry ii 3 116
Sweet, bid me hold my tongue, For in this rapture I shall surely speak The thing I shall repent iii 2 137
Bid them have patience; she shall come anon iv 4 54
Fair lady: Achilles bids you welcome iv 5 25
Bids thee, with most divine integrity, From heart of very heart, great Hector, welcome iv 5 170
I bid good night. Ajax commands the guard to tend on you v 1 78
Bid my trumpet sound.—No notes of sally, for the heavens, sweet brother v 3 13
Even in the fan and wind of your fair sword, You bid them rise, and live v 3 42
And bid the snail-paced Ajax arm for shame v 5 18
Tell Valeria, We are fit to bid her welcome *Coriolanus* i 3 47
Bid them wash their faces And keep their teeth clean ii 3 66
When I am forth, Bid me farewell, and smile iv 1 50
Bid them all home; he's gone, and we'll no further iv 2 1
Bid them home: Say their great enemy is gone iv 2 5
And beat the messenger who bids beware Of what is to be dreaded iv 6 54
Do not bid me Dismiss my soldiers, or capitulate Again with Rome's mechanics v 3 81
What he bids be done is finished with his bidding v 4 23
I am not bid to wait upon this bride *T. Andron.* i 1 338
This is the hole where Aaron bid us hide him ii 3 186
Bid him bury it; More hath it merited iii 1 196
To bid Æneas tell the tale twice o'er, How Troy was burnt iii 2 27
And bids thee christen it with thy dagger's point iv 2 70
For his safety, Bid him demand what pledge will please him best iv 4 106
Bid him come and banquet at thy house v 2 114
This is the feast that I have bid her to v 2 193
Bid a sick man in sadness make his will *Rom. and Jul.* i 1 208
'Twas no need, I trow, To bid me trudge i 3 34
It argues a distemper'd head So soon to bid good morrow to thy bed ii 3 34
Bid her devise Some means to come to shrift this afternoon ii 4 191
Give this ring to my true knight, And bid him come to take his last farewell iii 2 143
Bid her hasten all the house to bed iii 3 156
I'll tell my lady you will come.—Do so, and bid my sweet prepare to chide iii 3 162
Bid her, mark you me, on Wednesday next—But, soft! what day is this? iii 4 17
Bid me leap, rather than marry Paris, From off the battlements of yonder tower iv 1 77
Or bid me lurk Where serpents are; chain me with roaring bears iv 1 79
Or bid me go into a new-made grave And hide me with a dead man iv 1 84
Leave me, and do the thing I bid thee do v 1 30
Give me those flowers. Do as I bid thee, go v 3 9
Bid me devise some mean To rid her from this second marriage v 3 240
This letter he early bid me give his father v 3 275
He came with flowers to strew his lady's grave; And bid me stand aloof v 3 282
And being enfranchised, bid him come to me *T. of Athens* i 1 106
Fare thee well, fare thee well.—Thou art a fool to bid me farewell twice i 1 273
Thou mightst kill 'em and bid me to 'em! i 2 85
You have bid me Return so much, I have shook my head and wept ii 2 145
Men and men's fortunes could I frankly use As I can bid thee speak ii 2 189
Bid 'em send o' the instant A thousand talents to me ii 2 207
Bid him suppose some good necessity Touches his friend ii 2 236
Go, bid all my friends again, Lucius, Lucullus, and Sempronius iii 4 111
Thou gavest thine ears like tapsters that bid welcome To knaves iv 3 215
Ha! who calls?—Bid every noise be still: peace yet again! *J. Cæsar* i 2 14
What man is that?—A soothsayer bids you beware the ides of March i 2 19
He did bid Antonius Send word to you he would be there to-morrow i 3 37
Now bid me run, And I will strive with things impossible ii 1 324
Bid the priests do present sacrifice And bring me their opinions of success ii 2 5
For my dear dear love To your proceeding bids me tell you this ii 2 103
Bid them prepare within: I am to blame to be thus waited for ii 2 118
Thus, Brutus, did my master bid me kneel; Thus did Mark Antony bid me fall down iii 1 123
And bid me say to you by word of mouth—O Cæsar! iii 1 280
Show you sweet Cæsar's wounds, poor poor dumb mouths, And bid them speak for me iii 2 230
He must be taught and train'd and bid go forth; A barren-spirited fellow iv 1 35
Let us not wrangle; bid them move away iv 2 45
Bid our commanders lead their charges off A little from this ground iv 2 48
Bid the commanders Prepare to lodge their companies to-night iv 3 139
Bid him set on his powers betimes before, And we will follow iv 3 308
That whatsoever I did bid thee do, Thou shouldst attempt it v 3 39
They Put on my brows this wreath of victory, And bid me give it thee v 3 83
Take this garland on thy brow; Thy Brutus bid me give it thee v 3 86
Let's after him, Whose care is gone before to bid us welcome *Macbeth* i 4 57
Herein I teach you How you shall bid God 'ild us for your pains i 6 13
Go bid thy mistress, when my drink is ready, She strike upon the bell ii 1 31
Do not bid me speak; See, and then speak yourselves ii 3 77
Though I could With barefaced power sweep him from my sight And bid my will avouch it, yet I must not iii 1 120
But who did bid thee join with us?—Macbeth iii 3 1

Bid. Who can impress the forest, bid the tree Unfix his earth-bound root? *Macbeth* iv 1 95
The grief that does not speak Whispers the o'er-fraught heart and bids it break . iv 3 210
Bid them make haste.—I think I hear them . *Hamlet* i 1 13
I'll speak to it, though hell itself should gape And bid me hold my peace i 2 246
There was, for a while, no money bid for argument . ii 2 372
Bid the players make haste. Will you two help to hasten them? . iii 2 54
What shall I do?—Not this, by no means, that I bid you do . iii 4 181
Go, bid the soldiers shoot . v 2 414
Thus Kent, O princes, bids you all adieu . *Lear* i 1 189
Bid them farewell, Cordelia, though unkind . i 1 263
Bid farewell to your sisters . i 1 270
I will hold my tongue; so your face bids me, though you say nothing . i 4 215
Bid them come forth and hear me, Or at their chamber-door I'll beat the drum . ii 4 118
I do not bid the thunder-bearer shoot, Nor tell tales of thee . ii 4 230
What they may incense him to, being apt To have his ear abused, wisdom bids fear . ii 4 310
Bids the wind blow the earth into the sea . iii 1 5
Unbonneted he runs, And bids what will take all . iii 1 15
But better service have I never done you Than now to bid you hold . iii 7 75
Do as I bid thee, or rather do thy pleasure; Above the rest, be gone . iv 1 49
Go thou farther off; Bid me farewell, and let me hear thee going . iv 6 31
I am come To bid my king and master aye good night . v 3 235
You are one of those that will not serve God, if the devil bid you *Othello* i 1 109
So was I bid report here to the state . i 3 15
What handkerchief?—. . . That which so often you did bid me steal . iii 3 309
Bid him come hither: tell him I have moved my lord on his behalf . iii 4 18
I have sent to bid Cassio come speak with you . iii 4 50
She, dying, gave it me; And bid me, when my fate would have me wive, To give it her . iii 4 64
Bid her come hither: go. She says enough . iv 2 19
Seek no colour for your going, But bid farewell, and go . *Ant. and Cleo.* i 3 33
Then bid adieu to me, and say the tears Belong to Egypt . i 3 77
Bid him Report the feature of Octavia, her years, Her inclination . ii 5 111
Bid you Alexas Bring me word how tall she is . ii 5 117
Away! Do as I bid you. Where's this cup I call'd for? . ii 7 60
Let Neptune hear we bid a loud farewell To these great fellows . ii 7 139
Hark! the land bids me tread no more upon't; It is ashamed to bear me! iii 11 1
Bid them all fly; For when I am revenged upon my charm, I have done all. Bid them all fly . iv 12 15
Thy death and fortunes bid thy followers fly . iv 14 111
Bid that welcome Which comes to punish us, and we punish it . iv 14 136
Bid him yield; Being so frustrate, tell him he mocks The pauses that he makes . v 1 1
Bid her have good heart: She soon shall know of us . v 1 56
Bids thee study on what fair demands Thou mean'st to have him grant thee v 2 10
Those things I bid you do, get them dispatch'd . *Cymbeline* i 3 39
Without offence,—My conscience bids me ask . i 5 7
You are as welcome, worthy sir, as I Have words to bid you . i 6 30
Bid my woman Search for a jewel that too casually Hath left mine arm . ii 3 145
His majesty bids you welcome. Make pastime with us a day or two . iii 1 78
Bid my woman feign a sickness; say She'll home to her father . iii 2 76
Do as I bid thee: there's no more to say . iii 2 83
That is, what villany soe'er I bid thee do, to perform it directly and truly iii 5 112
Boys, bid him welcome . iii 6 69
In honesty, I bid for you as I'ld buy . iii 6 71
Command our present numbers Be muster'd: bid the captains look to't iv 2 344
I do not bid thee beg my life, good lad; And yet I know thou wilt . v 5 101
It fits thee not to ask the reason why, Because we bid it . *Pericles* i 1 158
Being bid to ask what he would of the king, desired he might know none of his secrets . i 3 5
If a king bid a man be a villain, he's bound by the indenture of his oath to be one . i 3 8
Do as I bid you, or you'll move me else . ii 3 71
Loath to bid farewell, we take our leaves . ii 5 13
Bidden. If he will not stand when he is bidden, he is none of the prince's subjects . *Much Ado* iii 3 32
Biddest. Thou bid'st me beg: this begging is not strange . *L. L. Lost* v 2 210
We shall not marry till thou bid'st us . *W. Tale* v 1 82
If thou, that bid'st me be content, wert grim . *K. John* iii 1 43
Bid'st thou me rage? why, now thou hast thy wish . 3 *Hen. VI.* i 4 143
Come, and be true.—Thou bid'st me to my loss . *Cymbeline* iii 5 163
Bidding. To thy strong bidding task Ariel and all his quality . *Tempest* i 2 192
Bidding the law make court'sy to their will . *Meas. for Meas.* ii 4 175
Was wont to tell me that I could do nothing without bidding *Mer. of Ven.* ii 5 9
Health, at your bidding, serve your majesty! . *All's Well* ii 1 18
And that at my bidding you could so stand up . ii 1 67
I shall not break your bidding, good my lord . ii 5 93
My legs do better understand me, sir, than I understand what you mean by bidding me taste my legs . *T. Night* iii 1 90
Go, do our bidding; hence! . *W. Tale* ii 1 125
Swear by this sword Thou wilt perform my bidding . ii 3 169
Leave me, And think upon my bidding . ii 3 207
Bidding me depend Upon thy stars, thy fortune and thy strength *K. John* iii 1 125
I know no cause Why I should welcome such a guest as grief, Save bidding farewell to so sweet a guest . *Richard II.* ii 2 8
His neigh is like the bidding of a monarch . *Hen. V.* iii 7 30
What he bids be done is finished with his bidding . *Coriolanus* v 4 24
Your bidding shall I do effectually . *T. Andron.* iv 4 107
Hang thyself!—No, I will do nothing at thy bidding . *T. of Athens* i 1 278
Take this garland on thy brow; Thy Brutus bid me give it thee, and I Will do his bidding . *J. Cæsar* v 3 87
How say'st thou, that Macduff denies his person At our great bidding? *Macbeth* iii 4 129
When the thunder would not peace at my bidding . *Lear* iv 6 104
Dismiss me!—It was his bidding . *Othello* iv 3 15
Thy biddings have been done . *Ant. and Cleo.* i 4 34
Thy beck might from the bidding of the gods Command me . iii 11 60
What art thou, fellow?—One that but performs The bidding of the fullest man . iii 13 87
Come, fellow, be thou honest: Do thou thy master's bidding *Cymbeline* iii 4 67
Do his bidding; strike: Thou mayst be valiant in a better cause . iii 4 73
Thou art too slow to do thy master's bidding, When I desire it too . iii 4 100
Perform my bidding, or thou livest in woe; Do it, and happy *Pericles* v 1 248
Biddy. Ay, Biddy, come with me . *T. Night* iii 4 128
Bide. Yet the gold bides still, That others touch . *Com. of Errors* ii 1 110
I'll keep what I have swore And bide the penance . *L. L. Lost* i 1 115
Lysander's love, that would not let him bide, Fair Helena *M. N. Dream* iii 2 186

Bide. For want of other idleness, I'll bide your proof . *T. Night* i 5 71
There is no woman's sides Can bide the beating of so strong a passion . ii 4 97
Say, My love can give no place, bide no denay . ii 4 127
To bide upon't, thou art not honest . *W. Tale* i 2 242
Wherein the fortune of ten thousand men Must bide the touch 1 *Hen. IV.* iv 4 10
In whose cold blood no spark of honour bides . 3 *Hen. VI.* i 1 184
Or bide the mortal fortune of the field . ii 2 83
Drag them from the pit unto the prison: There let them bide *T. Andron.* ii 3 284
What say you, boys? will you bide with him? . v 2 137
Nor bide the encounter of assailing eyes . *Rom. and Jul.* i 1 219
Safe in a ditch he bides, With twenty trenched gashes on his head *Macb.* iii 4 26
That bide the pelting of this pitiless storm . *Lear* iii 4 29
Bear me, good friends, where Cleopatra bides . *Ant. and Cleo.* iv 14 131
What shall I do the while? where bide? how live? . *Cymbeline* iii 4 131
If not at court, Then not in Britain must you bide . iii 4 138
Biding. With many bitter threats of biding there . *T. G. of Ver.* iii 1 236
Give me your hand, I'll lead you to some biding . *Lear* iv 6 228
Bier. Grace my mournings here; In weeping after this untimely bier *Richard II.* v 6 52
End motion here; And thou and Romeo press one heavy bier! *R. and J.* iii 2 60
In thy best robes uncover'd on the bier Thou shalt be borne . iv 1 110
They bore him barefaced on the bier; Hey non nonny . *Hamlet* iv 5 164
The bier at door, And a demand who is't shall die, I'ld say 'My father, not this youth' . *Cymbeline* iv 2 22
Bi-fold authority! where reason can revolt Without perdition *Tr. and Cr.* v 2 144
Big. A dog as big as ten of yours . *T. G. of Ver.* iv 4 62
He's too big to go in there. What shall I do? . *Mer. Wives* iii 3 142
There is no woman's gown big enough for him . iv 2 72
It will serve him; she's as big as he is . iv 2 80
If it be too big for your thief, your thief thinks it little enough *M. for M.* iv 2 48
She is too big, I hope, for me to compass . *Com. of Errors* iv 1 138
He is not so big as the end of his club . *L. L. Lost* v 1 111
I Pompey am, Pompey surnamed the Big,— The Great.—It is, 'Great,' sir v 2 553
His leg is too big for Hector's.—More calf, certain . v 2 644
His eye being big with tears . *Mer. of Venice* ii 8 46
The big round tears Coursed one another down his innocent nose *As Y. L.* ii 1 38
His big manly voice, Turning again toward childish treble . ii 7 161
Nay, look not big, nor stamp, nor stare, nor fret . *T. of Shrew* iii 2 230
My mind hath been as big as one of yours, My heart as great . v 2 170
The surplice of humility over the black gown of a big heart . *All's Well* i 3 99
No woman's heart So big, to hold so much . *T. Night* ii 4 99
Although the sheet were big enough for the bed of Ware in England . iii 2 50
Let her sport herself With that she's big with . *W. Tale* ii 1 61
The centre is not big enough to bear A school-boy's top . ii 1 102
If you had but looked big and spit at him, he'ld have run . iv 3 113
Boys, with women's voices, Strive to speak big . *Richard II.* iii 2 114
A home to fly unto, If that the devil and mischance look big 1 *Hen. IV.* iv 1 58
The big year, swoln with some other grief, Is thought with child by the stern tyrant war . 2 *Hen. IV.* Ind. 13
Advance ourselves To look with forehead bold and big enough . i 3 8
Care I for . . . the stature, bulk, and big assemblance of a man! . iii 2 277
Big Mars seems bankrupt in their beggar'd host . *Hen. V.* iv 2 43
Buckingham Shall lessen this big look . *Hen. VIII.* i 1 119
Full of protest, of oath and big compare . *Troi. and Cres.* iii 2 182
A carbuncle entire, as big as thou art, Were not so rich a jewel *Coriolanus* i 4 55
I mock at death With as big heart as thou . iii 2 128
A bump as big as a young cockerel's stone . *Rom. and Jul.* i 3 53
Not half so big as a round little worm Prick'd from the lazy finger of a maid . i 4 65
How big imagination Moves in this lip! . *T. of Athens* i 1 32
Thy heart is big, get thee apart and weep . *J. Cæsar* iii 1 282
Whilst I was big in clamour came there in a man . *Lear* v 3 208
Farewell the plumed troop, and the big wars! . *Othello* iii 3 349
His gentle lady, Big of this gentleman . *Cymbeline* i 1 39
It doth confirm Another stain, as big as hell can hold . ii 4 140
Have not I An arm as big as thine? a heart as big? . iv 2 77
Bigamy. Seduced the pitch and height of all his thoughts To base declension and loathed bigamy . *Richard III.* iii 7 189
Big-bellied. See the sails conceive And grow big-bellied . *M. N. Dream* ii 1 129
Big-boned. No big-boned men framed of the Cyclops' size *T. Andron.* iv 3 46
Biggen. As he whose brow with homely biggen bound . 2 *Hen. IV.* iv 5 27
Bigger. Teach me how To name the bigger light, and how the less *Tempest* i 2 335
All the more it seeks to hide itself, The bigger bulk it shows . iii 1 81
A planched gate, That makes his opening with this bigger key *M. for M.* iv 1 31
Away with it! come, let me have a bigger.—I'll have no bigger *T. of S.* iv 3 68
Fools are as like husbands as pilchards are to herrings; the husband's the bigger . *T. Night* iii 1 40
Thy crown, Whose compass is no bigger than thy head . *Richard II.* ii 1 101
With hearts in their bellies no bigger than pins' heads . 1 *Hen. IV.* iv 2 23
The spoons will be the bigger, sir . *Hen. VIII.* v 4 40
I'll run away till I am bigger, but then I'll fight . *Coriolanus* v 3 128
No less! nay, bigger; women grow by men . *Rom. and Jul.* i 3 95
She comes In shape no bigger than an agate-stone . i 4 55
Methinks he seems no bigger than his head . *Lear* iv 6 16
Great men, That had a court no bigger than this cave . *Cymbeline* iii 6 83
Thy words, I grant, are bigger, for I wear not My dagger in my mouth . iv 2 78
Biggest. With sighs shot through, and biggest tears o'er-shower'd *Pericles* iv 4 26
Bigness. Why does the prince love him so, then?—Because their legs are both of a bigness . 2 *Hen. IV.* ii 4 265
Bigot. I met Lord Bigot and Lord Salisbury . *K. John* iv 2 162
Big-swoln. Break off the parley; for scarce I can refrain The execution of my big-swoln heart . 3 *Hen. VI.* ii 2 111
If the winds rage, doth not the sea wax mad, Threatening the welkin with his big-swoln face? . *T. Andron.* iii 1 224
Bilberry. There pinch the maids as blue as bilberry . *Mer. Wives* v 5 49
Bilbo. I combat challenge of this latten bilbo . i 1 165
Next, to be compassed, like a good bilbo, in the circumference of a peck iii 5 112
Methought I lay Worse than the mutines in the bilboes . *Hamlet* v 2 6
Bilbow. De fingres, de nails, de arma, de bilbow . *Hen. V.* iii 4 31
Bill. Who writes himself 'Armigero,' in any bill, warrant, quittance *Mer. Wives* i 1 10
I'll exhibit a bill in the parliament for the putting down of men . ii 1 29
He set up his bills here in Messina and challenged Cupid . *Much Ado* i 1 39
Only, have a care that your bills be not stolen . iii 3 44
We are like to prove a goodly commodity, being taken up of these men's bills . iii 3 191
In the meantime I will draw a bill of properties . *M. N. Dream* i 2 108
The ousel cock so black of hue, With orange-tawny bill . iii 1 129
With bills on their necks, 'Be it known unto all men by these presents' *As Y. Like It* i 2 131

Bill. As pigeons bill, so wedlock would be nibbling . *As Y. Like It* iii 3 82
I have bills for money by exchange From Florence . *T. of Shrew* iv 2 89
Error i' the bill, sir; error i' the bill . iv 3 146
Take thou the bill, give me thy mete-yard, and spare not me . iv 3 153
How she holds up the neb, the bill to him! *W. Tale* i 2 183
Yea, distaff-women manage rusty bills Against thy seat . *Richard II.* iii 2 118
My lord, I'll tell you; that self bill is urged . *Hen. V.* i 1 1
A thousand pounds by the year: thus runs the bill . i 1 19
How now for mitigation of this bill Urged by the commons? . i 1 70
My lord, when shall we go to Cheapside and take up commodities upon our bills? . *2 Hen. VI.* iv 7 135
But for a sallet, my brain-pan had been cleft with a brown bill . iv 10 13
Clubs, bills, and partisans! strike! beat them down! . *Rom. and Jul.* i 1 80
Why then preferr'd you not your sums and bills? . *T. of Athens* iii 4 49
My lord, here is my bill.—Here's mine.—And mine, my lord . iii 4 86
All our bills.—Knock me down with 'em: cleave me to the girdle . iii 4 90
By proscription and bills of outlawry . *J. Cæsar* iv 3 173
Give these bills Unto the legions on the other side . v 2 1
Particular addition, from the bill That writes them all alike . *Macbeth* iii 1 100
There's my gauntlet; I'll prove it on a giant. Bring up the brown bills *Lear* iv 6 92
The ruddock would, With charitable bill,—O bill, sore-shaming Those rich-left heirs that let their fathers lie Without a monument!—bring thee all this . *Cymbeline* iv 2 225
Billet. They shall beat out my brains with billets . *Meas. for Meas.* iv 3 58
Billeted. The centurions and their charges, distinctly billeted *Coriolanus* iv 3 48
Go where thou art billeted: Away, I say . *Othello* ii 3 386
Billiards. Let's to billiards . *Ant. and Cleo.* ii 5 3
Billing. What, billing again? . *Troi. and Cres.* iii 2 60
Billow. Methought the billows spoke and told me of it . *Tempest* iii 3 96
Take the ruffian billows by the top, Curling their monstrous heads *2 Hen. IV.* iii 1 22
Behold A city on the inconstant billows dancing . *Hen. V.* iii Prol. 15
Overboard, Into the tumbling billows of the main . *Richard III.* i 4 20
Even the billows of the sea Hung their heads, and then lay by *Hen. VIII.* iii 1 10
Blow wind, swell billow and swim bark! The storm is up *J. Cæsar* v 1 67
The chidden billow seems to pelt the clouds . *Othello* ii 1 12
Their vessel shakes On Neptune's billow . *Pericles* iii Gower 45
But sea-room, an the brine and cloudy billow kiss the moon, I care not iii 1 46
I never saw so huge a billow, sir, As toss'd it upon shore . iii 2 58
Bind. To bind him to remember my good will . *T. G. of Ver.* iv 4 103
O, bind him, bind him! let him not come near me . *Com. of Errors* iv 4 109
Take his sword away: Bind Dromio too, and bear them to my house . v 1 35
Bind him fast And bear him home for his recovery . v 1 40
Chased us away, till raising of more aid We came again to bind them . v 1 154
Or to bind him up a rod, as being worthy to be whipped *Much Ado* ii 1 226
My kindness shall incite thee To bind our loves up in a holy band . iii 1 114
Fast bind, fast find; A proverb never stale in thrifty mind *Mer. of Venice* ii 5 54
They that reap must sheaf and bind . *As Y. Like It* iii 2 113
According as marriage binds and blood breaks . v 4 59
We will bind and hoodwink him so . *All's Well* iii 6 26
I saw your brother, Most provident in peril, bind himself . . . To a strong mast that lived upon the sea . *T. Night* i 2 12
Bind up those tresses. O, what love I note In the fair multitude of those her hairs! . *K. John* iii 4 61
Bind up your hairs.—Yes, that I will; and wherefore will I do it? . iii 4 68
Rush forth, And bind the boy which you shall find with me Fast to the chair . iv 1 4
Give me the iron, I say, and bind him here . iv 1 75
Go, bind thou up yon dangling apricocks . *Richard II.* iii 4 29
Now bind my brows with iron; and approach The ragged'st hour! *2 Hen. IV.* i 1 150
He is a man Who with a double surety binds his followers . i 1 191
A shelter to thy friends, A hoop of gold to bind thy brothers in . iv 4 43
The sooner to effect And surer bind this knot of amity . *1 Hen. VI.* v 1 16
As the butcher takes away the calf And binds the wretch and beats it when it strays . *2 Hen. VI.* iii 1 211
So shall you bind me to your highness' service . *3 Hen. VI.* iii 2 43
Give me another horse: bind up my wounds . *Richard III.* v 3 177
They told me they would bind me here Unto the body of a dismal yew *T. Andron.* ii 3 106
If there were reason for these miseries, Then into limits could I bind my woes . iii 1 221
Bind them, gentle Publius. Caius and Valentine, lay hands on them . v 2 158
Bind them sure, And stop their mouths, if they begin to cry . v 2 161
Is he sure bound? look that you bind them fast . v 2 166
I'll pay the debt, and free him.—Your lordship ever binds him *T. of Athens* i 1 104
From hence to Inverness, And bind us further to you . *Macbeth* i 4 43
Ingrateful fox! 'tis he.—Bind fast his corky arms . *Lear* iii 7 29
Do me no foul play, friends.—Bind him, I say.—Hard, hard . iii 7 32
To this chair bind him. Villain, thou shalt find . iii 7 34
Let me but bind it hard, within this hour It will be well . *Othello* ii 3 286
My leg is cut in two.—Marry, heaven forbid! Light, gentlemen: I'll bind it with my shirt . v 1 73
I bind, On pain of punishment, the world to weet . *Ant. and Cleo.* i 1 38
How the fear of us May cement their divisions and bind up The petty difference, we yet not know . ii 1 48
Bind the offender, And take him from our presence . *Cymbeline* v 5 300
Thou, that hast Upon the winds command, bind them in brass! *Pericles* iii 1 3
Bindeth. Since he affects her most, It most of all these reasons bindeth us *1 Hen. VI.* v 5 60
Biondello. If, Biondello, thou wert come ashore, We could at once put us in readiness . *T. of Shrew* i 1 42
When Biondello comes, he waits on thee . i 1 213
Is't he you mean?—Even he, Biondello.—Hark you, sir . i 2 224
I love no chiders, sir. Biondello, let's away . i 2 228
What is he, Biondello?—Master, a mercatante, or a pedant . iv 2 62
Sirrah Biondello, Now do your duty throughly, I advise you . iv 4 10
What sayest thou, Biondello?—You saw my master wink and laugh upon you?—Biondello, what of that? . iv 4 74
Hearest thou, Biondello?—I cannot tarry . iv 4 98
I fly, Biondello: but they may chance to need thee at home . v 1 3
Go, Biondello, bid your mistress come to me.—I go . v 2 76
Biondello, go and entreat my wife To come to me forthwith . v 2 86
Birch. As fond fathers, Having bound up the threatening twigs of birch, Only to stick it in their children's sight For terror, not to use *Meas. for Meas.* i 3 24
Bird. This was well done, my bird . *Tempest* iv 1 184
Shallow rivers, to whose falls Melodious birds sings madrigals *Mer. Wives* iii 1 18
We must not make a scarecrow of the law, Setting it up to fear the birds of prey . *Meas. for Meas.* ii 1 2
Bird. A bird of my tongue is better than a beast of yours *Much Ado* i 1 140
A school boy, who, being overjoyed with finding a birds' nest . ii 1 230
Why should proud summer boast Before the birds have any cause to sing? *L. L. Lost* i 1 102
About the sixth hour; when beasts most graze, birds best peck . i 1 239
Coughing drowns the parson's saw And birds sit brooding in the snow . v 2 933
Who would give a bird the lie, though he cry 'cuckoo' never so? *M. N. Dream* iii 1 138
Every elf and fairy sprite Hop as light as bird from brier . v 1 401
And Shylock, for his own part, knew the bird was fledged *Mer. of Venice* iii 1 32
And turn his merry note Unto the sweet bird's throat . *As Y. Like It* ii 5 4
And show the world what the bird hath done to her own nest . iv 1 208
When birds do sing, hey ding a ding, ding: Sweet lovers love the spring v 3 21
Am I your bird? I mean to shift my bush . *T. of Shrew* v 2 46
This bird you aim'd at, though you hit her not . v 2 50
That the soul of our grandam might haply inhabit a bird . *T. Night* iv 2 57
With heigh! the sweet birds, O, how they sing! . *W. Tale* iv 3 6
As confident as is the falcon's flight Against a bird . *Richard II.* i 3 62
Suppose the singing birds musicians . i 3 288
As that ungentle gull, the cuckoo's bird, Useth the sparrow . *1 Hen. IV.* v 1 60
Thou art a summer bird, Which ever in the haunch of winter sings The lifting up of day . *2 Hen. IV.* iv 4 91
I heard a bird so sing, Whose music, to my thinking, pleased the king . v 5 113
As duly, but not as truly, As bird doth sing on bough . *Hen. V.* iii 2 20
Myself have limed a bush for her, And placed a quire of such enticing birds, That she will light to listen . *2 Hen. VI.* i 3 92
Yea, man and birds are fain of climbing high . ii 1 8
'Tis but a base ignoble mind That mounts no higher than a bird can soar ii 1 14
Who finds the partridge in the puttock's nest, But may imagine how the bird was dead? . iii 2 192
My ashes, as the phœnix, may bring forth A bird that will revenge upon you all . *3 Hen. VI.* i 4 36
Nay, if thou be that princely eagle's bird, Show thy descent by gazing 'gainst the sun . ii 1 91
And of their feather many moe proud birds, Have wrought the easy-melting king like wax . ii 1 170
Both of you are birds of selfsame feather . iii 3 161
Such a pleasure as incaged birds Conceive . iv 6 12
The bird that hath been limed in a bush, With trembling wings misdoubteth every bush . v 6 13
And I, the hapless male to one sweet bird . v 6 15
The rod, and bird of peace, and all such emblems . *Hen. VIII.* iv 1 89
But as when The bird of wonder dies, the maiden phœnix, Her ashes new create another heir . v 5 41
The birds chant melody on every bush . *T. Andron.* ii 3 12
Hounds and horns and sweet melodious birds Be unto us as is a nurse's song Of lullaby . ii 3 27
Some say that ravens foster forlorn children, The whilst their own birds famish in their nests . ii 3 154
Like a sweet melodious bird, it sung Sweet varied notes . iii 1 85
The eagle suffers little birds to sing, And is not careful what they mean thereby . iv 4 83
Throw her forth to beasts and birds of prey . v 3 198
So bright That birds would sing and think it were not night *Rom. and Jul.* ii 2 22
I would have thee gone: And yet no further than a wanton's bird . ii 2 178
I would I were thy bird.—Sweet, so would I . ii 2 183
To fetch a ladder, by the which your love Must climb a bird's nest soon ii 5 76
We cannot live on grass, on berries, water, As beasts and birds and fishes.—Nor on the beasts themselves, the birds, and fishes; You must eat men . *T. of Athens* iv 3 426
Yesterday the bird of night did sit Even at noon-day upon the market-place, Hooting and shrieking . *J. Cæsar* i 3 26
Why birds and beasts from quality and kind, Why old men fool . i 3 64
No jutty, frieze, Buttress, nor coign of vantage, but this bird Hath made his pendent bed and procreant cradle . *Macbeth* i 6 7
The obscure bird Clamour'd the livelong night . ii 3 64
The poor wren, The most diminutive of birds, will fight . iv 2 10
And what will you do now? How will you live?—As birds do, mother iv 2 32
Poor bird! thou 'ldst never fear the net nor lime, The pitfall nor the gin.—Why should I, mother? Poor birds they are not set for . iv 2 34
The bird of dawning singeth all night long: And then, they say, no spirit dare stir abroad . *Hamlet* i 1 160
Hillo, ho, ho, my lord!—Hillo, ho, ho, boy! come, bird, come . i 5 116
Unpeg the basket on the house's top, Let the birds fly . iii 4 194
O, well flown, bird! i' the clout, i' the clout: hewgh! . *Lear* iv 6 92
We two alone will sing like birds i' the cage . v 3 9
O Antony! O thou Arabian bird! . *Ant. and Cleo.* iii 2 12
If she be furnish'd with a mind so rare, She is alone the Arabian bird *Cymbeline* i 6 17
Our cage We make a quire, as doth the prison'd bird, And sing our bondage freely . iii 3 43
The bird is dead That we have made so much on . iv 2 197
I saw Jove's bird, The Roman eagle, wing'd From the spongy south . iv 2 348
His royal bird Prunes the immortal wing and cloys his beak . v 4 117
Change me to the meanest bird That flies i' the purer air! . *Pericles* iv 6 108
With her neeld composes Nature's own shape, of bud, bird, branch, or berry . v Gower 6
Bird-bolt. And challenged him at the bird-bolt . *Much Ado* i 1 42
Thou hast thumped him with thy bird-bolt under the left pap *L. L. Lost* iv 3 25
Take those things for bird-bolts that you deem cannon-bullets *T. Night* i 5 100
Birding-pieces. Into the chimney.—There they always use to discharge their birding-pieces . *Mer. Wives* iv 2 59
Birdlime. I am about it; but indeed my invention Comes from my pate as birdlime does from frize . *Othello* ii 1 127
Birnam. Until Great Birnam wood to high Dunsinane hill Shall come *Macbeth* iv 1 93
Rebellion's head, rise never till the wood of Birnam rise . iv 1 98
Near Birnam wood Shall we well meet them . v 2 5
Make we our march towards Birnam . v 2 31
Till Birnam wood remove to Dunsinane, I cannot taint with fear . v 3 2
I will not be afraid of death and bane, Till Birnam forest come to Dunsinane . v 3 60
What wood is this before us?—The wood of Birnam . v 4 3
I look'd toward Birnam, and anon, methought, The wood began to move v 5 34
Fear not, till Birnam wood Do come to Dunsinane . v 5 44
Though Birnam wood be come to Dunsinane . v 8 30
Biron, Dumain, and Longaville, Have sworn for three years' term to live with me My fellow-scholars . *L. L. Lost* i 1 15
You swore to that, Biron, and to the rest.—By yea and nay, sir . i 1 53
Biron is like an envious sneaping frost . i 1 100

Biron. Go home, Biron: adieu.—No, my good lord; I have sworn to stay *L. L. Lost* i 1 110
Don Armado shall be your keeper. My Lord Biron, see him deliver'd o'er i 1 307
Biron they call him; but a merrier man, Within the limit of becoming mirth, I never spent an hour's talk withal ii 1 66
That last is Biron, the merry mad-cap lord ii 1 215
I have a letter from Monsieur Biron to one Lady Rosaline iv 1 53
One Monsieur Biron, one of the strange queen's lords iv 2 133
'Your ladyship's in all desired employment, Biron.' Sir Nathaniel, this Biron is one of the votaries with the king iv 2 140
O, would the king, Biron, and Longaville, Were lovers too! iv 3 123
What will Biron say when that he shall hear Faith so infringed? iv 3 145
It is Biron's writing, and here is his name iv 3 203
My eyes are then no eyes, nor I Biron iv 3 232
Good Biron, now prove Our loving lawful, and our faith not torn iv 3 284
Nay, I have verses too, I thank Biron: The numbers true v 2 34
That same Biron I'll torture ere I go v 2 60
Take thou this, my sweet, and give me thine, So shall Biron take me for Rosaline v 2 133
This pert Biron was out of countenance quite v 2 272
Biron did swear himself out of all suit v 2 275
The king is my love sworn.—And quick Biron hath plighted faith to me v 2 283
And Lord Biron, I thank him, is my dear v 2 457
Biron, they will shame us: let them not approach v 2 512
Oft have I heard of you, my Lord Biron, Before I saw you v 2 851
Birth. A birth indeed Which throes thee much to yield *Tempest* ii 1 230
Worthy his youth and nobleness of birth *T. G. of Ver.* i 3 33
But truer stars did govern Proteus' birth ii 7 74
What says she to my birth?—That you are well derived v 2 22
He doth object I am too great of birth *Mer. Wives* iii 4 4
Vile worm, thou wast o'erlook'd even in thy birth v 5 87
I pray you, dissuade him from her: she is no equal for his birth *Much Ado* ii 1 172
On this travail look for greater birth iv 1 215
Why should I joy in any abortive birth? *L. L. Lost* i 1 104
What was a month old at Cain's birth, that's not five weeks old as yet? iv 2 36
When great things labouring perish in their birth v 2 521
I do in birth deserve her, and in fortunes, In graces *Mer. of Venice* ii 7 32
Call you that keeping for a gentleman of my birth? *As Y. Like It* i 1 10
Civet is of a baser birth than tar iii 2 69
By birth a pedlar, by education a card-maker *T. of Shrew* Ind. 2 20
Bethink thee of thy birth, Call home thy ancient thoughts from banishment Ind. 2 32
She is of good esteem, Her dowry wealthy, and of worthy birth iv 5 65
You are more saucy with lords and honourable personages than the commission of your birth and virtue gives you heraldry *All's Well* ii 3 279
We will our celebration keep According to my birth *T. Night* iv 3 31
On the birth Of trembling winter *W. Tale* iv 4 80
She is as forward of her breeding as She is i' the rear our birth iv 4 592
Not full a month Between their births v 1 118
If love ambitious sought a match of birth *K. John* ii 1 430
Such as she is, in beauty, virtue, birth, Is the young Dauphin ii 1 432
At thy birth, dear boy, Nature and Fortune join'd to make thee great iii 1 51
Since the birth of Cain, . . . There was not such a gracious creature born iii 4 79
Fear'd by their breed and famous by their birth *Richard II.* ii 1 52
Myself, a prince by fortune of my birth, Near to the king in blood iii 1 16
At my birth The frame and huge foundation of the earth Shaked like a coward *1 Hen. IV.* iii 1 15
At your birth Our grandam earth, having this distemperature, In passion shook iii 1 33
At my birth The front of heaven was full of fiery shapes iii 1 37
Grant that our hopes, yet likely of fair birth, Should be still-born *2 Hen. IV.* i 3 63
Delivered o'er to the voice, the tongue, which is the birth, becomes excellent wit iv 3 110
Unfather'd heirs and loathly births of nature iv 4 122
In the derivation of my birth, and in other particularities *Hen. V.* iii 2 142
Poor and mangled Peace, Dear nurse of arts, plenties and joyful births v 2 35
I am by birth a shepherd's daughter, My wit untrain'd *1 Hen. VI.* i 2 72
A true-born gentleman And stands upon the honour of his birth ii 4 28
I was the next by birth and parentage ii 5 73
For your royal birth, Inferior to none but to his majesty iii 1 95
Doubting thy birth and lawful progeny iii 3 61
Knights of the garter were of noble birth, Valiant and virtuous iv 1 35
Neither in birth or for authority, The bishop will be overborne by thee v 1 59
You have suborn'd this man, Of purpose to obscure my noble birth v 4 22
Her peerless feature, joined with her birth, Approves her fit for none but for a king v 5 68
A cunning man did calculate my birth *2 Hen. VI.* iv 1 34
By her he had two children at one birth iv 2 147
Ignorant of his birth and parentage, Became a bricklayer iv 2 152
The sons of York, thy betters in their birth, Shall be their father's bail v 1 119
It ill befits thy state And birth, that thou shouldst stand *3 Hen. VI.* iii 3 3
The owl shriek'd at thy birth,—an evil sign v 6 44
Your state of fortune and your due of birth *Richard III.* iii 7 120
Your right of birth, your empery, your own iii 7 136
As my ripe revenue and due by birth iii 7 158
A grievous burthen was thy birth to me; Tetchy and wayward was thy infancy iv 4 167
Wrong not her birth, she is of royal blood iv 4 211
Her life is only safest in her birth iv 4 213
Lo, at their births good stars were opposite iv 4 215
Inter their bodies as becomes their births v 5 15
Birth, beauty, good shape, discourse, manhood, learning *Troi. and Cres.* i 2 275
The primogenitive and due of birth, Prerogative of age i 3 106
We will not name desert before his birth, and, being born, his addition shall be humble iii 2 101
For beauty, wit, High birth, vigour of bone, desert in service iii 3 172
Strangles our dear vows Even in the birth of our own labouring breath iv 4 40
Prodigious birth of love it is to me *Rom. and Jul.* i 5 142
Revolts from true birth, stumbling on abuse ii 3 20
Why rail'st thou on thy birth, the heaven, and earth? Since birth, and heaven, and earth, all three do meet In thee at once iii 3 119
Whose procreation, residence, and birth, Scarce is dividant *T. of Athens* iv 3 4
With all the abhorred births below crisp heaven iv 3 183
O error, soon conceived, Thou never comest unto a happy birth! *J. Cæsar* v 3 70
The son of Duncan, From whom this tyrant holds the due of birth *Macb.* iii 6 25
'Gainst that season comes Wherein our Saviour's birth is celebrated *Hamlet* i 1 159
His will is not his own; For he himself is subject to his birth i 3 18
Birth. Some vicious mole of nature in them, As, in their birth *Hamlet* i 4 25
Purpose is but the slave to memory, Of violent birth, but poor validity iii 2 199
Let me, if not by birth, have lands by wit *Lear* i 2 199
Hell and night Must bring this monstrous birth to the world's light *Othello* i 3 410
He that is approved in this offence, Though he had twinn'd with me, both at a birth, Shall lose me ii 3 212
What's his name and birth?—I cannot delve him to the root *Cymbeline* i 1 27
Beyond him in the advantage of the time, above him in birth iv 1 13
Not seeming So worthy as thy birth iv 2 94
Our Jovial star reign'd at his birth v 4 105
What, am I A mother to the birth of three? v 5 369
In the earth, From whence we had our being and our birth *Pericles* i 2 114
Our daughter, In honour of whose birth these triumphs are ii 2 5
Now, mild may be thy life! For a more blustrous birth had never babe iii 1 28
At her birth, Thetis, being proud, swallow'd some part o' the earth iv 4 38
Did you not name a tempest, A birth, and death? v 3 34
Birth-child. The earth, fearing to be o'erflow'd, Hath Thetis' birth-child on the heavens bestow'd iv 4 41
Birthday. This is my birth-day; as this very day Was Cassius born *J. Cæsar* v 1 72
It is my birth-day: I had thought to have held it poor *Ant. and Cleo.* iii 13 185
He hath a fair daughter, and to-morrow is her birth-day *Pericles* ii 1 114
Birthdom. Like good men Bestride our down-fall'n birthdom *Macb.* iv 3 4
Birthplace. My birth-place hate I *Coriolanus* iv 4 23
Birthright. And thy goodness Share with thy birthright! *All's Well* i 1 73
Bearing their birthrights proudly on their backs *K. John* ii 1 70
With honour of his birthright to the crown *2 Hen. VI.* ii 2 62
Hath he deserved to lose his birthright thus? *3 Hen. VI.* i 1 219
Pity that this goodly boy Should lose his birthright by his father's fault ii 2 35
Birth-strangled. Finger of birth-strangled babe *Macbeth* iv 1 30
Bis coctus. Twice-sod simplicity, bis coctus! *L. L. Lost* iv 2 23
Biscuit. As dry as the remainder biscuit After a voyage *As Y. Like It* ii 7 39
Pun thee into shivers with his fist, as a sailor breaks a biscuit *Tr. and Cr.* ii 1 43
Bishop. The bishop and Northumberland Are fifty thousand strong *2 Hen. IV.* iii 1 95
With you, lord bishop, It is even so iv 2 15
Ay, see the bishop be not overborne *1 Hen. VI.* iii 1 53
An uproar, I dare warrant, Begun through malice of the bishop's men iii 1 75
The bishop and the Duke of Gloucester's men, Forbidden late to carry any weapon, Have fill'd their pockets full of pebble stones iii 1 78
Sweet king! the bishop hath a kindly gird iii 1 131
Lord bishop, set the crown upon his head.—God save King Henry! iv 1 1
Neither in birth or for authority, The bishop will be overborne by thee v 1 60
Seven earls, twelve barons and twenty reverend bishops *2 Hen. VI.* i 1 8
I'll send some holy bishop to entreat; For God forbid so many simple souls Should perish! iv 4 9
Our king, my brother, Is prisoner to the bishop here *3 Hen. VI.* iv 5 5
Stand you thus close, to steal the bishop's deer? iv 5 17
Bishop, farewell: shield thee from Warwick's frown iv 5 28
And from the bishop's huntsmen rescued him iv 6 84
You left poor Henry at the Bishop's palace, And, ten to one, you'll meet him in the Tower.—'Tis even so v 1 45
With reverend fathers and well-learned bishops *Richard III.* iii 5 100
He, I mean the bishop, did require a respite *Hen. VIII.* ii 4 177
By which power You maim'd the jurisdiction of all bishops iii 2 312
What two reverend bishops Were those that went on each side of the queen? iv 1 99
This is about that which the bishop spake v 1 84
Bisson. What harm can your bisson conspectuities glean out of this character? *Coriolanus* ii 1 70
How shall this bisson multitude digest The senate's courtesy? iii 1 131
Threatening the flames With bisson rheum *Hamlet* ii 2 529
Bit. We have strict statutes and most biting laws, The needful bits and curbs to headstrong weeds *Meas. for Meas.* i 3 20
Dainty bits Make rich the ribs, but bankrupt quite the wits *L. L. Lost* i 1 26
Till he be first sufficed, Oppress'd with two weak evils, age and hunger, I will not touch a bit *As Y. Like It* ii 7 133
With a half-checked bit and a head-stall of sheep's leather *T. of Shrew* iii 2 57
There is ne'er a king christen could be better bit than I have been *1 Hen. IV.* ii 1 19
In their pale dull mouths the gimmal bit Lies foul with chew'd grass *Hen. V.* iv 2 49
Stop their mouths with stubborn bits, and spur 'em, Till they obey *Hen. VIII.* v 3 23
The bits and greasy relics Of her o'er-eaten faith *Troi. and Cres.* v 2 159
Follow your function, go, and batten on cold bits *Coriolanus* iv 5 36
As is the bud bit with an envious worm *Rom. and Jul.* i 1 157
The bounty of this lord! How many prodigal bits have slaves and peasants This night englutted! *T. of Athens* ii 2 174
That it had it head bit off by it young *Lear* i 4 236
Mine enemy's dog, Though he had bit me, should have stood that night Against my fire iv 7 37
Bitch. With as little remorse as they would have drowned a blind bitch's puppies *Mer. Wives* iii 5 11
The son and heir of a mongrel bitch *Lear* ii 2 24
Bitch-wolf. Thou bitch-wolf's son, canst thou not hear? *Troi. and Cres.* ii 1 11
Bite. Like apes that mow and chatter at me And after bite me *Tempest* ii 2 10
Bite him to death, I prithee iii 2 38
Like poison given to work a great time after, Now 'gins to bite the spirits iii 3 106
The green sour ringlets make, Whereof the ewe not bites v 1 38
The best is, she hath no teeth to bite *T. G. of Ver.* iii 1 349
I have a sword and it shall bite upon my necessity *Mer. Wives* ii 1 136
Has he affections in him, That thus can make him bite the law by the nose, When he would force it? *Meas. for Meas.* iii 1 109
If I had my mouth, I would bite *Much Ado* i 3 37
Bait the hook well; this fish will bite ii 3 114
Then the two bears will not bite one another when they meet ii 2 80
Sneaping frost That bites the first-born infants of the spring *L. L. Lost* i 1 101
It bites and blows upon my body *As Y. Like It* ii 1 8
Freeze, freeze, thou bitter sky, That dost not bite so nigh As benefits forgot ii 7 185
Thou canst not frown, thou canst not look askance, nor bite the lip *T. of Shrew* ii 1 250
It blots thy beauty as frosts do bite the meads v 2 139
My dagger muzzled, Lest it should bite its master *W. Tale* i 2 157
Gnarling sorrow hath less power to bite The man that mocks at it *Richard II.* i 3 292
Fell sorrow's tooth doth never rankle more Than when he bites, but lanceth not the sore i 3 303

Bite. Hope gives not so much warrant as despair That frosts will bite them *2 Hen. IV.* i 3 41
Bite, I pray you; it is good for your green wound *Hen. V.* v 1 43
Must I bite?—Yes, certainly, and out of doubt and out of question too v 1 46
So York must sit and fret and bite his tongue *2 Hen. VI.* i 1 230
Oft have I seen a hot o'erweening cur Run back and bite, because he was withheld v 1 152
If thou canst for blushing, view this face, And bite thy tongue *3 Hen. VI.* i 4 47
Teeth hadst thou in thy head when thou wast born, To signify thou camest to bite the world v 6 54
Which plainly signified That I should snarl and bite and play the dog v 6 77
Take heed of yonder dog! Look, when he fawns, he bites *Richard III.* i 3 290
Exceeding mad, in love too: But he would bite none *Hen. VIII.* i 4 29
He bites his lip, and starts; Stops on a sudden, looks upon the ground iii 2 113
Men that make Envy and crooked malice nourishment Dare bite the best v 3 45
Though you bite so sharp at reasons, You are so empty of them *Troi. and Cres.* ii 2 33
Bites his lip with a politic regard iii 3 254
Were it a casque composed by Vulcan's skill, My sword should bite it v 2 171
One bear will not bite another v 7 19
Yet, to bite his lip And hum at good Cominius, much unhearts me *Coriol.* v 1 48
Shall we bite our tongues, and in dumb shows Pass the remainder of our hateful days? What shall we do? *T. Andron.* iii 1 131
I will bite my thumb at them; which is a disgrace to them *Rom. and Jul.* i 1 48
Do you bite your thumb at us, sir?—I do bite my thumb, sir i 1 51
I do not bite my thumb at you, sir, but I bite my thumb, sir i 1 57
I will bite thee by the ear for that jest.—Nay, good goose, bite not ii 4 81
The air bites shrewdly; it is very cold *Hamlet* i 4 1
Like rats, oft bite the holy cords a-twain Which are too intrinse t' unloose *Lear* ii 2 80
The foul fiend bites my back iii 6 18
Be thy mouth or black or white, Tooth that poisons if it bite iii 6 70
Though I am mad, I will not bite him *Ant. and Cleo.* ii 5 80
Biting. I think to repay that money will be a biting affliction *Mer. Wives* v 5 178
Most biting laws, The needful bits and curbs to headstrong weeds *Meas. for Meas.* i 3 19
Guiltless here Under some biting error *Much Ado* iv 1 172
On a mountain top, Where biting cold would never let grass grow *2 Hen. VI.* iii 2 337
We are like to have biting statutes, unless his teeth be pulled out iv 7 19
If we use delay, Cold biting winter mars our hoped-for hay *3 Hen. VI.* iv 8 61
Grandam, this would have been a biting jest *Richard III.* ii 4 30
With my good biting falchion I would have made them skip *Lear* v 3 276
His biting is immortal *Ant. and Cleo.* v 2 247
How she died of the biting of it, what pain she felt v 2 254
Bitten. These are the youths that thunder at a playhouse, and fight for bitten apples *Hen. VIII.* v 4 64
Bitter. Punish'd me With bitter fasts *T. G. of Ver.* ii 4 131
When I was sick, you gave me bitter pills ii 4 149
With many bitter threats of biding there iii 1 236
It is a bitter deputy.—Not so, not so *Meas. for Meas.* iv 2 81
'Tis a physic That's bitter to sweet end iv 6 8
It is the base, though bitter, disposition of Beatrice *Much Ado* ii 1 215
Too bitter is thy jest. Are we betray'd thus to thy over-view? *L. L. Lost* iv 3 174
Thou grievest my gall.—Gall! bitter v 2 237
Lay breath so bitter on your bitter foe *M. N. Dream* iii 2 44
Do not be so bitter with me. I evermore did love you iii 2 306
Stir Demetrius up with bitter wrong iii 2 361
Thou bitter sky, That dost not bite so nigh As benefits forgot *As Y. L. It* ii 7 184
Fast as she answers thee with frowning looks, I'll sauce her with bitter words iii 5 69
I will be bitter with him and passing short iii 5 138
Pacing through the forest, Chewing the food of sweet and bitter fancy iv 3 102
O, how bitter a thing it is to look into happiness through another man's eyes! v 2 48
When did she cross thee with a bitter word? *T. of Shrew* ii 1 28
He was a frantic fool, Hiding his bitter jests in blunt behaviour iii 2 13
Since you have begun, Have at you for a bitter jest or two! v 2 45
This she delivered in the most bitter touch of sorrow *All's Well* i 3 122
'Tis bitter.—Find you that there? ii 3 78
If it end so meet, The bitter past, more welcome is the sweet v 3 334
His revenges must In that be made more bitter *W. Tale* i 2 457
Shall suffer what wit can make heavy and vengeance bitter iv 4 801
It is as bitter Upon thy tongue as in my thought v 1 18
Bitter shame hath spoil'd the sweet world's taste *K. John* iii 4 110
A woman's war, The bitter clamour of two eager tongues *Richard II.* i 1 49
Eating the bitter bread of banishment iii 1 21
Were nail'd For our advantage on the bitter cross *1 Hen. IV.* i 1 27
These are very bitter words *2 Hen. IV.* ii 4 185
And consecrate commotion's bitter edge iv 1 93
This bitter taste Yield his engrossments to the ending father iv 5 79
Sweeten the bitter mock you sent his majesty *Hen. V.* ii 4 122
Thou hast given me most bitter terms iv 8 44
Those bitter injuries Which Somerset hath offer'd to my house *1 Hen. VI.* ii 5 124
'Tis but his policy to counterfeit, Because he would avoid such bitter taunts *3 Hen. VI.* ii 6 66
I have too long borne Your blunt upbraidings and your bitter scoffs *Richard III.* i 3 104
I had thought That thou hadst call'd me all these bitter names i 3 236
Who pronounced The bitter sentence of poor Clarence' death? i 4 191
O bitter consequence, That Edward still should live! iv 2 15
Hoping the consequence Will prove as bitter, black, and tragical iv 4 7
In the breath of bitter words let's smother My damned son iv 4 133
His noble friends and fellows, whom to leave Is only bitter to him *Hen. VIII.* ii 1 74
To leave a thousand-fold more bitter than 'Tis sweet at first to acquire ii 3 8
How tastes it? is it bitter? forty pence, no ii 3 89
The bitter disposition of the time Will have it so *Troi. and Cres.* iv 1 48
You are too bitter to your countrywoman.—She's bitter to her country iv 1 67
These bitter tears, which now you see Filling the aged wrinkles in my cheeks *T. Andron.* iii 1 6
And made a brine-pit with our bitter tears iii 1 129
Losers will have leave To ease their stomachs with their bitter tongues iii 1 234
Preserve just so much strength in us As will revenge these bitter woes iii 2 3
Good grandsire, leave these bitter deep laments iii 2 46
So I might have your company in hell, But to torment you with my bitter tongue! v 1 150
Nor can I utter all our bitter grief v 3 89
Bitter. When it did taste the wormwood on the nipple Of my dug and felt it bitter, pretty fool, To see it tetchy! *Rom. and Jul.* i 3 31
This intrusion shall Now seeming sweet convert to bitter gall i 5 94
Thy wit is a very bitter sweeting; it is a most sharp sauce ii 4 83
Come, bitter conduct, come, unsavoury guide! v 3 116
'Tis bitter cold, And I am sick at heart *Hamlet* i 1 8
I am pigeon-liver'd and lack gall To make oppression bitter ii 2 606
And do such bitter business as the day Would quake to look on iii 2 409
This policy and reverence of age makes the world bitter to the best of our times *Lear* i 2 49
A bitter fool!—Dost thou know the difference, my boy, between a bitter fool and a sweet fool? i 4 150
The sweet and bitter fool Will presently appear i 4 158
My spirit and my place have in them power To make this bitter to thee *Othello* i 1 104
The bloody book of law You shall yourself read in the bitter letter i 3 68
Shall be to him shortly as bitter as coloquintida i 3 355
There's other work in hand: I see a thing Bitter to me as death *Cymbeline* v 5 104
Bitter torture shall Winnow the truth from falsehood v 5 133
Bitterest. I have deserved All tongues to talk their bitterest *W. Tale* iii 2 217
On a dissension of a doit, break out To bitterest enmity. *Coriolanus* iv 4 18
All the bitterest terms That ever ear did hear to such effect *T. Andron.* ii 3 110
Bitterly. My poor mistress, moved therewithal, Wept bitterly *T. G. of Ver.* iv 4 176
And she will speak most bitterly and strange *Meas. for Meas.* v 1 36
The north-east wind, Which then blew bitterly against our faces *Richard II.* i 4 7
I know not whether to depart in silence, Or bitterly to speak in your reproof, Best fitteth my degree *Richard III.* iii 7 142
More bitterly could I expostulate, Save that, for reverence to some alive iii 7 192
Hear me speak.—You speak too bitterly iv 4 180
They vent reproaches Most bitterly on you *Hen. VIII.* iv 2 24
A parlous knock; and it cried bitterly *Rom. and Jul.* i 3 54
Some consequence yet hanging in the stars Shall bitterly begin his fearful date With this night's revels i 4 108
Bitterness. Joy could not show itself modest enough without a badge of bitterness *Much Ado* i 1 23
Say that you love me not, but say not so In bitterness *As Y. Like It* iii 5 3
Contempt nor bitterness Were in his pride or sharpness *All's Well* i 2 36
It yields nought but shame and bitterness *K. John* iii 4 111
You do measure the heat of our livers with the bitterness of your galls *2 Hen. IV.* i 2 198
His curses, then from bitterness of soul Denounced against thee *Rich. III.* i 3 179
Shall we be thus afflicted in his wreaks, His fits, his frenzy, and his bitterness? *T. Andron.* iv 4 12
And what's to come of my despised time Is nought but bitterness *Othello* i 1 163
The bitterness of it I now belch from my heart *Cymbeline* iii 5 137
Bitter-searching. I would invent as bitter-searching terms *2 Hen. VI.* iii 2 311
Bitumed. We have a chest beneath the hatches, caulked and bitumed ready *Pericles* iii 1 72
How close 'tis caulk'd and bitumed! iii 2 56
Blab. When my tongue blabs, then let mine eyes not see *T. Night* i 2 63
Beaufort's red sparkling eyes blab his heart's malice *2 Hen. VI.* iii 1 154
Cannot choose But they must blab— Hath he said any thing? *Othello* iv 1 29
Blabbed. Why have I blabb'd? who shall be true to us? *Troi. and Cres.* iii 2 132
O, that delightful engine of her thoughts, That blabb'd them with such pleasing eloquence! *T. Andron.* iii 1 83
Blabbing. The gaudy, blabbing and remorseful day *2 Hen. VI.* iv 1 1
Black. Though ne'er so black, say they have angels' faces *T. G. of Ver.* iii 1 103
Why, man, how black?—Why, as black as ink iii 1 287
Now she is become as black as I iv 4 161
Fairies, black, grey, green, and white *Mer. Wives* v 5 41
If black, why, Nature drawing of an antique, Made a foul blot *Much Ado* iii 1 63
Which indeed is not under white and black v 1 314
No face is fair that is not full so black *L. L. Lost* iv 3 253
Black is the badge of hell, The hue of dungeons and the suit of night iv 3 254
O, if in black my lady's brows be deck'd iv 3 258
Therefore is she born to make black fair iv 3 261
Therefore red, that would avoid dispraise, Paints itself black, to imitate her brow iv 3 265
To look like her are chimney-sweepers black iv 3 266
Beetles black, approach not near *M. N. Dream* ii 2 22
The ousel cock so black of hue, With orange-tawny bill iii 1 128
O grim-look'd night! O night with hue so black! v 1 171
All the pictures fairest lined Are but black to Rosalind *As Y. Like It* iii 2 98
He said mine eyes were black and my hair black iii 5 130
Black and fearful On the opposer *All's Well* iii 1 5
Not black in my mind, though yellow in my legs *T. Night* iii 4 28
Were they false As o'er-dyed blacks, as wind, as waters *W. Tale* i 2 132
Lawn as white as driven snow; Cyprus black as e'er was crow iv 4 221
Thou'rt damn'd as black—nay, nothing is so black *K. John* iv 3 121
Whose black contagious breath Already smokes v 4 33
News fitting to the night, Black, fearful, comfortless and horrible v 6 20
So heinous, black, obscene a deed! *Richard II.* iv 1 131
Mourn with me for that I do lament, And put on sullen black incontinent v 6 48
Hung be the heavens with black, yield day to night! *1 Hen. VI.* i 1 1
We mourn in black: why mourn we not in blood? i 1 17
What colour is my gown of?—Black, forsooth: coal-black as jet *2 Hen. VI.* ii 1 112
His face is black and full of blood, His eyeballs further out than when he lived iii 2 168
And wrap our bodies in black mourning gowns *3 Hen. VI.* ii 1 161
I spy a black, suspicious, threatening cloud v 3 4
Hoping the consequence Will prove as bitter, black, and tragical *Richard III.* iv 4 7
That dye is on me Which makes my whitest part black *Hen. VIII.* i 1 209
Is become as black As if besmear'd in hell i 2 123
Our heads are some brown, some black, some auburn, some bald *Coriol.* ii 3 20
Aaron will have his soul black like his face *T. Andron.* iii 1 206
It was a black ill-favour'd fly, Like to the empress' Moor iii 2 66
A joyless, dismal, black, and sorrowful issue iv 2 66
Is black so base a hue? Sweet blowse, you are a beauteous blossom, sure iv 2 71
Black and portentous must this humour prove *Rom. and Jul.* i 1 147
These happy masks that kiss fair ladies' brows Being black put us in mind they hide the fair i 1 237
Come, civil night, Thou sober-suited matron, all in black iii 2 11
This [gold] will make black white, foul fair, Wrong right *T. of Athens* iv 3 28
Stars, hide your fires; Let not light see my black and deep desires *Macb* i 4 51
How now, you secret, black, and midnight hags! iv 1 48
The devil damn thee black, thou cream-faced loon! v 3 11

Black. Nor customary suits of solemn black . . . . . *Hamlet* i 2 78
He whose sable arms, Black as his purpose, did the night resemble . ii 2 475
Nay then, let the devil wear black, for I'll have a suit of sables . iii 2 138
Thoughts black, hands apt, drugs fit, and time agreeing . . . iii 2 266
There I see such black and grained spots As will not leave their tinct . iii 4 90
Look'd black upon me ; struck me with her tongue, Most serpent-like *Lear* ii 4 162
Be thy mouth or black or white, Tooth that poisons if it bite . . iii 6 69
Your son-in-law is far more fair than black . . . . *Othello* i 3 291
If she be black, and thereto have a wit, She'll find a white that shall her blackness fit . . . . ii 1 133
Haply, for I am black And have not those soft parts of conversation . iii 3 263
Her name, that was as fresh As Dian's visage, is now begrimed and black iii 3 387
Think on me, That am with Phœbus' amorous pinches black? *A. and C.* i 5 28
O damn'd paper ! Black as the ink that's on thee ! . . . *Cymbeline* iii 2 20
Black a day. Never was seen so black a day as this . *Rom. and Jul.* iv 5 53
Black agents. Whiles night's black agents to their preys do rouse *Macbeth* iii 2 53
Black and blue. Is beaten black and blue, that you cannot see a white spot about her . . . . *Mer. Wives* iv 5 115
What tellest thou me of black and blue? I was beaten myself into all the colours of the rainbow . . . . iv 5 117
They'll suck our breath or pinch us black and blue . *Com. of Errors* ii 2 194
We will fool him black and blue : shall we not? . . *T. Night* ii 5 12
Black and swart. And, whereas I was black and swart before, With those clear rays which she infused on me That beauty am I bless'd with which you see . . . . *1 Hen. VI.* i 2 84
Black and white. Though the truth of it stands off as gross As black and white . . . . *Hen. V.* ii 2 104
Black angel. Croak not, black angel ; I have no food for thee . *Lear* iii 6 33
Black as Acheron. With drooping fog as black as Acheron *M. N. Dream* iii 2 357
Black as death. O wretched state ! O bosom black as death ! *Hamlet* iii 3 67
Black as ebony. By heaven, thy love is black as ebony . . *L. L. Lost* iv 3 247
Black as hell. And that his soul may be as damn'd and black As hell, whereto it goes . . . . *Hamlet* iii 3 94
Black as incest. Her face was to mine eye beyond all wonder ; The rest—hark in thine ear—as black as incest . . . *Pericles* i 2 76
Black as ink. How black ?—Why, as black as ink . . *T. G. of Ver.* iii 1 288
Black as jet. Two proper palfreys, black as jet . . . *T. Andron.* v 2 50
Black as Vulcan in the smoke of war . . . . . *T. Night* v 1 56
Black beard. A black beard will turn white . . . . *Hen. V.* v 2 168
Black brows, they say, Become some women best . . . *W. Tale* ii 1 8
Here walk I in the black brow of night, To find you out . . *K. John* v 6 17
Black-browed. Must for aye consort with black-brow'd night *M. N. Dr.* iii 2 387
Come, gentle night, come, loving, black-brow'd night . *Rom. and Jul.* iii 2 20
Black cloud. Yond same black cloud, yond huge one, looks like a foul bombard . . . . *Tempest* ii 2 20
Black coffin. Not a flower sweet On my black coffin let there be strown *T. Night* ii 4 61
Black complexion. Hath now this dread and black complexion smear'd With heraldry more dismal . . . . *Hamlet* ii 2 477
Black-cornered. When the day serves, before black-corner'd night, Find what thou want'st . . . . *T. of Athens* v 1 47
Black day. A black day will it be to somebody . . *Richard III.* v 3 280
Black defiance. As black defiance As heart can think . *Troi. and Cres.* iv 1 12
Black despair. And from his bosom purge this black despair ! *2 Hen. VI.* iii 3 23
I'll join with black despair against my soul . . *Richard III.* ii 2 36
Black dog. Canst thou say all this, and never blush ?—Ay, like a black dog, as the saying is . . . . *T. Andron.* v 1 122
Black envy. No black envy Shall mark my grave . . *Hen. VIII.* ii 1 85
Black Ethiope. The device he bears upon his shield Is a black Ethiope reaching at the sun . . . . *Pericles* ii 2 20
Black eye. Stabbed with a white wench's black eye . *Rom. and Jul.* ii 4 14
Black-faced Clifford shook his sword at him . . *Richard III.* i 2 159
Black fate. This day's black fate on more days doth depend *R. and J.* iii 1 124
Black-Friars. The most convenient place that I can think of For such receipt of learning is Black-Friars . . . . *Hen. VIII.* ii 2 139
Black funeral. All things that we ordained festival, Turn from their office to black funeral . . . . *Rom. and Jul.* iv 5 85
Black George Barnes, and Francis Pickbone . . . *2 Hen. IV.* iii 2 22
Black gown. I'll change my black gown for a faithful friend . *L. L. Lost* v 2 844
The surplice of humility over the black gown of a big heart . *All's Well* i 3 99
Black Hecate. Ere to black Hecate's summons The shard-borne beetle with his drowsy hums Hath rung night's yawning peal . *Macbeth* iii 2 41
Black intelligencer. Richard yet lives, hell's black intelligencer *Richard III.* iv 4 71
Black legs. For all the water in the ocean Can never turn the swan's black legs to white . . . . *T. Andron.* iv 2 102
Black Macbeth Will seem as pure as snow . . . . *Macbeth* iv 3 52
Black magician. What black magician conjures up this fiend? *Richard III.* i 2 34
Black mantle. Cover'd with the night's black mantle . . *3 Hen. VI.* iv 2 22
Come, civil night, . . . Hood my unmann'd blood, bating in my cheeks, With thy black mantle . . . . . . *Rom. and Jul.* iii 2 15
Black masks. These black masks Proclaim an enshield beauty *M. for M.* ii 4 79
Black matter. If these men do not die well, it will be a black matter for the king that led them to it . . . . . . *Hen. V.* iv 1 151
Black men are pearls in beauteous ladies' eyes . . . *T. G. of Ver.* v 2 12
Black-Monday. Then it was not for nothing that my nose fell a-bleeding on Black-Monday . . . . *Mer. of Venice* ii 5 25
Black mouth. He had a black mouth that said other . . *Hen. VIII.* i 3 58
Black name. That black name, Edward, Black Prince . . *Hen. V.* ii 4 56
Black Nemesis. Your kingdom's terror and black Nemesis *1 Hen. VI.* iv 7 78
Black night o'ershade thy day, and death thy life ! . . *Richard III.* i 2 131
Acts of black night, abominable deeds . . . . *T. Andron.* v 1 64
Black ones. Told me I had white hairs in my beard ere the black ones were there . . . . *Lear* iv 6 99
Black-oppressing. I did commend the black-oppressing humour *L. L. Lost* i 1 234
Black Othello. To the health of black Othello . . . *Othello* ii 3 32
Black ousel. Alas, a black ousel, cousin Shallow ! . *2 Hen. IV.* iii 2 9
Black pagans. Streaming the ensign of the Christian cross Against black pagans . . . . *Richard II.* iv 1 95
Black Prince. What prince is that?—The black prince, sir ; alias, the prince of darkness . . . . *All's Well* iv 5 44
Rescued the Black Prince, that young Mars of men . *Richard II.* ii 3 101
Edward the Black Prince, Who on the French ground play'd a tragedy *Hen. V.* i 2 105
Captived by the hand Of that black name, Edward, Black Prince of Wales . . . . ii 4 56
Your great-uncle Edward the Black Prince of Wales . . . iv 7 97
Edward the Black Prince died before his father . . *2 Hen. VI.* ii 2 18
Black ram. An old black ram Is tupping your white ewe . *Othello* i 1 88
Black scandal. If black scandal or foul-faced reproach Attend the sequel of your imposition . . . . *Richard III.* iii 7 231
Black scruples. This noble passion, Child of integrity, hath from my soul Wiped the black scruples . . . . . *Macbeth* iv 3 116
Black scut. My doe with the black scut ! . . . *Mer. Wives* v 5 20
Black sentence. In our black sentence and proscription . *J. Cæsar* iv 1 17
Black silk. 'Tis not your inky brows, your black silk hair *As Y. Like It* iii 5 46
Black slave. Look, how the black slave smiles upon the father *T. Andron.* iv 2 120
Black soul. And a' said it was a black soul burning in hell-fire *Hen. V.* ii 3 44
Black storm. I will stir up in England some black storm *2 Hen. VI.* iii 1 349
Black spirits and white, Red spirits and grey . . . . *Macbeth* iv 1 43
Black strife. Some twenty of them fought in this black strife *R. and J.* iii 1 183
Black tidings. Letters came last night To a dear friend of the good Duke of York's, That tell black tidings . . . . *Richard II.* iii 4 71
Black toad. Engenders the black toad and adder blue . *T. of Athens* iv 3 181
Black vapour. Like the south Borne with black vapour . . *2 Hen. IV.* ii 4 393
Black veil. These eyes, that now are dimm'd with death's black veil *3 Hen. VI.* v 2 16
Black vengeance. Arise, black vengeance, from thy hollow cell ! *Othello* iii 3 447
Black vesper's. They are black vesper's pageants . . *Ant. and Cleo.* iv 14 8
Black villany. No visor does become black villany So well as soft and tender flattery . . . . *Pericles* iv 4 44
Black weight. Best in despair die under their black weight . *K. John* iii 1 297
Black word. Turn'd that black word death to banishment *Rom. and Jul.* iii 3 27
Black-a-moor. I care not an she were a black-a-moor . *Troi. and Cres.* i 1 80
Blackberries. If reasons were as plentiful as blackberries . *1 Hen. IV.* ii 4 265
Shall the blessed sun of heaven prove a micher and eat blackberries? . ii 4 450
Blackberry. Is not proved worth a blackberry . . . *Troi. and Cres.* v 4 13
Blacker. Such Ethiope words, blacker in their effect Than in their countenance . . . . *As Y. Like It* iv 3 35
Your brows are blacker ; yet black brows, they say, Become some women . . . . *W. Tale* ii 1 8
How his piety Does my deeds make the blacker ! . . . . iii 2 173
O, the more angel she, And you the blacker devil ! . . *Othello* v 2 131
Those men Blush not in actions blacker than the night . *Pericles* i 1 135
Blackest. The blackest news that ever thou heardest . *T. G. of Ver.* iii 1 285
Vows, to the blackest devil ! Conscience and grace, to the profoundest pit ! . . . . *Hamlet* iv 5 131
When devils will the blackest sins put on, They do suggest at first with heavenly shows . . . . *Othello* ii 3 357
Blackheath. You may imagine him upon Blackheath . *Hen. V.* v Prol. 16
Blackmere. Lord Strange of Blackmere, Lord Verdun of Alton *1 Hen. VI.* iv 7 65
Blackness. The raven chides blackness . . . *Troi. and Cres.* ii 3 221
If she be black, and thereto have a wit, She'll find a white that shall her blackness fit . . . . *Othello* ii 1 134
Seem as the spots of heaven, More fiery by night's blackness *A. and C.* i 4 13
To keep his bed of blackness unlaid ope . . . . *Pericles* i 2 89
Bladder. A plague of sighing and grief ! it blows a man up like a bladder *1 Hen. IV.* ii 4 366
Like little wanton boys that swim on bladders . . *Hen. VIII.* iii 2 359
Bladders full of imposthume, sciaticas, limekilns i' the palm *Tr. and Cr.* v 1 24
Green earthen pots, bladders and musty seeds . . *Rom. and Jul.* v 1 46
Blade. You break jests as braggarts do their blades, which, God be thanked, hurt not . . . . *Much Ado* v 1 190
Whereat, with blade, with bloody blameful blade, He bravely broach'd his boiling bloody breast . . . . . *M. N. Dream* v 1 147
Come, trusty sword ; Come, blade, my breast imbrue . . . v 1 351
Between two blades, which bears the better temper . *1 Hen. VI.* ii 4 13
And this thy son's blood cleaving to my blade Shall rust upon my weapon, till thy blood, Congeal'd with this, do make me wipe off both . . . . *3 Hen. VI.* i 3 50
With thy treacherous blade Unrip'dst the bowels of thy sovereign's son *Richard III.* i 4 211
Old Montague is come, And flourishes his blade in spite of me *R. and J.* i 1 85
Of breaches, ambuscadoes, Spanish blades, Of healths five-fathom deep i 4 84
A very good blade ! a very tall man ! . . . . . ii 4 31
I see thee still, And on thy blade and dudgeon gouts of blood *Macbeth* ii 1 46
Let fall thy blade on vulnerable crests ; I bear a charmed life . . v 8 11
Bladed. Decking with liquid pearl the bladed grass . *M. N. Dream* i 1 211
Though bladed corn be lodged and trees blown down . . *Macbeth* iv 1 55
Blain. Itches, blains, Sow all the Athenian bosoms ! . *T. of Athens* iv 1 28
Blame. I cannot blame thee, Who am myself attach'd with weariness *Tempest* iii 3 4
The one ne'er got me credit, the other mickle blame *Com. of Errors* iii 1 45
And I, to blame, have held him here too long . . . . iv 1 47
Then if she fear, or be to blame, By this you shall not know . *L. L. Lost* i 2 108
He hath made me a Christian.—Truly, the more to blame he *Mer. of Ven.* iii 5 23
You were to blame, I must be plain with you . . . . v 1 166
If this be so, why blame you me to love you? . . *As Y. Like It* v 2 109
I cannot blame thee now to weep ; For such an injury would vex a very saint, Much more a shrew . . . . . . *T. of Shrew* iii 2 27
Hath amazed me more Than I dare blame my weakness . *All's Well* ii 1 88
He has much worthy blame laid upon him for shaking off so good a wife iv 3 7
Shall render you no blame But rather make you thank your pains for it v 1 32
My high-repented blames, Dear sovereign, pardon to me . . . v 3 36
Whether I have been to blame or no, I know not . . . . v 3 129
Blame not this haste of mine. If you mean well, Now go with me *T. Night* iv 3 22
Nay, then I cannot blame his cousin king, That wish'd him on the barren mountains starve . . . . *1 Hen. IV.* i 3 158
I feel me much to blame, So idly to profane the precious time *2 Hen. IV.* ii 4 390
And gave me up to tears.—I blame you not . . . *Hen. V.* iv 6 32
Can you blame her then, being a maid yet rosed over with the virgin crimson of modesty? . . . . v 2 322
Must I still prevail, Or will you blame and lay the fault on me? *1 Hen. VI.* ii 1 57
Tush, that was but his fancy, blame him not . . . . iv 1 178
And shall my youth be guilty of such blame? . . . . iv 5 47
I cannot blame them all : what is't to them? . . . *2 Hen. VI.* i 1 220
Blame me not : 'Tis love I bear thy glories makes me speak *3 Hen. VI.* ii 1 157
I blame not her, she could say little less ; She had the wrong . iv 1 101
Yet in this one thing let me blame your grace, For choosing me . iv 6 30
Did not offend, nor were not worthy blame . . . . v 5 54
Are you all afraid? Alas, I blame you not ; for you are mortal *Rich. III.* i 2 44
I cannot blame her : by God's holy mother, She hath had too much wrong . . . . i 3 306
The king my uncle is to blame for this . . . . . ii 2 13
I'll bear thy blame And take thy office from thee, on my peril . v 1 25
Wrong hath but wrong, and blame the due of blame . . . v 1 29
I cannot blame his conscience . . . . . . *Hen. VIII.* ii 1 47
You are to blame, Knowing she will not lose her wonted greatness . iv 2 101

Blame. As I live, If the king blame me for't, I'll lay ye all By the heels . . . *Hen. VIII.* v 4 82
You blame Marcius for being proud? . . . *Coriolanus* ii 1 35
Who is't can blame him? Your enemies and his find something in him iv 6 105
If you fail in our request, the blame May hang upon your hardness . v 3 90
His own impatience Takes from Aufidius a great part of blame . v 6 147
You are to blame, my lord, to rate her so . . . . *Rom. and Jul.* iii 5 170
Ye've got a humour there Does not become a man; 'tis much to blame . . . *T. of Athens* i 2 27
Thou art true and honest; ingeniously I speak, No blame belongs to thee . . . ii 2 231
I am to blame to be thus waited for . . . . . . *J. Cæsar* ii 2 119
I blame you not for praising Cæsar so; But what compact mean you to have with us? . . . iii 1 214
You shall not in your funeral speech blame us, But speak all good you can devise of Cæsar . . . iii 1 245
Thou speak'st drowsily? Poor knave, I blame thee not; thou art o'er-watch'd. . . . iv 3 241
Even by the rule of that philosophy By which I did blame Cato . v 1 102
His absence, sir, Lays blame upon his promise . . *Macbeth* iii 4 44
Here abjure The taints and blames I laid upon myself . . . iv 3 124
Who then shall blame His pester'd senses to recoil and start? . . v 2 22
We are oft to blame in this . . . . *Hamlet* iii 1 46
Young men will do't, if they come to't; By cock, they are to blame . iv 5 62
And for his death no wind of blame shall breathe . . . iv 7 67
Thy mother's poison'd: I can no more: the king, the king's to blame . v 2 331
The contents, as in part I understand them, are to blame . *Lear* i 2 44
The duke's to blame in this; 'twill be ill taken . . . ii 2 166
'Tis on such ground, and to such wholesome end, As clears her from all blame . . . ii 4 147
'Tis his own blame; hath put himself from rest, And must needs taste his folly . . . ii 4 293
His wits begin to unsettle.—Canst thou blame him? His daughters seek his death . . . iii 4 167
Which men May blame, but not control . . . . . iii 7 27
Leave, gentle wax; and, manners, blame us not . . . . iv 6 264
To lay the blame upon her own despair, That she fordid herself . v 3 254
Destruction on my head, if my bad blame Light on the man! *Othello* i 3 177
Who let us not therefore blame . . . . . . ii 3 16
He thought 'twas witchcraft—but I am much to blame . . iii 3 211
I am to blame.—Why do you speak so faintly? Are you not well? . iii 3 282
The handkerchief!—In sooth, you are to blame . . . iii 4 97
If haply you my father do suspect An instrument of this your calling back, Lay not your blame on me . . . iv 2 46
Let nobody blame him; his scorn I approve,—Nay, that's not next . iv 3 52
But, heavens know, Some men are much to blame . . *Cymbeline* i 6 77
Our great court Made me to blame in memory . . . . iii 5 51
And brings the dire occasion in his arms Of what we blame him for . iv 2 197
No blame be to you, sir; for all was lost, But that the heavens fought. v 3 3
Though you did love this youth, I blame ye not; You had a motive for't v 5 267
He will . . . Blame both my lord and me, that we have taken No care to your best courses . . . *Pericles* iv 1 38

Blamed. When the players are all dead, there need none to be blamed . . . *M. N. Dream* v 1 364
That was not to be blamed in the command of the service . *All's Well* iii 6 54
More it would content me To have her honour true than your suspicion, Be blamed for't how you might . . . *W. Tale* ii 1 161
You that are blamed for it alike with us, Know you of this? . *Hen. VIII.* i 2 39
Which I have rather blamed as mine own jealous curiosity . *Lear* i 4 74

Blameful. With bloody blameful blade, He bravely broach'd his boiling bloody breast . . . *M. N. Dream* v 1 147
Thy mother took into her blameful bed Some stern untutor'd churl . . . *2 Hen. VI.* iii 2 212
Is not the causer of the timeless deaths Of these Plantagenets, Henry and Edward, As blameful as the executioner? . . *Richard III.* i 2 119

Blameless. And so far blameless proves my enterprise . *M. N. Dream* iii 2 350
Hermione is chaste; Polixenes blameless . . . *W. Tale* iii 2 134

Blanc. From Port le Blanc, a bay In Brittany . . . *Richard II.* ii 1 277

Blanch. That daughter there of Spain, the Lady Blanch . . *K. John* ii 1 423
If lusty love should go in quest of beauty, Where should he find it fairer than in Blanch? . . . ii 1 427
If zealous love should go in search of virtue, Where should he find it purer than in Blanch? . . . ii 1 429
Whose veins bound richer blood than Lady Blanch? . . . ii 1 431
Shall Lewis have Blanch, and Blanch those provinces? It is not so . iii 1 3
Lewis marry Blanch! O boy, then where art thou? . . . iii 1 34
You, in the right of Lady Blanch your wife, May then make all the claim that Arthur did . . . iii 4 142
Tray, Blanch, and Sweet-heart, see, they bark at me . . *Lear* iii 6 66

Blanched. When now I think you can behold such sights, And keep the natural ruby of your cheeks, When mine is blanch'd with fear *Macb.* iii 4 116

Blank. He hath a thousand of these letters, writ with blank space for different names . . . *Mer. Wives* ii 1 77
And what's her history?—A blank, my lord . . . *T. Night* ii 4 113
For his thoughts, Would they were blanks, rather than fill'd with me! iii 1 115
Out of the blank And level of my brain, plot-proof. . . *W. Tale* ii 3 5
Our substitutes at home shall have blank charters . . *Richard II.* i 4 48
Daily new exactions are devised, As blanks, benevolences . . ii 1 250
Omission to do what is necessary Seals a commission to a blank of danger; And danger, like an ague, subtly taints . *Troi. and Cres.* iii 3 231
The one almost as infinite as all, The other blank as nothing . iv 5 81
It is lots to blanks, My name hath touch'd your ears . *Coriolanus* v 2 10
Each opposite that blanks the face of joy Meet what I would have well and it destroy! . . . *Hamlet* iii 2 230
Whose whisper o'er the world's diameter, As level as the cannon to his blank, Transports his poison'd shot, may miss our name . . . iv 1 42
Let me still remain The true blank of thine eye . . *Lear* i 1 161
And stood within the blank of his displeasure For my free speech *Othello* iii 4 128

Blank verse. Run smoothly in the even road of a blank verse *Much Ado* v 2 34
Nay, then, God be wi' you, an you talk in blank verse . *As Y. Like It* iv 1 32
The lady shall say her mind freely, or the blank verse shall halt for't . . . *Hamlet* ii 2 339

Blanket. A rascally slave! I will toss the rogue in a blanket *2 Hen. IV.* ii 4 241
Nor heaven peep through the blanket of the dark, To cry 'Hold!' *Macbeth* i 5 54
A blanket, in the alarm of fear caught up . . . *Hamlet* ii 2 532
My face I'll grime with filth; Blanket my loins . . *Lear* ii 3 10
He reserved a blanket, else we had been all shamed . . iii 4 67
If Cæsar can hide the sun from us with a blanket . *Cymbeline* iii 1 44

Blaspheme. You do blaspheme the good in mocking me . *Meas. for Meas.* i 4 38
Brother of England, you blaspheme in this . . . *K. John* iii 1 161
Stands accursed, And does blaspheme his breed . *Macbeth* iv 3 108

Blaspheming God and cursing men on earth . . . . *2 Hen. VI.* iii 2 372
Liver of blaspheming Jew, Gall of goat, and slips of yew *Macbeth* iv 1 26

Blasphemous. You bawling, blasphemous, incharitable dog! . *Tempest* i 1 43

Blasphemy, That swear'st grace o'erboard . . . . . v 1 218
That in the captain's but a choleric word, Which in the soldier is flat blasphemy.—Art avised o' that? . . *Meas. for Meas.* ii 2 131
I would speak blasphemy ere bid you fly: But fly you must . *2 Hen. VI.* v 2 85

Blasts the tree and takes the cattle And makes milch-kine yield blood . . . *Mer. Wives* iv 4 32
So lean, that blasts of January Would blow you through and through . . . *W. Tale* iv 4 111
The fann'd snow that's bolted By the northern blasts twice o'er . iv 4 376
But when the blast of war blows in our ears, Then imitate the action of the tiger; Stiffen the sinews . . . *Hen. V.* iii 1 5
Now let the general trumpet blow his blast! . . *2 Hen. VI.* v 2 43
Lest with my sighs or tears I blast or drown King Edward's fruit . . . *3 Hen. VI.* iv 4 23
And of our labours thou shalt reap the gain.—I'll blast his harvest . v 7 21
They that stand high have many blasts to shake them . *Richard III.* i 3 259
Come, blow thy blast . . . . *Coriolanus* i 4 12
And pity, like a naked new-born babe, Striding the blast . *Macbeth* i 7 22
Lo, where it comes again! I'll cross it, though it blast me . *Hamlet* i 1 127
Bring with thee airs from heaven or blasts from hell . . . i 4 41
This project Should have a back or second, that might hold, If this should blast . . . iv 7 155
Blasts and fogs upon thee! . . . . *Lear* i 4 321
Infect her beauty, You fen-suck'd fogs, drawn by the powerful sun, To fall and blast her pride! . . . ii 4 170
Which the impetuous blasts, with eyeless rage, Catch in their fury iii 1 8
For one blast of thy minikin mouth, Thy sheep shall take no harm . iii 6 45
The wretch that thou hast blown unto the worst Owes nothing to thy blasts . . . iv 1 9
A fuller blast ne'er shook our battlements . . . *Othello* ii 1 6
Trumpeters, With brazen din blast you the city's ear . *Ant. and Cleo.* iv 8 36
A spark, To which that blast gives heat and stronger glowing *Pericles* i 2 41
Virtue preserved from fell destruction's blast, Led on by heaven v 3 Gower 89

Blasted. Every part about you blasted with antiquity . . *2 Hen. IV.* i 2 208
Thus are my blossoms blasted in the bud . . . *2 Hen. VI.* iii 1 89
Behold mine arm Is, like a blasted sapling, wither'd up . *Richard III.* iii 4 71
Be men like blasted woods, And may diseases lick up their false bloods! . . . *T. of Athens* iv 3 538
Or why Upon this blasted heath you stop our way? . . *Macbeth* i 3 77
That unmatch'd form and feature of blown youth Blasted with ecstasy . . . *Hamlet* iii 1 168
With Hecate's ban thrice blasted, thrice infected . . . iii 2 269
To see't mine eyes are blasted . . . . . *Ant. and Cleo.* iii 10 4
You were half blasted ere I knew you . . . . . iii 13 105
And find Our paragon to all reports thus blasted . . . *Pericles* iv 1 36

Blasting in the bud, Losing his verdure even in the prime *T. G. of Ver.* i 1 48
Shall we thus permit A blasting and a scandalous breath to fall On him so near us? . . . *Meas. for Meas.* v 1 122
Your husband; like a mildew'd ear, Blasting his wholesome brother . . . *Hamlet* iii 4 65

Blastment. Contagious blastments are most imminent . . . . i 3 42

Blaze. Natural rebellion, done i' the blaze of youth . . *All's Well* v 3 6
His rash fierce blaze of riot cannot last . . . *Richard II.* ii 1 33
I need not add more fuel to your fire, For well I wot ye blaze *3 Hen. VI.* v 4 71
Hector in his blaze of wrath subscribes To tender objects *Troi. and Cres.* iv 5 105
And their blaze Shall darken him for ever . . . *Coriolanus* i 1 274
The main blaze of it is past, but a small thing would make it flame again iv 3 20
Till we can find a time To blaze your marriage . . *Rom. and Jul.* iii 3 151
The heavens themselves blaze forth the death of princes *J. Cæsar* ii 2 31
These blazes, daughter, Giving more light than heat, extinct in both . . . *Hamlet* i 3 117
I have a speech of fire, that fain would blaze, But that this folly douts it iv 7 191

Blazed. And ever, as it blazed, they threw on him Great pails of puddled mire . . . *Com. of Errors* v 1 172
When every room Hath blazed with lights and bray'd with minstrelsy . . . *T. of Athens* ii 2 170

Blazing. An we might have a good woman born but one every blazing star, or at an earthquake . . . *All's Well* i 3 91
Each one already blazing by our meeds . . . *3 Hen. VI.* ii 1 36

Blazon. With loyal blazon, evermore be blest! . . *Mer. Wives* v 5 68
I think your blazon to be true . . . . . *Much Ado* ii 1 307
Thy limbs, actions and spirit, Do give thee five-fold blazon . *T. Night* i 5 312
If the measure of thy joy Be heap'd like mine and that thy skill be more To blazon it . . . *Rom. and Jul.* ii 6 26
This eternal blazon must not be To ears of flesh and blood . *Hamlet* i 5 21

Blazonest. Thou divine Nature, how thyself thou blazon'st In these two princely boys! . . . *Cymbeline* iv 2 170

Blazoning our injustice every where . . . *T. Andron.* iv 4 18
One that excels the quirks of blazoning pens . . . *Othello* ii 1 63

Bleach. And maidens bleach their summer smocks . *L. L. Lost* v 2 916

Bleaching. Behold what honest clothes you send forth to bleaching! . . . *Mer. Wives* iv 2 126
The white sheet bleaching on the hedge . . . *W. Tale* iv 3 5

Bleak. Thou liest in the bleak air: come, I will bear thee to some shelter . . . *As Y. Like It* ii 6 16
When virtue's steely bones Look bleak i' the cold wind . . *All's Well* i 1 115
Nor entreat the north To make his bleak winds kiss my parched lips . . . *K. John* v 7 40
What, think'st That the bleak air, thy boisterous chamberlain, Will put thy shirt on warm? . . . *T. of Athens* iv 3 222
Alack, the night comes on, and the bleak winds Do sorely ruffle . *Lear* ii 4 303
Our lodgings, standing bleak upon the sea, Shook . . *Pericles* iii 2 14

Bleared. Dardanian wives, With bleared visages . . *Mer. of Venice* iii 2 59
While counterfeit supposes blear'd thine eyne . . *T. of Shrew* v 1 120
The bleared sights Are spectacled to see him . . *Coriolanus* ii 1 221

Bleat. Will never answer a calf when he bleats . . *Much Ado* iii 3 76
Much like to you, for you have just his bleat . . . v 4 51
Bleat softly then; the butcher hears you cry . . *L. L. Lost* v 2 255
You may as well use question with the wolf Why he hath made the ewe bleat for the lamb . . . *Mer. of Venice* iv 1 74
We were as twinn'd lambs that did frisk i' the sun, And bleat the one at the other . . . *W. Tale* i 2 68

Bleated. Jupiter Became a bull, and bellow'd; the green Neptune A ram, and bleated . . . iv 4 29

Bled. The lioness had torn some flesh away, Which all this while had bled . . . *As Y. Like It* iv 3 149

Bled. For that I have not wash'd My nose that bled *Coriolanus* i 9 48
I urged our old acquaintance, and the drops That we have bled together v 1 11
Bleed. My heart bleeds To think o' the teen that I have turn'd you to *Tempest* i 2 63
If you prick us, do we not bleed? if you tickle us, do we not laugh? *Mer. of Venice* iii 1 67
Have by some surgeon, Shylock, on your charge, To stop his wounds, lest he do bleed to death . . . . . . iv 1 258
Scratching her legs that one shall swear she bleeds . . *T. of Shrew* Ind. 2 60
Weep I cannot, But my heart bleeds; and most accursed am I *W. Tale* iii 3 52
I would fain say, bleed tears, for I am sure my heart wept blood . v 2 96
Bleed France, and peace ascend to heaven . *K. John* ii 1 86
Retaining but a quantity of life, Which bleeds away . . . v 4 24
Our doctors say this is no month to bleed . *Richard II.* i 1 157
To tickle our noses with spear-grass to make them bleed . 1 *Hen. IV.* ii 4 341
Go you with him.—Not I, my lord, unless I did bleed too . v 4 4
My heart bleeds inwardly that my father is so sick . 2 *Hen. IV.* ii 2 51
Have brought ourselves into a burning fever, And we must bleed for it iv 1 57
That they lost France and made his England bleed . *Hen. V.* Epil. 12
If I, my lord, for my opinion bleed, Opinion shall be surgeon to my hurt . . . . . . 1 *Hen. VI.* ii 4 52
Dead Henry's wounds Open their congeal'd mouths and bleed afresh! *Richard III.* i 2 56
Let Paris bleed: 'tis but a scar to scorn *Troi. and Cres.* i 1 114
A good quarrel to draw emulous factions and bleed to death upon ii 3 80
Look, how thy wounds do bleed at many vents! . v 3 82
Can the son's eye behold his father bleed? There's meed for meed! *T. Andron.* v 3 65
O heavens! O wife, look how our daughter bleeds! . *Rom. and Jul.* v 3 202
I bleed inwardly for my lord . . . . . *T. of Athens* i 2 211
But, alas, Cæsar must bleed for it! . . . *J. Cæsar* ii 1 171
How many times shall Cæsar bleed in sport! . . . iii 1 114
Did not great Julius bleed for justice' sake? . . . iv 3 19
If he do bleed, I'll gild the faces of the grooms withal *Macbeth* ii 2 55
Bleed, bleed, poor country! Great tyranny! lay thou thy basis sure iv 3 31
I think our country sinks beneath the yoke; It weeps, it bleeds . iv 3 40
As easy mayst thou the intrenchant air With thy keen sword impress as make me bleed . . . . . v 8 10
They bleed on both sides . . . . *Hamlet* v 2 315
How does the queen?—She swounds to see them bleed . . v 2 319
Look, sir, I bleed.—Where is the villain? . . *Lear* ii 1 43
Regan, I bleed apace: Untimely comes this hurt: give me your arm iii 7 97
Bless thy sweet eyes, they bleed . . . . iv 1 56
At this time We sweat and bleed . . . . v 3 55
I bleed still; I am hurt to the death . . *Othello* ii 3 164
Nobody come? then shall I bleed to death . . . v 1 45
I bleed, sir; but not kill'd . . . . . v 2 288
The manner of their deaths? I do not see them bleed *Ant. and Cleo.* v 2 341
Which read and not expounded, 'tis decreed, As these before thee thou thyself shalt bleed . . . *Pericles* i 1 58
Bleedest. Withdraw thyself; thou bleed'st too much 1 *Hen. IV.* v 4 2
Worthy sir, thou bleed'st; Thy exercise hath been too violent *Coriolanus* i 5 15
Thou dost breathe; Hast heavy substance; bleed'st not; speak'st *Lear* iv 6 52
Thou bleed'st apace.—I had a wound here that was like a T, but now 'tis made an H . . . *Ant. and Cleo.* iv 7 6
Bleedeth. If God doth give successful end To this debate that bleedeth at our doors . . . . . 2 *Hen. IV.* iv 4 2
Bleeding. Then it was not for nothing that my nose fell a-bleeding on Black-Monday last at six o'clock i' the morning *Mer. of Venice* ii 5 25
Whose sons lie scattered on the bleeding ground . *K. John* ii 1 304
And spit it bleeding in his high disgrace . *Richard II.* i 1 194
He is come to open The purple testament of bleeding war . iii 3 94
And to the fire-eyed maid of smoky war All hot and bleeding will we offer them . . . . . 1 *Hen. IV.* iv 1 115
I saw him dead, Breathless and bleeding on the ground . . v 4 137
He doth bestride a bleeding land, Gasping for life . . 2 *Hen. IV.* i 1 207
That never war advance His bleeding sword . *Hen. V.* v 2 383
Prick not your finger as you pluck it off, Lest bleeding you do paint the white rose red . . . . 1 *Hen. VI.* ii 4 50
Well, I'll find friends to wear my bleeding roses . . ii 4 72
Who finds the heifer dead and bleeding fresh? . 2 *Hen. VI.* iii 2 188
Overgorged With gobbets of thy mother's bleeding heart . iv 1 85
Tears in her eyes, The bleeding witness of her hatred by *Richard III.* i 2 234
So she may live unscarr'd of bleeding slaughter . iv 4 209
Send to her, by the man that slew her brothers, A pair of bleeding hearts . . . . . . iv 4 272
Dismiss the controversy bleeding . *Coriolanus* ii 1 86
Five times he hath return'd Bleeding to Rome . *T. Andron.* i 1 34
And Juliet bleeding, warm, and newly dead *Rom. and Jul.* v 3 175
Nor sight of priests in holy vestments bleeding, Shall pierce a jot *T. of Athens* iv 3 125
See you but our hands And this the bleeding business they have done *J. Cæsar* iii 1 168
O, pardon me, thou bleeding piece of earth, That I am meek and gentle iii 1 254
Would to the bleeding and the grim alarm Excite the mortified man *Macbeth* v 2 4
With less remorse than Pyrrhus' bleeding sword Now falls on Priam *Hamlet* ii 2 513
I'll fetch some flax and whites of eggs To apply to his bleeding face *Lear* iii 7 107
Met I my father with his bleeding rings, Their precious stones new lost v 3 189
The testimonies whereof lie bleeding in me . . *Cymbeline* iii 4 23
Thou movest no less with thy complaining than Thy master in bleeding iv 2 376
Bleeding-new. So they were bleeding-new, my lord, there's no meat like em . . . . . *T. of Athens* i 2 80
Blemish. On their sustaining garments not a blemish *Tempest* i 2 218
His integrity Stands without blemish . . *Meas. for Meas.* v 1 108
In nature there's no blemish but the mind . *T. Night* iii 4 401
I'll give no blemish to her honour, none . *W. Tale* i 2 341
Whilst I remember Her and her virtues, I cannot forget My blemishes in them . . . . . . v 1 8
Speaking thick, which nature made his blemish . 2 *Hen. IV.* ii 3 24
You should not blemish it, if I stood by *Richard III.* i 2 128
Say this becomes him,—As his composure must be rare indeed Whom these things cannot blemish . . *Ant. and Cleo.* i 4 23
Read not my blemishes in the world's report . . ii 3 5
Therefore, he Does pity, as constrained blemishes, Not as deserved . iii 13 59
Vanish, or I shall give thee thy deserving, And blemish Cæsar's triumph iv 12 33
Blemish'd his gracious dam . . . *W. Tale* iii 2 199
Redeem from broking pawn the blemish'd crown . *Richard II.* ii 1 293
To the corruption of a blemish'd stock . . *Richard III.* iii 7 122

Blemished. The garter, blemish'd, pawn'd his knightly virtue *Richard III.* iv 4 370
Blench. Sometimes you do blench from this to that . *Meas. for Meas.* iv 5 5
Would I do this? Could man so blench? . . *W. Tale* i 2 333
Patience herself, what goddess e'er she be, Doth lesser blench at sufferance than I do . . . *Troi. and Cres.* i 1 28
There can be no evasion To blench from this and to stand firm by honour ii 2 68
I'll tent him to the quick: if he but blench, I know my course *Hamlet* ii 2 626
Blended. This blended knight, half Trojan and half Greek *Troi. and Cres.* iv 5 86
Both your voices blended, the great'st taste Most palates theirs *Coriol.* iii 1 103
Blent. Where every something, being blent together, Turns to a wild of nothing, save of joy . . *Mer. of Venice* iii 2 183
'Tis beauty truly blent, whose red and white Nature's own sweet and cunning hand laid on . . . *T. Night* i 5 257
Bless. That would not bless our Europe with your daughter . *Tempest* ii 1 124
Go with me To bless this twain, that they may prosperous be . iv 1 104
God bless them and make them his servants! . *Mer. Wives* ii 2 53
Bless you, sir! . . . . . . ii 2 160; iii 5 61
Bless thee, bully doctor! . . . . . ii 3 18
I will break thy pate across.—And he will bless that cross with other beating . . . . . *Com. of Errors* ii 1 79
If I can cross him any way, I bless myself every way *Much Ado* i 3 70
God bless me from a challenge! . . . . . v 1 145
God bless my ladies! are they all in love? . *L. L. Lost* ii 1 77
God bless the king!—What present hast thou there? . iv 3 189
In that hour, my lord, They did not bless us with one happy word v 2 370
Bless thee, Bottom! bless thee! thou art translated *M. N. Dream* iii 1 121
Bless it to all fair prosperity . . . . iv 1 95
You must say 'paragon:' a paramour is, God bless us, a thing of naught . . . . iv 2 14
He for a man, God warrant us; she for a woman, God bless us v 1 327
Hand in hand, with fairy grace, Will we sing, and bless this place v 1 407
And each several chamber bless, Through this palace, with sweet peace v 1 424
To him, father.—God bless your worship! *Mer. of Venice* ii 2 127
In religion, What damned error, but some sober brow Will bless it? iii 2 79
Bless you with such grace As 'longeth to a lover's blessed case! *T. of Shrew* iv 2 44
Bless our poor virginity from underminers and blowers up! *All's Well* i 1 131
Bless you, my fortunate lady! . . . . iii 4 14
Bless him at home in peace . . . . . iii 4 10
What angel shall Bless this unworthy husband? . . iii 4 26
O dear heaven, bless! Or, ere they meet, in me, O nature, cesse! v 3 71
Bless you, fair shrew.—And you too, sir . *T. Night* i 3 50
Now bless thyself: thou mettest with things dying . *W. Tale* iii 3 116
I bless the time When my good falcon made her flight across Thy father's ground . . . . . . iv 4 14
Bless me from marrying a usurer! . . . . iv 4 271
To bless the bed of majesty again With a sweet fellow to't . v 1 33
God bless your expedition! . . . 2 *Hen. IV.* i 2 249
You would bless you to hear what he said . . . ii 4 103
Now, the Lord bless that sweet face of thine! . . ii 4 317
The Lord bless you! God prosper your affairs! . . iii 2 312
God bless thy lungs, good knight . . . . v 5 9
The Lord in heaven bless thee, noble Harry! . *Hen. V.* iv 1 33
Why gentle Peace Should not expel these inconveniences And bless us with her former qualities . . . . . v 2 67
Which word thou shalt no sooner bless mine ear withal, but I will tell thee . . . . v 2 257
Saint Denis bless this happy stratagem! 1 *Hen. VI.* iii 2 18
O Lord bless me! I pray God! . . . 2 *Hen. VI.* ii 3 77
And himself Likely in time to bless a regal throne 3 *Hen. VI.* iv 6 74
O, Jesus bless us, he is born with teeth! . . . v 6 75
God bless your grace with health and happy days! *Richard III.* ii 1 18
God bless your grace! we see it, and will say it . iii 7 237
I, by attorney, bless thee from thy mother . . v 3 83
To taint that honour every good tongue blesses *Hen. VIII.* iii 1 55
Some spirit put this paper in the packet, To bless your eye withal iii 2 130
Heaven forgive me! Ever God bless your highness! . iii 2 136
Heaven bless thee! Thou hast the sweetest face I ever look'd on iv 1 42
The God of heaven Both now and ever bless her! . v 1 165
Bless me, what a fry of fornication is at door! . v 4 36
She shall be loved and fear'd: her own shall bless her . v 5 31
Our children's children Shall see this, and bless heaven . v 5 56
Heaven bless thee from a tutor! . *Troi. and Cres.* ii 3 32
You bless me, gods! . . . . *Coriolanus* iv 5 141
The gods bless you for your tidings . . . . v 4 61
O, bless me here with thy victorious hand! . . *T. Andron.* i 1 163
Commend me to thy mistress.—Now God in heaven bless thee! *Rom. and Jul.* ii 4 206
God in heaven bless her! You are to blame . . iii 5 169
So the gods bless me . . . . *T. of Athens* ii 2 166
Assurance bless your thoughts? . . . . ii 2 189
My present friends, as they are to me nothing, so in nothing bless them iii 6 94
This yellow slave [gold] Will knit and break religions, bless the accursed iv 3 34
One cried 'God bless us!' and 'Amen' the other *Macbeth* ii 2 27
I could not say 'Amen,' When they did say 'God bless us!' . ii 2 30
Bless you, fair dame! I am not to you known . . iv 2 65
God bless you, sir.—Let him bless thee too.—He shall, sir, an't please him . . . . *Hamlet* iv 6 6
Bless thy five wits! Tom's a-cold,—O, do de, do de, do de . *Lear* iii 4 59
Bless thee from whirlwinds, star-blasting, and taking! . . iii 4 60
Bless thy sweet eyes, they bleed . . . . iv 1 56
Bless thee, good man's son, from the foul fiend! . . iv 1 60
That he may bless this bay with his tall ship . . *Othello* ii 1 79
Heaven bless the isle of Cyprus and our noble general! . ii 2 12
That the holy priests Bless her when she is riggish . *Ant. and Cleo.* ii 2 245
When I shall pray, 'O, bless my lord and husband!' Undo that prayer, by crying out as loud, 'O, bless my brother!' . . . iii 4 16
To this great fairy I'll commend thy acts, Make her thanks bless thee . iv 8 13
The gods protect you! And bless the good remainders of the court! *Cymbeline* i 1 129
If you will bless me, sir, and give me leave, I'll take the better care iv 4 44
Now, the gods to bless your honour! . . . *Pericles* iv 6 23
I am wild in my beholding. O heavens bless my girl! . v 1 225
Pure Dian, bless thee for thy vision! . . . v 3 69
God bless thee (you)! *All's Well* iv 3; *T. Night* i 5; *Richard III.* ii 2; *Hamlet* iii 2; iv 6
Bless the mark. He had not been there—bless the mark! *T. G. of Ver.* iv 4 20
My master, who, God bless the mark, is a kind of devil *Mer. of Venice* ii 2 25
And I—God bless the mark!—his Moorship's ancient . *Othello* i 1 33

Blessed. What foul play had we, that we came from thence? Or blessed was 't we did? . . . . *Tempest* i 2 61
Do curse the grace that with such grace hath bless'd them *T. G. of Ver.* iii 1 146
Blessed be your royal grace! . . . . . . *Meas. for Meas.* v 1 137
God hath blessed you with a good name . . . . *Much Ado* iii 3 14
Blessed are clouds, to do as such clouds do! . . . . *L. L. Lost* v 2 204
She hath blessed and attractive eyes . . . . *M. N. Dream* ii 2 91
To the best bride-bed will we, Which by us shall blessed be . . v 1 411
Is the single man therefore blessed? No . . . *As Y. Like It* iii 3 59
Now blessed be the great Apollo!—Praised! . . . *W. Tale* iii 2 138
How blessed are we that are not simple men! . . . . . iv 4 772
Now blessed be the hour, by night or day! . . . . *K. John* i 1 165
With a blessed and unvex'd retire . . . . ii 1 253
Blessed shall he be that doth revolt From his allegiance to an heretic . iii 1 174
Whom they doted on And bless'd and graced indeed . . 2 *Hen. IV.* iv 1 139
Blessed are they that have been my friends . . . . . v 3 144
We are blessed in the change . . . . . . *Hen. V.* i 1 37
He was a king bless'd of the King of kings . . . 1 *Hen. VI.* i 1 28
That beauty am I bless'd with which you see . . . . . i 2 86
Whet not on these furious peers; For blessed are the peacemakers on earth.—Let me be blessed for the peace I make! . . 2 *Hen VI.* ii 1 35
The heavens have bless'd you with a goodly son, To be your comforter *Richard III.* i 3 9
Our princely father York Bless'd his three sons with his victorious arm i 4 242
My babes were destined to a fairer death, If grace had bless'd thee with a fairer life . . . . iv 4 220
Tell him, in death I bless'd him, For so I will . . *Hen. VIII.* iv 2 163
And, touching hers, make blessed my rude hand . *Rom. and Jul.* i 5 53
Bless'd, to be most accursed, Rich, only to be wretched . *T. of Athens* iv 2 42
When you are desirous to be bless'd, I'll blessing beg of you . *Hamlet* iii 4 171
And little bless'd with the soft phrase of peace . . *Othello* i 3 82
If she had been blessed, she would never have loved the Moor . . ii 1 257
Blessed live you long! A lady to the worthiest sir that ever Country call'd his! . . . . *Cymbeline* i 6 159
To have bless'd mine eyes with her . . . . . *Pericles* iii 3 9
Make me blessed in your care In bringing up my child . . iii 3 31
Blessed a disposition. She is of so free, so kind, so apt, so blessed a disposition . . . . *Othello* ii 3 326
Blessed beams. Till the eastern gate, all fiery-red, Opening on Neptune with fair blessed beams . . . . . *M. N. Dream* iii 2 392
Blessed bond. O blessed bond of board and bed! . . *As Y. Like It* v 4 148
Blessed candles. By these blessed candles of the night . *Mer. of Venice* v 1 220
Blessed case. Bless you with such grace As 'longeth to a lover's blessed case! . . . . *T. of Shrew* iv 2 45
Blessed condition. She's full of most blessed condition . *Othello* ii 1 255
Blessed cross. Under whose blessed cross We are impressed . 1 *Hen. IV.* i 1 20
Blessed crown. Look down, you gods, And on this couple drop a blessed crown! . . . . *Tempest* v 1 202
Blessed day. This blessed day Ever in France shall be kept festival *K. John* iii 1 75
Blessed feet. In those holy fields Over whose acres walk'd those blessed feet . . . . 1 *Hen. IV.* i 1 25
Blessed fellow. Thou art a blessed fellow to think as every man thinks 2 *Hen. IV.* ii 2 61
Blessed fig's-end! the wine she drinks is made of grapes . . *Othello* ii 1 256
Blessed gods. The blessed gods Purge all infection from our air! *W. Tale* v 1 168
The bless'd gods, as angry with my fancy, . . . take thee from me *Troi. and Cres.* iv 4 27
Blessed hap. More blessed hap did ne'er befall our state 1 *Hen. VI.* i 6 10
Blessed heavens. O blessed heavens! . . . . *Coriolanus* iv 2 20
Blessed hour. This is the period of my ambition: O this blessed hour! *Mer. Wives* iii 3 48
Blessed labour. A blessed labour, my most sovereign liege *Richard III.* ii 1 52
Blessed land. And that the people of this blessed land May not be punish'd . . . . 3 *Hen. VI.* iv 6 21
Blessed lottery. Octavia is A blessed lottery to him . *Ant. and Cleo.* ii 2 248
Blessed man. He is the half part of a blessed man . . *K. John* ii 1 437
I bear no hatred, blessed man . . . . *Rom. and Jul.* ii 3 53
Blessed marriage. Fell jealousy, Which troubles oft the bed of blessed marriage . . . . *Hen. V.* v 2 392
Blessed martyr. Then if thou fall'st, O Cromwell, Thou fall'st a blessed martyr! . . . . *Hen. VIII.* iii 2 449
Blessed Mary's Son. The world's ransom blessed Mary's Son *Richard II.* ii 1 56
Blessed Milford. How far it is To this same blessed Milford . *Cymbeline* iii 2 61
Blessed ministers above, Keep me in patience! . . *Meas. for Meas.* v 1 115
Blessed moon. By yonder blessed moon I swear . *Rom. and Jul.* ii 2 107
Be witness to me, O thou blessed moon! . . . *Ant. and Cleo.* iv 9 7
Blessed night. O blessed, blessed night! I am afeard, Being in night, all this is but a dream . . . . . . *Rom. and Jul.* ii 2 139
Blessed part. He gave his honours to the world again, His blessed part to heaven . . . . *Hen. VIII.* iv 2 30
Blessed plot, this earth, this realm, this England *Richard II.* ii 1 50
Blessed power. Some blessed power deliver us! . *Com. of Errors* iv 3 44
Blessed pudding. If she had been blessed, she would never have loved the Moor. Blessed pudding! . . . . . . *Othello* ii 1 258
Blessed saint. We'll set thy statue in some holy place, And have thee reverenced like a blessed saint . . . . 1 *Hen VI.* iii 3 15
Blessed sanctuary. God in heaven forbid We should infringe the holy privilege Of blessed sanctuary! . . . *Richard III.* iii 1 42
Blessed shore. Bid them blow towards England's blessed shore 2 *Hen. VI.* iii 2 90
Blessed soul. And there I'll rest, as after much turmoil A blessed soul doth in Elysium . . . . . . *T. G. of Ver.* ii 7 38
Blessed spirit. In thee some blessed spirit doth speak . *All's Well* ii 1 178
Whose white investments figure innocence, The dove and very blessed spirit of peace . . . . 2 *Hen. IV.* iv 1 46
Blessed sun. It is the blessed sun.—Then, God be bless'd, it is the blessed sun . . . . *T. of Shrew* iv 5 17
The blessed sun himself a fair hot wench in flame-coloured taffeta 1 *Hen. IV.* i 2 10
Shall the blessed sun of heaven prove a micher and eat blackberries? . ii 4 449
O blessed breeding sun, draw from the earth Rotten humidity! *T. of Athens* iv 3 1
Blessed thing. Thou blessed thing! Jove knows what man thou mightst have made . . . . *Cymbeline* iv 2 206
Blessed time. Then was a blessed time.—As thine is now *T. of Athens* v 3 78
Had I but died an hour before this chance, I had lived a blessed time *Macbeth* ii 3 97
Blessed troop. Saw you not, even now, a blessed troop Invite me to a banquet? . . . . *Hen. VIII.* iv 2 87
Blessed wings. And shade thy person Under their blessed wings! . v 1 161
Blessed youth. For all thy blessed youth Becomes as aged *Meas. for Meas.* iii 1 34
Blessedly. By foul play, as thou say'st, were we heaved thence, But blessedly holp hither . . . . *Tempest* i 2 63
The time was blessedly lost wherein such preparation was gained *Hen. V.* iv 1 191
Blessedness. Grows, lives and dies in single blessedness *M. N. Dream* i 1 78
And found the blessedness of being little . . *Hen. VIII.* iv 2 66
So shall she leave her blessedness to one, When heaven shall call her . v 5 44
Blesseth. It [mercy] blesseth him that gives and him that takes *Mer. of Venice* iv 1 187
Blessing. Juno sings her blessings on you . . . . *Tempest* iv 1 109
Scarcity and want shall shun you; Ceres' blessing so is on you . iv 1 117
Now all the blessings Of a glad father compass thee about! . . v 1 179
Now come I to my father; Father, your blessing . *T. G. of Ver.* ii 3 27
Thereof comes the proverb: 'Blessing of your heart, you brew good ale' iii 1 306
Blessing on your heart for't! . . . . . . *Mer. Wives* ii 2 112
Blessing of his heart! . . . . iv 1 13
It [hair] is a blessing that he bestows on beasts *Com. of Errors* ii 2 80
You should hear reason.—And when I have heard it, what blessing brings it? . . . . *Much Ado* i 3 8
For the which blessing I am at him upon my knees every morning and evening . . . . ii 1 30
God's blessing on your beard! . . . . . . *L. L. Lost* ii 1 203
And thrift is blessing, if men steal it not . *Mer. of Venice* i 3 91
Well, old man, I will tell you news of your son: give me your blessing . ii 2 83
Let's have no more fooling about it, but give me your blessing . ii 2 89
I feel too much thy blessing: make it less, For fear I surfeit . . iii 2 114
Having such a blessing in his lady, He finds the joys of heaven here on earth . . . . iii 5 80
Charged my brother, on his blessing, to breed me well . *As Y. Like It* i 1 4
I shall never have the blessing of God till I have issue o' my body *All's Well* i 3 27
They say barnes are blessings . . . . i 3 28
I'll stay at home And pray God's blessing into thy attempt . . i 3 260
Blessing upon your vows! and in your bed Find fairer fortune! . ii 3 97
Commends it to your blessing . . . . . . *W. Tale* ii 3 66
Blessing Against this cruelty fight on thy side, Poor thing, condemn'd to loss! . . . . ii 3 190
Tell me what blessings I have here alive, That I should fear to die? . iii 2 108
Please you to interpose, fair madam: kneel And pray your mother's blessing . . . . v 3 120
My blessing go with thee! . . . . *K. John* iii 3 71
And with thy blessings steel my lance's point . . *Richard II.* i 3 74
Blessing on his heart that gives it me! For 'tis a sign of love . v 5 64
O thou fond many, with what loud applause Didst thou beat heaven with blessing Bolingbroke! . . . . 2 *Hen. IV.* i 3 92
God's blessing of your good heart! and so she is, by my troth . ii 4 329
Upon my blessing, I command thee go.—To fight I will, but not to fly the foe . . . . 1 *Hen. VI.* iv 5 36
Kneel down and take my blessing, good my girl . . . . v 4 25
Thou hast given me in this beauteous face A world of earthly blessings to my soul . . . . 2 *Hen. VI.* i 1 22
Charity, Which renders good for bad, blessings for curses *Richard III.* i 2 69
Humbly on my knee I crave your blessing . . . . . ii 2 106
Make me die a good old man! That is the butt-end of a mother's blessing ii 2 110
And, till my soul forsake, Shall cry for blessings on him . *Hen. VIII.* ii 1 90
His curses and his blessings Touch me alike, they're breath I not believe in . . . . ii 2 53
Eminence, wealth, sovereignty; Which, to say sooth, are blessings . ii 3 30
You bear a gentle mind, and heavenly blessings Follow such creatures . ii 3 57
I persuade me, from her Will fall some blessing to this land . . iii 2 51
When he has run his course and sleeps in blessings . . . . iii 2 398
The dews of heaven fall thick in blessings on her! . . . . iv 2 133
With this kiss take my blessing: God protect thee! Into whose hand I give thy life . . . . v 5 11
Now promises Upon this land a thousand thousand blessings . . v 5 20
And steal immortal blessing from her lips . . *Rom. and Jul.* iii 3 37
A pack of blessings lights upon thy back; Happiness courts thee . iii 3 141
These wants of mine are crown'd, That I account them blessings *T. of Athens* ii 2 191
I had most need of blessing, and 'Amen' Stuck in my throat *Macbeth* ii 2 32
That a swift blessing May soon return to this our suffering country . iii 6 47
My pretty cousin, Blessing upon you! . . . . . . iv 2 26
Sundry blessings hang about his throne, That speak him full of grace . iv 3 158
A double blessing is a double grace . . . . . *Hamlet* i 3 53
My blessing with thee! And these few precepts in thy memory See thou character . . . . i 3 57
Farewell: my blessing season this in thee! . . . . . . i 3 81
Conception is a blessing: but not as your daughter may conceive . . ii 2 186
When you are desirous to be bless'd, I'll blessing beg of you . . iii 4 172
This fellow has banished two on's daughters, and did the third a blessing against his will . . . . *Lear* i 4 115
Good nuncle, in, and ask thy daughters' blessing . . . . iii 2 12
When thou dost ask me blessing, I'll kneel down, And ask of thee forgiveness . . . . v 3 10
I ask'd his blessing, and from first to last Told him my pilgrimage . v 3 195
Flow, flow, You heavenly blessings, on her! . . *Cymbeline* iii 5 167
Now, blessing on thee! rise; thou art my child . . . *Pericles* v 1 215
Blest. Let me be blest to make this happy close *T. G. of Ver.* v 4 117
I am blest in your acquaintance . . . . . *Mer. Wives* ii 2 279
With loyal blazon, evermore be blest! . . . . v 5 68
No night is now with hymn or carol blest . . *M. N. Dream* ii 1 102
And the owner of it blest Ever shall in safety rest . . . . v 1 426
This was a way to thrive, and he was blest: And thrift is blessing *Mer. of Venice* i 3 90
Good fortune then! To make me blest or cursed'st among men . ii 1 46
It [mercy] is twice blest; It blesseth him that gives and him that takes iv 1 186
I thank ye; and be blest for your good comfort! *As Y. Like It* ii 7 135
Be thou blest, Bertram, and succeed thy father In manners! *All's Well* i 1 70
Rest Unquestion'd welcome and undoubted blest . . . . ii 1 211
How blest am I In my just censure, in my true opinion! . *W. Tale* ii 1 36
Alack, for lesser knowledge! how accursed In being so blest! . . ii 1 39
Now be you blest for it! . . . . ii 2 54
We are blest in this man, as I may say, even blest . . . iv 4 858
By my free leave?—Never, Paulina; so be blest my spirit! . . v 1 71
And your father's blest, As he from heaven merits it . . . v 1 174
We shall be blest To do your pleasure and continue friends *K. John* iii 1 251
So blest a son, A son who is the theme of honour's tongue . 1 *Hen. IV.* i 1 80
Blest with a goodly son . . . . 3 *Hen. VI.* ii 2 23
As likely to be blest in peace and war . . . . . . iv 6 35
Having lands, and blest with beauteous wives . . *Richard III.* v 3 321
And have been blest With many children . . . *Hen. VIII.* ii 4 36

Blest. Which the rather We shall be blest to do, if he remember A kinder value of the people . . . *Coriolanus* ii 2 62
O, stand up blest! Whilst, with no softer cushion than the flint, I kneel before thee . . . v 3 52
Be blest For making up this peace! . . . v 3 139
Is she not proud? doth she not count her blest, Unworthy as she is? *Rom. and Jul.* iii 5 144
We scarce thought us blest That God had lent us but this only child . iii 5 165
If thou hatest curses, Stay not; fly, whilst thou are blest and free *T. of Athens* iv 3 542
This Cæsar was a tyrant.—Nay, that's certain: We are blest that Rome is rid of him . . . . . *J. Cæsar* iii 2 75
Blest are those Whose blood and judgement are so well commingled *Hamlet* iii 2 73
A wonderful piece of work; which not to have been blest withal would have discredited your travel . . . *Ant. and Cleo.* i 2 161
O blest, that I might not! I chose an eagle, And did avoid a puttock *Cymbeline* i 1 139
Blest be those, How mean soe'er, that have their honest wills . i 6 7
Blest be You bees that make these locks of counsel! . . iii 2 35
Do your best wills, And make me blest to obey! . . . v 1 17
Away! and, to be blest, Let us with care perform his great behest . v 4 121
Blest pray you be, That, after this strange starting from your orbs, You may reign in them now! . . . . . v 5 370
Blest, and mine own! . . . . . *Pericles* v 3 48
Blest altars. Let our crooked smokes climb to their nostrils From our blest altars . . . . . *Cymbeline* v 5 478
Blest beams. I am ashamed To look upon the holy sun, to have The benefit of his blest beams . . . . . iv 4 42
Blest fields. His ascension is More sweet than our blest fields . v 4 117
Blest gods. It would discredit the blest gods, proud man, To answer such a question . . . . *Troi. and Cres.* iv 5 247
O the blest gods! so will you wish on me . . . *Lear* ii 4 171
Blest infusions. The blest infusions That dwell in vegetives, in metals, stones . . . . . *Pericles* iii 2 35
Blest lovers. Some donation freely to estate On the blest lovers *Tempest* iv 1 86
Blest mother. God's blest mother! I swear he is true-hearted *Hen. VIII.* v 1 153
Blest order. Bound by my charity and my blest order . *Meas. for Meas.* ii 3 3
Blest secrets. All blest secrets, All you unpublish'd virtues of the earth, Spring with my tears! . . . . . *Lear* iv 4 15
Blew. It was my breath that blew this tempest up . *K. John* v 1 17
The north-east wind, Which then blew bitterly against our faces *Richard II.* i 4 7
What wind blew you hither, Pistol? . . . 2 *Hen. IV.* v 3 89
Ye blew the fire that burns ye: now have at ye! . . *Hen. VIII.* v 3 113
Blind. I see her beautiful.—If you love her, you cannot see her.—Why?—Because Love is blind . . . . *T. G. of Ver.* ii 1 76
My grandam, having no eyes, look you, wept herself blind at my parting . . . . ii 3 14
Then he should be blind; and, being blind, How could he see his way? ii 4 93
When I look on her perfections, There is no reason but I shall be blind ii 4 212
While truth the while Doth falsely blind the eyesight of his look *L. L. Lost* i 1 76
Strucken blind Kisses the base ground with obedient breast . iv 3 224
A lover's eyes will gaze an eagle blind . . . . iv 3 334
Therefore is wing'd Cupid painted blind . . . *M. N. Dream* i 1 235
But love is blind and lovers cannot see The pretty follies that themselves commit . . . . *Mer. of Venice* ii 6 36
That blind rascally boy that abuses every one's eyes because his own are out . . . . . *As Y. Like It* iv 1 218
And all eyes Blind with the pin and web but theirs . *W. Tale* i 2 291
Forgive the comment that my passion made Upon thy feature; for my rage was blind . . . . . *K. John* iv 2 264
Yet salt water blinds them not so much But they can see a sort of traitors here . . . . . *Richard II.* iv 1 245
Make blind itself with foolish tenderness . . 1 *Hen. IV.* iii 2 91
The blind and bloody soldier with foul hand . . *Hen. V.* iii 3 34
That goddess blind, That stands upon the rolling restless stone . iii 6 29
Fortune is painted blind, with a muffler afore her eyes, to signify to you that Fortune is blind . . . . . . iii 6 32
In his true likeness, he must appear naked and blind . . v 2 322
Yet they do wink and yield, as love is blind and enforces . v 2 328
Like flies at Bartholomew-tide, blind, though they have their eyes . v 2 336
So I shall catch the fly, your cousin, in the latter end and she must be blind too . . . . v 2 341
His brandish'd sword did blind men with his beams 1 *Hen. VI.* i 1 10
Hast thou been long blind and now restored?—Born blind . 2 *Hen. VI.* ii 1 76
I would be blind with weeping, sick with groans . . iii 2 62
And bid mine eyes be packing with my heart And call'd them blind and dusky spectacles . . . . . . iii 2 112
Let our hearts and eyes, like civil war, Be blind with tears 3 *Hen. VI.* ii 5 78
And made them blind with weeping . . . *Richard III.* i 2 167
And art thou yet to thy own soul so blind, That thou wilt war with God by murdering me? . . . . i 4 259
Who's so blind, but says he sees it not? . . . . iii 6 12
The dumb men throng to see him and The blind to hear him speak *Coriol.* ii 1 279
Come, let us go, and make thy father blind; For such a sight will blind a father's eye . . . . . *T. Andron.* ii 4 52
Make them blind with tributary tears . . . . iii 1 270
Kill'd her, for whom my tears have made me blind . . v 3 49
He that is strucken blind cannot forget The precious treasure of his eyesight lost . . . . *Rom. and Jul.* i 1 238
Blind is his love and best befits the dark . . . ii 1 32
If love be blind, love cannot hit the mark . . . ii 1 33
If love be blind, It best agrees with night . . . iii 2 9
Fathers that wear rags Do make their children blind . *Lear* ii 4 49
'Tis the times' plague, when madmen lead the blind . . iv 1 48
For nature so preposterously to err, Being not deficient, blind, or lame of sense, Sans witchcraft could not . . . *Othello* i 3 63
I'll wake mine eye-balls blind first . . . *Cymbeline* iii 4 104
Our very eyes Are sometimes like our judgements, blind . iv 2 302
Blind bitch. With as little remorse as they would have drowned a blind bitch's puppies . . . . *Mer. Wives* iii 5 11
Blind bow-boy. Cleft with the blind bow-boy's butt-shaft *Rom. and Jul.* ii 4 16
Blind boy. Her and her blind boy's scandal'd company I have forsworn.—Of her society Be not afraid . . *Tempest* iv 1 90
Blind brothers. When three or four of his blind brothers and sisters went to it . . . . . . *T. G. of Ver.* iv 4 4
Blind cave. Into the blind cave of eternal night *Richard III.* v 3 62
Blind Cupid. Hang me up at the door of a brothel-house for the sign of blind Cupid . . . . . . *Much Ado* i 1 256
No, do thy worst, blind Cupid; I'll not love . . . *Lear* iv 6 141

Blind fear, that seeing reason leads, finds safer footing than blind reason stumbling without fear . . . *Troi. and Cres.* iii 2 76
Blind fortune. So may I, blind fortune leading me, Miss that which one unworthier may attain . . . *Mer. of Venice* ii 1 36
Why, noble lords, Will you be put in mind of his blind fortune? *Coriol.* v 6 118
Blind harper. Nor woo in rhyme, like a blind harper's song *L. L. Lost* v 2 405
Blind man. Ho! now you strike like the blind man . *Much Ado* ii 1 205
He knows me as the blind man knows the cuckoo, By the bad voice *Mer. of Venice* v 1 112
So evident That it will glimmer through a blind man's eye 1 *Hen. VI.* ii 4 24
Forsooth, a blind man at Saint Alban's shrine, Within this half-hour, hath received his sight . . . . . . 2 *Hen. VI.* ii 1 63
All that follow their noses are led by their eyes but blind men *Lear* ii 4 71
Blind mole. That the blind mole may not Hear a foot fall *Tempest* iv 1 194
I will bring these two moles, these blind ones, aboard him . *W. Tale* iv 4 868
The blind mole casts Copp'd hills towards heaven . *Pericles* i 1 100
Blind oblivion. And blind oblivion swallow'd cities up *Troi. and Cres.* iii 2 194
Blind priest. That blind priest, like the eldest son of fortune, Turns what he list . . . . *Hen. VIII.* ii 2 21
Blind puppies. Come, be a man. Drown thyself! drown cats and blind puppies . . . . *Othello* i 3 341
Blind reason stumbling without fear . . *Troi. and Cres.* iii 2 77
Blind sight, dead life, poor mortal living ghost . *Richard III.* iv 4 26
Blind traitor. If you do chance to hear of that blind traitor . *Lear* iv 5 37
Blind waves. Whom the blind waves and surges have devour'd *T. Night* v 1 236
Blind woman. The bountiful blind woman doth most mistake in her gifts to women . . . . . . *As Y. Like It* i 2 38
Blind-worm. Newts and blind-worms, do no wrong . *M. N. Dream* ii 2 11
Adder's fork and blind-worm's sting, Lizard's leg and howlet's wing *Macbeth* iv 1 16
Blinded. If this fond Love were not a blinded god . *T. G. of Ver.* iv 4 201
That eye shall be his heed And give him light that it was blinded by *L. L. Lost* i 1 83
What peremptory eagle-sighted eye Dares look upon the heaven of her brow, That is not blinded by her majesty? . . . . iv 3 228
He hath no eyes, the dust hath blinded them . 2 *Hen. VI.* iii 3 14
Blindfold. My inch of taper will be burnt and done, And blindfold death not let me see my son . . . . . . *Richard II.* i 3 224
Blinding. Sorrow's eye, glazed with blinding tears, Divides one thing entire to many objects . . . . ii 2 16
You nimble lightnings, dart your blinding flames Into her scornful eyes! . . . . *Lear* ii 4 167
Blindly. The brother blindly shed the brother's blood . *Richard III.* v 5 24
Blindness. Love doth to her eyes repair, To help him of his blindness, And, being help'd, inhabits there . . *T. G. of Ver.* iv 2 47
Muffle your false love with some show of blindness . *Com. of Errors* iii 2 8
You may, some of you, thank love for my blindness . *Hen. V.* v 2 344
What an infinite mock is this, that a man should have the best use of eyes to see the way of blindness! . . . *Cymbeline* v 4 197
Blink. Show me thy chink, to blink through with mine eyne! *M. N. Dr.* v 1 178
Blinking. What's here? the portrait of a blinking idiot! *Mer. of Venice* ii 9 54
Pretty, fond, adoptious christendoms, That blinking Cupid gossips *A. W.* i 1 189
Bliss and goodness on you! . . . . *Meas. for Meas.* ii 2 228
Thus have you heard me sever'd from my bliss . *Com. of Errors* i 1 119
O, let me kiss This princess of pure white, this seal of bliss! *M. N. Dream* iii 2 144
O wicked wall, through whom I see no bliss! . . . v 1 181
Some there be that shadows kiss; Such have but a shadow's bliss *Mer. of Venice* ii 9 67
If you be well pleased with this And hold your fortune for your bliss . iii 2 137
I have arrived at the last Unto the wished haven of my bliss *T. of Shrew* v 1 131
Whereas the contrary bringeth bliss . . . 1 *Hen. VI.* v 5 64
If thou think'st on heaven's bliss, Hold up thy hand . 2 *Hen. VI.* iii 3 27
To wear a crown; Within whose circuit is Elysium And all that poets feign of bliss and joy . . . . . 3 *Hen. VI.* i 2 31
I here protest, in sight of heaven, And by the hope I have of heavenly bliss . . . . iii 3 182
This pretty lad will prove our country's bliss . . . iv 6 70
As far from help as Limbo is from bliss! . . *T. Andron.* iii 1 149
I shall never come to bliss Till all these mischiefs be return'd again . iii 1 273
Wisely too fair, To merit bliss by making me despair . *Rom. and Jul.* i 1 228
Bliss be upon you! . . . . v 3 124
Thou art a soul in bliss; but I am bound Upon a wheel of fire . *Lear* iv 7 46
That cuckold lives in bliss Who, certain of his fate, loves not his wronger *Othello* iii 3 167
So come my soul to bliss, as I speak true . . . . v 2 250
Eternity was in our lips and eyes, Bliss in our brows' bent *Ant. and Cleo.* i 3 36
Blister. A south-west blow on ye And blister you all o'er! . *Tempest* i 2 324
A blister on his sweet tongue, with my heart! . . *L. L. Lost* v 2 335
If I prove honey-mouth'd, let my tongue blister . . *W. Tale* ii 2 33
Which oft the angry Mab with blisters plagues, Because their breaths with sweetmeats tainted are . . . . *Rom. and Jul.* i 4 75
Speak, and be hang'd: For each true word, a blister! . *T. of Athens* v 1 135
This tyrant, whose sole name blisters our tongues . *Macbeth* iv 3 12
Takes off the rose From the fair forehead of an innocent love And sets a blister there . . . . *Hamlet* iii 4 44
Blistered. Who, falling in the flaws of her own youth, Hath blister'd her report . . . . . . *Meas. for Meas.* ii 3 12
Tall stockings, Short blister'd breeches, and those types of travel *Hen. VIII.* i 3 31
Blister'd be thy tongue For such a wish! . . *Rom. and Jul.* iii 2 90
Blithe. Sigh not so, but let them go, And be you blithe and bonny *M. Ado* ii 3 69
Bardolph, be blithe: Nym, rouse thy vaunting veins . *Hen. V.* ii 3 4
Be blithe again, And bury all thy fear in my devices . *T. Andron.* iv 4 111
So buxom, blithe, and full of face, As heaven had lent her all his grace *Pericles* i Gower 23
Blither. Crickets sing at the oven's mouth, E'er the blither for their drouth . . . . iii Gower 8
Blithild, which was daughter to King Clothair . . *Hen. V.* i 2 67
Bloat. Let the bloat king tempt you again to bed . *Hamlet* iii 4 182
Block. I understand thee not.—What a block art thou! . *T. G. of Ver.* ii 5 27
Had he twenty heads to tender down On twenty bloody blocks *M. for M.* ii 4 181
Provide your block and your axe to-morrow four o'clock . iv 2 55
Is the axe upon the block, sirrah?—Very ready, sir. . . iv 3 39
After him, fellows; bring him to the block . . . iv 3 69
We do condemn thee to the very block Where Claudio stoop'd to death v 1 419
As the fashion of his hat; it ever changes with the next block *Much Ado* i 1 77
O, she misused me past the endurance of a block! . . . ii 1 247
If speaking, why, a vane blown with all winds; If silent, why, a block moved with none . . . . iii 1 67
That which here stands up Is but a quintain, a mere lifeless block *As Y. Like It* i 2 263

Block. Thy conceit is soaking, will draw in More than the common blocks *W. Tale* i 2 225
The block of death, Treason's true bed and yielder up of death *2 Hen. IV.* iv 2 122
Rather let my head Stoop to the block than these knees bow to any *2 Hen. VI.* iv 1 125
Come, lead me to the block; bear him my head *Richard III.* iii 4 108
What tongueless blocks were they! would they not speak? . iii 7 42
Convey me to the block of shame; Wrong hath but wrong . v 1 28
Who, like a block, hath denied my access to thee . *Coriolanus* v 2 85
You blocks, you stones, you worse than senseless things! *J. Cæsar* i 1 40
This' a good block; It were a delicate stratagem, to shoe A troop of horse with felt . *Lear* iv 6 187
The viol once more: how thou stirr'st, thou block! *Pericles* iii 2 90
Blockhead. Your wit will not so soon out as another man's will; 'tis strongly wedged up in a block-head . *Coriolanus* ii 3 31
Blockish. Let blockish Ajax draw The sort to fight with Hector *Tr. and Cr.* i 3 375
Blois. Maine, Blois, Poictiers, and Tours, are won away *1 Hen. VI.* iv 3 45
Blomer. After your highness had reproved the duke About Sir William Blomer . *Hen. VIII.* i 2 190
Blood. The strongest oaths are straw To the fire i' the blood *Tempest* iv 1 53
Flesh and blood, You, brother mine . v 1 74
Thy pulse Beats as of flesh and blood . v 1 114
Hath more mind to feed on your blood than live in your air *T. G. of Ver.* ii 4 28
Now, as thou art a gentleman of blood, Advise me . iii 1 121
Takes the cattle And makes milch-kine yield blood . *Mer. Wives* iv 4 33
Stands at a guard with envy; scarce confesses That his blood flows *Meas. for Meas.* i 3 52
A man whose blood Is very snow-broth . i 4 57
The resolute acting of your blood Could have attain'd the effect . ii 1 12
Blood, thou art blood: Let's write good angel on the devil's horn . ii 4 15
O heavens! Why does my blood thus muster to my heart? . ii 4 20
He hath fall'n by prompture of the blood . ii 4 178
Such a warped slip of wilderness Ne'er issued from his blood . iii 1 143
In the heat of blood, And lack of temper'd judgement afterward . v 1 477
Have seal'd his rigorous statutes with their bloods *Com. of Errors* i 1 9
My blood is mingled with the crime of lust . ii 2 143
Some devils ask but the parings of one's nail, A rush, a hair, a drop of blood . iv 3 73
Even for the blood That then I lost for thee, now grant me justice . v 1 193
And all the conduits of my blood froze up . v 1 313
I thank God and my cold blood, I am of your humour for that *Much Ado* i 1 131
Prove that ever I lose more blood with love than I will get again with drinking . i 1 253
It better fits my blood to be disdained of all . i 3 30
Beauty is a witch Against whose charms faith melteth into blood . ii 1 187
Wisdom and blood combating in so tender a body, we have ten proofs to one that blood hath the victory . ii 3 170
There's no true drop of blood in him, to be truly touched with love . iii 2 19
How giddily a' [fashion] turns about all the hot bloods between fourteen and five-and-thirty . iii 3 141
Comes not that blood as modest evidence To witness simple virtue? . iv 1 38
You are more intemperate in your blood Than Venus . iv 1 60
Could she here deny The story that is printed in her blood? . iv 1 124
Time hath not yet so dried this blood of mine . iv 1 195
I pray thee, peace. I will be flesh and blood . v 1 34
Runs not this speech like iron through your blood? . v 1 252
I would see his own person in flesh and blood . *L. L. Lost* i 1 186
Thou art quick in answers: thou heatest my blood . i 2 32
Is the fool sick?—Sick at the heart.—Alack, let it blood . ii 1 186
As I for praise alone now seek to spill The poor deer's blood . iv 1 35
The deer was, as you know, sanguis, in blood . iv 2 4
I would forget her; but a fever she Reigns in my blood and will remember'd be.—A fever in your blood! why, then incision Would let her out in saucers . iv 3 96
As true we are as flesh and blood can be: The sea will ebb and flow . iv 3 215
Young blood doth not obey an old decree . iv 3 217
For native blood is counted painting now . iv 3 263
The blood of youth burns not with such excess As gravity's revolt . v 2 73
Ay, if a' have no more man's blood in's belly than will sup a flea . v 2 697
Sweet bloods, I both may and will . v 2 714
Change not your offer made in heat of blood . v 2 810
When blood is nipp'd and ways be foul, Then nightly sings the staring owl . v 2 926
Know of your youth, examine well your blood . *M. N. Dream* i 1 68
Thrice-blessed they that master so their blood, To undergo such maiden pilgrimage . i 1 74
The course of true love never did run smooth; But, either it was different in blood,— O cross! too high to be enthrall'd to low . i 1 135
Dead? or asleep? I see no blood, no wound . ii 2 101
Being o'er shoes in blood, plunge in the deep, And kill me too . iii 2 48
And pale of cheer, With sighs of love, that costs the fresh blood dear . iii 2 97
Thy mantle good, What, stain'd with blood! . v 1 288
Why should a man, whose blood is warm within, Sit like his grandsire cut in alabaster? . *Mer. of Venice* i 1 83
The brain may devise laws for the blood, but a hot temper leaps o'er a cold decree . i 2 20
Let us make incision for your love, To prove whose blood is reddest . ii 1 7
If thou be Launcelot, thou art mine own flesh and blood . ii 2 98
Though I am a daughter to his blood, I am not to his manners . ii 3 18
My own flesh and blood to rebel!—Out upon it, old carrion! rebels it at these years? . iii 1 37
I say, my daughter is my flesh and blood . iii 1 40
More [difference] between your bloods than there is between red wine and rhenish . iii 1 43
You have bereft me of all words, Only my blood speaks to you in my veins . iii 2 178
The Jew shall have my flesh, blood, bones and all, Ere thou shalt lose for me one drop of blood . iv 1 113
This bond doth give thee here no jot of blood . iv 1 306
If thou dost shed One drop of Christian blood, thy lands and goods Are, by the laws of Venice, confiscate . iv 1 310
Shed thou no blood, nor cut thou less nor more But just a pound of flesh iv 1 325
Bellowing and neighing loud, Which is the hot condition of their blood v 1 74
In the gentle condition of blood, you should so know me *As Y. Like It* i 1 48
The same tradition takes not away my blood, were there twenty brothers betwixt us . i 1 51
I rather will subject me to the malice Of a diverted blood . ii 3 37
In my youth I never did apply Hot and rebellious liquors in my blood . ii 3 49
Give this napkin Dyed in his blood unto the shepherd youth. . iv 3 156
Many will swoon when they do look on blood . iv 3 159

Blood. According as marriage binds and blood breaks *As Y. Like It* v 4 59
So workmanly the blood and tears are drawn . *T. of Shrew* Ind. 2 62
I will therefore tarry in despite of the flesh and the blood . Ind. 2 130
Seeing too much sadness hath congeal'd your blood . Ind. 2 134
Thy blood and virtue Contend for empire in thee! *All's Well* i 1 71
A wicked creature, as you and all flesh and blood are . i 3 38
He that comforts my wife is the cherisher of my flesh and blood; he that cherishes my flesh and blood loves my flesh and blood; he that loves my flesh and blood is my friend . i 3 50
Our blood to us, this to our blood is born . i 3 137
Does it curd thy blood To say I am thy mother? . i 3 155
To choose from forth the royal blood of France . ii 1 199
Too young, too happy, and too good, To make yourself a son out of my blood . ii 3 103
Strange is it that our bloods, Of colour, weight, and heat, pour'd all together, Would quite confound distinction, yet stand off In differences so mighty . ii 3 125
Whose great decision hath much blood let forth And more thirsts after iii 1 3
He was my son; But I do wash his name out of my blood . iii 2 70
Now his important blood will nought deny That she'll demand . iii 7 21
Am not I consanguineous? am I not of her blood? . *T. Night* ii 3 83
Thy Fates open their hands; let thy blood and spirit embrace them . ii 5 159
And you find so much blood in his liver as will clog the foot of a flea . iii 2 66
This does make some obstruction in the blood, this cross-gartering . iii 4 22
Any taint of vice whose strong corruption Inhabits our frail blood . iii 4 391
I must have an ounce or two of this malapert blood from you . iv 1 47
Put your grace in your pocket, sir, for this once, and let your flesh and blood obey it . v 1 36
Had it been the brother of my blood, I must have done no less . v 1 217
Right noble is his blood . v 1 271
And our weak spirits ne'er been higher rear'd With stronger blood *W. Tale* i 2 73
To mingle friendship far is mingling bloods . i 2 109
His varying childness cures in me Thoughts that would thick my blood . i 2 171
Give scandal to the blood o' the prince my son . i 2 330
O, then my best blood turn To an infected jelly! . i 2 417
He does bear some signs of me, yet you Have too much blood in him . ii 1 58
I'll pawn the little blood which I have left To save the innocent . ii 3 166
Comes in the sweet o' the year; For the red blood reigns in the winter's pale . iv 3 4
Your youth, And the true blood which peepeth fairly through't . iv 4 148
He tells her something That makes her blood look out . iv 4 160
We'll bar thee from succession; Not hold thee of our blood . iv 4 441
She being none of your flesh and blood, your flesh and blood has not offended . iv 4 710
Then your blood had been the dearer by I know how much an ounce . iv 4 724
I would fain say, bleed tears, for I am sure my heart wept blood . v 2 97
Would you not deem it breathed? and that those veins Did verily bear blood? . v 3 65
Here have we war for war and blood for blood. *K. John* i 1 19
That great forerunner of thy blood, Richard . ii 1 2
Wade to the market-place in Frenchmen's blood . ii 1 42
Lest unadvised you stain your swords with blood . ii 1 45
We shall repent each drop of blood That hot rash haste so indirectly shed . ii 1 48
An Ate, stirring him to blood and strife . ii 1 63
When living blood doth in these temples beat . ii 1 108
We will bear home that lusty blood again . ii 1 255
Shall we give the signal to our rage And stalk in blood to our possession? ii 1 266
As many and as well-born bloods as those . ii 1 278
Blood hath bought blood and blows have answer'd blows . ii 1 329
France, hast thou yet more blood to cast away? . ii 1 334
England, thou hast not saved one drop of blood In this hot trial . ii 1 341
How high thy glory towers, When the rich blood of kings is set on fire! ii 1 351
Till then, blows, blood and death! . ii 1 360
Whose veins bound richer blood than Lady Blanch? . ii 1 431
What cannoneer begot this lusty blood? . ii 1 461
She in beauty, education, blood, Holds hand with any princess of the world . ii 1 493
Gone to be married! gone to swear a peace! False blood to false blood join'd! . iii 1 2
So lately purged of blood, So newly join'd in love . iii 1 239
Upon thy wedding-day? Against the blood that thou hast married? . iii 1 301
The sun's o'ercast with blood: fair day, adieu! . iii 1 326
Nothing can allay, nothing but blood, The blood, and dearest-valued blood . iii 1 342
Thy rage shall burn thee up, and thou shalt turn To ashes, ere our blood shall quench that fire . iii 1 345
That surly spirit, melancholy, Had baked thy blood and made it heavy-thick . iii 3 43
Your mind is all as youthful as your blood . iii 4 125
He that steeps his safety in true blood Shall find but bloody safety and untrue . iii 4 147
That blood which owed the breadth of all this isle, Three foot of it doth hold . iv 2 99
There is no sure foundation set on blood . iv 2 104
Where is that blood That I have seen inhabit in those cheeks? . iv 2 106
This confine of blood and breath . iv 2 246
An innocent hand, Not painted with the crimson spots of blood . iv 2 253
Foul imaginary eyes of blood Presented thee more hideous than thou art iv 2 265
The foot That leaves the print of blood where'er it walks . iv 3 26
Swearing allegiance and the love of soul To stranger blood . v 1 11
Where these two Christian armies might combine The blood of malice in a vein of league . v 2 38
Full of warm blood, of mirth, of gossiping . v 2 59
By all the blood that ever fury breathed, The youth says well . v 2 127
It is too late: the life of all his blood Is touch'd corruptibly . v 7 1
A fiend confined to tyrannize On unreprievable condemned blood . v 7 48
The blood is hot that must be cool'd for this . *Richard II.* i 1 51
Setting aside his high blood's royalty . i 1 58
And lay aside my high blood's royalty . i 1 71
Sluiced out his innocent soul through streams of blood . i 1 103
Which blood, like sacrificing Abel's, cries, Even from the tongueless caverns of the earth . i 1 104
Till I have told this slander of his blood . i 1 113
Such neighbour nearness to our sacred blood Should nothing privilege him . i 1 119
Even in the best blood chamber'd in his bosom . i 1 149
Let's purge this choler without letting blood . i 1 153
Hath love in thy old blood no living fire? . i 2 10
Edward's seven sons . . . Were as seven vials of his sacred blood. . i 2 12

Blood. Ah, Gaunt, his blood was thine! *Richard II.* i 2 22
Farewell, my blood; which if to-day thou shed, Lament we may . i 3 57
O thou, the earthly author of my blood . i 3 69
Rouse up thy youthful blood, be valiant and live . i 3 83
For that our kingdom's earth should not be soil'd With that dear blood which it hath fostered . i 3 126
Fright fair peace And make us wade even in our kindred's blood . i 3 138
Make pale our cheek, chasing the royal blood With fury from his native residence . ii 1 118
That blood already, like the pelican, Hast thou tapp'd out . ii 1 126
Witness good That thou respect'st not spilling Edward's blood . ii 1 131
His hands were guilty of no kindred blood, But bloody with the enemies of his kin . ii 1 182
To wash your blood From off my hands . iii 1 5
A happy gentleman in blood and lineaments . iii 1 9
Near to the king in blood, and near in love . iii 1 17
Leaving me no sign, Save men's opinions and my living blood . iii 1 26
But now the blood of twenty thousand men Did triumph in my face . iii 2 76
Till so much blood thither come again, Have I not reason to look pale and dead? . iii 2 78
Cover your heads and mock not flesh and blood With solemn reverence iii 2 171
And lay the summer's dust with showers of blood . iii 3 43
No hand of blood and bone Can gripe the sacred handle of our sceptre . iii 3 79
And bedew Her pastures' grass with faithful English blood . iii 3 100
By the royalties of both your bloods, Currents that spring from one most gracious head . iii 3 107
Lest, being over-proud in sap and blood, With too much riches it confound itself . iii 4 59
The blood of English shall manure the ground, And future ages groan for this foul act . iv 1 137
Thy fierce hand Hath with the king's blood stain'd the king's own land v 5 111
As full of valour as of royal blood: Both have I spill'd . v 5 114
My soul is full of woe, That blood should sprinkle me to make me grow v 6 46
I'll make a voyage to the Holy Land, To wash this blood off from my guilty hand . v 6 50
No more the thirsty entrance of this soil Shall daub her lips with her own children's blood . *1 Hen. IV.* i 1 6
Ten thousand bold Scots, two and twenty knights, Balk'd in their own blood . i 1 69
Thou camest not of the blood royal, if thou darest not stand for ten shillings . i 2 157
My blood hath been too cold and temperate, Unapt to stir at these indignities . i 3 1
I'll empty all these veins, And shed my dear blood drop by drop in the dust . i 3 134
Was not he proclaim'd By Richard that dead is the next of blood? . i 3 146
O, the blood more stirs To rouse a lion than to start a hare! . i 3 197
Why hast thou lost the fresh blood in thy cheeks? . ii 3 47
And then to beslubber our garments with it and swear it was the blood of true men . ii 4 342
Art thou not horribly afraid? doth not thy blood thrill at it? . ii 4 406
Amend this fault: Though sometimes it show greatness, courage, blood iii 1 181
Charming your blood with pleasing heaviness . iii 1 218
Out of my blood He'll breed revengement and a scourge for me . iii 2 6
An alien to the hearts Of all the court and princes of my blood . iii 2 35
I will wear a garment all of blood And stain my favours in a bloody mask . iii 2 135
The mailed Mars shall on his altar sit Up to the ears in blood . iv 1 117
Steps me a little higher than his vow Made to my father, while his blood was poor . iv 3 76
To save the blood on either side, Try fortune with him in a single fight v 1 99
It hath the excuse of youth and heat of blood . v 2 17
Better consider what you have to do Than I, that have not well the gift of tongue, Can lift your blood up with persuasion . v 2 79
A sword, whose temper I intend to stain With the best blood that I can meet . v 2 95
Embowell'd will I see thee by and by: Till then in blood by noble Percy lie . v 4 110
Quenching the flame of bold rebellion Even with the rebels' blood *2 Hen. IV.* Ind. 27
And doth enlarge his rising with the blood Of fair King Richard . i 1 204
A kind of lethargy, an't please your lordship; a kind of sleeping in the blood . i 2 128
I had thought weariness durst not have attached one of so high blood . ii 2 4
Never prick their finger but they say, 'There's some of the king's blood spilt' . ii 2 122
In military rules, humours of blood, He was the mark and glass . ii 3 30
It perfumes the blood ere one can say 'What's this?' . ii 4 31
By this light flesh and corrupt blood, thou art welcome . ii 4 320
Turning your books to graves, your ink to blood, Your pens to lances . iv 1 50
Whose memory is written on the earth With yet appearing blood . iv 1 82
And swear here, by the honour of my blood . iv 2 55
For thin drink doth so over-cool their blood . iv 3 99
The second property of your excellent sherris is, the warming of the blood . iv 3 112
The cold blood he did naturally inherit of his father . iv 3 128
Chide him for faults, and do it reverently, When you perceive his blood inclined to mirth . iv 4 38
The united vessel of their blood, Mingled with venom of suggestion . iv 4 44
The blood weeps from my heart when I do shape In forms imaginary the unguided days And rotten times that you shall look upon . iv 4 58
When rage and hot blood are his counsellors . iv 4 63
Thy due from me Is tears and heavy sorrows of the blood . iv 5 38
Which, as immediate from thy place and blood, Derives itself to me . iv 5 42
Tyranny, which never quaff'd but blood . iv 5 86
If it did infect my blood with joy, Or swell my thoughts . iv 5 170
The tide of blood in me Hath proudly flow'd in vanity till now . v 2 129
Many now in health Shall drop their blood in approbation . *Hen. V.* i 2 19
Never two such kingdoms did contend Without much fall of blood . i 2 25
Stood smiling to behold his lion's whelp Forage in blood . i 2 110
The blood and courage that renowned them Runs in your veins . i 2 118
You should rouse yourself, As did the former lions of your blood . i 2 124
With blood and sword and fire to win your right . i 2 131
That hath so cowarded and chased your blood Out of appearance . ii 2 75
Constant in spirit, not swerving with the blood . ii 2 133
Like horse-leeches, my boys, To suck, to suck, the very blood to suck! ii 3 58
The widows' tears, the orphans' cries, The dead men's blood . ii 4 107
Summon up the blood, Disguise fair nature with hard-favour'd rage . iii 1 7
On, on, you noblest English, Whose blood is fet from fathers of war-proof! . iii 1 18

Blood. Be copy now to men of grosser blood, And teach them how to war *Hen. V.* iii 1 24
Can sodden water . . . Decoct their cold blood to such valiant heat? And shall our quick blood, spirited with wine, Seem frosty? . iii 5 20
With pennons painted in the blood of Harfleur . iii 5 49
For the effusion of our blood, the muster of his kingdom too faint a number . iii 6 138
We shall your tawny ground with your red blood Discolour . iii 6 170
How can they charitably dispose of any thing, when blood is their argument? . iv 1 150
Bestow'd more contrite tears Than from it issued forced drops of blood iv 1 314
Twice a-day their wither'd hands hold up Toward heaven, to pardon blood . iv 1 317
Make incision in their hides, That their hot blood may spin in English eyes . iv 2 10
Will you have them weep our horses' blood? How shall we, then, behold their natural tears? . iv 2 12
Scarce blood enough in all their sickly veins To give each naked curtle-axe a stain . iv 2 20
For he to-day that sheds his blood with me Shall be my brother . iv 3 61
As I suck blood, I will some mercy show . iv 4 68
From helmet to the spur all blood he was . iv 6 6
With blood he seal'd A testament of noble-ending love . iv 6 26
Many of our princes—woe the while!—Lie drown'd and soak'd in mercenary blood . iv 7 79
So do our vulgar drench their peasant limbs In blood of princes . iv 7 81
Knights, squires, And gentlemen of blood and quality . iv 8 95
Grow like savages,—as soldiers will That nothing do but meditate on blood . v 2 60
I dare not swear thou lovest me; yet my blood begins to flatter me that thou dost . v 2 239
From her blood raise up Issue to me . v 2 376
We mourn in black: why mourn we not in blood? . *1 Hen. VI.* i 1 17
Blood will I draw on thee, thou art a witch . i 5 6
His trespass yet lives guilty in thy blood . ii 4 94
I dare say This quarrel will drink blood another day . ii 4 134
To be restored to my blood, Or make my ill the advantage of my good . ii 5 128
Be at peace, except ye thirst for blood . iii 1 117
Our pleasure is That Richard be restored to his blood . iii 1 159
One drop of blood drawn from thy country's bosom Should grieve thee more than streams of foreign gore . iii 3 54
Or else this blow should broach thy dearest blood . iii 4 40
Like a hedge-born swain That doth presume to boast of gentle blood . iv 1 44
Let us not forego That for a trifle that was bought with blood! . iv 1 150
If we be English deer, be then in blood . iv 2 48
The world will say, he is not Talbot's blood . iv 5 16
The ireful bastard Orleans, that drew blood From thee, my boy . iv 6 16
Contaminated, base And misbegotten blood I spill of thine, Mean and right poor, for that pure blood of mine . iv 6 22
In that sea of blood my boy did drench His over-mounting spirit . iv 7 14
Did flesh his puny sword in Frenchmen's blood . iv 7 36
As the only means To stop effusion of our Christian blood . v 1 9
Where I was wont to feed you with my blood, I'll lop a member off . v 3 14
Base ignoble wretch! I am descended of a gentler blood . v 4 8
Stain'd with the guiltless blood of innocents . v 4 44
Whose maiden blood, thus rigorously effused, Will cry for vengeance at the gates of heaven . v 4 52
My sword should shed hot blood, mine eyes no tears . *2 Hen. VI.* i 1 118
He is the next of blood, And heir apparent . i 1 151
Bear that proportion to my flesh and blood . i 1 233
Were I a man, a duke, and next of blood, I would remove these . i 2 63
Red, master; red as blood.—Why, that's well said . ii 1 110
Before his chaps be stain'd with crimson blood . iii 1 259
Kerns of Ireland are in arms And temper clay with blood of Englishmen iii 1 311
See how the blood is settled in his face . iii 2 160
His face is black and full of blood, His eye-balls further out than when he lived . iii 2 168
Thou shalt be waking while I shed thy blood . iii 2 227
Or with their blood stain this discolour'd shore . iv 1 11
King Henry's blood, The honourable blood of Lancaster . iv 1 50
Drones suck not eagles' blood but rob bee-hives . iv 1 109
Angry, wrathful, and inclined to blood . iv 2 134
Brave thee! ay, by the best blood that ever was broached . iv 10 39
Ne'er shall this blood be wiped from thy point . iv 10 74
And shame thine honourable age with blood? . v 1 170
That this is true, father, behold his blood . *3 Hen. VI.* i 1 13
I'll have more lives Than drops of blood were in my father's veins . i 1 97
Write up his title with usurping blood . i 1 169
In whose cold blood no spark of honour bides . i 1 184
Or nourish'd him as I did with my blood . i 1 222
Even in the lukewarm blood of Henry's heart . i 2 34
My father's blood Hath stopp'd the passage where thy words should enter . i 3 21
And this thy son's blood cleaving to my blade Shall rust upon my weapon, till thy blood, Congeal'd with this, do make me wipe off both . i 3 50
With purple falchion, painted to the hilt In blood . i 4 13
I stain'd this napkin with the blood . i 4 79
That face of his the hungry cannibals Would not have touch'd, would not have stain'd with blood . i 4 153
This cloth thou dip'dst in blood of my sweet boy, And I with tears do wash the blood away . i 4 157
Take me from the world: My soul to heaven, my blood upon your heads! . i 4 168
Who thunders to his captives blood and death . ii 1 127
If thou deny, their blood upon thy head . ii 2 129
Till we have hewn thee down, Or bathed thy growing with our heated bloods . ii 2 169
Thy brother's blood the thirsty earth hath drunk . ii 3 15
Steeds, That stain'd their fetlocks in his smoking blood . ii 3 21
Let the earth be drunken with our blood . ii 3 23
The one his purple blood right well resembles . ii 5 99
The air hath got into my deadly wounds, And much effuse of blood doth make me faint . ii 6 28
This hand should chop it off, and with the issuing blood Stifle the villain . ii 6 82
You twain, of all the rest, Are near to Warwick by blood and by alliance iv 1 136
Write in the dust this sentence with thy blood . v 1 56
Both shall buy this treason Even with the dearest blood your bodies bear . v 1 69

Blood. I will not ruinate my father's house, Who gave his blood to lime the stones together *3 Hen. VI.* v 1 84
My blood, my want of strength, my sick heart shows, That I must yield my body to the earth v 2 8
The wrinkles in my brows, now fill'd with blood, Were liken'd oft to kingly sepulchres v 2 19
Lo, now my glory smear'd in dust and blood! v 2 23
Thy tears would wash this cold congealed blood That glues my lips v 2 37
They that stabb'd Cæsar shed no blood at all v 5 53
Murder is thy alms-deed; Petitioners for blood thou ne'er put'st back v 5 80
What, will the aspiring blood of Lancaster Sink in the ground? v 6 61
We sit in England's royal throne, Repurchased with the blood of enemies v 7 2
Poor key-cold figure of a holy king! Pale ashes of the house of Lancaster! Thou bloodless remnant of that royal blood! *Richard III.* i 2 7
Cursed the blood that let this blood from hence! i 2 16
'Tis thy presence that exhales this blood From cold and empty veins, where no blood dwells i 2 58
O God, which this blood madest, revenge his death! O earth, which this blood drink'st, revenge his death! i 2 62
Earth, gape open wide and eat him quick, As thou dost swallow up this good king's blood! i 2 66
Thy murderous falchion smoking in his blood i 2 94
To royalise his blood I spilt mine own.—Yea, and much better blood than his i 3 125
Steep'd in the faultless blood of pretty Rutland i 3 178
As it was won with blood, lost be it so! i 3 272
Thy garments are not spotted with our blood i 3 283
A shadow like an angel, with bright hair Dabbled in blood i 4 54
As you hope to have redemption By Christ's dear blood i 4 195
Less noble and less loyal, Nearer in bloody thoughts, but not in blood ii 1 92
Blood against blood, Self against self ii 4 62
His ancient knot of dangerous adversaries To-morrow are let blood iii 1 183
We give thee up our guiltless blood to drink iii 3 14
Be satisfied, dear God, with our true blood, Which, as thou know'st, unjustly must be spilt iii 3 21
Successively from blood to blood, Your right of birth, your empery, your own iii 7 135
When scarce the blood was well wash'd from his hands Which issued from my other angel husband iv 1 68
I am in So far in blood that sin will pluck on sin iv 2 65
England's lawful earth, Unlawfully made drunk with innocents' blood! iv 4 30
That dog, that had his teeth before his eyes, To worry lambs and lap their gentle blood iv 4 50
I have no moe sons of the royal blood For thee to murder iv 4 199
Wrong not her birth, she is of royal blood iv 4 211
Present to her,—as sometime Margaret Did to thy father, steep'd in Rutland's blood,—A handkerchief iv 4 275
I will beget Mine issue of your blood upon your daughter iv 4 298
As children but one step below, Even of your mettle, of your very blood iv 4 302
Swills your warm blood like wash v 2 9
One raised in blood, and one in blood establish'd v 3 247
Spur your proud horses hard, and ride in blood; Amaze the welkin! v 3 340
The brother blindly shed the brother's blood v 5 24
And make poor England weep in streams of blood! v 5 37
A beggar's book Outworths a noble's blood *Hen. VIII.* i 1 123
For then my guiltless blood must cry against 'em ii 1 68
I now seal it; And with that blood will make 'em one day groan for't ii 1 106
Tied by blood and favour to her ii 2 90
Would I had no being, If this salute my blood a jot: it faints me ii 3 103
And those about her From her shall read the perfect ways of honour, And by those claim their greatness, not by blood v 5 39
The princes orgulous, their high blood chafed *Troi. and Cres.* Prol. 2
Helen must needs be fair, When with your blood you daily paint her thus i 1 94
I'll prove this truth with my three drops of blood i 3 301
Is your blood So madly hot that no discourse of reason, Nor fear of bad success in a bad cause, Can qualify the same? ii 2 115
The reasons you allege do more conduce To the hot passion of distemper'd blood ii 2 169
I would not wish a drop of Trojan blood Spent more in her defence ii 2 197
Let thy blood be thy direction till thy death! ii 3 33
Imagined worth Holds in his blood such swoln and hot discourse ii 3 183
I'll let his humours blood.—He will be the physician that should be the patient ii 3 222
He eats nothing but doves, love, and that breeds hot blood iii 1 141
With a mind That doth renew swifter than blood decays iii 2 170
They will almost Give us a prince of blood iii 3 26
Our bloods are now in calm; and, so long, health! iv 1 15
No kin, no love, no blood, no soul so near me As the sweet Troilus iv 2 104
Come, stretch thy chest, and let thy eyes spout blood iv 5 10
The obligation of our blood forbids A gory emulation 'twixt us twain iv 5 122
My mother's blood Runs on the dexter cheek, and this sinister Bounds in my father's iv 5 127
The fall of every Phrygian stone will cost A drop of Grecian blood iv 5 224
I'll heat his blood with Greekish wine to-night, Which with my scimitar I'll cool to-morrow v 1 1
With too much blood and too little brain, these two may run mad; but, if with too much brain and too little blood they do, I'll be a curer of madmen v 1 53
Art thou of blood and honour?—No, no, I am a rascal v 4 29
Patroclus' wounds have roused his drowsy blood v 5 32
I'll take good breath: Rest, sword; thou hast thy fill of blood and death v 8 4
If you do remember, I send it through the rivers of your blood *Coriolanus* i 1 139
Thou rascal, that art worst in blood to run, Lead'st first to win some vantage i 1 163
His bloody brow! O Jupiter, no blood! i 3 41
Than Hector's forehead when it spit forth blood At Grecian sword, contemning i 3 45
The blood I drop is rather physical Than dangerous to me i 5 19
Come I too late?—Ay, if you come not in the blood of others, But mantled in your own i 6 28
By the blood we have shed together, by the vows We have made i 6 57
'Tis not my blood Wherein thou seest me mask'd i 8 9
My mother, Who has a charter to extol her blood i 9 14
The blood upon your visage dries; 'tis time It should be look'd to: come i 9 93
From face to foot He was a thing of blood ii 2 113
For my country I have shed my blood iii 1 76

Blood. The blood he hath lost—Which, I dare vouch, is more than that he hath, By many an ounce *Coriolanus* iii 1 299
Which else would put you to your fortune and The hazard of much blood iii 2 61
The extreme dangers and the drops of blood Shed for my thankless country iv 5 75
Drawn tuns of blood out of thy country's breast iv 5 105
They shall see, sir, his crest up again, and the man in blood iv 5 225
The veins unfill'd, our blood is cold, and then We pout upon the morning v 1 51
When we have stuff'd These pipes and these conveyances of our blood v 1 54
Back, I say, go; lest I let forth your half-pint of blood v 2 61
And in her hand The grandchild to her blood v 3 24
And bear the palm for having bravely shed Thy wife and children's blood v 3 118
He sold the blood and labour Of our great action v 6 47
Stain not thy tomb with blood *T. Andron.* i 1 116
Blood and revenge are hammering in my head ii 3 39
Make pillage of her chastity And wash their hands in Bassianus' blood ii 3 45
Rude-growing briers, Upon whose leaves are drops of new-shed blood ii 3 200
Look down into this den, And see a fearful sight of blood and death ii 3 216
So pale did shine the moon on Pyramus When he by night lay bathed in maiden blood ii 3 232
A crimson river of warm blood, Like to a bubbling fountain ii 4 22
Notwithstanding all this loss of blood ii 4 29
All my blood in Rome's great quarrel shed iii 1 4
Let my tears stanch the earth's dry appetite; My sons' sweet blood will make it shame and blush iii 1 15
My youth can better spare my blood than you iii 1 166
And see their blood, or die with this reproach iv 1 94
Let no man but I Do execution on my flesh and blood iv 2 84
Touch not the boy; he is of royal blood v 1 49
Lavinia 'tween her stumps doth hold The basin that receives your guilty blood v 2 184
I will grind your bones to dust And with your blood and it I'll make a paste v 2 188
Lavinia, come, Receive the blood v 2 198
That have preserved her welfare in my blood v 3 110
Where civil blood makes civil hands unclean *Rom. and Jul.* Prol. 4
Had she affections and warm youthful blood, She would be as swift in motion as a ball ii 5 12
Now comes the wanton blood up in your cheeks ii 5 72
For now, these hot days, is the mad blood stirring iii 1 4
O cousin! husband! O, the blood is spilt Of my dear kinsman! iii 1 152
Prince, as thou art true, For blood of ours, shed blood of Montague iii 1 154
Romeo slew him, he slew Mercutio; Who now the price of his dear blood doth owe? iii 1 188
My blood for your rude brawls doth lie a-bleeding iii 1 194
Hood my unmann'd blood, bating in my cheeks, With thy black mantle iii 2 14
Pale, pale as ashes, all bedaub'd in blood, All in gore-blood iii 2 55
O God! did Romeo's hand shed Tybalt's blood?—It did, it did iii 2 71
Now I have stain'd the childhood of our joy With blood removed but little from her own iii 3 96
Dry sorrow drinks our blood. Adieu, adieu! iii 5 59
Her blood is settled, and her joints are stiff iv 5 26
Alack, what blood is this, which stains The stony entrance of this sepulchre? v 3 140
Romeo! O, pale! Who else? what, Paris too? And steep'd in blood? v 3 145
It grieves me to see so many dip their meat in one man's blood *T. of Athens* i 2 42
Their blood is caked, 'tis cold, it seldom flows ii 2 225
Tell out my blood.—Five thousand crowns, my lord.—Five thousand drops pays that iii 4 95
In hot blood, Hath stepp'd into the law, which is past depth iii 5 11
Be pitifully good: Who cannot condemn rashness in cold blood? iii 5 53
Friend or brother, He forfeits his own blood that spills another iii 5 88
Strange, unusual blood, When man's worst sin is, he does too much good! iv 2 38
With man's blood paint the ground, gules, gules iv 3 59
Go, suck the subtle blood o' the grape, Till the high fever seethe your blood to froth iv 3 432
Be men like blasted woods, And may diseases lick up their false bloods! iv 3 539
And do you now strew flowers in his way That comes in triumph over Pompey's blood? *J. Cæsar* i 1 56
Age, thou art shamed! Rome, thou hast lost the breed of noble bloods! i 2 151
When every drop of blood That every Roman bears, and nobly bears, Is guilty ii 1 136
In the spirit of men there is no blood ii 1 168
Which drizzled blood upon the Capitol ii 2 21
Like a fountain with an hundred spouts, Did run pure blood ii 2 78
Your statue spouting blood in many pipes, In which so many smiling Romans bathed, Signifies that from you great Rome shall suck Reviving blood ii 2 85
These lowly courtesies Might fire the blood of ordinary men iii 1 37
To think that Cæsar bears such rebel blood That will be thaw'd from the true quality With that which melteth fools iii 1 40
Men are flesh and blood, and apprehensive iii 1 67
Let us bathe our hands in Cæsar's blood Up to the elbows iii 1 106
I know not, gentlemen, what you intend, Who else must be let blood iii 1 152
Made rich With the most noble blood of all this world iii 1 156
Had I as many eyes as thou hast wounds, Weeping as fast as they stream forth thy blood iii 1 201
Woe to the hand that shed this costly blood! iii 1 258
Blood and destruction shall be so in use And dreadful objects so familiar iii 1 265
Go and kiss dead Cæsar's wounds And dip their napkins in his sacred blood iii 2 138
As he pluck'd his cursed steel away, Mark how the blood of Cæsar follow'd it iii 2 182
At the base of Pompey's statua, Which all the while ran blood, great Cæsar fell iii 2 193
Nor utterance, nor the power of speech, To stir men's blood iii 2 227
I had rather coin my heart, And drop my blood for drachmas iv 3 73
When grief, and blood ill-temper'd, vexeth him iv 3 115
I know young bloods look for a time of rest iv 3 262
Art thou some god, some angel, or some devil, That makest my blood cold? iv 3 280
O setting sun, As in thy red rays thou dost sink to night, So in his red blood Cassius' day is set! v 3 62
Make thick my blood; Stop up the access and passage to remorse! *Macbeth* i 5 44
Will it not be received, When we have mark'd with blood those sleepy two Of his own chamber and used their very daggers, That they have done't? i 7 75
I see thee still, And on thy blade and dudgeon gouts of blood ii 1 46

Blood. Go carry them; and smear The sleepy grooms with blood.—I'll go no more . . . . *Macbeth* ii 2 50
Will all great Neptune's ocean wash this blood Clean from my hand? . ii 2 60
The fountain of your blood Is stopp'd; the very source of it is stopp'd. ii 3 103
Their hands and faces were all badged with blood; So were their daggers ii 3 107
Here lay Duncan, His silver skin laced with his golden blood . . ii 3 118
There's daggers in men's smiles: the near in blood, The nearer bloody. ii 3 146
There's blood upon thy face . . . . iii 4 12
Blood hath been shed ere now, i' the olden time . . . . iii 4 75
Let the earth hide thee! Thy bones are marrowless, thy blood is cold. iii 4 94
It will have blood; they say, blood will have blood . . . iii 4 122
Augurs and understood relations have By magot-pies and choughs and rooks brought forth The secret'st man of blood . . . . iii 4 126
I am in blood Stepp'd in so far that, should I wade no more, Returning were as tedious as go o'er . . . . iii 4 136
Cool it with a baboon's blood, Then the charm is firm and good . iv 1 37
Pour in sow's blood, that hath eaten Her nine farrow . . . iv 1 64
Who would have thought the old man to have had so much blood in him? v 1 44
Here's the smell of the blood still . . . . v 1 56
Those clamorous harbingers of blood and death . . . . v 6 10
Get thee back; my soul is too much charged With blood of thine already v 8 6
As stars with trains of fire and dews of blood, Disasters in the sun *Hamlet* i 1 117
Hold it a fashion and a toy in blood, A violet in the youth of primy nature i 3 6
When the blood burns, how prodigal the soul Lends the tongue vows i 3 116
Whose lightest word Would harrow up thy soul, freeze thy young blood i 5 16
But this eternal blazon must not be To ears of flesh and blood . i 5 22
Whose effect Holds such an enmity with blood of man . . . i 5 65
And curd, like eager droppings into milk, The thin and wholesome blood i 5 70
A savageness in unreclaimed blood, Of general assault . . . ii 1 34
Horridly trick'd With blood of fathers, mothers, daughters, sons . ii 2 480
Blest are those Whose blood and judgement are so well commingled . iii 2 74
Now could I drink hot blood, And do such bitter business as the day Would quake to look on . . . . iii 2 408
What if this cursed hand Were thicker than itself with brother's blood? iii 3 44
At your age The hey-day in the blood is tame, it's humble . . iii 4 69
What I have to do Will want true colour: tears perchance for blood . iii 4 130
For like the hectic in my blood he rages, And thou must cure me . iv 3 68
Excitements of my reason and my blood . . . . . . iv 4 58
That drop of blood that's calm proclaims me bastard . . . iv 5 117
Like the kind life-rendering pelican, Repast them with my blood . . iv 5 147
Where it draws blood no cataplasm so rare . . . . . iv 7 144
Here I disclaim all my paternal care, Propinquity and property of blood *Lear* i 1 116
Some blood drawn on me would beget opinion Of my more fierce endeavour ii 1 35
Are they inform'd of this? My breath and blood! . . . . ii 4 104
But yet thou art my flesh, my blood, my daughter . . . . ii 4 224
Thou art a boil, A plague-sore, an embossed carbuncle, In my corrupted blood . . . . ii 4 228
I am a gentleman of blood and breeding . . . . . . iii 1 40
Our flesh and blood is grown so vile, my lord, That it doth hate what gets it . . . . iii 4 150
I had a son, Now outlaw'd from my blood; he sought my life, But lately iii 4 172
Fie, foh, and fum, I smell the blood of a British man . . . iii 4 189
I will persevere in my course of loyalty, though the conflict be sore between that and my blood . . . . iii 5 24
Were't my fitness To let these hands obey my blood . . . iv 2 64
I am no less in blood than thou art, Edmund . . . . . v 3 167
O heaven! How got she out? O treason of the blood! . *Othello* i 1 170
With some mixtures powerful o'er the blood . . . . . i 3 104
As truly as to heaven I do confess the vices of my blood . . . i 3 123
The blood and baseness of our natures would conduct us to most preposterous conclusions . . . . i 3 332
It is merely a lust of the blood and a permission of the will . . i 3 339
When the blood is made dull with the act of sport . . . . ii 1 229
Now, by heaven, My blood begins my safer guides to rule . . . ii 3 205
With a little act upon the blood, Burn like the mines of sulphur . iii 3 328
O, blood, blood, blood!—Patience, I say; your mind perhaps may change . . . . iii 3 451
Is it his use? Or did the letters work upon his blood? . . . iv 1 286
Thy bed, lust-stain'd, shall with lust's blood be spotted . . . v 1 36
I'll not shed her blood; Nor scar that whiter skin of hers than snow . v 2 3
Thou blushest, Antony; and that blood of thine Is Cæsar's homager *Ant. and Cleo.* i 1 30
High in name and power, Higher than both in blood and life . . i 2 197
You'll heat my blood: no more.—You can do better yet; but this is meetly . . . . i 3 80
The borders maritime Lack blood to think on't, and flush youth revolt i 4 52
My salad days, When I was green in judgement: cold in blood . . i 5 74
Whilst yet with Parthian blood thy sword is warm, The fugitive Parthians follow . . . . iii 1 6
If from the field I shall return once more To kiss these lips, I will appear in blood . . . . iii 13 174
I will live, Or bathe my dying honour in the blood Shall make it live again . . . . iv 2 6
Before the sun shall see's, we'll spill the blood That has to-day escaped iv 8 3
I robb'd his wound of it; behold it stain'd With his most noble blood . v 1 26
But yet let me lament, With tears as sovereign as the blood of hearts v 1 41
Here, on her breast, There is a vent of blood and something blown . v 2 352
Our bloods No more obey the heavens than our courtiers Still seem as does the king . . . . *Cymbeline* i 1 1
Away! Thou'rt poison to my blood. . . . . i 1 128
Let her languish A drop of blood a day; and, being aged, Die of this folly! . . . . i 1 157
How! that I should murder her? Upon the love and truth and vows which I Have made to thy command? I, her? her blood? . . iii 2 13
Thus I set my foot on's neck; even then The princely blood flows in his cheek . . . . iii 3 93
To gain his colour I'ld let a parish of such Clotens blood, And praise myself . . . . iv 2 168
Yet as rough, Their royal blood enchafed, as the rudest wind . . iv 2 174
O! Give colour to my pale cheek with thy blood, That we the horrider may seem . . . . iv 2 330
Scarce ever look'd on blood, But that of coward hares, hot goats! . iv 4 36
Their blood thinks scorn, Till it fly out and show them princes born . iv 4 53
We should not, when the blood was cool, have threaten'd Our prisoners with the sword . . . . v 5 77
Save him, sir, And spare no blood beside . . . . . . v 5 92
That paragon, thy daughter,—For whom my heart drops blood . . v 5 148
They are the issue of your loins, my liege, And blood of your begetting v 5 331

Blood. How many worthy princes' bloods were shed, To keep his bed of blackness unlaid ope . . . . *Pericles* i 2 88
Drew sleep out of mine eyes, blood from my cheeks, Musings into my mind . . . . i 2 96
We'll mingle our bloods together in the earth, From whence we had our being . . . . i 2 113
The king my father, sir, has drunk to you.—I thank him.—Wishing it so much blood unto your life . . . . ii 3 77
May be, nor can I think the contrary, As great in blood as I myself . ii 5 80
If you love me, sir.—Even as my life my blood that fosters it . . ii 5 89
Do not Consume your blood with sorrowing: you have A nurse of me . iv 1 24
Pray, walk softly, do not heat your blood . . . . . . iv 1 49
O lady, Much less in blood than virtue, yet a princess To equal any single crown o' the earth! . . . . iv 3 7
For flesh and blood, sir, white and red, you shall see a rose . . iv 6 37
But are you flesh and blood? Have you a working pulse? . . v 1 154
Blood-bespotted Neapolitan, Outcast of Naples! . . . *2 Hen. VI.* v 1 117
Blood-boltered. The blood-bolter'd Banquo smiles upon me . *Macbeth* iv 1 123
Blood-consuming. Heart-offending groans Or blood-consuming sighs *2 Hen. VI.* iii 2 61
Blood-drinking. This pale and angry rose, As cognizance of my blood-drinking hate . . . . *1 Hen. VI.* ii 4 108
Look pale as primrose with blood-drinking sighs . . . *2 Hen. VI.* iii 2 63
In this detested, dark, blood-drinking pit . . . . *T. Andron.* ii 3 224
Bloodhound. You rogue, come; bring me to a justice.—Ay, come, you starved blood-hound . . . . *2 Hen. IV.* v 4 31
Bloodied. Stopp'd by me to breathe his bloodied horse . . . . i 1 38
Look you how his sword is bloodied! . . . . *Troi. and Cres.* i 2 253
Bloodier. Thou bloodier villain Than terms can give thee out! *Macbeth* v 8 7
Bloodiest. This is the bloodiest shame, The wildest savagery . *K. John* iv 3 47
Bloodily. How bloodily the sun begins to peer Above yon busky hill! the day looks pale . . . . *1 Hen. IV.* v 1 1
Kisses the gashes That bloodily did yawn upon his face . . *Hen. V.* iv 6 14
How they at Pomfret bloodily were butcher'd . . . *Richard III.* iii 4 92
That thou so many princes at a shot So bloodily hast struck? *Hamlet* v 2 378
Bloodless. But silence, like a Lucrece knife, With bloodless stroke my heart doth gore . . . . *T. Night* ii 5 117
A timely-parted ghost, Of ashy semblance, meagre, pale and bloodless *2 Hen. VI.* iii 2 162
Thou bloodless remnant of that royal blood! . . . *Richard III.* i 2 7
Grows to an envious fever Of pale and bloodless emulation *Troi. and Cres.* i 3 134
With this dear sight Struck pale and bloodless . . *T. Andron.* iii 1 258
Blood-sacrifice. Cannot my body nor blood-sacrifice Entreat you? *1 Hen. VI.* v 3 20
Bloodshed. And prove a deadly bloodshed but a jest, Exampled by this heinous spectacle . . . . *K. John* iv 3 55
Which daily grew to quarrel and to bloodshed . . *2 Hen. IV.* iv 5 195
Bloodshedding. These hands are free from guiltless blood-shedding *2 Hen. VI.* iv 7 108
Bloodstained. The hollow bank Bloodstained with these valiant combatants . . . . *1 Hen. IV.* i 3 107
Help me out From this unhallowed and blood-stained hole *T. Andron.* ii 3 210
These sorrowful drops upon thy blood-stain'd face . . . . v 3 154
Bloodsucker. Pernicious blood-sucker of sleeping men! . *2 Hen. VI.* iii 2 226
A knot you are of damned blood-suckers . . . . *Richard III.* iii 3 6
Bloodsucking. And stop the rising of blood-sucking sighs *3 Hen. VI.* iv 4 22
Bloodthirsty. Prisoner! to whom?—To me, blood-thirsty lord *1 Hen. VI.* ii 3 34
Bloody. Nor set A mark so bloody on the business . . . *Tempest* i 2 142
Thy desires Are wolvish, bloody, starved and ravenous *Mer. of Venice* iv 1 138
Full of despite, bloody as the hunter . . . . . *T. Night* iii 4 243
The most skilful, bloody and fatal opposite . . . . . iii 4 293
Whom thou, in terms so bloody and so dear, Hast made thine enemies . v 1 74
Which being so horrible, so bloody, must Lead on to some foul issue *W. Tale* ii 3 152
His hands were guilty of no kindred blood, But bloody with the enemies of his kin . . . . *Richard II.* ii 1 183
Bloody with spurring, fiery-red with haste . . . . . . ii 3 58
The pale-faced moon looks bloody on the earth . . . . . ii 4 10
Shall see thee wither'd, bloody, pale and dead . . *1 Hen. VI.* iv 2 38
Thy age confirm'd, proud, subtle, bloody, treacherous *Richard III.* iv 4 171
Bloody thou art, bloody will be thy end . . . . . . iv 4 194
Bloody and guilty, guiltily awake, And in a bloody battle end thy days! v 3 146
I'm sure Thou hast a cruel nature and a bloody . . . *Hen. VIII.* v 3 129
Arm'd, and bloody in intent . . . . . . *Troi. and Cres.* v 3 8
It is the humane way: the other course Will prove too bloody *Coriolanus* iii 1 328
May prove More stern and bloody than the Centaurs' feast *T. Andron.* v 2 204
The ground is bloody; search about the churchyard *Rom. and Jul.* v 3 172
The fault's Bloody; 'tis necessary he should die *T. of Athens* iii 5 2
Like the work we have in hand, Most bloody, fiery, and most terrible *J. Cæsar* i 3 130
Our course will seem too bloody, Caius Cassius, To cut the head off and then hack the limbs . . . . ii 1 162
Beg not your death of us. Though now we must appear bloody and cruel iii 1 165
There's daggers in men's smiles: the near in blood, The nearer bloody *Macbeth* ii 3 147
With thy bloody and invisible hand Cancel and tear to pieces that great bond Which keeps me pale! . . . . iii 2 48
Be bloody, bold, and resolute; laugh to scorn The power of man . iv 1 79
I grant him bloody, Luxurious, avaricious, false, deceitful . . iv 3 57
From this time forth, My thoughts be bloody, or be nothing worth! *Hamlet* iv 4 66
So shall you hear Of carnal, bloody, and unnatural acts . . . v 2 392
False of heart, light of ear, bloody of hand . . . . *Lear* iii 4 95
The arbitrement is like to be bloody . . . . iv 7 95
Swords out, and tilting one at other's breast, In opposition bloody *Othello* ii 3 184
I will be found most cunning in my patience; But—dost thou hear?—most bloody . . . . iv 1 92
If my shirt were bloody, then to shift it . . . . *Cymbeline* i 2 6
Bloody accidents. These bloody accidents must excuse my manners *Othello* v 1 94
Bloody affirmation. Upon warrant of bloody affirmation . *Cymbeline* i 4 63
Bloody argument. The quality of the time and quarrel Might well have given us bloody argument . . . . *T. Night* iii 3 32
Bloody axe. By envy's hand and murder's bloody axe . . *Richard II.* i 2 21
I will free myself, Or hew my way out with a bloody axe *3 Hen. VI.* iii 2 181
Bloody battle. To bloody battles and to bruising arms . *1 Hen. IV.* iii 2 105
And in a bloody battle end thy days! . . . . . *Richard III.* v 3 147
Bloody battle-axe. Rear'd aloft the bloody battle-axe . . *T. Andron.* iii 1 169
Bloody blocks. Had he twenty heads to tender down On twenty bloody blocks . . . . *Meas. for Meas.* ii 4 181

Bloody boar. In the sty of this most bloody boar . . *Richard III.* iv 5 2
The wretched, bloody, and usurping boar . . . . v 2 7
Bloody book. This lawless bloody book Of forged rebellion 2 *Hen. IV.* iv 1 91
The bloody book of law You shall yourself read in the bitter letter *Othello* i 3 67
Bloody breast. With bloody blameful blade, He bravely broach'd his boiling bloody breast . . . . . . *M. N. Dream* v 1 148
Bloody brother. I rather will subject me to the malice Of a diverted blood and bloody brother . . . . *As Y. Like It* ii 3 37
Bloody brow. His bloody brow With his mail'd hand then wiping *Coriol.* i 3 37
His bloody brow! O Jupiter, no blood! . . . . i 3 41
Bloody business. It is the bloody business which informs Thus to mine eyes . . . . *Macbeth* ii 1 48
Let him command, And to obey shall be in me remorse, What bloody business ever . . . . *Othello* iii 3 469
Bloody cannibals. Butchers and villains! bloody cannibals! 3 *Hen. VI.* v 5 61
Bloody Clifford. Ah, tutor, look where bloody Clifford comes! i 3 2
Come, bloody Clifford, rough Northumberland . . . i 4 27
Bloody cloth, I'll keep thee, for I wish'd Thou shouldst be colour'd thus *Cymbeline* v 1 1
Bloody colours. Sound trumpets! let our bloody colours wave! 3 *Hen. VI.* ii 2 173
Bloody constraint. Or else what follows?—Bloody constraint *Hen. V.* ii 4 97
Bloody corse. A piteous corse, a bloody piteous corse . *Rom. and Jul.* iii 2 54
Bloody course. Write, that from the bloody course of war My dearest master, your dear son, may hie . . . *All's Well* iii 4 8
Each heart being set On bloody courses, the rude scene may end 2 *Hen. IV.* i 1 159
Bloody cousins. Our bloody cousins are bestow'd In England *Macbeth* iii 1 30
Bloody coxcomb. If a bloody coxcomb be a hurt, you have hurt me *T. Night* v 1 193
I think you set nothing by a bloody coxcomb . . . . v 1 195
Bloody creditor. I shall hardly spare a pound of flesh To-morrow to my bloody creditor . . . . . *Mer. of Venice* iii 3 34
Bloody crowns. Ten thousand bloody crowns of mothers' sons *Richard II.* iii 3 96
Bloody daggers. When my son Was stabb'd with bloody daggers *Richard III.* i 3 212
Bloody darts. Like a wild Morisco, Shaking the bloody darts 2 *Hen. VI.* iii 1 366
Bloody day. He would make this a bloody day to somebody 2 *Hen. IV.* v 4 14
We should have found a bloody day of this . . . 1 *Hen. IV.* iv 7 34
That would reduce these bloody days again . . . *Richard III.* v 5 36
Bloody deed. This is the man should do the bloody deed . *K. John* iv 2 69
Whose bloody deeds shall make all Europe quake . 1 *Hen. VI.* iv 1 156
And God, not we, hath plagued thy bloody deed . *Richard III.* i 3 181
A bloody deed, and desperately dispatch'd! . . . . i 4 278
The tyrannous and bloody deed is done . . . . iv 3 1
Dream on, dream on, of bloody deeds and death! . . v 3 171
Performers of this heinous, bloody deed . . . *T. Andron.* iv 1 80
Is't known who did this more than bloody deed? . . *Macbeth* ii 4 22
O, what a rash and bloody deed is this! . . . . *Hamlet* iii 4 27
How shall this bloody deed be answer'd? It will be laid to us . iv 1 16
Bloody distance. In such bloody distance, That every minute of his being thrusts Against my near'st of life . . *Macbeth* iii 1 116
Bloody dogs, Melting with tenderness and kind compassion *Richard III.* iv 3 6
The day is ours, the bloody dog is dead . . . . v 5 2
Bloody Douglas. That furious Scot, The bloody Douglas . 2 *Hen. IV.* i 1 127
Bloody drops. Will you sterner be Than he that dies and lives by bloody drops? . . . . *As Y. Like It* iii 5 7
Bloody England into England gone, O'erbearing interruption *K. John* iii 4 8
Bloody execution. His brandish'd steel, Which smoked with bloody execution . . . . *Macbeth* i 2 18
Bloody-faced. In a theme so bloody-faced as this . . 2 *Hen. IV.* i 3 22
Bloody field. In a bloody field by Shrewsbury . . . . Ind. 24
Sword and shield, In bloody field, Doth win immortal fame *Hen. V.* iii 2 10
That we may wander o'er this bloody field To look our dead . iv 7 75
Bloody finger. Shaking the bloody fingers of thy foes . *J. Cæsar* iii 1 198
Upon his bloody finger he doth wear A precious ring . *T. Andron.* ii 3 226
Bloody fingers' ends. Out of the bloody fingers' ends of John *K. John* iii 4 168
Bloody fire. Lust is but a bloody fire, Kindled with unchaste desire *Mer. Wives* v 5 99
Bloody flag. Stand for your own; unwind your bloody flag *Hen. V.* i 2 101
Set up the bloody flag against all patience . . *Coriolanus* ii 1 84
Bloody fray. Death hath not struck so fat a deer to-day, Though many dearer, in this bloody fray . . . . 1 *Hen. IV.* v 4 108
After the bloody fray at Wakefield fought . . . 3 *Hen. VI.* ii 1 107
Who began this bloody fray? . . . . *Rom. and Jul.* iii 1 156
Bloody hand. In liberty of bloody hand shall range With conscience wide as hell . . . . *Hen. V.* iii 3 12
And may ye both be suddenly surprised By bloody hands! 1 *Hen. VI.* v 3 41
From those bloody hands Throw your mistemper'd weapons *R. and J.* i 1 93
Let each man render me his bloody hand . . . *J. Cæsar* iii 1 184
Hide thee, thou bloody hand . . . . . . *Lear* iii 2 53
Thou rascal beadle, hold thy bloody hand! . . . . iv 6 164
Set on there! Never was a war did cease, Ere bloody hands were wash'd, with such a peace . . . . . *Cymbeline* v 5 485
Bloody Hector. When I have the bloody Hector found, Empale him with your weapons round about . . . *Troi. and Cres.* v 7 4
Bloody homicide. I am with child, ye bloody homicides . 1 *Hen. VI.* v 4 62
To fight against that bloody homicide . . . . *Richard III.* v 2 18
Bloody host. And on the marriage-bed Of smiling peace to march a bloody host . . . . *K. John* iii 1 246
Bloody hounds. Turn on the bloody hounds with heads of steel 1 *Hen. VI.* iv 2 51
Bloody hour. Where they did spend a sad and bloody hour 1 *Hen. IV.* i 1 56
Bloody house. A warrant To break within the bloody house of life *K. John* iv 2 210
Bloody-hunting. Herod's bloody-hunting slaughtermen . *Hen. V.* iii 3 41
Bloody inclination. And their gentle hearts To fierce and bloody inclination . . . . *K. John* v 2 158
Bloody instructions, which, being taught, return To plague the inventor *Macbeth* i 7 9
Bloody insurrection. To dress the ugly form Of base and bloody insurrection . . . . 2 *Hen. IV.* iv 1 40
Bloody issue. Must With fearful bloody issue arbitrate . *K. John* i 1 38
Bloody kind. Two of thy whelps, fell curs of bloody kind *T. Andron.* iii 3 281
Bloody king. To bring this tidings to the bloody king *Richard III.* iv 3 22
Bloody knife. This bloody knife Shall play the umpire . *Rom. and Jul.* iv 1 62
What means that bloody knife?—'Tis hot, it smokes . . *Lear* v 3 223
Bloody knives. Free from our feasts and banquets bloody knives *Macbeth* iii 6 35
Bloody lines. What I mean to do See here in bloody lines I have set down *T. Andron.* v 2 14
Bloody looks. Affrighted with their bloody looks . . 1 *Hen. IV.* i 3 104
Bloody man. Save me! my eyes are out Even with the fierce looks of these bloody men . . . . *K. John* iv 1 74

Bloody man. How the people take The cruel issue of these bloody men *J. Cæsar* iii 1 294
What bloody man is that? He can report, As seemeth by his plight *Macbeth* i 2 1
These flowers are like the pleasures of the world; This bloody man, the care on't. I hope I dream . . . . . . *Cymbeline* iv 2 297
Bloody marks. My tears shall wipe away these bloody marks 3 *Hen. VI.* ii 5 71
Bloody mask. I will wear a garment all of blood And stain my favours in a bloody mask . . . . . . 1 *Hen. IV.* iii 2 136
Bloody massacre. In all our bloody massacre, I muse we met not with the Dauphin's grace . . . . 1 *Hen. VI.* ii 2 18
Bloody mind. Thou wast provoked by thy bloody mind . *Richard III.* i 2 99
That bloody mind, I think, they learn'd of me . . *T. Andron.* v 1 101
Bloody-minded. Yet let not this make thee be bloody-minded 2 *Hen. VI.* iv 1 36
Some troops pursue the bloody-minded queen . . . 3 *Hen. VI.* ii 6 33
Bloody minister. Who made thee, then, a bloody minister? *Richard III.* i 4 226
Bloody mouth. Which Lion vile with bloody mouth did stain *M. N. Dr.* v 1 144
Bloody murder. Where bloody murder or detested rape Can couch for fear . . . . *T. Andron.* v 2 37
Bloody murderer. Unless it were a bloody murderer 2 *Hen. VI.* iii 1 128
Bloody napkin. He sends this bloody napkin . . . *As Y. Like It* iv 3 94
But, for the bloody napkin?—By and by . . . . . iv 3 139
Bloody nature. The offence is not of such a bloody nature . *T. Night* iii 3 30
Bloody Neroes, ripping up the womb Of your dear mother England *K. John* v 2 152
Bloody noses. We must have bloody noses and crack'd crowns 1 *Hen. IV.* ii 3 96
Bloody nurser. He lies inhearsed in the arms Of the most bloody nurser of his harms! . . . . 1 *Hen. VI.* iv 7 46
Bloody office. Who perform'd The bloody office of his timeless end *Richard II.* iv 1 5
Bloody parliament. The bloody parliament shall this be call'd 3 *Hen. VI.* i 1 39
Bloody passage. And With bloody passage led your wars *Coriolanus* v 6 76
Bloody passion. Some bloody passion shakes your very frame *Othello* v 2 44
Bloody payment. Even with the bloody payment of your deaths 1 *Hen. IV.* i 3 186
Bloody period. O bloody period!—All that's spoke is marr'd . *Othello* v 2 357
Bloody piece of work. Let us meet, And question this most bloody piece of work . . . . *Macbeth* ii 3 134
Bloody pillow. Who is this Thou makest thy bloody pillow? *Cymbeline* iv 2 363
Bloody point. Turn face to face and bloody point to point . *K. John* ii 1 390
Bloody pole. And sooner dance upon a bloody pole Than stand uncover'd to the vulgar groom . . . . . . 2 *Hen. VI.* iv 1 127
Bloody power. I'll withdraw me and my bloody power . 1 *Hen. VI.* iv 2 8
And wide havoc made For bloody power to rush upon your peace *K. John* ii 1 221
Bloody prison. O Pomfret, Pomfret! O thou bloody prison! *Richard III.* iii 3 9
Bloody proclamation. The bloody proclamation to escape *Lear* v 3 183
Bloody question. So jump upon this bloody question . *Hamlet* v 2 386
Bloody red. Shall dye your white rose in a bloody red . 1 *Hen. VI.* ii 4 61
Bloody Richard. O bloody Richard! miserable England *Richard III.* iii 4 105
Bloody safety. He that steeps his safety in true blood Shall find but bloody safety and untrue . . . . *K. John* iii 4 148
Bloody-sceptered. O nation miserable, With an untitled tyrant bloody-scepter'd . . . . *Macbeth* iv 3 104
Bloody scourge. Our nation's terror and their bloody scourge 1 *Hen. VI.* v 2 16
Outcast of Naples, England's bloody scourge! . . 2 *Hen. VI.* v 1 118
Bloody sheet. Liest thou there in thy bloody sheet? . *Rom. and Jul.* v 3 97
Bloody side. By his bloody side, Yoke-fellow to his honour-owing wounds, The noble Earl of Suffolk . . . . . . *Hen. V.* iv 6 8
Bloody siege. All preparation for a bloody siege . . *K. John* ii 1 213
Bloody sight. O traitors, villains!—O most bloody sight! *J. Cæsar* iii 2 206
Bloody sign. Their bloody sign of battle is hung out . . . v 1 14
I'll give but notice you are dead and send him Some bloody sign of it *Cymbeline* iii 4 128
Bloody sin. Murder indeed, that bloody sin, I tortured Above the felon or what trespass else . . . . . . 2 *Hen. VI.* iii 1 131
Bloody slaughter-house. Bearing it to the bloody slaughter-house . iii 1 212
Bloody soldier. The blind and bloody soldier with foul hand *Hen. V.* iii 3 34
Bloody spectacle. O barbarous and bloody spectacle! 2 *Hen. VI.* iv 1 144
Bloody spoil. Thou dost shame That bloody spoil . . *K. John* iii 1 115
Having bought love with such a bloody spoil . . *Richard III.* iv 4 290
Bloody spur. But when they should endure the bloody spur, They fall their crests . . . . *J. Cæsar* iv 2 25
Bloody stage. Thou seest, the heavens, as troubled with man's act, Threaten his bloody stage . . . . *Macbeth* ii 4 6
Bloody state. These mine eyes saw him in bloody state . 2 *Hen. IV.* i 1 107
Bloody steel grasp'd in their ireful hands . . 3 *Hen. VI.* v 5 132
Bloody strain. He is bred out of that bloody strain That haunted us in our familiar paths . . . . *Hen. V.* ii 4 51
Bloody strife. That such immanity and bloody strife Should reign among professors of one faith . . . . . . 1 *Hen. VI.* v 1 13
Bloody stroke. Put thy fortune to the arbitrement Of bloody strokes *Richard III.* v 3 90
Let me say, Before I strike this bloody stroke, farewell . *Ant. and Cleo.* iv 14 91
Bloody succeeding. A most harsh one, and not to be understood without bloody succeeding . . . . *All's Well* ii 3 199
Bloody supper. To make a bloody supper in the Tower . 3 *Hen. VI.* v 5 85
Bloody sweat. Drops bloody sweat from his war-wearied limbs 1 *Hen. VI.* iv 4 18
Bloody sword. His bloody sword he brandish'd over me . 1 *Hen. VI.* iv 7 6
Bloody Talbot. All will be ours, now bloody Talbot's slain . . iv 7 96
Bloody teeth. I will give thee bloody teeth . . *Ant. and Cleo.* i 5 70
Bloody thieves. Where be these bloody thieves? . . . *Othello* v 1 63
Bloody thoughts. I do begin to have bloody thoughts . . *Tempest* iv 1 221
Being transported by my jealousies To bloody thoughts . . *W. Tale* iii 2 160
Nearer in bloody thoughts, but not in blood . . . *Richard III.* ii 1 92
Even so my bloody thoughts, with violent pace, Shall ne'er look back *Othello* iii 3 457
Bloody times. O piteous spectacle! O bloody times! . . 3 *Hen. VI.* ii 5 73
Bloody toil. After such bloody toil, we bid good night . *K. John* v 5 6
Bloody treason. And all of us fell down, Whilst bloody treason flourish'd over us . . . . *J. Cæsar* iii 2 196
Bloody trial. By this one bloody trial of sharp war *Richard III.* v 2 16
Bloody turbulence. I have dream'd Of bloody turbulence *Troi. and Cres.* v 3 11
Bloody Tybalt. Where bloody Tybalt, yet but green in earth, Lies festering in his shroud . . . . *Rom. and Jul.* iv 3 42
Bloody tyranny. My father's execution Was nothing less than bloody tyranny . . . . 1 *Hen. VI.* ii 5 100
Bloody tyrant. A bloody tyrant and a homicide; One raised in blood *Richard III.* v 3 246
Bloody veins. Like the Trojan horse was stuff'd within With bloody veins . . . . *Pericles* i 4 94

Bloody villain. I leave you both: like bloody villains T. Andron. iv 2 17
Bloody, bawdy villain! Remorseless, treacherous, lecherous, kindless villain! . . . . Hamlet ii 2 608
Bloody villany. Finding thee fit for bloody villany, Apt K. John iv 2 225
Bloody war. The proud control of fierce and bloody war . i 1 17
I myself, Rather than bloody war shall cut them short, Will parley 2 Hen. VI. iv 4 12
So thrive I in my enterprise And dangerous success of bloody wars! Richard III. iv 4 236
Bloody work. It is a damned and a bloody work K. John iv 3 57
Bloody wretch. This long-usurped royalty From the dead temples of this bloody wretch Have I pluck'd off Richard III. v 5 5
Bloody wrongs. To quit the bloody wrongs upon her foes T. Andron. i 1 141
Bloody youth. Led on by bloody youth, guarded with rags 2 Hen. IV. iv 1 34
Bloom. His May of youth and bloom of lustihood Much Ado v 1 76
No sun to ripe The bloom that promiseth a mighty fruit K. John ii 1 473
Bloomed. Thy promises are like Adonis' gardens That one day bloom'd and fruitful were the next 1 Hen. VI. i 6 7
Blossom. Merrily shall I live now Under the blossom that hangs on the bough Tempest v 1 94
Spied a blossom passing fair Playing in the wanton air L. L. Lost iv 3 103
If frosts and fasts, hard lodging and thin weeds Nip not the gaudy blossoms of your love v 2 812
Thou prunest a rotten tree, That cannot so much as a blossom yield As Y. Like It ii 3 64
Blossom, speed thee well! There lie, and there thy character W. Tale iii 3 46
Already appearing in the blossoms of their fortune . v 2 135
O, that this good blossom could be kept from cankers! . 2 Hen. IV. ii 2 101
Then for the truth and plainness of the case, I pluck this pale and maiden blossom here 1 Hen. VI. ii 4 47
And there died, My Icarus, my blossom, in his pride . iv 7 16
Thus are my blossoms blasted in the bud . 2 Hen. VI. iii 1 89
To-day he puts forth The tender leaves of hopes; to-morrow blossoms Hen. VIII. iii 2 353
Sweet blowse, you are a beauteous blossom, sure T. Andron. iv 2 72
Cut off even in the blossoms of my sin, Unhousel'd, disappointed Hamlet i 5 76
Yet fruits that blossom first will first be ripe . Othello ii 3 383
Blossoming. As blossoming time That from the seedness the bare fallow brings To teeming foison Meas. for Meas. i 4 41
Do discandy, melt their sweets On blossoming Cæsar Ant. and Cleo. iv 12 23
Blot. It is the lesser blot, modesty finds, Women to change their shapes than men their minds T. G. of Ver. v 4 108
I am possess'd with an adulterate blot Com. of Errors ii 2 142
If black, why, Nature, drawing of an antique, Made a foul blot Much Ado iii 1 64
Who can blot that name With any just reproach? . iv 1 81
Hero itself can blot out Hero's virtue . iv 1 83
She passes praise; then praise too short doth blot L. L. Lost iv 3 241
And the blots of Nature's hand Shall not in their issue stand M. N. Dream v 1 416
It blots thy beauty as frosts do bite the meads T. of Shrew v 2 139
To look into the blots and stains of right K. John ii 1 114
There's a good mother, boy, that blots thy father.—There's a good grandam, boy, that would blot thee . ii 1 132
Full of unpleasing blots and sightless stains . iii 1 45
Bound in with shame, With inky blots and rotten parchment bonds Richard II. ii 1 64
All souls that will be safe fly from my side, For time hath set a blot upon my pride . iii 2 81
Mark'd with a blot, damn'd in the book of heaven . iv 1 236
Is there no plot To rid the realm of this pernicious blot? . iv 1 325
Thy abundant goodness shall excuse This deadly blot in thy digressing son v 3 66
For his sake wear the detested blot Of murderous subornation 1 Hen. IV. i 3 162
Thy fall hath left a kind of blot, To mark the full-fraught man Hen. V. ii 2 138
This blot that they object against your house Shall be wiped out 1 Hen. VI. ii 4 116
Never yet did base dishonour blur our name, But with our sword we wiped away the blot 2 Hen. VI. iv 1 40
Have caused him, by new act of parliament, To blot out me 3 Hen. VI. i 2 92
Your mere enforcement shall acquittance me From all the impure blots and stains thereof Richard III. iii 7 234
Ah, beastly creature! The blot and enemy to our general name! T. And. ii 3 183
Even such heaps and sums of love and wealth As shall to thee blot out what wrongs were theirs T. of Athens v 1 156
It is no vicious blot, murder, or foulness, No unchaste action Lear i 1 230
Blotted. The unpleasant'st words That ever blotted paper! Mer. of Venice iii 2 255
If ever I were traitor, My name be blotted from the book of life! Rich. II. i 3 202
Forth of my heart those charms, thine eyes, are blotted . Othello v 1 35
Blotting your names from books of memory 2 Hen. VI. i 1 100
Blow, till thou burst thy wind, if room enough! . Tempest i 1 8
A south-west blow on ye And blister you all o'er! i 2 323
Continue and laugh at nothing still.—What a blow was there given! ii 1 180
And would no more endure This wooden slavery than to suffer The flesh-fly blow my mouth iii 1 63
I do beseech thy greatness, give him blows And take his bottle from him iii 2 72
The most forward bud Is eaten by the canker ere it blow T. G. of Ver. i 1 46
Be calm, good wind, blow not a word away Till I have found each letter i 2 118
Whose flames aspire As thoughts do blow them, higher and higher Mer. Wives v 5 102
There is a vice that most I do abhor, And most desire should meet the blow of justice Meas. for Meas. ii 2 30
He struck so plainly, I could too well feel his blows Com. of Errors ii 1 53
An you use these blows long, I must get a sconce for my head ii 2 37
He did buffet thee and in his blows Denied my house for his . ii 2 160
If the skin were parchment and the blows you gave were ink iii 1 13
Thou art an ass.—Marry, so it doth appear By the wrongs I suffer and the blows I bear iii 1 16
Well struck! there was blow for blow iii 1 56
If the wind blow any way from shore, I will not harbour in this town to-night iii 2 153
The ship is in her trim; the merry wind Blows fair from land iv 1 91
I would I were senseless, sir, that I might not feel your blows iv 4 27
Thou art sensible in nothing but blows, and so is an ass. iv 4 29
And have nothing at his hands for my service but blows iv 4 33
Air, quoth he, thy cheeks may blow; Air, would I might triumph so! L. L. Lost iv 3 109
And leap for joy, though they are lame with blows . v 2 291
Blow like sweet roses in this summer air.—How blow? how blow? v 2 293
When icicles hang by the wall And Dick the shepherd blows his nail v 2 923
When all aloud the wind doth blow And coughing drowns the parson's saw v 2 931
I know a bank where the wild thyme blows . M. N. Dream ii 1 249

Blow. My wind cooling my broth, Would blow me to an ague Mer. of Ven. i 1 23
The four winds blow in from every coast Renowned suitors . i 1 168
It bites and blows upon my body, Even till I shrink with cold As Y. Like It ii 1 8
As large a charter as the wind, To blow on whom I please ii 7 49
Blow, blow, thou winter wind, Thou art not so unkind As man's ingratitude ii 7 174
Their love is not so great, Hortensio, but we may blow our nails together, and fast it fairly out T. of Shrew i 1 109
What happy gale Blows you to Padua here? i 2 49
Not half so great a blow to hear As will a chestnut in a farmer's fire i 2 209
Though little fire grows great with little wind, Yet extreme gusts will blow out fire and all ii 1 136
As mountains are for winds, That shake not, though they blow perpetually ii 1 142
Man, sitting down before you, will undermine you and blow you up All's Well i 1 130
Is there no military policy, how virgins might blow up men? i 1 133
Look how imagination blows him T. Night ii 5 48
And does not Toby take you a blow o' the lips then? ii 5 75
A good note; that keeps you from the blow of the law iii 4 169
Blow No sneaping winds at home W. Tale i 2 12
I am a feather for each wind that blows ii 3 154
So lean, that blasts of January Would blow you through and through iv 4 112
Though full of our displeasure, yet we free thee From the dead blow of it iv 4 445
Slaves of chance and flies Of every wind that blows iv 4 552
Your sorrow was too sore laid on, Which sixteen winters cannot blow away v 3 50
Hath she no husband That will take pains to blow a horn before her? K. John i 1 219
Blood hath bought blood and blows have answer'd blows ii 1 329
Till then, blows, blood and death! ii 1 360
Shall blow each dust, each straw, each little rub, Out of the path iii 4 128
Let thy blows, doubly redoubled, Fall like amazing thunder Richard II. i 3 80
Basely yielded upon compromise That which his noble ancestors achieved with blows ii 1 254
I come To change blows with thee for our day of doom iii 2 189
Hath sorrow struck So many blows upon this face of mine, And made no deeper wounds? iv 1 278
What wards, what blows, what extremities he endured 1 Hen. IV. i 2 212
Let the hours be short Till fields and blows and groans applaud our sport! i 3 302
A plague of sighing and grief! it blows a man up like a bladder ii 4 366
Thou hast a sigh to blow away this praise 2 Hen. IV. i 1 80
It was your presurmise, That, in the dole of blows, your son might drop i 1 169
O my poor kingdom, sick with civil blows! iv 5 134
What wind blew you hither, Pistol?—Not the ill wind which blows no man to good v 3 90
But when the blast of war blows in our ears, Then imitate the action of the tiger Hen. V. iii 1 5
Let us but blow on them, The vapour of our valour will o'erturn them iv 2 23
I will not answer thee with words, but blows 1 Hen. VI. i 3 69
Or else this blow should broach thy dearest blood iii 4 40
Interchanging blows I quickly shed Some of his bastard blood iv 6 19
O Lord, have mercy upon me! I shall never be able to fight a blow 2 Hen. VI. i 3 220
Come, leave your drinking, and fall to blows ii 3 81
Have at thee with a downright blow! ii 3 93
Some black storm Shall blow ten thousand souls to heaven or hell iii 1 350
And bid them blow towards England's blessed shore iii 2 90
Tut, when struck'st thou one blow in the field? iv 7 84
Now let the general trumpet blow his blast! v 2 43
I cleft his beaver with a downright blow 3 Hen. VI. i 1 12
By words or blows here let us win our right i 1 37
I will not bandy with thee word for word, But buckle with thee blows i 4 50
For raging wind blows up incessant showers i 4 145
Tears then for babes; blows and revenge for me ii 1 86
For strokes received, and many blows repaid, Have robb'd my strong-knit sinews of their strength ii 3 3
Ill blows the wind that profits nobody ii 5 55
Give me thy gold, . . . For I have bought it with an hundred blows ii 5 81
Look, as I blow this feather from my face, And as the air blows it to me again, Obeying with my wind when I do blow, And yielding to another when it blows iii 1 84
Fight closer, or, good faith, you'll catch a blow iii 2 23
Strike now, or else the iron cools.—I had rather chop this hand off at a blow v 1 50
A little gale will soon disperse that cloud And blow it to the source from whence it came v 3 11
There is my purse to cure that blow of thine Richard III. iv 4 516
He stands there, like a mortar-piece, to blow us Hen. VIII. v 4 48
If I cannot ward what I would not have hit, I can watch you for telling how I took the blow Troi. and Cres. i 2 294
Trumpet, blow loud, Send thy brass voice through all these lazy tents i 3 256
More bright in zeal than the devotion which Cold lips blow to their deities iv 4 29
Blow, villain, till thy sphered bias cheek Outswell the colic of puff'd Aquilon iv 5 8
His blows are well disposed iv 5 116
Beat loud the tabourines, let the trumpets blow iv 5 275
To help our fielded friends! Come, blow thy blast. Coriolanus i 4 12
Who have their provand Only for bearing burdens, and sore blows For sinking under them ii 1 268
Yet oft, When blows have made me stay, I fled from words ii 2 76
Abated captives to some nation That won you without blows! iii 3 133
Fortune's blows, When most struck home, being gentle wounded, craves A noble cunning iv 1 7
Hadst thou foxship To banish him that struck more blows for Rome Than thou hast spoken words? iv 2 19
More noble blows than ever thou wise words iv 2 21
Can you think to blow out the intended fire your city is ready to flame in, with such weak breath as this? v 2 48
I am the sea; hark, how her sighs do blow! T. Andron. iii 1 226
The angry northern wind Will blow these sands, like Sibyl's leaves, abroad iv 1 105
Gregory, remember thy swashing blow Rom. and Jul. i 1 70
While we were interchanging thrusts and blows i 1 120
This wind, you talk of, blows us from ourselves i 4 104
But one word with one of us? couple it with something; make it a word and a blow iii 1 43
What storm is this that blows so contrary? iii 2 64
That shall demonstrate these quick blows of Fortune's T. of Athens i 1 91
And let his very breath, whom thou'lt observe, Blow off thy cap . iv 3 213

Blow. Left me open, bare For every storm that blows . *T. of Athens* iv 3 266
Words before blows: is it so, countrymen?—Not that we love words better, as you do . *J. Cæsar* v 1 27
The posture of your blows are yet unknown . . . v 1 33
Why, now, blow wind, swell billow and swim bark! . . . v 1 67
And the very ports they blow, All the quarters that they know *Macbeth* i 3 15
That but this blow Might be the be-all and the end-all here . i 7 4
Shall blow the horrid deed in every eye, That tears shall drown the wind i 7 24
Whom the vile blows and buffets of the world Have so incensed . iii 1 109
Blow, wind! come, wrack! At least we'll die with harness on our back . . . . v 5 51
It is, as the air, invulnerable, And our vain blows malicious mockery *Ham.* i 1 146
Senseless Ilium, Seeming to feel this blow, with flaming top Stoops to his base . . . . ii 2 497
Breaks my pate across? Plucks off my beard, and blows it in my face? . ii 2 600
I will delve one yard below their mines, And blow them at the moon . iii 4 209
Do but blow them to their trial, the bubbles are out . . v 2 201
Bids the wind blow the earth into the sea, Or swell the curled waters *Lear* iii 1 5
Blow, winds, and crack your cheeks! rage! blow! . . . iii 2 1
Through the sharp hawthorn blows the cold wind. Hum! go to thy cold bed . . . . iii 4 47
You are not worth the dust which the rude wind Blows in your face . iv 2 31
Milk-liver'd man! That bear'st a cheek for blows, a head for wrongs . iv 2 51
A most poor man, made tame to fortune's blows . . . iv 6 225
If after every tempest come such calms, May the winds blow till they have waken'd death . . . . . . *Othello* ii 1 188
I found them close together, At blow and thrust . . . ii 3 238
All my fond love thus do I blow to heaven . . . . . iii 3 445
Blow me about in winds! roast me in sulphur! . . . v 2 279
The blow thou hadst Shall make thy peace for moving me to rage *Ant. and Cleo.* ii 5 69
When Cæsar and your brother were at blows, Your mother came to Sicily ii 6 45
Then shall the sighs of Octavia blow the fire up in Cæsar . ii 6 135
The least wind i' the world will blow them down . . . ii 7 3
Fortune knows We scorn her most when most she offers blows . iii 11 74
This blows my heart: If swift thought break it not, a swifter mean Shall outstrike thought . . . . . . iv 6 34
Rather on Nilus' mud Lay me stark naked, and let the water-flies Blow me into abhorring! . . . . v 2 60
Thus ready for the way of life or death, I wait the sharpest blow *Pericles* i 1 55
Like the wandering wind, Blows dust in others' eyes, to spread itself . i 1 97
For flattery is the bellows blows up sin . . . . i 2 39
I have ground the axe myself; Do you but strike the blow . . i 2 59
When all, for mine, if I may call offence, Must feel war's blow . i 2 93
That were to blow at fire in hope to quench it . . . . i 4 4
For now the wind begins to blow; Thunder above and deeps below ii Gower 29
Slack the bolins there! Thou wilt not, wilt thou? Blow, and split thyself . . . . iii 1 44
See how she gins to blow Into life's flower again! . . . iii 2 95
The pregnant instrument of wrath Prest for this blow . iv Gower 45
Thou hast sworn to do't: 'Tis but a blow, which never shall be known iv 1 2
Is this wind westerly that blows?—South-west . . . iv 1 51
A strong wind will blow it to pieces, they are so pitifully sodden . . iv 2 20
Blowed. I would have blowed up the town, so Chrish save me, la! *Hen. V.* iii 2 96
Blower up. Bless our poor virginity from underminers and blowers up! Is there no military policy? . . . . . *All's Well* i 1 132
Blowest. Come, stretch thy chest, and let thy eyes spout blood; Thou blow'st for Hector . . . . . *Troi. and Cres.* iv 5 11
Blowing. Here's Mistress Page at the door, sweating and blowing and looking wildly . . . . *Mer. Wives* iii 3 94
But I, with blowing the fire, shall warm myself . *T. of Shrew* iv 1 9
Marry, in blowing him down again, with the breach yourselves made, you lose your city . . . . . . *All's Well* i 1 135
And the loud trumpet blowing them together . *2 Hen. IV.* iv 1 122
What time the shepherd, blowing of his nails, Can neither call it perfect day nor night . . . . *3 Hen. VI.* ii 5 3
As summer flies are in the shambles, That quicken even with blowing *Othello* iv 2 67
As gentle As zephyrs blowing below the violet . *Cymbeline* iv 2 172
Blown with restless violence round about The pendent world *Meas. for Meas.* iii 1 125
If speaking, why, a vane blown with all winds . *Much Ado* iii 1 66
As Dian in her orb, As chaste as is the bud ere it be blown . . iv 1 59
Dismask'd, their damask sweet commixture shown, Are angels vailing clouds, or roses blown . . . . . *L. L. Lost* v 2 297
These summer-flies Have blown me full of maggot ostentation . v 2 409
Virginity being blown down, man will quicklier be blown up . *All's Well* i 1 134
Behold him with flies blown to death . . . *W. Tale* iv 4 820
The breath of heaven hath blown his spirit . . *K. John* iv 1 110
This shower, blown up by tempest of the soul, Startles mine eyes . . v 2 50
'Tis far too huge to be blown out With that same weak wind which enkindled it . . . . v 2 86
Rumour is a pipe Blown by surmises, jealousies, conjectures *2 Hen. IV.* Ind. 16
This your air of France Hath blown that vice in me . *Hen. V.* iii 6 161
Think'st thou the fiery fever will go out With titles blown from adulation? . . . . iv 1 271
Was ever feather so lightly blown to and fro as this multitude? *2 Hen. VI.* iv 8 57
What showers arise, Blown with the windy tempest of my heart! *3 Hen. VI.* ii 5 86
What though the mast be now blown overboard, The cable broke? . v 4 3
It is you Have blown this coal betwixt my lord and me. . *Hen. VIII.* ii 4 79
You charge me That I have blown this coal; I do deny it . . ii 4 94
The seeded pride That hath to this maturity blown up . *Troi. and Cres.* i 3 317
Where are my tears? rain, to lay this wind, or my heart will be blown up by the root . . . . iv 4 56
I have been blown out of your gates with sighs . *Coriolanus* v 2 80
Where we lay, Our chimneys were blown down . *Macbeth* ii 3 60
Though bladed corn be lodged and trees blown down . . iv 1 55
With all his crimes broad blown, as flush as May . *Hamlet* iii 3 81
The wretch that thou hast blown unto the worst Owes nothing to thy blasts . . . . *Lear* iv 1 8
I have seen the cannon, When it hath blown his ranks into the air *Othello* iii 4 135
Good morrow, general.—'Tis well blown, lads . . *Ant. and Cleo.* iv 4 25
Here, on her breast, There is a vent of blood and something blown . v 2 352
Blown ambition. No blown ambition doth our arms incite, But love *Lear* iv 4 27
Blown Jack. How now, blown Jack! how now, quilt! . *1 Hen. IV.* iv 2 53
Blown rose. Against the blown rose may they stop their nose That kneel'd unto the buds . . . . . . *Ant. and Cleo.* iii 13 39
Blown sails. Toward Ephesus From our blown sails . *Pericles* v 1 256
Blown surmises. When I shall turn the business of my soul To such exsufflicate and blown surmises . . . . *Othello* iii 3 182

Blown tide. Ne'er through an arch so hurried the blown tide *Coriolanus* v 4 50
Blown youth. That unmatch'd form and feature of blown youth Blasted with ecstasy . . . . *Hamlet* iii 1 167
Blowse. Sweet blowse, you are a beauteous blossom, sure *T. Andron.* iv 2 72
Blubbered. Run, good Doll: come. [*She comes blubbered.*] . *2 Hen. IV.* ii 4 421
Blubbering. Even so lies she, Blubbering and weeping *Rom. and Jul.* iii 3 87
Blue. With each end of thy blue bow dost crown My bosky acres *Tempest* iv 1 80
Beaten black and blue, that you cannot see a white spot *Mer. Wives* iv 5 115
What tellest thou me of black and blue? I was beaten myself into all the colours of the rainbow . . . . iv 5 117
There pinch the maids as blue as bilberry . . . . v 5 49
In emerald tufts, flowers purple, blue, and white . . . v 5 74
They'll suck our breath or pinch us black and blue *Com. of Errors* ii 2 194
And violets blue And lady-smocks all silver-white . *L. L. Lost* v 2 904
A blue eye and sunken, which you have not . *As Y. Like It* iii 2 393
Gartered with a red and blue list . . . *T. of Shrew* iii 2 69
Let their heads be sleekly combed, their blue coats brushed . . iv 1 93
We will fool him black and blue: shall we not? . *T. Night* ii 5 12
What colour are your eyebrows?—Blue, my lord.—Nay, that's a mock: I have seen a lady's nose That has been blue, but not her eyebrows *W. Tale* ii 1 13
Draw, men, for all this privileged place; Blue coats to tawny coats *1 Hen. VI.* i 3 47
The lights burn blue. It is now dead midnight . *Richard III.* v 3 180
Make him fall His crest that prouder than blue Iris bends *Troi. and Cres.* i 3 380
Engenders the black toad and adder blue . . *T. of Athens* iv 3 181
The cross blue lightning seem'd to open The breast of heaven *J. Cæsar* i 3 50
To o'ertop old Pelion, or the skyish head Of blue Olympus . *Hamlet* v 1 277
Even till we make the main and the aerial blue An indistinct regard *Oth.* ii 1 39
A forked mountain, or blue promontory . . *Ant. and Cleo.* iv 14 5
White and azure laced With blue of heaven's own tinct . *Cymbeline* ii 2 23
The yellows, blues, The purple violets, and marigolds . *Pericles* iv 1 15
Blue-bottle. You blue-bottle rogue, you filthy famished correctioner *2 Hen. IV.* v 4 22
Blue-cap. One Mordake, and a thousand blue-caps more . *1 Hen. IV.* ii 4 392
Blue-eyed. This blue-eyed hag was hither brought with child *Tempest* i 2 269
Bluest. There is gold, and here My bluest veins to kiss . *Ant. and Cleo.* ii 5 29
Bluish. And skirts, round underborne with a bluish tinsel . *Much Ado* iii 4 22
Blunt. I'll quickly cross By some sly trick blunt Thurio's dull proceeding. Love, lend me wings! . . . . . *T. G. of Ver.* ii 6 41
Doth rebate and blunt his natural edge With profits of the mind *M. for M.* i 4 60
Unkindness blunts it more than marble hard . *Com. of Errors* ii 1 93
Foolish, blunt, unkind, Stigmatical in making, worse in mind . . iv 2 21
His wits are not so blunt as, God help, I would desire they were *M. Ado* iii 5 12
As blunt as the fencer's foils, which hit, but hurt not . . v 2 13
A sharp wit match'd with too blunt a will . . *L. L. Lost* ii 1 49
Dull lead, with warning all as blunt . . *Mer. of Venice* ii 7 8
You are too blunt: go to it orderly . . . *T. of Shrew* ii 1 45
Hiding his bitter jests in blunt behaviour . . . . iii 2 13
Though he be blunt, I know him passing wise . . . . iii 2 24
A good blunt fellow . . . . *K. John* i 1 71
I have to London sent The heads of Oxford, Salisbury, Blunt *Richard II.* v 6 8
Here is a dear, a true industrious friend, Sir Walter Blunt *1 Hen. IV.* i 1 63
How now, good Blunt? thy looks are full of speed . . . iii 2 162
Welcome, Sir Walter Blunt; and would to God You were of our determination! . . . . iv 3 32
The noble Westmoreland and warlike Blunt; And many moe corrivals iv 4 30
I know this face full well: A gallant knight he was, his name was Blunt . . . . v 3 20
Who are you? Sir Walter Blunt: there's honour for you! . . . v 3 33
The spirits Of valiant Shirley, Stafford, Blunt, are in my arms . v 4 41
The blunt monster with uncounted heads, The still-discordant wavering multitude, Can play upon it . . . . *2 Hen. IV.* Ind. 18
And both the Blunts Kill'd by the hand of Douglas . . . i 1 16
Blunt not his love, Nor lose the good advantage of his grace . . iv 4 27
And blunt the sword That guards the peace and safety of your person . v 2 87
As I judge By his blunt bearing he will keep his word . *Hen. V.* iv 7 185
Base slave, thy words are blunt and so art thou . *2 Hen. VI.* iv 1 67
With hasty Germans and blunt Hollanders . . *3 Hen. VI.* iv 8 2
Why, trow'st thou, Warwick, That Clarence is so harsh, so blunt? . v 1 86
I have too long borne Your blunt upbraidings . . *Richard III.* i 3 104
The murderous knife was dull and blunt Till it was whetted on thy stone-hard heart . . . . iv 4 226
Sir James Blunt, And Rice ap Thomas, with a valiant crew . . iv 5 11
Good Captain Blunt, bear my good-night to him . . . . v 3 30
Yet one thing more, good Blunt, before thou go'st . . . v 3 33
Good night, good Captain Blunt . . . . . . v 3 44
Blunt wedges rive hard knots . . . . *Troi. and Cres.* i 3 316
What a blunt fellow is this grown to be! . . . *J. Cæsar* i 2 299
I am no orator, as Brutus is; But, as you know me all, a plain blunt man . . . . iii 2 222
Let grief Convert to anger; blunt not the heart, enrage it . *Macbeth* iv 3 229
I am too blunt and saucy: here's my knee . . *Cymbeline* v 5 325
Blunted. With such eyes As, sick and blunted with community, Afford no extraordinary gaze . . . . *1 Hen. IV.* iii 2 77
This visitation Is but to whet thy almost blunted purpose *Hamlet* iii 4 111
Bluntest. He is the bluntest wooer in Christendom . *3 Hen. VI.* iii 2 83
Bluntly. No more but, plain and bluntly, 'To the king!' *1 Hen. VI.* iv 1 51
Good news or bad, that thou comest in so bluntly? . *Richard III.* iv 3 45
Deliver a plain message bluntly . . . . . *Lear* i 4 36
Bluntness. Who, having been praised for bluntness, doth affect A saucy roughness . . . . ii 2 102
Blunt-witted lord, ignoble in demeanour! . . *2 Hen. VI.* iii 2 210
Blur. Never yet did base dishonour blur our name . . . iv 1 39
Such an act That blurs the grace and blush of modesty . *Hamlet* iii 4 41
Blurred. Time hath nothing blurr'd those lines of favour *Cymbeline* iv 2 104
Blurted. Whilst ours was blurted at and held a malkin Not worth the time of day . . . . *Pericles* iv 3 34
Blush. O Proteus, let this habit make thee blush! . *T. G. of Ver.* v 4 104
I think the boy hath grace in him; he blushes . . . v 4 165
Lay by all nicety and prolixious blushes . . *Meas. for Meas.* ii 4 162
Behold how like a maid she blushes here! . . . *Much Ado* iv 1 35
Her blush is guiltiness, not modesty . . . . . iv 1 43
A thousand innocent shames In angel whiteness beat away those blushes . . . . iv 1 163
I should blush, I know, To be o'erheard and taken napping so *L. L. Lost* iv 3 129
Come, sir, you blush; as his your case is such . . . iv 3 131
And mark'd you both and for you both did blush . . . iv 3 138
Cupid himself would blush To see me thus transformed to a boy *Mer. of Venice* ii 6 38

Blush. Should I anatomize him to thee as he is, I must blush and weep . *As Y. Like It* i 1 163
Than with safety of a pure blush thou mayst in honour come off again . i 2 32
Let gentleness my strong enforcement be: In the which hope I blush . ii 7 119
The blushes in my cheeks thus whisper me, 'We blush that thou shouldst choose' . . . . *All's Well* ii 3 75
Rust, sword! cool, blushes! and, Parolles, live! . . . iv 3 373
I blush to say it, he won me . . . . . . v 3 140
He blushes, and 'tis it . . . . v 3 195
I doubt not then but innocence shall make False accusation blush *W. Tale* iii 2 32
I should blush To see you so attired . . . . . iv 4 12
Come, quench your blushes and present yourself That which you are . iv 4 67
For this I'll blush you thanks . . . . . . iv 4 595
You will but make it blush And glow with shame . . . *K. John* iv 1 113
O, he is bold and blushes not at death . . . . . iv 3 76
You bloody Neroes, ripping up the womb Of your dear mother England, blush for shame . . . . v 2 153
The sun of heaven methought was loath to set, But stay'd and made the western welkin blush . . . . v 5 2
You bashful fool, must you be blushing? wherefore blush you now? *2 Hen. IV.* ii 2 81
This was a merry message.—We hope to make the sender blush at it *Hen. V.* i 2 299
I said so, dear Katharine; and I must not blush to affirm it . . v 2 117
Put off your maiden blushes; avouch the thoughts of your heart . v 2 253
Thy cheeks Blush for pure shame to counterfeit our roses . *1 Hen. VI.* ii 4 66
But be thou mild and blush not at my shame . . *2 Hen. VI.* ii 4 48
Thou shalt not see me blush Nor change my countenance . . iii 1 98
Ne'er returneth To blush and beautify the cheek again . . iii 2 167
I would assay, proud queen, to make thee blush . . *3 Hen. VI.* i 4 118
And not bewray thy treason with a blush . . . . iii 3 97
Blush, blush, thou lump of foul deformity! . . . *Richard III.* i 2 57
Now, if you can blush and cry 'guilty,' cardinal, You'll show a little honesty.—Speak on, sir . . . . . *Hen. VIII.* iii 2 305
If I blush, It is to see a nobleman want manners . . . iii 2 307
Bid the cheek be ready with a blush Modest as morning *Troi. and Cres.* i 3 228
She does so blush, and fetches her wind so short . . . iii 2 33
Come, come, what need you blush? shame's a baby . . . iii 2 42
I will go wash; And when my face is fair, you shall perceive Whether I blush or no . . . . *Coriolanus* i 9 70
It is a part That I shall blush in acting . . . . . ii 2 149
Here do we make his friends Blush that the world goes well . . iv 6 5
My sons' sweet blood will make it shame and blush . *T. Andron.* iii 1 15
I blush to think upon this ignomy . . . . . . iv 2 115
What, canst thou say all this, and never blush? . . . . v 1 121
Here are the beetle brows shall blush for me . . *Rom. and Jul.* i 4 32
The mask of night is on my face, Else would a maiden blush bepaint my cheek . . . . ii 2 86
Even in pure and vestal modesty, Still blush, as thinking their own kisses sin . . . . iii 3 39
Loved and delicate wooer [gold], Whose blush doth thaw the consecrated snow That lies on Dian's lap! . . . . *T. of Athens* iv 3 386
Such an act That blurs the grace and blush of modesty . . *Hamlet* iii 4 41
O shame! where is thy blush? Rebellious hell, If thou canst mutine in a matron's bones . . . . iii 4 82
O I follow'd that I blush to look upon: My very hairs do mutiny *Ant. and Cleo.* iii 11 12
Nay, blush not, Cleopatra; I approve Your wisdom in the deed . v 2 149
Those men Blush not in actions blacker than the night . . *Pericles* i 1 135
What may make him blush in being known, He'll stop the course by which it might be known . . . . i 2 22
These blushes of hers must be quenched . . . . . iv 2 135
Blushed. I blushed to hear his monstrous devices . . . *1 Hen. IV.* ii 4 344
And ever since thou hast blushed extempore . . . . ii 4 347
There was such laughing! and Helen so blushed, and Paris so chafed *Troi. and Cres.* i 2 180
Pages blush'd at him and men of heart Look'd wondering . *Coriolanus* v 6 99
I have so often blushed to acknowledge him, that now I am brazed to it *Lear* i 1 10
Of spirit so still and quiet, that her motion Blush'd at herself *Othello* i 3 96
Blushest. Thou blushest, Antony; and that blood of thine Is Cæsar's homager . . . . *Ant. and Cleo.* i 1 30
Blushing. I have mark'd A thousand blushing apparitions To start into her face . . . . *Much Ado* iv 1 161
Blushing cheeks by faults are bred And fears by pale white shown *L. L. Lost* i 2 106
I do betray myself with blushing . . . . . . i 2 138
His treasons will sit blushing in his face . . . *Richard II.* iii 2 51
As doth the blushing discontented sun From out the fiery portal of the east . . . . iii 3 63
He made a blushing cital of himself . . . . . *1 Hen. IV.* v 2 62
You virtuous ass, you bashful fool, must you be blushing? . *2 Hen. IV.* ii 2 81
About the rose I wear; Saying, the sanguine colour of the leaves Did represent my master's blushing cheeks . . . *1 Hen. VI.* iv 1 93
If thou canst for blushing, view this face, And bite thy tongue *3 Hen. VI.* i 4 46
I defy thee, And to my brother turn my blushing cheeks . . . v 1 99
A blushing shamefast spirit [conscience] that mutinies in a man's bosom *Richard III.* i 4 141
For more than blushing comes to . . . . . *Hen. VIII.* ii 3 42
Speak my thanks and my obedience, As from a blushing handmaid . ii 3 72
To-morrow blossoms, And bears his blushing honours thick upon him . iii 2 354
What, blushing still? have you not done talking yet? . *Troi. and Cres.* iii 2 108
Yet do thy cheeks look red as Titan's face Blushing to be encounter'd with a cloud. Shall I speak for thee? . . . . *T. Andron.* ii 4 32
Betray with blushing The close enacts and counsels of the heart . . iv 2 117
My lips, two blushing pilgrims, ready stand . . . *Rom. and Jul.* i 5 97
Bluster. The skies look grimly And threaten present blusters *W. Tale* iii 3 4
And those kin Which in the bluster of thy wrath must fall *T. of Athens* v 4 41
Blustering. And make fair weather in your blustering land . *K. John* v 1 21
Hollow whistling in the leaves Foretells a tempest and a blustering day . . . . *1 Hen. IV.* v 1 6
Early in blustering morn this lady was Thrown upon this shore *Pericles* v 3 22
Blustrous. Now, mild may be thy life! For a more blustrous birth had never babe . . . . iii 1 28
Boar. Be it ounce, or cat, or bear, Pard, or boar with bristled hair *M. N. Dream* ii 2 31
Heard the sea puff'd up with winds Rage like an angry boar *T. of Shrew* i 2 203
Where sups he? doth the old boar feed in the old frank? . *2 Hen. IV.* ii 2 159
He dreamt to-night the boar had razed his helm . . *Richard III.* iii 2 11

Boar. To fly the boar before the boar pursues, Were to incense the boar to follow us . . . . *Richard III.* iii 2 28
The boar will use us kindly . . . . iii 2 33
Fear you the boar, and go so unprovided? . . . . . iii 2 75
Stanley did dream the boar did raze his helm; But I disdain'd it . . iii 4 84
In the sty of this most bloody boar My son George Stanley is frank'd up iv 5 2
The wretched, bloody, and usurping boar, That spoil'd your summer fields . . . . v 2 7
Good angels guard thee from the boar's annoy! . . . . v 3 156
The chafed boar, the mountain lioness, The ocean swells not so *T. Andron.* iv 2 138
Who, like a boar too savage, doth root up His country's peace *T. of Athens* v 1 168
The boar of Thessaly Was never so emboss'd . . . *Ant. and Cleo.* iv 13 2
Like a full-acorn'd boar, a German one, Cried 'O!' . . *Cymbeline* ii 5 16
Board. Bear up, and board 'em . . . . . . *Tempest* iii 2 3
'Tis double wrong to truant with your bed And let her read it in thy looks at board . . . . *Com. of Errors* iii 2 18
At board he fed not for my urging it . . . . . . v 1 64
I was as willing to grapple as he was to board . . . *L. L. Lost* ii 1 218
More than to us Wait in your royal walks, your board, your bed! *M. N. Dream* v 1 31
Ships are but boards, sailors but men . . . . *Mer. of Venice* i 3 22
Wedding is great Juno's crown: O blessed bond of board and bed! *As Y. Like It* v 4 148
I will board her, though she chide as loud As thunder . . *T. of Shrew* i 2 95
'Accost' is front her, board her, woo her, assail her . . *T. Night* i 3 60
This is he that did the Tiger board, When your young nephew Titus lost his leg . . . . v 1 65
We cannot lodge and board a dozen or fourteen gentlewomen *Hen. V.* ii 1 35
How often hast thou Waited at my cup, Fed from my trencher, kneel'd down at the board . . . . *2 Hen. VI.* iv 1 57
And his own letter, The honourable board of council out, Must fetch him in he papers . . . . *Hen. VIII.* i 1 79
Away, I do beseech you, both away: I'll board him presently *Hamlet* ii 2 170
His bed shall seem a school, his board a shrift . . . *Othello* iii 3 24
Here's money for my meat: I would have left it on the board *Cymbeline* iii 6 51
Boarded. I boarded the king's ship . . . . . . *Tempest* i 2 196
Unless he know some strain in me, that I know not myself, he would never have boarded me in this fury . . . . . *Mer. Wives* ii 1 92
I would he had boarded me . . . . . . *Much Ado* ii 1 149
I liked her, And boarded her i' the wanton way of youth *All's Well* v 3 211
Like to a ship that, having 'scaped a tempest, Is straightway calm'd and boarded with a pirate . . . . *2 Hen. VI.* iv 9 33
We put on a compelled valour, and in the grapple I boarded them *Ham.* iv 6 18
He to-night hath boarded a land carack . . . . *Othello* i 2 50
'Boarding,' call you it? I'll be sure to keep him above deck *Mer. Wives* ii 1 93
Boarish. In his anointed flesh stick boarish fangs . . . *Lear* iii 7 58
Boar-pig. Thou whoreson little tidy Bartholomew boar-pig . *2 Hen. IV.* ii 4 251
Boar-spear. A gallant curtle-axe upon my thigh, A boar-spear in my hand . . . . *As Y. Like It* i 3 120
Come on, come on; where is your boar-spear, man? Fear you the boar, and go so unprovided? . . . . . . *Richard III.* iii 2 74
Boast. Do not smile at me that I boast her off . . . *Tempest* iv 1 9
My duty will I boast of; nothing else . . . . *T. G. of Ver.* ii 4 111
Give God thanks, and make no boast of it . . . . *Much Ado* iii 3 20
Why should proud summer boast Before the birds have any cause to sing? Why should I joy? . . . . *L. L. Lost* i 1 102
And, which is more than all these boasts can be, I am beloved *M. N. Dr.* i 1 103
But I give heaven thanks and make no boast of them . *As Y. Like It* ii 5 38
It is no boast, being ask'd, to say we are . . . . . iv 3 91
And boasts himself To have a worthy feeding . . . *W. Tale* iv 4 168
Every present time doth boast itself Above a better gone . . . v 1 96
Thou mayst with lilies boast And with the half-blown rose . *K. John* iii 1 53
Yet can I not of such tame patience boast As to be hush'd *Richard II.* i 1 52
Boast of nothing else But that I was a journeyman to grief . . . i 3 273
Boast of this I can, Though banish'd, yet a trueborn Englishman . . i 3 308
It is a conquest for a prince to boast of . . . *1 Hen. IV.* i 1 77
I could make as true a boast as that, if I had a sow to my mistress *Hen. V.* iii 7 66
Be it death proclaimed through our host To boast of this or take that praise from God Which is his only . . . . iv 8 120
She may boast she hath beheld the man Whose glory fills the world with loud report . . . . *1 Hen. VI.* ii 2 42
Nor should that nation boast it so with us . . . . . iii 3 23
Like a hedge-born swain That doth presume to boast of gentle blood . iv 1 44
Upon my death the French can little boast; In yours they will . . iv 5 24
Keep thou the napkin, and go boast of this . . . *3 Hen. VI.* i 4 159
Cannot make boast to have that which he hath . . *Troi. and Cres.* iii 3 98
Look'st thou sad, When every thing doth make a gleeful boast? *T. Andron.* ii 3 11
Where they boast To have well-armed friends . . . . . *Lear* iii 7 19
But, O vain boast! Who can control his fate? . . . . *Othello* v 2 264
Now boast thee, death, in thy possession lies A lass unparallel'd *Ant. and Cleo.* v 2 318
A gentlewoman's son.—That's more Than some, whose tailors are as dear as yours, Can justly boast of . . . . . *Cymbeline* ii 3 85
I hate you; which I had rather You felt than make't my boast . . ii 3 116
Further to boast were neither true nor modest, Unless I add, we are honest . . . . v 5 18
For beauty that made barren the swell'd boast Of him that best could speak . . . . v 5 162
With other virtues, which I'll keep from boast . . . *Pericles* iv 6 195
Boasted. Where is the patience now, That you so oft have boasted? *Lear* iii 6 62
Boastful. Steed threatens steed, in high and boastful neighs *Hen. V.* iv Prol. 10
Boasting. And set upon our boasting enemy . . . . *1 Hen. VI.* iii 2 103
To such as boasting show their scars A mock is due . *Troi. and Cres.* iv 5 290
And topping all others in boasting . . . . . *Coriolanus* ii 1 23
No boasting like a fool; This deed I'll do before this purpose cool *Macb.* iv 1 153
Which, when I know that boasting is an honour, I shall promulgate *Oth.* i 2 20
Boat. A rotten carcass of a boat, not rigg'd . . . . *Tempest* i 2 146
If the wind were down, I could drive the boat with my sighs *T. G. of Ver.* ii 3 60
The sailors sought for safety by our boat, And left the ship *Com. of Err.* i 1 77
When you and those poor number saved with you Hung on our driving boat, I saw your brother . . . . *T. Night* i 2 11
O, too much folly is it, well I wot, To hazard all our lives in one small boat . . . . *1 Hen. VI.* iv 6 33
Richmond, in Dorsetshire, sent out a boat Unto the shore *Richard III.* iv 4 524
The sea being smooth, How many shallow bauble boats dare sail Upon her patient breast! . . . . *Troi. and Cres.* i 3 35
Where's then the saucy boat Whose weak untimber'd sides but even now Co-rivall'd greatness? . . . . i 3 42
Light boats sail swift, though greater hulks draw deep . . . . ii 3 277

Boat. When the sea was calm all boats alike Show'd mastership in floating *Coriolanus* iv 1 6
Her boat hath a leak, And she must not speak . . . . *Lear* iii 6 28
My boat sails freely, both with wind and stream . . *Othello* ii 3 65
Come, down into the boat.—Take heed you fall not . *Ant. and Cleo.* ii 7 136
Cydnus swell'd above the banks, or for The press of boats or pride *Cymb.* ii 4 72
With sands that will not bear your enemies' boats, But suck them up to the topmast . . . . iii 1 21
Fortune brings in some boats that are not steer'd . . . . iv 3 46
Convey thy deity Aboard our dancing boat! . . . . *Pericles* iii 1 13
Boatswain!—Here, master: what cheer?—Good, speak to the mariners *Tempest* i 1 1
Good boatswain have care. Where's the master? Play the men . i 1 10
The master, the swabber, the boatswain and I, The gunner and his mate . . . . ii 2 48
The master and the boatswain Being awake, enforce them to this place v 1 99
The boatswain whistles, and The master calls . . . *Pericles* iv 1 64
Bob. Against her lips I bob And on her wither'd dewlap pour the ale *M. N. Dream* ii 1 49
He that a fool doth very wisely hit Doth very foolishly, although he smart, Not to seem senseless of the bob . . . *As Y. Like It* ii 7 55
You shall not bob us out of our melody . . *Troi. and Cres.* iii 1 75
Bobbed. Whom our fathers Have in their own land beaten, bobb'd, and thump'd . . . . *Richard III.* v 3 334
I have bobbed his brain more than he has beat my bones *Troi. and Cres.* ii 1 76
He calls me to a restitution large Of gold and jewels that I bobb'd from him, As gifts to Desdemona . . . . *Othello* v 1 16
Boblibindo chicurmurco . . . . *All's Well* iv 3 143
Bobtail. Hound or spaniel, brach or lym, Or bobtail tike . *Lear* iii 6 73
Bocchus. He hath assembled Bocchus, the king of Libya *Ant. and Cleo.* iii 6 69
Bode. I pray God his bad voice bode no mischief . . *Much Ado* ii 3 83
A' brushes his hat o' mornings; what should that bode? . . iii 2 42
I wonder what it bodes.—Marry, peace it bodes, and love and quiet life *T. of Shrew* v 2 107
This was my dream: what it doth bode, God knows . *2 Hen. VI.* i 2 31
Whate'er it bodes, henceforward will I bear Upon my target three fair-shining suns.—Nay, bear three daughters . . . *3 Hen. VI.* ii 1 39
I would croak like a raven; I would bode, I would bode *Troi. and Cres.* v 2 191
My sight is very dull, whate'er it bodes . . . *T. Andron.* ii 3 195
And bakes the elf-locks in foul sluttish hairs, Which once untangled much misfortune bodes . . . . . . *Rom. and Jul.* i 4 91
This bodes some strange eruption to our state . . . *Hamlet* i 1 69
Mine eyes do itch; Doth that bode weeping?—'Tis neither here nor there *Othello* iv 3 59
What did thy song bode, lady? Hark, canst thou hear me? . . v 2 246
Boded. Invert What best is boded me to mischief! . . *Tempest* iii 1 71
What boded this, but well forewarning wind Did seem to say? *2 Hen. VI.* iii 2 85
Bodement. This foolish, dreaming, superstitious girl Makes all these bodements . . . . *Troi. and Cres.* v 3 80
Sweet bodements! good! . . . . *Macbeth* iv 1 96
Bodged. We charged again: but, out, alas! We bodged again *3 Hen. VI.* i 4 19
Bodies. He is a curer of souls, and you a curer of bodies . *Mer. Wives* ii 3 40
By gar, nor I too: there is no bodies . . . . iii 3 228
Strange that sheeps' guts should hale souls out of men's bodies *M. Ado* ii 3 62
So, with two seeming bodies, but one heart . . *M. N. Dream* iii 2 212
As imagination bodies forth The forms of things unknown . . . v 1 14
Why are our bodies soft and weak and smooth, Unapt to toil? *T. of Shrew* v 2 165
Souls and bodies hath he divorced three . . . . *T. Night* iii 4 259
Bring me To the dead bodies of my queen and son . . *W. Tale* iii 2 236
I will not vex your souls—Since presently your souls must part your bodies—With too much urging . . . . . . *Richard II.* iii 1 3
For what can we bequeath Save our deposed bodies to the ground? . iii 2 150
As the soldiers bore dead bodies by, He call'd them untaught knaves *1 Hen. IV.* i 3 42
Told me I had unloaded all the gibbets and pressed the dead bodies . iv 2 41
Rebellion, did divide The action of their bodies from their souls *2 Hen. IV.* i 1 195
Loyal subjects, Whose hearts have left their bodies here in England *Hen. V.* i 2 128
O, let their bodies follow, my dear liege, With blood and sword . i 2 130
They will give their bodies to the lust of English youth To new-store France . . . . iii 5 30
Where, wretches, their poor bodies Must lie and fester . . . iv 2 87
A many of our bodies shall no doubt Find native graves . . . iv 3 95
To view the field in safety and dispose Of their dead bodies . . iv 7 86
All will fight And have our bodies slaughter'd by thy foes *1 Hen. VI.* iii 1 101
Give me their bodies, that I may bear them hence . . . . . iv 7 85
Go, take their bodies hence . . . . iv 7 91
And sold their bodies for their country's benefit . . . . v 4 106
The bodies shall be dragged at my horse heels . . *2 Hen. VI.* iv 3 14
And wrap our bodies in black mourning gowns . . *3 Hen. VI.* ii 1 161
And all the unlook'd for issue of their bodies . . . . . iii 2 131
Even with the dearest blood your bodies bear . . . . . . v 1 69
Methought their souls, whose bodies Richard murder'd, Came to my tent, and cried on victory . . . . *Richard III.* v 3 230
Inter their bodies as becomes their births . . . . . . v 5 15
Why, had your bodies No heart among you? . . . *Coriolanus* i 3 211
Our raiment And state of bodies would bewray what life We have led . v 3 95
Here is come to do some villanous shame To the dead bodies . *R. and J.* v 3 53
Then are our beggars bodies, and our monarchs and outstretched heroes the beggars' shadows . . . . *Hamlet* ii 2 269
Most holy and religious fear it is To keep those many many bodies safe iii 3 9
Conceit in weakest bodies strongest works . . . . . . iii 4 114
Give order that these bodies High on a stage be placed to the view . v 2 388
Take up the bodies: such a sight as this Becomes the field . . . v 2 412
Produce their bodies, be they alive or dead . . . . . *Lear* v 3 230
Our bodies are our gardens, to the which our wills are gardeners *Othello* i 3 323
We do lance Diseases in our bodies . . . . . *Ant. and Cleo.* v 1 37
A fire from heaven came and shrivell'd up Their bodies . . *Pericles* ii 4 10
Bodiless. This bodiless creation ecstasy Is very cunning in . *Hamlet* iii 4 138
Bodily. How doth the martlemas, your master?—In bodily health *2 Hen. IV.* ii 2 111
What ever have been thought on in this state, That could be brought to bodily act ere Rome Had circumvention? . . . . *Coriolanus* i 2 5
I thought you had received some bodily wound; there is more sense in that than in reputation . . . . *Othello* ii 3 267
That I have enjoyed the dearest bodily part of your mistress *Cymbeline* i 4 162
Boding. And boding screech-owls make the concert full! *2 Hen. VI.* iii 2 327
O, it comes o'er my memory, As doth the raven o'er the infected house, Boding to all . . . . *Othello* iv 1 22

Bodkin. A cittern-head.—The head of a bodkin . . *L. L. Lost* v 2 615
Betwixt the firmament and it you cannot thrust a bodkin's point *W. Tale* iii 3 87
When he himself might his quietus make With a bare bodkin . *Hamlet* iii 1 76
Body. As with age his body uglier grows, So his mind cankers *Tempest* iv 1 191
I embrace thy body; And to thee and thy company I bid A hearty welcome . . . . v 1 109
That I, unworthy body as I am, Should censure thus . . *T. G. of Ver.* i 2 18
I hold him but a fool that will endanger His body for a girl that loves him not . . . . v 4 134
If he do, i' faith, and find any body in the house . . . *Mer. Wives* i 4 4
'Tis a great charge to come under one body's hand . . . . . i 4 105
Go thy ways; I'll make more of thy old body than I have done . . ii 2 145
Or, to redeem him, Give up your body to such sweet uncleanness *Meas. for Meas.* ii 4 54
Sir, believe this, I had rather give my body than my soul . . . ii 4 56
Lay down the treasures of your body To this supposed, or else to let him suffer . . . . ii 4 96
Ere I'ld yield My body up to shame . . . . ii 4 104
Redeem thy brother By yielding up thy body to my will . . . ii 4 164
Before his sister should her body stoop To such abhorr'd pollution . ii 4 182
The damned'st body to invest and cover In prenzie guards! . . . iii 1 96
But grace, being the soul of your complexion, shall keep the body of it ever fair . . . . iii 1 188
Hath any body inquired for me here to-day? . . . . . . iv 1 16
A deflower'd maid! And by an eminent body that enforced The law against it! . . . . iv 4 25
He would not, but by gift of my chaste body To his concupiscible intemperate lust, Release my brother . . . . v 1 97
Who thinks he knows that he ne'er knew my body, But knows he thinks that he knows Isabel's . . . . v 1 203
This is the body That took away the match from Isabel . . . . v 1 210
Soul-killing witches that deform the body, Disguised cheaters *C. of Err.* i 2 100
That this body, consecrate to thee, By ruffian lust should be contaminate! ii 2 134
What is she?—A very reverent body . . . . iii 2 91
In what part of her body stands Ireland? . . . . iii 2 118
Show'd me silks that he had bought for me And therewithal took measure of my body . . . . iv 3 9
The body of your discourse is sometime guarded with fragments *M. Ado* i 1 287
Wisdom and blood combating in so tender a body, we have ten proofs to one that blood hath the victory . . . . ii 3 171
Else it were pity but they should suffer salvation, body and soul . . iii 3 3
I will deal in this As secretly and justly as your soul Should with your body . . . . iv 1 251
I'll prove it on his body, if he dare, Despite his nice fence . . v 1 74
The mind shall banquet, though the body pine . . *L. L. Lost* i 1 25
My soul's earth's god, and body's fostering patron . . . . i 1 223
'Thus must thou speak,' and 'thus thy body bear' . . . . v 2 100
My little body is aweary of this great world . . *Mer. of Venice* i 2 2
An equal pound Of your fair flesh, to be cut off and taken In what part of your body pleaseth me . . . . i 3 152
Here is a letter, lady; The paper as the body of my friend . . . iii 2 267
I never knew so young a body with so old a head . . . . iv 1 164
I'll not deny him any thing I have, No, not my body nor my husband's bed . . . . v 1 228
I once did lend my body for his wealth . . . . v 1 249
It bites and blows upon my body, Even till I shrink with cold *As Y. L. It* ii 1 8
Thus most invectively he pierceth through The body of the country, city, court . . . . ii 1 59
I will through and through Cleanse the foul body of the infected world ii 7 60
Heaven Nature charged That one body should be fill'd With all graces . iii 2 150
A body would think this was well counterfeited! . . . . . iv 3 166
Bear your body more seeming . . . . v 4 72
The tailor stays thy leisure, To deck thy body with his ruffling treasure *T. of Shrew* iv 3 60
'Tis the mind that makes the body rich . . . . iv 3 174
For thy maintenance commits his body To painful labour . . . v 2 148
What's pity?—That wishing well had not a body in't . . *All's Well* i 1 195
I shall never have the blessing of God till I have issue o' my body . i 3 27
Tell me thy reason why thou wilt marry.—My poor body, madam, requires it . . . . i 3 30
I grow to you, and our parting is a tortured body . . . . . ii 1 37
Show me a child begotten of thy body that I am father to . . . iii 2 61
Of as able body as when he numbered thirty . . . . . . iv 5 86
The fabric of his folly, whose foundation Is piled upon his faith and will continue The standing of his body . . . . . . *W. Tale* i 2 431
I do in justice charge thee, On thy soul's peril and thy body's torture . ii 3 181
My second joy And first-fruits of my body . . . . . . iii 2 98
Or hoop his body more with thy embraces . . . . . . iv 4 450
Never such a power For any foreign preparation Was levied in the body of a land . . . . *K. John* iv 2 112
Nay, in the body of this fleshly land, This kingdom . . . . iv 2 245
And part this body and my soul With contemplation and devout desires v 4 47
From the organ-pipe of frailty sings His soul and body to their lasting rest . . . . v 7 24
At Worcester must his body be interr'd; For so he will'd it . . . v 7 99
For what I speak My body shall make good upon this earth *Richard II.* i 1 37
Here do stand in arms, To prove, by God's grace and my body's valour . i 3 37
Commit'st thy anointed body to the cure Of those physicians that first wounded thee . . . . ii 1 98
My father hath a power; inquire of him, And learn to make a body of a limb . . . . iii 2 187
There at Venice gave His body to that pleasant country's earth, And his pure soul unto his captain Christ . . . . iv 1 98
I have given here my soul's consent To undeck the pompous body of a king . . . . iv 1 250
With clog of conscience and sour melancholy Hath yielded up his body to the grave . . . . v 6 21
Let not us that are squires of the night's body be called thieves of the day's beauty: let us be Diana's foresters . . . . *1 Hen. IV.* i 2 28
When that this body did contain a spirit, A kingdom for it was too small a bound . . . . v 4 89
But what need I thus My well-known body to anatomize Among my household? Why is Rumour here? . . . . . *2 Hen. IV.* Ind. 21
Come, we will all put forth, body and goods . . . . . . i 1 186
Holy in his thoughts, He's followed both with body and with mind . i 1 203
I think we are a body strong enough, Even as we are . . . . i 3 66
Begin to patch up thine old body for heaven . . . . . . ii 4 253
Other gambol faculties a' has, that show a weak mind and an able body ii 4 274
You perceive the body of our kingdom How foul it is . . . . iii 1 38
As a body yet distemper'd; Which to his former strength may be restored iii 1 41

Body. The care on thee depending Hath fed upon the body of my father *2 Hen. IV.* iv 5 160
To spurn at your most royal image And mock your workings in a second body v 2 90
That the great body of our state may go In equal rank with the best govern'd nation v 2 136
Make less thy body hence, and more thy grace; Leave gormandizing v 5 56
Here I promised you I would be and here I commit my body to your mercies Epil. 15
The breath no sooner left his father's body *Hen. V.* i 1 25
Leaving his body as a paradise, To envelope and contain celestial spirits i 1 30
Model to thy inward greatness, Like little body with a mighty heart ii Prol. 17
I beseech your highness to forgive, Although my body pay the price of it ii 2 154
My fault, but not my body, pardon, sovereign ii 2 165
Never any body saw it but his lackey iii 7 121
Who with a body fill'd and vacant mind Gets him to rest iv 1 286
I Richard's body have interred new iv 1 312
Bear hence his body; I will help to bury it *1 Hen. VI.* i 4 87
Bring forth the body of old Salisbury ii 2 4
You did mistake The outward composition of his body ii 3 75
Leaving no heir begotten of his body ii 5 72
My body shall Pay recompense, if you will grant my suit iii 3 18
Cannot my body nor blood-sacrifice Entreat you? v 3 20
Then take my soul, my body, soul and all v 3 22
Throws away his crutch Before his legs be firm to bear his body *2 Hen. VI.* iii 1 190
My body round engirt with misery, For what's more miserable than discontent? iii 1 200
Rear up his body; wring him by the nose iii 2 34
The sea received it, And so I wish'd thy body might my heart iii 2 109
Come hither, gracious sovereign, view this body iii 2 149
Stop my mouth; So shouldst thou either turn my flying soul, Or I should breathe it so into thy body iii 2 398
There let his head and lifeless body lie iv 1 142
His body will I bear unto the king: If he revenge it not, yet will his friends iv 1 145
But where's the body that I should embrace? iv 4 6
And as I thrust thy body in with my sword, So wish I, I might thrust thy soul to hell iv 10 84
My soul and body on the action both! v 2 26
Like rich hangings in a homely house, So was his will in his old feeble body v 3 13
That this my body Might in the ground be closed up in rest! *3 Hen. VI.* ii 1 75
All my body's moisture Scarce serves to quench my furnace-burning heart ii 1 79
If with thy will it stands That to my foes this body must be prey ii 3 39
His body couched in a curious bed ii 5 53
I fear thy overthrow More than my body's parting with my soul! ii 6 4
I'll make my heaven in a lady's lap, And deck my body in gay ornaments iii 2 149
An envious mountain on my back, Where sits deformity to mock my body iii 2 158
We'll yoke together, like a double shadow To Henry's body iv 6 50
But when the fox hath once got in his nose, He'll soon find means to make the body follow iv 7 26
Do but answer this: What is the body when the head is off? v 1 41
My mangled body shows, My blood, my want of strength, my sick heart shows, That I must yield my body to the earth v 2 9
Of all my lands Is nothing left me but my body's length v 2 26
Since the heavens have shaped my body so, Let hell make crook'd my mind v 6 78
I'll throw thy body in another room And triumph, Henry v 6 92
Thou hadst but power over his mortal body, His soul thou canst not have; therefore, be gone *Richard III.* i 2 47
Entertain some score or two of tailors, To study fashions to adorn my body i 2 258
Now must I hide his body in some hole i 4 287
Have prevail'd Upon my body with their hellish charms iii 4 64
Not sleeping, to engross his idle body, But praying, to enrich his watchful soul iii 7 77
I thank thee, that this carnal cur Preys on the issue of his mother's body iv 4 57
Which, say to her, did drain The purple sap from her sweet brother's body iv 4 277
All-Souls' day is my body's doomsday v 1 12
My anointed body By thee was punched full of deadly holes v 3 124
Who set the body and the limbs Of this great sport together? *Hen. VIII.* i 1 46
'Tis a sufferance panging As soul and body's severing ii 3 16
Of his own body he was ill, and gave The clergy ill example iv 2 43
Body o' me, where is it? v 2 22
I would my heart were in her body *Troi. and Cres.* i 2 85
Time, force, and death, Do to this body what extremes you can iv 2 108
Her wanton spirits look out At every joint and motive of her body iv 5 57
In which part of his body Shall I destroy him? iv 5 242
Go, bear Patroclus' body to Achilles v 5 17
Come, tie his body to my horse's tail; Along the field I will the Trojan trail v 8 21
A time when all the body's members Rebell'd against the belly *Coriolanus* i 1 99
Like a gulf it did remain I' the midst o' the body i 1 102
Unto the appetite and affection common Of the whole body i 1 108
Because I am the store-house and the shop Of the whole body i 1 138
He received in the repulse of Tarquin seven hurts i' the body ii 1 166
We do request your kindest ears, and after, Your loving motion toward the common body, To yield what passes here ii 2 57
Your liberties and the charters that you bear I' the body of the weal ii 3 189
Wish To jump a body with a dangerous physic That's sure of death without it iii 1 154
And by my body's action teach my mind A most inherent baseness iii 2 122
Think Upon the wounds his body bears, which show Like graves iii 3 50
Let me twine Mine arms about that body, where against My grained ash an hundred times hath broke iv 5 113
After your way his tale pronounced shall bury His reasons with his body v 6 59
Bear from hence his body; And mourn you for him v 6 143
A better head her glorious body fits Than his that shakes for age *T. And.* i 1 187
Your swarth Cimmerian Doth make your honour of his body's hue ii 3 73
As any mortal body hearing it Should straight fall mad ii 3 103
They told me they would bind me here Unto the body of a dismal yew ii 3 107
Tumble me into some loathsome pit, Where never man's eye may behold my body ii 3 177
Have lopp'd and hew'd and made thy body bare Of her two branches ii 4 17
What shall I do Now I behold thy lively body so? iii 1 105
Let me teach you how to knit again This scatter'd corn into one mutual sheaf, These broken limbs again into one body v 3 72

Body. Sheathing the steel in my adventurous body *T. Andron.* v 3 112
For a hand, and a foot, and a body, though they be not to be talked on, yet they are past compare *Rom. and Jul.* ii 5 42
Bear hence this body and attend our will iii 1 201
Not body's death, but body's banishment iii 3 11
To wreak the love I bore my cousin Upon his body that hath slaughter'd him iii 5 103
In one little body Thou counterfeit'st a bark, a sea, a wind iii 5 131
The bark thy body is, Sailing in this salt flood; the winds, thy sighs iii 5 134
Without a sudden calm, will overset Thy tempest-tossed body iii 5 138
Methinks I see my cousin's ghost Seeking out Romeo, that did spit his body Upon a rapier's point iv 3 56
Her body sleeps in Capel's monument, And her immortal part with angels lives v 1 18
The public body, which doth seldom Play the recanter *T. of Athens* v 1 148
And Cassius is A wretched creature and must bend his body *J. Cæsar* i 2 117
Produce his body to the market-place iii 1 228
Mark Antony, here, take you Cæsar's body iii 1 244
Prepare the body then, and follow us iii 1 253
Here comes his body, mourned by Mark Antony iii 2 45
Stand from the hearse, stand from the body iii 2 169
Burn his body in the holy place, And with the brands fire the traitors' houses. Take up the body iii 2 259
What villain touch'd his body, that did stab, And not for justice? iv 3 20
Where, where, Messala, doth his body lie? v 3 91
Come, therefore, and to Thasos send his body v 3 104
Where is Duncan's body?—Carried to Colmekill *Macbeth* ii 4 32
I would not have such a heart in my bosom for the dignity of the whole body v 1 62
Before my body I throw my warlike shield v 8 32
Ere those shoes were old With which she follow'd my poor father's body *Hamlet* i 2 148
Unto the voice and yielding of that body Whereof he is the head i 3 23
Makes each petty artery in this body As hardy as the Nemean lion's nerve i 4 82
Swift as quicksilver it courses through The natural gates and alleys of the body i 5 67
A most instant tetter bark'd about, Most lazar-like, with vile and loathsome crust, All my smooth body i 5 73
The very age and body of the time his form and pressure iii 2 26
O, such a deed As from the body of contraction plucks The very soul iii 4 46
Where is he gone?—To draw apart the body he hath kill'd iv 1 24
Bring the body Into the chapel iv 1 36
What have you done, my lord, with the dead body?—Compounded it with dust iv 2 5
You must tell us where the body is, and go with us to the king iv 2 28
The body is with the king, but the king is not with the body iv 2 29
I have sent to seek him, and to find the body iv 3 1
Where the dead body is bestow'd, my lord, We cannot get from him iv 3 12
Your water is a sore decayer of your whoreson dead body v 1 189
From her derogate body never spring A babe to honour her! *Lear* i 4 302
With his prepared sword, he charges home My unprovided body ii 1 54
Nature, being oppress'd, commands the mind To suffer with the body ii 4 110
When the mind's free, The body's delicate iii 4 12
Thou wert better in thy grave than to answer with thy uncovered body this extremity of the skies iii 4 106
Like an old lecher's heart; a small spark, all the rest on's body cold iii 4 118
Who hath had three suits to his back, six shirts to his body, horse to ride iii 4 142
To thee a woman's services are due: My fool usurps my body iv 2 28
If ever thou wilt thrive, bury my body iv 6 253
When she is sated with his body, she will find the error of her choice *Othello* i 3 357
I'll pour this pestilence into his ear, That she repeals him for her body's lust ii 3 363
I had been happy, if the general camp, Pioneers and all, had tasted her sweet body, So I had nothing known iii 3 346
I'll not expostulate with her, lest her body and beauty unprovide my mind again iv 1 217
Cough, or cry 'hem,' if any body come iv 2 29
Demand that demi-devil Why he hath thus ensnared my soul and body v 2 302
This common body, Like to a vagabond flag upon the stream *Ant. and Cleo.* i 4 44
Bear the king's son's body Before our army iii 1 3
She shows a body rather than a life, A statue than a breather iii 3 23
The soul and body rive not more in parting Than greatness going off iv 13 5
My good knave Eros, now thy captain is Even such a body iv 14 13
The arm of mine own body, and the heart Where mine his thoughts did kindle v 1 45
Hurt him! his body's a passable carcass, if he be not hurt *Cymbeline* i 2 10
Some natural notes about her body, Above ten thousand meaner moveables Would testify ii 2 28
His meanest garment, That ever hath but clipp'd his body, is dearer ii 3 139
My body's mark'd With Roman swords iii 3 56
He on the ground, my speech of insultment ended on his dead body iii 5 145
The lines of my body are as well drawn as his; no less young, more strong iv 1 10
We do fear this body hath a tail More perilous than the head iv 2 144
His body's hostage For his return iv 2 185
Thersites' body is as good as Ajax', When neither are alive iv 2 252
He'll then instruct us of this body iv 2 360
To prepare This body, like to them, to what I must *Pericles* i 1 44
Makes both my body pine and soul to languish i 2 31
Go thy ways, good mariner: I'll bring the body presently ii 1 82
The common body, By you relieved, would force me to my duty iii 3 21
Body-curer. Soul-curer and body-curer *Mer. Wives* iii 1 100
Bodykins, Master Page ii 3 46
Use them according to their desert.—God's bodykins, man, much better *Hamlet* ii 2 554
Body public. Whether that the body public be A horse whereon the governor doth ride *Meas. for Meas.* i 2 163
Bog. All the infections that the sun sucks up From bogs, fens, flats, on Prosper fall! *Tempest* ii 2 2
I found it [Ireland] out by the bogs *Com. of Errors* iii 2 121
Through bog, through bush, through brake, through brier *M. N. Dream* iii 1 110
They that ride so and ride not warily, fall into foul bogs *Hen. V.* iii 7 61
Through ford and whirlipool, o'er bog and quagmire *Lear* iii 4 54
Boggle. You boggle shrewdly, every feather starts you *All's Well* v 3 232
Boggler. You have been a boggler ever *Ant. and Cleo.* iii 13 110
Bohemia. If you shall chance, Camillo, to visit Bohemia *W. Tale* i 1 2
As I have said, great difference betwixt our Bohemia and your Sicilia i 1 4

Bohemia. Sicilia means to pay Bohemia the visitation which he justly owes him *W. Tale* i 1 7
Sicilia cannot show himself over-kind to Bohemia i 1 24
Tell him, you are sure All in Bohemia's well i 2 31
When at Bohemia You take my lord, I'll give him my commission i 2 40
I think most understand Bohemia stays here longer i 2 230
The covering sky is nothing ; Bohemia nothing ; My wife is nothing i 2 294
Who does infect her ?—Why, he that wears her like her medal, hanging About his neck, Bohemia i 2 308
I must believe you, sir : I do ; and will fetch off Bohemia for't i 2 334
Keep with Bohemia And with your queen i 2 344
Our ship hath touch'd upon The deserts of Bohemia iii 3 2
Places remote enough are in Bohemia iii 3 31
Imagine me, Gentle spectators, that I now may be In fair Bohemia iv 1 21
Not a more cowardly rogue in all Bohemia iv 3 112
Points more than all the lawyers in Bohemia can learnedly handle iv 4 207
Not for Bohemia, nor the pomp that may Be thereat glean'd iv 4 499
We are not furnish'd like Bohemia's son, Nor shall appear in Sicilia iv 4 599
Who for Bohemia bend, to signify Not only my success in Libya v 1 165
Please you, great sir, Bohemia greets you from himself by me v 1 181
Where's Bohemia ? speak.—Here in your city v 1 185
Bohemia stops his ears, and threatens them With divers deaths in death v 1 201
Then asks Bohemia forgiveness ; then embraces his son-in-law v 2 57
Thou art as honest a true fellow as any is in Bohemia v 2 170
Bohemian. A Bohemian born, but here nursed up and bred *Meas. for Meas.* iv 2 134
Bohemian-Tartar. Here's a Bohemian-Tartar *Mer. Wives* iv 5 21
Bohun. I was lord high constable And Duke of Buckingham ; now, poor Edward Bohun *Hen. VIII.* ii 1 103
Boil. Where I have seen corruption boil and bubble *Meas. for Meas.* v 1 320
And doth boil, As 'twere from forth us all, a man distill'd Out of our virtues *Troi. and Cres.* i 3 349
How if he had boils ? full, all over, generally ? ii 1 2
And those boils did run ? say so ii 1 5
Boils and plagues Plaster you o'er, that you may be abhorr'd. *Coriolanus* i 4 31
Swelter'd venom sleeping got, Boil thou first i' the charmed pot *Macbeth* iv 1 9
Fillet of a fenny snake, In the cauldron boil and bake iv 1 13
For a charm of powerful trouble, Like a hell-broth boil and bubble iv 1 19
Thou art a boil, A plague-sore, an embossed carbuncle, In my corrupted blood *Lear* ii 4 226
Boiled. Cure thy brains, Now useless, boil'd within thy skull ! *Tempest* v 1 60
Let me be boiled to death with melancholy *T. Night* ii 5 3
Would any but these boiled brains of nineteen and two-and-twenty hunt this weather ? *W. Tale* iii 3 64
Such boil'd stuff As well might poison poison ! *Cymbeline* i 6 125
Boiling. He bravely broach'd his boiling bloody breast *M. N. Dream* v 1 148
What wheels ? racks ? fires ? what flaying ? boiling ? In leads or oils ? *W. Tale* iii 2 177
Boiling choler chokes The hollow passage of my poison'd voice *1 Hen. VI.* v 4 120
Boisterous. With a base and boisterous sword enforce A thievish living on the common road *As Y. Like It* ii 3 32
'Tis a boisterous and a cruel style, A style for challengers iv 3 31
Feeling what small things are boisterous there [in the eye] *K. John* iv 1 95
Here to make good the boisterous late appeal *Richard II.* i 1 4
Roused up with boisterous untuned drums i 3 134
Into the harsh and boisterous tongue of war *2 Hen. IV.* iv 1 49
It seem'd in me But as an honour snatch'd with boisterous hand iv 5 192
O Clifford, boisterous Clifford ! thou hast slain The flower of Europe *3 Hen. VI.* ii 1 70
As, by proof, we see The waters swell before a boisterous storm *Rich. III.* ii 3 44
Is love a tender thing ? it is too rough, Too rude, too boisterous *Rom. and Jul.* i 4 26
What, think'st That the bleak air, thy boisterous chamberlain, Will put thy shirt on warm ? *T. of Athens* iv 3 222
Each small annexment, petty consequence, Attends the boisterous ruin *Hamlet* iii 3 22
Be content to slubber the gloss of your new fortunes with this more stubborn and boisterous expedition *Othello* i 3 228
Boisterously. A sceptre snatch'd with an unruly hand Must be as boisterously maintain'd as gain'd *K. John* iii 4 136
Boisterous-rough. What need you be so boisterous-rough ? I will not struggle. iv 1 76
Boitier. Vetch me in my closet un boitier vert, a box, a green-a box *Mer. Wives* i 4 47
Bold. May I be bold To think these spirits ? *Tempest* iv 1 119
I'll be so bold to break the seal for once *T. G. of Ver.* iii 1 139
I dare be bold With our discourse to make your grace to smile v 4 162
I make bold to press with so little preparation upon you. *Mer. Wives* ii 2 162
I will first make bold with your money ; next, give me your hand. ii 2 262
A fat woman, gone up into his chamber : I'll be so bold as stay iv 5 13
May I be bold to say so, sir ?—Ay, sir ; like who more bold iv 5 54
Let me be bold ; I do arrest your words *Meas. for Meas.* ii 4 133
Virtue is bold, and goodness never fearful iii 1 215
I will only be bold with Benedick for his company *Much Ado* iii 2 8
Bold of your worthiness, we single you As our best-moving fair solicitor *L. L. Lost* ii 1 28
I know not by what power I am made bold *M. N. Dream* i 1 59
If I cut my finger, I shall make bold with you. iii 1 187
Thou art too wild, too rude and bold of voice *Mer. of Venice* ii 2 190
Had you been as wise as bold, Young in limbs, in judgement old ii 7 70
O, then be bold to say Bassanio's dead ! iii 2 187
Young gentleman, your spirits are too bold for your years *As Y. Like It* i 2 184
Therefore let me be thus bold with you *T. of Shrew* i 2 104
If I may be bold, Tell me, I beseech you i 2 219
Let me be so bold as ask you, Did you yet ever see Baptista's daughter ? i 2 251
Am bold to show myself a forward guest Within your house ii 1 51
May I be so bold to know the cause of your coming ? ii 1 88
May I be bold to acquaint his grace you are gone about it ? *All's Well* iii 6 84
Be bold you do so grow in my requital As nothing can unroot you v 1 5
That may you be bold to say in your foolery *T. Night* i 5 12
O, he is bold and blushes not at death *K. John* iv 3 76
Norfolk, sprightfully and bold, Stays but the summons *Richard II.* i 3 3
On pain of death, no person be so bold Or daring-hardy as to touch the lists i 3 42
Speaking so, Thy words are but as thoughts ; therefore, be bold ii 1 276
Your presence is too bold and peremptory *1 Hen. IV.* i 3 17
In the closing of some glorious day Be bold to tell you that I am your son iii 2 134
More active-valiant or more valiant-young, More daring or more bold v 1 91
To look with forehead bold and big enough *2 Hen. IV.* i 3 8
Happy am I, that have a man so bold, That dares do justice on my proper son v 2 108
Bold. With the like bold, just and impartial spirit As you have done 'gainst me *2 Hen. IV.* v 2 116
'Fore God, his grace is bold, to trust these traitors *Hen. V.* ii 2 1
I will be so bold as to tell you I know the disciplines of war iii 2 152
I'll be so bold to take what they have left *1 Hen. VI.* ii 1 78
Madam, I have been bold to trouble you ii 3 25
List to me ; For I am bold to counsel you in this *2 Hen. VI.* i 3 96
Weapons drawn Here in our presence ! dare you be so bold ? iii 2 238
The trust I have is in mine innocence, And therefore am I bold and resolute iv 4 60
Dare any be so bold to sound retreat or parley, when I command them kill ? iv 8 4
Were he as famous and as bold in war As he is famed for mildness, peace, and prayer *3 Hen. VI.* ii 1 155
Becomes it thee to be thus bold in terms ? ii 2 85
And what makes robbers bold but too much lenity ? ii 6 22
I have true-hearted friends, Not mutinous in peace, yet bold in war iv 8 10
O, 'tis a parlous boy ; Bold, quick, ingenious, forward, capable *Rich. III.* iii 1 155
I am thus bold to put your grace in mind Of what you promised me iv 2 113
Thy prime of manhood daring, bold, and venturous iv 4 170
Make bold her bashful years with your experience iv 4 326
Jockey of Norfolk, be not too bold, For Dickon thy master is bought and sold v 3 304
And dare be bold to weep for Buckingham *Hen. VIII.* ii 1 72
Ye are too bold : Go to ; I'll make ye know your times of business ii 2 71
I will be bold with time and your attention ii 4 168
You made bold To carry into Flanders the great seal iii 2 318
May I be bold to ask what that contains, That paper in your hand ? iv 1 13
A bold brave gentleman iv 1 40
The bold and coward, The wise and fool, the artist and unread, The hard and soft, seem all affined and kin *Troi. and Cres.* i 3 23
Rails on our state of war, Bold as an oracle i 3 192
I will be bold to take my leave of you *Coriolanus* iii 1 106
God forbid I should be so bold to press to heaven in my young days *T. Andron.* iv 3 90
Be bold in us : we'll follow where thou lead'st v 1 13
I will answer it. I am too bold, 'tis not to me she speaks *Rom. and Jul.* ii 2 14
One of your nine lives ; that I mean to make bold withal iii 1 81
Till strange love, grown bold, Think true love acted simple modesty iii 2 15
Flies an eagle flight, bold and forth on, Leaving no tract behind *T. of Athens* i 1 49
I have been bold—For that I knew it the most general way ii 2 208
I think we are too bold upon your rest *J. Cæsar* ii 1 86
Cæsar was mighty, bold, royal, and loving iii 1 127
That which hath made them drunk hath made me bold *Macbeth* ii 2 1
I'll make so bold to call, For 'tis my limited service ii 3 56
Be bloody, bold, and resolute ; laugh to scorn The power of man iv 1 79
If my duty be too bold, my love is too unmannerly *Hamlet* iii 2 363
Making so bold, My fears forgetting manners v 2 16
Men so disorder'd, so debosh'd and bold *Lear* i 4 263
Bold in the quarrel's right ii 1 56
For this business, It toucheth us, as France invades our land, Not bolds the king v 1 26
He is bold in his defence v 3 114
If this be known to you and your allowance, We then have done you bold and saucy wrongs *Othello* i 1 129
A maiden never bold ; Of spirit so still and quiet i 3 94
I have made bold, Iago, To send in to your wife iii 1 35
As—to be bold with you—Not to affect many proposed matches Of her own clime iii 3 228
Be near at hand ; I may miscarry in't.—Here, at thy hand : be bold v 1 7
I will make bold To send them to you, only for this night *Cymbeline* i 6 197
I would I were so sure To win the king as I am bold her honour Will remain hers ii 4 2
Which I'll make bold your highness Cannot deny v 5 89
Alas, my father, it befits not me Unto a stranger knight to be so bold *Pericles* ii 3 67
Bold a herald. At first I stuck my choice upon her, ere my heart Durst make too bold a herald of my tongue *All's Well* v 3 46
Bold a persuasion. You are a great deal abused in too bold a persuasion *Cymbeline* i 4 124
Bold adversity. Ring'd about with bold adversity *1 Hen. VI.* iv 4 14
Bold advertisement. Yet doth he give us bold advertisement *1 Hen. IV.* iv 1 36
Bold attempt. The ransom of my bold attempt Shall be this cold corpse on the earth's cold face *Richard III.* v 3 265
Bold bad man. Eyes, that so long have slept upon This bold bad man *Hen. VIII.* ii 2 44
Bold-beating. Your red-lattice phrases, and your bold-beating oaths *Mer. Wives* ii 2 28
Bold champion. Like a bold champion, I assume the lists *Pericles* i 1 61
Bold charter. Of that I have made a bold charter *All's Well* iv 5 97
Bold conspiracy. O heinous, strong and bold conspiracy ! *Richard II.* v 3 59
Bold cure. Therefore my hopes, not surfeited to death, Stand in bold cure *Othello* ii 1 51
Bold deeds. Stopping my greedy ear with their bold deeds *2 Hen. IV.* i 1 78
Bold enterprise. What hath this bold enterprise brought forth ? i 1 178
So is he now in execution Of any bold or noble enterprise *J. Cæsar* i 2 302
Bold-faced. It warm'd thy father's heart with proud desire Of bold-faced victory *1 Hen. VI.* iv 6 12
Bold fears. All these bold fears Thou see'st with peril I have answered *2 Hen. IV.* v 5 196
Bold flood. Pouring war Into the bowels of ungrateful Rome, Like a bold flood o'er-bear *Coriolanus* iv 5 137
Bold gentleman, Prosperity be thy page ! i 5 23
Bold head. His bold head 'Bove the contentious waves he kept *Tempest* ii 1 117
Bold hostility. Whereupon You conjure from the breast of civil peace Such bold hostility *1 Hen. IV.* iv 3 44
Bold Iachimo. Under the conduct of bold Iachimo *Cymbeline* iv 2 340
Bold Iago. Left in the conduct of the bold Iago *Othello* ii 1 75
Bold intent. To set a gloss upon his bold intent *1 Hen. VI.* iv 1 103
Bold language. I shall remember this bold language.—Do. Remember your bold life too *Hen. VIII.* v 3 84
Bold Leander. So bold Leander would adventure it *T. G. of Ver.* iii 1 120
Bold life. I shall remember this bold language.—Do. Remember your bold life too *Hen. VIII.* v 3 85
Bold malice. You shall do small respect, show too bold malice *Lear* ii 2 137
Bold Mercutio. But that he tilts With piercing steel at bold Mercutio's breast *Rom. and Jul.* iii 1 164
Bold mouths. This makes bold mouths *Hen. VIII.* i 2 60
Bold one. Are you a man ?—Ay, and a bold one, that dare look on that Which might appal the devil *Macbeth* iii 4 59

Bold one. That The Britons have razed out. though with the loss Of many a bold one . . . *Cymbeline* v 5 71
Bold oxlips and The crown imperial; lilies of all kinds . . *W. Tale* iv 4 125
Bold peasant, Darest thou support a publish'd traitor? . . *Lear* iv 6 235
Bold power. To break the heart of generosity, And make bold power look pale . . . . *Coriolanus* i 1 216
Bold rebellion. Quenching the flame of bold rebellion Even with the rebels' blood . . . . 2 *Hen. IV.* Ind. 26
Bold Scots. Ten thousand bold Scots, two and twenty knights 1 *Hen. IV.* i 1 68
Bold show. 'Tis my breeding That gives me this bold show of courtesy *Othello* ii 1 100
Bold son. Hast thou, according to thy oath and band, Brought hither Henry Hereford thy bold son? . . . . . *Richard II.* i 1 3
Bold spirit. A jewel in a ten-times-barr'd-up chest Is a bold spirit in a loyal breast . . . . i 1 181
With bold spirit relate what you . . . have collected . *Hen. VIII.* i 2 129
Bold verdict. Must your bold verdict enter talk with lords? 1 *Hen. VI.* iii 1 63
Bold wag. Making the bold wag by their praises bolder . *L. L. Lost* v 2 108
Bold waves. The most mighty Neptune Seem to besiege and make his bold waves tremble . . . . *Tempest* i 2 205
Bold way. As an offender to your father, I gave bold way to my authority 2 *Hen. IV.* v 2 82
Bold winds. A silence in the heavens, the rack stand still, The bold winds speechless . . . . *Hamlet* ii 2 507
Bold yeomen. Fight bold yeomen! Draw, archers! . . *Richard III.* v 3 338
Boldened. Art thou thus bolden'd, man, by thy distress? *As Y. Like It* ii 7 91
Bolden'd Under your promised pardon . . . . *Hen. VIII.* i 2 55
Bolder. You swinged me for my love, which makes me the bolder to chide you for yours . . . . *T. G. of Ver.* ii 1 89
Making the bold wag by their praises bolder . . *L. L. Lost* v 2 108
I ne'er heard yet That any of these bolder vices wanted Less impudence to gainsay what they did . . . . . *W. Tale* iii 2 56
Makes me the bolder to salute my king With ruder terms . 2 *Hen. VI.* i 1 29
Than my Lord Hastings no man might be bolder . . *Richard III.* iii 4 30
He's the devil.—Bolder, though not so subtle . . *Coriolanus* i 10 17
Boldest. Put on Your boldest suit of mirth . . *Mer. of Venice* ii 2 211
Even as bad as those That vulgars give bold'st titles . . *W. Tale* ii 1 94
We will grace his heels With the most boldest and best hearts of Rome *J. Cæsar* iii 1 121
Boldly. Look you speak justly.—Boldly, at least . . *Meas. for Meas.* v 1 299
Yet thus far I will boldly publish her . . . . *T. Night* ii 1 30
We should have answer'd heaven Boldly 'not guilty' . . *W. Tale* i 2 74
Which in myself I boldly will defend . . . . *Richard II.* i 1 145
If it be so, out with it boldly, man . . . . . . ii 1 233
Robbers range abroad unseen In murders and in outrage, boldly here . iii 2 40
Stirr'd up by God, thus boldly for his king . . . . iv 1 133
We may boldly spend upon the hope of what Is to come in 1 *Hen. IV.* iv 1 54
And boldly did outdare The dangers of the time . . . . v 1 40
He shall not hide his head, But boldly stand and front him . 2 *Hen. VI.* v 1 86
What's he approacheth boldly to our presence? . 3 *Hen. VI.* iii 3 44
Sound drums and trumpets boldly and cheerfully . . *Richard III.* v 3 269
Out with it boldly: truth loves open dealing . . *Hen. VIII.* iii 1 39
You shall know many dare accuse you boldly . . . . v 3 56
Let's kill him boldly, but not wrathfully . . . . *J. Cæsar* ii 1 172
Hear it apart.—None but friends: say boldly . . *Ant. and Cleo.* iii 13 47
Boldness. In the boldness of my cunning, I will lay my self in hazard *Meas. for Meas.* iv 2 165
Pardon me, sir, the boldness is mine own . . . *T. of Shrew* ii 1 89
A strumpet's boldness, a divulged shame . . . *All's Well* ii 1 174
'Tis but the boldness of his hand, haply, which his heart was not consenting to . . . . iii 2 79
Why appear you with this ridiculous boldness? . . *T. Night* iii 4 41
What foolish boldness brought thee to their mercies? . . . v 1 73
Arms her with the boldness of a wife To her allowing husband! *W. Tale* i 2 184
If wit flow from 't As boldness from my bosom, let't not be doubted I shall do good . . . . ii 2 53
Howe'er the business goes, you have made fault I' the boldness of your speech . . . . iii 2 219
Show boldness and aspiring confidence . . . . *K. John* v 1 56
You call honourable boldness impudent sauciness . 2 *Hen. IV.* ii 1 134
And spurn upon thee, beggar, for thy boldness . . *Richard III.* i 2 42
The tidings that I bring Will make my boldness manners . *Hen. VIII.* v 1 159
Boldness comes to me now, and brings me heart . . *Troi. and Cres.* iii 2 121
Boldness be my friend! Arm me, audacity, from head to foot! *Cymbeline* i 6 18
Bolin. Slack the bolins there! Thou wilt not, wilt thou? . *Pericles* iii 1 43
Bolingbroke, as low as to thy heart, Through the false passage of thy throat, thou liest . . . . *Richard II.* i 1 124
Nor the prevention of poor Bolingbroke About his marriage . . ii 1 167
The banish'd Bolingbroke repeals himself . . . . . ii 2 49
All the household servants fled with him To Bolingbroke . . ii 2 61
Green, thou art the midwife to my woe, And Bolingbroke my sorrow's dismal heir . . . . ii 2 63
We three here part that ne'er shall meet again.—That's as York thrives to beat back Bolingbroke . . . . ii 2 144
More welcome is the stroke of death to me Than Bolingbroke to England iii 1 32
Bolingbroke, through our security, Grows strong and great . . iii 2 34
This thief, this traitor, Bolingbroke . . . . . . iii 2 47
For every man that Bolingbroke hath press'd To lift shrewd steel against our golden crown, God for his Richard hath in heavenly pay A glorious angel . . . . iii 2 58
All the Welshmen, hearing thou wert dead, Are gone to Bolingbroke . iii 2 74
Strives Bolingbroke to be as great as we? Greater he shall not be . iii 2 97
So high above his limits swells the rage Of Bolingbroke . . . iii 2 110
I warrant they have made peace with Bolingbroke . . . . iii 2 127
Our lands, our lives and all are Bolingbroke's . . . . . iii 2 151
Proud Bolingbroke, I come To change blows with thee . . . iii 2 188
York is join'd with Bolingbroke, And all your northern castles yielded up iii 2 200
Let them hence away, From Richard's night to Bolingbroke's fair day . iii 2 218
Henry Bolingbroke On both his knees doth kiss King Richard's hand . iii 3 35
Far off from the mind of Bolingbroke It is . . . . . iii 3 45
Tell Bolingbroke—for yond methinks he stands—That every stride he makes upon my land Is dangerous treason . . . . . . iii 3 91
Thy thrice noble cousin Harry Bolingbroke doth humbly kiss thy hand iii 3 104
Northumberland comes back from Bolingbroke . . . . . iii 3 142
What says King Bolingbroke? will his majesty Give Richard leave to live till Richard die? . . . . iii 3 173
You make a leg, and Bolingbroke says ay . . . . . . iii 3 175
Pluck'd up root and all by Bolingbroke . . . . . . iii 4 52
Bolingbroke Hath seized the wasteful king . . . . . . iii 4 54
King Richard, he is in the mighty hold Of Bolingbroke . . . . iii 4 84

Bolingbroke. In the balance of great Bolingbroke, Besides himself, are all the English peers . . . . *Richard II.* iii 4 87
What, was I born to this, that my sad look Should grace the triumph of great Bolingbroke? . . . . iii 4 99
The resignation of thy state and crown To Henry Bolingbroke . . iv 1 180
O that I were a mockery king of snow, Standing before the sun of Bolingbroke! . . . . iv 1 261
Was this the face that faced so many follies, And was at last out-faced by Bolingbroke? . . . . iv 1 286
Hath Bolingbroke deposed Thine intellect? hath he been in thy heart? v 1 27
The mind of Bolingbroke is changed; You must to Pomfret . . v 1 51
Northumberland, thou ladder wherewithal The mounting Bolingbroke ascends my throne . . . . *Richard II.* v 1 56; 2 *Hen. IV.* iii 1 71
The duke, great Bolingbroke, Mounted upon a hot and fiery steed *Rich. II.* v 2 7
Whilst all tongues cried 'God save thee, Bolingbroke!' . . . v 2 11
Jesu preserve thee! welcome, Bolingbroke! . . . . . . v 2 17
To Bolingbroke are we sworn subjects now . . . . . . v 2 39
Never will I rise up from the ground Till Bolingbroke have pardon'd thee v 2 117
Then am I king'd again: and by and by Think that I am unking'd by Bolingbroke, And straight am nothing . . . . . . v 5 37
But my time Runs posting on in Bolingbroke's proud joy . . . v 5 59
That coronation-day, When Bolingbroke rode on roan Barbary . . v 5 78
So proud that Bolingbroke was on his back! . . . . . . v 5 84
I bear a burthen like an ass, Spurr'd, gall'd and tired by jauncing Bolingbroke . . . . v 5 94
This ingrate and canker'd Bolingbroke . . . 1 *Hen. IV.* i 3 137
To put down Richard, that sweet lovely rose, And plant this thorn, this canker, Bolingbroke . . . . i 3 176
All studies here I solemnly defy, Save how to gall and pinch this Bolingbroke . . . . i 3 229
Nettled and stung with pismires, when I hear Of this vile politician, Bolingbroke . . . . i 3 241
This king of smiles, this Bolingbroke . . . . i 3 246
Three times hath Henry Bolingbroke made head Against my power . iii 1 64
'This is he;' Others would say 'Where, which is Bolingbroke?' . iii 2 49
A bleeding land, Gasping for life under great Bolingbroke . 2 *Hen. IV.* i 1 208
With what loud applause Did'st thou beat heaven with blessing Bolingbroke! . . . . i 3 92
He came sighing on After the admired heels of Bolingbroke . . i 3 105
Henry Bolingbroke and he, Being mounted and both roused in their seats iv 1 117
When there was nothing could have stay'd My father from the breast of Bolingbroke . . . . iv 1 124
Then threw he down himself and all their lives That by indictment and by dint of sword Have since miscarried under Bolingbroke . . iv 1 129
When Henry the Fifth, Succeeding his father Bolingbroke 1 *Hen. VI.* ii 5 83
Roger Bolingbroke, the conjurer . . . . . 2 *Hen. VI.* i 2 76
Henry Bolingbroke, Duke of Lancaster, The eldest son and heir of John of Gaunt, Crown'd by the name of Henry the Fourth . . . . ii 2 21
This Edmund, in the reign of Bolingbroke, As I have read, laid claim unto the crown . . . . ii 2 39
Bolster. And here I'll fling the pillow, there the bolster . *T. of Shrew* iv 1 204
Damn them then, If ever mortal eyes do see them bolster! . *Othello* iii 3 399
Bolt. And rifted Jove's stout oak With his own bolt . . *Tempest* v 1 46
I'll make a shaft or a bolt on't: 'slid, 'tis but venturing *Mer. Wives* iii 4 24
With thy sharp and sulphurous bolt Split'st the unwedgeable and gnarled oak Than the soft myrtle . . . . *Meas. for Meas.* ii 2 115
Away with him to prison! lay bolts enough upon him . . . v 1 350
Yet mark'd I where the bolt of Cupid fell . . . *M. N. Dream* ii 1 165
According to the fool's bolt, sir, and such dulcet diseases *As Y. Like It* v 4 67
Bolts and shackles! . . . . *T. Night* ii 5 62
You are the better at proverbs, by how much 'A fool's bolt is soon shot' *Hen. V.* iii 7 132
With massy staples And corresponsive and fulfilling bolts *Troi. and Cres.* Prol. 18
To charge thy sulphur with a bolt That should but rive an oak *Coriolanus* v 3 152
And in conclusion to oppose the bolt Against my coming in . . *Lear* ii 4 179
It is great To do that thing that ends all other deeds; Which shackles accidents and bolts up change . . . . *Ant. and Cleo.* v 2 6
A bolt of nothing, shot at nothing, Which the brain makes of fumes *Cymbeline* iv 2 300
Give me The penitent instrument to pick that bolt, Then, free for ever! . v 4 10
The thunderer, whose bolt, you know, Sky-planted batters all rebelling coasts . . . . v 4 95
No bolts for the dead . . . . v 4 205
Bolted. Such and so finely bolted didst thou seem . . *Hen. V.* ii 2 137
Or the fann'd snow that's bolted By the northern blasts twice o'er *W. Tale* iv 4 375
And is ill school'd In bolted language . . . . *Coriolanus* iii 1 322
Bolter. I have given them away to bakers' wives, and they have made bolters of them . . . . 1 *Hen. IV.* iii 3 81
Bolting. Have I not tarried?—Ay, the grinding; but you must tarry the bolting . . . . *Troi. and Cres.* i 1 18
Have I not tarried?—Ay, the bolting, but you must tarry the leavening i 1 20
Bolting-hutch of beastliness, that swollen parcel of dropsies 1 *Hen. IV.* ii 4 495
Bombard. Looks like a foul bombard that would shed his liquor *Tempest* ii 2 21
That huge bombard of sack, that stuffed cloak-bag of guts 1 *Hen. IV.* ii 4 497
And here ye lie baiting of bombards, when Ye should do service *Hen. VIII.* v 4 85
Bombast. As bombast and as lining to the time . . *L. L. Lost* v 2 791
Here comes bare-bone. How now, my sweet creature of bombast! 1 *Hen. IV.* ii 4 359
With a bombast circumstance Horribly stuff'd with epithets of war *Othello* i 1 13
Bon. How say you by the French lord, Monsieur Le Bon? *Mer. of Venice* i 2 59
Je pense que je suis le bon écolier . . . . . *Hen. V.* iii 4 13
C'est bien dit, madame; il est fort bon Anglois . . . . iii 4 19
Bona. And ask the Lady Bona for thy queen . . . 3 *Hen. VI.* ii 6 90
That virtuous Lady Bona, thy fair sister . . . . . . iii 3 56
Tell me for truth the measure of his love Unto our sister Bona . iii 3 121
Be a witness That Bona shall be wife to the English king . . . iii 3 139
For mocking him About the marriage of the Lady Bona . . . . iv 1 31
But what said Lady Bona to my marriage? . . . . . . iv 1 97
I'll follow you, and tell what answer Lewis and the Lady Bona send to him . . . . iv 3 56
Bona-roba. We knew where the bona-robas were . . 2 *Hen. IV.* iii 2 26
She was then a bona-roba. Doth she hold her own well? . . iii 2 217
Bona terra. What say you of Kent?—Nothing but this; 'tis 'bona terra, mala gens' . . . . 2 *Hen. VI.* iv 7 61
Bond. His words are bonds, his oaths are oracles . . *T. G. of Ver.* ii 7 75
You make my bonds still greater . . . . *Meas. for Meas.* v 1 8
I will discharge my bond and thank you too . . *Com. of Errors* iv 1 13
I am here enter'd in bond for you . . . . iv 4 128
Gnawing with my teeth my bonds in sunder, I gain'd my freedom . v 1 249
Whoever bound him, I will loose his bonds . . . . . . v 1 339

Bond. The sealing-day betwixt my love and me, For everlasting bond of fellowship . . . *M. N. Dream* i 1 85
I would I had your bond, for I perceive A weak bond holds you . . iii 2 267
Three thousand ducats ; I think I may take his bond . *Mer. of Venice* i 3 28
Well then, your bond ; and let me see ; but hear you . . i 3 69
Go with me to a notary, seal me there Your single bond . . i 3 146
I'll seal to such a bond And say there is much kindness in the Jew . i 3 153
A month before This bond expires, I do expect return Of thrice three times the value of this bond . . i 3 160
Yes, Shylock, I will seal unto this bond . . i 3 172
Meet me forthwith at the notary's ; Give him direction for this merry bond . . ii 3 174
O, ten times faster Venus' pigeons fly To seal love's bonds new-made ! . ii 6 6
For the Jew's bond which he hath of me, Let it not enter in your mind of love . . ii 8 41
Let him look to his bond : he was wont to call me usurer ; let him look to his bond : he was wont to lend money for a Christian courtesy ; let him look to his bond . . iii 1 50
None can drive him from the envious plea Of forfeiture, of justice and his bond . . iii 2 285
Pay him six thousand, and deface the bond . . iii 2 301
My creditors grow cruel, my estate is very low, my bond to the Jew is forfeit . . iii 2 319
I'll have my bond ; speak not against my bond : I have sworn an oath that I will have my bond . . iii 3 4
I'll have my bond ; I will not hear thee speak . . iii 3 12
I'll have no speaking : I will have my bond . . iii 3 17
By our holy Sabbath have I sworn To have the due and forfeit of my bond . . iv 1 37
I would not draw them ; I would have my bond . . iv 1 87
Till thou canst rail the seal from off my bond, Thou but offend'st thy lungs . . iv 1 139
Do you confess the bond ?—I do.—Then must the Jew be merciful . iv 1 181
I crave the law, The penalty and forfeit of my bond . . iv 1 207
I pray you, let me look upon the bond . . iv 1 225
Why, this bond is forfeit . . iv 1 230
Be merciful : Take thrice thy money ; bid me tear the bond . . iv 1 234
There is no power in the tongue of man To alter me : I stay here on my bond . . iv 1 242
The intent and purpose of the law Hath full relation to the penalty, Which here appeareth due upon the bond . . iv 1 249
So says the bond : doth it not, noble judge ? 'Nearest his heart' . iv 1 253
Is it so nominated in the bond ?—It is not so express'd : but what of that ? . . iv 1 259
I cannot find it ; 'tis not in the bond . . iv 1 262
This bond doth give thee here no jot of blood ; The words expressly are 'a pound of flesh :' Take then thy bond, take thou thy pound of flesh . . iv 1 306
I take this offer, then ; pay the bond thrice And let the Christian go . iv 1 318
He shall have merely justice and his bond . . iv 1 339
Whose loves Are dearer than the natural bond of sisters *As Y. Like It* i 2 288
Wedding is great Juno's crown : O blessed bond of board and bed ! . v 4 148
My love hath in't a bond, Whereof the world takes note . *All's Well* i 3 194
Words are very rascals since bonds disgraced them . . *T. Night* iii 1 25
A contract of eternal bond of love, Confirm'd by mutual joinder of your hands . . v 1 159
Besides you know Prosperity's the very bond of love . . *W. Tale* iv 4 584
I tore them from their bonds and cried aloud . . *K. John* iii 4 70
I envy at their liberty, And will again commit them to their bonds . iii 4 74
Bound in with shame, With inky blots and rotten parchment bonds *Richard II.* ii 1 64
There is my bond of faith, To tie thee to my strong correction . . iv 1 76
'Tis nothing but some bond, that he is enter'd into For gay apparel . v 2 65
Bound to himself ! what doth he with a bond That he is bound to ? . v 2 67
Three or four bonds of forty pound a-piece . . *1 Hen. IV.* iii 3 117
Coupled in bonds of perpetuity . . *1 Hen. VI.* iv 7 20
Cancel his bond of life, dear God, I pray ! . *Richard III.* iv 4 77
If . . . you can report, And prove it too, against mine honour aught, My bond to wedlock . . *Hen. VIII.* ii 4 40
Should, notwithstanding that your bond of duty, As 'twere in love's particular, be more To me, your friend, than any . . iii 2 188
A bond of air, strong as the axle-tree On which heaven rides *Tr. and Cr.* i 3 66
Cressid is mine, tied with the bonds of heaven . . v 2 154
The bonds of heaven are slipp'd, dissolved, and loosed . . v 2 156
But, out, affection ! All bond and privilege of nature, break ! *Coriolanus* v 3 25
This gentleman of mine hath served me long : To build his fortune I will strain a little, For 'tis a bond in men . . *T. of Athens* i 1 144
Grant I may never prove so fond, To trust man on his oath or bond . i 2 66
Take the bonds along with you, And have the dates in compt . . ii 1 34
I am thus encounter'd With clamorous demands of date-broke bonds . ii 2 38
To grace in captive bonds his chariot-wheels . *J. Cæsar* i 1 39
What other bond Than secret Romans, that have spoke the word ? . ii 1 124
Within the bond of marriage, tell me, Brutus, Is it excepted I should know no secrets That appertain to you ? . . ii 1 280
Cancel and tear to pieces that great bond Which keeps me pale ! *Macbeth* iii 2 49
I'll make assurance double sure, And take a bond of fate . . iv 1 84
I love your majesty According to my bond ; nor more nor less *Lear* i 1 95
In countries, discord ; in palaces, treason ; and the bond cracked 'twixt son and father . . i 2 118
Spoke, with how manifold and strong a bond The child was bound to the father . . ii 1 49
Thou better know'st The offices of nature, bond of childhood, Effects of courtesy . . ii 4 181
Doubt not, sir ; I knew it for my bond . *Ant. and Cleo.* i 4 84
And sear up my embracements from a next With bonds of death ! *Cymb.* i 1 117
Lovers And men in dangerous bonds pray not alike . . iii 2 37
Every good servant does not all commands : No bond but to do just ones v 1 7
If you will take this audit, take this life, And cancel these cold bonds . v 4 28
That he could not But think her bond of chastity quite crack'd . v 5 207
All o'erjoy'd, Save these in bonds : let them be joyful too . . v 5 402
Bondage. The harmony of their tongues hath into bondage Brought my too diligent ear . . *Tempest* iii 1 41
With a heart as willing As bondage e'er of freedom . . iii 1 89
I will pray, Pompey, to increase your bondage . *Meas. for Meas.* iii 2 79
Translate thy life into death, thy liberty into bondage . *As Y. Like It* v 1 59
Thou shalt find what it is to be proud of thy bondage . *All's Well* ii 3 239
'Tis a hard bondage to become the wife Of a detesting lord . . iii 5 67
It will also be the bondage of certain ribbons and gloves . *W. Tale* iv 4 235
Never did captive with a freer heart Cast off his chains of bondage *Richard II.* i 3 89
Bondage. Would you not suppose Your bondage happy, to be made a queen ?—To be a queen in bondage is more vile Than is a slave in base servility . . *1 Hen. VI.* v 3 111
Bondage is hoarse, and may not speak aloud . *Rom. and Jul.* ii 2 161
Cassius from bondage will deliver Cassius : Therein, ye gods, you make the weak most strong . . *J. Cæsar* i 3 90
Where is thy master ?—Free from the bondage you are in . . v 5 54
I begin to find an idle and fond bondage in the oppression of aged tyranny . . *Lear* i 2 52
Doting on his own obsequious bondage, Wears out his time . *Othello* i 1 46
Can my sides hold, to think that man, who knows By history, report, or his own proof, What woman is, yea, what she cannot choose But must be, will his free hours languish for Assured bondage ? *Cymbeline* i 6 73
The vows of women Of no more bondage be, to where they are made, Than they are to their virtues . . ii 4 111
Our cage We make a quire, as doth the prison'd bird, And sing our bondage freely . . iii 3 44
Most welcome, bondage ! for thou art a way, I think, to liberty . v 4 3
Let his arms alone ; They were not born for bondage . . v 5 306
Bon Dieu ! les langues des hommes sont pleines de tromperies . *Hen. V.* v 2 118
Bondmaid. Wrong me not, nor wrong yourself, To make a bondmaid and a slave of me . . *T. of Shrew* ii 1 2
Bondman. With him his bondman, all as mad as he . *Com. of Errors* v 1 141
Is not that your bondman, Dromio ?—Within this hour I was his bondman . . v 1 287
Bend low and in a bondman's key, With bated breath *Mer. of Venice* i 3 124
So can I : So every bondman in his own hand bears The power to cancel his captivity . . *J. Cæsar* i 3 101
I perhaps speak this Before a willing bondman . . i 3 113
Who is here so base that would be a bondman ? If any, speak . iii 2 32
Hated by one he loves ; braved by his brother ; Check'd like a bondman iv 3 97
Where did you leave him ?—All disconsolate, With Pindarus his bondman v 3 56
He has Hipparchus, my enfranched bondman, whom He may at pleasure whip, or hang, or torture . . *Ant. and Cleo.* iii 13 149
Bondmen. And all the peers and nobles of the realm Have been as bondmen to thy sovereignty . . *2 Hen. VI.* i 3 130
If I were a man, Their mother's bed-chamber should not be safe For these bad bondmen to the yoke of Rome . *T. Andron.* iv 1 109
Fret till your proud heart break ; Go show your slaves how choleric you are, And make your bondmen tremble . *J. Cæsar* iv 3 44
You show'd your teeth like apes, and fawn'd like hounds, And bow'd like bondmen . . v 1 42
Bond-slave. Thy state of law is bondslave to the law . *Richard II.* ii 1 114
Shall I play my freedom at tray-trip, and become thy bond-slave? *T. Night* ii 5 209
If such actions may have passage free, Bond-slaves and pagans shall our statesmen be . . *Othello* i 2 99
Bone. I'll rack thee with old cramps, Fill all thy bones with aches *Tempest* i 2 370
Full fathom five thy father lies ; Of his bones are coral made . i 2 397
By'r lakin, I can go no further, sir ; My old bones ache . . iii 3 2
I have been in such a pickle since I saw you last that, I fear me, will never out of my bones . . v 1 284
Thy bones are hollow ; impiety has made a feast of thee . *Meas. for Meas.* i 2 56
As fast lock'd up in sleep as guiltless labour When it lies starkly in the traveller's bones . . iv 2 70
My bones bear witness, That since have felt the vigour of his rage *Com. of Errors* iv 4 80
Hang her an epitaph upon her tomb And sing it to her bones *Much Ado* v 1 294
Now, unto thy bones good night ! . . v 3 22
Smiles on every one, To show his teeth as white as whale's bone *L. L. Lost* v 2 332
Beat not the bones of the buried : when he breathed, he was a man . v 2 667
Let's have the tongs and the bones . . *M. N. Dream* iv 1 32
I had rather be married to a death's-head with a bone in his mouth *Mer. of Venice* i 2 56
The Jew shall have my flesh, blood, bones and all, Ere thou shalt lose for me one drop of blood . . iv 1 112
When virtue's steely bones Look bleak i' the cold wind . *All's Well* i 1 114
Where dust and damn'd oblivion is the tomb Of honour'd bones indeed ii 3 148
And the free maids that weave their thread with bones . *T. Night* ii 4 46
Not a friend greet My poor corpse, where my bones shall be thrown . ii 4 63
I desire to lay my bones there . . *W. Tale* iv 2 6
To die upon the bed my father died, To lie close by his honest bones . iv 4 467
Fair fall the bones that took the pains for me ! . *K. John* i 1 78
We'll lay before this town our royal bones . . ii 1 41
I will kiss thy detestable bones And put my eyeballs in thy vaulty brows iii 4 29
Heaven take my soul, And England keep my bones ! . . iv 3 10
Now for the bare-pick'd bone of majesty Doth dogged war bristle his angry crest . . iv 3 148
Whose hollow womb inherits nought but bones . *Richard II.* ii 1 83
The barren earth Which serves as paste and cover to our bones . iii 2 154
No hand of blood and bone Can gripe the sacred handle of our sceptre . iii 3 79
By the honourable tomb he swears, That stands upon your royal grandsire's bones . . iii 3 106
Over-careful fathers Have broke their sleep with thoughts, their brains with care, Their bones with industry . . *2 Hen. IV.* iv 5 70
Ay, come, you starved blood-hound.—Goodman death, goodman bones ! v 4 32
Or lay these bones in an unworthy urn, Tombless . . *Hen. V.* i 2 228
Yon island carrions, desperate of their bones, Ill-favouredly become the morning field . . iv 2 39
Bid them achieve me and then sell my bones . . iv 3 91
Those that leave their valiant bones in France, Dying like men . iv 3 98
Know'st thou not That I have fined these bones of mine for ransom ? iv 7 72
Rot but by degree, Till bones and flesh and sinews fall away *1 Hen. VI.* iii 1 193
Hew them to pieces, hack their bones asunder . . iv 7 47
By these ten bones, my lords, he did speak them to me . *2 Hen. VI.* i 3 193
Would he were wasted, marrow, bones and all ! *3 Hen. VI.* iii 2 125
I seek for thee, That Warwick's bones may keep thine company . v 2 4
And mock'd the dead bones that lay scatter'd by . . *Richard III.* i 4 33
Then would I hide my bones, not rest them here . . iv 4 33
That his bones, When he has run his course and sleeps in blessings, May have a tomb of orphans' tears wept on 'em ! . *Hen. VIII.* iii 2 397
An old man, broken with the storms of state, Is come to lay his weary bones among ye ; Give him a little earth for charity ! . . iv 2 22
Nerve and bone of Greece, Heart of our numbers . *Troi. and Cres.* i 3 55
Pride alone Must tarre the mastiffs on, as 'twere their bone . . i 3 392
I have bobbed his brain more than he has beat my bones . . ii 1 76
High birth, vigour of bone, desert in service, Love, friendship, charity, are subjects all To envious and calumniating time . . iii 3 172
Such an ache in my bones that, unless a man were cursed, I cannot tell what to think on't . . v 3 106
Here lies thy heart, thy sinews, and thy bone . . v 8 12

Bone. A goodly medicine for my aching bones! O world! world! world! *Troi. and Cres.* v 10 35
Yet give some groans, Though not for me, yet for your aching bones . v 10 51
Hence, rotten thing! or I shall shake thy bones Out of thy garments *Coriolanus* iii 1 179
Hew his limbs, and on a pile Ad manes fratrum sacrifice his flesh, Before this earthy prison of their bones . *T. Andron.* i 1 99
Let us withdraw.—Not I, till Mutius' bones be buried . . i 1 369
There lie thy bones, sweet Mutius, with thy friends . . i 1 387
I will grind your bones to dust And with your blood and it I'll make a paste . . . . v 2 187
When that they are dead, Let me go grind their bones to powder small v 2 199
Her whip of cricket's bone, the lash of film . . *Rom. and Jul.* i 4 63
They cannot sit at ease on the old bench? O, their bones, their bones! ii 4 37
Fie, how my bones ache! what a jaunt have I had! . . . ii 5 26
I would thou hadst my bones, and I thy news . . . . ii 5 27
Is this the poultice for my aching bones? . . . . . ii 5 65
With dead men's rattling bones, With reeky shanks and yellow chapless skulls . . . . iv 1 82
Where, for these many hundred years, the bones Of all my buried ancestors are pack'd . . . . iv 3 40
With some great kinsman's bone, As with a club, dash out my desperate brains . . . . iv 3 53
Meagre were his looks, Sharp misery had worn him to the bones . v 1 41
Now the gods keep you old enough; that you may live Only in bone! *T. of Athens* iii 5 105
I feel't upon my bones . . . . iii 6 130
Consumptions sow In hollow bones of man . . . . . iv 3 152
Let the famish'd flesh slide from the bone, Ere thou relieve the beggar iv 3 535
The evil that men do lives after them; The good is oft interred with their bones; So let it be with Cæsar . . . *J. Cæsar* iii 2 81
My bones would rest, That have but labour'd to attain this hour . v 5 41
Within my tent his bones to-night shall lie, Most like a soldier . v 5 78
Sacred storehouse of his predecessors, And guardian of their bones *Macb.* ii 4 35
Let the earth hide thee! Thy bones are marrowless, thy blood is cold iii 4 94
I'll fight till from my bones my flesh be hack'd. Give me my armour . v 3 32
But tell Why thy canonized bones, hearsed in death, Have burst their cerements . . . . *Hamlet* i 4 47
Rebellious hell, If thou canst mutine in a matron's bones . . iii 4 83
No trophy, sword, nor hatchment o'er his bones, No noble rite . iv 5 214
Did these bones cost no more the breeding, but to play at loggats with 'em? . . . . v 1 99
Strike her young bones, You taking airs, with lameness! . . *Lear* ii 4 165
Apt enough to dislocate and tear Thy flesh and bones . . . iv 2 66
A halter pardon him! and hell gnaw his bones! . . *Othello* iv 2 136
Full surfeits, and the dryness of his bones, Call on him for't *A. and C.* i 4 27
For a monument upon thy bones, And e'er-remaining lamps, the belching whale And humming water must o'erwhelm thy corpse *Pericles* iii 1 62
Bone-ache. Or rather, the bone-ache! for that, methinks, is the curse dependant on those that war for a placket . . *Troi. and Cres.* ii 3 20
Limekilns i' the palm, incurable bone-ache . . . . . v 1 26
Boneless. I would, while it was smiling in my face, Have pluck'd my nipple from his boneless gums . . . . . . *Macbeth* i 7 57
Bonfire. The news, Rogero?—Nothing but bonfires . . . *W. Tale* v 2 24
Bonfires in France forthwith I am to make . . . *1 Hen. VI.* i 1 153
Make bonfires And feast and banquet in the open streets . . i 6 12
Ring, bells, aloud; burn, bonfires, clear and bright . *2 Hen. VI.* v 1 3
That go the primrose way to the everlasting bonfire . *Macbeth* ii 3 22
Some to dance, some to make bonfires, each man to what sport and revels his addiction leads him . . . . . . *Othello* ii 2 5
Bonfire-light. Thou art a perpetual triumph, an everlasting bonfire-light! *1 Hen. IV.* iii 3 47
Bon jour, Monsieur Le Beau: what's the news? . *As Y. Like It* i 2 104
With horn and hound we'll give your grace bonjour . *T. Andron.* i 1 494
Bon jour! there's a French salutation to your French slop *Rom. and Jul.* ii 4 46
Bonne maison. Je suis gentilhomme de bonne maison . *Hen. V.* iv 4 44
Bonne qualité. Je pense que vous êtes gentilhomme de bonne qualité . iv 4 3
Bonnet. He bought his doublet in Italy, his round hose in France, his bonnet in Germany . . . . *Mer. of Venice* i 2 81
Your bonnet unbanded, your sleeve unbuttoned . *As Y. Like It* iii 2 398
Off goes his bonnet to an oyster-wench . . . . *Richard II.* i 4 31
Give me any gage of thine, and I will wear it in my bonnet . *Hen. V.* iv 1 224
Go to them, with this bonnet in thy hand . . . *Coriolanus* iii 2 73
Put your bonnet to his right use; 'tis for the head . . . *Hamlet* v 2 95
Bonneted. Who, having been supple and courteous to the people, bonneted, without any further deed . . . . *Coriolanus* ii 2 30
Bonny. Sigh not so, but let them go, And be you blithe and bonny *M. Ado* ii 3 69
Wherefore are you gentle, strong and valiant? Why would you be so fond to overcome The bonny priser of the humorous duke? *As Y. L. It* ii 3 8
You are call'd plain Kate, And bonny Kate . . *T. of Shrew* ii 1 187
But for my bonny Kate, she must with me . . . . . iii 2 229
And made a prey for carrion kites and crows Even of the bonny beast he loved so well . . . . *2 Hen. VI.* v 2 12
Shore's wife hath a pretty foot, A cherry lip, a bonny eye *Richard III.* i 1 94
For bonny sweet Robin is all my joy . . . . *Hamlet* iv 5 187
Bonos dies. Jove bless thee, master Parson.—Bonos dies, Sir Toby *T. Night* iv 2 14
Bonville. The heir Of the Lord Bonville . . . *3 Hen. VI.* iv 1 57
Book. Knowing I loved my books, he furnish'd me From mine own library with volumes . . . . *Tempest* i 2 166
Come, swear to that; kiss the book . . . . . . ii 2 145
I'll to my book, For yet ere supper-time must I perform Much business iii 1 94
There thou mayst brain him, Having first seized his books . . iii 2 97
Possess his books; for without them He's but a sot, as I am . . iii 2 100
Burn but his books . . . . iii 2 103
Deeper than did ever plummet sound I'll drown my book . . v 1 57
On a love-book pray for my success?—Upon some book I love *T. G. of Ver.* i 1 20
I had rather than forty shillings I had my Book of Songs and Sonnets here . . . . *Mer. Wives* i 1 206
You have not the Book of Riddles about you, have you? . . . i 1 209
I'll be sworn on a book, she loves you . . . . . . i 4 156
Keep a gamester from the dice, and a good student from his book . iii 1 38
My husband says my son profits nothing in the world at his book . iv 1 15
I'll be supposed upon a book, his face is the worst thing about him *Meas. for Meas.* ii 1 162
I see, lady, the gentleman is not in your books.—No; an he were, I would burn my study . . . . *Much Ado* i 1 79
Thou wilt be like a lover presently, And tire the hearer with a book of words . . . . i 1 309
In my chamber-window lies a book: bring it hither to me . . . ii 3 3

Book. Which with experimental seal doth warrant The tenour of my book *Much Ado* iv 1 169
As, painfully to pore upon a book To seek the light of truth *L. L. Lost* i 1 74
Small have continual plodders ever won Save base authority from others' books . . . . i 1 87
He hath never fed of the dainties that are bred in a book . . iv 2 25
Study his bias leaves and makes his book thine eyes . . . iv 2 113
O, who can give an oath? where is a book? That I may swear . . iv 3 250
In that each of you have forsworn his book, Can you still dream and pore and thereon look? . . . . iv 3 297
The books, the academes From whence doth spring the true Promethean fire . . . . iv 3 303
We have made a vow to study, lords, And in that vow we have forsworn our books . . . . iv 3 319
They [women's eyes] are the books, the arts, the academes, That show, contain and nourish all the world . . . . iv 3 352
Where I o'erlook Love's stories written in love's richest book *M. N. Dr.* ii 2 122
If any man in Italy have a fairer table which doth offer to swear upon a book, I shall have good fortune . . . *Mer. of Venice* ii 2 168
We turned o'er many books together: he is furnished with my opinion iv 1 157
Tongues in trees, books in the running brooks, Sermons in stones *As Y. Like It* ii 1 16
These trees shall be my books And in their barks my thoughts I'll character . . . . iii 2 5
We quarrel in print, by the book; as you have books for good manners v 4 95
My books and instruments shall be my company . . *T. of Shrew* i 1 82
Keep house and ply his book, welcome his friends, Visit his countrymen i 1 201
I'll have them very fairly bound: All books of love, see that at any hand . . . . i 2 147
Well read in poetry And other books, good ones, I warrant ye . . i 2 171
This small packet of Greek and Latin books . . . . . ii 1 101
Take you the lute, and you the set of books . . . . . ii 1 107
O, put me in thy books! . . . . ii 1 225
Your father prays you leave your books . . . . . . iii 1 82
Swore so loud, That, all-amazed, the priest let fall the book . . iii 2 163
Took him such a cuff That down fell priest and book and book and priest . . . . iii 2 166
Speaks three or four languages word for word without book . *T. Night* i 3 28
I have unclasp'd To thee the book even of my secret soul . . i 4 14
An affectioned ass, that cons state without book and utters it by great swarths . . . . ii 3 161
Let me be unrolled and my name put in the book of virtue! . *W. Tale* iv 3 131
If . . . thy princely son, Can in this book of beauty read 'I love' *K. John* ii 1 485
Bell, book, and candle shall not drive me back . . . . iii 3 12
If ever I were traitor, My name be blotted from the book of life! *Rich. II.* i 3 202
Mark'd with a blot, damn'd in the book of heaven . . . iv 1 236
I'll read enough, When I do see the very book indeed Where all my sins are writ, and that's myself . . . . iv 1 274
Say no more: And now I will unclasp a secret book . . *1 Hen. IV.* i 3 188
I'll be sworn upon all the books in England, I could find in my heart ii 4 56
I'll sit and hear her sing: By that time will our book, I think, be drawn iii 1 224
By this our book is drawn; we'll but seal, And then to horse immediately . . . . iii 1 270
Thou thinkest me as far in the devil's book as thou . *2 Hen. IV.* ii 2 49
He was the mark and glass, copy and book, That fashion'd others . ii 3 31
O God! that one might read the book of fate, And see the revolution of the times! . . . . iii 1 45
Would shut the book, and sit him down and die . . . . iii 1 56
Turning your books to graves, your ink to blood, Your pens to lances . iv 1 50
Seal this lawless bloody book Of forged rebellion with a seal divine . iv 1 91
Who hath not heard it spoken How deep you were within the books of God? . . . . iv 2 17
In the book of Numbers is it writ, When the man dies, let the inheritance Descend unto the daughter . . . . . . *Hen. V.* i 2 98
Unless my study and my books be false, The argument you held was wrong in you . . . . *1 Hen. VI.* ii 4 56
I'll note you in my book of memory, To scourge you for this apprehension . . . . ii 4 101
Fitter is my study and my books Than wanton dalliance . . . v 1 22
Blotting your names from books of memory . . *2 Hen. VI.* i 1 100
For sins Such as by God's book are adjudged to death . . . ii 3 4
Here's a villain!—Has a book in his pocket with red letters in't . iv 2 97
Our forefathers had no other books but the score and the tally . iv 7 38
Large gifts have I bestow'd on learned clerks, Because my book preferr'd me . . . . iv 7 77
What, at your book so hard? . . . . . . *3 Hen. VI.* v 6 1
Made him my book, wherein my soul recorded The history of all her secret thoughts . . . . *Richard III.* iii 5 27
A book of prayer in his hand, True ornaments to know a holy man . iii 7 98
A book of prayers on their pillow lay . . . . . . iv 3 14
By the book He should have braved the east an hour ago . . . v 3 278
A beggar's book Outworths a noble's blood . . . *Hen. VIII.* i 1 122
But, I think, thy horse will sooner con an oration than thou learn a prayer without a book . . . . . . *Troi. and Cres.* ii 1 19
O, like a book of sport thou'lt read me o'er . . . . . iv 5 239
Renowned Rome, whose gratitude Towards her deserved children is enroll'd In Jove's own book . . . . . . *Coriolanus* iii 1 293
I have been The book of his good acts, whence men have read His fame v 2 15
Which made me down to throw my books, and fly . *T. Andron.* iv 1 25
Some book there is that she desires to see . . . . . iv 1 31
What book is that she tosseth so? . . . . iv 1 41
Perhaps you have learned it without book . . . *Rom. and Jul.* i 2 62
This precious book of love, this unbound lover, To beautify him, only lacks a cover . . . . i 3 87
That book in many's eyes doth share the glory, That in gold clasps locks in the golden story . . . . i 3 91
You kiss by the book . . . . i 5 112
Love goes toward love, as schoolboys from their books . . . ii 2 157
A rogue, a villain, that fights by the book of arithmetic! . . . iii 1 106
Was ever book containing such vile matter So fairly bound? . . iii 2 83
O, give me thy hand, One writ with me in sour misfortune's book! . v 3 82
When comes your book forth?—Upon the heels of my presentment *T. of Athens* i 1 26
He is so kind that he now Pays interest for't; his land's put to their books . . . . i 2 206
Bade the Romans Mark him and write his speeches in their books *J. C.* i 2 126
Here's the book I sought for so; I put it in the pocket of my gown . iv 3 252
Your face, my thane, is as a book where men May read strange matters *Macbeth* i 5 63
I'll wipe away all trivial fond records, All saws of books . *Hamlet* i 5 100

Book. Thy commandment all alone shall live Within the book and volume of my brain . . . *Hamlet* i 5 103
Read on this book; That show of such an exercise may colour Your loneliness . . . iii 1 44
Keep thy foot out of brothels, thy hand out of plackets, thy pen from lenders' books, and defy the foul fiend . . . *Lear* iii 4 101
The bloody book of law You shall yourself read in the bitter letter *Oth.* i 3 67
Was this fair paper, this most goodly book, Made to write 'whore' upon? . . . iv 2 71
In nature's infinite book of secrecy A little I can read . *Ant. and Cleo.* i 2 9
Such gain the cap of him that makes 'em fine, Yet keeps his book uncross'd: no life to ours . . . *Cymbeline* iii 3 26
A book? O rare one! Be not, as is our fangled world . . . v 4 133
Your neck, sir, is pen, book and counters . . . v 4 173
Her face the book of praises . . . *Pericles* i 1 15
Who has a book of all that monarchs do, He's more secure to keep it shut than shown . . . i 1 94
Booked. Let it be booked with the rest of this day's deeds . 2 *Hen. IV.* iv 3 50
Bookful. A whole bookful of these quondam carpet-mongers . *Much Ado* v 2 32
Bookish. Though I am not bookish, yet I can read . . . *W. Tale* iii 3 73
Whose bookish rule hath pull'd fair England down . 2 *Hen. VI.* i 1 259
Unless the bookish theoric, Wherein the toged consuls can propose As masterly as he . . . *Othello* i 1 24
Bookmate. One that makes sport To the prince and his bookmates *L. L. Lost* iv 1 102
Bookmen. This civil war of wits were much better used On Navarre and his book-men . . . ii 1 227
You two are book-men: can you tell me by your wit? . . . iv 2 35
Book-oath. I put thee now to thy book-oath: deny it, if thou canst 2 *Hen. IV.* ii 1 111
Boon. A smaller boon than this I cannot beg . . . *T. G. of Ver.* v 4 24
For your daughter's sake, To grant one boon that I shall ask of you . v 4 150
I'll beg one boon, And then be gone and trouble you no more *Richard II.* iv 1 302
But you will take exceptions to my boon . . . 3 *Hen. VI.* iii 2 46
For divers unknown reasons, I beseech you, Grant me this boon *Rich. III.* i 2 219
A boon, my sovereign, for my service done! . . . ii 1 95
Upon my feeble knee I beg this boon, with tears . . . *T. Andron.* ii 3 289
My boon I make it, that you know me not Till time and I think meet *Lear* iv 7 10
This is not a boon; 'Tis as I should entreat you wear your gloves *Othello* iii 3 76
Ask of Cymbeline what boon thou wilt, Fitting my bounty . *Cymbeline* v 5 97
My boon is, that this gentleman may render Of whom he had this ring v 5 135
This, my last boon, give me, For such kindness must relieve me *Pericles* v 2 268
Boor. What wouldst thou have, boor? . . . *Mer. Wives* iv 5 1
Let boors and franklins say it, I'll swear it . . . *W. Tale* v 2 173
Boorish. Abandon,—which is in the vulgar leave,—the society,—which in the boorish is company . . . *As Y. Like It* v 1 53
Boot. You are over boots in love . . . *T. G. of Ver.* i 1 24
Over the boots? nay, give me not the boots.—No, I will not, for it boots thee not . . . i 1 27
That my leg is too long?—No; that it is too little.—I'll wear a boot, to make it somewhat rounder . . . v 2 6
They would melt me out of my fat drop by drop and liquor fishermen's boots with me . . . *Mer. Wives* iv 5 101
My gravity . . . Could I with boot change for an idle plume *M. for Meas.* ii 4 11
A pair of boots that have been candle-cases . . . *T. of Shrew* iii 2 45
There lies your way; You may be jogging whiles your boots are green . iii 2 213
Off with my boots, you rogues! . . . iv 1 147
Then vail your stomachs, for it is no boot . . . v 2 176
You have made shift to run into't, boots and spurs and all . *All's Well* ii 5 39
He will look upon his boot and sing; mend the ruff and sing . . . iii 2 6
These clothes are good enough to drink in; and so be these boots *T. Night* i 3 12
Grace to boot! Of this make no conclusion . . . *W. Tale* i 2 80
It shall scarce boot me To say 'not guilty' . . . iii 2 26
Though the pennyworth on his side be the worst, yet hold thee, there's some boot . . . iv 4 651
What an exchange had this been without boot! What a boot is here with this exchange! . . . iv 4 690
Norfolk, throw down, we bid; there is no boot . . . *Richard II.* i 1 164
It boots thee not to be compassionate . . . i 3 174
What I have I need not to repeat; And what I want it boots not to complain . . . iii 4 18
Give me my boots, I say; saddle my horse . . . v 2 77
Bring me my boots: I will unto the king . . . v 2 84
They ride up and down on her and make her their boots.—What, the commonwealth their boots? . . . 1 *Hen. IV.* ii 1 91
Home without boots, and in foul weather too! How 'scapes he agues? iii 1 68
By my sceptre and my soul to boot . . . iii 2 97
Wears his boots very smooth, like unto the sign of the leg . 2 *Hen. IV.* ii 4 270
With all appliances and means to boot . . . iii 1 29
Come, come, come, off with your boots . . . v 1 61
I am fortune's steward—get on thy boots: we'll ride all night . . . v 3 137
Boot, boot, Master Shallow: I know the young king is sick for me . v 3 141
Armed in their stings, Make boot upon the summer's velvet buds *Hen. V.* i 2 194
Then talk no more of flight, it is no boot . . . 1 *Hen. VI.* iv 6 52
And thou that art his mate, make boot of this . 2 *Hen. VI.* iv 1 13
It needs not, nor it boots thee not, proud queen . 3 *Hen. VI.* i 4 125
It boots not to resist both wind and tide . . . iv 3 59
Young York he is but boot . . . *Richard III.* iv 4 65
This, and Saint George to boot! What think'st thou, Norfolk? . . . v 3 301
I warrant, Helen, to change, would give an eye to boot . *Troi. and Cres.* i 2 260
I'll give you boot, I'll give you three for one . . . iv 5 40
What boots it thee to call thyself a sun? . . . *T. Andron.* v 3 18
I would not be the villain that thou think'st For the whole space that's in the tyrant's grasp, And the rich East to boot . . . *Macbeth* iv 3 37
Pull off my boots: harder, harder . . . *Lear* iv 6 177
The bounty and the benison of heaven To boot, and boot! . . . iv 6 229
With boot, and such addition as your honours Have more than merited v 3 301
I will boot thee with what gift beside Thy modesty can beg *Ant. and Cleo.* ii 5 71
Give him no breath, but now Make boot of his distraction . . . iv 1 9
Think what a chance thou changest on, but think Thou hast thy mistress still, to boot, my son . . . *Cymbeline* i 5 69
Which horse-hairs and calves'-guts, nor the voice of unpaved eunuch to boot, can never amend . . . ii 3 35
All curses madded Hecuba gave the Greeks, And mine to boot, be darted on thee! . . . iv 2 314
Nor boots it me to say I honour him, If he suspect I may dishonour him *Pericles* i 2 20
Boot-hose. A linen stock on one leg and a kersey boot-hose on the other, gartered with a red and blue list . . . *T. of Shrew* iii 2 68
Booties. She drops booties in my mouth . . . *W. Tale* iv 4 863
Bootless. You have often Begun to tell me what I am, but stopp'd And left me to a bootless inquisition . . . *Tempest* i 2 35
And spend his prodigal wits in bootless rhymes . . . *L. L. Lost* v 2 64
And bootless make the breathless housewife churn . *M. N. Dream* ii 1 37
Bootless speed, When cowardice pursues and valour flies . . . ii 1 233
I'll follow him no more with bootless prayers . *Mer. of Venice* iii 3 20
But this our purpose now is twelve month old, And bootless 'tis to tell you we will go . . . 1 *Hen. IV.* i 1 29
Thrice from the banks of Wye And sandy-bottom'd Severn have I sent him Bootless home . . . iii 1 67
As bootless spend our vain command Upon the enraged soldiers *Hen. V.* iii 3 24
As I have seen a swan With bootless labour swim against the tide 3 *Hen. VI.* i 4 20
Whither shall we fly?—Bootless is flight, they follow us with wings ii 3 12
Bootless are plaints, and cureless are my wounds . . . ii 6 23
Clifford, repent in bootless penitence . . . ii 6 70
Come, come, dispatch; 'tis bootless to exclaim . *Richard III.* iii 4 104
It shall be therefore bootless That longer you desire the court *Hen. VIII.* ii 4 61
They would not pity me, yet plead I must; And bootless unto them *T. Andron.* iii 1 36
In bootless prayer have they been held up . . . iii 1 75
Doth not Brutus bootless kneel? . . . *J. Cæsar* iii 1 75
Vain it is That we present us to him.—Very bootless . . . *Lear* v 3 294
He robs himself that spends a bootless grief . . . *Othello* i 3 209
But bootless is your sight: he will not speak To any . . . *Pericles* v 1 33
Booty. And when they have the booty, if you and I do not rob them, cut this head off . . . 1 *Hen. IV.* i 2 184
So triumph thieves upon their conquer'd booty . 3 *Hen. VI.* i 4 63
Here comes a parcel of our hopeful booty . . . *T. Andron.* ii 3 49
Bo-peep. That such a king should play bo-peep, And go the fools among *Lear* i 4 193
Borachio. What is your name, friend?—Borachio . . . *Much Ado* iv 2 12
Border. When the morning sun shall raise his car Above the border of this horizon . . . 3 *Hen. VI.* iv 7 81
The borders maritime Lack blood to think on't . . . *Ant. and Cleo.* i 4 51
Bordered. That nature, which contemns it origin, Cannot be border'd certain in itself . . . *Lear* iv 2 33
Borderer. A wall sufficient to defend Our inland from the pilfering borderers . . . *Hen. V.* i 2 142
Bore. So dear the love my people bore me . . . *Tempest* i 2 141
They hurried us aboard a bark, Bore us some leagues to sea . . . i 2 145
O, that you bore The mind that I do! . . . ii 1 266
My wrath shall far exceed the love I ever bore my daughter *T. G. of Ver.* iii 1 167
Bore many gentlemen, myself being one, In hand and hope of action *Meas. for Meas.* i 4 51
They fell upon me, bound me, bore me thence . . . *Com. of Errors* v 1 246
Æmilia What bore thee at a burden two fair sons . . . v 1 343
Thy father's father wore it, And thy father bore it . . . *As Y. Like It* iv 2 17
She bore a mind that envy could not but call fair . . . *T. Night* ii 1 30
And with a little pin Bores through his castle wall . *Richard II.* iii 2 170
As the soldiers bore dead bodies by, He call'd them untaught knaves 1 *Hen. IV.* i 3 42
Thou knowest my old ward; here I lay, and thus I bore my point . ii 4 216
He bore him in the thickest troop As doth a lion in a herd of neat 3 *Hen. VI.* ii 1 13
Some tardy cripple bore the countermand . . . *Richard III.* ii 1 89
At this instant He bores me with some trick . . . *Hen. VIII.* i 1 128
Out of his noble nature, Zeal and obedience he still bore your grace . iii 1 63
Your franchises, whereon you stood, confined Into an auger's bore *Coriol.* iv 6 87
To wreak the love I bore my cousin Upon his body . *Rom. and Jul.* iii 5 102
Those milk-paps, That through the window-bars bore at men's eyes *T. of Athens* iv 3 116
The queen that bore thee, Oftener upon her knees than on her feet, Died every day she lived . . . *Macbeth* iv 3 109
They bore him barefaced on the bier; Hey non nonny . . . *Hamlet* iv 5 164
Yet are they much too light for the bore of the matter . . . iv 6 26
And, mermaid-like, awhile they bore her up . . . iv 7 177
A' was the first that ever bore arms . . . v 1 37
He led our powers; Bore the commission of my place and person . *Lear* v 3 64
It had been pity you should have been put together with so mortal a purpose as then each bore . . . *Cymbeline* i 4 44
She that bore you was no queen, and you Recoil from your great stock . i 6 127
Love's counsellor should fill the bores of hearing, To the smothering of the sense . . . iii 2 59
Your daughter, whom she bore in hand to love With such integrity . v 5 43
Whose towers bore heads so high they kiss'd the clouds . . . *Pericles* i 4 24
Boreas. Let the ruffian Boreas once enrage The gentle Thetis *Tr. and Cr.* i 3 38
Bored. I'll believe as soon This whole earth may be bored and that the moon May through the centre creep . . . *M. N. Dream* iii 2 53
Borest. Thou borest thy ass on thy back o'er the dirt . . . *Lear* i 4 176
Boring. The ship boring the moon with her main-mast . . . *W. Tale* iii 3 93
Born. If he be not born to be hanged, our case is miserable . *Tempest* i 1 35
Where was she born? speak; tell me . . . i 2 260
A devil, a born devil, on whose nature Nurture can never stick . iv 1 188
And a gentleman born, master parson . . . *Mer. Wives* i 1 9
Yet I live like a poor gentleman born . . . i 1 287
As my mother was, the first hour I was born . . . ii 2 39
Where were you born, friend?—Here in Vienna . *Meas. for Meas.* ii 1 202
New-conceived, And so in progress to be hatch'd and born . . . ii 2 97
I had rather my brother die by the law than my son should be unlawfully born . . . iii 1 196
Usurp the beggary he was never born to . . . iii 2 100
A Bohemian born, but here nursed up and bred . . . iv 2 134
If any born at Ephesus be seen At any Syracusian marts and fairs; Again: if any Syracusian born Come to the bay of Ephesus, he dies *Com. of Errors* i 1 17
In Syracusa was I born, and wed Unto a woman . . . i 1 37
Being, as thou sayest thou art, born under Saturn . . . *Much Ado* i 3 12
I was born to speak all mirth and no matter . . . ii 1 343
Out of question, you were born in a merry hour . . . ii 1 347
There was a star danced, and under that was I born . . . ii 1 350
I was not born under a rhyming planet, nor I cannot woo in festival terms v 2 40
For every man with his affects is born, Not by might master'd *L. L. Lost* i 1 152
You were born to do me shame . . . iv 3 204
We cannot cross the cause why we were born . . . iv 3 218
Therefore is she born to make black fair . . . iv 3 261
Longaville was for my service born . . . v 2 284
Wherefore was I to this keen mockery born? . . . *M. N. Dream* ii 2 123
When I vow, I weep; and vows so born, In their nativity all truth appears . . . iii 2 124

Born. What stuff 'tis made of, whereof it is born, I am to learn *Mer. of Venice* i 1 4
Bring me the fairest creature northward born ii 1 4
Begot of thought, conceived of spleen and born of madness *As Y. L. It* iv 1 218
Take thou no scorn to wear the horn; It was a crest ere thou wast born iv 2 15
Wast born i' the forest here?—Ay, sir, I thank God v 1 24
For I am he am born to tame you Kate *T. of Shrew* ii 1 278
That we, the poorer born, Whose baser stars do shut us up in wishes, Might with effects of them follow our friends *All's Well* i 1 196
You were born under a charitable star.—Under Mars, I. i 1 204
The wars have so kept you under that you must needs be born under Mars i 1 210
An we might have a good woman born but one every blazing star i 3 91
Our blood to us, this to our blood is born i 3 137
That is honour's scorn, Which challenges itself as honour's born ii 3 141
Who, so ennobled, Is as 'twere born so ii 3 180
I was well born, Nothing acquainted with these businesses iii 7 4
I was bred and born Not three hours' travel from this very place *T. Night* i 2 22
What shall we do else? were we not born under Taurus? i 3 147
I can tell thee where that saying was born i 5 10
He left behind him myself and a sister, both born in an hour ii 1 20
Some are born great, some achieve greatness and some have greatness thrust upon 'em ii 5 157; iii 4 45; v 1 378
Makes old hearts fresh: they that went on crutches ere he was born desire yet their life to see him a man *W. Tale* i 1 45
Temptations have since then been born to's i 2 77
'Tis safer to Avoid what's grown than question how 'tis born i 2 433
Either thou art most ignorant by age, Or thou wert born a fool ii 1 174
O that ever I was born! iv 3 53
There shall not at your father's house these seven years Be born another such iv 4 590
Every wink of an eye some new grace will be born v 2 120
Thy sons and daughters will be all gentlemen born v 2 138
See you these clothes? say you see them not and think me still no gentleman born v 2 142
Give me the lie, do, and try whether I am not now a gentleman born v 2 145
A gentleman Born in Northamptonshire *K. John* i 1 51
Why, being younger born, Doth he lay claim to thine inheritance? i 1 71
That Geffrey was thy elder brother born, And this his son ii 1 104
A widow, husbandless, subject to fears, A woman, naturally born to fears iii 1 15
There was not such a gracious creature born iii 4 81
This act so evilly born shall cool the hearts Of all his people iii 4 149
That we, the sons and children of this isle, Were born to see so sad an hour v 2 26
You are born To set a form upon that indigest v 7 25
We were not born to sue, but to command *Richard II.* i 1 196
Wherefore was I born? ii 3 122
What, was I born to this? iii 4 98
Since thou, created to be awed by man, Wast born to bear v 5 92
I say the earth did shake when I was born *1 Hen. IV.* iii 1 21
I was not born a yielder, thou proud Scot v 3 11
I was born about three of the clock in the afternoon, with a white head *2 Hen. IV.* i 2 210
To brother born an household cruelty, I make my quarrel in particular iv 1 95
And so success of mischief shall be born iv 2 47
What call you the town's name where Alexander the Pig was born? *Hen. V.* iv 7 14
I think Alexander the Great was born in Macedon iv 7 20
That Henry born at Monmouth should win all And Henry born at Windsor lose all *1 Hen. VI.* iii 1 198
I take my leave of thee, fair son, Born to eclipse thy life this afternoon iv 5 53
Young Talbot was not born To be the pillage of a giglot wench iv 7 40
Hast thou been long blind and now restored?—Born blind *2 Hen. VI.* ii 1 77
Where wert thou born?—At Berwick in the north ii 1 82
How long hast thou been blind?—O, born so ii 1 98
If thou hadst been born blind ii 1 126
You, madam, for you are more nobly born, Despoiled of your honour ii 3 9
There was he born, under a hedge, for his father had never a house but the cage iv 2 55
I think this word 'sallet' was born to do me good iv 10 11
I am far better born than is the king, More like a king, more kingly v 1 28
Thy father hath.—But 'twas ere I was born *3 Hen. VI.* i 3 39
They have demean'd themselves Like men born to renown by life or death i 4 8
More than I seem, and less than I was born to iii 1 56
I'll plague ye for that word.—Ay, thou wast born to be a plague to men v 5 28
Many a thousand . . . Shall rue the hour that ever thou wast born v 6 43
Teeth hadst thou in thy head when thou wast born, To signify thou camest to bite the world v 6 53
And the women cried 'O, Jesus bless us, he is born with teeth!' v 6 75
But I was born so high, Our aery buildeth in the cedar's top *Richard III.* i 3 263
More than the infant that is born to-night ii 1 71
His nurse! why, she was dead ere thou wert born ii 4 33
'Tis better to be lowly born, And range with humble livers in content *Hen. VIII.* ii 3 19
I am a most poor woman, and a stranger, Born out of your dominions ii 4 16
She's noble born; And, like her true nobility, she has Carried herself towards me ii 4 141
He will weep you, an 'twere a man born in April *Troi. and Cres.* i 2 189
We will not name desert before his birth, and, being born, his addition shall be humble iii 2 102
Would thou hadst ne'er been born! I knew thou wouldst be his death iv 2 90
You were got in fear, Though you were born in Rome *Coriolanus* i 3 37
He was not born to shame: Upon his brow shame is ashamed to sit *Rom. and Jul.* iii 2 91
Well, we were born to die iii 4 4
Help, help! my lady's dead! O, well-a-day, that ever I was born! iv 5 15
We are born to do benefits *T. of Athens* i 2 105
O joy, e'en made away ere't can be born! i 2 110
Go; thou wast born a bastard, and thou't die a bawd ii 2 88
And came into the world When sects and factions were newly born iii 5 30
By killing of villains, Thou wast born to conquer iv 3 106
If thou hadst not been born the worst of men, Thou hadst been a knave iv 3 275
Let me behold thy face. Surely, this man Was born of woman iv 3 501
I was born free as Cæsar; so were you: We both have fed as well *J. Cæsar* i 2 97
I was not born to die on Brutus' sword v 1 58
This is my birth-day; as this very day Was Cassius born v 1 73
For none of woman born Shall harm Macbeth *Macbeth* iv 1 80
What's the boy Malcolm? Was he not born of woman? v 3 4

Born. Fear not, Macbeth; no man that's born of woman Shall e'er have power upon thee *Macbeth* v 3 6
What's he That was not born of woman? Such a one Am I to fear, or none v 7 3
Thou wast born of woman. But swords I smile at, weapons laugh to scorn, Brandish'd by man that's of a woman born v 7 11
I bear a charmed life, which must not yield To one of woman born v 8 13
Though I am native here And to the manner born *Hamlet* i 4 15
The time is out of joint: O cursed spite, That ever I was born to set it right! i 5 190
It was the very day that young Hamlet was born v 1 161
Better thou Hadst not been born than not to have pleased me better *Lear* i 1 237
All thy other titles thou hast given away; that thou wast born with i 4 164
The hot-blooded France, that dowerless took Our youngest born ii 4 216
When we are born, we cry that we are come To this great stage of fools iv 6 186
Thou hadst been better have been born a dog *Othello* iii 3 362
I think the sun where he was born Drew all such humours from him iii 4 30
'Tis a monster Begot upon itself, born on itself iii 4 162
The sense aches at thee, would thou hadst ne'er been born! iv 2 69
Why do you send so thick?—Who's born that day When I forget to send to Antony, Shall die a beggar *Ant. and Cleo.* i 5 63
Every time Serves for the matter that is then born in't ii 2 10
That he quit being, and his gentle lady, Big of this gentleman our theme, deceased As he was born *Cymbeline* i 1 40
Let it die as it was born, and, I pray you, be better acquainted i 4 131
Certainties Either are past remedies, or, timely knowing, The remedy then born i 6 98
Why should excuse be born or e'er begot? iii 2 67
Not born where't grows, But worn a bait for ladies iii 4 58
Their blood thinks scorn, Till it fly out and show them princes born iv 4 54
Gone! they went hence so soon as they were born v 4 126
In Cambria are we born, and gentlemen v 5 17
My boy, a Briton born, Let him be ransom'd v 5 84
Being born your vassal, Am something nearer v 5 113
Let his arms alone; They were not born for bondage v 5 306
You, born in these latter times, When wit's more ripe *Pericles* i Gower 11
Marina, whom, For she was born at sea, I have named so iii 3 13
Give her princely training, that she may be Manner'd as she is born iii 3 17
Ay me! poor maid, Born in a tempest, when my mother died iv 1 19
When I was born, the wind was north iv 1 52
When was this?—When I was born: Never was waves nor wind more violent iv 1 59
If you were born to honour, show it now iv 6 99
Hang you! She's born to undo us iv 6 158
Where were you born? And wherefore call'd Marina?—Call'd Marina For I was born at sea v 1 156
My mother was the daughter of a king; Who died the minute I was born v 1 160
Thou that wast born at sea, buried at Tarsus, And found at sea again! v 1 198
Borne. Good wombs have borne bad sons *Tempest* i 2 120
I should have borne the humoured letter to her *Mer. Wives* ii 1 134
'Tis well borne up *Meas. for Meas.* iv 1 48
Hence hath offence his quick celerity, When it is borne in high authority iv 2 114
Hath he borne himself penitently in prison? iv 2 147
We were encounter'd by a mighty rock; Which being violently borne upon, Our helpful ship was splitted in the midst *Com. of Errors* i 1 103
Let him be brought forth and borne hence for help v 1 160
Witness you, That he is borne about invisible v 1 187
He hath borne himself beyond the promise of his age *Much Ado* i 1 13
The conference was sadly borne ii 3 229
If over-boldly we have borne ourselves *L. L. Lost* v 2 744
Still have I borne it with a patient shrug *Mer. of Venice* i 3 110
Which never tender lady hath borne greater *W. Tale* ii 2 24
You have heard of my poor services, i' the love That I have borne your father? iv 4 528
This must not be thus borne: this will break out To all our sorrows *K. John* iv 2 101
What penny hath Rome borne? v 2 97
Woe doth the heavier sit, Where it perceives it is but faintly borne *Richard II.* i 3 281
Afore God, 'tis shame such wrongs are borne In him ii 1 238
Had he done so, himself had borne the crown iii 4 65
The seeming sufferances that you had borne *1 Hen. IV.* v 1 51
If like a Christian thou hadst truly borne Betwixt our armies true intelligence v 5 9
I have borne, and borne, and borne, and have been fubbed off, and fubbed off, and fubbed off *2 Hen. IV.* ii 1 36
Like the south Borne with black vapour, doth begin to melt ii 4 393
If your father had been victor there, He ne'er had borne it out of Coventry iv 1 135
How this action hath been borne Here at more leisure may your highness read iv 4 88
That action, hence borne out, May waste the memory of the former days iv 5 215
So may a thousand actions, once afoot, End in one purpose, and be all well borne Without defeat *Hen. V.* i 2 212
Her sceptre so fantastically borne By a vain, giddy, shallow, humorous youth ii 4 27
Behold the threaden sails, Borne with the invisible and creeping wind iii Prol. 11
Consider of his ransom; which must proportion the losses we have borne iii 6 134
Where they feared the death, they have borne life away iv 1 181
Blackheath; Where that his lords desire him to have borne His bruised helmit v Prol. 17
Your eyes, which hitherto have borne in them . . . The fatal balls v 2 15
O my dear lord, lo, where your son is borne! *1 Hen. VI.* iv 7 17
While all is shared and all is borne away *2 Hen. VI.* i 1 228
Even so remorseless have they borne him hence iii 1 213
We will have the mayor's sword borne before us iv 3 16
With these borne before us, instead of maces, will we ride iv 7 143
Their colours, often borne in France, And now in England *3 Hen. VI.* i 1 127
Would I had died a maid, And never seen thee, never borne thee son! i 1 217
I have too long borne Your blunt upbraidings *Richard III.* i 3 103
If he were proud,— Or covetous of praise,— Ay, or surly borne *Troi. and Cres.* ii 3 249
The beauty that is borne here in the face The bearer knows not iii 3 103
Troilus had rather Troy were borne to Greece Than Cressid borne from Troy iv 1 46
And giddy censure Will then cry out of Marcius 'O, if he Had borne the business!' *Coriolanus* i 1 274
Either Had borne the action of yourself, or else To him had left it solely iv 7 15
Report to the Volscian lords, how plainly I have borne this business v 3 4
Hast not thou full often struck a doe, And borne her cleanly by the keeper's nose? *T. Andron.* ii 1 94
These miseries are more than may be borne iii 1 244

Borne. I know from whence this same device proceeds: May this be borne? . . . . *T. Andron.* iv 4 53
Thou shalt be borne to that same ancient vault . . *Rom. and Jul.* iv 1 111
Yet, stay awhile; Thou shalt not back till I have borne this corse Into the market-place . . . . *J. Cæsar* iii 1 291
This Duncan Hath borne his faculties so meek . . *Macbeth* i 7 17
How you were borne in hand, how cross'd, the instruments, Who wrought with them . . . . iii 1 81
Only, I say, Things have been strangely borne . . . . . iii 6 3
So that, I say, He has borne all things well . . . . . iii 6 17
I came hither to transport the tidings, Which I have heavily borne . iv 3 182
That so his sickness, age and impotence Was falsely borne in hand *Hamlet* ii 2 67
I could accuse me of such things that it were better my mother had not borne me . . . . iii 1 126
He hath borne me on his back a thousand times . . . . v 1 205
The hard rein which both of them have borne Against the old kind king *Lear* iii 1 27
The oldest hath borne most . . . . v 3 325
Borne so like a soldier, that thy cheek So much as lank'd not *Ant. and Cleo.* i 4 70
The trees by the way Should have borne men . . . . . iii 6 47
No more a soldier: bruised pieces, go; You have been nobly borne . iv 14 43
Yet I not doing this, the fool had borne My head as I do his *Cymbeline* iv 2 116
Knighthoods and honours, borne As I wear mine, are titles but of scorn v 2 6
I'll show the virtue I have borne in arms . . . . *Pericles* ii 1 151
Borough. Met him in boroughs, cities, villages . . 1 *Hen. IV.* iv 3 69
King of England shalt thou be proclaim'd In every borough . 3 *Hen. VI.* ii 1 195
Borrows his wit from your ladyship's looks, and spends what he borrows kindly in your company . . . . . . *T. G. of Ver.* ii 4 38
Sit you down: We'll borrow place of him . . . *Meas for Meas.* v 1 367
Beg thou, or borrow, to make up the sum, And live . *Com. of Errors* i 1 154
Go borrow me a crow.—A crow without feather? . . . . iii 1 80
Borrows money in God's name, the which he hath used so long and never paid that now men grow hard-hearted . . . *Much Ado* v 1 319
I bepray you, let me borrow my arms again . . . *L. L. Lost* v 2 702
I neither lend nor borrow By taking nor by giving of excess *Mer. of Venice* i 3 62
Methought you said you neither lend nor borrow Upon advantage . i 3 70
You must borrow me Gargantua's mouth first . . *As Y. Like It* iii 2 238
She comes to borrow nothing of them . . . . *T. of Shrew* iv 1 107
You cannot, By the good aid that I of you shall borrow, Err in bestowing it.—I should believe you . . . . . *All's Well* iii 7 11
Of your royal presence I'll adventure The borrow of a week . *W. Tale* i 2 39
Inferior eyes, That borrow their behaviours from the great . *K. John* v 1 51
I could weep, madam, would it do you good.—And I could sing, would weeping do me good, And never borrow any tear of thee *Richard II.* iii 4 23
Coming in to borrow a mess of vinegar . . . . 2 *Hen. IV.* ii 1 103
I dare swear you borrow not that face Of seeming sorrow . . v 2 28
The sun borrows of the moon, when Diomed keeps his word *Tr. and Cr.* v 1 101
Borrow Cupid's wings, And soar with them above a common bound *Rom. and Jul.* i 4 17
When men come to borrow of your masters, they approach sadly, and go away merry; but they enter my mistress' house merrily *T. of Athens* ii 2 105
One of his men was with the Lord Lucullus to borrow so many talents iii 2 13
I am sorry, when he sent to borrow of me, that my provision was out . iii 6 17
Were you godheads to borrow of men, men would forsake the gods . iii 6 84
Stay, I will lend thee money, borrow none . . . . . iii 6 111
Renew I could not, like the moon; There were no suns to borrow of . iv 3 69
If but as well I other accents borrow, That can my speech defuse . *Lear* i 4 1
But he bears both the sentence and the sorrow That, to pay grief, must of poor patience borrow . . . . *Othello* i 3 215
If you borrow one another's love for the instant, you may *Ant. and Cleo.* ii 6 130
With what imitation you can borrow From youth of such a season *Cymb.* iii 4 174
Borrowed. Pluck the borrowed veil of modesty . . *Mer. Wives* iii 2 42
Articles are borrowed of the pronoun . . . . iv 1 41
He borrowed a box of the ear of the Englishman and swore he would pay him again . . . . *Mer. of Venice* i 2 86
I would have him help to waste His borrow'd purse . . . ii 5 51
Youth is bought more oft than begg'd or borrow'd . . *T. Night* iii 4 3
In these my borrow'd flaunts . . . . . . *W. Tale* iv 4 23
The majesty, The borrow'd majesty, of England here.—A strange beginning: 'borrow'd majesty!' . . . . . . *K. John* i 1 4
Paid money that I borrowed, three or four times . . 1 *Hen. IV.* iii 3 20
A borrow'd title hast thou bought too dear . . . . . v 3 23
I would have bestowed the thousand pound I borrowed of you 2 *Hen. IV.* v 5 13
Divest yourself, and lay apart The borrow'd glories . . *Hen. V.* ii 4 79
Seems he a dove? his feathers are but borrow'd . . 2 *Hen. VI.* iii 1 75
And in this borrow'd likeness of shrunk death Thou shalt continue two and forty hours . . . . *Rom. and Jul.* iv 1 104
Help to take her from her borrow'd grave . . . . . v 3 248
Why do you dress me In borrow'd robes? . . . . . *Macbeth* i 3 109
Thirty dozen moons with borrow'd sheen . . . . *Hamlet* iii 2 167
Must take me up for swearing; as if I borrowed mine oaths of him and might not spend them at my pleasure . . . . *Cymbeline* ii 1 5
This borrow'd passion stands for true old woe . . . *Pericles* iv 4 24
Borrowedst. That any drop thou borrow'dst from thy mother, My sacred aunt, should by my mortal sword Be drain'd! . . *Troi. and Cres.* iv 5 133
Borrower. The answer is as ready as a borrower's cap . 2 *Hen. IV.* ii 2 125
I must become a borrower of the night For a dark hour or twain *Macbeth* iii 1 27
Neither a borrower nor a lender be; For loan oft loses both itself and friend, And borrowing dulls the edge of husbandry . . . *Hamlet* i 3 75
Borrowing. Shut his bosom Against our borrowing prayers . *All's Well* iii 1 9
No remedy against this consumption of the purse; borrowing only lingers and lingers it out, but the disease is incurable . 2 *Hen. IV.* i 2 265
Try the argument of hearts by borrowing . . . . *T. of Athens* ii 2 187
And borrowing dulls the edge of husbandry . . . . . *Hamlet* i 3 77
Bosko chimurcho . . . . *All's Well* iv 3 142
Boskos thromuldo boskos . . . . iv 1 75
Boskos vauvado: I understand thee . . . . iv 1 81
Bosky. My bosky acres and my unshrubb'd down . . . *Tempest* iv 1 81
Bosom. I feel not This deity in my bosom . . . . . . ii 1 278
My bosom as a bed Shall lodge thee . . . . . *T. G. of Ver.* i 2 114
My herald thoughts in thy pure bosom rest them . . . . iii 1 144
Shall be deliver'd Even in the milk-white bosom of thy love . . iii 1 250
Who should be trusted, when one's own right hand Is perjured to the bosom? . . . . v 4 68
Throw away that thought; Believe not that the dribbling dart of love Can pierce a complete bosom . . . . . *Meas. for Meas.* i 3 3
Go to your bosom; Knock there, and ask your heart what it doth know ii 2 136
And you shall have your bosom on this wretch . . . . iv 3 139
Your desert speaks loud; and I should wrong it, To lock it in the wards of covert bosom . . . . v 1 10

Bosom. In her bosom I'll unclasp my heart And take her hearing prisoner *Much Ado* i 1 325
Through the transparent bosom of the deep . . . *L. L. Lost* iv 3 31
Lay his wreathed arms athwart His loving bosom to keep down his heart . . . . iv 3 136
This man hath bewitch'd the bosom of my child . . *M. N. Dream* i 1 27
Upon faint primrose-beds were wont to lie, Emptying our bosoms of their counsel sweet . . . . i 1 216
One heart, one bed, two bosoms and one troth . . . . . ii 2 42
Two bosoms interchained with an oath; So then two bosoms and a single troth . . . . ii 2 49
Nature shows art, That through thy bosom makes me see thy heart . ii 2 105
From brassy bosoms and rough hearts of flint . . *Mer. of Venice* iv 1 31
You must prepare your bosom for his knife . . . . . iv 1 245
Therefore lay bare your bosom.—Ay, his breast: So says the bond . iv 1 252
Join her hand with his Whose heart within his bosom is . *As Y. Like It* v 4 121
Tempting kisses, And with declining head into his bosom *T. of Shrew* Ind. 1 119
Stall this in your bosom; and I thank you for your honest care *All's Well* i 3 131
Would in so just a business shut his bosom Against our borrowing prayers . . . . iii 1 8
Betake thee to thy faith, for seventeen poniards are at thy bosom . . iv 1 84
Which gratitude Through flinty Tartar's bosom would peep forth . iv 4 7
Where lies your text?—In Orsino's bosom.—In his bosom! In what chapter of his bosom? . . . . *T. Night* i 5 241
Fare ye well at once: my bosom is full of kindness . . . ii 1 40
A cypress, not a bosom, Hideth my heart . . . . . iii 1 132
I have one heart, one bosom and one truth, And that no woman has . iii 1 170
Derive a liberty From heartiness, from bounty, fertile bosom *W. Tale* i 2 113
O, that is entertainment My bosom likes not, nor my brows! . . i 2 119
How sometimes nature will betray its folly, Its tenderness, and make itself a pastime To harder bosoms! . . . . i 2 153
Priest-like, thou Hast cleansed my bosom . . . . . . i 2 238
If wit flow from't As boldness from my bosom, let't not be doubted I shall do good . . . . ii 2 53
He shall not perceive But that you have your father's bosom there . iv 4 574
We from the west will send destruction Into this city's bosom *K. John* ii 1 410
Thy voluntary oath Lives in this bosom, dearly cherished . . iii 3 24
Despite of brooded watchful day, I would into thy bosom pour my thoughts . . . . iii 3 53
When I strike my foot Upon the bosom of the ground, rush forth . iv 1 3
His words do take possession of my bosom . . . . . . iv 1 32
Within this bosom never enter'd yet The dreadful motion of a murderous thought . . . . iv 2 254
Wherein we step after a stranger march Upon her gentle bosom . . v 2 28
Great affections wrestling in thy bosom Doth make an earthquake of nobility . . . . v 2 41
There is so hot a summer in my bosom, That all my bowels crumble up to dust . . . . v 7 30
Nor let my kingdom's rivers take their course Through my burn'd bosom v 7 39
Even in the best blood chamber'd in his bosom . . *Richard II.* i 1 149
Be Mowbray's sins so heavy in his bosom, That they may break his foaming courser's back! . . . . i 2 50
Why have they dared to march So many miles upon her peaceful bosom? ii 3 93
The king is left behind, And in my loyal bosom lies his power . . ii 3 98
When they from thy bosom pluck a flower, Guard it, I pray thee, with a lurking adder . . . . iii 2 19
And with rainy eyes Write sorrow on the bosom of the earth . . iii 2 147
Sweet peace conduct his sweet soul to the bosom Of good old Abraham! iv 1 103
To whose flint bosom my condemned lord Is doom'd a prisoner . . v 1 3
What seal is that, that hangs without thy bosom? . . . . v 2 56
I tore it from the traitor's bosom . . . . v 3 55
Shall secretly into the bosom creep Of that same noble prelate 1 *Hen. IV.* i 3 266
There's no room for faith, truth, nor honesty in this bosom of thine . iii 3 174
Like a thunderbolt Against the bosom of the Prince of Wales . . iv 1 121
Taught us how to cherish such high deeds Even in the bosom of our adversaries . . . . v 5 31
Let one spirit of the first-born Cain Reign in all bosoms! . 2 *Hen. IV.* i 1 158
Whose bosom burns With an incensed fire of injuries . . . . i 3 13
So, so, thou common dog, didst thou disgorge Thy glutton bosom . . i 3 98
There is a thing within my bosom tells me . . . . . . iv 1 183
A nest of hollow bosoms, which he fills With treacherous crowns *Hen. V.* ii Prol. 21
As if allegiance in their bosoms sat, Crowned with faith . . . ii 2 4
Your own reasons turn into your bosoms, As dogs upon their masters . ii 2 82
He's in Arthur's bosom, if ever man went to Arthur's bosom . . . ii 3 10
I and my bosom must debate awhile, And then I would no other company . . . . iv 1 31
Gored the gentle bosom of peace with pillage and robbery . . . iv 1 174
Plant neighbourhood and Christian-like accord In their sweet bosoms . v 2 382
And in his bosom spend my latter gasp . . . . 1 *Hen. VI.* ii 5 38
One drop of blood drawn from thy country's bosom Should grieve thee more than streams of foreign gore . . . . iii 3 54
The vulture of sedition Feeds in the bosom of such great commanders . iv 3 48
And from his bosom purge this black despair! . . . 2 *Hen. VI.* iii 3 23
The gaudy, blabbing and remorseful day Is crept into the bosom of the sea . . . . iv 1 2
Throw in the frozen bosoms of our part Hot coals of vengeance! . . v 2 35
I stain'd this napkin with the blood That valiant Clifford, with his rapier's point, Made issue from the bosom of the boy . 3 *Hen. VI.* i 4 81
I stabb'd your fathers' bosoms, split my breast . . . . . ii 6 30
And all the clouds that lour'd upon our house In the deep bosom of the ocean buried . . . . *Richard III.* i 1 4
So I might live one hour in your sweet bosom . . . . . i 2 124
'Tis [conscience] a blushing shamefast spirit that mutinies in a man's bosom . . . . i 4 143
The sons of Edward sleep in Abraham's bosom . . . . . iv 3 38
Like a poor bark, of sails and tackling reft, Rush all to pieces on thy rocky bosom . . . . iv 4 234
Thus doth he force the swords of wicked men To turn their own points on their masters' bosoms . . . . v 1 24
And makes his trough In your embowell'd bosoms, this foul swine . v 2 10
Awake, and think our wrongs in Richard's bosom Will conquer him! . v 3 144
Let us be lead within thy bosom, Richard, And weigh thee down to ruin! v 3 152
A thousand hearts are great within my bosom: Advance our standards v 3 347
Bosom up my counsel, You'll find it wholesome . . . *Hen. VIII.* i 1 112
This respite shook The bosom of my conscience . . . . . ii 4 182
And not wholesome to Our cause, that she should lie i' the bosom of Our hard-ruled king . . . . iii 2 100
The bounded waters Should lift their bosoms higher than the shores *Troi. and Cres.* i 3 112

Bosom. Should once set footing in your generous bosoms *Troi. and Cres.* ii 2 155
Even such a passion doth embrace my bosom: My heart beats thicker than a feverous pulse . . . iii 2 37
Syllables Of no allowance to your bosom's truth . . *Coriolanus* iii 2 57
Friends now fast sworn, Whose double bosoms seem to wear one heart . iv 4 13
Put up.—Not I, till I have sheathed My rapier in his bosom *T. Andron.* ii 1 54
And stain the sun with fog, as sometime clouds When they do hug him in their melting bosoms . . . . iii 1 214
Thou'lt do thy message, wilt thou not?—Ay, with my dagger in their bosoms . . . . iv 1 118
And from her bosom took the enemy's point . . . . . v 3 111
And more inconstant than the wind, who wooes Even now the frozen bosom of the north . . . . . . *Rom. and Jul.* i 4 101
Bestrides the lazy-pacing clouds And sails upon the bosom of the air . ii 2 32
From her womb children of divers kind We sucking on her natural bosom find . . . . ii 3 12
Rests me his minim rest, one, two, and the third in your bosom . . ii 4 23
Go, counsellor; Thou and my bosom henceforth shall be twain . . iii 5 240
My bosom's lord sits lightly in his throne . . . . . v 1 3
Thy husband in thy bosom there lies dead . . . . . v 3 155
This dagger hath mista'en,—for, lo, his house Is empty on the back of Montague,—And it mis-sheathed in my daughter's bosom! . . . v 3 205
All kind of natures, That labour on the bosom of this sphere *T. of Athens* i 1 66
The five best senses Acknowledge thee their patron; and come freely To gratulate thy plenteous bosom . . . . . . i 2 131
Itches, blains, Sow all the Athenian bosoms; and their crop Be general leprosy! . . . . iv 1 29
Yield him, who all thy human sons doth hate, From forth thy plenteous bosom, one poor root! . . . . iv 3 186
Know his gross patchery, love him, feed him, Keep in your bosom . v 1 100
As you see, Have bared my bosom to the thunder-stone . . *J. Cæsar* i 3 49
By and by thy bosom shall partake The secrets of my heart . . . ii 1 305
I am in their bosoms, and I know Wherefore they do it . . . . v 1 7
With this good sword, That ran through Cæsar's bowels, search this bosom . . . . v 3 42
Still keep My bosom franchised and allegiance clear . *Macbeth* ii 1 28
I will put that business in your bosoms, Whose execution takes your enemy off . . . . iii 1 104
Seek out some desolate shade, and there Weep our sad bosoms empty . iv 3 2
I would not have such a heart in my bosom for the dignity of the whole body . . . . v 1 62
Cleanse the stuff'd bosom of that perilous stuff Which weighs upon the heart . . . . v 3 44
Leave her to heaven And to those thorns that in her bosom lodge *Hamlet* i 5 87
In her excellent white bosom . . . . ii 2 113
Let not ever The soul of Nero enter this firm bosom . . . . iii 2 412
O wretched state! O bosom black as death! O limed soul! . . . iii 3 67
Shall to my bosom Be as well neighbour'd, pitied, and relieved . *Lear* i 1 120
Use well our father: To your professed bosoms I commit him . . i 1 275
Our good old friend, Lay comforts to your bosom . . . . . ii 1 128
I know you are of her bosom . . . . iv 5 26
Whose age has charms in it, whose title more, To pluck the common bosom on his side . . . . v 3 49
To the sooty bosom Of such a thing as thou . . . . . *Othello* i 2 70
I will bestow you where you shall have time To speak your bosom freely iii 1 58
Swell, bosom, with thy fraught, For 'tis of aspics' tongues! . . . iii 3 449
If you think other, Remove your thought; it doth abuse your bosom . iv 2 14
Her hand on her bosom, her head on her knee, Sing willow, willow, willow . . . . iv 3 43
My great office will sometimes Divide me from your bosom *Ant. and Cleo.* ii 3 2
In my bosom shall she never come, To make my heart her vassal . . ii 6 56
Whose bosom was my crownet, my chief end . . . . . iv 12 27
The heaviness and guilt within my bosom Takes off my manhood . *Cymb.* v 2 1
When I waked, I found This label on my bosom . . . . . v 5 430
Let not conscience, Which is but cold, inflaming love i' thy bosom, Inflame too nicely . . . . *Pericles* iv 1 5
My heart Leaps to be gone into my mother's bosom . . . . v 3 45

Bosom interest. No more that thane of Cawdor shall deceive Our bosom interest . . . . *Macbeth* i 2 64

Bosom lover. This Antonio, Being the bosom lover of my lord, Must needs be like my lord . . . . *Mer. of Venice* iii 4 17

Bosomed. I am doubtful that you have been conjunct And bosom'd with her, as far as we call hers . . . . *Lear* v 1 13

Bossed. Fine linen, Turkey cushions boss'd with pearl . *T. of Shrew* ii 1 355

Bosworth. Here pitch our tents, even here in Bosworth field *Richard III.* v 3 1

Botch. Do botch and bungle up damnation With patches . *Hen. V.* ii 2 115
Leave no rubs nor botches in the work . . . . *Macbeth* iii 1 134
And botch the words up fit to their own thoughts . . . *Hamlet* iv 5 10

Botched. Many fruitless pranks This ruffian hath botch'd up . *T. Night* iv 1 60
'Tis not well mended so, it is but botch'd . . . *T. of Athens* iv 3 285

Botcher. I know him: a' was a botcher's 'prentice in Paris . *All's Well* iv 3 211
If he cannot, let the botcher mend him . . . . *T. Night* i 5 51
Deserve not so honourable a grave as to stuff a botcher's cushion *Coriol.* ii 1 98

Botchy. Were not that a botchy core? . . . . . *Troi. and Cres.* ii 1 6

Both. What foul play had we, that we came from thence? Or blessed was't we did?—Both, both, my girl . . . . . . *Tempest* i 2 61
Having both the key Of officer and office . . . . . . i 2 83
The time 'twixt six and now Must by us both be spent most preciously i 2 241
This music crept by me upon the waters, Allaying both their fury and my passion . . . . i 2 392
They are both in either's powers . . . . i 2 450
Then let us both be sudden . . . . ii 1 306
Sour-eyed disdain and discord shall bestrew The union of your bed with weeds so loathly That you shall hate it both . . . . . iv 1 22
I will pay thy graces Home both in word and deed . . . . . v 1 71
O heavens, that they were living both in Naples! . . . . v 1 149
We look to hear from you.—We 'll both attend upon your ladyship *T. G. of Ver.* ii 4 121
Are they broken?—No, they are both as whole as a fish . . . ii 5 20
Friar Laurence met them both, As he in penance wander'd through the forest . . . . v 2 37
I will be cheater to them both, and they shall be exchequers to me; they shall be my East and West Indies, and I will trade to them both *Mer. Wives* i 3 77
Wilt thou revenge?—By welkin and her star!—With wit or steel?—With both the humours, I . . . . i 3 103
He wooes both high and low, both rich and poor, Both young and old . ii 1 117
He may come and go between you both . . . . . . ii 2 130
Fare thee well: commend me to them both . . . . . ii 2 138
What, the sword and the word! do you study them both? . . . iii 1 45
Both. Boys of art, I have deceived you both . . . *Mer. Wives* iii 1 110
Did he send you both these letters at an instant? . . . . iv 4 3
The devil take one party and his dam the other! and so they shall be both bestowed . . . . iv 5 109
Neither singly can be manifested, Without the show of both . . iv 6 16
Which means she to deceive, father or mother?—Both, my good host . iv 6 47
Both the proofs are extant . . . . v 5 126
Both thanks and use . . . . *Meas. for Meas.* i 1 41
I will, as 'twere a brother of your order, Visit both prince and people . i 3 45
Why does my blood thus muster to my heart, Making both it unable for itself? . . . . ii 4 21
Hooking both right and wrong to the appetite, To follow as it draws! . ii 4 176
Thou hast nor youth nor age, But, as it were, an after-dinner's sleep, Dreaming on both . . . . iii 1 34
Correction and instruction must both work Ere this rude beast will profit . . . . iii 2 33
For the which you are to do me both a present and a dangerous courtesy iv 2 171
Angelo hath seen them both, and will discover the favour . . iv 2 184
You know the character, I doubt not; and the signet is not strange to you.—I know them both . . . . iv 2 210
Many and hearty thankings to you both . . . . . . v 1 4
Both in the heat of blood, And lack of temper'd judgement afterward . v 1 477
Decreed, Both by the Syracusians and ourselves . . *Com. of Errors* i 1 14
Fortune had left to both of us alike What to delight in, what to sorrow for . . . . i 1 106
Not a thousand marks between you both . . . . . . i 2 84
Both in mind and in my shape . . . . ii 2 199
O villain! thou hast stolen both mine office and my name . . . iii 1 44
Both wind and tide stays for this gentleman . . . . . iv 1 46
Both one and other he denies me now . . . . . . iv 3 86
Both man and master is possess'd; I know it by their pale and deadly looks . . . . iv 4 95
Dissembling villain, thou speak'st false in both . . . . . iv 4 103
My master and his man are both broke loose . . . . . v 1 169
They are both forsworn: In this the madman justly chargeth them . v 1 212
I am sure you both of you remember me.—Ourselves we do remember . v 1 291
The duke, my husband and my children both . . . . . v 1 403
You are both sure, and will assist me?—To the death . *Much Ado* i 3 71
He both pleases men and angers them, and then they laugh at him . ii 1 146
Intend a kind of zeal both to the prince and Claudio . . . ii 2 36
Both which, master constable,— You have: I knew it would be your answer . . . . iii 3 17
Both strength of limb and policy of mind, Ability in means . . . iv 1 200
'Fore God, they are both in a tale . . . . iv 2 33
Good den, good den.—Good day to both of you . . . . . v 1 46
Gentlemen both, we will not wake your patience . . . . . v 1 102
I came to seek you both.—We have been up and down to seek thee . v 1 121
And she alone is heir to both of us . . . . v 1 299
To hear meekly, sir, and to laugh moderately; or to forbear both *L. L. Lost* i 1 200
You are a gentleman and a gamester, sir.—I confess both: they are both the varnish of a complete man . . . . i 2 46
And mark'd you both and for you both did blush . . . . iv 3 138
Well bandied both; a set of wit well play'd . . . . . v 2 29
Sweet bloods, I both may and will . . . . v 2 714
We to ourselves prove false, By being once false for ever to be true To those that make us both . . . . v 2 784
I have some private schooling for you both . . . *M. N. Dream* i 1 116
Brief as the lightning in the collied night, That, in a spleen, unfolds both heaven and earth . . . . i 1 146
One turf shall serve as pillow for us both . . . . . . ii 2 41
Your vows to her and me, put in two scales, Will even weigh, and both as light as tales . . . . iii 2 133
You both are rivals, and love Hermia; And now both rivals, to mock Helena . . . . iii 2 155
Created both one flower, Both on one sampler, sitting on one cushion, Both warbling of one song, both in one key . . . . . iii 2 204
You, ladies, you . . . May now perchance both quake and tremble here v 1 224
Good signiors both, when shall we laugh? say, when? . *Mer. of Venice* i 1 66
By adventuring both I oft found both . . . . i 1 143
Or to find both Or bring your latter hazard back again . . . . i 1 150
One speak for both. What would you?—Serve you, sir . . . . ii 2 150
My master Antonio is at his house and desires to speak with you both . iii 1 78
Having made one [eye], Methinks it should have power to steal both his iii 2 126
When we are both accoutred like young men, I'll prove the prettier . iii 4 63
I fear you are damned both by father and mother . . . . iii 5 18
Antonio and old Shylock, both stand forth . . . . . . iv 1 175
In the morning early will we both Fly toward Belmont . . . . iv 1 456
Stand you both forth now: stroke your chins . . . *As Y. Like It* i 2 75
That tripped up the wrestler's heels and your heart both in an instant . iii 2 225
The oath of a lover is no stronger than the word of a tapster; they are both the confirmer of false reckonings . . . . iii 4 35
By giving love your sorrow and my grief Were both extermined . . iii 5 89
Orlando doth commend him to you both . . . . . . iv 3 92
Consent with both that we may enjoy each other . . . . . v 2 10
Both in a tune, like two gipsies on a horse . . . . . . v 3 15
Was converted Both from his enterprise and from the world . . . v 4 168
If either of you both love Katharina . . . . . *T. of Shrew* i 1 52
It toucheth us both, that we may yet again have access to our fair mistress . . . . i 1 118
Both our inventions meet and jump in one . . . . . . i 1 195
Has my fellow Tranio stolen your clothes? Or you stolen his? or both? i 1 229
Sufficeth, my reasons are both good and weighty . . . . . i 1 253
To my daughters; and tell them both, These are their tutors . . ii 1 110
He of both That can assure my daughter greatest dower Shall have my Bianca's love . . . . ii 1 344
And so, I take my leave, and thank you both . . . . . ii 1 400
Take it not unkindly, pray, That I have been thus pleasant with you both . . . . iii 1 58
Farewell, sweet masters both; I must be gone . . . . . iii 1 85
My master riding behind my mistress,— Both of one horse? . . . iv 1 71
Better 'twere that both of us did fast . . . . iv 1 176
Then both, or one, or any thing thou wilt . . . . . . iv 3 29
Or both dissemble deeply their affections . . . . . . iv 4 42
For both our sakes, I would that word were true . . . . . v 2 15
Commits his body To painful labour both by sea and land . . . v 2 149
But on us both did haggish age steal on And wore us out of act *All's Well* i 2 29
O'er whom both sovereign power and father's voice I have to use . . ii 3 60
Which both thy duty owes and our power claims . . . . . ii 3 168
Both my revenge and hate Loosing upon thee, in the name of justice . ii 3 171

Both. Which of them both Is dearest to me, I have no skill in sense To make distinction *All's Well* iii 4 38
The duke shall both speak of it, and extend to you what further becomes iii 6 73
Where both not sin, and yet a sinful fact iii 7 47
For which live long to thank both heaven and me! You may so in the end iv 2 67
Dost thou put upon me at once both the office of God and the devil? v 2 52
Whose age and honour Both suffer under this complaint v 3 163
Courage and hope both teaching him the practice *T. Night* i 2 13
If both break, your gaskins fall i 5 27
He left behind him myself and a sister, both born in an hour ii 1 20
Your true love's coming, That can sing both high and low ii 3 42
This will so fright them both that they will kill one another by the look iii 4 214
Not a minute's vacancy, Both day and night did we keep company v 1 99
If spirits can assume both form and suit You come to fright us v 1 242
If nothing lets to make us happy both But this v 1 256
You are betroth'd both to a maid and man v 1 270
Thou shalt be both the plaintiff and the judge Of thine own cause v 1 362
A charge and trouble: to save both, Farewell, our brother *W. Tale* i 2 26
A hovering temporizer, that Canst with thine eyes at once see good and evil, Inclining to them both i 2 304
I mean to utter it, or both yourself and me Cry lost, and so good night! i 2 410
Are both landed, Hasting to the court ii 3 196
Which not to have done I think had been in me Both disobedience and ingratitude iii 2 69
One grave shall be for both iii 2 237
Which may, if fortune please, both breed thee, pretty, And still rest thine iii 3 48
How the poor gentleman roared and the bear mocked him, both roaring louder than the sea or weather iii 3 103
Both joy and terror Of good and bad, that makes and unfolds error iv 1 1
She was both pantler, butler, cook, Both dame and servant iv 4 56
Grace and remembrance be to you both! iv 4 76
We can both sing it: if thou'lt bear a part, thou shalt hear iv 4 298
I'll buy for you both. Pedlar, let's have the first choice iv 4 319
He would not stir his pettitoes till he had both tune and words iv 4 619
Having both their country quitted With this young prince v 1 192
Both your pardons, That e'er I put between your holy looks My ill suspicion v 3 147
Be judge yourself. If old Sir Robert did beget us both *K. John* i 1 80
When I have said, make answer to us both ii 1 235
We for the worthiest hold the right from both ii 1 282
The onset and retire Of both your armies ii 1 327
Both are alike; and both alike we like. One must prove greatest ii 1 331
Both conjointly bend Your sharpest deeds of malice on this town ii 1 379
So lately purged of blood, So newly join'd in love, so strong in both iii 1 240
Which is the side that I must go withal? I am with both iii 1 328
I will both hear and grant you your requests iv 2 46
Both for myself and them, but, chief of all, Your safety iv 2 49
The deed, which both our tongues held vile to name iv 2 241
Both they and we, perusing o'er these notes v 2 5
High-stomach'd are they both, and full of ire *Richard II.* i 1 18
We thank you both: yet one but flatters us i 1 25
Mine honour is my life; both grow in one i 1 182
Both to defend my loyalty and truth To God, my king and my succeeding issue i 3 19
Ask yonder knight in arms, Both who he is and why he cometh hither i 3 27
Both to defend himself and to approve Henry of Hereford . . . disloyal i 3 112
Lay by their helments and their spears, And both return back to their chairs i 3 120
Let them die that age and sullens have; For both hast thou, and both become the grave ii 1 140
Barely in title, not in revenue.—Richly in both ii 1 227
Both young and old rebel, And all goes worse than I have power to tell ii 2 119
Henry Bolingbroke On both his knees doth kiss King Richard's hand iii 3 36
By the royalties of both your bloods iii 3 107
I'll give thee scope to beat, Since foes have scope to beat both thee and me iii 3 141
Will no man say amen? Am I both priest and clerk? well then, amen iv 1 173
What, is my Richard both in shape and mind Transform'd and weaken'd? v 1 26
And hate turns one or both To worthy danger and deserved death v 1 67
Banish us both and send the king with me v 1 83
As dissolute as desperate; yet through both I see some sparks of better hope v 3 20
Against them both my true joints bended be v 3 98
As full of valour as of royal blood: Both have I spill'd v 5 115
Did gage them both in an unjust behalf *1 Hen. IV.* i 3 173
Poins! Hal! a plague upon you both! ii 2 22
O, we are undone, both we and ours for ever! ii 2 91
So majestically, both in word and matter ii 4 479
A true face and good conscience.—Both which I have had ii 4 552
Both he and they and you, yea, every man Shall be my friend v 1 107
But we rose both at an instant and fought a long hour by Shrewsbury clock v 4 150
Both the Blunts Kill'd by the hand of Douglas *2 Hen. IV.* i 1 16
He's followed both with body and with mind i 1 203
And made her serve your uses both in purse and in person ii 1 127
I must be fain to pawn both my plate and the tapestry ii 1 153
You are both, i' good truth, as rheumatic as two dry toasts ii 4 62
Their legs are both of a bigness, and a' plays at quoits well ii 4 265
A peace indeed, Concurring both in name and quality iv 1 87
Bolingbroke and he, Being mounted and both roused in their seats iv 1 118
In sight of both our battles we may meet iv 1 179
Both against the peace of heaven and him iv 2 29
Of capital treason I attach you both.—Is this proceeding just? iv 2 109
Both which we doubt not but your majesty Shall soon enjoy iv 4 101
For women are shrews, both short and tall v 3 36
Come, I charge you both go with me v 4 18
Gentlemen both, you will mistake each other *Hen. V.* iii 2 146
You talk of horse and armour?—You are as well provided of both as any prince in the world iii 7 9
Early stirrers, Which is both healthful and good husbandry iv 1 7
Brothers both, Commend me to the princes in our camp iv 1 24
He is as full of valour as of kindness; Princely in both iv 3 16
And there is salmons in both iv 7 33
Bring me just notice of the numbers dead On both our parts iv 7 123
My duty to you both, on equal love v 2 23
Losing both beauty and utility v 2 53
Shall this night appear How much in duty I am bound to both *1 Hen. VI.* ii 1 37
Arm in arm they both came swiftly running ii 2 29

Both. What is that wrong whereof you both complain? *1 Hen. VI.* iv 1 87
Good cousins both, of York and Somerset, Quiet yourselves, I pray iv 1 114
Both are my kinsmen, and I love them both iv 1 155
And now they meet where both their lives are done iv 3 38
If we both stay, we both are sure to die iv 5 20
If death be so apparent, then both fly iv 5 44
I always thought It was both impious and unnatural v 1 12
Your purpose is both good and reasonable v 1 36
And may ye both be suddenly surprised By bloody hands! v 3 40
Such fierce alarums both of hope and fear v 5 85
Ay, grief, I fear me, both at first and last v 5 102
But I will rule both her, the king and realm v 5 108
Anjou and Maine! myself did win them both *2 Hen. VI.* i 1 119
You shall go near To call them both a pair of crafty knaves i 2 103
Rue my shame, And ban thine enemies, both mine and thine? ii 4 25
Both of you were vow'd Duke Humphrey's foes iii 2 182
Cut both the villains' throats; for die you shall iv 1 20
And bring them both upon two poles hither iv 7 119
Of one or both of us the time is come v 2 13
My soul and body on the action both! v 2 26
You both have vow'd revenge On him, his sons, his favourites *3 Hen. VI.* i 1 55
He is both king and Duke of Lancaster i 1 87
How hast thou injured both thyself and us! i 1 179
I here divorce myself Both from thy table, Henry, and thy bed i 1 248
Murder not this innocent child, Lest thou be hated both of God and man! i 3 9
This thy son's blood cleaving to my blade Shall rust upon my weapon, till thy blood, Congeal'd with this, do make me wipe off both i 3 52
My uncles both are slain in rescuing me i 4 2
King of Naples, Of both the Sicils and Jerusalem i 4 122
To London all the crew are gone, To frustrate both his oath and what beside ii 1 175
Both bound to revenge, Wert thou environ'd with a brazen wall ii 4 3
Both tugging to be victors, breast to breast ii 5 11
Swearing both They prosper best of all when I am thence ii 5 17
And I, that haply take them from him now, May yet ere night yield both my life and them ii 5 59
So shalt thou sinew both these lands together ii 6 91
I'll stay above the hill, so both may shoot iii 1 5
Here stand we both, and aim we at the best iii 1 8
Herein your highness wrongs both them and me iii 2 75
I can tell you both Her suit is granted for her husband's lands iii 2 116
Our people and our peers are both misled, Our treasure seized iii 3 35
For this is he that moves both wind and tide iii 3 48
With my talk and tears, Both full of truth iii 3 159
Both of you are birds of selfsame feather iii 3 161
Tell me if you love Warwick more than me? If it be so, then both depart to him iv 1 138
It boots not to resist both wind and tide iv 3 59
Give me both your hands: Now join your hands iv 6 38
I make you both protectors of this land iv 6 41
We shall soon persuade Both him and all his brothers unto reason iv 7 34
Yet, as we may, we'll meet both thee and Warwick iv 7 86
Thou and thy brother both shall buy this treason v 1 68
Two of thy name, both Dukes of Somerset, Have sold their lives v 1 73
'Good Gloucester' and 'good devil' were alike, And both preposterous v 6 5
Love my lovely queen; And kiss your princely nephew, brothers both v 7 27
I beseech your graces both to pardon me *Richard III.* i 1 84
Black night o'ershade thy day, and death thy life!—Curse not thyself, fair creature; thou art both i 2 132
To both their deaths thou shalt be accessary i 2 192
I would I knew thy heart.—'Tis figured in my tongue.—I fear me both are false i 2 195
Wear both of them, for both of them are thine i 2 206
When we both lay in the field Frozen almost to death ii 1 114
Alas for both, both mine, Edward and Clarence! ii 2 73
The king Had virtuous uncles to protect his grace.—Why, so hath this, both by the father and mother ii 3 22
Uncle, my brother mocks both you and me iii 1 129
Effect this business soundly.—My good lords both, with all the heed I may iii 1 187
At Crosby Place, there shall you find us both iii 1 190
The princes both make high account of you iii 2 71
Both are ready in their offices, At any time, to grace my stratagems iii 5 10
And you my good lords, both have well proceeded, To warn false traitors iii 5 48
Doubt you not, right noble princes both, But I'll acquaint our duteous citizens iii 5 64
Bid them both Meet me within this hour at Baynard's Castle iii 5 104
Both in your form and nobleness of mind iii 7 14
God give your graces both A happy and a joyful time of day! iv 1 5
Thus both are gone with conscience and remorse; They could not speak; and so I left them both iv 3 20
Because both they Match not the high perfection of my loss iv 4 65
We must both give and take, my gracious lord v 3 6
And, being present both, 'Twas said they saw but one *Hen. VIII.* i 1 31
This holy fox, Or wolf, or both,—for he is equal ravenous i 1 159
Both Fell by our servants, by those men we loved most ii 1 121
Well met, my lord chamberlain.—Good day to both your graces ii 2 14
Forgetting, like a good man, your late censure Both of his truth and him iii 1 65
My lords, I thank you both for your good wills iii 1 68
'Twill be much Both for your honour better and your cause iii 1 95
He tells you rightly.—Ye tell me what ye wish for both,—my ruin iii 1 98
He would say untruths; and be ever double Both in his words and meaning iv 2 39
That so long Have follow'd both my fortunes faithfully iv 2 141
In all the progress Both of my life and office I have labour'd v 3 33
Both in his private conscience and his place v 3 40
If your will pass, I shall both find your lordship judge and juror v 3 60
Applause and approbation . . . I give to both your speeches *Tr. and Cr.* i 3 62
Let it please both, Thou great, and wise, to hear Ulysses speak i 3 68
Both our honour and our shame in this Are dogg'd i 3 364
In kissing, do you render or receive?—Both take and give iv 5 37
His heart and hand both open and both free iv 5 100
Both taxing me and gaging me to keep An oath that I have sworn v 1 46
He is both ass and ox: to an ox, were nothing; he is both ox and ass v 1 65
Come, both you cogging Greeks; have at you both! v 6 11
My ladies both, good day to you *Coriolanus* i 3 51
How do you both? you are manifest house-keepers i 3 54

Both. Both our powers, with smiling fronts encountering . *Coriolanus* i 6 8
Whom We met here both to thank and to remember With honours . ii 2 51
And till we call'd Both field and city ours, he never stood To ease his breast . ii 2 125
Both observe and answer The vantage of his anger . ii 3 267
When, both your voices blended, the great'st taste Most palates theirs . iii 1 103
How soon confusion May enter 'twixt the gap of both . iii 1 111
Since that to both It stands in like request . iii 2 50
The gods preserve you both !—God-den, our neighbours . iv 6 20
Peace, both, and hear me speak . v 6 111
Would it offend you, then, That both should speed? . *T. Andron.* ii 1 101
When ye have the honey ye desire, Let not this wasp outlive, us both to sting . ii 3 132
He and his lady both are at the lodge Upon the north side . ii 3 254
He for the same Will send thee hither both thy sons alive . iii 1 155
O, none of both but are of high desert . iii 1 171
Let me redeem my brothers both from death . iii 1 181
I'll deceive them both : Lend me thy hand, and I will give thee mine . iii 1 187
Carry from me to the empress' sons Presents that I intend to send them both . iv 1 116
And pray the Roman gods confound you both ! . iv 2 6
What's the news?—That you are both decipher'd, that's the news . iv 2 8
And so I leave you both : like bloody villains . iv 2 17
Give the mother gold, And tell them both the circumstance of all . iv 2 156
Gave Aries such a knock That down fell both the Ram's horns . iv 3 72
Yet should both ear and heart obey my tongue . iv 4 99
But where the bull and cow are both milk-white, They never do beget a coal-black calf . v 1 31
Both her sweet hands, her tongue, and that more dear Than hands or tongue . v 2 176
Why, there they are both, baked in that pie . v 3 60
Of honourable reckoning are you both . *Rom. and Jul.* i 2 4
The more I give to thee, The more I have, for both are infinite . ii 2 135
Both our remedies Within thy help and holy physic lies . ii 3 51
Doth not rosemary and Romeo begin both with a letter?—Ay, nurse; what of that? both with an R . ii 4 220
Romeo shall thank thee, daughter, for us both . ii 6 22
Unfold the imagined happiness that both Receive in either . ii 6 28
Either thou, or I, or both, must go with him . iii 1 134
Why follow'd not, when she said 'Tybalt's dead,' Thy father, or thy mother, nay, or both? . iii 2 119
Poor ropes, you are beguiled, Both you and I . iii 2 133
Unseemly woman in a seeming man! Or ill-beseeming beast in seeming both! . iii 3 113
Thy wit, that ornament to shape and love, Mis-shapen in the conduct of them both . iii 3 131
We both were in a house Where the infectious pestilence did reign . v 2 9
I stand, both to impeach and purge Myself condemned and myself excused . v 3 226
I know the merchant.—I know them both; th' other's a jeweller *T. of A.* i 1 8
More to move you, Take my deserts to his, and join 'em both . iii 5 79
With all my heart, gentlemen both ; and how fare you? . iii 6 27
The gods confound—hear me, you good gods all—The Athenians both within and out that wall! . iv 1 38
Now, thieves?—Soldiers, not thieves.—Both too; and women's sons . iv 3 417
If it be aught toward the general good, Set honour in one eye and death i' the other, And I will look on both indifferently . *J. Cæsar* i 2 87
We both have fed as well, and we can both Endure the winter's cold as well . i 2 98
I will with patience hear, and find a time Both meet to hear and answer . i 2 170
You shall confess that you are both deceived . ii 1 105
Before the eyes of both our armies here . . . Let us not wrangle . iv 2 43
So well thy words become thee as thy wounds; They smack of honour both . *Macbeth* i 2 44
That the proportion both of thanks and payment Might have been mine! . i 4 19
Greater than both, by the all-hail hereafter! . i 5 56
I am his kinsman and his subject, Strong both against the deed . i 7 14
Nor time nor place Did then adhere, and yet you would make both . i 7 52
An equivocator, that could swear in both the scales against either scale . ii 3 10
Our separated fortune Shall keep us both the safer . ii 3 145
Your good advice, Which still hath been both grave and prosperous . iii 1 22
Both of you Know Banquo was your enemy . iii 1 114
Yet I must not, For certain friends that are both his and mine . iii 1 121
Present him eminence, both with eye and tongue . iii 2 31
Now, good digestion wait on appetite, And health on both! . iii 4 39
Both more and less have given him the revolt . v 4 12
Both in time, Form of the thing, each word made true and good *Hamlet* i 2 209
For loan oft loses both itself and friend . i 3 76
These blazes, daughter, Giving more light than heat, extinct in both . i 3 118
I entreat you both, . . . That you vouchsafe your rest here in our court . ii 2 10
We both obey, And here give up ourselves, in the full bent . ii 2 29
I hold my duty, as I hold my soul, Both to my God and to my gracious king . ii 2 45
Good lads, how do ye both?—As the indifferent children of the earth . ii 2 230
Your virtues Will bring him to his wonted way again, To both your honours . iii 1 42
And after we will both our judgements join In censure of his seeming . iii 2 91
Like a man to double business bound, I stand in pause where I shall first begin, And both neglect . iii 3 43
Mad as the sea and wind, when both contend Which is the mightier . iv 1 7
We must, with all our majesty and skill, Both countenance and excuse . iv 1 32
Friends both, go join you with some further aid . iv 1 33
Let them know, both what we mean to do, And what's untimely done . iv 1 39
You will draw both friend and foe, Winner and loser . iv 5 142
Weigh what convenience both of time and means May fit us to our shape . iv 7 150
I do not fear it; I have seen you both . v 2 273
We will divest us, both of rule, Interest of territory, cares of state *Lear* i 1 50
It is not a little I have to say of what most nearly appertains to us both . i 1 287
It is both he and she; Your son and daughter . ii 4 13
Good morrow to you both.—Hail to your grace! . ii 4 129
Both charge and danger Speak 'gainst so great a number . ii 4 242
A poor old man, As full of grief as age; wretched in both! . ii 4 276
I will have such revenges on you both . ii 4 282
Or the hard rein which both of them have borne Against the old kind king . iii 1 27
To come seek you out, And bring you where both fire and food is ready . iii 4 158
Where thou shalt meet Both welcome and protection . iii 6 99
Both stile and gate, horse-way and foot-path . iv 1 58
To both these sisters have I sworn my love . v 1 55
Both. Which of them shall I take? Both? one? or neither? Neither can be enjoy'd, If both remain alive . *Lear* v 1 58
I was contracted to them both: all three Now marry in an instant . v 3 228
Hold your hands, Both you of my inclining, and the rest . *Othello* i 2 82
My life and education both do learn me How to respect you . i 3 183
But he bears both the sentence and the sorrow That, to pay grief, must of poor patience borrow . i 3 214
My boat sails freely, both with wind and stream . ii 3 65
Though he had twinn'd with me, both at a birth . ii 3 212
They see and smell And have their palates both for sweet and sour . iv 3 96
Such full license as both truth and malice Have power to utter *A. and C.* i 2 112
High in name and power, Higher than both in blood and life . i 2 197
He was not sad, . . . he was not merry, . . . but between both: O heavenly mingle! . i 5 58
Lepidus flatters both, Of both is flatter'd . ii 1 14
Let witchcraft join with beauty, lust with both! . ii 1 22
To lend me arms and aid when I required them; The which you both denied . ii 2 89
Her love to both Would, each to other and all loves to both, Draw after her . ii 2 137
Till I shall see you in your soldier's dress, Which will become you both ii 4 5
He plied them both with excellent praises . iii 2 14
Both he loves.—They are his shards, and he their beetle . iii 2 19
We perceived, both how you were wrong led, And we in negligent danger iii 6 80
Vantage like a pair of twins appear'd, Both as the same . iii 10 13
This if she perform, She shall not sue unheard. So to them both . iii 12 24
With that which makes him both without and within . *Cymbeline* i 4 10
Would by all likelihood have confounded one the other, or have fallen both . i 4 55
Would hazard the winning both of first and last . i 4 102
Seeing these effects will be Both noisome and infectious . i 5 26
That tub Both fill'd and running . i 6 49
Discover to me What both you spur and stop . i 6 99
If you'll be patient, I'll no more be mad; That cures us both . ii 3 109
Not the wronger Of her or you, having proceeded but By both your wills ii 4 56
Gains or loses Your sword or mine, or masterless leaves both . ii 4 60
Some villain . . . Hath done you both this cursed injury . iii 4 125
Grief and patience, rooted in him both, Mingle their spurs together . iv 2 57
Both their eyes And ears so cloy'd importantly as now . iv 4 18
Purse and brain both empty . v 4 166
Whom heavens, in justice, both on her and hers, Have laid most heavy hand . v 5 464
Where now you're both a father and a son . *Pericles* i 1 127
And both like serpents are . i 1 132
Makes both my body pine and soul to languish . i 2 31
I'll take thy word for faith, not ask thine oath: Who shuns not to break one will sure crack both . i 2 121
That time of both this truth shall ne'er convince . i 2 123
That will prove awful both in deed and word . ii Gower 4
A man whom both the waters and the wind, In that vast tennis-court, have made the ball For them to play upon . ii 1 63
What, are you both pleased?—Yes, if you love me, sir.—Even as my life ii 5 88
Which makes her both the heart and place Of general wonder . iv Gower 10
Blame both my lord and me, that we have taken No care to your best courses . iv 1 38
We should have both lord and lown . iv 6 19
Hath endured a grief Might equal yours, if both were justly weigh'd . v 1 89
Thou thought'st thy griefs might equal mine, If both were open'd . v 1 133
Both agreed. What, are you both agreed?—Yes . ii 5 90
Both alike. Male twins, both alike . *Com. of Errors* i 1 56
Both are alike; and both alike we like . *K. John* ii 1 331
The situations, look you, is both alike . *Hen. V.* iv 7 27
Who, in your thoughts, merits fair Helen best, Myself or Menelaus?—Both alike . *Troi. and Cres.* iv 1 54
Two households, both alike in dignity . *Rom. and Jul.* Prol. 1
Clay and clay differs in dignity, Whose dust is both alike . *Cymbeline* iv 2 5
Both at once. Open your purse, that the money and the matter may be both at once delivered . *T. G. of Ver.* i 1 138
That war, or peace, or both at once, may be As things acquainted . 2 *Hen. IV.* v 2 138
Good night and welcome, both at once, to those That go or tarry . *Troi. and Cres.* v 1 84
Both away. My father and Glendower being both away . 1 *Hen. IV.* iv 1 131
Away, I do beseech you, both away . *Hamlet* ii 2 169
Both ends. The middle of humanity thou never knewest, but the extremity of both ends . *T. of Athens* iv 3 301
Both hands full. Will Fortune never come with both hands full? . 2 *Hen. IV.* iv 4 103
Both here and hence. All members of our cause, both here and hence, That are insinew'd to this action . iv 1 171
Both here and hence pursue me lasting strife, If, once a widow, ever I be wife! . *Hamlet* iii 2 232
Both in one, or one in both . *L. L. Lost* iv 1 79
Both kinds. Two of both kinds makes up four . *M. N. Dream* iii 2 438
Both merits poised, each weighs nor less nor more . *Troi. and Cres.* iv 1 65
Both mine ears. I have such a heart that both mine ears Must not in haste abuse . *Cymbeline* i 6 130
Both my [mine] **eyes.** In both my eyes he doubly sees himself . *Mer. of Venice* v 1 244
Must you with hot irons burn out both mine eyes? . *K. John* iv 1 39
Laugh'd so heartily, That both mine eyes were rainy . *T. Andron.* v 1 117
Both now and ever. The God of heaven Both now and ever bless her! 'tis a girl . *Hen. VIII.* v 1 165
Both numbers. Within thine eyes sat twenty thousand deaths, In thy hands clutch'd as many millions, In Thy lying tongue both numbers, I would say 'Thou liest' . *Coriolanus* iii 3 72
Both one. Though to have her and death were both one thing *As Y. L. It* v 4 17
Howsome'er their hearts are severed . . ., their heads are both one *A. W.* i 3 58
Both or none. She which marries you must marry me, Either both or none . v 3 175
Both or nothing. Either both or nothing . *Cymbeline* v 4 147
Both parties nobly are subdued, And neither party loser . 2 *Hen. IV.* iv 2 90
Both parts. Your mightiness on both parts best can witness . *Hen. V.* v 2 28
To show a noble grace to both parts Than seek the end of one *Coriolanus* v 3 121
Thou clovest thy crown i' the middle, and gavest away both parts *Lear* i 4 176
For better might we Have loved without this mean, if on both parts This be not cherish'd . *Ant. and Cleo.* iii 2 32
A more unhappy lady, If this division chance, ne'er stood between, Praying for both parts . iii 4 14
Both sides. Writ o' both sides the leaf, margent and all . *L. L. Lost* v 2 8

Both sides. Our cake's dough on both sides . . . . *T. of Shrew* i 1 110
Damnable both-sides rogue! . . . . . . *All's Well* iv 3 251
If that the injuries be justly weigh'd That have on both sides pass'd *T. Night* v 1 376
Our battles join'd, and both sides fiercely fought . . *3 Hen. VI.* ii 1 121
Peace, rude sounds! Fools on both sides! . . . *Troi. and Cres.* i 1 93
On both sides more respect . . . . . . *Coriolanus* iii 1 181
Both sides are even: here I'll sit i' the midst . . . *Macbeth* iii 4 10
The tyrant's people on both sides do fight . . . . . v 7 25
'Faith, there has been much to do on both sides . . . *Hamlet* ii 2 370
They bleed on both sides . . . . v 2 315
Thou hast pared thy wit o' both sides, and left nothing i' the middle *Lear* i 4 205
To sugar, or to gall, Being strong on both sides, are equivocal . *Othello* i 3 217
Both the parties. All the peace you make in their cause is, calling both the parties knaves . . . . . . *Coriolanus* ii 1 88
Both the princes had been breathing here. . . . *Richard III.* iv 4 384
Both the sides. There is expectance here from both the sides *Tr. and Cr.* iv 5 146
Both the worlds. But let the frame of things disjoint, both the worlds suffer . . . . *Macbeth* iii 2 16
That both the worlds I give to negligence, Let come what comes *Hamlet* iv 5 134
Both together. And, having both together heaved it up, We'll both together lift our heads to heaven . . . . . *2 Hen. VI.* i 2 13
We will both together to the Tower . . . . . *Richard III.* iii 2 32
I would they were in Afric both together . . . . *Cymbeline* i 1 167
Both twain. Neither of either; I remit both twain . . *L. L. Lost* v 2 459
Both ways. Well, you are gone both ways . . . *Mer. of Venice* iii 5 20
Their residence, both in reputation and profit, was better both ways *Ham.* ii 2 345
Both your houses. A plague o' both your houses! . . *Rom. and Jul.* iii 1 103
Bots. Stark spoiled with the staggers, begnawn with the bots *T. of Shrew* iii 2 56
That is the next way to give poor jades the bots . . *1 Hen. IV.* ii 1 11
Ha! bots on't, 'tis come at last . . . . . *Pericles* ii 1 124
Bottle. He shall taste of my bottle: if he have never drunk wine afore *Tempest* ii 2 77
If all the wine in my bottle will recover him, I will help his ague . . ii 2 97
Swear by this bottle how thou camest hither . . . . . ii 2 125
I escaped upon a butt of sack which the sailors heaved o'erboard, by this bottle! . . . . ii 2 127
I'll swear upon that bottle to be thy true subject . . . . ii 2 130
When's god's asleep, he'll rob his bottle . . . . . ii 2 155
We will inherit here: here; bear my bottle . . . . . ii 2 180
Give him blows And take his bottle from him . . . . iii 2 73
A pox o' your bottle! this can sack and drinking do . . . iii 2 87
Ay, but to lose our bottles in the pool . . . . . iv 1 208
I will fetch off my bottle, though I be o'er ears for my labour . . iv 1 213
I will rather trust . . . an Irishman with my aqua-vitæ bottle *Mer. Wives* ii 2 319
For filling a bottle with a tun-dish . . . . *Meas. for Meas.* iii 2 182
Hang me in a bottle like a cat and shoot at me . . . *Much Ado* i 1 259
Methinks I have a great desire to a bottle of hay: good hay *M. N. Dream* iv 1 37
As wine comes out of a narrow-mouthed bottle . . . *As Y. Like It* iii 2 211
Fill me a bottle of sack . . . . . . *1 Hen. IV.* iv 2 2
This bottle makes an angel.—An if it do, take it for thy labour . . iv 2 6
If it be a hot day, and I brandish any thing but a bottle . . *2 Hen. IV.* i 2 237
Among foaming bottles and ale-washed wits . . . . *Hen. V.* iii 6 82
His cold thin drink out of his leather bottle . . . *3 Hen. VI.* ii 5 48
I'll beat the knave into a twiggen bottle . . . . *Othello* ii 3 152
Bottle-ale houses. The Myrmidons are no bottle-ale houses . *T. Night* ii 3 29
Bottle-ale rascal! Away, you bottle-ale rascal! . . . *2 Hen. IV.* ii 4 140
Bottled. Why strew'st thou sugar on that bottled spider? *Richard III.* i 3 242
Help me curse That bottled spider, that foul bunch-back'd toad! . . iv 4 81
Bottom. Ebbing men, indeed, Most often do so near the bottom run *Tempest* ii 1 227
As you unwind her love from him, Lest it should ravel and be good to none, You must provide to bottom it on me . . *T. G. of Ver.* iii 2 53
If the bottom were as deep as hell, I should down . . *Mer. Wives* iii 5 13
It concerns me To look into the bottom of my place . *Meas. for Meas.* i 1 79
Nick Bottom, the weaver.—Ready . . . . . *M. N. Dream* i 2 18
You, Nick Bottom, are set down for Pyramus . . . . . i 2 22
Peter Quince,— What sayest thou, bully Bottom? . . . . iii 1 8
Tell them that I Pyramus am not Pyramus, but Bottom the weaver . iii 1 21
You can never bring in a wall. What say you, Bottom? . . . iii 1 68
O Bottom, thou art changed! what do I see on thee? . . . iii 1 117
Bless thee, Bottom! bless thee! thou art translated . . . iii 1 121
It shall be called Bottom's Dream, because it hath no bottom . . iv 1 221
Have you sent to Bottom's house? is he come home yet? . . . iv 2 1
O, sweet bully Bottom! Thus hath he lost sixpence a day during his life . . . . iv 2 19
Bottom! O most courageous day! O most happy hour . . . iv 2 27
Let us hear, sweet Bottom.—Not a word of me . . . . iv 2 33
My ventures are not in one bottom trusted . . . *Mer. of Venice* i 1 42
My affection hath an unknown bottom, like the bay of Portugal *As Y. Like It* iv 1 212
West of this place, down in the neighbour bottom . . . . iv 3 79
Beat me to death with a bottom of brown thread . . *T. of Shrew* iv 3 138
When your lordship sees the bottom of his success . . *All's Well* iii 6 38
Now I see The bottom of your purpose . . . . . . iii 7 29
With which such scathful grapple did he make With the most noble bottom of our fleet . . . . *T. Night* v 1 60
A braver choice of dauntless spirits Than now the English bottoms have waft o'er Did never float upon the swelling tide . *K. John* ii 1 73
Or dive into the bottom of the deep, Where fathom-line could never touch the ground . . . . *1 Hen. IV.* i 3 203
It shall not wind with such a deep indent, To rob me of so rich a bottom here.—Not wind? it shall, it must . . . . . . iii 1 105
Therein should we read The very bottom and the soul of hope . . iv 1 50
I do see the bottom of Justice Shallow . . . *2 Hen. IV.* iii 2 324
Much too shallow To sound the bottom of the after-times . . iv 2 51
Fill the cup, and let it come; I'll pledge you a mile to the bottom . v 3 57
As is the ooze and bottom of the sea With sunken wreck *Hen. V.* i 2 164
The key of all my counsels, That knew'st the very bottom of my soul . ii 2 97
Draw the huge bottoms through the furrow'd sea . . . iii Prol. 12
We then should see the bottom Of all our fortunes . . *2 Hen. VI.* v 2 78
Unvalued jewels, All scatter'd in the bottom of the sea *Richard III.* i 4 28
Reflecting gems, Which woo'd the slimy bottom of the deep . . i 4 32
The tent that searches To the bottom of the worst . *Troi. and Cres.* ii 2 17
Finds bottom in the uncomprehensive deeps, Keeps place with thought iii 3 198
My mind is troubled, like a fountain stirr'd; And I myself see not the bottom of it . . . . iii 3 312
But the bottom of the news is, our general is cut i' the middle *Coriolanus* iv 5 209
Now to the bottom dost thou search my wound . . *T. Andron.* ii 3 262
Is not my sorrow deep, having no bottom? . . . . . iii 1 217
Bottom. O God, I have an ill-divining soul! Methinks I see thee, now thou art below, As one dead in the bottom of a tomb *Rom. and Jul.* iii 5 56
Is there no pity sitting in the clouds, That sees into the bottom of my grief? . . . . iii 5 199
But there's no bottom, none, In my voluptuousness . . *Macbeth* iv 3 60
Like the crimson drops I' the bottom of a cowslip . . *Cymbeline* ii 2 39
And mine ear, Therein false struck, can take no greater wound, Nor tent to bottom that . . . . iii 4 118
O melancholy! Who ever yet could sound thy bottom? . . . iv 2 204
I'll hear you more, to the bottom of your story, And never interrupt *Pericles* v 1 166
Bottomless, that as fast as you pour affection in, it runs out *As Y. Like It* iv 1 214
Do not break into these deep extremes.—Is not my sorrow deep, having no bottom? Then be my passions bottomless with them *T. Andron.* iii 1 218
Bouciqualt. John Duke of Bourbon, and Lord Bouciqualt . *Hen. V.* iv 8 82
Bough. Under the blossom that hangs on the bough . . *Tempest* v 1 94
Under the shade of melancholy boughs . . . *As Y. Like It* ii 7 111
Upon the fairest boughs, Or at every sentence end, Will I Rosalinda write . . . . iii 2 143
Under an oak, whose boughs were moss'd with age . . . . iv 3 105
I, an old turtle, Will wing me to some wither'd bough . . *W. Tale* v 3 133
Superfluous branches We lop away, that bearing boughs may live *Richard II.* iii 4 64
As duly, but not as truly, As bird doth sing on bough . *Hen. V.* iii 2 20
Cometh Andronicus, bound with laurel boughs, To re-salute his country with his tears . . . . *T. Andron.* i 1 74
With one winter's brush Fell from their boughs . . *T. of Athens* iv 3 265
Let every soldier hew him down a bough And bear't before him *Macbeth* v 4 4
On the pendent boughs her coronet weeds Clambering to hang *Hamlet* iv 7 173
Then was I as a tree Whose boughs did bend with fruit . *Cymbeline* iii 3 61
Bought. To be in love, where scorn is bought with groans *T. G. of Ver.* i 1 29
But a folly bought with wit, Or else a wit by folly vanquished . . i 1 34
Not only bought many presents to give her, but have given largely to many to know what she would have given . . . *Mer. Wives* ii 2 206
Those . . . I bought and brought up to attend my sons *Com. of Errors* i 1 58
It would make a man mad as a buck, to be so bought and sold . iii 1 72
I have bought The oil, the balsamum and aqua-vitæ . . . iv 1 88
Call'd me in his shop And show'd me silks that he had bought for me . iv 3 8
Beauty is bought by judgement of the eye . . . *L. L. Lost* ii 1 15
The boy's fat l'envoy, the goose that you bought . . . . iii 1 110
That can never be.—Then cannot we be bought . . . . v 2 226
I think he bought his doublet in Italy . . . *Mer. of Venice* i 2 80
These things being bought and orderly bestow'd, Return in haste . . ii 2 179
Since you are dear bought, I will love you dear . . . . iii 2 315
Which, like your asses and your dogs and mules, You use in abject and in slavish parts, Because you bought them . . . . . iv 1 93
The pound of flesh, which I demand of him, Is dearly bought . . iv 1 100
He hath bought a pair of cast lips of Diana . . *As Y. Like It* iii 4 16
He hath bought the cottage and the bounds That the old carlot once was master of . . . . iii 5 107
Creaking my shoes on the plain masonry, Till honour be bought up *All's Well* ii 1 32
He might have bought me at a common price . . . . . v 3 190
I had that which any inferior might At market-price have bought . v 3 219
Youth is bought more oft than begg'd or borrow'd . . *T. Night* iii 4 3
Blood hath bought blood and blows have answer'd blows . *K. John* ii 1 329
Fly, noble English, you are bought and sold . . . . . v 4 10
Trouble me no more with vanity. I would to God thou and I knew where a commodity of good names were to be bought . *1 Hen. IV.* i 2 94
The sack that thou hast drunk me would have bought me lights as good cheap at the dearest chandler's in Europe . . . . . iii 3 51
I bought you a dozen of shirts to your back . . . . . iii 3 77
They have bought out their services . . . . iv 2 24
To fill up the rooms of them that have bought out their services . iv 2 35
The Lord of Stafford dear to-day hath bought Thy likeness . . v 3 7
A borrow'd title hast thou bought too dear . . . . . v 3 23
I bought him in Paul's, and he'll buy me a horse in Smithfield *2 Hen. IV.* i 2 58
Let us not forego That for a trifle that was bought with blood! *1 Hen. VI.* iv 1 150
From bought and sold Lord Talbot . . . . . . iv 4 13
Bought with such a shame, To save a paltry life . . . . iv 6 44
And bought his climbing very dear . . . . *2 Hen. VI.* ii 1 100
Bid the apothecary Bring the strong poison that I bought of him . iii 3 18
Thou that so stoutly hast resisted me, Give me thy gold, if thou hast any gold; For I have bought it with an hundred blows *3 Hen. VI.* ii 5 81
Shine out, fair sun, till I have bought a glass, That I may see my shadow as I pass . . . . *Richard III.* i 2 263
She cannot choose but hate thee, Having bought love with such a bloody spoil . . . . iv 4 290
Dickon thy master is bought and sold . . . . . . v 3 305
That little thought, when she set footing here, She should have bought her dignities so dear . . . . . . *Hen. VIII.* iii 1 184
Thou art bought and sold among those of any wit . *Troi. and Cres.* ii 1 51
And yet dear too, because I bought mine own . . *T. Andron.* iii 1 200
I have bought the mansion of a love, But not possess'd it *Rom. and Jul.* iii 2 26
I have bought Golden opinions from all sorts of people . . *Macbeth* i 7 32
So great a day as this is cheaply bought . . . . . . v 8 37
I bought an unction of a mountebank . . . . . *Hamlet* iv 7 142
Corrupted By spells and medicines bought of mountebanks . . *Othello* i 3 61
She hath bought the name of whore thus dearly . . . *Cymbeline* ii 4 128
Before I enter'd here, I call'd; and thought To have begg'd or bought what I have took . . . . iii 6 48
And yet the end of all is bought thus dear . . . . *Pericles* i 1 98
Boult!—Sir?—Search the market narrowly . . . . . iv 2 1
Boult, take her away; use her at thy pleasure . . . . . iv 6 150
Bounce. He speaks plain cannon fire, and smoke and bounce . *K. John* ii 1 462
'Bounce' would a' say; and away again would a' go . *2 Hen. IV.* iii 2 304
Bounced. When I saw the porpus how he bounced and tumbled *Pericles* ii 1 26
Bouncing. The bouncing Amazon, Your buskin'd mistress *M. N. Dream* ii 1 70
Bound. Which had indeed no limit, A confidence sans bound . *Tempest* i 2 97
Upon the Mediterranean flote, Bound sadly home . . . . . i 2 235
My spirits, as in a dream, are all bound up . . . . . i 2 486
Contract, succession, Bourn, bound of land, tilth, vineyard . . ii 1 152
Lest it should burn above the bounds of reason . . *T. G. of Ver.* ii 7 23
So shall I evermore be bound to thee . . . . *Mer. Wives* iv 6 54
As fond fathers, Having bound up the threatening twigs of birch *Meas. for Meas.* i 3 24
Bound by my charity and my blest order . . . . . . ii 3 3
I am bound to call upon you; and, I pray you, your name? . . . iii 2 167
I am always bound to you.—Very well met . . . . . . iv 1 25
And that, by great injunctions, I am bound To enter publicly . . iv 3 100

Bound. To him one of the other twins was bound . . *Com. of Errors* i 1 82
Roaming clean through the bounds of Asia . . . . i 1 134
There's nothing situate under heaven's eye But hath his bound, in earth, in sea, in sky . . . . ii 1 17
I am bound To Persia and want guilders for my voyage . . . . iv 1 3
See him presently discharged, For he is bound to sea and stays but for it . . . . iv 1 33
They must be bound and laid in some dark room . . . . . iv 4 97
Wherefore dost thou mad me?—Will you be bound for nothing? . . iv 4 130
Let's call more help to have them bound again . . . . . iv 4 149
Once did I get him bound and sent him home . . . . . . v 1 145
And bound the doctor, Whose beard they have singed off . . . v 1 170
All together They fell upon me, bound me . . . . . . v 1 246
There left me and my man, both bound together . . . . . v 1 248
For lately we were bound, as you are now . . . . . . v 1 293
And whatsoever a man denies, you are now bound to believe him . . v 1 305
Who hath bound him here?—Whoever bound him, I will lose his bonds v 1 338
Master constable, let these men be bound . . . . *Much Ado* iv 2 67
How now? two of my brother's men bound! . . . . . . v 1 215
Who have you offended, masters, that you are thus bound to your answer? . . . . v 1 233
I am more bound to you than your fellows . . . *L. L. Lost* i 2 156
One part of Aquitaine is bound to us, Although not valued to the money's worth . . . . ii 1 136
The packet is not come Where that and other specialties are bound . ii 1 165
Thou wert immured, restrained, captivated, bound . . . . iii 1 126
Break up this capon.—I am bound to serve . . . . . iv 1 56
Thou drivest me past the bounds Of maiden's patience . *M. N. Dream* iii 2 65
For the which, as I told you, Antonio shall be bound.—Antonio shall become bound; well . . . . . . *Mer. of Venice* i 3 5
Three thousand ducats for three months and Antonio bound . . . i 3 10
He hath an argosy bound to Tripolis, another to the Indies . . . i 3 18
I am not bound to please thee with my answers . . . . . iv 1 65
Gratify this gentleman, For, in my mind, you are much bound to him . iv 1 407
Youthful and unhandled colts, Fetching mad bounds . . . . v 1 73
To whom I am so infinitely bound.—You should in all sense be much bound to him, For, as I hear, he was much bound for you . . . v 1 135
I dare be bound again, My soul upon the forfeit . . . . . v 1 251
His animals on his dunghills are as much bound to him as I *As Y. Like It* i 1 16
Besides, his cote, his flocks and bounds of feed Are now on sale . . ii 4 83
He hath bought the cottage and the bounds That the old carlot once was master of . . . . iii 5 107
Brief, I recover'd him, bound up his wound . . . . . . iv 3 151
I'll have them very fairly bound: All books of love . . *T. of Shrew* i 2 146
Bound I am to Padua; there to visit A son of mine . . . . iv 5 56
When they are bound to serve, love and obey . . . . . . v 2 164
You would answer very well to a whipping, if you were but bound to't.—I ne'er had worse luck in my life . . . . . *All's Well* ii 2 58
If ever thou be'st bound in thy scarf and beaten . . . . . ii 3 238
Which should sustain the bound and high curvet Of Mars's fiery steed . ii 3 299
Why, these balls bound; there's noise in it . . . . . . ii 3 314
Whither are you bound?—To Saint Jaques le Grand . . . . iii 5 36
And leap all civil bounds Rather than make unprofited return *T. Night* i 4 21
Let me yet know of you whither you are bound . . . . . ii 1 10
I am bound to the Count Orsino's court . . . . ii 1 43
I am bound to your niece, sir; I mean, she is the list of my voyage . iii 1 85
We'll have him in a dark room and bound . . . . . . iii 4 149
I shall be much bound to you for't . . . . iii 4 297
If one jot beyond The bound of honour . . . . *W. Tale* iii 2 52
How would he look, to see his work so noble Vilely bound up? . . iv 4 22
I am bound to you: There is some sap in this . . . . . iv 4 575
I am a soldier and now bound to France . . . . . *K. John* i 1 150
Whose veins bound richer blood than Lady Blanch? . . . . . ii 1 431
O, two such silver currents, when they join, Do glorify the banks that bound them in . . . . ii 1 442
Like a proud river peering o'er his bounds . . . . . . iii 1 23
And leave those woes alone which I alone Am bound to under-bear . iii 1 65
For heaven sake, Hubert, let me not be bound! . . . . . iv 1 78
Stoop low within those bounds we have o'erlook'd . . . . . v 4 55
England, bound in with the triumphant sea . . . . *Richard II.* ii 1 61
Bound in with shame, With inky blots and rotten parchment bonds . ii 1 63
But heaven hath a hand in these events, To whose high will we bound our calm contents . . . . v 2 38
Bound to himself! what doth he with a bond That he is bound to? . v 2 67
Drives him beyond the bounds of patience . . . . *1 Hen. IV.* i 3 200
The thieves have bound the true men . . . . ii 2 98
And bound them.—No, no, they were not bound.—You rogue, they were bound, every man of them . . . . ii 4 195
And all the fertile land within that bound . . . . . . iii 1 77
The very list, the very utmost bound Of all our fortunes . . . iv 1 51
A kingdom for it was too small a bound . . . . v 4 90
I am bound to thee, reverend Feeble . . . . . *2 Hen. IV.* iii 2 181
As he whose brow with homely biggen bound Snores out the watch . iv 5 27
No less for bounty bound to us Than Cambridge is . . . *Hen. V.* ii 2 92
He bounds from the earth, as if his entrails were hairs . . . . iii 7 13
The king is not bound to answer the particular endings of his soldiers . iv 1 163
If I might buffet for my love, or bound my horse for her favours . . v 2 146
Like captives bound to a triumphant car . . . . *1 Hen. VI.* i 1 22
And drive the English forth the bounds of France . . . . . i 2 54
Shall this night appear How much in duty I am bound to both . . ii 1 37
I am bound to you, That you on my behalf would pluck a flower . . ii 4 128
A heart it was, bound in with diamonds . . . . *2 Hen. VI.* iii 2 107
Who can be bound by any solemn vow To do a murderous deed, And have no other reason for this wrong But that he was bound by a solemn oath? . . . . v 1 184
Bound to revenge, Wert thou environ'd with a brazen wall . *3 Hen. VI.* ii 4 3
Now are our brows bound with victorious wreaths . . *Richard III.* i 1 5
Hath he set bounds betwixt their love and me? I am their mother . iv 1 21
I am bound by oath, and therefore pardon me . . . . . . iv 1 28
Bound with triumphant garlands will I come . . . . . . iv 4 333
A most rare speaker; To nature none more bound . . . *Hen. VIII.* i 2 112
For where I am robb'd and bound, There must I be unloosed . . . ii 4 146
And, if you may confess it, say withal, If you are bound to us or no . iii 2 165
With thee and all thy best parts bound together, Weigh'd not a hair of his . . . . iii 2 258
How much are we bound to heaven In daily thanks . . . . . v 3 114
But to the sport abroad: are you bound thither?—In all swift haste *Troi. and Cres.* i 1 118
My mother's blood Runs on the dexter cheek, and this sinister Bounds in my father's . . . . iv 5 129

Bound. Shall I, sweet lord, be bound to you so much? . *Troi. and Cres.* iv 5 284
The bits and greasy relics Of her o'er-eaten faith are bound to Diomed . v 2 160
From whence he returned, his brows bound with oak . . *Coriolanus* i 3 16
I, that now Refused most princely gifts, am bound to beg . . . i 9 80
If you will pass To where you are bound, you must inquire your way . iii 1 54
Ourselves, our wives, and children, on our knees, Are bound to pray for you both . . . . iv 6 23
What he would do, He sent in writing after me; what he would not, Bound with an oath to yield to his conditions . . . . . . v 1 69
Alas, how can we for our country pray, Whereto we are bound, together with thy victory, Whereto we are bound? . . . . v 3 108
There's no man in the world More bound to's mother . . . . v 3 159
Cometh Andronicus, bound with laurel boughs, To re-salute his country with his tears . . . . *T. Andron.* i 1 74
Faster bound to Aaron's charming eyes Than is Prometheus tied to Caucasus . . . . ii 1 16
My grief was at the height before thou camest, And now, like Nilus, it disdaineth bounds. Give me a sword . . . . iii 1 71
For this care of Tamora, Herself and hers are highly bound to thee . iv 2 171
Is he sure bound? look that you bind them fast . . . . . v 2 166
Come, come, Lavinia; look, thy foes are bound . . . . . v 2 167
But Montague is bound as well as I, In penalty alike . *Rom. and Jul.* i 2 1
Why, Romeo, art thou mad?—Not mad, but bound more than a madman is . . . . i 2 55
Borrow Cupid's wings, And soar with them above a common bound . i 4 18
So bound, I cannot bound a pitch above dull woe . . . . . i 4 20
Was ever book containing such vile matter So fairly bound? . . iii 2 84
There is no end, no limit, measure, bound, In that word's death . . iii 2 125
Not stepping o'er the bounds of modesty . . . . iv 2 27
All our whole city is much bound to him . . . . iv 2 32
And like the current flies Each bound it chafes . . *T. of Athens* i 1 25
In grateful virtue I am bound To your free heart . . . . . i 2 5
We are so virtuously bound— And so Am I to you . . . . i 2 232
Or offend the stream Of regular justice in your city's bounds . . . v 4 61
Which, taken at the flood, leads on to fortune; Omitted, all the voyage of their life Is bound in shallows and in miseries . . *J. Cæsar* iv 3 221
Think not, thou noble Roman, That ever Brutus will go bound to Rome v 1 112
Now I am cabin'd, cribb'd, confined, bound in To saucy doubts and fears *Macbeth* iii 4 24
Bound In filial obligation for some term To do obsequious sorrow *Hamlet* i 2 90
Speak; I am bound to hear.—So art thou to revenge, when thou shalt hear . . . . i 5 6
The single and peculiar life is bound, With all the strength and armour of the mind, To keep itself from noyance . . . . iii 3 11
Like a man to double business bound, I stand in pause where I shall first begin, And both neglect . . . . iii 3 41
Revenge should have no bounds . . . . iv 7 129
Of all these bounds, even from this line to this . . . . *Lear* i 1 64
To plainness honour's bound, When majesty stoops to folly . . . i 1 150
Thou, nature, art my goddess; to thy law My services are bound . . i 2 2
With how manifold and strong a bond The child was bound to the father ii 1 50
Infirmity doth still neglect all office Whereto our health is bound . ii 4 108
The revenges we are bound to take upon your traitorous father are not fit for your beholding . . . . iii 7 8
A most festinate preparation: we are bound to the like . . . . iii 7 11
Thou art a soul in bliss; but I am bound Upon a wheel of fire . . iv 7 46
By the law of arms thou wast not bound to answer An unknown opposite v 3 152
If she in chains of magic were not bound . . . . . *Othello* i 2 65
To you I am bound for life and education . . . . i 3 182
Speak your bosom freely.—I am much bound to you . . . . iii 1 58
Though I am bound to every act of duty, I am not bound to that all slaves are free to. Utter my thoughts? . . . . iii 3 134
Therefore, as I am bound, Receive it from me. I speak not yet of proof iii 3 195
I am bound to thee for ever . . . . iii 3 213
I will show you such a necessity in his death that you shall think yourself bound to put it on him . . . . iv 2 248
Go to, charm your tongue.—I will not charm my tongue; I am bound to speak . . . . v 2 184
When poison'd hours had bound me up From mine own knowledge *Ant. and Cleo.* ii 2 90
He's bound unto Octavia.—For what good turn? . . . . . ii 5 58
If I were bound to divine of this unity, I would not prophesy so . . ii 6 124
To whom I have been often bound for no less than my life . *Cymbeline* i 4 27
I chiefly, That set thee on to this desert, am bound To load thy merit richly . . . . i 5 73
Whilst I am bound to wonder, I am bound To pity too . . . . i 6 81
You are most bound to the king, Who lets go by no vantages that may Prefer you to his daughter . . . . ii 3 49
She should that duty leave unpaid to you, Which daily she was bound to proffer . . . . iii 5 49
Well or ill, I am bound to you.—And shalt be ever . . . . . iv 2 46
I dare be bound he's true and shall perform All parts of his subjection iv 3 18
For if a king bid a man be a villain, he's bound by the indenture of his oath to be one . . . . *Pericles* i 3 9
A man whom I am bound to.—If he govern the country, you are bound to him indeed . . . . iv 6 58
And to the world and awkward casualties Bound me in servitude . . v 1 95
Whereto being bound, The interim, pray you, all confound . . . v 2 278
Bound humbleness. I come to tender it and my appliance With all bound humbleness . . . . *All's Well* ii 1 117
Bound in charity. How much, methinks, I could despise this man, But that I am bound in charity against it! . . . . . *Hen. VIII.* iii 2 298
Bound in honour. She is bound in honour still to do . . *K. John* ii 1 522
Bound servants, steal! Large-handed robbers your grave masters are, And pill by law . . . . *T. of Athens* iv 1 10
Bounded. How are we park'd and bounded in a pale! . *1 Hen. VI.* iv 2 45
The bounded waters Should lift their bosoms higher than the shores *Troi. and Cres.* i 3 111
O God, I could be bounded in a nut-shell and count myself a king of infinite space, were it not that I have bad dreams . . *Hamlet* ii 2 260
Bounden. I rest much bounden to you . . . . *As Y. Like It* i 2 298
I am much bounden to your majesty . . . . . . *K. John* iii 3 29
Boundeth. Grief boundeth where it falls, Not with the empty hollowness, but weight . . . . *Richard II.* i 2 58
Bounding. Speak terms of manage to thy bounding steed . *1 Hen. IV.* ii 3 52
Bounding between the two moist elements, Like Perseus' horse *Troi. and Cres.* i 3 41
Boundless. A callat Of boundless tongue, who late hath beat her husband! *W. Tale* ii 3 91
Beyond the infinite and boundless reach Of mercy . . . *K. John* iv 3 117

Boundless. The desire is boundless and the act a slave to limit
Troi. and Cres. iii 2 89
My bounty is as boundless as the sea, My love as deep . *Rom. and Jul.* ii 2 133
There is boundless theft In limited professions . . *T. of Athens* iv 3 430
Boundless intemperance In nature is a tyranny . *Macbeth* iv 3 66
Be my helps . . . To compass such a boundless happiness ! . *Pericles* i 1 24
Bounteous. Ceres, most bounteous lady . . . . . *Tempest* iv 1 60
How does my bounteous sister? . . . . . . iv 1 103
Most bounteous sir, Look, if it please you, on this man . *Meas. for Meas.* v 1 448
A debt Which with a bounteous hand was kindly lent . *Richard III.* ii 2 93
That churchman bears a bounteous mind indeed . . *Hen. VIII.* i 3 55
Call him bounteous Buckingham, The mirror of all courtesy . . ii 1 52
Ere we depart, we'll share a bounteous time In different pleasures
T. of Athens i 1 263
Doors, that were ne'er acquainted with their wards Many a bounteous year . . . . iii 3 39
More counsel with more money, bounteous Timon . . . iv 3 167
The bounteous housewife, nature, on each bush Lays her full mess . iv 3 423
According to the gift which bounteous nature Hath in him closed *Macb.* iii 1 98
You yourself Have of your audience been most free and bounteous *Hamlet* i 3 93
But to be free and bounteous to her mind . . . *Othello* i 3 266
I greet thy love, Not with vain thanks, but with acceptance bounteous iii 3 470
Let's to-night Be bounteous at our meal . . . . *Ant. and Cleo.* iv 2 10
Well-sailing ships and bounteous winds have brought This king *Pericles* iv 4 17
Bounteously. I'll pay thee bounteously, Conceal me what I am *T. Night* i 2 52
Bounties. Have not alone Employ'd you . . . , But pared my present havings, to bestow My bounties upon you . . *Hen. VIII.* iii 2 160
As Hector's leisure and your bounties shall Concur together *Tr. and Cr.* iv 5 273
Hail to thee, worthy Timon, and to all That of his bounties taste !
T. of Athens i 2 129
I never tasted Timon in my life, Nor came any of his bounties over me iii 2 85
If that ever my low fortune's better, I'll pay your bounties . *Pericles* ii 1 149
Bountiful Fortune, Now my dear lady, hath mine enemies Brought to this shore . . . . *Tempest* i 2 178
Her benefits are mightily misplaced, and the bountiful blind woman doth most mistake in her gifts to women . . *As Y. Like It* i 2 38
That's a bountiful answer that fits all questions . . *All's Well* ii 2 15
Wondrous affable and as bountiful As mines of India . 1 *Hen. IV.* iii 1 168
I will counterfeit the bewitchment of some popular man and give it bountiful to the desires . . . . . *Coriolanus* ii 3 109
Thy very bountiful good lord and master . . *T. of Athens* iii 1 10
Thy lord's a bountiful gentleman : but thou art wise . . iii 1 42
Bountifully. Commend me bountifully to his good lordship . . iii 2 58
Bounty. She is a region in Guiana, all gold and bounty *Mer. Wives.* i 3 77
To testify your bounty, I thank you, you have testerned me *T. G. of Ver.* i 1 152
The gentleman Is full of virtue, bounty, worth and qualities . . iii 1 65
Prouder of the work Than customary bounty can enforce you *M. of Ven.* iii 4 9
Who had even tuned his bounty to sing happiness to him . *All's Well* iv 3 12
It may awake my bounty further . . . . *T. Night* v 1 47
Marry, sir, lullaby to your bounty till I come again . . v 1 48
Let your bounty take a nap, I will awake it anon . . . v 1 51
Derive a liberty From heartiness, from bounty . . *W. Tale* i 2 113
If your lass Interpretation should abuse and call this Your lack of love or bounty, you were straited For a reply . . . . . iv 4 365
Which, till my infant fortune comes to years, Stands for my bounty
Richard II. ii 3 67
I thank thee, king, For thy great bounty . . . . iv 1 300
To you This honourable bounty shall belong . . 1 *Hen. IV.* v 5 26
No less for bounty bound to us Than Cambridge is . *Hen. V.* ii 2 92
May Iden live to merit such a bounty ! . . . 2 *Hen. VI.* v 1 81
Your discipline in war, wisdom in peace, Your bounty *Richard III.* iii 7 17
As my hand has open'd bounty to you, My heart dropp'd love *Hen. VIII.* iii 2 184
Yet gives he not till judgement guide his bounty . *Troi. and Cres.* iv 5 102
My bounty is as boundless as the sea, My love as deep . *Rom. and Jul.* ii 2 133
See, Magic of bounty ! all these spirits thy power Hath conjured
T. of Athens i 1 6
Come, shall we in, And taste Lord Timon's bounty? . . . i 1 285
'Tis pity bounty had not eyes behind . . . . . i 2 169
O, he's the very soul of bounty ! . . . . . . i 2 215
Heavens, have I said, the bounty of this lord ! . . . ii 2 173
Sermon me no further : No villanous bounty yet hath pass'd my heart . ii 2 182
That thought is bounty's foe ; Being free itself, it thinks all others so . ii 2 241
For bounty, that makes gods, does still mar men . . . iv 2 41
Having often of your open bounty tasted . . . . . v 1 61
The king-becoming graces, As justice, verity, temperance, stableness, Bounty, perseverance, mercy . . . . . *Macbeth* iv 3 93
The less they deserve, the more merit is in your bounty . . *Hamlet* ii 2 558
Which of you shall we say doth love us most? That we our largest bounty may extend . . . . *Lear* i 1 53
The bounty and the benison of heaven To boot, and boot ! . . iv 6 229
Antony Hath after thee sent all thy treasure, with His bounty *A. and C.* iv 6 22
Thou mine of bounty, how wouldst thou have paid My better service ! . iv 6 32
Do not abuse my master's bounty by The undoing of yourself . v 2 43
For his bounty, There was no winter in't . . . . . v 2 86
Heaven's bounty towards him might Be used more thankfully *Cymbeline* i 6 78
Ask of Cymbeline what boon thou wilt, Fitting my bounty . . v 5 98
Pupils lacks she none of noble race, Who pour their bounty on her
Pericles v Gower 10
Fair one, all goodness that consists in bounty Expect even here . v 1 70
Bourbier. Et la truie lavée au bourbier . . . . *Hen. V.* iii 7 69
Bourbon. You Dukes of Orleans, Bourbon, and of Berri . . iii 5 41
He that will not follow Bourbon now, Let him go hence . . iv 5 12
John Duke of Bourbon, and Lord Bouciqualt . . . . iv 8 82
And thou, Lord Bourbon, our high admiral, Shalt waft them over
3 *Hen. VI.* iii 3 252
Bourdeaux. Herein all breathless lies The mightiest of thy greatest enemies, Richard of Bordeaux . . . . . *Richard II.* v 6 33
There's a whole merchant's venture of Bourdeaux stuff in him 2 *Hen. IV.* ii 4 69
Go to the gates of Bourdeaux, trumpeter . . 1 *Hen. VI.* iv 2 1
Give it out That he is march'd to Bourdeaux with his power . . iv 3 4
Which join'd with him and made their march for Bourdeaux . . iv 3 8
To Bourdeaux, warlike duke ! to Bourdeaux, York ! . . . iv 3 22
France hath flaw'd the league, and hath attach'd Our merchants' goods at Bourdeaux . . . . *Hen. VIII.* i 1 96
Bourn. Contract, succession, Bourn, bound of land, tilth *Tempest* ii 1 152
By one that fixes No bourn 'twixt his and mine . . *W. Tale* i 2 134
I will not praise thy wisdom, Which, like a bourn, a pale, a shore, confines Thy spacious and dilated parts . . . *Troi. and Cres.* ii 3 260
The undiscover'd country from whose bourn No traveller returns *Hamlet* iii 1 79
Come o'er the bourn, Bessy to me . . . . . . *Lear* iii 6 27

Bourn. From the dread summit of this chalky bourn . . *Lear* iv 6 57
I'll set a bourn how far to be beloved . . . *Ant. and Cleo.* i 1 16
To take your imagination, From bourn to bourn, region to region *Pericles* iv 4 4
Bout. The gentleman will, for his honour's sake, have one bout with you
T. Night iii 4 337
I'll have a bout with thee ; Devil or devil's dam . . 1 *Hen. VI.* i 5 4
Damsel, I'll have a bout with you again . . . . . . iii 2 56
Welcome, gentlemen ! ladies that have their toes Unplagued with corns will have a bout with you . . . . . *Rom. and Jul.* i 5 19
When in your motion you are hot and dry—As make your bouts more violent to that end . . . . *Hamlet* iv 7 159
Give him the cup.—I'll play this bout first . . . . v 2 295
Bow. The fair soul herself Weigh'd between loathness and obedience, at Which end o' the beam should bow . . . . *Tempest* ii 1 131
With each end of thy blue bow dost crown My bosky acres . . iv 1 80
Tell me, heavenly bow, If Venus or her son, as thou dost know, Do now attend the queen? . . . . iv 1 86
But come, the bow : now mercy goes to kill . . . *L. L. Lost* iv 1 24
She that bears the bow. Finely put off ! . . . . . iv 1 111
Wide o' the bow hand ! i' faith, your hand is out . . . iv 1 135
At the first opening of the gorgeous east, Bows not his vassal head . iv 3 224
The moon, like to a silver bow, New-bent in heaven . *M. N. Dream* i 1 9
I swear to thee, by Cupid's strongest bow, By his best arrow . . . i 1 169
Loosed his love-shaft smartly from his bow . . . . . ii 1 159
Look how I go, Swifter than arrow from the Tartar's bow . . iii 2 101
Then music is Even as the flourish when true subjects bow To a new-crowned monarch . . . . . . *Mer. of Venice* iii 2 49
As the ox hath his bow, sir, the horse his curb *As Y. Like It* iii 3 80
He hath ta'en his bow and arrows and is gone forth to sleep . . iv 3 4
Am I your bird? I mean to shift my bush ; And then pursue me as you draw your bow . . . . *T. of Shrew* v 2 47
Courteous feathers, which bow the head and nod at every man *All's Well* iv 5 112
And yet, to crush this a little, it would bow to me . . *T. Night* ii 5 153
Here is my throne, bid kings come bow to it . . *K. John* iii 1 74
Thy very beadsmen learn to bend their bows Of double-fatal yew against thy state . . . . *Richard II.* iii 2 116
I hardly yet have learn'd To insinuate, flatter, bow, and bend my limbs iv 1 165
A' drew a good bow ; and dead ! a' shot a fine shoot 2 *Hen. IV.* iii 2 48
And God forbid, my dear and faithful lord, That you should fashion, wrest, or bow your reading . . . . *Hen. V.* i 2 14
Which in weight to re-answer, his pettiness would bow under . iii 6 137
But, if I bow, they'll say it was for fear . . . 1 *Hen. VI.* iv 5 29
Rather let my head Stoop to the block than these knees bow to any
2 *Hen. VI.* iv 1 125
First let me ask of these, If they can brook I bow a knee to man . v 1 110
Why, Warwick, hath thy knee forgot to bow? . . . . v 1 161
In duty bend thy knee to me That bows unto the grave with mickle age v 1 174
A crown for York ! and, lords, bow low to him . . 3 *Hen. VI.* i 4 94
I am his king, and he should bow his knee . . . . . ii 2 87
If not, that, I being queen, you bow like subjects . . *Richard III.* i 3 161
The mountain tops that freeze, Bow themselves when he did sing
Hen. VIII. iii 1 5
My legs, like loaden branches, bow to the earth . . . . iv 2 2
Limbs are his instruments, In no less working than are swords and bows Directive by the limbs . . . . . *Troi. and Cres.* i 3 355
For, O, love's bow Shoots buck and doe . . . . . iii 1 126
O noble fellow ! Who sensibly outdares his senseless sword, And, when it bows, stands up . . . . *Coriolanus* i 4 54
My mother bows ; As if Olympus to a molehill should In supplication nod v 3 29
O, here I lift this one hand up to heaven, And bow this feeble ruin to the earth : If any power pities wretched tears, To that I call !
T. Andron. iii 1 208
From love's weak childish bow she lives unharm'd . *Rom. and Jul.* i 1 217
We'll have no Cupid hoodwink'd with a scarf, Bearing a Tartar's painted bow of lath . . . . i 4 5
Such a case as yours constrains a man to bow in the hams . . ii 4 57
By all the gods that Romans bow before, I here discard my sickness !
J. Cæsar ii 1 320
My thoughts and wishes bend again toward France And bow them to your gracious leave and pardon . . . . . *Hamlet* i 2 56
Help, angels ! Make assay ! Bow, stubborn knees ! . . . iii 3 70
Reverted to my bow again, And not where I had aim'd them . . iv 7 23
The bow is bent and drawn, make from the shaft . . *Lear* i 1 145
Think'st thou that duty shall have dread to speak, When power to flattery bows? . . . . i 1 150
How light and portable my pain seems now, When that which makes me bend makes the king bow ! . . . . iii 6 116
That fellow handles his bow like a crow-keeper : draw me a clothier's yard . . . . iv 6 88
Before the gods my knee shall bow my prayers To them for you *A. and C.* ii 3 3
The flame o' the taper Bows towards her, and would under-peep her lids
Cymbeline ii 2 20
This gate Instructs you how to adore the heavens and bows you To a morning's holy office . . . . iii 3 3
Train'd up thus meanly I' the cave wherein they bow . . . iii 3 83
Bow your knees. Arise my knights o' the battle . . . . v 5 19
Do it, and happy ; by my silver bow ! . . . . *Pericles* v 1 249
Bow-boy. The very pin of his heart cleft with the blind bow-boy's butt-shaft . . . . *Rom. and Jul.* ii 4 16
Bow-case. You tailor's-yard, you sheath, you bow-case . 1 *Hen. IV.* ii 4 273
Bowed. O'er his wave-worn basis bow'd, As stooping to relieve him
Tempest ii 1 120
Those thoughts to me were oaks, to thee like osiers bow'd . *L. L. Lost* iv 2 112
She mistook her frets, And bow'd her hand to teach her fingering
T. of Shrew ii 1 151
And bow'd his eminent top to their low ranks . . . *All's Well* i 2 43
She did approach My cabin where I lay ; thrice bow'd before me *W. Tale* iii 3 24
Where I first bow'd my knee Unto this king of smiles . 1 *Hen. IV.* i 3 245
I had no such intent, But that necessity so bow'd the state 2 *Hen. IV.* iii 1 73
A three-pence bow'd would hire me, Old as I am, to queen it *Hen. VIII.* ii 3 36
Then rose again and bow'd her to the people . . . . iv 1 85
My arm'd knees, Who bow'd but in my stirrup, bend like his That hath received an alms ! . . . . *Coriolanus* iii 2 119
To this end, He bow'd his nature, never known before But to be rough, unswayable and free . . . . v 6 25
All this uttered With gentle breath, calm look, knees humbly bow'd
Rom. and Jul. iii 1 161
Fawn'd like hounds, And bow'd like bondmen . . . *J. Cæsar* v 1 42
Whose heavy hand hath bow'd you to the grave . . . *Macbeth* iii 1 90
A young foolish sapling, and must be bowed . . . . *Pericles* iv 2 94

Bowels. Thine own bowels, which do call thee sire, The mere effusion of thy proper loins, Do curse the gout — *Meas. for Meas.* iii 1 29
The cannons have their bowels full of wrath — *K. John* ii 1 210
A resolved villain, Whose bowels suddenly burst out — v 6 30
So hot a summer in my bosom, That all my bowels crumble up to dust — v 7 31
Great pity, so it was, This villanous salt-petre should be digg'd Out of the bowels of the harmless earth — *1 Hen. IV.* i 3 61
God keep lead out of me! I need no more weight than mine own bowels — v 3 36
I do retort the 'solus' in thy bowels — *Hen. V.* ii 1 54
And bids you, in the bowels of the Lord, Deliver up the crown — ii 4 102
Cried out amain And rush'd into the bowels of the battle — *1 Hen. VI.* i 1 129
A viperous worm That gnaws the bowels of the commonwealth — iii 1 73
Rushing in the bowels of the French, He left me proudly, as unworthy fight — iv 7 42
Unrip'dst the bowels of thy sovereign's son — *Richard III.* i 4 212
Ready, with every nod, to tumble down Into the fatal bowels of the deep — iii 4 103
Thus far into the bowels of the land Have we march'd on — v 2 3
And tell what thou art by inches, thou thing of no bowels — *Troi. and Cres.* ii 1 54
There is no lady of more softer bowels, More spongy to suck in the sense of fear — ii 2 11
Pouring war Into the bowels of ungrateful Rome — *Coriolanus* iv 5 136
The husband and the father tearing His country's bowels out — v 3 103
Wave by wave, Expecting ever when some envious surge Will in his brinish bowels swallow him — *T. Andron.* iii 1 97
My bowels cannot hide her woes, But like a drunkard must I vomit them — iii 1 231
Sooner this sword shall plough thy bowels up — iv 2 87
With this good sword, That ran through Cæsar's bowels — *J. Cæsar* v 3 42

Bower. Bid her steal into the pleached bower — *Much Ado* iii 1 7
Come, wait upon him; lead him to my bower — *M. N. Dream* iii 1 202
Near to her close and consecrated bower — iii 2 7
Her fairy sent To bear him to my bower in fairy land — iv 1 66
Love-thoughts lie rich when canopied with bowers — *T. Night* i 1 41
Ditties highly penn'd, Sung by a fair queen in a summer's bower — *1 Hen. IV.* iii 1 210
I know thou hadst rather Follow thine enemy in a fiery gulf Than flatter him in a bower — *Coriolanus* iii 2 92
O nature, what hadst thou to do in hell, When thou didst bower the spirit of a fiend In mortal paradise of such sweet flesh? — *R. and J.* iii 2 81

Bowing. Plants with goodly burthen bowing — *Tempest* iv 1 113
Bowing his head against the steepy mount — *T. of Athens* i 1 75

Bowl. She's too hard for you at pricks, sir: challenge her to bowl — *L. L. L.* iv 1 140
When roasted crabs hiss in the bowl — v 2 935
Sometime lurk I in a gossip's bowl — *M. N. Dream* ii 1 47
Thus the bowl should run, And not unluckily against the bias — *T. of Shrew* iv 5 24
We'll play at bowls.—'Twill make me think the world is full of rubs — *Richard II.* iii 4 3
So, I am satisfied. Give me a bowl of wine — *Richard III.* v 3 72
Your grace is noble: Let me have such a bowl may hold my thanks, And save me so much talking — *Hen. VIII.* i 4 39
Like to a bowl upon a subtle ground, I have tumbled past the throw — *Coriolanus* v 2 20
Peace, you mumbling fool! Utter your gravity o'er a gossip's bowl — *Rom. and Jul.* iii 5 175
Give me a bowl of wine. In this I bury all unkindness — *J. Cæsar* iv 3 158
Bowl the round nave down the hill of heaven, As low as to the fiends! — *Hamlet* ii 2 518
Fill our bowls once more; Let's mock the midnight bell — *Ant. and Cleo.* iii 13 184
What got he by that? You have broke his pate with your bowl — *Cymbeline* ii 1 8
What I have lost to-day at bowls I'll win to-night of him — ii 1 54

Bowled. Set quick i' the earth And bowl'd to death with turnips! — *Mer. Wives* iii 4 91

Bowler. He is a marvellous good neighbour, faith, and a very good bowler — *L. L. Lost* v 2 587

Bowling. If it be not too rough for some that know little but bowling, it will please plentifully — *W. Tale* iv 4 338

Bowsprit. On the topmast, The yards and bowsprit, would I flame distinctly, Then meet and join — *Tempest* i 2 200

Bowstring. He hath twice or thrice cut Cupid's bow-string — *Much Ado* iii 2 11
Enough; hold or cut bow-strings — *M. N. Dream* i 2 114

Bow-wow. Hark, hark! Bow-wow. The watch-dogs bark: Bow-wow — *Tempest* i 2 382

Box. Vetch me in my closet un boitier vert, a box, a green-a box — *Mer. Wives* i 4 47
He wears his honour in a box unseen — *All's Well* ii 3 296
What's i' the fardel? Wherefore that box? — *W. Tale* iv 4 782
Such secrets in this fardel and box, which none must know but the king — iv 4 784
Who keeps the tent now?—The surgeon's box, or the patient's wound — *Troi. and Cres.* v 1 12
Why, thou damnable box of envy, thou, what meanest thou to curse thus? — v 1 29
About his shelves A beggarly account of empty boxes — *Rom. and Jul.* v 1 45
'Faith, nothing but an empty box, sir — *T. of Athens* iii 1 16
The very conveyances of his lands will hardly lie in this box — *Hamlet* v 1 120
Here is a box; I had it from the queen — *Cymbeline* iii 4 191
If That box I gave you was not thought by me A precious thing — v 5 241
Make a fire within: Fetch hither all my boxes in my closet — *Pericles* iii 2 81

Box of the ear. If he took you a box o' the ear, you might have your action of slander too — *Meas. for Meas.* ii 1 189
He borrowed a box of the ear of the Englishman — *Mer. of Venice* i 2 86
For the box of the ear that the prince gave you, he gave it like a rude prince, and you took it like a sensible lord — *2 Hen. IV.* i 2 218
I have sworn to take him a box o' th' ear — *Hen. V.* iv 7 133
May haply purchase him a box o' th' ear — iv 7 181
Give him a box o' the ear and that will make 'em red again — *2 Hen. VI.* iv 7 91

Box on the ear. I will take thee a box on the ear — *Hen. V.* iv 1 231

Box-tree. Get ye all three into the box-tree — *T. Night* ii 5 18

Boy. Then to sea, boys, and let her go hang! — *Tempest* ii 2 56
When we were boys, Who would believe that there were mountaineers Dew-lapp'd like bulls? — iii 3 43
Her and her blind boy's scandal'd company I have forsworn — iv 1 90
Swears he will shoot no more but play with sparrows And be a boy right out — iv 1 101
Not so fair, boy, as well-favoured — *T. G. of Ver.* ii 1 54
Belike, boy, then, you are in love — ii 1 85
Are they not lamely writ?—No, boy, but as well as I can do them — ii 1 98
Sir Thurio frowns on you.—Ay, boy, it's for love — ii 4 4
Run, boy, run, run, and seek him out — iii 1 188
If thou seest my boy, Bid him make haste — iii 1 257
I'll after, to rejoice in the boy's correction — iii 1 395
The other squirrel was stolen from me by the hangman boys — iv 4 60
Look to the boy.—Why, boy! why, wag! how now! — v 4 85
Where is that ring, boy?—Here 'tis; this is it — v 4 91

Boy. I think the boy hath grace in him; he blushes.—I warrant you, my lord, more grace than boy — *T. G. of Ver.* v 4 165
I keep but three men and a boy yet, till my mother be dead — *Mer. Wives* i 1 285
As many devils entertain; and 'To her, boy,' say I — i 3 62
Here, boys, here, here! shall we wag? — ii 1 238
The boy never need to understand any thing — ii 2 132
Boy, go along with this woman — ii 2 139
Thou art a Castalion-King-Urinal. Hector of Greece, my boy! — ii 3 35
You are a flattering boy: now I see you'll be a courtier — iii 2 7
This boy will carry a letter twenty mile, as easy as a cannon will shoot point-blank twelve score — iii 2 32
Now she's going to my wife, and Falstaff's boy with her — iii 2 37
Thou 'rt a good boy: this secrecy of thine shall be a tailor to thee — iii 3 33
Help to cover your master, boy — iii 3 151
O boy, thou hadst a father!—I had a father, Mistress Anne — iii 4 36
Master Slender is let the boys leave to play.—Blessing of his heart! — iv 1 11
Get you home, boy. Come, we stay too long — iv 1 87
And she's a great lubberly boy — v 5 195
Would I might never stir!—and 'tis a postmaster's boy — v 5 199
I think so, when I took a boy for a girl — v 5 203
And yet it was not Anne, but a postmaster's boy — v 5 212
By gar, I am cozened: I ha' married un garçon, a boy; un paysan, by gar, a boy — v 5 218
Ay, by gar, and 'tis a boy: by gar, I'll raise all Windsor — v 5 222
My wife, not meanly proud of two such boys — *Com. of Errors* i 1 59
My youngest boy, and yet my eldest care — i 1 125
By my troth, your town is troubled with unruly boys — iii 1 62
'Twas the boy that stole your meat, and you'll beat the post — *Much Ado* ii 1 206
Boy!—Signor?—In my chamber-window lies a book — ii 3 1
If thou kill'st me, boy, thou shalt kill a man — v 1 79
Come, follow me, boy; come, sir boy, come, follow me: Sir boy, I'll whip you — v 1 83
Boys, apes, braggarts, Jacks, milksops! — v 1 91
Scambling, out-facing, fashion-monging boys, That lie and cog and flout — v 1 94
Fare you well, boy: you know my mind — v 1 187
Boy, what sign is it when a man of great spirit grows melancholy? — *L. L. Lost* i 2 1
Comfort me, boy: what great men have been in love? — i 2 68
More authority, dear boy, name more — i 2 71
Is there not a ballad, boy, of the King and the Beggar? — i 2 114
Boy, I do love that country girl — i 2 122
Sing, boy; my spirit grows heavy in love — i 2 127
His disgrace is to be called boy; but his glory is to subdue men — i 2 186
Learn her by heart.—By heart and in heart, boy — iii 1 37
The boy hath sold him a bargain, a goose, that's flat — iii 1 102
Then the boy's fat l'envoy, the goose that you bought — iii 1 110
A domineering pedant o'er the boy — iii 1 179
This wimpled, whining, purblind, wayward boy — iii 1 181
That was a man when King Pepin of France was a little boy — iv 1 123
And Nestor play at push-pin with the boys — iv 3 169
He teaches boys the horn-book — v 1 49
He hath been five thousand years a boy — v 2 11
The boy replied, 'An angel is not evil' — v 2 105
The pedant, the braggart, the hedge-priest, the fool and the boy — v 2 546
As waggish boys in game themselves forswear, So the boy Love is perjured every where — *M. N. Dream* i 1 241
She as her attendant hath A lovely boy, stolen from an Indian king — ii 1 22
She perforce withholds the loved boy, Crowns him with flowers — ii 1 26
I do but beg a little changeling boy, To be my henchman — ii 1 120
But she, being mortal, of that boy did die; And for her sake do I rear up her boy — ii 1 135
Give me that boy, and I will go with thee.—Not for thy fairy kingdom — ii 1 143
I'll to my queen and beg her Indian boy — iii 2 375
Now I have the boy, I will undo This hateful imperfection of her eyes — iv 1 67
The boy was the very staff of my age, my very prop — *Mer. of Venice* ii 2 69
Is my boy, God rest his soul, alive or dead? — ii 2 74
Pray you, sir, stand up: I am sure you are not Launcelot, my boy — ii 2 87
Your boy that was, your son that is, your child that shall be — ii 2 90
Here's my son, sir, a poor boy,— Not a poor boy, sir, but the rich Jew's man — ii 2 129
Cupid himself would blush To see me thus transformed to a boy — ii 6 39
So are you, sweet, Even in the lovely garnish of a boy — ii 6 45
All the boys in Venice follow him, Crying, his stones, his daughter — ii 8 23
We'll play with them the first boy for a thousand ducats — iii 2 216
Speak between the change of man and boy With a reed voice — iii 4 66
A kind of boy, a little scrubbed boy, No higher than thyself — v 1 162
A prating boy, that begg'd it as a fee: I could not for my heart deny it him — v 1 164
The boy, his clerk, That took some pains in writing, he begg'd mine — v 1 181
That same scrubbed boy, the doctor's clerk — v 1 261
Nothing remains but that I kindle the boy thither — *As Y. Like It* i 1 179
Boys and women are for the most part cattle of this colour — iii 2 434
'Tis but a peevish boy; yet he talks well; But what care I for words? — iii 5 110
That blind rascally boy that abuses every one's eyes because his own are out — iv 1 218
The boy is fair, Of female favour, and bestows himself Like a ripe sister — iv 3 86
Dost thou believe, Orlando, that the boy Can do all this? — v 4 1
I do remember in this shepherd boy Some lively touches of my daughter's favour — v 4 26
This boy is forest-born, And hath been tutor'd in the rudiments Of many desperate studies by his uncle — v 4 30
I'll not budge an inch, boy: let him come — *T. of Shrew* Ind. 1 14
Saw'st thou not, boy, how Silver made it good At the hedge-corner? — Ind. 1 19
If the boy have not a woman's gift To rain a shower of commanded tears, An onion will do well — Ind. 1 124
The boy will well usurp the grace, Voice, gait and action of a gentlewoman — Ind. 1 131
Would I were so too!—So could I, faith, boy — i 1 244
Tush, tush! fear boys with bugs — i 2 211
An old Italian fox is not so kind, my boy — ii 1 405
The news.—Why, 'Jack, boy! ho! boy!' and as much news as will thaw — iv 1 43
Here comes your boy; 'Twere good he were school'd — iv 4 8
My boy shall fetch the scrivener presently — iv 4 59
An thy mind stand to't, boy, steal away bravely — *All's Well* ii 1 29
I'ld give bay Curtal and his furniture, My mouth no more were broken than these boys', And writ as little beard — ii 3 66
These boys are boys of ice, they'll none have her — ii 3 99
Here, take her hand, Proud scornful boy, unworthy this good gift — ii 3 158
To the wars, my boy, to the wars! — ii 3 295

Boy. This is not well, rash and unbridled boy . . . *All's Well* iii 2 30
She deserves a lord That twenty such rude boys might tend upon . iii 2 84
A foolish idle boy, but for all that very ruttish . . . iv 3 242
A dangerous and lascivious boy . . . . . . iv 3 248
Men are to mell with, boys are not to kiss . . . iv 3 257
That lascivious young boy the count . . . . iv 3 334
Not yet old enough for a man, nor young enough for a boy *T. Night* i 5 166
'Tis with him in standing water, between boy and man . . i 5 168
Come hither, boy: if ever thou shalt love, In the sweet pangs of it remember me . . . . ii 4 15
Thine eye Hath stay'd upon some favour that it loves: Hath it not, boy? . . . . ii 4 26
For, boy, however we do praise ourselves, Our fancies are more giddy . ii 4 33
But died thy sister of her love, my boy? . . . . . ii 4 122
Did she see thee the while, old boy? tell me that . . . iii 2 9
A very dishonest paltry boy, and more a coward than a hare . . iii 4 420
That most ingrateful boy there by your side, From the rude sea's enraged and foamy mouth Did I redeem . . . . . v 1 80
Come, boy, with me; my thoughts are ripe in mischief . . . v 1 132
When that I was and a little tiny boy, With hey, ho . . . v 1 398
I'll question you Of my lord's tricks and yours when you were boys *W. Tale* i 2 61
But such a day to-morrow as to-day, And to be boy eternal . . i 2 65
Art thou my boy?—Ay, my good lord.—I' fecks! Why, that's my bawcock . . . . i 2 120
Yet were it true To say this boy were like me . . . . i 2 135
Looking on the lines Of my boy's face, methoughts I did recoil Twenty-three years, and saw myself unbreech'd . . . . . i 2 154
Go, play, boy, play: thy mother plays, and I Play too . . . i 2 187
How now, boy!—I am like you, they say.—Why, that's some comfort . i 2 207
Take the boy to you: he so troubles me, 'Tis past enduring . . ii 1 1
Give me the boy: I am glad you did not nurse him . . . ii 1 56
Bear the boy hence; he shall not come about her; Away with him! . ii 1 59
A boy?—A daughter, and a goodly babe, Lusty and like to live . . ii 2 26
How does the boy?—He took good rest to-night . . . . ii 3 9
Fancies too weak for boys, too green and idle For girls of nine . iii 2 182
A very pretty barne! A boy or a child, I wonder? A pretty one . iii 3 71
I have seen two such sights, by sea and by land! . . .—Why, boy, how is it? . . . . iii 3 88
Name of mercy, when was this, boy?—Now, now: I have not winked since . . . . iii 3 105
Heavy matters! but look thee here, boy. Now bless thyself . . iii 3 116
Take up, take up, boy; open't. So, let's see . . . . iii 3 120
This is fairy gold, boy, and 'twill prove so: up with't, keep it close . iii 3 127
We are lucky, boy; and to be so still requires nothing but secrecy . iii 3 129
Come, good boy, the next way home.—Go you the next way with your findings . . . . iii 3 131
'Tis a lucky day, boy, and we'll do good deeds on't . . . iii 3 142
For thee, fond boy, If I may ever know thou dost but sigh That thou no more shalt see this knack, as never I mean thou shalt, we'll bar thee from succession . . . . iv 4 437
Come, boy; I am past moe children . . . . . . v 2 137
And so have I, boy.—So you have . . . . . . v 2 149
Sir Robert's son! Ay, thou unreverend boy . . . *K. John* i 1 227
A noble boy! Who would not do thee right? . . . . . ii 1 18
Till then, fair boy, Will I not think of home, but follow arms . . ii 1 30
We'll lay before this town our royal bones, Wade to the market-place in Frenchmen's blood, But we will make it subject to this boy . . ii 1 43
That judge hath made me guardian to this boy . . . . ii 1 115
This boy Liker in feature to his father Geffrey Than thou and John in manners; being as like As rain to water . . . . . ii 1 125
My boy a bastard! By my soul, I think His father never was so true begot . . . . ii 1 129
There's a good mother, boy, that blots thy father.—There's a good grandam, boy, that would blot thee . . . . . . ii 1 132
Submit thee, boy.—Come to thy grandam, child . . . . ii 1 159
His mother shames him so, poor boy, he weeps . . . . ii 1 166
Usurp The dominations, royalties and rights Of this oppressed boy . ii 1 177
Yon green boy shall have no sun to ripe The bloom that promiseth a mighty fruit . . . . ii 1 472
What say'st thou, boy? look in the lady's face . . . . ii 1 495
Lewis marry Blanch! O boy, then where art thou? . . . iii 1 34
At thy birth, dear boy, Nature and Fortune join'd to make thee great . iii 1 51
Hubert, keep this boy. Philip, make up . . . . . iii 2 5
Hubert, throw thine eye On yon young boy . . . . . iii 3 60
If that be true, I shall see my boy again . . . . . iii 4 78
My boy, my Arthur, my fair son! My life, my joy, my food, my all the world! . . . . iii 4 103
Rush forth, And bind the boy which you shall find with me Fast to the chair . . . . iv 1 4
Young boy, I must.—And will you?—And I will.—Have you the heart? iv 1 40
Boy, prepare yourself.—Is there no remedy?—None, but to lose your eyes . . . . iv 1 90
The instrument is cold And would not harm me.—I can heat it, boy . iv 1 105
Yet am I sworn and I did purpose, boy . . . . . iv 1 124
Shall a beardless boy, A cocker'd silken wanton, brave our fields? . v 1 69
Have you forgot the Duke of Hereford, boy? . . . *Richard II.* ii 3 36
Foolish boy, the king is left behind, And in my loyal bosom lies his power . . . . ii 3 97
Boys, with women's voices, Strive to speak big . . . . iii 2 113
Dishonourable boy! That lie shall lie so heavy on my sword . . iv 1 65
Boy, let me see the writing.—I do beseech you, pardon me; I may not show it . . . . v 2 69
Strike him, Aumerle. Poor boy, thou art amazed . . . . v 2 85
Young wanton and effeminate boy . . . . v 3 10
Bid me joy, By pardoning Rutland, my transgressing boy . . . v 3 96
The boy shall lead our horses down the hill . . . *1 Hen. IV.* ii 2 82
A Corinthian, a lad of mettle, a good boy, by the Lord, so they call me ii 4 13
Gallants, lads, boys, hearts of gold, all the titles of good fellowship . ii 4 307
Swearest thou, ungracious boy? henceforth ne'er look on me . . ii 4 490
Laugh at gibing boys and stand the push Of every beardless vain comparative . . . . iii 2 66
I have inquired, so has my husband, man by man, boy by boy . . iii 3 65
O, this boy Lends mettle to us all! . . . . . . v 4 23
I have two boys Seek Percy and thyself about the field . . . v 4 31
Boy, tell him I am deaf.—You must speak louder; my master is deaf *2 Hen. IV.* i 2 77
Boy!—Sir?—What money is in my purse?—Seven groats and two pence i 2 260
And the boy that I gave Falstaff: a' had him from me Christian . ii 2 75
Has not the boy profited? . . . . ii 2 90

Boy. Althæa's dream, away!—Instruct us, boy; what dream, boy? *2 Hen. IV.* ii 2 95
A crown's worth of good interpretation: there 'tis, boy . . . . ii 2 100
Sirrah, you boy, and Bardolph, no word to your master that I am yet come to town . . . . ii 2 176
Rides the wild-mare with the boys, and jumps upon joined-stools . ii 4 268
I love thee better than I love e'er a scurvy young boy of them all . ii 4 296
No abuse, Hal: none, Ned, none: no, faith, boys, none . . ii 4 351
Is thine hostess here of the wicked? or is thy boy of the wicked? . ii 4 356
For the boy, there is a good angel about him; but the devil outbids him too . . . . ii 4 362
Then was Jack Falstaff, now Sir John, a boy, and page to Thomas Mowbray . . . . iii 2 28
Our watch-word was 'Hem boys!' . . . . iii 2 232
Bloody youth, guarded with rags, And countenanced by boys and beggary . . . . iv 1 35
This same young sober-blooded boy doth not love me . . . iv 3 94
There's never none of these demure boys come to any proof . . iv 3 97
Cherish it, my boy, And noble offices thou mayst effect . . . iv 4 23
Rouse thy vaunting veins: Boy, bristle thy courage up . . *Hen. V.* ii 3 5
Let us to France; like horse-leeches, my boys . . . . . ii 3 57
I am boy to them all three: but all they three, though they would serve me, could not be man to me . . . . iii 2 30
Come hither, boy: ask me this slave in French What is his name . iv 4 24
Expound unto me, boy . . . . iv 4 62
There is none to guard it but boys . . . . iv 4 82
'Tis certain there's not a boy left alive . . . . . iv 7 5
The English beach Pales in the flood with men, with wives and boys v Prol. 10
Compound a boy, half French, half English, that shall go to Constantinople . . . . v 2 221
Promise, Kate, you will endeavour for your French part of such a boy . v 2 228
I scorn thee and thy fashion, peevish boy . . . . *1 Hen. VI.* ii 4 76
Dear boy, mount on my swiftest horse; And I'll direct thee how thou shalt escape . . . . iv 5 9
The ireful bastard Orleans, that drew blood From thee, my boy . . iv 6 17
That pure blood of mine Which thou didst force from Talbot, my brave boy . . . . iv 6 24
How dost thou fare? Wilt thou yet leave the battle, boy, and fly? . iv 6 28
Like me to the peasant boys of France, To be shame's scorn! . . iv 6 48
And in that sea of blood my boy did drench His over-mounting spirit . iv 7 14
Poor boy! he smiles, methinks, as who should say, Had death been French, then death had died to-day . . . . iv 7 27
We took him setting of boys' copies . . . . *2 Hen. VI.* iv 2 95
Henry the Fifth, in whose time boys went to span-counter for French crowns . . . . iv 2 165
The bastard boys of York Shall be the surety for their traitor father . v 1 115
Bane to those That for my surety will refuse the boys! . . . v 1 121
The crown of England, father, which is yours.—Mine, boy? . *3 Hen. VI.* i 2 10
Let me live.—In vain thou speak'st, poor boy . . . . . i 3 21
Dicky your boy, that with his grumbling voice Was wont to cheer his dad in mutinies . . . . i 4 76
I stain'd this napkin with the blood That valiant Clifford, with his rapier's point, Made issue from the bosom of the boy . . . . i 4 81
Were it not pity that this goodly boy Should lose his birthright by his father's fault? . . . . ii 2 34
Go, rate thy minions, proud insulting boy! . . . . . ii 2 84
Ah, boy, if any life be left in thee, Throw up thine eye! . . . ii 5 84
O boy, thy father gave thee life too soon, And hath bereft thee of thy life too late! . . . . ii 5 92
My heart, sweet boy, shall be thy sepulchre . . . . . ii 5 115
Peace, wilful boy, or I will charm your tongue . . . . v 5 31
Speak to thy mother, boy! Canst thou not speak? . . . . v 5 51
I, Dædalus; my poor boy, Icarus; Thy father, Minos . . . v 6 21
The sun that sear'd the wings of my sweet boy . . . . v 6 23
Come hither, Bess, and let me kiss my boy . . . . . v 7 15
Tell me, good grandam, is our father dead?—No, boy . *Richard III.* ii 2 2
Think you my uncle did dissemble, grandam?—Ay, boy . . . ii 2 32
A parlous boy: go to, you are too shrewd . . . . . ii 4 35
Come, come, my boy; we will to sanctuary . . . . . ii 4 66
O, 'tis a parlous boy; Bold, quick, ingenious, forward, capable . iii 1 154
I will converse with iron-witted fools And unrespective boys . . iv 2 29
The boy is foolish, and I fear not him . . . . . . iv 2 56
Henry the Sixth Did prophesy that Richmond should be king, When Richmond was a little peevish boy . . . . iv 2 100
But that still use of grief makes wild grief tame, My tongue should to thy ears not name my boys . . . . iv 4 230
If your back Cannot vouchsafe this burthen, 'tis too weak Ever to get a boy.—How you do talk! . . . . . . *Hen. VIII.* ii 3 44
I have ventured, Like little wanton boys that swim on bladders . iii 2 359
It's one o'clock, boy, is't not?—It hath struck . . . . v 1 1
Is the queen deliver'd? Say, ay; and of a boy.—Ay, ay, my liege; And of a lovely boy . . . . v 1 163
'Tis a girl, Promises boys hereafter . . . . . . v 1 166
A fellow-counsellor, 'Mong boys, grooms, and lackeys . . . v 2 18
A file of boys behind 'em, loose shot, delivered such a shower of pebbles v 4 59
Good boy, tell him I come. I doubt he be hurt . *Troi. and Cres.* i 2 301
Virgins and boys, mid-age and wrinkled eld, Soft infancy . . ii 2 104
If my lord get a boy of you, you'll give him me . . . . iii 2 113
Prithee, be silent, boy; I profit not by thy talk . . . . v 1 16
Unarm thee, go, and doubt thou not, brave boy, I'll stand to-day for thee and me . . . . v 3 35
O' my word, the father's son: I'll swear, 'tis a very pretty boy *Coriolanus* i 3 63
My boy Marcius approaches; for the love of Juno, let's go . . ii 1 110
Lest that thy wives with spits and boys with stones In puny battle slay me . . . . iv 4 5
With no less confidence Than boys pursuing summer butterflies . . iv 6 94
My young boy Hath an aspect of intercession, which Great nature cries 'Deny not' . . . . v 3 31
Your knee, sirrah.—That's my brave boy! . . . . . v 3 76
That brought you forth this boy, to keep your name Living to time . v 3 126
Speak thou, boy: Perhaps thy childishness will move him more Than can our reasons . . . . v 3 156
This boy, that cannot tell what he would have . . . . v 3 174
Boy! O slave! Pardon me, lords, 'tis the first time that ever I was forced to scold . . . . v 6 104
Boy! false hound! If you have writ your annals true, 'tis there, That, like an eagle in a dove-cote, I Flutter'd your Volscians in Corioli: Alone I did it. Boy! . . . . v 6 113
What, villain boy! Barr'st me my way in Rome? . . *T. Andron.* i 1 290
Why, boy, . . . Are you so desperate grown, to threat your friends? . ii 1 38

Boy. Full well shalt thou perceive how much I dare.—Ay, boy, grow ye so brave? . . . . *T. Andron.* ii 1 45
There speak, and strike, brave boys, and take your turns . . ii 1 129
You shall know, my boys, Your mother's hand shall right your mother's wrong . . . . ii 3 120
Remember, boys, I pour'd forth tears in vain, To save your brother . iii 3 163
This object kills me!—Faint-hearted boy, arise, and look upon her . iii 1 65
As for thee, boy, go get thee from my sight; Thou art an exile . iii 1 284
The tender boy, in passion moved, Doth weep to see his grandsire's heaviness . . . . iii 2 48
Come, boy, and go with me: thy sight is young, And thou shalt read . iii 2 84
Do not fear thine aunt.—She loves thee, boy, too well to do thee harm . iv 1 6
Ah, boy, Cornelia never with more care Read to her sons than she hath read to thee . . . . iv 1 12
Some book there is that she desires to see. Which is it, girl, of these? Open them, boy . . . . iv 1 32
Lavinia, kneel; And kneel, sweet boy, the Roman Hector's hope . iv 1 88
And where's your lesson, then? Boy, what say you? . . . iv 1 106
That's my boy! thy father hath full oft For his ungrateful country done the like.—And, uncle, so will I . . . . iv 1 110
My boy, Shalt carry from me to the empress' sons Presents . . iv 1 114
No, boy, not so; I'll teach thee another course . . . . iv 1 119
By the burning tapers of the sky, That shone so brightly when this boy was got . . . . iv 2 90
Ye sanguine, shallow-hearted boys! Ye white-limed walls! . . iv 2 97
Sir boy, now let me see your archery; Look ye draw home enough . iv 3 2
Here, boy, to Pallas: here, to Mercury: To Saturn, Caius . . iv 3 55
To it, boy! Marcus, loose when I bid . . . . . . iv 3 58
Now, masters, draw. O, well said, Lucius! Good boy, in Virgo's lap . iv 3 64
Touch not the boy; he is of royal blood.—Too like the sire for ever being good . . . . v 1 49
Thou shalt vow . . . To save my boy, to nourish and bring him up . v 1 84
Come hither, boy; come, come, and learn of us To melt in showers . v 3 160
Ay, boy, ready.—You are looked for and called for . . *Rom. and Jul.* i 5 12
Cheerly, boys; be brisk awhile, and the longer liver take all . . i 5 16
This, by his voice, should be a Montague. Fetch me my rapier, boy . i 5 57
He shall be endured: What, goodman boy! I say, he shall: go to; Am I the master here, or you? . . . . i 5 79
You are a saucy boy: is't so, indeed? This trick may chance to scathe you . . . . i 5 85
Thou, wretched boy, that didst consort him here, Shalt with him hence iii 1 135
Give me thy torch, boy: hence, and stand aloof: Yet put it out . v 3 1
The boy gives warning something doth approach . . . . v 3 18
Wilt thou provoke me? then have at thee, boy! . . . . v 3 70
Lead, boy: which way?—Yea, noise? then I'll be brief . . . v 3 168
Good boy, wink at me, and say thou sawest me not . *T. of Athens* iii 1 47
Is not to-morrow, boy, the ides of March?—I know not, sir *J. Cæsar* ii 1 40
Boy! Lucius! Fast asleep? It is no matter; Enjoy the honey-heavy dew of slumber: Thou hast no figures nor no fantasies . . ii 1 229
Boy, stand aside. Caius Ligarius! how?—Vouchsafe good morrow . ii 1 312
Boy, run to the senate-house; Stay not to answer me, but get thee gone ii 4 1
Yes, bring me word, boy, if thy lord look well, For he went sickly forth ii 4 13
Hark, boy! what noise is that?—I hear none, madam . . . ii 4 16
Sure, the boy heard me . . . . ii 4 42
Bear with me, good boy, I am much forgetful . . . . . iv 3 255
A strain or two?—Ay, my lord, an't please you.—It does, my boy . iv 3 258
O murderous slumber, Lay'st thou thy leaden mace upon my boy? . iv 3 268
Good boy, good night. Let me see, let me see; is not the leaf turn'd down Where I left reading? . . . . iv 3 272
How goes the night, boy?—The moon is down . . . . *Macbeth* ii 1 1
What's the boy Malcolm? Was he not born of woman? . . . v 3 3
Go prick thy face, and over-red thy fear, Thou lily-liver'd boy . v 3 15
Hillo, ho, ho, my lord!—Hillo, ho, ho, boy! come, bird, come *Hamlet* i 5 116
There has been much throwing about of brains.—Do the boys carry it away? . . . . ii 2 377
I have been sexton here, man and boy, thirty years . . . v 1 177
Would I had two coxcombs and two daughters!—Why, my boy? . *Lear* i 4 119
Can you make no use of nothing, nuncle?—Why, no, boy . . i 4 145
Dost thou know the difference, my boy, between a bitter fool and a sweet fool? . . . . i 4 151
Dost thou call me fool, boy?—All thy other titles thou hast given away i 4 162
If a man's brains were in's heels, were't not in danger of kibes?—Ay, boy i 5 10
I can tell what I can tell.—Why, what canst thou tell, my boy? . i 5 17
Loyal and natural boy, I'll work the means To make thee capable . ii 1 86
With you, goodman boy, an you please: come, I'll flesh ye; come on . ii 2 48
Come on, my boy: how dost, my boy? art cold? I am cold myself . iii 2 68
True, my good boy. Come, bring us to this hovel . . . . iii 2 78
But I'll go in. In, boy; go first. You houseless poverty,—Nay, get thee in . . . . iii 4 26
Dolphin my boy, my boy, sessa! let him trot by . . . . iii 4 104
He's mad that trusts in the tameness of a wolf, a horse's health, a boy's love . . . . iii 6 20
As flies to wanton boys, are we to the gods, They kill us for their sport iv 1 38
Why, then, let a soldier drink. Some wine, boys! . . *Othello* ii 3 76
Prithee, how many boys and wenches must I have? . *Ant. and Cleo.* i 2 36
As we rate boys, who, being mature in knowledge, Pawn their experience to their present pleasure . . . . i 4 31
Pretty dimpled boys, like smiling Cupids, With divers-colour'd fans . ii 2 207
All take hands. Make battery to our ears with the loud music: The while I'll place you: then the boy shall sing . . . . . ii 7 116
To the boy Cæsar send this grizzled head, And he will fill thy wishes . iii 13 17
Of late, when I cried 'Ho!' Like boys unto a muss, kings would start forth . . . . iii 13 91
Whip him, fellows, Till, like a boy, you see him cringe his face, And whine aloud for mercy . . . . iii 13 100
He calls me boy; and chides, as he had power To beat me out of Egypt iv 1 1
The witch shall die: To the young Roman boy she hath sold me . iv 12 48
Young boys and girls Are level now with men; the odds is gone . . iv 15 65
You laugh when boys or women tell their dreams; Is't not your trick? v 2 74
I shall see Some squeaking Cleopatra boy my greatness I' the posture of a whore . . . . v 2 220
Stoop, boys; this gate Instructs you how to adore the heavens *Cymb.* iii 3 2
O boys, this story The world may read in me . . . . . iii 3 55
These boys know little they are sons to the king . . . . iii 3 80
Behold divineness No elder than a boy! . . . . . . iii 6 45
Boys, bid him welcome . . . . iii 6 69
Boys, we'll go dress our hunt. Fair youth, come in: Discourse is heavy, fasting . . . . iii 6 90
I had no mind To hunt this day: the boy Fidele's sickness Did make my way long forth . . . . iv 2 148

Boy. Divine Nature, how thyself thou blazon'st In these two princely boys! . . . . *Cymbeline* iv 2 171
Lamenting toys Is jollity for apes and grief for boys . . . iv 2 194
Thou diedst, a most rare boy, of melancholy . . . . . iv 2 208
Cloten Is quite forgot. He was a queen's son, boys . . . iv 2 244
Let's see the boy's face.—He's alive, my lord . . . . iv 2 359
My friends, The boy hath taught us manly duties . . . . iv 2 397
Have with you, boys! . . . . iv 4 50
Away, boy, from the troops, and save thyself . . . . . v 2 14
This was strange chance: A narrow lane, an old man, and two boys . v 3 52
Two boys, an old man twice a boy, a lane, Preserved the Britons, was the Romans' bane . . . . v 3 57
Hath my poor boy done aught but well, Whose face I never saw? . v 4 35
My boy, a Briton born, Let him be ransom'd . . . . . v 5 84
Boy, Thou hast look'd thyself into my grace . . . . . v 5 93
I know not why, wherefore, To say 'live, boy' . . . . . v 5 96
The boy disdains me, He leaves me, scorns me: briefly die their joys That place them on the truth of girls and boys . . . . . v 5 105
What wouldst thou, boy? I love thee more and more . . . v 5 108
Is not this boy revived from death? . . . . v 5 120
Step you forth; Give answer to this boy, and do it freely . . v 5 131
My boys, There was our error . . . . v 5 259
Boys of art, I have deceived you both . . . . *Mer. Wives* iii 1 109
Boys of ice. These boys are boys of ice . . . . *All's Well* ii 3 99
Boy of tears. Name not the god, thou boy of tears! . *Coriolanus* v 6 101
Boy-queller. Come, come, thou boy-queller, show thy face *Troi. and Cres.* v 5 45
Boy's play. You shall find no boy's play here, I can tell you . 1 *Hen. IV.* v 4 76
Boyet. Good Lord Boyet, my beauty, though but mean, Needs not the painted flourish of your praise . . . . . *L. L. Lost* ii 1 13
Good Boyet, You are not ignorant, all-telling fame Doth noise abroad . ii 1 20
Boyet, you can produce acquittances For such a sum . . . ii 1 161
Come to our pavilion: Boyet is disposed . . . . . . ii 1 249
Boyet, you can carve; Break up this capon . . . . . iv 1 55
You still wrangle with her, Boyet, and she strikes at the brow . iv 1 119
Here comes Boyet, and mirth is in his face . . . . . v 2 79
O, I am stabb'd with laughter! Where's her grace?—Thy news, Boyet? v 2 81
Pay him the due of honey-tongued Boyet . . . . . . v 2 334
Boyet, prepare; I will away to-night . . . . . . v 2 737
Boyish. This unhair'd sauciness and boyish troops . . . *K. John* v 2 133
I ran it through, even from my boyish days . . . . *Othello* i 3 132
Boys. I am the youngest son of Sir Rowland de Boys . *As Y. Like It* i 1 60
Brabant. Did not I dance with you in Brabant once? . *L. L. Lost* ii 1 114
Dukes of Berri and of Bretagne, Of Brabant and of Orleans *Hen. V.* ii 4 5
Anthony Duke of Brabant, The brother to the Duke of Burgundy . iv 8 101
Brabantio. What, ho, Brabantio! Signior Brabantio, ho! . . *Othello* i 1 78
Most grave Brabantio, In simple and pure soul I come to you . i 1 106
It is Brabantio. General, be advised; He comes to bad intent . i 2 55
Here comes Brabantio and the valiant Moor . . . . . i 3 47
Good Brabantio, Take up this mangled matter at the best . . i 3 172
Brabble. In private brabble did we apprehend him . . *T. Night* v 1 68
This petty brabble will undo us all . . . . *T. Andron.* ii 1 62
Brabbler. Fare thee well; We hold our time too precious to be spent With such a brabbler . . . . *K. John* v 2 162
He will spend his mouth, and promise, like Brabbler the hound *Troi. and Cres.* v 1 99
Brace. But you, my brace of lords, were I so minded, I here could pluck his highness' frown upon you . . . . . . *Tempest* v 1 126
I implore so much expense of thy royal sweet breath as will utter a brace of words . . . . *L. L. Lost* v 2 524
Hold your tongue.—Hubert, the utterance of a brace of tongues Must needs want pleading for a pair of eyes . . . . *K. John* iv 1 98
A brace of draymen bid God speed him well . . . *Richard II.* i 4 32
Like a brace of greyhounds Having the fearful flying hare in sight 3 *Hen. VI.* ii 5 129
Not dallying with a brace of courtezans, But meditating *Richard III.* iii 7 74
You brace of warlike brothers, welcome hither . *Troi. and Cres.* iv 5 175
A brace of unmeriting, proud, violent, testy magistrates, alias fools *Coriolanus* ii 1 46
Here comes a brace. You know the cause . . . . . ii 3 67
I could myself Take up a brace o' the best of them . . . iii 1 244
I for winking at your discords too Have lost a brace of kinsmen *R. and J.* v 3 295
And has sent your honour two brace of greyhounds . *T. of Athens* i 2 195
Then was a blessed time.—As thine is now, held with a brace of harlots iv 3 79
It stands not in such warlike brace . . . . . *Othello* i 3 24
Here without are a brace of Cyprus gallants . . . . . ii 3 31
Your ring may be stolen too: so your brace of unprizable estimations *Cymbeline* i 4 99
'It hath been a shield 'Twixt me and death;'—and pointed to this brace *Pericles* ii 1 133
Braced. Even at hand a drum is ready braced . . . *K. John* v 2 169
Bracelet. With bracelets of thy hair, rings, gawds . . *M. N. Dream* i 1 33
With amber bracelets, beads and all this knavery . . *T. of Shrew* iv 3 58
Bugle bracelet, necklace amber, Perfume for a lady's chamber *W. Tale* iv 4 224
Ballad, knife, tape, glove, shoe-tie, bracelet . . . . iv 4 611
Averring notes Of chamber-hanging, pictures, this her bracelet,—O cunning, how I got it! . . . . *Cymbeline* v 5 204
And here the bracelet of the truest princess That ever swore her faith v 5 416
Brach Merriman, the poor cur is emboss'd . . . *T. of Shrew* Ind. 1 17
And couple Clowder with the deep-mouth'd brach . . . Ind. 1 18
I had rather hear Lady, my brach, howl in Irish . . 1 *Hen. IV.* iii 1 240
I will hold my peace when Achilles' brach bids me, shall I? *Tr. and Cr.* ii 1 126
He must be whipped out, when Lady the brach may stand by the fire *Lear* i 4 125
Hound or spaniel, brach or lym, Or bobtail tike or trundle-tail . iii 6 72
Bracy. Here was Sir John Bracy from your father . . 1 *Hen. IV.* ii 4 367
Brag. Thou shalt not live to brag what we have offer'd . *T. G. of Ver.* iv 1 69
What simple thief brags of his own attaint? . . *Com. of Errors* iii 2 16
As under privilege of age to brag What I have done being young *Much Ado* v 1 60
The child brags in her belly already . . . . *L. L. Lost* v 2 683
Cæsar's thrasonical brag of 'I came, saw, and overcame' *As Y Like It* v 2 34
Dares yet do more Than you have heard him brag to you he will *T. Night* iii 4 348
What a fool art thou, A ramping fool, to brag and stamp and swear! *K. John* iii 1 122
Forgive me, God, That I do brag thus! . . . . *Hen. V.* iii 6 160
Who would trot as well, were some of your brags dismounted . iii 7 83
Pardon me this brag; His insolence draws folly from my lips *Troi. and Cres.* iv 5 257
To brag unto them, thus I did, and thus . . . *Coriolanus* ii 2 151
Agree these deeds with that proud brag of thine . . *T. Andron.* i 1 306
Verona brags of him To be a virtuous and well-govern'd youth *R. and J.* i 5 69
Brags of his substance, not of ornament . . . . . . ii 6 31

Brag. Renown and grace is dead; The wine of life is drawn, and the mere lees Is left this vault to brag of . . . . . *Macbeth* ii 3 101
If fortune brag of two she loved and hated, One of them we behold *Lear* v 3 280
A kind of conquest Cæsar made here; but made not here his brag Of 'Came' and 'saw' and 'overcame' . . . . *Cymbeline* iii 1 23
He brags his service As if he were of note . . . . v 3 93
Either our brags Were crack'd of kitchen-trulls . . . v 5 176
Braggardism. What braggardism is this? . . . . *T. G. of Ver.* ii 4 164
Braggart. Boys, apes, braggarts, Jacks, milksops! . . . *Much Ado* v 1 91
You break jests as braggarts do their blades . . . v 1 189
The pedant, the braggart, the hedge-priest, the fool and the boy *L. L. Lost* v 2 545
Rating myself at nothing, you shall see How much I was a braggart *Mer. of Venice* iii 2 261
Who knows himself a braggart, Let him fear this, for it will come to pass That every braggart shall be found an ass . . . . *All's Well* iv 3 370
O braggart vile and damned furious wight! . . . *Hen. V.* ii 1 64
Will you be put in mind of his blind fortune, Which was your shame, by this unholy braggart? . . . . . *Coriolanus* v 6 119
To scratch a man to death! a braggart, a rogue, a villain! *Rom. and Jul.* iii 1 105
Let the unscarr'd braggarts of the war Derive some pain from you *T. of Athens* iv 3 161
O, I could play the woman with mine eyes And braggart with my tongue! *Macbeth* iv 3 231
You stubborn ancient knave, you reverend braggart, We'll teach you *Lear* ii 2 133
Bragged. May be the knave bragged of that he could not compass *Mer. Wives* iii 3 212
Wert thou the Hector That was the whip of your bragg'd progeny, Thou shouldst not 'scape me here . . . . *Coriolanus* i 8 12
Bragging. Thou coward, art thou bragging to the stars? . *M. N. Dream* iii 2 407
Speak of frays Like a fine bragging youth, and tell quaint lies *Mer. of Ven.* iii 4 69
I have within my mind A thousand raw tricks of these bragging Jacks iii 4 77
Threaten the threatener and outface the brow Of bragging horror *K. John* v 1 50
A rascal bragging slave! the rogue fled from me like quicksilver *2 Hen. IV.* ii 4 247
And fig me, like The bragging Spaniard . . . . . v 3 125
Under the correction of bragging be it spoken . . . *Hen. V.* v 2 144
Loved the Moor, but for bragging and telling her fantastical lies *Othello* ii 1 225
Bragless. If it be so, yet bragless let it be . . . *Troi. and Cres.* v 9 5
Braid. Since Frenchmen are so braid, Marry that will, I live and die a maid . . . . *All's Well* iv 2 73
Few love to hear the sins they love to act; 'Twould braid yourself too near for me to tell it . . . . *Pericles* i 1 93
Brain. Thou mayst brain him, Having first seized his books . *Tempest* iii 2 96
My old brain is troubled: Be not disturb'd with my infirmity . iv 1 159
A solemn air and the best comforter To an unsettled fancy cure thy brains! . . . . v 1 59
Has Page any brains? hath he any eyes? hath he any thinking? *M. Wives* iii 2 30
I'll have my brains ta'en out and buttered, and give them to a dog . iii 5 7
He's not here I seek for.—No, nor nowhere else but in your brain . iv 2 166
If it be but to scrape the figures out of your husband's brains . iv 2 231
Have I laid my brain in the sun and dried it, that it wants matter? v 5 143
They shall beat out my brains with billets . . *Meas. for Meas.* iv 3 58
Shall quips and sentences and these paper bullets of the brain awe a man from the career of his humour? . . . . *Much Ado* ii 3 250
A paper written in his hand, A halting sonnet of his own pure brain . v 4 87
If a man will be beaten with brains, a' shall wear nothing handsome . v 4 104
That hath a mint of phrases in his brain . . . *L. L. Lost* i 1 166
Other slow arts entirely keep the brain . . . . . iv 3 324
Love, first learned in a lady's eyes, Lives not alone immured in the brain iv 3 328
Weed this wormwood from your fruitful brain . . . . v 2 857
Lovers and madmen have such seething brains . . *M. N. Dream* v 1 4
The brain may devise laws for the blood, but a hot temper leaps o'er a cold decree: such a hare is madness the youth . . *Mer. of Venice* i 2 19
His brain, Which is as dry as the remainder biscuit After a voyage *As Y. Like It* ii 7 38
Troilus had his brains dashed out with a Grecian club . . . iv 1 98
With pure love and troubled brain . . . . . . iv 3 4
Women's gentle brain Could not drop forth such giant-rude invention . iv 3 33
The brains of my Cupid's knocked out, and I begin to love . *All's Well* iii 2 16
I know his brains are forfeit to the next tile that falls . . iv 3 216
Liver, brain, and heart These sovereign thrones . . . *T. Night* i 1 37
Till his brains turn o' the toe like a parish-top . . . . i 3 44
That's as much to say as I wear not motley in my brain . . . i 5 63
An ordinary fool that has no more brain than a stone . . . i 5 92
As if thy eldest son should be a fool; whose skull Jove cram with brains! i 5 122
I'll ne'er believe a madman till I see his brains . . . iv 2 126
To the infection of my brains And hardening of my brows . *W. Tale* i 2 145
Quite beyond mine arm, out of the blank And level of my brain, plot-proof . . . . ii 3 6
The bastard brains with these my proper hands Shall I dash out . . ii 3 139
Would any but these boiled brains of nineteen and two-and-twenty hunt this weather? . . . . iii 3 64
Here is more matter for a hot brain . . . . . . iv 4 700
His pure brain, Which some suppose the soul's frail dwelling-house *K. John* v 7 2
My brain I'll prove the female to my soul, My soul the father *Richard II.* v 5 6
An I were now by this rascal, I could brain him with his lady's fan *1 Hen. IV.* ii 3 24
The brain of this foolish-compounded clay, man, is not able to invent any thing that tends to laughter . . . . . *2 Hen. IV.* i 2 8
It hath it original from much grief, from study and perturbation of the brain . . . . i 2 132
And rock his brains In cradle of the rude imperious surge . . iii 1 19
It [sherris] ascends me into the brain; dries me there all the foolish and dull and crudy vapours . . . . iv 3 105
And now my sight fails, and my brain is giddy: O me! come near me . iv 4 110
Over-careful fathers Have broke their sleep with thoughts, their brains with care . . . . iv 5 69
Enjoys it; but in gross brain little wots What watch the king keeps to maintain the peace . . . . *Hen. V.* iv 1 299
And make a quagmire of your mingled brains . . . *1 Hen. VI.* i 4 109
Do pelt so fast at one another's pate That many have their giddy brains knock'd out . . . . iii 1 83
Undermine the duchess And buz these conjurations in her brain *2 Hen. VI.* i 2 99
My brain more busy than the labouring spider Weaves tedious snares . iii 1 339
I would to God that the inclusive verge Of golden metal that must round my brow Were red-hot steel, to sear me to the brain! *Richard III.* iv 1 61
Beside forfeiting Our own brains, and the opinion that we bring *Hen. VIII.* Prol. 20
Some strange commotion Is in his brain: he bites his lip, and starts . iii 2 113
Your hand and heart, Your brain, and every function of your power . iii 2 187

Brain. Is there no way to cure this? No new device to beat this from his brains? . . . . *Hen. VIII.* iii 2 217
I have a young conception in my brain . . . *Troi. and Cres.* i 3 312
Were his brain as barren As banks of Libya . . . . . i 3 327
Thou hast no more brain than I have in mine elbows . . . ii 1 48
I have bobbed his brain more than he has beat my bones . . ii 1 76
Hector shall have a great catch, if he knock out either of your brains . ii 1 111
Were your days As green as Ajax' and your brain so temper'd . . ii 3 265
Hath no arithmetic but her brain to set down her reckoning . . iii 3 253
What music will be in him when Hector has knocked out his brains, I know not . . . . iii 3 304
With too much blood and too little brain, these two may run mad; but, if with too much brain and too little blood they do, I'll be a curer of madmen . . . . v 1 54
One that loves quails; but he has not so much brain as ear-wax . v 1 58
I send it through the rivers of your blood, Even to the court, the heart, to the seat o' the brain . . . . *Coriolanus* i 1 140
More of your conversation would infect my brain . . . . ii 1 105
But yet a brain that leads my use of anger To better vantage . . iii 2 30
Cast us down, And on the ragged stones beat forth our brains *T. Andron.* v 3 133
Nay, I do bear a brain . . . . . . *Rom. and Jul.* i 3 29
In this state she gallops night by night Through lovers' brains . i 4 71
True, I talk of dreams, Which are the children of an idle brain . i 4 97
Where unbruised youth with unstuff'd brain Doth couch his limbs . ii 3 37
With some great kinsman's bone, As with a club, dash out my desperate brains . . . . iv 3 54
Whither art going?—To knock out an honest Athenian's brains *T. of Athens* i 1 193
Pluck the lined crutch from thy old limping sire, With it beat out his brains! . . . . iv 1 15
Scorn'dst our brain's flow and those our droplets which From niggard nature fall . . . . v 4 76
Thou hast no figures nor no fantasies, Which busy care draws in the brains of men; Therefore thou sleep'st so sound . . *J. Cæsar* ii 1 232
Your favour: my dull brain was wrought With things forgotten *Macbeth* i 3 149
Pluck'd my nipple from his boneless gums, And dash'd the brains out . i 7 58
That memory, the warder of the brain, Shall be a fume . . . i 7 65
A false creation, Proceeding from the heat-oppressed brain . . ii 1 39
The time has been, That, when the brains were out, the man would die iii 4 79
Pluck from the memory a rooted sorrow, Raze out the written troubles of the brain . . . . v 3 42
The very place puts toys of desperation, Without more motive, into every brain That looks so many fathoms to the sea . . *Hamlet* i 4 76
Thy commandment all alone shall live Within the book and volume of my brain . . . . i 5 103
This brain of mine Hunts not the trail of policy so sure As it hath used to do . . . . ii 2 46
There has been much throwing about of brains.—Do the boys carry it away? . . . . ii 2 376
Fie upon't! foh! About, my brain! . . . . . . ii 2 617
Whereon his brains still beating puts him thus From fashion of himself iii 1 182
Sleep rock thy brain; And never come mischance between us twain! . iii 2 237
This is the very coinage of your brain . . . . . . iii 4 137
O heat, dry up my brains! tears seven times salt, Burn out the sense and virtue of mine eye! . . . . iv 5 154
Cudgel thy brains no more about it . . . . v 1 63
Ere I could make a prologue to my brains, They had begun the play . v 2 30
Had he a hand to write this? a heart and brain to breed it in? . *Lear* i 2 61
If a man's brains were in's heels, were't not in danger of kibes? . i 5 8
I'll look no more; Lest my brain turn, and the deficient sight Topple down . . . . iv 6 23
Let me have surgeons; I am cut to the brains . . . . . iv 6 197
It plucks out brains and all: but my Muse labours . . . *Othello* ii 1 128
I have very poor and unhappy brains for drinking . . . . ii 3 35
That men should put an enemy in their mouths to steal away their brains! . . . . ii 3 92
As if thou then hadst shut up in thy brain Some horrible conceit . iii 3 114
Are his wits safe? is he not light of brain?—He's that he is . . iv 1 280
By making him uncapable of Othello's place; knocking out his brains . iv 2 236
Tie up the libertine in a field of feasts, Keep his brain fuming *A. and C.* ii 1 24
It's monstrous labour, when I wash my brain, And it grows fouler . ii 7 105
Take from his brain, from's time, What should not then be spared . iii 7 12
I see still, A diminution in our captain's brain Restores his heart . iii 13 198
Yet ha' we A brain that nourishes our nerves . . . . . iv 8 21
As I told you always, her beauty and her brain go not together *Cymbeline* i 2 32
A woman that Bears all down with her brain . . . . . ii 1 59
Not Hercules Could have knock'd out his brains, for he had none . iv 2 115
'Twas but a bolt of nothing, shot at nothing, Which the brain makes of fumes . . . . iv 2 301
To taint his nobler heart and brain With needless jealousy . . v 4 65
'Tis still a dream, or else such stuff as madmen Tongue and brain not . v 4 147
Purse and brain both empty; the brain the heavier for being too light . v 4 166
Which I will add To you, the liver, heart and brain of Britain . v 5 14
Mine Italian brain 'Gan in your duller Britain operate Most vilely . v 5 196
Brained. If th' other two be brained like us, the state totters . *Tempest* iii 2 7
That brain'd my purpose . . . . . . *Meas. for Meas.* v 1 401
Brainish. And, in this brainish apprehension, kills The unseen good old man . . . . *Hamlet* iv 1 11
Brainless. If the dull brainless Ajax come safe off, We'll dress him up in voices? . . . . *Troi. and Cres.* i 3 381
Brain-pan. Many a time, but for a sallet, my brain-pan had been cleft with a brown bill . . . . *2 Hen. VI.* iv 10 13
Brainsick. What madness rules in brainsick men! . . . *1 Hen. VI.* iv 1 111
Vaunts of his nobility, Did instigate the bedlam brain-sick duchess *2 Hen. VI.* iii 1 51
Shame to thy silver hair, Thou mad misleader of thy brain-sick son! . v 1 163
Her brain-sick raptures Cannot distaste the goodness of a quarrel *Troi. and Cres.* ii 2 122
Whate'er I forge to feed his brain-sick fits, Do you uphold *T. Andron.* v 2 71
Brainsickly. You do unbend your noble strength, to think So brainsickly of things . . . . *Macbeth* ii 2 46
Brake. Some run from brakes of ice, and answer none . *Meas. for Meas.* ii 1 39
Till this afternoon his passion Ne'er brake into extremity of rage *Com. of Errors* v 1 48
I'll run from thee and hide me in the brakes . . . *M. N. Dream* ii 1 227
Enter into that brake: and so every one according to his cue . . iii 1 77
Through bog, through bush, through brake, through brier . . . iii 1 110
Forsook his scene and enter'd in a brake . . . . . . iii 2 15
It seems then that the tidings of this broil Brake off our business *1 Hen. IV.* i 1 48
Under this thick-grown brake we'll shroud ourselves . . *3 Hen. VI.* iii 1 1

Brake. And even here brake off, and came away . . . *Richard III.* iii 7 41
The fate of place, and the rough brake That virtue must go through *Hen. VIII.* i 2 75
Brakenbury, You may partake of any thing we say . *Richard III.* i 1 88
We know thy charge, Brakenbury, and will obey . . . i 1 105
O Brakenbury, I have done those things, Which now bear evidence against my soul . . . . i 4 66
Bramble. Hangs odes upon hawthorns and elegies on brambles *As Y. Like It* iii 2 380
Bran. I am fain to dine and sup with water and bran *Meas. for Meas.* iv 3 160
You shall fast a week with bran and water . . *L. L. Lost* i 1 303
Chaff and bran! porridge after meat! . . *Troi. and Cres.* i 2 263
I can make my audit up, that all From me do back receive the flour of all, And leave me but the bran . . . *Coriolanus* i 1 150
Meal and bran together He throws without distinction . . . iii 1 322
Nature hath meal and bran, contempt and grace . . *Cymbeline* iv 2 27
Branch. It is a branch and parcel of mine oath . . . *Com. of Errors* v 1 106
In every lineament, branch, shape, and form . . *Much Ado* v 1 14
Strike his honour down That violates the smallest branch herein *L. L. Lost* i 1 21
The Sisters Three and such branches of learning . *Mer. of Venice* ii 2 66
To set the deer's horns upon his head, for a branch of victory *As Y. Like It* iv 2 5
With any branch or image of thy state . . . *All's Well* ii 1 201
Such an affection, which cannot choose but branch now . . *W. Tale* i 1 27
That wear upon your virgin branches yet Your maidenheads growing . iv 4 115
Seven fair branches springing from one root: Some of those seven are dried by nature's course, Some of those branches by the Destinies cut *Richard II.* i 2 13
One flourishing branch of his most royal root . . . Is hack'd down . i 2 18
Superfluous branches We lop away, that bearing boughs may live . iii 4 63
Not to break peace or any branch of it . . *2 Hen. IV.* iv 1 85
This most memorable line, In every branch truly demonstrative *Hen. V.* ii 4 89
As a branch and member of this royalty . . . . v 2 5
Like to a wither'd vine That droops his sapless branches to the ground *1 Hen. VI.* ii 5 12
Not contented that he lopp'd the branch In hewing Rutland when his leaves put forth . . . . *3 Hen. VI.* ii 6 47
That from his loins no hopeful branch may spring, To cross me from the golden time I look for! . . . . . . iii 2 126
To whom the heavens in thy nativity Adjudged an olive branch . . iv 6 34
Why grow the branches now the root is wither'd? . . *Richard III.* ii 2 41
My legs, like loaden branches, bow to the earth . *Hen. VIII.* iv 2 2
And, like a mountain cedar, reach his branches To all the plains about him . . . . v 5 54
What stern ungentle hands Have lopp'd and hew'd and made thy body bare Of her two branches? . . . . *T. Andron.* ii 4 18
An act hath three branches; it is, to act, to do, and to perform *Hamlet* v 1 12
Branches, which, being dead many years, shall after revive *Cymb.* v 4 141; v 5 438
This fierce abridgement Hath to it circumstantial branches . . v 5 383
Thy lopp'd branches point Thy two sons forth . . . v 5 454
A wither'd branch, that's only green at top . . *Pericles* ii 2 43
With her neeld composes Nature's own shape, of bud, bird, branch v Gower 6
Branched. In my branched velvet gown . . *T. Night* ii 5 54
Branchless. Better I were not yours Than yours so branchless *A. and C.* iii 4 24
Brand. Whose beard they have singed off with brands of fire *Com. of Errors* v 1 171
Now the wasted brands do glow . . . *M. N. Dream* v 1 382
The hum or ha, these petty brands That calumny doth use *W. Tale* ii 1 71
The senseless brands will sympathize The heavy accent of thy moving tongue And in compassion weep the fire out . *Richard II.* v 1 46
Bear that proportion to my flesh and blood As did the fatal brand Althæa burn'd Unto the prince's heart of Calydon . . *2 Hen. VI.* i 1 234
A brand to the end o' the world . . . *Coriolanus* iii 1 304
If he were putting to my house the brand That should consume it iv 6 115
We'll burn his body in the holy place, And with the brands fire the traitors' houses . . . . . . *J. Cæsar* iii 2 260
Tear him, tear him! Come, brands, ho! fire-brands! . . iii 3 41
Brands the harlot Even here, between the chaste unsmirched brow Of my true mother . . . . *Hamlet* iv 5 118
Why brand they us With base? with baseness? . . *Lear* i 2 9
He that parts us shall bring a brand from heaven, And fire us hence . v 3 22
Two winking Cupids Of silver, each on one foot standing, nicely Depending on their brands . . . . . *Cymbeline* ii 4 91
Branded. A woman, I dare say without vain-glory, Never yet branded with suspicion . . . . . . *Hen. VIII.* iii 1 128
Whilst the wheel'd seat Of fortunate Cæsar, drawn before him, branded His baseness that ensued . . . *Ant. and Cleo.* iv 14 76
Brandish. And never brandish more revengeful steel . *Richard II.* iv 1 50
If it be a hot day, and I brandish any thing but a bottle, I would I might never spit white again . . . . . *2 Hen. IV.* i 2 236
Comets, . . . Brandish your crystal tresses in the sky! . . *1 Hen. VI.* i 1 3
Brandished. His brandish'd sword did blind men with his beams . i 1 10
When he perceived me shrink and on my knee, His bloody sword he brandish'd over me . . . . iv 7 6
His brandish'd steel, Which smoked with bloody execution . *Macbeth* i 2 17
But swords I smile at, weapons laugh to scorn, Brandish'd by man that's of a woman born . . . . v 7 13
Brandon. Sir William Brandon, you shall bear my standard *Richard III.* v 3 22
What men of name are slain on either side?—. . . Sir William Brandon v 5 14
Bras. Dites-moi l'Anglois pour le bras.—De arm, madame *Hen. V.* iii 4 21
Est-il impossible d'échapper la force de ton bras? . . . iv 4 18
Brass. It deserves, with characters of brass, A forted residence 'gainst the tooth of time And razure of oblivion . . *Meas. for Meas.* v 1 11
Can any face of brass hold longer out? . . *L. L. Lost* v 2 395
Pewter and brass and all things that belong To house . *T. of Shrew* ii 1 357
Nor brass nor stone nor parchment bears not one . *W. Tale* i 2 360
As if this flesh which walls about our life Were brass impregnable *Richard II.* iii 2 168
Let it pry through the portage of the head Like the brass cannon *Hen. V.* iii 1 11
Upon the which, I trust, Shall witness live in brass of this day's work . iv 3 97
Brass, cur! Thou damned and luxurious mountain goat, Offer'st me brass? . . . . iv 4 19
Men's evil manners live in brass; their virtues We write in water *Hen. VIII.* iv 2 45
Your speeches, which were such As Agamemnon and the hand of Greece Should hold up high in brass . . . *Troi. and Cres.* i 3 64
Trumpet, blow loud, Send thy brass voice through all these lazy tents . i 3 257
I will go get a leaf of brass, And with a gad of steel will write these words, And lay it by . . . . *T. Andron.* iv 1 102
Nor walls of beaten brass, Nor airless dungeon, nor strong links of iron, Can be retentive to the strength of spirit . . *J. Cæsar* i 3 93
Thou, that hast Upon the winds command, bind them in brass! *Pericles* iii 1 3

Brassed. If damned custom have not brass'd it so . . *Hamlet* iii 4 37
Brassy. From brassy bosoms and rough hearts of flint . *Mer. of Venice* iv 1 31
Brat. I bear it on my shoulders, as a beggar wont her brat *Com. of Errors* iv 4 40
This brat is none of mine . . . . . *W. Tale* ii 3 92
What will you adventure To save this brat's life? . . . ii 3 163
Thy brat hath been cast out, like to itself, No father owning it . . iii 2 88
Strumpet, thy words condemn thy brat and thee . . *1 Hen. VI.* v 4 84
As for the brat of this accursed duke, Whose father slew my father, he shall die . . . . *3 Hen. VI.* i 3 4
By heaven, brat, I'll plague ye for that word . . . . v 5 27
My woful banishment, Could all but answer for that peevish brat? *Richard III.* i 3 194
To take some privy order, To draw the brats of Clarence out of sight . iii 5 107
They follow him, Against us brats, with no less confidence Than boys pursuing summer butterflies . . . . *Coriolanus* iv 6 93
Did not thy hue bewray whose brat thou art . . *T. Andron.* v 1 28
On whom there is no more dependency But brats and beggary *Cymbeline* ii 3 124
Brave. O brave new world, That has such people in't! . *Tempest* v 1 183
All's brave that youth mounts and folly guides . *As Y. Like It* iii 4 48
Sirrah, I will not bear these braves of thine . . *T. of Shrew* iii 1 15
Brave not me; I will neither be faced or braved . . . . iv 3 126
Darest thou brave a nobleman?—Not for my life . . *K. John* iv 3 87
Shall a beardless boy, A cocker'd silken wanton, brave our fields? . v 1 70
There end thy brave, and turn thy face in peace . . . v 2 159
A rascal! to brave me!—Ah, you sweet little rogue! . *2 Hen. IV.* ii 4 232
Le plus brave, vaillant, et très distingué . . . *Hen. V.* iv 4 60
Now where's the Bastard's braves, and Charles his gleeks? *1 Hen. VI.* iii 2 123
Brave death by speaking, whether he will or no . . . iv 7 25
Be brave, then; for your captain is brave, and vows reformation *2 Hen. VI.* iv 2 69
O, brave!—But is not this braver? . . . . . . iv 7 137
What, Buckingham and Clifford, are ye so brave? . . . iv 8 21
Thou wilt brave me with these saucy terms?—Brave thee! ay, by the best blood that ever was broached . . . . . iv 10 38
Is Lewis so brave! belike he thinks me Henry . . *3 Hen. VI.* iv 1 96
We must be brief when traitors brave the field . *Richard III.* v 3 57
Is't not a gallant man too, is't not? Why, this is brave now *Tr. and Cr.* i 2 232
This brave shall oft make thee to hide thy head . . . iv 4 139
Are you so brave! I'll have you talked with anon . *Coriolanus* iv 5 18
Demetrius, thou dost over-ween in all; And so in this, to bear me down with braves . . . . *T. Andron.* ii 1 30
Ay, boy, grow ye so brave? . . . . ii 1 45
And with that painted hope braves your mightiness . . ii 3 126
Lucius and I'll go brave it at the court . . . . iv 1 121
It did me good, before the palace gate To brave the tribune . . iv 2 36
But if you brave the Moor, The chafed boar, the mountain lioness, The ocean swells not so as Aaron storms . . . . . iv 2 137
This brave o'erhanging firmament . . . . *Hamlet* ii 2 312
Why, what an ass am I! This is most brave . . . . ii 2 611
He made him Brave me upon the watch . . . . *Othello* v 2 326
If fortune be not ours to-day, it is Because we brave her *Ant. and Cleo.* iv 4 5
What's brave, what's noble, Let's do it after the high Roman fashion . iv 15 86
Brave a lass. Is it so brave a lass?—Ay, lord . . *Tempest* iii 2 111
Brave acts. By his light Did all the chivalry of England move To do brave acts . . . . *2 Hen. IV.* ii 3 21
Brave Archibald, That ever-valiant and approved Scot . *1 Hen. IV.* i 1 53
Brave army. 'Tis a brave army, And full of purpose *Ant. and Cleo.* iv 3 11
Brave attendants near him when he wakes . . *T. of Shrew* Ind. 1 40
Brave Austria. Before Angiers well met, brave Austria . . *K. John* ii 1 1
Brave bears. Call hither to the stake my two brave bears *2 Hen. VI.* v 1 144
The two brave bears, Warwick and Montague . . *3 Hen. VI.* v 7 10
Brave bearing. With thy brave bearing should I be in love, But that thou art so fast mine enemy . . . . . *2 Hen. VI.* v 2 20
Brave beast. Incorpsed and demi-natured With the brave beast *Hamlet* iv 7 89
Brave boy. Doubt thou not, brave boy, I'll stand to-day for thee and me and Troy . . . . *Troi. and Cres.* v 3 35
Your knee, sirrah.—That's my brave boy! . . *Coriolanus* v 3 76
There speak, and strike, brave boys, and take your turns *T. Andron.* ii 1 129
Brave brood. She will become thy bed, I warrant. And bring thee forth brave brood . . . . *Tempest* iii 2 113
Brave Burgundy. And now no more ado, brave Burgundy *1 Hen. VI.* iii 2 101
Brave Burgundy, undoubted hope of France! . . . iii 3 41
Brave Cæsar. O that brave Cæsar! . . . *Ant. and Cleo.* i 5 67
Brave Caius. O, what a time have you chose out, brave Caius, To wear a kerchief! . . . . *J. Cæsar* ii 1 314
Brave captain. Welcome, brave captain and victorious lord! *1 Hen. VI.* iii 4 16
Brave Cassius. Why didst thou send me forth, brave Cassius? *J. Cæsar* v 3 80
Brave conquerors,—for so you are, That war against your own affections *L. L. Lost* i 1 8
Brave crowns. Owy, cuppele gorge, permafoy, Peasant, unless thou give me crowns, brave crowns . . . . . *Hen. V.* iv 4 40
Brave death, when princes die with us! . . . *1 Hen. IV.* v 2 87
If any think brave death outweighs bad life . . *Coriolanus* i 6 71
Brave deed. You have done a brave deed . . . . . iv 2 38
Brave defiance. To arms! for I have thrown A brave defiance in King Henry's teeth . . . . *1 Hen. IV.* v 2 43
Brave duke. By this brave duke came early to his grave . *K. John* ii 1 5
Welcome, brave duke! thy friendship makes us fresh *1 Hen. VI.* iii 3 86
Brave earl. Welcome, brave earl, into our territories . . v 3 146
With all the friends that thou, brave Earl of March, Amongst the loving Welshmen canst procure . . . . *3 Hen. VI.* ii 1 179
Brave Egyptians. Together with my brave Egyptians all *Ant. and Cleo.* iii 13 164
Brave emperor. Ha, my brave emperor! Shall we dance now? . . ii 7 109
O my brave emperor, this is fought indeed! . . . . iv 7 4
Brave father. Then I lost—All mine own folly—the society, Amity too, of your brave father . . . . *W. Tale* v 1 136
Where your brave father breathed his latest gasp . . *3 Hen. VI.* ii 1 108
Brave fellow. This is a brave fellow . . . . *W. Tale* iv 4 202
A brave fellow; but he's vengeance proud . . *Coriolanus* ii 2 5
His mother, wife, his child, And this brave fellow too . . v 1 30
A brave fellow! he keeps his tides well . . *T. of Athens* i 2 56
Brave fleet. And his brave fleet With silken streamers the young Phœbus fanning . . . . *Hen. V.* iii Prol. 5
Brave followers, yonder stands the thorny wood . *3 Hen. VI.* v 4 67
Brave form. It carries a brave form. But 'tis a spirit . *Tempest* i 2 411
Brave friend. Hail, brave friend! Say to the king the knowledge of the broil . . . . *Macbeth* i 2 5
Brave Gaunt, thy father, and myself Rescued the Black Prince *Rich. II.* ii 3 100
Brave gentleman. A bold brave gentleman . . *Hen. VIII.* iv 1 40
Brave god. That's a brave god and bears celestial liquor . *Tempest* ii 2 122

Brave hart. Here wast thou bay'd, brave hart . . . *J. Cæsar* iii 1 204
Brave Hector. Speak, brave Hector: we are much delighted . *L. L. Lost* v 2 671
O brave Hector! Look how he looks! there's a countenance *Tr. and Cr.* i 2 217
I presume, brave Hector would not lose So rich advantage . . ii 2 203
As if his foot were on brave Hector's breast And great Troy shrieking . iii 3 140
Welcome, brave Hector; welcome, princes all . . . . v 1 77
Brave Iago. O brave Iago, honest and just! . . . *Othello* v 1 31
Brave instruction. My queen and Eros Have by their brave instruction got upon me A nobleness in record . . . *Ant. and Cleo.* iv 14 98
Brave judge. I'll be a brave judge.—Thou judgest false already *1 Hen. IV.* i 2 73
Brave kingdom. This will prove a brave kingdom to me . *Tempest* iii 2 153
Brave lords! when we join in league, I am a lamb . . *T. Andron.* iv 2 136
There's hope in't yet.—That's my brave lord! . . *Ant. and Cleo.* iii 13 177
Brave Macbeth—well he deserves that name . . . *Macbeth* i 2 16
Brave man. That's a brave man! he writes brave verses, speaks brave words, swears brave oaths . . . . . . *As Y. Like It* iii 4 43
Is not that a brave man? he's one of the flowers of Troy . *Troi. and Cres.* i 2 202
There's a countenance! is't not a brave man?—O, a brave man! . . i 2 219
The brave man Holds honour far more precious-dear than life . . v 3 27
Brave manage. Full merrily Hath this brave manage, this career, been run . . . . *L. L. Lost* v 2 482
Brave Mark Antony. How goes it with my brave Mark Antony? *Ant. and Cleo.* i 5 38
Brave Master Shooty the great traveller . . . *Meas. for Meas.* iv 3 18
Brave Mercutio. There lies the man, slain by young Romeo, That slew thy kinsman, brave Mercutio . . . . *Rom. and Jul.* iii 1 150
Brave mettle. You are gentlemen of brave mettle . . *Tempest* ii 1 182
Brave mind. 'Rouse up a brave mind,' says the fiend . *Mer. of Venice* ii 2 12
There's no better sign of a brave mind than a hard hand *2 Hen. VI.* iv 2 22
Brave monster. O brave monster! Lead the way . . . *Tempest* ii 2 192
He were a brave monster indeed, if they were set in his tail . . iii 2 12
Brave Montgomery. Thanks, brave Montgomery; and thanks unto you all . . . . *3 Hen. VI.* iv 7 77
Brave Moor. Adieu, brave Moor; use Desdemona well . . *Othello* i 3 292
Brave night. This is a brave night to cool a courtezan . *Lear* iii 2 79
Brave oaths. Swears brave oaths and breaks them bravely *As Y. Like It* iii 4 44
Brave Oliver. O brave Oliver, Leave me not behind thee . . iii 3 102
Brave Othello. To throw out our eyes for brave Othello . *Othello* ii 1 38
Brave Oxford, wondrous well beloved . . . . *3 Hen. VI.* iv 8 17
Brave pavilions. The fresh and yet unbruised Greeks do pitch Their brave pavilions . . . . *Troi. and Cres.* Prol. 15
Brave peers of England, pillars of the state . . *2 Hen. VI.* i 1 75
Brave Percy. Thou art dust, And food for— For worms, brave Percy *1 Hen. IV.* v 4 87
Brave Plantagenet. We, the sons of brave Plantagenet . *3 Hen. VI.* ii 1 35
Gallant-springing brave Plantagenet, That princely novice *Richard III.* i 4 227
Brave prince. Hath she forgot already that brave prince? . . i 2 240
Brave punishments. I'll devise thee brave punishments for him *Much Ado* v 4 130
Brave respect. What a noble combat hast thou fought Between compulsion and a brave respect! . . . . . . *K. John* v 2 44
Brave sir! I would they were in Afric both together . *Cymbeline* i 1 166
Brave slip, sprung from the great Andronicus . . *T. Andron.* v 1 9
Brave soldier, pardon me . . . . *K. John* v 6 13
In which array, brave soldier, doth he lie, Larding the plain . *Hen. V.* iv 6 7
Come on, brave soldiers: doubt not of the day . . *3 Hen. VI.* iv 7 87
Brave son. The Duke of Milan And his brave son . . *Tempest* i 2 438
Soul of Rome! Brave son, derived from honourable loins! . *J. Cæsar* ii 1 322
Brave spirit. These be brave spirits indeed! . . . *Tempest* v 1 261
O brave spirit!—Via! les eaux et la terre . . . *Hen. V.* iv 2 3
Brave squares. And no practice had In the brave squares of war *Ant. and Cleo.* iii 11 40
Brave Talbot. Ascend, brave Talbot; we will follow thee *1 Hen. VI.* ii 1 28
Then God take mercy on brave Talbot's soul! . . . . iv 3 34
If he be dead, brave Talbot, then adieu! . . . . iv 4 45
Brave Timon. I have but little gold of late, brave Timon *T. of Athens* iv 3 90
Brave Titinius! Look, whether he have not crown'd dead Cassius! *J. Cæsar* v 3 96
Brave Titus. Advance, brave Titus: They do disdain us. . *Coriolanus* i 4 25
Brave touch! Could not a worm, an adder, do so much? *M. N. Dream* iii 2 70
Brave town. Welcome, my lord, to this brave town of York *3 Hen. VI.* ii 2 1
Brave Troilus! the prince of chivalry! . . . *Troi. and Cres.* i 2 248
Brave utensils. He has brave utensils,—for so he calls them . *Tempest* iii 2 104
Brave verses. He writes brave verses, speaks brave words *As Y. Like It* iii 4 43
Brave vessel. A brave vessel, Who had, no doubt, some noble creature in her, Dash'd all to pieces . . . . *Tempest* i 2 6
Brave warriors, Clifford and Northumberland . . *3 Hen. VI.* i 4 66
Why then it sorts, brave warriors, let's away . . . . ii 1 209
Brave wars. O, 'tis brave wars!—Most admirable . . *All's Well* ii 1 25
Brave Warwick! What brings thee to France? . . . *3 Hen. VI.* iii 3 46
Brave words. He writes brave verses, speaks brave words *As Y. Like It* iii 4 44
Brave world. Rare words! brave world! Hostess, my breakfast *1 Hen. IV.* iii 3 229
Brave York. I beg The leading of the vaward.—Take it, brave York *Hen. V.* iv 3 131
Brave young prince! thy famous grandfather Doth live again in thee *3 Hen. VI.* v 4 52
Braved in mine own house with a skein of thread? . *T. of Shrew* iv 3 111
Face not me: thou hast braved many men; brave not me . . iv 3 125
I will neither be faced nor braved . . . . . . iv 3 127
That damned villain Tranio, That faced and braved me in this matter so v 1 124
My state is braved, Even at my gates, with ranks of foreign powers *K. John* iv 2 243
How I am braved and must perforce endure it! . *1 Hen. VI.* i 4 115
By the book He should have braved the east an hour ago *Richard III.* v 3 279
Hated by one he loves; braved by his brother. . *J. Cæsar* iv 3 96
Bravely the figure of this harpy hast thou Perform'd . . *Tempest* iii 3 83
Tight and yare and bravely rigg'd . . . . . . v 1 224
Bravely, my diligence. Thou shalt be free . . . . v 1 241
'Twas bravely done, if you bethink you of it . . *Much Ado* v 1 280
He bravely broach'd his boiling bloody breast . . *M. N. Dream* v 1 148
Swears brave oaths and breaks them bravely . . *As Y. Like It* iii 4 45
Return unto thy father's house And revel it as bravely as the best *T. of Shrew* iv 3 54
An thy mind stand to't, boy, steal away bravely . . *All's Well* ii 1 29
Therefore away, and leave her bravely . . . . . ii 3 316
Away, and for our flight.—Bravely, coragio! . . . . ii 5 97
Whatsome'er he is, He's bravely taken here . . . . iii 5 55
The manner how she came to't bravely confessed . . *W. Tale* v 2 93
O, bravely came we off! . . . . *K. John* v 5 4
Full bravely hast thou flesh'd Thy maiden sword . . *1 Hen. IV.* v 4 133
Bravely. For to serve bravely is to come halting off, you know *2 Hen. IV.* ii 4 54
To come off the breach with his pike bent bravely, and to surgery bravely . . . . ii 4 56
Who came off bravely, who was shot, who disgraced . *Hen. V.* iii 6 77
The French are bravely in their battles set . . . . iv 3 69
She takes upon her bravely at first dash . . . *1 Hen. VI.* i 2 71
Pucelle hath bravely play'd her part in this . . . . i 3 88
When I have been dry and bravely marching . . *2 Hen. VI.* iv 10 15
March on, join bravely, let us to't pell-mell . . *Richard III.* v 3 312
Here we may see most bravely . . . . *Troi. and Cres.* i 2 198
But our great Ajax bravely beat down him . . . . iii 3 213
Bear the palm for having bravely shed Thy wife and children's blood *Coriolanus* v 3 117
See you do it bravely.—I warrant you, sir . . *T. Andron.* iv 3 113
Why, now thou diest as bravely as Titinius . . *J. Cæsar* v 4 10
The noble thanes do bravely in the war . . . *Macbeth* v 7 26
I will die bravely, like a bridegroom . . . . *Lear* iv 6 202
O happy horse, to bear the weight of Antony! Do bravely, horse! *Ant. and Cleo.* i 5 22
How bravely thou becomest thy bed, fresh lily! . . *Cymbeline* ii 2 15
A piece of work So bravely done . . . . . . ii 4 73
In our country's cause Fell bravely and were slain . . . v 4 72
Braver. The Duke of Milan And his more braver daughter . *Tempest* i 2 439
And wear my dagger with the braver grace . . *Mer. of Venice* iii 4 65
In brief, a braver choice of dauntless spirits . . *K. John* ii 1 72
A braver place In my heart's love hath no man than yourself *1 Hen. IV.* iv 1 7
A braver gentleman, More active-valiant or more valiant-young, More daring . . . . v 1 89
A braver soldier never couched lance . . . *1 Hen. VI.* iii 2 134
Two braver men Ne'er spurr'd their coursers . . *3 Hen. VI.* v 7 8
A nobler man, a braver warrior, Lives not this day . *T. Andron.* i 1 25
Bravery. That says his bravery is not on my cost . *As Y. Like It* ii 7 80
Assemblies Where youth, and cost, and witless bravery keeps *M. for M.* i 3 10
With scarfs and fans and double change of bravery . *T. of Shrew* iv 3 57
And come down With fearful bravery . . . . *J. Cæsar* v 1 10
The bravery of his grief did put me Into a towering passion . *Hamlet* v 2 79
Upon malicious bravery, dost thou come To start my quiet . . *Othello* i 1 100
The natural bravery of your isle, which stands As Neptune's park *Cymbeline* iii 1 18
Bravest. And was Discipled of the bravest . . . . *All's Well* i 2 28
When The bravest questant shrinks, find what you seek . . ii 1 16
Bravest at the last, She levell'd at our purposes . *Ant. and Cleo.* v 2 338
From this most bravest vessel of the world Struck the main-top! *Cymb.* iv 2 319
Braving. Fought with equal fortune and continue A braving war *All's Well* i 2 3
Here art come . . . In braving arms against thy sovereign *Richard II.* ii 3 112
But in this kind to come, in braving arms, Be his own carver . . ii 3 143
Brawl. But, like a shrew, you first begin to brawl . *Com. of Errors* iv 1 51
Thou say'st his sports were hinder'd by thy brawls . . . v 1 77
Will you win your love with a French brawl? . . *L. L. Lost* iii 1 9
With thy brawls thou hast disturb'd our sport . *M. N. Dream* ii 1 87
Peeps out Upon the brook that brawls along this wood . *As Y. Like It* ii 1 32
If she chance to nod I'll rail and brawl . . . *T. of Shrew* iv 1 209
He is a devil in private brawl . . . . . . *T. Night* iii 4 259
Let no quarrel nor no brawl to come Taint the condition of this present hour . . . . v 1 364
For his divisions, as the times do brawl, Are in three heads . *2 Hen. IV.* i 3 70
Be gone, good ancient: this will grow to a brawl anon . . ii 4 187
Right ill-disposed in brawl ridiculous . . . *Hen. V.* iv Prol. 51
This brawl to-day, Grown to this faction in the Temple-garden *1 Hen. VI.* ii 4 124
I do the wrong, and first begin to brawl . . . *Richard III.* i 3 324
Here none but soldiers and Rome's servitors Repose in fame; none basely slain in brawls . . . . *T. Andron.* i 1 353
To take up a matter of brawl betwixt my uncle and one of the emperial's men . . . . iv 3 93
Three civil brawls, bred of an airy word . . . *Rom. and Jul.* i 1 96
The day is hot, the Capulets abroad, And, if we meet, we shall not 'scape a brawl . . . . iii 1 3
I can discover all The unlucky manage of this fatal brawl . . iii 1 148
My blood for your rude brawls doth lie a-bleeding . . . iii 1 194
For Christian shame, put by this barbarous brawl . . *Othello* ii 3 172
Silence those whom this vile brawl distracted . . . . ii 3 256
Brawl'd down The flinty ribs of this contemptuous city . *K. John* ii 1 383
Brawling. Whose advice Hath often still'd my brawling discontent *Meas. for Meas.* iv 1 9
Will you win your love with a French brawl?—How meanest thou? brawling in French? . . . . *L. L. Lost* iii 1 10
I know she is an irksome brawling scold . . . *T. of Shrew* i 2 188
Giddy for lack of sleep, With oaths kept waking and with brawling fed iv 3 10
Peace, ye fat-kidneyed rascal! what a brawling dost thou keep! *1 Hen. IV.* ii 2 6
What are you brawling here? Doth this become your place? *2 Hen. IV.* ii 1 71
Why, then, O brawling love! O loving hate! . *Rom. and Jul.* i 1 182
Brawn. The quatch-buttock, the brawn buttock, or any buttock *All's Well* ii 2 19
I'll play Percy, and that damned brawn shall play Dame Mortimer his wife . . . . *1 Hen. IV.* ii 4 123
Harry Monmouth's brawn, the hulk Sir John, Is prisoner . *2 Hen. IV.* i 1 19
In my vantbrace put this wither'd brawn . . . *Troi. and Cres.* i 3 297
I had purpose Once more to hew thy target from thy brawn *Coriolanus* iv 5 126
His foot Mercurial; his Martial thigh; The brawns of Hercules *Cymb.* iv 2 311
Bray. With harsh-resounding trumpets' dreadful bray . *Richard II.* i 3 135
The kettle-drum and trumpet thus bray out The triumph of his pledge *Hamlet* i 4 11
Brayed. When every room Hath blazed with lights and bray'd with minstrelsy, I have retired me . . . . . . *T. of Athens* ii 2 170
Braying trumpets and loud churlish drums, Clamours of hell . *K. John* iii 1 303
Brazed. I have so often blushed to acknowledge him, that now I am brazed to it.—I cannot conceive you . . . . . . *Lear* i 1 11
Brazen. Let fame, that all hunt after in their lives, Live register'd upon our brazen tombs . . . . *L. L. Lost* i 1 2
The midnight bell Did, with his iron tongue and brazen mouth, Sound on into the drowsy race of night . . . . . . *K. John* iii 3 38
Through brazen trumpet send the breath of parley . *Richard II.* iii 3 33
I had rather hear a brazen canstick turn'd, Or a dry wheel grate on the axle-tree . . . . *1 Hen. IV.* iii 1 131
His loves Are brazen images of canonized saints . . *2 Hen. VI.* i 3 63
Cursed the gentle gusts And he that loosed them forth their brazen caves . . . . iii 2 89
Yet that thy brazen gates of heaven may ope, And give sweet passage to my sinful soul! . . . . *3 Hen. VI.* ii 3 40
Bound to revenge, Wert thou environ'd with a brazen wall . . ii 4 4
Now crack thy lungs, and split thy brazen pipe . . *Troi. and Cres.* iv 5 7

Brazen. Why such daily cast of brazen cannon? *Hamlet* i 1 73
Trumpeters, With brazen din blast you the city's ear *Ant. and Cleo.* iv 8 36
Brazen-face. Well said, brazen-face! hold it out *Mer. Wives* iv 2 141
Brazen-faced. What a brazen-faced varlet art thou! *Lear* ii 2 30
Brazier. He should be a brazier by his face *Hen. VIII.* v 4 42
Breach. You use this dalliance to excuse Your breach of promise *Com. of Errors* iv 1 49
As honour without breach of honour may Make tender of *L. L. Lost* ii 1 170
With the breach yourselves made, you lose your city *All's Well* i 1 136
Some hour before you took me from the breach of the sea *T. Night* ii 1 23
Patches set upon a little breach Discredit more in hiding of the fault *K. John* iv 2 32
To come off the breach with his pike bent bravely *2 Hen. IV.* ii 4 55
Came pouring, like the tide into a breach *Hen. V.* i 2 149
Once more unto the breach, dear friends, once more iii 1 1
On, on, on! to the breach, to the breach! iii 2 1
Up to the breach, you dogs! avaunt, you cullions! iii 2 21
The town is beseeched, and the trumpet call us to the breach iii 2 116
At such and such a sconce, at such a breach, at such a convoy iii 6 76
They found some place But weakly guarded, where the breach was made *1 Hen. VI.* ii 1 74
Through which our policy must make a breach iii 2 2
But I in danger for the breach of law *2 Hen. VI.* ii 4 66
A breach that craves a quick expedient stop! iii 1 288
This breach now in our fortunes made May readily be stopp'd v 2 82
It should be put To no apparent likelihood of breach *Richard III.* ii 2 136
That this tempest, Dashing the garment of this peace, aboded The sudden breach on't *Hen. VIII.* i 1 94
Our breach of duty this way Is business of estate ii 2 69
However, yet there is no great breach iv 1 106
Make distinct the very breach whereout Hector's great spirit flew *Troi. and Cres.* iv 5 245
Then dreams he of cutting foreign throats, Of breaches *Rom. and Jul.* i 4 84
His gash'd stabs look'd like a breach in nature *Macbeth* ii 3 119
It is a custom More honour'd in the breach than the observance *Hamlet* i 4 16
Nuptial breaches, and I know not what *Lear* i 2 162
O you kind gods, Cure this great breach in his abused nature! iv 7 15
Of hair-breadth 'scapes i' the imminent deadly breach *Othello* i 3 136
There's fall'n between him and my lord An unkind breach iv 1 236
If thy faith be not tainted with the breach of hers *Cymbeline* iii 4 27
Stick to your journal course: the breach of custom Is breach of all iv 2 10
Bread. An honest maid as ever broke bread *Mer. Wives* i 4 161
I love not the humour of bread and cheese, and there's the humour of it ii 1 140
His appetite Is more to bread than stone *Meas. for Meas.* i 3 53
He would mouth with a beggar, though she smelt brown bread and garlic iii 2 195
An honest soul, i' faith, sir; by my troth he is, as ever broke bread *Much Ado* iii 5 42
A crew of patches, rude mechanicals, That work for bread *M. N. Dream* iii 2 10
His kissing is as full of sanctity as the touch of holy bread *As Y. Like It* iii 4 15
Eating the bitter bread of banishment *Richard II.* iii 1 21
I live with bread like you, feel want, Taste grief, need friends iii 2 175
That jade hath eat bread from my royal hand v 5 85
O monstrous! but one half-pennyworth of bread to this intolerable deal of sack! *1 Hen. IV.* ii 4 592
Would have made a good pantler, a' would ha' chipped bread well *2 Hen. IV.* ii 4 259
Gets him to rest, cramm'd with distressful bread *Hen. V.* iv 1 287
Good morrow, gallants! want ye corn for bread? *1 Hen. VI.* iii 2 41
I speak this in hunger for bread, not in thirst for revenge *Coriolanus* i 1 25
God's bread! it makes me mad *Rom. and Jul.* iii 5 177
The fellow that sits next him now, parts bread with him *T. of Athens* i 2 48
He took my father grossly, full of bread; With all his crimes *Hamlet* iii 3 80
I'll prove it on thy heart, Ere I taste bread *Lear* v 3 94
A housewife that by selling her desires Buys herself bread and clothes *Othello* iv 1 96
Those palates who, not yet two summers younger, Must have inventions to delight the taste, Would now be glad of bread *Pericles* i 4 41
With corn to make your needy bread, And give them life i 4 95
Bread-chipper. To dispraise me, and call me pantler and bread-chipper and I know not what *2 Hen. IV.* ii 4 342
Breadth. I profess requital to a hair's breadth *Mer. Wives* iv 2 4
Then she bears some breadth? *Com. of Errors* iii 2 114
Measure his woe the length and breadth of mine *Much Ado* v 1 11
If there be breadth enough in the world, I will hold a long distance *All's Well* iii 2 26
That blood which owed the breadth of all this isle, Three foot of it doth hold: bad world the while! *K. John* iv 2 99
The spacious breadth of this division Admits no orifex *Troi. and Cres.* v 2 150
The length and breadth of a pair of indentures *Hamlet* v 1 119
It is shaped, sir, like itself; and it is as broad as it hath breadth *Ant. and Cleo.* ii 7 48
He will repent the breadth of his great voyage *Pericles* iv 1 37
Break. I had rather crack my sinews, break my back *Tempest* iii 1 26
If thou dost break her virgin-knot before iv 1 15
My charms I'll break, their senses I'll restore v 1 31
I'll break my staff, Bury it certain fathoms in the earth v 1 54
Now can I break my fast, dine, sup and sleep *T. G. of Ver.* ii 4 141
I'll be so bold to break the seal for once iii 1 139
Which he will break As easily as I do tear his paper iv 4 135
Lovers break not hours, Unless it be to come before their time v 1 4
What they think in their hearts they may effect, they will break their hearts but they will effect *Mer. Wives* ii 2 323
Break their talk, Mistress Quickly iii 4 22
Her brother's ghost his paved bed would break *Meas. for Meas.* v 1 440
I shall break that merry sconce of yours That stands on tricks *Com. of Errors* i 2 79
Back, slave, or I will break thy pate across ii 1 78
But, too unruly deer, he breaks the pale And feeds from home ii 1 100
And from my false hand cut the wedding-ring And break it with a deep-divorcing vow ii 2 140
Let none enter, lest I break your pate ii 2 220
Break any breaking here, and I'll break your knave's pate iii 1 74
A man may break a word with you, sir, and words are but wind iii 1 75
He that brings any man to answer it that breaks his band iv 3 31
Then after to her father will I break *Much Ado* i 1 328
He'll but break a comparison or two on me ii 1 152
You break jests as braggarts do their blades, which, God be thanked, hurt not v 1 189
Break. Or, having sworn too hard a keeping oath, Study to break it and not break my troth *L. L. Lost* i 1 66
This article, my liege, yourself must break i 1 134
He that breaks them in the least degree Stands in attainder of eternal shame i 1 157
Why, will shall break it; will and nothing else ii 1 100
'Tis deadly sin to keep that oath, my lord, And sin to break it ii 1 106
Break the neck of the wax, and every one give ear iv 1 59
I, that hold it sin To break the vow I am engaged in iv 3 178
The virtue of your eye must break my oath v 2 348
For virtue's office never breaks men's troth v 2 350
Despise me, when I break this oath of mine v 2 441
And shivering shocks Shall break the locks *M. N. Dream* i 2 35
And make him with fair Ægle break his faith ii 1 79
Have a care the honey-bag break not iv 1 16
To supply the ripe wants of my friend, I'll break a custom *Mer. of Venice* i 3 65
Who, if he break, thou mayst with better face Exact the penalty i 3 137
If he should break his day, what should I gain? i 3 165
There came divers of Antonio's creditors in my company to Venice, that swear he cannot choose but break iii 1 120
By my soul I swear I never more will break an oath with thee v 1 248
I had as lief thou didst break his neck as his finger *As Y. Like It* i 1 153
When I break that oath, let me turn monster i 2 23
I shall ne'er be ware of mine own wit till I break my shins against it ii 4 60
Speaks brave words, swears brave oaths and breaks them bravely iii 4 45
Break an hour's promise in love! He that will divide a minute into a thousand parts and break but a part of the thousandth part iv 1 44
If you break one jot of your promise or come one minute behind your hour iv 1 194
According as marriage binds and blood breaks v 4 59
You break into some merry passion And so offend him *T. of Shrew* Ind. 1 97
Then thou canst not break her to the lute?—Why, no; for she hath broke the lute to me ii 1 148
My tongue will tell the anger of my heart, Or else my heart concealing it will break iv 3 78
Like pleasant travellers, to break a jest Upon the company you overtake iv 5 72
If I break time, or flinch in property Of what I spoke *All's Well* ii 1 190
I shall not break your bidding, good my lord ii 5 93
I am resolved on two points.—That if one break, the other will hold; or, if both break, your gaskins fall *T. Night* i 5 26
Nay, patience, or we break the sinews of our plot ii 5 83
Since then You have not dared to break the holy seal *W. Tale* iii 2 130
O, cut my lace, lest my heart, cracking it, Break too! iii 2 175
The fury spent, anon Did this break from her iii 3 27
Mean mischief and break a foul gap into the matter iv 4 198
The tortures he shall feel, will break the back of man, the heart of monster iv 4 797
As monstrous to our human reason As my Antigonus to break his grave v 1 42
That broker, that still breaks the pate of faith *K. John* ii 1 568
No bargains break that are not this day made! iii 1 93
Move the murmuring lips of discontent To break into this dangerous argument iv 2 54
His passion is so ripe, it needs must break.—And when it breaks, I fear will issue thence The foul corruption of a sweet child's death iv 2 79
A warrant To break within the bloody house of life iv 2 210
If e'er those eyes of yours Behold another day break in the east v 4 32
Be Mowbray's sins so heavy in his bosom, That they may break his foaming courser's back! *Richard II.* i 2 51
My heart is great; but it must break with silence ii 1 228
And let him ne'er see joy that breaks that oath! ii 3 151
I am loath to break our country's laws ii 3 169
They break their faith to God as well as us iii 2 101
Ere foul sin gathering head Shall break into corruption v 1 59
You told me you would tell the rest, When weeping made you break the story off v 2 2
Open the door, or I will break it open v 3 45
Would he not fall down, Since pride must have a fall, and break the neck Of that proud man? v 5 88
Why, what a wasp-stung and impatient fool Art thou to break into this woman's mood! *1 Hen. IV.* i 3 237
An 'twere not as good deed as drink, to break the pate on thee ii 1 33
If I travel but four foot by the squier further afoot, I shall break my wind ii 2 13
I'll break thy little finger, Harry, An if thou wilt not tell me all things true ii 3 90
And withal Break with your wives of your departure hence iii 1 144
And I will die a hundred thousand deaths Ere break the smallest parcel of this vow iii 2 159
Nay, an I do, I pray God my girdle break iii 3 171
For you my staff of office did I break In Richard's time v 1 34
Breaks like a fire Out of his keeper's arms *2 Hen. IV.* i 1 142
The time will come, that foul sin, gathering head, Shall break into corruption iii 1 77
I see him break Skogan's head at the court-gate iii 2 33
Will you thus break your faith? iv 2 112
These tardy tricks of yours will, on my life, One time or other break some gallows' back iv 3 32
Pluck down my officers, break my decrees iv 5 118
I break, and you, my gentle creditors, lose Epil. 13
We'll bend it to our awe, Or break it all to pieces *Hen. V.* i 2 225
By the means whereof a' breaks words, and keeps whole weapons iii 2 37
Whiles the mad mothers with their howls confused Do break the clouds iii 3 40
Is not that the morning which breaks yonder? iv 1 88
Downright oaths, which I never use till urged, nor never break for urging v 2 152
Break thy mind to me in broken English v 2 265
I'll be no breaker of the law: But we shall meet, and break our minds at large *1 Hen. VI.* i 3 81
The day begins to break, and night is fled ii 2 1
Break a lance, And run a tilt at death within a chair iii 2 50
He dies, we lose; I break my warlike word iv 3 31
Till mischief and despair Drive you to break your necks or hang yourselves v 4 91
Break thou in pieces and consume to ashes! v 4 92
Take this compact of a truce, Although you break it when your pleasure serves v 4 164
He that breaks a stick of Gloucester's grove Shall lose his head *2 Hen. VI.* i 2 33
My lord, break we off; we know your mind at full ii 2 77
My burthen'd heart would break, Should I not curse them iii 2 320
Let them break your backs with burthens, take your houses over your heads iv 8 30

Break. I would break a thousand oaths to reign one year . 3 *Hen. VI.* i 2 17
Ah, would she break from hence, that this my body Might in the ground be closed up in rest! . . . . . . ii 1 75
Be blind with tears, and break o'ercharged with grief . . . ii 5 78
But did you never swear, and break an oath? . . . . . . iii 1 72
But do not break your oaths; for of that sin My mild entreaty shall not make you guilty . . . . iii 1 90
With patience calm the storm, While we bethink a means to break it off iii 3 39
And heave it shall some weight, or break my back . . . . v 7 24
Sorrow breaks seasons and reposing hours . . . *Richard III.* i 4 76
He holds vengeance in his hands, To hurl upon their heads that break his law . . . . i 4 205
And, like a traitor to the name of God, Didst break that vow . i 4 211
You break not sanctuary in seizing him . . . . . iii 1 47
Then, taking him from thence that is not there, You break no privilege iii 1 54
Harp on it still shall I till heartstrings break . . . . iv 4 365
God's wrong is most of all. If thou hadst fear'd to break an oath by Him . . . . iv 4 378
The silent hours steal on, And flaky darkness breaks within the east . v 3 86
And like a glass Did break i' the rinsing . . . *Hen. VIII.* i 1 167
That he would please to alter the king's course, And break the foresaid peace . . . . i 1 190
Language unmannerly, yea, such which breaks The sides of loyalty . i 2 27
Yet my duty, As doth a rock against the chiding flood, Should the approach of this wild river break . . . . . iii 2 198
Go, break among the press, and find a way out . . . . v 4 88
Upon a lazy bed the livelong day Breaks scurril jests . *Troi. and Cres.* i 3 148
He would pun thee into shivers with his fist, as a sailor breaks a biscuit ii 1 43
The fool slides o'er the ice that you should break . . . iii 3 215
If Hector break not his neck i' the combat, he'll break 't himself in vain-glory . . . . iii 3 259
Crack my clear voice with sobs and break my heart With sounding Troilus . . . . iv 2 114
An oath that I have sworn. I will not break it . . . . v 1 47
I must not break my faith. You know me dutiful . . . . v 3 71
A plague break thy neck for frighting me! . . . . . v 4 34
To break the heart of generosity, And make bold power look pale *Coriol.* i 1 215
We'll break our walls, Rather than they shall pound us up . . i 4 16
And that is there which looks With us to break his neck . . iii 3 30
Yet he hath left undone That which shall break his neck or hazard mine iv 7 25
All bond and privilege of nature, break! Let it be virtuous to be obstinate . . . . v 3 25
We respected not them; and, he returning to break our necks, they respect not us . . . . v 4 36
Prepare thy aged eyes to weep; Or, if not so, thy noble heart to break: I bring consuming sorrow to thine age . . *T. Andron.* iii 1 60
Speak with possibilities, And do not break into these deep extremes . iii 1 216
Make poor men's cattle break their necks . . . . . v 1 132
Break the parle; These quarrels must be quietly debated . . v 3 19
But floods of tears will drown my oratory, And break my utterance . v 3 91
From ancient grudge break to new mutiny . . *Rom. and Jul.* Prol. 3
What light through yonder window breaks? It is the east . . ii 2 2
O, break, my heart! poor bankrupt, break at once! . . . iii 2 57
The world affords no law to make thee rich; Then be not poor, but break it . . . . v 1 74
But must not break my back to heal his finger . *T. of Athens* ii 1 24
This yellow slave Will knit and break religions . . . . iv 3 34
And pursy insolence shall break his wind With fear and horrid flight . v 4 12
Here lies the east: doth not the day break here? . . *J. Cæsar* ii 1 101
If he do break the smallest particle Of any promise that hath pass'd . ii 1 139
All this! ay, more: fret till your proud heart break . . . iv 3 42
As whence the sun 'gins his reflection Shipwrecking storms and direful thunders break . . . . *Macbeth* i 2 26
What beast was't, then, That made you break this enterprise to me? . i 7 48
Give sorrow words: the grief that does not speak Whispers the o'er-fraught heart and bids it break . . . . iv 3 210
That keep the word of promise to our ear, And break it to our hope . v 8 22
Peace, break thee off; look, where it comes again! . . *Hamlet* i 1 40
Break we our watch up . . . . i 1 168
But break, my heart; for I must hold my tongue . . . . i 2 159
Take away her power; Break all the spokes and fellies from her wheel . ii 2 517
Am I a coward? Who calls me villain? breaks my pate across? . . ii 2 599
You think what now you speak; But what we do determine oft we break iii 2 197
If she should break it now!—'Tis deeply sworn . . . . iii 2 234
To try conclusions, in the basket creep, And break your own neck down iii 4 196
That inward breaks, and shows no cause without Why the man dies . iv 4 28
Break not your sleeps for that . . . . iv 7 30
Thou hast sought to make us break our vow, Which we durst never yet *Lear* i 1 171
These hot tears, which break from me perforce, Should make thee worth them . . . . i 4 320
Let go thy hold when a great wheel runs down a hill, lest it break thy neck . . . . ii 4 74
This heart Shall break into a hundred thousand flaws, Or ere I'll weep . ii 4 288
Wilt break my heart?—I had rather break mine own . . . iii 4 4
I would not take this from report; it is, And my heart breaks at it . iv 6 145
Plate sin with gold, And the strong lance of justice hurtless breaks . iv 6 170
Break, heart; I prithee, break! . . . . v 3 312
Balmy breath, that dost almost persuade Justice to break her sword! *Oth.* v 2 17
These strong Egyptian fetters I must break, Or lose myself *Ant. and Cleo.* i 2 120
I shall break The cause of our expedience to the queen . . . i 2 184
Those mouth-made vows, Which break themselves in swearing . . i 3 31
This blows my heart: If swift thought break it not, a swifter mean Shall outstrike thought . . . . iv 6 35
Being dried with grief, will break to powder, And finish all foul thoughts iv 9 17
Then in the midst a tearing groan did break The name of Antony . iv 14 31
Let me rail so high, That the false housewife Fortune break her wheel . iv 15 44
O, break! O, break!—As sweet as balm, as soft as air, as gentle,— O Antony! . . . . v 2 313
Wherefore breaks that sigh From the inward of thee? . . *Cymbeline* iii 4 5
If sleep charge nature, To break it with a fearful dream . . . iv 4 45
I'll take thy word for faith, not ask thine oath: Who shuns not to break one will sure crack both . . . . . . *Pericles* i 2 121
This by the eye of Cynthia hath she vow'd, And on her virgin honour will not break it . . . . ii 5 12
Break away. Fear me not, man; I will not break away *Com. of Errors* iv 4 1
Break faith. If I break faith, this word shall speak for me . *L. L. Lost* i 1 154
You would for paradise break faith and troth . . . . . iv 3 143
Your lord Will never more break faith advisedly . *Mer. of Venice* v 1 253
Since kings break faith upon commodity, Gain, be my lord . *K. John* ii 1 597

Break forth. On my life, his malice 'gainst the lady Will suddenly break forth . . . . *As Y. Like It* i 2 295
Diseased nature oftentimes breaks forth In strange eruptions 1 *Hen. IV.* iii 1 27
Within this mile break forth a hundred springs . . *T. of Athens* iv 3 421
Break in. I'll break in: go borrow me a crow . . . *Com. of Errors* iii 1 80
If by strong hand you offer to break in Now in the stirring passage of the day, A vulgar comment will be made of it . . . . . iii 1 98
Then how or which way should they first break in? . . 1 *Hen. VI.* ii 1 71
An answer from the king, or we will all break in! . . 2 *Hen. VI.* iii 2 278
Break into. And then break into his son-in-law's house . . . iv 7 117
Is't not enough to break into my garden, And, like a thief, to come to rob my grounds? . . . . iv 10 35
Break loose. No, no; he'll . . . Seem to break loose . *M. N. Dream* iii 2 258
Break of day. And those eyes, the break of day, Lights that do mislead the morn . . . . *Meas. for Meas.* iv 1 3
Here will I rest me till the break of day . . . *M. N. Dream* ii 2 446
Now, until the break of day, Through this house each fairy stray . v 1 408
Trip away; make no stay; Meet me all by break of day . . . v 1 429
Such it is As are those dulcet sounds in break of day . *Mer. of Venice* iii 2 51
My mistress will before the break of day Be here at Belmont . . . v 1 29
Either be gone before the watch be set, Or by the break of day *Rom. and Jul.* iii 3 168
When canst thou reach it?—By break of day . . . *Pericles* iii 1 77
Break off thy song, and haste thee quick away . . *Meas. for Meas.* iv 1 7
Do not break off so; For we may pity, though not pardon thee *C. of Err.* i 1 97
Not one word more, my maids; break off, break off . *L. L. Lost* v 2 262
Women and fools, break off your conference . . . *K. John* ii 1 150
Deep shame had struck me dumb, made me break off . . . iv 2 235
And so break off; the day is almost spent . . . 2 *Hen. VI.* iii 1 325
Break off the parley; for scarce I can refrain The execution of my big-swoln heart . . . . 3 *Hen. VI.* ii 2 110
Break off your talk, And give us notice of his inclination *Richard III.* iii 1 177
Break off betimes, And every man hence to his idle bed . *J. Cæsar* ii 1 116
I must from this enchanting queen break off . *Ant. and Cleo.* i 2 132
Break ope. I'll break ope the gate.—Break any breaking here, And I'll break your knave's pate . . . *Com. of Errors* iii 1 73
Which will in time Break ope the locks o' the senate . *Coriolanus* iii 1 138
Break open the gaols and let out the prisoners . . 2 *Hen. VI.* iv 3 18
To Athens go, Break open shops . . . . . *T. of Athens* iv 3 450
Break out. Did he break out into tears?—In great measure . *Much Ado* i 1 24
This will break out To all our sorrows . . . . *K. John* iv 2 101
So thin that life looks through and will break out . . 2 *Hen. IV.* iv 4 120
Like to the bullet's grazing, Break out into a second course of mischief *Hen. V.* iv 3 106
Burns under feigned ashes of forged love And will at last break out into a flame . . . . 1 *Hen. VI.* iii 1 191
Poor queen! how love to me and to her son Hath made her break out into terms of rage! . . . . 3 *Hen. VI.* i 1 265
The new-heal'd wound of malice should break out . . *Richard III.* ii 2 125
You shake, my lord, at something: will you go? You will break out *Troi. and Cres.* v 2 51
Lest parties, as he is beloved, break out, And sack great Rome *Coriol.* iii 1 315
On a dissension of a doit, break out To bitterest enmity . . . iv 4 17
He foams at mouth and by and by Breaks out to savage madness *Othello* iv 1 56
Or else break out in peevish jealousies, Throwing restraint upon us . iv 3 90
The which he hearing—As it is like him—might break out . *Cymbeline* iv 2 140
Break peace. Not to break peace or any branch of it . 2 *Hen. IV.* iv 1 85
Break promise. And then to break promise with him and make a fool of him . . . . *T. Night* ii 3 137
Break the ice. If you break the ice and do this feat . *T. of Shrew* i 2 267
Break the peace. If he break the peace, he ought to enter into a quarrel with fear and trembling . . . . *Much Ado* ii 3 202
Fie, lords! that you, being supreme magistrates, Thus contumeliously should break the peace! . . . . 1 *Hen. VI.* i 3 58
Breaks through. As the sun breaks through the darkest clouds *T. of Shr.* iv 3 175
Break up. You can carve; Break up this capon . . *L. L. Lost* iv 1 56
An it shall please you to break up this, it shall seem to signify *Mer. of Venice* ii 4 10
Break up the seals and read . . . . . . *W. Tale* iii 2 132
The organs, though defunct and dead before, Break up their drowsy grave . . . . *Hen. V.* iv 1 22
Break up the gates, I'll be your warrantize . . . 1 *Hen. VI.* i 3 13
And spirits walk and ghosts break up their graves . . 2 *Hen. VI.* i 4 22
Break up the court: I say, set on . . . . *Hen. VIII.* ii 4 240
Break up the senate till another time, When Cæsar's wife shall meet with better dreams . . . . *J. Cæsar* ii 2 98
Break with. In good time! now will we break with him. *T. G. of Ver.* i 3 44
I am to break with thee of some affairs That touch me near . . iii 1 59
I would not break with her for more money than I'll speak of *Mer. Wives* iii 2 57
I will break with her and with her father And thou shalt have her *Much Ado* i 1 311
He meant to take the present time by the top and instantly break with you of it . . . . i 2 16
And hath withdrawn her father to break with him about it . . . ii 1 162
For my life, to break with him about Beatrice . . . . . iii 2 76
It cannot be The Volsces dare break with us . . . *Coriolanus* iv 6 48
O, name him not: let us not break with him . . . *J. Cæsar* ii 1 150
Breaker. He was never yet a breaker of proverbs . . . 1 *Hen. IV.* i 2 132
I'll be no breaker of the law: But we shall meet, and break our minds 1 *Hen. VI.* i 3 80
Breakest. If thou dost nod, thou break'st thy instrument . *J. Cæsar* iv 3 271
Breakfast. Not a relation for a breakfast . . . . . *Tempest* v 1 164
That fault may be mended with a breakfast . . . *T. G. of Ver.* iii 1 329
Had I been seized by a hungry lion, I would have been a breakfast to the beast . . . . v 4 34
I do invite you to-morrow morning to my house to breakfast *Mer. Wives* iii 3 246
He that kills me some six or seven dozen of Scots at a breakfast 1 *Hen. IV.* ii 4 116
Go, make ready breakfast; love thy husband, look to thy servants . iii 3 193
I will bestow a breakfast to make you friends . . . *Hen. V.* ii 1 12
That's a valiant flea that dare eat his breakfast on the lip of a lion . iii 7 156
A sorry breakfast for my lord protector . . . . 2 *Hen. VI.* i 4 79
Humphrey Hour, that call'd your grace To breakfast once *Richard III.* iv 4 176
And then to breakfast with What appetite you have . *Hen. VIII.* iii 2 202
You had rather be at a breakfast of enemies than a dinner of friends *T. of Athens* i 2 78
If thou wert the ass, thy dulness would torment thee, and still thou livedst but as a breakfast to the wolf . . . . iv 3 336
Eight wild-boars roasted whole at a breakfast . . . *Ant. and Cleo.* ii 2 184
Is not worth a breakfast in the cheapest country under the cope *Pericles* iv 6 131

Breaking. How I have been forsworn In breaking faith . *T. G. of Ver.* iv 2 11
As easy mayst thou fall A drop of water in the breaking gulf *Com. of Err.* ii 2 128
Break any breaking here, and I'll break your knave's pate . . iii 1 74
It seems thou want'st breaking : out upon thee, hind ! . . . iii 1 77
Are good at such eruptions and sudden breaking out of mirth *L. L. Lost* v 1 121
So much I hate a breaking cause to be Of heavenly oaths . . v 2 355
The first time that ever I heard breaking of ribs was sport for ladies *As Y. L. It* i 2 146
I would the cutting of my garments would serve the turn, or the breaking of my Spanish sword . . . *All's Well* iv 1 51
He professes not keeping of oaths ; in breaking 'em he is stronger than Hercules . . . iv 3 282
The army breaking, My husband hies him home . . . iv 4 11
A note infallible Of breaking honesty . . . *W. Tale* i 2 288
Pardon me, That any accent breaking from thy tongue Should 'scape the true acquaintance of mine ear . . . *K. John* v 6 14
After your late tossing on the breaking seas . . *Richard II.* iii 2 3
He may be more wonder'd at, By breaking through the foul and ugly mists Of vapours that did seem to strangle him . . *1 Hen. IV.* i 2 226
Like a broken limb united, Grow stronger for the breaking *2 Hen. IV.* iv 1 223
To keep the horsemen off from breaking in . . . *1 Hen. VI.* i 1 119
And breaking in Were by the swords of common soldiers slain *3 Hen. VI.* i 1 8
O heart, heavy heart, Why sigh'st thou without breaking *Troi. and Cres.* iv 4 18
And is almost mature for the violent breaking out . *Coriolanus* iv 3 27
Breaking his oath and resolution like A twist of rotten silk . . v 6 95
Then this breaking of his has been but a try for his friends *T. of Athens* v 1 10
Oft breaking down the pales and forts of reason . . *Hamlet* i 4 28
Breaking forth In rank and not-to-be-endured riots . . . *Lear* i 4 222
Welcome hither : Your letters did withhold our breaking forth *A. and C.* iii 6 79
The breaking of so great a thing should make A greater crack . v 1 14
Break-neck. To do't, or no, is certain To me a break-neck . *W. Tale* i 2 363
Break-promise. I will think you the most pathetical break-promise and the most hollow lover . . . *As Y. Like It* iv 1 196
Break-vow. That daily break-vow, he that wins of all . *K. John* ii 1 569
Breast. Thy groans Did make wolves howl and penetrate the breasts Of ever angry bears . . . *Tempest* i 2 288
Such men Whose heads stood in their breasts . . . . iii 3 47
O thou that dost inhabit in my breast, Leave not the mansion so long tenantless, Lest, growing ruinous, the building fall ! *T. G. of Ver.* v 4 7
If my breast had not been made of faith and my heart of steel *C. of Err.* iii 2 150
Your fair self should make A yielding 'gainst some reason in my breast *L. L. Lost* ii 1 152
Where lies thy pain ? And where my liege's ? all about the breast . iv 3 173
A gait, a state, a brow, a breast, a waist, A leg, a limb . . . iv 3 185
Kisses the base ground with obedient breast . . . . iv 3 225
Hence ever then my heart is in thy breast . . . . v 2 826
Do thy best To pluck this crawling serpent from my breast ! *M. N. Dream* ii 2 146
With bloody blameful blade He bravely broach'd his boiling bloody breast v 1 148
Come, trusty sword ; Come, blade, my breast imbrue . . v 1 351
Therefore lay bare your bosom.—Ay, his breast : So says the bond *Mer. of Venice* iv 1 252
You must cut this flesh from off his breast : The law allows it . iv 1 302
I set him there ; Whoever charges on his forward breast, I am the caitiff that do hold him to't . . . *All's Well* iii 2 116
By my troth, the fool has an excellent breast . . . *T. Night* ii 3 20
Is from my breast, The innocent milk in it most innocent mouth, Haled out to murder . . . *W. Tale* iii 2 100
That stirs good thoughts In any breast of strong authority . *K. John* ii 1 113
What means that hand upon that breast of thine ? . . . iii 1 21
That close aspect of his Does show the mood of a much troubled breast iv 2 73
A jewel in a ten-times-barr'd-up chest Is a bold spirit in a loyal breast. Mine honour is my life . . . *Richard II.* i 1 181
That which in mean men we intitle patience Is pale cold cowardice in noble breasts. Whall shall I say ? . . . i 2 34
Sit my husband's wrongs on Hereford's spear, That it may enter butcher Mowbray's breast ! . . . i 2 48
As gentle and as jocund as to jest Go I to fight : truth hath a quiet breast i 3 96
To serve me last, that I may longest keep Thy sorrow in my breast . iii 4 96
I have a thousand spirits in one breast, To answer twenty thousand such as you . . . iv 1 58
His words come from his mouth, ours from our breast . . . v 3 102
You conjure from the breast of civil peace Such bold hostility *1 Hen. IV.* iv 3 43
Nothing could have stay'd My father from the breast of Bolingbroke *2 Hen. IV.* iv 1 124
Honour's thought Reigns solely in the breast of every man *Hen. V.* ii Prol. 4
My breast I'll burst with straining of my courage . *1 Hen. VI.* i 5 10
I will lock his counsel in my breast ; And what I do imagine let that rest ii 5 118
That engenders thunder in his breast And makes him roar these accusations . . . iii 1 39
Undaunted spirit in a dying breast ! . . . . iii 2 99
Most unnatural wounds, Which thou thyself hast given her woful breast iii 3 51
Thy friendship makes us fresh.—And doth beget new courage in our breasts . . . iii 3 87
I would the milk Thy mother gave thee when thou suck'dst her breast Had been a little ratsbane for thy sake ! . . . v 4 28
I feel such sharp dissension in my breast, Such fierce alarums . . v 5 84
I fear me you but warm the starved snake, Who, cherish'd in your breasts, will sting your hearts . . . *2 Hen. VI.* iii 1 344
Thinks he that the chirping of a wren, By crying comfort from a hollow breast, Can chase away the first-conceived sound ? . . . iii 2 43
Here may his head lie on my throbbing breast . . . iv 4 5
These hands are free from guiltless blood-shedding, This breast from harbouring foul deceitful thoughts . . . iv 7 109
For selfsame wind that I should speak withal Is kindling coals that fires all my breast . . . *3 Hen. VI.* ii 1 83
This may plant courage in their quailing breasts ; For yet is hope . ii 3 54
Both tugging to be victors, breast to breast . . . . ii 5 11
My sighing breast shall be thy funeral bell . . . . ii 5 117
I stabb'd your fathers' bosoms, split my breast . . . . ii 6 30
Her sighs will make a battery in his breast . . . . iii 1 37
Infuse his breast with magnanimity And make him, naked, foil a man at arms . . . v 4 41
My breast can better brook thy dagger's point Than can my ears that tragic history . . . v 6 27
Advance thy halberd higher than my breast, Or, by Saint Paul, I'll strike thee to my foot . . . *Richard III.* i 2 40
The which thou once didst bend against her breast . . . . i 2 95
Look, how this ring encompasseth thy finger, Even so thy breast encloseth my poor heart . . . i 2 205
Why do you wring your hands, and beat your breast ? . . . ii 2 3
Breast. With one hand on his dagger, Another spread on's breast *Hen. VIII.* i 2 205
Enter'd me, Yea, with a splitting power, and made to tremble The region of my breast . . . ii 4 184
Then stops again, Strikes his breast hard . . . . iii 2 117
He has a loyal breast, For you have seen him open't . . . iii 2 200
The sea being smooth, How many shallow bauble boats dare sail Upon her patient breast ! . . . *Troi. and Cres.* i 3 36
As if his foot were on brave Hector's breast And great Troy shrieking . iii 3 140
The breasts of Hecuba, When she did suckle Hector, look'd not lovelier *Coriolanus* i 3 43
He never stood To ease his breast with panting . . . ii 2 126
What his breast forges, that his tongue must vent . . . iii 1 258
Drawn tuns of blood out of thy country's breast . . . iv 5 105
Though I owe My revenge properly, my remission lies In Volscian breasts v 2 91
This poor right hand of mine Is left to tyrannize upon my breast *T. And.* iii 2 8
Danced thee on his knee, Sung thee asleep, his loving breast thy pillow v 3 163
Griefs of mine own lie heavy in my breast . . *Rom. and Jul.* i 1 192
Expire the term Of a despised life closed in my breast By some vile forfeit . . . i 4 110
As sweet repose and rest Come to thy heart as that within my breast ! . ii 2 124
Sleep dwell upon thine eyes, peace in thy breast ! . . . ii 2 187
He tilts With piercing steel at bold Mercutio's breast . . . iii 1 164
I saw the wound, I saw it with mine eyes,—God save the mark !—here on his manly breast . . . iii 2 53
Common mother, thou, Whose womb unmeasurable, and infinite breast, Teems, and feeds all . . . *T. of Athens* iv 3 178
In whose breast Doubt and suspect, alas, are placed too late . iv 3 518
This breast of mine hath buried Thoughts of great value . *J. Cæsar* i 2 49
The cross blue lightning seem'd to open The breast of heaven . . i 3 51
There is my dagger, And here my naked breast . . . iv 3 101
Come to my woman's breasts, And take my milk for gall ! . *Macbeth* i 5 48
O my breast, Thy hope ends here ? . . . . iv 3 113
Is it a fee-grief Due to some single breast ? . . . . iv 3 197
Such love must needs be treason in my breast . . . *Hamlet* iii 2 188
Swords out, and tilting one at other's breast, In opposition bloody *Othello* ii 3 183
Who has a breast so pure, But some uncleanly apprehensions Keep leets ? iii 3 138
Man but a rush against Othello's breast, And he retires . . . v 2 270
In the scuffles of great fights hath burst The buckles on his breast *Ant. and Cleo.* i 1 8
Dost thou not see my baby at my breast, That sucks the nurse asleep ? v 2 312
Here, on her breast, There is a vent of blood and something blown : The like is on her arm . . . v 2 351
On her left breast A mole cinque-spotted . . . *Cymbeline* ii 2 37
Under her breast—Worthy the pressing—lies a mole . . . ii 4 134
This tablet lay upon his breast . . . . . v 4 109
Whose naked breast Stepp'd before targes of proof . . . v 5 4
You gods that made me man, and sway in love, That have inflamed desire in my breast ! . . . *Pericles* i 1 20
Joy and all comfort in your sacred breast ! . . . . i 2 33
No din but snores the house about, Made louder by the o'er-fed breast iii Gower 3
Breast-deep. Set him breast-deep in earth, and famish him *T. Andron.* v 3 179
Breasted. He trod the water, Whose enmity he flung aside, and breasted The surge . . . *Tempest* ii 1 116
Breasting. Draw the huge bottoms through the furrow'd sea, Breasting the lofty surge . . . *Hen. V.* iii Prol. 13
Breastplate. What stronger breastplate than a heart untainted ! *2 Hen. VI.* iii 2 232
Breath. Side-stitches that shall pen thy breath up *Tempest* i 2 326
Their eyes do offices of truth, their words Are natural breath . . v 1 157
Gentle breath of yours my sails Must fill, or else my project fails . Epil. 11
Here's my mother's breath up and down . . . *T. G. of Ver.* ii 3 32
She is not to be kissed fasting, in respect of her breath . . . iii 1 327
She hath a sweet mouth.—That makes amends for her sour breath . iii 1 332
A breath thou art, Servile to all the skyey influences . *Meas. for Meas.* iii 1 8
Shall we thus permit A blasting and a scandalous breath to fall On him ? v 1 122
As there comes light from heaven and words from breath . . v 1 225
They'll suck our breath or pinch us black and blue . *Com. of Errors* ii 2 194
When the sweet breath of flattery conquers strife . . . iii 2 28
Where Spain ?—Faith, I saw it not ; but I felt it hot in her breath . iii 2 135
Sapphires, declining their rich aspect to the hot breath of Spain . iii 2 139
Fie, now you run this humour out of breath . . . . iv 1 57
How hast thou lost thy breath ?—By running fast . . . iv 2 30
Every word stabs : if her breath were as terrible as her terminations, there were no living near her . . . *Much Ado* ii 1 256
Rather than she will bate one breath of her accustomed crossness . iii 3 184
Art thou the slave that with thy breath hast kill'd Mine innocent child ? v 1 273
Foul words is but foul wind, and foul wind is but foul breath, and foul breath is noisome . . . v 2 53
The endeavour of this present breath may buy That honour . *L. L. Lost* i 1 5
Vows are but breath, and breath a vapour is . . . . iv 3 68
That the lover, sick to death, Wish himself the heaven's breath . iv 3 108
What are they That charge their breath against us ? . . . v 2 88
Tapers they are, with your sweet breaths puff'd out . . . v 2 267
I implore so much expense of thy royal sweet breath as will utter a brace of words . . . v 2 524
For mine own part, I breathe free breath . . . . v 2 733
If over-boldly we have borne ourselves In the converse of breath . . v 2 745
Such dulcet and harmonious breath That the rude sea grew civil *M. N. Dream* ii 1 151
O, I am out of breath in this fond chase ! . . . . ii 2 88
Odours savours sweet : So hath thy breath, my dearest Thisby . . iii 1 87
Why rebuke you him that loves you so ? Lay breath so bitter on your bitter foe . . . iii 2 44
Never did mockers waste more idle breath . . . . iii 2 168
Most dear actors, eat no onions nor garlic, for we are to utter sweet breath . . . iv 2 44
In a bondman's key, With bated breath and whispering humbleness *Mer. of Venice* i 3 125
Besides commends and courteous breath, Gifts of rich value . . ii 9 90
Here are sever'd lips, Parted with sugar breath . . . . iii 2 119
One in whom The ancient Roman honour more appears Than any that draws breath in Italy . . . iii 2 298
Thy tooth is not so keen, Because thou art not seen, Although thy breath be rude . . . *As Y. Like It* ii 7 179
Complexions that liked me and breaths that I defied not . . Epil. 20
As many as have good beards or good faces or sweet breaths . . Epil. 22
And Cytherea all in sedges hid, Which seem to move and wanton with her breath . . . *T. of Shrew* Ind. 2 54
I saw her coral lips to move, And with her breath she did perfume the air . . . i 1 180
Inspired merit so by breath is barr'd . . . . *All's Well* ii 1 151

Breath. Made a groan of her last breath, and now she sings in heaven . . . *All's Well* iv 3 62
I had rather than forty shillings I had such a leg, and so sweet a breath to sing . . . *T. Night* ii 3 21
A contagious breath.—Very sweet and contagious, i' faith . . . ii 3 56
Fly away, fly away, breath; I am slain by a fair cruel maid . . . ii 4 54
Till our very pastime, tired out of breath, prompt us to have mercy on him . . . iii 4 152
If you can bring Tincture or lustre in her lip, her eye, Heat outwardly or breath within, I'll serve you . . . *W. Tale* iii 2 207
Violets dim, But sweeter than the lids of Juno's eyes Or Cytherea's breath . . . iv 4 122
That Shall be when your first queen's again in breath . . . v 1 83
Who, had he himself eternity and could put breath into his work, would beguile Nature of her custom . . . v 2 107
What fine chisel Could ever yet cut breath? . . . v 3 79
What cracker is this same that deafs our ears With this abundance of superfluous breath? . . . *K. John* ii 1 148
Melted by the windy breath Of soft petitions, pity and remorse . . . ii 1 477
For thy word Is but the vain breath of a common man . . . iii 1 8
What earthy name to interrogatories Can task the free breath of a sacred king? . . . iii 1 148
The latest breath that gave the sound of words Was deep-sworn faith . . . iii 1 230
Holding the eternal spirit, against her will, In the vile prison of afflicted breath . . . iii 4 19
And stop this gap of breath with fulsome dust . . . iii 4 32
O fair affliction, peace!—No, no, I will not, having breath to cry . . . iii 4 37
Even the breath of what I mean to speak Shall blow each dust, each straw . . . iii 4 127
Entertain an hour, One minute, nay, one quiet breath of rest . . . iii 4 134
The breath of heaven hath blown his spirit out . . . iv 1 110
But with my breath I can revive it, boy . . . iv 1 112
This kingdom, this confine of blood and breath . . . iv 2 246
That sweet breath Which was embounded in this beauteous clay . . . iv 3 136
It was my breath that blew this tempest up, Upon your stubborn usage . . . v 1 17
And on our actions set the name of right With holy breath . . . v 2 68
Your breath first kindled the dead coal of wars . . . v 2 83
But even this night, whose black contagious breath Already smokes . . . v 4 33
But lusty, young, and cheerly drawing breath . . . *Richard II.* i 3 66
In our country's cradle Draws the sweet infant breath of gentle sleep . . . i 3 133
Which robs my tongue from breathing native breath . . . i 3 173
Such is the breath of kings . . . i 3 215
But dead, thy kingdom cannot buy my breath . . . i 3 232
Strive not with your breath; For all in vain comes counsel to his ear . . . ii 1 3
Direct not him whose way himself will choose: 'Tis breath thou lack'st, and that breath wilt thou lose . . . ii 1 30
And sigh'd my English breath in foreign clouds . . . iii 1 20
The breath of worldly men cannot depose The deputy elected by the Lord . . . iii 2 56
Allowing him a breath, a little scene, To monarchize, be fear'd . . . iii 2 164
Where fearing dying pays death servile breath . . . iii 2 185
Through brazen trumpet send the breath of parley Into his ruin'd ears . . . iii 3 33
Be judged by subject and inferior breath, And he himself not present? . . . iv 1 128
With mine own breath release all duty's rites . . . iv 1 210
Speak; Recover breath; tell us how near is danger, That we may arm . . . v 3 47
Giving him breath, The traitor lives, the true man's put to death . . . v 3 72
In thy face strange motions have appear'd, Such as we see when men restrain their breath On some great sudden hest . . . *1 Hen. IV.* ii 3 64
O for breath to utter what is like thee! . . . ii 4 272
Hark, how hard he fetches breath . . . ii 4 579
That no man might draw short breath to-day But I and Harry Monmouth! . . . v 2 49
I grant you I was down and out of breath; and so was he . . . v 4 150
He sure means brevity in breath, short-winded . . . *2 Hen. IV.* ii 2 136
The block of death, Treason's true bed and yielder up of breath . . . iv 2 123
By his gates of breath There lies a downy feather which stirs not . . . iv 5 31
When I here came in, And found no course of breath within your majesty, How cold it struck my heart! . . . iv 5 151
The breath no sooner left his father's body . . . *Hen. V.* i 1 25
A night is but small breath and little pause To answer matters of this consequence . . . ii 4 145
Hold hard the breath and bend up every spirit To his full height . . . iii 1 16
O hard condition, Twin-born with greatness, subject to the breath Of every fool! . . . iv 1 251
If that my fading breath permit . . . *1 Hen. VI.* ii 5 61
Vexation almost stops my breath . . . iii 3 41
Pause, and take thy breath; I gave thee life and rescued thee from death . . . iv 6 4
Speak to thy father ere thou yield thy breath! . . . iv 7 24
So am I driven by breath of her renown . . . v 5 7
And would have kept so long as breath did last . . . *2 Hen. VI.* i 1 211
His breath stinks with eating toasted cheese . . . iv 7 13
Canst thou quake, and change thy colour, Murder thy breath in middle of a word? . . . *Richard III.* iii 5 2
Give me some breath, some little pause, my lord, Before I positively speak . . . iv 2 24
Hath he so long held out with me untired, And stops he now for breath? . . . iv 2 45
A breath, a bubble, A sign of dignity, a garish flag . . . iv 4 88
In the breath of bitter words let's smother My damned son . . . iv 4 133
Fainting, despair; despairing, yield thy breath! . . . v 3 172
Just as I do now, He would kiss you twenty with a breath . . . *Hen. VIII.* i 4 30
His curses and his blessings Touch me alike, they're breath I not believe in . . . ii 2 54
That breath fame blows; that praise, sole pure, transcends . . . *Troi. and Cres.* i 3 244
Your breath of full consent bellied his sails . . . ii 2 74
But for your health and your digestion sake, An after-dinner's breath . . . ii 3 121
She fetches her breath as short as a new-ta'en sparrow . . . iii 2 35
An operation more divine Than breath or pen can give expressure to . . . iii 3 204
Since she could speak, She hath not given so many good words breath . . . iv 1 73
Strangles our dear vows Even in the birth of our own labouring breath . . . iv 4 40
With distinct breath and consign'd kisses to them . . . iv 4 47
Either to the uttermost, Or else a breath . . . iv 5 92
Nor dignifies an impair thought with breath . . . iv 5 103
I have seen thee pause and take thy breath . . . iv 5 192
Strike not a stroke, but keep yourselves in breath . . . v 7 3
Now is my day's work done; I'll take good breath . . . v 8 3
They say poor suitors have strong breaths: they shall know we have strong arms too . . . *Coriolanus* i 1 61
What I think I utter, and spend my malice in my breath . . . ii 1 59
Showing, as the manner is, his wounds To the people, beg their stinking breaths . . . ii 1 252

Breath. As if I had received them for the hire Of their breath only! . . . *Coriolanus* ii 2 154
I am out of breath; Confusion's near; I cannot speak . . . iii 1 189
Whose breath I hate As reek o' the rotten fens . . . iii 3 120
I loved the maid I married; never man Sigh'd truer breath . . . iv 5 121
You that stood so much Upon the voice of occupation and The breath of garlic-eaters! . . . iv 6 98
Can you think to blow out the intended fire your city is ready to flame in, with such weak breath as this? . . . v 2 50
Coming and going with thy honey breath . . . *T. Andron.* ii 4 25
Which oft the angry Mab with blisters plagues, Because their breaths with sweetmeats tainted are . . . *Rom. and Jul.* i 4 76
This bud of love, by summer's ripening breath, May prove a beauteous flower . . . ii 2 121
Can you not stay awhile? Do you not see that I am out of breath?—How art thou out of breath, when thou hast breath To say to me that thou art out of breath? . . . ii 5 30
Then sweeten with thy breath This neighbour air . . . ii 6 26
All this uttered With gentle breath, calm look, knees humbly bow'd . . . iii 1 161
Unless the breath of heart-sick groans, Mist-like, infold me from the search of eyes . . . iii 3 72
No warmth, no breath, shall testify thou livest . . . iv 1 98
That the life-weary taker may fall dead And that the trunk may be discharged of breath . . . v 1 63
Death, that hath suck'd the honey of thy breath, Hath had no power yet upon thy beauty . . . v 3 92
And, lips, O you The doors of breath, seal with a righteous kiss! . . . v 3 114
Grief of my son's exile hath stopp'd her breath . . . v 3 211
My short date of breath Is not so long as is a tedious tale . . . v 3 229
Parts bread with him, pledges the breath of him in a divided draught . . . *T. of Athens* i 2 49
Give me breath. I do beseech you, good my lords, keep on . . . ii 2 34
Were it all yours to give it in a breath, How quickly were it gone! . . . ii 2 162
When the means are gone that buy this praise, The breath is gone whereof this praise is made . . . ii 2 179
They have e'en put my breath from me, the slaves. Creditors? devils! . . . iii 4 104
Breath infect breath, That their society, as their friendship, may Be merely poison! . . . iv 1 30
He whose pious breath seeks to convert you . . . iv 3 140
And let his very breath, whom thou'lt observe, Blow off thy cap . . . iv 3 212
Thou shouldst desire to die, being miserable.—Not by his breath that is more miserable . . . iv 3 249
And uttered such a deal of stinking breath . . . *J. Cæsar* i 2 248
And what seem'd corporal melted As breath into the wind . . . *Macbeth* i 3 82
Almost dead for breath, had scarcely more Than would make up his message . . . i 5 37
The heaven's breath Smells wooingly here . . . i 6 5
Words to the heat of deeds too cold breath gives . . . ii 1 61
Shall live the lease of nature, pay his breath To time and mortal custom . . . iv 1 99
Curses, not loud but deep, mouth-honour, breath . . . v 3 27
Make all our trumpets speak; give them all breath . . . v 6 9
Nor windy suspiration of forced breath . . . *Hamlet* i 2 79
Words of so sweet breath composed As made the things more rich . . . iii 1 98
Give it breath with your mouth, and it will discourse most eloquent music . . . iii 2 374
If words be made of breath, And breath of life, I have no life to breathe . . . iii 4 197
Why do we wrap the gentleman in our more rawer breath? . . . v 2 129
The king shall drink to Hamlet's better breath . . . v 2 282
He's fat, and scant of breath . . . v 2 298
And in this harsh world draw thy breath in pain, To tell my story . . . v 2 359
A love that makes breath poor, and speech unable . . . *Lear* i 1 61
Then 'tis like the breath of an unfee'd lawyer; you gave me nothing for't . . . i 4 142
What is your difference? speak.—I am scarce in breath, my lord . . . ii 2 57
Are they inform'd of this? My breath and blood! . . . ii 4 104
You ever-gentle gods, take my breath from me! . . . iv 6 221
If that her breath will mist or stain the stone, Why, then she lives . . . v 3 262
Why should a dog, a horse, a rat, have life, And thou no breath at all? . . . v 3 307
And swell his sail with thine own powerful breath! . . . *Othello* ii 1 78
They met so near with their lips that their breaths embraced together . . . ii 1 266
And weigh'st thy words before thou givest them breath . . . iii 3 119
And then I heard Each syllable that breath made up between them . . . iv 2 5
Ah, balmy breath, that dost almost persuade Justice to break her sword! . . . v 2 16
There lies your niece, Whose breath, indeed, these hands have newly stopp'd . . . v 2 202
And having lost her breath, she spoke, and panted, That she did make defect perfection, And, breathless, power breathe forth . . . *Ant. and Cleo.* ii 2 235
Our fortune on the sea is out of breath, And sinks most lamentably . . . iii 10 25
Tell him, from his all-obeying breath I hear The doom of Egypt . . . iii 13 77
Give him no breath, but now Make boot of his distraction . . . iv 1 8
In their thick breaths, Rank of gross diet, shall we be enclouded . . . v 2 211
The cutter Was as another nature, dumb; outwent her, Motion and breath left out . . . *Cymbeline* ii 4 85
'Tis slander, . . . whose breath Rides on the posting winds . . . iii 4 37
The leaf of eglantine, whom not to slander, Out-sweeten'd not thy breath . . . iv 2 224
So I'll die For thee, O Imogen, even for whom my life Is every breath a death . . . v 1 27
On either side I come to spend my breath; Which neither here I'll keep nor bear again . . . v 3 81
He came in thunder; his celestial breath Was sulphurous to smell . . . v 4 114
Death remember'd should be like a mirror, Who tells us life's but breath, to trust it error . . . *Pericles* i 1 46
And yet the end of all is bought thus dear, The breath is gone . . . i 1 99
Let your breath cool yourself, telling your haste . . . i 1 161
Our eyes do weep, Till tongues fetch breath that may proclaim them louder . . . i 4 15
I'll then discourse our woes, felt several years, And wanting breath to speak help me with tears . . . i 4 19
And left me breath Nothing to think on but ensuing death . . . ii 1 6
Let us salute him, Or know what ground's made happy by his breath . . . ii 4 28

Breathe. The air breathes upon us here most sweetly . . . *Tempest* ii 1 46
It shall be said so again while Stephano breathes at nostrils . . . ii 2 65
Before you can say 'come' and 'go,' And breathe twice and cry 'so, so' . . . iv 1 45
Breathe it in mine ear, As ending anthem of my endless dolour . . . *T. G. of Ver.* iii 1 239
I dare thee but to breathe upon my love . . . v 4 131
Speak, breathe, discuss; brief, short, quick, snap . . . *Mer. Wives* iv 5 2
O, think on that; And mercy then will breathe within your lips . . . *Meas. for Meas.* ii 2 78
For mine own part, I breathe free breath . . . *L. L. Lost* v 2 732

Breathe. What's here? one dead, or drunk? See, doth he breathe? *T. of Shrew* Ind. 1 31
Here let us breathe and haply institute A course of learning . i 1 8
A medicine That's able to breathe life into a stone . *All's Well* ii 1 76
I think thou wast created for men to breathe themselves upon thee ii 3 271
Like the sweet sound, That breathes upon a bank of violets *T. Night* i 1 6
Alas the day!—What thriftless sighs shall poor Olivia breathe! . ii 2 40
O, hear me breathe my life Before this ancient sir! . *W. Tale* iv 4 371
Or let the church, our mother, breathe her curse . *K. John* iii 1 256
Austria's head lie there, While Philip breathes . iii 2 4
Now I breathe again Aloft the flood, and can give audience To any tongue iv 2 138
You breathe these dead news in as dead an ear . v 7 65
The hopeless word of 'never to return' Breathe I against thee *Richard II.* i 3 153
When the tongue's office should be prodigal To breathe the abundant dolour of the heart . . . . i 3 257
Will the king come, that I may breathe my last? . . ii 1 1
For they breathe truth that breathe their words in pain . . ii 1 8
Thou diest, though I the sicker be.—I am in health, I breathe, and see thee ill . . . . ii 1 92
Little joy have I To breathe this news; yet what I say is true . iii 4 82
If I dare eat, or drink, or breathe, or live, I dare meet Surrey . iv 1 73
Breathe short-winded accents of new broils To be commenced 1 *Hen. IV.* i 1 3
When you breathe in your watering, they cry 'hem!' and bid you play it off . . . . ii 4 17
Well, breathe awhile, and then to it again . . ii 4 275
No man so potent breathes upon the ground But I will beard him . iv 1 11
O Hal, I prithee, give me leave to breathe awhile . v 3 46
We breathe too long: come, cousin Westmoreland, Our duty this way lies v 4 15
Stay, and breathe awhile: Thou hast redeem'd thy lost opinion v 4 47
Stopp'd by me to breathe his bloodied horse . 2 *Hen. IV.* i 1 38
And hear, I think, the very latest counsel That ever I shall breathe iv 5 184
And suffer you to breathe in fruitful peace 1 *Hen. VI.* v 4 127
He shall not breathe infection in this air But three days longer 2 *Hen. VI.* iii 2 287
Here could I breathe my soul into the air . . iii 2 391
With thy lips to stop my mouth; So shouldst thou either turn my flying soul, Or I should breathe it so into thy body . iii 2 398
And from their misty jaws Breathe foul contagious darkness in the air iv 1 7
By giving the house of Lancaster leave to breathe, It will outrun you 3 *Hen. VI.* i 2 13
So desperate thieves, all hopeless of their lives, Breathe out invectives . i 4 43
And, whilst we breathe, take time to do him dead . i 4 108
As runners with a race, I lay me down a little while to breathe . ii 3 2
Now breathe we, lords: good fortune bids us pause . ii 6 31
Why, am I dead? do I not breathe a man? . . iii 1 82
Ha! durst the traitor breathe out so proud words? . iv 1 112
If she have time to breathe, be well assured Her faction will be full as strong as ours . . . . v 3 16
Clarence still breathes; Edward still lives and reigns *Richard III.* i 1 161
His better doth not breathe upon the earth . i 2 140
Curses never pass The lips of those that breathe them in the air . i 3 286
Else wherefore breathe I in a Christian land? . . iii 7 116
Breathe you, my friends: well fought; we are come off Like Romans *Coriolanus* i 6 1
With our sighs we'll breathe the welkin dim, And stain the sun with fog *T. Andron.* iii 1 212
That ever death should let life bear his name, Where life hath no more interest but to breathe! . . . . iii 1 250
To breathe such vows as lovers use to swear . *Rom. and Jul.* ii Prol. 10
Stifled in the vault, To whose foul mouth no healthsome air breathes in iv 3 34
He's truly valiant that can wisely suffer The worst that man can breathe, and make his wrongs His outsides *T. of Athens* iii 5 32
You breathe in vain.—In vain! . . . iii 5 59
Breathe his faults so quaintly That they may seem the taints of liberty *Hamlet* ii 1 31
Having ever seen in the prenominate crimes The youth you breathe of guilty . . . . ii 1 44
When churchyards yawn and hell itself breathes out Contagion to this world . . . . iii 2 407
I have no life to breathe What thou hast said to me . iii 4 198
And for his death no wind of blame shall breathe . iv 7 67
Thou dost breathe; Hast heavy substance; bleed'st not; speak'st *Lear* iv 6 51
Thy tongue some say of breeding breathes . . v 3 144
He's that he is: I may not breathe my censure What he might be *Othello* iv 1 281
She did make defect perfection, And, breathless, power breathe forth *Ant. and Cleo.* ii 2 237
Sues To let him breathe between the heavens and earth, A private man iii 12 14
Dangerous fellow, hence! Breathe not where princes are . *Cymbeline* v 5 238
Nature awakes; a warmth Breathes out of her *Pericles* iii 2 94
Breathed. I have not breathed almost since I did see it . *Com. of Errors* v 1 181
A man so breathed, that certain he would fight . *L. L. Lost* v 2 659
Beat not the bones of the buried: when he breathed, he was a man . v 2 668
I have toward heaven breathed a secret vow To live in prayer *Mer. of Ven.* iii 4 27
I am not yet well breathed . . . *As Y. Like It* i 2 230
Thy greyhounds are as swift As breathed stags . *T. of Shrew* Ind. 2 50
My soul the faithfull'st offerings hath breathed out That e'er devotion tender'd! What shall I do? . . . *T. Night* v 1 117
See, my lord, Would you not deem it breathed? . *W. Tale* v 3 64
Before you were new crown'd, We breathed our counsel . *K. John* iv 2 36
By all the blood that ever fury breathed, The youth says well . v 2 127
No balm can cure but his heart-blood Which breathed this poison *Richard II.* i 1 173
Three times they breathed and three times did they drink 1 *Hen. IV.* i 3 102
What thing, in honour, had my father lost, That need to be revived and breathed in me? . . . 2 *Hen. IV.* iv 1 114
A thousand sighs are breathed for thee . . 2 *Hen. VI.* iii 2 345
Where your brave father breathed his latest gasp . 3 *Hen. VI.* ii 1 108
Ah, Warwick! Montague hath breathed his last . . 40
Thus have you breathed your curse against yourself *Richard III.* i 240
The plainest harmless creature That breathed upon this earth a Christian iii 5 26
Thrust these reproachful speeches down his throat That he hath breathed in my dishonour here . *T. Andron.* ii 1 56
Which, as he breathed defiance to my ears, He swung about his head and cut the winds . . . *Rom. and Jul.* i 1 117
Breathed such life with kisses in my lips, That I revived . v 1 8
Breathed, as it were, To an untirable and continuate goodness *T. of Athens* i 1 10
And breathed Our sufferance vainly . . . v 4 7
This day I breathed first: time is come round, And where I did begin, there shall I end . . . *J. Cæsar* v 3 23
I will be treble-sinew'd, hearted, breathed, And fight maliciously *Ant. and Cleo.* iii 13 178

Breather. That no particular scandal once can touch But it confounds the breather . . . *Meas. for Meas.* iv 4 31
I will chide no breather in the world but myself . *As Y. Like It* iii 2 297
She shows a body rather than a life, A statue than a breather *A. and C.* iii 3 24
Breathest. Thou livest and breathest, Yet art thou slain in him *Richard II.* i 2 24
Breathing. So full of valour that they smote the air For breathing in their faces . . . *Tempest* iv 1 173
You shake the head at so long a breathing . *Much Ado* ii 1 378
No sighs but of my breathing; no tears but of my shedding *Mer. of Venice* iii 1 100
Welcome to our house: It must appear in other ways than words, Therefore I scant this breathing courtesy . . v 1 141
A nursery to our gentry, who are sick For breathing and exploit *All's Well* i 2 17
Rescue those breathing lives to die in beds, That here come sacrifices for the field . . . *K. John* ii 1 419
Breathing to his breathless excellence The incense of a vow . . iv 3 66
Even this ill night, your breathing shall expire . v 4 36
Speechless death, Which robs my tongue from breathing native breath *Richard II.* i 3 173
To prove it on thee to the extremest point Of mortal breathing . iv 1 48
A breathing valiant man, Of an invincible unconquer'd spirit! 1 *Hen. VI.* iv 2 31
Be my last breathing in this mortal world! . 2 *Hen. VI.* i 2 21
Sent before my time Into this breathing world . *Richard III.* i 1 21
Like dumb statuas or breathing stones, Gazed each on other . iii 7 25
Airy succeeders of intestate joys, Poor breathing orators of miseries! . iv 4 129
And both the princes had been breathing here . iv 4 384
The sun begins to set; How ugly night comes breathing at his heels *Troi. and Cres.* v 8 6
Breathing like sanctified and pious bawds, The better to beguile *Hamlet* i 3 130
'Tis the breathing time of day with me . . v 2 181
I am sorry to give breathing to my purpose *Ant. and Cleo.* i 3 14
Comes in my father And like the tyrannous breathing of the north Shakes all our buds from growing *Cymbeline* i 3 36
'Tis her breathing that Perfumes the chamber thus . ii 2 18
Here is a lady that wants breathing too . *Pericles* ii 3 101
Breathing-while. Cannot be quiet scarce a breathing-while *Richard III.* i 3 60
Breathless. And bootless make the breathless housewife churn *M. N. Dr.* ii 1 37
Breathing to his breathless excellence The incense of a vow *K. John* iv 3 66
Herein all breathless lies The mightiest of thy greatest enemies *Richard II.* v 6 31
I was dry with rage and extreme toil, Breathless and faint 1 *Hen. IV.* i 3 32
Here breathless lies the king.—Where?—Here . . v 3 16
I saw him dead, Breathless and bleeding on the ground . . v 4 137
View his breathless corpse, And comment then upon his sudden death 2 *Hen. VI.* iii 2 132
Now breathless wrong Shall sit and pant in your great chairs *T. of Athens* v 4 10
Why are you breathless? and why stare you so? *J. Cæsar* i 3 2
Came there a reeking post, Stew'd in his haste, half breathless . *Lear* ii 4 31
She spoke, and panted, That she did make defect perfection, And, breathless, power breathe forth . *Ant. and Cleo.* ii 2 237
Brecknock. Let me think on Hastings, and be gone To Brecknock, while my fearful head is on! . . . *Richard III.* iv 2 126
Bred. A Bohemian born, but here nursed up and bred *Meas. for Meas.* iv 2 135
Ill digestions; Thereof the raging fire of fever bred . *Com. of Errors* v 1 75
That advance their pride Against that power that bred it *Much Ado* iii 1 10
Blushing cheeks by faults are bred And fears by pale white shown *L. L. L.* i 2 106
He hath never fed of the dainties that are bred in a book . iv 2 25
My hounds are bred out of the Spartan kind, So flew'd, so sanded *M. N. Dr.* iv 1 124
The burnish'd sun, To whom I am a neighbour and near bred *Mer. of Ven.* ii 1 3
Tell me where is fancy bred, Or in the heart or in the head? . iii 2 63
The skull that bred them in the sepulchre . iii 2 96
Happier than this, She is not bred so dull but she can learn . iii 2 164
His horses are bred better . . . *As Y. Like It* i 1 11
Being ever from their cradles bred together . i 1 114
Yet am I inland bred And know some nurture . . ii 7 96
I was bred and born Not three hours' travel from this very place *T. Night* i 2 22
Would not a pair of these have bred, sir? . . iii 1 55
The sweet'st companion that e'er man Bred his hopes out of *W. Tale* v 1 12
Your father might have kept This calf bred from his cow from all the world; In sooth he might . . *K. John* i 1 124
All of one nature, of one substance bred . 1 *Hen. IV.* i 1 11
A gentleman well bred and of good name . 2 *Hen. IV.* i 1 26
Bred out of that bloody strain That haunted us in our familiar paths *Hen. V.* ii 4 51
Our madams mock at us, and plainly say Our mettle is bred out . iii 5 29
Records, England all Olivers and Rowlands bred . 1 *Hen. VI.* i 2 30
The wound that bred this meeting here Cannot be cured by words 3 *Hen. VI.* ii 2 121
When we saw our sunshine made thy spring, And that thy summer bred us no increase . . . . . ii 2 164
From deceit bred by necessity . . . . iii 3 68
The urging of that word 'judgement' hath bred a kind of remorse in me *Richard III.* i 4 110
He has been bred i' the wars Since he could draw a sword *Coriolanus* iii 1 320
Being bred in broils Hast not the soft way which, thou dost confess, Were fit . . . . iii 2 81
Eating the flesh that she herself hath bred . *T. Andron.* v 3 62
Three civil brawls, bred of an airy word *Rom. and Jul.* i 1 96
I have bred her at my dearest cost In qualities of the best *T. of Athens* i 1 124
The strain of man's bred out Into baboon and monkey . . i 1 259
A slave, whom Fortune's tender arm With favour never clasp'd; but bred a dog . . . . iv 3 251
You have begot me, bred me, loved me: I Return those duties back *Lear* i 1 98
A servant that he bred, thrill'd with remorse, Opposed against the act . iv 2 73
Your serpent of Egypt is bred now of your mud by the operation of your sun: so is your crocodile . . *Ant. and Cleo.* ii 7 29
Must I be unfolded With one that I have bred? The gods! it smites me Beneath the fall I have . . . . . v 2 171
Sir, It is your fault that I have loved Posthumus: You bred him as my playfellow . . . . . *Cymbeline* i 1 145
One bred of alms and foster'd with cold dishes, With scraps . iii 3 119
All love the womb that their first being bred *Pericles* i 1 107
Where were you bred? And how achieved you these endowments? . v 1 116
Well: where were you bred? I'll hear you more, to the bottom of your story . . . . v 1 165
Breech. You might still have worn the petticoat, And ne'er have stol'n the breech . . . . 3 *Hen. VI.* v 5 24
Breeched. Their daggers Unmannerly breech'd with gore *Macbeth* ii 3 122
Breeches. What fashion, madam, shall I make your breeches? *T. G. of Ver.* ii 7 49
An old jerkin, a pair of old breeches thrice turned . *T. of Shrew* iii 2 44
Well, ruffian, I must pocket up these wrongs, Because— Your breeches best may carry them . . . *K. John* iii 1 201

Breeches. Though in this place most master wear no breeches 2 *Hen. VI.* i 3 149
Tall stockings, Short blister'd breeches, and those types of travel *Hen. VIII.* i 3 31
When thou gavest them the rod, and put'st down thine own breeches *Lear* i 4 190
King Stephen was a worthy peer, His breeches cost him but a crown *Othello* ii 3 93
Breeching. I am no breeching scholar in the schools . *T. of Shrew* iii 1 18
Breed. Heavens rain grace On that which breeds between 'em! *Tempest* iii 1 76
How use doth breed a habit in a man! . . . . *T. G. of Ver.* v 4 1
She speaks, and 'tis Such sense, that my sense breeds with it *M. for M.* ii 2 142
Why are you thus out of measure sad?—There is no measure in the occasion that breeds . . . . . *Much Ado* i 3 4
Are these the breed of wits so wonder'd at . . . *L. L. Lost* v 2 266
Is your gold and silver ewes and rams?—I cannot tell; I make it breed as fast . . . . *Mer. of Venice* i 3 97
When did friendship take A breed for barren metal of his friend? . i 3 135
Charged my brother, on his blessing, to breed me well . *As Y. Like It* i 1 4
Let her never nurse her child herself, for she will breed it like a fool! . iv 1 179
Virginity breeds mites, much like a cheese . . . *All's Well* i 1 154
And choice breeds A native slip to us from foreign seeds . . . i 3 151
She is young, wise, fair; In these to nature she's immediate heir, And these breed honour . . . . ii 3 140
This letter, being so excellently ignorant, will breed no terror in the youth *T. Night* iii 4 207
Sir, that's to-morrow. I am question'd by my fears, of what may chance Or breed upon our absence . . . . . . *W. Tale* i 2 12
Which may, if fortune please, both breed thee, pretty, And still rest thine . . . . iii 3 48
No more than were I painted I would wish This youth should say 'twere well and only therefore Desire to breed by me . . . . . iv 4 103
Twice fifteen thousand hearts of England's breed . . . *K. John* ii 1 275
O, what better matter breeds for you Than I have named! . . . iii 4 170
This happy breed of men, this little world . . . *Richard II.* ii 1 45
Fear'd by their breed and famous by their birth, Renowned for their deeds . . . . ii 1 52
Watching breeds leanness, leanness is all gaunt . . . . ii 1 78
Your chamber-lie breeds fleas like a loach . . . . 1 *Hen. IV.* ii 1 23
Out of my blood He'll breed revengement and a scourge for me . . iii 2 7
May turn the tide of fearful faction And breed a kind of question . . iv 1 68
And breeds no bate with telling of discreet stories . . . 2 *Hen. IV.* ii 4 271
If you knew what pains I have bestow'd to breed this present peace . iv 2 74
Lest example Breed, by his sufferance, more of such a kind . *Hen. V.* ii 2 46
That island of England breeds very valiant creatures . . . . iii 7 150
The smell whereof shall breed a plague in France . . . . iv 3 103
It was in a place where I could not breed no contention with him . . v 1 11
So will this base and envious discord breed . . . 1 *Hen. VI.* iii 1 194
One sudden foil shall never breed distrust . . . . . iii 3 11
'Tis much when sceptres are in children's hands; But more when envy breeds unkind division . . . . iv 1 193
Her virtues graced with external gifts Do breed love's settled passions . v 5 4
Because in York this breeds suspicion . . . . 2 *Hen. VI.* i 3 210
In that nest of spicery they shall breed Selves of themselves *Richard III.* iv 4 424
Might, through their amity, Breed him some prejudice . . *Hen. VIII.* i 1 182
They were young and handsome, and of the best breed in the north . ii 2 4
I am sorry my integrity should breed, And service to his majesty and you, So deep suspicion . . . . iii 1 51
Or, shedding, breed a nursery of like evil, To overbulk us *Troi. and Cres.* i 3 319
He eats nothing but doves, love, and that breeds hot blood . . . iii 1 141
Out of whorish loins Are pleased to breed out your inheritors . . iv 1 64
Peace is nothing, but to rust iron, increase tailors, and breed ballad-makers.—Let me have war, say I . . . . . *Coriolanus* iv 5 235
Here nothing breeds, Unless the nightly owl or fatal raven *T. Andron.* ii 3 96
Yet every mother breeds not sons alike . . . . . . ii 3 146
No gift to him, But breeds the giver a return exceeding . *T. of Athens* i 1 290
The earth's a thief, That feeds and breeds by a composture stolen . iv 3 444
Make war breed peace, make peace stint war . . . . . v 4 83
Rome, thou hast lost the breed of noble bloods! . . . *J. Cæsar* i 2 151
It is impossible that ever Rome Should breed thy fellow . . . . v 3 101
Where they most breed and haunt, I have observed, The air is delicate *Macbeth* i 6 9
The worm that's fled Hath nature that in time will venom breed . iii 4 30
By his own interdiction stands accursed, And does blaspheme his breed iv 3 108
Unnatural deeds Do breed unnatural troubles . . . . . v 1 80
If the sun breed maggots in a dead dog, being a god kissing carrion *Hamlet* ii 2 181
Nay, good my lord, this courtesy is not of the right breed . . iii 2 327
And many more of the same breed that I know the drossy age dotes on . v 2 197
Had he a hand to write this? a heart and brain to breed it in? . *Lear* i 2 61
I would breed from hence occasions, and I shall, That I may speak . i 3 24
See what breeds about her heart . . . . iii 6 81
Or breed itself so out of circumstance . . . . *Othello* iii 3 16
From hence I'll love no friend, sith love breeds such offence . . . iii 3 380
The worms were hallow'd that did breed the silk . . . . iii 4 73
Is it sport? I think it is: and doth affection breed it? I think it doth iv 3 99
Equality of two domestic powers Breed scrupulous faction *Ant. and Cleo.* i 3 48
Breeds him and makes him of his bed-chamber . . . *Cymbeline* i 1 42
Plenty and peace breeds cowards: hardness ever Of hardiness is mother iii 6 21
O noble strain! O worthiness of nature! breed of greatness! . . iv 2 25
The imperious seas breed monsters, for the dish Poor tributary rivers as sweet fish . . . . iv 2 35
I am no viper, yet I feed On mother's flesh which did me breed *Pericles* i 1 65
Like serpents are, who though they feed On sweetest flowers, yet they poison breed . . . . i 1 133
Or peaceful night, The tomb where grief should sleep, can breed me quiet i 2 5
Breed-bate. I warrant you, no tell-tale nor no breed-bate . *Mer. Wives* i 4 12
Breeder. Time is the nurse and breeder of all good . *T. G. of Ver.* iii 1 243
When the work of generation was Between these woolly breeders *Mer. of Venice* i 3 84
You love the breeder better than the male . . . . 3 *Hen. VI.* ii 1 42
See where comes the breeder of my sorrow! . . . . . iii 3 43
As loathsome as a toad Amongst the fairest breeders of our clime *T. Andron.* iv 2 68
Give sentence on this execrable wretch, That hath been breeder of these dire events . . . . v 3 178
Get thee to a nunnery: why wouldst thou be a breeder of sinners? *Hamlet* iii 1 123
Breeding. A gentleman of excellent breeding, admirable discourse *Mer. Wives* ii 2 234
That's the lady: I do in birth deserve her, and in fortunes, In graces and in qualities of breeding . . . . *Mer. of Venice* ii 7 33
He that hath learned no wit by nature nor art may complain of good breeding or comes of a very dull kindred . . *As Y. Like It* iii 2 31
Breeding. Will you, being a man of your breeding, be married under a bush like a beggar? . . . . *As Y. Like It* iii 3 85
I shall now put you to the height of your breeding . . . *All's Well* ii 2 2
She had her breeding at my father's charge . . . . . . ii 3 121
Gives him out to be of good capacity and breeding . . . *T. Night* iii 4 204
So far beneath your soft and tender breeding . . . . . . v 1 331
Speeds from me and So leaves me to consider what is breeding That changeth thus his manners . . . . *W. Tale* i 2 374
She is as forward of her breeding as She is i' the rear our birth . iv 4 591
The place of your dwelling, your names, your ages, of what having, breeding . . . . iv 4 741
The affection of nobleness which nature shows above her breeding . v 2 41
It shall serve among wits of no higher breeding than thine 2 *Hen. IV.* ii 2 39
Honest gentlemen, I know not your breeding.—Why then, lament therefore . . . . v 3 112
Let us swear That you are worth your breeding . . . *Hen. V.* iii 1 28
Beseeching him to give her virtuous breeding . . . *Hen. VIII.* iv 2 134
O blessed breeding sun, draw from the earth Rotten humidity! *T. of Athens* iv 3 1
Did these bones cost no more the breeding, but to play at loggats with 'em? mine ache to think on't . . . . . . *Hamlet* v 1 100
Your son, my lord?—His breeding, sir, hath been at my charge . *Lear* i 1 9
I am a gentleman of blood and breeding . . . . . . iii 1 40
Thy tongue some say of breeding breathes . . . . . . v 3 143
Such accommodation and besort As levels with her breeding . . *Othello* i 3 240
'Tis my breeding That gives me this bold show of courtesy . . . ii 1 99
Much is breeding, Which, like the courser's hair, hath yet but life, And not a serpent's poison . . . . . . *Ant. and Cleo.* i 2 199
Who find in my exile the want of breeding . . . . *Cymbeline* iv 4 26
Who deserved So long a breeding as his white beard came to . . . v 3 17
My breeding was, sir, as Your highness knows . . . . . v 5 339
Breese. In her ray and brightness The herd hath more annoyance by the breese Than by the tiger . . . . . . *Troi. and Cres.* i 3 48
The breese upon her, like a cow in June, Hoists sails and flies *A. and C.* iii 10 14
Breff. That is the breff and the long . . . . . . *Hen. V.* iii 2 126
Brentford. My maid's aunt, the fat woman of Brentford . *Mer. Wives* iv 2 78
He cannot abide the old woman of Brentford . . . . . iv 2 88
Let's go dress him like the witch of Brentford . . . . . iv 2 100
Why, it is my maid's aunt of Brentford . . . . . . iv 2 179
Pray you, sir, was't not the wise woman of Brentford? . . . . iv 5 28
I was like to be apprehended for the witch of Brentford . . . . iv 5 120
Bretagne. Arthur of Bretagne, yield thee to my hand . . *K. John* ii 1 156
Arthur of Bretagne England's king and yours . . . . . ii 1 311
We'll create young Arthur Duke of Bretagne And Earl of Richmond . ii 1 551
All these well furnish'd by the Duke of Bretagne . . *Richard II.* ii 1 285
The Dukes of Orleans, Calaber, Bretagne and Alençon . . 2 *Hen. VI.* i 1 7
A paltry fellow, Long kept in Bretagne at our mother's cost *Richard III.* v 3 324
Brethren. Adam's sons are my brethren; and, truly, I hold it a sin to match in my kindred . . . . *Much Ado* ii 1 67
My friends and brethren in these great affairs . . . 2 *Hen. IV.* iv 1 6
Thou mayst effect . . . mediation, after I am dead, Between his greatness and thy other brethren . . . . iv 4 26
The mayor and all his brethren in best sort . . . *Hen. V.* v Prol. 25
Had I thy brethren here, their lives and thine Were not revenge sufficient for me . . . . 3 *Hen. VI.* i 3 25
Will not the mayor then and his brethren come? . . *Richard III.* iii 7 44
I, her frail son, amongst my brethren mortal . . . *Hen. VIII.* ii 2 148
My good lord mayor, And your good brethren, I am much beholding . v 5 71
Yet ne'ertheless, My spritely brethren, I propend to you *Troi. and Cres.* ii 2 190
Brethren and sisters of the hold-door trade . . . . . . v 10 52
Your brethren roar'd and ran From the noise of our own drums *Coriol.* ii 3 59
Make way to lay them by their brethren . . . . . *T. Andron.* i 1 89
These are their brethren, whom you Goths beheld Alive and dead, and for their brethren slain Religiously they ask a sacrifice . . . i 1 122
Lo, at this tomb my tributary tears I render, for my brethren's obsequies i 1 160
Give Mutius burial with our brethren . . . . i 1 348
He must be buried with his brethren.—And shall, or him we will accompany . . . . i 1 357
I train'd thy brethren to that guileful hole . . . . . . v 1 104
Breton. The Breton Richmond aims At young Elizabeth *Richard III.* iv 3 40
The Breton navy is dispersed by tempest . . . . . . iv 4 523
A scum of Bretons, and base lackey peasants . . . . . v 3 317
If we be conquer'd, let men conquer us, And not these bastard Bretons v 3 333
Brevis. They say, my lords, 'ira furor brevis est' . . *T. of Athens* i 2 28
Brevity. I will imitate the honourable Romans in brevity . 2 *Hen. IV.* ii 2 135
He sure means brevity in breath, short-winded . . . . . ii 2 135
With the rude brevity and discharge of one [sigh] . . *Troi. and Cres.* iv 4 43
Brevity is the soul of wit, And tediousness the limbs . . *Hamlet* ii 2 90
Brew. She brews good ale . . . . *T. G. of Ver.* iii 1 304
Blessing of your heart, you brew good ale . . . . . . iii 1 306
I wash, wring, brew, bake, scour, dress meat and drink, make the beds *Mer. Wives* i 4 101
Go brew me a pottle of sack finely . . . . iii 5 29
If I could temporise with my affection, Or brew it to a weak and colder palate, The like allayment could I give my grief . *Troi. and Cres.* iv 4 7
Brewage. I'll no pullet-sperm in my brewage . . . *Mer. Wives* iii 5 33
Brewed. Even then that sunshine brew'd a shower for him 3 *Hen. VI.* ii 1 156
She drinks no other drink but tears, Brew'd with her sorrow *T. Andron.* iii 2 38
Our tears are not yet brew'd . . . . *Macbeth* ii 3 130
Brewer. I am a peppercorn, a brewer's horse . . . 1 *Hen. IV.* iii 3 10
Come off and on swifter than he that gibbets on the brewer's bucket 2 *Hen. IV.* iii 2 282
When brewers mar their malt with water . . . . . . *Lear* iii 2 82
Brew-house. Be ready here hard by in the brew-house . *Mer. Wives* iii 3 10
Brewing. Another storm brewing; I hear it sing i' the wind . *Tempest* ii 2 19
There is some ill a-brewing towards my rest, For I did dream of money-bags to-night . . . . *Mer. of Venice* ii 5 17
Briareus. He is a gouty Briareus, many hands and no use *Troi. and Cres.* i 2 30
Bribe. Hark how I'll bribe you: good my lord, turn back.—How! bribe me?—Ay, with such gifts that heaven shall share with you *M. for M.* ii 2 145
'Tis thought, my lord, that you took bribes of France . 2 *Hen. VI.* iii 1 104
Nor ever had one penny bribe from France . . . . . . iii 1 109
She did corrupt frail nature with some bribe . . . 3 *Hen. VI.* iii 2 155
But cannot make my heart consent to take A bribe to pay my sword *Cor.* i 9 38
You have condemn'd and noted Lucius Pella For taking bribes *J. Cæsar* iv 3 3
Shall we now Contaminate our fingers with base bribes? . . . iv 3 24
Bribe buck. Divide me like a bribe buck, each a haunch . *Mer. Wives* v 5 27
Bribed. With these crystal beads heaven shall be bribed . . *K. John* ii 1 171
No, I'll nothing: for if I should be bribed too, there would be none left to rail upon thee . . . . *T. of Athens* i 2 244

Briber. His service done At Lacedæmon and Byzantium Were a sufficient briber for his life . . . . *T. of Athens* iii 5 61
Brick. He hath a garden circummured with brick . . *Meas. for Meas.* iv 1 28
He made a chimney in my father's house, and the bricks are alive at this day to testify it . . . . . . *2 Hen. VI.* iv 2 157
Bricklayer. He was an honest man, and a good bricklayer . . . iv 2 43
Ignorant of his birth and parentage, Became a bricklayer . . . iv 2 153
Brick-wall. In the hottest day prognostication proclaims, shall he be set against a brick-wall . . . . *W. Tale* iv 4 818
On a brick wall have I climbed into this garden . . . *2 Hen. VI.* iv 10 7
Bridal. Gentlemen, forward to the bridal dinner . . . *T. of Shrew* iii 2 221
Come, I will bring thee to thy bridal chamber . . . . . . iv 1 181
Shall gild her bridal bed and make her rich In titles, honours *K. John* ii 1 491
Make the bridal bed In that dim monument where Tybalt lies *Rom. and Jul.* iii 5 202
Our bridal flowers serve for a buried corse . . . . . . iv 5 89
Sweet flower, with flowers thy bridal bed I strew . . . . . v 3 12
We must think men are not gods, Nor of them look for such observances As fit the bridal . . . . *Othello* iii 4 150
Bridal-day. And graced thy poor sire with his bridal-day . *3 Hen. VI.* ii 2 155
Bride. If I must die, I will encounter darkness as a bride *Meas. for Meas.* iii 1 84
And you, brides and bridegrooms all, With measure heap'd in joy, to the measures fall . . . . *As Y. Like It* v 4 184
On the Sunday following, shall Bianca Be bride to you . *T. of Shrew* ii 1 398
But where is Kate? where is my lovely bride? . . . . . iii 2 94
See not your bride in these unreverent robes . . . . . iii 2 114
What a fool am I to chat with you, When I should bid good morrow to my bride! . . . . iii 2 124
And is the bride and bridegroom coming home? . . . . . iii 2 153
He took the bride about the neck And kiss'd her lips with such a clamorous smack . . . . iii 2 179
Obey the bride, you that attend on her . . . . . . iii 2 225
Though bride and bridegroom wants For to supply the places at the table . . . . iii 2 248
Shall sweet Bianca practise how to bride it? . . . . . iii 2 253
Ay, mistress bride, hath that awaken'd you? . . . . . . v 2 42
To-night, When I should take possession of the bride . . *All's Well* ii 5 28
The devil tempts thee here In likeness of a new untrimmed bride *K. John* iii 1 209
To be the princely bride of such a lord . . . . *1 Hen. VI.* v 3 152
Surfeiting in joys of love, With his new bride . . . *2 Hen. VI.* i 1 252
'Tis not his new-made bride shall succour him . . . *3 Hen. VI.* iii 3 207
Lewis of France is sending over masquers To revel it with him and his new bride . . . . iii 3 225; iv 1 95
Here comes the king.—And his well-chosen bride . . . . iv 1 7
To give the heir and daughter of Lord Scales Unto the brother of your loving bride . . . . iv 1 53
In your bride you bury brotherhood . . . . iv 1 55
Behold, I choose thee, Tamora, for my bride . . . . *T. Andron.* i 1 319
I will not re-salute the streets of Rome, Or climb my palace, till from forth this place I lead espoused my bride along with me . . . i 1 328
Accompany Your noble emperor and his lovely bride . . . . i 1 334
I am not bid to wait upon this bride . . . . i 1 338
You have play'd your prize: God give you joy, sir, of your gallant bride! . . . . i 1 400
If the emperor's court can feast two brides, You are my guest . . i 1 489
Let us make a bay And wake the emperor and his lovely bride . . ii 2 4
Let two more summers wither in their pride, Ere we may think her ripe to be a bride . . . . *Rom. and Jul.* i 2 11
At Saint Peter's Church, Shall happily make thee there a joyful bride. —Now, by Saint Peter's Church and Peter too, He shall not make me there a joyful bride . . . . iii 5 116
Why, love, I say! madam! sweet-heart! why, bride! What, not a word? . . . . iv 5 3
Come, is the bride ready to go to church?—Ready to go, but never to return . . . . iv 5 33
The maid is fair, o' the youngest for a bride . . . *T. of Athens* i 1 123
In quarter, and in terms like bride and groom Devesting them for bed *Othello* ii 3 180
Clothed like a bride, For the embracements even of Jove himself *Pericles* i 1 6
Hymen hath brought the bride to bed . . . . . . iii Gower 9
Your bride goes to that with shame which is her way to go with warrant . . . . iv 2 138
Bride-bed. I thought thy bride-bed to have deck'd, sweet maid *Hamlet* v 1 268
To the best bride-bed will we, Which by us shall blessed be *M. N. Dream* v 1 410
Bridegroom. Those dulcet sounds in break of day That creep into the dreaming bridegroom's ear . . . . . . *Mer. of Venice* iii 2 52
And you, brides and bridegrooms all, With measure heap'd in joy, to the measures fall . . . . *As Y. Like It* v 4 184
What will be said? what mockery will it be, To want the bridegroom when the priest attends! . . . . *T. of Shrew* iii 2 5
And is the bride and bridegroom coming home?—A bridegroom say you? 'tis a groom indeed, A grumbling groom . . . . . . iii 2 153
This mad-brain'd bridegroom took him such a cuff That down fell priest and book and book and priest . . . . iii 2 165
Though bride and bridegroom wants For to supply the places at the table . . . . iii 2 248
Lucentio, you shall supply the bridegroom's place . . . . . iii 2 251
Neat, and trimly dress'd, Fresh as a bridegroom . . . *1 Hen. IV.* i 3 34
Make ready straight.—Yea, with a bridegroom's fresh alacrity *Tr. and Cr.* iv 4 147
So worthy a gentleman to be her bridegroom . . . *Rom. and Jul.* iii 5 146
When the bridegroom in the morning comes To rouse thee from thy bed . . . . iv 1 107
The bridegroom he is come already: Make haste . . . . . iv 4 26
Whose untimely death Banish'd the new-made bridegroom from this city . . . . v 3 235
Bellona's bridegroom, lapp'd in proof, Confronted him . . *Macbeth* i 2 54
I will die bravely, like a bridegroom. What! I will be jovial . *Lear* iv 6 202
I will be A bridegroom in my death . . . . . *Ant. and Cleo.* iv 14 100
Bridge. What need the bridge much broader than the flood? . *Much Ado* i 1 318
Attended him on bridges, stood in lanes, Laid gifts before him *1 Hen. IV.* iv 3 70
How now, Captain Fluellen! come you from the bridge? . . *Hen. V.* iii 6 2
There is very excellent services committed at the bridge . . . iii 6 4
Here, at the bulwark of the bridge . . . . . . *1 Hen. VI.* i 4 67
Jack Cade hath gotten London bridge . . . . . *2 Hen. VI.* iv 4 49
They have won the bridge, killing all those that withstand them . . iv 5 3
The princes both make high account of you; For they account his head upon the bridge . . . . *Richard III.* iii 2 72
Down with the nose, Down with it flat; take the bridge quite away *T. of Athens* iv 3 158
To ride on a bay trotting-horse over four-inched bridges . . . *Lear* iii 4 58

Bridgenorth. Our meeting Is Bridgenorth . . . . . *1 Hen. IV.* iii 2 175
Some twelve days hence Our general forces at Bridgenorth shall meet . iii 2 178
Bridget. Mistress Bridget lost the handle of her fan . . *Mer. Wives* ii 2 11
Does Bridget paint still, Pompey, ha? . . . . . *Meas. for Meas.* iii 2 83
Maud, Bridget, Marian, Cicely, Gillian, Ginn! . . . *Com. of Errors* iii 1 31
Bridle. O, know he is the bridle of your will.—There's none but asses will be bridled so . . . . ii 1 13
How I cried, how the horses ran away, how her bridle was burst *T. of Shrew* iv 1 83
To bridle and suppress The pride of Suffolk . . . *2 Hen. VI.* i 1 200
I feel remorse in myself with his words; but I'll bridle it . . . iv 7 112
This is it that makes me bridle passion And bear with mildness *3 Hen. VI.* iv 4 19
Bridled. There's none but asses will be bridled so . . *Com. of Errors* ii 1 14
Mine was not bridled.—O then belike she was old and gentle *Hen. V.* iii 7 54
Brief. Come, come, open the matter in brief: what said she? *T. G. of Ver.* i 1 135
But what says she to me? be brief, my good she-Mercury *Mer. Wives* ii 2 81
Sir, I hear you are a scholar,—I will be brief with you . . . ii 2 187
Give your men the charge; we must be brief . . . . . iii 3 8
Speak, breathe, discuss; brief, short, quick, snap . . . . iv 5 2
The goodness that is cheap in beauty makes beauty brief in goodness *Meas. for Meas.* iii 1 186
I have possess'd him my most stay Can be but brief . . . . iv 1 45
Relate your wrongs; in what? by whom? be brief . . . . . v 1 26
The matter; proceed.—In brief, to set the needless process by . . v 1 92
Say in brief the cause Why thou departed'st . . . *Com. of Errors* i 1 29
A time too brief, too, to have all things answer my mind . *Much Ado* ii 1 375
Brief, I pray you; for you see it is a busy time with me . . . iii 5 5
Be brief; only to the plain form of marriage . . . . . . iv 1 1
Short as any dream; Brief as the lightning in the collied night *M. N. Dr.* i 1 145
There is a brief how many sports are ripe . . . . . . v 1 42
Tedious and brief! That is, hot ice and wondrous strange snow . . v 1 58
Some ten words long, Which is as brief as I have known a play . . v 1 62
I hope she will be brief . . . . v 1 323
In very brief, the suit is impertinent to myself . . *Mer. of Venice* ii 2 146
With all brief and plain conveniency Let me have judgement . . . iv 1 82
How brief the life of man Runs his erring pilgrimage . *As Y. Like It* iii 2 137
Brief, I recover'd him, bound up his wound . . . . . . iv 3 151
In brief, sir, study what you most affect . . . . . *T. of Shrew* i 1 40
In brief, sir, sith it your pleasure is, And I am tied to be obedient . i 1 216
Well, sir, in brief, the gown is not for me . . . . iv 3 156
'Tis very strange, that is the brief and the tedious of it . . *All's Well* ii 3 34
Whose ceremony Shall seem expedient on the now-born brief . . . ii 3 186
She told me, In a sweet verbal brief . . . . v 3 137
If you be not mad, be gone; if you have reason, be brief . . *T. Night* i 5 212
Go, write it in a martial hand; be curst and brief . . . . . iii 2 46
Very brief, and to exceeding good sense—less . . . . . . iii 4 174
The hand of time Shall draw this brief into as huge a volume . *K. John* ii 1 103
In brief, we are the king of England's subjects . . . . . . ii 1 267
I must be brief, lest resolution drop Out at mine eyes . . . . iv 1 35
A thousand businesses are brief in hand, And heaven itself doth frown . iv 3 158
Brief, then; and what's the news? . . . . v 6 18
Your grace mistakes; only to be brief, Left I his title out *Richard II.* iii 3 9
Would you have been so brief with him, he would Have been so brief with you . . . . iii 3 11
Come, come, in wooing sorrow let's be brief, Since, wedding it, there is such length in grief . . . . v 1 93
Bear this sealed brief With winged haste . . . . . *1 Hen. IV.* iv 4 1
In brief, Tell me their words as near as thou canst guess them *3 Hen. VI.* ii 1 9
Are you so brief?—O, sir, it is better to be brief than tedious *Richard III.* i 4 88
If you will live, lament; if die, be brief . . . . ii 2 43
What sayest thou? speak suddenly; be brief . . . . . . iv 2 20
We must be brief when traitors brave the field . . . . . iv 3 57
And brief, good mother; for I am in haste . . . . iv 4 161
Be brief, lest that the process of thy kindness Last longer telling than thy kindness' date . . . . iv 4 253
In brief,—for so the season bids us be . . . . v 3 87
Night hath been too brief . . . . *Troi. and Cres.* iv 2 11
Nay, I have done already.—Thou art too brief . . . . . . iv 5 257
Thus then in brief: The valiant Paris seeks you for his love *Rom. and Jul.* i 3 73
But that a joy past joy calls out on me, It were a grief, so brief to part with thee . . . . iii 3 174
Yea, noise? then I'll be brief. O happy dagger! . . . . . v 3 169
I will be brief, for my short date of breath Is not so long as is a tedious tale . . . . v 3 229
But, soft! methinks I scent the morning air; Brief let me be *Hamlet* i 5 59
Since brevity is the soul of wit, And tediousness the limbs and outward flourishes, I will be brief . . . . ii 2 92
'Tis brief, my lord.—As woman's love . . . . iii 2 163
In brief, Sorrow would be a rarity most beloved . . . . *Lear* iv 3 24
Quickly send, Be brief in it, to the castle . . . . v 3 245
When I came back—For this was brief—I found them close together *Oth.* ii 3 237
Masters, play here; I will content your pains; Something that's brief iii 1 2
Well, do it, and be brief; I will walk by . . . . iv 2 30
This is the brief of money, plate, and jewels, I am possess'd of *A. and C.* v 2 138
And, to be brief, my practice so prevailed . . . . . *Cymbeline* v 5 199
Brief abstract and record of tedious days . . . . *Richard III.* iv 4 28
Brief authority. But man, proud man, Drest in a little brief authority, Most ignorant of what he's most assured . . *Meas. for Meas.* ii 2 118
Brief candle. Out, out, brief candle! Life's but a walking shadow *Macb.* v 5 23
Brief chronicles. The abstract and brief chronicles of the time *Hamlet* ii 2 548
Brief discourse. Give me advantage of some brief discourse . *Othello* iii 1 55
Brief farewell. Come, leave your tears: a brief farewell . . *Coriolanus* iv 1 1
Brief mortality. Give edge unto the swords That make such waste in brief mortality . . . . *Hen. V.* i 2 28
Brief nature. Postures beyond brief nature . . . . *Cymbeline* v 5 165
Brief plagues. At once let your brief plagues be mercy! *Troi. and Cres.* v 10 8
Brief scene. A tedious brief scene of young Pyramus And his love Thisbe *M. N. Dream* v 1 56
Brief sounds determine of my weal or woe . . . . *Rom. and Jul.* iii 2 51
Brief span. You have scarce time To steal from spiritual leisure a brief span . . . . *Hen. VIII.* iii 2 140
Brief tale. List a brief tale; And when 'tis told, O, that my heart would burst! . . . . *Lear* v 3 181
Brief wars. They nothing doubt prevailing and to make it brief wars *Coriolanus* i 3 112
Brief world. The sweet degrees that this brief world affords To such as may the passive drugs of it Freely command . . . *T. of Athens* iv 3 253
Briefer. To teach you gamut in a briefer sort . . . *T. of Shrew* iii 1 67
Briefest. Ah, women, women! come; we have no friend But resolution, and the briefest end . . . . *Ant. and Cleo.* iv 15 91

Briefly, I do mean to make love to Ford's wife . . . . *Mer. Wives* i 3 47
Briefly, I have pursued her as love hath pursued me . . . ii 2 208
Show me briefly how . . . . *Much Ado* ii 2 11
Briefly, I desire nothing but the reward of a villain . . v 1 250
Instance, briefly; come, instance . . . *As Y. Like It* iii 2 53
What England says, say briefly, gentle lord . . *K. John* ii 1 52
So the question stands. Briefly to this end . . *2 Hen. IV* iv 1 54
Whose tenours and particular effects You have enscheduled briefly *Hen. V.* v 2 73
Briefly we heard their drums . . . *Coriolanus* i 6 16
Speak briefly then; For we are peremptory . . . iii 1 285
Speak briefly, can you like of Paris' love? . . *Rom. and Jul.* i 3 96
Answer every man directly.—Ay, and briefly.—Ay, and wisely *J. Cæsar* iii 3 11
To answer every man directly and briefly, wisely and truly: wisely I say, I am a bachelor . . . iii 3 17
For your dwelling,—briefly.—Briefly, I dwell by the Capitol . . iii 3 26
Let's briefly put on manly readiness, And meet i' the hall *Macbeth* ii 3 139
Briefly thyself remember: the sword is out That must destroy thee *Lear* iv 6 233
Go put on thy defences.—Briefly, sir . . *Ant. and Cleo.* iv 4 10
Briefly die their joys That place them on the truth of girls and boys *Cymbeline* v 5 106
Time that is so briefly spent With your fine fancies quaintly eche *Pericles* iii Gower 12
Therefore briefly yield her; for she must overboard straight . . iii 1 53
Briefness. I have one thing, of a queasy question, Which I must act: briefness and fortune, work! . . *Lear* ii 1 20
Welcome, sir.—I hope the briefness of your answer made The speediness of your return . . *Cymbeline* ii 4 30
In feather'd briefness sails are fill'd . . *Pericles* v 2 280
Brier. Through Tooth'd briers, sharp furzes, pricking goss *Tempest* iv 1 180
If aught possess thee from me, it is dross, Usurping ivy, brier *C. of Errors* ii 2 180
Thorough bush, thorough brier, Over park, over pale *M. N. Dream* ii 1 3
Most lily-white of hue, Of colour like the red rose on triumphant brier iii 1 96
Through bog, through bush, through brake, through brier . . iii 1 110
Briers and thorns at their apparel snatch; Some sleeves, some hats iii 2 29
Bedabbled with the dew and torn with briers, I can no further crawl . iii 2 443
Every elf and fairy sprite Hop as light as bird from brier . . v 1 401
O, how full of briers is this working-day world! *As Y. Like It* i 3 12
When briers shall have leaves as well as thorns . *All's Well* iv 4 32
I'll have thy beauty scratch'd with briers, and made More homely *W. Tale* iv 4 436
From off this brier pluck a white rose with me . *1 Hen. VI.* ii 4 30
Scratches with briers, Scars to move laughter only . *Coriolanus* iii 3 51
Whose mouth is cover'd with rude-growing briers . *T. Andron.* ii 3 199
The oaks bear mast, the briers scarlet hips . *T. of Athens* iv 3 422
Bright. She is too bright to be looked against . *Mer. Wives* ii 2 254
Wisdom wishes to appear most bright When it doth tax itself *M. for M.* ii 4 78
Nor shines the silver moon one half so bright . *L. L. Lost* iv 3 30
Since her time are colliers counted bright . . iv 3 267
As sweet and musical As bright Apollo's lute, strung with his hair . iv 3 343
Vouchsafe, bright moon, and these thy stars, to shine . . v 2 205
So quick bright things come to confusion . *M. N. Dream* i 1 149
How came her eyes so bright? Not with salt tears . . ii 2 92
Look as bright, as clear, As yonder Venus in her glimmering sphere . iii 2 60
I thank thee, Moon, for shining now so bright . . v 1 278
The moon shines bright: in such a night as this . *Mer. of Venice* v 1 1
Look how the floor of heaven Is thick inlaid with patines of bright gold v 1 59
She robs thee of thy name; And thou wilt show more bright and seem more virtuous When she is gone . *As Y. Like It* i 3 83
If the scorn of your bright eyne Have power to raise such love in mine. iv 3 50
Good Lord, how bright and goodly shines the moon! *T. of Shrew* iv 5 2
I say it is the moon that shines so bright.—I know it is the sun that shines so bright . . iv 5 4
'Twere all one That I should love a bright particular star *All's Well* i 1 97
In his bright radiance and collateral light Must I be comforted . . i 1 99
Ere they can behold Bright Phœbus in his strength *W. Tale* iv 4 124
The most peerless piece of earth, I think, That e'er the sun shone bright on . . v 1 95
Your sword is bright, sir; put it up again *K. John* iv 3 79
With hard bright steel and hearts harder than steel *Richard II.* iii 2 111
To stain the track Of his bright passage to the occident . . iii 3 67
Behold, his eye, As bright as is the eagle's . . iii 3 69
Like bright metal on a sullen ground . *1 Hen. IV.* i 2 236
It were an easy leap, To pluck bright honour from the pale-faced moon. i 3 202
The sun and not the moon; for it shines bright and never changes *Hen. V.* v 2 172
A far more glorious star thy soul will make Than Julius Cæsar or bright *1 Hen. VI.* i 1 56
Bright star of Venus, fall'n down on the earth . . i 2 144
To save a paltry life and slay bright fame . . iv 6 45
Ring, bells, aloud; burn, bonfires, clear and bright . *2 Hen. VI.* v 1 3
Whose bright out-shining beams thy cloudy wrath Hath in eternal darkness folded up . . *Richard III.* i 3 268
A shadow like an angel, with bright hair Dabbled in blood . i 4 53
By the bright track of his fiery car, Gives signal of a goodly day to-morrow . . v 3 20
I shall fall Like a bright exhalation in the evening . *Hen. VIII.* iii 2 226
Whose bright faces Cast thousand beams upon me, like the sun . iv 2 88
Wherever the bright sun of heaven shall shine . . v 5 51
Perseverance, dear my lord, Keeps honour bright . *Troi. and Cres.* iii 3 151
Tear my bright hair and scratch my praised cheeks . iv 2 113
More bright in zeal than the devotion which Cold lips blow to their deities iv 4 28
On whose bright crest Fame with her loud'st Oyes Cries 'This is he'. iv 5 143
And tapers burn so bright and every thing In readiness . *T. Andron.* i 1 324
I will be bright, and shine in pearl and gold . . ii 1 19
The moon is bright and grey, The fields are fragrant . . ii 2 1
Feather of lead, bright smoke, cold fire, sick health! *Rom. and Jul.* i 1 186
O, she doth teach the torches to burn bright! . . i 5 46
I conjure thee by Rosaline's bright eyes, By her high forehead ii 1 17
Her eyes in heaven Would through the airy region stream so bright ii 2 21
She speaks: O, speak again, bright angel! . . ii 2 26
Thou bright defiler [gold] Of Hymen's purest bed! *T. of Athens* iv 3 383
It is the bright day that brings forth the adder *J. Cæsar* ii 1 14
Sleek o'er your rugged looks; Be bright and jovial among your guests *Macbeth* iii 2 28
Angels are bright still, though the brightest fell . . iv 3 22
Keep up your bright swords, for the dew will rust them *Othello* i 2 59
The bright day is done, And we are for the dark *Ant. and Cleo.* v 2 193
Made Lud's town with rejoicing fires bright . *Cymbeline* iii 1 32
Her eyelids . . Begin to part their fringes of bright gold *Pericles* iii 2 101
By bright Diana, whom we honour . . iii 3 28
Bright-burning. What fool hath added water to the sea, Or brought a faggot to bright-burning Troy? . . *T. Andron.* iii 1 69

Brighten. There were two honours lost, yours and your son's. For yours, the God of heaven brighten it! . *2 Hen. IV.* ii 3 17
Brightest. To the brightest beams Distracted clouds give way *All's Well* v 3 34
O for a Muse of fire, that would ascend The brightest heaven of invention, A kingdom for a stage! . . *Hen. V.* Prol. 2
Thus sometimes hath the brightest day a cloud . *2 Hen. VI.* ii 4 1
Angels are bright still, though the brightest fell . *Macbeth* iv 3 22
Brightly. So doth the greater glory dim the less: A substitute shines brightly as a king Until a king be by . *Mer. of Venice* v 1 94
Now, by the burning tapers of the sky, That shone so brightly *T. Andron.* iv 2 90
Brightness. In her ray and brightness The herd hath more annoyance by the breese Than by the tiger *Troi. and Cres.* i 3 47
The brightness of her cheek would shame those stars *Rom. and Jul.* ii 2 19
Bright-shining. In the midst of this bright-shining day . *3 Hen. VI.* v 3 3
Brim. Banks with pioned and twilled brims . . *Tempest* iv 1 64
Which they distil now in the curbed time, To make the coming hour o'erflow with joy And pleasure drown the brim . *All's Well* ii 4 48
Bring me but to the very brim of it . . *Lear* iv 1 78
He will fill thy wishes to the brim With principalities . *Ant. and Cleo.* iii 13 18
Here, with a cup that's stored unto the brim *Pericles* ii 3 50
Brimful of sorrow and dismay . . *Tempest* v 1 14
With his eye brimful of tears *2 Hen. IV.* iii 2 67
Our legions are brim-full, our cause is ripe *J. Cæsar* iv 3 215
In a town of war, Yet wild, the people's hearts brimful of fear *Othello* ii 3 214
Brim fulness. With ample and brim fulness *Hen. V.* i 2 150
Brimstone. Fire and brimstone!—O, peace, peace! . *T. Night* ii 5 56
To put fire in your heart, and brimstone in your liver . iii 2 22
Fire and brimstone!—My lord?—Are you wise? . *Othello* iv 1 245
Brinded. Thrice the brinded cat hath mew'd *Macbeth* iv 1 1
Brine. All but mariners Plunged in the foaming brine *Tempest* i 2 211
Take his bottle from him: when that's gone He shall drink nought but brine . . iii 2 74
Your commendations, madam, get from her tears.—'Tis the best brine a maiden can season her praise in . *All's Well* i 1 55
Water once a day her chamber round With eye-offending brine *T. Night* i 1 30
What a deal of brine Hath wash'd thy sallow cheeks for Rosaline! *R. and J.* ii 3 69
Thou shalt be whipp'd with wire, and stew'd in brine *Ant. and Cleo.* ii 5 65
But sea-room, an the brine and cloudy billow kiss the morn, I care not *Pericles* iii 1 45
Brine-pit. The fresh springs, brine-pits *Tempest* i 2 338
And made a brine-pit with our bitter tears *T. Andron.* iii 1 129
Bring her to try with main-course . *Tempest* i 1 38
Hear a little further And then I'll bring thee to the present business i 2 136
Milan and Naples have Moe widows in them of this business' making Than we bring men to comfort them . . ii 1 134
You rub the sore, When you should bring the plaster . ii 1 139
Do not torment me, prithee; I'll bring my wood home faster ii 2 74
I prithee, let me bring thee where crabs grow . . ii 2 171
I'll bring thee To clustering filberts . . ii 2 174
Canst thou bring me to the party? . iii 2 67
She will become thy bed, I warrant. And bring thee forth brave brood iii 2 113
Each putter-out of five for one will bring us Good warrant of . iii 3 48
Go bring the rabble, O'er whom I give thee power . iv 1 37
Bring a corollary, Rather than want a spirit . iv 1 57
The trumpery in my house, go bring it hither, For stale to catch these thieves . iv 1 186
The prize I'll bring thee to Shall hoodwink this mischance . iv 1 205
In the morn I'll bring you to your ship . v 1 307
And thither will I bring thee, Valentine *T. G. of Ver.* i 1 55
Come, go with us, we'll bring thee to our crews . iv 1 74
I'll bring you where you shall hear music . iv 2 30
Then to Silvia let us sing, . . . To her let us garlands bring . iv 2 53
Be my mean To bring me where to speak with Madam Silvia . iv 4 114
Bring my picture there. Go give your master this . iv 4 122
Come, come, Be patient; we must bring you to our captain . v 3 2
Bring her away.—Where is the gentleman that was with her? v 3 5
Come, I must bring you to our captain's cave . v 3 12
I will bring the doctor about by the fields *Mer. Wives* ii 3 81
I will bring thee where Mistress Anne Page is, at a farmhouse a-feasting ii 3 90
He promise to bring me where is Anne Page . iii 1 126
What I have suffered to bring this woman to evil for your good iii 5 97
I'll but bring my young man here to school . iv 1 8
I'll bring linen for him straight . iv 2 102
Let us two devise to bring him thither iv 4 27
Good hearts, what ado here is to bring you together! iv 5 129
Bring you the maid, you shall not lack a priest iv 6 53
We'll bring you to Windsor, to one Master Brook v 5 174
That we may bring you something on the way. *Meas. for Meas.* i 1 62
The heavens give safety to your purposes!—Lead forth and bring you back in happiness! . i 1 75
Can you so stead me As bring me to the sight of Isabella? i 4 18
That from the seedness the bare fallow brings To teeming foison i 4 42
Bring him his confessor, let him be prepared ii 1 35
I know no law: bring them away ii 1 44
Look you bring me in the names of some six or seven ii 1 286
Bring me to hear them speak iii 1 52
He would never bring them to light iii 2 188
But my kisses bring again, bring again; Seals of love, but seal'd in vain iv 1 5
To bring you thus together, 'tis no sin iv 1 73
Sirrah, bring Barnardine hither.—Master Barnardine! you must rise iv 3 22
After him, fellows; bring him to the block iv 3 69
Bid them bring the trumpets to the gate iv 5 9
So, bring us to our palace; where we'll show What's yet behind v 1 544
And that to-morrow you will bring it home *Com. of Errors* iii 1 5
Bring it, I pray you, to the Porpentine; For there's the house iii 1 116
Get thee gone; Buy thou a rope and bring it home to me iv 1 20
Then you will bring the chain to her yourself?—No; bear it with you. iv 1 40
There's the money, bear it straight, And bring thy master home immediately . iv 2 64
He that brings any man to answer it that breaks his band iv 3 31
Here comes my man; I think he brings the money . iv 4 8
Come, gaoler, bring me where the goldsmith is iv 4 145
Let your servants bring my husband forth v 1 93
Parted with me to go fetch a chain, Promising to bring it to the Porpentine . v 1 222
This purse of ducats I received from you And Dromio my man did bring them . v 1 386
And when I have heard it, what blessing brings it? *Much Ado* i 3 8
I will fetch you a toothpicker now from the furthest inch of Asia, bring you the length of Prester John's foot . ii 1 275

Bring. To bring Signior Benedick and the Lady Beatrice into a mountain of affection . . . *Much Ado* ii 1 381
And bring them to see this the very night before the intended wedding . ii 2 45
Bring it hither to me in the orchard.—I am here already . . iii 3 4
I'll bring you thither, my lord, if you'll vouchsafe me . . iii 2 3
You'll be made bring Deformed forth, I warrant you . . iii 3 185
Take their examination yourself and bring it me . . . iii 5 54
Bid him bring his pen and inkhorn to the gaol . . . iii 5 63
Bring him away . . . . iv 2 89
Bring me a father that so loved his child . . . . v 1 8
Bring him yet to me, And I of him will gather patience . . v 1 18
Come, bring away the plaintiffs . . . . . v 1 261
Bring you these fellows on. . . . . . . v 1 340
And shall, at the least of thy sweet notice, bring her to trial *L. L. Lost* i 1 279
Give enlargement to the swain, bring him festinately hither . iii 1 5
They do not mark me, and that brings me out . . . v 2 172
The news I bring Is heavy in my tongue . . . . v 2 726
I take my leave.—No, madam ; we will bring you on your way . v 2 883
As a surfeit of the sweetest things The deepest loathing to the stomach brings, . . . So thou, my surfeit . . *M. N. Dream* ii 2 138
There is two hard things ; that is, to bring the moonlight into a chamber . . . . iii 1 49
Tie up my love's tongue, bring him silently . . . . iii 1 206
By some illusion see thou bring her here . . . . iii 2 98
And, good mounsieur, bring me the honey-bag . . . iv 1 13
Go, bring them in : and take your places, ladies . . . v 1 84
Or to find both Or bring your latter hazard back again *Mer. of Venice* i 1 151
Bring me the fairest creature northward born . . . ii 1 4
Come, bring me unto my chance . . . . . . ii 1 43
I must freely have the half of anything That this same paper brings you iii 2 253
When it is paid, bring your true friend along . . . iii 2 310
Bring them, I pray thee, with imagined speed . . . iii 4 52
Bring us the letters ; call the messenger . . . . iv 1 110
In christening shalt thou have two godfathers : Had I been judge, thou shouldst have had ten more, To bring thee to the gallows, not the font . . . . iv 1 400
Bring him, if thou canst, Unto Antonio's house . . . iv 1 453
Bring your music forth into the air . . . . . v 1 53
I'll bring you to him straight . . . . *As Y. Like It* ii 1 69
If he be absent, bring his brother to me ; I'll make him find him . ii 2 18
Let not search and inquisition quail To bring again these foolish runaways . . . . ii 2 21
Bring us where we may rest ourselves and feed . . . ii 4 73
I will either be food for it or bring it for food to thee . . ii 6 7
If I bring thee not something to eat, I will give thee leave to die . ii 6 11
Bring him dead or living Within this twelvemonth . . . iii 1 6
That is another simple sin in you, to bring the ewes and the rams together . . . . iii 2 83
When I think, I must speak. Sweet, say on.—You bring me out . iii 2 265
Bring us to this sight, and you shall say I'll prove a busy actor in their play . . . . iii 4 61
Besides, he brings his destiny with him . . . . iv 1 57
He that brings this love to thee Little knows this love in me . iv 3 56
Left on your right hand brings you to the place . . . iv 3 81
And you say, you will have her, when I bring her? . . . v 4 9
I am the second son of old Sir Roland, That bring these tidings . v 4 159
Well, bring our lady hither to our sight . . . *T. of Shrew* Ind. 2 76
I am he am born to tame you Kate, And bring you from a wild Kate to a Kate Conformable as other household Kates . . . ii 1 279
'Twas a commodity lay fretting by you : 'Twill bring you gain, or perish ii 1 331
I'll bring mine action on the proudest he That stops my way . iii 2 236
How durst you, villains, bring it from the dresser, And serve it thus? . iv 1 166
Come, I will bring thee to thy bridal chamber . . . iv 1 181
Thou see'st how diligent I am To dress thy meat myself and bring it thee . . . . iv 3 40
Bring our horses unto Long-lane end . . . . . iv 3 187
What if a man bring him a hundred pound or two? . . . v 1 22
Away, I say, and bring them hither straight . . . . v 2 105
See where she comes and brings your froward wives . . . v 2 119
The mightiest space in fortune nature brings To join like likes *All's Well* i 1 237
Ere twice the horses of the sun shall bring Their fiery torches his diurnal ring . . . . ii 1 164
But follows it, my lord, to bring me down Must answer for your raising? . . . . ii 3 119
I write man ; to which title age cannot bring thee . . . ii 3 209
Bring him forth : has sat i' the stocks all night . . . iv 3 116
It lies in you, my lord, to bring me in some grace, for you did bring me out . . . . v 2 49
One brings thee in grace and the other brings thee out . . . v 2 53
Seek these suitors : Go speedily and bring again the count . . v 3 152
Both suffer under this complaint we bring . . . . v 3 163
I saw the man to-day, if man he be.—Find him, and bring him hither . v 3 204
I pray you, bring your hand to the buttery-bar and let it drink *T. Night* i 3 74
I bring no overture of war, no taxation of homage . . . i 5 224
Come, bring us, bring us where he is . . . . . ii 2 90
We will bring the device to the bar and crown thee for a finder of madmen . . . . iii 4 153
Bring her along with you, it may awake my bounty further . . v 1 46
I'll bring you to a captain in this town, Where lie my maiden weeds v 1 261
The captain that did bring me first on shore Hath my maid's garments v 1 281
Fourteen they shall not see, To bring false generations *W. Tale* ii 1 148
Now from the oracle They will bring all . . . . . ii 1 186
Put apart these your attendants, I Shall bring Emilia forth . . ii 2 15
I come to bring him sleep . . . . ii 3 33
If you can bring Tincture or lustre in her lip, her eye . . . iii 2 205
Prithee, bring me To the dead bodies of my queen and son . . iii 2 235
Shall I bring thee on the way ?—No, good-faced sir ; no, sweet sir . iv 3 122
She shall bring him that Which he not dreams of . . . iv 4 179
Come, bring away thy pack after me . . . . . iv 4 317
Strive to qualify And bring him up to liking . . . . iv 4 544
I'll bring you where he is aboard, tender your persons to his presence iv 4 825
And leave this young man in pawn till I bring it you . . iv 4 839
I will bring these two moles, these blind ones, aboard him . . iv 4 867
Bring them to our embracement . . . . . . v 1 114
Thy speeches Will bring me to consider that which may Unfurnish me of reason . . . . v 1 122
What brings you here to court so hastily? . . . *K. John* i 1 221
May from England bring That right in peace which here we urge in war ii 1 46
I bring you witnesses, Twice fifteen thousand hearts . . . ii 1 274

Bring. The yearly course that brings this day about Shall never see it but a holiday . . . . *K. John* iii 1 81
For very little pains Will bring this labour to an happy end . . iii 2 10
I have a way to win their loves again ; Bring them before me . iv 2 169
Answer not, but to my closet bring The angry lords . . . iv 2 267
And brings from him such offers of our peace As we with honour and respect may take . . . . v 7 84
Ere the six years that he hath to spend Can change their moons and bring their times about . . . . . *Richard II.* i 3 220
Come, come, my son, I'll bring thee on thy way . . . i 3 304
Provide some carts And bring away the armour that is there . . ii 2 107
Where no man never comes but that sad dog That brings me food . v 5 71
He call'd them untaught knaves, unmannerly, To bring a slovenly unhandsome corse Betwixt the wind and his nobility . *1 Hen. IV.* i 3 44
Only stays but to behold the face Of that occasion that shall bring it on i 3 276
Bid the ostler bring my gelding out of the stable . . . ii 1 105
And bring him out that is but woman's son . . . . iii 1 47
If thou have power to raise him, bring him hither . . . iii 1 60
In the morning early shall my uncle Bring him our purposes . . iv 3 111
Which cannot choose but bring him quickly on . . . . v 2 45
Come, bring your luggage nobly on your back . . . . v 4 160
Not a man of them brings other news Than they have learn'd of me *2 Hen. IV.* Ind. 38
From Rumour's tongues They bring smooth comforts false . . Ind. 40
Noble earl, I bring you certain news from Shrewsbury . . . i 1 12
Approach The ragged'st hour that time and spite dare bring ! . i 1 151
A rescue !—Good people, bring a rescue or two . . . ii 1 62
The powers that you already have sent forth Shall bring this prize in very easily . . . . iii 1 101
Our thighs pack'd with wax, our mouths with honey, We bring it to the hive . . . . iv 5 78
Tidings do I bring and lucky joys And golden times . . . v 3 99
What ! I do bring good news . . . . . . v 3 134
Come, you rogue, come ; bring me to a justice . . . . v 4 29
Thence to France shall we convey you safe, And bring you back *Hen. V.* ii Prol. 38
Honey-sweet husband, let me bring thee to Staines . . . ii 3 2
We'll give them present audience. Go, and bring them . . ii 4 67
To whom expressly I bring greeting . . . . . . ii 4 112
And in a captive chariot into Rouen Bring him our prisoner . . iii 5 55
Bring me just notice of the numbers dead On both our parts . . iv 7 122
Pray thee, go seek him, and bring him to my tent . . . iv 7 175
Till Harry's back-return again to France : There must we bring him v Prol. 42
To bring your most imperial majesties Unto this bar . . . v 2 26
Sad tidings bring I to you out of France . . . *1 Hen. VI.* i 1 58
To quell the Dauphin utterly, Or bring him in obedience to your yoke i 1 164
Succour is at hand : A holy maid hither with me I bring . . i 2 51
And when you have done so, bring the keys to me . . . . ii 3 2
He From John of Gaunt doth bring his pedigree . . . . ii 5 77
Perceive how I will work To bring this matter to the wished end . iii 3 28
When sapless age and weak unable limbs Should bring thy father to his drooping chair . . . . iv 5 5
To match with her that brings no vantages . . . *2 Hen. VI.* i 1 131
Dame Eleanor gives gold to bring the witch . . . . i 2 91
Bring him near the king ; His highness' pleasure is to talk with him ii 1 72
This dishonour in thine age Will bring thy head with sorrow to the ground ! ii 3 19
I rather would have lost my life betimes Than bring a burthen of dishonour home . . . . iii 1 298
Bring me unto my trial when you will . . . . . iii 3 8
Bid the apothecary Bring the strong poison that I bought of him . . iii 3 18
Strike off his head, and bring them both upon two poles hither . iv 7 118
He that brings his head unto the king Shall have a thousand crowns . iv 8 69
Or dare to bring thy force so near the court . . . . v 1 22
Then what intends these forces thou dost bring? . . . . v 1 60
If thou darest bring them to the baiting place . . . . v 1 150
Brings a thousand-fold more care to keep Than in possession any jot of pleasure . . . . *3 Hen. VI.* ii 2 52
Would bring white hairs unto a quiet grave . . . . . ii 5 40
Brave Warwick ! What brings thee to France? . . . . iii 3 46
I was the chief that raised him to the crown, And I'll be chief to bring him down again . . . . iii 3 263
The bruit thereof will bring you many friends . . . . iv 7 64
See, he brings the mayor along . . . . *Richard III.* iii 5 13
If you thrive well, bring them to Baynard's Castle . . . iii 5 98
No doubt we'll bring it to a happy issue . . . . . iii 7 54
Bring me to their sights ; I'll bear thy blame . . . . iv 1 25
Take that, until thou bring me better news . . . . . iv 4 510
Reward to him that brings the traitor in . . . . . iv 4 518
Yet this good comfort bring I to your grace . . . . iv 4 522
Bid him bring his power Before sunrising . . . . . v 3 60
Call up Lord Stanley, bid him bring his power . . . . v 3 290
You sleeping safe, they bring to you unrest . . . . v 3 320
What says Lord Stanley? will he bring his power? . . . . v 3 342
Beside forfeiting Our own brains, and the opinion that we bring *Hen. VIII.* Prol. 20
May bring his plain-song And have an hour of hearing . . . i 3 45
To bring my whole cause 'fore his holiness, And to be judged by him ii 4 120
Is this your comfort? The cordial that ye bring a wretched lady? . iii 1 106
Bring me a constant woman to her husband . . . . . iii 1 134
He brings his physic After his patient's death . . . . iii 2 40
I know A way, if it take right, in spite of fortune Will bring me off again iii 2 220
How sleek and wanton Ye appear in every thing may bring my ruin ! . iii 2 242
I should have ta'en some pains to bring together Yourself and your accusers . . . . v 1 119
The tidings that I bring Will make my boldness manners . . . v 1 158
A thousand thousand blessings, Which time shall bring to ripeness . v 5 21
Three or four hairs on his chin,— Indeed, a tapster's arithmetic may soon bring his particulars therein to a total . *Troi. and Cres.* i 2 124
I'll be with you, niece, by and by.—To bring, uncle?—Ay, a token . i 2 305
The worthiness of praise distains his worth, If that the praised himself bring the praise forth . . . . i 3 242
I bring a trumpet to awake his ear . . . . . . i 3 251
I have a young conception in my brain ; Be you my time to bring it to some shape . . . . i 3 313
Whom may you else oppose, That can from Hector bring his honour off? i 3 334
I propose not merely to myself The pleasures such a beauty brings with it ii 2 147
Bring action hither, this cannot go to war . . . . . ii 3 145
Tell him so.—I shall ; and bring his answer presently . . . ii 3 148
Walk here i' the orchard, I'll bring her straight . . . . iii 2 17
Boldness comes to me now, and brings me heart . . . . iii 2 121
I have taken such pains to bring you together . . . . . iii 2 207

Bring. Let Diomedes bear him, And bring us Cressid hither *Tr. and Cr.* iii 3 31
His purpose meets you: 'twas to bring this Greek To Calchas' house . iv 1 36
You bring me to do, and then you flout me too . . . iv 2 27
Walk into her house; I'll bring her to the Grecian presently. . . iv 3 6
Come you hither; And bring Æneas and the Grecian with you . . iv 4 102
I'll bring you to your father . . . . . . iv 5 53
Let these threats alone, Till accident or purpose bring you to't . . iv 5 262
Shall I, sweet lord, be bound to you so much, After we part from Agamemnon's tent, To bring me thither? . . . . . . iv 5 286
I'll bring you to the gates.—Accept distracted thanks . . . v 2 188
I'll be ta'en too, Or bring him off: fate, hear me what I say! . . v 6 25
Briefly we heard their drums: How couldst thou in a mile confound an hour, And bring thy news so late? . . . *Coriolanus* i 6 18
Brings a' victory in his pocket? the wounds become him . . ii 1 135
Of the which we being members, should bring ourselves to be monstrous members . . . . ii 3 13
I cannot bring My tongue to such a pace . . . . . ii 3 56
That is the way to lay the city flat; To bring the roof to the foundation iii 1 205
I'll go to him, and undertake to bring him Where he shall answer . iii 1 324
If you bring not Marcius, we'll proceed In our first way.—I'll bring him iii 1 333
Bring me but out at gate . . . . iv 1 47
Mark what mercy his mother shall bring from him . . . . v 4 29
If The Roman ladies bring not comfort home, They'll give him death by inches . . . . v 4 41
These that I bring unto their latest home . . . *T. Andron.* i 1 83
Follow, my lord, and I'll soon bring her back . . . . i 1 289
As is a nurse's song Of lullaby to bring her babe asleep . . . ii 3 29
Bring thou her husband: This is the hole where Aaron bid us hide him ii 3 185
Straight will I bring you to the loathsome pit . . . . ii 3 193
Then all too late I bring this fatal writ . . . . . ii 3 264
Some bring the murder'd body, some the murderers . . . ii 3 300
I bring consuming sorrow to thine age.—Will it consume me? . . iii 1 61
And bring you up To be a warrior . . . . . . iv 2 179
To save my boy, to nourish and bring him up . . . . v 1 84
And bring with him Some of the chiefest princes of the Goths . . v 2 124
So, now bring them in, for I'll play the cook . . . . v 2 205
Come, thou reverend man of Rome, And bring our emperor gently in thy hand . . . . v 3 138
My man shall be with thee, And bring thee cords *Rom. and Jul.* ii 4 201
O, here comes my nurse, And she brings news . . . . iii 2 32
Will you go to them? I will bring you thither . . . . iii 2 129
I bring thee tidings of the prince's doom . . . . . iii 3 8
Could to no issue of true honour bring . . . . . iv 1 65
For shame, bring Juliet forth; her lord is come . . . iv 5 22
Dost thou not bring me letters from the friar? . . . . v 1 13
I could not send it,—here it is again,—Nor get a messenger to bring it thee . . . . v 2 15
Get me an iron crow, and bring it straight Unto my cell . . . v 2 21
A glooming peace this morning with it brings . . . . v 3 305
The little casket bring me hither . . . *T. of Athens* i 2 164
Your words have took such pains as if they labour'd To bring manslaughter into form . . . . iii 5 27
And ne'er prefer his injuries to his heart, To bring it into danger . iii 5 35
O, the fierce wretchedness that glory brings us! . . . iv 2 30
What viler thing upon the earth than friends Who can bring noblest minds to basest ends! . . . . iv 3 471
Bring us to his cave: It is our part and promise to the Athenians To speak with Timon . . . . v 1 122
Bring us to him, And chance it as it may . . . . . v 1 128
My long sickness Of health and living now begins to mend, And nothing brings me all things . . . . v 1 191
We stand much hazard, if they bring not Timon . . . . v 2 5
Bring me into your city, And I will use the olive with my sword . v 4 81
Wherefore rejoice? What conquest brings he home? *J. Cæsar* i 1 37
I can give his humour the true bent, And I will bring him to the Capitol ii 1 211
Bring me their opinions of success . . . . . . ii 2 6
A bustling rumour, like a fray, And the wind brings it from the Capitol ii 4 19
Bring him with triumph home unto his house . . . . iii 2 54
We'll bring him to his house With shouts and clamours . . . iii 2 57
Bring me to Octavius . . . . iii 2 276
Bring Messala with you Immediately to us . . . . . iv 3 141
Give him tending; He brings great news . . . . *Macbeth* i 5 39
Why did you bring these daggers from the place? . . . . ii 2 48
I'll bring you to him.—I know this is a joyful trouble to you . . ii 3 52
They are, my lord, without the palace gate.—Bring them before us . iii 1 48
Where are these gentlemen? Come, bring me where they are . . iv 1 156
Front to front Bring thou this fiend of Scotland and myself . . iv 3 233
Bring me no more reports; let them fly all . . . . . v 3 1
Your royal preparation Makes us hear something.—Bring it after me . v 3 58
Bring with thee airs from heaven or blasts from hell . . *Hamlet* i 4 41
Go, some of you, And bring these gentlemen where Hamlet is . . ii 2 37
Thyself do grace to them, and bring them in . . . . . ii 2 53
Keeps aloof, When we would bring him on to some confession . . iii 1 9
I hope your virtues Will bring him to his wonted way again . . iii 1 41
Bring me to the test, And I the matter will re-word . . . iii 4 142
Speak fair, and bring the body Into the chapel . . . . iv 1 36
The king is a thing— A thing, my lord!—Of nothing: bring me to him iv 2 32
Bring him before us.—Ho, Guildenstern! bring in my lord . . iv 3 15
These good fellows will bring thee where I am . . . . iv 6 27
Bring you in fine together And wager on your heads . . . iv 7 134
The unruly waywardness that infirm and choleric years bring with them *Lear* i 1 302
I will fitly bring you to hear my lord speak . . . . . i 2 184
Bring oil to fire, snow to their colder moods . . . . ii 2 83
Come, bring away the stocks! . . . . ii 2 146
I entreat you To bring but five and twenty: to no more Will I give place ii 4 251
My good boy. Come, bring us to this hovel . . . . . iii 2 78
To come seek you out, And bring you where both fire and food is ready iii 4 158
Pinion him like a thief, bring him before us . . . . . iii 7 23
Bring some covering for this naked soul . . . . . iv 1 46
I'll bring him the best 'parel that I have . . . . . iv 1 51
Bring me but to the very brim of it . . . . . . iv 1 78
I'll bring you to our master Lear, And leave you to attend him . . iv 3 52
Search every acre in the high-grown field, And bring him to our eye . iv 4 8
He's full of alteration And self-reproving: bring his constant pleasure v 1 4
If ever I return to you again, I'll bring you comfort . . . v 2 4
He that parts us shall bring a brand from heaven, And fire us hence like foxes . . . . v 3 22
Time will bring it out: 'Tis past, and so am I . . . . . v 3 163
Upon some present business of the state To bring me to him . *Othello* i 2 91

Bring. Bring him away: Mine's not an idle cause . . *Othello* i 2 94
Leave some officer behind, And he shall our commission bring to you . i 3 282
Let thy wife attend on her; And bring them after in the best advantage i 3 298
Hell and night Must bring this monstrous birth to the world's light . i 3 410
Give renew'd fire to our extincted spirits, And bring all Cyprus comfort! ii 1 82
Bring thou the master to the citadel; He is a good one . . . ii 1 211
I will do this, if I can bring it to any opportunity . . . ii 1 289
And bring him jump when he may Cassio find Soliciting his wife . ii 3 392
And needs no other suitor but his likings To take the safest occasion by the front To bring you in again . . . . iii 1 53
To have so much to do To bring him in! Trust me, I could do much,—Prithee, no more . . . . iii 3 74
It were a tedious difficulty, I think, To bring them to that prospect . iii 3 398
I pray you, bring me on the way a little, And say if I shall see you soon at night.—'Tis but a little way that I can bring you; For I attend here . . . . iii 4 197
Where is that viper? bring the villain forth . . . . v 2 285
Bring him away.—Soft you; a word or two before you go . . v 2 337
Seek him, and bring him hither . . . *Ant. and Cleo.* i 2 89
We use To say the dead are well: bring it to that, The gold I give thee will I melt and pour Down thy ill-uttering throat . . . ii 5 33
Gracious madam, I that do bring the news made not the match . ii 5 67
Though it be honest, it is never good To bring bad news . . . ii 5 86
The April's in her eyes: it is love's spring, And these the showers to bring it on . . . . iii 2 44
Thou shalt bring him to me Where I will write . . . . iii 3 49
'Twill be naught: But let it be. Bring me to Antony . . . iii 5 24
Bring him through the bands . . . . iii 12 25
Tug him away: being whipp'd, Bring him again . . . . iii 13 103
You that will fight, Follow me close; I'll bring you to't . . iv 4 34
And bring me how he takes my death . . . . . . iv 13 10
With your speediest bring us what she says, And how you find of her . v 1 67
Bring our crown and all . . . . v 2 232
Will not be denied your highness' presence: He brings you figs . . v 2 235
What poor an instrument May do a noble deed! he brings me liberty . v 2 237
He would not suffer me To bring him to the haven . . *Cymbeline* i 1 171
I will bring from thence that honour of hers which you imagine so reserved . . . . i 4 142
If I bring you no sufficient testimony . . . . . . i 4 160
Bring this apparel to my chamber; that is the second thing . . iii 5 156
Not Absolute madness could so far have raved To bring him here alone iv 2 136
I'll stay Till hasty Polydore return, and bring him To dinner presently iv 2 165
Still it's strange What Cloten's being here to us portends, Or what his death will bring us . . . . iv 2 183
Here he comes, And brings the dire occasion in his arms . . . iv 2 196
Bring thee all this; Yea, and furr'd moss besides . . . . iv 2 227
He brags his service As if he were of note: bring him to the king . v 3 94
Knock off his manacles; bring your prisoner to the king . . . v 4 199
And that to hear an old man sing May to your wishes pleasure bring *Pericles* i Gower 14
Are arms to princes, and bring joys to subjects . . . . . i 2 74
One sorrow never comes but brings an heir, That may succeed . . i 4 63
They bring us peace, And come to us as favourers, not as foes . . i 4 72
But bring they what they will and what they can, What need we fear? . i 4 76
Here have you seen a mighty king His child, I wis, to incest bring ii Gower 2
Ha, come and bring away the nets! . . . . . . ii 1 13
I'll bring thee to the court myself . . . . . . ii 1 170
I'll tame you; I'll bring you in subjection . . . . . ii 5 75
Bid Nestor bring me spices, ink and paper, My casket and my jewels; and bid Nicander Bring me the satin coffer . . . . . iii 1 66
Go thy ways, good mariner: I'll bring the body presently . . iii 1 82
We'll bring your grace e'en to the edge o' the shore . . . iii 3 35
Come, bring me to some private place . . . . . iv 6 97

Bring about. How many hours bring about the day . 3 *Hen. VI.* ii 5 27

Bring along these rascal knaves with thee . . *T. of Shrew* iv 1 134

Brings back. His majesty commended him to you by young Osric, who brings back to him, that you attend him in the hall . . *Hamlet* v 2 204

Bring down. He lends out money gratis and brings down The rate of usance . . . . *Mer. of Venice* i 3 45
Bring down the devil; for he must not die So sweet a death as hanging *T. Andron.* v 1 145
Bring down rose-cheeked youth To the tub-fast and the diet *T. of Athens* iv 3 86

Bring forth. And, sowing the kernels of it in the sea, bring forth more islands . . . . *Tempest* ii 1 93
Nature should bring forth, Of it own kind, all foison, all abundance . ii 1 162
I will requite you with as good a thing; At least bring forth a wonder . v 1 170
Come, bring forth this counterfeit module . . . *All's Well* iv 3 113
The heavens have thought well on thee, Lafeu, To bring forth this discovery . . . . v 3 151
Bring forth, And in Apollo's name, his oracle . . . *W. Tale* iii 2 118
Bring forth these men. . . . . . . *Richard II.* iii 1 1
I see some sparks of better hope, which elder years May happily bring forth . . . . v 3 22
On this unworthy scaffold to bring forth So great an object . *Hen. V.* Prol. 10
Bring forth the body of old Salisbury . . . 1 *Hen. VI.* ii 2 4
Bring forth that sorceress condemn'd to burn . . . . v 4 1
Therefore bring forth the soldiers of our prize . . 2 *Hen. VI.* iv 1 8
My ashes, as the phœnix, may bring forth A bird that will revenge upon you all . . . . 3 *Hen. VI.* i 4 35
Bring forth that fatal screech-owl to our house . . . . ii 6 56
Bring forth the gallant, let us hear him speak . . . . v 5 12
I am not barren to bring forth complaints . . . *Richard III.* ii 2 67
Come, bring forth the prisoners. . . . . . . iii 3 1
Bring forth the parties of suspicion . . . *Rom. and Jul.* v 3 222
It is the bright day that brings forth the adder . . *J. Cæsar* ii 1 14
Bring forth men-children only . . . . . *Macbeth* i 7 72
We bring forth weeds, When our quick minds lie still . *Ant. and Cleo.* i 2 113
Your old smock brings forth a new petticoat . . . . . i 2 175
'But yet' is as a gaoler to bring forth Some monstrous malefactor . ii 5 52

Bring home. A victory is twice itself when the achiever brings home full numbers . . . . *Much Ado* i 1 9
Since I nor wax nor honey can bring home . . . *All's Well* i 2 65
Which pillage they with merry march bring home . . . *Hen. V.* i 2 195
I'll bring home some to-night . . . . . . *Pericles* iv 2 156

Bring in here before your good honour two notorious benefactors *Meas. for Meas.* ii 1 49
Four happy days bring in Another moon . . . *M. N. Dream* i 1 2
To bring in—God shield us!—a lion among ladies, is a most dreadful thing . . . . iii 1 31
You can never bring in a wall. What say you, Bottom? . . . iii 1 67

Bring in. If I bring in your Rosalind, You will bestow her on Orlando? *As Y. Like It* v 4 6
Bring in the admiration . . . . . . *All's Well* ii 1 91
Thus your own proper wisdom Brings in the champion Honour on my part, Against your vain assault . . . . iv 2 50
And thus the whirligig of time brings in his revenges . *T. Night* v 1 385
Got with swearing 'Lay by' and spent with crying 'Bring in' 1 *Hen. IV.* i 2 41
Such a mighty sum As never did the clergy at one time Bring in *Hen. V.* i 2 135
But thou, 'gainst all proportion, didst bring in Wonder to wait on treason ii 2 109
And every tongue brings in a several tale . . . *Richard III.* v 3 194
And bring in The crows to peck the eagles . . *Coriolanus* iii 1 138
I will bring in the empress and her sons, The emperor himself *T. Andron.* v 2 116
And bring in cloudy night immediately . . . . *Rom. and Jul.* iii 2 4
Come, bring in all together.—All covered dishes! . *T. of Athens* iii 6 53
Then, dear countryman, Bring in thy ranks, but leave without thy rage v 4 39
I'll see their trial first. Bring in the evidence . . *Lear* iii 6 37
Bring in the banquet quickly . . . . *Ant. and Cleo.* i 2 11
Fortune brings in some boats that are not steer'd . . *Cymbeline* iv 3 46
Bring in our daughter, clothed like a bride . . . *Pericles* i 1 6
Bring on. With the word the time will bring on summer . *All's Well* iv 4 31
Bring out. If I make not this cheat bring out another . *W. Tale* iv 3 129
Let it no more bring out ingrateful man! . . . *T. of Athens* iv 3 188
Bring to light. These are petty faults to faults unknown, Which time will bring to light . . . . . . 2 *Hen VI.* iii 1 65
Bring to pass. A thing not in his power to bring to pass *Mer. of Venice* i 3 93
Which to bring to pass, As I before imparted . . . *T. of Shrew* iii 2 131
Bring up. My heart's dear Harry Threw many a northward look to see his father Bring up his powers . . . . . 2 *Hen. IV.* ii 3 14
If they set down before's, for the remove Bring up your army *Coriolanus* i 2 29
There's my gauntlet; I'll prove it on a giant. Bring up the brown bills *Lear* iv 6 91
Brings word the prince his master will be here to-night *Mer. of Venice* i 2 138
I bring word My mistress will before the break of day Be here . v 1 28
Bring word if Hector will to-morrow Be answer'd in his challenge *Troi. and Cres.* iii 3 34
Bring (me, thee, us, you) **word.** Bring me word how thou findest him *T. Night* iv 2 71
Within this hour bring me word 'tis done, And by good testimony *W. Tale* ii 3 136
So tell your cousin, and bring me word What he will do . . 1 *Hen. IV.* v 1 109
And quickly bring us word of England's fall . . . *Hen. V.* iii 5 68
If thou spy'st any, run and bring me word . . 1 *Hen. VI.* i 4 19
'Tis south the city mills—bring me word thither How the world goes *Coriolanus* i 10 31
Look in the calendar, and bring me word . . . *J. Cæsar* ii 1 42
Bring me word, boy, if thy lord look well, For he went sickly forth . ii 4 13
Come to me again, And bring me word what he doth say to thee . ii 4 46
Bring us word unto Octavius' tent How every thing is chanced . v 4 31
'Tis two or three, my lord, that bring you word Macduff is fled to England *Macbeth* iv 1 141
The colour of her hair: bring me word quickly . . *Ant. and Cleo.* ii 5 114
Bid your Alexas Bring me word how tall she is . . . ii 5 118
I'll bring thee word Straight, how 'tis like to go . . . iv 12 2
When thou shalt bring me word she loves my son . *Cymbeline* i 5 49
Again; and bring me word how 'tis with her . . . iv 3 1
Bringer. If it would but apprehend some joy, It comprehends some bringer of that joy . . . . . . *M. N. Dream* v 1 20
The first bringer of unwelcome news Hath but a losing office . 2 *Hen. IV.* i 1 100
I tell you true: best you safed the bringer Out of the host *Ant. and Cleo.* iv 6 26
Bringest. Thou bringest me out of tune . . . *As Y. Like It* iii 2 262
Thou bring'st me happiness and peace . . . 2 *Hen. IV.* iv 5 228
Thou canst not die by traitors' hands, Unless thou bring'st them with thee.—So I hope . . . . . . *J. Cæsar* v 1 57
Thou bring'st good news; I am called to be made free . *Cymbeline* v 4 201
Speak out thy sorrows which thou bring'st in haste . *Pericles* i 4 58
Bringeth. From whom he bringeth sensible regreets . *Mer. of Venice* ii 9 89
Whereas the contrary bringeth bliss . . . . 1 *Hen. VI.* v 5 64
Bringing. To torment me For bringing wood in slowly . *Tempest* ii 2 16
I should have chid you for not bringing it . . *Com. of Errors* iv 1 50
Bringing rebellion broached on his sword . . . *Hen. V.* v Prol. 32
In bringing them to civil discipline . . . . 2 *Hen. VI.* i 1 195
All's now done, but the ceremony Of bringing back the prisoner *Hen. VIII.* ii 1 5
Our drums Are bringing forth our youth . . . *Coriolanus* i 4 16
O, pardon me for bringing these ill news, Since you did leave it for my office, sir . . . . *Rom. and Jul.* v 1 22
And the bringing home Of bell and burial . . . *Hamlet* v 1 256
He which finds him shall deserve our thanks, Bringing the murderous coward to the stake . . . . *Lear* ii 1 64
Bringings-forth. Let him be but testimonied in his own bringings-forth, and he shall appear to the envious a scholar . *Meas. for Meas.* iii 2 153
Bringing up. Witness good bringing up . . . *T. G. of Ver.* iv 4 74
Liberal To mine own children in good bringing up . *T. of Shrew* i 1 99
A plague on my bringing up! . . . . . 1 *Hen. IV.* ii 4 547
Make me blessed in your care In bringing up my child . *Pericles* iii 3 32
'Tis not our bringing up of poor bastards,—as, I think, I have brought up some eleven— Ay, to eleven . . . . . iv 2 14
Brinish. Nero will be tainted with remorse, To hear and see her plaints, her brinish tears . . . . 3 *Hen. VI.* iii 1 41
Wave by wave, Expecting ever when some envious surge Will in his brinish bowels swallow him . . . . *T. Andron.* iii 1 97
Brink. I have no strength to pluck thee to the brink . . ii 3 241
You witch me in it; Surprise me to the very brink of tears *T. of Athens* v 1 159
Brisk. These most brisk and giddy-paced times . . *T. Night* ii 4 6
He made me mad To see him shine so brisk and smell so sweet 1 *Hen. IV.* i 3 54
A cup of wine that's brisk and fine . . . 2 *Hen. IV.* v 3 48
Cheerly, boys; be brisk awhile, and the longer liver take all *Rom. and Jul.* i 5 16
Brisky. Most brisky juvenal and eke most lovely Jew . *M. N. Dream* iii 1 97
Bristle. I will not open my lips so wide as a bristle may enter *T. Night* i 5 3
Now for the bare-pick'd bone of majesty Doth dogged war bristle his angry crest And snarleth . . . . . . *K. John* iv 3 149
And bristle up The crest of youth against your dignity . 1 *Hen. IV.* i 1 98
Rouse thy vaunting veins: Boy, bristle thy courage up . . *Hen. V.* ii 3 5
Bristled. Pard, or boar with bristled hair . . . *M. N. Dream* ii 2 31
When with his Amazonian chin he drove The bristled lips before him *Coriolanus* ii 2 96
Bristol. Ay, all of them at Bristol lost their heads . . *Richard II.* iii 2 142
Who bears hard His brother's death at Bristol . . 1 *Hen. IV.* i 3 271
Within fourteen days At Bristol I expect my soldiers . 2 *Hen. VI.* iii 1 328
Bristol castle. I will for refuge straight to Bristol castle *Richard II.* ii 2 135
We must win your grace to go with us To Bristol castle . . . ii 3 164

Britain. When Queen Guinover of Britain was a little wench . *L. L. Lost* iv 1 126
Is this the government of Britain's isle, And this the royalty of Albion's king? . . . . 2 *Hen. VI.* i 3 47
And, to-morrow, they Made Britain India . . . *Hen. VIII.* i 1 21
Believe it, sir, I have seen him in Britain . . . *Cymbeline* i 4 1
Something too fair and too good for any lady in Britain . . . i 4 77
My lord, I fear, Has forgot Britain . . . . i 6 113
In our not-fearing Britain . . . . ii 4 19
Was Caius Lucius in the Britain court When you were there? . ii 4 37
I'll make a journey twice as far, to enjoy A second night of such sweet shortness which Was mine in Britain . . . . . . ii 4 45
When Julius Cæsar . . . was in this Britain And conquer'd it . iii 1 4
Britain is A world by itself; and we will nothing pay For wearing our own noses . . . . iii 1 12
The first of Britain which did put His brows within a golden crown and call'd Himself a king . . . . iii 1 60
This Polydore, The heir of Cymbeline and Britain . . . . iii 3 87
If not at court, Then not in Britain must you bide . . . iii 4 138
Hath Britain all the sun that shines? Day, night, Are they not but in Britain? I' the world's volume Our Britain seems as of it, but not in't; In a great pool a swan's nest: prithee, think There's livers out of Britain . . . . iii 4 139
From whence he moves His war for Britain . . . . . iii 5 26
'Tis enough That, Britain, I have kill'd thy mistress . . . v 1 20
If that thy gentry, Britain, go before This lout as he exceeds our lords, the odds Is that we scarce are men and you are gods . . . v 2 8
Our Britain's harts die flying, not our men . . . . v 3 24
In Britain where was he That could stand up his parallel? . . v 4 53
Then shall . . . Britain be fortunate and flourish in peace and plenty v 4 144; v 5 441
Which I will add To you, the liver, heart and brain of Britain . v 5 14
You look like Romans, And not o' the court of Britain . . . v 5 25
Away to Britain Post I in this design . . . . . . v 5 191
Mine Italian brain 'Gan in your duller Britain operate Most vilely . v 5 197
Whose issue Promises Britain peace and plenty . . . . v 5 458
British. Fie, foh, and fum, I smell the blood of a British man . *Lear* iii 4 189
The British powers are marching hitherward . . . . iv 4 21
Seek him out Upon the British party . . . . . . iv 6 256
She being down, I have the placing of the British crown . *Cymbeline* iii 5 65
Let A Roman and a British ensign wave Friendly together . . v 5 480
Briton. Here comes the Briton: let him be so entertained amongst you as suits, with gentlemen . . . . i 4 28
So merry and so gamesome: he is call'd The Briton reveller . . . i 6 61
Whiles the jolly Briton—Your lord, I mean—laughs from's free lungs . i 6 67
Made Lud's town with rejoicing fires bright And Britons strut with courage . . . . iii 1 33
A precedent Which not to read would show the Britons cold . . iii 1 76
Your valiant Britons have their wishes in it . . . . . iii 5 20
The legions now in Gallia are Full weak to undertake our wars against The fall'n-off Britons . . . . iii 7 6
This was my master, A very valiant Briton and a good . . . iv 2 369
This way, the Romans Must or for Britons slay us . . . . iv 4 5
I'll disrobe me Of these Italian weeds and suit myself As does a Briton peasant . . . . v 1 24
And but the backs of Britons seen, all flying Through a strait lane . v 3 6
Two boys, an old man twice a boy, a lane, Preserved the Britons . . v 3 58
For being now a favourer to the Briton, No more a Briton, I have resumed again The part I came in . . . . v 3 74
Great the slaughter is Here made by the Roman; great the answer be Britons must take . . . . v 3 80
Thou comest not, Caius, now for tribute; that The Britons have razed out v 5 70
My boy, a Briton born, Let him be ransom'd . . . . . v 5 84
He hath done no Briton harm, Though he have served a Roman . v 5 90
Brittany. From Port le Blanc, a bay In Brittany . *Richard II.* ii 1 278
And then to Brittany I'll cross the sea . . . 3 *Hen. VI.* ii 6 97
We'll send him hence to Brittany, Till storms be past of civil enmity . iv 6 97
It shall be so; he shall to Brittany . . . . . . iv 6 101
Brittle. A brittle glory shineth in this face: As brittle as the glory is the face . . . . *Richard II.* iv 1 287
I better brook the loss of brittle life Than those proud titles . 1 *Hen. IV.* v 4 78
My kingdom stands on brittle glass . . . . *Richard III.* iv 2 62
Broach. Or else this blow should broach thy dearest blood 1 *Hen. VI.* iii 4 40
Whether ever I Did broach this business to your highness *Hen. VIII.* ii 4 149
I'll broach the tadpole on my rapier's point . . *T. Andron.* iv 2 85
If I would broach the vessels of my love, And try the argument of hearts by borrowing . . . . *T. of Athens* ii 2 186
Broached. He bravely broach'd his boiling bloody breast *M. N. Dream* v 1 148
Since we are stepp'd thus far in, I will continue that I broach'd in jest *T. of Shrew* i 2 84
And a portent Of broached mischief to the unborn times . 1 *Hen. IV.* v 1 21
Bringing rebellion broached on his sword . . . *Hen. V.* v Prol. 32
Brave thee! ay, by the best blood that ever was broached 2 *Hen. VI.* iv 10 40
For what hath broach'd this tumult but thy pride? . 3 *Hen. VI.* ii 2 159
Broach'd with the steely point of Clifford's lance . . . ii 3 16
That for her love such quarrels may be broach'd Without controlment *T. Andron.* ii 1 67
The business she hath broached in the state Cannot endure my absence. —And the business you have broached here cannot be without you *Ant. and Cleo.* i 2 178
Broad. They'll be for the flowery way that leads to the broad gate and the great fire . . . . *All's Well* iv 5 57
I'll canvass thee in thy broad cardinal's hat . . 1 *Hen. VI.* i 3 36
Distinction, with a broad and powerful fan, Puffing at all *Troi. and Cres.* i 3 27
In full as proud a place As broad Achilles . . . . . i 3 190
I have been broad awake two hours and more . . *T. Andron.* ii 2 17
O, here's a wit of cheveril, that stretches from an inch narrow to an ell broad!—I stretch it out for that word 'broad;' which added to the goose, proves thee far and wide a broad goose . *Rom. and Jul.* ii 4 88
Be patient, for the world is broad and wide . . . . iii 3 16
Honours deep and broad wherewith Your majesty loads our house *Macb.* i 6 17
Founded as the rock, As broad and general as the casing air . . iii 4 23
From broad words and 'cause he fail'd His presence at the tyrant's feast iii 6 21
With all his crimes broad blown, as flush as May . . . *Hamlet* iii 3 81
Tell him his pranks have been too broad to bear with . . . iii 4 2
It is as broad as it hath breadth: it is just so high as it is *Ant. and Cleo.* ii 7 48
Broader. What need the bridge much broader than the flood? *Much Ado* i 1 318
Who can speak broader than he that has no house to put his head in? *T. of Athens* iii 4 64
Broad-fronted Cæsar, When thou wast here above the ground, I was A morsel for a monarch . . . . *Ant. and Cleo.* i 5 29

Broadside. Fear we broadsides? no, let the fiend give fire . 2 *Hen. IV.* ii 4 196
Broad-spreading. The weeds which his broad-spreading leaves did shelter *Richard II.* iii 4 50
Glory is like a circle in the water, Which never ceaseth to enlarge itself Till by broad spreading it disperse to nought . 1 *Hen. VI.* i 2 135
Brocas. I have from Oxford sent to London The heads of Brocas and Sir Bennet Seely *Richard II.* v 6 14
Brock. Marry, hang thee, brock! *T. Night* ii 5 114
Brogue. I thought he slept, and put My clouted brogues from off my feet, whose rudeness Answer'd my steps too loud *Cymbeline* iv 2 214
Broil. And breathe short-winded accents of new broils . 1 *Hen. IV.* i 1 3
The tidings of this broil Brake off our business for the Holy Land . i 1 47
Prosper this realm, keep it from civil broils! 1 *Hen. VI.* i 1 53
Leave this peevish broil And set this unaccustom'd fight aside . iii 1 92
Who should study to prefer a peace, If holy churchmen take delight in broils? iii 1 111
More furious raging broils Than yet can be imagined or supposed . iv 1 185
Moved with remorse of these outrageous broils . v 4 97
Already in this civil broil I see them lording it in London streets 2 *Hen. VI.* iv 8 46
Now here a period of tumultuous broils . 3 *Hen. VI.* v 5 1
Domestic broils Clean over-blown *Richard III.* ii 4 60
Our play Leaps o'er the vaunt and firstlings of those broils *Troi. and Cres.* Prol. 27
That will physic the great Myrmidon Who broils in loud applause . i 3 379
Stop, Or all will fall in broil *Coriolanus* iii 1 33
Being bred in broils Hast not the soft way . iii 2 81
Say to the king the knowledge of the broil As thou didst leave it *Macbeth* i 2 6
These domestic and particular broils Are not the question here . *Lear* v 1 30
Little of this great world can I speak, More than pertains to feats of broil and battle . *Othello* i 3 87
Broiled. How say you to a fat tripe finely broil'd? . *T. of Shrew* iv 3 20
And notched him like a carbonado.—An he had been cannibally given, he might have broiled and eaten him too *Coriolanus* iv 5 201
Broiling. God save you, sir! where have you been broiling? *Hen. VIII.* iv 1 56
Broke. O my father, I have broke your hest to say so! *Tempest* iii 1 37
Her waspish-headed son has broke his arrows, Swears he will shoot no more . iv 1 99
I broke your head: what matter have you against me? . *Mer. Wives* i 1 125
Women are frail too.—Ay, as the glasses where they view themselves; Which are as easy broke as they make forms . *Meas. for Meas.* ii 4 126
You have no stomach having broke your fast . *Com. of Errors* i 2 50
He broke from those that had the guard of him . v 1 149
I have broke with her father, and his good will obtained . *Much Ado* ii 1 310
Give him another staff: this last was broke cross . v 1 139
Fell over the threshold, and broke my shin . *L. L. Lost* iii 1 118
Vows for thee broke deserve not punishment . iv 3 63
If by me broke, what fool is not so wise To lose an oath to win a paradise? iv 3 72
Your oath once broke, you force not to forswear . v 2 440
By all the vows that ever men have broke, In number more than ever women spoke *M. N. Dream* i 1 175
In a moment threw him and broke three of his ribs . *As Y. Like It* i 2 135
If thou hast not broke from company Abruptly, as my passion now makes me, Thou hast not loved . ii 4 40
When I was in love I broke my sword upon a stone . ii 4 47
She hath broke the lute to me . *T. of Shrew* ii 1 149
So I had broke thy pate, And ask'd thee mercy for't . *All's Well* ii 1 68
Brokes with all that can in such a suit Corrupt the tender honour of a maid . iii 5 74
He has broke my head across . *T. Night* v 1 178
You broke my head for nothing . v 1 188
Sir Robert might have eat his part in me Upon Good-Friday and ne'er broke his fast . *K. John* i 1 235
I faintly broke with thee of Arthur's death . iv 2 227
Worcester Hath broke his staff, resign'd his stewardship *Richard II.* ii 2 59
Made a divorce betwixt his queen and him, Broke the possession of a royal bed . iii 1 13
God pardon all oaths that are broke to me! . iv 1 214
How sour sweet music is, When time is broke and no proportion kept! v 5 43
Here have I the daintiness of ear To check time broke in a disorder'd string . v 5 46
Broke oath on oath, committed wrong on wrong . 1 *Hen. IV.* iv 3 101
The prince broke thy head for liking his father to a singing-man 2 *Hen. IV.* ii 1 97
You broke your word, When you were more endear'd to it than now ii 3 10
The foolish over-careful fathers Have broke their sleep with thoughts . iv 5 69
What was the impediment that broke this off? . *Hen. V.* v 2 65
For a' never broke any man's head but his own . iii 2 42
Do not run away.—Why, all our ranks are broke . iv 5 6
Then broke I from the officers that led me . 1 *Hen. VI.* i 4 44
The regent hath with Talbot broke his word . iv 6 2
Unequal odds, And therefore may be broke without offence . v 5 35
Broke be my sword, my arms torn and defaced! 2 *Hen. VI.* iv 1 42
A thousand men have broke their fasts to-day, That ne'er shall dine unless thou yield the crown . 3 *Hen. VI.* ii 2 127
Our ranks are broke, and ruin follows us . ii 3 10
Tell me, then, have you not broke your oaths? . iii 1 79
What though the mast be now blown overboard, The cable broke? . v 4 4
How canst thou urge God's dreadful law to us, When thou hast broke it in so dear degree? . *Richard III.* i 4 215
Many Have broke their backs with laying manors on 'em . *Hen. VIII.* i 1 84
A thing inspired; and, not consulting, broke Into a general prophecy . i 1 91
My high-blown pride At length broke under me . iii 2 362
Here is good broken music.—You have broke it, cousin . *Troi. and Cres.* iii 1 53
I would they had broke 's neck! . v 2 79
Sigh'd forth proverbs, That hunger broke stone walls . *Coriolanus* i 1 210
Whose passions and whose plots have broke their sleep . iv 4 19
That body, where against My grained ash an hundred times hath broke iv 5 114
And almost broke my heart with extreme laughter . *T. Andron.* v 1 113
Even the day before, she broke her brow . *Rom. and Jul.* i 3 38
The day is broke; be wary, look about . iii 5 40
Such a house broke! So noble a master fall'n! All gone! *T. of Athens* iv 2 5
How has the ass broke the wall, that thou art out of the city? . iv 3 354
Shame that they wanted cunning, in excess Hath broke their hearts . v 4 29
Broke their stalls, flung out, Contending 'gainst obedience . *Macbeth* ii 4 16
You have displaced the mirth, broke the good meeting, With most admired disorder . iii 4 109
At no time broke my faith, would not betray The devil to his fellow . iv 3 128
The doors are broke.—Where is this king? . *Hamlet* iv 5 111
There, on the pendent boughs her coronet weeds Clambering to hang, an envious sliver broke . iv 7 174
Broke. Swore as many oaths as I spake words, and broke them in the sweet face of heaven . *Lear* iii 4 91
The day had broke Before we parted . *Othello* iii 1 34
I would have broke mine eye-strings; crack'd them, but To look upon him . *Cymbeline* i 3 17
What got he by that? You have broke his pate with your bowl . ii 1 8
If his wit had been like him that broke it, it would have run all out . ii 1 10
Broke bread. An honest maid as ever broke bread . *Mer. Wives* i 4 161
An honest soul, i' faith, sir; by my troth he is, as ever broke bread *M. Ado* iii 5 42
Broke down. Our windows are broke down in every street 1 *Hen. VI.* iii 1 84
Broke loose. My master and his man are both broke loose *Com. of Errors* v 1 169
Contention, like a horse Full of high feeding, madly hath broke loose 2 *Hen. IV.* i 1 10
Broke off. There was some speech of marriage Betwixt myself and her; which was broke off . *Meas. for Meas.* v 1 218
In conclusion dumbly have broke off, Not paying me a welcome *M. N. Dr.* v 1 98
Broke ope. Most sacrilegious murder hath broke ope The Lord's anointed temple! . *Macbeth* ii 3 72
Broke open. You have beaten my men, killed my deer, and broke open my lodge . *Mer. Wives* i 1 115
Broke out. I left him almost speechless; and broke out To acquaint you with this evil . *K. John* v 6 24
Broke through. Hath my sword therefore broke through London gates, that you should leave me? . 2 *Hen. VI.* iv 8 24
Broke up. Like a school broke up, Each hurries toward his home 2 *Hen. IV.* iv 2 104
Broken. What, are they broken?—No, they are both as whole as a fish *T. G. of Ver.* ii 5 19
Unheedful vows may heedfully be broken . ii 6 11
I may chance have some odd quirks and remnants of wit broken on me *Much Ado* ii 3 245
Here's a costard broken in a shin . *L. L. Lost* iii 1 71
He that escapes me without some broken limb shall acquit him well *As Y. Like It* i 1 134
Is there any else longs to see this broken music in his sides? . i 2 150
Wherefore do you look Upon that poor and broken bankrupt there? ii 1 57
To glean the broken ears after the man That the main harvest reaps . iii 5 102
That you might excuse His broken promise . iv 3 155
An old rusty sword ta'en out of the town-armoury, with a broken hilt, and chapeless; with two broken points . *T. of Shrew* iii 2 48
I'ld give bay Curtal and his furniture, My mouth no more were broken than these boys', And writ as little beard . *All's Well* ii 3 66
I am sorry, Most sorry, you have broken from his liking . *W. Tale* v 1 212
I make a broken delivery of the business . v 2 10
Such a deal of wonder is broken out within this hour . v 2 26
Upon our sides it never shall be broken . *K. John* v 2 8
The king's grown bankrupt, like a broken man *Richard II.* ii 1 257
Imp out our drooping country's broken wing . ii 1 292
He hath forsook the court, Broken his staff of office . ii 3 27
Their points being broken,— Down fell their hose . 1 *Hen. IV.* ii 4 238
Wouldst thou have thy head broken?—No.—Then be still . iii 1 242
Is not your voice broken? your wind short? . 2 *Hen. IV.* i 2 206
Like a broken limb united, Grow stronger for the breaking . iv 1 222
Beguiling virgins with the broken seals of perjury . *Hen. V.* iv 1 172
Come, your answer in broken music; for thy voice is music and thy English broken . v 2 263
Break thy mind to me in broken English; wilt thou have me? . v 2 265
False king! why hast thou broken faith with me, Knowing how hardly I can brook abuse? . 2 *Hen. VI.* v 1 91
Hither we have broken in by force . 3 *Hen. VI.* i 1 29
For a kingdom any oath may be broken . i 2 16
Trust not him that hath once broken faith . iv 4 30
Methoughts that I had broken from the Tower . *Richard III.* i 4 9
The broken rancour of your high-swoln hearts . ii 2 117
The unity the king thy brother made Had not been broken . iv 4 380
Thy broken faith hath made a prey for worms . iv 4 386
Amaze the welkin with your broken staves! . v 3 341
You have now a broken banquet; but we'll mend it . *Hen. VIII.* i 4 61
An old man, broken with the storms of state . iv 2 21
With which they moved Have broken with the king . iv 1 47
Here is good broken music . *Troi. and Cres.* iii 1 52
Scants us with a single famish'd kiss, Distasted with the salt of broken tears . iv 4 50
Admits no orifex for a point as subtle As Ariachne's broken woof to enter v 2 152
Your plaintain-leaf is excellent for that.—For what, I pray thee?—For your broken shin . *Rom. and Jul.* i 2 53
All broken implements of a ruin'd house . *T. of Athens* iv 2 16
Tears in his eyes, distraction in 's aspect, A broken voice . *Hamlet* ii 2 582
A knave; a rascal; an eater of broken meats . *Lear* ii 2 15
Oppressed nature sleeps: This rest might yet have balm'd thy broken sinews . iii 6 105
Men do their broken weapons rather use Than their bare hands . *Othello* i 3 174
This broken joint between you and her husband entreat her to splinter ii 3 328
You have broken The article of your oath . *Ant. and Cleo.* ii 2 81
The king himself Of his wings destitute, the army broken . *Cymbeline* v 3 5
Who of their broken debtors take a third, A sixth, a tenth . v 4 19
Has done no more than other knights have done; Has broken a staff or so . *Pericles* ii 3 35
Brokenly. Confess it brokenly with your English tongue . *Hen. V.* v 2 106
Broker. Now, by my modesty, a goodly broker! . *T. G. of Ver.* i 2 41
That sly devil, That broker, that still breaks the pate of faith *K. John* ii 1 568
This bawd, this broker, this all-changing word . ii 1 582
They say 'A crafty knave does need no broker' . 2 *Hen. VI.* i 2 100
You shall give me leave To play the broker in mine own behalf 3 *Hen. VI.* iv 1 63
Do not believe his vows; for they are brokers . *Hamlet* i 3 127
Broker-between. Let all constant men be Troiluses, all false women Cressids, and all brokers-between Pandars! . *Troi. and Cres.* iii 2 211
Broker-lackey. Hence, broker-lackey! ignomy and shame Pursue thy life, and live aye with thy name! . v 10 33
Broking. Redeem from broking pawn the blemish'd crown *Richard II.* ii 1 293
Brooch. Saint George's half-cheek in a brooch.—Ay, and in a brooch of lead . *L. L. Lost* v 2 620
Richly suited, but unsuitable: just like the brooch and the tooth-pick, which wear not now . *All s Well* i 1 171
Brooch, table-book, ballad, knife, tape, glove . *W. Tale* iv 4 610
Love to Richard Is a strange brooch in this all-hating world *Richard II.* v 5 66
Your brooches, pearls, and ouches . 2 *Hen. IV.* ii 4 53
He is the brooch indeed And gem of all the nation . *Hamlet* iv 7 94
Brooched. Not the imperious show Of the full-fortuned Cæsar ever shall Be brooch'd with me . *Ant. and Cleo.* iv 15 25

Brood. She will become thy bed, I warrant. And bring thee forth brave brood . . . . *Tempest* iii 2 113
Such things become the hatch and brood of time . . 2 *Hen. IV.* iii 1 86
Why, what a brood of traitors have we here! . 2 *Hen. VI.* v 1 141
Doves will peck in safeguard of their brood . . 3 *Hen. VI.* ii 2 18
She, poor hen, fond of no second brood, Has cluck'd thee to the wars and safely home . . . . . . *Coriolanus* v 3 162
Not Enceladus, With all his threatening band of Typhon's brood *T. Andron.* iv 2 94
There's something in his soul, O'er which his melancholy sits on brood *Hamlet* iii 1 173
Brooded. In despite of brooded watchful day . . . . *K. John* iii 3 52
Brooding. And birds sit brooding in the snow . . *L. L. Lost* v 2 933
Brook. You nymphs, call'd Naiads, of the windring brooks *Tempest* iv 1 128
Ye elves of hills, brooks, standing lakes and groves . . . v 1 33
A thousand more mischances than this one Have learn'd me how to brook this patiently . . . . *T. G. of Ver.* v 3 4
Unfrequented woods, I better brook than flourishing peopled towns . v 4 3
Tell him my name is Brook ; only for a jest . *Mer. Wives* ii 1 224
There's one Master Brook below would fain speak with you . ii 2 150
Brook is his name?—Ay, sir.—Call him in . . . . ii 2 154
Such Brooks are welcome to me, that o'erflow such liquor . ii 2 157
I am a gentleman that have spent much ; my name is Brook . ii 2 167
Good Master Brook, I desire more acquaintance of you . . ii 2 168
Speak, good Master Brook : I shall be glad to be your servant . ii 2 184
Master Brook, I will first make bold with your money . . ii 2 262
Want no Mistress Ford, Master Brook ; you shall want none . . ii 2 270
Master Brook, thou shalt know I will predominate over the peasant . ii 2 293
Thou, Master Brook, shalt know him for knave and cuckold . . ii 2 297
I marvel I hear not of Master Brook . . . . . . iii 5 58
Master Brook, you come to know what hath passed between me and Ford's wife? . . . . iii 5 62
Master Brook, I will not lie to you . . . . . . iii 5 65
And sped you, sir?—Very ill-favouredly, Master Brook . . iii 5 68
Did she change her determination?—No, Master Brook . . . iii 5 71
Master Brook, there was the rankest compound of villanous smell . iii 5 92
You shall hear, Master Brook, what I have suffered to bring this woman to evil for your good . . . . iii 5 96
But mark the sequel, Master Brook . . . . . . iii 5 109
Think of that,—hissing hot,—think of that, Master Brook . . iii 5 124
Master Brook, I will be thrown into Etna, as I have been into Thames, ere I will leave her thus . . . . iii 5 128
'Twixt eight and nine is the hour, Master Brook . . . iii 5 133
You shall have her, Master Brook ; Master Brook, you shall cuckold Ford . . . . iii 5 139
Send to Falstaff straight.—Nay, I'll to him again in name of Brook . iv 4 76
Master Brook, the matter will be known to-night, or never . . v 1 10
I went to her, Master Brook, as you see, like a poor old man : but I came from her, Master Brook, like a poor old woman . . . v 1 16
Her husband, hath the finest mad devil of jealousy in him, Master Brook v 1 20
In the shape of man, Master Brook, I fear not Goliath with a weaver's beam . . . . v 1 23
Go along with me : I'll tell you all, Master Brook . . . v 1 26
Follow. Strange things in hand, Master Brook! . . . . v 1 32
Master Brook, Falstaff's a knave, a cuckoldly knave . . . v 5 114
Here are his horns, Master Brook : and, Master Brook, he hath enjoyed nothing of Ford's but his buck-basket, his cudgel . . . v 5 115
Twenty pounds of money, which must be paid to Master Brook ; his horses are arrested for it, Master Brook . . . . . v 5 118
One Master Brook, that you have cozened of money . . . v 5 175
To Master Brook you yet shall hold your word . . . . v 5 258
My business cannot brook this dalliance . . . *Com. of Errors* iv 1 59
Many can brook the weather that love not the wind . . *L. L. Lost* iv 2 34
In dale, forest or mead, By paved fountain or by rushy brook *M. N. Dr.* ii 1 84
They come, As o'er a brook, to see fair Portia . . *Mer. of Venice* ii 7 47
Empties itself, as doth an inland brook Into the main of waters . v 1 96
That either you might stay him from his intendment or brook such disgrace well as he shall run into . . . . . *As Y. Like It* i 1 140
Tongues in trees, books in the running brooks, Sermons in stones . ii 1 16
Whose antique root peeps out Upon the brook that brawls along this wood . . . . ii 1 32
Stood on the extremest verge of the swift brook, Augmenting it with tears . . . . ii 1 42
He is drowned in the brook : look but in, and you shall see him . iii 2 305
Adonis painted by a running brook . . . . *T. of Shrew* Ind. 2 52
I cannot brook thy sight : This news hath made thee a most ugly man *K. John* iii 1 36
How brooks your grace the air, After your late tossing on the breaking seas?—Needs must I like it well . . . . *Richard II.* iii 2 2
The quality and hair of our attempt Brooks no division . 1 *Hen. IV.* iv 1 62
Nor can one England brook a double reign . . . . . v 4 66
I can no longer brook thy vanities . . . . v 4 74
I better brook the loss of brittle life Than those proud titles . . v 4 78
Then brook abridgement, and your eyes advance . *Hen. V.* v Prol. 44
Arrogant Winchester, that haughty prelate, Whom Henry, our late sovereign, ne'er could brook . . . . . . 1 *Hen. VI.* i 3 24
Let him perceive how ill we brook his treason . . . . iv 1 74
This weighty business will not brook delay . . 2 *Hen. VI.* i 1 170
For flying at the brook, I saw not better sport these seven years' day . ii 1 1
Smooth runs the water where the brook is deep . . . . iii 1 53
Be not too rough in terms ; For he is fierce and cannot brook hard language . . . . iv 9 45
Why hast thou broken faith with me, Knowing how hardly I can brook abuse? . . . . v 1 92
First let me ask of these, If they can brook I bow a knee to man . v 1 110
Whose warlike ears could never brook retreat . . 3 *Hen. VI.* i 1 5
My heart for anger burns ; I cannot brook it . . . . i 1 60
I cannot brook delay : May it please your highness to resolve me now . iii 2 18
You are the fount that makes small brooks to flow . . . iv 8 54
My breast can better brook thy dagger's point Than can my ears that tragic history . . . . v 6 27
In that you brook it ill, it makes him worse . . *Richard III.* i 3 3
I had rather hide me from my greatness, Being a bark to brook no mighty sea . . . . iii 7 162
I have a touch of your condition, Which cannot brook the accent of reproof . . . . iv 4 158
I do wonder His insolence can brook to be commanded . *Coriolanus* i 1 266
Know ye not, in Rome How furious and impatient they be, And cannot brook competitors in love? . . . . . . *T. Andron.* ii 1 77
Soldiers should brook as little wrongs as gods . . *T. of Athens* iii 5 117
Brook. Will the cold brook, Candied with ice, caudle thy morning taste? *T. of Athens* iv 3 225
There is a willow grows aslant a brook, That shows his hoar leaves in the glassy stream . . . . *Hamlet* iv 7 167
When down her weedy trophies and herself Fell in the weeping brook . iv 7 176
Brooked. The nature of our quarrel yet never brooked parle . *T. of Shrew* i 1 117
How hath your lordship brook'd imprisonment? . . *Richard III.* i 1 125
There was a Brutus once that would have brook'd The eternal devil to keep his state in Rome As easily as a king . . . *J. Cæsar* i 2 159
Broom. Not a mouse Shall disturb this hallow'd house : I am sent with broom before, To sweep the dust behind the door . *M. N. Dream* v 1 396
Broom-groves, Whose shadow the dismissed bachelor loves . *Tempest* iv 1 66
Broom-staff. At length they came to the broom-staff to me ; I defied 'em still . . . . *Hen. VIII.* v 4 57
Broth. My wind cooling my broth Would blow me to an ague *Mer. of Ven.* i 1 22
And sauced our broths, as Juno had been sick . . *Cymbeline* iv 2 50
Brothel. Maid, to thy master's bed ; Thy mistress is o' the brothel! *T. of Athens* iv 1 13
I saw him enter such a house of sale, Videlicit, a brothel . *Hamlet* ii 1 61
Epicurism and lust Make it more like a tavern or a brothel Than a graced palace . . . . *Lear* i 4 266
Keep thy foot out of brothels, thy hand out of plackets . . iii 4 99
Marina thus the brothel 'scapes, and chances Into an honest house *Pericles* v Gower 1
Brothel-house. And hang me up at the door of a brothel-house for the sign of blind Cupid . . . . *Much Ado* i 1 256
Brother. Farewell my wife and children!—Farewell, brother . *Tempest* i 1 66
I pray thee, mark me—that a brother should Be so perfidious! . i 2 67
The government I cast upon my brother And to my state grew stranger i 2 75
In my false brother Awaked an evil nature . . . . . i 2 92
Then tell me If this might be a brother . . . . . . i 2 118
Naples, being an enemy To me inveterate, hearkens my brother's suit . i 2 122
And confer fair Milan With all the honours on my brother . . i 2 127
'Tis true, my brother's daughter's queen of Tunis . . . ii 1 255
My brother's servants Were then my fellows . . . . ii 1 273
Here lies your brother, No better than the earth he lies upon . ii 1 280
The king, His brother and yours, abide all three distracted . . v 1 12
Thy brother was a furtherer in the act . . . . . . v 1 73
You, brother mine, that entertain'd ambition, Expell'd remorse and nature . . . . v 1 75
Whom to call brother Would even infect my mouth . . . v 1 130
What sad talk was that Wherewith my brother held you? *T. G. of Ver.* i 3 2
One that I saved from drowning, when three or four of his blind brothers and sisters went to it . . . . iv 4 4
Three of Master Ford's brothers watch the door with pistols *Mer. Wives* iv 2 52
I will, as 'twere a brother of your order, Visit both prince and people *Meas. for Meas.* i 3 44
Why 'her unhappy brother'? let me ask . . . . . i 4 21
Gentle and fair, your brother kindly greets you . . . . i 4 24
Under whose heavy sense your brother's life Falls into forfeit . . i 4 65
I humbly thank you: Commend me to my brother . . . . i 4 88
I have a brother is condemn'd to die . . . . . . ii 2 34
Let it be his fault, And not my brother . . . . . ii 2 36
O just but severe law! I had a brother, then . . . . ii 2 42
Your brother is a forfeit of the law, And you but waste your words . ii 2 71
It is the law, not I condemn your brother . . . . . ii 2 80
Were he my kinsman, brother, or my son, It should be thus with him . ii 2 81
Your brother dies to-morrow; be content . . . . . ii 2 105
We cannot weigh our brother with ourself . . . . . ii 2 126
Ask your heart what it doth know That's like my brother's fault . ii 2 138
Let it not sound a thought upon your tongue Against my brother's life . ii 2 141
Your brother cannot live . . . . ii 4 33
Which had you rather, that the most just law Now took your brother's life; or, to redeem him, Give up your body? . . . . ii 4 53
I, now the voice of the recorded law, Pronounce a sentence on your brother's life . . . . ii 4 62
Might there not be a charity in sin To save this brother's life? . . ii 4 64
I'll speak more gross : Your brother is to die . . . . ii 4 83
Could fetch your brother from the manacles Of the all-building law . ii 4 93
What would you do?—As much for my poor brother as myself . . ii 4 99
Then must your brother die.—And 'twere the cheaper way . . ii 4 104
Better it were a brother died at once, Than that a sister, by redeeming him, Should die for ever . . . . ii 4 106
Rather proved the sliding of your brother A merriment than a vice . ii 4 115
We are all frail.—Else let my brother die . . . . . ii 4 121
My brother did love Juliet, And you tell me that he shall die for it . ii 4 142
Sign me a present pardon for my brother . . . . . ii 4 152
Redeem thy brother By yielding up thy body to my will . . . ii 4 163
I'll to my brother : Though he hath fall'n by prompture of the blood . ii 4 177
Then, Isabel, live chaste, and, brother, die : More than our brother is our chastity . . . . ii 4 184
Yes, brother, you may live . . . . iii 1 64
There spake my brother; there my father's grave Did utter forth a voice iii 1 86
What says my brother?—Death is a fearful thing . . . . iii 1 116
What sin you do to save a brother's life, Nature dispenses with the deed so far That it becomes a virtue . . . . iii 1 134
How will you do to content this substitute, and to save your brother? . iii 1 193
I had rather my brother die by the law than my son should be unlawfully born . . . . iii 1 195
Redeem your brother from the angry law . . . . . iii 1 207
There she lost a noble and renowned brother . . . . iii 1 228
Not only saves your brother, but keeps you from dishonour in doing it . iii 1 246
By this, is your brother saved, your honour untainted . . . iii 1 264
If my brother wrought by my pity, it should not be so with him . . iii 2 222
I am a brother Of gracious order, late come from the See . . iii 2 231
Whose persuasion is I come about my brother . . . . iv 1 48
Soft and low, 'Remember now my brother' . . . . . iv 1 70
The one has my pity; not a jot the other, Being a murderer, though he were my brother . . . . iv 2 65
Hath yet the deputy sent my brother's pardon? . . . . iv 3 118
By my troth, Isabel, I loved thy brother . . . . . iv 3 163
She hath been a suitor to me for her brother Cut off by course of justice v 1 34
I, in probation of a sisterhood, Was sent to by my brother . . v 1 73
He would not, but by gift of my chaste body To his concupiscible intemperate lust, Release my brother . . . . v 1 99
His purpose surfeiting, he sends a warrant For my poor brother's head . v 1 103
If he had so offended, He would have weigh'd thy brother by himself . v 1 111
Your brother's death, I know, sits at your heart . . . . v 1 394
Make it your comfort, So happy is your brother . . . . v 1 404
For your brother's life,—The very mercy of the law cries out . . v 1 411

Brother. Should she kneel down in mercy of this fact, Her brother's ghost his paved bed would break *Meas. for Meas.* v 1 440
Look, if it please you, on this man condemn'd, As if my brother lived v 1 450
My brother had but justice, In that he did the thing for which he died v 1 453
If he be like your brother, for his sake Is he pardon'd v 1 495
Give me your hand and say you will be mine, He is my brother too v 1 498
At eighteen years became inquisitive After his brother *Com. of Errors* i 1 127
Importuned me That his attendant—so his case was like, Reft of his brother, but retain'd his name—Might bear him company i 1 129
So I, to find a mother and a brother, In quest of them, unhappy, lose myself i 2 39
Fie, brother! how the world is changed with you! ii 2 154
Then, gentle brother, get you in again iii 2 25
I would not spare my brother in this case, If he should scorn me so iv 1 77
Embrace thy brother there; rejoice with him v 1 413
Methinks you are my glass, and not my brother v 1 417
We came into the world like brother and brother v 1 424
He hath every month a new sworn brother *Much Ado* i 1 73
Being reconciled to the prince your brother, I owe you all duty i 1 157
You have of late stood out against your brother i 3 23
It is your brother's right hand i 3 51
Sure my brother is amorous on Hero ii 1 161
You are very near my brother in his love ii 1 169
Hath your grace ne'er a brother like you? ii 1 336
As,—in love of your brother's honour, who hath made this match ii 2 37
My lord and brother, God save you!—Good den, brother iii 2 82
For my brother, I think he holds you well iii 2 100
But, as a brother to his sister, show'd Bashful sincerity and comely love iv 1 54
Stand I here? Is this the prince? is this the prince's brother? iv 1 71
Myself, my brother and this grieved count Did see her iv 1 90
This is flat perjury, to call a prince's brother villain iv 2 44
As I am a gentleman, I will.—Brother,— Content yourself v 1 86
Come, brother; away! I will be heard.—And shall v 1 108
Your brother the bastard is fled from Messina v 1 192
Did he not say, my brother was fled? v 1 209
How now? two of my brother's men bound! v 1 214
Your brother incensed me to slander the Lady Hero v 1 242
But did my brother set thee on to this? v 1 254
My brother hath a daughter, Almost the copy of my child that's dead v 1 297
You must be father to your brother's daughter v 4 15
Are you yet determined To-day to marry with my brother's daughter? v 4 37
The moon May through the centre creep and so displease Her brother's noontide with the Antipodes *M. N. Dream* iii 2 55
If they should speak, would almost damn those ears Which, hearing them, would call their brothers fools *Mer. of Venice* i 1 99
Charged my brother, on his blessing, to breed me well *As Y. Like It* i 1 4
I, his brother, gain nothing under him but growth i 1 14
He lets me feed with his hinds, bars me the place of a brother i 1 21
Yonder comes my master, your brother i 1 28
I am helping you to mar that which God made, a poor unworthy brother of yours, with idleness i 1 36
You are my eldest brother; and, in the gentle condition of blood, you should so know me i 1 47
Tradition takes not away my blood, were there twenty brothers betwixt us i 1 52
Come, come, elder brother, you are too young in this i 1 56
Wert thou not my brother, I would not take this hand from thy throat till this other had pulled out thy tongue for saying so i 1 62
The old duke is banished by his younger brother i 1 105
Your brother is but young and tender i 1 135
I had myself notice of my brother's purpose herein and have by underhand means laboured to dissuade him from it i 1 145
A secret and villanous contriver against me his natural brother i 1 151
Thus must I from the smoke into the smother; From tyrant duke unto a tyrant brother i 2 300
Now, my co-mates and brothers in exile ii 1 1
Send to his brother; fetch that gallant hither; If he be absent, bring his brother to me ii 2 17
Your brother—no, no brother; yet the son—Yet not the son, I will not call him son Of him I was about to call his father ii 3 19
I rather will subject me to the malice Of a diverted blood and bloody brother ii 3 37
Find out thy brother, wheresoe'er he is iii 1 5
Till thou canst quit thee by thy brother's mouth Of what we think against thee iii 1 11
I never loved my brother in my life.—More villain thou iii 1 14
Here comes young Master Ganymede, my new mistress's brother iii 2 92
Simply your having in beard is a younger brother's revenue iii 2 397
The woman low And browner than her brother iv 3 89
Orlando did approach the man And found it was his brother, his elder brother.—O, I have heard him speak of that same brother iv 3 121
Are you his brother?—Was't you he rescued? iv 3 134
Committing me unto my brother's love iv 3 145
Tell your brother how well I counterfeited iv 3 168
I must bear answer back How you excuse my brother iv 3 181
God save you, brother.—And you, fair sister v 2 20
Did your brother tell you how I counterfeited to swoon? v 2 28
Your brother and my sister no sooner met but they looked v 2 35
I shall think my brother happy in having what he wishes for v 2 51
When your brother marries Aliena, shall you marry her v 2 70
The first time that I ever saw him Methought he was a brother to your daughter v 4 29
And they shook hands and swore brothers v 4 107
Purposely to take His brother here and put him to the sword v 4 164
His crown bequeathing to his banish'd brother v 4 169
Thou offer'st fairly to thy brothers' wedding v 4 173
The Count Rousillon cannot be my brother *All's Well* i 3 161
He must not be my brother.—Nor I your mother? i 3 166
So that my lord your son were not my brother,—Indeed my mother! i 3 168
Can't no other, But, I your daughter, he must be my brother? i 3 172
With his own hand he slew the duke's brother iii 5 7
Your brother he shall go along with me iii 6 116
He excels his brother for a coward, yet his brother is reputed one of the best that is iv 3 321
All this to season A brother's dead love *T. Night* i 1 31
To pay this debt of love but to a brother, How will she love! i 1 34
My brother he is in Elysium i 2 4
I saw your brother, Most provident in peril i 2 11
What a plague means my niece, to take the death of her brother thus? i 3 2
Why mournest thou?—Good fool, for my brother's death i 5 73

Brother. The more fool, madonna, to mourn for your brother's soul being in heaven *T. Night* i 5 77
I am all the daughters of my father's house, And all the brothers too ii 4 124
Prove true, imagination, O, prove true, That I, dear brother, be now ta'en for you! iii 4 410
I my brother know Yet living in my glass; even such and so In favour was my brother iii 4 414
Had it been the brother of my blood, I must have done no less v 1 217
I never had a brother; Nor can there be that deity in my nature, Of here and every where v 1 233
Such a Sebastian was my brother too v 1 240
Time as long again Would be fill'd up, my brother, with our thanks *W. Tale* i 2 4
We are tougher, brother, Than you can put us to't i 2 15
My stay To you a charge and trouble: to save both, Farewell, our brother i 2 27
What cheer? how is't with you, best brother? i 2 148
How thou lovest us, show in our brother's welcome i 2 174
What a fool Honesty is! and Trust, his sworn brother, a very simple gentleman! iv 4 607
Were I but twenty one, Your father's image is so hit in you, His very air, that I should call you brother v 1 128
Give you all greetings that a king, at friend, Can send his brother v 1 141
Meets he on the way The father of this seeming lady and Her brother v 1 192
The king's son took me by the hand, and called me brother; and then the two kings called my father brother; and then the prince my brother and the princess my sister called my father father v 2 152
Your crown'd brother and these your contracted Heirs of your kingdoms v 3 5
Look upon my brother: both your pardons, That e'er I put between your holy looks My ill suspicion v 3 147
That is my brother's plea and none of mine *K. John* i 1 67
What doth move you to claim your brother's land? i 1 91
Your brother did employ my father much i 1 96
Your brother is legitimate; Your father's wife did after wedlock bear him i 1 116
Tell me, how if my brother, Who, as you say, took pains to get this son, Had of your father claim'd this son for his? i 1 120
Hadst thou rather be a Faulconbridge And like thy brother? i 1 135
An if my brother had my shape, And I had his i 1 138
Brother, take you my land, I'll take my chance i 1 151
Brother by the mother's side, give me your hand i 1 163
Where is that slave, thy brother? where is he? i 1 222
Hast thou conspired with thy brother too? i 1 241
Young Plantagenet, Son to the elder brother of this man ii 1 239
I was never so bethump'd with words Since I first call'd my brother's father dad ii 1 467
Impartial are our eyes and ears: Were he my brother, nay, my kingdom's heir, As he is but my father's brother's son *Richard II.* i 1 116
Thou dost consent In some large measure to thy father's death, In that thou seest thy wretched brother die i 2 27
In suffering thus thy brother to be slaughter'd, Thou showest the naked pathway to thy life i 2 30
Thy sometimes brother's wife With her companion grief must end her life i 2 54
Commend me to thy brother, Edmund York i 2 62
Wert thou not brother to great Edward's son ii 1 121
I would to God . . . The king had cut off my head with my brother's ii 2 102
I am sworn brother, sweet, To grim Necessity v 1 20
When I urged the ransom once again Of my wife's brother, then his cheek look'd pale *1 Hen. IV.* i 3 142
Who bears hard His brother's death i 3 271
Farewell, good brother: we shall thrive, I trust i 3 300
I am sworn brother to a leash of drawers ii 4 7
Thy place in council thou hast rudely lost, Which by thy younger brother is supplied iii 2 33
Younger sons to younger brothers iv 2 31
It was myself, my brother and his son v 1 39
Unless a brother should a brother dare To gentle exercise v 2 54
How doth my son and brother? Thou tremblest *2 Hen. IV.* i 1 67
This thou wouldst say, 'Your son did thus and thus; Your brother thus' i 1 77
Brother, son, and all are dead i 1 81
The worst that they can say of me is that I am a second brother ii 2 71
JACK FALSTAFF with my familiars, JOHN with my brothers and sisters ii 2 145
A bastard son of the king's? And art not thou Poins his brother? ii 4 308
Who like a brother toil'd in my affairs iii 1 62
As if he had been sworn brother to him iii 2 345
Where is the prince your brother?—I think he's gone to hunt iv 4 13
How chance thou art not with the prince thy brother? iv 4 20
Thou hast a better place in his affection Than all thy brothers iv 4 23
A shelter to thy friends, A hoop of gold to bind thy brothers in iv 4 43
I am here, brother, full of heaviness iv 5 8
We left the prince my brother here, my liege iv 5 52
Brothers, you mix your sadness with some fear v 2 46
Yet be sad, good brothers, For, by my faith, it very well becomes you v 2 49
Entertain no more of it, good brothers, Than a joint burden laid upon us all v 2 54
I bid you be assured, I'll be your father and your brother too v 2 57
We'll be all three sworn brothers to France *Hen. V.* ii 1 13
Nym and Bardolph are sworn brothers in filching iii 2 47
If, look you, he were my brother, I would desire the duke to use his good pleasure iii 6 56
We are in God's hand, brother, not in theirs iii 6 178
Bids them good morrow with a modest smile And calls them brothers iv Prol. 34
Brothers both, Commend me to the princes in our camp iv 1 24
Go with my brothers to my lords of England iv 1 30
We few, we happy few, we band of brothers iv 3 60
He to-day that sheds his blood with me Shall be my brother iv 3 62
Nor this I have not, brother, so denied v 2 371
Apparel them all in one livery, that they may agree like brothers *2 Hen. VI.* iv 2 81
Sir Humphrey Stafford and his brother are hard by iv 2 121
Stafford and his brother's death Hath given them heart and courage iv 4 34
Brother, though I be youngest, give me leave *3 Hen. VI.* i 2 1
Why, how now, sons and brother! at a strife? i 2 4
Brother, I go; I'll win them, fear it not i 2 60
How fares my brother? why is he so sad? ii 1 8
I think it cites us, brother, to the field ii 1 34
And for your brother, he was lately sent From your kind aunt ii 1 145
And ne'er was Agamemnon's brother wrong'd By that false woman, as this king by thee ii 2 148

Brother. Thy brother's blood the thirsty earth hath drunk *3 Hen. VI.* ii 3 15
Warwick, revenge! brother, revenge my death! ii 3 19
Brother, give me thy hand; and, gentle Warwick, Let me embrace thee ii 3 44
And cheers these hands that slew thy sire and brother ii 4 9
Brothers, you muse what chat we two have had iii 2 109
Well, jest on, brothers: I can tell you both Her suit is granted iii 2 116
And go we, brothers, to the man that took him, To question of his apprehension iii 2 121
My elder brother, the Lord Aubrey Vere, Was done to death iii 3 102
These letters are for you, Sent from your brother iii 3 164
Hath not our brother made a worthy choice? iv 1 3
Your grace hath not done well, To give the heir and daughter of Lord Scales Unto the brother of your loving bride iv 1 53
And leave your brothers to go speed elsewhere iv 1 58
Edward will be king, And not be tied unto his brother's will iv 1 66
Clarence, Edward's brother, Were but a feigned friend to our proceedings iv 2 10
Thy brother being carelessly encamp'd iv 2 14
How to use your brothers brotherly iv 3 38
See that forthwith Duke Edward be convey'd Unto my brother iv 3 53
The Bishop of York, Fell Warwick's brother iv 4 12
Our king, my brother, Is prisoner to the bishop here iv 5 4
Brother, the time and case requireth haste iv 5 18
Edward is escaped from your brother, And fled iv 6 78
My brother was too careless of his charge iv 6 86
The gates made fast! Brother, I like not this iv 7 10
We shall soon persuade Both him and all his brothers unto reason iv 7 34
Why, brother, wherefore stand you on nice points? iv 7 58
Brother, we will proclaim you out of hand iv 7 63
How evil it beseems thee, To flatter Henry and forsake thy brother! iv 7 85
'Twas I that gave the kingdom to thy brother v 1 34
Thou and thy brother both shall buy this treason Even with the dearest blood your bodies bear v 1 68
Clarence sweeps along, Of force enough to bid his brother battle v 1 77
With whom an upright zeal to right prevails More than the nature of a brother's love! v 1 79
So blunt, unnatural, To bend the fatal instruments of war Against his brother? v 1 88
To deserve well at my brother's hands, I here proclaim myself thy mortal foe v 1 93
I defy thee, And to my brother turn my blushing cheeks v 1 99
Sweet brother, take my hand, And with thy lips keep in my soul awhile! v 2 34
Thou lovest me not; for, brother, if thou didst, Thy tears would wash this cold congealed blood v 2 36
Commend me to my valiant brother v 2 42
There's no hoped-for mercy with the brothers v 4 35
Excuse me to the king my brother v 5 46
I have no brother, I am like no brother v 6 80
And kiss your princely nephew, brothers both v 7 27
Thanks, noble Clarence; worthy brother, thanks v 7 30
Now am I seated as my soul delights, Having my country's peace and brothers' loves v 7 36
Since that our brother dubb'd them gentlewomen *Richard III.* i 1 82
No man shall have private conference, Of what degree soever, with his brother i 1 87
But that thy brothers beat aside the point i 2 96
Make atonement Betwixt the Duke of Gloucester and your brothers i 3 37
Your interior hatred . . Against my kindred, brothers, and myself i 3 67
Our brother is imprison'd by your means, Myself disgraced i 3 78
It is the queen and her allies That stir the king against the duke my brother i 3 331
For whose sake did I that ill deed? For Edward, for my brother, for his sake i 4 217
Who made thee then, a bloody minister . . ?—My brother's love i 4 229
Thy brother's love, our duty, and thy fault, Provoke us hither now i 4 230
O, if you love my brother, hate not me; I am his brother, and I love him well i 4 232
I would he knew that I had saved his brother! i 4 283
Brother, we have done deeds of charity ii 1 49
Have I a tongue to doom my brother's death? ii 1 102
My brother slew no man; his fault was thought ii 1 104
He rescued me, And said, 'Dear brother, live, and be a king' ii 1 113
But for my brother not a man would speak ii 1 126
And the queen's sons and brothers haught and proud ii 3 28
My uncle Rivers talk'd how I did grow More than my brother ii 4 12
Send the Duke of York Unto his princely brother presently iii 1 34
If our brother come, Where shall we sojourn till our coronation? iii 1 61
How fares our loving brother?—Well, my dread lord iii 1 96
The prince my brother hath outgrown me far iii 1 104
A beggar, brother?—Of my kind uncle, that I know will give iii 1 112
Uncle, my brother mocks both you and me iii 1 129
The moveables Whereof the king my brother stood possess'd iii 1 196
You say that Edward is your brother's son iii 7 177
Loath to depose the child, your brother's son iii 7 209
Your brother's son shall never reign our king iii 7 215
I must be married to my brother's daughter iv 2 61
Murder her brothers, and then marry her! Uncertain way of gain! iv 2 63
The Breton Richmond aims At young Elizabeth, my brother's daughter iv 3 41
Where is thy husband now? where be thy brothers? iv 4 92
And the dire death of my two sons and brothers iv 4 143
Her life is only safest in her birth.—And only in that safety died her brothers iv 4 214
So from thy soul's love didst thou love her brothers iv 4 259
Send to her, by the man that slew her brothers iv 4 271
Did drain The purple sap from her sweet brother's body iv 4 277
The king, that calls your beauteous daughter wife, Familiarly shall call thy Dorset brother iv 4 316
Her father's brother Would be her lord? or shall I say, her uncle? Or, he that slew her brothers and her uncles? iv 4 337
The unity the king thy brother made Had not been broken, nor my brother slain iv 4 379
His brother there, With many moe confederates, are in arms iv 4 503
The brother blindly shed the brother's blood v 5 24
What's the cause?—It seems the marriage with his brother's wife Has crept too near his conscience *Hen. VIII.* ii 2 17
Learn this, brother, We live not to be grip'd by meaner persons ii 2 135
The dowager, Sometimes our brother's wife ii 4 181
You a brother of us, It fits we thus proceed v 1 106
The tribulation of Tower-hill, or the limbs of Limehouse, their dear brothers v 4 66
Brother, she is not worth what she doth cost The holding *Troi. and Cres.* ii 2 51

Brother. Our firebrand brother, Paris, burns us all *Troi. and Cres.* ii 2 110
You'll remember your brother's excuse?—To a hair iii 1 156
Let me confirm my princely brother's greeting: You brace of warlike brothers, welcome hither iv 5 174
His brother, the bull,—the primitive statue, and oblique memorial of cuckolds v 1 59
A thrifty shoeing-horn in a chain, hanging at his brother's leg v 1 62
No notes of sally, for the heavens, sweet brother v 3 14
Brother, you have a vice of mercy in you v 3 37
Nor you, my brother, with your true sword drawn, Opposed to hinder me, should stop my way, But by my ruin v 3 56
O, well fought, my youngest brother! v 6 12
Were it At home, upon my brother's guard, even there, Against the hospitable canon, would I Wash my fierce hand in 's heart *Coriolanus* i 10 25
I will, sir, flatter my sworn brother, the people, to earn a dearer estimation of them ii 3 102
Unworthy brother, and unworthy sons! *T. Andron.* i 1 346
Brother, for in that name doth nature plead i 1 370
For thy sake and thy brother's here i 1 482
Lavinia is thine elder brother's hope ii 1 74
Though Bassianus be the emperor's brother, Better than he have worn Vulcan's badge ii 1 88
The king my brother shall have note of this ii 3 85
I pour'd forth tears in vain, To save your brother from the sacrifice ii 3 164
Speak, brother, hast thou hurt thee with the fall?—O brother, with the dismall'st object hurt! ii 3 203
May give a likely guess How these were they that made away his brother ii 3 208
O brother, help me with thy fainting hand—If fear hath made thee faint ii 3 233
My brother dead! I know thou dost but jest ii 3 253
Fell curs of bloody kind, Have here bereft my brother of his life ii 3 282
For thy brothers let me plead iii 1 30
To rescue my two brothers from their death iii 1 49
And here my brother, weeping at my woes iii 1 100
And for his death Thy brothers are condemn'd, and dead by this iii 1 109
When I did name her brothers, then fresh tears Stood on her cheeks iii 1 111
Had she a tongue to speak, now would she say That to her brother which I said to thee iii 1 145
My youth can better spare my blood than you; And therefore mine shall save my brothers' lives iii 1 167
Let me redeem my brothers both from death iii 1 181
Now let me show a brother's love to thee iii 1 183
O brother, speak with possibilities iii 1 215
And thy brother, I, Even like a stony image, cold and numb iii 1 258
Come, brother, take a head; And in this hand the other will I bear iii 1 280
A deed of death done on the innocent Becomes not Titus' brother iii 2 57
It did me good, before the palace gate To brave the tribune in his brother's hearing iv 2 36
Murderous villains! will you kill your brother? iv 2 88
He is your brother, lords, sensibly fed Of that self-blood that first gave life to you iv 2 122
He is your brother by the surer side iv 2 126
His traitorous sons, That died by law for murder of our brother iv 4 54
Stay with me; Or else I'll call my brother back again v 2 135
For that vile fault Two of her brothers were condemn'd to death v 2 174
Chiron and Demetrius Were they that murdered our emperor's brother v 3 98
For their fell faults our brothers were beheaded v 3 100
O my brother's child! O prince! O cousin! *Rom. and Jul.* iii 1 151
But for the sunset of my brother's son It rains downright iii 5 128
Holy Franciscan friar! brother, ho! v 2 1
Going to find a bare-foot brother out, One of our order v 2 5
What a precious comfort 'tis, to have so many, like brothers, commanding one another's fortunes! *T. of Athens* i 2 109
I do not always follow lover, elder brother and woman; sometime the philosopher ii 2 130
Welcome, good brother. What do you think the hour? iii 4 7
Friend or brother, He forfeits his own blood that spills another iii 5 87
Twinn'd brothers of one womb, Whose procreation, residence, and birth, Scarce is dividant iv 3 3
Thy brother by decree is banished *J. Cæsar* iii 1 44
Is there no voice . . For the repealing of my banish'd brother? iii 1 51
Our arms, in strength of malice, and our hearts Of brothers' temper, do receive you in With all kind love iii 1 175
Their names are prick'd.—Your brother too must die iv 1 2
Most noble brother, you have done me wrong iv 2 37
Wrong I mine enemies? And, if not so, how should I wrong a brother? iv 2 39
Hated by one he loves; braved by his brother iv 3 96
Hear me, good brother.—Under your pardon iv 3 212
O my dear brother! This was an ill beginning of the night iv 3 233
Good night, good brother.—Good night, Lord Brutus iv 3 237
Who knows if Donalbain be with his brother? *Macbeth* v 2 7
Though yet of Hamlet our dear brother's death The memory be green *Hamlet* i 2 1
Or thinking by our late dear brother's death Our state to be disjoint i 2 19
Importing the surrender of those lands . . To our most valiant brother i 2 25
My father's brother, but no more like my father Than I to Hercules i 2 152
By a brother's hand Of life, of crown, of queen, at once dispatch'd i 5 74
It hath the primal eldest curse upon 't, A brother's murder iii 3 38
What if this cursed hand Were thicker than itself with brother's blood? iii 3 44
You are the queen, your husband's brother's wife iii 4 15
Almost as bad, good mother, As kill a king, and marry with his brother iii 4 29
Look here, upon this picture, and on this, The counterfeit presentment of two brothers iii 4 54
Here is your husband; like a mildew'd ear, Blasting his wholesome brother iii 4 65
My brother shall know of it: and so I thank you for your good counsel iv 5 71
Her brother is in secret come from France iv 5 88
Forty thousand brothers Could not, with all their quantity of love, Make up my sum v 1 292
I have shot mine arrow o'er the house, And hurt my brother v 2 255
I embrace it freely; And will this brother's wager frankly play v 2 264
I am some twelve or fourteen moonshines Lag of a brother *Lear* i 2 6
It is a letter from my brother, that I have not all o'er-read i 2 38
I hope, for my brother's justification, he wrote this but as an essay or taste of my virtue i 2 46
And live the beloved of your brother i 2 57
You know the character to be your brother's?—If the matter were good, my lord, I durst swear it were his i 2 67

Brother. Please you to suspend your indignation against my brother *Lear* i 2 87
Love cools, friendship falls off, brothers divide . i 2 116
If you do stir abroad, go armed.—Armed, brother! . i 2 187
Brother, I advise you to the best; go armed . i 2 188
A credulous father! and a brother noble! . i 2 195
My father hath set guard to take my brother . ii 1 18
Brother, a word; descend: brother, I say! . ii 1 21
Light, ho, here! Fly, brother. Torches, torches! . ii 1 34
'Twas her brother that, in pure kindness to his horse, buttered his hay . ii 4 126
Your brother's evil disposition made him seek his death . iii 5 7
Could my good brother suffer you to do it? . iv 2 44
But are my brother's powers set forth? . iv 5 1
Have you never found my brother's way To the forfended place? . v 1 10
By your patience, I hold you but a subject of this war, Not as a brother v 3 61
The which immediacy may well stand up, And call itself your brother . v 3 66
False to thy gods, thy brother, and thy father . v 3 134
Call up my brother. O, would you had had her! . *Othello* i 1 176
Any of my brothers of the state Cannot but feel this wrong as 'twere their own . i 2 96
And, like the devil, from his very arm Puff'd his own brother . iii 4 137
How is't, brother!—My leg is cut in two . v 1 71
My brother never Did urge me in his act . *Ant. and Cleo.* ii 2 45
To hold you in perpetual amity, To make you brothers . ii 2 128
From this hour The heart of brothers govern in our loves! . ii 2 150
A sister I bequeath you, whom no brother Did ever love so dearly . ii 2 152
When Cæsar and your brother were at blows, Your mother came to Sicily ii 6 45
What, are the brothers parted? . iii 2 1
Undo that prayer, by crying out as loud, 'O bless my brother!' . iii 4 18
Husband win, win brother, Prays, and destroys the prayer . iii 4 18
Mean time, lady, I'll raise the preparation of a war Shall stain your brother . iii 4 27
Had I been thief-stol'n, As my two brothers, happy! . *Cymbeline* i 6 6
I'll make't my comfort He is a man; I'll love him as my brother . iii 6 72
Be sprightly, for you fall 'mongst friends.—'Mongst friends, If brothers iii 6 76
Brother, stay here: Are we not brothers?—So man and man should be . iv 2 2
If it be sin to say so, sir, I yoke me In my good brother's fault . iv 2 20
Brother, farewell.—I wish ye sport . iv 2 30
You and my brother search What companies are near . iv 2 68
I wish my brother made good time with him, You say he is so fell . iv 2 108
Howsoe'er, My brother hath done well . iv 2 147
O sweetest, fairest lily! My brother wears thee not the one half so well As when thou grew'st thyself . iv 2 202
I and my brother are not known . iv 4 32
Sleep, . . . thou hast created A mother and two brothers: but, O scorn! Gone! . v 4 125
O my gentle brothers, Have we thus met? . v 5 374
You call'd me brother, When I was but your sister; I you brothers, When ye were so indeed . v 5 376
How parted with your brothers? how first met them? . v 5 386
She, like harmless lightning, throws her eye On him, her brothers . v 5 395
Thou art my brother; so we'll hold thee ever . v 5 399
You holp us, sir, As you did mean indeed to be our brother . v 5 423
Brother Abel. Be thou cursed Cain, To slay thy brother Abel 1 *Hen. VI.* i 3 40
Brother Angelo. My brother Angelo will not be altered *Meas. for Meas.* iii 2 219
Brother Antony,— Hold you content . *Much Ado* v 1 91
But, brother Antony,— Come, 'tis no matter . v 1 100
Brother Bedford. And did my brother Bedford toil his wits? 2 *Hen. VI.* i 1 83
Brother born. Geffrey was thy elder brother born . *K. John* ii 1 104
To brother born an household cruelty, I make my quarrel in particular 2 *Hen. IV.* iv 1 95
Brother cardinals. The heads of all thy brother cardinals, With thee *Hen. VIII.* iii 2 257
Brother Cassius. It may be I shall raise you by and by On business to my brother Cassius . *J. Cæsar* iv 3 248
Go and commend me to my brother Cassius . iv 3 307
Brother Clarence, what think you Of this new marriage? . 3 *Hen. VI.* iv 1 1
To set my brother Clarence and the king In deadly hate *Richard III.* i 1 34
Brother Claudio. The fair sister To her unhappy brother Claudio.—Why 'her unhappy brother'? . *Meas. for Meas.* i 4 20
Brother Edward. O, spare me not, my brother Edward's son, For that I was his father Edward's son . *Richard II.* ii 1 124
Brother England. From our brother England?—From him . *Hen. V.* ii 4 75
To-morrow shall you bear our full intent Back to our brother England . ii 4 115
Right joyous are we to behold your face, Most worthy brother England v 2 10
So happy be the issue, brother England, Of this good day . v 2 12
Brother father. 'Bless you, good father friar.—And you, good brother father . *Meas. for Meas.* iii 2 14
Brother France. Unto our brother France, and to our sister, Health and fair time of day! . *Hen. V.* v 2 2
Brother Geffrey. In right and true behalf Of thy deceased brother Geffrey's son . *K. John* ii 1 8
Look here upon thy brother Geffrey's face . ii 1 99
Brother general. My brother general, the commonwealth, To brother born an household cruelty . 2 *Hen. IV.* iv 1 94
Brother Gloucester, plain well-meaning soul . *Richard II.* ii 1 128
I will send you to my brother Gloucester, Who shall reward you *Rich. III.* i 4 235
You are deceived, your brother Gloucester hates you . i 4 238
Brother Hector. Lift as much as his brother Hector . *Troi. and Cres.* i 2 126
Brother Henry. What! did my brother Henry spend his youth? 2 *Hen. VI.* i 1 78
Brother Jaques. My brother Jaques he keeps at school . *As Y. Like It* i 1 5
Brother John. Your brother John is ta'en in flight . *Much Ado* v 4 127
Bear this letter to Lord John of Lancaster, to my brother John 1 *Hen. IV.* iii 3 219
Come, brother John; full bravely hast thou flesh'd Thy maiden sword . v 4 133
Brother John Bates, is not that the morning which breaks yonder? *Hen. V.* iv 1 87
Brother justice. My brother justice have I found so severe *M. for M.* iii 2 267
Brother king. Your brother kings and monarchs of the earth Do all expect that you should rouse yourself . *Hen. V.* i 2 122
Now, brother king, farewell, and sit you fast . 3 *Hen. VI.* iv 1 119
Brother Montague. My brother Montague shall post to London . i 2 55
How far off is our brother Montague? . iv 1 4
O brother Montague, give me thy hand . *Rom. and Jul.* v 3 296
Brother Mortimer. I fear my brother Mortimer doth stir About his title 1 *Hen. IV.* iii 3 84
Brother of England, how may we content This widow lady? . *K. John* ii 1 547
Brother of England, you blaspheme in this . iii 1 161
Brother of Gloucester, at Saint Alban's field This lady's husband, Sir Richard Grey, was slain . 3 *Hen. VI.* iii 2 1
Brother Orlando. Your younger brother Orlando hath a disposition to come in disguised against me to try a fall . *As Y. Like It* i 1 130
Brother Petruchio, sister Katharina . *T. of Shrew* v 2 6

Brother priest. You are for dreams and slumbers, brother priest; You fur your gloves with reason . *Troi and Cres.* ii 2 37
Brother Prospero. You did supplant your brother Prospero . *Tempest* ii 1 271
Brother Richard. Though before his face I speak the words, Your brother Richard mark'd him for the grave . 3 *Hen. VI.* ii 6 40
Now, brother Richard, will you stand by us? . iv 1 145
Brother Rutland. Thou didst kill our tender brother Rutland . ii 2 115
And this the hand that slew thy brother Rutland . ii 4 7
Brother Troilus!—Good brother, come you hither . *Troi. and Cres.* iv 4 101
Brother Worcester. Young Harry Percy, Sent from my brother Worcester *Richard II.* ii 3 22
Brother York, thy acts in Ireland, In bringing them to civil discipline, . . . Have made thee fear'd . 2 *Hen. VI.* i 1 194
Brotherhood. Finds brotherhood in thee no sharper spur? . *Richard II.* i 2 9
Friendship shall combine, and brotherhood . *Hen. V.* ii 1 114
In your bride you bury brotherhood . 3 *Hen. VI.* iv 1 55
Meantime, this deep disgrace in brotherhood Touches me deeper than you can imagine . *Richard III.* i 1 111
Who spake of brotherhood? who spake of love? . ii 1 108
Communities, Degrees in schools and brotherhoods in cities *Troi. and Cres.* i 3 104
By my brotherhood, The letter was not nice . *Rom. and Jul.* v 2 17
Brother-in-law. To go about to make me the king's brother-in-law *W. Tale* iv 4 720
Our trusty brother-in-law and the abbot . *Richard II.* v 3 137
At our own charge shall ransom straight His brother-in-law 1 *Hen. IV.* i 3 80
Brother-like. Welcome, good Clarence; this is brother-like . 3 *Hen. VI.* v 1 105
Brother-love. Embrace and love this man.—With a true heart and brother-love I do it . *Hen. VIII.* v 3 173
Brotherly. I speak but brotherly of him . *As Y. Like It* i 1 162
Nor how to use your brothers brotherly . 3 *Hen. VI.* iv 3 38
I love thee brotherly, but envy much Thou hast robb'd me of this deed *Cymbeline* iv 2 158

Brought. Bountiful Fortune, Now my dear lady, hath mine enemies Brought to this shore . *Tempest* i 2 180
This blue-eyed hag was hither brought with child . i 2 269
The harmony of their tongues hath into bondage Brought my too diligent ear . iii 1 42
Is she the goddess that hath sever'd us, And brought us thus together? v 1 188
It is you that have chalk'd forth the way Which brought us hither . v 1 204
Even in a dream, were we divided from them And were brought moping hither . v 1 240
Being so hard to me that brought your mind, I fear she'll prove as hard to you in telling your mind . *T. G. of Ver.* i 1 147
Till the last step have brought me to my love . ii 7 36
Here have I brought him back again.—What, didst thou offer her this? iv 4 57
You have brought her into such a canaries as 'tis wonderful . *Mer. Wives* ii 2 61
When you have brought him thither, What shall be done with him? . iv 4 44
Cursed hours, Which forced marriage would have brought upon her . v 5 243
As that the sin hath brought you to this shame . *Meas. for Meas.* ii 3 31
That brought you home The head of Ragozine . v 1 538
Why, sir, I brought you word an hour since . *Com. of Errors* iv 3 37
Till I have brought him to his wits again . v 1 96
Along with them They brought one Pinch, a hungry lean-faced villain . v 1 237
Brought to this town by that most famous warrior, Duke Menaphon . v 1 367
That she brought me up, I likewise give her most humble thanks *Much Ado* i 1 241
How you were brought into the orchard and saw me court Margaret . v 1 243
This naughty man Shall face to face be brought to Margaret . v 1 307
Your brother John is ta'en in flight, And brought with armed men back v 4 128
Mine ear, I thank it, brought me to thy sound . *M. N. Dream* iii 2 182
How dost thou and thy master agree? I have brought him a present *Mer. of Venice* ii 2 107
Hymen from heaven brought her, Yea, brought her hither *As Y. Like It* v 4 118
Because she brought stone jugs and no seal'd quarts . *T. of Shrew* Ind. 2 90
What's this? mutton?—Ay.—Who brought it?—I . iv 1 163
His daughter is to be brought by you to the supper . iv 4 85
Now we are undone and brought to nothing . v 1 45
I have brought him up ever since he was three years old . v 1 85
Let me never have a cause to sigh, Till I be brought to such a silly pass! v 2 124
Here's a man stands, that has brought his pardon . *All's Well* ii 1 65
Brought you this letter, gentlemen? . iii 2 65
Doubt not but heaven Hath brought me up to be your daughter's dower iv 4 19
He brought me out o' favour with my lady about a bear-baiting *T. Night* ii 5 8
What foolish boldness brought thee to their mercies? . v 1 73
The good queen, For she is good, hath brought you forth a daughter *W. Tale* ii 3 65
And from thence have brought This seal'd-up oracle . iii 2 127
I witness to The times that brought them in . iv 1 12
As if my trinkets had been hallowed and brought a benediction to the buyer . iv 4 613
I brought the old man and his son aboard the prince . v 2 124
Painfully with much expedient march Have brought a countercheck *K. John* ii 1 224
Whom zeal and charity brought to the field As God's own soldier . ii 1 565
And here's a prophet, that I brought with me . iv 2 147
And brought in matter that should feed this fire . v 2 85
This news was brought to Richard but even now . v 3 12
The lords are all come back, And brought Prince Henry . v 6 34
That, being brought into the open air, It would allay the burning quality Of that fell poison which assaileth him . v 7 7
Let him be brought into the orchard here . v 7 10
Hast thou . . . Brought hither Henry Hereford thy bold son? *Richard II.* i 1 3
How far brought you high Hereford on his way?—I brought high Hereford, if you call him so, But to the next highway . i 4 2
He hath brought us smooth and welcome news . 1 *Hen. IV.* i 1 66
There's a franklin in the wild of Kent hath brought three hundred marks . ii 1 60
Hath Butler brought those horses from the sheriff? . ii 3 70
That brought you home and boldly did outdare The dangers of the time v 1 40
And show'd thou makest some tender of my life, In this fair rescue thou hast brought to me . v 4 50
Let him be brought in to his answer . 2 *Hen. IV.* ii 1 34
What the devil hast thou brought there? . ii 4 1
Surfeiting and wanton hours Have brought ourselves into a burning fever . iv 1 56
Fondly brought here and foolishly sent hence . iv 2 119
Hastings and all Are brought to the correction of your law . iv 4 85
That this fair action may on foot be brought . *Hen. V.* i 2 310
The even mead, that erst brought sweetly forth The freckled cowslip . v 2 48
Whom with my bare fists I would execute, If I now had him brought into my power . 1 *Hen. VI.* i 4 37

Brought. Had York and Somerset brought rescue in, We should have found a bloody day of this . . . . . 1 *Hen. VI.* iv 7 33
See them guarded And safely brought to Dover . . . v 1 49
Till we have brought Duke Humphrey in disgrace . 2 *Hen. VI.* i 3 99
Be brought against me at my trial-day . . . . . iii 1 114
This spark will prove a raging fire, If wind and fuel be brought to feed it with . . . . iii 1 303
The cause why I have brought this army hither Is to remove proud Somerset . . . . v 1 35
Tidings, as swiftly as the posts could run, Were brought me . 3 *Hen. VI.* ii 1 110
Your foe is taken, And brought your prisoner to your palace gate . . iii 2 119
When nature brought him to the door of death . . . iii 3 105
Stole to Rhesus' tents, And brought from thence the Thracian fatal steeds . . . . iv 2 21
Pass'd and now repass'd the seas And brought desired help from Burgundy . . . . iv 7 6
The queen from France hath brought a puissant power . . . v 2 31
That they who brought me in my master's hate, I live to look upon their tragedy . . . . . . *Richard III.* iii 2 58
Some one take order Buckingham be brought To Salisbury . . iv 4 539
He was brought to this By a vain prophecy . . *Hen. VIII.* i 2 146
None here, he hopes, In all this noble bevy, has brought with her One care . . . . i 4 4
Divers witnesses; which the duke desired To have brought vivâ voce to his face . . . . ii 1 18
When he was brought again to the bar, to hear His knell rung out . ii 1 31
In which you brought the king To be your servant . . . iii 2 315
Having brought the queen To a prepared place in the choir, fell off . iv 1 63
Brought him forward, As a man sorely tainted, to his answer . . iv 2 13
They promised me eternal happiness; And brought me garlands . . iv 2 91
I have brought my lord the archbishop, As you commanded me . . v 1 80
For an old aunt . . ., He brought a Grecian queen . *Troi. and Cres.* ii 2 78
Let her say what: what have I brought you to do? . . . iv 2 29
What ever have been thought on in this state, That could be brought to bodily act ere Rome Had circumvention? . . . *Coriolanus* i 2 5
I was forced to wheel Three or four miles about, else had I, sir, Half an hour since brought my report . . . . . . i 6 21
Tell us what hath brought you to 't.—Mine own desert . . ii 3 70
Our best water brought by conduits hither . . . . ii 3 250
Now this extremity Hath brought me to thy hearth . . . iv 5 85
You have brought A trembling upon Rome . . . .—Say not we brought it iv 6 120
Than to tread . . . on thy mother's womb, That brought thee to this world . . . . v 3 125
That brought you forth this boy, to keep your name Living to time . v 3 126
And brought to yoke the enemies of Rome . . *T. Andron.* i 1 69
Sufficeth not that we are brought to Rome, To beautify thy triumphs? i 1 109
Is she not then beholding to the man That brought her for this high good turn so far? . . . . i 1 397
Brought hither in a most unlucky hour . . . . ii 3 251
What fool hath added water to the sea, Or brought a faggot to bright-burning Troy? . . . . iii 1 69
We are not brought so low, But that between us we can kill a fly . iii 2 76
I have brought you a letter and a couple of pigeons here . . iv 4 43
Fetter him, Till he be brought unto the empress' face . . v 3 7
Brought the fatal engine in That gives our Troy, our Rome, the civil wound . . . . v 3 86
I brought my master news of Juliet's death . *Rom. and Jul.* v 3 272
Brought you Cæsar home? Why are you breathless? . *J. Cæsar* i 3 1
He hath brought many captives home to Rome . . . iii 2 93
And having brought our treasure where we will, Then take we down his load . . . . iv 1 24
He was but a fool that brought My answer back . . . iv 3 84
And hide thy spurs in him, Till he have brought thee up to yonder troops . . . . v 3 16
Then he is dead?—Ay, and brought off the field . *Macbeth* v 8 44
Direct me To him from whom you brought them . *Hamlet* iv 6 34
From Hamlet! who brought them?—Sailors, my lord . . iv 7 38
They were given me by Claudio; he received them Of him that brought them . . . . iv 7 41
To such wondrous doing brought his horse . . . . iv 7 87
Let the foils be brought, the gentleman willing . . . v 2 182
When came this to you? who brought it?—It was not brought me *Lear* i 2 62
Poorest shape That ever penury, in contempt of man, Brought near to beast . . . . ii 3 9
I could as well be brought To knee his throne . . . ii 4 216
Have his daughters brought him to this pass? Couldst thou save nothing? . . . . iii 4 65
Thou hast one daughter, Who redeems nature from the general curse Which twain have brought her to . . . . . iv 6 211
If you have victory, let the trumpet sound For him that brought it . v 1 42
This Moor, whom now, it seems, Your special mandate for the state-affairs Hath hither brought . . . . *Othello* i 3 73
Be you ruled by me: I have brought you from Venice . . ii 1 271
Would in action glorious I had lost Those legs that brought me to a part of it! . . . . ii 3 187
The merchandise which thou hast brought from Rome Are all too dear for me: lie they upon thy hand . . . *Ant. and Cleo.* ii 5 104
His guard have brought him thither . . . . . . iv 15 9
Antony Shall be brought drunken forth . . . . . v 2 219
Who was last with them?—A simple countryman, that brought her figs v 2 342
Their story is No less in pity than his glory which Brought them to be lamented . . . . v 2 366
Now, master doctor, have you brought those drugs? . *Cymbeline* i 5 4
Had I not brought The knowledge of your mistress home, I grant We were to question further . . . . ii 4 50
I am brought hither Among the Italian gentry . . . v 1 17
But tidings to the contrary Are brought your eyes . *Pericles* ii Gower 16
Hymen hath brought the bride to bed . . . . . iii Gower 9
The sum of this, Brought hither to Pentapolis . . . iii Gower 34
O your sweet queen! That the strict fates had pleased you had brought her hither! . . . . iii 3 8
Well-sailing ships and bounteous winds have brought This king to Tarsus . . . . iv 4 17
Her better stars Brought her to Mytilene; 'gainst whose shore Riding, her fortunes brought the maid aboard us . . . . . v 3 10
They shall be brought you to my house, Whither I invite you . . v 3 26

Brought about. Until the twelve celestial signs Have brought about the annual reckoning . . . . . . *L. L. Lost* v 2 808

Brought away. This insculpture, which With wax I brought away *T. of Athens* v 4 68

Brought forth. Let him be brought forth and borne hence *Com. of Errors* v 1 160
Let Time's news Be known when 'tis brought forth . . *W. Tale* iv 1 27
Now hath my soul brought forth her prodigy . . *Richard II.* ii 2 64
Or what hath this bold enterprise brought forth? . . 2 *Hen. IV.* i 1 178
Thy mother felt more than a mother's pain, And yet brought forth less than a mother's hope . . . . . 3 *Hen. VI.* v 6 50
Have By magot-pies and choughs and rooks brought forth The secret'st man of blood . . . . *Macbeth* iii 4 125
I was mortally brought forth, and am No other than I appear *Pericles* v 1 105
At sea in childbed died she, but brought forth A maid-child call'd Marina . . . . v 3 5

Brought home. Confess he brought home noble prize *Troi. and Cres.* ii 2 86
Our spoils we have brought home Do more than counterpoise *Coriolanus* v 6 77

Brought in. A foolish knight that you brought in one night . *T. Night* i 3 16
At many times I brought in my accounts . . . *T. of Athens* ii 2 142

Brought low. So are the horses of the enemy In general, journey-bated and brought low . . . . . 1 *Hen. IV.* iv 3 26
Poor honest lord, brought low by his own heart! . *T. of Athens* iv 2 37

Brought to bed. A usurer's wife was brought to bed of twenty money-bags . . . . *W. Tale* iv 4 266
She is deliver'd.—To whom?—I mean, she is brought a-bed *T. Andron.* iv 2 62
His wife but yesternight was brought to bed . . . . iv 2 153

Brought to know. If your grace Could but be brought to know *Hen. VIII.* iii 1 154

Brought to light. What your wisdoms could not discover, these shallow fools have brought to light . . . . . . *Much Ado* v 1 240
Since God so graciously hath brought to light This dangerous treason *Hen. V.* ii 2 185
Prodigious, and untimely brought to light . . *Richard III.* i 2 22

Brought to pass. We do not know what's brought to pass under the profession of fortune-telling . . . . *Mer. Wives* iv 2 183

Brought up. One that I brought up of a puppy . . *T. G. of Ver.* iv 4 3
Bought and brought up to attend my sons . . *Com. of Errors* i 1 58
Vincentio's son brought up in Florence . . . *T. of Shrew* i 1 14
Young and beauteous, Brought up as best becomes a gentlewoman . i 2 87
I have been so well brought up that I can write my name 2 *Hen. VI.* iv 2 113
Hanged! by'r lady, then I have brought up a neck to a fair end *T. Andron.* iv 4 48
Being of so young days brought up with him . . *Hamlet* ii 2 11
Whom thou fought'st against, Though daintily brought up *Ant. and Cleo.* i 4 60
I have brought up some eleven— Ay, to eleven; and brought them down again . . . . *Pericles* iv 2 15

Brow. How angerly I taught my brow to frown, When inward joy enforced my heart to smile! . . . . . . *T. G. of Ver.* i 2 62
Thou hast the right arched beauty of the brow . . *Mer. Wives* iii 3 60
A plain kerchief, Sir John: my brows become nothing else . . iii 3 63
There is written in your brow, provost, honesty and constancy *Meas. for Meas.* iv 2 163
Speak you this with a sad brow? or do you play the flouting Jack? *Much Ado* i 1 185
But, in faith, honest as the skin between his brows . . . iii 5 14
With a velvet brow, With two pitch-balls stuck in her face for eyes *L. L. Lost* iii 1 198
Never paint me now: Where fair is not, praise cannot mend the brow . iv 1 17
She strikes at the brow.—But she herself is hit lower . . . iv 1 119
A gait, a state, a brow, a breast, a waist, A leg, a limb . . iv 3 185
What peremptory eagle-sighted eye Dares look upon the heaven of her brow? . . . . iv 3 227
If in black my lady's brows be deck'd . . . . . iv 3 258
Therefore red, that would avoid dispraise, Paints itself black, to imitate her brow . . . . iv 3 265
Help, hold his brows! he'll swoon! Why look you pale? . . v 2 392
Though the mourning brow of progeny Forbid the smiling courtesy of love . . . . v 2 754
Till o'er their brows death-counterfeiting sleep With leaden legs and batty wings doth creep . . . . . . *M. N. Dream* iii 2 364
The lover, all as frantic, Sees Helen's beauty in a brow of Egypt . v 1 11
In religion, What damned error, but some sober brow Will bless it? *Mer. of Venice* iii 2 78
To view with hollow eye and wrinkled brow An age of poverty . . iv 1 270
The devil take mocking: speak, sad brow and true maid *As Y. Like It* iii 2 227
So is the forehead of a married man more honourable than the bare brow of a bachelor . . . . iii 3 62
'Tis not your inky brows, your black silk hair, Your bugle eyeballs . iii 5 46
As I guess By the stern brow and waspish action . . . iv 3 9
Fie, fie! unknit that threatening unkind brow . . *T. of Shrew* v 2 136
To sit and draw His arched brows, his hawking eye . . *All's Well* i 1 105
My father had a mole upon his brow.—And so had mine *T. Night* v 1 249
O, that is entertainment My bosom likes not, nor my brows! *W. Tale* i 2 119
I find it, And that to the infection of my brains And hardening of my brows . . . . i 2 146
You look As if you held a brow of much distraction . . . i 2 149
Black brows, they say, Become some women best . . . ii 1 8
Take your sweetheart's hat And pluck it o'er your brows . . iv 4 665
Our cannon shall be bent Against the brows of this resisting town *K. John* ii 1 38
These eyes, these brows, were moulded out of his . . . ii 1 100
Hang'd in the frowning wrinkle of her brow! And quarter'd in her heart! . . . . ii 1 505
And make a riot on the gentle brow Of true sincerity . . . iii 1 247
I will kiss thy detestable bones And put my eyeballs in thy vaulty brows . . . . iii 4 30
When your head did but ache, I knit my handkercher about your brows iv 1 42
Why do you bend such solemn brows on me? Think you I bear the shears of destiny? . . . . iv 2 90
With wrinkled brows, with nods, with rolling eyes . . . iv 2 192
Threaten the threatener and outface the brow Of bragging horror . . v 1 49
Lift up thy brow, renowned Salisbury, And with a great heart heave away this storm . . . . v 2 54
Here walk I in the black brow of night, To find you out . . v 6 17
Face to face, And frowning brow to brow, ourselves will hear *Richard II.* i 1 16
I see your brows are full of discontent, Your hearts of sorrow . . iv 1 331
See riot and dishonour stain the brow Of my young Harry . 1 *Hen. IV.* i 1 85
Majesty might never yet endure The moody frontier of a servant brow . i 3 19
Beads of sweat have stood upon thy brow, Like bubbles . . ii 3 61
By this face, This seeming brow of justice, did he win The hearts of all iv 3 83
This man's brow, like to a title-leaf, Foretells the nature of a tragic volume: So looks the strand . . . . . 2 *Hen. IV.* i 1 60
Now bind my brows with iron . . . . i 1 150
It is not a confident brow, nor the throng of words that come . . ii 1 122
He whose brow with homely biggen bound Snores out the watch of night iv 5 27

Brow. O, it is much that a lie with a slight oath and a jest with a sad brow will do! . . . 2 *Hen. IV.* v 1 92
Let the brow o'erwhelm it As fearfully as doth a galled rock O'erhang and jutty his confounded base . *Hen. V.* iii 1 11
The duke Hath banish'd moody discontented fury, As by his smoothed brows it doth appear . . . . . . 1 *Hen. VI.* iii 1 124
See, how the ugly witch doth bend her brows! . . . . . v 3 34
Knit his brows, As frowning at the favours of the world . 2 *Hen. VI.* i 2 3
He knits his brow and shows an angry eye . . . . . iii 1 15
And Suffolk's cloudy brow his stormy hate . . . . . iii 1 155
That gold must round engirt these brows of mine . . . . v 1 99
Like a gallant in the brow of youth, Repairs him with occasion . v 3 4
Thou smiling while he knit his angry brows . . 3 *Hen. VI.* ii 2 20
The widow likes him not, she knits her brows . . . . iii 2 82
The wrinkles in my brows, now fill'd with blood, Were liken'd oft to kingly sepulchres . . . . v 2 19
And who durst smile when Warwick bent his brow? . . . v 2 22
Now are our brows bound with victorious wreaths . *Richard III.* i 1 5
When thou didst crown his warlike brows with paper . . . i 3 175
I would to God that the inclusive verge Of golden metal that must round my brow Were red-hot steel! . . . . iv 1 60
This long-usurped royalty From the dead temples of this bloody wretch Have I pluck'd off, to grace thy brows withal . . . . v 5 6
Things now, That bear a weighty and a serious brow . *Hen. VIII.* Prol. 2
To a cruel war I sent him; from whence he returned, his brows bound with oak . . . . *Coriolanus* i 3 16
His bloody brow With his mail'd hand then wiping . . . i 3 37
The wounds become him.—On's brows . . . . . . ii 1 137
Prepare thy brow to frown: know'st thou me yet? . . . . iv 5 69
These happy masks that kiss fair ladies' brows . . *Rom. and Jul.* i 1 236
Even the day before, she broke her brow . . . . . . i 3 38
It had upon its brow A bump as big as a young cockerel's stone . i 3 52
Here are the beetle brows shall blush for me . . . . . i 4 32
He was not born to shame: Upon his brow shame is ashamed to sit . iii 2 92
Yon grey is not the morning's eye, 'Tis but the pale reflex of Cynthia's brow . . . . iii 5 20
In tatter'd weeds, with overwhelming brows, Culling of simples . . v 1 39
Look you, Cassius, The angry spot doth glow on Cæsar's brow *J. Cæsar* i 2 183
O conspiracy, Shamest thou to show thy dangerous brow by night? . ii 1 78
All my engagements I will construe to thee, All the charactery of my sad brows . . . . ii 1 308
Did not they Put on my brows this wreath of victory, And bid me give it thee? . . . . v 3 82
But, hold thee, take this garland on thy brow; Thy Brutus bid me give it thee . . . . v 3 85
Thy hair, Thou other gold-bound brow, is like the first . *Macbeth* iv 1 114
Though all things foul would wear the brows of grace, Yet grace must still look so . . . . iv 3 23
What, man! ne'er pull your hat upon your brows; Give sorrow words iv 3 208
And our whole kingdom To be contracted in one brow of woe *Hamlet* i 2 4
With his other hand thus o'er his brow, He falls to such perusal of my face . . . . ii 1 89
See, what a grace was seated on this brow; Hyperion's curls . . iii 4 55
The chaste unsmirched brow Of my true mother . . . . iv 5 119
He's fat, and scant of breath. Here, Hamlet, take my napkin, rub thy brows . . . . v 2 299
Let it stamp wrinkles in her brow of youth . . . . *Lear* i 4 306
Hast not in thy brows an eye discerning Thine honour from thy suffering iv 2 52
On the brow o' the sea Stand ranks of people . . . *Othello* ii 1 53
Thou criedst 'Indeed!' And didst contract and purse thy brow together iii 3 113
Eternity was in our lips and eyes, Bliss in our brows' bent *Ant. and Cleo.* i 3 36
Would stand and make his eyes grow in my brow . . . . . i 5 32
The first of Britain which did put His brows within a golden crown *Cymbeline* iii 1 61
Thou Hast moved us: what seest thou in our looks?—An angry brow *Pericles* i 2 52
My queen's square brows; Her stature to an inch; as wand-like straight v 1 109
Brow-bound. For his meed Was brow-bound with the oak . *Coriolanus* ii 2 102
Brown. Long heath, brown furze, any thing . . . . *Tempest* i 1 70
She has brown hair, and speaks small like a woman . *Mer. Wives* i 1 48
We shall have all the world drink brown and white bastard *M. for M.* iii 2 4
He's in for a commodity of brown paper and old ginger . . . iv 3 5
She's too low for a high praise, too brown for a fair praise *Much Ado* i 1 174
As brown in hue As hazel nuts and sweeter than the kernels *T. of Shrew* ii 1 256
Beat me to death with a bottom of brown thread . . . . iv 3 138
Why, then, your brown bastard is your only drink . . 1 *Hen. IV.* ii 4 82
When the brown wench Lay kissing in your arms . . *Hen. VIII.* iii 2 295
Helen herself swore th' other day, that Troilus, for a brown favour—for so 'tis, I must confess,—not brown neither,— No, but brown.— 'Faith, to say truth, brown and not brown . . *Troi. and Cres.* i 2 101
Not that our heads are some brown, some black, some auburn *Coriolanus* ii 3 20
Her hair, what colour?—Brown, madam . . . *Ant. and Cleo.* iii 3 36
My very hairs do mutiny; for the white Reprove the brown for rashness, and they them For fear and doting . . . . iii 11 14
Though grey Do something mingle with our younger brown . . iv 8 20
Brown bill. Bring up the brown bills . . . . . *Lear* iv 6 92
But for a sallet, my brain-pan had been cleft with a brown bill 2 *Hen. VI.* iv 10 13
Brown bread. Though she smelt brown bread and garlic *Meas. for Meas.* iii 2 194
Browner. I like the new tire within excellently, if the hair were a thought browner . . . . *Much Ado* iii 4 14
His very hair is of the dissembling colour.—Something browner than Judas's: marry, his kisses are Judas's own children *As Y. Like It* iii 4 9
The woman low And browner than her brother . . . . . iv 3 89
Brownist. I had as lief be a Brownist as a politician . *T. Night* iii 2 34
Browse. There is cold meat i' the cave; we'll browse on that . *Cymbeline* iii 6 38
Browsedest. The barks of trees thou browsed'st . . *Ant. and Cleo.* i 4 66
Browsing. By the seaside, browsing of ivy . . . . *W. Tale* iii 3 69
Bruise. Let us be keen, and rather cut a little, Than fall, and bruise to death . . . . *Meas. for Meas.* ii 1 6
With grey hairs and bruise of many days, Do challenge thee to trial *Much Ado* v 1 65
Dart thy skill at me; Bruise me with scorn . . *L. L. Lost* v 2 397
Nor bruise her flowerets with the armed hoofs Of hostile paces 1 *Hen. IV.* i 1 8
The sovereign'st thing on earth Was parmaceti for an inward bruise . i 3 58
To us all That feel the bruises of the days before . . 2 *Hen. IV.* iv 1 100
But that we thought not good to bruise an injury till it were full ripe *Hen. V.* iii 6 129
The law shall bruise him . . . . *T. of Athens* iii 5 4
Which, for they yet glance by and scarcely bruise . . . . *Lear* v 3 148
Bruised. I bruised my shin th' other day with playing at sword and dagger *Mer. Wives* i 1 294
A wretched soul, bruised with adversity . . . . *Com. of Errors* ii 1 34
Falling from a hill, he was so bruised That the pursuers took him 1 *Hen. IV.* v 5 21
His lords desire him to have borne His bruised helmet and his bended sword Before him . . . . *Hen. V.* v Prol. 18
Our bruised arms hung up for monuments . . . *Richard III.* i 1 6
Bruised underneath the yoke of tyranny . . . . v 2 2
But words are words; I never yet did hear That the bruised heart was pierced through the ear . . . . *Othello* i 3 219
No more a soldier: bruised pieces, go; You have been nobly borne *Ant. and Cleo.* iv 14 42
Bruising. I throw thy name against the bruising stones . *T. G. of Ver.* i 2 111
To bloody battles and to bruising arms . . . 1 *Hen. IV.* iii 2 105
Put in their hands thy bruising irons of wrath . . *Richard III.* v 3 110
Do you think That his contempt shall not be bruising to you? *Coriolanus* ii 3 210
Bruit. The bruit thereof will bring you many friends . 3 *Hen. VI.* iv 7 64
The bruit is, Hector's slain, and by Achilles . . *Troi. and Cres.* v 9 4
Rejoices in the common wreck, As common bruit doth put it *T. of Athens* v 1 196
The king's rouse the heavens shall bruit again, Re-speaking earthly thunder . . . . *Hamlet* i 2 127
Bruited. Being bruited once, took fire and heat away From the best-temper'd courage in his troops . . . . . 2 *Hen. IV.* i 1 114
I find thou art no less than fame hath bruited . . 1 *Hen. VI.* ii 3 68
By this great clatter, one of greatest note Seems bruited . *Macbeth* v 7 22
Brundusium. From Tarentum and Brundusium He could so quickly cut the Ionian sea . . . . *Ant. and Cleo.* iii 7 22
Brunt. In the brunt of seventeen battles since He lurch'd all swords of the garland . . . . *Coriolanus* ii 2 104
Brush. A' brushes his hat o' mornings; what should that bode? *Much Ado* iii 2 41
Who in rage forgets Aged contusions and all brush of time . 2 *Hen. VI.* v 3 3
Let grow thy sinews till their knots be strong, And tempt not yet the brushes of the war . . . . *Troi. and Cres.* v 3 34
With one winter's brush Fell from their boughs and left me open *T. of Athens* iv 3 264
Brushed. As wicked dew as e'er my mother brush'd With raven's feather from unwholesome fen . . . . *Tempest* i 2 321
Let their heads be sleekly combed, their blue coats brushed *T. of Shrew* iv 1 94
Brute. Et tu, Brute! Then fall, Cæsar! . . . . *J. Cæsar* iii 1 77
It was a brute part of him to kill so capital a calf . . *Hamlet* iii 2 110
Brutish. Wouldst gabble like A thing most brutish . . . *Tempest* i 2 357
A libertine, As sensual as the brutish sting itself . . *As Y. Like It* ii 7 66
All this from my remembrance brutish wrath Sinfully pluck'd *Rich. III.* ii 1 118
O judgement! thou art fled to brutish beasts . . . *J. Cæsar* iii 2 109
Unnatural, detested, brutish villain! worse than brutish! . . *Lear* i 2 82
Brutus. Her name is Portia, nothing undervalued To Cato's daughter, Brutus' Portia . . . . *Mer. of Venice* i 1 166
His vanities forespent Were but the outside of the Roman Brutus *Hen. V.* ii 4 37
Brutus' bastard hand Stabb'd Julius Cæsar; savage islanders Pompey the Great . . . . 2 *Hen. VI.* iv 1 136
One's Junius Brutus, Sicinius Velutus, and I know not—'Sdeath! *Coriol.* i 1 220
And swear with me, as, with the woful fere And father of that chaste dishonour'd dame, Lord Junius Brutus sware for Lucrece' rape *T. Andron.* iv 1 91
Brutus, I do observe you now of late . . . . . *J. Cæsar* i 2 32
Poor Brutus, with himself at war, Forgets the shows of love to other men i 2 46
Then, Brutus, I have much mistook your passion . . . . . i 2 48
Tell me, good Brutus, can you see your face? . . . . . . i 2 51
It is very much lamented, Brutus, That you have no such mirrors as will turn Your hidden worthiness into your eye . . . . i 2 55
I have heard, Where many of the best respect in Rome, Except immortal Cæsar, speaking of Brutus And groaning underneath this age's yoke, Have wish'd that noble Brutus had his eyes . . . . . . i 2 60
Therefore, good Brutus, be prepared to hear . . . . . . i 2 66
Be not jealous on me, gentle Brutus . . . . i 2 71
I know that virtue to be in you, Brutus, As well as I do know your outward favour . . . . i 2 90
The fault, dear Brutus, is not in our stars, But in ourselves . . . i 2 140
Brutus and Cæsar: what should be in that 'Cæsar'? Why should that name be sounded more than yours? . . . . i 2 142
Conjure with 'em, Brutus will start a spirit as soon as Cæsar . . i 2 147
There was a Brutus once that would have brook'd The eternal devil to keep his state in Rome As easily as a king . . . . i 2 159
Brutus had rather be a villager Than to repute himself a son of Rome Under these hard conditions . . . . i 2 172
I am glad that my weak words Have struck but thus much show of fire from Brutus . . . . i 2 177
Brutus, thou art noble; yet, I see, Thy honourable metal may be wrought i 2 312
Cæsar doth bear me hard; but he loves Brutus . . . . . i 2 317
If I were Brutus now and he were Cassius, He should not humour me . i 2 318
O Cassius, if you could But win the noble Brutus to our party . . i 3 141
Take this paper, And look you lay it in the prætor's chair, Where Brutus may but find it . . . . i 3 144
Throw this In at his window; set this up with wax Upon old Brutus' statue . . . . i 3 146
You and I will yet ere day See Brutus at his house . . . . . i 3 154
'Brutus, thou sleep'st: awake!' Such instigations have been often dropp'd Where I have took them up . . . . ii 1 48
I make thee promise; If the redress will follow, thou receivest Thy full petition at the hand of Brutus! . . . . ii 1 58
Good morrow, Brutus; do we trouble you? . . . . . . ii 1 87
This, Decius Brutus.—He is welcome too. . . . . . . ii 1 95
The morning comes upon's: we'll leave you, Brutus . . . . ii 1 221
You've ungently, Brutus, Stole from my bed . . . . . . ii 1 237
Could it work so much upon your shape As it hath much prevail'd on your condition, I should not know you, Brutus . . . . . . ii 1 255
Brutus is wise, and, were he not in health, He would embrace the means to come by it . . . . ii 1 258
Is Brutus sick? and is it physical To walk unbraced? . . . . ii 1 261
What, is Brutus sick, And will he steal out of his wholesome bed? . ii 1 263
No, my Brutus; You have some sick offence within your mind . . ii 1 267
Kneel not, gentle Portia.—I should not need, if you were gentle Brutus ii 1 279
Within the bond of marriage, tell me, Brutus, Is it excepted I should know no secrets That appertain to you? . . . . ii 1 280
If it be no more, Portia is Brutus' harlot, not his wife . . . . ii 1 287
I grant I am a woman; but withal A woman that Lord Brutus took to wife . . . . ii 1 293
I am not sick, if Brutus have in hand Any exploit worthy the name of honour . . . . ii 1 316

Brutus. I follow you, To do I know not what: but it sufficeth That Brutus leads me on *J. Cæsar* ii 1 334
Here's Decius Brutus, he shall tell them so ii 2 57
What, Brutus, are you stirr'd so early too? ii 2 110
That every like is not the same, O Cæsar, The heart of Brutus yearns to think upon! ii 2 129
Cæsar, beware of Brutus; take heed of Cassius; come not near Casca ii 3 1
Mark well Metellus Cimber: Decius Brutus loves thee not ii 3 4
O Brutus, The heavens speed thee in thine enterprise! ii 4 40
Brutus hath a suit That Cæsar will not grant ii 4 42
Be sudden, for we fear prevention. Brutus, what shall be done? iii 1 20
Look you, Brutus, He draws Mark Antony out of the way iii 1 25
Doth not Brutus bootless kneel? iii 1 75
Go to the pulpit, Brutus.—And Cassius too iii 1 84
Brutus shall lead; and we will grace his heels With the most boldest and best hearts of Rome iii 1 120
Thus, Brutus, did my master bid me kneel iii 1 123
Brutus is noble, wise, valiant, and honest; Cæsar was mighty, bold, royal, and loving iii 1 126
Say I love Brutus, and I honour him; Say I fear'd Cæsar, honour'd him iii 1 128
If Brutus will vouchsafe that Antony May safely come to him iii 1 130
Mark Antony shall not love Cæsar dead So well as Brutus living iii 1 134
Will follow The fortunes and affairs of noble Brutus Thorough the hazards of this untrod state iii 1 135
Let each man render me his bloody hand: First, Marcus Brutus iii 1 185
Next, Caius Cassius, do I take your hand; Now, Decius Brutus, yours iii 1 187
Brutus, a word with you. You know not what you do iii 1 231
I will hear Brutus speak.—I will hear Cassius; and compare their reasons iii 2 8
The noble Brutus is ascended: silence! iii 2 11
To him I say, that Brutus' love to Cæsar was no less than his iii 2 20
If then that friend demand why Brutus rose against Cæsar, this is my answer iii 2 21
I pause for a reply.—None, Brutus, none iii 2 38
I have done no more to Cæsar than you shall do to Brutus iii 2 40
Live, Brutus! live, live!—Bring him with triumph home iii 2 53
Cæsar's better parts Shall be crown'd in Brutus iii 2 57
My countrymen,— Peace, silence! Brutus speaks iii 2 59
What does he say of Brutus?—He says, for Brutus' sake, He finds himself beholding to us all.—'Twere best he speak no harm of Brutus here iii 2 71
The noble Brutus Hath told you Cæsar was ambitious iii 2 82
Here, under leave of Brutus and the rest—For Brutus is an honourable man; So are they all, all honourable men iii 2 86
But Brutus says he was ambitious; And Brutus is an honourable man iii 2 91
I speak not to disprove what Brutus spoke, But here I am to speak what I do know iii 2 105
I should do Brutus wrong, and Cassius wrong, Who, you all know, are honourable men iii 2 128
Through this the well-beloved Brutus stabb'd iii 2 180
Mark how the blood of Cæsar follow'd it, As rushing out of doors, to be resolved If Brutus so unkindly knock'd, or no; For Brutus, as you know, was Cæsar's angel iii 2 184
I am no orator, as Brutus is; But, as you know me all, a plain blunt man iii 2 221
But were I Brutus, And Brutus Antony, there were an Antony Would ruffle up your spirits iii 2 230
We'll burn the house of Brutus.—Away, then! iii 2 236
Brutus and Cassius Are rid like madmen through the gates of Rome iii 2 273
Come, brands, ho! fire-brands: to Brutus', to Cassius' iii 3 41
Brutus and Cassius Are levying powers: we must straight make head iv 1 41
Brutus, this sober form of yours hides wrongs iv 2 40
You know that you are Brutus that speak this, Or, by the gods, this speech were else your last iv 3 13
Brutus, bay not me; I'll not endure it: you forget yourself iv 3 28
You wrong me, Brutus; I said, an elder soldier, not a better iv 3 55
When Marcus Brutus grows so covetous, To lock such rascal counters from his friends iv 3 79
Brutus hath rived my heart iv 3 85
A friend should bear his friend's infirmities, But Brutus makes mine greater iv 3 87
Hath Cassius lived To be but mirth and laughter to his Brutus? iv 3 114
O Brutus!—What's the matter?—Have not you love enough to bear with me? iv 3 118
Henceforth, When you are over-earnest with your Brutus, He'll think your mother chides iv 3 122
Bear with him, Brutus; 'tis his fashion iv 3 135
I cannot drink too much of Brutus' love iv 3 162
Never come such division 'tween our souls! Let it not, Brutus iv 3 236
Good night, good brother.—Good night, Lord Brutus iv 3 238
Speak to me what thou art.—Thy evil spirit, Brutus iv 3 282
In your bad strokes, Brutus, you give good words v 1 30
Flatterers! Now, Brutus, thank yourself v 1 45
I was not born to die on Brutus' sword v 1 58
Now, most noble Brutus, The gods to-day stand friendly v 1 93
Think not, thou noble Roman, That ever Brutus will go bound to Rome v 1 112
For ever, and for ever, farewell, Brutus! If we do meet again, we'll smile indeed v 1 120
O Cassius, Brutus gave the word too early v 3 5
Octavius Is overthrown by noble Brutus' power v 3 52
Piercing steel and darts envenomed Shall be as welcome to the ears of Brutus As tidings of this sight v 3 77
Take this garland on thy brow; Thy Brutus bid me give it thee v 3 86
I am Brutus, Marcus Brutus, I; Brutus, my country's friend; know me for Brutus! v 4 7
Kill Brutus, and be honour'd in his death v 4 14
Tell Antony, Brutus is ta'en.—I'll tell the news v 4 16
Brutus is safe enough: I dare assure thee that no enemy Shall ever take alive the noble Brutus v 4 20
When you do find him, or alive or dead, He will be found like Brutus v 4 25
This is not Brutus, friend; but, I assure you, A prize no less in worth v 4 26
What ill request did Brutus make to thee?—To kill him v 5 11
For Brutus' tongue Hath almost ended his life's history v 5 39
Brutus only overcame himself, And no man else hath honour by his death v 5 56
So Brutus should be found. I thank thee, Brutus, That thou hast proved Lucilius' saying true v 5 58
All that served Brutus, I will entertain them v 5 60
I did enact Julius Cæsar: I was killed i' the Capitol; Brutus killed me *Hamlet* iii 2 109
Since Julius Cæsar, Who at Philippi the good Brutus ghosted *A. and C.* ii 6 13

Brutus. The all-honour'd, honest Roman, Brutus, With the arm'd rest, courtiers of beauteous freedom *Ant. and Cleo.* ii 6 16
He wept When at Philippi he found Brutus slain iii 2 56
I struck The lean and wrinkled Cassius; and 'twas I That the mad Brutus ended iii 11 38

Bubble. Where I have seen corruption boil and bubble *Meas. for Meas.* v 1 320
Seeking the bubble reputation Even in the cannon's mouth *As Y. Like It* ii 7 152
On my life, my lord, a bubble *All's Well* iii 6 5
That beads of sweat have stood upon thy brow, Like bubbles in a late-disturbed stream *1 Hen. IV.* ii 3 62
A dream of what thou wert, a breath, a bubble, A sign of dignity *Richard III.* iv 4 88
The earth hath bubbles, as the water has, And these are of them *Macbeth* i 3 79
Double, double toil and trouble; Fire burn, and cauldron bubble iv 1 11
For a charm of powerful trouble, Like a hell-broth boil and bubble iv 1 19
Do but blow them to their trial, the bubbles are out *Hamlet* v 2 202

Bubbling. A crimson river of warm blood, Like to a bubbling fountain stirr'd with wind *T. Andron.* ii 4 23

Bubukle. His face is all bubukles, and whelks, and knobs *Hen. V.* iii 6 108

Buck! I would I could wash myself of the buck! Buck, buck, buck! Ay, buck; I warrant you, buck; and of the season too *Mer. Wives* iii 3 167
Divide me like a bribe buck, each a haunch v 5 27
It would make a man mad as a buck, to be so bought and sold *C. of Err.* iii 1 72
I assure ye, it was a buck of the first head *L. L. Lost* iv 2 10
She washes bucks here at home *2 Hen. VI.* iv 2 51
For, O, love's bow Shoots buck and doe *Troi. and Cres.* iii 1 127

Buck-basket. Quickly, quickly! Is the buck-basket— I warrant *Mer. Wives* iii 3 2
They conveyed me into a buck-basket.—A buck-basket!—By the Lord, a buck-basket! iii 5 88
This 'tis to be married! this 'tis to have linen and buck-baskets! iii 5 145
He hath enjoyed nothing of Ford's but his buck-basket, his cudgel v 5 117

Bucket. To dive like buckets in concealed wells *K. John* v 2 139
Like a deep well That owes two buckets, filling one another, The emptier ever dancing in the air, The other down, unseen and full of water: That bucket down and full of tears am I *Richard II.* iv 1 185
Swifter than he that gibbets on the brewer's bucket *2 Hen. IV.* iii 2 283
Now, sir, a new link to the bucket must needs be had v 1 23

Bucking. He may creep in here; and throw foul linen upon him, as if it were going to bucking *Mer. Wives* iii 3 140

Buckingham. Somerset, Buckingham, And grumbling York *2 Hen. VI.* i 3 72
Show some reason, Buckingham, Why Somerset should be preferred in this i 3 116
Lord Buckingham, methinks, you watch'd her well i 4 58
What tidings with our cousin Buckingham? ii 1 165
Wink at the Duke of Suffolk's insolence, At Beaufort's pride, at Somerset's ambition, At Buckingham and all the crew of them ii 2 72
Sharp Buckingham unburthens with his tongue The envious load that lies upon his heart iii 1 156
What, Buckingham and Clifford, are ye so brave? iv 8 20
Why, Buckingham, is the traitor Cade surprised? iv 9 8
Buckingham, go and meet him, And ask him what's the reason of these arms iv 9 36
Whom have we here? Buckingham, to disturb me? v 1 12
Humphrey of Buckingham, I accept thy greeting. Art thou a messenger? v 1 15
Buckingham, I prithee, pardon me, That I have given no answer v 1 32
Then, Buckingham, I do dismiss my powers v 1 44
Buckingham, doth York intend no harm to us, That thus he marcheth with thee arm in arm? v 1 56
See, Buckingham, Somerset comes with the queen v 1 83
Call Buckingham, and bid him arm himself.—Call Buckingham, and all the friends thou hast, I am resolved for death or dignity v 1 192
Duke of Buckingham Is either slain or wounded dangerously *3 Hen. VI.* i 1 10
In Buckingham, Northampton and in Leicestershire, shalt find Men iv 8 14
Here come the lords of Buckingham and Derby *Richard III.* i 3 17
The Duke of Buckingham and I Are come from visiting his majesty i 3 31
O princely Buckingham, I'll kiss thy hand, In sign of league and amity i 3 280
O Buckingham, take heed of yonder dog! i 3 289
What doth she say, my Lord of Buckingham? i 3 295
I do beweep to many simple gulls; Namely, to Hastings, Derby, Buckingham i 3 329
Yourself are not exempt in this, Nor your son Dorset, Buckingham, nor you ii 1 19
Now, princely Buckingham, seal thou this league With thy embracements ii 1 29
Whenever Buckingham doth turn his hate On you or yours, but with all duteous love Doth cherish you and yours, God punish me! ii 1 32
A pleasing cordial, princely Buckingham, Is this thy vow ii 1 41
My noble cousin Buckingham, If ever any grudge were lodged between us ii 1 64
Why with some little train, my Lord of Buckingham? ii 2 123
I say with noble Buckingham, That it is meet so few should fetch the prince ii 2 138
Who hath committed them?—The mighty dukes Gloucester and Buckingham ii 4 45
My Lord of Buckingham, if my weak oratory Can from his mother win the Duke of York, Anon expect him here iii 1 37
I'll tell you what, my cousin Buckingham,— What, my gracious lord? iii 1 89
Myself and my good cousin Buckingham Will to your mother iii 1 137
Who, as thou know'st, are dear To princely Richard and to Buckingham iii 2 70
Then cursed she Hastings, then cursed she Buckingham, Then cursed she Richard iii 3 17
Cousin of Buckingham, a word with you iii 4 37
Cousin of Buckingham, and you sage, grave men iii 7 227
Cousin of Buckingham!—My gracious sovereign?—Give me thy hand iv 2 1
O Buckingham, now do I play the touch, To try if thou be current gold indeed iv 2 8
High-reaching Buckingham grows circumspect iv 2 31
The deep-revolving witty Buckingham No more shall be the neighbour to my counsel iv 2 42
Buckingham, back'd with the hardy Welshman, Is in the field iv 3 47
Ely with Richmond troubles me more near Than Buckingham and his rash-levied army iv 3 50
The petty rebel, dull-brain'd Buckingham iv 4 332
There they hull, expecting but the aid Of Buckingham to welcome them iv 4 439
Stirr'd up by Dorset, Buckingham, and Ely, He makes for England iv 4 468
The army of the Duke of Buckingham— Out on you, owls! iv 4 508
Buckingham's army is dispersed and scatter'd iv 4 513
They came from Buckingham Upon his party iv 4 527

Buckingham. My liege, the Duke of Buckingham is taken *Richard III.* iv 4 533
Some one take order Buckingham be brought To Salisbury . iv 4 539
In the battle think on Buckingham, And die in terror of thy guiltiness! v 3 169
The Duke of Buckingham's surveyor, ha? Where's his examination? *Hen. VIII.* i 1 115
And Buckingham Shall lessen this big look . . . . . . i 1 118
I am the shadow of poor Buckingham, Whose figure even this instant cloud puts on, By darkening my clear sun. i 1 224
Let be call'd before us That gentleman of Buckingham's. . . i 2 5
I am sorry that the Duke of Buckingham Is run in your displeasure . i 2 109
Relate what you, Most like a careful subject, have collected Out of the Duke of Buckingham . . . . i 2 131
To the hall, to hear what shall become Of the great Duke of Buckingham ii 1 3
Call him bounteous Buckingham, The mirror of all courtesy . . ii 1 52
You few that loved me, And dare be bold to weep for Buckingham . ii 1 72
If he speak of Buckingham, pray, tell him You met him half in heaven ii 1 87
When I came hither, I was lord high constable And Duke of Buckingham ii 1 103
Henry of Buckingham, Who first raised head against usurping Richard ii 1 107
Thy ambition, Thou scarlet sin, robb'd this bewailing land Of noble Buckingham, my father-in-law . . . . iii 2 256
At our last encounter, The Duke of Buckingham came from his trial . iv 1 5
Buckle. The stretching of a span Buckles in his sum of age *As Y. Like It* iii 2 140
As the wretch, whose fever-weaken'd joints, Like strengthless hinges, buckle under life . . . . *2 Hen. IV.* i 1 141
You live in great infamy.—He that buckles him in my belt cannot live in less . . . . i 2 157
In single combat thou shalt buckle with me . . . *1 Hen. VI.* i 2 95
And hell too strong for me to buckle with . . . . . v 3 28
I will not bandy with thee word for word, But buckle with thee blows, twice two for one . . . . *3 Hen. VI.* i 4 50
Since you will buckle fortune on my back . . . *Richard III.* iii 7 228
Your friends are up, and buckle on their armour . . . . v 3 211
Buckle in a waist most fathomless With spans and inches *Troi. and Cres.* ii 2 30
His stubborn buckles, With these your white enchanting fingers touch'd iii 1 163
He cannot buckle his distemper'd cause Within the belt of rule *Macbeth* v 2 15
His captain's heart, Which in the scuffles of great fights hath burst The buckles on his breast . . . . . . *Ant. and Cleo.* i 1 8
Buckled below fair knighthood's bending knee *Mer. Wives* v 5 76
A pair of boots that have been candle-cases, one buckled, another laced, an old rusty sword . . . . . . *T. of Shrew* iii 2 46
Whose armour conscience buckled on . . . . *K. John* ii 1 564
Too rashly plotted: all our general force Might with a sally of the very town Be buckled with . . . . *1 Hen. VI.* iv 4 5
When we have our armours buckled on . . . *Troi. and Cres.* v 3 46
Is not this buckled well?—Rarely, rarely . . *Ant. and Cleo.* iv 4 11
Buckler. I give thee the bucklers.—Give us the swords; we have bucklers of our own . . . . *Much Ado* v 2 17
I'll buckler thee against a million . . . . *T. of Shrew* iii 2 241
My buckler cut through and through; my sword hacked *1 Hen. IV.* ii 4 186
But that the guilt of murder bucklers thee . . *2 Hen. VI.* iii 2 216
Can Oxford, that did ever fence the right, Now buckler falsehood with a pedigree? . . . . *3 Hen. VI.* iii 3 99
Bucklersbury. Smell like Bucklersbury in simple time . *Mer. Wives* iii 3 79
Buckram. I have cases of buckram for the nonce . . *1 Hen. IV.* i 2 201
Two I am sure I have paid, two rogues in buckram suits . . ii 4 213
Four rogues in buckram let drive at me— What, four? thou saidst but two even now . . . . ii 4 217
There were but four even now.—In buckram?—Ay, four, in buckram suits . . . . ii 4 227
It is worth the listening to. These nine in buckram that I told thee of ii 4 236
O monstrous! eleven buckram men grown out of two! . . . ii 4 243
Thou say, thou serge, nay, thou buckram lord! . *2 Hen. VI.* iv 7 28
Buck-washing. You were best meddle with buck-washing *Mer. Wives* iii 3 166
Bud. In the sweetest bud The eating canker dwells . *T. G. of Ver.* i 1 42
The most forward bud Is eaten by the canker ere it blow . . i 1 45
Blasting in the bud, Losing his verdure even in the prime . . i 1 48
As Dian in her orb, As chaste as is the bud ere it be blown . *Much Ado* iv 1 59
Fair ladies mask'd are roses in their bud . . . *L. L. Lost* v 2 295
When wheat is green, when hawthorn buds appear . . *M. N. Dream* i 1 185
An odorous chaplet of sweet summer buds Is, as in mockery, set . ii 1 110
Some to kill cankers in the musk-rose buds . . . . . . ii 2 3
That same dew, which sometime on the buds Was wont to swell like round and orient pearls . . . . iv 1 58
Dian's bud o'er Cupid's flower Hath such force and blessed power . iv 1 78
Confounds thy fame as whirlwinds shake fair buds . *T. of Shrew* v 2 140
Let concealment, like a worm i' the bud, Feed on her damask cheek *T. Night* ii 4 114
Make conceive a bark of baser kind By bud of nobler race . *W. Tale* iv 4 95
Now will canker sorrow eat my bud . . . . . *K. John* iii 4 82
Live so in hope as in an early spring We see the appearing buds *2 Hen. IV.* i 3 39
Armed in their stings, Make boot upon the summer's velvet buds *Hen. V.* i 2 194
Thus are my blossoms blasted in the bud And caterpillars eat my leaves away; But I will remedy this gear ere long . *2 Hen. VI.* iii 1 89
As is the bud bit with an envious worm . . . . *Rom. and Jul.* i 1 157
Even such delight Among fresh female buds . . . . . . i 2 29
This bud of love, by summer's ripening breath, May prove a beauteous flower when next we meet . . . . ii 2 121
See, my women! Against the blown rose may they stop their nose That kneel'd unto the buds . . . . *Ant. and Cleo.* iii 13 40
Comes in my father And like the tyrannous breathing of the north Shakes all our buds from growing . . . . *Cymbeline* i 3 37
With her neeld composes Nature's own shape, of bud, bird, branch or berry . . . . *Pericles* v Gower 6
Budded. Which is budded out . . . . . . *Hen. VIII.* i 1 94
Budding. Young budding virgin, fair and fresh and sweet *T. of Shrew* iv 5 37
And all the budding honours on thy crest I'll crop, to make a garland for my head . . . . *1 Hen. IV.* v 4 72
Budge. They cannot budge till you release . . . *Tempest* v 1 11
'Budge,' says the fiend. 'Budge not,' says my conscience. 'Conscience,' say I, 'you counsel well' . . . *Mer. of Venice* ii 2 20
I'll not budge an inch, boy: let him come, and kindly . *T. of Shrew* Ind. 1 14
But afoot he will not budge a foot.—Yes, Jack, upon instinct *1 Hen. IV.* ii 4 388
Stand thou back; I will not budge a foot. . . . *1 Hen. VI.* i 3 38
Here pitch our battle; hence we will not budge . *3 Hen. VI.* v 4 66
The mouse ne'er shunn'd the cat as they did budge . *Coriolanus* i 6 44
Let them gaze; I will not budge for no man's pleasure, I *Rom. and Jul.* iii 1 58
Must I budge? Must I observe you? must I stand and crouch Under your testy humour? . . . . *J. Cæsar* iv 3 44
Come, come, and sit you down; you shall not budge . . *Hamlet* iii 4 18
Budger. Let the first budger die the other's slave! . . . *Coriolanus* i 8 5

Budget. I come to her in white, and cry 'mum;' she cries 'budget' *Mer. Wives* v 2 7; v 5 210
What needs either your 'mum' or her 'budget'? . . . . . v 2 10
If tinkers may have leave to live, And bear the sow-skin budget *W. Tale* iv 3 20
Buff. A wolf, nay, worse, a fellow all in buff *Com. of Errors* iv 2 36
He's in a suit of buff which 'rested him . . . . . . iv 2 45
And is not a buff jerkin a most sweet robe of durance? . *1 Hen. IV.* i 2 48
What a plague have I to do with a buff jerkin? . . . . . i 2 52
Buffet. And so buffets himself on the forehead . . . *Mer. Wives* iv 2 25
He did buffet thee and in his blows Denied my house for his *C. of Err.* ii 2 160
Not a word of his But buffets better than a fist . . *K. John* ii 1 465
O, I could divide myself and go to buffets! . . . *1 Hen. IV.* ii 3 35
If I might buffet for my love, or bound my horse for her favours *Hen. V.* v 2 146
The torrent roar'd, and we did buffet it With lusty sinews *J. Cæsar* i 2 107
Whom the vile blows and buffets of the world Have so incensed *Macbeth* iii 1 109
A man that fortune's buffets and rewards Hast ta'en with equal thanks *Hamlet* iii 2 72
And stand the buffet With knaves that smell of sweat *Ant. and Cleo.* i 4 20
Buffeting. Why, then, it is like, if there come a hot June and this civil buffeting hold . . . . *1 Hen. IV.* ii 4 397
Bug. Tush, tush! fear boys with bugs . . . . *T. of Shrew* i 2 211
Spare your threats: The bug which you would fright me with I seek *W. Tale* iii 2 93
Warwick was a bug that fear'd us all . . . . *3 Hen. VI.* v 2 2
With, ho! such bugs and goblins in my life . . . *Hamlet* v 2 22
Those that would die or ere resist are grown The mortal bugs o' the field.— This was strange chance . . . . *Cymbeline* v 3 51
Bugbear. Would he not, a naughty man, let it sleep? a bugbear take him! *Troi. and Cres.* iv 2 34
Bugle. I will have a recheat winded in my forehead, or hang my bugle in an invisible baldrick . . . . *Much Ado* i 1 243
Your black silk hair, Your bugle eyeballs . . . . *As Y. Like It* iii 5 47
Bugle bracelet, necklace amber, Perfume for a lady's chamber *W. Tale* iv 4 224
Build. To build upon a foolish woman's promise . . *Mer. Wives* iii 5 42
Sparrows must not build in his house-eaves . . *Meas. for Meas.* iii 2 186
Will it serve for any model to build mischief on? . . . *Much Ado* i 3 48
Like the martlet, Builds in the weather on the outward wall *Mer. of Ven.* ii 9 29
'Tis only title thou disdain'st in her, the which I can build up *All's Well* ii 3 125
Then, build me thy fortunes upon the basis of valour . . *T. Night* iii 2 35
If I mistake In those foundations which I build upon, The centre is not big enough to bear A school-boy's top . . . . *W. Tale* ii 1 101
When the kite builds, look to lesser linen. . . . . . . iv 3 23
When we mean to build, We first survey the plot . . . *2 Hen. IV.* i 3 41
Like one that draws the model of a house Beyond his power to build it i 3 59
That you should have an inch of any ground To build a grief on . iv 1 110
A pretty plot, well chosen to build upon! . . . . *2 Hen. VI.* i 4 59
In thy shoulder do I build my seat . . . . . *3 Hen. VI.* ii 6 100
Did Julius Cæsar build that place [the Tower], my lord? *Richard III.* iii 1 69
Who builds his hopes in air of your good looks, Lives like a drunken sailor on a mast . . . . iii 4 100
Nor build their evils on the graves of great men . . *Hen. VIII.* ii 1 67
A kiss in fee-farm! build there, carpenter . . . *Troi. and Cres.* iii 2 53
O, why should nature build so foul a den? . . . . *T. Andron.* iv 1 59
To build his fortune I will strain a little, For 'tis a bond in men *T. of A.* i 1 143
Thou shalt build from men; Hate all, curse all, show charity to none . iv 3 533
He must build churches, then; or else shall he suffer not thinking on *Ham.* iii 2 142
What is he that builds stronger than either the mason, the shipwright, or the carpenter?—The gallows-maker . . . . v 1 46
Who builds stronger than a mason, a shipwright, or a carpenter? . . v 1 57
If on my credit you dare build so far . . . . . . *Lear* iii 1 35
And bawds and whores do churches build . . . . . . iii 2 90
Take no notice, nor build yourself a trouble Out of his scattering and unsure observance . . . . *Othello* iii 3 150
Even from this instant do build on thee a better opinion than ever before iv 2 208
The cuckoo builds not for himself . . . . . *Ant. and Cleo.* ii 6 28
Build his statue to make him glorious . . . . *Pericles* ii Gower 14
Builded. The piece of virtue, which is set Betwixt us as the cement of our love, To keep it builded . . . . . . *Ant. and Cleo.* iii 2 30
Buildeth. An habitation giddy and unsure Hath he that buildeth on the vulgar heart . . . . *2 Hen. IV.* i 3 90
Our aery buildeth in the cedar's top, And dallies with the wind *Rich. III.* i 3 264
Your aery buildeth in our aery's nest . . . . i 3 270
Building. Leave not the mansion so long tenantless, Lest, growing ruinous, the building fall . . . . *T. G. of Ver.* v 4 9
Peruse the traders, gaze upon the buildings . . *Com. of Errors* i 2 13
Shall love, in building, grow so ruinous? . . . . . . iii 2 4
Surveys The singing masons building roofs of gold . . *Hen. V.* i 2 198
Thy sumptuous buildings and thy wife's attire Have cost a mass of public treasury . . . . *2 Hen. VI.* i 3 133
The strong base and building of my love Is as the very centre of the earth, Drawing all things to it . . . . *Troi. and Cres.* iv 2 109
I have lived To see inherited my very wishes And the buildings of my fancy: only There's one thing wanting . . . *Coriolanus* ii 1 216
I earnestly did fix mine eye Upon the wasted building . *T. Andron.* v 1 23
Who can speak broader than he that has no house to put his head in? such may rail against great buildings . . . . . *T. of Athens* iii 4 65
Stole thence The life o' the building!—What is't you say? . *Macbeth* ii 3 74
May all the building in my fancy pluck Upon my hateful life! . *Lear* iv 2 86
The ruin speaks that sometime It was a worthy building . *Cymbeline* iv 2 355
I am clothed in steel; And, spite of all the rapture of the sea, This jewel holds his building on my arm . . . . *Pericles* ii 1 162
Like goodly buildings left without a roof Soon fall to ruin . . . ii 4 36
Built. And built so shelving that one cannot climb it *T. G. of Ver.* iii 1 115
Like a fair house built on another man's ground . . *Mer. Wives* ii 2 224
His apparel is built upon his back . . . . . . *2 Hen. IV.* iii 2 155
I have built Two chantries, where the sad and solemn priests Sing still for Richard's soul. . . . . *Hen. V.* iv 1 317
Thou hast caused printing to be used, and, contrary to the king, his crown and dignity, thou hast built a paper-mill . *2 Hen. VI.* iv 7 41
Is it upon record, or else reported Successively from age to age, he built it?—Upon record . . . . *Richard III.* iii 1 73
On him erect A second hope, as fairly built as Hector *Troi. and Cres.* iv 5 109
Ladies, you deserve To have a temple built you . . . *Coriolanus* v 3 207
He was a gentleman on whom I built An absolute trust . . *Macbeth* i 4 13
Thou dost ill to say the gallows is built stronger than the church *Hamlet* v 1 54
Swallows have built In Cleopatra's sails their nests . . . *Ant. and Cleo.* iv 12 3
What shalt thou expect, To be depender on a thing that leans, Who cannot be new built? . . . . *Cymbeline* i 5 59
Antiochus the Great Built up, this city, for his chiefest seat *Pericles* i Gower 18
Hath built Lord Cerimon Such strong renown as time shall ne'er decay . iii 2 47

Bulk. All the more it seeks to hide itself, The bigger bulk it shows *Tempest* iii 1 81
My authority bears of a credent bulk . . . *Meas. for Meas.* iv 4 29
A bawbling vessel was he captain of, For shallow draught and bulk unprizable . . . *T. Night* v 1 58
She is spread of late Into a goodly bulk . . . *W. Tale* ii 1 20
Grew by our feeding to so great a bulk . . . *1 Hen. IV.* v 1 62
Care I for the limb, the thewes, the stature, bulk, and big assemblance of a man! Give me the spirit . . . *2 Hen. IV.* iii 2 277
Smother'd it within my panting bulk, Which almost burst to belch it . . . *Richard III.* i 4 40
I wonder That such a keech can with his very bulk Take up the rays o' the beneficial sun . . . *Hen. VIII.* i 1 55
The sea being smooth, How many shallow bauble boats dare sail Upon her patient breast, making their way With those of nobler bulk! . . . *Troi. and Cres.* i 3 37
Though the great bulk Achilles be thy guard, I'll cut thy throat . . . iv 4 130
Stalls, bulks, windows, Are smother'd up, leads fill'd . . . *Coriolanus* ii 1 226
I am rapt and cannot cover The monstrous bulk of this ingratitude With any size of words . . . *T. of Athens* v 1 68
For nature, crescent, does not grow alone In thews and bulk . . . *Hamlet* i 3 12
A sigh so piteous and profound As it did seem to shatter all his bulk . . . ii 1 95
Here, stand behind this bulk; straight will he come . . . *Othello* v 1 1
With half the bulk o' the world play'd as I pleased . . . *Ant. and Cleo.* iii 11 64

Bull. We heard a hollow burst of bellowing Like bulls, or rather lions . . . *Tempest* ii 1 312
Dew-lapp'd like bulls, whose throats had hanging at 'em Wallets of flesh iii 3 45
Remember, Jove, thou wast a bull for thy Europa . . . *Mer. Wives* v 5 3
In time the savage bull doth bear the yoke.—The savage bull may; but if ever the sensible Benedick bear it, pluck off the bull's horns and set them in my forehead . . . *Much Ado* i 1 263
When shall we set the savage bull's horns on the sensible Benedick's head? . . . v 1 184
I think he thinks upon the savage bull . . . v 4 43
Bull Jove, sir, had an amiable low . . . v 4 48
Some such strange bull leap'd your father's cow . . . v 4 49
Be it on lion, bear, or wolf, or bull . . . *M. N. Dream* ii 1 180
Crook-knee'd, and dew-lapp'd like Thessalian bulls . . . iv 1 127
Jupiter Became a bull, and bellow'd . . . *W. Tale* iv 4 28
You dried neat's tongue, you bull's pizzle, you stock-fish! *1 Hen. IV.* ii 4 271
Wanton as youthful goats, wild as young bulls . . . iv 1 103
Even such kin as the parish heifers are to the town bull . *2 Hen. IV.* ii 2 172
From a God to a bull? a heavy descension! it was Jove's case . . . ii 2 192
All your friends are fled, And Warwick rages like a chafed bull *3 Hen. VI.* ii 5 126
The goodly transformation of Jupiter there, his brother, the bull . . . *Troi. and Cres.* v 1 60
Now, bull! now, dog! 'Loo, Paris, 'loo! . . . v 7 10
The bull has the game: ware horns, ho! . . . v 7 12
The Bull, being gall'd, gave Aries such a knock . . . *T. Andron.* iv 3 71
But where the bull and cow are both milk-white, They never do beget a coal-black calf . . . v 1 31

Bull-bearing Milo his addition yield To sinewy Ajax . . . *Troi. and Cres.* ii 3 258

Bull-beeves. They want their porridge and their fat bull-beeves *1 Hen. VI.* i 2 9

Bull-calf. And still run and roared, as ever I heard bull-calf *1 Hen. IV.* ii 4 287
Peter Bullcalf o' the green!—Yea, marry, let's see Bullcalf *2 Hen. IV.* iii 2 183
'Fore God, a likely fellow! Come, prick me Bullcalf till he roar again . iii 2 187
I have three pound to free Mouldy and Bullcalf . . . iii 2 261
Do you choose for me.—Marry, then, Mouldy, Bullcalf, Feeble and Shadow . . . iii 2 266
For your part, Bullcalf, grow till you come unto it . . . iii 2 270

Bullen. An 't please your grace, Sir Thomas Bullen's daughter *Hen. VIII.* i 4 92
A creature of the queen's, Lady Anne Bullen . . . iii 2 36
Anne Bullen! No; I'll no Anne Bullens for him: There's more in 't than fair visage. Bullen! No, we'll no Bullens . . . iii 2 87

Bullet. Quips and sentences and these paper bullets of the brain *M. Ado* ii 3 249
He reputes me a cannon; and the bullet, that's he . . . *L. L. Lost* iii 1 65
Their conceits have wings Fleeter than arrows, bullets, wind, thought . v 2 261
Instead of bullets wrapp'd in fire . . . , They shoot but calm words *K. John* ii 1 227
Our thunder from the south Shall rain their drift of bullets . . . ii 1 412
I will discharge upon her, Sir John, with two bullets . *2 Hen. IV.* ii 4 124
I'll drink no proofs nor no bullets . . . iv 4 127
Do you think me a swallow, an arrow, or a bullet? . . . iv 3 36
Like to the bullet's grazing, Break out into a second course of mischief . . . *Hen. V.* iv 3 105
O, were mine eye-balls into bullets turn'd, That I in rage might shoot them at your faces! . . . *1 Hen. VI.* iv 7 79

Bullock. Spoken like an honest drover: so they sell bullocks *Much Ado* ii 1 202
How a good yoke of bullocks at Stamford fair? . . . *2 Hen. IV.* iii 2 42

Bully. Discard, bully Hercules; cashier: let them wag . *Mer. Wives* i 3 6
He shall tap: said I well, bully Hector? . . . i 3 11
My hand, bully; thou shalt have egress and regress . . . ii 1 225
Bless thee, bully doctor!—Save you, Master Doctor Caius! . . . ii 3 18
Ha! is he dead, bully stale? is he dead? . . . ii 3 30
Mock-water, in our English tongue, is valour, bully . . . ii 3 63
He will clapper-claw thee tightly, bully . . . ii 3 68
Bully knight! bully Sir John! speak from thy lungs military . . . iv 5 17
Peter Quince,— What sayest thou, bully Bottom? . . . *M. N. Dream* iii 1 8
O sweet bully Bottom! . . . iv 2 19
From heart-string I love the lovely bully . . . *Hen. V.* iv 1 48

Bully-monster. Coragio, bully-monster, coragio! . . . *Tempest* v 1 258

Bully-rook. What says my bully-rook? speak scholarly . . . *Mer. Wives* i 3 2
How now, bully-rook! thou'rt a gentleman . . . ii 1 200
Tell him, cavaleiro-justice; tell him, bully-rook . . . ii 1 207
Mine host o' the Garter, a word with you.—What sayest thou, my bully-rook? . . . ii 1 213

Bulwark. That water-walled bulwark, still secure And confident *K. John* ii 1 27
Some, making the wars their bulwark . . . *Hen. V.* iv 1 173
And I, here, at the bulwark of the bridge . . . *1 Hen. VI.* i 4 67
In whose conquering name Let us resolve to scale their flinty bulwarks ii 1 27
Now, Rouen, I'll shake thy bulwarks to the ground . . . iii 2 17
The prayers of holy saints and wronged souls, Like high-rear'd bulwarks, stand before our faces . . . *Richard III.* v 3 242
If damned custom have not brass'd it so That it be proof and bulwark against sense . . . *Hamlet* iii 4 38

Bum. Troth, and your bum is the greatest thing about you *Meas. for Meas.* ii 1 228
Then slip I from her bum, down topples she . . . *M. N. Dream* ii 1 53
What a coil's here! Serving of becks and jutting-out of bums! *T. of Athens* i 2 237

Bum-baily. Go, Sir Andrew; scout me for him at the corner of the orchard like a bum-baily . . . *T. Night* iii 4 194

Bump. I warrant, it had upon its brow A bump as big as a young cockerel's stone . . . *Rom. and Jul.* i 3 53

Bunch. Vines with clustering bunches growing . . . *Tempest* iv 1 112
In the Bunch of Grapes, where indeed you have a delight to sit *M. for M.* ii 1 133
If I fought not with fifty of them, I am a bunch of radish . *1 Hen. IV.* ii 4 205
Nothing but high shoes, and bunches of keys at their girdles . *2 Hen. IV.* i 2 44

Bunch-backed. The time will come when thou shalt wish for me To help thee curse that poisonous bunch-back'd toad *Richard III.* i 3 246; iv 4 81

Bung. Away, you cut-purse rascal! you filthy bung, away! . *2 Hen. IV.* ii 4 138

Bung-hole. Why may not imagination trace the noble dust of Alexander, till he find it stopping a bung-hole? . . . *Hamlet* v 1 226

Bungle. Do botch and bungle up damnation With patches, colours *Hen V.* ii 2 115

Bunting. I took this lark for a bunting . . . *All's Well* ii 5 7

Buoy. A buoy Almost too small for sight . . . *Lear* iv 6 19

Buoyed. The sea, with such a storm as his bare head In hell-black night endured, would have buoy'd up, And quench'd the stelled fires . iii 7 60

Burden—Burthen. When I have deck'd the sea with drops full salt, Under my burden groan'd . . . *Tempest* i 2 156
Foot it featly here and there; And, sweet sprites, the burthen bear . i 2 381
Vines with clustering bunches growing, Plants with goodly burthen bowing . . . iv 1 113
Let us not burthen our remembrance with A heaviness that's gone . v 1 199
Sing it to the tune of 'Light o' love.'—It is too heavy for so light a tune.—Heavy! belike it hath some burden then? . . . *T. G. of Ver.* i 2 85
A meaner woman was delivered Of such a burden, male twins *Com. of Err.* i 1 56
So befall my soul As this is false he burdens me withal! . . . v 1 209
So help me Heaven! And this is false you burden me withal . . . v 1 268
A wife once call'd Æmilia That bore thee at a burden two fair sons . v 1 343
Thirty-three years have I but gone in travail Of you, my sons; and till this present hour My heavy burthen ne'er delivered . . . v 1 402
Clap's into 'Light o' love;' that goes without a burden . . . *Much Ado* iii 4 45
Why sweat they under burthens? . . . *Mer. of Venice* iv 1 95
Set down your venerable burden And let him feed . . . *As Y. Like It* ii 7 167
I would sing my song without a burden: thou bringest me out of tune . iii 2 261
One lacking the burden of lean and wasteful learning . . . iii 2 341
Knowing no burden of heavy tedious penury . . . iii 2 342
As wealth is burden of my wooing dance . . . *T. of Shrew* i 2 68
Alas! good Kate, I will not burden thee . . . ii 1 203
Dissuade me from believing thee a vessel of too great a burthen *All's Well* ii 3 216
Nine changes of the watery star hath been The shepherd's note since we have left our throne Without a burthen . . . *W. Tale* i 2 3
While she lives My heart will be a burthen to me . . . ii 3 206
With such delicate burthens of dildos and fadings . . . iv 4 195
A usurer's wife was brought to bed of twenty money-bags at a burthen iv 4 267
With burden of our armour here we sweat . . . *K. John* ii 1 92
But, ass, I'll take that burthen from your back, Or lay on that shall make your shoulders crack . . . ii 1 145
Let wives with child Pray that their burthens may not fall this day . iii 1 90
Bear not along The clogging burthen of a guilty soul . . . *Richard II.* i 3 200
I was not made a horse; And yet I bear a burthen like an ass . . . v 5 93
A joint burden laid upon us all . . . *2 Hen. IV.* v 2 55
The poor mechanic porters crowding in Their heavy burdens . *Hen. V.* i 2 201
I rather would have lost my life betimes Than bring a burthen of dishonour home . . . *2 Hen. VI.* iii 1 298
Let them break your backs with burthens, take your houses over your heads . . . iv 8 30
Nor can my tongue unload my heart's great burthen . . . *3 Hen. VI.* ii 1 81
Since you will buckle fortune on my back, To bear her burthen, whether I will or no . . . *Richard III.* iii 7 229
I slip my weary neck, And leave the burthen of it all on thee . . . iv 4 113
A grievous burthen was thy birth to me . . . iv 4 167
If your back Cannot vouchsafe this burthen, 'tis too weak Ever to get a boy.—How you do talk! . . . *Hen. VIII.* ii 3 43
Take heed, lest at once The burthen of my sorrows fall upon ye . . . iii 1 111
Too much honour: O, 'tis a burthen, Cromwell, 'tis a burthen Too heavy for a man that hopes for heaven! . . . iii 2 384
My legs, like loaden branches, bow to the earth, Willing to leave their burthen . . . iv 2 3
God safely quit her of her burthen, and With gentle travail! . . . v 1 70
That matter needless, of importless burden, Divide thy lips . *Tr. and Cr.* i 3 71
'Tis a burden Which I am proud to bear . . . iii 3 36
Who have their provand Only for bearing burdens, and sore blows For sinking under them . . . *Coriolanus* ii 1 268
Under love's heavy burden do I sink . . . *Rom. and Jul.* i 4 22
I am the drudge and toil in your delight, But you shall bear the burden soon at night . . . ii 5 78
Thatch your poor thin roofs With burthens of the dead . *T. of Athens* iv 3 145
I, to bear this, That never knew but better, is some burden . . . iv 3 267
O heavy burthen! . . . *Hamlet* iii 1 54
At whose burthen The anger'd ocean foams . . . *Ant. and Cleo.* ii 6 20
Thy burden at the sea, and call'd Marina For she was yielded there *Per.* v 3 47

Burdened With lesser weight but not with lesser woe *Com. of Errors* i 1 108
Were we burden'd with like weight of pain, As much or more we should ourselves complain . . . ii 1 36
My burthen'd heart would break, Should I not curse them *2 Hen. VI.* iii 2 320
Now thy proud neck bears half my burthen'd yoke . *Richard III.* iv 4 111

Burdening. Weak shoulders, overborne with burthening grief *1 Hen VI.* ii 5 10

Burdenous. His burthenous taxations notwithstanding . *Richard II.* ii 1 260

Bur-docks, hemlock, nettles, cuckoo-flowers . . . *Lear* iv 4 4

Burgher. But that a wise burgher put in for them . *Meas. for Meas.* i 2 103
With portly sail, Like signiors and rich burghers on the flood *Mer. of Ven.* i 1 10
The poor dappled fools, Being native burghers of this desert city . . . *As Y. Like It* ii 1 23

Burglary. Flat burglary as ever was committed . . . *Much Ado* iv 2 52

Burgomasters and great oneyers, such as can hold in . *1 Hen. IV.* ii 1 84

Burgonet. That I'll write upon thy burgonet . . . *2 Hen. VI.* v 1 200
I'll wear aloft my burgonet, As on a mountain top the cedar shows . v 1 204
From thy burgonet I'll rend thy bear And tread it under foot . . . v 1 208
The demi-Atlas of this earth, the arm And burgonet of men *Ant. and Cleo.* i 5 24

Burgundy. Duke of Brabant, The brother to the Duke of Burgundy . . . *Hen. V.* iv 8 102
We do salute you, Duke of Burgundy; And, princes French, and peers v 2 7
If, Duke of Burgundy, you would the peace, Whose want gives growth to the imperfections Which you have cited . . . v 2 68
My Lord of Burgundy, we'll take your oath, And all the peers' . . . v 2 399
Lord Regent, and redoubted Burgundy . . . *1 Hen. VI.* ii 1 8
The Duke of Burgundy will fast Before he'll buy again at such a rate . iii 2 42
Vow, Burgundy, by honour of thy house . . . iii 2 77
This is a double honour, Burgundy . . . iii 2 116
Warlike and martial Talbot, Burgundy Enshrines thee in his heart . iii 2 118
We will entice the Duke of Burgundy To leave the Talbot and to follow us . . . iii 3 19

Burgundy. A parley with the Duke of Burgundy!—Who craves a parley with the Burgundy? *1 Hen. VI.* iii 3 36
Brave Burgundy, undoubted hope of France! . . . iii 3 41
They set him free without his ransom paid, In spite of Burgundy . iii 3 73
A letter was deliver'd to my hands, Writ to your grace from the Duke of Burgundy.—Shame to the Duke of Burgundy and thee! . iv 1 12
View the letter Sent from our uncle Duke of Burgundy . . . iv 1 49
What! doth my uncle Burgundy revolt? . . . . . iv 1 64
Burgundy, Alençon, Reignier, compass him about . . . iv 4 26
When came George from Burgundy to England? . . *3 Hen. VI.* ii 1 143
He was lately sent From your kind aunt, Duchess of Burgundy . ii 1 146
Edward is escaped from your brother, And fled, as he hears since, to Burgundy . . . . iv 6 79
Doubtless Burgundy will yield him help . . . . . iv 6 90
Pass'd and now repass'd the seas And brought desired help from Burgundy . . . . iv 7 6
Methoughts that I had broken from the Tower, And was embark'd to cross to Burgundy . . . . . . *Richard III.* i 4 10
Attend the lords of France and Burgundy, Gloucester . . *Lear* i 1 35
France and Burgundy, Great rivals in our youngest daughter's love . i 1 46
To whose young love The vines of France and milk of Burgundy Strive to be interess'd . . . . i 1 86
Call France; who stirs? Call Burgundy . . . . . i 1 129
Here's France and Burgundy, my noble lord.—My lord of Burgundy . i 1 191
Right noble Burgundy, When she was dear to us, we did hold her so . i 1 198
My lord of Burgundy, What say you to the lady? . . . . i 1 240
Here I take Cordelia by the hand, Duchess of Burgundy . . i 1 247
Peace be with Burgundy! Since that respects of fortune are his love, I shall not be his wife . . . . i 1 250
Not all the dukes of waterish Burgundy Can buy this unprized precious maid . . . . i 1 261
Be gone Without our grace, our love, our benison. Come, noble Burgundy . . . . i 1 269

Burial. Do all rites That appertain unto a burial . . . *Much Ado* iv 1 210
Damned spirits all, That in crossways and floods have burial . *M. N. Dr.* iii 2 383
Vailing her high-top lower than her ribs To kiss her burial *Mer. of Venice* i 1 29
Take hence the rest, and give them burial here . . *Richard II.* v 5 119
I myself Will see his burial better than his life . . *1 Hen. VI.* ii 5 121
Bear them hence And give them burial as beseems their worth . iv 7 86
Hide his body in some hole, Until the duke take order for his burial *Richard III.* i 4 288
I bring unto their latest home, With burial amongst their ancestors *T. Andron.* i 1 84
Let us give him burial, as becomes . . . . . . i 1 347
Give him burial in his father's grave . . . . . v 3 192
No mournful bell shall ring her burial . . . . . v 3 197
Our wedding cheer to a sad burial feast . . . *Rom. and Jul.* iv 5 87
That this foul deed shall smell above the earth With carrion men, groaning for burial . . . . *J. Cæsar* iii 1 275
According to his virtue let us use him, With all respect and rites of burial . . . . v 5 77
Nor would we deign him burial of his men . . . . *Macbeth* i 2 60
Is she to be buried in Christian burial that wilfully seeks her own salvation?—I tell thee she is . . . . . . *Hamlet* v 1 2
The crowner hath sat on her, and finds it Christian burial . . v 1 5
If this had not been a gentlewoman, she should have been buried out o' Christian burial . . . . v 1 28
Her maiden strewments and the bringing home Of bell and burial . v 1 257
Here many sink, yet those which see them fall Have scarce strength left to give them burial . . . . *Pericles* i 4 49
That all those eyes adored them ere their fall Scorn now their hand should give them burial . . . . ii 4 12

Buried. To weep, like a young wench that had buried her grandam *T. G. of Ver.* ii 1 24
I am sure she is not buried.—Say that she be . . . . iv 2 108
In his grave Assure thyself my love is buried . . . . iv 2 115
His act did not o'ertake his bad intent, And must be buried but as an intent That perish'd by the way . . . *Meas. for Meas.* v 1 457
Hath he not lost much wealth by wreck of sea? Buried some dear friend? *Com. of Errors* v 1 50
She shall be buried with her face upwards . . . *Much Ado* iii 2 70
She lies buried with her ancestors; O, in a tomb where never scandal slept! . . . . v 1 69
I will live in thy heart, die in thy lap and be buried in thy eyes . v 2 105
Beat not the bones of the buried . . . . *L. L. Lost* v 2 667
Where the carcases of many a tall ship lie buried . *Mer. of Venice* iii 1 6
Well, the beginning, that is dead and buried . . *As Y. Like It* i 2 124
Should be buried in highways out of all sanctified limit . . *All's Well* i 1 152
I'll lie with him When I am buried . . . . . . iv 2 73
Buried a wife, mourned for her . . . . iv 3 101
Not to be buried, But quick and in mine arms. . . *W. Tale* iv 4 131
Such grief That words seem'd buried in my sorrow's grave . *Richard II.* i 4 15
By the buried hand of warlike Gaunt . . . . . . iii 3 109
Or I'll be buried in the king's highway, Some way of common trade . iii 3 155
On my heart they tread now whilst I live; And buried once, why not upon my head? . . . . iii 3 159
Great king, within this coffin I present Thy buried fear . . . v 6 31
If I begin the battery once again, I will not leave the half-achieved Harfleur Till in her ashes she lie buried . . . . . *Hen. V.* iii 3 9
Though buried in your dunghills, They shall be famed . . . iv 3 99
In this late-betrayed town Great Cœur-de-lion's heart was buried *1 Hen. VI.* iii 2 83
Between my soul's desire and me—The lustful Edward's title buried *3 Hen. VI.* iii 2 129
And all the clouds that lour'd upon our house In the deep bosom of the ocean buried . . . . *Richard III.* i 1 4
That came too lag to see him buried . . . . . . ii 1 90
But didst thou see them dead?—I did, my lord.—And buried? . iv 3 28
Buried them; But how or in what place I do not know . . . iv 3 29
Buried this sigh in wrinkle of a smile . . . *Troi. and Cres.* i 1 38
Buried one and twenty valiant sons, Knighted in field . . *T. Andron.* i 1 195
He must be buried with his brethren.—And shall, or him we will accompany . . . . i 1 357
And this shall all be buried by my death . . . . . . v 1 67
Where . . . the bones Of all my buried ancestors are pack'd . *R. and J.* iv 3 41
Alack! my child is dead; And with my child my joys are buried . iv 5 64
Our bridal flowers serve for a buried corse . . . . . iv 5 89
And Juliet bleeding, warm, and newly dead, Who here hath lain these two days buried . . . . v 3 176
So his familiars to his buried fortunes Slink all away . . *T. of Athens* iv 2 10

Buried. This breast of mine hath buried Thoughts of great value *J. Cæsar* i 2 49
Their hats are pluck'd about their ears, And half their faces buried in their cloaks . . . . ii 1 74
Our youths and wildness shall no whit appear, But all be buried in his gravity . . . . ii 1 149
I tell you yet again, Banquo's buried; he cannot come out on's grave *Macbeth* v 1 70
That fair and warlike form In which the majesty of buried Denmark Did sometimes march . . . . *Hamlet* i 1 48
Is she to be buried in Christian burial that wilfully seeks her own salvation? . . . . v 1 1
If this had not been a gentlewoman, she should have been buried out o' Christian burial . . . . v 1 28
Who is to be buried in't?—One that was a woman . . . v 1 145
Alexander died, Alexander was buried, Alexander returneth into dust . v 1 232
Be buried quick with her, and so will I . . . . . v 1 302
Lie graveless, till the flies and gnats of Nile Have buried them *A. and C.* iii 13 167
She render'd life, Thy name so buried in her . . . . iv 14 34
She shall be buried by her Antony: No grave upon the earth shall clip in it A pair so famous . . . . v 2 361
When I am dead, For that I am a man, pray see me buried . *Pericles* ii 1 81
Thou that wast born at sea, buried at Tarsus, And found at sea again! v 1 198
O, come, be buried A second time within these arms . . . v 3 43

Burier. And darkness be the burier of the dead! . *2 Hen. IV.* i 1 160

Burly-boned. Steel, if thou turn the edge, or cut not out the burly-boned clown in chines of beef . . . . . *2 Hen. VI.* iv 10 60

Burn. Sometime I'ld divide, And burn in many places . . *Tempest* i 2 199
Teach me how To name the bigger light, and how the less, That burn by day and night . . . . i 2 336
When this burns, 'Twill weep for having wearied you . . . iii 1 18
Burn but his books . . . . iii 2 103
Fire that's closest kept burns most of all . . . *T. G. of Ver.* i 2 30
I tell thee, I care not though he burn himself in love . . . ii 5 56
But qualify the fire's extreme rage, Lest it should burn above the bounds of reason . . . . ii 7 23
The more thou damm'st it up, the more it burns . . . . ii 7 24
Wilt thou aspire to guide the heavenly car And with thy daring folly burn the world? . . . . iii 1 155
We burn daylight: here, read, read . . . . *Mer. Wives* ii 1 54
Let the supposed fairies pinch him sound And burn him with their tapers iv 4 62
I will be like a jack-an-apes also, to burn the knight with my taber . iv 4 68
Burn him, and turn him about, Till candles and starlight and moonshine be out . . . . v 5 105
The capon burns, the pig falls from the spit . *Com. of Errors* i 2 44
'Tis dinner-time,' quoth I; 'My gold!' quoth he: 'Your meat doth burn,' quoth I . . . . ii 1 63
I warrant, her rags and the tallow in them will burn a Poland winter iii 2 100
Light is an effect of fire, and fire will burn; ergo, light wenches will burn iv 3 57
I see, lady, the gentleman is not in your books.—No; an he were, I would burn my study . . . . *Much Ado* i 1 80
And in her eye there hath appear'd a fire, To burn the errors . . iv 1 165
The blood of youth burns not with such excess As gravity's revolt to wantonness . . . . *L. L. Lost* v 2 73
And neigh, and bark, and grunt, and roar, and burn . *M. N. Dream* iii 1 113
This night he means To burn the lodging where you use to lie *As Y. L. It* ii 3 23
The property of rain is to wet and fire to burn . . . . iii 2 28
And burn sweet wood to make the lodging sweet . . *T. of Shrew* Ind. 1 49
I burn, I pine, I perish, Tranio, If I achieve not this young modest girl i 1 160
I' the blaze of youth; When oil and fire, too strong for reason's force, O'erbears it and burns on . . . . *All's Well* v 3 8
Come, come, I'll go burn some sack; 'tis too late to go to bed now *T. Night* ii 3 206
But I have That honourable grief lodged here which burns Worse than tears drown . . . . *W. Tale* ii 1 111
It is an heretic that makes the fire, Not she which burns in't . . ii 3 116
Better burn it now Than curse it then . . . . . . ii 3 156
Since my desires Run not before mine honour, nor my lusts Burn hotter than my faith . . . . iv 4 35
Thy rage shall burn thee up . . . . . . *K. John* iii 1 344
Must you with hot irons burn out both mine eyes? . . . . iv 1 39
I have sworn to do it; And with hot irons must I burn them out . iv 1 59
They burn in indignation . . . . iv 2 103
Ay me! this tyrant fever burns me up . . . . . . v 3 14
Cannot last, For violent fires soon burn out themselves . . *Richard II.* ii 1 34
That hand shall burn in never-quenching fire That staggers thus my person . . . . v 5 109
Whose bosom burns With an incensed fire of injuries . . *2 Hen. IV.* i 3 13
Honest Bardolph, whose zeal burns in his nose . . . . . ii 4 357
She is in hell already, and burns poor souls . . . . . ii 4 366
Impatiently I burn with thy desire . . . . . *1 Hen. VI.* i 2 108
And like thee, Nero, Play on the lute, beholding the towns burn . . i 4 96
Burns under feigned ashes of forged love . . . . . . iii 3 190
Bring forth that sorceress condemn'd to burn . . . . . v 4 1
O, burn her, burn her! hanging is too good . . . . . v 4 33
Now the house of York . . . Burns with revenging fire . *2 Hen. VI.* iv 1 97
Burn all the records of the realm: my mouth shall be the parliament of England . . . . iv 7 16
Ring, bells, aloud; burn, bonfires, clear and bright . . . v 1 3
Take heed, lest by your heat you burn yourselves . . . . v 1 160
My heart for anger burns; I cannot brook it . . . *3 Hen. VI.* i 1 60
And burns me up with flames that tears would quench . . . ii 1 84
Here burns my candle out; ay, here it dies . . . . . ii 6 1
I need not add more fuel to your fire, For well I wot ye blaze to burn them out . . . . v 4 71
Earth gapes, hell burns, fiends roar, saints pray . . *Richard III.* iv 4 75
The lights burn blue. It is now dead midnight . . . . v 3 180
This candle burns not clear: 'tis I must snuff it . . *Hen. VIII.* iii 2 96
Ye blew the fire that burns ye: now have at ye! . . . . v 3 113
Stay the cooling too, or you may chance to burn your lips *Troi. and Cres.* i 1 26
Our firebrand brother, Paris, burns us all . . . . . ii 2 110
Add more coals to Cancer when he burns With entertaining great Hyperion . . . . ii 3 206
Let them hang.—Ay, and burn too . . . . *Coriolanus* iii 2 24
If he could burn us all into one coal, We have deserved it . . iv 6 137
He does sit in gold, his eye Red as 'twould burn Rome . . . v 1 64
Tapers burn so bright and every thing In readiness for Hymenæus *T. Andron.* i 1 324
First thrash the corn, then after burn the straw . . . . ii 3 123
Sorrow concealed, like an oven stopp'd, Doth burn the heart to cinders ii 4 37
If there be devils, would I were a devil, To live and burn in everlasting fire! . . . . v 1 148

Burn. One fire burns out another's burning *Rom. and Jul.* i 2 46
Come, we burn daylight, ho! i 4 43
O, she doth teach the torches to burn bright! i 5 46
This is the place; there, where the torch doth burn v 3 171
Burn, house! sink, Athens! henceforth hated be Of Timon! *T. of Athens* iii 6 114
Be strong in whore, allure him, burn him up iv 3 141
Thou sun, that comfort'st, burn! Speak, and be hang'd v 1 134
Which did flame and burn Like twenty torches join'd *J. Cæsar* i 3 16
Revenge! About! Seek! Burn! Fire! Kill! Slay! iii 2 208
We'll burn the house of Brutus iii 2 236
We'll burn his body in the holy place, And with the brands fire the traitors' houses iii 2 259
How ill this taper burns! iv 3 275
Double, double toil and trouble; Fire burn, and cauldron bubble *Macbeth* iv 1 11
Revenges burn in them v 2 3
When yond same star that's westward from the pole Had made his course to illume that part of heaven Where now it burns *Hamlet* i 1 38
When the blood burns, how prodigal the soul Lends the tongue vows i 3 116
Since frost itself as actively doth burn And reason pandars will iii 4 87
Tears seven times salt, Burn out the sense and virtue of mine eye! iv 5 155
Her eyes are fierce; but thine Do comfort and not burn *Lear* ii 4 176
My snuff and loathed part of nature should Burn itself out iv 6 40
But with a little act upon the blood, Burn like the mines of sulphur *Othello* iii 3 329
Make very forges of my cheeks, That would to cinders burn up modesty iv 2 75
Our overplus of shipping will we burn *Ant. and Cleo.* iii 7 51
Did desire you To burn this night with torches iv 2 41
O sun, Burn the great sphere thou movest in! iv 15 10
That him and his they in his palace burn *Pericles* v 3 Gower 97
Burned. By that fire which burn'd the Carthage queen *M. N. Dream* i 1 173
Art thou god to shepherd turn'd, That a maiden's heart hath burned? *As Y. Like It* iv 3 41
I am burn'd up with inflaming wrath *K. John* iii 1 340
Let my kingdom's rivers take their course Through my burn'd bosom v 7 39
The tackle of my heart is crack'd and burn'd v 7 52
They have burned and carried away all that was in the king's tent *Hen. V.* iv 7 7
The fatal brand Althæa burn'd Unto the prince's heart of Calydon *2 Hen. VI.* i 1 234
The witch in Smithfield shall be burn'd to ashes ii 3 7
When our nuptial day was done, And tapers burn'd to bedward *Coriolanus* i 6 32
What's the news?—Your temples burned in their cement iv 6 85
When I burned in desire to question them further, they made themselves air, into which they vanished *Macbeth* i 5 4
No heretics burn'd, but wenches' suitors *Lear* iii 2 84
The barge she sat in, like a burnish'd throne, Burn'd on the water *Ant. and Cleo.* ii 2 197
Burnet. The freckled cowslip, burnet and green clover *Hen. V.* v 2 49
Burneth. It burneth in the Capels' monument *Rom. and Jul.* v 3 127
The taper burneth in your closet, sir *J. Cæsar* ii 1 35
Burning. Thus have I shunn'd the fire for fear of burning, And drench'd me in the sea *T. G. of Ver.* i 3 78
Love my wife!—With liver burning hot *Mer. Wives* ii 1 121
More grave and wrinkled than the aims and ends Of burning youth *Meas. for Meas.* i 3 6
Let the devil Be sometime honour'd for his burning throne! v 1 295
That light we see is burning in my hall *Mer. of Venice* v 1 89
There is no malice in this burning coal *K. John* iv 1 109
The vaulty top of heaven Figured quite o'er with burning meteors v 2 53
The burning crest Of the old, feeble and day-wearied sun v 4 34
It would allay the burning quality Of that fell poison which assaileth him v 7 8
The front of heaven was full of fiery shapes, Of burning cressets *1 Hen. IV.* iii 1 15
Thou art the Knight of the Burning Lamp iii 3 30
There he is in his robes, burning, burning iii 3 37
The land is burning; Percy stands on high; And either we or they must lower lie iii 3 227
Wanton hours Have brought ourselves into a burning fever *2 Hen. IV.* iv 1 56
He is so shaked of a burning quotidian tertian *Hen. V.* ii 1 124
A' said it was a black soul burning in hell-fire ii 3 44
This is the happy wedding torch That joineth Rouen unto her country-men, But burning fatal to the Talbotites! *1 Hen. VI.* iii 2 28
The burning torch in yonder turret stands iii 2 30
Descend to darkness and the burning lake! False fiend, avoid! *2 Hen. VI.* i 4 42
His father's acts commenced in burning Troy iii 2 118
Thy burning car never had scorch'd the earth *3 Hen. VI.* ii 6 13
A burning devil take them! *Troi. and Cres.* v 2 196
To the wanton spoil Of Phœbus' burning kisses *Coriolanus* ii 1 234
Till he had forged himself a name o' the fire Of burning Rome v 1 15
By the burning tapers of the sky, That shone so brightly *T. Andron.* iv 2 89
I'll dive into the burning lake below, And pull her out of Acheron iv 3 43
Here's the base fruit of his burning lust v 1 43
That baleful burning night When subtle Greeks surprised King Priam's Troy v 3 83
One fire burns out another's burning *Rom. and Jul.* i 2 46
Ere the sun advance his burning eye, The day to cheer ii 3 5
Would have made milch the burning eyes of heaven *Hamlet* ii 2 540
Till our ground, Singeing his pate against the burning zone, Make Ossa like a wart! v 1 305
To have a thousand with red burning spits Come hissing in upon 'em *Lear* iii 6 16
These things sting His mind so venomously, that burning shame Detains him iv 3 48
There's the sulphurous pit, Burning, scalding, stench, consumption iv 6 131
The wind-shaked surge, with high and monstrous mane, Seems to cast water on the burning bear *Othello* ii 1 14
She's, like a liar, gone to burning hell: 'Twas I that kill'd her v 2 129
Take not away the taper, leave it burning *Cymbeline* ii 2 5
A burning torch that's turned upside down; The word, 'Quod me alit, me extinguit' *Pericles* ii 2 32
The cat, with eyne of burning coal iii Gower 5
Burning-glass. The appetite of her eye did seem to scorch me up like a burning-glass! *Mer. Wives* i 3 74
Burnished. Mislike me not for my complexion, The shadow'd livery of the burnish'd sun *Mer. of Venice* ii 1 2
The barge she sat in, like a burnish'd throne, Burn'd on the water *Ant. and Cleo.* ii 2 196
Burnt. I would the lightning had Burnt up those logs that you are en-join'd to pile! *Tempest* iii 1 17
I'll give you a pottle of burnt sack to give me recourse to him *M. Wives* ii 1 223
And let burnt sack be the issue iii 1 112

Burnt. 'Tis burnt; and so is all the meat *T. of Shrew* iv 1 164
I tell thee, Kate, 'twas burnt and dried away iv 1 173
I'll ha' thee burnt.—I care not *W. Tale* ii 3 114
My inch of taper will be burnt and done *Richard II.* i 3 223
Rash bavin wits, Soon kindled and soon burnt *1 Hen. IV.* iii 2 62
And would have told him half his Troy was burnt *2 Hen. IV.* i 1 73
What! you are as a candle, the better part burnt out i 2 178
He should stand in fear of fire, being burnt i' the hand for stealing *2 Hen. VI.* iv 2 67
Better Have burnt that tongue than said so *Hen. VIII.* iii 2 254
You are smelt Above the moon: we must be burnt for you *Coriolanus* v 1 32
Bid Æneas tell the tale twice o'er, How Troy was burnt *T. Andron.* iii 2 28
And these, who often drown'd could never die, Transparent heretics, be burnt for liars! *Rom. and Jul.* i 2 96
Night's candles are burnt out, and jocund day Stands tiptoe on the misty mountain tops iii 5 9
Confined to fast in fires, Till the foul crimes done in my days of nature Are burnt and purged away *Hamlet* i 5 13
Gentle lords, let's part; You see we have burnt our cheeks *Ant. and Cleo.* ii 7 129
Burr. I am a kind of burr; I shall stick *Meas. for Meas.* iv 3 189
Hang off, thou cat, thou burr! vile thing, let loose! *M. N. Dream* iii 2 260
They are but burs, cousin, thrown upon thee in holiday foolery *As Y. L. It* i 3 13
These burs are in my heart.—Hem them away i 3 17
Hateful docks, rough thistles, kecksies, burs *Hen. V.* v 2 52
They are burs, I can tell you; they'll stick where they are thrown *Troi. and Cres.* iii 2 119
Burrow. They will out of their burrows, like conies after rain *Coriolanus* iv 5 226
Burst. Blow, till thou burst thy wind, if room enough! *Tempest* i 1 9
Even now, we heard a hollow burst of bellowing Like bulls, or rather lions ii 1 311
You will not pay for the glasses you have burst?—No, not a denier *T. of Shrew* Ind. 1 8
Hath been often burst and now repaired with knots iii 2 60
How the horses ran away, how her bridle was burst iv 1 83
If my heart were great, 'Twould burst at this *All's Well* iv 3 367
The burst And the ear-deafening voice o' the oracle, Kin to Jove's thunder *W. Tale* iii 1 8
A resolved villain, Whose bowels suddenly burst out *K. John* v 6 30
I cannot speak; if my heart be not ready to burst,—well, sweet Jack, have a care of thyself *2 Hen. IV.* ii 4 410
And then he burst his head for crowding among the marshal's men iii 2 347
Will make him burst his lead and rise from death *1 Hen. VI.* i 1 64
We'll burst them open, if that you come not quickly i 3 28
My breast I'll burst with straining of my courage i 5 10
Had the passions of thy heart burst out, I fear we should have seen decipher'd there More rancorous spite iv 1 183
No, no, my heart will burst, an if I speak: And I will speak, that so my heart may burst *3 Hen. VI.* v 5 59
Smother'd it within my panting bulk, Which almost burst to belch it *Richard III.* i 4 41
I swound to see thee.—Would thou wouldst burst! *T. of Athens* iv 3 373
Then burst his mighty heart *J. Cæsar* iii 2 190
O, answer me! Let me not burst in ignorance *Hamlet* i 4 46
Tell Why thy canonized bones, hearsed in death, Have burst their cerements i 4 48
The instant burst of clamour that she made ii 2 538
Such sheets of fire, such bursts of horrid thunder *Lear* iii 2 46
List a brief tale; And when 'tis told, O, that my heart would burst! v 3 182
'Twixt two extremes of passion, joy and grief, Burst smilingly v 3 199
He fasten'd on my neck, and bellow'd out As he'ld burst heaven v 3 213
Your heart is burst, you have lost half your soul *Othello* i 1 87
In the scuffles of great fights hath burst The buckles on his breast *Ant. and Cleo.* i 1 7
The snatches in his voice, And burst of speaking, were as his *Cymbeline* iv 2 106
Endured a sea That almost burst the deck *Pericles* iv 1 57
Bursting. Such groans That their discharge did stretch his leathern coat Almost to bursting *As Y. Like It* ii 1 38
Burton. My moiety, north from Burton here, In quantity equals not one of yours *1 Hen. IV.* iii 1 96
Burton-heath. Old Sly's son of Burton-heath *T. of Shrew* Ind. 2 19
Bury. I'll break my staff, Bury it certain fathoms in the earth *Tempest* v 1 55
Then in dumb silence will I bury mine [my news] *T. G. of Ver.* iii 1 207
Moonshine and Lion are left to bury the dead *M. N. Dream* v 1 355
In delivering my son from me, I bury a second husband *All's Well* i 1 1
And deeper than oblivion we do bury The incensing relics of it v 3 24
We need no grave to bury honesty *W. Tale* ii 1 155
If there be any of him left, I'll bury it iii 3 136
Away toward Bury, to the Dauphin there! *K. John* iv 3 114
You shall not only take the sacrament To bury mine intents *Richard II.* iv 1 329
To look our dead, and then to bury them *Hen. V.* iv 7 76
Bear hence his body; I will help to bury it *1 Hen. VI.* i 4 87
I summon your grace to his majesty's parliament, Holden at Bury *2 Hen. VI.* ii 4 71
The traitorous Warwick with the men of Bury Set all upon me iii 2 240
There let his head and lifeless body lie, Until the queen his mistress bury it iv 1 143
But in your bride you bury brotherhood *3 Hen. VI.* iv 1 55
In your daughter's womb I bury them *Richard III.* iv 4 423
Doublets that hangmen would Bury with those that wore them *Coriol.* i 5 8
And bury all, which yet distinctly ranges, In heaps and piles of ruin iii 1 206
After your way his tale pronounced shall bury His reasons with his body v 6 58
Bury him where you can; he comes not here *T. Andron.* i 1 354
What, would you bury him in my despite? i 1 361
The Greeks upon advice did bury Ajax That slew himself i 1 379
Well, bury him, and bury me the next i 1 386
He that had wit would think that I had none, To bury so much gold under a tree ii 3 2
Bid him bury it; More hath it merited iii 1 196
Be blithe again, And bury all thy fear in my devices iv 4 112
Whose misadventured piteous overthrows Do with their death bury their parents' strife *Rom. and Jul.* Prol. 8
Bad'st me bury love.—Not in a grave, To lay one in, another out to have ii 3 83
I'll bury thee in a triumphant grave; A grave? O, no! a lantern v 3 83
Thou'rt quick, But yet I'll bury thee *T. of Athens* iv 3 45
Lend me your ears; I come to bury Cæsar, not to praise him *J. Cæsar* iii 2 79
Give me a bowl of wine. In this I bury all unkindness iv 3 159
If charnel-houses and our graves must send Those that we bury back, our monuments Shall be the maws of kites *Macbeth* iii 4 72
If ever thou wilt thrive, bury my body *Lear* iv 6 253
Good sirs, take heart: We'll bury him *Ant. and Cleo.* iv 15 86

Bury. Bury him, And not protract with admiration what Is now due debt *Cymbeline* iv 2 231
And though you took his life, as being our foe, Yet bury him as a prince iv 2 251
Burying. The earth that's nature's mother is her tomb; What is her burying grave that is her womb *Rom. and Jul.* ii 3 10
Who finds her, give her burying; She was the daughter of a king *Pericles* iii 2 72
Burying-place. Be henceforth a burying-place to all that do dwell in this house 2 *Hen. VI.* iv 10 68
Bush. Here's neither bush nor shrub, to bear off any weather at all *Temp.* ii 2 18
My mistress show'd me thee and thy dog and thy bush ii 2 144
We'll a-birding together; I have a fine hawk for the bush *Mer. Wives* iii 3 248
Where is the bush That we must stand and play the murderer in? *L. L. L.* iv 1 7
I have been closely shrouded in this bush And mark'd you both iv 3 137
Over hill, over dale, Thorough bush, thorough brier *M. N. Dream* ii 1 3
One must come in with a bush of thorns and a lanthorn iii 1 61
Through bog, through bush, through brake, through brier iii 1 110
Art thou fled? Speak! In some bush? Where dost thou hide thy head? iii 2 406
Art thou bragging to the stars, Telling the bushes that thou look'st for wars? iii 2 408
In the night, imagining some fear, How easy is a bush supposed a bear! v 1 22
This man, with lanthorn, dog, and bush of thorn, Presenteth Moonshine v 1 136
Be married under a bush like a beggar? *As Y. Like It* iii 3 85
Under which bush's shade A lioness, with udders all drawn dry, Lay couching iv 3 114
If it be true that good wine needs no bush Epil. 4
Yet to good wine they do use good bushes Epil. 6
Madam, myself have limed a bush for her 2 *Hen. VI.* i 3 91
Have all limed bushes to betray thy wings, And, fly thou how thou canst, they'll tangle thee ii 4 54
Suspicion always haunts the guilty mind; The thief doth fear each bush an officer 3 *Hen. VI.* v 6 12
The bird that hath been limed in a bush, With trembling wings misdoubteth every bush v 6 13
The birds chant melody on every bush *T. Andron.* ii 3 12
The bounteous housewife, nature, on each bush Lays her full mess before you. Want! why want? *T. of Athens* iv 3 423
For many miles about There's scarce a bush *Lear* ii 4 305
Which is the way?—I thank you.—By yond bush? *Cymbeline* iv 2 292
Bushel. His reasons are as two grains of wheat hid in two bushels of chaff: you shall seek all day ere you find them *Mer. of Venice* i 1 116
Bushy, Bagot here and Green Observed his courtship *Richard II.* i 4 23
Bushy, what news?—Old John of Gaunt is grievous sick i 4 53
Go, Bushy, to the Earl of Wiltshire straight ii 1 215
To Bristol castle, which they say is held By Bushy, Bagot and their complices ii 3 165
Bushy and Green, I will not vex your souls—Since presently your souls must part your bodies iii 1 2
Where is Bagot? What is become of Bushy? where is Green? iii 2 123
Is Bushy, Green, and the Earl of Wiltshire dead?—Ay, all of them iii 2 141
Busied. They are busied about a counterfeit assurance *T. of Shrew* iv 4 91
Who, busied in his majesty, surveys The singing masons building roofs of gold *Hen. V.* i 2 197
No more than if we heard that England Were busied with a Whitsun morris-dance ii 4 25
How is't with Titus Lartius?—As with a man busied about decrees *Coriolanus* i 6 34
Most are busied when they're most alone *Rom. and Jul.* i 1 134
Busily. Who, as we hear, are busily in arms 1 *Hen. IV.* v 5 38
See how busily she turns the leaves! *T. Andron.* iv 1 45
Business. And then I'll bring thee to the present business *Tempest* i 2 136
Nor set A mark so bloody on the business i 2 142
To do me business in the veins o' the earth i 2 255
There's other business for thee: Come, thou tortoise! when? i 2 315
Be quick, thou'rt best, To answer other business i 2 367
This is no mortal business, nor no sound That the earth owes i 2 406
This swift business I must uneasy make i 2 450
Milan and Naples have Moe widows in them of this business' making ii 1 133
They'll tell the clock to any business that We say befits the hour ii 1 289
Ere supper-time must I perform Much business iii 1 96
But remember—For that's my business to you iii 3 69
There is in this business more than nature Was ever conduct of v 1 243
Do not infest your mind with beating on The strangeness of this business v 1 247
Such a youth That can with some discretion do my business *T. G. of Ver.* iv 4 70
That, indeed, Sir John, is my business *Mer. Wives* ii 5 64
Turn you the key, and know his business of him *Meas. for Meas.* i 4 8
That's my pith of business 'Twixt you and your poor brother i 4 70
My business is a word or two with Claudio iii 1 48
If peradventure he shall ever return to have hearing of this business iii 1 211
The very stream of his life and the business he hath helmed iii 2 151
Late come from the See In special business from his holiness iii 2 233
When you have A business for yourself, pray heaven you then Be perfect v 1 81
My business in this state Made me a looker on here in Vienna v 1 318
As I was then Advertising and holy to your business v 1 388
My present business calls me from you now *Com. of Errors* i 2 29
Because their business still lies out o' door ii 1 11
Besides, I have some business in the town iv 1 35
My business cannot brook this dalliance iv 1 59
Sleep when I am drowsy and tend on no man's business *Much Ado* i 3 18
Whither?—Even to the next willow, about your own business ii 1 195
On serious business, craving quick dispatch *L. L. Lost* ii 1 31
I must employ you in some business Against our nuptial *M. N. Dream* i 1 124
Make no delay: We may effect this business yet ere day iii 2 395
I take it, your own business calls on you *Mer. of Venice* i 1 63
Fare you well: I have some business ii 2 213
Slubber not business for my sake, Bassanio, But stay the very riping of the time ii 8 39
O love, dispatch all business, and be gone! iii 2 325
I'll do the service of a younger man In all your business *As Y. Like It* ii 3 55
My business asketh haste, And every day I cannot come to woo *T. of Shrew* ii 1 115
We mean to look into, And watch our vantage in this business iii 2 146
If you knew my business, You would entreat me rather go than stay iii 2 193
So shall you stay Till you have done your business in the city iv 2 110
This night, We'll pass the business privately and well iv 4 57
Lest you be cony-catched in this business v 1 102
I am so full of businesses, I cannot answer thee acutely *All's Well* i 1 220
Wherein our dearest friend Prejudicates the business i 2 8
The business is for Helen to come hither i 3 100
Business. Will you see her, For that is her demand, and know her business? *All's Well* ii 1 89
Now, fair one, does your business follow us? ii 1 102
I know my business is but to the court.—To the court! ii 2 4
An end, sir; to your business ii 2 65
In such a business give me leave to use The help of mine own eyes ii 3 114
A very serious business calls on him ii 4 41
Prepared I was not For such a business; therefore am I found So much unsettled ii 5 67
Would in so just a business shut his bosom Against our borrowing prayers iii 1 8
He might at some great and trusty business in a main danger fail you iii 6 16
Confidently seems to undertake this business, which he knows is not to be done iii 6 94
I was well born, Nothing acquainted with these businesses iii 7 5
I have to-night dispatched sixteen businesses, a month's length a-piece iv 3 98
If the business be of any difficulty iv 3 107
I mean, the business is not ended, as fearing to hear of it hereafter iv 3 110
You never had a servant to whose trust Your business was more welcome iv 4 16
Let the justices make you and fortune friends: I am for other business v 2 36
Her business looks in her With an importing visage v 3 135
Their business might be every thing and their intent every where *T. Night* ii 4 79
He would not stay at your petitions; made His business more material *W. Tale* i 2 216
Lower messes Perchance are to this business purblind? say i 2 228
Your followers I will whisper to the business i 2 437
You smell this business with a sense as cold As is a dead man's nose ii 1 151
Come, follow us; We are to speak in public; for this business Will raise us all ii 1 197
The violent carriage of it Will clear or end the business iii 1 18
What is the business?—O sir, I shall be hated to report it! iii 2 143
Howe'er the business goes, you have made fault I' the boldness of your speech iii 2 218
I am glad at heart To be so rid o' the business iii 3 15
For this ungentle business, Put on thee by my lord iii 3 34
Made me businesses which none without thee can sufficiently manage iv 2 15
Prithee, be my present partner in this business iv 2 58
The father, all whose joy is nothing else But fair posterity, should hold some counsel In such a business iv 4 421
For some other reasons, my grave sir, Which 'tis not fit you know, I not acquaint My father of this business iv 4 424
I am so fraught with curious business That I leave out ceremony iv 4 525
I understand the business, I hear it iv 4 684
Thinkest thou, for that I insinuate, or toaze from thee thy business, I am therefore no courtier? iv 4 760
Please you, sir, to undertake the business for us, here is that gold I have iv 4 837
Are you a party in this business?—In some sort, sir iv 4 843
I will give you as much as this old man does when the business is performed iv 4 852
I make a broken delivery of the business v 2 11
Those that think it is unlawful business I am about, let them depart v 3 96
A thousand businesses are brief in hand, And heaven itself doth frown *K. John* iv 3 158
I, And such as to my claim are liable, Sweat in this business v 2 102
This afternoon will post To consummate this business happily v 7 95
Bid him repair to us to Ely House To see this business *Richard II.* ii 1 217
O, full of careful business are his looks! ii 2 75
It seems then that the tidings of this broil Brake off our business 1 *Hen. IV.* i 1 48
Happy man be his dole, say I: every man to his business ii 2 81
Some heavy business hath my lord in hand, And I must know it ii 3 66
In faith, I'll know your business, Harry, that I will ii 3 83
A business that this night may execute iii 1 82
Thy looks are full of speed.—So hath the business that I come to speak of iii 2 163
By which account, Our business valued iii 2 177
Our hands are full of business: let's away; Advantage feeds him fat iii 2 179
And since this business so fair is done, Let us not leave v 5 43
Doth this become your place, your time and business? 2 *Hen. IV.* ii 1 72
Upon thy sight My worldly business makes a period iv 5 231
Well conceited, Davy: about thy business, Davy v 1 39
We have now no thought in us but France, Save those to God, that run before our business *Hen. V.* i 2 303
You may call the business of the master the author of the servant's damnation iv 1 161
This weighty business will not brook delay 2 *Hen. VI.* i 1 170
Give no words but mum: The business asketh silent secrecy i 2 90
To-morrow toward London back again, To look into this business thoroughly ii 1 202
About your business straight; Go, go, dispatch *Richard III.* i 3 355
Will you go To give your censures in this weighty business? ii 2 144
Go, effect this business soundly iii 1 186
Catesby hath sounded Hastings in our business iii 4 38
Come, gentlemen, Let us consult upon to-morrow's business v 3 45
One, certes, that promises no element In such a business *Hen. VIII.* i 1 49
Why, all this business Our reverend cardinal carried i 1 99
I am sorry To see you ta'en from liberty, to look on The business present i 1 206
Give it quick consideration, for There is no primer business i 2 67
Cardinal Campeius is arrived, and lately; As all think, for this business ii 1 161
How holily he works in all his business! And with what zeal! ii 2 24
With some other business put the king From these sad thoughts ii 2 57
Our breach of duty this way Is business of estate ii 2 70
I'll make ye know your times of business: Is this an hour for temporal affairs? ii 2 72
Join'd with me their servant In the unpartial judging of this business ii 2 107
There ye shall meet about this weighty business ii 2 140
It was a gentle business, and becoming The action of good women ii 3 54
They had gather'd a wise council to them Of every realm, that did debate this business ii 4 52
I will not tarry; no, nor ever more Upon this business my appearance make ii 4 132
Declare whether ever I Did broach this business to your highness ii 4 149
You ever Have wish'd the sleeping of this business ii 4 163
I' the progress of this business, Ere a determinate resolution ii 4 175
What can be their business With me, a poor weak woman? iii 1 19
If your business Seek me out, and that way I am wife in, Out with it boldly iii 1 37
Full little, God knows, looking Either for such men or such business iii 1 76
If you please To trust us in your business, we are ready To use our utmost studies in your service iii 1 173
Cranmer's A worthy fellow, and hath ta'en much pain In the king's business iii 2 73
A time To think upon the part of business which I bear i' the state iii 2 145

Business. The Lord increase this business! *Hen. VIII.* iii 2 161
The letter, as I live, with all the business I writ to's holiness iii 2 221
'Tis all my business iv 1 4
The princess dowager? how goes her business? iv 1 23
Give your friend Some touch of your late business v 1 13
Affairs, that walk, As they say spirits do, at midnight, have In them a wilder nature than the business That seeks dispatch by day v 1 15
Speak to the business, master secretary: Why are we met in council? v 3 1
Because we have business of more moment, We will be short with you v 3 51
This day, no man think Has business at his house v 5 76
I will make a complimental assault upon him, for my business seethes. —Sodden business! there's a stewed phrase indeed! *Troi. and Cres.* iii 1 42
Nothing but heavenly business Should rob my bed-mate of my company iv 1 4
What business, lord, so early?—I was sent for to the king iv 1 34
I have important business, The tide whereof is now v 1 89
Our business is not unknown to the senate *Coriolanus* i 1 58
I'll lean upon one crutch and fight with t'other, Ere stay behind this business i 1 247
O, if he Had borne the business! i 1 274
But had he died in the business, madam; how then? i 3 20
The rest Shall bear the business in some other fight, As cause will be obey'd i 6 82
How! I inform them!—You are like to do such business iii 1 48
For in such business Action is eloquence iii 2 75
You have ended my business, and I will merrily accompany you home iv 3 41
Report to the Volscian lords, how plainly I have borne this business v 3 4
Perfidiously He has betray'd your business v 6 92
And set abroad new business for you all *T. Andron.* i 1 192
Two of the fairest stars in all the heaven, Having some business, do entreat her eyes To twinkle in their spheres till they return *Rom. and Jul.* ii 2 16
My business was great; and in such a case as mine a man may strain courtesy ii 4 53
You have your hands full all, In this so sudden business iv 3 12
What, You come for money?—Is't not your business too? *T. of Athens* ii 2 10
The time is unagreeable to this business: Your importunacy cease ii 2 41
One business does command us all; for mine Is money iii 4 4
In like manner was I in debt to my importunate business iii 6 16
Yet see you but our hands And this the bleeding business they have done: Our hearts you see not *J. Cæsar* iii 1 168
To groan and sweat under the business, Either led or driven iv 1 22
It may be I shall raise you by and by On business iv 3 248
O, that a man might know The end of this day's business ere it come! v 1 124
You shall put This night's great business into my dispatch *Macbeth* i 5 69
In every point twice done and then done double Were poor and single business i 6 16
We will proceed no further in this business i 7 31
When we can entreat an hour to serve, We would spend it in some words upon that business ii 1 23
It is the bloody business which informs Thus to mine eyes ii 1 48
What's the business, That such a hideous trumpet calls to parley The sleepers? ii 3 86
I will put that business in your bosoms, Whose execution takes your enemy off iii 1 104
Masking the business from the common eye For sundry weighty reasons iii 1 125
Great business must be wrought ere noon iii 5 22
Now for ourself and for this time of meeting: Thus much the business is *Hamlet* i 2 27
Giving to you no further personal power To business with the king i 2 37
Shake hands and part: You, as your business and desire shall point you i 5 129
For every man has business and desire, Such as it is i 5 130
We'll read, Answer, and think upon this business ii 2 82
This business is well ended ii 2 85
If not, your pardon and my return shall be the end of my business iii 2 330
And do such bitter business as the day Would quake to look on iii 3 409
Like a man to double business bound, I stand in pause where I shall first begin, And both neglect iii 3 41
Has this fellow no feeling of his business, that he sings at grave-making? v 1 73
It must be shortly known to him from England What is the issue of the business there v 2 72
'Tis our fast intent To shake all cares and business from our age *Lear* i 1 40
Hath he never heretofore sounded you in this business? i 2 75
Frame the business after your own wisdom i 2 107
I will seek him, sir, presently; convey the business as I shall find means i 2 110
Shall I hear from you anon?—I do serve you in this business i 2 194
I see the business. Let me, if not by birth, have lands by wit i 2 198
The better! best! This weaves itself perforce into my business ii 1 17
Bestow Your needful counsel to our business, Which craves the instant use ii 1 129
You have mighty business in hand iii 5 17
It is thy business that I go about iv 4 24
My lady charged my duty in this business iv 5 18
For him 'tis well That of thy death and business I can tell iv 6 285
For this business, It toucheth us v 1 24
If you miscarry, Your business of the world hath so an end v 1 45
Our present business Is general woe v 3 318
Another of his fathom they have none, To lead their business *Othello* i 1 154
It is a business of some heat i 2 40
Upon some present business of the state i 2 90
Now, what's the business? i 3 13
Neither my place nor aught I heard of business Hath raised me from my bed i 3 53
You think I will your serious and great business scant For she is with me i 3 268
That my disports corrupt and taint my business i 3 272
Gentlemen, let's look to our business. Do not think, gentlemen, I am drunk ii 3 117
That your converse and business May be more free iii 1 40
Exchange me for a goat, When I shall turn the business of my soul To such exsufflicate and blown surmises iii 3 181
And to obey shall be in me remorse, What bloody business ever iii 3 469
'Tis but his humour: The business of the state does him offence iv 2 166
The business she hath broached in the state Cannot endure my absence. —And the business you have broached here cannot be without you *Ant. and Cleo.* i 2 178
Till which encounter, It is my business too i 4 80
You do mistake your business ii 2 45
Ere we put ourselves in arms, dispatch we The business we have talk'd of ii 2 169
Let me request you off: our graver business Frowns at this levity ii 7 127
I will employ thee back again; I find thee Most fit for business iii 3 40
Business. Thy business?—The news is true, my lord *Ant. and Cleo.* iii 7 54
To business that we love we rise betime, And go to't with delight iv 4 20
The business of this man looks out of him; We'll hear him what he says v 1 50
Myself and other noble friends Are partners in the business *Cymbeline* i 6 184
Since I received command to do this business I have not slept one wink iii 4 102
'Tis not sleepy business; But must be look'd to speedily and strongly iii 5 26
We do incite The gentry to this business iii 7 7
There's business in these faces v 5 23
Buskined. The bouncing Amazon, Your buskin'd mistress *M. N. Dream* ii 1 71
Busky. How bloodily the sun begins to peer Above yon busky hill! *1 Hen. IV.* v 1 2
Buss. Come, grin on me, and I will think thou smilest And buss thee as thy wife *K. John* iii 4 35
Thou dost give me flattering busses *2 Hen. IV.* ii 4 291
Yond towers, whose wanton tops do buss the clouds *Troi. and Cres.* iv 5 220
Bussing. Thy knee bussing the stones—for in such business Action is eloquence *Coriolanus* iii 2 75
Bustle. And leave the world for me to bustle in *Richard III.* i 1 152
Come, bustle, bustle; caparison my horse v 3 289
Bustling. Listen well; I heard a bustling rumour, like a fray *J. Cæsar* ii 4 18
Busy. Most busy lest, when I do it *Tempest* iii 1 15
Hath he provided this music?—He is very busy about it *Much Ado* i 2 3
Have a care this busy time i 2 29
Brief, I pray you; for you see it is a busy time with me iii 5 6
On meddling monkey, or on busy ape *M. N. Dream* ii 1 181
You shall say I'll prove a busy actor in their play *As Y. Like It* iii 4 62
They're busy within; you were best knock louder *T. of Shrew* v 1 15
She is busy and she cannot come! Is that an answer? v 2 82
Be it thy course to busy giddy minds With foreign quarrels *2 Hen. IV.* iv 5 214
Whiles I was busy for the commonwealth v 2 76
With busy hammers closing rivets up *Hen. V.* iv Prol. 13
You be by her aloft, while we be busy below *2 Hen. VI.* i 4 11
My brain more busy than the labouring spider Weaves tedious snares iii 1 339
O, beat away the busy meddling fiend! iii 3 21
In those busy days Which here you urge to prove us enemies *Richard III.* i 3 145
Let's want no discipline, make no delay; For, lords, to-morrow is a busy day v 3 18
We are busy; go.—This priest has no pride in him? *Hen. VIII.* ii 2 81
The busy day, Waked by the lark, hath roused the ribald crows *Troi. and Cres.* iv 2 8
What, are you busy, ho? need you my help? *Rom. and Jul.* iv 3 6
Fantasies, Which busy care draws in the brains of men *J. Cæsar* ii 1 232
Take thy fortune; Thou find'st to be too busy is some danger *Hamlet* iii 4 33
Do you busy yourself about that? *Lear* i 2 155
In the mean time, Let me be thought too busy in my fears *Othello* iii 3 253
He did not call; he's busy in the paper iv 1 241
Some eternal villain, Some busy and insinuating rogue iv 2 131
But. The wills above be done! but I would fain die a dry death *Tempest* i 1 72
I have done nothing but in care of thee, Of thee, my dear one i 2 16
But how is it That this lives in thy mind? i 2 48
With that which, but by being so retired, O'er-prized all popular rate i 2 91
I should sin To think but nobly of my grandmother i 2 119
But With colours fairer painted their foul ends i 2 142
Whose influence If now I court not but omit, my fortunes Will ever after droop i 2 183
All but mariners Plunged in the foaming brine and quit the vessel i 2 210
But was not this nigh shore?—Close by, my master.—But are they, Ariel, safe? i 2 216
Thy charge Exactly is perform'd: but there's more work i 2 238
Subject To no sight but thine and mine i 2 302
And, but he's something stain'd With grief that's beauty's canker, thou mightst call him A goodly person i 2 414
Ambition cannot pierce a wink beyond, But doubt discovery there ii 1 243
Yond same cloud cannot choose but fall by pailfuls ii 2 24
Not a holiday fool there but would give a piece of silver ii 2 30
When that's gone He shall drink nought but brine iii 2 74
Will you troll the catch You taught me but while-ere? iii 2 127
Is nothing but heart-sorrow And a clear life ensuing iii 3 81
It shall go hard but I'll prove it by another *T. G. of Ver.* i 1 86
But tell me, dost thou know my lady Silvia? ii 1 44
I'll die on him that says so but yourself ii 4 114
But when I look on her perfections, There is no reason but I shall be blind ii 4 211
What lets but one may enter at her window? iii 1 113
Him we go to find: there's not a hair on's head but 'tis a Valentine iii 1 192
Have you any thing to take to?—Nothing but my fortune iv 1 43
But nobody but has his fault; but let that pass *Mer. Wives* i 4 14
Tells me 'tis a thing impossible I should love thee but as a property iii 4 10
Well, let it not be doubted but he'll come iv 4 43
Spirits are not finely touch'd But to fine issues *Meas. for Meas.* i 1 37
But, like a thrifty goddess, she determines Herself the glory of a creditor i 1 39
Your brother is a forfeit of the law, And you but waste your words ii 2 72
A man that apprehends death no more dreadfully but as a drunken sleep iv 2 150
Nay, but it is not so.—It is no other iv 3 121
Our soul Cannot but yield you forth to public thanks v 1 7
There had she not been long but she became A joyful mother *Com. of Err.* i 1 50
The one so like the other As could not be distinguish'd but by names i 1 53
But your reason was not substantial, why there is no time to recover ii 2 105
Else it could never be But I should know her as well as she knows me ii 2 204
And welcome more common; for that's nothing but words iii 1 25
There's not a man I meet but doth salute me iv 3 1
But seven years since, in Syracusa, boy, Thou know'st we parted v 1 320
It must not be denied but I am a plain-dealing villain *Much Ado* i 3 33
I do but stay till your marriage be consummate iii 2 1
I am much deceived but I remember the style *L. L. Lost* iv 1 98
Or ever, but in vizards, show their faces v 2 271
If thou follow me, do not believe But I shall do thee mischief *M. N. Dream* ii 1 237
It cannot be but thou hast murder'd him; So should a murderer look iii 2 56
Can you not hate me, as I know you do, But you must join in souls to mock me too? iii 2 150
Saint Valentine is past: Begin these wood-birds but to couple now? iv 1 145
But tell not me; I know, Antonio Is sad to think upon his merchandise. —Believe me, no *Mer. of Venice* i 1 39
I'll plead for you myself, but you shall have him *T. of Shrew* ii 1 15
How speed you with my daughter?—How but well, sir? how but well? ii 1 284
For, but I be deceived, Our fine musician groweth amorous iii 1 62
With no greater a run but my head and my neck iv [illegible] 16
And but I be deceived Signior Baptista may remember me iv [illegible] 2
Can't no other, But, I your daughter, he must be my brother? *All's Well* i 3 172

But. There were no further danger known but the modesty which is so lost *All's Well* iii 5 29
He hath known you but three days, and already you are no stranger *T. Night* i 4 3
Thou know'st no less but all i 4 13
That it cannot but turn him into a notable contempt ii 5 224
One that knows What she should shame to know herself But with her most vile principal *W. Tale* ii 1 92
Let them come in; but quickly now iv 4 350
But hear me *K. John* ii 1 421
Then speak again; not all thy former tale, But this one word iii 1 26
But on this day let seamen fear no wreck; No bargains break! iii 1 92
Your uncle must not know but you are dead iv 1 128
If thou didst but consent To this most cruel act, do but despair iv 3 125
We three are but thyself *Richard II.* ii 1 275
Let no man speak again To alter this, for counsel is but vain iii 2 214
Had only but the corpse, But shadows and the shows of men, to fight *2 Hen. IV.* i 1 192
My honour is at pawn; And, but my going, nothing can redeem it ii 3 8
What towns of any moment but we have? *1 Hen. VI.* i 2 5
I never read but England's kings have had Large sums of gold and dowries with their wives *2 Hen. VI.* i 1 128
I never saw but Humphrey Duke of Gloucester Did bear him like a noble gentleman i 1 183
The greatest man in England but the king ii 2 82
It cannot be but he was murder'd here iii 2 177
If thou be found by me, thou art but dead iii 2 387
My woful banishment, Could all but answer for that peevish brat? *Richard III.* i 3 194
Which of you But is four Volsces? *Coriolanus* i 6 78
None of you but is Able to bear against the great Aufidius A shield as hard as his i 6 78
He would miss it rather Than carry it but by the suit of the gentry ii 1 254
'I would be consul,' says he: 'aged custom, But by your voices, will not so permit me' ii 3 177
And but thou love me, let them find me here *Rom. and Jul.* ii 2 76
It cannot be But I am pigeon-liver'd and lack gall *Hamlet* ii 2 605
There's none so foul and foolish thereunto, But does foul pranks *Othello* ii 1 143
I do not think but Desdemona's honest.—Long live she so! iii 3 225
He hath, and is again to cope your wife: I say, but mark his gesture iv 1 88
Death will seize her, but Your comfort makes the rescue *Ant. and Cleo.* iii 11 47
But being charged, we will be still by land, Which, as I take 't, we shall iv 11 1
Not any, but abide the change of time *Cymbeline* ii 4 4
Other of them may have crook'd noses, but to owe such straight arms, none iii 1 38
Of his content, All but in that! iii 2 35
Were you a woman, youth, I should woo hard but be your groom iii 6 70
And, but she spoke it dying, I would not Believe her lips v 5 41
But even now worth this, And now worth nothing *Mer. of Venice* i 1 35
But ever. Would I might But ever see that man! *Tempest* i 2 169
But for. Which I was much unwilling to proceed in But for my duty *T. G. of Ver.* ii 1 113
Happy but for me, And by me, had not our hap been bad *Com. of Errors* i 1 38
But for staying on our controversy, Had hoisted sail v 1 20
Truly, she's very well indeed, but for two things *All's Well* ii 4 8
But for these vile guns, He would himself have been a soldier *1 Hen. IV.* i 3 63
And, but for shame, In such a parley should I answer thee iii 1 203
But for a sallet, my brain-pan had been cleft with a brown bill *2 Hen. VI.* iv 10 12
I'ld have beaten him like a dog, but for disturbing the lords within *Coriol.* iv 5 57
But for your company, I would have been a-bed an hour ago *R. and J.* iii 4 6
'Tis our match: The sweat of industry would dry and die, But for the end it works to *Cymbeline* iii 6 32
But now he parted hence, to embark for Milan *T. G. of Ver.* i 1 71
As if but now they waxed pale for woe iii 1 228
But now I was the lord Of this fair mansion *Mer. of Venice* iii 2 169
And even now, but now, This house, these servants and this same myself Are yours iii 2 171
My liege! my lord! but now a king, now thus *K. John* v 7 66
But now the Duke of Buckingham and I Are come from visiting *Richard III.* i 3 31
That she, that even but now was your best object, . . . should in this trice of time Commit a thing so monstrous *Lear* i 1 217
But only. Who but Rumour, who but only I, Make fearful musters? *2 Hen. IV.* Ind. 11
I say not, slaughter him, For I intend but only to surprise him *3 Hen. VI.* iv 2 25
But perhaps, my son, Thou shamest to acknowledge me in misery *Com. of Errors* v 1 321
But that. The sky, it seems, would pour down stinking pitch, But that the sea, mounting to the welkin's cheek, Dashes the fire out *Tempest* i 2 4
No news, my lord, but that he writes How happily he lives *T. G. of Ver.* i 3 56
But that his mistress Did hold his eyes lock'd in her crystal looks ii 4 88
Fear not but that she will love you iii 2 1
I had been drowned, but that the shore was shelvy and shallow *Mer. Wives* iii 5 15
For which I would not plead, but that I must; For which I must not plead, but that I am At war 'twixt will and will not *Meas. for Meas.* ii 2 31
But that you take what doth to you belong, It were a fault to snatch words from my tongue *L. L. Lost* v 2 381
Welcome, Mercade; But that thou interrupt'st our merriment v 2 725
I am not yet so low But that my nails can reach unto thine eyes *M. N. Dream* iii 2 298
That could give more, but that her hand lacks means *As Y. Like It* i 2 259
Cannot for all that dissuade succession, but that they are limed *All's Well* iii 5 25
I neither can nor will deny But that I know them v 3 167
But that it would be double-dealing, sir, I would you could *T. Night* v 1 32
He who shall speak for her is afar off guilty But that he speaks *W. Tale* ii 1 105
Peace itself should not so dull a kingdom, . . . But that defences, musters, preparations, Should be maintain'd *Hen. V.* ii 4 18
I would ne'er have fled, But that they left me 'midst my enemies *1 Hen. VI.* i 2 24
But that I am prevented, I should have begg'd I might have been employ'd iv 1 71
But that my heart's on future mischief set, I would speak blasphemy ere bid you fly *2 Hen. VI.* v 2 84
But that I hate thee deadly, I should lament thy miserable state *3 Hen. VI.* i 4 84
Think you, but that I know our state secure, I would be so triumphant as I am? *Richard III.* iii 2 83
I cannot promise But that you shall sustain moe new disgraces *Hen. VIII.* iii 2 5
I could despise this man, But that I am bound in charity against it! iii 2 298
But that I am forbid To tell the secrets of my prison-house, I could a tale unfold *Hamlet* i 5 13
It cannot be But that my master is abused *Cymbeline* iii 4 123
But that. But that it eats our victuals, I should think Here were a fairy *Cymbeline* iii 6 41
Whose life, But that her flight prevented it, she had Ta'en off by poison v 5 46
But then exactly do All points of my command *Tempest* i 2 499
But though we think it so, it is no matter *Hen. V.* ii 4 42
But till. And depart when you bid me.—O, stay but till then! *Much Ado* v 2 45
He only lived but till he was a man *Macbeth* v 8 40
But what. Not only with what my revenue yielded, But what my power might else exact *Tempest* i 2 99
Padua affords nothing but what is kind *T. of Shrew* v 2 14
Draw no swords but what are sanctified *2 Hen. IV.* iv 4 4
Nor answer have I none, But what should go by water *Othello* iv 2 104
And said nothing but what I protest intendment of doing iv 2 205
But yet. Well, I have done: but yet,— He will be talking *Tempest* ii 1 25
I shall miss thee; But yet thou shalt have freedom v 1 96
A gracious person: but yet I cannot love him *T. Night* i 5 281
But yet I'll make assurance double sure *Macbeth* iv 1 83
That's not amiss; But yet keep time in all *Othello* iv 1 93
I do not like 'But yet,' it does allay The good precedence *Ant. and Cleo.* ii 5 50
'But yet' is as a gaoler to bring forth Some monstrous malefactor ii 5 52
Butcher. Have I lived to be carried in a basket, like a barrow of butcher's offal? *Mer. Wives* iii 5 5
Bleat softly then; the butcher hears you cry *L. L. Lost* v 2 255
That eyes . . . Should be call'd tyrants, butchers, murderers! *As You Like It* iii 5 14
Is yet the cover of a fairer mind Than to be butcher of an innocent child *K. John* iv 2 259
To stir against the butchers of his life *Richard II.* i 2 3
Teaching stern murder how to butcher thee i 2 32
O, sit my husband's wrongs on Hereford's spear, That it may enter butcher Mowbray's breast! i 2 48
Goodwife Keech, the butcher's wife *2 Hen. IV.* ii 1 101
I could lay on like a butcher and sit like a jack-an-apes, never off *Hen. V.* v 2 147
As the butcher takes away the calf And binds the wretch *2 Hen. VI.* iii 1 210
Who finds the heifer dead and bleeding fresh And sees fast by a butcher with an axe, But will suspect 'twas he that made the slaughter? iii 2 189
Are you the butcher, Suffolk? Where's your knife? iii 2 195
Where's Dick, the butcher of Ashford? iv 3 1
And work in their shirt too; as myself, for example, that am a butcher iv 7 58
Are you there, butcher? O, I cannot speak! *3 Hen. VI.* i 2 95
Butchers and villains! bloody cannibals! How sweet a plant have you untimely cropp'd! You have no children, butchers! v 5 61
Where is that devil's butcher, Hard-favour'd Richard v 5 77
So first the harmless sheep doth yield his fleece And next his throat unto the butcher's knife v 6 9
The father rashly slaughter'd his own son, The son, compell'd, been butcher to the sire *Richard III.* v 5 26
This butcher's cur is venom-mouth'd, and I Have not the power to muzzle him; therefore best Not wake him *Hen. VIII.* i 1 120
Were he the butcher of my son, he should Be free as is the wind *Coriolanus* i 9 88
With no less confidence Than boys pursuing summer butterflies, Or butchers killing flies iv 6 95
The very butcher of a silk button, a duellist *Rom. and Jul.* ii 4 24
Let us be sacrificers, but not butchers, Caius *J. Cæsar* ii 1 166
O, pardon me, thou bleeding piece of earth, That I am meek and gentle with these butchers! iii 1 255
The cruel ministers Of this dead butcher and his fiend-like queen *Macbeth* v 8 69
Prithee, dispatch: The lamb entreats the butcher *Cymbeline* iii 4 99
Butchered. A thousand of his people butchered *1 Hen. IV.* i 1 42
Which his hell-govern'd arm hath butchered! *Richard III.* i 2 67
And shamefully by you my hopes are butcher'd i 3 276
How they at Pomfret bloodily were butcher'd iii 4 92
The parents live, whose children thou hast butcher'd iv 4 393
The wronged souls Of butcher'd princes fight in thy behalf v 3 122
Have by my means been butcher'd wrongfully! *T. Andron.* iv 4 55
Butcheries. Behold this pattern of thy butcheries *Richard III.* i 2 54
Provoked by thy bloody mind, Which never dreamt on aught but butcheries i 2 100
Butcherly. How butcherly, Erroneous, mutinous and unnatural! *3 Hen. VI.* ii 5 89
Butchery. This house is but a butchery: Abhor it, fear it *As Y. Like It* ii 3 27
In the intestine shock And furious close of civil butchery *1 Hen. IV.* i 1 13
Whom I did suborn To do this ruthless piece of butchery *Richard III.* iv 3 5
Butler. Is not this Stephano, my drunken butler? *Tempest* v 1 277
She was both pantler, butler, cook, Both dame and servant *W. Tale* iv 4 56
Hath Butler brought those horses from the sheriff? *1 Hen. IV.* ii 3 70
Bid Butler lead him forth into the park ii 3 75
Butt. I escaped upon a butt of sack which the sailors heaved o'erboard *Tempest* ii 2 126
Hast any more of this?—The whole butt, man: my cellar is in a rock by the sea-side ii 2 137
When the butt is out, we will drink water; not a drop before iii 2 1
Look, how you butt yourself in these sharp mocks! *L. L. Lost* v 2 251
Believe me, sir, they butt together well.—Head, and butt! an hasty-witted body Would say your head and butt were head and horn *T. of Shrew* v 2 39
To which is fixed, as an aim or butt, Obedience *Hen. V.* i 2 186
I am your butt, and I abide your shot *3 Hen. VI.* i 4 29
You ruinous butt, you whoreson indistinguishable cur *Troi. and Cres.* v 1 32
The beast With many heads butts me away *Coriolanus* iv 1 2
Here is my butt, And very sea-mark of my utmost sail *Othello* v 2 267
Butt-end. That is the butt-end of a mother's blessing *Richard III.* ii 2 110
Butter. I will rather trust a Fleming with my butter *Mer. Wives* ii 2 317
As subject to heat as butter; a man of continual dissolution and thaw iii 5 118
Not so much as will serve to be prologue to an egg and butter *1 Hen. IV.* i 2 23
They are up already, and call for eggs and butter ii 1 65
Didst thou never see Titan kiss a dish of butter? pitiful-hearted Titan! ii 4 134
A gross fat man.—As fat as butter ii 4 560
I think, to steal cream indeed, for thy theft hath already made thee butter iv 2 67
Buttered. I'll have my brains ta'en out and buttered *Mer. Wives* iii 5 8
'Twas her brother that, in pure kindness to his horse, buttered his hay *Lear* ii 4 127
Butterflies. Pluck the wings from painted butterflies To fan the moon-beams from his sleeping eyes *M. N. Dream* iii 1 175
Men, like butterflies, Show not their mealy wings but to the summer *Troi. and Cres.* iii 3 78
With no less confidence Than boys pursuing summer butterflies *Coriol.* iv 6 94
Laugh At gilded butterflies, and hear poor rogues Talk of court news *Lear* v 3 13
Butterfly. I saw him run after a gilded butterfly *Coriolanus* i 3 66

Butterfly. There is differency between a grub and a butterfly; yet your butterfly was a grub *Coriolanus* v 4 12
Buttering. I will henceforth eat no fish of fortune's buttering *All's Well* v 2 9
Butter-woman. Tongue, I must put you into a butter-woman's mouth iv 1 45
Butter-women. It is the right butter-women's rank to market *As Y. L. It* iii 2 103
Buttery. Take them to the buttery, And give them friendly welcome *T. of Shrew* Ind. 1 102
Buttery-bar. Bring your hand to the buttery-bar and let it drink *T. Night* i 3 74
Buttock. In what part of her body stands Ireland?—Marry, sir, in her buttocks *Com. of Errors* iii 2 120
It is like a barber's chair that fits all buttocks, the pin-buttock, the quatch-buttock, the brawn buttock, or any buttock *All's Well* ii 2 17
One that converses more with the buttock of the night than with the forehead of the morning *Coriolanus* ii 1 56
Button. 'Tis in his buttons; he will carry't *Mer. Wives* iii 2 71
The very butcher of a silk button, a duellist *Rom. and Jul.* ii 4 24
The canker galls the infants of the spring, Too oft before their buttons be disclosed *Hamlet* i 3 40
On fortune's cap we are not the very button.—Nor the soles of her shoe? ii 2 233
Thou'lt come no more, Never, never, never, never, never! Pray you, undo this button: thank you, sir *Lear* v 3 309
Buttoned. One whose hard heart is button'd up with steel *Com. of Errors* iv 2 34
Button-hole. Let me take you a botton-hole lower *L. L. Lost* v 2 706
Buttress. No jutty, frieze, Buttress, nor coign of vantage *Macbeth* i 6 7
Butts. 'Tis Butts, The king's physician *Hen. VIII.* v 2 10
I'll show your grace the strangest sight— What's that, Butts? v 2 20
By holy Mary, Butts, there's knavery v 2 33
Butt-shaft. Cupid's butt-shaft is too hard for Hercules' club *L. L. Lost* i 2 181
The very pin of his heart cleft with the blind bow-boy's butt-shaft *Rom. and Jul.* ii 4 16
Buxom. A soldier, firm and sound of heart, And of buxom valour *Hen. V.* iii 6 28
So buxom, blithe, and full of face *Pericles* i Gower 23
Buy. What things are these, my lord Antonio? Will money buy 'em? *Temp.* v 1 265
That will be excellent. I'll go buy them vizards *Mer. Wives* iv 4 69
That silk will I go buy iv 4 73
Money buys lands, and wives are sold by fate v 5 246
You will needs buy and sell men and women like beasts *Meas. for Meas.* iii 2 2
We do instate and widow you withal, To buy you a better husband v 1 430
Not being able to buy out his life According to the statute *Com. of Errors* i 2 5
Go thou And buy a rope's end iv 1 16
Get thee gone; Buy thou a rope and bring it home to me iv 1 20
You shall buy this sport as dear As all the metal in your shop will answer iv 1 81
Some offer me commodities to buy iv 3 6
Would you buy her, that you inquire after her?—Can the world buy such a jewel?—Yea, and a case to put it into *Much Ado* i 1 181
The endeavour of this present breath may buy That honour *L. L. Lost* i 1 5
His senses were lock'd in his eye, As jewels in crystal for some prince to buy ii 1 243
I will never buy and sell out of this word iii 1 143
How much carnation ribbon may a man buy for a remuneration? iii 1 147
If so, our copper buys no better treasure iv 3 386
An I had but one penny in the world, thou shouldst have it to buy gingerbread v 1 75
What buys your company?—Your absence only v 2 224
The fairy land buys not the child of me *M. N. Dream* ii 1 122
Thou shalt buy this dear, If ever I thy face by daylight see iii 2 426
They lose it that do buy it with much care *Mer. of Venice* i 1 75
I will buy with you, sell with you, talk with you, walk with you i 3 36
I say, To buy his favour, I extend this friendship i 3 169
With that I will go buy my fortunes *As Y. Like It* i 1 78
If that love or gold Can in this desert place buy entertainment ii 4 72
What is he that shall buy his flock and pasture? ii 4 88
If it stand with honesty, Buy thou the cottage ii 4 92
Buy it with your gold right suddenly ii 4 100
I will unto Venice, To buy apparel 'gainst the wedding-day *T. of Shrew* ii 1 317
Take this purse of gold, And let me buy your friendly help thus far *All's Well* iii 7 15
Yet in his idle fire, To buy his will, it would not seem too dear iii 7 27
And buy myself another [tongue] of Bajazet's mule iv 1 45
I will buy me a son-in-law in a fair v 3 148
Where did you buy it? or who gave it you?—It was not given me, nor I did not buy it v 3 272
What am I to buy for our sheep-shearing feast? *W. Tale* iv 3 39
I must go buy spices for our sheep-shearing iv 3 124
When you sing, I'ld have you buy and sell so, so give alms, Pray so iv 4 138
Come buy of me, come; come buy, come buy; Buy, lads, or else your lasses cry iv 4 230
What hast here? ballads?—Pray now, buy some iv 4 263
Let's first see moe ballads; we'll buy the other things anon iv 4 278
Bring away thy pack after me. Wenches, I'll buy for you both iv 4 318
Will you buy any tape, Or lace for your cape? iv 4 322
They throng who should buy first iv 4 612
Dreading the curse that money may buy out *K. John* iii 1 164
But dead, thy kingdom cannot buy my breath *Richard II.* i 3 232
Shall our coffers, then, Be emptied to redeem a traitor home? Shall we buy treason? *1 Hen. IV.* i 3 87
You may buy land now as cheap as stinking mackerel ii 4 394
We shall buy maidenheads as they buy hob-nails, by the hundreds ii 4 398
He's gone into Smithfield to buy your worship a horse *2 Hen. IV.* i 2 55
Saving your manhoods—to buy a saddle ii 1 29
They sell the pasture now to buy the horse *Hen. V.* ii Prol. 5
I will sell my dukedom, To buy a slobbery and a dirty farm iii 5 13
You shall be a woodmonger, and buy nothing of me but cudgels v 1 69
You must buy that peace With full accord to all our just demands v 2 70
Thou wouldst think I had sold my farm to buy my crown v 2 129
The Duke of Burgundy will fast Before he'll buy again at such a rate *1 Hen. VI.* iii 2 43
Ah! sancta majestas, who would not buy thee dear? *2 Hen. VI.* v 1 5
If this right hand would buy two hours' life *3 Hen. VI.* ii 6 80
Shall buy this treason Even with the dearest blood your bodies bear v 1 68
I would not spend another such a night, Though 'twere to buy a world of happy days *Richard III.* i 4 6
Hell's black intelligencer, Only reserved their factor, to buy souls iv 4 72
His own merit makes his way; A gift that heaven gives for him, which buys A place next to the king *Hen. VIII.* i 1 65
The cardinal Does buy and sell his honour as he pleases i 1 192
I will buy nine sparrows for a penny *Troi. and Cres.* ii 1 77
Let him be sent, great princes, And he shall buy my daughter iii 3 28
You do as chapmen do, Dispraise the thing that you desire to buy iv 1 76

Buy. We two, that with so many thousand sighs Did buy each other, must poorly sell ourselves *Troi. and Cres.* iv 4 42
I will the second time, As I would buy thee, view thee limb by limb iv 5 238
So, the good horse is mine.—I'll buy him of you *Coriolanus* i 4 5
Things created To buy and sell with groats iii 2 10
I would not buy Their mercy at the price of one fair word iii 3 90
Would half my wealth Would buy this for a lie! iv 6 161
An I were so apt to quarrel as thou art, any man should buy the fee-simple of my life for an hour and a quarter *Rom. and Jul.* iii 1 35
Buy food, and get thyself in flesh v 1 84
Here he writes that he did buy a poison Of a poor 'pothecary v 3 288
If I would sell my horse, and buy twenty more Better than he, why, give my horse to Timon *T. of Athens* ii 1 7
When the means are gone that buy this praise, The breath is gone whereof this praise is made ii 2 178
An honour in him which buys out his fault iii 5 17
His silver hairs Will purchase us a good opinion And buy men's voices to commend our deeds *J. Cæsar* ii 1 146
How will you do for a husband?—Why, I can buy me twenty at any market.—Then you'll buy 'em to sell again *Macbeth* iv 2 40
Costly thy habit as thy purse can buy, But not express'd in fancy *Hamlet* i 3 70
And oft 'tis seen the wicked prize itself Buys out the law iii 3 60
Not all the dukes of waterish Burgundy Can buy this unprized precious maid of me *Lear* i 1 262
Such a daughter Should sure to the slaughter, If my cap would buy a halter i 4 343
A housewife that by selling her desires Buys herself bread and clothes *Othello* iv 1 96
I never do him wrong, But he does buy my injuries, to be friends *Cymb.* i 1 105
If you buy ladies' flesh at a million a dram, you cannot preserve it from tainting i 4 147
Have mingled sums To buy a present i 6 187
'Tis gold Which buys admittance; oft it doth ii 3 73
In honesty, I bid for you as I'ld buy iii 6 71
A man may serve seven years for the loss of a leg, and have not money enough in the end to buy him a wooden one *Pericles* iv 6 183
Buyer. As if my trinkets had been hallowed and brought a benediction to the buyer *W. Tale* iv 4 614
This fellow might be in's time a great buyer of land *Hamlet* v 1 113
Buying. That young swain that you saw here but erewhile, That little cares for buying any thing *As Y. Like It* ii 4 90
Buzz. Should be! should—buzz! *T. of Shrew* ii 1 207
And buz these conjurations in her brain *2 Hen. VI.* i 2 99
Though they cannot greatly sting to hurt, Yet look to have them buzz to offend thine ears *3 Hen. VI.* ii 6 95
I will buz abroad such prophecies That Edward shall be fearful of his life v 6 86
There be moe wasps that buzz about his nose *Hen. VIII.* iii 2 55
How would he hang his slender gilded wings, And buzz lamenting doings in the air! Poor harmless fly! *T. Andron.* iii 2 62
However these disturbers of our peace Buz in the people's ears iv 4 7
On every dream, Each buzz, each fancy, each complaint, dislike *Lear* i 4 348
Buzzard. Well ta'en, and like a buzzard *T. of Shrew* ii 1 207
O slow-wing'd turtle! shall a buzzard take thee?—Ay, for a turtle, as he takes a buzzard ii 1 208
More pity that the eagle should be mew'd, While kites and buzzards prey at liberty *Richard III.* i 1 133
Buzzed. So it be new, there's no respect how vile—That is not quickly buzz'd into his ears *Richard II.* ii 1 26
Buzzer. And wants not buzzers to infect his ear *Hamlet* iv 5 90
Buzzing. Among the buzzing pleased multitude *Mer. of Venice* iii 2 182
And hush'd with buzzing night-flies to thy slumber *2 Hen. IV.* iii 1 11
Did you not of late days hear A buzzing of a separation? *Hen. VIII.* ii 1 148
Poor harmless fly, That, with his pretty buzzing melody, Came here to make us merry! *T. Andron.* iii 2 64
And soundless too; For you have stol'n their buzzing, Antony, And very wisely threat before you sting *J. Cæsar* v 1 37
By. But was not this nigh shore?—Close by *Tempest* i 2 216
This music crept by me upon the waters i 2 391
'Tis a chronicle of day by day, Not a relation for a breakfast v 1 163
Hast thou no mouth by land? What is the news? v 1 220
The story of my life And the particular accidents gone by v 1 305
Then speak the truth by her *T. G. of Ver.* ii 4 151
Except I be by Silvia in the night, There is no music in the nightingale iii 1 178
Shall I Sir Pandarus of Troy become, And by my side wear steel? *Mer. Wives* i 3 84
Be ready here hard by in the brew-house iii 3 10
To find the faults . . . , And let go by the actor *Meas. for Meas.* ii 2 41
Either send the chain or send me by some token *Com. of Errors* iv 1 56
An you be not turned Turk, there's no more sailing by the star *Much Ado* iii 4 58
O, one too much by thee! Why had I one? iv 1 131
Dost thou wear thy wit by thy side? v 1 126
Always hath been just and virtuous In any thing that I do know by her v 1 312
I would not have him know so much by me *L. L. Lost* iv 3 150
The letter is too long by half a mile v 2 54
Warily I stole into a neighbour thicket by v 2 94
Though my mocks come home by me, I will now be merry v 2 637
By day's approach look to be visited *M. N. Dream* iii 2 430
How say you by the French lord, Monsieur Le Bon? *Mer. of Venice* i 2 58
He attendeth here hard by, To know your answer iv 1 145
By how much defence is better than no skill, by so much *As Y. Like It* iii 3 62
The property by what it is should go, Not by the title *All's Well* ii 3 137
He can come no other way but by this hedge-corner iv 1 1
By him and by this woman here what know you? v 3 237
Dost thou live by thy tabor?—No, sir, I live by the church *T. Night* iii 1 2
What's that to us? The time goes by iii 4 398
Keep the peace, I say.—Stand by, or I shall gall you *K. John* iv 3 94
I'll not be by the while *Richard II.* ii 1 211
To-day, as I came by, I called there ii 2 94
Got with swearing 'Lay by' and spent with crying 'Bring in' *1 Hen. IV.* i 2 40
Ay, my lord cardinal? how think you by that? *2 Hen. VI.* ii 1 16
By so much is the wonder in extremes *3 Hen. VI.* ii 2 115
Tears in her eyes, The bleeding witness of her hatred by *Richard III.* i 2 234
By as much as a performance Does an irresolute purpose *Hen. VIII.* i 2 208
By day and night, He's traitor to the height i 2 213
Even the billows of the sea Hung their heads, and then lay by iii 1 11
Diomed, a whole week by days, Doth haunt you *Troi. and Cres.* iv 1 9
The worthiest of them tell me name by name iv 5 160
Come by him where he stands, by ones, by twos, and by threes *Coriol.* ii 3 47
And day by day I'll do this heavy task *T. Andron.* v 2 58
A rose By any other name would smell as sweet *Rom. and Jul.* ii 2 44

By. I did hear The galloping of horse: who was 't came by? . *Macbeth* iv 1 140
And by very much more handsome than fine . . *Hamlet* ii 2 466
This was but as a fly by an eagle . *Ant. and Cleo.* ii 2 186
He beats thee 'gainst the odds: thy lustre thickens, When he shines by ii 3 28
You have done well by water.—And you by land . ii 6 89
Who lets go by no vantages that may Prefer you . *Cymbeline* ii 3 50
This you might have heard of here, by me, Or by some other . ii 4 77
By all means . . . *Mer. Wives* iv 2 230; *T. Night* iii 2 62
By no means *Meas. for Meas.* iii 1; *Much Ado* ii 1; *M. N. Dream* i 1;
As Y. Like It iii 2; *T. of Athens* i 2; *J. Cæsar* ii 1; *Hamlet* i 3; i 4;
iii 1; *Lear* ii 1; ii 4; iv 3; *Pericles* ii 5
By and by. He's winding up the watch of his wit; by and by it will
strike . . . . *Tempest* ii 1 13
We'll fill him by and by again . . . ii 2 181
When Prospero is destroyed.—That shall be by and by . . iii 2 156
And by and by a cloud takes all away . *T. G. of Ver.* i 3 87
And by and by intend to chide myself . . . iv 2 103
I'll be with her by and by . . . . *Mer. Wives* iv 1 7
I would by and by have some speech with you. *Meas. for Meas.* iii 1 155
Heaven give your spirits comfort! By and by . . iv 2 73
By and by rude fishermen of Corinth By force took Dromio *Com. of Err.* v 1 351
By and by, disguised they will be here . . *L. L. Lost* v 2 96
And by and by I will to thee appear . *M. N. Dream* iii 1 89
By and by, with us These couples shall eternally be knit . iv 1 185
But, for the bloody napkin?—By and by . . *As Y. Like It* iv 3 139
He is now in some commerce with my lady, and will by and by depart
T. Night iii 4 192
Come by and by to my chamber . . . . iv 2 77
I'll hear you by and by . . . . . *W. Tale* iv 4 518
Then am I king'd again: and by and by Think that I am unking'd
Richard II. v 5 36
And by and by in as high a flow as the ridge of the gallows . 1 *Hen. IV.* i 2 42
Embowell'd will I see thee by and by . . . . v 4 109
They shall be apprehended by and by . . . *Hen. V.* ii 2 2
My lord protector will come this way by and by . 2 *Hen. VI.* i 3 2
Now fetch me a stool hither by and by . . . . ii 1 142
I'll be with you, niece, by and by . . *Troi. and Cres.* i 2 304
When, by and by, the din of war gan pierce His ready sense *Coriolanus* ii 2 119
Ay, by and by; But we will drink together . . . v 3 202
For thy hand Look by and by to have thy sons with thee *T. Andron.* iii 1 202
If one arm's embracement will content thee, I will embrace thee in it by
and by . . . . v 2 69
By and by, I come:—To cease thy suit, and leave me to my grief
Rom. and Jul. ii 2 152
Then Tybalt fled; But by and by comes back to Romeo . . iii 1 175
Run to my study. By and by! God's will, What simpleness is this! . iii 3 76
It is so very very late, That we may call it early by and by . iii 4 35
By and by my master drew on him; And then I ran away . . v 3 284
By and by thy bosom shall partake The secrets of my heart . *J. Cæsar* ii 1 305
It may be I shall raise you by and by On business . . iv 3 247
Then I will come to my mother by and by . . *Hamlet* iii 2 400
I will come by and by.—I will say so.—By and by is easily said . iii 2 402
I dare not drink yet, madam; by and by . . . v 2 304
Meet me by and by at the citadel . . . *Othello* ii 1 291
To be now a sensible man, by and by a fool, and presently a beast! . ii 3 309
He foams at mouth and by and by Breaks out to savage madness . iv 1 55
I would speak a word with you!—Yes: 'tis Emilia. By and by . v 2 91
Soft; by and by. Let me the curtains draw . . . v 2 104
I'll see you by and by . . . . . *Ant. and Cleo.* iii 11 24
By-dependencies. And all the other by-dependencies . *Cymbeline* v 5 390
By-drinking. For your diet and by-drinkings . . 1 *Hen. IV.* iii 3 84
By-gone. This satisfaction The by-gone day proclaim'd . *W. Tale* i 2 32
Stark mad! for all Thy by-gone fooleries were but spices of it . iii 2 185
By himself. The king's son have I landed by himself . *Tempest* i 2 221
By himself. Go, let him have a table by himself . *T. of Athens* i 2 30
By inches. They'll give him death by inches . . . *Coriolanus* v 4 42
By the minute feed on life and lingering By inches waste you *Cymbeline* v 5 52
By itself. Britain is A world by itself . . . . . iii 1 13
By moonlight. Thou hast by moonlight at her window sung *M. N. Dr.* i 1 30
By my head, here come the Capulets.—By my heel, I care not
Rom. and Jul. iii 1 38
By myself. On them to look and practise by myself . *T. of Shrew* i 1 83
By one. Better have none Than plural faith which is too much by one
T. G. of Ver. v 4 52
By ourselves. We'll have this song out anon by ourselves *W. Tale* iv 4 315
By-path. God knows, my son, By what by-paths and indirect crook'd
ways I met this crown . . . . . 2 *Hen. IV.* iv 5 185
By-peeping in an eye Base and unlustrous as the smoky light That's fed
with stinking tallow . . . . . . *Cymbeline* i 6 108
By'r lady. Not a whit.—Yes, py'r lady . . . *Mer. Wives* i 1 28
By'r lady, that I think a' cannot . . . . *Much Ado* iii 3 82
By'r lady, I think it be so . . . . iii 3 89
Nay, by'r lady, I am not such a fool to think what I list . . iii 4 82
Five year! by'r lady, a long lease . . . . 1 *Hen. IV.* ii 4 50
Now, sirs: by'r lady, you fought fair . . . . ii 4 329
His age some fifty, or, by'r lady, inclining to three score . . ii 4 467
By'r lady, he is a good musician . . . . . iii 1 235
By'r lady, I think a' be, but goodman Puff of Barson . 2 *Hen. IV.* v 3 93
Bad news, by'r lady; seldom comes the better *Richard III.* ii 3 4
And, by'r lady, Held current music too *Hen. VIII.* i 3 46
Hanged! by'r lady, then I have brought up a neck to a fair end *T. Andron.* iv 4 48
By'r lady, thirty years.—What, man! 'tis not so much *Rom. and Jul.* i 5 35
By'r lady, your ladyship is nearer to heaven than when I saw you last
Hamlet ii 2 445
But, by'r lady, he must build churches, then . . . iii 2 141
By'r lakin, I can go no further . . . . *Tempest* iii 3 1
By'r lakin, a parlous fear . . . . *M. N. Dream* iii 1 14
By-room. Do thou stand in some by-room . . 1 *Hen. IV.* ii 4 32
By the book. We quarrel in print, by the book . *As Y. Like It* v 4 94
A rogue, a villain, that fights by the book of arithmetic! *Rom. and Jul.* iii 1 106
By the church. I do live by the church; for I do live at my house, and
my house doth stand by the church.—So thou mayst say, the king
lies by a beggar, if a beggar dwell near him; or, the church stands
by thy tabor, if thy tabor stand by the church . . *T. Night* iii 1 5
By the ears. The Florentines and Senoys are by the ears . *All's Well* i 2 1
I come to draw you out by the ears . . . 2 *Hen. IV.* ii 4 314
Were half to half the world by the ears . . . *Coriolanus* i 1 237
He'll go, he says, and sowl the porter of Rome gates by the ears . iv 5 214
Will you pluck your sword out of his pilcher by the ears? *Rom. and Jul.* iii 1 84
By the hand. To pinch her by the hand . . *Mer. Wives* iv 6 44
Take, then, this your companion by the hand . *Meas. for Meas.* iv 1 55
Do you think you have fools in hand?—Sir, I have not you by the hand
T. Night i 3 70
We should not step too far Till we had his assistance by the hand 2 *Hen. IV.* i 3 21
By the hour. What expense by the hour Seems to flow from him!
Hen. VIII. iii 2 108
By the way. I can tell you that by the way . . . *Mer. Wives* i 4 150
An intent That perish'd by the way . . . . *Meas. for Meas.* v 1 458
By the way we met My wife, her sister . . . *Com. of Errors* v 1 235
And by the way let us recount our dreams . . *M. N. Dream* iv 1 204
Meeting with Salerio by the way, He did intreat me *Mer. of Venice* iii 2 231
This, by the way, I let you understand . . *T. of Shrew* iv 2 115
By the year. Besides two thousand ducats by the year . . ii 1 371
By-word. Whose cowardice Hath made us by-words to our enemies
3 *Hen. VI.* i 1 42
By yourselves. Withdraw into a chamber by yourselves . *Much Ado* v 4 11
Byzantium. His service done At Lacedæmon and Byzantium Were a
sufficient briber for his life . . . . *T. of Athens* iii 5 60

C

Cabbage. Good worts! good cabbage . . . *Mer. Wives* i 1 124
Cabin. You mar our labour: keep your cabins: you do assist the storm
Tempest i 1 15
To cabin: silence! trouble us not . . . . . i 1 18
Make yourself ready in your cabin for the mischance of the hour, if it
so hap . . . . i 1 28
Now in the waist, the deck, in every cabin, I flamed amazement . i 2 197
Why, what would you?—Make me a willow cabin at your gate *T. Night* i 5 287
In pure white robes, Like very sanctity, she did approach My cabin
W. Tale iii 3 24
Who from my cabin tempted me to walk Upon the hatches *Richard III.* i 4 12
Feed on curds and whey, and suck the goat, And cabin in a cave
T. Andron. iv 2 179
Up from my cabin, My sea-gown scarf'd about me . . *Hamlet* v 2 12
I'll not on shore.—No, to my cabin . . *Ant. and Cleo.* ii 7 137
Cabined. Now I am cabin'd, cribb'd, confined, bound in To saucy doubts
and fears . . . . *Macbeth* iii 4 24
Cable. Make the rope of his destiny our cable . . *Tempest* i 1 34
What though the mast be now blown overboard, The cable broke?
3 *Hen. VI.* v 4 4
The law, with all his might to enforce it on, Will give him cable *Othello* i 2 17
I confess me knit to thy deserving with cables of perdurable toughness i 3 343
Let me cut the cable; And, when we are put off, fall to their throats
Ant. and Cleo. ii 7 77
Cacaliban. 'Ban, 'Ban, Cacaliban Has a new master . . *Tempest* ii 2 188
Cackling. The nightingale, if she should sing by day, When every goose
is cackling . . . . *Mer. of Venice* v 1 105
If I had you upon Sarum plain, I'ld drive ye cackling home to Camelot!
Lear ii 2 90
Cacodemon. Hie thee to hell for shame, and leave the world, Thou
cacodemon! . . . . *Richard III.* i 3 144
Caddis-garter. Agate-ring, puke-stocking, caddis-garter . . 1 *Hen. IV.* ii 4 79
Caddisses. Inkles, caddisses, cambrics, lawns . . *W. Tale* iv 4 208
Cade. I have seduced a headstrong Kentishman, John Cade of Ashford
2 *Hen. VI.* iii 1 357
In Ireland have I seen this stubborn Cade Oppose himself against a
troop of kerns . . . . iii 1 360
Jack Cade the clothier means to dress the commonwealth, and turn it . iv 2 5
We John Cade, so termed of our supposed father,— Or rather, of steal-
ing a cade of herrings . . . . iv 2 33
Jack Cade, the Duke of York hath taught you this . . . iv 2 162
Throughout every town Proclaim them traitors that are up with Cade . iv 2 187
I myself, Rather than bloody war shall cut them short, Will parley with
Jack Cade . . . . iv 4 13
Lord Say, Jack Cade hath sworn to have thy head . . . iv 4 19
Jack Cade proclaims himself Lord Mortimer, Descended from the Duke
of Clarence' house . . . . iv 4 28
Jack Cade hath gotten London bridge: The citizens fly . . iv 4 49
Is Jack Cade slain?—No, my lord, nor likely to be slain . . iv 5 1
Jack Cade! Jack Cade!—Knock him down there . . . iv 6 8
If this fellow be wise, he'll never call ye Jack Cade more . . iv 6 11
Know, Cade, we come ambassadors from the king Unto the commons
whom thou hast misled . . . . iv 8 7
We'll follow Cade, we'll follow Cade! . . . . . iv 8 35
Is Cade the son of Henry the Fifth, That thus you do exclaim you'll go
with him? . . . . iv 8 36
Better ten thousand base-born Cades miscarry Than you should stoop
unto a Frenchman's mercy . . . . iv 8 49
Is the traitor Cade surprised? Or is he but retired to make him strong? iv 9 8
Thus stands my state, 'twixt Cade and York distress'd . . iv 9 31
But now is Cade driven back, his men dispersed . . . iv 9 34
The unconquered soul of Cade is fled . . . . . iv 10 69
Is't Cade that I have slain, that monstrous traitor? . . . iv 10 71
And fight against that monstrous rebel Cade . . . . v 1 62
Lo, I present your grace a traitor's head, The head of Cade . . v 1 67
The head of Cade! Great God, how just art Thou! . . . v 1 68

Cadence. But, for the elegancy, facility, and golden cadence of poesy, caret . . . . *L. L. Lost* iv 2 126
Cadent. With cadent tears fret channels in her cheeks . *Lear* i 4 307
Cadmus. I was with Hercules and Cadmus once . *M. N. Dream* iv 1 117
Caduceus. And, Mercury, lose all the serpentine craft of thy caduceus, if ye take not that ! . . . . *Troi. and Cres.* ii 3 14
Cadwal. The younger brother, Cadwal, Once Arviragus . *Cymbeline* iii 3 95
Cadwal and I Will play the cook and servant ; 'tis our match . . iii 6 29
It sounds ! But what occasion Hath Cadwal now to give it motion ? iv 2 188
Is Cadwal mad ?—Look, here he comes . . . . . iv 2 195
Nay, Cadwal, we must lay his head to the east . . . . iv 2 255
This gentleman, my Cadwal, Arviragus, Your younger princely son . v 5 359
Cadwallader. Not for Cadwallader and all his goats . *Hen. V.* v 1 29
Cælius. Marcus Octavius, Marcus Justeius, Publicola, and Cælius, are for sea . . . . *Ant. and Cleo.* iii 7 74
Caelo. Hangeth like a jewel in the ear of caelo, the sky, the welkin, the heaven . . . . *L. L. Lost* iv 2 5
Cæsar. Thou'rt an emperor, Cæsar, Keisar, and Pheezar . *Mer. Wives* i 3 9
I shall beat you to your tent, and prove a shrewd Cæsar to you *Meas. for Meas.* ii 1 263
What, at the wheels of Cæsar ? art thou led in triumph ? . . iii 2 46
The pommel of Cæsar's falchion . . . . *L. L. Lost* v 2 618
Cæsar's thrasonical brag of 'I came, saw, and overcame' *As Y. Like It* v 2 34
It was a disaster of war that Cæsar himself could not have prevented *All's Well* iii 6 56
This is the way To Julius Cæsar's ill-erected tower . *Richard II.* v 1 2
Came not till now to dignify the times, Since Cæsar's fortunes 2 *Hen. IV.* i 1 23
Compare with Cæsars, and with Cannibals, And Trojan Greeks . ii 4 180
Go forth and fetch their conquering Cæsar in . . *Hen. V.* v Prol. 28
A far more glorious star thy soul will make Than Julius Cæsar 1 *Hen. VI.* i 1 56
Like that proud insulting ship Which Cæsar and his fortune bare at once i 2 139
Brutus' bastard hand Stabb'd Julius Cæsar . . 2 *Hen. VI.* iv 1 137
Kent, in the Commentaries Cæsar writ, Is term'd the civil'st place iv 7 65
No bending knee will call thee Cæsar now . 3 *Hen. VI.* iii 1 18
They that stabb'd Cæsar shed no blood at all . . . . v 5 53
I do not like the Tower, of any place. Did Julius Cæsar build that place, my lord ?—He did . . . . *Richard III.* iii 1 69
That Julius Cæsar was a famous man . . . . . iii 1 84
She shall be sole victress, Cæsar's Cæsar . . . . . iv 4 336
If ever Bassianus, Cæsar's son, Were gracious in the eyes of royal Rome, Keep then this passage to the Capitol . . *T. Andron.* i 1 10
We make holiday, to see Cæsar and to rejoice in his triumph *J. Cæsar* i 1 35
Let no images Be hung with Cæsar's trophies . . . . i 1 74
These growing feathers pluck'd from Cæsar's wing Will make him fly an ordinary pitch . . . . i 1 77
Calpurnia !—Peace, ho ! Cæsar speaks . . . . . i 2 1
Antonius !—Cæsar, my lord ? . . . . i 2 5
When Cæsar says 'do this,' it is perform'd . . . . i 2 10
Cæsar !—Ha ! who calls ?—Bid every noise be still . . . i 2 12
I hear a tongue, shriller than all the music, Cry 'Cæsar !' Speak ; Cæsar is turn'd to hear . . . . i 2 17
Let me see his face.—Fellow, come from the throng ; look upon Cæsar . i 2 21
Many of the best repect in Rome, Except immortal Cæsar . . i 2 60
What means this shouting ? I do fear, the people Choose Cæsar for their king . . . . i 2 80
I was born free as Cæsar ; so were you : We both have fed as well . i 2 97
Cæsar said to me 'Darest thou, Cassius, now Leap in with me into this angry flood ?' . . . . i 2 102
Ere we could arrive the point proposed, Cæsar cried 'Help me, Cassius !' i 2 111
So from the waves of Tiber Did I the tired Cæsar . . . i 2 115
Cassius is A wretched creature and must bend his body, If Cæsar carelessly but nod on him . . . . i 2 118
These applauses are For some new honours that are heap'd on Cæsar i 2 134
Brutus and Cæsar : what should be in that 'Cæsar' ? Why should that name be sounded more than yours ? . . . . . i 2 142
Conjure with 'em, Brutus will start a spirit as soon as Cæsar . i 2 147
Upon what meat doth this our Cæsar feed, That he is grown so great ? i 2 149
The games are done and Cæsar is returning . . . . i 2 178
The angry spot doth glow on Cæsar's brow . . . . i 2 183
Antonius !—Cæsar ?—Let me have men about me that are fat . . i 2 191
Fear him not, Cæsar ; he's not dangerous . . . . i 2 196
I rather tell thee what is to be fear'd Than what I fear ; for always I am Cæsar . . . . i 2 212
Tell us what hath chanced to-day, That Cæsar looks so sad . . i 2 217
Uttered such a deal of stinking breath because Cæsar refused the crown that it had almost choked Cæsar . . . . . . i 2 248
But, soft, I pray you : what, did Cæsar swound ? . . . i 2 253
He hath the falling sickness.—No, Cæsar hath it not . . . i 2 257
I know not what you mean by that ; but, I am sure, Cæsar fell down . i 2 260
If Cæsar had stabbed their mothers, they would have done no less . i 2 277
Marullus and Flavius, for pulling scarfs off Cæsar's images, are put to silence . . . . i 2 289
Cæsar doth bear me hard ; but he loves Brutus . . . . i 2 317
Wherein obscurely Cæsar's ambition shall be glanced at . . . i 2 324
And after this let Cæsar seat him sure ; For we will shake him, or worse days endure . . . . i 2 325
Good even, Casca : brought you Cæsar home ? Why are you breathless ? i 3 1
Comes Cæsar to the Capitol to-morrow ? . . . . . i 3 36
'Tis Cæsar that you mean ; is it not, Cassius ? . . . . i 3 79
The senators to-morrow Mean to establish Cæsar as a king . . i 3 86
And why should Cæsar be a tyrant then ? Poor man ! . . . i 3 103
To illuminate So vile a thing as Cæsar ! . . . . . i 3 111
To speak truth of Cæsar, I have not known when his affections sway'd More than his reason . . . . ii 1 19
So Cæsar may. Then, lest he may, prevent . . . . . ii 1 27
Since Cassius first did whet me against Cæsar, I have not slept . . ii 1 61
Shall no man else be touch'd but only Cæsar ? . . . . ii 1 154
It is not meet, Mark Antony, so well beloved of Cæsar, Should outlive Cæsar . . . . ii 1 156
Let Antony and Cæsar fall together . . . . . . ii 1 161
Antony is but a limb of Cæsar . . . . ii 1 165
We all stand up against the spirit of Cæsar ; And in the spirit of men there is no blood . . . . ii 1 167
O, that we then could come by Cæsar's spirit, And not dismember Cæsar ! . . . . ii 1 169
But, alas, Cæsar must bleed for it ! . . . . . . ii 1 171
He can do no more than Cæsar's arm When Cæsar's head is off . . ii 1 182
If he love Cæsar, all that he can do Is to himself, take thought and die for Cæsar . . . . ii 1 186
It is doubtful yet, Whether Cæsar will come forth to-day, or no . . ii 1 194
Cæsar. Caius Ligarius doth bear Cæsar hard, Who rated him for speaking well of Pompey . . . . *J. Cæsar* ii 1 215
Thrice hath Calpurnia in her sleep cried out, 'Help, ho ! they murder Cæsar !' . . . . ii 2 3
What mean you, Cæsar ? think you to walk forth ? You shall not stir out of your house to-day . . . . ii 2 8
Cæsar shall forth : the things that threaten'd me Ne'er look'd but on my back . . . . ii 2 10
When they shall see The face of Cæsar, they are vanished . . ii 2 12
Cæsar, I never stood on ceremonies, Yet now they fright me . . ii 2 13
O Cæsar ! these things are beyond all use, And I do fear them . ii 2 25
Yet Cæsar shall go forth ; for these predictions Are to the world in general as to Cæsar . . . . ii 2 28
Cæsar should be a beast without a heart, If he should stay at home to-day for fear. No, Cæsar shall not . . . . . . ii 2 42
Danger knows full well That Cæsar is more dangerous than he . . ii 2 45
We are two lions litter'd in one day, And I the elder and more terrible : And Cæsar shall go forth . . . . ii 2 48
Cæsar, all hail ! good morrow, worthy Cæsar . . . . ii 2 58
Shall Cæsar send a lie ? . . . . ii 2 65
Go tell them Cæsar will not come.—Most mighty Cæsar, let me know some cause . . . . ii 2 68
The senate have concluded To give this day a crown to mighty Cæsar . ii 2 94
Break up the senate till another time, When Cæsar's wife shall meet with better dreams . . . . ii 2 99
If Cæsar hide himself, shall they not whisper 'Lo, Cæsar is afraid' ? . ii 2 100
Pardon me, Cæsar ; for my dear dear love To your proceeding bids me tell you this . . . . ii 2 102
Cæsar was ne'er so much your enemy As that same ague which hath made you lean . . . . ii 2 112
Cæsar, 'tis strucken eight.—I thank you for your pains and courtesy . ii 2 114
Good morrow, Antony.—So to most noble Cæsar . . . . ii 2 118
Be near me, that I may remember you.—Cæsar, I will . . . ii 2 124
That every like is not the same, O Cæsar, The heart of Brutus yearns to think upon ! . . . . ii 2 128
Cæsar, beware of Brutus ; take heed of Cassius ; come not near Casca . ii 3 1
There is but one mind in all these men, and it is bent against Cæsar . ii 3 7
Here will I stand till Cæsar pass along, And as a suitor will I give him this ii 3 11
If thou read this, O Cæsar, thou mayst live ; If not, the Fates with traitors do contrive . . . . ii 3 15
And take good note What Cæsar doth, what suitors press to him . ii 4 15
Is Cæsar yet gone to the Capitol ?—Madam, not yet . . . . ii 4 24
Thou hast some suit to Cæsar, hast thou not ? . . . . . ii 4 27
If it will please Cæsar To be so good to Cæsar as to hear me . . ii 4 28
The throng that follows Cæsar at the heels, Of senators, of prætors . ii 4 34
I'll get me to a place more void, and there Speak to great Cæsar as he comes along . . . . ii 4 38
Brutus hath a suit That Cæsar will not grant . . . . ii 4 43
The ides of March are come.—Ay, Cæsar ; but not gone . . . iii 1 2
Hail, Cæsar ! read this schedule . . . . iii 1 3
O Cæsar, read mine first ; for mine's a suit That touches Cæsar nearer : read it, great Cæsar . . . . iii 1 6
Delay not, Cæsar ; read it instantly.—What, is the fellow mad ? . iii 1 9
I fear our purpose is discovered.—Look how he makes to Cæsar : mark him . . . . iii 1 18
If this be known, Cassius or Cæsar never shall turn back, For I will slay myself . . . . iii 1 21
Look, he smiles, and Cæsar doth not change . . . . . iii 1 24
Let him go, And presently prefer his suit to Cæsar . . . . iii 1 28
What is now amiss That Cæsar and his senate must redress ? . . iii 1 32
Most high, most mighty, and most puissant Cæsar . . . . iii 1 33
Be not fond, To think that Cæsar bears such rebel blood That will be thaw'd from the true quality With that which melteth fools . . iii 1 40
Know, Cæsar doth not wrong, nor without cause Will he be satisfied . iii 1 47
Is there no voice more worthy than my own, To sound more sweetly in great Cæsar's ear ? . . . . iii 1 50
I kiss thy hand, but not in flattery, Cæsar . . . . . iii 1 52
What, Brutus !—Pardon, Cæsar ; Cæsar, pardon . . . . iii 1 55
O Cæsar,— Hence ! wilt thou lift up Olympus ? . . . . iii 1 74
Great Cæsar,— Doth not Brutus bootless kneel ? . . . . iii 1 75
Et tu, Brute ! Then fall, Cæsar !—Liberty ! Freedom ! Tyranny is dead ! iii 1 77
Stand fast together, lest some friend of Cæsar's Should chance— Talk not of standing . . . . iii 1 87
So are we Cæsar's friends, that have abridged His time of fearing death iii 1 104
Let us bathe our hands in Cæsar's blood Up to the elbows . . iii 1 106
How many times shall Cæsar bleed in sport ! . . . . . iii 1 114
Cæsar was mighty, bold, royal, and loving . . . . . iii 1 127
Say I fear'd Cæsar, honour'd him and loved him . . . . iii 1 129
Antony May safely come to him, and be resolved How Cæsar hath deserved to lie in death . . . . iii 1 132
Mark Antony shall not love Cæsar dead So well as Brutus living . . iii 1 133
O mighty Cæsar ! dost thou lie so low ? . . . . . . iii 1 148
There is no hour so fit As Cæsar's death's hour . . . . iii 1 154
No place will please me so, no mean of death, As here by Cæsar . . iii 1 162
Pity to the general wrong of Rome—As fire drives out fire, so pity pity —Hath done this deed on Cæsar . . . . iii 1 172
We will deliver you the cause, Why I, that did love Cæsar when I struck him, Have thus proceeded . . . . iii 1 182
That I did love thee, Cæsar, O, 'tis true . . . . . . iii 1 194
The enemies of Cæsar shall say this ; Then, in a friend, it is cold modesty iii 1 212
I blame you not for praising Cæsar so . . . . . . iii 1 214
Therefore I took your hands, but was, indeed, Sway'd from the point, by looking down on Cæsar . . . . iii 1 219
You shall give me reasons Why and wherein Cæsar was dangerous . . iii 1 222
That were you, Antony, the son of Cæsar, You should be satisfied . . iii 1 225
I will myself into the pulpit first, And show the reason of our Cæsar's death . . . . iii 1 237
We are contented Cæsar shall Have all true rites . . . . iii 1 240
Mark Antony, here, take you Cæsar's body . . . . . . iii 1 244
Speak all good you can devise of Cæsar, And say you do't by our permission . . . . iii 1 246
Cæsar's spirit, ranging for revenge, With Ate by his side come hot from hell iii 1 270
You serve Octavius Cæsar, do you not ?—I do, Mark Antony . . iii 1 276
Cæsar did write for him to come to Rome . . . . . . iii 1 278
O Cæsar !—Thy heart is big, get thee apart and weep . . . iii 1 281
Public reasons shall be rendered Of Cæsar's death . . . . iii 2 8
If there be any in this assembly, any dear friend of Cæsar's . . iii 2 19
To him I say, that Brutus' love to Cæsar was no less than his . . iii 2 20
If then that friend demand why Brutus rose against Cæsar, this is my answer . . . . iii 2 22

Cæsar. Not that I loved Cæsar less, but that I loved Rome more *J. Cæsar* iii 2 23
Had you rather Cæsar were living and die all slaves, than that Cæsar were dead, to live all free men? iii 2 24
As Cæsar loved me, I weep for him; as he was fortunate, I rejoice at it iii 2 26
I have done no more to Cæsar than you shall do to Brutus iii 2 40
Let him be Cæsar.—Cæsar's better parts Shall be crown'd in Brutus iii 2 56
Stay here with Antony: Do grace to Cæsar's corpse, and grace his speech Tending to Cæsar's glories iii 2 62
This Cæsar was a tyrant.—Nay, that's certain: We are blest that Rome is rid of him iii 2 74
I come to bury Cæsar, not to praise him iii 2 79
The good is oft interred with their bones; So let it be with Cæsar iii 2 82
The noble Brutus Hath told you Cæsar was ambitious iii 2 83
If it were so, it was a grievous fault, And grievously hath Cæsar answer'd it iii 2 85
Come I to speak in Cæsar's funeral. He was my friend, faithful and just to me iii 2 89
Did this in Cæsar seem ambitious? When that the poor have cried, Cæsar hath wept iii 2 95
My heart is in the coffin there with Cæsar, And I must pause iii 2 111
If thou consider rightly of the matter, Cæsar has had great wrong iii 2 115
But yesterday the word of Cæsar might Have stood against the world iii 2 123
But here's a parchment with the seal of Cæsar; I found it in his closet iii 2 133
They would go and kiss dead Cæsar's wounds And dip their napkins in his sacred blood, Yea, beg a hair of him for memory iii 2 137
It is not meet you know how Cæsar loved you iii 2 146
Being men, hearing the will of Cæsar, It will inflame you, it will make you mad iii 2 148
You shall read us the will, Cæsar's will iii 2 153
I fear I wrong the honourable men Whose daggers have stabb'd Cæsar iii 2 157
Then make a ring about the corpse of Cæsar, And let me show you him that made the will iii 2 162
You all do know this mantle: I remember The first time ever Cæsar put it on iii 2 175
As he pluck'd his cursed steel away, Mark how the blood of Cæsar follow'd it iii 2 182
Brutus, as you know, was Cæsar's angel: Judge, O you gods, how dearly Cæsar loved him! iii 2 185
When the noble Cæsar saw him stab, Ingratitude, more strong than traitors' arms, Quite vanquish'd him iii 2 188
Great Cæsar fell. O, what a fall was there, my countrymen! iii 2 193
Kind souls, what, weep you when you but behold Our Cæsar's vesture wounded? iii 2 200
O piteous spectacle!—O noble Cæsar!—O woful day!—O traitors, villains! iii 2 203
Show you sweet Cæsar's wounds, poor poor dumb mouths, And bid them speak iii 2 229
And put a tongue In every wound of Cæsar iii 2 233
You go to do you know not what: Wherein hath Cæsar thus deserved your loves? iii 2 241
Hear the will.—Here is the will, and under Cæsar's seal iii 2 245
Most noble Cæsar! We'll revenge his death.—O royal Cæsar! iii 2 248
Here was a Cæsar! when comes such another?—Never, never iii 2 257
He and Lepidus are at Cæsar's house iii 2 269
I dreamt to-night that I did feast with Cæsar, And things unluckily charge my fantasy iii 3 1
I am going to Cæsar's funeral.—As a friend or an enemy? iii 3 22
Go you to Cæsar's house; Fetch the will hither iv 1 7
When Cæsar lived, he durst not thus have moved me iv 3 58
Strike, as thou didst at Cæsar iv 3 105
Shall we give sign of battle?—No, Cæsar, we will answer on their charge v 1 24
In your bad strokes, Brutus, you give good words: Witness the hole you made in Cæsar's heart v 1 31
Villains, you did not so, when your vile daggers Hack'd one another in the sides of Cæsar v 1 40
Fawn'd like hounds, And bow'd like bondmen, kissing Cæsar's feet v 1 42
Whilst damned Casca, like a cur, behind Struck Cæsar on the neck v 1 44
When think you that the sword goes up again? Never, till Cæsar's three and thirty wounds Be well avenged; or till another Cæsar Have added slaughter to the sword of traitors v 1 53
Cæsar, thou canst not die by traitors' hands, Unless thou bring'st them with thee v 1 56
With this good sword, That ran through Cæsar's bowels, search this bosom v 3 42
Cæsar, thou art revenged, Even with the sword that kill'd thee v 3 45
O Julius Cæsar, thou art mighty yet! Thy spirit walks abroad v 3 94
The ghost of Cæsar hath appear'd to me Two several times by night v 5 17
Cæsar, now be still: I kill'd not thee with half so good a will v 5 50
All the conspirators save only he Did that they did in envy of great Cæsar v 5 70
My Genius is rebuked; as, it is said, Mark Antony's was by Cæsar *Macb.* iii 1 57
What did you enact?—I did enact Julius Cæsar: I was killed i' the Capitol; Brutus killed me *Hamlet* iii 2 108
Imperious Cæsar, dead and turn'd to clay, Might stop a hole to keep the wind away v 1 236
He is a soldier fit to stand by Cæsar And give direction *Othello* ii 3 127
Who knows If the scarce-bearded Cæsar have not sent His powerful mandate to you, 'Do this, or this' *Ant. and Cleo.* i 1 21
You must not stay here longer, your dismission Is come from Cæsar i 1 27
That blood of thine Is Cæsar's homager i 1 31
Is Cæsar with Antonius prized so slight? i 1 56
Find me to marry me with Octavius Cæsar i 2 29
The time's state Made friends of them, jointing their force 'gainst Cæsar i 2 96
Sextus Pompeius Hath given the dare to Cæsar i 2 191
It is not Cæsar's natural vice to hate Our great competitor i 4 2
Every hour, Most noble Cæsar, shalt thou have report How 'tis abroad i 4 35
It appears he is beloved of those That only have fear'd Cæsar i 4 38
To-morrow, Cæsar, I shall be furnish'd to inform you rightly i 4 76
Broad-fronted Cæsar, When thou wast here above the ground i 5 29
Did I, Charmian, Ever love Cæsar so?—O that brave Cæsar!—Be choked with such another emphasis! i 5 67
Say, the brave Antony.—The valiant Cæsar!—By Isis, I will give thee bloody teeth, If thou with Cæsar paragon again My man of men i 5 69
Cæsar gets money where He loses hearts ii 1 13
Cæsar and Lepidus Are in the field: a mighty strength they carry ii 1 16
I cannot hope Cæsar and Antony shall well greet together: His wife that's dead did trespasses to Cæsar ii 1 39
If Cæsar move him, Let Antony look over Cæsar's head And speak as loud as Mars ii 2 4
Here comes The noble Antony.—And yonder, Cæsar ii 2 14

Cæsar. My being in Egypt, Cæsar, What was't to you? *Ant. and Cleo.* ii 2 35
So much uncurable, her garboils, Cæsar, Made out of her impatience ii 2 67
Soft, Cæsar!—No, Lepidus, let him speak ii 2 83
But, on, Cæsar; The article of my oath ii 2 86
Give me leave, Cæsar,— Speak, Agrippa ii 2 118
I am not married, Cæsar: let me hear Agrippa further speak ii 2 125
Will Cæsar speak?—Not till he hears how Antony is touch'd With what is spoke already ii 2 141
The power of Cæsar, and His power unto Octavia ii 2 145
Welcome from Egypt, sir.—Half the heart of Cæsar, worthy Mecænas! ii 2 175
She made great Cæsar lay his sword to bed ii 2 232
Whose fortunes shall rise higher, Cæsar's or mine?—Cæsar's ii 3 16
Thy demon, that's thy spirit which keeps thee, is Noble, courageous, high, unmatchable, Where Cæsar's is not ii 3 21
If thou say Antony lives, is well, Or friends with Cæsar, or not captive to him, I'll set thee in a shower of gold ii 5 44
He's well.—Well said.—And friends with Cæsar ii 5 47
Cæsar and he are greater friends than ever ii 5 48
He's friends with Cæsar; In state of health thou say'st; and thou say'st free ii 5 55
In praising Antony, I have dispraised Cæsar.—Many times, madam ii 5 107
Julius Cæsar, Who at Philippi the good Brutus ghosted ii 6 12
When Cæsar and your brother were at blows, Your mother came to Sicily ii 6 45
I have heard that Julius Cæsar Grew fat with feasting there ii 6 65
Apollodorus carried . . . A certain queen to Cæsar in a mattress ii 6 71
Cæsar's sister is called Octavia.—True, sir ii 6 116
Then is Cæsar and he for ever knit together ii 6 122
He will to his Egyptian dish again: then shall the sighs of Octavia blow the fire up in Cæsar ii 6 136
Strike the vessels, ho! Here is to Cæsar! ii 7 104
Cæsar and Antony have ever won More in their officer than person iii 1 16
Octavia weeps To part from Rome; Cæsar is sad iii 2 4
'Tis a noble Lepidus.—A very fine one: O, how he loves Cæsar! iii 2 7
Cæsar? Why, he's the Jupiter of men.—What's Antony? The god of Jupiter iii 2 9
Spake you of Cæsar? How! the nonpareil! iii 2 11
Would you praise Cæsar, say 'Cæsar:' go no further iii 2 13
He plied them both with excellent praises.—But he loves Cæsar best iii 2 15
But as for Cæsar, Kneel down, kneel down, and wonder iii 2 18
Will Cæsar weep?—He has a cloud in's face iii 2 50
When Antony found Julius Cæsar dead, He cried almost to roaring iii 2 54
Cæsar and Lepidus have made wars upon Pompey.—This is old: what is the success? iii 5 4
Cæsar, having made use of him in the wars 'gainst Pompey, presently denied him rivality iii 5 7
Our great navy's rigg'd.—For Italy and Cæsar iii 5 21
Who does he accuse?—Cæsar iii 6 24
Hail, Cæsar, and my lord! hail, most dear Cæsar! iii 6 39
Why have you stol'n upon us thus? You come not Like Cæsar's sister iii 6 43
At Pharsalia, Where Cæsar fought with Pompey iii 7 33
In Cæsar's fleet Are those that often have 'gainst Pompey fought iii 7 37
I have sixty sails, Cæsar none better iii 7 50
From the head of Actium Beat the approaching Cæsar iii 7 53
Cæsar has taken Toryne.—Can he be there in person? iii 7 56
This speed of Cæsar's Carries beyond belief iii 7 75
Set we our squadrons on yond side o' the hill, In eye of Cæsar's battle iii 9 2
To Cæsar will I render My legions and my horse: six kings already Show me the way of yielding iii 10 33
Take that, divide it; fly, And make your peace with Cæsar iii 11 6
Know you him?—Cæsar, 'tis his schoolmaster iii 12 2
To the boy Cæsar send this grizzled head, And he will fill thy wishes iii 13 17
Whose ministers would prevail Under the service of a child as soon As i' the command of Cæsar iii 13 25
Like enough, high-battled Cæsar will Unstate his happiness, and be staged to the show, Against a sworder! iii 13 29
That he should dream, Knowing all measures, the full Cæsar will Answer his emptiness! iii 13 35
Cæsar, thou hast subdued His judgement too iii 13 36
Cæsar's will?—Hear it apart.—None but friends iii 13 46
Haply, are they friends to Antony.—He needs as many, sir, as Cæsar has iii 13 49
If Cæsar please, our master Will leap to be his friend iii 13 50
For us, you know Whose he is we are, and that is, Cæsar's iii 13 52
Cæsar entreats, Not to consider in what case thou stand'st, Further than he is Cæsar iii 13 53
Shall I say to Cæsar What you require of him? for he partly begs To be desired to give iii 13 65
Say to great Cæsar this: in deputation I kiss his conquering hand iii 13 74
Cæsar's father oft, When he hath mused of taking kingdoms in, Bestow'd his lips on that unworthy place, As it rain'd kisses iii 13 82
Whip him. Were't twenty of the greatest tributaries That do acknowledge Cæsar iii 13 97
This Jack of Cæsar's shall Bear us an errand to him iii 13 103
I found you as a morsel cold upon Dead Cæsar's trencher iii 13 117
Be thou sorry To follow Cæsar in his triumph, since Thou hast been whipp'd for following him iii 13 136
Get thee back to Cæsar, Tell him thy entertainment: look, thou say He makes me angry with him iii 13 139
To flatter Cæsar, would you mingle eyes With one that ties his points? iii 13 156
Cæsar sits down in Alexandria; where I will oppose his fate iii 13 168
Dares me to personal combat, Cæsar to Antony iv 1 4
Cæsar must think, When one so great begins to rage, he's hunted Even to falling iv 1 6
That he and Cæsar might Determine this great war in single fight! iv 4 36
Call for Enobarbus, He shall not hear thee; or from Cæsar's camp Say 'I am none of thine' iv 5 8
There did persuade Great Herod to incline himself to Cæsar, And leave his master Antony: for this pains Cæsar hath hang'd him iv 6 14
Cæsar himself has work, and our oppression Exceeds what we expected iv 7 2
Let's hear him, for the things he speaks May concern Cæsar iv 9 26
Melt their sweets On blossoming Cæsar iv 12 23
Vanish, or I shall give thee thy deserving, And blemish Cæsar's triumph iv 12 33
She, Eros, has Pack'd cards with Cæsar, and false-play'd my glory iv 14 19
Less noble mind Than she which by her death our Cæsar tells 'I am conqueror of myself' iv 14 61
The time is come: Thou strikest not me, 'tis Cæsar thou defeat'st. iv 14 68
Whilst the wheel'd seat Of fortunate Cæsar, drawn before him, branded His baseness that ensued iv 14 76
This sword but shown to Cæsar, with this tidings, Shall enter me with him iv 14 112

Cæsar. For when she saw—Which never shall be found—you did suspect She had disposed with Cæsar . . . . *Ant. and Cleo.* iv 14 123
Not Cæsar's valour hath o'erthrown Antony, But Antony's hath triumph'd on itself . . . . iv 15 14
Not the imperious show Of the full-fortuned Cæsar ever shall Be brooch'd with me . . . . iv 15 24
Sweet queen: Of Cæsar seek your honour, with your safety. O! . iv 15 46
None about Cæsar trust but Proculeius.—My resolution and my hands I'll trust; None about Cæsar . . . . iv 15 48
Take me to thee, as I was to him I'll be to Cæsar . . v 1 11
What is't thou say'st?—I say, O Cæsar, Antony is dead . . v 1 13
He is dead, Cæsar; Not by a public minister of justice, Nor by a hired knife . . . . v 1 19
Cæsar is touch'd.—When such a spacious mirror's set before him, He needs must see himself . . . . v 1 33
Cæsar cannot live To be ungentle . . . . v 1 59
'Tis paltry to be Cæsar; Not being Fortune, he's but Fortune's knave . v 2 2
Which sleeps, and never palates more the dug, The beggar's nurse and Cæsar's . . . . v 2 8
Cæsar sends greeting to the Queen of Egypt . . . v 2 9
You see how easily she may be surprised: Guard her till Cæsar come . v 2 36
This mortal house I'll ruin, Do Cæsar what he can . . . v 2 52
You do extend These thoughts of horror further than you shall Find cause in Cæsar . . . . v 2 64
What thou hast done thy master Cæsar knows, And he hath sent for thee v 2 65
To Cæsar I will speak what you shall please, If you'll employ me to him v 2 69
Know you what Cæsar means to do with me?—I am loath to tell you . v 2 106
See, Cæsar! O, behold, How pomp is follow'd! . . . v 2 150
O Cæsar, what a wounding shame is this! . . . v 2 159
Say, good Cæsar, That I some lady trifles have reserved, Immoment toys v 2 164
Cæsar's no merchant, to make prize with you Of things that merchants sold v 2 183
Cæsar through Syria Intends his journey . . . v 2 200
Adieu, good queen; I must attend on Cæsar . . . v 2 206
I hear him mock The luck of Cæsar . . . . v 2 289
O, couldst thou speak, That I might hear thee call great Cæsar ass Unpolicied! . . . . v 2 310
Cæsar hath sent— Too slow a messenger . . . v 2 324
Approach, ho! All's not well: Cæsar's beguiled . . . v 2 326
Cæsar, thy thoughts Touch their effects in this . . . v 2 332
A way there, a way for Cæsar! . . . . . v 2 335
O Cæsar, This Charmian lived but now; she stood and spake . v 2 343
Our countrymen Are men more order'd than when Julius Cæsar Smiled at their lack of skill . . . . *Cymbeline* ii 4 21
Now say, what would Augustus Cæsar with us? . . . iii 1 1
Julius Cæsar, whose remembrance yet Lives in men's eyes . . iii 1 2
Cassibelan, thine uncle,—Famous in Cæsar's praises . . iii 1 6
There be many Cæsars, Ere such another Julius . . . iii 1 11
A kind of conquest Cæsar made here; but made not here his brag Of 'Came' and 'saw' and 'overcame' . . . . iii 1 23
The famed Cassibelan, who was once at point—O giglot fortune!—to master Cæsar's sword . . . . iii 1 31
There is no moe such Cæsars: other of them may have crook'd noses, but to owe such straight arms, none . . . iii 1 37
If Cæsar can hide the sun from us with a blanket, or put the moon in his pocket, we will pay him tribute for light . . iii 1 43
Cæsar's ambition, Which swell'd so much that it did almost stretch The sides o' the world . . . . . . iii 1 49
Say, then, to Cæsar, Our ancestor was that Mulmutius which Ordain'd our laws, whose use the sword of Cæsar Hath too much mangled iii 1 54
Augustus Cæsar—Cæsar, that hath more kings his servants than Thyself domestic officers . . . . . . iii 1 63
War and confusion In Cæsar's name pronounce I 'gainst thee . . iii 1 67
Thy Cæsar knighted me; my youth I spent Much under him . iii 1 70
A precedent Which not to read would show the Britons cold: So Cæsar shall not find them . . . . . . iii 1 77
We submit to Cæsar, And to the Roman empire . . . v 5 460
Which foreshow'd our princely eagle, The imperial Cæsar . . v 5 474
Cæsarion, whom they call my father's son . *Ant. and Cleo.* iii 6 6
The first stone Drop in my neck: as it determines, so Dissolve my life! The next Cæsarion smite! . . . . . iii 13 162
Cage. Therefore I have decreed not to sing in my cage . *Much Ado* i 3 36
In which cage of rushes I am sure you are not prisoner . *As Y. Like It* iii 2 389
There was he born, under a hedge, for his father had never a house but the cage . . . . . *2 Hen. VI.* iv 2 56
O, that delightful engine of her thoughts, That blabb'd them with such pleasing eloquence, Is torn from forth that pretty hollow cage! *T. Andron.* iii 1 84
I must up-fill this osier cage of ours With baleful weeds . *Rom. and Jul.* ii 3 7
We two alone will sing like birds i' the cage . . *Lear* v 3 9
Our cage We make a quire, as doth the prison'd bird . *Cymbeline* iii 3 42
Caged. Apollo plays And twenty caged nightingales do sing *T. of Shrew* Ind. 2 38
Cain. What was a month old at Cain's birth, that's not five weeks old as yet? . . . . . . *L. L. Lost* iv 2 36
For since the birth of Cain, the first male child, To him that did but yesterday suspire, There was not such a gracious creature born *K. John* iii 4 79
With Cain go wander thorough shades of night, And never show thy head by day nor light . . . . *Richard II.* v 6 43
Let one spirit of the first-born Cain Reign in all bosoms! . *2 Hen. IV.* i 1 157
Be thou cursed Cain, To slay thy brother Abel, if thou wilt . *1 Hen. VI.* i 3 39
How the knave jowls it to the ground, as if it were Cain's jaw-bone, that did the first murder! . . . . . *Hamlet* v 1 85
Cain-coloured. A little yellow beard, a Cain-coloured beard . *Mer. Wives* i 4 23
Caitiff. O thou caitiff! O thou varlet! O thou wicked Hannibal! *Meas. for Meas.* ii 1 182
What is't your worship's pleasure I shall do with this wicked caitiff? . ii 1 193
The wicked'st caitiff on the ground May seem as shy, as grave, as just, as absolute As Angelo . . . . . . v 1 53
I went To this pernicious caitiff deputy . . . . v 1 88
Whoever charges on his forward breast, I am the caitiff that do hold him to't . . . . . . *All's Well* iii 2 117
A caitiff recreant to my cousin Hereford! . . *Richard II.* i 2 53
For queen, a very caitiff crown'd with care . . *Richard III.* iv 4 100
Here lives a caitiff wretch would sell it him . *Rom. and Jul.* v 1 52
Thou flatter'st misery.—I flatter not; but say thou art a caitiff *T. of Athens* iv 3 235
Seek not my name: a plague consume you wicked caitiffs left! . v 4 71
Caitiff, to pieces shake, That under covert and convenient seeming Hast practised on man's life . . . . . *Lear* iii 2 55
Alas, poor caitiff!—Look, how he laughs already! . . *Othello* iv 1 109
O the pernicious caitiff! . . . . v 2 318

Caius. Ask of Doctor Caius' house which is the way . *Mer. Wives* i 2 2
See if you can see my master, Master Doctor Caius, coming . . i 4 3
Sir Hugh the Welsh priest and Caius the French doctor . . ii 1 209
Master Doctor Caius, the renowned French physician . . iii 1 61
If Anne Page be my daughter, she is, by this, Doctor Caius' wife v 5 186
Here, to Mercury: To Saturn, Caius, not to Saturnine *T. Andron.* iv 3 56
Publius, come hither, Caius, and Valentine! . . . v 2 151
Where is your servant Caius?—He's a good fellow, I can tell you that *Lear* v 3 283
Caius Cassius. Our course will seem too bloody, Caius Cassius *J. Cæsar* ii 1 162
Let us be sacrificers, but not butchers, Caius . . . ii 1 166
Next, Caius Cassius, do I take your hand . . . . ii 1 186
Pardon me, Caius Cassius: The enemies of Cæsar shall say this . iii 1 211
Was that done like Cassius? Should I have answer'd Caius Cassius so? iv 3 78
Brutus, come apace, And see how I regarded Caius Cassius . . v 3 88
Caius Ligarius doth bear Cæsar hard . . . . ii 1 215
Here is a sick man that would speak with you.—Caius Ligarius . ii 1 311
Caius Ligarius! how?—Vouchsafe good morrow from a feeble tongue.—O, what a time have you chose out, brave Caius, To wear a kerchief! ii 1 312
What it is, my Caius, I shall unfold to thee, as we are going . ii 1 329
Caius Ligarius, Cæsar was ne'er so much your enemy As that same ague ii 2 111
Decius Brutus loves thee not: thou hast wronged Caius Ligarius . ii 3 5
Caius Marcius. First, you know Caius Marcius is chief enemy to the people.—We know't, we know't . . . . *Coriolanus* i 1 7
Would you proceed especially against Caius Marcius?—Against him first i 1 27
Where's Caius Marcius?—Here: what's the matter? . . . i 1 227
If we and Caius Marcius chance to meet, 'Tis sworn between us we shall ever strike Till one can do no more . . . . i 2 34
Therefore, be it known, As to us, to all the world, that Caius Marcius Wears this war's garland . . . . . i 9 59
Call him, With all the applause and clamour of the host, CAIUS MARCIUS CORIOLANUS! . . . . i 9 65
He hath won, With fame, a name to Caius Marcius . . . ii 1 181
My gentle Marcius, worthy Caius . . . . . ii 1 189
Report A little of that worthy work perform'd By Caius Marcius Coriolanus . . . . ii 2 50
My name is Caius Marcius, who hath done To thee particularly and to all the Volsces Great hurt and mischief . . . . iv 5 71
Here's he that was wont to thwack our general, Caius Marcius . iv 5 189
Caius Marcius was A worthy officer i' the war; but insolent . iv 6 29
A fearful army, led by Caius Marcius Associated with Aufidius . iv 6 75
When, Caius, Rome is thine, Thou art poor'st of all; then shortly art thou mine . . . . iv 7 56
Ay, traitor, Marcius!—Marcius!—Ay, Marcius, Caius Marcius . v 6 88
Cake. Your cake there is warm withim; you stand here in the cold *Com. of Errors* iii 1 71
Our cake's dough on both sides . . . *T. of Shrew* i 1 110
My cake is dough; but I'll in among the rest, Out of hope of all . v 1 145
Dost thou think, because thou art virtuous, there shall be no more cakes and ale? . . . . . . *T. Night* ii 3 124
He lives upon mouldy stewed prunes and dried cakes . *2 Hen. IV.* ii 4 159
Do you look for ale and cakes here, you rude rascals? *Hen. VIII.* v 4 11
He that will have a cake out of the wheat must needs tarry the grinding *Troi. and Cres.* i 1 15
The making of the cake, the heating of the oven and the baking . i 1 24
Remnants of packthread and old cakes of roses *Rom. and Jul.* v 1 47
Caked. Their blood is caked, 'tis cold, it seldom flows *T. of Athens* ii 2 225
Calaber. The Dukes of Orleans, Calaber, Bretagne and Alençon *2 Hen. VI.* i 1 7
Calais. On toward Calais, ho! . . . . *K. John* iii 3 73
Three parts of that receipt I had for Calais Disbursed I duly . *Richard II.* i 1 126
From the restful English court As far as Calais . . . iv 1 13
Send two of thy men To execute the noble duke at Calais . . iv 1 82
In Calais they stole a fire-shovel . . . . *Hen. V.* iii 2 48
The winter coming on and sickness growing Upon our soldiers, we will retire to Calais . . . . iii 3 56
I do not seek him now; But could be willing to march on to Calais iii 6 150
And then to Calais; and to England then . . . iv 8 130
Now we bear the king Toward Calais . . . . v Prol. 7
As I rode from Calais, To haste unto your coronation . *1 Hen. VI.* iv 1 9
My lord protector and the rest After some respite will return to Calais iv 1 170
Warwick is chancellor and the lord of Calais . . *3 Hen. VI.* i 1 238
Calamities. His wits Are drown'd and lost in his calamities *T. of Athens* iv 3 89
Calamity. As there is no true cuckold but calamity, so beauty's a flower . . . . *T. Night* i 5 57
Too well, too well I feel The different plague of each calamity *K. John* iii 4 60
Like true, inseparable, faithful loves, Sticking together in calamity iii 4 67
So arm'd To bear the tidings of calamity . . . . *Richard II.* iii 2 105
Will'd me to leave my base vocation And free my country from calamity *1 Hen. VI.* i 2 81
Why should calamity be full of words? . . *Richard III.* iv 4 126
You are transported by calamity Thither where more attends you *Coriol.* i 1 77
We must find An evident calamity, though we had Our wish, which side should win . . . . v 3 112
Affliction is enamour'd of thy parts, And thou art wedded to calamity *Rom. and Jul.* iii 3 3
There's the respect That makes calamity of so long life . *Hamlet* iii 1 69
Calchas shall have What he requests of us . . *Troi. and Cres.* iii 3 31
Bring this Greek To Calchas' house . . . . . iv 1 37
Is not yond Diomed, with Calchas' daughter? . . . . iv 5 13
In what place of the field doth Calchas keep? . . . . iv 5 278
Follow his torch; he goes to Calchas' tent . . . . v 1 92
He keeps a Trojan drab, and uses the traitor Calchas' tent . . v 1 105
Calchas, I think. Where's your daughter? . . . . v 2 3
Calculate. A cunning man did calculate my birth And told me that by water I should die . . . . . *2 Hen. VI.* iv 1 34
Why old men fool and children calculate . . . . *J. Cæsar* i 3 65
Calendar. And you the calendars of their nativity *Com. of Errors* v 1 404
A calendar! look in the almanac; find out moonshine . *M. N. Dream* iii 1 54
I wish might be found in the calendar of my past endeavours *All's Well* i 3 4
In golden letters should be set Among the high tides in the calendar? *K. John* iii 1 86
Give me a calendar. Who saw the sun to-day? *Richard III.* v 3 276
Look in the calendar, and bring me word . . *J. Cæsar* ii 1 42
Let this pernicious hour Stand aye accursed in the calendar! . *Macbeth* iv 1 134
To speak feelingly of him, he is the card or calendar of gentry *Hamlet* v 2 114
If it be a day fits you, search out of the calendar, and nobody look after it . . . . *Pericles* ii 1 58
Calf. The ewe that will not hear her lamb when it baes will never answer a calf when he bleats . . . . . *Much Ado* iii 3 76
I thank him; he hath bid me to a calf's head and a capon . v 1 156
Some such strange bull leap'd your father's cow, And got a calf . v 4 50

Calf. He clepeth a calf, cauf; half, hauf; neighbour vocatur nebour *L. L. Lost* v 1 25
Veal, quoth the Dutchman. Is not 'veal' a calf? . . v 2 247
A calf, fair lady!—No, a fair lord calf . . v 2 248
Will you give horns, chaste lady? do not so.—Then die a calf, before your horns do grow . . v 2 253
His leg is too big for Hector's—More calf, certain . . v 2 645
The steer, the heifer and the calf Are all call'd neat *W. Tale* i 2 124
How now, you wanton calf! Art thou my calf? . . i 2 126
Your father might have kept This calf bred from his cow from all the world *K. John* i 1 124
As the butcher takes away the calf And binds the wretch and beats it when it strays *2 Hen. VI.* iii 1 210
Then is sin struck down like an ox, and iniquity's throat cut like a calf iv 2 29
As fox to lamb, as wolf to heifer's calf, Pard to the hind *Troi. and Cres.* iii 2 200
But where the bull and cow are both milk-white, They never do beget a coal-black calf *T. Andron.* v 1 32
It was a brute part of him to kill so capital a calf *Hamlet* iii 2 111
Calf-like. So I charm'd their ears That calf-like they my lowing follow'd *Tempest* iv 1 179
Calf's-skin. He that goes in the calf's skin that was killed for the Prodigal *Com. of Errors* iv 3 18
Thou wear a lion's hide! doff it for shame, And hang a calf's-skin on those recreant limbs *K. John* iii 1 129
Hang nothing but a calf's-skin, most sweet lout . . iii 1 220
Will not a calf's-skin stop that mouth of thine? . . iii 1 299
Is not parchment made of sheep-skins?—Ay, my lord, and of calf-skins too *Hamlet* v 1 124
Caliban her son.—Dull thing, I say so; he, that Caliban Whom now I keep in service *Tempest* i 2 284
We'll visit Caliban my slave, who never Yields us kind answer . . i 2 308
What, ho! slave! Caliban! Thou earth, thou! speak . . i 2 313
Thou didst prevent me; I had peopled else This isle with Calibans . . i 2 351
Thou think'st there is no more such shapes as he, Having seen but him and Caliban: foolish wench! . . i 2 479
To the most of men this is a Caliban And they to him are angels . . i 2 480
I had forgot that foul conspiracy Of the beast Caliban and his confederates iv 1 140
Spirit, We must prepare to meet with Caliban . . iv 1 166
And I, thy Caliban, For aye thy foot-licker . . iv 1 218
Set Caliban and his companions free . . v 1 252
Calipolis. Then feed, and be fat, my fair Calipolis *2 Hen. IV.* ii 4 193
Caliver. Fear the report of a caliver worse than a struck fowl *1 Hen. IV.* iv 2 21
Put me a caliver into Wart's hand, Bardolph *2 Hen. IV.* iii 2 289
Come, manage me your caliver . . iii 2 292
Call. Thou mightst call him A goodly person *Tempest* i 2 415
I might call him A thing divine, for nothing natural I ever saw so noble i 2 417
Doth thy other mouth call me? Mercy, Mercy! . . ii 2 101
Nor have I seen More that I may call men than you . . iii 1 51
He has brave utensils,—for so he calls them . . iii 2 104
He himself Calls her a nonpareil . . iii 2 108
Do not approach Till thou dost hear me call . . iv 1 50
Whom to call brother Would even infect my mouth . . v 1 130
Supportable To make the dear loss, have I means much weaker Than you may call to comfort you . . v 1 147
You should wrangle, And I would call it fair play . . v 1 175
It were a shame to call her back again *T. G. of Ver.* i 2 51
Your father calls for you: He is in haste . . i 3 88
She is not within hearing, sir.—Why, sir, who bade you call her? . . ii 1 9
I was sent to call thee.—Sir, call me what thou darest . . ii 3 62
She is an earthly paragon.—Call her divine . . ii 4 147
Fie, fie, unreverend tongue! to call her bad . . ii 6 14
A sea of melting pearl, which some call tears . . iii 1 224
Go to thy lady's grave and call hers thence . . iv 2 117
Entreated me to call and know her mind . . iv 3 2
Who calls?—Your servant and your friend . . iv 3 4
'Convey,' the wise it call. 'Steal!' foh! a fico for the phrase! *Mer. Wives* i 3 32
I may call him my master, look you . . i 4 100
I wrong him to call him poor . . ii 2 282
That calls himself doctor of physic . . iii 1 4
What do you call your knight's name, sirrah? . . iii 2 21
And when I suddenly call you, come forth . . iii 3 11
Be not amazed; call all your senses to you . . iii 3 125
She calls you, coz: I'll leave you . . iii 4 54
Somebody call my wife . . iv 2 121
Ay, sir; I'll call them to you . . iv 3 9
Go knock and call . . iv 5 9
The knight may be robbed: I'll call . . iv 5 17
What, is't murder?—No.—Lechery?—Call it so *Meas. for Meas.* ii 1 144
Who's that which calls?—It is a man's voice . . i 4 6
He calls again; I pray you, answer him . . i 4 14
Peace and prosperity! Who is't that calls? . . i 4 15
I, that do speak a word, May call it back again . . ii 2 58
Nay, call us ten times frail; For we are soft as our complexions are ii 4 128
For thine own bowels, which do call thee sire . . iii 1 29
Do you call, sir?—Sirrah, here's a fellow will help you . . iv 2 22
Do you call, sir, your occupation a mystery? . . iv 2 35
Call your executioner, and off with Barnardine's head . . iv 2 222
I'll call you at your house . . iv 4 18
Go call at Flavius' house, And tell him where I stay . . iv 5 6
Call that same Isabel here once again . . v 1 270
And in the witness of his proper ear, To call him villain . . v 1 311
My present business calls me from you now *Com. of Errors* i 2 29
I will beat this method in your sconce.—Sconce call you it? . . ii 2 35
Thou art thus estranged from thyself? Thyself I call it, being strange to me . . ii 2 123
How can she thus then call us by our names? . . ii 2 168
Comfort my sister, cheer her, call her wife . . iii 2 26
Why call you me love? call my sister so . . iii 2 59
Call thyself sister, sweet, for I am thee . . iii 2 66
She that doth call me husband, even my soul Doth for a wife abhor . iii 2 163
And every one doth call me by my name . . iv 3 3
Let's call more help to have them bound again . . iv 4 149
This fair gentlewoman, her sister here, Did call me brother . . v 1 374
And presently call the rest of the watch together *Much Ado* iii 3 30
Call at all the alehouses, and bid those that are drunk get them to bed iii 3 44
If you hear a child cry in the night, you must call to the nurse . iii 3 70
What kind of catechising call you this? . . iv 1 79
This is flat perjury, to call a prince's brother villain . . iv 2 44
This plaintiff here, the offender, did call me ass . . v 1 315
I will call Beatrice to you, who I think hath legs . . v 2 23
Call. Being else by faith enforced To call young Claudio to a reckoning *Much Ado* v 4 9
One more than two.—Which the base vulgar do call three *L. L. Lost* i 2 51
Do not call it sin in me, That I am forsworn for thee . . iv 3 115
Too odd, as it were, too peregrinate, as I may call it . . v 1 16
The posteriors of this day, which the rude multitude call the afternoon v 1 95
You were best call it 'daughter-beamed eyes' . . v 2 171
The ladies call him sweet; The stairs, as he treads on them, kiss his feet . . v 2 329
I dare not call them fools . . v 2 371
Call you me fair? that fair again unsay *M. N. Dream* i 1 181
You were best to call them generally, man by man . . i 2 2
Masters, spread yourselves.—Answer as I call you . . i 2 18
Those that Hobgoblin call you and sweet Puck . . ii 1 40
He murder cries and help from Athens calls . . iii 2 26
To call me goddess, nymph, divine and rare, Precious, celestial . iii 2 226
When I come where he calls, then he is gone . . iii 2 414
Music call; and strike more dead Than common sleep of all these five the sense . . iv 1 86
When my cue comes, call me, and I will answer . . iv 1 205
We will make amends ere long; Else the Puck a liar call . . v 1 442
I take it, your own business calls on you And you embrace the occasion to depart *Mer. of Venice* i 1 63
Would call their brothers fools . . i 1 99
You call me misbeliever, cut-throat dog, And spit upon my Jewish gaberdine . . i 3 112
I am as like to call thee so again, To spit on thee again . . i 3 131
Who bids thee call? I do not bid thee call . . ii 5 7
Call you? what is your will?—I am bid forth to supper . . ii 5 10
The Goodwins, I think they call the place . . iii 1 5
He was wont to call me usurer; let him look to his bond . . iii 1 50
First go with me to church and call me wife . . iii 2 305
Go one, and call the Jew into the court . . iv 1 14
Call you that keeping for a gentleman of my birth? *As. Y Like It* i 1 9
What shall I call thee when thou art a man? . . i 3 125
Look you call me Ganymede. But what will you be call'd? . . i 3 127
I will not call him son Of him I was about to call his father . . ii 3 20
Who calls?—Your betters, sir . . ii 4 67
Come, more; another stanzo: call you 'em stanzos? . . ii 5 19
That they call compliment is like the encounter of two dog-apes . . ii 5 26
A Greek invocation, to call fools into a circle . . ii 5 61
Call me not fool till heaven hath sent me fortune . . ii 7 19
Thy lands and all things that thou dost call thine Worth seizure do we seize . . iii 1 9
I would cure you, if you would but call me Rosalind . . iii 2 446
With all my heart, good youth.—Nay, you must call me Rosalind . iii 2 455
Good even, good Master What-ye-call't: how do you, sir? . . iii 3 75
And I am your Rosalind.—It pleases him to call you so . . iv 1 66
She calls me proud, and that she could not love me . . iv 3 16
Can a woman rail thus?—Call you this railing? . . iv 3 43
Call you this chiding? . . iv 3 64
The shepherd youth That he in sport doth call his Rosalind . . iv 3 157
Neither call the giddiness of it in question . . v 2 6
Call him 'madam,' do him obeisance *T. of Shrew* Ind. 1 108
Call not me 'honour' nor 'lordship' . . Ind. 2 5
Are you my wife and will not call me husband? My men should call me 'lord' . . Ind. 2 106
What must I call her?—Madam . . Ind. 2 110
'Madam,' and nothing else: so lords call ladies . . Ind. 2 113
She may perhaps call him half a score knaves or so . . i 2 110
Whence are you, sir? what may I call your name? . . ii 1 67
'Frets, call you these?' quoth she; 'I'll fume with them' . . ii 1 153
She did call me rascal fiddler And twangling Jack . . ii 1 158
They call me Katharine that do talk of me . . ii 1 185
Call you me daughter? now, I promise you You have show'd a tender fatherly regard . . ii 1 287
Call you this gamut? tut, I like it not . . iii 1 79
After many ceremonies done, He calls for wine . . iii 2 172
My haste doth call me hence . . iii 2 189
Who is that calls so coldly?—A piece of ice . . iv 1 13
Thou, it seems, that calls for company to countenance her . . iv 1 104
Another way I have to man my haggard, To make her come and know her keeper's call . . iv 1 197
Go, call my men, and let us straight to him . . iv 3 186
Please it you that I call?—Ay, what else? . . iv 4 1
An if you please to call it a rush-candle, Henceforth I vow it shall be so for me . . iv 5 14
Fie! what a foolish duty call you this? . . v 2 125
All That happiness and prime can happy call *All's Well* ii 1 185
You shall read it in—what do ye call there? . . ii 3 25
Go, call before me all the lords in court . . ii 3 52
You are not worth another word, else I'ld call you knave . . ii 3 281
A very serious business calls on him . . ii 4 41
Then call me husband: but in such a 'then' I write a 'never' . iii 2 62
She deserves a lord That twenty such rude boys might tend upon And call her hourly mistress . . iii 2 85
Thou shalt live as freely as thy lord, To call his fortunes thine *T. Night* i 4 40
She bore a mind that envy could not but call fair . . ii 1 31
I shall be constrained in't to call thee knave . . ii 3 69
'Tis not the first time I have constrained one to call me knave . ii 3 72
Where shall I find you?—We'll call thee at the cubiculo . . iii 2 56
Wonder not, nor admire not in thy mind, why I do call thee so . iii 4 166
Thou dishonest Satan! I call thee by the most modest terms . iv 2 35
O thou thing! Which I'll not call a creature of thy place *W. Tale* ii 1 83
Our prerogative Calls not your counsels . . ii 1 164
Then 'twere past all doubt You'ld call your children yours . . ii 3 81
I'll not call you tyrant . . ii 3 116
Were I a tyrant, Where were her life? she durst not call me so . ii 3 123
Shall I live on to see this bastard kneel And call me father? . ii 3 156
Streak'd gillyvors, Which some call nature's bastards . . iv 4 83
Then make your garden rich in gillyvors, And do not call them bastards iv 4 99
They call themselves Saltiers . . iv 4 334
This is desperate, sir.—So call it . . iv 4 497
That I may call thee something more than man And after that trust to thee . . iv 4 546
Should I now meet my father, He would not call me son . . iv 4 672
Let him call me rogue for being so far officious . . iv 4 871
Your father's image is so hit in you, His very air, that I should call you brother . . v 1 128
I am thy grandam, Richard; call me so . . *K. John* i 1 168

Call. And if his name be George, I'll call him Peter . . . *K. John* i 1 186
Call for our chiefest men of discipline, To cull the plots of best advantages ii 1 39
Who is it thou dost call usurper, France? . . . ii 1 120
Thou monstrous injurer of heaven and earth! Call not me slanderer . ii 1 175
Call them meteors, prodigies and signs, Abortives . . . iii 4 157
They would be as a call To train ten thousand English to their side . iii 4 174
You may think my love was crafty love And call it cunning . . iv 1 54
Then call them to our presence; face to face . . . *Richard II.* i 1 15
I spit at him; Call him a slanderous coward and a villain . . i 1 61
Call it not patience, Gaunt; it is despair . . . i 2 29
Call it a travel that thou takest for pleasure . . . i 3 262
I brought high Hereford, if you call him so, But to the next highway . i 4 3
'Tis doubt, When time shall call him home from banishment . . i 4 21
Unless you call it good to pity him . . . ii 1 236
Barkloughly castle call they this at hand? . . . iii 2 1
Nothing can we call our own but death And that small model of the barren earth . . . iii 2 152
Base court, where kings grow base, To come at traitors' calls . . iii 3 181
My Lord of Hereford here, whom you call king . . . iv 1 134
I have worn so many winters out, And know not now what name to call myself! . . . iv 1 259
And, madam, you must call him Rutland now . . . v 2 43
Did I ever call for thee to pay thy part? . . . *1 Hen. IV.* i 2 57
An I do not, call me villain and baffle me . . . i 2 113
In Richard's time,—what do you call the place? . . . i 3 242
They are up already, and call for eggs and butter . . . ii 1 65
Call them all by their christen names, as Tom, Dick, and Francis . ii 4 8
A good boy, by the Lord, so they call me . . . ii 4 14
They call drinking deep, dyeing scarlet . . . ii 4 16
Away, you rogue! dost thou not hear them call? . . . ii 4 89
An ye call me coward, by the Lord, I'll stab thee . . . ii 4 159
I call thee coward! I'll see thee damned ere I call thee coward . ii 4 161
Call you that backing of your friends? A plague upon such backing! . ii 4 165
Fought you with them all?—All! I know not what you call all . . ii 4 204
If I tell thee a lie, spit in my face, call me horse . . . ii 4 215
What a plague call you him? . . . ii 4 373
Never call a true piece of gold a counterfeit . . . ii 4 539
Which calls me pupil, or hath read to me . . . iii 1 46
I can call spirits from the vasty deep.—Why, so can I, or so can any man; But will they come when you do call for them? . . . iii 1 52
I will call him to so strict account, That he shall render every glory up iii 2 149
How! poor? look upon his face; what call you rich? . . . iii 3 90
Setting thy knighthood aside, thou art a knave to call me so . . iii 3 138
Unless you call three fingers on the ribs bare . . . iv 2 79
What need I be so forward with him that calls not on me? . . v 1 130
And will you yet call yourself young? . . . *2 Hen. IV.* i 2 209
Saying that ere long they should call me madam . . . ii 1 109
You call honourable boldness impudent sauciness . . . ii 1 134
One it pleases me, for fault of a better, to call my friend . . ii 2 45
A' calls me e'en now, my lord, through a red lattice . . . ii 2 85
Althæa dreamed she was delivered of a fire-brand; and therefore I call him her dream . . . ii 2 98
Call him up, drawer.—Cheater, call you him? . . . ii 4 109
Call me pantler and bread-chipper and I know not what? . . . ii 4 341
Phrase call you it? by this good day, I know not the phrase . . iii 2 81
Let them appear as I call; let them do so . . . iii 2 109
To the place of difference call the swords Which must decide it . . iv 1 181
Now call we our high court of parliament . . . v 2 134
If thou wantest any thing, and wilt not call, beshrew thy heart . . v 3 59
He'll call you to so hot an answer . . . *Hen. V.* ii 4 123
They will steal any thing, and call it purchase . . . iii 2 45
The town is beseeched, and the trumpet call us to the breach . . iii 2 116
Poor we may call them in their native lords . . . iii 5 26
What do you call him? . . . iii 6 18
All other jades you may call beasts . . . iii 7 26
You may call the business of the master the author of the servant's damnation . . . iv 1 161
They call it Agincourt.—Then call we this the field of Agincourt . iv 7 92
Call yonder fellow hither . . . iv 7 123
Upon that I kiss your hand, and I call you my queen . . . v 2 272
Open the gates; 'tis Gloucester that calls . . . *1 Hen. VI.* i 3 4
I'll call for clubs, if you will not away . . . i 3 84
Which of this princely train Call ye the warlike Talbot? . . . ii 2 35
Call we to mind, and mark but this for proof . . . iii 3 68
English John Talbot, captains, calls you forth . . . iv 2 3
Call my sovereign yours, And do him homage as obedient subjects . iv 2 6
O, that I could but call these dead to life! . . . iv 7 81
I'll call for pen and ink, and write my mind . . . v 3 66
You shall go near To call them both a pair of crafty knaves . *2 Hen. VI.* i 2 103
Many time and oft Myself have heard a voice to call him so . . ii 1 94
Call these foul offenders to their answers . . . ii 1 203
If it be fond, call it a woman's fear . . . iii 1 36
Go, call our uncle to our presence straight . . . iii 2 15
I'll call him presently, my noble lord . . . iii 2 18
Ungentle queen, to call him gentle Suffolk! . . . iii 2 290
Sometime he calls the king And whispers to his pillow as to him . . iii 2 374
The false revolting Normans thorough thee Disdain to call us lord . iv 1 88
And calls your grace usurper openly . . . iv 4 30
All scholars, lawyers, courtiers, gentlemen, They call false caterpillars iv 4 37
It shall be treason for any that calls me other than Lord Mortimer . iv 6 6
If this fellow be wise, he'll never call ye Jack Cade more . . iv 6 10
Thou hast appointed justices of peace, to call poor men before them . iv 7 46
King did I call thee? no, thou art not king . . . v 1 93
What a brood of traitors have we here!—Look in a glass, and call thy image so . . . v 1 142
Call Buckingham, and bid him arm himself . . . v 1 192
Call Buckingham, and all the friends thou hast . . . v 1 193
Clifford of Cumberland, 'tis Warwick calls . . . v 2 1
The king is fled to London, To call a present court of parliament . v 3 25
And call them pillars that will stand to us . . . *3 Hen. VI.* i 3 51
Can neither call it perfect day nor night . . . ii 5 4
No bending knee will call thee Cæsar now . . . iii 1 18
'Twill grieve your grace my sons should call you father.—No more than when my daughters call thee mother . . . iii 2 100
Call Edward king.—Call him my king? . . . iii 3 100
Humbly bend thy knee, Call Edward king and at his hands beg mercy . v 1 23
Call Warwick patron and be penitent . . . v 1 27
Come, Clarence, come; thou wilt, if Warwick call . . . v 1 80
And this word 'love,' which greybeards call divine, Be resident in men like one another And not in me . . . v 6 81

Call. Were it to call King Edward's widow sister, I will perform it *Richard III.* i 1 109
Richard!—Ha!—I call thee not . . . i 3 234
His majesty doth call for you; And for your grace . . . i 3 320
Why do you look on us, and shake your head, And call us wretches? . ii 2 6
My dread lord; so must I call you now . . . iii 1 97
I would, that I might thank you as you call me.—How?—Little . iii 1 123
Call them again, my lord, and accept their suit . . . iii 7 221
Well, call them again. I am not made of stones . . . iii 7 224
The king that calls your beauteous daughter wife, Familiarly shall call thy Dorset brother . . . iv 4 315
Good mother,—I must call you so—Be the attorney of my love to her . iv 4 412
Call for some men of sound direction . . . v 3 16
He is attach'd; Call him to present trial . . . *Hen. VIII.* i 2 211
It calls, I fear, too many curses on their heads That were the authors . ii 1 137
She's going away.—Call her again . . . ii 4 125
My robe, And my integrity to heaven, is all I dare now call mine own . iii 2 454
You must no more call it York-place, that's past . . . iv 1 95
It is not you I call for: Saw ye none enter since I slept? . . iv 2 85
When heaven shall call her from this cloud of darkness . . . v 5 45
Call here my varlet; I'll unarm again . . . *Troi. and Cres.* i 1 1
They call him Ajax.—Good; and what of him? . . . i 2 14
Do you with cheeks abash'd behold our works, And call them shames? . i 3 19
Which, slanderer, he imitation calls . . . i 3 150
They tax our policy, and call it cowardice . . . i 3 197
How many hands shall strike, When fitness calls them on . . . i 3 202
They call this bed-work, mappery, closet-war . . . i 3 205
Sir, you of Troy, call you yourself Æneas? . . . i 3 245
And will to-morrow with his trumpet call . . . i 3 277
To-morrow morning call some knight to arms That hath a stomach . ii 1 136
You may call it melancholy, if you will favour the man . . . ii 3 94
Shall I call you father?—Ay, my good son . . . iii 3 267
That if the king call for him at supper, you will make his excuse . iii 1 84
She'll bereave you o' the deeds too, if she call your activity in question iii 2 60
Call them all Pandars . . . iii 2 209
The advantage of the time prompts me aloud To call for recompense . iii 3 3
I constantly do think—Or rather, call my thought a certain knowledge iv 1 41
I'll call mine uncle down; He shall unbolt the gates . . . iv 2 2
A kind of godly jealousy—Which, I beseech you, call a virtuous sin . iv 4 83
In this I do not call your faith in question So mainly as my merit . iv 4 86
The dreadful spout Which shipmen do the hurricano call . . . v 2 172
Call him noble that was now your hate, Him vile that was your garland *Coriolanus* i 1 187
Methinks I see him stamp thus, and call thus . . . i 3 35
Call him, With all the applause and clamour of the host, CAIUS MARCIUS CORIOLANUS! . . . i 9 63
I cannot call you Lycurguses . . . ii 1 60
Coriolanus must I call thee? . . . ii 1 191
We call a nettle but a nettle and The faults of fools but folly . . ii 1 207
Call Coriolanus.—He doth appear . . . ii 2 134
He himself stuck not to call us the many-headed multitude . . . ii 3 17
Custom calls me to't: What custom wills, in all things should we do't ii 3 124
Call't not a plot: The people cry you mock'd them . . . iii 1 41
We debase The nature of our seats and make the rabble Call our cares fears . . . iii 1 137
Go, call the people: in whose name myself Attach thee . . . iii 1 174
I muse my mother Does not approve me further, who was wont To call them woollen vassals . . . iii 2 9
The fires i' the lowest hell fold-in the people! Call me their traitor! . iii 3 69
Yet one time he did call me by my name . . . v 1 9
Call all your tribes together, praise the gods, And make triumphant fires . . . v 5 2
Please it your honours To call me to your senate . . . v 6 141
Rape, call you it, my lord, to seize my own? . . . *T. Andron.* i 1 405
Call for sweet water, wash thy hands . . . ii 4 6
She hath no tongue to call, nor hands to wash . . . ii 4 7
Let fools do good, and fair men call for grace . . . iii 1 205
If any power pities wretched tears, To that I call! . . . iii 1 210
Or else I'll call my brother back again . . . v 2 135
What boots it thee to call thyself a sun? . . . v 3 18
A crutch, a crutch! why call you for a sword? . . . *Rom. and Jul.* i 1 83
Examine other beauties.—'Tis the way To call hers exquisite, in question more . . . i 1 235
Who calls?—Your mother.—Madam, I am here. What is your will? . i 3 5
That which we call a rose By any other name would smell as sweet . ii 2 43
Call me but love, and I'll be new baptized . . . ii 2 50
I have forgot why I did call thee back.—Let me stand here till thou remember . . . ii 2 171
Then love-devouring death do what he dare; It is enough I may but call her mine . . . ii 6 8
Your worship in that sense may call him 'man' . . . iii 1 62
O rude unthankfulness! Thy fault our law calls death . . . iii 3 25
And now falls on her bed; and then starts up, And Tybalt calls . iii 3 101
And call thee back With twenty hundred thousand times more joy . iii 3 152
It is so very very late, That we may call it early by and by . . iii 4 35
O fortune, fortune! all men call thee fickle . . . iii 5 60
Who is't that calls? is it my lady mother? . . . iii 5 66
Thy eyes, which I may call the sea, Do ebb and flow with tears . . iii 5 133
Do thou but call my resolution wise . . . iv 1 53
I'll call them back again to comfort me: Nurse! What should she do here? . . . iv 3 17
They call for dates and quinces in the pastry . . . iv 4 2
Fetch drier logs: Call Peter, he will show thee where they are . . iv 4 16
Who calls so loud?—Come hither, man . . . v 1 57
O Lord, they fight! I will go call the watch . . . v 3 71
Which their keepers call A lightning before death: O, how may I Call this a lightning? . . . v 3 89
What misadventure is so early up, That calls our person from our morning's rest? . . . v 3 189
Call the man before thee.—Attends he here, or no? . . . *T. of Athens* i 1 113
I call the gods to witness . . . i 1 137
Why dost thou call them knaves? thou know'st them not . . . i 1 181
It hath pleased the gods to remember my father's age, And call him to long peace . . . i 2 3
I'll call to you.—O, none so welcome . . . i 2 223
Call me before the exactest auditors And set me on the proof . . ii 2 165
Who can call him His friend that dips in the same dish? . . . iii 2 72
He goes away in a cloud: call him, call him . . . iii 4 42
Call me to your remembrances.—What!—I cannot think but your age has forgot me . . . iii 5 92

Call. Praise his most vicious strain, And call it excellent *T. of Athens* iv 3 214
Call the creatures Whose naked natures live in all the spite Of wreakful heaven iv 3 227
Ha! who calls?—Bid every noise be still: peace yet again! *J. Cæsar* i 2 13
Call it my fear That keeps you in the house, and not your own ii 2 50
Call the field to rest; and let's away, To part the glories of this happy day v 5 80
Paddock calls.—Anon.—Fair is foul, and foul is fair *Macbeth* i 1 9
He bade me, from him, call thee thane of Cawdor i 3 105
Get on your nightgown, lest occasion call us, And show us to be watchers ii 2 70
I'll make so bold to call, For 'tis my limited service ii 3 56
Now go to the door, and stay there till we call iii 1 73
Our masters?—Call 'em; let me see 'em iv 1 63
What need we fear who knows it, when none can call our power to account? v 1 43
Others that lesser hate him Do call it valiant fury v 2 14
Do you believe his tenders, as you call them? *Hamlet* i 3 103
Ay, fashion you may call it; go to, go to i 3 112
I'll call thee Hamlet, King, father, royal Dane i 4 44
So call it, Sith nor the exterior nor the inward man Resembles that it was ii 2 5
Your noble son is mad: Mad call I it ii 2 93
The common stages—so they call them ii 2 358
If you call me Jephthah, my lord, I have a daughter that I love ii 2 430
Am I a coward? Who calls me villain? breaks my pate across? ii 2 599
What do you call the play?—The Mouse-trap iii 2 246
Call me what instrument you will, though you can fret me, yet you cannot play upon me iii 2 387
An act That blurs the grace and blush of modesty, Calls virtue hypocrite iii 4 42
You cannot call it love; for at your age The hey-day in the blood is tame iii 4 68
Pinch wanton on your cheek; call you his mouse iii 4 183
What noise? who calls on Hamlet? iv 2 3
The rabble call him lord iv 5 102
You must sing a-down a-down, An you call him a-down-a iv 5 171
We will our kingdom give, Our crown, our life, and all that we call ours iv 5 208
I must call't in question iv 5 217
Even his mother shall uncharge the practice And call it accident iv 7 69
And that he calls for drink, I'll have prepared him A chalice for the nonce iv 7 160
But our cold maids do dead men's fingers call them iv 7 172
What call you the carriages? v 2 161
Why is this 'imponed,' as you call it? v 2 171
Let us haste to hear it, And call the noblest to the audience v 2 398
Call France; who stirs? Call Burgundy *Lear* i 1 128
Let pride, which she calls plainness, marry her i 1 131
Like a sister am most loath to call Your faults as they are named i 1 273
You have that in your countenance which I would fain call master i 4 30
What says the fellow there? Call the clotpoll back i 4 50
That then necessity Will call discreet proceeding i 4 233
Saddle my horses; call my train together i 4 274
Since I came hither, Which I can call but now ii 1 89
Why dost thou call him knave? What's his offence? ii 2 95
I am too old to learn: Call not your stocks for me ii 2 135
Thou art my flesh, my blood, my daughter; Or rather a disease that's in my flesh, Which I must needs call mine ii 4 226
Let shame come when it will, I do not call it ii 4 229
Why might not you, my lord, receive attendance From those that she calls servants or from mine? ii 4 247
He calls to horse; but will I know not whither ii 4 300
But yet I call you servile ministers iii 2 21
You have been conjunct And bosom'd with her, as far as we call hers v 1 13
The which immediacy may well stand up, And call itself your brother v 3 66
Call by thy trumpet: he that dares approach, On him, on you, who not? v 3 99
My master calls me, I must not say no v 3 322
Here is her father's house; I'll call aloud *Othello* i 1 74
At every house I'll call; I may command at most i 1 181
To prison, till fit time Of law and course of direct session Call thee to answer i 2 87
Whereof I take this that you call love to be a sect or scion i 3 336
If thou hast no name to be known by, let us call thee devil! ii 3 284
I prithee, call him back.—Went he hence now? iii 3 51
Good love, call him back.—Not now, sweet Desdemona iii 3 54
O curse of marriage, That we can call these delicate creatures ours, And not their appetites! iii 3 269
I do beseech your lordship, call her back iv 1 260
Is this the noble Moor whom our full senate Call all in all sufficient? iv 1 276
Remember; And call thy husband hither iv 2 106
Why should he call her whore? who keeps her company? iv 2 137
He calls me to a restitution large Of gold and jewels that I bobb'd from him v 1 15
Thou dost stone my heart, And makest me call what I intend to do A murder v 2 64
We cannot call her winds and waters sighs and tears *Ant. and Cleo.* i 2 153
Your honour calls you hence; Therefore be deaf to my unpitied folly i 3 97
Full surfeits, and the dryness of his bones, Call on him for't i 4 27
'Where's my serpent of old Nile?' For so he calls me i 5 26
All the east, Say thou, shall call her mistress i 5 47
Call the slave again: Though I am mad, I will not bite him: call ii 5 79
At the feet sat Cæsarion, whom they call my father's son iii 6 6
Who, queasy with his insolence Already, will their good thoughts call from him iii 6 21
That ever I should call thee castaway!—You have not call'd me so, nor have you cause iii 6 40
Call to me All my sad captains; fill our bowls once more iii 13 183
Call all his noble captains to my lord iii 13 189
He calls me boy; and chides, as he had power To beat me out of Egypt iv 1 1
Too late, good Diomed: call my guard, I prithee iv 14 128
The guard, what, ho! Come, your lord calls! iv 14 130
Methinks I hear Antony call v 2 287
That I might hear thee call great Cæsar ass Unpolicied! v 2 310
Call my women: Think on my words *Cymbeline* i 5 74
If thou canst awake by four o' the clock, I prithee, call me ii 2 7
If you will make't an action, call witness to't ii 3 156
That most venerable man which I Did call my father ii 5 4
Call her before us; for We have been too slight in sufferance iii 5 34
I were best not call; I dare not call iii 6 19

Call. These two young gentlemen, that call me father And think they are my sons *Cymbeline* v 5 328
Whom I call Polydore, Most worthy prince, as yours, is true Guiderius v 5 357
When all, for mine, if I may call offence, Must feel war's blow *Pericles* i 2 92
Call it by what you will, the day is yours ii 3 13
Even in his throat—unless it be the king—That calls me traitor, I return the lie ii 5 57
Hundreds call themselves Your creatures iii 2 44
The boatswain whistles, and The master calls iv 1 65
Though you call my course unnatural iv 3 36
Thou little know'st how thou dost startle me, To call thyself Marina v 1 148
Call And give them repetition to the life v 1 246
Call back. O, call back yesterday, bid time return! *Richard II.* iii 2 69
Shall we call back Northumberland? iii 3 129
To call back her appeal She intends unto his holiness *Hen. VIII.* ii 4 234
Call forth the watch that are their accusers *Much Ado* iv 2 36
Call forth your actors by the scroll *M. N. Dream* i 2 15
Call forth Nathaniel, Joseph, Nicholas *T. of Shrew* iv 1 91
Call forth an officer iv 1 94
Call forth the holy father *T. Night* v 1 145
Call forth Bagot. Now, Bagot, freely speak thy mind *Richard II.* iv 1 1
Were our tears wanting to this funeral, These tidings would call forth their flowing tides 1 *Hen. VI.* i 1 83
Call forth my household servants; let's to-night Be bounteous *Ant. and Cleo.* iv 2 9
Call forth your soothsayer *Cymbeline* v 5 426
Well, call forth, call forth *Pericles* iv 6 36
Call (her, him, them) forth *Much Ado* v 4; *L. L. Lost* v 2; *T. of Shrew* iv 1; 1 *Hen. IV.* ii 4; *Rom. and Jul.* i 3
Call him hither *As Y. Like It* i 2; *All's Well* v 3; *T. Night* iii 4; *Hen. V.* iv 7; *Richard III.* iv 2; *Coriolanus* i 6
Call hither, I say, bid come before us Angelo *Meas. for Meas.* i 1 15
Call hither Clifford; bid him come amain 2 *Hen. VI.* v 1 114
Call hither to the stake my two brave bears v 1 144
Call home thy ancient thoughts from banishment *T. of Shrew* Ind. 2 33
This fair alliance quickly shall call home To high promotions *Richard III.* iv 4 313
Call in. Let him approach: call in my gentlewoman *T. Night* i 5 172
Call in the letters patent that he hath *Richard II.* ii 1 202
Call in ribs, call in tallow 1 *Hen. IV.* ii 4 125
Call in the sheriff. Now, master sheriff, what is your will with me? ii 4 554
Follow no further now: Call in the powers 2 *Hen. IV.* iv 3 28
Sirrah, call in my sons to be my bail 2 *Hen. VI.* v 1 111
I must to bed; Call in more women *Hen. VIII.* iv 2 167
Call (her, him) in *Mer. Wives* ii 2; iii 5; *Much Ado* ii 3; *As Y. Like It* i 1; 1 *Hen. VI.* i 2
Call in question. You call in question the continuance of his love *T. Night* i 4 6
Now sit we close about this taper here, And call in question our necessities *J. Cæsar* iv 3 165
Call it what you will. Let it do something, my good lord, that may do me good, and call it what you will 2 *Hen. IV.* iv 3 66
A storm or robbery, call it what you will *Cymbeline* iii 3 62
Call me cut. If thou hast her not i' the end, call me cut *T. Night* ii 3 203
Call me fool *T. G. of Ver.* i 1; *Much Ado* iv 1; *T. Night* ii 5; *Lear* i 4; *Cymbeline* ii 3
Call out. Sometimes you would call out for Cicely Hacket *T. of Shrew* Ind. 2 91
But that a joy past joy calls out on me, It were a grief, so brief to part with thee *Rom. and Jul.* iii 3 173
Call thither all the officers o' the town *Coriolanus* i 5 28
Call together. Please it our great general To call together all his state of war *Troi. and Cres.* ii 3 271
Call to mind. When I call to mind your gracious favours *T. G. of Ver.* iii 1 6
Call to mind That I have been your wife *Hen. VIII.* ii 4 34
Call up. Look, the unfolding star calls up the shepherd *Meas. for Meas.* iv 2 219
An there be any matter of weight chances, call up me *Much Ado* iii 3 91
Call up the right master constable iii 3 178
We'll call up the gentlemen 1 *Hen. IV.* ii 1 50
Come, Gertrude, we'll call up our wisest friends *Hamlet* iv 1 38
Call up her father, Rouse him: make after him *Othello* i 1 67
Strike on the tinder, ho! Give me a taper! call up all my people! i 1 142
Call up my brother. O, would you had had her! i 1 176
Call up some gentlemen.—Ho, gentlemen! my lord calls *Pericles* v 1 6
Call upon. At that place call upon me *Meas. for Meas.* iii 1 278
I am bound to call upon you iii 2 167
May be I will call upon you anon iv 1 23
I made my promise Upon the heavy middle of the night To call upon him iv 1 36
Speak not you to him till we call upon you v 1 287
I'll not be long before I call upon thee *W. Tale* iii 3 9
He is much sorry, If any thing more than your sport and pleasure Did move your greatness and this noble state To call upon him *Troi. and Cres.* ii 3 119
It is my soul that calls upon my name *Rom. and Jul.* ii 2 165
My master is awaked by great occasion To call upon his own *T. of Athens* ii 2 22
Our time does call upon 's *Macbeth* iii 1 37
I'll call upon you straight: abide within iii 1 140
And what needful else That calls upon us v 8 72
Time calls upon 's *Ant. and Cleo.* ii 2 160
Callat. A callat Of boundless tongue, who late hath beat her husband! *W. Tale* ii 3 90
Shall I not live to be avenged on her? Contemptuous base-born callet 2 *Hen. VI.* i 3 86
A wisp of straw were worth a thousand crowns, To make this shameless callet know herself 3 *Hen. VI.* ii 2 145
A beggar in his drink Could not have laid such terms upon his callat *Othello* iv 2 121
Called. Spirits, which by mine art I have from their confines call'd *Temp.* iv 1 121
You nymphs, call'd Naiads, of the windring brooks iv 1 128
I have bedimm'd The noontide sun, call'd forth the mutinous winds v 1 42
Be gone, and come when you are called *Mer. Wives* iii 3 20
His hinds were called forth by their mistress iii 5 100
Who call'd here of late?—None, since the curfew rung *Meas. for Meas.* iv 2 77
He must stay until the officer Arise to let him in: he is call'd up iv 2 94
If thy name be call'd Luce,—Luce, thou hast answer'd him well *Com. of Errors* iii 1 53
Called me Dromio; swore I was assured to her iii 2 145
Even now a tailor call'd me in his shop And show'd me silks iv 3 7
Let him be clapped on the shoulder, and called Adam *Much Ado* i 1 261
That jealousy shall be called assurance ii 2 50
You have been always called a merciful man, partner iii 3 64
And men sit down to that nourishment which is called supper *L. L. Lost* i 1 240

Called. So is the weaker vessel called which I apprehended with the aforesaid swain *L. L. Lost* i 1 276
His disgrace is to be called boy; but his glory is to subdue men i 2 186
Then call'd you for the l'envoy.—True, and I for a plantain iii 1 108
A lady of France that he call'd Rosaline iv 1 107
Who is intituled, nominated, or called v 1 8
And trow you what he call'd me?—Qualm, perhaps v 2 279
It shall be called Bottom's Dream, because it hath no bottom *M. N. Dr.* iv 1 221
I think, he was so called.—True, madam *Mer. of Venice* i 2 128
You spurn'd me such a day; another time You call'd me dog i 3 129
What will you be call'd?—Something that hath a reference to my state *As Y. Like It* i 3 128
It may well be called Jove's tree, when it drops forth such fruit iii 2 249
Here comes a pair of very strange beasts, which in all tongues are called fools v 4 38
This is called the Retort Courteous v 4 76
You are call'd plain Kate, And bonny Kate *T. of Shrew* ii 1 186
Æacides Was Ajax, call'd so from his grandfather iii 1 53
This is to feel a tale, not to hear a tale.—And therefore 'tis called a sensible tale iv 1 66
How called you the man you speak of? *All's Well* i 1 27
I cannot give thee less, to be call'd grateful ii 1 132
Whose dear perfection hearts that scorn'd to serve Humbly call'd mistress v 3 19
She call'd the saints to surety v 3 108
My name is Sebastian, which I called Roderigo *T. Night* ii 1 17
If my lady have not called up her steward ii 3 77
Their love may be call'd appetite, No motion of the liver, but the palate ii 4 100
'Twas never merry world Since lowly feigning was call'd compliment iii 1 110
None can be call'd deform'd but the unkind iii 4 402
Since you call'd me master for so long, Here is my hand v 1 332
And yet the steer, the heifer and the calf Are all call'd neat *W. Tale* i 2 125
This news which is called true is so like an old tale v 2 30
How comes it then that thou art call'd a king? *K. John* ii 1 107
Our trumpet call'd you to this gentle parle ii 1 205
Since I first call'd my brother's father dad ii 1 467
And meritorious shall that hand be call'd iii 1 176
To-day, as I came by, I called there *Richard II.* ii 2 94
And this land be call'd The field of Golgotha iv 1 143
Let not us that are squires of the night's body be called thieves of the day's beauty *1 Hen. IV.* i 2 28
Thou hast called her to a reckoning many a time and oft i 2 55
As the soldiers bore dead bodies by, He call'd them untaught knaves i 3 43
I was never called so in mine own house before iii 3 72
He called you Jack, and said he would cudgel you iii 3 158
Art thou not ashamed to be called captain? *2 Hen. IV.* ii 4 152
The undeserver may sleep, when the man of action is called on ii 4 407
You were called 'lusty Shallow' then, cousin iii 2 17
By the mass, I was called any thing iii 2 19
Here is two more called than your number iii 2 200
What is this forest call'd?—'Tis Gaultree Forest iv 1 1
'Tis call'd Jerusalem, my noble lord iv 5 235
I would his majesty had call'd me with him v 2 6
The king hath call'd his parliament v 5 109
Is at this day in Germany call'd Meisen *Hen. V.* i 2 53
Now attest That those whom you call'd fathers did beget you iii 1 23
My name is Pistol call'd.—It sorts well with your fierceness iv 1 62
This day is call'd the feast of Crispian iv 3 40
His father was called Philip of Macedon, as I take it iv 7 21
There is also moreover a river at Monmouth: it is called Wye iv 7 29
What is this castle call'd that stands hard by? iv 7 91
You called me yesterday mountain-squire v 1 36
They call'd us for our fierceness English dogs *1 Hen. VI.* i 5 25
Is my Lord of Winchester install'd, And call'd unto a cardinal's degree? v 1 29
An earl I am, and Suffolk am I call'd v 3 53
To be call'd but viceroy of the whole v 4 143
Being call'd A hundred times and oftener, in my sleep *2 Hen. VI.* ii 1 89
Have you not beadles in your town, and things called whips? ii 1 136
And call'd them blind and dusky spectacles iii 2 112
How art thou call'd? and what is thy degree? iv 1 73
The bloody parliament shall this be call'd *3 Hen. VI.* i 1 39
As if a channel should be call'd the sea ii 2 141
My crown is called content: A crown it is that seldom kings enjoy iii 1 64
I had thought That thou hadst call'd me all these bitter names *Rich. III.* i 3 236
Are you call'd forth from out a world of men To slay the innocent? i 4 186
In common wordly things, 'tis call'd ungrateful, With dull unwillingness to repay a debt ii 2 91
The mayor in courtesy show'd me the castle, And call'd it Rougemont iv 2 108
I call'd thee then vain flourish of my fortune iv 4 82
I call'd thee then poor shadow, painted queen iv 4 83
Humphrey Hour, that call'd your grace To breakfast once forth of my company iv 4 175
You have a daughter call'd Elizabeth, Virtuous and fair iv 4 203
Nor call'd upon For high feats done to the crown *Hen. VIII.* i 1 60
Let be call'd before us That gentleman of Buckingham's i 2 4
You are call'd back.—What need you note it? pray you, keep your way: When you are call'd, return ii 4 127
Katharine no more Shall be call'd queen, but princess dowager iii 2 70
That title's lost: 'Tis now the king's, and call'd Whitehall iv 1 97
Your grace must wait till you be call'd for v 2 7
Let it be call'd the wild and wandering flood *Troi. and Cres.* i 1 105
We have, great Agamemnon, here in Troy A prince call'd Hector i 3 261
Modest doubt is call'd The beacon of the wise ii 2 15
Let all pitiful goers-between be called to the world's end after my name [Pandarus] iii 2 208
Hark! you are call'd: some say the Genius so Cries 'come' to him that instantly must die iv 4 52
She is as far high-soaring o'er thy praises As thou unworthy to be call'd her servant iv 4 127
What he will he does, and does so much That proof is call'd impossibility v 5 29
Let him that will a screech-owl aye be call'd, Go in to Troy, and say there, Hector's dead v 10 16
And till we call'd Both field and city ours, he never stood To ease his breast with panting *Coriolanus* ii 2 124
He's right noble: Let him be call'd for ii 2 134
He himself stuck not to call us the many-headed multitude.—We have been called so of many ii 3 19
His gracious promise, which you might, As cause had call'd you up, have held him to ii 3 202
Called. Would pawn his fortunes To hopeless restitution, so he might Be call'd your vanquisher *Coriolanus* iii 1 17
Scandal'd the suppliants for the people, call'd them Time-pleasers iii 1 44
Manhood is call'd foolery, when it stands Against a falling fabric iii 1 246
He call'd me father: But what o' that? v 1 3
And then they call'd me foul adulteress *T. Andron.* ii 3 109
Revenge it, as you love your mother's life, Or be ye not henceforth call'd my children ii 3 115
O Tamora, be call'd a gentle queen, And with thine own hands kill me! ii 3 168
If that be call'd deceit, I will be honest iii 1 189
I know thou art religious And hast a thing within thee called conscience v 1 75
The guests are come, supper served up, you called *Rom. and Jul.* i 3 101
You are looked for and called for, asked for and sought for i 5 13
So Romeo would, were he not Romeo call'd, Retain that dear perfection which he owes Without that title ii 2 45
I call'd thee by thy name.—Thou art proud *T. of Athens* i 1 186
These debts may well be called desperate ones, for a madman owes 'em iii 4 103
Call'd you, my lord?—Get me a taper in my study *J. Cæsar* ii 1 6
Did from the streets of Rome The Tarquin drive, when he was call'd a king ii 1 54
To the common eyes, We shall be call'd purgers, not murderers ii 1 180
So oft as that shall be, So often shall the knot of us be call'd The men that gave their country liberty iii 1 117
How far is't call'd to Forres? *Macbeth* i 3 39
The close contriver of all harms, Was never call'd to bear my part iii 5 8
What's the disease he means?—'Tis call'd the evil iv 3 146
It cannot Be call'd our mother, but our grave iv 3 166
Still am I call'd. Unhand me, gentlemen *Hamlet* i 4 84
Called it an honest method, as wholesome as sweet ii 2 465
Why came not the slave back to me when I called him? *Lear* i 4 57
I never gave you kingdom, call'd you children, You owe me no subscription iii 2 17
He call'd me sot, And told me I had turn'd the wrong side out iv 2 8
You have been hotly call'd for *Othello* i 2 44
He held them sixpence all too dear, With that he call'd the tailor lown ii 3 95
I will not leave him now till Cassio Be call'd to him ii 4 33
I call'd my love false love; but what said he then? iv 3 55
Name Cleopatra as she is call'd in Rome *Ant. and Cleo.* i 2 110
Thanks to you, That call'd me timelier than my purpose hither ii 6 52
To be called into a huge sphere, and not to be seen to move in't ii 7 16
Where's this cup I call'd for? ii 7 60
That ever I should call thee castaway!—You have not call'd me so iii 6 41
This grave charm,—Whose eye beck'd forth my wars, and call'd them home iv 12 26
His father Was called Sicilius *Cymbeline* i 1 29
He is call'd The Briton reveller i 6 60
A lady to the worthiest sir that ever Country call'd his! i 6 161
The first of Britain which did put His brows within a golden crown and call'd Himself a king iii 1 61
The heir of Cymbeline and Britain, who The king his father call'd Guiderius iii 3 88
Before I enter'd here, I call'd; and thought To have begg'd or bought what I have took iii 6 47
You shall be called to no more payments, fear no more tavern-bills v 4 160
Thou bring'st good news; I am called to be made free v 4 201
Every villain Be call'd Posthumus Leonatus! v 5 224
Thou hadst, great king, a subject who Was call'd Belarius v 5 317
You call'd me brother, When I was but your sister v 5 376
Ay, sir; and he deserves so to be called *Pericles* ii 1 108
Thou, that hast Upon the winds command, bind them in brass, Having call'd them from the deep! iii 1 4
Marina was she call'd; and at her birth, Thetis, being proud, swallow'd some part o' the earth iv 4 38
How! a king's daughter? And call'd Marina? v 1 152
And wherefore call'd Marina?—Call'd Marina For I was born at sea v 1 157
At sea in childbed died she, but brought forth A maid-child call'd Marina v 3 6
Flesh of thy flesh, Thaisa; Thy burden at the sea, and call'd Marina v 3 47
Can you remember what I call'd the man? I have named him oft v 3 52
Calledst. Thou call'dst me up at midnight to fetch dew From the still-vex'd Bermoothes *Tempest* i 2 228
Thou call'dst me dog before thou hadst a cause *Mer. of Venice* iii 3 6
When we parted, Thou call'dst me king *3 Hen. VI.* iv 3 31
Callest. Dost thou conjure for wenches, that thou call'st for such store? *Com. of Errors* iii 1 34
'The hobby-horse is forgot.'—Callest thou my love 'hobby-horse'? *L. L. Lost* iii 1 31
Why, what, i' devil's name, tailor, call'st thou this? *T. of Shrew* iv 3 92
Or I'll seize thy life, With what thou else call'st thine *W. Tale* ii 3 137
That penitent, as thou callest him iv 2 25
How now, mine host Pistol!—Base tike, call'st thou me host? *Hen. V.* ii 1 31
Cruel child-killer.—I slew thy father, call'st thou him a child? *3 Hen. VI.* ii 2 113
Thou spokest well of me.—Call'st thou that harm? *T. of Athens* iv 3 173
What is thy name?—Thou'lt be afraid to hear it.—No; though thou call'st thyself a hotter name Than any is in hell *Macbeth* v 7 6
Thou call'st on him that hates thee *Lear* iii 7 88
Calling. You have paid the heavens your function, and the prisoner the very debt of your calling *Meas. for Meas.* iii 2 265
Trust not my age, My reverence, calling, nor divinity *Much Ado* iv 1 170
Would not change that calling, To be adopted heir to Frederick *As Y. Like It* i 2 246
Ne'er a fantastical knave of them all shall flout me out of my calling iii 3 109
Calling my officers about me, in my branched velvet gown *T. Night* ii 5 53
And do thou never leave calling 'Francis' *1 Hen. IV.* ii 4 34
What, standest thou still, and hearest such a calling? ii 4 91
I seek not to advance Or raise myself, but keep my wonted calling *1 Hen. VI.* iii 1 32
What though the common people favour him, Calling him 'Humphrey, the good Duke of Gloucester' *2 Hen. VI.* i 1 159
Clifford of Cumberland, Warwick is hoarse with calling thee to arms v 2 7
You sign your place and calling, in full seeming, With meekness and humility *Hen. VIII.* ii 4 108
I could say more, But reverence to your calling makes me modest v 3 69
All the peace you make in their cause is, calling both the parties knaves *Coriolanus* ii 1 88
Calling death banishment, Thou cutt'st my head off with a golden axe, And smilest upon the stroke *Rom. and Jul.* iii 3 21
As calling home our exiled friends abroad *Macbeth* v 8 66
If haply you my father do suspect An instrument of this your calling back, Lay not your blame on me *Othello* iv 2 45
Neither is our profession any trade; it's no calling *Pericles* iv 2 43

Calm. And promise you calm seas, auspicious gales *Tempest* v 1 314
Be calm, good wind, blow not a word away Till I have found each letter *T. G. of Ver.* i 2 118
What dangerous action, stood it next to death, Would I not undergo for one calm look! v 4 42
The seas wax'd calm, and we discovered Two ships *Com. of Errors* i 1 92
They shoot but calm words folded up in smoke *K. John* ii 1 229
Heaven hath a hand in these events, To whose high will we bound our calm contents *Richard II.* v 2 38
The cankers of a calm world and a long peace 1 *Hen. IV.* iv 2 32
Sick of a calm; yea, good faith.—So is all her sect; an they be once in a calm, they are sick 2 *Hen. IV.* ii 4 40
Do calm the fury of this mad-bred flaw 2 *Hen. VI.* iii 1 354
He dares not calm his contumelious spirit iii 2 204
Some troops pursue the bloody-minded queen, That led calm Henry 3 *Hen. VI.* ii 6 34
With patience calm the storm, While we bethink a means to break it off iii 3 38
I know you have a gentle, noble temper, A soul as even as a calm *Hen. VIII.* iii 1 166
Rend and deracinate The unity and married calm of states *Troi. and Cres.* i 3 100
Our bloods are now in calm; and, so long, health! iv 1 15
Have you not set them on?—Be calm, be calm *Coriolanus* iii 1 37
Let's be calm.—The people are abused; set on iii 1 57
When the sea was calm all boats alike Show'd mastership in floating iv 1 6
How fair the tribune speaks to calm my thoughts *T. Andron.* i 1 46
Till I find the stream To cool this heat, a charm to calm these fits ii 1 134
O, calm thee, gentle lord ii 1 83
To calm this tempest whirling in the court iv 2 160
Commander of my thoughts, Calm thee, and bear the faults of Titus' age iv 4 29
O calm, dishonourable, vile submission! *Rom. and Jul.* iii 1 76
All this uttered With gentle breath, calm look, knees humbly bow'd iii 1 161
Without a sudden calm, will overset Thy tempest-tossed body iii 5 137
That drop of blood that's calm proclaims me bastard *Hamlet* iv 5 117
How much I had to do to calm his rage! iv 7 193
If after every tempest come such calms, May the winds blow! *Othello* ii 1 187
How calm and gentle I proceeded still In all my writings *Ant. and Cleo.* v 1 75
Therein He was as calm as virtue *Cymbeline* v 5 174
Calmed. Myself have calm'd their spleenful mutiny 2 *Hen. VI.* iii 2 128
Like to a ship that, having 'scaped a tempest, Is straightway calm'd and boarded with a pirate iv 9 33
Not soon provoked nor being provoked soon calm'd *Troi. and Cres.* iv 5 99
Must be be-lee'd and calm'd By debitor and creditor *Othello* i 1 30
Till the rough seas, that spare not any man, Took it in rage, though calm'd have given't again *Pericles* ii 1 138
Calmest. In the calmest and most stillest night 2 *Hen. IV.* iii 1 28
Calmie. Qualtitie calmie custure me! *Hen. V.* iv 4 4
Calmly. And calmly run on in obedience *K. John* v 4 56
Calmly, I do beseech you.—Ay, as an ostler, that for the poorest piece Will bear the knave by the volume *Coriolanus* iii 3 31
Calmly, good Laertes *Hamlet* iv 5 116
Calmness. Defend yourself By calmness or by absence *Coriolanus* iii 2 95
Calpurnia!—Peace, ho! Cæsar speaks.—Calpurnia!—Here, my lord *J. Cæsar* i 2 1
Forget not, in your speed, Antonius, To touch Calpurnia i 2 7
Calpurnia's cheek is pale; and Cicero Looks with such ferret and such fiery eyes i 2 185
Thrice hath Calpurnia in her sleep cried out, 'Help, ho! they murder Cæsar!' ii 2 2
Calpurnia here, my wife, stays me at home: She dreamt to-night ii 2 75
This by Calpurnia's dream is signified ii 2 90
How foolish do your fears seem now, Calpurnia! I am ashamed I did yield to them ii 2 105
Calumniate. Deceptious functions, Created only to calumniate *Troi. and Cres.* v 2 124
Calumniating. Subjects all To envious and calumniating time iii 3 174
Calumnious. Wilt thou ever be a foul-mouthed and calumnious knave? *All's Well* i 3 61
There's none stands under more calumnious tongues Than I *Hen. VIII.* v 1 112
Virtue itself 'scapes not calumnious strokes *Hamlet* i 3 38
Calumny. You shall stifle in your own report And smell of calumny *Meas. for Meas.* ii 4 159
Back-wounding calumny The whitest virtue strikes iii 2 197
The shrug, the hum or ha, these petty brands That calumny doth use— O, I am out—That mercy does, for calumny will sear Virtue itself *W. Tale* ii 1 72
Be thou as chaste as ice, as pure as snow, thou shalt not escape calumny *Hamlet* iii 1 141
Calved. Not Romans—as they are not, Though calved i' the porch o' the Capitol *Coriolanus* iii 1 240
Calves. They are sheep and calves which seek out assurance in that *Ham.* v 1 125
Calves'-guts. It is a vice in her ears, which horse-hairs and calves'-guts, nor the voice of unpaved eunuch to boot, can never amend *Cymbeline* ii 3 34
Calydon. As did the fatal brand Althæa burn'd Unto the prince's heart of Calydon 2 *Hen. VI.* i 1 235
Cambio. His name is Cambio; pray, accept his service *T. of Shrew* ii 1 83
It shall go hard if Cambio go without her iv 4 109
Why, tell me, is not this my Cambio?—Cambio is changed into Lucentio v 1 125
Cambria. I am in Cambria, at Milford-Haven: what your own love will out of this advise you, follow *Cymbeline* iii 2 44
Sir, In Cambria are we born, and gentlemen v 5 17
Cambric. Inkles, caddisses, cambrics, lawns *W. Tale* iv 4 208
I would your cambric were sensible as your finger *Coriolanus* i 3 95
When she would with sharp needle wound The cambric *Pericles* iv Gower 24
Cambridge. Three corrupted men, One, Richard Earl of Cambridge *Hen. V.* ii Prol. 23
My Lord of Cambridge, and my kind Lord of Masham, And you, my gentle knight, give me your thoughts ii 2 13
We'll yet enlarge that man, Though Cambridge, Scroop and Grey, in their dear care And tender preservation of our person, Would have him punish'd ii 2 58
Then, Richard Earl of Cambridge, there is yours ii 2 66
My Lord of Cambridge here, You know ii 2 85
To the which This knight, no less for bounty bound to us Than Cambridge is, hath likewise sworn ii 2 93
I arrest thee of high treason, by the name of Richard Earl of Cambridge ii 2 146
Was not thy father, Richard Earl of Cambridge, For treason executed? 1 *Hen. VI.* ii 4 90
Declare the cause My father, Earl of Cambridge, lost his head ii 5 54
Cambridge. Thy father, Earl of Cambridge, then derived From famous Edmund Langley 1 *Hen. VI.* ii 5 84
Anne, My mother, being heir unto the crown, Married Richard Earl of Cambridge 2 *Hen. VI.* ii 2 45
Cambyses. That it may be thought I have wept; for I must speak in passion, and I will do it in King Cambyses' vein 1 *Hen. IV.* ii 4 425
Came. Canst thou remember A time before we came unto this cell? *Temp.* i 2 39
What foul play had we, that we came from thence? Or blessed was't we did? i 2 60
How came we ashore?—By Providence divine i 2 158
This is unwonted Which now came from him i 2 498
Not since widow Dido's time.—Widow! a pox o' that! How came that widow in? ii 1 77
Your daughter, who is now queen.—And the rarest that e'er came there ii 1 99
I not doubt He came alive to land ii 1 122
Now trust me, madam, it came hardly off *T. G. of Ver.* ii 1 115
Now, tell me, how do all from whence you came? ii 4 122
Unhappy were you, madam, ere I came v 4 29
Hear the truth of it: he came of an errand to me *Mer. Wives* i 4 80
You might slip away ere he came iv 2 55
So soon as I came beyond Eton, they threw me off iv 5 68
I came from her, Master Brook, like a poor old woman v 1 17
I came yonder at Eton to marry Mistress Anne Page v 5 194
This we came not to, Only for propagation of a dower *Meas. for Meas.* i 2 153
Came not to an undoubtful proof iv 2 142
But ere they came,—O, let me say no more! *Com. of Errors* i 1 95
Let him walk from whence he came, lest he catch cold on's feet iii 1 37
But neither chain nor goldsmith came to me iv 1 24
Belike you thought our love would last too long, If it were chain'd together, and therefore came not iv 1 26
He that came behind you, sir, like an evil angel iv 3 19
I sent you money to redeem you, By Dromio here, who came in haste for it iv 4 87
He came to me and I deliver'd it iv 4 91
Your husband all in rage to-day Came to my house iv 4 141
I never came within these abbey-walls v 1 265
Thou camest from Corinth first?—No, sir, not I; I came from Syracuse v 1 363
Never came trouble to my house in the likeness of your grace *Much Ado* i 1 99
I came yonder from a great supper i 3 44
How came you to this? i 3 59
There was never counterfeit of passion came so near the life of passion ii 3 110
I came to seek you both.—We have been up and down to seek thee v 1 121
Yet, ere I go, let me go with that I came v 2 47
Until the goose came out of door, And stay'd the odds by adding four *L. L. Lost* iii 1 92
Thus came your argument in iii 1 109
He came, saw, and overcame: he came, one; saw, two; overcame, three iv 1 70
Who came? the king: why did he come? to see: why did he see? to overcome: to whom came he? iv 1 72
The moon was a month old when Adam was no more, And raught not to five weeks when he came to five-score iv 2 41
Madame, came nothing else along with that?—Nothing but this! v 2 5
Lord Longaville said, I came o'er his heart v 2 278
How came her eyes so bright? Not with salt tears *M. N. Dream* ii 2 92
I wonder if Titania be awaked; Then, what it was that next came in her eye iii 2 2
How came these things to pass? iv 1 83
Tell me how it came this night That I sleeping here was found iv 1 105
Hearing our intent, Came here in grace of our solemnity iv 1 139
But as yet, I swear, I cannot truly say how I came here iv 1 153
And now I do bethink me, so it is,—I came with Hermia hither iv 1 156
It was play'd When I from Thebes came last a conqueror v 1 51
And so the lion vanished.—And then came Pyramus v 1 276
With one fool's head I came to woo, But I go away with two *M. of Ven.* ii 9 75
A day in April never came so sweet, To show how costly summer was at hand ii 9 93
Hast thou found my daughter?—I often came where I did hear of her, but cannot find her iii 1 85
Came you from Padua, from Bellario?—From both, my lord iv 1 119
In the instant that your messenger came iv 1 152
I came to acquaint you with a matter *As Y. Like It* i 1 128
I was seven of the nine days out of the wonder before you came iii 2 185
Every one fault seeming monstrous till his fellow-fault came to match it iii 2 373
What wit could wit have to excuse that?—Marry, to say she came to seek you iv 1 174
Cæsar's thrasonical brag of 'I came, saw, and overcame' v 2 35
Though Paris came in hope to speed alone *T. of Shrew* i 2 247
If whilst I live she will be only mine.—That 'only' came well in ii 1 365
Didst thou not say he comes?—Who? that Petruchio came?—Ay, that Petruchio came iii 2 79
Came you from the church?—As willingly as e'er I came from school iii 2 151
And I seeing this came thence for very shame iii 2 182
We met him thitherward; for thence we came *All's Well* iii 2 55
You came, I think, from France?—I did so iii 5 49
They will say, 'Came you off with so little?' iv 1 42
Thence it came That she whom all men praised and whom myself, Since I have lost, have loved, was in mine eye The dust that did offend it v 3 52
It came o'er my ear like the sweet sound, That breathes upon a bank of violets, Stealing and giving odour! *T. Night* i 1 5
When came he to this town?—To-day, my lord v 1 96
But when I came to man's estate, With hey, ho, the wind and the rain. v 1 402
But when I came, alas! to wive, With hey, ho &c. v 1 406
But when I came unto my beds, With hey, ho, &c. v 1 410
It is a gentleman of the greatest promise that ever came into my note *W. Tale* i 1 40
How came the posterns So easily open? ii 1 52
As by strange fortune It came to us ii 3 180
Where's Bohemia? speak.—Here in your city; I now came from him v 1 186
We came To see the statue of our queen v 3 9
But we saw not That which my daughter came to look upon v 3 13
You came not of one mother then, it seems *K. John* i 1 58
By this brave duke came early to his grave ii 1 5
We will bear home that lusty blood again Which here we came to spout against your town ii 1 256
In her right we came; Which we, God knows, have turn'd another way ii 1 548
O, bravely came we off! v 5 4
Your son was gone before I came.—He was? *Richard II.* ii 2 86
An hour before I came, the duchess died ii 2 97
Letters came last night To a dear friend of the good Duke of York's iii 4 69

Came. She came adorned hither like sweet May . . . *Richard II.* v 1 79
When all athwart there came A post from Wales . . . 1 *Hen. IV.* i 1 36
More uneven and unwelcome news Came from the north . . . i 1 51
Came there a certain lord, neat, and trimly dress'd, Fresh as a bridegroom i 3 33
Who therewith angry, when it next came there, Took it in snuff . i 3 40
Three misbegotten knaves in Kendal green came at my back . ii 4 246
How came Falstaff's sword so hacked ? . . . . . ii 4 335
He came but to be Duke of Lancaster . . . . . iv 3 61
Tut, I came not to hear this . . . . iv 3 89
Came not till now to dignify the times, Since Cæsar's fortunes 2 *Hen. IV.* i 1 22
Saw you the field ? came you from Shrewsbury ? . . . . i 1 24
After him came spurring hard A gentleman . . . . . i 1 36
When through proud London he came sighing on . . . . i 3 104
So came I a widow . . . . ii 3 57
A' came ever in the rearward of the fashion . . . . iii 2 339
If that rebellion Came like itself, in base and abject routs . . iv 1 33
I may justly say, with the hook-nosed fellow of Rome, 'I came, saw, and overcame' . . . . iv 3 45
He came not through the chamber where we stay'd . . . iv 5 57
At that very moment Consideration, like an angel, came . *Hen. V.* i 1 28
Never came reformation in a flood, With such a heady currance . i 1 33
The Scot on his unfurnish'd kingdom Came pouring, like the tide into a breach . . . . i 2 149
As ever you came of women, come in quickly . . . . ii 1 122
Upon these words I came and cheer'd him up . . . . iv 6 20
All my mother came into mine eyes And gave me up to tears . . iv 6 31
I was not angry since I came to France Until this instant . . iv 7 58
All offences, my lord, come from the heart: never came any from mine that might offend your majesty . . . . iv 8 50
Your majesty came not like yourself . . . . . . iv 8 53
Arm in arm they both came swiftly running . . . 1 *Hen. VI.* ii 2 29
We came but to tell you That we are here . . . . . iii 2 73
Stout Pendragon in his litter sick Came to the field and vanquished his foes . . . . iii 2 96
As we hither came in peace, So let us still continue peace and love iv 1 160
As I was cause Your highness came to England, so will I In England work your grace's full content . . . . . 2 *Hen. VI.* i 3 69
Came he right now to sing a raven's note . . . . . iii 2 40
And I unto the sea from whence I came . . . 3 *Hen. VI.* i 1 209
And thrice cried 'Courage, father ! fight it out !' And full as oft came Edward to my side . . . . i 4 11
Their weapons like to lightning came and went . . . . ii 1 129
Why, therefore Warwick came to seek you out . . . . ii 1 166
My father, being the Earl of Warwick's man, Came on the part of York . ii 5 66
Therefore I came unto your majesty . . . . . . iii 2 41
My father came untimely to his death . . . . . . iii 3 187
I came from Edward as ambassador, But I return his sworn and mortal foe . . . . iii 3 256
I came to serve a king and not a duke . . . . . iv 7 49
Where is the post that came from valiant Oxford ? . . . v 1 1
Never came poison from so sweet a place . . . *Richard III.* i 2 147
What ! were you snarling all before I came ? . . . . i 3 188
If two such murderers as yourselves came to you, Would not entreat for life ? . . . . i 4 268
Both by the father and mother.—Better it were they all came by the father . . . . ii 3 23
When I met this holy man, Those men you talk of came into my mind . iii 2 118
Yet had not we determined he should die, Until your lordship came . iii 5 53
When he that is my husband now Came to me, as I follow'd Henry's corse . . . . iv 1 67
And came I not at last to comfort you ? . . . . . iv 4 164
They came from Buckingham Upon his party . . . . . iv 4 527
Methought the souls of all that I had murder'd Came to my tent . v 3 205
Methought their souls, whose bodies Richard murder'd, Came to my tent v 3 231
He came To whisper Wolsey,—here makes visitation . *Hen. VIII.* i 1 178
I'll tell you in a little. The great duke Came to the bar . . ii 1 12
Thus it came ; give heed to't . . . . ii 4 169
How came His practices to light ? . . . . iii 2 28
The cardinal's letters to the pope miscarried, And came to the eye o' the king . . . . iii 2 31
At our last encounter, The Duke of Buckingham came from his trial . iv 1 5
At length her grace rose, and with modest paces Came to the altar . iv 1 83
At last, with easy roads, he came to Leicester . . . . iv 2 17
Came you from the king, my lord ?—I did . . . . . v 1 6
I am glad I came this way so happily . . . . . . v 2 9
At length they came to the broom-staff to me . . . . v 4 57
What were you talking of when I came ? . . . *Troi. and Cres.* i 2 48
She came to him th' other day into the compassed window . . i 2 119
She came and puts me her white hand to his cloven chin— Juno have mercy ! how came it cloven ? . . . . i 2 131
Who said he came hurt home to-day ? he's not hurt . . . . i 2 233
I came to kill thee, cousin, and bear hence A great addition earned in thy death . . . . iv 5 140
With a kind of smile, Which ne'er came from the lungs . . *Coriolanus* i 1 112
There came news from him last night . . . . . . i 3 104
His doubled spirit Re-quicken'd what in flesh was fatigate, And to the battle came he . . . . ii 2 122
Saw you Aufidius ?—On safe-guard he came to me . . . . iii 1 9
He came unto my hearth ; Presented to my knife his throat . . v 6 30
Poor harmless fly, That, with his pretty buzzing melody, Came here to make us merry ! . . . . *T. Andron.* iii 2 65
Didst thou not come from heaven ?—From heaven ! alas, sir, I never came there . . . . iv 3 89
In the instant came The fiery Tybalt . . . . *Rom. and Jul.* i 1 115
Came more and more and fought on part and part, Till the prince came i 1 121
Marry, that 'marry' is the very theme I came to talk of . . . i 3 64
Came he not home to-night ?—Not to his father's . . . . ii 4 2
Why the devil came you between us ? . . . . . . iii 1 107
I dreamt my lady came and found me dead . . . . . v 1 6
Came I to take her from her kindred's vault . . . . . v 3 254
When I came, some minute ere the time Of her awaking . . . v 3 257
He came with flowers to strew his lady's grave . . . . v 3 281
And therewithal Came to this vault to die . . . . . v 3 290
Nor came any of his bounties over me, To mark me for his friend *T. of Athens* iii 2 85
How came the noble Timon to this change ? . . . . . iv 3 66
So it is said, my noble lord ; but therefore Came not my friend nor I . v 1 82
And after that, he came, thus sad, away ?—Ay . . . *J. Cæsar* i 2 279
With her death That tidings came . . . . iv 3 155
As thick as hail Came post with post . . . . . *Macbeth* i 3 98

Came. Whiles I stood rapt in the wonder of it, came missives from the king . . . . *Macbeth* i 5 6
Came they not by you ?—No, indeed, my lord . . . . . iv 1 137
How came she by that light ?—Why, it stood by her . . . v 1 25
My lord, I came to see your father's funeral . . . *Hamlet* i 2 176
Came this from Hamlet to her ? . . . . ii 2 114
Then came each actor on his ass . . . . ii 2 414
How came he dead ? I'll not be juggled with . . . . iv 5 130
How came he mad ?—Very strangely, they say . . . . v 1 171
When came this to you ? who brought it ? . . . . . *Lear* i 2 61
Why came not the slave back to me when I called him ? . . . i 4 56
How came my man i' the stocks ? . . . . ii 4 201
My son Came then into my mind . . . . iv 1 36
When the rain came to wet me once, and the wind to make me chatter . iv 6 102
We came crying hither : Thou know'st, the first time that we smell the air, We wawl and cry . . . . iv 6 182
What means that bloody knife ?—'Tis hot, it smokes ; It came even from the heart of—O, she's dead ! . . . . v 3 224
Came it by request and such fair question As soul to soul affordeth ? *Oth.* i 3 113
But you are now well enough : how came you thus recovered ? . ii 3 296
What ! Michael Cassio, That came a-wooing with you ! . . . iii 3 71
O Cassio, whence came this ? . . . . iii 4 180
Cassio came hither : I shifted him away . . . . . . iv 1 79
How came you, Cassio, by that handkerchief That was my wife's ? . v 2 319
Whereon it came That I was cast . . . . v 2 326
Fulvia thy wife first came into the field . . . *Ant. and Cleo.* i 2 92
I came before you here a man prepared To take this offer . . ii 6 41
When Cæsar and your brother were at blows, Your mother came to Sicily . . . . ii 6 46
We came hither to fight with you . . . . ii 6 107
The messenger Came on my guard . . . . iv 6 23
Why came you from your master ?—On his command . . *Cymbeline* i 1 169
Made not here his brag Of 'Came' and 'saw' and 'overcame' . . iii 1 24
Thou told'st me, when we came from horse, the place Was near at hand iii 4 1
And though he came our enemy, remember He was paid for that . . iv 2 245
I have resumed again The part I came in . . . . . . v 3 76
Came crying 'mongst his foes, A thing of pity ! . . . . . v 4 46
For this from stiller seats we came, Our parents and us twain . . v 4 69
He came in thunder ; his celestial breath Was sulphurous to smell . v 4 114
Came to me With his sword drawn . . . . v 5 275
And when came you to serve our Roman captive ? . . . . v 5 385
My riches to the earth from whence they came . . . *Pericles* i 1 52
With thousand doubts How I might stop this tempest ere it came . i 2 98
How Thaliard came full bent with sin And had intent to murder him ii Gower 23
A fire from heaven came and shrivell'd up Their bodies . . . ii 4 9
I came unto your court for honour's cause, And not to be a rebel to her state . . . . ii 5 61
But there never came her like in Mytilene . . . . . iv 6 31
She's such a one, that, were I well assured Came of a gentle kind and noble stock, I'ld wish no better choice . . . . v 1 68
How came you in these parts ? where were you bred ? . . . . v 1 171
Came I hither *Meas. for Meas.* v 1 ; *T. of Shrew* i 2 ; *Rom. and Jul.* v 3
Came into the world *Com. of Errors* v 1 ; *K. John* i 1 ; 3 *Hen. VI.* v 6 ; *T. of Athens* iii 5 ; *Lear* i 1
How came you hither ? . . . . . . *Tempest* v 1 228 ; *Richard III.* i 4 85
I came hither *Much Ado* iii 2 ; *As Y. Like It* i 1 ; *Richard III.* i 4 ; *Hen. VIII.* ii 1 ; *Macbeth* iv 3 ; *Lear* ii 1
Whence came you ? . . . . . . *T. G. of Ver.* iv 1 18 ; *T. Night* i 5 189
Came aboard. Alas ! too soon We came aboard . . . *Com. of Errors* i 1 62
Came about. Let me speak to the yet unknowing world How these things came about . . . . *Hamlet* v 2 391
Came along. As I came along, I met and overtook a dozen captains 2 *Hen. IV.* ii 4 386
Came ashore. In a quarrel since I came ashore I kill'd a man *T. of Shrew* i 1 236
Came away. I saw our party to their trenches driven, And then I came away . . . . *Coriolanus* i 6 13
Came back. When you and he came back from Ravenspurgh . 1 *Hen. IV.* i 3 248
When I came back—For this was brief . . . . . *Othello* ii 3 236
Came by. To-day, as I came by, I called there. . . . *Richard II.* ii 2 94
How I came by the crown, O God forgive ! . . . . 2 *Hen. IV.* iv 5 219
Who was't came by ?—'Tis two or three, my lord . . . *Macbeth* iv 1 140
Came by it. How I caught it, found it, or came by it, What stuff 'tis made of, whereof it is born, I am to learn . . . *Mer. of Venice* i 1 3
Who knows if one of her women, being corrupted, Hath stol'n it from her ?—Very true ; And so, I hope, he came by't . . . *Cymbeline* ii 4 118
Came down. Now I begin : Imprimis, we came down a foul hill *T. of Shr.* iv 1 69
Came home. When you cast out, it still came home . . . *W. Tale* i 2 214
Came in. Even as you came in to me, her assistant or go-between parted from me . . . . *Mer. Wives* ii 2 273
Sir, she came in great with child . . . . . *Meas. for Meas.* ii 1 91
We came in with Richard Conqueror . . . . . *T. of Shrew* Ind. 1 4
But I followed me close, came in foot and hand . . . 1 *Hen. IV.* ii 4 241
The more and less came in with cap and knee . . . . . iv 3 68
When I here came in, And found no course of breath within your majesty, How cold it struck my heart ! . . . . . . 2 *Hen. IV.* iv 5 150
Here, purposing the Bastard to destroy, Came in strong rescue 1 *Hen. VI.* iv 6 26
For my own part, I came in late . . . . *Troi. and Cres.* i 2 54
Belike Iago in the interim Came in and satisfied him . . . *Othello* v 2 318
Enough of this : it came in too suddenly ; let it die as it was born *Cymb.* i 4 130
Came it. How came it that the absent duke had not either delivered him to his liberty or executed him ? . . . . . . *Meas. for Meas.* iv 2 136
How came it Claudio was beheaded At an unusual hour ? . . . iv 2 462
And thereof came it that the man was mad . . . *Com. of Errors* v 1 68
How came't, Camillo, That he did stay ? . . . . . *W. Tale* i 2 219
What's thy interest In this sad wreck ? How came it ? Who is it ? *Cymb.* iv 2 366
Came off. Who came off bravely, who was shot . . . . *Hen. V.* iii 6 77
Aidless came off, And with a sudden re-inforcement struck Corioli *Coriol.* ii 2 116
Came on. It was the swift celerity of his death, Which I did think with slower foot came on, That brain'd my purpose . . . *Meas. for Meas.* v 1 400
Came short. Her promised proportions Came short of composition . . v 1 220
Came to. Who deserved So long a breeding as his white beard came to *Cymbeline* v 3 17
Came to age. When his infant fortune came to age . . . 1 *Hen. IV.* i 3 253
Became a bricklayer when he came to age . . . . 2 *Hen. VI.* iv 2 153
Came to himself. What said he when he came unto himself ?— . . . When he came to himself again, he said, If he had done or said any thing amiss, he desired their worships to think it was his infirmity *J. Cæsar* i 2 271
Came to it. At the relation of the queen's death, with the manner how she came to't . . . . *W. Tale* v 2 93
I came to't that day that our last king Hamlet overcame Fortinbras *Hamlet* v 1 155

Came to pass. So it came to pass, Titania waked and straightway loved an ass *M. N. Dream* iii 2 33
Then, you know, 'It came to pass, as most like it was' *Hamlet* ii 2 437
Came too lag to see him buried *Richard III.* ii 1 90
Came too late. He came too late, the ship was under sail *Mer. of Venice* ii 8 6
Came up. It was never merry world in England since gentlemen came up *2 Hen. VI.* iv 2 10

Camel. It is as hard to come as for a camel To thread the postern of a small needle's eye *Richard II.* v 5 16
Achilles! a drayman, a porter, a very camel *Troi. and Cres.* i 2 271
Mars his idiot! do, rudeness; do, camel; do, do ii 1 58
Of no more soul nor fitness for the world Than camels in the war *Coriol.* ii 1 267
Do you see yonder cloud that's almost in shape of a camel?—By the mass, and 'tis like a camel, indeed *Hamlet* iii 2 394
Camelot. Goose, if I had you upon Sarum plain, I'ld drive ye cackling home to Camelot *Lear* ii 2 90
Camest. If thou remember'st aught ere thou camest here, How thou camest here thou mayst *Tempest* i 2 51
When thou camest first, Thou strokedst me and madest much of me i 2 332
How camest thou to be the siege of this moon-calf? ii 2 110
How camest thou hither? swear by this bottle how thou camest hither ii 2 124
Arise, and say how thou camest here v 1 181
How camest thou in this pickle? v 1 281
But how camest thou by this ring? *T. G. of Ver.* v 4 96
Say by whose advice Thou camest here to complain *Meas. for Meas.* v 1 114
And for what cause thou camest to Ephesus *Com. of Errors* i 1 31
Thou camest from Corinth first?—No, sir, not I; I came from Syracuse v 1 362
It was she First told me thou wast mad; then camest in smiling *T. Night* v 1 357
Say, where, when, and how, Camest thou by this ill tidings? *Richard II.* iii 4 80
Thou camest not of the blood royal, if thou darest not stand for ten shillings *1 Hen. IV.* i 2 156
How now, Fluellen! camest thou from the bridge? *Hen. V.* iii 6 93
Camest thou here by chance, Or of devotion? *2 Hen. VI.* ii 1 87
Art thou lame?—Ay, God Almighty help me!—How camest thou so? ii 1 96
To tell thee whence thou camest, of whom derived, Were shame enough to shame thee *3 Hen. VI.* i 4 119
To signify thou camest to bite the world v 6 54
If the rest be true which I have heard, Thou camest— I'll hear no more v 6 56
Thou camest on earth to make the earth my hell *Richard III.* iv 4 166
Yet camest thou to a morsel of this feast, Having fully dined before *Coriolanus* i 9 10
My grief was at the height before thou camest *T. Andron.* iii 1 70
How camest thou hither, tell me, and wherefore? *Rom. and Jul.* ii 2 62
Uncomfortable time, why camest thou now! iv 5 60
Whence camest thou, worthy thane?—From Fife, great king *Macbeth* i 2 48
Camest thou from where they made the stand? *Cymbeline* v 3 1
Didst thou not say . . . that thou camest From good descending? *Pericles* v 1 128
Camillo. If you shall chance, Camillo, to visit Bohemia *W. Tale* i 1 1
What, Camillo there?—Ay, my good lord i 2 209
Camillo, this great sir will yet stay longer i 2 212
How came't, Camillo, That he did stay? i 2 219
I have trusted thee, Camillo, With all the nearest things to my heart i 2 235
Ha' not you seen, Camillo,—But that's past doubt, you have i 2 267
I say thou liest, Camillo, and I hate thee i 2 300
Good Camillo, Your changed complexions are to me a mirror i 2 380
Camillo,—As you are certainly a gentleman, thereto Clerk-like experienced i 2 390
Dost thou hear, Camillo, I conjure thee, by all the parts of man i 2 399
On, good Camillo.—I am appointed him to murder you.—By whom, Camillo? i 2 411
Come, Camillo; I will respect thee as a father if Thou bear'st my life off hence i 2 460
Was he met there? his train? Camillo with him? ii 1 33
Camillo was his help in this, his pandar ii 1 46
She's a traitor and Camillo is A federary with her ii 1 89
Camillo's flight, Added to their familiarity ii 1 174
Camillo and Polixenes Laugh at me, make their pastime at my sorrow ii 3 23
Conspiring with Camillo to take away the life of our sovereign lord the king iii 2 16
All I know of it Is that Camillo was an honest man iii 2 75
Camillo a true subject; Leontes a jealous tyrant iii 2 134
Recall the good Camillo, Whom I proclaim a man of truth iii 2 157
I chose Camillo for the minister to poison My friend Polixenes: which had been done, But that the good mind of Camillo tardied My swift command iii 2 161
Nor was't much, Thou wouldst have poison'd good Camillo's honour iii 2 189
I pray thee, good Camillo, be no more importunate iv 2 1
As thou lovest me, Camillo, wipe not out the rest of thy services by leaving me now iv 2 11
I have considered so much, Camillo, and with some care iv 2 39
My best Camillo! We must disguise ourselves iv 2 61
I not purpose it. I think, Camillo?—Even he, my lord iv 4 484
Camillo, Not for Bohemia, nor the pomp that may Be thereat glean'd iv 4 498
Now, good Camillo; I am so fraught with curious business that I leave out ceremony iv 4 524
How, Camillo, May this, almost a miracle, be done? iv 4 544
Worthy Camillo, What colour for my visitation shall I Hold up before him? iv 4 565
My good Camillo, She is as forward of her breeding as She is i' the rear our birth iv 4 590
Camillo, Preserver of my father, now of me iv 4 596
Fortune speed us! Thus we set on, Camillo, to the sea-side iv 4 682
Camillo has betray'd me; Whose honour and whose honesty till now Endured all weathers v 1 193
He's with the king your father.—Who? Camillo?—Camillo, sir v 1 196
But the changes I perceived in the king and Camillo were very notes of admiration v 2 12
Come, Camillo, And take her by the hand v 3 143
Camlet. You i' the camlet, get up o' the rail *Hen. VIII.* v 4 93
Camomile, the more it is trodden on the faster it grows *1 Hen. IV.* ii 4 441
Camp. O, let me live! And all the secrets of our camp I'll show *All's Well* iv 1 93
You shall demand of him, whether one Captain Dumain be i' the camp iv 3 200
Is this captain in the duke of Florence's camp? iv 3 219
She's impudent, my lord, And was a common gamester to the camp v 3 188
He gave it to a commoner o' the camp, If I be one v 3 194
This sickness doth infect The very life-blood of our enterprise; 'Tis catching hither, even to our camp *1 Hen. IV.* iv 1 30
Whose spirit lent a fire Even to the dullest peasant in his camp *2 Hen. IV.* i 1 113
For I shall sutler be Unto the camp, and profits will accrue *Hen. V.* ii 1 117

Camp. And what a beard of the general's cut and a horrid suit of the camp will do *Hen. V.* iii 6 81
From camp to camp through the foul womb of night The hum of either army stilly sounds iv Prol. 4
Commend me to the princes in our camp iv 1 25
There is no tiddle taddle nor pibble pabble in Pompey's camp iv 1 72
Your nobles, jealous of your absence, Seek through your camp to find you iv 1 303
I must stay with the lackeys, with the luggage of our camp iv 4 80
After this, the vengeance of the whole camp! or rather, the bone-ache! *Troi. and Cres.* ii 3 20
Our guider, come; to the Roman camp conduct us *Coriolanus* i 7 7
My noble steed, known to the camp, I give him, With all his trim belonging i 9 61
As Tarquin erst, That left the camp to sin in Lucrece' bed *T. Andron.* iv 1 64
And bring you up To be a warrior, and command a camp iv 2 180
There's not a whittle in the unruly camp But I do prize it at my love before The reverend'st throat in Athens *T. of Athens* v 1 183
His funerals shall not be in our camp, Lest it discomfort us *J. Cæsar* v 3 105
I had been happy, if the general camp, Pioners and all, had tasted her sweet body, So I had nothing known *Othello* iii 3 345
Call for Enobarbus, He shall not hear thee; or from Cæsar's camp Say 'I am none of thine' *Ant. and Cleo.* iv 5 8
We have beat him to his camp: run one before, And let the queen know iv 8 1
Had our great palace the capacity To camp this host iv 8 33
Campeius. To confirm this too, Cardinal Campeius is arrived *Hen. VIII.* ii 1 160
This good man, This just and learned priest, Cardinal Campeius ii 2 97
Cardinal Campeius Is stol'n away to Rome; hath ta'en no leave iii 2 56
Camping. With camping foes to live *All's Well* iii 4 14
Can. If you can command these elements to silence *Tempest* i 1 23
Canst thou remember A time before we came unto this cell?—Certainly, sir, I can i 2 41
Made thee more profit Than other princesses can that have more time i 2 173
Lords that can prate As amply and unnecessarily ii 1 263
The strong'st suggestion Our worser genius can iv 1 27
All I can is nothing To her whose worth makes other worthies nothing *T. G. of Ver.* ii 4 165
Here can I sit alone, unseen of any v 4 4
But can you, if you would?—Look, what I will not, that I cannot do *Meas. for Meas.* ii 2 51
Grow this to what adverse issue it can, I will put it in practice *Much Ado* ii 2 53
What fire is in mine ears? Can this be true? iii 1 107
The wind, All unseen, can passage find *L. L. Lost* iv 3 106
Yet this I will not do, do how I can *As Y. Like It* ii 3 35
Do what you can, yours will not be entreated *T. of Shrew* v 2 89
Can't no other, But, I your daughter, he must be my brother? *All's Well* i 3 171
A false conclusion: I hate it as an unfilled can *T. Night* ii 3 7
Nothing that can be can come between me and the full prospect of my hopes iii 4 90
I can call spirits from the vasty deep.—Why, so can I, or so can any man; But will they come? *1 Hen. IV.* iii 1 52
Look how we can, or sad or merrily, Interpretation will misquote our looks v 2 12
No more my fortune can, But curse the cause I cannot aid the man *1 Hen. VI.* iv 3 43
O gross and miserable ignorance!—Nay, answer, if you can *2 Hen. VI.* iv 2 179
Secure us By what we can, which can no more but fly v 2 77
Shall we after them?—After them! nay, before them, if we can v 3 28
For what, alas, can these my single arms? *Troi. and Cres.* ii 2 135
I have done As you have done; that's what I can *Coriolanus* i 9 16
Cannot be! We have record that very well it can iv 6 49
Come what sorrow can, It cannot countervail the exchange of joy *Rom. and Jul.* ii 6 3
Can such things be, And overcome us like a summer's cloud, Without our special wonder? *Macbeth* iii 4 110
Try what repentance can: what can it not? Yet what can it when one can not repent? *Hamlet* iii 3 65
And they can well on horseback iv 7 85
What can man's wisdom In the restoring his bereaved sense? *Lear* iv 4 8
Something you can deny for your own safety *Ant. and Cleo.* ii 6 95
Can we, with manners, ask what was the difference? *Cymbeline* i 4 56
What Can it [gold] not do and undo? ii 3 78
And on it said a century of prayers, Such as I can, twice o'er iv 2 392
But bring they what they will and what they can, What need we fear? *Pericles* i 4 76
Where each man Thinks all is writ he speken can ii Gower 12
And every one with claps can sound, 'Our heir-apparent is a king!' iii Gower 36
I can no more *2 Hen. VI.* iii 2; *Hen. VIII.* iv 2; *Hamlet* v 2; *Ant. and Cleo.* iv 15
I can tell (them, you) *Tempest* ii 2; *Mer. Wives* i 4; *Meas. for Meas.* ii 1; *As Y. Like It* i 2; *W. Tale* iv 4; *1 Hen. IV.* i 2; iv 2; v 4; *Hen. V.* iv 7; iv 8; *3 Hen. VI.* iii 2; *Hen. VIII.* iv 1; *Troi. and Cres.* i 2; iii 2; *Coriolanus* iv 3; *Rom. and Jul.* ii 4; *T. of Athens* iii 2; *Lear* v 3
Can do it. Do not think I have wit enough to lie straight in my bed: I know I can do it *T. Night* ii 3 148
Ha, ha, ha! you can do it, sir; you can do it *2 Hen. IV.* iii 2 157
But if we fail, We then can do't at land *Ant. and Cleo.* iii 7 54
Can it be That so degenerate a strain as this Should once set footing in your generous bosoms? *Troi. and Cres.* ii 2 153
Canakin. Some wine, ho! And let me the canakin clink, clink; And let me the canakin clink *Othello* ii 3 71
Canaries. You have brought her into such a canaries *Mer. Wives* ii 2 61
But, i' faith, you have drunk too much canaries; and that's a marvellous searching wine *2 Hen. IV.* ii 4 29
Canary. The best courtier of them all, when the court lay at Windsor, could never have brought her to such a canary *Mer. Wives* ii 2 64
I will to my honest knight Falstaff, and drink canary with him iii 2 89
Canary to it with your feet, humour it with turning up your eyelids *L. L. Lost* iii 1 12
And make you dance canary With spritely fire and motion *All's Well* ii 1 77
Thou lackest a cup of canary: when did I see thee so put down?—Never in your life, I think; unless you see canary put me down *T. Night* i 3 85
Cancel. I here forget all former griefs, Cancel all grudge *T. G. of Ver.* v 4 143
The end of life cancels all bands *1 Hen. IV.* iii 2 157
Cancel his bond of life, dear God, I pray! *Richard III.* iv 4 77
Every bondman in his own hand bears The power to cancel his captivity *J. Cæsar* i 3 102
Cancel and tear to pieces that great bond Which keeps me pale! *Macbeth* iii 2 49

Cancel. If you will take this audit, take this life, And cancel these cold bonds . . . . *Cymbeline* v 4 28
Your exposition misinterpreting, We might proceed to cancel of your days . . . . *Pericles* i 1 113
Cancelled. His subjects slain, His statutes cancell'd . 3 *Hen. VI.* v 4 79
And what says My conceal'd lady to our cancell'd love? *Rom. and Jul.* iii 3 98
Cancelling. Fatal this marriage, cancelling your fame . . 2 *Hen. VI.* i 1 99
Cancer. And add more coals to Cancer . . . *Troi. and Cres.* ii 3 206
Candidatus. Be candidatus then, and put it on . . *T. Andron.* i 1 185
Candied be they And melt ere they molest! . . . . *Tempest* ii 1 279
Will the cold brook, Candied with ice, caudle thy morning taste? *T. of Athens* iv 3 226
Let the candied tongue lick absurd pomp . . . *Hamlet* iii 2 65
Candle. Burn him, and turn him about, Till candles and starlight and moonshine be out . . . . . . *Mer. Wives* v 5 106
Dark needs no candles now, for dark is light . . *L. L. Lost* iv 3 269
He dares not come there for the candle; for, you see, it is already in snuff . . . . *M. N. Dream* v 1 253
What, must I hold a candle to my shames? . . *Mer. of Venice* ii 6 41
Thus hath the candle singed the moth. O, these deliberate fools! ii 9 79
How far that little candle throws his beams! So shines a good deed in a naughty world . . . . v 1 90
When the moon shone, we did not see the candle . . . . v 1 92
By these blessed candles of the night . . . . . . v 1 220
Seek him with candle; bring him dead or living . *As Y. Like It* iii 1 6
I see no more in you Than without candle may go dark to bed . iii 5 39
Help me to a candle, and pen, ink and paper . . . *T. Night* iv 2 87
Bell, book, and candle shall not drive me back . . *K. John* iii 3 12
Time enough to go to bed with a candle, I warrant thee . 1 *Hen. IV.* ii 1 49
You are as a candle, the better part burnt out . . 2 *Hen. IV.* i 2 177
A wassail candle, my lord, all tallow: if I did say of wax, my growth would approve the truth . . . . i 2 179
Drinks off candles' ends for flap-dragons, and rides the wild-mare . ii 4 267
Here burns my candle out; ay, here it dies . . . 3 *Hen. VI.* ii 6 1
This candle burns not clear: 'tis I must snuff it; Then out it goes *Hen. VIII.* iii 2 96
Night's candles are burnt out, and jocund day Stands tiptoe on the misty mountain tops . . . . . *Rom. and Jul.* iii 5 9
There's husbandry in heaven; Their candles are all out . *Macbeth* ii 1 5
Out, out, brief candle! Life's but a walking shadow, a poor player v 5 23
So, out went the candle, and we were left darkling . . . *Lear* i 4 237
Candle-case. A pair of boots that have been candle-cases *T. of Shrew* iii 2 45
Candle-holder. I'll be a candle-holder, and look on . *Rom. and Jul.* i 4 38
Candle-mine. You whoreson candle-mine, you! . . 2 *Hen. IV.* ii 4 326
Candlestick. The horsemen sit like fixed candlesticks . *Hen. V.* iv 2 45
Candle-waster. Make misfortune drunk With candle-wasters *Much Ado* v 1 18
Candy. This is that Antonio That took the Phœnix and her fraught from Candy . . . . *T. Night* v 1 64
Why, what a candy deal of courtesy This fawning greyhound then did proffer me! . . . . 1 *Hen. IV.* i 3 251
Canidius. Is it not strange, Canidius? . . . . *Ant. and Cleo.* iii 7 21
Canidius, we Will fight with him by sea . . . . . iii 7 28
Canidius, Our nineteen legions thou shalt hold by land . . iii 7 58
Canidius and the rest That fell away have entertainment, but No honourable trust . . . . iv 6 16
Canis. Whose club kill'd Cerberus, that three-headed canis *L. L. Lost.* v 2 593
Canker. Stain'd With grief that's beauty's canker . . *Tempest* i 2 415
As with age his body uglier grows, So his mind cankers . . . iv 1 192
In the sweetest bud The eating canker dwells . . *T. G. of Ver.* i 1 43
The most forward bud Is eaten by the canker ere it blow . . . i 1 46
I had rather be a canker in a hedge than a rose in his grace . *Much Ado* i 3 28
Some to kill cankers in the musk-rose buds . . . *M. N. Dream* ii 2 3
Now will canker sorrow eat my bud . . . . . *K. John* iii 4 82
And heal the inveterate canker of one wound By making many . . v 2 14
To put down Richard, that sweet lovely rose, And plant this thorn, this canker, Bolingbroke . . . . . . 1 *Hen. IV.* i 3 176
The cankers of a calm world and a long peace . . . . iv 2 32
O, that this good blossom could be kept from cankers! . . 2 *Hen. IV.* ii 2 102
Hath not thy rose a canker, Somerset? . . . 1 *Hen. VI.* ii 4 68
Whiles thy consuming canker eats his falsehood . . . . ii 4 71
Banish the canker of ambitious thoughts . . . . 2 *Hen. VI.* i 2 18
Full soon the canker death eats up that plant . . *Rom. and Jul.* ii 3 30
The canker gnaw thy heart, For showing me again the eyes of man! *T. of Athens* iv 3 49
The canker galls the infants of the spring, Too oft before their buttons be disclosed . . . . *Hamlet* i 3 39
Is't not to be damn'd, To let this canker of our nature come In further evil? . . . . v 2 69
Canker-bit. My name is lost; By treason's tooth bare-gnawn and canker-bit . . . . *Lear* v 3 122
Canker-blossom. You canker-blossom! You thief of love! *M. N. Dream* iii 2 282
Cankered. A woman's will; a canker'd grandam's will! . *K. John* ii 1 194
This ingrate and canker'd Bolingbroke . . . 1 *Hen. IV.* i 3 137
And piled up The canker'd heaps of strange-achieved gold 2 *Hen. IV.* iv 5 72
I will fight Against my canker'd country with the spleen Of all the under fiends . . . . *Coriolanus* iv 5 97
To wield old partisans, in hands as old, Canker'd with peace, to part your canker'd hate . . . . *Rom. and Jul.* i 1 102
Cannibal. Compare with Cæsars, and with Cannibals . 2 *Hen. IV.* ii 4 180
That face of his the hungry cannibals Would not have touch'd 3 *Hen. VI.* i 4 152
Bloody cannibals! How sweet a plant have you untimely cropp'd! . v 5 61
And of the Cannibals that each other eat . . . . *Othello* i 3 143
Cannibally. An he had been cannibally given, he might have broiled and eaten him too . . . . *Coriolanus* iv 5 200
Cannon. As easy as a cannon will shoot point-blank twelve score *Mer. Wives* iii 2 33
Sweet smoke of rhetoric! He reputes me a cannon . . *L. L. Lost* iii 1 65
Seeking the bubble reputation Even in the cannon's mouth *As Y. Like It* ii 7 153
The thunder of my cannon shall be heard . . . . *K. John* i 1 26
Our cannon shall be bent Against the brows of this resisting town . ii 1 37
The cannons have their bowels full of wrath . . . . . ii 1 210
Our cannons' malice vainly shall be spent . . . . . ii 1 251
Their battering cannon charged to the mouths . . . . ii 1 382
He speaks plain cannon fire, and smoke and bounce . . . ii 1 462
Thou hast talk'd . . . Of basilisks, of cannon, culverin . 1 *Hen. IV.* ii 3 56
The nimble gunner With linstock now the devilish cannon touches *Hen. V.* iii Prol. 33
Let it pry through the portage of the head Like the brass cannon . iii 1 11
'Tis as much impossible—Unless we sweep 'em from the door with cannons—To scatter 'em . . . . . . *Hen. VIII.* v 4 13
Cannon. As violently as hasty powder fired Doth hurry from the fatal cannon's womb . . . . *Rom. and Jul.* v 1 65
They were As cannons overcharged with double cracks . *Macbeth* i 2 37
And why such daily cast of brazen cannon? . . . *Hamlet* i 1 73
But the great cannon to the clouds shall tell . . . . . i 2 126
As level as the cannon to his blank, Transports his poison'd shot . . iv 1 42
The phrase would be more german to the matter, if we could carry cannon by our sides . . . . v 2 166
The cannons to the heavens, the heavens to earth . . . v 2 288
I have seen the cannon, When it hath blown his ranks into the air *Oth.* iii 4 134
Cannon-bullet. Take those things for bird-bolts that you deem cannon-bullets . . . . *T. Night* i 5 100
Cannoneer. What cannoneer begot this lusty blood? . *K. John* ii 1 461
Let the kettle to the trumpet speak, The trumpet to the cannoneer *Ham.* v 2 287
Cannon-shot. These haughty words of hers Have batter'd me like roaring cannon-shot . . . . 1 *Hen. VI.* iii 3 79
Cannot. Use your authority: if you cannot, give thanks . *Tempest* i 1 26
So high a hope that even Ambition cannot pierce a wink beyond . ii 1 242
Yond same cloud cannot choose but fall by pailfuls . . . ii 2 24
So glad of this as they I cannot be, Who are surprised withal . iii 1 92
Our soul Cannot but yield you forth to public thanks . *Meas. for Meas.* v 1 7
I cannot, nor I will not, hold me still . . *Com. of Errors* iv 2 17
Not to be so odd and from all fashions As Beatrice is, cannot be commendable: But who dare tell her so? . . . . *Much Ado* iii 1 73
You may stay him.—Nay, by'r lady, that I think a' cannot . iii 3 83
An I cannot, cannot, cannot, An I cannot, another can . *L. L. Lost* iv 1 129
Cannot a plain man live and think no harm, But thus his simple truth must be abused? . . . . *Richard III.* i 3 51
Cannot thy master sleep these tedious nights? . . . . ii 2 6
Look, what is done cannot be now amended . . . . . iv 4 291
I cannot tell what you and other men Think of this life . *J. Cæsar* i 2 93
Cannot, is false, and that I dare not, falser . . . . ii 2 63
I cannot but remember such things were . . . *Macbeth* iv 3 222
Though it cannot be denied what I have done by land . *Ant. and Cleo.* ii 6 92
Cannot be. To move wild laughter in the throat of death? It cannot be; it is impossible . . . . *L. L. Lost* v 2 866
It cannot be but he was murder'd here . . . 2 *Hen. VI.* iii 2 177
It cannot be The Volsces dare break with us.—Cannot be! We have record that very well it can . . . . . . *Coriolanus* iv 6 47
Tell not me: I know this cannot be.—Not possible . . . iv 6 56
It cannot be But I am pigeon-liver'd and lack gall . . *Hamlet* ii 2 604
For't cannot be We shall remain in friendship . . *Ant. and Cleo.* ii 2 114
It cannot be But that my master is abused . . . *Cymbeline* iii 4 122
Canon. Contrary to thy established proclaimed edict and continent canon *L. L. Lost* i 1 263
Self-love, which is the most inhibited sin in the canon . *All's Well* i 1 158
The canon of the law is laid on him . . . . . *K. John* ii 1 180
Against the hospitable canon, would I Wash my fierce hand in's heart *Coriolanus* i 10 26
Mark you His absolute 'shall'?—'Twas from the canon . . iii 1 90
Religious canons, civil laws are cruel; Then what should war be? *T. of Athens* iv 3 60
That the Everlasting had not fix'd His canon 'gainst self-slaughter! *Ham.* i 2 132
Canonize. And fame in time to come canonize us . . *Troi. and Cres.* ii 2 202
Canonized and worshipp'd as a saint . . . . *K. John* iii 1 177
Preach some philosophy to make me mad, And thou shalt be canonized iii 4 52
His loves Are brazen images of canonized saints . . 2 *Hen. VI.* i 3 63
But tell Why thy canonized bones, hearsed in death, Have burst their cerements . . . . *Hamlet* i 4 47
Canopied. Love-thoughts lie rich when canopied with bowers *T. Night* i 1 41
To see the enclosed lights, now canopied Under these windows *Cymbeline* ii 2 21
Canopies. Costly apparel, tents, and canopies, Fine linen *T. of Shrew* ii 1 354
Under the canopies of costly state . . . . 2 *Hen. IV.* iii 1 13
Canopy. Than doth a rich embroider'd canopy To kings . 3 *Hen. VI.* ii 5 44
Where dwellest thou?—Under the canopy . . . *Coriolanus* iv 5 41
O woe! thy canopy is dust and stones . . . *Rom. and Jul.* v 3 13
Their shadows seem A canopy most fatal . . . . *J. Cæsar* v 1 88
This most excellent canopy, the air, look you . . . *Hamlet* ii 2 311
Canst thou remember A time before we came unto this cell? I do not think thou canst . . . . *Tempest* i 2 38
'Tis a good dulness, And give it way: I know thou canst not choose . i 2 186
How now? moody? What is't thou canst demand? . . . i 2 245
Say what thou canst, I'll go along with thee . . *As Y. Like It* i 3 107
List if thou canst hear the tread of travellers . . 1 *Hen. IV.* ii 2 34
Canst thou, when thou command'st the beggar's knee, Command the health of it? . . . . *Hen. V.* iv 1 273
Not fit to govern and rule multitudes, Which darest not, no, nor canst not rule a traitor . . . . 2 *Hen. VI.* v 1 95
Canst thou quake, and change thy colour? . . . *Richard III.* iii 5 1
Soft infancy, that nothing canst but cry . . . *Troi. and Cres.* ii 2 105
Canst thou not minister to a mind diseased? . . . . *Macbeth* v 3 40
Canstick. I had rather hear a brazen canstick turn'd . 1 *Hen. IV.* iii 1 131
Can't. I can't say your worships have delivered the matter well *Coriolanus* ii 1 62
Canterbury. Stephen Langton, chosen archbishop Of Canterbury *K. John* iii 1 144
There are pilgrims going to Canterbury with rich offerings . 1 *Hen. IV.* i 2 140
Where is my gracious Lord of Canterbury?—Not here in presence *Hen. V.* i 2 1
I then moved you, My Lord of Canterbury . . . . *Hen. VIII.* ii 4 218
Cranmer is return'd with welcome, Install'd lord archbishop of Canterbury . . . . iii 2 401
The Archbishop Of Canterbury, accompanied with other Learned and reverend fathers of his order . . . . iv 1 25
By the Archbishop of Canterbury She had all the royal makings of a queen . . . . iv 1 86
Ha! Canterbury?—Ay, my good lord . . . . v 1 81
Pray you, arise, My good and gracious Lord of Canterbury . . . v 1 92
Stand up, good Canterbury: Thy truth and thy integrity is rooted In us, thy friend . . . . v 1 113
His grace of Canterbury; Who holds his state at door, 'mongst pursuivants . . . . v 2 23
My Lord of Canterbury, I have a suit which you must not deny me . v 3 160
Do my Lord of Canterbury A shrewd turn, and he is your friend for ever . . . . v 3 177
Cantle. Cuts me from the best of all my land A huge half-moon, a monstrous cantle out . . . . 1 *Hen. IV.* iii 1 100
The greater cantle of the world is lost With very ignorance; we have kiss'd away Kingdoms . . . . *Ant. and Cleo.* iii 10 6
Canton. Write loyal cantons of contemned love . . . *T. Night* i 5 289
Canvas. Your white canvas doublet will sully . . . 1 *Hen. IV.* ii 4 84

Canvas-climber. Never was waves nor wind more violent; And from the ladder-tackle washes off A canvas-climber . . . . *Pericles* iv 1 62
Canvass. I'll canvass thee between a pair of sheets . . . . 2 *Hen. IV.* ii 4 243
I'll canvass thee in thy broad cardinal's hat, If thou proceed in this thy insolence . . . . 1 *Hen. VI.* i 3 36
Canzonet. Let me supervise the canzonet . . . . *L. L. Lost* iv 2 124
Cap. In faith, hath not the world one man but he will wear his cap with suspicion? . . . . *Much Ado* i 1 200
Doth not my wit become me rarely?—It is not seen enough, you should wear it in your cap . . . . iii 4 72
What's her name in the cap?—Rosaline, by good hap *L. L. Lost* ii 1 209
A brooch of lead.—Ay, and worn in the cap of a tooth-drawer . v 2 622
With silken coats and caps and golden rings, With ruffs and cuffs *T. of Shrew* iv 3 55
Here is the cap your worship did bespeak.—Why, this was moulded on a porringer . . . . iv 3 63
'Tis a cockle or a walnut-shell, A knack, a toy, a trick, a baby's cap . iv 3 67
This doth fit the time, And gentlewomen wear such caps as these . iv 3 70
It is a paltry cap, A custard-coffin, a bauble, a silken pie . . iv 3 81
I like the cap; And it I will have, or I will have none . . iv 3 84
I see she's like to have neither cap nor gown . . . iv 3 93
That cap of yours becomes you not: Off with that bauble, throw it under-foot . . . . v 2 121
Wears her cap out of fashion: richly suited, but unsuitable . *All's Well* i 1 170
Be more expressive to them: for they wear themselves in the cap of the time . . . . ii 1 55
He that cannot make a leg, put off's cap, kiss his hand and say nothing, has neither leg, hands, lip, nor cap . . . ii 2 10
The more and less came in with cap and knee . . 1 *Hen. IV.* iv 3 68
Thou art fitter to be worn in my cap than to wait at my heels 2 *Hen. IV.* i 2 17
The answer is as ready as a borrower's cap . . . ii 2 125
I shall receive money o' Thursday: shalt have a cap to-morrow . ii 4 298
I will cap that proverb with 'There is flattery in friendship' *Hen. V.* iii 7 124
Do not you wear your dagger in your cap that day, lest he knock that . iv 1 57
This will I also wear in my cap . . . . . . iv 1 229
And with his cap in hand, Like a base pandar, hold the chamber-door . iv 5 13
Wearing leeks in their Monmouth caps . . . . iv 7 104
Why wearest thou that glove in thy cap? . . . . iv 7 126
Wear thou this favour for me and stick it in thy cap . . iv 7 161
I met this man with my glove in his cap . . . . iv 8 33
Wear it for an honour in thy cap Till I do challenge it . . iv 8 63
I will be so bold as to wear it in my cap till I see him once again . v 1 13
If once he come to be a cardinal, He'll make his cap co-equal with the crown . . . . 1 *Hen. VI.* v 1 33
Who loves the king and will embrace his pardon, Fling up his cap 2 *Hen. VI.* iv 8 15
He that throws not up his cap for joy Shall for the fault make forfeit of his head . . . . . . 3 *Hen. VI.* ii 1 196
Some followers of mine own, At the lower end of the hall, hurl'd up their caps, And some ten voices cried . . *Richard III.* iii 7 35
Let his grace go forward, And dare us with his cap like larks *Hen. VIII.* iii 2 282
They threw their caps As they would hang them on the horns o' the moon . . . . *Coriolanus* i 1 216
You are ambitious for poor knaves' caps and legs . . ii 1 77
Take my cap, Jupiter, and I thank thee . . . . ii 1 115
The commons made A shower and thunder with their caps and shouts . ii 1 283
When you cast Your stinking greasy caps in hooting at Coriolanus' exile . . . . iv 6 131
As many coxcombs As you threw caps up will he tumble down . iv 6 135
And the cap Plays in the right hand, thus . . *T. of Athens* ii 1 18
'Faith, I perceive our masters may throw their caps at their money . iii 4 102
Time's flies, Cap and knee slaves, vapours, and minute-jacks! . iii 6 107
Did you see my cap?—I have lost my gown . . . iii 6 119
Did you see my cap?—Here 'tis . . . . . iii 6 125
And let his very breath, whom thou'lt observe, Blow off thy cap . iv 3 213
Thou art the cap of all the fools alive . . . . iv 3 363
Good men's lives Expire before the flowers in their caps . *Macbeth* iv 3 172
On fortune's cap we are not the very button . . *Hamlet* ii 2 233
Caps, hands, and tongues, applaud it to the clouds . . iv 5 107
A very riband in the cap of youth, Yet needful too . . iv 7 78
Should sure to the slaughter, If my cap would buy a halter . *Lear* i 4 343
Proud in heart and mind; that curled my hair; wore gloves in my cap iii 4 88
I would not do such a thing for a joint-ring, nor for measures of lawn, nor for gowns, petticoats, nor caps . . . *Othello* iv 3 74
I have ever held my cap off to thy fortunes . . *Ant. and Cleo.* ii 7 63
Ho! says a'. There's my cap.—Ho! Noble captain, come . ii 7 141
Yonder They cast their caps up and carouse together Like friends long lost . . . . iv 12 12
Such gain the cap of him that makes 'em fine . . *Cymbeline* iii 3 25
Capability. Gave us not That capability and god-like reason To fust in us unused . . . . . . *Hamlet* iv 4 38
Capable. Which any print of goodness wilt not take, Being capable of all ill! . . . . *Tempest* i 2 353
If their daughters be capable, I will put it to them . . *L. L. Lost* iv 2 82
The cicatrice and capable impressure Thy palm some moment keeps *As Y. Like It* iii 5 23
Heart too capable Of every line and trick of his sweet favour *All's Well* i 1 106
So thou wilt be capable of a courtier's counsel . . . . i 1 223
If thou beest capable of things serious . . . *W. Tale* iv 4 791
Urge them while their souls Are capable of this ambition *K. John* ii 1 476
For I am sick and capable of fears, Oppress'd with wrongs . . iii 1 12
You were advised his flesh was capable Of wounds and scars . 2 *Hen. IV.* i 1 172
'Tis a parlous boy; Bold, quick, ingenious, forward, capable *Richard III.* iii 1 155
We all are men, In our own natures frail, and capable Of our flesh *Hen. VIII.* v 3 11
His horse; for that's the more capable creature . *Troi. and Cres.* iii 3 310
Are capable of nothing but inexplicable dumb-shows and noise *Hamlet* iii 2 13
His form and cause conjoin'd, preaching to stones, Would make them capable . . . . iii 4 127
Of my land . . . I'll work the means To make thee capable . *Lear* ii 1 87
Till that a capable and wide revenge Swallow them up . . *Othello* iii 3 459
Capacities. You that are old consider not the capacities of us that are young . . . . 2 *Hen. IV.* i 2 197
Capacity. I will description the matter to you, if you be capacity of it *Mer. Wives* i 1 223
God comfort thy capacity! . . . . . *L. L. Lost* iv 2 44
Your capacity Is of that nature that to your huge store Wise things seem foolish and rich things but poor . . . . v 2 376
And tongue-tied simplicity In least speak most, to my capacity *M. N. Dr.* v 1 105
Notwithstanding thy capacity Receiveth as the sea, nought enters *T. Night* i 1 10
Capacity. Why, this is evident to any formal capacity; there is no obstruction in this . . . . *T. Night* ii 5 128
The young gentleman gives him out to be of good capacity and breeding iii 4 204
The capacity Of your soft cheveril conscience would receive, If you might please to stretch it . . . . . *Hen. VIII.* ii 3 31
Tuned too sharp in sweetness, For the capacity of my ruder powers *Troi. and Cres.* iii 2 26
In human action and capacity, Of no more soul nor fitness for the world Than camels in the war . . . . . *Coriolanus* ii 1 265
Had our great palace the capacity To camp this host, we all would sup together . . . . . . *Ant. and Cleo.* iv 8 32
Cap-a-pe. I am courtier cap-a-pe . . . . . . *W. Tale* iv 4 761
A figure like your father, Armed at point exactly, cap-a-pe . *Hamlet* i 2 200
Caparison. With die and drab I purchased this caparison . *W. Tale* iv 3 27
Come, bustle, bustle; caparison my horse . . . *Richard III.* v 3 289
O general, Here is the steed, we the caparison . . *Coriolanus* i 9 12
Caparisoned. Dost thou think, though I am caparisoned like a man, I have a doublet and hose in my disposition? . . *As Y. Like It* iii 2 205
O, sir, his lackey, for all the world caparisoned like the horse *T. of Shrew* iii 2 67
Cape. With a small compassed cape:—I confess the cape . . iv 3 140
Will you buy any tape, Or lace for your cape? . . *W. Tale* iv 4 323
But a little charge will trench him here And on this north side win this cape of land . . . . . . 1 *Hen. IV.* iii 1 113
What from the cape can you discern at sea? . . . *Othello* ii 1 1
Capel. Her body sleeps in Capel's monument . . *Rom. and Jul.* v 1 18
What torch is yond, that vainly lends his light To grubs and eyeless skulls? as I discern, It burneth in the Capels' monument . . v 3 127
Caper. He capers, he dances, he has eyes of youth . *Mer. Wives* iii 2 68
One Master Caper, at the suit of Master Three-pile the mercer *M. for M.* iv 3 10
We that are true lovers run into strange capers . *As Y. Like It* ii 4 55
Faith, I can cut a caper.—And I can cut the mutton to't . *T. Night* i 3 129
Let me see thee caper: ha! higher: ha, ha! excellent! . . i 3 150
He that will caper with me for a thousand marks, let him lend me the money, and have at him! . . . . . 2 *Hen. IV.* i 2 216
I have seen Him caper upright like a wild Morisco . . 2 *Hen. VI.* iii 1 365
Capers nimbly in a lady's chamber To the lascivious pleasing of a lute *Richard III.* i 1 12
He offered to cut a caper at the proclamation . . . *Pericles* iv 2 116
Capered. He caper'd, and cried, 'All goes well' . . *L. L. Lost* v 2 113
Capering. Our master Capering to eye her . . . *Tempest* v 1 238
If a throstle sing, he falls straight a capering . . *Mer. of Venice* i 2 66
Carded his state, Mingled his royalty with capering fools 1 *Hen. IV.* iii 2 63
Capet. Hugh Capet also, who usurp'd the crown . . . *Hen. V.* i 2 69
Also King Lewis the Tenth, Who was sole heir to the usurper Capet . i 2 78
Hugh Capet's claim, King Lewis his satisfaction, all appear To hold in right and title of the female . . . . . . i 2 87
Caphis, ho! Caphis, I say!—Here, sir . . . *T. of Athens* ii 1 13
Capilet. A wretched Florentine, Derived from the ancient Capilet *All's Well* v 3 159
Let him let the matter slip, and I'll give him my horse, grey Capilet *T. Night* iii 4 315
Capitaine. Suivez-vous le grand capitaine . . . . *Hen. V.* iv 4 70
Capital. But what talk we of these traitorly rascals, whose miseries are to be smiled at, their offences being so capital? . . *W. Tale* iv 4 823
And, for your pains, Of capital treason we arrest you here . *Rich II.* iv 1 151
Holds from all soldiers chief majority And military title capital 1 *Hen. IV.* iii 2 110
And you, lord archbishop, and you, lord Mowbray, Of capital treason I attach you both . . . . 2 *Hen. IV.* iv 2 109
How shall we stretch our eye When capital crimes, chew'd, swallow'd and digested, Appear before us? . . . . *Hen. V.* ii 2 56
She is our capital demand, comprised Within the fore-rank of our articles . . . . v 2 96
I arrest thee, York, Of capital treason 'gainst the king and crown 2 *Hen. VI.* v 1 107
So criminal and in such capital kind, Deserves the extremest death *Coriol.* iii 3 81
And to poor we Thine enmity's most capital . . . . v 3 104
But treasons capital, confess'd and proved, Have overthrown him *Macbeth* i 3 115
It was a brute part of him to kill so capital a calf . *Hamlet* iii 2 111
These feats, So crimeful and so capital in nature . . iv 7 7
Edmund, I arrest thee On capital treason . . . . *Lear* v 3 83
This heinous capital offence . . . . . *Pericles* ii 4 5
Capite. Men shall hold of me in capite . . . 2 *Hen. VI.* iv 7 131
Capitol. They'll sit by the fire, and presume to know What's done i' the Capitol . . . . *Coriolanus* i 1 196
Your company to the Capitol; where, I know, Our greatest friends attend us . . . . i 1 248
Nor fane nor Capitol, The prayers of priests nor times of sacrifice . i 10 20
A perfecter giber for the table than a necessary bencher in the Capitol . ii 1 92
What's the matter?—You are sent for to the Capitol . . ii 1 276
Let's to the Capitol; And carry with us ears and eyes for the time . ii 1 284
When you have drawn your number, Repair to the Capitol . . ii 3 262
To the Capitol, come: We will be there before the stream o' the people ii 3 268
Not Romans—as they are not, Though calved i' the porch o' the Capitol iii 1 240
As far as doth the Capitol exceed The meanest house in Rome . iv 2 39
Let's to the Capitol. Would half my wealth Would buy this for a lie! iv 6 160
See you yon coign o' the Capitol, yon corner-stone? . . . v 4 1
Keep then this passage to the Capitol And suffer not dishonour to approach The imperial seat . . . . . . *T. Andron.* i 1 12
Thou great defender of this Capitol, Stand gracious to the rites that we intend! . . . . i 1 77
Go you down that way towards the Capitol; This way will I *J. Cæsar* i 1 68
And Cicero Looks with such ferret and such fiery eyes As we have seen him in the Capitol . . . . i 2 187
Against the Capitol I met a lion, Who glared upon me, and went surly by . . . . i 3 20
Comes Cæsar to the Capitol to-morrow?—He doth . . . . i 3 36
And roars As doth the lion in the Capitol . . . . i 3 75
The high east Stands, as the Capitol, directly here . . . ii 1 111
The persuasion of his augurers May hold him from the Capitol to-day ii 1 201
Let me work; For I can give his humour the true bent, And I will bring him to the Capitol . . . . ii 1 211
Which drizzled blood upon the Capitol . . . . . ii 2 21
What should I do? Run to the Capitol, and nothing else? . . ii 4 11
I heard a bustling rumour, like a fray, And the wind brings it from the Capitol . . . . ii 4 19
Is Cæsar yet gone to the Capitol?—Madam, not yet . . . ii 4 24
I go to take my stand, To see him pass on to the Capitol . . ii 4 26
What, urge you your petitions in the street? Come to the Capitol . iii 1 12
The question of his death is enrolled in the Capitol . . . iii 2 41
For your dwelling,—briefly.—Briefly, I dwell by the Capitol . . iii 3 27

Capitol. What, shall I find you here?—Or here, or at the Capitol *J. Cæsar* iv 1 11
I did enact Julius Cæsar: I was killed i' the Capitol . *Hamlet* iii 2 109
What Made the all-honour'd, honest Roman, Brutus, With the arm'd rest, courtiers of beauteous freedom, To drench the Capitol? *Ant. and Cleo.* ii 6 18
With lips as common as the stairs That mount the Capitol . *Cymbeline* i 6 106
Capitulate. Douglas, Mortimer, Capitulate against us and are up *1 Hen. IV.* iii 2 120
Do not bid me Dismiss my soldiers, or capitulate Again with Rome's mechanics *Coriolanus* v 3 82
Capocchia. Alas, poor wretch! ah, poor capocchia! . *Troi. and Cres.* iv 2 33
Capon. He steps me to her trencher and steals her capon's leg *T. G. of Ver.* iv 4 10
The capon burns, the pig falls from the spit . *Com. of Errors* i 2 44
Mome, malt-horse, capon, coxcomb, idiot, patch! . iii 1 32
He hath bid me to a calf's head and a capon . *Much Ado* v 1 156
You can carve; Break up this capon . *L. L. Lost* iv 1 56
Then the justice, In fair round belly with good capon lined *As Y. Like It* ii 7 154
Unless hours were cups of sack and minutes capons . *1 Hen. IV.* i 2 8
A cup of Madeira and a cold capon's leg . i 2 129
Wherein neat and cleanly, but to carve a capon and eat it? . ii 4 502
I eat the air, promise-crammed: you cannot feed capons so *Hamlet* iii 2 100
You are cock and capon too; and you crow, cock, with your comb on *Cymbeline* ii 1 25
Cappadocia. Archelaus, Of Cappadocia . *Ant. and Cleo.* iii 6 70
Capriccio. Will this capriccio hold in thee? art sure? . *All's Well* ii 3 310
Capricious. The most capricious poet, honest Ovid *As Y. Like It* iii 3 8
Captain. Wilt thou be of our consort? Say ay, and be the captain of us all . *T. G. of Ver.* iv 1 65
Be patient; we must bring you to our captain . v 3 2
I must bring you to our captain's cave . v 3 12
'Twas a commandment to command the captain . *M. for Meas.* i 2 13
That in the captain's but a choleric word, Which in the soldier is flat blasphemy.—Art avised o' that? . ii 2 130
Captain of our fairy band, Helena is here at hand . *M. N. Dream* iii 2 110
A phœnix, captain and an enemy . *All's Well* i 1 182
Observe his reports for me.—We shall, noble captain . ii 1 47
You are undone, captain, all but your scarf; that has a knot on't yet iv 3 358
Captain I'll be no more; But I will eat and drink, and sleep as soft As captain shall . iv 3 367
A bawbling vessel was he captain of . *T. Night* v 1 57
I'll bring you to a captain in this town, Where lie my maiden weeds v 1 261
The captain that did bring me first on shore Hath my maid's garments v 1 281
He hath not told us of the captain yet . v 1 390
His pure soul unto his captain Christ, Under whose colours he had fought so long . *Richard II.* iv 1 99
The figure of God's majesty, His captain, steward, deputy-elect iv 1 126
Discharge yourself of our company, Pistol.—No, good Captain Pistol; not here, sweet captain . *2 Hen. IV.* ii 4 149
Captain! thou abominable damned cheater, art thou not ashamed to be called captain? . ii 4 151
An captains were of my mind, they would truncheon you out, for taking their names . ii 4 153
You a captain! you slave, for what? . ii 4 156
He a captain! hang him, rogue! he lives upon mouldy stewed prunes . ii 4 157
A captain! God's light, these villains will make the word as odious as the word 'occupy' . ii 4 159
Therefore captains had need look to't . ii 4 162
By my troth, captain, these are very bitter words . ii 4 184
Have we not Hiren here?—O' my word, captain, there's none such here ii 4 190
As I came along, I met and overtook a dozen captains . ii 4 387
A dozen captains stay at door for you . ii 4 402
My captain, sir, commends him to you; my captain, Sir John Falstaff iii 2 66
Good my lord captain,— What, dost thou roar before thou art pricked? iii 2 188
Good master corporal captain, for my old dame's sake, stand my friend iii 2 244
Go, captain, and deliver to the army This news of peace . iv 2 69
And then the vital commoners and inland petty spirits muster me all to their captain, the heart . iv 3 120
Here a' comes; and the Scots captain, Captain Jamy . *Hen. V.* iii 2 79
It sall be vary gud, gud feith, gud captains bath . iii 2 110
O now, who will behold The royal captain of this ruin'd band! iv Prol. 29
Under what captain serve you?—Under Sir Thomas Erpingham . iv 1 95
Gower is a good captain, and is good knowledge and literatured in the wars . iv 7 156
Enough, captain: you have astonished him . v 1 40
Being captain of the watch to-night . *1 Hen. VI.* ii 1 61
Away, captains! let's get us from the walls . iii 2 71
Welcome, brave captain and victorious lord! . iii 4 16
Ill beseeming any common man, Much more a knight, a captain and a leader . iv 1 32
English John Talbot, captains, calls you forth . iv 2 3
Whiles the honourable captain there Drops bloody sweat from his war-wearied limbs . iv 4 17
Hear ye, captain, are you not at leisure? . v 3 97
Then call our captains and our colours forth . v 3 128
After the slaughter of so many peers, So many captains . v 4 104
Speak, captain, shall I stab the forlorn swain? . *2 Hen. VI.* iv 1 65
This villain here, Being captain of a pinnace, threatens more Than Bargulus the strong Illyrian . iv 1 107
Be brave, then; for your captain is brave, and vows reformation . iv 2 69
Where's Captain Margaret, to fence you now? . *3 Hen. VI.* ii 6 75
A wise stout captain, and soon persuaded! . iv 7 30
O Thou, whose captain I account myself, Look on my forces with a gracious eye! . *Richard III.* v 3 108
He was a soldier good; But, by great Mars, the captain of us all, Never like thee . *Troi. and Cres.* iv 5 198
If thy captain knew I were here, he would use me with estimation *Coriol.* v 2 55
My captain knows you not.—I mean, thy general . v 2 57
Here is a captain, let him tell the tale. . *T. Andron* v 3 94
O, he is the courageous captain of complements . *Rom. and Jul.* ii 4 20
Under favour, pardon me, If I speak like a captain. . *T. of Athens* iii 5 41
The ass more captain than the lion . iii 5 49
Is this the balsam that the usuring senate Pours into captains' wounds? iii 5 111
Our captain hath in every figure skill, An aged interpreter . v 3 7
Dismay'd not this Our captains, Macbeth and Banquo? . *Macbeth* i 2 34
Go, captain, from me greet the Danish king . *Hamlet* iv 4 1
Let four captains Bear Hamlet, like a soldier, to the stage . v 2 406
He's married.—To who?—Marry, to—Come, captain, will you go? *Othello* i 2 53
She that I spake of, our great captain's captain . ii 1 74
I shall not dine at home; I meet the captains at the citadel . iii 3 59

Captain. His captain's heart, Which in the scuffles of great fights hath burst The buckles on his breast . *Ant. and Cleo.* i 1 6
Shall become you well, to entreat your captain To soft and gentle speech ii 2 2
There's my cap.—Ho! Noble captain, come . ii 7 142
So thy grand captain Antony Shall set thee on triumphant chariots . iii 1 9
Who does i' the wars more than his captain can Becomes his captain's captain . iii 1 22
Call to me All my sad captains; fill our bowls once more . iii 13 184
Call all his noble captains to my lord . iii 13 189
I see still, A diminution in our captain's brain Restores his heart . iii 13 198
My captain, and my emperor, let me say, Before I strike this bloody stroke, farewell . iv 14 90
Command our present numbers Be muster'd; bid the captains look to't *Cymbeline* iv 2 344
Captain-general. Six-or-seven-times-honoured captain-general *Tr. and Cr.* iii 3 279
Captainship. Take The captainship, thou shalt be met with thanks *T. of Athens* v 1 164
The itch of his affection should not then Have nick'd his captainship *Ant. and Cleo.* iii 13 8
Captious. Yet in this captious and intenible sieve I still pour in the waters of my love . *All's Well* i 3 208
Captivate. And sent our sons and husbands captivate . *1 Hen. VI.* ii 3 42
Tush, women have been captivate ere now . v 3 107
How ill-beseeming is it in thy sex To triumph, like an Amazonian trull, Upon their woes whom fortune captivates! . *3 Hen. VI.* i 4 115
Captivated. Thou wert immured, restrained, captivated, bound *L. L. Lost* iii 1 126
Captive. The captive is enriched: on whose side? the beggar's . iv 1 76
Beware of being captives, Before you serve . *All's Well* ii 1 21
Whose words all ears took captive . v 3 17
Never did captive with a freer heart Cast off his chains . *Richard II.* i 3 88
In a captive chariot into Rouen Bring him our prisoner . *Hen. V.* iii 5 54
Like captives bound to a triumphant car . *1 Hen. VI.* i 1 22
Who thunders to his captives blood and death . *3 Hen. VI.* ii 1 127
Turn'd my captive state to liberty, My fear to hope . iv 6 3
For God's sake, take away this captive scold . v 5 29
My woman's heart Grossly grew captive to his honey words *Richard III.* iv 1 80
And for an old aunt whom the Greeks held captive, He brought a Grecian queen . *Troi. and Cres.* ii 2 77
When many times the captive Grecian falls, Even in the fan and wind of your fair sword, You bid them rise, and live. . v 3 40
As most Abated captives to some nation That won you without blows! *Cor.* iii 3 132
Captive to thee and to thy Roman yoke . *T. Andron* i 1 111
Was't not a happy star Led us to Rome, strangers, and more than so, Captives, to be advanced to this height? . iv 2 34
To grace in captive bonds his chariot-wheels . *J. Cæsar* i 1 39
He hath brought many captives home to Rome . iii 2 93
You have the captives That were the opposites of this day's strife *Lear* v 3 41
If thou say Antony lives, is well, Or friends with Cæsar, or not captive to him, I'll set thee in a shower of gold . *Ant. and Cleo.* ii 5 44
Whose kinsmen have made suit That their good souls may be appeased with slaughter Of you their captives . *Cymbeline* v 5 73
How lived you? And when came you to serve our Roman captive? v 5 385
Captived. When Cressy battle fatally was struck, And all our princes captived . *Hen. V.* ii 4 55
Captivity. Triumphant death, smear'd with captivity . *1 Hen. VI.* iv 7 3
Who kept him in captivity till he died . *2 Hen. VI.* ii 2 42
He shall here find his friends with horse and men To set him free from his captivity . *3 Hen. VI.* iv 5 13
So can I: So every bondman in his own hand bears The power to cancel his captivity . *J. Cæsar* i 3 102
Who like a good and hardy soldier fought 'Gainst my captivity *Macbeth* i 2 5
Given to captivity me and my utmost hopes . *Othello* iv 2 51
Captum. Redime te captum quam queas minimo . *T. of Shrew* i 1 167
Capucius. My royal nephew, and your name Capucius . *Hen. VIII.* iv 2 110
Capulet. Down with the Capulets! down with the Montagues! *R. and J.* i 1 81
Thou villain Capulet,—Hold me not, let me go . i 1 86
Three civil brawls, bred of an airy word, By thee, old Capulet, and Montague, Have thrice disturb'd the quiet of our streets . i 1 97
You, Capulet, shall go along with me: And, Montague, come you . i 1 106
My master is the great rich Capulet . i 2 84
At this same ancient feast of Capulet's Sups the fair Rosaline . i 2 87
Nay, sit, good cousin Capulet; For you and I are past our dancing days i 5 32
Is she a Capulet? O dear account! my life is my foe's debt . i 5 119
Be but sworn my love, And I'll no longer be a Capulet . ii 2 36
My heart's dear love is set On the fair daughter of rich Capulet . ii 3 58
Tybalt, the kinsman of old Capulet . ii 4 6
The day is hot, the Capulets abroad, And, if we meet, we shall not 'scape a brawl . iii 1 2
By my head, here come the Capulets.—By my heel, I care not . iii 1 38
Good Capulet,—which name I tender As dearly as my own,—be satisfied iii 1 74
The time is very short.—My father Capulet will have it so . iv 1 2
That same ancient vault Where all the kindred of the Capulets lie . iv 1 112
Run to the Capulets: Raise up the Montagues . v 3 177
Capulet! Montague! See, what a scourge is laid upon your hate . v 3 291
Car. Wilt thou aspire to guide the heavenly car? . *T. G. of Ver.* iii 1 154
And Phibbus' car Shall shine from far And make and mar *M. N. Dream* i 2 37
Though our silence be drawn from us with cars, yet peace . *T. Night* ii 5 71
Like captives bound to a triumphant car . *1 Hen. VI.* i 1 22
Now Phaëthon hath tumbled from his car, And made an evening at the noontide prick . *3 Hen. VI.* i 4 33
O Phœbus, hadst thou never given consent That Phaëthon should check thy fiery steeds, Thy burning car never had scorch'd the earth! . ii 6 13
When the morning sun shall raise his car Above the border of this horizon iv 7 80
The weary sun hath made a golden set, And, by the bright track of his fiery car, Gives signal of a goodly day to-morrow . *Richard III.* v 3 20
The duke's confessor, John de la Car . *Hen. VIII.* i 1 218
John de la Car, my chaplain . i 2 162
Sir Gilbert Peck his chancellor; and John Car, Confessor to him . ii 1 20
When thy car is loaden with their heads, I will dismount *T. Andron.* v 2 53
He has deserved it, were it carbuncled Like holy Phœbus' car *Ant. and Cleo.* iv 8 29
And would so, had it been a carbuncle Of Phœbus' wheel, and might so safely, had it Been all the worth of 's car . *Cymbeline* v 5 191
Carack. Whole armadoes of caracks to be ballast at her nose *C. of Err.* iii 2 140
He to-night hath boarded a land carack . *Othello* i 2 50
Carat. How much your chain weighs to the utmost carat *Com. of Err.* iv 1 28
Other, less fine in carat, is more precious . *2 Hen. IV.* iv 5 162
Caraway. Pippin of my own graffing, with a dish of caraways . v 3 3
Carbonado. Let him make a carbonado of me . *1 Hen. IV.* v 3 61
He scotched him and notched him like a carbonado . *Coriolanus* iv 5 199
Draw, you rogue, or I'll so carbonado your shanks . *Lear* ii 2 41

Carbonadoed. It is your carbonadoed face . *All's Well* iv 5 107
How she longed to eat adders' heads and toads carbonadoed . *W. Tale* iv 4 268
Carbuncle. All o'er embellished with rubies, carbuncles *Com. of Errors* iii 2 138
A carbuncle entire, as big as thou art, Were not so rich a jewel *Coriolanus* i 4 55
O'er-sized with coagulate gore, With eyes like carbuncles . *Hamlet* ii 2 485
Thou art a boil, A plague-sore, an embossed carbuncle . *Lear* ii 4 227
Had it been a carbuncle Of Phœbus' wheel . . . . *Cymbeline* v 5 189
Carbuncled. Were it carbuncled Like holy Phœbus' car *Ant. and Cleo.* iv 8 28
Carcanet. Say that I linger'd with you at your shop To see the making of her carcanet . . . *Com. of Errors* iii 1 4
Carcass. A rotten carcass of a boat, not rigg'd . *Tempest* i 2 146
I had rather give his carcass to my hounds . . *M. N. Dream* iii 2 64
Where the carcases of many a tall ship lie buried . *Mer. of Venice* iii 1 6
That shakes the rotten carcass of old Death Out of his rags . *K. John* ii 1 456
Whose loves I prize As the dead carcasses of unburied men *Coriolanus* iii 3 122
Carve him as a dish fit for the gods, Not hew him as a carcass *J. Cæsar* ii 1 174
Hurt him! his body's a passable carcass, if he be not hurt . *Cymbeline* i 2 11
To-day how many would have given their honours To have saved their carcases! . . . . v 3 67
Card. Yet I have faced it with a card of ten . *T. of Shrew* ii 1 407
Have I not here the best cards for the game, To win this easy match? *K. John* v 2 105
There all is marr'd; there lies a cooling card . 1 *Hen. VI.* v 3 83
As sure a card as ever won the set . . . *T. Andron.* v 1 100
All the quarters that they know I' the shipman's card . *Macbeth* i 3 17
We must speak by the card, or equivocation will undo us . *Hamlet* v 1 149
Indeed, to speak feelingly of him, he is the card or calendar of gentry v 2 114
She, Eros, has Pack'd cards with Cæsar, and false-play'd my glory *Ant. and Cleo.* iv 14 19
Carded his state, Mingled his royalty with capering fools . 1 *Hen. IV.* iii 2 62
Carder. The spinsters, carders, fullers, weavers . *Hen. VIII.* i 2 33
Cardinal. I Pandulph, of fair Milan cardinal . *K. John* iii 1 138
Thou canst not, cardinal, devise a name So slight, unworthy and ridiculous . . . . iii 1 149
Good father cardinal, cry thou amen To my keen curses . iii 1 181
King Philip, listen to the cardinal . . . . iii 1 198
Philip, what say'st thou to the cardinal?—What should he say, but as the cardinal? . . . . iii 1 202
Preach some philosophy to make me mad, And thou shalt be canonized, cardinal . . . . iii 4 52
Father cardinal, I have heard you say That we shall see and know our friends in heaven . . . . iii 4 76
Who brought that letter from the cardinal? . . . iv 3 14
Perchance the cardinal cannot make your peace . . v 1 74
Put his cause and quarrel To the disposing of the cardinal . v 7 92
I'll canvass thee in thy broad cardinal's hat . 1 *Hen. VI.* i 3 36
Under my feet I stamp thy cardinal's hat . . . i 3 49
This cardinal's more haughty than the devil . . i 3 85
Is my Lord of Winchester install'd, And call'd unto a cardinal's degree? v 1 29
If once he come to be a cardinal, He'll make his cap co-equal with the crown . . . . v 1 32
Yet let us watch the haughty cardinal . 2 *Hen. VI.* i 1 174
Or thou or I, Somerset, will be protector, Despite Duke Humphrey or the cardinal . . . . i 1 179
The haughty cardinal, More like a soldier than a man o' the church . i 1 185
I have forgot, But, as I think, it was by the cardinal . i 2 27
Yet have I gold flies from another coast; I dare not say, from the rich cardinal . . . . i 2 94
A crafty knave does need no broker; Yet am I Suffolk and the cardinal's broker . . . . i 2 101
John Goodman, my lord cardinal's man . . . i 3 19
I would the college of the cardinals Would choose him pope . i 3 64
Although we fancy not the cardinal, Yet must we join with him . i 3 97
Let thy betters speak.—The cardinal's not my better in the field . i 3 113
What, cardinal, is your priesthood grown peremptory? . ii 1 23
Cardinal, I am with you . . . . . ii 1 49
I do arrest you in his highness' name; And here commit you to my lord cardinal To keep . . . . . . iii 1 137
Lord cardinal, he is your prisoner . . . . iii 1 187
Lord cardinal, if thou think'st on heaven's bliss, Hold up thy hand . iii 3 27
Why, all this business Our reverend cardinal carried . *Hen. VIII.* i 1 100
The state takes notice of the private difference Betwixt you and the cardinal . . . . i 1 102
That you read The cardinal's malice and his potency Together . i 1 105
This cunning cardinal The articles o' the combination drew As himself pleased . . . . i 1 168
He privily Deals with our cardinal . . . . i 1 184
Thus the cardinal Does buy and sell his honour as he pleases . i 1 191
The o'er-great cardinal Hath show'd him gold . . i 1 222
My good lord cardinal, they vent reproaches Most bitterly on you . i 2 23
My lord cardinal, You that are blamed for it alike with us, Know you of this taxation? . . . . i 2 38
My learn'd lord cardinal, Deliver all with charity . . i 2 142
The cardinal's and Sir Thomas Lovell's heads Should have gone off . i 2 185
Whither were you a-going?—To the cardinal's . . i 3 50
Had the cardinal But half my lay thoughts in him . . i 4 10
You are a churchman, or, I'll tell you, cardinal, I should judge now unhappily . . . . i 4 88
Let's be merry: Good my lord cardinal . . . i 4 105
Certainly The cardinal is the end of this . . . ii 1 40
Whoever the king favours, The cardinal instantly will find employment, And far enough from court too . . . . ii 1 48
The cardinal Will have his will, and she must fall . ii 1 166
A man of my lord cardinal's, by commission and main power, took 'em from me . . . . ii 2 6
This is the cardinal's doing, the king-cardinal . . ii 2 20
My good lord cardinal? O my Wolsey, The quiet of my wounded conscience ii 2 74
Cardinal, Prithee, call Gardiner to me, my new secretary ii 2 115
There's an ill opinion spread then Even of yourself, lord cardinal . ii 2 126
Lord cardinal, To you I speak.—Your pleasure, madam? ii 4 68
My lord cardinal, I do excuse you . . . . ii 4 155
I speak my good lord cardinal to this point . . ii 4 166
I may perceive These cardinals trifle with me . . ii 4 236
The two great cardinals Wait in the presence . . iii 1 16
Lord cardinal, The willing'st sin I ever yet committed May be absolved in English . . . . iii 1 48
If you will now unite in your complaints, And force them with a constancy, the cardinal Cannot stand under them . . iii 2 2
The cardinal's letters to the pope miscarried, And came to the eye o' the king . . . . iii 2 30

Cardinal. The cardinal did entreat his holiness To stay the judgement o' the divorce . . . . . *Hen. VIII.* iii 2 32
Will the king Digest this letter of the cardinal's? . iii 2 53
And Is posted, as the agent of our cardinal, To second all his plot . iii 2 59
Saw you the cardinal?—My lord, we have . . . iii 2 111
Hear the king's pleasure, cardinal: who commands you To render up the great seal presently . . . . iii 2 228
The heads of all thy brother cardinals, With thee and all thy best parts bound together, Weigh'd not a hair of his . . iii 2 257
Yes, that goodness Of gleaning all the land's wealth into one, Into your own hands, cardinal, by extortion . . . iii 2 285
When the brown wench Lay kissing in your arms, lord cardinal . iii 2 296
If you can blush and cry 'guilty,' cardinal, You'll show a little honesty iii 2 305
So fare you well, my little good lord cardinal . . iii 2 349
For, since the cardinal fell, that title's lost . . iv 1 96
This cardinal, Though from an humble stock, undoubtedly Was fashion'd to much honour from his cradle . . . . . iv 2 48
Cardinal sins. But cardinal sins and hollow hearts I fear ye: Mend 'em, for shame . . . . iii 1 104
Cardinal virtues. Holy men I thought ye, Upon my soul, two reverend cardinal virtues . . . . iii 1 103
Cardinally. If she had been a woman cardinally given . *Meas. for Meas.* ii 1 81
Cardmaker. By birth a pedlar, by education a cardmaker *T. of Shrew* Ind. 2 20
Carduus Benedictus. I am sick.—Get you some of this distilled Carduus Benedictus . . . . . *Much Ado* iii 4 73
Care. Good boatswain, have care . . . *Tempest* i 1 10
What cares these roarers for the name of king? . . i 1 17
I have done nothing but in care of thee, Of thee, my dear one . i 2 16
I have used thee, Filth as thou art, with human care . . i 2 346
If of life you keep a care, Shake off slumber, and beware . ii 1 303
Every man shift for all the rest, and let no man take care for himself . v 1 257
And yet I will not name it; and yet I care not . *T. G. of Ver.* ii 1 123
I care not though he burn himself in love . . . ii 5 55
I thank thee for thine honest care; Which to requite, command me while I live . . . . iii 1 22
What need a man care for a stock with a wench, when she can knit him a stock? . . . . iii 1 311
She hath no teeth.—I care not for that neither, because I love crusts iii 1 345
You dote on her that cares not for your love . . iv 4 87
I care not for her, I: I hold him but a fool that will endanger His body for a girl that loves him not . . . . . v 4 132
He cares not what he puts into the press . . *Mer. Wives* ii 1 79
She shall not dismay me: I care not for that, but that I am afeard iii 4 27
Thanks, provost, for thy care and secrecy . *Meas. for Meas.* v 1 536
The great care of goods at random left Drew me from kind embracements of my spouse . . . . . *Com. of Errors* i 1 43
My wife and I, Fixing our eyes on whom our care was fix'd . i 1 85
My youngest boy, and yet my eldest care . . . i 1 125
When I am dull with care and melancholy, Lightens my humour with his merry jests . . . . i 2 20
It seems he hath great care to please his wife . . ii 1 56
The heedful slave Is wander'd forth, in care to seek me . ii 2 3
My only son Knows not my feeble key of untuned cares . v 1 310
I thank it, poor fool, it keeps on the windy side of care . *Much Ado* ii 1 327
What though care killed a cat, thou hast mettle enough in thee to kill care v 1 133
I thank thee for thy care and honest pains . . . v 1 323
Dost thou think I care for a satire or an epigram? . . v 4 103
By the world, I would not care a pin . . *L. L. Lost* iv 3 18
You weigh me not? O, that's you care not for me . . v 2 27
Great reason; for 'past cure is still past care' . . v 2 28
We will turn it finely off, sir; we will take some care . v 2 511
Effect it with some care . . . . *M. N. Dream* ii 1 265
They lose it that do buy it with much care . *Mer. of Venice* i 1 75
My chief care Is to come fairly off from the great debts . i 1 127
Pray God, Bassanio come To see me pay his debt, and then I care not! iii 3 36
I care not for my spirits, if my legs were not weary . *As Y. Like It* ii 4 2
That little cares for buying any thing . . . . ii 4 90
I care not for their names; they owe me nothing . . ii 5 21
What care I for words? yet words do well When he that speaks them pleases . . . . iii 5 111
To show the letter that I writ to you.—I care not if I have . v 2 85
Her care should be To comb your noddle with a three-legg'd stool *T. of Shr.* i 1 63
He took some care To get her cunning schoolmasters to instruct her . i 1 191
Yet you are wither'd.—'Tis with cares.—I care not . . ii 1 240
I intend That all is done in reverend care of her . . iv 1 207
Go and get me some repast; I care not what, so it be wholesome food iv 3 16
I am content, in a good father's care, To have him match'd . iv 4 31
One that cares for thee, And for thy maintenance commits his body To painful labour . . . . v 2 147
The care I have had to even your content . . . *All's Well* i 3 3
I thank you for your honest care: I will speak with you further anon i 3 132
You ne'er oppress'd me with a mother's groan, Yet I express to you a mother's care . . . . i 3 154
I care no more for than I do for heaven . . . i 3 170
I will throw thee from my care for ever Into the staggers . ii 3 169
I have now found thee; when I lose thee again, I care not . ii 3 217
Undone, and forfeited to cares for ever . . . ii 3 284
I am sure care's an enemy to life . . . *T. Night* i 3 3
Let him be the devil, an he will, I care not: give me faith, say I . i 5 137
Ay, ay: I care not for good life . . . . ii 3 39
I do care for something; but in my conscience, sir, I do not care for you iii 1 32
If that be to care for nothing, sir, I would it would make you invisible iii 1 34
Let some of my people have a special care of him . . iii 4 69
I care not who knows so much of my mettle . . . iii 4 299
I'll ha' thee burnt.—I care not . . . *W. Tale* ii 3 114
I have considered so much, Camillo, and with some care . iv 2 40
Of that kind Our rustic garden 's barren; and I care not To get slips . iv 4 84
You were straited For a reply, at least if you make a care Of happy holding her . . . . iv 4 366
I told you what would come of this: beseech you, Of your own state take care . . . . iv 4 459
It is my father's music To speak your deeds, not little of his care To have them recompensed as thought on . . . . . iv 4 530
It shall be so my care To have you royally appointed . . iv 4 602
Care not for issue: The crown will find an heir . . v 1 46
I would not care, I then would be content . . *K. John* iii 1 48
Where is my mother's care, That such an army could be drawn in France? iv 2 117
Keep good quarter and good care to-night . . . v 5 20
We are on the earth, Where nothing lives but crosses, cares and grief *Richard II.* ii 2 79

Care. Things past redress are now with me past care *Richard II.* ii 3 171
Take special care my greetings be deliver'd iii 1 39
Why, 'twas my care; And what loss is it to be rid of care? iii 2 95
To drive away the heavy thought of care iii 4 2
Part of your cares you give me with your crown iv 1 194
Your cares set up do not pluck my cares down iv 1 195
My care is loss of care, by old care done; Your care is gain of care, by new care won iv 1 196
The cares I give I have, though given away iv 1 198
I know not, nor I greatly care not: God knows I had as lief be none as one v 2 48
So shaken as we are, so wan with care *1 Hen. IV.* i 1 1
I'll be a traitor then, when thou art king.—I care not i 2 166
Love! I love thee not, I care not for thee, Kate ii 3 94
You are straight enough in the shoulders, you care not who sees your back ii 4 165
You shall have Trent turn'd.—I do not care: I'll give thrice so much land iii 1 137
Beseech your lordship to have a reverent care of your health *2 Hen. IV.* i 2 113
I care not if I do become your physician i 2 142
In good faith, he cares not what mischief he does ii 1 16
If I can close with him, I care not for his thrust ii 1 20
Whether I shall ever see thee again or no, there is nobody cares ii 4 73
For mine own part, sir, I do not care; but rather, because I am unwilling iii 2 239
I did not care, for mine own part, so much iii 2 242
I care not; a man can die but once: we owe God a death iii 2 250
Care I for the limb, the thewes, the stature, bulk, and big assemblance of a man! iii 2 276
Which, by mine honour, I will perform with a most Christian care iv 2 115
I shall observe him with all care and love iv 4 49
The incessant care and labour of his mind Hath wrought the mure that should confine it in So thin that life looks through iv 4 118
Golden care! That keep'st the ports of slumber open wide To many a watchful night! iv 5 23
Have broke their sleep with thoughts, their brains with care iv 5 69
When that my care could not withhold thy riots, What wilt thou do when riot is thy care? iv 5 135
The care on thee depending Hath fed upon the body of my father iv 5 159
His cares are now all ended.—I hope, not dead v 2 3
Let me but bear your love, I'll bear your cares v 2 58
For my part, I care not: I say little *Hen. V.* ii 1 5
Alas, your too much love and care of me Are heavy orisons 'gainst this poor wretch! ii 2 52
Their dear care And tender preservation of our person ii 2 58
The cares of it, and the forms of it, and the sobriety of it iv 1 73
There is much care and valour in this Welshman iv 1 86
I am not covetous for gold, Nor care I who doth feed upon my cost iv 3 25
I care not who know it; I will confess it to all the 'orld iv 7 117
Take you no care; I'll never trouble you *1 Hen. VI.* i 4 21
These grey locks, the pursuivants of death, Nestor-like aged in an age of care ii 5 6
The rest I wish thee gather: But yet be wary in thy studious care ii 5 97
Care is no cure, but rather corrosive, For things that are not to be remedied iii 3 3
Speak, thy father's care, Art thou not weary? iv 6 26
Till you do return, I rest perplexed with a thousand cares v 5 95
I care not which; Or Somerset or York, all's one to me *2 Hen. VI.* i 3 104
So cares and joys abound, as seasons fleet ii 4 4
Take me hence; I care not whither, for I beg no favour ii 4 92
The reverent care I bear unto my lord Made me collect these dangers iii 1 34
The care you have of us, To mow down thorns that would annoy our foot, Is worthy praise iii 1 66
Those that care to keep your royal person From treason's secret knife iii 1 173
Like an angry hive of bees That want their leader, scatter up and down And care not who they sting iii 2 127
In care of your most royal person iii 2 254
Tell them all from me, I thank them for their tender loving care iii 2 280
'Tis not the land I care for, wert thou thence iii 2 359
Gaultier or Walter, which it is, I care not iv 1 38
I seek not to wax great by others' waning, Or gather wealth, I care not, with what envy iv 10 23
As brings a thousand-fold more care to keep Than in possession any jot of pleasure *3 Hen. VI.* ii 2 52
Couched in a curious bed, When care, mistrust, and treason waits on him ii 5 54
Sad-hearted men, much overgone with care, Here sits a king more woful ii 5 123
Fills mine eyes with tears And stops my tongue, while heart is drown'd in cares iii 3 14
What youth is that, Of whom you seem to have so tender care? iv 6 66
For unfelt imagination, They often feel a world of restless cares *Rich. III.* i 4 81
Alas, why would you heap these cares on me? I am unfit for state iii 7 204
Would you enforce me to a world of care? iii 7 223
Full of wise care is this your counsel, madam. Take all the swift advantage of the hours iv 1 48
For queen, a very caitiff crown'd with care iv 4 100
My life itself, and the best heart of it, Thanks you for this great care *Hen. VIII.* i 2 2
Things done well, And with a care, exempt themselves from fear i 2 89
Pray, look to't; I put it to your care i 2 102
None here, he hopes, In all this noble bevy, has brought with her One care abroad i 4 5
The horses your lordship sent for, with all the care I had, I saw well chosen ii 2 2
Have great care I be not found a talker ii 2 78
Heaven's peace be with him! That's Christian care enough ii 2 131
In sweet music is such art, Killing care and grief of heart iii 1 13
I care not, so much I am happy Above a number iii 1 33
Who hath so far Given ear to our complaint, of his great grace And princely care v 1 49
I care not an she were a black-a-moor; 'tis all one to me *Troi. and Cres.* i 1 79
Say I she is not fair?—I do not care whether you do or no i 1 82
He cares not; an the devil come to him, it's all one i 2 227
Nay, I care not for such words; no, no iii 1 82
He cares not; he'll obey conditions iv 5 72
Or a herring without a roe, I would not care; but to be Menelaus! v 1 69
I care not to be the louse of a lazar, so I were not Menelaus v 1 71
Advantageous care Withdrew me from the odds of multitude v 4 22
With such a careless force and forceless care v 5 40
I tell you, friends, most charitable care Have the patricians of you *Coriolanus* i 1 67
You slander The helms o' the state, who care for you like fathers i 1 79
Care for us! True, indeed! They ne'er cared for us yet i 1 81
Examine Their counsels and their cares, digest things rightly i 1 154
We cannot keep the town.—Fear not our care, sir i 7 5

Care. Neither to care whether they love or hate him *Coriolanus* ii 2 14
He did not care whether he had their love or no ii 2 18
And make the rabble Call our cares fears iii 1 137
My general cares not for you. Back, I say, go v 2 59
I neither care for the world nor your general v 2 108
Daughter, speak you: He cares not for your weeping v 3 156
I care not, I, knew she and all the world: I love Lavinia *T. Andron.* ii 1 71
For our father's sake and mother's care, Now let me show a brother's love to thee iii 1 182
Cornelia never with more care Read to her sons than she hath read to thee iv 1 12
For this care of Tamora, Herself and hers are highly bound to thee iv 2 170
Witness these trenches made by grief and care v 2 23
What care I What curious eye doth quote deformities? *Rom. and Jul.* i 4 30
Care keeps his watch in every old man's eye ii 3 35
And where care lodges, sleep will never lie ii 3 36
By my head, here come the Capulets.—By my heel, I care not iii 1 39
I have more care to stay than will to go: Come, death, and welcome! iii 5 23
Alone, in company, still my care hath been To have her match'd iii 5 179
No care, no stop! so senseless of expense *T. of Athens* ii 2 1
Takes no account How things go from him, nor resumes *no* care ii 2 4
Be't not in thy care; go iii 4 117
Why this spade? this place? This slave-like habit? and these looks of care? iv 3 205
If he care not for't, he will supply us easily iv 3 407
Duty and zeal to your unmatched mind, Care of your food and living iv 3 524
I cannot choose but tell him, that I care not, And let him take't at worst v 1 180
Their knives care not, While you have throats to answer v 1 181
They are all welcome. What watchful cares do interpose themselves Betwixt your eyes and night? *J. Cæsar* ii 1 98
No figures nor no fantasies Which busy care draws in the brains of men ii 1 232
Did I say 'better'?—If you did, I care not iv 3 57
Let's after him, Whose care is gone before to bid us welcome *Macbeth* i 4 57
The innocent sleep, Sleep that knits up the ravell'd sleave of care ii 2 37
How say you? Why, what care I? If thou canst nod, speak too iii 4 70
Be lion-mettled, proud; and take no care Who chafes, who frets iv 1 90
'Tis our fast intent To shake all cares and business from our age *Lear* i 1 40
Now we will divest us, both of rule, Interest of territory, cares of state i 1 51
That lord whose hand must take my plight shall carry Half my love with him, half my care and duty i 1 104
Here I disclaim all my paternal care, Propinquity and property of blood i 1 115
Thou wast a pretty fellow when thou hadst no need to care for her frowning i 4 211
I love thee not.—Why, then, I care not for thee ii 2 8
If I had thee in Lipsbury pinfold, I would make thee care for me ii 2 10
O, I have ta'en Too little care of this! iii 4 33
I'll never care what wickedness I do, If this man come to good iii 7 99
Nor doth the general care Take hold on me *Othello* i 3 54
Look with care about the town, And silence those whom this vile brawl distracted ii 3 255
As they say, to hear music the general does not greatly care iii 1 18
I care not for thy sword; I'll make thee known, Though I lost twenty lives v 2 165
He neither loves, Nor either cares for him *Ant. and Cleo.* ii 1 16
In thy fats our cares be drown'd, With thy grapes our hairs be crown'd ii 7 122
Noblest of men, woo't die? Hast thou no care of me? iv 15 60
I do not greatly care to be deceived, That have no use for trusting v 2 14
Our care and pity is so much upon you, That we remain your friend v 2 188
Take thou no care; it shall be heeded v 2 269
A court He little cares for and a daughter who He not respects at all *Cymbeline* i 6 154
I care not for you, And am so near the lack of charity—To accuse myself—I hate you ii 3 113
Care no more to clothe and eat iv 2 266
These flowers are like the pleasures of the world; This bloody man, the care on't iv 2 297
If you will bless me, sir, and give me leave, I'll take the better care iv 4 45
No reason I, since of your lives you set So slight a valuation, should reserve My crack'd one to more care iv 4 50
Be not with mortal accidents opprest; No care of yours it is v 4 100
Away! and, to be blest, Let us with care perform his great behest v 4 122
And so much For my peculiar care v 5 83
Good sooth, I care not for you *Pericles* i 1 86
The passions of the mind, That have their first conception by mis-dread, Have after-nourishment and life by care i 2 13
What was first but fear what might be done, Grows elder now and cares it be not done i 2 15
Care of them, not pity of myself i 2 29
Let your cares o'erlook What shipping and what lading's in our haven i 2 48
The care I had and have of subjects' good On thee I lay i 2 118
But sea-room, an the brine and cloudy billow kiss the moon, I care not iii 1 46
I charge your charity withal, leaving her The infant of your care iii 3 15
Make me blessed in your care In bringing up my child iii 3 31
Blame both my lord and me, that we have taken No care to your best courses iv 1 39
Care not for me; I can go home alone iv 1 42
Her epitaphs In glittering golden characters express A general praise to her, and care in us At whose expense 'tis done iv 3 45
Have a care *Mer. Wives* iv 5; *Much Ado* i 2; iii 3; *M. N. Dream* iv 1; *T. Night* iii 4; *2 Hen. IV.* ii 4; *Pericles* iv 1

Care-crazed. A care-crazed mother of a many children *Richard III.* iii 7 184

Cared. But none of us cared for Kate *Tempest* ii 2 51
For the which she wept heartily and said she cared not *Much Ado* v 1 176
He said he cared not who knew it *Hen. V.* iv 7 117
Care for us! True, indeed! They ne'er cared for us yet *Coriolanus* i 1 82

Career. Shall quips and sentences and these paper bullets of the brain awe a man from the career of his humour? *Much Ado* ii 3 250
I shall meet your wit in the career, an you charge it against me v 1 135
Full merrily Hath this brave manage, this career, been run *L. L. Lost* v 2 482
Stopping the career Of laughter with a sigh *W. Tale* i 2 286
Or, if misfortune miss the first career *Richard II.* i 2 49
It must be as it may; he passes some humours and careers *Hen. V.* ii 1 132
What rein can hold licentious wickedness When down the hill he holds his fierce career? iii 3 23

Careful. Made thee more profit Than other princesses can that have more time For vainer hours and tutors not so careful *Tempest* i 2 174
My wife, more careful for the latter-born *Com. of Errors* i 1 79

Careful. Careful hours with time's deformed hand Have written strange defeatures in my face . . . . *Com. of Errors* v 1 298
A careful man and a great scholar . . . . . *T. Night* iv 2 11
Every shop, church, session, hanging, yields a careful man work *W. Tale* iv 4 701
O, full of careful business are his looks! . . . *Richard II.* ii 2 75
In which doing, I have done the part of a careful friend . . 2 *Hen. IV.* ii 4 348
Our lives, our souls, Our debts, our careful wives, Our children *Hen. V.* iv 1 248
By Him that raised me to this careful height . . *Richard III.* i 3 83
Madam, bethink you, like a careful mother . . . . . ii 2 96
Use careful watch, choose trusty sentinels . . . . . v 3 54
Relate what you, Most like a careful subject, have collected . *Hen. VIII.* i 2 130
Pray be careful all, And leave you not a man-of-war unsearch'd *T. And.* iv 3 21
Feed his humour kindly as we may, Till time beget some careful remedy iv 3 30
The eagle suffers little birds to sing, And is not careful what they mean iv 4 84
Ceremonies, Which I have seen thee careful to observe . . . v 1 77
The feast is ready, which the careful Titus Hath ordain'd to an honourable end . . . . v 3 21
Well, well, thou hast a careful father, child . . *Rom. and Jul.* iii 5 108
There is some strange thing toward, Edmund; pray you, be careful *Lear* iii 3 21
Soldiers, have careful watch . . . . . *Ant. and Cleo.* iv 3 7
I hither fled, Under the covering of a careful night . . *Pericles* i 2 81
By many a dern and painful perch Of Pericles the careful search iii Gower 16
There I'll leave it At careful nursing . . . . . . iii 1 81
Carefully. I promised to inquire carefully About a schoolmaster *T. of Shr.* i 2 166
That horse that I so carefully have dress'd . . . *Richard II.* v 5 80
And more than carefully it us concerns . . . . *Hen. V* ii 4 2
Attend the emperor's person carefully . . . . *T. Andron.* ii 2 8
It highly us concerns By day and night to attend him carefully . . iv 3 28
You come most carefully upon your hour.—'Tis now struck twelve *Hamlet* i 1 6
It shall lose thee nothing; do it carefully . . . . . *Lear* i 2 125
Some good man bear him carefully from hence . . . *Othello* v 1 99
Careire. And so conclusions passed the careires . . *Mer. Wives* i 1 184
Careless. Sleep she as sound as careless infancy . . . . . v 5 56
Careless, reckless, and fearless of what's past, present, or to come *Meas. for Meas.* iv 2 150
Anon a careless herd, Full of the pasture, jumps along by him *As Y. L. It* ii 1 52
Every thing about you demonstrating a careless desolation . . . iii 2 400
And come to Padua, careless of your life? . . . *T. of Shrew* iv 2 79
Into the staggers and the careless lapse Of youth and ignorance *All's Well* ii 3 170
And thou, too careless patient as thou art . . . *Richard II.* ii 1 97
By seeming cold or careless of his will . . . 2 *Hen. IV.* iv 4 29
What my great-grandfather and grandsire got My careless father fondly gave away . . . . 3 *Hen. VI.* ii 2 38
My brother was too careless of his charge . . . . . iv 6 86
With such a careless force and forceless care . . . *Troi. and Cres.* v 5 40
Titus, unkind and careless of thine own . . . *T. Andron.* i 1 86
To throw away the dearest thing he owed, As 'twere a careless trifle *Macbeth* i 4 11
Youth no less becomes The light and careless livery that it wears *Hamlet* iv 7 80
Virtue and cunning were endowments greater Than nobleness and riches: careless heirs May the two latter darken and expend *Pericles* iii 2 28
Carelessly. Fleet the time carelessly, as they did in the golden world *As Y. Like It* i 1 124
Carelessly encamp'd, His soldiers lurking in the towns about 3 *Hen. VI.* iv 2 14
It may be thought we held him carelessly . . . *Rom. and Jul.* iii 4 25
And make his wrongs His outsides, to wear them like his raiment, carelessly . . . . *T. of Athens* iii 5 33
Must bend his body, If Cæsar carelessly but nod on him *J. Cæsar* i 2 118
Carelessness. Out of his noble carelessness lets them plainly see't *Coriol.* ii 2 16
Carest. Thou art a merry fellow and carest for nothing . . *T. Night* iii 1 31
Caret. Focative is caret.—And that's a good root . . *Mer. Wives* iv 1 55
For the elegancy, facility, and golden cadence of poesy, caret *L. L. Lost* iv 2 127
Care-tuned. Than can my care-tuned tongue deliver . . *Richard II.* iii 2 92
Cargo, cargo, cargo, villianda par corbo, cargo . . . *All's Well* iv 1 72
Carl. Or could this carl, A very drudge of nature's, have subdued me? *Cymb.* v 2 4
Carlisle. O, belike it is the Bishop of Carlisle . . . *Richard II.* iii 3 30
Here is Carlisle living, to abide Thy kingly doom . . . . . v 6 22
Carlisle, this is your doom . . . . v 6 24
Carlot. The bounds That the old carlot once was master of *As Y. Like It* iii 5 108
Carman. Let carman whip his jade: The valiant heart's not whipt out of his trade . . . . *Meas. for Meas.* ii 1 269
Carmen. And sung those tunes to the over-scutched huswives that he heard the carmen whistle . . . . 2 *Hen. IV.* iii 2 341
Carnal. This carnal cur Preys on the issue of his mother's body! *Richard III.* iv 4 56
So shall you hear Of carnal, bloody, and unnatural acts . . . *Hamlet* v 2 392
We have reason to cool our raging motions, our carnal stings . *Othello* i 3 335
Carnally. Know you this woman?—Carnally, she says . *Meas. for Meas.* v 1 214
Carnarvonshire. I myself Would for Carnarvonshire, although there 'long'd No more to the crown but that . . . . *Hen. VIII.* ii 3 48
Carnation. How much carnation ribbon may a man buy for a remuneration? . . . . *L. L. Lost* iii 1 146
The fairest flowers o' the season Are our carnations . . *W. Tale* iv 4 82
A' could never abide carnation; 'twas a colour he never liked *Hen. V.* ii 3 35
Carol. No night is now with hymn or carol blest . . *M. N. Dream* ii 1 102
This carol they began that hour, With a hey, and a ho . *As Y. Like It* v 3 27
Carouse. And quaff carouses to our mistress' health . . . *T. of Shrew* i 2 277
Carouse full measure to her maidenhead . . . . . . iii 2 227
The queen carouses to thy fortune, Hamlet . . . . *Hamlet* v 2 300
Sup together, And drink carouses to the next day's fate *Ant. and Cleo.* iv 8 34
They cast their caps up and carouse together Like friends long lost . iv 12 12
Caroused. That blood already, like the pelican, Hast thou tapp'd out and drunkenly caroused . . . . *Richard II.* ii 1 127
Having all day caroused and banqueted . . . . 1 *Hen. VI.* ii 1 12
To Desdemona hath to-night caroused Potations pottle-deep . *Othello* ii 3 55
Carousing to his mates After a storm . . . . . *T. of Shrew* iii 2 173
'Faith, sir, we were carousing till the second cock . . *Macbeth* ii 3 26
Carp. Pray you, sir, use the carp as you may . . . *All's Well* v 2 24
See you now; Your bait of falsehood takes this carp of truth *Hamlet* ii 1 63
Other of your insolent retinue Do hourly carp and quarrel . . *Lear* i 4 222
Carped. If we shall stand still, In fear our motion will be mock'd or carp'd at, We should take root here . . . . *Hen. VIII.* i 2 86
Carpenter. And Vulcan a rare carpenter . . . . . *Much Ado* i 1 187
A wooden thing!—He talks of wood: it is some carpenter . 1 *Hen. VI.* v 3 90
A kiss in fee-farm! build there, carpenter; the air is sweet *Tr. and Cr.* iii 2 53
What trade art thou?—Why, sir, a carpenter.—Where is thy leather apron and thy rule? . . . . *J. Cæsar* i 1 6
What is he that builds stronger than either the mason, the shipwright, or the carpenter?—The gallows-maker . . . . *Hamlet* v 1 48
Who builds stronger than a mason, a shipwright, or a carpenter? . . v 1 58

Carper. Shame not these woods, By putting on the cunning of a carper. Be thou a flatterer now . . . . *T. of Athens* iv 3 209
Carpet. The carpets laid, and every thing in order . . *T. of Shrew* iv 1 52
Knight, dubbed with unhatched rapier and on carpet consideration *T. Night* iii 4 258
While here we march Upon the grassy carpet of this plain *Richard II.* iii 3 50
The purple violets, and marigolds, Shall as a carpet hang upon thy grave, While summer-days do last . . . . . *Pericles* iv 1 17
Carpet-monger. A whole bookful of these quondam carpet-mongers *Much Ado* v 2 32
Carping. Sure, sure, such carping is not commendable . . . iii 1 71
This fellow here, with envious carping tongue, Upbraided me 1 *Hen. VI.* iv 1 90
To avoid the carping censures of the world . . . *Richard III.* iii 5 68
Carriage. Time Goes upright with his carriage . . . . *Tempest* v 1 3
Take all, or half, for easing me of the carriage . . . *Mer. Wives* ii 2 179
Teach sin the carriage of a holy saint . . . *Com. of Errors* iii 2 14
It better fits my blood to be disdained of all than to fashion a carriage to rob love from any . . . . *Much Ado* i 3 31
A man of good repute, carriage, bearing, and estimation . *L. L. Lost* i 1 272
Let them be men of good repute and carriage . . . . . i 2 72
Samson, master: he was a man of good carriage, great carriage . . i 2 74
And their rough carriage so ridiculous . . . . . . v 2 306
A sad face, a reverend carriage, a slow tongue . . . *T. Night* iii 4 81
The violent carriage of it Will clear or end the business . . *W. Tale* iii 1 17
Many carriages he hath dispatch'd To the sea-side . . . *K. John* v 7 90
A cheerful look, a pleasing eye and a most noble carriage . 1 *Hen. IV.* ii 4 466
Wise bearing or ignorant carriage is caught, as men take diseases, one of another . . . . 2 *Hen. IV.* v 1 84
Behold the ordnance on their carriages, With fatal mouths gaping *Hen. V.* iii Prol. 26
Ay, utterly Grow from the king's acquaintance, by this carriage *Hen. VIII.* iii 1 161
For virtue and true beauty of the soul, For honesty and decent carriage iv 2 145
As if The passage and whole carriage of this action Rode on his tide *Troi. and Cres.* ii 3 140
Learns them first to bear, Making them women of good carriage *Rom. and Jul.* i 4 94
For his right noble mind, illustrious virtue And honourable carriage *T. of Athens* iii 2 88
By the same covenant, And carriage of the article design'd . *Hamlet* i 1 94
Three of the carriages, in faith, are very dear to fancy . . . v 2 158
Most delicate carriages, and of very liberal conceit . . . . v 2 160
What call you the carriages? . . . . v 2 161
The carriages, sir, are the hangers . . . . v 2 164
Against six French swords, their assigns, and three liberal-conceited carriages . . . . v 2 169
How this Herculean Roman does become The carriage of his chafe *Ant. and Cleo.* i 3 85
Lest, being miss'd, I be suspected of Your carriage from the court *Cymbeline* iii 4 190
Carried. I carried Mistress Silvia the dog you bade me . *T. G. of Ver.* iv 4 49
Have I lived to be carried in a basket? . . . . *Mer. Wives* iii 5 4
Swears he was carried out, the last time he searched for him, in a basket . . . . iv 2 32
There's one yonder arrested and carried to prison . . *Meas. for Meas.* i 2 61
I saw him arrested, saw him carried away . . . . . . i 2 68
Yonder man is carried to prison.—Well; what has he done? . . . i 2 87
Already he hath carried Notice . . . . iv 3 134
Floating straight, obedient to the stream, Was carried towards Corinth *Com. of Errors* i 1 88
With lesser weight but not with lesser woe, Was carried with more speed . . . . i 1 110
This well carried shall on her behalf Change slander to remorse *M. Ado* iv 1 212
He carried the town-gates on his back like a porter . . *L. L. Lost* i 2 74
This sport, well carried, shall be chronicled . . . *M. N. Dream* iii 2 240
He is carried into the leaguer of the adversaries . . . *All's Well* iii 6 27
Like a remorseful pardon slowly carried . . . . . . v 3 58
You carried your guts away as nimbly . . . . 1 *Hen. IV.* ii 4 285
Thou art violently carried away from grace . . . . . ii 4 491
And carried you a forehand shaft a fourteen and fourteen and a half 2 *Hen. IV.* iii 2 52
They have burned and carried away all that was in the king's tent *Hen. V.* iv 7 8
Why, all this business Our reverend cardinal carried . . *Hen. VIII.* i 1 100
Like her true nobility, she has Carried herself towards me . . . ii 4 143
By the jealous queen of heaven, that kiss I carried from thee, dear *Coriol.* v 3 47
The army marvell'd at it, and, in the last, When he had carried Rome . v 6 43
Where is Duncan's body?—Carried to Colmekill . . . *Macbeth* ii 4 33
And I have heard, Apollodorus carried— No more of that: he did so *Ant. and Cleo.* ii 6 69
He was carried From off our coast, twice beaten . . . *Cymbeline* iii 1 25
Carrier. This punk is one of Cupid's carriers . . . *Mer. Wives* ii 2 141
Good morrow, carriers. What's o'clock? . . . . 1 *Hen. IV.* ii 1 36
Sirrah carrier, what time do you mean to come to London? . . . ii 1 46
Art not thou the carrier?—Ay, of my pigeons, sir . . *T. Andron.* iv 3 86
Carries. Believe me, sir, It carries a brave form . . . *Tempest* i 2 411
One that before the judgement carries poor souls to hell *Com. of Errors* iv 2 40
No, I'll give you a remuneration: why, it carries it . . *L. L. Lost* iii 1 141
And the fox carries the goose . . . . . . *M. N. Dream* v 1 237
The second, silver, which this promise carries . . *Mer. of Venice* ii 7 6
A snail; for though he comes slowly, he carries his house on his head *As Y. Like It* iv 1 55
For where an unclean mind carries virtuous qualities, there commendations go with pity . . . . *All's Well* i 1 48
My imagination Carries no favour in't but Bertram's . . . . i 1 94
It must be a very plausive invention that carries it . . . . iv 1 30
What is it carries you away!—Why, my horse, my love, my horse 1 *Hen. IV.* ii 3 78
An unlick'd bear-whelp That carries no impression like the dam 3 *Hen. VI.* iii 2 162
She that carries up the train Is that old noble lady, Duchess of Norfolk *Hen. VIII.* iv 1 51
Not ever The justice and the truth o' the question carries The due o' the verdict with it . . . . v 1 131
Nor any man an attaint but he carries some stain of it *Troi. and Cres.* i 2 26
Carries on the stream of his dispose Without observance or respect of any . . . . ii 3 174
Before him he carries noise, and behind him he leaves tears *Coriolanus* ii 1 175
But that's no matter, the greater part carries it . . . . . ii 3 42
Vile submission! Alla stoccata carries it away . . *Rom. and Jul.* iii 1 77

Carries. The noblest mind he carries That ever govern'd man *T. of Athens* i 1 291
You are yoked with a lamb That carries anger as the flint bears fire *J. Cæsar* iv 3 111
Which carries them through and through the most fond and winnowed opinions *Hamlet* v 2 200
This speed of Cæsar's Carries beyond belief *Ant. and Cleo.* iii 7 76

Carrion. Shall we send that foolish carrion, Mistress Quickly, to him? *Mer. Wives* iii 3 205
Do as the carrion does, not as the flower *Meas. for Meas.* ii 2 167
A carrion Death, within whose empty eye There is a written scroll! *Mer. of Venice* ii 7 63
Out upon it, old carrion! rebels it at these years? iii 1 38
Why I rather choose to have A weight of carrion flesh than to receive Three thousand ducats iv 1 41
And be a carrion monster like thyself *K. John* iii 4 33
'Tis seldom when the bee doth leave her comb In the dead carrion *2 Hen. IV.* iv 4 80
Yon island carrions, desperate of their bones, Ill-favouredly become the morning field *Hen. V.* iv 2 39
And made a prey for carrion kites and crows Even of the bonny beast he loved so well *2 Hen. VI.* v 2 11
For every scruple Of her contaminated carrion weight, A Trojan hath been slain *Troi. and Cres.* iv 1 71
Out, you green-sickness carrion! out, you baggage! *Rom. and Jul.* iii 5 157
Old feeble carrions and such suffering souls That welcome wrongs *J. C.* ii 1 130
This foul deed shall smell above the earth With carrion men iii 1 275
If the sun breed maggots in a dead dog, being a god kissing carrion *Ham.* ii 2 182

Carrion-flies. More courtship lives In carrion-flies than Romeo *Rom. and Jul.* iii 3 35

Carry. I think he will carry this island home in his pocket *Tempest* ii 1 90
Pray, give me that; I'll carry it iii 1 25
Go to, carry this.—And this.—Ay, and this iv 1 253
Henceforth carry your letters yourself *T. G. of Ver.* i 1 154
She can fetch and carry. Why, a horse can do no more: nay, a horse cannot fetch, but only carry iii 1 274
By his master's command, he must carry for a present to his lady iv 2 79
To carry that which I would have refused iv 4 106
Nay, daughter, carry the wine in; we'll drink within *Mer. Wives* i 1 195
Can you carry your good will to the maid? i 1 238
You must speak possitable, if you can carry her your desires towards her i 1 244
This boy will carry a letter twenty mile, as easy as a cannon will shoot point-blank twelve score iii 2 32
Carry them to the laundress in Datchet-mead iii 3 156
I must carry her word quickly: she'll make you amends iii 5 48
To carry me in the name of foul clothes to Datchet-lane iii 5 100
I'll appoint my men to carry the basket again iv 2 97
Repent you, fair one, of the sin you carry? *Meas. for Meas.* ii 3 19
If you think well to carry this as you may iii 1 267
We have very oft awaked him, as if to carry him to execution iv 2 159
And that must your daughter and her gentlewomen carry *Much Ado* ii 3 223
Fetch hither the swain: he must carry me a letter *L. L. Lost* iii 1 50
I do weep: No drop but as a coach doth carry thee iv 3 34
His valour cannot carry his discretion *M. N. Dream* v 1 237
His discretion, I am sure, cannot carry his valour v 1 239
No lawful means can carry me Out of his envy's reach *Mer. of Venice* iv 1 9
Carry him gently to my fairest chamber *T. of Shrew* Ind. 1 46
Carry this mad knave to the gaol v 1 95
Carry me to the gaol!—Stay, officer: he shall not go to prison v 1 97
He wooes your daughter, Lays down his wanton siege before her beauty, Resolved to carry her *All's Well* iii 7 19
How does he carry himself?—I have told your lordship already, the stocks carry him iv 3 120
Carry his water to the wise woman *T. Night* iii 4 114
We enjoin thee, As thou art liege-man to us, that thou carry This female bastard hence *W. Tale* ii 3 174
Why should I carry lies abroad? iv 4 274
I must pocket up these wrongs, Because— Your breeches best may carry them *K. John* iii 1 201
Carry Master Silence to bed *2 Hen. IV.* v 3 135
Go, carry Sir John Falstaff to the Fleet v 5 97
'Tis your thoughts that now must deck our kings, Carry them here and there *Hen. V.* Prol. 29
We carry not a heart with us from hence That grows not in a fair consent with ours ii 2 21
Thy scarlet robes as a child's bearing-cloth I'll use to carry thee out of this place *1 Hen. VI.* i 3 43
Pray God she prove not masculine ere long, If underneath the standard of the French She carry armour as she hath begun ii 1 24
Gloucester's men, Forbidden late to carry any weapon, Have fill'd their pockets full of pebble stones iii 1 79
I would the college of the cardinals Would choose him pope and carry him to Rome *2 Hen. VI.* i 3 65
Thither go these news, as fast as horse can carry them i 4 78
Words cannot carry Authority so weighty *Hen. VIII.* iii 2 233
You made bold To carry into Flanders the great seal iii 2 319
Still in thy right hand carry gentle peace, To silence envious tongues iii 2 445
By the flame of yonder glorious heaven, He shall not carry him *T. and C.* v 6 24
This will I carry to Rome.—And I this *Coriolanus* i 5 1
Carry with us ears and eyes for the time, But hearts for the event ii 1 285
I beseech you, think you he'll carry Rome? iv 7 27
He was A noble servant to them; but he could not Carry his honours even iv 7 37
And shall she carry this unto her grave? *T. Andron.* ii 3 127
My boy, Shalt carry from me to the empress' sons Presents iv 1 115
I will carry no crotchets: I'll re you, I'll fa you *Rom. and Jul.* iv 5 120
Why did you bring these daggers from the place? They must lie there: go carry them *Macbeth* ii 2 49
And some I see That two-fold balls and treble sceptres carry iv 1 121
Do the boys carry it away?—Ay, that they do *Hamlet* ii 2 377
Speaks things in doubt, That carry but half sense iv 5 7
The phrase would be more german to the matter, if we could carry cannon by our sides v 2 166
That lord whose hand must take my plight shall carry Half my love *Lear* i 1 103
If our father carry authority with such dispositions as he bears i 1 308
My good intent May carry through itself to that full issue For which I razed my likeness i 4 3
Man's nature cannot carry The affliction nor the fear iii 2 48
And hardly shall I carry out my side, Her husband being alive v 1 61
A mighty strength they carry *Ant. and Cleo.* ii 1 17

Carry. Take me up: I have led you oft: carry me now, good friends, And have my thanks for all *Ant. and Cleo.* iv 14 139
Only I carry winged time Post on the lame feet of my rhyme *Pericles* iv Gower 47

Carry back to Sicily much tall youth *Ant. and Cleo.* ii 6 7

Carry coals. I knew by that piece of service the men would carry coals *Hen. V.* iii 2 50
We'll not carry coals.—No, for then we should be colliers *Rom. and Jul.* i 1 1

Carry it. He will carry't, he will carry't; 'tis in his buttons; he will carry't *Mer. Wives* iii 2 70
Slight ones will not carry it; they will say, 'Came you off with so little?' and great ones I dare not give *All's Well* iv 1 42
We may carry it thus, for our pleasure *T. Night* iii 4 150
If the king Should without issue die, he'll carry it so To make the sceptre his *Hen. VIII.* i 2 134
Shall the elephant Ajax carry it thus? *Troi. and Cres.* ii 3 3
Shall pride carry it?—An 'twould, you'ld carry half ii 3 228
He would miss it rather Than carry it but by the suit of the gentry *Coriolanus* ii 1 254
'Tis thought of every one Coriolanus will carry it ii 2 4
Women are more valiant That stay at home, if bearing carry it *T. of Athens* iii 5 48
Mark, I say, instantly; and carry it so As I have set it down *Lear* v 3 36
What a full fortune does the thick-lips owe, If he can carry 't thus! *Othello* i 1 67

Carrying. Less than a pound shall serve me for carrying your letter *T. G. of Ver.* i 1 112
'Tis threefold too little for carrying a letter to your lover i 1 116
Strong-jointed Samson! I do excel thee in my rapier as much as thou didst me in carrying gates *L. L. Lost* i 2 79
Get a thousand crowns of the king by carrying my head to him *2 Hen. VI.* iv 10 29
Carrying, I say, the stamp of one defect *Hamlet* i 4 31

Carry-tale. Some carry-tale, some please-man, some slight zany *L. L. Lost* v 2 463

Cart. They that reap must sheaf and bind; Then to cart with Rosalind *As Y. Like It* iii 2 114
Leave shall you have to court her at your pleasure.—To cart her rather *T. of Shrew* i 1 55
Provide some carts And bring away the armour *Richard II.* ii 2 106
If I become not a cart as well as another man, a plague! *1 Hen. IV.* ii 4 546
Full thirty times hath Phœbus' cart gone round Neptune's salt wash and Tellus' orbed ground *Hamlet* iii 2 165
May not an ass know when the cart draws the horse? *Lear* i 4 244
I cannot draw a cart, nor eat dried oats; If it be man's work, I'll do't v 3 38

Carter. There is three carters, three shepherds, three neat-herds *W. Tale* iv 4 331
Your carters or your waiting-vassals Have done a drunken slaughter *Richard III.* ii 1 121
Let me be no assistant for a state, But keep a farm and carters *Hamlet* ii 2 167

Carthage. She was of Carthage, not of Tunis.—This Tunis, sir, was Carthage.—Carthage?—I assure you, Carthage *Tempest* ii 1 82
By that fire which burn'd the Carthage queen *M. N. Dream* i 1 173
And waft her love To come again to Carthage *Mer. of Venice* v 1 12
As secret and as dear As Anna to the queen of Carthage was *T. of Shrew* i 1 159

Carve. She discourses, she carves, she gives the leer of invitation *M. Wives* i 3 49
If I do not carve most curiously, say my knife's naught *Much Ado* v 1 157
You can carve; Break up this capon *L. L. Lost* iv 1 55
A' can carve too, and lisp v 2 323
Carve on every tree The fair, the chaste and unexpressive she *As Y. Like It* iii 2 9
Wherein neat and cleanly, but to carve a capon and eat it? *1 Hen. IV.* ii 4 502
To carve out dials quaintly, point by point *3 Hen. VI.* ii 5 24
Carve him as a dish fit for the gods, Not hew him as a carcass *J. Cæsar* ii 1 173
He may not, as unvalued persons do, Carve for himself *Hamlet* i 3 20
He that stirs next to carve for his own rage Holds his soul light *Othello* ii 3 173

Carved. That never meat sweet-savour'd in thy taste, Unless I spake, or look'd, or touch'd, or carved to thee *Com. of Errors* ii 2 120
Wondering how thy name should be hanged and carved upon these trees *As Y. Like It* iii 2 182
What, up and down, carved like an apple-tart? *T. of Shrew* iv 3 89
My subjects for a pair of carved saints *Richard II.* iii 3 152
Like a forked radish, with a head fantastically carved upon it *2 Hen. IV.* iii 2 335
And on their skins, as on the bark of trees, Have with my knife carved in Roman letters *T. Andron.* v 1 139
Like valour's minion carved out his passage *Macbeth* i 2 19

Carved-bone. The carved-bone face on a flask *L. L. Lost* v 2 619

Carver. So much the more our carver's excellence *W. Tale* v 3 30
Be his own carver and cut out his way *Richard II.* ii 3 144

Carving. Now will he lie ten nights awake, carving the fashion of a new doublet *Much Ado* ii 3 18
Abuses our young plants with carving 'Rosalind' on their barks *As Y. Like It* iii 2 379

Casa. Alla nostra casa ben venuto *T. of Shrew* i 2 25

Casca. As they pass by, pluck Casca by the sleeve *Jul. Cæsar* i 2 179
Casca will tell us what the matter is i 2 189
Ay, Casca; tell us what hath chanced to-day i 2 216
You were with him, were you not?—I should not then ask Casca what had chanced i 2 219
Tell us the manner of it, gentle Casca i 2 234
But you and I And honest Casca, we have the falling sickness i 2 258
Will you sup with me to-night, Casca?—No, I am promised forth i 2 292
Good even, Casca: brought you Cæsar home? Why are you breathless? i 3 1
Good night then, Casca: this disturbed sky Is not to walk in i 3 39
Who's there?—A Roman.—Casca, by your voice i 3 41
Thus unbraced, Casca, as you see, Have bared my bosom to the thunder-stone i 3 48
You are dull, Casca, and those sparks of life That should be in a Roman you do want, Or else you use not i 3 57
Now could I, Casca, name to thee a man Most like this dreadful night i 3 72
You speak to Casca, and to such a man That is no fleering tell-tale i 3 116
Casca, I have moved already Some certain of the noblest-minded Romans i 3 121
It is Casca; one incorporate To our attempts i 3 135
Come, Casca, you and I will yet ere day See Brutus at his house i 3 153
This, Casca; this, Cinna; and this, Metellus Cimber.—They are all welcome ii 1 96
Welcome, Publius. What, Brutus, are you stirr'd so early too? Good morrow, Casca ii 2 111
Come not near Casca; have an eye to Cinna; trust not Trebonius ii 3 2
Casca, be sudden, for we fear prevention. Brutus, what shall be done? iii 1 19
Casca, you are the first that rears your hand iii 1 30
I take your hand . . .; and, my valiant Casca, yours iii 1 188
See what a rent the envious Casca made iii 2 179
Some to Decius' house, and some to Casca's iii 3 43
Whilst damned Casca, like a cur, behind Struck Cæsar on the neck v 1 43

Case. If he be not born to be hanged, our case is miserable . *Tempest* i 1 35
Let's assist them, For our case is as theirs . . . . i 1 58
Thy case, dear friend, Shall be my precedent . . . ii 1 290
I am in case to justle a constable . . . . . iii 2 29
In any case have a nay-word, that you may know one another's mind *Mer. Wives* ii 2 131
Well, what is your accusative case?—Accusativo, hinc . . iv 1 46
What is the focative case, William?—O,—vocativo, O . . iv 1 53
What is your genitive case plural, William?—Genitive case!—Ay.—Genitive,—horum, harum, horum . . . . . iv 1 59
Hast thou no understandings for thy cases and the numbers of the genders? . . . . iv 1 72
How often dost thou with thy case, thy habit, Wrench awe from fools! *Meas. for Meas.* ii 4 13
I may make my case as Claudio's, to cross this in the smallest iv 2 178
His case was like, Reft of his brother . . *Com. of Errors* i 1 128
If I last in this service, you must case me in leather . ii 1 85
I would not spare my brother in this case . . . . iv 1 77
What observation madest thou in this case Of his heart's meteors? iv 2 5
He is 'rested on the case.—What, is he arrested? Tell me at whose suit iv 2 42
I understand thee not.—No? why, 'tis a plain case . . . iv 3 22
Can the world buy such a jewel?—Yea, and a case to put it into *M. Ado* i 1 184
For God defend the lute should be like the case! . . . ii 1 98
Pause awhile, And let my counsel sway you in this case . . iv 1 203
You blush; as his your case is such . . . . . *L. L. Lost* iv 3 131
O, they were all in lamentable cases! . . . . . v 2 273
That vizard; that superfluous case That hid the worse and show'd the better face . . . . v 2 387
According to our law Immediately provided in that case *M. N. Dream* i 1 45
That I may know The worst that may befall me in this case . . i 1 63
In any case, let Thisby have clean linen . . . . iv 2 40
What a case am I in then! . . . . . *As Y. Like It* Epil. 7
Bless you with such grace As 'longeth to a lover's blessed case! *T. of Shrew* iv 2 45
Hold your own, in any case, With such austerity as 'longeth to a father iv 4 6
I do beg your good will in this case.—In what case? . . *All's Well* i 3 23
We'll make you some sport with the fox ere we case him . . iii 6 111
My life, sir, in any case: not that I am afraid to die . . iv 3 270
What wilt thou be When time hath sow'd a grizzle on thy case? *T. Night* v 1 168
He holds Belzebub at the staves's end as well as a man in his case may do v 1 292
But, for me, What case stand I in? . . . . . *W. Tale* i 2 352
As the case now stands, it is a curse He cannot be compell'd to't ii 3 87
But though my case be a pitiful one, I hope I shall not be flayed out of it.—O, that's the case of the shepherd's son . . . . iv 4 844
They seemed almost, with staring on one another, to tear the cases of their eyes . . . . v 2 14
I would not be sir Nob in any case . . . . . *K. John* i 1 147
To my own disgrace Neglected my sworn duty in that case *Richard II.* i 1 134
I have cases of buckram for the nonce . . . . 1 *Hen IV.* i 2 201
Case ye, case ye; on with your vizards . . . . . ii 2 55
Let not Harry know, In any case, the offer of the king . . v 2 25
Give it me: what, is it in the case? . . . . . . v 3 54
Indeed It was young Hotspur's case at Shrewsbury . . 2 *Hen. IV.* i 3 26
Since my exion is entered and my case so openly known to the world . ii 1 33
She hath been in good case, and the truth is, poverty hath distracted her ii 1 115
From a God to a bull? a heavy descension! it was Jove's case . . ii 2 193
The case of a treble hautboy was a mansion for him . . . iii 2 351
A rotten case abides no handling . . . . . . iv 1 161
Make the case yours; Be now the father and propose a son . . v 2 91
In cases of defence 'tis best to weigh The enemy more mighty than he seems . . . . *Hen. V.* ii 4 43
The knocks are too hot; and, for mine own part, I have not a case of lives iii 2 5
Question, my lords, no further of the case, How or which way 1 *Hen. VI.* ii 1 72
What means this silence? Dare no man answer in a case of truth? . ii 4 2
Then for the truth and plainness of the case . . . . ii 4 46
This day, in argument upon a case, Some words there grew . . ii 5 45
I could be well content To be mine own attorney in this case . . v 3 166
I cannot fight; for God's sake, pity my case . . 2 *Hen. VI.* i 3 218
Even so myself bewails good Gloucester's case . . . . iii 1 217
In any case, be not too rough in terms . . . . . iv 9 44
Thou call'dst me king.—Ay, but the case is alter'd . 3 *Hen. VI.* iv 3 31
Thus stands the case . . . . iv 5 4
The time and case requireth haste . . . . iv 5 18
To let you understand, If case some one of you would fly from us . v 4 34
The extreme peril of the case . . . . . *Richard III.* iii 5 44
I do beseech your lordships, That, in this case of justice, my accusers, Be what they will, may stand forth face to face . . *Hen. VIII.* v 3 46
And case thy reputation in thy tent . . . . . *Troi. and Cres.* iii 3 187
Have the gods envy?—Ay, ay, ay, ay; 'tis too plain a case . . iv 4 31
In such a case the gods will not be good unto us . . *Coriolanus* v 4 34
An 'twere my case, I should go hang myself . . *T. Andron.* ii 4 9
Is not this a heavy case, To see thy noble uncle thus distract? . iv 3 25
Come you this afternoon, To know our further pleasure in this case *Rom. and Jul.* i 1 108
Give me a case to put my visage in: A visor for a visor! . . i 4 29
In such a case as mine a man may strain courtesy . . . ii 4 54
Such a case as yours constrains a man to bow in the hams . . ii 4 56
O, he is even in my mistress' case, Just in her case! . . . iii 3 84
Since the case so stands as now it doth, I think it best you married iii 5 218
This is a pitiful case.—Ay, by my troth, the case may be amended . iv 5 99
Would most resemble sweet instruments hung up in cases *T. of Athens* i 2 103
What a strange case was that! now, before the gods, I am ashamed on't iii 2 18
You wrong'd yourself to write in such a case . . . *J. Cæsar* iv 3 6
But in these cases We still have judgement here . . . *Macbeth* i 7 7
Where be his quiddities now, his quillets, his cases, his tenures? *Hamlet* v 1 108
Whose motive, in this case, should stir me most To my revenge . v 2 256
And leave his horns without a case . . . . . . *Lear* i 5 34
When every case in law is right; No squire in debt, nor no poor knight iii 2 85
Read.—What, with the case of eyes? . . . . . . iv 6 147
Your eyes are in a heavy case, your purse in a light . . . iv 6 150
As in these cases, where the aim reports, 'Tis oft with difference *Othello* i 3 6
It grieves my husband, As if the case were his . . . . iii 3 4
In such cases Men's natures wrangle with inferior things . . iii 4 143
Your case is better . . . . iv 1 70
If there were no more women but Fulvia, then had you indeed a cut, and the case to be lamented . . . . . . *Ant. and Cleo.* i 2 174
Do So far ask pardon as befits mine honour To stoop in such a case . ii 2 98
Cæsar entreats, Not to consider in what case thou stand'st, Further than he is Cæsar . . . . iii 13 54
Heart, once be stronger than thy continent, Crack thy frail case! . . iv 14 41
This case of that huge spirit now is cold . . . *Ant. and Cleo.* iv 15 89
Tell thy mistress how The case stands with her . . *Cymbeline* i 5 67
Idiots in this case of favour would Be wisely definite . . . . i 6 42
I will make One of her women lawyer to me, for I yet not understand the case myself . . . . ii 3 80
Those that are betray'd Do feel the treason sharply, yet the traitor Stands in worse case of woe . . . . iii 4 89
Behold, Her eyelids, cases to those heavenly jewels. . . *Pericles* iii 2 99

Cased. Like a cunning instrument cased up . . . *Richard II.* i 3 163
With faces fit for masks, or rather fairer Than those for preservation cased, or shame . . . . *Cymbeline* v 3 22
Her eyes as jewel-like And cased as richly . . . . *Pericles* v 1 112

Casement. Go to the casement, and see if you can see my master *Mer. Wives* i 4 2
Then may you leave a casement of the great chamber window, where we play, open, and the moon may shine in at the casement *M. N. Dream* iii 1 57
Clamber not you up to the casements then, Nor thrust your head into the public street . . . . *Mer. of Venice* ii 5 31
Stop my house's ears, I mean my casements . . . . ii 5 34
Make the doors upon a woman's wit and it will out at the casement *As Y. Like It* iv 1 163
Thy casement I need not open, for I look through thee . . *All's Well* ii 3 225
In Florence was it from a casement thrown me . . . . v 3 93
The story then goes false, you threw it him Out of a casement . v 3 230
Young and old Through casements darted their desiring eyes *Rich. II.* v 2 14
I found it thrown in at the casement of my closet . . *Lear* i 2 65
Let her beauty Look through a casement to allure false hearts *Cymbeline* ii 4 34

Cash. I shall have my noble?—In cash most justly paid . . *Hen. V.* ii 1 120

Cashier: let them wag; trot, trot . . . . . *Mer. Wives* i 3 6

Cashiered. And being fap, sir, was, as they say, cashiered . . . i 1 184
What does his cashiered worship mutter?—No matter what; he's poor, and that's revenge enough . . . . . . *T. of Athens* iii 4 60
Wears out his time, much like his master's ass, For nought but provender, and when he's old, cashier'd . . . . . *Othello* i 1 48
Cassio hath beaten thee, And thou, by that small hurt, has cashier'd Cassio ii 3 381

Casing. As broad and general as the casing air. . . *Macbeth* iii 4 23

'Casion. Chill not let go, zir, without vurther 'casion . . *Lear* iv 6 240

Cask. A jewel, lock'd into the wofull'st cask That ever did contain a thing of worth . . . . 2 *Hen. VI.* iii 2 409

Casket. If he should offer to choose, and choose the right casket *Mer. of Ven.* i 2 100
For fear of the worst, I pray thee, set a deep glass of rhenish wine on the contrary casket . . . . i 2 105
Unless you may be won by some other sort than your father's imposition depending on the caskets . . . . i 2 115
Lead me to the caskets To try my fortune . . . . . ii 1 23
Here, catch this casket; it is worth the pains . . . . ii 6 33
Draw aside the curtains and discover The several caskets . . ii 7 2
What says this leaden casket? . . . . ii 7 15
Behold, there stand the caskets, noble prince . . . . . ii 9 4
Never to unfold to any one Which casket 'twas I chose; next, if I fail Of the right casket, never in my life To woo a maid in way of marriage ii 9 11
But let me to my fortune and the caskets . . . . . iii 2 39
Your fortune stood upon the casket there, And so did mine too . iii 2 203
They found him dead and cast into the streets, An empty casket *K. John* v 1 40
The little casket bring me hither . . . . . *T. of Athens* i 2 164
Fair glass of light, I loved you, and could still, Were not this glorious casket stored with ill . . . . *Pericles* i 1 77
Bid Nestor bring me spices, ink and paper, My casket and my jewels iii 1 67

Casketed. I have writ my letters, casketed my treasure . . *All's Well* ii 5 26

Casque. Let thy blows, doubly redoubled, Fall like amazing thunder on the casque Of thy adverse pernicious enemy . . . *Richard II.* i 3 81
The very casques That did affright the air at Agincourt . . *Hen. V.* Prol. 13
Were it a casque composed by Vulcan's skill, My sword should bite it *Troi. and Cres.* v 2 170
Not moving From the casque to the cushion . . . *Coriolanus* iv 7 43

Cassado. You sent a large commission To Gregory de Cassado *Hen. VIII.* iii 2 321

Cassandra. I will not dispraise your sister Cassandra's wit *Tr. and Cr.* i 1 47
And Cassandra laughed.—But there was more temperate fire under the pot of her eyes . . . . i 2 159
Nor once deject the courage of our minds, Because Cassandra's mad . ii 2 122
Cassandra, call my father to persuade . . . . . . v 3 30
Thy mother hath had visions; Cassandra doth foresee . . . v 3 64

Cassibelan. His father Was called Sicilius, who did join his honour Against the Romans with Cassibelan . . . . . *Cymbeline* i 1 30
Cassibelan, thine uncle,—Famous in Cæsar's praises, no whit less Than in his feats deserving it . . . . iii 1 5
The famed Cassibelan, who was once at point—O giglot fortune!—to master Cæsar's sword . . . . iii 1 30
Many among us can gripe as hard as Cassibelan . . . . iii 1 41

Cassio. A great arithmetician, One Michael Cassio, a Florentine . *Othello* i 1 20
Cassio's a proper man: let me see now: To get his place . . i 3 398
Michael Cassio, Lieutenant to the warlike Moor Othello . . ii 1 26
This same Cassio, though he speak of comfort Touching the Turkish loss, yet he looks sadly . . . . ii 1 31
I thank you, valiant Cassio. What tidings can you tell me of my lord? ii 1 87
How say you, Cassio? is he not a most profane and liberal counsellor? ii 1 164
With as little a web as this will I ensnare as great a fly as Cassio . ii 1 170
Who stands so eminent in the degree of this fortune as Cassio does? . ii 1 241
Cassio knows you not. I'll not be far from you . . . . ii 1 272
Find some occasion to anger Cassio, either by speaking too loud, or tainting his discipline . . . . ii 1 274
Whose qualification shall come into no true taste again but by the displanting of Cassio . . . . ii 1 284
That Cassio loves her, I do well believe it; That she loves him, 'tis apt ii 1 295
I'll have our Michael Cassio on the hip, Abuse him to the Moor . ii 1 314
For I fear Cassio with my night-cap too . . . . . ii 1 316
'Mongst this flock of drunkards, Am I to put our Cassio in some action That may offend the isle . . . . ii 3 62
Prizes the virtue that appears in Cassio, And looks not on his evils . ii 3 139
I do love Cassio well; and would do much To cure him of this evil . ii 3 148
I had rather have this tongue cut from my mouth Than it should do offence to Michael Cassio . . . . ii 3 222
There comes a fellow crying out for help; And Cassio following him with determined sword, To execute upon him . . . . . ii 3 227
Sir, this gentleman Steps in to Cassio, and entreats his pause . ii 3 229
I heard the clink and fall of swords, And Cassio high in oath . ii 3 235
Though Cassio did some little wrong to him, As men in rage strike those that wish them best . . . . ii 3 242
Cassio, I believe, received From him that fled some strange indignity . ii 3 244
Iago, Thy honesty and love doth mince this matter, Making it light to Cassio . . . . ii 3 248

Cassio. Cassio, I love thee; But never more be officer of mine *Othello* ii 3 248
How am I then a villain To counsel Cassio to this parallel course, Directly to his good? ii 3 355
Cassio hath beaten thee, And thou, by that small hurt, hast cashier'd Cassio ii 3 380
My wife must move for Cassio to her mistress; I'll set her on ii 3 389
And bring him jump when he may Cassio find Soliciting his wife ii 3 392
Tell her there's one Cassio entreats her a little favour of speech iii 1 28
Be thou assured, good Cassio, I will do All my abilities in thy behalf iii 3 1
Do not doubt, Cassio, But I will have my lord and you again As friendly as you were iii 3 5
Whatever shall become of Michael Cassio, He's never any thing but your true servant iii 3 8
I'll intermingle every thing he does With Cassio's suit: therefore be merry, Cassio iii 3 26
Was not that Cassio parted from my wife?—Cassio, my lord! No, sure, I cannot think it iii 3 37
Who is't you mean?—Why, your lieutenant, Cassio iii 3 45
What! Michael Cassio, That came a-wooing with you! iii 3 70
Did Michael Cassio, when you woo'd my lady, Know of your love? iii 3 94
I heard thee say even now, thou likedst not that, When Cassio left my wife iii 3 110
For Michael Cassio, I dare be sworn I think that he is honest iii 3 124
Men should be what they seem.—Why, then, I think Cassio's an honest man iii 3 129
Look to your wife; observe her well with Cassio; Wear your eye thus iii 3 197
Cassio's my worthy friend—My lord, I see you're moved iii 3 223
It be fit that Cassio have his place, For, sure, he fills it up with great ability iii 3 246
I will in Cassio's lodging lose this napkin, And let him find it iii 3 321
I found not Cassio's kisses on her lips iii 3 341
I lay with Cassio lately; And, being troubled with a raging tooth, I could not sleep iii 3 413
There are a kind of men so loose of soul, That in their sleeps will mutter their affairs: One of this kind is Cassio iii 3 418
Such a handkerchief—I am sure it was your wife's—did I to-day See Cassio wipe his beard with iii 3 439
Within these three days let me hear thee say That Cassio's not alive iii 3 473
Do you know, sirrah, where Lieutenant Cassio lies? iii 4 2
I will not leave him now till Cassio Be call'd to him iii 4 32
I have sent to bid Cassio come speak with you iii 4 50
Pray you, let Cassio be received again iii 4 88
The handkerchief!—I pray, talk me of Cassio iii 4 92
Look you, Cassio and my husband! iii 4 106
How now, good Cassio! what's the news with you? iii 4 109
Alas, thrice-gentle Cassio! My advocation is not now in tune iii 4 122
Cassio, walk hereabout: If I do find him fit, I'll move your suit iii 4 165
Save you, friend Cassio!—What make you from home? iii 4 169
I was coming to your house.—And I was going to your lodging, Cassio iii 4 172
O Cassio, whence came this? This is some token from a newer friend iii 4 180
How now, Cassio!—What's the matter? iv 1 49
Whilst you were here o'erwhelmed with your grief—A passion most unsuiting such a man—Cassio came hither iv 1 79
Now will I question Cassio of Bianca iv 1 94
It is a creature That dotes on Cassio iv 1 97
Jealousy must construe Poor Cassio's smiles, gestures and light behaviour, Quite in the wrong iv 1 103
Do you hear, Cassio?—Now he importunes him To tell it o'er iv 1 114
Crying 'O dear Cassio!' as it were: his gesture imports it iv 1 141
For Cassio, let me be his undertaker: you shall hear more by midnight iv 1 224
How does Lieutenant Cassio?—Lives, sir iv 1 234
Is there division 'twixt my lord and Cassio?—A most unhappy one iv 1 242
I would do much To atone them, for the love I bear to Cassio iv 1 244
As I think, they do command him home, Deputing Cassio in his government iv 1 248
Hence, avaunt! Cassio shall have my place iv 1 272
Yes, you have seen Cassio and she together iv 2 3
Especial commission come from Venice to depute Cassio in Othello's place iv 2 226
Wherein none can be so determinate as the removing of Cassio iv 2 233
Whether he kill Cassio, Or Cassio him, or each do kill the other, Every way makes my gain v 1 12
If Cassio do remain, He hath a daily beauty in his life That makes me ugly v 1 18
The voice of Cassio: Iago keeps his word v 1 28
I cry you mercy. Here's Cassio hurt by villains.—Cassio! v 1 69
O my dear Cassio! my sweet Cassio! O Cassio, Cassio, Cassio! v 1 76
Cassio, may you suspect Who they should be that have thus mangled you? v 1 78
Alas, he faints! O Cassio, Cassio, Cassio! v 1 84
Patience awhile, good Cassio. Come, come; Lend me a light v 1 87
How do you, Cassio? O, a chair, a chair! v 1 96
He that lies slain here, Cassio, Was my dear friend v 1 101
Cassio hath here been set on in the dark By Roderigo v 1 112
Alas, good gentleman! alas, good Cassio! v 1 115
Go know of Cassio where he supp'd to-night v 1 117
Kind gentlemen, let's go see poor Cassio dress'd v 1 124
That handkerchief which I so loved and gave thee Thou gavest to Cassio v 2 49
Never loved Cassio But with such general warranty of heaven As I might love v 2 59
'Tis like she comes to speak of Cassio's death v 2 92
Cassio, my lord, hath kill'd a young Venetian Call'd Roderigo v 2 112
Roderigo kill'd! And Cassio kill'd!—No, Cassio is not kill'd v 2 114
Not Cassio kill'd! then murder's out of tune, And sweet revenge grows harsh v 2 115
Cassio did top her; ask thy husband else v 2 136
That she was false to wedlock?—Ay, with Cassio v 2 143
She false with Cassio!—did you say with Cassio?—With Cassio, mistress v 2 182
That she with Cassio hath the act of shame A thousand times committed v 2 211
Cassio confess'd it: And she did gratify his amorous works With that recognizance and pledge of love v 2 212
She give it Cassio! no, alas! I found it, And I did give't my husband v 2 230
Did you and he consent in Cassio's death?—Ay v 2 297
One of them imports The death of Cassio to be undertook By Roderigo v 2 311
How came you, Cassio, by that handkerchief That was my wife's? v 2 319
Your power and your command is taken off, And Cassio rules in Cyprus v 2 332
Cassius. Let me not hinder, Cassius, your desires; I'll leave you *J. Cæsar* i 2 30
Cassius, Be not deceived: if I have veil'd my look i 2 36
Let not therefore my good friends be grieved—Among which number, Cassius, be you one i 2 44
Tell me, good Brutus, can you see your face?—No, Cassius i 2 52
Cassius. Into what dangers would you lead me, Cassius? *J. Cæsar* i 2 63
You would not have it so.—I would not, Cassius; yet I love him well i 2 82
Darest thou, Cassius, now Leap in with me into this angry flood? i 2 102
Cæsar cried 'Help me, Cassius, or I sink!' i 2 111
Cassius is A wretched creature and must bend his body, If Cæsar carelessly but nod on him i 2 116
But, look you, Cassius, The angry spot doth glow on Cæsar's brow i 2 182
Yond Cassius has a lean and hungry look; He thinks too much i 2 194
I do not know the man I should avoid So soon as that spare Cassius i 2 201
If I were Brutus now and he were Cassius, He should not humour me i 2 318
Cassius, what night is this!—A very pleasing night to honest men i 3 42
'Tis Cæsar that you mean; is it not, Cassius? i 3 79
I know where I will wear this dagger then; Cassius from bondage will deliver Cassius i 3 90
Since Cassius first did whet me against Cæsar, I have not slept ii 1 61
'Tis your brother Cassius at the door, Who doth desire to see you ii 1 70
Our course will seem too bloody, Caius Cassius ii 1 162
Alas, good Cassius, do not think of him ii 1 185
Cæsar, beware of Brutus; take heed of Cassius; come not near Casca ii 3 2
If this be known, Cassius or Cæsar never shall turn back iii 1 21
Cassius, be constant: Popilius Lena speaks not of our purposes iii 1 22
As low as to thy foot doth Cassius fall, To beg enfranchisement for Publius Cimber iii 1 56
Ambition's debt is paid.—Go to the pulpit, Brutus.—And Cassius too iii 1 84
Next, Caius Cassius, do I take your hand; Now, Decius Brutus, yours iii 1 186
Pardon me, Caius Cassius: The enemies of Cæsar shall say this iii 1 211
Cassius, go you into the other street, And part the numbers iii 2 3
Those that will hear me speak, let 'em stay here; Those that will follow Cassius, go with him iii 2 6
I will hear Brutus speak.—I will hear Cassius; and compare their reasons iii 2 9
I should do Brutus wrong, and Cassius wrong, Who, you all know, are honourable men iii 2 128
Look, in this place ran Cassius' dagger through iii 2 178
Brutus and Cassius Are rid like madmen through the gates of Rome iii 2 273
Brands, ho! fire-brands: to Brutus', to Cassius'; burn all iii 3 41
Brutus and Cassius Are levying powers: we must straight make head iv 1 41
Is Cassius near?—He is at hand; and Pindarus is come To do you salutation iv 2 3
The greater part, the horse in general, Are come with Cassius iv 2 30
Cassius, be content; Speak your griefs softly: I do know you well iv 2 41
In my tent, Cassius, enlarge your griefs, And I will give you audience iv 2 46
Cassius, you yourself Are much condemn'd to have an itching palm iv 3 9
The name of Cassius honours this corruption iv 3 15
Go to; you are not, Cassius.—I am.—I say you are not iv 3 32
There is no terror, Cassius, in your threats, For I am arm'd so strong in honesty That they pass by me as the idle wind iv 3 66
Was that done like Cassius? Should I have answer'd Caius Cassius so? iv 3 77
Revenge yourselves alone on Cassius, For Cassius is aweary of the world; Hated by one he loves iv 3 94
When thou didst hate him worst, thou lovedst him better Than ever thou lovedst Cassius iv 3 107
O Cassius, you are yoked with a lamb That carries anger as the flint bears fire iv 3 110
Hath Cassius lived To be but mirth and laughter to his Brutus? iv 3 113
Yes, Cassius; and, from henceforth, When you are over-earnest with your Brutus, He'll think your mother chides, and leave you so iv 3 121
O Cassius, I am sick of many griefs iv 3 144
Give me a bowl of wine. In this I bury all unkindness, Cassius iv 3 159
Noble, noble Cassius, Good night, and good repose iv 3 232
It may be I shall raise you by and by On business to my brother Cassius iv 3 248
Go and commend me to my brother Cassius iv 3 307
This tongue had not offended so to-day, If Cassius might have ruled v 1 47
Old Cassius still! v 1 63
This is my birth-day; as this very day Was Cassius born v 1 73
No, Cassius, no: think not, thou noble Roman, That ever Brutus will go bound to Rome v 1 111
For ever, and for ever, farewell, Cassius! If we do meet again, why, we shall smile v 1 117
O Cassius, Brutus gave the word too early v 3 5
Fly, therefore, noble Cassius, fly far off v 3 11
O Cassius, Far from this country Pindarus shall run v 3 48
Octavius Is overthrown by noble Brutus' power, As Cassius' legions are by Antony v 3 53
These tidings will well comfort Cassius.—Where did you leave him? v 3 54
No, this was he, Messala, But Cassius is no more v 3 60
O setting sun, As in thy red rays thou dost sink to-night, So in his red blood Cassius' day is set; The sun of Rome is set! v 3 62
Why didst thou send me forth, brave Cassius? v 3 80
Brutus, come apace, And see how I regarded Caius Cassius v 3 88
This is a Roman's part: Come, Cassius' sword, and find Titinius' heart v 3 90
Look, whether he have not crown'd dead Cassius! v 3 97
I shall find time, Cassius, I shall find time v 3 103
What was't That moved pale Cassius to conspire? *Ant. and Cleo.* ii 6 15
I struck The lean and wrinkled Cassius; and 'twas I That the mad Brutus ended iii 11 37
Cassock. Half of the which dare not shake the snow from off their cassocks, lest they shake themselves to pieces *All's Well* iv 3 192
Cast. The government I cast upon my brother *Tempest* i 2 75
We all were sea-swallow'd, though some cast again ii 1 251
Wouldst thou have me cast my love on him? *T. G. of Ver.* i 2 25
His filth within being cast, he would appear A pond as deep as hell *Meas. for Meas.* iii 1 93
To cast thy wandering eyes on every stale *T. of Shrew* iii 1 90
And therefore fire, fire; cast on no water iv 1 21
Cast thy humble slough and appear fresh *T. Night* ii 5 161; iii 4 75
Hear me this: Since you to non-regardance cast my faith v 1 124
Cast your good counsels Upon his passion *W. Tale* iv 4 506
They found him dead and cast into the streets *K. John* iv 2 39
However God or fortune cast my lot *Richard II.* i 3 85
To set the exact wealth of all our states All at one cast *1 Hen. IV.* iv 1 47
You cast the event of war *2 Hen. IV.* i 1 166
So full of him, That thou provokest thyself to cast him up i 3 96
The smith's note for shoeing and plough-irons.—Let it be cast and paid v 1 21
Goes against my weak stomach, and therefore I must cast it up *Hen. V.* iii 2 57
I'll rather keep That which I have than, coveting for more, Be cast from possibility of all *1 Hen. VI.* v 4 146
To whom do lions cast their gentle looks? *3 Hen. VI.* i 2 11
I have set my life upon a cast, And I will stand the hazard *Richard III.* v 4 9
Your colt's tooth is not cast yet *Hen. VIII.* i 3 48

Cast. A noble spirit, As yours was put into you, ever casts Such doubts, as false coin, from it . . . . *Hen. VIII.* iii 1 170
Strikes his breast hard, and anon he casts His eye against the moon . iii 2 117
And saint-like Cast her fair eyes to heaven and pray'd devoutly . iv 1 84
Whose bright faces Cast thousand beams upon me . . . . iv 2 89
As he pass'd along, How earnestly he cast his eyes upon me! . . v 2 12
Win straying souls with modesty again, Cast none away . . . v 3 65
There's one thing wanting, which I doubt not but Our Rome will cast upon thee . . . . *Coriolanus* ii 1 218
You must Cast your election on him . . . . . . ii 3 237
And from thence Into destruction cast him . . . . . iii 1 214
That made the air unwholesome, when you cast Your stinking greasy caps . . . . iv 6 130
Go sound the ocean, and cast your nets . . . . *T. Andron.* iv 3 7
All headlong cast us down, And on the ragged stones beat forth our brains . . . . v 3 132
Her vestal livery is but sick and green And none but fools do wear it; cast it off . . . . *Rom. and Jul.* ii 2 9
O, sweet my mother, cast me not away! . . . . . iii 5 200
She, whom the spital-house and ulcerous sores Would cast the gorge at *T. of Athens* iv 3 40
Look pale and gaze And put on fear and cast yourself in wonder *J. Cæsar* i 3 60
Set in a note-book, learn'd, and conn'd by rote, To cast into my teeth . iv 3 99
He took up my legs sometime, yet I made a shift to cast him *Macbeth* ii 3 46
If thou couldst, doctor, cast The water of my land, find her disease v 3 50
Why such daily cast of brazen cannon, And foreign mart for implements of war? . . . . *Hamlet* i 1 73
Cast thy nighted colour off, And let thine eye look like a friend . i 2 68
Hath oped his ponderous and marble jaws, To cast thee up again . . i 4 51
It is as proper to our age To cast beyond ourselves in our opinions . ii 1 115
Thus the native hue of resolution Is sicklied o'er with the pale cast of thought . . . . iii 1 85
With what poor judgement he hath now cast her off appears too grossly *Lear* i 1 294
And cast you, with the waters that you lose, To temper clay . . i 4 325
How fearful And dizzy 'tis, to cast one's eyes so low! . . . iv 6 12
The state, However this may gall him with some check, Cannot with safety cast him . . . . *Othello* i 1 150
The wind-shaked surge, with high and monstrous mane, Seems to cast water on the burning bear . . . . ii 1 14
Our general cast us thus early for the love of his Desdemona . . ii 3 14
You are but now cast in his mood, a punishment more in policy than in malice . . . . ii 3 273
Whereon it came That I was cast . . . . v 2 327
It were pity to cast them away for nothing *Ant. and Cleo.* i 2 142
The city cast Her people out upon her . . . . . ii 2 218
To scourge the ingratitude that despiteful Rome Cast on my noble father ii 6 23
I know not What counts harsh fortune casts upon my face . . ii 6 55
Scribes, bards, poets, cannot Think, speak, cast, write, sing, number, ho! His love to Antony . . . . iii 2 17
They cast their caps up and carouse together Like friends long lost . iv 12 12
Forfeiters you cast in prison, yet You clasp young Cupid's tables *Cymb.* iii 2 38
Thrown From Leonati seat, and cast From her his dearest one, Sweet Imogen . . . . v 4 60
Spit, and throw stones, cast mire upon me . . . . . v 5 222
The blind mole casts Copp'd hills towards heaven . . *Pericles* i 1 100
Alas, the sea hath cast me on the rocks, Wash'd me from shore to shore ii 1 5
He should never have left, till he cast bells, steeple, church, and parish, up again . . . . ii 1 46
What a drunken knave was the sea to cast thee in our way! . . ii 1 62
By misfortune of the seas Bereft of ships and men, cast on this shore . ii 3 89
Straight Must cast thee, scarcely coffin'd, in the ooze . . iii 1 61
Did the sea cast it up?—I never saw so huge a billow, sir, As toss'd it upon shore . . . . iii 2 57
None would look on her, But cast their gazes on Marina's face . iv 3 33

Cast accompt. He can write and read and cast accompt.—O monstrous! 2 *Hen. VI.* iv 2 93

Cast ashore. By this bottle! which I made of the bark of a tree with mine own hands since I was cast ashore . . . *Tempest* ii 2 129

Cast aside. Which would be worn now in their newest gloss, Not cast aside so soon . . . . *Macbeth* i 7 35

Cast away. Wouldst thou have me cast my love on him?—Ay, if you thought your love not cast away . . . *T. G. of Ver.* i 2 26
'Nay,' said I, 'will you cast away your child on a fool?' *Mer. Wives* iii 4 100
Unless you play the honest Troyan, the poor wench is cast away *L. L. Lost* v 2 682
Ill luck?—Hath an argosy cast away, coming from Tripolis *Mer. of Ven.* iii 1 105
Thy words are too precious to be cast away upon curs *As Y. Like It* i 3 5
I will not cast away my physic but on those that are sick . . iii 2 376
To cast away honesty upon a foul slut were to put good meat into an unclean dish . . . . iii 3 35
That flattering tongue of yours won me: 'tis but one cast away . iv 1 189
I would be loath to cast away my speech . . . . *T. Night* i 5 184
Hast thou yet more blood to cast away? . . . . *K. John* ii 1 334
Cast away and sunk on Goodwin Sands . . . . . . v 5 13
Do not cast away an honest man for a villain's accusation . 2 *Hen. VI.* i 3 205
Let us cast away nothing, for we may live to have need . *Troi. and Cres.* iv 4 22
Thou hast cast away thyself, being like thyself . . *T. of Athens* iv 3 220
He is gone, he is gone, And we cast away moan . . . *Hamlet* iv 5 198
Be it lawful I take up what's cast away . . . . . *Lear* i 1 256
I am thinking of the poor men that were cast away before us even now *Pericles* ii 1 19

Cast by. Ancient citizens Cast by their grave beseeming ornaments, To wield old partisans . . . . . . *Rom. and Jul.* i 1 100

Cast down. For thee, oppressed king, am I cast down . . *Lear* v 3 5

Cast forth. Not so deep a maim As to be cast forth in the common air *Richard II.* i 3 157

Cast lips. He hath bought a pair of cast lips of Diana . *As Y. Like It* iii 4 16

Cast off. His dignity and duty both cast off . . . . *W. Tale* v 1 183
How fares your majesty?—Poison'd,—ill fare—dead, forsook, cast off *K. John* v 7 35
Never did captive with a freer heart Cast off his chains of bondage *Richard II.* i 3 89
The prince will in the perfectness of time Cast off his followers 2 *Hen. IV.* iv 4 75
Are we undone? cast off? nothing remaining? . . *T. of Athens* iv 2 2
I'll resume the shape which thou dost think I have cast off for ever *Lear* i 4 332
Nor let pity, which Even women have cast off, melt thee . *Pericles* iv 1 7

Cast out. You had much ado to make his anchor hold: When you cast out, it still came home . . . . *W. Tale* i 2 214
Thy brat hath been cast out, like to itself, No father owning it . . iii 2 88

Cast up. A ladder quaintly made of cords, To cast up, with a pair of anchoring hooks . . . . *T. G. of Ver.* iii 1 118
Who digs hills because they do aspire Throws down one mountain to cast up a higher . . . . *Pericles* i 4 6

Castalion. Thou art a Castalion-King-Urinal . . . *Mer. Wives* ii 3 34

Castaway. And call us wretches, orphans, castaways . *Richard III.* ii 2 6
Like a forlorn and desperate castaway, Do shameful execution on herself *T. Andron.* v 3 75
That ever I should call thee castaway!—You have not call'd me so *Ant. and Cleo.* iii 6 40

Casted. With casted slough and fresh legerity . . . . *Hen. V.* iv 1 23

Castigate. If thou didst put this sour-cold habit on To castigate thy pride, 'twere well . . . . *T. of Athens* iv 3 240

Castigation. Requires A sequester from liberty, fasting and prayer, Much castigation, exercise devout . . . . . *Othello* iii 4 41

Castiliano. What, wench! Castiliano vulgo! . . . . *T. Night* i 3 45

Casting. Wolves and bears, they say, Casting their savageness aside have done Like offices of pity . . . . . *W. Tale* ii 3 188
Whereof I reckon The casting forth to crows thy baby-daughter To be or none or little . . . . iii 2 192
There was casting up of eyes, holding up of hands . . . . v 2 51

Castle. For the wealth of Windsor Castle . . . . *Mer. Wives* iii 3 232
There's his chamber, his house, his castle . . . . . iv 5 7
Search Windsor Castle, elves, within and out . . . . v 5 60
All Kent hath yielded; nothing there holds out But Dover castle *K. John* v 1 31
I will for refuge straight to Bristol castle . . . *Richard II.* ii 2 135
There stands the castle, by yon tuft of trees . . . . ii 3 53
Fare you well; Unless you please to enter in the castle And there repose you . . . . ii 3 160
We must win your grace to go with us To Bristol castle . . . ii 3 164
Barkloughly castle call they this at hand? . . . . . iii 2 1
Comes at the last and with a little pin Bores through his castle wall . iii 2 170
All your northern castles yielded up . . . . . . iii 2 201
Go to Flint castle: there I'll pine away . . . . . iii 2 209
What, will not this castle yield?—The castle royally is mann'd . iii 3 20
Go to the rude ribs of that ancient castle . . . . . iii 3 32
From this castle's tatter'd battlements . . . . . . iii 3 52
As the honey of Hybla, my old lad of the castle . . . 1 *Hen. IV.* i 2 48
We steal as in a castle, cock-sure . . . . ii 1 95
Girding with grievous siege castles and towns . . . *Hen. V.* i 2 152
Mock mothers from their sons, mock castles down . . . . i 2 286
What is this castle call'd that stands hard by? . . . . iv 7 91
Entreats, great lord, thou wouldst vouchsafe To visit her poor castle 1 *Hen. VI.* ii 2 41
As an outlaw in a castle keeps And useth it to patronage his theft . iii 1 47
At your father's castle walls We'll crave a parley . . . . v 3 129
Let him shun castles; Safer shall he be upon the sandy plains Than where castles mounted stand . . . . 2 *Hen. VI.* i 4 70
Underneath an alehouse' paltry sign, The Castle in Saint Alban's . v 2 68
Farewell, my gracious lord; I'll to my castle . . . 3 *Hen. VI.* i 1 206
All the northern earls and lords Intend here to besiege you in your castle i 2 50
Away with Oxford to Hames Castle straight . . . . . v 5 2
His ancient knot of dangerous adversaries To-morrow are let blood at Pomfret-castle . . . . *Richard III.* iii 1 183
If you thrive well, bring them to Baynard's Castle . . . iii 5 98
Bid them both Meet me within this hour at Baynard's Castle . . iii 5 105
The mayor in courtesy show'd me the castle, And call'd it Rougemont iv 2 107
Stand fast, and wear a castle on thy head! . . . *Troi. and Cres.* v 2 187
Writing destruction on the enemy's castle . . . *T. Andron.* iii 1 170
This castle hath a pleasant seat . . . . *Macbeth* i 6 1
Though castles topple on their warders' heads . . . . iv 1 56
The castle of Macduff I will surprise; Seize upon Fife . . . iv 1 150
Your castle is surprised; your wife and babes Savagely slaughter'd iv 3 204
Our castle's strength Will laugh a siege to scorn . . . . v 5 2
The castle's gently render'd: The tyrant's people on both sides do fight v 7 24
Quickly send, Be brief in it, to the castle . . . . *Lear* v 3 245

Castle-ditch. We'll couch i' the castle-ditch till we see the light of our fairies . . . . *Mer. Wives* v 2 1

Casual. Of accidental judgements, casual slaughters . . *Hamlet* v 2 393
So your brace of unprizable estimations; the one is but frail and the other casual . . . . *Cymbeline* i 4 100

Casually. Bid my woman Search for a jewel that too casually Hath left mine arm . . . . ii 3 146

Casualties. Turn'd her To foreign casualties . . . . *Lear* iv 3 46
Time hath rooted out my parentage, And to the world and awkward casualties Bound me in servitude . . . . . *Pericles* v 1 94

Casualty. Even in the force and road of casualty . *Mer. of Venice* ii 9 30

Cat. They'll take suggestion as a cat laps milk . . . *Tempest* ii 1 288
Here is that which will give language to you, cat . . . . ii 2 86
My sister crying, our maid howling, our cat wringing her hands *T. G. of Ver.* ii 3 8
If I do, hang me in a bottle like a cat and shoot at me . *Much Ado* i 1 259
What though care killed a cat, thou hast mettle enough in thee to kill care . . . . v 1 133
I could play Ercles rarely, or a part to tear a cat in, to make all split *M. N. Dream* i 2 32
Be it ounce, or cat, or bear, Pard, or boar with bristled hair . . ii 2 30
Hang off, thou cat, thou burr! vile thing, let loose, Or I will shake thee! iii 2 260
Some, that are mad if they behold a cat . . . *Mer. of Venice* iv 1 48
There is no firm reason to be render'd, Why he cannot abide a gaping pig; Why he, a harmless necessary cat . . . . iv 1 55
Civet is of a baser birth than tar, the very uncleanly flux of a cat *As Y. Like It* iii 2 70
If the cat will after kind, So be sure will Rosalind . . . . iii 2 109
She shall have no more eyes to see withal than a cat . *T. of Shrew* i 2 116
I could endure any thing before but a cat, and now he's a cat to me *All's Well* iv 3 267
A pox upon him for me, he's more and more a cat . . . . iv 3 295
A pox on him, he's a cat still . . . . iv 3 307
Here is a purr of fortune's, sir, or of fortune's cat,—but not a musk-cat v 2 20
'Sblood, I am as melancholy as a gib cat or a lugged bear . 1 *Hen. IV.* i 2 83
So it would have done at the same season, if your mother's cat had but kittened . . . . iii 1 19
A clip-wing'd griffin and a moulten raven, A couching lion and a ramping cat . . . . iii 1 153
Tut, never fear me: I am as vigilant as a cat to steal cream . . iv 2 65
Playing the mouse in absence of the cat, To tear and havoc more than she can eat . . . . *Hen. V.* i 2 172
It follows then the cat must stay at home: Yet that is but a crush'd necessity . . . . i 2 174

Cat. To be a dog, a mule, a cat, a fitchew, a toad . *Troi. and Cres.* v 1 67
The mouse ne'er shunn'd the cat as they did budge . *Coriolanus* i 6 44
Cats, that can judge as fitly of his worth As I can of those mysteries which heaven Will not have earth to know . iv 2 34
What is Tybalt?—More than prince of cats, I can tell you *Rom. and Jul.* ii 4 19
What wouldst thou have with me?—Good king of cats, nothing but one of your nine lives . iii 1 80
'Zounds, a dog, a rat, a mouse, a cat, to scratch a man to death! . iii 1 104
Every cat and dog And little mouse, every unworthy thing, Live here in heaven and may look on her . iii 3 30
Letting 'I dare not' wait upon 'I would,' Like the poor cat i' the adage *Macbeth* i 7 45
Thrice the brinded cat hath mew'd.—Thrice and once the hedge-pig whined . iv 1 1
Let Hercules himself do what he may, The cat will mew and dog will have his day . *Hamlet* v 1 315
Thou owest the worm no silk, the beast no hide, the sheep no wool, the cat no perfume . *Lear* iii 4 109
Pur! the cat is gray.—Arraign her first; 'tis Goneril . iii 6 47
Come, be a man. Drown thyself! drown cats and blind puppies *Othello* i 3 341
She'll prove on cats and dogs, Then afterward up higher *Cymbeline* i 5 38
Killing creatures vile, as cats and dogs, Of no esteem . v 5 252
The cat, with eyne of burning coal, Now couches fore the mouse's hole *Pericles* iii Gower 5
Cataian. I will not believe such a Cataian . *Mer. Wives* ii 1 148
My lady's a Cataian, we are politicians . *T. Night* ii 3 80
Catalogue. I am your mother; And put you in the catalogue of those That were enwombed mine . *All's Well* i 3 149
Have you a catalogue Of all the voices that we have procured? *Coriol.* iii 3 9
We are men, my liege.—Ay, in the catalogue ye go for men . *Macbeth* iii 1 92
Though the catalogue of his endowments had been tabled by his side and I to peruse him by items . *Cymbeline* i 4 5
Cataplasm. No cataplasm so rare, Collected from all simples that have virtue Under the moon, can save the thing from death *Hamlet* iv 7 144
Cataracts and hurricanoes, spout Till you have drench'd our steeples! *Lear* iii 2 2
Catarrhs, loads o' gravel i' the back, lethargies . *Troi. and Cres.* v 1 22
Catastrophe. The catastrophe is a nuptial . *L. L. Lost* iv 1 77
This his good melancholy oft began, On the catastrophe and heel of pastime, When it was out . *All's Well* i 2 57
You fustilarian! I'll tickle your catastrophe . 2 *Hen. IV.* ii 1 66
Pat he comes like the catastrophe of the old comedy . *Lear* i 2 146
Catch. Will you troll the catch You taught me but while-ere? *Tempest* iii 2 126
This is the tune of our catch, played by the picture of Nobody . iii 2 135
Go bring it hither, For stale to catch these thieves . iv 1 187
O cunning enemy, that, to catch a saint, With saints dost bait thy hook! . *Meas. for Meas.* ii 2 180
Thy wit is as quick as the greyhound's mouth; it catches *Much Ado* v 2 12
His eye begets occasion for his wit; For every object that the one doth catch The other turns to a mirth-moving jest *L. L. Lost* ii 1 70
Sickness is catching: O, were favour so, Yours would I catch, fair Hermia, ere I go . *M. N. Dream* i 1 187
My ear should catch your voice, my eye your eye . i 1 188
The mild hind Makes speed to catch the tiger . ii 1 233
Some sleeves, some hats, from yielders all things catch . iii 2 30
If I can catch him once upon the hip, I will feed fat the ancient grudge I bear him . *Mer. of Venice* i 3 47
Here, catch this casket; it is worth the pains . ii 6 33
I would I were invisible, to catch the strong fellow by the leg *As Y. L. It* i 2 223
If we walk not in the trodden paths, our very petticoats will catch them . i 3 15
Too light for such a swain as you to catch . *T. of Shrew* ii 1 205
No doubt but he hath got a quiet catch . ii 1 333
Like his greyhound, Which runs himself and catches for his master . v 2 53
Even so quickly may one catch the plague? . *T. Night* i 5 314
Shall we rouse the night-owl in a catch that will draw three souls out of one weaver? . ii 3 60
I am dog at a catch.—By'r lady, sir, and some dogs will catch well . ii 3 64
Most certain. Let our catch be, 'Thou knave' . ii 3 66
Ye squeak out your coziers' catches without any mitigation . ii 3 97
We did keep time, sir, in our catches . ii 3 100
And have is have, however men do catch . *K. John* i 1 173
What the devil art thou?—One that will play the devil, sir, with you, An a' may catch your hide and you alone . ii 1 136
I'll smoke your skin-coat, an I catch you right . ii 1 139
When thou rannest up Gadshill in the night to catch my horse 1 *Hen. IV.* iii 3 43
We catch of you, Doll, we catch of you . 2 *Hen. IV.* ii 4 49
We have locks to safeguard necessaries, And pretty traps to catch the petty thieves . *Hen. V.* i 2 177
And so I shall catch the fly, your cousin . v 2 340
Suddenly a grievous sickness took him, That makes him gasp and stare and catch the air . 2 *Hen. VI.* iii 2 371
It stands upright, Like lime-twigs set to catch my winged soul . iii 3 16
Fight closer, or, good faith, you'll catch a blow . 3 *Hen. VI.* iii 2 23
Ready to catch each other by the throat . *Richard III.* i 3 189
Be brief, That our swift-winged souls may catch the king's . ii 2 44
And am right glad to catch this good occasion . *Hen. VIII.* v 1 109
Hector shall have a great catch, if he knock out either of your brains *Troi. and Cres.* ii 1 110
Since things in motion sooner catch the eye Than what not stirs . iii 3 183
I with great truth catch mere simplicity . iv 4 106
Think'st thou to catch my life so pleasantly? . iv 5 249
Those measles, Which we disdain should tetter us, yet sought The very way to catch them . *Coriolanus* iii 1 80
Cast your nets; Happily you may catch her in the sea . *T. Andron.* iv 3 8
To catch my death with jaunting up and down *Rom. and Jul.* ii 5 53
Something hath been amiss—a noble nature May catch a wrench *T. of A.* ii 2 218
I will fear to catch it and give way . iv 3 358
And would send them back the plague, Could I but catch it for them . v 1 141
I fear thy nature; It is too full o' the milk of human kindness To catch the nearest way . *Macbeth* i 5 19
If the assassination Could trammel up the consequence, and catch With his surcease success . i 7 3
There hangs a vaporous drop profound; I'll catch it ere it come to ground . iii 5 25
Springes to catch woodcocks . *Hamlet* i 3 115
The play's the thing Wherein I'll catch the conscience of the king . ii 2 634
Tears his white hair, Which the impetuous blasts, with eyeless rage, Catch in their fury . *Lear* iii 1 9
Excellent wretch! Perdition catch my soul, But I do love thee! *Othello* iii 3 90
Be pleased to catch at mine intent By what did here befal me *A. and C.* ii 2 41
Catch. I'll catch thine eyes, Though they had wings: slave, soulless villain! *Ant. and Cleo.* v 2 156
Saucy lictors Will catch at us, like strumpets . v 2 215
She looks like sleep, As she would catch another Antony In her strong toil v 2 350
Canst thou catch any fishes, then?—I never practised it . *Pericles* ii 1 70
Catch cold. Let him walk from whence he came, lest he catch cold on's feet . *Com. of Errors* iii 1 37
You will catch cold, and curse me . *Troi. and Cres.* iv 2 15
An thou canst not smile as the wind sits, thou'lt catch cold shortly *Lear* i 4 113
Lest the bargain should catch cold and starve . *Cymbeline* i 4 180
Catched. None are so surely caught, when they are catch'd *L. L. Lost* v 2 69
What, pale again? My fear hath catch'd your fondness . *All's Well* i 3 176
And over and over he comes, and up again; catched it again . *Coriolanus* i 3 68
But one thing to rejoice and solace in, And cruel death hath catch'd it from my sight! . *Rom. and Jul.* iv 5 48
Catching. A maid, and stuffed! there's goodly catching of cold *M. Ado* iii 4 66
Sickness is catching: O, were favour so, Yours would I catch *M. N. Dr.* i 1 186
This sickness doth infect The very life-blood of our enterprise; 'Tis catching hither . 1 *Hen. IV.* iv 1 30
'Tis time to give 'em physic, their diseases Are grown so catching *Hen. VIII.* i 3 37
Lest his infection, being of catching nature, Spread further *Coriolanus* iii 1 310
Thy heart is big, get thee apart and weep. Passion, I see, is catching *J. Cæsar* iii 1 283
Cleopatra, catching but the least noise of this, dies instantly *Ant. and Cleo.* i 2 144
Catching cold. Here they shall not lie, for catching cold *T. G. of Ver.* i 2 136
Catechising. What kind of catechising call you this? . *Much Ado* iv 1 79
Catechism. To say ay and no to these particulars is more than to answer in a catechism . *As Y. Like It* iii 2 241
Honour is a mere scutcheon: and so ends my catechism . 1 *Hen. IV.* v 1 144
Catechize. I must catechize you for it, madonna . *T. Night* i 5 68
Then I suck my teeth and catechize My picked man of countries *K. John* i 1 192
I will catechize the world for him; that is, make questions, and by them answer . *Othello* iii 4 16
Cate-log. Here is the cate-log of her condition . *T. G. of Ver.* iii 1 273
Cater. He that doth the ravens feed, Yea, providently caters for the sparrow, Be comfort to my age! . *As Y. Like It* ii 3 44
Cater-cousin. His master and he, saving your worship's reverence, are scarce cater-cousins . *Mer. of Venice* ii 2 139
Caterpillars of the commonwealth, Which I have sworn to weed *Rich. II.* ii 3 166
Her wholesome herbs Swarming with caterpillars . iii 4 47
Ah! whoreson caterpillars! bacon-fed knaves! . 1 *Hen. IV.* ii 2 88
Thus are my blossoms blasted in the bud And caterpillars eat my leaves away . 2 *Hen. VI.* iii 1 90
All scholars, lawyers, courtiers, gentlemen, They call false caterpillars iv 4 37
A courtesy Which if we should deny, the most just gods For every graff would send a caterpillar . *Pericles* v 1 60
Caterwauling. What a caterwauling do you keep here! . *T. Night* ii 3 76
Why, what a caterwauling dost thou keep! . *T. Andron.* iv 2 57
Cates. But though my cates be mean, take them in good part *C. of Err.* iii 1 28
I had rather live With cheese and garlic in a windmill, far, Than feed on cates and have him talk to me . 1 *Hen. IV.* iii 1 163
That we may Taste of your wine and see what cates you have 1 *Hen. VI.* ii 3 79
These cates resist me, she but thought upon . *Pericles* ii 3 29
Catesby, we come. Lords, will you go with us? . *Richard III.* i 3 322
Well, let them rest. Come hither, Catesby . iii 1 157
Go, gentle Catesby, And, as it were far off, sound thou Lord Hastings . iii 1 169
Tell him, Catesby, His ancient knot of dangerous adversaries To-morrow are let blood at Pomfret-castle . iii 1 181
Good Catesby, go, effect this business soundly . iii 1 186
Shall we hear from you, Catesby, ere we sleep? . iii 1 188
His honour and myself are at the one, And at the other is my servant Catesby . iii 2 22
Good morrow, Catesby; you are early stirring . iii 2 36
I tell thee, Catesby,— What, my lord? . iii 2 60
Catesby hath sounded Hastings in our business . iii 4 38
But what, is Catesby gone?—He is . iii 5 12
Hark! a drum.—Catesby, o'erlook the walls . iii 5 17
Eleven hours I spent to write it over, For yesternight by Catesby was it brought me . iii 6 6
How now, Catesby, what says your lord? . iii 7 83
Catesby!—My lord?—Rumour it abroad That Anne, my wife, is sick and like to die . iv 2 49
Ratcliff, thyself, or Catesby; where is he?—Here, my lord.—Fly to the duke . iv 4 441
What from your grace I shall deliver to him.—O, true, good Catesby . iv 4 448
Cathedral. Methought I sat in seat of majesty In the cathedral church of Westminster . 2 *Hen. VI.* i 2 37
Catlike. A lioness, with udders all drawn dry, Lay couching, head on ground, with catlike watch . *As Y. Like It* iv 3 116
Catling. Unless the fiddler Apollo get his sinews to make catlings on *Troi. and Cres.* iii 3 306
What say you, Simon Catling? . *Rom. and Jul.* iv 5 132
Cat o' mountain. More pinch-spotted make them Than pard or cat o' mountain . *Tempest* iv 1 262
Your cat-a-mountain looks, your red-lattice phrases *Mer. Wives* ii 2 27
Cato. Her name is Portia, nothing undervalued To Cato's daughter, Brutus' Portia . *Mer. of Venice* i 1 166
Thou wast a soldier Even to Cato's wish . *Coriolanus* i 4 57
I grant I am a woman; but withal A woman well-reputed, Cato's daughter . *J. Cæsar* ii 1 295
Even by the rule of that philosophy By which I did blame Cato . v 1 102
And come, young Cato; let us to the field . v 3 107
I am the son of Marcus Cato, ho! . v 4 4
O young and noble Cato, art thou down? . v 4 9
Thou diest as bravely as Titinius; And mayst be honour'd, being Cato's son v 4 11
Cattle. And there he blasts the tree and takes the cattle *Mer. Wives* iv 4 32
To offer to get your living by the copulation of cattle *As Y. Like It* iii 2 85
Boys and women are for the most part cattle of this colour . iii 2 435
Make poor men's cattle break their necks . *T. Andron.* v 1 132
Caucasus. Who can hold a fire in his hand By thinking on the frosty Caucasus? . *Richard II.* i 3 295
And faster bound to Aaron's charming eyes Than is Prometheus tied to Caucasus . *T. Andron.* ii 1 17
Caudle. Where lies thy pain? And where my liege's? all about the breast: A caudle, ho! . *L. L. Lost* iv 3 174
Ye shall have a hempen caudle then and the help of hatchet 2 *Hen. VI.* iv 7 95
Caudle thy morning taste, To cure thy o'er-night's surfeit *T. of Athens* iv 3 226
Caught. Have I caught thee, my heavenly jewel? . *Mer. Wives* iii 3 45
He is sooner caught than the pestilence . *Much Ado* i 1 87

Caught. If he have caught the Benedick, it will cost him a thousand pound . . . *Much Ado* i 1 89
She's limed, I warrant you: we have caught her . . . iii 1 104
None are so surely caught, when they are catch'd, As wit turn'd fool *L. L. Lost* v 2 69
They have the plague, and caught it of your eyes . . . v 2 421
How I caught it, found it, or came by it, What stuff 'tis made of, whereof it is born, I am to learn . . . *Mer. of Venice* i 1 3
And all the embossed sores and headed evils, That thou with license of free foot hast caught . . . *As Y. Like It* ii 7 68
I have caught extreme cold . . . *T. of Shrew* iv 1 46
I must go look my twigs: he shall be caught . . . *All's Well* iii 6 115
We have caught the woodcock, and will keep him muffled . . . iv 1 100
Here comes the trout that must be caught with tickling . . . *T. Night* ii 5 25
I cannot name the disease; and it is caught Of you that yet are well *W. Tale* i 2 386
How! caught of me! Make me not sighted like the basilisk . . . i 2 387
I shall report, For most it caught me, the celestial habits . . . iii 1 4
That which angled for mine eyes, caught the water though not the fish v 2 90
A cough, sir, which I caught with ringing in the king's affairs *2 Hen. IV.* iii 2 194
Wise bearing or ignorant carriage is caught, as men take diseases . . . v 1 85
Where my poor young was limed, was caught and kill'd . . . *3 Hen. VI.* v 6 17
Beauty and honour in her are so mingled That they have caught the king *Hen. VIII.* ii 3 77
And when he caught it, he let it go again . . . *Coriolanus* i 3 66
Will or exceed the common or be caught With cautelous baits and practice iv 1 32
Has caught me in his eye: I will present My honest grief unto him *T. of A.* iv 3 476
A blanket, in the alarm of fear caught up . . . *Hamlet* ii 2 532
Hold off the earth awhile, Till I have caught her once more in mine arms v 1 273
A fox, when one has caught her, And such a daughter . . . *Lear* i 4 340
Have I caught thee? He that parts us shall bring a brand from heaven v 3 21
Thus credulous fools are caught . . . *Othello* iv 1 46
As I draw them up, I'll think them every one an Antony, And say 'Ah, ha! you're caught' . . . *Ant. and Cleo.* ii 5 15
I saw you lately, When you caught hurt in parting two that fought *Pericles* iv 1 88

Cauldron. Round about the cauldron go; In the poison'd entrails throw *Macbeth* iv 1 4
Double, double toil and trouble; Fire burn, and cauldron bubble . . . iv 1 11
Fillet of a fenny snake, In the cauldron boil and bake . . . iv 1 13
Add thereto a tiger's chaudron, For the ingredients of our cauldron . . . iv 1 34
And now about the cauldron sing, Like elves and fairies in a ring . . . iv 1 41
Let me know. Why sinks that cauldron? and what noise is this? . . . iv 1 106

Caulked. We have a chest beneath the hatches, caulked and bitumed *Pericles* iii 1 72
How close 'tis caulk'd and bitumed! Did the sea cast it up? . . . iii 2 56

Cause. Be merry; you have cause, So have we all, of joy . . . *Tempest* ii 1 1
Who hath cause to wet the grief on't . . . ii 1 127
I have cursed them without cause . . . v 1 179
And that's her cause of sorrow . . . *T. G. of Ver.* iv 4 152
We will afterwards ork upon the cause with as great discreetly as we can *Mer. Wives* i 1 148
He's as far from jealousy as I am from giving him cause . . . ii 1 108
There is reasons and causes for it . . . iii 1 48
Having an honest man to your husband, to give him such cause of suspicion!—What cause of suspicion?—What cause of suspicion! Out upon you! . . . iii 3 108
If I suspect without cause, why then make sport at me . . . iii 3 160
I suspect without cause, mistress, do I? . . . iv 2 138
What was done to Elbow's wife, that he hath cause to complain of? *Meas. for Meas.* ii 1 121
I'll take my leave, And leave you to the hearing of the cause; Hoping you'll find good cause to whip them all . . . ii 1 141
He's hearing of a cause; he will come straight . . . ii 2 1
I believe I know the cause of his withdrawing.—What, I prithee, might be the cause? . . . iii 2 140
Forbear it therefore; give your cause to heaven . . . iv 3 129
Her cause and yours I'll perfect him withal . . . iv 3 145
Though sometimes you do blench from this to that, As cause doth minister iv 5 6
In this I'll be impartial; be you judge Of your own cause . . . v 1 167
I would he had some cause To prattle for himself . . . v 1 181
Is the duke gone? Then is your cause gone too . . . v 1 302
Say in brief the cause Why thou departed'st from thy native home *Com. of Errors* i 1 29
They can be meek that have no other cause . . . ii 1 33
Her sober virtue, years and modesty, Plead on her part some cause to you unknown . . . iii 1 91
I must be sad when I have cause and smile at no man's jests *Much Ado* i 3 15
I am sorry for her, as I have just cause . . . ii 3 173
Beshrew my hand, If it should give your age such cause of fear . . . v 1 56
Why should proud summer boast Before the birds have any cause to sing? *L. L. Lost* i 1 103
Be it as the style shall give us cause to climb in the merriness . . . i 1 202
The first and second cause will not serve my turn . . . i 2 184
We cannot cross the cause why we were born . . . iv 3 218
I hate a breaking cause to be Of heavenly oaths, vow'd with integrity . . . v 2 355
The extreme parts of time extremely forms All causes to the purpose of his speed . . . v 2 751
If for my love, as there is no such cause, You will do aught . . . v 2 802
I'll be an auditor; An actor too perhaps, if I see cause . . . *M. N. Dream* iii 1 82
Thou, I fear, hast given me cause to curse . . . iii 2 46
The noise they make Will cause Demetrius to awake . . . iii 2 117
The Jew, having done me wrong, doth cause me, as my father, being, I hope, an old man, shall frutify unto you . . . *Mer. of Venice* ii 2 141
Thou call'dst me dog before thou hadst a cause . . . iii 3 6
I acquainted him with the cause in controversy between the Jew and Antonio . . . iv 1 155
I am informed throughly of the cause . . . iv 1 173
You give your wife too unkind a cause of grief . . . v 1 175
I have more cause.—Thou hast not, cousin . . . *As Y. Like It* i 3 95
And that a great cause of the night is lack of the sun . . . iii 2 29
Have I not cause to weep?—As good cause as one would desire . . . iii 4 4
I have more cause to hate him than to love him . . . iii 5 128
We met, and found the quarrel was upon the seventh cause.—How seventh cause? . . . v 4 52
But, for the seventh cause; how did you find the quarrel on the seventh cause? . . . v 4 69
If this be not lawful cause for me to leave his service *T. of Shrew* i 2 29
May I be so bold to know the cause of your coming? . . . ii 1 88
Ass, that never read so far To know the cause why music was ordain'd! iii 1 10
I must be gone.—Faith, mistress, then I have no cause to stay . . . iii 1 86

Cause. 'Tis death for any one in Mantua To come to Padua. Know you not the cause? . . . *T. of Shrew* iv 2 82
Made me acquainted with a weighty cause Of love . . . iv 4 26
Let me never have a cause to sigh, Till I be brought to such a silly pass! v 2 123
Was this fair face the cause, quoth she, Why the Grecians sacked Troy? *All's Well* i 3 74
Hearing your high majesty is touch'd With that malignant cause wherein the honour Of my dear father's gift stands chief in power . . . ii 1 114
And, though I kill him not, I am the cause His death was so effected . . . iii 2 118
Alas, our frailty is the cause, not we! For such as we are made of, such we be . . . *T. Night* ii 2 32
On that vice in him will my revenge find notable cause to work . . . ii 3 166
Do not extort thy reasons from this clause, For that I woo, thou therefore hast no cause . . . iii 1 166
You drew your sword upon me without cause . . . v 1 191
Thou shalt be both the plaintiff and the judge Of thine own cause . . . v 1 363
Be't known, From him that has most cause to grieve . . . *W. Tale* ii 1 77
Do not weep, good fools; There is no cause . . . ii 1 119
If the cause were not in being,—part o' the cause, She the adulteress . . . ii 3 3
Such as you Nourish the cause of his awaking . . . ii 3 36
Upon them shall The causes of their death appear, unto Our shame perpetual . . . iii 2 238
I think it not uneasy to get the cause of my son's resort thither . . . iv 2 56
Now Jove afford you cause! To me the difference forges dread . . . iv 4 16
Had she such power, She had just cause . . . v 1 61
Let him that was the cause of this have power To take off so much grief from you as he Will piece up in himself . . . v 3 54
You think them false That give you cause to prove my saying true *K. John* iii 1 28
You shall have no cause To curse the fair proceedings of this day . . . iii 1 96
Thou hast no cause to say so yet, But thou shalt have . . . iii 3 30
Such temperate order in so fierce a cause Doth want example . . . iii 4 12
No common wind, no customed event, But they will pluck away his natural cause And call them meteors . . . iii 4 156
I had a mighty cause To wish him dead, but thou hadst none to kill him . . . iv 2 205
I must withdraw and weep Upon the spot of this enforced cause . . . v 2 30
And put his cause and quarrel To the disposing of the cardinal . . . v 7 91
Yet one but flatters us, As well appeareth by the cause you come *Richard II.* i 1 26
'Tis not the trial of a woman's war, The bitter clamour of two eager tongues, Can arbitrate this cause . . . i 1 50
Demand of yonder champion The cause of his arrival here in arms . . . i 3 8
Ask him his name and orderly proceed To swear him in the justice of his cause . . . i 3 10
As thy cause is right, So be thy fortune in this royal fight! . . . i 3 55
God in thy good cause make thee prosperous! . . . i 3 78
Had I thy youth and cause, I would not stay . . . i 3 305
Unavoided is the danger now, For suffering so the causes of our wreck . . . ii 1 269
I know no cause Why I should welcome such a guest as grief . . . ii 2 6
Here in the view of men I will unfold some causes of your deaths . . . iii 1 7
Madam, I'll sing.—'Tis well that thou hast cause . . . iii 4 19
Vauntingly thou spakest it, That thou wert cause of noble Gloucester's death . . . iv 1 37
That not only givest Me cause to wail but teachest me the way How to lament the cause . . . iv 1 301
Stay thy revengeful hand; thou hast no cause to fear . . . v 3 42
For this cause awhile we must neglect Our holy purpose to Jerusalem *1 Hen. IV.* i 1 101
Turn the tide of fearful faction And breed a kind of question in our cause . . . iv 1 68
Never yet did insurrection want Such water-colours to impaint his cause . . . v 1 80
And God befriend us, as our cause is just! . . . v 1 120
Derives from heaven his quarrel and his cause . . . *2 Hen. IV.* i 1 206
I am not only witty in myself, but the cause that wit is in other men . . . i 2 11
I have read the cause of his effects in Galen: it is a kind of deafness . . . i 2 133
Thus have you heard our cause and known our means . . . i 3 1
A cause on foot Lives so in hope as in an early spring We see the appearing buds . . . i 3 37
I am well acquainted with your manner of wrenching the true cause the false way . . . ii 1 121
Our cause the best; Then reason will our hearts should be as good . . . iv 1 156
All members of our cause, both here and hence . . . iv 1 171
Every slight and false-derived cause, Yea, every idle, nice and wanton reason . . . iv 1 190
If I be measured rightly, Your majesty hath no just cause to hate me . . . v 2 66
No prince nor peer shall have just cause to say, God shorten Harry's happy life one day! . . . v 2 144
Turn him to any cause of policy, The Gordian knot of it he will unloose *Hen. V.* i 1 45
In regard of causes now in hand . . . i 1 77
They know your grace hath cause and means and might . . . i 2 125
And some are yet ungotten and unborn That shall have cause to curse . . . i 2 288
And to put forth My rightful hand in a well-hallow'd cause . . . i 2 293
We therefore have great cause of thankfulness . . . ii 2 32
And now to our French causes: Who are the late commissioners? . . . ii 2 60
Working so grossly in a natural cause, That admiration did not hoop at them . . . ii 2 107
What is't to me, when you yourselves are cause? . . . iii 3 19
But we have no great cause to desire the approach of day . . . iv 1 90
His cause being just and his quarrel honourable . . . iv 1 133
If his cause be wrong, our obedience to the king wipes the crime of it out of us . . . iv 1 138
But if the cause be not good, the king himself hath a heavy reckoning to make . . . iv 1 140
Be his cause never so spotless . . . iv 1 167
There is occasions and causes why and wherefore in all things . . . v 1 3
If Henry were recall'd to life again, These news would cause him once more yield the ghost . . . *1 Hen. VI.* i 1 67
And for that cause I train'd thee to my house . . . ii 3 35
That cause, fair nephew, that imprison'd me . . . ii 5 55
Discover more at large what cause that was . . . ii 5 59
Upon especial cause, Moved with compassion of my country's wreck . . . iv 1 55
When for so slight and frivolous a cause Such factious emulations shall arise! . . . iv 1 112
I charge you, as you love our favour, Quite to forget this quarrel and the cause . . . iv 1 136
No more my fortune can, But curse the cause I cannot aid the man . . . iv 3 44
Sweet madam, give me hearing in a cause . . . v 3 106

Cause. And so says York, for he hath greatest cause . . . *2 Hen. VI.* i 1 207
Make merry, man, With thy confederates in this weighty cause . . i 2 86
I was cause Your highness came to England . . . i 3 68
Injurious duke, that threatest where's no cause . . . i 4 51
Poise the cause in justice' equal scales, Whose beam stands sure, whose rightful cause prevails . . . . ii 1 204
What counsel give you in this weighty cause . . . iii 1 289
Thou shalt have cause to fear before I leave thee . . . iv 1 118
Long sitting to determine poor men's causes Hath made me full of sickness and diseases . . . . iv 7 93
The cause why I have brought this army hither Is to remove proud Somerset . . . . v 1 35
Thou hast no cause.—No cause! Thy father slew my father . *3 Hen. VI.* i 3 45
For a thousand causes I would prolong awhile the traitor's life . i 4 51
I cheer'd them up with justice of our cause, With promise of high pay . ii 1 133
So I say, I'll cut the causes off, Flattering me with impossibilities . iii 2 142
Such a cause as fills mine eyes with tears And stops my tongue . iii 3 13
Suppose they take offence without a cause . . . iv 1 14
To the Tower.—Upon what cause?—Because my name is George *Richard III.* i 1 46
I shall live, my lord, to give them thanks That were the cause of my imprisonment . . . . i 1 128
Thou art the cause, and most accursed effect . . . i 2 120
Leave these sad designs To him that hath more cause to be a mourner . i 2 212
You may deny that you were not the cause Of my Lord Hastings' late imprisonment . . . . i 3 90
God pardon them that are the cause of it! . . . i 3 315
O, what cause have I, Thine being but a moiety of my grief, To overgo thy plaints and drown thy cries! . . . ii 2 59
All of us have cause To wail the dimming of our shining star . ii 2 101
I'll go along with you.—You have no cause . . . ii 4 68
Supposed their state was sure, And they indeed had no cause to mistrust . . . . iii 2 87
The cause why we are met Is, to determine of the coronation . . iii 4 1
I'll acquaint our duteous citizens With all your just proceedings in this cause . . . . iii 5 66
O, who hath any cause to mourn but I? . . . iv 4 34
Though far more cause, yet much less spirit to curse Abides in me; I say amen to all . . . . iv 4 196
You have no cause to hold my friendship doubtful . . . iv 4 493
Yet remember this, God and our good cause fight upon our side . v 3 240
I do not think he fears death.—Sure, he does not: He never was so womanish; the cause He may a little grieve at . *Hen. VIII.* ii 1 38
I left him private, Full of sad thoughts and troubles.—What's the cause? . . . . ii 2 16
What cause Hath my behaviour given to your displeasure? . . ii 4 19
The elect o' the land, who are assembled To plead your cause . . ii 4 61
Appeal unto the pope, To bring my whole cause 'fore his holiness . ii 4 120
We shall give you The full cause of our coming . . . iii 1 29
A strange tongue makes my cause more strange, suspicious . . iii 1 45
And to deliver, Like free and honest men, our just opinions And comforts to your cause . . . . iii 1 61
Let me have time and counsel for my cause . . . iii 1 79
Put your main cause into the king's protection . . . iii 1 93
'Twill be much Both for your honour better and your cause . . iii 1 95
Put my sick cause into his hands that hates me? . . . iii 1 118
Why should we, good lady, Upon what cause, wrong you? . . iii 1 156
Has left the cause o' the king unhandled . . . iii 2 58
And not wholesome to Our cause, that she should lie i' the bosom of Our hard-ruled king . . . . iii 2 100
Ever may your highness yoke together, As I will lend you cause, my doing well With my well saying! . . . iii 2 151
Cause the musicians play me that sad note I named my knell . iv 2 78
The chief cause concerns his grace of Canterbury . . . v 3 3
I take my cause Out of the gripes of cruel men, and give it To a most noble judge, the king . . . . v 3 99
His royal self in judgement comes to hear The cause betwixt her and this great offender . . . . v 3 121
What was his cause of anger?—The noise goes, this. *Troi. and Cres.* i 2 11
He is melancholy without cause, and merry against the hair . . i 2 27
I know the cause too: he'll lay about him to-day, I can tell them that i 2 57
No discourse of reason, Nor fear of bad success in a bad cause . ii 2 117
And on the cause and question now in hand Have glozed, but superficially . . . . ii 2 164
A cause that hath no mean dependance Upon our joint and several dignities . . . . ii 2 192
But why, why? let him show us the cause . . . ii 3 96
We have had pelting wars, since you refused The Grecians' cause . iv 5 268
O madness of discourse, That cause sets up with and against itself! . v 2 143
Shall bear the business in some other fight, As cause will be obey'd *Coriol.* i 6 83
You wear out a good wholesome forenoon in hearing a cause between an orange-wife and a fosset-seller . . . ii 1 78
All the peace you make in their cause is, calling both the parties knaves ii 1 87
Marcius is coming home: he has more cause to be proud . . ii 1 161
But they Upon their ancient malice will forget With the least cause these his new honours . . . . ii 1 245
You know the cause, sir, of my standing here.—We do, sir . . ii 3 68
From him pluck'd Either his gracious promise, which you might, As cause had call'd you up, have held him to. . . . ii 3 202
I wish I had a cause to seek him there, To oppose his hatred fully . iii 1 19
All cause unborn, could never be the motive Of our so frank donation . iii 1 129
Where one part does disdain with cause, the other Insult without all reason . . . . iii 1 143
Noble friend, home to thy house; Leave us to cure this cause . . iii 1 235
Insisting on the old prerogative And power i' the truth o' the cause . iii 3 18
If the time thrust forth A cause for thy repeal . . . iv 1 41
You have told them home; And, by my troth, you have cause . . iv 2 49
You take my part from me, sir; I have the most cause to be glad of yours . . . . iv 3 56
What cause, do you think, I have to swoon? . . . v 2 106
I'll back with you; and pray you, Stand to me in this cause . . v 3 199
We have all Great cause to give great thanks . . . v 4 63
Patrons of my right, Defend the justice of my cause with arms *T. Andron.* i 1 2
Ten years are spent since first he undertook This cause of Rome . i 1 32
To my fortunes and the people's favour Commit my cause . . i 1 55
And to the love and favour of my country Commit myself, my person and the cause . . . . i 1 59
Must my sons be slaughter'd in the streets, For valiant doings in their country's cause? . . . . i 1 113
That died in honour and Lavinia's cause . . . . i 1 377

Cause. He lives in fame that died in virtue's cause . . . *T. Andron.* i 1 390
I would not for a million of gold The cause were known to them it most concerns . . . . ii 1 50
Arm, arm, my lord;—Rome never had more cause . . . iv 4 62
And what not done, that thou hast cause to rue, Wherein I had no stroke of mischief in it? . . . . v 1 109
Rapine and Murder; therefore called so, Cause they take vengeance of such kind of men . . . . v 2 63
I am as woful as Virginius was, And have a thousand times more cause than he To do this outrage . . . . v 3 51
Now judge what cause had Titus to revenge . . . v 3 125
Black and portentous must this humour prove, Unless good counsel may the cause remove . . . *Rom. and Jul.* i 1 148
Do you know the cause?—I neither know it nor can learn of him . i 1 149
A gentleman of the very first house, of the first and second cause . ii 4 26
Up so early? What unaccustom'd cause procures her hither? . . iii 5 68
I have watch'd ere now All night for lesser cause, and ne'er been sick . iv 4 10
It is a cause worthy my spleen and fury, That I may strike at Athens *T. of Athens* iii 5 113
Warr'st thou 'gainst Athens?—Ay, Timon, and have cause . . iv 3 102
With letters of entreaty, which imported His fellowship i' the cause against your city . . . . v 2 12
Ere thou hadst power or we had cause of fear, We sent to thee, to give thy rages balm . . . . v 4 15
If you would consider the true cause . . . . *J. Cæsar* i 3 62
For my part, I know no personal cause to spurn at him, But for the general . . . . ii 1 11
What need we any spur but our own cause, To prick us to redress? . ii 1 123
Unto bad causes swear Such creatures as men doubt . . . ii 1 131
To think that or our cause or our performance Did need an oath . ii 1 135
Dear my lord, Make me acquainted with your cause of grief . . ii 1 256
Let me know some cause, Lest I be laugh'd at when I tell them so . ii 2 69
The cause is in my will: I will not come; That is enough . . ii 2 71
Know, Cæsar doth not wrong, nor without cause Will he be satisfied . iii 1 47
We will deliver you the cause, Why I, that did love Cæsar when I struck him, Have thus proceeded . . . iii 1 181
Hear me for my cause, and be silent, that you may hear . . iii 2 14
You all did love him once, not without cause: What cause withholds you then, to mourn for him? . . . iii 2 107
Hath given me some worthy cause to wish Things done, undone . . iv 2 8
We have tried the utmost of our friends, Our legions are brim-full, our cause is ripe . . . . iv 3 215
Come, the cause: if arguing make us sweat, The proof of it will turn to redder drops . . . . v 1 48
But of that to-morrow, When therewithal we shall have cause of state Craving us jointly . . . *Macbeth* iii 1 34
For mine own good, All causes shall give way . . . iii 4 136
'Cause he fail'd His presence at the tyrant's feast, I hear Macduff lives in disgrace . . . . iii 6 21
What concern they? The general cause? or is it a fee-grief Due to some single breast? . . . . iv 3 196
Their dear causes Would to the bleeding and the grim alarm Excite the mortified man . . . . v 2 3
He cannot buckle his distemper'd cause Within the belt of rule . . v 2 15
Your cause of sorrow Must not be measured by his worth, for then It hath no end . . . . v 8 44
I have found The very cause of Hamlet's lunacy . . . *Hamlet* ii 2 49
And now remains That we find out the cause of this effect, Or rather say, the cause of this defect, For this effect defective comes by cause . . . . ii 2 101
Peak, Like John-a-dreams, unpregnant of my cause, And can say nothing ii 2 595
But from what cause he will by no means speak . . . iii 1 6
I do wish That your good beauties be the happy cause Of Hamlet's wildness . . . . iii 1 39
Good my lord, what is your cause of distemper? . . . iii 2 350
His form and cause conjoin'd, preaching to stones, Would make them capable . . . . iii 4 126
That inward breaks, and shows no cause without Why the man dies . iv 4 28
Sith I have cause and will and strength and means To do't . . iv 4 45
Fight for a plot Whereon the numbers cannot try the cause . . iv 4 63
What is the cause, Laertes, That thy rebellion looks so giant-like? . iv 5 120
For, by the image of my cause, I see The portraiture of his . . v 2 77
Report me and my cause aright To the unsatisfied . . . v 2 350
Of deaths put on by cunning and forced cause . . . v 2 394
Of that I shall have also cause to speak . . . . v 2 402
Now, gods that we adore, whereof comes this?—Never afflict yourself to know the cause . . . . *Lear* i 4 313
Old fond eyes, Beweep this cause again, I'll pluck ye out . . i 4 324
If your sweet sway Allow obedience, if yourselves are old, Make it your cause; send down, and take my part! . . . ii 4 195
You think I'll weep; No, I'll not weep: I have full cause of weeping . ii 4 287
Of how unnatural and bemadding sorrow The king hath cause to plain . iii 1 39
Let me talk with this philosopher. What is the cause of thunder? . iii 4 160
Is there any cause in nature that makes these hard hearts? . . iii 6 81
Some dear cause Will in concealment wrap me up awhile . . iv 3 53
What was thy cause? Adultery? Thou shalt not die . . . iv 6 111
Though that the queen on special cause is here, Her army is moved on iv 6 219
You have some cause, they have not.—No cause, no cause . . iv 7 75
Others, whom, I fear, Most just and heavy causes make oppose . . v 1 27
Mine's not an idle cause . . . . . *Othello* i 2 95
Little shall I grace my cause In speaking for myself . . . i 3 88
My cause is hearted; thine hath no less reason . . . i 3 373
You have little cause to say so . . . . . ii 1 109
Even out of that will I cause these of Cyprus to mutiny . . ii 1 281
Thy solicitor shall rather die Than give thy cause away . . iii 3 28
Let me be thought too busy in my fears—As worthy cause I have to fear I am . . . . iii 3 254
Sith I am enter'd in this cause so far, Prick'd to't by foolish honesty and love, I will go on . . . . iii 3 411
I never gave him cause.—But jealous souls will not be answer'd so . iii 4 158
They are not ever jealous for the cause, But jealous for they are jealous . iii 4 160
To the felt absence now I feel a cause: Is't come to this? . . iii 4 182
It is the cause, it is the cause, my soul,—Let me not name it to you, you chaste stars! . . . . v 2 1
I never gave you cause.—I do believe it, and I ask you pardon . v 2 299
Between them [women] and a great cause, they should be esteemed nothing . . . . *Ant. and Cleo.* i 2 143
I shall break The cause of our expedience to the queen . . . i 2 185
They have entertained cause enough To draw their swords . . ii 1 46
And make the wars alike against my stomach, Having alike your cause ii 2 51

Cause. That I, your partner in the cause 'gainst which he fought, Could not with graceful eyes attend those wars *Ant. and Cleo.* ii 2 60
We have cause to be glad that matters are so well digested ii 2 178
You shall not find, Though you be therein curious, the least cause For what you seem to fear iii 2 35
That ever I should call thee castaway!—You have not call'd me so, nor have you cause iii 6 41
My sword, made weak by my affection, would Obey it on all cause iii 11 68
I have savage cause; And to proclaim it civilly, were like A halter'd neck which does the hangman thank For being yare about him iii 13 128
Say that I wish he never find more cause To change a master iv 5 15
Have fought Not as you served the cause, but as 't had been Each man's like mine iv 8 6
Our size of sorrow, Proportion'd to our cause, must be as great As that which makes it iv 15 5
You do extend These thoughts of horror further than you shall Find cause v 2 64
I cannot project mine own cause so well To make it clear v 2 121
Weep no more, lest I give cause To be suspected of more tenderness Than doth become a man *Cymbeline* i 1 93
Your cause doth strike my heart With pity, that doth make me sick i 6 118
Thou mayst be valiant in a better cause; But now thou seem'st a coward iii 4 74
He goes hence frowning: but it honours us That we have given him cause iii 5 19
The effect of judgement Is oft the cause of fear iv 2 112
That striking in our country's cause Fell bravely and were slain v 4 71
To the judgement of your eye I give, My cause who best can justify *Pericles* I Gower 42
On what cause I know not—Took some displeasure at him i 3 20
Be resolved he lives to govern us, Or dead, give's cause to mourn his funeral ii 4 32
For honour's cause, forbear your suffrages ii 4 41
I came unto your court for honour's cause ii 5 61
That is the cause we trouble you so early; 'Tis not our husbandry iii 2 19
The rough and woeful music that we have, Cause it to sound iii 2 89
Once more Let me entreat to know at large the cause Of your king's sorrow v 1 62
Caused. The never-surfeited sea Hath caused to belch up you *Tempest* iii 3 56
God's substitute, His deputy anointed in His sight, Hath caused his death *Richard II.* i 2 39
Hath caused every soldier to cut his prisoner's throat *Hen. V.* iv 7 9
Thou hast caused printing to be used *2 Hen. VI.* iv 7 39
You, that are king, though he do wear the crown, Have caused him, by new act of parliament, To blot out me *3 Hen. VI.* ii 2 91
You cannot guess who caused your father's death *Richard III.* ii 2 19
You have caused Your holy hat to be stamp'd on the king's coin *Hen. VIII.* iii 2 324
Patience, is that letter, I caused you write, yet sent away? iv 2 128
And that it was which caused Our swifter composition *Coriolanus* ii 1 2
Have comfort, for I know your plight is pitied Of him that caused it *Ant. and Cleo.* v 2 34
That caused a lesser villain than myself, A sacrilegious thief, to do't *Cymbeline* v 5 219
Causeless. To make modern and familiar, things supernatural and causeless *All's Well* ii 3 3
With the rest, Causeless have laid disgraces on my head *2 Hen. VI.* iii 1 162
Which made me down to throw my books, and fly,—Causeless, perhaps *T. Andron.* iv 1 26
Causer. And study too, the causer of your vow *L. L. Lost* iv 3 311
Is not the causer of the timeless deaths Of these Plantagenets, Henry and Edward, As blameful as the executioner? *Richard III.* i 2 117
Bettering thy loss makes the bad causer worse iv 4 122
Causest. The evil that thou causest to be done, That is thy means to live *Meas. for Meas.* iii 2 21
Causeth. The grief is fine, full, perfect, that I taste, And violenteth in a sense as strong As that which causeth it *Troi. and Cres.* iv 4 5
Cautel. No soil nor cautel doth besmirch The virtue of his will *Hamlet* i 3 15
Cautelous. Be caught With cautelous baits and practice *Coriolanus* iv 1 33
Swear priests and cowards and men cautelous, Old feeble carrions *J. Cæsar* ii 1 129
Cauterizing. For each true word, a blister! and each false Be as a cauterizing to the root o' the tongue, Consuming it with speaking! *T. of Athens* v 1 136
Caution. A certainty, vouch'd from our cousin Austria, With caution *All's Well* i 2 6
Many mazed considerings did throng And press'd in with this caution *Hen. VIII.* ii 4 186
My caution was more pertinent Than the rebuke you give it *Coriolanus* ii 2 67
That well might Advise him to a caution, to hold what distance His wisdom can provide *Macbeth* iii 6 44
Whate'er thou art, for thy good caution, thanks iv 1 73
In way of caution, I must tell you, You do not understand yourself *Hamlet* i 3 95
Inform'd of them; and with such cautions, That if they come to sojourn at my house, I'll not be there *Lear* ii 1 104
Cavaleiro. Master Page, and eke Cavaleiro Slender *Mer. Wives* ii 3 77
Cavaleiro-justice. Thou'rt a gentleman. Cavaleiro-justice, I say! ii 1 201
Tell him, cavaleiro-justice; tell him, bully-rook ii 1 206
Cavalero. I'll drink to Master Bardolph, and to all the cavaleros about London *2 Hen. IV.* v 3 62
Cavalery. Help Cavalery Cobweb to scratch *M. N. Dream* iv 1 25
Cavalier. These cull'd and choice-drawn cavaliers *Hen. V.* iii Prol. 24
She'll disfurnish us of all our cavaliers *Pericles* iv 6 12
Cave. I must bring you to our captain's cave *T. G. of Ver.* v 3 12
Like an o'ergrown lion in a cave, That goes not out to prey *M. for Meas.* i 3 22
The residue of your fortune, Go to my cave and tell me *As Y. Like It* ii 7 197
Who led me instantly unto his cave, There stripp'd himself iv 3 146
What you would have I'll stay to know at your abandon'd cave v 4 202
Ungracious wretch, Fit for the mountains and the barbarous caves, Where manners ne'er were preach'd! *T. Night* iv 1 52
Caves and womby vaultages of France Shall chide your trespass *Hen. V.* ii 4 124
Cursed the gentle gusts And he that loosed them forth their brazen caves *2 Hen. VI.* iii 2 89
Lean-faced Envy in her loathsome cave iii 2 315
Into the blind cave of eternal night *Richard III.* v 3 62
When with a happy storm they were surprised And curtain'd with a counsel-keeping cave *T. Andron.* ii 3 24
Then which way shall I find Revenge's cave? iii 1 271
And feed on curds and whey, and suck the goat, And cabin in a cave iv 2 179
There's not a hollow cave or lurking-place, No vast obscurity or misty vale, Where bloody murder or detested rape Can couch for fear, but I will find them out v 2 35
Cave. And find out murderers in their guilty caves *T. Andron.* v 2 52
Bondage is hoarse, and may not speak aloud; Else would I tear the cave where Echo lies *Rom. and Jul.* ii 2 162
Did ever dragon keep so fair a cave? Beautiful tyrant! fiend angelical! iii 2 74
Bring us to his cave *T. of Athens* v 1 122
Here is his cave. Peace and content be here! v 1 129
This man was riding From Alcibiades to Timon's cave v 2 10
The wrathful skies Gallow the very wanderers of the dark, And make them keep their caves *Lear* iii 2 45
These fig-leaves Have slime upon them, such as the aspic leaves Upon the caves of Nile *Ant. and Cleo.* v 2 356
How, In this our pinching cave, shall we discourse The freezing hours away? *Cymbeline* iii 3 38
Though train'd up thus meanly I' the cave wherein they bow, their thoughts do hit The roofs of palaces iii 3 83
Great men, That had a court no bigger than this cave iii 6 83
It may be heard at court that such as we Cave here, hunt here, are outlaws iv 2 138
Cave-keeper. I hope I dream; For so I thought I was a cave-keeper, And cook to honest creatures iv 2 298
Cavern. Even from the tongueless caverns of the earth *Richard II.* i 1 105
O, then by day Where wilt thou find a cavern dark enough To mask thy monstrous visage? *J. Cæsar* ii 1 80
Caveto. Therefore, Caveto be thy counsellor. Go, clear thy crystals *Hen. V.* ii 3 55
Caviare. The play, I remember, pleased not the million; 'twas caviare to the general *Hamlet* ii 2 457
Cavil. 'Tis love you cavil at: I am not Love *T. G. of Ver.* i 1 38
That's but a cavil: he is old, I young *T. of Shrew* ii 1 392
I'll give thrice so much . . . : But in the way of bargain, mark ye me, I'll cavil on the ninth part of a hair *1 Hen. IV.* iii 1 140
You do not well in obstinacy To cavil in the course of this contract *1 Hen. VI.* v 4 156
You cavil, widow: I did mean, my queen *3 Hen. VI.* iii 2 99
Cavilling. Let's fight it out and not stand cavilling thus ii 1 117
Cawdor. That most disloyal traitor The thane of Cawdor *Macbeth* i 2 53
No more that thane of Cawdor shall deceive Our bosom interest i 2 63
All hail, Macbeth! hail to thee, thane of Cawdor! i 3 49
But how of Cawdor? the thane of Cawdor lives, A prosperous gentleman i 3 72
To be king Stands not within the prospect of belief, No more than to be Cawdor i 3 75
You shall be king.—And thane of Cawdor too: went it not so? i 3 87
He bade me, from him, call thee thane of Cawdor i 3 105
The thane of Cawdor lives: why do you dress me In borrow'd robes? i 3 108
Glamis, and thane of Cawdor! The greatest is behind i 3 116
Those that gave the thane of Cawdor to me Promised no less to them i 3 119
That trusted home Might yet enkindle you unto the crown, Besides the thane of Cawdor i 3 122
Is execution done on Cawdor? Are not Those in commission yet return'd? i 4 1
My worthy Cawdor!—The Prince of Cumberland! i 4 47
'Thane of Cawdor;' by which title, before, these weird sisters saluted me i 5 8
Glamis thou art, and Cawdor; and shalt be What thou art promised i 5 16
Great Glamis! worthy Cawdor! Greater than both, by the all-hail hereafter! i 5 55
Where's the thane of Cawdor? We coursed him at the heels i 6 20
Glamis hath murder'd sleep, and therefore Cawdor Shall sleep no more ii 2 42
Thou hast it now: king, Cawdor, Glamis, all, As the weird women promised iii 1 1
Cawing. Russet-pated choughs, many in sort, Rising and cawing at the gun's report *M. N. Dream* iii 2 22
Cease. Here cease more questions *Tempest* i 2 184
At which time, my lord, You said our work should cease v 1 5
Cease to persuade, my loving Proteus *T. G. of Ver.* i 1 1
I would you were set, so your affection would cease ii 1 92
Cease to lament for that thou canst not help iii 1 241
Cease thy counsel, Which falls into mine ears as profitless As water in a sieve *Much Ado* v 1 3
Heaven cease this idle humour in your honour! *T. of Shrew* Ind. 2 14
Both suffer under this complaint we bring, And both shall cease, without your remedy *All's Well* v 3 164
Cease; no more. You smell this business with a sense as cold As is a dead man's nose *W. Tale* ii 1 150
Have I not ever said How that ambitious Constance would not cease? *K. John* i 1 32
May cease their hatred, and this dear conjunction Plant neighbourhood and Christian-like accord *Hen. V.* v 2 380
Cease, cease these jars and rest your minds in peace *1 Hen. VI.* i 1 44
Here sound retreat, and cease our hot pursuit ii 2 3
And this fell tempest shall not cease to rage *2 Hen. VI.* iii 1 351
He dares not calm his contumelious spirit Nor cease to be an arrogant controller iii 2 205
Cease, gentle queen, these execrations iii 2 305
O, let me entreat thee cease. Give me thy hand iii 2 339
Think therefore on revenge and cease to weep. But who can cease to weep and look on this? iv 4 3
Now let the general trumpet blow his blast, Particularities and petty sounds To cease! v 2 45
Conditionally, that here thou take an oath To cease this civil war *3 Hen. VI.* i 1 197
When the lion fawns upon the lamb, The lamb will never cease to follow him iv 8 50
Are you lords o' the field? If not, why cease you till you are so? *Coriolanus* i 6 48
And when such time they have begun to cry, Let them not cease ii 3 20
I have not the face To say 'Beseech you, cease' iv 6 117
Sweet father, cease your tears *T. Andron.* iii 1 136
Too unadvised, too sudden; Too like the lightning, which doth cease to be Ere one can say 'It lightens' *Rom. and Jul.* ii 2 119
By and by, I come:—To cease thy suit, and leave me to my grief ii 2 153
Being the time the potion's force should cease v 3 249
No stop! so senseless of expense, That he will neither know how to maintain it, Nor cease his flow of riot *T. of Athens* ii 2 3
Your importunacy cease till after dinner ii 2 42
Things at the worst will cease, or else climb upward To what they were before *Macbeth* iv 2 24
The cease of majesty Dies not alone; but, like a gulf, doth draw What's near it with it *Hamlet* iii 3 15
What is it ye would see? If aught of woe or wonder, cease your search v 2 374
The orbs From whom we do exist, and cease to be *Lear* i 1 114
What, in the least, Will you require in present dower with her, Or cease your quest of love? i 1 196
Bids the wind blow the earth into the sea, Or swell the curled waters 'bove the main, That things might change or cease iii 1 7

Cease. Your business of the world hath so an end, And machination ceases . . . *Lear* v 1 46
Is this the promised end?—Or image of that horror?—Fall, and cease! v 3 264
Quarrel no more, but be prepared to know The purposes I bear; which are, or cease, As you shall give the advice . *Ant. and Cleo.* i 3 67
Than be so Better to cease to be . . . . *Cymbeline* iv 4 31
A certain stuff, which, being ta'en, would cease The present power of life v 5 255
Never was a war did cease, Ere bloody hands were wash'd, with such a peace . . . . v 5 484
Yet cease your ire, you angry stars of heaven! . *Pericles* ii 1 1
When canst thou reach it?—By break of day, if the wind cease . iii 1 77
Patience, good sir, Or here I'll cease . . . . . v 1 146
Ceased. She ceased In heavy satisfaction . . *All's Well* v 3 99
Miracles are ceased; And therefore we must needs admit the means How things are perfected . . . . . *Hen. V.* i 1 67
Importune him for my moneys; be not ceased With slight denial *T. of Athens* ii 1 16
Ceaseth. Glory is like a circle in the water, Which never ceaseth to enlarge itself . . . . . 1 *Hen. VI.* i 2 134
Cedar. And by the spurs pluck'd up The pine and cedar . *Tempest* v 1 48
As upright as the cedar . . . . . *L. L. Lost* iv 3 89
I'll wear aloft my burgonet, As on a mountain top the cedar shows 2 *Hen. VI.* v 1 205
Thus yields the cedar to the axe's edge . . . 3 *Hen VI.* v 2 11
Our aery buildeth in the cedar's top, And dallies with the wind *Richard III.* i 3 264
Like a mountain cedar, reach his branches To all the plains . *Hen. VIII.* v 5 54
Let the mutinous winds Strike the proud cedars 'gainst the fiery sun *Coriolanus* v 3 60
We are but shrubs, no cedars we, No big-boned men . *T. Andron.* iv 3 45
When from a stately cedar shall be lopped branches, which, being dead many years, shall after revive . . . . *Cymbeline* v 4 141
The lofty cedar, royal Cymbeline, Personates thee . . . v 5 453
For many years thought dead, are now revived, To the majestic cedar join'd . . . . v 5 457
Cedius. The pashed corses of the kings Epistrophus and Cedius *Troi. and Cres.* v 5 11
Celebrate. A contract of true love to celebrate . *Tempest* iv 1 84
Come, temperate nymphs, and help to celebrate A contract of true love iv 1 132
My dancing soul doth celebrate This feast of battle . *Richard II.* i 3 91
To celebrate the joy that God hath given us . . 1 *Hen. VI.* i 6 14
Witchcraft celebrates Pale Hecate's offerings . . *Macbeth* ii 1 51
Dance now the Egyptian Bacchanals, And celebrate our drink *Ant. and Cleo.* ii 7 111
Yet there, my queen, We'll celebrate their nuptials . . *Pericles* v 3 80
Celebrated. The heaven sets spies upon us, will not have Our contract celebrated . . . . . . *W. Tale* v 1 204
Ever 'gainst that season comes Wherein our Saviour's birth is celebrated *Hamlet* i 1 159
Celebration. To take away The edge of that day's celebration *Tempest* iv 1 29
It shall come to note, What time we will our celebration keep *T. Night* iv 3 30
Celebration of that nuptial which We two have sworn shall come *W. Tale* iv 4 50
They are ever forward—In celebration of this day with shows *Hen. VIII.* iv 1 10
Besides these beneficial news, it is the celebration of his nuptial *Othello* ii 2 7
Celerity. Hence hath offence his quick celerity *Meas. for Meas.* iv 2 113
It was the swift celerity of his death, Which I did think with slower foot came on, That brain'd my purpose . . . . v 1 399
In motion of no less celerity Than that of thought . *Hen. V.* iii Prol. 2
With great speed of judgement, Ay, with celerity . *Troi. and Cres.* i 3 330
She hath such a celerity in dying . . *Ant. and Cleo.* i 2 149
Celerity is never more admired Than by the negligent . . iii 7 25
Celestial. That's a brave god and bears celestial liquor *Tempest* ii 2 122
But now I worship a celestial sun . . . *T. G. of Ver.* ii 6 10
He meaneth with a corded ladder To climb celestial Silvia's chamber-window . . . . iii 6 34
Give me thy hand, terrestrial; so. Give me thy hand, celestial; so *Mer. Wives* iii 1 109
Celestial as thou art, O, pardon love this wrong . *L. L. Lost* iv 2 121
Until the twelve celestial signs Have brought about the annual reckoning v 2 807
To call me goddess, nymph, divine and rare, Precious, celestial *M. N. Dream* iii 2 227
The celestial habits, Methinks I so should term them . *W. Tale* iii 1 4
Leaving his body as a paradise, To envelope and contain celestial spirits *Hen. V.* i 1 31
Chosen from above, By inspiration of celestial grace . 1 *Hen. VI.* v 4 40
And is a pattern of celestial peace . . . . v 5 65
Whilst I sit meditating On that celestial harmony I go to *Hen. VIII.* iv 2 80
So lust, though to a radiant angel link'd, Will sate itself in a celestial bed, And prey on garbage . . . . . *Hamlet* i 5 56
To the celestial and my soul's idol, the most beautified Ophelia . ii 2 109
He came in thunder; his celestial breath Was sulphurous to smell *Cymbeline* v 4 114
To taste the fruit of yon celestial tree, Or die in the adventure *Pericles* i 1 21
Celestial Dian, goddess argentine, I will obey thee . . v 1 251
Celia. Dear Celia, I show more mirth than I am mistress of *As Y. Like It* i 2 3
Dear sovereign, hear me speak.—Ay, Celia; we stay'd her for your sake i 3 69
Something that hath a reference to my state; No longer Celia, but Aliena i 3 130
Cell. Prospero, master of a full poor cell, And thy no greater father *Tempest* i 2 20
Canst thou remember A time before we came unto this cell? . i 2 39
I have used thee, Filth as thou art, with human care, and lodged thee In mine own cell . . . . i 2 347
If you be pleased, retire into my cell And there repose . . iv 1 161
I left them I' the filthy-mantled pool beyond your cell . . iv 1 182
We now are near his cell . . . . . . iv 1 195
See'st thou here, This is the mouth o' the cell . . . iv 1 216
In the line-grove which weather-fends your cell . . . v 1 10
Fetch me the hat and rapier in my cell . . . . v 1 84
Welcome, sir; This cell's my court . . . . . v 1 166
Go, sirrah, to my cell; Take with you your companions . . v 1 291
I invite your highness and your train To my poor cell . . v 1 301
Where shall I meet you?—At Friar Patrick's cell . *T. G. of Ver.* iv 3 43
And now it is about the very hour That Silvia, at Friar Patrick's cell, should meet me . . . . v 1 3
She did intend confession At Patrick's cell this even . . v 2 42
O sacred receptacle of my joys, Sweet cell of virtue and nobility! *T. Andron.* i 1 93
Hence will I to my ghostly father's cell, His help to crave *Rom. and Jul.* ii 2 189
And there she shall at Friar Laurence' cell Be shrived and married ii 4 193
Hie you hence to Friar Laurence' cell; There stays a husband to make you a wife . . . . ii 5 70
Hie you to the cell.—Hie to high fortune! Honest nurse, farewell ii 5 79
I'll to him; he is hid at Laurence' cell . . . . iii 2 141
Cell. Tell my lady I am gone, Having displeased my father, to Laurence' cell, To make confession . . . *Rom. and Jul.* iii 5 232
Look, sir, here comes the lady towards my cell . . . iv 1 17
I met the youthful lord at Laurence' cell . . . . iv 2 25
Get me an iron crow, and bring it straight Unto my cell . . v 2 22
And keep her at my cell till Romeo come . . . . v 2 29
Meaning to keep her closely at my cell, Till I conveniently could send to Romeo . . . . v 3 255
O proud death, What feast is toward in thine eternal cell? . *Hamlet* v 2 376
Arise, black vengeance, from thy hollow cell! . . . *Othello* iii 3 447
Unto us it is A cell of ignorance; travelling a-bed . . *Cymbeline* iii 3 33
Cellar. My cellar is in a rock by the sea-side where my wine is hid *Temp.* ii 2 137
Cellarage. Come on—you hear this fellow in the cellarage . *Hamlet* i 5 151
Celsa. Hic steterat Priami regia celsa senis . *T. of Shrew* iii 1 29
'Celsa senis,' that we might beguile the old pantaloon . . iii 1 36
'Regia,' presume not, 'celsa senis,' despair not . . . iii 1 44
Cement. Your temples burned in their cement . . . *Coriolanus* iv 6 85
The fear of us May cement their divisions . . *Ant. and Cleo.* ii 1 48
Set Betwixt us as the cement of our love, To keep it builded . iii 2 29
Censer. Like to a censer in a barber's shop . . *T. of Shrew* iv 3 91
You thin man in a censer, I will have you as soundly swinged for this 2 *Hen. IV.* v 4 21
Censor. Twice being [by the people chosen] censor . . *Coriolanus* ii 3 252
[Censorinus,] nobly named so, Twice being [by the people chosen] censor ii 3 251
Censure. 'Tis a passing shame That I, unworthy body as I am, Should censure thus on lovely gentlemen . . . . *T. G. of Ver.* i 2 19
Whether you had not sometime in your life Err'd in this point which now you censure him . . . . . . *Meas. for Meas.* ii 1 15
But rather tell me, When I, that censure him, do so offend . . ii 1 29
No might nor greatness in mortality Can censure 'scape . . . iii 2 197
Betray themselves to every modern censure worse than drunkards *As Y. Like It* iv 1 7
Therefore beware my censure and keep your promise . . . iv 1 200
How blest am I In my just censure, in my true opinion! . *W. Tale* ii 1 37
Fain would mine eyes be witness with mine ears, To give their censure of these rare reports . . . . 1 *Hen. VI.* ii 3 10
If you do censure me by what you were, Not what you are . . v 5 97
The king is old enough himself To give his censure . . 2 *Hen. VI.* i 3 120
Say you consent and censure well the deed, And I'll provide his executioner . . . . iii 1 275
Will you go To give your censures in this weighty business? *Richard III.* ii 2 144
To avoid the carping censures of the world . . . . iii 5 68
And no discerner Durst wag his tongue in censure . . . *Hen. VIII.* i 1 33
Forgetting, like a good man, your late censure Both of his truth and him, which was too far . . . . iii 1 64
And giddy censure Will then cry out of Marcius 'O, if he Had borne the business!' . . . . *Coriolanus* i 1 272
To suffer lawful censure for such faults As shall be proved upon you . iii 3 46
I'll deliver Myself your loyal servant, or endure Your heaviest censure v 6 143
Censure me in your wisdom, and awake your senses . . *J. Cæsar* iii 2 16
Let our just censures Attend the true event . . . *Macbeth* v 4 14
Take each man's censure, but reserve thy judgement . . *Hamlet* i 3 69
Shall in the general censure take corruption From that particular fault i 4 35
The censure of the which one must in your allowance o'erweigh a whole theatre of others . . . . iii 2 30
We will both our judgements join In censure of his seeming . . iii 2 92
The fault Would not 'scape censure, nor the redresses sleep . . *Lear* i 4 229
Until their greater pleasures first be known That are to censure them . v 3 3
Your name is great In mouths of wisest censure . . . *Othello* ii 3 193
He's that he is: I may not breathe my censure What he might be . iv 1 281
To you, lord governor, Remains the censure of this hellish villain . . v 2 368
Many times, Doth ill deserve by doing well; what's worse, Must court'sy at the censure . . . . *Cymbeline* iii 3 55
Fear not slander, censure rash;—Thou hast finish'd joy and moan . . iv 2 272
Whose death indeed's the strongest in our censure . . *Pericles* ii 4 34
Censured. Doth he so seek his life?—Has censured him Already *Meas. for Meas.* i 4 72
I hear how I am censured . . . . . . *Much Ado* ii 3 233
Whose equality By our best eyes cannot be censured . . *K. John* ii 1 328
Do you two know how you are censured here in the city, I mean of us o' the right-hand file? . . . . *Coriolanus* ii 1 25
Why, how are we censured? . . . . ii 1 27
How, my lord, I may be censured, that nature thus gives way to loyalty, something fears me to think of . . . . . . *Lear* iii 5 3
Censurer. We must not stint Our necessary actions, in the fear To cope malicious censurers . . . . *Hen. VIII.* i 2 78
Censuring. Shall they hoist me up And show me to the shouting varletry Of censuring Rome? . . . . . . *Ant. and Cleo.* v 2 57
Cent. Je vous donnerai deux cents écus . . . *Hen. V.* iv 4 45
Centaur. Go bear it to the Centaur, where we host *Com. of Errors* i 2 9
I'll to the Centaur, to go seek this slave . . . . i 2 104
The gold I gave to Dromio is laid up Safe at the Centaur . . ii 2 2
You know no Centaur? you received no gold? . . . . ii 2 9
Come to the Centaur; fetch our stuff from thence . . . iv 4 153
What stuff of mine hast thou embark'd?—Your goods that lay at host, sir, in the Centaur . . . . v 1 410
The battle with the Centaurs, to be sung By an Athenian eunuch *M. N. Dream* v 1 44
Which I wish may prove More stern and bloody than the Centaurs' feast *T. Andron.* v 2 204
Down from the waist they are Centaurs, Though women all above *Lear* iv 6 126
Centre. I'll believe as soon This whole earth may be bored and that the moon May through the centre creep . . . *M. N. Dream* iii 2 54
Affection! thy intention stabs the centre . . . . *W. Tale* i 2 138
The centre is not big enough to bear A school-boy's top . . ii 1 102
As many lines close in the dial's centre . . . . *Hen. V.* i 2 210
In the market-place, The middle centre of this cursed town 1 *Hen. VI.* ii 2 6
This foul swine Lies now even in the centre of this isle *Richard III.* v 2 11
The heavens themselves, the planets and this centre Observe degree, priority and place . . . . *Troi. and Cres.* i 3 85
As iron to adamant, as earth to the centre . . . . iii 2 186
The strong base and building of my love Is as the very centre of the earth . . . . iv 2 110
'Tis you must dig with mattock and with spade, And pierce the inmost centre of the earth . . . . *T. Andron.* iv 3 12
Turn back, dull earth, and find thy centre out . *Rom. and Jul.* ii 1 2
If circumstances lead me, I will find Where truth is hid, though it were hid indeed Within the centre . . . . *Hamlet* ii 2 159
Centuries. Dispatch Those centuries to our aid . . *Coriolanus* i 7 3
Centurion. The centurions and their charges, distinctly billeted . iv 3 47

Century. A century send forth; Search every acre . . . *Lear* iv 4 6
I ha' strew'd his grave, And on it said a century of prayers . *Cymbeline* iv 2 391
Cerberus. Whose club kill'd Cerberus, that three-headed canis *L. L. Lost* v 2 593
Nay, rather damn them with King Cerberus; and let the welkin roar *2 Hen. IV.* ii 4 182
Thou art as full of envy at his greatness as Cerberus is at Proserpina's beauty . . . *Troi. and Cres.* ii 1 37
And fell asleep, As Cerberus at the Thracian poet's feet . *T. Andron.* ii 4 51
Cerecloth. To rib her cerecloth in the obscure grave . *Mer. of Venice* ii 7 51
Cerement. Tell Why thy canonized bones, hearsed in death, Have burst their cerements . . . *Hamlet* i 4 48
Ceremonial. The priest attends To speak the ceremonial rites of marriage *T. of Shrew* iii 2 6
Ceremonies. Before All sanctimonious ceremonies . . *Tempest* iv 1 16
After many ceremonies done, He calls for wine . . *T. of Shrew* iii 2 171
The ceremonies of the wars, and the cares of it, and the forms of it *Hen. V.* iv 1 73
His ceremonies laid by, in his nakedness he appears but a man . iv 1 109
With twenty popish tricks and ceremonies . . . *T. Andron.* v 1 76
Disrobe the images, If you do find them deck'd with ceremonies *J. Cæsar* i 1 70
Quite from the main opinion he held once Of fantasy, of dreams and ceremonies . . . . ii 1 197
I never stood on ceremonies, Yet now they fright me . . . ii 2 13
We are contented Cæsar shall Have all true rites and lawful ceremonies iii 1 241
Ceremonious. How ceremonious, solemn and unearthly It was i' the offering! . . . . *W. Tale* iii 1 7
Let us take a ceremonious leave And loving farewell . . *Richard II.* i 3 50
Throw away respect, Tradition, form and ceremonious duty . iii 2 173
You are too senseless-obstinate, my lord, Too ceremonious *Richard III.* iii 1 45
The leisure and the fearful time Cuts off the ceremonious vows of love . v 3 98
This Trojan scorns us; or the men of Troy Are ceremonious courtiers *Troi. and Cres.* i 3 234
To my judgement, your highness is not entertained with that ceremonious affection as you were wont . . . *Lear* i 4 63
Ceremoniously let us prepare Some welcome . . *Mer. of Venice* v 1 37
Ceremony. In all the accoutrement, complement and ceremony of it *Mer. Wives* iv 2 6
In the lawful name of marrying, To give our hearts united ceremony iv 6 51
No ceremony that to great ones 'longs . . *Meas. for Meas.* ii 2 59
Not sorting with a nuptial ceremony . . . . *M. N. Dream* v 1 55
Wanted the modesty To urge the thing held as a ceremony *Mer. of Venice* v 1 206
Use a more spacious ceremony to the noble lords . . *All's Well* ii 1 51
Whose ceremony Shall seem expedient on the now-born brief . ii 3 185
And all the ceremony of this compact Seal'd in my function . *T. Night* v 1 163
I am so fraught with curious business that I leave out ceremony *W. Tale* iv 4 526
What have kings, that privates have not too, Save ceremony, save general ceremony? . . . . . . *Hen. V.* iv 1 256
And what art thou, thou idol ceremony? What kind of god art thou? iv 1 257
What are thy comings in? O ceremony, show me but thy worth! . iv 1 261
O, be sick, great greatness, And bid thy ceremony give thee cure! iv 1 269
No, not all these, thrice-gorgeous ceremony, Not all these, laid in bed majestical, Can sleep so soundly as the wretched slave . . iv 1 283
All's now done, but the ceremony . . . . *Hen. VIII.* ii 1 4
You saw The ceremony?—That I did . . . . iv 1 60
Neither will they bate One jot of ceremony . . . *Coriolanus* ii 2 145
Ceremony was but devised at first To set a gloss on faint deeds *T. of Athens* i 2 15
Set on; and leave no ceremony out . . . . *J. Cæsar* i 2 11
When love begins to sicken and decay, It useth an enforced ceremony iv 2 21
To feed were best at home; From thence the sauce to meat is ceremony *Macbeth* iii 4 36
The appurtenance of welcome is fashion and ceremony . *Hamlet* ii 2 389
What ceremony else?—Her obsequies have been as far enlarged As we have warranty . . . . v 1 248
A messenger from Cæsar.—What, no more ceremony? *Ant. and Cleo.* iii 13 38
Ceres, most bounteous lady, thy rich leas Of wheat, rye, barley *Tempest* iv 1 60
Approach, rich Ceres, her to entertain . . . . iv 1 75
Scarcity and want shall shun you; Ceres' blessing so is on you . iv 1 117
Like over-ripen'd corn, Hanging the head at Ceres' plenteous load *2 Hen. VI.* i 2 2
Cerimon. Your purse, still open, hath built Lord Cerimon Such strong renown as time shall ne'er decay . . . *Pericles* iii 2 47
Lord Cerimon, my lord; this man, Through whom the gods have shown their power . . . . v 3 59
Lord Cerimon hath letters of good credit, sir, My father's dead . v 3 77
Lord Cerimon, we do our longing stay To hear the rest untold . v 3 83
In reverend Cerimon there well appears The worth that learned charity aye wears . . . . v 3 Gower 93
'Cern. What 'cerns it you if I wear pearl and gold? . . *T. of Shrew* v 1 77
Certain. That will not let you Believe things certain . *Tempest* v 1 125
Know for certain That I am Prospero . . . . v 1 158
I would send for certain of my creditors . . *Meas. for Meas.* i 2 136
And what thou hast, forget'st. Thou art not certain . . . iii 1 23
It is certain that when he makes water his urine is congealed ice . iii 2 117
It is certain I am loved of all ladies, only you excepted . *Much Ado* i 1 126
'Tis certain so; the prince wooes for himself . . . . ii 1 181
Said I, 'the gentleman is wise:' 'Certain,' said she, 'a wise gentleman' v 1 166
Some certain special honours . . . . *L. L. Lost* v 1 112
His leg is too big for Hector's.—More calf, certain . . . v 2 645
A man so breathed, that certain he would fight . . . . v 2 659
Be out of hope, of question, of doubt; Be certain, nothing truer *M. N. Dream* iii 2 280
This beauteous lady Thisby is certain . . . . . v 1 131
Lorenzo, certain, and my love indeed, For who love I so much? *Mer. of Venice* ii 6 29
Here I read for certain that my ships Are safely come to road . v 1 287
I would do the man what honour I can, but of this I am not certain *All's Well* iv 3 304
To do't, or no, is certain To me a break-neck . . *W. Tale* i 2 362
Be certain what you do, sir, lest your justice Prove violence . ii 1 127
Nothing so certain as your anchors . . . . . iv 4 581
Looks he not for supply?—So do we.—His is certain, ours is doubtful *1 Hen. IV.* iv 3 4
You are too great to be by me gainsaid: Your spirit is too true, your fears too certain . . . *2 Hen. IV.* i 1 92
I hear for certain, and do speak the truth . . . . i 1 188
Certain, 'tis certain; very sure, very sure: death, as the Psalmist saith, is certain to all . . . . iii 2 40
Death is certain. Is old Double of your town living yet? . . iii 2 45
She cannot choose but be old; certain she's old . . . iii 2 221
This apoplexy will certain be his end . . . . . iv 4 130

Certain. It is certain that either wise bearing or ignorant carriage is caught . . . . *2 Hen. IV.* v 1 84
It is best, certain . . . . v 5 24
I will live so long as I may, that's the certain of it . . *Hen. V.* ii 1 16
It is certain, corporal, that he is married . . . . ii 1 19
'Tis certain he hath pass'd the river Somme . . . iii 5 1
'Tis certain, every man that dies ill, the ill upon his own head . iv 1 197
'Tis certain there's not a boy left alive . . . . iv 7 5
Believe my words, For they are certain and unfallible . . *1 Hen. VI.* i 2 59
Yet, you that hear me, This from a dying man receive as certain *Hen. VIII.* ii 1 125
And held for certain The king will venture at it . . . ii 1 155
We are a queen, or long have dream'd so, certain The daughter of a king ii 4 71
For certain, This is of purpose laid by some that hate me . v 2 13
'Tis now too certain: How much more is his life in value with him? v 3 107
Exposed myself, From certain and possess'd conveniences, To doubtful fortunes . . . . . . *Troi. and Cres.* iii 3 7
'Tis certain, greatness, once fall'n out with fortune, Must fall out with men too . . . . iii 3 75
A letter for me!—Yes, certain, there's a letter for you . . *Coriolanus* ii 1 123
Some certain of your brethren roar'd and ran From the noise of our own drums . . . . iii 3 59
The end of war's uncertain, but this certain . . . . v 3 141
Is it most certain?—As certain as I know the sun is fire . . . v 4 48
If money were as certain as your waiting, 'Twere sure enough *T. of Athens* iii 4 47
Does the rumour hold for true, that he's so full of gold?—Certain . v 1 5
I have moved already Some certain of the noblest-minded Romans *J. Cæsar* i 3 122
He would not take the crown; Therefore 'tis certain he was not ambitious . . . . iii 2 118
For certain she is dead, and by strange manner . . . iv 3 189
A thing most strange and certain . . . . *Macbeth* ii 4 14
For certain, sir, he is not . . . . v 2 8
For certain, He cannot buckle his distemper'd cause Within the belt of rule . . . . v 2 14
If the matter of this paper be certain, you have mighty business . *Lear* iii 5 16
That nature, which contemns it origin, Cannot be border'd certain in itself iv 2 33
And prays you to believe him.—'Tis certain, then, for Cyprus . *Othello* i 3 43
Certain, men should be what they seem . . . . iii 3 128
That cuckold lives in bliss Who, certain of his fate, loves not his wronger iii 3 168
O, thou art wise; 'tis certain . . . . . . iv 1 75
This is most certain that I shall deliver . . . *Ant. and Cleo.* ii 1 28
I know you could not lack, I am certain on't . . . . ii 2 57
Is this certain?—Or I have no observance . . . . iii 3 24
I speak not out of weak surmises, but from proof as strong as my grief and as certain as I expect my revenge . . . . *Cymbeline* iii 4 25
If thou fear to strike and to make me certain it is done, thou art the pandar to her dishonour . . . . iii 4 31
'Tis certain she is fled. Go in and cheer the king: he rages . iii 5 66
If it be true that I interpret false, Then were it certain you were not so bad . . . . *Pericles* i 1 125
And it is said For certain in our story . . . . iv Gower 19
Certain it is . . . . *All's Well* iii 6 98; v 3 210
Most certain *T. Night* i 5; *W. Tale* iv 4; *K. John* i 1; *Lear* iv 7; *Ant. and Cleo.* iii 6; iv 5
That's certain *T. G. of Ver.* ii 1; *Meas. for Meas.* iv 3; *Much Ado* ii 3; iv 2; *Mer. of Venice* iii 1; *T. Night* iii 1; iii 4; *1 Hen. IV.* ii 3; v 4; *Hen. V.* iii 2; *J. Cæsar* iii 2; *Othello* iv 1; *Ant. and Cleo.* v 2
That's most certain *Tempest* iii 2; *Hamlet* v 2; *Lear* i 1
'Tis most certain *Mer. Wives* iii 3; *Ant. and Cleo.* v 2; *Pericles* v 3
Certain aim. A certain aim he took At a fair vestal throned by the west *M. N. Dream* ii 1 157
Certain condolements. There are certain condolements . *Pericles* ii 1 156
Certain convocation. A certain convocation of politic worms are e'en at him . . . . *Hamlet* iv 3 21
Certain course. You shall run a certain course . . . *Lear* i 2 89
Certain courtier. I did dislike the cut of a certain courtier's beard *As Y. Like It* v 4 73
Certain death. To eject him hence Were but one danger, and to keep him here Our certain death . . . . *Coriolanus* iii 1 289
Certain dregs of conscience are yet within me . . *Richard III.* i 4 124
Certain drops. And given up, For certain drops of salt, your city Rome *Coriolanus* v 6 93
Certain ducats. Sent my peasant home For certain ducats *Com. of Errors* v 1 232
Certain dues. My lord, here is a note of certain dues . *T. of Athens* ii 2 16
Certain dukedoms. His true titles to some certain dukedoms *Hen. V.* i 1 87
Your highness, lately sending into France, Did claim some certain dukedoms . . . . i 2 247
Certain edicts. And now, forsooth, takes on him to reform Some certain edicts . . . . *1 Hen. IV.* iv 3 79
Certain falling. The art o' the court, As hard to leave as keep; whose top to climb Is certain falling . . . . *Cymbeline* iii 3 48
Certain father. As a certain father saith . . *L. L. Lost* iv 2 153
Certain fathoms. I'll break my staff, Bury it certain fathoms in the earth *Tempest* v 1 55
Certain French. Where Charles the Great, having subdued the Saxons, There left behind and settled certain French . . . *Hen. V.* i 2 47
Certain friends that are both his and mine . . . *Macbeth* iii 1 121
Certain half-caps and cold-moving nods . . *T. of Athens* ii 2 221
Certain horse Of my cousin Vernon's are not yet come up *1 Hen. IV.* iv 3 19
Certain hours. Ere I could tell him How I would think on him at certain hours . . . . *Cymbeline* i 3 27
Certain instance. I have received A certain instance that Glendower is dead . . . . *2 Hen. IV.* iii 1 103
Certain issue strokes must arbitrate . . . . *Macbeth* v 4 20
Certain jewels. This letter, and some certain jewels, Lay with you in your coffer . . . . *Pericles* iii 4 1
Certain king. Until our fears, resolved, Be by some certain king purged and deposed . . . . *K. John* ii 1 372
Certain knight. Where learned you that oath, fool?—Of a certain knight *As Y. Like It* i 2 66
Certain knowledge. But for the certain knowledge of that truth I put you o'er to heaven and to my mother . . . *K. John* i 1 61
I constantly do think—Or rather, call my thought a certain knowledge *Troi. and Cres.* iv 1 41
Certain ladies most desirous of admittance . . *T. of Athens* i 2 121
Certain life. No certain life achieved by others' death *K. John* iv 2 105
Certain loathing. More than a lodged hate and a certain loathing *Mer. of Venice* iv 1 60
Certain lord. A certain lord, neat, and trimly dress'd . *1 Hen. IV.* i 3 33
Certain men. A hue and cry Hath follow'd certain men unto this house ii 4 557
Certain merchants. I am invited, sir, to certain merchants *C. of Errors* i 2 24

Certain money. We wait for certain money here *T. of Athens* iii 4 46
Certain news. I bring you certain news from Shrewsbury *2 Hen. IV.* i 1 12
Certain nobles of the senate Newly alighted *T. of Athens* i 2 180
Certain notice. I have no certain notice *2 Hen. IV.* i 3 85
Certain number. A certain number, Though thanks to all, must I select from all *Coriolanus* i 6 80
Certain ones. Nay, not sure, in a thing falsing.—Certain ones then *Com. of Errors* ii 2 96
Certain players We o'er-raught on the way *Hamlet* iii 1 16
Certain princess. In your tears There is no certain princess that appears *L. L. Lost* iv 3 156
Certain pupil. I do dine to-day at the father's of a certain pupil of mine iv 2 159
Certain queen. Apollodorus carried— No more of that: he did so.— What, I pray you?—A certain queen to Cæsar in a mattress *Ant. and Cleo.* ii 6 71
Certain question. Stubbornly he did repugn the truth About a certain question in the law *1 Hen. VI.* ii 4 95
Certain ribbons. It will also be the bondage of certain ribbons and gloves *W. Tale* iv 4 236
Certain right. Yield Thy crazed title to my certain right *M. N. Dream* i 1 92
Certain scales. They take the flow o' the Nile By certain scales i' the pyramid *Ant. and Cleo.* ii 7 21
Certain shot. Nor never welcome to a place till some certain shot be paid *T. G. of Ver.* ii 5 6
Certain snatch. Then, it seems, some certain snatch or so Would serve your turns *T. Andron.* ii 1 95
Certain speeches utter'd By the Bishop of Bayonne *Hen. VIII.* ii 4 171
Certain stars shot madly from their spheres *M. N. Dream* ii 1 153
Certain stuff. I, dreading that her purpose Was of more danger, did compound for her A certain stuff *Cymbeline* v 5 255
Certain sums. I did send to you For certain sums of gold *J. Cæsar* iv 3 70
Certain term. I am thy father's spirit, Doom'd for a certain term to walk the night *Hamlet* i 5 10
Certain text. What must be shall be.—That's a certain text *R. and J.* iv 1 21
Certain tidings. Upon certain tidings now arrived *Othello* ii 2 2
Certain treason. What present hast thou there?—Some certain treason *L. L. Lost* iv 3 190
Certain vails. There are certain condolements, certain vails *Pericles* ii 1 157
Certain Venetians. I was the other day talking on the sea-bank with certain Venetians *Othello* iv 1 138
Certain wands. The skilful shepherd peel'd me certain wands *Mer. of Venice* i 3 85
Certain word. I'll send him certain word of my success *Meas. for Meas.* i 4 89
For certain words he spake against your grace v 1 129
'Twould prove the verity of certain words Spoke by a holy monk *Hen. VIII.* i 2 159
Certainer. Another Hero!—Nothing certainer *Much Ado* v 4 62
Certainly. No wonder, sir; But certainly a maid *Tempest* i 2 428
None but mine own people.—Indeed!—No, certainly *Mer. Wives* iv 2 16
Certainly, while she is here, a man may live as quiet in hell *Much Ado* ii 1 265
Certainly it were not good She knew his love, lest she make sport at it iii 1 57
Certainly my conscience will serve me *Mer. of Venice* ii 2 1
Certainly the Jew is the very devil incarnal ii 2 28
But Antonio is certainly undone.—Nay, that's true iii 1 129
Certainly, there is no truth in him.—Do you think so? *As Y. Like It* iii 4 22
Certainly a woman's thought runs before her actions iv 1 140
You are certainly a gentleman, thereto Clerk-like experienced *W. Tale* i 2 391
He was certainly whipped out of the court iv 3 94
The king is certainly possess'd Of all our purposes *1 Hen. IV.* iv 1 40
Certainly she did you wrong; for you were troth-plight to her *Hen. V.* ii 1 20
Certainly, aunchient, it is not a thing to rejoice at iii 6 55
Certainly thou art so near the gulf, Thou needs must be englutted iv 3 82
Certainly, and out of doubt and out of question too, and ambiguities v 1 47
And therefore are we certainly resolved To draw conditions *1 Hen. VI.* v 1 37
Certainly The cardinal is the end of this *Hen. VIII.* ii 1 39
We'll hear you sing, certainly *Troi. and Cres.* iii 1 66
Certainly He flouted us downright *Coriolanus* ii 3 167
Our sister's man is certainly miscarried *Lear* v 1 5
He went hence but now, And certainly in strange unquietness *Othello* iii 4 133
Certainly, I have heard the Ptolemies' pyramises are very goodly things *Ant. and Cleo.* ii 7 39
This chanced to-night.—Most likely, sir.—Nay, certainly *Pericles* iii 2 78
Certainties. He is furnish'd with no certainties More than he haply may retail from me *2 Hen. IV.* i 1 31
O, doubt not that; I speak from certainties *Coriolanus* i 2 31
For certainties Either are past remedies, or, timely knowing, The remedy then born *Cymbeline* i 6 96
Certainty. Not a resemblance, but a certainty *Meas. for Meas.* iv 2 203
Who are you? Tell me, for more certainty, Albeit I'll swear that I do know your tongue *Mer. of Venice* ii 6 26
Nay, 'tis most credible; we here receive it A certainty *All's Well* i 2 5
Upon thy certainty and confidence What darest thou venture? ii 1 172
I will presently pen down my dilemmas, encourage myself in my certainty iii 6 81
Many other evidences proclaim her with all certainty *W. Tale* v 2 42
If you desire to know the certainty Of your dear father's death *Hamlet* iv 5 140
Find in my exile the want of breeding, The certainty of this hard life *Cymbeline* iv 4 27
Certes. For, certes, these are people of the island *Tempest* iii 3 30
Did not her kitchen-maid rail, taunt and scorn me?—Certes, she did *Com. of Errors* iv 4 78
And, certes, the text most infallibly concludes it *L. L. Lost* iv 2 169
One, certes, that promises no element In such a business *Hen. VIII.* i 1 48
'Certes,' says he, 'I have already chose my officer' *Othello* i 1 16
Certificate. Why, this is a certificate *2 Hen. IV.* ii 2 132
Certified. Antonio certified the duke *Mer. of Venice* ii 8 10
What infamy will there arise, When foreign princes shall be certified! *1 Hen. VI.* iv 1 144
Certify. For that she's in a wrong belief, I go to certify her ii 3 32
Cesario. If the duke continue these favours towards you, Cesario, you are like to be much advanced *T. Night* i 4 2
Who saw Cesario, ho?—On your attendance, my lord; here i 4 10
Cesario, Thou know'st no less but all i 4 12
Now, good Cesario, but that piece of song, That old and antique song we heard last night ii 4 2
Mark it, Cesario, it is old and plain ii 4 44
Once more, Cesario, Get thee to yond same sovereign cruelty ii 4 82
What is your name?—Cesario is your servant's name iii 1 108
Cesario, by the roses of the spring, By maidhood, honour, truth and every thing, I love thee so iii 1 161
Cesario. Your name is not Master Cesario; nor this is not my nose neither *T. Night* iv 1 8
Out of my sight! Be not offended, dear Cesario iv 1 54
Cesario, you do not keep promise with me v 1 106
What do you say, Cesario? Good my lord,— My lord would speak; my duty hushes me v 1 109
Where goes Cesario?—After him I love v 1 137
Cesario, husband, stay.—Husband!—Ay, husband: can he that deny? v 1 146
Fear not, Cesario; take thy fortunes up; Be that thou know'st thou art v 1 151
Who has done this, Sir Andrew?—The count's gentleman, one Cesario v 1 183
He's the very devil incardinate.—My gentleman, Cesario? v 1 186
Cesario, come; For so you shall be, while you are a man v 1 394
Cess. Poor jade, is wrung in the withers out of all cess *1 Hen. IV.* ii 1 8
Cesse. Or, ere they meet, in me, O nature, cesse! *All's Well* v 3 72
Chace. All the courts of France will be disturb'd With chaces *Hen. V.* i 2 266
Chafe. He will chafe at the doctor's marrying my daughter *Mer. Wives* v 3 9
I chafe you, if I tarry: let me go *T. of Shrew* ii 1 243
I would you did but see how it chafes, how it rages! *W. Tale* iii 3 89
Fain would I go to chafe his paly lips With twenty thousand kisses *2 Hen. VI.* iii 2 141
Do not chafe thee, cousin *Troi. and Cres.* iv 5 260
And like the current flies Each bound it chafes *T. of Athens* i 1 25
Be lion-mettled, proud; and take no care Who chafes, who frets *Macbeth* iv 1 91
The murmuring surge, That on the unnumber'd idle pebbles chafes *Lear* iv 6 21
How this Herculean Roman does become The carriage of his chafe *Ant. and Cleo.* i 3 85
Chafed. Besides, her intercession chafed him so *T. G. of Ver.* iii 1 233
Rage like an angry boar chafed with sweat *T. of Shrew* i 2 203
Thou mayst hold a serpent by the tongue, A chafed lion by the mortal paw, A fasting tiger safer by the tooth *K. John* iii 1 259
And Warwick rages like a chafed bull *3 Hen. VI.* ii 5 126
What, are you chafed? Ask God for temperance *Hen. VIII.* i 1 123
So looks the chafed lion Upon the daring huntsman that has gall'd him; Then makes him nothing iii 2 206
The princes orgulous, their high blood chafed *Troi. and Cres.* Prol. 2
And Helen so blushed, and Paris so chafed i 2 181
Being once chafed, he cannot Be rein'd again to temperance *Coriol.* iii 3 27
The chafed boar, the mountain lioness, The ocean swells not so as Aaron storms *T. Andron.* iv 2 138
Chaff. His reasons are as two grains of wheat hid in two bushels of chaff: you shall seek all day ere you find them *Mer. of Venice* i 1 116
Pick'd from the chaff and ruin of the times To be new-varnish'd ii 9 48
And scared my choughs from the chaff *W. Tale* iv 4 630
Even our corn shall seem as light as chaff *2 Hen. IV.* iv 1 195
Where my chaff And corn shall fly asunder *Hen. VIII.* v 1 110
Chaff and bran! porridge after meat! *Troi. and Cres.* i 2 262
He could not stay to pick them in a pile Of noisome musty chaff *Coriol.* v 1 26
We are the grains: You are the musty chaff v 1 31
Chaffless. The gods made you, Unlike all others, chaffless *Cymbeline* i 6 178
Chafing. Once, upon a raw and gusty day, The troubled Tiber chafing with her shores *J. Cæsar* i 2 101
Chain. Several noises Of roaring, shrieking, howling, jingling chains, And moe diversity of sounds *Tempest* v 1 233
Were't not affection chains thy tender days *T. G. of Ver.* i 1 3
I have seen Sackerson loose twenty times, and have taken him by the chain *Mer. Wives* i 1 308
And makes milch-kine yield blood and shakes a chain iv 4 33
To know, sir, whether one Nym, sir, that beguiled him of a chain, had the chain or no iv 5 34
The very same man that beguiled Master Slender of his chain cozened him of it iv 5 38
I'll provide you a chain; and I'll do what I can to get you a pair of horns v 1 6
He promised me a chain; Would that alone, alone he would detain! *Com. of Errors* ii 1 106
Get you home And fetch the chain iii 1 115
That chain will I bestow—Be it for nothing but to spite my wife iii 1 117
Here is the chain. I thought to have ta'en you at the Porpentine: The chain unfinish'd made me stay thus long iii 2 171
No man is so vain That would refuse so fair an offer'd chain iii 2 186
In the instant that I met with you He had of me a chain iv 1 10
Here's the note How much your chain weighs to the utmost carat iv 1 28
A chain, a chain! Do you not hear it ring?—What, the chain?—No, no, the bell iv 2 51
Is that the chain you promised me to-day? iv 3 47
Give me the ring of mine you had at dinner, Or, for my diamond, the chain you promised iv 3 70
But she, more covetous, would have a chain iv 3 75
If you give it her, The devil will shake her chain and fright us with it iv 3 77
How grows it due?—Due for a chain your husband had of him iv 4 138
He did bespeak a chain for me, but had it not iv 4 139
The ring I saw upon his finger now—Straight after did I meet him with a chain iv 4 143
He had the chain of me, Though most dishonestly he doth deny it v 1 2
That self chain about his neck Which he forswore most monstrously to have v 1 10
So to deny This chain which now you wear so openly v 1 17
This chain you had of me; can you deny it?—I think I had v 1 22
Parted with me to go fetch a chain, Promising to bring it to the Porpentine v 1 221
There did this perjured goldsmith swear me down That I this day of him received the chain v 1 228
But had he such a chain of thee or no?—He had v 1 256
When he ran in here, These people saw the chain about his neck v 1 258
I will be sworn these ears of mine Heard you confess you had the chain v 1 260
I never saw the chain, so help me Heaven! And this is false v 1 267
That is the chain, sir, which you had of me.—I think it be, sir v 1 377
And you, sir, for this chain arrested me.—I think I did, sir v 1 380
What fashion will you wear the garland of? about your neck, like an usurer's chain? *Much Ado* ii 1 197
Dost thou not wish in heart The chain were longer and the letter short? *L. L. Lost* v 2 56
His speech was like a tangled chain; nothing impaired, but all disordered *M. N. Dream* v 1 125
And a chain, that you once wore, about his neck *As Y. Like It* iii 2 191
Go, sir, rub your chain with crums *T. Night* ii 3 129
I could have filed keys off that hung in chains *W. Tale* iv 4 624
Never did captive with a freer heart Cast off his chains of bondage *Richard II.* i 3 89
Yea, joy, our chains and our jewels *2 Hen. IV.* ii 4 52

Chain. I will chain these legs and arms of thine — *1 Hen. VI.* ii 3 39
That with the very shaking of their chains They may astonish these fell-lurking curs — *2 Hen. VI.* v 1 145
We'll bait thy bears to death, And manacle the bear-ward in their chains — v 1 149
If I digg'd up thy forefathers' graves And hung their rotten coffins up in chains, It could not slake mine ire — *3 Hen. VI.* i 3 28
I do bend my knee with thine; And in this vow do chain my soul to thine! — ii 3 34
The two brave bears, Warwick and Montague, That in their chains fetter'd the kingly lion — v 7 11
A thrifty shoeing-horn in a chain, hanging at his brother's leg *Tr. and Cr.* v 1 62
Provide more piercing statutes daily, to chain up and restrain the poor — *Coriolanus* i 1 87
Hast prisoner held, fetter'd in amorous chains — *T. Andron.* ii 1 15
Or bid me lurk Where serpents are; chain me with roaring bears — *Rom. and Jul.* iv 1 80
Thou hast enchanted her; For I'll refer me to all things of sense, If she in chains of magic were not bound — *Othello* i 2 65
O thou day o' the world, Chain mine arm'd neck! — *Ant. and Cleo.* iv 8 14
Rather make My country's high pyramides my gibbet, And hang me up in chains! — v 2 62

Chained. When I shall think, or Phœbus' steeds are founder'd, Or Night kept chain'd below — *Tempest* iv 1 31
Belike you thought our love would last too long, If it were chain'd together, and therefore came not — *Com. of Errors* iv 1 26
Old Nevil's crest, The rampant bear chain'd to the ragged staff *2 Hen. VI.* v 1 203

Chair. The several chairs of order look you scour — *Mer. Wives* v 5 65
He, sir, sitting, as I say, in a lower chair, sir — *Meas. for Meas.* ii 1 132
It is like a barber's chair that fits all buttocks — *All's Well* ii 2 17
Bind the boy which you shall find with me Fast to the chair — *K. John* iv 1 5
Let them lay by their helmets and their spears, And both return back to their chairs again — *Richard II.* i 3 120
This chair shall be my state, this dagger my sceptre — *1 Hen. IV.* ii 4 415
Dost thou so hunger for mine empty chair? — *2 Hen. IV.* iv 5 95
Break a lance, And run a tilt at death within a chair — *1 Hen. VI.* iii 2 51
When sapless age and weak unable limbs Should bring thy father to his drooping chair — iv 5 5
In that chair where kings and queens are crown'd — *2 Hen. VI.* i 2 38
Look where the sturdy rebel sits, Even in the chair of state — *3 Hen. VI.* i 1 51
And over the chair of state, where now he sits, Write up his title with usurping blood — i 1 168
This is he that took King Henry's chair, And this is he was his adopted heir — i 4 97
His name that valiant duke hath left with thee; His dukedom and his chair with me is left — ii 1 90
For chair and dukedom, throne and kingdom say; Either that is thine, or else thou wert not his — ii 1 93
And thou this day hadst kept thy chair in peace — ii 6 20
Resign thy chair, and where I stand kneel thou — v 5 19
Is the chair empty? is the sword unsway'd? Is the king dead? *Rich. III.* iv 4 470
A base foul stone, made precious by the foil Of England's chair — v 3 251
Sat down To rest awhile, some half an hour or so, In a rich chair of state — *Hen. VIII.* iv 1 67
Reach a chair: So; now, methinks, I feel a little ease — iv 2 3
I'm very sorry To sit here at this present, and behold That chair stand empty — v 3 10
The honour'd gods Keep Rome in safety, and the chairs of justice Supplied with worthy men! — *Coriolanus* iii 3 34
Hath not a tomb so evident as a chair To extol what it hath done — iv 7 52
Breathless wrong Shall sit and pant in your great chairs of ease — *T. of Athens* v 4 11
Look you lay it in the prætor's chair, Where Brutus may but find it — *J. Cæsar* i 3 143
Let us hear Mark Antony.—Let him go up into the public chair — iii 2 68
To this chair bind him. Villain, thou shalt find — *Lear* iii 7 34
Fellows, hold the chair. Upon these eyes of thine I'll set my foot — iii 7 67
O, for a chair, To bear him easily hence! — *Othello* v 1 82
How do you, Cassio? O, a chair, a chair! — v 1 96
Cleopatra and himself in chairs of gold Were publicly enthroned — *Ant. and Cleo.* iii 6 4

Chair-days. In thy reverence and thy chair-days — *2 Hen. VI.* v 2 48

Chalice. Take away these chalices. Go brew me a pottle of sack — *Mer. Wives* iii 5 29
Commends the ingredients of our poison'd chalice To our own lips *Macbeth* i 7 11
And that he calls for drink, I'll have prepared him A chalice for the nonce — *Hamlet* iv 7 161

Chaliced. His steeds to water at those springs On chaliced flowers that lies — *Cymbeline* ii 3 25

Chalk. Not propp'd by ancestry, whose grace Chalks successors their way — *Hen. VIII.* i 1 60

Chalked. It is you that have chalk'd forth the way — *Tempest* v 1 203

Chalky. Where England?—I looked for the chalky cliffs, but I could find no whiteness in them — *Com. of Errors* iii 2 129
As far as I could ken thy chalky cliffs — *2 Hen. VI.* iii 2 101
From the dread summit of this chalky bourn — *Lear* iv 6 57

Challenge. I combat challenge of this latten bilbo — *Mer. Wives* i 1 165
It is a shallenge: I will cut his troat in de park — i 4 114
My uncle's fool, reading the challenge, subscribed for Cupid — *Much Ado* i 1 41
Enough, I am engaged; I will challenge him — iv 1 335
With grey hairs and bruise of many days, Do challenge thee to trial of a man — v 1 66
God bless me from a challenge! — v 1 145
I must tell thee plainly, Claudio undergoes my challenge — v 2 57
She's too hard for you at pricks, sir: challenge her to bowl — *L. L. Lost* iv 1 140
When she shall challenge this, you will reject her — v 2 438
By the north pole, I do challenge thee — v 2 699
You may not deny it: Pompey hath made the challenge — v 2 713
Come challenge me, challenge me by these deserts — v 2 815
That is honour's scorn, Which challenges itself as honour's born — *All's Well* ii 3 141
To challenge him the field, and then to break promise with him and make a fool of him — *T. Night* ii 3 136
I'll write thee a challenge — ii 3 140
Challenge me the count's youth to fight with him — iii 2 36
Will either of you bear me a challenge to him? — iii 2 43
Here's the challenge, read it: I warrant there's vinegar and pepper in't iii 4 157
But thou liest in thy throat; that is not the matter I challenge thee for iii 4 173
I will deliver his challenge by word of mouth — iii 4 209
I will meditate the while upon some horrid message for a challenge — iii 4 220
I am a subject, And I challenge law — *Richard II.* ii 3 134
I never in my life Did hear a challenge urged more modestly — *1 Hen. IV.* v 2 53
If ever I live to see it, I will challenge it — *Hen. V.* iv 1 233
Who, if alive and ever dare to challenge this glove, I have sworn to take him a box o' th' ear — iv 7 132
If any man challenge this, he is a friend to Alençon — iv 7 163
I know the glove is a glove.—I know this; and thus I challenge it — iv 8 9
Wear it for an honour in thy cap Till I do challenge it — iv 8 64
Accept the title thou usurp'st, Of benefit proceeding from our king And not of any challenge of desert — *1 Hen. VI.* v 4 153
All her perfections challenge sovereignty — *3 Hen. VI.* iii 2 86
Subjects may challenge nothing of their sovereigns — iv 6 6
I challenge nothing but my dukedom — iv 7 23
By this I challenge him to single fight — iv 7 75
No, Exeter, these graces challenge grace — iv 8 48
And make my challenge You shall not be my judge — *Hen. VIII.* ii 4 77
And dare avow her beauty and her worth In other arms than hers,—to him this challenge — *Troi. and Cres.* i 3 272
This challenge that the gallant Hector sends — i 3 321
A roisting challenge sent amongst The dull and factious nobles of the Greeks — ii 2 208
Bring word if Hector will to-morrow Be answer'd in his challenge — iii 3 35
To-morrow will I wear it on my helm, And grieve his spirit that dares not challenge it — v 2 94
A challenge, on my life.—Romeo will answer it — *Rom. and Jul.* ii 4 8
All the world to nothing, That he dares ne'er come back to challenge you iii 5 216
Who may I rather challenge for unkindness Than pity for mischance! — *Macbeth* iii 4 42
That we our largest bounty may extend Where nature doth with merit challenge — *Lear* i 1 54
Read thou this challenge; mark but the penning of it — iv 6 141
So much I challenge that I may profess Due to the Moor my lord *Othello* i 3 188
He is a good one, and his worthiness Does challenge much respect — ii 1 213
I have many other ways to die; meantime Laugh at his challenge — *Ant. and Cleo.* iv 1 6

Challenged. He set up his bills here in Messina and challenged Cupid at the flight — *Much Ado* i 1 40
Subscribed for Cupid, and challenged him at the bird-bolt — i 1 42
For the love of Beatrice.—And hath challenged thee.—Most sincerely — v 1 200
Young man, have you challenged Charles the wrestler? — *As Y. L. It* i 2 178
I'ld have seen him damned ere I'ld have challenged him — *T. Night* iii 4 313
Shall your city call us lord, In that behalf which we have challenged it? — *K. John* ii 1 264
And, nephew, challenged you to single fight — *1 Hen. IV.* v 2 47
When these suns—For so they phrase 'em—by their heralds challenged The noble spirits to arms — *Hen. VIII.* i 1 34
To walk alone, Dishonour'd thus, and challenged of wrongs — *T. Andron.* i 1 340
Had you not been their father, these white flakes Had challenged pity — *Lear* iv 7 31

Challenger. In pity of the challenger's youth I would fain dissuade him — *As Y. Like It* i 2 170
Monsieur the challenger, the princesses call for you — i 2 175
He is the general challenger — i 2 180
'Tis a boisterous and a cruel style, A style for challengers — iv 3 32
And with that He would unhorse the lustiest challenger — *Richard II.* v 3 19
Stood challenger on mount of all the age For her perfections — *Hamlet* iv 7 28

Cham. Fetch you a hair off the great Cham's beard — *Much Ado* ii 1 277

Chamber. Go with me to my chamber, In these affairs to aid me with thy counsel — *T. G. of Ver.* ii 4 184
Go with me to my chamber, To take a note of what I stand in need of — ii 7 83
Her chamber is aloft, far from the ground — iii 1 114
Vouchsafe me yet your picture for my love, The picture that is hanging in your chamber — iv 2 122
But all the chamber smelt him — iv 4 21
He makes me no more ado, but whips me out of the chamber — iv 4 31
Give her that ring and therewithal This letter. That's her chamber — iv 4 91
Your message done, hie home unto my chamber — iv 4 93
One Julia, that his changing thoughts forget, Would better fit his chamber than this shadow — iv 4 125
I would I might never come in mine own great chamber again else — *Mer. Wives* i 1 157
Here be my keys: ascend my chambers; search, seek, find out — iii 3 173
If there be any pody in the house, and in the chambers — iii 3 225
My husband will come into the chamber — iv 2 176
There's his chamber, his house, his castle — iv 5 6
There's an old woman, a fat woman, gone up into his chamber — iv 5 13
My chambers are honourable: fie! privacy? fie! — iv 5 23
Let me speak with you in your chamber — iv 5 126
Come up into my chamber — iv 5 131
You gentlewomen all, Withdraw into a chamber by yourselves *Much Ado* v 4 11
Two hard things; that is, to bring the moonlight into a chamber — *M. N. Dream* iii 1 50
We must have a wall in the great chamber — iii 1 64
And each several chamber bless, Through this palace, with sweet peace v 1 424
The ladies, her attendants of her chamber, Saw her a-bed *As Y. Like It* ii 2 5
Carry him gently to my fairest chamber And hang it round with all my wanton pictures — *T. of Shrew* Ind. 1 46
Conduct him to the drunkard's chamber — Ind. 1 107
For though you lay here in this goodly chamber, Yet would you say ye were beaten out of door — Ind. 2 86
Did ever Dian so become a grove As Kate this chamber? — ii 1 261
Go to my chamber; put on clothes of mine — iii 2 115
Come, I will bring thee to thy bridal chamber — iv 1 181
Where is he?—In her chamber, making a sermon of continency to her — iv 1 185
Go with me to my chamber, and advise me — *All's Well* ii 3 311
And water once a day her chamber round With eye-offending brine *T. Night* i 1 29
Come by and by to my chamber — iv 2 77
On your allegiance, Out of the chamber with her! — *W. Tale* ii 3 122
Bugle bracelet, necklace amber, Perfume for a lady's chamber — iv 4 225
We were all commanded out of the chamber — v 2 6
Shall that victorious hand be feebled here, That in your chambers gave you chastisement? — *K. John* v 2 147
To venture upon the charged chambers bravely — *2 Hen. IV.* ii 4 57
In the perfumed chambers of the great — iii 1 12
Bear me hence Into some other chamber — iv 4 132
He came not through the chamber where we stay'd — iv 5 57
Depart the chamber, leave us here alone — iv 5 91
But bear me to that chamber; there I'll lie — iv 5 240
We sent unto the Temple, unto his chamber — *1 Hen. VI.* ii 5 19
Enter his chamber, view his breathless corpse — *2 Hen. VI.* iii 2 132

Chamber. He capers nimbly in a lady's chamber *Richard III.* i 1 12
Ill rest betide the chamber where thou liest! i 2 112
Welcome, sweet prince, to London, to your chamber iii 1 1
An untimely ague Stay'd me a prisoner in my chamber *Hen. VIII.* i 1 5
All the whole time I was my chamber's prisoner i 1 13
Is the banquet ready I' the privy chamber? i 4 99
There's fresher air, my lord, In the next chamber i 4 102
May it please you, noble madam, to withdraw Into your private chamber iii 1 28
Whereupon I will show you a chamber with a bed *Troi. and Cres.* iii 2 216
Cupid grant all tongue-tied maidens here Bed, chamber, Pandar to provide this gear! iii 2 220
My lord, come you again into my chamber iv 2 37
Away from light steals home my heavy son, And private in his chamber pens himself *Rom. and Jul.* i 1 144
You are looked for and called for, asked for and sought for, in the great chamber i 5 14
Hie to your chamber: I'll find Romeo To comfort you iii 2 138
Go, get thee to thy love, as was decreed, Ascend her chamber iii 3 147
Light to my chamber, ho! Afore me! iii 4 33
Your lady mother is coming to your chamber iii 5 39
Let not thy nurse lie with thee in thy chamber iv 1 92
He's much out of health, and keeps his chamber *T. of Athens* iii 4 73
Many do keep their chambers are not sick iii 4 74
He has almost supp'd: why have you left the chamber? *Macbeth* i 7 29
When we have mark'd with blood those sleepy two Of his own chamber i 7 76
Hark! Who lies i' the second chamber?—Donalbain ii 2 20
I hear a knocking At the south entry: retire we to our chamber ii 2 66
Approach the chamber, and destroy your sight With a new Gorgon ii 3 76
Those of his chamber, as it seem'd, had done't ii 3 106
I hope the days are near at hand That chambers will be safe v 4 2
But, good Laertes, Will you do this, keep close within your chamber *Hamlet* iv 7 130
Now get you to my lady's chamber, and tell her, let her paint an inch thick v 1 213
Straight satisfy yourself: If she be in her chamber or your house *Othello* i 1 139
I found it in my chamber. I like the work well iii 4 188
Now he tells how she plucked him to my chamber iv 1 146
A likely piece of work, that you should find it in your chamber! iv 1 157
I have another weapon in this chamber; It is a sword of Spain v 2 252
How came you, Cassio, by that handkerchief That was my wife's?—I found it in my chamber v 2 320
Lead me to my chamber *Ant. and Cleo.* ii 5 119
Come, I'll to my chamber *Cymbeline* i 2 36
'Tis her breathing that Perfumes the chamber thus ii 2 19
But my design, To note the chamber: I will write all down ii 2 24
Your lady's person: is she ready?—Ay, To keep her chamber ii 3 87
The chimney Is south the chamber, and the chimney-piece Chaste Dian ii 4 81
The roof o' the chamber With golden cherubins is fretted ii 4 87
The description Of what is in her chamber nothing saves The wager ii 4 94
Her chambers are all lock'd; and there's no answer That will be given iii 5 43
Bring this apparel to my chamber; that is the second thing iii 5 156
It is not vain-glory for a man and his glass to confer in his own chamber iv 1 9
You are of our chamber, and our mind partakes Her private actions to your secrecy *Pericles* i 1 152
She hath so strictly tied Her to her chamber ii 5 9
Lend me your hands; to the next chamber bear her iii 2 108
Chamber-council. I have trusted thee, Camillo, With all the nearest things to my heart, as well My chamber-councils *W. Tale* i 2 237
Chamber-door. Like a base pandar, hold the chamber-door *Hen. V.* iv 5 14
'Twas time, I trow, to wake and leave our beds, Hearing alarums at our chamber-doors *1 Hen. VI.* ii 1 42
Wait like a lousy footboy At chamber-door *Hen. VIII.* v 3 140
Then up he rose, and donn'd his clothes, And dupp'd the chamber-door *Hamlet* iv 5 53
Bid them come forth and hear me, Or at their chamber-door I'll beat the drum Till it cry sleep to death *Lear* ii 4 119
Chambered. Even in the best blood chamber'd in his bosom *Richard II.* i 1 149
Chamberer. And have not those soft parts of conversation That chamberers have *Othello* iii 3 265
Chamber-hanging. Averring notes Of chamber-hanging, pictures *Cymb.* v 5 204
Chamberlain. What, ho! chamberlain!—At hand, quoth pick-purse.—That's even as fair as—at hand, quoth the chamberlain *1 Hen. IV.* ii 1 52
Humbly complaining to her deity Got my lord chamberlain his liberty *Richard III.* i 1 77
Good time of day unto my gracious lord!—As much unto my good lord chamberlain! i 1 123
What, talking with a priest, lord chamberlain? iii 2 114
Good lord chamberlain, Go, give 'em welcome *Hen. VIII.* i 4 56
Say, lord chamberlain, They have done my poor house grace i 4 72
My lord chamberlain, Prithee, come hither: what fair lady's that? i 4 90
What, think'st That the bleak air, thy boisterous chamberlain, Will put thy shirt on warm? *T. of Athens* iv 3 222
His two chamberlains Will I with wine and wassail so convince *Macbeth* i 7 63
Chamber-lie. Your chamber-lie breeds fleas like a loach *1 Hen. IV.* ii 1 23
Chamber-maid. My niece's chambermaid *T. Night* i 3 54
Here will I remain With worms that are thy chamber-maids *Rom. and Jul.* v 3 109
Who since possesses chambermaids and waiting-women *Lear* iv 1 65
Chamber-pot. Roaring for a chamber-pot *Coriolanus* ii 1 85
Chamber-window. This night he meaneth with a corded ladder To climb celestial Silvia's chamber-window *T. G. of Ver.* ii 6 34
They have devised a mean How he her chamber-window will ascend iii 1 39
Visit by night your lady's chamber-window With some sweet concert iii 2 83
Appoint her to look out at her lady's chamber window *Much Ado* ii 2 18
In my chamber-window lies a book ii 3 3
Get us some excellent music; for to-morrow night we would have it at the Lady Hero's chamber-window ii 3 89
You shall see her chamber-window entered, even the night before her wedding-day iii 2 116
She leans me out at her mistress' chamber-window iii 3 156
This grieved count Did see her, hear her, at that hour last night Talk with a ruffian at her chamber-window iv 1 92
Leave a casement of the great chamber window, where we play, open *M. N. Dream* iii 1 58
When midnight comes, knock at my chamber-window *All's Well* iv 2 54
Chameleon. Though the chameleon Love can feed on the air *T. G. of Ver.* ii 1 178
Do you change colour?—Give him leave, madam; he is a kind of chameleon ii 4 26
I can add colours to the chameleon, Change shapes with Proteus *3 Hen. VI.* iii 2 191
Of the chameleon's dish: I eat the air, promise-crammed *Hamlet* iii 2 98
Champ. Say his name, good friend.—Richard du Champ *Cymbeline* iv 2 377
Champagne. Guienne, Champagne, Rheims, Orleans *1 Hen. VI.* i 1 60
Champain. Daylight and champain discovers not more *T. Night* ii 5 174
With shadowy forests and with champains rich'd *Lear* i 1 65
Champion. Thus your own proper wisdom Brings in the champion Honour on my part *All's Well* iv 2 50
Thou Fortune's champion that dost never fight But when her humourous ladyship is by To teach thee safety! *K. John* iii 1 118
Therefore to arms! be champion of our church iii 1 255
To God, the widow's champion and defence *Richard II.* i 2 43
The champions are prepared i 3 5
Demand of yonder champion The cause of his arrival here in arms i 3 7
His new-come champion, virtuous Joan of Arc *1 Hen. VI.* ii 2 20
A stouter champion never handled sword iii 4 19
His champions are the prophets and apostles, His weapons holy saws of sacred writ *2 Hen. VI.* i 3 60
The most complete champion that ever I heard! iv 10 59
And now will I be Edward's champion *3 Hen. VI.* iv 7 68
Three Dukes of Somerset, threefold renown'd For hardy and undoubted champions v 7 6
Rome's best champion, Successful in the battles that he fights *T. Andron.* i 1 65
Rome's readiest champions, repose you here in rest, Secure from wordly chances and mishaps! i 1 151
Come fate into the list, And champion me to the utterance! *Macbeth* iii 1 72
I can produce a champion that will prove What is avouched there *Lear* v 1 43
Like a bold champion, I assume the lists *Pericles* i 1 61
Chance. Bear my lady's train, lest the base earth Should from her vesture chance to steal a kiss *T. G. of Ver.* ii 4 160
There is divinity in odd numbers, either in nativity, chance, or death *Mer. Wives* v 1 4
How chance you went not with Master Slender? v 5 230
It chances The stealth of our most mutual entertainment With character too gross is writ on Juliet *Meas. for Meas.* i 2 157
Not of this country, though my chance is now To use it for my time iii 2 230
Wherein if he chance to fail, he hath sentenced himself iii 2 271
By chance, nothing of what is writ iv 2 218
What now? how chance thou art return'd so soon? *Com. of Errors* i 2 42
I may chance have some odd quirks and remnants of wit broken on me *Much Ado* ii 3 244
An there be any matter of weight chances, call up me iii 3 91
They have writ the style of gods And made a push at chance and sufferance v 1 38
Since you are strangers and come here by chance, We'll not be nice *L. L. Lost* v 2 218
Travelling along this coast, I here am come by chance v 2 557
Why is your cheek so pale? How chance the roses there do fade so fast? *M. N. Dream* i 1 129
How chance Moonshine is gone before Thisbe comes back and finds her lover? v 1 318
You must take your chance *Mer. of Venice* ii 1 38
Come, bring me unto my chance ii 1 43
You that choose not by the view, Chance as fair and choose as true! iii 2 133
If he chance to speak, be ready straight *T. of Shrew* Ind. 1 52
Why, this's a heavy chance 'twixt him and you i 2 46
Here is a gentleman whom by chance I met i 2 182
And if she chance to nod I'll rail and brawl iv 1 209
They may chance to need thee at home; therefore leave us v 1 3
To comfort you with chance *T. Night* i 2 8
Where if it be thy chance to kill me,— Good.—Thou killest me like a rogue iii 4 177
If you shall chance, Camillo, to visit Bohemia *W. Tale* i 1 1
I am question'd by my fears, of what may chance Or breed upon our absence i 2 11
Commend it strangely to some place Where chance may nurse or end it ii 3 183
We profess Ourselves to be the slaves of chance and flies Of every wind iv 4 551
Though I am not naturally honest, I am so sometimes by chance iv 4 733
Brother, take you my land, I'll take my chance *K. John* i 1 151
By chance but not by truth; what though? i 1 169
Those her hairs! Where but by chance a silver drop hath fallen iii 4 63
And so by chance Did grace our hollow parting with a tear *Richard II.* i 4 8
He never did fall off, my sovereign liege, But by the chance of war *1 Hen. IV.* i 3 95
This all-praised knight And your unthought-of Harry chance to meet iii 2 141
And summ'd the account of chance *2 Hen. IV.* i 1 167
It may chance cost some of us our lives, for he will stab ii 1 12
How chances mock, And changes fill the cup of alteration With divers liquors! iii 1 51
A man may prophesy, With a near aim, of the main chance of things As yet not come to life iii 1 83
Against ill chances men are ever merry; But heaviness foreruns the good event iv 2 81
How chance thou art not with the prince thy brother? iv 4 20
What chance is this that suddenly hath cross'd us? *1 Hen. VI.* i 4 72
If it chance the one of us do fail, The other yet may rise against their force ii 1 31
And, now it is my chance to find thee out, Must I behold thy timeless cruel death? v 4 4
Main chance, father, you meant; but I meant Maine *2 Hen. VI.* i 1 212
Camest thou here by chance, Or of devotion, to this holy shrine? ii 1 87
How will the country for these woful chances Misthink the king and not be satisfied! *3 Hen. VI.* ii 5 107
I fear her not, unless she chance to fall iii 2 24
But if you ever chance to have a child, Look in his youth to have him so cut off v 5 65
How chance the prophet could not at that time Have told me, I being by, that I should kill him? *Richard III.* iv 2 103
If I chance to talk a little wild, forgive me *Hen. VIII.* i 4 26
If they shall chance, In charging you with matters, to commit you v 1 145
Now good or bad, 'tis but the chance of war *Troi. and Cres.* Prol. 31
You must stay the cooling too, or you may chance to burn your lips i 1 26
In the reproof of chance Lies the true proof of men i 3 33
How chance my brother Triolus went not? iii 1 151
An act that very chance doth throw upon him iii 3 131
We met by chance; you did not find me here iv 2 73
Injury of chance Puts back leave-taking, justles roughly by All time of pause iv 4 35
If I might in entreaties find success—As seld I have the chance iv 5 150
If we and Caius Marcius chance to meet, 'Tis sworn between us we shall ever strike Till one can do no more *Coriolanus* i 2 34
If you chance to be pinched with the colic, you make faces like mummers ii 1 82

Chance. Enforce the present execution Of what we chance to sentence *Coriolanus* iii 3 22
That common chances common men could bear . . . . iv 1 5
Determine on some course, More than a wild exposure to each chance iv 1 36
By some chance, Some trick not worth an egg, shall grow dear friends iv 4 20
Lest you shall chance to whip your information . . . . iv 6 53
Defect of judgement, To fail in the disposing of those chances Which he was lord of . . . . iv 7 40
His wife is in Corioli and his child Like him by chance . . . . v 3 180
Repose you here in rest, Secure from worldly chances and mishaps! *T. Andron.* i 1 152
And triumphs over chance in honour's bed . . . . . . i 1 178
Though chance of war hath wrought this change of cheer . . . i 1 264
Woe to her chance, and damn'd her loathed choice! . . . iv 2 78
This trick may chance to scathe you, I know what . *Rom. and Jul.* i 5 86
He shall signify from time to time Every good hap to you that chances here . . . . iii 3 171
Well, he may chance to do some good on her . . . . . iv 2 13
Ah, what an unkind hour Is guilty of this lamentable chance! . . v 3 146
Bring us to him, And chance it as it may . . . . *T. of Athens* v 1 129
Know'st thou any harm's intended towards him?—None that I know will be, much that I fear may chance . . . *J. Cæsar* ii 4 32
Stand fast together, lest some friend of Cæsar's Should chance— Talk not of standing . . . . iii 1 88
If chance will have me king, why, chance may crown me *Macbeth* i 3 143
Had I but died an hour before this chance, I had lived a blessed time . ii 3 96
I would set my life on any chance, To mend it, or be rid on't . iii 1 113
And the chance of goodness Be like our warranted quarrel! . . iv 3 136
So, oft it chances in particular men . . . . . . *Hamlet* i 4 23
How chances it they travel? their residence, both in reputation and profit, was better both ways . . . . ii 2 343
If he by chance escape your venom'd stuck, Our purpose may hold there iv 7 162
You that look pale and tremble at this chance . . . . . v 2 345
Thy dowerless daughter, king, thrown to my chance, Is queen of us, of ours, and our fair France . . . . *Lear* i 1 259
How chance the king comes with so small a train? . . . . . ii 4 64
Nay, then, come on, and take the chance of anger . . . . iii 7 79
If you do chance to hear of that blind traitor, Preferment falls on him that cuts him off . . . . iv 5 37
It is a chance which does redeem all sorrows That ever I have felt . v 3 266
Wherein I spake of most disastrous chances, Of moving accidents by flood and field . . . . *Othello* i 3 134
I may chance to see you; for I would very fain speak with you . iv 1 174
Whose solid virtue The shot of accident, nor dart of chance, Could neither graze nor pierce . . . . iv 1 278
In our sports my better cunning faints Under his chance *Ant. and Cleo.* ii 3 35
A more unhappy lady, If this division chance, ne'er stood between, Praying for both parts . . . . iii 4 13
Give up yourself merely to chance and hazard, From firm security . iii 7 48
I'll yet follow The wounded chance of Antony . . . . . iii 10 36
Wisdom and fortune combating together, If that the former dare but what it can, No chance may shake it . . . . iii 13 81
The record of what injuries you did us, Though written in our flesh, we shall remember As things but done by chance . . . . . v 2 120
I shall show the cinders of my spirits Through the ashes of my chance v 2 174
Think what a chance thou changest on, but think Thou hast thy mistress still, to boot, my son . . . . *Cymbeline* i 5 68
That we the horrider may seem to those Which chance to find us . iv 2 332
Wilt take thy chance with me? . . . . iv 2 382
But We grieve at chances here. Away! . . . . iv 3 35
If in your country wars you chance to die, That is my bed too, lads iv 4 51
This was strange chance: A narrow lane, an old man, and two boys v 3 51
So am I, That have this golden chance and know not why . . v 4 132
Consider, sir, the chance of war: the day Was yours by accident . v 5 75
And all the other by-dependencies, From chance to chance . . v 5 391
How chance my daughter is not with you? . . . . *Pericles* iv 1 23
Marina thus the brothel 'scapes, and chances Into an honest house v Gower 1
Chanced. You shall not know by what strange accident I chanced on this letter . . . . *Mer. of Venice* v 1 279
He that but fears the thing he would not know Hath by instinct knowledge from others' eyes That what he fear'd is chanced *2 Hen. IV.* i 1 87
And omit All the occurrences, whatever chanced . . . *Hen. V.* v Prol. 40
And go read with thee Sad stories chanced in the times of old *T. Andron.* iii 2 83
Tell us what hath chanced to-day, That Cæsar looks so sad *J. Cæsar* i 2 216
Post back with speed, and tell him what hath chanced . . . iii 1 287
Bring us word unto Octavius' tent How every thing is chanced . v 4 32
Think upon what hath chanced . . . . *Macbeth* i 3 153
If then they chanced to slack you, We could control them . . *Lear* ii 4 248
This chanced to-night.—Most likely, sir . . . . . *Pericles* iii 2 77
Chancellor. Warwick is chancellor and the lord of Calais *3 Hen. VI.* i 1 238
One Gilbert Peck, his chancellor . . . . . *Hen. VIII.* i 1 219; ii 1 20
Sir Thomas More is chosen Lord chancellor in your place . . iii 2 394
Chandler. The sack that thou hast drunk me would have bought me lights as good cheap at the dearest chandler's in Europe *1 Hen. IV.* iii 3 52
Change. Do you change colour?—Give him leave, madam; he is a kind of chameleon . . . . *T. G. of Ver.* ii 4 23
You are already Love's firm votary And cannot soon revolt and change your mind . . . . iii 2 59
Hark, what fine change is in the music!—Ay, that change is the spite . iv 2 68
If the gentle spirit of moving words Can no way change you to a milder form . . . . v 4 56
It is the lesser blot, modesty finds, Women to change their shapes than men their minds . . . . v 4 109
Did she change her determination? . . . . . *Mer. Wives* iii 5 69
Why, here's a change indeed in the commonwealth! . *Meas. for Meas.* i 2 107
Though you change your place, you need not change your trade . i 2 110
Hence shall we see, If power change purpose, what our seemers be . i 3 54
As school-maids change their names By vain though apt affection . i 4 47
My gravity . . . Could I with boot change for an idle plume . . ii 4 11
You must, sir, change persons with me, ere you make that my report . v 1 339
Dark-working sorcerers that change the mind . . *Com. of Errors* i 2 99
As the fashion of his hat; it ever changes with the next block *Much Ado* i 1 76
If my passion change not shortly, God forbid it should be otherwise . i 1 221
It would better fit your honour to change your mind . . . iii 2 119
Or that I yesternight Maintain'd the change of words with any creature iv 1 185
Change slander to remorse; that is some good . . . . . iv 1 213
By this light, he changes more and more . . . . v 1 140
So shall Biron take me for Rosaline. And change you favours too *L. L. Lost* v 2 134
Then, in our measure do but vouchsafe one change . . . . . v 2 209
Change. Thus change I like the moon . . . . . *L. L. Lost* v 2 212
Will you vouchsafe with me to change a word? . . . . . . v 2 238
Therefore change favours; and, when they repair, Blow like sweet roses v 2 292
The ladies did change favours . . . . v 2 468
These four will change habits, and present the other five . . . v 2 542
Change not your offer made in heat of blood . . . . . . v 2 810
I'll change my black gown for a faithful friend . . . . . v 2 844
The spring, the summer, The childing autumn, angry winter, change Their wonted liveries . . . . *M. N. Dream* ii 1 112
Who will not change a raven for a dove? . . . . ii 2 114
Why are you grown so rude? what change is this? . . . . . iii 2 262
I am aweary of this moon: would he would change! . . . . v 1 256
I would not change this hue, Except to steal your thoughts *Mer. of Ven.* ii 1 11
Speak between the change of man and boy With a reed voice . . iii 4 66
I would she were in heaven, so she could Entreat some power to change this currish Jew . . . . iv 1 292
But music for the time doth change his nature . . . . . v 1 82
Would not change that calling, To be adopted heir to Frederick *As Y. Like It* i 2 246
Whither wilt thou go? Wilt thou change fathers? . . . . . i 3 93
Do not seek to take your change upon you, To bear your griefs yourself i 3 104
I would not change it . . . . ii 1 18
Change you colour?—I prithee, who? . . . . iii 2 192
'Tis a fault I will not change for your best virtue . . . . iii 2 301
Maids are May when they are maids, but the sky changes when they are wives . . . . iv 1 149
I am not so nice, To change true rules for old inventions *T. of Shrew* iii 1 81
I can change these poor accoutrements . . . . iii 2 121
With scarfs and fans and double change of bravery . . . . iv 3 57
And the moon changes even as your mind . . . . . . iv 5 20
We serve you, madam, In that and all your worthiest affairs.—Not so, but as we change our courtesies . . . . . . *All's Well* iii 2 100
Change it, change it; Be not so holy-cruel . . . . . . iv 2 31
Nine changes of the watery star hath been The shepherd's note *W. Tale* i 2 1
We beg, As recompense of our dear services Past and to come, that you do change this purpose . . . . ii 3 151
You must change this purpose, Or I my life . . . . . . iv 4 39
This is an art Which does mend nature, change it rather, but The art itself is nature . . . . iv 4 96
Sure this robe of mine Does change my disposition . . . . . iv 4 135
This follows, if you will not change your purpose . . . . iv 4 553
Change garments with this gentleman . . . . iv 4 649
Power no jot Hath she to change our loves . . . . . . v 1 218
The changes I perceived in the king and Camillo were very notes of admiration . . . . v 2 11
This day, all things begun come to ill end, Yea, faith itself to hollow falsehood change! . . . . *K. John* iii 1 95
And kiss the lips of unacquainted change . . . . iii 4 166
Fresh expectation troubled not the land With any long'd-for change . iv 2 8
Their thimbles into armed gauntlets change . . . . . . v 2 156
Lions make leopards tame.—Yea, but not change his spots . *Richard II.* i 1 175
Ere the six years that he hath to spend Can change their moons . . i 3 220
And lean-look'd prophets whisper fearful change . . . . . ii 4 11
I come To change blows with thee for our day of doom . . . iii 2 189
Change the complexion of her maid-pale peace To scarlet indignation . iii 3 98
They'll talk of state; for every one doth so Against a change . . iii 4 28
Our vizards we will change after we leave them . . . . *1 Hen. IV.* i 2 200
And changes fill the cup of alteration With divers liquors! *2 Hen. IV.* iii 1 52
The seasons change their manners . . . . iv 4 123
His eye is hollow, and he changes much . . . . iv 5 6
And never live to show the incredulous world The noble change that I have purposed . . . . iv 5 155
And now my death Changes the mode . . . . iv 5 200
We are blessed in the change . . . . *Hen. V.* i 1 37
Look ye, how they change! Their cheeks are paper . . . . . ii 2 73
I will not change my horse with any that treads but on four pasterns . iii 7 12
And he that I gave it to in change promised to wear it in his cap . iv 8 30
'Tis a good silling, I warrant you, or I will change it . . . iv 8 77
This day Shall change all griefs and quarrels into love . . . . v 2 20
Rather the sun and not the moon; for it shines bright and never changes . . . . v 2 173
Comets, importing change of times and states . . . *1 Hen. VI.* i 1 2
Four of their lords I'll change for one of ours . . . . . i 1 151
Doth bend her brows, As if with Circe she would change my shape! . v 3 35
Well pleased To change two dukedoms for a duke's fair daughter *2 Hen. VI.* i 1 219
Thou shalt not see me blush Nor change my countenance . . . iii 1 99
Steel thy fearful thoughts, And change misdoubt to resolution . . iii 1 332
Whose smile and frown, like to Achilles' spear, Is able with the change to kill and cure . . . . v 1 101
I can add colours to the chameleon, Change shapes with Proteus for advantages . . . . *3 Hen. VI.* iii 2 192
Madam, what makes you in this sudden change? . . . . . iv 4 1
Wind-changing Warwick now can change no more . . . . . v 1 57
I hope my holy humour will change . . . . . . *Richard III.* i 4 121
Ye cannot reason almost with a man That looks not heavily and full of fear.—Before the times of change, still is it so . . . . . ii 3 41
Quake, and change thy colour, Murder thy breath in middle of a word . iii 5 1
Moreover, urge his hateful luxury, And bestial appetite in change of lust . . . . iii 5 81
Helen, to change, would give an eye to boot . . . *Troi. and Cres.* i 2 260
Frights, changes, horrors, Divert and crack, rend and deracinate . . i 3 98
Give us a prince of blood, a son of Priam, In change of him . . . iii 3 27
It is prodigious, there will come some change . . . . . . v 1 101
Go, wind, to wind, there turn and change together . . . . . v 3 110
Trust ye? With every minute you do change a mind . . *Coriolanus* i 1 186
I have received not only greetings, But with them change of honours . ii 1 214
May I change these garments?—You may, sir . . . . . . ii 3 154
It will be dangerous to go on: no further.—What makes this change? . iii 1 27
That love the fundamental part of state More than you doubt the change on't . . . . iii 1 152
Though chance of war hath wrought this change of cheer . *T. Andron.* i 1 264
My child is yet a stranger in the world; She hath not seen the change of fourteen years . . . . *Rom. and Jul.* i 2 9
The inconstant moon, That monthly changes in her circled orb . . ii 2 110
What a change is here! Is Rosaline, whom thou didst love so dear, So soon forsaken? . . . . ii 3 65
Some say the lark and loathed toad change eyes . . . . . iii 5 31
Our solemn hymns to sullen dirges change, Our bridal flowers serve for a buried corse, And all things change them to the contrary . . iv 5 88

Change. When Fortune in her shift and change of mood Spurns down her late beloved . . . . *T. of Athens* i 1 84
How came the noble Timon to this change?—As the moon does, by wanting light to give . . . . iv 3 66
A poor unmanly melancholy sprung From change of fortune . . . iv 3 204
Why all these things change from their ordinance Their natures *J. Cæsar* i 3 66
That which would appear offence in us, His countenance, like richest alchemy, Will change to virtue and to worthiness . . . i 3 160
How that might change his nature, there's the question . . . ii 1 13
If you shall send them word you will not come, Their minds may change . . . . ii 2 96
For, look, he smiles, and Cæsar doth not change . . . iii 1 24
Pindarus, In his own change, or by ill officers, Hath given me some worthy cause to wish Things done, undone . . . . iv 2 7
Now I change my mind, And partly credit things that do presage . v 1 78
It is but change, Titinius . . . . v 3 51
Your poor servant ever.—Sir, my good friend; I'll change that name with you . . . . *Hamlet* i 2 163
'Tis not strange That even our loves should with our fortunes change . iii 2 211
For use almost can change the stamp of nature . . . iii 4 168
For this 'would' changes And hath abatements and delays . . iv 7 120
You see how full of changes his age is . . . . *Lear* i 1 291
Bids the wind blow the earth into the sea, Or swell the curled waters 'bove the main, That things might change or cease . . . iii 1 7
The lamentable change is from the best; The worst returns to laughter iv 1 5
I must change arms at home, and give the distaff Into my husband's hands iv 2 17
Change places; and, handy-dandy, which is the justice, which is the thief? . . . . iv 6 156
Or whether since he is advised by aught To change the course . v 1 3
Throw such changes of vexation on't, As it may lose some colour *Othello* i 1 72
How say you by this change?—This cannot be, By no assay of reason . i 3 17
I would change my humanity with a baboon . . . . i 3 317
She must change for youth . . . . i 3 356
She must have change, she must: therefore put money in thy purse . i 3 358
She that in wisdom never was so frail To change the cod's head for the salmon's tail . . . . ii 1 156
To follow still the changes of the moon With fresh suspicions . iii 3 178
The Moor already changes with my poison . . . . iii 3 325
O, blood, blood, blood!—Patience, I say; your mind perhaps may change . . . . iii 3 452
Here's a change indeed! . . . . iv 2 106
What is it that they do When they change us for others? Is it sport? . iv 3 98
Quietness, grown sick of rest, would purge By any desperate change *Ant. and Cleo.* i 3 54
Hereditary, Rather than purchased; what he cannot change, Than what he chooses . . . . i 4 14
Since I saw you last, There is a change upon you . . . ii 6 54
That he his high authority abused, And did deserve his change . iii 6 34
Say that I wish he never find more cause To change a master . iv 5 16
The miserable change now at my end Lament nor sorrow at . . iv 15 51
It is great To do that thing that ends all other deeds; Which shackles accidents and bolts up change . . . . v 2 6
You shall find A benefit in this change . . . . . v 2 128
Change you, madam? The worthy Leonatus is in safety *Cymbeline* i 6 11
Not I, Inclined to this intelligence, pronounce The beggary of his change . . . . i 6 115
Abide the change of time, Quake in the present winter's state . ii 4 4
Ambitions, covetings, change of prides, disdain, Nice longing, slanders ii 5 25
You must forget to be a woman; change Command into obedience . iii 4 157
Pardon me, gods! I'ld change my sex to be companion with them . iii 6 88
I think he would change places with his officer . . . iv 4 180
This change of thoughts, The sad companion, dull-eyed melancholy *Pericles* i 2 1
Though they did change me to the meanest bird That flies i' the purer air iv 6 108
A place, for which the pained'st fiend Of hell would not in reputation change . . . . iv 6 174

Changeable. Be effeminate, changeable, longing and liking *As Y. Like It* iii 2 431
And the tailor make thy doublet of changeable taffeta . *T. Night* ii 4 76
Report is changeable . . . . *Lear* iv 7 92
These Moors are changeable in their wills . . . *Othello* i 3 352

Changed 'em, Or else new form'd 'em . . . . . . *Tempest* i 2 82
At the first sight They have changed eyes . . . . . i 2 441
Besides, the fashion of the time is changed . . *T. G. of Ver.* iii 1 86
How the world is changed with you! . . . . *Com. of Errors* ii 2 154
If thou art changed to aught, 'tis to an ass . . . . iii 2 201
Thou wouldst have changed thy face for a name . . . iii 1 47
O, grief hath changed me since you saw me last . . . v 1 297
You took the moon at full, but now she's changed . *L. L. Lost* v 2 214
Run when you will, the story shall be changed . *M. N. Dream* ii 1 230
O Bottom, thou art changed! what do I see on thee? . . . iii 1 117
Believe me, you are marvellously changed . . *Mer. of Venice* i 1 76
Lord, how art thou changed! . . . . ii 2 106
She is changed, as she had never been . . . *T. of Shrew* v 2 115
On the reading it he changed almost into another man . *All's Well* iv 3 5
What we changed Was innocence for innocence . . *W. Tale* i 2 68
Your changed complexions are to me a mirror Which shows me mine changed too . . . . i 2 381
Who was most marble there changed colour . . . . v 2 98
She is corrupted, changed and won from thee . . *K. John* iii 1 55
My lord, the mind of Bolingbroke is changed . . . *Richard II.* v 1 51
Our scene is alter'd from a serious thing, And now changed to 'The Beggar and the King' . . . . v 3 80
What means his grace, that he hath changed his style? . *1 Hen. VI.* iv 1 50
Changed to a worser shape thou canst not be . . . . v 3 36
Our stern alarums changed to merry meetings . . *Richard III.* i 1 7
'Which once,' quoth Forrest, 'almost changed my mind' . . iv 3 15
My mind is changed, sir, my mind is changed . . . . iv 4 456
The sorrow that delivers us thus changed Makes you think so *Coriol.* v 3 39
And art thou changed? pronounce this sentence then, Women may fall, when there's no strength in men . . . *Rom. and Jul.* ii 3 79
Some say the lark and loathed toad change eyes; O, now I would they had changed voices too! . . . . iii 5 32
I beseech you instantly to visit My too much changed son *Hamlet* ii 2 36
You will say they are Persian attire; but let them be changed *Lear* iii 6 86
Where's your master?—Madam, within; but never man so changed . iv 2 3
Thou changed and self-cover'd thing, for shame, Be-monster not thy feature . . . . iv 2 62
In nothing am I changed But in my garments . . . . iv 6 9
I am changed: I'll go sell all my land . . . . *Othello* i 3 388
He is much changed.—Are his wits safe? is he not light of brain? . iv 1 279
How your favour's changed With this unprofitable woe! . *Pericles* iv 1 25

Changeful. Sometimes we are devils to ourselves, When we will tempt the frailty of our powers, Presuming on their changeful potency *Troi. and Cres.* iv 4 99

Changeling. She never had so sweet a changeling . . *M. N. Dream* ii 1 23
I do but beg a little changeling boy, To be my henchman . . ii 1 120
I then did ask of her her changeling child . . . . iv 1 64
This is some changeling: open't. What's within, boy? . . *W. Tale* iii 3 122
She's a changeling and none of your flesh and blood . . . iv 4 704
Of fickle changelings and poor discontents . . . *1 Hen. IV.* v 1 76
Yet his nature In that's no changeling . . . . *Coriolanus* iv 7 11
Subscribed it, gave't the impression, placed it safely, The changeling never known . . . . *Hamlet* v 2 53

Changest. Think what a chance thou changest on . . . *Cymbeline* i 5 68

Changeth. So leaves me to consider what is breeding That changeth thus his manners . . . . *W. Tale* i 2 375

Changing. You would lift the moon out of her sphere, if she would continue in it five weeks without changing . . . *Tempest* ii 1 184
One Julia, that his changing thoughts forget . . . *T. G. of Ver.* iv 4 124
Not changing heart with habit . . . . . *Meas. for Meas.* v 1 389
But in this changing what is your intent? . . . *L. L. Lost* v 2 137
If once I find thee ranging, Hortensio will be quit with thee by changing *T. of Shrew* iii 1 92
Sweet love, I see, changing his property, Turns to the sourest and most deadly hate . . . . *Richard II.* iii 2 135
He did confound the best part of an hour In changing hardiment with great Glendower . . . . *1 Hen. IV.* i 3 101
Relenting fool, and shallow, changing woman! . . *Richard III.* iv 4 431
Go, give that changing piece To him that flourish'd for her *T. Andron.* i 1 309
Even to vice They are not constant, but are changing still One vice, but of a minute old, for one Not half so old as that . . . *Cymbeline* ii 5 30

Channel. You nymphs, call'd Naiads, of the windring brooks, . . . Leave your crisp channels . . . . *Tempest* iv 1 130
Whose passage, vex'd with thy impediment, Shall leave his native channel *K. John* ii 1 337
No more shall trenching war channel her fields . . *1 Hen. IV.* i 1 7
Here the smug and silver Trent shall run In a new channel, fair and evenly . . . . iii 1 103
Throw the quean in the channel.—Throw me in the channel! I'll throw thee in the channel . . . . *2 Hen. IV.* ii 1 52
I charge thee waft me safely cross the Channel . *2 Hen. VI.* iv 1 114
As if a channel should be call'd the sea . . . . . *3 Hen. VI.* ii 2 141
He'll turn your current in a ditch, And make your channel his *Coriol.* iii 1 97
Weep your tears Into the channel, till the lowest stream Do kiss the most exalted shores of all . . . . *J. Cæsar* i 1 64
With cadent tears fret channels in her cheeks . . . . *Lear* i 4 307

Chanson. The first row of the pious chanson will show you more *Hamlet* ii 2 438

Chant. The free maids that weave their thread with bones Do use to chant it . . . . *T. Night* ii 4 47
The lark, that tirra-lyra chants . . . . . . *W. Tale* iv 3 9
He so chants to the sleeve-hand and the work about the square on't . iv 4 211
This pale faint swan, Who chants a doleful hymn to his own death *K. John* v 7 22
The birds chant melody on every bush . . . . *T. Andron.* ii 3 12

Chanted. Which time she chanted snatches of old tunes . . *Hamlet* iv 7 178

Chanticleer. I hear The strain of strutting chanticleer . . *Tempest* i 2 385
My lungs began to crow like chanticleer . . . *As Y. Like It* ii 7 30

Chanting faint hymns to the cold fruitless moon . *M. N. Dream* i 1 73

Chantries. I have built Two chantries, where the sad and solemn priests Sing still for Richard's soul . . . . *Hen. V.* iv 1 318

Chantry. Now go with me and with this holy man Into the chantry *T. Night* iv 3 24

Chaos. Like to a chaos, or an unlick'd bear-whelp . . *3 Hen. VI.* iii 2 161
This chaos, when degree is suffocate, Follows the choking *Troi. and Cres.* i 3 125
Serious vanity! Mis-shapen chaos of well-seeming forms! *Rom. and Jul.* i 1 185
But I do love thee! and when I love thee not, Chaos is come again *Othello* iii 3 92

Chape. In the chape of his dagger . . . . . . *All's Well* iv 3 164

Chapel. Let wonder seem familiar, And to the chapel let us presently *Much Ado* v 4 71
If to do were as easy as to know what were good to do, chapels had been churches and poor men's cottages princes' palaces *Mer. of Venice* i 2 14
Will you dispatch us here under this tree, or shall we go with you to your chapel? . . . . *As Y. Like It* iii 3 67
Once a day I'll visit The chapel where they lie . . *W. Tale* iii 2 240
Quit presently the chapel, or resolve you For more amazement . . v 3 86
At Saint Mary's chapel presently The rites of marriage shall be solemnized . . . . *K. John* ii 1 538
This day was view'd in open as his queen, Going to chapel *Hen. VIII.* iii 2 405
Go seek him out; speak fair, and bring the body Into the chapel *Hamlet* iv 1 37
Tell us where 'tis, that we may take it thence And bear it to the chapel iv 2 8
And be her sense but as a monument, Thus in a chapel lying! *Cymbeline* ii 2 33

Chapeless. An old rusty sword ta'en out of the town-armoury, with a broken hilt, and chapeless . . . . *T. of Shrew* iii 2 48

Chap-fallen. Not one now, to mock your own grinning? quite chap-fallen? *Hamlet* v 1 212

Chaplain, away! thy priesthood saves thy life . . *3 Hen. VI.* i 3 3
The chaplain of the Tower hath buried them . . *Richard III.* iv 3 29
That what he spoke My chaplain to no creature living, but To me, should utter . . . . *Hen. VIII.* i 2 166
Filling The whole realm, by your teaching and your chaplains, For so we are inform'd, with new opinions . . . . v 3 16

Chapless. With dead men's rattling bones, With reeky shanks and yellow chapless skulls . . . . *Rom. and Jul.* iv 1 83
Chapless, and knocked about the mazzard with a sexton's spade *Hamlet* v 1 97

Chaplet. An odorous chaplet of sweet summer buds *M. N. Dream* ii 1 110

Chapmen. Not utter'd by base sale of chapmen's tongues *L. L. Lost* ii 1 16
As chapmen do, Dispraise the thing that you desire to buy *Troi. and Cres.* iv 1 75

Chaps. You cannot tell who's your friend: open your chaps again *Tempest* ii 2 89
O, now doth Death line his dead chaps with steel . . *K. John* ii 1 352
I'll thrust my knife in your mouldy chaps . . . *2 Hen. IV.* ii 4 139
Before his chaps be stain'd with crimson blood . *2 Hen. VI.* iii 1 259
My frosty signs and chaps of age, Grave witnesses of true experience *T. Andron.* v 3 77
He unseam'd him from the nave to the chaps . . . *Macbeth* i 2 22
Then, world, thou hast a pair of chaps, no more . *Ant. and Cleo.* iii 5 14

Chapt. O, give me always a little, lean, old, chapt, bald shot *2 Hen. IV.* iii 2 294

Chapter. In his bosom! In what chapter of his bosom? . *T. Night* i 5 242

Charact. Even so may Angelo, In all his dressings, characts, titles, forms, Be an arch-villain . . . . . . *Meas. for Meas.* v 1 56

Character. There is a kind of character in thy life, That to the observer doth thy history Fully unfold . . . . i 1 28

Character. The stealth of our most mutual entertainment With character too gross is writ on Juliet . . . *Meas. for Meas.* i 2 159
You know the character, I doubt not; and the signet is not strange to you . . . iv 2 208
With characters of brass, A forted residence 'gainst the tooth of time . v 1 11
These trees shall be my books And in their barks my thoughts I'll character . . . *As Y. Like It* iii 2 6
Thou hast a mind that suits With this thy fair and outward character *T. Night* i 2 51
This is not my writing, Though, I confess, much like the character . v 1 354
Blossom, speed thee well! There lie, and there thy character *W. Tale* iii 3 47
The letters of Antigonus found with it which they know to be his character . . . . v 2 38
That are written down old with all the characters of age . 2 *Hen. IV.* i 2 203
Razing the characters of your renown, Defacing monuments . 2 *Hen. VI.* i 1 101
I say, without characters, fame lives long . . *Richard III.* iii 1 81
The purpose is perspicuous even as substance, Whose grossness little characters sum up . . . *Troi. and Cres.* i 3 325
In characters as red as Mars his heart Inflamed with Venus . v 2 164
What harm can your bisson conspectuities glean out of this character? *Coriolanus* ii 1 71
I paint him in the character . . . . v 4 28
What's on this tomb I cannot read; the character I'll take with wax *T. of Athens* v 3 6
And these few precepts in thy memory See thou character . *Hamlet* i 3 59
Know you the hand?—'Tis Hamlet's character . . . iv 7 52
You know the character to be your brother's?—If the matter were good, my lord, I durst swear it were his . . . . *Lear* i 2 66
Ay, though thou didst produce My very character . . . ii 1 74
Learn'd indeed were that astronomer That knew the stars as I his characters; He'ld lay the future open . . . *Cymbeline* iii 2 28
He cut our roots In characters, And sauced our broths . . iv 2 49
A passport too! Apollo, perfect me in the characters! . . *Pericles* iii 2 67
Know you the character?—It is my lord's . . . . iii 4 3
Her epitaphs In glittering golden characters express A general praise to her . . . . iv 3 44
Charactered. Who art the table wherein all my thoughts Are visibly character'd and engraved . . . *T. G. of Ver.* ii 7 4
Show me one scar character'd on thy skin. . . 2 *Hen. VI.* iii 1 300
Characterless. And mighty states characterless are grated To dusty nothing . . . . . *Troi. and Cres.* iii 2 195
Charactery. Fairies use flowers for their charactery . *Mer. Wives* v 5 77
All my engagements I will construe to thee, All the charactery of my sad brows . . . . . *J. Cæsar* ii 1 308
Charbon. Young Charbon the puritan and old Poysam the papist *All's Well* i 3 55
Chare. As the maid that milks And does the meanest chares *Ant. and Cleo.* iv 15 75
When thou hast done this chare, I'll give thee leave To play till doomsday . . . . v 2 231
Charge. Thy charge Exactly is perform'd: but there's more work *Tempest* i 2 237
One word more; I charge thee That thou attend me . . i 2 452
Go charge my goblins that they grind their joints . . iv 1 259
Confined together In the same fashion as you gave in charge . v 1 8
My Ariel, chick, That is thy charge . . . . . v 1 317
'Tis a great charge to come under one body's hand . *Mer. Wives* i 4 104
Are you avised o' that? you shall find it a great charge . i 4 107
I desire more acquaintance of you.—Good Sir John, I sue for yours: not to charge you. . . . . . . ii 2 171
Give your men the charge; we must be brief . . . . iii 3 7
I do it not in evil disposition, But from Lord Angelo by special charge *Meas. for Meas.* i 2 123
My lord hath sent you this note; and by me this further charge . iv 2 106
And charges him, my lord, with such a time When I'll depose I had him in mine arms . . . . v 1 197
Charges she more than me?—Not that I know. . . v 1 200
How darest thou trust So great a charge from thine own custody? *Com. of Errors* i 2 61
Where is the gold I gave in charge to thee? . . . i 2 70
Tell me how thou hast disposed thy charge.—My charge was but to fetch you from the mart . . . . i 2 73
And charge you in the duke's name to obey me . . . iv 1 70
Satan, avoid! I charge thee, tempt me not . . . iv 3 48
I charge thee, Satan, housed within this man, To yield possession to my holy prayers . . . . iv 4 57
Beside the charge, the shame, imprisonment, You have done wrong . v 1 18
You embrace your charge too willingly . . . *Much Ado* i 1 103
Constrain me to tell.—I charge thee on thy allegiance . . i 1 210
Well, give them their charge, neighbour Dogberry . . . iii 3 7
This is your charge: you shall comprehend all vagrom men . iii 3 25
This is the end of the charge . . . . . . iii 3 78
Well, masters, we hear our charge: let us go sit here . . iii 3 94
We charge you, in the prince's name, stand! . . . iii 3 176
We charge you let us obey you to go with us . . . iii 3 188
I charge you, on your souls, to utter it . . . . iv 1 14
I charge thee do so, as thou art my child . . . . iv 1 77
Masters, I charge you, in the prince's name, accuse these men . iv 2 39
I shall meet your wit in the career, an you charge it against me . v 1 136
Why they are committed; and, to conclude, what you lay to their charge v 1 228
What are they That charge their breath against us? . *L. L. Lost* v 2 88
I charge thee, hence, and do not haunt me thus . *M. N. Dream* ii 2 85
I charge you by the law, Whereof you are a well-deserving pillar *Mer. of Venice* iv 1 238
Have by some surgeon, Shylock, on your charge, To stop his wounds . iv 1 257
Therefore thou must be hang'd at the state's charge . . iv 1 367
Let us go in; And charge us there upon inter'gatories . . v 1 298
I charge thee, be not thou more grieved than I am . *As Y. Like It* i 3 94
Can you remember any of the principal evils that he laid to the charge of women? . . . . iii 2 370
I charge her to love thee; if she will not, I will never have her . iv 3 72
I charge you, O women, for the love you bear to men . . Epil. 12
I charge you, O men, for the love you bear to women . . Epil. 15
Huntsman, I charge thee, tender well my hounds . *T. of Shrew* Ind. 1 16
Wait you on him, I charge you, as becomes . . . . i 1 238
I promised we would be contributors And bear his charge of wooing . i 2 216
Of all thy suitors, here I charge thee, tell Whom thou lovest best . ii 1 8
Lay hold on him, I charge you, in the duke's name. . . v 1 91
I charge you see that he be forthcoming . . . . v 1 96
I charge thee, tell these headstrong women What duty they do owe their lords . . . . v 2 130

Charge. I charge thee, As heaven shall work in me for thine avail, To tell me truly . . . . *All's Well* i 3 189
She had her breeding at my father's charge . . . . ii 3 121
Whoever charges on his forward breast, I am the caitiff that do hold him to't . . . . iii 2 116
It is A charge too heavy for my strength, but yet We'll strive to bear it iii 3 4
The charge and thanking Shall be for me . . . . iii 5 101
Excellent command,—to charge in with our horse upon our own wings! iii 6 52
My integrity ne'er knew the crafts That you do charge men with . iv 2 34
Now will I charge you in the band of truth . . . . iv 2 56
I know them: do they charge me further? . . . . . v 3 167
Tell me, sirrah, but tell me true, I charge you. . . . v 3 234
Therefore it charges me in manners the rather to express myself *T. Night* ii 1 15
On thy life I charge thee, hold! . . . . . . iv 1 49
Father, I charge thee, by thy reverence, Here to unfold . . v 1 154
My stay To you a charge and trouble . . . . *W. Tale* i 2 26
You, sir, Charge him too coldly . . . . . . i 2 30
And, might we lay the old proverb to your charge, So like you, 'tis the worse . . . . ii 3 96
I do in justice charge thee, On thy soul's peril and thy body's torture ii 3 180
I have about me many parcels of charge . . . . iv 4 261
We have cross'd, To execute the charge my father gave me . . v 1 162
Lay't so to his charge: He's with the king your father . . v 1 195
Our abbeys and our priories shall pay This expedition's charge *K. John* i 1 49
Heaven lay not my transgression to my charge! . . . i 1 256
Thou canst not, cardinal, devise a name So slight, unworthy and ridiculous, To charge me to an answer . . . . iii 1 151
I do fearfully believe 'tis done, What we so fear'd he had a charge to do iv 2 75
Is't not I That undergo this charge? who else but I? . . v 2 100
What doth our cousin lay to Mowbray's charge? . *Richard II.* i 1 84
For these great affairs do ask some charge . . . . ii 1 159
Be it your charge To keep him safely till his day of trial . iv 1 152
This haste was hot in question, And many limits of the charge set down but yesternight . . . . 1 *Hen. IV.* i 1 35
That we at our own charge shall ransom straight His brother-in-law . i 3 79
They will along with company, for they have great charge . . ii 1 51
A kind of auditor; one that hath abundance of charge too, God knows what . . . . ii 1 64
But a little charge will trench him here . . . . iii 1 112
Thou shalt have charge and sovereign trust herein . . . iii 2 161
Charge an honest woman with picking thy pocket! . . . iii 3 176
There shalt thou know thy charge; and there receive Money and order iii 3 225
And now my whole charge consists of ancients, corporals, lieutenants iv 2 25
But to my charge. The king hath sent to know The nature of your griefs . . . . iv 3 41
Hence, therefore, every leader to his charge . . . . v 1 118
As I hear, is now going with some charge. . . 2 *Hen. IV.* i 2 72
Here, Pistol, I charge you with a cup of sack . . . ii 4 121
I will charge you.—Charge me! I scorn you, scurvy companion . ii 4 131
A' shall charge you and discharge you with the motion of a pewterer's hammer. . . . . iii 2 280
Their armed staves in charge, their beavers down . . . iv 1 120
The leaders, having charge from you to stand, Will not go off . iv 2 99
Come, I charge you both go with me . . . . . . v 4 18
Be it your charge, my lord, To see perform'd the tenour of our word . v 5 74
Nicely charge your understanding soul With opening titles miscreate *Hen. V.* i 2 15
We charge you, in the name of God, take heed. . . . i 2 23
Give us leave Freely to render what we have in charge . . i 2 238
Upon this charge Cry 'God for Harry, England, and Saint George!' . iii 1 33
And we give express charge, that in our marches through the country, there be nothing compelled from the villages . . . . iii 6 114
God be wi' you, princes all; I'll to my charge . . . iv 3 6
The French are bravely in their battles set, And will with all expedience charge on us. . . . . iv 3 70
I charge you in his majesty's name, apprehend him . . iv 8 17
We charge and command you, in his highness' name, to repair to your several dwelling-places . . . . . . 1 *Hen. VI.* i 3 76
Being captain of the watch to-night, Did look no better to that weighty charge . . . . ii 1 62
Porter, remember what I gave in charge . . . . . ii 3 1
If thou canst accuse, Or aught intend'st to lay unto my charge, Do it without invention . . . . iii 1 4
We charge you, on allegiance to ourself, To hold your slaughtering hands iii 1 86
I charge you, as you love our favour, Quite to forget this quarrel and the cause . . . . iv 1 135
Thy father's charge shall clear thee from that stain . . iv 5 42
For your expenses and sufficient charge, Among the people gather up a tenth . . . . v 5 92
As by your high imperial majesty I had in charge at my depart 2 *Hen. VI.* i 1 2
She sent over of the King of England's own proper cost and charges . i 1 61
That Suffolk should demand a whole fifteenth For costs and charges! . i 1 134
So am I given in charge, may't please your grace . . . i 4 80
But mightier crimes are laid unto your charge . . . iii 1 134
A charge, Lord York, that I will see perform'd . . . iii 1 321
And charge that no man should disturb your rest . . . iii 2 256
I charge thee waft me safely cross the Channel . . . iv 1 114
And we charge and command that their wives be as free as heart can wish iv 7 131
Richard cried, 'Charge! and give no foot of ground!' . 3 *Hen. VI.* i 4 15
And once again cry 'Charge upon our foes!' But never once again turn back . . . . ii 1 184
We charge you, in God's name, and the king's, To go with us . iii 1 97
Matter of marriage was the charge he gave me, But dreadful war shall answer his demand . . . . iii 3 258
And Warwick, doing what you gave in charge, Is now dishonoured by this new marriage . . . . iv 1 32
My brother was too careless of his charge . . . . iv 6 86
Why not Ned and I For once allow'd the skilful pilot's charge? . v 4 20
Away, I say; I charge ye, bear her hence . . . . v 5 81
His majesty hath straitly given in charge That no man shall have private conference, Of what degree soever . . . *Richard III.* i 1 85
We know thy charge, Brakenbury, and will obey . . . i 1 105
I'll be at charges for a looking-glass . . . . . i 2 256
The secret mischiefs that I set abroach I lay unto the grievous charge of others . . . . i 3 326
Signify to him That thus I have resign'd my charge to you . i 4 98
I charge you, as you hope to have redemption By Christ's dear blood . i 4 194
We heartily solicit Your gracious self to take on you the charge . iii 7 131
If to have done the thing you gave in charge Beget your happiness, be happy . . . . iv 3 25

Charge. Limit each leader to his several charge . . . *Richard III.* v 3 25
Hie thee to thy charge ; Use careful watch, choose trusty sentinels . v 3 53
Go, gentlemen, every man unto his charge . . . v 3 307
For the most part such To whom as great a charge as little honour He meant to lay upon . . . *Hen. VIII.* i 1 77
Take good heed You charge not in your spleen a noble person . . i 2 174
Place you that side ; I'll take the charge of this . . . i 4 20
Give my charge up to Sir Nicholas Vaux, Who undertakes you to your end . . . . ii 1 96
You charge me That I have blown this coal . . . . ii 4 93
Cromwell, I charge thee, fling away ambition . . . . iii 2 440
Till further trial in those charges Which will require your answer . . v 1 103
I charge you, Embrace and love this man . . . . v 3 171
As doth a battle, when they charge on heaps The enemy flying *Troi. and Cres.* iii 2 29
With such a hell of pain and world of charge . . . iv 1 57
I charge thee use her well, even for my charge . . . iv 4 128
I'll nothing do on charge : to her own worth She shall be prized . iv 4 135
How now, my charge !—Now, my sweet guardian ! . . . v 2 6
Mend and charge home, Or, by the fires of heaven, I'll leave the foe And make my wars on you . . . *Coriolanus* i 4 38
Obey, I charge thee, And follow to thine answer . . . iii 1 176
In this point charge him home, that he affects Tyrannical power . iii 3 1
We charge you, that you have contrived to take From Rome all season'd office . . . . iii 3 63
Peace ! We need not put new matter to his charge . . . iii 3 76
The centurions and their charges, distinctly billeted . . iv 3 48
And yet to charge thy sulphur with a bolt That should but rive an oak v 3 152
Answering us With our own charge . . . . . v 6 68
Our spoils we have brought home Do more than counterpoise a full third part The charges of the action . . . . . v 6 79
Let it be your charge, as it is ours, To attend the emperor's person carefully . . . . *T. Andron.* ii 2 7
Hold, hold ; meanwhile here's money for thy charges . . iv 3 105
Go with me ; I charge thee in the prince's name, obey *Rom. and Jul.* iii 1 145
The letter was not nice but full of charge Of dear import . . v 2 18
I charge thee, Whate'er thou hear'st or seest, stand all aloof . . v 3 25
I'm weary of this charge, the gods can witness . *T. of Athens* iii 4 25
Go, I charge thee, invite them all . . . . iii 4 118
Things unluckily charge my fantasy . . . *J. Cæsar* iii 3 2
Fetch the will hither, and we shall determine How to cut off some charge in legacies . . . . iv 1 9
Bid our commanders lead their charges off A little from this ground . iv 2 48
Shall we give sign of battle?—No, Cæsar, we will answer on their charge . . . . v 1 24
Speak, I charge you . . . . . . *Macbeth* i 3 78
The surfeited grooms Do mock their charge with snores . . ii 2 6
A good and virtuous nature may recoil In an imperial charge . . iv 3 20
By heaven I charge thee, speak !—It is offended.—See, it stalks away ! *Hamlet* i 1 49
Stay ! speak, speak ! I charge thee, speak !—'Tis gone, and will not answer . . . . i 1 51
Look to't, I charge you : come your ways.—I shall obey, my lord . i 3 135
That would dishonour him.—'Faith, no ; as you may season it in the charge . . . . ii 1 28
And by what more dear a better proposer could charge you withal . ii 2 297
Proclaim no shame When the compulsive ardour gives the charge . iii 4 86
Witness this army of such mass and charge Led by a delicate and tender prince . . . . iv 4 47
And many such-like 'As'es of great charge . . . . v 2 43
Is not this your son, my lord?—His breeding, sir, hath been at my charge . . . . *Lear* i 1 10
To lay his goatish disposition to the charge of a star ! . . i 2 139
With his prepared sword, he charges home My unprovided body . ii 1 53
Sith that both charge and danger Speak 'gainst so great a number . ii 4 242
Where will you that I go To answer this your charge? . . . *Othello* i 2 85
Speak, who began this? on thy love, I charge thee . . . ii 3 178
You charge me most unjustly.—With nought but truth . . iv 2 186
O, did he so? I charge you, go with me . . . . v 1 120
What, are you mad? I charge you, get you home . . . v 2 194
O, that I knew this husband, which, you say, must charge his horns with garlands ! . . . . *Ant. and Cleo.* i 2 5
You have broken The article of your oath ; which you shall never Have tongue to charge me with . . . . ii 2 83
A charge we bear i' the war, And, as the president of my kingdom, will Appear there for a man . . . . . . iii 7 17
Welcome : Thou look'st like him that knows a warlike charge . . iv 4 19
Send his treasure after ; do it ; Detain no jot, I charge thee . . iv 5 13
Go charge Agrippa Plant those that have revolted in the van . . iv 6 8
If sleep charge nature, To break it with a fearful dream of him *Cymbeline* iii 4 44
With this strict charge, even as he left his life, 'Keep it, my Pericles' *Pericles* ii 1 131
Patience, good sir, Even for this charge . . . . iii 1 27
Here I charge your charity withal, leaving her The infant of your care . iii 3 14

Charge of foot. I'll procure this fat rogue a charge of foot . 1 *Hen. IV.* iii 4 597

Charged. My master charged me to deliver a ring . . *T. G. of Ver.* v 4 88
That I beat him And charged him with a thousand marks in gold *Com. of Errors* iii 1 8
She was charged with nothing But what was true . . *Much Ado* v 1 104
Charged my brother, on his blessing, to breed me well . *As Y. Like It* i 1 3
My father charged you in his will to give me good education . . i 1 70
Heaven Nature charged That one body should be fill'd With all graces . iii 2 149
Your physicians have expressly charged . . . *T. of Shrew* Ind. 2 123
For so your father charged me at our parting . . . . i 1 218
I will tell you ; Since I am charged in honour . . . *W. Tale* i 2 407
I charged thee that she should not come about me . . . ii 3 43
Their battering cannon charged to the mouths . . *K. John* ii 1 382
Send him to answer thee, or any man, For any thing he shall be charged withal . . . . 1 *Hen. IV.* ii 4 566
I can purge Myself of many I am charged withal . . . iii 2 21
To venture upon the charged chambers bravely . . 2 *Hen. IV.* ii 4 57
His soul Shall stand sore charged for the wasteful vengeance *Hen. V.* i 2 283
All abreast, Charged our main battle's front . . . 3 *Hen. VI.* i 1 8
With this, we charged again : but, out, alas ! We bodged again . . i 4 18
Charged us from his soul to love each other . . *Richard III.* i 4 243
The king hath straitly charged the contrary . . . . iv 1 17
Believe me, sirs, We shall be charged again . . . *Coriolanus* i 6 4
Shall I be charged no further than this present? Must all determine here? iii 3 42
They charged him even As those should do that had deserved his hate iv 6 112
What a sigh is there ! The heart is sorely charged . . . *Macbeth* v 1 60

Charged. Get thee back ; my soul is too much charged With blood of thine already . . . . *Macbeth* v 8 5
Charged me, on pain of their perpetual displeasure, neither to speak of him, entreat for him, nor any way sustain him . . . *Lear* iii 3 4
Wherefore to Dover? Wast thou not charged at peril . . . iii 7 52
My lady charged my duty in this business . . . . iv 5 18
What you have charged me with, that have I done ; And more, much more . . . . v 3 162
I have charged thee not to haunt about my doors . . . *Othello* i 1 96
What mighty magic, For such proceeding I am charged withal . . i 3 93
Being charged, we will be still by land . . . *Ant. and Cleo.* iv 11 1
The king Hath charged you should not speak together . . *Cymbeline* i 1 83
Or have charged him, At the sixth hour of morn, at noon, at midnight, To encounter me with orisons . . . . i 3 30

Chargeful. The fineness of the gold and chargeful fashion *Com. of Errors* iv 1 29

Charge-house. Do you not educate youth at the charge-house on the top of the mountain? . . . . *L. L. Lost* v 1 87

Chargeth. They are both forsworn : In this the madman justly chargeth them . . . . *Com. of Errors* v 1 213

Charging. If they shall chance, In charging you with matters, to commit you . . . . *Hen. VIII.* v 1 146

Chariest. The chariest maid is prodigal enough, if she unmask her beauty to the moon . . . . *Hamlet* i 3 36

Chariness. That may not sully the chariness of our honesty *Mer. Wives* ii 1 102

Charing-cross. Two razes of ginger, to be delivered as far as Charing-cross 1 *Hen. IV.* ii 1 27

Chariot. In a captive chariot into Rouen Bring him our prisoner *Hen. V.* iii 5 54
I consecrate My sword, my chariot and my prisoners . . *T. Andron.* i 1 249
Horse and chariots let us have, And to our sport . . . ii 2 18
Her chariot is an empty hazel-nut Made by the joiner squirrel *Rom. and Jul.* i 4 67
And when you saw his chariot but appear, Have you not made an universal shout, That Tiber trembled? . . . . . *J. Cæsar* i 1 48
Thy grand captain Antony Shall set thee on triumphant chariots *Ant. and Cleo.* iii 1 10
Follow his chariot, like the greatest spot Of all thy sex . . iv 12 35
It fits us therefore ripely Our chariots and our horsemen be in readiness *Cymbeline* iii 5 23
He was seated in a chariot Of an inestimable value . . *Pericles* ii 4 7

Chariot-wheel. That erst did follow thy proud chariot-wheels 2 *Hen. VI.* ii 4 13
Stab them, or tear them on thy chariot-wheels . . *T. Andron.* v 2 47
What conquest brings he home? What tributaries follow him to Rome, To grace in captive bonds his chariot-wheels? . . . *J. Cæsar* i 1 39

Charitable. Let him be furnished with divines, and have all charitable preparation . . . . *Meas. for Meas.* iii 2 222
A charitable duty of my order . . . . . *Com. of Errors* v 1 107
Why had I not with charitable hand Took up a beggar's issue? *Much Ado* iv 1 133
You were born under a charitable star.—Under Mars, I . . *All's Well* i 1 205
You ha' done me a charitable office . . . . *W. Tale* iv 3 80
The peace of heaven is theirs that lift their swords In such a just and charitable war . . . . *K. John* ii 1 36
I come to thee for charitable license . . . . *Hen. V.* iv 7 74
What black magician conjures up this fiend, To stop devoted charitable deeds? . . . . *Richard III.* i 2 35
Most charitable care Have the patricians of you . . . *Coriolanus* i 1 67
Do this, and be a charitable murderer . . . . *T. Andron.* ii 3 178
Pardon me for reprehending thee, For thou hast done a charitable deed iii 2 70
A charitable wish and full of love . . . . . v 2 43
Why have you that charitable title from thousands? . *T. of Athens* i 2 94
He does deny him, in respect of his, What charitable men afford to beggars iii 2 82
Bring with thee airs from heaven or blasts from hell, Be thy intents wicked or charitable . . . . *Hamlet* i 4 42
For charitable prayers, Shards, flints and pebbles should be thrown on her . . . . v 1 253
The ruddock would, With charitable bill,—O bill, sore-shaming Those rich-left heirs that let their fathers lie Without a monument ! *Cymbeline* iv 2 225

Charitably. How can they charitably dispose of any thing, when blood is their argument? . . . . *Hen. V.* iv 1 149

Charities. As your charities Shall best instruct you, measure me *W. Tale* ii 1 113

Charity. Out of his charity . . . did give us . . . . *Tempest* i 2 162
Thou hast not so much charity in thee as to go to the ale with a Christian *T. G. of Ver.* ii 5 60
Bound by my charity and my blest order . . . *Meas. for Meas.* ii 3 3
Might there not be a charity in sin To save this brother's life . . ii 4 63
I'll take it as a peril to my soul, It is no sin at all, but charity . . ii 4 66
To do't at peril of your soul, Were equal poise of sin and charity . ii 4 68
Sir, induced by my charity . . . . . . iv 3 53
Thy love is far from charity, That in love's grief desirest society *L. L. Lost* iv 3 127
For charity itself fulfils the law, And who can sever love from charity? iv 3 364
He hath a neighbourly charity in him . . . *Mer. of Venice* i 2 85
But what of that? 'Twere good you do so much for charity . . iv 1 261
He that knows better how to tame a shrew, Now let him speak : 'tis charity to show . . . . *T. of Shrew* iv 1 214
If not, elsewhere they meet with charity . . . . iv 3 6
Of charity, what kin are you to me? . . . . . *T. Night* v 1 237
There your charity would have lacked footing . . . *W. Tale* iii 3 113
Whom zeal and charity brought to the field . . . *K. John* ii 1 565
Ransacking the church, Offending charity . . . . iii 4 173
I will not vex your souls—Since presently your souls must part your bodies—With too much urging your pernicious lives, For 'twere no charity . . . . *Richard II.* iii 1 5
A tear for pity and a hand Open as day for melting charity 2 *Hen. IV.* iv 4 32
The dead with charity enclosed in clay . . . *Hen. V.* iv 8 129
Virtue is choked with foul ambition And charity chased hence by rancour's hand . . . . 2 *Hen. VI.* iii 1 144
Fie ! charity, for shame ! speak not in spite . . . . v 1 213
'Twas sin before, but now 'tis charity . . . 3 *Hen. VI.* v 5 76
Sweet saint, for charity, be not so curst . . . *Richard III.* i 2 49
You know no rules of charity, Which renders good for bad, blessings for curses . . . . i 2 68
Have done ! for shame, if not for charity . . . . i 3 273
Urge neither charity nor shame to me : Uncharitably with me have you dealt . . . . i 3 274
My charity is outrage, life my shame . . . . . i 3 277
Brother, we have done deeds of charity ; Made peace of enmity . . ii 1 49
Put meekness in thy mind, Love, charity, obedience, and true duty ! . ii 2 108
My learn'd lord cardinal, Deliver all with charity . . *Hen. VIII.* i 2 143
You speak not like yourself ; who ever yet Have stood to charity . ii 4 86
I will not wish ye half my miseries ; I have more charity . . . iii 1 109
I could despise this man, But that I am bound in charity against it ! . iii 2 298

Charity. Is come to lay his weary bones among ye; Give him a little earth for charity! . . . *Hen. VIII.* iv 2 23
Give me leave to speak him, And yet with charity . . iv 2 33
Love, friendship, charity, are subjects all To envious and calumniating time . . . *Troi. and Cres.* iii 3 173
We would give much, to use violent thefts, And rob in the behalf of charity . . . v 3 22
A man by his own alms empoison'd, And with his charity slain *Coriol.* v 6 12
This was but a deed of charity To that which thou shalt hear of me *T. Andron.* v 1 89
Thou art a soldier, therefore seldom rich; It comes in charity to thee *T. of Athens* i 2 229
Thou shalt build from men; Hate all, curse all, show charity to none . iv 3 534
By Gis and by Saint Charity, Alack, and fie for shame! . *Hamlet* iv 5 59
Sometime with lunatic bans, sometime with prayers, Enforce their charity . . . *Lear* ii 3 20
Talk with the duke, that my charity be not of him perceived . iii 3 17
Do poor Tom some charity, whom the foul fiend vexes . . iii 4 61
Let's exchange charity. I am no less in blood than thou art . v 3 166
Bear some charity to my wit; do not think it so unwholesome *Othello* iv 1 123
I care not for you, And am so near the lack of charity—To accuse myself—I hate you . . . *Cymbeline* ii 3 114
I'ld let a parish of such Clotens blood, And praise myself for charity . iv 2 169
O, the charity of a penny cord! it sums up thousands in a trice . v 4 170
And finding little comfort to relieve them, I thought it princely charity to grieve them . . . *Pericles* i 2 100
Your honour has through Ephesus pour'd forth Your charity . iii 2 44
Besides this treasure for a fee, The gods requite his charity! . iii 2 75
Here I charge your charity withal, leaving her The infant of your care iii 3 14
In reverend Cerimon there well appears The worth that learned charity aye wears . . . v 3 Gower 94
Charlemain. Nay, To give great Charlemain a pen in's hand And write to her a love-line . . . *All's Well* ii 1 80
The Lady Lingare, Daughter to Charlemain . . . *Hen. V.* i 2 75
Charles. Was not Charles, the duke's wrestler, here? *As Y. Like It* i 1 94
Good Monsieur Charles, what's the new news at the new court? . i 1 101
Charles, I thank thee for thy love to me . . . i 1 143
I'll tell thee, Charles: it is the stubbornest young fellow of France . i 1 148
Farewell, good Charles. Now will I stir this gamester . . i 1 169
The eldest of the three wrestled with Charles, the duke's wrestler; which Charles in a moment threw him and broke three of his ribs . i 2 134
Young man, have you challenged Charles the wrestler? . . i 2 178
How dost thou, Charles?—He cannot speak . . . i 2 231
O poor Orlando, thou art overthrown! Or Charles or something weaker masters thee . . . i 2 272
The wrestler That did but lately foil the sinewy Charles . . ii 2 14
Hugh Capet also, who usurp'd the crown Of Charles the duke of Lorraine *Hen. V.* i 2 70
The Lady Ermengare, Daughter to Charles the foresaid duke of Lorraine i 2 83
Charles Delabreth, high constable of France . . . iii 5 40; iv 8 97
Charles Duke of Orleans, nephew to the king . . . iv 8 81
The Dauphin Charles is crowned king in Rheims . . 1 *Hen. VI.* i 1 92
Here cometh Charles: I marvel how he sped . . . ii 1 48
Wherefore is Charles impatient with his friend? . . . ii 1 54
I'll by a sign give notice to our friends, That Charles the Dauphin may encounter them . . . iii 2 9
See, noble Charles, the beacon of our friend . . . iii 2 29
Now where's the Bastard's braves, and Charles his gleeks? . iii 2 123
Who craves a parley with the Burgundy?—The princely Charles of France . . . iii 3 38
What say'st thou, Charles? for I am marching hence . . iii 3 39
Return, thou wandering lord; Charles and the rest will take thee in their arms . . . iii 3 77
And join'd with Charles, the rightful King of France . . iv 1 60
I hope ere long To be presented, by your victories, With Charles, Alençon and that traitorous rout . . . iv 1 173
Charles, Burgundy, Alençon, Reignier, compass him about . iv 4 26
Earl of Armagnac, near knit to Charles, A man of great authority in France . . . v 1 17
Then march to Paris, royal Charles of France . . . v 2 4
Command the conquest, Charles, it shall be thine . . . v 2 19
O, Charles the Dauphin is a proper man . . . v 3 37
A plaguing mischief light on Charles and thee! . . . v 3 39
We'll have no bastards live; Especially since Charles must father it v 4 71
'Twas neither Charles nor yet the duke I named . . . v 4 77
Charles, and the rest, it is enacted thus . . . v 4 123
And, Charles, upon condition thou wilt swear To pay him tribute v 4 129
Insulting Charles! hast thou by secret means Used intercession to obtain a league? . . . v 4 147
How say'st thou, Charles? shall our condition stand? . . v 4 165
So the Earl of Armagnac may do, Because he is near kinsman unto Charles . . . v 5 45
Here are the articles of contracted peace Between our sovereign and the French king Charles . . . 2 *Hen. VI.* i 1 41
It is agreed between the French king Charles, and William de la Pole . i 1 44
Charles the emperor, Under pretence to see the queen his aunt *Hen. VIII.* i 1 176
Charles, I will play no more to-night; My mind's not on't . v 1 56
Sir, I did never win of you before.—But little, Charles . . v 1 59
'Tis midnight, Charles; Prithee, to bed . . . v 1 72
Charles the Great, having subdued the Saxons, There left behind and settled certain French . . . *Hen. V.* i 2 46
Charles the Great Subdued the Saxons, and did seat the French Beyond the river Sala, in the year Eight hundred five . . . i 2 61
Charles the duke of Lorraine, sole heir male Of the true line and stock of Charles the Great . . . i 2 71
Charlemain, who was the son To Lewis the emperor, and Lewis the son Of Charles the Great . . . i 2 77
By the which marriage the line of Charles the Great Was re-united to the crown of France . . . i 2 84
Charles' wain is over the new chimney . . . 1 *Hen. IV.* ii 1 2
Charm. Who, with a charm join'd to their suffer'd labour, I have left asleep . . . *Tempest* i 2 231
All the charms Of Sycorax, toads, beetles, bats, light on you! . i 2 339
My meaner ministers Their several kinds have done. My high charms work iii 3 88
Here thought they to have done Some wanton charm upon this man and maid . . . iv 1 95
Now does my project gather to a head: My charms crack not . v 1 2
Your charm so strongly works 'em . . . v 1 17
My charms I'll break, their senses I'll restore, And they shall be themselves . . . v 1 31
Charm. When I have required Some heavenly music, which even now I do, To work mine end upon their senses that This airy charm is for, I'll break my staff . . . *Tempest* v 1 54
The charm dissolves apace . . . v 1 64
Now my charms are all o'erthrown, And what strength I have's mine own . . . Epil. 1
Surely I think you have charms, la; yes, in truth *Mer. Wives* ii 2 107
Setting the attraction of my good parts aside I have no other charms . ii 2 111
She works by charms, by spells, by the figure, and such daubery . iv 2 185
Music oft hath such a charm To make bad good, and good provoke to harm . . . *Meas. for Meas.* iv 1 14
Beauty is a witch Against whose charms faith melteth into blood *Much Ado* ii 1 187
Yet is this no charm for the toothache . . . iii 2 72
Charm ache with air and agony with words . . . v 1 26
Ere I take this charm from off her sight, As I can take it *M. N. Dream* ii 1 183
Never harm, Nor spell, nor charm, Come our lovely lady nigh . ii 2 17
Churl, upon thy eyes I throw All the power this charm doth owe . ii 2 79
I'll charm his eyes against she do appear . . . iii 2 99
I will charm him first to keep his tongue . . *T. of Shrew* i 1 214
To tame a shrew and charm her chattering tongue . . . iv 2 58
Unchain your spirits now with spelling charms . . 1 *Hen. VI.* v 3 31
This hand of mine hath writ in thy behalf And therefore shall it charm thy riotous tongue . . . 2 *Hen. VI.* iv 1 64
Peace, wilful boy, or I will charm your tongue . . 3 *Hen. VI.* v 5 31
Have done thy charm, thou hateful wither'd hag! . *Richard III.* i 3 215
That have prevail'd Upon my body with their hellish charms . iii 4 64
Now the fair goddess, Fortune, Fall deep in love with thee; and her great charms Misguide thy opposers' swords! . . . *Coriolanus* i 5 22
This siren, that will charm Rome's Saturnine . . *T. Andron.* ii 1 23
Till I find . . . a charm to calm these fits, Per Styga, per manes vehor ii 1 134
Is beloved and loves again, Alike bewitched by the charm of looks *Rom. and Jul.* ii Prol. 6
Upon my knees, I charm you, by my once-commended beauty *J. Cæsar* ii 1 271
Peace! the charm's wound up . . . *Macbeth* i 3 37
I, the mistress of your charms, The close contriver of all harms . iii 5 6
Your vessels and your spells provide, Your charms and every thing beside . . . iii 5 19
For a charm of powerful trouble, Like a hell-broth boil and bubble . iv 1 18
Cool it with a baboon's blood, Then the charm is firm and good . iv 1 38
I'll charm the air to give a sound, While you perform your antic round iv 1 129
Despair thy charm . . . v 8 13
No fairy takes, nor witch hath power to charm . . *Hamlet* i 1 163
Mumbling of wicked charms, conjuring the moon . . *Lear* ii 1 41
Whose age has charms in it, whose title more, To pluck the common bosom on his side . . . v 3 48
Is there not charms By which the property of youth and maidhood May be abused? . . . *Othello* i 1 172
Thou hast practised on her with foul charms . . . i 2 73
What drugs, what charms, What conjuration and what mighty magic . i 3 91
Forth of my heart those charms, thine eyes, are blotted . . v 1 35
Go to, charm your tongue.—I will not charm my tongue; I am bound to speak . . . v 2 183
All the charms of love, Salt Cleopatra, soften thy waned lip! *A. and C.* ii 1 20
When I am revenged upon my charm, I have done all . . . iv 12 16
O this false soul of Egypt! this grave charm . . . iv 12 25
'Tis your graces That from my mutest conscience to my tongue Charms this report out . . . *Cymbeline* i 6 117
No exorciser harm thee!—Nor no witchcraft charm thee! . iv 2 277
Charmed. I charm'd their ears That calf-like they my lowing follow'd *Tempest* iv 1 178
And then I will her charmed eye release From monster's view *M. N. Dr.* iii 2 376
Fortune forbid my outside have not charm'd her! . *T. Night* ii 2 19
Whose dangerous eyes may well be charm'd asleep . 2 *Hen. IV.* iv 2 39
Has almost charmed me from my profession, by persuading me to it *T. of Athens* iv 3 454
Swelter'd venom sleeping got, Boil thou first i' the charmed pot *Macbeth* iv 1 9
I bear a charmed life, which must not yield To one of woman born . v 8 12
I, in mine own woe charm'd, Could not find death where I did hear him groan . . . *Cymbeline* v 3 68
Charmer. She was a charmer, and could almost read The thoughts of people . . . *Othello* iii 4 57
Charmeth. Music, ho! music, such as charmeth sleep! *M. N. Dream* iv 1 88
Charmian. Help me away, dear Charmian; I shall fall . *Ant. and Cleo.* i 3 15
Cut my lace, Charmian, come . . . i 3 71
Look, prithee, Charmian, How this Herculean Roman does become The carriage of his chafe . . . i 3 96
Charmian!—Madam?—Ha, ha! Give me to drink mandragora . i 5 1
O Charmian, Where think'st thou he is now? . . . i 5 18
Note him, good Charmian, 'tis the man; but note him . . i 5 54
Ink and paper, Charmian . . . i 5 65
Did I, Charmian, Ever love Cæsar so? . . . i 5 66
Let's to billiards: come, Charmian.—My arm is sore; best play with Mardian . . . ii 5 3
I am pale, Charmian . . . ii 5 59
I faint: O Iras, Charmian! 'tis no matter . . . ii 5 110
Let him for ever go:—let him not—Charmian, Though he be painted one way like a Gorgon, The other way's a Mars . . . ii 5 115
Pity me, Charmian, But do not speak to me . . . ii 5 118
Like her! O Isis! 'tis impossible.—I think so, Charmian . . iii 3 19
Madam, She was a widow,— Widow! Charmian, hark . . iii 3 30
I have one thing more to ask him yet, good Charmian: But 'tis no matter . . . iii 3 48
O Charmian, I will never go from hence . . . iv 15 1
Help, Charmian, help, Iras, help; Help, friends below . . iv 15 12
Why, how now, Charmian! My noble girls! Ah, women, women, look! . . . iv 15 83
He words me, that I should not Be noble to myself: but, hark thee, Charmian . . . v 2 192
Now, Charmian! Show me, my women, like a queen . . v 2 226
Now, noble Charmian, we'll dispatch indeed . . . v 2 230
Come then, and take the last warmth of my lips. Farewell, kind Charmian . . . v 2 295
What work is here! Charmian, is this well done? . . . v 2 328
O Cæsar, This Charmian lived but now; she stood and spake . v 2 344
Charming your blood with pleasing heaviness . . 1 *Hen. IV.* iii 1 218
Charming the narrow seas To give you gentle pass . . *Hen. V.* ii Prol. 38
Now help, ye charming spells and periapts . . 1 *Hen. VI.* v 3 2
Faster bound to Aaron's charming eyes Than is Prometheus tied to Caucasus . . . *T. Andron.* ii 1 16

Charming. That parting kiss which I had set Betwixt two charming words *Cymbeline* i 3 35
More charming With their own nobleness, which could have turn'd A distaff to a lance v 3 32
Charmingly. This is a most majestic vision, and Harmonious charmingly *Tempest* iv 1 119
Charneco. Neighbour, here's a cup of charneco 2 *Hen. VI.* ii 3 63
Charnel-house. Or shut me nightly in a charnel-house *Rom. and Jul.* iv 1 81
If charnel-houses and our graves must send Those that we bury back, our monuments Shall be the maws of kites *Macbeth* iii 4 71
Charolois. Foix, Lestrale, Bouciqualt, and Charolois *Hen. V.* iii 5 45
Charon. O, be thou my Charon, And give me swift transportance to those fields Where I may wallow in the lily-beds! *Troi. and Cres.* iii 2 11
Charter. If you deny it, let the danger light Upon your charter and your city's freedom *Mer. of Venice* iv 1 39
I must have liberty Withal, as large a charter as the wind *As Y. Like It* ii 7 48
Of that I have made a bold charter *All's Well* iv 5 97
Our substitutes at home shall have blank charters *Richard II.* i 4 48
And take from Time His charters and his customary rights ii 1 196
You break no privilege nor charter there *Richard III.* iii 1 54
My mother, Who has a charter to extol her blood *Coriolanus* i 9 14
Ever spake against Your liberties and the charters that you bear ii 3 188
Let me find a charter in your voice, To assist my simpleness *Othello* i 3 246
Chartered. When he speaks, The air, a charter'd libertine, is still *Hen. V.* i 1 48
Chartreux. A monk o' the Chartreux.—O, Nicholas Hopkins? *Hen. VIII.* i 1 221
What was that Hopkins?—Sir, a Chartreux friar i 2 148
Charybdis. Thus when I shun Scylla, your father, I fall into Charybdis, your mother *Mer. of Venice* iii 5 19
Chase. Ye that on the sands with printless foot Do chase the ebbing Neptune and do fly him When he comes back *Tempest* v 1 35
Their rising senses Begin to chase the ignorant fumes that mantle Their clearer reason v 1 67
Have some unhappy passenger in chase *T. G. of Ver.* v 4 15
Apollo flies, and Daphne holds the chase *M. N. Dream* ii 1 231
O, I am out of breath in this fond chase! ii 2 88
By this kind of chase, I should hate him *As Y. Like It* i 3 33
Big round tears Coursed one another down his innocent nose In piteous chase ii 1 40
Poor lord! is't I That chase thee from thy country? *All's Well* iii 2 106
I did send, After the last enchantment you did here, A ring in chase of you *T. Night* iii 1 124
This is the chase: I am gone for ever *W. Tale* iii 3 57
Whiles he was hastening, in the chase, it seems, Of this fair couple v 1 189
Though Fortune, visible an enemy, Should chase us with my father v 1 217
Where is he, That holds in chase mine honour up and down? *K. John* i 1 223
And chase the native beauty from his cheek iii 4 83
To rouse his wrongs and chase them to the bay *Richard II.* ii 3 128
Whose arms were moulded in their mothers' womb To chase these pagans 1 *Hen. IV.* i 1 24
You see this chase is hotly follow'd *Hen. V.* ii 4 68
Thee I'll chase hence, thou wolf in sheep's array 1 *Hen. VI.* i 3 55
Thinks he that the chirping of a wren, By crying comfort from a hollow breast, Can chase away the first-conceived sound? 2 *Hen. VI.* iii 2 44
Seek thee out some other chase, For I myself must hunt this deer to death v 2 14
Single out some other chase; For I myself will hunt this wolf to death 3 *Hen. VI.* ii 4 12
And make pursuit where he did mean no chase *Richard III.* iii 2 30
To chase us to our graves iv 4 54
Spies of the Volsces Held me in chase, that I was forced to wheel *Coriol.* i 6 19
I have dogs, my lord, Will rouse the proudest panther in the chase *T. Andron.* ii 2 21
Both are at the lodge Upon the north side of this pleasant chase ii 3 255
If thy wits run the wild-goose chase, I have done *Rom. and Jul.* ii 4 75
The barren, touched in this holy chase, Shake off their sterile curse *J. Cæsar* i 2 8
A pirate of very warlike appointment gave us chase *Hamlet* iv 6 16
I do follow here in the chase, not like a hound that hunts, but one that fills up the cry *Othello* ii 3 369
Warlike as the wolf for what we eat; Our valour is to chase what flies *Cymbeline* iii 3 42
Chased. Love hath chased sleep from my enthralled eyes *T. G. of Ver.* ii 4 134
When night-dogs run, all sorts of deer are chased *Mer. Wives* v 5 252
Met us again and madly bent on us Chased us away *Com. of Errors* v 1 153
All things that are, Are with more spirit chased than enjoy'd *Mer. of Venice* ii 6 13
That hath so cowarded and chased your blood Out of appearance *Hen. V.* ii 2 75
Alas, she hath from France too long been chased v 2 38
When I have chased all thy foes from hence, Then will I think upon a recompense 1 *Hen. VI.* i 2 115
And charity chased hence by rancour's hand 2 *Hen. VI.* iii 1 144
You forget That we are those which chased you from the field 3 *Hen. VI.* i 1 90
Ten, chased by one, Are now each one the slaughter-man of twenty *Cymbeline* v 3 48
Chaser. Then began A stop i' the chaser, a retire, anon A rout v 3 40
Chaseth. A woman clad in armour chaseth them 1 *Hen. VI.* i 5 3
Chasing the royal blood With fury from his native residence *Richard II.* ii 1 118
Chaste. To make cold nymphs chaste crowns *Tempest* iv 1 66
I will find you twenty lascivious turtles ere one chaste man *Mer. Wives* ii 1 83
With trial-fire touch me his finger-end: If he be chaste, the flame will back descend v 5 89
Then, Isabel, live chaste, and, brother, die *Meas. for Meas.* ii 4 184
He would not, but by gift of my chaste body To his concupiscible intemperate lust, Release my brother v 1 97
As Dian in her orb, As chaste as is the bud ere it be blown *Much Ado* iv 1 59
Will you give horns, chaste lady? do not so *L. L. Lost* v 2 252
Quench'd in the chaste beams of the watery moon *M. N. Dream* ii 1 162
If I live to be as old as Sibylla, I will die as chaste as Diana *Mer. of Venice* i 2 117
And thou, thrice-crowned queen of night, survey With thy chaste eye, from thy pale sphere above *As Y. Like It* iii 2 3
Carve on every tree The fair, the chaste and unexpressive she iii 2 10
And then let Kate be chaste and Dian sportful *T. of Shrew* ii 1 263
Of a most chaste renown *All's Well* iv 3 18
As continent, as chaste, as true, As I am now unhappy *W. Tale* iii 2 35
Hermione is chaste; Polixenes blameless iii 2 133
Their transformations Were never for a piece of beauty rarer, Nor in a way so chaste iv 4 33
Our noble and chaste mistress the moon 1 *Hen. IV.* i 2 30
Chaste and immaculate in very thought 1 *Hen. VI.* v 4 51
At your command; Command, I mean, of virtuous chaste intents v 5 20
Chaste. I have commended to his goodness The model of our chaste loves *Hen. VIII.* iv 2 132
Strew me over With maiden flowers, that all the world may know I was a chaste wife to my grave iv 2 170
Tell him that my lady Was fairer than his grandam and as chaste As may be in the world *Troi. and Cres.* i 3 299
Chaste as the icicle That's curdied by the frost from purest snow *Coriol.* v 3 65
Lucrece was not more chaste Than this Lavinia *T. Andron.* ii 1 108
And father of that chaste dishonour'd dame iv 1 90
Then she hath sworn that she will still live chaste?—She hath *Rom. and Jul.* i 1 223
Or your chaste treasure open To his unmaster'd importunity. *Hamlet* i 3 31
Be thou as chaste as ice, as pure as snow, thou shalt not escape calumny iii 1 140
The chaste unsmirched brow Of my true mother iv 5 119
Many worthy and chaste dames even thus, All guiltless, meet reproach *Othello* iv 1 47
O, 'tis the spite of hell, the fiend's arch-mock, To lip a wanton in a secure couch, And to suppose her chaste! iv 1 73
If she be not honest, chaste, and true, There's no man happy iv 2 17
It is the cause, my soul,—Let me not name it to you, you chaste stars! v 2 2
Moor, she was chaste; she loved thee, cruel Moor v 2 249
Virtuous, wise, chaste, constant-qualified *Cymbeline* i 4 64
And the chimney-piece Chaste Dian bathing ii 4 82
I thought her As chaste as unsunn'd snow ii 5 13
Where I was taught Of your chaste daughter the wide difference 'Twixt amorous and villanous v 5 194
It gives a good report to a number to be chaste *Pericles* iv 6 44
Chastely. Wish chastely and love dearly *All's Well* i 3 218
Herself most chastely absent iii 7 34
No, though it were as virtuous to lie as to live chastely *Coriolanus* v 2 28
Chastise. I am afraid He will chastise me *Tempest* v 1 263
Under whose warrant I impeach thy wrong And by whose help I mean to chastise it *K. John* ii 1 117
O, then how quickly should this arm of mine, Now prisoner to the palsy, chastise thee! *Richard II.* ii 3 104
I will chastise this high-minded strumpet. 1 *Hen. VI.* i 5 12
And chastise with the valour of my tongue All that impedes thee *Macb.* i 5 28
Chastised. Your breath first kindled the dead coal of wars Between this chastised kingdom and myself *K. John* v 2 84
When this arm of mine hath chastised The petty rebel *Richard III.* iv 4 331
Tell her I have chastised the amorous Trojan *Troi. and Cres.* v 5 4
Chastised with arms Our enemies' pride *T. Andron.* i 1 32
Nor once be chastised with the sober eye Of dull Octavia *Ant. and Cleo.* v 2 54
Chastisement. Do with your injuries as seems you best, In any chastisement: I for a while will leave you *Meas. for Meas.* v 1 257
Shall that victorious hand be feebled here, That in your chambers gave you chastisement? *K. John* v 2 147
Cries To me for justice and rough chastisement *Richard II.* i 1 106
Shall I so much dishonour my fair stars, On equal terms to give him chastisement? iv 1 22
He now doth lack The very instruments of chastisement 2 *Hen. IV.* iv 1 217
Talk with him And give him chastisement for this abuse 1 *Hen. VI.* iv 1 69
Make us thy ministers of chastisement, That we may praise thee in the victory! *Richard III.* v 3 113
And chastisement doth therefore hide his head *J. Cæsar* iv 3 16
Chastity. Upon whose grave thou vow'dst pure chastity. *T. G. of Ver.* iv 3 21
More than our brother is our chastity *Meas. for Meas.* ii 4 185
In double violation Of sacred chastity and of promise-breach v 1 410
There is not chastity enough in language Without offence to utter them *Much Ado* iv 1 98
When she weeps, weeps every little flower, Lamenting some enforced chastity *M. N. Dream* iii 1 205
The very ice of chastity is in them [his kisses]. *As Y. Like It* iii 4 18
For patience she will prove a second Grissel, And Roman Lucrece for her chastity *T. of Shrew* ii 1 298
My chastity's the jewel of our house, Bequeathed down. *All's Well* iv 2 46
To rob a man, To force a spotless virgin's chastity 2 *Hen. VI.* v 1 186
Thy sons make pillage of her chastity *T. Andron.* ii 3 44
This minion stood upon her chastity, Upon her nuptial vow, her loyalty ii 3 124
And that more dear Than hands or tongue, her spotless chastity v 2 177
In strong proof of chastity well arm'd, From love's weak childish bow she lives unharm'd *Rom. and Jul.* i 1 216
Cold, cold, my girl! Even like thy chastity *Othello* v 2 276
There's a palm presages chastity, if nothing else *Ant. and Cleo.* i 2 47
For your ill opinion and the assault you have made to her chastity you shall answer me with your sword *Cymbeline* i 4 176
Our Tarquin thus Did softly press the rushes, ere he waken'd The chastity he wounded ii 2 14
To the purpose.—Your daughter's chastity—there it begins v 5 179
That he could not But think her bond of chastity quite crack'd v 5 207
Your peevish chastity, which is not worth a breakfast in the cheapest country under the cope *Pericles* iv 6 130
Marry, come up, my dish of chastity with rosemary and bays! iv 6 160
Chat. I myself could make A chough of as deep chat *Tempest* ii 1 266
I familiarly sometimes Do use you for my fool and chat with you *Com. of Errors* ii 2 27
Then leave this chat *L. L. Lost* iv 3 284
If you deny to dance, let's hold more chat v 2 228
O, how I long to have some chat with her! *T. of Shrew* ii 1 163
Setting all this chat aside, Thus in plain terms ii 1 270
But what a fool am I to chat with you! iii 2 123
Pray you, sit down; For now we sit to chat as well as eat v 2 11
This bald unjointed chat of his, my lord, I answer'd indirectly 1 *Hen. IV.* i 3 65
Come, come, no more of this unprofitable chat iii 1 63
You muse what chat we two have had 3 *Hen. VI.* iii 2 109
Into a rapture lets her baby cry While she chats him *Coriolanus* ii 1 224
Go and trim her up; I'll go and chat with Paris *Rom. and Jul.* iv 4 25
Chatham. The clerk of Chatham: he can write and read and cast accompt 2 *Hen. VI.* iv 2 92
Chatillon. Now, say, Chatillon, what would France with us? *K. John* i 1 1
My Lord Chatillon may from England bring That right in peace ii 1 46
Lo, upon thy wish, Our messenger Chatillon is arrived! ii 1 51
What England says, say briefly, gentle lord; We coldly pause for thee; Chatillon, speak ii 1 53
Jaques Chatillon, Rambures, Vaudemont *Hen. V.* iii 5 43
Jacques of Chatillon, admiral of France iv 8 98
Chattel. She is my goods, my chattels; she is my house. *T. of Shrew* iii 2 232
Look to my chattels and my movables: Let senses rule *Hen. V.* ii 3 50
To forfeit all your goods, lands, tenements, Chattels, and whatsoever *Hen. VIII.* iii 2 343

Chatter. Sometime like apes that mow and chatter at me . *Tempest* ii 2 9

When the rain came to wet me once, and the wind to make me chatter *Lear* iv 6 103

Apes and monkeys 'Twixt two such shes would chatter this way and Contemn with mows the other . . . . . *Cymbeline* i 6 40

Chattering. To tame a shrew and charm her chattering tongue *T. of Shr.* iv 2 58

And chattering pies in dismal discords sung . . . 3 *Hen. VI.* v 6 48

Chaud. Ma foi, il fait fort chaud . . . . *Mer. Wives* i 4 53

Chaudron. Make the gruel thick and slab: Add thereto a tiger's chaudron, For the ingredients of our cauldron . . . *Macbeth* iv 1 33

Cheap. The goodness that is cheap in beauty makes beauty brief in goodness . . . . *Meas. for Meas.* iii 1 185

I hold your dainties cheap, sir, and your welcome dear *Com. of Errors* iii 1 21

Let what is dear in Sicily be cheap . . . . *W. Tale* i 2 175

You may buy land now as cheap as stinking mackerel . 1 *Hen. IV.* ii 4 394

So stale and cheap to vulgar company . . . . . . iii 2 41

Would have bought me lights as good cheap at the dearest chandler's . iii 3 51

When flesh is cheap and females dear . . . 2 *Hen. IV.* v 3 20

And hold their manhoods cheap . . . . . *Hen. V.* iv 3 66

Pirates may make cheap pennyworths of their pillage . 2 *Hen. VI.* i 1 222

Who, in a cheap estimation, is worth all your predecessors *Coriolanus* ii 1 100

I hope to see Romans as cheap as Volscians . . . . iv 5 249

A pair of tribunes that have rack'd for Rome, To make coals cheap . v 1 17

A few drops of women's rheum, which are As cheap as lies . v 6 47

Allow not nature more than nature needs, Man's life's as cheap as beast's *Lear* ii 4 270

Cheapen. Virtuous, or I'll never cheapen her . *Much Ado* ii 3 33

She would make a puritan of the devil, if he should cheapen a kiss of her *Pericles* iv 6 10

Cheaper. 'Twere the cheaper way . . . *Meas. for Meas.* ii 4 105

Cheapest. The cheapest of us is ten groats too dear. *Richard II.* v 5 68

Your peevish chastity, which is not worth a breakfast in the cheapest country under the cope . . . . . . *Pericles* iv 6 131

Cheaply. So great a day as this is cheaply bought . *Macbeth* v 8 37

Cheapside. In Cheapside shall my palfry go to grass 2 *Hen. VI.* iv 2 74

When shall we go to Cheapside and take up commodities upon our bills? . . . . iv 7 134

Cheat. I hope you do not mean to cheat me so. *Com. of Errors* iv 3 79

Some tricks, some quillets, how to cheat the devil . *L. L. Lost* iv 3 288

I purchased this caparison, and my revenue is the silly cheat *W. Tale* iv 3 28

If I make not this cheat bring out another . . . iv 3 129

Maids, Who, having no external thing to lose But the word 'maid,' cheats the poor maid of that . . . *K. John* ii 1 572

Cheated. We are merely cheated of our lives by drunkards *Tempest* i 1 59

A sorcerer, that by his cunning hath cheated me . . iii 2 49

Cheated of feature by dissembling nature, Deform'd, unfinish'd *Richard III.* i 1 19

Cheater. I will be cheater to them both, and they shall be exchequers to me . . . . *Mer. Wives* i 3 77

Disguised cheaters, prating mountebanks . *Com. of Errors* i 2 101

A tame cheater, i' faith; you may stroke him as gently as a puppy greyhound . . . . 2 *Hen. IV.* ii 4 106

I will bar no honest man my house, nor no cheater . ii 4 111

Thou abominable damned cheater, art thou not ashamed to be called captain? . . . . ii 4 152

I play'd the cheater for thy father's hand . *T. Andron.* v 1 111

Cheating. You poor, base, rascally, cheating, lack-linen mate! 2 *Hen. IV.* ii 4 133

Check. If I can check my erring love, I will . *T. G. of Ver.* ii 4 213

Against all checks, rebukes and manners, I must advance *Mer. Wives* iii 4 84

That in this spleen ridiculous appears, To check their folly, passion's solemn tears . . . . . . *L. L. Lost* v 2 118

Wit, whither wilt?—Nay, you might keep that check for it till you met your wife's wit going to your neighbour's bed *As Y. Like It* iv 1 169

So devote to Aristotle's checks As Ovid be an outcast quite abjured *T. of Shrew* i 1 32

Check thy contempt: Obey our will, which travails in thy good *All's Well* ii 3 164

And with what wing the staniel checks at it! . *T. Night* ii 5 125

Like the haggard, check at every feather That comes before his eye iii 1 71

Thou mayst be a queen, and check the world . . *K. John* ii 1 123

That none so small advantage shall step forth To check his reign . iii 4 152

Mocking the air with colours idly spread, And find no check . v 1 73

And here have I the daintiness of ear To check time broke *Richard II.* v 5 46

Meeting the check of such another day . . . . . 1 *Hen. IV.* v 5 42

I never knew yet but rebuke and check was the reward of valour 2 *Hen. IV.* iv 3 34

Hardly can I check my eyes from tears . . . . . 3 *Hen. VI.* i 4 151

O Phœbus, hadst thou never given consent That Phaëthon should check thy fiery steeds! . . . . ii 6 12

This earth affords no joy to me, But to command, to check, to o'erbear iii 2 166

He cannot swear, but it [conscience] checks him . . *Richard III.* i 4 140

Checks and disasters Grow in the veins of actions highest rear'd *Troi. and Cres.* i 3 5

Posts, like the commandment of a king, Sans check to good and bad . i 3 94

Nor check my courage for what they can give . . *Coriolanus* iii 3 92

I did endure Not seldom, nor no slight checks . . *T. of Athens* ii 2 149

Lay thou thy basis sure, For goodness dare not check thee . *Macbeth* iv 3 33

In thy best consideration, check This hideous rashness . . *Lear* i 1 152

Old fools are babes again; and must be used With checks as flatteries . i 3 20

His fault is much, and the good king his master Will check him for't . ii 2 149

The state, However this may gall him with some check, Cannot with safety cast him . . . . *Othello* i 1 149

I am desperate of my fortunes if they check me here . . . ii 3 338

Is not almost a fault To incur a private check . . . . . iii 3 67

That even his stubbornness, his checks, his frowns,—Prithee, unpin me,—have grace and favour in them . . . . iv 3 20

Rebukeable And worthy shameful check it were . . *Ant. and Cleo.* iv 4 31

O, this life Is nobler than attending for a check . . . *Cymbeline* iii 3 22

Checked. Be check'd for silence, But never tax'd for speech . *All s Well* i 1 76

I have checked him for it, and the young lion repents . . 2 *Hen. IV.* i 2 220

Check'd and rated by Northumberland . . . . . . iii 1 68

Next time I'll keep my dreams unto myself, And not be check'd 2 *Hen. VI.* i 2 54

Then, on the other side, I check'd my friends . . . *Richard III.* iii 7 150

Hated by one he loves; braved by his brother; Check'd like a bondman *J. Cæsar* iv 3 97

Checkered. Or as the snake roll'd in a flowering bank, With shining checker'd slough . . . . 2 *Hen. VI.* iii 1 229

Checking. If he be now return'd, As checking at his voyage . *Hamlet* iv 7 63

Cheek. The sea, mounting to the welkin's cheek, Dashes the fire out *Temp.* i 2 4

The setting of thine eye and cheek proclaim A matter from thee . . ii 1 229

The air hath starved the roses in her cheeks . . . *T. G. of Ver.* iv 4 159

Cheek. The clock hath strucken twelve upon the bell; My mistress made it one upon my cheek . . . . . *Com. of Errors* i 2 46

Hath homely age the alluring beauty took From my poor cheek? . ii 1 90

The old ornament of his cheek hath already stuffed tennis-balls *Much Ado* iii 2 46

Blushing cheeks by faults are bred And fears by pale white shown *L. L. Lost* i 2 106

For still her cheeks possess the same Which native she doth owe . i 2 110

The night of dew that on my cheeks down flows . . . . iv 3 29

Air, quoth he, thy cheeks may blow . . . . . . iv 3 109

Of all complexions the cull'd sovereignty Do meet, as at a fair, in her fair cheek . . . . iv 3 235

Some Dick, That smiles his cheek in years . . . . . v 2 465

Why is your cheek so pale? How chance the roses there do fade so fast?—Belike for want of rain . . . . *M. N. Dream* i 1 128

Follow! nay, I'll go with thee, cheek by jole . . . . iii 2 338

Sit thee down upon this flowery bed, While I thy amiable cheeks do coy iv 1 2

This cherry nose, These yellow cowslip cheeks . . . . v 1 339

Is like a villain with a smiling cheek . . . . *Mer. of Venice* i 3 101

There are some shrewd contents in yon same paper, That steals the colour from Bassanio's cheek . . . . iii 2 247

Helen's cheek, but not her heart . . . . . *As Y. Like It* iii 2 153

What were his marks?—A lean cheek, which you have not . iii 2 392

If ever,—as that ever may be near,—You meet in some fresh cheek the power of fancy . . . . iii 5 29

Your black silk hair, Your bugle eyeballs, nor your cheek of cream . iii 5 47

A little riper and more lusty red Than that mix'd in his cheek . iii 5 122

Such war of white and red within her cheeks! . *T. of Shrew* iv 5 30

The tyranny of her sorrows takes all livelihood from her cheek *All's Well* i 1 58

Your date is better in your pie and your porridge than in your cheek . i 1 173

'Tis so; for, look, thy cheeks Confess it, th' one to th' other . i 3 182

His cicatrice, an emblem of war, here on his sinister cheek . . ii 1 44

The blushes in my cheeks thus whisper me, 'We blush that thou shouldst choose; but, be refused, Let the white death sit on thy cheek for ever' . . . . ii 3 75

His left cheek is a cheek of two pile and a half, but his right cheek is worn bare . . . . iv 5 102

She never told her love, But let concealment, like a worm i' the bud, Feed on her damask cheek . . . . . *T. Night* ii 4 115

Were you a woman, as the rest goes even, I should my tears let fall upon your cheek . . . . v 1 247

Is whispering nothing? Is leaning cheek to cheek? . *W. Tale* i 2 285

The pretty dimples of his chin and cheek . . . . ii 3 101

I think affliction may subdue the cheek, But not take in the mind . iv 4 587

Upon thy cheek lay I this zealous kiss . . . . *K. John* ii 1 19

To save unscratch'd your city's threaten'd cheeks . . . ii 1 225

Making that idiot, laughter, keep men's eyes And strain their cheeks to idle merriment . . . . iii 3 46

Now will canker sorrow eat my bud And chase the native beauty from his cheek . . . . iii 4 83

Where is that blood That I have seen inhabit in those cheeks? . . iv 2 107

Let me wipe off this honourable dew, That silvery doth progress on thy cheeks . . . . v 2 46

Darest with thy frozen admonition Make pale our cheek . *Richard II.* ii 1 118

Nor my own disgrace Have ever made me sour my patient cheek . . ii 1 169

And stain'd the beauty of a fair queen's cheeks With tears . . iii 1 14

Their thundering shock At meeting tears the cloudy cheeks of heaven . iii 3 57

Then his cheek look'd pale, And on my face he turn'd an eye of death 1 *Hen. IV.* i 3 142

Why hast thou lost the fresh blood in thy cheeks? . . . . ii 3 47

His cheek looks pale and with A rising sigh he wisheth you in heaven . iii 1 9

Let them coin his nose, let them coin his cheeks: I'll not pay a denier iii 3 91

The whiteness in thy cheek Is apter than thy tongue to tell thy errand 2 *Hen. IV.* i 1 68

I will sooner have a beard grow in the palm of my hand than he shall get one on his cheek . . . . i 2 25

Have you not a moist eye? a dry hand? a yellow cheek? a white beard? i 2 204

Washing with kindly tears his gentle cheeks . . . . iv 5 84

Look ye, how they change! Their cheeks are paper . . *Hen. V.* ii 2 74

Their gesture sad Investing lank-lean cheeks and war-worn coats . iv Prol. 26

Whilst I waited on my tender lambs, And to sun's parching heat display'd my cheeks . . . . 1 *Hen. VI.* i 2 77

Here by the cheeks I'll drag thee up and down . . . . i 3 51

One of thy eyes and thy cheek's side struck off! Accursed tower! . i 4 75

Meantime your cheeks do counterfeit our roses . . . . ii 4 62

'Tis not for fear but anger that thy cheeks Blush for pure shame . ii 4 65

O, tell me when my lips do touch his cheeks, That I may kindly give one fainting kiss . . . . ii 5 39

The sanguine colour of the leaves Did represent my master's blushing cheeks . . . . iv 1 93

And ne'er returneth To blush and beautify the cheek again 2 *Hen. VI.* iii 2 167

These cheeks are pale for watching for your good . . . . iv 7 90

I give thee this to dry thy cheeks withal . . . . . 3 *Hen. VI.* i 4 83

The ruthless queen gave him to dry his cheeks A napkin . . . ii 1 61

Wet my cheeks with artificial tears, And frame my face to all occasions iii 2 184

I defy thee, And to my brother turn my blushing cheeks . . . v 1 99

These nails should rend that beauty from my cheeks . *Richard III.* i 2 126

All the standers-by had wet their cheeks, Like trees bedash'd with rain i 2 163

No one in this presence But his red colour hath forsook his cheeks . ii 1 85

He wept, And hugg'd me in his arm, and kindly kiss'd my cheek . ii 2 24

The red wine first must rise In their fair cheeks . . . *Hen. VIII.* i 4 44

Pour'st in the open ulcer of my heart Her eyes, her hair, her cheek, her gait, her voice . . . . *Troi. and Cres.* i 1 54

What grief hath set the jaundice on your cheeks? . . . . i 3 2

Why then, you princes, Do you with cheeks abash'd behold our works? i 3 18

Bid the cheek be ready with a blush Modest as morning . . . . i 3 228

Scratch my praised cheeks, Crack my clear voice with sobs . . iv 2 113

The lustre in your eye, heaven in your cheek, Pleads your fair usage . iv 4 120

Blow, villain, till thy sphered bias cheek Outswell the colic of puff'd Aquilon . . . . iv 5 8

There's language in her eye, her cheek, her lip, Nay, her foot speaks . iv 5 55

My mother's blood Runs on the dexter cheek, and this sinister Bounds in my father's . . . . iv 5 128

She strokes his cheek! . . . . v 2 51

The war of white and damask in Their nicely-gawded cheeks *Coriolanus* ii 1 233

The smiles of knaves Tent in my cheeks, and schoolboys' tears take up The glasses of my sight! . . . . iii 2 116

To tear with thunder the wide cheeks o' the air . . . . . v 3 151

Which, like a taper in some monument, Doth shine upon the dead man's earthy cheeks . . . . *T. Andron.* ii 3 229

Cheek. Thy cheeks look red as Titan's face Blushing to be encounter'd with a cloud . . . *T. Andron.* ii 4 31
These bitter tears, which now you see Filling the aged wrinkles in my cheeks . . . . iii 1 7
To behold our cheeks How they are stain'd, as meadows, yet not dry . iii 1 124
Ah, my Lavinia, I will wipe thy cheeks . . . . iii 1 142
His napkin, with his true tears all bewet, Can do no service on her sorrowful cheeks . . . . iii 1 147
Tears, Brew'd with her sorrow, mesh'd upon her cheeks . . iii 2 38
She hangs upon the cheek of night Like a rich jewel . *Rom. and Jul.* i 5 47
The brightness of her cheek would shame those stars . . ii 2 19
See, how she leans her cheek upon her hand! O, that I were a glove upon that hand, That I might touch that cheek! . . . . ii 2 23
The mask of night is on my face, Else would a maiden blush bepaint my cheek . . . . ii 2 86
What a deal of brine Hath wash'd thy sallow cheeks for Rosaline! . ii 3 70
Lo, here upon thy cheek the stain doth sit Of an old tear . . ii 3 75
Now comes the wanton blood up in your cheeks, They'll be in scarlet straight at any news . . . . ii 5 72
Hood my unmann'd blood, bating in my cheeks, With thy black mantle iii 2 14
The roses in thy lips and cheeks shall fade To paly ashes . . iv 1 99
Famine is in thy cheeks, Need and oppression starveth in thine eyes . v 1 69
Beauty's ensign yet Is crimson in thy lips and in thy cheeks . . v 3 95
Let not the virgin's cheek Make soft thy trenchant sword *T. of Athens* iv 3 114
Calpurnia's cheek is pale . . . . *J. Cæsar* i 2 185
You can behold such sights, And keep the natural ruby of your cheeks, When mine is blanch'd with fear . . . . . *Macbeth* iii 4 115
Those linen cheeks of thine Are counsellors to fear . . . v 3 16
The harlot's cheek, beautied with plastering art, Is not more ugly *Hamlet* iii 1 51
Let the bloat king tempt you again to bed; Pinch wanton on your cheek iii 4 183
With cadent tears fret channels in her cheeks . . . *Lear* i 4 307
Let not women's weapons, water-drops, Stain my man's cheeks! . ii 4 281
Blow, winds, and crack your cheeks! rage! blow! . . . iii 2 1
Milk-liver'd man! That bear'st a cheek for blows, a head for wrongs iv 2 51
And now and then an ample tear trill'd down Her delicate cheek . iv 3 15
I should make very forges of my cheeks, That would to cinders burn up modesty, Did I but speak thy deeds . . . . *Othello* iv 2 74
Else so thy cheek pays shame When shrill-tongued Fulvia scolds *Ant. and Cleo.* i 1 31
Was borne so like a soldier, that thy cheek So much as lank'd not . i 4 70
Divers-colour'd fans, whose wind did seem To glow the delicate cheeks ii 2 209
The holes where eyes should be, which pitifully disaster the cheeks . ii 7 19
Gentle lords, let's part; You see we have burnt our cheeks . . ii 7 129
Put colour in thy cheek . . . . iv 14 69
Had I this cheek To bathe my lips upon . . . . *Cymbeline* i 6 99
Even then The princely blood flows in his cheek, he sweats . . iii 3 93
You must Forget that rarest treasure of your cheek, Exposing it . . iii 4 163
O! Give colour to my pale cheek with thy blood, That we the horrider may seem . . . . iv 2 330
Who with wet cheeks Were present when she finish'd . . . v 5 35
With dead cheeks advise thee to desist For going on death's net *Pericles* i 1 39
Drew sleep out of mine eyes, blood from my cheeks, Musings into my mind . . . . i 2 96
Is not this true?—Our cheeks and hollow eyes do witness it . . i 4 51
There is something glows upon my cheek, And whispers in mine ear 'Go not' . . . . v 1 96
Cheek-roses. Hail, virgin, if you be, as those cheek-roses Proclaim you are no less! . . . . *Meas. for Meas.* i 4 16
Cheer. Boatswain!—Here, master: what cheer? . . . *Tempest* i 1 2
I have good cheer at home; and I pray you all go with me *Mer. Wives* iii 2 53
Besides your cheer, you shall have sport . . . . . iii 2 81
Our cheer May answer my good will and your good welcome here *Com. of Errors* iii 1 19
Small cheer and great welcome makes a merry feast . . . iii 1 26
Better cheer may you have, but not with better heart . . . iii 1 29
Here is neither cheer, sir, nor welcome: we would fain have either . iii 1 66
Comfort my sister, cheer her, call her wife . . . . iii 2 26
There, take it; and much thanks for my good cheer . . . v 1 392
Their cheer is the greater that I am subdued . . *Much Ado* i 3 74
Well, I will meet you, so I may have good cheer . . . v 1 153
What cheer, my love? . . . . . . *M. N. Dream* i 1 122
All fancy-sick she is and pale of cheer, With sighs of love . . iii 2 96
The fairest dame That lived, that loved, that liked, that look'd with cheer . . . . v 1 299
Nerissa, cheer yon stranger; bid her welcome . . *Mer. of Venice* iii 2 240
Bid your friends welcome, show a merry cheer . . . . iii 2 314
Therefore be of good cheer, for truly I think you are damned . . iii 5 6
Good cheer, Antonio! What, man, courage yet! . . . . iv 1 111
Live a little; comfort a little; cheer thyself a little . *As Y. Like It* ii 6 5
Be of good cheer, youth: you a man! you lack a man's heart . iv 3 164
I fare well; for here is cheer enough . . . *T. of Shrew* Ind. 2 103
And have prepared great store of wedding cheer . . . . iii 2 188
What cheer?—Faith, as cold as can be . . . . . iv 3 37
Welcome! one mess is like to be your cheer . . . . iv 4 70
And, by all likelihood, some cheer is toward . . . . iv 5 14
My banquet is to close our stomachs up, After our great good cheer . v 2 10
I prithee, lady, have a better cheer . . . . *All's Well* iii 2 67
What cheer? how is't with you, best brother? . . . *W. Tale* i 2 148
My sovereign lord, cheer up yourself, look up . *2 Hen. IV.* iv 4 113
Quoth-a, we shall Do nothing but eat, and make good cheer . . v 3 18
What, man! be o' good cheer . . . . . . *Hen. V.* ii 3 19
Methinks your looks are sad, your cheer appall'd . *1 Hen. VI.* i 2 48
Salisbury, cheer thy spirit with this comfort . . . . i 4 90
Go, go, cheer up thy hungry-starved men . . . . . i 5 16
These news, my lords, may cheer our drooping spirits . . . v 2 1
With his grumbling voice Was wont to cheer his dad in mutinies *3 Hen. VI.* i 4 77
Doth not the object cheer your heart, my lord?—Ay, as the rocks cheer them that fear their wreck . . . . ii 2 4
My lord, cheer up your spirits: our foes are nigh . . . ii 2 56
Cheer these noble lords And hearten those that fight in your defence . ii 2 78
And cheers these hands that slew thy sire and brother To execute the like upon thyself . . . . ii 4 9
This cheers my heart, to see your forwardness . . . . iv 8 65
And cheer his grace with quick and merry words *Richard III.* i 3 5
Now cheer each other in each other's love . . . . ii 2 114
Be of good cheer: mother, how fares your grace? . . . iv 1 38
I have not that alacrity of spirit, Nor cheer of mind, that I was wont to have . . . . v 3 74
But cheer thy heart, and be thou not dismay'd . . . v 3 174
Cheer your neighbours. Ladies, you are not merry . . *Hen. VIII.* i 4 41
Cheer. Be of good cheer; They shall no more prevail than we give way to *Hen. VIII.* v 1 142
Go in and cheer the town: we'll forth and fight . *Troi. and Cres.* v 3 92
Though chance of war hath wrought this change of cheer . *T. Andron.* i 1 264
Take up this good old man, and cheer the heart That dies in tempest of thy angry frown . . . . i 1 457
Ne'er let my heart know merry cheer indeed, Till all the Andronici be made away . . . . ii 3 188
Then cheer thy spirit . . . . iv 4 88
Although the cheer be poor, 'Twill fill your stomachs; please you eat of it v 3 28
Now, ere the sun advance his burning eye, The day to cheer *Rom. and Jul.* ii 3 6
For this, being smelt, with that part cheers each part . . ii 3 25
Our instruments to melancholy bells, Our wedding cheer to a sad burial feast . . . . iv 5 87
And all the madness is, he cheers them up too . *T. of Athens* i 2 43
I'll cheer up My discontented troops, and lay for hearts . . iii 5 114
Ah, my good friend, what cheer? . . . . . . iii 6 44
All covered dishes!—Royal cheer, I warrant you.—Doubt not that, if money and the season can yield it . . . . . . iii 6 56
Publius, good cheer; There is no harm intended to your person *J. Cæsar* iii 1 89
My royal lord, You do not give the cheer . . . *Macbeth* iii 4 33
Come, sisters, cheer we up his sprites, And show the best of our delights iv 1 127
Receive what cheer you may: The night is long that never finds the day iv 3 239
This push Will cheer me ever, or disseat me now . . . v 3 21
Remain Here, in the cheer and comfort of our eye . . *Hamlet* i 2 116
You are so sick of late, So far from cheer and from your former state, That I distrust you . . . . iii 2 174
An anchor's cheer in prison be my scope! . . . . . iii 2 229
Cheer your heart: Be you not troubled with the time *Ant. and Cleo.* iii 6 81
How do you, women? What, what! good cheer! . . . iv 15 83
Be of good cheer; You're fall'n into a princely hand, fear nothing . v 2 21
Go in and cheer the king: he rages; none Dare come about him *Cymb.* iii 5 67
You shall have better cheer Ere you depart; and thanks to stay and eat it . . . . iii 6 67
Cheered. A cry more tuneable Was never holla'd to, nor cheer'd with horn . . . . *M. N. Dream* iv 1 130
Still and anon cheer'd up the heavy time . . . . *K. John* iv 1 47
Upon these words I came and cheer'd him up . . . *Hen. V.* iv 6 20
Northumberland, Whose warlike ears could never brook retreat, Cheer'd up the drooping army . . . . . . *3 Hen. VI.* i 1 6
I cheer'd them up with justice of our cause, With promise of high pay . ii 1 133
As all the world is cheer'd by the sun, So I by that; it is my day, my life . . . . *Richard III.* i 2 129
Therefore be cheer'd; Make not your thoughts your prisons *A. and C.* v 2 184
Cheerer. Her vine, the merry cheerer of the heart . . *Hen. V.* v 2 41
Cheerest. How cheer'st thou, Jessica? . . . *Mer. of Venice* iii 5 75
Cheerful. You do look, my son, in a moved sort, As if you were dismay'd: be cheerful, sir . . . . *Tempest* iv 1 147
Be cheerful And think of each thing well . . . . . v 1 250
Yet be cheerful, knight: thou shalt eat a posset to-night at my house *Mer. Wives* v 5 179
Prithee, be cheerful . . . . *As Y. Like It* i 3 96
And looked upon, I hope, with cheerful eyes . . *K. John* iv 2 2
You promised . . . To . . . entertain a cheerful disposition *Richard II.* ii 2 4
Of a cheerful look, a pleasing eye and a most noble carriage *1 Hen. IV.* ii 4 465
How they shout!—This had been cheerful after victory . *2 Hen. IV.* iv 2 88
Freshly looks and over-bears attaint With cheerful semblance *Hen. V.* iv Prol. 40
With one cheerful voice welcome my love . . . *2 Hen. VI.* i 1 36
O cheerful colours! see where Oxford comes! . . *3 Hen. VI.* v 1 58
Be cheerful, Richmond; for the wronged souls Of butcher'd princes fight in thy behalf . . . . *Richard III.* v 3 121
The snake lies rolled in the cheerful sun . . . *T. Andron.* ii 3 13
All this day an unaccustom'd spirit Lifts me above the ground with cheerful thoughts . . . . *Rom. and Jul.* v 1 5
Be cheerful; wipe thine eyes . . . . . . *Cymbeline* iv 2 402
Go, I pray you, Walk, and be cheerful once again . . . *Pericles* iv 1 40
Cheerfully. Pluck up thy spirits; look cheerfully upon me *T. of Shrew* iv 3 38
God-a-mercy, old heart! thou speak'st cheerfully . . . *Hen. V.* iv 1 34
Ay, he said so, to make us fight cheerfully . . . . iv 1 204
Go cheerfully together and digest Your angry choler *1 Hen. VI.* iv 1 167
Madam, good hope; his grace speaks cheerfully . *Richard III.* i 3 34
His grace looks cheerfully and smooth to-day . . . . iii 4 50
Sound drums and trumpets boldly and cheerfully . . . v 3 269
Look you, how cheerfully my mother looks, and my father died within these two hours . . . . *Hamlet* iii 2 134
How cheerfully on the false trail they cry! . . . . iv 5 109
Cheering a rout of rebels with your drum . . *2 Hen. IV.* iv 2 9
Went through the army, cheering up the soldiers . *Richard III.* v 3 71
Cheerless. All's cheerless, dark, and deadly . . . *Lear* v 3 290
Cheerly. Heigh, my hearts! cheerly, cheerly, my hearts! . *Tempest* i 1 6
Cheerly, good hearts! Out of our way, I say . . . . i 1 29
Well said! thou lookest cheerly . . . . *As Y. Like It* ii 6 14
Cheerly, good Adam! . . . . ii 6 19
But lusty, young, and cheerly drawing breath . *Richard II.* i 3 66
Cheerly, my lord: how fares your grace? . . *1 Hen. IV.* v 4 44
Cheerly to sea; the signs of war advance . . . *Hen. V.* ii 2 192
Wise men ne'er sit and wail their loss, But cheerly seek how to redress their harms . . . . *3 Hen. VI.* v 4 2
In God's name, cheerly on, courageous friends . *Richard III.* v 2 14
Cheerly, boys; be brisk awhile, and the longer liver take all *Rom. and Jul.* i 5 16
For shame! I'll make you quiet. What, cheerly, my hearts! . . i 5 90
Prithee, man, look cheerly . . . . . . *T. of Athens* ii 2 223
Cheese. You Banbury cheese! . . . . . . *Mer. Wives* i 1 130
I will make an end of my dinner; there's pippins and cheese to come . i 2 13
I love not the humour of bread and cheese, and there's the humour of it ii 1 140
I will rather trust a Fleming with my butter, Parson Hugh the Welshman with my cheese . . . . ii 2 318
Defend me from that Welsh fairy, lest he transform me to a piece of cheese! . . . . v 5 86
'Tis time I were choked with a piece of toasted cheese . . . v 5 147
Virginity breeds mites, much like a cheese . . . *All's Well* i 1 154
I had rather live With cheese and garlic in a windmill . *1 Hen. IV.* iii 1 162
It will toast cheese, and it will endure cold as another man's sword *Hen. V.* ii 1 9
His breath stinks with eating toasted cheese . . . *2 Hen. VI.* iv 7 14
Art thou come? why, my cheese, my digestion . *Troi. and Cres.* ii 3 44
That stale old mouse-eaten dry cheese, Nestor . . . . v 4 12
Look, look, a mouse! Peace, peace; this piece of toasted cheese will do't . . . . *Lear* iv 6 90

Cheese-paring. Like a man made after supper of a cheese-paring *2 Hen. IV.* iii 2 332
Chequered. The green leaves quiver with the cooling wind And make a chequer'd shadow on the ground *T. Andron.* ii 3 15
Chequering the eastern clouds with streaks of light *Rom. and Jul.* ii 3 2
Chequin. Three or four thousand chequins were as pretty a proportion to live quietly *Pericles* iv 2 28
Cher. Mon très cher et devin déesse *Hen. V.* v 2 231
Notre très-cher fils Henri, Roi d'Angleterre v 2 368
Cherish. O, If you but knew how you the purpose cherish Whiles thus you mock it! *Tempest* ii 1 224
Thou gentle nymph, cherish thy forlorn swain! *T. G. of Ver.* v 4 12
If thou dost love fair Hero, cherish it *Much Ado* i 1 310
He that cherishes my flesh and blood loves my flesh and blood *All's Well* i 3 51
There's no virtue whipped out of the court: they cherish it *W. Tale* iv 3 97
This juggling witchcraft with revenue cherish *K. John* iii 1 169
That none so small advantage shall step forth To check his reign, but they will cherish it iii 4 152
You that do abet him in this kind Cherish rebellion *Richard II.* ii 3 147
Love thy husband, look to thy servants, cherish thy guests *1 Hen. IV.* iii 3 194
Hath taught us how to cherish such high deeds Even in the bosom of our adversaries v 5 30
Cherish it, my boy, And noble offices thou mayst effect *2 Hen. IV.* iv 4 23
And, as we may, cherish Duke Humphrey's deeds *2 Hen. VI.* i 1 203
For what doth cherish weeds but gentle air? *3 Hen. VI.* ii 6 21
Whom thou wert sworn to cherish and defend *Richard III.* i 4 213
With all duteous love Doth cherish you and yours i 1 34
Love thyself last: cherish those hearts that hate thee *Hen. VIII.* iii 2 443
Killing that love which thou hast vow'd to cherish *Rom. and Jul.* iii 3 129
He has been known to commit outrages, And cherish factions *T. of Athens* iii 5 73
Cherished. The remnant of mine age Should have been cherish'd by her child-like duty *T. G. of Ver.* iii 1 75
If I be not by her fair influence Foster'd, illumined, cherish'd, kept alive iii 1 184
Our virtues would be proud, if our faults whipped them not; and our crimes would despair, if they were not cherished by our virtues *All's Well* iv 3 86
Thy voluntary oath Lives in this bosom, dearly cherished *K. John* iii 3 24
Who, ne'er so tame, so cherish'd and lock'd up, Will have a wild trick of his ancestors *1 Hen. IV.* v 2 10
Feed like oxen at a stall, The better cherish'd, still the nearer death v 2 15
I fear me you but warm the starved snake, Who, cherish'd in your breasts, will sting your hearts *2 Hen. VI.* iii 1 344
Must gently be preserved, cherish'd, and kept *Richard III.* ii 2 119
Better might we Have loved without this mean, if on both parts This be not cherish'd *Ant. and Cleo.* iii 2 33
Cherisher. He that comforts my wife is the cherisher of my flesh and blood *All's Well* i 3 50
Cherishing. He seems indifferent, Or rather swaying more upon our part Than cherishing the exhibiters against us *Hen. V.* i 1 74
I would I were thy bird.—Sweet, so would I: Yet I should kill thee with much cherishing *Rom. and Jul.* ii 2 184
Cherries. O, how ripe in show Thy lips, those kissing cherries! *M. N. Dr.* iii 2 140
Cherry. We grew together, Like to a double cherry, seeming parted iii 2 209
My cherry lips have often kiss'd thy stones v 1 192
This cherry nose, These yellow cowslip cheeks v 1 338
Give grandam kingdom, and it grandam will Give it a plum, a cherry, and a fig: There's a good grandam *K. John* ii 1 162
A pretty foot, A cherry lip, a bonny eye *Richard III.* i 1 94
'Tis as like you As cherry is to cherry *Hen. VIII.* v 1 169
Her inkle, silk, twin with the rubied cherry *Pericles* v Gower 8
Cherry-pit. 'Tis not for gravity to play at cherry-pit with Satan *T. Night* iii 4 129
Cherry-stone. A drop of blood, a pin, A nut, a cherry-stone *Com. of Err.* iv 3 74
Chertsey. Come, now towards Chertsey with your holy load *Richard III.* i 2 29
After I have solemnly interr'd At Chertsey monastery this noble king i 2 215
Sirs, take up the corse.—Towards Chertsey, noble lord? i 2 226
Cherub. I see a cherub that sees them *Hamlet* iv 3 50
Cherubim. Heaven's cherubim, horsed Upon the sightless couriers of the air *Macbeth* i 7 22
Cherubin. A cherubin Thou wast that did preserve me *Tempest* i 2 152
Still quiring to the young-eyed cherubins *Mer. of Venice* v 1 62
Their dwarfish pages were As cherubins, all gilt *Hen. VIII.* i 1 23
Fears make devils of cherubins; they never see truly *Troi. and Cres.* iii 2 74
In her more destruction than thy sword, For all her cherubin look *T. of Athens* iv 3 63
Patience, thou young and rose-lipp'd cherubin *Othello* iv 2 63
The roof o' the chamber With golden cherubins is fretted *Cymbeline* ii 4 88
Cheshu. By Cheshu, I think a' will plow up all *Hen. V.* iii 2 67
By Cheshu, he is an ass, as in the world iii 2 74
By Cheshu, he will maintain his argument as well as any military man iii 2 84
Chest. Neither press, coffer, chest, trunk, well, vault *Mer. Wives* iv 2 62
The lottery, that he hath devised in these three chests of gold, silver and lead *Mer. of Venice* i 2 33
What says the golden chest? ha! let me see ii 9 23
In cypress chests my arras counterpoints *T. of Shrew* ii 1 353
To lie like pawns lock'd up in chests and trunks *K. John* v 2 141
A jewel in a ten-times-barr'd-up chest Is a bold spirit in a loyal breast *Richard II.* i 1 180
Are my chests fill'd up with extorted gold? Is my apparel sumptuous? *2 Hen. VI.* iv 7 105
From his deep chest laughs out a loud applause *Troi. and Cres.* i 3 163
Come, stretch thy chest, and let thy eyes spout blood iv 5 10
I would not have been so fidiused for all the chests in Corioli, and the gold that's in them *Coriolanus* ii 1 144
And so repose, sweet gold, for their unrest That have their alms out of the empress' chest *T. Andron.* ii 3 9
His chests and treasure He has not with him *Ant. and Cleo.* iv 5 10
We have a chest beneath the hatches, caulked and bitumed ready *Pericles* iii 1 71
Even now Did the sea toss upon our shore this chest iii 2 50
Chester. He ask'd the way to Chester; and of him I did demand what news from Shrewsbury *2 Hen. IV.* i 1 39
Chestnut. Your chestnut was ever the only colour *As Y. Like It* iii 4 12
Not half so great a blow to hear As will a chestnut in a farmer's fire *T. of Shrew* i 2 210
A sailor's wife had chestnuts in her lap, And munch'd, and munch'd *Macbeth* i 3 4
Chetas. Priam's six-gated city, Dardan, and Tymbria, Helias, Chetas, Troien, And Antenorides *Troi. and Cres.* Prol. 16
Cheval. Le cheval volant, the Pegasus, chez les narines de feu! *Hen. V.* iii 7 14
Montez à cheval!. My horse! varlet! laquais! ha! iv 2 2
Chevalier. Mount, chevaliers! to arms! *K. John* ii 1 287
Et je m'estime heureux que je suis tombé entre les mains d'un chevalier *Hen. V.* iv 4 59
Cheveril. A sentence is but a cheveril glove to a good wit *T. Night* iii 1 13
Saving your mincing, the capacity Of your soft cheveril conscience would receive, If you might please to stretch it *Hen. VIII.* ii 3 32
O, here's a wit of cheveril, that stretches from an inch narrow to an ell broad! *Rom. and Jul.* ii 4 87
Chew. Heaven in my mouth, As if I did but only chew his name *M. for M.* ii 4 5
Till then, my noble friend, chew upon this *J. Cæsar* i 2 171
Chewed. I am the veriest varlet that ever chewed with a tooth *1 Hen. IV.* ii 2 26
When capital crimes, chew'd, swallow'd, and digested, Appear before us *Hen. V.* ii 2 56
The gimmal bit Lies foul with chew'd grass, still and motionless iv 2 50
Chewet. Peace, chewet, peace! *1 Hen. IV.* v 1 29
Chewing the food of sweet and bitter fancy *As Y. Like It* iv 3 102
Chick. Ariel, chick, That is thy charge: then to the elements Be free *Temp.* v 1 316
Chicken. Were't not all one, an empty eagle were set To guard the chicken from a hungry kite? *2 Hen. VI.* iii 1 249
So the poor chicken should be sure of death iii 1 251
You would eat chickens i' the shell *Troi. and Cres.* i 2 147
She's e'en setting on water to scald such chickens as you are *T. of Athens* ii 2 72
What, all my pretty chickens and their dam At one fell swoop? *Macbeth* iv 3 218
Forthwith they fly Chickens, the way which they stoop'd eagles *Cymbeline* v 3 42
Chid. It were a shame to call her back again And pray her to a fault for which I chid her *T. G. of Ver.* i 2 52
How churlishly I chid Lucetta hence, When willingly I would have had her here! i 2 60
When you chid at Sir Proteus for going ungartered ii 1 78
I should have chid you for not bringing it *Com. of Errors* iv 1 50
Chid I for that at frugal nature's frame? *Much Ado* iv 1 130
When we have chid the hasty-footed time For parting us *M. N. Dream* iii 2 200
He hath chid me hence and threaten'd me iii 2 312
Whiles you chid me, I did love; How then might your prayers move! *As Y. Like It* iv 3 54
Alas, I then have chid away my friend! *K. John* iv 1 87
Thou wilt be horribly chid to-morrow when thou comest to thy father *1 Hen. IV.* ii 4 410
And chid his truant youth with such a grace v 2 63
Thus upbraided, chid and rated at *2 Hen. VI.* iii 1 175
Margaret my queen, and Clifford too, Have chid me from the battle *3 Hen. VI.* ii 5 17
He chid Andromache and struck his armorer *Troi. and Cres.* i 2 6
Look, who comes here: will you be chid? *T. of Athens* i 2 176
He chid the sisters When first they put the name of king upon me *Macbeth* iii 1 57
He might have chid me so; for, in good faith, I am a child to chiding *Othello* iv 2 113
But to confound such time, That drums him from his sport, and speaks as loud As his own state and ours,—'tis to be chid *Ant. and Cleo.* i 4 30
Chidden. You'll still be too forward.—And yet I was last chidden for being too slow *T. G. of Ver.* ii 1 12
Fly like chidden Mercury from Jove, Or like a star disorb'd *Troi. and Cres.* ii 2 45
And all the rest look like a chidden train *J. Cæsar* i 2 184
The chidden billow seems to pelt the clouds *Othello* ii 1 12
Chiddest. Thou chid'st me oft for loving Rosaline.—For doting, not for loving, pupil mine *Rom. and Jul.* ii 3 81
Chide. One word more Shall make me chide thee, if not hate thee *Tempest* i 2 476
I thank you, you swinged me for my love, which makes me the bolder to chide you for yours *T. G. of Ver.* ii 1 89
If she do chide, 'tis not to have you gone iii 1 98
By and by intend to chide myself Even for this time I spend in talking to thee iv 2 103
You chide at him, offending twice as much *L. L. Lost* iv 3 132
That, when he plays at tables, chides the dice In honourable terms v 2 326
We shall chide downright, if I longer stay *M. N. Dream* ii 1 145
Now I but chide; but I should use thee worse iii 2 45
'Tis not maidenly: Our sex, as well as I, may chide you for it iii 2 218
I will chide no breather in the world but myself *As Y. Like It* iii 2 297
Sweet youth, I pray you, chide a year together: I had rather hear you chide than this man woo iii 5 64
Almost chide God for making you that countenance you are iv 1 36
It is no time to chide you now *T. of Shrew* i 1 164
I will board her, though she chide as loud As thunder i 2 95
Not her that chides, sir, at any hand, I pray.—I love no chiders i 2 227
It nothing steads us To chide him from our eaves *All's Well* iii 7 42
Since you make your pleasure of your pains, I will no further chide you *T. Night* iii 3 3
My gracious lord, To chide at your extremes it not becomes me *W. Tale* iv 4 6
The one He chides to hell and bids the other grow Faster than thought or time iv 4 564
Chide me, dear stone, that I may say indeed Thou art Hermione; or rather, thou art she In thy not chiding v 3 24
The sea That chides the banks of England, Scotland, Wales *1 Hen. IV.* iii 1 45
Chide him for faults, and do it reverently *2 Hen. IV.* iv 4 37
Find him, my Lord of Warwick; chide him hither iv 5 63
For, God before, We'll chide this Dauphin at his father's door *Hen. V.* i 2 308
That caves and womby vaultages of France Shall chide your trespass ii 4 125
And chide the cripple tardy-gaited night iv Prol. 20
Nay, Eleanor, then must I chide outright *2 Hen. VI.* i 2 41
And chides the sea that sunders him from thence *3 Hen. VI.* iii 2 138
And so I chide the means that keeps me from it iii 2 141
As good to chide the waves as speak them fair v 4 24
Oh, who shall hinder me to wail and weep, To chide my fortune? *Richard III.* ii 2 35
Can he not be sociable?—The raven chides blackness *Troi. and Cres.* ii 3 221
Be true to my lord: if he flinch, chide me for it iii 2 114
What vice is that, good Troilus? chide me for it v 3 39
Mother, I am going to the market-place; Chide me no more *Coriolanus* iii 2 132
I pray thee, chide not: she whom I love now Doth grace for grace and love for love allow *Rom. and Jul.* ii 3 85
So smile the heavens upon this holy act, That after hours with sorrow chide us not! ii 6 2
O, what a beast was I to chide at him! iii 2 95
I'll tell my lady you will come.—Do so, and bid my sweet prepare to chide iii 3 162
Thou wilt undertake A thing like death to chide away this shame iv 1 74
Stir up their servants to an act of rage, And after seem to chide 'em *J. Cæsar* ii 1 177
When you are over-earnest with your Brutus, He'll think your mother chides iv 3 123

Chide. Do you not come your tardy son to chide? *Hamlet* iii 4 106
But I'll not chide thee; Let shame come when it will, I do not call it *Lear* ii 4 228
She puts her tongue a little in her heart, And chides with thinking *Othello* ii 1 108
What do you here alone?—Do not you chide; I have a thing for you iii 3 301
The business of the state does him offence, And he does chide with you iv 2 167
Whom every thing becomes, to chide, to laugh, To weep *Ant. and Cleo.* i 1 49
Chides, as he had power To beat me out of Egypt iv 1 1
With Mars fall out, with Juno chide *Cymbeline* v 4 32
Chider. I love no chiders, sir *T. of Shrew* i 2 228
Chidest. Thou chidest me well *Richard II.* iii 2 188
Chiding. Better a little chiding than a great deal of heart-break *Mer. Wives* v 3 11
Never did I hear Such gallant chiding *M. N. Dream* iv 1 120
As the icy fang And churlish chiding of the winter's wind *As Y. Like It* ii 1 7
Would I do but good?—Most mischievous foul sin, in chiding sin ii 7 64
Call you this chiding? iv 3 64
Chide me, dear stone, that I may say indeed Thou art Hermione; or rather, thou art she In thy not chiding *W. Tale* v 3 26
As doth a rock against the chiding flood *Hen. VIII.* iii 2 197
In selfsame key Retorts to chiding fortune *Troi. and Cres.* i 3 54
Did my father strike my gentleman for chiding of his fool? *Lear* i 3 1
He might have chid me so; for, in good faith, I am a child to chiding *Othello* iv 2 114
As chiding a nativity As fire, air, water, earth, and heaven can make *Pericles* iii 1 32
Chief. Out with 't, and place it for her chief virtue *T. G. of Ver.* iii 1 340
But in chief For that her reputation was disvalued In levity *M. for Meas.* v 1 220
Are not you the chief woman? you are the thickest here *L. L. Lost* iv 1 51
Yet my chief humour is for a tyrant *M. N. Dream* i 2 30
My chief care Is to come fairly off *Mer. of Venice* i 1 127
Wherein the honour Of my dear father's gift stands chief in power *All's Well* ii 1 115
Both for myself and them, but, chief of all, Your safety *K. John* iv 2 49
Holds from all soldiers chief majority *1 Hen. IV.* iii 2 109
Unto your grace do I in chief address The substance of my speech *2 Hen. IV.* iv 1 31
Whom all France with their chief assembled strength Durst not presume to look once in the face *1 Hen. VI.* i 1 139
Chief master-gunner am I of this town i 4 6
Will not you maintain the thing you teach, But prove a chief offender? iii 1 130
King Henry's peers and chief nobility Destroy'd themselves iv 1 146
The chief perfections of that lovely dame, Had I sufficient skill to utter them, Would make a volume v 5 12
I was the chief that raised him to the crown, And I'll be chief to bring him down again *3 Hen. VI.* iii 3 262
But why commands the king That his chief followers lodge in towns about him? iv 3 13
But, with the first of all your chief affairs, Let me entreat iv 6 58
The chief cause concerns his grace of Canterbury *Hen. VIII.* v 3 3
One that, in all obedience, makes the church The chief aim of his honour v 3 118
You know Caius Marcius is chief enemy to the people *Coriolanus* i 1 8
I have ever verified my friends, Of whom he's chief v 2 18
An irreligious Moor, Chief architect and plotter of these woes *T. Andron.* v 3 122
Thy great fortunes Are made thy chief afflictions *T. of Athens* iv 2 44
Great nature's second course, Chief nourisher in life's feast *Macbeth* ii 2 40
Here's our chief guest.—If he had been forgotten, It had been as a gap iii 1 11
The chief head Of this post-haste and romage in the land *Hamlet* i 1 106
They in France of the best rank and station Are of a most select and generous chief in that i 3 74
What is a man, If his chief good and market of his time Be but to sleep and feed? a beast, no more iv 4 34
The senators alone of this great world, Chief factors for the gods *Ant. and Cleo.* ii 6 10
Whose bosom was my crownet, my chief end iv 12 27
Farewell, great chief. Shall I strike now?—Now, Eros iv 14 93
Were I chief lord of all this spacious world, I'ld give it to undo the deed *Pericles* iv 3 5
Chiefest. Employ your chiefest thoughts To courtship *Mer. of Venice* ii 8 43
Call for our chiefest men of discipline *K. John* ii 1 39
The king from Eltham I intend to steal And sit at chiefest stern of public weal *1 Hen. VI.* i 1 177
Within their chiefest temple I'll erect A tomb ii 2 12
Their chiefest prospect murdering basilisks! *2 Hen. VI.* iii 2 324
'Tis the Lord Hastings, the king's chiefest friend *3 Hen. VI.* iv 3 11
Why I drew you hither, Into this chiefest thicket of the park iv 5 3
Shall be well winged with our chiefest horse *Richard III.* v 3 300
That's one of the chiefest of them too *Troi. and Cres.* i 2 292
It is held That valour is the chiefest virtue *Coriolanus* ii 2 88
Take him up. Help, three o' the chiefest soldiers v 6 150
And bring with him Some of the chiefest princes of the Goths *T. Andron.* v 2 125
Security Is mortals' chiefest enemy *Macbeth* iii 5 33
Our chiefest courtier, cousin, and our son *Hamlet* i 2 117
Antiochus the Great Built up, this city, for his chiefest seat *Pericles* i Gower 18
Chief-justice. How now, my lord chief-justice! whither away? *2 Hen. IV.* v 2 1
Blessed are they that have been my friends; and woe to my lord chief-justice! v 3 145
My lord chief-justice, speak to that vain man v 5 48
Chiefly that I might set it in my prayers—What is your name? *Tempest* iii 1 35
Chiefly Him that you term'd, sir, 'The good old lord' v 1 14
But chiefly for thy face and thy behaviour *T. G. of Ver.* iv 4 72
But chiefly by my villany *Much Ado* iii 3 168
On's bed of death Many receipts he gave me; chiefly one *All's Well* ii 1 108
But chiefly a villanous trick of thine eye *1 Hen. IV.* ii 4 445
And chiefly therefore I thank God and thee *3 Hen. VI.* iv 6 17
Partly to behold my lady's face; But chiefly to take thence from her dead finger A precious ring *Rom. and Jul.* v 3 30
Did not you chiefly belong to my heart? *T. of Athens* i 2 95
One speech in it I chiefly loved *Hamlet* ii 2 467
I Should say myself offended, and with you Chiefly i' the world *Ant. and Cleo.* ii 2 33
And then myself, I chiefly, That set thee on to this desert, am bound To load thy merit richly *Cymbeline* i 5 72
Chien. Le chien est retourné à son propre vomissement, et la truie lavée au bourbier *Hen. V.* iii 7 68
Child. This blue-eyed hag was hither brought with child *Tempest* i 2 269
Lodged thee In mine own cell, till thou didst seek to violate The honour of my child i 2 348
Exposed unto the sea, which hath requit it, Him and his innocent child iii 3 72
How oddly will it sound that I Must ask my child forgiveness! v 1 198
Neither regarding that she is my child Nor fearing me as if I were her father *T. G. of Ver.* iii 1 70

Child. Love is like a child, That longs for every thing that he can come by *T. G. of Ver.* iii 1 124
Good Master Fenton, come not to my child *Mer. Wives* iii 4 76
'Nay,' said I, 'will you cast away your child on a fool, and a physician?' iii 4 100
I pray you, have your remembrance, child iv 1 49
Vengeance of Jenny's case! fie on her! never name her, child iv 1 65
You do ill to teach the child such words: he teaches him to hick and to hack iv 1 67
It is for getting Madam Julietta with child *Meas. for Meas.* i 2 74
What, is there a maid with child by him? i 2 92
With child, perhaps?—Unhappily, even so i 2 160
He hath got his friend with child i 4 29
Some one with child by him? My cousin Juliet? i 4 45
Sir, she came in great with child ii 1 91
This Mistress Elbow, being, as I say, with child ii 1 101
The time is yet to come that she was ever respected with man, woman, or child ii 1 177
She is with child; And he that got it, sentenced ii 3 12
Mistress Kate Keepdown was with child by him in the duke's time iii 2 212
His child is a year and a quarter old, come Philip and Jacob iii 2 213
I was once before him for getting a wench with child iv 3 180
I have heard him swear himself there's one Whom he begot with child v 1 517
For then were you a child.—You have it full *Much Ado* i 1 109
Hath Leonato any son, my lord?—No child but Hero i 1 297
As to show a child his new coat and forbid him to wear it iii 2 7
If you hear a child cry in the night, you must call to the nurse and bid her still it iii 3 69
Depart in peace, and let the child wake her with crying iii 3 74
I charge thee do so, as thou art my child iv 1 77
Bring me a father that so loved his child, Whose joy of her is overwhelm'd like mine, And bid him speak of patience v 1 8
I say thou hast belied mine innocent child v 1 67
Canst thou so daff me? Thou hast kill'd my child v 1 78
Art thou the slave that with thy breath hast kill'd Mine innocent child? v 1 274
My brother hath a daughter, Almost the copy of my child that's dead v 1 298
With a child of our grandmother Eve, a female *L. L. Lost* i 1 266
And, sweet my child, let them be men of good repute and carriage i 2 71
Sweet invocation of a child; most pretty and pathetical! i 2 102
Warble, child; make passionate my sense of hearing iii 1 1
On my privilege I have with the parents of the foresaid child or pupil iv 2 163
Her shoulder is with child iv 3 90
True wit!—Offered by a child to an old man; which is wit-old v 1 65
And when he was a babe, a child, a shrimp, Thus did he strangle serpents v 2 594
She's quick: the child brags in her belly already v 2 683
Love is full of unbefitting strains, All wanton as a child, skipping and vain v 2 771
Full of vexation come I, with complaint Against my child *M. N. Dream* i 1 23
This man hath bewitch'd the bosom of my child i 1 27
Thou hast given her rhymes And interchanged love-tokens with my child i 1 29
I have a widow aunt, a dowager Of great revenue, and she hath no child i 1 158
Therefore is Love said to be a child, Because in choice he is so oft beguiled i 1 238
And jealous Oberon would have the child Knight of his train ii 1 24
Set your heart at rest: The fairy land buys not the child of me ii 1 122
Come, recreant; come, thou child; I'll whip thee with a rod iii 2 409
I then did ask of her her changeling child iv 1 64
Like a child on a recorder; a sound, but not in government v 1 123
It is a wise father that knows his own child *Mer. of Venice* ii 2 81
Your boy that was, your son that is, your child that shall be ii 2 91
What heinous sin is it in me To be ashamed to be my father's child! ii 3 17
The Moor is with child by you, Launcelot iii 5 42
My father hath no child but I, nor none is like to have *As Y. Like It* i 2 18
Is all this for your father?—No, some of it is for my child's father i 3 11
A man's good wit seconded with the forward child Understanding iii 3 14
Let her never nurse her child herself, for she will breed it like a fool! iv 1 178
In this case of wooing, A child shall get a sire *T. of Shrew* ii 1 413
Speak I will; I am no child, no babe iv 3 74
Happy the parents of so fair a child! iv 5 39
His sole child, my lord, and bequeathed to my overlooking *All's Well* i 1 44
Show me a child begotten of thy body that I am father to iii 2 61
I do wash his name out of my blood, And thou art all my child iii 2 71
He was whipped for getting the shrieve's fool with child iv 3 213
At that time he got his wife with child v 3 302
It is a gallant child; one that indeed physics the subject *W. Tale* i 1 42
We do not know How he may soften at the sight o' the child ii 2 40
This child was prisoner to the womb and is By law and process of great nature thence Freed and enfranchised ii 2 59
Thou, traitor, hast set on thy wife to this. My child? away with't! ii 3 132
There is nothing in the between but getting wenches with child iii 3 62
A boy or a child, I wonder? A pretty one iii 3 71
Look thee, a bearing-cloth for a squire's child! iii 3 119
King Leontes shall not have an heir Till his lost child be found v 1 40
Methought I heard the shepherd say, he found the child v 2 8
What, pray you, became of Antigonus, that carried hence the child? v 2 65
So that all the instruments which aided to expose the child were even then lost when it was found v 2 78
Shall then my father's will be of no force To dispossess that child which is not his? *K. John* i 1 131
Come to thy grandam, child.—Do, child, go to it grandam, child ii 1 159
Thy sins are visited in this poor child ii 1 179
All punish'd in the person of this child, And all for her ii 1 189
Being no further enemy to you Than the constraint of hospitable zeal In the relief of this oppressed child ii 1 245
Let wives with child Pray that their burthens may not fall this day iii 1 89
Law cannot give my child his kingdom here, For he that holds his kingdom holds the law iii 1 187
I envy at their liberty, And will again commit them to their bonds, Because my poor child is a prisoner iii 4 75
For since the birth of Cain, the first male child, To him that did but yesterday suspire, There was not such a gracious creature born iii 4 79
You are as fond of grief as of your child.—Grief fills the room up of my absent child iii 4 92
And, pretty child, sleep doubtless and secure, That Hubert, for the wealth of all the world, Will not offend thee iv 1 130
I fear will issue thence The foul corruption of a sweet child's death iv 2 81
We heard how near his death he was Before the child himself felt he was sick iv 2 88
And find the inheritance of this poor child, His little kingdom of a forced grave iv 2 97

Child. Which, howsoever rude exteriorly, Is yet the cover of a fairer mind Than to be butcher of an innocent child . . . . *K. John* iv 2 259
There is not yet so ugly a fiend of hell As thou shalt be, if thou didst kill this child . . . . iv 3 124
Bear away that child And follow me with speed . . . . . iv 3 156
O, had it been a stranger, not my child, To smooth his fault I should have been more mild . . . . . *Richard II.* i 3 239
As a long-parted mother with her child Plays fondly with her tears and smiles . . . . iii 2 8
Let it not be so, Lest child, child's children, cry against you 'woe!' . iv 1 149
The big year, swoln with some other grief, Is thought with child by the stern tyrant war . . . . *2 Hen. IV.* Ind. 14
He will spare neither man, woman, nor child . . . . ii 1 19
An the child I now go with do miscarry, thou wert better thou hadst struck thy mother . . . . v 4 10
A' made a finer end and went away an it had been any christom child *Hen. V.* ii 3 12
Thy scarlet robes as a child's bearing-cloth I'll use to carry thee out of this place . . . . *1 Hen. VI.* i 3 42
Alas, there is a child, a silly dwarf! . . . . . ii 3 22
What, shall a child instruct you what to do? . . . . . iii 1 133
Happy for so sweet a child, Fit to be made companion with a king . v 3 148
I am with child, ye bloody homicides . . . . . v 4 62
Now heaven forfend! the holy maid with child! . . . . v 4 65
My child is none of his: It was Alençon that enjoy'd my love . v 4 72
I see no reason why a king of years Should be to be protected like a child *2 Hen. VI.* ii 3 29
Or as the snake roll'd in a flowering bank, With shining checker'd slough, doth sting a child That for the beauty thinks it excellent iii 1 229
Murder not this innocent child, Lest thou be hated both of God and man! . . . . *3 Hen. VI.* i 3 8
How couldst thou drain the life-blood of the child, To bid the father wipe his eyes withal? . . . . i 4 138
And long hereafter say unto his child, 'What my great-grandfather and grandsire got My careless father fondly gave away' . . . ii 2 36
I slew thy father, call'st thou him a child? . . . . . ii 2 113
I think he means to beg a child of her . . . . . iii 2 27
He was a man; this, in respect, a child: And men ne'er spend their fury on a child . . . . v 5 56
If you ever chance to have a child, Look in his youth to have him so cut off . . . . v 5 65
If ever he have child, abortive be it! . . . . *Richard III.* i 2 21
When thy warlike father, like a child, Told the sad story of my father's death . . . . i 2 160
Bade me rely on him as on my father, And he would love me dearly as his child . . . . ii 2 26
I, like a child, will go by thy direction . . . . . ii 2 153
Woe to that land that's govern'd by a child! . . . . ii 3 11
Good madam, be not angry with the child . . . . . ii 4 36
When that my mother went with child Of that unsatiate Edward . . iii 5 86
As, in love and zeal, Loath to depose the child . . . . iii 7 209
What dignity, what honour, Canst thou demise to any child of mine? . iv 4 247
All I have; yea, and myself and all, Will I withal endow a child of thine . . . . iv 4 249
The imperial metal, circling now thy brow, Had graced the tender temples of my child . . . . iv 4 383
That my lady's womb, If it conceived a male child by me, should Do no more offices of life to't than The grave does to the dead *Hen. VIII.* ii 4 189
Never, before This happy child, did I get any thing . . . v 5 66
When I am in heaven I shall desire To see what this child does . v 5 69
One on's father's moods.—Indeed, la, tis a noble child . *Coriolanus* i 3 73
His mother, wife, his child, And this brave fellow too, we are the grains v 1 29
Wife, mother, child, I know not. My affairs Are servanted to others v 2 88
Unproperly Show duty, as mistaken all this while Between the child and parent . . . . v 3 56
Not of a woman's tenderness to be, Requires nor child nor woman's face to see . . . . v 3 130
His wife is in Corioli and his child Like him by chance . . . v 3 179
Ne'er till now Was I a child to fear I know not what . *T. Andron.* ii 3 221
Save thou the child, so we may all be safe . . . . iv 2 131
How many women saw this child of his? . . . . . iv 2 135
But say, again, how many saw the child? . . . . . iv 2 140
His child is like to her, fair as you are . . . . . iv 2 154
Tell them both the circumstance of all; And how by this their child shall be advanced . . . . iv 2 157
Suddenly I heard a child cry underneath a wall . . . . v 1 24
First hang the child, that he may see it sprawl . . . . v 1 51
Lucius, save the child, And bear it from me to the empress . . v 1 53
Thy child shall live, and I will see it nourish'd . . . . v 1 60
And this shall all be buried by my death, Unless thou swear to me my child shall live . . . . v 1 68
Tell on thy mind; I say thy child shall live . . . . v 1 69
Behold this child: Of this was Tamora delivered . . . . v 3 119
Like a loving child, Shed yet some small drops from thy tender spring v 3 166
My child is yet a stranger in the world . . . *Rom. and Jul.* i 2 8
My husband—God be with his soul! A' was a merry man—took up the child . . . . i 3 40
Tybalt, my cousin! O my brother's child! . . . . . iii 1 151
So tedious is this day As is the night before some festival To an impatient child that hath new robes And may not wear them . . iii 2 30
I will make a desperate tender Of my child's love: I think she will be ruled . . . . iii 4 13
Well, well, thou hast a careful father, child . . . . iii 5 108
What day is that?—Marry, my child, early next Thursday morn . iii 5 113
We scarce thought us blest That God had lent us but this only child . iii 5 166
O me! My child, my only life, Revive, look up, or I will die with thee! iv 5 19
But one, poor one, one poor and loving child, But one thing to rejoice and solace in, And cruel death hath catch'd it from my sight! . iv 5 46
O child! O child! my soul, and not my child! Dead art thou! . . iv 5 62
Alack! my child is dead; And with my child my joys are buried . iv 5 63
O, in this love, you love your child so ill, That you run mad, seeing that she is well . . . . iv 5 75
Whose self-same mettle, Whereof thy proud child, arrogant man, is puff'd, Engenders the black toad . . . *T. of Athens* iv 3 180
O hateful error, melancholy's child! . . . . *J. Cæsar* v 3 67
Wife and child, Those precious motives, those strong knots of love *Macb.* iv 3 26
They say an old man is twice a child . . . . . *Hamlet* ii 2 404
Why, now you speak Like a good child and a true gentleman . . iv 5 148
As much as child e'er loved, or father found . . . *Lear* i 1 60
The king falls from bias of nature; there's father against child . . i 2 121

Child. As of unnaturalness between the child and the parent . . *Lear* i 2 158
Ingratitude, thou marble-hearted fiend, More hideous when thou show'st thee in a child Than the sea-monster! . . . . . i 4 282
If she must teem, Create her child of spleen; that it may live, And be a thwart disnatured torment to her! . . . . . i 4 304
How sharper than a serpent's tooth it is To have a thankless child! . i 4 311
Spoke, with how manifold and strong a bond The child was bound to the father . . . . ii 1 50
I prithee, daughter, do not make me mad: I will not trouble thee, my child . . . . ii 4 222
I have served you ever since I was a child; But better service have I never done you Than now to bid you hold . . . . . iii 7 73
As I am a man, I think this lady To be my child Cordelia . . iv 7 70
I had rather to adopt a child than get it . . . . *Othello* i 3 191
I am glad at soul I have no other child . . . . . i 3 196
He might have chid me so; for, in good faith, I am a child to chiding . iv 2 114
Let me have a child at fifty, to whom Herod of Jewry may do homage *Ant. and Cleo.* i 2 27
Be a child o' the time.—Possess it, I'll make answer . . . ii 7 106
Whose ministers would prevail Under the service of a child as soon As i' the command of Cæsar . . . . iii 13 24
To the more mature A glass that feated them, and to the graver A child that guided dotards . . . . . *Cymbeline* i 1 50
Is she sole child to the king?—His only child. He had two sons . . i 1 56
How now, my flesh, my child! What, makest thou me a dullard in this act? . . . . v 5 264
Bad child; worse father! to entice his own To evil should be done by none . . . . . *Pericles* i Gower 27
He's father, son, and husband mild; I mother, wife, and yet his child . i 1 69
You're both a father and a son, By your untimely claspings with your child . . . . i 1 128
Here have you seen a mighty king His child, I wis, to incest bring ii Gower 2
Like beauty's child, whom nature gat For men to see, and seeing wonder at . . . . ii 2 6
His queen with child makes her desire—Which who shall cross? . iii Gower 40
Thou art the rudeliest welcome to this world That ever was prince's child iii 1 31
Fear not, my lord, but think Your grace . . . Must in your child be thought on . . . . iii 3 20
Make me blessed in your care In bringing up my child . . . iii 3 32
I think You'll turn a child again . . . . . iv 3 4
What canst thou say When noble Pericles shall demand his child? . iv 3 13
She did distain my child, and stood between Her and her fortunes . iv 3 31
Though you call my course unnatural, You not your child well loving . iv 3 37
Now, blessing on thee! rise; thou art my child. Give me fresh garments . . . . v 1 215
Child of conscience. Now is Cupid a child of conscience; he makes restitution . . . . . *Mer. Wives* v 5 32
Child of fancy. This child of fancy that Armado hight . . *L. L. Lost* i 1 171
Child of hell. Horrid night, the child of hell . . . *Hen. V.* iv 1 288
Child of honour. This same child of honour and renown, This gallant Hotspur . . . . . . *1 Hen. IV.* iii 2 139
The great child of honour, Cardinal Wolsey . . . *Hen. VIII.* iv 2 6
Child of integrity. This noble passion, Child of integrity, hath from my soul Wiped the black scruples . . . . *Macbeth* iv 3 115
Child-bed. The child-bed privilege denied, which 'longs To women of all fashion . . . . . . *W. Tale* iii 2 104
A terrible childbed hast thou had, my dear; No light, no fire *Pericles* iii 1 57
At sea in childbed died she . . . . v 3 5
Child-changed. The untuned and jarring senses, O, wind up Of this child-changed father! . . . . . . *Lear* iv 7 17
Childed. That which makes me bend makes the king bow, He childed as I father'd . . . . iii 6 117
Childeric. King Pepin, which deposed Childeric . . . *Hen. V.* i 2 65
Childhood. O, is it all forgot? All school-days' friendship, childhood innocence? . . . . . . *M. N. Dream* iii 2 202
An idle gawd Which in my childhood I did dote upon . . . iv 1 173
I urge this childhood proof, Because what follows is pure innocence. I owe you much . . . . . *Mer. of Venice* i 1 144
They were trained together in their childhoods . . . *W. Tale* i 1 25
Now I have stain'd the childhood of our joy . . *Rom. and Jul.* iii 3 95
'Tis the eye of childhood That fears a painted devil . . *Macbeth* ii 2 54
Thou better know'st The offices of nature, bond of childhood . *Lear* ii 4 181
Childing. The childing autumn, angry winter . . *M. N. Dream* ii 1 112
Childish. His big manly voice Turning again toward childish treble, pipes And whistles in his sound . . . . *As Y. Like It* ii 7 162
And again does nothing But what he did being childish . *W. Tale* iv 4 413
Nor hold the sceptre in his chidish fist, Nor wear the diadem *2 Hen. VI.* i 1 245
What cannot be avoided 'Twere childish weakness to lament . *3 Hen. VI.* v 4 38
Shamed their aspect with store of childish drops . . *Richard III.* i 2 155
If we suffer, Out of our easiness and childish pity To one man's honour, this contagious sickness, Farewell all physic . . . *Hen. VIII.* v 3 25
Of such childish friendliness To yield your voices . . *Coriolanus* ii 3 183
From love's weak childish bow she lives unharm'd . . *Rom. and Jul.* i 1 217
Childish-foolish. I am too childish-foolish for this world *Richard III.* i 3 142
Childishness. Second childishness and mere oblivion *As Y. Like It* ii 7 165
Perhaps thy childishness will move him more Than can our reasons *Coriolanus* v 3 157
Though age from folly could not give me freedom, It does from childishness: can Fulvia die? . . . . . *Ant. and Cleo.* i 3 58
Child-killer. Clifford, that cruel child-killer . . . *3 Hen. VI.* ii 2 112
Child-like. The remnant of mine age Should have been cherish'd by her child-like duty . . . . . . *T. G. of Ver.* iii 1 75
I hear that you have shown your father A child-like office . *Lear* ii 1 108
Childness. His varying childness cures in me Thoughts that would thick my blood . . . . *W. Tale* i 2 170
Children. Farewell my wife and children!—Farewell, brother! *Tempest* i 1 65
'Tis not good that children should know any wickedness *Mer. Wives* ii 2 133
The children must Be practised well to this, or they'll ne'er do't . iv 4 64
I will teach the children their behaviours . . . . iv 4 66
As fond fathers, Having bound up the threatening twigs of birch, Only to stick it in their children's sight For terror, not to use *Meas. for Meas.* i 3 25
The children thus disposed, my wife and I, Fixing our eyes on whom our care was fix'd, Fasten'd ourselves at either end the mast *Com. of Errors* i 1 84
These are the parents to these children, Which accidentally are met together . . . . v 1 360
The duke, my husband and my children both . . . . v 1 403
Therein do men from children nothing differ . . . *Much Ado* v 1 33
Never mole, hare lip, nor scar, Nor mark prodigious, such as are Despised in nativity, Shall upon their children be . . . *M. N. Dream* v 1 421

Children. The sins of the father are to be laid upon the children *Mer. of Venice* iii 5 2
Marry, his kisses are Judas's own children *As Y. Like It* iii 4 10
'Tis such fools as you That makes the world full of ill-favour'd children iii 5 53
Liberal To mine own children in good bringing up *T. of Shrew* i 1 99
Fathers commonly Do get their children . . . . ii 1 412
'Tis a good hearing when children are toward . . . . v 2 182
That's the loss of men, though it be the getting of children *All's Well* iii 2 45
Then 'twere past all doubt You 'ld call your children yours *W. Tale* ii 3 81
Lest she suspect, as he does, Her children not her husband's . . ii 3 108
I'll speak of her no more, nor of your children . . . iii 2 230
Whose loss of his most precious queen and children are even now to be afresh lamented . . . . . iv 2 27
Had our prince, Jewel of children, seen this hour . . . v 1 116
I am past moe children, but thy sons and daughters will be all gentle-men born . . . . . v 2 137
Of that I doubt, as all men's children may *K. John* i 1 63
And leave your children, wives and you in peace . . ii 1 257
So jest with heaven, Make such unconstant children of ourselves . iii 1 243
Is't not pity, O my grieved friends, That we, the sons and children of this isle, Were born to see so sad an hour . . . v 2 25
The pleasure that some fathers feed upon, Is my strict fast; I mean, my children's looks . . . . . *Richard II.* ii 1 80
That will the king severely prosecute 'Gainst us, our lives, our children ii 1 245
They shall strike Your children yet unborn and unbegot . . iii 3 88
Yon dangling apricocks, Which, like unruly children, make their sire Stoop with oppression of their prodigal weight . . . iii 4 30
Lest child, child's children, cry against you 'woe!' . . iv 1 149
The children yet unborn Shall feel this day as sharp to them as thorn iv 1 322
No more the thirsty entrance of this soil Shall daub her lips with her own children's blood . . . . *1 Hen. IV.* i 1 6
O that it could be proved That some night-tripping fairy had exchanged In cradle-clothes our children! . . . . . i 1 88
That men would tell their children 'This is he' . . . iii 2 48
The midwives say the children are not in the fault . *2 Hen. IV.* ii 2 28
What mightst thou do, that honour would thee do, Were all thy children kind and natural! . . . . *Hen. V.* ii Prol. 19
Their children rawly left . . . . . . iv 1 147
Let us our lives, our souls, Our debts, our careful wives, Our children and our sins lay on the king! . . . . iv 1 249
Ourselves and children Have lost, or do not learn for want of time . v 2 56
The scarecrow that affrights our children so . *1 Hen. VI.* i 4 43
We and our wives and children all will fight . . . iii 1 100
'Tis much when sceptres are in children's hands . . . iv 1 192
By her he had two children at one birth . *2 Hen. VI.* iv 2 147
May, even in their wives' and children's sight, Be hang'd up for example iv 2 189
How many children hast thou, widow? tell me *3 Hen. VI.* iii 2 26
Now tell me, madam, do you love your children?—Ay, fully as dearly as I love myself . . . . . . iii 2 35
Therein thou wrong'st thy children mightily . . . iii 2 74
Thou art a widow, and thou hast some children . . . iii 2 102
Women and children of so high a courage, And warriors faint! . v 4 50
You have no children, butchers! if you had, The thought of them would have stirr'd up remorse . . . . . v 5 63
Long mayst thou live to wail thy children's loss! *Richard III.* i 3 204
O, spare my guiltless wife and my poor children! . . . i 4 72
Peace, children, peace! the king doth love you well . . ii 2 17
Thou art a mother, And hast the comfort of thy children left thee ii 2 56
Oft have I heard of sanctuary men; But sanctuary children ne'er till now . . . . iii 1 57
Infer the bastardy of Edward's children . . . . iii 5 75
A care-crazed mother of a many children . . . . iii 7 184
Thy mother's name is ominous to children . . . . iv 1 41
Wept like two children in their deaths' sad stories . . iv 3 8
Where are thy children? wherein dost thou joy? . . . iv 4 93
The little souls of Edward's children Whisper the spirits of thine enemies . . . . iv 4 191
The advancement of your children, gentle lady.—Up to some scaffold? iv 4 241
They are as children but one step below, Even of your mettle . iv 4 301
Your children were vexation to your youth, But mine shall be a comfort to your age . . . . iv 4 305
The children live, whose parents thou hast slaughter'd, Ungovern'd youth, to wail it in their age . . . . . iv 4 391
The parents live, whose children thou hast butcher'd, Old wither'd plants, to wail it with their age . . . . iv 4 393
But thou didst kill my children . . . . . iv 4 422
Hastings, and Edward's children, Rivers, Grey, Holy King Henry . v 1 3
If you do free your children from the sword, Your children's children quit it in your age . . . . . . v 3 261
And have been blest With many children by you . *Hen. VIII.* ii 4 37
Our children's children Shall see this, and bless heaven . . v 5 55
My thoughts were like unbridled children . . *Troi. and Cres.* iii 2 130
See him pluck Aufidius down by the hair, As children from a bear *Coriolanus* i 3 34
Have I had children's voices? . . . . . . iii 1 30
Rome, whose gratitude Towards her deserved children is enroll'd . iii 1 292
Peace is a very apoplexy . . . .; a getter of more bastard children than war's a destroyer of men . . . . . . iv 5 240
Ourselves, our wives, and children, on our knees, Are bound to pray for you . . . . iv 6 22
Bear the palm for having bravely shed Thy wife and children's blood . v 3 118
And patient fools, Whose children he hath slain, their base throats tear With giving him glory . . . . v 6 53
Revenge it, as you love your mother's life, Or be ye not henceforth call'd my children . . . . . *T. Andron.* ii 3 115
Some say that ravens foster forlorn children . . . . ii 3 153
The continuance of their parents' rage, Which, but their children's end, nought could remove . . . *Rom. and Jul.* Prol. 11
True, I talk of dreams, Which are the children of an idle brain . i 4 97
Children of divers kind We sucking on her natural bosom find . ii 3 11
Matrons, turn incontinent! Obedience fail in children! . *T. of Athens* iv 1 4
Why old men fool and children calculate . . . *J. Cæsar* i 3 65
Turn pre-ordinance and first decree Into the law of children . . iii 1 39
Men, wives and children stare, cry out and run As it were doomsday . iii 1 97
Your children shall be kings.—You shall be king *Macbeth* i 3 86
Do you not hope your children shall be kings? . . . . i 3 118
Our duties Are to your throne and state children and servants . . i 4 25
How does my wife?—Why, well.—And all my children?—Well too . iv 3 177
My children too?—Wife, children, servants, all That could be found . iv 3 211
He has no children. All my pretty ones? Did you say all? . . iv 3 216

Children. If thou be'st slain and with no stroke of mine, My wife and children's ghosts will haunt me still . . . . *Macbeth* v 7 16
How do ye both?—As the indifferent children of the earth *Hamlet* ii 2 231
An aery of children, little eyases, that cry out on the top of question . ii 2 354
What, are they children? who maintains 'em? how are they escoted? . ii 2 361
Fathers that wear rags Do make their children blind *Lear* ii 4 49
But fathers that bear bags Shall see their children kind . . ii 4 51
I never gave you kingdom, call'd you children, You owe me no subscription iii 2 17
I shall see The winged vengeance overtake such children . . iii 7 66
Belike my children shall have no names . . *Ant. and Cleo.* i 2 35
And put your children To that destruction which I'll guard them from v 2 131
And within three days You with your children will he send before . v 2 202
That a king's children should be so convey'd, So slackly guarded! *Cymb.* i 1 63
Is't enough I am sorry? So children temporal fathers do appease . v 4 12
Their nurse, Euriphile, Whom for the theft I wedded, stole these children v 5 341
I lost my children: If these be they, I know not how to wish A pair of worthier sons . . . . v 5 354
Be it our wives, our children, or ourselves, The curse of heaven and men succeed their evils! . . . . . . *Pericles* i 4 103
Child Rowland to the dark tower came . . . . *Lear* iii 4 187
Chill. But the many will be too chill and tender . . *All's Well* iv 5 56
Chill not let go, zir, without vurther 'casion . . . *Lear* iv 6 239
Chill pick your teeth, zir: come; no matter vor your foins . iv 6 250
My veins are chill, And have no more of life than may suffice To give my tongue that heat to ask your help . . . . *Pericles* ii 1 77
Chilling. A chilling sweat o'er-runs my trembling joints . *T. Andron.* ii 3 212
Chime. We have heard the chimes at midnight . . *2 Hen. IV.* iii 2 228
When he speaks, 'Tis like a chime a-mending . *Troi. and Cres.* i 3 159
Hell only danceth at so harsh a chime . . . . *Pericles* i 1 85
Chimney. I'll creep up into the chimney . . . *Mer. Wives* iv 2 57
Cricket, to Windsor chimneys shalt thou leap . . . . v 5 47
'Twill fly with the smoke out at the chimney . . *As Y. Like It* iv 1 166
Charles' wain is over the new chimney . . . *1 Hen. IV.* ii 1 3
They will allow us ne'er a jordan, and then we leak in your chimney ii 1 22
He made a chimney in my father's house, and the bricks are alive at this day to testify it . . . . . . *2 Hen. VI.* iv 2 156
Where we lay, Our chimneys were blown down . . . *Macbeth* ii 3 60
The chimney Is south the chamber . . . . . *Cymbeline* ii 4 80
Chimney-piece. The chimney-piece Chaste Dian bathing. . . ii 4 81
Chimney-sweeper. To look like her are chimney-sweepers black *L. L. Lost* iv 3 266
Golden lads and girls all must, As chimney-sweepers, come to dust *Cymbeline* iv 2 263
Chimney-top. The raven rook'd her on the chimney's top . *3 Hen. VI.* v 6 47
Yea, to chimney-tops, Your infants in your arms . . *J. Cæsar* i 1 44
Chin. Till new-born chins Be rough and razorable . . . *Tempest* ii 1 249
I' the filthy-mantled pool beyond your cell, There dancing up to the chins . . . . iv 1 183
I guess it stood in her chin, by the salt rheum . *Com. of Errors* iii 2 131
Thou hast got more hair on thy chin than Dobbin my fill-horse has on his tail . . . . *Mer. of Venice* ii 2 100
Wear yet upon their chins The beards of Hercules and frowning Mars iii 2 84
Stroke your chins, and swear by your beards . *As Y. Like It* i 2 76
Is his head worth a hat, or his chin worth a beard? . . . iii 2 217
Let me stay the growth of his beard, if thou delay me not the knowledge of his chin . . . . iii 2 223
Item, one neck, one chin, and so forth . . . *T. Night* i 5 267
I am almost sick for one [a beard]; though I would not have it grow on my chin . . . . iii 1 54
The pretty dimples of his chin and cheek, His smiles . . *W. Tale* ii 3 101
His chin new reap'd Show'd like a stubble-land . . *1 Hen. IV.* i 3 34
Whose chin is not yet fledged . . . . . *2 Hen. IV.* i 2 23
Your chin double? your wit single? . . . . . . i 2 207
Whom I have weekly sworn to marry since I perceived the first white hair on my chin . . . . i 2 271
Whose chin is but enrich'd With one appearing hair *Hen. V.* iii Prol. 22
De nick. Et le menton?—De chin.—De sin . . . . iii 4 37
He has not past three or four hairs on his chin . . *Troi. and Cres.* i 2 122
She came and puts me her white hand to his cloven chin . . i 2 132
I cannot choose but laugh, to think how she tickled his chin . . i 2 150
And she takes upon her to spy a white hair on his chin . . . i 2 154
Alas, poor chin! many a wart is richer . . . . . i 2 155
At what was all this laughing?—Marry, at the white hair that Helen spied on Troilus' chin . . . . i 2 165
Here's but two and fifty hairs on your chin, and one of them is white . i 2 172
When with his Amazonian chin he drove The bristled lips . *Coriolanus* ii 2 95
These hairs, which thou dost ravish from my chin, Will quicken *Lear* iii 7 38
If you did wear a beard upon your chin, I'd shake it on this quarrel iii 7 76
China. They are not China dishes, but very good dishes . *Meas. for Meas.* ii 1 97
Chine. And like to mose in the chine. . . . . *T. of Shrew* iii 2 51
Or cut not out the burly-boned clown in chines of beef . *2 Hen. VI.* iv 10 61
Let me ne'er hope to see a chine again . . . . *Hen. VIII.* v 4 26
Chink. Talk through the chink of a wall . . . . *M. N. Dream* iii 1 66
And through Wall's chink, poor souls, they are content To whisper . v 1 134
Such a wall, as I would have you think, That had in it a crannied hole or chink . . . . v 1 159
Show me thy chink, to blink through with mine eyne! . . . v 1 178
Now will I to the chink, To spy an I can hear my Thisby's face . v 1 194
I tell you, he that can lay hold of her Shall have the chinks . *R. and J.* i 5 119
Chipped. Would have made a good pantler, a' would ha' chipped bread well . . . . *2 Hen. IV.* ii 4 258
That noseless, handless, hack'd and chipp'd, come to him *Troi. and Cres.* v 5 34
Chiron, thy years want wit, thy wit wants edge, And manners *T. Andron.* ii 1 26
Chiron, we hunt not, we, with horse nor hound . . . . ii 2 25
O, do ye read, my lord, what she hath writ? 'Stuprum. Chiron. Demetrius' . . . . iv 1 78
The empress' sons, I take them, Chiron and Demetrius . . . v 2 154
O villains, Chiron and Demetrius! . . . . . . v 2 170
'Twas Chiron and Demetrius: They ravish'd her, and cut away her tongue . . . . v 3 56
Cursed Chiron and Demetrius Were they that murdered our emperor's brother . . . . v 3 97
Chirping. Thinks he that the chirping of a wren, By crying comfort from a hollow breast, Can chase away the first-conceived sound? *2 Hen. VI.* iii 2 42
Chirrah!—Quare chirrah, not sirrah? . . . . *L. L. Lost* v 1 35
Chirurgeonly. And most chirurgeonly . . . . *Tempest* ii 1 140
Chisel. What fine chisel Could ever yet cut breath? . . *W. Tale* v 3 78
Chitopher. Mine own company, Chitopher, Vaumond, Bentii *All's Well* iv 3 187
Chivalrous. I'll answer thee in any fair degree, Or chivalrous design of knightly trial . . . . *Richard II.* i 1 81

Chivalry. We shall see Justice design the victor's chivalry . *Richard II.* i 1 203

For Christian service and true chivalry . ii 1 54

I may speak it to my shame, I have a truant been to chivalry 1 *Hen. IV.* v 1 94

Did all the chivalry of England move To do brave acts . 2 *Hen. IV.* ii 3 20

When all her chivalry hath been in France . *Hen. V.* i 2 157

In this glorious and well-foughten field We kept together in our chivalry iv 6 19

Now thou art seal'd the son of chivalry . 1 *Hen. VI.* iv 6 29

Thou hast slain The flower of Europe for his chivalry . 3 *Hen. VI.* ii 1 71

Brave Troilus! The prince of chivalry! . *Troi. and Cres.* i 2 249

The glory of our Troy doth this day lie On his fair worth and single chivalry . iv 4 150

I am to-day i' the vein of chivalry . v 3 32

His device, a wreath of chivalry; The word, 'Me pompæ provexit apex' *Pericles* ii 2 29

Choice. This is my father's choice . *Mer. Wives* iii 4 31

We have with a leaven'd and prepared choice Proceeded to you *M. for M.* i 1 52

Policy of mind, Ability in means and choice of friends . *Much Ado* iv 1 201

If you yield not to your father's choice, You can endure the livery of a nun . *M. N. Dream* i 1 69

Too old to be engaged to young.—Or else it stood upon the choice of friends . i 1 139

If there were a sympathy in choice, War, death, or sickness did lay siege to it . i 1 141

Therefore is Love said to be a child, Because in choice he is so oft beguiled . i 1 239

Is not this the day That Hermia should give answer of her choice? . iv 1 141

Many sports are ripe: Make choice of which your highness will see first . v 1 43

In terms of choice I am not solely led By nice direction of a maiden's eyes; Besides, the lottery of my destiny Bars me . *Mer. of Venice* ii 1 13

Now make your choice . ii 7 3

If I do fail in fortune of my choice . ii 9 15

But to my choice: 'Who chooseth me shall get as much as he deserves' ii 9 49

Let music sound while he doth make his choice . iii 2 43

Faith, as you say, there's small choice in rotten apples . *T. of Shrew* i 1 138

You do me double wrong, To strive for that which resteth in my choice iii 1 17

And choice breeds A native slip to us from foreign seeds . *All's Well* i 3 151

Make the choice of thy own time, for I, Thy resolved patient, on thee still rely . ii 1 206

Make choice; and, see, Who shuns thy love shuns all his love in me . ii 3 78

I had rather be in this choice than throw ames-ace for my life . ii 3 84

This ring he holds In most rich choice . iii 7 26

Admiringly, my liege, at first I stuck my choice upon her . v 3 45

I'll buy for you both. Pedlar, let's have the first choice *W. Tale* iv 4 319

He shall not need to grieve At knowing of thy choice . iv 4 427

Sorry Your choice is not so rich in worth as beauty . v 1 214

A braver choice of dauntless spirits Than now the English bottoms have waft o'er Did never float . *K. John* ii 1 72

Five and twenty thousand men of choice . 2 *Hen. IV.* i 3 11

The commonwealth is sick of their own choice . i 3 87

I shall be well content with any choice Tends to God's glory . 1 *Hen. VI.* v 1 26

I unworthy am To woo so fair a dame to be his wife And have no portion in the choice myself . v 3 125

So full-replete with choice of all delights . v 5 17

Hath not our brother made a worthy choice? . 3 *Hen. VI.* iv 1 3

How like you our choice, That you stand pensive, as half malcontent? iv 1 9

Here I'll make My royal choice . *Hen. VIII.* i 4 86

You have here, lady, And of your choice, these reverend fathers . ii 4 58

Had I a sister were a grace, or a daughter a goddess, he should take his choice . *Troi. and Cres.* i 2 258

And choice, being mutual act of all our souls, Makes merit her election i 3 348

Five tribunes to defend their vulgar wisdoms, Of their own choice *Coriol.* i 1 220

Take your choice of those That best can aid your action . i 6 65

To be ta'en forth, Before the common distribution, at Your only choice i 9 36

Since the wisdom of their choice is rather to have my hat than my heart . ii 3 105

At thy choice, then . iii 2 123

And, Romans, fight for freedom in your choice . *T. Andron.* i 1 17

If thou be pleased with this my sudden choice, Behold, I choose thee . i 1 318

Queen of Goths, dost thou applaud my choice? . i 1 321

Youngling, learn thou to make some meaner choice . ii 1 73

Come, and take choice of all my library, And so beguile thy sorrow . iv 1 34

Woe to her chance, and damn'd her loathed choice! . iv 2 78

Within her scope of choice Lies my consent and fair according voice *Rom. and Jul.* i 2 18

You have made a simple choice; you know not how to choose a man . ii 5 38

The choice and master spirits of this age . *J. Cæsar* iii 1 163

On his choice depends The safety and health of this whole state *Hamlet* i 3 20

Therefore must his choice be circumscribed Unto the voice and yielding of that body Whereof he is the head . i 3 22

Since my dear soul was mistress of her choice And could of men distinguish . iii 2 68

Sense to ecstasy was ne'er so thrall'd But it reserved some quantity of choice . iii 4 75

Make choice of whom your wisest friends you will, And they shall hear and judge . iv 5 204

Equalities are so weighed, that curiosity in neither can make choice of either's moiety . *Lear* i 1 7

Most rich, being poor; Most choice, forsaken; and most loved, despised! . i 1 254

Men of choice and rarest parts, That all particulars of duty know . i 4 285

At your choice, sir.—I prithee, daughter, do not make me mad . ii 4 220

When she is sated with his body, she will find the error of her choice *Othello* i 3 358

Very nature will instruct her in it and compel her to some second choice ii 1 238

Rather makes choice of loss, Than gain which darkens him *Ant. and Cleo.* iii 1 23

Your choice agrees with mine; I like that well . *Pericles* ii 5 18

Well, I do commend her choice; And will no longer have it be delay'd ii 5 21

I 'ld wish no better choice, and think me rarely wed . v 1 69

Choice-drawn. These cull'd and choice-drawn cavaliers . *Hen. V.* iii Prol. 24

Choice epithet. A most singular and choice epithet . *L. L. Lost* v 1 17

Choice hour. A choice hour To hear from him a matter of some moment *Hen. VIII.* i 2 162

Choice Italian. The story is extant, and writ in choice Italian *Hamlet* iii 2 274

Choice love. She's the choice love of Signior Gremio . *T. of Shrew* i 2 236

Choice spirits. Now help, ye charming spells and periapts; And ye choice spirits that admonish me . 1 *Hen. VI.* v 3 3

Choicely. To Ireland will you lead a band of men, Collected choicely, from each county some? . 2 *Hen. VI.* iii 1 313

Choicest. With all the choicest music of the kingdom . *Hen. VIII.* iv 1 91

Choir. Having brought the queen To a prepared place in the choir *Hen. VIII.* iv 1 64

The choir, With all the choicest music of the kingdom, Together sung 'Te Deum' . iv 1 90

Choke. Might reproach your life And choke your good to come *M. for M.* v 1 427

So much as you may take upon a knife's point and choke a daw withal *Much Ado* ii 3 264

Why, that's the way to choke a gibing spirit . *L. L. Lost* v 2 868

Having that, do choke their service up Even with the having *As Y. Like It* ii 3 61

To choke his days With barbarous ignorance . *K. John* iv 2 58

With eager feeding food doth choke the feeder . *Richard II.* ii 1 37

Leaving their earthly parts to choke your clime . *Hen. V.* iv 3 102

I trust ere long to choke thee with thine own . 1 *Hen. VI.* iii 2 46

Boiling choler chokes The hollow passage of my poison'd voice . v 4 120

They'll o'ergrow the garden And choke the herbs for want of husbandry 2 *Hen. VI.* iii 1 33

But he has a merit, To choke it in the utterance . *Coriolanus* iv 7 49

My tears will choke me, if I ope my mouth . *T. Andron.* v 3 175

I scorn thy meat; 'twould choke me, for I should ne'er flatter thee *T. of Athens* i 2 38

And fearful scouring Doth choke the air with dust . v 2 16

As two spent swimmers, that do cling together And choke their art *Macbeth* i 2 9

To deny each article with oath Cannot remove nor choke the strong conception That I do groan withal . *Othello* v 2 55

When to my good lord I prove untrue, I'll choke myself . *Cymbeline* i 5 87

Choked. 'Tis time I were choked with a piece of toasted cheese *Mer. Wives* v 5 147

What, have I choked you with an argosy? . *T. of Shrew* ii 1 378

Her fairest flowers choked up, Her fruit-trees all unpruned *Richard II.* iii 4 44

The gain proposed Choked the respect of likely peril fear'd 2 *Hen. IV.* i 1 184

Go forward and be choked with thy ambition! . 1 *Hen. VI.* ii 4 112

Choked with ambition of the meaner sort . ii 5 123

Virtue is choked with foul ambition . 2 *Hen VI.* iii 1 143

I stood i' the level Of a full-charged confederacy, and give thanks To you that choked it . *Hen. VIII.* i 2 4

Uttered such a deal of stinking breath because Cæsar refused the crown that it had almost choked Cæsar . *J. Cæsar* i 2 249

All pity choked with custom of fell deeds . iii 1 269

O that brave Cæsar!—Be choked with such another emphasis! *A. and C.* i 5 68

Slanders so her judgement That what's else rare is choked . *Cymbeline* iii 5 77

Choking. This chaos, when degree is suffocate, Follows the choking *Troi. and Cres.* i 3 126

A madness most discreet, A choking gall and a preserving sweet *R. and J.* i 1 200

Choler. Sheathe thy impatience, throw cold water on thy choler *Mer. Wives* ii 3 89

Nay, my choler is ended . *L. L. Lost* ii 1 206

It engenders choler, planteth anger . *T. of Shrew* iv 1 175

Let's purge this choler without letting blood . *Richard II.* i 1 153

What, drunk with choler? stay and pause awhile . 1 *Hen. IV.* i 3 129

Choler, my lord, if rightly taken.—No, if rightly taken, halter . ii 4 356

I beseek you now, aggravate your choler . 2 *Hen. IV.* ii 4 176

In his rages, and his furies, and his wraths, and his cholers . *Hen. V.* iv 7 38

Valiant And, touch'd with choler, hot as gunpowder . iv 7 188

Digest Your angry choler on your enemies . 1 *Hen. VI.* iv 1 168

Boiling choler chokes The hollow passage of my poison'd voice . v 4 120

My choler being over-blown With walking once about the quadrangle 2 *Hen. VI.* i 3 155

Scarce can I speak, my choler is so great . v 1 23

Let your reason with your choler question What 'tis you go about *Hen. VIII.* i 1 130

He was stirr'd With such an agony, he sweat extremely, And something spoke in choler . ii 1 34

So putting him to rage, You should have ta'en the advantage of his choler *Coriolanus* ii 3 206

Let the people know't.—What, what? his choler?—Choler! Were I as patient as the midnight sleep, By Jove, 'twould be my mind! . iii 1 83

Go about it. Put him to choler straight . iii 3 25

An we be in choler, we'll draw.—Ay, while you live, draw your neck out o' the collar . *Rom. and Jul.* i 1 4

Patience perforce with wilful choler meeting Makes my flesh tremble in their different greeting . i 5 91

Choler does kill me that thou art alive; I swound to see thee *T. of Athens* iv 3 372

Must I give way and room to your rash choler? . *J. Cæsar* iv 3 39

Is in his retirement marvellous distempered.—With drink, sir?—No, my lord, rather with choler . *Hamlet* iii 2 315

To put him to his purgation would perhaps plunge him into far more choler . iii 2 319

Kent banish'd thus! and France in choler parted! . *Lear* i 2 23

He is rash and very sudden in choler, and haply may strike at you *Othello* ii 1 279

Choleric. That in the captain's but a choleric word, Which in the soldier is flat blasphemy . *Meas. for Meas.* ii 2 130

Lest it make you choleric and purchase me another dry basting *Com. of Errors* ii 2 63

I durst have denied that, before you were so choleric . ii 2 68

Since, of ourselves, ourselves are choleric . *T. of Shrew* iv 1 177

I fear it is too choleric a meat . iv 3 19

I cannot tell; I fear 'tis choleric . iv 3 22

Are you so choleric With Eleanor, for telling but her dream? 2 *Hen. VI.* i 2 51

Go show your slaves how choleric you are . *J. Cæsar* iv 3 43

The unruly waywardness that infirm and choleric years bring with them *Lear* i 1 302

To the choleric fisting of every rogue Thy ear is liable . *Pericles* iv 6 177

Chollor. How full of chollors I am, and trempling of mind! *Mer. Wives* iii 1 11

Choose. Give it way: I know thou canst not choose . *Tempest* i 2 186

Yond same cloud cannot choose but fall by pailfuls . ii 2 24

Why dost thou cry 'alas'?—I cannot choose But pity her *T. G. of Ver.* iv 4 82

By cock and pie, you shall not choose, sir! come, come . *Mer. Wives* i 1 316

That cannot choose but amaze him . v 3 18

As they are chosen, they are glad to choose me for them *Meas. for Meas.* ii 1 283

This course I fittest choose; For forty ducats is too much to lose *Com. of Errors* iv 3 96

I pray you choose another subject . *Much Ado* v 1 136

Yet I must speak. Choose your revenge yourself . v 1 282

Who is your deer?—If we choose by the horns, yourself come not near *L. L. Lost* iv 1 117

O hell! to choose love by another's eyes . *M. N. Dream* i 1 140

But this reasoning is not in the fashion to choose me a husband *Mer. of Venice* i 2 23

O me, the word 'choose!' I may neither choose whom I would nor refuse whom I dislike . i 2 24

Is it not hard, Nerissa, that I cannot choose one nor refuse none? . i 2 28

Choose. The lottery, that he hath devised in these three chests of gold, silver and lead, whereof who chooses his meaning chooses you, will, no doubt, never be chosen by any rightly but one who shall rightly love . . . . . . *Mer. of Venice* i 2 34
He doth nothing but frown, as who should say 'If you will not have me, choose' . . . . . . i 2 51
If he should offer to choose, and choose the right casket, you should refuse to perform your father's will, if you should refuse to accept him . . . . . . i 2 99
If the devil be within and that temptation without, I know he will choose it . . . . . . i 2 106
You must take your chance, And either not attempt to choose at all Or swear before you choose, if you choose wrong Never to speak to lady afterward In way of marriage . . . . . . ii 1 39
How shall I know if I do choose the right? . . . . . . ii 7 10
If you choose that, then I am yours withal . . . . . . ii 7 12
Here do I choose, and thrive I as I may! . . . . . . ii 7 60
Let all of his complexion choose me so . . . . . . ii 7 79
If you choose that wherein I am contain'd, Straight shall our nuptial rites be solemnized . . . . . . ii 9 5
The fool multitude, that choose by show . . . . . . ii 9 26
I will not choose what many men desire . . . . . . ii 9 31
Seven times tried that judgement is, That did never choose amiss . . ii 9 65
O, these deliberate fools! when they do choose, They have the wisdom by their wit to lose . . . . . . ii 9 80
That swear he cannot choose but break . . . . . . iii 1 120
I could teach you How to choose right, but I am then forsworn . . iii 2 11
Let me choose; For as I am, I live upon the rack . . . . iii 2 24
And here choose I: joy be the consequence! . . . . iii 2 107
You that choose not by the view, Chance as fair and choose as true! . iii 2 132
You'll ask me, why I rather choose to have A weight of carrion flesh than to receive Three thousand ducats . . . . . . iv 1 40
Believe me, lord, I think he cannot choose . . . *T. of Shrew* Ind. 1 42
I choose her for myself: If she and I be pleased, what's that to you? . ii 1 304
You shall not choose but drink before you go . . . . . v 1 12
I hope I may choose, sir . . . . . . v 1 48
Keep it not; you cannot choose but lose by't . . . *All's Well* i 1 158
Give pity To her, whose state is such that cannot choose . . . i 3 220
Exempted be from me the arrogance To choose from forth the royal blood of France . . . . . . ii 1 199
Thy frank election make; Thou hast power to choose, and they none to forsake . . . . . . ii 3 62
The blushes in my cheeks thus whisper me, 'We blush that thou shouldst choose' . . . . . . ii 3 76
Thou wrong'st thyself, if thou shouldst strive to choose . . . ii 3 153
Choose thou thy husband, and I'll pay thy dower . . . . v 3 328
Thou canst not choose but know who I am . . . *T. Night* ii 5 189
Thou shalt not choose but go: Do not deny . . . . . iv 1 61
There rooted betwixt them then such an affection, which cannot choose but branch now . . . . . . *W. Tale* i 1 26
There is not half a kiss to choose Who loves another best . . . iv 4 175
Reason my son Should choose himself a wife . . . . . iv 4 418
Give me the office To choose you a queen . . . . . v 1 78
Direct not him whose way himself will choose . . . *Richard II.* ii 1 29
Let's choose executors and talk of wills . . . . . iii 2 148
Choose out some secret place, some reverend room, More than thou hast v 6 25
Why, it cannot choose but be a noble plot . . . *1 Hen. IV.* i 3 279
How you cross my father!—I cannot choose . . . . . iii 1 148
Which cannot choose but bring him quickly on . . . . . v 2 45
She cannot choose but be old; certain she's old . . *2 Hen. IV.* iii 2 221
Which four will you have?—Do you choose for me . . . . iii 2 265
Will you tell me, Master Shallow, how to choose a man? . . . iii 2 276
Let us choose such limbs of noble counsel . . . . . v 2 135
Choose what office thou wilt in the land, 'tis thine . . . . v 3 129
And rather choose to hide them in a net . . . *Hen. V.* i 2 93
To choose for wealth and not for perfect love . . *1 Hen. VI.* v 5 50
I would the college of the cardinals Would choose him pope . *2 Hen. VI.* i 3 65
And I choose Clarence only for protector . . . *3 Hen. VI.* iv 6 37
Indeed she cannot choose but hate thee . . . . *Richard III.* iv 4 289
Use careful watch, choose trusty sentinels . . . . . v 3 54
I cannot choose but laugh, to think how she tickled his chin *Troi. and Cres.* i 2 149
Have you thus Given Hydra here to choose an officer? *Coriolanus* iii 1 93
They choose their magistrate . . . . . . iii 1 104
Aufidius will appear well in these wars . . .—He cannot choose . iv 3 39
Let him choose Out of my files, his projects to accomplish, My best and freshest men . . . . . . v 6 33
Of the hue That I would choose, were I to choose anew . . *T. Andron.* i 1 262
And told the Moor he should not choose But give them to his master . iv 3 74
Hold thy peace.—Yes, madam: yet I cannot choose but laugh *R. and J.* i 3 50
You have made a simple choice; you know not how to choose a man . ii 5 39
Feeling so the loss, I cannot choose but ever weep the friend . . iii 5 78
I will choose Mine heir from forth the beggars of the world *T. of Athens* i 1 137
I cannot choose but tell him, that I care not, And let him take't at worst v 1 180
I do fear, the people Choose Cæsar for their king . . . *J. Cæsar* i 2 80
I rather choose To wrong the dead, to wrong myself and you . . iii 2 130
In their birth—wherein they are not guilty, Since nature cannot choose his origin . . . . . . *Hamlet* i 4 26
I cannot choose but weep, to think they should lay him i' the cold ground . . . . . . iv 5 69
They cry 'Choose we: Laertes shall be king' . . . . . iv 5 106
Under the which he shall not choose but fall . . . . . iv 7 66
You may choose A sword unbated, and in a pass of practice Requite him iv 7 138
To fight when I cannot choose; and to eat no fish . . . *Lear* i 4 18
Rather I abjure all roofs, and choose To wage against the enmity o' the air . . . . . . ii 4 211
Cannot choose But they must blab— Hath he said anything? *Othello* iv 1 28
If you were but an inch of fortune better than I, where would you choose it? . . . . . . *Ant. and Cleo.* i 2 62
What he cannot change, Than what he chooses . . . . . i 4 15
Choose your own company, and command what cost Your heart has mind to . . . . . . iii 4 37
What lady would you choose to assail? . . . *Cymbeline* i 4 136
What woman is, yea, what she cannot choose But must be . . . i 6 71
He cannot choose but take this service I have done fatherly . . . iii 3 38

Chooser. Who mutually hath answer'd my affection, So far forth as herself might be her chooser . . . . *Mer. Wives* iv 6 11

Chooseth. Who chooseth me shall gain what many men desire *Mer. of Ven.* ii 7 5
Who chooseth me shall get as much as he deserves . . . . ii 7 7
Who chooseth me must give and hazard all he hath . . . . ii 7 9

Choosing. The lottery of my destiny Bars me the right of voluntary choosing . . . . . . *Mer. of Venice* ii 1 16
In choosing wrong, I lose your company . . . . . iii 2 2
In choosing for yourself, you show'd your judgement . . *3 Hen. VI.* iv 1 61
Let me blame your grace, For choosing me when Clarence is in place . iv 6 31

Chop. I'll hang you for going.—You will, chops? . . *1 Hen. IV.* i 2 151
Let me wipe thy face; come on, you whoreson chops . *2 Hen. IV.* ii 4 235
Let him to the Tower, And chop away that factious pate of his *2 Hen. VI.* v 1 135
If this right hand would buy two hours' life, That I in all despite might rail at him, This hand should chop it off . . . *3 Hen. VI.* ii 6 82
I had rather chop this hand off at a blow . . . . . v 1 50
Then we will chop him in the malmsey-butt in the next room *Richard III.* i 4 160
Chop off his head, man; somewhat we will do . . . . iii 1 193
Give me a sword, I'll chop off my hands too . . . *T. Andron.* iii 1 72
Lucius, or thyself, old Titus, Or any one of you, chop off your hand . iii 1 153
Good Aaron, wilt thou help to chop it off?—Stay, father! . . . iii 1 162
I will chop her into messes . . . . . *Othello* iv 1 211

Chopine. Your ladyship is nearer to heaven than when I saw you last, by the altitude of a chopine . . . . . *Hamlet* ii 2 447

Chop-logic. How now, how now, chop-logic! What is this? *Rom. and Jul.* iii 5 150

Chopped. Within these three days his head to be chopped off *M. for M.* i 2 70
When all those legs and arms and heads, chopped off in a battle, shall join together at the latter day . . . . *Hen. V.* iv 1 142
The rabblement hooted and clapped their chopped hands . *J. Cæsar* i 2 246

Chopping. The chopping French we do not understand . *Richard II.* v 3 124

Choppy. You seem to understand me, By each at once her choppy finger laying Upon her skinny lips . . . . . *Macbeth* i 3 44

Chopt. Her pretty chopt hands . . . . *As Y. Like It* ii 4 50

Chorus. For the which supply, Admit me Chorus to this history *Hen. V.* Prol. 32
You are as good as a chorus, my lord . . . . *Hamlet* iii 2 255

Chose. I chose her when I could not ask my father For his advice *Tempest* v 1 190
I rather chose To cross my friend in his intended drift . *T. G. of Ver.* iii 1 17
A man of complements, whom right and wrong Have chose as umpire *L. L. Lost* i 1 170
The word is well culled, chose, sweet and apt . . . . . v 1 98
What if I stray'd no further, but chose here? . . *Mer. of Venice* ii 7 35
First, never to unfold to any one Which casket 'twas I chose . . ii 9 11
Mark Her eye, and tell me for what dull part in't You chose her *W. Tale* v 1 65
Out of a great deal of old iron I chose forth . . *1 Hen. VI.* i 2 101
How may I avoid, Although my will distaste what it elected, The wife I chose? . . . . . . *Troi. and Cres.* ii 2 67
How now, my masters! have you chose this man? . . *Coriolanus* ii 3 163
They have chose a consul that will from them take Their liberties . ii 3 222
Say, you chose him More after our commandment . . . . ii 3 237
O, what a time have you chose out, brave Caius, To wear a kerchief! *J. Cæsar* ii 1 314
'Certes,' says he, 'I have already chose my officer' . . . *Othello* i 1 17
Nor from mine own weak merits will I draw The smallest fear or doubt of her revolt; For she had eyes, and chose me . . . . iii 3 189
I chose an eagle, And did avoid a puttock . . . . *Cymbeline* i 1 139

Chosen. As they are chosen, they are glad to choose me for them *Meas. for Meas.* ii 1 283
Being chosen for the prince's watch . . . . *Much Ado* iii 3 6
Will, no doubt, never be chosen by any rightly but one who shall rightly love . . . . . . *Mer. of Venice* i 2 35
The most hollow lover and the most unworthy of her you call Rosalind that may be chosen out of the gross band of the unfaithful *As Y. Like It* iv 1 198
That she's the chosen of Signior Hortensio . . . *T. of Shrew* i 2 237
A guard of chosen shot I had That walked about me every minute *1 Hen. VI.* i 4 53
Chosen from above, By inspiration of celestial grace . . . . v 4 39
A pretty plot, well chosen to build upon! . . . *2 Hen. VI.* i 4 59
I were loath To link with him that were not lawful chosen *3 Hen. VI.* iii 3 115
With some few bands of chosen soldiers . . . . . iii 3 204
To rank our chosen truth with such a show . . . *Hen. VIII.* Prol. 18
The horses your lordship sent for, with all the care I had, I saw well chosen . . . . . . ii 2 2
Sir Thomas More is chosen Lord chancellor in your place . . . iii 2 393
Peace, plenty, love, truth, terror, That were the servants to this chosen infant . . . . . . v 5 49
When we were chosen tribunes for the people . . . *Coriolanus* i 1 258
In a rebellion, When what's not meet, but what must be, was law, Then were they chosen . . . . . . iii 1 169
Be chosen with proclamations to-day, To-morrow yield up rule *T. Andron.* i 1 190
With her sweet harmony And other chosen attractions . . . *Pericles* v 1 46

Chough. I myself could make A chough of as deep chat . . *Tempest* ii 1 266
Russet-pated choughs, many in sort, Rising and cawing *M. N. Dream* iii 2 21
Choughs' language, gabble enough, and good enough . . *All's Well* iv 1 22
And scared my choughs from the chaff . . . . *W. Tale* iv 4 630
Augurs and understood relations have By magot-pies and choughs and rooks brought forth The secret'st man of blood . . . *Macbeth* iii 4 125
'Tis a chough; but, as I say, spacious in the possession of dirt *Hamlet* v 2 89
The crows and choughs that wing the midway air Show scarce so gross as beetles . . . . . . *Lear* iv 6 13

Chrish. By Chrish, la! tish ill done . . . . . *Hen. V.* iii 2 93
I would have blowed up the town, so Chrish save me, la! . . . iii 2 97
It is no time to discourse, so Chrish save me . . . . . iii 2 112
We talk, and, be Chrish, do nothing . . . . . . iii 2 117
So Chrish save me, I will cut off your head . . . . . iii 2 144

Christ. Fought For Jesu Christ in glorious Christian field *Richard II.* iv 1 93
And his pure soul unto his captain Christ . . . . . . iv 1 99
Did they not sometime cry, 'all hail!' to me? So Judas did to Christ iv 1 170
As far as to the sepulchre of Christ . . . . *1 Hen. IV.* i 1 19
Through all the kingdoms that acknowledge Christ . . . . iii 2 111
So! in the name of Jesu Christ, speak lower . . . . *Hen. V.* iv 1 65
Christ's mother helps me, else I were too weak . . *1 Hen. VI.* i 2 106
Speak not in spite, For you shall sup with Jesu Christ to-night *2 Hen. VI.* v 1 214
As you hope to have redemption By Christ's dear blood . *Richard III.* i 4 195

Christen. There is ne'er a king christen could be better bit than I have been since the first cock . . . . . *1 Hen. IV.* ii 1 19
Call them all by their christen names, as Tom, Dick, and Francis . . ii 4 8
And bids thee christen it with thy dagger's point . . *T. Andron.* iv 2 70

Christendom. The lyingest knave in Christendom . . *T. of Shrew* Ind. 2 26
The prettiest Kate in Christendom . . . . . . ii 1 188
With a world Of pretty, fond, adoptious christendoms . . *All's Well* i 1 188
To do offence and scath in Christendom . . . . *K. John* ii 1 75
Though you and all the kings of Christendom Are led so grossly by this meddling priest . . . . . . iii 1 162
By my christendom. So I were out of prison and kept sheep . . . iv 1 16

Christendom. I'll be damned for never a king's son in Christendom 1 *Hen. IV.* i 2 109
I had rather . . . , far, Than feed on cates and have him talk to me In any summer-house in Christendom iii 1 164
I'll maintain my words On any plot of ground in Christendom 1 *Hen. VI.* ii 4 89
The states of Christendom, Moved with remorse v 4 96
Sit there, the lyingest knave in Christendom 2 *Hen. VI.* ii 1 126
He is the bluntest wooer in Christendom 3 *Hen. VI.* iii 2 83
Never a man in Christendom That can less hide his love or hate *Richard III.* iii 4 53
Their clothes are after such a pagan cut too, That, sure, they've worn out Christendom *Hen. VIII.* i 3 15
Committing freely Your scruple to the voice of Christendom ii 2 88
Together with all famous colleges Almost in Christendom iii 2 67
And still so rising, That Christendom shall ever speak his virtue iv 2 63
An older and a better soldier none That Christendom gives out *Macbeth* iv 3 192
Christened. There was no thought of pleasing you when she was christened *As Y. Like It* iii 2 284
Christening. In christening shalt thou have two godfathers *Mer. of Venice* iv 1 398
I'll scratch your heads: you must be seeing christenings? *Hen. VIII.* v 4 10
This one christening will beget a thousand v 4 38
We shall have Great store of room, no doubt, left for the ladies, When they pass back from the christening v 4 78
The trumpets sound; They're come already from the christening v 4 87
Christian. A Jew, and not worth the name of a Christian *T. G. of Ver.* ii 5 58
Thou hast not so much charity in thee as to go to the ale with a Christian ii 5 61
More qualities than a water-spaniel; which is much in a bare Christian iii 1 272
It is spoke as a Christians ought to speak *Mer. Wives* i 1 103
As I am a Christians soul now, look you iii 1 96
Thou art as foolish Christian creatures as I would desires iv 1 73
Void of all profanation in the world that good Christians ought to have *Meas. for Meas.* ii 1 56
Now, as I am a Christian, answer me *Com. of Errors* i 2 77
I hate him for he is a Christian *Mer. of Venice* i 3 43
O father Abram, what these Christians are, Whose own hard dealings teaches them suspect The thoughts of others! i 3 162
The Hebrew will turn Christian: he grows kind i 3 180
If a Christian did not play the knave and get thee, I am much deceived ii 3 11
I shall end this strife, Become a Christian and thy loving wife ii 3 21
Whither goest thou?—Marry, sir, to bid my old master the Jew to sup to-night with my new master the Christian ii 4 19
But yet I'll go in hate, to feed upon The prodigal Christian ii 5 15
Nor thrust your head into the public street To gaze on Christian fools with varnish'd faces ii 5 33
There will come a Christian by, Will be worth a Jewess' eye ii 5 42
O my ducats! O my daughter! Fled with a Christian! O my Christian ducats! ii 8 16
He was wont to lend money for a Christian courtesy iii 1 52
Warmed and cooled by the same winter and summer as a Christian is iii 1 66
If a Jew wrong a Christian, what is his humility? Revenge iii 1 71
If a Christian wrong a Jew, what should his sufferance be by Christian example? Why, revenge iii 1 72
I'll not be made a soft and dull-eyed fool, To shake the head, relent, and sigh, and yield To Christian intercessors iii 3 16
I shall be saved by my husband; he hath made me a Christian iii 5 22
Christians enow before; e'en as many as could well live, one by another iii 5 24
This making of Christians will raise the price of hogs iii 5 25
In converting Jews to Christians, you raise the price of pork iii 5 38
These be the Christian husbands iv 1 295
Would any of the stock of Barrabas Had been her husband rather than a Christian! iv 1 297
If thou dost shed One drop of Christian blood, thy lands and goods Are, by the laws of Venice, confiscate iv 1 310
Pay the bond thrice And let the Christian go iv 1 319
Two things provided more, that, for this favour, He presently become a Christian iv 1 387
She defies me, Like Turk to Christian *As Y. Like It* iv 3 33
Not like a Christian footboy or a gentleman's lackey *T. of Shrew* iii 2 72
One of the greatest in the Christian world Shall be my surety *All's Well* iv 4 2
Methinks sometimes I have no more wit than a Christian or an ordinary man has *T. Night* i 3 89
For there is no Christian, that means to be saved by believing rightly, can ever believe such impossible passages iii 2 75
Unto a pagan shore; Where these two Christian armies might combine *K. John* v 2 37
Renowned for their deeds as far from home, For Christian service and true chivalry, As is the sepulchre in stubborn Jewry Of the world's ransom, blessed Mary's son *Richard II.* ii 1 54
Fought For Jesu Christ in glorious Christian field, Streaming the ensign of the Christian cross Against black pagans iv 1 93
That in a Christian climate souls refined Should show so heinous, black, obscene a deed! iv 1 130
If like a Christian thou hadst truly borne Betwixt our armies true intelligence 1 *Hen. IV.* v 5 9
The boy that I gave Falstaff: a' had him from me Christian 2 *Hen. IV.* ii 2 76
Which, by mine honour, I will perform with a most Christian care iv 2 115
We are no tyrant, but a Christian king *Hen. V.* i 2 241
Following the mirror of all Christian kings ii Prol. 6
Upon no Christian soul but English Talbot 1 *Hen. VI.* iv 2 30
The only means To stop effusion of our Christian blood v 1 9
I do embrace thee, as I would embrace The Christian prince, King Henry v 3 172
Such abominable words as no Christian ear can endure to hear 2 *Hen. VI.* iv 7 44
As I am a Christian faithful man, I would not spend another such a night, Though 'twere to buy a world of happy days *Richard III.* i 4 4
The plainest harmless creature That breathed upon this earth a Christian iii 5 26
Between two clergymen!—Two props of virtue for a Christian prince iii 7 96
Pardon us the interruption Of thy devotion and right Christian zeal iii 7 103
Amend that fault!—Else wherefore breathe I in a Christian land? iii 7 116
To thee, herself, and many a Christian soul, Death, desolation, ruin iv 4 408
Those that sought it I could wish more Christians *Hen. VIII.* i 3 64
All the clerks, I mean the learned ones, in Christian kingdoms Have their free voices ii 2 93
Heaven's peace be with him! That's Christian care enough ii 2 131
Is this your Christian counsel? out upon ye! Heaven is above all yet iii 1 99
Follow your envious courses, men of malice; You have Christian warrant for 'em iii 2 244
As you wish Christian peace to souls departed iv 2 156
I long To have this young one made a Christian v 3 180
On my Christian conscience, this one christening will beget a thousand v 4 37
Susan and she—God rest all Christian souls!—Were of an age *Rom. and Jul.* i 3 18
Christian. Neither having the accent of Christians nor the gait of Christian, pagan, nor man *Hamlet* iii 2 35
God ha' mercy on his soul! And of all Christian souls, I pray God iv 5 200
Is she to be buried in Christian burial that wilfully seeks her own salvation? v 1 1
The crowner hath sat on her, and finds it Christian burial v 1 5
If this had not been a gentlewoman, she should have been buried out o' Christian burial v 1 28
The more pity that great folk should have countenance in this world to drown or hang themselves, more than their even Christian v 1 32
I, of whom his eyes had seen the proof At Rhodes, at Cyprus and on other grounds Christian and heathen *Othello* i 1 30
For Christian shame, put by this barbarous brawl ii 3 172
Are not you a strumpet?—No, as I am a Christian iv 2 82
Christian-like. Undertakes them with a most Christian-like fear *Much Ado* ii 3 199
Plant neighbourhood and Christian-like accord *Hen. V.* v 2 381
Yet he most Christian-like laments his death 2 *Hen. VI.* iii 2 58
A virtuous and a Christian-like conclusion *Richard III.* i 3 316
Christmas. At Christmas I no more desire a rose Than wish a snow in May's new-fangled mirth *L. L. Lost* i 1 105
Dash it like a Christmas comedy v 2 462
Is not a comonty a Christmas gambold or a tumbling-trick? *T. of Shrew* Ind. 2 140
Christom child. A' made a finer end and went away an it had been any christom child *Hen. V.* ii 3 12
Christopher. Am not I Christopher Sly, old Sly's son? *T. of Shrew* Ind. 2 19
Sir Christopher, tell Richmond this from me *Richard III.* iv 5 1
Christophero. I am Christophero Sly; call not me 'honour' nor 'lordship' *T. of Shrew* Ind. 2 5
Upon my life, I am a lord indeed And not a tinker nor Christophero Sly Ind. 2 75
Chronicle. No more yet of this; For 'tis a chronicle of day by day, Not a relation for a breakfast *Tempest* v 1 163
The Slys are no rogues; look in the chronicles *T. of Shrew* Ind. 1 4
Shall it for shame be spoken in these days, Or fill up chronicles? 1 *Hen. IV.* i 3 171
Spoke your deservings like a chronicle, Making you ever better than his praise v 2 58
And the old folk, time's doting chronicles, Say it did so 2 *Hen. IV.* iv 4 126
And make her chronicle as rich with praise As is the ooze and bottom of the sea With sunken wreck *Hen. V.* i 2 163
Edward the Plack Prince of Wales, as I have read in the chronicles, fought a most prave pattle here in France iv 7 98
Traduced by ignorant tongues, which neither know My faculties nor person, yet will be The chronicles of my doing *Hen. VIII.* i 2 74
Pride is his own glass, his own trumpet, his own chronicle *Troi. and Cres.* ii 3 166
Good old chronicle, That hast so long walk'd hand in hand with time iv 5 202
Whose chronicle thus writ: 'The man was noble, But with his last attempt he wiped it out' *Coriolanus* v 3 145
They are the abstract and brief chronicles of the time *Hamlet* ii 2 549
To suckle fools and chronicle small beer *Othello* ii 1 161
I and my sword will earn our chronicle: There's hope in't yet *A. and C.* iii 13 175
Chronicled. He that is so yoked by a fool, Methinks, should not be chronicled for wise *T. G. of Ver.* i 1 41
This sport, well carried, shall be chronicled *M. N. Dream* iii 2 240
For now the devil, that told me I did well, Says that this deed is chronicled in hell *Richard II.* v 5 117
Chronicler. But such an honest chronicler as Griffith *Hen. VIII.* iv 2 72
Chrysolite. If heaven would make me such another world Of one entire and perfect chrysolite *Othello* v 2 145
Chuck. The king would have me present the princess, sweet chuck, with some delightful ostentation *L. L. Lost* v 1 117
Sweet chucks, beat not the bones of the buried v 2 667
Why, how now, my bawcock! how dost thou, chuck? *T. Night* iii 4 126
Good bawcock, bate thy rage; use lenity, sweet chuck! *Hen. V.* iii 2 26
Be innocent of the knowledge, dearest chuck, Till thou applaud the deed *Macbeth* iii 2 45
Come now, your promise.—What promise, chuck? *Othello* iii 4 49
Pray, chuck, come hither.—What is your pleasure? iv 2 24
Sleep a little.—No, my chuck. Eros, come; mine armour, Eros! *Ant. and Cleo.* iv 4 2
Chuff. Hang ye, gorbellied knaves, are ye undone? No, ye fat chuffs 1 *Hen. IV.* ii 2 94
Church. I am of the church, and will be glad to do my benevolence to make atonements *Mer. Wives* i 1 32
And here it rests, that you'll procure the vicar To stay for me at church iv 6 49
If it had not been i' the church, I would have swinged him v 5 196
I have a good eye, uncle; I can see a church by daylight *Much Ado* ii 1 86
When mean you to go to church?—To-morrow, my lord ii 1 371
All the gallants of the town are come to fetch you to church iii 4 97
Should I go to church And see the holy edifice of stone, And not bethink me straight of dangerous rocks? *Mer. of Venice* i 1 29
Chapels had been churches and poor men's cottages princes' palaces i 2 14
First go with me to church and call me wife iii 2 305
The 'why' is plain as way to parish church *As Y. Like It* ii 7 52
If ever been where bells have knoll'd to church ii 7 114
We have seen better days, And have with holy bell been knoll'd to church ii 7 121
Get you to church, and have a good priest that can tell you what marriage is iii 3 86
The morning wears, 'tis time we were at church *T. of Shrew* iii 2 113
We will persuade him, be it possible, To put on better ere he go to church iii 2 128
Signior Gremio, came you from the church? iii 2 151
And kiss'd her lips with such a clamorous smack That at the parting all the church did echo iii 2 181
The old priest of Saint Luke's church is at your command at all hours iv 4 88
To the church; take the priest, clerk, and some sufficient honest witnesses iv 4 94
I'll see the church o' your back; and then come back to my master's v 1 5
I have seen them in the church together v 1 42
Why dost thou not go to church in a galliard? *T. Night* i 3 136
Dost thou live by thy tabor?—No, sir, I live by the church iii 1 3
I do live by the church; for I do live at my house, and my house doth stand by the church iii 1 6
The church stands by thy tabor, if thy tabor stand by the church iii 1 10
Like a pedant that keeps a school i' the church iii 2 81
Every shop, church, session, hanging, yields a careful man work *W. Tale* iv 4 700
Why thou against the church, our holy mother, So wilfully dost spurn *K. John* iii 1 141
Be champion of our church, Or let the church, our mother, breathe her curse, A mother's curse, on her revolting son iii 1 255
Ransacking the church, Offending charity iii 4 172
His spirit is come in, That so stood out against the holy church v 2 71
An I have not forgotten what the inside of a church is made of 1 *Hen. IV.* iii 3 9

Church. Proclaim'd at market-crosses, read in churches *1 Hen. IV.* v 1 73
What company?—Ephesians, my lord, of the old church *2 Hen. IV.* ii 2 164
I' faith, and thou followedst him like a church ii 4 250
All the temporal lands which men devout By testament have given to the church Would they strip from us *Hen. V.* i 1 10
A true lover of the holy church.—The courses of his youth promised it not i 1 23
Lost never a man, but one that is like to be executed for robbing a church iii 6 106
The church's prayers made him so prosperous.—The church! where is it? *1 Hen. VI.* i 1 32
Ne'er throughout the year to church thou go'st Except it be to pray against thy foes i 1 42
In spite of pope or dignities of church i 3 50
And am not I a prelate of the church?—Yes, as an outlaw in a castle iii 1 46
More like a soldier than a man o' the church *2 Hen. VI.* i 1 186
Methought I sat in seat of majesty In the cathedral church of Westminster i 2 37
In all obedience, makes the church The chief aim of his honour *Hen. VIII.* v 3 117
Hie you to church; I must another way *Rom. and Jul.* ii 5 74
You shall not stay alone Till holy church incorporate two in one ii 6 37
The County Paris, at Saint Peter's Church, Shall happily make thee there a joyful bride iii 5 115
Now, by Saint Peter's Church and Peter too, He shall not make me there a joyful bride iii 5 117
Go with Paris to Saint Peter's Church, Or I will drag thee on a hurdle iii 5 155
Get thee to church o' Thursday, Or never after look me in the face iii 5 162
Go, nurse, go with her: we'll to church to-morrow iv 2 37
Come, is the bride ready to go to church?—Ready to go, but never to return iv 5 33
And, as the custom is, In all her best array bear her to church iv 5 81
Though you untie the winds and let them fight Against the churches *Macbeth* iv 1 53
He must build churches, then; or else shall he suffer not thinking on *Hamlet* iii 2 142
To cut his throat i' the church.—No place, indeed, should murder sanctuarize iv 7 127
Thou dost ill to say the gallows is built stronger than the church v 1 55
And bawds and whores do churches build *Lear* iii 2 90
Never leave gaping till they've swallowed the whole parish, church, steeple, bells, and all *Pericles* ii 1 38
He should never have left, till he cast bells, steeple, church, and parish, up again ii 1 47
Church-bench. Let us go sit here upon the church-bench till two *M. Ado* iii 3 95
Church-door. 'Tis not so deep as a well, nor so wide as a church-door; but 'tis enough *Rom. and Jul.* iii 1 100
Church-like. Whose church-like humours fits not for a crown *2 Hen. VI.* i 1 247
Churchman. Sir Hugh hath shown himself a wise and patient churchman *Mer. Wives* ii 3 57
Art thou a churchman?—No such matter, sir *T. Night* iii 1 4
Beaufort The imperious churchman *2 Hen. VI.* i 3 72
Ambitious churchman, leave to afflict my heart ii 1 182
That churchman bears a bounteous mind indeed *Hen. VIII.* i 3 55
You are a churchman, or, I'll tell you, cardinal, I should judge now unhappily i 4 88
Love and meekness, lord, Become a churchman better than ambition v 3 63
Churchmen. We are justices and doctors and churchmen *Mer. Wives* ii 3 49
Had not churchmen pray'd, His thread of life had not so soon decay'd *1 Hen. VI.* i 1 33
Thy wife is proud; she holdeth thee in awe, More than God or religious churchmen may i 1 40
Who should study to prefer a peace, If holy churchmen take delight in broils? iii 1 111
Churchmen so hot? good uncle, hide such malice *2 Hen. VI.* ii 1 25
Get a prayer-book in your hand, And stand betwixt two churchmen *Richard III.* iii 7 48
If you have any justice, any pity; If ye be any thing but churchmen's habits *Hen. VIII.* iii 1 117
Church-way. In the church-way paths to glide *M. N. Dream* v 1 389
Church-window. Like god Bel's priests in the old church-window *M. Ado* iii 3 144
Churchyard. At whose approach, ghosts, wandering here and there, Troop home to churchyards *M. N. Dream* iii 2 382
There was a man . . . Dwelt by a churchyard: I will tell it softly *W. Tale* ii 1 30
If this same were a churchyard where we stand *K. John* iii 3 40
At Touraine, in Saint Katharine's churchyard *1 Hen. VI.* i 2 100
Think Upon the wounds his body bears, which show Like graves i' the holy churchyard *Coriolanus* iii 3 51
So shall no foot upon the churchyard tread, Being loose, unfirm, with digging up of graves, But thou shalt hear it *Rom. and Jul.* v 3 5
I am almost afraid to stand alone Here in the churchyard v 3 11
I will tear thee joint by joint And strew this hungry churchyard with thy limbs v 3 36
The ground is bloody; search about the churchyard v 3 172
Here's Romeo's man; we found him in the churchyard v 3 182
We took this mattock and this spade from him, As he was coming from this churchyard side v 3 186
When churchyards yawn and hell itself breathes out Contagion *Hamlet* iii 2 407
Churl. Good meat, sir, is common; that every churl affords *Com. of Errors* iii 1 24
Churl, upon thy eyes I throw All the power this charm doth owe *M. N. Dream* ii 2 78
Thou churl, for this time, Though full of our displeasure, yet we free thee From the dead blow of it *W. Tale* iv 4 443
Thy mother took into her blameful bed Some stern untutor'd churl *2 Hen. VI.* iii 2 213
Though you left me like a churl, I found a friend *T. Andron.* i 1 486
O churl! drunk all, and left no friendly drop To help me after? *R. and J.* v 3 163
Thou'rt a churl; ye've got a humour there Does not become a man *T. of Athens* i 2 26
Think us no churls, nor measure our good minds By this rude place we live in *Cymbeline* iii 6 65
Churlish. A sea of melting pearl, which some call tears: Those at her father's churlish feet she tender'd *T. G. of Ver.* iii 1 225
As the icy fang And churlish chiding of the winter's wind *As Y. Like It* ii 1 7
My master is of churlish disposition ii 4 80
This is called the Reply Churlish v 4 81
The third, the Reply Churlish; the fourth, the Reproof Valiant v 4 98
The cunning of her passion Invites me in this churlish messenger *T. Night* ii 2 24
The interruption of their churlish drums Cuts off more circumstance *K. John* ii 1 76
Nothing do I see in you, Though churlish thoughts themselves should be your judge, That I can find should merit any hate ii 1 519
Churlish. Braying trumpets and loud churlish drums, Clamours of hell, be measures to our pomp *K. John* iii 1 303
Will you again unknit This churlish knot of all-abhorred war? *1 Hen. IV.* v 1 16
And waste for churlish winter's tyranny *2 Hen. IV.* i 3 62
A good soft pillow for that good white head Were better than a churlish turf of France *Hen. V.* iv 1 15
Doth this churlish superscription Pretend some alteration in good will? *1 Hen. VI.* iv 1 53
Valiant as the lion, churlish as the bear, slow as the elephant *Tr. and Cr.* i 2 21
I tell thee, churlish priest, A ministering angel shall my sister be, When thou liest howling *Hamlet* v 1 263
Churlishly. How churlishly I chid Lucetta hence! *T. G. of Ver.* i 2 60
Churn. And bootless make the breathless housewife churn *M. N. Dream* ii 1 37
Chus. I have heard him swear To Tubal and to Chus, his countrymen *Mer. of Venice* iii 2 287
Cicatrice. Lean but upon a rush, The cicatrice and capable impressure Thy palm some moment keeps *As Y. L. It* iii 5 23
His cicatrice, an emblem of war, here on his sinister cheek *All's Well* ii 1 43
There will be large cicatrices to show the people, when he shall stand for his place *Coriolanus* ii 1 164
Since yet thy cicatrice looks raw and red After the Danish sword *Hamlet* iv 3 62
Cicely. Maud, Bridget, Marian, Cicely, Gillian, Ginn! *Com. of Errors* iii 1 31
Sometimes you would call out for Cicely Hacket *T. of Shrew* Ind. 2 91
Cicero Looks with such ferret and such fiery eyes *J. Cæsar* i 2 185
Did Cicero say any thing?—Ay, he spoke Greek.—To what effect? i 2 281
O Cicero, I have seen tempests, when the scolding winds Have rived the knotty oaks i 3 4
This disturbed sky Is not to walk in.—Farewell, Cicero i 3 40
But what of Cicero? shall we sound him? ii 1 141
Our letters do not well agree; Mine speak of seventy senators that died By their proscriptions, Cicero being one.—Cicero one!—Cicero is dead iv 3 178
Cicester. The rebels have consumed with fire Our town of Cicester in Gloucestershire *Richard II.* v 6 3
Ciel, cousin Orleans. Now, my lord constable! *Hen. V.* iv 2 6
Cilicia. To Ptolemy he assign'd Syria, Cilicia, and Phœnicia *Ant. and Cleo.* iii 6 16
Cimber. Who's that? Metellus Cimber?—No, it is Casca *J. Cæsar* i 3 134
All but Metellus Cimber; and he's gone To seek you at your house i 3 149
He is welcome too.—This, Casca; this, Cinna; and this, Metellus Cimber ii 1 96
Mark well Metellus Cimber: Decius Brutus loves thee not ii 3 4
Most puissant Cæsar, Metellus Cimber throws before thy seat An humble heart,— I must prevent thee, Cimber iii 1 34
Desiring thee that Publius Cimber may Have an immediate freedom of repeal iii 1 53
To thy foot doth Cassius fall, To beg enfranchisement for Publius Cimber iii 1 57
I was constant Cimber should be banish'd, And constant do remain to keep him so iii 1 72
Cimmerian. Your swarth Cimmerian Doth make your honour of his body's hue, Spotted, detested, and abominable *T. Andron.* ii 3 72
Cincture. Happy he whose cloak and cincture can Hold out this tempest *K. John* iv 3 155
Cinder. O'ershine you as much as the full moon doth the cinders of the element *2 Hen. IV.* iv 3 58
Sorrow concealed, like an oven stopp'd, Doth burn the heart to cinders where it is *T. Andron.* ii 4 37
I should make very forges of my cheeks, That would to cinders burn up modesty, Did I but speak thy deeds *Othello* iv 2 75
Prithee, go hence; Or I shall show the cinders of my spirits Through the ashes of my chance *Ant. and Cleo.* v 2 173
Cinna. 'Tis Cinna; I do know him by his gait *J. Cæsar* i 3 132
Cinna, where haste you so?—To find out you i 3 133
Am I not stay'd for, Cinna?—I am glad on't i 3 136
Good Cinna, take this paper, And look you lay it in the prætor's chair i 3 142
This, Casca; this, Cinna; and this, Metellus Cimber.—They are all welcome ii 1 96
Have an eye to Cinna; trust not Trebonius; mark well Metellus Cimber ii 3 3
Truly, my name is Cinna.—Tear him to pieces; he's a conspirator iii 3 29
I am Cinna the poet.—Tear him for his bad verses iii 3 32
I am not Cinna the conspirator.—It is no matter, his name's Cinna iii 3 36
Cinque pace. A Scotch jig, a measure, and a cinque pace *Much Ado* ii 1 77
Falls into the cinque pace faster and faster, till he sink into his grave ii 1 82
Cinque-ports. Four barons Of the Cinque-ports *Hen. VIII.* iv 1 49
Cinque-spotted, like the crimson drops I' the bottom of a cowslip *Cymb.* ii 2 38
Cipher. Mine were the very cipher of a function *Meas. for Meas.* ii 2 39
There I shall see mine own figure.—Which I take to be either a fool or a cipher *As Y. Like It* iii 2 308
Like a cipher, Yet standing in rich place *W. Tale* i 2 6
Let us, ciphers to this great accompt, On your imaginary forces work *Hen. V.* Prol. 17
Circe. I think you all have drunk of Circe's cup *Com. of Errors* v 1 270
As if with Circe she would change my shape! *1 Hen. VI.* v 3 35
Circle. 'Tis a Greek invocation, to call fools into a circle *As Y. Like It* ii 5 62
A great magician, Obscured in the circle of this forest v 4 34
Thus have I yielded up into your hand The circle of my glory *K. John* v 1 2
And is well prepared To whip this dwarfish war, these pigmy arms, From out the circle of his territories v 2 136
If you would conjure in her, you must make a circle *Hen. V.* v 2 320
Glory is like a circle in the water, Which never ceaseth to enlarge itself *1 Hen. VI.* i 2 133
With Henry's death the English circle ends i 2 136
You heavy people, circle me about, That I may turn me to each one of you *T. Andron.* iii 1 277
'Twould anger him To raise a spirit in his mistress' circle Of some strange nature *Rom. and Jul.* ii 1 24
'Tis true; The wheel is come full circle; I am here *Lear* v 3 174
Of thee craves The circle of the Ptolemies for her heirs *Ant. and Cleo.* iii 12 18
Circled. Until thy head be circled with the same *2 Hen. VI.* i 2 10
Modest Dian circled with her nymphs *3 Hen. VI.* iv 8 21
The inconstant moon, That monthly changes in her circled orb *R. and J.* ii 2 110
Circling. The imperial metal, circling now thy brow, Had graced the tender temples of my child *Richard III.* iv 4 382
Whose circling shadows kings have sought to sleep in *T. Andron.* ii 4 19
Circuit. Until the golden circuit on my head, Like to the glorious sun's transparent beams, Do calm the fury of this mad-bred flaw *2 Hen. VI.* iii 1 352
How sweet a thing it is to wear a crown; Within whose circuit is Elysium And all that poets feign of bliss and joy *3 Hen. VI.* i 2 30
Circum circa. I will whip about your infamy circum circa *L. L. Lost* v 1 72

Circumcised. I took by the throat the circumcised dog, And smote him, thus *Othello* v 2 355

Circumference. In the circumference of a peck, hilt to point, heel to head *Mer. Wives* iii 5 113

He is no crescent, and his horns are invisible within the circumference *M. N. Dream* v 1 247

Though all these English and their discipline Were harbour'd in their rude circumference *K. John* ii 1 262

Circummured. He hath a garden circummured with brick *Meas. for Meas.* iv 1 28

Circumscribed. From where he circumscribed with his sword, And brought to yoke, the enemies of Rome *T. Andron.* i 1 68

Therefore must his choice be circumscribed Unto the voice and yielding of that body Whereof he is the head *Hamlet* i 3 22

Circumscription. I would not my unhoused free condition Put into circumscription and confine For the sea's worth *Othello* i 2 27

Circumspect. Be wise and circumspect *2 Hen. VI.* i 1 157

High-reaching Buckingham grows circumspect *Richard III.* iv 2 31

Circumstance. So, by your circumstance, you call me fool.—So, by your circumstance, I fear you'll prove *T. G. of Ver.* i 1 36

Nay, that I can deny by a circumstance i 1 84

Therefore it must with circumstance be spoken iii 2 36

Neither in time, matter, or other circumstance *Meas. for Meas.* iv 2 108

With circumstance and oaths so to deny This chain *Com. of Errors* v 1 16

And, circumstances shortened, for she has been too long a talking of, the lady is disloyal *Much Ado* iii 2 105

Herein spend but time To wind about my love with circumstance *Mer. of Venice* i 1 154

The sixth, the Lie with Circumstance *As Y. Like It* v 4 100

In all these circumstances I'll instruct you *T. of Shrew* iv 2 119

Leave frivolous circumstances, I pray you v 1 28

No obstacle, no incredulous or unsafe circumstance *T. Night* iii 4 89

I know the knight is incensed against you, even to a mortal arbitrement; but nothing of the circumstance more iii 4 287

Till each circumstance Of place, time, fortune, do cohere and jump v 1 258

All other circumstances Made up to the deed *W. Tale* ii 1 178

The pretence whereof being by circumstances partly laid open iii 2 18

His approach, So out of circumstance and sudden v 1 90

Most true, if ever truth were pregnant by circumstance v 2 34

The interruption of their churlish drums Cuts off more circumstance *K. John* ii 1 77

The circumstance consider'd, good my lord *1 Hen. IV.* i 3 70

The circumstance I'll tell you more at large *1 Hen. VI.* i 1 109

If your grace mark every circumstance, You have great reason to do Richard right iii 1 153

What means this passionate discourse, This peroration with such circumstance? *2 Hen. VI.* i 1 105

Tell us hear the circumstance, That we for thee may glorify the Lord ii 1 74

Hath not essentially but by circumstance The name of valour v 2 39

Give me leave, By circumstance, but to acquit myself *Richard III.* i 2 77

Give me leave, By circumstance, to curse thy cursed self i 2 80

The respects thereof are nice and trivial, All circumstances well considered iii 7 176

I do believe, Induced by potent circumstances, that You are mine enemy *Hen. VIII.* ii 4 76

Who, in his circumstance, expressly proves That no man is the lord of any thing *Troi. and Cres.* iii 3 114

And tell them both the circumstance of all *T. Andron.* iv 2 156

Answer to that; Say either, and I'll stay the circumstance *Rom. and Jul.* ii 5 36

But the true ground of all these piteous woes We cannot without circumstance descry v 3 181

You speak like a green girl, Unsifted in such perilous circumstance *Hamlet* i 3 102

Without more circumstance at all, I hold it fit that we shake hands and part i 5 127

If circumstances lead me, I will find Where truth is hid ii 2 157

Can you, by no drift of circumstance, Get from him why he puts on this confusion? iii 1 1

One scene of it comes near the circumstance Which I have told thee of iii 2 81

But in our circumstance and course of thought, 'Tis heavy with him iii 3 83

You do remember all the circumstance?—Remember it, my lord! v 2 2

With a bombast circumstance Horribly stuff'd with epithets of war *Othello* i 1 13

Or feed upon such nice and waterish diet, Or breed itself so out of circumstance iii 3 16

All quality, Pride, pomp and circumstance of glorious war! iii 3 354

Strong circumstances, Which lead directly to the door of truth iii 3 406

My circumstances, Being so near the truth as I will make them, Must first induce you to believe *Cymbeline* ii 4 61

Circumstanced. 'Tis very good; I must be circumstanced *Othello* iii 4 201

Circumstantial. So to the Lie Circumstantial and the Lie Direct *As Y. Like It* v 4 85

This fierce abridgement Hath to it circumstantial branches *Cymbeline* v 5 383

Circumvent. One that would circumvent God *Hamlet* v 1 88

Circumvention. So abundant scarce, it will not in circumvention deliver a fly from a spider *Troi. and Cres.* ii 3 17

What ever have been thought on in this state, That could be brought to bodily act ere Rome Had circumvention? *Coriolanus* i 2 6

Cistern. Could not fill up The cistern of my lust *Macbeth* iv 3 63

Keep it as a cistern for foul toads To knot and gender in! *Othello* iv 2 61

So half my Egypt were submerged and made A cistern for scaled snakes! *Ant. and Cleo.* ii 5 95

Citadel. I swore I leaped from the window of the citadel *All's Well* iv 1 61

They give their greeting to the citadel *Othello* ii 1 95

Bring thou the master to the citadel ii 1 211

Meet me by and by at the citadel ii 1 292

I shall not dine at home; I meet the captains at the citadel iii 3 59

Run you to the citadel, And tell my lord and lady what hath happ'd v 1 126

A tower'd citadel, a pendent rock, A forked mountain *Ant. and Cleo.* iv 14 4

Cital. He made a blushing cital of himself *1 Hen. IV.* v 2 62

Cite. I need not cite him to it *T. G. of Ver.* ii 4 85

We cite our faults, That they may hold excused our lawless lives iv 1 53

The devil can cite Scripture for his purpose *Mer. of Venice* i 3 99

Whose aged honour cites a virtuous youth *All's Well* i 3 216

I think it cites us, brother, to the field *3 Hen. VI.* ii 1 34

Cited. Whose want gives growth to the imperfections Which you have cited *Hen. V.* v 2 70

Had I not been cited so by them, Yet did I purpose as they do entreat *2 Hen. VI.* iii 2 281

We look'd toward England, And cited up a thousand fearful times *Richard III.* i 4 14

To which She was often cited by them, but appear'd not *Hen. VIII.* iv 1 29

As truth's authentic author to be cited *Troi. and Cres.* iii 2 188

Cities. Met him in boroughs, cities, villages *1 Hen. IV.* iv 3 69

You see them perspectively, the cities turned into a maid *Hen. V.* v 2 348

I am content, so the maiden cities you talk of may wait on her v 2 353

Razeth your cities and subverts your towns *1 Hen. VI.* ii 3 65

Look on fertile France, And see the cities and the towns defaced iii 3 45

Twelve cities and seven walled towns of strength iii 4 7

Are the cities, that I got with wounds, Deliver'd up again with peaceful words? *2 Hen. VI.* i 1 121

It [conscience] is turned out of all towns and cities for a dangerous thing *Richard III.* i 4 146

Degrees in schools and brotherhoods in cities *Troi. and Cres.* i 3 104

And blind oblivion swallow'd cities up iii 2 194

Let courts and cities be Made all of false-faced soothing! *Coriolanus* i 9 43

In cities, mutinies; in countries, discord; in palaces, treason *Lear* i 2 116

As when, by night and negligence, the fire Is spied in populous cities *Othello* i 1 77

And o'er green Neptune's back With ships made cities *Ant. and Cleo.* iv 14 59

Those cities that of plenty's cup And her prosperities so largely taste *Pericles* i 4 52

Citing. I do digress too much, Citing my worthless praise *T. Andron.* v 3 117

Citizen. The generous and gravest citizens Have hent the gates *Meas. for Meas.* iv 6 13

His bondman, all as mad as he,—Doing displeasure to the citizens *Com. of Errors* v 1 142

If it be proved against an alien That by direct or indirect attempts He seek the life of any citizen *Mer. of Venice* iv 1 351

Sweep on, you fat and greasy citizens; 'Tis just the fashion *As Y. Like It* ii 1 55

Pisa renown'd for grave citizens *T. of Shrew* i 1 10; iv 2 95

Which trust accordingly kind citizens *K. John* ii 1 231

Speak, citizens, for England; who's your king? ii 1 362

Citizens of Angiers, ope your gates, Let in that amity which you have made ii 1 536

The civil citizens kneading up the honey *Hen. V.* i 2 199

How London doth pour out her citizens! v Prol. 24

A foe to citizens, One that still motions war and never peace *1 Hen. VI.* i 3 62

Command the citizens make bonfires And feast and banquet in the open streets i 6 12

Slain our citizens And sent our sons and husbands captivate ii 3 41

The citizens fly and forsake their houses *2 Hen. VI.* iv 4 50

You might well have signified the same Unto the citizens *Richard III.* iii 5 60

I'll acquaint our duteous citizens With all your just proceedings in this cause iii 5 65

Tell them how Edward put to death a citizen iii 5 76

How now, my lord, what say the citizens? iii 7 1

The citizens are mum and speak not a word iii 7 3

Thanks, gentle citizens and friends iii 7 38

The mayor and citizens, In deep designs and matters of great moment iii 7 66

He wonders to what end you have assembled Such troops of citizens iii 7 85

Consorted with the citizens, Your very worshipful and loving friends iii 7 137

Do, good my lord, your citizens entreat you iii 7 201

Come, citizens: 'zounds! I'll entreat no more iii 7 219

The citizens, I am sure, have shown at full their royal minds *Hen. VIII.* iv 1 7

We are accounted poor citizens, the patricians good *Coriolanus* i 1 15

Thy news?—The citizens of Corioli have issued i 6 10

Help, ye citizens!—On both sides more respect iii 1 180

I am content.—Lo, citizens, he says he is content iii 3 48

When he speaks not like a citizen, You find him like a soldier iii 3 53

O, bless me here with thy victorious hand, Whose fortunes Rome's best citizens applaud! *T. Andron.* i 1 164

But the citizens favour Lucius, And will revolt from me to succour him iv 4 79

Ancient citizens Cast by their grave beseeming ornaments, To wield old partisans, in hands as old *Rom. and Jul.* i 1 99

Romeo, away, be gone! The citizens are up, and Tybalt slain iii 1 138

I will this night, In several hands, in at his windows throw, As if they came from several citizens, Writings *J. Cæsar* i 2 321

To every Roman citizen he gives, To every several man, seventy-five drachmas iii 2 246

Arise, arise; Awake the snorting citizens with the bell *Othello* i 1 90

The round world Should have shook lions into civil streets, And citizens to their dens *Ant. and Cleo.* v 1 17

So sick I am not, yet I am not well; But not so citizen a wanton as To seem to die ere sick *Cymbeline* iv 2 8

Cittern-head. A cittern-head.—The head of a bodkin *L. L. Lost* v 2 614

City. Let us into the city presently *T. G. of Ver.* iii 2 91

The nature of our people, Our city's institutions *Meas. for Meas.* i 1 11

And what shall become of those in the city? i 2 101

Does your worship mean to geld and splay all the youth of the city? ii 1 243

Meet me at the consecrated fount A league below the city iv 3 103

Proclaim it, provost, round about the city v 1 514

I will go lose myself And wander up and down to view the city *Com. of Errors* i 2 31

How is the man esteem'd here in the city? v 1 4

Highly beloved, Second to none that lives here in the city v 1 7

All that know me in the city Can witness with me v 1 323

I hear as good exclamation on your worship as of any man in the city *Much Ado* iii 5 29

If we meet in the city, we shall be dogged with company *M. N. Dream* i 2 106

You do impeach your modesty too much, To leave the city ii 1 215

The trade and profit of the city Consisteth of all nations *Mer. of Venice* iii 3 30

Let the danger light Upon your charter and your city's freedom iv 1 39

Being native burghers of this desert city *As Y. Like It* ii 1 23

Thus most invectively he pierceth through The body of the country, city, court ii 1 59

What woman in the city do I name, When that I say the city-woman? ii 7 74

The boldness is mine own, That, being a stranger in this city here, Do make myself a suitor to your daughter *T. of Shrew* ii 1 90

My house within the city Is richly furnished with plate and gold ii 1 348

So shall you stay Till you have done your business in the city iv 2 110

A' means to cozen somebody in this city under my countenance v 1 40

In blowing him down again, with the breach yourselves made, you lose your city *All's Well* i 1 137

If they do approach the city, we shall lose all the sight iii 5 2

The memorials and the things of fame That do renown this city *T. Night* iii 3 24

By twos and threes at several posterns Clear them o' the city *W. Tale* i 2 439

Where's Bohemia? speak.—Here in your city v 1 186

Merciless proceeding by these French Confronts your city's eyes *K. John* ii 1 215

To save unscratch'd your city's threatened cheeks ii 1 225

Then tell us, shall your city call us lord? ii 1 263

The flinty ribs of this contemptuous city ii 1 384

We from the west will send destruction Into this city's bosom ii 1 410

City. Win you this city without stroke or wound . . . *K. John* ii 1 418
Not Death himself In mortal fury half so peremptory, As we to keep this city . . . . ii 1 455
Speak England first, that hath been forward first To speak unto this city . . . . ii 1 483
Except this city now by us besieged . . . . . ii 1 489
'Tis hot; there's that will sack a city . . . . . *1 Hen. IV.* v 3 56
Behold A city on the inconstant billows dancing . . *Hen. V.* iii Prol. 15
Desire him to have borne His bruised helmet and his bended sword Before him through the city . . . . v Prol. 19
How many would the peaceful city quit, To welcome him! . . v Prol. 33
Who cannot see many a fair French city for one fair French maid . v 2 345
In yonder tower to overpeer the city . . . . . *1 Hen. VI.* i 4 11
This city must be famish'd, Or with light skirmishes enfeebled . i 4 68
O, my good lords, and virtuous Henry, Pity the city of London, pity us! . . . . iii 1 77
Our sacks shall be a mean to sack the city . . . . . iii 2 10
In the famous ancient city Tours . . . . . *2 Hen. VI.* i 1 5
When in the city Tours Thou ran'st a tilt in honour of my love . . i 3 53
In this city will I stay And live alone as secret as I may . . iv 4 47
And they jointly swear To spoil the city and your royal court . . iv 4 53
The lord mayor craves aid of your honour from the Tower to defend the city from the rebels . . . . iv 5 6
Now is Mortimer lord of this city . . . . . . iv 6 1
I charge and command that, of the city's cost, the pissing-conduit run nothing but claret wine . . . . iv 6 3
Soldiers, defer the spoil of the city until night . . . . iv 7 142
Ah, know you not the city favours them? . . . *3 Hen. VI.* i 1 67
And with colours spread March'd through the city to the palace gates i 1 92
The city being but of small defence, We'll quickly rouse the traitors v 1 64
I have done some offence That seems disgracious in the city's eyes *Richard III.* iii 7 112
They'll say 'tis naught: others, to hear the city Abused extremely, and to cry 'That's witty!'. . . . . . . *Hen. VIII.* Epil. 5
Priam's six-gated city, Dardan, and Tymbria, Helias, Chetas, Troien, And Antenorides . . . . . . *Troi. and Cres.* Prol. 15
I wonder now how yonder city stands When we have here her base and pillar . . . . iv 5 211
The other side o' the city is risen . . . . . *Coriolanus* i 1 48
What's the matter, That in these several places of the city You cry against the noble senate? . . . . i 1 189
Corn at their own rates; whereof, they say, The city is well stored . i 1 194
The rabble should have first unroof'd the city, Ere so prevail'd with me i 1 222
They fear us not, but issue forth their city . . . . . i 4 23
He is himself alone, To answer all the city . . . . . i 4 52
Then, valiant Titus, take Convenient numbers to make good the city . i 5 13
Of all The treasure in this field achieved and city, We render you the tenth . . . . i 9 33
Go you to the city; Learn how 'tis held . . . . . i 10 27
Do you two know how you are censured here in the city? . . . ii 1 25
Alone he enter'd The mortal gate of the city . . . . . ii 2 115
Till we call'd Both field and city ours, he never stood To ease his breast ii 2 125
To unbuild the city and to lay all flat.—What is the city but the people?—True, The people are the city . . . . . . iii 1 198
That is the way to lay the city flat; To bring the roof to the foundation iii 1 204
Where is this viper That would depopulate the city and Be every man himself? . . . . iii 1 264
There's no remedy: Unless, by not so doing, our good city Cleave in the midst . . . . iii 2 27
Even from this instant, banish him our city . . . . . iii 3 101
Despising, For you, the city, thus I turn my back . . . . iii 3 134
Let a guard Attend us through the city . . . . . . iii 3 141
A goodly city is this Antium. City, 'Tis I that made thy widows . iv 4 1
I' the city of kites and crows . . . . iv 5 45
Gave way unto your clusters, Who did hoot him out o' the city . iv 6 123
Can you think to blow out the intended fire your city is ready to flame in, with such weak breath as this? . . . . . . v 2 49
I am hush'd until our city be afire, And then I'll speak a little . v 3 181
There is no more mercy in him than there is milk in a male tiger; that shall our poor city find . . . . v 4 31
This Volumnia Is worth of consuls, senators, patricians, A city full . v 4 57
They are near the city?—Almost at point to enter . . . v 4 63
Go tell the lords o' the city I am here . . . . . v 6 1
And given up, For certain drops of salt, your city Rome, I say 'your city' v 6 93
In this city he Hath widow'd and unchilded many a one . . v 6 152
Why should you fear? is not your city strong? . *T. Andron.* iv 4 78
The grove of sycamore That westward rooteth from the city's side *Rom. and Jul.* i 1 129
This reverend holy friar, All our whole city is much bound to him . iv 2 32
One of our order, to associate me, Here in this city visiting the sick v 2 7
Whose untimely death Banish'd the new-made bridegroom from this city v 3 235
Be as a planetary plague, when Jove Will o'er some high-viced city hang his poison In the sick air . . . . *T. of Athens* iv 3 109
How has the ass broke the wall, that thou art out of the city? . iv 3 355
With letters of entreaty, which imported His fellowship i' the cause against your city . . . . v 2 12
So did we woo Transformed Timon to our city's love By humble message v 4 19
March, noble lord, Into our city with thy banners spread . . . v 4 30
Or offend the stream Of regular justice in your city's bounds . . v 4 61
Bring me into your city, And I will use the olive with my sword . v 4 81
Even those you were wont to take delight in, the tragedians of the city *Hamlet* ii 2 342
Do they hold the same estimation they did when I was in the city? . ii 2 349
Three great ones of the city, In personal suit to make me his lieutenant *Othello* i 1 8
There's many a beast then in a populous city, And many a civil monster iv 1 64
The city cast Her people out upon her . . . . *Ant. and Cleo.* ii 2 218
Enter the city, clip your wives, your friends, Tell them your feats . iv 8 8
Trumpeters, With brazen din blast you the city's ear . . . iv 8 36
Our foot Upon the hills adjoining to the city Shall stay with us . . iv 10 5
Did you but know the city's usuries And felt them knowingly *Cymbeline* iii 3 45
Antiochus the Great Built up, this city, for his chiefest seat *Pericles* 1 Gower 18
A city on whom plenty held full hand, For riches strew'd herself even in the streets . . . . i 4 22
I doubt not but this populous city will Yield many scholars . . iv 6 197
The city strived God Neptune's annual feast to keep . . . v Gower 16
To rage the city turn, That him and his they in his palace burn v 3 Gower 97

City feast. Make not a city feast of it . . . . *T. of Athens* iii 6 75

City gate. Come, I'll convey thee through the city-gate . *T. G. of Ver.* iii 1 252
These are the city gates, the gates of Rouen . . . *1 Hen. VI.* iii 2 1

City gate. Open your city gates; Be humble to us . . . *1 Hen. VI.* iv 2 5
Now, Warwick, wilt thou ope the city gates? . . . . *3 Hen. VI.* v 1 21

City leads. You have holp to ravish your own daughters and To melt the city leads upon your pates . . . . . *Coriolanus* iv 6 82

City mills. At the cypress grove: I pray you—'Tis south the city mills i 10 31

City ports. Him I accuse The city ports by this hath enter'd . v 6 6

City walls. Crave harbourage within your city walls . . *K John* ii 1 234
A nobler man, a braver warrior, Lives not this day within the city walls *T. Andron.* i 1 26

City wives. The insatiate greediness of his desires, And his enforcement of the city wives . . . . *Richard III.* iii 7 8

City woman. What woman in the city do I name, When that I say the city-woman?. . . . . *As Y. Like It* ii 7 75

Civet. Rubs himself with civet: can you smell him out by that? *Much Ado* iii 2 50
The courtier's hands are perfumed with civet . . *As Y. Like It* iii 2 66
Civet is of a baser birth than tar, the very uncleanly flux of a cat . . iii 2 69
Give me an ounce of civet, good apothecary, to sweeten my imagination *Lear* iv 6 132

Civil. They are reformed, civil, full of good . . . *T. G. of Ver.* v 4 156
I'll ne'er be drunk whilst I live again, but in honest, civil, godly company . . . . *Mer. Wives* i 1 187
She's as fartuous a civil modest wife . . . . . . ii 2 101
Civil as an orange, and something of that jealous complexion *Much Ado* ii 1 304
This civil war of wits were much better used . . . *L. L. Lost* ii 1 226
That the rude sea grew civil at her song . . . *M. N. Dream* ii 1 152
If you were civil and knew courtesy, You would not do me thus much injury . . . . iii 2 147
By my soul, No woman had it, but a civil doctor . *Mer. of Venice* v 1 210
Tongues I'll hang on every tree, That shall civil sayings show *As Y. Like It* iii 2 136
Be clamorous and leap all civil bounds . . . . . *T. Night* i 4 21
He is sad and civil, And suits well for a servant with my fortunes . iii 4 5
And like a civil war set'st oath to oath . . . . *K. John* iii 1 264
Civil tumult reigns Between my conscience and my cousin's death . iv 2 247
Our eyes do hate the dire aspect Of civil wounds . . *Richard II.* i 3 128
The king of heaven forbid our lord the king Should so with civil and uncivil arms Be rush'd upon! . . . . iii 3 102
In the intestine shock And furious close of civil butchery . *1 Hen. IV.* i 1 13
And whereupon You conjure from the breast of civil peace Such bold hostility . . . . iv 3 43
'Neighbour Quickly,' says he, 'receive those that are civil' . *2 Hen. IV.* ii 4 97
Even now before this honest, virtuous, civil gentlewoman! . . . ii 4 328
You, lord archbishop, Whose see is by a civil peace maintain'd . iv 1 42
O my poor kingdom, sick with civil blows! . . . . . iv 5 134
We bear our civil swords and native fire As far as France . . v 5 112
The civil citizens kneading up the honey . . . . *Hen. V.* i 2 199
He was thinking of civil wars when he got me . . . . v 2 243
Prosper this realm, keep it from civil broils! . . . *1 Hen. VI.* i 1 53
Civil dissension is a viperous worm That gnaws the bowels of the commonwealth . . . . iii 1 72
Thy acts in Ireland, In bringing them to civil discipline *2 Hen. VI.* i 1 195
Already in this civil broil I see them lording it in London streets . iv 8 46
Conditionally, that here thou take an oath To cease this civil war *3 Hen. VI.* i 1 197
Let our hearts and eyes, like civil war, Be blind with tears . . ii 5 77
Send him hence to Brittany, Till storms be past of civil enmity . iv 6 98
Now civil wounds are stopp'd, peace lives again . *Richard III.* v 5 40
Or who hath brought the fatal engine in That gives our Troy, our Rome, the civil wound . . . . *T. Andron.* v 3 87
Where civil blood makes civil hands unclean . . *Rom. and Jul.* Prol. 4
Three civil brawls, bred of an airy word . . . . . i 1 96
Come, civil night, Thou sober-suited matron, all in black . . iii 2 10
Civil laws are cruel; Then what should war be? *T. of Athens* iv 3 60
Either there is a civil strife in heaven, Or else the world, too saucy with the gods, Incenses them to send destruction . . . *J. Cæsar* i 3 11
Domestic fury and fierce civil strife Shall cumber all the parts of Italy iii 1 263
Putting on the mere form of civil and humane seeming . . *Othello* ii 1 243
You were wont be civil; The gravity and stillness of your youth The world hath noted . . . . ii 3 190
There's many a beast then in a populous city, And many a civil monster iv 1 65
Our Italy Shines o'er with civil swords . . . *Ant. and Cleo.* i 3 45
The round world Should have shook lions into civil streets . . v 1 16
Ho! who's here? If any thing that's civil, speak . . *Cymbeline* iii 6 23

Civilest. Kent, in the Commentaries Cæsar writ, Is term'd the civil'st place of all this isle . . . . *2 Hen. VI.* iv 7 66

Civility. Any madness I ever yet beheld seemed but tameness, civilty and patience, to this his distemper . . . . . *Mer. Wives* iv 2 28
Use all the observance of civility, Like one well studied *Mer. of Venice* ii 2 204
In civility thou seem'st so empty . . . . . *As Y. Like It* ii 7 93
The thorny point Of bare distress hath ta'en from me the show Of smooth civility . . . . ii 7 96
Do not believe That, from the sense of all civility, I thus would play and trifle with your reverence . . . . . . *Othello* i 1 132
Royalty unlearn'd, honour untaught, Civility not seen from other *Cymbeline* iv 2 179

Civilly. I have savage cause; And to proclaim it civilly, were like A halter'd neck which does the hangman thank For being yare about him . . . . *Ant. and Cleo.* iii 13 129

Clack-dish. His use was to put a ducat in her clack-dish *Meas. for Meas.* iii 2 135

Clad. A spirit I am indeed; But am in that dimension grossly clad *T. Night* v 1 244
Say who thou art And why thou comest thus knightly clad in arms *Richard II.* i 3 12
A woman clad in armour chaseth them . . . . *1 Hen. VI.* i 5 3
But, look, the morn, in russet mantle clad, Walks o'er the dew of yon high eastward hill. . . . . *Hamlet* i 1 166

Claim. Tell my lady I claim the promise for her heavenly picture *T. G. of Ver.* iv 4 92
I claim her not, and therefore she is thine . . . . . v 4 135
My sole earth's heaven and my heaven's claim . *Com. of Errors* iii 2 64
One that claims me, one that haunts me, one that will have me . . iii 2 82
What claim lays she to thee?—Marry, sir, such claim as you would lay to your horse . . . . iii 2 84
To conclude, this drudge, or diviner, laid claim to me . . . iii 2 144
That is where we dined, Where Dowsabel did claim me for her husband iv 1 110
But for the mountain of mad flesh that claims marriage of me, I could find in my heart to stay here . . . . iv 4 159
Turn you where your lady is And claim her with a loving kiss *Mer. of Venice* iii 2 139

Claim. And lawfully by this the Jew may claim A pound of flesh *Mer. of Venice* iv 1 231
There is a youth here in the forest lays claim to you . *As Y. Like It* v 1 7
That obedient right Which both thy duty owes and our power claims *All's Well* ii 3 168
Which, as your due, time claims, he does acknowledge . . . . ii 4 43
All the honour That good convenience claims . . . . . iii 2 75
Arthur Plantagenet lays most lawful claim To this fair island *K. John* i 1 9
Why, being younger born, Doth he lay claim to thine inheritance? . i 1 72
What doth move you to claim your brother's land? . . . . i 1 91
If he were my brother's, My brother might not claim him . . . i 1 126
In right of Arthur do I claim of thee . . . . . . ii 1 153
Some bastards too.—Stand in his face to contradict his claim . . ii 1 280
You, in the right of Lady Blanch your wife, May then make all the claim that Arthur did . . . . iii 4 143
I, by the honour of my marriage-bed, After young Arthur, claim this land for mine . . . . v 2 94
Who else but I, And such as to my claim are liable, Sweat in this business? . . . . v 2 101
Personally I lay my claim To my inheritance of free descent *Richard II.* ii 3 135
Nor claim no further than your new-fall'n right . 1 *Hen. IV.* v 1 44
Unfold Why the law Salique that they have in France Or should, or should not, bar us in our claim . . . . . . *Hen. V.* i 2 12
There is no bar To make against your highness' claim to France . . i 2 36
May I with right and conscience make this claim? . . . . i 2 96
Go, my dread lord, to your great-grandsire's tomb, From whom you claim . . . . i 2 104
Desires you let the dukedoms that you claim Hear no more of you . i 2 256
No awkward claim, Pick'd from the worm-holes of long-vanish'd days . ii 4 85
This is his claim, his threatening and my message . . . . ii 4 110
Only reserved, you claim no interest In any of our towns of garrison 1 *Hen. VI.* v 4 167
A day will come when York shall claim his own . . . 2 *Hen. VI.* i 1 239
And, when I spy advantage, claim the crown . . . . . i 1 242
If thy claim be good, The Nevils are thy subjects to command . . ii 2 7
The third son, Duke of Clarence, from whose line I claim the crown . ii 2 35
This Edmund, in the reign of Bolingbroke, As I have read, laid claim unto the crown . . . . ii 2 40
By her I claim the kingdom: she was heir . . . . . . ii 2 47
Henry doth claim the crown from John of Gaunt, The fourth son; York claims it from the third . . . . ii 2 54
By this I shall perceive the commons' mind, How they affect the house and claim of York . . . . iii 1 375
Thus comes York to claim his right, And pluck the crown . . . v 1 1
Resolve thee, Richard; claim the English crown . . . 3 *Hen. VI.* i 1 49
Plantagenet, for all the claim thou lay'st, Think not that Henry shall be so deposed . . . . i 1 152
God forbid your grace should be forsworn.—I shall be, if I claim by open war . . . . i 2 19
And we, in pity of the gentle king, Had slipp'd our claim until another age . . . . ii 2 162
When we grow stronger, then we'll make our claim . . . . iv 7 59
Those who have the wit to claim the place . . . *Richard III.* iii 1 50
I'll claim that promise at your grace's hands . . . . . iii 1 197
I claim your gift, my due by promise, For which your honour and your faith is pawn'd . . . . iv 2 91
He makes for England, there to claim the crown . . . . . iv 4 469
'Tis the list Of those that claim their offices this day *Hen. VIII.* iv 1 15
The Duke of Suffolk is the first, and claims To be high-steward . iv 1 17
And those about her From her shall read the perfect ways of honour, And by those claim their greatness . . . . v 5 39
I am your debtor, claim it when 'tis due . . *Troi. and Cres.* iv 5 51
His worthy deeds did claim no less Than what he stood for . *Coriolanus* ii 3 194
Were fit for thee to use as they to claim . . . . . . iii 2 83
Why do we hold our tongues, That most may claim this argument for ours? *Macbeth* ii 3 126
I have some rights of memory in this kingdom, Which now to claim my vantage doth invite me . . . . *Hamlet* v 2 401
For your claim, fair sister, I bar it in the interest of my wife . *Lear* v 3 84
Whose beauty claims No worse a husband than the best of men *Ant. and Cleo.* ii 2 130

Claimed. Tell me, how if my brother, Who, as you say, took pains to get this son, Had of your father claim'd this son for his? *K. John* i 1 122
This prince hath neither claim'd it nor deserved it . *Richard III.* iii 1 51

Claiming. Howbeit they would hold up this Salique law To bar your highness claiming from the female . . . . . *Hen. V.* i 2 92

Clamber not you up to the casements then. . . . *Mer. of Venice* ii 5 31

Clambering the walls to eye him. . . . . . . *Coriolanus* ii 1 226
There, on the pendent boughs her coronet weeds Clambering to hang, an envious sliver broke . . . . *Hamlet* iv 7 174

Clamorous. The clamorous owl that nightly hoots . *M. N. Dream* ii 2 6
More clamorous than a parrot against rain . . . *As Y. Like It* iv 1 151
And kiss'd her lips with such a clamorous smack . *T. of Shrew* iii 2 180
She never will admit me.—Be clamorous and leap all civil bounds Rather than make unprofited return . . . . . . *T. Night* i 4 21
The sound that tells what hour it is Are clamorous groans *Richard II.* v 5 56
The herds Were strangely clamorous to the frighted fields 1 *Hen. IV.* iii 1 40
Are you not ashamed With this immodest clamorous outrage? 1 *Hen. VI.* iv 1 126
Entreat me fair, Or with the clamorous report of war Thus will I drown your exclamations . . . . *Richard III.* iv 4 152
I am thus encounter'd With clamorous demands of date-broke bonds *T. of Athens* ii 2 38
Those clamorous harbingers of blood and death . . . *Macbeth* v 6 10
One whom I will beat into clamorous whining . . . . *Lear* ii 2 25

Clamour. The venom clamours of a jealous woman Poisons more deadly than a mad dog's tooth . . . . *Com. of Errors* v 1 69
An hour in clamour and a quarter in rheum . . . . *Much Ado* v 2 84
Sickly ears, Deaf'd with the clamours of their own dear groans *L. L. Lost* v 2 874
I'll rail and brawl And with the clamour keep her still awake *T. of Shrew* iv 1 210
Contempt and clamour Will be my knell . . . . . *W. Tale* i 2 189
I never saw The heavens so dim by day. A savage clamour! . . . iii 3 56
Clamour your tongues, and not a word more . . . . . iv 4 250
Their soul-fearing clamours have brawl'd down The flinty ribs of this contemptuous city . . . . *K. John* ii 1 383
Shall braying trumpets and loud churlish drums, Clamours of hell, be measures to our pomp? . . . . iii 1 304
Do but start An echo with the clamour of thy drum . . . . v 2 168
'Tis not the trial of a woman's war, The bitter clamour of two eager tongues, Can arbitrate this cause . . . . . *Richard II.* i 1 49
Hanging them With deafening clamour in the slippery clouds 2 *Hen. IV.* iii 1 24
Why, what tumultuous clamour have we here? 2 *Hen. VI.* iii 2 239
And more he spoke, Which sounded like a clamour in a vault, That mought not be distinguish'd . . . . 3 *Hen. VI.* v 2 44
Peace, you ungracious clamours! peace, rude sounds! . *Troi. and Cres.* i 1 92
Soft infancy, that nothing canst but cry, Add to my clamours! . . ii 2 106
Shall dizzy with more clamour Neptune's ear . . . . . v 2 174
With all the applause and clamour of the host . . . *Coriolanus* i 9 64
We'll bring him to his house With shouts and clamours . *J. Cæsar* ii 2 58
As we shall make our griefs and clamour roar Upon his death *Macbeth* i 7 78
The instant burst of clamour that she made, Unless things mortal move them not at all, Would have made milch the burning eyes of heaven *Hamlet* ii 2 538
Whilst I can vent clamour from my throat, I'll tell thee thou dost evil *Lear* i 1 168
She shook The holy water from her heavenly eyes, And clamour moisten'd . . . . iv 3 33
Whilst I was big in clamour came there in a man . . . . v 3 208
Lest by his clamour—as it so fell out—The town might fall in fright *Othello* ii 3 231
You mortal engines, whose rude throats The immortal Jove's dread clamours counterfeit . . . . iii 3 356

Clamoured. The obscure bird Clamour'd the livelong night . *Macbeth* ii 3 65

Clang. Loud 'larums, neighing steeds, and trumpets' clang *T. of Shrew* i 2 207

Clangor. Like to a dismal clangor heard from far . . 3 *Hen. VI.* ii 3 18

Clap on more sails; pursue . . . . *Mer. Wives* ii 2 142
I would desire you to clap into your prayers . . *Meas. for Meas.* iv 3 43
Clap's into 'Light o' love;' that goes without a burden. *Much Ado* iii 4 44
Shall we clap into't roundly, without hawking or spitting? *As Y. Like It* v 3 11
Clap upon you two or three probable lies. . . . . *All's Well* iii 6 106
Ere I could make thee open thy white hand And clap thyself my love *W Tale* i 2 104
No longer than we well could wash our hands To clap this royal bargain up of peace . . . . *K. John* iii 1 235
Strive to speak big and clap their female joints In stiff unwieldy arms *Richard II.* iii 2 114
Clap to the doors: watch to-night, pray to-morrow . 1 *Hen. IV.* ii 4 305
Whose shouts and claps out-voice the deep-mouth'd sea *Hen. V.* v Prol. 11
Give me your answer; i' faith, do: and so clap hands and a bargain v 2 133
And on your heads Clap round fines for neglect . . . *Hen. VIII.* v 4 84
All the best men are ours; for 'tis ill hap, If they hold when their ladies bid 'em clap . . . . Epil. 14
Why, even already They clap the lubber Ajax on the shoulder *Troi. and Cres.* iii 3 139
One of those fellows that when he enters the confines of a tavern claps me his sword upon the table . . . . . *Rom. and Jul.* iii 1 6
Clap him and hiss him, according as he pleased and displeased them *J. Cæsar* i 2 261
What, fifty of my followers at a clap! . . . . . . *Lear* i 4 316
Antony Claps on his sea-wing, and, like a doting mallard, Leaving the fight in height, flies after her . . . . . *Ant. and Cleo.* iii 10 20
And every one with claps can sound, 'Our heir-apparent is a king!' *Pericles* iii Gower 36

Clapped. And—how we know not—all clapp'd under hatches *Tempest* v 1 231
Let him be clapped on the shoulder, and called Adam . *Much Ado* i 1 261
With that, all laugh'd and clapp'd him on the shoulder . *L. L. Lost* v 2 107
Cupid hath clapped him o' the shoulder . . . *As Y. Like It* iv 1 48
Was ever match clapp'd up so suddenly? . . . . *T. of Shrew* ii 1 327
This all-changing word, Clapp'd on the outward eye of fickle France *K. John* ii 1 583
This pennyworth of sugar, clapped even now into my hand 1 *Hen. IV.* ii 4 25
A' would have clapped i' the clout at twelve score . 2 *Hen. IV.* iii 2 51
Let them be clapp'd up close, And kept asunder . . . 2 *Hen. VI.* i 4 53
Clapp'd his tail between his legs and cried . . . . . . v 1 154
The new proclamation That's clapp'd upon the court-gate . *Hen. VIII.* i 3 18
The very thought of this fair company Clapp'd wings to me . . . i 4 9
You all clapp'd your hands, And cried 'Inestimable!' . *Tr. and Cr.* ii 2 87
Who, upon the sudden, Clapp'd to their gates . . . *Coriolanus* i 4 51
The rabblement hooted and clapped their chopped hands . *J. Cæsar* i 2 246
Little eyases, that cry out on the top of question, and are most tyrannically clapped for't . . . . *Hamlet* ii 2 356
I wish I could be made so many men, And all of you clapp'd up together in An Antony . . . . *Ant. and Cleo.* iv 2 17

Clapper. He hath a heart as sound as a bell and his tongue is the clapper *Much Ado* iii 2 13

Clapper-claw. He will clapper-claw thee tightly, bully . *Mer. Wives* ii 3 67

Clapper-clawing. Now they are clapper-clawing one another *Trio. and Cres.* v 4 1

Clapper-de-claw! vat is dat? . . . . *Mer. Wives* ii 3 69
By gar, me do look he shall clapper-de-claw me . . . . . ii 3 71

Clapping. This hand hath made him proud with clapping him *Rich. II.* v 5 86
Clapping their hands, and crying with loud voice . 2 *Hen. VI.* i 1 160

Clare. The sisterhood, the votarists of Saint Clare . *Meas. for Meas.* i 4 5

Clarence. Is not his brother, Thomas of Clarence, with him? 2 *Hen. IV.* iv 4 16
What would my lord and father?—Nothing but well to thee, Thomas of Clarence . . . . iv 4 19
Who saw the Duke of Clarence?—I am here, brother, full of heaviness iv 5 7
Warwick! Gloucester! Clarence!—Doth the king call? . . . iv 5 48
Lionel Duke of Clarence, Third son to the third Edward King of England . . . . 1 *Hen. VI.* ii 4 83; ii 5 75
Duke of Clarence, from whose line I claim the crown . 2 *Hen. VI.* ii 2 34
Philippe, Sole daughter unto Lionel Duke of Clarence . . . . ii 2 50
Edmund Mortimer, Earl of March, Married the Duke of Clarence' daughter . . . . iv 2 145
Jack Cade proclaims himself Lord Mortimer, Descended from the Duke of Clarence' house . . . . iv 4 29
I will create thee Duke of Gloucester, And George, of Clarence 3 *Hen. VI.* ii 6 104
Let me be Duke of Clarence, George of Gloucester . . . . ii 6 106
You'ld think it strange if I should marry her.—To whom, my lord?—Why, Clarence, to myself . . . . iii 2 112
Between my soul's desire and me . . . Is Clarence, Henry, and his son iii 2 130
As for Clarence, as my letters tell me, He's very likely now to fall from him . . . . iii 3 208
Now tell me, brother Clarence, what think you Of this new marriage? iv 1 1
Now, brother of Clarence, how like you our choice? . . . . iv 1 9
She better would have fitted me or Clarence . . . . . . iv 1 54
Alas, poor Clarence! is it for a wife That thou art malcontent? . iv 1 59
Prince Edward marries Warwick's daughter.—Belike the elder; Clarence will have the younger . . . . iv 1 118
Clarence and Somerset both gone to Warwick! . . . . . iv 1 127
But see where Somerset and Clarence comes! . . . . . . iv 2 3

Clarence. Gentle Clarence, welcome unto Warwick; And welcome, Somerset . . . *3 Hen. VI.* iv 2 6
Else might I think that Clarence, Edward's brother, Were but a feigned friend to our proceedings: But welcome, sweet Clarence; my daughter shall be thine . . . iv 2 10
Clarence, art thou here too? Nay, then I see that Edward needs must down . . . iv 3 41
Let me blame your grace, For choosing me when Clarence is in place . iv 6 31
And I choose Clarence only for protector . . . iv 6 37
Warwick and Clarence, give me both your hands: Now join your hands iv 6 38
What answers Clarence to his sovereign's will? . . . iv 6 45
And, Clarence, now then it is more than needful Forthwith that Edward be pronounced a traitor . . . iv 6 53
Ay, therein Clarence shall not want his part . . . iv 6 57
Ah, froward Clarence! how evil it beseems thee, To flatter Henry and forsake thy brother! . . . iv 7 84
Those will I muster up: and thou, son Clarence, Shalt stir up in Suffolk iv 8 11
Well-minded Clarence, be thou fortunate! . . . iv 8 27
By thy guess, how nigh is Clarence now? . . . v 1 8
Then Clarence is at hand; I hear his drum.—It is not his . . . v 1 11
And lo, where George of Clarence sweeps along, Of force enough to bid his brother battle . . . v 1 76
Come, Clarence, come; thou wilt, if Warwick call . . . v 1 80
Why, trow'st thou, Warwick, That Clarence is so harsh, so blunt, unnatural? . . . v 1 86
Welcome, good Clarence; this is brother-like.—O passing traitor! . v 1 105
What is Edward but a ruthless sea? What Clarence but a quicksand of deceit? . . . v 4 26
Clarence, excuse me to the king my brother . . . v 5 46
I'll pardon thee my death: What, wilt thou not? then, Clarence, do it thou . . . v 5 71
Good Clarence, do; sweet Clarence, do thou do it . . . v 5 73
Clarence, beware; thou keep'st me from the light . . . v 6 84
Clarence, thy turn is next, and then the rest, Counting myself but bad till I be best . . . v 6 90
Clarence and Gloucester, love my lovely queen; And kiss your princely nephew . . . v 7 26
Thanks, noble Clarence; worthy brother, thanks . . . v 7 30
To set my brother Clarence and the king In deadly hate the one against the other . . . *Richard III.* i 1 34
This day should Clarence closely be mew'd up, About a prophecy . i 1 38
Dive, thoughts, down to my soul: here Clarence comes . . . i 1 41
But what's the matter, Clarence? may I know? . . . i 1 51
'Tis not the king that sends you to the Tower; My Lady Grey his wife, Clarence, 'tis she . . . i 1 64
We are not safe, Clarence; we are not safe . . . i 1 70
Go, tread the path that thou shalt ne'er return, Simple, plain Clarence! i 1 118
I shall live, my lord, to give them thanks That were the cause of my imprisonment.—No doubt, no doubt; and so shall Clarence too . i 1 129
I'll in, to urge his hatred more to Clarence . . . i 1 147
If I fail not in my deep intent, Clarence hath not another day to live . i 1 150
Clarence still breathes; Edward still lives and reigns . . . i 1 161
I never did incense his majesty Against the Duke of Clarence . . i 3 86
Poor Clarence did forsake his father, Warwick; Yea, and forswore himself . . . i 3 135
Marry, as for Clarence, he is well repaid . . . i 3 313
Clarence, whom I, indeed, have laid in darkness, I do beweep to many simple gulls . . . i 3 327
Do not hear him plead; For Clarence is well-spoken, and perhaps May move your hearts to pity, if you mark him . . . i 3 348
What scourge for perjury Can this dark monarchy afford false Clarence? i 4 51
Clarence is come; false, fleeting, perjured Clarence, That stabb'd me in the field by Tewksbury . . . i 4 55
How came you hither?—I would speak with Clarence, and I came hither on my legs . . . i 4 86
I am, in this, commanded to deliver The noble Duke of Clarence to your hands . . . i 4 93
Who pronounced The bitter sentence of poor Clarence' death? . . i 4 191
I do beseech your majesty To take our brother Clarence to your grace . ii 1 76
Is Clarence dead? the order was reversed . . . ii 1 86
God grant that some, less noble and less loyal, Nearer in bloody thoughts, but not in blood, Deserve not worse than wretched Clarence did! . . . ii 1 93
Hastings, help me to my closet. Oh, poor Clarence! . . . ii 1 133
Mark'd you not How that the guilty kindred of the queen Look'd pale when they did hear of Clarence' death? . . . ii 1 136
Why do you wring your hands, and beat your breast, And cry 'O Clarence, my unhappy son!' . . . ii 2 4
And pluck'd two crutches from my feeble limbs, Edward and Clarence ii 2 59
Oh for our father, for our dear lord Clarence! . . . ii 2 72
Alas for both, both mine, Edward and Clarence! . . . ii 2 73
What stay had we but Clarence? and he's gone . . . ii 2 75
She for an Edward weeps, and so do I; I for a Clarence weep, so doth not she: These babes for Clarence weep, and so do I . . . ii 2 83
What should you fear?—Marry, my uncle Clarence' angry ghost . iii 1 144
To take some privy order, To draw the brats of Clarence out of sight . iii 5 107
Inquire me out some mean-born gentleman, Whom I will marry straight to Clarence' daughter . . . iv 2 55
The son of Clarence have I pent up close; His daughter meanly have I match'd in marriage . . . iv 3 36
Thou hadst a Clarence too, and Richard kill'd him . . . iv 4 46
Thy Clarence he is dead that kill'd my Edward . . . iv 4 67
Thou toad, thou toad, where is thy brother Clarence? . . . iv 4 145
Tell her thou madest away her uncle Clarence . . . iv 4 281
Poor Clarence, by thy guile betrayed to death! . . . v 3 133

Claret. I charge and command that, of the city's cost, the pissing-conduit run nothing but claret wine . . . *2 Hen. VI.* iv 6 4

Claribel. At the marriage of the king's fair daughter Claribel to the King of Tunis . . . *Tempest* ii 1 70
Who's the next heir of Naples?—Claribel . . . ii 1 245
How shall that Claribel Measure us back to Naples? . . . ii 1 258
In one voyage Did Claribel her husband find at Tunis . . . v 1 209

Clasp. Most reverend Nestor, I am glad to clasp thee . *Troi. and Cres.* iv 5 204
That in gold clasps locks in the golden story . . . *Rom. and Jul.* i 3 92
To the gross clasps of a lascivious Moor . . . *Othello* i 1 127
Though forfeiters you cast in prison, yet You clasp young Cupid's tables . . . *Cymbeline* iii 2 39
Then you love us, we you, and we'll clasp hands . . . *Pericles* ii 4 57

Clasped. Whom Fortune's tender arm With favour never clasp'd . . . *T. of Athens* iv 3 251

Clasping. By your untimely claspings with your child . . . *Pericles* i 1 128
Clasping to the mast, endured a sea That almost burst the deck . . iv 1 56

Clatter. By this great clatter, one of greatest note Seems bruited *Macbeth* v 7 21

Claudio. That's Claudio, Signior Claudio.—Claudio to prison? 'tis not so.—Nay, but I know 'tis so . . . *Meas. for Meas.* i 2 64
Here comes Signior Claudio, led by the provost to prison . . . i 2 118
Why, how now, Claudio! whence comes this restraint? . . . i 2 128
What's thy offence, Claudio?—What but to speak of would offend again i 2 139
A novice of this place and the fair sister To her unhappy brother Claudio i 4 20
See that Claudio Be executed by nine to-morrow morning . . . ii 1 33
It grieves me for the death of Claudio; But there's no remedy . . ii 1 294
But yet,—poor Claudio! There is no remedy. Come, sir . . . ii 1 299
Is it your will Claudio shall die to-morrow? . . . ii 2 7
My business is a word or two with Claudio . . . iii 1 48
O, I do fear thee, Claudio; and I quake, Lest thou a feverous life shouldst entertain . . . iii 1 74
Dost thou think, Claudio? If I would yield him my virginity, Thou mightst be freed . . . iii 1 97
Be ready, Claudio, for your death to-morrow . . . iii 1 107
Canst thou tell if Claudio die to-morrow or no? . . . iii 2 180
Marry, this Claudio is condemned for untrussing . . . iii 2 190
Claudio must die to-morrow: let him be furnished with divines . . iii 2 220
Let me desire to know how you find Claudio prepared . . . iii 2 254
To-morrow morning are to die Claudio and Barnardine . . . iv 2 8
Call hither Barnardine and Claudio: The one has my pity; not a jot the other . . . iv 2 63
Look, here's the warrant, Claudio, for thy death . . . iv 2 66
I hope it is some pardon or reprieve For the most gentle Claudio . . iv 2 75
What comfort is for Claudio?—There's some in hope . . . iv 2 80
Have you no countermand for Claudio yet? . . . iv 2 95
And here comes Claudio's pardon . . . iv 2 104
Let Claudio be executed by four of the clock . . . iv 2 124
Let me have Claudio's head sent me by five . . . iv 2 126
Claudio, whom here you have warrant to execute, is no greater forfeit to the law than Angelo . . . iv 2 166
I may make my case as Claudio's, to cross this in the smallest . . iv 2 178
A man of Claudio's years; his beard and head Just of his colour . . iv 3 76
Satisfy the deputy with the visage Of Ragozine, more like to Claudio . iv 3 80
How shall we continue Claudio, To save me from the danger that might come If he were known alive? . . . iv 3 88
Put them in secret holds, both Barnardine and Claudio . . . iv 3 91
Unhappy Claudio! wretched Isabel! Injurious world! . . . iv 3 126
What would you say?—I am the sister of one Claudio . . . v 1 69
I came to her from Claudio, and desired her To try her gracious fortune v 1 75
An Angelo for Claudio, death for death! . . . v 1 414
We do condemn thee to the very block Where Claudio stoop'd to death v 1 420
O Isabel, will you not lend a knee?—He dies for Claudio's death . . v 1 448
How came it Claudio was beheaded At an unusual hour? . . . v 1 462
I would thou hadst done so by Claudio . . . v 1 473
This is another prisoner that I saved, Who should have died when Claudio lost his head; As like almost to Claudio as himself . . v 1 493
She, Claudio, that you wrong'd, look you restore . . . v 1 531
Forgive him, Angelo, that brought you home The head of Ragozine for Claudio's . . . v 1 539
A young Florentine called Claudio . . . *Much Ado* i 1 11
He is most in the company of the right noble Claudio . . . i 1 85
God help the noble Claudio! if he have caught the Benedick . . . i 1 89
Signior Claudio and Signior Benedick, my dear friend Leonato hath invited you all . . . i 1 148
You hear, Count Claudio: I can be secret as a dumb man . . . i 1 211
She's his only heir. Dost thou affect her, Claudio? . . . i 1 298
Tell fair Hero I am Claudio, And in her bosom I'll unclasp my heart . i 1 324
The prince and Count Claudio, walking in a thick-pleached alley . . i 2 9
The prince discovered to Claudio that he loved my niece . . . i 2 12
The most exquisite Claudio?—Even he.—A proper squire! . . . i 3 52
Comes me the prince and Claudio, hand in hand . . . i 3 62
That the prince should woo Hero for himself, and having obtained her, give her to Count Claudio . . . i 3 66
And that is Claudio: I know him by his bearing . . . ii 1 165
But hear these ill news with the ears of Claudio . . . ii 1 180
Count Claudio?—Yea, the same.—Come, will you go with me?—Whither? ii 1 190
I have brought Count Claudio, whom you sent me to seek . . . ii 1 296
Claudio, I have wooed in thy name, and fair Hero is won . . . ii 1 309
County Claudio, when mean you to go to church? . . . ii 1 370
I warrant thee, Claudio, the time shall not go dully by us . . . ii 1 378
The Count Claudio shall marry the daughter of Leonato . . . ii 2 1
He hath wronged his honour in marrying the renowned Claudio . . ii 2 24
Proof enough to misuse the prince, to vex Claudio, to undo Hero . . ii 2 29
Find me a meet hour to draw Don Pedro and the Count Claudio alone . ii 2 34
Intend a kind of zeal both to the prince and Claudio . . . ii 2 36
Hear me call Margaret Hero, hear Margaret term me Claudio . . ii 2 45
And such a man is Claudio . . . ii 3 13
There shalt thou find my cousin Beatrice Proposing with the prince and Claudio . . . iii 1 3
He is the only man of Italy, Always excepted my dear Claudio . . iii 1 93
Count Claudio may hear; for what I would speak of concerns him . iii 2 87
Claudio and my master, planted and placed and possessed by my master iii 3 158
Thought they Margaret was Hero?—Two of them did, the prince and Claudio . . . iii 3 165
Away went Claudio enraged; swore he would meet her . . . iii 3 170
Would the two princes lie, and Claudio lie? . . . iv 1 154
So will it fare with Claudio . . . iv 1 224
You know my inwardness and love Is very much unto the prince and Claudio . . . iv 1 248
Come, bid me do any thing for thee.—Kill Claudio . . . iv 1 291
Is Claudio thine enemy?—Is he not approved in the height a villain? . iv 1 302
Think you in your soul the Count Claudio hath wronged Hero? . . iv 1 331
By this hand, Claudio shall render me a dear account . . . iv 1 337
My soul doth tell me Hero is belied; And that shall Claudio know . v 1 43
Here comes the prince and Claudio hastily . . . v 1 45
Know, Claudio, to thy head . . . v 1 62
My villany?—Thine, Claudio; thine, I say . . . v 1 72
I do embrace your offer; and dispose For henceforth of poor Claudio . v 1 304
With knowing what hath passed between you and Claudio.—Only foul words . . . v 2 49
But I must tell thee plainly, Claudio undergoes my challenge . . v 2 57
Hero hath been falsely accused, the prince and Claudio mightily abused v 2 100
Did I not tell you she was innocent?—So are the prince and Claudio . v 4 2
So am I, being else by faith enforced To call young Claudio to a reckoning . . . v 4 9

Claudio. The prince and Claudio promised by this hour To visit me . *Much Ado* v 4 13
You must be father to your brother's daughter, And give her to young Claudio . . . v 4 16
Why, then your uncle and the prince and Claudio Have been deceived . . v 4 75
For thy part, Claudio, I did think to have beaten thee . . . . v 4 110
They were given me by Claudio . . . . . *Hamlet* iv 7 40
Claudius. Call Claudius and some other of my men . . . *J. Cæsar* iv 3 242
Varro and Claudius!—Calls my lord? . . . . . iv 3 244
Boy, Lucius! Varro! Claudius! Sirs, awake! Claudius! . . . iv 3 290
Sleep again, Lucius. Sirrah Claudius! Fellow thou, awake! . . . iv 3 300
Clause. Do not extort thy reasons from this clause . . . *T. Night* iii 1 165
Claw. Laugh when I am merry and claw no man in his humour *Much Ado* i 3 18
If a talent be a claw, look how he claws him with a talent *L. L. Lost* iv 2 65
Let not him that plays the lion pare his nails, for they shall hang out for the lion's claws . . . . *M. N. Dream* iv 2 42
I thought thy heart had been wounded with the claws of a lion *As Y. Like It* v 2 26
Clawed. Look, whether the withered elder hath not his poll clawed like a parrot . . . . *2 Hen. IV.* ii 4 282
Age, with his stealing steps, Hath claw'd me in his clutch . *Hamlet* v 1 80
Clay. That sweet breath Which was embounded in this beauteous clay *K. John* iv 3 137
What hope, what stay, When this was now a king, and now is clay? . v 7 69
Men are but gilded loam or painted clay . . . *Richard II.* i 1 179
The brain of this foolish-compounded clay, man, is not able to invent any thing that tends to laughter . . *2 Hen. IV.* i 2 8
The dead with charity enclosed in clay . . . . *Hen. V.* iv 8 129
Yet are these feet, whose strengthless stay is numb, Unable to support this lump of clay . . . . . . *1 Hen. VI.* ii 5 14
The uncivil kerns of Ireland are in arms And temper clay with blood of Englishmen . . . . *2 Hen. VI.* iii 1 311
O, a pit of clay for to be made For such a guest is meet . *Hamlet* v 1 104
Imperious Cæsar, dead and turn'd to clay, Might stop a hole to keep the wind away . . . . v 1 236
Beweep this cause again, I'll pluck ye out, And cast you, with the waters that you lose, To temper clay . . . . *Lear* i 4 326
Kingdoms are clay: our dungy earth alike Feeds beast as man *Ant. and Cleo.* i 1 35
But clay and clay differs in dignity, Whose dust is both alike *Cymb.* iv 2 4
Clay-brained. Thou clay-brained guts, thou knotty-pated fool *1 Hen. IV.* ii 4 251
Clean. She can milk; look you, a sweet virtue in a maid with clean hands *T. G. of Ver.* iii 1 278
Roaming clean through the bounds of Asia . *Com. of Errors* i 1 134
Swart, like my shoe, but her face nothing like so clean kept . . iii 2 105
The wide sea Hath drops too few to wash her clean again! . *Much Ado* iv 1 143
In any case, let Thisby have clean linen . . *M. N. Dream* iv 2 40
As clean as a sound sheep's heart . . . . *As Y. Like It* iii 2 442
I will never trust a man again for keeping his sword clean . *All's Well* iv 3 166
By you unhappied and disfigured clean . . . . *Richard II.* iii 1 10
Though not clean past your youth . . . . . *2 Hen. IV.* i 2 110
Will he wipe his tables clean And keep no tell-tale to his memory . . iv 1 201
I am the besom that must sweep the court clean of such filth as thou art *2 Hen. VI.* iv 7 34
And domestic broils Clean over-blown . . . *Richard III.* ii 4 61
Renouncing clean The faith they have in tennis, and tall stockings *Hen. VIII.* i 3 29
Bid them wash their faces And keep their teeth clean . . *Coriolanus* ii 3 67
This is clean kam.—Merely awry . . . . iii 1 304
Let's hew his limbs till they be clean consumed . . *T. Andron.* i 1 129
Would thou wert clean enough to spit upon! . . *T. of Athens* iv 3 364
Men may construe things after their fashion, Clean from the purpose of the things themselves . . . . . . *J. Cæsar* i 3 35
Will all great Neptune's ocean wash this blood Clean from my hand? *Macbeth* ii 2 61
What, will these hands ne'er be clean?—No more o' that, my lord . v 1 49
It is clean out of the way . . . . *Othello* i 3 366
Yet famine, Ere clean it o'erthrow nature, makes it valiant *Cymbeline* iii 6 20
Cleanliest. The cleanliest shift is to kiss . . *As Y. Like It* iv 1 77
Cleanly. We must be neat; not neat, but cleanly . . *W. Tale* i 2 123
Wherein neat and cleanly, but to carve a capon and eat it? . *1 Hen. IV.* ii 4 502
And live cleanly as a nobleman should do . . . . . v 4 169
Hast not thou full often struck a doe, And borne her cleanly by the keeper's nose? . . . . *T. Andron.* ii 1 94
Cleanse. I will through and through Cleanse the foul body of the infected world . . . . *As Y. Like It* ii 7 60
With some sweet oblivious antidote Cleanse the stuff'd bosom of that perilous stuff Which weighs upon the heart . . . *Macbeth* v 3 44
Cleansed. Wherein, priest-like, thou Hast cleansed my bosom *W. Tale* i 2 238
Cleansing. Unto mine eyes, the outward watch, Whereto my finger, like a dial's point, Is pointing still, in cleansing them from tears *Richard II.* v 5 54
Clean-timbered. I think Hector was not so clean-timbered . *L. L. Lost* v 2 642
Clear. If you know yourself clear, why, I am glad of it . *Mer. Wives* iii 3 123
He in time may come to clear himself . . . *Meas. for Meas.* v 1 150
And what he with his oath And all probation will make up full clear . v 1 157
Gaze where you should, and that will clear your sight . *Com. of Errors* iii 2 57
And now they never meet in grove or green, By fountain clear *M. N. Dr.* ii 1 29
As clear As yonder Venus in her glimmering sphere . . . iii 2 60
How to get clear of all the debts I owe . . . *Mer. of Venice* i 1 134
This wrestler shall clear all . . . . . . *As Y. Like It* i 1 178
She looks as clear As morning roses newly wash'd with dew *T. of Shrew* ii 1 173
My remembrance is very free and clear from any image of offence *T. Night* iii 4 249
Thou art a foolish fellow: Let me be clear of thee . . . . iv 1 4
With a countenance as clear As friendship wears at feasts . *W. Tale* i 2 343
By twos and threes at several posterns Clear them o' the city . . i 2 439
These lords, my noble fellows, if they please, Can clear me in't . . ii 3 143
The violent carriage of it Will clear or end the business . . . iii 1 18
But my letters, by this means being there So soon as you arrive, shall clear that doubt . . . . iv 4 633
So foul a sky clears not without a storm . . . *K. John* iv 2 108
As clear as is the summer's sun . . . . . *Hen. V.* i 2 86
Go, clear thy crystals. Yoke-fellows in arms, Let us to France . . ii 3 56
So clear, so shining and so evident That it will glimmer through a blind man's eye . . . . *1 Hen. VI.* ii 4 23
Thy father's charge shall clear thee from that stain . . . iv 5 42
The purest spring is not so free from mud As I am clear from treason *2 Hen. VI.* iii 1 102
'Tis my special hope That you will clear yourself from all suspect . . iii 1 140
Ring, bells, aloud; burn, bonfires, clear and bright . . . v 1 3
Clear. I am clear from this misdeed of Edward's . . *3 Hen. VI.* iii 3 183
Proofs as clear as founts in July when We see each grain of gravel *Hen. VIII.* i 1 154
I speak my good lord cardinal to this point, And thus far clear him . ii 4 167
This candle burns not clear: 'tis I must snuff it . . . iii 2 96
I shall clear myself, Lay all the weight ye can upon my patience . v 3 65
So, 'tis clear They'll say 'tis naught . . . . Epil. 4
Would the fountain of your mind were clear again! . *Troi. and Cres.* iii 3 314
Understand more clear, What's past and what's to come is strew'd with husks . . . . iv 5 165
The sun not yet thy sighs from heaven clears . . . *Rom. and Jul.* ii 3 73
Till we can clear these ambiguities, And know their spring, their head . v 3 217
I cannot think but, in the end, the villanies of man will set him clear *T. of Athens* iii 3 31
You cannot make gross sins look clear . . . . . . iii 5 38
Only look up clear; To alter favour ever is to fear . . *Macbeth* i 5 72
Hath borne his faculties so meek, hath been So clear in his great office . i 7 18
But still keep My bosom franchised and allegiance clear . . . ii 1 28
A little water clears us of this deed: How easy is it, then! . . ii 2 67
Were I from Dunsinane away and clear, Profit again should hardly draw me here . . . . v 3 61
On the instant they got clear of our ship . . . . *Hamlet* iv 6 19
On such ground, and to such wholesome end, As clears her from all blame *Lear* ii 4 147
I cannot project mine own cause so well To make it clear *Ant. and Cleo* v 2 122
And the sore eyes see clear To stop the air would hurt them *Pericles* i 1 99
Lest my life be cropp'd to keep you clear, By flight I'll shun the danger which I fear . . . . i 1 141
Clear as day. Thou see'st not well.—Yes, master, clear as day *2 Hen. VI.* ii 1 107
Clear dawn. Come away; it is almost clear dawn . *Meas. for Meas.* iv 2 226
Clear excuse. I would I could Quit all offences with as clear excuse *1 Hen. IV.* iii 2 19
Clear eye. Mine own self's better part, Mine eye's clear eye *C. of Err.* iii 2 62
Clear heavens. I am no idle votarist: roots, you clear heavens! *T. of Athens* iv 3 27
Clear honour. That clear honour Were purchased by the merit of the wearer! . . . . *Mer. of Venice* ii 9 42
Clear judgements. In our own filth drop our clear judgements *Ant. and Cleo.* iii 13 113
Clear life. Nothing but heart-sorrow And a clear life ensuing *Tempest* iii 3 82
Clear lights. Tell me, in the modesty of honour, Why you have given me such clear lights of favour . . . . . *T. Night* v 1 344
Clear rays. With those clear rays which she infused on me . *1 Hen. VI.* i 2 85
Clear remembrance. By her own most clear remembrance . *Pericles* v 3 12
Clear-shining. In a pale clear-shining sky . . . *3 Hen. VI.* ii 1 28
Clear sky. And I in the clear sky of fame o'ershine you *2 Hen. IV.* iv 3 56
Clear spirit. Hath puddled his clear spirit . . . *Othello* iii 4 143
Clear sun. Whose figure even this instant cloud puts on, By darkening my clear sun . . . . *Hen. VIII.* i 1 226
Clear up, fair queen, that cloudy countenance . . . *T. Andron.* i 1 263
Clear voice. Crack my clear voice with sobs . . *Troi. and Cres.* iv 2 114
Clear way. Methinks he should the sooner pay his debts, And make a clear way to the gods . . . . . . *T. of Athens* iii 4 77
Persever in that clear way thou goest, And the gods strengthen thee! *Pericles* iv 6 113
Cleared. All debts are cleared between you and I, if I might but see you at my death . . . . *Mer. of Venice* iii 2 321
The imposition clear'd Hereditary ours . . . . *W. Tale* i 2 74
Let us be clear'd Of being tyrannous . . . . . iii 2 4
See the coast clear'd, and then we will depart . . . *1 Hen. VI.* i 3 89
When he was poor, Imprison'd and in scarcity of friends, I clear'd him with five talents . . . . *T. of Athens* ii 2 235
All other doubts, by time let them be clear'd . . *Cymbeline* iv 3 45
The sea works high, the wind is loud, and will not lie till the ship be cleared of the dead . . . . *Pericles* iii 1 49
Clearer. Their rising senses Begin to chase the ignorant fumes that mantle Their clearer reason . . . . *Tempest* v 1 68
How will this grieve you, When you shall come to clearer knowledge! *W. Tale* ii 1 97
Your mind is the clearer, Ajax, and your virtues the fairer *Tr. and Cr.* ii 3 163
Clearest. Think that the clearest gods, who make them honours Of men's impossibilities, have preserved thee . . . . *Lear* iv 6 73
Clearly. If she, my liege, can make me know this clearly . *All's Well* v 3 316
A most extracting frenzy of mine own From my remembrance clearly banish'd his . . . . *T. Night* v 1 289
'Tis strange to think how much King John hath lost In this which he accounts so clearly won . . . . . . *K. John* iii 4 122
Wound our tattering colours clearly up, Last in the field, and almost lords of it! . . . . v 5 7
You do not understand yourself so clearly As it behoves my daughter and your honour . . . . *Hamlet* i 3 96
Clearness. Then we wound our modesty and make foul the clearness of our deservings, when of ourselves we publish them . *All's Well* i 3 6
And in the fountain shall we gaze so long Till the fresh taste be taken from that clearness . . . . *T. Andron.* iii 1 128
Always thought That I require a clearness . . . *Macbeth* iii 1 133
Cleave. Thy thoughts I cleave to. What's thy pleasure? . *Tempest* iv 1 165
Such remedy as, to save a head, To cleave a heart in twain *Meas. for Meas.* iii 1 63
My tongue cleave to my roof within my mouth . . *Richard II.* v 3 31
There's no remedy; Unless, by not so doing, our good city Cleave in the midst, and perish . . . . *Coriolanus* iii 2 28
I'll call my brother back again, And cleave to no revenge but Lucius *T. Andron.* v 2 136
All our bills.—Knock me down with 'em: cleave me to the girdle *T. of A.* iii 4 91
New honours come upon him, Like our strange garments, cleave not to their mould But with the aid of use . . . . . *Macbeth* i 3 145
If you shall cleave to my consent, when 'tis, It shall make honour for you . . . . ii 1 25
And cleave the general ear with horrid speech . . . *Hamlet* ii 2 589
Wars 'twixt you twain would be As if the world should cleave, and that slain men Should solder up the rift . . . *Ant. and Cleo.* iii 4 31
O, cleave, my sides! Heart, once be stronger than thy continent, Crack thy frail case! . . . . iv 14 39
Cleaving. Then will she get the upshot by cleaving the pin *L. L. Lost* iv 1 138
This thy son's blood cleaving to my blade Shall rust upon my weapon *3 Hen. VI.* i 3 50
Clef. 'D sol re,' one clef, two notes have I . . . *T. of Shrew* iii 1 77
Cleft. How oft hast thou with perjury cleft the root! . *T. G. of Ver.* v 4 103
She would have made Hercules have turned spit, yea, and have cleft his club to make the fire too . . . . *Much Ado* ii 1 261

Cleft. An apple, cleft in two, is not more twin Than these two creatures *T. Night* v 1 230
Whose honourable thoughts, Thoughts high for one so tender, cleft the heart *W. Tale* iii 2 197
But for a sallet, my brain-pan had been cleft with a brown bill 2 *Hen. VI.* iv 10 13
I cleft his beaver with a downright blow . . . . . . 3 *Hen. VI.* i 1 12
The very pin of his heart cleft with the blind bow-boy's butt-shaft *Rom. and Jul.* ii 4 16
O Hamlet, thou hast cleft my heart in twain . . . . *Hamlet* iii 4 156

Cleitus. Alexander . . . did, in his ales and his angers, look you, kill his best friend, Cleitus *Hen. V.* iv 7 41
Alexander killed his friend Cleitus, being in his ales and his cups . iv 7 48

Clemency. Here stooping to your clemency, We beg your hearing patiently *Hamlet* iii 2 160

Clement. I know you are more clement than vile men . *Cymbeline* v 4 18

Clement's Inn. I was once of Clement's Inn, where I think they will talk of mad Shallow yet . . . . 2 *Hen. IV.* iii 2 15
Before I came to Clement's Inn.—That's fifty five year ago . . iii 2 223
I remember at Mile-end Green, when I lay at Clement's Inn . . . iii 2 299
I do remember him at Clement's Inn . . . . . . iii 2 331

Cleomenes and Dion, whom you know Of stuff'd sufficiency . *W. Tale* ii 1 184
Cleomenes and Dion, Being well arrived from Delphos, are both landed ii 3 195
You, Cleomenes and Dion, have Been both at Delphos . . . . iii 2 126
Go, Cleomenes; Yourself, assisted with your honour'd friends, Bring them . . . . v 1 112

Cleon. Make for Tarsus! There will I visit Cleon . . . *Pericles* iii 1 79
Most honour'd Cleon, I must needs be gone . . . . . iii 3 1
And by Cleon train'd In music, letters . . . . . iv Gower 7
And in this kind hath our Cleon One daughter . . . . iv Gower 15
Cleon's wife, with envy rare, A present murderer does prepare . iv Gower 37
My father did in Tarsus leave me; Till cruel Cleon, with his wicked wife, Did seek to murder me . . . . v 1 173
She is not dead at Tarsus, as she should have been, By savage Cleon . v 1 218
My purpose was for Tarsus, there to strike The inhospitable Cleon . v 1 254
She at Tarsus Was nursed with Cleon . . . . . . v 3 8

Cleopatra's majesty, Atalanta's better part . . *As Y. Like It* iii 2 154
Cleopatra a gipsy; Helen and Hero hildings and harlots *Rom. and Jul.* ii 4 44
Antony Will be himself.—But stirr'd by Cleopatra . *Ant. and Cleo.* i 1 43
Bring in the banquet quickly; wine enough Cleopatra's health to drink i 2 12
Name Cleopatra as she is call'd in Rome; Rail thou in Fulvia's phrase i 2 110
Cleopatra, catching but the least noise of this, dies instantly i 2 144
The business you have broached here cannot be without you; especially that of Cleopatra's . . . . i 2 182
Cleopatra,— Why should I think you can be mine and true? . i 3 26
'Tis sweating labour To bear such idleness so near the heart As Cleopatra this . . . . i 3 95
Is not more manlike Than Cleopatra; nor the queen of Ptolemy More womanly than he . . . . i 4 6
But all the charms of love, Salt Cleopatra, soften thy waned lip! . . ii 1 21
If Cleopatra heard you, your reproof Were well deserved of rashness . ii 2 123
The air; which, but for vacancy, Had gone to gaze on Cleopatra . ii 2 222
We looked not for Mark Antony here: pray you, is he married to Cleopatra? . . . . ii 6 115
On a tribunal silver'd, Cleopatra and himself in chairs of gold . . iii 6 4
No, my most wronged sister; Cleopatra Hath nodded him to her . . iii 6 65
Cleopatra does confess thy greatness; Submits her to thy might . iii 12 16
To try thy eloquence, now 'tis time: dispatch; From Antony win Cleopatra . . . . iii 12 27
So saucy with the hand of she here,—what's her name, Since she was Cleopatra? . . . . iii 13 99
Since my lord Is Antony again, I will be Cleopatra . . . . iii 13 187
Swallows have built In Cleopatra's sails their nests . . . iv 12 4
I will o'ertake thee, Cleopatra, and Weep for my pardon . . . iv 14 44
Since Cleopatra died, I have lived in such dishonour, that the gods Detest my baseness . . . . iv 14 55
Most absolute lord, My mistress Cleopatra sent me to thee . . . iv 14 118
Bear me, good friends, where Cleopatra bides; 'Tis the last service that I shall command you . . . . iv 14 131
O Cleopatra! thou art taken, queen . . . . v 2 38
Cleopatra, Do not abuse my master's bounty . . . . . v 2 42
Cleopatra!—Think you there was, or might be, such a man As this? . v 2 92
Cleopatra, know, We will extenuate rather than enforce . . . v 2 124
You shall advise me in all for Cleopatra . . . . . . v 2 137
Nay, blush not, Cleopatra; I approve Your wisdom in the deed . v 2 149
Cleopatra, Not what you have reserved, nor what acknowledged, Put we i' the roll of conquest . . . . v 2 179
And I shall see Some squeaking Cleopatra boy my greatness I' the posture of a whore . . . . v 2 220
The story Proud Cleopatra, when she met her Roman, And Cydnus swell'd above the banks . . . . *Cymbeline* ii 4 70

Clepe. They clepe us drunkards, and with swinish phrase Soil our addition *Hamlet* i 4 19

Clepeth. He clepeth a calf, cauf; half, hauf . . . . . *L. L. Lost* v 1 24

Clept. Spaniels, curs, Shoughs, water-rugs and demi-wolves are clept All by the name of dogs . . . . *Macbeth* iii 1 94

Clergy. To give a greater sum Than ever at one time the clergy yet Did to his predecessors part withal . . . . *Hen. V.* i 1 80
Such a mighty sum As never did the clergy at one time Bring in . . i 2 134
The clergy's bags Are lank and lean with thy extortions . 2 *Hen. VI.* i 3 131
Of his own body he was ill, and gave The clergy ill example *Hen. VIII.* iv 2 44

Clergyman. A clergyman Of holy reverence . . . *Richard II.* iii 3 28

Clergymen. How I have sped among the clergymen, The sums I have collected shall express . . . . *K. John* iv 2 141
You holy clergymen, is there no plot To rid the realm of this pernicious blot? . . . . *Richard II.* iv 1 324
See, where he stands between two clergymen!—Two props of virtue for a Christian prince . . . . *Richard III.* iii 7 95

Clerk. Answer, clerk.—No more words: the clerk is answered *Much Ado* ii 1 114
Great clerks have purposed To greet me with premeditated welcomes *M. N. Dream* v 1 93
I am content.—Clerk, draw a deed of gift . . . *Mer. of Venice* iv 1 394
In faith, I gave it to the judge's clerk . . . . v 1 143
Gave it a judge's clerk! no, God's my judge, The clerk will ne'er wear hair on's face that had it . . . . v 1 157
A little scrubbed boy, No higher than thyself, the judge's clerk . . v 1 163
The boy, his clerk, That took some pains in writing, he begg'd mine . v 1 181
I'll mar the young clerk's pen . . . . v 1 237
You shall find that Portia was the doctor, Nerissa there her clerk . v 1 270
Were you the clerk that is to make me cuckold?—Ay, but the clerk that never means to do it, Unless he live until he be a man . . v 1 281
My clerk hath some good comforts too for you . *Mer. of Venice* v 1 289
I should wish it dark, That I were couching with the doctor's clerk . v 1 305
Take the priest, clerk, and some sufficient honest witnesses *T. of Shrew* iv 4 94
Will no man say amen? Am I both priest and clerk? . *Richard II.* iv 1 173
If they meet not with Saint Nicholas' clerks, I'll give thee this neck 1 *Hen. IV.* ii 1 68
The clerk of Chatham:—he can write and read and cast accompt 2 *Hen. VI.* iv 2 92
Large gifts have I bestow'd on learned clerks . . . . . iv 7 76
All the clerks, I mean the learned ones, in Christian kingdoms Have their free voices . . . . *Hen. VIII.* ii 2 92
Deep clerks she dumbs . . . . *Pericles* v Gower 5

Clerk-like. Thereto Clerk-like experienced . . . . *W. Tale* i 2 392

Clerkly. I thank you, gentle servant: 'tis very clerkly done *T. G. of Ver.* ii 1 114
Thou art clerkly, thou art clerkly . . . . . *Mer. Wives* iv 5 58
With ignominious words, though clerkly couch'd . . 2 *Hen. VI.* iii 1 179

Clew. You have wound a goodly clew . . . . *All's Well* i 3 188

Client. Fear not you: good counsellors lack no clients *Meas. for Meas.* i 2 110
Windy attorneys to their client woes, Airy succeeders of intestate joys *Richard III.* iv 4 127
When she should do for clients her fitment . . . *Pericles* iv 6 6

Cliff. Where England?—I looked for the chalky cliffs, but I could find no whiteness in them . . . . *Com. of Errors* iii 2 129
As far as I could ken thy chalky cliffs . . . 2 *Hen. VI.* iii 2 101
Any man may sing her, if he can take her cliff . *Troi. and Cres.* v 2 11
The dreadful summit of the cliff That beetles o'er his base into the sea *Hamlet* i 4 70
There is a cliff, whose high and bending head Looks fearfully in the confined deep . . . . *Lear* iv 1 76
Upon the crown o' the cliff, what thing was that Which parted from you? . . . . iv 6 67

Clifford. What, Buckingham and Clifford, are ye so brave? 2 *Hen. VI.* iv 8 20
A Clifford! a Clifford! we'll follow the king and Clifford . . . iv 8 55
Call hither Clifford; bid him come amain . . . . . v 1 114
And here comes Clifford to deny their bail . . . . . v 1 123
I thank thee, Clifford; say, what news with thee? . . . . v 1 125
We are thy sovereign, Clifford, kneel again . . . . . v 1 127
Clifford, I say, come forth and fight with me: Proud northern lord, Clifford of Cumberland, Warwick is hoarse with calling thee to arms v 2 5
The deadly-handed Clifford slew my steed . . . . . v 2 9
As I intend, Clifford, to thrive to-day, It grieves my soul to leave thee unassail'd . . . . v 2 17
Come, thou new ruin of old Clifford's house . . . . . v 2 61
Himself, Lord Clifford and Lord Stafford, all abreast, Charged our main battle's front . . . . 3 *Hen. VI.* i 1 7
He slew thy father, And thine, Lord Clifford; and you both have vow'd revenge . . . . i 1 55
The hope thereof makes Clifford mourn in steel . . . . i 1 58
Poor Clifford! how I scorn his worthless threats! . . . . i 1 101
Be thy title right or wrong, Lord Clifford vows to fight in thy defence i 1 160
O Clifford, how thy words revive my heart! . . . . . i 1 163
Look where bloody Clifford comes! . . . . i 3 2
Ah, Clifford, murder not this innocent child, Lest thou be hated both of God and man! . . . . i 3 8
Ah, gentle Clifford, kill me with thy sword, And not with such a cruel threatening look. Sweet Clifford, hear me speak before I die . i 3 16
He is a man, and, Clifford, cope with him . . . . . . i 3 24
Sweet Clifford, pity me!—Such pity as my rapier's point affords . . i 3 36
Come, bloody Clifford, rough Northumberland, I dare your quenchless fury . . . . i 4 27
O Clifford, but bethink thee once again, And in thy thought o'er-run my former time! . . . . i 4 44
Hold, valiant Clifford! for a thousand causes I would prolong awhile the traitor's life . . . . i 4 51
Hold, Clifford! do not honour him so much To prick thy finger, though to wound his heart . . . . i 4 54
Brave warriors, Clifford and Northumberland, Come, make him stand upon this molehill here . . . . i 4 66
I stain'd this napkin with the blood That valiant Clifford, with his rapier's point, Made issue from the bosom of the boy . . . i 4 80
And every drop cries vengeance for his death, 'Gainst thee, fell Clifford i 4 149
Hard-hearted Clifford, take me from the world . . . . i 4 167
Or whether he be 'scaped away or no From Clifford's and Northumberland's pursuit . . . . ii 1 3
I saw him in the battle range about; And watch'd him how he singled Clifford forth . . . . ii 1 12
Slaughter'd by the ireful arm Of unrelenting Clifford . . . ii 1 58
Sweet young Rutland, by rough Clifford slain . . . . . ii 1 63
O Clifford, boisterous Clifford! thou hast slain The flower of Europe for his chivalry . . . . ii 1 70
Is by the stern Lord Clifford done to death . . . . . ii 1 103
Or more than common fear of Clifford's rigour . . . . ii 1 126
The proud insulting queen, With Clifford and the haught Northumberland ii 1 169
Then, Clifford, were thy heart as hard as steel, As thou hast shown it flinty by thy deeds, I come to pierce it . . . . . . ii 1 201
Full well hath Clifford play'd the orator . . . . . ii 2 43
But, Clifford, tell me, didst thou never hear That things ill-got had ever bad success? . . . . ii 2 45
Yet you fled.—'Twas not your valour, Clifford, drove me thence . ii 2 107
Clifford, that cruel child-killer . . . . ii 2 112
I am resolved That Clifford's manhood lies upon his tongue . . ii 2 125
Thy brother's blood the thirsty earth hath drunk, Broach'd with the steely point of Clifford's lance . . . . ii 3 16
Now, Clifford, I have singled thee alone . . . . . . ii 4 1
For Margaret my queen, and Clifford too, Have chid me from the battle ii 5 16
But think you, lords, that Clifford fled with them? . . . . ii 6 37
Let him be gently used.—Revoke that doom of mercy, for 'tis Clifford ii 6 46
From off the gates of York fetch down the head, Your father's head, which Clifford placed there . . . . ii 6 53
Speak, Clifford, dost thou know who speaks to thee? . . . . ii 6 61
Clifford, ask mercy and obtain no grace.—Clifford, repent in bootless penitence.—Clifford, devise excuses for thy faults . . . ii 6 69
They mock thee, Clifford: swear as thou wast wont.—What, not an oath? nay, then the world goes hard When Clifford cannot spare his friends an oath . . . . ii 6 76
Two Cliffords, as the father and the son . . . . . . v 7 7
To hear the piteous moan that Rutland made When black-faced Clifford shook his sword at him . . . . . . *Richard III.* i 2 159

Clifton. Sir Nicholas Gawsey hath for succour sent, And so hath Clifton: I'll to Clifton straight . . . . 1 *Hen. IV.* v 4 46
Make up to Clifton: I'll to Sir Nicholas Gawsey . . . . . v 4 58

Climate. What a strange drowsiness possesses them!—It is the quality o' the climate . . . . . *Tempest* ii 1 200
Leave it . . . to it own protection And favour of the climate . *W. Tale* ii 3 179
The climate's delicate, the air most sweet . . . . iii 1 1
The blessed gods Purge all infection from our air whilst you Do climate here! . . . . v 1 170
By this hand I swear, That sways the earth this climate overlooks *K. John* ii 1 344
That in a Christian climate souls refined Should show so heinous, black, obscene a deed! . . . . . . *Richard II.* iv 1 130
Is not their climate foggy, raw and dull? . . . *Hen. V.* iii 5 16
They are portentous things Unto the climate that they point upon *J. Cæsar* i 3 32
Though he in a fertile climate dwell, Plague him with flies . *Othello* i 1 70
Climature. Have heaven and earth together demonstrated Unto our climatures and countrymen . . . . . *Hamlet* i 1 125
Climb. How I must climb her window . . . . *T. G. of Ver.* ii 4 181
He meaneth with a corded ladder To climb celestial Silvia's chamber-window . . . . ii 6 34
One cannot climb it Without apparent hazard of his life . . . iii 1 115
Climb o'er the house to unlock the little gate . . *L. L. Lost* i 1 109
Be it as the style shall give us cause to climb in the merriness . i 1 202
In these degrees have they made a pair of stairs to marriage which they will climb incontinent . . . . . *As Y. Like It* v 2 42
What, and wouldst climb a tree? . . . . *2 Hen. VI.* ii 1 98
My wife desired some damsons, And made me climb, with danger of my life . . . . ii 1 103
Fearless minds climb soonest unto crowns . . . *3 Hen. VI.* iv 7 62
To climb steep hills Requires slow pace at first . . *Hen. VIII.* i 1 131
This neglection of degree it is That by a pace goes backward, with a purpose It hath to climb . . . . *Troi. and Cres.* i 3 129
I will not re-salute the streets of Rome, Or climb my palace *T. Andron.* i 1 327
I have dogs, my lord, Will rouse the proudest panther in the chase, And climb the highest promontory top . . . . . ii 2 22
Nor I no strength to climb without thy help . . . . ii 3 242
The orchard walls are high and hard to climb . . *Rom. and Jul.* ii 2 63
To fetch a ladder, by the which your love Must climb a bird's nest soon ii 5 76
Bowing his head against the steepy mount To climb his happiness *T. of Athens* i 1 76
Things at the worst will cease, or else climb upward To what they were before . . . . *Macbeth* iv 2 24
When shall we come to the top of that same hill?—You do climb up it now . . . . *Lear* iv 6 2
Let the labouring bark climb hills of seas Olympus-high! . *Othello* ii 1 189
The art o' the court, As hard to leave as keep; whose top to climb Is certain falling . . . . *Cymbeline* iii 3 47
Let our crooked smokes climb to their nostrils From our blest altars . v 5 477
Climbed. I climbed into this garden, to see if I can eat grass *2 Hen. VI.* iv 10 8
Make war with him that climb'd unto their nest . . . *3 Hen. VI.* ii 2 31
Many a time and oft Have you climb'd up to walls and battlements *J. Cæsar* i 1 43
Climber-upward. Lowliness is young ambition's ladder, Whereto the climber-upward turns his face . . . . ii 1 23
Climbeth. Now climbeth Tamora Olympus' top . . *T. Andron.* ii 1 1
Climbing. Is not Love a Hercules, Still climbing trees in the Hesperides? *L. L. Lost* iv 3 341
Behold Upon the hempen tackle ship-boys climbing . *Hen. V.* iii Prol. 8
Lean famine, quartering steel, and climbing fire . *1 Hen. VI.* iv 2 11
Yea, man and birds are fain of climbing high . . *2 Hen. VI.* ii 1 8
And bought his climbing very dear . . . . . . ii 1 100
Like a thief, to come to rob my grounds, Climbing my walls in spite of me . . . . iv 10 37
Down, thou climbing sorrow, Thy element's below! . . *Lear* ii 4 57
Clime. The best-regarded virgins of our clime Have loved it too *Mer. of Venice* ii 1 10
And thou art flying to a fresher clime . . . . *Richard II.* i 3 285
Towards the north, Where shivering cold and sickness pines the clime. v 1 77
Leaving their earthly parts to choke your clime . *Hen. V.* iv 3 102
And twice by awkward wind from England's bank Drove back again unto my native clime . . . . . . *2 Hen. VI.* iii 2 84
As loathsome as a toad Amongst the fairest breeders of our clime *T. Andron.* iv 2 68
Not to affect many proposed matches Of her own clime . *Othello* iii 3 230
We commit no crime To use one language in each several clime *Pericles* iv 4 6
Cling. Doubtful it stood; As two spent swimmers, that do cling together And choke their art . . . . . . *Macbeth* i 2 8
Upon the next tree shalt thou hang alive, Till famine cling thee . v 5 40
Clink. Some wine, ho! And let me the canakin clink, clink . *Othello* ii 3 71
I heard the clink and fall of swords, And Cassio high in oath . ii 3 234
Clinking. Five year! by'r lady, a long lease for the clinking of pewter *1 Hen. IV.* ii 4 51
Clinquant. To-day the French, All clinquant, all in gold, like heathen gods, Shone down the English . . . . . *Hen. VIII.* i 1 19
Clip. Who, with their drowsy, slow and flagging wings, Clip dead men's graves . . . . *2 Hen. VI.* iv 1 6
O, let me clip ye In arms as sound as when I woo'd! . *Coriolanus* i 6 29
Here I clip The anvil of my sword . . . . . . iv 5 115
Witness, you ever-burning lights above, You elements that clip us round about . . . . *Othello* iii 3 464
Enter the city, clip your wives, your friends . *Ant. and Cleo.* iv 8 8
No grave upon the earth shall clip in it A pair so famous . . v 2 362
And now, This ornament Makes me look dismal will I clip to form *Pericles* v 3 74
Clipp'd in with the sea That chides the banks of England, Scotland, Wales *1 Hen. IV.* iii 1 44
All my reports go with the modest truth; Nor more nor clipp'd, but so *Lear* iv 7 6
His meanest garment, That ever hath but clipp'd his body, is dearer In my respect . . . . *Cymbeline* ii 3 139
Were clipp'd about With this most tender air . . . . . v 5 451
Clipper. It is no English treason to cut French crowns, and to-morrow the king himself will be a clipper . . . . *Hen. V.* iv 1 246
Clippeth. That Neptune's arms, who clippeth thee about . *K. John* v 2 34
Clipping. Then again worries he his daughter with clipping her *W. Tale* v 2 59
Clipt. Judas Maccabæus clipt is plain Judas . . *L. L. Lost* v 2 603
Clip-winged. A clip-wing'd griffin and a moulten raven . *1 Hen. IV.* iii 1 152
Clitus. Sit thee down, Clitus: slaying is the word; It is a deed in fashion. Hark thee, Clitus . . . . . . *J. Cæsar* v 5 4
O Clitus!—What ill request did Brutus make to thee?—To kill him, Clitus . . . . v 5 10

Cloak. You may bear it Under a cloak that is of any length *T. G. of Ver.* iii 1 130
A cloak as long as thine will serve the turn? . . . . iii 1 131
Let me see thy cloak: I'll get me one of such another length . iii 1 132
Why, any cloak will serve the turn . . . . . . iii 1 134
How shall I fashion me to wear a cloak? I pray thee, let me feel thy cloak upon me . . . . iii 1 135
An old cloak makes a new jerkin . . . . . *Mer. Wives* i 3 18
The fashion of a doublet, or a hat, or a cloak, is nothing to a man *Much Ado* iii 3 126
Uncase thee; take my colour'd hat and cloak . . *T. of Shrew* i 1 212
A silken doublet! a velvet hose! a scarlet cloak! . . . v 1 69
We will not line his thin bestained cloak With our pure honours *K. John* iv 3 24
Happy he whose cloak and cincture can Hold out this tempest . . iv 3 155
The cloak of night being pluck'd from off their backs, Stand bare and naked, trembling at themselves . . . . . *Richard II.* iii 2 45
What said Master Dombledon about the satin for my short cloak? *2 Hen. IV.* i 2 34
Give me my sword and cloak . . . . ii 4 395
O, you shall see him laugh till his face be like a wet cloak ill laid up! . v 1 95
Lend me thy cloak, Sir Thomas . . . . . *Hen. V.* iv 1 24
What colour is this cloak of?—Red, master; red as blood . *2 Hen. VI.* ii 1 109
Jet did he never see.—But cloaks and gowns, before this day, a many . ii 1 115
Thou oughtest not to let thy horse wear a cloak, when honester men than thou go in their hose and doublets . . . . . iv 7 55
When clouds appear, wise men put on their cloaks . . *Richard III.* ii 3 32
Hats, cloaks,—Doublets, I think,—flew up . . . *Hen. VIII.* iv 1 73
I have night's cloak to hide me from their sight . *Rom. and Jul.* ii 2 75
What is your pleasure?—Get on your cloak . . *T. of Athens* i 1 15
What hast thou there under thy cloak? . . . . . iii 1 14
You pull'd me by the cloak; would you speak with me? . *J. Cæsar* i 2 215
And half their faces buried in their cloaks . . . . . ii 1 74
'Tis not alone my inky cloak, good mother . . . *Hamlet* i 2 77
Then take thine auld cloak about thee . . . . *Othello* ii 3 99
Cloak-bag. That stuffed cloak-bag of guts . . . . *1 Hen. IV.* ii 4 497
I have already fit—'Tis in my cloak-bag—doublet, hat, hose, all *Cymb.* iii 4 172
Clock. They'll tell the clock to any business that We say . *Tempest* ii 1 289
By seven o'clock I'll get you such a ladder . . . *T. G. of Ver.* iii 1 126
Eleven o'clock the hour. I will prevent this, detect my wife *Mer. Wives* ii 2 324
Vat is de clock, Jack?—'Tis past the hour . . . . . ii 3 3
The clock gives me my cue, and my assurance bids me search . . iii 2 46
Let him be sent for to-morrow, eight o'clock, to have amends . . iii 3 210
It hath struck ten o'clock.—The night is dark . . . . v 2 12
Away; disperse: but till 'tis one o'clock . . . . . v 5 78
What's o'clock, think you?—Eleven, sir . . . *Meas. for Meas.* ii 1 290
Provide your block and your axe to-morrow four o'clock . . . iv 2 56
Let Claudio be executed by four of the clock . . . . . iv 2 124
The clock hath strucken twelve upon the bell . . *Com. of Errors* i 2 45
Methinks your maw, like mine, should be your clock And strike you home . . . . i 2 66
At five o'clock I shall receive the money for the same . . . iv 1 10
It was two ere I left him, and now the clock strikes one . . . iv 2 54
'Tis almost five o'clock, cousin; 'tis time you were ready *Much Ado* iii 4 52
Like a German clock, Still a-repairing, ever out of frame . *L. L. Lost* iii 1 192
Shepherds pipe on oaten straws And merry larks are ploughmen's clocks v 2 914
That supper be ready at the farthest by five of the clock *Mer. of Venice* ii 2 123
'Tis now but four o'clock: we have two hours To furnish us . . ii 4 8
My nose fell a-bleeding on Black-Monday last at six o'clock i' the morning . . . . ii 5 25
He out-dwells his hour, For lovers ever run before the clock . . ii 6 4
Where are all the rest? 'Tis nine o'clock: our friends all stay for you ii 6 63
'It is ten o'clock: Thus we may see,' quoth he, 'how the world wags' *As Y. Like It* ii 7 22
I pray you, what is't o'clock?—You should ask me what time o' day: there's no clock in the forest . . . . iii 2 317
Groaning every hour would detect the lazy foot of Time as well as a clock . . . . iii 2 323
By two o'clock I will be with thee again.—Ay, go your ways . . iv 1 185
How say you now? Is it not past two o'clock? . . . . iv 3 2
Let's see; I think 'tis now some seven o'clock, And well we may come there by dinner-time . . . . . . *T. of Shrew* iv 3 189
I will not go to-day; and ere I do, It shall be what o'clock I say it is . iv 3 197
His honour, Clock to itself, knew the true minute . . *All's Well* i 2 39
Ten o'clock: within these three hours 'twill be time enough to go home iv 1 27
The clock upbraids me with the waste of time . . . *T. Night* iii 1 141
I love thee not a jar o' the clock behind What lady-she her lord *W. Tale* i 2 43
Wishing clocks more swift? Hours, minutes? noon, midnight? . . i 2 289
Now hath time made me his numbering clock . . . *Richard II.* v 5 50
While I stand fooling here, his Jack o' the clock . . . . v 5 60
Unless hours were cups of sack and minutes capons and clocks the tongues of bawds . . . . *1 Hen. IV.* i 2 8
Good morrow, carriers. What's o'clock?—I think it be two o'clock . ii 1 36
Since the old days of goodman Adam to the pupil age of this present twelve o'clock at midnight . . . . ii 4 107
Meet me to-morrow in the temple hall at two o'clock in the afternoon . iii 3 224
We rose both at an instant and fought a long hour by Shrewsbury clock v 4 152
I was born about three of the clock in the afternoon . *2 Hen. IV.* i 2 211
Is it good morrow, lords?—'Tis one o'clock, and past . . . iii 1 34
'Twill be two o'clock ere they come from the coronation . . . v 5 3
Is it four o'clock?—It is.—Then go we in . . . . *Hen. V.* i 1 93
It is now two o'clock: but, let me see, by ten We shall have each a hundred Englishmen . . . . iii 7 168
The country cocks do crow, the clocks do toll, And the third hour of drowsy morning name . . . . iv Prol. 15
Their arms are set like clocks, still to strike on . . *1 Hen. VI.* i 2 42
Sirs, what's o'clock?—Ten, my lord.—Ten is the hour . *2 Hen. VI.* i 4 5
What is't o'clock?—Upon the stroke of four.—Cannot thy master sleep these tedious nights? . . . . *Richard III.* iii 2 4
Towards three or four o'clock Look for the news that the Guildhall affords . . . . iii 5 101
Well, but what's o'clock?—Upon the stroke of ten.—Well, let it strike iv 2 114
Tell the clock there. Give me a calendar. Who saw the sun to-day? v 3 276
If to-morrow be a fair day, by eleven o'clock it will go one way or other *Troi. and Cres.* iii 3 297
At what o'clock to-morrow Shall I send to thee? . . *Rom. and Jul.* ii 2 168
The clock struck nine when I did send the nurse . . . . ii 5 1
The curfew-bell hath rung, 'tis three o'clock . . . . . iv 4 4
Peace! count the clock.—The clock hath stricken three.—'Tis time to part . . . . *J. Cæsar* ii 1 192
What is't o'clock?—Cæsar, 'tis strucken eight.—I thank you . . ii 2 114
What is't o'clock?—About the ninth hour, lady . . . . ii 4 23

Clock. 'Tis three o'clock; and, Romans, yet ere night We shall try fortune in a second fight . . . J. Cæsar v 3 109
The moon is down; I have not heard the clock . . . Macbeth ii 1 2
By the clock, 'tis day, And yet dark night strangles the travelling lamp . . . ii 4 6
'Tis not yet ten o' the clock. Our general cast us thus early for the love of his Desdemona . . . Othello ii 3 14
If thou canst awake by four o' the clock, I prithee, call me . Cymbeline ii 2 6
Where horses have been nimbler than the sands That run i' the clock's behalf . . . iii 2 75
What is it to be false? To lie in watch there and to think on him? To weep 'twixt clock and clock? . . . iii 4 44
Upon a time,—unhappy was the clock That struck the hour! . . . v 5 153
Clock-setter. Old Time the clock-setter, that bald sexton Time K. John iii 1 324
Clod. This sensible warm motion to become A kneaded clod . M. for M. iii 1 121
To make an account of her life to a clod of wayward marl . Much Ado ii 1 65
All this thou seest is but a clod And module of confounded royalty K. John v 7 57
Cloddy earth. Turning with splendour of his precious eye The meagre cloddy earth to glittering gold . . . iii 1 80
Clodpole. He will find it comes from a clodpole . . . T. Night iii 4 208
Clog. I am trusted with a muzzle and enfranchised with a clog Much Ado i 3 35
Here comes my clog . . . All's Well ii 5 58
So much blood in his liver as will clog the foot of a flea . T. Night iii 2 66
Stealing away from his father with his clog at his heels . W. Tale iv 4 695
With clog of conscience and sour melancholy . . . Richard II. v 6 20
You'll rue the time That clogs me with this answer . . Macbeth iii 6 43
I am glad at soul I have no other child; For thy escape would teach me tyranny, To hang clogs on them . . . Othello i 3 198
Gutter'd rocks and congregated sands,—Traitors ensteep'd to clog the guiltless keel . . . ii 1 70
Clogging. Bear not along The clogging burthen of a guilty soul Rich. II. i 3 200
Cloister. What sad talk was that Wherewith my brother held you in the cloister? . . . T. G. of Ver. i 3 2
This day my sister should the cloister enter . . . Meas. for Meas. i 2 182
For aye to be in shady cloister mew'd . . . M. N. Dream i 1 71
He will steal, sir, an egg out of a cloister . . . All's Well iv 3 280
Hie thee to France And cloister thee in some religious house Richard II. v 1 23
Cloistered. Ere the bat hath flown His cloister'd flight . . Macbeth iii 2 41
Cloistress. Like a cloistress, she will veiled walk . . T. Night i 1 28
Close. Here follow her vices.—Close at the heels of her virtues T. G. of Ver. iii 1 325
Let me be blest to make this happy close . . . v 4 117
He arrests him on it; And follows close the rigour of the statute Meas. for Meas. i 4 67
How the villain would close now, after his treasonable abuses! . . v 1 346
Stand thee close, then, under this pent-house . . . Much Ado iii 3 110
I thought to close mine eyes some half an hour . . L. L. Lost v 2 90
Near to her close and consecrated bower . . . M. N. Dream iii 2 7
Whilst this muddy vesture of decay Doth grossly close it in Mer. of Venice v 1 65
My banquet is to close our stomachs up, After our great good cheer T. of Shrew v 2 9
And she is dead; which nothing, but to close Her eyes myself, could win me to believe, More than to see this ring . . . All's Well v 3 118
Nature with a beauteous wall Doth oft close in pollution . T. Night i 2 49
Close, in the name of jesting! . . . ii 5 23
Attested by the holy close of lips . . . v 1 161
Keep it close: home, home, the next way . . W. Tale iii 3 128
He seems to be of great authority: close with him, give him gold . iv 4 830
Young princes, close your hands.—And your lips too . . K. John ii 1 533
The setting sun, and music at the close, As the last taste of sweets, is sweetest last . . . Richard II. ii 1 12
In the intestine shock And furious close of civil butchery . 1 Hen. IV. i 1 13
Lay thine ear close to the ground and list if thou canst hear the tread of travellers . . . ii 2 34
But I followed me close, came in foot and hand . . . ii 4 241
What there is else, keep close; we'll read it at more advantage . ii 4 593
Wait close; I will not see him . . . 2 Hen. IV. ii 2 65
If I can close with him, I care not for his thrust . . . ii 1 20
Doth not make thee wrong this virtuous gentlewoman to close with us ii 4 354
Congreeing in a full and natural close, Like music . . Hen. V. i 2 182
As many lines close in the dial's centre . . . i 2 210
Let housewifery appear: keep close, I thee command . . . ii 3 65
Or close the wall up with our English dead . . . iii 1 2
As looks the mother on her lowly babe When death doth close his tender dying eyes . . . 1 Hen. VI. iii 3 48
Let them be clapp'd up close, And kept asunder . . 2 Hen. VI. i 4 53
I vow by heaven these eyes shall never close . . 3 Hen. VI. i 1 24
Is he dead already? or is it fear That makes him close his eyes? . . i 3 11
Defy them then, or else hold close thy lips . . . ii 2 118
Stand you thus close, to steal the bishop's deer? . . . iv 5 17
I will take order for her keeping close . . . Richard III. iv 2 53
The son of Clarence have I pent up close . . . iv 3 36
Let 'em alone, and draw the curtain close . . . Hen. VIII. v 2 34
Keep the door close, sirrah . . . v 4 30
An 'twere dark, you'ld close sooner . . . Troi. and Cres. iii 2 51
Even with the vail and darking of the sun, To close the day up . v 8 8
Stop close their mouths, let them not speak a word . T. Andron. v 2 165
So secret and so close, So far from sounding and discovery Rom. and Jul. i 1 155
Close our hands with holy words, Then love-devouring death do what he dare . . . ii 6 6
Follow me close, for I will speak to them . . . iii 1 40
Lay thee all along, Holding thine ear close to the hollow ground . . v 3 4
I have shook my head and wept; Yea, 'gainst the authority of manners, pray'd you To hold your hand more close . . T. of Athens ii 2 148
I have a tree, which grows here in my close, That mine own use invites me to cut down . . . v 1 208
It would become me better than to close In terms of friendship with thine enemies . . . J. Cæsar iii 1 202
Now sit we close about this taper here, And call in question our necessities . . . iv 3 164
We have scotch'd the snake, not kill'd it: She'll close and be herself Macbeth iii 2 14
Be assured He closes with you in this consequence . . Hamlet ii 1 45
He closes thus: 'I know the gentleman' . . . ii 1 55
This must be known; which, being kept close, might move More grief to hide than hate to utter love . . . ii 1 118
Follow her close; give her good watch . . . iv 5 75
Keep close within your chamber. Hamlet return'd shall know you are come home . . . iv 7 130

Close. Whose power Will close the eye of anguish . . . Lear iv 4 15
To seel her father's eyes up close as oak . . . Othello iii 3 210
You that will fight, Follow me close . . . Ant. and Cleo. iv 4 34
Downy windows, close; And golden Phœbus never be beheld Of eyes again so royal! . . . v 2 319
And will continue fast to your affection, Still close as sure . Cymbeline i 6 139
She pray'd me to excuse her keeping close, Whereto constrain'd by her infirmity . . . iii 5 46
The marble pavement closes, he is enter'd His radiant roof . . v 4 120
How close 'tis caulk'd and bitumed! Did the sea cast it up? Pericles iii 2 56
Stand close Much Ado iii 3; M. N. Dream iii 2; 1 Hen. IV. ii 2; 2 Hen. VI. i 3; Hen. VIII. ii 1; iv 1; J. Cæsar i 3; Macbeth v 1; Ant. and Cleo. iv 9
Close aspect. That close aspect of his Does show the mood of a much troubled breast . . . K. John iv 2 72
Close by. Was not this nigh shore?—Close by, my master . Tempest i 2 216
In the muddy ditch close by the Thames side . . Mer. Wives iii 3 16
Look where Beatrice, like a lapwing, runs Close by the ground M. Ado iii 1 25
To die upon the bed my father died, To lie close by his honest bones W. Tale iv 4 467
Where was this lane?—Close by the battle . . . Cymbeline v 3 14
Close contriver. The close contriver of all harms . . Macbeth iii 5 7
Close conveyed. An onion will do well for such a shift, Which in a napkin being close convey'd . . . T. of Shrew Ind. 1 127
Close curtain. Spread thy close curtain, love-performing night R. and J. iii 2 5
Close dealing. And my consent ne'er ask'd herein before! This is close dealing . . . 2 Hen. VI. ii 4 73
Close delations. They are close delations, working from the heart Othello iii 3 123
Close earth. For all the sun sees or The close earth wombs . W. Tale iv 4 501
Close enacts. Fie, treacherous hue, that will betray with blushing The close enacts and counsels of the heart! . . . T. Andron. iv 2 118
Close exploit. Know'st thou not any whom corrupting gold Would tempt unto a close exploit of death? . . . Richard III. iv 2 35
Close fighting. Here were the servants of your adversary, And yours, close fighting ere I did approach . . . Rom. and Jul. i 1 114
Close fire. Let your close fire predominate his smoke . T. of Athens iv 3 142
Close impossibilities. Thou visible god [gold], That solder'st close impossibilities, And makest them kiss! . . . iv 3 388
Close intent. Not all so much for love As for another secret close intent Richard III. i 1 158
Close intrenched. The English, in the suburbs close intrench'd 1 Hen. VI i 4 9
Close night. The close night doth play the runaway . Mer. of Venice ii 6 47
Close patience. Show your wisdom, daughter, In your close patience Meas. for Meas. iv 3 123
Close pent-up guilts, Rive your concealing continents . . Lear iii 2 57
Close prison. To close prison he commanded her . . T. G. of Ver. iii 1 235
Close prisoner. You shall close prisoner rest, Till that the nature of your fault be known . . . Othello v 2 335
Close-stool. Your lion, that holds his poll-axe sitting on a close-stool, will be given to Ajax . . . L. L. Lost v 2 580
A paper from fortune's close-stool to give to a nobleman! All's Well v 2 18
Close together. I found them close together, At blow and thrust Othello ii 3 237
Close up. The sudden hand of death close up mine eye! . . L. L. Lost v 2 825
Where, from thy sight, I should be raging mad And cry out for thee to close up mine eyes . . . 2 Hen. VI. iii 2 395
Close up his eyes and draw the curtain close; And let us all to meditation . . . iii 3 32
No sleep close up that deadly eye of thine! . . . Richard III. i 3 225
You great fellow, Stand close up, or I'll make your head ache Hen. VIII. v 4 92
Close villain, I'll have this secret from thy heart . . Cymbeline iii 5 85
Close walk. Give me leave In this close walk to satisfy myself 2 Hen. VI. ii 2 3
Closed. After they closed in earnest, they parted very fairly in jest.—But shall she marry him? . . . T. G. of Ver. ii 5 13
That this my body Might in the ground be closed up in rest! 3 Hen. VI. ii 1 76
Till either death hath closed these eyes of mine Or fortune given me measure of revenge . . . ii 3 31
My father and Lavinia shall forthwith Be closed in our household's monument . . . T. Andron. v 3 194
And expire the term Of a despised life closed in my breast Rom. and Jul. i 4 110
Poor living corse, closed in a dead man's tomb! . . . v 2 30
What's here? a cup, closed in my true love's hand? . . . v 3 161
Every one According to the gift which bounteous nature Hath in him closed . . . Macbeth iii 1 99
Closely. I have been closely shrouded in this bush . . L. L. Lost iv 3 137
And therefore has he closely mew'd her up . . . T. of Shrew i 1 188
Go closely in with me: Much danger do I undergo for thee . K. John iv 1 133
My brother Gloucester, Follow Fluellen closely at the heels . Hen. V. iv 7 179
This day should Clarence closely be mew'd up, About a prophecy Richard III. i 1 38
Thou art sworn as deeply to effect what we intend As closely to conceal what we impart . . . iii 1 159
Meaning to keep her closely at my cell . . . Rom. and Jul. v 3 255
We have closely sent for Hamlet hither . . . Hamlet iii 1 29
Closeness. All dedicated To closeness and the bettering of my mind Tempest i 2 90
Closer. And for secrecy, No lady closer . . . 1 Hen. IV. ii 3 113
Fight closer, or, good faith, you'll catch a blow . . 3 Hen. VI. iii 2 23
Closest. Fire that's closest kept burns most of all . . T. G. of Ver. i 2 30
Closet. Run in here, good young man; go into this closet . Mer. Wives i 4 39
Vetch me in my closet un boitier vert . . . i 4 46
Dere is some simples in my closet . . . i 4 66
O diable, diable! vat is in my closet? . . . i 4 70
What shall de honest man do in my closet? . . . i 4 77
To my closet bring The angry lords with all expedient haste . K. John iv 2 267
When you come into your closet, you'll question this gentlewoman about me . . . Hen. V. v 2 211
And, in thy closet pent up, rue my shame . . . 2 Hen. VI. ii 4 24
Come, Hastings, help me to my closet . . . Richard III. ii 1 133
I'll to thy closet; and go read with thee . . . T. Andron. iii 2 82
Nurse, will you go with me into my closet? . . . Rom. and Jul. iv 2 33
The taper burneth in your closet, sir . . . J. Cæsar ii 1 35
Here's a parchment with the seal of Cæsar; I found it in his closet . iii 2 134
I have seen her rise from her bed, throw her nightgown upon her, unlock her closet . . . Macbeth v 1 6
As I was sewing in my closet, Lord Hamlet, with his doublet all unbraced; No hat upon his head . . . Hamlet ii 1 77
She desires to speak with you in her closet, ere you go to bed . . iii 2 344
He's going to his mother's closet: Behind the arras I'll convey myself . iii 3 27
Hamlet in madness hath Polonius slain, And from his mother's closet hath he dragg'd him . . . iv 1 35
I found it thrown in at the casement of my closet . . . Lear i 2 65

Closet. I have locked the letter in my closet . . . . *Lear* iii 3 12
A subtle whore, A closet lock and key of villanous secrets . *Othello* iv 2 22
The violets, cowslips, and the primroses, Bear to my closet . *Cymbeline* i 5 84
Make a fire within: Fetch hither all my boxes in my closet . *Pericles* iii 2 81
Closet-war. They call this bed-work, mappery, closet-war *Troi. and Cres.* i 3 205
Closing. In the closing of some glorious day . . . 1 *Hen. IV.* iii 2 133
With busy hammers closing rivets up . . . . *Hen. V.* iv Prol. 13
Be this dismal sight The closing up of our most wretched eyes *T. Andron.* iii 1 263
This closing with him fits his lunacy . . . . v 2 70
Closure. Within the guilty closure of thy walls Richard the Second here was hack'd to death . . . . . . *Richard III.* iii 3 11
Beat forth our brains, And make a mutual closure of our house *T. Andron.* v 3 134
Cloten, whose love-suit hath been to me As fearful as a siege *Cymbeline* iii 4 136
'Tis Cloten, the son o' the queen. I fear some ambush . iv 2 65
What's thy name?—Cloten, thou villain.—Cloten, thou double villain, be thy name, I cannot tremble at it . . . . . . iv 2 88
I am absolute 'Twas very Cloten . . . . iv 2 107
This Cloten was a fool, an empty purse; There was no money in't . iv 2 113
What hast thou done?—I am perfect what: cut off one Cloten's head . iv 2 118
Let it to the sea, And tell the fishes he's the queen's son, Cloten . iv 2 153
I'ld let a parish of such Clotens blood, And praise myself for charity . iv 2 168
Yet still it's strange What Cloten's being here to us portends . iv 2 182
I have sent Cloten's clotpoll down the stream, In embassy to his mother . . . . iv 2 184
Great griefs, I see, medicine the less; for Cloten Is quite forgot . iv 2 243
Thou, Conspired with that irregulous devil, Cloten . . . . iv 2 315
How should this be? Pisanio? 'Tis he and Cloten . . . . iv 2 324
This is Pisanio's deed, and Cloten's . . . . iv 2 329
For Cloten, There wants no diligence in seeking him . . . iv 3 19
Neither know I What is betid to Cloten; but remain Perplex'd in all . iv 3 40
Cloten's death . . . may drive us to a render Where we have lived . iv 4 10
Many years, Though Cloten then but young, you see, not wore him From my remembrance . . . . iv 4 23
Lord Cloten, Upon my lady's missing, came to me With his sword drawn v 5 274
And hath More of thee merited than a band of Clotens Had ever scar for v 5 304
Cloth. You will be scraped out of the painted cloth for this . *L. L. Lost* v 2 579
I answer you right painted cloth, from whence you have studied your questions . . . . *As Y. Like It* iii 2 291
As ragged as Lazarus in the painted cloth . . . 1 *Hen. IV.* iv 2 28
Doth, like a miser, spoil his coat with scanting A little cloth *Hen. V.* ii 4 48
This cloth thou dip'dst in blood of my sweet boy . . 3 *Hen. VI.* i 4 157
Good traders in the flesh, set this in your painted cloths *Troi. and Cres.* v 10 47
This must be patch'd With cloth of any colour . . *Coriolanus* iii 1 253
A base slave, A hilding for a livery, a squire's cloth, A pantler *Cymbeline* ii 3 128
Yea, bloody cloth, I'll keep thee, for I wish'd Thou shouldst be colour'd thus v 1 1
Well said, well said; the fire and cloths . . . . *Pericles* iii 2 87
Cloth o' gold, and cuts, and laced with silver . . . *Much Ado* iii 4 19
She did lie In her pavilion—cloth-of-gold of tissue . *Ant. and Cleo.* ii 2 204
Cloth of honour. They that bear The cloth of honour over her, are four barons . . . . *Hen. VIII.* iv 1 48
Cloth of state. Shrouded in cloth of state . . . *Pericles* iii 2 65
Clothair. Descended Of Blithild, which was daughter to King Clothair *Hen. V.* i 2 67
Clotharius. You would swear directly Their very noses had been counsellers To Pepin or Clotharius . . . . . *Hen. VIII.* i 3 10
Clothe. Omitting the sweet benefit of time To clothe mine age *T. G. of Ver.* ii 4 66
Do thou but think What 'tis to cram a maw or clothe a back From such a filthy vice . . . . *Meas. for Meas.* iii 2 23
Go with me to clothe you as becomes you . . . *T. of Shrew* iv 2 120
Thus I clothe my naked villany With old odd ends stolen out of holy writ; And seem a saint . . . . . . *Richard III.* i 3 336
That no revenue hast but thy good spirits, To feed and clothe thee *Hamlet* iii 2 64
So shall I clothe me in a forced content . . . . *Othello* iii 4 120
Care no more to clothe and eat; To thee the reed is as the oak *Cymbeline* iv 2 266
Clothed. Bring in our daughter, clothed like a bride . *Pericles* i 1 6
By your futherance I am clothed in steel . . . . . ii 1 160
Clothes. Go take up these clothes here quickly . *Mer. Wives* iii 3 155
His hinds were called forth by their mistress to carry me in the name of foul clothes to Datchet-lane . . . . iii 5 101
On went he for a search, and away went I for foul clothes . . iii 5 108
Stinking clothes that fretted in their own grease . . . . iii 5 115
Behold what honest clothes you send forth to bleaching! . . . iv 2 126
Are you not ashamed? let the clothes alone . . . . . iv 2 145
Will you take up your wife's clothes? Come away . . . . iv 2 148
Honest in nothing but in his clothes . . . . *Meas. for Meas.* v 1 264
Wrapp'd in sweet clothes, rings put upon his fingers . *T. of Shrew* Ind. 1 38
Has my fellow Tranio stolen your clothes? Or you stolen his? or both? i 1 229
Put on clothes of mine.—Not I, believe me . . . . . iii 2 115
To me she's married, not unto my clothes . . . . . iii 2 119
The soul of this man is his clothes . . . . . *All's Well* ii 5 48
Or to drown my clothes, and say I was stripped . . . . iv 1 57
When I have held familiarity with fresher clothes . . . . v 2 4
These clothes are good enough to drink in; and so be these boots *T. Night* i 3 11
See you these clothes? say you see them not and think me still no gentleman born . . . . *W. Tale* v 2 141
This Hotspur, Mars in swathling clothes . . . . 1 *Hen. IV.* iii 2 112
So a' bade me lay more clothes on his feet . . . *Hen. V.* ii 3 24
Their clothes are after such a pagan cut too, That, sure, they've worn out Christendom . . . . *Hen. VIII.* i 3 14
Yet my mind gave me his clothes made a false report of him *Coriolanus* iv 5 157
What, dress'd! and in your clothes! and down again! . *Rom. and Jul.* iv 5 12
A fool in good clothes, and something like thee . . *T. of Athens* ii 2 114
Then up he rose, and donn'd his clothes . . . . *Hamlet* iv 5 52
Her clothes spread wide; And, mermaid-like, awhile they bore her up iv 7 176
Through tatter'd clothes small vices do appear; Robes and furr'd gowns hide all . . . . *Lear* iv 6 168
A housewife that by selling her desires Buys herself bread and clothes *Othello* iv 1 96
To vex her I will execute in the clothes that she so praised . *Cymbeline* iii 5 147
Thou villain base, Know'st me not by my clothes?—No, nor thy tailor, rascal, Who is thy grandfather: he made those clothes, Which, as it seems, make thee . . . . iv 2 81
She has a good face, speaks well, and has excellent good clothes *Pericles* iv 2 52
Clothier. Jack Cade the clothier means to dress the commonwealth, and turn it, and set a new nap upon it . . . 2 *Hen. VI.* iv 2 5
Upon these taxations, The clothiers all, not able to maintain The many to them 'longing, have put off The spinsters, carders, fullers, weavers *Hen. VIII.* i 2 31
That fellow handles his bow like a crow-keeper: draw me a clothier's yard . . . . *Lear* iv 6 88

Clothing. For clothing me in these grave ornaments . . 1 *Hen. VI.* v 1 54
Clotpoll. I will see you hanged, like clotpoles, ere I come *Troi. and Cres.* ii 1 128
What says the fellow there? Call the clotpoll back . . . *Lear* i 4 51
I have sent Cloten's clotpoll down the stream, In embassy to his mother *Cymbeline* iv 2 184
Cloud. To swim, to dive into the fire, to ride On the curl'd clouds *Tempest* i 2 192
Yond same black cloud, yond huge one, looks like a foul bombard that would shed his liquor . . . . ii 2 20
Yond same cloud cannot choose but fall by pailfuls . . . . ii 2 24
The clouds methought would open and show riches Ready to drop upon me . . . . iii 2 150
I met her deity Cutting the clouds towards Paphos . . . . iv 1 93
An April day, Which now shows all the beauty of the sun, And by and by a cloud takes all away . . . . . . *T. G. of Ver.* i 3 87
Blessed are clouds, to do as such clouds do! . . . . *L. L. Lost* v 2 204
Vouchsafe, bright moon, and these thy stars, to shine, Those clouds removed . . . . v 2 206
Are angels vailing clouds, or roses blown . . . . . . v 2 297
Worthies, away! the scene begins to cloud . . . . . . v 2 731
For night's swift dragons cut the clouds full fast . . *M. N. Dream* iii 2 379
Small and undistinguishable, Like far-off mountains turned into clouds iv 1 193
Though she chide as loud As thunder when the clouds in autumn crack *T. of Shrew* i 2 96
As the sun breaks through the darkest clouds, So honour peereth in the meanest habit . . . . iv 3 175
To the brightest beams Distracted clouds give way . . . *All's Well* v 3 35
Against the invulnerable clouds of heaven . . . . *K. John* ii 1 252
The more fair and crystal is the sky, The uglier seem the clouds that in it fly . . . . *Richard II.* i 1 42
And sigh'd my English breath in foreign clouds . . . . . iii 1 20
When he perceives the envious clouds are bent To dim his glory . iii 3 65
My master, God omnipotent, Is mustering in his clouds on our behalf . iii 3 86
Herein will I imitate the sun, Who doth permit the base contagious clouds To smother up his beauty from the world . . 1 *Hen. IV.* i 2 222
As if an angel dropp'd down from the clouds, To turn and wind a fiery Pegasus . . . . iv 1 108
Leaves his part-created cost A naked subject to the weeping clouds 2 *Hen. IV.* i 3 61
And the spirits of the wise sit in the clouds and mock us . . . ii 2 156
Hanging them With deafening clamour in the slippery clouds . . iii 1 24
The filthy and contagious clouds Of heady murder . . . *Hen. V.* iii 3 31
Whiles the mad mothers with their howls confused Do break the clouds iii 3 40
Our scions, put in wild and savage stock, Spirt up so suddenly into the clouds . . . . iii 5 8
He would be above the clouds . . . . . . 2 *Hen. VI.* ii 1 15
Thus sometimes hath the brightest day a cloud . . . . . ii 4 1
And with the southern clouds contend in tears . . . . . iii 2 384
Each one a perfect sun; Not separated with the racking clouds, But sever'd in a pale clear-shining sky . . . . . 3 *Hen. VI.* ii 1 27
When dying clouds contend with growing light . . . . . ii 5 2
So your dislike, to whom I would be pleasing, Doth cloud my joys . iv 1 74
I spy a black, suspicious, threatening cloud . . . . . . v 3 4
A little gale will soon disperse that cloud . . . . . . v 3 10
For every cloud engenders not a storm . . . . v 3 13
And all the clouds that lour'd upon our house In the deep bosom of the ocean buried . . . . *Richard III.* i 1 3
Can curses pierce the clouds and enter heaven? . . . . . i 3 195
When clouds appear, wise men put on their cloaks . . . . ii 3 32
If that your moody discontented souls Do through the clouds behold this present hour, Even for revenge mock my destruction! . . v 1 8
Whose figure even this instant cloud puts on . . . *Hen. VIII.* i 1 225
O, he smiles valiantly.—Does he not?—O yes, an 'twere a cloud in autumn *Troi. and Cres.* i 2 139
Yond towers, whose wanton tops do buss the clouds . . . . iv 5 220
By yond clouds, Let me deserve so ill as you . . . *Coriolanus* iii 1 50
If Jupiter Should from yond cloud speak divine things, And say ''Tis true,' I'ld not believe . . . . iv 5 110
Yet do thy cheeks look red as Titan's face Blushing to be encounter'd with a cloud . . . . *T. Andron.* ii 4 32
And stain the sun with fog, as sometime clouds When they do hug him in their melting bosoms . . . . iii 1 213
Adding to clouds more clouds with his deep sighs . . *Rom. and Jul.* i 1 139
He bestrides the lazy-pacing clouds And sails upon the bosom of the air ii 2 31
Chequering the eastern clouds with streaks of light . . . . ii 3 2
That gallant spirit hath aspired the clouds . . . . . . iii 1 122
Look, love, what envious streaks Do lace the severing clouds in yonder east . . . . iii 5 8
Is there no pity sitting in the clouds? . . . . iii 5 198
She is advanced Above the clouds, as high as heaven itself . . iv 5 74
One cloud of winter showers, These flies are couch'd . . *T. of Athens* ii 2 180
He goes away in a cloud: call him, call him . . . . . iii 4 42
I have seen The ambitious ocean swell and rage and foam, To be exalted with the threatening clouds . . . . *J. Cæsar* i 3 8
Looks in the clouds, scorning the base degrees By which he did ascend ii 1 26
Yon gray lines That fret the clouds are messengers of day . . . ii 1 104
Fierce fiery warriors fought upon the clouds, In ranks and squadrons . ii 2 19
Our day is gone; Clouds, dews, and dangers come; our deeds are done! v 3 64
Can such things be, And overcome us like a summer's cloud? *Macbeth* iii 4 111
My little spirit, see, Sits in a foggy cloud, and stays for me . . iii 5 36
How is it that the clouds still hang on you? . . . . *Hamlet* i 2 66
The great cannon to the clouds shall tell . . . . . . i 2 126
Do you see yonder cloud that's almost in shape of a camel? . . iii 2 393
Feeds on his wonder, keeps himself in clouds . . . . . iv 5 89
Caps, hands, and tongues, applaud it to the clouds . . . . iv 5 107
The chidden billow seems to pelt the clouds . . . . *Othello* ii 1 12
Will Cæsar weep?—He has a cloud in's face . . . *Ant. and Cleo.* iii 2 51
Sometime we see a cloud that's dragonish; A vapour sometime like a bear or lion . . . . iv 14 2
Dissolve, thick cloud, and rain; that I may say, The gods themselves do weep! . . . . v 2 302
Why cloud they not their sights perpetually, If this be true? *Pericles* i 1 74
Whose towers bore heads so high they kiss'd the clouds . . . i 4 24
An hand environed with clouds, Holding out gold that's by the touch-stone tried . . . . ii 2 36
Cloud of darkness. When heaven shall call her from this cloud of darkness . . . . *Hen. VIII.* v 5 45
Cloud of dignity. My cloud of dignity Is held from falling with so weak a wind That it will quickly drop . . . . 2 *Hen. IV.* iv 5 99
Cloud of sorrow. Since love's argument was first on foot, Let not the cloud of sorrow justle it . . . . *L. L. Lost* v 2 758

Cloud-capp'd towers, the gorgeous palaces, The solemn temples *Tempest* iv 1 152
Clouded. My face is but a moon, and clouded too . . . *L. L. Lost* v 2 203
I would not be a stander-by to hear My sovereign mistress clouded so *W. Tale* i 2 280
One day too late, I fear me, noble lord, Hath clouded all thy happy days on earth . . . *Richard. II.* iii 2 68
This world frowns, and Edward's sun is clouded . . 3 *Hen. VI.* ii 3 7
Cloudiness. What's the matter, That you have such a February face, So full of frost, of storm and cloudiness? . . . *Much Ado* v 4 42
Cloudy. It is foul weather in us all, good sir, When you are cloudy *Tempest* ii 1 142
The elements Of fire and water, when their thundering shock At meeting tears the cloudy cheeks of heaven . . . . *Richard II.* iii 3 57
Render'd such aspect As cloudy men use to their adversaries 1 *Hen. IV.* iii 2 83
Beaufort's red sparkling eyes blab his heart's malice, And Suffolk's cloudy brow his stormy hate . . . . . 2 *Hen. VI.* iii 1 155
Dark cloudy death o'ershades his beams of life . . . 3 *Hen. VI.* ii 6 62
Whose bright out-shining beams thy cloudy wrath Hath in eternal darkness folded up . . . . . *Richard III.* i 3 268
You cloudy princes and heart-sorrowing peers . . . . . ii 2 112
Clear up, fair queen, that cloudy countenance . . . *T. Andron.* i 1 263
My silence and my cloudy melancholy . . . . ii 3 33
Such a waggoner As Phaethon would whip you to the west, And bring in cloudy night immediately . . . *Rom. and Jul.* iii 2 4
With an absolute 'Sir, not I,' The cloudy messenger turns me his back *Macbeth* iii 6 41
But sea-room, and the brine and cloudy billow kiss the moon, I care not *Pericles* iii 1 46
Clout. A' must shoot nearer, or he'll ne'er hit the clout . *L. L. Lost* iv 1 136
If I were mad, I should forget my son, Or madly think a babe of clouts were he . . . . . . *K. John* iii 4 58
A' would have clapped i' the clout at twelve score . 2 *Hen. IV.* iii 2 51
A clout Steep'd in the faultless blood of pretty Rutland *Richard III.* i 3 177
When I say so, she looks as pale as any clout in the versal world *Rom. and Jul.* ii 4 218
A clout upon that head Where late the diadem stood . *Hamlet* ii 2 529
O, well flown, bird! i' the clout, i' the clout: hewgh! . . *Lear* iv 6 92
This is fought indeed! Had we done so at first, we had droven them home With clouts about their heads . . . *Ant. and Cleo.* iv 7 6
Clouted. Spare none but such as go in clouted shoon . 2 *Hen VI.* iv 2 195
I thought he slept, and put My clouted brogues from off my feet *Cymb.* iv 2 214
Clove. A gilt nutmeg.—A lemon.—Stuck with cloves . . *L. L. Lost* v 2 654
Cloven. She did confine thee, By help of her more potent ministers And in her most unmitigable rage, Into a cloven pine . *Tempest* i 2 277
All wound with adders who with cloven tongues Do hiss me into madness . . . . ii 2 13
A lemon.—Stuck with cloves.—No, cloven . . *L. L. Lost* v 2 655
She came and puts me her white hand to his cloven chin— Juno have mercy! how came it cloven?—Why, you know, 'tis dimpled *Tr. and Cr.* i 2 132
List, what work he makes Amongst your cloven army *Coriolanus* i 4 21
Clover. The freckled cowslip, burnet and green clover . . *Hen. V.* v 2 49
Clovest. When thou clovest thy crown i' the middle, and gavest away both parts, thou borest thy ass on thy back o'er the dirt *Lear* i 4 175
Clowder. And couple Clowder with the deep-mouth'd brach *T. of Shrew* Ind. 1 18
Clown. A most simple clown! . . . . . *L. L. Lost* iv 1 142
The clown bore it, the fool sent it, and the lady hath it: sweet clown, sweeter fool, sweetest lady! . . . . . . iv 3 17
The roynish clown, at whom so oft Your grace was wont to laugh *As Y. Like It* ii 2 8
Holla, you clown!—Peace, fool: he's not thy kinsman . . . ii 4 66
It is meat and drink to me to see a clown . . . . v 1 12
Therefore, you clown, abandon,—which is in the vulgar leave . v 1 52
Abandon the society of this female, or, clown, thou perishest . v 1 56
My clown, who wants but something to be a reasonable man *W. Tale* iv 4 616
Or cut not out the burly-boned clown in chines of beef . 2 *Hen. VI.* iv 10 60
The clown shall make those laugh whose lungs are tickle o' the sere *Hamlet* ii 2 336
Let those that play your clowns speak no more than is set down for them iii 2 43
Clownish. What if we assay'd to steal The clownish fool out of your father's court? . . . . *As Y. Like It* i 3 132
Cloy the hungry edge of appetite By bare imagination of a feast *Richard II.* i 3 296
I am hungry for revenge, And now I cloy me with beholding it *Rich. III.* iv 4 62
Other women cloy The appetites they feed; but she makes hungry Where most she satisfies . . . *Ant. and Cleo.* ii 2 241
His royal bird Prunes the immortal wing and cloys his beak *Cymbeline* v 4 118
Cloyed. If you be not too much cloyed with fat meat 2 *Hen. IV.* Epil. 28
Whom he hath dull'd and cloy'd with gracious favours . *Hen. V.* ii 2 9
They are cloy'd With long continuance in a settled place 1 *Hen. VI.* iv 5 105
Mine eyes are cloy'd with view of tyranny . . *T. Andron.* ii 2 55
The cloyed will, That satiate yet unsatisfied desire . . *Cymbeline* i 6 47
Both their eyes And ears so cloy'd importantly as now . . iv 4 19
Cloyless. Epicurean cooks Sharpen with cloyless sauce his appetite *Ant. and Cleo.* ii 1 25
Cloyment. No motion of the liver, but the palate, That suffer surfeit, cloyment and revolt . . . . . . *T. Night* ii 4 102
Club. She would have made Hercules have turned spit, yea, and have cleft his club to make the fire too . . . *Much Ado* ii 1 262
His codpiece seems as massy as his club . . . . iii 3 147
Cupid's butt-shaft is too hard for Hercules' club . . *L. L. Lost* i 2 182
He is not so big as the end of his club . . . . v 1 139
Great Hercules is presented by this imp, Whose club kill'd Cerberus . v 2 593
Troilus had his brains dashed out with a Grecian club . *As Y. Like It* iv 1 98
Clubs cannot part them . . . . v 2 44
I'll call for clubs, if you will not away . . . 1 *Hen. VI.* i 3 84
I missed the meteor once, and hit that woman; who cried out 'Clubs!' *Hen. VIII.* v 4 53
What work's, my countrymen, in hand? where go you With bats and clubs? . . . . *Coriolanus* i 1 57
But make you ready your stiff bats and clubs . . . . i 1 165
Clubs, clubs! these lovers will not keep the peace . *T. Andron.* ii 1 37
Clubs, bills, and partisans! strike! beat them down! . *Rom. and Jul.* i 1 80
With some great kinsman's bone, As with a club, dash out my desperate brains . . . . iv 3 54
And with those hands, that grasp'd the heaviest club, Subdue my worthiest self . . . . . . *Ant. and Cleo.* iv 12 46
Clucked. She, poor hen, fond of no second brood, Has cluck'd thee to the wars and safely home, Loaden with honour . . *Coriolanus* v 3 163
Clung. When they lighted, how they clung In their embracement *Hen. VIII.* i 1 9
Cluster. Like beasts And cowardly nobles, gave way unto your clusters *Coriolanus* iv 6 122
Here come the clusters . . . . iv 6 128
Clustering. I'll bring thee To clustering filberts . . . *Tempest* ii 2 175
Vines with clustering bunches growing . . . . . iv 1 112
Into the clustering battle of the French . . . 1 *Hen. VI.* iv 7 13
Clutch. Not that I have the power to clutch my hand, When his fair angels would salute my palm . . . . . . *K. John* ii 1 589
Come, let me clutch thee. I have thee not, and yet I see thee still *Macb.* ii 1 34
Age, with his stealing steps, Hath claw'd me in his clutch . *Hamlet* v 1 80
Clutched. For putting the hand in the pocket and extracting it clutched *Meas. for Meas.* iii 2 49
Within thine eyes sat twenty thousand deaths, In thy hands clutch'd as many millions . . . . *Coriolanus* iii 3 71
Clyster-pipe. Yet again your fingers to your lips? would they were clyster-pipes for your sake! . . . . . . *Othello* ii 1 178
Cneius Pompey. Nay, you were a fragment Of Cneius Pompey's *A. and C.* iii 13 118
Coach. And lords, and gentlemen, with their coaches, I warrant you, coach after coach . . . . *Mer. Wives* ii 2 66
Thou shinest in every tear that I do weep: No drop but as a coach doth carry thee . . . . *L. L. Lost* iv 3 34
Your eyes do make no coaches . . . . . . iv 3 155
I'll tell thee all my whole device When I am in my coach *Mer. of Venice* iii 4 82
Gallops the zodiac in his glistering coach . . . *T. Andron.* ii 1 7
Come, my coach! Good night, ladies; good night, sweet ladies *Hamlet* iv 5 72
Coach-fellow. You and your coach-fellow Nym . . *Mer. Wives* ii 2 7
Coach-maker. Made by the joiner squirrel or old grub, Time out o' mind the fairies' coachmakers . . . . . *Rom. and Jul.* i 4 69
Co-act. But if I tell how these two did co-act, Shall I not lie in publishing a truth? . . . . *Troi. and Cres.* v 2 118
Coactive. With what's unreal thou coactive art . . *W. Tale* i 2 141
Coagulate. And thus o'er-sized with coagulate gore . . *Hamlet* ii 2 484
Coal. We shall not shortly have a rasher on the coals for money *Mer. of Venice* iii 5 28
Stars, stars, And all eyes else dead coals! . . . *W. Tale* v 1 68
There is no malice in this burning coal . . . *K. John* iv 1 109
Your breath first kindled the dead coal of wars . . . v 2 83
They stole a fire-shovel: I knew by that piece of service the men would carry coals . . . . *Hen. V.* iii 2 50
His lips blows at his nose, and it is like a coal of fire, sometimes plue and sometimes red . . . . iii 6 110
Throw in the frozen bosoms of our part Hot coals of vengeance! 2 *Hen. VI.* v 2 36
For selfsame wind that I should speak withal Is kindling coals that fires all my breast . . . . 3 *Hen. VI.* ii 1 83
It is you Have blown this coal betwixt my lord and me . *Hen. VIII.* ii 4 79
You charge me That I have blown this coal: I do deny it . . ii 4 94
That were to enlard his fat already pride And add more coals to Cancer *Troi. and Cres.* ii 3 206
You are no surer, no, Than is the coal of fire upon the ice, Or hailstone in the sun . . . . *Coriolanus* i 1 177
If he could burn us all into one coal, We have deserved it . . iv 6 137
A pair of tribunes that have rack'd for Rome, To make coals cheap,—a noble memory! . . . . v 1 17
We'll not carry coals.—No, for then we should be colliers *Rom. and Jul.* i 1 2
The cat, with eyne of burning coal, Now couches fore the mouse's hole *Pericles* iii Gower 5
Coal-black. And some will mourn in ashes, some coal-black *Richard II.* v 1 49
Black, forsooth: coal-black as jet . . . . 2 *Hen. VI.* ii 1 112
This hand, fast wound about thy coal-black hair . . 3 *Hen. VI.* v 1 54
We are not brought so low, But that between us we can kill a fly That comes in likeness of a coal-black Moor . . *T. Andron.* iii 2 78
Coal-black is better than another hue, In that it scorns to bear another hue . . . . iv 2 99
But where the bull and cow are both milk-white, They never do beget a coal-black calf . . . . v 1 32
Coarse. Now I feel Of what coarse metal ye are moulded, envy *Hen. VIII.* iii 2 239
Coarsely. There is a gentleman that serves the count Reports but coarsely of her . . . . *All's Well* iii 5 60
Coast. Travelling along this coast, I here am come by chance *L. L. Lost* v 2 557
The four winds blow in from every coast Renowned suitors *Mer. of Venice* i 1 168
Ballad of a fish, that appeared upon the coast on Wednesday the four-score of April . . . . *W. Tale* iv 4 280
Who lately landed With some few private friends upon this coast *Richard II.* iii 3 4
See the coast clear'd, and then we will depart . . . 1 *Hen. VI.* i 3 89
Yet have I gold flies from another coast . . . 2 *Hen. VI.* i 2 93
Losing ken of Albion's wished coast . . . . . iii 2 113
Spare England, for it is your native coast . . . . iv 8 52
I'll undertake to land them on our coast . . . 3 *Hen. VI.* iii 3 205
Those powers that the queen Hath raised in Gallia have arrived our coast . . . . v 3 8
On the western coast Rideth a puissant navy . . *Richard III.* iv 4 433
How he coasts And hedges his own way . . . *Hen. VIII.* iii 2 38
He was carried From off our coast, twice beaten . . *Cymbeline* iii 1 26
Find The ooze, to show what coast thy sluggish crare Might easiliest harbour in . . . . iv 2 205
The Roman legions, all from Gallia drawn, Are landed on your coast . iv 3 25
The thunderer, whose bolt, you know, Sky-planted batters all rebelling coasts . . . . v 4 96
He, good prince, having all lost, By waves from coast to coast is tost *Pericles* ii Gower 34
May see the sea hath cast upon your coast . . . . ii 1 60
Mariner, say what coast is this? . . . . . . iii 1 73
And on this coast Suppose him now at anchor . . . v Gower 15
I threw her overboard with these very arms.—Upon this coast . v 3 20
Coasting. And, coasting homeward, came to Ephesus *Com. of Errors* i 1 135
Coat. The dozen white luces in their coat.—It is an old coat.—The dozen white louses do become an old coat well . . . *Mer. Wives* i 1 17
The luce is the fresh fish; the salt fish is an old coat . . . i 1 23
If he has a quarter of your coat, there is but three skirts for yourself . i 1 29
There's a hole made in your best coat, Master Ford . . . iii 5 144
Each fair instalment, coat, and several crest, With loyal blazon, ever-more be blest! . . . . v 5 67
Neither my coat, integrity, nor persuasion can with ease attempt you *Meas. for Meas.* iv 2 204
As to show a child his new coat and forbid him to wear it . *Much Ado* iii 2 7
Cowslips tall her pensioners be: In their gold coats spots you see *M. N. Dream* ii 1 11
Some war with rere-mice for their leathern wings, To make my small elves coats . . . . ii 2 5
Like coats in heraldry, Due but to one and crowned with one crest . iii 2 213
I could shake them off my coat: these burs are in my heart *As Y. Like It* i 3 16
Did stretch his leathern coat Almost to bursting . . . . ii 1 37

Coat. O that I were a fool! I am ambitious for a motley coat *As Y. Like It* ii 7 43
Let their heads be sleekly combed, their blue coats brushed *T. of Shrew* iv 1 94
Nathaniel's coat, sir, was not fully made . iv 1 135
With silken coats and caps and golden rings, With ruffs and cuffs iv 3 55
I would not be in some of your coats for two pence . *T. Night* iv 1 33
And saw myself unbreech'd, In my green velvet coat . *W. Tale* i 2 156
If this be a horseman's coat, it hath seen very hot service . iv 3 71
Steel my lance's point, That it may enter Mowbray's waxen coat *Richard II.* i 3 75
The lining of his coffers shall make coats To deck our soldiers . i 4 61
From my own windows torn my household coat, Razed out my imprese iii 1 24
Glittering in golden coats, like images . *1 Hen. IV.* iv 1 100
Thrown over the shoulders like a herald's coat without sleeves . iv 2 49
The king hath many marching in his coats . v 3 25
Bardolph, give the soldiers coats . *2 Hen. IV.* iii 2 311
Covering discretion with a coat of folly . *Hen. V.* ii 4 38
Like a miser, spoil his coat with scanting A little cloth . ii 4 47
If I find a hole in his coat, I will tell him my mind . iii 6 89
Their gesture sad Investing lank-lean cheeks and war-worn coats . iv Prol. 26
They will pluck The gay new coats o'er the French soldiers' heads iv 3 118
Cropp'd are the flower-de-luces in your arms; Of England's coat one half is cut away . *1 Hen. VI.* i 1 81
Regent I am of France. Give me my steeled coat. I'll fight for France i 1 85
Draw, men, for all this privileged place; Blue coats to tawny coats i 3 47
Out, tawny coats! out, scarlet hypocrite! . i 3 56
Either renew the fight, Or tear the lions out of England's coat . i 5 28
He need not fear the sword; for his coat is of proof *2 Hen. VI.* iv 2 65
Wear it as a herald's coat, To emblaze the honour that thy master got iv 10 75
Shall we go throw away our coats of steel, And wrap our bodies in black mourning gowns? . *3 Hen. VI.* ii 1 160
A fellow In a long motley coat guarded with yellow *Hen. VIII.* Prol. 16
Your long coat, priest, protects you . iii 2 276
And when they have lined their coats Do themselves homage *Othello* i 1 53
That thrust had been mine enemy indeed, But that my coat is better than thou know st . v 1 25
What mean you, sir?—To beg of you, kind friends, this coat of worth *Pericles* ii 1 142
Cobble. Mend me, thou saucy fellow!—Why, sir, cobble you . *J. Cæsar* i 1 22
Cobbled. Making parties strong And feebling such as stand not in their liking Below their cobbled shoes *Coriolanus* i 1 200
Cobbler. I am but, as you would say, a cobbler . *J. Cæsar* i 1 11
Thou art a cobbler, art thou?—Truly, sir, all that I live by is with the awl i 1 23
Cobham. Harry Duke of Hereford, Rainold Lord Cobham *Richard II.* ii 1 279
Stand forth, Dame Eleanor Cobham, Gloucester's wife *2 Hen. VI.* ii 3 1
You, Edward, shall unto my Lord Cobham . *3 Hen. VI.* i 2 40
Cobloaf. Thou shouldst strike him.—Cobloaf! . *Troi. and Cres.* ii 1 41
Cobweb. Peaseblossom! Cobweb! Moth! and Mustard-seed! *M. N. Dream* iii 1 165
I shall desire you of more acquaintance, good Master Cobweb: if I cut my finger, I shall make bold with you . iii 1 186
Where s Mounsieur Cobweb?—Ready . iv 1 8
Mounsieur Cobweb, good mounsieur, get you your weapons in your hand iv 1 10
Help Cavalery Cobweb to scratch . iv 1 25
Here in her hairs ... hath woven A golden mesh to entrap the hearts of men Faster than gnats in cobwebs . *Mer. of Venice* iii 2 123
The house trimmed, rushes strewed, cobwebs swept . *T. of Shrew* iv 1 48
Cock. The old cock.—The cockerel . *Tempest* ii 1 30
You were wont, when you laughed, to crow like a cock . *T. G. of Ver.* ii 1 28
And look thou meet me ere the first cock crow . *M. N. Dream* ii 1 267
The ousel cock so black of hue, With orange-tawny bill . iii 1 128
Of what kind should this cock come of? . *As Y. Like It* ii 7 90
What is your crest? a coxcomb?—A combless cock . *T. of Shrew* ii 1 227
No cock of mine: you crow too like a craven . ii 1 228
If the springe hold, the cock's mine . *W. Tale* iv 3 36
I have no pheasant, cock nor hen . iv 4 770
There is ne'er a king christen could be better bit than I have been since the first cock . *1 Hen. IV.* ii 1 20
Pistol's cock is up, And flashing fire will follow . *Hen. V.* ii 1 55
The country cocks do crow, the clocks do toll, And the third hour of drowsy morning name . iv Prol. 15
The early village-cock Hath twice done salutation to the morn *Richard III.* v 3 209
Come, stir, stir, stir! the second cock hath crow'd, The curfew-bell hath rung, 'tis three o'clock . *Rom. and Jul.* iv 4 3
I have retired me to a wasteful cock, And set mine eyes at flow *T. of Athens* ii 2 171
We were carousing till the second cock . *Macbeth* ii 3 27
It was about to speak, when the cock crew . *Hamlet* i 2 147
The cock, that is the trumpet to the morn . i 1 150
It faded on the crowing of the cock . i 1 157
The morning cock crew loud, And at the sound it shrunk in haste away i 2 218
Young men will do't, if they come to't; By cock, they are to blame . iv 5 62
Spout Till you have drench'd our steeples, drown'd the cocks! *Lear* iii 2 3
He begins at curfew, and walks till the first cock . iii 4 121
The fishermen, that walk upon the beach, Appear like mice; and yond tall anchoring bark, Diminish'd to her cock; her cock, a buoy Almost too small for sight . iv 6 19
His cocks do win the battle still of mine, When it is all to nought *Ant. and Cleo.* ii 3 36
I must go up and down like a cock that nobody can match *Cymbeline* ii 1 24
You are cock and capon too; and you crow, cock, with your comb on ii 1 25
Cock-a-diddle-dow. I hear The strain of strutting chanticleer Cry, Cock-a-diddle-dow *Tempest* i 2 386
Cock-a-hoop. You'll make a mutiny among my guests! You will set cock-a-hoop! you'll be the man! *Rom. and Jul.* i 5 83
Cock and pie. By cock and pie, you shall not choose, sir! *Mer. Wives* i 1 316
By cock and pie, sir, you shall not away to-night . *2 Hen. IV.* v 1 1
Cockatrice. They will kill one another by the look, like cockatrices *T. Night* iii 4 215
A cockatrice hast thou hatch'd to the world, Whose unavoided eye is murderous *Richard III.* iv 1 55
Shall poison more Than the death-darting eye of cockatrice *Rom. and Jul.* iii 2 47
Cockered. Shall a beardless boy, A cocker'd silken wanton, brave our fields? . *K. John* v 1 70
Cockerel. The old cock.—The cockerel *Tempest* ii 1 31
It had upon its brow A bump as big as a young cockerel's stone *Rom. and Jul.* i 3 53
Cockle. Sow'd cockle reap'd no corn . *L. L. Lost* iv 3 383
'Tis a cockle or a walnut-shell, A knack, a toy, a trick, a baby's cap *T. of Shrew* iv 3 66
The cockle of rebellion, insolence, sedition *Coriolanus* iii 1 70
Sail seas in cockles, have an wish but for't . *Pericles* iv 4 2
Cockle hat. By his cockle hat and staff, And his sandal shoon *Hamlet* iv 5 25
Cockled snails. The tender horns of cockled snails . *L. L. Lost* iv 3 338

Cockney. I am afraid this great lubber, the world, will prove a cockney *T. Night* iv 1 15
As the cockney did to the eels when she put 'em i' the paste alive *Lear* ii 4 123
Cock-pigeon. I will be more jealous of thee than a Barbary cock-pigeon over his hen *As Y. Like It* iv 1 151
Cockpit. Can this cockpit hold The vasty fields of France? *Hen. V.* Prol. 11
Cockshut. Much about cock-shut time . *Richard III.* v 3 70
Cock's passion, silence! I hear my master . *T. of Shrew* iv 1 121
Cock-sure. We steal as in a castle, cock-sure . *1 Hen. IV.* ii 1 95
Coctus. Twice-sod simplicity, bis coctus! . *L. L. Lost* iv 2 23
Cocytus. This fell devouring receptacle, As hateful as Cocytus' misty mouth . *T. Andron.* ii 3 236
Cod. I remember the wooing of a peascod instead of her, from whom I took two cods . *As Y. Like It* ii 4 53
She that in wisdom never was so frail To change the cod's head for the salmon's tail . *Othello* ii 1 156
Codding. That codding spirit had they from their mother *T. Andron.* v 1 99
Codling. Or a codling when 'tis almost an apple . *T. Night* i 5 167
Codpiece. You must needs have them with a codpiece *T. G. of Ver.* ii 7 53
A round hose, madam, now's not worth a pin, Unless you have a cod-piece to stick pins on . ii 7 56
For the rebellion of a codpiece to take away the life of a man! *M. for M.* iii 2 122
His codpiece seems as massy as his club . *Much Ado* iii 3 146
Dread prince of plackets, king of codpieces . *L. L. Lost* iii 1 186
'Twas nothing to geld a codpiece of a purse . *W. Tale* iv 4 623
The cod-piece that will house Before the head has any, The head and he shall louse . *Lear* iii 2 27
Here's grace and a cod-piece; that's a wise man and a fool . iii 2 40
Cœlestibus. Tantæne animis cœlestibus iræ? *2 Hen. VI.* ii 1 24
Co-equal. If once he come to be a cardinal, He'll make his cap co-equal with the crown . *1 Hen. VI.* v 1 33
Cœur-de-lion. By the honour-giving hand Of Cœur-de-lion knighted *K. John* i 1 54
He hath a trick of Cœur-de-lion's face; The accent of his tongue . i 1 85
The reputed son of Cœur-de-lion, Lord of thy presence and no land beside . i 1 136
King Richard Cœur-de-lion was thy father . i 1 253
God shall forgive you Cœur-de-lion's death . ii 1 12
In this late-betrayed town Great Cœur-de-lion's heart was buried *1 Hen. VI.* iii 2 83
Coffer. I will use her as the key of the cuckoldly rogue's coffer *Mer. Wives* ii 2 286
My bed shall be abused, my coffers ransacked . ii 2 306
In the chambers, and in the coffers, and in the presses . iii 3 225
Neither press, coffer, chest, trunk, well, vault . iv 2 62
A dower Remaining in the coffer of her friends . *Meas. for Meas.* i 2 155
The other half Comes to the privy coffer of the state *Mer. of Venice* iv 1 354
In ivory coffers I have stuff'd my crowns . *T. of Shrew* ii 1 352
Hold, there's half my coffer . *T. Night* iii 4 381
Our coffers, with too great a court And liberal largess, are grown somewhat light . *Richard II.* i 4 43
The lining of his coffers shall make coats To deck our soldiers . i 4 61
Shall our coffers, then, Be emptied to redeem a traitor home? *1 Hen. IV.* i 3 85
His coffers sound With hollow poverty and emptiness *2 Hen. IV.* i 3 74
And to the coffers of the king beside, A thousand pounds by the year *Hen. V.* i 1 18
And from his coffers Received the golden earnest of our death ii 2 168
An urn more precious Than the rich-jewel'd coffer of Darius *1 Hen. VI.* i 6 25
He commands us to provide, and give great gifts, And all out of an empty coffer . *T. of Athens* i 2 199
He hath brought many captives home to Rome, Whose ransoms did the general coffers fill . *J. Cæsar* iii 2 94
Go to the bay and disembark my coffers: Bring thou the master *Othello* ii 1 210
To be partner'd With tomboys hired with that self exhibition Which your own coffers yield! . *Cymbeline* i 6 123
Bid Nicander Bring me the satin coffer . *Pericles* iii 1 68
This letter, and some certain jewels, Lay with you in your coffer . iii 4 2
Coffin. Would she were hearsed at my foot, and the ducats in her coffin! *Mer. of Venice* iii 1 94
Not a flower sweet On my black coffin let there be strown *T. Night* ii 4 61
Great king, within this coffin I present Thy buried fear . *Richard II.* v 6 30
Upon a wooden coffin we attend, And death's dishonourable victory We with our stately presence glorify . *1 Hen. VI.* i 1 19
If I digg'd up thy forefathers' graves And hung their rotten coffins up in chains, It could not slake mine ire, nor ease my heart *3 Hen. VI.* i 3 28
My lord, stand back, and let the coffin pass *Richard III.* i 2 38
Five times he hath return'd Bleeding to Rome, bearing his valiant sons In coffins . *T. Andron.* i 1 35
With your blood and it I'll make a paste, And of the paste a coffin I will rear . v 2 189
My heart is in the coffin there with Cæsar . *J. Cæsar* iii 2 111
'Tis like a coffin, sir.—Whate'er it be, 'Tis wondrous heavy . *Pericles* iii 1 52
Here I give to understand, If e'er this coffin drive a-land . iii 2 69
I oped the coffin, Found there rich jewels . v 3 23
Coffined. Wouldst thou have laugh'd had I come coffin'd home, That weep'st to see me triumph? . *Coriolanus* ii 1 193
Straight Must cast thee, scarcely coffin'd, in the ooze *Pericles* iii 1 61
Cog. I cannot cog, I cannot prate . *Mer. Wives* iii 3 50
I cannot cog and say thou art this and that . iii 3 76
Fashion-monging boys, That lie and cog and flout *Much Ado* v 1 95
Since you can cog, I'll play no more with you . *L. L. Lost* v 2 235
I cannot flatter and speak fair, Smile in men's faces, smooth, deceive and cog . *Richard III.* i 3 48
I'll mountebank their loves, Cog their hearts from them *Coriolanus* iii 2 133
You hear him cog, see him dissemble, Know his gross patchery *T. of Athens* v 1 98
Cogging. This same scall, scurvy, cogging companion . *Mer. Wives* iii 1 123
Come, both you cogging Greeks; have at you both! *Troi. and Cres.* v 6 11
Some busy and insinuating rogue, Some cogging, cozening slave *Othello* iv 2 132
Cogitation Resides not in that man that does not think *W. Tale* i 2 271
This breast of mine hath buried Thoughts of great value, worthy cogitations . *J. Cæsar* i 2 50
Cognition. I will not be myself, nor have cognition Of what I feel: I am all patience . *Troi. and Cres.* v 2 63
Cognizance. This pale and angry rose, As cognizance of my blood-drinking hate . *1 Hen. VI.* ii 4 108
Great men shall press For tinctures, stains, relics and cognizance *J. Cæsar* ii 2 89
The cognizance of her incontinency Is this *Cymbeline* ii 4 127
Cogscomb. I will knog your urinals about your knave's cogscomb *Mer. Wives* iii 1 91

Co-heir. They are co-heirs; And I had rather glib myself than they Should not produce fair issue *W. Tale* ii 1 148

Cohere. Till each circumstance Of place, time, fortune, do cohere *T. Night* v 1 259

Cohered. Had time cohered with place or place with wishing *M. for M.* ii 1 11

Coherence. It is a wonderful thing to see the semblable coherence of his men's spirits and his . 2 *Hen. IV.* v 1 73

Coherent. How she shall persever, That time and place with this deceit so lawful May prove coherent *All's Well* iii 7 39

Cohort. Banishment of friends, dissipation of cohorts *Lear* i 2 162

Coign. See you yon coign o' the Capitol, yon corner-stone? *Coriolanus* v 4 1

No jutty, frieze, Buttress, nor coign of vantage *Macbeth* i 6 7

By the four opposing coigns Which the world together joins *Pericles* iii Gower 17

Coil. Who was so firm, so constant, that this coil Would not infect his reason? *Tempest* i 2 207

Here is a coil with protestation! *T. G. of Ver.* i 2 99

What a coil is there, Dromio? *Com. of Errors* iii 1 48

The wedding being there to-morrow, their is a great coil to-night *M. Ado* iii 3 100

Yonder's old coil at home v 2 98

All this coil is 'long of you *M. N. Dream* iii 2 339

I am commanded here, and kept a coil with 'Too young' and 'the next year' and ''tis too early' *All's Well* ii 1 27

I would that I were low laid in my grave: I am not worth this coil that's made for me *K. John* ii 1 165

And wilt thou have a reason for this coil? *T. Andron.* iii 1 225

Here's such a coil! come, what says Romeo? *Rom. and Jul.* ii 5 67

What a coil's here! Serving of becks and jutting-out of bums! *T. of Athens* i 2 236

What dreams may come When we have shuffled off this mortal coil *Ham.* iii 1 67

Coin. That do coin heaven's image In stamps that are forbid *Meas. for Meas.* ii 4 45

The face of an old Roman coin, scarce seen *L. L. Lost* v 2 617

A coin that bears the figure of an angel Stamped in gold *Mer. of Venice* ii 7 56

We pay them for it with stamped coin, not stabbing steel *W. Tale* iv 4 747

Full thirty thousand marks of English coin *K. John* ii 1 530

We do seize to us The plate, coin, revenues and moveables *Richard II.* ii 1 161

Yea, and elsewhere, so far as my coin would stretch 1 *Hen. IV.* i 2 61

For all the coin in thy father's exchequer ii 2 38

What call you rich? let them coin his nose, let them coin his cheeks iii 3 90

What! did my brother Henry spend his youth, His valour, coin and people, in the wars? 2 *Hen. VI.* i 1 79

A noble spirit, As yours was put into you, ever casts Such doubts, as false coin, from it *Hen. VIII.* iii 1 171

You have caused Your holy hat to be stamp'd on the king's coin iii 2 325

A slave whose gall coins slanders like a mint *Troi. and Cres.* i 3 193

So shall my lungs Coin words till their decay against those measles *Coriolanus* iii 1 78

Know that this gold must coin a stratagem *T. Andron.* ii 3 5

If I want gold, steal but a beggar's dog, And give it Timon, why, the dog coins gold *T. of Athens* ii 1 6

Let molten coin be thy damnation, Thou disease of a friend, and not himself! iii 1 55

Who bates mine honour shall not know my coin iii 3 26

While they have told their money and let out Their coin upon large interest, I myself Rich only in large hurts iii 5 108

I had rather coin my heart, And drop my blood for drachmas *J. Cæsar* iv 3 72

His coin, ships, legions, May be a coward's *Ant. and Cleo.* iii 13 22

Coinage. I'll answer the coinage 1 *Hen. IV.* iv 2 9

This is the very coinage of your brain *Hamlet* iii 4 137

Coined. Almost mightst have coin'd me into gold *Hen. V.* ii 2 98

Though 'Tis not so dear, yet 'tis a life; you coin'd it *Cymbeline* v 4 23

Coiner. Some coiner with his tools Made me a counterfeit ii 5 5

Coining. No, they cannot touch me for coining; I am the king *Lear* iv 6 83

A mother hourly coining plots *Cymbeline* ii 1 64

Coistrel. Thou art the damned doorkeeper to every Coistrel *Pericles* iv 6 176

Co-join. 'Tis very credent Thou mayst co-join with something *W. Tale* i 2 143

Col. Comment appelez-vous le col?—De neck, madame.—De nick *Hen. V.* iii 4 34

Colbrand the giant, that same mighty man *K. John* i 1 225

I am not Samson, nor Sir Guy, nor Colbrand, To mow 'em down before me *Hen. VIII.* v 4 22

Colchos. Which makes her seat of Belmont Colchos' strand, And many Jasons come in quest of her *Mer. of Venice* i 1 171

Cold. To prayers! all lost!—What, must our mouths be cold? *Tempest* i 1 56

The white cold virgin snow upon my heart Abates the ardour of my liver iv 1 55

Yet here they shall not lie, for catching cold *T. G. of Ver.* i 2 136

Methinks my zeal to Valentine is cold, And that I love him not as I was wont ii 4 203

I hope my master's suit will be but cold iv 4 186

My belly's as cold as if I had swallowed snowballs for pills *Mer. Wives* iii 5 23

I rather will suspect the sun with cold Than thee with wantonness iv 4 7

Old, cold, withered and of intolerable entrails v 5 161

You are too cold; if you should need a pin, You could not with more tame a tongue desire it *Meas. for Meas.* ii 2 45

He's sentenced; 'tis too late.—You are too cold.—Too late? why, no ii 2 56

She is so hot because the meat is cold *Com. of Errors* i 2 47

Let him walk from whence he came, lest he catch cold on's feet iii 1 37

Your cake there is warm within; you stand here in the cold iii 1 71

When I am cold, he heats me with beating iv 4 34

A maid, and stuffed! there's goodly catching of cold *Much Ado* iii 4 66

Your suit is cold.—Cold, indeed; and labour lost *Mer. of Venice* ii 7 73

It bites and blows upon my body, Even till I shrink with cold *As Y. Like It* ii 1 9

Were he not warm'd with ale, This were a bed but cold to sleep so soundly *T. of Shrew* Ind. 1 33

Considering the weather, a taller man than I will take cold iv 1 11

Therefore fire; for I have caught extreme cold iv 1 47

Mistress, what cheer?—Faith, as cold as can be iv 3 37

To watch the night in storms, the day in cold v 2 150

I spoke with her but once And found her wondrous cold *All's Well* iii 6 121

When you are dead, you should be such a one As you are now, for you are cold and stern iv 2 8

You smell this business with a sense as cold As is a dead man's nose *W. Tale* ii 1 151

The men are not yet cold under water iii 3 107

The grappling vigour and rough frown of war Is cold in amity *K. John* iii 1 105

I muse your majesty doth seem so cold, When such profound respects do pull you on iii 1 317

The instrument is cold And would not harm me iv 1 104

Entreat the north To make his bleak winds kiss my parched lips And comfort me with cold v 7 41

The nobles they are fled, the commons they are cold *Richard II.* ii 2 88

I towards the north, Where shivering cold and sickness pines the clime v 1 77

Cold. My blood hath been too cold and temperate, Unapt to stir at these indignities 1 *Hen. IV.* i 3 1

I then, all smarting with my wounds being cold i 3 49

'Tis dangerous to take a cold, to sleep, to drink ii 3 9

He told me that rebellion had bad luck And that young Harry Percy's spur was cold 2 *Hen. IV.* i 1 42

Said he young Harry Percy's spur was cold? Of Hotspur Coldspur? i 1 49

What disease hast thou?—A whoreson cold, sir, a cough, sir iii 2 193

Thou shalt go to the wars in a gown; we will have away thy cold iii 2 197

Which, before cold and settled, left the liver white and pale iv 3 112

Blunt not his love, Nor lose the good advantage of his grace By seeming cold iv 4 29

How cold it struck my heart! iv 5 152

All out of work and cold for action! *Hen. V.* i 2 114

It will endure cold as another man's sword will ii 1 10

Then I felt to his knees, and they were as cold as any stone ii 3 27

As cold a night as 'tis, he could wish himself in Thames up to the neck iv 1 119

Constrain'd to watch in darkness, rain and cold 1 *Hen. VI.* ii 1 7

In winter's cold and summer's parching heat 2 *Hen. VI.* i 1 81

After summer evermore succeeds Barren winter, with his wrathful nipping cold ii 4 3

My lord is cold in great affairs, Too full of foolish pity iii 1 224

Naked on a mountain top, Where biting cold would never let grass grow iii 2 337

And, if we use delay, Cold biting winter mars our hoped-for hay 3 *Hen. VI.* iv 8 61

'Tis thy presence that exhales this blood From cold and empty veins *Richard III.* i 2 59

I was too hot to do somebody good, That is too cold in thinking of it now i 3 312

This do I beg of God, When I am cold in zeal to you or yours ii 1 40

In to our tent; the air is raw and cold v 3 46

Cold fearful drops stand on my trembling flesh. What do I fear? myself? v 3 181

One that never in his life Felt so much cold as over shoes in snow v 3 326

How pale she looks, And of an earthy cold? Mark her eyes! *Hen. VIII.* iv 2 98

Trouble not yourself: the morn is cold *Troi. and Cres.* iv 2 1

You will catch cold, and curse me iv 2 15

The veins unfill'd, our blood is cold, and then We pout upon the morning, are unapt To give or to forgive *Coriolanus* v 1 51

Even like a stony image, cold and numb *T. Andron.* iii 1 259

This field-bed is too cold for me to sleep *Rom. and Jul.* ii 1 40

Presently through all thy veins shall run A cold and drowsy humour iv 1 96

Stiff and stark and cold, appear like death iv 1 103

Alas! she's cold; Her blood is settled, and her joints are stiff iv 5 25

Their blood is caked, 'tis cold, it seldom flows; 'Tis lack of kindly warmth they are not kind *T. of Athens* ii 2 225

We both have fed as well, and we can both Endure the winter's cold as well as he *J. Cæsar* i 2 99

Carries anger as the flint bears fire; Who, much enforced, shows a hasty spark, And straight is cold again iv 3 113

Art thou some god, some angel, or some devil, That makest my blood cold and my hair to stare? iv 3 280

Where the Norweyan banners flout the sky And fan our people cold *Macb.* i 2 50

But this place is too cold for hell ii 3 19

Thy blood is cold; Thou hast no speculation in those eyes Which thou dost glare with! iii 4 94

You may Convey your pleasures in a spacious plenty, And yet seem cold iv 3 72

For this relief much thanks: 'tis bitter cold, And I am sick at heart *Hamlet* i 1 8

The air bites shrewdly; it is very cold.—It is a nipping and an eager air i 4 1

'Tis very cold; the wind is northerly.—It is indifferent cold v 2 98

An thou canst not smile as the wind sits, thou'lt catch cold shortly *Lear* i 4 113

How dost, my boy? art cold? I am cold myself iii 2 68

Tom's a-cold,—O do de, do de, do de iii 4 59

Like an old lecher's heart; a small spark, all the rest on's body cold iii 4 118

Cold, cold, my girl! Even like thy chastity *Othello* v 2 275

Like to the time o' the year between the extremes Of hot and cold *Ant. and Cleo.* i 5 52

My salad days, When I was green in judgement: cold in blood i 5 74

Octavia is of a holy, cold, and still conversation ii 6 131

When perforce he could not But pay me terms of honour, cold and sickly He vented them iii 4 7

I found you as a morsel cold upon Dead Cæsar's trencher iii 13 116

Come, away: This case of that huge spirit now is cold iv 15 89

Lest the bargain should catch cold and starve *Cymbeline* i 4 180

It would make any man cold to lose.—But not every man patient ii 3 4

A precedent Which not to read would show the Britons cold iii 1 76

He spake of her, as Dian had hot dreams, And she alone were cold v 5 181

A man throng'd up with cold: my veins are chill *Pericles* ii 1 77

Let not conscience, Which is but cold, inflaming love i' thy bosom, Inflame too nicely iv 1 5

She sent him away as cold as a snowball; saying his prayers too iv 6 149

Cold a companion. 'Tis [virginity] too cold a companion; away with't! *All's Well* i 1 144

Cold an adieu. You have restrained yourself within the list of too cold an adieu ii 1 53

Cold bed. Faintness constraineth me To measure out my length on this cold bed *M. N. Dream* iii 2 429

Go to thy cold bed, and warm thee *T. of Shrew.* Ind. 1 10; *Lear* iii 4 48

Cold bits. Follow your function, go, and fatten on cold bits *Coriolanus* iv 5 36

Cold blood. I thank God and my cold blood *Much Ado* i 1 131

The cold blood he did naturally inherit of his father 2 *Hen. IV.* iv 3 128

Can sodden water, A drench for sur-rein'd jades their barley-broth, Decoct their cold blood to such valiant heat? *Hen. V.* iii 5 20

In whose cold blood no spark of honour bides 3 *Hen. VI.* i 1 184

Who cannot condemn rashness in cold blood? *T. of Athens* iii 5 53

Cold-blooded slave, Hast thou not spoke like thunder on my side? *K. John* iii 1 123

Cold bonds. If you will take this audit, take this life, And cancel these cold bonds *Cymbeline* v 4 28

Cold breath. Words to the heat of deeds too cold breath gives *Macbeth* ii 1 61

Cold brook. Will the cold brook, Candied with ice, caudle thy morning taste, To cure thy o'er-night's surfeit? *T. of Athens* iv 3 225

Cold capon. A cup of Madeira and a cold capon's leg 1 *Hen. IV.* i 2 128

Cold comfort. I do not ask you much, I beg cold comfort *K. John* v 7 42

To thy cold comfort, for being slow in thy hot office *T. of Shrew* iv 1 33

Cold conqueror. Sleeping neglection doth betray to loss The conquest of our scarce cold conqueror 1 *Hen. VI.* iv 3 50

Cold considerance. After this cold considerance, sentence me 2 *Hen. IV.* v 2 98

Cold corpse. For me, the ransom of my bold attempt Shall be this cold corpse on the earth's cold face *Richard III.* v 3 266

Cold cowardice. That which in mean men we intitle patience Is pale cold cowardice in noble breasts . . . . . . *Richard II.* i 2 34
Cold death. With one hand beats Cold death aside . *Rom. and Jul.* iii 1 167
Cold decree. But a hot temper leaps o'er a cold decree . *Mer. of Venice* i 2 20
Cold demeanour. I perceive But cold demeanour in Octavius' wing *J. Cæsar* v 2 4
Cold dew. Herbs that have on them cold dew o' the night *Cymbeline* iv 2 284
Cold dishes. One bred of alms and foster'd with cold dishes ii 3 119
Cold drops. Take pain To allay with some cold drops of modesty Thy skipping spirit . . . *Mer. of Venice* ii 2 195
Cold face. Ere my knee rise from the earth's cold face . 3 *Hen. VI.* ii 3 35
For me, the ransom of my bold attempt Shall be this cold corpse on the earth's cold face . . . . . *Richard III.* v 3 266
Cold fear. His liberal eye doth give to every one, Thawing cold fear *Hen. V.* iv Prol. 45
A faint cold fear thrills through my veins . . *Rom. and Jul.* iv 3 15
Cold field. His chief followers lodge in towns about him, While he himself keeps in the cold field 3 *Hen. VI.* iv 3 14
Cold fire. Feather of lead, bright smoke, cold fire, sick health! Still-waking sleep! . . . . *Rom. and Jul.* i 1 186
Cold fish. It was thought she was a woman and was turned into a cold fish *W. Tale* iv 4 284
Cold friends to Richard . . *Richard III.* iv 4 485
Cold gradation. By cold gradation and well-balanced form, We shall proceed . . . . *Meas. for Meas.* iv 3 104
Cold ground. That barefoot plod I the cold ground upon . *All's Well* iii 4 6
I cannot choose but weep, to think they should lay him i' the cold ground *Hamlet* iv 5 70
Cold hand. The earthy and cold hand of death Lies on my tongue 1 *Hen. IV.* v 4 84
Cold heart. You shall see now in very sincerity of fear and cold heart . ii 3 33
You do not counsel well: You speak it out of fear and cold heart . iv 3 7
Tongues spit their duties out, and cold hearts freeze Allegiance in them *Hen. VIII.* i 2 61
If I be so, From my cold heart let heaven engender hail . *Ant. and Cleo.* iii 13 159
Cold-hearted. Not know me yet?—Cold-hearted toward me? . . iii 13 158
Cold intent. Their cold intent, tenour and substance, thus 2 *Hen. IV.* iv 1 9
Cold lips. More bright in zeal than the devotion which Cold lips blow to their deities . . . . *Troi. and Cres.* iv 4 29
O, take this warm kiss on thy pale cold lips! . *T. Andron.* v 3 153
Cold looks. Gave me cold looks . . . . *Lear* ii 4 37
Cold maids. Our cold maids do dead men's fingers call them *Hamlet* iv 7 172
Cold marble. When I am forgotten, as I shall be, And sleep in dull cold marble . . . . *Hen. VIII.* iii 2 433
Cold meat. There is cold meat i' the cave; we'll browse on that *Cymb.* iii 6 38
Cold modesty. The enemies of Cæsar shall say this; Then, in a friend, it is cold modesty . . . *J. Cæsar* iii 1 213
Cold moon. Chanting faint hymns to the cold fruitless moon *M. N. Dream* i 1 73
Flying between the cold moon and the earth, Cupid all arm'd ii 1 156
Cold-moving. With certain half-caps and cold-moving nods They froze me into silence . . . *T. of Athens* ii 2 221
Cold news for me, for I had hope of France 2 *Hen. VI.* i 1 237; iii 1 87
Cold news, Lord Somerset: but God's will be done! . . iii 1 86
Cold night. This cold night will turn us all to fools and madmen . *Lear* iii 4 80
Cold nymphs. To make cold nymphs chaste crowns *Tempest* iv 1 66
Cold obstruction. To lie in cold obstruction and to rot . *Meas. for Meas.* iii 1 119
Cold palsies, raw eyes, dirt-rotten livers, wheezing lungs . *Troi. and Cres.* v 1 23
Cold porridge. He receives comfort like cold porridge . . *Tempest* ii 1 10
Cold premeditation. A cold premeditation for my purpose! 3 *Hen. VI.* iii 2 133
Cold purses. What think you they portend?—Hot livers and cold purses 1 *Hen. IV.* ii 4 355
Cold scent. He is now at a cold scent . . *T. Night* ii 5 134
Cold sciatica. Thou cold sciatica, Cripple our senators! . *T. of Athens* iv 1 23
Cold sheets. Should he make me Live, like Diana's priest, betwixt cold sheets? . . . . . *Cymbeline* i 6 133
Cold snow melts with the sun's hot beams . 2 *Hen. VI.* iii 1 223
Cold soldier. He's like to be a cold soldier . 2 *Hen. IV.* iii 2 134
Cold statues. Make wells and Niobes of the maids and wives, Cold statues of the youth . . . *Troi. and Cres.* v 10 20
Cold stone. Toad, that under cold stone Days and nights has thirty one *Macbeth* iv 1 6
Cold thin drink. The shepherd's homely curds, His cold thin drink 3 *Hen. VI.* ii 5 48
Cold water. Throw cold water on thy choler . . . *Mer. Wives* ii 3 89
Can you eat roots, and drink cold water? . *T. of Athens* iv 1 77
Cold ways. Those cold ways, That seem like prudent helps, are very poisonous Where the disease is violent *Coriolanus* iii 1 220
Cold weather. Two women placed together makes cold weather *Hen. VIII.* i 4 22
Cold wind. When virtue's steely bones Look bleak i' the cold wind *All's Well* i 1 115
Through the sharp hawthorn blows the cold wind . . *Lear* iii 4 47
Cold wisdom. Full oft we see Cold wisdom waiting on superfluous folly *All's Well* i 1 116
Cold words. Let not my cold words here accuse my zeal . *Richard II.* i 1 47
Cold world. How goes the world?—A cold world . . *T. of Shrew* iv 1 37
Colder. Your writing now Is colder than that theme . *W. Tale* v 1 100
Colder tidings, yet they must be told . . *Richard III.* iv 4 536
If I could temporise with my affection, Or brew it to a weak and colder palate . . . . . . *Troi. and Cres.* iv 4 7
Desire not To allay my rages and revenges with Your colder reasons *Coriolanus* v 3 86
Let his knights have colder looks among you . . *Lear* i 3 22
Bring oil to fire, snow to their colder moods . . ii 2 83
Coldest. Saw'st thou not, boy, how Silver made it good At the hedge-corner, in the coldest fault? . . *T. of Shrew* Ind. 1 20
Oft it hits Where hope is coldest and despair most fits . *All's Well* ii 1 147
Though no man be assured what grace to find, You stand in coldest expectation . . . . . 2 *Hen. IV.* v 2 31
'Tis strange that from their cold'st neglect My love should kindle to inflamed respect . . . . . . *Lear* i 1 257
The most patient man in loss, the most coldest that ever turned up ace *Cymbeline* ii 3 2
Coldly. Yet will I woo for him, but yet so coldly As, heaven it knows, I would not have him speed . . . *T. G. of Ver.* iv 4 111
If he were mad, he would not plead so coldly *Com. of Errors* v 1 272
Bear it coldly but till midnight, and let the issue show itself *Much Ado* iii 2 132
Who is that calls so coldly?—A piece of ice . *T. of Shrew* iv 1 13
You, sir, Charge him too coldly . . . . *W. Tale* i 2 30
O, thus she stood, Even with such life of majesty, warm life, As now it coldly stands! . . . . v 3 36

Coldly. We coldly pause for thee . . . . *K. John* ii 1 53
Grovelling lies, Coldly embracing the discolour'd earth . . . ii 1 306
The French fight coldly, and retire themselves . . . v 3 13
Modest as morning when she coldly eyes The youthful Phœbus *Tr. and Cr.* i 3 229
It lies as coldly in him as fire in a flint . . . iii 3 257
Reason coldly of your grievances, Or else depart *Rom. and Jul.* iii 1 55
The funeral baked meats Did coldly furnish forth the marriage tables *Hamlet* i 2 181
Thou mayst not coldly set Our sovereign process . . iv 3 64
Coldness. Whether 'twas the coldness of the king . 3 *Hen VI.* ii 1 122
Dull not device by coldness and delay . . . *Othello* ii 3 394
Coldspur. Said he young Harry Percy's spur was cold? Of Hotspur Coldspur? . . . . . . 2 *Hen. IV.* i 1 50
Colebrook. The hosts of Readins, of Maidenhead, of Colebrook *Mer. Wives* iv 5 80
Colevile. I am a knight, sir; and my name is Colevile of the dale 2 *Hen. IV.* iv 3 4
Well, then, Colevile is your name, a knight is your degree, and your place the dale: Colevile shall be still your name, a traitor your degree, and the dungeon your place . . . . iv 3 5
Have, in my pure and immaculate valour, taken Sir John Colevile of the dale . . . . iv 3 42
I will have it in a particular ballad else, with mine own picture on the top on't, Colevile kissing my foot . . iv 3 53
Is thy name Colevile?—It is, my lord.—A famous rebel art thou, Colevile iv 3 67
Colic. Oft the teeming earth Is with a kind of colic pinch'd 1 *Hen. IV.* iii 1 29
Blow, villain, till thy sphered bias cheek Outswell the colic of puff'd Aquilon . . . . . *Troi. and Cres.* iv 5 9
If you chance to be pinched with the colic, you make faces like mummers *Coriolanus* ii 1 83
Collar. Ay, while you live, draw your neck out o' the collar *Rom. and Jul.* i 1 6
The collars of the moonshine's watery beams . . . i 4 62
Collateral. In his bright radiance and collateral light Must I be comforted, not in his sphere . . . *All's Well* i 1 99
If by direct or by collateral hand They find us touch'd . *Hamlet* iv 5 206
Colleagued with the dream of his advantage . . . i 2 21
Collect. Affrighted much, I did in time collect myself . *W. Tale.* iii 3 38
Collect them all together at my tent: I'll be before thee *Hen. V.* iv 1 304
The reverent care I bear unto my lord Made me collect these dangers 2 *Hen. VI.* iii 1 35
Collected. Be collected: No more amazement . . *Tempest* i 2 13
Such as his reading And manifest experience had collected . *All's Well* i 3 229
How I have sped among the clergymen, The sums I have collected shall express . . . . . *K. John* iv 2 142
Our navy is address'd, our power collected . 2 *Hen. IV.* iv 4 5
Let our proportions for these wars Be soon collected *Hen. V.* i 2 305
Defences, musters, preparations, Should be maintain'd, assembled and collected . . . . . . ii 4 19
You withhold his levied host, Collected for this expedition 1 *Hen. VI.* iv 4 32
A band of men, Collected choicely, from each county some 2 *Hen. VI.* iii 1 313
Relate what you, Most like a careful subject, have collected *Hen. VIII.* i 2 130
Produce the grand sum of his sins, the articles Collected from his life iii 2 294
Have you collected them by tribes? . . *Coriolanus* iii 3 11
Thou mixture rank, of midnight weeds collected . *Hamlet* iii 2 268
Collected from all simples that have virtue Under the moon . iv 7 145
Collection. The unshaped use of it doth move The hearers to collection iv 5 9
A kind of yesty collection, which carries them through and through the most fond and winnowed opinions . . . . v 2 199
Whose containing Is so from sense in hardness, that I can Make no collection of it . . . . . . *Cymbeline* v 5 432
College. A college of wit-crackers cannot flout me out of my humour *Much Ado* v 4 101
The congregated college have concluded . . *All's Well* ii 1 120
I would the college of the cardinals Would choose him pope . 2 *Hen. VI.* i 3 64
Together with all famous colleges Almost in Christendom *Hen. VIII.* iii 2 66
Collied. Brief as the lightning in the collied night *M. N. Dream* i 1 145
Passion, having my best judgement collied, Assays to lead the way *Othello* ii 3 206
Collier. Since her time are colliers counted bright . *L. L. Lost* iv 3 267
Hang him, foul collier! . . . . *T. Night* iii 4 130
We'll not carry coals.—No, for then we should be colliers *Rom. and Jul.* i 1 3
Collop. Sweet villain! Most dear'st! my collop! . *W. Tale* i 2 137
God knows thou art a collop of my flesh . . 1 *Hen. VI.* v 4 18
Collusion. The collusion holds in the exchange . *L. L. Lost* iv 2 43
Colme's inch. Till he disbursed at Saint Colme's inch Ten thousand dollars . . . . *Macbeth* i 2 61
Colmekill, The sacred storehouse of his predecessors . . ii 4 33
Coloquintida. Shall be to him shortly as bitter as coloquintida . *Othello* i 3 355
Colossus. Nothing but a colossus can do thee that friendship . 1 *Hen. IV.* v 1 123
He doth bestride the narrow world Like a Colossus . *J. Cæsar* i 2 136
Colossus-wise. And stands colossus-wise, waving his beam *Troi. and Cres.* v 5 9
Colour. With colours fairer painted their foul ends . *Tempest* i 2 143
Do you change colour?—Give him leave, madam; he is a kind of chameleon *T. G. of Ver.* ii 4 24
Under the colour of commending him, I have access my own love to prefer . . . . iv 2 3
I must advance the colours of my love And not retire *Mer. Wives* iii 4 85
If I find not what I seek, show no colour for my extremity . iv 2 168
I was beaten myself into all the colours of the rainbow . . iv 5 118
Howsoever you colour it in being a tapster . *Meas. for Meas.* ii 1 231
His beard and head Just of his colour . . . . iv 3 77
And her hair shall be of what colour it please God . . *Much Ado* ii 3 37
Green indeed is the colour of lovers . . . *L. L. Lost* i 2 90
Most maculate thoughts, master, are masked under such colours . i 2 98
I to be a corporal of his field, And wear his colours like a tumbler's hoop! . . . . iii 1 190
I do fear colourable colours . . . . . iv 2 156
Your mistresses dare never come in rain, For fear their colours should be wash'd away . . . . iv 3 271
Of colour like the red rose on triumphant brier . *M. N. Dream* iii 1 96
There are some shrewd contents in yon same paper, That steals the colour from Bassanio's cheek . . . *Mer. of Venice* iii 2 247
Sport! of what colour?—What colour, madam! how shall I answer you? *As Y. Like It* i 2 107
Change you colour?—I prithee, who? . . . . iii 2 192
Boys and women are for the most part cattle of this colour . iii 2 435
His very hair is of the dissembling colour.—Something browner than Judas's . . . . iii 4 8
An excellent colour: your chestnut was ever the only colour . iii 4 12
There was no link to colour Peter's hat . *T. of Shrew* iv 1 137
Strange is it that our bloods, Of colour, weight, and heat, pour'd all together, Would quite confound distinction *All's Well* ii 3 126
My course, Which holds not colour with the time . . . ii 5 64

Colour. Whose villanous saffron would have made all the unbaked and doughy youth of a nation in his colour . . . *All's Well* iv 5 4
Scorn'd a fair colour, or express'd it stolen . . . v 3 50
He that is well hanged in this world needs to fear no colours . *T. Night* i 5 6
I can tell thee where that saying was born, of 'I fear no colours' . . i 5 10
By the colour of his beard, the shape of his leg, the manner of his gait . ii 3 169
My purpose is, indeed, a horse of that colour . . . . . ii 3 182
He will come to her in yellow stockings, and 'tis a colour she abhors . ii 5 220
He went Still in this fashion, colour, ornament, For him I imitate . iii 4 417
What colour are your eyebrows?—Blue, my lord . . *W. Tale* ii 1 13
'Mongst all colours No yellow in't! . . . . . . ii 3 106
I must have saffron to colour the warden pies . . . . . iv 3 48
He hath ribbons of all the colours i' the rainbow . . . . iv 4 205
What colour for my visitation shall I Hold up before him? . . . iv 4 566
Who was most marble there changed colour; some swooned . . . v 2 98
The statue is but newly fix'd, the colour's Not dry . . . . v 3 47
At our importance hither is he come, To spread his colours . *K. John* ii 1 8
Our colours do return in those same hands That did display them when we first march'd forth . . . . ii 1 319
Dissever your united strengths, And part your mingled colours once again ii 1 389
The colour of the king doth come and go Between his purpose and his conscience . . . . iv 2 76
Mocking the air with colours idly spread, And find no check . . . v 1 72
And follow unacquainted colours here . . . . . . v 2 32
Therefore thy threatening colours now wind up . . . . . v 2 73
And wound our tattering colours clearly up . . . . . v 5 7
Unto his captain Christ, Under whose colours he had fought so long *Richard II.* iv 1 100
Never did base and rotten policy Colour her working with such deadly wounds . . . . 1 *Hen. IV.* i 3 109
Of no right, nor colour like to right . . . . . . iii 2 100
With some fine colour that may please the eye Of fickle changelings . v 1 75
I am the Douglas, fatal to all those That wear those colours on them . v 4 27
'Tis no matter if I do halt; I have the wars for my colour 2 *Hen. IV.* i 2 275
How might we see Falstaff bestow himself to-night in his true colours? ii 2 187
Your colour, I warrant you, is as red as any rose, in good truth, la! . ii 4 27
This that you heard was but a colour.—A colour that I fear you will die in . . . . v 5 91
Whose right Suits not in native colours with the truth . . *Hen. V.* i 2 17
Do botch and bungle up damnation With patches, colours, and with forms . . . . ii 2 116
A' could never abide carnation; 'twas a colour he never liked . . ii 3 36
He's of the colour of the nutmeg.—And of the heat of the ginger . iii 7 20
Nor doth he dedicate one jot of colour Unto the weary and all-watched night . . . . iv Prol. 37
Advance our waving colours on the walls . . . 1 *Hen. VI.* i 6 1
I love no colours, and without all colour Of base insinuating flattery I pluck this white rose . . . . ii 4 34
And know us by these colours for thy foes . . . . . ii 4 105
There goes the Talbot, with his colours spread . . . . iii 3 31
You, that were so hot at sea, Disgracing of these colours that I wear iii 4 29
The sanguine colour of the leaves Did represent my master's blushing cheeks . . . . iv 1 92
Prosper our colours in this dangerous fight! . . . . . iv 2 56
Then call our captains and our colours forth . . . . . v 3 128
What colour is my gown of?—Black, forsooth . . 2 *Hen. VI.* ii 1 111
Thou mightst as well have known all our names as thus to name the several colours we do wear . . . . ii 1 128
That he should die is worthy policy; But yet we want a colour for his death . . . . iii 1 236
Whose hopeful colours Advance our half-faced sun . . . . iv 1 97
With colours spread March'd through the city to the palace gates 3 *Hen. VI.* i 1 91
Their colours, often borne in France, And now in England to our heart's great sorrow, Shall be my winding-sheet . . . . . i 1 127
The northern lords that have forsworn thy colours Will follow mine . i 1 251
Let our bloody colours wave! And either victory, or else a grave . . ii 2 173
The red rose and the white are on his face, The fatal colours of our striving houses . . . . ii 5 98
I can add colours to the chameleon, Change shapes with Proteus . . iii 2 191
If about this hour he make this way Under the colour of his usual game iv 5 11
O cheerful colours! see where Oxford comes! . . . . . v 1 58
No one in this presence But his red colour hath forsook his cheeks *Richard III.* ii 1 85
Canst thou quake, and change thy colour, Murder thy breath in middle of a word? . . . . iii 5 1
Unless I have mista'en his colours much . . . . . . v 3 35
'Twas indeed his colour, but he came To whisper Wolsey . *Hen. VIII.* i 1 178
His complexion is higher than his; he having colour enough *Trio. and Cres.* i 2 112
This must be patch'd With cloth of any colour . . *Coriolanus* iii 1 253
This god did shake: His coward lips did from their colour fly *J. Cæsar* i 2 122
Since the quarrel Will bear no colour for the thing he is, Fashion it thus ii 1 29
My hands are of your colour; but I shame To wear a heart so white *Macb.* ii 2 64
There, the murderers, Steep'd in the colours of their trade . . . ii 3 121
Cast thy nighted colour off, And let thine eye look like a friend *Hamlet* i 2 68
Which your modesties have not craft enough to colour . . . ii 2 290
Look, whether he has not turned his colour and has tears in's eyes . ii 2 543
That show of such an exercise may colour Your loneliness . . . iii 1 45
Then what I have to do Will want true colour; tears perchance for blood . . . . iii 4 130
This is a fellow of the self-same colour Our sister speaks of . . *Lear* ii 2 145
Though that his joy be joy, Yet throw such changes of vexation on't, As it may lose some colour . . . . *Othello* i 1 73
Seek no colour for your going, But bid farewell, and go . *Ant. and Cleo.* i 3 32
Let him not leave out The colour of her hair . . . . . ii 5 114
What colour is it of?—Of it own colour too.—'Tis a strange serpent . ii 7 52
Her hair, what colour?—Brown, madam . . . . . . iii 3 35
Put colour in thy cheek . . . . iv 14 69
The approbation of those that weep this lamentable divorce under her colours are wonderfully to extend him . . . *Cymbeline* i 4 20
Against all colour here Did put the yoke upon's . . . . . iii 1 51
To gain his colour I'ld let a parish of such Clotens blood, And praise myself . . . . iv 2 167
O! Give colour to my pale cheek with thy blood, That we the horrider may seem . . . . iv 2 330
Take you the marks of her, the colour of her hair . . *Pericles* iv 2 62
Colourable. I do fear colourable colours . . . *L. L. Lost* iv 2 156
Coloured. I'll get me such a colour'd periwig . . *T. G. of Ver.* iv 4 196
Uncase thee; take my colour'd hat and cloak . . . *T. of Shrew* i 1 212

Coloured. These eyes, that see thee now well coloured, Shall see thee wither'd, bloody, pale and dead . . . . . 1 *Hen. VI.* iv 2 37
Our wits are so diversely coloured . . . . . *Coriolanus* ii 3 22
Yea, bloody cloth, I'll keep thee, for I wish'd Thou shouldst be colour'd thus . . . . *Cymbeline* v 1 2
Colouring. Here's such ado to make no stain a stain As passes colouring *W. Tale* ii 2 20
Colt. Like unback'd colts, they prick'd their ears . . *Tempest* iv 1 176
The hobby-horse is but a colt . . . . . *L. L. Lost* iii 1 33
He hath rid his prologue like a rough colt . . . *M. N. Dream* v 1 120
That's a colt indeed, for he doth nothing but talk of his horse *Mer. of Ven.* i 2 44
Race of youthful and unhandled colts, Fetching mad bounds . . . v 1 72
For young hot colts being raged do rage the more . . *Richard II.* ii 1 70
What a plague mean ye to colt me thus?—Thou liest; thou art not colted, thou art uncolted . . . . 1 *Hen. IV.* ii 2 39
Your colt's tooth is not cast yet . . . . . . *Hen. VIII.* i 3 48
Colted. Thou liest; thou art not colted, thou art uncolted . 1 *Hen. IV.* ii 2 41
Never talk on't; She hath been colted by him . . . *Cymbeline* ii 4 133
Columbine. I am that flower,— That mint.—That columbine *L. L. Lost* v 2 661
There's fennel for you, and columbines: there's rue for you . *Hamlet* iv 5 180
Comagene. Mithridates, king of Comagene . . . *Ant. and Cleo.* iii 6 74
Co-mate. Now, my co-mates and brothers in exile . . *As Y. Like It* ii 1 1
Comb. To comb your noddle with a three-legg'd stool . *T. of Shrew* i 1 64
'Tis seldom when the bee doth leave her comb In the dead carrion 2 *Hen. IV.* iv 4 79
Comb down his hair; look, look! it stands upright . 2 *Hen. VI.* iii 3 15
You are cock and capon too; and you crow, cock, with your comb on *Cymbeline* ii 1 26
Combat. I combat challenge of this latten bilbo . . . *Mer. Wives* i 1 165
Do you not see Pompey is uncasing for the combat? . *L. L. Lost* v 2 708
Gentlemen and soldiers, pardon me; I will not combat in my shirt . v 2 711
I say good queen; And would by combat make her good, so were I A man, the worst about you . . . . *W. Tale* ii 3 60
But O, the noble combat that 'twixt joy and sorrow was fought in Paulina! . . . . v 2 79
What a noble combat thou hast fought Between compulsion and a brave respect! . . . . *K. John* v 2 43
Prosper this realm, keep it from civil broils, Combat with adverse planets in the heavens! . . . . 1 *Hen. VI.* i 1 54
My courage try by combat, if thou darest . . . . . . i 2 89
This proof I'll of thy valour make, In single combat thou shalt buckle with me . . . . i 2 95
Grant me the combat, gracious sovereign.—And me, my lord, grant me the combat too . . . . iv 1 78
And wherefore crave you combat? or with whom? . . . . iv 1 84
Peace be amongst them, if they turn to us; Else, ruin combat with their palaces! . . . . v 2 7
Let these have a day appointed them For single combat . 2 *Hen. VI.* i 3 212
And I accept the combat willingly . . . . i 3 216
The day of combat shall be the last of the next month . . . . i 3 224
This is the day appointed for the combat . . . . . . ii 3 48
Took odds to combat a poor famish'd man . . . . . iv 10 47
A traitor's head, The head of Cade, whom I in combat slew . . . v 1 67
Now sways it this way, like a mighty sea Forced by the tide to combat with the wind . . . . 3 *Hen. VI.* ii 5 6
Though't be a sportful combat, Yet in the trial much opinion dwells *Troi. and Cres.* i 3 335
Invite the Trojan lords after the combat To see us here unarm'd . . iii 3 236
If Hector break not his neck i' the combat, he'll break't himself in vain-glory . . . . iii 3 259
Thereto prick'd on by a most emulate pride, Dared to the combat *Hamlet* i 1 84
Dares me to personal combat, Cæsar to Antony . *Ant. and Cleo.* iv 1 3
Combatant. Sound, trumpets; and set forward, combatants *Richard II.* i 3 117
Bloodstained with these valiant combatants . . 1 *Hen. IV.* i 3 107
Come hither, you that would be combatants . 1 *Hen. VI.* iv 1 134
Sound, trumpets, alarum to the combatants! . . 2 *Hen. VI.* ii 3 95
That the appalled air May pierce the head of the great combatant *Troi. and Cres.* iv 5 5
The combatants being kin Half stints their strife before their strokes begin . . . . iv 5 92
Combated. Such was the very armour he had on When he the ambitious Norway combated . . . . *Hamlet* i 1 61
Combating. Wisdom and blood combating in so tender a body *Much Ado* ii 3 170
His face still combating with tears and smiles . . *Richard II.* v 2 32
Wisdom and fortune combating together, If that the former dare but what it can, No chance may shake it . . . *Ant. and Cleo.* iii 13 79
Combed. Let their heads be sleekly combed . . . *T. of Shrew* iv 1 93
Combinate. Her combinate husband . . . . *Meas. for Meas.* iii 1 231
Combination. A solemn combination shall be made Of our dear souls *T. Night* v 1 392
The articles o' the combination drew As himself pleased . *Hen. VIII.* i 1 169
A combination and a form indeed, Where every god did seem to set his seal . . . . *Hamlet* iii 4 60
Combine. Thy faith my fancy to thee doth combine . *As Y. Like It* v 4 156
Where these two Christian armies might combine The blood of malice in a vein of league . . . . *K. John* v 2 37
And friendship shall combine, and brotherhood . . . *Hen. V.* ii 1 114
God, the best maker of all marriages, Combine your hearts in one! . v 2 388
And tell me, In peace what each of them by the other lose, That they combine not there . . . . *Coriolanus* iii 2 45
And all combined, save what thou must combine By holy marriage *Rom. and Jul.* ii 3 60
Combine together 'gainst the enemy . . . . . . *Lear* v 1 29
Combined. I am combined by a sacred vow And shall be absent *M. for M.* iv 3 149
And all combined, save what thou must combine By holy marriage *Rom. and Jul.* ii 3 60
Let our alliance be combined, Our best friends made . . *J. Cæsar* iv 1 43
Whether he was combined With those of Norway, or did line the rebel With hidden help and vantage . . . . . *Macbeth* i 3 111
Thy knotted and combined locks to part And each particular hair to stand an end . . . . *Hamlet* i 5 18
Noble friends, That which combined us was most great, and let not A leaner action rend us . . . . . . *Ant. and Cleo.* ii 2 18
Combless. What is your crest? a coxcomb?—A combless cock *T. of Shrew* ii 1 227
Combustion. For kindling such a combustion in the state *Hen. VIII.* v 4 51
Dire combustion and confused events New hatch'd to the woeful time *Macbeth* ii 3 63
Come. The hour's now come . . . . *Tempest* i 2 36
I come To answer thy best pleasure . . . . i 2 189
Go take this shape And hither come in't . . . . . . i 2 304

Come unto these yellow sands, And then take hands *Tempest* i 2 375
Come from thy ward, For I can here disarm thee with this stick i 2 471
When every grief is entertain'd that's offer'd, Comes to the entertainer—A dollar.—Dolour comes to him, indeed ii 1 17
Whereof what's past is prologue, what to come In yours and my discharge ii 1 253
Here on this grass-plot, in this very place, To come and sport iv 1 74
Spring come to you at the farthest In the very end of harvest! iv 1 114
The minute of their plot Is almost come iv 1 142
Come with a thought. I thank thee, Ariel: come iv 1 164
You are stay'd for.—Go; I come, I come *T. G. of Ver.* ii 2 20
Now come I to my father; Father, your blessing ii 3 26
Now come I to my mother: O, that she could speak now like a wood woman! ii 3 29
Now come I to my sister; mark the moan she makes ii 3 32
Far behind his worth Comes all the praises that I now bestow ii 4 72
If Proteus like your journey when you come, No matter who's displeased when you are gone ii 7 65
Pray heaven he prove so, when you come to him! ii 7 79
The youthful lover now is gone And this way comes he with it presently iii 1 42
And thereof comes the proverb iii 1 305
No grief did ever come so near thy heart iv 3 19
They will not sit till you come *Mer. Wives* i 1 289
There's pippins and cheese to come i 2 13
'Tis a great charge to come under one body's hand i 4 105
If it were not for one trifling respect, I could come to such honour! ii 1 45
If he come under my hatches, I'll never to sea again ii 1 95
Ere summer comes or cuckoo-birds do sing ii 1 127
You'll come to dinner, George ii 1 161
Look who comes yonder: she shall be our messenger ii 1 163
Come a little nearer this ways ii 2 50
You may come and see the picture, she says, that you wot of ii 2 89
Could I come to her with any detection in my hand, my desires had instance ii 2 255
By gar, he has save his soul, dat he is no come ii 3 7
He has pray his Pible well, dat he is no come ii 3 8
He is dead already, if he be come ii 3 9
Me have stay six or seven, two, tree hours for him, and he is no come ii 3 38
I am come to fetch you home ii 3 54
We are come to you to do a good office iii 1 49
Be gone, and come when you are called iii 3 19
Lisping hawthorn-buds, that come like women in men's apparel iii 3 78
May be he tells you true.—No, heaven so speed me in my time to come! iii 4 12
Master Slender would speak a word with you.—I come to him iii 4 31
Ay, that I will, come cut and long-tail iii 4 47
She desires you once more to come to her iii 5 47
No, I'll come no more i' the basket. May I not go out ere he come? iv 2 50
We'll come dress you straight iv 2 84
Come you and the old woman down; my husband will come into the chamber iv 2 174
What duke should that be comes so secretly? iv 3 5
Fie, fie! he'll never come iv 4 20
Methinks there should be terrors in him that he should not come iv 4 24
Devise but how you'll use him when he comes iv 4 27
Let it not be doubted but he'll come iv 4 43
Sure, he'll come.—Fear not you that iv 4 77
None but he shall have her, Though twenty thousand worthier come to crave her iv 4 90
Come up into my chamber iv 5 131
I come to her in white, and cry 'mum;' she cries 'budget' v 2 6
I pray you, come, hold up the jest no higher v 5 109
Whence comes this restraint?—From too much liberty *Meas. for Meas.* i 2 128
Let mine own judgement pattern out my death, And nothing come in partial ii 1 31
The time is yet to come that she was ever respected with man, woman ii 1 175
' come to visit the afflicted spirits Here in the prison ii 3 4
So play the foolish throngs with one that swoons; Come all to help him, and so stop the air ii 4 25
What's your will, father?—That now you are come, you will be gone iii 1 179
His neck will come to your waist iii 2 42
His child is a year and a quarter old, come Philip and Jacob iii 2 214
I am a brother Of gracious order, late come from the See iii 2 232
The time is come even now. I shall crave your forbearance a little iv 1 22
Very well met, and well come iv 1 26
I have a servant comes with me iv 1 46
Whose persuasion is I come about my brother iv 1 48
Be acquainted with this maid; She comes to do you good iv 1 52
I believe there comes No countermand iv 2 99
Careless, reckless, and fearless of what's past, present, or to come iv 2 152
Clap into your prayers; for, look you, the warrant's come iv 3 45
I am come to advise you, comfort you and pray with you iv 3 54
If you have any thing to say to me, come to my ward iv 3 66
To save me from the danger that might come If he were known alive iv 3 89
Might in the times to come have ta'en revenge iv 4 33
Well, he in time may come to clear himself iv 6 150
As there comes light from heaven and words from breath v 1 225
We shall entreat you to abide here till he come v 1 267
Come you to seek the lamb here of the fox? v 1 300
Put your trial in the villain's mouth Which here you come to accuse v 1 305
Might reproach your life And choke your good to come v 1 427
And all my life to come I'll lend you all my life to do you service v 1 436
Take this mercy to provide For better times to come v 1 490
If any Syracusian born Come to the bay of Ephesus, he dies *Com. of Err.* i 1 20
Weeping before for what she saw must come i 1 72
Stay there, Dromio, till I come to thee i 2 10
I from my mistress come to you in post i 2 63
Time is their master, and when they see time They'll go or come ii 1 9
And about evening come yourself alone iii 1 96
Come to the mart, Where I will walk till thou return to me iii 2 155
On, officer, to prison till it come iv 1 108
Have you not heard men say, That Time comes stealing on by night and day? iv 2 60
And thereof comes that the wenches say 'God damn me' iv 3 53
They are loose again.—And come with naked swords iv 4 148
My tears and prayers Have won his grace to come in person hither v 1 116
The duke himself in person Comes this way v 1 120
Courtesy itself must convert to disdain, if you come in her presence *Much Ado* i 1 124
In their rooms Come thronging soft and delicate desires i 1 305
And then comes repentance ii 1 81

Come. But till all graces be in one woman, one woman shall not come in my grace *Much Ado* ii 3 31
I had as lief have heard the night-raven, come what plague could have come after it ii 3 84
They say I will bear myself proudly, if I perceive the love come from her ii 3 234
If it had been painful, I would not have come ii 3 261
I'll make her come, I warrant you, presently iii 1 14
All the gallants of the town are come to fetch you to church iii 4 97
To be married to her: friar, you come to marry her iv 1 7
These things, come thus to light, Smother her spirits up iv 1 112
And every lovely organ of her life Shall come apparell'd in more precious habit iv 1 229
What, bear her in hand until they come to take hands! iv 1 306
You are almost come to part almost a fray v 1 114
To-morrow morning come you to my house v 1 295
You, who I think hath legs.—And therefore will come v 2 25
Wouldst thou come when I called thee?—Yea, signior, and depart when you bid v 2 42
Will you come presently? v 2 101
Item, That no woman shall come within a mile of my court *L. L. Lost* i 1 120
This article is made in vain, Or vainly comes the admired princess i 1 141
Whose will still wills It should none spare that come within his power ii 1 51
The packet is not come Where that and other specialties are bound ii 1 164
You may not come, fair princess, in my gates ii 1 172
I will come to your worship to-morrow morning iii 1 161
The princess comes to hunt here in the park iii 1 165
Why did he come? to see: why did he see? to overcome iv 1 72
When it comes so smoothly off, so obscenely, as it were, so fit iv 1 145
Your mistresses dare never come in rain iv 3 270
We shall be rich ere we depart, If fairings come thus plentifully in v 2 2
But what, but what, come they to visit us? v 2 119
Ergo I come with this apology v 2 597
Then, at the expiration of the year, Come challenge me v 2 815
Come when the king doth to my lady come v 2 839
And milk comes frozen home in pail v 2 925
Full of vexation come I, with complaint Against my child *M. N. Dream* i 1 22
Why art thou here, Come from the farthest steppe of India? ii 1 69
And you come To give their bed joy and prosperity ii 1 72
And this same progeny of evils comes From our debate ii 1 115
Nor spell nor charm, Come our lovely lady nigh ii 2 18
Say he comes to disfigure, or to present, the person of Moonshine iii 1 61
Anon his Thisbe must be answered, And forth my mimic comes iii 2 19
Look, where thy love comes; yonder is thy dear iii 2 176
Let me come to her.—Get you gone, you dwarf iii 2 328
When I come where he calls, then he is gone iii 2 414
Yet but three? Come one more; Two of both kinds makes up four iii 2 437
Come, sit thee down upon this flowery bed iv 1 1
When my cue comes, call me, and I will answer iv 1 205
Where I have come, great clerks have purposed To greet me v 1 93
We come but in despite. We do not come as minding to content you v 1 112
It will fall pat as I told you. Yonder she comes v 1 189
'Tide life, 'tide death, I come without delay v 1 205
With mirth and laughter let old wrinkles come *Mer. of Venice* i 1 80
My chief care Is to come fairly off from the great debts i 1 128
If e'er the Jew her father come to heaven, It will be for his gentle daughter's sake ii 4 34
There will come a Christian by, Will be worth a Jewess' eye ii 5 42
What, art thou come? On, gentlemen; away! ii 6 58
From the four corners of the earth they come, To kiss this shrine ii 7 39
Are as throughfares now For princes to come view fair Portia ii 7 43
But they come, As o'er a brook, to see fair Portia ii 7 46
To these injunctions every one doth swear That comes to hazard ii 9 18
I long to see Quick Cupid's post that comes so mannerly ii 9 100
A beggar, that was used to come so smug upon the mart iii 1 49
What demi-god Hath come so near creation? iii 2 117
He did intreat me, past all saying nay, To come with him along iii 2 233
If your love do not persuade you to come, let not my letter iii 2 324
In reason he should never come to heaven iii 5 83
Thou art come to answer A strong adversary iv 1 3
A messenger with letters from the doctor, New come from Padua iv 1 109
And here, I take it, is the doctor come iv 1 168
The other half Comes to the privy coffer of the state iv 1 354
I would out-night you, did no body come v 1 23
Who comes so fast in silence of the night? v 1 25
Tell him there's a post come from my master v 1 46
There is come a messenger before, To signify their coming v 1 117
But were the day come, I should wish it dark v 1 304
Yonder comes my master, your brother *As Y. Like It* i 1 28
If he come to-morrow, I'll give him his payment i 1 166
There comes an old man and his three sons i 2 125
I come but in, as others do, to try with him the strength i 2 181
Your praise is come too swiftly home before you ii 3 9
He was furnished like a hunter.—O, ominous! he comes to kill my heart iii 2 260
Soft! comes he not here?—'Tis he: slink by, and note him iii 2 265
Come every day to my cote and woo me iii 2 447
Why did he swear he would come this morning, and comes not? iii 4 20
But till that time Come not thou near me: and when that time comes, Afflict me with thy mocks, pity me not iii 5 32
An you serve me such another trick, never come in my sight more iv 1 41
I come within an hour of my promise iv 1 42
Ay, of a snail; for though he comes slowly, he carries his house on his head iv 1 54
He comes armed in his fortune iv 1 60
'Tis but one cast away, and so, come, death! iv 1 190
If you break one jot of your promise or come one minute behind your hour iv 1 195
I'll go find a shadow and sigh till he come iv 1 223
Undress you and come now to bed *T. of Shrew* Ind. 2 119
If, Biondello, thou wert come ashore, We could at once put us in readiness i 1 42
A good matter, surely: comes there any more of it? i 1 256
I come to wive it wealthily in Padua; If wealthily, then happily i 2 75
My business asketh haste, And every day I cannot come to woo ii 1 116
I will attend her here, And woo her with some spirit when she comes ii 1 170
Is he come?—Why, no, sir.—What then?—He is coming iii 2 35
Who comes with him?—O, sir, his lackey iii 2 65
I am glad he's come, howsoe'er he comes iii 2 76
Didst thou not say he comes?—Who? that Petruchio came?—Ay, that Petruchio came.—No, sir; I say his horse comes, with him on his back iii 2 78
First were we sad, fearing you would not come; Now sadder, that you come so unprovided iii 2 100

Come. I am come to keep my word — *T. of Shrew* iii 2 108
I must away to-day, before night come — iii 2 192
Why, she comes to borrow nothing of them — iv 1 107
Another way I have to man my haggard, To make her come — iv 1 197
Of Mantua, sir? marry, God forbid! And come to Padua? — iv 2 79
'Tis death for any one in Mantua To come to Padua — iv 2 82
But that you are but newly come, You might have heard it else proclaim'd — iv 2 86
Beggars, that come unto my father's door, Upon entreaty have a present alms — iv 3 4
Bid the priest be ready to come against you come with your appendix — iv 4 104
Forward, I pray, since we have come so far — iv 5 12
He whose wife is most obedient To come at first when he doth send for her, Shall win the wager — v 2 68
She is busy and she cannot come.—How! she is busy and she cannot come! — v 2 81
O, ho! entreat her! Nay, then she needs must come — v 2 88
She will not come; she bids you come to her — v 2 92
She will not come! O vile, Intolerable, not to be endured! — v 2 93
If they deny to come, Swinge me them soundly forth unto their husbands — v 2 103
And Florence is denied before he comes — *All's Well* i 2 12
The knaves come to do that for me which I am aweary of — i 3 46
I come to tender it and my appliance With all bound humbleness — ii 1 116
Go thou toward home; where I will never come — ii 5 95
Let me see what he writes, and when he means to come — iii 2 12
You shall hear I am run away: know it before the report come — iii 2 25
Come thou home, Rousillon, Whence honour but of danger wins a scar, As oft it loses all — iii 2 123
Come, night; end, day! For with the dark, poor thief, I'll steal away — iii 2 131
Hark you! they come this way — iii 5 41
Every night he comes With musics of all sorts — iii 7 39
He can come no other way but by this hedge-corner — iv 1 1
When midnight comes, knock at my chamber-window — iv 2 54
We will not meddle with him till he come — iv 3 42
Her death itself, which could not be her office to say is come, was faithfully confirmed — iv 3 68
Give a favour from you To sparkle in the spirits of my daughter, That she may quickly come — v 3 76
Unless she gave it to yourself in bed, Where you have never come — v 3 111
How have you come so early by this lethargy? — *T. Night* i 5 131
Come to what is important in't — i 5 204
If that the youth will come this way to-morrow, I'll give him reasons for't — i 5 324
What's to come is still unsure — ii 3 50
Come kiss me, sweet and twenty, Youth's a stuff will not endure — ii 3 52
And I have heard herself come thus near — ii 5 29
He will come to her in yellow stockings — ii 5 219
I will construe to them whence you come — iii 1 64
I come to whet your gentle thoughts On his behalf — iii 1 116
Look, where the youngest wren of nine comes — iii 2 71
Come, bring us, bring us where he is — iii 2 90
I have sent after him: he says he'll come — iii 4 1
Your ladyship were best to have some guard about you, if he come — iii 4 13
It did come to his hands, and commands shall be executed — iii 4 29
To bed! ay, sweet-heart, and I'll come to thee — iii 4 33
Ay, Biddy, come with me — iii 4 128
This comes with seeking you: But there's no remedy — iii 4 366
I am not sent to you by my lady, to bid you come speak with her — iv 1 7
The curate, who comes to visit Malvolio the lunatic — iv 2 25
If spirits can assume both form and suit You come to fright us — v 1 243
Bade me come smiling and cross-garter'd to you — v 1 345
Let no quarrel nor no brawl to come Taint the condition of this present hour — v 1 364
How will this grieve you, When you shall come to clearer knowledge! — *W. Tale* ii 1 97
Whose ignorant credulity will not Come up to the truth — ii 1 193
Please you, come something nearer — ii 2 55
Not so hot, good sir: I come to bring him sleep — ii 3 33
I Do come with words as medicinal as true — ii 3 37
I say, I come From your good queen.—Good queen! — ii 3 57
As recompense of our dear services Past and to come — ii 3 151
Posts From those you sent to the oracle are come An hour since — ii 3 194
The testimony on my part no other But what comes from myself — iii 2 26
To prate and talk for life and honour 'fore Who please to come and hear — iii 2 43
To me comes a creature, Sometimes her head on one side, some another — iii 3 19
Tarry till my son come; he hallooed but even now — iii 3 78
For the life to come, I sleep out the thought of it — iv 3 31
Fifteen hundred shorn, what comes the wool to? — iv 3 35
Celebration of that nuptial which We two have sworn shall come — iv 4 51
Points more than all the lawyers in Bohemia can learnedly handle, though they come to him by the gross — iv 4 207
Come to the pedlar; Money's a medler — iv 4 328
Let myself and fortune Tug for the time to come — iv 4 508
He shall know within this hour, if I may come to the speech of him — iv 4 786
Though removed fifty times, shall all come under the hangman — iv 4 803
Still, methinks, There is an air comes from her — v 3 78
Here is the strangest controversy Come from the country — *K. John* i 1 45
Brother, adieu: good fortune come to thee! — i 1 180
And then comes answer like an Absey book — i 1 196
But who comes in such haste in riding-robes? — i 1 217
At our importance hither is he come — ii 1 7
With him along is come the mother-queen — ii 1 62
Come to thy grandam, child — ii 1 159
And, like a jolly troop of huntsmen, come Our lusty English — ii 1 321
Rescue those breathing lives to die in beds, That here come sacrifices for the field — ii 1 420
Here is my throne, bid kings come bow to it — iii 1 74
This day, all things begun come to ill end! — iii 1 94
The tidings comes that they are all arrived — iv 2 115
That you shall think the devil is come from hell — iv 3 100
Grapple with him ere he come so nigh — v 1 61
And come ye now to tell me John hath made His peace with Rome? — v 2 91
I come, to learn how you have dealt for him — v 2 121
Befriend me so much as to think I come one way of the Plantagenets — v 6 11
I doubt he will be dead or ere I come — v 6 44
None of you will bid the winter come To thrust his icy fingers in my maw — v 7 36
O cousin, thou art come to set mine eye — v 7 51
Come the three corners of the world in arms, And we shall shock them — v 7 116
Yet one but flatters us, As well appeareth by the cause you come — *Rich. II.* i 1 26

Come. Who hither come engaged by my oath — *Richard II.* i 3 17
Will the king come, that I may breathe my last In wholesome counsel? — ii 1 1
All in vain comes counsel to his ear — ii 1 4
The king is come: deal mildly with his youth — ii 1 69
He is gone to save far off, Whilst others come to make him lose at home — ii 2 81
Now comes the sick hour that his surfeit made — ii 2 84
And I am come to seek that name in England — ii 3 71
To you, my lord, I come, what lord you will — ii 3 76
Thou art a banish'd man, and here art come Before the expiration of thy time — ii 3 110
But as I come, I come for Lancaster — ii 3 114
But in this kind to come, in braving arms, Be his own carver — ii 3 143
Thy sun sets weeping in the lowly west, Witnessing storms to come — ii 4 22
Comes at the last and with a little pin Bores through his castle wall — iii 2 169
Fear, and be slain; no worse can come to fight — iii 2 183
Hither come Even at his feet to lay my arms and power — iii 3 38
He is come to open The purple testament of bleeding war — iii 3 93
Yet he is come.—Stand all apart — iii 3 186
I come but for mine own.—Your own is yours, and I am yours, and all — iii 3 196
I come to thee From plume-pluck'd Richard — iv 1 107
Read o'er this paper while the glass doth come — iv 1 269
Fiend, thou torment'st me ere I come to hell! — iv 1 270
A woeful pageant have we here beheld.—The woe's to come — iv 1 322
This way the king will come — v 1 1
Hence, villain! never more come in my sight — v 2 86
Let your mother in: I know she is come to pray for your foul sin — v 3 82
His words come from his mouth, ours from our breast — v 3 102
As thus, 'Come, little ones,' and then again, 'It is as hard to come as for a camel To thread the postern of a small needle's eye' — v 5 15
Where no man never comes but that sad dog That brings me food — v 5 70
But come yourself with speed to us again — *1 Hen. IV.* i 1 105
But when they seldom come, they wish'd for come — i 2 230
An if the devil come and roar for them, I will not send them — i 3 125
Or fill up chronicles in time to come — i 3 171
What time do you mean to come to London? — ii 1 47
All the titles of good fellowship come to you! — ii 4 308
He says he comes from your father — ii 4 319
It is like, if there come a hot June — ii 4 396
They are come to search the house — ii 4 537
I can call spirits from the vasty deep.—Why, so can I, or so can any man; But will they come when you do call for them? — iii 1 54
And in my conduct shall your ladies come — iii 1 92
The time will come, That I shall make this northern youth exchange His glorious deeds for my indignities — iii 2 144
These letters come from your father.—Letters from him! why comes he not himself?—He cannot come, my lord — iv 1 14
Who leads his power? Under whose government come they along? — iv 1 19
Let them come; They come like sacrifices in their trim — iv 1 112
O that Glendower were come! — iv 1 124
Tattered prodigals lately come from swine-keeping — iv 2 37
Certain horse Of my cousin Vernon's are not yet come up — iv 3 20
If he do come in my way, so: if he do not, if I come in his willingly, let him make a carbonado of me — v 3 60
Give me life: which if I can save, so; if not, honour comes unlooked for, and there's an end — v 3 64
The hour is come To end the one of us — v 4 68
The posts come tiring on — *2 Hen. IV.* Ind. 37
What good tidings comes with you? — i 1 33
You would not come when I sent for you — i 2 121
I sent for you, when there were matters against you for your life, to come speak with me — i 2 151
Past and to come seems best; things present worst — i 3 108
An I but fist him once; an a' come but within my vice — ii 1 23
A' comes continuantly to Pie-corner — ii 1 28
Yonder he comes; and that arrant malmsey-nose knave, Bardolph — ii 1 42
It is not a confident brow, nor the throng of words that come with such — ii 1 122
For to serve bravely is to come halting off, you know — ii 4 54
Shut the door; there comes no swaggerers here — ii 4 83
Come we to full points here; and are etceteras nothing? — ii 4 198
The music is come, sir.—Let them play — ii 4 245
And I come to draw you out by the ears — ii 4 313
O Jesu, are you come from Wales? — ii 4 318
There are twenty weak and wearied posts Come from the north — ii 4 386
Run, good Doll: come. [*She comes blubbered.*] Yea, will you come, Doll? — ii 4 420
But, ere they come, bid them o'er-read these letters — iii 1 2
'The time shall come,' thus did he follow it, 'The time will come, that foul sin, gathering head, Shall break into corruption' — iii 1 75
Bullcalf, grow till you come unto it: I will none of you — iii 2 270
'Bounce' would a' say; and away again would a' go, and again would a' come — iii 2 305
This offer comes from mercy, not from fear — iv 1 150
We come within our awful banks again — iv 1 176
Set forward.—Before, and greet his grace: my lord, we come — iv 1 228
Sudden sorrow Serves to say thus, 'some good thing comes to-morrow' — iv 2 84
When every thing is ended, then you come — iv 3 30
When you come to court, Stand my good lord, pray, in your good report — iv 3 88
There's never none of these demure boys come to any proof — iv 3 97
Till these rebels, now afoot, Come underneath the yoke of government — iv 4 10
Comes to no further use But to be known and hated — iv 4 72
May they fall As those that I am come to tell you of! — iv 4 96
Will Fortune never come with both hands full? — iv 4 103
For now a time is come to mock at form — iv 5 119
Come, come, come, off with your boots — v 1 60
There's one Pistol come from the court with news — v 3 85
If, sir, you come with news from the court, I take it there's but two ways, either to utter them, or to conceal them — v 3 114
O the Lord, that Sir John were come! — v 4 13
Well, of sufferance comes ease — v 4 28
Come, you rogue, come; bring me to a justice — v 4 29
'Twill be two o'clock ere they come from the coronation — v 5 4
If like an ill venture it come unluckily home, I break — Epil. 13
The hour, I think, is come To give him hearing — *Hen. V.* i 1 92
To her unguarded nest the weasel Scot Comes sneaking — i 2 171
You must come to my master, and you, hostess — ii 1 85
It is most lamentable to behold. Sweet men, come to him — ii 1 125
Thus comes the English with full power upon us — ii 4 1
Knocks go and come; God's vassals drop and die — iii 2 8
You must come presently to the mines — iii 2 58
Tell you the duke, it is not so good to come to the mines — iii 2 62

Come. As bootless spend our vain command Upon the enraged soldiers in their spoil As send precepts to the leviathan To come ashore *Hen. V.* iii 3 27
Come, come, away! The sun is high and we outwear the day iv 2 62
And York, all haggled over, Comes to him, where in gore he lay iv 6 12
I come to thee for charitable license iv 7 74
Soldier, you must come to the king iv 7 124
All offences, my lord, come from the heart iv 8 49
When I come to woo ladies, I fright them v 2 245
What's past and what's to come she can descry 1 *Hen. VI.* i 2 57
Come, come from behind; I know thee well, though never seen before i 2 66
Come, o' God's name; I fear no woman i 2 102
I am come to survey the Tower this day i 3 1
A holy prophetess new risen up Is come with a great power i 4 103
Farewell; thy hour is not yet come i 5 13
According as your ladyship desired, By message craved, so is Lord Talbot come ii 3 13
But tell me, keeper, will my nephew come? ii 5 17
Like the vulgar sort of market men That come to gather money for their corn iii 2 5
Poor market folks that come to sell their corn iii 2 15
Will ye, like soldiers, come and fight it out? iii 2 66
Now in the rearward comes the duke and his iii 3 33
There comes the ruin, there begins confusion iv 1 194
Too late comes rescue: he is ta'en or slain iv 4 42
Now thou art come unto a feast of death iv 5 7
Now the time is come That France must vail her lofty-plumed crest v 3 24
We come to be informed by yourselves v 4 118
Come, let us in, and with all speed provide To see her coronation 2 *Hen. VI.* i 1 73
A day will come when York shall claim his own i 1 239
Come, Nell, thou wilt ride with us? i 2 59
My lord protector will come this way by and by i 3 2
Come, my masters; the duchess, I tell you, expects performance of your promises i 4 1
Come with thy two-hand sword ii 1 46
A miracle!—Come to the king and tell him what miracle ii 1 62
Simpcox, come, Come, offer at my shrine, and I will help thee ii 1 92
Let them be whipped through every market-town, till they come to Berwick ii 1 159
I think she comes; and I'll prepare My tear-stain'd eyes to see her miseries ii 4 15
Come you, my lord, to see my open shame? ii 4 19
I muse my Lord of Gloucester is not come iii 1 1
And yet, good Humphrey, is the hour to come That e'er I proved thee false iii 1 204
Faster than spring-time showers comes thought on thought iii 1 337
From Ireland come I with my strength And reap the harvest which that rascal sow'd iii 1 380
Come, basilisk, And kill the innocent gazer with thy sight iii 2 52
Come, Warwick, come, good Warwick, go with me iii 2 298
Come, soldiers, show what cruelty ye can iv 1 132
Therefore come you with us and let him go iv 1 141
Come, and get thee a sword, though made of a lath iv 2 1
Come, come, let's fall in with them iv 2 32
Over whom, in time to come, I hope to reign iv 2 138
The bodies shall be dragged at my horse heels till I do come to London iv 3 15
Come, then, let's go fight with them iv 6 15
We come ambassadors from the king Unto the commons iv 8 7
The Duke of York is newly come from Ireland iv 9 24
Here's the lord of the soil come to seize me for a stray iv 10 26
And, like a thief, to come to rob my grounds iv 10 36
I have eat no meat these five days; yet, come thou and thy five men iv 10 42
From Ireland thus comes York to claim his right v 1 1
Of one or both of us the time is come v 2 13
Come, thou new ruin of old Clifford's house v 2 61
Shall be eternized in all age to come v 3 31
When the king comes, offer him no violence 3 *Hen. VI.* i 1 33
Come, son, let's away; Our army is ready; come, we'll after them i 1 255
Come, son, away; we may not linger thus i 1 263
You are come to Sandal in a happy hour i 2 63
Look where bloody Clifford comes! i 3 2
And so he comes, to rend his limbs asunder i 3 15
Why come you not? what! multitudes, and fear? i 4 39
Come, make him stand upon this molehill here i 4 67
And in thy need such comfort come to thee As now I reap! i 4 165
I come to tell you things sith then befall'n ii 1 106
Norfolk and myself, In haste, post-haste, are come to join with you ii 1 139
Through this laund anon the deer will come iii 1 2
Ay, but she's come to beg, Warwick, to give iii 1 42
We will consider of your suit; And come some other time to know our mind iii 2 17
Am come to crave thy just and lawful aid iii 3 32
I come, in kindness and unfeigned love iii 3 51
Then I degraded you from being king, And come now to create you Duke of York iv 3 34
I am inform'd that he comes towards London iv 4 26
Come, therefore, let us fly while we may fly iv 4 34
Come then, away; let's ha' no more ado iv 5 27
Come, therefore, let's about it speedily iv 6 102
But why come you in arms?—To help King Edward iv 7 42
And be gone To keep them back that come to succour you iv 7 56
Shall rest in London till we come to him iv 8 22
O unbid spite! is sportful Edward come? v 1 18
Come, Warwick, take the time; kneel down, kneel down v 1 48
O cheerful colours! see where Oxford comes! v 1 58
Come quickly, Montague, or I am dead v 2 39
And lo, where youthful Edward comes! v 5 11
So come to you and yours, as to this prince! v 5 82
But wherefore dost thou come? is't for my life? v 6 29
Dive, thoughts, down to my soul: here Clarence comes *Richard III.* i 1 41
He is in heaven, where thou shalt never come i 2 106
But now the Duke of Buckingham and I Are come from visiting his majesty i 3 32
The time will come when thou shalt wish for me To help thee curse i 3 245
Catesby, we come. Lords, will you go with us? i 3 322
Are you now going to dispatch this deed?—We are, my lord; and come to have the warrant i 3 342
And he squeak'd out aloud, 'Clarence is come' i 4 55
How if it [conscience] come to thee again?—I'll not meddle with it i 4 136
Wherefore do you come?—To, to, to— To murder me? i 4 177
Come. O, if thine eye be not a flatterer, Come thou on my side, and entreat for me *Richard III.* i 4 272
The king is dead.—Bad news, by'r lady; seldom comes the better ii 3 4
The mayor of London comes to greet you iii 1 17
Will our mother come?—On what occasion, God he knows, not I iii 1 25
The tender prince Would fain have come with me to meet your grace iii 1 29
If our brother come, Where shall we sojourn till our coronation? iii 1 61
Come the next Sabbath, and I will content you iii 2 113
Will not the mayor then and his brethren come? iii 7 44
Are come to have some conference with his grace iii 7 69
By heaven, I come in perfect love to him iii 7 90
You come to reprehend my ignorance iii 7 113
In this just suit come I to move your grace iii 7 140
And, in good time, here the lieutenant comes iv 1 12
Let me have open means to come to them iv 2 77
O, thou didst prophesy the time would come! iv 4 79
Bound with triumphant garlands will I come iv 4 333
What canst thou swear by now?—The time to come iv 4 387
Swear not by time to come; for that thou hast Misused ere used iv 4 395
Unless for that he comes to be your liege, You cannot guess wherefore the Welshman comes iv 4 476
About the mid of night come to my tent And help to arm me v 3 77
Will he bring his power?—My lord, he doth deny to come v 3 343
Enrich the time to come with smooth-faced peace v 5 33
Only they That come to hear a merry bawdy play *Hen. VIII.* Prol. 14
Lo, where comes that rock That I advise your shunning i 1 113
The subjects' grief Comes through commissions i 2 57
Through our intercession this revokement And pardon comes i 2 107
Made suit to come in's presence i 2 197
You that thus far have come to pity me, Hear what I say ii 1 56
The queen shall be acquainted Forthwith for what you come ii 2 109
We are contented To wear our mortal state to come with her ii 4 228
You come to take your stand here iv 1 2
Yet there is no great breach; when it comes, Cranmer will find a friend iv 1 106
An old man, broken with the storms of state, Is come to lay his weary bones among ye iv 2 22
Come, come, give me your hand v 1 94
His royal self in judgement comes to hear The cause v 3 120
Some strange Indian with the great tool come to court v 4 35
Besides the running banquet of two beadles that is to come v 4 70
Some come to take their ease, And sleep an act or two Epil. 2
To Tenedos they come *Troi. and Cres.* Prol. 11
When fair Cressid comes into my thoughts,—So, traitor! 'When she comes!' When is she thence? i 1 30
I cannot come to Cressid but by Pandar i 1 98
Troilus will not come far behind him i 2 59
When comes Troilus? I'll show you Troilus anon i 2 209
Swords! any thing, he cares not; an the devil come to him, it's all one i 2 228
Yonder comes Paris, yonder comes Paris i 2 229
What sneaking fellow comes yonder? i 2 246
Good boy, tell him I come. I doubt he be hurt i 2 301
'Tis for Agamemnon's ears.—He hears nought privately that comes from Troy i 3 249
The baby figure of the giant mass Of things to come at large i 3 346
Dog!—Then would come some matter from him ii 1 9
I will see you hanged, like clotpoles, ere I come any more to your tents ii 1 129
Let us pay betimes A moiety of that mass of moan to come ii 2 107
And fame in time to come canonize us ii 2 202
Art thou come? why, my cheese, my digestion ii 3 43
And here's a lord,—come knights from east to west, And cull their flower ii 3 274
They're come from field iii 1 161
True swains in love shall in the world to come Approve their truths by Troilus iii 2 180
Which, you say, live to come in my behalf iii 3 16
What, comes the general to speak with me? iii 3 55
Come as humbly as they used to creep To holy altars iii 3 73
Invite the most valorous Hector to come unarmed to my tent iii 3 276
I come from the worthy Achilles iii 3 283
My lord, come you again into my chamber iv 2 37
The hour prefix'd Of her delivery to this valiant Greek Comes fast upon iv 3 3
Some say the Genius so Cries 'come' to him that instantly must die iv 4 53
Come, stretch thy chest, and let thy eyes spout blood iv 5 10
So glib of tongue, That give accosting welcome ere it comes! iv 5 59
Half heart, half hand, half Hector comes to seek This blended knight iv 5 85
What's past and what's to come is strew'd with husks And formless ruin iv 5 166
It is prodigious, there will come some change v 1 101
What, shall I come? the hour?—Ay, come:—O Jove!—do come v 2 104
Believe, I come to lose my arm, or win my sleeve v 3 96
Noseless, handless, hack'd and chipp'd, come to him, Crying on Hector v 5 34
Come, both you cogging Greeks; have at you both! v 6 11
How the sun begins to set; How ugly night comes breathing at his heels v 8 6
It proceeds or comes from them to you And no way from yourselves *Coriolanus* i 1 157
The Lady Valeria is come to visit you i 3 29
Over and over he comes, and up again; catched it again i 3 68
Yonder comes news. A wager they have met i 4 1
Come I too late?—Ay, if you come not in the blood of others, But mantled in your own i 6 27
He comes the third time home with the oaken garland ii 1 137
Wouldst thou have laugh'd had I come coffin'd home? ii 1 193
To Coriolanus come all joy and honour! ii 2 158
He must come, Or what is worst will follow iii 1 335
Come all to ruin iii 2 125
What, will he come?—He's coming iii 3 6
Some news is come That turns their countenances iv 6 58
When he shall come to his account, he knows not What I can urge against him iv 7 18
He hath left undone That which shall break his neck or hazard mine, Whene'er we come to our account iv 7 26
Bury him where you can; he comes not here *T. Andron.* i 1 354
Had you not by wondrous fortune come ii 3 112
Thou canst not come to me: I come to thee ii 3 245
But who comes with our brother Marcus here? iii 1 58
Plot some device of further misery, To make us wonder'd at in time to come iii 1 135
Come, agree whose hand shall go along, For fear they die before their pardon come iii 1 175

Come. And threat me I shall never come to bliss . . *T. Andron.* iii 1 273
Between us we can kill a fly That comes in likeness of a coal-black Moor iii 2 78
See how swift she comes . . . iv 1 3
When you come to Pluto's region, I pray you, deliver him this petition iv 3 13
The post is come. Sirrah, what tidings? . . . iv 3 77
Why, didst thou not come from heaven? . . . iv 3 88
When you come to him, at the first approach you must kneel . . iv 3 110
Few come within the compass of my curse . . . v 1 126
We will come. March away . . . v 1 165
Tell him Revenge is come to join with him . . . v 2 7
Titus, I am come to talk with thee.—No, not a word . . . v 2 16
Do me some service, ere I come to thee . . . v 2 44
Then I'll come and be thy waggoner, And whirl along with thee . . v 2 48
These are my ministers, and come with me . . . v 2 60
O sweet Revenge, now do I come to thee . . . v 2 67
Bid him come and banquet at thy house . . . v 2 114
I'll play the cook, And see them ready 'gainst their mother comes . v 2 206
Old Montague is come, And flourishes his blade in spite of me *R. and J.* i 1 84
Come you this afternoon, To know our further pleasure in this case . i 1 107
A fair assembly: whither should they come? . . . i 2 75
I pray, come and crush a cup of wine . . . i 2 85
At twelve year old, I bade her come . . . i 3 3
Come Lammas-eve at night shall she be fourteen . . . i 3 17
The guests are come, supper served up . . . i 3 100
She comes In shape no bigger than an agate-stone . . . i 4 54
Sometime comes she with a tithe-pig's tail . . . i 4 79
Come pentecost as quickly as it will . . . i 5 38
As sweet repose and rest Come to thy heart as that within my breast! . ii 2 124
Send me word to-morrow, By one that I'll procure to come to thee . ii 2 145
Madam!—By and by, I come . . . ii 2 152
I would have made it short: for I was come to the whole depth of my tale . . . ii 4 104
Will you come to your father's? we'll to dinner, thither . . . ii 4 147
From nine till twelve Is three long hours, yet she is not come . . ii 5 11
O God, she comes! O honey nurse, what news? . . . ii 5 18
Now comes the wanton blood up in your cheeks . . . ii 5 72
But come what sorrow can, It cannot countervail the exchange of joy . ii 6 3
Come, come with me, and we will make short work . . . ii 6 35
Come, night; come, Romeo; come, thou day in night . . . iii 2 17
Come, gentle night, come, loving, black-brow'd night, Give me my Romeo . . . iii 2 20
Shame come to Romeo!—Blister'd be thy tongue For such a wish! . iii 2 90
And bid him come to take his last farewell . . . iii 2 143
I come, I come! Who knocks so hard? whence come you? what's your will? . . . iii 3 77
My lord, I'll tell my lady you will come . . . iii 3 161
All these woes shall serve For sweet discourses in our time to come . iii 5 53
O, how my heart abhors To hear him named, and cannot come to him! iii 5 101
I wonder at this haste; that I must wed Ere he, that should be husband, comes to woo . . . iii 5 120
Come you to make confession to this father? . . . iv 1 22
Shall I come to you at evening mass? . . . iv 1 38
Come weep with me; past hope, past cure, past help! . . . iv 1 45
When the bridegroom in the morning comes To rouse thee from thy bed iv 1 107
Hither shall he come: and he and I Will watch thy waking . . iv 1 115
How if, when I am laid into the tomb, I wake before the time that Romeo Come to redeem me? . . . iv 3 32
And there die strangled ere my Romeo comes . . . iv 3 35
Romeo, I come! this do I drink to thee . . . iv 3 58
For shame, bring Juliet forth; her lord is come . . . iv 5 22
Keep her at my cell till Romeo come . . . v 2 28
And here is come to do some villanous shame To the dead bodies . . v 3 52
Lady, come from that nest Of death, contagion, and unnatural sleep . v 3 151
Search, seek, and know how this foul murder comes . . . v 3 198
Then comes she to me, And, with wild looks, bid me devise some mean To rid her from this second marriage . . . v 3 239
I writ to Romeo, That he should hither come . . . v 3 247
Anon comes one with light to ope the tomb . . . v 3 283
When comes your book forth? . . . *T. of Athens* i 1 26
I come to have thee thrust me out of doors . . . i 2 25
I come to observe; I give thee warning on't.—I take no heed of thee . i 2 33
There comes with them a forerunner . . . i 2 124
They only now come but to feast thine eyes . . . i 2 133
Hoy-day, what a sweep of vanity comes this way! They dance! . . i 2 137
Farewell; and come with better music . . . i 2 252
When men come to borrow of your masters, they approach sadly . . ii 2 105
Come with me, fool, come.—I do not always follow lover . . ii 2 129
Which, in my lord's behalf, I come to entreat your honour to supply . iii 1 17
Yonder comes a poet and a painter: the plague of company light upon thee! . . . iv 3 356
Suspect still comes where an estate is least . . . iv 3 521
We are hither come to offer you our service . . . v 1 75
Thither come, And let my grave-stone be your oracle . . . v 1 221
And do you now strew flowers in his way That comes in triumph over Pompey's blood? . . . *J. Cæsar* i 1 56
Let me see his face.—Fellow, come from the throng . . . i 2 21
Come on my right hand, for this ear is deaf . . . i 2 213
Comes Cæsar to the Capitol to-morrow?—He doth . . . i 3 36
Come and call me here.—I will, my lord . . . ii 1 8
It seems to me most strange that men should fear; Seeing that death, a necessary end, Will come when it will come . . . ii 2 37
I come to fetch you to the senate-house.—And you are come in very happy time . . . ii 2 59
Bear my greeting to the senators And tell them that I will not come to-day; Cannot, is false, and that I dare not, falser: I will not come to-day . . . ii 2 62
Tell them Cæsar will not come.—Most mighty Cæsar, let me know some cause . . . ii 2 68
The cause is in my will: I will not come; That is enough . . . ii 2 71
If you shall send them word you will not come, Their minds may change . . . ii 2 95
Look where Publius is come to fetch me . . . ii 2 108
The ides of March are come.—Ay, Cæsar; but not gone . . . iii 1 1
What, urge you your petitions in the street? Come to the Capitol . iii 1 12
If Brutus will vouchsafe that Antony May safely come to him . . iii 1 131
Tell him, so please him come unto this place, He shall be satisfied . iii 1 140
With Ate by his side come hot from hell . . . iii 1 271
Cæsar did write for him to come to Rome . . . iii 1 278
I come to bury Cæsar, not to praise him . . . iii 2 79
Come I to speak in Cæsar's funeral . . . iii 2 89

Come. I fear there will a worse come in his place . . . *J. Cæsar* iii 2 116
Here was a Cæsar! when comes such another? . . . iii 2 257
Comes his army on?—They mean this night in Sardis to be quarter'd . iv 2 27
The greater part, the horse in general, Are come with Cassius . . iv 2 30
Let no man Come to our tent till we have done our conference . . iv 2 51
You shall not come to them.—Nothing but death shall stay me . . iv 3 127
Come yourselves, and bring Messala with you Immediately to us . . iv 3 141
Never come such division 'tween our souls! Let it not, Brutus . . iv 3 235
If you dare fight to-day, come to the field . . . v 1 65
O, that a man might know The end of this day's business ere it come! . v 1 124
Our day is gone; Clouds, dews, and dangers come; our deeds are done! v 3 64
I know my hour is come . . . v 5 20
I come, Graymalkin!—Paddock calls . . . *Macbeth* i 1 8
So from that spring whence comfort seem'd to come Discomfort swells i 2 27
Here I have a pilot's thumb, Wreck'd as homeward he did come . . i 3 29
A drum, a drum! Macbeth doth come . . . i 3 31
Come, you spirits That tend on mortal thoughts, unsex me here! . . i 5 41
Come to my woman's breasts, And take my milk for gall! . . . i 5 48
Come, thick night, And pall thee in the dunnest smoke of hell! . . i 5 51
Which shall to all our nights and days to come Give solely sovereign sway . . . i 5 70
But here, upon this bank and shoal of time, We'ld jump the life to come i 7 7
If there come truth from them—As upon thee, Macbeth, their speeches shine . . . iii 1 6
Rather than so, come fate into the list, And champion me to the utterance! . . . iii 1 71
Resolve yourselves apart: I'll come to you anon . . . iii 1 139
Fleance is 'scaped.—Then comes my fit again . . . iii 4 21
Fly to the court of England and unfold His message ere he come . . iii 6 47
By the pricking of my thumbs, Something wicked this way comes . iv 1 45
Come, high or low; Thyself and office deftly show! . . . iv 1 67
Show his eyes, and grieve his heart; Come like shadows, so depart! . iv 1 111
Not in the legions Of horrid hell can come a devil more damn'd In evils iv 3 56
Comes the king forth, I pray you? . . . iv 3 140
I will set down what comes from her, to satisfy my remembrance . . v 1 37
To bed, to bed! there's knocking at the gate: come, come, come, come v 1 74
The cry is still 'They come:' our castle's strength Will laugh a siege to scorn . . . v 5 2
'Fear not, till Birnam wood Do come to Dunsinane:' and now a wood Comes toward Dunsinane . . . v 5 45
Though Birnam wood be come to Dunsinane, And thou opposed, being of no woman born, Yet I will try . . . v 8 30
You come most carefully upon your hour.—'Tis now struck twelve *Hamlet* i 1 6
If again this apparition come, He may approve our eyes and speak to it i 1 28
Well may it sort that this portentous figure Comes armed through our watch . . . i 1 110
Ever 'gainst that season comes Wherein our Saviour's birth is celebrated i 1 158
Would the night were come! Till then sit still, my soul . . . i 2 256
Look, my lord, it comes!—Angels and ministers of grace defend us! . i 4 38
Have after. To what issue will this come? . . . i 4 89
My hour is almost come, When I to sulphurous and tormenting flames Must render up myself . . . i 5 2
Hillo, ho, ho, my lord!—Hillo, ho, ho, boy! come, bird, come . . i 5 116
There needs no ghost, my lord, come from the grave To tell us this . i 5 125
Come you more nearer Than your particular demands will touch it . ii 1 11
Rather say, the cause of this defect, For this effect defective comes by cause . . . ii 2 103
Look, where sadly the poor wretch comes reading . . . ii 2 168
I think their inhibition comes by the means of the late innovation . ii 2 346
That great baby you see there is not yet out of his swaddling-clouts.—Happily he's the second time come to them . . . ii 2 402
I will prophesy he comes to tell me of the players . . . ii 2 405
For look, where my abridgement comes . . . ii 2 439
Say on: come to Hecuba . . . ii 2 523
For in that sleep of death what dreams may come . . . iii 1 66
Sleep rock thy brain; And never come mischance between us twain! . iii 2 238
Then I will come to my mother by and by . . . iii 2 400
Do you not come your tardy son to chide? . . . iii 4 106
Confess yourself to heaven; Repent what's past; avoid what is to come iii 4 150
Go seek him there.—He will stay till you come . . . iv 3 41
Her brother is in secret come from France . . . iv 5 88
There's a letter for you, sir; it comes from the ambassador . . iv 6 9
But my revenge will come.—Break not your sleeps for that . . iv 7 29
There with fantastic garlands did she come . . . iv 7 169
But if the water come to him and drown him, he drowns not himself . v 1 20
The toe of the peasant comes so near the heel of the courtier . . v 1 152
Let her paint an inch thick, to this favour she must come . . v 1 214
Is't not to be damn'd, To let this canker of our nature come In further evil? . . . v 2 69
Sir, here is newly come to court Laertes . . . v 2 110
It would come to immediate trial, if your lordship would vouchsafe the answer . . . v 2 175
If it be now, 'tis not to come; if it be not to come, it will be now; if it be not now, yet it will come: the readiness is all . . . v 2 232
Part them; they are incensed.—Nay, come, again . . . v 2 314
This villain of mine comes under the prediction . . . *Lear* i 2 119
And pat he comes like the catastrophe of the old comedy . . i 2 146
So may it come, thy master, whom thou lovest, Shall find thee full of labours . . . i 4 6
Woe, that too late repents,—O, sir, are you come? Is it your will? . i 4 279
Acquaint my daughter no further with any thing you know than comes from her demand out of the letter . . . i 5 3
My worthy arch and patron comes to-night . . . ii 1 61
I know not why he comes. All ports I'll bar . . . ii 1 81
If they come to sojourn at my house, I'll not be there . . . ii 1 105
You rascal: you come with letters against the king . . . ii 2 38
How chance the king comes with so small a train? . . . ii 4 64
She would soon be here. Is your lady come? . . . ii 4 187
Dismissing half your train, come then to me . . . ii 4 207
Let shame come when it will, I do not call it . . . ii 4 229
What, must I come to you With five and twenty, Regan? said you so? ii 4 256
From France there comes a power Into this scatter'd kingdom . . iii 1 30
Then shall the realm of Albion Come to great confusion . . . iii 2 92
Then comes the time, who lives to see't, That going shall be used with feet iii 2 93
To have a thousand with red burning spits Come hissing in upon 'em . iii 6 17
Perforce must wither And come to deadly use . . . iv 2 36
If that the heavens do not their visible spirits Send quickly down to tame these vile offences, It will come . . . iv 2 48
Where was his son when they did take his eyes?—Come with my lady hither . . . iv 2 90

Come. When shall we come to the top of that same hill? . *Lear* iv 6 1
When we are born, we cry that we are come To this great stage of fools . iv 6 186
Sir, this I hear; the king is come to his daughter . v 1 21
Yet am I noble as the adversary I come to cope . v 3 124
The wheel is come full circle; I am here . v 3 174
I am come To bid my king and master aye good night . v 3 234
What comfort to this great decay may come Shall be applied . v 3 297
Upon malicious bravery, dost thou come To start my quiet . *Othello* i 1 100
In simple and pure soul I come to you . i 1 107
Because we come to do you service and you think we are ruffians . i 1 110
I am one, sir, that comes to tell you . i 1 116
But, look! what lights come yond? . i 2 28
Be advised; He comes to bad intent . i 2 56
And, till she come, as truly as to heaven I do confess the vices of my blood . i 3 122
O, behold, The riches of the ship is come on shore! . ii 1 83
My invention Comes from my pate as birdlime does from frize . ii 1 127
Let's meet him and receive him.—Lo, where he comes! . ii 1 183
If after every tempest come such calms, May the winds blow till they have waken'd death! . ii 1 187
Hard at hand comes the master and main exercise . ii 1 268
That profit's yet to come 'tween me and you . ii 3 10
When shall he come? Tell me, Othello . iii 3 67
Let him come when he will; I will deny thee nothing . iii 3 75
Farewell, my Desdemona: I'll come to thee straight . iii 3 87
I hope you will consider what is spoke Comes from my love . iii 3 217
Desdemona comes: If she be false, O, then heaven mocks itself! . iii 3 277
I have sent to bid Cassio come speak with you . iii 4 50
Thither comes the bauble, and, by this hand, she falls me thus about my neck . iv 1 139
An you'll come to supper to-night, you may; an you will not, come when you are next prepared for . iv 1 166
Shut the door; Cough, or cry 'hem,' if any body come . iv 2 29
How comes this trick upon him?—Nay, heaven doth know . iv 2 129
Stand behind this bulk; straight will be come . v 1 1
Nobody come? then shall I bleed to death . v 1 45
Here's one comes in his shirt, with light and weapons . v 1 47
Will you come to bed, my lord?—Have you pray'd to-night? . v 2 24
She comes more nearer earth than she was wont, And makes men mad . v 2 110
O, are you come, Iago? you have done well . v 2 169
So come my soul to bliss, as I speak true . v 2 250
Your dismission Is come from Cæsar . *Ant. and Cleo.* i 1 27
You may go: Would she had never given you leave to come! . i 3 21
Ne'er loved till ne'er worth love, Comes dear'd by being lack'd . i 4 44
I have not kept my square; but that to come Shall all be done by the rule . ii 3 6
You do wish yourself in Egypt?—Would I had never come from thence! ii 3 11
Thou shouldst come like a Fury crown'd with snakes . ii 5 40
But in my bosom shall she never come, To make my heart her vassal . ii 6 56
Come, thou monarch of the vine, Plumpy Bacchus with pink eyne! . ii 7 120
Where is the fellow?—Half afeard to come . iii 3 1
There's strange news come, sir . iii 5 2
But you are come A market-maid to Rome . iii 6 50
To come thus was I not constrain'd, but did On my free will . iii 6 56
'Tis easy to't; and there I will attend What further comes . iii 10 33
Let him appear that's come from Antony . iii 12 1
Such as I am, I come from Antony . iii 12 7
Come thee on.—I'll halt after . iv 7 16
That, when the exigent should come, which now Is come indeed . iv 14 63
That, on my command, Thou then wouldst kill me; do't; the time is come . iv 14 67
Come, then; for with a wound I must be cured . iv 14 78
Draw, and come.—Turn from me, then, that noble countenance . iv 14 84
I am come, I dread, too late . iv 14 126
Bid that welcome Which comes to punish us, and we punish it . iv 14 137
Yet come a little,—Wishers were ever fools,—O, come, come, come! iv 15 37
Is it sin To rush into the secret house of death, Ere death dare come to us? . iv 15 82
Guard her till Cæsar come . v 2 36
Where art thou, death? Come hither, come! come, come, and take a queen! . v 2 47
Husband, I come: Now to that name my courage prove my title! . v 2 290
So; have you done? Come then, and take the last warmth of my lips . v 2 294
If the king come, I shall incur I know not How much . *Cymbeline* i 1 102
And every day that comes comes to decay A day's work in him . i 5 56
A noble gentleman of Rome, Comes from my lord with letters . i 6 11
Did you hear of a stranger that's come to court to-night? . ii 1 36
I would this music would come . ii 3 12
A worthy fellow, Albeit he comes on angry purpose now . ii 3 61
He never can meet more mischance than come To be but named of thee ii 3 137
And wish That warmer days would come . ii 4 6
I would these garments were come . iii 5 136
We'll come to you after hunting . iv 2 2
Let ordinance Come as the gods foresay it . iv 2 146
With female fairies will his tomb be haunted, And worms will not come to thee . iv 2 218
Come more, for more you're ready . iv 3 30
So I'll fight Against the part I come with . v 1 25
You, it seems, come from the fliers . v 3 2
On either side I come to spend my breath . v 3 81
Of what's past, is, and to come, the discharge . v 4 172
I stand on fire: Come to the matter.—All too soon I shall . v 5 169
Thief, any thing That's due to all the villains past, in being, To come! v 5 213
Does the world go round?—How come these staggers on me? . v 5 233
From him I come With message . *Pericles* i 3 32
One sorrow never comes but brings an heir . i 4 63
They bring us peace, And come to us as favourers, not as foes . i 4 73
We attend him here, To know for what he comes, and whence he comes i 4 80
Nor come we to add sorrow to your tears, But to relieve them . i 4 90
They ne'er come but I look to be washed . ii 1 28
And there are princes and knights come from all parts of the world . ii 1 115
He comes To an honour'd triumph strangely furnished . ii 2 52
Like gods above, Who freely give to every one that comes To honour them . ii 3 60
Come you between, And save poor me, the weaker . iv 1 90
Would she had never come within my doors! . iv 6 157
The damned doorkeeper to every Coistrel that comes inquiring for his Tib . iv 6 176
Falseness cannot come from thee . v 1 121

Come. Bid her (him) come hither *Much Ado* iii 4; *2 Hen. IV.* v 1; *Othello* iii 4; iv 2
Come away *Tempest* i 2; *Mer. Wives* iv 2; *Meas. for Meas.* iv 2; *W. Tale* v 3; *1 Hen. IV.* ii 1; *Coriolanus* iii 1; *T. of Athens* ii 2; *Hamlet* iv 1; *Pericles* ii 1
Come forth *Tempest* i 2; ii 2; *Mer. Wives* iii 3; iv 2; *Meas. for Meas.* iv 1; *K. John* iv 1; *Rom. and Jul.* iii 3; *Lear* iii 4
Come hither *Tempest* v 1; *Mer. Wives* iv 1; *Meas. for Meas.* ii 1; iv 2; v 1; *Much Ado* ii 3; iii 3; *M. N. Dream* ii 1; iii 2; *T. of Shrew* i 1; v 1; *All's Well* ii 1; v 3; *T. Night* ii 4; *K. John* iii 3; *1 Hen. IV.* ii 4; *2 Hen. IV.* ii 1; iv 5; *Hen. V.* iv 4; *1 Hen. VI.* ii 2; iv 1; *2 Hen. VI.* iii 2; iv 2; *3 Hen. VI.* iv 6; v 7; *Richard III.* iii 1; *Hen. VIII.* i 4; ii 2; *Troi. and Cres.* v 2; *T. Andron.* iii 1; v 2; v 3; *Rom. and Jul.* i 5; *J. Cæsar* ii 4; v 3; v 5; *Hamlet* i 5; iii 2; *Lear* iii 6; *Othello* i 3; ii 1; iv 2; *Ant. and Cleo.* iii 3; iii 11; v 1; v 2; *Pericles* iv 2; v 1
Come now *M. N. Dream* v 1; *J. Cæsar* v 3; *Pericles* iv 6
Come on *Tempest* i 2; ii 2; iii 2; *T. G. of Ver.* i 3; ii 5; *Mer. Wives* i 1; iv 1; *Meas. for Meas.* ii 1; iv 2; v 1; *Com. of Errors* i 2; *L. L. Lost* i 1; v 2; *Mer. of Venice* i 3; iii 4; *As Y. Like It* i 2; *T. of Shrew* i 1; iv 5; v 2; *All's Well* ii 2; iv 1; v 3; *T. Night* ii 3; iii 4; iv 1; *W. Tale* ii 1; iv 4; *Richard II.* ii 1; *2 Hen. IV.* v 4; *1 Hen. VI.* ii 4; *2 Hen. VI.* ii 1; *3 Hen. VI.* iv 3; iv 7; *Richard III.* iii 2; *Coriolanus* i 3; i 4; *T. Andron.* ii 2; *Rom. and Jul.* i 5; *Macbeth* iii 2; *Hamlet* i 5; v 2; *Lear* ii 2; iii 7; iv 6; *Othello* ii 1; *Ant. and Cleo.* iv 2; iv 9; *Cymbeline* ii 3; iv 2
Come you hither *Much Ado* iv 2; *W. Tale* ii 3; *Troi. and Cres.* iv 4; *Lear* i 4
Come your (thy) ways *Meas. for Meas.* iii 2; *As Y. Like It* i 2; ii 3; *All's Well* ii 1; *T. Night* ii 5; *Troi. and Cres.* iii 2; *Hamlet* i 3; *Lear* ii 2; *Pericles* iv 2; iv 6
Here comes *Tempest* ii 2; *T. G. of Ver.* iv 2; *Mer. Wives* i 1; i 4; iii 1; iii 3; v 5; *Meas. for Meas.* i 2; iv 1; iv 2; iv 3; v 1; *Com. of Errors* i 2; *Much Ado* ii 3; v 1; v 4; *L. L. Lost* i 1; ii 1; iv 1; v 2; *M. N. Dream* i 1; ii 1; iii 2; v 1; *Mer. of Venice* ii 6; iii 1; *As Y. L. It* i 2; iii 2; iii 3; iv 3; v 2; v 3; v 4; *T. of Shrew* i 1; iv 4; v 2; *All's Well* ii 5; iii 5; *T. Night* i 3; i 4; i 5; ii 5; iii 4; v 1; *W. Tale* i 2; v 2; *K. John* iii 1; *Richard II.* ii 3; iii 4; v 2; *1 Hen. IV.* i 3; ii 4; iii 1; v 2; *2 Hen. IV.* i 1; i 2; ii 2; iii 2; iv 1; iv 3; iv 5; v 2; *Hen. V.* ii 1; iv 7; *2 Hen. VI.* ii 1; v 1; *3 Hen. VI.* i 1; *Richard III.* i 3; ii 4; iii 1; iii 7; *Troi. and Cres.* i 2; ii 3; v 1; v 4; *Coriolanus* ii 3; iv 2; iv 6; *T. Andron.* ii 3; *Rom. and Jul.* i 1; ii 4; iii 1; iii 2; *T. of Athens* ii 2; v 2; *J. Cæsar* iii 1; v 4; *Macbeth* ii 4; v 8; *Lear* iii 4; v 3; *Othello* ii 1; i 3; *Ant. and Cleo.* i 2; i 3; ii 2; iii 7; *Cymbeline* i 4; i 5; *Pericles* ii 5; iv 2; iv 6
Here comes a (my, the, your) man *Meas. for Meas.* iv 1; *Com. of Errors* ii 1; iv 4; *Much Ado* v 1; *Mer. of Venice* ii 2; *As Y. Like It* v 1; *T. Night* v 1; *3 Hen. VI.* ii 1; *Rom. and Jul.* iii 1
Here comes my (your) father *T. G. of Ver.* ii 4; *T. of Shrew* ii 1; *Hen. V.* v 2; *Rom. and Jul.* iii 5; *Hamlet* i 3
Here comes my (the) lord *Richard II.* ii 3; *2 Hen. VI.* iii 2; *Richard III.* i 3; *Coriolanus* v 6; *Lear* iv 2; *Othello* iii 3; *Pericles* i 3; iv 6
Here comes one *Meas. for Meas.* ii 3; *Much Ado* v 2; *L. L. Lost* iv 3; *M. N. Dream* iii 2; *Rom. and Jul.* i 1; *J. Cæsar* i 3; *Lear* i 4
Here comes the duke *T. G. of Ver.* v 2; *As Y. Like It* i 3; *Richard II.* ii 2; *Richard III.* ii 1; iii 1; iii 4
Here comes the fool . *T. Night* ii 3 15; *T. of Athens* ii 2 47
Here comes the gentleman . *T. G. of Ver.* ii 4 99; *Cymbeline* i 1 68
Here comes the king *All's Well* ii 3; *3 Hen. VI.* iv 1; *Hamlet* v 1; *Cymbeline* ii 3
Here comes the lady *T. Night* iv 3; *Rom. and Jul.* ii 6; iv 1; *Othello* i 3
Here he (she) comes *T. G. of Ver.* ii 1; *Mer. Wives* iii 4; iii 5; *Com. of Errors* ii 2; iv 3; *Much Ado* ii 1; iii 4; *L. L. Lost* v 2; *M. N. Dream* iii 2; v 1; *Mer. of Venice* iii 1; iii 5; *T. of Shrew* ii 1; *All's Well* ii 5; iii 6; iv 1; v 2; *T. Night* i 5; iii 4; *Hen. V.* iii 2; v 1; *1 Hen. VI.* i 5; *2 Hen. VI.* i 3; *Richard III.* iv 3; *Troi. and Cres.* iii 2; iv 4; *Coriolanus* ii 3; iii 3; *T. Andron.* v 2; *T. of Athens* iii 6; *Macbeth* ii 3; v 1; *Othello* iv 1; *Cymbeline* iii 2; iv 2; *Pericles* ii Gower; ii 5; iv 1
Here they come . *All's Well* iii 2 45; *Hamlet* iv 2 4
How comes that? . *2 Hen. IV.* ii 2 123; *Lear* ii 1 6
Is it to come to this? *Much Ado* i 1; *J. Cæsar* iv 3; *Lear* i 4; *Othello* iii 3; iii 4; *Ant. and Cleo.* iii 13
Let her (him, them, us) come in *Com. of Errors* v 1; *W. Tale* iv 4; *2 Hen. IV.* v 3; *Hen. VIII.* v 3; *Hamlet* iv 5; iv 6; *Ant. and Cleo.* v 2
Let him (it, them) come *T. of Shrew* Ind. 1; *1 Hen. IV.* iv 1; *2 Hen. IV.* v 3; *2 Hen. VI.* ii 3; *Coriolanus* v 3; *Hamlet* iv 7; *Cymbeline* v 5
Look where he (she) comes *Mer. Wives* ii 1; *Meas. for Meas.* i 1; *2 Hen. VI.* v 3; *Othello* iii 3; iii 4; iv 1
Look (see) where they come . *2 Hen. VI.* v 1 122; *Ant. and Cleo.* i 1 10
Marry, come up . *Rom. and Jul.* ii 5 64; *Pericles* iv 6 159
See where he (she) comes *T. G. of Ver.* v 1; *Rom. and Jul.* i 1; iv 2; *Pericles* i 1
What (who) is he comes here? *L. L. Lost* iv 3; *Mer. of Venice* i 3; *All's Well* i 2
Whence come you? *Mer. Wives* iv 5; *1 Hen. IV.* ii 4; *Rom. and Jul.* iii 3
Who comes here? *Meas. for Meas.* iii 2; *Much Ado* i 3; *M. N. Dream* ii 1; *Mer. of Venice* iii 2; *As Y. Like It* ii 4; ii 7; iii 4; iv 3; *T. of Shrew* ii 1; *All's Well* i 1; *K. John* iii 4; *Richard II.* ii 3; iii 2; iii 3; v 3; *1 Hen. IV.* v 3; *Richard III.* i 1; iv 4; *Hen. VIII.* ii 3; *Troi. and Cres.* ii 3; *Coriolanus* i 1; *T. Andron.* iv 2; v 1; *T. of Athens* i 1; *J. Cæsar* iii 1; iv 3; *Macbeth* ii 2; iv 3; *Hamlet* v 2; *Lear* ii 4; iv 1; iv 6

Comes a frost. The third day comes a frost, a killing frost *Hen. VIII.* iii 2 355
Come a little. Yet come a little,—Wishers were ever fools *Ant. and Cleo.* iv 15 36
Come a time. She hopes there will come a time . *Mer. Wives* ii 2 106
Come aboard. There is a bark of Epidamnum That stays but till her owner comes aboard . *Com. of Errors* iv 1 86
The governor, Who craves to come aboard . *Pericles* v 1 5
Gentlemen, there's some of worth would come aboard . v 1 9
Come about. The wind is come about . *Mer. of Venice* ii 6 64
Bear the boy hence; he shall not come about her . *W. Tale* ii 1 59
That he should come about your royal person . *2 Hen. VI.* iii 1 26
To see, now, how a jest shall come about! . *Rom. and Jul.* i 3 45
Sometime, in his better tune, remembers What we are come about *Lear* iv 3 42
He rages; none Dare come about him . *Cymbeline* iii 5 68

Come abroad. I do wonder, Thou naughty gaoler, that thou art so fond
To come abroad with him . . . *Mer. of Venice* iii 3 10
And so am come abroad to see the world . . . *T. of Shrew* i 2 58
Is he ready To come abroad?—I think, by this he is . *Hen. VIII.* iii 2 83
Come after. All his ancestors that come after him may . *Mer. Wives* i 1 15
Take-a your rapier, and come after my heel . . . i 4 62
I had as lief have heard the night-raven, come what plague could have
come after it. . . . *Much Ado* ii 3 85
I will come after you with what good speed Our means will make us
means . . . *All's Well* v 1 34
But tell me, Jack, whose fellows are these that come after? 1 *Hen. IV.* iv 2 68
All that I can do is nothing worth, Since that my penitence comes after
all, Imploring pardon . . . *Hen. V.* iv 1 321
If you mark Alexander's life well, Harry of Monmouth's life is come
after it indifferent well . . . iv 7 34
Stay not to expostulate, make speed; Or else come after . 3 *Hen. VI.* ii 5 136
Come again. Alas, the storm is come again! . . . *Tempest* ii 2 39
I will bethink me: come again to-morrow . *Meas. for Meas.* ii 2 144
To-day here you must not; come again when you may . *Com. of Errors* iii 1 41
He goes but to see a noise that he heard, and is to come again
M. N. Dream iii 1 94
But, till I come, again, No bed shall e'er be guilty of my stay
Mer. of Venice iii 2 327
And waft her love To come again to Carthage . . . v 1 12
Nay, come again, Good Kate; I am a gentleman . . *T. of Shrew* ii 1 219
And one thing more, that you be never so hardy to come again *T. Night* ii 2 10
Yet come again; for thou perhaps mayst move That heart . . iii 1 175
I beseech you come again to-morrow . . . iii 4 230
Well, come again to-morrow: fare thee well . . . iii 4 236
Marry, sir, lullaby to your bounty till I come again . . v 1 49
To break his grave And come again to me . . *W. Tale* v 1 43
And, till so much blood thither come again, Have I not reason to look
pale and dead? . . . *Richard II.* iii 2 78
I fear thou 'lt once more come again for ransom . *Hen. V.* iv 3 128
The liquid drops of tears that you have shed Shall come again, trans-
form'd to orient pearl . . *Richard III.* iv 4 322
Till Lucius come again, He leaves his pledges dearer than his life
T. Andron. iii 1 291
Stay but a little, I will come again . . *Rom. and Jul.* ii 2 138
And come again to supper to him . . *T. of Athens* iii 1 26
Peace, break thee off; look, where it comes again! . . *Hamlet* i 1 40
But soft, behold! lo, where it comes again! . . . i 1 126
And will he not come again? No, no, he is dead . . iv 5 191
He never will come again . . . iv 5 194
Which ever as she could with haste dispatch, She'ld come again *Othello* i 3 149
But I do love thee! and when I love thee not, Chaos is come again . iii 3 92
Come against. And come against us in full puissance . 2 *Hen. IV.* i 3 77
Let ten thousand devils come against me . . 2 *Hen. VI.* iv 10 65
It fits we thus proceed, or else no witness Would come against you
Hen. VIII. v 1 108
Until Great Birnam wood to high Dunsinane hill Shall come against him
Macbeth iv 1 94
Come alone. Yet is't not probable To come alone . . *Cymbeline* iv 2 142
Come along. This is the gentleman I told your ladyship Had come
along with me . . . *T. G. of Ver.* ii 4 88
Still proclaimeth, as he comes along . . . 2 *Hen VI.* iv 9 28
Away! for vengeance comes along with them . . 3 *Hen. VI.* ii 5 134
With thy approach, I know, My comfort comes along . *Hen. VIII.* ii 4 240
Know I these men that come along with you? . *J. Cæsar* ii 1 89
And there Speak to great Cæsar as he comes along . . ii 4 38
Come already. They're come already from the christening . *Hen. VIII.* v 4 87
The bridegroom he is come already: Make haste, I say . *Rom. and Jul.* iv 4 26
Come amain. Great lords, from Ireland am I come amain 2 *Hen. VI.* iii 1 282
Call hither Clifford; bid him come amain . . . v 1 114
Come amiss. Nothing comes amiss, so money comes withal . *T. of Shrew* i 2 82
Gold cannot come amiss, were she a devil . . 2 *Hen. VI.* i 2 92
Come and go. Before you can say 'come' and 'go,' And breathe twice
Tempest iv 1 44
O, could their master come and go as lightly! . . *T. G. of Ver.* iii 1 142
He may come and go between you both . . *Mer. Wives* ii 2 130
The colour of the king doth come and go Between his purpose and his
conscience . . . *K. John* iv 2 76
Come anon. Go home, John Rugby; I come anon . . *Mer. Wives* iii 2 87
Come anon to my lodging . . . *Mer. of Venice* ii 2 124
Bid them have patience; she shall come anon . *Troi. and Cres.* iv 4 54
Madam!—I come, anon.—But if thou mean'st not well . *Rom. and Jul.* ii 2 150
Prithee, hie thee; he'll come anon . . . *Othello* iv 3 50
Come apace, good Audrey . . . *As Y. Like It* iii 3 1
Sunday comes apace . . . *T. of Shrew* ii 1 324
Look, where the holy legate comes apace . . *K. John* v 2 65
I beseech you now, come apace to the king . . *Hen. V.* iv 8 3
The future comes apace: What shall defend the interim? *T. of Athens* ii 2 157
Brutus, come apace, And see how I regarded Caius Cassius *J. Cæsar* v 3 87
Come at him. Commanded None should come at him . *W. Tale* ii 3 32
Come at last. Ha! bots on't, 'tis come at last . *Pericles* ii 1 125
Come at my heels, Jack Rugby . . . *Mer. Wives* iii 3 102
Come at once; For the close night doth play the runaway *M. of Venice* ii 6 46
Comes athwart. Whatsoever comes athwart his affection ranges evenly
with mine . . . *Much Ado* ii 2 6
Come away. Mistress, you must come away to your father *As Y. Like It* i 2 60
Come away, come away, death, And in sad cypress let me be laid *T. Night* ii 4 52
All's well now, sweeting; come away to bed . . *Othello* ii 3 252
Comes a-wooing. Lucentio that comes a-wooing . . *T. of Shrew* iii 1 35
Come back. Do fly him When he comes back . . *Tempest* v 1 36
The hours come back! that did I never hear . *Com. of Errors* iv 2 55
How chance Moonshine is gone before Thisbe comes back? *M. N. Dream* v 1 319
I'll see the church o' your back; and then come back . *T. of Shrew* v 1 6
He hath a stern look, but a gentle heart: Let him come back *K. John* iv 1 89
Know you not? the lords are all come back . . . v 6 33
Suppose the ambassador from the French comes back . *Hen. V.* iii Prol. 28
I'll be the first, sure.—Come back, fool . . 2 *Hen. VI.* i 3 9
Come back: what mean you?—I'll not come back . *Hen. VIII.* i 1 157
This day is ominous: Therefore, come back . . *Troi. and Cres.* v 3 67
Nurse, come back again; I have remember'd me . *Rom. and Jul.* i 3 8
Then Tybalt fled; But by and by comes back to Romeo . . iii 1 175
All the world to nothing, That he dares ne'er come back to challenge
you . . . iii 5 216
Bear with me; My heart is in the coffin there with Cæsar, And I must
pause till it come back to me . . *J. Cæsar* iii 2 112
My liege, They are not yet come back . . *Macbeth* i 4 3

Come back. But, to the quick o' the ulcer:—Hamlet comes back *Hamlet* iv 7 125
We sent our schoolmaster; Is he come back? . . *Ant. and Cleo.* iii 11 72
Come before. For lovers break not hours, Unless it be to come before
their time . . . *T. G. of Ver.* v 1 5
I come before to tell you . . . *Mer. Wives* iii 3 122
Bid come before us Angelo . . *Meas. for Meas.* ii 1 16
If he be a whoremonger, and comes before him, he were as good go a
mile on his errand . . . iii 2 37
Are you there, wife? you might have come before . *Com. of Errors* iii 1 63
Let them come before master constable.—Yea, marry, let them come
before me. What is your name? . . *Much Ado* iv 2 8
One that comes before To signify the approaching of his lord
Mer. of Venice ii 9 87
Like the haggard, check at every feather That comes before his eye
T. Night iii 1 72
Daffodils, That come before the swallow dares . . *W. Tale* iv 4 119
You shall This morning come before us . . *Hen. VIII.* v 1 101
As if he had been loosed out of hell To speak of horrors,—he comes
before me . . . *Hamlet* ii 1 84
Yield: come before my father. Light, ho, here! . . *Lear* ii 1 33
Come behind. And then I comes behind . . *T. Night* ii 5 147
O monstrous coward! what, to come behind folks? 2 *Hen. VI.* iv 7 89
Come better. He could never come better; he shall come in *W. Tale* iv 4 187
Come between. Nothing that can be can come between me and the full
prospect of my hopes . . . *T. Night* iii 4 90
When you have said 'she's goodly,' come between Ere you can say
'she's honest' . . . *W. Tale* ii 1 75
Come between us, good Benvolio; my wits faint . *Rom. and Jul.* ii 4 71
'Tis dangerous when the baser nature comes Between the pass and fell
incensed points Of mighty opposites . . . *Hamlet* v 2 60
With strain'd pride To come between our sentence and our power *Lear* i 1 173
I would they had not come between us . . . *Cymbeline* i 2 23
Comes blubbered. [*She comes blubbered*] . . . 2 *Hen. IV.* ii 4 421
Come buy of me, come; come buy, come buy . . *W. Tale* iv 4 230
Come by. As thou got'st Milan, I'll come by Naples . *Tempest* ii 1 292
Love is like a child, That longs for every thing that he can come by
T. G. of Ver. iii 1 125
Your father got excellent husbands, if a maid could come by them
Much Ado ii 1 338
By heart you love her, because your heart cannot come by her *L. L. Lost* iii 1 43
Superfluity comes sooner by white hairs . . *Mer. of Venice* i 2 9
And then I know after who comes by the worst . . *T. of Shrew* i 2 14
Ere I should come by a fire to thaw me . . . iv 1 9
Wouldst thou not be glad to have the niggardly rascally sheep-biter
come by some notable shame? . . . *T. Night* ii 5 6
Are you not ashamed to enforce a poor widow to so rough a course to
come by her own? . . . 2 *Hen. IV.* ii 1 89
I will leer upon him as a' comes by . . . v 5 7
One that made means to come by what he hath *Richard III.* v 3 248
We are not to stay all together, but to come by him where he stands
Coriolanus ii 3 46
O, they eat lords; so they come by great bellies *T. of Athens* i 1 209
O, that we then could come by Cæsar's spirit, And not dismember
Cæsar! But, alas, Cæsar must bleed for it! . . *J. Cæsar* ii 1 169
And, were he not in health, He would embrace the means to come by it ii 1 259
The stone's too hard to come by . . . *Cymbeline* ii 4 46
Come by and by to my chamber . . . *T. Night* iv 2 77
I will come by and by.—I will say so . . *Hamlet* iii 2 402
Come by chance. Travelling along this coast, I here am come by chance
L. L. Lost v 2 557
Comes by destiny. Your marriage comes by destiny . *All's Well* i 3 66
Comes by fits. 'Tis said a woman's fitness comes by fits . *Cymbeline* iv 1 6
Comes by nature. To write and read comes by nature . *Much Ado* iii 3 16
Come by night. What, have you come by night And stolen my love's
heart from him? . . . *M. N. Dream* iii 2 283
Come by note. I come by note, to give and to receive . *Mer. of Venice* iii 2 141
Come current. Let not his report Come current for an accusation
1 *Hen. IV.* i 3 68
Come down, you witch, you hag, you; come down, I say! *Mer. Wives* iv 2 187
I'll be so bold as stay, sir, till she come down; I come to speak with
her . . . iv 5 14
May it please you to come down.—Down, down I come . *Richard II.* iii 3 177
In the base court? Come down? Down, court! down, king! . iii 3 182
Bid them come down, Or void the field . . *Hen. V.* iv 7 61
For shame, come down . . . 3 *Hen. VI.* i 1 77
Come down, and welcome me to this world's light . *T. Andron.* v 2 33
'Tis very late, she'll not come down to-night . *Rom. and Jul.* iii 4 5
Shall I descend? and will you give me leave?—Come down *J. Cæsar* iii 2 165
Young Octavius and Mark Antony Come down upon us with a mighty
power . . . iv 3 169
You said the enemy would not come down, But keep the hills . v 1 2
And come down With fearful bravery . . . v 1 9
Ride, ride, Messala: let them all come down . . v 2 6
Come down, behold no more. O, coward that I am, to live so long! . v 3 33
It will be rain to-night.—Let it come down . . *Macbeth* iii 3 16
Come first. But small to greater matters must give way.—Not if the
small come first . . . *Ant. and Cleo.* ii 2 12
Come for. Vat be all you, one, two, tree, four, come for? *Mer. Wives* ii 3 23
I was bid to come for you . . . *As Y. Like It* i 2 64
But as I come, I come for Lancaster . . . *Richard II.* ii 3 114
No, not a man comes for redress of thee . . 3 *Hen. VI.* iii 1 20
What, You come for money?—Is't not your business too?—It is
T. of Athens ii 2 10
Come for me. And creep time ne'er so slow, Yet it shall come for me to
do thee good . . . *K. John* iii 3 32
Comes foremost. My wife comes foremost . . *Coriolanus* v 3 22
Come forth. Let the watch come forth . . . *Much Ado* iv 2 39
With bleared visages, come forth to view The issue *Mer. of Venice* iii 2 59
Till the king come forth, and not till then . . *Hen. V.* ii Prol. 41
Dare ye come forth and meet us in the field? . . 1 *Hen. VI.* iii 2 61
Clifford, I say, come forth and fight with me . . 2 *Hen. VI.* v 2 5
Cressid comes forth to him . . . *Troi. and Cres.* v 2 6
She wakes; and I entreated her come forth . . *Rom. and Jul.* v 3 260
Pray, is my lord ready to come forth? . . *T. of Athens* ii 4 35
It is doubtful yet, Whether Cæsar will come forth to-day, or no *J. Cæsar* ii 1 194
Bid them come forth and hear me . . . *Lear* ii 4 118
Uncle, I must come forth . . . *Othello* v 2 254
Let the world see His nobleness well acted, which your death Will
never let come forth . . . *Ant. and Cleo.* v 2 46
Come freely To gratulate thy plenteous bosom . . *T. of Athens* i 2 130

Come here. Who's this comes here? *T. G. of Ver.* v 4 18
Like one that comes here to besiege his court *L. L. Lost* ii 1 86
Since you are strangers and come here by chance v 2 218
Our queen and all her elves come here anon *M. N. Dream* ii 1 17
To determine this, Come here to-day *Mer. of Venice* iv 1 107
Will day by day Come here for physic *All's Well* iii 1 19
Lest that our king Come here himself to question our delay *Hen. V.* ii 4 142
Come here about me, you my Myrmidons *Troi. and Cres.* v 7 1
What is your tidings?—The king comes here to-night *Macbeth* i 5 32
Duncan comes here to-night.—And when goes hence? i 5 60
Dost thou come here to whine? *Hamlet* v 1 300
I had rather than twice the worth of her she had ne'er come here *Pericles* iv 6 1
Come hereafter. Praised be the gods for thy foulness! sluttishness may come hereafter *As Y. Like It* iii 3 41
Come hither from the furrow and be merry: Make holiday *Tempest* iv 1 135
She's come to know If yet her brother's pardon be come hither *Meas. for Meas.* iv 3 112
You come hither, my lord, to marry this lady *Much Ado* iv 1 4
Lady, you come hither to be married to this count iv 1 9
When I send for you, come hither mask'd v 4 12
If to come hither you have measured miles *L. L. Lost* v 2 191
If you think I come hither as a lion, it were pity of my life *M. N. Dream* iii 1 44
And turn his merry note Unto the sweet bird's throat, Come hither, come hither, come hither *As Y. Like It* ii 5 5
The business is for Helen to come hither *All's Well* ii 3 101
If thou'lt see a thing to talk on when thou art dead and rotten, come hither. What ailest thou, man? *W. Tale* iii 3 83
Swaggering rascal! let him not come hither *2 Hen. IV.* ii 4 77
This Sir John, cousin, that comes hither anon about soldiers iii 2 30
I am come hither, as it were, upon my man's instigation *2 Hen. VI.* ii 3 87
I am happily come hither *Hen. VIII.* v 1 85
How more unfortunate than all living women Are we come hither *Coriol.* v 3 98
As if it were the Moor Come hither purposely to poison me *T. Andron.* iii 2 73
What dares the slave Come hither, cover'd with an antic face? *R. and J.* i 5 58
I come hither arm'd against myself v 3 65
Hold him in safety, till the prince come hither v 3 183
Whoso please To stop affliction, let him take his haste, Come hither *T. of Athens* v 1 214
Here's an English tailor come hither, for stealing out of a French hose *Macbeth* ii 3 15
The actors are come hither, my lord *Hamlet* ii 2 411
Why does the drum come hither? v 2 372
Come home. The duke comes home to-morrow *Meas. for Meas.* iv 3 132
She that doth fast till you come home to dinner *Com. of Errors* i 2 89
Till he come home again, I would forbear ii 1 31
When I desired him to come home to dinner, He ask'd me for a thousand marks in gold ii 1 60
'Will you come home?' quoth I; 'My gold!' quoth he ii 1 64
Though my mocks come home by me, I will now be merry *L. L. Lost* v 2 637
Have you sent to Bottom's house? is he come home yet? *M. N. Dream* iv 2 2
My ships come home a month before the day *Mer. of Venice* i 3 183
That thou and the proudest of you all shall find when he comes home *T. of Shrew* iv 1 90
Why dost thou not go to church in a galliard and come home in a coranto? *T. Night* i 3 137
Let my prophecy Come home to ye! *W. Tale* iv 4 663
Now these her princes are come home again, Come the three corners of the world in arms *K. John* v 7 115
Come home with me to supper *Richard II.* iv 1 333
Good husband, come home presently *Hen. V.* ii 1 93
Employ'd you where high profits might come home *Hen. VIII.* iii 2 158
Is he not wounded? he was wont to come home wounded *Coriolanus* ii 1 131
And come home beloved Of all the trades in Rome iii 2 133
I will come home to you; or, if you will, Come home to me *J. Cæsar* i 2 309
Hamlet return'd shall know you are come home *Hamlet* iv 7 131
Comes hunting. And, often but attended with weak guard, Comes hunting this way *3 Hen. VI.* iv 5 8
Come in. By these gloves, did he, or I would I might never come in mine own great chamber again else *Mer. Wives* i 1 157
Will't please your worship to come in? i 1 275
Dere is no honest man dat shall come in my closet i 4 77
My master, Sir John, is come in at your back-door iii 3 24
Peace here; grace and good company!—Who's there? come in *M. for M.* ii 1 45
Against my will I am sent to bid you come in to dinner *Much Ado* ii 3 257
He comes in like a perjure, wearing papers *L. L. Lost* iv 3 47
I make no doubt The rest will ne'er come in, if he be out v 2 152
One must come in with a bush of thorns and a lanthorn *M. N. Dream* iii 1 60
Serve in the meat, and we will come in to dinner *Mer. of Venice* iii 5 65
I will ne'er come in your bed Until I see the ring v 1 190
Hath a disposition to come in disguised against me to try a fall *As Y. Like It* i 1 131
I would be loath to foil him, as I must, for my own honour, if he come in i 1 137
Who can come in and say that I mean her? ii 7 77
By my troth, Sir Toby, you must come in earlier o' nights *T. Night* i 3 4
Why, then comes in the sweet o' the year *W. Tale* iv 3 3
He could never come better; he shall come in iv 4 188
Had not the old man come in with a whoo-bub against his daughter iv 4 628
Upon which better part our prayers come in *K. John* iii 1 293
His spirit is come in, That so stood out against the holy church v 2 70
Fresh men set upon us— And unbound the rest, and then come in the other *1 Hen. IV.* ii 4 201
And so, come in when ye will iii 1 266
We may boldly spend upon the hope of what Is to come in iv 1 55
For God's sake, cousin, stay till all come in iv 3 29
Did not goodwife Keech, the butcher's wife, come in then? *2 Hen. IV.* ii 1 102
The room where they supped is too hot; they'll come in straight ii 4 15
Now comes in the sweetest morsel of the night ii 4 396
Now comes in the sweet o' the night v 3 52
As ever you came of women, come in quickly *Hen. V.* ii 1 122
Come in, and let us banquet royally *1 Hen. VI.* i 6 30
Good Thersites, come in and rail *Troi. and Cres* ii 3 26
Come in, come in: I'll go get a fire ii 2 62
Pray you, come in: I would not for half Troy have you seen here iv 2 41
But come in: Let me commend thee first to those that shall Say yea to thy desires *Coriolanus* iv 5 149
Let me come in, and you shall know my errand *Rom. and Jul.* iii 3 79
O, come in, equivocator *Macbeth* ii 3 13
Come in, tailor; here you may roast your goose ii 3 16
Come in, without there!—What's your grace's will? iv 1 135
Even but now, demanding after you, Denied me to come in *Lear* iii 2 66

Come in. Let's to the seaside, ho! As well to see the vessel that's come in As to throw out our eyes for brave Othello *Othello* ii 1 37
Come in: I will bestow you where you shall have time To speak your bosom freely iii 1 56
Let's think't unsafe To come in to the cry without more help v 1 44
What are you there? come in, and give some help v 1 59
Shall she come in? were't good?—I think she stirs again:—no. What's best to do? v 2 94
If she come in, she'll sure speak to my wife v 2 96
I had forgot thee: O, come in, Emilia: Soft; by and by v 2 103
Where air comes out, air comes in *Cymbeline* i 2 3
Ere I could Give him that parting kiss which I had set Betwixt two charming words, comes in my father i 3 35
Fair youth, come in: Discourse is heavy, fasting iii 6 90
You come in faint for want of meat, depart reeling with too much drink v 4 163
Comes in charity. It comes in charity to thee *T. of Athens* i 2 229
Comes in his head. He's sudden, if a thing comes in his head *3 Hen. VI.* v 5 86
Come in house. An honest, willing, kind fellow, as ever servant shall come in house *Mer. Wives* i 4 11
Come in quest. Many Jasons come in quest of her *Mer. of Venice* i 1 172
Come in spite. A villain that is hither come in spite *Rom. and Jul.* i 5 64
Come in strife. If I should as lion come in strife Into this place, 'twere pity on my life *M. N. Dream* v 1 228
Come in tears. Scorn and derision never come in tears iii 2 123
Come in time; have napkins enow about you *Macbeth* ii 3 6
Come into. I never come into any room in a taphouse, but I am drawn in *Meas. for Meas.* ii 1 219
You will come into the court and swear that I have a poor pennyworth in the English *Mer. of Venice* i 2 75
Aid me with that store of power you have To come into his presence *All's Well* v 1 21
And makest conjectural fears to come into me, Which I would fain shut out v 3 114
To offer to have his daughter come into grace! *W. Tale* iv 4 806
This murder had not come into my mind *K. John* iv 2 223
When you come into your closet, you'll question this gentlewoman about me *Hen. V.* v 2 210
Say, Henry King of England, come into the court *Hen. VIII.* ii 4 6
Say, Katharine Queen of England, come into the court ii 4 11
When fair Cressid comes into my thoughts,—So, traitor! 'When she comes!' When is she thence? *Troi. and Cres.* i 1 30
Whose qualification shall come into no true taste again *Othello* ii 1 283
Antony Is come into the field *Ant. and Cleo.* iv 6 8
Do you know this house to be a place of such resort, and will come into't? *Pericles* iv 6 86
Comes it. How comes it now, my husband, O, how comes it, That thou art thus estranged from thyself? *Com. of Errors* ii 2 121
And thereof comes it that his head is light v 1 72
Hence comes it that your kindred shuns your house *T. of Shrew* Ind. 2 30
So comes it, lady, you have been mistook *T. Night* v 1 266
Comes it not something near? *W. Tale* v 3 23
How comes it then that thou art call'd a king? *K. John* ii 1 107
You have not sought it! how comes it, then? *1 Hen. IV.* v 1 27
Hereof comes it that Prince Harry is valiant *2 Hen. IV.* iv 3 127
How comes't that you Have holp to make this rescue? *Coriolanus* iii 1 276
How comes it that the subtle Queen of Goths Is of a sudden thus advanced in Rome? *T. Andron.* i 1 392
How comes it? do they grow rusty? *Hamlet* ii 2 352
How comes it, Michael, you are thus forgot? *Othello* ii 3 188
How comes it he is to sojourn with you? *Cymbeline* i 4 24
Come last. I will come last. 'Tis like he'll question me *Troi. and Cres.* iii 3 42
Come me to what was done to her *Meas. for Meas.* ii 1 121
Comes me the prince and Claudio, hand in hand *Much Ado* i 3 61
See how this river comes me cranking in *1 Hen. IV.* iii 1 98
Comes me in. Her husband, Master Brook, dwelling in a continual 'larum of jealousy, comes me in the instant of our encounter *Mer. Wives* iii 5 73
Come near the house, I pray you i 4 140
Pray you, come near: if I suspect without cause, why then make sport at me iii 3 159
Bind him! let him not come near me *Com. of Errors* iv 4 109
Let not that doctor e'er come near my house *Mer. of Venice* v 1 223
O, ho! do you come near me now? *T. Night* iii 4 71
To souse annoyance that comes near his nest *K. John* v 2 150
Indeed, you come near me now *1 Hen. IV.* i 2 14
That ever our love durst not come near your sight v 1 63
O me! come near me; now I am much ill *2 Hen. IV.* iv 4 111
Not to come near our person by ten mile v 5 69
None durst come near for fear of sudden death *1 Hen. VI.* i 4 48
Could I come near your beauty with my nails, I'ld set my ten commandments in your face *2 Hen. VI.* i 3 144
Nay, for a need, thus far come near my person *Richard III.* iii 5 85
Pray their graces To come near *Hen. VIII.* iii 1 19
She, I'll swear, hath corns; am I come near ye now? *Rom. and Jul.* i 5 22
One scene of it comes near the circumstance Which I have told thee *Hamlet* iii 2 81
If it touch not you, it comes near nobody *Othello* iv 1 210
Ghost unlaid forbear thee!—Nothing ill come near thee! *Cymbeline* iv 2 279
Provided That none but I and my companion maid Be suffer'd to come near him *Pericles* v 1 79
Come nearer. I have often wished myself poorer, that I might come nearer to you *T. of Athens* i 2 105
What, dost thou weep? Come nearer iv 3 489
Come nearer; No further halting *Cymbeline* v 5 91
Come no more. No, I'll come no more i' the basket *Mer. Wives* iv 2 50
An you be so tardy, come no more in my sight *As Y. Like It* iv 1 51
I come no more to make you laugh *Hen. VIII.* Prol. 1
Thou'lt come no more, Never, never, never, never, never! *Lear* v 3 307
Come not within the measure of my wrath *T. G. of Ver.* v 4 127
Come not to my child.—She is no match for you *Mer. Wives* iii 4 76
If the duke with the other dukes come not to composition *Meas. for Meas.* i 2 1
The meat is cold because you come not home; You come not home because you have no stomach *Com. of Errors* i 2 48
Bear it with you, lest I come not time enough iv 1 41
Light wenches will burn. Come not near her iv 3 58
Fair, or I'll never look on her; mild, or come not near me *Much Ado* ii 3 34
Comes not that blood as modest evidence To witness simple virtue? iv 1 38
Who is your deer?—If we choose by the horns, yourself come not near *L. L. Lost* iv 1 117
Take heed the queen come not within his sight *M. N. Dream* ii 1 19

Come not. Newts and blind-worms, do no wrong, Come not near our fairy queen . . . *M. N. Dream* ii 2 12
Weaving spiders, come not here; Hence, you long-legg'd spinners! ii 2 20
Take on as you would follow, But yet come not . . . iii 2 259
Lead these testy rivals so astray As one come not within another's way iii 2 359
If he come not, then the play is marred . . . iv 2 5
We come not to offend, But with good will . . . v 1 109
O unhappy youth! Come not within these doors . *As Y. Like It* ii 3 17
No matter whither, so you come not here . . . ii 3 30
Why did he swear he would come this morning, and comes not? . . iii 4 21
But till that time Come not thou near me . . . iii 5 32
Why, sir, he comes not.—Didst thou not say he comes? . *T. of Shrew* iii 2 77
You are welcome, sir.—And yet I come not well . . . iii 2 90
I marvel Cambio comes not all this while . . . v 1 7
See that you come Not to woo honour, but to wed it . *All's Well* ii 1 14
It hath happened all as I would have had it, save that he comes not along with her . . . iii 2 2
Then, till the fury of his highness settle, Come not before him *W. Tale* iv 4 483
He comes not Like to his father's greatness . . . v 1 88
And comes not in, o'er-ruled by prophecies . . *1 Hen. IV.* iv 4 18
We'll burst them open, if that you come not quickly . *1 Hen. VI.* i 3 28
What a slug is Hastings, that he comes not To tell us whether they will come or no! . . . *Richard III.* iii 1 22
We come not by the way of accusation . . *Hen. VIII.* iii 1 54
I come not To hear such flattery now . . . . v 3 123
Nor I from Troy come not to whisper him . . *Troi. and Cres.* i 3 250
Heaven bless thee from a tutor, and discipline come not near thee! . . ii 3 33
Come I too late?—Ay, if you come not in the blood of others, But mantled in your own . . . *Coriolanus* i 6 28
Bury him where you can; he comes not here . . *T. Andron.* i 1 354
Banishment! It comes not ill; I hate not to be banish'd *T. of Athens* iii 5 112
If where thou art two villains shall not be, Come not near him . v 1 113
Come not to me again . . . . . . v 1 217
Come not near Casca; have an eye to Cinna . . *J. Cæsar* ii 3 2
I come not, friends, to steal away your hearts . . iii 2 220
When sorrows come, they come not single spies, But in battalions *Ham.* iv 5 78
Mine and my father's death come not upon thee, Nor thine on me! . v 2 341
Come not between the dragon and his wrath . . *Lear* i 1 124
Nor cutpurses come not to throngs . . . . iii 2 88
Come not in here, nuncle, here's a spirit . . . . iii 4 39
Come not near th' old man; keep out . . . . iv 6 245
You come not Like Cæsar's sister . . . *Ant. and Cleo.* iii 6 42
Stay; come not in. But that it eats our victuals, I should think Here were a fairy . . . *Cymbeline* iii 6 40
O, our credit comes not in like the commodity . . *Pericles* iv 2 33
Come of. She comes of errands, does she? . . *Mer. Wives* iv 2 182
Of what kind should this cock come of? . . *As Y. Like It* ii 7 90
Or comes of a very dull kindred . . . . . iii 2 32
Vincentio, come of the Bentivolii . . . *T. of Shrew* i 1 13
I told you what would come of this . . . *W. Tale* iv 4 458
Accommodated! it comes of 'accommodo' . . *2 Hen. IV* iii 2 78
And this valour comes of sherris . . . . iv 3 122
Art thou a messenger, or come of pleasure? . . *2 Hen. VI.* v 1 16
If you should, O, what would come of it! . . *J. Cæsar* iii 2 151
Nothing will come of nothing: speak again . . *Lear* i 1 92
And what's to come of my despised time Is nought but bitterness *Othello* i 1 162
Come off. They must come off; I'll sauce them . . *Mer. Wives* iv 3 13
This comes off well; here's a wise officer . . *Meas. for Meas.* ii 1 57
Nor no further in sport neither than with safety of a pure blush thou mayst in honour come off again . . . *As Y. Like It* i 2 32
The ring upon my finger which never shall come off . *All's Well* iii 2 60
To come off the breach with his pike bent bravely . *2 Hen. IV.* ii 4 55
No, he's settled, Not to come off, in his displeasure . *Hen. VIII.* iii 2 23
We are come off Like Romans . . . . *Coriolanus* i 6 1
This comes off well and excellent . . . *T. of Athens* i 1 29
If I come off, and leave her in such honour as you have trust in, she your jewel, this your jewel, and my gold are yours . . *Cymbeline* i 4 164
Come off, come off: As slippery as the Gordian knot was hard! . ii 2 33
Come off and on swifter than he that gibbets on the brewer's bucket *2 Hen. IV.* iii 2 281
Come on your ways . . . . . *Tempest* ii 2 85
To sue to live, I find I seek to die; And, seeking death, find life: let it come on . . . . . . *Meas. for Meas.* iii 1 43
When once she is my wife.—That 'once,' I see by your good father's speed, Will come on very slowly . . . . *W. Tale* v 1 211
Bell, book, and candle shall not drive me back, When gold and silver becks me to come on . . . . . *K. John* iii 3 13
Come on, come on, come on, sir; give me your hand, sir *2 Hen. IV.* iii 2 1
In goodly form comes on the enemy . . . . iv 1 20
Yet, God before, tell him we will come on . . *Hen. V.* iii 6 165
Come on refresh'd, new-added, and encouraged . *J. Cæsar* iv 3 209
The enemy comes on in gallant show . . . . v 1 13
Alack, the night comes on, and the bleak winds Do sorely ruffle . *Lear* ii 4 303
Come on't. I'll bring him the best 'parel that I have, Come on't what will . . . . iv 1 52
Come out. As wine comes out of a narrow-mouthed bottle *As Y. Like It* iii 2 211
When you shall know your mistress Has deserved prison, then abound in tears, As I come out . . . . . *W. Tale* ii 1 121
Come out of that fat room, and lend me thy hand to laugh a little *1 Hen. IV.* ii 4 1
That the laws of England may come out of your mouth . *2 Hen. VI.* iv 7 8
Banquo's buried; he cannot come out on's grave . . . *Macbeth* v 1 70
My Regan counsels well: come out o' the storm . . *Lear* ii 4 312
Where air comes out, air comes in . . . *Cymbeline* i 2 3
'Twill hardly come out. Ha! bots on't, 'tis come at last . *Pericles* ii 1 124
Come over. In so high a style, Margaret, that no man living shall come over it . . . . *Much Ado* v 2 7
Thou deservest it.—To have no man come over me! . . v 2 9
How he comes o'er us with our wilder days . . *Hen. V.* i 2 267
Come o'er the bourn, Bessy, to me,— Her boat hath a leak, And she must not speak Why she dares not come over to thee . *Lear* iii 6 27
It comes o'er my memory, As doth the raven o'er the infected house *Oth.* iv 1 20
Come pat. Nor could Come pat betwixt too early and too late *Hen. VIII.* ii 3 84
Comes post. His highness comes post from Marseilles . *All's Well* iv 5 85
Come round. Time is come round . . . . *J. Cæsar* v 3 23
Come roundly. Shall I then come roundly to thee? . . *T. of Shrew* i 2 59
Comes rushing. What a tide of woes Comes rushing on this woeful land at once! . . . . *Richard II.* ii 2 99
Comes safe home. He that outlives this day, and comes safe home, Will stand a tip-toe when this day is named . . *Hen. V.* iv 3 41

Come safe off. If the dull brainless Ajax come safe off, We'll dress him up in voices . . . . *Troi. and Cres.* i 3 381
Come see. There is nothing That you will feed on; but what is, come see . . . . *As Y. Like It* ii 4 86
Come seek. Yet have I ventured to come seek you out . . *Lear* iii 4 157
Come short. Who hath for four or five removes come short To tender it herself . . . . *All's Well* v 3 131
Shall furnish us For our affairs in hand: if that come short, Our substitutes at home shall have blank charters . . *Richard II.* i 4 47
That we come short of our suppose so far . . *Troi. and Cres.* i 3 11
That I, in forgery of shapes and tricks, Come short of what he did *Ham.* iv 7 91
Come slack. If you come slack of former services, You shall do well *Lear* i 3 9
Come straight. He's hearing of a cause; he will come straight *M. for M.* ii 2 1
She's making her ready, she'll come straight . . *Troi. and Cres.* iii 2 31
He will come straight. Look you lay home to him . . *Hamlet* iii 4 1
Come suddenly. Mistress Ford desires you to come suddenly *Mer. Wives* iv 1 6
Come tardy off. Now this overdone, or come tardy off, though it make the unskilful laugh, cannot but make the judicious grieve *Hamlet* iii 2 28
Come there. He dares not come there for the candle . . *M. N. Dream* v 1 253
And well we may come there by dinner-time . . . *T. of Shrew* iv 3 190
'Twill be supper-time ere you come there . . . . iv 3 192
We'll ne'er come there again . . . . . *All's Well* ii 3 78
Let him not come there, To seek out sorrow that dwells every where *Richard II.* i 2 71
Ere ye come there, be sure to hear some news . . . *3 Hen. VI.* v 5 48
Comes this. Now, gods that we adore, whereof comes this? . . *Lear* i 4 312
Come thither. That many wearing rapiers are afraid of goose-quills and dare scarce come thither . . . . *Hamlet* ii 2 360
Come to. I have purchased as many diseases under her roof as come to— To what, I pray? . . . . . . *Meas. for Meas.* i 2 47
What prodigal portion have I spent, that I should come to such penury? *As Y. Like It* i 1 42
A million of beating may come to a great matter . . *W. Tale* iv 3 63
In Barbary, sir, it cannot come to so much . . . *1 Hen. IV.* ii 4 85
Besides, there is no king, be his cause never so spotless, if it come to the arbitrement of swords, can try it out with all unspotted soldiers *Hen. V.* iv 1 168
For more than blushing comes to . . . . *Hen. VIII.* ii 3 42
What will this come to? . . . . . *T. of Athens* i 2 197
Tell him, so much the rent of his land comes to . . *Lear* i 4 148
How look I, That I should seem to lack humanity So much as this fact comes to? . . . . *Cymbeline* iii 2 17
Come to be. If once he come to be a cardinal, He'll make his cap coequal with the crown . . . . *1 Hen. VI.* v 1 32
Come to confusion. So quick bright things come to confusion *M. N. Dr.* i 1 149
Come to dust. Golden lads and girls all must, As chimney-sweepers, come to dust . . . . *Cymbeline* iv 2 263
The sceptre, learning, physic, must All follow this, and come to dust . iv 2 269
All lovers young, and lovers must Consign to thee, and come to dust . iv 2 275
Come to fall. And what's in prayer but this two-fold force, To be forestalled ere we come to fall, Or pardon'd being down? . . *Hamlet* iii 3 49
Come to good. It is not nor it cannot come to good . . . i 2 158
I'll never care what wickedness I do, If this man come to good . *Lear* iii 7 100
Come to ground. There hangs a vaporous drop profound; I'll catch it ere it come to ground . . . . *Macbeth* iii 5 25
Come to harbour. Three of your argosies Are richly come to harbour suddenly . . . . *Mer. of Venice* v 1 277
Come to harvest. When wit and youth is come to harvest, Your wife is like to reap a proper man . . . . . *T. Night* iii 1 143
The seedsman Upon the slime and ooze scatters his grain, And shortly comes to harvest . . . . . . *Ant. and Cleo.* ii 7 26
Come to it. But you shall come to it, by your honour's leave *M. for M.* ii 1 125
Now I come to't, my lord . . . . v 1 194
Th' other's not come to't; you shall tell me another tale, when th' other's come to't . . . . . . *Troi. and Cres.* i 2 90
Young men will do't, if they come to't . . . *Hamlet* iv 5 61
Come to judgement. A Daniel come to judgement! . *Mer. of Venice* iv 1 223
Come to know what service It is your pleasure to command *T. G. of Ver.* iv 3 9
You come to know what hath passed between me and Ford's wife? *Mer. Wives* iii 5 62
I come to know your pleasure . . . *Meas. for Meas.* i 1 27; ii 4 31
She's come to know If yet her brother's pardon be come hither . iv 3 111
All faults I make, when I shall come to know them, I do repent *W. Tale* iii 2 220
Once more I come to know of thee . . . . *Hen. V.* iv 3 79
I come to know what prisoners thou hast ta'en . . *1 Hen. VI.* iv 7 56
We come To know your royal pleasure . . . *Hen. VIII.* ii 2 70
Meet me i' the morning: thither he Will come to know his destiny *Macbeth* iii 5 17
By that which you profess, Howe'er you come to know it, answer me iv 1 51
Come to knowledge. Being come to knowledge that there was complaint Intended . . . . *Meas. for Meas.* v 1 153
Come to life. A man may prophesy, With a near aim, of the main chance of things As yet not come to life . . . . *2 Hen. IV.* iii 1 84
Come to light. Truth will come to light . . . *Mer. of Venice* ii 2 83
A most contagious treason come to light, look you . . *Hen. V.* iv 8 22
Come to me, And I'll be sworn 'tis true . . . *Tempest* iii 3 25
Come to me, With commendation from great potentates . *T. G. of Ver.* ii 4 78
Come to me soon at night . . . . . . *Mer. Wives* ii 2 295
Come to me at your convenient leisure, and you shall know . iii 5 136
Well; come to me to-morrow.—Go to; 'tis well . *Meas. for Meas.* ii 2 155
O Sisters Three, Come, come to me . . . . *M. N. Dream* v 1 344
You come to me, and you say 'Shylock, we would have moneys' *Mer. of Venice* i 3 116
Here shall he see Gross fools as he, An if he will come to me *As Y. Like It* ii 5 59
You are come to me in happy time . . . . *T. of Shrew* Ind. 1 90
Go and entreat my wife To come to me forthwith . . . v 2 87
Go to your mistress; Say, I command her come to me . . . v 2 96
Unless, perchance, you come to me again, To tell me how he takes it *T. Night* i 5 300
Say that she were gone, Given to the fire, a moiety of my rest Might come to me again . . . . *W. Tale* ii 3 8
More than mistress of Which comes to me in name of fault, I must not At all acknowledge . . . . iii 2 61
An if an angel should have come to me And told me . . *K. John* iv 1 68
If ever thou come to me and say, after to-morrow, 'This is my glove' *Hen. V.* iv 1 230
He is come to me and prings me pread and salt yesterday . . v 1 9
Conversed with the enemy, And undiscover'd come to me again *2 Hen. VI.* iii 1 369
Ah, who is nigh? come to me, friend or foe . . . *3 Hen. VI.* v 2 5

Come to me. Go, bid thy master rise and come to me . *Richard III.* iii 2 31
Come to me, Tyrrel, soon at after supper . . . . . iv 3 31
Boldness comes to me now, and brings me heart . . *Troi. and Cres.* iii 2 121
Thou canst not come to me: I come to thee . . . *T. Andron.* ii 3 245
And being enfranchised, bid him come to me . . . *T. of Athens* i 1 106
Confound them by some course, and come to me, I'll give you gold enough . . . v 1 106
Come to me again, And bring me word what he doth say . *J. Cæsar* ii 4 45
Come to me, that of this I may speak more . . . *Lear* i 2 54
I have eyes upon him, And his affairs come to me on the wind *Ant. and Cleo.* iii 6 63
Come to meet. Yet, as they are, here are they come to meet you *T. of Shrew* iv 1 141
Great Agamemnon comes to meet us here . . *Troi. and Cres.* iv 5 159
Come to note. He shall conceal it Whiles you are willing it shall come to note . . . *T. Night* iv 3 29
Come to nought. Bad is the world; and all will come to nought *Richard III.* iii 6 13
Come to pass. If you live to see this come to pass, say Pompey told you so . . . *Meas. for Meas.* ii 1 256
If it do come to pass That any man turn ass . . *As Y. Like It* ii 5 52
For it will come to pass That every braggart shall be found an ass *All's Well* iv 3 371
For it comes to pass oft . . . *T. Night* iii 4 196
It's come to pass, This tractable obedience is a slave . . *Hen. VIII.* i 2 63
She had a prophesying fear Of what hath come to pass . *Ant. and Cleo.* iv 14 121
Come to prime. Lest you be cropp'd before you come to prime *Richard II.* v 2 51
Come to question. I'ld have it come to question . . . *Lear* i 3 13
Come to road. My ships Are safely come to road . . *Mer. of Venice* v 1 288
Come to see. You are come to see my daughter? . . *Mer. Wives* ii 1 167
Pray God, Bassanio come To see me pay his debt! . . *Mer. of Venice* iii 3 35
Whether our kinsman come to see his friends . . . *Richard II.* i 4 22
Those that come to see Only a show or two . . . *Hen. VIII.* Prol. 9
Who, hearing of your melancholy state, Did come to see you . *Pericles* v 1 223
Come to shrift. Bid her devise Some means to come to shrift this afternoon *Rom. and Jul.* ii 4 192
Come to speak. I come to speak with Sir John Falstaff . *Mer. Wives* iv 5 4
I'll be so bold as stay, sir, till she come down; I come to speak with her iv 5 14
He seems to have a foreknowledge of that too, and therefore comes to speak with you . . . *T. Night* i 5 152
Thy looks are full of speed.—So hath the business that I come to speak of *1 Hen. IV.* iii 2 163
Go and tell him, We come to speak with him . . . *Troi. and Cres.* ii 3 131
In second voice we'll not be satisfied; We come to speak with him . ii 3 150
I come to speak with Paris from the Prince Troilus . . . iii 1 40
I am an officer of state, and come To speak with Coriolanus *Coriolanus* v 2 3
'Tis like she comes to speak of Cassio's death . . . *Othello* v 2 92
Come to that. Your honour cannot come to that yet . *Meas. for Meas.* ii 1 123
I am exceeding weary.—Is't come to that? . . . *2 Hen. IV.* ii 2 2
Faith, holy uncle, would 'twere come to that! . . . *2 Hen. VI.* ii 1 38
Come to the ear. If it should come to the ear of the court *Mer. Wives* iv 5 97
Come to the full. My powers are crescent, and my auguring hope Says it will come to the full . . . *Ant. and Cleo.* ii 1 11
Come to this. Is all your strict preciseness come to this? *1 Hen. VI.* v 4 67
That it should come to this! But two months dead: nay, not so much, not two . . . *Hamlet* i 2 137
Hast thou given all to thy two daughters? And art thou come to this? *Lear* iii 4 50
Even here Do we shake hands. All come to this? . . *Ant. and Cleo.* iv 12 20
Come to town. There is a friend of mine come to town . *Mer. Wives* iv 5 78
No word to your master that I am yet come to town . . *2 Hen. IV.* ii 2 177
Come to words. Most meet That first we come to words *Ant. and Cleo.* ii 6 3
Come to years. Till my infant fortune comes to years . *Richard II.* ii 3 66
Come too late. He comes too late; And so tell your master *Com. of Errors* iii 1 49
Love that comes too late, Like a remorseful pardon slowly carried *All's Well* v 3 57
After our sentence plaining comes too late . . . *Richard II.* i 3 175
Pray God we may make haste, and come too late! . . . i 4 64
That comfort comes too late . . . *Hen. VIII.* iv 2 120
Supper is done, and we shall come too late . . *Rom. and Jul.* i 4 105
Then do we sin against our own estate, When we may profit meet, and come too late . . . *T. of Athens* v 1 45
Our affairs from England come too late . . . *Hamlet* v 2 379
Comes too near. This comes too near the praising of myself *Mer. of Ven.* iii 4 22
Come too short. Indeed, neighbour, he comes too short of you *M. Ado* iii 5 45
Your reputation comes too short for my daughter . . *All's Well* v 3 176
My endeavours Have ever come too short of my desires . *Hen. VIII.* iii 2 170
I find she names my very deed of love; Only she comes too short *Lear* i 1 74
If it be true, all vengeance comes too short . . . ii 1 90
He comes too short of that great property . . . *Ant. and Cleo.* i 1 58
When good will is show'd, though 't come too short, The actor may plead pardon . . . ii 5 8
Come too soon. Know that thou art come too soon . *2 Hen. VI.* iii 1 95
Come upon. Shall I come upon thee with an old saying? . . *L. L. Lost* iv 1 121
Thou seest, thou wicked varlet, now, what's come upon thee *M. for M.* ii 1 199
I have an exposition of sleep come upon me . . . *M. N. Dream* iv 1 44
I hope they will not come upon us now . . . *Hen. V.* iii 6 177
Had not you come upon your cue . . . *Richard III.* iii 4 27
The last hour Of my long weary life is come upon me . *Hen. VIII.* ii 1 133
And hope to come upon them in the heat of their division *Coriolanus* iv 3 18
Behold now presently, and swoon for what's to come upon thee . v 2 73
Fear comes upon me: O, much I fear some ill unlucky thing *R. and J.* v 3 135
The morning comes upon 's: we'll leave you . . *J. Cæsar* ii 1 221
He comes upon a wish. Fortune is merry . . . iii 2 271
It comes upon me. Art thou any thing? . . . iv 3 278
New honours come upon him, Like our strange garments *Macbeth* i 3 144
Comes well. This unlooked-for sport comes well *Rom. and Jul.* i 5 31
And joy comes well in such a needy time . . . iii 5 106
Come what come may, Time and the hour runs through the roughest day *Macbeth* i 3 146
Let come what comes; only I'll be revenged Most thoroughly *Hamlet* iv 5 135
Come what may, I do adore thee so, That danger shall seem sport *T. Night* ii 1 48
Come what will. Via! we will do't, come what will come *L. L. Lost* v 2 112
Well, come what will, I'll tarry at home . . . *1 Hen. IV.* i 2 162
Come you in. About and about, and come you in and come you in *2 Hen. IV.* iii 2 302
Come you now with, 'knocking at the gate'? . . . *T. of Shrew* i 2 42
Comedian. Are you a comedian? . . . *T. Night* i 5 194
The quick comedians Extemporally will stage us . . *Ant. and Cleo.* v 2 216

Comedy. As it were, spoke the prologue of our comedy . *Mer. Wives* iii 5 76
Here was a consent, Knowing aforehand of our merriment, To dash it like a Christmas comedy . . . *L. L. Lost* v 2 462
These ladies' courtesy Might well have made our sport a comedy . . v 2 886
Our play is, The most lamentable comedy, and most cruel death of Pyramus and Thisby . . . *M. N. Dream* i 2 12
There are things in this comedy of Pyramus and Thisby that will never please . . . iii 1 9
I do not doubt but to hear them say, it is a sweet comedy . . . iv 2 45
Are come to play a pleasant comedy . . . *T. of Shrew* Ind. 2 132
The best actors in the world, either for tragedy, comedy, history *Hamlet* ii 2 416
For if the king like not the comedy, Why then, belike, he likes it not, perdy . . . iii 2 304
Pat he comes like the catastrophe of the old comedy . . . *Lear* i 2 147
Comeliness. When youth with comeliness plucked all gaze his way *Coriolanus* i 3 7
Comely. Show'd bashful sincerity and comely love . . *Much Ado* iv 1 55
In most comely truth, thou deservest it . . . v 2 7
What a world is this, when what is comely Envenoms him that bears it!—Why, what's the matter? . . . *As Y. Like It* ii 3 14
This is a happier and more comely time . . . *Coriolanus* iv 6 27
He is a man, setting his fate aside, Of comely virtues . *T. of Athens* iii 5 15
Comer. Stood as fair As any comer I have look'd on yet . *Mer. of Venice* ii 1 21
With his arms outstretch'd, as he would fly, Grasps in the comer *Troi. and Cres.* iii 3 168
Comest. Coward, why comest thou not? . . . *M. N. Dream* iii 2 421
Thou comest to the lady Olivia, and in my sight she uses thee kindly *T. Night* iii 4 170
Say who thou art And why thou comest thus knightly clad in arms *Richard II.* i 3 12
What is thy name? and wherefore comest thou hither? . . . i 3 31
Against whom comest thou? and what's thy quarrel? . . . i 3 33
Imagine it To lie that way thou go'st, not whence thou comest . . i 3 287
Comest thou because the anointed king is hence? . . . ii 3 96
What art thou? and how comest thou hither? . . . v 5 69
Thou wilt be horribly chid to-morrow when thou comest to thy father *1 Hen. IV.* ii 4 411
Comest thou again for ransom? . . . *Hen. V.* iv 7 73
Comest thou with deep premeditated lines, With written pamphlets? *1 Hen. VI.* iii 1 1
Curse, miscreant, when thou comest to the stake . . . v 3 44
That, when thou comest to kneel at Henry's feet, Thou mayst bereave him of his wits with wonder . . . v 3 194
What news? why comest thou in such haste? . . . *2 Hen. VI.* iv 4 26
What news? Why comest thou in such post? . . . *3 Hen. VI.* i 2 48
Good news or bad, that thou comest in so bluntly? . . *Richard III.* iv 3 45
When thou comest thither,—Dull, unmindful villain, Why stand'st thou still? . . . iv 4 444
Whence comest thou? what wouldst thou? thy name? . *Coriolanus* iv 5 58
Thou comest not to be made a scorn in Rome . . . *T. Andron.* i 1 265
Thou wilt fall backward when thou comest to age . . *Rom. and Jul.* i 3 56
Thou knowest well enough, although thou comest to me *T. of Athens* iii 1 44
Why comest thou?—To tell thee thou shalt see me at Philippi *J. Cæsar* iv 3 283
O error, soon conceived, Thou never comest unto a happy birth! . . v 3 70
Thou comest to use thy tongue; thy story quickly . . . *Macbeth* v 5 29
Thou comest in such a questionable shape That I will speak to thee *Hamlet* i 4 43
Comest thou to beard me in Denmark? . . . ii 2 443
Thou out of heaven's benediction comest To the warm sun! . . *Lear* ii 2 168
Comest thou smiling from The world's great snare uncaught? *A. and C.* iv 8 17
Thou comest not, Caius, now for tribute . . . *Cymbeline* v 5 69
Comet. Wherefore gaze this goodly company, As if they saw some wondrous monument, Some comet or unusual prodigy? . *T. of Shrew* iii 2 98
By being seldom seen, I could not stir But like a comet I was wonder'd at *1 Hen. IV.* iii 2 47
Comets, importing change of times and states, Brandish your crystal tresses in the sky! . . . *1 Hen. VI.* i 1 2
The burning torch in yonder turret stands.—Now shine it like a comet of revenge! . . . iii 2 31
When beggars die, there are no comets seen . . . *J. Cæsar* ii 2 30
That ne'er before invited eyes, But have been gazed on like a comet *Pericles* v 1 87
Cometh. Ask yonder knight in arms, Both who he is and why he cometh hither . . . *Richard II.* i 3 27
Whence cometh this alarum and the noise? . . . *1 Hen. VI.* i 4 99
Here cometh Charles: I marvel how he sped . . . ii 1 48
Cometh Andronicus, bound with laurel boughs . . . *T. Andron.* i 1 74
Comfect. Count Comfect; a sweet gallant, surely! . . . *Much Ado* iv 1 318
Comfit-maker. You swear like a comfit-maker's wife . *1 Hen. IV.* iii 1 253
Comfort. I have great comfort from this fellow . . . *Tempest* i 1 30
Wipe thou thine eyes; have comfort . . . i 2 25
Be of comfort; My father's of a better nature, sir, Than he appears by speech . . . i 2 495
Then wisely, good sir, weigh Our sorrow with our comfort . . ii 1 9
He receives comfort like cold porridge . . . ii 1 10
Milan and Naples have Moe widows in them of this business' making Than we bring men to comfort them . . . ii 1 134
Well, here's my comfort . . . ii 2 47
This is a scurvy tune too: but here's my comfort . . . ii 2 57
Supportable To make the dear loss, have I means much weaker Than you may call to comfort you . . . v 1 147
To thy great comfort in this mystery of ill opinions . *Mer. Wives* ii 1 73
Give him a show of comfort in his suit and lead him on . . ii 1 98
I thank you for that good comfort . . . iii 4 54
A life, whose very comfort Is still a dying horror! . . *Meas. for Meas.* ii 3 41
What's the comfort?—Why, As all comforts are; most good, most good indeed . . . iii 1 54
Left her in her tears, and dried not one of them with his comfort . . iii 1 235
I thank you for this comfort . . . iii 1 280
I spy comfort; I cry bail . . . iii 2 43
Here comes a man of comfort . . . iv 1 8
Heaven give your spirits comfort! . . . iv 2 73
What comfort is for Claudio?—There's some in hope . . . iv 2 80
I am come to advise you, comfort you and pray with you . . iv 3 55
To make her heavenly comforts of despair, When it is least expected . iv 3 114
I conjure thee, as thou believest There is another comfort than this world . . . v 1 49
Make it your comfort, So happy is your brother . . . v 1 403
Yet this my comfort: when your words are done, My woes end likewise *Com. of Errors* i 1 27
Get you in again; Comfort my sister, cheer her, call her wife . . iii 2 26

Comfort. I am press'd down with conceit—Conceit, my comfort and my injury *Com. of Errors* iv 2 66
For trouble being gone, comfort should remain *Much Ado* i 1 101
Have comfort, lady.—Dost thou look up? iv 1 119
Go, comfort your cousin: I must say she is dead iv 1 339
Men Can counsel and speak comfort to that grief Which they themselves not feel v 1 21
Comfort me, boy: what great men have been in love? *L. L. Lost* i 2 67
God comfort thy capacity! iv 2 44
I could put thee in comfort iv 3 52
Take comfort: he no more shall see my face *M. N. Dream* i 1 202
And tarry for the comfort of the day ii 2 38
Shine comforts from the east iii 2 432
My clerk hath some good comforts too for you *Mer. of Venice* v 1 289
Would he not be a comfort to our travel? *As Y. Like It* i 3 133
He that doth the ravens feed, Yea, providently caters for the sparrow, Be comfort to my age! ii 3 45
I must comfort the weaker vessel, as doublet and hose ought to show itself courageous to petticoat ii 4 6
Live a little; comfort a little; cheer thyself a little ii 6 5
I thank ye; and be blest for your good comfort! ii 7 135
This contents: The rest will comfort *T. of Shrew* i 1 169
Thou shalt soon feel, to thy cold comfort, for being slow in thy hot office iv 1 33
He that comforts my wife is the cherisher of my flesh and blood *All's Well* i 3 49
Nay, there is some comfort in the news, some comfort iii 2 38
How mightily sometimes we make us comforts of our losses! iv 3 77
I do pity his distress in my similes of comfort v 2 26
And, to comfort you with chance, Assure yourself *T. Night* i 2 8
God comfort thee! Why dost thou smile so and kiss thy hand so oft? iii 4 35
You stand amazed; But be of comfort iii 4 372
You have an unspeakable comfort of your young prince *W. Tale* i 1 38
Nay, there's comfort in't i 2 196
I am like you, they say.—Why, that's some comfort i 2 208
Good expedition be my friend, and comfort The gracious queen! i 2 458
The queen receives Much comfort in't ii 2 28
The crown and comfort of my life, your favour, I do give lost iii 2 95
My third comfort, Starr'd most unluckily, is from my breast, The innocent milk in it most innocent mouth, Haled out to murder iii 2 99
To greet him and to give him comforts iv 4 568
He'll be made an example.—Comfort, good comfort! iv 4 848
For present comfort and for future good v 2 32
O grave and good Paulina, the great comfort That I have had of thee! v 3 1
Makes her As she lived now.—As now she might have done, So much to my good comfort, as it is Now piercing to my soul v 3 33
For this affliction has a taste as sweet As any cordial comfort v 3 77
Courage and comfort! all shall yet go well *K. John* iii 4 4
Patience, good lady! comfort, gentle Constance! iii 4 22
Had you such a loss as I, I could give better comfort than you do iii 4 100
The fire is dead with grief, Being create for comfort, to be used In undeserved extremes iv 1 107
Be of good comfort v 3 9; v 7 25
Entreat the north To make his bleak winds kiss my parched lips And comfort me with cold v 7 41
I do not ask you much, I beg cold comfort v 7 42
This must my comfort be, That sun that warms you here shall shine on me *Richard II.* i 3 144
What comfort, man? how is't? ii 1 72
I dare not say How near the tidings of our comfort is ii 1 272
Comfort's in heaven; and we are on the earth ii 2 78
My comfort is that heaven will take our souls And plague injustice iii 1 33
Nor with thy sweets comfort his ravenous sense iii 2 13
Comfort, my liege: why looks your grace so pale? iii 2 75
Comfort, my liege; remember who you are iii 2 82
Of comfort no man speak: Let's talk of graves, of worms and epitaphs iii 2 144
I'll hate him everlastingly That bids me be of comfort any more iii 2 208
A comfort of retirement lives in this *1 Hen. IV.* iv 1 56
They bring smooth comforts false, worse than true wrongs *2 Hen. IV.* Ind. 40
You muddy rascal, is that all the comfort you give me? ii 4 43
To comfort you the more, I have received A certain instance that Glendower is dead iii 1 102
Our news shall go before us to his majesty, Which, cousin, you shall bear to comfort him iv 3 85
Comfort, your majesty!—O my royal father! iv 4 112
Now I, to comfort him, bid him a' should not think of God *Hen. V.* ii 3 21
That every wretch, pining and pale before, Beholding him, plucks comfort from his looks iv Prol. 42
My comfort is, that old age, that ill layer up of beauty, can do no more spoil upon my face v 2 247
Cheer thy spirit with this comfort *1 Hen. VI.* i 4 90
Swift-winged with desire to get a grave, As witting I no other comfort have ii 5 16
God comfort him in this necessity! iv 3 15
My son, the comfort of my age *2 Hen. VI.* i 1 190
God be praised, that to believing souls Gives light in darkness, comfort in despair! ii 1 67
Great is his comfort in this earthly vale, Although by his sight his sin be multiplied ii 1 70
All comfort go with thee! For none abides with me: my joy is death ii 4 87
Comfort, my sovereign! gracious Henry, comfort! iii 2 38
What, doth my Lord of Suffolk comfort me? iii 2 39
Is all thy comfort shut in Gloucester's tomb? iii 2 78
And in thy need such comfort come to thee As now I reap! *3 Hen. VI.* i 4 165
Comfort, my lord; and so I take my leave iv 8 28
For God's sake, entertain good comfort *Richard III.* i 3 4
Let us in, To comfort Edward with our company ii 1 139
And I for comfort have but one false glass, Which grieves me when I see my shame in him ii 2 53
Thou art a mother, And hast the comfort of thy children left thee ii 2 56
Comfort, dear mother: God is much displeased That you take with unthankfulness his doing ii 2 89
Let him be crown'd; in him your comfort lives ii 2 98
Have comfort: all of us have cause To wail the dimming of our shining star ii 2 101
And came I not at last to comfort you? iv 4 164
Cozen'd Of comfort, kingdom, kindred, freedom, life iv 4 223
Your children were vexation to your youth, But mine shall be a comfort to your age iv 4 306
Yet this good comfort bring I to your grace iv 4 522

Comfort. Lines of fair comfort and encouragement *Richard III.* v 2 6
All comfort that the dark night can afford Be to thy person! v 3 80
Harry, that prophesied thou shouldst be king, Doth comfort thee in thy sleep v 3 130
With thy approach, I know, My comfort comes along *Hen. VIII.* ii 4 240
Deliver, Like free and honest men, our just opinions And comforts to your cause iii 1 61
They are, as all my other comforts, far hence iii 1 90
Is this your comfort? The cordial that ye bring a wretched lady? iii 1 105
If your grace Could but be brought to know our ends are honest, You'ld feel more comfort iii 1 155
She is going, wench: pray, pray.—Heaven comfort her! iv 2 99
That comfort comes too late; 'Tis like a pardon after execution iv 2 120
But now I am past all comforts here, but prayers iv 2 123
Keep comfort to you; and this morning see You do appear before them v 1 144
All comfort, joy, in this most gracious lady, Heaven ever laid up to make parents happy, May hourly fall upon ye! v 5 7
This oracle of comfort has so pleased me, That when I am in heaven I shall desire To see what this child does v 5 67
Strike a free march to Troy! with comfort go *Troi. and Cres.* v 10 30
Will Lose those he hath won.—In that there's comfort *Coriolanus* ii 1 242
Which should Make our eyes flow with joy, hearts dance with comforts v 3 99
Thou barr'st us Our prayers to the gods, which is a comfort That all but we enjoy v 3 105
Alack, or we must lose The country, our dear nurse, or else thy person, Our comfort in the country v 3 111
If The Roman ladies bring not comfort home, They'll give him death by inches v 4 41
He comforts you Can make you greater than the Queen of Goths *T. Andron.* i 1 268
But dawning day new comfort hath inspired ii 2 10
Why dost not comfort me, and help me out? ii 3 209
Rather comfort his distressed plight Than prosecute the meanest or the best iv 4 32
Whose name was once our terror, now our comfort v 1 10
Such comfort as do lusty young men feel When well-apparell'd April on the heel Of limping winter treads *Rom. and Jul.* i 2 26
All this is comfort; wherefore weep I then? iii 2 107
Hie to your chamber: I'll find Romeo To comfort you iii 2 139
Adversity's sweet milk, philosophy, To comfort thee iii 3 56
Ascend her chamber, hence and comfort her iii 3 147
How well my comfort is revived by this! iii 3 165
Comfort me, counsel me iii 5 210
Hast thou not a word of joy? Some comfort, nurse iii 5 214
I'll call them back again to comfort me: Nurse! What should she do here? iv 3 17
O, play me some merry dump, to comfort me iv 5 108
Which failing, Periods his comfort *T. of Athens* i 1 99
O, what a precious comfort 'tis, to have so many, like brothers, commanding one another's fortunes! i 2 108
Lend me a fool's heart and a woman's eyes, And I'll beweep these comforts v 1 161
To keep with you at meals, comfort your bed, And talk to you *J. Cæsar* ii 1 284
These tidings will well comfort Cassius v 3 54
From that spring whence comfort seem'd to come Discomfort swells *Macbeth* i 2 27
There's comfort yet; they are assailable; Then be thou jocund iii 2 39
Be't their comfort We are coming thither iv 3 188
Would I could answer This comfort with the like! iv 3 193
Here comes newer comfort v 8 53
Bend you to remain Here, in the cheer and comfort of our eye *Hamlet* i 2 116
Our good old friend, Lay comforts to your bosom *Lear* ii 1 128
Her eyes are fierce; but thine Do comfort and not burn ii 4 176
I will piece out the comfort with what addition I can iii 6 2
Thy comforts can do me no good at all; Thee they may hurt iv 1 17
'Twas yet some comfort, When misery could beguile the tyrant's rage, And frustrate his proud will iv 6 62
If ever I return to you again, I'll bring you comfort v 2 4
What comfort to this great decay may come Shall be applied v 3 297
He bears the sentence well that nothing bears But the free comfort *Othello* i 3 213
Though he speak of comfort Touching the Turkish loss, yet he looks sadly ii 1 31
Give renew'd fire to our extincted spirits, And bring all Cyprus comfort! ii 1 82
Not another comfort like to this Succeeds in unknown fate ii 1 194
Our loves and comforts should increase, Even as our days do grow ii 1 196
I prattle out of fashion, and I dote In mine own comforts ii 1 209
Or that I do not yet . . . love him dearly, Comfort forswear me! iv 2 159
And returned me expectations and comforts of sudden respect and acquaintance iv 2 192
The elements be kind to thee, and make Thy spirits all of comfort! *Ant. and Cleo.* iii 2 41
Best of comfort; And ever welcome to us iii 6 89
Nay, gentle madam, to him, comfort him iii 11 25
Her head's declined, and death will seize her, but Your comfort makes the rescue iii 11 48
You take me in too dolorous a sense; For I spake to you for your comfort iv 2 40
I will reward thee Once for thy spritely comfort, and ten-fold For thy good valour iv 7 15
All strange and terrible events are welcome, But comforts we despise iv 15 4
Give her what comforts The quality of her passion shall require v 1 62
Have comfort, for I know your plight is pitied Of him that caused it v 2 33
Make yourself some comfort Out of your best advice *Cymbeline* i 1 155
Blest be those, How mean soe'er, that have their honest wills, Which seasons comfort i 6 9
Often, to our comfort, shall we find The sharded beetle in a safer hold Than is the full-wing'd eagle iii 3 19
In my life what comfort, when I am Dead to my husband? iii 4 132
Thou art all the comfort The gods will diet me with iii 4 182
I'll make't my comfort He is a man; I'll love him as my brother iii 6 71
Society is no comfort To one not sociable iv 2 12
Imogen, The great part of my comfort, gone; my queen Upon a desperate bed iv 3 5
It strikes me, past The hope of comfort iv 3 9
His comforts thrive, his trials well are spent v 4 104
The comfort is, you shall be called to no more payments, fear no more tavern-bills v 4 160
All o'erjoy'd, Save these in bonds: let them be joyful too, For they shall taste our comfort v 5 403

Comfort. Neither pleasure's art can joy my spirits, Nor yet the other's distance comfort me *Pericles* i 2 10
Joy and all comfort in your sacred breast! i 2 33
Finding little comfort to relieve them, I thought it princely charity to grieve them i 2 99
That, if heaven slumber while their creatures want, They may awake their helps to comfort them i 4 17
Comfort is too far for us to expect i 4 59
A little daughter: for the sake of it, Be manly, and take comfort iii 1 22
Men must comfort you, men must feed you iv 2 97
Comfortable. For my sake be comfortable *As Y. L. It* ii 6 9
Be comfortable to my mother, your mistress, and make much of her *All's Well* i 1 86
A comfortable doctrine, and much may be said of it *T. Night* i 5 239
For God's sake, speak comfortable words.—Should I do so, I should belie my thoughts *Richard II.* ii 2 76
What comfortable hour canst thou name, That ever graced me in thy company? *Richard III.* iv 4 173
Daughter, sing; or express yourself in a more comfortable sort *Coriolanus* i 3 2
O comfortable friar! where is my lord? *Rom. and Jul.* v 3 148
His comfortable temper has forsook him; he's much out of health *T. of Athens* iii 4 71
Had I steward So true, so just, and now so comfortable? iv 3 498
Yet have I left a daughter, Who, I am sure, is kind and comfortable *Lear* i 4 32[?]
That by thy comfortable beams I may Peruse this letter ii 2 171
Keep your mind, till you return to us, Peaceful and comfortable! *Pericles* i 2 35
Comforted. In his bright radiance and collateral light Must I be comforted *All's Well* i 1 100
Well, thou hast comforted me marvellous much *Rom. and Jul.* iii 5 230
Be comforted: Let's make us medicines of our great revenge. *Macbeth* iv 3 213
Be comforted, good madam: the great rage, You see, is kill'd in him *Lear* iv 7 78
Be comforted, dear madam.—No, I will not *Ant. and Cleo.* iv 15 2
Not comforted to live, But that there is this jewel in the world That I may see again *Cymbeline* i 1 90
Comforter. Do not omit the heavy offer of it: It seldom visits sorrow; when it doth, It is a comforter *Tempest* ii 1 196
A solemn air and the best comforter To an unsettled fancy v 1 58
Give not me counsel; Nor let no comforter delight mine ear *Much Ado* v 1 6
The heavens have bless'd you with a goodly son, To be your comforter *Richard III.* i 3 10
Comfortest. Thou sun, that comfort'st, burn! Speak, and be hang'd *T. of Athens* v 1 134
Comforting. Your most obedient counsellor, yet that dare Less appear so in comforting your evils *W. Tale* ii 3 56
Times to repair our nature With comforting repose *Hen VIII.* v 1 4
If I find him comforting the king, it will stuff his suspicion more fully *Lear* iii 5 21
Comforting therein, that when old robes are worn out, there are members to make new. *Ant. and Cleo.* i 2 170
Comfortless. Moody and dull melancholy, Kinsman to grim and comfortless despair *Com. of Errors* v 1 80
News fitting to the night, Black, fearful, comfortless and horrible *K. John* v 6 20
The queen is comfortless, and we forgetful In our long absence *Hen. VIII.* ii 3 105
That kiss is comfortless As frozen water to a starved snake *T. Andron.* iii 1 251
Out, vile jelly! Where is thy lustre now?—All dark and comfortless *Lear* iii 7 85
Comic. I see our wars Will turn unto a peaceful comic sport *1 Hen. VI.* ii 2 45
With stately triumphs, mirthful comic shows *3 Hen. VI.* v 7 43
Coming thence, My son is lost *Tempest* ii 1 108
Once more adieu! my father at the road Expects my coming *T. G. of Ver.* i 1 54
My father stays my coming; answer not; The tide is now ii 2 13
When will you go?—This evening coming iv 3 42
Unhappy were you, madam, ere I came; But by my coming I have made you happy v 4 30
See if you can see my master, Master Doctor Caius, coming *Mer. Wives* i 4 3
Trust me, I was coming to you ii 2 35
Yonder he is coming, this way iii 1 27
Your husband's coming hither, woman, with all the officers iii 3 113
But 'tis most certain your husband's coming iii 3 121
She's coming; to her, coz. O boy, thou hadst a father! iii 4 36
But is my husband coming?—Ay, in good sadness, is he iv 2 92
Here's a Bohemian-Tartar tarries the coming down of thy fat woman iv 5 22
Who knew of your intent and coming hither? *Meas. for Meas.* v 1 124
I prithee, is he coming home? *Com. of Errors* ii 1 55
Go along; my wife is coming yonder iv 4 43
He not coming thither, I went to seek him v 1 224
To-morrow then I will expect your coming *Much Ado* v 1 305
Vouchsafe to read the purpose of my coming *L. L. Lost* ii 1 109
Why look you pale? Sea-sick, I think, coming from Muscovy v 2 393
There are Worthies a-coming will speak their mind in some other sort v 2 589
Excuse me so, coming too short of thanks v 2 748
Let not me play a woman; I have a beard coming *M. N. Dream* i 2 50
The trusty Thisby, coming first by night, Did scare away v 1 141
I fear we shall out-sleep the coming morn v 1 372
Ill luck?—Hath an argosy cast away, coming from Tripolis *Mer. of Ven.* iii 1 105
Sweet soul, let's in, and there expect their coming v 1 49
But there is come a messenger before, To signify their coming v 1 118
I confess, your coming before me is nearer to his reverence *As Y. Like It* i 1 54
And here, where you are, they are coming to perform it i 2 122
And bid him take that for coming a-night to Jane Smile ii 4 48
There is, sure, another flood toward, and these couples are coming to the ark v 4 36
May I be so bold to know the cause of your coming? *T. of Shrew* ii 1 88
Why, is it not news, to hear of Petruchio's coming? iii 2 34
Is he come?—Why, no, sir.—What then?—He is coming iii 2 38
Petruchio is coming in a new hat and an old jerkin iii 2 43
And is the bride and bridegroom coming home? iii 2 153
And after me, I know, the rout is coming iii 2 183
I am sent before to make a fire, and they are coming after to warm them iv 1 5
Is my master and his wife coming? iv 1 18
But at last I spied An ancient angel coming down the hill iv 2 61
But, soft! company is coming here iv 5 26
The solemn feast Shall more attend upon the coming space, Expecting absent friends *All's Well* ii 3 188
To make the coming hour o'erflow with joy And pleasure drown the brim ii 4 47
Your true love's coming, That can sing both high and low *T. Night* ii 3 41
Malvolio's coming down this walk ii 5 19
Shall I vent to her that thou art coming? iv 1 18
I think, this coming summer *W. Tale* i 1 6
He is not guilty of her coming hither ii 3 144

Coming. Your guests are coming: Lift up your countenance *W. Tale* iv 4 48
And, ere our coming, see thou shake the bags Of hoarding abbots *K. John* iii 3 7
Some unborn sorrow, ripe in fortune's womb, Is coming towards me *Richard II.* ii 2 11
The noble duke hath sworn his coming is But for his own ii 3 148
His coming hither hath no further scope Than for his lineal royalties iii 3 112
When weeping made you break the story off, Of our two cousins coming v 2 3
There's money of the king's coming down the hill *1 Hen. IV.* ii 2 56
Stand close; I hear them coming ii 2 103
Since your coming hither have done enough To put him quite beside his patience iii 1 178
Coming in to borrow a mess of vinegar *2 Hen. IV.* ii 1 103
He heard of your grace's coming to town: there's a letter for you ii 2 108
What doth concern your coming? iv 1 30
Coming to look on you, thinking you dead iv 5 156
I am coming on, To venge me as I may *Hen. V.* i 2 291
In fierce tempest is he coming, In thunder and in earthquake ii 4 99
The winter coming on and sickness growing iii 3 55
From Ireland coming, Bringing rebellion v Prol. 31
The emperor's coming in behalf of France v Prol. 38
And here I will expect thy coming *1 Hen. VI.* v 3 145
To watch the coming of my punish'd duchess *2 Hen. VI.* ii 4 7
Now get thee hence: the king, thou know'st, is coming iii 2 386
And duly waited for my coming forth iv 1 62
She was coming with a full intent To dash our late decree *3 Hen. VI.* ii 1 117
Before thy coming Lewis was Henry's friend iii 3 143
We were forewarned of your coming iv 7 17
To White-Friars; there attend my coming *Richard III.* i 2 227
I do not like their coming *Hen. VIII.* iii 1 21
We shall give you The full cause of our coming iii 1 29
I am not such a truant since my coming, As not to know the language iii 1 43
From all parts they are coming, As if we kept a fair here! v 4 72
They are coming from the field: shall we stand up here? *Troi. and Cres.* i 2 192
Ha! Marcius coming home! *Coriolanus* ii 1 112
Hoo! Marcius coming home!—Nay, 'tis true ii 1 116
Coming and going with thy honey breath *T. Andron.* ii 4 25
Is not thy coming for my other hand? v 2 27
Hasten all the house to bed . . . : Romeo is coming *Rom. and Jul.* iii 3 158
Your lady mother is coming to your chamber iii 5 39
Stay not to question, for the watch is coming v 3 158
We took this mattock and this spade from him, As he was coming from this churchyard side v 3 186
I have told my lord of you; he is coming down to you *T. of Athens* iii 1 1
He would embrace no counsel, take no warning by my coming iii 1 28
Tell him of an intent that's coming toward him v 1 23
He did receive his letters, and is coming *J. Cæsar* iii 1 279
Is thy master coming?—He lies to-night within seven leagues of Rome iii 1 285
Coming from Sardis, on our former ensign Two mighty eagles fell v 1 80
So please you, it is true: our thane is coming *Macbeth* i 5 35
He that's coming Must be provided for i 5 67
Be't their comfort We are coming thither iv 3 189
That way are they coming v 2 6
Within this three mile may you see it coming; I say, a moving grove v 5 37
And prologue to the omen coming on *Hamlet* i 1 123
And hither are they coming, to offer you service ii 2 331
I hear him coming: let's withdraw iii 1 55
Fear me not: withdraw, I hear him coming iii 4 7
He could nothing do but wish and beg Your sudden coming o'er iv 7 106
The king and queen and all are coming down v 2 212
I hear my father coming: pardon me *Lear* ii 1 30
Which way Thou mightst deserve, or they impose, this usage, Coming from us ii 4 27
I told him you were coming; His answer was 'The worse' iv 2 5
Which since his coming forth is thought of iv 3 4
Men must endure Their going hence, even as their coming hither v 2 10
That he would steal away so guilty-like, Seeing you coming *Othello* iii 3 40
I' faith, sweet love, I was coming to your house iii 4 171
I hear him coming.—I know his gait, 'tis he v 1 22
Coming from him, that great medicine hath With his tinct gilded thee *Ant. and Cleo.* i 5 36
Thyself art coming To see perform'd the dreaded act which thou So sought'st to hinder v 2 333
May This night forestall him of the coming day! *Cymbeline* iii 5 69
And stay your coming to present themselves *Pericles* ii 2 3
The knights are coming: we will withdraw ii 2 58
You have fortunes coming upon you iv 2 126
He is coming *Meas. for Meas.* ii 2; iv 3; *T. Night* iii 4; *Coriolanus* iii 3; iv 6; *Lear* i 3
He is coming hither *T. of Shrew* iv 1; *2 Hen. IV.* iv 5; *Lear* ii 1
The duke is coming *M. N. Dream* iv 2 15; *Hen. VIII.* ii 1 98
The king is coming *All's Well* v 2; *Hen. V.* iii 6; *Lear* i 1
The queen is coming *3 Hen. VI.* ii 1 207; *Hen. VIII.* iv 1 36
They are coming *As Y. Like It* i 2; *Coriolanus* ii 2; *Hamlet* iii 2
Coming in. Eleven widows and nine maids is a simple coming-in for one man *Mer. of Venice* ii 2 171
For your coming in to dinner, sir, why, let it be as humours and conceits shall govern iii 5 68
What are thy comings in? O ceremony, show me but thy worth! *Hen. V.* iv 1 260
And in conclusion to oppose the bolt Against my coming in *Lear* ii 4 180
Coming on. In a more coming-on disposition *As Y. Like It* iv 1 113
In coming on he has the cramp *All's Well* iv 3 324
The men do sympathize with the mastiffs in robustious and rough coming on *Hen. V.* iii 7 159
Referred me to the coming on of time, with 'Hail, king that shalt be!' *Macbeth* i 5 9
Cominius. Attend upon Cominius to these wars *Coriolanus* i 1 241
Lead you on. Follow Cominius; we must follow you i 1 250
I do wonder His insolence can brook to be commanded Under Cominius i 1 267
Opinion that so sticks on Marcius shall Of his demerits rob Cominius i 1 276
Half all Cominius' honours are to Marcius, Though Marcius earn'd them not i 1 277
The Volsces have an army forth; against whom Cominius the general is gone i 3 108
Whilst I, with those that have the spirit, will haste To help Cominius i 5 15
Speak, good Cominius: Leave nothing out for length ii 2 52
Please you To hear Cominius speak? ii 2 66
Worthy Cominius, speak. Nay, keep your place.—Sit, Coriolanus ii 2 70
Proceed, Cominius.—I shall lack voice ii 2 85
Hath he not pass'd the noble and the common?—Cominius, no iii 1 30
Here is Cominius.—I have been i' the market-place iii 2 92

Cominius. Cominius, Droop not; adieu. Farewell, my wife, my mother *Coriolanus* iv 1 19
Whither wilt thou go? Take good Cominius With thee awhile iv 1 34
Nay, if he coy'd To hear Cominius speak, I'll keep at home v 1 7
Return me, as Cominius is return'd, Unheard v 1 42
Yet, to bite his lip And hum at good Cominius, much unhearts me v 1 49
Comma. No levell'd malice Infects one comma in the course *T. of Athens* i 1 48
Peace should still her wheaten garland wear And stand a comma 'tween their amities *Hamlet* v 2 42
Command. If you can command these elements to silence *Tempest* i 1 23
Thou wast a spirit too delicate To act her earthy and abhorr'd commands i 2 273
I will be correspondent to command And do my spiriting gently i 2 297
If thou neglect'st or dost unwillingly What I command, I'll rack thee with old cramps i 2 369
But then exactly do All points of my command i 2 500
He's but a sot, as I am, nor hath not One spirit to command iii 2 102
Juno does command: Come, temperate nymphs iv 1 131
Graves at my command Have waked their sleepers v 1 48
One so strong That could control the moon, make flows and ebbs, And deal in her command without her power v 1 271
So it stead you, I will write, Please you command *T. G. of Ver.* ii 1 120
Which to requite, command me while I live iii 1 23
By his master's command, he must carry for a present to his lady iv 2 79
Your friend; One that attends your ladyship's command iv 3 5
Thus early come to know what service It is your pleasure to command me in iv 3 10
Let us command to know that of your mouth or of your lips *Mer. Wives* i 1 235
They have had my house a week at command iv 3 12
'Twas a commandment to command the captain *Meas. for Meas.* i 2 13
Or whether that the body public be A horse whereon the governor doth ride, Who, newly in the seat, that it may know He can command, lets it straight feel the spur i 2 166
This bigger key: This other doth command a little door iv 1 32
Having the hour limited, and an express command, under penalty iv 2 176
See this be done, And sent according to command iv 3 84
Command these fretting waters from your eyes With a light heart iv 3 151
With thy command Let him be brought forth *Com. of Errors* v 1 159
I, sir, am Dromio: command him away v 1 335
Will your grace command me any service to the world's end? *Much Ado* ii 1 271
Shall I command thy love? I may: shall I enforce thy love? I could *L. L. Lost* iv 1 82
At the king's command iv 1 128
Please it your majesty Command me any service? v 2 312
My heels are at your command *Mer. of Venice* ii 2 33
How many then should cover that stand bare! How many be commanded that command! ii 9 45
I shall obey you in all fair commands iii 4 36
Take upon command what help we have *As Y. Like It* ii 7 125
So fare you well: I have left you commands v 2 131
With a low submissive reverence Say 'What is it your honour will command?' *T. of Shrew* Ind. 1 54
What is't your honour will command, Wherein your lady and your humble wife May show her duty? Ind. 1 115
Or what you will command me will I do ii 1 6
Go, fool, and whom thou keep'st command ii 1 259
They shall go forward, Kate, at thy command iii 2 224
Why, so this gallant will command the sun iv 3 198
The old priest of Saint Luke's church is at your command at all hours iv 4 89
I think I shall command your welcome here v 1 13
Say, I command her come to me.—I know her answer v 2 96
I must attend his majesty's command, to whom I am now in ward *All's Well* i 1 5
That man should be at woman's command, and yet no hurt done! i 3 96
Give me with thy kingly hand What husband in thy power I will command ii 1 197
What more commands he? ii 4 52
There was excellent command,—to charge in with our horse upon our own wings! iii 6 51
That was not to be blamed in the command of the service iii 6 55
Cæsar himself could not have prevented, if he had been there to command iii 6 57
I am a poor man, and at your majesty's command v 3 252
I may command where I adore *T. Night* ii 5 115
'I may command where I adore.' Why, she may command me: I serve her ii 5 126
It did come to his hands, and commands shall be executed iii 4 29
If 'twere so, She could not sway her house, command her followers iv 3 17
It is in mine authority to command The keys *W. Tale* i 2 463
Which often hath no less prevail'd than so On your command ii 1 55
The good mind of Camillo tardied My swift command iii 2 164
I willingly obey your command iv 2 60
Whereupon I command thee to open thy affair iv 4 763
By his command Have I here touch'd Sicilia v 1 138
At your best command; At your employment; at your service, sir *K. John* i 1 197
It shall be so; and at the other hill Command the rest to stand ii 1 299
Command thy son and daughter to join hands ii 1 532
My life thou shalt command, but not my shame *Richard II.* i 1 166
We were not born to sue, but to command i 1 196
Command our officers at arms Be ready i 1 204
If my word be sterling yet in England, Let it command a mirror hither straight iv 1 265
Sir Pierce of Exton, who lately came from the king, commands the contrary v 5 101
When I am king of England, I shall command all the good lads in East-cheap *1 Hen. IV.* ii 4 15
Why, I can teach you, cousin, to command The devil iii 1 55
And many moe corrivals and dear men Of estimation and command in arms iv 4 32
A soldier-like word, and a word of exceeding good command *2 Hen. IV.* iii 2 84
No man could better command his servants v 1 83
Will you command me to use my legs? Epil. 19
Keep close, I thee command *Hen. V.* ii 3 65
As bootless spend our vain command Upon the enraged soldiers in their spoil iii 3 24
Take pity of your town and of your people, Whiles yet my soldiers are in my command iii 3 29
A servant, under his master's command transporting a sum of money iv 1 158
Canst thou, when thou command'st the beggar's knee, Command the health of it? iv 1 274
Virtue he had, deserving to command *1 Hen. VI.* i 1 9
Command. Thou art protector And lookest to command the prince and realm *1 Hen. VI.* i 1 38
Peel'd priest, dost thou command me to be shut out? i 3 30
We charge and command you, in his highness' name i 3 76
Command the citizens make bonfires And feast and banquet in the open streets i 6 12
This place commands my patience iii 1 8
Compassion on the king commands me stoop iii 1 119
And then your highness shall command a peace iv 1 117
Upon my blessing, I command thee go iv 5 36
Command the conquest, Charles, it shall be thine v 2 19
Command in Anjou what your honour pleases v 3 147
She is content to be at your command; Command, I mean, of virtuous chaste intents v 5 19
Hast thou not worldly pleasure at command? *2 Hen. VI.* i 2 45
The Nevils are thy subjects to command ii 2 8
Suffolk's imperial tongue is stern and rough, Used to command iv 1 122
Command silence.—Silence! iv 2 39
Such aid as I can spare you shall command iv 5 7
I charge and command that, of the city's cost, the pissing-conduit run nothing but claret wine iv 6 3
Away with him! and do as I command ye iv 7 125
We charge and command that their wives be as free as heart can wish or tongue can tell iv 7 132
Dare any be so bold to sound retreat or parley, when I command them kill? iv 8 5
Was ever king that joy'd an earthly throne, And could command no more content than I? iv 9 2
Command my eldest son, nay, all my sons, As pledges v 1 49
Stern Falconbridge commands the narrow seas *3 Hen. VI.* i 1 239
As doth a sail, fill'd with a fretting gust, Command an argosy to stem the waves ii 6 36
The king shall be commanded; And be you kings, command, and I'll obey iii 1 93
What service wilt thou do me, if I give them?—What you command iii 2 45
Why, then I will do what your grace commands iii 2 49
Since this earth affords no joy to me, But to command, to check, to o'erbear iii 2 166
Margaret Must strike her sail and learn awhile to serve Where kings command iii 3 6
Why commands the king That his chief followers lodge in towns about him? iv 3 12
Let me entreat, for I command no more iv 6 59
Unmanner'd dog! stand thou, when I command *Richard III.* i 2 39
What we will do, we do upon command i 4 198
He may command me as my sovereign; But you have power in me as in a kinsman iii 1 108
Say that the king, which may command, entreats iv 4 345
Out of anger He sent command to the lord mayor straight *Hen. VIII.* ii 1 151
That good fellow, if I command him, follows my appointment ii 2 134
Hear the king's pleasure, cardinal: who commands you To render up the great seal iii 2 228
Ye shall be my guests: Something I can command iv 1 116
You may command us, sir iv 1 117
The eastern tower, Whose height commands as subject all the vale *Troi. and Cres.* i 2 3
Achievement is command; ungain'd, beseech i 2 319
Agamemnon commands Achilles; Achilles is my lord ii 3 56
Agamemnon is a fool to offer to command Achilles ii 3 67
Disguise the holy strength of their command ii 3 136
To Diomed You shall be mistress, and command him wholly iv 4 122
What shall be done To him that victory commands? iv 5 66
Shall I, sweet lord, be bound to you so much . . . ?—You shall command me, sir iv 5 286
Ajax commands the guard to tend on you v 1 79
Four shall quickly draw out my command, Which men are best inclined *Coriolanus* i 6 84
Necessity Commands me name myself iv 5 63
Thou hast a grim appearance, and thy face Bears a command in't iv 5 67
I parted hence, but still subsisting Under your great command v 6 74
And bring you up To be a warrior, and command a camp *T. Andron.* iv 2 180
He commands us to provide, and give great gifts, And all out of an empty coffer *T. of Athens* i 2 198
One business does command us all; for mine Is money iii 4 4
Nor has he with him to Supply his life, or that which can command it iv 2 47
The sweet degrees that this brief world affords To such as may the passive drugs of it Freely command iv 3 255
He did command me to call timely on him *Macbeth* ii 3 51
Let your highness Command upon me iii 1 16
We shall, my lord, Perform what you command us iii 1 127
What I am truly, Is thine and my poor country's to command iv 3 132
She has light by her continually; 'tis her command v 1 27
Those he commands move only in command, Nothing in love v 2 19
Set your entreatments at a higher rate Than a command to parley *Hamlet* i 3 123
As you did command, I did repel his letters ii 1 108
Put your dread pleasures more into command Than to entreaty ii 2 28
His antique sword, Rebellious to his arm, lies where it falls, Repugnant to command ii 2 493
Such answer as I can make, you shall command iii 2 335
These are the stops.—But these cannot I command to any utterance of harmony iii 2 377
The front of Jove himself; An eye like Mars, to threaten and command iii 4 57
That, lapsed in time and passion, lets go by The important acting of your dread command iii 4 108
Who commands them, sir?—The nephew to old Norway iv 4 13
And, but that great command o'ersways the order, She should in ground unsanctified have lodged v 1 251
An exact command, Larded with many several sorts of reasons v 2 19
The dear father Would with his daughter speak, commands her service *Lear* ii 4 103
When nature, being oppress'd, commands the mind To suffer with the body ii 4 109
How, in one house, Should many people, under two commands, Hold amity? ii 4 244
What need you five and twenty, ten, or five, To follow in a house where twice so many Have a command to tend you? ii 4 266
My duty cannot suffer To obey in all your daughters' hard commands iii 4 154
To hear, If you dare venture in your own behalf, A mistress's command iv 2 21
And turn our impress'd lances in our eyes Which do command them v 3 51
At every house I'll call; I may command at most *Othello* i 1 182

Command. You shall more command with years Than with your weapons *Othello* i 2 60
I have served him, and the man commands Like a full soldier ii 1 35
Watch you to-night; for the command, I'll lay't upon you ii 1 272
Let him command, And to obey shall be in me remorse, What bloody business ever iii 3 467
She might lie by an emperor's side and command him tasks iv 1 196
As I think, they do command him home, Deputing Cassio in his government iv 1 247
Your power and your command is taken off, And Cassio rules in Cyprus v 2 331
Sextus Pompeius Hath given the dare to Cæsar, and commands The empire of the sea *Ant. and Cleo.* i 2 191
The strong necessity of time commands Our services awhile i 3 42
That Herod's head I'll have: but how, when Antony is gone Through whom I might command it? iii 3 6
Choose your own company, and command what cost Your heart has mind to. iii 4 37
Leave me, I pray, a little: pray you now: Nay, do so; for, indeed, I have lost command iii 11 23
Thy beck might from the bidding of the gods Command me iii 11 61
Whose ministers would prevail Under the service of a child as soon As i' the command of Cæsar iii 13 25
One that but performs The bidding of the fullest man, and worthiest To have command obey'd iii 13 88
Make as much of me As when mine empire was your fellow too, And suffer'd my command iv 2 23
That, on my command, Thou then wouldst kill me. iv 14 66
'Tis the last service that I shall command you iv 14 132
As thereto sworn by your command, Which my love makes religion to obey v 2 198
If after this command thou fraught the court With thy unworthiness, thou diest *Cymbeline* i 1 126
You have done Not after our command. Away with her, And pen her up i 1 152
Why came you from your master?—On his command i 1 170
Left these notes Of what commands I should be subject to i 1 172
That you in all obey her, Save when command to your dismission tends iii 5 57
How! that I should murder her? Upon the love and truth and vows which I Have made to thy command? iii 2 13
By her own command Shall give thee opportunity iii 2 18
Since I received command to do this business I have not slept one wink iii 4 102
You must forget to be a woman; change Command into obedience iii 4 158
Command our present numbers Be muster'd iv 2 343
Every good servant does not all commands: No bond but to do just ones v 1 6
And thou, that hast Upon the winds command, bind them in brass! *Pericles* iii 1 3
Certain jewels Lay with you in your coffer: which are now At your command iii 4 3
Get this done as I command you.—Performance shall follow iv 2 66
Neither of these are so bad as thou art, Since they do better thee in their command iv 6 172
To perform thy just command, I here confess myself the king v 3 1
Commande. Il me commande de vous dire que vous faites vous prêt *Hen. V.* iv 4 36
Commanded. To close prison he commanded her *T. G. of Ver.* iii 1 235
Her father hath commanded her to slip Away *Mer. Wives* iv 6 23
It was commanded so.—Had you a special warrant? *Meas. for Meas.* v 1 463
How many be commanded that command! *Mer. of Venice* ii 9 45
A woman's gift To rain a shower of commanded tears *T. of Shrew* Ind. 1 125
I commanded the sleeves should be cut out and sewed up again iv 3 147
I am commanded here, and kept a coil with 'Too young' and 'the next year' and ''tis too early' *All's Well* ii 1 27
I have, sir, as I was commanded from you, Spoke with the king ii 5 59
He hath not slept to-night; commanded None should come at him *W. Tale* ii 3 31
With a love even such, So and no other, as yourself commanded iii 2 67
We were all commanded out of the chamber v 2 6
I beg no favour, Only convey me where thou art commanded *2 Hen. VI.* ii 4 93
We have dispatch'd the duke, as he commanded iii 2 2
Commanded always by the greater gust *3 Hen. VI.* iii 1 88
The king shall be commanded; And be you kings, command, and I'll obey iv 6 92
I am commanded, with your leave and favour, Humbly to kiss your hand iii 3 60
I am, in this, commanded to deliver The noble Duke of Clarence to your hands *Richard III.* i 4 92
What we will do, we do upon command.—And he that hath commanded is the king i 4 199
The great King of kings Hath in the tables of his law commanded That thou shalt do no murder i 4 201
They have not been commanded, mighty sovereign iv 4 487
To be commanded For ever by your grace, whose hand has raised me *Hen. VIII.* ii 2 119
Let silence be commanded.—What's the need? ii 4 2
I stood not in the smile of heaven; who had Commanded nature ii 4 188
Hath commanded To-morrow morning to the council-board He be convented v 1 50
I could not personally deliver to her What you commanded me v 1 63
I have brought my lord the archbishop, As you commanded me v 1 81
Achilles is a fool to be commanded of Agamemnon *Troi. and Cres.* ii 3 68
I do wonder His insolence can brook to be commanded *Coriolanus* i 1 266
We are the empress' sons.—And therefore do we what we are commanded *T. Andron.* v 2 164
But one word more,— He will not be commanded *Macbeth* iv 1 75
And here give up ourselves, in the full bent To lay our service freely at your feet, To be commanded *Hamlet* ii 2 32
Commanded me to follow, and attend The leisure of their answer *Lear* ii 4 36
I am commanded home. Get you away *Othello* iv 1 269
He hath commanded me to go to bed, And bade me to dismiss you iv 3 13
E'en a woman, and commanded By such poor passion as the maid that milks And does the meanest chares *Ant. and Cleo.* iv 15 73
Wherefore you have Commanded of me these most poisonous compounds *Cymbeline* i 5 8
I am ignorant in what I am commanded iii 2 23
'Tis commanded I should do so iii 4 128
That is the second thing that I have commanded thee iii 5 157
Commander. We must prepare to meet with Caliban.—Ay, my commander *Tempest* iv 1 167
Be ruled by thee, Love thee as our commander and our king *T. G. of Ver.* iv 1 67
When in the world I lived, I was the world's commander *L. L. Lost* v 2 565
It is reported that he has taken their greatest commander *All's Well* iii 5 6
Commander. The troops are all scattered, and the commanders very poor rogues *All's Well* iv 3 153
Commander of this hot malicious day *K. John* ii 1 314
Such fellows are perfect in the great commanders' names *Hen. V.* iii 6 74
A good old commander and a most kind gentleman iv 1 97
While the vulture of sedition Feeds in the bosom of such great commanders *1 Hen. VI.* iv 3 48
Royal commanders, be in readiness *3 Hen. VI.* ii 2 67
Agamemnon, Thou great commander, nerve and bone of Greece *Tr. and Cr.* i 3 55
What's Agamemnon?—Thy commander, Achilles ii 3 47
To Saturnine, King and commander of our commonweal. *T. Andron.* i 1 247
Lord of my life, commander of my thoughts iv 4 28
Bid our commanders lead their charges off A little from this ground *J. Cæsar* iv 2 48
Bid the commanders Prepare to lodge their companies to-night iv 3 139
I will rather sue to be despised than to deceive so good a commander *Othello* ii 3 279
Commandest. Canst thou, when thou command'st the beggar's knee, Command the health of it? *Hen. V.* iv 1 273
Shalt find Men well inclined to hear what thou command'st *3 Hen. VI.* iv 8 15
Commanding. Subjected tribute to commanding love *K. John* i 1 264
He speaks with such a proud commanding spirit *1 Hen. VI.* iv 7 88
The great commanding Warwick Is thither gone *3 Hen. VI.* iii 1 29
Where every horse bears his commanding rein *Richard III.* ii 2 128
For one being fear'd of all, now fearing one; For one commanding all, obey'd of none iv 4 104
By whose virtue, The court of Rome commanding *Hen. VIII.* ii 2 105
Wife-like government, Obeying in commanding ii 4 139
Commanding peace Even with the same austerity and garb As he controll'd the war *Coriolanus* iv 7 43
O, what a precious comfort 'tis, to have so many, like brothers, commanding one another's fortunes! *T. of Athens* i 2 109
Commandment. Like the sanctimonious pirate, that went to sea with the Ten Commandments, but scraped one out of the table *M. for M.* i 2 8
Why, 'twas a commandment to command the captain and all the rest from their functions i 2 12
Let his deservings and my love withal Be valued 'gainst your wife's commandment *Mer. of Venice* iv 1 451
Therefore put I on the countenance Of stern commandment *As Y. Like It* ii 7 109
To the contrary I have express commandment *W. Tale* ii 2 8
Have I commandment on the pulse of life? *K. John* iv 2 92
Had the best of them all at commandment *2 Hen. IV.* iii 2 27
The laws of England are at my commandment v 3 143
From him I have express commandment *1 Hen. VI.* i 3 20
I'ld set my ten commandments in your face *2 Hen. VI.* i 3 145
And posts, like the commandment of a king, Sans check to good and bad *Troi. and Cres.* i 3 93
Say, you chose him More after our commandment than as guided By your own true affections *Coriolanus* ii 3 238
Thy commandment all alone shall live Within the book and volume of my brain *Hamlet* i 5 102
If it shall please you to make me a wholesome answer, I will do your mother's commandment iii 2 329
Tell him his commandment is fulfill'd v 2 381
He never gave commandment for their death v 2 385
Commence. Many a wooer doth commence his suit To her he thinks not worthy, yet he wooes *Much Ado* ii 3 52
Most shallowly did you these arms commence *2 Hen. IV.* iv 2 118
Sack commences it and sets it in act and use iv 3 125
And, like a hungry lion, did commence Rough deeds of rage *1 Hen. VI.* iv 7 7
Thy nature did commence in sufferance, time Hath made thee hard in't *T. of Athens* iv 3 268
Never did my actions yet commence A deed might gain her love or your displeasure *Pericles* ii 5 53
Commenced. And breathe short-winded accents of new broils To be commenced in strands afar remote *1 Hen. IV.* i 1 4
Still unfold The acts commenced on this ball of earth *2 Hen. IV.* Ind. 5
When he to madding Dido would unfold His father's acts commenced in burning Troy *2 Hen. VI.* iii 2 118
Commencement. The origin and commencement of his grief Sprung from neglected love *Hamlet* iii 1 185
It was a violent commencement, and thou shalt see an answerable sequestration *Othello* i 3 350
Commencing. Why hath it given me earnest of success, Commencing in a truth? *Macbeth* i 3 133
Commend thy grievance to my holy prayers *T. G. of Ver.* i 1 17
I'll commend you to my master i 1 155
To salute the emperor And to commend their service to his will i 3 42
Flatter and praise, commend, extol their graces iii 1 102
When to her beauty I commend my vows, She bids me think how I have been forsworn iv 2 9
What is she, That all our swains commend her? iv 2 40
If thou seest her before me, commend me *Mer. Wives* i 4 168
My desires had instance and argument to commend themselves ii 2 256
Sir, I commend you to your own content.—He that commends me to mine own content Commends me to the thing I cannot get *Com. of Err.* i 2 32
I did commend the black-oppressing humour to the most wholesome physic of thy health-giving air *L. L. Lost* i 1 234
Lady, I will commend you to mine own heart ii 1 180
And to her white hand see thou do commend This seal'd-up counsel iii 1 169
Well learned is that tongue that well can thee commend iv 2 116
Besides commends and courteous breath, Gifts of rich value *Mer. of Ven.* ii 9 90
This letter from Bellario doth commend A young and learned doctor iv 1 143
Bettered with his own learning, the greatness whereof I cannot enough commend iv 1 159
Your daughter and her cousin much commend The parts and graces of the wrestler *As Y. Like It* ii 2 12
I pray you, commend my counterfeiting to him iv 3 183
Say she be mute and will not speak a word; Then I'll commend her volubility *T. of Shrew* ii 1 176
They shall be no more than needful there, if they were more than they can commend *All's Well* iv 3 94
Commend the paper to his gracious hand v 1 31
She did commend my yellow stockings *T. Night* ii 5 180
Commend my best obedience to the queen *W. Tale* ii 2 36
Hath brought you forth a daughter; Here 'tis; commends it to your blessing ii 3 66
Commend it strangely to some place Where chance may nurse or end it ii 3 182
Commend them and condemn them to her service Or to their own perdition iv 4 388

Commend. Commend these waters to those baby eyes That never saw the giant world enraged *K. John* v 2 56
Therefore commend me; let him not come there . . . *Richard II.* i 2 71
Tell her I send to her my kind commends . . . . . iii 1 38
His glittering arms he will commend to rust . . . . iii 3 116
Speak to his gentle hearing kind commends . . . . iii 3 126
York commends the plot and the general course of the action 1 *Hen. IV.* ii 3 22
I commend me to thee, I commend thee, and I leave thee . 2 *Hen. IV.* ii 2 136
You can do it: I commend you well . . . . . . iii 2 158
Commend my service to my sovereign . . . . *Hen. V.* iv 6 23
I commend this kind submission . . . . . 2 *Hen. VI.* v 1 54
First, he commends him to your noble lordship.—And then? *Richard III.* iii 2 8
To thee I do commend my watchful soul, Ere I let fall the windows of mine eyes . . . . v 3 115
The king's majesty Commends his good opinion of you . *Hen. VIII.* ii 3 61
I love you; And durst commend a secret to your ear . . . v 1 17
But what the repining enemy commends, That breath fame blows *Troi. and Cres.* i 3 243
Commends himself most affectionately to you . . . . . iii 1 73
The beauty that is borne here in the face The bearer knows not, but commends itself To others' eyes . . . . iii 3 104
We'll but commend what we intend to sell . . . . . iv 1 78
She's well, but bade me not commend her to you . . . iv 5 180
Commend my service to her beauty . . . . . . v 5 3
We did commend To your remembrances . . . . *Coriolanus* ii 3 255
Let me commend thee first to those that shall Say yea to thy desires . iv 5 150
Commend me to their loves . . . . . . *T. of Athens* ii 2 199
Commend me bountifully to his good lordship . . . . iii 2 58
His silver hairs Will purchase us a good opinion And buy men's voices to commend our deeds . . . . *J. Cæsar* ii 1 146
Commends the ingredients of our poison'd chalice To our own lips *Macb.* i 7 11
I wish your horses swift and sure of foot; And so I do commend you to their backs . . . . iii 1 39
O, well done! I commend your pains; And every one shall share i' the gains . . . . iv 1 39
Farewell, and let your haste commend your duty . . . *Hamlet* i 2 39
So, gentlemen, With all my love I do commend me to you . . . i 5 184
I commend my duty to your lordship . . . . . . v 2 189
He does well to commend it himself; there are no tongues else for's turn . . . . v 2 191
Whose virtue and obedience doth this instant So much commend itself *Lear* ii 1 116
I did commend your highness' letters to them . . . . ii 4 28
And dare, upon the warrant of my note, Commend a dear thing to you . iii 1 19
To this great fairy I'll commend thy acts . . . *Ant. and Cleo.* iv 8 12
Commend unto his lips thy favouring hand: Kiss it, my warrior . . iv 8 23
Whom I commend to you as a noble friend of mine . . *Cymbeline* i 4 32
To your protection I commend me, gods . . . . . . i 2 8
For this immediate levy, he commends His absolute commission . . iii 7 9
He had need mean better than his outward show Can any way speak in his just commend . . . . *Pericles* ii 2 49
Or more than's fit, Since every worth in show commends itself . . ii 3 6
Well, I do commend her choice; And will no longer have it be delay'd . ii 5 21
It is your grace's pleasure to commend; Not my desert . . . ii 5 29
The unborn event I do commend to your content . . . iv Gower 46
Commends him *Mer. of Venice* iii 2; *As Y. Like It* iv 3; *Richard II.* ii 1; 2 *Hen. IV.* iii 2; *Hen. V.* iv 6
Commend me to *M. N. Dream* iii 1; *Mer. Wives* ii 2; *Much Ado* i 1; *T. of Shrew* iv 3; *All's Well* ii 2; *K. John* v 4; *Richard II.* i 2; 2 *Hen. IV.* i 2; *Hen. V.* iv 1; 3 *Hen. VI.* v 2; *Richard III.* iii 1; iv 5; *Hen. VIII.* ii 1; *Coriolanus* iii 2; *Rom. and Jul.* ii 4; iii 4; *T. of Athens* i 1; ii 1; ii 2; iii 2; v 1; *J. Cæsar* ii 4; iv 3; *Othello* v 2; *Cymbeline* i 4

Commendable. Sure, sure, such carping is not commendable *Much Ado* iii 1 71
Not to be so odd and from all fashions As Beatrice is, cannot be commendable . . . . iii 1 73
Silence is only commendable In a neat's tongue dried and a maid not vendible . . . . *Mer. of Venice* i 1 111
The best grace of wit will shortly turn into silence, and discourse grow commendable in none only but parrots . . . . . iii 5 50
More quaint, more pleasing, nor more commendable . *T. of Shrew* iv 3 102
Good phrases are surely, and ever were, very commendable 2 *Hen. IV.* iii 2 77
And, commendable proved, let's die in pride . . 1 *Hen. VI.* iv 6 57
And power, unto itself most commendable, Hath not a tomb so evident as a chair To extol what it hath done . . . . *Coriolanus* iv 7 51
'Tis sweet and commendable in your nature . . . *Hamlet* i 2 87

Commendation. 'Tis a word or two Of commendations . *T. G. of Ver.* i 3 53
This gentleman is come to me, With commendation from great potentates . . . . ii 4 79
Mistress Page hath her hearty commendations to you . *Mer. Wives* ii 2 99
Only this commendation I can afford her . . . . *Much Ado* i 1 175
The commendation is not in his wit, but in his villany . . . ii 1 145
I will commend you to mine own heart.—Pray you, do my commendations . . . . *L. L. Lost* ii 1 181
Whose trial shall better publish his commendation . *Mer. of Venice* iv 1 166
You have deserved High commendation, true applause and love *As Y. Like It* i 2 275
Where an unclean mind carries virtuous qualities, there commendations go with pity . . . . *All's Well* i 1 49
Your commendations, madam, get from her tears . . . . i 1 53
This is not much.—Not much commendation to them . . . ii 2 70
The duke hath offered him letters of commendations . . . iv 3 92
There is no love-broker in the world can more prevail in man's commendation with woman than report of valour . . *T. Night* iii 2 40
Beguiling them of commendation . . . . . 1 *Hen. IV.* iii 1 189
Such commendations as becomes a maid, A virgin and his servant 1 *Hen. VI.* v 3 177
By me Sends you his princely commendations . . *Hen. VIII.* iv 2 118
You were ever good at sudden commendations . . . . . v 3 122
A mere satiety of commendations . . . . . *T. of Athens* i 1 166
In his commendations I am fed; It is a banquet to me . . *Macbeth* i 4 55
I have your commendation for my more free entertainment *Cymbeline* i 4 166
My mother, having power of his testiness, shall turn all into my commendations . . . . iv 1 23
It pleaseth you, my royal father, to express My commendations great, whose merit's less . . . . *Pericles* ii 2 9

Commended. Your friends are well and have them much commended *T. G. of Ver.* ii 4 123
The priest o' the town commended him for a true man . *Mer. Wives* ii 1 149
Remember who commended thy yellow stockings . *T. Night* ii 5 166; iii 4 52

Commended. To the hazard Of all incertainties himself commended *W. Tale* iii 2 170
I have commended to his goodness The model of our chaste loves *Hen. VIII.* iv 2 131
I had as lief Helen's golden tongue had commended Troilus for a copper nose . . . . *Troi. and Cres.* i 2 115
His majesty commended him to you . . . . . *Hamlet* v 2 203
We have no reason to desire it, Commended to our master, not to us *Per.* i 3 38

Commending. Under the colour of commending him, I have access my own love to prefer . . . . *T. G. of Ver.* iv 2 3

Comment. Not an eye that sees you but is a physician to comment on your malady . . . . ii 1 42
A vulgar comment will be made of it . . . *Com. of Errors* iii 1 100
Forgive the comment that my passion made Upon thy feature *K. John* iv 2 263
Doth by the idle comments that it makes Foretell the ending of mortality v 7 4
View his breathless corpse, And comment then upon his sudden death 2 *Hen. VI.* iii 2 133
It is not meet That every nice offence should bear his comment *J. Cæsar* iv 3 8
Even with the very comment of thy soul Observe mine uncle *Hamlet* iii 2 84

Commentaries. Kent, in the Commentaries Cæsar writ, Is term'd the civil'st place of all this isle . . . . . . 2 *Hen. VI.* iv 7 65

Commenting. Weeping and commenting Upon the sobbing deer *As Y. Like It* ii 1 65
Fearful commenting Is leaden servitor to dull delay . *Richard III.* iv 3 51

Commerce. He is now in some commerce with my lady . *T. Night* iii 4 191
Peaceful commerce from dividable shores . . . *Troi. and Cres.* i 3 105
All the commerce that you have had with Troy As perfectly is ours as yours . . . . iii 3 205
Could beauty, my lord, have better commerce than with honesty *Hamlet* iii 1 110

Commingled. Blest are those Whose blood and judgement are so well commingled . . . . iii 2 74

Commiseration. Have commiseration on thy heroical vassal *L. L. Lost* iv 1 64
And pluck commiseration of his state From brassy bosoms *Mer. of Ven.* iv 1 30
Lending your kind commiseration . . . . . *T. Andron.* v 3 93

Commission. There is our commission, From which we would not have you warp . . . . *Meas. for Meas.* i 1 14
Take thy commission . . . . i 1 48
To the hopeful execution do I leave you Of your commissions . . i 1 51
You'll be glad to give out a commission for more heads . . . ii 1 253
I might ask you for your commission . . . . *As Y. Like It* iv 1 138
You are more saucy with lords and honourable personages than the commission of your birth and virtue gives you heraldry *All's Well* ii 3 279
But this is from my commission . . . . . . *T. Night* i 5 201
Have you any commission from your lord to negotiate with my face? . i 5 249
I'll give him my commission To let him there a month behind the gest Prefix'd for's parting . . . . *W. Tale* i 2 40
Thou mayst co-join with something; and thou dost, And that beyond commission . . . . i 2 144
From whom hast thou this great commission? . . . *K. John* ii 1 110
Use our commission in his utmost force . . . . . . iii 3 11
It is my cousin Silence, in commission with me . . 2 *Hen. IV.* iii 2 97
Hath the Prince John a full commission, In very ample virtue of his father? . . . . iv 1 162
I do greet your excellence With letters of commission from the king 1 *Hen. VI.* v 4 95
Let not her penance exceed the king's commission . . . 2 *Hen. VI.* ii 4 75
Here my commission stays . . . . ii 4 76
Shew him our commission; talk no more . . . . *Richard III.* i 4 90
There have been commissions Sent down among 'em, which hath flaw'd the heart Of all their loyalties . . . . *Hen. VIII.* i 2 20
The subjects' grief Comes through commissions . . . . . i 2 57
Have you a precedent Of this commission? I believe, not any . . i 2 92
With Free pardon to each man that has denied The force of this commission i 2 101
A man of my lord cardinal's, by commission and main power, took 'em from me . . . . ii 2 6
To your highness' hand I tender my commission . . . . ii 2 104
Whilst our commission from Rome is read, Let silence be commanded . ii 4 1
Is warranted By a commission from the consistory . . . . ii 4 92
Where's your commission, lords? words cannot carry Authority so weighty . . . . iii 2 233
Item, you sent a large commission To Gregory de Cassado . . . iii 2 320
Did my commission Bid ye so far forget yourselves? . . . . v 3 141
Omission to do what is necessary Seals a commission to a blank of danger *Troi. and Cres.* iii 3 231
Take your commission; hie you to your bands . . . *Coriolanus* i 2 26
Take The one half of my commission . . . . iv 5 144
Yet I wish, sir,—I mean for your particular,—you had not Join'd in commission with him . . . . iv 7 14
Arbitrating that Which the commission of thy years and art Could to no issue of true honour bring . . . . . . *Rom. and Jul.* iv 1 64
Is execution done on Cawdor? Are not Those in commission yet return'd? . . . . *Macbeth* i 4 2
Gives him three thousand crowns in annual fee, And his commission *Hamlet* ii 2 74
I your commission will forthwith dispatch, And he to England shall along with you . . . . iii 3 3
Making so bold, My fears forgetting manners, to unseal Their grand commission . . . . v 2 18
Here's the commission: read it at more leisure . . . . . v 2 26
I sat me down, Devised a new commission, wrote it fair . . . v 2 32
You are o' the commission, Sit you too . . . . . *Lear* iii 6 40
He led our powers; Bore the commission of my place and person . . v 3 64
He hath commission from thy wife and me To hang Cordelia . . . v 3 252
Leave some officer behind, And he shall our commission bring to you *Othello* i 3 282
And is in full commission here for Cyprus . . . . . . ii 1 29
Sir, there is especial commission come from Venice . . . . iv 2 225
Your commission's ready; Follow me, and receive't . *Ant. and Cleo.* ii 3 41
Caius Lucius Will do's commission throughly . . . *Cymbeline* ii 4 12
For this immediate levy, he commends His absolute commission . . iii 7 10
The words of your commission Will tie you to the numbers and the time Of their dispatch . . . . iii 7 14
His seal'd commission, left in trust with me, Doth speak sufficiently he's gone to travel . . . . *Pericles* i 3 13
My commission Is not to reason of the deed, but do it . . . . iv 1 83

Commissioner. Who are the late commissioners? . . . *Hen. V.* ii 2 61

Commit. I do as truly suffer As e'er I did commit . . *T. G. of Ver.* v 4 77
And so I commit you— To the tuition of God . . . *Much Ado* i 1 282
You do impeach your modesty too much, To leave the city and commit yourself Into the hands of one that loves you not . *M. N. Dream* ii 1 215

Commit. Lovers cannot see The pretty follies that themselves commit *Mer. of Venice* ii 6 37
Happiest of all is that her gentle spirit Commits itself to yours to be directed . . . iii 2 166
I commit into your hands The husbandry and manage of my house . . . iii 4 24
And for thy maintenance commits his body To painful labour *T. of Shrew* v 2 148
You lack not folly to commit them, and have ability enough . *All's Well* i 3 11
There's honour in the theft.—Commit it, count . . . ii 1 34
What else may hap to time I will commit . *T. Night* i 2 60
Which is for me less easy to commit Than you to punish *W. Tale* i 2 58
Unless he take the course that you have done, Commit me for committing honour . . . ii 3 49
Hence with it, and together with the dam Commit them to the fire! . ii 3 95
I envy at their liberty, And will again commit them to their bonds *K. John* iii 4 74
I do commit his youth To your direction . . iv 2 67
Rob, murder, and commit The oldest sins the newest kind of ways *2 Hen. IV* iv 5 126
I gave bold way to my authority And did commit you . . v 2 83
You did commit me: For which, I do commit into your hand The unstained sword that you have used to bear . . v 2 112
And here I commit my body to your mercies . . Epil. 15
Where inshipp'd Commit them to the fortune of the sea . *1 Hen. VI.* v 1 50
A fouler fact Did never traitor in the land commit . *2 Hen. VI.* i 3 177
And here commit you to my lord cardinal To keep . . iii 1 137
To the Tower; And, Somerset, we will commit thee thither . iv 9 39
That fault is none of yours; He should, for that, commit your godfathers *Richard III.* i 1 48
Such like toys as these Have moved his highness to commit me . i 1 61
If they shall chance, In charging you with matters, to commit you *Hen. VIII.* v 1 146
What folly I commit, I dedicate to you . *Troi. and Cres.* iii 2 110
Commit the war of white and damask in Their nicely-gawded cheeks to the wanton spoil Of Phœbus' burning kisses . *Coriolanus* ii 1 232
And to my fortunes and the people's favour Commit my cause *T. Andron.* i 1 55
And to the love and favour of my country Commit myself, my person . i 1 59
Bid him farewell; commit him to the grave . . v 3 170
In that beastly fury He has been known to commit outrages *T. of Athens* iii 5 72
It is not for your health thus to commit Your weak condition to the raw cold morning . . *J. Cæsar* ii 1 235
Should in this trice of time Commit a thing so monstrous . *Lear* i 1 220
Use well our father: To your professed bosoms I commit him . i 1 275
Commit not with man's sworn spouse . . iii 4 83
I do think there is mettle in death, which commits some loving act upon her . . *Ant. and Cleo.* i 2 148
When we debate Our trivial difference loud, we do commit Murder in healing wounds . . ii 2 21
It is fit I should commit offence to my inferiors . *Cymbeline* ii 1 32
Lads more like to run The country base than to commit such slaughter v 3 20
You must seem to do that fearfully which you commit willingly *Pericles* iv 2 128
We commit no crime To use one language in each several clime . iv 4 5
Committed. Forgive them what they have committed here *T. G. of Ver.* v 4 154
If Sir John Falstaff have committed disparagements . *Mer. Wives* i 1 31
The offence is holy that she hath committed . . v 5 238
Bear me to prison, where I am committed . *Meas. for Meas.* i 2 121
Who is it that hath died for this offence? There's many have committed it . . . ii 2 89
So then it seems your most offenceful act Was mutually committed? . ii 3 27
And sent him home, Whilst to take order for the wrongs I went That here and there his fury had committed *Com. of Errors* v 1 147
Flat burglary as ever was committed.—Yea, by mass, that it is *M. Ado* iv 2 52
They have committed false report; moreover, they have spoken untruths v 1 219
I ask thee what's their offence; sixth and lastly, why they are committed . . . v 1 227
Beseech you, sir, to pardon me all the faults I have committed *W. Tale* v 2 161
Grievous crimes Committed by your person and your followers *Rich. II.* iv 1 224
Intended or committed was this fault? . . v 3 33
Broke oath on oath, committed wrong on wrong *1 Hen. IV.* iv 3 101
Here comes the nobleman that committed the prince for striking him *2 Hen. IV.* i 2 63
We shall see wilful adultery and murder committed . *Hen. V.* ii 1 40
Enlarge the man committed yesterday, That rail'd against our person . ii 2 40
I assure you, there is very excellent services committed at the bridge . iii 6 4
And, as I further have to understand, Is new committed *3 Hen. VI.* iv 4 11
If I unwittingly, or in my rage, Have aught committed that is hardly borne By any in this presence *Richard III.* ii 1 57
Who hath committed them?—The mighty dukes Gloucester and Buckingham . . . ii 4 44
Why or for what these nobles were committed Is all unknown to me . ii 4 47
Alas, I rather hate myself For hateful deeds committed by myself! . v 3 190
'If,' quoth he, 'I for this had been committed, As, to the Tower, I thought, I would have play'd The part' . *Hen. VIII.* i 2 193
I committed The daring'st counsel which I had to doubt . ii 4 214
The willing'st sin I ever yet committed May be absolved in English . iii 1 49
For better trial of you, From hence you be committed to the Tower . v 3 54
I shall never come to bliss Till all these mischiefs be return'd again Even in their throats that have committed them *T. Andron.* iii 1 275
Who committed treason enough for God's sake, yet could not equivocate to heaven . . *Macbeth* ii 3 11
Alas, what ignorant sin have I committed? *Othello* iv 2 70
What committed! Committed! O thou public commoner! . iv 2 72
What committed! Heaven stops the nose at it and the moon winks . iv 2 76
What committed! Impudent strumpet! . . iv 2 80
That she with Cassio hath the act of shame A thousand times committed v 2 212
Committest. Still thou mistakest, Or else committ'st thy knaveries wilfully . . *M. N. Dream* iii 2 346
And thou, too careless patient as thou art, Committ'st thy anointed body to the cure Of those physicians that first wounded thee *Richard II.* ii 1 98
Committing me unto my brother's love *As Y. Like It* iv 3 145
Commit me for committing honour . . *W. Tale* ii 3 49
Arraigned of high treason, in committing adultery with Polixenes . iii 2 14
In committing freely Your scruple to the voice of Christendom *Hen. VIII.* ii 2 87
Commix. To commix With winds that sailors rail at . *Cymbeline* iv 2 55
Commixtion. Were thy commixtion Greek and Trojan . *Troi. and Cres.* iv 5 124
Commixture. Dismask'd, their damask sweet commixture shown, Are angels vailing clouds . . *L. L. Lost* v 2 296
And, now I fall, thy tough commixture melts . *3 Hen. VI.* ii 6 6
Commodious. The parrot will not do more for an almond than he for a commodious drab . . *Troi. and Cres.* v 2 194

Commodities. Some offer me commodities to buy . *Com. of Errors* iv 3 6
Shall we go to Cheapside and take up commodities upon our bills? *2 Hen. VI.* iv 7 135
Our means secure us, and our mere defects Prove our commodities *Lear* iv 1 23
Commodity. He's in for a commodity of brown paper and old ginger *Meas. for Meas.* iv 3 5
We are like to prove a goodly commodity, being taken up of these men's bills.—A commodity in question, I warrant you . *Much Ado* iii 3 190
Neither have I money nor commodity To raise a present sum *Mer. of Ven.* i 1 178
For the commodity that strangers have With us in Venice, if it be denied, Will much impeach the justice of his state . . iii 3 27
'Twas a commodity lay fretting by you *T. of Shrew* ii 1 330
'Tis a commodity will lose the gloss with lying *All's Well* i 1 166
Now Jove, in his next commodity of hair, send thee a beard! *T. Night* iii 1 50
To me can life be no commodity *W. Tale* iii 2 94
That smooth-faced gentleman, tickling Commodity . *K. John* ii 1 573
Commodity, the bias of the world, The world, who of itself is peised well ii 1 574
This sway of motion, this Commodity, Makes it take head from all indifferency . . ii 1 578
This Commodity, This bawd, this broker, this all-changing word . ii 1 581
Why rail I on this Commodity? But for because he hath not woo'd me yet . . ii 1 587
Since kings break faith upon commodity, Gain, be my lord . ii 1 597
I would to God thou and I knew where a commodity of good names were to be bought . *1 Hen. IV.* i 2 93
Such a commodity of warm slaves, as had as lieve hear the devil as a drum . . iv 2 19
A good wit will make use of any thing: I will turn diseases to commodity *2 Hen. IV.* i 2 278
Our credit comes not in like the commodity, nor the commodity wages not with the danger . *Pericles* iv 2 34
Common. Our hint of woe Is common *Tempest* ii 1 4
All things in common nature should produce Without sweat or endeavour . . ii 1 159
You know the course is common . *Meas. for Meas.* iv 2 190
And make a common of my serious hours *Com. of Errors* ii 2 29
Good meat, sir, is common; that every churl affords.—And welcome more common . . iii 1 24
My lips are no common, though several they be *L. L. Lost* ii 1 223
This female,—which in the common is woman . *As Y. Like It* v 1 54
Like a common and an outward man . *All's Well* iii 1 11
Young Arthur's death is common in their mouths . *K. John* iv 2 187
It was alway yet the trick of our English nation, if they have a good thing, to make it too common . *2 Hen. IV.* i 2 242
As common as the way between Saint Alban's and London . ii 2 184
'Tis ever common That men are merriest when they are from home *Hen. V.* i 2 271
Art thou officer? Or art thou base, common and popular? . iv 1 38
Against the Duke of Suffolk, for enclosing the commons of Melford *2 Hen. VI.* i 3 24
All the realm shall be in common . . iv 2 74
And henceforward all things shall be in common . iv 7 21
Unto the appetite and affection common Of the whole body . *Coriolanus* i 1 108
Digest things rightly Touching the weal o' the common . i 1 155
Account me the more virtuous that I have not been common in my love ii 3 101
Hath he not pass'd the noble and the common? . iii 1 29
Your son Will or exceed the common or be caught With cautelous baits iv 1 32
Like to the empty ass, to shake his ears, And graze in commons *J. Cæsar* iv 1 27
Thou know'st 'tis common; all that lives must die . *Hamlet* i 2 72
It is common.—If it be, Why seems it so particular with thee? . i 2 74
What we know must be and is as common As any the most vulgar thing to sense . . i 2 98
It is common for the younger sort To lack discretion . ii 1 116
Slaver with lips as common as the stairs That mount the Capitol *Cymb.* i 6 105
Common air. Not so deep a maim As to be cast forth in the common air *Richard II.* i 3 157
Common arbitrator. That old common arbitrator, Time *Troi. and Cres.* iv 5 225
Common blocks. Thy conceit is soaking, will draw in More than the common blocks . . *W. Tale* i 2 225
Common body. We do request your kindest ears, and after, Your loving motion toward the common body *Coriolanus* ii 2 57
This common body, Like to a vagabond flag upon the stream, Goes to and back . . *Ant. and Cleo.* i 4 44
If neglection Should therein make me vile, the common body, By you relieved, would force me to my duty . *Pericles* iii 3 21
Common bosom. To pluck the common bosom on his side . *Lear* v 3 49
Common bound. Borrow Cupid's wings, And soar with them above a common bound . . *Rom. and Jul.* i 4 18
Common bruit. And am not One that rejoices in the common wreck, As common bruit doth put it . . *T. of Athens* v 1 196
Common chances. That common chances common men could bear *Coriolanus* iv 1 5
Common course. As in the common course of all treasons . *All's Well* iv 3 26
Common cry. You common cry of curs! whose breath I hate *Coriolanus* iii 3 120
Common curse. The common curse of mankind, folly and ignorance *Troi. and Cres.* ii 3 30
Common customer. I think thee now some common customer *All's Well* v 3 287
Common distribution. To be ta'en forth, Before the common distribution *Coriolanus* i 9 35
Common dog. So, so, thou common dog, didst thou disgorge Thy glutton bosom . . *2 Hen. IV.* i 3 97
Common drudge. Thou pale and common drudge 'Tween man and man *Mer. of Venice* iii 2 103
Common ear. So I have strew'd it in the common ear *Meas. for Meas.* i 3 15
Common enemy. And mine eternal jewel Given to the common enemy of man . . *Macbeth* iii 1 69
Common executioner. Here is in our prison a common executioner *Meas. for Meas.* iv 2 9
The common executioner, Whose heart the accustom'd sight of death makes hard, Falls not the axe *As Y. Like It* iii 5 3
Common eye. Which so appearing to the common eyes, We shall be call'd purgers, not murderers . *J. Cæsar* ii 1 179
Masking the business from the common eye For sundry weighty reasons *Macbeth* iii 1 125
Common fear. Or more than common fear of Clifford's rigour *3 Hen. VI.* ii 1 126
Common ferry. Bring them, I pray thee, with imagined speed Unto the tranect, to the common ferry . . *Mer. of Venice* iii 4 53
Common file. But for our gentlemen, The common file—a plague! *Coriolanus* i 6 43
Common fools. If you are learn'd, Be not as common fools . iii 1 100

Common friend. Thou common friend, that's without faith or love! *T. G. of Ver.* v 4 62
Hear me, my masters, and my common friends *Coriolanus* iii 3 108
Common gamester. Was a common gamester to the camp . *All's Well* v 3 188
Common good. As you respect the common good . *Hen. VIII.* iii 2 290
He only, in a general honest thought And common good to all, made one of them . . . . *J. Cæsar* v 5 72
Common grace. To sue, and be denied such common grace *T. of Athens* iii 5 95
Common grief. Your grief, the common grief of all the land . *2 Hen. VI.* i 1 77
Woe above woe! grief more than common grief! . *3 Hen. VI.* ii 5 94
Common-hackneyed. So common-hackney'd in the eyes of men, So stale and cheap . . . . *1 Hen. IV.* iii 2 40
Common hangman. Serve by indenture to the common hangman *Pericles* iv 6 187
Common herd. When he perceived the common herd was glad he refused the crown, he plucked me ope his doublet . *J. Cæsar* i 2 266
Common hire. A knave of common hire, a gondolier . *Othello* i 1 126
Common houses. That do nothing but use their abuses in common houses . . . . *Meas. for Meas.* ii 1 43
Common joy. O, rejoice Beyond a common joy . *Tempest* v 1 207
Common judgement-place. To old Free-town, our common judgement-place . . . . *Rom. and Jul.* i 1 109
Common justice. The terms For common justice, you're as pregnant in As art and practice hath enriched any . *Meas. for Meas.* i 1 12
Common-kissing. To the greedy touch Of common-kissing Titan *Cymb.* iii 4 166
Common lag. Together with the common lag of people . *T. of Athens* iii 6 90
Common 'larum-bell. A watch-case or a common 'larum-bell *2 Hen. IV.* iii 1 17
Common laugher. Were I a common laugher . . *J. Cæsar* i 2 72
Common liar. I am full sorry That he approves the common liar, who Thus speaks of him . . . . *Ant. and Cleo.* i 1 60
Common man. Thy word Is but the vain breath of a common man *K. John* iii 1 8
All the courses of my life do show I am not in the roll of common men *1 Hen. IV.* iii 1 43
To sort our nobles from our common men . . *Hen. V.* iv 7 77
You appeared to me but as a common man . . . iv 8 54
Knights and squires, Full fifteen hundred, besides common men . iv 8 84
Ill beseeming any common man, Much more a knight . *1 Hen. VI.* iv 1 31
Commanded always by the greater gust; Such is the lightness of you common men . . . . . . *3 Hen. VI.* iii 1 89
That common chances common men could bear . *Coriolanus* iv 1 5
Since the common men are now in action . . . . *Cymbeline* iii 7 2
Common mother, thou, Whose womb unmeasurable, and infinite breast, Teems, and feeds all . . . *T. of Athens* iv 3 177
Common mouth. These are the tribunes of the people, The tongues o' the common mouth . . . . *Coriolanus* iii 1 22
Common muck. And look'd upon things precious as they were The common muck of the world . . . . . . ii 2 130
Common name. 'Homo' is a common name to all men . *1 Hen. IV.* ii 1 104
Common ounces. Weigh you the worth and honour of a king So great as our dread father in a scale Of common ounces? *Troi. and Cres.* ii 2 28
Common pain. With more than with a common pain . *2 Hen. IV.* iv 5 224
Common part. And stand upon my common part with those That have beheld the doing . . . . . . *Coriolanus* i 9 39
Common passage. It is no act of common passage . *Cymbeline* iii 4 94
Common people. Observed his courtship to the common people *Rich. II.* i 4 24
What though the common people favour him . *2 Hen. VI.* i 1 158
The common people swarm like summer flies . *3 Hen. VI.* ii 6 8
The common people by numbers swarm to us . . . iv 2 2
He's vengeance proud, and loves not the common people . *Coriolanus* ii 2 6
'Tis he the common people love so much *T. Andron.* iv 4 73
Common players. If they should grow themselves to common players *Hamlet* ii 2 365
Common pleasures. He hath left them you, And to your heirs for ever, common pleasures . . . . *J. Cæsar* iii 2 255
Common praise. Much surpassing The common praise it bears *W. Tale* iii 1 3
Common price. He might have bought me at a common price *All's Well* v 3 190
Common profit. He loves the land, And common profit of his country *2 Hen. VI.* i 1 206
Common proof. 'Tis a common proof, That lowliness is young ambition's ladder . . . . *J. Cæsar* ii 1 21
Common pulpits. Some to the common pulpits, and cry out 'Liberty, freedom!' . . . . iii 1 80
Common rate. I am a spirit of no common rate . *M. N. Dream* iii 1 157
Common reason. His trespass, in our common reason, . . is not almost a fault . . . . *Othello* iii 3 64
Common recreation. And make him a common recreation . *T. Night* ii 3 146
Common right. Do me the common right To let me see them *M. for M.* ii 3 5
Common road. Enforce A thievish living on the common road *As Y. L. It* ii 3 33
Common rout. And that supposed by the common rout Against your yet ungalled estimation . . . *Com. of Errors* iii 1 101
Common rumours. Which I hear from common rumours . *T. of Athens* iii 2 5
Common saw. Good king, that must approve the common saw, Thou out of heaven's benediction comest To the warm sun! . . *Lear* ii 2 167
Common sense. Things hid and barr'd, you mean, from common sense? *L. L. Lost* i 1 57
Study where to meet some mistress fine, When mistresses from common sense are hid . . . . i 1 64
What impossibility would slay In common sense, sense saves another way . . . . *All's Well* ii 1 181
The time misorder'd doth, in common sense, Crowd us and crush us *2 Hen. IV.* iv 2 33
Common shores. Old receptacles, or common shores, of filth . *Pericles* iv 6 186
Common show-place. I' the common show-place, where they exercise *Ant. and Cleo.* iii 6 12
Common sight. Not an eye But is a-weary of thy common sight *1 Hen. IV.* iii 2 88
Common slave. A common slave—you know him well by sight *J. Cæsar* i 3 15
Common sleep. And strike more dead Than common sleep of all these five the sense . . . . . *M. N. Dream* iv 1 87
Common soldiers. Were by the swords of common soldiers slain *3 Hen. VI.* i 1 9
Common sons. Of thy deep duty more impression show Than that of common sons . . . . *Coriolanus* v 3 52
Common sort. Discharge the common sort With pay and thanks *3 Hen. VI.* v 5 87
Common speech Gives him a worthy pass . . . *All's Well* ii 5 57
Common spirits. I will not jump with common spirits . *Mer. of Venice* ii 9 32
Common stages. And so berattle the common stages . *Hamlet* ii 2 358
Common stale. To link my dear friend to a common stale . *Much Ado* iv 1 66
Common stocks. The knave constable had set me i' the stocks, i' the common stocks . . . . . . *Mer. Wives* iv 5 123
Common streets. Grew a companion to the common streets *1 Hen. IV.* iii 2 68
Common stroke. We were not all unkind, nor all deserve The common stroke of war . . . . . . *T. of Athens* v 4 22
Common suitors. Of senators, of prætors, common suitors . *J. Cæsar* ii 4 35
Common talk. And practise rhetoric in your common talk . *T. of Shrew* i 1 35
Common tall. I am more than common tall . *As Y. Like It* i 3 117
Common thanks. With more than common thanks I will receive it *T. of Athens* i 2 214
Common theme. Whose common theme Is death of fathers . *Hamlet* i 2 103
Common thing. A thing for me? it is a common thing— Ha!—To have a foolish wife . . . . *Othello* iii 3 302
Common tongue. He speaks the common tongue . . *T. of Athens* i 1 174
Common trade. I'll be buried in the king's highway, Some way of common trade . . . . *Richard II.* iii 3 156
Common trespasses. Pilferings and most common trespasses . *Lear* ii 2 151
Common view. That in common view He may surrender *Richard II.* iv 1 155
Common voice. The common voice, I see, is verified *Hen. VIII.* v 3 176
Have, by common voice, In election for the Roman empery, Chosen Andronicus . . . . *T. Andron.* i 1 21
The common voice do cry it shall be so . . . . . v 3 140
Common whore. Damned earth, Thou common whore of mankind *T. of Athens* iv 3 42
Common wind. No common wind, no customed event . *K. John* iii 4 155
Common worldly things. In common worldly things, 'tis call'd ungrateful . . . . *Richard III.* ii 2 91
Common wreck. Am not One that rejoices in the common wreck *T. of A.* v 1 195
Commonalty. Bid him strive To gain the love o' the commonalty *Hen. VIII.* i 2 170
He's a very dog to the commonalty . . *Coriolanus* i 1 29
Commoner. He gave it to a commoner o' the camp, If I be one *All's Well* v 3 194
The vital commoners and inland petty spirits muster me all to their captain, the heart . . . *2 Hen. IV.* iv 3 119
Doubt not The commoners, for whom we stand . . . *Coriolanus* ii 1 243
What committed! Committed! O thou public commoner! . *Othello* iv 2 73
Commonest. He would unto the stews, And from the common'st creature pluck a glove . . . . *Richard II.* v 3 17
Commonly. Fathers commonly Do get their children . *T. of Shrew* ii 1 411
I am not prone to weeping, as our sex Commonly are . *W. Tale* ii 1 109
More than in women commonly is seen . . . *1 Hen. VI.* v 5 71
Here's a young and sweating devil here, That commonly rebels *Othello* iii 4 43
Commons. The commons hath he pill'd with grievous taxes *Richard II.* ii 1 246
The nobles they are fled, the commons they are cold . . ii 2 88
That's the wavering commons: for their love Lies in their purses . ii 2 129
For little office The hateful commons will perform for us . ii 2 138
May it please you, lords, to grant the commons' suit . . iv 1 154
The commons will not then be satisfied.—They shall be satisfied . iv 1 272
Till that the nobles and the armed commons Have of their puissance made a little taste . . . . *2 Hen. IV.* ii 3 51
How now for mitigation of this bill Urged by the commons? *Hen. V.* i 1 71
Thy housekeeping Hath won the greatest favour of the commons *2 Hen. VI.* i 1 192
The commons hast thou rack'd; the clergy's bags Are lank and lean . i 3 131
By flattery hath he won the common's hearts . . . iii 1 28
Many a pound of mine own proper store, Because I would not tax the needy commons, Have I dispursed . . . . . iii 1 116
The commons haply rise, to save his life . . . iii 1 240
By this I shall perceive the commons' mind . . . iii 1 374
The commons, like an angry hive of bees That want their leader, scatter up and down . . . . iii 2 125
Dread lord, the commons send you word by me . . . iii 2 243
'Tis like the commons, rude unpolish'd hinds . . iii 2 271
The commons here in Kent are up in arms . . . . iv 1 100
And you that love the commons, follow me . . . iv 2 192
We come ambassadors from the king Unto the commons whom thou hast misled . . . . iv 8 8
The grieved commons Hardly conceive of me . *Hen. VIII.* i 2 104
All the commons Hate him perniciously . . . . ii 1 49
The commons made A shower and thunder with their caps and shouts *Coriolanus* ii 1 282
It shall be so I' the right and strength o' the commons . iii 3 14
Even in theirs and in the commons' ears, Will vouch the truth of it . v 6 4
Let but the commons hear this testament—Which, pardon me, I do not mean to read . . . . *J. Cæsar* iii 2 135
Commonweal. If these be good people in a commonweal that do nothing but use their abuses in common houses, I know no law *M. for M.* ii 1 42
So kind a father of the commonweal . . . . *1 Hen. VI.* iii 1 98
Oft have I seen the haughty cardinal . . . Swear like a ruffian and demean himself Unlike the ruler of a commonweal . *2 Hen. VI.* i 1 189
The king and commonweal Are deeply indebted for this piece of pains . i 4 46
Dangerous peer, That smooth'st it so with king and commonweal! . ii 1 22
To heaven I do appeal, How I have loved my king and commonweal . ii 1 191
If to fight for king and commonweal Were piety in thine, it is in these *T. Andron.* i 1 114
And ripen justice in this commonweal . . . . . i 1 227
King and commander of our commonweal, The wide world's emperor . i 1 247
This siren, that will charm Rome's Saturnine, And see his shipwreck and his commonweal's . . . . ii 1 24
Commonwealth. I' the commonwealth I would by contraries Execute all things . . . . *Tempest* ii 1 147
The latter end of his commonwealth forgets the beginning . ii 1 157
Here's a change indeed in the commonwealth! . *Meas. for Meas.* i 2 108
We have here recovered the most dangerous piece of lechery that ever was known in the commonwealth . . . . . *Much Ado* iii 3 181
Here comes a member of the commonwealth . . . *L. L. Lost* iv 1 41
You are a good member of the commonwealth . . . iv 2 79
He says, you are no good member of the commonwealth *Mer. of Venice* iii 5 37
I shall answer that better to the commonwealth than you can . iii 5 40
It is not politic in the commonwealth of nature to preserve virginity *All's Well* i 1 137
Caterpillars of the commonwealth, Which I have sworn to weed *Richard II.* ii 3 166
Like an executioner, Cut off the heads of too fast growing sprays, That look too lofty in our commonwealth . . . . . . iii 4 35
They pray continually to their saint, the commonwealth . *1 Hen. IV.* ii 1 89
What, the commonwealth their boots? will she hold out water in foul way? . . . . ii 1 92
Some strait decrees That lie too heavy on the commonwealth . iv 3 80
The commonwealth is sick of their own choice . . . *2 Hen. IV.* i 3 87
My brother general, the commonwealth, To brother born an household cruelty, I make my quarrel in particular . . . . . iv 1 94
Whiles I was busy for the commonwealth . . . . v 2 76
Hear him debate of commonwealth affairs . . . *Hen. V.* i 1 41

Commonwealth. Civil dissension is a viperous worm That gnaws the bowels of the commonwealth . . . . . 1 *Hen. VI.* iii 1 73
The commonwealth hath daily run to wreck . . 2 *Hen. VI.* i 3 127
I come to talk of commonwealth affairs . . . . i 3 157
Means to dress the commonwealth, and turn it, and set a new nap upon it . . . . iv 2 6
Lord Say hath gelded the commonwealth, and made it an eunuch . iv 2 174
Such alliance Would more have strengthen'd this our commonwealth . . . . 3 *Hen. VI.* iv 1 37
The commonwealth doth stand, and so would do, Were he more angry at it . . . . *Coriolanus* iv 6 14
One fit to bandy with thy lawless sons, To ruffle in the commonwealth of Rome . . . . *T. Andron.* i 1 313
The commonwealth of Athens is become a forest of beasts *T. of Athens* iv 3 352
Receive the benefit of his dying, a place in the commonwealth *J. Cæsar* iii 2 48
Commotion. When tempest of commotion, like the south Borne with black vapour, doth begin to melt . . 2 *Hen. IV.* ii 4 392
If damn'd commotion so appear'd, In his true, native and most proper shape . . . . iv 1 36
And consecrate commotion's bitter edge . . . . iv 1 93
And when he please to make commotion, 'Tis to be fear'd they all will follow him . . . . . 2 *Hen. VI.* iii 1 29
To make commotion, as full well he can . . . . iii 1 358
Some strange commotion Is in his brain: he bites his lip *Hen. VIII.* iii 2 112
What follows then? Commotions, uproars, with a general taint Of the whole state . . . . v 3 28
What raging of the sea! shaking of earth! Commotion in the winds! *Troi. and Cres.* i 3 98
Kingdom'd Achilles in commotion rages And batters down himself ii 3 185
Commune. I would commune with you of such things That want no ear but yours . . . . . . *Meas. for Meas.* iv 3 109
You may stay; For I have more to commune with Bianca *T. of Shrew* i 1 101
Why, what need we Commune with you of this? . . . *W. Tale* ii 1 162
I must commune with your grief, Or you deny me right *Hamlet* iv 5 202
Communicate. Whose weakness married to thy stronger state Makes me with thy strength to communicate . . . *Com. of Errors* ii 2 178
Alone she was, and did communicate to herself her own words to her own ears . . . . *All's Well* i 3 112
No man is the lord of any thing, Though in and of him there be much consisting, Till he communicate his parts to others *Troi. and Cres.* iii 3 117
Communicatest with dreams . . . . . *W. Tale* i 2 140
Communication. In the way of argument, look you, and friendly communication . . . . *Hen. V.* iii 2 104
What did this vanity But minister communication of A most poor issue? *Hen. VIII.* i 1 86
Communities, Degrees in schools and brotherhoods in cities *Tr. and Cr.* i 3 103
Community. Such eyes As, sick and blunted with community, Afford no extraordinary gaze . . . 1 *Hen. IV.* iii 2 77
Commutual. Since love our hearts and Hymen did our hands Unite commutual in most sacred bands . . . . *Hamlet* iii 2 170
Comonty. Is not a comonty a Christmas gambold or a tumbling-trick? *T. of Shrew* Ind. 2 140
Compact. Pernicious woman, Compact with her that's gone *M. for M.* v 1 242
What is the course and drift of your compact? *Com. of Errors* ii 2 163
Make us but believe, Being compact of credit, that you love us . iii 2 22
The lunatic, the lover and the poet Are of imagination all compact *M. N. Dream* v 1 8
If he, compact of jars, grow musical, We shall have shortly discord in the spheres . . . . *As Y. Like It* ii 7 5
Patience once more, whiles our compact is urged . . . v 4 5
And all the ceremony of this compact Seal'd in my function . *T. Night* v 1 163
Therefore take this compact of a truce, Although you break it when your pleasure serves . . . . . . 1 *Hen. VI.* v 4 163
The compact is firm and true in me . . . *Richard III.* ii 2 133
My heart is not compact of flint nor steel . . *T. Andron.* v 3 88
But what compact mean you to have with us? . . *J. Cæsar* iii 1 215
A seal'd compact, Well ratified by law and heraldry . . *Hamlet* i 1 86
My dimensions are as well compact, My mind as generous . *Lear* i 2 7
Thereto add such reasons of your own As may compact it more . i 4 362
Companies. 'Tis a foul thing when a cur cannot keep himself in all companies! . . . . *T. G. of Ver.* iv 4 12
To seek new friends and stranger companies . . *M. N. Dream* i 1 219
I advise You use your manners discreetly in all kind of companies *T. of Shrew* i 1 247
Gentle kinsman, go, And thrust thyself into their companies *K. John* iv 2 167
Ancients, corporals, lieutenants, gentlemen of companies 1 *Hen. IV.* iv 2 27
His companies unletter'd, rude and shallow . . . *Hen. V.* i 1 55
I'll give you gold, Rid me these villains from your companies *T. of Athens* v 1 104
Bid the commanders Prepare to lodge their companies to-night *J. Cæsar* iv 3 140
So by your companies To draw him on to pleasures . . *Hamlet* ii 2 14
You and my brother search What companies are near . *Cymbeline* iv 2 69
No companies abroad?—None in the world . . . . iv 2 101
Companion. I would not wish Any companion in the world but you *Tempest* iii 1 55
Set Caliban and his companions free . . . . . . v 1 252
To my cell; Take with you your companions . . . . v 1 292
His companion, youthful Valentine, Attends the emperor *T. G. of Ver.* i 3 26
This same scall, scurvy, cogging companion . . *Mer. Wives* iii 1 123
And at his heels a rabble of his companions . . . . iii 5 77
Take, then, this your companion by the hand. Who hath a story ready for your ear . . . . *Meas. for Meas.* iv 1 55
Away with those giglots too, and with the other confederate companion! v 1 352
Did this companion with the saffron face Revel and feast it at my house to-day? . . . . *Com. of Errors* iv 4 64
Who is his companion now? He hath every month a new sworn brother *Much Ado* i 1 72
But, I pray you, who is his companion? . . . . . i 1 81
The flat transgression of a school-boy, who, being overjoyed with finding a birds' nest, shows it his companion, and he steals it . ii 1 231
I did converse this quondam day with a companion . *L. L. Lost* v 1 7
I abhor such fanatical phantasimes, such insociable and point-devise companions . . . . v 1 21
Toward that shade I might behold addrest The king and his companions v 2 93
Turn melancholy forth to funerals; The pale companion is not for our pomp *M. N. Dream* i 1 16
Companions That do converse and waste the time together *Mer. of Ven.* iii 4 11
Now, my spruce companions, is all ready, and all things neat? *T. of Shrew* iv 1 116
'Tis too cold a companion; away with't! . . . . *All's Well* i 1 144
Companion. Are you companion to the Count Rousillon? *All's Well* ii 3 200
How you have been solicited by a gentleman his companion . . iii 5 16
What an equivocal companion is this! . . . . . v 3 250
The sweet'st companion that e'er man Bred his hopes out of . *W. Tale* v 1 11
With her companion grief must end her life . . *Richard II.* i 2 55
Most mighty liege, and my companion peers . . . . i 3 93
There, they say, he daily doth frequent, With unrestrained loose companions . . . . v 3 7
A tun of man is thy companion . . . . . 1 *Hen. IV.* ii 4 494
Grew a companion to the common streets, Enfeoff'd himself to popularity . . . . iii 2 68
God send the prince a better companion!—God send the companion a better prince! . . . . 2 *Hen. IV.* i 2 224
'Receive,' says he, 'no swaggering companions' . . . ii 4 102
Charge me! I scorn you, scurvy companion . . . . ii 4 132
The prince but studies his companions Like a strange tongue . iv 4 68
Happy for so sweet a child, Fit to be made companion with a king 1 *Hen. VI.* v 3 149
Not whom we will, but whom his grace affects, Must be companion of his nuptial bed . . . . v 5 58
Why, rude companion, whatsoe'er thou be, I know thee not 2 *Hen. VI.* iv 10 33
Sure, in that I deem you an ill husband, and am glad To have you therein my companion . . . . . . *Hen. VIII.* iii 2 143
Has the porter his eyes in his head, that he gives entrance to such companions? . . . . *Coriolanus* iv 5 14
Now, you companion, I'll say an errand for you . . . v 2 65
As we do turn our backs From our companion thrown into his grave *T. of Athens* iv 2 9
What should the wars do with these jigging fools? Companion, hence! *J. Cæsar* iv 3 138
Why do you keep alone, Of sorriest fancies your companions making? *Macbeth* iii 2 9
Companions noted and most known To youth and liberty . *Hamlet* ii 1 23
Was he not companion with the riotous knights? . . *Lear* ii 1 96
O heaven, that such companions thou 'ldst unfold! . . *Othello* iv 2 141
Marry me with Octavius Cæsar, and companion me with my mistress *Ant. and Cleo.* i 2 29
My mate in empire, Friend and companion in the front of war . v 1 44
There is a Frenchman his companion . . . . *Cymbeline* i 6 64
It is not fit your lordship should undertake every companion that you give offence to . . . . ii 1 29
I'ld change my sex to be companion with them . . . . iii 6 88
I create you Companions to our person and will fit you With dignities becoming your estates . . . . v 5 21
And I must lose Two of the sweet'st companions in the world . v 5 349
And testy wrath Could never be her mild companion . . *Pericles* i 1 18
The sad companion, dull-eyed melancholy . . . . i 2 2
Provided That none but I and my companion maid Be suffer'd To come near him . . . . v 1 78
My companion friends, If this but answer to my just belief, I'll well remember you . . . . v 1 238
Companionship. How is it less or worse, That it shall hold companionship in peace With honour, as in war? . . . *Coriolanus* iii 2 49
'Tis Alcibiades, and some twenty horse, All of companionship *T. of Athens* i 1 251
Company. The king and all our company else being drowned, we will inherit here . . . . *Tempest* ii 2 179
Her and her blind boy's scandal'd company I have forsworn . iv 1 90
To thee and thy company I bid A hearty welcome . . . . v 1 110
The best news is, that we have safely found Our king and company v 1 222
There are yet missing of your company Some few odd lads . . v 1 254
Entreat thy company To see the wonders of the world abroad *T. G. of Ver.* i 1 5
Good company; with them shall Proteus go . . . . i 3 43
And spends what he borrows kindly in your company . . ii 4 40
And oftentimes have purposed to forbid Sir Valentine her company iii 1 27
She hath despised me most, Forsworn my company and rail'd at me iii 2 4
Such as the fury of ungovern'd youth Thrust from the company of awful men . . . . iv 1 46
Peace! stand aside: the company parts . . . . . iv 2 81
I do desire thy worthy company, Upon whose faith and honour I repose iv 3 25
Bear me company and go with me . . . . . . iv 3 34
He thrusts me himself into the company of three or four gentlemanlike dogs . . . . iv 4 18
And Eglamour is in her company . . . . . . v 2 36
I'll ne'er be drunk whilst I live again, but in honest, civil, godly company . . . . *Mer. Wives* i 1 187
The dinner is on the table; my father desires your worships' company . i 1 271
I shall never laugh but in that maid's company! . . . i 4 163
Why, he hath not been thrice in my company! . . . . ii 1 27
She was in his company at Page's house . . . . . ii 1 243
Take your rapier.—Forbear; here's company . . . . ii 3 17
Is she at home?—Ay; and as idle as she may hang together, for want of company . . . . iii 2 14
The gentleman is of no having: he kept company with the wild prince iii 2 73
Sir John is come in at your back-door, Mistress Ford, and requests your company . . . . iii 3 25
If there is one, I shall make two in the company . . . . iii 3 251
And hath drawn him and the rest of their company from their sport iv 2 35
Peace here; grace and good company! . . . *Meas. for Meas.* iii 1 44
My mind promises with my habit no loss shall touch her by my company iii 1 182
Say, by this token, I desire his company . . . . iv 3 144
Sir, your company is fairer than honest . . . . iv 3 185
Might bear him company in the quest of him . *Com. of Errors* i 1 130
His company must do his minions grace, Whilst I at home starve for a merry look . . . . ii 1 87
More company! The fiend is strong within him . . . iv 4 110
Alone, it was the subject of my theme; In company I often glanced it . v 1 66
In the street I met him And in his company that gentleman . . v 1 226
Go keep us company, And we shall make full satisfaction . . v 1 398
With me in your company?—I may say so, when I please . *Much Ado* ii 1 94
I offered him my company to a willow-tree . . . . ii 1 225
You have no employment for me?—None, but to desire your good company . . . . ii 1 282
I will only be bold with Benedick for his company . . . iii 2 8
Let him show himself what he is and steal out of your company . iii 3 63
For your many courtesies I thank you: I must discontinue your company v 1 192
I say, sing.—Forbear till this company be past . *L. L. Lost* i 2 131
By whom shall I send this?—Company! stay . . . . iv 3 77
I am betray'd, by keeping company With men like men of inconstancy iv 3 179
What buys your company?—Your absence only . . . . v 2 224

Company. 'Tis some policy To have one show worse than the king's and his company . . . . *L. L. Lost* v 2 514
Is all our company here?—You were best to call them generally *M. N. Dream* i 2 1
We shall be dogged with company, and our devices known . i 2 106
I have forsworn his bed and company . . . . ii 1 62
Nor doth this wood lack worlds of company, For you in my respect are all the world . . . . ii 1 223
To say the truth, reason and love keep little company together now-a-days . . . . iii 1 147
I will not trust you, I, Nor longer stay in your curst company . iii 2 341
That I may back to Athens by daylight, From these that my poor company detest . . . . iii 2 434
And sleep, that sometimes shuts up sorrow's eye, Steal me awhile from mine own company . . . . iii 2 436
A Bergomask dance between two of our company . . . v 1 361
Fare ye well: We leave you now with better company . *Mer. of Venice* i 1 59
Keep me company but two years moe, Thou shalt not know the sound of thine own tongue . . . . i 1 108
A soldier, that came hither in company of the Marquis of Montferrat . i 2 125
O that I had a title good enough to keep his name company! . iii 1 16
There came divers of Antonio's creditors in my company to Venice iii 1 119
In choosing wrong, I lose your company . . . . iii 2 3
And doth entreat Your company at dinner . . . . iv 2 8
Detain'd by her usurping uncle, To keep his daughter company *As Y. Like It* i 2 287
I cannot live out of her company . . . . . i 3 88
Thus misery doth part The flux of company . . . . ii 1 52
Wherever they are gone, That youth is surely in their company . ii 2 16
If thou hast not broke from company Abruptly, as my passion now makes me, Thou hast not loved . . . . . . ii 4 40
He is too disputable for my company . . . . . ii 5 36
What a life is this, That your poor friends must woo your company? ii 7 10
I thank you for your company; but, good faith, I had as lief have been myself alone . . . . iii 2 268
God 'ild you for your last company: I am very glad to see you . iii 3 76
Thy company, which erst was irksome to me, I will endure . . iii 5 95
Not a word; for here comes more company . . . . iv 3 75
The society,—which in the boorish is company . . . v 1 54
Arm'd with his good will and thy good company . *T. of Shrew* i 1 6
But stay a while: what company is this? . . . . i 1 46
My books and instruments shall be my company, On them to look . i 1 82
I see you do not mean to part with her, Or else you like not of my company . . . . i 1 65
'Tis bargain'd 'twixt us twain, being alone, That she shall still be curst in company . . . . ii 1 307
Wherefore gaze this goodly company, As if they saw some wondrous monument? . . . . iii 2 96
Honest company, I thank you all, That have beheld me give away myself . . . . iii 2 195
Thou, it seems, that calls for company to countenance her . iv 1 104
To-morrow't shall be mended, And, for this night, we'll fast for company . . . . iv 1 180
Come, Mistress Kate, I'll bear you company . . . iv 3 49
But, soft! company is coming here . . . . . iv 5 26
If along with us, We shall be joyful of thy company . . iv 5 52
Like pleasant travellers, to break a jest Upon the company you overtake iv 5 73
We shall not then have his company to-night? . . *All's Well* iv 3 33
I would gladly have him see his company anatomized . . iv 3 37
Mine own company, Chitopher, Vaumond, Bentii, two hundred and fifty each . . . . iv 3 187
She hath abjured the company And sight of men . *T. Night* i 2 40
Moreover, he's drunk nightly in your company . . . i 3 39
I would not undertake her in this company . . . . i 3 62
I myself am best When least in company . . . . i 4 38
No interim, not a minute's vacancy, Both day and night did we keep company . . . . v 1 99
In whose company I shall review Sicilia . . . *W. Tale* iv 4 679
Shall we thither and with our company piece the rejoicing? . v 2 117
The lords are all come back, And brought Prince Henry in their company . . . . *K. John* v 6 34
Your company, Which, I protest, hath very much beguiled The tediousness and process of my travel *Richard II.* ii 3 10
Of much less value is my company Than your good words . ii 3 19
They will along with company, for they have great charge . 1 *Hen. IV.* ii 1 51
I heard him tell it to one of his company last night at supper . ii 1 62
I am accursed to rob in that thief's company . . . . ii 2 10
I have forsworn his company hourly any time this two and twenty years, and yet I am bewitched with the rogue's company . . ii 2 16
This pitch, as ancient writers do report, doth defile; so doth the company thou keepest . . . . ii 4 456
There is a virtuous man whom I have often noted in thy company . ii 4 461
Banish not him thy Harry's company . . . . ii 4 525
So stale and cheap to vulgar company . . . . . iii 2 41
Company, villanous company, hath been the spoil of me . . iii 3 10
But a shirt and a half in all my company; and the half shirt is two napkins . . . . iv 2 46
Keeping such vile company as thou art hath in reason taken from me all ostentation of sorrow . . . . 2 *Hen. IV.* ii 2 53
What company?—Ephesians, my lord, of the old church . . ii 2 163
There am I, Till time and vantage crave my company . . ii 3 68
Discharge yourself of our company, Pistol . . . . ii 4 147
Therefore let men take heed of their company . . . . v 1 87
I have turn'd away my former self; So will I those that kept me company . . . . v 5 63
Take all his company along with him . . . . . v 5 98
I and my bosom must debate a while, And then I would no other company *Hen. V.* iv 1 32
I am a gentleman of a company . . . . . . iv 1 39
I could not die any where so contented as in the king's company . iv 1 133
I will do it, though I take thee in the king's company . . iv 1 237
We would not die in that man's company That fears his fellowship to die with us . . . . iv 3 38
My soul shall thine keep company to heaven . . . . iv 6 16
To join with witches and the help of hell!—Traitors have never other company . . . . 1 *Hen. VI.* ii 1 19
Will not your honours bear me company?—No, truly; it is more than manners will . . . . ii 2 53
Rouen hangs her head for grief That such a valiant company are fled . iii 2 125
Conduct me where, from company, I may revolve and ruminate my grief v 5 100
Company. Waking and in my dreams, In courtly company or at my beads 2 *Hen. VI.* i 1 27
I banish her my bed and company And give her as a prey to law and shame . . . . ii 1 197
Heart's discontent and sour affliction Be playfellows to keep you company! . . . . iii 2 302
A wilderness is populous enough, So Suffolk had thy heavenly company iii 2 361
He shall die.—And I, my lord, will bear him company . 3 *Hen. VI.* i 3 6
And craves your company for speedy counsel . . . . ii 1 208
I seek for thee, That Warwick's bones may keep thine company . v 2 4
And, in my company, my brother Gloucester . . *Richard III.* i 4 11
Let us in, To comfort Edward with our company . . . ii 1 139
No apparent likelihood of breach, Which haply by much company might be urged . . . . ii 2 137
We were sent for to the justices.—And so was I: I'll bear you company iii 3 47
What comfortable hour canst thou name, That ever graced me in thy company?—Faith, none, but Humphrey Hour, that call'd your grace To breakfast once forth of my company . . . . . iv 4 174
Fare you well!—Nay, he must bear you company . *Hen. VIII.* i 1 212
Good company, good wine, good welcome, Can make good people . i 4 6
The very thought of this fair company Clapp'd wings to me . i 4 8
A noble company! what are their pleasures? . . . . i 4 64
My lord, you'll bear us company?—Excuse me . . . ii 2 59
Leave me alone; For I must think of that which company Would not be friendly to . . . . v 1 75
Fair be to you, my lord, and to all this fair company! . *Troi. and Cres.* iii 1 47
What offends you, lady?—Sir, mine own company . . . iii 2 152
Nothing but heavenly business Should rob my bed-mate of my company iv 1 5
Let's have your company, or, if you please, Haste there before us iv 1 39
And you too, Diomed, Keep Hector company an hour or two . . v 1 88
I'll keep you company.—Sweet sir, you honour me . . . v 1 93
Your company to the Capitol; where, I know, Our greatest friends attend us . . . . *Coriolanus* i 1 248
I'll keep you company. Will you along? . . . . ii 3 157
Let me desire your company . . . . iii 1 335
Heartily well met, and most glad of your company . . . iv 3 54
Get thee gone; I see thou art not for my company . *T. Andron.* iii 2 58
Would I were a devil, To live and burn in everlasting fire, So I might have your company in hell! . . . . v 1 149
The empress never wags But in her company there is a Moor . v 2 88
I shall forget, to have thee still stand there, Remembering how I love thy company . . . . *Rom. and Jul.* ii 2 174
Mercutio's soul Is but a little way above our heads, Staying for thine to keep him company . . . . iii 1 133
Too familiar Is my dear son with such sour company . . . iii 3 7
But for your company, I would have been a-bed an hour ago . . iii 4 6
He shall soon keep Tybalt company: And then, I hope, thou wilt be satisfied . . . . iii 5 92
Alone, in company, still my care hath been To have her match'd . iii 5 179
Shall we in?—I'll keep you company . . . *T. of Athens* i 1 294
He does neither affect company, nor is he fit for't, indeed . . i 2 30
Entreats your company to-morrow to hunt with him . . . i 2 194
What do you in this wise company? . . . . . ii 2 77
I will mend thy feast.—First mend my company, take away thyself . iv 3 283
Yonder comes a poet and a painter: the plague of company light upon thee! . . . . iv 3 357
You that way and you this, but two in company . . . v 1 109
Each man apart, all single and alone, Yet an arch-villain keeps him company . . . . v 1 111
He is given To sports, to wildness and much company . *J. Cæsar* ii 1 189
Fleance his son, that keeps him company, Whose absence is no less material to me Than is his father's . . . . *Macbeth* iii 1 135
Please't your highness To grace us with your royal company . . iii 4 45
What means, and where they keep, What company, at what expense *Hamlet* ii 1 9
Take you some company, and away to horse . . . *Lear* i 4 359
What, hath your grace no better company? . . . . iii 4 147
Beseech your grace,— O, cry you mercy, sir. Noble philosopher, your company . . . . iii 4 177
Keep you our sister company . . . . iii 7 7
Do you perceive in all this noble company Where most you owe obedience? . . . . *Othello* i 3 179
O, but I fear—How lost you company? . . . . . ii 1 91
My wife is fair, feeds well, loves company, Is free of speech, sings, plays iii 3 184
Well, I must leave her company . . . . . . iv 1 148
Who keeps her company? What place? what time? what form? . iv 2 137
Let us, Lepidus, Not lack your company . . *Ant. and Cleo.* ii 2 172
Choose your own company, and command what cost Your heart has mind to . . . . iii 4 37
The queen, madam, Desires your highness' company . *Cymbeline* i 3 38
Your very goodness and your company O'erpays all I can do . . ii 4 9
What company Discover you abroad? . . . . . iv 2 129
I am, sir, The soldier that did company these three In poor beseeming . v 5 408
At Ephesus, the temple see, Our king and all his company . *Pericles* v 2 283
Comparative. And art indeed the most comparative, rascalliest, sweet young prince . . . . 1 *Hen. IV.* i 2 90
And stand the push Of every beardless vain comparative . . iii 2 67
Thou wert dignified enough, Even to the point of envy, if 'twere made Comparative for your virtues, to be styled The under-hangman of his kingdom . . . . *Cymbeline* ii 3 134
Compare. What wicked and dissembling glass of mine Made me compare with Hermia's sphery eyne? . . . . . *M. N. Dream* ii 2 99
To what, my love, shall I compare thine eyne? Crystal is muddy . iii 2 138
Now I perceive that she hath made compare Between our statures . iii 2 290
Our strength as weak, our weakness past compare . *T. of Shrew* v 2 174
And yet I will not compare with an old man . . . *T. Night* i 3 126
Make no compare Between that love a woman can bear me And that I owe . . . . ii 4 104
Compare our faces and be judge yourself . . . *K. John* i 1 79
York is too far gone with grief, Or else he never would compare between *Richard II.* ii 1 185
I have been studying how I may compare This prison where I live unto the world . . . . v 5 1
Compare with Cæsars, and with Cannibals, And Trojan Greeks 2 *Hen. IV.* ii 4 180
Compare dead happiness with living woe . . *Richard III.* iv 4 119
Their rhymes, Full of protest, of oath and big compare, Want similes *Troi. and Cres.* iii 2 182
With unattainted eye, Compare her face with some that I shall show *Rom. and Jul.* i 2 91

Compare. And for a hand, and a foot, and a body, though they be not to be talked on, yet they are past compare . . . *Rom. and Jul.* ii 5 43
To dispraise my lord with that same tongue Which she hath praised him with above compare So many thousand times . . . . iii 5 238
What things in the world canst thou nearest compare to thy flatterers? *T. of Athens* iv 3 319
Compare their reasons, When severally we hear them rendered *J. Cæsar* iii 2 9
I dare not confess that, lest I should compare with him in excellence *Hamlet* v 2 146
To seek through the regions of the earth For one his like, there would be something failing In him that should compare . *Cymbeline* i 1 22
I can compare our rich misers to nothing so fitly as to a whale *Pericles* ii 1 32
A princess To equal any single crown o' the earth I' the justice of compare! . . . . iv 3 9
Compared. I am compared to twenty thousand fairs *L. L. Lost* v 2 37
Thy leg a stick compared with this truncheon . 2 *Hen. VI.* iv 10 52
Esteem him as a lamb, being compared With my confineless harms *Macbeth* iv 3 54
Comparing. Such-like trifles, nothing comparing to his . *T. of Athens* iii 2 24
Comparison. He'll but break a comparison or two on me . *Much Ado* ii 1 152
Comparisons are odorous: palabras, neighbour Verges . iii 5 18
For so stands the comparison . . . . *L. L. Lost* iv 1 80
A man replete with mocks, Full of comparisons and wounding flouts . v 2 854
That the comparison May stand more proper . *Mer. of Venice* iii 2 45
When thou hast tired thyself in base comparisons, hear me speak 1 *Hen. IV.* ii 4 277
You sall find, in the comparisons between Macedon and Monmouth, that the situations, look you, is both alike . . *Hen. V.* iv 7 26
I speak but in the figures and comparisons of it . . . iv 7 47
Stand'st thou aloof upon comparison? . . 1 *Hen. VI.* iv 4 150
Go to—there were no more comparison between the women *Troi. and Cres.* i 1 43
Her hand, in whose comparison all whites are ink . . . i 1 56
O Jupiter! there's no comparison . . . . . . i 2 65
Whose gall coins slanders like a mint, To match us in comparisons with dirt . . . . i 3 194
After all comparisons of truth, As truth's authentic author to be cited . iii 2 187
I dare him therefore To lay his gay comparisons apart, And answer me declined, sword against sword . . *Ant. and Cleo.* iii 13 26
As fair and as good—a kind of hand-in-hand comparison *Cymbeline* i 4 76
Compass. Now all the blessings Of a glad father compass thee about! *Tempest* v 1 180
If I can check my erring love, I will; If not, to compass her I'll use my skill . . . . *T. G. of Ver.* ii 4 214
What compass will you wear your farthingale? . . . iv 7 51
What's your will?—That I may compass yours . . . iv 2 92
May be the knave bragged of that he could not compass *Mer. Wives* iii 3 212
Meadow-fairies, look you sing, Like to the Garter's compass, in a ring . v 5 70
And draw within the compass of suspect The unviolated honour *Com. of Errors* iii 1 87
She is too big, I hope, for me to compass . . . . iv 1 111
We the globe can compass soon, Swifter than the wandering moon *M. N. Dream* iv 1 102
That were hard to compass; Because she will admit no kind of suit *T. Night* i 2 44
Within thy crown, Whose compass is no bigger than thy head *Richard II.* ii 1 101
Why should we in the compass of a pale Keep law and form and due proportion? . . . . iii 4 40
Now I live out of all order, out of all compass . 1 *Hen. IV.* iii 3 23
You must needs be out of all compass, out of all reasonable compass . iii 3 25
Alençon, Reignier, compass him about, And Talbot perisheth 1 *Hen. VI.* iv 4 27
A thing impossible To compass wonders but by help of devils . v 4 48
Pleasure at command, Above the reach or compass of thy thought 2 *Hen. VI.* i 2 46
My mind exceeds the compass of her wheel . 3 *Hen. VI.* iv 3 47
Nor thou within the compass of my curse . . *Richard III.* i 3 284
They did perform Beyond thought's compass . . *Hen. VIII.* i 1 36
Fall into the compass of a præmunire . . . . . iii 2 340
A lady, wiser, fairer, truer, Than ever Greek did compass in his arms *Troi. and Cres.* i 3 276
To all the points o' the compass . . . . *Coriolanus* ii 3 26
I curse the day—and yet, I think, Few come within the compass of my curse—Wherein I did not some notorious ill . . *T. Andron.* v 1 126
I already know thy grief; It strains me past the compass of my wits *Rom. and Jul.* iv 1 47
Where I did begin, there shall I end; My life is run his compass *J. Cæsar* v 3 25
You would sound me from my lowest note to the top of my compass *Hamlet* iii 2 384
To do this is within the compass of man's wit . . . *Othello* ii 4 21
That had number'd in the world The sun to course two hundred compasses . . . . iii 4 71
Well, what is it? is it within reason and compass? . . . iv 2 224
To compass such a boundless happiness! . . . *Pericles* i 1 24
Compassed. How now shall this be compassed? . . *Tempest* iii 2 66
To be compassed, like a good bilbo, in the circumference of a peck *Mer. Wives* iii 5 112
With a small compassed cape . . . . *T. of Shrew* iv 3 140
Then he compassed a motion of the Prodigal Son . *W. Tale* iv 3 102
She came to him th' other day into the compassed window *Troi. and Cres.* i 2 120
I see thee compass'd with thy kingdom's pearl . . *Macbeth* v 8 56
Compassing. O, not to-day, think not upon the fault My father made in compassing the crown! . . . . . *Hen. V.* iv 1 311
Seek thou rather to be hanged in compassing thy joy than to be drowned and go without her . . . . . . *Othello* i 3 367
For the better compassing of his salt and most hidden loose affection . ii 1 244
Compassion. Which touch'd The very virtue of compassion in thee *Tempest* i 2 27
Let him come back, that his compassion may Give life to yours *K. John* iv 1 89
And in compassion weep the fire out . . . . *Richard. II.* v 1 48
Compassion on the king commands me stoop 1 *Hen. VI.* iii 1 119
Moved with compassion of my country's wreck . . . v 1 56
Gives consent, Of mere compassion and of lenity . . . v 4 125
Melting with tenderness and kind compassion . *Richard III.* iv 3 7
It is no little thing to make Mine eyes to sweat compassion . *Coriolanus* v 3 196
O heavens, can you hear a good man groan, And not relent, or not compassion him? . . . . *T. Andron.* iv 1 124
Honour, health, and compassion to the senate! *T. of Athens* iii 5 5
Compassionate. It boots thee not to be compassionate . *Richard II.* i 3 174
My compassionate heart Will not permit mine eyes once to behold The thing whereat it trembles by surmise *T. Andron.* ii 3 217
Compeer. In my rights, By me invested, he compeers the best . *Lear* v 3 69

Compel. It may compel him to her recompense *Meas. for Meas.* iii 1 262
Thou canst compel no more than she entreat . *M. N. Dream* iii 2 249
An I were not a very coward, I'ld compel it of you . . *All's Well* iv 3 357
He hath forced us to compel this offer . . . . 2 *Hen. IV.* iv 1 147
If requiring fail, he will compel . . . . *Hen. V.* ii 4 101
Which compel from each The sixth part of his substance *Hen. VIII.* i 2 57
You will compel me, then, to read the will? . . *J. Cæsar* iii 2 161
Very nature will instruct her in it and compel her to some second choice *Othello* ii 1 238
Strange it is, That nature must compel us to lament Our most persisted deeds . . . . *Ant. and Cleo.* v 1 29
Compelled. Our compell'd sins Stand more for number than for accompt *Meas. for Meas.* ii 4 57
He does acknowledge; But puts it off to a compell'd restraint *All's Well* ii 4 44
I prithee, do not strive against my vows: I was compell'd to her . iv 2 15
As the case now stands, it is a curse He cannot be compell'd to't *W. Tale* ii 3 88
Like a dog that is compell'd to fight . . . *K. John* iv 1 116
I had no such intent, But that necessity so bow'd the state That I and greatness were compell'd to kiss . . . . 2 *Hen. IV.* iii 1 74
As the state stood then, Was force perforce compell'd to banish him . iv 1 116
Say you not then our offer is compell'd . . . . . iv 1 158
Nothing compelled from the villages, nothing taken but paid for *Hen. V.* iii 6 116
And we for fear compell'd to shut our shops . 1 *Hen. VI.* iii 1 85
The son, compell'd, been butcher to the sire . *Richard III.* v 5 26
Compell'd by hunger And lack of other means . . *Hen. VIII.* i 2 34
Fie, fie, fie upon This compell'd fortune! . . . . . ii 3 87
As Pompey was, am I compell'd to set Upon one battle all our liberties *J. Cæsar* v 1 75
Compell'd these skipping kerns to trust their heels . *Macbeth* i 2 30
We ourselves compell'd, Even to the teeth and forehead of our faults, To give in evidence . . . . *Hamlet* iii 3 62
We put on a compelled valour, and in the grapple I boarded them . iv 6 17
'Tis most strange, Nature should be so conversant with pain, Being thereto not compell'd . . . . . . *Pericles* iii 2 26
Compelling. Under a compelling occasion, let women die *Ant. and Cleo.* i 2 141
Compensation. If I have too austerely punish'd you, Your compensation makes amends . . . . *Tempest* iv 1 2
Competence. For competence of life I will allow you, That lack of means enforce you not to evil . . . . 2 *Hen. IV.* v 5 70
Competency. Superfluity comes sooner by white hairs, but competency lives longer . . . . . . *Mer. of Venice* i 2 9
From me receive that natural competency Whereby they live *Coriolanus* i 1 143
Competent. His indignation derives itself out of a very competent injury *T. Night* iii 4 270
Against the which, a moiety competent Was gaged by our king *Hamlet* i 1 90
Competitor. Myself in counsel, his competitor . . *T. G. of Ver.* ii 6 35
He and his competitors in oath Were all address'd to meet you *L. L. Lost* ii 1 82
The competitors enter . . . . *T. Night* iv 2 12
And every hour more competitors Flock to their aid *Richard III.* iv 4 506
Let me in.—Tribunes, and me, a poor competitor . . *T. Andron.* i 1 63
Know ye not, in Rome How furious and impatient they be, And cannot brook competitors in love? . . . . ii 1 77
It is not Cæsar's natural vice to hate Our great competitor *Ant. and Cleo.* i 4 3
These three world-sharers, these competitors, Are in thy vessel . ii 7 76
Thou, my brother, my competitor, In top of all design . . v 1 42
Compile. Did never sonnet for her sake compile . *L. L. Lost* iv 3 134
Compiled. A huge translation of hypocrisy, Vilely compiled . . v 2 52
Will you hear the dialogue that the two learned men have compiled? . v 2 896
Complain. You'll complain of me to the king? . . *Mer. Wives* i 1 112
What was done to Elbow's wife, that he hath cause to complain of? *Meas. for Meas.* ii 1 121
To whom should I complain? Did I tell this, Who would believe me? ii 4 171
Say by whose advice Thou camest here to complain . . v 1 114
Were we burden'd with like weight of pain, As much or more we should ourselves complain . . . . . . *Com. of Errors* ii 1 37
Complain unto the duke of this indignity . . . . . v 1 113
Let us complain to them what fools were here . . *L. L. Lost* v 2 302
He that hath learned no wit by nature nor art may complain of good breeding . . . . *As Y. Like It* iii 2 31
Will thou make a fire, or shall I complain on thee? . *T. of Shrew* iv 1 31
Where then, alas, may I complain myself?—To God . *Richard II.* i 2 42
What I want it boots not to complain . . . . . iii 4 18
I promised you redress of these same grievances Whereof you did complain . . . . 2 *Hen. IV.* iv 2 114
What is that wrong whereof you both complain? . 1 *Hen. VI.* iv 1 87
Who are they that complain unto the king? . . *Richard III.* i 3 43
If they did complain, What could the belly answer? . *Coriolanus* i 1 127
But to his foe supposed he must complain . *Rom. and Jul.* ii Prol. 7
Complained. The shepherd that complain'd of love . *As Y. Like It* iii 4 51
Complainer. Speechless complainer, I will learn thy thought *T. Andron.* iii 2 39
Complainest. And yet complainest thou of obstruction? *T. Night* iv 2 43
Complaining. So prettily He couples it to his complaining names *T. G. of Ver.* i 2 127
And to the nightingale's complaining notes Tune my distresses . v 4 5
Humbly complaining to her deity Got my lord chamberlain his liberty *Richard III.* i 1 76
Poor heart, adieu! I pity thy complaining . . . . iv 1 88
With these shreds They vented their complainings . . *Coriolanus* i 1 213
Thou movest no less with thy complaining than Thy master in bleeding *Cymbeline* iv 2 375
Complaint. I advise you, let me not find you before me again upon any complaint whatsoever . . . . . . *Meas. for Meas.* ii 1 261
To have a dispatch of complaints, and to deliver us from devices hereafter . . . . iv 4 14
Till you have heard me in my true complaint And given me justice . v 1 24
Being come to knowledge that there was complaint Intended . . v 1 153
He indeed Hath set the women on to this complaint . . . v 1 251
Full of vexation come I, with complaint Against my child *M. N. Dream* i 1 22
The complaints I have heard of you I do not all believe . *All's Well* i 3 9
I am her mother, sir, whose age and honour Both suffer under this complaint . . . . v 3 163
I know not what impediment this complaint may be . . *W. Tale* iv 4 730
The complaint they have to the king concerns him nothing . . iv 4 869
The complaints I hear of thee are grievous . . 1 *Hen. IV.* ii 4 486
There is many complaints, Davy, against that Visor . 2 *Hen. IV.* v 1 44
Whose guiltless drops Are every one a woe, a sore complaint *Hen. V.* i 2 26
With the pitiful complaints Of such as your oppression feeds upon 1 *Hen. VI.* iv 1 57
This late complaint Will make but little for his benefit . . 2 *Hen. VI.* i 3 100

Complaint. Cannot be quiet scarce a breathing-while, But you must trouble him with lewd complaints . . . *Richard III.* i 3 61
Give me no help in lamentation; I am not barren to bring forth complaints . . . ii 2 67
And lost your office On the complaint o' the tenants . . . *Hen. VIII.* i 2 173
Unite in your complaints, And force them with a constancy . . . iii 2 1
Hath so far Given ear to our complaint . . . v 1 48
I have, and most unwillingly, of late Heard many grievous, I do say, my lord, Grievous complaints of you . . . v 1 99
Said to be something imperfect in favouring the first complaint *Coriolanus* ii 1 54
Each buzz, each fancy, each complaint, dislike . . . *Lear* i 4 348
Let him do his spite: My services which I have done the signiory Shall out-tongue his complaints . . . *Othello* i 2 19
Complement. In all the accoutrement, complement and ceremony of it *Mer. Wives* iv 2 5
A man of complements, whom right and wrong Have chose as umpire of their mutiny . . . *L. L. Lost* i 1 169
These are complements, these are humours; these betray nice wenches iii 1 23
Garnish'd and deck'd in modest complement . . . *Hen. V.* ii 2 134
O, he is the courageous captain of complements . . . *Rom. and Jul.* ii 4 20
Complete in feature and in mind With all good grace . *T. G. of Ver.* ii 4 73
Believe not that the dribbling dart of love Can pierce a complete bosom *Meas. for Meas.* i 3 3
A maid of grace and complete majesty . . . *L. L. Lost* i 1 137
They are both the varnish of a complete man . . . i 2 47
Brawling in French?—No, my complete master . . . iii 1 11
Such as she is, in beauty, virtue, birth, Is the young Dauphin every way complete: If not complete of, say he is not she . . . *K. John* ii 1 433
In complete glory she reveal'd herself . . . 1 *Hen. VI.* i 2 83
The most complete champion that ever I heard! . . . 2 *Hen. VI.* iv 10 58
Thereby to see the minutes how they run, How many make the hour full complete . . . 3 *Hen. VI.* ii 5 26
Take with thee my most heavy curse; Which, in the day of battle, tire thee more Than all the complete armour that thou wear'st! *Rich. III.* iv 4 189
This man so complete, Who was enroll'd 'mongst wonders . *Hen. VIII.* i 2 118
She is a gallant creature, and complete In mind and feature . . . iii 2 49
Then marvel not, thou great and complete man . . . *Troi. and Cres.* iii 3 181
A thousand complete courses of the sun . . . iv 1 27
And how does that honourable, complete, free-hearted gentleman? *T. of Athens* iii 1 9
The one is filling still, never complete; The other, at high wish . iv 3 244
Again in complete steel Revisit'st thus the glimpses of the moon *Hamlet* i 4 52
A pestilent complete knave; and the woman hath found him already *Oth.* ii 1 252
Complexion. His complexion is perfect gallows . . . *Tempest* i 1 32
So curses all Eve's daughters, of what complexion soever *Mer. Wives* iv 2 25
How near the god drew to the complexion of a goose! . . . v 5 9
We are soft as our complexions are, And credulous to false prints *Meas. for Meas.* ii 4 129
Thy complexion shifts to strange effects, After the moon . . . iii 1 24
Grace, being the soul of your complexion, shall keep the body of it ever fair . . . iii 1 187
What complexion is she of?—Swart, like my shoe . *Com. of Errors* iii 2 103
How sweetly you do minister to love, That know love's grief by his complexion! . . . *Much Ado* i 1 315
Civil as an orange, and something of that jealous complexion . . . ii 1 305
A woman, master.—Of what complexion?—Of all the four . *L. L. Lost* i 2 82
Tell me precisely of what complexion.—Of the sea-water green, sir.—Is that one of the four complexions? . . . i 2 85
Of all complexions the cull'd sovereignty Do meet, as at a fair, in her fair cheek . . . iv 3 234
And Ethiopes of their sweet complexion crack . . . iv 3 268
If he have the condition of a saint and the complexion of a devil *Mer. of Venice* i 2 143
Mislike me not for my complexion, The shadow'd livery of the burnish'd sun . . . ii 1 1
Let all of his complexion choose me so . . . ii 7 79
It is the complexion of them all to leave the dam . . . iii 1 32
Good my complexion! . . . *As Y. Like It* iii 2 204
Between the pale complexion of true love And the red glow of scorn . iii 4 56
He'll make a proper man: the best thing in him Is his complexion . iii 5 116
There is too great testimony in your complexion that it was a passion of earnest.—Counterfeit, I assure you . . . iv 3 171
Complexions that liked me and breaths that I defied not . . . Epil. 20
The expressure of his eye, forehead, and complexion . . . *T. Night* ii 3 172
What kind of woman is't?—Of your complexion . . . ii 4 27
That, should she fancy, it should be one of my complexion . . . ii 5 30
Your changed complexions are to me a mirror Which shows me mine changed too . . . *W. Tale* i 2 381
Whose fresh complexion and whose heart together Affliction alters . iv 4 585
Men judge by the complexion of the sky The state and inclination of the day . . . *Richard II.* iii 2 194
Change the complexion of her maid-pale peace To scarlet indignation iii 3 98
It discolours the complexion of my greatness to acknowledge it 2 *Hen. IV.* ii 2 6
What see you in those papers that you lose So much complexion? *Hen. V.* ii 2 73
Impious war . . . with his smirch'd complexion . . . iii 3 17
She praised his complexion above Paris . . . *Troi. and Cres.* i 2 107
His complexion is higher than his; he having colour enough, and the other higher, is too flaming a praise for a good complexion . . . i 2 111
Ridges horsed With variable complexions . . . *Coriolanus* ii 1 228
The complexion of the element In favour's like the work we have *J. Cæsar* i 3 128
By the o'ergrowth of some complexion . . . *Hamlet* i 4 27
Hath now this dread and black complexion smear'd With heraldry more dismal . . . ii 2 477
But yet methinks it is very sultry and hot for my complexion . . . v 2 102
Not to affect many proposed matches Of her own clime, complexion, and degree . . . *Othello* iii 3 230
Turn thy complexion there, Patience, thou young and rose-lipp'd cherubin . . . iv 2 62
That excellent complexion, which did steal The eyes of young and old *Pericles* iv 1 41
Take you the marks of her, the colour of her hair, complexion, height iv 2 62
You shall have the difference of all complexions . . . iv 2 85
Complice. Their complices, The caterpillars of the commonwealth *Richard II.* ii 3 165
Away, To fight with Glendower and his complices . . . iii 1 43
The lives of all your loving complices Lean on your health . 2 *Hen. IV.* i 1 163
To quell the rebels and their complices . . . 2 *Hen. VI.* v 1 212
In despite of all mischance, Of thee thyself and all thy complices 3 *Hen. VI.* iv 3 44
Compliment. Manhood is melted into courtesies, valour into compliment *Much Ado* iv 1 322
Thine, in all compliments of devoted and heart-burning heat of duty *L. L. Lost* i 1 279
Stay not thy compliment; I forgive thy duty: adieu . . . iv 2 147
That they call compliment is like the encounter of two dog-apes *As Y. Like It* ii 5 26
'Twas never merry world Since lowly feigning was call'd compliment *T. Night* iii 1 110
Even now I met him With customary compliment . . . *W. Tale* i 2 371
Saving in dialogue of compliment . . . *K. John* i 1 201
Come, come; sans compliment, what news abroad? . . . v 6 16
But farewell compliment! Dost thou love me? . . . *Rom. and Jul.* ii 2 89
There is further compliment of leave-taking . . . *Lear* i 1 306
The time will not allow the compliment Which very manners urges . v 3 233
The native act and figure of my heart In compliment extern . *Othello* i 1 63
Worthy shameful check it were, to stand On more mechanic compliment *Ant. and Cleo.* iv 4 32
Complimental. I will make a complimental assault upon him *Tr. and Cr.* iii 1 42
Complot. Never by advised purpose meet To plot, contrive, or complot any ill . . . *Richard II.* i 3 189
I know their complot is to have my life . . . 2 *Hen. VI.* iii 1 147
Lord Hastings will not yield to our complots . . . *Richard III.* iii 1 192
Let us sup betimes, that afterwards We may digest our complots in some form . . . iii 1 200
I bring this fatal writ, The complot of this timeless tragedy *T. Andron.* ii 3 265
Complots of mischief, treason, villanies Ruthful to hear . . . v 1 65
Revenge now goes To lay a complot to betray thy foes . . . v 2 147
Complotted. All the treasons for these eighteen years Complotted and contrived in this land . . . *Richard II.* i 1 96
Comply. Let me comply with you in this garb . . . *Hamlet* ii 2 390
He did comply with his dug, before he sucked it . . . v 2 195
Nor to comply with heat—the young affects In me defunct . *Othello* i 3 264
Compose. Thy undaunted mettle should compose Nothing but males *Macbeth* i 7 73
If we compose well here, to Parthia . . . *Ant. and Cleo.* ii 2 15
And with her neeld composes Nature's own shape, of bud, bird *Pericles* v Gower 5
Composed. He's composed of harshness . . . *Tempest* iii 1 9
Whose composed rhymes Should be full-fraught with serviceable vows *T. G. of Ver.* iii 2 69
He is composed and framed of treachery . . . *Much Ado* v 1 257
One that composed your beauties . . . *M. N. Dream* i 1 48
Frank nature, rather curious than in haste, Hath well composed thee *All's Well* i 2 21
With musics of all sorts and songs composed To her unworthiness . iii 7 40
Then did they imitate that which I composed to my courser . *Hen. V.* iii 7 46
They're loving, well composed with gifts of nature . *Troi. and Cres.* iv 4 79
Were it a casque composed by Vulcan's skill, My sword should bite it v 2 170
Words of so sweet breath composed As made the things more rich *Hamlet* iii 1 98
Composition. If the duke with the other dukes come not to composition *Meas. for Meas.* i 2 2
Her promised proportions Came short of composition . . . v 1 220
The composition that your valour and fear makes in you is a virtue of a good wing . . . *All's Well* i 1 217
And thinks himself made in the unchaste composition . . . iv 3 22
Do you not read some tokens of my son In the large composition of this man? . . . *K. John* i 1 88
Mad world! mad kings! mad composition! . . . ii 1 561
Aged Gaunt?—O, how that name befits my composition! *Richard II.* ii 1 73
A prince should not be so loosely studied as to remember so weak a composition . . . 2 *Hen. IV.* ii 2 10
You did mistake The outward composition of his body . 1 *Hen. VI.* ii 3 75
That it was which caused Our swifter composition . . . *Coriolanus* iii 1 3
Sweno, the Norway's king, craves composition . . . *Macbeth* i 2 59
Who, in the lusty stealth of nature, take More composition . . . *Lear* i 2 12
Art nothing but the composition of a knave, beggar, coward . . . ii 2 22
There is no composition in these news That gives them credit . *Othello* i 3 1
I crave our composition may be written, And seal'd between us *Ant. and Cleo.* ii 6 59
Compost. Do not spread the compost on the weeds, To make them ranker *Hamlet* iii 4 151
Composture. The earth's a thief, That feeds and breeds by a composture stolen From general excrement . . . *T. of Athens* iv 3 444
Composure. It was a strong composure a fool could disunite *Troi. and Cres.* ii 3 109
Thank the heavens, lord, thou art of sweet composure . . . iii 3 251
His composure must be rare indeed Whom these things cannot blemish *Ant. and Cleo.* i 4 22
Compound. There was the rankest compound of villanous smell that ever offended nostril . . . *Mer. Wives* iii 5 93
If you think it meet, compound with him by the year *Meas. for Meas.* iv 2 25
We will compound this quarrel . . . *T. of Shrew* i 2 27
I will compound this strife: 'Tis deeds must win the prize . . . ii 1 343
Compound whose right is worthiest . . . *K. John* ii 1 281
If thou didst, then behold that compound . . . 1 *Hen. IV.* ii 4 136
Compound me with forgotten dust . . . 2 *Hen. IV.* iv 5 116
As manhood shall compound: push home . . . *Hen. V.* ii 1 103
I come to know of thee, King Harry, If for thy ransom thou wilt now compound . . . iv 3 80
I must perforce compound With mistful eyes, or they will issue too . iv 6 33
Compound a boy, half French, half English . . . v 2 221
I pray, my lords, let me compound this strife . . . 2 *Hen. VI.* ii 1 58
I find the ass in compound with the major part of your syllables *Coriolanus* ii 1 64
There is thy gold, worse poison to men's souls, Doing more murders in this loathsome world, Than these poor compounds that thou mayst not sell . . . *Rom. and Jul.* v 1 82
To have his pomp and all what state compounds But only painted, like his varnish'd friends? . . . *T. of Athens* iv 2 35
This solidity and compound mass . . . *Hamlet* iii 4 49
Most poisonous compounds, Which are the movers of a languishing death *Cymbeline* i 5 8
I will try the forces Of these thy compounds on such creatures as We count not worth the hanging . . . i 5 19
I, dreading that her purpose Was of more danger, did compound for her A certain stuff . . . v 5 254
Compound of majesty. Thou whoreson mad compound of majesty 2 *Hen. IV.* ii 4 319
Compounded. It is a melancholy of mine own, compounded of many simples . . . *As Y. Like It* iv 1 16
I would to God all strifes were well compounded . . . *Richard III.* ii 1 74
What four throned ones could have weigh'd Such a compounded one? *Hen. VIII.* i 1 12

Compounded. We here deliver, . . . Together with the seal o' the senate, what We have compounded on . . . *Coriolanus* v 6 84
Who in spite put stuff To some she beggar and compounded thee Poor rogue hereditary . . . . *T. of Athens* iv 3 273
What have you done, my lord, with the dead body?—Compounded it with dust, whereto 'tis kin . . . *Hamlet* iv 2 6
My father compounded with my mother under the dragon's tail *Lear* i 2 139
From every one The best she hath, and she, of all compounded, Outsells them all . . . . *Cymbeline* iii 5 73
Comprehend. You shall comprehend all vagrom men . *Much Ado* iii 3 25
Thine eyes, Where all those pleasures live that art would comprehend *L. L. Lost* iv 2 114
Fantasies, that apprehend More than cool reason ever comprehends *M. N. Dream* v 1 6
If it would but apprehend some joy, It comprehends some bringer of that joy . . . . v 1 20
Comprehended. Our watch, sir, have indeed comprehended two aspicious persons . . . . *Much Ado* iii 5 50
Compremise. And will be glad to do my benevolence to make atonements and compremises between you . . . . . *Mer. Wives* i 1 33
Comprised. She is our capital demand, comprised Within the fore-rank of our articles . . . . *Hen. V.* v 2 96
Comprising all that may be sworn or said *Richard II.* iii 3 111
Compromise. Send fair-play orders and make compromise . *K. John* v 1 67
But basely yielded upon compromise That which his noble ancestors achieved with blows . . . . . *Richard II.* ii 1 253
Now the matter grows to compromise, Stand'st thou aloof? . 1 *Hen. VI.* v 4 149
Compromised. When Laban and himself were compromised *Mer. of Venice* i 3 79
Compt. That thou didst love her, strikes some scores away From the great compt . . . . *All's Well* v 3 57
Take the bonds along with you, And have the dates in compt *T. of Athens* ii 1 35
Your servants ever Have theirs, themselves and what is theirs, in compt, To make their audit . . . . . *Macbeth* i 6 26
When we shall meet at compt, This look of thine will hurl my soul from heaven, And fiends will snatch at it . . . *Othello* v 2 273
Comptible. I am very comptible, even to the least sinister usage *T. Night* i 5 187
Comptroller. I was spoke to, with Sir Henry Guildford This night to be comptrollers . . . . *Hen. VIII.* i 3 67
Compulsatory. By strong hand And terms compulsatory . *Hamlet* i 1 103
Compulsion. Then must the Jew be merciful.—On what compulsion must I? tell me that . . . . . *Mer. of Venice* iv 1 183
In the highest compulsion of base fear . . . . *All's Well* iii 6 31
By the compulsion of their ordinance . . . . *K. John* ii 1 218
What a brave noble combat hast thou fought Between compulsion and a brave respect! . . . . v 2 44
An I were at the strappado, or all the racks in the world, I would not tell you on compulsion . . . . 1 *Hen. IV.* ii 4 263
Give you a reason on compulsion! if reasons were as plentiful as blackberries, I would give no man a reason upon compulsion . . . ii 4 264
To deliver her possession up On terms of base compulsion! *Troi. and Cres.* ii 2 153
As if we were villains by necessity; fools by heavenly compulsion *Lear* i 2 133
Compulsive. Proclaim no shame When the compulsive ardour gives the charge . . . . *Hamlet* iii 4 86
Whose icy current and compulsive course Ne'er feels retiring ebb *Othello* iii 3 454
Compunctious. That no compunctious visitings of nature Shake my fell purpose . . . . *Macbeth* i 5 46
Computation. In care to seek me out By computation . *Com. of Errors* ii 2 4
By just computation of the time . . . . *Richard III.* iii 5 89
Comrade. The nimble-footed madcap Prince of Wales, And his comrades 1 *Hen. IV.* iv 1 96
Do not dull thy palm with entertainment Of each new-hatch'd, unfledged comrade . . . . *Hamlet* i 3 65
To be a comrade with the wolf and owl,—Necessity's sharp pinch! *Lear* ii 4 213
Con. Here are your parts: and I am to entreat you, request you and desire you, to con them . . . . *M. N. Dream* i 2 102
But I con him no thanks for't, in the nature he delivers it *All's Well* iv 3 174
It is excellently well penned, I have taken great pains to con it *T. Night* i 5 186
An affectioned ass, that cons state without book . . . ii 3 161
And this they con perfectly in the phrase of war . *Hen. V.* iii 6 79
Thy horse will sooner con an oration than thou learn a prayer without book . . . . *Troi. and Cres.* ii 1 18
Yet thanks I must you con That you are thieves profess'd *T. of Athens* iv 3 428
Concave. I do think him as concave as a covered goblet *As Y. Like It* iii 4 26
Tiber trembled underneath her banks, To hear the replication of your sounds Made in her concave shores . . . *J. Cæsar* i 1 52
Concavities. The concavities of it is not sufficient . *Hen. V.* iii 2 64
Conceal. That which I would discover The law of friendship bids me to conceal . . . . *T. G. of Ver.* iii 1 5
I may not conceal them, sir.—Conceal them, or thou diest *Mer. Wives* iv 5 45
You may conceal her, As best befits her wounded reputation *Much Ado* iv 1 242
A time that lovers' flights doth still conceal . *M. N. Dream* i 1 212
I'll pay thee bounteously, Conceal me what I am . *T. Night* i 2 53
He shall conceal it Whiles you are willing it shall come to note . iv 3 28
I hold it the more knavery to conceal it . . . *W. Tale* iv 4 697
Thou fond mad woman, Wilt thou conceal this dark conspiracy? *Richard II.* v 2 96
There's but two ways, either to utter them, or to conceal them 2 *Hen. IV.* v 3 116
'Tis wisdom to conceal our meaning . . . 3 *Hen. VI.* iv 7 60
Thou art sworn as deeply to effect what we intend As closely to conceal what we impart . . . . *Richard III.* iii 1 159
This secret is so weighty, 'twill require A strong faith to conceal it *Hen. VIII.* ii 1 145
He that conceals him, death . . . . *Lear* ii 1 65
I am glad to be constrain'd to utter that Which torments me to conceal *Cymbeline* v 5 142
Who wanteth food, and will not say he wants it, Or can conceal his hunger till he famish? . . . . . . *Pericles* i 4 12
Concealed. Bring me to hear them speak, where I may be concealed *Meas. for Meas.* iii 1 53
That thou mightst pour this concealed man out of thy mouth *As Y. Like It* iii 2 210
Very good; let it be concealed awhile . . . *All's Well* ii 3 283
To dive like buckets in concealed wells . . . *K. John* v 2 139
Sorrow concealed, like an oven stopp'd, Doth burn the heart to cinders *T. Andron.* ii 4 36
What says My conceal'd lady to our cancell'd love? *Rom. and Jul.* iii 3 98
I pray you all, If you have hitherto conceal'd this sight, Let it be tenable in your silence still . . . . . . *Hamlet* i 2 247
Concealing. By concealing it, heap on your head A pack of sorrows *T. G. of Ver.* iii 1 19

Concealing. My tongue will tell the anger of my heart, Or else my heart concealing it will break . . . *T. of Shrew* iv 3 78
Close pent-up guilts, Rive your concealing continents . . . *Lear* iii 2 58
Concealment. She never told her love, But let concealment, like a worm i' the bud, Feed on her damask cheek . . . *T. Night* ii 4 114
Imprison't not In ignorant concealment . . . *W. Tale* i 2 397
Exceedingly well read, and profited In strange concealments 1 *Hen. IV.* iii 1 167
'Twere a concealment Worse than a theft, no less than a traducement *Coriolanus* i 9 21
Some dear cause Will in concealment wrap me up awhile . *Lear* iv 3 54
Conceit. The good conceit I hold of thee . . *T. G. of Ver.* iii 2 17
Lay open to my earthy-gross conceit, Smother'd in errors *Com. of Errors* iii 2 34
I am press'd down with conceit—Conceit, my comfort and my injury iv 2 65
If he be so, his conceit is false . . . . . *Much Ado* ii 1 309
His fair tongue, conceit's expositor . . . . . *L. L. Lost* ii 1 72
A good lustre of conceit in a turf of earth; fire enough for a flint . iv 2 90
Their conceits have wings Fleeter than arrows, bullets, wind, thought . v 2 260
Cut me to pieces with thy keen conceit . . . . . . v 2 399
With bracelets of thy hair, rings, gawds, conceits . *M. N. Dream* i 1 33
To be dress'd in an opinion Of wisdom, gravity, profound conceit *Mer. of Venice* i 1 92
You have a noble and a true conceit Of god-like amity . . . iii 4 2
Let it be as humours and conceits shall govern . . . . iii 5 69
Thy conceit is nearer death than thy powers . *As Y. Like It* ii 6 8
I know you are a gentleman of good conceit . . . . . v 2 59
The conceit is deeper than you think for . . *T. of Shrew* iv 3 163
Thy conceit is soaking, will draw in More than the common blocks *W. Tale* i 2 224
The prince your son, with mere conceit and fear Of the queen's speed, is gone . . . . iii 2 145
Using conceit alone, Without eyes, ears and harmful sound of words *K. John* iii 3 50
'Tis nothing but conceit, my gracious lady . . *Richard II.* ii 2 33
Conceit is still derived From some forefather grief . . . ii 2 34
Infusing him with self and vain conceit . . . . . iii 2 166
There's no more conceit in him than is in a mallet . 2 *Hen. IV.* ii 4 263
With forged quaint conceit To set a gloss upon his bold intent 1 *Hen. VI.* iv 1 102
A volume of enticing lines, Able to ravish any dull conceit . . v 5 15
There's some conceit or other likes him well . *Richard III.* iii 4 51
I shall not fail to approve the fair conceit The king hath of you *Hen. VIII.* ii 3 74
Like a strutting player, whose conceit Lies in his hamstring *Troi. and Cres.* i 3 153
She would applaud Andronicus' conceit . . . *T. Andron.* iv 2 30
Conceit, more rich in matter than in words, Brags of his substance *Rom. and Jul.* ii 6 30
The horrible conceit of death and night, Together with the terror of the place . . . . iv 3 37
Noble and young, When thy first griefs were but a mere conceit *T. of Athens* v 4 14
Rich conceit Taught thee to make vast Neptune weep for aye On thy low grave . . . . v 4 77
One of two bad ways you must conceit me . . *J. Cæsar* iii 1 192
In a dream of passion, Could force his soul so to his own conceit *Hamlet* ii 2 579
A broken voice, and his whole function suiting With forms to his conceit . . . . ii 2 583
Conceit in weakest bodies strongest works . . . . iii 4 114
Conceit upon her father . . . . iv 5 45
Most delicate carriages, and of very liberal conceit . . . v 2 160
I know not how conceit may rob The treasury of life . . *Lear* iv 6 42
As if thou then hadst shut up in thy brain Some horrible conceit *Othello* iii 3 115
That your wisdom yet, From one that so imperfectly conceits, Would take no notice . . . . iii 3 149
Dangerous conceits are, in their natures, poisons . . . iii 3 326
A thing too young for such a place, Who, if it had conceit, would die *Pericles* iii 1 16
Conceited. He was gotten in drink: is not the humour conceited? *Mer. Wives* i 3 26
The youth's a devil.—He is as horribly conceited of him *T. Night* iii 4 322
Thou talkest of an admirable conceited fellow . . . *W. Tale* iv 4 204
Well conceited, Davy: about thy business, Davy . 2 *Hen. IV.* v 1 39
Our great need of him You have right well conceited . *J. Cæsar* i 3 162
Conceitless. Think'st thou I am so shallow, so conceitless, To be seduced by thy flattery? . . . . . *T. G. of Ver.* iv 2 96
Conceive. Do not approach Till thou dost hear me call.—Well, I conceive *Tempest* iv 1 50
Nay, conceive me, conceive me, sweet coz . . . *Mer. Wives* i 1 250
Plainly conceive, I love you . . . . *Meas. for Meas.* ii 4 141
'Fair' in 'all hail' is foul, as I conceive . . *L. L. Lost* v 2 340
We have laugh'd to see the sails conceive And grow big-bellied with the wanton wind . . . . *M. N. Dream* ii 1 128
Man's hand is not able to taste, his tongue to conceive . . iv 1 219
If you did know for whom I gave the ring And would conceive for what I gave the ring . . . . . . *Mer. of Venice* v 1 195
What he is indeed, More suits you to conceive than I to speak of *As Y. Like It* i 2 279
Sir, you say well and well you do conceive . . *T. of Shrew* i 2 271
Thus I conceive by him.—Conceives by me! . . . . v 2 22
My widow says, thus she conceives her tale . . . . v 2 24
He does conceive He is dishonour'd by a man which ever Profess'd to him . . . . *W. Tale* i 2 454
Whose honourable thoughts, Thoughts high for one so tender, cleft the heart That could conceive a gross and foolish sire Blemish'd his gracious dam . . . . iii 2 198
And make conceive a bark of baser kind By bud of nobler race . iv 4 94
'How comes that?' says he, that takes upon him not to conceive 2 *Hen. IV.* ii 2 124
Conceives by idleness and nothing teems But hateful docks . *Hen. V.* v 2 51
Ay, such a pleasure as incaged birds Conceive . . 3 *Hen. VI.* iv 6 13
The grieved commons Hardly conceive of me . . . *Hen. VIII.* i 2 105
What counterfeit did I give you?—The slip, sir, the slip; can you not conceive? . . . . *Rom. and Jul.* ii 4 51
I hope his honour will conceive the fairest of me . *T. of Athens* iii 2 60
But time will—and so— I do conceive . . . . . iii 6 72
Tongue nor heart Cannot conceive nor name thee! . *Macbeth* ii 3 70
Conception is a blessing: but not as your daughter may conceive *Hamlet* ii 2 186
I cannot conceive you.—Sir, this young fellow's mother could *Lear* i 1 12
Conceive, and fare thee well . . . . iv 2 24
Alas, what does this gentleman conceive? . . . . *Othello* iv 2 95

Conceive. We shall, As I conceive the journey, be at the Mount Before you . . . . *Ant. and Cleo.* ii 4 6
She's my good lady, and will conceive, I hope, But the worst of me *Cymbeline* ii 3 158
Conceived. That a woman conceived me, I thank her . . *Much Ado* i 1 240
Begot of thought, conceived of spleen and born of madness *As Y. Like It* iv 1 217
It shall become to serve all hopes conceived . . *T. of Shrew* i 1 15
To stop up the displeasure he hath conceived against your son *All's Well* iv 5 80
Set this device against Malvolio here, Upon some stubborn and uncourteous parts We had conceived against him . . . *T. Night* v 1 370
Who had Commanded nature, that my lady's womb, If it conceived a male child by me, should Do no more offices of life to't than The grave does to the dead . . . . . *Hen. VIII.* ii 4 189
'Tis conceived to scope . . . . . . *T. of Athens* i 1 72
O error, soon conceived, Thou never comest unto a happy birth! *J. Cæsar* v 3 69
Conceiving. The fulsome ewes, Who then conceiving did in eaning time Fall parti-colour'd lambs . . . . *Mer. of Venice* i 3 88
Conceiving the dishonour of his mother, He straight declined *W. Tale* ii 3 13
She did print your royal father off, Conceiving you . . . v 1 126
Strikes life into my speech and shows much more His own conceiving *Cymbeline* iii 3 98
Conception. And in my heart the strong and swelling evil Of my conception . . . . *Meas. for Meas.* ii 4 7
Note This dangerous conception in this point . . *Hen. VIII.* i 2 139
I have a young conception in my brain . . . . *Troi. and Cres.* i 3 312
Joy had the like conception in our eyes . . . *T. of Athens* i 2 115
Conceptions only proper to myself . . . . *J. Cæsar* i 2 41
Conception is a blessing: but not as your daughter may conceive *Hamlet* ii 2 185
Thou but rememberest me of mine own conception . . *Lear* i 4 73
Pray heaven it be state-matters, as you think, And no conception nor no jealous toy Concerning you . . . . *Othello* iii 4 156
Cannot remove nor choke the strong conception That I do groan withal v 2 55
At whose conception, till Lucina reign'd, Nature this dowry gave *Pericles* i 1 8
The passions of the mind, That have their first conception by mis-dread i 2 12
Conceptious. Ensear thy fertile and conceptious womb, Let it no more bring out ingrateful man! . . . *T. of Athens* iv 3 187
Concern. Let it lie for those that it concerns.—Madam, it will not lie where it concerns . . . . . . *T. G. of Ver.* i 2 76
Confer at large Of all that may concern thy love-affairs . iii 1 254
It concerns me To look into the bottom of my place *Meas. for Meas.* i 1 78
My noble and well-warranted cousin, Whom it concerns to hear this matter forth . . . . v 1 255
What I would speak of concerns him . . . *Much Ado* iii 2 88
It may concern much. Stay not thy compliment . *L. L. Lost* iv 2 146
Pardon me. I know not by what power I am made bold, Nor how it may concern my modesty . . . . . *M. N. Dream* i 1 60
And confer with you Of something nearly that concerns yourselves . i 1 126
In the loss that may happen, it concerns you something to know it *All's Well* i 3 125
She told me, In a sweet verbal brief, it did concern Your highness with herself . . . . v 3 137
Speak your office.—It alone concerns your ear . . *T. Night* i 5 224
Which to deny concerns more than avails . . *W. Tale* iii 2 87
Shall nothing benefit your knowledge, nor Concern me the reporting . iv 4 515
The complaint they have to the king concerns him nothing . iv 4 870
What doth concern your coming? . . . *2 Hen. IV.* iv 1 30
And more than carefully it us concerns . . . *Hen. V.* ii 4 2
These tidings would call forth their flowing tides.—Me they concern *1 Hen. VI.* i 1 84
Why, what concerns his freedom unto me? . . . v 3 116
About what?—About that which concerns your grace and us *3 Hen. VI.* i 2 8
Please your honours, The chief cause concerns his grace *Hen. VIII.* v 3 3
I would not for a million of gold The cause were known to them it most concerns . . . . *T. Andron.* ii 1 50
It highly us concerns By day and night to attend him carefully . iv 3 27
Vouchsafe me a word; it does concern you near . *T. of Athens* i 2 183
What concern they? The general cause? or is it a fee-grief? *Macbeth* iv 3 195
As it more concerns the Turk than Rhodes, So may he with more facile question bear it . . . . *Othello* i 3 22
We must not think the Turk is so unskilful To leave that latest which concerns him first . . . . i 3 28
The nature of bad news infects the teller.—When it concerns the fool or coward . . . . *Ant. and Cleo.* i 2 100
You take things ill which are not so, Or being, concern you not . ii 2 30
Let's hear him, for the things he speaks May concern Cæsar . iv 9 26
You do seem to know Something of me, or what concerns me *Cymb.* i 6 94
A small request, And yet of moment too, for it concerns Your lord . i 6 182
Concernancy. The concernancy, sir? why do we wrap the gentleman in our more rawer breath? . . . . *Hamlet* v 2 128
Concerned. That I should Once name you derogately, when to sound your name It not concern'd me . . . . *Ant. and Cleo.* ii 2 35
Concerneth. To her love concerneth us to add Her father's liking *T. of Shrew* iii 2 130
Concerning. And is that paper nothing?—Nothing concerning me *T. G. of Ver.* i 2 75
That is not the question: the question is concerning your marriage *Mer. Wives* i 1 228
As time and our concernings shall importune . . *Meas. for Meas.* i 1 57
Are there no other tokens Between you 'greed concerning her observance? . . . . iv 1 42
The matter is to me, sir, as concerning Jaquenetta . . *L. L. Lost* i 1 203
As concerning some entertainment of time . . . v 1 125
What is the opinion of Pythagoras concerning wild fowl? *T. Night* iv 2 54
Some things of weight That task our thoughts, concerning us *Hen. V.* i 2 6
Did of me demand What was the speech among the Londoners Concerning the French journey . . . . . *Hen. VIII.* i 2 155
What was purposed Concerning his imprisonment . . . v 3 150
From a paddock, from a bat, a gib, Such dear concernings hide *Hamlet* iii 4 191
No conception nor no jealous toy Concerning you . . *Othello* iii 4 157
Proceed you in your tears. Concerning this, sir,—O well-painted passion! . . . . iv 1 268
Concert. Visit by night your lady's chamber-window With some sweet concert . . . . *T. G. of Ver.* iii 2 84
And boding screech-owls make the concert full! . *2 Hen. VI.* iii 2 327
Conclave. And thank the holy conclave for their loves . *Hen. VIII.* ii 2 100
Conclude. You conclude that my master is a shepherd then and I a sheep?—I do . . . . *T. G. of Ver.* i 1 76
Why, thou didst conclude hairy men plain dealers without wit *Com. of Errors* ii 2 87
Conclude. Conclude, conclude he is in love.—Nay, but I know who loves him . . . . *Much Ado* iii 2 64
The text most infallibly concludes it . . . *L. L. Lost* iv 2 170
Cut thread and thrum; Quail, crush, conclude, and quell! *M. N. Dream* v 1 292
This concludes; My mother's son did get your father's heir *K. John* i 1 127
Forget, forgive; conclude and be agreed . . . *Richard II.* i 1 156
Concludes in hearty prayers That your attempts may overlive the hazard . . . . *2 Hen. IV.* iv 1 14
Wicked and vile; and so her death concludes . . *1 Hen. VI.* v 4 16
Shall we at last conclude effeminate peace? . . . . v 4 107
If we conclude a peace, It shall be with such strict and severe covenants v 4 113
And here conclude with me That Margaret shall be queen . . v 5 77
Reprove my allegation, if you can; Or else conclude my words effectual *2 Hen. VI.* iii 1 41
For thousands more, that yet suspect no peril, Will not conclude their plotted tragedy . . . . iii 1 153
But, to conclude with truth . . . . *3 Hen. VI.* ii 1 128
Then, grandam, you conclude that he is dead . . *Richard III.* ii 2 12
Grievingly I think, The peace between the French and us not values The cost that did conclude it . . . . *Hen. VIII.* i 1 89
To conclude, Without the king's will or the state's allowance, A league iii 2 321
O, then conclude Minds sway'd by eyes are full of turpitude *Tr. and Cr.* v 2 111
Cannot conclude but by the yea and no Of general ignorance *Coriolanus* iii 1 145
His fault concludes but what the law should end . *Rom. and Jul.* iii 1 190
In that point I will conclude to hate her . . . *Cymbeline* iii 5 78
And, to conclude *Much Ado* v 1; *T. of Shrew* ii 1; *1 Hen. IV.* ii 3; *2 Hen. VI.* iv 1; *3 Hen. VI.* ii 5; *Macbeth* i 2
To conclude . . . . *Com. of Errors* iii 2 144; *1 Hen. IV.* iv 4 19
Concluded. Yet at last she concluded with a sigh . . *Much Ado* v 1 173
The congregated college have concluded . . . *All's Well* ii 1 120
There is an overture of peace.—Nay, I assure you, a peace concluded iv 3 47
Be it concluded, No barricado for a belly . . . *W. Tale* i 2 203
They humbly sue unto your excellence To have a godly peace concluded of . . . . *1 Hen. VI.* v 1 5
For eighteen months concluded by consent . . . *2 Hen. VI.* i 1 42
Suffolk concluded on the articles, The peers agreed . . . i 1 217
Is it concluded he shall be protector?—It is determined, not concluded yet . . . . *Richard III.* i 3 14
But, I hope, My absence doth neglect no great designs, Which by my presence might have been concluded . . . . . . iii 4 26
Is it so concluded? . . . . . . *Troi. and Cres.* iv 2 68
The senate have concluded To give this day a crown to mighty Cæsar *J. Cæsar* ii 2 93
It is concluded. Banquo, thy soul's flight, If it find heaven, must find it out to-night . . . . *Macbeth* iii 1 141
Alack, I had forgot: 'tis so concluded on . . . *Hamlet* iii 4 201
'Tis wonder that thy life and wits at once Had not concluded all . *Lear* iv 7 42
Being cruel to the world, concluded Most cruel to herself . *Cymbeline* v 5 32
Concludest. Thou concludest like the sanctimonious pirate *Meas. for Meas.* i 2 7
Concluding. And left me to a bootless inquisition, Concluding 'Stay: not yet' . . . . *Tempest* i 2 36
Conclusion. In conclusion, I stand affected to her . *T. G. of Ver.* ii 1 90
The conclusion is then that it will . . . . . ii 5 39
And so conclusions passed the careires . . . *Mer. Wives* i 1 184
And the conclusion shall be crowned with your enjoying her . . iii 5 138
The vile conclusion I now begin with grief and shame to utter *M. for M.* v 1 95
In conclusion, he did beat me there . . . *Com. of Errors* ii 1 74
I knew 'twould be a bald conclusion . . . . . . ii 2 110
And the conclusion is, she shall be thine . . . *Much Ado* i 1 329
Man is a giddy thing, and this is my conclusion . . . v 4 110
The conclusion is victory: on whose side? the king's . *L. L. Lost* iv 1 75
Beauteous as ink; a good conclusion.—Fair as a text B in a copy-book v 2 41
And in conclusion dumbly have broke off . . . *M. N. Dream* v 1 98
'Tis I must make conclusion Of these most strange events *As Y. Like It* v 4 132
And in conclusion she shall watch all night . *T. of Shrew* iv 1 208
A false conclusion: I hate it as an unfilled can . . *T. Night* ii 3 6
So that, conclusions to be as kisses . . . . . v 1 23
But in conclusion put strange speech upon me . . . . v 1 70
Grace to boot! Of this make no conclusion . . . *W. Tale* i 2 81
It draws toward supper in conclusion so . . . . *K. John* i 1 204
And in conclusion drove us to seek out This head of safety *1 Hen. IV.* iv 3 102
There must be conclusions. Well, I cannot tell . . *Hen. V.* ii 1 27
And tell him, for conclusion, he hath betrayed his followers . iii 6 142
And in conclusion wins the king from her . . . *3 Hen. VI.* iii 1 50
A virtuous and a Christian-like conclusion . . . *Richard III.* i 3 316
In conclusion, equivocates him in a sleep . . . *Macbeth* ii 3 38
Like the famous ape, To try conclusions, in the basket creep *Hamlet* iii 4 195
And in conclusion to oppose the bolt Against my coming in . *Lear* ii 4 179
And, in conclusion, Nonsuits my mediators . . . . *Othello* i 1 15
The blood and baseness of our natures would conduct us to most preposterous conclusions . . . . i 3 333
O most lame and impotent conclusion! . . . . . . ii 1 162
Hard at hand comes the master and main exercise, the incorporate conclusion . . . . ii 1 269
But this denoted a foregone conclusion . . . . . iii 3 428
With her modest eyes And still conclusion . . . *Ant. and Cleo.* iv 15 28
She hath pursued conclusions infinite Of easy ways to die . . v 2 358
Is't not meet That I did amplify my judgement in Other conclusions? *Cymbeline* i 5 18
Scorning advice, read the conclusion, then . . . . *Pericles* i 1 56
Concolinel.—Sweet air! . . . . *L. L. Lost* iii 1 3
Concord. And mar the concord with too harsh a descant *T. G. of Ver.* i 2 94
How comes this gentle concord in the world? . *M. N. Dream* iv 1 148
How shall we find the concord of this discord? . . . . v 1 60
The man that hath no music in himself, Nor is not moved with concord of sweet sounds . . . . *Mer. of Venice* v 1 84
His jarring concord, and his discord dulcet . . . *All's Well* i 1 186
But for the concord of my state and time Had not an ear to hear my true time broke . . . . *Richard II.* v 5 47
Had I power, I should Pour the sweet milk of concord into hell *Macbeth* iv 3 98
Concubine. I know I am too mean to be your queen, And yet too good to be your concubine . . . . *3 Hen. VI.* iii 2 98
Concupiscible. To his concupiscible intemperate lust . *Meas. for Meas.* v 1 98
Concupy. He'll tickle it for his concupy . . . . *Troi. and Cres.* v 2 177
Concur. This concurs directly with the letter . . . *T. Night* iii 4 73
As Hector's leisure and your bounties shall Concur together *Tr. and Cr.* iv 5 274
Concurring both in name and quality . . . *2 Hen. IV.* iv 1 87
Condemn. Travellers ne'er did lie, Though fools at home condemn 'em *Temp.* iii 3 27
Condemn the fault, and not the actor of it? . . . *Meas. for Meas.* ii 2 37
It is the law, not I condemn your brother . . . . . . ii 2 80

Condemn. We do condemn thee to the very block Where Claudio stoop'd to death . . . *Meas. for Meas.* v 1 419
Well, we cannot greatly condemn our success . . . *All's Well* iii 6 58
I could condemn it as an improbable fiction . . . *T. Night* iii 4 141
Commend them and condemn them to her service Or to their own perdition . . . *W. Tale* iv 4 388
This and much more, much more than twice all this, Condemns you to the death . . . *Richard II.* iii 1 29
Thy words condemn thy brat and thee: Use no entreaty . . . *1 Hen. VI.* v 4 84
I cannot justify whom the law condemns . . . *2 Hen. VI.* ii 3 16
I shall not want false witness to condemn me . . . iii 1 168
God forbid any malice should prevail, That faultless may condemn a nobleman! . . . iii 2 24
And every tale condemns me for a villain . . . *Richard III.* v 3 195
You might condemn us, As poisonous of your honour . . . *Coriolanus* v 3 134
Who cannot condemn rashness in cold blood? . . . *T. of Athens* iii 5 53
All that is within him does condemn Itself for being there . . . *Macbeth* v 2 24
This milky gentleness and course of yours Though I condemn not . . . *Lear* i 4 365
Being done unknown, I should have found it afterwards well done; But must condemn it now . . . *Ant. and Cleo.* ii 7 86
Condemn myself to lack The courage of a woman . . . iv 14 59
Away! I do condemn mine ears that have So long attended thee . . . *Cymb.* i 6 141
Condemnation. O perilous mouths, That bear in them one and the self-same tongue, Either of condemnation or approof! . . . *Meas. for Meas.* ii 4 174
He hath betrayed his followers, whose condemnation is pronounced . . . *Hen. V.* iii 6 143
Speak, or thy silence on the instant is Thy condemnation . . . *Cymbeline* iii 5 98
Condemned. Some run from brakes of ice, and answer none: And some condemned for a fault alone . . . *Meas. for Meas.* ii 1 40
Here is the sister of the man condemn'd Desires access to you . . . ii 2 18
I have a brother is condemn'd to die . . . ii 2 34
Why, every fault's condemn'd ere it be done . . . ii 2 38
Marry, this Claudio is condemned for untrussing . . . iii 2 190
Condemn'd upon the act of fornication To lose his head; condemn'd by Angelo . . . v 1 70
Look, if it please you, on this man condemn'd, As if my brother lived . . . v 1 449
Thou 'rt condemn'd: But, for those earthly faults, I quit them all . . . v 1 487
Therefore by law thou art condemn'd to die . . . *Com. of Errors* i 1 26
Stand I condemn'd for pride and scorn so much? . . . *Much Ado* iii 1 108
Thou wilt be condemned into everlasting redemption for this . . . iv 2 58
Nor shall you be safer Than one condemn'd by the king's own mouth . . . *W. Tale* i 2 445
Blessing Against this cruelty fight on thy side, Poor thing, condemn'd to loss! . . . ii 3 192
If I shall be condemn'd Upon surmises, all proofs sleeping else But what your jealousies awake, I tell you 'Tis rigour and not law . . . iii 2 112
And there the poison Is as a fiend confined to tyrannize On unreprievable condemned blood . . . *K. John* v 7 48
Wherein the king stands generally condemn'd . . . *Richard II.* ii 2 132
Will you permit that I shall stand condemn'd A wandering vagabond? . . . ii 3 119
To whose flint bosom my condemned lord Is doom'd a prisoner . . . v 1 3
The poor condemned English, Like sacrifices . . . *Hen. V.* iv Prol. 22
Condemn'd to die for treason, but no traitor . . . *1 Hen. VI.* ii 4 97
Bring forth that sorceress condemn'd to burn . . . v 4 1
First, let me tell you whom you have condemn'd . . . v 4 36
'Tis meet he be condemn'd by course of law . . . *2 Hen. VI.* iii 1 237
Even thus two friends condemn'd Embrace and kiss and take ten thousand leaves . . . iii 2 353
Is he found guilty?—Yes, truly is he, and condemn'd upon't . . . *Hen. VIII.* ii 1 8
I stand condemn'd for this . . . *Troi. and Cres.* iii 3 219
You have shamed me In your condemned seconds . . . *Coriolanus* i 8 15
I would not be a Roman, of all nations; I had as lieve be a condemned man . . . iv 5 186
Prepare for your execution? you are condemned . . . v 2 52
Be pitiful to my condemned sons, Whose souls are not corrupted . . . *T. And.* iii 1 8
Thy brothers are condemn'd, and dead by this . . . iii 1 109
For that vile fault Two of her brothers were condemn'd to death . . . v 2 174
Condemned villain, I do apprehend thee . . . *Rom. and Jul.* v 3 56
Here I stand, both to impeach and purge Myself condemned and myself excused . . . v 3 227
You have condemn'd and noted Lucius Pella For taking bribes . . . *J. Cæsar* iv 3 2
You yourself Are much condemn'd to have an itching palm . . . iv 3 10
If thou canst serve where thou dost stand condemn'd . . . *Lear* i 4 5
The condemn'd Pompey, Rich in his father's honour, creeps apace Into the hearts of such as have not thrived . . . *Ant. and Cleo.* i 3 49
By thine own tongue thou art condemn'd, and must Endure our law . . . *Cymbeline* v 5 298
Condemning some to death, and some to exile . . . *Coriolanus* i 6 35
Were nature's piece 'gainst fancy, Condemning shadows quite . . . *A. and C.* v 2 100
Condescend. And give it you In earnest of a further benefit, So you do condescend to help me now . . . *1 Hen. VI.* v 3 17
If thou wilt condescend to be my— What?—His love . . . v 3 120
Condign. In thy condign praise . . . *L. L. Lost* i 2 27
I never gave them condign punishment . . . *2 Hen. VI.* iii 1 130
Condition. Mark his condition and the event . . . *Tempest* i 2 117
Now the condition . . . i 2 120
I am in my condition A prince . . . iii 1 59
Here is the cate-log of her condition . . . *T. G. of Ver.* iii 1 273
And leave her on such slight conditions . . . v 4 138
Our haste from hence is of so quick condition That it prefers itself . . . *Meas. for Meas.* i 1 54
I warrant, one that knows him not.—Yes, and his ill conditions . . . *M. Ado* iii 2 68
A light condition in a beauty dark . . . *L. L. Lost* v 2 20
If he have the condition of a saint and the complexion of a devil . . . *Mer. of Venice* i 2 143
Such sum or sums as are Express'd in the condition . . . i 3 149
Which is the hot condition of their blood . . . v 1 74
In the gentle condition of blood, you should so know me . . . *As Y. Like It* i 1 48
Well, I will forget the condition of my estate, to rejoice in yours . . . i 2 16
Such is now the duke's condition That he misconstrues all that you have done . . . i 2 276
I had as lief take her dowry with this condition . . . *T. of Shrew* i 1 136
Our soft conditions and our hearts Should well agree with our external parts . . . v 2 167
Your oaths Are words and poor conditions . . . *All's Well* iv 2 30
Demand of him my condition, and what credit I have . . . iv 3 196
They know his conditions and lay him in straw . . . iv 3 288
Let no quarrel nor no brawl to come Taint the condition of this present hour . . . *T. Night* v 1 365
Your affairs there, what, with whom, the condition of that fardel . . . *W. Tale* iv 4 739

Condition. A rage whose heat hath this condition, That nothing can allay . . . *K. John* iii 1 341
Let me know my fault: On what condition stands it and wherein?—Even in condition of the worst degree, In gross rebellion . . . *Richard II.* ii 3 107
Rather be myself, Mighty and to be fear'd, than my condition . . . *1 Hen. IV.* i 3 6
So went on, Foretelling this same time's condition . . . *2 Hen. IV.* iii 1 78
And suffer the condition of these times To lay a heavy and unequal hand Upon our honours . . . iv 1 101
To hear and absolutely to determine Of what conditions we shall stand upon . . . iv 1 165
A thing within my bosom tells me That no conditions of our peace can stand . . . iv 1 184
Upon such large terms and so absolute As our conditions shall consist upon . . . iv 1 187
What's your name, sir? of what condition are you, and of what place? . . . iv 3 1
I, in my condition, Shall better speak of you than you deserve . . . iv 3 90
And do arm myself To welcome the condition of the time . . . v 2 11
You shall be soon dispatch'd with fair conditions . . . *Hen. V.* ii 4 144
All his senses have but human conditions . . . iv 1 108
O hard condition, Twin-born with greatness! . . . iv 1 250
Be he ne'er so vile, This day shall gentle his condition . . . iv 3 63
Let a Welsh correction teach you a good English condition . . . v 1 83
Our tongue is rough, coz, and my condition is not smooth . . . v 2 314
It were, my lord, a hard condition for a maid to consign to . . . v 2 326
Therefore are we certainly resolved To draw conditions of a friendly peace . . . *1 Hen. VI.* v 1 38
Upon condition I may quietly Enjoy mine own . . . v 3 153
We come to be informed by yourselves What the conditions of that league must be . . . v 4 119
Upon condition thou wilt swear To pay him tribute . . . v 4 129
Shall our condition stand?—It shall . . . v 4 165
If one so rude and of so mean condition May pass into the presence of a king . . . *2 Hen. VI.* v 1 64
I had rather be a country servant-maid Than a great queen, with this condition, To be thus taunted . . . *Richard III.* i 3 108
Best fitteth my degree or your condition . . . iii 7 143
I have a touch of your condition, Which cannot brook the accent of reproof . . . iv 4 157
I am solicited, not by a few, And those of true condition . . . *Hen. VIII.* i 2 19
For so run the conditions . . . i 3 24
Suited In like conditions as our argument . . . *Troi. and Cres.* Prol. 25
Condition, I had gone barefoot to India . . . i 2 80
All That time, acquaintance, custom and condition Made tame . . . iii 3 9
He cares not; he 'll obey conditions . . . iv 5 72
'Twill be deliver'd back on good condition.—Condition! . . . *Coriolanus* i 10 2
Condition! What good condition can a treaty find I' the part that is at mercy? . . . i 10 5
'Tis a condition they account gentle . . . ii 3 103
What he would not, Bound with an oath to yield to his conditions . . . v 1 69
Though I show'd sourly to him, once more offer'd The first conditions . . . v 3 14
Which we, On like conditions, will have counter-seal'd . . . v 3 205
Is't possible that so short a time can alter the condition of a man? . . . v 4 10
How all conditions, how all minds, As well of glib and slippery creatures as Of grave and austere quality, tender down Their services . . . *T. of Athens* i 1 52
Would be well express'd In our condition . . . i 1 77
Spare your oaths, I 'll trust to your conditions . . . iv 3 139
Under these hard conditions as this time Is like to lay upon us . . . *J. Cæsar* i 2 174
It is not for your health thus to commit Your weak condition to the raw cold morning . . . ii 1 236
Could it work so much upon your shape As it hath much prevail'd on your condition, I should not know you . . . ii 1 254
Prick him down, Antony.—Upon condition Publius shall not live . . . iv 1 4
I am a soldier, I, Older in practice, abler than yourself To make conditions . . . iv 3 32
Election makes not up on such conditions . . . *Lear* i 1 209
Not alone the imperfections of long-engraffed condition . . . i 1 301
It is the stars, The stars above us, govern our conditions . . . iv 3 35
Would I were assured Of my condition! . . . iv 7 57
I would not my unhoused free condition Put into circumscription . . . *Othello* i 2 26
She's full of most blessed condition.—Blessed fig's-end! . . . ii 1 255
As the time, the place, and the condition of this country stands . . . ii 3 302
And then, of so gentle a condition!—Ay, too gentle . . . iv 1 204
For't cannot be We shall remain in friendship, our conditions So differing in their acts . . . *Ant. and Cleo.* ii 2 115
I embrace these conditions; let us have articles betwixt us . . . *Cymbeline* i 4 168
For condition, A shop of all the qualities that man Loves woman for . . . v 5 165
Mild may be thy life! . . . Quiet and gentle thy conditions! . . . *Pericles* iii 1 29
Conditionally, that here thou take an oath . . . *3 Hen. VI.* i 1 196
Conditioned. Go, live rich and happy; But thus condition'd . . . *T. of Athens* iv 3 533
Condole. I will move storms, I will condole in some measure . . . *M. N. Dream* i 2 29
Let us condole the knight . . . *Hen. V.* ii 1 133
Condolement. To persever In obstinate condolement is a course Of impious stubbornness . . . *Hamlet* i 2 93
There are certain condolements, certain vails . . . *Pericles* ii 1 156
Condoling. A lover is more condoling . . . *M. N. Dream* i 2 43
Conduce. The reasons you allege do more conduce To the hot passion of distemper'd blood . . . *Troi. and Cres.* ii 2 168
Within my soul there doth conduce a fight Of this strange nature . . . v 2 147
Conduct. There is in this business more than nature Was ever conduct of . . . *Tempest* v 1 244
I will be welcome, then: conduct me thither . . . *L. L. Lost* ii 1 96
From the park let us conduct them thither . . . iv 3 374
Some three or four of you Go give him courteous conduct to this place . . . *Mer. of Venice* iv 1 148
Go hence a little and I shall conduct you, If you will mark it . . . *As Y. Like It* iii 4 58
Address'd a mighty power; which were on foot, In his own conduct . . . v 4 163
Conduct him to the drunkard's chamber . . . *T. of Shrew* Ind. 1 107
I will conduct you where you shall be lodged . . . *All's Well* iii 5 44
I will return again into the house and desire some conduct of the lady . . . *T. Night* iii 4 265
Pray you then, Conduct me to the queen . . . *W. Tale* ii 2 7
An honourable conduct let him have . . . *K. John* i 1 29
Under whose conduct came those powers of France? . . . iv 2 129
Conduct me to the king; I doubt he will be dead or ere I come . . . v 6 43
Sweet peace conduct his sweet soul to the bosom Of good old Abraham! . . . *Richard II.* iv 1 103
I will be his conduct . . . iv 1 157
And in my conduct shall your ladies come . . . *1 Hen. IV.* iii 1 92

Conduct. My aunt Percy Shall follow in your conduct speedily 1 *Hen. IV.* iii 1 197
Under the conduct of young Lancaster And Westmoreland . 2 *Hen. IV.* i 1 134
Led by the impartial conduct of my soul . . . . v 2 36
Convey them with safe conduct . . . . *Hen. V.* i 2 297
Herald, conduct me to the Dauphin's tent . 1 *Hen. VI.* iv 7 51
Conduct me where, from company, I may revolve and ruminate my grief . . . . v 5 100
Better than I fare, Although thou hast been conduct of my shame 2 *Hen. VI.* ii 4 101
Will he conduct you through the heart of France? . . . iv 8 38
Hath appointed This conduct to convey me to the Tower *Richard III.* i 1 45
Come, I'll conduct you to the sanctuary . . . . ii 4 73
Good lords, conduct him to his regiment . . . . v 3 103
And, under your fair conduct, Crave leave to view these ladies *Hen. VIII.* i 4 70
To the water side I must conduct your grace . . . ii 1 95
I take to-day a wife, and my election Is led on in the conduct of my will *Troi. and Cres.* ii 2 62
He stays for you to conduct him thither . . . . . iii 2 3
Your guard stays to conduct you home . . . . . v 2 184
Our guider, come; to the Roman camp conduct us . *Coriolanus* i 7 7
They hither march amain, under conduct Of Lucius *T. Andron.* iv 4 65
Away to heaven, respective lenity, And fire-eyed fury be my conduct now! . . . . . *Rom. and Jul.* iii 1 129
Thy wit, that ornament to shape and love, Mis-shapen in the conduct of them both . . . . iii 3 131
Come, bitter conduct, come, unsavoury guide! . . . v 3 116
Conduct me to mine host: we love him highly . *Macbeth* i 6 29
Follow me, that will to some provision Give thee quick conduct . *Lear* iii 6 104
Hasten his musters and conduct his powers . . . iv 2 16
Ancient, conduct them; you best know the place *Othello* i 3 121
The blood and baseness of our natures would conduct us to most preposterous conclusions . . . . . . i 3 333
Our great captain's captain, Left in the conduct of the bold Iago . ii 1 75
I desire of you A conduct over-land to Milford-Haven *Cymbeline* iii 5 8
They come Under the conduct of bold Iachimo . . . iv 2 340
Pages and lights, to conduct These knights unto their several lodgings! *Pericles* ii 3 109
Conducted. Stay awhile, And you shall be conducted . *Meas. for Meas.* ii 3 18
I could wish You were conducted to a gentle bath . *Coriolanus* i 6 63
If foul desire had not conducted you . . *T. Andron.* ii 3 79
Conductor. Who is conductor of his people? . . . *Lear* iv 7 88
Conduit. All the conduits of my blood froze up . *Com. of Errors* v 1 313
Like a weather-bitten conduit . . . . *W. Tale* v 2 60
That our best water brought by conduits hither . *Coriolanus* ii 3 250
As from a conduit with three issuing spouts . . *T. Andron.* ii 4 30
How now! a conduit, girl? what, still in tears? *Rom. and Jul.* iii 5 130
Confection. Our great king himself doth woo me oft For my confections *Cymbeline* i 5 15
That confection Which I gave him for cordial . . . v 5 246
Confectionary. Myself, Who had the world as my confectionary *T. of A.* iv 3 260
Confederacy. Lo, she is one of this confederacy! . *M. N. Dream* iii 2 192
He hath heard of our confederacy . . . . 1 *Hen. IV.* iv 4 38
Under the countenance and confederacy Of Lady Eleanor . 2 *Hen. VI.* ii 1 168
I stood i' the level Of a full-charged confederacy . *Hen. VIII.* i 2 3
What confederacy have you with the traitors Late footed in the kingdom? *Lear* iii 7 44
Confederates—So dry he was for sway—wi' the King of Naples *Tempest* i 2 111
I had forgot that foul conspiracy Of the beast Caliban and his confederates . . . . iv 1 140
Away with those giglots too, and with the other confederate companion! *Meas. for Meas.* v 1 352
Buy a rope's end: that will I bestow Among my wife and her confederates . . . . *Com. of Errors* iv 1 17
Thou art false in all And art confederate with a damned pack . . iv 4 105
My wife, her sister, and a rabble more Of vile confederates . . v 1 237
My heart is not confederate with my hand *Richard II.* v 3 53
Send Colevile with his confederates To York 2 *Hen. IV.* iv 3 79
Joan of Arc, Nor any of his false confederates . 1 *Hen. VI.* ii 1 21
Make merry, man, With thy confederates in this weighty cause 2 *Hen. VI.* i 2 86
His brother there, With many moe confederates, are in arms *Richard III.* iv 4 504
All the swords In Italy, and her confederate arms, Could not have made this peace . . . . . . *Coriolanus* v 3 208
Confederates all thus to dishonour me . *T. Andron.* i 1 303
Confederates in the deed That hath dishonour'd all our family . i 1 344
I think she means that there was more than one Confederate in the fact iv 1 39
Confederate with the queen and her two sons . . . v 1 108
Confederate season, else no creature seeing . *Hamlet* iii 2 267
Swore to Cymbeline I was confederate with the Romans . *Cymbeline* iii 3 68
Confer fair Milan With all the honours on my brother . *Tempest* i 2 126
I'll leave you to confer of home affairs . . . *T. G. of Ver.* ii 4 119
We have some secrets to confer about . . . . . iii 1 2
Ere I part with thee, confer at large Of all that may concern thy love-affairs . . . . iii 1 253
For thou hast shown some sign of good desert—Makes me the better to confer with thee . . . . iii 2 19
Shall you have access Where you with Silvia may confer at large . . iii 2 61
And confer with you Of something nearly that concerns yourselves *M. N. Dream* i 1 125
We'll crave a parley, to confer with him . . . 1 *Hen. VI.* v 3 130
The Dauphin and his train Approacheth, to confer about some matter . v 4 101
Leave us to ourselves: we must confer . . 3 *Hen. VI.* v 1 6
Did you confer with him?—Madam, we did . . *Richard III.* i 3 35
Confer with me of murder and of death . . *T. Andron.* v 2 34
One only daughter have I, no kin else, On whom I may confer what I have got . . . . . . *T. of Athens* i 1 122
I will place you where you shall hear us confer of this . . *Lear* i 2 98
It is not vain-glory for a man and his glass to confer in his own chamber *Cymbeline* iv 1 9
Conference. It was the copy of our conference . *Com. of Errors* v 1 62
Comes me the prince and Claudio, hand in hand, in sad conference *Much Ado* i 3 62
Rather than hold three words' conference with this harpy . . ii 1 279
This can be no trick: the conference was sadly borne . . ii 3 229
Beatrice, like a lapwing, runs Close by the ground, to hear our conference iii 1 25
Importunes personal conference with his grace . *L. L. Lost* ii 1 32
So sensible Seemeth their conference . . . . . v 2 260
I am invisible; And I will overhear their conference . *M. N. Dream* ii 1 187
Love takes the meaning in love's conference . . . ii 2 46
I cannot speak to her, yet she urged conference . . *As Y. Like It* i 2 270
With gentle conference, soft and affable . . . *T. of Shrew* ii 1 253
Conference. I must be present at your conference . . . *W. Tale* ii 2 17
But needful conference About some gossips for your highness ii 3 40
Women and fools, break off your conference . . *K. John* ii 1 150
I do beseech your majesty, To have some conference with your grace alone . . . . *Richard II.* v 3 27
The Prince of Wales and I Must have some private conference 1 *Hen. IV.* iii 2 2
The mutual conference that my mind hath had, By day, by night 2 *Hen. VI.* i 1 25
In this resolution, I defy thee; Not willing any longer conference 3 *Hen. VI.* ii 2 171
Vouchsafe, at our request, to stand aside, While I use further conference iii 3 111
That no man shall have private conference, Of what degree soever *Richard III.* i 1 86
Forbear your conference with the noble duke . . . i 1 104
The mayor and citizens . . . Are come to have some conference with his grace . . . . iii 7 69
I would your grace would give us but an hour Of private conference *Hen. VIII.* ii 2 81
What were't worth to know The secret of your conference? . ii 3 51
Being cross'd in conference by some senators . . *J. Cæsar* i 2 188
Nor with such free and friendly conference As he hath used of old . iv 2 17
Let no man Come to our tent till we have done our conference . iv 2 51
This I made good to you In our last conference . . *Macbeth* iii 1 80
And I'll be placed, so please you, in the ear Of all their conference *Hamlet* iii 1 193
Let's not confound the time with conference harsh . *Ant. and Cleo.* i 1 45
With no more advantage than the opportunity of a second conference *Cymbeline* i 4 141
Not a man in private conference Or council has respect with him but he *Pericles* ii 4 17
Conferr'd by testament to the sequent issue . . . *All's Well* v 3 197
Hast thou as yet conferr'd With Margery Jourdain? . . 2 *Hen. VI.* i 2 74
No less in space, validity, and pleasure, Than that conferr'd on Goneril *Lear* i 1 84
Conferring. They sit conferring by the parlour fire . *T. of Shrew* v 2 102
'Tis our fast intent To shake all cares and business from our age; Conferring them on younger strengths . . . . . *Lear* i 1 41
Confess. I confess There is no woe to his correction . *T. G. of Ver.* ii 4 137
You'll not confess, you'll not confess.—That he will not . *Mer. Wives* i 1 94
He doth in some sort confess it.—If it be confessed, it is not redressed . i 1 106
I will confess thy father's wealth Was the first motive that I woo'd thee iii 4 13
Scarce confesses That his blood flows . . . *Meas. for Meas.* i 3 51
If it confess A natural guiltiness such as is his, Let it not sound a thought upon your tongue . . . . ii 2 138
I do confess it, and repent it, father.—'Tis meet so, daughter . . ii 3 29
Confess the truth, and say by whose advice Thou camest here to complain . . . . v 1 113
Her shall you hear disproved to her eyes, Till she herself confess it . v 1 162
My lord, I do confess I ne'er was married; And I confess besides I am no maid . . . . v 1 184
I must confess I know this woman . . . . . v 1 216
I think, if you handled her privately, she would sooner confess . . v 1 277
I confess, sir, that we were lock'd out . *Com. of Errors* iv 4 102
These ears of mine Heard you confess you had the chain . . v 1 260
If you dare not trust that you see, confess not that you know *Much Ado* iii 2 123
Believe me not; and yet I lie not; I confess nothing, nor I deny nothing iv 1 274
What say you to this?—Sir, I confess the wench . *L. L. Lost* i 1 286
Did you hear the proclamation?—I do confess much of the hearing it . i 1 288
You are a gentleman and a gamester, sir.—I confess both . . i 2 46
I will hereupon confess I am in love . . . . . . i 2 60
And wrong the reputation of your name, In so unseeming to confess receipt . . . . ii 1 156
Guilty, my lord, guilty! I confess, I confess . . . . iv 3 205
Let us confess and turn it to a jest . . . . . v 2 390
I must confess that I have heard so much . . . *M. N. Dream* i 1 111
I must confess I thought you lord of more true gentleness . . ii 2 131
I must confess, Made mine eyes water . . . . . v 1 68
Confess What treason there is mingled with your love . *Mer. of Venice* iii 2 26
Promise me life, and I'll confess the truth.—Well then, confess and live iii 2 34
'Confess' and 'love' Had been the very sum of my confession . . iii 2 35
Do you confess the bond?—I do . . . . . . iv 1 181
I confess, your coming before me is nearer to his reverence *As Y. Like It* i 1 53
Wherein I confess me much guilty, to deny so fair and excellent ladies i 2 196
The princess' gentlewoman Confesses that she secretly o'erheard Your daughter . . . . ii 2 11
I warrant, she is apter to do than to confess she does . . . iii 2 408
You lack a man's heart.—I do so, I confess it . . . . iv 3 166
And now in plainness do confess to thee . . *T. of Shrew* i 1 157
Myself am struck in years, I must confess . . . . ii 1 362
I must confess your offer is the best . . . . . ii 1 388
With a small compassed cape:—I confess the cape . . iv 3 141
With a trunk sleeve:—I confess two sleeves . . . iv 3 143
Confess, confess, hath he not hit you here?—A' has a little gall'd me, I confess . . . . v 2 59
For, look, thy cheeks Confess it, th' one to th' other . *All's Well* i 3 183
I confess, Here on my knee, before high heaven and you . . i 3 197
My heart Will not confess he owes the malady That doth my life besiege ii 1 9
I will confess what I know without constraint . . . iv 3 139
We'll see what may be done, so you confess freely . . . iv 3 276
Confess 'twas hers, and by what rough enforcement You got it from her v 3 107
My lord, I do confess the ring was hers . . . . . v 3 231
Antonio never yet was thief or pirate, Though I confess, on base and ground enough, Orsino's enemy . . . . . *T. Night* v 1 78
This is not my writing, Though, I confess, much like the character . v 1 354
Most freely I confess, Myself and Toby Set this device . . v 1 367
If thou wilt confess, Or else be impudently negative . *W. Tale* i 2 273
I do confess I loved him as in honour he required . . iii 2 63
I must confess to you, sir, I am no fighter . . . iv 3 115
Sir Robert could do well: marry, to confess, Could he get me? *K. John* i 1 236
And though thou now confess thou didst but jest, With my vex'd spirits I cannot take a truce . . . . iii 1 16
For that my grandsire was an Englishman, Awakes my conscience to confess all this . . . . v 4 43
But ere I last received the sacrament I did confess it . *Richard II.* i 1 140
Confess thy treasons ere thou fly the realm . . . i 3 198
I cannot mend it, I must needs confess, Because my power is weak . ii 3 153
You confess then, you picked my pocket? . . . 1 *Hen. IV.* iii 3 189
We that are in the vaward of our youth, I must confess, are wags too 2 *Hen. IV.* i 2 200
That I am a second brother and that I am a proper fellow of my hands; and those two things, I confess, I cannot help . . . . . ii 2 73

Confess. I shall drive you then to confess the wilful abuse 2 *Hen. IV.* ii 4 338
I do confess my fault; And do submit me to your highness' mercy *Hen. V.* ii 2 76
Though 'tis no wisdom to confess so much Unto an enemy of craft and vantage . . . . iii 6 152
I care not who know it; I will confess it to all the 'orld iv 7 117
I will be glad to hear you confess it brokenly with your English tongue v 2 106
And yet thy tongue will not confess thy error . . 1 *Hen. VI.* ii 4 67
Hold! I confess, I confess treason . . . . . 2 *Hen. VI.* ii 3 96
O, torture me no more! I will confess . . . . iii 3 11
I was, I must confess, Great Albion's queen in former golden days 3 *Hen. VI.* iii 3 6
Yet I confess that often ere this day, When I have heard your king's desert recounted, Mine ear hath tempted judgment to desire . . iii 3 131
You must all confess That I was not ignoble of descent . . . iv 1 69
These news I must confess are full of grief . . . . iv 4 13
Confess who set thee up and pluck'd thee down . . . v 1 26
We would have had you heard The traitor speak, and timorously confess *Richard III.* iii 5 57
I will confess she was not Edward's daughter . . . iv 4 210
What say they?—Such a one, they all confess, There is indeed *Hen. VIII.* i 4 82
Must now confess, if they have any goodness . . . . iii 2 91
If you may confess it, say withal, If you are bound to us or no iii 2 164
I confess your royal graces, Shower'd on me daily . . . iii 2 166
A brown favour—for so 'tis, I must confess,—not brown neither *Troi. and Cres.* i 2 101
She has a marvellous white hand, I must needs confess . . i 2 151
Confess he brought home noble prize—As you must needs . . iii 2 86
If I confess much, you will play the tyrant . . . iii 2 127
You must Confess yourselves wondrous malicious, Or be accused of folly *Coriolanus* ii 1 91
That for their tongues to be silent, and not confess so much, were a kind of ingrateful injury . . . . ii 2 35
Which, thou dost confess, Were fit for thee to use as they to claim iii 2 82
I should have been more strange, I must confess . *Rom. and Jul.* ii 2 102
Come you to make confession to this father?—To answer that, I should confess to you . . . . iv 1 23
Do not deny to him that you love me.—I will confess to you that I love him . . . . iv 1 25
I must needs confess, I have received some small kindnesses from him *T. of Athens.* iii 2 22
They confess Toward thee forgetfulness too general, gross . . v 1 146
You shall confess that you are both deceived . . *J. Cæsar* ii 1 105
Do you confess so much? Give me your hand.—And my heart too iv 3 117
Yet now, I must confess, that duty done . . . . *Hamlet* i 2 54
He does confess he feels himself distracted; But from what cause he will by no means speak . . . . iii 1 5
Confess yourself to heaven; Repent what's past; avoid what is to come iii 4 149
If thou answerest me not to the purpose, confess thyself . . v 1 44
You are not ignorant of what excellence Laertes is— I dare not confess that . . . . v 2 145
Another hit; what say you?—A touch, a touch, I do confess . . v 2 297
Dear daughter, I confess that I am old; Age is unnecessary . . *Lear* ii 4 156
It is a judgement maim'd and most imperfect That will confess perfection so could err Against all rules of nature . . *Othello* i 3 100
As truly as to heaven I do confess the vices of my blood . . i 3 123
If she confess that she was half the wooer, Destruction on my head, if my bad blame Light on the man! . . . . . . i 3 176
I confess it is my shame to be so fond; but it is not in my virtue to amend it . . . . i 3 319
I confess me knit to thy deserving with cables of perdurable toughness i 3 342
Confess yourself freely to her; importune her help to put you in your place again . . . . ii 3 323
I confess, it is my nature's plague To spy into abuses . . . iii 3 146
To confess, and be hanged for his labour;—first, to be hanged, and then to confess . . . . iv 1 38
Pish! Noses, ears, and lips.—Is't possible?—Confess—handkerchief!—O devil! . . . . iv 1 43
Did he confess it?—Good sir, be a man . . . . . iv 1 66
But not yet to die.—Yes, presently: Therefore confess thee freely of thy sin . . . . v 2 53
Let him confess a truth.—He hath confess'd . . . . v 2 68
Cleopatra does confess thy greatness; Submits her to thy might *Ant. and Cleo.* iii 12 16
But do confess I have Been laden with like frailties . . . v 2 122
I confess, I slept not, but profess Had that was well worth watching *Cymbeline* ii 4 67
She did confess Was as a scorpion to her sight . . . . v 5 44
She did confess she had For you a mortal mineral . . . v 5 49
I here confess myself the king of Tyre . . . . *Pericles* v 3 2
Confessed. If it be confessed, it is not redressed . . *Mer. Wives* i 1 107
Did you set these women on to slander Lord Angelo? they have confessed you did . . . . . . *Meas. for Meas.* v 1 290
I have confess'd her and I know her virtue . . . . v 1 533
Most like a liberal villain, Confess'd the vile encounters they have had *Much Ado* iv 1 94
He hath confessed himself . . . . . . *All's Well* iv 3 124
And what think you he hath confessed?—Nothing of me, has a'? . iv 3 128
With the manner how she came to't bravely confessed . . *W. Tale* v 2 93
He hath confessed: away with him! he's a villain and a traitor 2 *Hen. VI.* iv 2 114
Ho, ho, confess'd it! hang'd it, have you not? . . *T. of Athens* i 2 22
But treasons capital, confess'd and proved, Have overthrown him *Macbeth* i 3 115
Very frankly he confess'd his treasons, Implored your highness' pardon i 4 5
Her sister By her is poisoned; she hath confess'd it . . . *Lear* v 3 227
He hath confess'd.—What, my lord?—That he hath used thee *Othello* v 2 68
That she with Cassio hath the act of shame A thousand times committed; Cassio confess'd it . . . . v 2 212
This wretch hath part confess'd his villany: Did you and he consent? . v 2 296
Himself confess'd but even now That there he dropp'd it for a special purpose . . . . v 2 321
What she confess'd I will report, so please you . . *Cymbeline* v 5 33
She confess'd she never loved you, only Affected greatness got by you, not you . . . . v 5 37
O gods! I left out one thing which the queen confess'd . . v 5 244
Confesseth. 'If that the king Have any way your good deserts forgot, Which he confesseth to be manifold, He bids you name your griefs 1 *Hen. IV.* iv 3 47
Confessing. In the night overheard me confessing to this man *Much Ado* v 1 241
That, by confessing them, the souls of men May deem that you are worthily deposed . . . . *Richard II.* iv 1 226
Not confessing Their cruel parricide . . . . . *Macbeth* iii 1 31

Confession. Where I intend holy confession . . . *T. G. of Ver.* iv 3 44
She did intend confession At Patrick's cell this even . . . v 2 41
I will, out of thine own confession, learn to begin thy health *M. for M.* i 2 39
No longer session hold upon my shame, But let my trial be mine own confession . . . . v 1 377
Thou and I are too wise to woo peaceably.—It appears not in this confession . . . . *Much Ado* v 2 75
Some fair excuse.—The fairest is confession . . . *L. L. Lost* v 2 432
'Confess' and 'love' Had been the very sum of my confession *Mer. of Venice* iii 2 36
His confession is taken, and it shall be read to his face . *All's Well* iv 3 130
I see a strange confession in thine eye . . . 2 *Hen. IV.* i 1 94
In person I'll hear him his confessions justify . . *Hen. VIII.* i 2 6
Under the confession's seal He solemnly had sworn . . . i 2 164
Urged on the examinations, proofs, confessions Of divers witnesses . ii 1 16
That loves his mistress more than in confession *Troi. and Cres.* i 3 269
And fell so roundly to a large confession, To angle for your thoughts . iii 2 161
Riddling confession finds but riddling shrift . . *Rom. and Jul.* ii 3 56
To make confession and to be absolved . . . . . iii 5 233
Come you to make confession to this father?—To answer that, I should confess to you . . . . iv 1 22
There is a kind of confession in your looks . . . *Hamlet* ii 2 288
With a crafty madness, keeps aloof, When we would bring him on to some confession Of his true state . . . . iii 1 9
He made confession of you, And gave you such a masterly report . iv 7 96
Handkerchief—confessions—handkerchief!—To confess, and be hanged for his labour . . . . *Othello* iv 1 37
Confessor. Bring him his confessor, let him be prepared *Meas. for Meas.* ii 1 35
I am confessor to Angelo, and I know this to be true . . . iii 1 168
One of our covent, and his confessor, Gives me this instance . iv 3 133
The duke's confessor, John de la Car . . . . *Hen. VIII.* i 1 218
A Chartreux friar, His confessor . . . . . . i 2 149
O, that your lordship were but now confessor To one or two of these! i 4 15
Sir Gilbert Peck his chancellor; and John Car, Confessor to him . ii 1 21
All the royal makings of a queen; As holy oil, Edward Confessor's crown iv 1 88
Good even to my ghostly confessor . . . . *Rom. and Jul.* ii 6 21
Being a divine, a ghostly confessor, A sin-absolver, and my friend profess'd . . . . iii 3 49
Confidence. Which had indeed no limit, A confidence sans bound *Tempest* i 2 97
The next time we have confidence . . . . . *Mer. Wives* i 4 172
I would have some confidence with you that decerns you nearly *M. Ado* iii 5 3
Upon thy certainty and confidence What darest thou venture? *All's Well* ii 1 172
He thinks, nay, with all confidence he swears, As he had seen't *W. Tale* i 2 414
Show boldness and aspiring confidence . . . . *K. John* v 1 56
The king reposeth all his confidence in thee . . . *Richard II.* ii 4 6
Otherwise I renounce all confidence . . . . 1 *Hen. VI.* i 2 97
With demure confidence, This pausingly ensued . . . *Hen. VIII.* i 2 167
But not in confidence Of author's pen or actor's voice *Troi. and Cres.* Prol. 23
With no less confidence Than boys pursuing summer butterflies *Coriol.* iv 6 93
If you be he, sir, I desire some confidence with you *Rom. and Jul.* ii 4 133
It should seem by the sum, Your master's confidence was above mine *T. of Athens* iii 4 31
Alas, my lord, Your wisdom is consumed in confidence . . *J. Cæsar* ii 2 49
Nay, in all confidence, he's not for Rhodes . . . *Othello* i 3 31
I make my wager rather against your confidence than her reputation *Cymbeline* i 4 121
Confident. A man may be too confident . . . *Mer. Wives* ii 1 194
Yet confident I'll keep what I have swore . . . *L. L. Lost* i 1 114
My art is not past power nor you past cure.—Art thou so confident? *All's Well* ii 1 162
That water-walled bulwark, still secure And confident . . *K. John* ii 1 28
His forces strong, his soldiers confident . . . . . ii 1 61
The sea enraged is not half so deaf, Lions more confident . . . ii 1 452
As confident as is the falcon's flight Against a bird *Richard II.* i 3 61
Be confident to speak, Northumberland: We three are but thyself . ii 1 274
Both together Are confident against the world in arms . 1 *Hen. IV.* v 1 117
It is not a confident brow, nor the throng of words . 2 *Hen. IV.* ii 1 121
Too confident To give admittance to a thought of fear . . . iv 1 152
Secure in soul, The confident and over-lusty French Do the low-rated English play at dice . . . . *Hen V.* iv Prol. 18
I do not talk much.—I am confident . . . . *Hen. VIII.* ii 1 146
We are confident, When rank Thersites opes his mastic jaws, We shall hear music, wit and oracle . . . . . *Troi. and Cres.* i 3 72
Be as just and gracious unto me As I am confident and kind to thee *T. Andron.* i 1 61
The confident tyrant Keeps still in Dunsinane . . . *Macbeth* v 4 8
Confident I am Last night 'twas on mine arm . . . *Cymbeline* ii 3 150
These three, Three thousand confident, in act as many . . . v 3 29
He, true knight, No lesser of her honour confident That I did truly find her . . . . v 5 187
Confidently. Which you hear him so confidently undertake to do *All's Well* iii 6 21
Is not this a strange fellow, my lord, that so confidently seems to undertake this business? . . . . iii 6 93
Confine. She did confine thee, By help of her more potent ministers And in her most unmitigable rage, Into a cloven pine . . . *Tempest* i 2 274
Spirits, which by mine art I have from their confines call'd . . iv 1 121
Being native burghers of this desert city, Should in their own confines with forked heads Have their round haunches gored *As Y. Like It* ii 1 24
You must confine yourself within the modest limits of order.—Confine! I'll confine myself no finer than I am . . . . *T. Night* i 3 8
This kingdom, this confine of blood and breath . . . *K. John* iv 2 246
Might from our quiet confines fright fair peace . . *Richard II.* i 3 137
They have let the dangerous enemy Measure our confines with such peaceful steps . . . . iii 2 125
The incessant care and labour of his mind Hath wrought the mure that should confine it in So thin that life looks through . 2 *Hen. IV.* iv 4 119
Now, neighbour confines, purge you of your scum . . . . iv 5 124
Here in these confines slily have I lurk'd . . . *Richard III.* iv 4 3
And to confine yourself To Asher House . . . . *Hen. VIII.* iii 2 230
I will not praise thy wisdom, Which, like a bourn, a pale, a shore, confines Thy spacious and dilated parts . . . *Troi. and Cres.* ii 3 260
Fie, you confine yourself most unreasonably . . . *Coriolanus* i 3 84
One of those fellows that when he enters the confines of a tavern claps me his sword upon the table . . . . . *Rom. and Jul.* iii 1 6
Shall in these confines with a monarch's voice Cry 'Havoc' *J. Cæsar* iii 1 272
The extravagant and erring spirit hies To his confine . . *Hamlet* i 1 155
In which there are many confines, wards and dungeons . . . ii 2 252
To England send him, or confine him where Your wisdom best shall think . . . . iii 1 194

Confine. Nature in you stands on the very verge Of her confine . Lear ii 4 150
I would not my unhoused free condition Put into circumscription and confine For the sea's worth . Othello i 2 27
Stand you awhile apart ; Confine yourself but in a patient list . iv 1 76
Seizes him : so the poor third is up, till death enlarge his confine Ant. and Cleo. iii 5 13
Wherein Our pleasure his full fortune doth confine . Cymbeline v 4 110
Confined. Therefore wast thou Deservedly confined into this rock Tempest i 2 361
Confined together In the same fashion as you gave in charge . v 1 7
Let me embrace thine age, whose honour cannot Be measured or confined . v 1 122
Now, 'tis true, I must be here confined by you, Or sent to Naples . Epil. 4
We thought it good From our free person she should be confined W. Tale ii 1 194
And there the poison Is as a fiend confined to tyrannize On unreprievable condemned blood . K. John v 7 47
Now let not Nature's hand Keep the wild flood confined ! . 2 Hen. IV. i 1 154
And present execution of our wills To us and to our purposes confined . iv 1 175
Suppose within the girdle of these walls Are now confined two mighty monarchies . Hen. V. Prol. 20
You and I cannot be confined within the weak list of a country's fashion v 2 295
That the will is infinite and the execution confined . Troi. and Cres. iii 2 89
Your franchises, whereon you stood, confined Into an auger's bore Coriolanus iv 6 86
I am cabin'd, cribb'd, confined, bound in To saucy doubts and fears Macbeth iii 4 24
And for the day confined to fast in fires Hamlet i 5 11
And the king gone to-night ! subscribed his power ! Confined to exhibition ! All this done Upon the gad ! . Lear i 2 25
A cliff, whose high and bending head Looks fearfully in the confined deep . iv 1 77
The queen my mistress, Confined in all she has, her monument A. and C. v 1 53
Confineless. And the poor state Esteem him as a lamb, being compared With my confineless harms . Macbeth iv 3 55
Confiner. The confiners And gentlemen of Italy, most willing spirits, That promise noble service . Cymbeline iv 2 337
Confining. O'erswell With course disturb'd even thy confining shores K. John ii 1 338
In little room confining mighty men . Hen. V. Epil. 3
Confirm his welcome with some special favour . T. G. of Ver. ii 4 101
These likelihoods confirm her flight from hence . v 2 43
Is not your husband mad ?—His incivility confirms no less Com. of Errors iv 4 49
But chiefly by my villany, which did confirm any slander Much Ado iii 3 169
You did ; and to confirm it plain, You gave me this . L. L. Lost v 2 452
His employment between his lord and my niece confirms no less T. Night iii 4 205
Which to confirm, I'll bring you to a captain in this town . v 1 260
Let confusion of one part confirm The other's peace K. John ii 1 359
Our souls religiously confirm thy words . iv 3 73
Which elder days shall ripen and confirm To more approved service Richard II. ii 3 43
What she says I'll confirm . 1 Hen. VI. ii 2 128
Confirm it so, mine honourable lord.—Confirm it so ! . iv 1 122
Of such great authority in France As his alliance will confirm our peace v 5 42
Our authority is his consent, And what we do establish he confirms 2 Hen. VI. iii 1 317
Confirm the crown to me and to mine heirs . 3 Hen. VI. i 1 172
And lastly, to confirm that amity With nuptial knot . iii 3 54
Thou dost confirm his happiness for ever . Richard III. i 2 209
This, to confirm my welcome ; And to you all, good health Hen. VIII. i 4 37
To confirm this too, Cardinal Campeius is arrived . ii 1 159
And, to confirm his goodness, Tied it by letters-patents . iii 2 249
Let me confirm my princely brother's greeting . Troi. and Cres. iv 5 174
I would the gods had nothing else to do But to confirm my curses ! Coriolanus iv 2 46
And thus far I confirm you . T. of Athens i 2 98
Having no witness to confirm my speech . Macbeth v 1 21
Which to confirm, This coronet part betwixt you . Lear i 1 140
Yet do they all confirm A Turkish fleet, and bearing up to Cyprus Othello i 3 7
Whose strength I will confirm with oath . Cymbeline ii 4 64
It doth confirm Another stain, as big as hell can hold . ii 4 139
You shall be miss'd at court, And that will well confirm it . iii 4 130
That confirms it home . iv 2 328
Confirmation. Receive The confirmation of my promised gift All's Well ii 3 56
The particular confirmations, point from point, to the full arming of the verity . iv 3 71
Yet, for a greater confirmation, For in an act of this importance 'twere Most piteous to be wild . W. Tale ii 1 180
To thee it shall descend with better quiet, Better opinion, better confirmation . 2 Hen. IV. iv 5 189
Let heaven Witness, how dear I hold this confirmation . Hen. VIII. v 3 174
For confirmation that I am much more Than my out-wall, open this purse, and take What it contains . Lear iii 1 44
Trifles light as air Are to the jealous confirmations strong As proofs of holy writ . Othello iii 3 323
Which hath Honour'd with confirmation your great judgement Cymb. i 6 174
Still confirmation : Embrace him, dear Thaisa . Pericles v 3 54
Confirmed. Of approved valour and confirmed honesty . Much Ado ii 1 395
Confirm'd, confirm'd ! O, that is stronger made Which was before barr'd up with ribs of iron ! . iv 1 152
Which I will do with confirm'd countenance . v 4 17
Until confirm'd, sign'd, ratified by you . Mer. of Venice iii 2 149
Was faithfully confirmed by the rector of the place . All's Well iv 3 69
Confirm'd by mutual joinder of your hands . T. Night v 1 160
O guilt indeed !—Confirm'd conspiracy . Hen. V. ii Prol. 27
Thy age confirm'd, proud, subtle, bloody, treacherous . Richard III. iv 4 171
Has such a confirmed countenance . Coriolanus i 3 65
He's not confirm'd ; we may deny him yet . ii 3 217
All is confirm'd, my lord, which was reported . Macbeth v 3 31
The which no sooner had his prowess confirm'd In the unshrinking station where he fought, But like a man he died . v 8 41
For truth can never be confirm'd enough . Pericles v 1 203
Confirmer. The oath of a lover is no stronger than the word of a tapster; they are both the confirmer of false reckonings As Y. Like It iii 4 35
Be these sad signs confirmers of thy words ? . K. John iii 1 24
Confirmities. You cannot one bear with another's confirmities 2 Hen. IV. ii 4 64
Confiscate. His goods confiscate to the duke's dispose . Com. of Errors i 1 21
Lest that your goods too soon be confiscate . i 2 2
If thou dost shed One drop of Christian blood, thy lands and goods Are, by the laws of Venice, confiscate . Mer. of Venice iv 1 311
Confiscate. If the scale do turn But in the estimation of a hair, Thou diest and all thy goods are confiscate . Mer. of Venice iv 1 332
Be pronounced a traitor, And all his lands and goods be confiscate 3 Hen. VI. iv 6 55
And let it be confiscate all, so soon As I have received it . Cymbeline v 5 323
Confiscation. For his possessions, Although by confiscation they are ours, We do instate and widow you withal Meas. for Meas. v 1 428
Confixed. Or else for ever be confixed here, A marble monument ! . v 1 232
Conflict. In our last conflict four of his five wits went halting off M. Ado i 1 66
But be first advised, In conflict that you get the sun of them L. L. Lost iv 3 369
Who, in the conflict that it holds with death, Attracts the same for aidance 'gainst the enemy . 2 Hen. VI. iii 2 164
O God ! it is my father's face, Whom in this conflict I unwares have kill'd . 3 Hen. VI. ii 5 62
So doth my heart misgive me, in these conflicts What may befall him . iv 6 94
After conflict such as was supposed The wandering prince and Dido once enjoy'd . T. Andron. ii 3 21
How full of valour did he bear himself In the last conflict ! T. of Athens iii 5 66
Assisted by that most disloyal traitor, The thane of Cawdor, began a dismal conflict . Macbeth i 2 53
I will persevere in my course of loyalty, though the conflict be sore between that and my blood . Lear iii 5 24
But his flaw'd heart, Alack, too weak the conflict to support ! . v 3 197
Conflicting. Whose bare unhoused trunks, To the conflicting elements exposed, Answer mere nature . T. of Athens iv 3 230
The to-and-fro-conflicting wind and rain . Lear iii 1 11
Confluence. This confluence, this great flood of visitors . T. of Athens i 1 42
Conflux. As knots, by the conflux of meeting sap, Infect the sound pine and divert his grain . Troi. and Cres. i 3 7
Conform. And to my humble seat conform myself . 3 Hen. VI. iii 3 11
Conformable as other household Kates . T. of Shrew ii 1 280
A true and humble wife, At all times to your will conformable Hen. VIII. ii 4 24
Confound. My shame and guilt confounds me . T. G. of Ver. v 4 73
That no particular scandal once can touch But it confounds the breather Meas. for Meas. iv 4 31
Unseen, inquisitive, confounds himself . Com. of Errors i 2 38
Bruise me with scorn, confound me with a flout . L. L. Lost v 2 397
Come, tears, confound ; Out, sword, and wound The pap of Pyramus M. N. Dream v 1 300
Never did I know A creature, that did bear the shape of man, So keen and greedy to confound a man . Mer. of Venice iii 2 278
Confounds thy fame as whirlwinds shake fair buds . T. of Shrew v 2 140
Pour'd all together, Would quite confound distinction, yet stand off In differences so mighty . All's Well ii 3 127
When workmen strive to do better than well, They do confound their skill in covetousness . K. John iv 2 29
Which, in their throng and press to that last hold, Confound themselves v 7 20
With too much riches it confound itself . Richard II. iii 4 60
Shall kin with kin and kind with kind confound . iv 1 141
This let alone will all the rest confound . v 3 86
He did confound the best part of an hour . 1 Hen. IV. i 3 100
Being moody, give him line and scope, Till that his passions, like a whale on ground, Confound themselves with working 2 Hen. IV. iv 4 41
Confounds the tongue and makes the senses rough . 1 Hen. VI. v 3 71
Lest he that is the supreme King of kings Confound your hidden falsehood . Richard III. ii 1 14
Be not so hasty to confound my meaning . iv 4 261
Myself myself confound ! Heaven and fortune bar me happy hours ! . iv 4 399
The dry serpigo on the subject ! and war and lechery confound all ! Troi. and Cres. ii 3 82
The shaft confounds, Not that it wounds, But tickles still the sore . iii 1 128
How couldst thou in a mile confound an hour ? . Coriolanus i 6 17
And pray the Roman gods confound you both ! . T. Andron. iv 2 6
The sweetest honey Is loathsome in his own deliciousness And in the taste confounds the appetite . Rom. and Jul. ii 6 13
Traffic confound thee, if the gods will not !—If traffic do it, the gods do it . T. of Athens i 1 244
Traffic's thy god ; and thy god confound thee ! . i 1 247
The gods confound—hear me, you good gods all—The Athenians ! . iv 1 37
If thou dost perform, confound thee, for thou art a man ! . iv 3 75
The gods confound them all in thy conquest ; And thee after ! . iv 3 103
Wert thou the unicorn, pride and wrath would confound thee . iv 3 339
Steal no less for this I give you ; and gold confound you howsoe'er ! . iv 3 452
Confound them by some course, and come to me, I'll give you gold enough . v 1 106
The attempt and not the deed Confounds us . Macbeth ii 2 12
Though the yesty waves Confound and swallow navigation up . iv 1 54
Uproar the universal peace, confound All unity on earth . iv 3 99
Make mad the guilty and appal the free, Confound the ignorant Hamlet ii 2 591
And haply one as kind For husband shalt thou— O, confound the rest ! iii 2 187
Let's not confound the time with conference harsh . Ant. and Cleo. i 1 45
But to confound such time, That drums him from his sport . i 4 28
The gods confound thee ! dost thou hold there still ?—Should I lie, madam ? . ii 5 92
What willingly he did confound he wail'd, Believe't, till I wept too . iii 2 58
Whereto being bound, The interim, pray you, all confound . Pericles v 2 279
Confounded. Their form confounded makes most form in mirth L. L. Lost v 2 520
All this thou seest is but a clod And module of confounded royalty K. John v 7 58
As doth a galled rock O'erhang and jutty his confounded base Hen. V. iii 1 13
Mort de ma vie ! all is confounded, all ! . iv 5 3
Confounded be your strife ! And perish ye, with your audacious prate ! 1 Hen. VI. iv 1 123
Make large confusion ; and, thy fury spent, Confounded be thyself ! T. of Athens iv 3 128
Where's Publius ?—Here, quite confounded with this mutiny J. Cæsar iii 1 86
Such two that would by all likelihood have confounded one the other, or have fallen both . Cymbeline i 4 54
Confounding. Then fate o'er-rules, that, one man holding troth, A million fail, confounding oath on oath . M. N. Dream iii 2 93
Degrees, observances, customs, and laws, Decline to your confounding contraries, And let confusion live ! . T. of Athens iv 1 20
Set them into confounding odds, that beasts May have the world in empire ! . iv 3 392
Confront. All preparation for a bloody siege And merciless proceeding by these French Confronts your city's eyes . K. John ii 1 215
Shall dunghill curs confront the Helicons ? . 2 Hen. IV. v 3 108
Whereto serves mercy But to confront the visage of offence ? . Hamlet iii 3 47

Confronted. We four indeed confronted were with four In Russian habit . . . . *L. L. Lost* v 2 367
Strength match'd with strength, and power confronted power *K. John* ii 1 330
Was ever seen An emperor in Rome thus overborne, Troubled, confronted thus? . . . . . . *T. Andron.* iv 4 3
Confronted him with self-comparisons, Point against point *Macbeth* i 2 55
Confused. I never heard a passion so confused . . . *Mer. of Venice* ii 8 12
For the health and physic of our right, We cannot deal but with the very hand Of stern injustice and confused wrong . *K. John* v 2 23
Hear the shrill whistle which doth order give To sounds confused *Hen. V.* iii Prol. 10
Whiles the mad mothers with their howls confused Do break the clouds iii 3 39
With a din confused Enforce the present execution . *Coriolanus* iii 3 20
Such fearful and confused cries . . . . . . *T. Andron.* ii 3 102
Dire combustion and confused events New hatch'd to the woeful time *Macbeth* ii 3 63
'Tis here, but yet confused : Knavery's plain face is never seen till used *Othello* ii 1 320
Confusedly. Sharp stakes pluck'd out of hedges They pitched in the ground confusedly . . . . 1 *Hen. VI.* i 1 118
Confusion. Infect thy sap and live on thy confusion . *Com. of Errors* ii 2 182
So quick bright things come to confusion . . . *M. N. Dream* i 1 149
Mark the musical confusion Of hounds and echo in conjunction . iv 1 115
I will try confusions with him . . . *Mer. of Venice* ii 2 39
There is such confusion in my powers . . . . iii 2 179
Peace, ho! I bar confusion : 'Tis I must make conclusion *As Y. Like It* v 4 131
Then let confusion of one part confirm The other's peace *K. John* ii 1 359
Vast confusion waits, As doth a raven on a sick-fall'n beast, The imminent decay . . . . iv 3 152
Like perspectives, which rightly gazed upon Show nothing but confusion . . . . *Richard II.* ii 2 19
Moody beggars, starving for a time Of pellmell havoc and confusion 1 *Hen. IV.* v 1 82
In heart desiring still You may behold confusion of your foes 1 *Hen. VI.* iv 1 77
When envy breeds unkind division ; There comes the ruin, there begins confusion . . . . iv 1 194
Heaping confusion on their own heads . 2 *Hen. VI.* ii 1 187
Shame and confusion ! all is on the rout ; Fear frames disorder . v 2 31
My soul aches To know, when two authorities are up, Neither supreme, how soon confusion May enter 'twixt the gap of both *Coriolanus* iii 1 110
I am out of breath ; Confusion's near ; I cannot speak . iii 1 190
These fellows ran about the streets, Crying confusion . . iv 6 29
Confusion fall— Nay, then I'll stop your mouth *T. Andron.* ii 3 184
Tell him Revenge is come to join with him, And work confusion on his enemies . . . . v 2 8
Peace, ho, for shame ! confusion's cure lives not In these confusions *Rom. and Jul.* iv 5 65
Degrees, observances, customs, and laws, Decline to your confounding contraries, And let confusion live ! . . *T. of Athens* iv 1 21
Make large confusion ; and, thy fury spent, Confounded be thyself ! . iv 3 127
Wouldst thou have thyself fall in the confusion of men, and remain a beast with the beasts ? . . . . iv 3 326
That thou wilt use the wars as thy redress And not as our confusion . v 4 52
Confusion now hath made his masterpiece ! . . *Macbeth* ii 3 71
Such artificial sprites As by the strength of their illusion Shall draw him on to his confusion . . . . iii 5 29
Can you, by no drift of circumstance, Get from him why he puts on this confusion ? . . . . *Hamlet* iii 1 2
Vengeance ! plague ! death ! confusion ! Fiery ? what quality ? *Lear* ii 4 96
Then shall the realm of Albion Come to great confusion . . iii 2 92
Laugh at's, while we strut To our confusion . *Ant. and Cleo.* iii 13 115
War and confusion In Cæsar's name pronounce I 'gainst thee *Cymbeline* iii 1 66
To thy further fear, Nay, to thy mere confusion, thou shalt know . iv 2 92
Then began A stop i' the chaser, a retire, anon A rout, confusion thick v 3 41
The boatswain whistles, and The master calls, and trebles their confusion . . . . *Pericles* iv 1 65
Confutation. In confutation of which rude reproach 1 *Hen. VI.* iii 1 98
Confute. My sisterly remorse confutes mine honour . *Meas. for Meas.* v 1 100
Nothing confutes me but eyes, and nobody sees me . 1 *Hen. IV.* v 4 129
Congeal. Cool and congeal again to what it was *K. John* ii 1 479
Congealed ice . . . . . . *Meas. for Meas.* iii 2 118
That pure congealed white, high Taurus' snow . *M. N. Dream* iii 2 141
Seeing too much sadness hath congeal'd your blood *T. of Shrew* Ind. 2 134
As sudden As flaws congealed in the spring of day . 2 *Hen. IV.* iv 4 35
And this thy son's blood cleaving to my blade Shall rust upon my weapon, till thy blood, Congeal'd with this, do make me wipe off both . . . . 3 *Hen. VI.* i 3 52
Thy tears would wash this cold congealed blood That glues my lips . v 2 37
Dead Henry's wounds Open their congeal'd mouths and bleed afresh ! *Richard III.* i 2 56
Congealment. Whilst they with joyful tears Wash the congealment from your wounds . . . . . *Ant. and Cleo.* iv 8 10
Conger. Hang yourself, you muddy conger, hang yourself ! . 2 *Hen. IV.* ii 4 58
A' plays at quoits well, and eats conger and fennel . . . . ii 4 266
Congied. I have congied with the duke . . . . *All's Well* iv 3 100
Congratulate. It is the king's most sweet pleasure and affection to congratulate the princess . . . . . . *L. L. Lost* v 1 93
Congreeing in a full and natural close, Like music . . . *Hen. V.* i 2 182
Congreeted. Face to face and royal eye to eye, You have congreeted . v 2 31
Congregate. Even there where merchants most do congregate *Mer. of Ven.* i 3 50
Congregated. The congregated college have concluded . *All's Well* ii 1 120
The gutter'd rocks and congregated sands,—Traitors ensteep'd *Othello* ii 1 69
Congregation. In the congregation, where I should wed, there will I shame her . . . . *Much Ado* iii 2 127
And there, before the whole congregation, shame her . . . iii 3 173
To show bare heads In congregations, to yawn, be still and wonder *Coriolanus* iii 2 11
Than a foul and pestilent congregation of vapours . . *Hamlet* ii 2 315
Congruent. As a congruent epitheton appertaining to thy young days *L. L. Lost* i 2 14
Is liable, congruent and measurable for the afternoon . . . . v 1 97
Congruing. Imports at full, By letters congruing to that effect *Hamlet* iv 3 66
Conies. They will out of their burrows, like conies after rain *Coriolanus* iv 5 226
Conjectural. Makest conjectural fears to come into me, Which I would fain shut out . . . . *All's Well* v 3 114
Side factions and give out Conjectural marriages . *Coriolanus* i 1 198
Conjecture. In my simple conjectures : but that is all one . *Mer. Wives* i 1 30
On my eyelids shall conjecture hang, To turn all beauty into thoughts of harm . . . . *Much Ado* iv 1 107
As gross as ever touch'd conjecture, That lack'd sight only *W. Tale* ii 1 176

Conjecture. Rumour is a pipe Blown by surmises, jealousies, conjectures 2 *Hen. IV.* Ind. 16
Conjecture, expectation, and surmise Of aids incertain should not be admitted . . . . i 3 23
Now entertain conjecture of a time When creeping murmur and the poring dark Fills the wide vessel of the universe . *Hen. V.* iv Prol. 1
'Tis likely, By all conjectures . . . . . . *Hen. VIII.* ii 1 41
To prenominate in nice conjecture Where thou wilt hit me dead *Troi. and Cres.* iv 5 250
She may strew Dangerous conjectures in ill-breeding minds . *Hamlet* iv 5 15
Conjoin. This part of his conjoins with my disease, And helps to end me 2 *Hen. IV.* iv 5 64
By God's fair ordinance conjoin together ! . . . *Richard III.* v 5 31
Conjoined. If either of you know any inward impediment why you should not be conjoined . . . . . *Much Ado* iv 1 13
This day to be conjoin'd In the state of honourable marriage . . v 4 29
I perceive they have conjoin'd all three To fashion this false sport *M. N. Dream* iii 2 193
The English army, that divided was Into two parties, is now conjoin'd in one . . . . 1 *Hen. VI.* v 2 12
His form and cause conjoin'd, preaching to stones, Would make them capable . . . . *Hamlet* iii 4 126
Conjointly. Be friends awhile and both conjointly bend Your sharpest deeds of malice on this town . . . . . *K. John* ii 1 379
When these prodigies Do so conjointly meet, let not men say 'These are their reasons ; they are natural' . . . *J. Cæsar* i 3 29
Conjunct. He, conjunct, and flattering his displeasure, Tripp'd me *Lear* ii 2 125
I am doubtful that you have been conjunct And bosom'd with her . v 1 12
Conjunction. Mark the musical confusion Of hounds and echo in conjunction . . . . *M. N. Dream* iv 1 116
List to this conjunction, make this match . . *K. John* ii 1 468
The conjunction of our inward souls Married in league . . iii 1 227
That with our small conjunction we should on . . 1 *Hen. IV.* iv 1 37
Saturn and Venus this year in conjunction ! what says the almanac to that ! . . . . 2 *Hen. IV.* ii 4 286
Their spirits are so married in conjunction with the participation of society . . . . v 1 77
And this dear conjunction Plant neighbourhood and Christian-like accord . . . . *Hen. V.* v 2 380
Smile heaven upon this fair conjunction ! . . . . *Richard III.* v 5 20
Now, all my joy Trace the conjunction ! . . . *Hen. VIII.* iii 2 45
Conjunctive. She's so conjunctive to my life and soul . *Hamlet* iv 7 14
Let us be conjunctive in our revenge against him . . . *Othello* i 3 374
Conjuration. Mock not my senseless conjuration, lords . *Richard II.* iii 2 23
Under this conjuration speak, my lord . . . . . *Hen. V.* i 2 29
And buz these conjurations in her brain . . . . . 2 *Hen. VI.* i 2 99
I do defy thy conjurations . . . . . *Rom. and Jul.* v 3 68
An earnest conjuration from the king . . . . *Hamlet* v 2 38
What drugs, what charms, What conjuration and what mighty magic *Othello* i 3 92
Conjure. And even in kind love I do conjure thee . . *T. G. of Ver.* ii 7 2
I'll conjure you, I'll fortune-tell you . . . *Mer. Wives* iv 2 195
I conjure thee, as thou believest There is another comfort than this world . . . . *Meas. for Meas.* v 1 48
Dost thou conjure for wenches, that thou call'st for such store? *Com. of Errors* iii 1 34
I conjure thee to leave me and be gone . . . . . . iv 3 68
I conjure thee by all the saints in heaven ! . . . . . iv 4 60
I would to God some scholar would conjure her . . *Much Ado* ii 1 264
A manly enterprise, To conjure tears up in a poor maid's eyes ! *M. N. Dream* iii 2 158
My way is to conjure you ; and I'll begin with the women *As Y. Like It* Epil. 11
I conjure thee, by all the parts of man Which honour does acknowledge *W. Tale* i 2 400
I conjure thee but slowly ; run more fast . . . . *K. John* iv 2 269
You conjure from the breast of civil peace Such bold hostility 1 *Hen. IV.* iv 3 43
I am not Barbason ; you cannot conjure me . . *Hen. V.* ii 1 57
I cannot so conjure up the spirit of love in her, that he will appear in his true likeness . . . . v 2 316
If you would conjure in her, you must make a circle . . . v 2 319
I'll have a bout with thee ; Devil or devil's dam, I'll conjure thee 1 *Hen. VI.* i 5 5
I am resolved to bear a greater storm Than any thou canst conjure up 2 *Hen. VI.* v 1 199
What black magician conjures up this fiend ? . . . *Richard III.* i 2 34
I'll learn to conjure and raise devils, but I'll see some issue *Tr. and Cr.* ii 3 6
Was Cressid here?—I cannot conjure, Trojan . . . . v 2 125
And conjure thee to pardon Rome, and thy petitionary countrymen *Coriolanus* v 2 81
Nay, I'll conjure too. Romeo ! humours ! madman ! passion ! lover ! *Rom. and Jul.* ii 1 6
The ape is dead, and I must conjure him. I conjure thee by Rosaline's bright eyes . . . . ii 1 16
And in his mistress' name I conjure only but to raise up him . ii 1 29
Conjure with 'em, Brutus will start a spirit as soon as Cæsar *J. Cæsar* i 2 146
I conjure you, by that which you profess, Howe'er you come to know it, answer me . . . . *Macbeth* iv 1 50
Let me conjure you, by the rights of our fellowship . . *Hamlet* ii 2 294
Whose phrase of sorrow Conjures the wandering stars . . . v 1 279
She conjures : away with her ! . . . . . . *Pericles* iv 6 156
Conjured. To eat of the habitation which your prophet the Nazarite conjured the devil into . . . . . *Mer. of Venice* i 3 35
There's magic in thy majesty, which has My evils conjured to remembrance . . . . *W. Tale* v 3 40
Letting it there stand Till she had laid it and conjured it down *Rom. and Jul.* ii 1 26
All these spirits thy power Hath conjured to attend . *T. of Athens* i 1 7
But he hath conjured me beyond them, and I must needs appear . iii 6 13
Thou, like an exorcist, hast conjured up My mortified spirit *J. Cæsar* ii 1 323
Or with some dram conjured to this effect, He wrought upon her *Othello* i 3 105
But she so loves the token, For he conjured her she should ever keep it iii 3 294
Conjurer. You are a conjurer ; Establish him in his true sense again *Com. of Errors* iv 4 50
Unless you send some present help, Between them they will kill the conjurer . . . . v 1 177
This pernicious slave, Forsooth, took on him as a conjurer . . v 1 242
Shall we think the subtle-witted French Conjurers and sorcerers? 1 *Hen. VI.* i 1 26
Roger Bolingbroke, the conjurer . . . . 2 *Hen. VI.* i 2 76
Dealing with witches and with conjurers . . . . . . ii 1 172

Conjurer. Has a book in his pocket with red letters in't.—Nay, then, he is a conjurer *2 Hen. VI.* iv 2 99
Conjuring the moon To stand auspicious mistress *Lear* ii 1 41
Conned. That well by heart hath conn'd his embassage *L. L. Lost* v 2 98
Extremely stretch'd and conn'd with cruel pain *M. N. Dream* v 1 80
Have you not been acquainted with goldsmiths' wives, and conned them out of rings? *As Y. Like It* iii 2 289
With precepts that would make invincible The heart that conn'd them *Coriolanus* iv 1 11
All his faults observed, Set in a note-book, learn'd, and conn'd by rote *J. Cæsar* iv 3 98
Connive. Sure the gods do this year connive at us *W. Tale* iv 4 692
Conquer. When the sweet breath of flattery conquers strife *Com. of Errors* iii 2 28
That England, that was wont to conquer others, Hath made a shameful conquest of itself *Richard II.* ii 1 65
It is as easy for me, Kate, to conquer the kingdom as to speak so much more French *Hen. V.* v 2 195
A witch, by fear, not force, like Hannibal, Drives back our troops and conquers as she lists *1 Hen. VI.* i 5 22
The regent conquers, and the Frenchmen fly v 3 1
To conquer France, his true inheritance *2 Hen. VI.* i 1 82
Were there hope to conquer them again, My sword should shed hot blood i 1 117
Those provinces these arms of mine did conquer i 1 120
That I may conquer fortune's spite By living low *3 Hen. VI.* iv 6 19
Awake, and think our wrongs in Richard's bosom Will conquer him! *Richard III.* v 3 145
Awake, awake! Arm, fight, and conquer, for fair England's sake! v 3 150
If we be conquer'd, let men conquer us, And not these bastard Bretons v 3 332
He hath been used Ever to conquer, and to have his worth Of contradiction *Coriolanus* iii 3 26
If thou conquer Rome, the benefit Which thou shalt thereby reap is such a name, Whose repetition will be dogg'd with curses v 3 142
That, by killing of villains, Thou wast born to conquer my country *T. of Athens* iv 3 106
We Have used to conquer, standing on the earth, And fighting foot to foot *Ant. and Cleo.* iii 7 66
He that can endure To follow with allegiance a fall'n lord Does conquer him that did his master conquer, And earns a place i' the story iii 13 45
So it should be, that none but Antony Should conquer Antony; but woe 'tis so! iv 15 17
That's the way To fool their preparation, and to conquer Their most absurd intents v 2 225
Conquered. When you have conquer'd my yet maiden bed, Remain there but an hour, nor speak to me *All's Well* iv 2 57
He ne'er lift up his hand but conquered *1 Hen. VI.* i 1 16
Have we not lost most part of all the towns, By treason, falsehood and by treachery, Our great progenitors had conquered? v 4 110
Defacing monuments of conquer'd France, Undoing all *2 Hen. VI.* i 1 102
So triumph thieves upon their conquer'd booty *3 Hen. VI.* i 4 63
Both tugging to be victors, breast to breast, Yet neither conqueror nor conquered ii 5 12
Henry the Fifth, Who by his prowess conquered all France iii 3 86
If we be conquer'd, let men conquer us *Richard III.* v 3 332
Whose wisdom hath her fortune conquered *T. Andron.* i 1 336
Death, that hath suck'd the honey of thy breath, Hath had no power yet upon thy beauty: Thou art not conquer'd *Rom. and Jul.* v 3 94
The gods confound them all in thy conquest; And thee after, when thou hast conquer'd! *T. of Athens* iv 3 104
For what I have conquer'd, I grant him part; but then, in his Armenia, And other of his conquer'd kingdoms, I Demand the like *Ant. and Cleo.* iii 6 34
Mine honour was not yielded, But conquer'd merely iii 13 62
If he please To give me conquer'd Egypt for my son v 2 19
When Julius Cæsar ... was in this Britain And conquer'd it *Cymbeline* iii 1 5
The device he bears upon his shield Is an arm'd knight that's conquer'd by a lady *Pericles* ii 2 26
Conquering. By east, west, north, and south, I spread my conquering might *L. L. Lost* v 2 566
Go forth and fetch their conquering Cæsar in *Hen. V.* v Prol. 28
God is our fortress, in whose conquering name Let us resolve to scale their flinty bulwarks *1 Hen. VI.* ii 1 26
And now to Paris, in this conquering vein: All will be ours iv 7 95
What heart receives from hence the conquering part? *Troi. and Cres.* i 3 352
His conquering banner shook from Syria To Lydia and to Ionia *Ant. and Cleo.* i 2 106
Till that the conquering wine hath steep'd our sense In soft and delicate Lethe ii 7 113
Say to great Cæsar this: in deputation I kiss his conquering hand iii 13 75
Conqueror. Brave conquerors,—for so you are, That war against your own affections *L. L. Lost* i 1 8
The conqueror is dismay'd. Proceed v 2 570
Take away the conqueror, take away Alisander v 2 575
O, sir, you have overthrown Alisander the conqueror! v 2 578
A conqueror, and afeard to speak! run away for shame v 2 582
It was play'd When I from Thebes came last a conqueror *M. N. Dream* v 1 51
Let's present him to the duke, like a Roman conqueror *As Y. Like It* iv 2 4
We came in with Richard Conqueror *T. of Shrew* Ind. 1 5
The dancing banners of the French, Who are at hand, triumphantly display'd, To enter conquerors *K. John* ii 1 310
England never did, nor never shall, Lie at the proud foot of a conqueror v 7 113
As sure as English Henry lives And as his father here was conqueror *1 Hen. VI.* iii 2 81
Sleeping neglection doth betray to loss The conquest of our scarce cold conqueror iv 3 50
For Henry, son unto a conqueror, Is likely to beget more conquerors v 5 73
Both tugging to be victors, breast to breast, Yet neither conqueror nor conquered *3 Hen. VI.* ii 5 12
Sir Richard Grey was slain, His lands then seized on by the conqueror iii 2 3
Themselves, the conquerors, Make war upon themselves *Richard III.* ii 4 61
Death makes no conquest of this conqueror iii 1 87
Ere from this war thou turn a conqueror iv 4 184
Bound with triumphant garlands will I come And lead thy daughter to a conqueror's bed iv 4 334
Virtuous and holy, be thou conqueror! v 3 128
If you do fight in safeguard of your wives, Your wives shall welcome home the conquerors v 3 260
Gracious conqueror, Victorious Titus, rue the tears I shed *T. Andron.* i 1 104
The conquerors can but make a fire of him *J. Cæsar* v 5 55
Did forfeit, with his life, all those his lands Which he stood seized of, to the conqueror *Hamlet* i 1 89
There is nothing done, if he return the conqueror *Lear* iv 6 271

Conqueror. You did know How much you were my conqueror *Ant. and Cleo.* iii 11 66
She which by her death our Cæsar tells 'I am conqueror of myself' iv 14 62
You shall find A conqueror that will pray in aid for kindness, Where he for grace is kneel'd to v 2 27
Conquest. Better conquest never canst thou make Than arm thy constant and thy nobler parts Against these giddy loose suggestions *K. John* iii 1 290
To outlook conquest and to win renown Even in the jaws of danger v 2 115
That England, that was wont to conquer others, Hath made a shameful conquest of itself *Richard II.* ii 1 66
It is a conquest for a prince to boast of *1 Hen. IV.* i 1 77
The head Which princes, flesh'd with conquest, aim to hit *2 Hen. IV.* i 1 149
A peace is of the nature of a conquest; For then both parties nobly are subdued iv 2 89
Nor leave not one behind that doth not wish Success and conquest to attend on us *Hen. V.* ii 2 24
Here had the conquest fully been seal'd up, If Sir John Fastolfe had not play'd the coward *1 Hen. VI.* i 1 130
Ascribes the glory of his conquest got First to my God and next unto your grace iii 4 11
O, think upon the conquest of my father, My tender years! iv 1 148
Sleeping neglection doth betray to loss The conquest of our scarce cold conqueror iv 3 50
Command the conquest, Charles, it shall be thine v 2 19
Shall Henry's conquest, Bedford's vigilance, Your deeds of war and all our counsel die? *2 Hen. VI.* i 1 96
Henry the Fourth by conquest got the crown *3 Hen. VI.* i 1 132
My mind presageth happy gain and conquest v 1 71
I must yield my body to the earth And, by my fall, the conquest to my foe v 2 10
Death makes no conquest of this conqueror *Richard III.* iii 1 87
To whom I will retail my conquest won, And she shall be sole victress iv 4 335
The gods confound them all in thy conquest; And thee after, when thou hast conquer'd! *T. of Athens* iv 3 103
Wert thou the unicorn, pride and wrath would confound thee and make thine own self the conquest of thy fury iv 3 340
Wherefore rejoice? What conquest brings he home? *J. Cæsar* i 1 37
Have I in conquest stretch'd mine arm so far To be afeard to tell graybeards the truth? ii 2 66
Are all thy conquests, glories, triumphs, spoils, Shrunk to this little measure? iii 1 149
I shall have glory by this losing day More than Octavius and Mark Antony By this vile conquest shall attain unto v 5 38
Young Fortinbras, with conquest come from Poland *Hamlet* v 2 361
We, Your scutcheons and your signs of conquest, shall Hang in what place you please *Ant. and Cleo.* v 2 135
Not what you have reserved, nor what acknowledged, Put we i' the roll of conquest v 2 181
A kind of conquest Cæsar made here; but made not here his brag Of 'Came' and 'saw' and 'overcame' *Cymbeline* iii 1 22
And make a conquest of unhappy me, Whereas no glory's got to overcome *Pericles* i 4 69
Conrade. What, Conrade!—Peace! stir not *Much Ado* iii 3 102
Conrade, I say!—Here, man; I am at thy elbow iii 3 104
I am a gentleman, sir, and my name is Conrade.—Write down, master gentleman Conrade iv 2 16
Consanguineous. Am not I consanguineous? am I not of her blood? *T. Night* ii 3 82
Consanguinity. I know no touch of consanguinity *Troi. and Cres.* iv 2 103
Conscience. Thy conscience Is so possess'd with guilt *Tempest* i 2 470
But, for your conscience?—Ay, sir; where lies that? if 'twere a kibe, 'Twould put me to my slipper: but I feel not This deity in my bosom ii 1 275
Twenty consciences, That stand 'twixt me and Milan, candied be they And melt ere they molest! ii 1 278
I suffer for it.—You suffer for a pad conscience *Mer. Wives* iii 3 235
With the warrant of womanhood and the witness of a good conscience iv 2 221
Now is Cupid a child of conscience; he makes restitution v 5 32
I'll teach you how you shall arraign your conscience *Meas. for Meas.* ii 3 21
Ere you flout old ends any further, examine your conscience *Much Ado* i 1 291
If Don Worm, his conscience, find no impediment to the contrary v 2 86
Done in the testimony of a good conscience *L. L. Lost* iv 2 2
Consciences, that will not die in debt v 2 333
A very gentle beast, and of a good conscience *M. N. Dream* v 1 230
Certainly my conscience will serve me to run from this Jew *Mer. of Venice* ii 2 1
My conscience says 'No; take heed, honest Launcelot'. ii 2 6
My conscience, hanging about the neck of my heart, says very wisely to me ii 2 13
My conscience says 'Launcelot, budge not.' 'Budge,' says the fiend ii 2 19
'Budge not,' says my conscience. 'Conscience,' say I, 'you counsel well' ii 2 21
To be ruled by my conscience, I should stay with the Jew my master ii 2 23
In my conscience, my conscience is but a kind of hard conscience ii 2 29
One of the points in the which women still give the lie to their consciences *As Y. Like It* iii 2 410
Were my worth as is my conscience firm, You should find better dealing *T. Night* iii 3 17
I appeal To your own conscience *W. Tale* iii 2 47
But I cannot with conscience take it iv 4 660
So much my conscience whispers in your ear *K. John* i 1 42
Whose armour conscience buckled on ii 1 564
The colour of the king doth come and go Between his purpose and his conscience iv 2 77
Thou, to be endeared to a king, Made it no conscience to destroy a prince iv 2 229
Hostility and civil tumult reigns Between my conscience and my cousin's death iv 2 248
That my grandsire was an Englishman, Awakes my conscience to confess all this v 4 43
Whom conscience and my kindred bids to right *Richard II.* ii 2 115
With clog of conscience and sour melancholy Hath yielded up his body to the grave v 6 20
The guilt of conscience take thou for thy labour v 6 41
Now, my masters, for a true face and good conscience *1 Hen. IV.* ii 4 551
Now, for our consciences, the arms are fair, When the intent of bearing them is just v 2 88
But a good conscience will make any possible satisfaction *2 Hen. IV.* Epil. 21
What you speak is in your conscience wash'd As pure as sin with baptism *Hen. V.* i 2 31
Could not keep quiet in his conscience, Wearing the crown of France i 2 79
May I with right and conscience make this claim? i 2 96

Conscience. In liberty of bloody hand shall range With conscience wide as hell — *Hen. V.* iii 3 13
I think in my very conscience he is as valiant a man as Mark Antony — iii 6 14
Besides, they are our outward consciences, And preachers to us all — iv 1 8
Is it meet, think you, . . . ? in your conscience, now? — iv 1 81
I will speak my conscience of the king — iv 1 123
Do as every sick man in his bed, wash every mote out of his conscience — iv 1 189
Yes, my conscience, he did us great good — iv 8 126
But, shall I speak my conscience — *2 Hen. VI.* iii 1 68
My conscience tells me you are innocent — iii 1 141
And he but naked, though lock'd up in steel, Whose conscience with injustice is corrupted — iii 2 235
My conscience tells me he is lawful king — *3 Hen. VI.* i 1 150
Tell me, even upon thy conscience — iii 3 113
Having God, her conscience, and these bars against me — *Richard III.* i 2 235
The worm of conscience still begnaw thy soul! — i 3 222
'Faith, some certain dregs of conscience are yet within me — i 4 124
Where is thy conscience now?—In the Duke of Gloucester's purse — i 4 130
So when he opens his purse to give us our reward, thy conscience flies out — i 4 133
It [conscience] is a dangerous thing: it makes a man a coward: a man cannot steal, but it accuseth him; he cannot swear, but it checks him — i 4 137
It [conscience] fills one full of obstacles: it made me once restore a purse of gold that I found; it beggars any man that keeps it: it is turned out of all towns and cities for a dangerous thing; and every man that means to live well endeavours to trust to himself and to live without it — i 4 143
This argues conscience in your grace — iii 7 174
Albeit against my conscience and my soul — iii 7 226
Both are gone with conscience and remorse; They could not speak — iv 3 20
Every man's conscience is a thousand swords — v 2 17
Soft! I did but dream. O coward conscience, how dost thou afflict me! — v 3 179
My conscience hath a thousand several tongues — v 3 193
Conscience is but a word that cowards use, Devised at first to keep the strong in awe — v 3 309
Our strong arms be our conscience, swords our law — v 3 311
If I have a conscience, let it sink me, Even as the axe falls, if I be not faithful! — *Hen. VIII.* ii 1 60
The marriage with his brother's wife Has crept too near his conscience. —No, his conscience Has crept too near another lady — ii 2 18
Dangers, doubts, wringing of the conscience, Fears, and despairs — ii 2 28
O my Wolsey, The quiet of my wounded conscience — ii 2 75
But, conscience, conscience! O, 'tis a tender place; and I must leave her — ii 2 143
Your soft cheveril conscience would receive, If you might please to stretch it — ii 3 32
My conscience first received a tenderness, Scruple, and prick — ii 4 170
This respite shook The bosom of my conscience, enter'd me, Yea, with a splitting power — ii 4 182
Thus hulling in The wild sea of my conscience, I did steer — ii 4 200
That's to say, I meant to rectify my conscience — ii 4 203
By what means got, I leave to your own conscience — iii 2 327
I feel within me A peace above all earthly dignities, A still and quiet conscience — iii 2 380
And do justice For truth's sake and his conscience — iii 2 397
I cannot blame his conscience — iv 1 47
Yet my conscience says She's a good creature — v 1 24
Both in his private conscience and his place — v 3 40
I make as little doubt, as you do conscience In doing daily wrongs — v 3 67
On my Christian conscience, this one christening will beget a thousand — v 4 37
I'll haunt thee like a wicked conscience still — *Troi. and Cres.* v 10 28
Would return for conscience sake — *Coriolanus* ii 3 36
Thou art religious And hast a thing within thee called conscience — *T. Andron.* v 1 75
Canst thou the conscience lack, To think I shall lack friends? *T. of Athens* ii 2 184
Men must learn now with pity to dispense; For policy sits above conscience — iii 2 94
A trade, sir, that, I hope, I may use with a safe conscience — *J. Cæsar* i 1 14
The play's the thing Wherein I'll catch the conscience of the king *Hamlet* ii 2 634
How smart a lash that speech doth give my conscience! — iii 1 50
Thus conscience does make cowards of us all — iii 1 83
Vows, to the blackest devil! Conscience and grace, to the profoundest pit! — iv 5 132
Now must your conscience my acquittance seal — iv 7 1
They did make love to this employment; They are not near my conscience — v 2 58
Is't not perfect conscience, To quit him with this arm? — v 2 67
And yet 'tis almost 'gainst my conscience — v 2 307
Though in the trade of war I have slain men, Yet do I hold it very stuff o' the conscience To do no contrived murder — *Othello* i 2 2
Their best conscience Is not to leave't undone, but keep't unknown — iii 3 203
Dost thou in conscience think,—tell me, Emilia,—That there be women do abuse their husbands In such gross kind? — iv 3 61
I beseech your grace, without offence,—My conscience bids me ask *Cymb.* i 5 7
'Tis your graces That from my mutest conscience to my tongue Charms this report out — i 6 116
This will witness outwardly, As strongly as the conscience does within — ii 2 36
Heaven and my conscience knows Thou didst unjustly banish me — iii 3 99
I false! Thy conscience witness — iii 4 48
And had the virtue Which their own conscience seal'd them — iii 6 85
My conscience, thou art fetter'd More than my shanks and wrists — v 4 8
My heavy conscience sinks my knee, As then your force did — v 5 413
Let not conscience, Which is but cold, inflaming love i' thy bosom, Inflame too nicely — *Pericles* iv 1 4
If there be not a conscience to be used in every trade, we shall never prosper — iv 2 11
They're too unwholesome, o' conscience — iv 2 23
In (on) my conscience *Mer. of Venice* ii 2; *T. Night* iii 1; *W. Tale* iii 3; *Hen. V.* iv 7; *2 Hen. VI.* v 1; *Hen. VIII.* ii 1; iii 1; iii 2; v 4; *T. of Athens* iii 3; *Cymbeline* v 4
In your conscience, now — *Hen. V.* iv 7 4; iv 8 40

Conscionable. No further conscionable than in putting on the mere form of civil and humane seeming — *Othello* ii 1 242

Consecrate. And that this body, consecrate to thee, By ruffian lust should be contaminate! — *Com. of Errors* ii 2 134
With this field-dew consecrate, Every fairy take his gait — *M. N. Dream* v 1 422
And consecrate commotion's bitter edge — *2 Hen. IV.* iv 1 93
We'll consecrate the steps that Ajax makes When they go from Achilles — *Troi. and Cres.* ii 3 193

Consecrate. To virtue consecrate, To justice, continence and nobility — *T. Andron.* i 1 14
To Saturnine, King and commander of our commonweal, The wide world's emperor, do I consecrate My sword, my chariot and my prisoners — i 1 248
Her sacred wit To villany and vengeance consecrate — ii 1 121
To his honours and his valiant parts Did I my soul and fortunes consecrate — *Othello* i 3 255

Consecrated. Meet me at the consecrated fount — *Meas. for Meas.* iv 3 102
Near to her close and consecrated bower — *M. N. Dream* iii 2 7
There, before him, And underneath that consecrated roof, Plight me the full assurance of your faith — *T. Night* iv 3 25
Whose blush doth thaw the consecrated snow That lies on Dian's lap! — *T. of Athens* iv 3 386

Consent. They fell together all, as by consent — *Tempest* ii 1 203
O, that our fathers would applaud our loves, To seal our happiness with their consents! — *T. G. of Ver.* i 3 49
I give consent to go along with you, Recking as little what betideth me iv 3 39
I will consent to act any villany against him — *Mer. Wives* ii 1 101
Win her to consent to you: if any man may, you may as soon as any — ii 2 245
'Tis in his buttons; he will carry 't.—Not by my consent — iii 2 72
The wealth I have waits on my consent, and my consent goes not that way — iii 2 78
Is here now in the house by your consent — iii 3 116
The maid hath given consent to go with him — iv 6 45
Fit thy consent to my sharp appetite — *Meas. for Meas.* ii 4 161
It is not my consent, But my entreaty too — iv 1 67
I will not consent to die this day, that's certain — iv 3 59
I see the trick on't: here was a consent — *L. L. Lost* v 2 460
This man hath my consent to marry her — *M. N. Dream* i 1 25
Be it so she will not here before your grace Consent to marry with Demetrius, I beg the ancient privilege of Athens — i 1 40
Whose unwished yoke My soul consents not to give sovereignty — i 1 82
By your setting on, by your consent — iii 2 231
Thereby to have defeated you and me, You of your wife and me of my consent — iv 1 163
Some villains of my court Are of consent and sufferance in this — *As Y. Like It* ii 2 3
Come, woo me, woo me, for now I am in a holiday humour and like enough to consent — iv 1 69
For all your writers do consent that ipse is he — v 1 48
Consent with both that we may enjoy each other — v 2 10
You have my consent. Let your wedding be to-morrow — v 2 15
Quietly enjoy your hope, And marry sweet Bianca with consent — *T. of Shrew* iii 2 139
Me shall you find ready and willing With one consent to have her so bestow'd — iv 4 35
Your son shall have my daughter with consent — iv 4 47
Dear sir, to my endeavours give consent — *All's Well* ii 1 156
Let her in fine consent, As we'll direct her how 'tis best to bear it — iii 7 19
The main consents are had — v 3 69
Thou shouldst a husband take by my consent, As I by thine a wife — *W. Tale* v 3 136
Didst let thy heart consent, And consequently thy rude hand to act — *K. John* iv 2 239
If thou didst but consent To this most cruel act, do but despair — iv 3 125
If in act, consent, or sin of thought, Be guilty — iv 3 135
The other part reserved I by consent — *Richard II.* i 1 128
Thou dost consent In some large measure to thy father's death — i 2 25
I have given here my soul's consent To undeck the pompous body of a king — iv 1 249
Consent upon a sure foundation, Question surveyors — *2 Hen. IV.* i 3 52
They flock together in consent, like so many wild-geese — v 1 78
For government, though high and low and lower, Put into parts, doth keep in one consent — *Hen. V.* i 2 181
Many things, having full reference To our consent, may work contrariously — i 2 206
We are well persuaded We carry not a heart with us from hence That grows not in a fair consent with ours — ii 2 22
Teach your cousin to consent winking.—I will wink on her to consent — v 2 332
By my consent, we'll even let them alone.—Be it so — *1 Hen. VI.* i 2 44
Consent, and for thy honour give consent — v 3 136
In regard King Henry gives consent, Of mere compassion and of lenity — v 4 124
Give consent That Margaret may be England's royal queen.—So should I give consent to flatter sin — v 5 23
For eighteen months concluded by consent — *2 Hen. VI.* i 1 42
And my consent ne'er ask'd herein before! This is close dealing — ii 4 72
Say you consent and censure well the deed, And I'll provide his executioner — iii 1 275
Our authority is his consent, And what we do establish he confirms — iii 1 316
He swore consent to your succession, His oath enrolled — *3 Hen. VI.* ii 1 172
A king, blest with a goodly son, Didst yield consent to disinherit him — ii 2 24
I was adopted heir by his consent — ii 2 88
O Phœbus, hadst thou never given consent That Phaëthon should check thy fiery steeds! — ii 6 11
Never will I undertake the thing Wherein thy counsel and consent is wanting — ii 6 102
Therefore I yield thee my free consent — iv 6 36
What answers Clarence to his sovereign's will?—That he consents, if Warwick yield consent — iv 6 46
As he will lose his head ere give consent — *Richard III.* iii 4 40
Say, have I thy consent that they shall die? — iv 2 23
By particular consent proceeded Under your hands and seals *Hen. VIII.* ii 4 221
'Tis his highness' pleasure, And our consent — v 3 53
Do not consent That ever Hector and Achilles meet — *Troi. and Cres.* i 3 362
Your breath of full consent bellied his sails — ii 2 74
Your full consent Gave wings to my propension — ii 2 132
That all with one consent praise new-born gawds — iii 3 176
As you and Lord Æneas Consent upon the order of their fight, So be it iv 5 90
Give me leave To take that course by your consent and voice — v 3 74
But cannot make my heart consent to take A bribe to pay my sword *Cor.* i 9 37
Their consent of one direct way should be at once to all the points o' the compass — ii 3 24
By the consent of all, we were establish'd The people's magistrates — iii 1 201
The god of soldiers, With the consent of supreme Jove, inform Thy thoughts with nobleness! — v 3 71
Get her heart, My will to her consent is but a part — *Rom. and Jul.* i 2 17
An she agree, within her scope of choice Lies my consent — i 2 19
No more deep will I endart mine eye Than your consent gives strength to make it fly — i 3 99

Consent. But this I pray, That thou consent to marry us to-day *Rom. and Jul.* ii 3 64
Go home, be merry, give consent To marry Paris . . . . iv 1 89
My poverty, but not my will, consents.—I pay thy poverty, and not thy will . . . . v 1 75
If in her marriage my consent be missing . *T. of Athens.* i 1 136
The senators with one consent of love Entreat thee back . v 1 143
Do not consent That Antony speak in his funeral . *J. Cæsar* iii 1 232
Your brother too must die; consent you, Lepidus?—I do consent . iv 1 2
If you shall cleave to my consent, when 'tis, It shall make honour for you *Macbeth* ii 1 25
Do you consent we shall acquaint him with it? . . . *Hamlet* i 1 172
And at last Upon his will I seal'd my hard consent . . . i 2 60
Come on—you hear this fellow in the cellarage—Consent to swear . i 5 152
How in my words soever she be shent, To give them seals never, my soul, consent! . . . . iii 2 417
If't be your pleasure and most wise consent . . . . *Othello* i 1 122
I did consent, And often did beguile her of her tears . . . i 3 155
Did you and he consent in Cassio's death? . . . . v 2 297
Will you, not having my consent, Bestow your love and your affections Upon a stranger? . . . . *Pericles* ii 5 76
Who ever but his approbation added, Though not his prime consent, he did not flow From honourable sources . . . . iv 3 27
There's no going but by their consent . . . . . iv 6 209

Consented. Away with Slender and with him at Eton Immediately to marry: she hath consented . . . *Mer. Wives* iv 6 25
The smallest twine may lead me.—'Tis well consented . *Much Ado* iv 1 253
Your father hath consented That you shall be my wife . *T. of Shrew* ii 1 271
We have consented to all terms of reason . . *Hen. V.* v 2 357
Scourge the bad revolting stars That have consented unto Henry's death! . . . . 1 *Hen. VI.* i 1 5
You all consented unto Salisbury's death . . . . i 5 34
The queen hath heartily consented He shall espouse Elizabeth *Rich. III.* iv 5 17
Though we willingly consented to his banishment, yet it was against our will . . . . *Coriolanus* iv 6 144

Consenting. You consenting to't, Would bark your honour from that trunk you bear . . . . *Meas. for Meas.* iii 1 71
Consenting to the safeguard of your honour, I thought your marriage fit v 1 424
Neither call the giddiness of it in question, the poverty of her, the small acquaintance, my sudden wooing, nor her sudden consenting *As Y. Like It* v 2 8
'Tis but the boldness of his hand, haply, which his heart was not consenting to . . . . *All's Well* iii 2 80

Consequence. An unshunned consequence; it must be so *Meas. for Meas.* iii 2 62
The consequence is then thy jealous fits Have scared thy husband from the use of wits . . . . . . *Com. of Errors* v 1 85
Here choose I: joy be the consequence! . . *Mer. of Venice* iii 2 107
Trust him not in matter of heavy consequence . . *All's Well* iii 5 49
It is a matter of small consequence, Which for some reasons I would not have seen . . . . *Richard II.* v 2 61
A night is but small breath and little pause To answer matters of this consequence . . . . *Hen. V.* ii 4 146
O bitter consequence, That Edward still should live! *Richard III.* iv 2 15
Hoping the consequence Will prove as bitter, black, and tragical . iv 4 6
Bearing a state of mighty moment in't And consequence of dread *Hen. VIII.* iii 4 214
Some consequence yet hanging in the stars Shall bitterly begin his fearful date With this night's revels . . *Rom. and Jul.* i 4 107
An enterprise Of honourable-dangerous consequence . *J. Cæsar* i 3 124
Win us with honest trifles, to betray's In deepest consequence *Macbeth* i 3 126
If the assassination Could trammel up the consequence . . . i 7 3
The spirits that know All mortal consequences have pronounced me thus v 3 5
Be assured He closes with you in this consequence . . *Hamlet* ii 1 45
Where did I leave?—At 'closes in the consequence' . . . ii 1 52
At 'closes in the consequence,' ay, marry; He closes thus . . ii 1 54
Each small annexment, petty consequence, Attends the boisterous ruin iii 3 21
If consequence do but approve my dream, My boat sails freely *Othello* ii 3 64
You are curb'd from that enlargement by The consequence o' the crown *Cymbeline* ii 3 126

Consequently. And consequently sets down the manner how *T. Night* iii 4 79
Didst let thy heart consent, And consequently thy rude hand to act *K. John* iv 2 240
And consequently, like a traitor coward, Sluiced out his innocent soul *Richard II.* i 1 102

Conserve. Thou art too noble to conserve a life In base appliances *Meas. for Meas.* iii 1 88
Will't please your honour taste of these conserves? . *T. of Shrew* Ind. 2 3
If you give me any conserves, give me conserves of beef . . Ind. 2 7

Conserved. It was dyed in mummy which the skilful Conserved of maidens' hearts . . . . *Othello* iii 4 75

Consider. That most deeply to consider is The beauty of his daughter *Temp.* iii 2 106
Considers she my possessions?—O, ay; and pities them . *T. G. of Ver.* v 2 25
Bid her think what a man is: let her consider his frailty *Mer. Wives* iii 5 51
Consider how it stands upon my credit . . . *Com. of Errors* iv 1 68
Consider who the king your father sends, To whom he sends *L. L. Lost* ii 1 2
Consider what you first did swear unto, To fast, to study, and to see no woman . . . . iv 3 291
You ought to consider with yourselves . . . . *M. N. Dream* iii 1 30
Consider then we come but in despite . . . . . . v 1 112
Though justice be thy plea, consider this, That, in the course of justice, none of us Should see salvation . . . *Mer. of Venice* iv 1 198
But yet have the grace to consider that tears do not become a man *As Y. Like It* iii 4 3
When I consider What great creation and what dole of honour Flies where you bid it . . . . *All's Well* ii 3 175
Defy the devil: consider, he's an enemy to mankind *T. Night* iii 4 108
So leaves me to consider what is breeding That changeth thus his manners *W. Tale* i 2 374
Consider little What dangers, by his highness' fail of issue, May drop upon his kingdom . . . . v 1 26
Thy speeches Will bring me to consider that which may Unfurnish me of reason . . . . v 1 122
Better consider what you have to do Than I, that have not well the gift of tongue, Can lift your blood up with persuasion 1 *Hen. IV.* v 2 77
You that are old consider not the capacities of us that are young 2 *Hen. IV.* i 2 196
Bid them o'er-read these letters, And well consider of them . . iii 1 3
We consider It was excess of wine that set him on . . *Hen. V.* ii 2 41
For us, we will consider of this further . . . . . ii 4 113
Bid him therefore consider of his ransom . . . . . iii 6 133
Consider, lords, he is the next of blood . . . 2 *Hen. VI.* i 1 151
We will consider of your suit; And come some other time to know our mind . . . . 3 *Hen. VI.* iii 2 16
Consider, he that set you on To do this deed will hate you for the deed *Richard III.* i 4 261
To consider further that What his high hatred would effect wants not A minister in his power . . . . *Hen. VIII.* i 1 106
For goodness' sake, consider what you do; How you may hurt yourself iii 1 159
Consider you what services he has done for his country? *Coriolanus* i 1 30
Most likely 'tis for you: Consider of it . . . . . . i 2 17
Consider this: he has been bred i' the wars Since he could draw a sword iii 1 320
The warlike service he has done, consider; think Upon the wounds his body bears . . . . iii 3 49
Consider further, That when he speaks not like a citizen, You find him like a soldier . . . . iii 3 52
You must consider that a prodigal course Is like the sun's *T. of Athens* iii 4 12
What you have said I will consider . . . . *J. Cæsar* i 2 168
But if you would consider the true cause Why all these fires . . i 3 62
If thou consider rightly of the matter, Cæsar has had great wrong iii 2 114
Consider it not so deeply.—But wherefore could not I pronounce 'Amen'? *Macbeth* ii 2 30
'Twere to consider too curiously, to consider so . . . *Hamlet* v 1 227
Is man no more than this? Consider him well . . . *Lear* iii 4 107
Good my friends, consider You are my guests . . . . iii 7 30
When we consider The importancy of Cyprus to the Turk . *Othello* i 3 19
I hope you will consider what is spoke Comes from my love . . iii 3 216
Cæsar entreats, Not to consider in what case thou stand'st, Further than he is Cæsar . . . . *Ant. and Cleo.* iii 13 54
And then let her consider . . . . . . *Cymbeline* ii 3 20
If this penetrate, I will consider your music the better . . ii 3 32
Madam, you're best consider.—I see before me, man . . . iii 2 79
Consider, When you above perceive me like a crow, That it is place which lessens and sets off . . . . iii 3 11
But I consider, By medicine life may be prolong'd, yet death Will seize the doctor too . . . . v 5 28
Consider, sir, the chance of war: the day Was yours by accident v 5 75

Considerance. After this cold considerance, sentence me . 2 *Hen. IV.* v 2 98

Considerate. None are for me That look into me with considerate eyes *Richard III.* iv 2 30
Go to, then; your considerate stone . . . *Ant. and Cleo.* ii 2 112

Consideration. He is knight, dubbed with unhatched rapier and on carpet consideration . . . . *T. Night* iii 4 258
Startles and frights consideration, Makes sound opinion sick . *K. John* iv 2 25
Albeit considerations infinite Do make against it . . . 1 *Hen. IV.* v 1 102
Can thrust me from a level consideration . . . 2 *Hen. IV.* ii 1 124
These humble considerations make me out of love with my greatness ii 2 14
Consideration, like an angel, came And whipp'd the offending Adam out of him . . . . *Hen. V.* i 1 28
Give it quick consideration, for There is no primer business *Hen. VIII.* i 2 66
With liquorish draughts And morsels unctuous, greases his pure mind, That from it all consideration slips! . . . *T. of Athens* iv 3 196
In thy best consideration, check This hideous rashness . . *Lear* i 1 152
Let's to supper, come, And drown consideration . *Ant. and Cleo.* iv 2 45

Considered. I have consider'd well his loss of time . . *T. G. of Ver.* i 3 19
You that have worn your eyes almost out in the service, you will be considered . . . . *Meas. for Meas.* i 2 114
Which if I have not enough considered, as too much I cannot *W. Tale* iv 2 19
I have considered so much, Camillo, and with some care . . iv 2 39
Being something gently considered, I'll bring you where he is . iv 4 825
The circumstance consider'd, good my lord . . 1 *Hen. IV.* i 3 70
Your several suits Have been consider'd and debated on . 1 *Hen. VI.* v 1 35
I have consider'd with myself The title of this most renowned duke 2 *Hen. VI.* v 1 175
All circumstances well considered . . . . *Richard III.* iii 7 176
I have consider'd in my mind The late demand that you did sound me in iv 2 86
Grievous complaints of you; which, being consider'd, Have moved us *Hen. VIII.* v 1 99
Well then, now Have you consider'd of my speeches? . . *Macbeth* iii 1 76
At our more consider'd time we'll read, Answer, and think upon this business . . . . *Hamlet* ii 2 81
Though, in the mean time, some necessary question of the play be then to be considered . . . . iii 2 48
Which, if thou hast consider'd, let us know . . *Ant. and Cleo.* ii 6 5
But to win time To lose so bad employment; in the which I have consider'd of a course . . . . *Cymbeline* iii 4 114
There's more to be consider'd; but we'll even All that good time will give us . . . . iii 4 184
If thine consider'd prove the thousandth part Of my endurance *Pericles* v 1 136

Considering the weather, a taller man than I will take cold *T. of Shrew* iv 1 10
Many mazed considerings did throng And press'd in with this caution *Hen. VIII.* ii 4 185
His thinkings are below the moon, not worth His serious considering . iii 2 135
Considering how honour would become such a person . *Coriolanus* i 3 10
And the place death, considering who thou art . . *Rom. and Jul.* ii 2 64

Consign. Any thing in or out of our demands, And we'll consign thereto *Hen. V.* v 2 90
It were, my lord, a hard condition for a maid to consign to . . v 2 326
All lovers young, all lovers must Consign to thee, and come to dust *Cymbeline* iv 2 275

Consigned. As many farewells as be stars in heaven, With distinct breath and consign'd kisses to them . . . . *Troi. and Cres.* iv 4 47

Consigning. God consigning to my good intents . . 2 *Hen. IV.* v 2 143

Consist. If their purgation did consist in words, They are as innocent as grace itself . . . . *As Y. Like It* i 3 55
Does not our life consist of the four elements?—Faith, so they say; but I think it rather consists of eating and drinking . . *T. Night* ii 3 10
My whole charge consists of ancients, corporals, lieutenants 1 *Hen. IV.* iv 2 25
So absolute As our conditions shall consist upon . . 2 *Hen. IV.* iv 1 187
In her consists my happiness and thine . . . *Richard III.* iv 4 406
Distract your army, which doth most consist Of war-mark'd footmen *Ant. and Cleo.* iii 7 44
Welcome is peace, if he on peace consist . . . . *Pericles* i 4 83
Fair one, all goodness that consists in bounty Expect even here . v 1 70

Consisteth. Since that the trade and profit of the city Consisteth of all nations . . . . *Mer. of Venice* iii 3 31

Consisting equally of horse and foot . . . . *Richard III.* v 3 294
Expressly proves That no man is the lord of any thing, Though in and of him there be much consisting . . . *Troi. and Cres.* iii 3 116

Consistory. My other self, my counsel's consistory, My oracle! *Rich. III.* ii 2 151
Warranted By a commission from the consistory, Yea, the whole consistory of Rome . . . . *Hen. VIII.* ii 4 92

Consolate. I will be gone, That pitiful rumour may report my flight, To consolate thine ear . . . . *All's Well* iii 2 131
Consolation. Take this of me, Kate of my consolation . *T. of Shrew* ii 1 191
This grief is crowned with consolation . . . . *Ant. and Cleo.* i 2 175
Consonanacy. But then there is no consonancy in the sequel *T. Night* ii 5 141
By the rights of our fellowship, by the consonancy of our youth *Hamlet* ii 2 295
Consonant. Quis, quis, thou consonant? . . . . *L. L. Lost* v 1 55
Consort. What say'st thou? wilt thou be of our consort? *T. G. of Ver.* iv 1 64
I'll meet with you upon the mart And afterward consort you till bed-time *Com. of Errors* i 2 28
Sweet health and fair desires consort your grace! . . *L. L. Lost* ii 1 178
And must for aye consort with black-brow'd night . . *M. N. Dream* iii 2 387
Consort with me in loud and dear petition . . *Troi. and Cres.* v 3 9
Mercutio, thou consort'st with Romeo,— Consort! what, dost thou make us minstrels? . . . 'Zounds, consort! . *Rom. and Jul.* iii 1 49
Thou, wretched boy, that didst consort him here, Shalt with him hence iii 1 135
What will you do? Let's not consort with them . . *Macbeth* ii 3 141
He was of that consort.—No marvel, then, though he were ill affected *Lear* ii 1 99
Consorted. Sorted and consorted, contrary to thy established proclaimed edict . . . . *L. L. Lost* i 1 261
With all the rest of that consorted crew . . . *Richard II.* v 3 138
Two of the dangerous consorted traitors . . . . v 6 15
That monstrous witch, Consorted with that harlot strumpet Shore *Richard III.* iii 4 73
For this, consorted with the citizens, Your very worshipful and loving friends . . . . iii 7 137
To be consorted with the humorous night . . . *Rom. and Jul.* ii 1 31
Who to Philippi here consorted us . . . . *J. Cæsar* v 1 83
Consortest. Mercutio, thou consort'st with Romeo . *Rom. and Jul.* iii 1 48
Conspectuities. What harm can your bisson conspectuities glean out of this character? . . . . *Coriolanus* ii 1 70
Conspiracy. While you here do snoring lie, Open-eyed conspiracy His time doth take . . . . *Tempest* ii 1 301
I had forgot that foul conspiracy Of the beast Caliban and his confederates . . . . iv 1 139
There's a knot, a ging, a pack, a conspiracy against me . *Mer. Wives* iv 2 123
Now, for conspiracy, I know not how it tastes . . . *W. Tale* iii 2 72
Wilt thou conceal this dark conspiracy? . . . . *Richard II.* v 2 96
O heinous, strong and bold conspiracy! . . . . . v 3 59
Confirm'd conspiracy with fearful France . . . . *Hen. V.* ii Prol. 27
O conspiracy, Shamest thou to show thy dangerous brow by night? *J. Cæsar* ii 1 77
Where wilt thou find a cavern dark enough To mask thy monstrous visage? Seek none, conspiracy . . . . . . ii 1 81
Look about you: security gives way to conspiracy . . . . ii 3 8
Hum—conspiracy!—'Sleep till I waked him' . . . . *Lear* i 2 58
Conspirant 'gainst this high-illustrious prince . . . . v 3 135
Conspirator. The grand conspirator, Abbot of Westminster *Richard II.* v 6 19
Stand back, thou manifest conspirator . . . . . 1 *Hen. VI.* i 3 33
Cut off the proud'st conspirator that lives . . . *T. Andron.* iv 4 26
Away, then! come, seek the conspirators . . . *J. Cæsar* iii 2 237
Tear him to pieces; he's a conspirator . . . . . . iii 3 30
I am not Cinna the conspirator.—It is no matter, his name's Cinna . iii 3 36
Look; I draw a sword against conspirators . . . . . v 1 51
All the conspirators save only he Did that they did in envy of great Cæsar . . . . v 5 69
Conspire. To whisper and conspire against my youth . *T. G. of Ver.* i 2 43
John lays you plots; the times conspire with you . . . *K. John* iii 4 146
What mutter you, or what conspire you? . . . . 3 *Hen. VI.* i 1 165
Tell me what they deserve That do conspire my death with devilish plots? *Richard III.* iii 4 62
I would conspire against destiny . . . . *Troi. and Cres.* v 1 70
What further woe conspires against mine age? . . . *Rom. and Jul.* v 3 212
Thou dost conspire against thy friend, Iago, If thou but think'st him wrong'd and makest his ear A stranger to thy thoughts . *Othello* iii 3 142
What was't That moved pale Cassius to conspire? . . *Ant. and Cleo.* ii 6 15
Conspired. Have you conspired, have you with these contrived? *M. N. Dream* iii 2 196
So do I his.—And they have conspired together . . *Mer. of Venice* ii 5 22
Hast thou conspired with thy brother too? . . . . *K. John* i 1 241
Hath, for a few light crowns, lightly conspired . . *Hen. V.* ii 2 89
You have conspired against our royal person . . . . . ii 2 167
Thou, Conspired with that irregulous devil, Cloten . . *Cymbeline* iv 2 315
Conspirer. Be lion-mettled, proud; and take no care Who chafes, who frets, or where conspirers are . . . . . . *Macbeth* iv 1 91
Conspiring with Camillo to take away the life of our sovereign lord the king . . . . *W. Tale* iii 2 16
Constable. I am in case to justle a constable . . . *Tempest* iii 2 29
The knave constable had set me i' the stocks, i' the common stocks *Mer. Wives* iv 5 122
I am the poor duke's constable, and my name is Elbow *Meas. for Meas.* ii 1 48
It is a naughty house.—How dost thou know that, constable? . . ii 1 79
How could Master Froth do the constable's wife any harm? . . . ii 1 165
He's in the right. Constable, what say you to it? . . . . . ii 1 167
How long have you been in this place of constable? . . . . ii 1 273
Who think you the most desartless man to be constable? . *Much Ado* iii 3 10
To write and read comes by nature.—Both which, master constable,— You have . . . . iii 3 17
The most senseless and fit man for the constable of the watch . . iii 3 24
You, constable, are to present the prince's own person . . . . iii 3 79
Call up the right master constable . . . . iii 3 178
Let them come before master constable . . . . . . iv 2 8
Master constable, you go not the way to examine . . . . iv 2 35
Master constable,— Pray thee, fellow, peace: I do not like thy look . iv 2 45
Master constable, let these men be bound . . . . . iv 2 66
This learned constable is too cunning to be understood . . . . v 1 234
A critic, nay, a night-watch constable . . . . *L. L. Lost* iii 1 178
From below your duke to beneath your constable . . . *All's Well* ii 3 33
The constables have delivered her over to me . . . 2 *Hen. IV.* v 4 4
Well, 'tis not so, my lord high constable . . . . *Hen. V.* ii 4 41
Charles Delabreth, high constable of France . . . . iii 5 40; iv 8 97
Therefore, lord constable, haste on Montjoy . . . . . iii 5 61
Now forth, lord constable and princes all, And quickly bring us word of England's fall . . . . iii 5 67
My lord high constable, you talk of horse and armour? . . . . iii 7 8
I tell thee, constable, my mistress wears his own hair . . . iii 7 64
My lord constable, the armour that I saw in your tent to-night, are those stars or suns upon it? . . . . iii 7 73
My lord high constable, the English lie within fifteen hundred paces . iii 7 135
Constable. Now, my lord constable!—Hark, how our steeds for present service neigh! . . . . *Hen. V.* iv 2 7
The constable desires thee thou wilt mind Thy followers of repentance iv 3 84
Who hath sent thee now?—The Constable of France . . . iv 3 89
Tell the constable We are but warriors for the working-day . . iv 3 108
These my joints; Which if they have as I will leave 'em them, Shall yield them little, tell the constable . . . . iv 3 125
When I came hither, I was lord high constable . . *Hen. VIII.* ii 1 102
Dun's the mouse, the constable's own word . . *Rom. and Jul.* i 4 40
Constance. Have I not ever said How that ambitious Constance would not cease Till she had kindled France and all the world? . *K. John* i 1 32
Is not the Lady Constance in this troop? . . . . . . ii 1 540
Call the Lady Constance; Some speedy messenger bid her repair To our solemnity . . . . ii 1 553
Hear me, O, hear me!—Lady Constance, peace! . . . . . iii 1 112
The Lady Constance speaks not from her faith, But from her need . iii 1 210
Comfort, gentle Constance!—No, I defy all counsel . . . . iii 4 22
I am not mad: this hair I tear is mine; My name is Constance . . iii 4 46
As I hear, my lord, The Lady Constance in a frenzy died . . . iv 2 122
Constancies. Whose constancies Expire before their fashions . *All's Well* i 2 62
Constancy. Here is my hand for my true constancy . *T. G. of Ver.* ii 2 8
There is written in your brow, provost, honesty and constancy *Meas. for Meas.* iv 2 163
And grows to something of great constancy . . . *M. N. Dream* v 1 26
Her years, profession, Wisdom and constancy, hath amazed me *All's Well* ii 1 87
I would have men of such constancy put to sea . . *T. Night* ii 4 78
Take a fellow of plain and uncoined constancy . . . *Hen. V.* v 2 161
Unite in your complaints, And force them with a constancy *Hen. VIII.* iii 2 2
The protractive trials of great Jove To find persistive constancy in men *Troi. and Cres.* i 3 21
To keep her constancy in plight and youth, Outliving beauty's outward iii 2 168
With untired spirits and formal constancy . . . *J. Cæsar* ii 1 227
I have made strong proof of my constancy, Giving myself a voluntary wound . . . . ii 1 299
O constancy, be strong upon my side! . . . . ii 4 6
Your constancy Hath left you unattended . . . . *Macbeth* ii 2 68
What lady would you choose to assail?—Yours; whom in constancy you think stands so safe . . . . *Cymbeline* i 4 137
Constant. Who was so firm, so constant, that this coil Would not infect his reason? . . . . *Tempest* i 2 207
Do not turn me about; my stomach is not constant . . . . ii 2 120
I cannot now prove constant to myself . . . . *T. G. of Ver.* ii 6 31
O heaven! were man But constant, he were perfect . . . . v 4 111
What is in Silvia's face, but I may spy More fresh in Julia's with a constant eye? . . . . v 4 115
It is virtuous to be constant in any undertaking . *Meas. for Meas.* iii 2 239
Friendship is constant in all other things Save in the office and affairs of love . . . . *Much Ado* ii 1 182
Be you constant in the accusation, and my cunning shall not shame me ii 2 55
Men were deceivers ever, One foot in sea and one on shore, To one thing constant never . . . . ii 3 67
Wise, fair and true, Shall she be placed in my constant soul *Mer. of Ven.* ii 6 57
Nothing in the world Could turn so much the constitution Of any constant man . . . . iii 2 250
How well in thee appears The constant service of the antique world! *As Y. Like It* ii 3 57
'Twas just the difference Betwixt the constant red and mingled damask iii 5 123
Unstaid and skittish in all motions else, Save in the constant image of the creature That is beloved . . . . *T. Night* ii 4 19
Make the trial of it in any constant question . . . . . iv 2 53
Still so cruel?—Still so constant, lord . . . . . . v 1 114
To this I am most constant, Though destiny say no . . *W. Tale* iv 4 45
Therein am I constant to my profession . . . . . . iv 4 698
Better conquest never canst thou make Than arm thy constant and thy nobler parts Against these giddy loose suggestions . . *K. John* iii 1 291
A good plot as ever was laid; our friends true and constant 1 *Hen. IV.* ii 3 19
Constant you are, But yet a woman; and for secrecy, No lady closer . ii 3 111
I kiss thee with a most constant heart . . . . . 2 *Hen. IV.* ii 4 293
As if allegiance in their bosoms sat, Crowned with faith and constant loyalty . . . . *Hen. V.* ii 2 5
Constant in spirit, not swerving with the blood . . . . . ii 2 133
How modest in exception, and withal How terrible in constant resolution . . . . ii 4 35
This shall assure my constant loyalty . . . 3 *Hen. VI.* iii 3 240
What sorrow can befall thee, So long as Edward is thy constant friend? iv 1 77
Bring me a constant woman to her husband, One that ne'er dream'd a joy beyond his pleasure . . . . *Hen. VIII.* iii 1 134
Though they be long ere they are wooed, they are constant being won *Troi. and Cres.* iii 2 119
Let all constant men be Troiluses, all false women Cressids . . . iii 2 210
It is your former promise.—Sir, it is; And I am constant . *Coriolanus* i 1 243
Who resist Are mock'd for valiant ignorance, And perish constant fools iv 6 105
You keep a constant temper . . . . v 2 100
Cassius, be constant: Popilius Lena speaks not of our purposes *J. Cæsar* iii 1 22
I am constant as the northern star . . . . iii 1 60
I was constant Cimber should be banish'd, And constant do remain to keep him so . . . . iii 1 72
I am constant to my purposes . . . . *Hamlet* v 2 208
We have this hour a constant will to publish Our daughters' several dowers . . . . *Lear* i 1 44
Bring his constant pleasure . . . . v 1 4
Is of a constant, loving, noble nature . . . . . *Othello* ii 1 298
A sly and constant knave, Not to be shaked . . . . *Cymbeline* i 5 75
Even to vice They are not constant, but are changing still . . . ii 5 30
Which 'mulier' I divine Is this most constant wife . . . . v 5 449
Or when She would with rich and constant pen Vail to her mistress Dian . . . . *Pericles* iv Gower 28
Constantine. Helen, the mother of great Constantine, Nor yet Saint Philip's daughters, were like thee . . . . 1 *Hen. VI.* i 2 142
Constantinople. Go to Constantinople and take the Turk by the beard *Hen. V.* v 2 222
Constantly. I do constantly believe you . . . . *Meas. for Meas.* iv 1 21
The devil a puritan that he is, or any thing constantly, but a time-pleaser . . . . *T. Night* ii 3 160
I constantly do think—Or rather, call my thought a certain knowledge *Troi. and Cres.* iv 1 40
I am fresh of spirit and resolved To meet all perils very constantly *J. Cæsar* v 1 92
And fix'd his eyes upon you?—Most constantly . . . . *Hamlet* i 2 235

Constantly. Patiently and constantly thou hast stuck to the bare fortune of that beggar Posthumus — *Cymbeline* iii 5 119
Constant-qualified. More fair, virtuous, wise, chaste, constant-qualified — i 4 65
Constellation. I know thy constellation is right apt For this affair *T. Night* i 4 35
Constitution. Nothing in the world Could turn so much the constitution Of any constant man — *Mer. of Venice* iii 2 249
By the excellent constitution of thy leg — *T. Night* i 3 141
Constrain. I would your grace would constrain me to tell — *Much Ado* i 1 208
Constrains them weep and shake with fear and sorrow — *Coriolanus* v 3 100
Such a case as yours constrains a man to bow in the hams *Rom. and Jul.* ii 4 57
And constrains the garb Quite from his nature — *Lear* ii 2 103
Constrained. I shall be constrained in't to call thee knave, knight.—'Tis not the first time I have constrained one to call me knave *T. Night* ii 3 69
Constrain'd, As men drink potions — *2 Hen. IV.* i 1 196
Constrain'd to watch in darkness, rain and cold — *1 Hen. VI.* ii 1 7
Her spotless chastity, Inhuman traitors, you constrain'd and forced — *T. Andron.* v 2 178
None serve with him but constrained things Whose hearts are absent — *Macbeth* v 4 13
To come thus was I not constrain'd, but did On my free will *Ant. and Cleo.* iii 6 56
Therefore, he Does pity, as constrained blemishes, Not as deserved — iii 13 59
To excuse her keeping close, Whereto constrain'd by her infirmity *Cymb.* iii 5 47
Desired more than constrain'd — v 4 15
I am glad to be constrain'd to utter that Which torments me to conceal — v 5 141
Constraineth. Faintness constraineth me To measure out my length on this cold bed — *M. N. Dream* iii 2 428
Constraint. Better 'twere I met the ravin lion when he roar'd With sharp constraint of hunger — *All's Well* iii 2 121
I love thee By love's own sweet constraint — iv 2 16
I will confess what I know without constraint — iv 3 139
No further enemy to you Than the constraint of hospitable zeal *K. John* ii 1 244
I did suppose it should be on constraint; But, heaven be thank'd, it is but voluntary — v 1 28
Or else what follows?—Bloody constraint — *Hen. V.* ii 4 97
'Tis a good constraint of fortune it belches upon us — *Pericles* iii 2 55
Constringed in mass by the almighty sun — *Troi. and Cres.* v 2 173
Construction. She enlargeth her mirth so far that there is shrewd construction made of her — *Mer. Wives* ii 2 232
O illegitimate construction! I scorn that with my heels *Much Ado* iii 4 50
He shall find the letter: observe his construction of it — *T. Night* ii 3 190
Under your hard construction must I sit — iii 1 126
Only in The merciful construction of good women — *Hen. VIII.* Epil. 10
And my pretext to strike at him admits A good construction *Coriolanus* v 6 21
There's no art To find the mind's construction in the face — *Macbeth* i 4 12
Let him show His skill in the construction — *Cymbeline* v 5 433
Thou, Leonatus, art the lion's whelp; The fit and apt construction of thy name, Being Leo-natus, doth import so much — v 5 444
Construe. Since maids, in modesty, say 'no' to that Which they would have the profferer construe 'ay' — *T. G. of Ver.* i 2 56
I can construe the action of her familiar style — *Mer. Wives* i 3 50
Construe my speeches better, if you may — *L. L. Lost* v 2 341
Construe them.—'Hic ibat,' as I told you before, 'Simois,' I am Lucentio — *T. of Shrew* iii 1 30
Now let me see if I can construe it: 'Hic ibat Simois,' I know you not iii 1 41
I will construe to them whence you come — *T. Night* iii 1 63
Construe the times to their necessities — *2 Hen. IV.* iv 1 104
Nor construe any further my neglect, Than that poor Brutus, with himself at war, Forgets — *J. Cæsar* i 2 45
Men may construe things after their fashion, Clean from the purpose of the things themselves — i 3 34
All my engagements I will construe to thee — ii 1 307
His unbookish jealousy must construe Poor Cassio's smiles, gestures and light behaviour, Quite in the wrong — *Othello* iv 1 102
Consul. I warrant him consul.—Then our office may, During his power, go sleep — *Coriolanus* ii 1 238
I heard him swear, Were he to stand for consul, never would he Appear i' the market-place — ii 1 248
'Tis thought That Marcius shall be consul — ii 1 277
Desire The present consul, and last general In our well-found successes, to report — ii 2 47
He bestrid An o'er-press'd Roman and i' the consul's view Slew three opposers — ii 2 97
The senate, Coriolanus, are well pleased To make thee consul — ii 2 137
And to our noble consul Wish we all joy and honour — ii 2 156
If it may stand with the tune of your voices that I may be consul, I have here the customary gown — ii 3 92
Therefore, beseech you, I may be consul — ii 3 110
Your voices: Indeed, I would be consul — ii 3 138
Therefore let him be consul: the gods give him joy! — ii 3 141
God save thee, noble consul!—Worthy voices! — ii 3 144
And with his hat, thus waving it in scorn, 'I would be consul,' says he ii 3 176
They have chose a consul that will from them take Their liberties — ii 3 222
Made you against the grain To voice him consul — ii 3 242
They are worn, lord consul, so, That we shall hardly in our ages see Their banners wave again — iii 1 6
Why then should I be consul! — iii 1 50
You must inquire your way, Which you are out of, with a gentler spirit, Or never be so noble as a consul — iii 1 56
By Jove himself! It makes the consuls base — iii 1 108
Manifest treason.—This a consul? no.—The ædiles, ho! — iii 1 172
Marcius, Whom late you have named for consul — iii 1 196
As I do know the consul's worthiness, So can I name his faults — iii 1 278
Consul! what consul?—The consul Coriolanus.—He consul! — iii 1 279
Look, I am going: Commend me to my wife. I'll return consul — iii 2 135
What is the matter That being pass'd for consul with full voice, I am so dishonour'd that the very hour You take it off again? — iii 3 59
I have been consul, and can show for Rome Her enemies' marks upon me — iii 3 110
We should by this, to all our lamentation, If he had gone forth consul, found it so — iv 6 35
This Volumnia Is worth of consuls, senators, patricians, A city full — v 4 56
His stoutness When he did stand for consul, which he lost By lack of stooping — v 6 28
We here deliver, Subscribed by the consuls and patricians — v 6 82
Unless the bookish theoric, Wherein the toged consuls can propose As masterly as he — *Othello* i 1 25
Many of the consuls, raised and met, Are at the duke's already — i 2 43
Beaten from Modena, where thou slew'st Hirtius and Pansa, consuls — *Ant. and Cleo.* i 4 58
The Roman emperor's letters, Sent by a consul to me — *Cymbeline* iv 2 385

Consulship. How many stand for consulships? — *Coriolanus* ii 2 2
Well then, I pray, your price o' the consulship?—The price is to ask it kindly — ii 3 80
Consult. Let's consult together against this greasy knight *Mer. Wives* ii 1 111
Now part them again, lest they consult — *2 Hen. VI.* iv 7 140
Come, gentlemen, Let us consult upon to-morrow's business *Rich. III.* v 3 45
Then sit we down, and let us all consult — *T. Andron.* iv 2 132
Consulting. And, not consulting, broke Into a general prophecy *Hen. VIII.* i 1 91
Consume. Like cover'd fire, Consume away in sighs, waste inwardly — *Much Ado* iii 1 78
Where two raging fires meet together They do consume the thing that feeds their fury — *T. of Shrew* ii 1 134
Consumes itself to the very paring, and so dies with feeding — *All's Well* i 1 154
Nay, after that, consume away in rust — *K. John* iv 1 65
Break thou in pieces and consume to ashes! — *1 Hen. VI.* v 4 92
If he were putting to my house the brand That should consume it, I have not the face To say 'Beseech you, cease' — *Coriolanus* iv 6 116
I bring consuming sorrow to thine age.—Will it consume me? let me see it, then — *T. Andron.* iii 1 62
Like fire and powder, Which as they kiss consume — *Rom. and Jul.* ii 6 11
A plague consume you wicked caitiffs left! — *T. of Athens* v 4 71
Do not Consume your blood with sorrowing: you have A nurse of me — *Pericles* iv 1 24
Consumed. Not one word more of the consumed time — *All's Well* v 3 38
Take it hence And see it instantly consumed with fire — *W. Tale* ii 3 134
The rebels have consumed with fire Our town of Cicester — *Richard II.* v 6 2
He hath kept an evil diet long, And overmuch consumed his royal person — *Richard III.* i 1 140
Consumed In hot digestion of this cormorant war — *Troi. and Cres.* ii 2 5
O'erborne their way, consumed with fire, and took What lay before them — *Coriolanus* iv 6 78
Upon a pile of wood, Let's hew his limbs till they be clean consumed — *T. Andron.* i 1 129
Alas, my lord, Your wisdom is consumed in confidence — *J. Cæsar* ii 2 49
Consuming means, soon preys upon itself — *Richard II.* ii 1 39
Whiles thy consuming canker eats his falsehood — *1 Hen. VI.* ii 4 71
I bring consuming sorrow to thine age.—Will it consume me? *T. Andron.* iii 1 61
For each true word, a blister! and each false Be as a cauterizing to the root o' the tongue, Consuming it with speaking! — *T. of Athens* v 1 137
Consummate. Do you the office, friar; which consummate, Return him here again — *Meas. for Meas.* v 1 383
I do but stay till your marriage be consummate — *Much Ado* iii 2 2
This afternoon will post To consummate this business happily *K. John* v 7 95
There shall we consummate our spousal rites — *T. Andron.* i 1 337
Consummation. 'Tis a consummation Devoutly to be wish'd — *Hamlet* iii 1 63
Quiet consummation have; And renowned be thy grave! — *Cymbeline* iv 2 280
Consumption. I was told you were in a consumption — *Much Ado* v 4 97
I can get no remedy against this consumption of the purse — *2 Hen. IV.* i 2 264
Consumptions sow In hollow bones of man; strike their sharp shins — *T. of Athens* iv 3 151
Consumption catch thee! — iv 3 201
There's the sulphurous pit, Burning, scalding, stench, consumption *Lear* iv 6 131
Contagion. Strumpeted by thy contagion — *Com. of Errors* ii 2 146
To hear by the nose, it is dulcet in contagion — *T. Night* ii 3 59
All the contagion of the south light on you! — *Coriolanus* i 4 30
Lady, come from that nest Of death, contagion, and unnatural sleep — *Rom. and Jul.* v 3 152
To dare the vile contagion of the night — *J. Cæsar* ii 1 265
When churchyards yawn and hell itself breathes out Contagion *Hamlet* iii 2 408
I'll touch my point With this contagion — iv 7 148
Contagious. Suck'd up from the sea Contagious fogs — *M. N. Dream* ii 1 90
A contagious breath.—Very sweet and contagious, i' faith — *T. Night* ii 3 56
This night, whose black contagious breath Already smokes about the burning crest Of the old, feeble and day-wearied sun — *K. John* v 4 33
Herein will I imitate the sun, Who doth permit the base contagious clouds To smother up his beauty from the world — *1 Hen. IV.* i 2 222
In base durance and contagious prison — *2 Hen. IV.* v 5 36
The filthy and contagious clouds Of heady murder — *Hen. V.* iii 3 31
A most contagious treason come to light — iv 8 22
And from their misty jaws Breathe foul contagious darkness in the air — *2 Hen. VI.* iv 1 7
If we suffer, Out of our easiness and childish pity To one man's honour, this contagious sickness, Farewell all physic — *Hen. VIII.* v 3 26
In the morn and liquid dew of youth Contagious blastments are most imminent — *Hamlet* i 3 42
Contain. The academes, That show, contain and nourish all the world — *L. L. Lost* iv 3 353
The one of them contains my picture, prince — *Mer. of Venice* ii 7 11
One of these three contains her heavenly picture. Is't like that lead contains her? — ii 7 48
And others, when the bagpipe sings i' the nose, Cannot contain their urine — iv 1 50
Her worthiness that gave the ring, Or your own honour to contain the ring — v 1 201
We can contain ourselves, Were he the veriest antic in the world — *T. of Shrew* Ind. 1 100
This little abstract doth contain that large Which died in Geffrey *K. John* ii 1 101
Why, it contains no king?—Yes, my good lord, It doth contain a king — *Richard II.* iii 3 24
When that this body did contain a spirit, A kingdom for it was too small a bound — *1 Hen. IV.* v 4 89
This schedule, For this contains our general grievances — *2 Hen. IV.* iv 1 169
The manner and true order of the fight This packet, please it you, contains at large — iv 4 101
Leaving his body as a paradise, To envelope and contain celestial spirits — *Hen. V.* i 1 31
Your roof were not sufficient to contain't — *1 Hen. VI.* ii 3 56
Is that the worst this letter doth contain? — iv 1 66
A jewel, lock'd into the wofull'st cask That ever did contain a thing of worth — *2 Hen. VI.* iii 2 410
May I be bold to ask what that contains? — *Hen. VIII.* iv 1 13
O, contain yourself; Your passion draws ears hither — *Troi. and Cres.* v 2 180
Thou hast made my heart Too great for what contains it — *Coriolanus* v 6 104
Nay, good my lord,— Contain thyself, good friend — *T. of Athens* ii 2 26
If, after two days' shine, Athens contain thee, Attend our weightier judgement — iii 5 101
Open this purse, and take What it contains — *Lear* iii 1 46
Your Italy contains none so accomplished a courtier — *Cymbeline* i 4 103
Contained. If you choose that wherein I am contain'd, Straight shall our nuptial rites be solemnized — *Mer. of Venice* ii 9 5

Contained. Wrapp'd in a paper, which contain'd the name Of her that threw it . . . . . *All's Well* v 3 94
Let what is here contain'd relish of love, Of my lord's health *Cymbeline* iii 2 30
Containing. Writ in my cousin's hand, stolen from her pocket, Containing her affection unto Benedick . . . *Much Ado* v 4 90
Consume away in rust, But for containing fire to harm mine eye *K. John* iv 1 66
One heinous article, Containing the deposing of a king . *Richard II.* iv 1 234
Was ever book containing such vile matter So fairly bound? *R. and J.* iii 2 83
Last, and as much containing as all these, Her brother is in secret come *Hamlet* iv 5 87
This label on my bosom; whose containing Is so from sense in hardness, that I can Make no collection of it . . . *Cymbeline* v 5 430
Contaminate. And that this body, consecrate to thee, By ruffian lust should be contaminate! . . . *Com. of Errors* ii 2 135
Shall we now Contaminate our fingers with base bribes? *J. Cæsar* iv 3 24
Contaminated. A contaminated stale . . . . . *Much Ado* ii 2 25
Whilst by a slave, no gentler than my dog, His fairest daughter is contaminated . . . *Hen. V.* iv 5 16
Contaminated, base And misbegotten blood I spill of thine 1 *Hen. VI.* iv 6 21
For every scruple Of her contaminated carrion weight, A Trojan hath been slain . . . *Troi. and Cres.* iv 1 71
Strangle her in her bed, even the bed she hath contaminated *Othello* iv 1 221
Contemn. He will require them, As if he did contemn what he requested Should be in them to give . . . *Coriolanus* ii 2 161
That nature, which contemns it origin, Cannot be border'd certain in itself . . . *Lear* iv 2 32
Apes and monkeys 'Twixt two such shes would chatter this way and Contemn with mows the other . . . *Cymbeline* i 6 41
Contemned. Write loyal cantons of contemned love . *T. Night* i 5 289
That such a sore of time Should seek a plaster by contemn'd revolt *K. John* v 2 13
Better thus, and known to be contemn'd, Than still contemn'd and flatter'd . . . *Lear* iv 1 1
Contemnedest. Such as basest and contemned'st wretches For pilferings and most common trespasses Are punish'd with . ii 2 150
Contemning. I have done penance for contemning Love *T. G. of Ver.* ii 4 129
Look'd not lovelier Than Hector's forehead when it spit forth blood At Grecian sword, contemning . . . *Coriolanus* i 3 46
Contemning Rome, he has done all this, and more, In Alexandria *Ant. and Cleo.* iii 6 1
Contemplate. So many hours must I contemplate . . 3 *Hen. VI.* ii 5 33
Contemplation. In leaden contemplation . . . . *L. L. Lost* iv 3 321
Breathed a secret vow To live in prayer and contemplation *Mer. of Ven.* iii 4 28
Did you leave him in this contemplation? . . *As Y. Like It* ii 1 64
The sundry contemplation of my travels . . . . iv 1 18
Contemplation makes a rare turkey-cock of him . *T. Night* ii 5 35
And part this body and my soul With contemplation and devout desires *K. John* v 4 48
Obscured his contemplation Under the veil of wildness . *Hen. V.* i 1 63
'Tis hard to draw them thence, So sweet is zealous contemplation *Richard III.* iii 7 94
His contemplation were above the earth, And fix'd on spiritual object *Hen. VIII.* iii 2 131
Thou wouldst not have slipped out of my contemplation *Troi. and Cres.* ii 3 29
Who doth molest my contemplation? . . . *T. Andron.* v 2 9
What serious contemplation are you in? . . . . *Lear* i 2 151
He hath devoted and given up himself to the contemplation, mark, and denotement of her parts and graces . . . . *Othello* ii 3 322
Contemplative. Still and contemplative in living art . *L. L. Lost* i 1 14
I know this letter will make a contemplative idiot of him . *T. Night* ii 5 23
Contempt. In revenge of my contempt of love, Love hath chased sleep from my enthralled eyes . . . *T. G. of Ver.* ii 4 133
I hope, upon familiarity will grow more contempt . *Mer. Wives* i 1 258
But wrong not that wrong with a more contempt . *Com. of Errors* ii 2 174
Contempt, farewell! and maiden pride, adieu! . . *Much Ado* iii 1 109
The contempts thereof are as touching me . . *L. L. Lost* i 1 191
Contempt will kill the speaker's heart, And quite divorce his memory from his part . . . . v 2 149
Contempt nor bitterness Were in his pride or sharpness . *All's Well* i 2 36
What place make you special, when you put off that with such contempt? ii 2 6
Check thy contempt: Obey our will, which travails in thy good . ii 3 164
By the misprising of a maid too virtuous For the contempt of empire . iii 2 34
Contempt his scornful perspective did lend me . . . v 3 48
And let your fervour, like my master's, be Placed in contempt! *T. Night* i 5 307
If you prized my lady's favour at any thing more than contempt . ii 3 131
It is, in contempt of question, her hand . . . . ii 5 97
It cannot but turn him into a notable contempt . . . ii 5 224
O, what a deal of scorn looks beautiful In the contempt and anger of his lip! iii 1 158
Contempt and clamour Will be my knell . . . *W. Tale* i 2 189
Wafting his eyes to the contrary and falling A lip of much contempt . i 2 373
Whiles we, God's wrathful agent, do correct Their proud contempt that beats His peace to heaven . . . . . *K. John* ii 1 88
With much more contempt men's eyes Did scowl on gentle Richard *Richard II.* v 2 27
Revenge the jeering and disdain'd contempt Of this proud king 1 *Hen. IV.* i 3 183
How show'd his tasking? seem'd it in contempt? . . . v 2 51
His peers to servitude, His subjects to oppression and contempt *Hen. V.* ii 2 172
Contempt, And any thing that may not misbecome The mighty sender, doth he prize you at . . . . . ii 4 117
With a baser man of arms by far Once in contempt they would have barter'd me . . . . . 1 *Hen. VI.* i 4 31
Who in contempt shall hiss at thee again . . . 2 *Hen. VI.* iv 1 78
I'll rend thy bear And tread it under foot with all contempt . v 1 209
Teach not thy lips such scorn, for they were made For kissing, lady, not for such contempt . . . . *Richard III.* i 2 173
Myself disgraced, and the nobility Held in contempt . . . i 3 80
Rewards he my true service With such deep contempt? . . iv 2 124
Let the foul'st contempt Shut door upon me . . *Hen. VIII.* ii 4 42
He did solicit you in free contempt When he did need your loves, and do you think That his contempt shall not be bruising to you? *Coriolanus* ii 3 208
Forget not With what contempt he wore the humble weed . ii 3 229
And, for the extent Of egal justice, used in such contempt *T. Andron.* iv 4 4
Rather comfort his distressed plight Than prosecute the meanest or the best For these contempts . . . . . iv 4 34
Whose high exploits and honourable deeds Ingrateful Rome requites with foul contempt . . . . . . v 1 12
Contempt and beggary hangs upon thy back . . *Rom. and Jul.* v 1 71
With his disease of all-shunn'd poverty, Walks, like contempt, alone *T. of Athens* iv 2 15
Who would not wish to be from wealth exempt, Since riches point to misery and contempt? . . . . . . iv 2 32
Contempt. Not nature, To whom all sores lay siege, can bear great fortune, But by contempt of nature . . . *T. of Athens* iv 3 8
The senator shall bear contempt hereditary, The beggar native honour . iv 3 10
Turn all her mother's pains and benefits To laughter and contempt *Lear* i 4 309
The basest and most poorest shape That ever penury, in contempt of man, Brought near to beast . . . . . . ii 3 8
What our contempt doth often hurl from us, We wish it ours again *Ant. and Cleo.* i 2 127
And make me put into contempt the suits Of princely fellows *Cymbeline* iii 4 92
How Can her contempt be answer'd? . . . . iii 5 42
There shall she see my valour, which will then be a torment to her contempt . . . . iii 5 144
Nature hath meal and bran, contempt and grace . . . iv 2 27
Contemptible. The man, as you know all, hath a contemptible spirit *Much Ado* ii 3 187
Heaven and our Lady gracious hath it pleased To shine on my contemptible estate . . . . . . 1 *Hen. VI.* i 2 75
Contemptuous. The flinty ribs of this contemptuous city *K. John* ii 1 384
Contemptuous base-born callet as she is . . . 2 *Hen. VI.* i 3 86
Contemptuously. Trampling contemptuously on thy disdain *T. G. of Ver.* i 2 112
Contend. Now kiss, embrace, contend, do what you will . i 2 129
Thy blood and virtue Contend for empire in thee! *All's Well* i 1 72
For never two such kingdoms did contend Without much fall of blood *Hen. V.* i 2 24
And with the southern clouds contend in tears 2 *Hen. VI.* iii 2 384
When dying clouds contend with growing light . . 3 *Hen. VI.* ii 5 2
If you contend, a thousand lives must wither . . . ii 5 102
I would my arms could match thee in contention, As they contend with thee in courtesy . . . . *Troi. and Cres.* iv 5 206
As ever in ambitious strength I did Contend against thy valour *Coriol.* iv 5 119
His wonders and his praises do contend Which should be thine or his *Macbeth* i 3 92
Were poor and single business to contend Against those honours . i 6 16
That death and nature do contend about them, Whether they live or die ii 2 7
Mad as the sea and wind, when both contend Which is the mightier *Hamlet* iv 1 7
If we contend, Out of our question wipe him . *Ant. and Cleo.* ii 2 80
The next time I do fight, I'll make death love me; for I will contend Even with his pestilent scythe . . . . . iii 13 193
'Gainst whom I am too little to contend . . . *Pericles* i 2 17
Contend not, sir; for we are gentlemen . . . . ii 3 24
This Philoten contends in skill With absolute Marina . iv Gower 30
Contended. One that, above all other strifes, contended especially to know himself . . . . *Meas. for Meas.* iii 2 246
Contending. Like one of two contending in a prize . *Mer. of Venice* iii 2 142
What is she but a foul contending rebel? . . *T. of Shrew* v 2 159
The contending kingdoms Of France and England . . *Hen. V.* v 2 377
Broke their stalls, flung out, Contending 'gainst obedience *Macbeth* ii 4 17
Where's the king?—Contending with the fretful element *Lear* iii 1 4
Content. How does your content Tender your own good fortune? *Tempest* ii 1 269
For the like loss I have her sovereign aid And rest myself content v 1 144
At least bring forth a wonder, to content ye As much as me my dukedom v 1 170
A woman sometimes scorns what best contents her *T. G of Ver.* iii 1 93
We parley to you: Are you content to be our general? . . iv 1 61
Good master, be content.—Wherefore shall I be content-a? . *Mer. Wives* i 4 73
I have been content, sir, you should lay my countenance to pawn . ii 2 4
You shall hear how things go; and, I warrant, to your content . iv 5 127
How will you do to content this substitute? . . *Meas. for Meas.* iii 1 192
The image of it gives me content already . . . . iii 1 270
But yet I will be content to be a lawful hangman . . iv 2 17
I commend you to your own content.—He that commends me to mine own content Commends me to the thing I cannot get *Com. of Errors* i 2 32
Where zeal strives to content, and the contents Dies in the zeal of that which it presents . . . . . . *L. L. Lost* v 2 518
Hermia still loves you: then be content.—Content with Hermia! No *M. N. Dream* ii 2 110
We do not come as minding to content you . . . v 1 113
Content, i' faith: I'll seal to such a bond. . . *Mer. of Venice* i 3 153
I wish your ladyship all heart's content . . . . iii 4 42
Now go we in content To liberty and not to banishment. *As Y. Like It* i 3 139
Ere we have thy youthful wages spent, We'll light upon some settled low content . . . . ii 3 68
When I was at home, I was in a better place: but travellers must be content . . . . ii 4 18
He that wants money, means and content is without three good friends iii 2 26
Glad of other men's good, content with my harm . . . iii 2 79
Doth my simple feature content you? . . . . . iii 3 3
I will content you, if what pleases you contents you . v 2 126
Content you in my discontent . . . . *T. of Shrew* i 1 80
Gentlemen, content ye; I am resolved . . . . i 1 90
This contents: The rest will comfort, for thy counsel's sound . i 1 168
I am content to be Lucentio, Because so well I love Lucentio . i 1 221
Let me entreat you.—I am content.—Are you content to stay?—I am content you shall entreat me stay . . . . . iii 2 202
Is the adder better than the eel, Because his painted skin contents the eye? . . . . iv 3 180
I am content, in a good father's care, To have him match'd . iv 4 31
We will content you, go to. . . . . . . v 1 138
A hundred then.—Content.—A match! 'tis done . . v 2 74
The care I have had to even your content, I wish might be found in the calendar of my past endeavours . . . *All's Well* i 3 4
The general is content to spare thee yet . . . . iv 1 89
How does your ladyship like it?—With very much content . iv 5 83
All is well ended, if this suit be won, That you express content . Epil. 3
Would they else be content to die? . . . . *W. Tale* i 1 46
More it would content me To have her honour true than your suspicion ii 1 159
Your gallery Have we pass'd through, not without much content . v 3 11
What you can make her do, I am content to look on: what to speak, I am content to hear . . . . v 3 92
How may we content This widow lady? . . . *K. John* ii 1 547
Madam, be content.—If thou, that bid'st me be content wert grim, . . . I would not care, I then would be content . . . iii 1 42
Pardon me, if you please; if not, I, pleased Not to be pardon'd, am content withal . . . . *Richard II.* ii 1 188
Heaven hath a hand in these events, To whose high will we bound our calm contents . . . . v 2 38
Thoughts tending to content flatter themselves That they are not the first of fortune's slaves . . . . v 5 23
Which, for sport sake are content to do the profession some grace 1 *Hen. IV.* ii 1 78
Will this content you, Kate?—It must of force . . . ii 3 120
Shall we have a play extempore?—Content . . . . ii 4 310

Content. Examine me upon the particulars of my life.—Shall I? content 1 *Hen. IV.* ii 4 415
Yea, or to-night.—Content.—To-night, say I . . . . . iv 3 14
I could be well content To entertain the lag-end of my life With quiet hours . . . . v 1 23
I am content that he shall take the odds . . . . . . v 1 97
Il est content de vous donner la liberté, le franchisement . *Hen. V.* iv 4 55
It shall please him, Kate.—Den it sall also content me . . . v 2 270
How say you, my lord? are you not content?—Content, my liege! yes 1 *Hen. VI.* iv 1 70
I shall be well content with any choice Tends to God's glory . . . v 1 26
How say you, madam, are ye so content?—An if my father please, I am content . . . . v 3 126
I could be well content To be mine own attorney in this case . . v 3 165
She is content to be at your command . . . . . . v 5 19
Such is the fulness of my heart's content . . . . . 2 *Hen. VI.* i 1 35
So will I In England work your grace's full content . . . . i 3 70
These words content me much . . . . iii 2 26
I am content he shall reign; but I'll be protector over him . . . iv 2 167
Was ever king that joy'd an earthly throne, And could command no more content than I? . . . . iv 9 2
My crown is called content: A crown it is that seldom kings enjoy 3 *Hen. VI.* iii 1 64
If you be a king crown'd with content, Your crown content and you must be contented To go along with us . . . . . . iii 1 66
And murder whiles I smile, And cry 'Content' to that which grieves my heart . . . . iii 2 183
Why, then, though loath, yet must I be content . . . . . iv 6 48
I challenge nothing but my dukedom, As being well content with that alone . . . . iv 7 24
God hold it, to your honour's good content! . . . . *Richard III.* iii 2 107
Come the next Sabbath, and I will content you . . . . . iii 2 113
And all the ruins of distressful times Repair'd with double riches of content . . . . iv 4 319
This night he dedicates To fair content and you . . . . *Hen. VIII.* i 4 3
'Tis better to be lowly born, And range with humble livers in content . ii 3 20
Our content Is our best having . . . . ii 3 22
Almost forgot my prayers to content him? And am I thus rewarded? iii 1 132
Then though my heart's content firm love doth bear, Nothing of that shall from mine eyes appear . . . . . . *Troi. and Cres.* i 2 320
Could be content to give him good report for't, but that he pays himself with being proud . . . . *Coriolanus* i 1 32
Soft-conscienced men can be content to say it was for his country . i 1 38
I must be content to bear with those that say you are reverend grave men ii 1 65
Rewards His deeds with doing them, and is content To spend the time to end it . . . . ii 2 132
I'll direct you how you shall go by him.—Content, content . . . ii 3 53
And are content To suffer lawful censure for such faults As shall be proved . . . . iii 3 45
If one arm's embracement will content thee, I will embrace thee in it *T. Andron.* v 2 68
Examine every married lineament And see how one another lends content *Rom. and Jul.* i 3 84
I am content, so thou wilt have it so . . . . iii 5 18
Best state, contentless, Hath a distracted and most wretched being, Worse than the worst, content . . . . . . *T. of Athens* iv 3 247
Peace and content be here! . . . . v 1 130
They could be content To visit other places . . . . . *J. Cæsar* v 1 8
Shut up In measureless content . . . . *Macbeth* ii 1 17
Nought's had, all's spent, Where our desire is got without content . iii 2 5
It doth much content me To hear him so inclined . . . *Hamlet* iii 1 24
Be you content to lend your patience to us, And we shall jointly labour with your soul To give it due content . . . . . . iv 5 210
Let your study Be to content your lord . . . . . . *Lear* i 1 280
Those that mingle reason with your passion Must be content to think you old . . . . ii 4 238
Must make content with his fortunes fit, For the rain it raineth every day iii 2 76
Therefore be content to slubber the gloss of your new fortunes . *Othello* i 3 227
It gives me wonder great as my content To see you here before me . ii 1 185
My soul hath her content so absolute That not another comfort like to this Succeeds in unknown fate . . . . ii 1 193
I cannot speak enough of this content; It stops me here . . . ii 1 198
Nothing can or shall content my soul Till I am even'd with him . . ii 1 307
Masters, play here; I will content your pains; Something that's brief . iii 1 1
Poor and content is rich and rich enough, But riches fineless is as poor as winter To him that ever fears he shall be poor . . . . iii 3 172
O, now, for ever Farewell the tranquil mind! farewell content! . . iii 3 348
So shall I clothe me in a forced content . . . . . . iii 4 120
Be you not troubled with the time, which drives O'er your content these strong necessities . . . . *Ant. and Cleo.* iii 6 83
It shall content me best: be gentle to her . . . . . . v 2 68
Let what is here contain'd relish of love, Of my lord's health, of his content, yet not That we two are asunder; . . . of his content, All but in that! . . . . *Cymbeline* iii 2 31
Who but of late, earth, sea, and air, Were all too little to content and please . . . . *Pericles* i 4 35
Doth give me A more content in course of true delight Than to be thirsty after tottering honour . . . . iii 2 39
The unborn event I do commend to your content . . . . iv Gower 46
The gods for murder seemed so content To punish them . . . v 3 Gower 98
Be content *Mer. Wives* i 4; *Meas. for Meas.* ii 2; *Mer. of Venice* iii 2; *T. Night* v 1; *K. John* iii 1; *Richard II.* v 2; *Coriolanus* iii 2; *J. Cæsar* iv 2; *Othello* iii 3; iv 2; *Cymbeline* v 4
Be you content . . . . *Meas. for Meas.* ii 2 79; *J. Cæsar* i 3 142
Content thee (thyself, you, yourself) *Much Ado* v 1; *T. of Shrew* i 1; ii 1; iii 2; 3 *Hen. VI.* i 1; *Troi. and Cres.* ii 2; *T. Andron.* i 1; *Rom. and Jul.* i 5; *Othello* i 1; ii 3; *Cymbeline* i 5
I am content *Mer. of Venice* iv 1; *T. of Shrew* iii 2; *Hen. V.* v 2; 2 *Hen. VI.* iii 1; 3 *Hen. VI.* i 1; *Coriolanus* iii 3; *T. Andron.* v. 3; *Rom. and Jul.* iii 5
Contenta. Si fortuna me tormenta, spero contenta . . 2 *Hen. IV.* v 5 102
Contented. Be contented: you wrong yourself too much *Mer. Wives* iii 3 177
Art thou contented, Jew? what dost thou say?—I am content *Mer. of Venice* iv 1 393
Thither will I invite the duke and all's contented followers *As Y. Like It* v 2 17
The meat was well, if you were so contented . . . *T. of Shrew* iv 1 172
I will with you, if you be so contented, Forswear Bianca . . iv 2 25
I may, and will, if she be so contented . . . . . . iv 4 106
If men could be contented to be what they are, there were no fear in marriage . . . . *All's Well* i 3 54
Contented. Must he be deposed? The king shall be contented *Richard II.* iii 3 145
Are you contented to resign the crown?—Ay, no; no, ay . . . iv 1 200
In humours like the people of this world, For no thought is contented . v 5 11
Thus play I in one person many people, And none contented . . v 5 32
I could be well contented to be there, in respect of the love I bear your house . . . . 1 *Hen. IV.* ii 3 2
He could be contented: why is he not, then? . . . . . ii 3 3
If the deed were ill, Be you contented . . . . . 2 *Hen. IV.* v 2 84
Methinks I could not die any where so contented as in the king's company . . . . *Hen. V.* iv 1 132
Not contented that he lopp'd the branch . . . . . 3 *Hen. VI.* ii 6 47
Your crown content and you must be contented To go along with us . iii 1 67
Nor how to be contented with one wife . . . . . . iv 3 37
From that contented hap which I enjoy'd . . . . *Richard III.* i 3 84
We are contented To wear our mortal state to come with her *Hen. VIII.* ii 4 227
You must take Your patience to you, and be well contented . . v 1 105
We are contented Cæsar shall Have all true rites . . . *J. Cæsar* iii 1 240
Then, if we lose this battle, You are contented to be led in triumph Thorough the streets of Rome? . . . . v 1 109
Meet i' the hall together.—Well contented . . . . *Macbeth* ii 3 140
Prithee, nuncle, be contented; 'tis a naughty night to swim in . *Lear* iii 4 115
Contenteth. This small inheritance my father left me Contenteth me 2 *Hen. VI.* iv 10 21
Contention. In the very heat And pride of their contention 1 *Hen. IV.* i 1 60
Contention, like a horse Full of high feeding, madly hath broke loose 2 *Hen. IV.* i 1 9
Let this world no longer be a stage To feed contention in a lingering act i 1 156
It was in a place where I could not breed no contention with him *Hen. V.* v 1 11
No quarrel, but a slight contention . . . . . 3 *Hen. VI.* i 2 6
But when contention and occasion meet, By Jove, I'll play the hunter for thy life . . . . *Troi. and Cres.* iv 1 16
I would my arms could match thee in contention, As they contend with thee in courtesy . . . . iv 5 205
The great contention of the sea and skies Parted our fellowship *Othello* ii 1 92
'Twas a contention in public, which may, without contradiction, suffer the report . . . . *Cymbeline* i 4 58
Contentious. His bold head 'Bove the contentious waves he kept *Tempest* ii 1 118
Thou think'st 'tis much that this contentious storm Invades us to the skin *Lear* iii 4 6
Contentless. Best state, contentless, Hath a distracted and most wretched being, Worse than the worst, content . . . *T. of Athens* iv 3 245
Contento. Si fortune me tormente, sperato me contento . 2 *Hen. IV.* ii 4 195
Contents. Kiss the book: I will furnish it anon with new contents *Tempest* ii 2 146
Say, from whom?—That the contents will show . . *T. G. of Ver.* i 2 36
I have a letter from her Of such contents as you will wonder at *Mer. Wives* iv 6 13
The contents of this is the return of the duke . . *Meas. for Meas.* iv 2 211
Letters . . . whose contents Shall witness to him I am near at home iv 3 98
Under pardon, sir, what are the contents? . . . *L. L. Lost* iv 2 103
And the contents Dies in the zeal of that which it presents . . v 2 518
There are some shrewd contents in yon same paper . *Mer. of Venice* iii 2 246
No, I protest, I know not the contents . . . *As Y. Like It* iv 3 21
If truth holds true contents . . . . v 4 136
And for the contents' sake are sorry for our pains . . *All's Well* iii 2 66
When the oracle, Thus by Apollo's great divine seal'd up, Shall the contents discover, something rare . . . . . . *W. Tale* iii 1 20
These are the whole contents . . . . *Hen. VIII.* iv 2 154
On the view and knowing of these contents . . . . *Hamlet* v 2 44
The contents, as in part I understand them, are to blame . . *Lear* i 2 43
It is his hand, my lord; but I hope his heart is not in the contents . i 2 73
On whose contents, They summon'd up their meiny, straight took horse ii 4 34
The arras; figures, Why, such and such; and the contents o' the story *Cymbeline* ii 2 27
Contest. And do contest As hotly and as nobly with thy love As ever in ambitious strength I did Contend against thy valour *Coriolanus* iv 5 116
Contestation. Their contestation Was theme for you, you were the word of war . . . . *Ant. and Cleo.* ii 2 43
Continence. The imperial seat, to virtue consecrate, To justice, continence and nobility . . . . *T. Andron.* i 1 15
Continency. This ungenitured agent will unpeople the province with continency . . . . *Meas. for Meas.* iii 2 185
Where is he?—In her chamber, making a sermon of continency to her *T. of Shrew* iv 1 186
Continent. Contrary to thy established proclaimed edict and continent canon . . . . *L. L. Lost* i 1 262
Shall I teach you to know?—Ay, my continent of beauty . . iv 1 111
Which falling in the land Have every pelting river made so proud That they have overborne their continents . . . . *M. N. Dream* ii 1 92
Here's the scroll, The continent and summary of my fortune *Mer. of Venice* iii 2 131
As doth that orbed continent the fire That severs day from night *T. Night* v 1 278
My past life Hath been as continent, as chaste, as true, As I am now unhappy . . . . *W. Tale* iii 2 35
Gelding the opposed continent as much As on the other side it takes from you . . . . 1 *Hen. IV.* iii 1 110
Why, thou globe of sinful continents, what a life dost thou lead 2 *Hen. IV.* ii 4 309
And the continent, Weary of solid firmness, melt itself Into the sea! . iii 1 47
My desire All continent impediments would o'erbear That did oppose my will . . . . *Macbeth* iv 3 64
Which is not tomb enough and continent To hide the slain . *Hamlet* iv 4 64
You shall find in him the continent of what part a gentleman would see v 2 115
Have a continent forbearance till the speed of his rage goes slower *Lear* i 2 182
Close pent-up guilts, Rive your concealing continents . . . iii 2 58
Heart, once be stronger than thy continent, Crack thy frail case! *Ant. and Cleo.* iv 14 40
Continual. Dwelling in a continual 'larum of jealousy . *Mer. Wives* iii 5 73
As subject to heat as butter; a man of continual dissolution and thaw iii 5 118
Small have continual plodders ever won . . . . . *L. L. Lost* i 1 86
Upon my tongues continual slanders ride . . . . 2 *Hen. IV.* Ind. 6
Poins, and other his continual followers . . . . . . iv 4 53
To keep Prince Harry in continual laughter the wearing out of six fashions v 1 88
Setting endeavour in continual motion . . . . . . *Hen. V.* i 2 185
For what is wedlock forced but a hell, An age of discord and continual strife? . . . . 1 *Hen. VI.* v 5 63
Continual meditations, tears, and sorrows . . . . *Hen. VIII.* iv 2 28
Then must my earth with her continual tears Become a deluge *T. Andron.* iii 1 229
I have been in continual practice; I shall win at the odds . *Hamlet* v 2 221
They with continual action are even as good as rotten . . *Pericles* iv 2 8
Continually. They pray continually to their saint, the commonwealth 1 *Hen. IV.* ii 1 88
Thy mother, Who prays continually for Richmond's good *Richard III.* v 3 84
She has light by her continually; 'tis her command . . *Macbeth* v 1 27

Continuance. Honour, riches, marriage-blessing, Long continuance, and increasing . . . . *Tempest* iv 1 107
Hath yet in her the continuance of her first affection *Meas. for Meas.* iii 1 249
A bawd of eleven years' continuance . . . . iii 2 208
A more swelling port Than my faint means would grant continuance *Mer. of Venice* i 1 125
You either fear his humour or my negligence, that you call in question the continuance of his love . . . . *T. Night* i 4 6
Fierce extremes In their continuance will not feel themselves *K. John* v 7 14
To pry Into his title, the which we find Too indirect for long continuance *1 Hen. IV.* iv 3 105
Cloy'd With long continuance in a settled place . . . *1 Hen. VI.* ii 5 106
And the continuance of their parents' rage . . *Rom. and Jul.* Prol. 10
Continuantly. A' comes continuantly to Pie-corner . *2 Hen. IV.* ii 1 28
Continuate. A most incomparable man, breathed, as it were, To an untirable and continuate goodness . . . . *T. of Athens* i 1 11
I shall, in a more continuate time, Strike off this score of absence *Othello* iii 4 178
Continue. So you may continue and laugh at nothing still . *Tempest* ii 1 178
You would lift the moon out of her sphere, if she would continue in it five weeks without changing . . . . ii 1 184
She shall not long continue love to him . . . *T. G. of Ver.* iii 2 48
Let him continue in his courses till thou knowest what they are *Meas. for Meas.* ii 1 196
Thou art to continue now, thou varlet; thou art to continue . . . ii 1 200
And how shall we continue Claudio? . . . . iv 3 88
Continue then, And I will have you and that fault withal . *L. L. Lost* v 2 875
Glad that you thus continue your resolve To suck the sweets of sweet philosophy . . . . *T. of Shrew* i 1 27
Since we are stepp'd thus far in, I will continue that I broach'd in jest i 2 84
Have fought with equal fortune and continue A braving war *All's Well* i 2 2
I put you to The use of your own virtues, for the which I shall continue thankful . . . . v 1 17
If the duke continue these favours towards you . . . *T. Night* i 4 1
The heavens continue their loves! . . . . . . *W. Tale* i 1 35
If you first sinn'd with us and that with us You did continue fault . i 2 85
Whose foundation Is piled upon his faith and will continue The standing of his body . . . . i 2 430
And then we shall be blest To do your pleasure and continue friends *K. John* iii 1 252
If you be not too much cloyed with fat meat, our humble author will continue the story . . . . *2 Hen. IV.* Epil. 29
As we hither came in peace, So let us still continue peace and love *1 Hen. VI.* iv 1 161
Continue still in this so good a mind . . . . *2 Hen. VI.* iv 9 17
You peers, continue this united league . . . . *Richard III.* ii 1 2
I would not be so sick though for his place: But this cannot continue *Hen. VIII.* ii 2 84
What friend of mine That had to him derived your anger, did I Continue in my liking? . . . . ii 4 33
May he continue Long in his highness' favour! . . . . . iii 2 395
In this borrow'd likeness of shrunk death Thou shalt continue two and forty hours . . . . *Rom. and Jul.* iv 1 105
Takes no account How things go from him, nor resumes no care Of what is to continue . . . . . . *T. of Athens* ii 2 5
We love him highly, And shall continue our graces towards him *Macbeth* i 6 30
I have known her continue in this a quarter of an hour . . v 1 34
It cannot be that Desdemona should long continue her love to the Moor *Othello* i 3 348
Do but go after, And mark how he continues . . . . . . iv 1 292
Your emperor Continues still a Jove . . . . *Ant. and Cleo.* iv 6 29
Return he cannot, nor Continue where he is . . . . *Cymbeline* i 5 54
Continues well my lord? His health, beseech you?—Well, madam . i 6 56
And will continue fast to your affection, Still close as sure . . i 6 138
I hope you know that we Must not continue friends . . . . ii 4 49
Continued. I thought, by your readiness in the office, you had continued in it some time . . . . . . *Meas. for Meas.* ii 1 276
More than three hours the fight continued . . . *1 Hen. VI.* i 1 120
How youngly he began to serve his country, How long continued *Coriol.* ii 3 245
I would he had continued to his country As he began . . . iv 2 30
And at first meeting loved; Continued so, until we thought he died *Cymb.* v 5 380
Continuer. I would my horse had the speed of your tongue, and so good a continuer . . . . *Much Ado* i 1 143
Continuing. Extremity of weather continuing . . . . *W. Tale* v 2 129
Contract, succession, Bourn, bound of land, tilth, vineyard, none *Tempest* ii 1 151
No sweet aspersion shall the heavens let fall To make this contract grow iv 1 19
A contract of true love to celebrate; And some donation freely to estate . . . . iv 1 84
Come, temperate nymphs, and help to celebrate A contract of true love iv 1 133
Upon a true contract I got possession of Julietta's bed . *Meas. for Meas.* i 2 149
Between which time of the contract and limit of the solemnity . . iii 1 223
This is the hand which, with a vow'd contract, Was fast belock'd in thine . . . . v 1 209
He trots hard with a young maid between the contract of her marriage and the day it is solemnized . . . . . . *As Y. Like It* iii 2 332
Good fortune and the favour of the king Smile upon this contract *All's Well* ii 3 185
A contract of eternal bond of love, Confirm'd by mutual joinder of your hands . . . . *T. Night* v 1 159
But, come on, Contract us 'fore these witnesses . . . *W. Tale* iv 4 401
Mark our contract.—Mark your divorce, young sir . . . . . iv 4 428
The heaven sets spies upon us, will not have Our contract celebrated . v 1 204
How joyful am I made by this contract! . . . . *1 Hen. VI.* iii 1 143
In argument and proof of which contract, Bear her this jewel . . v 1 46
You do not well in obstinacy To cavil in the course of this contract . v 4 156
How shall we then dispense with that contract, And not deface your honour? . . . . v 5 28
His contract with Lady Lucy, And his contract by deputy in France *Richard III.* iii 7 5
First he was contract to Lady Lucy—Your mother lives a witness to that vow . . . . iii 7 179
Although I joy in thee, I have no joy of this contract to-night *Rom. and Jul.* ii 2 117
Aches contract and starve your supple joints! . . *T. of Athens* i 1 257
To contract, O, the time, for, ah, my behove, O, methought, there was nothing meet . . . . *Hamlet* v 1 71
Didst contract and purse thy brow together, As if thou then hadst shut up in thy brain Some horrible conceit . . . . . *Othello* iii 3 113
The contract you pretend with that base wretch, One bred of alms and foster'd with cold dishes, With scraps o' the court, it is no contract, none . . . . *Cymbeline* ii 3 118

Contracted. She and I, long since contracted, Are now so sure that nothing can dissolve us . . . . *Mer. Wives* v 5 236
Say, wast thou e'er contracted to this woman? . *Meas. for Meas.* v 1 380
Extended or contracted all proportions To a most hideous object *All's Well* v 3 51
You would have been contracted to a maid . . . *T. Night* v 1 268
And these your contracted Heirs of your kingdoms . . . *W. Tale* v 3 5
Inquire me out contracted bachelors, such as had been asked twice on the banns . . . . *1 Hen. IV.* iv 2 17
Here are the articles of contracted peace . . . . . *2 Hen. VI.* i 1 40
And our whole kingdom To be contracted in one brow of woe *Hamlet* i 2 4
I was contracted to them both: all three Now marry in an instant *Lear* v 3 228
Contracting. Pay with falsehood false exacting, And perform an old contracting . . . . *Meas. for Meas.* iii 2 296
Contraction. O, such a deed As from the body of contraction plucks The very soul . . . . *Hamlet* iii 4 46
Contradict. What I am to say must be but that Which contradicts my accusation . . . . *W. Tale* iii 2 24
Free from a stubborn opposite intent, As being thought to contradict your liking . . . . *2 Hen. VI.* iii 2 252
A greater power than we can contradict Hath thwarted our intents *Rom. and Jul.* v 3 153
Dear Duff, I prithee, contradict thyself, And say it is not so *Macbeth* ii 3 94
And I, her husband, contradict your bans . . . . . *Lear* v 3 87
Contradicted. When was the hour I ever contradicted your desire? *Hen. VIII.* ii 4 28
Contradiction. And all the number of his fair demands Shall be accomplish'd without contradiction . . . . . *Richard II.* iii 3 124
He hath been used Ever to conquer, and to have his worth Of contradiction . . . . *Coriolanus* iii 3 27
Without contradiction, I have heard that . . . *Ant. and Cleo.* ii 7 41
Which may, without contradiction, suffer the report *Cymbeline* i 4 59
Of this contradiction you shall now be quit . . . . . . v 4 169
Contraries. I would by contraries Execute all things . . *Tempest* ii 1 147
Is't good to soothe him in these contraries? *Com. of Errors* iv 4 82
Degrees, observances, customs, and laws, Decline to your confounding contraries, And let confusion live! . . . . *T. of Athens* iv 1 20
No contraries hold more antipathy Than I and such a knave . *Lear* ii 2 93
Contrarieties. He will be here, and yet he is not here: How can these contrarieties agree? . . . . *1 Hen. VI.* ii 3 59
Contrariety. Can no more atone Than violentest contrariety *Coriolanus* iv 6 73
Contrarious. Volumes of report Run with these false and most contrarious quests . . . . *Meas. for Meas.* iv 1 62
And the contrarious winds that held the king So long . *1 Hen. IV.* v 1 52
Contrariously. I this infer, That many things, having full reference To one consent, may work contrariously . . . . *Hen. V.* i 2 206
Contrary. A falsehood in its contrary as great As my trust was *Tempest* i 2 95
What seem I that I am not?—Wise.—What instance of the contrary?—Your folly . . . . *T. G. of Ver.* ii 4 16
'Tis pity love should be so contrary . . . . iv 4 88
You look very ill.—Nay, I'll ne'er believe that; I have to show to the contrary . . . . *Mer. Wives* ii 1 38
Well, I do then; yet I say I could show you to the contrary . . . ii 1 41
My merry host hath had the measuring of their weapons; and, I think, hath appointed them contrary places . . . . ii 1 217
Angelo hath to the public ear Profess'd the contrary *Meas. for Meas.* iv 2 103
Whatsoever you may hear to the contrary . . . . iv 2 123
I would scarce trust myself, though I had sworn the contrary *Much Ado* i 1 198
If Don Worm, his conscience, find no impediment to the contrary . v 2 87
Contrary to thy established proclaimed edict and continent canon *L. L. Lost* i 1 261
He speaks the mere contrary; crosses love not him . . . . i 2 35
And change you favours too; so shall your loves Woo contrary . . v 2 135
Set a deep glass of rhenish wine on the contrary casket *Mer. of Venice* i 2 105
Have you heard any imputation to the contrary? . . . . . i 3 14
As soon as thou canst, for thou hast to pull at a smack o' the contrary *All's Well* ii 3 237
We have lost our labour; they are gone a contrary way . . . iii 5 8
The better for my foes and the worse for my friends.—Just the contrary *T. Night* v 1 15
Wafting his eyes to the contrary and falling A lip of much contempt *W. Tale* i 2 372
To the contrary I have express commandment . . . . . ii 2 8
Contrary to the faith and allegiance of a true subject . . . iii 2 19
'Tis your counsel My lord should to the heavens be contrary . . . v 1 45
I have a king's oath to the contrary . . . . . *K. John* iii 1 10
Slippers, which his nimble haste Had falsely thrust upon contrary feet iv 2 198
Sir Pierce of Exton, who lately came from the king, commands the contrary . . . . *Richard II.* v 5 102
Wouldst thou turn our offers contrary? . . . . . *1 Hen. IV.* v 5 4
Contrary to the law; for the which I think thou wilt howl *2 Hen. IV.* ii 4 373
Banding themselves in contrary parts . . . . *1 Hen. VI.* iii 1 81
Whereas the contrary bringeth bliss, And is a pattern of celestial peace v 5 64
Did he not, contrary to form of law, Devise strange deaths for small offences done? . . . . *2 Hen. VI.* iii 1 58
Contrary to the king, his crown and dignity, thou hast built a paper-mill . . . . iv 7 40
I'll prove the contrary, if you'll hear me speak . . *3 Hen. VI.* i 2 20
'Tis virtue that doth make them most admired; The contrary doth make thee wonder'd at . . . . i 4 131
The king hath straitly charged the contrary . . . *Richard III.* iv 1 17
Lo, at their births good stars were opposite.—No, to their lives bad friends were contrary . . . . iv 4 216
The king's attorney on the contrary Urged on the examinations *Hen. VIII.* ii 1 15
In the divorce his contrary proceedings Are all unfolded . . . iii 2 26
The honour of it Does pay the act of it; as, i' the contrary, The foulness is the punishment . . . . iii 2 182
The best persuasions to the contrary Fail not to use . . . . v 1 147
You must contrary me! marry, 'tis time . . . . *Rom. and Jul.* i 5 87
What storm is this that blows so contrary? Is Romeo slaughter'd? . iii 2 64
And all things change them to the contrary . . . . . . iv 5 90
Yet may your pains, six months, Be quite contrary . *T. of Athens* iv 3 144
In thy rags thou knowest none, but art despised for the contrary . . iv 3 304
Our wills and fates do so contrary run That our devices still are overthrown . . . . *Hamlet* iii 2 221
I do not find that thou dealest justly with me.—What in the contrary? *Othello* iv 2 175
But tidings to the contrary Are brought your eyes . . *Pericles* ii Gower 15
Who, for aught I know, May be, nor can I think the contrary, As great in blood as I myself . . . . ii 5 79

Contribution. Sixth part of each? A trembling contribution! *Hen. VIII.* i 2 95
They have grudged us contribution . . . . . *J. Cæsar* iv 3 206
Contributor. I promised we would be contributors And bear his charge of wooing . . . . . *T. of Shrew* i 2 215
Contrite. And on it have bestow'd more contrite tears Than from it issued forced drops of blood . . . . *Hen. V.* iv 1 313
Contrive. The party 'gainst the which he doth contrive Shall seize one half his goods . . . . . *Mer. of Venice* iv 1 352
Was't you that did so oft contrive to kill him? . . *As Y. Like It* iv 3 135
Please ye we may contrive this afternoon . . . *T. of Shrew* i 2 276
So he that in this action contrives against his own nobility, in his proper stream o'erflows himself . . . . . *All's Well* iv 3 28
Nor never by advised purpose meet To plot, contrive, or complot any ill *Richard II.* i 3 189
The still and mental parts, That do contrive how many hands shall strike *Troi. and Cres.* i 3 201
If thou read this, O Cæsar, thou mayst live; If not, the Fates with traitors do contrive . . . . . *J. Cæsar* ii 3 16
Taint not thy mind, nor let thy soul contrive Against thy mother aught *Hamlet* i 5 85
And suddenly contrive the means of meeting between him and my daughter . . . . ii 2 216
Contrived. Have you conspired, have you with these contrived To bait me with this foul derision? . . . . *M. N. Dream* iii 2 196
Thou hast contrived against the very life Of the defendant *Mer. of Venice* iv 1 360
All the treasons for these eighteen years Complotted and contrived in this land . . . . . . *Richard II.* i 1 96
The guilt of premeditated and contrived murder . . . *Hen. V.* iv 1 171
As a branch and member of this royalty, By whom this great assembly is contrived, We do salute you . . . . . v 2 6
By magic verses have contrived his end . . . . *1 Hen. VI.* i 1 27
Accursed fatal hand That hath contrived this woful tragedy! . i 4 77
As fitting best to quittance their deceit Contrived by art and baleful sorcery . . . . ii 1 15
You have contrived to take From Rome all season'd office *Coriolanus* iii 3 63
Though in the trade of war I have slain men, Yet do I hold it very stuff o' the conscience To do no contrived murder . . . *Othello* i 2 3
Contrivedst. Thou that contrivedst to murder our dead lord *1 Hen. VI.* i 3 34
Contriver. A secret and villanous contriver against me . *As Y. Like It* i 1 151
Till the heavens Reveal the damn'd contriver of this deed *T. Andron.* iv 1 36
We shall find of him A shrewd contriver . . . *J. Cæsar* ii 1 158
And I, the mistress of your charms, The close contriver of all harms *Macbeth* iii 5 7
Contriving. Most generous and free from all contriving . *Hamlet* iv 7 136
One that slept in the contriving of lust, and waked to do it . *Lear* iii 4 92
The letters too Of many our contriving friends in Rome Petition us at home . . . . *Ant. and Cleo.* i 2 189
Control. His art is of such power, It would control my dam's god, Setebos, And make a vassal of him . . . . . *Tempest* i 2 373
His more braver daughter could control thee, If now 'twere fit to do't . i 2 439
One so strong That could control the moon, make flows and ebbs . . v 1 270
The beasts, the fishes and the winged fowls Are their males' subjects and at their controls . . . . *Com. of Errors* ii 1 19
Quenching my familiar smile with an austere regard of control *T. Night* ii 5 74
The proud control of fierce and bloody war . . . *K. John* i 1 17
I am too high-born to be propertied, To be a secondary at control . v 2 80
Even where his lustful eye or savage heart, Without control, listed to make his prey . . . . *Richard III.* iii 5 84
Not having the power to do the good it would, For the ill which doth control't . . . . *Coriolanus* iii 1 161
Give me a staff of honour for mine age, But not a sceptre to control the world . . . . *T. Andron.* i 1 199
Ah, now no more will I control thy griefs: Rend off thy silver hair . iii 1 260
If then they chanced to slack you, We could control them . *Lear* ii 4 249
Which men May blame, but not control . . . . . iii 7 27
But, O vain boast! Who can control his fate? . . . *Othello* v 2 265
Controlled. Commanding peace Even with the same austerity and garb As he controll'd the war . . . . . *Coriolanus* iv 7 45
Highly moved to wrath To be controll'd in that he frankly gave *T. Andron.* i 1 420
When soon I heard The crying babe controll'd with this discourse . v 1 26
Controller. He dares not calm his contumelious spirit Nor cease to be an arrogant controller . . . . . *2 Hen. VI.* iii 2 205
Saucy controller of our private steps! . . . . *T. Andron.* ii 3 60
Controlling. Two such controlling bounds shall you be . . *K. John* ii 1 444
His eye, As bright as is the eagle's, lightens forth Controlling majesty *Richard II.* iii 3 70
A hand to hold a sceptre up And with the same to act controlling laws *2 Hen. VI.* v 1 103
Controlment. Till you may do it without controlment . . *Much Ado* i 3 21
Here have we war for war and blood for blood, Controlment for controlment . . . . *K. John* i 1 20
That for her love such quarrels may be broach'd Without controlment *T. Andron.* ii 1 68
Controversy. Grace is grace, despite of all controversy . *Meas. for Meas.* i 2 26
Who, but for staying on our controversy, Had hoisted sail and put to sea *Com. of Errors* v 1 20
I acquainted him with the cause in controversy . . *Mer. of Venice* iv 1 155
Let's stand aside and see the end of this controversy . *T. of Shrew* v 1 64
Here is the strangest controversy Come from the country . *K. John* i 1 44
Fathers and betrothed lovers, That shall be swallow'd in this controversy *Hen. V.* ii 4 109
Rejourn the controversy of three pence to a second day of audience *Coriolanus* ii 1 80
Dismiss the controversy bleeding, the more entangled by your hearing ii 1 85
We did buffet it With lusty sinews, throwing it aside And stemming it with hearts of controversy . . . . . *J. Cæsar* i 2 109
The nation holds it no sin to tarre them to controversy . . *Hamlet* ii 2 371
Contumelious. With scoffs and scorns and contumelious taunts *1 Hen. VI.* i 4 39
He dares not calm his contumelious spirit . . . *2 Hen. VI.* iii 2 204
Giving our holy virgins to the stain Of contumelious, beastly, mad-brain'd war . . . . *T. of Athens* v 1 177
Contumeliously. Fie, lords! that you, being supreme magistrates, Thus contumeliously should break the peace! . . . *1 Hen. VI.* i 3 58
Contumely. The oppressor's wrong, the proud man's contumely *Hamlet* iii 1 71
Contusion. That winter lion, who in rage forgets Aged contusions and all brush of time . . . . *2 Hen. VI.* v 3 3
Convenience. And the place answer to convenience . *Meas. for Meas.* iii 1 258
I'll beat him, by my life, if I can meet him with any convenience *All's Well* ii 3 253
Will lay upon him all the honour That good convenience claims . iii 2 75

Convenience. Incurr'd a traitor's name; exposed myself, From certain and possess'd conveniences, To doubtful fortunes . *Troi. and Cres.* iii 3 7
Weigh what convenience both of time and means May fit us to our shape *Hamlet* iv 7 150
Which, if convenience will not allow, Stand in hard cure . . *Lear* iii 6 106
For want of these required conveniences, her delicate tenderness will find itself abused . . . . *Othello* ii 1 234
Conveniency. With all brief and plain conveniency . . *Mer. of Venice* iv 1 82
Keepest from me all conveniency than suppliest me with the least advantage of hope . . . . *Othello* iv 2 178
Convenient. Come to me at your convenient leisure . . *Mer. Wives* iii 5 136
'Tis not convenient you should be cozened . . . . . iv 5 83
I'll carry it myself.—Convenient is it . . . *Meas. for Meas.* iv 3 107
Here's a marvellous convenient place for our rehearsal . *M. N. Dream* iii 1 2
Madam, I go with all convenient speed . . . *Mer. of Venice* iii 4 56
Dispatch the most convenient messenger . . . . *All's Well* iii 4 34
To which place We have convenient convoy . . . . . iv 4 10
I should be angry with you, if the time were convenient . . *Hen. V.* iv 1 218
The garden here is more convenient . . . . . *1 Hen. VI.* ii 4 4
Let these have a day appointed them For single combat in convenient place . . . . *2 Hen. VI.* i 3 212
But it shall be convenient, Master Hume, that you be by her . . i 4 10
The most convenient place that I can think of . . . *Hen. VIII.* ii 2 138
Take Convenient numbers to make good the city . . . *Coriolanus* i 5 13
Though I cannot make true wars, I'll frame convenient peace . . v 3 191
It were convenient you had such a devil . . . . *T. Andron.* v 2 90
Caitiff, to pieces shake, That under covert and convenient seeming Hast practised on man's life . . . . *Lear* iii 2 56
More convenient is he for my hand Than for your lady's . . . iv 5 31
'Tis most convenient; pray you, go with us . . . . . v 1 36
Conveniently. And such fair ostents of love As shall conveniently become you there . . . . *Mer. of Venice* ii 8 45
If he may be conveniently delivered, I would he were . *T. Night* iv 2 73
Till I conveniently could send . . . . . *Rom. and Jul.* v 3 256
I this morning know Where we shall find him most conveniently *Hamlet* i 1 175
I nill relate, action may Conveniently the rest convey *Pericles* iii Gower 56
Convent. When that is known and golden time convents . *T. Night* v 1 391
Convented. And what he with his oath And all probation will make up full clear, Whensoever he's convented . . . . . *Meas. for Meas.* v 1 158
Hath commanded To-morrow morning to the council-board He be convented . . . . *Hen. VIII.* v 1 52
Convented Upon a pleasing treaty . . . . . . *Coriolanus* ii 2 58
Conventicle. Myself had notice of your conventicles . . *2 Hen. VI.* iii 1 166
Conversant. Never to be infected with delight, Nor conversant with ease and idleness . . . . *K. John* iv 3 70
Alike conversant in general services, and more remarkable in single oppositions . . . . *Cymbeline* iv 1 13
'Tis most strange, Nature should be so conversant with pain . *Pericles* iii 2 25
Conversation. What an unweighed behaviour hath this Flemish drunkard picked—with the devil's name!—out of my conversation? *Mer. Wives* ii 1 25
Had from the conversation of my thoughts Haply been absent then *All's Well* i 3 240
All are banish'd till their conversations Appear more wise and modest *2 Hen. IV.* v 5 106
His apparent open guilt omitted, I mean, his conversation with Shore's wife, He lived from all attainder of suspect . . . *Richard III.* iii 5 31
More of your conversation would infect my brain . . *Coriolanus* ii 1 104
Thou art e'en as just a man As e'er my conversation coped withal *Hamlet* iii 2 60
And have not those soft parts of conversation That chamberers have *Othello* iii 3 264
Octavia is of a holy, cold, and still conversation . . *Ant. and Cleo.* ii 6 131
With five times so much conversation, I should get ground of your fair mistress . . . . *Cymbeline* i 4 113
The good in conversation, To whom I give my benison . *Pericles* ii Gower 9
Converse. Hear sweet discourse, converse with noblemen . *T. G. of Ver.* i 3 31
Did you converse, sir, with this gentlewoman? . *Com. of Errors* ii 2 162
I did converse this quondam day with a companion . . *L. L. Lost* v 1 6
If over-boldly we have borne ourselves In the converse of breath . . v 2 745
Visit the speechless sick and still converse With groaning wretches v 2 861
A proper man's picture, but, alas, who can converse with a dumb-show? *Mer. of Venice* i 2 78
Companions That do converse and waste the time together . . iii 4 12
Why dost thou converse with that trunk of humours? . *1 Hen. IV.* ii 4 494
Let them practise and converse with spirits . . . *1 Hen. VI.* ii 1 25
I will converse with iron-witted fools And unrespective boys *Richard III.* iv 2 28
One that converses more with the buttock of the night than with the forehead of the morning . . . . *Coriolanus* ii 1 56
Your party in converse, him you would sound . . . *Hamlet* ii 1 42
To converse with him that is wise, and says little; to fear judgement *Lear* i 4 16
I'll devise a mean to draw the Moor Out of the way, that your converse and business May be more free . . . . . *Othello* iii 1 40
Conversed. From our infancy We have conversed and spent our hours together . . . . *T. G. of Ver.* ii 4 63
Prove you that any man with me conversed At hours unmeet *Much Ado* iv 1 183
I have, since I was three year old, conversed with a magician *As Y. L. It* v 2 66
And conversed with such As, like to pitch, defile nobility . *2 Hen. VI.* ii 1 195
Like a shag-hair'd crafty kern, Hath he conversed with the enemy . iii 1 368
Conversing. He, by conversing with them, is turned into a justice-like serving-man . . . . *2 Hen. IV.* v 1 75
We grace the yeoman by conversing with him . . . *1 Hen. VI.* ii 4 81
Conversion. I do not shame To tell you what I was, since my conversion So sweetly tastes, being the thing I am . . . *As Y. Like It* iv 3 137
'Tis too respective and too sociable For your conversion . *K. John* i 1 189
Convert. Courtesy itself must convert to disdain, if you come in her presence . . . . *Much Ado* i 1 123
The love of wicked men converts to fear; That fear to hate *Richard II.* v 1 66
Thy overflow of good converts to bad . . . . . v 3 64
That shall convert those tears By number into hours of happiness *2 Hen. IV.* v 2 60
This intrusion shall Now seeming sweet convert to bitter gall *R. and J.* i 5 94
To general filths Convert o' the instant, green virginity! *T. of Athens* iv 1 7
He whose pious breath seeks to convert you . . . . iv 3 140
Let grief Convert to anger; blunt not the heart, enrage it . *Macbeth* iv 3 229
Do not look upon me; Lest with this piteous action you convert My stern effects . . . . *Hamlet* iii 4 128
Like the spring that turneth wood to stone, Convert his gyves to graces . . . . iv 7 21
Converted. May I be so converted and see with these eyes? . *Much Ado* ii 3 23
How you may be converted I know not, but methinks you look with your eyes as other women do . . . . iii 4 91

Converted. Myself and what is mine to you and yours Is now converted *Mer. of Ven.* iii 2 169
Was converted Both from his enterprise and from the world *As Y. Like It* v 4 167
Why of that loam, whereto he was converted, might they not stop a beer-barrel? . . . . *Hamlet* v 1 234

Converting all your sounds of woe Into Hey nonny, nonny . *Much Ado* ii 3 70
In converting Jews to Christians, you raise the price of pork *Mer. of Ven.* iii 5 37
I am glad they are going, For, sure, there's no converting of 'em *Hen. VIII.* i 3 43

Convertite. Out of these convertites There is much matter to be heard and learn'd . . . . *As Y. Like It* v 4 190
Since you are a gentle convertite, My tongue shall hush again this storm of war . . . . *K. John* v 1 19

Convey. How shall I best convey the ladder thither? *T. G. of Ver.* iii 1 128
Come, I'll convey thee through the city-gate . . . . iii 1 252
'Convey,' the wise it call. 'Steal!' foh! a fico for the phrase! *Mer. Wives* i 3 32
If you have a friend here, convey, convey him out . . . iii 3 125
Did but convey unto our fearful minds A doubtful warrant *Com. of Errors* i 1 68
If seriously I may convey my thoughts In this my light deliverance *All's Well* ii 1 84
Convey what I will set down to my lady . . *T. Night* iv 2 118
Convey me to my bed, then to my grave . . *Richard II.* ii 1 137
Convey him to the Tower.—O, good! convey? conveyers are you all . iv 1 316
For God's sake, lords, convey my tristful queen . 1 *Hen. IV.* ii 4 434
Convey them with safe conduct . . . *Hen. V.* i 2 297
And thence to France shall we convey you safe, And bring you back ii Prol. 37
Convey me Salisbury into his tent . . . 1 *Hen. VI.* i 4 110
Convey him hence, and I myself Will see his burial better than his life . ii 5 120
I beg no favour, Only convey me where thou art commanded 2 *Hen. VI.* ii 4 93
Convey him hence and on our long-boat's side Strike off his head . iv 1 68
Hath appointed This conduct to convey me to the Tower *Richard III.* i 1 45
Look to your wife: if she convey Letters to Richmond, you shall answer it . . . . iv 2 95
Come, sirs, convey me to the block of shame; Wrong hath but wrong . v 1 28
Help to convey her hence away, And with my sword I'll keep this door safe . . . . *T. Andron.* ii 1 287
Whither wouldst thou convey This growing image of thy fiend-like face? v 1 44
Sirs, help our uncle to convey him in . . . v 3 15
Some loving friends convey the emperor hence . . v 3 191
I will omit no opportunity That may convey my greetings, love, to thee *Rom. and Jul.* iii 5 50
You may Convey your pleasures in a spacious plenty, And yet seem cold *Macbeth* iv 3 71
Behind the arras I'll convey myself, To hear the process *Hamlet* iii 3 28
Convey the business as I shall find means, and acquaint you withal *Lear* i 2 109
Into her womb convey sterility! Dry up in her the organs of increase! i 4 300
She is not well; convey her to my tent . . . v 3 106
With what haste The weight we must convey with's will permit *Ant. and Cleo.* iii 1 36
See, How I convey my shame out of thine eyes By looking back what I have left behind . . . . iii 11 52
I nill relate, action may Conveniently the rest convey *Pericles* iii Gower 56
Convey thy deity Aboard our dancing boat . . . . iii 1 12
Which never could I so convey, Unless your thoughts went on my way . . . . iv Gower 49

Conveyance. Bethink you of some conveyance: in the house you cannot hide him . . . . *Mer. Wives* iii 3 135
Huddling jest upon jest with such impossible conveyance upon me *Much Ado* ii 1 253
Since Henry's death, I fear, there is conveyance . 1 *Hen. VI.* i 3 2
Thy sly conveyance and thy lord's false love . . 3 *Hen. VI.* iii 3 160
For her sake, Madest quick conveyance with her good aunt Anne *Richard III.* iv 4 283
When we have stuff'd These pipes and these conveyances of our blood *Coriolanus* v 1 54
Craves the conveyance of a promised march Over his kingdom *Hamlet* iv 4 3
The very conveyances of his lands will hardly lie in this box . . v 1 119
To his conveyance I assign my wife, With what else needful . *Othello* i 3 286

Conveyed. And thence she cannot be convey'd away . *T. G. of Ver.* iii 1 37
They conveyed me into a buck-basket . . *Mer. Wives* iii 5 87
There was one conveyed out of my house yesterday in this basket . iv 2 152
The assault that Angelo hath made to you, fortune hath conveyed to my understanding . . . . . *Meas. for Meas.* iii 1 189
Our fraughtage, sir, I have convey'd aboard . *Com. of Errors* iv 1 88
See him safe convey'd Home to my house. . . . iv 4 125
What think you, if he were convey'd to bed? . *T. of Shrew* Ind. 1 37
An onion will do well for such a shift, Which in a napkin being close convey'd, Shall in despite enforce a watery eye. . . Ind. 1 127
Convey'd himself as heir to the Lady Lingare . *Hen. V.* i 2 74
See that he be convey'd unto the Tower . . 3 *Hen. VI.* iii 2 120
See that forthwith Duke Edward be convey'd Unto my brother . iv 3 52
But how made he escape?—He was convey'd by Richard Duke of Gloucester . . . . iv 6 81
Earth gapes, hell burns, fiends roar, saints pray, To have him suddenly convey'd away . . . . . . *Richard III.* iv 4 76
By all voices, that forthwith You be convey'd to the Tower a prisoner *Hen. VIII.* v 3 89
Where's the king?—My lord of Gloucester hath convey'd him hence *Lear* iii 7 15
That a king's children should be so convey'd, So slackly guarded! *Cymb.* i 1 63

Conveyers are you all, That rise thus nimbly by a true king's fall *Richard II.* iv 1 317

Conveying. By interims and conveying gusts we have heard The charges of our friends . . . . *Coriolanus* i 6 5

Convict. Before I be convict by course of law, To threaten me with death is most unlawful . . . . *Richard III.* i 4 192

Convicted. A whole armado of convicted sail . . . *K. John* iii 4 2

Convince. Though the mourning brow of progeny Forbid the smiling courtesy of love The holy suit which fain it would convince *L. L. Lost* v 2 756
Else might the world convince of levity As well my undertakings as your counsels . . . . *Troi. and Cres.* ii 2 130
Or that persuasion could but thus convince me . . . iii 2 171
His two chamberlains Will I with wine and wassail so convince *Macbeth* i 7 64
Their malady convinces The great assay of art. . . iv 3 142
Italy contains none so accomplished a courtier to convince the honour of my mistress . . . . *Cymbeline* i 4 104
Time of both this truth shall ne'er convince . . *Pericles* i 2 123

Convinced. Having, by their own importunate suit, Or voluntary dotage of some mistress, Convinced or supplied them . . . *Othello* iv 1 28

Convive. There in the full convive we . . *Troi. and Cres.* iv 5 272

Convocation. Upon our spiritual convocation . . *Hen. V.* i 1 76
A certain convocation of politic worms are e'en at him . *Hamlet* iv 3 21

Convoy. Entertained my convoy; and between these main parcels of dispatch effected many nicer needs . . . *All's Well* iv 3 103
To which place We have convenient convoy . . . iv 4 10
At such and such a sconce, at such a breach, at such a convoy *Hen. V.* iii 6 76
His passport shall be made And crowns for convoy put into his purse . iv 3 37
And this sailing Pandar Our doubtful hope, our convoy and our bark *Troi. and Cres.* i 1 107
Which to the high top-gallant of my joy Must be my convoy *R. and J.* ii 4 203
As the winds give benefit And convoy is assistant, do not sleep *Hamlet* i 3 3

Convulsion. Go charge my goblins that they grind their joints With dry convulsions . . . . *Tempest* iv 1 260

Cony. Are you native of this place?—As the cony that you see dwell where she is kindled . . . . . *As Y. Like It* iii 2 357
So doth the cony struggle in the net. . . . . 3 *Hen. VI.* i 4 62

Cony-catch. I must cony-catch; I must shift . *Mer. Wives* i 3 36

Cony-catched. Take heed, Signior Baptista, lest you be cony-catched in this business . . . . *T. of Shrew* v 1 102

Cony-catching. Your cony-catching rascals . . . *Mer. Wives* i 1 128
Come, you are so full of cony-catching! . . . *T. of Shrew* iv 1 45

Cook. Mistress Quickly, which is in the manner of his nurse, or his dry nurse, or his cook . . . . *Mer. Wives* i 2 4
Would the cook were of my mind! . . . . . *Much Ado* i 3 75
Where's the cook? is supper ready? . . . *T. of Shrew* iv 1 47
Where is the rascal cook? How durst you, villains, bring it from the dresser? . . . . iv 1 165
Upon This day she was both pantler, butler, cook . *W. Tale* iv 4 56
If the cook help to make the gluttony, you help to make the diseases 2 *Hen. IV.* ii 4 48
Yea, marry, William cook, bid him come hither . . . v 1 12
And any pretty little tiny kickshaws, tell William cook . . v 1 30
Let thine eye be thy cook . . . . . *Hen. V.* v 2 156
So, now bring them in, for I'll play the cook *T. Andron.* v 2 205
Go hire me twenty cunning cooks.—You shall have none ill, sir *Rom. and Jul.* iv 2 2
'Tis an ill cook that cannot lick his own fingers . . . iv 2 6
What's there?—Things for the cook, sir; but I know not what . iv 4 14
Let in the tide Of knaves once more; my cook and I'll provide *T. of A.* iii 4 119
Epicurean cooks Sharpen with cloyless sauce his appetite *Ant. and Cleo.* ii 1 24
Cadwal and I Will play the cook and servant . . *Cymbeline* iii 6 30
You and Fidele play the cooks: I'll stay Till hasty Polydore return . iv 2 164
I thought I was a cave-keeper, And cook to honest creatures: but 'tis not so . . . . iv 2 299

Cooked. We'll browse on that, Whilst what we have kill'd be cook'd . iii 6 39
Hanging is the word, sir: if you be ready for that, you are well cooked v 4 156

Cookery. Your fine Egyptian cookery Shall have the fame *Ant. and Cleo.* ii 6 64
But his neat cookery! he cuts our roots In characters . *Cymbeline* iv 2 49

Cool. My humour shall not cool . . . . *Mer. Wives* i 3 109
As cold as if I had swallowed snowballs for pills to cool the reins . iii 5 24
Shape it: I would not have things cool . . . . iv 2 240
Send me a cool rut-time, Jove . . . . . v 5 15
When I am cold, he heats me with beating; when I am warm, he cools me with beating . . . . . . *Com. of Error* iv 4 35
We will hear further of it by your daughter: let it cool the while *M. Ado* ii 3 212
Under the cool shade of a sycamore I thought to close mine eyes *L. L. Lost* v 2 89
Fantasies, that apprehend More than cool reason ever comprehends *M. N. Dream* v 1 6
Let my liver rather heat with wine Than my heart cool with mortifying groans . . . . *Mer. of Venice* i 1 82
Will't please your lordship cool your hands? . . *T. of Shrew* Ind. 1 58
Rust, sword! cool, blushes! and, Parolles, live Safest in shame! *All's Well* iv 3 373
Cool and congeal again to what it was . . . *K. John* ii 1 479
As fire cools fire Within the scorched veins of one new-burn'd . iii 1 277
This act so evilly born shall cool the hearts Of all his people. . iii 4 149
I saw a smith stand with his hammer, thus, The whilst his iron did on the anvil cool . . . . iv 2 194
Whiles yet the cool and temperate wind of grace O'erblows the filthy and contagious clouds Of heady murder . . . *Hen. V.* iii 3 30
'Twill make them cool in zeal unto your grace . . 2 *Hen. VI.* iii 1 177
Which with the heart there cools and ne'er returneth . . iii 2 166
Which is not amiss to cool a man's stomach this hot weather . iv 10 10
Strike now, or else the iron cools.—I had rather chop this hand off 3 *Hen. VI.* v 1 49
I'll heat his blood with Greekish wine to-night, Which with my scimitar I'll cool to-morrow . . . . *Troi. and Cres.* v 1 2
And lose advantage, which doth ever cool I' the absence of the needer *Coriolanus* iv 1 43
Sit fas aut nefas, till I find the stream To cool this heat *T. Andron.* ii 1 134
Now let hot Ætna cool in Sicily! . . . . . iii 1 242
To let the meat cool ere we can agree upon the first place *T. of Athens* iii 6 76
Cool it with a baboon's blood, Then the charm is firm and good *Macbeth* iv 1 37
No boasting like a fool; This deed I'll do before this purpose cool . iv 1 154
Upon the heat and flame of thy distemper Sprinkle cool patience *Hamlet* iii 4 124
Love cools, friendship falls off, brothers divide: in cities, mutinies *Lear* i 2 115
This is a brave night to cool a courtezan . . . iii 2 79
We have reason to cool our raging motions, our carnal stings . *Othello* i 3 334
And is become the bellows and the fan To cool a gipsy's lust *A. and C.* i 1 10
Fans, whose wind did seem To glow the delicate cheeks which they did cool . . . . ii 2 209
We should not, when the blood was cool, have threaten'd Our prisoners with the sword . . . . *Cymbeline* v 5 77
Let your breath cool yourself, telling your haste . . *Pericles* i 1 161

Cooled, glowing hot, in that surge, like a horse-shoe . *Mer. Wives* iii 5 122
Thwarted my bargains, cooled my friends, heated mine enemies *Mer. of Venice* iii 1 59
Warmed and cooled by the same winter and summer as a Christian is . iii 1 65
The blood is hot that must be cool'd for this . . *Richard II.* i 1 51
My Lord Northumberland will soon be cool'd . . 2 *Hen. IV.* iii 1 44
The time has been, my senses would have cool'd To hear a night-shriek *Macbeth* v 5 10

Cooling. Whom I left cooling of the air with sighs . . *Tempest* i 2 222
My wind cooling my broth Would blow me to an ague . *Mer. of Venice* i 1 22
There all is marr'd; there lies a cooling card . . 1 *Hen. VI.* v 3 83
You must stay the cooling too, or you may chance to burn your lips *Troi. and Cres.* i 1 25
The green leaves quiver with the cooling wind . . *T. Andron.* ii 3 14
Thou hast described A hot friend cooling . . . *J. Cæsar* iv 2 19

Coop. And coops from other lands her islanders . . *K. John* ii 1 25

Cooped. Alas, I am not coop'd here for defence! . . 3 *Hen. VI.* v 1 109

Copatain hat. A scarlet cloak! and a copatain hat! . . *T. of Shrew* v 1 69

Cope. We freely cope your courteous pains withal . *Mer. of Venice* iv 1 412
I love to cope him in these sullen fits, For then he's full of matter *As Y. Like It* ii 1 67
Unworthy though thou art, I'll cope with thee . . *2 Hen. VI.* iii 2 230
He is a man, and, Clifford, cope with him . . *3 Hen. VI.* i 3 24
Remember whom you are to cope withal . . . . *Richard III.* v 3 315
We must not stint Our necessary actions, in the fear To cope malicious censurers . . . *Hen. VIII.* i 2 78
Come knights from east to west, And cull their flower, Ajax shall cope the best . . . *Troi. and Cres.* ii 3 275
Yet am I noble as the adversary I come to cope . . . *Lear* v 3 124
How long ago, and when He hath, and is again to cope your wife *Othello* iv 1 87
Is not worth a breakfast in the cheapest country under the cope *Pericles* iv 6 132
Coped. March by us, that we may peruse the men We should have coped withal . . . *2 Hen. IV.* iv 2 95
He yesterday coped Hector in the battle and struck him down *Troi. and Cres.* i 2 34
Thou art e'en as just a man As e'er my conversation coped withal *Hamlet* iii 2 60
Copest. Who of force must know The royal fool thou copest with *W. Tale* iv 4 435
Thou wilt undertake A thing like death to chide away this shame, That copest with death himself to 'scape from it *Rom. and Jul.* iv 1 75
Cophetua. The magnanimous and most illustrate king Cophetua *L. L. Lost* iv 1 66
Let King Cophetua know the truth thereof . *2 Hen. IV.* v 3 106
He that shot so trim, When King Cophetua loved the beggar-maid! *Rom. and Jul.* ii 1 14
Copied. Let this be copied out, And keep it safe for our remembrance *K. John* v 2 1
All saws of books, all forms, all pressures past, That youth and observation copied there . . . *Hamlet* i 5 101
I'ld have it copied : Take it, and do't ; and leave me for this time *Othello* iii 4 190
Copies. We took him setting of boys' copies . *2 Hen. VI.* iv 2 95
How fairly this lord strives to appear foul! takes virtuous copies to be wicked . . . . *T. of Athens* iii 3 32
Copious. Be copious in exclaims . . . *Richard III.* iv 4 135
Copped. The blind mole casts Copp'd hills towards heaven . *Pericles* i 1 101
Copper. Our copper buys no better treasure . *L. L. Lost* iv 3 386
I have heard the prince tell him, I know not how oft, that that ring was copper! . . . *1 Hen. IV.* iii 3 98
If he said my ring was copper.—I say 'tis copper . . iii 3 162
Whilst some with cunning gild their copper crowns, With truth and plainness I do wear mine bear . *Troi. and Cres.* iv 4 107
Copper nose. I had as lief Helen's golden tongue had commended Troilus for a copper nose . . . i 2 115
Copper-spur. Master Copper-spur, and Master Starve-lackey *M. for M.* iv 3 14
Coppice. Upon the edge of yonder coppice . *L. L. Lost* iv 1 9
Copulation. To offer to get your living by the copulation of cattle *As Y. Like It* iii 2 84
Let copulation thrive . . . . . *Lear* iv 6 116
Copulative. I press in here, sir, amongst the rest of the country copulatives, to swear and to forswear . *As Y. Like It* v 4 58
Copy. It was the copy of our conference . *Com. of Errors* v 1 62
My brother hath a daughter, Almost the copy of my child that's dead *Much Ado* v 1 298
Such a man Might be a copy to these younger times . *All's Well* i 2 46
Will you give me a copy of the sonnet you writ to Diana? . iv 3 355
You are the cruell'st she alive, If you will lead these graces to the grave And leave the world no copy . . *T. Night* i 5 261
What, hast smutch'd thy nose? They say it is a copy out of mine *W. Tale* i 2 122
Although the print be little, the whole matter And copy of the father . ii 3 99
The copy of your speed is learn'd by them . *K. John* iv 2 113
He was the mark and glass, copy and book, That fashion'd others *2 Hen. IV.* ii 3 31
Be copy now to men of grosser blood, And teach them how to war *Hen. V.* iii 1 24
But in them nature's copy's not eterne . . *Macbeth* iii 2 38
Copy-book. Fair as a text B in a copy-book . *L. L. Lost* v 2 42
Coragio, bully-monster, coragio! . . . *Tempest* v 1 258
Away, and for our flight.—Bravely, coragio! . *All's Well* ii 5 97
Coral. Of his bones are coral made . . . *Tempest* i 2 397
I saw her coral lips to move . . . . *T. of Shrew* i 1 179
Coram. Justice of peace and 'Coram' . . . *Mer. Wives* i 1 6
Corambus, so many ; Jaques, so many . . *All's Well* iv 3 185
Coranto. Why, he's able to lead her a coranto . . ii 3 49
Why dost thou not go to church in a galliard and come home in a coranto? . . . . . *T. Night* i 3 137
And teach lavoltas high and swift corantos . *Hen. V.* iii 5 33
Cord. The ladder made of cords, and all the means Plotted *T. G. of Ver.* ii 4 182
A ladder quaintly made of cords, To cast up, with a pair of anchoring hooks . . . . . iii 1 117
His neck will come to your waist,—a cord, sir . *Meas. for Meas.* iii 2 42
But he, I thank him, gnaw'd in two my cords . *Com. of Errors* v 1 289
Thy wealth being forfeit to the state, Thou hast not left the value of a cord . . . . *Mer. of Venice* iv 1 366
If thou want'st a cord, the smallest thread That ever spider twisted from her womb Will serve to strangle thee . *K. John* iv 3 127
Being the agents, or base second means, The cords, the ladder, or the hangman rather . . . *1 Hen. IV.* i 3 166
Let not Bardolph's vital thread be cut With edge of penny cord *Hen. V.* iii 6 50
I should go hang myself.—If thou hadst hands to help thee knit the cord . . . . . *T. Andron.* ii 4 10
And bring thee cords made like a tackled stair . *Rom. and Jul.* ii 4 201
What hast thou there? the cords That Romeo bid thee fetch?—Ay, ay, the cords . . . . . iii 2 34
Take up those cords : poor ropes, you are beguiled, Both you and I iii 2 132
Come, cords, come, nurse ; I'll to my wedding-bed . iii 2 136
Like rats, oft bite the holy cords a-twain Which are too intrinse t'unloose . . . . . *Lear* ii 2 80
If there be cords, or knives, Poison, or fire, or suffocating streams, I'll not endure it . . . . *Othello* iii 3 388
O, the charity of a penny cord! it sums up thousands in a trice *Cymbeline* v 4 170
O, give me cord, or knife, or poison, Some upright justicer! . v 5 213
Corded. This night he meaneth with a corded ladder To climb celestial Silvia's chamber-window . . . *T. G. of Ver.* ii 6 33
He her chamber-window will ascend And with a corded ladder fetch her down . . . . . . iii 1 40

Cordelia. What shall Cordelia do? Love, and be silent . *Lear* i 1 63
Then poor Cordelia! And yet not so ; since, I am sure, my love's More richer than my tongue . . . . . i 1 78
How, how, Cordelia! mend your speech a little, Lest it may mar your fortunes . . . . . . i 1 96
Give but that portion which yourself proposed, And here I take Cordelia by the hand . . . . i 1 246
Fairest Cordelia, that art most rich, being poor ; Most choice, forsaken! i 1 253
Bid them farewell, Cordelia, though unkind : Thou losest here, a better where to find . . . . . i 1 263
The jewels of our father, with wash'd eyes Cordelia leaves you . i 1 272
Well may you prosper!—Come, my fair Cordelia . . i 1 285
O most small fault, How ugly didst thou in Cordelia show! . i 4 289
Peruse this letter! Nothing almost sees miracles But misery : I know 'tis from Cordelia . . . . . ii 2 173
If you shall see Cordelia,—As fear not but you shall,—show her this ring . . . . . . iii 1 46
That burning shame Detains him from Cordelia . . iv 3 49
Do not laugh at me ; For, as I am a man, I think this lady To be my child Cordelia.—And so I am, I am . . iv 7 70
The mercy Which he intends to Lear and to Cordelia . v 1 66
Upon such sacrifices, my Cordelia, The gods themselves throw incense v 3 20
The question of Cordelia and her father Requires a fitter place . v 3 58
Speak, Edmund, where's the king? and where's Cordelia? . v 3 237
My writ Is on the life of Lear and on Cordelia . . v 3 246
He hath commission from thy wife and me To hang Cordelia in the prison . . . . . . v 3 253
Cordelia, Cordelia! stay a little. Ha! What is't thou say'st? . v 3 271
Cordial. Which draught to me were cordial . *W. Tale* i 2 318
This affliction has a taste as sweet As any cordial comfort . v 3 77
A pleasing cordial, princely Buckingham, Is this thy vow unto my sickly heart . . . . *Richard III.* ii 1 41
Is this your comfort? The cordial that ye bring a wretched lady? *Hen. VIII.* iii 1 106
Kind Rome, that hast thus lovingly reserved The cordial of mine age to glad my heart! . . . *T. Andron.* i 1 166
Come, cordial and not poison, go with me To Juliet's grave *Rom. and Jul.* v 1 85
I do not know What is more cordial. Nay, I prithee, take it *Cymbeline* i 5 64
The drug he gave me, which he said was precious And cordial to me, have I not found it Murderous to the senses? . iv 2 327
That confection Which I gave him for cordial . . v 5 247
Cordis. I have tremor cordis on me : my heart dances *W. Tale* i 2 110
Core. Were not that a botchy core? *Troi. and Cres.* ii 1 7
How now, thou core of envy! Thou crusty batch of nature, what's the news? . . . . v 1 4
Most putrefied core, so fair without, Thy goodly armour thus hath cost thy life . . . . . . v 8 1
I will wear him In my heart's core, ay, in my heart of heart . *Hamlet* iii 2 78
Corin. In the shape of Corin sat all day, Playing on pipes of corn and versing love To amorous Phillida . . *M. N. Dream* ii 1 66
O Corin, that thou knew'st how I do love her! . *As Y. Like It* ii 4 23
No, Corin, being old, thou canst not guess . . ii 4 25
Corinth. Obedient to the stream, Was carried towards Corinth *C. of Err.* i 1 88
Two ships from far making amain to us, Of Corinth that, of Epidaurus this . . . . i 1 94
They three were taken up By fishermen of Corinth, as we thought . i 1 112
Rude fishermen of Corinth By force took Dromio and my son . v 1 351
Antipholus, thou camest from Corinth first?—No, sir, not I . v 1 362
I came from Corinth, my most gracious lord . . v 1 365
Would we could see you at Corinth! . . *T. of Athens* ii 2 73
Corinthian. A Corinthian, a lad of mettle, a good boy . *1 Hen. IV.* ii 4 13
Coriolanus. For what he did before Corioli, call him, With all the applause and clamour of the host, CAIUS MARCIUS CORIOLANUS! *Cor.* i 9 65
These In honour follows Coriolanus . . . ii 1 182
Welcome to Rome, renowned Coriolanus! . . . ii 1 183
Newly named,—What is it?—Coriolanus must I call thee? . ii 1 191
'Tis thought of every one Coriolanus will carry it . . ii 2 4
For Coriolanus neither to care whether they love or hate him manifests the true knowledge he has in their disposition . . ii 2 13
Report A little of that worthy work perform'd by Caius Marcius Coriolanus . . . . ii 2 50
Sit, Coriolanus ; never shame to hear What you have nobly done . ii 2 71
The deeds of Coriolanus Should not be utter'd feebly . . ii 2 86
The senate, Coriolanus, are well pleased To make thee consul . ii 2 136
To Coriolanus come all joy and honour! . . . ii 2 158
Where? at the senate-house?—There, Coriolanus . . ii 3 153
Nor has Coriolanus Deserved this so dishonour'd rub . . iii 1 59
What, ho! Sicinius! Brutus! Coriolanus! Citizens! Peace, peace, peace! . . . . iii 1 187
You, tribunes To the people! Coriolanus, patience! . . iii 1 191
Consul! what consul?—The consul Coriolanus.—He consul! . iii 1 280
The nobles receive so to heart the banishment of that worthy Coriolanus iv 3 23
Coriolanus banished!—Banished, sir.—You will be welcome with this intelligence . . . . iv 3 28
Coriolanus being now in no request of his country . . iv 3 37
I have deserved no better entertainment, In being Coriolanus . iv 5 11
Thereto witness may My surname, Coriolanus . . . iv 5 74
Your Coriolanus Is not much miss'd, but with his friends . iv 6 12
We wish'd Coriolanus Had loved you as we did . . iv 6 24
When you cast Your stinking greasy caps in hooting at Coriolanus' exile . . . . iv 6 132
Coriolanus He would not answer to : forbad all names . v 1 11
I am an officer of state, and come To speak with Coriolanus . v 2 4
You'll see your Rome embraced with fire before You'll speak with Coriolanus . . . . v 2 8
You shall perceive that a Jack guardant cannot office me from my son Coriolanus . . . . v 2 68
To his surname Coriolanus 'longs more pride Than pity to our prayers . v 3 170
Dost thou think I'll grace thee with that robbery, thy stol'n name Coriolanus in Corioli? . . . . . . v 6 90
Who threats, in course of this revenge, to do As much as ever Coriolanus did . . . . *T. Andron.* iv 4 68
Corioli. Hie you to your bands : Let us alone to guard Corioli *Coriolanus* i 2 27
Your lord and Titus Lartius are set down before their city Corioli i 3 111
Thy news?—The citizens of Corioli have issued . . i 6 10
Holding Corioli in the name of Rome . . . i 6 37
Alone I fought in your Corioli walls, And made what work I pleased i 8 8
For what he did before Corioli, call him, With all the applause and clamour of the host, CAIUS MARCIUS CORIOLANUS! . . i 9 63
You, Titus Lartius, Must to Corioli back . . . i 9 76

Corioli. I sometime lay here in Corioli At a poor man's house; he used me kindly . . . *Coriolanus* i 9 82
I would not have been so fidiused for all the chests in Corioli . ii 1 144
Know, Rome, that all alone Marcius did fight Within Corioli gates ii 1 180
Such eyes the widows in Corioli wear, And mothers that lack sons ii 1 195
For this last, Before and in Corioli, let me say, I cannot speak him home . . . ii 2 106
With a sudden re-inforcement struck Corioli like a planet . . ii 2 118
Before Corioli he scotched him and notched him like a carbonado . iv 5 198
This fellow had a Volscian to his mother; His wife is in Corioli v 3 179
Dost thou think I'll grace thee with that robbery, thy stol'n name Coriolanus in Corioli? . . . . . . v 6 90
Like an eagle in a dove-cote, I Flutter'd your Volscians in Corioli v 6 116
Co-rivalled. Where's then the saucy boat Whose weak untimber'd sides but even now Co-rivall'd greatness? . . . . *Troi. and Cres.* i 3 44
Cork. Take the cork out of thy mouth that I may drink thy tidings *As Y. Like It* iii 2 213
Swallowed with yest and froth, as you'ld thrust a cork into a hogshead *W. Tale* iii 3 95
Corky. Ingrateful fox! 'tis he.—Bind fast his corky arms *Lear* iii 7 29
Cormorant. Spite of cormorant devouring Time . *L. L. Lost* i 1 4
Light vanity, insatiate cormorant, Consuming means, soon preys upon itself . . . . *Richard II.* ii 1 38
And what else dear that is consumed In hot digestion of this cormorant war—Shall be struck off . . *Troi. and Cres.* ii 2 6
Should by the cormorant belly be restrain'd . *Coriolanus* i 1 125
Corn. No use of metal, corn, or wine, or oil . . . *Tempest* ii 1 153
Our corn's to reap, for yet our tithe's to sow . *Meas. for Meas.* iv 1 76
He weeds the corn and still lets grow the weeding . *L. L. Lost* i 1 96
Sow'd cockle reap'd no corn; And justice always whirls in equal measure . . . . iv 3 383
Playing on pipes of corn and versing love To amorous Phillida *M. N. Dr.* ii 1 67
The green corn Hath rotted ere his youth attain'd a beard . . ii 1 94
Our sighs and they shall lodge the summer corn, And make a dearth *Richard II.* iii 3 162
We shall be winnow'd with so rough a wind That even our corn shall seem as light as chaff . . . . *2 Hen. IV.* iv 1 195
Talk like the vulgar sort of market men That come to gather money for their corn . . . . . . *1 Hen. VI.* iii 2 5
Good morrow, gallants! want ye corn for bread? . . . iii 2 41
I trust ere long to choke thee with thine own And make thee curse the harvest of that corn . . . . . iii 2 47
Like over-ripen'd corn, Hanging the head at Ceres' plenteous load *2 Hen. VI.* i 2 1
His well-proportion'd beard made rough and rugged, Like to the summer's corn by tempest lodged . . . . . iii 2 176
What valiant foemen, like to autumn's corn, Have we mow'd down in tops of all their pride! . . . . *3 Hen. VI.* v 7 3
Throughly to be winnow'd, where my chaff And corn shall fly asunder *Hen. VIII.* v 1 111
Her foes shake like a field of beaten corn, And hang their heads with sorrow . . . . v 5 32
Let us kill him, and we'll have corn at our own price. Is't a verdict? *Coriolanus* i 1 11
What's their seeking?—For corn at their own rates . . i 1 193
That the gods sent not Corn for the rich men only . . . i 1 212
The Volsces have much corn; take these rats thither To gnaw their garners . . . . i 1 253
For once we stood up about the corn, he himself struck not to call us the many-headed multitude . . . . . ii 3 17
Of late, When corn was given them gratis, you repined . . iii 1 43
Tell me of corn! This was my speech, and I will speak't again— Not now . . . . iii 1 61
Whoever gave that counsel, to give forth The corn o' the storehouse gratis . . . . iii 1 114
They know the corn Was not our recompense, resting well assured They ne'er did service for't . . . . . . iii 1 120
This kind of service Did not deserve corn gratis . . . iii 1 125
First thrash the corn, then after burn the straw *T. Andron.* ii 3 123
Let me teach you how to knit again This scatter'd corn into one mutual sheaf . . . . v 3 71
Ladies that have their toes Unplagued with corns . *Rom. and Jul.* i 5 19
Which of you all Will now deny to dance? she that makes dainty, She, I'll swear, hath corns . . . . i 5 22
Though bladed corn be lodged and trees blown down . *Macbeth* iv 1 55
Shall of a corn cry woe, And turn his sleep to wake . *Lear* iii 2 33
Sleepest or wakest thou, jolly shepherd? Thy sheep be in the corn iii 6 44
Darnel, and all the idle weeds that grow In our sustaining corn . iv 4 6
With corn to make your needy bread, And give them life whom hunger starved half dead . . . . *Pericles* i 4 95
Your grace, that fed my country with your corn . . . iii 3 18
Cornelia never with more care Read to her sons than she hath read to thee Sweet poetry and Tully's Orator. . *T. Andron.* iv 1 12
How many saw the child?—Cornelia the midwife and myself . . iv 2 141
Cornelius. We here dispatch You, good Cornelius, and you, Voltimand, For bearers of this greeting to old Norway *Hamlet* i 2 34
What's this, Cornelius?—The queen, sir, very oft importuned me To temper poisons for her. . . . *Cymbeline* v 5 248
Corner. All corners else o' the earth Let liberty make use of . *Tempest* i 2 491
The old fantastical duke of dark corners *Meas. for Meas.* iv 3 164
I may sit in a corner and cry heigh-ho for a husband! . *Much Ado* ii 1 332
Is't possible? Sits the wind in that corner? . . . . ii 3 103
From the west corner of thy curious-knotted garden *L. L. Lost* i 1 249
From the four corners of the earth they come, To kiss this shrine *Mer. of Venice* ii 7 39
I shall grow jealous of you shortly, Launcelot, if you thus get my wife into corners . . . . iii 5 32
My old limbs lie lame And unregarded age in corners thrown *As Y. L. It* ii 3 42
Scout me for him at the corner of the orchard like a bum-baily *T. Night* iii 4 194
Skulking in corners? wishing clocks more swift? . *W. Tale* i 2 289
Even till that utmost corner of the west Salute thee for her king *K. John* ii 1 29
Come the three corners of the world in arms, And we shall shock them . v 7 116
I'll to yond corner.—And I to this . . . . *1 Hen. VI.* ii 1 33
And at every corner have them kiss . . . *2 Hen. VI.* iv 7 145
Up Fish Street! down Saint Magnus' Corner! . . . . iv 8 2
There's nothing I have done yet, o' my conscience, Deserves a corner *Hen. VIII.* iii 1 31
Upon the corner of the moon There hangs a vaporous drop profound *Macbeth* iii 5 23
He keeps them, like an ape, in the corner of his jaw . *Hamlet* iv 2 19
Than keep a corner in the thing I love For others' uses . *Othello* iii 3 272
Corner. Winds of all the corners kiss'd your sails, To make your vessel nimble . . . . *Cymbeline* ii 4 28
'Tis slander, . . . whose breath Rides on the posting winds and doth belie All corners of the world . . . . . . iii 4 39
Corner-cap. Thou makest the triumviry, the corner-cap of society *L. L. Lost* iv 3 53
Corner-stone. See you yon coign o' the Capitol, yon corner-stone? *Coriol.* v 4 2
Cornet. O God, that Somerset, who in proud heart Doth stop my cornets, were in Talbot's place! . . . . *1 Hen. VI.* iv 3 25
Cornfield. With a hey, and a ho, and a hey nonino, That o'er the green corn-field did pass . . . . *As Y. Like It* v 3 19
Cornish. Le Roy! a Cornish name: art thou of Cornish crew? *Hen. V.* iv 1 50
Cornuto. The peaking Cornuto her husband . . *Mer. Wives* iii 5 71
Cornwall. I thought the king had more affected the Duke of Albany than Cornwall . . . . *Lear* i 1 2
Our son of Cornwall, And you, our no less loving son of Albany . i 1 42
What says our second daughter, Our dearest Regan, wife to Cornwall? . i 1 69
Cornwall and Albany, With my two daughters' dowers digest this third i 1 129
The Duke of Cornwall and Regan his duchess will be here with him this night . . . . ii 1 4
Have you heard of no likely wars toward, 'twixt the Dukes of Cornwall and Albany? . . . . ii 1 12
Have you not spoken 'gainst the Duke of Cornwall? . . . ii 1 25
I'ld speak with the Duke of Cornwall and his wife.—Well, my good lord, I have inform'd them so . . . . ii 4 98
The king would speak with Cornwall; the dear father Would with his daughter speak . . . . ii 4 102
There is division, Although as yet the face of it be cover'd With mutual cunning, 'twixt Albany and Cornwall . . . . . iii 1 21
The Duke of Cornwall's dead; Slain by his servant, going to put out The other eye of Gloucester . . . . . . iv 2 70
Of Albany's and Cornwall's powers you heard not? . . . iv 3 50
Holds it true, sir, that the Duke of Cornwall was so slain? . . iv 7 86
Corollary. Bring a corollary, Rather than want a spirit . . *Tempest* iv 1 57
Coronation. Some reasons of this double coronation I have possess'd you with . . . . *K. John* iv 2 40
On Wednesday next we solemnly set down Our coronation *Richard II.* iv 1 320
Our coronation done, we will accite, As I before remember'd, all our state *2 Hen. IV.* v 2 141
'Twill be two o'clock ere they come from the coronation . . v 5 4
And in our coronation take your place . . . *1 Hen. VI.* iii 4 27
As I rode from Calais, To haste unto your coronation . . . iv 1 10
And with all speed provide To see her coronation be perform'd *2 Hen. VI.* i 1 74
First will I see the coronation; And then to Brittany . *3 Hen. VI.* ii 6 96
If our brother come, Where shall we sojourn till our coronation? *Richard III.* iii 1 62
Summon him to-morrow to the Tower, To sit about the coronation . iii 1 173
The cause why we are met Is, to determine of the coronation . iii 4 2
But, for his purpose in the coronation, I have not sounded him . iii 4 16
There's order given for her coronation . . . *Hen. VIII.* iii 2 46
Shortly, I believe, His second marriage shall be publish'd, and Her coronation . . . . iii 2 69
And the voice is now Only about her coronation . . . . iii 2 406
And behold The Lady Anne pass from her coronation . . . iv 1 3
'Tis the list Of those that claim their offices this day By custom of the coronation . . . . iv 1 16
Though willingly I came to Denmark, To show my duty in your coronation . . . . *Hamlet* i 2 53
Coronation-day. In London streets, that coronation-day, When Bolingbroke rode on roan Barbary . . . . . *Richard II.* v 5 77
A cough, sir, which I caught with ringing in the king's affairs upon his coronation-day, sir . . . . . . *2 Hen. IV.* iii 2 195
Coroner. The foolish coroners of that age . . . *As Y. Like It* iv 1 105
Coronet. Subject his coronet to his crown and bend The dukedom yet unbow'd . . . . *Tempest* i 2 114
With coronet of fresh and fragrant flowers . . . *M. N. Dream* iv 1 57
With crowns imperial, crowns and coronets . . . *Hen. V.* ii Prol. 10
And doth deserve a coronet of gold . . . . *1 Hen. VI.* iii 3 89
Adorn his temples with a coronet . . . . v 4 134
All the rest are countesses.—Their coronets say so . *Hen. VIII.* iv 1 54
I saw Mark Antony offer him a crown;—yet 'twas not a crown neither, 'twas one of these coronets . . . . *J. Cæsar* i 2 238
On the pendent boughs her coronet weeds Clambering to hang *Hamlet* iv 7 173
This coronet part betwixt you . . . . . . *Lear* i 1 141
Corporal. The poor beetle, that we tread upon, In corporal sufferance finds a pang as great As when a gaint dies . *Meas. for Meas.* iii 1 80
O my little heart!—And I to be a corporal of his field! . *L. L. Lost* iii 1 189
By earth, she is not, corporal . . . . iv 3 86
I would I had that corporal soundness now! . . . *All's Well* i 2 24
My whole charge consists of ancients, corporals, lieutenants *1 Hen. IV.* iv 2 26
Good master corporal captain, for my old dame's sake, stand my friend *2 Hen. IV.* iii 2 244
To relief of lazars and weak age, Of indigent faint souls past corporal toil . . . . *Hen. V.* i 1 16
It is certain, corporal, that he is married to Nell Quickly . . ii 1 19
Good corporal, be patient here . . . . ii 1 29
Good lieutenant! good corporal! offer nothing here . . . ii 1 41
Pray thee, corporal, stay: the knocks are too hot . . . iii 2 3
His corporal motion govern'd by my spirit . . . *J. Cæsar* iv 1 33
What seem'd corporal melted As breath into the wind . *Macbeth* i 3 81
I am settled, and bend up Each corporal agent to this terrible feat i 7 80
Render to me some corporal sign about her, More evident than this *Cymb.* ii 4 119
Corporal Nym. Away, Sir Corporal Nym! Believe it, Page; he speaks sense . . . . *Mer. Wives* ii 1 128
My name is Corporal Nym; I speak and I avouch; 'tis true . . i 1 137
Let it be so, good Corporal Nym.—Faith, I will live so long as I may *Hen. V.* ii 1 14
Corporal Nym, an thou wilt be friends, be friends . . . ii 1 107
Corporate. Good Master Corporate Bardolph, stand my friend; and here's four Harry ten shillings . . . . *2 Hen. IV.* iii 2 235
They answer, in a joint and corporate voice . . *T. of Athens* ii 2 213
Corpse. Not a friend, not a friend greet My poor corpse, where my bones shall be thrown . . . . *T. Night* ii 4 63
Therefore, no wife: one worse, And better used, would make her sainted spirit Again possess her corpse . . . . *W. Tale* v 1 58
Upon whose dead corpse there was such misuse . . *1 Hen. IV.* i 1 43
Had only but the corpse, But shadows and the shows of men, to fight *2 Hen. IV.* i 1 192
Within their chiefest temple I'll erect A tomb, wherein his corpse shall be interr'd . . . . *1 Hen. VI.* ii 2 13

Corpse. View his breathless corpse, And comment then upon his sudden death 2 *Hen. VI.* iii 2 132
For me, the ransom of my bold attempt Shall be this cold corpse on the earth's cold face *Richard III.* v 3 266
Stay here with Antony: Do grace to Cæsar's corpse *J. Cæsar* iii 2 62
Make a ring about the corpse of Cæsar, And let me show you him that made the will iii 2 162
The belching whale And humming water must o'erwhelm thy corpse *Pericles* iii 1 64
Corpulent. A goodly portly man, i' faith, and a corpulent 1 *Hen. IV.* ii 4 464
Correct. Were he meal'd with that Which he corrects, then were he tyrannous *Meas. for Meas.* iv 2 87
I beseech your worship to correct yourself, for the example of others *Much Ado* v 1 331
Whiles we, God's wrathful agent, do correct Their proud contempt *K. John* ii 1 87
But since correction lieth in those hands Which made the fault that we cannot correct, Put we our quarrel to the will of heaven *Richard II.* i 2 5
Where some, like magistrates, correct at home, Others, like merchants, venture trade abroad *Hen. V.* i 2 191
And when I did correct him for his fault the other day, he did vow upon his knees he would be even with me 2 *Hen. VI.* i 3 202
His faults lie open to the laws; let them, Not you, correct him *Hen. VIII.* iii 2 335
Whose medicinable eye Corrects the ill aspects of planets evil *Troi. and Cres.* i 3 92
What wouldst thou?—I would correct him v 6 3
To show his sorrow, he'ld correct himself *Pericles* i 3 23
Corrected. What is this? Your knees to me? to your corrected son? *Coriolanus* v 3 57
Correcting thy stout heart, Now humble as the ripest mulberry That will not hold the handling iii 2 78
Correction. There is no woe to his correction *T. G. of Ver.* ii 4 138
I'll after, to rejoice in the boy's correction iii 1 395
Under your good correction, I have seen, When, after execution, judgement hath Repented o'er his doom *Meas. for Meas.* ii 2 10
Correction and instruction must both work Ere this rude beast will profit iii 2 33
As it shall follow in my correction: and God defend the right! *L. L. Lost* i 1 215
Not so, sir; under correction, sir; I hope it is not so v 2 489
Under correction, sir, we know whereuntil it doth amount v 2 493
But since correction lieth in those hands Which made the fault that we cannot correct, Put we our quarrel to the will of heaven *Richard II.* i 2 4
Chastise thee And minister correction to thy fault iii 3 105
There is my bond of faith, To tie thee to my strong correction iv 7 77
And wilt thou, pupil-like, Take thy correction mildly, kiss the rod? v 1 32
But if he will not yield, Rebuke and dread correction wait on us And they shall do their office 1 *Hen. IV.* v 1 111
Holds his infant up And hangs resolved correction in the arm That was uprear'd to execution 2 *Hen. IV.* iv 1 213
Hastings and all Are brought to the correction of your law iv 4 85
Sir, You show great mercy, if you give him life, After the taste of much correction *Hen. V.* ii 2 51
Under your correction, there is not many of your nation— Of my nation! iii 2 130
Henceforth let a Welsh correction teach you a good English condition v 1 83
Under the correction of bragging be it spoken v 2 144
Were I the general, thou shouldst have my office Ere that correction *Troi. and Cres.* v 6 5
Your purposed low correction Is such as basest and contemned'st wretches For pilferings and most common trespasses Are punish'd with *Lear* ii 2 149
Correctioner. You filthy famished correctioner 2 *Hen. IV.* v 4 23
Correspondent. I will be correspondent to command And do my spiriting gently *Tempest* i 2 297
Corresponding. Well corresponding With your stiff age *Cymbeline* iii 3 31
Corresponsive. Massy staples And corresponsive and fulfilling bolts *Troi. and Cres.* Prol. 18
Corrigible. The power and corrigible authority of this lies in our wills *Othello* i 3 329
Bending down His corrigible neck, His face subdued *Ant. and Cleo.* iv 14 74
Corrival. Might wear Without corrival all her dignities 1 *Hen. IV.* i 3 207
Many moe corrivals and dear men Of estimation and command in arms iv 4 31
Corroborate. His heart is fracted and corroborate *Hen. V.* ii 1 130
Corrosive. Care is no cure, but rather corrosive, For things that are not to be remedied 1 *Hen. VI.* iii 3 3
Though parting be a fretful corrosive 2 *Hen. VI.* iii 2 403
Corrupt, corrupt, and tainted in desire! *Mer. Wives* v 5 94
Do as the carrion does, not as the flower, Corrupt with virtuous season *Meas. for Meas.* ii 2 168
Angelo had never the purpose to corrupt her iii 1 163
And the corrupt deputy scaled iii 1 265
In law, what plea so tainted and corrupt But, being season'd with a gracious voice, Obscures the show of evil? *Mer. of Venice* iii 2 75
You corrupt the song *All's Well* i 3 84
We must not So stain our judgement, or corrupt our hope ii 1 123
Disdain Rather corrupt me ever! ii 3 123
My son corrupts a well-derived nature With his inducement iii 2 90
Brokes with all that can in such a suit Corrupt the tender honour of a maid iii 5 75
I need not to ask you if gold will corrupt him to revolt iv 3 309
Thou hast damnable iteration and art indeed able to corrupt a saint 1 *Hen. IV.* i 2 102
By this light flesh and corrupt blood, thou art welcome 2 *Hen. IV.* ii 4 320
Corrupt and tainted with a thousand vices 1 *Hen. VI.* v 4 45
She did corrupt frail nature with some bribe, To shrink mine arm up 3 *Hen. VI.* iii 2 155
O, let her live, And I'll corrupt her manners, stain her beauty *Richard III.* iv 4 206
This top-proud fellow . . . I do know To be corrupt and treasonous *Hen. VIII.* i 1 156
The mind growing once corrupt, They turn to vicious forms i 2 116
Heaven is above all yet; there sits a judge That no king can corrupt iii 1 100
At what ease Might corrupt minds procure knaves as corrupt To swear against you? such things have been done v 1 133
I will corrupt the Grecian sentinels, To give thee nightly visitation *Troi. and Cres.* iv 4 74
I prize As the dead carcasses of unburied men That do corrupt my air *Coriolanus* iii 3 123
The fittest time to corrupt a man's wife is when she's fallen out with her husband iv 3 33
My disports corrupt and taint my business *Othello* i 3 272
Corrupted. Too holy, To be corrupted with my worthless gifts *T. G. of Ver.* iv 2 6
But if he start, It is the flesh of a corrupted heart *Mer. Wives* v 5 91

Corrupted. But Fortune, O, She is corrupted, changed and won from thee *K. John* iii 1 55
By the merit of vile gold, dross, dust, Purchase corrupted pardon of a man iii 1 166
Three corrupted men *Hen. V.* ii Prol. 22
Attainted, Corrupted, and exempt from ancient gentry 1 *Hen. VI.* ii 4 93
And he but naked, though lock'd up in steel, Whose conscience with injustice is corrupted 2 *Hen. VI.* iii 2 235
Corrupted the youth of the realm in erecting a grammar school iv 7 36
By underhand corrupted foul injustice *Richard III.* v 1 6
If this law Of nature be corrupted through affection *Troi. and Cres.* ii 2 177
Be pitiful to my condemned sons, Whose souls are not corrupted as 'tis thought *T. Andron.* iii 1 9
In the corrupted currents of this world Offence's gilded hand may shove by justice *Hamlet* iii 3 57
Thou art a boil, A plague-sore, an embossed carbuncle, In my corrupted blood *Lear* ii 4 228
Corrupted By spells and medicines bought of mountebanks *Othello* i 3 60
The jewels you have had from me to deliver to Desdemona would half have corrupted a votarist iv 2 190
O, my fortunes have Corrupted honest men! *Ant. and Cleo.* iv 5 17
Who knows if one of her women, being corrupted, Hath stol'n it from her? *Cymbeline* ii 4 116
Had I brought hither a corrupted mind, Thy speech had alter'd it *Pericles* iv 6 111
Corrupter. Not her fool, but her corrupter of words *T. Night* iii 1 41
Harbour more craft and more corrupter ends *Lear* ii 2 108
Away, away, Corrupters of my faith! *Cymbeline* iii 4 85
Corruptibly. The life of all his blood Is touch'd corruptibly *K. John* v 7 2
Corrupting. And all her husbandry doth lie on heaps, Corrupting in it own fertility *Hen. V.* v 2 40
Know'st thou not any whom corrupting gold Would tempt? *Richard III.* iv 2 34
Corruption. What corruption in this life, that it will let this man live! *Meas. for Meas.* iii 1 241
Where I have seen corruption boil and bubble Till it o'er-run the stew v 1 320
No man that hath a name, By falsehood and corruption doth it shame *Com. of Errors* ii 1 113
Babbling, drunkenness, Or any taint of vice whose strong corruption Inhabits our frail blood *T. Night* iii 4 390
I fear will issue thence The foul corruption of a sweet child's death *K. John* iv 2 81
Foul sin gathering head Shall break into corruption *Richard II.* v 1 59; 2 *Hen. IV.* iii 1 77
We did train him on, And, his corruption being ta'en from us, We, as the spring of all, shall pay for all 1 *Hen. IV.* v 2 22
To the corruption of a blemish'd stock *Richard III.* iii 7 122
From the corruption of abusing times iii 7 199
Corruption wins not more than honesty *Hen. VIII.* iii 2 444
No other speaker of my living actions, To keep mine honour from corruption iv 2 71
The name of Cassius honours this corruption *J. Cæsar* iv 3 15
Shall in the general censure take corruption From that particular fault *Hamlet* i 4 35
Stew'd in corruption, honeying and making love Over the nasty sty iii 4 93
Whiles rank corruption, mining all within, Infects unseen iii 4 148
Stop her there! Arms, arms, sword, fire! Corruption in the place! *Lear* iii 6 58
Corruptly. O, that estates, degrees and offices Were not derived corruptly! *Mer. of Venice* ii 9 42
Corse. Strew him o'er and o'er!—What, like a corse?—No, like a bank for love to lie and play on; Not like a corse *W. Tale* iv 4 129
He call'd them untaught knaves, unmannerly, To bring a slovenly unhandsome corse Betwixt the wind and his nobility 1 *Hen. IV.* i 3 44
Harry to Harry shall, hot horse to horse, Meet and ne'er part till one drop down a corse iv 1 123
What say'st thou, man, before dead Henry's corse? 1 *Hen. VI.* i 1 62
Stay, you that bear the corse, and set it down *Richard III.* i 2 33
Set down the corse; or, by Saint Paul, I'll make a corse of him that disobeys i 2 36
Sirs, take up the corse.—Towards Chertsey, noble lord?—No, to White-Friars i 2 226
You do him injury to scorn his corse ii 1 80
When he that is my husband now Came to me, as I follow'd Henry's corse iv 1 67
Then if she that lays thee out says thou art a fair corse, I'll be sworn and sworn upon't she never shrouded any but lazars *Troi. and Cres.* ii 3 35
Stands colossus-wise, waving his beam, Upon the pashed corses of the kings v 5 10
The most noble corse that ever herald Did follow to his urn *Coriolanus* v 6 145
A piteous corse, a bloody piteous corse; Pale, pale as ashes *Rom. and Jul.* iii 2 54
Where is my father, and my mother, nurse?—Weeping and wailing over Tybalt's corse iii 2 128
Dry up your tears, and stick your rosemary On this fair corse iv 5 80
Our bridal flowers serve for a buried corse iv 5 89
Every one prepare To follow this fair corse unto her grave iv 5 93
Poor living corse, closed in a dead man's tomb! v 2 29
Here lies a wretched corse, of wretched soul bereft: Seek not my name *T. of Athens* v 4 70
Making his peace, Shaking the bloody fingers of thy foes, Most noble! in the presence of thy corse? *J. Cæsar* iii 1 199
Thou shalt not back till I have borne this corse Into the market-place iii 1 291
Who still hath cried, From the first corse till he that died to-day, 'This must be so' *Hamlet* i 2 105
What may this mean, That thou, dead corse, again in complete steel Revisit'st thus the glimpses of the moon? i 4 52
We have many pocky corses now-a-days, that will scarce hold the laying in v 1 181
This doth betoken The corse they follow did with desperate hand Fordo it own life v 1 243
Yea, and furr'd moss besides, when flowers are none, To winter-ground thy corse *Cymbeline* iv 2 229
O you most potent gods! what's here? a corse! *Pericles* ii 2 63
Corslet. He is able to pierce a corslet with his eye *Coriolanus* v 4 21
Cosmo, Lodowick, and Gratii, two hundred and fifty each *All's Well* iv 3 186
Cost. That cost me two shilling and two pence a-piece *Mer. Wives* i 1 159
Assemblies Where youth, and cost, and witless bravery keeps *Meas. for Meas.* i 3 10
This jest shall cost me some expense *Com. of Errors* iii 1 123
It will cost him a thousand pound ere a' be cured *Much Ado* i 1 90
The fashion of the world is to avoid cost, and you encounter it i 1 98
I am for you, though it cost me ten nights' watchings ii 1 387

Cost. With sighs of love, that costs the fresh blood dear *M. N. Dream* iii 2 97
A diamond gone, cost me two thousand ducats! . . . *Mer. of Venice* iii 1 88
How little is the cost I have bestow'd In purchasing the semblance of my soul! . . . . iii 4 19
The city-woman bears The cost of princes on unworthy shoulders *As Y. Like It* ii 7 76
Or what is he of basest function That says his bravery is not on my cost? ii 7 80
The wisdom of your duty, fair Bianca, Hath cost me an hundred crowns *T. of Shrew* v 2 128
If she had partaken of my flesh, and cost me the dearest groans of a mother, I could not have owed her a more rooted love *All's Well* iv 5 11
Here at my house and at my proper cost . . . *T. Night* v 1 327
I shall never hold that man my friend Whose tongue shall ask me for one penny cost . . . . . . *1 Hen. IV.* i 3 91
When we see the figure of the house, Then must we rate the cost *2 Hen. IV.* i 3 44
Who, half through, Gives o'er and leaves his part-created cost A naked subject to the weeping clouds . . . . i 3 60
It may chance cost some of us our lives . . . . . ii 1 12
He is at Oxford still, is he not?—Indeed, sir, to my cost . iii 2 13
I am not covetous for gold, Nor care I who doth feed upon my cost *Hen. V.* iv 3 25
One would have lingering wars with little cost; Another would fly swift, but wanteth wings . . . . *1 Hen. VI.* i 1 74
We will meet; to thy cost, be sure . . . . . . i 3 82
Thou shalt see I'll meet thee to thy cost . . . . . iii 4 43
She sent over of the King of England's own proper cost . *2 Hen. VI.* i 1 61
That Suffolk should demand a whole fifteenth For costs and charges! i 1 134
Thy sumptuous buildings and thy wife's attire Have cost a mass of public treasury . . . . i 3 134
I charge and command that, of the city's cost . . . . iv 6 3
Whose haughty spirit, winged with desire, Will cost my crown *3 Hen. VI.* i 1 268
These words will cost ten thousand lives this day . . ii 2 177
Since I am crept in favour with myself, I will maintain it with some little cost . . . . *Richard III.* i 2 260
A paltry fellow, Long kept in Bretagne at our mother's cost . . v 3 324
Grievingly I think, The peace between the French and us not values The cost that did conclude it . . . . . *Hen. VIII.* i 1 89
She is not worth what she doth cost The holding . *Troi. and Cres.* ii 2 51
The fall of every Phrygian stone will cost A drop of Grecian blood . iv 5 223
Most putrefied core, so fair without, Thy goodly armour thus hath cost thy life . . . . v 8 2
Look to the baked meats, good Angelica: Spare not for cost *Rom. and Jul.* iv 4 6
I have bred her at my dearest cost In qualities of the best *T. of Athens* i 1 124
How dost thou like this jewel, Apemantus?—Not so well as plain-dealing, which will not cost a man a doit . . . . i 1 217
It would cost you a groaning to take off my edge . . *Hamlet* iii 2 259
Did these bones cost no more the breeding, but to play at loggats with 'em? . . . . v 1 100
The dark and vicious place where thee he got Cost him his eyes . *Lear* v 3 173
King Stephen was a worthy peer, His breeches cost him but a crown *Oth.* ii 3 93
I must come forth.—If thou attempt it, it will cost thee dear . v 2 255
Choose your own company, and command what cost Your heart has mind to . . . . *Ant. and Cleo.* iii 4 37
Whate'er it be, What pain it cost, what danger . . *Cymbeline* iii 6 81
I, King Pericles, have lost This queen, worth all our mundane cost *Per.* iii 2 71
Costard. I will knog his urinals about his knave's costard *Mer. Wives* iii 1 14
Costard the swain and he shall be our sport . . . *L. L. Lost* i 1 180
Not a word of Costard yet . . . . i 1 224
Which, as I remember, hight Costard . . . . . i 1 259
The rational hind Costard . . . . i 2 124
The duke's pleasure is, that you keep Costard safe . . . i 2 133
Here's a costard broken in a shin . . . . . . iii 1 71
How did this argument begin?—By saying that a costard was broken in a shin . . . . iii 1 107
I Costard, running out, that was safely within, Fell over the threshold, and broke my shin . . . . iii 1 117
Sirrah Costard, I will enfranchise thee.—O, marry me to one Frances iii 1 121
O, my good knave Costard! exceedingly well met . . . iii 1 144
Be so good as read me this letter: it was given me by Costard . iv 2 93
Good Costard, go with me. Sir, God save your life! . . . iv 2 149
Where hadst thou it?—Of Costard.—Where hadst thou it?—Of Dun Adramadio . . . . iv 3 197
Pompey the Great,— Your servant, and Costard . . . . v 2 574
Take him over the costard with the hilts of thy sword . *Richard III.* i 4 159
Keep out, che vor ye, or ise try whether your costard or my ballow be the harder . . . . *Lear* iv 6 247
Costermonger. Virtue is of so little regard in these costermonger times that true valour is turned bear-herd . . . *2 Hen. IV.* i 2 191
Costlier. Provide me presently A riding-suit, no costlier than would fit A franklin's housewife . . . . . . *Cymbeline* iii 2 78
Costly. Your grace is too costly to wear every day . . *Much Ado* iii 1 341
A day in April never came so sweet, To show how costly summer was at hand . . . . *Mer. of Venice* ii 9 94
Be ready with a costly suit And ask him what apparel he will wear *T. of Shrew* Ind. 1 59
Costly apparel, tents, and canopies, Fine linen, Turkey cushions . ii 1 354
Under the canopies of costly state . . . . *2 Hen. IV.* iii 1 13
I took a costly jewel from my neck, A heart it was, bound in with diamonds . . . . *2 Hen. VI.* iii 2 106
Suggests the king our master To this last costly treaty . *Hen. VIII.* i 1 165
With such a costly loss of wealth and friends . *Troi. and Cres.* iv 1 60
Woe to the hand that shed this costly blood! . . . *J. Cæsar* iii 1 258
Costly thy habit as thy purse can buy, But not express'd in fancy *Hamlet* i 3 70
Cote. His cote, his flocks and bounds of feed Are now on sale *As Y. L. It* ii 4 83
Come every day to my cote and woo me . . . . . iii 2 447
Coted. We coted them on the way; and hither are they coming *Hamlet* ii 2 330
Cot-quean. Go, you cot-quean, go, Get you to bed . *Rom. and Jul.* iv 4 6
Cotsall. How does your fallow greyhound, sir? I heard say he was outrun on Cotsall . . . . *Mer. Wives* i 1 92
Cotswold. I bethink me what a weary way From Ravenspurgh to Cotswold will be found . . . . *Richard II.* ii 3 9
Will Squele, a Cotswold man . . . . . . *2 Hen. IV.* iii 2 23
Cottage. If to do were as easy as to know what were good to do, chapels had been churches and poor men's cottages princes' palaces *Mer. of Venice* i 2 15
If it stand with honesty, Buy thou the cottage . . *As Y. Like It* ii 4 92
He hath bought the cottage and the bounds That the old carlot once was master of . . . . iii 5 107
The report of her is extended more than can be thought to begin from such a cottage . . . . *W. Tale* iv 2 50
Cottage. The selfsame sun that shines upon his court Hides not his visage from our cottage but Looks on alike . . . *W. Tale* iv 4 456
Home to your cottages, forsake this groom . . . *2 Hen. VI.* iv 2 132
Cotus. Where's Cotus? my master calls for him. Cotus! *Coriolanus* iv 5 3
Couch. In a cowslip's bell I lie; There I couch when owls do cry *Tempest* v 1 90
His dove will prove, his gold will hold, And his soft couch defile *M. Wives* i 3 108
We'll couch i' the castle-ditch till we see the light of our fairies . v 2 1
They are fairies; he that speaks to them shall die: I'll wink and couch v 5 52
Doth not the gentleman Deserve as full as fortunate a bed As ever Beatrice shall couch upon? . . . . . . *Much Ado* iii 1 46
Wilt thou sleep? we'll have thee to a couch . . . *T. of Shrew* Ind. 2 39
But couch, ho! here he comes . . . . *All's Well* iv 1 24
Arise forth from the couch of lasting night, Thou hate and terror to prosperity . . . . *K. John* iii 4 27
And leavest the kingly couch A watch-case or a common 'larum-bell *2 Hen. IV.* iii 1 16
England shall couch down in fear and yield . . . *Hen. V.* iv 2 37
No vast obscurity or misty vale, Where bloody murder or detested rape Can couch for fear, but I will find them out . . *T. Andron.* v 2 38
Where unbruised youth with unstuff'd brain Doth couch his limbs, there golden sleep doth reign . . . . . . *Rom. and Jul.* ii 3 38
Let not the royal bed of Denmark be A couch for luxury . . *Hamlet* i 5 83
Couch we awhile, and mark . . . . v 1 245
This night, wherein the cub-drawn bear would couch . . *Lear* iii 1 12
The tyrant custom, most grave senators, Hath made the flinty and steel couch of war My thrice-driven bed of down . . . . *Othello* i 3 231
O, 'tis the spite of hell, the fiend's arch-mock, To lip a wanton in a secure couch, And to suppose her chaste! . . . . . iv 1 72
If I court moe women, you'll couch with moe men . . . . iv 3 57
Where souls do couch on flowers, we'll hand in hand . *Ant. and Cleo.* iv 14 51
The cat, with eyne of burning coal, Now couches fore the mouse's hole *Pericles* iii Gower 6
Couched. They are all couched in a pit hard by . . *Mer. Wives* v 3 14
Who even now Is couched in the woodbine coverture . . *Much Ado* iii 1 30
Securely I espy Virtue with valour couched in thine eye . *Richard II.* i 3 98
A braver soldier never couched lance . . . . *1 Hen. VI.* iii 2 134
With ignominious words, though clerkly couch'd . . *2 Hen. VI.* iii 1 179
His body couched in a curious bed . . . . . *3 Hen. VI.* ii 5 53
Sorrow, that is couch'd in seeming gladness . . *Troi. and Cres.* i 1 39
One cloud of winter showers, These flies are couch'd . *T. of Athens* ii 2 181
He whose sable arms, Black as his purpose, did the night resemble When he lay couched in the ominous horse . . . . *Hamlet* ii 2 476
Couching. Were the day come, I should wish it dark, That I were couching with the doctor's clerk . . . . . . *Mer. of Venice* v 1 305
A lioness, with udders all drawn dry, Lay couching, head on ground *As Y. Like It* iv 3 116
A couching lion and a ramping cat . . . . . *1 Hen. IV.* iii 1 153
These couchings and these lowly courtesies Might fire the blood of ordinary men . . . . *J. Cæsar* iii 1 36
Coude. Dites-moi l'Anglois pour le bras.—De arm, madame.—Et le coude?—De elbow . . . . *Hen. V.* iii 4 23
Cough. Down topples she, And 'tailor' cries, and falls into a cough *M. N. Dream* ii 1 54
What disease hast thou?—A whoreson cold, sir, a cough, sir *2 Hen. IV.* iii 2 193
The faint defects of age Must be the scene of mirth; to cough and spit *Troi. and Cres.* i 3 173
Shut the door; Cough, or cry 'hem,' if any body come . . *Othello* iv 2 29
Thou didst drink The stale of horses, and the gilded puddle Which beasts would cough at . . . . *Ant. and Cleo.* i 4 63
Coughing. And coughing drowns the parson's saw . . *L. L. Lost* v 2 932
Thou hast quarrelled with a man for coughing in the street *Rom. and Jul.* iii 1 27
Could. Had that in't which good natures Could not abide to be with *Tempest* i 2 360
His more braver daughter could control thee, If now 'twere fit to do't . i 2 439
This is to make an ass of me; to fright me, if they could *M. N. Dream* iii 1 124
Some doubtful phrase, As 'Well, well, we know,' or 'We could, an if we would' . . . . *Hamlet* i 5 176
The hand could pluck her back that shoved her on . *Ant. and Cleo.* i 2 131
When perforce he could not But pay me terms of honour, cold and sickly He vented them . . . . iii 4 6
Coulter. The coulter rusts That should deracinate such savagery *Hen. V.* v 2 46
Council. The council shall hear it; it is a riot.—It is not meet the council hear a riot . . . . *Mer. Wives* i 1 35
The council, look you, shall desire to hear the fear of Got, and not to hear a riot . . . . i 1 37
The council shall know this.—'Twere better for you if it were known in counsel . . . . i 1 120
In our maiden council, rated them At courtship, pleasant jest *L. L. Lost* v 2 789
That the great figure of a council frames By self-unable motion *All's Well* iii 1 12
I perceive, by this demand, you are not altogether of his council . iv 3 53
Draw near, And list what with our council we have done *Richard II.* i 3 124
Let me hear . . . What yesternight our council did decree . *1 Hen. IV.* i 1 32
On Wednesday next our council we Will hold at Windsor . . i 1 103
An old lord of the council rated me the other day in the street about you i 2 95
Thy place in council thou hast rudely lost . . . . iii 2 32
Appoint some of your council presently To sit with us once more *Hen. V.* v 2 79
There is more eloquence in a sugar touch of them than in the tongues of the French council . . . . v 2 304
With all the learned council of the realm . . . . *2 Hen. VI.* i 1 89
Me seemeth then it is no policy . . . That he should come about your royal person Or be admitted to your highness' council . . iii 1 27
The king's council are no good workmen . . . . . iv 2 15
The queen this day here holds her parliament, But little thinks we shall be of her council . . . . *3 Hen. VI.* i 1 36
In his nonage council under him . . . . . *Richard III.* ii 3 13
We to-morrow hold divided councils, Wherein thyself shalt highly be employ'd . . . . iii 1 179
Besides, he says there are two councils held . . . iii 2 12
Bid him not fear the separated councils . . . . . iii 2 20
You may jest on, but, by the holy rood, I do not like these several councils . . . . iii 2 78
His own letter, The honourable board of council out, Must fetch him in he papers . . . . *Hen. VIII.* i 1 79
They had gather'd a wise council to them Of every realm . . ii 4 51
Without the knowledge Either of king or council . . . iii 2 317
I think I have Incensed the lords o' the council . . . v 1 43
Which, being consider'd, Have moved us and our council . . v 1 100
The gentleman, That was sent to me from the council, pray'd me To make great haste . . . . v 2 2

Council. Speak to the business, master secretary: Why are we met in council? *Hen. VIII.* v 3 2
I had thought I had had men of some understanding And wisdom of my council v 3 136
Go we to council. Let Achilles sleep *Troi. and Cres.* ii 3 276
The Genius and the mortal instruments Are then in council *J. Cæsar* ii 1 67
Let us presently go sit in council, How covert matters may be best disclosed iv 1 45
We should have else desired your good advice, Which still hath been both grave and prosperous, In this day's council *Macbeth* iii 1 23
How! the duke in council! In this time of the night! *Othello* i 2 93
And to that end Assemble we immediate council *Ant. and Cleo.* i 4 75
Not a man in private conference Or council has respect with him but he *Pericles* ii 4 18
Council-board. Rated mine uncle from the council-board 1 *Hen. IV.* iv 3 99
Hath commanded To-morrow morning to the council-board He be convented *Hen. VIII.* v 1 51
Council-house. Sat in the council-house Early and late, debating to and fro 2 *Hen. VI.* i 1 90
The subtle traitor This day had plotted, in the council-house To murder me *Richard III.* iii 5 38
Counsel. But wherefore waste I time to counsel thee, That art a votary to fond desire? *T. G. of Ver.* i 1 51
Made me neglect my studies, lose my time, War with good counsel i 1 68
Now we are alone, Wouldst thou then counsel me to fall in love? i 2 2
I like thy counsel; well hast thou advised i 3 34
Go with me to my chamber, In these affairs to aid me with thy counsel ii 4 185
Myself in counsel, his competitor ii 6 35
Counsel, Lucetta; gentle girl, assist me ii 7 1
The council shall know this.—'Twere better for you if it were known in counsel *Mer. Wives* i 1 122
O Mistress Page, give me some counsel!—What's the matter, woman? ii 1 42
Follow your friend's counsel iii 3 146
I will at the least keep your counsel iv 6 7
I thank your worship for your good counsel *Meas. for Meas.* ii 1 267
Let her wear it out with good counsel *Much Ado* ii 3 208
Counsel him to fight against his passion iii 1 83
And have thy counsel Which is the best to furnish me to-morrow iii 1 102
Keep your fellows' counsels and your own; and good night iii 3 92
What a Hero hadst thou been, If half thy outward graces had been placed About thy thoughts and counsels of thy heart! iv 1 103
Pause awhile, And let my counsel sway you in this case iv 1 203
Cease thy counsel, Which falls into mine ears as profitless As water in a sieve v 1 3
Give not me counsel; Nor let no comforter delight mine ear v 1 5
Men Can counsel and speak comfort to that grief Which they themselves not feel; but, tasting it, Their counsel turns to passion v 1 21
Give me no counsel: My griefs cry louder than advertisement v 1 31
To her white hand see thou do commend This seal'd-up counsel *L. L. Lost* iii 1 170
Their several counsels they unbosom shall To loves mistook v 2 141
Emptying our bosoms of their counsel sweet *M. N. Dream* i 1 216
To trust the opportunity of night And the ill counsel of a desert place ii 1 218
The counsel that we two have shared, The sisters' vows iii 2 198
Did ever keep your counsels, never wrong'd you iii 2 308
Such a hare is madness the youth, to skip o'er the meshes of good counsel the cripple *Mer. of Venice* i 2 22
'Conscience,' say I, 'you counsel well;' 'Fiend,' say I, 'you counsel well' ii 2 22
My conscience is but a kind of hard conscience, to offer to counsel me to stay ii 2 30
The fiend gives the more friendly counsel ii 2 32
You know yourself, Hate counsels not in such a quality iii 2 6
Fear of your adventure would counsel you to a more equal enterprise *As Y. Like It* i 2 187
I do in friendship counsel you To leave this place i 2 273
I would give him some good counsel iii 2 383
I profess curing it by counsel.—Did you ever cure any so? iii 2 425
Go thou with me, and let me counsel thee iii 3 96
I'll in to counsel them; haply my presence May well abate the over-merry spleen *T. of Shrew* Ind. 1 136
Counsel me, Tranio, for I know thou canst; Assist me, Tranio i 1 162
This contents: The rest will comfort, for thy counsel's sound i 1 169
Thou'ldst thank me but a little for my counsel i 2 61
So thou wilt be capable of a courtier's counsel *All's Well* i 1 224
And what to your sworn counsel I have spoken Is so from word to word iii 7 9
Two faults, madonna, that drink and good counsel will amend *T. Night* i 5 48
His counsel now might do me golden service iv 3 8
O, you give me ill counsel.—Put your grace in your pocket, sir, for this once v 1 34
Mark my counsel, Which must be even as swiftly follow'd as I mean to utter it *W. Tale* i 2 408
As or by oath remove or counsel shake The fabric of his folly i 2 428
Our prerogative Calls not your counsels, but our natural goodness Imparts this ii 1 164
Whose spiritual counsel had, Shall stop or spur me ii 1 186
Didst counsel and aid them, for their better safety, to fly away by night iii 2 20
The father, all whose joy is nothing else But fair posterity, should hold some counsel In such a business iv 4 420
Cast your good counsels Upon his passion iv 4 506
'Tis your counsel My lord should to the heavens be contrary v 1 44
O, that ever I Had squared me to thy counsel! v 1 52
I defy all counsel, all redress, But that which ends all counsel, true redress, Death, death *K. John* iii 4 23
Before you were new crown'd, We breathed our counsel iv 2 36
Will the king come, that I may breathe my last In wholesome counsel to his unstaid youth? *Richard II.* ii 1 2
Strive not with your breath; For all in vain comes counsel to his ear ii 1 4
Though Richard my life's counsel would not hear, My death's sad tale may yet undeaf his ear ii 1 15
Then all too late comes counsel to be heard, Where will doth mutiny with wit's regard ii 1 27
Let no man speak again To alter this, for counsel is but vain iii 2 214
When we need Your use and counsel, we shall send for you 1 *Hen. IV.* i 3 21
You do not counsel well: You speak it out of fear and cold heart iv 3 6
If well-respected honour bid me on, I hold as little counsel with weak fear As you iv 3 11
Counsel every man The aptest way for safety and revenge 2 *Hen. IV.* i 1 212
As I was then advised by my learned counsel in the laws i 2 153
I will take your counsel iii 1 106
Counsel. And hear, I think, the very latest counsel That ever I shall breathe 2 *Hen. IV.* iv 5 183
And let us choose such limbs of noble counsel v 2 135
By your own counsel is suppress'd and kill'd *Hen. V.* ii 2 80
Thou that didst bear the key of all my counsels ii 2 96
Well, I will lock his counsel in my breast 1 *Hen VI.* ii 5 118
Friendly counsel cuts off many foes iii 1 185
Shall Henry's conquest, Bedford's vigilance, Your deeds of war and all our counsel die? 2 *Hen. VI.* i 1 97
Madam, list to me; For I am bold to counsel you in this i 3 96
What counsel give you in this weighty cause? iii 1 289
And craves your company for speedy counsel 3 *Hen. VI.* iii 1 208
What counsel give you? whither shall we fly? iii 3 11
Never will I undertake the thing Wherein thy counsel and consent is wanting ii 6 102
What counsel, lords? iv 8 1
Good counsel, marry: learn it, learn it, marquess *Richard III.* i 3 261
What, dost thou scorn me for my gentle counsel? i 3 297
Hast thou that holy feeling in thy soul, To counsel me to make my peace with God, And art thou yet to thy own soul so blind? i 4 258
My other self, my counsel's consistory, My oracle, my prophet! ii 2 151
Then this land was famously enrich'd With politic grave counsel ii 3 20
If I may counsel you, some day or two Your highness shall repose you at the Tower iii 1 64
Full of wise care is this your counsel iv 1 48
Buckingham No more shall be the neighbour to my counsel iv 2 43
My counsel is my shield; We must be brief when traitors brave the field iv 3 56
Bosom up my counsel, You'll find it wholesome *Hen. VIII.* i 1 112
Where you are liberal of your loves and counsels Be sure you be not loose ii 1 126
And out of all these to restore the king, He counsels a divorce ii 2 31
Is not this course pious?—Heaven keep me from such counsel! ii 2 38
Spare me, till I may Be by my friends in Spain advised; whose counsel I will implore ii 4 55
I committed The daring'st counsel which I had to doubt ii 4 215
Offers, as I do, in a sign of peace, His service and his counsel iii 1 67
Let me have time and counsel for my cause iii 1 79
Can you think, lords, That any Englishman dare give me counsel? iii 1 84
I would your grace Would leave your griefs, and take my counsel iii 1 92
Is this your Christian counsel? out upon ye! Heaven is above all yet iii 1 99
Come, reverend fathers, Bestow your counsels on me iii 1 182
Truth shall nurse her, Holy and heavenly thoughts still counsel her v 5 30
Else might the world convince of levity As well my undertakings as your counsels *Troi. and Cres.* ii 2 131
Your silence, Cunning in dumbness, from my weakness draws My very soul of counsel! iii 2 141
'Twere better she were kiss'd in general.—And very courtly counsel iv 5 22
Examine Their counsels and their cares, digest things rightly *Coriolanus* i 1 154
So, your opinion is, Aufidius, That they of Rome are enter'd in our counsels i 2 2
Whoever gave that counsel, to give forth The corn o' the storehouse gratis iii 1 113
Never admitting Counsel o' the war v 6 97
Thy counsel, lad, smells of no cowardice *T. Andron.* ii 1 132
That will betray with blushing The close enacts and counsels of the heart iv 2 118
Two may keep counsel when the third's away iv 2 144
Black and portentous must this humour prove, Unless good counsel may the cause remove *Rom. and Jul.* i 1 148
Nurse, come back again; I have remember'd me, thou's hear our counsel i 3 9
What man art thou that thus bescreen'd in night So stumblest on my counsel? ii 2 53
Love, who first did prompt me to inquire; He lent me counsel and I lent him eyes ii 2 81
Did you ne'er hear say, Two may keep counsel, putting one away? ii 4 209
O Lord, I could have stay'd here all the night To hear good counsel iii 3 160
Comfort me, counsel me. Alack, alack, that heaven should practise stratagems Upon so soft a subject as myself! iii 5 210
Out of thy long-experienced time, Give me some present counsel iv 1 61
O, that men's ears should be To counsel deaf, but not to flattery! *T. of Athens* i 2 257
He would embrace no counsel, take no warning by my coming iii 1 28
Hast thou gold yet? I'll take the gold thou givest me, Not all thy counsel iv 3 130
More counsel with more money, bounteous Timon iv 3 167
Tell me your counsels, I will not disclose 'em *J. Cæsar* ii 1 298
How hard it is for women to keep counsel! ii 4 9
The players cannot keep counsel; they'll tell all *Hamlet* iii 2 152
Do not believe it.—Believe what?—That I can keep your counsel and not mine own iv 2 11
And so I thank you for your good counsel iv 5 72
I can keep honest counsel, ride, run, mar a curious tale in telling it *Lear* i 4 34
This man hath had good counsel:—a hundred knights! i 4 345
Bestow Your needful counsel to our business, Which craves the instant use ii 1 129
When a wise man gives thee better counsel, give me mine again ii 4 76
My Regan counsels well: come out o' the storm ii 4 312
We lack'd your counsel and your help to-night.—So did I yours *Othello* i 3 51
How am I then a villain To counsel Cassio to this parallel course? ii 3 355
When I told thee he was of my counsel In my whole course of wooing, thou criedst 'Indeed!' iii 3 111
There's money for your pains: I pray you, turn the key and keep our counsel iv 2 94
We intend so to dispose you as Yourself shall give us counsel *Ant. and Cleo.* v 2 187
We will have these things set down by lawful counsel *Cymbeline* i 4 178
Blest be You bees that make these locks of counsel! iii 2 36
Now for the counsel of my son and queen! I am amazed with matter iv 3 27
Counsel-keeper. His note-book, his counsel-keeper 2 *Hen. IV.* ii 4 290
Counsel-keeping. Curtain'd with a counsel-keeping cave *T. Andron.* ii 3 24
Counselled. Pray, be counsell'd *Coriolanus* iii 2 28
So I lose none In seeking to augment it, but still keep My bosom franchised and allegiance clear, I shall be counsell'd *Macbeth* ii 1 29
That lord that counsell'd thee To give away thy land *Lear* i 4 154
Counsellor. You are a counsellor *Tempest* i 1 23
As worthy for an empress' love As meet to be an emperor's counsellor *T. G. of Ver.* ii 4 77
For though Love use Reason for his physician, he admits him not for his counsellor *Mer. Wives* ii 1 6

Counsellor. Good counsellors lack no clients . . . . *Meas. for Meas.* i 2 109
These are counsellors That feelingly persuade me what I am *As Y. Like It* ii 1 10
A counsellor, a traitress, and a dear . . . . . *All's Well* i 1 184
Your loyal servant, your physician, Your most obedient counsellor *W. Tale* ii 3 55
When rage and hot blood are his counsellors . . . 2 *Hen. IV.* iv 4 63
Up, vanity! Down, royal state! all you sage counsellors, hence! . iv 5 121
Therefore, Caveto be thy counsellor . . . . . *Hen. V.* ii 3 55
How well supplied with noble counsellors, How modest in exception . ii 4 33
Can he that speaks with the tongue of an enemy be a good counsellor? 2 *Hen. VI.* iv 2 182
You would swear directly Their very noses had been counsellors To Pepin or Clotharius . . . . . . *Hen. VIII.* i 3 9
You are a counsellor, And, by that virtue, no man dare accuse you . v 3 49
I gave ye Power as he was a counsellor to try him, Not as a groom . v 3 143
The vigilant eye, The counsellor heart, the arm our soldier . *Coriolanus* i 1 120
But he, his own affections' counsellor, Is to himself—I will not say how true . . . . *Rom. and Jul.* i 1 153
Go, counsellor; Thou and my bosom henceforth shall be twain . iii 5 239
Those linen cheeks of thine Are counsellors to fear . . . *Macbeth* v 3 17
This counsellor Is now most still, most secret and most grave *Hamlet* iii 4 213
Is he not a most profane and liberal counsellor? . . . *Othello* ii 1 165
Love's counsellor should fill the bores of hearing, To the smothering of the sense . . . . *Cymbeline* iii 2 59
Fit counsellor and servant for a prince, Who by thy wisdom makest a prince thy servant . . . . *Pericles* i 2 63
Thou art a grave and noble counsellor, Most wise in general . . v 1 184
Count. The one is painted and the other out of all count.—How painted? and how out of count? . . . . . *T. G. of Ver.* ii 1 62
So painted, to make her fair, that no man counts of her beauty . ii 1 65
I must never trust thee more, But count the world a stranger for thy sake . . . . v 4 70
I will never take you for my love again; but I will always count you my deer . . . . *Mer. Wives* v 5 122
Now, signior, where's the count? did you see him? . . . *Much Ado* ii 1 218
Why, how now, count! wherefore are you sad?—Not sad, my lord . ii 1 298
The count is neither sad, nor sick, nor merry, nor well; but civil count, civil as an orange . . . . ii 1 303
Count, take of me my daughter, and with her my fortunes . . ii 1 313
These gloves the count sent me; they are an excellent perfume . iii 4 62
Lady, you come hither to be married to this count . . . . iv 1 10
My brother and this grieved count Did see her, hear her . . . iv 1 90
A goodly count, Count Comfect; a sweet gallant, surely! . . iv 1 318
Let this count kill me. I have deceived even your very eyes . . v 1 238
It is as easy to count atomies as to resolve the propositions of a lover *As Y. Like It* iii 2 245
I count it but time lost to hear such a foolish song . . . . v 3 40
How long is't, count, Since the physician at your father's died? *All's Well* i 2 69
Welcome, count; My son's no dearer.—Thank your majesty . . i 2 75
There's honour in the theft.—Commit it, count . . . . . ii 1 34
But most it is presumption in us when The help of heaven we count the act of men . . . . ii 1 155
Are you companion to the Count Rousillon?—To any count, to all counts, to what is man.—To what is count's man: count's master is of another style . . . . ii 3 200
They say the French count has done most honourable service . . iii 5 3
There is a gentleman that serves the count Reports but coarsely of her iii 5 59
In argument of praise, or to the worth Of the great count himself, she is too mean To have her name repeated . . . . . . iii 5 63
May be the amorous count solicits her In the unlawful purpose . iii 5 72
First, give me trust, the count he is my husband . . . . iii 7 8
The count he wooes your daughter, Lays down his wanton siege before her beauty . . . . iii 7 17
Dian, the count's a fool, and full of gold . . . . . . iv 3 238
I knew the young count to be a dangerous and lascivious boy . . iv 3 248
For count of this, the count's a fool, I know it . . . . iv 3 258
To beguile the supposition of that lascivious young boy the count . iv 3 334
Go speedily and bring again the count . . . . . . v 3 152
Come hither, count; do you know these women? . . . . v 3 165
A virtuous maid, the daughter of a count . . . . *T. Night* i 2 36
She'll none of me: the count himself here hard by wooes her . . i 3 113
She'll none o' the count: she'll not match above her degree . . i 3 115
If it be a suit from the count, I am sick, or not at home . . i 5 116
The youth of the count's was to-day with my lady . . . . i 5 143
I saw your niece do more favours to the count's serving-man than ever she bestowed upon me . . . . iii 2 7
Challenge me the count's youth to fight with him . . . . iii 2 36
Once, in a sea-fight, 'gainst the count his galleys I did some service . iii 3 26
Who has done this, Sir Andrew?—The count's gentleman, one Cesario . v 1 183
By whose gentle help I was preserved to serve this noble count . v 1 263
I'ld beg your precious mistress, Which he counts but a trifle *W. Tale* v 1 224
Alone do me oppose Against the pope and count his friends my foes *K. John* iii 1 171
Within this wall of flesh There is a soul counts thee her creditor . iii 3 21
Our weal, on you depending, Counts it your weal he have his liberty . iv 2 66
I count myself in nothing else so happy As in a soul remembering my good friends . . . . *Richard II.* ii 3 46
Go, count thy way with sighs; I mine with groans . . . . v 1 89
Here, through this grate, I count each one And view the Frenchmen 1 *Hen. VI.* i 4 60
Trow'st thou that e'er I'll look upon the world, Or count them happy that enjoy the sun? . . . . 2 *Hen. VI.* ii 4 39
When they are gone, then must I count my gains . *Richard III.* i 1 162
I would not be a young count in your way, For more than blushing comes too . . . . *Hen. VIII.* ii 3 41
Count wisdom as no member of the war . . *Troi. and Cres.* i 3 198
Do not count it holy To hurt by being just . . . . . v 3 19
By my count, I was your mother much upon these years That you are now a maid . . . . *Rom. and Jul.* i 3 71
They are but beggars that can count their worth . . . . ii 6 32
O, by this count I shall be much in years Ere I again behold my Romeo! iii 5 46
Doth she not count her blest, Unworthy as she is? . . . . iii 5 144
Her father counts it dangerous That she doth give her sorrow so much sway . . . . iv 1 9
I count it one of my greatest afflictions, say, that I cannot pleasure such an honourable gentleman . . . . . *T. of Athens* iii 2 62
Peace! count the clock.—The clock hath stricken three . *J. Cæsar* ii 1 192
I could be bounded in a nutshell and count myself a king of infinite space, were it not that I have bad dreams . . . . *Hamlet* ii 2 261
Count. So many journeys may the sun and moon Make us again count o'er ere love be done! . . . . *Hamlet* iii 2 172
The other motive, Why to a public count I might not go, Is the great love the general gender bear him . . . . iv 7 17
I know not What counts harsh fortune casts upon my face *A. and C.* ii 6 55
Such creatures as We count not worth the hanging . *Cymbeline* i 5 20
Spare your arithmetic: never count the turns; Once, and a million! . ii 4 142
Count-cardinal. But our count-cardinal Has done this, and 'tis well *Hen. VIII.* i 1 172
Count Comfect. A goodly count, Count Comfect; a sweet gallant! *Much Ado* iv 1 318
Counted. I am less proud to hear you tell my worth Than you much willing to be counted wise In spending your wit . . *L. L. Lost* ii 1 18
For native blood is counted painting now . . . . . . iv 3 263
And since her time are colliers counted bright . . . . . iv 3 267
Else thou must be counted A servant grafted in my serious trust And therein negligent . . . . *W. Tale* i 2 245
Mine integrity Being counted falsehood, shall, as I express it, Be so received . . . . iii 2 28
And, for the babe Is counted lost for ever, Perdita, I prithee, call't . iii 3 33
Nor mother, wife, nor England's counted queen . . *Richard III.* iv 1 47
If it be so to do good service, never Let me be counted serviceable *Cymbeline* iii 2 15
Countenance. You should lay my countenance to pawn . *Mer. Wives* ii 2 5
Unfold the evil which is here wrapt up In countenance! *Meas. for Meas.* v 1 118
Which I will do with confirm'd countenance . . . . *Much Ado* v 4 17
This pert Biron was out of countenance quite . . . *L. L. Lost* v 2 272
I will not be put out of countenance.—Because thou hast no face . v 2 611
We have put thee in countenance.—You have put me out of countenance . . . . v 2 623
The something that nature gave me his countenance seems to take from me . . . . *As Y. Like It* i 1 19
Therefore put I on the countenance Of stern commandment . . . ii 7 108
Almost chide God for making you that countenance you are . . iv 1 37
Such Ethiope words, blacker in their effect Than in their countenance iv 3 36
To save my life, Puts my apparel and my countenance on . *T. of Shrew* i 1 234
You must meet my master to countenance my mistress . . . iv 1 101
She hath a face of her own.—Who knows not that?—Thou, it seems, that calls for company to countenance her . . . . . . iv 1 105
Formal in apparel, In gait and countenance surely like a father . iv 2 65
And, sooth to say, In countenance somewhat doth resemble you . . iv 2 100
Set your countenance, sir . . . . iv 4 18
I believe a' means to cozen somebody in this city under my countenance v 1 41
While he did bear my countenance in the town . . . . . v 1 129
With a countenance as clear As friendship wears at feasts *W. Tale* i 2 343
The king hath on him such a countenance As he had lost some province i 2 368
Your guests are coming: Lift up your countenance . . . . iv 4 49
With countenance of such distraction that they were to be known by garment, not by favour . . . . v 2 52
Our noble and chaste mistress the moon, under whose countenance we steal . . . . 1 *Hen. IV.* i 2 33
The poor abuses of the time want countenance . . . . . i 2 175
O, the father, how he holds his countenance! . . . . . ii 4 432
And gave his countenance, against his name, To laugh at gibing boys . iii 2 65
By unkind usage, dangerous countenance, And violation of all faith . v 1 69
Would he abuse the countenance of the king, Alack, what mischiefs might he set abroach! . . . . 2 *Hen. IV.* iv 2 13
Employ the countenance and grace of heaven, As a false favourite doth his prince's name, In deeds dishonourable . . . . . . iv 2 24
To countenance William Visor of Woncot against Clement Perkes of the hill . . . . v 1 41
But a knave should have some countenance at his friend's request . v 1 49
Do but mark the countenance that he will give me . . . . v 5 8
His countenance enforces homage . . . . . *Hen V.* iii 7 30
My grisly countenance made others fly . . . 1 *Hen. VI.* i 4 47
Under the countenance and confederacy Of Lady Eleanor . 2 *Hen. VI.* i 1 168
Can you not see? or will ye not observe The strangeness of his alter'd countenance? . . . . iii 1 5
Thou shalt not see me blush Nor change my countenance . . . iii 1 99
Subject to your countenance, glad or sorry As I saw it inclined *Hen. VIII.* ii 4 26
He did it with a serious mind; a heed Was in his countenance . . iii 2 81
Look how he looks! there's a countenance! is't not a brave man? *Troi. and Cres.* i 2 218
But this thy countenance, still lock'd in steel, I never saw till now . iv 5 195
Has such a confirmed countenance . . . . . *Coriolanus* i 3 65
Some news is come That turns their countenances . . . . iv 6 59
He waged me with his countenance, as if I had been mercenary . v 6 40
Clear up, fair queen, that cloudy countenance . . . *T. Andron.* i 1 263
If I have veil'd my look, I turn the trouble of my countenance Merely upon myself . . . . *J. Cæsar* i 2 38
That which would appear offence in us, His countenance, like richest alchemy, Will change to virtue . . . . i 3 159
As from your graves rise up, and walk like sprites, To countenance this horror! . . . . *Macbeth* ii 3 85
Look'd he frowningly?—A countenance more in sorrow than in anger *Hamlet* i 2 232
And hath given countenance to his speech, my lord, With almost all the holy vows of heaven . . . . i 3 113
This vile deed We must, with all our majesty and skill, Both countenance and excuse . . . . iv 1 32
That soaks up the king's countenance, his rewards, his authorities . iv 2 16
And the more pity that great folk should have countenance in this world to drown or hang themselves . . . . v 1 30
Found you no displeasure in him by word or countenance? . . *Lear* i 2 172
You have that in your countenance which I would fain call master.—What's that?—Authority . . . . i 4 30
What's his offence?—His countenance likes me not.—No more, perchance, does mine, nor his, nor hers . . . . ii 2 96
Now then we'll use His countenance for the battle . . . . v 1 63
We did sleep day out of countenance, and made the night light *A. and C.* ii 2 181
Turn from me, then, that noble countenance, Wherein the worship of the whole world lies . . . . iv 14 85
If't be summer news, Smile to't before; if winterly, thou need'st But keep that countenance still . . . . *Cymbeline* iii 4 14
Countenanced. But faults so countenanced, that the strong statutes Stand like the forfeits in a barber's shop . *Meas. for Meas* v 1 322
Led on by bloody youth, guarded with rags, And countenanced by boys and beggary . . . . 2 *Hen. IV.* iv 1 35
The knave is mine honest friend, sir; therefore, I beseech your worship, let him be countenanced . . . . v 1 57

Counter. A hound that runs counter and yet draws dry-foot well *Com. of Errors* iv 2 39
What, for a counter, would I do but good? . . . . *As Y. Like It* ii 7 63
I cannot do't without counters . . . . *W. Tale* iv 3 38
You hunt counter: hence! avaunt! . . . . . *2 Hen. IV.* i 2 102
Will you with counters sum The past proportion of his infinite? *Troi. and Cres.* ii 2 28
So covetous To lock such rascal counters from his friends . *J. Cæsar* iv 3 80
How cheerfully on the false trail they cry! O, this is counter, you false Danish dogs! . . . . *Hamlet* iv 5 110
Your neck, sir, is pen, book and counters . . . *Cymbeline* v 4 174
Counter-caster. This counter-caster, He, in good time, must his lieutenant be . . . . *Othello* i 1 31
Counterchange. The counterchange Is severally in all . *Cymbeline* v 5 396
Countercheck. 'This is called the Countercheck Quarrelsome *As Y. Like It* v 4 84
The fourth, the Reproof Valiant; the fifth, the Countercheck Quarrelsome v 4 99
Who painfully with much expedient march Have brought a countercheck before your gates . . . . *K. John* ii 1 224
Counterfeit. Seem you that you are not?—Haply I do.—So do counterfeits *T. G. of Ver.* ii 4 12
Thou counterfeit to thy true friend!—In love Who respects friend? . v 4 53
How ill agrees it with your gravity To counterfeit thus grossly! *Com. of Errors* ii 2 171
To tell you true, I counterfeit him . . . . . *Much Ado* ii 1 121
May be she doth but counterfeit.—Faith, like enough.—O God, counterfeit! . . . . ii 3 107
There was never counterfeit of passion came so near the life of passion. ii 3 110
Counterfeit sad looks, Make mouths upon me when I turn my back *M. N. Dream* iii 2 237
Fie, fie! you counterfeit, you puppet, you!—Puppet? why so? . iii 2 288
What find I here? Fair Portia's counterfeit! . . *Mer. of Venice* iii 2 116
Now counterfeit to swoon; why now fall down . . *As Y. Like It* iii 5 17
This was not counterfeit: there is too great testimony in your complexion . . . . iv 3 170
Counterfeit, I assure you.—Well then, take a good heart and counterfeit to be a man . . . . iv 3 173
They are busied about a counterfeit assurance . . *T. of Shrew* iv 4 92
While counterfeit supposes blear'd thine eyne . . . . v 1 120
To what metal this counterfeit lump of ore will be melted *All's Well* iii 6 39
That he might take a measure of his own judgements, wherein so curiously he had set this counterfeit . . . . . . iv 3 39
Come, bring forth this counterfeit module, has deceived me . . iv 3 113
The knave counterfeits well; a good knave . . . *T. Night* iv 2 22
Are you not mad indeed? or do you but counterfeit? . . . iv 2 122
Not a counterfeit stone, not a ribbon, glass, pomander . . *W. Tale* iv 4 608
You have beguiled me with a counterfeit Resembling majesty *K. John* iii 1 99
Taught me craft To counterfeit oppression of such grief . *Richard II.* i 4 14
Never call a true piece of gold a counterfeit . . *1 Hen. IV.* ii 4 540
I fear thou art another counterfeit; And yet, in faith, thou bear'st thee like a king . . . . v 4 35
'Sblood, 'twas time to counterfeit . . . . v 4 114
Counterfeit? I lie, I am no counterfeit: to die, is to be a counterfeit . v 4 115
He is but the counterfeit of a man who hath not the life of a man . . v 4 117
To counterfeit dying, when a man thereby liveth, is to be no counterfeit v 4 118
By my faith, I am afraid he would prove the better counterfeit . v 4 126
Why, this is an arrant counterfeit rascal . . . . . *Hen. V.* iii 6 64
You are a counterfeit cowardly knave . . . . . . v 1 73
Your cheeks do counterfeit our roses . . . . *1 Hen. VI.* ii 4 62
Thy cheeks Blush for pure shame to counterfeit our roses . . ii 4 66
'Tis but his policy to counterfeit . . . . *3 Hen. VI.* ii 6 65
I can counterfeit the deep tragedian; Speak and look back *Richard III.* iii 5 5
This is the king's ring.—'Tis no counterfeit . . . *Hen. VIII.* v 3 102
If I could have remembered a gilt counterfeit, thou wouldst not have slipped out of my contemplation . . . . *Troi. and Cres.* ii 3 28
I will counterfeit the bewitchment of some popular man *Coriolanus* ii 3 108
You gave us the counterfeit fairly last night . . *Rom. and Jul.* ii 4 48
What counterfeit did I give you?—The slip, sir, the slip; can you not conceive? . . . . ii 4 49
Strike me the counterfeit matron; It is her habit only that is honest *T. of Athens* iv 3 112
Thou draw'st a counterfeit Best in all Athens . . . . v 1 83
Shake off this downy sleep, death's counterfeit, And look on death itself! *Macbeth* ii 3 81
The counterfeit presentment of two brothers . . . *Hamlet* iii 4 54
That has an eye can stamp and counterfeit advantages . . *Othello* ii 1 247
Whose rude throats The immortal Jove's dread clamours counterfeit . iii 3 356
These may be counterfeits: let's think't unsafe To come in to the cry . v 1 43
Some coiner with his tools Made me a counterfeit . . . *Cymbeline* ii 5 6
Counterfeited. A body would think this was well counterfeited! *As Y. Like It* iv 3 167
I pray you, tell your brother how well I counterfeited . . . iv 3 168
Did your brother tell you how I counterfeited to swoon? . . v 2 28
Under the counterfeited zeal of God . . . . *2 Hen. IV.* iv 2 27
As plays the sun upon the glassy streams, Twinkling another counterfeited beam . . . . *1 Hen. VI.* v 3 63
Counterfeitest. What art thou, That counterfeit'st the person of a king? *1 Hen. IV.* v 4 28
In one little body Thou counterfeit'st a bark, a sea, a wind *R. and J.* iii 5 132
Thou counterfeit'st most lively . . . . . . *T. of Athens* v 1 85
Counterfeiting. My counterfeiting the action of an old woman delivered me . . . . *Mer. Wives* iv 5 121
I pray you, commend my counterfeiting to him . . *As Y. Like It* iv 3 183
As if the tragedy Were play'd in jest by counterfeiting actors *3 Hen. VI.* ii 3 28
My tears begin to take his part so much, They'll mar my counterfeiting *Lear* iii 6 64
Counterfeitly. I will practise the insinuating nod and be off to them most counterfeitly . . . . *Coriolanus* ii 3 107
Counter-gate. Thou mightst as well say I love to walk by the Counter-gate . . . . *Mer. Wives* iii 3 85
Countermand. Have you no countermand for Claudio yet? *Meas. for Meas.* iv 2 95
Yet I believe there comes No countermand . . . . . iv 2 100
A shoulder-clapper, one that countermands The passages of alleys *Com. of Errors* iv 2 37
Some tardy cripple bore the countermand, That came too lag to see him buried . . . . *Richard III.* ii 1 89
Countermine. The duke, look you, is digt himself four yard under the countermines . . . . *Hen. V.* iii 2 67
Counterpoint. In cypress chests my arras counterpoints . *T. of Shrew* ii 1 353
Counterpoise. What have I to give you back, whose worth May counterpoise this rich and precious gift? . . . . . . *Much Ado* iv 1 29
Counterpoise. To whom I promise A counterpoise, if not to thy estate A balance more replete . . . . *All's Well* ii 3 182
Too light for the counterpoise of so great an opposition . . *1 Hen. IV.* ii 3 14
Do more than counterpoise a full third part The charges of the action *Coriolanus* v 6 78
Give him thy daughter: What you bestow, in him I'll counterpoise, And make him weigh with her . . . . . . *T. of Athens* i 1 145
Counterpoised. The lives of those which we have lost in fight Be counterpoised with such a petty sum! . . . . *2 Hen. VI.* iv 1 22
Touching the jointure that your king must make, Which with her dowry shall be counterpoised . . . . *3 Hen. VI.* iii 3 137
The man I speak of cannot in the world Be singly counterpoised *Coriolanus* ii 2 91
Counter-sealed. Which we, On like conditions, will have counter-seal'd . v 3 205
Countervail. It cannot countervail the exchange of joy That one short minute gives me in her sight . . . . . . *Rom. and Jul.* ii 6 4
Yon knight doth sit too melancholy, As if the entertainment in our court Had not a show might countervail his worth . . . *Pericles* ii 3 56
Countess. Here comes the countess: now heaven walks on earth *T. Night* v 1 100
The rest are countesses.—Their coronets say so . . *Hen. VIII.* iv 1 53
Counties. Princes and counties! Surely, a princely testimony! *M. Ado* iv 1 317
Our discontented counties do revolt . . . . . . *K. John* v 1 8
You loiter here too long, being you are to take soldiers up in counties as you go . . . . *2 Hen. IV.* ii 1 199
Discharge your powers unto their several counties, As we will ours . iv 2 61
Those two counties I will undertake Your grace shall well and quietly enjoy . . . . *1 Hen. VI.* v 3 158
These counties were the keys of Normandy . . . . *2 Hen. VI.* i 1 114
Counting myself but bad till I be best . . . . *3 Hen. VI.* v 6 91
Countless. O, were the sum of these that I should pay Countless and infinite, yet would I pay them! . . . . . . *T. Andron.* v 3 159
Her face, like heaven, enticeth thee to view Her countless glory *Pericles* i 1 31
O you powers That give heaven countless eyes to view men's acts! . i 1 73
Countries. She is spherical, like a globe; I could find out countries in her . . . . *Com. of Errors* iii 2 117
A Dutchman to-day, a Frenchman to-morrow, or in the shape of two countries at once . . . . *Much Ado* iii 2 34
Then I suck my teeth and catechize My picked man of countries *K. John* i 1 193
The rest of thy low countries have made a shift to eat up thy holland *2 Hen. IV.* ii 2 25
And so, with thanks and pardon to you all, I do dismiss you to your several countries . . . . *2 Hen. VI.* iv 9 21
Haply the seas and countries different With variable objects shall expel This something-settled matter in his heart . . *Hamlet* iii 1 179
In cities, mutinies; in countries, discord; in palaces, treason *Lear* i 2 117
Country. Wit shall not go unrewarded while I am king of this country *Tempest* iv 1 243
Some heavenly power guide us Out of this fearful country! . . v 1 106
He's a justice of peace in his country . . . . *Mer. Wives* i 1 226
Of whence are you?—Not of this country, though my chance is now To use it for my time . . . . *Meas. for Meas.* iii 2 230
There miscarried A vessel of our country richly fraught . *Mer. of Venice* ii 8 30
Thus most invectively he pierceth through The body of the country, city, court . . . . *As Y. Like It* ii 1 59
Good manners at the court are as ridiculous in the country as the behaviour of the country is most mockable at the court . . . iii 2 48
Graff it with a medlar: then it will be the earliest fruit i' the country iii 2 126
You lisp and wear strange suits, disable all the benefits of your own country . . . . iv 1 35
Our old ling and our Isbels o' the country are nothing like your old ling and your Isbels o' the court . . . . *All's Well* iii 2 14
Poor lord! is't I That chase thee from thy country? . . . iii 2 106
In that country he had the honour to be the officer at a place there called Mile-end . . . . iv 3 301
If you could find out a country where but women were that had received so much shame . . . . iv 3 361
I follow him to his country for justice: grant it me, O king! . . v 3 144
What country, friends, is this?—This is Illyria . . *T. Night* i 2 1
Know'st thou this country?—Ay, madam, well . . . . i 2 21
It is fifteen years since I saw my country . . . . *W. Tale* iv 2 5
Of that fatal country, Sicilia, prithee speak no more . . . iv 2 23
The father of this seeming lady and Her brother, having both their country quitted . . . . v 1 192
Here is the strangest controversy Come from the country . *K. John* i 1 45
To wake our peace, which in our country's cradle Draws the sweet infant breath of gentle sleep . . . . *Richard II.* i 3 132
Thus I turn me from my country's light, To dwell in solemn shades of endless night . . . . i 3 176
Shake off our slavish yoke, Imp out our drooping country's broken wing ii 1 292
But yet I'll pause; For I am loath to break our country's laws . ii 3 169
The bay-trees in our country are all wither'd . . . . ii 4 8
Gave His body to that pleasant country's earth, And his pure soul unto his captain Christ . . . . iv 1 98
Cries out upon abuses, seems to weep Over his country's wrongs *1 Hen. IV.* iv 3 82
All the country in a general voice Cried hate upon him *2 Hen. IV.* iv 1 136
And we give express charge, that in our marches through the country, there be nothing compelled from the villages . . . *Hen. V.* iii 6 115
The slave, a member of the country's peace, Enjoys it . . iv 1 298
If we are mark'd to die, we are enow To do our country loss . . iv 3 21
Have lost, or do not learn for want of time, The sciences that should become our country . . . . v 2 58
You and I cannot be confined within the weak list of a country's fashion v 2 295
For upholding the nice fashion of your country in denying me a kiss v 2 299
Will'd me to leave my base vocation And free my country from calamity *1 Hen. VI.* i 2 81
That hast by tyranny these many years Wasted our country . . ii 3 41
Look on thy country, look on fertile France . . . . . iii 3 44
One drop of blood drawn from thy country's bosom Should grieve thee more than streams of foreign gore . . . . iii 3 54
And wash away thy country's stained spots . . . . . iii 3 57
Forgive me, country, and sweet countrymen . . . . . iii 3 81
Moved with compassion of my country's wreck . . . . iv 1 56
Well content with any choice Tends to God's glory and my country's weal . . . . v 1 27
I'll either make thee stoop and bend thy knee, Or sack this country with a mutiny . . . . v 1 62
Upon condition I may quietly Enjoy mine own, the country Maine and Anjou . . . . v 3 154
Have I sought every country far and near, And, now it is my chance to find thee out, Must I behold thy timeless cruel death? . . . v 4 3

Country. May never glorious sun reflex his beams Upon the country where you make abode! . . . . *1 Hen. VI.* v 4 88
And sold their bodies for their country's benefit . . . . . . v 4 106
To ease your country of distressful war . . . . v 4 126
As he loves the land, And common profit of his country . *2 Hen. VI.* i 1 206
God in mercy so deal with my soul, As I in duty love my king and country! . . . . i 3 161
Live in your country here in banishment . . . . ii 3 12
Fight for your king, your country and your lives . . . . iv 5 12
Sweet is the country, because full of riches; The people liberal, valiant iv 7 67
You redeem'd your lives And show'd how well you love your prince and country . . . . iv 9 16
I'll yield myself to prison willingly, Or unto death, to do my country good . . . . iv 9 43
All the country is laid for me . . . . iv 10 4
How will the country for these woful chances Misthink the king! *3 Hen. VI.* ii 5 107
Where did you dwell when I was King of England?—Here in this country iii 1 75
Matching more for wanton lust than honour, Or than for strength and safety of our country . . . . iii 3 211
This pretty lad will prove our country's bliss . . . . . iv 6 70
Now am I seated as my soul delights, Having my country's peace and brothers' loves . . . . v 7 36
As little joy, my lord, as you suppose You should enjoy, were you this country's king . . . . *Richard III.* i 3 152
I bid them that did love their country's good Cry 'God save Richard!' iii 7 21
Your sleepy thoughts, Which here we waken to our country's good . iii 7 124
If you do fight against your country's foes, Your country's fat shall pay your pains the hire . . . . v 3 257
Base lackey peasants, Whom their o'er-cloyed country vomits forth . v 3 318
They are, as all my other comforts, far hence In mine own country *Hen. VIII.* iii 1 91
Let all the ends thou aim'st at be thy country's, Thy God's, and truth's iii 2 448
Thieves, . . . That in their country did them that disgrace, We fear to warrant in our native place! . . . . *Troi. and Cres.* ii 2 95
You are too bitter to your countrywoman.—She's bitter to her country iv 1 68
Consider you what services he has done for his country? . *Coriolanus* i 1 31
Soft-conscienced men can be content to say it was for his country . i 1 39
I had rather had eleven die nobly for their country than one voluptuously surfeit out of action . . . . i 3 27
If any think brave death outweighs bad life And that his country's dearer than himself . . . . i 6 72
I have done As you have done; that's what I can; induced As you have been; that's for my country . . . . i 9 17
He hath deserved worthily of his country . . . . ii 2 28
To gratify his noble service that Hath thus stood for his country . . ii 2 45
Look, sir, my wounds! I got them in my country's service . . . ii 3 58
You have deserved nobly of your country, and you have not deserved nobly . . . . ii 3 95
You have received many wounds for your country . . . . . ii 3 114
He should have show'd us His marks of merit, wounds received for's country . . . . ii 3 172
How youngly he began to serve his country, How long continued . . ii 3 244
As for my country I have shed my blood, Not fearing outward force . iii 1 76
Be that you seem, truly your country's friend . . . . . . iii 1 218
The blood he hath lost . . . he dropp'd it for his country; And what is left, to lose it by his country, Were to us all, that do't and suffer it, A brand to the end o' the world . . . . iii 1 301
When he did love his country, It honour'd him . . . . . . iii 1 305
I do love My country's good with a respect more tender, More holy and profound, than mine own life . . . . iii 3 112
He is banish'd, As enemy to the people and his country . . . . iii 3 118
I would he had continued to his country As he began . . . . iv 2 30
His great opposer, Coriolanus, being now in no request of his country . iv 3 38
If he give me way, I'll do his country service . . . . . . iv 4 26
The extreme dangers and the drops of blood Shed for my thankless country . . . . iv 5 76
And stop those maims Of shame seen through thy country . . . iv 5 93
I will fight Against my canker'd country with the spleen Of all the under fiends . . . . iv 5 97
Ever follow'd thee with hate, Drawn tuns of blood out of thy country's breast . . . . iv 5 105
Thou know'st Thy country's strength and weakness . . . . . iv 5 146
If you Would be your country's pleader, your good tongue, More than the instant army we can make, Might stop our countryman . . v 1 36
His noble mother, and his wife; Who, as I hear, mean to solicit him For mercy to his country . . . . v 1 73
Tearing His country's bowels out . . . . v 3 103
Alas, how can we for our country pray, Whereto we are bound, together with thy victory, Whereto we are bound? . . . . v 3 107
Alack, or we must lose The country, our dear nurse, or else thy person, Our comfort in the country . . . . v 3 110
Triumphantly tread on thy country's ruin . . . . v 3 116
Thou shalt no sooner March to assault thy country than to tread—Trust to't, thou shalt not—on thy mother's womb . . . . . v 3 123
Destroy'd his country, and his name remains To the ensuing age abhorr'd . . . . v 3 147
No more infected with my country's love Than when I parted hence . v 6 72
And to the love and favour of my country Commit myself, my person and the cause . . . . *T. Andron.* i 1 58
Cometh Andronicus, bound with laurel boughs, To re-salute his country with his tears . . . . i 1 75
And sleep in peace, slain in your country's wars! . . . . . i 1 91
Must my sons be slaughter'd in the streets, For valiant doings in their country's cause? . . . . i 1 113
Your fortunes are alike in all, That in your country's service drew your swords . . . . i 1 175
I have been thy soldier forty years, And led my country's strength successfully . . . . i 1 194
Slain manfully in arms, In right and service of their noble country . i 1 197
Thy father hath full oft For his ungrateful country done the like . . iv 1 111
As the manner of our country is . . . . . . *Rom. and Jul.* iv 1 109
That, by killing of villains, Thou wast born to conquer my country *T. of Athens* iv 3 106
Who, like a boar too savage, doth root up His country's peace . . v 1 169
I love my country, and am not One that rejoices in the common wreck v 1 194
So often shall the knot of us be call'd The men that gave their country liberty . . . . *J. Cæsar* iii 1 118
Who is here so vile that will not love his country? . . . . . iii 2 35
When it shall please my country to need my death . . . . . iii 2 51

Country. Far from this country Pindarus shall run, Where never Roman shall take note of him . . . . . . *J. Cæsar* v 3 49
I am the son of Marcus Cato, ho! A foe to tyrants, and my country's friend . . . . v 4 5
And I am Brutus, Marcus Brutus, I; Brutus, my country's friend . . v 4 8
Or that with both He labour'd in his country's wreck . . *Macbeth* i 3 114
Here had we now our country's honour roof'd, Were the graced person of our Banquo present . . . . iii 4 40
That a swift blessing May soon return to this our suffering country . iii 6 48
Bleed, bleed, poor country! Great tyranny! lay thou thy basis sure . iv 3 31
Our country sinks beneath the yoke; It weeps, it bleeds . . . iv 3 39
Yet my poor country Shall have more vices than it had before . . iv 3 46
What I am truly, Is thine and my poor country's to command . . iv 3 132
Stands Scotland where it did?—Alas, poor country! Almost afraid to know itself . . . . iv 3 164
Meet we the medicine of the sickly weal, And with him pour we in our country's purge Each drop of us . . . . v 2 28
Send out moe horses; skirr the country round; Hang those that talk of fear . . . . v 3 35
If thou art privy to thy country's fate, Which, happily, foreknowing may avoid, O, speak! . . . . *Hamlet* i 1 133
According to the phrase or the addition Of man and country . . . ii 1 48
The undiscover'd country from whose bourn No traveller returns . . iii 1 79
He'll shape his old course in a country new . . . . *Lear* i 1 190
The country gives me proof and precedent Of Bedlam beggars . . ii 3 13
In spite of nature, Of years, of country, credit, every thing . *Othello* i 3 97
'Tis pride that pulls the country down; Then take thine auld cloak about thee . . . . ii 3 98
As the time, the place, and the condition of this country stands, I could heartily wish this had not befallen . . . . ii 3 303
She forsook so many noble matches, Her father and her country and her friends . . . . iv 2 126
With a wound I must be cured. Draw that thy honest sword, which thou hast worn Most useful for thy country . *Ant. and Cleo.* iv 14 80
Rather make My country's high pyramides my gibbet, And hang me up in chains! . . . . v 2 61
A lady to the worthiest sir that ever Country call'd his! . *Cymbeline* i 6 161
These present wars shall find I love my country, Even to the note o' the king . . . . iv 3 43
I have belied a lady, The princess of this country, and the air on't Revengingly enfeebles me . . . . v 2 3
Who deserved So long a breeding as his white beard came to, In doing this for's country . . . . v 3 18
Striking in our country's cause Fell bravely and were slain . . . v 4 71
Here's them in our country of Greece gets more with begging than we can do with working . . . . *Pericles* ii 1 68
Your grace, that fed my country with your corn . . . . . iii 3 18
He's the governor of this country, and a man whom I am bound to . iv 6 57
If he govern the country, you are bound to him indeed . . . iv 6 59
Which is not worth a breakfast in the cheapest country under the cope . . . . iv 6 132
Who, frighted from my country, did wed At Pentapolis the fair Thaisa v 3 3
Country base. Lads more like to run The country base than to commit such slaughter . . . . *Cymbeline* v 3 20
Country cocks. The country cocks do crow, the clocks do toll *Hen. V.* iv Prol. 15
Country copulatives. I press in here, sir, amongst the rest of the country copulatives . . . . *As Y. Like It* v 4 58
Country disposition. I know our country disposition well . *Othello* iii 3 201
Country fire. And laugh this sport o'er by a country fire . *Mer. Wives* v 5 256
Country folks. These pretty country folks would lie, In spring time *As Y. Like It* v 3 25
Country footing. Your rye-straw hats put on And these fresh nymphs encounter every one In country footing . . . . *Tempest* iv 1 138
Country forms. Her will, recoiling to her better judgement, May fall to match you with her country forms . . . . . *Othello* iii 3 237
Country gentleman. Sure, he's a gallant gentleman.—He's but a country gentleman . . . . *Pericles* ii 3 33
Country girl. Boy, I do love that country girl . . . *L. L. Lost* i 2 122
Country lord. An honest country lord, as I am, beaten A long time out of play . . . . *Hen VIII.* i 3 44
Country maid. Bear this significant to the country maid Jaquenetta *L. L. Lost* iii 1 132
Country manners. Our country manners give our betters way *K. John* i 1 156
Country matters. Do you think I meant country matters? . *Hamlet* iii 2 123
Country mistresses. Each of us fell in praise of our country mistresses *Cymbeline* i 4 62
Country proverb. And the country proverb known, That every man should take his own . . . . *M. N. Dream* iii 2 458
Country servant-maid. I had rather be a country servant-maid Than a great queen, with this condition . . . . . . *Richard III.* i 3 107
Country wars. If in your country wars you chance to die, That is my bed too, lads, and there I'll lie . . . . *Cymbeline* iv 4 51
Countryman. Know ye Don Antonio, your countryman? *T. G. of Ver.* ii 4 54
Is your countryman According to our proclamation gone? . . . ii 2 11
What countryman?—Born in Verona, old Antonio's son . *T. of Shrew* i 2 190
What countryman, I pray?—Of Mantua . . . . iv 2 77
Here you shall see a countryman of yours That has done worthy service *All's Well* iii 5 50
What countryman? what name? what parentage? . . . *T. Night* v 1 238
I am Welsh, you know, good countryman . . . . . *Hen. V.* iv 7 110
Thanks, good my countryman.—By Jeshu, I am your majesty's countryman . . . . iv 7 115
Froissart, a countryman of ours, records, England all Olivers and Rowlands bred . . . . *1 Hen. VI.* i 2 29
The princely Charles of France, thy countryman . . . . . iii 3 38
Your good tongue, More than the instant army we can make, Might stop our countryman . . . . *Coriolanus* v 1 38
Not far, one Muli lives, my countryman . . . . . *T. Andron.* iv 2 152
Dear countryman, Bring in thy ranks, but leave without thy rage *T. of Athens* v 4 38
See, who comes here?—My countryman; but yet I know him not *Macbeth* iv 3 160
Alas, my friend and my dear countryman Roderigo! . . *Othello* v 1 89
Not cowardly put off my helmet to My countryman . *Ant. and Cleo.* iv 15 57
Who was last with them?—A simple countryman, that brought her figs . . . . v 2 342
I was glad I did atone my countryman and you . . . *Cymbeline* i 4 42
Countrymen. Our well-dealing countrymen . . . *Com. of Errors* i 1 7
Since the mortal and intestine jars 'Twixt thy seditious countrymen and us i 1 12

Countrymen. I bid my very friends and countrymen, Sweet Portia, welcome . . . . . . *Mer. of Venice* iii 2 226
I have heard him swear To Tubal and to Chus, his countrymen . . iii 2 287
Visit his countrymen and banquet them . . . . . *T. of Shrew* i 1 202
Thanks, my countrymen, my loving friends . . . . *Richard II.* i 4 34
We have stay'd ten days, And hardly kept our countrymen together . ii 4 2
Our countrymen are gone and fled, As well assured Richard their king is dead . . . . ii 4 16
Bespake them thus; 'I thank you, countrymen' . . . v 2 20
Forth, dear countrymen: let us deliver Our puissance into the hand of God . . . . *Hen. V.* ii 2 189
And calls them brothers, friends and countrymen . . . iv Prol. 34
Well have we done, thrice valiant countrymen: But all's not done . iv 6 1
Hark, countrymen! either renew the fight, Or tear the lions out of England's coat . . . . 1 *Hen. VI.* i 5 27
See here, my friends and loving countrymen, This token . . iii 1 137
This is the happy wedding torch That joineth Rouen unto her countrymen . . . . iii 2 27
Thou fight'st against thy countrymen And join'st with them will be thy slaughter-men . . . . iii 3 74
Forgive me, country, and sweet countrymen . . . . . iii 3 81
Stain to thy countrymen, thou hear'st thy doom! . . . . iv 1 45
Ah, countrymen! if when you make your prayers, God should be so obdurate as yourselves . . . . . . 2 *Hen. VI.* iv 7 121
What say ye, countrymen? will ye relent? . . . . . iv 8 11
More than I have said, loving countrymen . . . *Richard III.* v 3 237
What work's, my countrymen, in hand? where go you With bats and clubs? . . . . *Coriolanus* i 1 56
And conjure thee to pardon Rome, and thy petitionary countrymen . v 2 82
And, countrymen, my loving followers, Plead my successive title with your swords . . . . *T. Andron.* i 1 3
If Alcibiades kill my countrymen, Let Alcibiades know this of Timon, That Timon cares not . . . . *T. of Athens* v 1 172
Commend me to my loving countrymen . . . . . v 1 197
Go, go, good countrymen, and, for this fault, Assemble all the poor men of your sort . . . . *J. Cæsar* i 1 61
Then, countrymen, What need we any spur but our own cause? ii 1 122
Romans, countrymen, and lovers! hear me for my cause, and be silent iii 2 13
My countrymen,— Peace, silence! Brutus speaks. . . . iii 2 58
Good countrymen, let me depart alone, And, for my sake, stay here with Antony . . . . iii 2 60
Friends, Romans, countrymen, lend me your ears; I come to bury Cæsar, not to praise him . . . . iii 2 78
Great Cæsar fell. O, what a fall was there, my countrymen! . iii 2 194
Stay, countrymen.—Peace there! hear the noble Antony . . iii 2 210
Yet hear me, countrymen; yet hear me speak . . . . iii 2 238
Words before blows: is it so, countrymen?—Not that we love words better, as you do . . . . v 1 27
Yet, countrymen, O, yet hold up your heads! . . . . . v 4 1
Countrymen, My heart doth joy that yet in all my life I found no man but he was true to me . . . . v 5 33
Have heaven and earth together demonstrated Unto our climatures and countrymen . . . . *Hamlet* i 1 125
Our countrymen Are men more order'd than when Julius Cæsar Smiled at their lack of skill . . . . . . *Cymbeline* ii 4 20

Countrywoman. You are too bitter to your countrywoman *Troi. and Cres.* iv 1 67
Turn your eyes upon me. You are like something that—What countrywoman? . . . . *Pericles* v 1 103

County. In the county of Gloucester, justice of peace and 'Coram' *Mer. Wives* i 1 5
Whither?—Even to the next willow, about your own business, county *Much Ado* ii 1 195
A ring the county wears, That downward hath succeeded in his house *All's Well* iii 7 22
Run after that same peevish messenger, The county's man . *T. Night* i 5 320
A poor esquire of this county . . . . . . 2 *Hen. IV.* iii 2 64
The duchy of Anjou and the county of Maine shall be released 2 *Hen. VI.* i 1 51
To Ireland will you lead a band of men, Collected choicely, from each county some? . . . . iii 1 313
Our strength will be augmented In every county as we go along 3 *Hen. VI.* v 3 23
To every county Where this is question'd send our letters . *Hen. VIII.* i 2 98
We follow thee. Juliet, the county stays . . . *Rom. and Jul.* i 3 105
I think it best you married with the county . . . . iii 5 219
I hear thou must, and nothing may prorogue it, On Thursday next be married to this county . . . . iv 1 49
Send for the county; go tell him of this . . . . . . iv 2 23
Let me see the county; Ay, marry, go, I say, and fetch him hither iv 2 29
The county will be here with music straight . . . . . iv 4 21
Ay, let the county take you in your bed . . . . . . iv 5 10
Where is the county's page, that raised the watch? . . . v 3 279

County Palatine. Then there is the County Palatine *Mer. of Venice* i 2 49

County Paris. For the next night, I warrant, The County Paris hath set up his rest, That you shall rest but little . *Rom. and Jul.* iv 5 6
Let me peruse this face. Mercutio's kinsman, noble County Paris! . v 3 75

Couper. Car ce soldat ici est disposé tout à cette heure de couper votre gorge . . . . *Hen. V.* iv 4 38

Couple. I must Bestow upon the eyes of this young couple Some vanity of mine art . . . . *Tempest* iv 1 40
Look down, you gods, And on this couple drop a blessed crown! . v 1 202
So prettily He couples it to his complaining names . *T. G. of Ver.* i 2 127
A couple of Ford's knaves, his hinds . . . *Mer. Wives* iii 5 99
Ha' ta'en a couple of as arrant knaves as any in Messina *Much Ado* iii 5 34
Saint Valentine is past: Begin these wood-birds but to couple now? *M. N. Dream* iv 1 145
In the temple, by and by, with us These couples shall eternally be knit iv 1 186
So shall all the couples three Ever true in loving be . . v 1 414
Promised to meet me in this place of the forest and to couple us *As Y. Like It* iii 3 45
There is, sure, another flood toward, and these couples are coming to the ark . . . . v 4 36
And couple Clowder with the deep-mouth'd brach . *T. of Shrew* Ind. 1 18
Nay, let them go, a couple of quiet ones . . . . . i 2 242
I'll go in couples with her . . . . *W. Tale* ii 1 135
I lost a couple, that 'twixt heaven and earth Might thus have stood begetting wonder as You, gracious couple, do . . . . v 1 132
Whiles he was hastening, in the chase, it seems, Of this fair couple . v 1 190
A couple of short-legged hens, a joint of mutton . 2 *Hen. IV.* v 1 28
I have brought you a letter and a couple of pigeons . *T. Andron.* iv 4 44
Couple. Couple it with something; make it a word and a blow *Rom. and Jul.* iii 1 42
O all you host of heaven! O earth! what else? And shall I couple hell? . . . . *Hamlet* i 5 93

'Couple a gorge!' That is the word . . . . . . *Hen. V.* ii 1 75

Coupled. Like Juno's swans, Still we went coupled and inseparable *As Y. Like It* i 3 78
Honesty coupled to beauty is to have honey a sauce to sugar . iii 3 30
With slaughter coupled to the name of kings . . . *K. John* ii 1 349
Coupled and link'd together With all religious strength of sacred vows iii 1 228
Coupled in bonds of perpetuity . . . . . . 1 *Hen. VI.* iv 7 20
And let your mind be coupled with your words . . *Troi. and Cres.* v 2 15
His discontents are unremoveably Coupled to nature . *T. of Athens* v 1 228

Couplement. I wish you the peace of mind, most royal couplement! *L. L. Lost* v 2 535

Couplet. We'll whisper o'er a couplet or two of most sage saws *T. Night* iii 4 412
Anon, as patient as the female dove, When that her golden couplets are disclosed, His silence will sit drooping . . . . *Hamlet* v 1 310

Cour. Je m'en vais a la cour—la grande affaire . . *Mer. Wives* i 4 54

Courage! there will be pity taken on you . . . *Meas. for Meas.* i 2 112
If it be honest you have spoke, you have courage to maintain it . iii 2 166
Art thou sick, or angry?—What, courage, man! . . . *Much Ado* v 1 132
Good cheer, Antonio! What, man, courage yet! . . *Mer. of Venice* iv 1 111
Therefore courage, good Aliena! . . . . . . *As Y. Like It* ii 4 8
Courage! As horns are odious, they are necessary . . . iii 3 51
Beauty, wisdom, courage, all That happiness and prime can happy call *All's Well* ii 1 184
Courage and hope both teaching him the practice . . . *T. Night* i 2 13
For courage mounteth with occasion . . . . . *K. John* ii 1 82
Courage and comfort! all shall yet go well . . . . . iii 4 4
Away, then, with good courage! . . . . v 1 78
Speak terms of manage to thy bounding steed; Cry 'Courage! to the field!' . . . . 1 *Hen. IV.* ii 3 53
Amend this fault: Though sometimes it show greatness, courage, blood iii 1 181
Their courage with hard labour tame and dull . . . . iv 3 23
Took fire and heat away From the best-temper'd courage in his troops 2 *Hen. IV.* i 1 115
Who, great and puffed up with this retinue, doth any deed of courage . iv 3 122
The blood and courage that renowned them Runs in your veins *Hen. V.* i 2 118
Bardolph, be blithe: Nym, rouse thy vaunting veins: Boy, bristle thy courage up . . . . ii 3 5
With men of courage and with means defendant . . . . ii 4 8
Their mastiffs are of unmatchable courage . . . . . iii 7 152
We are in great danger; The greater therefore should our courage be . iv 1 2
He may show what outward courage he will . . . . . iv 1 118
That their hot blood may spin in English eyes, And dout them with superfluous courage . . . . iv 2 11
Lean raw-boned rascals! who would e'er suppose They had such courage? . . . . 1 *Hen. VI.* i 2 36
My courage try by combat, if thou darest . . . . . i 2 89
My breast I'll burst with straining of my courage . . . . i 5 10
Thy friendship makes us fresh.—And doth beget new courage in our breasts . . . . iii 3 87
Valiant and virtuous, full of haughty courage . . . . iv 1 35
Her valiant courage and undaunted spirit, More than in women commonly is seen . . . . v 5 70
Resembled thee In courage, courtship and proportion 2 *Hen. VI.* i 3 57
Fear you not her courage.—I have heard her reported to be a woman of an invincible spirit . . . . i 4 7
His brother's death Hath given them heart and courage to proceed . iv 4 35
Three times did Richard make a lane to me, And thrice cried 'Courage, father! fight it out!' . . . . 3 *Hen. VI.* i 4 10
Our foes are nigh, And this soft courage makes your followers faint . ii 2 57
This may plant courage in their quailing breasts; For yet is hope . ii 3 54
So weak of courage and in judgement That they'll take no offence at our abuse . . . . iv 1 12
Courage, my masters! honour now or never! . . . . . iv 3 24
Strike up the drum; cry 'Courage!' and away . . . . v 3 24
The ship splits on the rock, Which industry and courage might have saved . . . . v 4 11
Courage then! what cannot be avoided 'Twere childish weakness to lament or fear . . . . v 4 37
Women and children of so high a courage, And warriors faint! . v 4 50
Our ancient word of courage, fair Saint George, Inspire us! *Richard III.* v 3 349
Then the thing of courage As roused with rage with rage doth sympathize *Troi. and Cres.* i 3 51
Nor once deject the courage of our minds, Because Cassandra's mad . ii 2 121
Whose present courage may beat down our foes . . . . ii 2 201
But when I meet you arm'd, as black defiance As heart can think or courage execute . . . . iv 1 13
In appointment fresh and fair, Anticipating time with starting courage iv 5 2
O courage, courage, princes! great Achilles Is arming . . v 5 30
Nor check my courage for what they can give . . . *Coriolanus* iii 3 92
Nay, mother, Where is your ancient courage? you were used To say extremity was the trier of spirits . . . . iv 1 3
Courage, man; the hurt cannot be much.—No, 'tis not so deep as a well . . . . *Rom. and Jul.* iii 1 98
I'd such a courage to do him good . . . . . *T. of Athens* iii 3 24
Thinking by this face To fasten in our thoughts that they have courage *J. Cæsar* v 1 11
We fail! But screw your courage to the sticking-place, And we'll not fail . . . . *Macbeth* i 7 60
Who could refrain, That had a heart to love, and in that heart Courage to make's love known? . . . . ii 3 124
Devotion, patience, courage, fortitude, I have no relish of them . iv 3 94
I mean purpose, courage and valour . . . . . . *Othello* iv 2 218
Condemn myself to lack The courage of a woman . *Ant. and Cleo.* iv 14 60
That self hand, Which writ his honour in the acts it did, Hath, with the courage which the heart did lend it, Splitted the heart . v 1 23
Husband, I come: Now to that name my courage prove my title! . v 2 291
Winning will put any man into courage . . . . *Cymbeline* ii 3 8
When Julius Cæsar Smiled at their lack of skill, but found their courage Worthy his frowning at . . . . ii 4 22
Their discipline, Now mingled with their courages . . . ii 4 24
Made Lud's town with rejoicing fires bright And Britons strut with courage . . . . iii 1 33
Change . . . fear and niceness—The handmaids of all women, or, more truly, Woman it pretty self—into a waggish courage . . . iii 4 160
This attempt I am soldier to. and will abide it with A prince's courage iii 4 187
Nor ask advice of any other thought But faithfulness and courage *Pericles* i 1 63

Courage. Will look so huge, Amazement shall drive courage from the state . . . . *Pericles* i 2 26
Now, by the gods, I do applaud his courage . . . . . ii 5 58
What courage, sir? God save you!—Courage enough: I do not fear the flaw . . . . . iii 1 38
Courageous. He is very courageous mad about his throwing into the water . . . *Mer. Wives* iv 1 4
O most courageous day! O most happy hour! *M. N. Dream* iv 2 27
The most courageous fiend bids me pack *Mer. of Venice* ii 2 10
Doublet and hose ought to show itself courageous to petticoat *As Y. Like It* ii 4 7
Well said, courageous Feeble! . . . 2 *Hen. IV.* iii 2 170
Courageous Bedford, let us now persuade you . . . 1 *Hen. VI.* iii 2 93
In God's name, cheerly on, courageous friends . . . *Richard III.* v 2 14
Courageous Richmond, well hast thou acquit thee . . . v 5 3
O, he is the courageous captain of complements . . . *Rom. and Jul.* ii 4 20
Thy spirit which keeps thee is Noble, courageous, high, unmatchable *Ant. and Cleo.* ii 3 20
Courageously. There we may rehearse most obscenely and courageously *M. N. Dream* i 2 111
Courageously and with a free desire Attending but the signal to begin *Richard II.* i 3 115
Courier. I met a courier, one mine ancient friend . . . *T. of Athens* v 2 6
Horsed Upon the sightless couriers of the air . . . *Macbeth* i 7 23
Couronne. La fin couronne les œuvres . . . 2 *Hen. VI.* v 2 28
Course. Set her two courses off to sea again; lay her off . . . *Tempest* i 1 53
This Sir Prudence, who Should not upbraid our course . . . ii 1 287
When his fair course is not hindered, He makes sweet music with the enamell'd stones . . . *T. G. of Ver.* ii 7 27
Then let me go and hinder not my course . . . ii 7 33
She did so course o'er my exteriors with such a greedy intention *Mer. Wives* i 3 72
Let him continue in his courses till thou knowest what they are *Meas. for Meas.* ii 1 196
This being granted in course,—and now follows all . . . iii 1 259
Dangerous to be aged in any kind of course . . . iii 2 238
You know the course is common . . . iv 2 190
Trust not my holy order, If I pervert your course . . . iv 3 153
Therefore homeward did they bend their course . . . *Com. of Errors* i 1 118
What is the course and drift of your compact? . . . ii 2 163
This course I fittest choose; For forty ducats is too much to lose . iv 3 96
But not for that dream I on this strange course . . . *Much Ado* iv 1 214
Against her will, as it appears In the true course of all the question v 4 6
Therefore to's seemeth it a needful course, Before we enter his forbidden gates, To know his pleasure . . . *L. L. Lost* ii 1 25
With the motion of all elements, Courses as swift as thought in every power . . . iv 3 330
Your grace hath ta'en great pains to qualify His rigorous course *Mer. of Venice* iv 1 8
Say thou wilt course; thy greyhounds are as swift As breathed stags *T. of Shrew* Ind. 2 49
You must not marvel, Helen, at my course . . . *All's Well* ii 5 63
In the common course of all treasons, we still see them reveal themselves iv 3 26
The fine's the crown; Whate'er the course, the end is the renown . iv 4 36
As all impediments in fancy's course Are motives of more fancy . v 3 214
Which hoxes honesty behind, restraining From course required *W. Tale* i 2 245
Thou dost advise me Even so as I mine own course have set down . i 2 340
Unless he take the course that you have done . . . ii 3 48
Proceed in justice, which shall have due course . . . iii 2 6
What course I mean to hold Shall nothing benefit your knowledge . iv 4 513
A course more promising Than a wild dedication of yourselves To unpath'd waters . . . iv 4 576
And o'erswell With course disturb'd even thy confining shores *K. John* ii 1 338
Take head from all indifferency, From all direction, purpose, course, intent . . . ii 1 580
To solemnize this day the glorious sun Stays in his course . . . iii 1 78
The yearly course that brings this day about Shall never see it but a holiday . . . iii 1 81
That takes away by any secret course Thy hateful life . . . iii 1 178
Like a bated and retired flood, Leaving our rankness and irregular course . . . v 4 54
Nor let my kingdom's rivers take their course Through my burn'd bosom v 7 38
Some of those seven are dried by nature's course . . . *Richard II.* i 2 14
By bad courses may be understood That their events can never fall out good . . . ii 1 213
With slow but stately pace kept on his course . . . v 2 10
No further go in this Than I by letters shall direct your course 1 *Hen. IV.* i 3 293
My lord of York commends the plot and the general course of the action ii 3 23
All the courses of my life do show I am not in the roll of common men iii 1 42
Mark how he bears his course, and runs me up With like advantage on the other side . . . iii 1 108
Each heart being set On bloody courses . . . 2 *Hen. IV.* i 1 159
Are you not ashamed to enforce a poor widow to so rough a course to come by her own? . . . ii 1 89
Like youthful steers unyoked, they take their courses East, west, north, south . . . iv 2 103
To the which course if I be enforced . . . iv 3 54
The sherris warms it and makes it course from the inwards to the parts extreme . . . iv 3 115
Here at more leisure may your highness read, With every course in his particular . . . iv 4 90
I had forestall'd this dear and deep rebuke Ere you with grief had spoke and I had heard The course of it so far . . . iv 5 143
Be it thy course to busy giddy minds With foreign quarrels . . . iv 5 214
The courses of his youth promised it not . . . *Hen. V.* i 1 24
His addiction was to courses vain, His companies unletter'd, rude . i 1 54
By this sword, I will.—Sword is an oath, and oaths must have their course . . . ii 1 106
So appears this fleet majestical, Holding due course to Harfleur iii Prol. 17
Or rather the sun and not the moon; for it shines bright and never changes, but keeps his course . . . v 2 173
Mangling by starts the full course of their glory . . . Epil. 4
Let me persuade you take a better course . . . 1 *Hen. VI.* iv 1 132
You do not well in obstinacy To cavil in the course of this contract v 4 156
Let me embrace thee, sour adversity, For wise men say it is the wisest course . . . 3 *Hen. VI.* iii 1 25
And, lords, towards Coventry bend we our course . . . iv 8 58
Thus far our fortune keeps an upward course . . . v 3 1
They do hold their course toward Tewksbury . . . v 3 19
But keep our course, though the rough wind say no . . . v 4 22
Course. I, Dædalus; my poor boy, Icarus; Thy father, Minos, that denied our course . . . 3 *Hen. VI.* v 6 22
He needs no indirect nor lawless course To cut off those that have offended him . . . *Richard III.* i 4 224
Where every horse bears his commanding rein, And may direct his course as please himself . . . ii 2 129
What an indirect and peevish course Is this of hers! . . . iii 1 31
Unto a lineal true-derived course . . . iii 7 200
And towards London they do bend their course . . . iv 5 14
The emperor thus desired, That he would please to alter the king's course . . . *Hen. VIII.* i 1 189
Is not this course pious?—Heaven keep me from such counsel! . ii 2 37
After So many courses of the sun enthroned, Still growing in a majesty ii 3 6
If, in the course And process of this time, you can report, And prove it too . . . ii 4 37
And did entreat your highness to this course Which you are running here . . . ii 4 216
Follow your envious courses, men of malice . . . iii 2 243
When he has run his course and sleeps in blessings . . . iii 2 398
That my teaching And the strong course of my authority Might go one way . . . v 3 35
Insisture, course, proportion, season, form . . . *Troi. and Cres.* i 3 87
A thousand complete courses of the sun . . . iv 1 27
Give me leave To take that course by your consent and voice . v 3 74
Whose course will on The way it takes, cracking ten thousand curbs *Coriolanus* i 1 71
It is the humane way: the other course Will prove too bloody . iii 1 327
Determine on some course, More than a wild exposture to each chance iv 1 35
A speedier course than lingering languishment Must we pursue *T. Andron.* ii 1 110
No, boy, not so; I'll teach thee another course . . . iv 1 119
Who threats, in course of this revenge, to do As much as ever Coriolanus did . . . iv 4 67
But He, that hath the steerage of my course, Direct my sail! *R. and J.* i 4 112
Uneven is the course, I like it not . . . iv 1 5
Stand all aloof, And do not interrupt me in my course . . . v 3 27
No levell'd malice Infects one comma in the course I hold *T. of Athens* i 1 48
This is all a liberal course allows; Who cannot keep his wealth must keep his house . . . iii 3 41
Consider that a prodigal course Is like the sun's; but not, like his, recoverable . . . iii 4 12
Drown them in a draught, Confound them by some course . . . v 1 106
Stand you directly in Antonius' way, When he doth run his course *J. Cæsar* i 2 4
Will you go see the order of the course?—Not I.—I pray you, do i 2 25
Our course will seem too bloody, Caius Cassius, To cut the head off and then hack the limbs . . . ii 1 162
Mischief, thou art afoot, Take thou what course thou wilt! . . . iii 2 266
Balm of hurt minds, great nature's second course . . . *Macbeth* ii 2 39
They have tied me to a stake; I cannot fly, But, bear-like, I must fight the course . . . v 7 2
When yond same star that's westward from the pole Had made his course . . . *Hamlet* i 1 37
To persever In obstinate condolement is a course Of impious stubbornness i 2 93
Swift as quicksilver it courses through The natural gates and alleys of the body . . . i 5 66
I'll tent him to the quick: if he but blench, I know my course . . ii 2 627
Rosencrantz and Guildenstern hold their course for England . . iv 6 29
Ourself, by monthly course, With reservation of an hundred knights, By you to be sustain'd, shall our abode Make with you by due turns . . . *Lear* i 1 134
He'll shape his old course in a country new . . . i 1 190
You shall run a certain course . . . i 2 89
I'll write straight to my sister, To hold my very course . . . i 3 26
That you protect this course, and put it on By your allowance . . i 4 227
This milky gentleness and course of yours Though I condemn not . i 4 364
'Tis from Cordelia, Who hath most fortunately been inform'd Of my obscured course . . . ii 2 175
How unremoveable and fix'd he is In his own course . . . ii 4 95
To course his own shadow for a traitor . . . iii 4 58
I am tied to the stake, and I must stand the course . . . iii 7 54
Quit the house on purpose, that their punishment Might have the freer course . . . iv 2 95
Know of the duke if his last purpose hold, Or whether since he is advised by aught To change the course . . . v 1 3
Till fit time Of law and course of direct session Call thee to answer *Othello* i 2 86
Steering with due course towards the isle of Rhodes . . . i 3 34
Now they do re-stem Their backward course . . . i 3 38
Did you by indirect and forced courses Subdue and poison this young maid's affections? . . . i 3 111
Or tainting his discipline; or from what other course you please . ii 1 276
Probal to thinking and indeed the course To win the Moor again ii 3 344
How am I then a villain To counsel Cassio to this parallel course? ii 3 355
Like to the Pontic sea, Whose icy current and compulsive course Ne'er feels retiring ebb . . . iii 3 454
A sibyl, that had number'd in the world The sun to course two hundred compasses . . . iii 4 71
So shall I clothe me in a forced content, And shut myself up in some other course, To fortune's alms . . . iii 4 121
The lethargy must have his quiet course: If not, he foams at mouth iv 1 54
His own courses will denote him so That I may save my speech iv 1 290
We have done our course; there's money for your pains . . . iv 2 93
I have myself resolved upon a course Which has no need of you *Ant. and Cleo.* iii 11 9
'Twas a shame no less Than was his loss, to course your flying flags, And leave his navy gazing . . . iii 13 11
'Tis your noblest course . . . iii 13 78
A sun and moon, which kept their course, and lighted The little O, the earth . . . v 2 80
By taking Antony's course, you shall bereave yourself Of my good purposes . . . v 2 130
But to win time To lose so bad employment; in the which I have consider'd of a course . . . *Cymbeline* iii 4 114
You should tread a course Pretty and full of view . . . iii 4 149
Stick to your journal course: the breach of custom Is breach of all iv 2 10
If each of you should take this course, how many Must murder wives much better than themselves For wrying but a little! . . . v 1 3
Those men Blush not in actions blacker than the night, Will shun no course to keep them from the light . . . *Pericles* i 1 136
What may make him blush in being known, He'll stop the course by which it might be known . . . i 2 23
Gentle mariner, Alter thy course for Tyre . . . iii 1 76

Course. Doth give me A more content in course of true delight Than to be thirsty after tottering honour . . . . . . *Pericles* iii 2 39
Blame both my lord and me, that we have taken No care to your best courses . . . . iv 1 39
Though you call my course unnatural, You not your child well loving . iv 3 36
And bear his courses to be ordered By Lady Fortune . . . . iv 4 47
We must take another course with you . . . . . iv 6 130
Course of breath. When I here came in, And found no course of breath within your majesty, How cold it struck my heart! 2 *Hen. IV.* iv 5 151
Course of death. If she live long, And in the end meet the old course of death, Women will all turn monsters . . . . *Lear* iii 7 101
Course of fight. Thy exercise hath been too violent For a second course of fight . . . . *Coriolanus* i 5 17
Course of fortune. I have only been Silent so long and given way unto This course of fortune . . . . . . *Much Ado* iv 1 159
Course of gratitude. Thou canst not, in the course of gratitude, but be a diligent follower of mine . . . . . *Cymbeline* iii 5 121
Course of growth. And divert his grain Tortive and errant from his course of growth . . . . . . *Troi. and Cres.* i 3 9
Course of honour. I could not answer in that course of honour *All's Well* v 3 98
Course of justice. Cut off by course of justice,— By course of justice! *Meas. for Meas.* v 1 35
In the course of justice, none of us Should see salvation *Mer. of Venice* iv 1 199
Thus hath the course of justice wheel'd about . . *Richard III.* iv 4 105
Course of law. The duke cannot deny the course of law *Mer. of Venice* iii 3 26
To pluck down justice from your awful bench, To trip the course of law 2 *Hen. IV.* v 2 87
'Tis meet he be condemn'd by course of law . . 2 *Hen. VI.* iii 1 237
Before I be convict by course of law, To threaten me with death is most unlawful . . . . *Richard III.* i 4 192
Course of learning. A course of learning and ingenious studies *T. of Shr.* i 1 9
Course of love. This letter doth make good the friar's words, Their course of love . . . . . . *Rom. and Jul.* v 3 287
I will a round unvarnish'd tale deliver Of my whole course of love *Othello* i 3 91
Course of loyalty. I will persevere in my course of loyalty . . *Lear* iii 5 23
Course of mischief. Like to the bullet's grazing, Break out into a second course of mischief . . . . . . *Hen. V.* iv 3 106
Course of things. Admit the excuse Of time, of numbers and due course of things . . . . v Prol. 4
Course of thought. It makes the course of thoughts to fetch about *K. John* iv 2 24
In our circumstance and course of thought, 'Tis heavy with him *Hamlet* iii 3 83
Course of time. Experience is by industry achieved And perfected by the swift course of time . . . . . *T. G. of Ver.* i 3 23
He came into the world Full fourteen weeks before the course of time *K. John* i 1 113
Course of true love. The course of true love never did run smooth *M. N. Dream* i 1 134
Course of war. Write, write, that from the bloody course of war My dearest master, your dear son, may hie . . . *All's Well* iii 4 8
Course of wooing. When I told thee he was of my counsel In my whole course of wooing, thou criedst 'Indeed!' . . . *Othello* iii 3 112
Coursed. The big round tears Coursed one another down his innocent nose *As Y. Like It* ii 1 39
We coursed him at the heels, and had a purpose To be his purveyor *Macbeth* i 6 21
Courser. They may break his foaming courser's back . . *Richard II.* i 2 51
Their neighing coursers daring of the spur . 2 *Hen. IV.* iv 1 119
I have heard a sonnet begin so to one's mistress.—Then did they imitate that which I composed to my courser . . . *Hen. V.* iii 7 47
Two braver men Ne'er spurr'd their coursers at the trumpet's sound 3 *Hen. VI.* v 7 9
You gave Good words the other day of a bay courser I rode on *T. of Athens* i 2 217
You'll have coursers for cousins and gennets for germans . *Othello* i 1 113
Much is breeding, Which, like the courser's hair, hath yet but life, And not a serpent's poison . . . . *Ant. and Cleo.* i 2 200
A courser, whose delightful steps Shall make the gazer joy to see him tread . . . . *Pericles* ii 1 164
Coursing. I am coursing myself: they have pitched a toil *L. L. Lost* iv 3 2
We do not mean the coursing snatchers only . . *Hen. V.* i 2 143
Court. Whose influence If now I court not but omit, my fortunes Will ever after droop . . . . . . *Tempest* i 2 183
Welcome, sir; This cell's my court: here have I few attendants . v 1 166
Youthful Valentine Attends the emperor in his royal court *T. G. of Ver.* i 3 27
With the speediest expedition I will dispatch him to the emperor's court i 3 38
Thou shalt spend some time With Valentinus in the emperor's court . i 3 67
And am going with Sir Proteus to the Imperial's court . . . ii 3 5
Oftentimes have purposed to forbid Sir Valentine her company and my court . . . . iii 1 27
Doth but signify My health and happy being at your court . . iii 1 57
For long agone I have forgot to court . . . . . iii 1 85
Longer than swiftest expedition Will give thee time to leave our royal court . . . . iii 1 165
Take-a your rapier, and come after my heel to the court *Mer. Wives* i 4 62
Rugby, come to the court with me . . . . . . i 4 130
The best courtier of them all, when the court lay at Windsor, could never have brought her to such a canary . . . . . ii 2 63
I should be a pitiful lady!—Let the court of France show me such another . . . . iii 3 57
The duke himself will be to-morrow at court . . . . iv 3 3
I hear not of him in the court . . . . iv 3 6
The doctor is well money'd, and his friends Potent at court . . iv 4 89
Dere is no duke dat the court is know to come . . . . iv 5 90
If it should come to the ear of the court . . . . . iv 5 97
You were brought into the orchard and saw me court Margaret *Much Ado* v 1 244
Our court shall be a little Academe . . . . *L. L. Lost* i 1 13
To study with your grace And stay here in your court for three years' space . . . . i 1 52
Item, That no woman shall come within a mile of my court . . i 1 120
He shall endure such public shame as the rest of the court can possibly devise . . . . i 1 133
Our court, you know, is haunted With a refined traveller of Spain . i 1 163
No woman may approach his silent court . . . . . ii 1 24
Means to lodge you in the field, Like one that comes here to besiege his court . . . . ii 1 86
The roof of this court is too high to be yours . . . . ii 1 92
You shall be welcome, madam, to my court . . . . . ii 1 95
All his behaviours did make their retire To the court of his eye . ii 1 235
This Armado is a Spaniard, that keeps here in court . . iv 1 100
Their purpose is to parle, to court and dance . . . . v 2 122
Court. This favour thou shalt wear, And then the king will court thee for his dear . . . . *L. L. Lost* v 2 131
We came to visit you, and purpose now To lead you to our court . v 2 344
You will come into the court and swear that I have a poor pennyworth in the English . . . . *Mer. of Venice* i 2 76
Go one, and call the Jew into the court.—He is ready at the door . iv 1 14
Upon my power I may dismiss this court . . . . . iv 1 104
This letter from Bellario doth commend A young and learned doctor to our court . . . . iv 1 144
Meantime the court shall hear Bellario's letter . . . . iv 1 149
Are you acquainted with the difference That holds this present question in the court? . . . . iv 1 172
This strict court of Venice Must needs give sentence 'gainst the merchant there . . . . iv 1 204
Yes, here I tender it for him in the court; Yea, twice the sum . iv 1 209
Most heartily I do beseech the court To give the judgement . . iv 1 243
The court awards it, and the law doth give it . . . . iv 1 300
The law allows it, and the court awards it . . . . iv 1 303
He hath refused it in the open court: He shall have merely justice . iv 1 338
So please my lord the duke and all the court To quit the fine . iv 1 380
That he do record a gift, Here in the court, of all he dies possess'd, Unto his son . . . . iv 1 389
What's the new news at the new court?—There's no news at the court, sir, but the old news . . . . . . *As Y. Like It* i 1 102
She is at the court, and no less beloved of her uncle than his own daughter . . . . i 1 116
Dispatch you with your safest haste And get you from our court . i 3 44
If that thou be'st found So near our public court as twenty miles, Thou diest . . . . i 3 46
What if we assay'd to steal The clownish fool out of your father's court? i 3 132
Are not these woods More free from peril than the envious court? . ii 1 4
Thus most invectively he pierceth through The body of the country, city, court . . . . ii 1 59
Some villains of my court Are of consent and sufferance in this . ii 2 2
But in respect it is not in the court, it is tedious . . . iii 2 19
Wast ever in court, shepherd?—No, truly.—Then thou art damned . iii 2 34
If thou never wast at court, thou never sawest good manners . . iii 2 41
Good manners at the court are as ridiculous in the country as the behaviour of the country is most mockable at the court . . iii 2 47
You told me you salute not at the court, but you kiss your hands . iii 2 50
Hath put on a religious life And thrown into neglect the pompous court v 4 188
Leave shall you have to court her at your pleasure . . *T. of Shrew* i 1 54
Make love to her And unsuspected court her by herself . . i 2 137
Now, for my life, the knave doth court my love . . . iii 1 49
See, how they kiss and court! . . . . iv 2 27
Fie on her! see, how beastly she doth court him! . . . iv 2 34
The court's a learning place . . . . . . *All's Well* i 1 191
If I can remember thee, I will think of thee at court . . . i 1 203
My loving greetings To those of mine in court. . . . . i 3 259
My business is but to the court.—To the court! why, what place make you special, when you put off that with such contempt? But to the court! . . . . ii 2 4
If God have lent a man any manners, he may easily put it off at court . ii 2 9
Such a fellow, to say precisely, were not for the court . . . ii 2 13
Go, call before me all the lords in court . . . . . ii 3 52
I have no mind to Isbel since I was at court: our old ling and our Isbels o' the country are nothing like your old ling and your Isbels o' the court . . . . iii 2 14
After some dispatch in hand at court, Thither we bend again . . iii 2 56
And is it I That drive thee from the sportive court? . . . iii 2 109
He is the prince of the world; let his nobility remain in's court . iv 5 52
Sir, I have seen you in the court of France . . . . . v 1 10
Such a ring as this, The last that e'er I took her leave at court, I saw upon her finger . . . . v 3 79
You said You saw one here in court could witness it . . . v 3 200
I am bound to the Count Orsino's court: farewell . . . *T. Night* ii 1 44
I have many enemies in Orsino's court . . . . . . ii 1 47
For sealing The injury of tongues in courts and kingdoms . *W. Tale* i 2 338
I must Forsake the court: to do't, or no, is certain To me a break-neck i 2 362
What is the news i' the court?—None rare, my lord . . . i 2 367
No court in Europe is too good for thee; What dost thou then in prison? ii 2 3
Being well arrived from Delphos, are both landed, Hasting to the court iii 2 197
It is his highness' pleasure that the queen Appear in person here in court iii 2 10
Before Polixenes Came to your court, how I was in your grace . iii 2 48
And why he left your court, the gods themselves, Wotting no more than I, are ignorant . . . . iii 2 76
I have missingly noted, he is of late much retired from court . . iv 2 36
I cannot tell, good sir, for which of his virtues it was, but he was certainly whipped out of the court . . . . iv 3 95
There's no virtue whipped out of the court: they cherish it to make it stay . . . . iv 3 97
Mark thou my words: Follow us to the court . . . . . iv 4 443
The selfsame sun that shines upon his court Hides not his visage from our cottage . . . . iv 4 455
Seest thou not the air of the court in these enfoldings? . . . iv 4 755
To your court Whiles he was hastening, in the chase, it seems, Of this fair couple . . . . v 1 188
Are they returned to the court? . . . . v 2 101
Where hast thou been preserved? where lived? how found Thy father's court? . . . . v 3 125
What brings you here to court so hastily? . . . . *K. John* i 1 221
When I shall meet him in the court of heaven I shall not know him . iii 4 87
And, for our coffers, with too great a court And liberal largess, are grown somewhat light . . . . *Richard II.* i 4 43
He hath forsook the court, Broken his staff of office . . . ii 3 26
Within the hollow crown That rounds the mortal temples of a king Keeps Death his court . . . . iii 2 162
In the base court he doth attend To speak with you . . . iii 3 176
In the base court? Base court, where kings grow base . . . iii 3 180
In the base court? Come down? Down, court! down, king! . . iii 3 182
Is not my arm of length, That reacheth from the restful English court As far as Calais? . . . . iv 1 12
In some sort it jumps with my humour as well as waiting in the court 1 *Hen. IV.* i 2 79
There is a nobleman of the court at door would speak with you . ii 4 318
You must to the court in the morning . . . . . . ii 4 368
There let him sleep till day. I'll to the court in the morning . ii 4 594
I was train'd up in the English court . . . . . . iii 1 122
An alien to the hearts Of all the court and princes of my blood . iii 2 35
Now, Hal, to the news at court: for the robbery, lad, how is that answered? iii 3 197

Court. In rage dismiss'd my father from the court . . . 1 *Hen. IV.* iv 3 100
When Arthur first in court . . . 2 *Hen. IV.* ii 4 36
You must away to court, sir, presently; A dozen captains stay at door ii 4 401
A' must, then, to the inns o' court shortly . . . iii 2 14
You had not four such swinge-bucklers in all the inns o' court . iii 2 25
Peradventure I will with ye to the court . . . iii 2 316
The case of a treble hautboy was a mansion for him, a court . iii 2 352
Our grief, The which hath been with scorn shoved from the court iv 2 37
And now dispatch we toward the court . . . iv 3 82
When you come to court, Stand my good lord, pray, in your good report iv 3 88
And to the English court assemble now, From every region apes of idleness! . . . iv 5 122
A friend i' the court is better than a penny in purse . . . v 1 34
This is the English, not the Turkish court . . . v 2 47
There's one Pistol come from the court with news . . . v 3 85
If, sir, you come with news from the court, I take it there's but two ways, either to utter them, or to conceal them . . . v 3 115
All the courts of France will be disturb'd With chaces . *Hen. V.* i 2 265
But now thy uncle is removing hence; As princes do their courts 1 *Hen. VI.* ii 5 105
A gentler heart did never sway in court . . . iii 2 135
This shouldering of each other in the court . . . iv 1 189
This staff, mine office-badge in court, Was broke in twain . 2 *Hen. VI.* i 2 25
Is this the guise, Is this the fashion in the court of England? . i 3 46
She sweeps it through the court with troops of ladies . . . i 3 80
Humphrey's wife: Strangers in court do take her for the queen . i 3 82
Purposely therefore Left I the court, to see this quarrel tried . ii 3 53
All the court admired him for submission . . . iii 1 12
So shall my name with slander's tongue be wounded, And princes' courts be fill'd with my reproach . . . iii 2 69
And they jointly swear To spoil the city and your royal court . iv 4 53
Pull down the Savoy; others to the inns of court; down with them all iv 7 2
I am the besom that must sweep the court clean . . . iv 7 34
Who would live turmoiled in the court, And may enjoy such quiet walks as these? . . . iv 10 18
Or dare to bring thy force so near the court . . . v 1 22
And I, with grief and sorrow, to the court . . . 3 *Hen. VI.* i 1 210
Mirthful comic shows, Such as befits the pleasure of the court . v 7 44
Nor made to court an amorous looking-glass . . . *Richard III.* i 1 15
Fill the court with quarrels, talk, and tailors . . . *Hen. VIII.* i 3 20
Whoever the king favours, The cardinal instantly will find employment, And far enough from court too . . . ii 1 49
By whose virtue, The court of Rome commanding . . . ii 2 105
I have been begging sixteen years in court, Am yet a courtier beggarly ii 3 82
Henry King of England, come into the court . . . ii 4 7
Katharine Queen of England, come into the court . . . ii 4 11
It shall be therefore bootless That longer you desire the court . ii 4 62
Nor ever more Upon this business my appearance make In any of their courts . . . ii 4 133
Unsolicited I left no reverend person in this court . . . ii 4 220
'Tis a needful fitness That we adjourn this court till further day . ii 4 232
Break up the court: I say, set on . . . ii 4 240
Farewell The hopes of court! my hopes in heaven do dwell . iii 2 459
Held a late court at Dunstable, six miles off From Ampthill . iv 1 27
Ye shall go my way, which Is to the court . . . iv 1 115
Do you take the court for Paris-garden? ye rude slaves, leave your gaping . . . v 4 2
Some strange Indian with the great tool come to court . . . v 4 35
Through the rivers of your blood, Even to the court, the heart, to the seat o' the brain . . . *Coriolanus* i 1 140
Let courts and cities be Made all of false-faced soothing! . . . i 9 43
If the emperor's court can feast two brides, You are my guest *T. Andron.* i 1 489
Nor would your noble mother for much more Be so dishonour'd in the court of Rome . . . ii 1 52
Why should he despair that knows to court it With words, fair looks and liberality? . . . ii 1 91
The emperor's court is like the house of Fame, The palace full of tongues ii 1 126
Ring a hunter's peal, That all the court may echo with the noise . ii 2 6
Lucius and I'll go brave it at the court . . . iv 1 121
To calm this tempest whirling in the court . . . iv 2 160
Kinsmen, shoot all your shafts into the court . . . iv 3 61
The Bull, being gall'd, gave Aries such a knock That down fell both the Ram's horns in the court . . . iv 3 72
In the emperor's court There is a queen, attended by a Moor . v 2 104
Happiness courts thee in her best array . . . *Rom. and Jul.* iii 3 142
Is Banquo gone from court?—Ay, madam, but returns again to-night *Macbeth* iii 2 1
The rest That are within the note of expectation Already are i' the court iii 3 11
The son of Duncan, From whom this tyrant holds the due of birth, Lives in the English court . . . iii 6 26
Some holy angel Fly to the court of England and unfold His message ere he come! . . . iii 6 46
Virtue, as it never will be moved, Though lewdness court it in a shape of heaven . . . *Hamlet* i 5 54
Vouchsafe your rest here in our court Some little time . . . ii 2 13
Shall we to the court? for, by my fay, I cannot reason . . . ii 2 271
They are about the court, And, as I think, they have already order This night to play before him . . . iii 1 19
I'll court his favours . . . v 2 78
Great rivals in our youngest daughter's love, Long in our court have made their amorous sojourn . . . *Lear* i 1 48
This our court, infected with their manners, Shows like a riotous inn i 4 264
To manage private and domestic quarrel, In night, and on the court and guard of safety! 'Tis monstrous . . . *Othello* ii 3 216
If I court moe women, you'll couch with moe men . . . iv 3 57
I will not wait pinion'd at your master's court . *Ant. and Cleo.* v 2 53
Lived in court—Which rare it is to do—most praised, most loved *Cymb.* i 1 46
If after this command thou fraught the court With thy unworthiness, thou diest . . . i 1 126
The gods protect you! And bless the good remainders of the court! . i 1 129
Commend me to the court where your lady is . . . i 4 139
A saucy stranger in his court to mart As in a Romish stew . . . i 6 151
He hath a court He little cares for and a daughter who He not respects at all . . . i 6 153
Take my power i' the court for yours.—My humble thanks . . . i 6 179
Did you hear of a stranger that's come to court to-night? . . . ii 1 36
One bred of alms and foster'd with cold dishes, With scraps o' the court ii 3 120
Was Caius Lucius in the Britain court When you were there? . . . ii 4 37
O, that I had her here, to tear her limb-meal! I will go there and do't, i' the court, before Her father . . . ii 4 148

Court. Revolve what tales I have told you Of courts, of princes, of the tricks in war . . . *Cymbeline* iii 3 15
The art o' the court, As hard to leave as keep . . . iii 3 46
The perturb'd court, For my being absent . . . iii 4 108
You shall be miss'd at court, And that will well confirm it . . . iii 4 129
If you'll back to the court— No court, no father . . . iii 4 133
If not at court, Then not in Britain must you bide . . . iii 4 137
Lest, being miss'd, I be suspected of Your carriage from the court . iii 4 190
But our great court Made me to blame in memory . . . iii 5 50
To the court I'll knock her back, foot her home again . . . iii 5 148
Great men, That had a court no bigger than this cave . . . iii 6 83
What lies I have heard! Our courtiers say all's savage but at court . iv 2 33
It may be heard at court that such as we Cave here, hunt here, are outlaws . . . iv 2 137
You look like Romans, And not o' the court of Britain . . . v 5 25
Well may you, sir, Remember me at court . . . v 5 193
Why fled you from the court? and whither? . . . v 5 387
Here pleasures court mine eyes, and mine eyes shun them . *Pericles* i 2 6
So, this is Tyre, and this the court . . . i 3 1
How far is his court distant from this shore? . . . ii 1 111
Guide me to your sovereign's court . . . ii 1 146
I'll bring thee to the court myself . . . ii 1 170
Yon knight doth sit too melancholy, As if the entertainment in our court Had not a show might countervail his worth . . . ii 3 55
I came unto your court for honour's cause, And not to be a rebel to her state . . . ii 5 61
To the court of King Simonides Are letters brought . . . iii Gower 23
Court-contempt. Reflect I not on thy baseness court-contempt? *W. Tale* iv 4 759
Court-cupboard. Away with the joint-stools, remove the court-cupboard, look to the plate . . . *Rom. and Jul.* i 5 8
Court-gate. I see him break Skogan's head at the court-gate 2 *Hen. IV.* iii 2 33
The new proclamation That's clapp'd upon the court-gate . *Hen. VIII.* i 3 18
Court-hand. He can make obligations, and write court-hand 2 *Hen. VI.* iv 2 101
Court holy-water in a dry house is better than this rain-water out o' door *Lear* iii 2 10
Court-like. Generally allowed for your many war-like, court-like, and learned preparations . . . *Mer. Wives* ii 2 237
Court news. And hear poor rogues Talk of court news . *Lear* v 3 14
Court-odour. Receives not thy nose court-odour from me? . *W. Tale* iv 4 758
Court of guard. Let us have knowledge at the court of guard 1 *Hen. VI.* ii 1 4
The lieutenant to-night watches on the court of guard . *Othello* ii 1 220
If we be not relieved within this hour, We must return to the court of guard . . . *Ant. and Cleo.* iv 9 2
Let us bear him To the court of guard; he is of note . . . iv 9 32
Court of parliament. Now call we our high court of parliament 2 *Hen. IV.* v 2 134
The king is fled to London, To call a present court of parliament 2 *Hen. VI.* v 3 25
Court-word. Advocate's the court-word for a pheasant . *W. Tale* iv 4 768
Courted. I am courted now with a double occasion . . . iv 4 864
Courteous. Be kind and courteous to this gentleman . *M. N. Dream* iii 1 167
Thanks, courteous wall: Jove shield thee well for this! . . . v 1 179
Besides commends and courteous breath, Gifts of rich value *Mer. of Ven.* ii 9 90
Go give him courteous conduct to this place . . . iv 1 148
We freely cope your courteous pains withal . . . iv 1 412
This is called the Retort Courteous . . . *As Y. Like It* v 4 76
I will name you the degrees. The first, the Retort Courteous . v 4 97
An affable and courteous gentleman . . . *T. of Shrew* i 2 98
Thou art pleasant, gamesome, passing courteous, But slow in speech . ii 1 247
Delicate fine hats and most courteous feathers, which bow the head and nod at every man . . . *All's Well* iv 5 111
I beseech you, do me this courteous office . . . *T. Night* iii 4 278
They are soldiers, Witty, courteous, liberal, full of spirit . 3 *Hen. VI.* i 2 43
My courteous lord, adieu. Farewell, revolted fair! . *Troi. and Cres.* v 2 185
Having been supple and courteous to the people . . . *Coriolanus* ii 2 30
To bow in the hams.—Meaning, to court'sy.—Thou hast most kindly hit it.—A most courteous exposition . . . *Rom. and Jul.* ii 4 60
Like an honest gentleman, and a courteous, and a kind, and a handsome ii 5 57
The best friend I had! O courteous Tybalt! . . . iii 2 62
Courteous destroyers, affable wolves, meek bears! . *T. of Athens* iii 6 105
With what courteous action It waves you to a more removed ground *Ham.* i 4 60
Courteous lord, one word. Sir, you and I must part *Ant. and Cleo.* i 3 86
Our courteous Antony, Whom ne'er the word of 'No' woman heard speak . . . ii 2 227
You are right courteous knights . . . *Pericles* ii 3 27
Courteously. Thou dost not use me courteously . *Troi. and Cres.* iv 4 123
Courtesies. Outward courtesies would fain proclaim Favours that keep within . . . *Meas. for Meas.* v 1 15
Manhood is melted into courtesies, valour into compliment *Much Ado* iv 1 322
For your many courtesies I thank you: I must discontinue your company . . . v 1 191
Nod to him, elves, and do him courtesies . . . *M. N. Dream* iii 1 177
Another time You call'd me dog; and for these courtesies I'll lend you thus much moneys'? . . . *Mer. of Venice* i 3 129
The best-condition'd and unwearied spirit In doing courtesies . . . iii 2 296
We serve you, madam, In that and all your worthiest affairs.—Not so, but as we change our courtesies . . . *All's Well* iii 2 100
Let thy courtesies alone, they are scurvy ones . . . v 3 324
Toby approaches; courtesies there to me . . . *T. Night* ii 5 67
O'er courtiers' knees, that dream on court'sies straight . *Rom. and Jul.* i 4 72
Thus honest fools lay out their wealth on court'sies . *T. of Athens* i 2 241
These couchings and these lowly courtesies Might fire the blood of ordinary men . . . *J. Cæsar* iii 1 36
Sweet words, Low-crooked court'sies and base spaniel-fawning . iii 1 43
He hath laid strange courtesies and great Of late upon me *Ant. and Cleo.* ii 2 157
I have been debtor to you for courtesies, which I will be ever to pay and yet pay still . . . *Cymbeline* i 4 39
Courtesy. If thou scorn our courtesy, thou diest . . . *T. G. of Ver.* iv 1 68
Bidding the law make court'sy to their will . . . *Meas. for Meas.* ii 4 175
You are to do me both a present and a dangerous courtesy . . . iv 2 172
Courtesy itself must convert to disdain, if you come in her presence *Much Ado* i 1 123
Then is courtesy a turncoat. But it is certain I am loved of all ladies . i 1 125
And ransom him to any French courtier for a new-devised courtesy *L. L. Lost* i 2 66
Remember thy courtesy; I beseech thee, apparel thy head . . . v 1 103
This is he That kiss'd his hand away in courtesy . . . v 2 324
My lady, to the manner of the days, In courtesy gives undeserving praise . . . v 2 366
Though the mourning brow of progeny Forbid the smiling courtesy of love . . . v 2 755

Courtesy. In our maiden council, rated them At courtship, pleasant jest and courtesy . . . . *L. L. Lost* v 2 790
These ladies' courtesy Might well have made our sport a comedy . . v 2 885
But, gentle friend, for love and courtesy Lie further off . *M. N. Dream* ii 2 56
If you were civil and knew courtesy, You would not do me thus much injury . . . . iii 2 147
Pray you, leave your courtesy, good mounsieur . . . . . iv 1 21
Yet, in courtesy, in all reason, we must stay the time . . . . v 1 258
He was wont to lend money for a Christian courtesy . *Mer. of Venice* iii 1 52
Never train'd To offices of tender courtesy . . . . . iv 1 33
Welcome to our house: It must appear in other ways than words, Therefore I scant this breathing courtesy . . . . . v 1 141
I was enforced to send it after him; I was beset with shame and courtesy . . . . v 1 217
The courtesy of nations allows you my better, in that you are the first-born . . . . *As Y. Like It* i 1 49
That courtesy would be uncleanly, if courtiers were shepherds . . iii 2 51
With soft low tongue and lowly courtesy . . *T. of Shrew* Ind. 1 114
To do you courtesy, This will I do, and this I will advise you . . iv 2 91
If this be courtesy, sir, accept of it.—O sir, I do . . . . iv 2 111
Marry, hang you!—And your courtesy, for a ring-carrier! . *All's Well* iii 5 95
You have some hideous matter to deliver, when the courtesy of it is so fearful . . . . *T. Night* i 5 222
I am one of those gentle ones that will use the devil himself with courtesy . . . . iv 2 38
How he did seem to dive into their hearts With humble and familiar courtesy . . . . *Richard II.* i 4 26
Me rather had my heart might feel your love Than my unpleased eye see your courtesy . . . . iii 3 193
Why, what a candy deal of courtesy This fawning greyhound then did proffer me! . . . . *1 Hen. IV.* i 3 251
Though I be but Prince of Wales, yet I am the king of courtesy . . ii 4 11
Then I stole all courtesy from heaven, And dress'd myself in such humility . . . . iii 2 50
I will embrace him with a soldier's arm, That he shall shrink under my courtesy . . . . v 2 75
Some of us never shall A second time do such a courtesy . . . v 2 101
If thou wert sensible of courtesy, I should not make so dear a show of zeal . . . . v 4 94
I thank your grace for this high courtesy, Which I shall give away immediately . . . . v 5 32
If a man will make courtesy and say nothing, he is virtuous . *2 Hen. IV.* ii 1 135
It was more of his courtesy than your deserving . . . . iv 3 47
First my fear; then my courtesy; last my speech . . . . Epil. 1
My fear is, your displeasure; my courtesy, my duty . . . Epil. 2
Alone, since there's no remedy, I mean to prove this lady's courtesy *1 Hen. VI.* ii 2 58
And then I need not crave his courtesy . . . . v 3 105
Deceive and cog, Duck with French nods and apish courtesy *Richard III.* i 3 49
When last I was at Exeter, The mayor in courtesy show'd me the castle iv 2 107
Bounteous Buckingham, The mirror of all courtesy . . *Hen. VIII.* ii 1 53
The elephant hath joints, but none for courtesy . *Troi. and Cres.* ii 3 114
Weigh him well, And that which looks like pride is courtesy. . . iv 5 82
I would my arms could match thee in contention, As they contend with thee in courtesy . . . . iv 5 206
I do disdain thy courtesy, proud Trojan . . . . v 6 15
How shall this bisson multitude digest The senate's courtesy? *Coriol.* iii 1 132
Thou hast never in thy life Show'd thy dear mother any courtesy . . v 3 161
True nobility Warrants these words in princely courtesy . *T. Andron.* i 1 272
She whom mighty kingdoms court'sy to . . . . v 3 74
In such a case as mine a man may strain courtesy . . *Rom. and Jul.* ii 4 55
To bow in the hams.—Meaning, to court'sy.—Thou hast most kindly hit it . . . . ii 4 58
Nay, I am the very pink of courtesy.—Pink for flower . . . ii 4 61
He is not the flower of courtesy, but, I'll warrant him, as gentle as a lamb . . . . ii 5 44
That there should be small love 'mongst these sweet knaves, And all this courtesy! . . . . *T. of Athens* i 1 259
I thank you for your pains and courtesy . . . . *J. Cæsar* ii 2 115
With courtesy and with respect enough . . . . . . iv 2 15
This courtesy is not of the right breed . . . . *Hamlet* iii 2 326
Bond of childhood, Effects of courtesy, dues of gratitude . . *Lear* ii 4 182
Return, and force Their scanted courtesy . . . . . . iii 2 67
This courtesy, forbid thee, shall the duke Instantly know . . . iii 3 22
Our power Shall do a courtesy to our wrath, which men May blame . iii 7 26
They do discharge their shot of courtesy: Our friends at least *Othello* ii 1 56
'Tis my breeding That gives me this bold show of courtesy . . . ii 1 100
Very good; well kissed! an excellent courtesy! 'tis so, indeed . . ii 1 177
But that was but courtesy.—Lechery, by this hand . . . . ii 1 261
I could well wish courtesy would invent some other custom of entertainment . . . . ii 3 36
The queen shall then have courtesy, so she Will yield us up *A. and C.* iii 13 15
O Dissembling courtesy! How fine this tyrant Can tickle where she wounds! . . . . *Cymbeline* i 1 84
Many times, Doth ill deserve by doing well; what's worse, Must court'sy at the censure . . . . iii 3 55
Aye hopeless To have the courtesy your cradle promised . . . iv 4 28
How courtesy would seem to cover sin! . . . . . *Pericles* i 1 121
The which the knight himself With such a graceful courtesy deliver'd . ii 2 41
O, that's as much as you would be denied Of your fair courtesy . . ii 3 107
A courtesy Which if we should deny, the most just gods For every graff would send a caterpillar . . . . v 1 58

Courtezan. Scoff on, vile fiend and shameless courtezan! *1 Hen. VI.* iii 2 45
Pirates may make cheap pennyworths of their pillage And purchase friends and give to courtezans . . . . . . *2 Hen. VI.* i 1 223
Not dallying with a brace of courtezans, But meditating with two deep divines . . . . *Richard III.* iii 7 74
This is a brave night to cool a courtezan . . . . . *Lear* iii 2 79
Some Roman courtezan . . . . *Cymbeline* iii 4 126

Courtier. The best courtier of them all, when the court lay at Windsor, could never have brought her to such a canary . *Mer. Wives* ii 2 62
You are a flattering boy: now I see you'll be a courtier . . . iii 2 8
Thou wouldst make an absolute courtier . . . . . . iii 3 66
I would take Desire prisoner, and ransom him to any French courtier for a new-devised courtesy . . . . *L. L. Lost* i 2 65
O worthy fool! One that hath been a courtier . *As Y. Like It* ii 7 36
That courtesy would be uncleanly, if courtiers were shepherds . . iii 2 51
Do not your courtier's hands sweat? . . . . iii 2 56
The courtier's hands are perfumed with civet . . . . . iii 2 65

Courtier. I have neither the scholar's melancholy, which is emulation, nor the musician's, which is fantastical, nor the courtier's, which is proud . . . . *As Y. Like It* iv 1 12
He hath been a courtier, he swears . . . . v 4 42
I did dislike the cut of a certain courtier's beard . . . . v 4 73
'Tis an unseason'd courtier . . . . *All's Well* i 1 80
Virginity, like an old courtier, wears her cap out of fashion . . i 1 169
I will return perfect courtier; in the which, my instruction shall serve to naturalize thee, so thou wilt be capable of a courtier's counsel . i 1 222
So like a courtier, contempt nor bitterness Were in his pride or sharpness . . . . i 2 36
Ask me if I am a courtier: it shall do you no harm to learn . . ii 2 38
I pray you, sir, are you a courtier? . . . . ii 2 42
That youth's a rare courtier . . . . *T. Night* iii 1 97
Are you a courtier, an't like you, sir? . . . . *W. Tale* iv 4 753
This cannot be but a great courtier . . . . iv 4 775
All scholars, lawyers, courtiers, gentlemen, They call false caterpillars *2 Hen. VI.* iv 4 36
Think an English courtier may be wise, And never see the Louvre *Hen. VIII.* i 3 22
I have been begging sixteen years in court, Am yet a courtier beggarly ii 3 83
This Trojan scorns us; or the men of Troy Are ceremonious courtiers *Troi. and Cres.* i 3 234
Courtiers as free, as debonair, unarm'd, As bending angels . . . i 3 235
O'er courtiers' knees, that dream on court'sies straight . *Rom. and Jul.* i 4 72
Sometime she gallops o'er a courtier's nose, And then dreams he of smelling out a suit . . . . i 4 77
Thou 'ldst courtier be again, Wert thou not beggar . . *T. of Athens* iv 3 241
Our chiefest courtier, cousin, and our son . . . . *Hamlet* i 2 117
O, what a noble mind is here o'erthrown! The courtier's, soldier's, scholar's . . . . iii 1 159
Or of a courtier; which could say 'Good morrow, sweet lord!' . v 1 90
The toe of the peasant comes so near the heel of the courtier, he galls his kibe . . . . v 1 153
Here comes the king, The queen, the courtiers . . . . . v 1 241
Brutus, With the arm'd rest, courtiers of beauteous freedom *Ant. and Cleo.* ii 6 17
Our bloods No more obey the heavens than our courtiers Still seem as does the king . . . . *Cymbeline* i 1 2
Not a courtier, Although they wear their faces to the bent Of the king's looks, hath a heart that is not Glad at the thing they scowl at . i 1 12
A cunning thief, or a that way accomplished courtier, would hazard the winning . . . . i 4 101
Italy contains none so accomplished a courtier to convince the honour of my mistress . . . . i 4 104
What lies I have heard! Our courtiers say all's savage but at court . iv 2 33
Let thy effects So follow, to be most unlike our courtiers, As good as promise . . . . v 4 136

Courtly. You have too courtly a wit for me . . *As Y. Like It* iii 2 72
I, his despiteful Juno, sent him forth From courtly friends *All's Well* iii 4 14
In courtly company or at my beads . . . . . *2 Hen. VI.* i 1 27
I am too courtly and thou art too cunning . . *Troi. and Cres.* iii 1 30
'Twere better she were kiss'd in general.—And very courtly counsel . iv 5 22
To promise is most courtly and fashionable . . . *T. of Athens* v 1 29
She hath all courtly parts more exquisite Than lady, ladies, woman *Cymbeline* iii 5 71

Courtney. Sir Edward Courtney, and the haughty prelate Bishop of Exeter . . . . *Richard III.* iv 4 502

Courtship. Trim gallants, full of courtship and of state . *L. L. Lost* v 2 363
In our maiden council, rated them At courtship, pleasant jest and courtesy . . . . v 2 790
Be merry, and employ your chiefest thoughts To courtship *Mer. of Venice* ii 8 44
One that knew courtship too well, for there he fell in love *As Y. Like It* iii 2 364
Observed his courtship to the common people . . . *Richard II.* i 4 24
I thought King Henry had resembled thee In courage, courtship *2 Hen. VI.* i 3 57
More courtship lives In carrion-flies than Romeo . . *Rom. and Jul.* iii 3 34
Ay, smile upon her, do; I will gyve thee in thine own courtship *Othello* ii 1 171

Courtsied when you have and kiss'd The wild waves whist . *Tempest* i 2 378

Cousin. I will do a greater thing than that, upon your request, cousin *Mer. Wives* i 1 249
His meaning is good.—Ay, I think my cousin meant well . . . i 1 265
My cousin loves you.—Ay, that I do; as well as I love any woman . iii 4 42
Is she your cousin?—Adoptedly; as school-maids change their names *Meas. for Meas.* i 4 46
My very worthy cousin, fairly met! . . . . v 1 1
My noble and well-warranted cousin. . . . . . . v 1 254
My cousin means Signior Benedick of Padua . . . . *Much Ado* i 1 35
There's her cousin, an she were not possessed with a fury, exceeds her as much in beauty as the first of May doth the last of December . i 1 192
How now, brother! Where is my cousin, your son? . . . . i 2 2
Cousins, you know what you have to do . . . . . . i 2 25
Good cousin, have a care this busy time . . . . . . i 2 28
It is my cousin's duty to make curtsy . . . . . . ii 1 55
But yet for all that, cousin, let him be a handsome fellow . . ii 1 57
My cousin tells him in his ear that he is in her heart . . . ii 1 327
Cousins, God give you joy! . . . . ii 1 350
I will do any modest office, my lord, to help my cousin to a good husband . . . . ii 1 391
I will teach you how to humour your cousin . . . . . ii 1 396
I'll devise some honest slanders To stain my cousin with . . . iii 1 85
O, do not do your cousin such a wrong . . . . . . iii 1 87
Your cousin will say so.—My cousin 's a fool, and thou art another . iii 4 10
'Tis almost five o'clock, cousin; 'tis time you were ready . . iii 4 52
I am stuffed, cousin; I cannot smell. . . . . . . iii 4 64
Why, how now, cousin! wherefore sink you down? . . . . iv 1 111
O, on my soul, my cousin is belied! . . . . iv 1 148
Surely I do believe your fair cousin is wronged . . . . iv 1 261
I am sorry for my cousin . . . . iv 1 275
Go, comfort your cousin: I must say she is dead . . . . iv 1 339
Give her the right you should have given her cousin . . . . v 1 300
And now tell me, how doth your cousin? . . . . . . v 2 91
Come, cousin, I am sure you love the gentleman . . . . v 4 84
And here's another Writ in my cousin's hand . . . . . v 4 89
In that thou art like to be my kinsman, live unbruised and love my cousin . . . . v 4 113
Thou wilt be, if my cousin do not look exceeding narrowly to thee . v 4 118
See thou render this Into my cousin's hand . . . *Mer. of Venice* iii 4 50
Her cousin so loves her, being ever from their cradles bred together *As Y. Like It* i 1 113

Cousin. Shall we see this wrestling, cousin? *As Y. Like It* i 2 152
How now, daughter and cousin! are you crept hither to see the wrestling? i 2 164
Gentle cousin, Let us go thank him and encourage him i 2 251
Then there were two cousins laid up i 3 7
They are but burs, cousin, thrown upon thee in holiday foolery i 3 13
And get you from our court.—Me, uncle?—You, cousin i 3 44
Be not thou more grieved than I am.—I have more cause.—Thou hast not, cousin i 3 95
But, cousin, what if we assay'd to steal The clownish fool? i 3 131
Your daughter and her cousin much commend The parts and graces of the wrestler ii 2 12
Give us some music; and, good cousin, sing ii 7 173
Your cousin, my lady, takes great exceptions to your ill hours *T. Night* i 3 5
Cousin, cousin, how have you come so early by this lethargy? i 5 131
You have put me into darkness and given your drunken cousin rule over me v 1 313
Cousin, go draw our puissance together *K. John* iii 1 339
Cousin, look not sad: Thy grandam loves thee iii 3 2
Cousin, away for England! haste before iii 3 6
Farewell, gentle cousin.—Coz, farewell iii 3 17
Bear with me, cousin; for I was amazed Under the tide iv 2 137
O my gentle cousin, Hear'st thou the news abroad, who are arrived? iv 2 159
Hostility and civil tumult reigns Between my conscience and my cousin's death iv 2 248
O cousin, thou art come to set mine eye v 7 51
What doth our cousin lay to Mowbray's charge? *Richard II.* i 1 84
Cousin, throw up your gage; do you begin i 1 186
My loving lord, I take my leave of you; Of you, my noble cousin, Lord Aumerle i 3 64
Cousin, farewell; and, uncle, bid him so: Six years we banish him i 3 247
What said our cousin when you parted with him? i 4 10
He had none of me.—He is our cousin, cousin i 4 20
Why, cousin, wert thou regent of the world, It were a shame to let this land ii 1 109
Come, sister,—cousin, I would say,—pray, pardon me ii 2 105
Come, cousin, I'll Dispose of you ii 2 116
I have had feeling of my cousin's wrongs And laboured all I could to do him right ii 3 141
Discomfortable cousin! know'st thou not? iii 2 36
Beshrew thee, cousin, which didst lead me forth Of that sweet way I was in to despair! iii 2 204
Take not, good cousin, further than you should iii 3 15
Thy thrice noble cousin Harry Bolingbroke doth humbly kiss thy hand iii 3 103
Say thus the king returns: His noble cousin is right welcome hither iii 3 122
We do debase ourselves, cousin, do we not, To look so poorly? iii 3 127
Aumerle, thou weep'st, my tender-hearted cousin! iii 3 160
Fair cousin, you debase your princely knee iii 3 190
Up, cousin, up; your heart is up, I know, Thus high at least iii 3 194
Cousin, I am too young to be your father, Though you are old enough to be my heir iii 3 204
Set on towards London, cousin, is it so? iii 3 208
Cousin, stand forth, and look upon that man iv 1 7
Name it, fair cousin.—'Fair cousin'? I am greater than a king iv 1 304
Weeping made you break the story off, Of our two cousins v 2 3
What means our cousin, that he stares and looks So wildly? v 3 24
What is the matter with our cousin now? v 3 29
My dangerous cousin, let your mother in v 3 81
A gallant prize? ha, cousin, is it not?—In faith *1 Hen. IV.* i 1 75
Peace, cousin, say no more: And now I will unclasp a secret book i 3 187
Good cousin, give me audience for a while i 3 211
Look, 'when his infant fortune came to age,' And 'gentle Harry Percy,' and 'kind cousin' i 3 254
Cousin, farewell: no further go in this Than I by letters shall direct i 3 292
Cousin, of many men I do not bear these crossings iii 1 35
I can teach you, cousin, to command The devil iii 1 55
Shall I tell you, cousin? He holds your temper in a high respect? iii 1 169
Good cousin, be advised; stir not to-night iv 3 5
Even those we love That are misled upon your cousin's part v 1 105
So tell your cousin, and bring me word What he will do v 1 109
Good cousin, let not Harry know, In any case, the offer of the king v 2 24
Deliver what you will; I'll say 'tis so. Here comes your cousin v 2 27
Cousin, I think thou art enamoured On his follies v 2 70
I am the king's poor cousin, sir *2 Hen. IV.* ii 2 126
And how doth my cousin, your bedfellow? iii 2 6
You were called 'lusty Shallow' then, cousin iii 2 18
How many of my old acquaintance are dead!—We shall all follow, cousin iii 2 39
Now cousin, wherefore stands our army still? iv 2 98
Our news shall go before us to his majesty, Which, cousin, you shall bear iv 3 85
Shall we call in the ambassador, my liege?—Not yet, my cousin *Hen. V.* i 2 4
What's he that wishes so? My cousin Westmoreland? No, my fair cousin iv 3 19
My royal cousin, teach you our princess English?—I would have her learn, my fair cousin, how perfectly I love her v 2 308
Good my lord, teach your cousin to consent winking v 2 332
And so I shall catch the fly, your cousin v 2 341
Good cousins both, of York and Somerset, Quiet yourselves *1 Hen. VI.* iv 1 114
Well hast thou spoken, cousin: be it so *3 Hen. VI.* i 1 66
Come, cousin, let us tell the queen these news i 1 182
Come, cousin, you shall be the messenger i 1 272
My pretty cousins, you mistake me much *Richard III.* ii 2 8
My dear cousin, I, like a child, will go by thy direction ii 2 152
Why, my young cousin, it is good to grow ii 4 9
Welcome, dear cousin, my thoughts' sovereign iii 1 2
How fares our cousin, noble Lord of York? iii 1 101
Therefore is he idle?—O, my fair cousin, I must not say so iii 1 106
Give me this dagger.—My dagger, little cousin? with all my heart iii 1 111
A greater gift than that I'll give my cousin iii 1 115
My noble lords and cousins all, good morrow iii 4 23
Come, cousin, canst thou quake, and change thy colour? iii 5 1
Sorry I am my noble cousin should Suspect me, that I mean no good to him iii 7 88
Farewell, good cousin; farewell, gentle friends iii 7 247
Cousin, thou wert not wont to be so dull: Shall I be plain? iv 2 17
You speak as if that I had slain my cousins iv 4 221
Cousins, indeed; and by their uncle cozen'd Of comfort, kingdom, kindred, freedom, life iv 4 222
Dream on thy cousins smother'd in the Tower v 3 151

Cousin. Well, cousin, I told you a thing yesterday; think on't *Troi. and Cres.* i 2 185
Here is good broken music.—You have broke it, cousin iii 1 53
My cousin will fall out with you iii 1 92
Have you seen my cousin?—No, Pandarus iii 2 8
Here I hold your hand, here my cousin's. If ever you prove false iii 2 206
Cousin, all honour to thee!—I thank thee, Hector iv 5 138
I came to kill thee, cousin, and bear hence A great addition earned in thy death iv 5 140
I would desire My famous cousin to our Grecian tents iv 5 151
Give me thy hand, my cousin; I will go eat with thee iv 5 157
Do not chafe thee, cousin iv 5 260
Cousin, a word; where is your husband? *T. Andron.* ii 4 12
You, cousins, shall Go sound the ocean, and cast your nets iv 3 6
Good morrow, cousin.—Is the day so young? *Rom. and Jul.* i 1 166
In sadness, cousin, I do love a woman i 1 210
Tybalt, my cousin! O my brother's child! iii 1 151
O prince! O cousin! husband! O, the blood is spilt Of my dear kinsman! iii 1 152
Is Romeo slaughter'd, and is Tybalt dead? My dear-loved cousin, and my dearer lord? iii 2 66
Will you speak well of him that kill'd your cousin?—Shall I speak ill of him that is my husband? iii 2 96
But, wherefore, villain, didst thou kill my cousin? That villain cousin would have kill'd my husband iii 2 100
Evermore weeping for your cousin's death? iii 5 70
Would none but I might venge my cousin's death! iii 5 87
Methinks I see my cousin's ghost Seeking out Romeo iv 3 55
This is that banish d haughty Montague, That murder'd my love's cousin v 3 50
Forgive me, cousin! Ah, dear Juliet, Why art thou yet so fair? v 3 101
O valiant cousin! worthy gentleman! *Macbeth* i 2 24
Cousins, a word, I pray you i 3 127
O worthiest cousin! The sin of my ingratitude even now Was heavy on me i 4 14
We hear, our bloody cousins are bestow'd In England and in Ireland iii 1 30
My pretty cousin, Blessing upon you! iv 2 25
My ever-gentle cousin, welcome hither iv 3 161
Cousins, I hope the days are near at hand That chambers will be safe v 4 1
You, worthy uncle, Shall, with my cousin, your right-noble son, Lead our first battle v 6 3
Our chiefest courtier, cousin, and our son *Hamlet* i 2 117
You'll have coursers for cousins and gennets for germans *Othello* i 1 113
Cousin, there's fall'n between him and my lord An unkind breach iv 1 236
Cousin of Buckingham *2 Hen. VI.* i 1 172; *Richard III.* iii 4 37
Cousin of Exeter *3 Hen. VI.* i 1 72; iv 8 34
Cousin of Hereford *Richard II.* i 1 28; i 3 55
Cousin of Somerset *2 Hen. VI.* i 1 167
Cousin of York *1 Hen. VI.* iv 1 162; *2 Hen. VI.* i 1 65
Cousin Abraham Slender, can you love her? *Mer. Wives* i 1 239
Cousin Angelo; In this I'll be impartial *Meas. for Meas.* v 1 165
Cousin Aumerle, How far brought you high Hereford on his way? *Richard II.* i 4 1
Cousin Austria. A certainty, vouch'd from our cousin Austria *All's Well* i 2 5
Cousin Beatrice. Run thee to the parlour; There shalt thou find my cousin Beatrice *Much Ado* iii 1 2
Wake my cousin Beatrice, and desire her to rise iii 4 1
Cousin Cressid. Good morrow, cousin Cressid: what do you talk of? *Troi. and Cres.* i 2 44
Cousin Cressida. Love's invisible soul,— Who, my cousin Cressida? iii 1 36
Cousin Dauphin. Know the pleasure Of our fair cousin Dauphin *Hen. V.* i 2 235
Cousin Ferdinand. Bid my cousin Ferdinand come hither *T. of Shrew* iv 1 154
Cousin France. We marvel much our cousin France Would in so just a business shut his bosom *All's Well* iii 1 7
Cousin Ganymede. There is more in it. Cousin Ganymede! *As Y. L. It* iv 3 160
Cousin-german. My father's sister's son, A cousin-german to great Priam's seed *Troi. and Cres.* iv 5 121
Cousin Hamlet. But now, my cousin Hamlet, and my son,— A little more than kin, and less than kind *Hamlet* i 2 64
How fares our cousin Hamlet?—Excellent, i' faith iii 2 97
Cousin Hamlet, You know the wager?—Very well, my lord v 2 270
Cousin Hereford. To behold Our cousin Hereford and fell Mowbray fight *Richard II.* i 2 46
A caitiff recreant to my cousin Hereford! i 2 53
Cousin Hero. How now, cousin Hero!—Have comfort, lady *Much Ado* iv 1 118
Cousin Juliet. My cousin Juliet?—Is she your cousin? *Meas. for Meas.* i 4 45
Cousin Katharine. Joy and good wishes To our most fair and princely cousin Katharine! *Hen. V.* v 2 4
Yet leave our cousin Katharine here with us v 2 95
Cousin king. If that my cousin king be King of England, It must be granted I am Duke of Lancaster *Richard II.* iii 3 123
Then I cannot blame his cousin king *1 Hen. IV.* i 3 158
Cousin Marcus. He killed my cousin Marcus *Coriolanus* v 6 123
Cousin Percy. Peace, cousin Percy; you will make him mad *1 Hen. IV.* iii 1 51
Cousin Scroop. This to my cousin Scroop, and all the rest To whom they are directed iv 4 3
Cousin Shallow. Nay, I will do as my cousin Shallow says *Mer. Wives* i 1 224
For all you are my man, go wait upon my cousin Shallow i 1 282
Cousin Silence. And how doth my good cousin Silence?—Good morrow, good cousin Shallow *2 Hen. IV.* iii 2 4
Master Surecard, as I think?—No, Sir John; it is my cousin Silence iii 2 96
Cousin Slender. Justice of peace and 'Coram.'—Ay, cousin Slender, and 'Custalorum *Mer. Wives* i 1 7
About a match between Anne Page and my cousin Slender iii 2 59
Cousin Toby, my fortunes having cast me on your niece *T. Night* ii 5 77
Where's my cousin Toby? iii 4 68
Cousin Vernon. My cousin Vernon! welcome, by my soul *1 Hen. IV.* iv 1 86
Cousin Warwick. Good morrow, cousin Warwick, good morrow *2 Hen. IV.* v 2 20
Cousin Westmoreland. Then let me hear Of you, my gentle cousin Westmoreland *1 Hen. IV.* i 1 31
Come, cousin Westmoreland, Our duty this way lies v 4 15
What's he that wishes so? My cousin Westmoreland? *Hen. V.* iv 3 19
Cousin William. I dare say my cousin William is become a good scholar *2 Hen. IV.* iii 2 11
Coutume de France. Il n'est pas la coutume de France *Hen. V.* v 2 280
Covenant. Let specialties be therefore drawn between us, That covenants may be kept on either hand *T. of Shrew* ii 1 128
My heart this covenant makes, my hand thus seals it *Richard II.* ii 3 50
With such strict and severe covenants As little shall the Frenchmen gain *1 Hen. VI.* v 4 114
Post, my lord, to France; Agree to any covenants v 5 88

Covenant. By the same covenant, And carriage of the article design'd *Hamlet* i 1 93
Let there be covenants drawn between's . . . *Cymbeline* i 4 155
Your hand; a covenant: we will have these things set down by lawful counsel . . . i 4 177
We Must not continue friends.—Good sir, we must, If you keep covenant . . . ii 4 50

Covent. One of our covent, and his confessor, Gives me this instance *Meas. for Meas.* iv 3 133
Where the reverend abbot, With all his covent, honourably received him . . . *Hen. VIII.* iv 2 19

Coventry. Be ready, as your lives shall answer it, At Coventry *Rich. II.* i 1 199
To Coventry, there to behold Our cousin Hereford and fell Mowbray fight . . . i 2 45
I must to Coventry: As much good stay with thee as go with me! . i 2 56
Bardolph, get thee before to Coventry . . . *1 Hen. IV.* iv 2 1
I'll not march through Coventry with them, that's flat . . . iv 2 42
If your father had been victor there, He ne'er had borne it out of Coventry . . . *2 Hen. IV.* iv 1 135
Farewell, sweet lords: let's meet at Coventry . . . *3 Hen. VI.* iv 8 32
And, lords, towards Coventry bend we our course . . . iv 8 58
Brave warriors, march amain towards Coventry . . . iv 8 64

Cover. The cover of the salt hides the salt, and therefore it is more than the salt . . . *T. G. of Ver.* iii 1 369
The hair that covers the wit is more than the wit . . . iii 1 371
Help to cover your master, boy . . . *Mer. Wives* iii 3 151
The damned'st body to invest and cover In prenzie guards! *Meas. for Meas.* iii 1 96
They have a good cover; they show well outward . . . *Much Ado* i 2 8
O, what authority and show of truth Can cunning sin cover itself withal! . . . iv 1 37
Death is the fairest cover for her shame That may be wish'd for . iv 1 117
Why seek'st thou then to cover with excuse That which appears in proper nakedness? . . . iv 1 176
Now fair befall your mask!—Fair fall the face it covers! . *L. L. Lost* ii 1 125
The starry welkin cover thou anon With drooping fog . *M. N. Dream* iii 2 356
A tomb Must cover thy sweet eyes . . . v 1 336
How many then should cover that stand bare! . *Mer. of Venice* ii 9 44
Then bid them prepare dinner.—That is done too, sir; only 'cover' is the word.—Will you cover then, sir? . . . iii 5 57
Bid them cover the table, serve in the meat . . . iii 5 64
Sirs, cover the while; the duke will drink under this tree *As Y. Like It* ii 5 32
Cover thy head; nay, prithee, be covered . . . v 1 19
Howsoever rude exteriorly, Is yet the cover of a fairer mind . *K. John* iv 2 258
Nothing can we call our own but death And that small model of the barren earth Which serves as paste and cover to our bones *Rich. II.* iii 2 154
Cover your heads and mock not flesh and blood With solemn reverence iii 2 171
Why, then, cover, and set them down . . *2 Hen. IV.* ii 4 11
This unbound lover, To beautify him, only lacks a cover *Rom. and Jul.* i 3 88
The cover of the wings of grasshoppers . . . i 4 60
I am rapt and cannot cover The monstrous bulk of this ingratitude With any size of words . . . *T. of Athens* v 1 67
Who cover faults, at last shame them derides . . . *Lear* i 1 284
Even so. Cover their faces . . . v 3 242
Be not, as is our fangled world, a garment Nobler than that it covers *Cymbeline* v 4 135
How courtesy would seem to cover sin! . . . *Pericles* i 1 121

Covered. In the desk That's cover'd o'er with Turkish tapestry There is a purse of ducats . . . *Com. of Errors* iv 1 104
Let Benedick, like cover'd fire, Consume away in sighs . . *Much Ado* iii 1 77
For the meat, sir, it shall be covered . . . *Mer. of Venice* iii 5 67
Nay, pray be covered . . . *As Y. Like It* iii 3 78
I do think him as concave as a covered goblet or a worm-eaten nut . iii 4 26
Cover thy head; nay, prithee, be covered . . . v 1 19
Well cover'd with the night's black mantle . . . *3 Hen. VI.* iv 2 22
What good is cover'd with the face of heaven, To be discover'd, that can do me good? . . . *Richard III.* iv 4 239
Whose mouth is cover'd with rude-growing briers . . *T. Andron.* ii 3 199
What dares the slave Come hither, cover'd with an antic face, To fleer and scorn at our solemnity? . . . *Rom. and Jul.* i 5 58
All covered dishes!—Royal cheer, I warrant you . . *T. of Athens* iii 6 55
When my face is cover'd, as 'tis now, Guide thou the sword *J. Cæsar* v 3 44
There is division, Although as yet the face of it be cover'd . *Lear* iii 1 20
You'll have your daughter covered with a Barbary horse . *Othello* i 1 111

Covering. Why, then the world and all that's in't is nothing; The covering sky is nothing . . . *W. Tale* i 2 294
Covering your fearful land With hard bright steel . . *Richard II.* iii 2 110
Covering discretion with a coat of folly . . . *Hen. V.* ii 4 38
Bring some covering for this naked soul . . . *Lear* iv 1 46
The benediction of these covering heavens Fall on their heads! *Cymbeline* v 5 350
Without covering, save yon field of stars . . . *Pericles* i 1 37
I hither fled, Under the covering of a careful night . . . i 2 81

Coverlet. Here I'll fling the pillow, there the bolster, This way the coverlet, another way the sheets . . . *T. of Shrew* iv 1 205

Covert. To lock it in the wards of covert bosom . *Meas. for Meas.* v 1 10
You must retire yourself Into some covert . . . *W. Tale* iv 4 664
While covert enmity Under the smile of safety wounds the world *2 Hen. IV.* Ind. 9
In this covert will we make our stand . . . *3 Hen. VI.* iii 1 3
He was ware of me And stole into the covert of the wood *Rom. and Jul.* i 1 132
Sit in council, How covert matters may be best disclosed, And open perils surest answered . . . *J. Cæsar* iv 1 46
That under covert and convenient seeming Hast practised on man's life *Lear* iii 2 56

Covertest. He was the covert'st shelter'd traitor That ever lived *Richard III.* iii 5 33

Covertly. So covertly that no dishonesty shall appear in me *Much Ado* ii 2 9

Coverture. Who even now Is couched in the woodbine coverture . iii 1 30
In night's coverture . . . *3 Hen. VI.* iv 2 13
When steel grows soft as the parasite's silk, Let him be made a coverture for the wars! . . . *Coriolanus* i 9 46

Covet. But if it be a sin to covet honour, I am the most offending soul alive . . . *Hen. V.* iv 3 28
I had rather hide me from my greatness, Being a bark to brook no mighty sea, Than in my greatness covet to be hid . *Richard III.* iii 7 163
He covets less Than misery itself would give . . . *Coriolanus* ii 2 130

Coveted. Scarcely have coveted what was mine own . *Macbeth* iv 3 127

Coveting. I'll rather keep That which I have than, coveting for more, Be cast from possibility of all . . . *1 Hen. VI.* v 4 145
Ambitions, covetings, change of prides, disdain, Nice longing *Cymbeline* ii 5 25

Covetous. But she, more covetous, would have a chain *Com. of Errors* iv 3 75
I am not covetous for gold, Nor care I who doth feed upon my cost *Hen. V.* iv 3 24
If I were covetous, ambitious or perverse, As he will have me, how am I so poor? . . . *1 Hen. VI.* iii 1 29
Saba was never More covetous of wisdom and fair virtue . *Hen. VIII.* v 5 25
If he were proud,— Or covetous of praise . . . *Troi. and Cres.* ii 3 248
You must in no way say he is covetous . . . *Coriolanus* i 1 44
Is not thy kindness subtle, covetous, If not a usuring kindness? *T. of A.* iv 3 515
When Marcus Brutus grows so covetous, To lock such rascal counters from his friends . . . *J. Cæsar* iv 3 79

Covetously. If he covetously reserve it, how shall's get it? *T. of Athens* iv 3 408

Covetousness. I would have you.—Why, that were covetousness *As Y. Like It* iii 5 91
I would not have you to think that my desire of having is the sin of covetousness . . . *T. Night* v 1 51
They do confound their skill in covetousness . . . *K. John* iv 2 29
A man can no more separate age and covetousness than a' can part young limbs and lechery . . . *2 Hen. IV.* i 2 256

Cow. For it is said, 'God sends a curst cow short horns' . *Much Ado* ii 1 25
Some such strange bull leap'd your father's cow . . . v 4 49
The cow's dugs that her pretty chopt hands had milked *As Y. Like It* ii 4 50
Your father might have kept This calf bred from his cow from all the world; In sooth he might . . . *K. John* i 1 124
Let me ne'er hope to see a chine again; And that I would not for a cow, God save her! . . . *Hen. VIII.* v 4 27
But where the bull and cow are both milk-white, They never do beget a coal-black calf . . . *T. Andron.* v 1 31
The breese upon her, like a cow in June, Hoists sails and flies *Ant. and Cleo.* iii 10 14

Coward. Was there ever man a coward that hath drunk so much sack as I to-day? . . . *Tempest* iii 2 30
By gar, you are de coward, de Jack dog, John ape . *Mer. Wives* iii 1 85
O you beast! O faithless coward! O dishonest wretch! *Meas. for Meas.* iii 1 137
Was the duke a fleshmonger, a fool, and a coward, as you then reported him? . . . v 1 337
You, sirrah, that knew me for a fool, a coward, One all of luxury . v 1 505
I must shortly hear from him, or I will subscribe him a coward *Much Ado* v 2 59
Stand in your own defence; Or hide your heads like cowards *L. L. Lost* v 2 86
Speak again: Thou runaway, thou coward, art thou fled? *M. N. Dream* iii 2 405
Thou coward, art thou bragging to the stars? . . . iii 2 407
Ho, ho, ho! Coward, why comest thou not? . . . iii 2 421
How many cowards, whose hearts are all as false As stairs of sand, wear yet upon their chins The beards of Hercules and frowning Mars! *Mer. of Venice* iii 2 83
We'll have a swashing and a martial outside, As many other mannish cowards have . . . *As Y. Like It* i 3 123
Think him a great way fool, solely a coward . . . *All's Well* i 1 112
He's a most notable coward, an infinite and endless liar . . iii 6 11
He excels his brother for a coward, yet his brother is reputed one of the best that is . . . iv 3 321
An I were not a very coward, I'ld compel it of you . . . iv 3 356
He hath the gift of a coward to allay the gust he hath in quarrelling *T. Night* i 3 32
He's a coward and a coystrill that will not drink to my niece . . i 3 42
A very dishonest paltry boy, and more a coward than a hare . . iii 4 421
A coward, a most devout coward, religious in it . . . iii 4 424
We took him for a coward, but he's the very devil incardinate . . v 1 184
Thou art not honest, or, If thou inclinest that way, thou art a coward *W. Tale* i 2 243
Thou slave, thou wretch, thou coward! Thou little valiant! *K. John* iii 1 115
I do defy him, and I spit at him; Call him a slanderous coward *Richard II.* i 1 61
Pale trembling coward, there I throw my gage . . . i 1 69
Like a traitor coward, Sluiced out his innocent soul through streams of blood . . . i 1 102
Thou darest not, coward, live to see that day . . . iv 1 41
I know them to be as true-bred cowards as ever turned back *1 Hen. IV.* i 2 206
Will they not rob us?—What, a coward, Sir John Paunch? . . ii 2 69
I am not John of Gaunt, your grandfather; but yet no coward, Hal ii 2 71
An the Prince and Poins be not two arrant cowards, there's no equity stirring . . . ii 2 106
Darest thou be so valiant as to play the coward with thy indenture? . ii 4 52
A plague of all cowards, I say, and a vengeance too! . . . ii 4 127
A coward is worse than a cup of sack with lime in it. A villanous coward! ii 4 139
Are not you a coward? answer me to that: and Poins there? . . ii 4 157
I call thee coward! I'll see thee damned ere I call thee coward . . ii 4 161
This sanguine coward, this bed-presser . . . ii 4 268
Instinct is a great matter; I was now a coward on instinct . . . ii 4 301
And thou a natural coward, without instinct . . . ii 4 542
At my birth The frame and huge foundation of the earth Shaked like a coward . . . iii 1 17
They are generally fools and cowards . . . *2 Hen. IV.* iv 3 102
Puff! Puff in thy teeth, most recreant coward base! . . . v 3 96
He scorns to say his prayers, lest a' should be thought a coward *Hen. V.* iii 2 41
If Sir John Fastolfe had not play'd the coward . . . *1 Hen. VI.* i 1 131
Who ever saw the like? what men have I! Dogs! cowards! dastards! i 2 23
Coward of France! how much he wrongs his fame! . . . ii 1 16
Let him that is no coward nor no flatterer, But dare maintain the party of the truth, Pluck a red rose . . . ii 4 34
Or whether that such cowards ought to wear This ornament of knighthood . . . iv 1 28
Turn on the bloody hounds with heads of steel And make the cowards stand aloof at bay . . . iv 2 52
So should we save a valiant gentleman By forfeiting a traitor and a coward . . . iv 3 27
I would, false murderous coward, on thy knee Make thee beg pardon *2 Hen. VI.* iii 2 220
My arms torn and defaced, And I proclaim'd a coward through the world! . . . iv 1 43
O monstrous coward! what, to come behind folks? . . . iv 7 88
Exhort all the world to be cowards . . . iv 10 79
So cowards fight when they can fly no further . . . *3 Hen. VI.* i 4 40
Ay, like a dastard and a treacherous coward . . . ii 2 114
A woman of this valiant spirit Should, if a coward heard her speak these words, Infuse his breast with magnanimity . . . v 4 40
It [conscience] makes a man a coward . . . *Richard III.* i 4 138
I repent me that the duke is slain.—So do not I: go, coward as thou art i 4 286
Pray God, I say, I prove a needless coward! . . . iii 2 90
Conscience is but a word that cowards use . . . v 3 309
The bold and coward, The wise and fool, the artist and unread, The hard and soft, seem all affined and kin . . . *Troi. and Cres.* i 3 23

Coward. Troilus! thou coward Troilus . . . . . *Troi. and Cres.* v 5 43
Troilus, thou coward Troilus, show thy head! . . . . . v 6 1
The devil take thee, coward! . . . . v 7 24
Thou great-sized coward, No space of earth shall sunder our two hates v 10 26
You cowards! you were got in fear, Though you were born in Rome *Coriolanus* i 3 36
And by his rare example made the coward Turn terror into sport . . ii 2 108
Foul-spoken coward, that thunder'st with thy tongue, And with thy weapon nothing darest perform! *T. Andron.* ii 1 58
Peace! I hate the word, As I hate hell, all Montagues, and thee: Have at thee, coward! . . . . *Rom. and Jul.* i 1 79
Thus much of this [gold] will make black white, foul fair, Wrong right, base noble, old young, coward valiant . . *T. of Athens* iv 3 29
Sound to this coward and lascivious town Our terrible approach . . v 4 1
Bear fire enough To kindle cowards and to steel with valour The melting spirits of women . . . . *J. Cæsar* ii 1 121
Swear priests and cowards and men cautelous, Old feeble carrions . ii 1 129
Cowards die many times before their deaths . . . . . ii 2 32
One of two bad ways you must conceit me, Either a coward or a flatterer iii 1 193
This ensign here of mine was turning back; I slew the coward . . v 3 4
O, coward that I am, to live so long, To see my best friend ta'en! . v 3 34
And live a coward in thine own esteem, Letting 'I dare not' wait upon 'I would' . . . . *Macbeth* i 7 43
Then yield thee, coward, And live to be the show and gaze o' the time v 8 23
Am I a coward? Who calls me villain? breaks my pate across? *Hamlet* ii 2 598
Thus conscience does make cowards of us all . . . . . iii 1 83
Hath but one part wisdom And ever three parts coward . . . iv 4 43
Bringing the murderous coward to the stake . . . . . *Lear* ii 1 64
Art nothing but the composition of a knave, beggar, coward . . . ii 2 23
None of these rogues and cowards But Ajax is their fool . . . ii 2 131
The nature of bad news infects the teller.—When it concerns the fool or coward . . . . *Ant. and Cleo.* i 2 100
I have fled myself; and have instructed cowards To run . . . iii 11 7
His coin, ships, legions, May be a coward's . . . . . iii 13 23
Do his bidding; strike; Thou mayst be valiant in a better cause; But now thou seem'st a coward . . . . *Cymbeline* iii 4 75
Plenty and peace breeds cowards: hardness ever Of hardiness is mother iii 6 21
Cowards father cowards and base things sire base . . . . iv 2 26
Cowards living To die with lengthen'd shame . . . . . v 3 12
Some, turn'd coward But by example—O, a sin in war, Damn'd in the first beginners! . . . . v 3 35
Our cowards, Like fragments in hard voyages, became The life o' the need . . . . v 3 43
I do shame To think of what a noble strain you are, And of how coward a spirit . . . . *Pericles* iv 3 25
Coward conscience. Soft! I did but dream. O coward conscience, how dost thou afflict me! . . . . *Richard III.* v 3 179
Coward cries. He raised the house with loud and coward cries . *Lear* ii 4 43
Coward dogs Most spend their mouths when what they seem to threaten Runs far before them . . . . *Hen. V.* ii 4 69
Coward gates. Eyes, that are the frail'st and softest things, Who shut their coward gates on atomies . . . . . *As Y. Like It* iii 5 13
Coward hand. I'll give thee more Than e'er the coward hand of France can win . . . . *K. John* ii 1 158
Coward hares. Scarce ever look'd on blood, But that of coward hares, hot goats, and venison! . . . . *Cymbeline* iv 4 37
Coward horse. Before young Talbot from old Talbot fly, The coward horse that bears me fall and die! . . . . . *1 Hen. VI.* iv 6 47
Coward Jack priest. By gar, he is de coward Jack priest of de vorld *Mer. Wives* ii 3 32
Coward lips. His coward lips did from their colour fly . . . *J. Cæsar* i 2 122
Coward majesty. Awake, thou coward majesty! . . . . *Richard II.* iii 2 84
Coward woman. Fie, coward woman and soft-hearted wretch! *2 Hen. VI.* iii 2 307
Cowarded. What read you there, That hath so cowarded and chased your blood Out of appearance? . . . . *Hen. V.* ii 2 75
Cowardice. Falsehood, cowardice and poor descent, Three things that women highly hold in hate . . . . . . *T. G. of Ver.* iii 2 32
What says she to my valour?—O, sir, she makes no doubt of that.—She needs not, when she knows it cowardice . . . . . v 2 21
Do me right, or I will protest your cowardice . . . . *Much Ado* v 1 149
Bootless speed, When cowardice pursues and valour flies *M. N. Dream* ii 1 234
I am a right maid for my cowardice: Let her not strike me . . . iii 2 302
That which in mean men we intitle patience Is pale cold cowardice in noble breasts . . . . *Richard II.* i 2 34
See now, whether pure fear and entire cowardice doth not make thee wrong this virtuous gentlewoman? . . . . . *2 Hen. IV.* ii 4 353
White and pale, which is the badge of pusillanimity and cowardice . iv 3 114
Becomes it thee to taunt his valiant age And twit with cowardice a man half dead? . . . . *1 Hen. VI.* iii 2 55
Whose cowardice Hath made us by-words to our enemies *3 Hen. VI.* i 1 41
View this face, And bite thy tongue, that slanders him with cowardice i 4 47
I hold it cowardice To rest mistrustful where a noble heart Hath pawn'd an open hand in sign of love . . . . iv 2 7
They tax our policy, and call it cowardice . . . . *Troi. and Cres.* i 3 197
Thy counsel, lad, smells of no cowardice . . . . . *T. Andron.* ii 1 132
Nor did he soil the fact with cowardice—An honour in him *T. of Athens* iii 5 16
The gods do this in shame of cowardice . . . . . . *J. Cæsar* i 2 41
Cowardly. A cowardly knave as you would desires . . . *Mer. Wives* iii 1 68
That same cowardly giant-like ox-beef . . . . . *M. N. Dream* iii 1 197
Not a more cowardly rogue in all Bohemia . . . . . *W. Tale* iv 3 112
This villanous salt-petre . . ., Which many a good tall fellow had destroy'd So cowardly . . . . *1 Hen. IV.* i 3 63
You are a shallow cowardly hind, and you lie . . . . . ii 3 16
Cowardly rascals that ran from the battle ha' done this slaughter *Hen. V.* iv 7 6
Go, go; you are a counterfeit cowardly knave . . . . . v 1 73
Cowardly fled, not having struck one stroke . . . . *1 Hen. VI.* i 1 134
Cowardly knight! ill fortune follow thee . . . . . . iii 2 109
Then he will say 'twas done cowardly, when he wakes . *Richard III.* i 4 104
Relent! 'tis cowardly and womanish . . . . i 4 264
Abundantly they lack discretion, Yet are they passing cowardly *Coriolanus* i 1 207
Come off Like Romans, neither foolish in our stands, Nor cowardly in retire . . . . i 6 3
Like beasts And cowardly nobles, gave way unto your clusters . . iv 6 122
I do find it cowardly and vile, For fear of what might fall, so to prevent The time of life . . . . *J. Cæsar* v 1 104
You cowardly rascal, nature disclaims in thee . . . . . *Lear* ii 2 59
Not cowardly put off my helmet to My countryman . *Ant. and Cleo.* iv 15 56
Cowardship. For his cowardship, ask Fabian . . . . *T. Night* iii 4 423
Cow-dung. In the fury of his heart, when the foul fiend rages, eats cow-dung for sallets . . . . *Lear* iii 4 137

Cowed. It hath cow'd my better part of man . . . . *Macbeth* v 8 18
Cower. The French knight that cowers i' the hams . . . *Pericles* iv 2 113
Cowered. The splitting rocks cower'd in the sinking sands *2 Hen. VI.* iii 2 97
Cowish. The cowish terror of his spirit, That dares not undertake *Lear* iv 2 12
Cowl-staff. Where's the cowl-staff? look, how you drumble! *Mer. Wives* iii 3 156
Cowslip. In a cowslip's bell I lie . . . . . . *Tempest* v 1 89
The cowslips tall her pensioners be . . . . . *M. N. Dream* ii 1 10
Go seek some dewdrops here And hang a pearl in every cowslip's ear . ii 1 15
This cherry nose, These yellow cowslip cheeks . . . . . v 1 339
The freckled cowslip, burnet and green clover . . . . *Hen. V.* v 2 49
The violets, cowslips, and the primroses, Bear to my closet . *Cymbeline* i 5 83
On her left breast A mole cinque-spotted, like the crimson drops I' the bottom of a cowslip . . . . ii 2 39
Cox my passion! give me your hand. How does your drum? . *All's Well* v 2 42
Coxcomb. Am I ridden with a Welsh goat too? shall I have a coxcomb of frize? . . . . *Mer. Wives* v 5 146
Mome, malt-horse, capon, coxcomb, idiot, patch! . . *Com. of Errors* iii 1 32
Off, coxcomb!—God's my life, where's the sexton? let him write down the prince's officer coxcomb . . . . *Much Ado* iv 2 71
O most divine Kate!—O most profane coxcomb! . . . *L. L. Lost* iv 3 84
What is your crest? a coxcomb?—A combless cock . . *T. of Shrew* ii 1 226
I sent to her, By this same coxcomb that we have i' the wind *All's Well* iii 6 122
Broke my head across and has given Sir Toby a bloody coxcomb *T. Night* v 1 179
If a bloody coxcomb be a hurt, you have hurt me . . . . . v 1 193
I think you set nothing by a bloody coxcomb . . . . . v 1 195
A coxcomb and a knave, a thin-faced knave, a gull! . . . . v 1 213
If the enemy is an ass and a fool and a prating coxcomb, is it meet, think you, that we should also, look you, be an ass and a fool and a prating coxcomb? . . . . *Hen. V.* iv 1 79
Bite, I pray you; it is good for your green wound and your ploody coxcomb . . . . v 1 45
The skin is good for your broken coxcomb . . . . . . v 1 57
As many coxcombs As you threw caps up will he tumble down *Coriol.* iv 6 134
Let me hire him too: here's my coxcomb . . . . . . *Lear* i 4 105
My pretty knave! how dost thou?—Sirrah, you were best take my coxcomb . . . . i 4 109
Thou'lt catch cold shortly: there, take my coxcomb . . . . i 4 114
If thou follow him, thou must needs wear my coxcomb . . . . i 4 117
Would I had two coxcombs and two daughters! . . . . . i 4 118
If I gave them all my living, I'ld keep my coxcombs myself . . . i 4 121
She knapped 'em o' the coxcombs with a stick, and cried 'Down, wantons, down!' . . . . ii 4 125
O murderous coxcomb! what should such a fool Do with so good a woman? . . . . *Othello* v 2 233
Coy. To be in love, where scorn is bought with groans; Coy looks with heart-sore sighs . . . . *T. G. of Ver.* i 1 30
But she is nice and coy And nought esteems my aged eloquence . . iii 1 82
I know her spirits are as coy and wild As haggerds of the rock *Much Ado* iii 1 35
While I thy amiable cheeks do coy . . . . . *M. N. Dream* iv 1 2
'Twas told me you were rough and coy and sullen . . *T. of Shrew* ii 1 245
Coyed. If he coy'd To hear Cominius speak, I'll keep at home *Coriolanus* v 1 6
Coystrill. He's a coward and a coystrill that will not drink to my niece *T. Night* i 3 43
Coz. I may quarter, coz.—You may, by marrying . . . *Mer. Wives* i 1 24
Come, coz; we stay for you. A word with you, coz; marry, this, coz . i 1 213
Conceive me, sweet coz: what I do is to pleasure you, coz . . . i 1 251
She's coming; to her, coz. O boy, thou hadst a father! . . . iii 4 36
She calls you, coz: I'll leave you . . . . iii 4 54
Good morrow, coz.—Good morrow, sweet Hero . . . *Much Ado* iii 4 39
Help to dress me, good coz, good Meg, good Ursula . . . . iii 4 98
I pray thee, Rosalind, sweet my coz, be merry . . . *As Y. Like It* i 2 1
Be merry.—From henceforth I will, coz . . . . . . i 2 26
Were I my father, coz, would I do this? . . . . . . i 2 244
Shall we go, coz?—Ay. Fare you well, fair gentleman . . . i 2 260
Will you go, coz?—Have with you. Fare you well. . . . . i 2 267
Speak, sad brow and true maid.—I' faith, coz, 'tis he . . . iii 2 228
O coz, coz, coz, my pretty little coz! . . . . iv 1 209
Go thou and seek the crowner, and let him sit o' my coz . . *T. Night* i 5 143
Farewell, gentle cousin.—Coz, farewell . . . . . *K. John* iii 3 17
What think you, coz, Of this young Percy's pride? . . . *1 Hen. IV.* i 1 91
And I can teach thee, coz, to shame the devil . . . . . iii 1 58
And, dear coz, to you The remnant northward, lying off from Trent . iii 1 78
Heaviness foreruns the good event.—Therefore be merry, coz *2 Hen. IV.* iv 2 83
No, faith, my coz, wish not a man from England . . . *Hen. V.* iv 3 30
Our tongue is rough, coz, and my condition is not smooth . . . v 2 313
Dost thou not laugh?—No, coz, I rather weep . . . *Rom. and Jul.* i 1 189
Farewell, my coz.—Soft! I will go along . . . . . . i 1 201
A right fair mark, fair coz, is soonest hit. . . . . . . i 1 213
Content thee, gentle coz, let him alone . . . . . . i 5 67
My dearest coz, I pray you, school yourself . . . . *Macbeth* iv 2 14
Cozen. Who shall go about To cozen fortune and be honourable? *Mer. of Venice* ii 9 38
He stamp'd and swore, As if the vicar meant to cozen him *T. of Shrew* iii 2 170
I believe a' means to cozen somebody in this city under my countenance v 1 40
I think't no sin To cozen him that would unjustly win . *All's Well* iv 2 76
I would cozen the man of his wife . . . . iv 5 28
Cozenage. Out, alas, sir! cozenage, mere cozenage! . . *Mer. Wives* iv 5 64
They say this town is full of cozenage . . . . . *Com. of Errors* i 2 97
With such cozenage—is't not perfect conscience, To quit him? *Hamlet* v 2 67
Cozened. The very same man that beguiled Master Slender of his chain cozened him of it . . . . *Mer. Wives* iv 5 38
There is three cozen-germans that has cozened all the hosts of Readins iv 5 79
'Tis not convenient you should be cozened . . . . . . iv 5 84
I would all the world might be cozened; for I have been cozened and beaten too . . . . iv 5 95
One Master Brook, that you have cozened of money . . . . v 5 175
By gar, I am cozened: I ha' married un garçon, a boy . . . v 5 218
Who is thus like to be cozened with the semblance of a maid *Much Ado* iv 2 39
Saucy trusting of the cozen'd thoughts Defiles the pitchy night *All's Well* iv 4 23
I was cozened by the way and lost all my money . . . *W. Tale* iv 4 254
Cozen'd Of comfort, kingdom, kindred, freedom, life *Richard III.* iv 4 222
Despised, and basely cozen'd Of that true hand . . . *T. Andron.* v 3 101
What devil was't That thus hath cozen'd you at hoodman-blind? *Hamlet* iii 4 77
Thou art not vanquish'd, But cozen'd and beguiled . . . *Lear* v 3 154
Cozener. Run away with the cozeners . . . . . *Mer. Wives* iv 5 67
There are cozeners abroad; therefore it behoves men to be wary *W. Tale* iv 4 256
O, the devil take such cozeners! God forgive me! . . . *1 Hen. IV.* i 3 255
The usurer hangs the cozener . . . . *Lear* iv 6 167
Cozen-german. There is three cozen-germans that has cozened all the hosts of Readins . . . . *Mer. Wives* iv 5 79

Cozening. A witch, a quean, an old cozening quean! . *Mer. Wives* iv 2 180
I will despair, and be at enmity With cozening hope . *Richard II.* ii 2 69
Else he had been damned for cozening the devil 1 *Hen. IV.* i 2 136
Some busy and insinuating rogue, Some cogging, cozening slave *Othello* iv 2 132
Cozier. Do ye make an alehouse of my lady's house, that ye squeak out your coziers' catches? . *T. Night* ii 3 97
Crab. I prithee, let me bring thee where crabs grow . *Tempest* ii 2 171
I think Crab my dog be the sourest-natured dog that lives *T. G. of Ver.* ii 3 5
What's the unkindest tide?—Why, he that's tied here, Crab, my dog . ii 3 44
I, having been acquainted with the smell before, knew it was Crab . iv 4 26
Falleth like a crab on the face of terra, the soil, the land . *L. L. Lost* iv 2 6
When roasted crabs hiss in the bowl, Then nightly sings the staring owl v 2 935
In a gossip's bowl, In very likeness of a roasted crab . *M. N. Dream* ii 1 48
You must not look so sour.—It is my fashion, when I see a crab.— Why, here's no crab . *T. of Shrew* ii 1 230
Should be old as I am, if like a crab you could go backward *Hamlet* ii 2 206
She's as like this as a crab's like an apple . *Lear* i 5 16
She will taste as like this as a crab does to a crab . i 5 18
Crabbed. O, she is Ten times more gentle than her father's crabbed, And he's composed of harshness . *Tempest* iii 1 8
Something too crabbed that way . *Meas. for Meas.* iii 2 104
That was when Three crabbed months had sour'd themselves to death *W. Tale* i 2 102
Crab-tree. And noble stock Was graft with crab-tree slip 2 *Hen. VI.* iii 2 214
Fetch me a dozen crab-tree staves, and strong ones . *Hen. VIII.* v 4 8
We have some old crab-trees here at home . *Coriolanus* ii 1 205
Crack. The fire and cracks Of sulphurous roaring . *Tempest* i 2 203
I had rather crack my sinews, break my back, Than you should such dishonour undergo . iii 1 26
Now does my project gather to a head: My charms crack not . v 1 2
My heart is ready to crack with impatience . *Mer. Wives* ii 2 301
And Ethiopes of their sweet complexion crack . *L. L. Lost* iv 3 268
My love to thee is sound, sans crack or flaw . v 2 415
Though she chide as loud As thunder when the clouds in autumn crack *T. of Shrew* i 2 96
I cannot Believe this crack to be in my dread mistress . *W. Tale* i 2 322
He cracks his gorge, his sides, With violent hefts . ii 1 44
But, ass, I'll take that burthen from your back, Or lay on that shall make your shoulders crack . *K. John* ii 1 146
When a' was a crack not thus high . 2 *Hen. IV.* iii 2 34
My breast I'll burst with straining of my courage And from my shoulders crack my arms asunder 1 *Hen. VI.* i 5 11
Though all the world should crack their duty to you *Hen. VIII.* iii 2 193
Divert and crack, rend and deracinate The unity and married calm of states Quite from their fixure! *Troi. and Cres.* i 3 99
A' were as good crack a fusty nut with no kernel . ii 1 111
Crack my clear voice with sobs and break my heart . iv 2 114
Thou, trumpet, there's my purse. Now crack thy lungs . iv 5 7
Indeed, la, 'tis a noble child.—A crack, madam *Coriolanus* i 3 74
Sits aloft, Secure of thunder's crack or lightning flash . *T. Andron.* ii 1 3
Crack the lawyer's voice, That he may never more false title plead, Nor sound his quillets shrilly . *T. of Athens* iv 3 153
They were As cannons overcharged with double cracks . *Macbeth* i 2 37
Start, eyes! What, will the line stretch out to the crack of doom? . iv 1 117
Not to crack the wind of the poor phrase, Running it thus . *Hamlet* i 3 108
Now cracks a noble heart . v 2 370
Blow, winds, and crack your cheeks! rage! blow! . *Lear* iii 2 1
Crack nature's moulds, all germens spill at once, That make ingrateful man! . iii 2 8
His grief grew puissant, and the strings of life Began to crack . v 3 217
Had I your tongues and eyes, I'ld use them so That heaven's vault should crack . v 3 259
This crack of your love shall grow stronger than it was before *Othello* ii 3 330
Heart, once be stronger than thy continent, Crack thy frail case! *Ant. and Cleo.* iv 14 41
The breaking of so great a thing should make A greater crack . v 1 15
Though now our voices Have got the mannish crack . *Cymbeline* iv 2 236
Who shuns not to break one will sure crack both . *Pericles* i 2 121
Thou hast a heart That even cracks for woe! This chanced to-night . iii 2 77
Crack the glass of her virginity, and make the rest malleable . iv 6 151
Crack a quart. You'll crack a quart together, ha! . 2 *Hen. IV.* v 3 66
Cracked. Not know my voice! O time's extremity, Hast thou so crack'd and splitted my poor tongue? . *Com. of Errors* v 1 308
The tackle of my heart is crack'd and burn'd . *K. John* v 7 52
One flourishing branch of his most royal root Is crack'd *Richard II.* i 2 19
There it is, crack'd in a hundred shivers . iv 1 289
We must have bloody noses and crack'd crowns . 1 *Hen. IV.* ii 3 96
But now two mirrors of his princely semblance Are crack'd in pieces by malignant death *Richard III.* ii 2 52
He has crack'd the league . *Hen. VIII.* ii 2 25
See here these movers that do prize their hours At a crack'd drachma! *Coriolanus* i 5 6
This last old man, Whom with a crack'd heart I have sent to Rome, Loved me . v 3 9
Pray God, your voice, like a piece of uncurrent gold, be not cracked within the ring *Hamlet* ii 2 448
In palaces, treason; and the bond cracked 'twixt son and father *Lear* i 2 118
O, madam, my old heart is crack'd, is crack'd! . ii 1 92
I would have broke mine eye-strings; crack'd them, but To look upon him . *Cymbeline* i 3 17
Like egg-shells moved upon their surges, crack'd As easily 'gainst our rocks . iii 1 28
No reason I, since of your lives you set So slight a valuation, should reserve My crack'd one to more care . iv 4 50
Either our brags Were crack'd of kitchen-trulls, or his description Proved us unspeaking sots . v 5 177
That he could not But think her bond of chastity quite crack'd . v 5 207
Cracker. What cracker is this same that deafs our ears? . *K. John* ii 1 147
Crack-hemp. Come hither, crack-hemp . *T. of Shrew* v 1 46
Cracking the stones of the foresaid prunes . *Meas. for Meas.* ii 1 110
O, cut my lace, lest my heart, cracking it, Break too! . *W. Tale* iii 2 174
Cracking the strong warrant of an oath *Richard II.* iv 1 235
Whose course will on The way it takes, cracking ten thousand curbs *Coriolanus* i 1 72
Thou wilt quarrel with a man for cracking nuts . *Rom. and Jul.* iii 1 21
Cradle. Gives the crutch the cradle's infancy . *L. L. Lost* iv 3 245
What hempen home-spuns have we swaggering here, So near the cradle of the fairy queen? *M. N. Dream* iii 1 80
Fancy dies In the cradle where it lies . *Mer. of Venice* iii 2 69
Being ever from their cradles bred together . *As Y. Like It* i 1 113
Cradle. In our country's cradle Draws the sweet infant breath *Rich. II.* i 3 132
Rock his brains In cradle of the rude imperious surge . 2 *Hen. IV.* iii 1 20
No sooner was I crept out of my cradle But I was made a king 2 *Hen. VI.* iv 9 3
Rough cradle for such little pretty ones! Rude ragged nurse! *Richard III.* iv 1 101
Undoubtedly Was fashion'd to much honour from his cradle *Hen. VIII.* iv 2 50
In her cradle, yet now promises Upon this land a thousand thousand blessings . v 5 19
Keeps place with thought and almost, like the gods, Does thoughts unveil in their dumb cradles . *Troi. and Cres.* iii 3 200
Spare thy Athenian cradle and those kin . *T. of Athens* v 4 40
But this bird Hath made his pendent bed and procreant cradle *Macbeth* i 6 8
A son for her cradle ere she had a husband for her bed . *Lear* i 1 15
He'll watch the horologe a double set, If drink rock not his cradle *Oth.* ii 3 136
Aye hopeless To have the courtesy your cradle promised *Cymbeline* iv 4 28
Cradle-babe. As mild and gentle as the cradle-babe Dying with mother's dug between its lips . 2 *Hen. VI.* iii 2 392
Cradle-clothes. O that it could be proved That some night-tripping fairy had exchanged In cradle-clothes our children where they lay! 1 *Hen. IV.* i 1 88
Cradled. And husks Wherein the acorn cradled . *Tempest* i 2 464
Craft. And this deceit loses the name of craft . *Mer. Wives* v 5 239
Craft, being richer than innocency, stands for the facing *Meas. for Meas.* iii 2 10
Craft against vice I must apply . iii 2 291
My integrity ne'er knew the crafts That you do charge men with *All's Well* iv 2 33
Had you that craft, to reave her Of what should stead her most? . v 3 86
Will not else thy craft so quickly grow, That thine own trip shall be thine overthrow? . *T. Night* v 1 169
That taught me craft To counterfeit oppression of such grief *Richard II.* i 4 13
Wooing poor craftsmen with the craft of smiles . i 4 28
Wherein cunning, but in craft? wherein crafty, but in villany? 1 *Hen. IV.* ii 4 503
'Tis no wisdom to confess so much Unto an enemy of craft . *Hen. V.* iii 6 153
And, Mercury, lose all the serpentine craft of thy caduceus! *Tr. and Cr.* ii 3 13
Perchance, my lord, I show more craft than love . iii 2 160
Whiles others fish with craft for great opinion . iv 4 105
I'll potch at him some way Or wrath or craft may get him *Coriolanus* i 10 16
You have made fair hands, You and your crafts! you have crafted fair! iv 6 118
Which your modesties have not craft enough to colour . *Hamlet* ii 2 290
That I essentially am not in madness, But mad in craft . iii 4 188
O, 'tis most sweet, When in one line two crafts directly meet . iii 4 210
In this plainness Harbour more craft and more corrupter ends *Lear* ii 2 108
In time, When she had fitted you with her craft . *Cymbeline* v 5 55
Crafted. You have made fair hands, You and your crafts! you have crafted fair! *Coriolanus* iv 6 118
Craftier. A craftier Tereus, cousin, hast thou met . *T. Andron.* ii 4 41
Craftily. Either you are ignorant, Or seem so craftily . *Meas. for Meas.* ii 4 75
I have drunk but one cup to-night, and that was craftily qualified too *Othello* ii 3 41
Craft's master. He is not his craft's master; he doth not do it right 2 *Hen. IV.* iii 2 297
Craftsmen. Wooing poor craftsmen with the craft of smiles *Richard II.* i 4 28
Crafty. Of this matter Is little Cupid's crafty arrow made . *Much Ado* iii 1 22
A vengeance on your crafty wither'd hide! . *T. of Shrew* ii 1 406
You may think my love was crafty love And call it cunning . *K. John* iv 1 53
Wherein cunning, but in craft? wherein crafty, but in villany? 1 *Hen. IV.* ii 4 504
They say 'A crafty knave does need no broker' . 2 *Hen. VI.* i 2 100
You shall go near To call them both a pair of crafty knaves . i 2 103
Being accused a crafty murderer . iii 1 254
Full often, like a shag-hair'd crafty kern, Hath he conversed with the enemy . iii 1 367
The policy of those crafty swearing rascals . *Troi. and Cres.* v 4 10
But, with a crafty madness, keeps aloof . *Hamlet* iii 1 8
That such a crafty devil as is his mother Should yield the world this ass! *Cymbeline* ii 1 57
Crafty-sick. Old Northumberland Lies crafty-sick . 2 *Hen. IV.* Ind. 37
Cram. You cram these words into mine ears . *Tempest* ii 1 106
Do thou but think What 'tis to cram a maw or clothe a back *M. for M.* iii 2 23
Whose skull Jove cram with brains! . *T. Night* i 5 122
Cram's with praise, and make's As fat as tame things . *W. Tale* i 2 91
May we cram Within this wooden O the very casques That did affright the air at Agincourt? . *Hen. V.* Prol. 12
Injurious time now with a robber's haste Crams his rich thievery up, he knows not how . *Troi. and Cres.* iv 4 45
And, in despite, I'll cram thee with more food! . *Rom. and Jul.* v 3 48
Crammed. Being thus crammed in the basket . *Mer. Wives* iii 5 98
As much love in rhyme As would be cramm'd up in a sheet of paper *L. L. Lost* v 2 7
He hath strange places cramm'd With observation . *As Y. Like It* ii 7 40
So crammed, as he thinks, with excellencies . *T. Night* ii 3 163
Gets him to rest, cramm'd with distressful bread . *Hen. V.* iv 1 287
Your heart Is cramm'd with arrogancy, spleen, and pride . *Hen. VIII.* ii 4 110
Would they but fat their thoughts With this cramm'd reason *Tr. and Cr.* ii 2 49
Suffer us to famish, and their store-houses crammed with grain *Coriol.* i 1 83
Cramp. Thou shalt have cramps, Side-stitches . *Tempest* i 2 325
I'll rack thee with old cramps, Fill all thy bones with aches . i 2 369
Shorten up their sinews With aged cramps . iv 1 261
O, touch me not; I am not Stephano, but a cramp . v 1 286
Being taken with the cramp was drowned . *As Y. Like It* iv 1 105
In coming on he has the cramp . *All's Well* iv 3 324
Crank. Through the cranks and offices of man . *Coriolanus* i 1 141
Cranking. See how this river comes me cranking in . 1 *Hen. IV.* iii 1 98
Cranmer. My learn'd and well-beloved servant, Cranmer *Hen. VIII.* ii 4 238
When returns Cranmer?—He is return'd in his opinions . iii 2 63
Cranmer's A worthy fellow, and hath ta'en much pain In the king's business . iii 2 71
Again, there is sprung up An heretic, an arch one, Cranmer . iii 2 102
Cranmer is return'd with welcome, Install'd lord archbishop . iii 2 400
He of Winchester Is held no great good lover of the archbishop's, The virtuous Cranmer . iv 1 105
When it comes, Cranmer will find a friend will not shrink from him . iv 1 107
Till Cranmer, Cromwell, her two hands, and she, Sleep in their graves . v 1 31
Crannied. That had in it a crannied hole or chink . *M. N. Dream* v 1 159
Crannies. When the sun shines let foolish gnats make sport, But creep in crannies when he hides his beams . *Com. of Errors* ii 2 31
Cranny. Through that cranny shall Pyramus and Thisby whisper *M. N. Dream* iii 1 73
And this the cranny is, right and sinister, Through which the fearful lovers are to whisper . v 1 164

Crants. She is allow'd her virgin crants, Her maiden strewments *Hamlet* v 1 255

Crare. Find The ooze, to show what coast thy sluggish crare Might easiliest harbour in . . . . *Cymbeline* iv 2 205

Crash. With a hideous crash Takes prisoner Pyrrhus' ear . *Hamlet* ii 2 498

Crassus. Tell him where I stay: give the like notice To Valentinus, Rowland, and to Crassus . . . . *Meas. for Meas.* iv 5 8

Pleased fortune does of Marcus Crassus' death Make me revenger *Ant. and Cleo.* iii 1 2

Thy Pacorus, Orodes, Pays this for Marcus Crassus . . . iii 1 5

Crave. This must crave, An if this be at all, a most strange story *Tempest* v 1 116

He, none but he, shall have her, Though twenty thousand worthier come to crave her . . . . . . *Mer. Wives* iv 4 90

I crave your honour's pardon. What shall be done, sir? *Meas. for Meas.* ii 2 14

I shall crave your forbearance a little: may be I will call upon you . iv 1 22

I crave but four days' respite . . . . iv 2 170

If any crave redress of injustice . . . . . . iv 4 10

I crave no other, nor no better man.—Never crave him . . . v 1 431

I crave death more willingly than mercy; 'Tis my deserving . . v 1 481

I crave your pardon. Soon at five o'clock, Please you *Com. of Errors* i 2 26

Acquainted you withal, to the end to crave your assistance *L. L. Lost* v 1 123

I crave the law, The penalty and forfeit of my bond *Mer. of Venice* iv 1 206

I'll crave the day When I shall ask the banns . . *T. of Shrew* ii 1 180

Craves no other tribute at thy hands But love, fair looks . . v 2 152

I shall crave of you your leave that I may bear my evils alone *T. Night* ii 1 5

Wise enough to play the fool; And to do that well craves a kind of wit iii 1 68

Crave harbourage within your city walls . . . *K. John* ii 1 234

And craves to kiss your hand and take his leave . . *Richard II.* i 3 53

His designs crave haste, his haste good hope . . . . i 3 44

There am I, Till time and vantage crave my company . *2 Hen. IV.* ii 3 68

Do crave admittance to your majesty . . . . *Hen. V.* ii 4 66

Our wars Will turn unto a peaceful comic sport, When ladies crave to be encounter'd with . . . . . . *1 Hen. VI.* ii 2 46

My lady craves To know the cause of your abrupt departure . . ii 3 29

Nor other satisfaction do I crave . . . . . . ii 3 77

Who craves a parley with the Burgundy? . . . . . iii 3 37

I'll unto his majesty, and crave I may have liberty to venge this wrong iii 4 41

What makes you thus exclaim? And wherefore crave you combat? . iv 1 84

In defence of my lord's worthiness, I crave the benefit of law of arms iv 1 100

Then I need not crave his courtesy . . . . . . v 3 105

We'll crave a parley, to confer with him . . . . . v 3 130

A breach that craves a quick expedient stop! . . *2 Hen. VI.* iii 1 288

The lord mayor craves aid of your honour from the Tower . . iv 5 4

And craves your company for speedy counsel . . *3 Hen. VI.* ii 1 208

Warwick Is thither gone, to crave the French king's sister To wife for Edward . . . . iii 1 30

Am come to crave thy just and lawful aid . . . . . iii 3 32

To do greetings to thy royal person; And then to crave a league of amity iii 3 53

If an humble prayer may prevail, I then crave pardon of your majesty iv 6 8

Humbly on my knee I crave your blessing . . . *Richard III.* ii 2 106

Under your fair conduct, Crave leave to view these ladies . *Hen. VIII.* i 4 71

Nature craves All dues be render'd to their owners . *Troi. and Cres.* ii 2 173

Better to starve, Than crave the hire which first we do deserve *Coriol.* ii 3 121

My nobler friends, I crave their pardons . . . . . iii 1 65

I would crave a word or two; The which shall turn you to no further harm Than so much loss of time . . . . iii 1 283

The violent fit o' the time craves it as physic For the whole state . iii 2 33

Fortune's blows, When most struck home, being gentle wounded, craves A noble cunning . . . . iv 1 8

He craves a parley at your father's house . . . *T. Andron.* v 1 159

Madam, your mother craves a word with you.—What is her mother? *Rom. and Jul.* i 5 113

Hence will I to my ghostly father's cell, His help to crave . . ii 2 190

What sorrow craves acquaintance at my hand, That I yet know not? . iii 3 5

A kind of hope, Which craves as desperate an execution As that is desperate which we would prevent . . . . . . iv 1 69

Immortal gods, I crave no pelf; I pray for no man but myself *T. of Athens* i 2 63

Some good necessity Touches his friend, which craves to be remember'd ii 2 237

It is the bright day that brings forth the adder; And that craves wary walking . . . . *J. Cæsar* ii 1 15

Sweno, the Norways' king, craves composition . . . *Macbeth* i 2 59

I shall crave your pardon; That which you are my thoughts cannot transpose . . . . iv 3 20

Fortinbras Craves the conveyance of a promised march Over his kingdom *Hamlet* iv 4 3

I crave no more than what your highness offer'd, Nor will you tender less *Lear* i 1 197

Bestow Your needful counsel to our business, Which craves the instant use . . . . ii 1 130

This letter, madam, craves a speedy answer . . . . . iv 2 82

I crave fit disposition for my wife, Due reference of place . *Othello* i 3 237

He is married?—I crave your highness' pardon.—He is married? *Ant. and Cleo.* ii 5 98

I crave our composition may be written, And seal'd between us . . ii 6 59

Craves The circle of the Ptolemies for her heirs, Now hazarded to thy grace . . . . iii 12 17

Inform us of thy fortunes, for it seems They crave to be demanded *Cymbeline* iv 2 362

Know for what he comes, and whence he comes, And what he craves *Pericles* i 4 81

Here to have death in peace is all he'll crave . . . . ii 1 11

You said you could not beg.—I did but crave.—But crave! Then I'll turn craver too, and so I shall 'scape whipping. . . . . ii 1 91

And gives them what he will, not what they crave . . . . ii 3 47

The governor, Who craves to come aboard . . . . . v 1 5

Craved. The French ambassador upon that instant Craved audience *Hen. V.* i 1 92

And craved death Rather than I would be so vile-esteem'd . *1 Hen. VI.* i 4 32

As your ladyship desired, By message craved, so is Lord Talbot come . ii 3 13

Craven. No cock of mine; you crow too like a craven *T. of Shrew* ii 1 228

He is a craven and a villain else . . . . . *Hen. V.* iv 7 139

He bears him on the place's privilege, Or durst not, for his craven heart, say thus . . . . *1 Hen. VI.* ii 4 87

I vow'd, base knight, when I did meet thee next, To tear the garter from thy craven's leg . . . . iv 1 15

Whether it be Bestial oblivion, or some craven scruple . *Hamlet* iv 4 40

Against self-slaughter There is a prohibition so divine That cravens my weak hand . . . . *Cymbeline* iii 4 80

Craver. I did but crave.—But crave! Then I'll turn craver too, and so I shall 'scape whipping . . . . *Pericles* ii 1 92

Craveth. The Earl of Salisbury craveth supply, And hardly keeps his men from mutiny . . . . *1 Hen. VI.* i 1 159

Craving. On serious business, craving quick dispatch . . *L. L. Lost* ii 1 31

To satisfy myself, In craving your opinion of my title . *2 Hen. VI.* ii 2 4

She, on his left side, craving aid for Henry, He, on his right, asking a wife for Edward . . . . *3 Hen. VI.* iii 1 43

When therewithal we shall have cause of state Craving us jointly *Macbeth* iii 1 35

Crawl. I can no further crawl, no further go . . . *M. N. Dream* iii 2 444

Conferring them on younger strengths, while we Unburthen'd crawl toward death . . . . *Lear* i 1 42

Crawled. Hath crawl'd into the favour of the king, And is his oracle *Hen. VIII.* iii 2 103

Crawling. Do thy best To pluck this crawling serpent from my breast! *M. N. Dream* ii 2 146

What should such fellows as I do crawling between earth and heaven? *Hamlet* iii 1 130

Crazed. Yield Thy crazed title to my certain right . *M. N. Dream* i 1 92

So many miseries have crazed my voice . . . *Richard III.* iv 4 17

To half a soul and to a notion crazed Say 'Thus did Banquo' *Macbeth* iii 1 83

Truth to tell thee, The grief hath crazed my wits . . *Lear* iii 4 175

Crazy. We will bestow you in some better place, Fitter for sickness and for crazy age . . . . *1 Hen. VI.* iii 2 89

Creaking my shoes on the plain masonry . . . . *All's Well* ii 1 31

Let not the creaking of shoes nor the rustling of silks betray thy poor heart to woman . . . . *Lear* iii 4 97

Cream. There are a sort of men whose visages Do cream and mantle like a standing pond . . . . *Mer. of Venice* i 1 89

Your black silk hair, Your bugle eyeballs, nor your cheek of cream *As Y. Like It* iii 5 47

Good sooth, she is The queen of curds and cream . . *W. Tale* iv 4 161

I am as vigilant as a cat to steal cream.—I think, to steal cream indeed, for thy theft hath already made thee butter . . . *1 Hen. IV.* iv 2 65

Cream-faced. The devil damn thee black, thou cream-faced loon! *Macbeth* v 3 11

Create. Are you a god? would you create me new? . *Com. of Errors* iii 2 39

And the issue there create Ever shall be fortunate . . *M. N. Dream* v 1 412

If thou canst like this creature as a maid, I can create the rest *All's Well* ii 3 150

We'll create young Arthur Duke of Bretagne And Earl of Richmond *K. John* ii 1 551

The fire is dead with grief, Being create for comfort, to be used In undeserved extremes . . . . iv 1 107

We create, in absence of ourself, Our uncle York lord governor *Rich. II.* ii 1 219

Might create a perfect guess . . . . . *2 Hen. IV.* iii 1 88

With hearts create of duty and of zeal . . . . *Hen. V.* ii 2 31

We here create you Earl of Shrewsbury . . . . *1 Hen. VI.* iii 4 26

Kneel down: We here create thee the first duke of Suffolk *2 Hen. VI.* i 1 64

Richard, I will create thee Duke of Gloucester . . *3 Hen. VI.* ii 6 103

Then I degraded you from being king, And come now to create you Duke of York . . . . iv 3 34

Her ashes new create another heir, As great in admiration as herself *Hen. VIII.* v 5 42

This suit I make, That you create your emperor's eldest son, Lord Saturnine . . . . *T. Andron.* i 1 224

I choose thee, Tamora, for my bride, And will create thee empress of Rome . . . . i 1 320

O any thing, of nothing first create! O heavy lightness! *Rom. and Jul.* i 1 183

Your eye in Scotland Would create soldiers . . . *Macbeth* iv 3 187

Create her child of spleen; that it may live, And be a thwart disnatured torment to her! . . . . *Lear* i 4 304

Witness the world, that I create thee here My lord and master . . v 3 77

He creates Lucius proconsul . . . . . . *Cymbeline* iii 7 7

I create you Companions to our person . . . . . . v 5 20

Created. New created The creatures that were mine . . *Tempest* i 2 81

O you, So perfect and so peerless, are created Of every creature's best! iii 1 47

With our needles created both one flower, Both on one sampler *M. N. Dream* iii 2 204

I think thou wast created for men to breathe themselves upon thee *All's Well* ii 3 271

Thou, created to be awed by man, Wast born to bear . *Richard II.* v 5 91

Therefore was I created with a stubborn outside . . *Hen. V.* v 2 244

If thou be not then created York, I will not live to be accounted Warwick . . . . *1 Hen. VI.* ii 4 119

And rise created princely Duke of York . . . . . iii 1 173

Earl of Shrewsbury, Created, for his rare success in arms, Great Earl of Washford . . . . iv 7 62

'Twere not amiss He were created knight for his good service *2 Hen. VI.* v 1 77

Thou shalt rule no more O'er him whom heaven created for thy ruler v 1 105

Pass'd over to the end they were created . . . *3 Hen. VI.* ii 5 39

Deceptious functions, Created only to calumniate . *Troi. and Cres.* v 2 124

Things created To buy and sell with groats . . . *Coriolanus* iii 2 9

Thou hast created A mother and two brothers . . *Cymbeline* v 4 124

Creating. The most virtuous gentlewoman that ever nature had praise for creating . . . . *All's Well* iv 5 10

An art which in their piedness shares With great creating nature *W. Tale* iv 4 88

Art thou aught else but place, degree and form, Creating awe and fear in other men? . . . . *Hen. V.* iv 1 264

Go to the creating a whole tribe of fops, Got 'tween asleep and wake *Lear* i 2 14

Creation. Women! Help Heaven! men their creation mar In profiting by them . . . . *Meas. for Meas.* ii 4 127

After this downright way of creation . . . . . . iii 2 113

What demi-god Hath come so near creation? . . *Mer. of Venice* iii 2 117

What great creation and what dole of honour Flies where you bid it *All's Well* ii 3 176

The most replenished sweet work of nature, That from the prime creation e'er she framed . . . . *Richard III.* iv 3 19

A false creation, Proceeding from the heat-oppressed brain . *Macbeth* ii 1 38

This bodiless creation ecstasy Is very cunning in . . . *Hamlet* iii 4 138

In the essential vesture of creation Does tire the ingener . . *Othello* ii 1 64

Creator. And in devotion spend my latter days, To sin's rebuke and my Creator's praise . . . . *3 Hen. VI.* iv 6 44

Creature. A brave vessel, Who had, no doubt, some noble creature in her *Tempest* i 2 7

Not so much perdition as an hair Betid to any creature . . . i 2 31

New created The creatures that were mine . . . . . i 2 82

I'll carry it to the pile.—No, precious creature . . . . iii 1 25

O you, So perfect and so peerless, are created Of every creature's best! iii 1 48

Incensed the seas and shores, yea, all the creatures, Against your peace iii 3 74

How many goodly creatures are there here! How beauteous mankind is! v 1 182

Sovereign to all the creatures on the earth . . . *T. G. of Ver.* ii 4 153

She's a good creature . . . . *Mer. Wives* iii 2 56

I am not such a sickly creature, I give heaven praise . . . . iii 4 61

Thou art as foolish Christian creatures as I would desires . . iv 1 73

The virtuous creature, that hath the jealous fool to her husband! . iv 2 137

Creature. A creature unprepared, unmeet for death . *Meas. for Meas.* iv 3 71
If any ask you for your master, Say he dines forth and let no creature enter . . . . *Com. of Errors* ii 2 212
Teach me, dear creature, how to think and speak . . . iii 2 33
But that she, being a very beastly creature, lays claim to me . iii 2 88
No, not a creature enters in my house . . . . . v 1 92
It is all the wealth that he hath left, to be known a reasonable creature *Much Ado* i 1 71
Or that I yesternight Maintain'd the change of words with any creature iv 1 185
Will make or man or woman madly dote Upon the next live creature that it sees . . . . . . *M. N. Dream* ii 1 172
Bring me the fairest creature northward born . . . *Mer. of Venice* ii 1 4
Never did I know A creature, that did bear the shape of man, So keen . iii 2 278
When Nature hath made a fair creature, may she not by Fortune fall into the fire? . . . . *As Y. Like It* i 2 46
She was the fairest creature in the world . . *T. of Shrew* Ind. 2 68
Who were below him He used as creatures of another place . *All's Well* i 2 42
A wicked creature, as you and all flesh and blood are . . i 3 37
If thou canst like this creature as a maid, I can create the rest . ii 3 149
I warrant, good creature, wheresoe'er she is, Her heart weighs sadly . iii 5 69
She's a fair creature: Will you go see her? . . . . . iii 6 124
My heart hath the fear of Mars before it and of his creatures . . iv 1 34
Helen, that's dead, Was a sweet creature . . . . . v 3 78
A fond and desperate creature, Whom sometime I have laugh'd with . v 3 178
Unstaid and skittish in all motions else, Save in the constant image of the creature That is beloved . . . . . . *T. Night* ii 4 19
An apple, cleft in two, is not more twin Than these two creatures . v 1 231
This jealousy Is for a precious creature . . . . . *W. Tale* i 2 452
O thou thing! Which I'll not call a creature of thy place . . ii 1 83
The sweet'st, dear'st creature's dead, and vengeance for't Not dropp'd down yet . . . . iii 2 202
This place is famous for the creatures Of prey that keep upon't . . iii 3 12
To me comes a creature, Sometimes her head on one side, some another iii 3 19
This is a creature, Would she begin a sect, might quench the zeal Of all professors else . . . . v 1 106
The majesty of the creature in resemblance of the mother . . v 2 39
There was not such a gracious creature born . . . *K. John* iii 4 81
Creatures of note for mercy-lacking uses . . . . . . iv 1 121
He would unto the stews, And from the common'st creature pluck a glove *Richard II.* v 3 17
The world is populous And here is not a creature but myself . . v 5 4
Then am I no two-legged creature . . . . 1 *Hen. IV.* ii 4 208
Here comes bare-bone. How now, my sweet creature of bombast! . ii 4 359
A noble earl and many a creature else Had been alive this hour . v 5 7
I do now remember the poor creature, small beer . . 2 *Hen. IV.* ii 2 13
So work the honey-bees, Creatures that by a rule in nature teach The act of order . . . . *Hen. V.* i 2 188
Thou cruel, Ingrateful, savage and inhuman creature! . . . . ii 2 95
That island of England breeds very valiant creatures . . . iii 7 151
Divinest creature, Astræa's daughter, How shall I honour thee for this success? . . . . 1 *Hen. VI.* i 6 4
To see how God in all his creatures works! . . . . 2 *Hen. VI.* ii 1 7
Unreasonable creatures feed their young . . . . 3 *Hen. VI.* ii 2 26
Curse not thyself, fair creature . . . . *Richard III.* i 2 132
The plainest harmless creature That breathed upon this earth a Christian . . . . iii 5 25
Kings it makes gods, and meaner creatures kings . . . . v 2 24
There is no creature loves me; And if I die, no soul shall pity me . v 3 200
What he spoke My chaplain to no creature living, but To me, should utter, with demure confidence . . . . *Hen. VIII.* i 2 166
You bear a gentle mind, and heavenly blessings Follow such creatures . ii 3 58
The primest creature That's paragon'd o' the world . . . ii 4 229
My king is tangled in affection to A creature of the queen's, Lady Anne Bullen . . . . iii 2 36
She is a gallant creature, and complete In mind and feature . . iii 2 49
She's a good creature, and, sweet lady, does Deserve our better wishes v 1 25
Let me bear another to his horse; for that's the more capable creature *Troi. and Cres.* iii 3 310
Ah, beastly creature! The blot and enemy to our general name! *T. And.* ii 3 182
Thy niece and I, poor creatures, want our hands . . . . iii 2 5
With which grief, It is supposed, the fair creature died . *Rom. and Jul.* v 3 51
As well of glib and slippery creatures as Of grave and austere quality *T. of Athens* i 1 53
This thy creature By night frequents my house . . . . . i 1 116
The most needless creatures living, should we ne'er have use for 'em . i 2 101
The creatures Whose naked natures live in all the spite Of wreakful heaven . . . . iv 3 227
Hence! home, you idle creatures, get you home: Is this a holiday? *J. Cæsar* i 1 1
This man Is now become a god, and Cassius is A wretched creature . i 2 117
Unto bad causes swear Such creatures as men doubt . . . . ii 1 132
It is a creature that I teach to fight, To wind, to stop, to run directly on . . . . iv 1 31
I have heard That guilty creatures sitting at a play Have by the very cunning of the scene Been struck so to the soul that presently They have proclaim'd their malefactions . . . . . *Hamlet* ii 2 618
You jig, you amble, and you lisp, and nick-name God's creatures . . iii 1 151
Confederate season, else no creature seeing . . . . . . iii 2 267
We fat all creatures else to fat us, and we fat ourselves for maggots . iv 3 23
Or like a creature native and indued Unto that element . . . iv 7 180
Suspend thy purpose, if thou didst intend To make this creature fruitful! *Lear* i 4 299
Those wicked creatures yet do look well-favour'd, When others are more wicked . . . . ii 4 259
Mildews the white wheat, and hurts the poor creature of earth . . iii 4 124
Thou hast seen a farmer's dog bark at a beggar?—Ay, sir.—And the creature run from the cur? . . . . iv 6 161
Indeed, she's a most fresh and delicate creature . . . *Othello* ii 3 21
Come, come, good wine is a good familiar creature, if it be well used . ii 3 314
This honest creature doubtless Sees and knows more, much more, than he unfolds . . . . iii 3 242
O curse of marriage, That we can call these delicate creatures ours, And not their appetites! . . . . iii 3 269
And then, sir, would he gripe and wring my hand, Cry 'O sweet creature!' . . . . iii 3 422
Is true of mind and made of no such baseness As jealous creatures are . iii 4 28
It is a creature That dotes on Cassio . . . . iv 1 96
O, the world hath not a sweeter creature . . . . iv 1 194
Melt Egypt into Nile! and kindly creatures Turn all to serpents! *Ant. and Cleo.* ii 5 78

Creature. Why, methinks, by him, This creature's no such thing.—Nothing, madam . . . . *Ant. and Cleo.* iii 3 44
Most sovereign creature . . . . v 2 81
Is a creature such As, to seek through the regions of the earth For one his like, there would be something failing In him that should compare . . . . *Cymbeline* i 1 19
Such creatures as We count not worth the hanging . . . . . i 5 19
What do you pity, sir?—Two creatures heartily.—Am I one, sir? . . i 6 83
You, O the dearest of creatures, would even renew me with your eyes . iii 2 43
These are kind creatures. Gods, what lies I have heard! . . . iv 2 32
I thought I was a cave-keeper, And cook to honest creatures: but 'tis not so . . . . iv 2 299
Creatures may be alike: were't he, I am sure He would have spoke to us . . . . v 5 125
In killing creatures vile, as cats and dogs, Of no esteem . . . . v 5 252
That, if heaven slumber while their creatures want, They may awake their helps to comfort them . . . . *Pericles* i 4 16
Were all too little to content and please, Although they gave their creatures in abundance . . . . i 4 36
Hundreds call themselves Your creatures, who by you have been restored . . . . iii 2 45
Live, And make us weep to hear your fate, fair creature, Rare as you seem to be . . . . iii 2 104
She is a goodly creature.—The fitter, then, the gods should have her . iv 1 9
I never spake bad word, nor did ill turn To any living creature . . iv 1 77
We were never so much out of creatures . . . . iv 2 6
Is she not a fair creature? . . . . iv 6 47
The house you dwell in proclaims you to be a creature of sale . . iv 6 84
Credence. May plead For amplest credence . . . . *All's Well* i 2 11
Great in our hope, lay our best love and credence Upon thy promising fortune . . . . iii 3 2
There is a credence in my heart, An esperance so obstinately strong *Troi. and Cres.* v 2 120
Credent. For my authority bears of a credent bulk . *Meas. for Meas.* iv 4 29
Then 'tis very credent Thou mayst co-join with something . *W. Tale* i 2 142
If with too credent ear you list his songs, Or lose your heart. *Hamlet* i 3 30
Credible. So 'tis reported, sir.—Nay, 'tis most credible *All's Well* i 2 4
Credit. Made such a sinner of his memory, To credit his own lie *Tempest* i 2 102
Which is indeed almost beyond credit,— As many vouched rarities are ii 1 59
And what does else want credit, come to me, And I'll be sworn 'tis true iii 3 25
'Tis a goodly credit for you . . . . *Mer. Wives* iv 2 200
Such a person, Whose credit with the judge, or own great place, Could fetch your brother . . . . *Meas. for Meas.* ii 4 92
Think'st thou thy oaths, Though they would swear down each particular saint, Were testimonies against his worth and credit? . . v 1 244
Thou hast stolen both mine office and my name. The one ne'er got me credit, the other mickle blame . . . . . *Com. of Errors* iii 1 45
Make us but believe, Being compact of credit, that you love us . . iii 2 22
Consider how it stands upon my credit . . . . iv 1 68
Of credit infinite, highly beloved, Second to none that lives here in the city . . . . v 1 6
Thus will I save my credit in the shoot . . . . *L. L. Lost* iv 1 26
How canst thou thus for shame, Titania, Glance at my credit with Hippolyta? . . . . *M. N. Dream* ii 1 75
Therefore go forth; Try what my credit can in Venice do *Mer. of Venice* i 1 180
Swear by your double self, And there's an oath of credit . . . v 1 246
To-morrow, sir, I wrestle for my credit . . . . *As Y. Like It* i 1 133
I call them forth to credit her . . . . *T. of. Shrew* iv 1 106
His name and credit shall you undertake . . . . iv 2 106
You must hold the credit of your father . . . . . *All's Well* i 1 89
How shall they credit A poor unlearned virgin? . . . . . i 3 245
Or to dissever so Our great self and our credit . . . . . ii 1 126
Very poor rogues, upon my reputation and credit and as I hope to live . iv 3 154
Demand of him my condition, and what credit I have with the duke . iv 3 196
I was in that credit with them at that time that I knew of their going to bed . . . . v 3 262
There you lie.—This is much credit to you . . . . . *T. Night* iii 3 117
There I found this credit, That he did range the town to seek me out . iv 3 6
What! lack I credit?—I had rather you did lack than I . . *W. Tale* ii 1 157
Give us better credit: We have always truly served you . . . ii 3 146
That which I shall report will bear no credit, Were not the proof so nigh v 1 179
Like an old tale still, which will have matter to rehearse, though credit be asleep and not an ear open . . . . v 2 67
And, as I am a gentleman, I credit him . . . . . *Richard II.* iii 3 120
Where it would not, I have used my credit . . . . . 1 *Hen. IV.* i 2 63
That would, if matters should be looked into, for their own credit sake, make all whole . . . . ii 1 80
If I cannot once or twice in a quarter bear out a knave against an honest man, I have but a very little credit with your worship 2 *Hen. IV.* v 1 54
Such as were grown to credit by the wars . . . . 1 *Hen. VI.* iv 1 36
Fear not thy master: fight for credit of the 'prentices . . 2 *Hen. VI.* ii 3 71
And will you credit this base drudge's words, That speaks he knows not what? . . . . iv 2 159
Thereon I pawn my credit and mine honour . . . . 3 *Hen. VI.* iii 3 116
That former fabulous story, Being now seen possible enough, got credit, That Bevis was believed . . . . *Hen. VIII.* i 1 37
All else This talking lord can lay upon my credit, I answer is most false iii 2 265
My reliances on his fracted dates Have smit my credit . *T. of Athens* ii 1 23
Timon has been this lord's father, And kept his credit with his purse . iii 2 75
My credit now stands on such slippery ground . . . . *J. Cæsar* iii 1 191
Now I change my mind, And partly credit things that do presage . . v 1 79
If on my credit you dare build so far . . . . *Lear* iii 1 35
There is no composition in these news That gives them credit . *Othello* i 3 2
In spite of nature, Of years, of country, credit, every thing . . . i 3 97
That she loves him, 'tis apt and of great credit . . . . . . ii 1 296
By how much she strives to do him good, She shall undo her credit with the Moor . . . . ii 3 365
The credit that thy lady hath of thee Deserves thy trust, and thy most perfect goodness Her assured credit . . . . *Cymbeline* i 6 157
Our credit comes not in like the commodity . . . . . . *Pericles* iv 2 33
I will believe thee, And make my senses credit thy relation . . . v 1 124
Letters of good credit . . . . v 3 77
Creditor. The glory of a creditor, Both thanks and use *Meas. for Meas.* i 1 40
If I could speak so wisely under an arrest, I would send for certain of my creditors . . . . i 2 136
Bear me forthwith unto his creditor And, knowing how the debt grows, I will pay it . . . . *Com. of Errors* iv 4 123
There came divers of Antonio's creditors in my company to Venice, that swear he cannot choose but break . . . . *Mer. of Venice* iii 1 118

Creditor. My ships have all miscarried, my creditors grow cruel, my estate is very low . . . . . . *Mer. of Venice* iii 2 318
I shall hardly spare a pound of flesh To-morrow to my bloody creditor . iii 3 34
Within this wall of flesh There is a soul counts thee her creditor *K. John* iii 3 21
Which, if like an ill venture it come unluckily home, I break, and you, my gentle creditors, lose . . . . *2 Hen. IV.* Epil. 14
His means most short, his creditors most strait . . *T. of Athens* i 1 96
They have e'en put my breath from me, the slaves. Creditors? devils! iii 4 105
Must be be-lee'd and calm'd By debitor and creditor . . *Othello* i 1 31
You have no true debitor and creditor but it . . . *Cymbeline* v 4 172
Credo. Sir Nathaniel, haud credo.—'Twas not a haud credo . *L. L. Lost* iv 2 11
Credulity. Whose ignorant credulity will not Come up to the truth *W. T.* ii 1 192
Credulous. A most poor credulous monster! . . . *Tempest* ii 2 149
We are soft as our complexions are, And credulous to false prints *Meas. for Meas.* ii 4 130
If he be credulous and trust my tale . . . . *T. of Shrew* iv 2 67
But may not be so credulous of cure, When our most learned doctors leave us . . . . *All's Well* ii 1 118
Being credulous in this mad thought . . . . *T. Andron.* v 2 74
A credulous father! and a brother noble! . . . . *Lear* i 2 195
Work on, My medicine, work! Thus credulous fools are caught *Othello* iv 1 46
Ay me, most credulous fool, Egregious murderer! . . *Cymbeline* v 5 210
Creed. I love him not, nor fear him; there's my creed . . *Hen. VIII.* ii 2 51
Creek. One that countermands The passages of alleys, creeks *Com. of Err.* iv 2 38
I have ta'en His head from him: I'll throw't into the creek . *Cymbeline* iv 2 151
Creep. My best way is to creep under his gaberdine . . . *Tempest* ii 2 40
You know that love Will creep in service where it cannot go *T. G. of Ver.* iv 2 20
If he be of any reasonable stature, he may creep in here . *Mer. Wives* iii 3 138
I love thee. Help me away. Let me creep in here . . . iii 3 150
He cannot creep into a halfpenny purse, nor into a pepper-box . . iii 5 148
What shall I do? I'll creep up into the chimney . . . . . iv 2 56
Creep into the kiln-hole.—Where is it? . . . . . . iv 2 59
When the sun shines let foolish gnats make sport, But creep in crannies when he hides his beams . . . . *Com. of Errors* ii 2 31
Alas, poor hurt fowl! now will he creep into sedges . . *Much Ado* ii 1 209
The idea of her life shall sweetly creep Into his study of imagination . iv 1 226
That all their elves for fear Creep into acorn-cups and hide them there *M. N. Dream* ii 1 31
I'll believe as soon This whole earth may be bored and that the moon May through the centre creep . . . . iii 2 54
Till o'er their brows death-counterfeiting sleep With leaden legs and batty wings doth creep . . . . iii 2 365
The smallest monstrous mouse that creeps on floor . . . . v 1 223
Sleep when he wakes and creep into the jaundice By being peevish *Mer. of Venice* i 1 85
Dulcet sounds in break of day That creep into the dreaming bride-groom's ear . . . . iii 2 52
Here will we sit and let the sounds of music Creep in our ears . . v 1 56
I feel this youth's perfections With an invisible and subtle stealth To creep in at mine eyes . . . . *T. Night* i 5 317
'Tis such as you, That creep like shadows by him . . . *W. Tale* ii 3 34
Creep time ne'er so slow, Yet it shall come for me to do thee good *K. John* iii 3 31
Shall secretly into the bosom creep Of that same noble prelate *1 Hen. IV.* i 3 266
What is it, but to make thy sepulchre And creep into it far before thy time? . . . . *3 Hen. VI.* i 1 237
To come as humbly as they used to creep To holy altars *Troi. and Cres.* iii 3 73
How some men creep in skittish fortune's hall! . . . . . iii 3 134
Lust and liberty Creep in the minds and marrows of our youth! *T. of Athens* iv 1 26
To-morrow, and to-morrow, and to-morrow, Creeps in this petty pace from day to day *Macbeth* v 5 20
And, like the famous ape, To try conclusions, in the basket creep *Hamlet* iii 4 195
Rich in his father's honour, creeps apace Into the hearts of such as have not thrived Upon the present state . . . *Ant. and Cleo.* i 3 50
She creeps: Her motion and her station are as one . . . . iii 3 21
How comes it he is to sojourn with you? How creeps acquaintance? *Cymbeline* i 4 25
Creeping. As wild geese that the creeping fowler eye *M. N. Dream* iii 2 20
Lose and neglect the creeping hours of time . . *As Y. Like It* ii 7 112
Creeping like snail Unwillingly to school . . . . . ii 7 146
What incidency thou dost guess of harm Is creeping toward me *W. Tale* i 2 404
Behold the threaden sails, Borne with the invisible and creeping wind *Hen. V.* iii Prol. 11
Creeping murmur and the poring dark Fills the wide vessel of the universe . . . . iv Prol. 2
Or any creeping venom'd thing that lives . . . *Richard III.* i 2 20
He has wings; he's more than a creeping thing . . *Coriolanus* v 4 14
Crept. This music crept by me upon the waters . . . *Tempest* i 2 391
How now, Sir Proteus, are you crept before us? . *T. G. of Ver.* iv 2 18
His jesting spirit; which is now crept into a lute-string and now govern'd by stops . . . . *Much Ado* iii 2 61
Daughter and cousin! are you crept hither to see the wrestling? *As Y. Like It* i 2 165
I could have crept into any alderman's thumb-ring . . *1 Hen. IV.* ii 4 364
The gaudy, blabbing and remorseful day Is crept into the bosom of the sea . . . . *2 Hen. VI.* iv 1 2
Reproach and beggary Is crept into the palace of our king, And all by thee . . . . iv 1 102
No sooner was I crept out of my cradle But I was made a king . . iv 9 3
Since I am crept in favour with myself, I will maintain it with some little cost . . . . *Richard III.* i 2 259
In those holes Where eyes did once inhabit, there were crept, As 'twere in scorn of eyes, reflecting gems . . . . i 4 30
From forth the kennel of thy womb hath crept A hell-hound that doth hunt us all to death . . . . iv 4 47
The marriage with his brother's wife Has crept too near his conscience. —No, his conscience Has crept too near another lady *Hen. VIII.* ii 2 18
Their great general slept, Whilst emulation in the army crept *Tr. and Cr.* ii 2 212
Such a pother As if that whatsoever god who leads him Were slily crept into his human powers . . . . . . *Coriolanus* ii 1 236
The deep of night is crept upon our talk . . . . *J. Cæsar* iv 3 226
Crescent. He is no crescent, and his horns are invisible within the circumference . . . . *M. N. Dream* v 1 246
For nature, crescent, does not grow alone In thews and bulk *Hamlet* i 3 11
My powers are crescent, and my auguring hope Says it will come to the full . . . . *Ant. and Cleo.* ii 1 10
He was then of a crescent note . . . . *Cymbeline* i 4 2
Crescive. Unseen, yet crescive in his faculty . . . . *Hen. V.* i 1 66
Cresset. At my nativity The front of heaven was full of fiery shapes, Of burning cressets . . . . *1 Hen. IV.* iii 1 15

Cressid. Toward the Grecian tents, Where Cressid lay that night *Mer. of Venice* v 1 6
I am Cressid's uncle, That dare leave two together . . . *All's Well* ii 1 100
Fetch forth the lazar kite of Cressid's kind . . . . *Hen. V.* ii 1 80
When fair Cressid comes into my thoughts,—So, traitor! 'When she comes!' When is she thence? . . . . . *Troi. and Cres.* i 1 30
I tell thee I am mad In Cressid's love: thou answer'st 'she is fair' . i 1 52
O gods, how do you plague me! I cannot come to Cressid but by Pandar . . . . i 1 98
Tell me, Apollo, for thy Daphne's love, What Cressid is, what Pandar? i 1 102
Good morrow, cousin Cressid: what do you talk of? . . . i 2 44
From Cupid's shoulder pluck his painted wings, And fly with me to Cressid! . . . . iii 2 16
Troilus shall be such to Cressid as what envy can say worst shall be a mock for his truth . . . . iii 2 103
Why was my Cressid then so hard to win?—Hard to seem won . iii 2 124
For this time will I take my leave, my lord.—Your leave, sweet Cressid! . . . . iii 2 148
'Yea,' let them say, to stick the heart of falsehood, 'As false as Cressid' iii 2 203
Let all constant men be Troiluses, all false women Cressids . . iii 2 211
Desired my Cressid in right great exchange, Whom Troy hath still denied . . . . iii 3 21
Let Diomedes bear him, And bring us Cressid hither . . . iii 3 31
And there to render him, For the enfreed Antenor, the fair Cressid . iv 1 38
Troilus had rather Troy were borne to Greece Than Cressid borne from Troy . . . . iv 1 47
O foolish Cressid! I might have still held off, And then you would have tarried . . . . iv 2 17
Here, you maid! where's my cousin Cressid? . . . . . iv 2 25
Make Cressid's name the very crown of falsehood, If ever she leave Troilus! . . . . iv 2 106
Cressid, I love thee in so strain'd a purity . . . . . iv 4 26
A woful Cressid 'mongst the merry Greeks! When shall we see again? iv 4 58
Name Cressid, and thy life shall be as safe As Priam is in Ilion . iv 4 117
Fair Lady Cressid, So please you, save the thanks this prince expects . iv 4 118
Is this the Lady Cressid?—Even she.—Most dearly welcome to the Greeks, sweeet lady . . . . iv 5 17
Gives all gaze and bent of amorous view On the fair Cressid . . iv 5 283
Cressid comes forth to him.—How now, my charge! . . . . v 2 6
Was Cressid here?—I cannot conjure, Trojan.—She was not, sure . v 2 125
Cressid was here but now.—Let it not be believed for womanhood! . v 2 128
To square the general sex By Cressid's rule: rather think this not Cressid . . . . v 2 133
This is, and is not, Cressid . . . . v 2 146
Cressid is mine, tied with the bonds of heaven . . . . . v 2 154
As much as I do Cressid love, So much by weight hate I her Diomed . v 2 167
O Cressid! O false Cressid! false, false, false! Let all untruths stand by thy stained name, And they'll seem glorious . . . . v 2 178
Take thou Troilus' horse; Present the fair steed to my lady Cressid . v 5 2
Cressida. I would play Lord Pandarus of Phrygia, sir, to bring a Cressida to this Troilus . . . . *T. Night* iii 1 59
Cressida was a beggar . . . . iii 1 62
Do, sweet niece Cressida.—At your pleasure . . . *Troi. and Cres.* i 2 195
Love's invisible soul,— Who, my cousin Cressida?—No, sir, Helen . iii 1 36
It should seem, fellow that thou hast not seen the Lady Cressida . iii 1 40
Know where he sups.—I'll lay my life, with my disposer Cressida . iii 1 95
Why should you say Cressida? no, your poor disposer's sick . . iii 1 101
Where's thy master? at my cousin Cressida's? . . . . . iii 2 2
O Cressida, how often have I wished me thus! . . . . . iii 2 65
Are you a-weary of me?—O Cressida! . . . . iv 2 8
We must give up to Diomedes' hand The Lady Cressida . . . iv 2 68
As gentle tell me, of what honour was This Cressida in Troy? . . iv 5 288
This she? no, this is Diomed's Cressida . . . . . . v 2 137
Cressy. Witness our too much memorable shame When Cressy battle fatally was struck . . . . *Hen. V.* ii 4 54
Crest. Each fair instalment, coat, and several crest, With loyal blazon, evermore be blest! . . . . *Mer. Wives* v 5 67
Let's write good angel on the devil's horn; 'Tis not the devil's crest *Meas. for Meas.* ii 4 17
Beauty's crest becomes the heavens well . . . . *L. L. Lost* iv 3 256
Like coats in heraldry, Due but to one and crowned with one crest *M. N. Dream* iii 2 214
Take thou no scorn to wear the horn; It was a crest ere thou wast born *As Y. Like It* iv 2 15
What is your crest? a coxcomb?—A combless cock . . *T. of Shrew* ii 1 226
This is the very top, The height, the crest, or crest unto the crest *K. John* iv 3 46
Now for the bare-pick'd bone of majesty Doth dogged war bristle his angry crest . . . . iv 3 149
About the burning crest Of the old, feeble and day-wearied sun . . v 4 34
And bristle up The crest of youth against your dignity . *1 Hen. IV.* i 1 99
All the budding honours on thy crest I'll crop, to make a garland for my head . . . . v 4 72
His valour shown upon our crests to-day Hath taught us how to cherish such high deeds . . . . v 5 29
When from the Dauphin's crest thy sword struck fire, It warm'd thy father's heart with proud desire . . . . . *1 Hen. VI.* iv 6 10
Now the time is come That France must vail her lofty-plumed crest . v 3 25
Old Nevil's crest, The rampant bear chain'd to the ragged staff *2 Hen. VI.* v 1 202
Make him fall His crest that prouder than blue Iris bends *Troi. and Cres.* i 3 380
On whose bright crest Fame with her loud'st Oyes Cries 'This is he' . iv 5 143
When they shall see, sir, his crest up again, and the man in blood, they will out of their burrows . . . . *Coriolanus* iv 5 225
Even thou hast struck upon my crest . . . . . *T. Andron.* i 1 364
But when they should endure the bloody spur, They fall their crests *J. Cæsar* iv 2 26
Let fall thy blade on vulnerable crests; I bear a charmed life *Macbeth* v 8 11
Crested. His rear'd arm Crested the world . . . *Ant. and Cleo.* v 2 83
Crest-fallen. Till I were as crest-fallen as a dried pear . *Mer. Wives* iv 5 102
Shall I seem crest-fall'n in my father's sight? . . . *Richard II.* i 1 188
Remember it and let it make thee crest-fall'n . . . *2 Hen. VI.* i 1 59
Crestless. Spring crestless yeomen from so deep a root? . *1 Hen. VI.* ii 4 85
Cretan strand. When with his knees he kiss'd the Cretan strand *T. of Shrew* i 1 175
Crete. When in a wood of Crete they bay'd the bear . . *M. N. Dream* iv 1 118
A cry more tuneable Was never holla'd to, nor cheer'd with horn, In Crete, in Sparta, nor in Thessaly . . . . iv 1 131
O hound of Crete, think'st thou my spouse to get? . . . *Hen. V.* ii 1 77
Then follow thou thy desperate sire of Crete, Thou Icarus *1 Hen. VI.* iv 6 54
What a peevish fool was that of Crete, That taught his son the office of a fowl! And yet, for all his wings, the fool was drown'd *3 Hen. VI.* v 6 18

Crevice. I pry'd me through the crevice of a wall . . *T. Andron.* v 1 114

Crew. Come, go with us, we'll bring thee to our crews . *T. G. of Ver.* iv 1 74
A crew of patches, rude mechanicals, That work for bread *M. N. Dream* iii 2 9
Takes on the point of honour to support So dissolute a crew *Richard II.* v 3 12
The abbot, With all the rest of that consorted crew . . . v 3 138
Le Roy! a Cornish name: art thou of Cornish crew? . *Hen. V.* iv 1 50
At Buckingham and all the crew of them . . . 2 *Hen. VI.* ii 2 72
And now to London all the crew are gone . . . 3 *Hen. VI.* ii 1 174
A valiant crew; And many moe of noble fame and worth *Richard III.* iv 5 12
There are a crew of wretched souls That stay his cure . *Macbeth* iv 3 141
It was about to speak, when the cock crew . . *Hamlet* i 1 147
Then the morning cock crew loud, And at the sound it shrunk in haste away . . . i 2 218
A crew of pirates came and rescued me . . . *Pericles* v 1 176

Crib. Why rather, sleep, liest thou in smoky cribs? . . 2 *Hen. IV.* iii 1 9
Let a beast be lord of beasts, and his crib shall stand at the king's mess *Hamlet* v 2 88

Cribbed. Now I am cabin'd, cribb'd, confined, bound in To saucy doubts and fears . . . . *Macbeth* iii 4 24

Cricket, to Windsor chimneys shalt thou leap . *Mer. Wives* v 5 47
I will tell it softly; Yond crickets shall not hear it . . *W. Tale* ii 1 31
Shall we be merry?—As merry as crickets, my lad . . 1 *Hen. IV.* ii 4 100
Her whip of cricket's bone, the lash of film . . *Rom. and Jul.* i 4 63
I heard the owl scream and the crickets cry . . *Macbeth* ii 2 16
The crickets sing, and man's o'er-labour'd sense Repairs itself by rest *Cymbeline* ii 2 11
Crickets sing at the oven's mouth, E'er the blither for their drouth *Pericles* iii Gower 7

Cried, 'Hell is empty, And all the devils are here' . . . *Tempest* i 2 214
Which did awake me: I shaked you, sir, and cried . . . ii 1 319
When I waked, I cried to dream again . . . . . iii 2 152
The women have so cried and shrieked at it, that it passed . *Mer. Wives* i 1 309
Thou shalt woo her. Cried I aim? said I well? . . . ii 3 92
I went to her in white, and cried 'mum,' and she cried 'budget' . . v 5 209
You were born in a merry hour.—No, sure, my lord, my mother cried *Much Ado* ii 1 348
Another, with his finger and his thumb, Cried, 'Via! we will do't, come what will come;' The third he caper'd, and cried, 'All goes well' . . . . *L. L. Lost* v 2 112
And never cried 'Have patience, good people'! *As Y. Like It* iii 2 165
And now he fainted And cried, in fainting, upon Rosalind . . iv 3 150
He cried upon it at the merest loss And twice to-day pick'd out the dullest scent . . . . *T. of Shrew* Ind. 1 23
How I cried, how the horses ran away, how her bridle was burst . iv 1 82
That very envy and the tongue of loss Cried fame and honour on him *T. Night* v 1 62
How he cried to me for help . . . . . . *W. Tale* iii 3 97
Whilst all tongues cried 'God save thee, Bolingbroke!'. *Richard II.* v 2 11
No man cried 'God save him!' No joyful tongue gave him his welcome home . . . . v 2 28
The most omnipotent villain that ever cried 'Stand' to a true man 1 *Hen. IV.* i 2 122
I cried 'hum,' and 'well, go to,' But mark'd him not a word . . iii 1 158
All the country in a general voice Cried hate upon him . 2 *Hen. IV.* iv 1 137
Clapp'd his tail between his legs and cried . . 2 *Hen. VI.* v 1 154
And thrice cried 'Courage, father! fight it out!' . 3 *Hen. VI.* i 4 10
Richard cried 'Charge! and give no foot of ground!' And cried 'A crown, or else a glorious tomb!' . . . . i 4 15
In the very pangs of death he cried, Like to a dismal clangor heard from far . . . . ii 3 17
The night-crow cried, aboding luckless time . . . . v 6 45
And the women cried 'O, Jesus bless us, he is born with teeth!' . v 6 74
So Judas kiss'd his master, And cried 'all hail!' when as he meant all harm . . . . v 7 34
And some ten voices cried 'God save King Richard!' . *Richard III.* iii 7 36
Methought their souls, whose bodies Richard murder'd, Came to my tent, and cried on victory . . . . v 3 231
Now this masque Was cried incomparable . . . *Hen. VIII.* i 1 27
I do assure you The king cried Ha! at this . . . . iii 2 61
You must needs, for you all cried 'Go, go!' . *Troi. and Cres.* ii 2 85
You all clapp'd your hands, And cried 'Inestimable!' . . . ii 2 88
He used me kindly: He cried to me; I saw him prisoner . *Coriolanus* i 9 84
A parlous knock; and it cried bitterly . . . *Rom. and Jul.* i 3 54
Cæsar cried 'Help me, Cassius, or I sink!' . . *J. Cæsar* i 2 111
Alas, it cried 'Give me some drink, Titinius,' As a sick girl . . i 2 127
Three or four wenches, where I stood, cried 'Alas, good soul!' . i 2 275
When that the poor have cried, Cæsar hath wept . . . iii 2 96
There's one did laugh in's sleep, and one cried 'Murder!' . *Macbeth* ii 2 23
One cried 'God bless us!' and 'Amen' the other . . . ii 2 27
Still it cried 'Sleep no more!' to all the house . . . ii 2 41
Macbeth shall sleep no more.—Who was it that thus cried? . . ii 2 44
Who still hath cried, From the first corse till he that died to-day, 'This must be so' . . . . *Hamlet* i 2 104
Whose judgements in such matters cried in the top of mine . . ii 2 459
She knapped 'em o' the coxcombs with a stick, and cried 'Down, wantons, down!' . . . . *Lear* ii 4 126
Cried 'Sisters! sisters! Shame of ladies! sisters!' . . . iv 3 29
And then Cried 'Cursed fate that gave thee to the Moor!' . *Othello* iii 3 426
What is the matter, ho? who is't that cried?—Who is't that cried! . v 1 74
When Antony found Julius Cæsar dead, He cried almost to roaring *Ant. and Cleo.* iii 2 55
Of late, when I cried 'Ho!' Like boys unto a muss, kings would start forth . . . . iii 13 90
Cried he? and begg'd a' pardon?—He did ask favour . . . iii 13 132
He spoke not, but, Like a full-acorn'd boar, a German one, Cried 'O!' *Cymbeline* ii 5 17
Cried to those that fled, 'Our Britain's harts die flying, not our men' . v 3 23
Did never fear, But cried 'Good seamen!' to the sailors . *Pericles* iv 1 54
Hast thou cried her through the market?—I have cried her almost to the number of her hairs . . . . iv 2 99

Cried aloud 'O that these hands could so redeem my son!' . *K. John* iii 4 70
Cried aloud, 'What scourge for perjury Can this dark monarchy afford?' *Richard III.* i 4 50

Cried out. I, not remembering how I cried out then, Will cry it o'er again . . . . *Tempest* i 2 133
So a' cried out 'God, God, God!' three or four times . *Hen. V.* ii 3 19
They say he cried out of sack.—Ay, that a' did . . . ii 3 29
A Talbot! a Talbot! cried out amain And rush'd into the bowels of the battle . . . . 1 *Hen. VI.* i 1 128
And to the latest gasp cried out for Warwick . . . 3 *Hen. VI.* v 2 41

Cried out. I missed the meteor once, and hit that woman; who cried out 'Clubs!' . . . . *Hen. VIII.* v 4 53
Thrice hath Calpurnia in her sleep cried out, 'Help, ho! they murder Cæsar!' . . . . *J. Cæsar* ii 2 2
He cried out, 'twould be a sight indeed, If one could match you *Hamlet* iv 7 100

Cried up. What worst, as oft, Hitting a grosser quality, is cried up For our best act . . . . *Hen. VIII.* i 2 84

Criedst. Didst thou dream, Lucius, that thou so criedst out? . *J. Cæsar* iv 3 296
Thou criedst 'Indeed!' And didst contract and purse thy brow together . . . . *Othello* iii 3 112

Crier Hobgoblin, make the fairy oyes . . . . . *Mer. Wives* v 5 45
Peace!—Hear the crier.—What the devil art thou? . . *K. John* ii 1 134

Cries. I come to her in white, and cry 'mum;' she cries 'budget' . v 2 7
Far from her nest the lapwing cries away . . *Com. of Errors* iv 2 27
He cries for you and vows, if he can take you, To scorch your face . v 1 182
Ay me! says one; O Jove! the other cries . . *L. L. Lost* iv 3 141
Down topples she, And 'tailor' cries, and falls into a cough *M. N. Dream* ii 1 54
He murder cries and help from Athens calls . . . . iii 2 26
If you do love Rosalind so near the heart as your gesture cries it out *As Y. Like It* v 2 69
Our own love waking cries to see what's done . . . *All's Well* v 3 65
In his rage and his wrath, Cries, ah, ha! to the devil . *T. Night* iv 2 138
As if that joy were now become a loss, cries 'O, thy mother, thy mother!' . . . . *W. Tale* v 2 56
A widow cries; be husband to me, heavens! . . . *K. John* iii 1 108
Which blood, like sacrificing Abel's, cries . . . *Richard II.* i 1 104
On your head Turning the widows' tears, the orphans' cries . *Hen. V.* ii 4 106
And dead men's cries do fill the empty air . . 2 *Hen. VI.* v 2 4
And every drop cries vengeance for his death . . . 3 *Hen. VI.* i 4 148
Ne'er may he live to see a sunshine day, That cries 'Retire' . . ii 1 188
Thou hast made the happy earth thy hell, Fill'd it with cursing cries *Richard III.* i 2 52
Environ d me about, and howled in mine ears Such hideous cries . . i 4 60
O, what cause have I, Thine being but a moiety of my grief, To overgo thy plaints and drown thy cries! . . . . . . ii 2 61
From his deep chest laughs out a loud applause; Cries 'Excellent!' *Troi. and Cres.* i 3 164
Yet god Achilles still cries 'Excellent! 'Tis Nestor right' . . i 3 169
And at this sport Sir Valour dies; cries 'O, enough!' . . . i 3 176
On whose bright crest Fame with her loud'st Oyes Cries 'This is he' . iv 5 144
He was a thing of blood, whose every motion Was timed with dying cries *Coriolanus* ii 2 114
Hath an aspect of intercession, which Great nature cries 'Deny not' . v 3 33
Such fearful and confused cries As any mortal body hearing it Should straight fall mad, or else die suddenly . . . *T. Andron.* ii 3 102
Weke, weke! so cries a pig prepared to the spit . . . iv 2 146
And then on Romeo cries, And then down falls again . *Rom. and Jul.* iii 3 101
'Aroint thee, witch!' the rump-fed ronyon cries . . *Macbeth* i 3 6
That which cries 'Thus thou must do, if thou have it' . . . i 5 24
Harpier cries 'Tis time, 'tis time . . . . . . iv 1 3
Lay on, Macduff, And damn'd be him that first cries 'Hold, enough!' v 8 34
Whips out his rapier, cries, 'A rat, a rat!' . . . *Hamlet* iv 1 10
That drop of blood that's calm proclaims me bastard, Cries cuckold to my father . . . . iv 5 118
This quarry cries on havoc . . . . v 2 375
He raised the house with loud and coward cries . . . *Lear* ii 4 43
Hopdance cries in Tom's belly for two white herring . . . iii 6 32
The affair cries haste, And speed must answer it . . *Othello* i 3 277
Who's there? whose noise is this that cries on murder? . . . v 1 48
Spurns The rush that lies before him; cries, 'Fool Lepidus!' *Ant. and Cleo.* iii 5 18
Laughs from's free lungs, cries 'O, Can my sides hold?' . *Cymbeline* i 6 68
Poor souls, it grieved my heart to hear what pitiful cries they made to us to help them . . . . *Pericles* ii 1 22

Cries aloud 'Tarry, dear cousin Suffolk!' . . . *Hen. V.* iv 6 15
And I am sent to tell his majesty That even now he cries aloud for him 2 *Hen. VI.* iii 2 378
Romeo he cries aloud, 'Hold, friends! friends, part!' . *Rom. and Jul.* iii 1 169

Cries out. The very mercy of the law cries out Most audible *Meas. for Meas.* v 1 412
As 'twere, outfacing me, Cries out, I was possess'd . *Com. of Errors* v 1 245
Why, who cries out on pride, That can therein tax any private party? *As Y. Like It* ii 7 70
O, and there Where honourable rescue and defence Cries out! *K. John* v 2 19
For wisdom cries out in the streets, and no man regards it 1 *Hen. IV.* i 2 99
Cries out upon abuses, seems to weep Over his country's wrongs . . iv 3 81
Let us meet them like necessities: And that same word even now cries out on us . . . . 2 *Hen. IV.* iii 1 94
Who, ring'd about with bold adversity, Cries out for noble York and Somerset . . . . 1 *Hen. VI.* iv 4 15
Hark, how Troy roars! how Hecuba cries out! . . *Troi. and Cres.* v 3 83
Art thou a man? thy form cries out thou art . . *Rom. and Jul.* iii 3 109
My fate cries out, And makes each petty artery in this body As hardy as the Nemean lion's nerve . . . . *Hamlet* i 4 81
As they pinch one another by the disposition, he cries out 'No more' *Ant. and Cleo.* ii 7 8

Criest now 'O earth, yield us that king again, And take thou this!' 2 *Hen. IV.* i 3 106
Whiles thou, a moral fool, sit'st still, and criest 'Alack, why does he so?' *Lear* iv 2 58

Crime. As you from crimes would pardon'd be, Let your indulgence set me free . . . . *Tempest* Epil. 19
And I for such like petty crimes as these . . *T. G. of Ver.* iv 1 52
Make me know The nature of their crimes, that I may minister To them *Meas. for Meas.* ii 3 7
How may likeness made in crimes, Making practice on the times . . iii 2 287
My blood is mingled with the crime of lust . . *Com. of Errors* ii 2 143
So it is sometimes, Glory grows guilty of detested crimes . *L. L. Lost* iv 1 31
Our crimes would despair, if they were not cherished by our virtues *All's Well* iv 3 86
Impute it not a crime To me or my swift passage . . *W. Tale* iv 1 4
And these grievous crimes Committed by your person . *Richard II.* iv 1 223
How shall we stretch our eye When capital crimes, chew'd, swallow'd and digested, Appear before us? . . . . . . *Hen. V.* ii 2 56
If his cause be wrong, our obedience to the king wipes the crime of it out of us . . . . iv 1 139
In writing I preferr'd The manner of thy vile outrageous crimes 1 *Hen. VI.* iii 1 11
But mightier crimes are laid unto your charge . . 2 *Hen. VI.* iii 1 134
Who is man that is not angry? Weigh but the crime with this *T. of Athens* iii 5 58

Crime. If by this crime he owes the law his life, Why, let the war receive't in valiant gore . . . . . . *T. of Athens* iii 5 83
Crimes, like lands, Are not inherited . . . . . . v 4 37
I have no relish of them, but abound In the division of each several crime, Acting it many ways . . . . . *Macbeth* iv 3 96
Confined to fast in fires, Till the foul crimes done in my days of nature Are burnt and purged away . . . . . . *Hamlet* i 5 12
Having ever seen in the prenominate crimes The youth you breathe of guilty . . . . ii 1 43
He took my father grossly, full of bread; With all his crimes broad blown, as flush as May . . . . iii 3 81
Every hour He flashes into one gross crime or other . . *Lear* i 3 4
Tremble, thou wretch, That hast within thee undivulged crimes, Unwhipp'd of justice . . . . iii 2 52
You justicers, that these our nether crimes So speedily can venge! . iv 2 79
If you bethink yourself of any crime Unreconciled as yet to heaven *Othello* v 2 26
We commit no crime To use one language in each several clime *Pericles* iv 4 5
Crimeful. These feats, So crimeful and so capital in nature . *Hamlet* iv 7 7
Crimeless. So long as I am loyal, true and crimeless . 2 *Hen. VI.* ii 4 63
Criminal. Being criminal, in double violation Of sacred chastity and of promise-breach . . . . . . *Meas. for Meas.* v 1 409
Which is, indeed, More criminal in thee than it . . *W. Tale* iii 2 90
So criminal and in such capital kind, Deserves the extremest death *Coriolanus* iii 3 81
Crimson. Hoary-headed frosts Fall in the fresh lap of the crimson rose *M. N. Dream* ii 1 108
An innocent hand, Not painted with the crimson spots of blood *K. John* iv 2 253
Such crimson tempest should bedrench The fresh green lap of fair King Richard's land . . . . . *Richard II.* iii 3 46
I will fetch thy rim out at thy throat In drops of crimson blood *Hen. V.* iv 4 16
A maid yet rosed over with the virgin crimson of modesty . . v 2 323
Before his chaps be stain'd with crimson blood . . 2 *Hen. VI.* iii 1 259
That slanders me with murder's crimson badge . . . . iii 2 200
A crimson river of warm blood . . . . . *T. Andron.* ii 4 22
Witness this wretched stump, witness these crimson lines . . v 2 22
Beauty's ensign yet Is crimson in thy lips and in thy cheeks *Rom. and Jul.* v 3 95
On her left breast A mole cinque-spotted, like the crimson drops I' the bottom of a cowslip . . . . . . *Cymbeline* ii 2 38
Crimsoned. Here thy hunters stand, Sign'd in thy spoil, and crimson'd in thy lethe . . . . *J. Cæsar* iii 1 206
Cringe. Whip him, fellows, Till, like a boy, you see him cringe his face, And whine aloud for mercy . . . . . *Ant. and Cleo.* iii 13 100
Cripple. Such a hare is madness the youth, to skip o'er the meshes of good counsel the cripple . . . . . *Mer. of Venice* i 2 22
And chide the cripple tardy-gaited night . . *Hen. V.* iv Prol. 20
Would ye not think his cunning to be great, that could restore this cripple? . . . . 2 *Hen. VI.* ii 1 133
Some tardy cripple bore the countermand, That came too lag to see him buried . . . . *Richard III.* ii 1 89
Thou cold sciatica, Cripple our senators, that their limbs may halt As lamely as their manners! . . . . . . *T. of Athens* iv 1 24
Crisp. Leave your crisp channels and on this green land Answer your summons . . . . *Tempest* iv 1 130
And hid his crisp head in the hollow bank . . . 1 *Hen. IV.* i 3 106
With all the abhorred births below crisp heaven . *T. of Athens* iv 3 183
Crisped. Those crisped snaky golden locks . . *Mer. of Venice* iii 2 92
Crispian. This day is call'd the feast of Crispian . . *Hen. V.* iv 3 40
Will stand a tip-toe when this day is named, And rouse him at the name of Crispian . . . . iv 3 43
Will yearly on the vigil feast his neighbours, And say 'To-morrow is Saint Crispian' . . . . iv 3 46
And Crispin Crispian shall ne'er go by, From this day to the ending of the world, But we in it shall be remembered . . . . iv 3 57
Crispianus. Then call we this the field of Agincourt, Fought on the day of Crispin Crispianus . . . . iv 7 94
Crispin. Show his scars, And say 'These wounds I had on Crispin's day' iv 3 48
And Crispin Crispian shall ne'er go by, From this day to the ending of the world, But we in it shall be remembered . . . . iv 3 57
And hold their manhoods cheap whiles any speaks That fought with us upon Saint Crispin's day . . . . iv 3 67
Then call we this the field of Agincourt, Fought on the day of Crispin iv 7 94
Critic. A critic, nay, a night-watch constable . . *L. L. Lost* iii 1 178
Nestor play at push-pin with the boys, And critic Timon laugh at idle toys! . . . . iv 3 170
Do not give advantage To stubborn critics, apt, without a theme *Troi. and Cres.* v 2 131
Critical. That is some satire, keen and critical . . *M. N. Dream* v 1 54
Do not put me to't; For I am nothing, if not critical . *Othello* ii 1 120
Croak. I would croak like a raven; I would bode . *Troi. and Cres.* v 2 191
The raven himself is hoarse That croaks the fatal entrance of Duncan Under my battlements . . . . . . *Macbeth* i 5 40
Croak not, black angel; I have no food for thee . . *Lear* iii 6 33
Croaking. The croaking raven doth bellow for revenge . *Hamlet* iii 2 264
Crocodile. As the mournful crocodile With sorrow snares relenting passengers . . . . 2 *Hen. VI.* iii 1 226
Woo't drink up eisel? eat a crocodile? . . . . . *Hamlet* v 1 299
Each drop she falls would prove a crocodile . . . *Othello* iv 1 257
Your serpent of Egypt is bred now of your mud by the operation of your sun: so is your crocodile . . . . . *Ant. and Cleo.* ii 7 31
What manner o' thing is your crocodile?—It is shaped, sir, like itself . ii 7 46
Cromer. Break into his son-in-law's house, Sir James Cromer 2 *Hen. VI.* iv 7 118
Cromwell. Lord Cromwell of Wingfield . . . . 1 *Hen. VI.* iv 7 66
The packet, Cromwell, Gave't you the king? . . . *Hen. VIII.* iii 2 76
Why, how now, Cromwell!—I have no power to speak, sir . . iii 2 372
Never so truly happy, my good Cromwell. I know myself now . . iii 2 377
Too much honour: O, 'tis a burthen, Cromwell, 'tis a burthen Too heavy for a man that hopes for heaven! . . . . iii 2 384
O Cromwell, The king has gone beyond me . . . . . . iii 2 407
Go, get thee from me, Cromwell; I am a poor fall'n man, unworthy now To be thy lord and master . . . . iii 2 412
Good Cromwell, Neglect him not; make use now, and provide For thine own future safety . . . . iii 2 419
Bear witness, all that have not hearts of iron, With what a sorrow Cromwell leaves his lord . . . . iii 2 425
Cromwell, I did not think to shed a tear In all my miseries . . . iii 2 428
Let's dry our eyes: and thus far hear me, Cromwell . . . . iii 2 431
Cromwell, I charge thee, fling away ambition: By that sin fell the angels iii 2 440
Then if thou fall'st, O Cromwell, Thou fall'st a blessed martyr! . . iii 2 448
O Cromwell, Cromwell! Had I but served my God with half the zeal I served my king . . . . iii 2 454

Cromwell. Thomas Cromwell; A man in much esteem with the king *Hen. VIII.* iv 1 108
Till Cramner, Cromwell, her two hands, and she, Sleep in their graves v 1 31
As for Cromwell, Beside that of the jewel house, is made master O' the rolls, and the king's secretary . . . . v 1 33
Crone. Give't to thy crone . . . . *W. Tale* ii 3 76
Crook. And crook the pregnant hinges of the knee Where thrift may follow fawning . . . . *Hamlet* iii 2 66
Crook-back. Where's that valiant crook-back prodigy, Dicky your boy? 3 *Hen. VI.* i 4 75
Ay, crook-back, here I stand to answer thee, Or any he the proudest of thy sort . . . . ii 2 96
Take away this captive scold.—Nay, take away this scolding crook-back rather . . . . v 5 30
Crooked. If crooked fortune had not thwarted me . . *T. G. of Ver.* iv 1 22
He is deformed, crooked, old and sere . . . *Com. of Errors* iv 2 19
Lame, foolish, crooked, swart, prodigious . . . . *K. John* iii 1 46
And thy unkindness be like crooked age, To crop at once a too long wither'd flower . . . . *Richard II.* ii 1 133
By what by-paths and indirect crook'd ways I met this crown 2 *Hen. IV.* iv 5 185
A crooked figure may Attest in little place a million . . *Hen. V.* Prol. 15
Rather choose to hide them in a net Than amply to imbar their crooked titles . . . . i 2 94
Foul, indigested lump, As crooked in thy manners as thy shape! 2 *Hen. VI.* v 1 158
Then, since the heavens have shaped my body so, Let hell make crook'd my mind to answer it . . . . 3 *Hen. VI.* v 6 79
Men that make Envy and crooked malice nourishment Dare bite the best . . . . *Hen. VIII.* v 3 44
If the drink you give me touch my palate adversely, I make a crooked face at it . . . . *Coriolanus* ii 1 62
There is no moe such Cæsars: other of them may have crook'd noses, but to owe such straight arms, none . . . . *Cymbeline* iii 1 37
Let our crooked smokes climb to their nostrils From our blest altars . v 5 477
Crooked-pated. A crooked-pated, old, cuckoldly ram . *As Y. Like It* iii 2 86
Crook-knee'd, and dew-lapp'd like Thessalian bulls . *M. N. Dream* iv 1 127
Crop. The honey-bags steal from the humble-bees, And for night-tapers crop their waxen thighs . . . . iii 1 172
I shall think it a most plenteous crop To glean the broken ears after the man That the main harvest reaps . . . . *As Y. Like It* iii 5 101
He that ears my land spares my team and gives me leave to in the crop *All's Well* i 3 48
And thy unkindness be like crooked age, To crop at once a too long wither'd flower . . . . *Richard II.* ii 1 134
All the budding honours on thy crest I'll crop, to make a garland for my head . . . . 1 *Hen. IV.* v 4 73
Itches, blains, Sow all the Athenian bosoms; and their crop Be general leprosy! . . . . *T. of Athens* iv 1 29
Hath nature given them eyes To see this vaulted arch, and the rich crop Of sea and land? . . . . *Cymbeline* i 6 33
It is not for any standers-by to curtail his oaths, ha?—No, my lord; nor crop the ears of them . . . . ii 1 14
Valour That wildly grows in them, but yields a crop As if it had been sow'd . . . . iv 2 180
Crop-ear. What horse? a roan, a crop-ear, is it not? . . 1 *Hen. IV.* ii 3 72
Cropped. Bear you well in this new spring of time, Lest you be cropp'd before you come to prime . . . . . . *Richard II.* v 2 51
Cropp'd are the flower-de-luces in your arms; Of England's coat one half is cut away . . . . 1 *Hen. VI.* i 1 80
He upon whose side The fewest roses are cropp'd from the tree Shall yield the other in the right opinion . . . . ii 4 41
How sweet a plant have you untimely cropp'd! . . . 3 *Hen. VI.* v 5 62
That cropp'd the golden prime of this sweet prince . *Richard III.* i 2 248
Must or now be cropp'd, Or, shedding, breed a nursery of like evil, To overbulk us all . . . . *Troi. and Cres.* i 3 318
He plough'd her, and she cropp'd . . . . . *Ant. and Cleo.* ii 2 233
Lest my life be cropp'd to keep you clear, By flight I'll shun the danger which I fear . . . . *Pericles* i 1 141
Crosby Place. And presently repair to Crosby Place . *Richard III.* i 2 213
When you have done, repair to Crosby Place . . . . . i 3 345
At Crosby Place, there shall you find us . . . . . . iii 1 190
Cross. I'll quickly cross By some sly trick blunt Thurio's dull proceeding . . . . *T. G. of Ver.* ii 6 40
For my duty's sake, I rather chose To cross my friend in his intended drift . . . . iii 1 18
I will follow, more to cross that love Than hate for Silvia . . . v 2 55
He would never else cross me thus . . . . . *Mer. Wives* v 5 40
I am that way going to temptation, Where prayers cross *Meas. for Meas.* ii 2 159
I may make my case as Claudio's, to cross this in the smallest . iv 2 178
I will break thy pate across.—And he will bless that cross with other beating . . . . *Com. of Errors* ii 1 79
O, for my beads! I cross me for a sinner . . . . . . ii 2 190
If I can cross him any way, I bless myself every way . . *Much Ado* i 3 70
Claudio shall marry the daughter of Leonato.—Yea, my lord; but I can cross it . . . . ii 2 3
Any bar, any cross, any impediment will be medicinable to me . . ii 2 4
How canst thou cross this marriage?—Not honestly, my lord . . ii 2 8
Give him another staff: this last was broke cross . . . . v 1 139
He speaks the mere contrary; crosses love not him . . *L. L. Lost* i 2 36
We cannot cross the cause why we were born . . . . . iv 3 218
The effect of my intent is to cross theirs . . . . . . v 2 138
O cross! too high to be enthrall'd to low . . . . *M. N. Dream* i 1 136
Let us teach our trial patience, Because it is a customary cross . . i 1 153
Why should Titania cross her Oberon? . . . . ii 1 119
And never dare misfortune cross her foot . . . *Mer. of Venice* ii 4 36
Let me say 'amen' betimes, lest the devil cross my prayer . . . iii 1 23
She doth stray about By holy crosses, where she kneels and prays . v 1 31
I should bear no cross if I did bear you, for I think you have no money in your purse . . . . *As Y. Like It* ii 4 12
You and you no cross shall part: You and you are heart in heart . . v 4 137
When did she cross thee with a bitter word? . . . *T. of Shrew* ii 1 28
Nor hast thou pleasure to be cross in talk . . . . . . ii 1 251
We are on the earth, Where nothing lives but crosses, cares and grief *Richard II.* ii 2 79
Streaming the ensign of the Christian cross Against black pagans . . iv 1 94
You Pilates Have here deliver'd me to my sour cross . . . . iv 1 241
Under whose blessed cross We are impressed and engaged to fight 1 *Hen. IV.* i 1 20
Those blessed feet Which fourteen hundred years ago were nail'd For our advantage on the bitter cross . . . . i 1 27

Cross. Send danger from the east unto the west, So honour cross it from the north to south — 1 *Hen. IV.* i 3 196
And swore the devil his true liegeman upon the cross of a Welsh hook — ii 4 372
How you cross my father!—I cannot choose — iii 1 147
Curbs himself even of his natural scope When you come 'cross his humour — iii 1 172
You are too impatient to bear crosses — 2 *Hen. IV.* i 2 253
What perils past, what crosses to ensue — iii 1 55
Now will it best avail your majesty To cross the seas — 1 *Hen. VI.* iii 1 180
Whiles they each other cross, Lives, honours, lands and all hurry to loss — iv 3 52
That Lady Margaret do vouchsafe to come To cross the seas to England — v 5 90
I charge thee waft me safely cross the Channel — 2 *Hen. VI.* iv 1 114
And then to Brittany I'll cross the sea — 3 *Hen. VI.* ii 6 97
That from his loins no hopeful branch may spring, To cross me from the golden time I look for! — iii 2 127
Thou and Oxford, with five thousand men, Shall cross the seas — iii 3 235
That makes me bridle passion And bear with mildness my misfortune's cross — iv 4 20
And was embark'd to cross to Burgundy — *Richard III.* i 4 10
Our crosses on the way Have made it tedious, wearisome, and heavy — iii 1 4
My Lord of York will still be cross in talk — iii 1 126
If thou wilt outstrip death, go cross the seas — iv 1 42
What cross devil Made me put this main secret in the packet? — *Hen. VIII.* iii 2 214
Who dare cross 'em, Bearing the king's will from his mouth expressly? — iii 2 234
If You had not show'd them how ye were disposed Ere they lack'd power to cross you — *Coriolanus* iii 2 23
Bassianus comes: Be cross with him — *T. Andron.* ii 3 53
My state, Which, well thou know'st, is cross and full of sin — *Rom. and Jul.* iv 3 5
What cursed foot wanders this way to-night, To cross my obsequies? — v 3 20
The cross blue lightning seem'd to open The breast of heaven — *J. Cæsar* i 3 50
Why do you cross me in this exigent?—I do not cross you; but I will do so — v 1 19
Lo, where it comes again! I'll cross it, though it blast me — *Hamlet* i 1 127
In the most terrible and nimble stroke Of quick, cross lightning — *Lear* iv 7 35
I am old now, And these same crosses spoil me — v 3 278
In each thing give him way, cross him in nothing — *Ant. and Cleo.* i 3 9
Whom best I love I cross; to make my gift, The more delay'd, delighted — *Cymbeline* v 4 101
After all my crosses, Thou givest me somewhat to repair myself — *Pericles* ii 1 127
His queen with child makes her desire—Which who shall cross? — iii Gower 41
She died at night; I'll say so. Who can cross it? — iv 3 16
It is not good to cross him; give him way — v 1 232
To mourn thy crosses, with thy daughter's, call And give them repetition to the life — v 1 246
Cross-bow. The master of the cross-bows, Lord Rambures — *Hen. V.* iv 8 99
The noise of thy cross-bow Will scare the herd, and so my shoot is lost — 3 *Hen. VI.* iii 1 6
Crossed. How young Leander cross'd the Hellespont — *T. G. of Ver.* i 1 22
I have little wealth to lose: A man I am cross'd with adversity — iv 1 12
Sure, one of you does not serve heaven well, that you are so crossed — *Mer. Wives* iv 5 130
I love not to be crossed — *L. L. Lost* i 2 34
With your arms crossed on your thin-belly doublet like a rabbit on a spit — iii 1 19
If then true lovers have been ever cross'd, It stands as an edict in destiny — *M. N. Dream* i 1 150
But hadst thou not crossed me, thou shouldst have heard — *T. of Shrew* iv 1 75
Evermore cross'd and cross'd; nothing but cross'd! — iv 5 10
Your precious self had then not cross'd the eyes Of my young play-fellow — *W. Tale* i 2 79
We have cross'd, To execute the charge my father gave me — v 1 161
Lest that their hopes prodigiously be cross'd — *K. John* iii 1 91
What chance is this that suddenly hath cross'd us? — 1 *Hen. VI.* i 4 72
When all's spent, he'ld be cross'd then, an he could — *T. of Athens* i 2 168
The devil knew not what he did when he made man politic; he crossed himself by't — iii 3 29
Being cross'd in conference by some senators — *J. Cæsar* i 2 188
How 'scaped I killing when I cross'd you so? — iv 3 150
How you were borne in hand, how cross'd, the instruments — *Macbeth* iii 1 81
I cross'd the seas on purpose and on promise To see your grace *Cymbeline* i 6 202
Leave not the worthy Lucius, good my lords, Till he have cross'd the Severn — iii 5 17
This fool's speed Be cross'd with slowness; labour be his meed! — iii 5 168
The legions garrison'd in Gallia, After your will, have cross'd the sea — iv 2 334
Crossest. What is thy name, that in the battle thus Thou crossest me? — 1 *Hen. IV.* v 3 2
Cross-gartered. Remember who commended thy yellow stockings, and wished to see thee ever cross-gartered — *T. Night* ii 5 167
She did praise my leg being cross-gartered — ii 5 182
I will be strange, stout, in yellow stockings, and cross-gartered — ii 5 186
'Tis a colour she abhors, and cross-gartered, a fashion she detests — ii 5 220
He's in yellow stockings.—And cross-gartered?—Most villanously — iii 2 79
And wished to see thee cross-gartered.—Cross-gartered! — iii 4 55
Cross-gartering. This does make some obstruction in the blood, this cross-gartering — iii 4 22
Crossing. It is true, without any slips of prolixity or crossing the plain highway of talk — *Mer. of Venice* iii 1 13
Look, what I speak, or do, or think to do, You are still crossing it — *T. of Shrew* iv 3 195
Of many men I do not bear these crossings — 1 *Hen. IV.* iii 1 36
Crossing the sea from England into France — 1 *Hen. VI.* iv 1 89
The heavens do lour upon you for some ill; Move them no more by crossing their high will — *Rom. and Jul.* iv 5 95
There is no crossing him in's humour — *T. of Athens* i 2 166
Crossly to thy good all fortune goes — *Richard II.* ii 4 24
Crossness. She will die, if he woo her, rather than she will bate one breath of her accustomed crossness — *Much Ado* ii 3 184
Cross-row. From the cross-row plucks the letter G, And says a wizard told him that by G His issue disinherited should be — *Richard III.* i 1 55
Crossway. Damned spirits all, That in crossways and floods have burial — *M. N. Dream* iii 2 383
Crost. If my fortune be not crost, I have a father, you a daughter, lost — *Mer. of Venice* ii 5 56
Crotchet. Faith, thou hast some crotchets in thy head — *Mer. Wives* ii 1 159
The duke had crotchets in him — *Meas. for Meas.* iii 2 135
Why, these are very crotchets that he speaks — *Much Ado* ii 3 58

Crotchet. I will carry no crotchets: I'll re you, I'll fa you; do you note me? — *Rom. and Jul.* iv 5 120
Crouch. To crouch in litter of your stable planks — *K. John* v 2 140
Should famine, sword and fire Crouch for employment — *Hen. V.* Prol. 8
Must I stand and crouch Under your testy humour? — *J. Cæsar* iv 3 45
Crouching. Now the time is flush, When crouching marrow in the bearer strong Cries of itself 'No more' — *T. of Athens* v 4 9
Crow. For a good wager, first begins to crow — *Tempest* ii 1 29
You were wont, when you laughed, to crow like a cock — *T. G. of Ver.* ii 1 28
Go borrow me a crow.—A crow without feather? — *Com. of Errors* iii 1 80
If a crow help us in, sirrah, we'll pluck a crow together — iii 1 83
Go get thee gone; fetch me an iron crow — iii 1 84
I had rather hear my dog bark at a crow than a man swear he loves me — *Much Ado* i 1 133
And crows are fatted with the murrion flock — *M. N. Dream* ii 1 97
And look thou meet me ere the first cock crow — ii 1 267
High Taurus' snow, Fann'd with the eastern wind, turns to a crow When thou hold'st up thy hand — iii 2 142
The crow doth sing as sweetly as the lark When neither is attended — *Mer. of Venice* v 1 102
My lungs began to crow like chanticleer — *As Y. Like It* ii 7 30
You crow too like a craven — *T. of Shrew* ii 1 228
What's he?—E'en a crow o' the same nest — *All's Well* iv 3 319
I take these wise men, that crow so at these set kind of fools, no better than the fools' zanies — *T. Night* i 5 95
The casting forth to crows thy baby-daughter — *W. Tale* iii 2 192
Lawn as white as driven snow; Cyprus black as e'er was crow — iv 4 221
To thrill and shake Even at the crying of your nation's crow — *K. John* v 2 144
He'll yield the crow a pudding one of these days — *Hen. V.* ii 1 91
The country cocks do crow, the clocks do toll — iv Prol. 15
Their executors, the knavish crows, Fly o'er them, all impatient for their hour — iv 2 51
Leaving thy trunk for crows to feed upon — 2 *Hen. VI.* iv 10 90
And made a prey for carrion kites and crows Even of the bonny beast he loved so well — v 2 11
The eagles are gone: crows and daws, crows and daws! — *Troi. and Cres.* i 2 265
The busy day, Waked by the lark, hath roused the ribald crows — iv 2 9
Bring in The crows to peck the eagles — *Coriolanus* iii 1 139
I' the city of kites and crows — iv 5 45
I will make thee think thy swan a crow — *Rom. and Jul.* i 2 92
So shows a snowy dove trooping with crows, As yonder lady o'er her fellows shows — i 5 50
Get me an iron crow, and bring it straight Unto my cell — v 2 21
Ravens, crows and kites, Fly o'er our heads and downward look on us — *J. Cæsar* v 1 85
Light thickens; and the crow Makes wing to the rooky wood — *Macbeth* iii 2 50
The crows and choughs that wing the midway air Show scarce so gross as beetles — *Lear* iv 6 13
Thou shouldst have made him As little as a crow, or less, ere left To after-eye him — *Cymbeline* i 3 15
You are cock and capon too; and you crow, cock, with your comb on — ii 1 26
If you fall in the adventure, our crows shall fare the better for you — iii 1 83
Consider, When you above perceive me like a crow, That it is place which lessens and sets off — iii 3 12
A leg of Rome shall not return to tell What crows have peck'd them here — v 3 93
So With the dove of Paphos might the crow Vie feathers white — *Pericles* iv Gower 32
Crowd. And in obsequious fondness Crowd to his presence — *M. for M.* ii 4 29
The time misorder'd doth, in common sense, Crowd us and crush us to this monstrous form — 2 *Hen. IV.* iv 2 34
Where have you been broiling?—Among the crowd i' the Abbey — *Hen. VIII.* iv 1 57
Will crowd a feeble man almost to death — *J. Cæsar* ii 4 36
Crowded. A man into whom nature hath so crowded humours that his valour is crushed into folly — *Troi. and Cres.* i 2 23
Crowding. He burst his head for crowding among the marshal's men — 2 *Hen. IV.* iii 2 347
The poor mechanic porters crowding in Their heavy burdens — *Hen. V.* i 2 200
Crowed. The second cock hath crow'd, The curfew-bell hath rung — *Rom. and Jul.* iv 4 3
Crow-flower. There with fantastic garlands did she come Of crow-flowers, nettles, daisies, and long purples — *Hamlet* iv 7 170
Crowing as if he had writ man ever since his father was a bachelor — 2 *Hen. IV.* i 2 30
It faded on the crowing of the cock — *Hamlet* i 1 157
Crow-keeper. Scaring the ladies like a crow-keeper — *Rom. and Jul.* i 4 6
That fellow handles his bow like a crow-keeper: draw me a clothier's yard — *Lear* iv 6 88
Crown. Subject his coronet to his crown and bend The dukedom — *Tempest* i 2 114
My strong imagination sees a crown Dropping upon thy head — ii 1 208
And crown what I profess with kind event If I speak true! — iii 1 69
Which spongy April at thy hest betrims, To make cold nymphs chaste crowns — iv 1 66
And with each end of thy blue bow dost crown My bosky acres — iv 1 80
With your sedged crowns and ever-harmless looks — iv 1 129
From toe to crown he'll fill our skins with pinches, Make us strange stuff — iv 1 233
Look down, you gods, And on this couple drop a blessed crown! — v 1 202
Three thousand dolours a year.—Ay, and more.—A French crown more — *Meas. for Meas.* i 2 52
Not the king's crown, nor the deputed sword — ii 2 60
Against our laws, Against my crown, my oath, my dignity *Com. of Errors* i 1 144
From the crown of his head to the sole of his foot, he is all mirth — *Much Ado* iii 2 9
Madam, your father here doth intimate The payment of a hundred thousand crowns — *L. L. Lost* ii 1 130
For here he doth demand to have repaid A hundred thousand crowns — ii 1 144
And not demands, On payment of a hundred thousand crowns, To have his title live in Aquitaine — ii 1 145
Remuneration! why, it is a fairer name than French crown — iii 1 142
Some of your French crowns have no hair at all — *M. N. Dream* i 2 99
Crowns him with flowers and makes him all her joy — ii 1 27
On old Hiems' thin and icy crown An odorous chaplet of sweet summer buds — ii 1 109
It [mercy] becomes The throned monarch better than his crown — *Mer. of Venice* iv 1 189
Bequeathed me by will but poor a thousand crowns — *As Y. Like It* i 1 3
I will physic your rankness, and yet give no thousand crowns neither — i 1 92
I have five hundred crowns, The thrifty hire I saved under your father — ii 3 38

Crown. Wedding is great Juno's crown . . . *As Y. Like It* v 4 147

His crown bequeathing to his banish'd brother . . . v 4 169

Crowns in my purse I have and goods at home . . . *T. of Shrew* i 2 57

The one half of my lands, And in possession twenty thousand crowns . ii 1 123

In ivory coffers I have stuff'd my crowns . . . ii 1 352

What is the wager?—Twenty crowns.—Twenty crowns! v 2 70

And I will add Unto their losses twenty thousand crowns v 2 113

The wisdom of your duty, fair Bianca, Hath cost me an hundred crowns v 2 128

As fit as ten groats is for the hand of an attorney, as your French crown for your taffeta punk . . . *All's Well* ii 2 23

To marry her, I'll add three thousand crowns To what is past already iii 7 35

The fine's the crown; Whate'er the course, the end is the renown iv 4 35

And crown thee for a finder of madmen . . . *T. Night* iii 4 154

One day shall crown the alliance on't, so please you, Here at my house v 1 326

There is a plot against my life, my crown; All's true that is mistrusted *W. Tale* ii 1 47

The crown and comfort of my life, your favour, I do give lost iii 2 95

Each your doing, So singular in each particular, Crowns what you are doing in the present deed . . . iv 4 145

The crown will find an heir: great Alexander Left his to the worthiest v 1 47

There might you have beheld one joy crown another . . . v 2 48

And done a rape Upon the maiden virtue of the crown . . . *K. John* ii 1 98

How comes it then that thou art call'd a king, When living blood doth in these temples beat, Which owe the crown that thou o'ermasterest? . . . ii 1 109

Doth not the crown of England prove the king? . . . ii 1 273

By this knot thou shalt so surely tie Thy now unsured assurance to the crown . . . ii 1 471

Find liable to our crown and dignity . . . ii 1 490

For then I should not love thee, no, nor thou Become thy great birth nor deserve a crown . . . iii 1 50

That, ere the next Ascension-day at noon, Your highness should deliver up your crown . . . iv 2 152

And on that day at noon, whereon he says I shall yield up my crown, let him be hang'd . . . iv 2 157

Did not the prophet Say that before Ascension-day at noon My crown I should give off? . . . v 1 27

Have I not here the best cards for the game, To win this easy match play'd for a crown? . . . v 2 106

Until the heavens, envying earth's good hap, Add an immortal title to your crown . . . *Richard II.* i 1 24

A thousand flatterers sit within thy crown, Whose compass is no bigger than thy head . . . ii 1 100

Redeem from broking pawn the blemish'd crown . . . ii 1 293

To lift shrewd steel against our golden crown . . . iii 2 59

And clap their female joints In stiff unwieldy arms against thy crown . iii 2 115

Within the hollow crown That rounds the mortal temples of a king Keeps Death his court . . . iii 2 160

And threat the glory of my precious crown . . . iii 3 90

But ere the crown he looks for live in peace, Ten thousand bloody crowns of mothers' sons Shall ill become the flower of England's face iii 3 95

Had he done so, himself had borne the crown . . . iii 4 65

You say that you had rather refuse The offer of an hundred thousand crowns . . . iv 1 16

And if you crown him, let me prophesy: The blood of English shall manure the ground . . . iv 1 136

The resignation of thy state and crown To Henry Bolingbroke . . . iv 1 179

Give me the crown. Here, cousin, seize the crown . . . iv 1 181

Now is this golden crown like a deep well That owes two buckets . iv 1 184

I thought you had been willing to resign.—My crown I am; but still my griefs are mine . . . iv 1 191

Part of your cares you give me with your crown . . . iv 1 194

The cares I give I have, though given away; They tend the crown, yet still with me they stay . . . iv 1 199

Are you contented to resign the crown?—Ay, no; no, ay . . . iv 1 200

With mine own hands I give away my crown . . . iv 1 208

Our holy lives must win a new world's crown . . . v 1 24

Bad men, you violate A twofold marriage, 'twixt my crown and me . v 1 72

If you will go, I will stuff your purses full of crowns . *1 Hen. IV.* i 2 147

Proclaim my brother Edmund Mortimer Heir to the crown . . . i 3 157

You, that set the crown Upon the head of this forgetful man . . . i 3 160

We must have bloody noses and crack'd crowns, And pass them current . ii 3 96

This chair shall be my state, this dagger my sceptre, and this cushion my crown . . . ii 4 417

Thy state is taken for a joined-stool, thy golden sceptre for a leaden dagger, and thy precious rich crown for a pitiful bald crown! . ii 4 420

On your eyelids crown the god of sleep, Charming your blood . . . iii 1 217

Opinion, that did help me to the crown, Had still kept loyal to possession iii 2 42

A crown's worth of good interpretation . . . *2 Hen. IV.* ii 2 99

Die men like dogs! give crowns like pins! . . . ii 4 188

Then happy low, lie down! Uneasy lies the head that wears a crown . iii 1 31

Here's four Harry ten shillings in French crowns for you . . . iii 2 237

Set me the crown upon my pillow here . . . iv 5 5

Why doth the crown lie there upon his pillow, Being so troublesome a bedfellow? . . . iv 5 21

My due from thee is this imperial crown . . . iv 5 41

Where is the crown? who took it from my pillow? . . . iv 5 58

But wherefore did he take away the crown? . . . iv 5 89

There is your crown; And He that wears the crown immortally Long guard it yours! . . . iv 5 143

I spake unto this crown as having sense, And thus upbraided it . . . iv 5 158

God knows, my son, By what by-paths and indirect crook'd ways I met this crown . . . iv 5 186

How I came by the crown, O God forgive; And grant it may with thee in true peace live! . . . iv 5 219

Certain dukedoms And generally to the crown and seat of France *Hen. V.* i 1 88

Make claim and title to the crown of France . . . i 2 68

Could not keep quiet in his conscience, Wearing the crown of France . i 2 80

The line of Charles the Great Was re-united to the crown of France . i 2 85

By God's grace, play a set Shall strike his father's crown into the hazard i 2 263

A nest of hollow bosoms, which he fills With treacherous crowns . ii Prol. 22

This man Hath, for a few light crowns, lightly conspired . . . ii 2 89

The crown And all wide-stretched honours that pertain By custom and the ordinance of times Unto the crown of France . . . ii 4 81

He bids you then resign Your crown and kingdom, indirectly held From him . . . ii 4 94

For if you hide the crown Even in your hearts, there will he rake for it ii 4 97

And bids you, in the bowels of the Lord, Deliver up the crown . . . ii 4 103

The French may lay twenty French crowns to one, they will beat us . iv 1 243

It is no English treason to cut French crowns . . . iv 1 245

Crown. O, not to-day, think not upon the fault My father made in compassing the crown! . . . *Hen. V.* iv 1 311

His passport shall be made And crowns for convoy put into his purse . iv 3 37

Owy, cuppele gorge, permafoy, Peasant, unless thou give me crowns, brave crowns . . . iv 4 40

And for his ransom he will give you two hundred crowns . . . iv 4 49

Tell him my fury shall abate, and I The crowns will take . . . iv 4 51

Fill this glove with crowns, And give it to this fellow . . . iv 8 61

Give him the crowns: And, captain, you must needs be friends with him iv 8 64

Thou wouldst think I had sold my farm to buy my crown . . . v 2 129

His crown shall be the ransom of my friend . . . *1 Hen. VI.* i 1 150

And would have armour here out of the Tower, To crown himself king . i 3 68

'Tis Joan, not we, by whom the day is won; For which I will divide my crown with her . . . i 6 18

What a scandal is it to our crown, That two such noble peers as ye should jar! . . . iii 1 69

Lord bishop, set the crown upon his head . . . iv 1 1

As well they may upbraid me with my crown, Because, forsooth, the king of Scots is crown'd . . . iv 1 156

If once he come to be a cardinal, He'll make his cap co-equal with the crown . . . v 1 33

Put a golden sceptre in thy hand And set a precious crown upon thy head v 3 119

You shall become true liegemen to his crown . . . v 4 128

Never to disobey Nor be rebellious to the crown of England, Thou, nor thy nobles, to the crown of England . . . v 4 171

Espouse the Lady Margaret . . . and crown her Queen of England *2 Hen. VI.* i 1 48

He is the next of blood, And heir apparent to the English crown . i 1 152

And, when I spy advantage, claim the crown, For that's the golden mark I seek to hit . . . i 1 242

Whose church-like humours fits not for a crown . . . i 1 247

And, force perforce, I'll make him yield the crown . . . i 1 258

Saying that the Duke of York was rightful heir to the crown . . . i 3 30

Carry him to Rome, And set the triple crown upon his head . . . i 3 66

That Richard Duke of York was rightful heir unto the English crown . i 3 187

Thine eyes and thoughts Beat on a crown, the treasure of thy heart . ii 1 20

Now, by God's mother, priest, I'll shave your crown for this . . . ii 1 51

Craving your opinion of my title, Which is infallible, to England's crown ii 2 5

Thus got the house of Lancaster the crown.—Which now they hold by force . . . ii 2 29

The third son, Duke of Clarence, from whose line I claim the crown . ii 2 35

Edmund, in the reign of Bolingbroke, As I have read, laid claim unto the crown . . . ii 2 40

My mother, being heir unto the crown, Married Richard Earl of Cambridge . . . ii 2 44

Henry doth claim the crown from John of Gaunt . . . ii 2 54

In this private plot be we the first That shall salute our rightful sovereign With honour of his birthright to the crown . . . ii 2 62

A thousand crowns, or else lay down your head . . . iv 1 16

What, think you much to pay two thousand crowns, And bear the name and port of gentlemen? . . . iv 1 18

The house of York, thrust from the crown By shameful murder of a guiltless king . . . iv 1 94

In time to come, I hope to reign; For I am rightful heir unto the crown iv 2 139

Henry the Fifth, in whose time boys went to span-counter for French crowns . . . iv 2 166

Calls your grace usurper openly And vows to crown himself in Westminster . . . iv 4 31

Contrary to the king, his crown and dignity, thou hast built a paper-mill iv 7 40

He that brings his head unto the king Shall have a thousand crowns . iv 8 70

Ah, villain, thou wilt betray me, and get a thousand crowns of the king iv 10 29

And pluck the crown from feeble Henry's head . . . v 1 2

That head of thine doth not become a crown . . . v 1 96

I arrest thee, York, Of capital treason 'gainst the king and crown . v 1 107

Then, nobly, York; 'tis for a crown thou fight'st . . . v 2 16

Resolve thee, Richard; claim the English crown . . . *3 Hen. VI.* i 1 49

Belike he means, Back'd by the power of Warwick, that false peer, To aspire unto the crown . . . i 1 53

Thy father was a traitor to the crown.—Exeter, thou art a traitor to the crown . . . i 1 79

Will you we show our title to the crown? . . . i 1 102

What title hast thou, traitor, to the crown? . . . i 1 104

Father, tear the crown from the usurper's head . . . i 1 114

Henry the Fourth by conquest got the crown.—'Twas by rebellion . i 1 132

Richard, in the view of many lords, Resign'd the crown to Henry the Fourth . . . i 1 139

He rose against him, being his sovereign, And made him to resign his crown . . . i 1 142

Suppose, my lords, he did it unconstrain'd, Think you 'twere prejudicial to his crown? . . . i 1 144

He could not so resign his crown But that the next heir should succeed i 1 145

Henry of Lancaster, resign thy crown . . . i 1 164

Confirm the crown to me and to mine heirs, And thou shalt reign in quiet . . . i 1 172

I here entail The crown to thee and to thine heirs for ever . . . i 1 195

To entail him and his heirs unto the crown, What is it, but to make thy sepulchre And creep into it far before thy time? . . . i 1 235

That hateful duke, Whose haughty spirit, winged with desire, Will cost my crown . . . i 1 268

The crown of England, father, which is yours.—Mine, boy? not till King Henry be dead . . . i 2 9

Do but think How sweet a thing it is to wear a crown . . . i 2 29

A crown, or else a glorious tomb! A sceptre, or an earthly sepulchre! i 4 16

York cannot speak, unless he wear a crown. A crown for York! . . i 4 93

Off with the crown; and, with the crown, his head . . . i 4 107

There, take the crown, and, with the crown, my curse . . . i 4 164

Yonder's the head of that arch-enemy That sought to be encompass'd with your crown . . . ii 2 3

Ambitious York did level at thy crown, Thou smiling while he knit his angry brows . . . ii 2 19

Draw thy sword in right.—My gracious father, by your kingly leave, I'll draw it as apparent to the crown . . . ii 2 64

You, that are king, though he do wear the crown . . . ii 2 90

What say'st thou, Henry, wilt thou yield the crown? . . . ii 2 101

A thousand men have broke their fasts to-day, That ne'er shall dine unless thou yield the crown . . . ii 2 128

A wisp of straw were worth a thousand crowns, To make this shameless callet know herself . . . ii 2 144

And heap'd sedition on his crown at home . . . ii 2 158

This man, whom hand to hand I slew in fight, May be possessed with some store of crowns . . . ii 5 57

Crown. But, if thou be a king, where is thy crown? 3 *Hen. VI.* iii 1 61
My crown is in my heart, not on my head . iii 1 62
My crown is called content: A crown it is that seldom kings enjoy iii 1 64
If you be a king crown'd with content, Your crown content and you must be contented To go along with us iii 1 67
So do I wish the crown, being so far off; And so I chide the means that keeps me from it . . . . . iii 2 140
O miserable thought! and more unlikely Than to accomplish twenty golden crowns! . . . . . . iii 2 152
I'll make my heaven to dream upon the crown . . . . iii 2 168
Until my mis-shaped trunk that bears this head Be round impaled with a glorious crown . . . . . . iii 2 171
And yet I know not how to get the crown, For many lives stand between me and home . . . . . . iii 2 172
Torment myself to catch the English crown . . . iii 2 179
Can I do this, and cannot get a crown? . . . . iii 2 194
But if your title to the crown be weak, As may appear by Edward's good success, Then 'tis but reason that I be released From giving aid . . . . iii 3 145
Did I impale him with the regal crown? . . . . iii 3 189
I was the chief that raised him to the crown, And I'll be chief to bring him down again . . . . . . iii 3 262
But Henry now shall wear the English crown . . iv 3 49
Lest with my sighs or tears I blast or drown King Edward's fruit, true heir to the English crown . . . . . iv 4 24
He comes towards London, To set the crown once more on Henry's head iv 4 27
Shield thee from Warwick's frown; And pray that I may repossess the crown . . . . iv 5 29
Although my head still wear the crown, I here resign my government to thee . . . . iv 6 23
To whom the heavens in thy nativity Adjudged an olive branch and laurel crown . . . . iv 6 34
His head by nature framed to wear a crown . . . iv 6 72
If Edward repossess the crown, 'Tis like that Richmond with the rest shall down . . . . iv 6 99
Once more I shall interchange My waned state for Henry's regal crown iv 7 4
We now forget Our title to the crown and only claim Our dukedom . iv 7 46
We'll debate By what safe means the crown may be recover'd . iv 7 52
Fearless minds climb soonest unto crowns . . . iv 7 62
Went all afoot in summer's scalding heat, That thou mightst repossess the crown in peace . . . . v 7 19
To fight on Edward's party for the crown *Richard III.* i 3 138
When thou didst crown his warlike brows with paper . i 3 175
My husband lost his life to get the crown . . . ii 4 57
How! wear the garland! dost thou mean the crown? . iii 2 41
I'll have this crown of mine cut from my shoulders Ere I will see the crown so foul misplaced . . . . . . iii 2 43
Tell them how Edward put to death a citizen, Only for saying he would make his son Heir to the crown . . . . . iii 5 78
If all obstacles were cut away, And that my path were even to the crown . . . . iii 7 157
And, by that knot, looks proudly o'er the crown . . iv 3 42
Hidest thou that forehead with a golden crown, Where should be graven, if that right were right, The slaughter of the prince that owed that crown? . . . . iv 4 140
By my George, my garter, and my crown . . . iv 4 366
The crown, usurp'd, disgraced his kingly glory . . iv 4 371
He makes for England, there to claim the crown.—Is the chair empty? iv 4 469
The first was I that help'd thee to the crown . . v 3 167
Nor call'd upon For high feats done to the crown . *Hen. VIII.* i 1 61
How grounded he his title to the crown, Upon our fail? . . i 2 144
I myself Would for Carnarvonshire, although there 'long'd No more to the crown but that . . . . ii 3 49
And with his deed did crown His word upon you . . iii 2 155
She had all the royal makings of a queen; As holy oil, Edward Confessor's crown, The rod, and bird of peace . . . . iv 1 88
Many days shall see her, And yet no day without a deed to crown it . v 5 59
Crowns, sceptres, laurels, But by degree, stand in authentic place *Troi. and Cres.* i 3 107
Achilles, whom opinion crowns The sinew and the forehand of our host i 3 142
Who, as Ulysses says, opinion crowns With an imperial voice . i 3 186
Our head shall go bare till merit crown it . . . iii 2 99
'As true as Troilus' shall crown up the verse, And sanctify the numbers iii 2 189
Make Cressid's name the very crown of falsehood, If ever she leave Troilus! . . . . iv 2 106
Whilst some with cunning gild their copper crowns, With truth and plainness I do wear mine bare . . . . . . iv 4 107
The end crowns all . . . . iv 5 224
Now, the gods crown thee!—And live you yet? . . *Coriolanus* ii 1 196
Crown him, and say 'Long live our emperor!' . . *T. Andron.* i 1 229
Mine's three thousand crowns: what's yours? . *T. of Athens* iii 4 28
Five thousand crowns, my lord.—Five thousand drops pays that . iii 4 96
There was a crown offered him: and being offered him, he put it by with the back of his hand . . . . . *J. Cæsar* i 2 220
Was the crown offered him thrice?—Ay, marry, was't, and he put it by thrice . . . . i 2 228
Who offered him the crown?—Why, Antony . . . i 2 232
I saw Mark Antony offer him a crown;—yet 'twas not a crown neither, 'twas one of these coronets . . . . . . i 2 237
Uttered such a deal of stinking breath because Cæsar refused the crown i 2 248
When he perceived the common herd was glad he refused the crown i 2 267
He shall wear his crown by sea and land, In every place, save here in Italy . . . . i 3 87
Crown him?—that;—And then, I grant, we put a sting in him . ii 1 15
The senate have concluded To give this day a crown to mighty Cæsar . ii 2 94
You all did see that on the Lupercal I thrice presented him a kingly crown, Which he did thrice refuse . . . . . iii 2 101
He would not take the crown; Therefore 'tis certain he was not ambitious . . . . iii 2 117
That trusted home Might yet enkindle you unto the crown *Macbeth* i 3 121
If chance will have me king, why, chance may crown me, Without my stir . . . . i 3 143
Fill me from the crown to the toe top-full Of direst cruelty! . . i 5 43
Upon my head they placed a fruitless crown . . . iii 1 61
But now they rise again, With twenty mortal murders on their crowns iii 4 81
Down! Thy crown does sear mine eye-balls . . . iv 1 113
Even now, To crown my thoughts with acts, be it thought and done . iv 1 149
The serpent that did sting thy father's life Now wears his crown *Hamlet* i 5 40
By a brother's hand Of life, of crown, of queen, at once dispatch'd i 5 75
Gives him three thousand crowns in annual fee . . . ii 2 73

Crown. I am still possess'd Of those effects for which I did the murder, My crown, mine own ambition and my queen *Hamlet* iii 3 55
We will our kingdom give, Our crown, our life, and all that we call ours iv 5 208
Richer than that which four successive kings In Denmark's crown have worn . . . . v 2 285
Give me an egg, nuncle, and I'll give thee two crowns.—What two crowns shall they be? . . . . *Lear* i 4 171
After I have cut the egg i' the middle, and eat up the meat, the two crowns of the egg. . . . . i 4 174
When thou clovest thy crown i' the middle, and gavest away both parts, thou borest thy ass on thy back . . . . . i 4 175
Thou hadst little wit in thy bald crown, when thou gavest thy golden one away . . . . i 4 178
Upon the crown o' the cliff, what thing was that Which parted from you? . . . . iv 6 67
King Stephen was a worthy peer, His breeches cost him but a crown *Othello* ii 3 93
Yield up, O love, thy crown and hearted throne To tyrannous hate! . iii 3 448
Tell him, I am prompt To lay my crown at's feet, and there to kneel *Ant. and Cleo.* iii 13 76
How wouldst thou have paid My better service, when my turpitude Thou dost so crown with gold! . . . . iv 6 34
O, see, my women, The crown o' the earth doth melt . . iv 15 63
In his livery Walk'd crowns and crownets . . . . v 2 91
Go fetch My best attires. . . . Bring our crown and all . . v 2 232
Give me my robe, put on my crown; I have Immortal longings in me . v 2 283
Your crown's awry; I'll mend it, and then play . . . v 2 321
O, that husband! My supreme crown of grief! . . *Cymbeline* i 6 4
You are curb'd from that enlargement by The consequence o' the crown ii 3 126
The first of Britain which did put His brows within a golden crown . iii 1 61
She being down, I have the placing of the British crown . . iii 5 65
And in time When she had fitted you with her craft, to work Her son into the adoption of the crown . . . . v 5 56
And crown you king of this day's happiness . . *Pericles* ii 3 11
But, like lesser lights, Did vail their crowns to his supremacy . ii 3 42
You shall like diamonds sit about his crown . . . ii 4 53
The men of Tyrus on the head Of Helicanus would set on The crown of Tyre . . . . iii Gower 28
He, obedient to their dooms, Will take the crown . . . iii Gower 33
I know he will come in our shadow, to scatter his crowns in the sun iv 2 121
A princess To equal any single crown o' the earth I' the justice of compare! . . . . iv 3 8

Crown imperial. Bold oxslips and The crown imperial . *W. Tale* iv 4 126
With crowns imperial, crowns and coronets . . *Hen. V.* ii Prol. 10
The sword, the mace, the crown imperial . . . . iv 1 278

Crowned. The conclusion shall be crowned with your enjoying her *Mer. Wives* iii 5 138
Like coats in heraldry, Due but to one and crowned with one crest *M. N. Dream* iii 2 214
For love is crowned with the prime In spring time . . *As Y. Like It* v 3 33
Though you were crown'd The nonpareil of beauty . . *T. Night* i 5 272
Him will I tear out of that cruel eye, Where he sits crowned in his master's spite . . . . v 1 131
Were I crown'd the most imperial monarch . . . *W. Tale* iv 4 383
With your crown'd brother and these your contracted Heirs of your kingdoms . . . . iv 3 5
Here once again we sit, once again crown'd . . . *K. John* iv 2 1
You were crown'd before, And that high royalty was ne'er pluck'd off . iv 2 4
Anointed, crowned, planted many years . . . *Richard II.* iv 1 127
Even in the presence of the crowned king . . . 1 *Hen. IV.* iii 2 54
And bid the merry bells ring to thine ear That thou art crowned, not that I am dead . . . . 2 *Hen. IV.* iv 5 113
Harry the Fifth is crown'd: up, vanity! Down, royal state! . iv 5 120
As if allegiance in their bosoms sat, Crowned with faith and constant loyalty . . . . *Hen. V.* ii 2 5
On mountain standing, Up in the air, crown'd with the golden sun . iii 4 58
Henry the Sixth, in infant bands crown'd King . . . . Epil. 9
The Dauphin Charles is crowned king in Rheims . . 1 *Hen. VI.* i 1 92
The Dauphin crowned king! all fly to him! . . . . i 1 96
Now will it best avail your majesty To cross the seas and to be crown'd in France . . . . iii 1 180
As well they may upbraid me with my crown, Because, forsooth, the king of Scots is crown'd . . . . iv 1 157
And be crown'd King Henry's faithful and anointed queen . v 5 90
Had his highness in his infancy Crowned in Paris in despite of foes 2 *Hen. VI.* i 1 94
In that chair where kings and queens are crown'd . . . i 2 38
The eldest son and heir of John of Gaunt, Crown'd by the name of Henry the Fourth . . . . ii 2 23
But I am not your king Till I be crown'd. . . . . ii 2 65
Ay me, unhappy! To be a queen, and crown'd with infamy! . . iii 2 71
When I was crown'd I was but nine months old . . 3 *Hen. VI.* i 1 112
But how is it that great Plantagenet Is crown'd so soon? . . i 4 100
Who crown'd the gracious duke in high despite, Laugh'd in his face ii 1 59
Now to London with triumphant march, There to be crowned England's royal king . . . . ii 6 88
Well, if you be a king crown'd with content, Your crown content and you must be contented To go along with us . . . . iii 1 66
Send straight for him; Let him be crown'd . . . *Richard III.* ii 2 98
Forthwith from Ludlow the young prince be fetch'd Hither to London, to be crown'd our king . . . . ii 2 122
Henry the Sixth Was crown'd in Paris but at nine months old . ii 3 17
To-morrow will it please you to be crown'd? . . . . iii 7 242
You must straight to Westminster, There to be crowned Richard's royal queen . . . . iv 1 33
For queen, a very caitiff crown'd with care . . . . iv 4 100
Whose price hath launch'd above a thousand ships, And turn'd crown'd kings to merchants . . . . . *Troi. and Cres.* ii 2 83
Where honour may be crown'd Sole monarch of the universal earth *Rom. and Jul.* iii 2 93
In some sort these wants of mine are crown'd, That I account them blessings . . . . *T. of A.* ii 2 190
Willing misery Outlives incertain pomp, is crown'd before . iv 3 243
And thy saints for aye Be crown'd with plagues that thee alone obey! . v 1 56
He would be crown'd: How that might change his nature, there's the question . . . . *J. Cæsar* ii 1 12
Let him be Cæsar.—Cæsar's better parts Shall be crown'd in Brutus . iii 2 57
Look, whether he have not crown'd dead Cassius! . . . v 3 97
Which fate and metaphysical aid doth seem To have thee crown'd withal *Macbeth* i 5 31

Crowned. So, thanks to all at once and to each one, Whom we invite to see us crown'd at Scone *Macbeth* v 8 75
Crown'd with rank fumiter and furrow-weeds . *Lear* iv 4 3
This grief is crowned with consolation *Ant. and Cleo.* i 2 174
Thou shouldst come like a Fury crown'd with snakes, Not like a formal man . . . . ii 5 40
In thy fats our cares be drown'd, With thy grapes our hairs be crown'd ii 7 123
Thou seem'st a palace For the crown'd Truth to dwell in . *Pericles* v 1 123
Led on by heaven, and crown'd with joy at last . v 3 Gower 90
Crowner. Go thou and seek the crowner, and let him sit o' my coz *T. Night* i 5 142
The crowner hath sat on her, and finds it Christian burial *Hamlet* v 1 4
Is this law?—Ay, marry, is't; crowner's quest law. . v 1 24
Crownet. Sixty and nine, that wore Their crownets regal *Troi. and Cres.* Prol. 6
Whose bosom was my crownet, my chief end . . *Ant. and Cleo.* iv 12 27
In his livery Walk'd crowns and crownets . . . . v 2 91
Crowning. Your part,—I mean, your voice,—for crowning of the king *Richard III.* iii 4 29
Crudy. It [sherris] ascends me into the brain; dries me there all the foolish and dull and crudy vapours 2 *Hen. IV.* iv 3 106
Cruel. Were not you then as cruel as the sentence That you have slander'd so? *Meas. for Meas.* ii 4 109
Shame to him whose cruel striking Kills for faults of his own liking! . iii 2 281
There died this morning of a cruel fever One Ragozine . . iv 3 74
This is that face, thou cruel Angelo, Which once thou sworest was worth the looking on . . . . . . v 1 207
The most lamentable comedy, and most cruel death of Pyramus and Thisby . . . . . . *M. N. Dream* i 2 12
Methought a serpent eat my heart away, And you sat smiling at his cruel prey . . . . ii 2 150
Extremely stretch'd and conn'd with cruel pain . . v 1 80
My creditors grow cruel, my estate is very low *Mer. of Venice* iii 2 318
To do a great right, do a little wrong, And curb this cruel devil of his will . . . . iv 1 217
You have seen cruel proof of this man's strength *As Y. Like It* i 2 184
'Tis a boisterous and a cruel style, A style for challengers . iv 3 31
What a cruel father's he! . . . . *T. of Shrew* i 1 190
And my desires, like fell and cruel hounds, E'er since pursue me *T. Night* i 1 22
Fly away, fly away, breath; I am slain by a fair cruel maid . ii 4 55
Still so cruel?—Still so constant, lord . . . v 1 113
Him will I tear out of that cruel eye . . . v 1 130
This most cruel usage of your queen . . . *W. Tale* ii 3 117
I will devise a death as cruel for thee As thou art tender to't . iv 4 451
If thou didst but consent To this most cruel act, do but despair *K. John* iv 3 126
I do see the cruel pangs of death Right in thine eye . v 4 59
Thou cruel, Ingrateful, savage and inhuman creature! . *Hen. V.* ii 2 94
By cruel fate, And giddy Fortune's furious fickle wheel . . iii 6 28
The cities and the towns defaced By wasting ruin of the cruel foe 1 *Hen. VI.* iii 3 46
Now it is my chance to find thee out, Must I behold thy timeless cruel death? . . . . v 4 5
Kill me with thy sword, And not with such a cruel threatening look 3 *Hen. VI.* i 3 17
And in thy need such comfort come to thee As now I reap at thy too cruel hand! . . . . i 4 166
Clifford, that cruel child-killer . . . . . ii 2 112
His fault was thought, And yet his punishment was cruel death *Richard III.* ii 1 105
But is't not cruel That she should feel the smart of this? *Hen. VIII.* ii 1 165
By virtue of that ring, I take my cause Out of the gripes of cruel men . v 3 100
I'm sure Thou hast a cruel nature and a bloody . . . v 3 129
Ships, Fraught with the ministers and instruments Of cruel war *Troi. and Cres.* Prol. 5
Why should I war without the walls of Troy, That find such cruel battle here within? . . . . i 1 3
Labouring for destiny make cruel way, Through ranks of Greekish youth . . . . v 5 184
To a cruel war I sent him . . . . *Coriolanus* i 3 15
Too modest are you; More cruel to your good report than grateful To us . . . . i 9 54
O cruel, irreligious piety! . . . . *T. Andron.* i 1 130
The cruel father and his traitorous sons . . . . i 1 452
I will be cruel with the maids, and cut off their heads *Rom. and Jul.* i 1 27
And cruel death hath catch'd it from my sight! . . iv 5 48
Detestable death, by thee beguiled, By cruel cruel thee quite overthrown! . . . . iv 5 57
Religious canons, civil laws are cruel . . . *T. of Athens* iv 3 60
O you hard hearts, you cruel men of Rome! . . *J. Cæsar* i 1 41
Beg not your death of us. Though now we must appear bloody and cruel . . . . iii 1 165
There shall I try, In my oration, how the people take The cruel issue of these bloody men . . . . iii 1 294
Our royal master's murder'd!—Woe, alas! What, in our house?—Too cruel any where . . . . . . *Macbeth* ii 3 93
Not confessing Their cruel parricide, filling their hearers With strange invention . . . . iii 1 32
Cruel are the times, when we are traitors And do not know ourselves iv 2 18
The cruel ministers Of this dead butcher . . . v 8 68
Let me be cruel, not unnatural: I will speak daggers to her, but use none . . . . *Hamlet* iii 2 413
I must be cruel, only to be kind: Thus bad begins and worse remains behind . . . . iii 4 178
He wears cruel garters . . . . . *Lear* ii 4 7
I would not see thy cruel nails Pluck out his poor old eyes . iii 7 56
Thou shouldst have said 'Good porter, turn the key,' All cruels else subscribed . . . . iii 7 65
Give me some help! O cruel! O you gods! . . . iii 7 70
I must weep, But they are cruel tears: this sorrow's heavenly *Othello* v 2 21
I that am cruel am yet merciful; I would not have thee linger in thy pain . . . . v 2 86
Moor, she was chaste; she loved thee, cruel Moor . . . v 2 249
I have told him, Lepidus was grown too cruel . *Ant. and Cleo.* iii 6 32
A father cruel, and a step-dame false . . . *Cymbeline* i 6 1
Could not be so cruel to me, as you, O the dearest of creatures, would even renew me with your eyes . . . . . . iii 2 42
Being cruel to the world, concluded Most cruel to herself . . v 5 32
Cruel Cleon, with his wicked wife, Did seek to murder me *Pericles* v 1 173
Cruel-hearted. Yet did not this cruel-hearted cur shed one tear *T. G. of Ver.* ii 3 10
Crueller. Some death more long in spectatorship, and crueller in suffering *Coriolanus* v 2 71
Cruellest. Lady, you are the cruell'st she alive . . *T. Night* i 5 259
Cruelly. Most cruelly Didst thou, Alonso, use me and my daughter *Temp.* v 1 71
I am a man whom fortune hath cruelly scratched . *All's Well* v 2 29
The rather, gentle princess, because I love thee cruelly . *Hen. V.* v 2 216
Pity is the virtue of the law, And none but tyrants use it cruelly *T. of Athens* iii 5 9
Cruelty. Pierced through the heart with your stern cruelty *M. N. Dream* iii 2 59
More strange Than is thy strange apparent cruelty . *Mer. of Venice* iv 1 21
This is no answer, thou unfeeling man, To excuse the current of thy cruelty . . . . iv 1 64
Yet heard too much of Phebe's cruelty . . *As Y. Like It* iv 3 38
Farewell, fair cruelty . . . . . . *T. Night* i 5 307
Get thee to yond same sovereign cruelty . . . . ii 4 83
The youth bears in his visage no great presage of cruelty . iii 2 69
Blessing Against this cruelty fight on thy side, Poor thing, condemn'd to loss! . . . . *W. Tale* ii 3 191
Teaching his duteous land Audacious cruelty . 1 *Hen. IV.* iv 3 45
To brother born an household cruelty, I make my quarrel in particular 2 *Hen. IV.* iv 1 95
When lenity and cruelty play for a kingdom, the gentler gamester is the soonest winner . . . . *Hen. V.* iii 6 119
Thy cruelty in execution Upon offenders hath exceeded law . 2 *Hen. VI.* i 3 135
Soldiers, show what cruelty ye can, That this my death may never be forgot! . . . . iv 1 132
In cruelty will I seek out my fame . . . . v 2 60
'Tis a cruelty To load a falling man . . . *Hen. VIII.* v 3 76
The cruelty and envy of the people, Permitted by our dastard nobles *Coriolanus* iv 5 80
Fill me from the crown to the toe top-full Of direst cruelty! . *Macbeth* i 5 44
To fright you thus, methinks, I am too savage; To do worse to you were fell cruelty . . . . iv 2 71
If there be any cunning cruelty That can torment him much and hold him long, It shall be his . . . . . *Othello* v 2 333
If you seek To lay on me a cruelty, by taking Antony's course *A. and C.* v 2 129
Crum. Go, sir, rub your chain with crums . . *T. Night* ii 3 129
He that keeps nor crust nor crum, Weary of all, shall want some *Lear* i 4 217
Crumble. All my bowels crumble up to dust . . *K. John* v 7 31
Crupper. To pay the saddler for my mistress' crupper *Com. of Errors* i 2 56
A woman's crupper of velure . . . *T. of Shrew* iii 2 61
How I lost my crupper, with many things of worthy memory iv 1 84
Crusadoes. I had rather have lost my purse Full of crusadoes *Othello* iii 4 26
Crush. Then crush this herb into Lysander's eye . *M. N. Dream* iii 2 366
Cut thread and thrum; Quail, crush, conclude, and quell! . v 1 292
And yet, to crush this a little, it would bow to me . *T. Night* ii 5 152
Let nature crush the sides o' the earth together And mar the seeds within! . . . . *W. Tale* iv 4 489
To crush our old limbs in ungentle steel . . 1 *Hen. IV.* v 1 13
The time misorder'd doth, in common sense, Crowd us and crush us to this monstrous form . . . . 2 *Hen. IV.* iv 2 34
That they may crush down with a heavy fall The usurping helmets! *Richard III.* v 3 111
We did our main opinion crush In taint of our best man. *Troi. and Cres.* i 3 373
For where I thought to crush him in an equal force, True sword to sword, I'll potch at him some way Or wrath or craft may get him *Coriolanus* i 10 14
And do you think That his contempt shall not be bruising to you, When he hath power to crush? . . . . ii 3 211
I pray, come and crush a cup of wine . . *Rom. and Jul.* i 2 86
Crush him together rather than unfold His measure duly *Cymbeline* i 1 26
Crushed. Who cannot be crushed with a plot? . . *All's Well* iv 3 360
And have their heads crushed like rotten apples . *Hen. V.* iii 7 155
A man into whom nature hath so crowded humours that his valour is crushed into folly . . . . *Troi. and Cres.* i 2 23
Crushed necessity. Yet that is but a crush'd necessity . *Hen. V.* ii 2 175
Crushest. Now thou crushest the snake! . . . *L. L. Lost* v 1 146
Crushing penury Persuades me I was better when a king . *Richard II.* v 5 34
Crust. She hath no teeth.—I care not for that neither, because I love crusts . . . . *T. G. of Ver.* iii 1 346
Grew so fast That he could gnaw a crust at two hours old *Richard III.* ii 4 28
Of man and beast the infinite malady Crust you quite o'er! *T. of Athens* iii 6 109
A most instant tetter bark'd about, Most lazar-like, with vile and loathsome crust, All my smooth body . . . . . *Hamlet* i 5 72
He that keeps nor crust nor crum, Weary of all, shall want some . *Lear* i 4 217
Crusty. Thou crusty batch of nature, what's the news? *Troi. and Cres.* v 1 5
Crutch. Time goes on crutches till love have all his rites . *Much Ado* ii 1 373
Beauty doth varnish age, as if new-born, And gives the crutch the cradle's infancy . . . . *L. L. Lost* iv 3 245
They that went on crutches ere he was born desire yet their life to see him a man . . . . *W. Tale* i 1 44
If the king had no son, they would desire to live on crutches till he had one i 1 50
Hence, therefore, thou nice crutch! . . . . 2 *Hen IV.* i 1 145
Throws away his crutch Before his legs be firm to bear his body 2 *Hen. VI.* iii 1 189
Till youth take leave and leave you to the crutch . 3 *Hen. VI.* iii 2 35
Death hath snatch'd my husband from mine arms, And pluck'd two crutches from my feeble limbs . . . . . *Richard III.* ii 2 58
To as much end As give a crutch to the dead . . . *Hen. VIII.* i 1 172
Hold him fast: He is thy crutch . . . *Troi. and Cres.* v 3 60
I'll lean upon one crutch and fight with t' other, Ere stay behind *Coriol.* i 1 246
Give me my long sword, ho!—A crutch, a crutch! why call you for a sword?—My sword, I say! . . . . . . *Rom. and Jul.* i 1 83
Son of sixteen, Pluck the lined crutch from thy old limping sire, With it beat out his brains! . . . . *T. of Athens* iv 1 14
I had rather Have skipp'd from sixteen years of age to sixty, To have turn'd my leaping-time into a crutch, Than have seen this *Cymbeline* iv 2 200
Cry. O, the cry did knock Against my very heart! . . *Tempest* i 2 8
Not so much perdition as an hair Betid to any creature in the vessel Which thou heard'st cry . . . . i 2 32
I, not remembering how I cried out then, Will cry it o'er again . i 2 134
There they hoist us, To cry to the sea that roar'd to us . . . i 2 149
For she had a tongue with a tang, Would cry to a sailor, Go hang! ii 2 53
Before you can say 'come' and 'go,' And breathe twice and cry 'so, so' iv 1 45
In a cowslip's bell I lie; There I couch when owls do cry . v 1 90
Such another proof will make me cry 'baa' . *T. G. of Ver.* i 1 97
Alas!—Why dost thou cry 'alas'?—I cannot choose . . iv 4 82
'Tis pity love should be so contrary; And thinking on it makes me cry 'alas!' . . . . iv 4 89
Mercy on me! I have a great dispositions to cry . *Mer. Wives* iii 1 22
A wretched soul, bruised with adversity, We bid be quiet when we hear it cry . . . . *Com. of Errors* ii 1 35
You'll cry for this, minion, if I beat the door down . . . iii 1 59

Cry. Will you be bound for nothing? be mad, good master: cry 'The devil!' . . . . *Com. of Errors* iv 4 131
If you hear a child cry in the night, you must call to the nurse *Much Ado* iii 3 69
My griefs cry louder than advertisement . . . . . . v 1 32
If any of the audience hiss, you may cry 'Well done!' . *L. L. Lost* v 1 145
Bleat softly then; the butcher hears you cry . . . . v 2 255
Who would give a bird the lie, though he cry 'cuckoo' never so? *M. N. Dream* iii 1 139
I cry your worships mercy, heartily . . . . . . iii 1 182
The skies, the fountains, every region near Seem'd all one mutual cry iv 1 122
A cry more tuneable Was never holla'd to, nor cheer'd with horn . iv 1 129
It is now our time, That have stood by and seen our wishes prosper, To cry, good joy . . . . . . *Mer. of Venice* iii 2 190
I could find in my heart to disgrace my man's apparel and to cry like a woman; but I must comfort the weaker vessel . *As Y. Like It* ii 4 5
Cry the man mercy; love him; take his offer . . . iii 5 61
When The bravest questant shrinks, find what you seek, That fame may cry you loud . . . . *All's Well* ii 1 17
O Lord, sir! spare not me.—Do you cry, 'O Lord, Sir!' at your whipping? . . . . ii 2 54
Sowter will cry upon't for all this, though it be as rank as a fox *T. Night* ii 5 135
O, the most piteous cry of the poor souls! . . . *W. Tale* iii 3 91
Come buy, come buy; Buy, lads, or else your lasses cry . . iv 4 231
Peace!—No, no, I will not, having breath to cry . . . *K. John* iv 3 37
Lest child, child's children, cry against you 'woe!' . . *Richard II.* iv 1 149
Did they not sometime cry, 'all hail!' to me? So Judas did to Christ . iv 1 169
What shrill-voiced suppliant makes this eager cry? . . . v 3 75
Speak terms of manage to thy bounding steed; Cry 'Courage!' 1 *Hen. IV.* ii 3 53
Upon this charge Cry 'God for Harry, England, and Saint George!' *Hen. V.* iii 1 34
Let him cry 'Praise and glory on his head!' . . . . iv Prol. 31
Join together at the latter day and cry all 'We died at such a place' . iv 1 144
Winchester goose, I cry, a rope! a rope! . . . 1 *Hen. VI.* i 3 53
No longer on Saint Denis will we cry . . . . . . i 6 28
The cry of Talbot serves me for a sword . . . . . ii 1 79
Will cry for vengeance at the gates of heaven . . . . v 4 53
The time when screech-owls cry and ban-dogs howl . 2 *Hen. VI.* i 4 21
And therefore do they cry, though you forbid . . . . iii 2 264
Or as a bear, encompass'd round with dogs, Who having pinch'd a few and made them cry, The rest stand all aloof . . . 3 *Hen. VI.* ii 1 16
Once again cry 'Charge upon our foes!' But never once again turn back and fly . . . . ii 1 184
Unsheathe your sword, good father; cry 'Saint George!' . . ii 2 80
And cry 'Content' to that which grieves my heart . . . iii 2 183
Strike up the drum; cry 'Courage!' and away . . . . v 3 24
Why do you wring your hands, and beat your breast, And cry 'O Clarence, my unhappy son!' . . . . . . *Richard III.* ii 2 4
Cry 'God save Richard, England's royal king!' . . . iii 7 22
For then my guiltless blood must cry against 'em . . *Hen. VIII.* ii 1 68
And, till my soul forsake, Shall cry for blessings on him . . ii 1 90
The king cried Ha! at this.—Now, God incense him, And let him cry Ha! louder! . . . . iii 2 62
Now, if you can blush and cry 'guilty,' cardinal, You'll show a little honesty . . . . iii 2 305
Methinks I could Cry the amen . . . . v 1 24
I cry your honour mercy; you may, worst Of all this table, say so . v 3 78
Others, to hear the city Abused extremely, and to cry 'That's witty!' Epil. 6
Hark! do you not hear the people cry? . . . *Troi. and Cres.* i 2 244
Cry, Trojans, cry! lend me ten thousand eyes, And I will fill them . ii 2 101
Soft infancy, that nothing canst but cry, Add to my clamours! . . ii 2 105
Cry, Trojans, cry! practise your eyes with tears! . . . ii 2 108
Cry, Trojans, cry! a Helen and a woe: Cry, cry! Troy burns, or else let Helen go . . . . ii 2 111
He is so plaguy proud that the death-tokens of it Cry 'No recovery' . ii 3 188
These lovers cry Oh! oh! they die! . . . . . . iii 1 131
The cry went once on thee, And still it might, and yet it may again iii 3 184
And all cry, Hector! Hector's dead! O Hector! . . . . v 3 87
On, Myrmidons, and cry you all amain, 'Achilles hath the mighty Hector slain' . . . . v 8 13
What's the matter, That in these several places of the city You cry against the noble senate? . . . . . . *Coriolanus* i 1 190
Your prattling nurse Into a rapture lets her baby cry While she chats him . . . . ii 1 223
Had you tongues to cry Against the rectorship of judgement? . . ii 3 212
Call't not a plot: The people cry you mock'd them . . . iii 1 42
If I say fine, cry 'Fine;' if death, cry 'Death' . . . iii 3 16
And when such time they have begun to cry, Let them not cease . iii 3 19
You have made Good work, you and your cry! . . . . iv 6 148
Give the all-hail to thee, and cry 'Be blest For making up this peace!' v 3 139
Repeal him with the welcome of his mother; Cry 'Welcome, ladies, welcome!' . . . . v 5 6
Suddenly I heard a child cry underneath a wall . . *T. Andron.* v 1 24
Bind them sure, And stop their mouths, if they begin to cry . . v 2 162
For well I know The common voice do cry it shall be so . . v 3 140
There let him stand, and rave, and cry for food . . . . v 3 180
Cry but 'Ay me!' pronounce but 'love' and 'dove' *Rom. and Jul.* ii 1 10
Switch and spurs, switch and spurs; or I'll cry a match . . ii 4 74
The people in the street cry Romeo, Some Juliet, and some Paris . v 3 191
Tell him, My uses cry to me, I must serve my turn Out of mine own *T. of Athens* ii 1 20
I hear a tongue, shriller than all the music, Cry 'Cæsar!' . *J. Cæsar* i 2 17
They shouted thrice: what was the last cry for? . . . i 2 226
Run hence, proclaim, cry it about the streets . . . . iii 1 79
Let's all cry 'Peace, freedom and liberty!' . . . . iii 1 110
My lord, I do not know that I did cry.—Yes, that thou didst . iv 3 297
I am faint, my gashes cry for help . . . . . *Macbeth* i 2 42
Nor heaven peep through the blanket of the dark, To cry 'Hold, hold!' i 5 55
I heard the owl scream and the crickets cry . . . . ii 2 16
Methought I heard a voice cry 'Sleep no more!' . . . . ii 2 35
Each new morn New widows howl, new orphans cry . . iv 3 5
Hang out our banners on the outward walls; The cry is still 'They come' . . . . v 5 2
What is that noise?—It is the cry of women, my good lord . . v 5 8
Wherefore was that cry?—The queen, my lord, is dead . . . v 5 15
They cry 'Choose we: Laertes shall be king' . . . *Hamlet* iv 5 106
How cheerfully on the false trail they cry! . . . . iv 5 109
Cry to be heard, as 'twere from heaven to earth . . . iv 5 216
At their chamber-door I'll beat the drum Till it cry sleep to death *Lear* ii 4 120
Cry to it, nuncle, as the cockney did to the eels when she put 'em i' the paste alive . . . . ii 4 123

Cry. Rive your concealing continents, and cry These dreadful summoners grace . . . . *Lear* iii 2 58
Thou know'st, the first time that we smell the air, We wawl and cry . iv 6 184
When we are born, we cry that we are come To this great stage of fools iv 6 186
When time shall serve, let but the herald cry, And I'll appear again . v 1 48
On the brow o' the sea Stand ranks of people, and they cry 'A sail!' *Othello* ii 1 54
Away, I say; go out, and cry a mutiny . . . . . . ii 3 157
I do follow here in the chase, not like a hound that hunts, but one that fills up the cry . . . . ii 3 370
Then, sir, would he gripe and wring my hand, Cry 'O sweet creature!' iii 3 422
'Faith, the cry goes that you shall marry her . . . . iv 1 126
'Tis some mischance; the cry is very direful . . . . . v 1 38
Let's think't unsafe To come in to the cry without more help . . v 1 44
Did not you hear a cry?—Here, here! for heaven's sake, help me! . v 1 49
What are you here that cry so grievously? . . . . . v 1 53
I cry you gentle pardon . . . . v 1 93
O, falsely, falsely murder'd!—Alas, what cry is that? . . . v 2 117
Kings would start forth, And cry 'Your will?' . *Ant. and Cleo.* iii 13 92
I'll strike, and cry 'Take all.'—Well said; come on . . . iv 2 8
If sleep charge nature, To break it with a fearful dream of him And cry myself awake . . . . *Cymbeline* iii 4 46
We poor ghosts will cry To the shining synod of the rest Against thy deity . . . . v 4 88
Divinest patroness, and midwife gentle To those that cry by night *Per.* iii 1 12
Cry 'He that will give most shall have her first' . . . . iv 2 63
Cry you (thee) mercy *T. G. of Ver.* v 4; *Mer. Wives* iii 5; *Meas. for Meas.* iv 1; *Much Ado* ii 1; 1 *Hen. IV.* i 3; iv 2; 1 *Hen. VI.* v 3; 2 *Hen. VI.* i 3; *Rich. III.* i 3; ii 2; iv 4; *Rom. and Jul.* iv 5; *Lear* iii 4; iii 6; *Othello* iv 2; v 1

Cry aim. To these violent proceedings all my neighbours shall cry aim *Mer. Wives* iii 2 45
It ill beseems this presence to cry aim To these ill-tuned repetitions *K. John* ii 1 196

Cry amen. I say my prayers aloud.—I love you the better: the hearers may cry, Amen . . . . *Much Ado* ii 1 110
Strong as a tower in hope, I cry amen . . . . *Richard II.* i 3 102
To cry amen to that, thus we appear . . . . . *Hen. V.* v 2 21

Cry bail. I cry bail. Here's a gentleman and a friend of mine *M. for M.* iii 2 43

Cry down. I'll to the king; And from a mouth of honour quite cry down This Ipswich fellow's insolence . . . . . *Hen. VIII.* i 1 137

Cry fie. And my near'st of kin Cry fie upon my grave! . *W. Tale* iii 2 55

Cry 'Havoc,' and let slip the dogs of war . . . *J. Cæsar* iii 1 273
Why stand these royal fronts amazed thus? Cry, 'havoc!' kings *K. John* ii 1 357
Do not cry havoc, where you should but hunt With modest warrant *Coriolanus* iii 1 275

Cry heigh-ho. I may sit in a corner and cry heigh-ho for a husband! *Much Ado* ii 1 332

Cry 'hem.' Bid sorrow wag, cry 'hem!' when he should groan . v 1 16
I would try, if I could cry 'hem' and have him . *As Y. Like It* i 3 19
And when you breathe in your watering, they cry 'hem!' . 1 *Hen. IV.* ii 4 18
Cough, or cry 'hem,' if any body come . . . . *Othello* iv 2 29

Cry 'holla' to thy tongue, I prithee . . . . *As Y. Like It* iii 2 257

Cry lost. Or both yourself and me Cry lost, and so good night! *W. Tale* i 2 411

Cry mercy, lords and watchful gentlemen, That you have ta'en a tardy sluggard here . . . . *Richard III.* v 3 224

Cry mew. I had rather be a kitten and cry mew . . 1 *Hen. IV.* iii 1 129

Cry 'mum.' I come to her in white, and cry 'mum;' she cries 'budget' *Mer. Wives* v 2 6

Cry O. I'll cudgel him, and make him cry O! . . . *T. Night* ii 5 146

Cry of curs. You common cry of curs! whose breath I hate As reek o' the rotten fens . . . . *Coriolanus* iii 3 120

Cry of players. Get me a fellowship in a cry of players, sir . *Hamlet* iii 2 289

Cry out. A space whose every cubit Seems to cry out . . *Tempest* ii 1 258
If I cry out thus upon no trail, never trust me when I open again *Mer. Wives* iv 2 208
And make the babbling gossip of the air Cry out . . . *T. Night* i 5 293
Whereof the execution did cry out Against the non-performance *W. Tale* i 2 260
Your drums, being beaten, will cry out . . . . *K. John* v 2 166
I should be raging mad And cry out for thee to close up mine eyes 2 *Hen. VI.* iii 2 395
More ready to cry out 'Who knows what follows?' . *Troi. and Cres.* ii 2 13
And giddy censure Will then cry out of Marcius 'O, if he Had borne the business!' . . . . *Coriolanus* i 1 273
Some to the common pulpits, and cry out 'Liberty, freedom!' *J. Cæsar* iii 1 80
Men, wives and children stare, cry out and run As it were doomsday . iii 1 97
Why did you so cry out, sirs, in your sleep?—Did we? . . . iv 3 304
Little eyases, that cry out on the top of question . . *Hamlet* ii 2 355
Henceforth I'll bear Affliction till it do cry out itself 'Enough, enough,' and die . . . . *Lear* iv 6 76
With others whom the rigour of our state Forced to cry out . . v 1 23
I may wander From east to occident, cry out for service, Try many *Cymbeline* iv 2 372
And for an honest attribute cry out 'She died by foul play' . *Pericles* iv 3 18

Cry shame. Doth not every earthly thing Cry shame upon her? *Much Ado* iv 1 123
Let heaven and men and devils, let them all, All, all, cry shame against me, yet I'll speak . . . . *Othello* v 2 222

Cry woe. But the last,—O lords, When I have said, cry 'woe!' *W. Tale* iii 2 201
Cry woe, destruction, ruin and decay; The worst is death *Richard II.* iii 2 102
You live that shall cry woe for this hereafter . . *Richard III.* iii 3 7
The man that makes his toe What he his heart should make Shall of a corn cry woe . . . . *Lear* iii 2 33

Crying. Hurried thence Me and thy crying self . . . *Tempest* i 2 132
My mother weeping, my father wailing, my sister crying *T. G. of Ver.* ii 3 8
And so buffets himself on the forehead, crying, 'Peer out, peer out!' *Mer. Wives* iv 2 26
Let the child wake her with crying . . . . . . *Much Ado* iii 3 74
All the boys in Venice follow him, Crying, his stones, his daughter, and his ducats . . . . *Mer. of Venice* ii 8 24
Crying, 'That's good that's gone' . . . . . . *All's Well* v 3 60
Places remote enough are in Bohemia, There weep and leave it crying *W. Tale* iii 3 32
To thrill and shake Even at the crying of your nation's crow *K. John* v 2 144
Got with swearing 'Lay by' and spent with crying 'Bring in' 1 *Hen. IV.* i 2 41
Some swearing, some crying for a surgeon . . . *Hen. V.* iv 1 145
They call'd us for our fierceness English dogs; Now, like to whelps, we crying run away . . . . 1 *Hen. VI.* i 5 26
Crying with loud voice, 'Jesu maintain your royal excellence!' 2 *Hen. VI.* i 1 160
By crying comfort from a hollow breast . . . . . . iii 2 43
I see them lording it in London streets, Crying 'Villiago!' . . . iv 8 48

Crying. All several sins, all used in each degree, Throng to the bar, crying all, Guilty! guilty! I shall despair . . *Richard III.* v 3 199
To pray for her? what, is she crying out? . . *Hen. VIII.* v 1 67
Hack'd and chipp'd, come to him, Crying on Hector . *Troi. and Cres.* v 5 35
These fellows ran about the streets, Crying confusion . *Coriolanus* iv 6 29
Soon I heard The crying babe controll'd with this discourse *T. Andron.* v 1 26
The pretty wretch left crying and said 'Ay . . . *Rom. and Jul.* i 3 44
I cannot choose but laugh, To think it should leave crying and say 'Ay' i 3 51
Witness the hole you made in Cæsar's heart, Crying 'Long live!' *J. Cæsar* v 1 32
Thou must be patient; we came crying hither . . *Lear* iv 6 182
There comes a fellow crying out for help; And Cassio following him with determined sword . . . . *Othello* ii 3 226
Myself the crying fellow did pursue, Lest by his clamour—as it so fell out—The town might fall in fright . . . . ii 3 230
She falls me thus about my neck— Crying 'O dear Cassio!' as it were iv 1 141
Undo that prayer, by crying out as loud, 'O, bless my brother!' *Ant. and Cleo.* iii 4 17
Came crying 'mongst his foes, A thing of pity! . *Cymbeline* v 4 46
Crystal. His mistress Did hold his eyes lock'd in her crystal looks *T. G. of Ver.* ii 4 89
Methought all his senses were lock'd in his eye, As jewels in crystal *L. L. Lost* ii 1 243
One, her hairs were gold, crystal the other's eyes . . . . iv 3 142
To what, my love, shall I compare thine eyne? Crystal is muddy *M. N. Dream* iii 2 139
With these crystal beads heaven shall be bribed To do him justice *K. John* ii 1 171
The more fair and crystal is the sky, The uglier seem the clouds that in it fly . . . . . . *Richard II.* i 1 41
Go, clear thy crystals . . . . . . *Hen. V.* ii 3 56
Comets, importing change of times and states, Brandish your crystal tresses in the sky! . . . . 1 *Hen. VI.* i 1 3
But in that crystal scales let there be weigh'd Your lady's love against some other maid . . . . . . *Rom. and Jul.* i 2 101
Thy crystal window ope; look out . . . . *Cymbeline* v 4 81
Crystal-button. Wilt thou rob this leathern jerkin, crystal-button? 1 *Hen. IV.* ii 4 78
Crystalline. Mount, eagle, to my palace crystalline . . *Cymbeline* v 4 113
Cub. Pluck the young sucking cubs from the she-bear . *Mer. of Venice* ii 1 29
O thou dissembling cub! what wilt thou be When time hath sow'd a grizzle on thy case? . . . . . . *T. Night* v 1 167
Cub-drawn. This night, wherein the cub-drawn bear would couch *Lear* iii 1 12
Cubiculo. Where shall I find you?—We'll call thee at the cubiculo *T. Night* iii 2 56
Cubit. A space whose every cubit Seems to cry out . . *Tempest* ii 1 257
Cuckold. I will awe him with my cudgel: it shall hang like a meteor o'er the cuckold's horns . . . . *Mer. Wives* ii 2 293
Thou, Master Brook, shalt know him for knave and cuckold . . ii 2 298
Wittol!—Cuckold! the devil himself hath not such a name . . ii 2 313
Fie, fie, fie! cuckold! cuckold! cuckold! . . . . . ii 2 328
But fate, ordaining he should be a cuckold, held his hand . . iii 5 106
Master Brook, you shall cuckold Ford . . . . . iii 5 140
Now, sir, who's a cuckold now? . . . . . . v 5 113
Do not recompense me in making me a cuckold . *Meas. for Meas.* v 1 523
Like an old cuckold, with horns on his head . . *Much Ado* ii 1 46
A gig of a cuckold's horn . . . . . *L. L. Lost* v 1 73
What, are we cuckolds ere we have deserved it? . *Mer. of Venice* v 1 265
Were you the clerk that is to make me cuckold? . . . v 1 281
If I be his cuckold, he's my drudge . . . . . *All's Well* i 3 49
As the nail to his hole, the cuckold to his horn . . . ii 2 26
As there is no true cuckold but calamity, so beauty's a flower *T. Night* i 5 56
There have been, Or I am much deceived, cuckolds ere now *W. Tale* i 2 191
Your eye-glass Is thicker than a cuckold's horn . . . i 2 269
Gave Amamon the bastinado and made Lucifer cuckold . 1 *Hen. IV.* ii 4 371
Either young or old, He or she, cuckold or cuckold-maker *Hen. VIII.* v 4 25
All the argument is a cuckold and a whore . . *Troi. and Cres.* ii 3 78
What, does the cuckold scorn me? . . . . . iii 3 64
He, like a puling cuckold, would drink up The lees and dregs of a flat tamed piece . . . . iv 1 61
The primitive statue, and oblique memorial of cuckolds . . . v 1 61
The cuckold and the cuckold-maker are at it . . . . v 7 9
It cannot be denied but peace is a great maker of cuckolds *Coriolanus* iv 5 244
That drop of blood that's calm proclaims me bastard, Cries cuckold to my father . . . . *Hamlet* iv 5 118
If thou canst cuckold him, thou dost thyself a pleasure, me a sport *Othello* i 3 375
That cuckold lives in bliss Who, certain of his fate, loves not his wronger . . . . iii 3 167
I will chop her into messes: cuckold me!—O, 'tis foul in her . . iv 1 211
But, for the whole world,—why, who would not make her husband a cuckold to make him a monarch? . . . . . iv 3 76
And let worse follow worse, till the worst of all follow him laughing to his grave, fifty-fold a cuckold! . . . . *Ant. and Cleo.* i 2 70
If it lay in their hands to make me a cuckold . . . . . i 2 81
And I will kill thee, if thou dost deny Thou'st made me cuckold *Cymb.* ii 4 146
Cuckoldly. Hang him, poor cuckoldly knave! . . *Mer. Wives* ii 2 281
I will use her as the key of the cuckoldly rogue's coffer . . . ii 2 286
Falstaff's a knave, a cuckoldly knave . . . . . v 5 114
A crooked-pated, old, cuckoldly ram . . . *As Y. Like It* iii 2 87
Cuckold-mad. I mean not cuckold-mad; But, sure, he is stark mad *Com. of Errors* ii 1 58
Cuckold-maker. Either young or old, He or she, cuckold or cuckold-maker . . . . *Hen. VIII.* v 4 25
The cuckold and the cuckold-maker are at it . *Troi. and Cres.* v 7 9
Cuckoo. Will you hear the dialogue that the two learned men have compiled in praise of the owl and the cuckoo? . . *L. L. Lost* v 2 896
This side is Hiems, Winter, this Ver, the Spring; the one maintained by the owl, the other by the cuckoo . . . . v 2 903
The cuckoo then, on every tree, Mocks married men; for thus sings he, Cuckoo; Cuckoo, cuckoo: O word of fear, Unpleasing to a married ear! . . . . v 2 908
The plain-song cuckoo gray . . . . *M. N. Dream* iii 1 134
Who would give a bird the lie, though he cry 'cuckoo' never so? . . iii 1 139
He knows me as the blind man knows the cuckoo, By the bad voice *Mer. of Venice* v 1 112
Your marriage comes by destiny, Your cuckoo sings by kind . *All's Well* i 3 67
O' horseback, ye cuckoo; but afoot he will not budge a foot . 1 *Hen. IV.* ii 4 387
He was but as the cuckoo is in June, Heard, not regarded . . . iii 2 75
As that ungentle gull, the cuckoo's bird, Useth the sparrow . . . v 1 60
The hedge-sparrow fed the cuckoo so long, That it had it head bit off by it young . . . . *Lear* i 4 235
Since the cuckoo builds not for himself . . . *Ant. and Cleo.* ii 6 28
Cuckoo-bird. Take heed, ere summer comes or cuckoo-birds do sing *Mer. Wives* ii 1 127
Cuckoo-buds of yellow hue Do paint the meadows with delight *L. L. Lost* v 2 906
Cuckoo-flower. Bur-docks, hemlock, nettles, cuckoo-flowers . . *Lear* iv 4 4
Cucullus non facit monachum *Meas. for Meas.* v 1 263; *T. Night* i 5 62
Cudgel. I will awe him with my cudgel . . . *Mer. Wives* ii 2 292
Heaven guide him to thy husband's cudgel, and the devil guide his cudgel afterwards! . . . . iv 2 91
I'll have the cudgel hallowed and hung o'er the altar . . iv 2 216
He hath enjoyed nothing of Ford's but his buck-basket, his cudgel, and twenty pounds of money . . . . v 5 117
Do I look like a cudgel or a hovel-post, a staff or a prop? *Mer. of Venice* ii 2 71
Ay, or I'll cudgel him, and make him cry O! . . . *T. Night* ii 5 145
That hand which had the strength, even at your door, To cudgel you *K. John* v 2 138
An he were here, I would cudgel him like a dog, if he would say so 1 *Hen. IV.* iii 3 100
And said he would cudgel you.—What! he did not? . . . iii 3 123
He called you Jack, and said he would cudgel you . . . iii 3 159
Quiet thy cudgel; thou dost see I eat . . . . *Hen. V.* v 1 54
If I owe you any thing, I will pay you in cudgels . . . . v 1 69
You shall be a woodmonger, and buy nothing of me but cudgels . . v 1 70
As much as one sound cudgel of four foot—You see the poor remainder—could distribute, I made no spare . . . *Hen. VIII.* v 4 19
By my hand, I had thought to have strucken him with a cudgel *Coriol.* iv 5 156
Cudgel thy brains no more about it . . . . *Hamlet* v 1 63
Cudgelled. If it should come to the ear of the court, how I have been transformed and how my transformation hath been washed and cudgelled . . . . *Mer. Wives* iv 5 99
I might have cudgelled thee out of thy single life . . *Much Ado* v 4 115
Our ears are cudgell'd; not a word of his But buffets better than a fist *K. John* ii 1 464
Old I do wax; and from my weary limbs Honour is cudgell'd *Hen. V.* v 1 90
And patches will I get unto these cudgell'd scars . . . v 1 93
My money is almost spent; I have been to-night exceedingly well cudgelled . . . . *Othello* ii 3 372
Cudgelling. So prophetically proud of an heroical cudgelling *Troi. and Cres.* iii 3 249
Cue. The clock gives me my cue, and my assurance bids me search *Mer. Wives* iii 2 46
Remember you your cue.—I warrant thee . . . . iii 3 39
Speak, count, 'tis your cue . . . . . . *Much Ado* ii 1 316
And so every one according to his cue . . . *M. N. Dream* iii 1 78
You speak all your part at once, cues and all . . . . iii 1 102
When my cue comes, call me, and I will answer . . . . iv 1 205
'Deceiving me' is Thisby's cue . . . . v 1 186
Now we speak upon our cue, and our voice is imperial . . *Hen. V.* iii 6 130
Had not you come upon your cue, my lord, William Lord Hastings had pronounced your part . . . . . *Richard III.* iii 4 27
What would he do, Had he the motive and the cue for passion That I have? . . . . *Hamlet* ii 2 587
My cue is villanous melancholy, with a sigh like Tom o' Bedlam *Lear* i 2 147
Were it my cue to fight, I should have known it Without a prompter *Othello* i 2 83
Cuff. I swear I'll cuff you, if you strike again . . *T. of Shrew* ii 1 221
The mad-brain'd bridegroom took him such a cuff That down fell priest and book and book and priest . . . . . . iii 2 165
This cuff was but to knock at your ear, and beseech listening . . iv 1 67
With ruffs and cuffs and fardingales and things . . . . iv 3 56
Cuff him soundly, but never draw thy sword . . . *T. Night* iii 4 428
Beware your beard; I mean to tug it and to cuff you soundly 1 *Hen. VI.* i 3 48
Unless the poet and the player went to cuffs in the question . *Hamlet* ii 2 373
Cuique. 'Suum cuique' is our Roman justice . . . *T. Andron.* i 1 280
Cuisses. His cuisses on his thighs, gallantly arm'd . . 1 *Hen. IV.* iv 1 105
Cull. Call for our chiefest men of discipline, To cull the plots of best advantages . . . . *K. John* ii 1 40
Fortune shall cull forth Out of one side her happy minion . . ii 1 391
Come knights from east to west, And cull their flower *Troi. and Cres.* ii 3 275
Approach the fold and cull the infected forth, But kill not all together *T. of Athens* v 4 43
And do you now cull out a holiday? . . . . *J. Cæsar* i 1 54
Culled. Of all complexions the cull'd sovereignty Do meet . *L. L. Lost* iv 3 234
The word is well culled, chose, sweet and apt, I do assure you . . v 1 98
And cull'd these fiery spirits from the world . . . *K. John* v 2 114
These cull'd and choice-drawn cavaliers . . . *Hen. V.* iii Prol. 24
Familiar spirits, that are cull'd Out of the powerful regions under earth 1 *Hen. VI.* v 3 10
For love of her that's gone, Perhaps she cull'd it from among the rest *T. Andron.* iv 1 44
We have cull'd such necessaries As are behoveful for our state *Rom. and Jul.* iv 3 7
Culling. Like the bee, culling from every flower The virtuous sweets 2 *Hen. IV.* iv 5 75
In this covert will we make our stand, Culling the principal of all the deer . . . . 3 *Hen. VI.* iii 1 4
In tatter'd weeds, with overwhelming brows, Culling of simples *R. and J.* v 1 40
Cullion. And makes a god of such a cullion . . . *T. of Shrew* iv 2 20
Up to the breach, you dogs! avaunt, you cullions! . . . *Hen. V.* iii 2 22
Away, base cullions! . . . . 2 *Hen. VI.* i 3 43
Cullionly. You whoreson cullionly barber-monger . . . . *Lear* ii 2 36
Culpable. Than from true evidence of good esteem He be approved in practice culpable . . . . 2 *Hen. VI.* iii 2 22
Culverin. Of basilisks, of cannon, culverin . . . . 1 *Hen. IV.* ii 3 56
Cum privilegio ad imprimendum solum . . . *T. of Shrew* iv 4 93
Cumber. Let it not cumber your better remembrance . *T. of Athens* iii 6 52
Domestic fury and fierce civil strife Shall cumber all the parts of Italy *J. Cæsar* iii 1 264
Cumberland. Clifford of Cumberland, 'tis Warwick calls . 2 *Hen. VI.* v 2 1
Clifford of Cumberland, Warwick is hoarse with calling thee to arms . v 2 6
We will establish our estate upon Our eldest, Malcolm, whom we name hereafter The Prince of Cumberland . . . . *Macbeth* i 4 39
The Prince of Cumberland! that is a step On which I must fall down, or else o'erleap, For in my way it lies . . . . . . i 4 48
Cunning. Hence, bashful cunning! And prompt me, plain and holy innocence! I am your wife . . . . . . *Tempest* iii 1 81
A sorcerer, that by his cunning hath cheated me of the island . . iii 2 49
Our marriage-hour, With all the cunning manner of our flight *T. G. of Ver.* ii 4 180
I will so plead That you shall say my cunning drift excels . . iv 2 83
O cunning enemy, that, to catch a saint, With saints dost bait thy hook! *Meas. for Meas.* ii 2 180

Cunning. O 'tis the cunning livery of hell! *Meas. for Meas.* iii 1 95
In the boldness of my cunning, I will lay myself in hazard iv 2 165
Be cunning in the working this *Much Ado* ii 2 53
Be you constant in the accusation, and my cunning shall not shame me ii 2 56
O, what authority and show of truth Can cunning sin cover itself withal! iv 1 37
This learned constable is too cunning to be understood v 1 234
To sell a bargain well is as cunning as fast and loose *L. L. Lost* iii 1 104
With cunning hast thou filch'd my daughter's heart *M. N. Dream* i 1 36
You do advance your cunning more and more iii 2 128
The seeming truth which cunning times put on *Mer. of Venice* iii 2 100
I have some sport in hand Wherein your cunning can assist me much *T. of Shrew* Ind. 1 92
To cunning men I will be very kind, and liberal To mine own children i 1 97
He took some care To get her cunning schoolmasters to instruct her i 1 192
Cunning in music and the mathematics ii 1 56
Cunning in Greek, Latin, and other languages ii 1 81
In this case of wooing, A child shall get a sire, if I fail not of my cunning ii 1 413
Whose red and white Nature's own sweet and cunning hand laid on *T. Night* i 5 258
The cunning of her passion Invites me in this churlish messenger ii 2 23
To force that on you, in a shameful cunning, Which you knew none of yours iii 1 127
An I thought he had been valiant and so cunning in fence iii 4 312
His false cunning, Not meaning to partake with me in danger, Taught him to face me out of his acquaintance v 1 89
You may think my love was crafty love And call it cunning *K. John* iv 1 54
Trust not those cunning waters of his eyes iv 3 107
Like a cunning instrument cased up *Richard II.* i 3 163
What cunning match have you made with this jest of the drawer? *1 Hen. IV.* ii 4 101
Wherein cunning, but in craft? wherein crafty, but in villany? ii 4 503
Whatsoever cunning fiend it was That wrought upon thee so preposterously *Hen. V.* ii 2 111
I have no cunning in protestation; only downright oaths v 2 150
Is this thy cunning, thou deceitful dame? *1 Hen. VI.* ii 1 50
We have been guided by thee hitherto And of thy cunning had no diffidence iii 3 10
Margery Jourdain, the cunning witch *2 Hen. VI.* i 2 75
Would ye not think his cunning to be great, that could restore this cripple to his legs again? ii 1 132
A cunning man did calculate my birth And told me that by water I should die iv 1 34
So cunning and so young is wonderful *Richard III.* iii 1 135
This cunning cardinal The articles o' the combination drew As himself pleased; and they were ratified *Hen. VIII.* i 1 168
I am a simple woman, much too weak To oppose your cunning ii 4 107
Friend, we understand not one another: I am too courtly and thou art too cunning *Troi. and Cres.* iii 1 30
See, see, your silence, Cunning in dumbness, from my weakness draws My very soul of counsel! iii 2 140
Whilst some with cunning gild their copper crowns, With truth and plainness I do wear mine bare iv 4 107
As if that luck, in every spite of cunning, Bade him win all v 5 41
Fortune's blows, When most struck home, being gentle wounded, craves A noble cunning *Coriolanus* iv 1 9
I'll find some cunning practice out of hand *T. Andron.* v 2 77
I'll prove more true Than those that have more cunning to be strange *Rom. and Jul.* ii 2 101
Go hire me twenty cunning cooks.—You shall have none ill, sir iv 2 2
Shame not these woods, By putting on the cunning of a carper *T. of Athens* iv 3 209
Shame that they wanted cunning, in excess Hath broke their hearts v 4 28
Well digested in the scenes, set down with as much modesty as cunning *Hamlet* ii 2 461
I have heard That guilty creatures sitting at a play Have by the very cunning of the scene Been struck so to the soul that presently They have proclaim'd their malefactions ii 2 619
This bodiless creation ecstasy Is very cunning in iii 4 139
Soft! let me see: We'll make a solemn wager on your cunnings iv 7 156
Of deaths put on by cunning and forced cause v 2 394
Time shall unfold what plaited cunning hides *Lear* i 1 283
There's the cunning of it i 2 64
In cunning I must draw my sword upon you: Draw; seem to defend yourself ii 1 31
There is division, Although as yet the face of it be cover'd With mutual cunning iii 1 21
Cunning.—And false iii 7 49
Must be driven To find out practices of cunning hell *Othello* i 3 102
If he be not one that truly loves you, That errs in ignorance and not in cunning, I have no judgement iii 3 49
I will be found most cunning in my patience; But—dost thou hear?—most bloody iv 1 91
I took you for that cunning whore of Venice That married with Othello iv 2 89
If there be any cunning cruelty That can torment him much and hold him long, It shall be his v 2 333
She is cunning past man's thought *Ant. and Cleo.* i 2 150
This cannot be cunning in her; if it be, she makes a shower of rain as well as Jove i 2 155
In our sports my better cunning faints Under his chance ii 3 34
Try thy cunning, Thyreus; Make thine own edict for thy pains iii 12 31
A cunning thief, or a that way accomplished courtier, would hazard the winning *Cymbeline* i 4 100
This her bracelet,—O cunning, how I got it! v 5 205
Virtue and cunning were endowments greater Than nobleness and riches *Pericles* iii 2 27
Cunningest. Thou cunning'st pattern of excelling nature *Othello* v 2 11
Cunningly. Do it so cunningly That my discovery be not aimed at *T. G. of Ver.* iii 1 44
Will out, Though ne'er so cunningly you smother it *1 Hen. VI.* iv 1 110
A still and dumb-discoursive devil That tempts most cunningly *Troi. and Cres.* iv 4 93
Which, cunningly effected, will beget A very excellent piece of villany *T. Andron.* ii 3 6
Cuore. Con tutto il cuore, ben trovato *T. of Shrew* i 2 24
Cup. They could never get her so much as sip on a cup with the proudest of them *Mer. Wives* ii 2 77
I think you all have drunk of Circe's cup *Com. of Errors* v 1 270
Therefore welcome the sour cup of prosperity! *L. L. Lost* i 1 315
That drink, being poured out of a cup into a glass, by filling the one doth empty the other *As Y. Like It* v 1 46
Cup. Will't please your lordship drink a cup of sack? *T. of Shrew* Ind. 2 2
There, take it to you, trenchers, cups, and all iv 1 168
Thou lackest a cup of canary: when did I see thee so put down? *T. Night* i 3 85
Mightst bespice a cup, To give mine enemy a lasting wink *W. Tale* i 2 316
There may be in the cup A spider steep'd, and one may drink ii 1 39
Unless hours were cups of sack and minutes capons *1 Hen. IV.* i 2 8
A cup of Madeira and a cold capon's leg i 2 128
Let a cup of sack be my poison ii 2 49
Give me a cup of sack, boy ii 4 129
A coward is worse than a cup of sack with lime in it ii 4 139
O villain, thou stolest a cup of sack eighteen years ago ii 4 345
Give me a cup of sack to make my eyes look red ii 4 423
I charge you with a cup of sack: do you discharge upon mine hostess *2 Hen. IV.* ii 4 121
How chances mock, And changes fill the cup of alteration With divers liquors! iii 1 52
A cup of wine, sir?—A cup of wine that's brisk and fine v 3 47
Fill the cup, and let it come; I'll pledge you a mile to the bottom v 3 56
This would drink deep.—'Twould drink the cup and all *Hen. V.* i 1 20
Be in their flowing cups freshly remember'd iv 3 55
Alexander killed his friend Cleitus, being in his ales and his cups iv 7 48
I drink to you in a cup of sack *2 Hen. VI.* ii 3 60
Here, neighbour, here's a cup of charneco ii 3 62
How often hast thou waited at my cup, Fed from my trencher? iv 1 56
Far beyond a prince's delicates, His viands sparkling in a golden cup *3 Hen. VI.* ii 5 52
Give me a cup of wine.—You shall have wine enough, my lord, anon *Richard III.* i 4 166
One that loves a cup of hot wine with not a drop of allaying Tiber in't *Coriolanus* ii 1 52
I pray, come and crush a cup of wine *Rom. and Jul.* i 2 86
And by the operation of the second cup draws it on the drawer iii 1 9
What's here? a cup, closed in my true love's hand? v 3 161
Fill, Lucius, till the wine o'erswell the cup *J. Cæsar* iv 3 161
And in the cup an union shall he throw *Hamlet* v 2 283
Give me the cups; And let the kettle to the trumpet speak v 2 285
Give him the cup.—I'll play this bout first; set it by awhile v 2 294
It is the poison'd cup: it is too late v 2 303
As thou'rt a man, Give me the cup: let go; by heaven, I'll have't v 2 354
All friends shall taste The wages of their virtue, and all foes The cup of their deservings *Lear* v 3 304
I have drunk but one cup to-night, and that was craftily qualified too *Othello* ii 3 40
If I can fasten but one cup upon him, With that which he hath drunk to-night already ii 3 50
Have I to-night fluster'd with flowing cups ii 3 60
Every inordinate cup is unblessed and the ingredient is a devil ii 3 311
Do as I bid you. Where's this cup I call'd for? *Ant. and Cleo.* ii 7 60
Hast thou drunk well?—No, Pompey, I have kept me from the cup ii 7 72
Fill till the cup be hid ii 7 93
Cup us, till the world go round, Cup us, till the world go round! ii 7 124
Well, my good fellows, wait on me to-night: Scant not my cups iv 2 21
Being an ugly monster, 'Tis strange he hides him in fresh cups, soft beds, Sweet words *Cymbeline* v 3 71
Those cities that of plenty's cup And her prosperities so largely taste *Pericles* i 4 52
Here, with a cup that's stored unto the brim,—As you do love, fill to your mistress' lips ii 3 50
Cupbearer. Thou, His cup-bearer, . . . mightst bespice a cup *W. Tale* i 2 313
I am his cupbearer: If from me he have wholesome beverage, Account me not your servant i 2 345
Cupboarding. Idle and unactive, Still cupboarding the viand *Coriolanus* i 1 103
Cupid. This punk is one of Cupid's carriers *Mer. Wives* ii 2 141
Now is Cupid a child of conscience; he makes restitution v 5 32
He set up his bills here in Messina and challenged Cupid at the flight *Much Ado* i 1 40
My uncle's fool, reading the challenge, subscribed for Cupid i 1 41
Do you play the flouting Jack, to tell us Cupid is a good hare-finder? i 1 186
For the sign of blind Cupid i 1 256
If Cupid have not spent all his quiver in Venice, thou wilt quake for this shortly i 1 273
If we can do this, Cupid is no longer an archer: his glory shall be ours ii 1 400
Of this matter Is little Cupid's crafty arrow made, That only wounds by hearsay iii 1 22
Then loving goes by haps: Some Cupid kills with arrows, some with traps iii 1 106
He hath twice or thrice cut Cupid's bow-string and the little hangman dare not shoot at him iii 2 11
I think scorn to sigh: methinks I should outswear Cupid *L. L. Lost* i 2 67
Cupid's butt-shaft is too hard for Hercules' club i 2 181
He is Cupid's grandfather and learns news of him ii 1 254
This senior-junior, giant-dwarf, Dan Cupid; Regent of love-rhymes, lord of folded arms iii 1 182
It is a plague That Cupid will impose for my neglect Of his almighty dreadful little might iii 1 204
Shot, by heaven! Proceed, sweet Cupid: thou hast thumped him with thy bird-bolt iv 3 23
Rhymes are guards on wanton Cupid's hose: Disfigure not his slop iv 3 58
Saint Cupid, then! and, soldiers, to the field! iv 3 366
Writ o' both sides the leaf, margent and all, That he was fain to seal on Cupid's name v 2 9
Saint Denis to Saint Cupid! What are they? v 2 87
I swear to thee, by Cupid's strongest bow, By his best arrow *M. N. Dream* i 1 169
Love looks not with the eyes, but with the mind; And therefore is wing'd Cupid painted blind i 1 235
Flying between the cold moon and the earth Cupid all arm'd ii 1 157
Cupid's fiery shaft Quench'd in the chaste beams of the watery moon ii 1 161
Yet mark'd I where the bolt of Cupid fell: It fell upon a little western flower ii 1 165
Hit with Cupid's archery, Sink in apple of his eye iii 2 103
Cupid is a knavish lad, Thus to make poor females mad iii 2 440
Dian's bud o'er Cupid's flower Hath such force and blessed power iv 1 78
Cupid himself would blush To see me thus transformed to a boy *M. of V.* ii 6 38
I long to see Quick Cupid's post that comes so mannerly ii 9 100
Cupid have mercy! not a word?—Not one to throw at a dog *As Y. Like It* i 3 1
It may be said of him that Cupid hath clapped him o' the shoulder iv 1 48
A world Of pretty, fond, adoptious christendoms, That blinking Cupid gossips *All's Well* i 1 189
The brains of my Cupid's knocked out iii 2 16
This love will undo us all. O Cupid, Cupid, Cupid! *Troi. and Cres.* iii 1 120

Cupid. From Cupid's shoulder pluck his painted wings . *Troi. and Cres.* iii 2 15
In all Cupid's pageant there is presented no monster . . iii 2 81
Cupid grant all tongue-tied maidens here Bed, chamber, Pandar! . . iii 2 219
The weak wanton Cupid Shall from your neck unloose his amorous fold iii 3 222
She'll not be hit With Cupid's arrow; she hath Dian's wit *Rom. and Jul.* i 1 215
We'll have no Cupid hoodwink'd with a scarf . . . . . . i 4 4
Borrow Cupid's wings, And soar with them above a common bound . i 4 17
Young Adam Cupid, he that shot so trim, When King Cophetua loved the beggar-maid! . . . . ii 1 13
Therefore do nimble-pinion'd doves draw love, And therefore hath the wind-swift Cupid wings . . . . ii 5 8
No, do thy worst, blind Cupid; I'll not love . . . . *Lear* iv 6 141
When light-wing'd toys Of feather'd Cupid seel with wanton dullness My speculative and officed instruments . . . . *Othello* i 3 270
Pretty dimpled boys, like smiling Cupids, With divers-colour'd fans *Ant. and Cleo.* ii 2 207
Her andirons—I had forgot them—were two winking Cupids Of silver *Cymbeline* ii 4 89
Though forfeiters you cast in prison, yet You clasp young Cupid's tables . . . . iii 2 39
Here they stand martyrs, slain in Cupid's wars . . . *Pericles* i 1 38
Cuppele. Owy, cuppele gorge, permafoy . . . . *Hen. V.* iv 4 39
Cur. Hang, cur! hang, you whoreson, insolent noisemaker! . *Tempest* i 1 46
Yet did not this cruel-hearted cur shed one tear . *T. G. of Ver.* ii 3 10
When a man's servant shall play the cur with him, look you, it goes hard iv 4 2
'Tis a foul thing when a cur cannot keep himself in all companies! . iv 4 11
'Out with the dog!' says one: 'What cur is that?' says another . . iv 4 23
She says your dog was a cur, and tells you currish thanks is good enough for such a present . . . . iv 4 52
'Tis a good dog.—A cur, sir . . . . *Mer. Wives* i 1 97
Out, cur! thou drivest me past the bounds Of maiden's patience *M. N. Dream* iii 2 65
And foot me as you spurn a stranger cur Over your threshold *Mer. of Ven.* i 3 119
Is it possible A cur can lend three thousand ducats? . . . . i 3 123
It is the most impenetrable cur That ever kept with men . . . iii 3 18
Thy words are too precious to be cast away upon curs . *As Y. Like It* i 3 5
Brach Merriman, the poor cur is emboss'd . . *T. of Shrew* Ind. 1 17
Did not I say he would work it out? the cur is excellent at faults *T. Night* ii 5 140
Except like curs to tear us all to pieces . . . *Richard II.* ii 2 139
Shall dunghill curs confront the Helicons? . . . *2 Hen. IV.* v 3 108
Pish for thee, Iceland dog! thou prick-ear'd cur of Iceland! *Hen. V.* ii 1 44
Foolish curs, that run winking into the mouth of a Russian bear! . iii 7 153
Yield, cur!—Je pense que vous êtes gentilhomme de bonne qualité . iv 4 1
Brass, cur! Thou damned and luxurious mountain goat, Offer'st me brass? . . . . iv 4 19
Mazed with a yelping kennel of French curs . . . *1 Hen. VI.* iv 2 47
Small curs are not regarded when they grin . . *2 Hen. VI.* iii 1 18
They may astonish these fell-lurking curs . . . . . v 1 146
Oft have I seen a hot o'erweening cur Run back and bite, because he was withheld . . . . v 1 151
What valour were it, when a cur doth grin, For one to thrust his hand between his teeth? . . . . *3 Hen. VI.* i 4 56
This carnal cur Preys on the issue of his mother's body . *Richard III.* iv 4 56
This butcher's cur is venom-mouth'd, and I Have not the power to muzzle him . . . . *Hen. VIII.* i 1 120
But, like to village-curs, Bark when their fellows do . . . . ii 4 159
Two curs shall tame each other . . . . *Troi. and Cres.* i 3 391
You whoreson cur!—Do, do.—Thou stool for a witch! . . . ii 1 44
You cur!—Mars his idiot! do, rudeness; do, camel; do, do . . ii 1 57
O thou damned cur! I shall— Will you set your wit to a fool's? . ii 1 93
You ruinous butt, you whoreson indistinguishable cur . . . v 1 33
They set me up, in policy, that mongrel cur, Ajax, against that dog of as bad a kind, Achilles: and now is the cur Ajax prouder than the cur Achilles . . . . v 4 14
What would you have, you curs, That like nor peace nor war? *Coriolanus* i 1 172
You common cry of curs! whose breath I hate as reek o' the rotten fens iii 3 120
Your judgements, my grave lords, Must give this cur the lie . . v 6 107
Two of thy whelps, fell curs of bloody kind, Have here bereft my brother of his life . . . . *T. Andron.* ii 3 281
I spurn thee like a cur out of my way . . . *J. Cæsar* iii 1 46
Whilst damned Casca, like a cur, behind Struck Cæsar on the neck . v 1 43
As hounds and greyhounds, mongrels, spaniels, curs . . *Macbeth* iii 1 93
You slave! you cur!—I am none of these, my lord . . . *Lear* i 4 89
Avaunt, you curs! Be thy mouth or black or white, Tooth that poisons if it bite . . . . iii 6 68
And the creature run from the cur . . . . iv 6 161
Curan. Save thee, Curan.—And you, sir . . . . . . ii 1 1
Curate. The curate and your sweet self are good at such eruptions and sudden breaking out of mirth . . . . . . *L. L. Lost* v 1 120
The parish curate, Alexander; Armado's page, Hercules . . . v 2 538
Make him believe thou art Sir Topas the curate . . *T. Night* iv 2 3
Who calls there?—Sir Topas the curate, who comes to visit Malvolio the lunatic . . . . iv 2 25
Curb. Strict statutes and most biting laws, The needful bits and curbs to headstrong weeds . . . . . . *Meas. for Meas.* i 3 20
To do a great right, do a little wrong, And curb this cruel devil of his will . . . . *Mer. of Venice* iv 1 217
As the ox hath his bow, sir, the horse his curb and the falcon her bells *As Y. Like It* iii 3 81
Thus I'll curb her mad and headstrong humour . *T. of Shrew* iv 1 212
Curbs me From giving reins and spurs to my free speech *Richard II.* i 1 54
With the rusty curb of old father antic the law . . *1 Hen. IV.* i 2 68
Curbs himself even of his natural scope When you come 'cross his humour iii 1 171
When his headstrong riot hath no curb . . . *2 Hen. IV.* iv 4 62
Curb those raging appetites that are Most disobedient and refractory *Troi. and Cres.* ii 2 181
Cracking ten thousand curbs Of more strong link asunder *Coriolanus* i 1 72
It is a purposed thing, and grows by plot, To curb the will of the nobility iii 1 39
Each thing's a thief: The laws, your curb and whip, in their rough power Have uncheck'd theft . . . . . . *T. of Athens* iv 3 446
Virtue itself of vice must pardon beg, Yea, curb and woo for leave to do him good . . . . *Hamlet* iii 4 155
My sanctity Will to my sense bend no licentious ear, But curb it *Pericles* v 3 31
Curbed. So is the will of a living daughter curbed by the will of a dead father . . . . *Mer. of Venice* i 2 26
Strew'd with sweets, Which they distil now in the curbed time *All's Well* ii 4 46
The fifth Harry from curb'd license plucks The muzzle of restraint *2 Hen. IV.* iv 5 131
You are curb'd from that enlargement by The consequence o' the crown *Cymbeline* ii 3 125

Curbing his lavish spirit . . . . *Macbeth* i 2 57
Curd. Does it curd thy blood To say I am thy mother? . . *All's Well* i 3 155
Good sooth, she is The queen of curds and cream . . *W. Tale* iv 4 161
The shepherd's homely curds, His cold thin drink . . *3 Hen. VI.* ii 5 47
And feed on curds and whey, and suck the goat . . *T. Andron.* iv 2 178
Doth posset And curd, like eager droppings into milk . . *Hamlet* i 5 69
Curdied. Chaste as the icicle That's curdied by the frost from purest snow And hangs on Dian's temple . . . . . . *Coriolanus* v 3 66
Cure. Your tale, sir, would cure deafness . . . . *Tempest* i 2 106
A solemn air and the best comforter To an unsettled fancy cure thy brains! . . . . v 1 59
Irreparable is the loss, and patience Says it is past her cure . . . v 1 141
That such a one and such a one were past cure *Meas. for Meas.* ii 1 115
It is a rupture that you may easily heal: and the cure of it not only saves your brother, but keeps you from dishonour in doing it . . iii 1 245
It is too general a vice, and severity must cure it . . . . iii 2 107
There is so great a fever on goodness, that the dissolution of it must cure it . . . . iii 2 236
For to strange sores strangely they strain the cure . . . *Much Ado* iv 1 254
Thy grace being gain'd cures all disgrace in me . . *L. L. Lost* iv 3 67
For 'past cure is still past care' . . . . v 2 28
I profess curing it by counsel.—Did you ever cure any so? *As Y. Like It* iii 2 426
I would cure you, if you would but call me Rosalind . . . . iii 2 446
Past cure of the fives, stark spoiled with the staggers . *T. of Shrew* iii 2 54
There is a remedy, approved, set down, To cure the desperate languishings . . . . *All's Well* i 3 235
I'ld venture The well-lost life of mine in his grace's cure . . . i 3 254
We thank you, maiden; But may not be so credulous of cure . . ii 1 118
And think I know most sure My art is not past power nor you past cure ii 1 161
Within what space Hopest thou my cure? . . . . . . ii 1 163
And with his varying childness cures in me Thoughts that would thick my blood . . . . *W. Tale* i 2 170
This league that we have made Will give her sadness very little cure *K. John* ii 1 546
And falsehood falsehood cures, as fire cools fire . . . . iii 1 277
My widow-comfort, and my sorrows' cure! . . . . . . iii 4 105
Arthur is deceased to-night.—Indeed we fear'd his sickness was past cure iv 2 86
No balm can cure but his heart-blood Which breathed this poison *Richard II.* i 1 172
Too careless patient as thou art, Commit'st thy anointed body to the cure Of those physicians that first wounded thee . . . . . ii 1 98
O, be sick, great greatness, And bid thy ceremony give thee cure! *Hen. V.* iv 1 269
Care is no cure, but rather corrosive, For things that are not to be remedied . . . . *1 Hen. VI.* iii 3 3
Like to Achilles' spear, Is able with the change to kill and cure *2 Hen. VI.* v 1 101
None can cure their harms by wailing them . . . *Richard III.* ii 2 103
There is my purse to cure that blow of thine . . . . . iv 4 516
For my little cure, Let me alone . . . . . . *Hen. VIII.* i 4 33
Thou art a cure fit for a king . . . . ii 2 76
In him It lies to cure me: and the cure is, to Remove these thoughts from you . . . . ii 4 101
We are to cure such sorrows, not to sow 'em . . . . . iii 1 158
Is there no way to cure this? No new device to beat this from his brains? . . . . iii 2 216
To fear the worst oft cures the worse . . . *Troi. and Cres.* iii 2 78
Leave us to cure this cause.—For 'tis a sore upon us *Coriolanus* iii 1 235
O, he's a limb that has but a disease; Mortal, to cut it off; to cure it, easy . . . . iii 1 297
Could we but learn from whence his sorrows grow, We would as willingly give cure as know . . . . *Rom. and Jul.* i 1 161
One desperate grief cures with another's languish . . . . i 2 49
Come weep with me; past hope, past cure, past help! . . . iv 1 45
Peace, ho, for shame! confusion's cure lives not In these confusions . iv 5 65
His friends, like physicians, Thrive, give him over: must I take the cure upon me? . . . . *T. of Athens* iii 3 12
Will the cold brook, Candied with ice, caudle thy morning taste To cure thy o'er-night's surfeit? . . . . iv 3 227
There are a crew of wretched souls That stay his cure . *Macbeth* iv 3 142
He cures, Hanging a golden stamp about their necks, Put on with holy prayers . . . . iv 3 152
Let's make us medicines of our great revenge, To cure this deadly grief iv 3 215
Cure her of that. Canst thou not minister to a mind diseased? . v 3 39
For like the hectic in my blood he rages, And thou must cure me *Hamlet* iv 3 69
Which, if convenience will not allow, Stand in hard cure . *Lear* iii 6 107
Why I do trifle thus with his despair Is done to cure it . . . iv 6 34
O you kind gods, Cure this great breach in his abused nature! . iv 7 15
Therefore my hopes, not surfeited to death, Stand in bold cure *Othello* ii 1 51
A jealousy so strong That judgement cannot cure . . . . ii 1 311
I do love Cassio well; and would do much To cure him of this evil . ii 3 149
If you'll be patient, I'll no more be mad; That cures us both *Cymbeline* iii 3 109
The cure whereof, my lord, 'Tis time must do . . . . . iii 5 37
I can speak of the disturbances That nature works, and of her cures *Pericles* iii 2 38
Cured. It will cost him a thousand pound ere a' be cured *Much Ado* iii 1 90
The reason why they are not so punished and cured is, that the lunacy is so ordinary . . . . *As Y. Like It* iii 2 423
And thus I cured him . . . . iii 2 442
That there shall not be one spot of love in't.—I would not be cured, youth . . . . iii 2 446
Will you be cured of your infirmity? . . . . . *All's Well* ii 1 71
Good my lord, be cured Of this diseased opinion, and betimes *W. Tale* i 2 296
Of this madness cured, Stoop tamely to the foot of majesty *2 Hen. IV.* iv 2 41
The wound that bred this meeting here Cannot be cured by words *3 Hen. VI.* ii 2 122
The king has cured me, I humbly thank his grace . *Hen. VIII.* iii 2 380
That gentle physic, given in time, had cured me . . . . iv 2 122
Come, then; for with a wound I must be cured . *Ant. and Cleo.* iv 14 78
Had rather Groan so in perpetuity than be cured By the sure physician, death . . . . *Cymbeline* v 4 6
Cureless. Repair thy wit, good youth, or it will fall To cureless ruin *Mer. of Venice* iv 1 142
Bootless are plaints, and cureless are my wounds . . *3 Hen. VI.* ii 6 23
Curer. He is a curer of souls, and you a curer of bodies *Mer. Wives* iii 3 40
I'll be a curer of madmen . . . . . . *Troi. and Cres.* v 1 55
Curfew. That rejoice To hear the solemn curfew . . . *Tempest* v 1 40
Who call'd here of late?—None, since the curfew rung *Meas. for Meas.* iv 2 78
He begins at curfew, and walks till the first cock . . . *Lear* iii 4 121
Curfew-bell. The second cock hath crow'd, The curfew-bell hath rung, 'tis three o'clock . . . . *Rom. and Jul.* iv 4 4

Curing. I profess curing it by counsel.—Did you ever cure any so? *As You Like It* iii 2 425
Before the curing of a strong disease, Even in the instant of repair and health, The fit is strongest . *K. John* iii 4 112
Curio. Will you go hunt, my lord?—What, Curio?—The hart . *T. Night* i 1 16
Curiosity. When thou wast in thy gilt and thy perfume, they mocked thee for too much curiosity . . . . *T. of Athens* iv 3 303
Equalities are so weighed, that curiosity in neither can make choice of either's moiety . . . . . . *Lear* i 1 6
Wherefore should I Stand in the plague of custom, and permit The curiosity of nations to deprive me? . . . . i 2 4
I have rather blamed as mine own jealous curiosity than as a very pretence . . . . i 4 75
Curious I cannot be with you, Signior Baptista, of whom I hear so well *T. of Shrew* iv 4 36
Frank nature, rather curious than in haste, Hath well composed thee *All's Well* i 2 20
I am so fraught with curious business that I leave out ceremony *W. Tale* iv 4 525
His body couched in a curious bed . . . *3 Hen. VI.* ii 5 53
What too curious dreg espies my sweet lady in the fountain of our love? *Troi. and Cres.* iii 2 70
What care I What curious eye doth quote deformities? *Rom. and Jul.* i 4 31
Mar a curious tale in telling it, and deliver a plain message bluntly *Lear* i 4 35
You shall not find, Though you be therein curious, the least cause For what you seem to fear . . . *Ant. and Cleo.* iii 2 35
And I am something curious, being strange, To have them in safe stowage *Cymbeline* i 6 191
A most curious mantle, wrought by the hand Of his queen mother . v 5 361
Her face the book of praises, where is read Nothing but curious pleasures *Pericles* i 1 16
Those mothers who, to nousle up their babes, Thought nought too curious i 4 43
Curious-knotted. From the west corner of thy curious-knotted garden *L. L. Lost* i 1 249
Curiously. If I do not carve most curiously, say my knife's naught *Much Ado* v 1 157
The sleeves curiously cut . . . . *T. of Shrew* iv 3 144
Wherein so curiously he had set this counterfeit . *All's Well* iv 3 39
'Twere to consider too curiously, to consider so . *Hamlet* v 1 227
Curl. His arched brows, his hawking eye, his curls . *All's Well* i 1 105
For thou seest it will not curl by nature . . *T. Night* i 3 105
See, what a grace was seated on this brow; Hyperion's curls *Hamlet* iii 4 56
Curled. To dive into the fire, to ride On the curl'd clouds *Tempest* i 2 192
A curled pate will grow bald; a fair face will wither . *Hen. V.* v 2 169
Or swell the curled waters 'bove the main . . *Lear* iii 1 6
A serving-man, proud in heart and mind; that curled my hair . iii 4 83
She shunn'd The wealthy curled darlings of our nation . *Othello* i 2 68
If she first meet the curled Antony, He'll make demand of her *A. and C.* v 2 304
Curled-pate. Make curl'd-pate ruffians bald . *T. of Athens* iv 3 160
Curling. Who take the ruffian billows by the top, Curling their monstrous heads . . . *2 Hen. IV.* iii 1 23
Currance. Never came reformation in a flood, With such a heady currance, scouring faults . . . . *Hen. V.* i 1 34
Currant. Three pound of sugar, five pound of currants . *W. Tale* iv 3 40
Current. The current that with gentle murmur glides *T. G. of Ver.* ii 7 25
Like an impediment in the current, made it more violent and unruly *Meas. for Meas.* iii 1 251
This is no answer, thou unfeeling man, To excuse the current of thy cruelty . . . . . *Mer. of Venice* iv 1 64
Say, shall the current of our right run on? . . *K. John* ii 1 335
O, two such silver currents, when they join, Do glorify the banks that bound them in . . . . . . ii 1 441
Thy word is current with him for my death . *Richard II.* i 3 231
Currents that spring from one most gracious head . iii 3 108
Through muddy passages Hath held his current and defiled himself v 3 63
Speak 'pardon' as 'tis current in our land . . v 3 123
Let not his report Come current for an accusation . *1 Hen. IV.* i 3 68
As to o'er-walk a current roaring loud On the unsteadfast footing of a spear . . . . i 3 192
It holds current that I told you yesternight . . ii 1 59
And all the currents of a heady fight . . . ii 3 58
We must have bloody noses and crack'd crowns, And pass them current too . . . . ii 3 97
I'll have the current in this place damm'd up . . iii 1 101
As not a soldier of this season's stamp Should go so general current through the world . . . . iv 1 5
The one you may do with sterling money, and the other with current repentance . . . . . *2 Hen. IV.* ii 1 132
Thou canst make No excuse current, but to hang thyself *Richard III.* i 2 84
Your fire-new stamp of honour is scarce current . i 3 256
And yet go current from suspicion! . . . i 3 94
All springs reduce their currents to mine eyes . . . ii 2 68
Now do I play the touch, To try if thou be current gold indeed iv 2 9
And, by'r lady, Held current music too . . *Hen. VIII.* i 3 47
He'll turn your current in a ditch, And make your channel his *Coriolanus* iii 1 96
Provokes itself and like the current flies Each bound it chafes *T. of Athens* i 1 24
We must take the current when it serves, Or lose our ventures *J. Cæsar* iv 3 223
With this regard their currents turn awry, And lose the name of action *Hamlet* iii 1 87
In the corrupted currents of this world Offence's gilded hand may shove by justice . . . . iii 3 57
Whose icy current and compulsive course Ne'er feels retiring ebb *Othello* iii 3 454
The fountain from the which my current runs, Or else dries up . iv 2 59
Currish thanks is good enough for such a present . *T. G. of Ver.* iv 4 53
Thy currish spirit Govern'd a wolf . . *Mer. of Venice* iv 1 133
Entreat some power to change this currish Jew . . iv 1 292
A good swift simile, but something currish . *T. of Shrew* v 2 54
His currish riddles sort not with this place . *3 Hen. VI.* v 5 26
Curry. I would curry with Master Shallow that no man could better command his servants . . . . *2 Hen. IV.* v 1 82
Curse. You taught me language; and my profit on't Is, I know how to curse . . . . *Tempest* i 2 364
His spirits hear me And yet I needs must curse . . ii 2 4
Do curse the grace that with such grace hath bless'd them *T. G. of Ver.* iii 1 146
Because myself do want my servants' fortune: I curse myself . iii 1 148
O, 'tis the curse in love, and still approved, When women cannot love where they're beloved! . . . . v 4 43
So curses all Eve's daughters, of what complexion soever *Mer. Wives* iv 2 24
Do curse the gout, serpigo, and the rheum, For ending thee no sooner *Meas. for Meas.* iii 1 31
My heart prays for him, though my tongue do curse . *Com. of Errors* iv 2 28

Curse. Weeps, sobs, beats her heart, tears her hair, prays, curses *M. Ado* ii 3 154
I give him curses, yet he gives me love . . . . *M. N. Dream* i 1 196
Thou, I fear, hast given me cause to curse . . . iii 2 46
The wall, methinks, being sensible, should curse again . . v 1 184
The curse never fell upon our nation till now; I never felt it till now *Mer. of Venice* iii 1 89
I doubt it not, sir; but you will curse your wooing . *T. of Shrew* ii 1 75
It is a curse He cannot be compell'd to't . . *W. Tale* ii 3 87
Better burn it now Than curse it then . . . ii 3 157
The curses he shall have, the tortures he shall feel, will break the back of man . . . . iv 4 796
You shall have no cause To curse the fair proceedings of this day *K. John* iii 1 97
Dreading the curse that money may buy out . . . iii 1 164
O, lawful let it be That I have room with Rome to curse awhile . iii 1 180
Good father cardinal, cry thou amen To my keen curses . . iii 1 182
Without my wrong There is no tongue hath power to curse him right . iii 1 183
There's law and warrant, lady, for my curse.—And for mine too . iii 1 184
Since law itself is perfect wrong, How can the law forbid my tongue to curse? . . . . iii 1 190
Philip of France, on peril of a curse, Let go the hand of that arch-heretic iii 1 191
A heavy curse from Rome, Or the light loss of England for a friend . iii 1 205
Forego the easier.—That's the curse of Rome . . . iii 1 207
Be champion of our church, Or let the church, our mother, breathe her curse, A mother's curse, on her revolting son . . . . . iii 1 256
The peril of our curses light on thee So heavy as thou shalt not shake them off, But in despair die under their black weight . . iii 1 295
I will denounce a curse upon his head.—Thou shalt not need . iii 1 319
It is the curse of kings to be attended By slaves that take their humours for a warrant . . . . iv 2 208
Those whom you curse Have felt the worst of death's destroying wound *Richard II.* iii 2 138
So that thy state might be no worse, I would my skill were subject to thy curse . . . . iii 4 103
Shall it be, That you a world of curses undergo? . *1 Hen. IV.* i 3 164
Both the degrees prevent my curses . . . *2 Hen. IV.* i 2 260
Some are yet ungotten and unborn That shall have cause to curse the Dauphin's scorn . . . . . . *Hen. V.* i 2 288
What! shall we curse the planets of mishap? . . *1 Hen. VI.* i 1 23
And make thee curse the harvest of that corn . . . iii 2 47
No more my fortune can, But curse the cause I cannot aid the man . iv 3 44
Give me leave to curse awhile.—Curse, miscreant, when thou comest to the stake . . . . v 3 43
Then lead me hence; with whom I leave my curse . . v 4 86
That dread King that took our state upon him To free us from his father's wrathful curse . . . . *2 Hen. VI.* iii 2 155
Soft-hearted wretch! Hast thou not spirit to curse thine enemy? . iii 2 308
Wherefore should I curse them? Would curses kill, as doth the mandrake's groan, I would invent as bitter-searching terms . . iii 2 309
Ay, every joint should seem to curse and ban . . . iii 2 319
Even now my burthen'd heart would break, Should I not curse them . iii 2 321
These dread curses, like the sun 'gainst glass, Or like an overcharged gun, recoil . . . . iii 2 330
Well could I curse away a winter's night, Though standing naked on a mountain top . . . . iii 2 335
Ignorance is the curse of God, Knowledge the wing wherewith we fly to heaven . . . . iv 7 78
And so, God's curse light upon you all! . . . . iv 8 33
For yet may England curse my wretched reign . . . iv 9 49
Die, damned wretch, the curse of her that bare thee . . iv 10 83
There, take the crown, and, with the crown, my curse . *3 Hen. VI.* i 4 164
But ere sunset I'll make thee curse the deed . . . ii 2 116
You know no rules of charity, Which renders good for bad, blessings for curses . . . . *Richard III.* i 2 69
But to give me leave, By circumstance, to curse thy cursed self . i 2 80
Curse not thyself, fair creature; thou art both . . . i 2 132
In her heart's extremest hate, With curses in her mouth, tears in her eyes i 2 233
The curse my noble father laid on thee . . . . i 3 174
His curses, then from bitterness of soul Denounced against thee, are all fall'n upon thee . . . . i 3 179
Did York's dread curse prevail so much with heaven? . . i 3 191
Can curses pierce the clouds and enter heaven? Why, then, give way, dull clouds, to my quick curses! . . . . . . i 3 195
O, let me make the period to my curse! . . . . i 3 238
Thus have you breathed your curse against yourself . . i 3 240
The time will come when thou shalt wish for me To help thee curse that poisonous bunch-back'd toad . . . . . . i 3 246
False-boding woman, end thy frantic curse . . . i 3 247
Thy garments are not spotted with our blood, Nor thou within the compass of my curse . . . . i 3 284
Curses never pass The lips of those that breathe them in the air . i 3 285
My hair doth stand on end to hear her curses . . . i 3 304
Now Margaret's curse is fall'n upon our heads . . . iii 3 15
O Margaret, Margaret, now thy heavy curse Is lighted on poor Hastings' wretched head! . . . . iii 4 94
Make me die the thrall of Margaret's curse . . . . iv 1 46
Ere I can repeat this curse again, Even in so short a space . iv 1 78
And proved the subject of my own soul's curse . . . iv 1 81
Help me curse That bottled spider, that foul bunch-back'd toad! . iv 4 80
O thou well skill'd in curses, stay awhile, And teach me how to curse mine enemies! . . . . iv 4 116
Revolving this will teach thee how to curse . . . iv 4 123
Take with thee my most heavy curse; Which, in the day of battle, tire thee more Than all the complete armour that thou wear'st! . iv 4 187
Though far more cause, yet much less spirit to curse Abides in me iv 4 196
Now Margaret's curse is fallen upon my head . . . v 1 25
Their curses now Live where their prayers did . . *Hen. VIII.* i 2 62
It calls, I fear, too many curses on their heads That were the authors ii 1 138
His curses and his blessings Touch me alike, they're breath I not believe in . . . . ii 2 53
All your studies Make me a curse like this.—Your fears are worse . iii 1 124
Or rather, the bone-ache! for that, methinks, is the curse dependant on those that war for a placket . . . *Troi. and Cres.* ii 3 21
The common curse of mankind, folly and ignorance, be thine in great revenue! . . . . ii 3 30
You will catch cold, and curse me . . . . . iv 2 15
Thou damnable box of envy, thou, what meanest thou to curse thus? v 1 30
You slander The helms o' the state, who care for you like fathers, When you curse them as enemies . . . . *Coriolanus* i 1 80
Your virtue is To make him worthy whose offence subdues him And curse that justice did it . . . . i 1 180

Curse. A curse begin at very root on's heart, That is not glad to see thee! *Coriolanus* ii 1 202
Your voices might Be curses to yourselves ii 3 193
Saw you Aufidius?—On safe-guard he came to me; and did curse Against the Volsces iii 1 9
I would the gods had nothing else to do But to confirm my curses! iv 2 46
Such a name, Whose repetition will be dogg'd with curses v 3 144
I curse the day—and yet, I think, Few come within the compass of my curse—Wherein I did not some notorious ill *T. Andron.* v 1 125
Some devil whisper curses in mine ear, And prompt me! v 3 11
But now I see this one is one too much, And that we have a curse in having her *Rom. and Jul.* iii 5 168
Dost thou, or dost thou not, heaven's curse upon thee! *T. of Athens* iv 3 131
If thou wilt curse, thy father, that poor rag, Must be thy subject iv 3 271
A plague on thee! thou art too bad to curse iv 3 365
Thou redeem'st thyself: but all, save thee, I fell with curses iv 3 508
Thou shalt build from men; Hate all, curse all, show charity to none iv 3 534
If thou hatest curses, Stay not; fly, whilst thou art blest and free iv 3 541
Pass by and curse thy fill, but pass and stay not here thy gait v 4 73
The barren, touched in this holy chase, Shake off their sterile curse *J. Cæsar* i 2 9
A curse shall light upon the limbs of men iii 1 262
I will be satisfied: deny me this, And an eternal curse fall on you! *Macbeth* iv 1 105
Curses, not loud but deep, mouth-honour, breath v 3 27
To be baited with the rabble's curse v 8 29
It hath the primal eldest curse upon't, A brother's murder *Hamlet* iii 3 37
Dower'd with our curse, and stranger'd with our oath *Lear* i 1 207
The untented woundings of a father's curse Pierce every sense about thee! i 4 322
My curses on her!—O, sir, you are old ii 4 148
Thou hast one daughter, Who redeems nature from the general curse Which twain have brought her to iv 6 210
'Tis the curse of service, Preferment goes by letter and affection *Othello* i 1 35
O curse of marriage, That we can call these delicate creatures ours, And not their appetites! iii 3 268
Let heaven requite it with the serpent's curse! iv 2 16
Curse his better angel from his side, And fall to reprobation v 2 208
I'll write against them, Detest them, curse them *Cymbeline* ii 5 33
All curses madded Hecuba gave the Greeks, And mine to boot, be darted on thee! iv 2 313
The curse of heaven and men succeed their evils! *Pericles* i 4 104
A curse upon him, die he like a thief, That robs thee of thy goodness! iv 6 121

Cursed be I that did so! *Tempest* i 2 339
I have cursed them without cause v 1 179
Therein she doth evitate and shun A thousand irreligious cursed hours *Mer. Wives* v 5 242
Cursed be thy stones for thus deceiving me! *M. N. Dream* v 1 182
Cursed be my tribe, If I forgive him! *Mer. of Venice* i 3 52
O cursed wretch, That knew'st this was the prince, and wouldst adventure To mingle faith with him! *W. Tale* iv 4 469
Thou shalt stand cursed and excommunicate *K. John* iii 1 173
What canst thou say but will perplex thee more, If thou stand excommunicate and cursed? iii 1 223
What serpent hath suggested thee To make a second fall of cursed man? *Richard II.* iii 4 76
It will the woefullest division prove That ever fell upon this cursed earth iv 1 147
To thick-eyed musing and cursed melancholy *1 Hen. IV.* ii 3 49
Be thou cursed Cain, To slay thy brother Abel, if thou wilt *1 Hen. VI.* i 3 39
Here advance it in the market-place, The middle centre of this cursed town ii 2 6
Was cursed instrument of his decease ii 5 58
Now cursed be the time Of thy nativity! v 4 26
Dost thou deny thy father, cursed drab? v 4 32
What did I then, but cursed the gentle gusts? *2 Hen. VI.* iii 2 88
Cursed be the hand that made these fatal holes! Cursed be the heart that had the heart to do it! Cursed the blood that let this blood from hence! *Richard III.* i 2 14
Give me leave, By circumstance, to curse thy cursed self i 2 80
For had I cursed now, I had cursed myself i 3 319
Then cursed she Hastings, then cursed she Buckingham, Then cursed she Richard iii 3 17
Unless a man were cursed, I cannot tell what to think on't *Tr. and Cr.* v 3 106
Cursed be that heart that forced us to this shift! *T. Andron.* iv 1 72
And be avenged on cursed Tamora v 1 16
A pair of cursed hell-hounds and their dam! v 2 144
Cursed Chiron and Demetrius Were they that murdered our emperor's brother v 3 97
The nurse cursed in the pantry, and every thing in extremity *Rom. and Jul.* i 3 102
That name's cursed hand Murder'd her kinsman iii 3 104
What cursed foot wanders this way to-night? v 3 19
There's nothing level in our cursed natures, But direct villainy *T. of Athens* iv 3 19
Cursed Athens, mindless of thy worth, Forgetting thy great deeds iv 3 93
Through this the well-beloved Brutus stabb'd; And as he pluck'd his cursed steel away, Mark how the blood of Cæsar follow'd it *J. Cæsar* iii 2 181
Merciful powers, Restrain in me the cursed thoughts that nature Gives way to in repose! *Macbeth* ii 1 8
Behold, where stands The usurper's cursed head v 8 55
With juice of cursed hebenon in a vial *Hamlet* i 5 62
The time is out of joint: O cursed spite, That ever I was born to set it right! i 5 189
What if this cursed hand Were thicker than itself with brother's blood? iii 3 43
O, treble woe Fall ten times treble on that cursed head! v 1 270
The best quarrels, in the heat, are cursed By those that feel their sharpness *Lear* v 3 56
And then cried 'Cursed fate that gave thee to the Moor!' *Othello* iii 3 426
O cursed slave! Whip me, ye devils, From the possession of this heavenly sight! v 2 276
Some villain, ay, and singular in his art, Hath done you both this cursed injury *Cymbeline* iii 4 125
And cursed be he that will not second it *Pericles* ii 4 20
Cursed Dionyza hath The pregnant instrument of wrath Prest for this blow iv Gower 43
And her gain She gives the cursed bawd v Gower 11
When fame Had spread their cursed deed Gower v 3 96

Cursedest. Good fortune then! To make me blest or cursed'st among men *Mer. of Venice* ii 1 46

Cursing. Nay, an you be a cursing hypocrite once, you must be looked to *Much Ado* v 1 212
Blaspheming God and cursing men on earth *2 Hen. VI.* iii 2 372
Thou hast made the happy earth thy hell, Fill'd it with cursing cries *Richard III.* i 2 52
Great Achilles Is arming, weeping, cursing, vowing vengeance *Troi. and Cres.* v 5 31
Beating your officers, cursing yourselves *Coriolanus* iii 3 78
Unpack my heart with words, And fall a-cursing, like a very drab *Hamlet* ii 2 615

Cursorary. I have but with a cursorary eye O'erglanced the articles *Hen. V.* v 2 77

Curst. She is curst.—Well, the best is, she hath no teeth to bite *T. G. of Ver.* iii 1 347
In faith, she's too curst.—Too curst is more than curst *Much Ado* ii 1 22
'God sends a curst cow short horns;' but to a cow too curst he sends none ii 1 25
By being too curst, God will send you no horns ii 1 27
Do not curst wives hold that self-sovereignty Only for praise sake? *L. L. Lost* iv 1 36
I was never curst; I have no gift at all in shrewishness *M. N. Dream* iii 2 300
I will not trust you, I, Nor longer stay in your curst company iii 2 341
Here she comes, curst and sad iii 2 439
Her elder sister is so curst and shrewd *T. of Shrew* i 1 185
As old as Sibyl and as curst and shrewd As Socrates' Xanthippe i 2 70
Her only fault, and that is faults enough, Is that she is intolerable curst i 2 89
Katharine the curst! A title for a maid of all titles the worst i 2 129
Will undertake to woo curst Katharine, Yea, and to marry her i 2 184
You are call'd plain Kate, And bonny Kate and sometimes Kate the curst ii 1 187
If she be curst, it is for policy, For she's not froward ii 1 294
'Tis bargain'd twixt us twain, being alone, That she shall still be curst in company ii 1 307
Now, go thy ways; thou hast tamed a curst shrew v 2 188
Go, write it in a martial hand; be curst and brief *T. Night* iii 2 46
They are never curst but when they are hungry *W. Tale* iii 3 135
I would invent as bitter-searching terms, As curst, as harsh *2 Hen. VI.* iii 2 312
Sweet saint, for charity, be not so curst *Richard III.* i 2 49
With curst speech I threaten'd to discover him *Lear* ii 1 67

Curster than she? why, 'tis impossible *T. of Shrew* iii 2 156

Curstest. When men and women are alone, A meacock wretch can make the curstest shrew ii 1 315

Curstness. Touch you the sourest points with sweetest terms, Nor curstness grow to the matter *Ant. and Cleo.* ii 2 25

Curtail. When a gentleman is disposed to swear, it is not for any standers-by to curtail his oaths *Cymbeline* ii 1 12

Curtailed. I, that am curtail'd of this fair proportion *Richard III.* i 1 18

Curtain. The fringed curtains of thine eye advance *Tempest* i 2 408
Go draw aside the curtains and discover The several caskets *Mer. of Venice* ii 7 1
A gentle riddance. Draw the curtains, go ii 7 78
Quick, quick, I pray thee; draw the curtain straight ii 9 1
Come, draw the curtain, Nerissa ii 9 84
Wherefore have these gifts a curtain before 'em? *T. Night* i 3 134
We will draw the curtain and show you the picture i 5 251
Do not draw the curtain.—No longer shall you gaze on't *W. Tale* v 3 59
I'll draw the curtain: My lord's almost so far transported that He'll think anon it lives v 3 68
Shall I draw the curtain?—No, not these twenty years v 3 83
This absence of your father's draws a curtain, That shows the ignorant a kind of fear Before not dreamt of *1 Hen. IV.* iv 1 73
Drew Priam's curtain in the dead of night *2 Hen. IV.* i 1 72
Their ragged curtains poorly are let loose *Hen. V.* iv 2 41
Close up his eyes and draw the curtain close *2 Hen. VI.* iii 3 32
Let 'em alone, and draw the curtain close: We shall hear more anon *Hen. VIII.* v 2 34
Come, draw this curtain, and let's see your picture *Troi. and Cres.* iii 2 49
Soon as the all-cheering sun Should in the furthest east begin to draw The shady curtains from Aurora's bed *Rom. and Jul.* i 1 142
Spread thy close curtain, love-performing night iii 2 5
Make no noise, make no noise; draw the curtains *Lear* iii 6 90
Let me the curtains draw. Where art thou? *Othello* v 2 104

Curtain'd with a counsel-keeping cave *T. Andron.* ii 3 24
Nature seems dead, and wicked dreams abuse The curtain'd sleep *Macbeth* ii 1 51

Curtal. I'ld give bay Curtal and his furniture, My mouth no more were broken than these boys' *All's Well* ii 3 65

Curtal dog. Hope is a curtal dog in some affairs *Mer. Wives* ii 1 114
She had transform'd me to a curtal dog and made me turn i' the wheel *Com. of Errors* iii 2 151

Curtis. Holla, ho! Curtis.—Who is that calls so coldly? *T. of Shrew* iv 1 12
A fire, good Curtis iv 1 17
Is my master and his wife coming, Grumio?—O, ay, Curtis, ay: and therefore fire, fire iv 1 20
Is she so hot a shrew as she's reported?—She was, good Curtis, before this frost iv 1 23
It hath tamed my old master and my new mistress and myself, fellow Curtis iv 1 26
How goes the world?—A cold world, Curtis, in every office but thine iv 1 37

Curtle-axe. A gallant curtle-axe upon my thigh *As Y. Like It* i 3 119
Scarce blood enough in all their sickly veins To give each naked curtle-axe a stain *Hen. V.* iv 2 21

Curtsy. It is my cousin's duty to make curtsy and say 'Father, as it please you' *Much Ado* ii 1 56
Let him be a handsome fellow, or else make another curtsy and say 'Father, as it please me' ii 1 58
Curtsy, sweet hearts; and so the measure ends *L. L. Lost* v 2 221
Do overpeer the petty traffickers, That curtsy to them *Mer. of Venice* i 1 13
For my kind offer, when I make curtsy, bid me farewell *As Y. Like It* Epil. 23
Let them curtsy with their left legs *T. of Shrew* iv 1 95
To dog his heels and curtsy at his frowns *1 Hen. IV.* iii 2 127
Nice customs curtsy to great kings *Hen. V.* v 2 293
The match is made; she seals it with a curtsy *3 Hen. VI.* iii 2 57
What is that curt'sy worth? or those doves' eyes? *Coriolanus* v 3 27

Curvet. Cry 'holla' to thy tongue, I prithee; it curvets unseasonably *As Y. Like It* iii 2 258
The bound and high curvet Of Mars's fiery steed *All's Well* ii 3 299

Cushion. O, a stool and a cushion for the sexton *Much Ado* iv 2 2
Both on one sampler, sitting on one cushion *M. N. Dream* iii 2 205

Cushion. Fine linen, Turkey cushions boss'd with pearl . *T. of Shrew* ii 1 355
This chair shall be my state, this dagger my sceptre, and this cushion my crown . . . 1 *Hen. IV.* ii 4 416
You shall have a dozen of cushions again; you have but eleven now 2 *Hen. IV.* v 4 17
Cushions, leaden spoons, Irons of a doit *Coriolanus* i 5 6
Your beards deserve not so honourable a grave as to stuff a botcher's cushion . . . ii 1 98
If you are learn'd, Be not as common fools; if you are not, Let them have cushions by you . . . iii 1 101
Not to be other than one thing, not moving From the casque to the cushion . . . iv 7 43
Stand up blest! Whilst, with no softer cushion than the flint, I kneel before thee . . . v 3 53
I'll have them sleep on cushions in my tent . . . *J. Cæsar* iv 3 243
Will you lie down and rest upon the cushions? . *Lear* iii 6 36
His right cheek Reposing on a cushion . *Cymbeline* iv 2 212
Custalorum. Ay, cousin Slender, and 'Custalorum.'—Ay, and 'Ratolorum' too . . . *Mer. Wives* i 1 7
Custard. You have made shift to run into't, boots and spurs and all, like him that leaped into the custard . *All's Well* ii 5 41
Custard-coffin. It is a paltry cap, A custard-coffin, a bauble *T. of Shrew* iv 3 82
Custody. Gaoler, take him to thy custody *Com. of Errors* i 1 156
How darest thou trust So great a charge from thine own custody? . i 2 61
I'll know thy thoughts.—You cannot, if my heart were in your hand; Nor shall not, whilst 'tis in my custody . . . *Othello* iii 3 164
Custom. I am more serious than my custom . *Tempest* ii 1 219
'Tis a custom with him, I' th' afternoon to sleep . iii 2 95
Our dance of custom round about the oak Of Herne the hunter *M. Wives* v 5 79
Till custom make it Their perch and not their terror . *Meas. for Meas.* ii 1 3
Would you have me speak after my custom? . *Much Ado* i 1 169
Yet, to supply the ripe wants of my friend, I'll break a custom *Mer. of Venice* i 3 65
For herein Fortune shows herself more kind Than is her custom . iv 1 268
Hath not old custom made this life more sweet Than that of painted pomp? . . . *As Y. Like It* ii 1 2
You shall hop without my custom, sir . *T. of Shrew* iv 3 99
In one self-born hour To plant and o'erwhelm custom . *W. Tale* iv 1 9
Our feasts In every mess have folly and the feeders Digest it with a custom . . . iv 4 12
Would beguile Nature of her custom, so perfectly he is her ape . v 2 108
By custom and the ordinance of times . *Hen. V.* ii 4 83
Nice customs curtsy to great kings . v 2 293
New customs, Though they be never so ridiculous, Nay, let 'em be unmanly, yet are follow'd . *Hen. VIII.* i 3 2
The list Of those that claim their offices this day By custom of the coronation . iv 1 16
Had I not known those customs, I should have been beholding to your paper . iv 1 20
Office and custom, in all line of order . *Troi. and Cres.* i 3 88
All That time, acquaintance, custom and condition Made tame . iii 3 9
Shall lift up Their rotten privilege and custom 'gainst My hate *Coriol.* i 10 23
I do beseech you, Let me o'erleap that custom . ii 2 140
Go fit you to the custom and Take to you, as your predecessors have, Your honour with your form . ii 2 146
Custom calls me to't: What custom wills, in all things should we do't ii 3 124
The custom of request you have discharged . ii 3 150
'I would be consul,' says he: 'aged custom, But by your voices, will not so permit me' . ii 3 176
As the custom is, In all her best array bear her to church *Rom. and Jul.* iv 5 80
Degrees, observances, customs, and laws, Decline to your confounding contraries, And let confusion live! . *T. of Athens* iv 1 19
All pity choked with custom of fell deeds . *J. Cæsar* iii 1 269
Think of this, good peers, But as a thing of custom: 'tis no other *Macb.* iii 4 97
Shall live the lease of nature, pay his breath To time and mortal custom iv 1 100
Is it a custom?—Ay, marry, is't . *Hamlet* i 4 12
It is a custom more honour'd in the breach than the observance . i 4 15
Sleeping within my orchard, My custom always of the afternoon . i 5 60
Lost all my mirth, forgone all custom of exercises . ii 2 308
If damned custom have not brass'd it so That it be proof and bulwark against sense . iii 4 37
That monster, custom, who all sense doth eat, Of habits devil, is angel yet in this . iii 4 161
As the world were now but to begin, Antiquity forgot, custom not known . iv 5 104
Nature her custom holds, Let shame say what it will . iv 7 188
Custom hath made it in him a property of easiness . v 1 75
Wherefore should I Stand in the plague of custom? . *Lear* i 2 3
The tyrant custom, most grave senators . *Othello* i 3 230
I could well wish courtesy would invent some other custom of entertainment . ii 3 36
Such things in a false disloyal knave Are tricks of custom . iii 3 122
Age cannot wither her, nor custom stale Her infinite variety *Ant. and Cleo.* ii 2 240
This is but a custom in your tongue; you bear a graver purpose, I hope *Cymbeline* i 4 150
Stick to your journal course: the breach of custom Is breach of all . iv 2 10
But custom what they did begin Was with long use account no sin *Pericles* i Gower 29
With us at sea it hath been still observed: and we are strong in custom iii 1 53
You'll lose nothing by custom . iv 2 150
Customary. Let us teach our trial patience, Because it is a customary cross . *M. N. Dream* i 1 153
I know you would be prouder of the work Than customary bounty can enforce you . *Mer. of Venice* iii 4 9
Even now I met him With customary compliment . *W. Tale* i 2 371
Take from Time His charters and his customary rights . *Richard II.* ii 1 196
I have here the customary gown . *Coriolanus* ii 3 93
'Tis not alone my inky cloak, good mother, Nor customary suits of solemn black . *Hamlet* i 2 78
Customed. No common wind, no customed event . *K. John* iii 4 155
To wring the widow from her custom'd right . 2 *Hen. VI.* v 1 188
Customer. Here be many of her old customers . *Meas. for Meas.* iv 3 4
You minion, you, are these your customers? . *Com. of Errors* iv 4 63
I think thee now some common customer . *All's Well* v 3 287
No milliner can so fit his customers with gloves . *W. Tale* iv 4 192
I marry her! what? a customer! . *Othello* iv 1 122
If the peevish baggage would but give way to customers . *Pericles* iv 6 21
Custom-shrunk. What with poverty, I am custom-shrunk *Meas. for Meas.* i 2 85
Custure. Qualtitie calmie custure me! . *Hen. V.* iv 4 4

Cut. Paunch him with a stake, Or cut his wezand with thy knife *Temp.* iii 2 99
Why, then, your ladyship must cut your hair *T. G. of Ver.* ii 7 44
I will cut his troat in de park . *Mer. Wives* i 4 114
I will cut all his two stones; by gar, he shall not have a stone to throw at his dog . i 4 118
Scurvy jack-dog priest! by gar, me vill cut his ears . iii 3 66
Let us be keen, and rather cut a little, Than fall . *Meas. for Meas.* ii 1 5
He would have weigh'd thy brother by himself And not have cut him off . v 1 112
And from my false hand cut the wedding-ring . *Com. of Errors* ii 2 139
How shall we try it?—We'll draw cuts for the senior . v 1 422
The pleasant'st angling is to see the fish Cut with her golden oars the silver stream . *Much Ado* iii 1 27
If tall, a lance ill-headed; If low, an agate very vilely cut . iii 1 65
He hath twice or thrice cut Cupid's bow-string . iii 2 11
Cloth o' gold, and cuts, and laced with silver . iii 4 19
A sharp wit match'd with too blunt a will; Whose edge hath power to cut . *L. L. Lost* ii 1 50
Cut me to pieces with thy keen conceit . v 2 399
Enough; hold or cut bow-strings . *M. N. Dream* i 2 114
Good Master Cobweb: if I cut my finger, I shall make bold with you . iii 1 186
Night's swift dragons cut the clouds full fast . iii 2 379
O Fates, come, come, Cut thread and thrum . v 1 291
Sit like his grandsire cut in alabaster . *Mer. of Venice* i 1 84
Why dost thou whet thy knife so earnestly?—To cut the forfeiture . iv 1 122
From which lingering penance Of such misery doth she cut me off . iv 1 272
If the Jew do cut but deep enough, I'll pay it presently with all my heart . iv 1 280
And you must cut this flesh from off his breast: The law allows it . iv 1 302
Shed thou no blood, nor cut thou less nor more But just a pound of flesh . iv 1 325
I were best to cut my left hand off And swear I lost the ring defending it . v 1 177
If he fail of that, He will have other means to cut you off *As Y. Like It* ii 3 25
With eyes severe and beard of formal cut, Full of wise saws . ii 7 155
I did dislike the cut of a certain courtier's beard: he sent me word, if I said his beard was not cut well, he was in the mind it was . v 4 73
If I sent him word again 'it was not well cut,' he would send me word, he cut it to please himself . v 4 77
Here's snip and nip and cut and slish and slash . *T. of Shrew* iv 3 90
With needle and thread.—But did you not request to have it cut? . iv 3 122
I bid thy master cut out the gown; but I did not bid him cut it to pieces . iv 3 127
The sleeves curiously cut.—Ay, there's the villany . iv 3 144
And cut the entail from all remainders . *All's Well* iv 3 313
I can cut a caper.—And I can cut the mutton to't . *T. Night* i 3 129
If thou hast her not i' the end, call me cut . ii 3 203
O, cut my lace, lest my heart, cracking it, Break too! . *W. Tale* iii 2 174
I picked and cut most of their festival purses . iv 4 627
What fine chisel Could ever yet cut breath? . v 3 79
Cut him to pieces.—Keep the peace, I say . *K. John* iv 3 93
Some of those branches by the Destinies cut . *Richard II.* i 2 15
The edge of war, like an ill-sheathed knife, No more shall cut his master . 1 *Hen. IV.* i 1 18
If you and I do not rob them, cut this head off from my shoulders . i 2 185
Strike; down with them; cut the villains' throats . ii 2 87
My buckler cut through and through . ii 4 186
This river comes me cranking in, And cuts me from the best of all my land . iii 1 99
Cut me off the heads Of all the favourites . iv 3 85
I thank him, that he cuts me from my tale, For I profess not talking . v 2 91
Cut me off the villain's head . 2 *Hen. IV.* ii 1 50
Which to avoid, I cut them off . iv 5 210
I will cut thy throat, one time or other, in fair terms . *Hen. V.* ii 1 73
Why the devil should we keep knives to cut one another's throats? . ii 1 96
The powers we bear with us Will cut their passage through the force of France . ii 2 16
And there is throats to be cut, and works to be done . iii 2 119
Let not Bardolph's vital thread be cut With edge of penny cord . iii 6 49
And what a beard of the general's cut and a horrid suit of the camp will do . iii 6 81
When our throats are cut, he may be ransomed, and we ne'er the wiser iv 1 205
It is no English treason to cut French crowns . iv 1 245
Bid him prepare; for I will cut his throat . iv 4 34
The king, most worthily, hath caused every soldier to cut his prisoner's throat . iv 7 10
We'll cut the throats of those we have . iv 7 66
The ruthless flint doth cut my tender feet . 2 *Hen. VI.* ii 4 34
Cut both the villains' throats; for die you shall . iv 1 20
Then is sin struck down like an ox, and iniquity's throat cut like a calf iv 2 29
I myself, Rather than bloody war shall cut them short, Will parley with Jack Cade . iv 4 12
Steel, if thou turn the edge, or cut not out the burly-boned clown . iv 10 60
Into as many gobbets will I cut it As wild Medea young Absyrtus did . v 2 58
From whence shall Warwick cut the sea to France . 3 *Hen. VI.* ii 6 89
And so I say, I'll cut the causes off, Flattering me with impossibilities iii 2 142
I'll have this crown of mine cut from my shoulders Ere I will see the crown so foul misplaced . *Richard III.* iii 2 43
O, cut my lace in sunder, that my pent heart May have some scope to beat! . iv 1 34
Their clothes are after such a pagan cut too . *Hen. VIII.* i 3 14
The strong-ribb'd bark through liquid mountains cut . *Troi. and Cres.* i 3 40
Though the great bulk Achilles be thy guard, I'll cut thy throat . iv 4 131
O, he's a limb that has but a disease; Mortal, to cut it off; to cure it, easy . *Coriolanus* iii 1 297
Present My throat to thee and to thy ancient malice; Which not to cut would show thee but a fool . iv 5 103
Our general is cut i' the middle and but one half of what he was yesterday . iv 5 210
Cut me to pieces, Volsces; men and lads, Stain all your edges on me . v 6 112
Easy it is Of a cut loaf to steal a shive, we know . *T. Andron.* ii 1 87
Speak, Who 'twas that cut thy tongue and ravish'd thee . ii 4 2
And, lest thou shouldst detect him, cut thy tongue . ii 4 27
But, lovely niece, that mean is cut from thee . ii 4 40
And he hath cut those pretty fingers off . ii 4 42
All the service I require of them Is that the one will help to cut the other . iii 1 78
They cut thy sister's tongue and ravish'd her And cut her hands . v 1 92
She was wash'd and cut and trimm'd, and 'twas Trim sport for them . v 1 95
This one hand yet is left to cut your throats . v 2 182

Cut. He swung about his head and cut the winds . . . *Rom. and Jul.* i 1 118
Beauty starved with her severity Cuts beauty off from all posterity . . i 1 226
When he shall die, Take him and cut him out in little stars . . iii 2 22
O, what more favour can I do to thee, Than with that hand that cut thy youth in twain To sunder his that was thine enemy? . . . v 3 99
Cut my heart in sums.—Mine, fifty talents.—Tell out my blood *T. of A.* iii 4 93
And let the foes quietly cut their throats, Without repugnancy . . iii 5 44
Out with your knifes, And cut your trusters' throats! . . . iv 1 10
A bastard, whom the oracle Hath doubtfully pronounced thy throat shall cut . . . . iv 3 121
Cut throats; All that you meet are thieves . . . . iv 3 448
He plucked me ope his doublet and offered them his throat to cut *J. Cæsar* i 2 268
To cut the head off and then hack the limbs . . . . ii 1 163
This was the most unkindest cut of all . . . . iii 2 187
From which advantage shall we cut him off . . . . iv 3 210
His throat is cut; that I did for him.—Thou art the best o' the cut-throats . . . . . . *Macbeth* iii 4 16
What would you undertake . . . ?—To cut his throat i' the church *Hamlet* iv 7 127
After I have cut the egg i' the middle . . . . *Lear* i 4 173
Shall not be a maid long, unless things be cut shorter . . i 5 56
Preferment falls on him that cuts him off . . . . iv 5 38
Let me have surgeons; I am cut to the brains . . . . iv 6 197
You have many opportunities to cut him off . . . . iv 6 268
I had rather have this tongue cut from my mouth Than it should do offence to Michael Cassio . . . . *Othello* ii 3 221
My leg is cut in two.—Marry, heaven forbid! Light, gentlemen . v 1 72
If there were no more women but Fulvia, then had you indeed a cut, and the case to be lamented . . . *Ant. and Cleo.* i 2 173
Cut my lace, Charmian, come; But let it be: I am quickly ill, and well, So Antony loves . . . . i 3 71
Let me cut the cable; And, when we are put off, fall to their throats . ii 7 77
He could so quickly cut the Ionian sea, And take in Toryne . . iii 7 23
Draw my sword? the paper Hath cut her throat already . *Cymbeline* iii 4 35
Thy garments cut to pieces before thy face . . . . iv 1 19
But his neat cookery! he cut our roots In characters . . . iv 2 48
Or till the Destinies do cut his thread of life . . . *Pericles* i 2 108
Their vessel shakes On Neptune's billow; half the flood Hath their keel cut . . . . iii Gower 46
Thou mayst cut a morsel off the spit . . . . . iv 2 142
He swears Never to wash his face, nor cut his hairs: He puts on sackcloth iv 4 28
Cut a caper. I can cut a caper.—And I can cut the mutton to't *T. Night* i 3 129
He offered to cut a caper at the proclamation . . . *Pericles* iv 2 116
Cut and long-tail. Ay, that I will, come cut and long-tail *Mer. Wives* iii 4 47
Cut away. Of England's coat one half is cut away . . 1 *Hen. VI.* i 1 81
If all obstacles were cut away . . . . . *Richard III.* iii 7 156
He's a disease that must be cut away . . . *Coriolanus* iii 1 295
Shall we cut away our hands, like thine? . . . *T. Andron.* iii 1 130
They ravish'd her, and cut away her tongue . . . . v 3 57
Cut down. I have a tree, which grows here in my close, That mine own use invites me to cut down . . . . . *T. of Athens* v 1 209
Cut off. Can you cut off a man's head? . . . *Meas. for Meas.* iv 2 1
I can never cut off a woman's head . . . . . iv 2 5
She hath been a suitor to me for her brother Cut off by course of justice v 1 35
Let the forfeit Be nominated for an equal pound Of your fair flesh, to be cut off . . . . . . *Mer. of Venice* i 3 151
A pound of flesh, to be by him cut off Nearest the merchant's heart . iv 1 232
Therefore prepare thee to cut off the flesh . . . . iv 1 324
Hath not Fortune sent in this fool to cut off the argument? *As Y. Like It* i 2 49
And, to cut off all strife, here sit we down . . *T. of Shrew* iii 1 21
The interruption of their churlish drums Cuts off more circumstance *K. John* ii 1 77
Thou hast under-wrought his lawful king, Cut off the sequence of posterity . . . . ii 1 96
Another lean unwash'd artificer Cuts off his tale and talks of Arthur's death . . . . iv 2 202
I would to God, So my untruth had not provoked him to it, The king had cut off my head . . . . . . *Richard II.* ii 2 102
Go thou, and like an executioner, Cut off the heads of too fast growing sprays . . . . iii 4 34
This fester'd joint cut off, the rest rest sound . . . . v 3 85
Would not this nave of a wheel have his ears cut off? . 2 *Hen. IV.* ii 4 279
So Chrish save me, I will cut off your head . . . *Hen. V.* iii 2 144
We would have all such offenders so cut off . . . . iii 6 114
And there my rendezvous is quite cut off . . . . v 1 88
For friendly counsel cuts off many foes . . . 1 *Hen. VI.* iii 1 185
Unto a dunghill which shall be thy grave, And there cut off thy most ungracious head . . . . 2 *Hen. VI.* iv 10 88
I, that did never weep, now melt with woe That winter should cut off our spring-time so . . . . . . 3 *Hen. VI.* ii 3 47
Shall, whiles thy head is warm and new cut off, Write in the dust this sentence with thy blood . . . . v 1 55
But if you ever chance to have a child, Look in his youth to have him so cut off . . . . v 5 66
God, I pray him, That none of you may live your natural age, But by some unlook'd accident cut off! . . . . *Richard III.* i 3 214
He needs no indirect nor lawless course To cut off those that have offended him . . . . i 4 225
The leisure and the fearful time Cuts off the ceremonious vows of love . v 3 98
Your full consent Gave wings to my propension and cut off All fears attending on so dire a project . . . . . *Troi. and Cres.* ii 2 133
You'll rejoice That he is thus cut off . . . . *Coriolanus* v 6 140
As she in fury shall Cut off the proud'st conspirator that lives *T. Andron.* iv 4 26
My hand cut off and made a merry jest . . . . . v 2 175
I will be cruel with the maids, and cut off their heads . *Rom. and Jul.* i 1 27
He that cuts off twenty years of life Cuts off so many years of fearing death . . . . *J. Cæsar* iii 1 102
No place will please me so, no mean of death, As here by Cæsar, and by you cut off . . . . iii 1 162
Fetch the will hither, and we shall determine How to cut off some charge in legacies . . . . iv 1 9
Were I king, I should cut off the nobles for their lands . *Macbeth* iv 3 79
Cut off even in the blossoms of my sin, Unhousel'd, disappointed *Hamlet* i 5 76
'Tis not in thee To grudge my pleasures, to cut off my train . *Lear* ii 4 177
What hast thou done?—I am perfect what: cut off one Cloten's head *Cymb.* iv 2 118
Conspired with that irregulous devil, Cloten, Hast here cut off my lord iv 2 316
I cut off's head; And am right glad he is not standing here To tell . v 5 295
Cut out. I bid thy master cut out the gown; but I did not bid him cut it to pieces . . . . *T. of Shrew* iv 3 127
I commanded the sleeves should be cut out and sewed up again . . iv 3 147
By the pattern of mine own thoughts I cut out The purity of his *W. Tale* iv 4 393
Cut out. Or, Hubert, if you will, cut out my tongue, So I may keep mine eyes . . . . *K. John* iv 1 101
Be his own carver and cut out his way . . . *Richard II.* ii 3 144
I shall cut out your tongue.—'Tis no matter; I shall speak as much as thou afterwards . . . . . . *Troi. and Cres.* ii 1 121
Cut short. But, gentle heavens, Cut short all intermission . *Macbeth* iv 3 232
Cutler. For all the world like cutler's poetry Upon a knife *Mer. of Venice* v 1 149
Cutpurse. An open ear, a quick eye, and a nimble hand, is necessary for a cut-purse . . . . *W. Tale* iv 4 686
Away, you cut-purse rascal! you filthy bung, away! . 2 *Hen. IV.* ii 4 137
I remember him now; a bawd, a cut-purse . . . *Hen. V.* iii 6 65
Bawd I'll turn, And something lean to cutpurse of quick hand . v 1 91
A vice of kings; A cutpurse of the empire and the rule . *Hamlet* iii 4 99
When slanders do not live in tongues; Nor cutpurses come not to throngs . . . . *Lear* iii 2 88
Cut's saddle. Beat Cut's saddle, put a few flocks in the point 1 *Hen. IV.* ii 1 6
Cutter. The cutter Was as another nature, dumb . *Cymbeline* ii 4 83
Cutter-off. When Fortune makes Nature's natural the cutter-off of Nature's wit . . . . *As Y. Like It* i 2 53
Cuttest. If thou cut'st more Or less than a just pound . *Mer. of Venice* iv 1 326
Thou cutt'st my head off with a golden axe . . *Rom. and Jul.* iii 3 22
Cut-throat. You call me misbeliever, cut-throat dog . *Mer. of Venice* i 3 112
Thou art the best o' the cut-throats: yet he's good . . *Macbeth* iii 4 17
Cutting. I met her deity Cutting the clouds towards Paphos . *Tempest* iv 1 93
Cutting a smaller hair than may be seen, Above the sense of sense *L. L. Lost* v 2 258
Take thou thy pound of flesh; But, in the cutting it, if thou dost shed One drop of Christian blood, thy lands and goods Are, by the laws of Venice, confiscate . . . . . . *Mer. of Venice* iv 1 309
I would the cutting of my garments would serve the turn . *All's Well* iv 1 50
He means to recompense the pains you take By cutting off your heads *K. John* v 4 16
The welfare of us all Hangs on the cutting short that fraudful man 2 *Hen. VI.* iii 1 81
It will not in circumvention deliver a fly from a spider, without drawing their massy irons and cutting the web . . . *Troi. and Cres.* ii 3 19
Sometime she driveth o'er a soldier's neck, And then dreams he of cutting foreign throats . . . . . . *Rom. and Jul.* i 4 83
Cuttle. I'll thrust my knife in your mouldy chaps, an you play the saucy cuttle with me . . . . 2 *Hen. IV.* ii 4 139
Cyclops. No big-boned men framed of the Cyclops' size *T. Andron.* iv 3 46
Never did the Cyclops' hammers fall On Mars's armour forged for proof eterne With less remorse . . . . . . *Hamlet* ii 2 511
Cydnus. When she first met Mark Antony, she pursed up his heart, upon the river of Cydnus . . . . *Ant. and Cleo.* ii 2 192
I am again for Cydnus, To meet Mark Antony . . . . v 2 228
And Cydnus swell'd above the banks, or for The press of boats or pride *Cymbeline* ii 4 71
Cygnet. I am the cygnet to this pale faint swan . . *K. John* v 7 21
So doth the swan her downy cygnets save . . . 1 *Hen. VI.* v 3 56
To whose soft seizure The cygnet's down is harsh *Troi. and Cres.* i 1 58
Cymbal. Tabors and cymbals and the shouting Romans Make the sun dance . . . . *Coriolanus* v 4 53
Cymbeline loved me, And when a soldier was the theme, my name Was not far off . . . . *Cymbeline* iii 3 58
Swore to Cymbeline I was confederate with the Romans . . iii 3 67
These boys know little they are sons to the king; Nor Cymbeline dreams that they are alive . . . . iii 3 81
This Polydore, The heir of Cymbeline and Britain . . . iii 3 87
O Cymbeline! heaven and my conscience knows Thou didst unjustly banish me . . . . iii 3 99
Like hardiment Posthumus hath To Cymbeline perform'd . . v 4 76
Ask of Cymbeline what boon thou wilt, Fitting my bounty and thy state v 5 97
The lofty cedar, royal Cymbeline, Personates thee . . . v 5 453
The imperial Cæsar should again unite His favour with the radiant Cymbeline . . . . v 5 475
Cyme. What rhubarb, cyme, or what purgative drug, Would scour these English hence? . . . . *Macbeth* v 3 55
Cynic. Ha ha! how vilely doth this cynic rhyme! . . *J. Cæsar* iv 3 133
Cynthia. 'Tis but the pale reflex of Cynthia's brow . *Rom. and Jul.* iii 5 20
This by the eye of Cynthia hath she vow'd . . . *Pericles* ii 5 11
Cypress. In cypress chests my arras counterpoints . *T. of Shrew* ii 1 353
Come away, come away, death, And in sad cypress let me be laid *T. Night* ii 4 53
A cypress, not a bosom, Hideth my heart . . . . iii 1 132
Their sweetest shade a grove of cypress trees! . . . 2 *Hen. VI.* iii 2 323
I am attended at the cypress grove . . . . *Coriolanus* i 10 30
Cyprus black as e'er was crow . . . . . *W. Tale* iv 4 221
At Rhodes, at Cyprus and on other grounds Christian and heathen *Othello* i 1 29
He's embark'd With such loud reason to the Cyprus wars . . i 1 151
What is the matter, think you?—Something from Cyprus, as I may divine i 2 39
They all confirm A Turkish fleet, and bearing up to Cyprus . . i 3 8
When we consider The importancy of Cyprus to the Turk . . i 3 20
Bearing with frank appearance Their purposes toward Cyprus . . i 3 39
'Tis certain, then, for Cyprus . . . . i 3 43
So let the Turk of Cyprus us beguile; We lose it not, so long as we can smile . . . . i 3 210
The Turk with a most mighty preparation makes for Cyprus . . i 3 222
The Moor himself at sea, And is in full commission here for Cyprus . ii 1 29
Give renew'd fire to our extincted spirits, And bring all Cyprus comfort! ii 1 82
Behold, The riches of the ship is come on shore! Ye men of Cyprus, let her have your knees . . . . ii 1 84
You shall be well desired in Cyprus; I have found great love amongst them ii 1 206
Come, Desdemona, Once more, well met at Cyprus . . . . ii 1 214
Even out of that will I cause these of Cyprus to mutiny . . ii 1 282
Heaven bless the isle of Cyprus and our noble general Othello! . ii 2 12
A brace of Cyprus gallants that would fain have a measure to the health of black Othello . . . . ii 3 31
Three lads of Cyprus, noble swelling spirits . . . . ii 3 57
He you hurt is of great fame in Cyprus And great affinity . . iii 1 48
Some unhatch'd practice Made demonstrable here in Cyprus . . iii 4 142
I am very glad to see you, signior; Welcome to Cyprus . . iv 1 232
I do entreat that we may sup together: You are welcome, sir, to Cyprus iv 1 274
Your power and your command is taken off, And Cassio rules in Cyprus v 2 332
Made her Of lower Syria, Cyprus, Lydia, Absolute queen *Ant. and Cleo.* iii 6 10
Cyrus. I shall as famous be by this exploit As Scythian Tomyris by Cyrus' death . . . . 1 *Hen. VI.* ii 3 6
Cytherea. And Cytherea all in sedges hid . . . *T. of Shrew* Ind. 2 53
Sweeter than the lids of Juno's eyes Or Cytherea's breath *W. Tale* iv 4 122
Cytherea, How bravely thou becomest thy bed, fresh lily, And whiter than the sheets! . . . . *Cymbeline* ii 2 14

D

Dabbled. A shadow like an angel, with bright hair Dabbled in blood *Richard III.* i 4 54
Dace. If the young dace be a bait for the old pike . *2 Hen. IV.* iii 2 356
Dad. Like a mad lad, Pare thy nails, dad . *T. Night* iv 2 140
I was never so bethump'd with words Since I first call'd my brother's father dad *K. John* ii 1 467
Dicky your boy, that with his grumbling voice Was wont to cheer his dad in mutinies *3 Hen. VI.* i 4 77
Dædalus. I, Dædalus; my poor boy, Icarus; Thy father, Minos, that denied our course v 6 21
Daff. Canst thou so daff me? *Much Ado* v 1 78
He that unbuckles this, till we do please To daff 't for our repose, shall hear a storm. *Ant. and Cleo.* iv 4 13
Daffed. I would have daffed all other respects . *Much Ado* ii 3 176
That daff'd the world aside, And bid it pass *1 Hen. IV.* iv 1 96
Daffest. Every day thou daffest me with some device *Othello* iv 2 176
Daffodil. When daffodils begin to peer *W. Tale* iv 3 1
Daffodils, That come before the swallow dares, and take The winds of March with beauty iv 4 118
Dagger. Playing at sword and dagger with a master of fence . *Mer. Wives* i 1 295
Hath no man's dagger here a point for me? *Much Ado* iv 1 110
And Thisby, tarrying in mulberry shade, His dagger drew, and died *M. N. Dream* v 1 150
Thou stickest a dagger in me: I shall never see my gold again *Mer. of Venice* iii 1 115
I'll prove the prettier fellow of the two, And wear my dagger with the braver grace. iii 4 65
And Walter's dagger was not come from sheathing . *T. of Shrew* iv 1 138
That had the whole theoric of war in the knot of his scarf, and the practice in the chape of his dagger *All's Well* iv 3 164
Hold, sir, or I'll throw your dagger o'er the house . *T. Night* iv 1 30
Who, with dagger of lath, In his rage and his wrath, Cries, ah, ha! to the devil iv 2 136
My dagger muzzled, Lest it should bite its master . *W Tale* i 2 156
If I do not beat thee out of thy kingdom with a dagger of lath *1 Hen. IV.* ii 4 151
How came Falstaff's sword so hacked?—Why, he hacked it with his dagger ii 4 336
This chair shall be my state, this dagger my sceptre ii 4 416
Thy state is taken for a joined-stool, thy golden sceptre for a leaden dagger ii 4 419
And now is this Vice's dagger become a squire . *2 Hen. IV.* iii 2 343
Thou hidest a thousand daggers in thy thoughts iv 5 107
Do not you wear your dagger in your cap that day . *Hen. V.* iv 1 56
That every one may pare his nails with a wooden dagger iv 4 77
And not to wear, handle, or use any sword, weapon, or dagger *1 Hen. VI.* i 3 79
My breast can better brook thy dagger's point Than can my ears that tragic history *3 Hen. VI.* v 6 27
When my son Was stabb'd with bloody daggers *Richard III.* i 3 212
Uncle, give me this dagger.—My dagger, little cousin? with all my heart iii 1 110
With one hand on his dagger, Another spread on's breast *Hen. VIII.* i 2 204
Thou'lt do thy message, wilt thou not?—Ay, with my dagger in their bosoms . *T. Andron.* iv 1 118
And bids thee christen it with thy dagger's point iv 2 70
Then will I lay the serving-creature's dagger on your pate *Rom. and Jul.* iv 5 120
Pray you, put up your dagger, and put out your wit iv 5 123
I will dry-beat you with an iron wit, and put up my iron dagger iv 5 127
O happy dagger! This is thy sheath; there rust, and let me die v 3 169
This dagger hath mista'en,—for, lo, his house Is empty on the back of Montague,—And it mis-sheathed in my daughter's bosom! v 3 203
I know where I will wear this dagger then *J. Cæsar* i 3 89
As I slew my best lover for the good of Rome, I have the same dagger for myself iii 2 50
I fear I wrong the honourable men Whose daggers have stabb'd Cæsar iii 2 157
Look, in this place ran Cassius' dagger through iii 2 178
There is my dagger, And here my naked breast iv 3 100
Sheathe your dagger: Be angry when you will, it shall have scope iv 3 107
When your vile daggers Hack'd one another in the sides of Cæsar v 1 39
We have mark'd with blood those sleepy two Of his own chamber and used their very daggers *Macbeth* i 7 76
Is this a dagger which I see before me, The handle toward my hand? ii 1 33
Or art thou but A dagger of the mind, a false creation? ii 1 38
Hark! I laid their daggers ready; He could not miss 'em ii 2 12
Why did you bring these daggers from the place? They must lie there ii 2 48
Infirm of purpose! Give me the daggers: the sleeping and the dead Are but as pictures ii 2 53
Their hands and faces were all badged with blood; So were their daggers, which unwiped we found Upon their pillows ii 3 108
Their daggers Unmannerly breech'd with gore ii 3 121
Where we are, There's daggers in men's smiles ii 3 146
This is the air-drawn dagger which, you said, Led you to Duncan iii 4 62
I will speak daggers to her, but use none *Hamlet* iii 2 414
Speak to me no more; These words, like daggers, enter in mine ears iii 4 95
What's his weapon?—Rapier and dagger.—That's two of his weapons v 2 152
Thy words, I grant, are bigger, for I wear not My dagger in my mouth *Cymbeline* iv 2 79
Dagger man. Master Starve-lackey the rapier and dagger man *M. for M.* iv 3 16
Dagonet. I was then Sir Dagonet in Arthur's show *2 Hen. IV.* iii 2 300
Daily. Well beloved And daily graced by the emperor *T. G. of Ver.* i 3 58
With nightly tears and daily heart-sore sighs ii 4 132
Made daily motions for our home return *Com. of Errors* i 1 60
O, what men dare do! what men may do! what men daily do! *Much Ado* iv 1 20
So long I daily vow to use it *W. Tale* iii 2 243
That daily break-vow, he that wins of all, Of kings, of beggars *K. John* ii 1 569
And daily new exactions are devised *Richard II.* ii 1 249
For there, they say, he daily doth frequent v 3 6
Being daily swallow'd by men's eyes *1 Hen. IV.* iii 2 70
Daily grew to quarrel and to bloodshed, Wounding supposed peace *2 Hen. IV.* iv 5 195
We mourn, France smiles; we lose, they daily get *1 Hen. VI.* iv 3 32
Such massacre And ruthless slaughters as are daily seen v 4 161
The commonwealth hath daily run to wreck *2 Hen. VI.* i 3 127
What stratagems . . . This deadly quarrel daily doth beget! *3 Hen. VI.* ii 5 91
For hunting was his daily exercise iv 6 85
Daily. Whilst many fair promotions Are daily given *Richard III.* i 3 81
God will revenge it; whom I will importune With daily prayers ii 2 15
Your royal graces, Shower'd on me daily *Hen. VIII.* iii 2 167
I make as little doubt, as you do conscience In doing daily wrongs v 3 68
How much are we bound to heaven In daily thanks v 3 115
Helen must needs be fair, When with your blood you daily paint her thus *Troi. and Cres.* i 1 94
Repeal daily any wholesome act established against the rich . *Coriolanus* i 1 84
Provide more piercing statutes daily, to chain up and restrain the poor i 1 86
Whether 'twas pride, Which out of daily fortune ever taints The happy man iv 7 38
The want whereof doth daily make revolt *T. of Athens* iv 3 91
Call'st thou that harm?—Men daily find it iv 3 174
Lie where the light foam of the sea may beat Thy grave-stone daily iv 3 380
And why such daily cast of brazen cannon! *Hamlet* i 1 73
He hath a daily beauty in his life That makes me ugly *Othello* v 1 19
That duty leave unpaid to you, Which daily she was bound to proffer *Cymbeline* iii 5 49
Daintier. The hand of little employment hath the daintier sense *Hamlet* v 1 78
Dainties. I hold your dainties cheap, sir, and your welcome dear *Com. of Errors* iii 1 21
He hath never fed of the dainties that are bred in a book *L. L. Lost* iv 2 25
My super-dainty Kate, For dainties are all Kates *T. of Shrew* ii 1 190
Daintiest. The daintiest last, to make the end most sweet *Richard II.* i 3 68
Gall, worse than gall, the daintiest that they taste! *2 Hen. VI.* iii 2 322
Daintily. Baked in that pie; Whereof their mother daintily hath fed *T. Andron.* v 3 61
Whom thou fought'st against, Though daintily brought up *Ant. and Cleo.* i 4 60
Daintiness. Here have I the daintiness of ear To check time broke *Richard II.* v 5 45
Daintry. Where is the post that came from Montague?—By this at Daintry. *3 Hen. VI.* v 1 6
Dainty. Why, that's my dainty Ariel! I shall miss thee *Tempest* v 1 95
A table full of welcome makes scarce one dainty dish *Com. of Errors* iii 1 23
Dainty bits Make rich the ribs, but bankrupt quite the wits *L. L. Lost* i 1 26
O, a most dainty man! To see him walk before a lady and to bear her fan! iv 1 146
If the streets were paved with thine eyes, Her feet were much too dainty for such tread! iv 3 279
Love's tongue proves dainty Bacchus gross in taste iv 3 339
O dainty duck! O dear! *M. N. Dream* v 1 286
Basins and ewers to lave her dainty hands *T. of Shrew* ii 1 350
Will you buy any tape, Or lace for your cape, My dainty duck, my dear-a? *W. Tale* iv 4 324
The king is weary Of dainty and such picking grievances *2 Hen. IV.* iv 1 198
No shape but his can please your dainty eye *1 Hen. VI.* v 3 38
By heaven, she is a dainty one *Hen. VIII.* i 4 94
Having his ear full of his airy fame, Grows dainty of his worth *Tr. and Cr.* i 3 145
And takes my glove, And gives memorial dainty kisses to it v 2 80
Pleased with this dainty bait, thus goes to bed v 8 20
Single you thither then this dainty doe *T. Andron.* ii 1 117
We hunt not, we, with horse nor hound, But hope to pluck a dainty doe to ground ii 2 26
She that makes dainty, She, I'll swear, hath corns *Rom. and Jul.* i 5 21
Let us not be dainty of leave-taking, But shift away *Macbeth* ii 3 150
Forget Your laboursome and dainty trims *Cymbeline* iii 4 167
Daisied. Let us Find out the prettiest daisied plot we can iv 2 398
Daisies pied and violets blue And lady-smocks all silver-white *L. L. Lost* v 2 904
Daisies, and long purples That liberal shepherds give a grosser name *Hamlet* iv 7 170
Daisy. There's a daisy: I would give you some violets, but they withered iv 5 184
Dale. On hill, in dale, forest or mead *M. N. Dream* ii 1 83
With heigh! the doxy over the dale *W. Tale* iv 3 2
My name is Colevile of the dale *2 Hen. IV.* iv 3 4
Colevile is your name, a knight is your degree, and your place the dale iv 3 6
Dalliance. Do not give dalliance Too much the rein *Tempest* iv 1 51
You use this dalliance to excuse Your breach of promise *Com. of Errors* iv 1 48
My business cannot brook this dalliance iv 1 59
Silken dalliance in the wardrobe lies: Now thrive the armourers *Hen. V.* ii Prol. 2
And fitter is my study and my books Than wanton dalliance *1 Hen. VI.* v 1 23
Keep not back your powers in dalliance v 2 5
Himself the primrose path of dalliance treads, And recks not his own rede *Hamlet* i 3 50
Dallied. That high All-Seer that I dallied with. *Richard III.* v 1 20
Dallies. And dallies with the innocence of love, Like the old age *T. Night* ii 4 48
Our aery buildeth in the cedar's top, And dallies with the wind, and scorns the sun *Richard III.* i 3 265
Dally. Tell me, and dally not *Com. of Errors* i 2 59
Thus, dally with my excrement, with my mustachio *L. L. Lost* v 1 109
Dally not with the gods *T. of Shrew* iv 4 68
They that dally nicely with words may quickly make them wanton *T. Night* iii 1 16
Her name's a word; and to dally with that word might make my sister wanton iii 1 23
What, is it a time to jest and dally now? *1 Hen. IV.* v 3 57
Escape By sudden flight: come, dally not, be gone *1 Hen. VI.* iv 5 11
Take heed you dally not before your king *Richard III.* ii 1 12
You but dally; I pray you, pass with your best violence *Hamlet* v 2 308
If thou shouldst dally half an hour, his life, With thine, and all that offer to defend him, Stand in assured loss *Lear* iii 6 100
Dallying. Not dallying with a brace of courtezans, But meditating with two deep divines *Richard III.* iii 7 74
I could interpret between you and your love, if I could see the puppets dallying *Hamlet* iii 2 257
Dalmatian. I am perfect That the Pannonians and Dalmatians for Their liberties are now in arms *Cymbeline* iii 1 74
The common men are now in action 'Gainst the Pannonians and Dalmatians iii 7 3
Dam. Poisonous slave, got by the devil himself Upon thy wicked dam! *Tempest* i 2 320
His art is of such power, It would control my dam's god, Setebos . i 2 373
No more dams I'll make for fish; Nor fetch in firing At requiring ii 2 184

Dam. I never saw a woman, But only Sycorax my dam and she *Tempest* iii 2 109
The devil take one party and his dam the other! *Mer. Wives* iv 5 108
It is the devil.—Nay, she is worse, she is the devil's dam *Com. of Errors* iv 3 52
I, one Snug the joiner, am A lion-fell, nor else no lion's dam *M. N. Dream* v 1 227
It is the complexion of them all to leave the dam *Mer. of Venice* iii 1 33
And, whilst thou lay'st in thy unhallow'd dam, Infused itself in thee iv 1 136
You may go to the devil's dam *T. of Shrew* i 1 106
Why, she's a devil, a devil, the devil's dam iii 2 158
Most dear'st! my collop! Can thy dam?—may't be?—Affection! *W. Tale* i 2 137
Hence with it, and together with the dam Commit them to the fire! ii 3 94
That could conceive a gross and foolish sire Blemish'd his gracious dam iii 2 199
Being as like As rain to water, or devil to his dam *K. John* ii 1 128
Devil or devil's dam, I'll conjure thee 1 *Hen. VI.* i 5 5
And as the dam runs lowing up and down, Looking the way her harmless young one went 2 *Hen. VI.* iii 1 214
Now will I dam up this thy yawning mouth For swallowing the treasure of the realm iv 1 73
Thou art neither like thy sire nor dam 3 *Hen. VI.* ii 2 135
An unlick'd bear-whelp That carries no impression like the dam iii 2 162
Which, as I take it, is a kind of puppy To the old dam, treason *Hen. VIII.* i 1 176
Like an unnatural dam Should now eat up her own! *Coriolanus* iii 1 293
When did the tiger's young ones teach the dam? *T. Andron.* ii 3 142
But if you hunt these bear-whelps, then beware: The dam will wake iv 1 97
What hath he sent her?—A devil.—Why, then she is the devil's dam iv 2 65
Peace, tawny slave, half me and half thy dam! v 1 27
A pair of cursed hell-hounds and their dam! v 2 144
And bid that strumpet, your unhallow'd dam, Like to the earth swallow her own increase v 2 191
What, all my pretty chickens and their dam At one fell swoop? *Macbeth* iv 3 218
What do you mean by this haunting of me?—Let the devil and his dam haunt you! *Othello* iv 1 153
Damage. To stop all hopes whose growth may damage me *Richard III.* iv 2 60
It can do me no damage *Hen. VIII.* ii 2 183
All damage else—As honour, loss of time, travail, expense *Tr. and Cr.* ii 2 3
Damascus. This be Damascus, be thou cursed Cain, To slay thy brother Abel, if thou wilt 1 *Hen. VI.* i 3 39
Damask sweet commixture *L. L. Lost* v 2 296
Just the difference Betwixt the constant red and mingled damask *As Y. Like It* iii 5 123
Let concealment, like a worm i' the bud, Feed on her damask cheek *T. Night* ii 4 115
Gloves as sweet as damask roses; Masks for faces and for noses *W. Tale* iv 4 222
The war of white and damask in Their nicely-gawded cheeks *Coriolanus* ii 1 232
Dame. Plead you to me, fair dame? I know you not *Com. of Errors* ii 2 149
A holy parcel of the fairest dames *L. L. Lost* v 2 160
The fairest dame That lived, that loved, that liked *M. N. Dream* v 1 298
Why, how now, dame! whence grows this insolence? *T. of Shrew* ii 1 23
She was both pantler, butler, cook, Both dame and servant *W. Tale* iv 4 57
My old dame will be undone now for one to do her husbandry 2 *Hen. IV.* iii 2 123
For my old dame's sake, stand my friend iii 2 245
Les dames et demoiselles pour être baisées devant leur noces, il n'est pas la coutume de France *Hen. V.* v 2 279
Is this thy cunning, thou deceitful dame? 1 *Hen. VI.* ii 1 50
I unworthy am To woo so fair a dame to be his wife v 3 124
The chief perfections of that lovely dame, Had I sufficient skill to utter them, Would make a volume of enticing lines v 5 12
Presumptuous dame, ill-nurtured Eleanor 2 *Hen. VI.* i 2 42
That proud dame, the lord protector's wife i 3 79
I long till Edward fall by war's mischance, For mocking marriage with a dame of France 3 *Hen. VI.* iii 3 255
The Grecian dames are sunburnt and not worth The splinter of a lance *Troi. and Cres.* i 3 282
Our veil'd dames Commit the war of white and damask in Their nicely-gawded cheeks to the wanton spoil Of Phœbus' burning kisses *Coriolanus* ii 1 231
Dost overshine the gallant'st dames of Rome *T. Andron.* i 1 317
Father of that chaste dishonour'd dame iv 1 90
I would we had a thousand Roman dames At such a bay iv 2 41
Bless you, fair dame! I am not to you known *Macbeth* iv 2 65
We have willing dames enough iv 3 73
Yond simpering dame, Whose face between her forks presages snow *Lear* iv 6 120
Shut your mouth, dame, Or with this paper shall I stop it v 3 154
Many worthy and chaste dames even thus, All guiltless, meet reproach *Othello* iv 1 47
Fare thee well, dame, whate'er becomes of me *Ant. and Cleo.* iv 4 29
The beauty of this sinful dame Made many princes thither frame *Pericles* i Gower 31
Whose men and dames so jetted and adorn'd, Like one another's glass i 4 26
Dames d'honneur. Gros, et impudique, et non pour les dames d'honneur *Hen. V.* iii 4 57
Dame Mortimer. I'll play Percy, and that damned brawn shall play Dame Mortimer his wife 1 *Hen. IV.* ii 4 123
Dame Partlet. How now, Dame Partlet the hen! iii 3 60
Thou art woman-tired, unroosted By thy dame Partlet here *W. Tale* ii 3 75
Dammed. I'll have the current in this place damm'd up 1 *Hen. IV.* iii 1 101
The strait pass was damm'd With dead men *Cymbeline* v 3 11
Dammest. The more thou damm'st it up, the more it burns *T. G. of Ver.* ii 7 24
Damn. Thereof comes that the wenches say 'God damn me' *Com. of Err.* iv 3 54
If they should speak, would almost damn those ears Which, hearing them, would call their brothers fools *Mer. of Venice* i 1 98
Damns himself to do and dares better be damned than to do't *All's Well* iii 6 95
But wilt thou faithfully?—If I do not, damn me iv 1 96
Nay, rather damn them with King Cerberus; and let the welkin roar 2 *Hen. IV.* ii 4 181
There's more gold: Do you damn others, and let this damn you *T. of Athens* iv 3 165
He shall not live; look, with a spot I damn him *J. Cæsar* iv 1 6
The devil damn thee black, thou cream-faced loon! *Macbeth* v 3 11
Out of my weakness and my melancholy, As he is very potent with such spirits, Abuses me to damn me *Hamlet* ii 2 632
If thou wilt needs damn thyself, do it a more delicate way than drowning *Othello* i 3 360
Damn them then, If ever mortal eyes do see them bolster! iii 3 398
Let her live.—Damn her, lewd minx! O, damn her! iii 3 475
Swear it, damn thyself; Lest, being like one of heaven, the devils themselves Should fear to seize thee iv 2 35
Perform't, or else we damn thee *Ant. and Cleo.* i 1 24
Hence, vile instrument! Thou shalt not damn my hand *Cymbeline* iii 4 76
Damnable. If it were damnable, he being so wise, Why would he for the momentary trick Be perdurably fined? *Meas. for Meas.* iii 1 113
Damnable. To transport him in the mind he is Were damnable *Meas. for Meas.* iv 3 73
O thou damnable fellow! Did not I pluck thee by the nose? v 1 342
A magician, most profound in his art and yet not damnable *As Y. Like It* v 2 68
Is it not meant damnable in us, to be trumpeters of our unlawful intents? *All's Well* iv 3 31
Damnable both-sides rogue! iv 3 251
That did but show thee, of a fool, inconstant And damnable ingrateful *W. Tale* iii 2 188
Thou hast damnable iteration and art indeed able to corrupt a saint 1 *Hen. IV.* i 2 101
The deed you undertake is damnable *Richard III.* i 4 197
Thou damnable box of envy, thou, what meanest thou to curse thus? *Troi. and Cres.* v 1 29
Leave thy damnable faces, and begin *Hamlet* iii 2 263
Damnably. I have misused the king's press damnably 1 *Hen. IV.* iv 2 14
Damnation. Our revolted wives share damnation together *Mer. Wives* iii 2 40
She will not add to her damnation A sin of perjury *Much Ado* iv 1 174
'Twere damnation To think so base a thought *Mer. of Venice* ii 7 49
If thou never sawest good manners, then thy manners must be wicked; and wickedness is sin, and sin is damnation *As Y. Like It* iii 2 45
Then shall this hand and seal Witness against us to damnation! *K. John* iv 2 218
Do botch and bungle up damnation With patches, colours *Hen. V.* ii 2 115
You may call the business of the master the author of the servant's damnation iv 1 162
No more is the king guilty of their damnation iv 1 184
Ancient damnation! O most wicked fiend! *Rom. and Jul.* iii 5 235
Let molten coin be thy damnation, Thou disease of a friend! *T. of Athens* iii 1 55
His virtues Will plead like angels, trumpet-tongued, against The deep damnation of his taking-off *Macbeth* i 7 20
Conscience and grace, to the profoundest pit! I dare damnation *Hamlet* iv 5 133
For nothing canst thou to damnation add Greater than that *Othello* iii 3 372
Death and damnation! O!—It were a tedious difficulty, I think iii 3 396
Damned. This damn'd witch Sycorax *Tempest* i 2 263
It was a torment To lay upon the damn'd i 2 290
I am damned in hell for swearing *Mer. Wives* ii 2 9
What a damned Epicurean rascal is this! ii 2 300
I think the devil will not have me damned v 5 38
Injurious world! most damned Angelo! *Meas. for Meas.* iv 3 127
Thou art false in all And art confederate with a damned pack *Com. of Err.* iv 4 105
Damned spirits all, That in crossways and floods have burial *M. N. Dream* iii 2 382
She is damned for it.—That's certain, if the devil may be her judge *Mer. of Venice* iii 1 34
In religion, What damned error, but some sober brow Will bless it? iii 2 78
Therefore be of good cheer, for truly I think you are damned iii 5 6
Truly then I fear you are damned both by father and mother iii 5 17
O, be thou damn'd, inexecrable dog! And for thy life let justice be accused iv 1 128
Wast ever in court, shepherd?—No, truly.—Then thou art damned *As Y. Like It* iii 2 36
Truly, thou art damned, like an ill-roasted egg, all on one side iii 2 38
Wilt thou rest damned? God help thee, shallow man! iii 2 74
If thou beest not damned for this, the devil himself will have no shepherds iii 2 88
Where is that damned villain Tranio? *T. of Shrew* v 1 131
'Tis not so well that I am poor, though many of the rich are damned *All's Well* i 3 18
Where dust and damn'd oblivion is the tomb Of honour'd bones indeed ii 3 147
Damns himself to do and dares better be damned than to do't iii 6 96
I'ld have seen him damned ere I'ld have challenged him *T. Night* iii 4 313
You are abused and by some putter-on That will be damn'd for't *W. Tale* ii 1 142
It is a damned and a bloody work *K. John* iv 3 57
Thou'rt damn'd as black—nay, nothing is so black; Thou art more deep damn'd than Prince Lucifer iv 3 121
Where the jewel of life By some damn'd hand was robb'd and ta'en away v 1 41
We will untread the steps of damned flight v 4 52
O villains, vipers, damn'd without redemption! *Richard II.* iii 2 129
Thou art damn'd to hell for this iv 1 43
Mark'd with a blot, damn'd in the book of heaven iv 1 236
I'll be damned for never a king's son in Christendom 1 *Hen. IV.* i 2 109
Then art thou damned for keeping thy word with the devil.—Else he had been damned for cozening the devil i 2 134
Against that great magician, damn'd Glendower i 3 83
I'll play Percy, and that damned brawn shall play Dame Mortimer his wife ii 4 123
I call thee coward! I'll see thee damned ere I call thee coward ii 4 161
If to be old and merry be a sin, then many an old host that I know is damned ii 4 519
Let him be damned, like the glutton! 2 *Hen. IV.* i 2 39
Captain! thou abominable damned cheater, art thou not ashamed? ii 4 151
I'll see her damned first; to Pluto's damned lake ii 4 169
I owe her money; and whether she be damned for that, I know not ii 4 367
If damn'd commotion so appear'd, In his true, native and most proper shape iv 1 36
Thou damned tripe-visaged rascal v 4 9
O braggart vile and damned furious wight! *Hen. V.* ii 1 64
I do at this hour joy o'er myself, Prevented from a damned enterprise ii 2 164
He hath stolen a pax, and hanged must a' be: A damned death! iii 6 43
Die and be damn'd! and figo for thy friendship! iii 6 60
Thou damned and luxurious mountain goat iv 4 20
Pucelle, that witch, that damned sorceress 1 *Hen. VI.* iii 2 38
Die, damned wretch, the curse of her that bare thee 2 *Hen. VI.* iv 10 83
God grant me too Thou mayst be damned for that wicked deed! *Richard III.* i 2 103
But to be damned for killing him, from which no warrant can defend us i 4 113
O, preposterous And frantic outrage, end thy damned spleen! ii 4 64
A knot you are of damned blood-suckers iii 3 6
With devilish plots Of damned witchcraft iii 4 63
If! thou protector of this damned strumpet, Tellest thou me of 'ifs'? iii 4 76
In the breath of bitter words let's smother My damned son iv 4 134
O thou damned cur! I shall— Will you set your wit to a fool's? *Troi. and Cres.* ii 1 93
Here no envy swells, Here grow no damned grudges *T. Andron.* i 1 154
Beguile thy sorrow, till the heavens Reveal the damn'd contriver of this deed iv 1 36
Woe to her chance, and damn'd her loathed choice! iv 2 78
See justice done on Aaron, that damn'd Moor v 3 201
A damned saint, an honourable villain! *Rom. and Jul.* iii 2 79

Damned. But, O, it presses to my memory, Like damned guilty deeds to sinners' minds . . . . *Rom. and Jul.* iii 2 111
'Banished'? O friar, the damned use that word in hell; Howlings attend it . . . . iii 3 47
Wilt thou slay thyself? And slay thy lady too that lives in thee, By doing damned hate upon thyself? . . . . . . iii 3 118
Fly, damned baseness, To him that worships thee! . *T. of Athens* iii 1 50
Come, damned earth, Thou common whore of mankind . . . iv 3 41
Whilst damned Casca, like a cur, behind Struck Cæsar on the neck *J. Cæsar* v 1 43
Fortune, on his damned quarrel smiling, Show'd like a rebel's whore *Macbeth* i 2 14
To kill their gracious father? damned fact! How it did grieve Macbeth! . . . . iii 6 10
Infected be the air whereon they ride; And damn'd all those that trust them! . . . . iv 1 139
Not in the legions Of horrid hell can come a devil more damn'd In evils iv 3 56
Out, damned spot! out, I say!—One: two: why, then 'tis time to do't v 1 39
Lay on, Macduff, And damn'd be him that first cries 'Hold, enough!' v 8 34
Be thou a spirit of health or goblin damn'd . . . *Hamlet* i 4 40
Let not the royal bed of Denmark be A couch for luxury and damned incest . . . . i 5 83
O villain, villain, smiling, damned villain! . . . . . . i 5 106
That lend a tyrannous and damned light To their lord's murder . ii 2 482
Upon whose property and most dear life A damn'd defeat was made . ii 2 598
It is a damned ghost that we have seen . . . . . . iii 2 87
That his soul may be as damn'd and black As hell, whereto it goes . iii 3 94
If damned custom have not brass'd it so . . . . . . iii 4 37
Or paddling in your neck with his damn'd fingers . . . . . iii 4 185
Is't not to be damn'd, To let this canker of our nature come In further evil? . . . . v 2 68
Here, thou incestuous, murderous, damned Dane, Drink off this potion v 2 336
I'ld turn it all To thy suggestion, plot, and damned practice. . *Lear* ii 1 75
A fellow almost damn'd in a fair wife . . . . . *Othello* i 1 21
Where hast thou stow'd my daughter? Damn'd as thou art, thou hast enchanted her . . . . i 2 63
But, O, what damned minutes tells he o'er Who dotes, yet doubts! . iii 3 169
Ay, let her rot, and perish, and be damned to-night . . . . iv 1 192
Therefore be double damn'd: Swear thou art honest.—Heaven doth truly know it . . . . iv 2 37
O damn'd Iago! O inhuman dog! . . . . v 1 62
I were damn'd beneath all depth in hell, But that I did proceed upon just grounds To this extremity . . . . v 2 137
You told a lie; an odious, damned lie; Upon my soul, a lie, a wicked lie . . . . v 2 180
I'll after that same villain, For 'tis a damned slave . . . . v 2 243
O thou Othello, that wert once so good, Fall'n in the practice of a damned slave, What shall be said to thee? . . . . . . v 2 292
This, it seems, Roderigo meant to have sent this damned villain . v 2 316
If it be a sin to make a true election, she is damned . . *Cymbeline* i 2 30
And will not trust one of her malice with A drug of such damn'd nature i 5 36
Should I, damn'd then, Slaver with lips as common as the stairs That mount the Capitol . . . . i 6 104
O damn'd paper! Black as the ink that's on thee . . . . . iii 2 19
Damn'd Pisanio Hath with his forged letters,—damn'd Pisanio—From this most bravest vessel of the world Struck the main-top! . . . iv 2 317
Some, turn'd coward But by example—O, a sin in war, Damn'd in the first beginners! . . . . v 3 37
Avaunt, thou damned door-keeper! . . . . . . *Pericles* iv 6 126
Thou art the damned doorkeeper to every Coistrel . . . . . iv 6 175

Damnedest. The damned'st body to invest and cover In prenzie guards! *Meas. for Meas.* iii 1 96

Damon. For thou dost know, O Damon dear, This realm dismantled was Of Jove himself . . . . *Hamlet* iii 2 292

Damosella. But, damosella virgin, was this directed to you? *L. L. Lost* iv 2 132

Damp. In murk and occidental damp . . . . . . *All's Well* ii 1 166
The poisonous damp of night disponge upon me . . *Ant. and Cleo.* iv 9 13

Damsel. I was taken with a damsel . . . . . . *L. L. Lost* i 1 292
For this damsel, I must keep her at the park . . . . . . i 2 135
Damsel, I'll have a bout with you again . . . *1 Hen. VI.* iii 2 56
Damsel of France, I think I have you fast . . . . . . v 3 30

Damson. My wife desired some damsons, And made me climb *2 Hen. VI.* ii 1 102

Dance. Huge leviathans Forsake unsounded deeps to dance on sands *T. G. of Ver.* iii 2 81
He capers, he dances, he has eyes of youth . . . . *Mer. Wives* iii 2 68
I shall drink in pipe-wine first with him; I'll make him dance . . iii 2 91
Our dance of custom round about the oak Of Herne the hunter, let us not forget . . . . v 5 79
And meant to acknowledge it this night in a dance . . *Much Ado* i 2 14
Tell him there is measure in every thing and so dance out the answer . ii 1 75
God keep him out of my sight when the dance is done! . . . . ii 1 114
Do you sing it, and I'll dance it . . . . iii 4 46
Let's have a dance ere we are married, that we may lighten our own hearts and our wives' heels . . . . v 4 120
Did not I dance with you in Brabant once? . . . *L. L. Lost* ii 1 114
For revels, dances, masks and merry hours Forerun fair Love . . iv 3 379
I'll make one in a dance, or so; or I will play On the tabor to the Worthies, and let them dance the hay . . . . v 1 160
Their purpose is to parle, to court and dance . . . . . v 2 122
But shall we dance, if they desire us to't? . . . . . . v 2 145
Not yet! no dance! Thus change I like the moon.—Will you not dance? . . . . v 2 212
Take hands. We will not dance.—Why take we hands, then? . . . v 2 219
If you deny to dance, let's hold more chat . . . . . . v 2 228
And I will wish thee never more to dance . . . . . . v 2 400
To dance our ringlets to the whistling wind . . *M. N. Dream* ii 1 86
If you will patiently dance in our round And see our moonlight revels, go with us . . . . ii 1 140
Lull'd in these flowers with dances and delight . . . . . ii 1 254
To-morrow midnight solemnly Dance in Duke Theseus' house triumphantly . . . . iv 1 94
What dances shall we have, To wear away this long age of three hours? . v 1 32
Will it please you to see the epilogue, or to hear a Bergomask dance? . v 1 361
And this ditty, after me, Sing, and dance it trippingly . . . . v 1 403
As wealth is burden of my wooing dance . . . *T. of Shrew* i 2 68
I must dance bare-foot on her wedding day . . . . . . ii 1 33
Till honour be bought up and no sword worn But one to dance with! *All's Well* ii 1 33
I have seen a medicine That's able to breathe life into a stone, Quicken a rock, and make you dance canary . . . . ii 1 77
Dance. But shall we make the welkin dance indeed? . . . *T. Night* ii 3 59
My heart dances; But not for joy; not joy . . . . *W. Tale* i 2 110
Welcomed all, served all; Would sing her song and dance her turn . iv 4 58
When you do dance, I wish you A wave o' the sea . . . . . iv 4 140
But come; our dance, I pray . . . . iv 4 153
What fair swain is this Which dances with your daughter? . . . iv 4 167
She dances featly.—So she does any thing . . . . . . iv 4 176
If you did but hear the pedlar at the door, you would never dance again after a tabor and pipe . . . . iv 4 182
They have a dance which the wenches say is a gallimaufry of gambols . iv 4 334
Thy steps no more Than a delightful measure or a dance . *Richard II.* i 3 291
Rich men look sad and ruffians dance and leap . . . . . ii 4 12
Madam, we'll dance.—My legs can keep no measure in delight . . iii 4 6
Have you a ruffian that will swear, drink, dance, Revel the night? *2 Hen. IV.* iv 5 125
That were but light payment, to dance out of your debt . . . Epil. 20
If you would put me to verses or to dance for your sake . *Hen. V.* v 2 138
And sooner dance upon a bloody pole Than stand uncover'd to the vulgar groom . . . . *2 Hen. VI.* iv 1 127
Stamp, rave, and fret, that I may sing and dance . *3 Hen. VI.* i 4 91
I have some of 'em in Limbo Patrum, and there they are like to dance these three days . . . . *Hen. VIII.* v 4 68
More dances my rapt heart Than when I first my wedded mistress saw Bestride my threshold . . . . *Coriolanus* iv 5 122
Which should Make our eyes flow with joy, hearts dance with comforts v 3 99
Tabors and cymbals and the shouting Romans Make the sun dance . v 4 54
Nay, gentle Romeo, we must have you dance.—Not I, believe me *Rom. and Jul.* i 4 13
Which of you all Will now deny to dance? she that makes dainty, She, I'll swear, hath corns . . . . i 5 21
What's he that follows there, that would not dance? . . . . i 5 134
Here's my fiddlestick; here's that shall make you dance . . . iii 1 52
What a sweep of vanity comes this way! They dance! they are mad women . . . . *T. of Athens* i 2 138
I should fear those that dance before me now Would one day stamp upon me . . . . i 2 148
Some to dance, some to make bonfires . . . . . *Othello* ii 2 5
Feeds well, loves company, Is free of speech, sings, plays and dances well . . . . iii 3 185
Shall we dance now the Egyptian Bacchanals, And celebrate our drink? *Ant. and Cleo.* ii 7 110
Even in your armours, as you are address'd, Will very well become a soldier's dance . . . . *Pericles* ii 3 95
I can sing, weave, sew, and dance, With other virtues . . . . iv 6 194
She sings like one immortal, and she dances As goddess-like . . . v Gower 3

Dance attendance. I dance attendance here . . . *Richard III.* iii 7 56
To dance attendance on their lordships' pleasures . . *Hen. VIII.* v 2 31

Danced. The gentleman that danced with her told her . . *Much Ado* ii 1 244
There was a star danced, and under that was I born . . . . ii 1 349
One three of them, by their own report, sir, hath danced before the king *W. Tale* iv 4 346
I danced attendance on his will Till Paris was besieged, famish'd, and lost *2 Hen. VI.* i 3 174
Many a time he danced thee on his knee, Sung thee asleep *T. Andron.* v 3 162
What's this?—A rhyme I learn'd even now Of one I danced withal *Rom. and Jul.* i 5 145

Dancer. God match me with a good dancer! . . . . . *Much Ado* ii 1 111
He at Philippi kept His sword e'en like a dancer . . *Ant. and Cleo.* iii 11 36

Danceth. Hell only danceth at so harsh a chime . . . . *Pericles* i 1 85

Dancing. There dancing up to the chins . . . . . . *Tempest* iv 1 183
We'll have dancing afterward . . . . *Much Ado* v 4 122
The dancing horse will tell you . . . . *L. L. Lost* i 2 57
To your pleasures: I am for other than for dancing measures *As Y. Like It* v 4 199
I would I had bestowed that time in the tongues that I have in fencing, dancing and bear-baiting . . . . *T. Night* i 3 98
And victory, with little loss, doth play Upon the dancing banners of the French . . . . *K. John* ii 1 308
My dancing soul doth celebrate This feast of battle with mine adversary *Richard II.* i 3 91
Therefore, no dancing, girl; some other sport . . . . . . iii 4 9
Like a deep well That owes two buckets, filling one another, The emptier ever dancing in the air . . . . iv 1 185
A city on the inconstant billows dancing . . . . *Hen. V.* iii Prol. 15
Your grace, I fear, with dancing is a little heated . . *Hen. VIII.* i 4 100
You have dancing shoes With nimble soles: I have a soul of lead *R. and J.* i 4 14
For you and I are past our dancing days . . . . i 5 33
If you find him sad, Say I am dancing; if in mirth, report That I am sudden sick . . . . *Ant. and Cleo.* i 3 4
Convey thy deity Aboard our dancing boat . . . . . *Pericles* iii 1 13

Dancing-rapier. Although our mother, unadvised, Gave you a dancing-rapier by your side, Are you so desperate grown, to threat your friends? . . . . *T. Andron.* ii 1 39

Dancing-school. They bid us to the English dancing-schools . *Hen. V.* iii 5 32

Dan Cupid. This senior-junior, giant-dwarf, Dan Cupid . . *L. L. Lost* iii 1 182

Dandle. She'll hamper thee, and dandle thee like a baby . *2 Hen. VI.* i 3 148
Let the emperor dandle him for his own . . . . . *T. Andron.* iv 2 161

Dane. German, or Dane, low Dutch, Italian, or French . . *All's Well* iv 1 78
Who's there?—Friends to this ground.—And liegemen to the Dane *Hamlet* i 1 15
You cannot speak of reason to the Dane, And lose your voice . . i 2 44
I'll call thee Hamlet, King, father, royal Dane: O, answer me! . . i 4 45
This is I, Hamlet the Dane . . . . v 1 281
Here, thou incestuous, murderous, damned Dane, Drink off this potion v 2 336
I am more an antique Roman than a Dane . . . . v 2 352
Your Dane, your German, and your swag-bellied Hollander—Drink, ho!—are nothing to your English . . . . *Othello* ii 3 79
Why, he drinks you, with facility, your Dane dead drunk . . . ii 3 85

Danger. My master through his art forsees the danger . . *Tempest* ii 1 297
Run into no further danger . . . . iii 2 76
In thy danger, If ever danger do environ thee, Commend thy grievance to my holy prayers . . . . *T. G. of Ver.* i 1 15
As thou lovest Silvia, though not for thyself, Regard thy danger . . iii 1 256
Acquaint her with the danger of my state . . *Meas. for Meas.* i 2 184
How shall we continue Claudio, To save me from the danger that might come? . . . . iv 3 89
I see thy age and dangers make thee dote . . . *Com. of Errors* v 1 329
Let the danger light Upon your charter and your city's freedom *Mer. of Venice* iv 1 38
You stand within his danger, do you not? . . . . iv 1 180
Thou hast incurr'd The danger formerly by me rehearsed . . . iv 1 362

Danger. What danger will it be to us, Maids as we are, to travel forth so far! *As Y. Like It* i 3 110
To set her before your eyes to-morrow human as she is and without any danger v 2 75
The schools, Embowell'd of their doctrine, have left off The danger to itself *All's Well* i 3 248
The danger is in standing to't iii 2 43
Whence honour but of danger wins a scar, As oft it loses all iii 2 124
Where death and danger dogs the heels of worth iii 4 15
Though there were no further danger known but the modesty which is so lost iii 5 29
He might at some great and trusty business in a main danger fail you iii 6 17
To beguile the supposition of that lascivious young boy the count, have I run into this danger iv 3 334
Come what may, I do adore thee so, That danger shall seem sport *T. Night* ii 1 49
I do not without danger walk these streets iii 3 25
For his sake Did I expose myself, pure for his love, Into the danger of this adverse town v 1 87
His false cunning, Not meaning to partake with me in danger v 1 90
I Will stand betwixt you and danger *W. Tale* ii 2 66
Save him from danger, do him love and honour iv 4 521
What dangers, by his highness' fail of issue, May drop upon his kingdom v 1 27
She would pin her to her heart that she might no more be in danger of losing *W. Tale* v 2 85
Much danger do I undergo for thee *K John* iv 1 134
Fit for bloody villany, Apt, liable to be employ'd in danger iv 2 226
Nor tempt the danger of my true defence iv 3 84
And lose my way Among the thorns and dangers of this world iv 3 141
To win renown Even in the jaws of danger and of death v 2 116
Strike up our drums, to find this danger out v 2 179
Some apparent danger seen in him Aim'd at your highness *Richard II.* i 1 13
You pluck a thousand dangers on your head ii 1 205
And unavoided is the danger now ii 1 268
And hate turns one or both To worthy danger and deserved death v 1 68
Tell us how near is danger, That we may arm us to encounter it v 3 47
Get thee gone; for I do see Danger and disobedience in thine eye 1 *Hen. IV.* i 3 16
Send danger from the east unto the west, So honour cross it from the north to south, And let them grapple i 3 195
Out of this nettle, danger, we pluck this flower, safety ii 3 10
Without the taste of danger and reproof iii 1 175
And boldly did outdare The dangers of the time v 1 41
His forward spirit Would lift him where most trade of danger ranged 2 *Hen. IV.* i 1 174
I must go and meet with danger there, Or it will seek me in another place ii 3 48
What rank diseases grow, And with what danger, near the heart of it iii 1 40
The dangers of the days but newly gone iv 1 80
Sit patiently and inly ruminate The morning's danger *Hen. V.* iv Prol. 25
'Tis true that we are in great danger iv 1 1
A terrible and unavoided danger 1 *Hen. VI.* iv 5 8
My wife desired some damsons, And made me climb, with danger of my life 2 *Hen. VI.* ii 1 103
Yet thy scandal were not wiped away, But I in danger for the breach of law ii 4 66
The reverent care I bear unto my lord Made me collect these dangers iii 1 35
So might your grace's person be in danger iv 4 45
But still, where danger was, still there I met him v 3 11
Look, therefore, Lewis, that by this league and marriage Thou draw not on thy danger and dishonour 3 *Hen. VI.* iii 3 75
Your dislike, to whom I would be pleasing, Doth cloud my joys with danger iv 1 74
Men that stumble at the threshold Are well foretold that danger lurks within iv 7 12
O, full of danger is the Duke of Gloucester! *Richard III.* ii 3 27
By a divine instinct men's minds mistrust Ensuing dangers ii 3 43
To shun the danger that his soul divines iii 2 18
The king enacts more wonders than a man, Daring an opposite to every danger v 4 3
Are all in uproar, And danger serves among them *Hen. VIII.* i 2 37
Men fear'd the French would prove perfidious, To the king's danger i 2 157
Dangers, doubts, wringing of the conscience, Fears, and despairs ii 2 28
I weigh'd the danger which my realms stood in By this my issue's fail ii 4 197
You take a precipice for no leap of danger, And woo your own destruction v 1 140
How rank soever rounded in with danger *Troi. and Cres.* i 3 196
Omission to do what is necessary Seals a commission to a blank of danger iii 3 231
Danger, like an ague, subtly taints Even then when we sit idly in the sun iii 3 232
O, you shall be exposed, my lord, to dangers As infinite as imminent! iv 4 70
I'll grow friend with danger iv 4 72
But dare all imminence that gods and men Address their dangers in v 10 14
Was pleased to let him seek danger where he was like to find fame *Coriolanus* i 3 14
To eject him hence Were but one danger, and to keep him here Our certain death iii 1 288
The extreme dangers and the drops of blood Shed for my thankless country iv 5 75
We'll deliver you Of your great danger v 6 15
The great danger Which this man's life did owe you v 6 138
Tell him it was a hand that warded him From thousand dangers *T. Andron.* iii 1 196
The neglecting it May do much danger *Rom. and Jul.* v 2 20
And ne'er prefer his injuries to his heart, To bring it into danger *T. of Athens* iii 5 35
A surgeon to old shoes; when they are in great danger, I recover them *J. Cæsar* i 1 28
Into what dangers would you lead me, Cassius? i 2 63
I am arm'd, And dangers are to me indifferent i 3 115
Then, I grant, we put a sting in him, That at his will he may do danger with ii 1 17
Danger knows full well That Cæsar is more dangerous than he ii 2 44
Our day is gone; Clouds, dews, and dangers come; our deeds are done! v 3 64
Whilst our poor malice Remains in danger of her former tooth *Macbeth* iii 2 15
I doubt some danger does approach you nearly iv 2 67
Keep you in the rear of your affection, Out of the shot and danger of desire *Hamlet* i 3 35
And I do doubt the hatch and the disclose Will be some danger iii 1 175
Take thy fortune; Thou find'st to be too busy is some danger iii 4 33
To all that fortune, death and danger dare, Even for an egg-shell iv 4 52
That we can let our beard be shook with danger And think it pastime iv 7 32

Danger. And to no further pretence of danger *Lear* i 2 95
If a man's brains were in's heels, were't not in danger of kibes? i 5 9
Sith that both charge and danger Speak 'gainst so great a number ii 4 242
If you will come to me,—For now I spy a danger ii 4 250
Which imports to the kingdom so much fear and danger iv 3 6
It is danger To make him even o'er the time he has lost iv 7 79
Neglecting an attempt of ease and gain, To wake and wage a danger profitless *Othello* i 3 30
She loved me for the dangers I had pass'd, And I loved her that she did pity them i 3 167
Worthy Othello, I am hurt to danger ii 3 197
A man that all his time Hath founded his good fortunes on your love, Shared dangers with you iii 4 95
Whose quality, going on, The sides o' the world may danger *Ant. and Cleo.* i 2 199
All great fears, which now import their dangers, Would then be nothing ii 2 135
We perceived, both how you were wrong led, And we in negligent danger iii 6 81
There is No danger in what show of death it makes *Cymbeline* i 5 40
A pain that only seems to seek out danger I' the name of fame and honour iii 3 50
What he learns by this May prove his travel, not her danger iii 5 103
Would I could free't!—Or I, whate'er it be, What pain it cost, what danger iii 6 81
We'll hunt no more to-day, nor seek for danger Where there's no profit *Cymbeline* iv 2 162
A fever with the absence of her son, A madness, of which her life's in danger iv 3 3
I, dreading that her purpose Was of more danger, did compound for her A certain stuff v 5 254
Your danger's ours.—And our good his.—Have at it then v 5 314
You have at large received The danger of the task you undertake *Pericles* i 1 2
By flight I'll shun the danger which I fear i 1 142
Danger, which I fear'd, is at Antioch, Whose arm seems far too short to hit me here i 2 7
How have I offended, Wherein my death might yield her any profit, Or my life imply her any danger? iv 1 82
The commodity wages not with the danger iv 2 35
Dangerous. For the ways are dangerous to pass *T. G. of Ver.* iv 3 24
What dangerous action, stood it next to death, Would I not undergo for one calm look! v 4 41
For the revolt of mine is dangerous *Mer. Wives* i 3 112
Most dangerous Is that temptation that doth goad us on To sin in loving virtue *Meas. for Meas.* ii 2 181
Dangerous to be aged in any kind of course, as it is virtuous to be constant iii 2 237
For the which you are to do me both a present and a dangerous courtesy iv 2 171
His riotous youth, with dangerous sense, Might in the times to come have ta'en revenge iv 4 32
The most dangerous piece of lechery that ever was known *Much Ado* iii 3 179
Show outward hideousness, And speak off half a dozen dangerous words v 1 97
They are dangerous weapons for maids v 2 21
A dangerous law against gentility! *L. L. Lost* i 1 129
A dangerous rhyme, master, against the reason of white and red i 2 112
And not bethink me straight of dangerous rocks *Mer. of Venice* i 1 31
A very dangerous flat and fatal iii 1 5
Thus ornament is but the guiled shore To a most dangerous sea iii 2 98
All pretty oaths that are not dangerous *As Y. Like It* iv 1 194
And my state that way is dangerous, since I cannot yet find in my heart to repent *All's Well* ii 5 12
I knew the young count to be a dangerous and lascivious boy iv 3 248
So prove, As ornaments oft do, too dangerous *W. Tale* i 1 158
Be cured Of this diseased opinion, and betimes; For 'tis most dangerous i 2 298
These dangerous unsafe lunes i' the king, beshrew them! ii 2 30
To break into this dangerous argument *K. John* iv 2 54
To know the meaning Of dangerous majesty iv 2 213
He is a traitor, foul and dangerous *Richard II.* i 3 39
That they have let the dangerous enemy Measure our confines iii 2 124
Every stride he makes upon my land Is dangerous treason iii 3 93
My dangerous cousin, let your mother in v 3 81
Two of the dangerous consorted traitors v 6 15
I'll read your matter deep and dangerous 1 *Hen. IV.* i 3 190
'The purpose you undertake is dangerous;'—why, that's certain: 'tis dangerous to take a cold, to sleep, to drink ii 3 8
Nor did he think it meet To lay so dangerous and dear a trust On any soul iv 1 34
Dangerous countenance, And violation of all faith and troth v 1 69
Knew that we ventured on such dangerous seas 2 *Hen. IV.* i 1 181
Not a dangerous action can peep out his head but I am thrust upon it i 2 238
Whose dangerous eyes may well be charm'd asleep iv 2 39
Never did faithful subject more rejoice At the discovery of most dangerous treason *Hen. V.* ii 2 162
Since God so graciously hath brought to light This dangerous treason ii 2 186
Defer no time, delays have dangerous ends 1 *Hen. VI.* iii 2 33
To rive their dangerous artillery Upon no Christian soul but English Talbot iv 2 29
Prosper our colours in this dangerous fight! iv 2 56
For all this flattering gloss, He will be found a dangerous protector 2 *Hen. VI.* i 1 164
Dangerous peer, That smooth'st it so with king and commonweal! ii 1 21
Do you as I do in these dangerous days ii 2 69
Ah, what's more dangerous than this fond affiance! iii 1 74
These days are dangerous iii 1 142
'Tis the more honour, because more dangerous 3 *Hen. VI.* iv 3 15
I like it better than a dangerous honour iv 3 17
Plots have I laid, inductions dangerous *Richard III.* i 1 32
I'll not meddle with it [conscience]: it is a dangerous thing i 4 138
It [conscience] is turned out of all towns and cities for a dangerous thing i 4 146
So much the more dangerous, By how much the estate is green ii 2 126
Those uncles which you want were dangerous iii 1 12
His ancient knot of dangerous adversaries To-morrow are let blood iii 1 182
That ignoble traitor, The dangerous and unsuspected Hastings iii 5 23
A garish flag, To be the aim of every dangerous shot iv 4 90
So thrive I in my enterprise And dangerous success of bloody wars! iv 4 236
So thrive I in my dangerous attempt Of hostile arms! iv 4 398
Note This dangerous conception in this point *Hen. VIII.* i 2 139
'Twas dangerous for him To ruminate on this so far i 2 179
With new opinions, Divers and dangerous v 3 18
I told ye all, When we first put this dangerous stone a-rolling, 'Twould fall upon ourselves v 3 104
Two traded pilots 'twixt the dangerous shores Of will and judgement *Troi. and Cres.* ii 2 64

Dangerous. Manly as Hector, but more dangerous . *Troi. and Cres.* iv 5 104
This place is dangerous; The time right deadly . v 2 38
The blood I drop is rather physical Than dangerous to me . *Coriolanus* i 5 20
Pass no further.—Ha! what is that?—It will be dangerous to go on . iii 1 26
Then vail your ignorance; if none, awake Your dangerous lenity . iii 1 99
And wish To jump a body with a dangerous physic . iii 1 154
You may salve so, Not what is dangerous present, but the loss Of what is past . iii 2 71
Let Thy mother rather feel thy pride than fear Thy dangerous stoutness iii 2 127
Think you not how dangerous It is to jet upon a prince's right? *T. Andron.* ii 1 63
Stay! For pity of mine age, whose youth was spent In dangerous wars iii 1 3
With words more sweet, and yet more dangerous, Than baits to fish . iv 4 90
Her father counts it dangerous That she doth give her sorrow so much sway . *Rom. and Jul.* iv 1 9
Lest they should spy my windpipe's dangerous notes . *T. of Athens* i 2 52
'Tis inferr'd to us, His days are foul and his drink dangerous . iii 5 74
It almost turns my dangerous nature mild . iv 3 499
If you know That I profess myself in banqueting To all the rout, then hold me dangerous . *J. Cæsar* i 2 78
He thinks too much: such men are dangerous.—Fear him not, Cæsar; he's not dangerous . i 2 195
And therefore are they very dangerous . i 2 210
O conspiracy, Shamest thou to show thy dangerous brow by night? . ii 1 78
Danger knows full well That Cæsar is more dangerous than he! . ii 2 45
You shall give me reasons Why and wherein Cæsar was dangerous . iii 1 222
Here is a mourning Rome, a dangerous Rome . iii 1 288
This earthly world; where to do harm Is often laudable, to do good sometime Accounted dangerous folly . *Macbeth* iv 2 77
Grating so harshly all his days of quiet With turbulent and dangerous lunacy . *Hamlet* iii 1 4
How dangerous is it that this man goes loose! . iv 3 2
She may strew Dangerous conjectures in ill-breeding minds . iv 5 15
Though I am not splenitive and rash, Yet have I something in me dangerous . v 1 285
'Tis dangerous when the baser nature comes Between the pass and fell incensed points Of mighty opposites . v 2 60
I have received a letter this night; 'tis dangerous to be spoken . *Lear* iii 3 11
Stay with us; The ways are dangerous . iv 5 17
I have lost him on a dangerous sea . *Othello* ii 1 46
Dangerous conceits are, in their natures, poisons . iii 3 326
Lovers And men in dangerous bonds pray not alike . *Cymbeline* iii 2 37
Dangerous fellow, hence! Breathe not where princes are . v 5 237
I must, For mine own part, unfold a dangerous speech . v 5 313
Before thee stands this fair Hesperides, With golden fruit, but dangerous to be touch'd . *Pericles* i 1 28
For that's an article within our law, As dangerous as the rest . i 1 89
If I do it not, I am sure to be hanged at home: 'tis dangerous . i 3 3
Dangerously. Do prophesy upon it dangerously . *K. John* iv 2 186
Have practised dangerously against your state . 2 *Hen. VI.* ii 1 171
Is either slain or wounded dangerously . 3 *Hen. VI.* i 1 11
Most dangerously you have with him prevail'd . *Coriolanus* v 3 188
Dangling. Go, bind thou up yon dangling apricocks . *Richard II.* iii 4 29
Daniel. A Daniel come to judgement! yea, a Daniel! *Mer. of Venice* iv 1 223
A second Daniel, a Daniel, Jew! Now, infidel, I have you on the hip . iv 1 333
A Daniel, still say I, a second Daniel! I thank thee, Jew, for teaching me that word . iv 1 340
Danish. Since yet thy cicatrice looks raw and red After the Danish sword . *Hamlet* iv 3 63
Go, captain, from me greet the Danish king . iv 4 1
O, this is counter, you false Danish dogs! . iv 5 110
I had my father's signet in my purse, Which was the model of that Danish seal . v 2 50
That's the French bet against the Danish . v 2 170
Dank. Sleeping sound, On the dank and dirty ground . *M. N. Dream* ii 2 75
Peas and beans are as dank here as a dog . 1 *Hen. IV.* ii 1 9
Now, ere the sun advance his burning eye, The day to cheer and night's dank dew to dry . *Rom. and Jul.* ii 3 6
Is it physical To walk unbraced and suck up the humours Of the dank morning? . *J. Cæsar* ii 1 263
Dankish. In a dark and dankish vault at home There left me . *Com. of Errors* v 1 247
Dansker. Inquire me first what Danskers are in Paris . *Hamlet* ii 1 7
Daphne. Apollo flies, and Daphne holds the chase . *M. N. Dream* ii 1 231
Daphne roaming through a thorny wood, scratching her legs . *T. of Shrew* Ind. 2 59
Tell me, Apollo, for thy Daphne's love, What Cressid is, what Pandar, and what we? . *Troi. and Cres.* i 1 101
Dapple. Round about Dapples the drowsy east with spots of grey . *Much Ado* v 3 27
Dappled. The poor dappled fools . *As Y. Like It* ii 1 22
Dardan. On Dardan plains The fresh and yet unbruised Greeks do pitch Their brave pavilions . *Troi. and Cres.* Prol. 13
Priam's six-gated city, Dardan, and Tymbria, Helias, Chetas, Troien, And Antenorides . Prol. 16
Dardanian. The Dardanian wives, With bleared visages . *Mer. of Venice* iii 2 58
Dardanius. I'll rather kill myself.—Hark thee, Dardanius.—Shall I do such a deed?—O Dardanius! . *J. Cæsar* v 5 8
Dare you presume to harbour wanton lines? . *T. G. of Ver.* i 2 42
We dare trust you in this kind . iii 2 56
I dare thee but to breathe upon my love . v 4 131
I dare be bold With our discourse to make your grace to smile . v 4 162
That he dares in this manner assay me . *Mer. Wives* ii 1 25
In their so sacred paths he dares to tread . iv 4 59
How might she tongue me! Yet reason dares her no . *Meas. for Meas.* iv 4 28
The duke Dare no more stretch this finger of mine than he Dare rack his own . v 1 316
I dare, and do defy thee for a villain . *Com. of Errors* v 1 32
I dare swear he is no hypocrite, but prays from his heart . *Much Ado* i 1 152
Who dare tell her so? If I should speak, She would mock me into air . iii 1 74
I dare make his answer, none.—O, what men dare do! . iv 1 18
You dare easier be friends with me than fight with mine enemy . iv 1 300
I'll prove it on his body, if he dare, Despite his nice fence . v 1 74
That dare as well answer a man indeed As I dare take a serpent by the tongue . v 1 89
I will make it good how you dare, with what you dare, and when you dare . v 1 147
What peremptory eagle-sighted eye Dares look upon the heaven of her brow, That is not blinded? . *L. L. Lost* iv 3 227
Your mistresses dare never come in rain . iv 3 270
He goes before me and still dares me on . *M. N. Dream* iii 2 413
Dare. And never dare misfortune cross her foot . *Mer. of Venice* ii 4 36
A prodigal, who dare scarce show his head on the Rialto . iii 1 47
I dare be sworn for him he would not leave it . v 1 172
I dare be bound again, My soul upon the forfeit . v 1 251
And here she stands, touch her whoever dare . *T. of Shrew* iii 2 235
I dare assure you, sir, 'tis almost two . iv 3 191
I dare swear this is the right Vincentio.—Swear, if thou darest.—Nay, I dare not swear it . v 1 102
She thought, I dare vow for her, they touched not any stranger sense . *All's Well* i 3 113
Amazed me more Than I dare blame my weakness . ii 1 88
I am Cressid's uncle, That dare leave two together . ii 1 101
What I dare too well do, I dare not do . ii 3 210
I am not worthy of the wealth I owe, Nor dare I say 'tis mine, and yet it is . ii 5 85
Damns himself to do and dares better be damned than to do't . iii 6 96
For his love dares yet do more Than you have heard him brag *T. Night* iii 4 347
I dare lay any money 'twill be nothing yet . iii 4 432
If therefore you dare trust my honesty . *W Tale* i 2 434
I dare my life lay down and will do't, sir . ii 1 130
I am innocent as you.—I dare be sworn . ii 2 29
If she dares trust me with her little babe, I'll show't the king . ii 2 37
Your most obedient counsellor, yet that dare Less appear so . ii 3 55
Daffodils, That come before the swallow dares . iv 4 119
I cannot speak, nor think, Nor dare to know that which I know . iv 4 463
Who lives and dares but say thou didst not well . *K. John* i 1 271
But yet I dare defend My innocent life against an emperor . iv 3 88
And dares him to set forward to the fight . *Richard II.* i 3 109
How dare thy joints forget To pay their awful duty to our presence? . iii 3 75
How dares thy harsh rude tongue sound this unpleasing news? . iii 4 74
If I dare eat, or drink, or breathe, or live, I dare meet Surrey in a wilderness . iv 1 73
Thou knowest, as thou art but man, I dare . 1 *Hen. IV.* iii 3 166
It lends a lustre and more great opinion, A larger dare to our great enterprise . iv 1 78
By my life, And I dare well maintain it with my life . iv 3 9
So dare we venture thee, Albeit considerations infinite Do make against it . v 1 101
Unless a brother should a brother dare To gentle exercise and proof of arms . v 2 54
Now bind my brows with iron; and approach The ragged'st hour that time and spite dare bring! . 2 *Hen. IV.* i 1 151
I dare swear you borrow not that face Of seeming sorrow . v 2 28
Happy am I, that have a man so bold, That dares do justice . v 2 109
You must not dare, for shame, to talk of mercy . *Hen. V.* ii 2 81
That's a valiant flea that dare eat his breakfast on the lip of a lion . iii 7 156
For our approach shall so much dare the field That England shall couch down in fear and yield . iv 2 36
We'll try what these dastard Frenchmen dare . 1 *Hen. VI.* i 4 111
Dare no man answer in a case of truth? . ii 4 2
No coward nor no flatterer, But dare maintain the party of the truth . ii 4 32
An uproar, I dare warrant, Begun through malice . iii 1 74
Do what ye dare, we are as resolute . iii 1 91
Dare ye come forth and meet us in the field? . iii 2 61
As well as you dare patronage The envious barking of your saucy tongue . iii 4 32
I dare presume, sweet prince, he thought no harm . iv 1 179
Though Suffolk dare him twenty thousand times . 2 *Hen. VI.* iii 2 206
Here in our presence! dare you be so bold? . iii 2 238
More can I bear than you dare execute . iv 1 130
Dare any be so bold to sound retreat? . iv 8 4
Here they be that dare and will disturb thee . iv 8 6
Or dare to bring thy force so near the court . v 1 22
Nor he that loves him best . . . Dares stir a wing, if Warwick shake his bells. I'll plant Plantagenet, root him up who dares 3 *Hen. VI.* i 1 47
I dare your quenchless fury to more rage . i 4 28
How now, long-tongued Warwick! dare you speak? . ii 2 102
Dare he presume to scorn us in this manner? . iii 3 178
Edward dares, and leads the way. Lords, to the field . v 1 112
I dare adventure to be sent to the Tower . *Richard III.* i 3 116
Although the king have mercies More than I dare make faults *Hen. VIII.* ii 1 71
You few that loved me, And dare be bold to weep for Buckingham . ii 1 72
All that dare Look into these affairs see this main end . ii 2 40
How dare you thrust yourselves Into my private meditations? . ii 2 65
Can you think, lords, That any Englishman dare give me counsel? . iii 1 84
Who dare cross 'em, Bearing the king's will from his mouth expressly? iii 2 234
Know, officious lords, I dare and must deny it . iii 2 238
Dare mate a sounder man than Surrey can be . iii 2 274
Let his grace go forward, And dare us with his cap like larks . iii 2 282
Speak on, sir; I dare your worst objections . iii 2 307
More miseries and greater far Than my weak-hearted enemies dare offer iii 2 390
My robe, And my integrity to heaven, is all I dare now call mine own . iii 2 454
I dare avow, And now I should not lie . iv 2 142
And who dare speak One syllable against him?—Yes, yes, Sir Thomas, There are that dare . v 1 38
Men that make Envy and crooked malice nourishment Dare bite the best . v 3 45
You are a counsellor, And, by that virtue, no man dare accuse you . v 3 50
Being but a private man again, You shall know many dare accuse you boldly . v 3 56
Now let me see the proudest He, that dares most, but wag his finger at thee . v 3 131
The sea being smooth, How many shallow bauble boats dare sail! . *Troi. and Cres.* i 3 35
And dare avow her beauty and her worth In other arms than hers . i 3 271
And such a one that dare Maintain—I know not what: 'tis trash . ii 1 137
Without a heart to dare or sword to draw . ii 2 157
But dare all imminence that gods and men Address their dangers in . v 10 13
Let Titan rise as early as he dare . v 10 25
Yet dare I never Deny your asking . *Coriolanus* i 6 64
The blood he hath lost—Which, I dare vouch, is more than that he hath . iii 1 300
It cannot be The Volsces dare break with us . iv 6 48
As he hath spices of them all, not all, For I dare so far free him . iv 7 47
I was moved withal.—I dare be sworn you were . v 3 194
Dare I undertake For good Lord Titus' innocence in all . *T. Andron.* i 1 436
With the little skill I have, Full well shalt thou perceive how much I dare . ii 1 44
So near the emperor's palace dare you draw, And maintain such a quarrel openly? . ii 1 46

Dare. Let them take it as they list.—Nay, as they dare . *Rom. and Jul.* i 1 48
What dares the slave Come hither, cover'd with an antic face, To fleer and scorn at our solemnity? . . . . i 5 57
Stony limits cannot hold love out, And what love can do that dares love attempt . . . . ii 2 68
Nay, he will answer the letter's master, how he dares, being dared ii 4 12
I dare draw as soon as another man, if I see occasion in a good quarrel, and the law on my side . . . . ii 4 167
Then love-devouring death do what he dare . . . . . ii 6 7
And all the world to nothing, That he dares ne'er come back to challenge you . . . . iii 5 216
I dare no longer stay . . . . v 3 159
If our betters play at that game, we must not dare To imitate them *T. of Athens* i 2 12
I wonder men dare trust themselves with men . . . . i 2 44
Do you dare our anger? 'Tis in few words, but spacious in effect . . iii 5 96
Who, then, dares to be half so kind again? . . . . . iv 2 40
Who dares, who dares, In purity of manhood stand upright, And say 'This man's a flatterer'? . . . . iv 3 13
To dare the vile contagion of the night . . . . . *J. Cæsar* ii 1 265
If you dare fight to-day, come to the field . . . . . v 1 65
I dare assure thee that no enemy Shall ever take alive the noble Brutus v 4 21
I dare do all that may become a man; Who dares do more is none *Macbeth* i 7 46
Who dares receive it other, As we shall make our griefs and clamour roar? . . . . i 7 77
'Tis much he dares; And, to that dauntless temper of his mind, He hath a wisdom . . . . iii 1 51
A bold one, that dare look on that Which might appal the devil . . iii 4 59
What man dare, I dare: Approach thou like the rugged Russian bear . iii 4 99
Or be alive again, And dare me to the desert with thy sword . . . iii 4 104
How did you dare To trade and traffic with Macbeth In riddles and affairs of death? . . . . iii 5 3
Heaven preserve you! I dare abide no longer . . . . iv 2 73
And then, they say, no spirit dare stir abroad . . . . *Hamlet* i 1 161
Many wearing rapiers are afraid of goose-quills and dare scarce come thither . . . . ii 2 360
To all that fortune, death and danger dare, Even for an egg-shell . . iv 4 52
Conscience and grace, to the profoundest pit! I dare damnation . . iv 5 133
I dare pawn down my life for him . . . . . . *Lear* i 2 92
Is this well spoken?—I dare avouch it, sir . . . . . ii 4 240
And dare, upon the warrant of my note, Commend a dear thing to you iii 1 18
If on my credit you dare build so far . . . . . . iii 1 35
If you dare venture in your own behalf . . . . . . iv 2 20
Call by thy trumpet: he that dares approach, On him, on you, who not? . . . . v 3 99
I dare think he'll prove to Desdemona A most dear husband . . *Othello* ii 1 299
I dare be sworn I think that he is honest.—I think so too . . . ii 3 125
What I can do I will; and more I will Than for myself I dare . . iii 4 131
There's millions now alive That nightly lie in those unproper beds Which they dare swear peculiar . . . . iv 1 70
That you would have me to do?—Ay, if you dare do yourself a profit . iv 2 238
Sextus Pompeius Hath given the dare to Cæsar . . *Ant. and Cleo.* i 2 191
He dares us to't.—So hath my lord dared him to single fight . . . iii 7 30
I dare him therefore To lay his gay comparisons apart, And answer me declined . . . . iii 13 25
If that the former dare but what it can, No chance may shake it . . iii 13 80
My messenger He hath whipp'd with rods; dares me to personal combat iv 1 3
Is it sin To rush into the secret house of death, Ere death dare come to us? . . . . iv 15 82
I dare lay mine honour He will remain so . . . . *Cymbeline* i 1 174
I dare thereupon pawn the moiety of my estate to your ring . . . i 4 118
I dare you to this match: here's my ring.—I will have it no lay . . i 4 157
A prison for a debtor, that not dares To stride a limit . . . . iii 3 34
He rages; none Dare come about him . . . . iii 5 68
I dare speak it to myself—for it is not vain-glory . . . . iv 1 7
I dare be bound he's true . . . . iv 3 18
How dare you ghosts Accuse the thunderer? . . . . . . v 4 94
And if Jove stray, who dares say Jove doth ill? . . . . *Pericles* i 1 104
How dare the plants look up to heaven? . . . . i 2 55
I dare say 2 *Hen. IV.* iii 2; *Hen. V.* iv 1; 1 *Hen. VI.* ii 4; *Hen. VIII.* iii 1
Dare not offer What I desire to give . . . . . . *Tempest* iii 1 77
Revenge it on him,—for I know thou darest, But this thing dare not . iii 2 63
I dare not say I have one friend alive . . . . *T. G. of Ver.* iv 4 65
The folly of my soul dares not present itself . . . *Mer. Wives* ii 2 253
I dare not for my head fill my belly . . . . *Meas. for Meas.* iv 3 160
The little hangman dare not shoot at him . . . . . *Much Ado* iii 2 12
If you dare not trust that you see, confess not that you know . . iii 2 122
Peace!—Be to me and every man that dares not fight! . . *L. L. Lost* i 1 229
I dare not call them fools; but this I think . . . . . . v 2 371
The plain-song cuckoo gray, Whose note full many a man doth mark, And dares not answer nay . . . . . . *M. N. Dream* iii 1 136
He dares not come there for the candle; for, you see, it is already in snuff . . . . v 1 253
No, no, forsooth; I dare not for my life . . . . *T. of Shrew* iv 3 1
Swear, if thou darest.—Nay, I dare not swear it . . . . . v 1 105
I dare not say I take you . . . . *All's Well* ii 3 109
What I dare too well do, I dare not do . . . . . . ii 3 210
Therefore dare not Say what I think of it . . . . iii 1 13
Slight ones will not carry it; . . . and great ones I dare not give . . iv 1 43
Half of the which dare not shake the snow from off their cassocks . . iv 3 191
Shall I bid him go, and spare not?—'O no, no, no, no, you dare not' *T. Night* ii 3 121
I dare not know, my lord.—How! dare not! do not. Do you know, and dare not? Be intelligent to me . . . . *W. Tale* i 2 376
What you do know, you must, And cannot say, you dare not . . . i 2 380
I Have utter'd truth: which if you seek to prove, I dare not stand by . i 2 444
Mark your divorce, young sir, Whom son I dare not call . . . iv 4 429
Who dares not stir by day must walk by night . . . . *K. John* i 1 172
I dare not say How near the tidings of our comfort is . . *Richard II.* ii 1 271
What my tongue dares not, that my heart shall say . . . . v 5 97
Taste of it first, as thou art wont to do.—My lord, I dare not . . v 5 100
The thieves are all scattered and possess'd with fear So strongly that they dare not meet each other . . . . 1 *Hen. IV.* ii 2 113
I dare not fight; but I will wink and hold out mine iron . . *Hen. V.* ii 1 7
And dare not avouch in your deeds any of your words . . . . . v 1 76
By which honour I dare not swear thou lovest me . . . . . v 2 238
Where false Plantagenet dare not be seen . . . . . 1 *Hen. VI.* ii 4 74
And dare not take up arms like gentlemen . . . . iii 2 70

Dare not. Fain would I woo her, yet I dare not speak . . 1 *Hen. VI.* v 3 65
Ready to starve and dare not touch his own . . . 2 *Hen. VI.* i 1 229
Yet have I gold flies from another coast; I dare not say, from the rich cardinal . . . . i 2 94
What dares not Warwick, if false Suffolk dare him?—He dares not calm his contumelious spirit . . . . iii 2 203
Thrifty honest men and such As would, but that they dare not, take our parts . . . . iv 2 197
But such as I, without your special pardon, Dare not relate 3 *Hen. VI.* iv 1 88
My lord, I dare not make myself so guilty . . . . *Hen. VIII.* iii 1 139
Let him be told so; lest perchance he think We dare not move *Troi. and Cres.* ii 3 89
And grieve his spirit that dares not challenge it . . . . . v 2 94
Go with me to the vault.—I dare not, sir . . . . *Rom. and Jul.* v 3 131
Cannot, is false, and that I dare not, falser: I will not come to-day *J. Cæsar* ii 2 63
Letting 'I dare not' wait upon 'I would,' Like the poor cat i' the adage *Macbeth* i 7 44
I am afraid to think what I have done; Look on't again I dare not . . ii 2 52
I dare not speak much further . . . . iv 2 17
Great tyranny! lay thou thy basis sure, For goodness dare not check thee . . . . iv 3 33
I think, but dare not speak . . . . v 1 87
Which the poor heart would fain deny, and dare not . . . . v 3 28
I dare not confess that, lest I should compare with him . . . *Hamlet* v 2 145
I dare not drink yet, madam; by and by . . . . . . v 2 304
She must not speak Why she dares not come over to thee . . *Lear* iii 6 30
It is the cowish terror of his spirit, That dares not undertake . . iv 2 13
In Venice they do let heaven see the pranks They dare not show their husbands . . . . *Othello* iii 3 203
I dare not say he lies any where . . . . iii 4 3
Dare not look upon you But when you are well pleased . *Ant. and Cleo.* iii 3 3
Look grimly, And dare not speak their knowledge . . . . . iv 12 6
I dare not, dear,—Dear my lord, pardon,—I dare not, Lest I be taken . iv 15 21
They dare not fight with me, because of the queen my mother *Cymbeline* ii 1 21
I dare not call: yet famine, Ere clean it o'erthrow nature, makes it valiant . . . . iii 6 19
The fellow dares not deceive me . . . . iv 1 27
Who dares not stand his foe, I'll be his friend . . . . . . v 3 60
Dared. Those many had not dared to do that evil . . *Meas. for Meas.* ii 2 91
You have not dared to break the holy seal Nor read the secrets in't *W. Tale* iii 2 130
Why have those banish'd and forbidden legs Dared once to touch a dust of England's ground? . . . . *Richard II.* ii 3 91
Why have they dared to march So many miles upon her peaceful bosom? . . . . ii 3 92
Pardon, gentles all, The flat unraised spirits that have dared On this unworthy scaffold to bring forth So great an object . . *Hen. V.* Prol. 9
What! am I dared and bearded to my face? . . . . . 1 *Hen. VI.* i 3 45
He will answer the letter's master, how he dares, being dared *R. and J.* ii 4 12
Thereto prick'd on by a most emulate pride, Dared to the combat *Hamlet* i 1 84
He dares us to't.—So hath my lord dared him to single fight *A. and C.* iii 7 31
Dareful. We might have met them dareful, beard to beard . *Macbeth* v 5 6
Darest. Who makest a show but darest not strike . . . *Tempest* i 2 470
I know thou darest, But this thing dare not . . . . . iii 2 62
I was sent to call thee.—Sir, call me what thou darest . *T. G. of Ver.* ii 3 63
Darest thou die? The sense of death is most in apprehension *Meas. for Meas.* iii 1 77
How darest thou trust So great a charge from thine own custody? *Com. of Errors* i 2 60
Arrest me, foolish fellow, if thou darest . . . . . . iv 1 75
If thou darest stand.—I dare, and do defy thee for a villain . . v 1 31
Follow, if thou darest, to try whose right, Of thine or mine, is most *M. N. Dream* iii 2 336
Abide me, if thou darest; for well I wot, Thou runn'st before me, shifting every place, And darest not stand . . . . iii 2 422
Swear, if thou darest.—Nay, I dare not swear it . . . *T. of Shrew* v 1 104
Upon thy certainty and confidence What darest thou venture? *All's Well* ii 1 173
If thou darest tempt me further, draw thy sword . . . *T. Night* iv 1 45
If I do not wonder how thou darest venture to be drunk . . *W. Tale* v 2 184
Thou darest not say so, villain, for thy life . . . . *K. John* ii 1 132
Out, dunghill! darest thou brave a nobleman? . . . . . iv 3 87
Darest with thy frozen admonition Make pale our cheek . *Richard II.* ii 1 117
Darest thou, thou little better thing than earth, Divine his downfal? . iii 4 78
Thou darest not, coward, live to see that day . . . . . iv 1 41
Seize it, if thou darest.—An if I do not, may my hands rot off! . . iv 1 48
Thou camest not of the blood royal, if thou darest not stand for ten shillings . . . . 1 *Hen. IV.* i 2 157
Darest thou be so valiant as to play the coward with thy indenture? . ii 4 51
Darest thou be as good as thy word now? . . . . iii 3 163
I will toss the rogue in a blanket.—Do, an thou darest for thy heart 2 *Hen. IV.* ii 4 242
If ever thou darest acknowledge it, I will make it my quarrel *Hen. V.* iv 1 225
I will challenge it.—Thou darest as well be hanged . . . . . iv 1 235
My courage try by combat, if thou darest . . . . 1 *Hen. VI.* i 2 89
Do what thou darest; I beard thee to thy face . . . . . i 3 44
Darest thou maintain the former words thou spakest? . . . . . iii 4 31
Would 'twere come to that!—Marry, when thou darest . 2 *Hen. VI.* ii 1 39
In thine own person answer thy abuse.—Ay, where thou darest not peep: an if thou darest, This evening . . . . ii 1 42
Say, if thou darest, proud Lord of Warwickshire, That I am faulty . iii 2 201
If from this presence thou darest go with me . . . . . . iii 2 228
Strike off his head.—Thou darest not, for thy own . . . . . iv 1 69
Which darest not, no, nor canst not rule a traitor . . . . . v 1 95
If thou darest bring them to the baiting place . . . . . . v 1 150
And bid thee battle, Edward, if thou darest . . . . 3 *Hen. VI.* v 1 111
Darest thou resolve to kill a friend of mine? . . . . *Richard III.* iv 2 70
If so be Thou darest not this and that to prove more fortunes Thou'rt tired, then, in a word, I also am Longer to live most weary *Coriol.* iv 5 99
Foul-spoken coward, that thunder'st with thy tongue, And with thy weapon nothing darest perform! . . . . *T. Andron.* ii 1 59
And, if thou darest, I'll give thee remedy . . . *Rom. and Jul.* iv 1 76
Darest thou, Cassius, now Leap in with me into this angry flood? *J. Cæsar* i 2 102
What have I done, that thou darest wag thy tongue In noise so rude against me? . . . . *Hamlet* iii 4 39
Bold peasant, Darest thou support a publish'd traitor? . . . *Lear* iv 6 236
Thou art, if thou darest be, the earthly Jove . . . *Ant. and Cleo.* ii 7 73
Wherefore is that? and what art thou that darest Appear thus to us? . v 1 4
Daring. And with thy daring folly burn the world . . . *T. G. of Ver.* iii 1 155
Outbrave the heart most daring on the earth . . . *Mer. of Venice* ii 1 28

Daring. Not daring the reports of my tongue *All's Well* iv 1 34
Your daring tongue Scorns to unsay what once it hath deliver'd *Richard II.* iv 1 8
More active-valiant or more valiant-young, More daring or more bold *1 Hen. IV.* v 1 91
Their neighing coursers daring of the spur . . *2 Hen. IV.* iv 1 119
They that of late were daring with their scoffs Are glad and fain by flight to save themselves *1 Hen. VI.* iii 2 113
And wedded be thou to the hags of hell, For daring to affy a mighty lord . . . . . *2 Hen. VI.* iv 1 80
Thy prime of manhood daring, bold, and venturous *Richard III.* iv 4 170
The king enacts more wonders than a man, Daring an opposite to every danger . . . . v 4 3
In desperate manner Daring the event to the teeth . *Hen. VIII.* i 2 36
So looks the chafed lion Upon the daring huntsman that has gall'd him . . . . iii 2 207
Daringest. I committed The daring'st counsel which I had to doubt ii 4 215
Daring-hardy. No person be so bold Or daring-hardy *Richard II.* i 3 43
Darius. More precious Than the rich-jewel'd coffer of Darius *1 Hen. VI.* i 6 25
Dark. Nor lead me, like a firebrand, in the dark Out of my way *Tempest* ii 2 6
The night is dark; light and spirits will become it well *Mer. Wives* v 2 13
None, but only a repair i' the dark . . *Meas. for Meas.* iv 1 43
And in a dark and dankish vault at home There left me . *Com. of Errors* v 1 247
Your light grows dark by losing of your eyes . *L. L. Lost* i 1 79
Dark needs no candles now, for dark is light . . iv 3 269
A light condition in a beauty dark.—We need more light to find your meaning . . . . v 2 20
Look, what you do, you do it still i' the dark . . v 2 24
A light for Monsieur Judas! it grows dark, he may stumble . v 2 633
Fallen am I in dark uneven way, And here will rest me . *M. N. Dream* iii 2 417
And his affections dark as Erebus . . . . *Mer. of Venice* v 1 87
But were the day come, I should wish it dark . . . iii 1 304
I see no more in you Than without candle may go dark to bed *As Y. Like It* iii 5 39
Come, night; end, day! For with the dark, poor thief, I'll steal away *All's Well* iii 2 132
Till then I'll keep him dark and safely lock'd . . iv 1 105
Sayest thou that house is dark?—As hell . *T. Night* iv 2 38
I say to you, this house is dark . . . . . iv 2 45
This house is as dark as ignorance, though ignorance were as dark as hell . . . . iv 2 49
It was so dark, Hal, that thou couldst not see thy hand . *1 Hen. IV.* ii 4 247
How couldst thou know these men in Kendal green, when it was so dark thou couldst not see thy hand? . . . ii 4 257
A time When creeping murmur and the poring dark Fills the wide vessel of the universe . . . . *Hen. V.* iv Prol. 2
No; dark shall be my light and night my day . *2 Hen. VI.* ii 4 40
Dark cloudy death o'ershades his beams of life . *3 Hen. VI.* ii 6 62
How loath you are to offend daylight! an't were dark, you'ld close sooner . . . . . . *Troi. and Cres.* iii 2 51
In this detested, dark, blood-drinking pit.—If it be dark, how dost thou know 'tis he? . . . . . *T. Andron.* ii 3 224
Blind is his love and best befits the dark . *Rom. and Jul.* ii 1 32
By the which your love Must climb a bird's nest soon when it is dark . ii 5 76
More light and light; more dark and dark our woes! . iii 5 36
And that the lean abhorred monster keeps Thee here in dark . v 3 105
Nor heaven peep through the blanket of the dark, To cry 'Hold!' *Macbeth* i 5 54
Root of hemlock digg'd i' the dark, Liver of blaspheming Jew . iv 1 25
My sea-gown scarf'd about me, in the dark Groped I to find out them *Hamlet* v 2 13
Here stood he in the dark, his sharp sword out . *Lear* ii 1 40
The wrathful skies Gallow the very wanderers of the dark . . iii 2 44
Out, vile jelly! Where is thy lustre now?—All dark and comfortless . iii 7 85
The dark and vicious place where thee he got Cost him his eyes . v 3 172
All's cheerless, dark, and deadly . . . . . v 3 290
No, by this heavenly light!—Nor I neither by this heavenly light; I might do't as well i' the dark . . . . . *Othello* iv 3 67
Kill men i' the dark!—Where be these bloody thieves?—How silent is this town! . . . . v 1 63
Cassio hath here been set on in the dark . . . v 1 112
The bright day is done, And we are for the dark . *Ant. and Cleo.* v 2 194
If you could wear a mind Dark as your fortune is . . *Cymbeline* iii 4 147
This so darks In Philoten all graceful marks *Pericles* iv Gower 35
Dark backward. What seest thou else In the dark backward and abysm of time? . . . . *Tempest* i 2 50
Dark conspiracy. Thou fond mad woman, Wilt thou conceal this dark conspiracy? . . . . *Richard II.* v 2 96
Dark corners. The old fantastical duke of dark corners *Meas. for Meas.* iv 3 164
Dark December. When we shall hear The rain and wind beat dark December . . . . *Cymbeline* iii 3 37
Dark deeds. The duke yet would have dark deeds darkly answered *Meas. for Meas.* iii 2 187
Dark dishonour. But my fair name, Despite of death that lives upon my grave, To dark dishonour's use thou shalt not have *Richard II.* i 1 169
Dark enough. O, then by day Where wilt thou find a cavern dark enough To mask thy monstrous visage . . . . . . *J. Cæsar* ii 1 80
Dark-eyed. Threading dark-eyed night . . . *Lear* ii 1 121
Dark heaven. Earth-treading stars that make dark heaven light *Rom. and Jul.* i 2 25
Dark hour. I must become a borrower of the night For a dark hour or twain . . . . *Macbeth* iii 1 28
Must embrace the fate Of that dark hour . . . . iii 1 138
Dark house. Love is merely a madness, and, I tell you, deserves as well a dark house and a whip as madmen do *As Y. Like It* iii 2 421
War is no strife To the dark house and the detested wife . *All's Well* ii 3 309
Why have you suffer'd me to be imprison'd, Kept in a dark house? *T. Night* v 1 350
Dark meaning. What's your dark meaning, mouse, of this light word? *L. L. Lost* v 2 19
Dark monarchy. What scourge for perjury Can this dark monarchy afford false Clarence . . . . . . *Richard III.* i 4 51
Dark night. Partly by the dark night, which did deceive them *Much Ado* iii 3 167
And make a dark night too of half the day . *L. L. Lost* i 1 45
Dark night, that from the eye his function takes . *M. N. Dream* iii 2 177
Deep night, dark night, the silent of the night . *2 Hen. VI.* i 4 19
All comfort that the dark night can afford Be to thy person! *Richard III.* v 3 80
Pardon me, And not impute this yielding to light love, Which the dark night hath so discovered . . . *Rom. and Jul.* ii 2 106
By the clock, 'tis day, And yet dark night strangles the travelling lamp *Macbeth* ii 4 7
Dark oblivion. In the swallowing gulf Of blind forgetfulness and dark oblivion *Richard III.* iii 7 129
Dark room. They must be bound and laid in some dark room *C. of Err.* iv 4 97
We'll have him in a dark room and bound . *T. Night* iii 4 148
Dark-seated. All the foul terrors in dark-seated hell . *2 Hen. VI.* iii 2 328
Dark spirit. Death, that dark spirit, in's nervy arm doth lie . *Coriolanus* ii 1 177
Dark tower. Child Rowland to the dark tower came . . *Lear* iii 4 187
Dark-working sorcerers that change the mind . *Com. of Errors* i 2 99
Darken. I prithee, darken not The mirth o' the feast . . *W. Tale* iv 4 41
And their blaze Shall darken him for ever . . . *Coriolanus* ii 1 275
I must not think there are Evils enow to darken all his goodness *Ant. and Cleo.* i 4 11
Ambition, The soldier's virtue, rather makes choice of loss, Than gain which darkens him . . . . iii 1 24
Nobleness and riches: careless heirs May the two latter darken and expend . . . . *Pericles* iii 2 29
Darkened. If your knowledge be more it is much darkened in your malice . . . . *Meas. for Meas.* iii 2 157
You are darken'd in this action, sir, Even by your own . *Coriolanus* iv 7 5
Darkening. Whose figure even this instant cloud puts on, By darkening my clear sun. . . . . *Hen. VIII.* i 1 226
Darker. An her hair were not somewhat darker than Helen's—well, go to *Troi. and Cres.* i 1 41
Meantime we shall express our darker purpose . . *Lear* i 1 37
Darkest. And as the sun breaks through the darkest clouds, So honour peereth in the meanest habit . . . . *T. of Shrew* iv 3 175
Your skill shall, like a star i' the darkest night, Stick fiery off indeed *Hamlet* v 2 267
Darking. Even with the vail and darking of the sun . *Troi. and Cres.* v 8 7
Darkling. O, wilt thou darkling leave me? do not so . *M. N. Dream* ii 2 86
So, out went the candle, and we were left darkling . *Lear* i 4 237
Darkling stand The varying shore o' the world . *Ant. and Cleo.* iv 15 10
Darkly. The duke yet would have dark deeds darkly answered *Meas. for Meas.* iii 2 188
I will go darkly to work with her.—That's the way . v 1 279
Therefore I'll darkly end the argument . . *L. L. Lost* v 2 23
I will tell you a thing, but you shall let it dwell darkly with you *All's Well* iv 3 13
My stars shine darkly over me . . . . . *T. Night* ii 1 4
Hadst thou but shook thy head or made a pause When I spake darkly *K. John* iv 2 232
How darkly and how deadly dost thou speak! . *Richard III.* i 4 175
Darkness. I' the dead of darkness . . . . *Tempest* i 2 130
As the morning steals upon the night, Melting the darkness . v 1 66
This thing of darkness I Acknowledge mine . . . v 1 275
If I must die, I will encounter darkness as a bride . *Meas. for Meas.* iii 1 84
Yield possession to my holy prayers And to thy state of darkness hie thee straight . . . . *Com. of Errors* iv 4 59
Ere you find where light in darkness lies, Your light grows dark by losing of your eyes . . . . *L. L. Lost* i 1 78
Ere a man hath power to say 'Behold!' The jaws of darkness do devour it up . . . . *M. N. Dream* i 1 148
From the presence of the sun, Following darkness like a dream . v 1 393
The black prince, sir; alias, the prince of darkness; alias, the devil *All's Well* iv 5 45
They have laid me here in hideous darkness . . *T. Night* iv 2 34
Madman, thou errest: I say, there is no darkness but ignorance . iv 2 47
Remain thou still in darkness . . . . . . iv 2 62
Keep me in darkness, send ministers to me, asses . . iv 2 100
We intended To keep in darkness what occasion now Reveals before 'tis ripe . . . . v 1 156
You have put me into darkness and given your drunken cousin rule over me. . . . . v 1 312
They are villains and the sons of darkness . *1 Hen. IV.* ii 4 191
And wert indeed, but for the light in thy face, the son of utter darkness iii 3 42
The rude scene may end, And darkness be the burier of the dead! *2 Hen. IV.* i 1 160
Constrain'd to watch in darkness, rain and cold . *1 Hen. VI.* ii 1 7
But darkness and the gloomy shade of death Environ you! . . v 4 89
Descend to darkness and the burning lake! . . . *2 Hen. VI.* i 4 42
Now, God be praised, that to believing souls Gives light in darkness, comfort in despair . . . . ii 1 67
From their misty jaws Breathe foul contagious darkness in the air . iv 1 7
Whose bright out-shining beams thy cloudy wrath Hath in eternal darkness folded up . . . . *Richard III.* i 3 269
Clarence, whom I, indeed, have laid in darkness, I do beweep . i 3 327
The silent hours steal on, And flaky darkness breaks within the east . v 3 86
When heaven shall call her from this cloud of darkness . *Hen. VIII.* v 5 45
Flecked darkness like a drunkard reels From forth day's path *Rom. and Jul.* ii 3 3
Some six or seven, who did hide their faces Even from darkness *J. Cæsar* ii 1 278
To win us to our harm, The instruments of darkness tell us truths *Macbeth* i 3 124
Darkness does the face of earth entomb, When living light should kiss it . . . . ii 4 9
Darkness and devils! Saddle my horses; call my train together . *Lear* i 4 273
And did the act of darkness with her . . . . iii 4 90
The prince of darkness is a gentleman: Modo he's call'd, and Mahu iii 4 148
Nero is an angler in the lake of darkness . . . . iii 6 8
There's hell, there's darkness, there's the sulphurous pit . iv 6 130
I'll set my teeth, And send to darkness all that stop me *Ant. and Cleo.* iii 13 182
To darkness fleet souls that fly backwards . . . *Cymbeline* v 3 25
Now his son's like a glow-worm in the night, The which hath fire in darkness, none in light . . . . *Pericles* ii 3 44
If she'ld do the deed of darkness . . . . . iv 6 32
Darling. And his and mine loved darling . . . *Tempest* iii 3 93
The dearest issue of his practice, And of his old experience the only darling . . . . *All's Well* ii 1 110
And can do nought but wail her darling's loss . *2 Hen. VI.* ii 1 216
Where is your darling Rutland? . . . . *3 Hen. VI.* i 4 78
She shunn'd The wealthy curled darlings of our nation . *Othello* i 2 68
Take heed on't; Make it a darling like your precious eye . . iii 4 66
Are ready now To eat those little darlings whom they loved . *Pericles* i 4 44
Darnel. Her fallow leas The darnel, hemlock and rank fumitory Doth root upon . . . . *Hen. V.* v 2 45
'Twas full of darnel; do you like the taste? . . *1 Hen. VI.* iii 2 44
Darnel, and all the idle weeds that grow In our sustaining corn *Lear* iv 4 5
Darraign your battle, for they are at hand . . *3 Hen. VI.* ii 2 72
Dart. Believe not that the dribbling dart of love Can pierce a complete bosom . . . . *Meas. for Meas.* i 3 2

Dart. Here stand I: lady, dart thy skill at me; Bruise me with scorn *L. L. Lost* v 2 396
Dart not scornful glances from those eyes, To wound thy lord *T. of Shr.* v 2 137
And darts his light through every guilty hole . *Richard II.* iii 2 43
Till that his thighs with darts Were almost like a sharp-quill'd porpentine *2 Hen. VI.* iii 1 362
Like a wild Morisco, Shaking the bloody darts as he his bells . . iii 1 366
It reaches far, and where 'twill not extend, Thither he darts it *Hen. VIII.* i 1 112
Filling the air with swords advanced and darts, We prove this very hour *Coriolanus* i 6 61
Piercing steel and darts envenomed Shall be as welcome to the ears of Brutus As tidings of this sight . . . . . *J. Cæsar* v 3 76
You nimble lightnings, dart your blinding flames Into her scornful eyes! *Lear* ii 4 167
Whose solid virtue The shot of accident, nor dart of chance, Could neither graze nor pierce . . . . *Othello* iv 1 278
Shall I do that which all the Parthian darts, Though enemy, lost aim, and could not? . . . . *Ant. and Cleo.* iv 14 70
Thus smiling, as some fly had tickled slumber, Not as death's dart, being laugh'd at . . . . *Cymbeline* iv 2 211
If there be such a dart in princes' frowns, How durst thy tongue move anger to our face? . . . . *Pericles* i 2 53
Darted. Mine eyes, Which I have darted at thee, hurt thee not *As Y. Like It* iii 5 25
Young and old Through casements darted their desiring eyes *Richard II.* v 2 14
All curses madded Hecuba gave the Greeks, And mine to boot, be darted on thee! . . . . *Cymbeline* iv 2 314
Darting. Now, darting Parthia, art thou struck . . *Ant. and Cleo.* iii 1 1
Dash. The sea, mounting to the welkin's cheek, Dashes the fire out *Temp.* i 2 5
To dash it like a Christmas comedy . . . . . *L. L. Lost* v 2 462
The bastard brains with these my proper hands Shall I dash out *W. Tale* ii 3 140
Now, had I not the dash of my former life in me, would preferment drop on my head . . . . v 2 122
Thus do the hopes we have in him touch ground And dash themselves to pieces . . . . *2 Hen. IV.* iv 1 18
She takes upon her bravely at first dash . . . . *1 Hen. VI.* i 2 71
The splitting rocks cower'd in the sinking sands And would not dash me with their ragged sides . . . . . *2 Hen. VI.* iii 2 98
To dash our late decree in parliament . . . . *3 Hen. VI.* ii 1 118
And if they fall, they dash themselves to pieces . . *Richard III.* i 3 260
And, in this rage, with some great kinsman's bone, As with a club, dash out my desperate brains . . . . . *Rom. and Jul.* iv 3 54
Be ready, gods, with all your thunderbolts; Dash him to pieces! *J. Cæsar* iv 3 82
Dashed. A brave vessel, Who had, no doubt, some noble creature in her, Dash'd all to pieces . . . . *Tempest* i 2 8
A foolish mild man; an honest man, look you, and soon dashed *L. L. Lost* v 2 585
Troilus had his brains dashed out with a Grecian club *As Y. Like It* iv 1 98
When that we have dash'd them to the ground, Why then defy each other *K. John* ii 1 405
Your fathers taken by the silver beards, And their most reverend heads dash'd to the walls . . . . *Hen. V.* iii 3 37
Have pluck'd my nipple from his boneless gums, And dash'd the brains out . . . . *Macbeth* i 7 58
I see this hath a little dash'd your spirits.—Not a jot, not a jot *Othello* iii 3 214
Dashing. That this tempest, Dashing the garment of this peace, aboded The sudden breach on't . . . . *Hen. VIII.* i 1 93
Thou desperate pilot, now at once run on The dashing rocks thy sea-sick weary bark! . . . . *Rom. and Jul.* v 3 118
Dastard. With pale beggar-fear impeach my height Before this out-dared dastard . . . . *Richard II.* i 1 190
Such a worthy leader, wanting aid, Unto his dastard foemen is betray'd *1 Hen. VI.* i 1 144
Who ever saw the like? what men have I! Dogs! cowards! dastards! i 2 23
And then we'll try what these dastard Frenchmen dare . . i 4 111
This dastard, at the battle of Patay, . . . did run away . . iv 1 19
You are all recreants and dastards . . . . *2 Hen. VI.* iv 8 28
Like a dastard and a treacherous coward . . . *3 Hen. VI.* ii 2 114
The cruelty and envy of the people, Permitted by our dastard nobles *Coriolanus* iv 5 81
Datchet-lane. To carry me in the name of foul clothes to Datchet-lane *Mer. Wives* iii 5 101
Datchet-mead. Carry it among the whitsters in Datchet-mead . iii 3 15
Send him by your two men to Datchet-mead . . . . iii 3 141
Carry them to the laundress in Datchet-mead . . . . iii 3 157
Date. Here comes the almanac of my true date *Com. of Errors* i 2 41
With league whose date till death shall never end . *M. N. Dream* iii 2 373
Your date is better in your pie and your porridge than in your cheek *All's Well* i 1 172
I must have saffron to colour the warden pies; mace; dates?—none *W. Tale* iv 3 49
I loved him, and will weep My date of life out for his sweet life's loss *K. John* iv 3 106
Is not my teeming date drunk up with time? . . *Richard II.* v 2 91
A true face and good conscience.—Both which I have had: but their date is out . . . . *1 Hen. IV.* ii 4 552
Despite of fate, To my determined time thou gavest new date *1 Hen. VI.* iv 6 9
Be brief, lest that the process of thy kindness Last longer telling than thy kindness' date . . . . *Richard III.* iv 4 254
To be baked with no date in the pie, for then the man's date's out *Troi. and Cres.* i 2 280
Outlive thy father's days, And fame's eternal date, for virtue's praise! *T. Andron.* i 1 168
The date is out of such prolixity . . . . *Rom. and Jul.* i 4 3
Some consequence yet hanging in the stars Shall bitterly begin his fearful date With this night's revels . . . . . i 4 108
They call for dates and quinces in the pastry . . . iv 4 2
My short date of breath Is not so long as is a tedious tale . v 3 229
My reliances on his fracted dates Have smit my credit *T. of Athens* ii 1 22
Take the bonds along with you, And have the dates in compt . ii 1 35
Where you may abide till your date expire . . . *Pericles* iii 4 14
Date-broke. Clamorous demands of date-broke bonds . *T. of Athens* ii 2 38
Dateless. The sly slow hours shall not determinate The dateless limit of thy dear exile . . . . *Richard II.* i 3 151
Seal with a righteous kiss A dateless bargain to engrossing death! *Rom. and Jul.* v 3 115
Daub. No more the thirsty entrance of this soil Shall daub her lips with her own children's blood . . . . . . *1 Hen. IV.* i 1 6
Daub the walls of a jakes with him . . . . . *Lear* ii 2 71
Poor Tom's a-cold. I cannot daub it further . . . . iv 1 54

Daubed. So smooth he daub'd his vice with show of virtue *Richard III.* iii 5 29
Daubery. Such daubery as this is, beyond our element . *Mer. Wives* iv 2 186
Daughter. I have done nothing but in care of thee, Of thee, my dear one, thee, my daughter . . . . *Tempest* i 2 17
Thy mother was a piece of virtue, and She said thou wast my daughter i 2 57
The Duke of Milan And his more braver daughter could control thee . i 2 439
At the marriage of the king's fair daughter Claribel . . . ii 1 70
When we were at Tunis at the marriage of your daughter . . ii 1 98
I wore it at your daughter's marriage . . . . . ii 1 105
Would I had never Married my daughter there! . . . ii 1 108
Would not bless our Europe with your daughter, But rather lose her to an African . . . . ii 1 124
'Tis true, my brother's daughter's queen of Tunis . . . ii 1 255
And that most deeply to consider is The beauty of his daughter . iii 2 107
I will kill this man: his daughter and I will be king and queen . iii 2 114
As my gift and thine own acquisition Worthily purchased, take my daughter . . . . iv 1 14
Since they did plot The means that dusky Dis my daughter got . iv 1 89
Most cruelly Didst thou, Alonso, use me and my daughter . . v 1 72
I Have lost my daugher.—A daughter? . . . . v 1 148
When did you lose your daughter?—In this last tempest . . v 1 152
She Is daughter to this famous Duke of Milan . . . v 1 192
For Thurio, he intends, shall wed his daughter . . *T. G. of Ver.* ii 6 39
My friend This night intends to steal away your daughter . . iii 1 11
Thurio whom your gentle daughter hates . . . . iii 1 14
I have sought To match my friend Sir Thurio to my daughter . iii 1 62
Bounty, worth and qualities Beseeming such a wife as your fair daughter iii 1 66
My wrath shall far exceed the love I ever bore my daughter . . iii 1 167
My daughter takes his going grievously . . . . iii 2 14
How willingly I would effect The match between Sir Thurio and my daughter . . . . iii 2 23
Saw you my daughter?—Neither . . . . . . v 2 33
I now beseech you, for your daughter's sake, To grant one boon . v 4 149
Anne Page, which is daughter to Master Thomas Page . *Mer. Wives* i 1 46
But not kissed your keeper's daughter?—Tut, a pin! . . . i 1 116
Nay, daughter, carry the wine in; we'll drink within . . . i 1 195
I told you, sir, my daughter is disposed of . . . . iii 4 74
I love your daughter In such a righteous fashion . . . iii 4 82
My daughter will I question how she loves you, And as I find her, so am I affected . . . . iii 4 94
So curses all Eve's daughters, of what complexion soever . . iv 2 24
Nan Page my daughter and my little son And three or four more . iv 4 47
Remember, son Slender, my daughter . . . . . v 2 3
My daughter is in green: when you see your time, take her by the hand v 3 1
He will chafe at the doctor's marrying my daughter . . . v 3 10
Tell her Master Slender hath married her daughter . . . v 5 183
If Anne Page be my daughter, she is, by this, Doctor Caius' wife . v 5 185
Did not I tell you how you should know my daughter by her garments? v 5 207
I knew of your purpose; turned my daughter into green . . v 5 214
I do confess it, and repent it, father.—'Tis meet so, daughter *M. for M.* ii 3 30
Fear me not.—Nor, gentle daughter, fear you not at all . . iv 1 71
Good morning to you, fair and gracious daughter . . . iv 3 116
Show your wisdom, daughter, In your close patience . . . iv 3 122
I think this is your daughter.—Her mother hath many times told me so *Much Ado* i 1 104
Didst thou note the daughter of Signior Leonato?—I noted her not . i 1 163
How short his answer is;—With Hero, Leonato's short daughter . i 1 216
He loved my niece your daughter and meant to acknowledge it . i 2 13
I will acquaint my daughter withal, that she may be the better prepared i 2 22
Which way looks he?—Marry, on Hero, the daughter and heir of Leonato . . . . i 3 56
Daughter, remember what I told you . . . . . ii 1 69
Take of me my daughter, and with her my fortunes . . . ii 1 313
I have heard my daughter say, she hath often dreamed of unhappiness ii 1 360
The Count Claudio shall marry the daughter of Leonato . . ii 2 2
She will sit you, you heard my daughter tell you how . . ii 3 116
'Tis true, indeed; so your daughter says . . . . ii 3 131
My daughter tells us all . . . . ii 3 138
I remember a pretty jest your daughter told us of . . . ii 3 141
She doth indeed; my daughter says so . . . . . ii 3 156
My daughter is sometime afeard she will do a desperate outrage to herself . . . . ii 3 158
We will hear further of it by your daughter . . . . ii 3 212
And that must your daughter and her gentlewomen carry . . ii 3 222
They stay for you to give your daughter to her husband . . iii 5 60
Will you with free and unconstrained soul Give me this maid, your daughter? . . . . iv 1 26
Let me but move one question to your daughter . . . iv 1 74
Your daughter here the princes left for dead . . . . iv 1 204
My heart is sorry for your daughter's death . . . . v 1 103
The old man's daughter told us all . . . . . v 1 179
I thank you, princes, for my daughter's death . . . . v 1 278
I cannot bid you bid my daughter live; That were impossible . . v 1 288
My brother hath a daughter, Almost the copy of my child that's dead. v 1 297
Daughter, and you gentlewomen all, Withdraw into a chamber by yourselves . . . . v 4 10
Brother, You must be father to your brother's daughter . . v 4 15
Your niece regards me with an eye of favour.—That eye my daughter lent her . . . . v 4 23
Are you yet determined To-day to marry with my brother's daughter? . v 4 37
Here comes in embassy The French king's daughter . *L. L. Lost* i 1 136
The daughter of the King of France, On serious business, craving quick dispatch . . . . ii 1 30
Pray you, sir, whose daughter?—Her mother's, I have heard . . ii 1 201
Their daughters profit very greatly under you . . . . iv 2 77
If their daughters be capable, I will put it to them . . . iv 2 81
With cunning hast thou filch'd my daughter's heart . *M. N. Dream* i 1 36
This is my daughter here asleep . . . . . . iv 1 133
Her name is Portia, nothing undervalued To Cato's daughter, Brutus' Portia . . . . *Mer. of Venice* i 1 166
So is the will of a living daughter curbed by the will of a dead father i 2 26
But though I am a daughter to his blood, I am not to his manners . ii 3 18
If e'er the Jew her father come to heaven, It will be for his gentle daughter's sake . . . . ii 4 35
If my fortune be not crost, I have a father, you a daughter, lost . ii 5 57
My daughter! O my ducats! O my daughter! Fled with a Christian! ii 8 15
O my Christian ducats! Justice! the law! my ducats, and my daughter! ii 8 17
A sealed bag, two sealed bags of ducats, Of double ducats, stolen from me by my daughter! . . . . ii 8 19
Stolen by my daughter! Justice! find the girl . . . . ii 8 21

Daughter. All the boys in Venice follow him, Crying, his stones, his daughter, and his ducats *Mer. of Venice* ii 8 24
You knew, none so well, none so well as you, of my daughter's flight iii 1 28
I say, my daughter is my flesh and blood iii 1 40
What news from Genoa? hast thou found my daughter? iii 1 84
I would my daughter were dead at my foot, and the jewels in her ear! iii 1 92
Your daughter spent in Genoa, as I heard, in one night fourscore ducats iii 1 113
One of them showed me a ring that he had of your daughter for a monkey iii 1 124
You may partly hope . . . that you are not the Jew's daughter iii 5 13
He tells me flatly, there is no mercy for me in heaven, because I am a Jew's daughter iii 5 36
I have a daughter; Would any of the stock of Barrabas Had been her husband rather than a Christian! iv 1 295
The gentleman That lately stole his daughter iv 1 385
That he do record a gift, Here in the court, of all he dies possess'd, Unto his son Lorenzo and his daughter iv 1 390
Can you tell if Rosalind, the duke's daughter, be banished? *As Y. Like It* i 1 111
And no less beloved of her uncle than his own daughter i 1 117
How now, daughter and cousin! are you crept hither to see the wrestling? i 2 164
Which of the two was daughter of the duke That here was at the wrestling? i 2 281
Neither his daughter, if we judge by manners i 2 283
Daughter to the banish'd duke, And here detain'd by her usurping uncle, To keep his daughter company i 2 285
Thou art thy father's daughter; there's enough i 3 60
Know'st thou not, the duke Hath banish'd me, his daughter? i 3 97
Your daughter and her cousin much commend The parts and graces of the wrestler ii 2 12
Keep you your word, O duke, to give your daughter; You yours, Orlando, to receive his daughter v 4 19
I do remember in this shepherd boy Some lively touches of my daughter's favour v 4 27
The first time that I ever saw him Methought he was a brother to your daughter v 4 29
Good duke, receive thy daughter: Hymen from heaven brought her v 4 117
If there be truth in sight, you are my daughter v 4 124
Dear niece, welcome thou art to me! Even daughter, welcome, in no less degree v 4 154
How I firmly am resolved you know; That is, not to bestow my youngest daughter Before I have a husband for the elder *T. of Shrew* i 1 50
By helping Baptista's eldest daughter to a husband we set his youngest free i 1 142
I saw sweet beauty in her face, Such as the daughter of Agenor had i 1 173
That Lucentio indeed had Baptista's youngest daughter i 1 245
His youngest daughter, beautiful Bianca i 2 120
He that has the two fair daughters: is't he you mean? i 2 222
Fair Leda's daughter had a thousand wooers i 2 244
Did you yet ever see Baptista's daughter? i 2 252
The youngest daughter whom you hearken for Her father keeps from all access of suitors i 2 260
Have you not a daughter Call'd Katharina, fair and virtuous?—I have a daughter, sir, called Katharina ii 1 42
A stranger in this city here, Do make myself a suitor to your daughter ii 1 91
Toward the education of your daughters, I here bestow a simple instrument ii 1 99
Lead these gentlemen To my daughters ii 1 110
If I get your daughter's love, What dowry shall I have with her to wife? ii 1 120
What, will my daughter prove a good musician? ii 1 145
Proceed in practice with my younger daughter; She's apt to learn ii 1 165
How speed you with my daughter?—How but well, sir? ii 1 283
Call you me daughter? now, I promise you You have show'd a tender fatherly regard ii 1 287
But now, Baptista, to your younger daughter ii 1 334
And he of both That can assure my daughter greatest dower Shall have my Bianca's love ii 1 345
If I may have your daughter to my wife, I'll leave her houses three or four ii 1 367
To pass assurance of a dower in marriage 'Twixt me and one Baptista's daughter iv 2 118
A weighty cause Of love between your daughter and himself iv 4 27
For the good report I hear of you And for the love he beareth to your daughter iv 4 29
Your son Lucentio here Doth love my daughter and she loveth him iv 4 41
And pass my daughter a sufficient dower, The match is made iv 4 45
Your son shall have my daughter with consent iv 4 47
Send for your daughter by your servant here iv 4 58
His daughter is to be brought by you to the supper iv 4 85
That have by marriage made thy daughter mine v 1 119
Have you married my daughter without asking my good will? v 1 137
Another dowry to another daughter, For she is changed, as she had never been v 2 114
Was this gentlewoman the daughter of Gerard de Narbon? *All's Well* i 1 42
Why? that you are my daughter?—That I am not i 3 159
Can't no other, But, I your daughter, he must be my brother? i 3 172
You might be my daughter-in-law: God shield you mean it not! daughter and mother So strive upon your pulse i 3 174
A poor physician's daughter my wife! ii 3 122
If she be All that is virtuous, save what thou dislikest, A poor physician's daughter, thou dislikest Of virtue for the name ii 3 130
The count he wooes your daughter, Lays down his wanton siege before her beauty iii 7 17
It is no more, But that your daughter, ere she seems as won, Desires this ring iii 7 31
Instruct my daughter how she shall persever iii 7 37
Doubt not but heaven Hath brought me up to be your daughter's dower iv 4 19
I moved the king my master to speak in the behalf of my daughter iv 5 76
What says he to your daughter? have you spoke? v 3 28
You remember The daughter of this lord? v 3 43
Give a favour from you To sparkle in the spirits of my daughter v 3 75
Your reputation comes too short for my daughter v 3 177
A virtuous maid, the daughter of a count *T. Night* i 2 36
My father had a daughter loved a man ii 4 110
I am all the daughters of my father's house, And all the brothers too ii 4 123
I have three daughters; the eldest is eleven; The second and the third, nine, and some five *W. Tale* ii 1 144
A daughter, and a goodly babe, Lusty and like to live ii 2 26
The good queen, For she is good, hath brought you forth a daughter ii 3 65

Daughter. The party tried The daughter of a king *W. Tale* iii 2 3
A great king's daughter, The mother to a hopeful prince iii 2 40
O that he were alive, and here beholding His daughter's trial! iii 2 122
A shepherd's daughter, And what to her adheres, which follows after iv 1 27
A man, who hath a daughter of most rare note iv 2 48
Fie, daughter! when my old wife lived, upon This day she was both pantler, butler, cook iv 4 55
What fair swain is this Which dances with your daughter? iv 4 167
He says he loves my daughter: I think so too iv 4 171
Never gazed the moon Upon the water as he'll stand and read As 'twere my daughter's eyes iv 4 174
But, my daughter, Say you the like to him? iv 4 390
You shall bear witness to't: I give my daughter to him iv 4 396
O, that must be I' the virtue of your daughter iv 4 398
Come, your hand; And, daughter, yours iv 4 402
Had not the old man come in with a whoo-bub against his daughter iv 4 629
His son, that should have married a shepherd's daughter iv 4 794
An old sheep-whistling rogue, a ram-tender, to offer to have his daughter come into grace! iv 4 806
He must know 'tis none of your daughter nor my sister iv 4 850
From him, whose daughter His tears proclaim'd his, parting with her v 1 159
What might I have been, Might I a son and daughter now have look'd on, Such goodly things as you! v 1 177
Fled from his father, from his hopes, and with A shepherd's daughter v 1 185
Is this the daughter of a king?—She is, When once she is my wife v 1 208
The oracle is fulfilled; the king's daughter is found v 2 25
Many other evidences proclaim her with all certainty to be the king's daughter v 2 43
Our king, being ready to leap out of himself for joy of his found daughter v 2 55
Then again worries he his daughter with clipping her v 2 58
How attentiveness wounded his daughter v 2 95
He at that time, over-fond of the shepherd's daughter v 2 127
Thy sons and daughters will be all gentlemen born v 2 138
That which my daughter came to look upon, The statue of her mother v 3 13
From thy admiring daughter took the spirits, Standing like stone with thee v 3 41
You gods, look down And from your sacred vials pour your graces Upon my daughter's head! v 3 123
Who, heavens directing, Is troth-plight to your daughter v 3 151
That daughter there of Spain, the Lady Blanch *K. John* ii 1 423
If thou be pleased withal, Command thy son and daughter to join hands ii 1 532
'Tis true, fair daughter; and this blessed day Ever in France shall be kept festival iii 1 75
Whose daughter, as we hear, the Earl of March Hath lately married *1 Hen. IV.* i 3 84
I am afraid my daughter will run mad iii 1 145
My daughter weeps: she will not part with you iii 1 194
Loving wife, and gentle daughter, Give even way unto my rough affairs *2 Hen. IV.* ii 3 1
Beshrew your heart, Fair daughter, you do draw my spirits from me ii 3 46
How doth my cousin, your bedfellow? and your fairest daughter and mine? iii 2 7
Being descended Of Blithild, which was daughter to King Clothair *Hen. V.* i 2 67
As heir to the Lady Lingare, Daughter to Charlemain i 2 75
Lady Ermengare, Daughter to Charles the foresaid duke of Lorraine i 2 83
When the man dies, let the inheritance Descend unto the daughter i 2 100
Tells Harry that the king doth offer him Katharine his daughter iii Prol. 30
See The blind and bloody soldier with foul hand Defile the locks of your shrill-shrieking daughters iii 3 35
Whilst by a slave, no gentler than my dog, His fairest daughter is contaminated iv 5 16
His daughter first, and then in sequel all v 2 361
Thereupon give me your daughter.—Take her, fair son v 2 375
I am by birth a shepherd's daughter, My wit untrain'd *1 Hen. VI.* i 2 72
Nor yet Saint Philip's daughters were like thee i 2 143
Divinest creature, Astræa's daughter, How shall I honour thee for this? i 6 4
A man of great authority in France, Proffers his only daughter to your grace v 1 19
Margaret my name, and daughter to a king v 3 51
See, Reignier, see, thy daughter prisoner! v 3 131
And for thy honour give consent, Thy daughter shall be wedded to my king v 3 137
This her easy-held imprisonment Hath gain'd thy daughter princely liberty v 3 140
My daughter shall be Henry's, if he please v 3 156
A poor earl's daughter is unequal odds v 5 34
Whom should we match with Henry, being a king, But Margaret, that is daughter to a king? v 5 67
Henry shall espouse the Lady Margaret, daughter unto Reignier *2 Hen. VI.* i 1 47
Henry was well pleased To change two dukedoms for a duke's fair daughter i 1 219
Till Suffolk gave two dukedoms for his daughter i 3 90
Philippe, a daughter, Who married Edmund Mortimer, Earl of March ii 2 35
Philippe, Sole daughter unto Lionel Duke of Clarence ii 2 50
For daring to affy a mighty lord Unto the daughter of a worthless king iv 1 81
She was, indeed, a pedler's daughter, and sold many laces iv 2 49
Edmund Mortimer, Earl of March, Married the Duke of Clarence' daughter iv 2 145
Ravish your wives and daughters before your faces iv 8 32
Henceforward will I bear Upon my target three fair-shining suns.—Nay, bear three daughters *3 Hen. VI.* ii 1 41
'Twill grieve your grace my sons should call you father.—No more than when my daughters call thee mother iii 2 101
I'll join mine eldest daughter and my joy To him forthwith in holy wedlock iii 3 242
Thy faith irrevocable, That only Warwick's daughter shall be thine iii 3 248
Young Prince Edward marries Warwick's daughter iv 1 117
Sit you fast, For I will hence to Warwick's other daughter iv 1 120
Welcome, sweet Clarence; my daughter shall be thine iv 2 12
To keep that oath were more impiety Than Jephthah's, when he sacrificed his daughter v 1 91
Then I'll marry Warwick's youngest daughter *Richard III.* i 1 153
Which stretched to their servants, daughters, wives iii 5 82
Daughter, well met.—God give your graces both A happy and a joyful time of day! iv 1 5
Inquire me out some mean-born gentleman, Whom I will marry straight to Clarence' daughter iv 2 55
I must be married to my brother's daughter, Or else my kingdom stands on brittle glass iv 2 61

Daughter. The son of Clarence have I pent up close; His daughter meanly have I match'd in marriage *Richard III.* iv 3 37
The Breton Richmond aims At young Elizabeth, my brother's daughter iv 3 41
For my daughters, Richard, They shall be praying nuns, not weeping queens iv 4 200
You have a daughter call'd Elizabeth, Virtuous and fair, royal and gracious iv 4 203
I will confess she was not Edward's daughter.—Wrong not her birth iv 4 210
Then know, that from my soul I love thy daughter.—My daughter's mother thinks it with her soul iv 4 255
What do you think?—That thou dost love my daughter from thy soul iv 4 258
I mean, that with my soul I love thy daughter, And mean to make her queen iv 4 262
This is not the way To win your daughter iv 4 285
If I did take the kingdom from your sons, To make amends, I'll give it to your daughter iv 4 295
I will beget Mine issue of your blood upon your daughter iv 4 298
The loss you have is but a son being king, And by that loss your daughter is made queen iv 4 308
The king, that calls your beauteous daughter wife, Familiarly shall call thy Dorset brother iv 4 315
Go, then, my mother, to thy daughter go; Make bold her bashful years iv 4 325
Bound with triumphant garlands will I come And lead thy daughter to a conqueror's bed iv 4 334
Thy beauteous princely daughter! In her consists my happiness and thine iv 4 405
But thou didst kill my children.—But in your daughter's womb I bury them iv 4 423
Shall I go win my daughter to thy will?—And be a happy mother by the deed iv 4 426
The queen hath heartily consented He shall espouse Elizabeth her daughter iv 5 18
Shall these enjoy our lands? lie with our wives? Ravish our daughters? v 3 337
What fair lady's that?—An't please your grace, Sir Thomas Bullen's daughter *Hen. VIII.* i 4 92
We are a queen, or long have dream'd so, certain The daughter of a king ii 4 72
Wherein he might the king his lord advertise Whether our daughter were legitimate ii 4 179
The late queen's gentlewoman, a knight's daughter, To be her mistress' mistress! iii 2 94
The model of our chaste loves, his young daughter iv 2 132
Although unqueen'd, yet like A queen, and daughter to a king, inter me iv 2 172
Had I a sister were a grace, or a daughter a goddess, he should take his choice *Troi. and Cres.* i 2 257
Let him be sent, great princes, And he shall buy my daughter iii 3 28
'Tis known, Achilles, that you are in love With one of Priam's daughters iii 3 194
Is not yond Diomed, with Calchas' daughter? iv 5 13
Set them down For sluttish spoils of opportunity And daughters of the game iv 5 63
Here is a letter from Queen Hecuba, A token from her daughter, my fair love v 1 45
Where's your daughter?—She comes to you v 2 3
Daughter, sing; or express yourself in a more comfortable sort *Coriol.* i 3 1
I tell thee, daughter, I sprang not more in joy at first hearing he was a man-child i 3 16
That Ancus Marcius, Numa's daughter's son ii 3 247
You have holp to ravish your own daughters iv 6 81
The easy groans of old women, the virginal palms of your daughters v 2 46
Daughter, speak you: He cares not for your weeping v 3 155
He killed my son. My daughter. He killed my cousin Marcus v 6 122
This was thy daughter.—Why, Marcus, so she is *T. Andron.* iii 1 63
See, thy two sons' heads, Thy warlike hand, thy mangled daughter here iii 1 256
For worse than Philomel you used my daughter v 2 195
Was it well done of rash Virginius To slay his daughter with his own right hand? v 3 37
Why hast thou slain thine only daughter thus? v 3 55
Signior Martino and his wife and daughters *Rom. and Jul.* i 2 67
Mine uncle Capulet, his wife, and daughters i 2 71
Nurse, where's my daughter? call her forth to me i 3 1
Thou know'st my daughter's of a pretty age i 3 10
I nursed her daughter, that you talk'd withal; I tell you, he that can lay hold of her Shall have the chinks i 5 117
My heart's dear love is set On the fair daughter of rich Capulet ii 3 58
Romeo shall thank thee, daughter, for us both ii 6 22
Things have fall'n out, sir, so unluckily, That we have had no time to move our daughter iii 4 2
Madam, good night: commend me to your daughter iii 4 9
Ho, daughter! are you up? iii 5 65
My leisure serves me, pensive daughter, now iv 1 39
Hold, daughter: I do spy a kind of hope iv 1 68
What, is my daughter gone to Friar Laurence? iv 2 11
Death is my son-in-law, Death is my heir; My daughter he hath wedded iv 5 39
O heavens! O wife, look how our daughter bleeds! v 3 202
This dagger hath mista'en,—for, lo, his house Is empty on the back of Montague,—And it mis-sheathed in my daughter's bosom! v 3 205
O brother Montague, give me thy hand: This is my daughter's jointure v 3 297
One only daughter have I, no kin else, On whom I may confer what I have got *T. of Athens* i 1 121
His honesty rewards him in itself; It must not bear my daughter i 1 131
Give him thy daughter: What you bestow, in him I'll counterpoise i 1 144
I grant I am a woman; but withal A woman well-reputed, Cato's daughter *J. Cæsar* ii 1 295
Your wives, your daughters, Your matrons and your maids, could not fill up The cistern of my lust *Macbeth* iv 3 61
You do not understand yourself so clearly As it behoves my daughter *Ham.* i 3 97
These blazes, daughter, Giving more light than heat, extinct in both, Even in their promise, as it is a-making, You must not take for fire i 3 117
I have a daughter—have while she is mine—Who, in her duty and obedience, mark, Hath given me this ii 2 106
This, in obedience, hath my daughter shown me, And more above ii 2 125
I perceived it, I must tell you that, Before my daughter told me ii 2 134
I'll loose my daughter to him: Be you and I behind an arras then ii 2 162
Have you a daughter?—I have, my lord.—Let her not walk i' the sun ii 2 183
Conception is a blessing: but not as your daughter may conceive ii 2 186
Still harping on my daughter: yet he knew me not at first ii 2 189
And suddenly contrive the means of meeting between him and my daughter ii 2 217

Daughter. One fair daughter, and no more, The which he loved passing well. *Hamlet* ii 2 426
Still on my daughter.—Am I not i' the right, old Jephthah? ii 2 428
If you call me Jephthah, my lord, I have a daughter that I love passing well ii 2 431
Horridly trick'd With blood of fathers, mothers, daughters, sons ii 2 480
They say the owl was a baker's daughter iv 5 42
It is the false steward, that stole his master's daughter iv 5 173
We have this hour a constant will to publish Our daughters' several dowers *Lear* i 1 45
Great rivals in our youngest daughter's love i 1 47
Tell me, my daughters, . . . Which of you shall we say doth love us most? i 1 49
What says our second daughter, Our dearest Regan, wife to Cornwall? i 1 68
Shall to my bosom Be as well neighbour'd, pitied, and relieved, As thou my sometime daughter i 1 122
Cornwall and Albany, With my two daughters' dowers digest this third i 1 130
Answer my life my judgement, Thy youngest daughter does not love thee least i 1 154
You, who with this king Hath rivall'd for our daughter i 1 194
Thy dowerless daughter, king, thrown to my chance, Is queen of us, of ours, and our fair France i 1 259
For we Have no such daughter, nor shall ever see That face of hers again i 1 266
You, you, sirrah, where's my daughter? i 4 48
He says, my lord, your daughter is not well i 4 54
There's a great abatement of kindness appears as well in the general dependants as in the duke himself also and your daughter i 4 67
Go you, and tell my daughter I would speak with her i 4 82
This fellow has banished two on's daughters, and did the third a blessing against his will i 4 115
There's mine; beg another of thy daughters.—Take heed, sirrah; the whip i 4 122
I have used it, nuncle, ever since thou madest thy daughters thy mother i 4 188
I marvel what kin thou and thy daughters are i 4 199
How now, daughter! what makes that frontlet on? Methinks you are too much of late i' the frown i 4 207
Are you our daughter?—Come, sir i 4 238
By the marks of sovereignty, knowledge, and reason, I should be false persuaded I had daughters i 4 254
I'll not trouble thee: Yet have I left a daughter i 4 276
Yet have I left a daughter, Who, I am sure, is kind and comfortable i 4 327
A fox, when one has caught her, And such a daughter, Should sure to the slaughter i 4 341
Acquaint my daughter no further with any thing you know i 5 2
Shalt see thy other daughter will use thee kindly i 5 14
I can tell why a snail has a house.—Why?—Why, to put his head in; not to give it away to his daughters i 5 33
It is both he and she; Your son and daughter ii 4 14
Your son and daughter found this trespass worth The shame ii 4 44
Thou shalt have as many dolours for thy daughters as thou canst tell in a year ii 4 55
Where is this daughter?—With the earl, sir, here within ii 4 58
The dear father Would with his daughter speak, commands her service ii 4 103
Dear daughter, I confess that I am old; Age is unnecessary ii 4 156
I prithee, daughter, do not make me mad: I will not trouble thee, my child ii 4 221
We'll no more meet, no more see one another: But yet thou art my flesh, my blood, my daughter ii 4 224
If it be you that stir these daughters' hearts Against their father, fool me not so much To bear it tamely ii 4 277
Good nuncle, in, and ask thy daughters' blessing iii 2 12
Nor rain, wind, thunder, fire, are my daughters: I tax not you, you elements, with unkindness iii 2 15
Yet I call you servile ministers, That have with two pernicious daughters join'd iii 2 22
Hast thou given all to thy two daughters? And art thou come to this? iii 4 49
What, have his daughters brought him to this pass? iii 4 65
Now, all the plagues that in the pendulous air Hang fated o'er men's faults light on thy daughters!—He hath no daughters, sir iii 4 70
Nothing could have subdued nature To such a lowness but his unkind daughters iii 4 73
Judicious punishment! 'twas this flesh begot Those pelican daughters iii 4 77
My duty cannot suffer To obey in all your daughters' hard commands iii 4 154
His wits begin to unsettle.—Canst thou blame him? His daughters seek his death iii 4 168
Tigers, not daughters, what have you perform'd? iv 2 40
And by no means Will yield to see his daughter iv 3 43
Gave her dear rights To his dog-hearted daughters iv 3 47
Gloucester's bastard son Was kinder to his father than my daughters iv 6 117
Sir, Your most dear daughter— No rescue? What, a prisoner? iv 6 193
Thou hast one daughter, Who redeems nature from the general curse Which twain have brought her to iv 6 209
Sir, this I hear; the king is come to his daughter v 1 21
King Lear hath lost, he and his daughter ta'en v 2 6
Shall we not see these daughters and these sisters? v 3 7
Your eldest daughters have fordone themselves, And desperately are dead v 3 291
Thieves! thieves! Look to your house, your daughter and your bags! *Othello* i 1 80
In honest plainness thou hast heard me say My daughter is not for thee i 1 98
You'll have your daughter covered with a Barbary horse i 1 111
Your daughter and the Moor are now making the beast with two backs i 1 117
Your fair daughter, At this odd-even and dull watch o' the night i 1 123
Your daughter, if you have not given her leave, I say again, hath made a gross revolt i 1 134
Fathers, from hence trust not your daughters' minds By what you see them act i 1 171
O thou foul thief, where hast thou stow'd my daughter? i 2 62
Why, what's the matter?—My daughter! O, my daughter!—Dead? i 3 59
Whoe'er he be that in this foul proceeding Hath thus beguiled your daughter of herself i 3 66
That I have ta'en away this old man's daughter, It is most true i 3 78
For such proceeding I am charged withal, I won his daughter i 3 94
I think this tale would win my daughter too i 3 171
I am hitherto your daughter: but here's my husband i 3 185
If that thy father live, let him repent Thou wast not made his daughter *Ant. and Cleo.* iii 13 135

Daughter. His daughter, and the heir of's kingdom, whom He purposed to his wife's sole son *Cymbeline* i 1 4
You shall not find me, daughter, After the slander of most stepmothers i 1 70
Would I were A neat-herd's daughter, and my Leonatus Our neighbour shepherd's son! i 1 149
Beseech your patience. Peace, Dear lady daughter, peace! i 1 154
This matter of marrying his king's daughter i 4 15
He hath a court He little cares for and a daughter who He not respects at all i 6 154
Attend you here the door of our stern daughter? ii 3 42
Who lets go by no vantages that may Prefer you to his daughter ii 3 51
But, my gentle queen, Where is our daughter? iii 5 30
Your daughter, whom she bore in hand to love With such integrity v 5 43
Yet, O my daughter! That it was folly in me, thou mayst say, And prove it v 5 66
That paragon, thy daughter,—For whom my heart drops blood v 5 147
Give me leave; I faint.—My daughter! what of her? Renew thy strength v 5 150
Nay, nay, to the purpose.—Your daughter's chastity—there it begins v 5 179
Where I was taught Of your chaste daughter the wide difference 'Twixt amorous and villanous v 5 194
I am Posthumus, That kill'd thy daughter v 5 218
The piece of tender air, thy virtuous daughter v 5 446
Bring in our daughter, clothed like a bride *Pericles* i 1 6
He hath a fair daughter, and to-morrow is her birth-day ii 1 113
Our daughter, In honour of whose birth these triumphs are ii 2 4
'Tis now your honour, daughter, to explain ii 2 14
Come, queen o' the feast,—For, daughter, so you are ii 3 18
He was seated in a chariot Of an inestimable value, and his daughter with him ii 4 8
From my daughter this I let you know ii 5 2
Now to my daughter's letter: She tells me here, she'll wed the stranger knight ii 5 15
Let me ask you one thing: What do you think of my daughter, sir? ii 5 33
My daughter thinks very well of you; Ay, so well, that you must be her master ii 5 37
Never aim'd so high to love your daughter, But bent all offices to honour her ii 5 47
Thou hast bewitch'd my daughter, and thou art A villain ii 5 49
Here comes my daughter, she can witness it ii 5 66
Antiochus and his daughter dead iii Gower 25
A little daughter: for the sake of it, Be manly, and take comfort iii 1 21
Who finds her, give her burying; She was the daughter of a king iii 2 73
And in this kind hath our Cleon One daughter iv Gower 16
A present murderer does prepare For good Marina, that her daughter Might stand peerless iv Gower 39
Why do you keep alone? How chance my daughter is not with you? iv 1 23
It greets me as an enterprise of kindness Perform'd to your sole daughter iv 3 39
Attended on by many a lord and knight, To see his daughter, all his life's delight iv 4 12
So with his steerage shall your thoughts grow on,—To fetch his daughter home iv 4 20
She was of Tyrus the king's daughter iv 4 36
Let Pericles believe his daughter's dead iv 4 46
While our scene must play His daughter's woe iv 4 49
Driven before the winds, he is arrived Here where his daughter dwells v Gower 15
The main grief springs from the loss Of a beloved daughter and a wife v 1 30
My dearest wife was like this maid, and such a one My daughter might have been v 1 109
How! a king's daughter? And call'd Marina? v 1 151
My mother was the daughter of a king; Who died the minute I was born v 1 159
This cannot be: My daughter's buried v 1 165
I am the daughter to King Pericles, If good King Pericles be v 1 180
Is it no more to be your daughter than To say my mother's name was Thaisa? v 1 211
Tell him O'er, point by point, for yet he seems to doubt, How sure you are my daughter v 1 228
To mourn thy crosses, with thy daughter's, call And give them repetition v 1 246
You shall prevail, Were it to woo my daughter v 1 263
By her own most clear remembrance, she Made known herself my daughter v 3 13
Thaisa, This prince, the fair-betrothed of your daughter, Shall marry her v 3 71
Our son and daughter shall in Tyrus reign v 3 82
In Antiochus and his daughter you have heard Of monstrous lust the due and just reward v 3 Gower 85
In Pericles, his queen and daughter, seen, Although assail'd with fortune fierce and keen, Virtue preserved from fell destruction's blast v 3 Gower 87
Daughter Anne. You are come to see my daughter Anne? *Mer. Wives* ii 1 167
Now, Master Slender: love him, daughter Anne iii 4 71
Daughter Hermia. With complaint Against my child, my daughter Hermia *M. N. Dream* i 1 23
Daughter Joan. Ah, Joan, sweet daughter Joan, I'll die with thee! 1 *Hen. VI.* v 4 6
Daughter Juliet, How stands your disposition to be married? *Rom. and Jul.* i 3 64
Daughter Kate. Will you go with us, Or shall I send my daughter Kate to you? *T. of Shrew* ii 1 168
Daughter Katharine. But for my daughter Katharine, this I know, She is not for your turn, the more my grief ii 1 62
How now, daughter Katharine! in your dumps? ii 1 286
On Sunday next you know My daughter Katharine is to be married iii 1 396
Daughter Mary. A marriage 'twixt the Duke of Orleans and Our daughter Mary *Hen. VIII.* ii 4 175
Daughter Silvia. Now, daughter Silvia, you are hard beset *T. G. of Ver.* ii 4 49
Daughter-beamed. You were best call it 'daughter-beamed eyes' *L. L. L.* v 2 171
Daughter-in-law. Yes, Helen, you might be my daughter-in-law *All's Well* i 3 173
I have sent you a daughter-in-law iii 2 21
Your daughter-in-law had been alive at this hour iv 5 4
Daunt. Think you a little din can daunt mine ears? *T. of Shrew* i 2 200
Let not discontent Daunt all your hopes *T. Andron.* i 1 268
Daunted. Wilt thou be daunted at a woman's sight? 1 *Hen. VI.* v 3 69
A heart unspotted is not easily daunted 2 *Hen. VI.* iii 1 100
What, are ye daunted now? now will ye stoop? iv 1 119
Dauntless. A braver choice of dauntless spirits Than now the English bottoms have waft o'er Did never float *K. John* ii 1 72
Grow great by your example and put on The dauntless spirit of resolution v 1 53
Let thy dauntless mind Still ride in triumph over all mischance 3 *Hen. VI.* iii 3 17
And, to that dauntless temper of his mind, He hath a wisdom *Macbeth* iii 1 52
Dauphin. Look upon the years Of Lewis the Dauphin and that lovely maid *K. John* ii 1 425
Such as she is, in beauty, virtue, birth, Is the young Dauphin every way ii 1 433
If that the Dauphin there, thy princely son, Can in this book of beauty read 'I love' ii 1 484
Speak then, prince Dauphin; can you love this lady? ii 1 524
Thou virtuous Dauphin, alter not the doom Forethought by heaven! iii 1 311
O noble Dauphin, Go with me to the king iii 4 177
Under whose conduct came those powers of France...?—Under the Dauphin iv 2 131
Whose private with me of the Dauphin's love Is much more general than these lines import iv 3 16
Away toward Bury, to the Dauphin there! iv 3 114
London hath received, Like a kind host, the Dauphin and his powers v 1 32
He hath promised to dismiss the powers Led by the Dauphin v 1 65
And, noble Dauphin, albeit we swear A voluntary zeal and an unurged faith v 2 9
The Dauphin is too wilful-opposite, And will not temporize v 2 124
Strike up our drums, to find this danger out.—And thou shalt find it, Dauphin v 2 180
The great supply That was expected by the Dauphin here, Are wreck'd v 3 10
Where is my prince, the Dauphin?—Here: what news? v 5 9
The Dauphin is preparing hitherward v 7 59
The Dauphin rages at our very heels v 7 80
The Cardinal Pandulph is within at rest, Who half an hour since came from the Dauphin v 7 83
Call in the messengers sent from the Dauphin *Hen. V.* i 2 221
Now are we well prepared to know the pleasure Of our fair cousin Dauphin i 2 235
Shall we sparingly show you far off The Dauphin's meaning? i 2 240
With frank and with uncurbed plainness Tell us the Dauphin's mind i 2 245
Desires you let the dukedoms that you claim Hear no more of you. This the Dauphin speaks i 2 257
We are glad the Dauphin is so pleasant with us i 2 259
But tell the Dauphin I will keep my state i 2 273
I will dazzle all the eyes of France, Yea, strike the Dauphin blind i 2 280
And some are yet ungotten and unborn That shall have cause to curse the Dauphin's scorn i 2 288
Tell you the Dauphin I am coming on, To venge me as I may i 2 291
Tell the Dauphin His jest will savour but of shallow wit i 2 294
For, God before, We'll chide this Dauphin at his father's door i 2 308
Orleans shall make forth, And you, Prince Dauphin ii 4 6
O peace, Prince Dauphin! You are too much mistaken in this king ii 4 29
This is his claim, his threatening and my message; Unless the Dauphin be in presence here ii 4 111
For the Dauphin, I stand here for him: what to him from England? ii 4 115
The Dauphin, whom of succours we entreated, Returns us that his powers are yet not ready iii 3 45
Prince Dauphin, you shall stay with us in Rouen iii 5 64
The Dauphin longs for morning.—He longs to eat the English iii 7 98
The Dauphin Charles is crowned king in Rheims 1 *Hen. VI.* i 1 92
The Dauphin crowned king! all fly to him! i 1 96
A base Walloon, to win the Dauphin's grace, Thrust Talbot with a spear into the back i 1 137
I'll hale the Dauphin headlong from his throne i 1 149
Either to quell the Dauphin utterly, Or bring him in obedience to your yoke i 1 163
Where's the Prince Dauphin? I have news for him i 2 46
Reignier, stand thou as Dauphin in my place: Question her proudly i 2 61
Reignier, is't thou that thinkest to beguile me? Where is the Dauphin? i 2 66
Dauphin, I am by birth a shepherd's daughter i 2 72
Let me thy servant and not sovereign be: 'Tis the French Dauphin sueth i 2 112
The Dauphin, with one Joan la Pucelle join'd i 4 101
Dauphin, command the citizens make bonfires And feast and banquet i 6 12
I muse we met not with the Dauphin's grace, His new-come champion ii 2 19
Am sure I scared the Dauphin and his trull ii 2 28
I'll by a sign give notice to our friends, That Charles the Dauphin may encounter them iii 2 9
Enter, and cry 'The Dauphin!' presently, And then do execution on the watch iii 2 34
We'll pull his plumes and take away his train, If Dauphin and the rest will be but ruled iii 3 8
The Dauphin, well appointed, Stands with the snares of war to tangle thee iv 2 21
The Dauphin's drum, a warning bell, Sings heavy music to thy timorous soul iv 2 39
Are not the speedy scouts return'd again, That dogg'd the mighty army of the Dauphin? iv 3 2
Discovered Two mightier troops than that the Dauphin led iv 3 7
When from the Dauphin's crest thy sword struck fire, It warm'd thy father's heart with proud desire iv 6 10
Herald, conduct me to the Dauphin's tent iv 7 51
Submission, Dauphin! 'tis a mere French word iv 7 54
O, Charles the Dauphin is a proper man v 3 37
She and the Dauphin have been juggling v 4 68
And here at hand the Dauphin and his train Approacheth v 4 100
The Dauphin hath prevail'd beyond the seas 2 *Hen. VI.* i 3 128
Till France be won into the Dauphin's hands i 3 173
For giving up of Normandy unto Monsieur Basimecu, the dauphin of France iv 7 31
I am the son of Henry the Fifth, Who made the Dauphin and the French to stoop 3 *Hen. VI.* i 1 108
Tamed the king, and made the dauphin stoop ii 2 151
Daventry. The red-nose innkeeper of Daventry 1 *Hen. IV.* iv 2 51
Davy, Davy, Davy, Davy, let me see, Davy; let me see, Davy; let me see 2 *Hen. IV.* v 1 10
Shall we sow the headland with wheat?—With red wheat, Davy v 1 17
Some pigeons, Davy, a couple of short-legged hens, a joint of mutton v 1 27
Use his men well, Davy; for they are arrant knaves, and will backbite v 1 35
Well conceited, Davy: about thy business, Davy v 1 39
There is many complaints, Davy, against that Visor v 1 44
I say he shall have no wrong. Look about, Davy v 1 59
Spread, Davy; spread, Davy: well said, Davy v 3 10
This Davy serves you for good uses; he is your serving-man and your husband v 3 11
Give Master Bardolph some wine, Davy v 3 27
I hope to see London once ere I die.—An I might see you there, Davy v 3 65
Tell him, I'll knock his leek about his pate Upon Saint Davy's day *Hen. V.* iv 1 55

Davy. Earl of Suffolk, Sir Richard Ketly, Davy Gam, esquire: None else of name *Hen. V.* iv 8 109
Why wear you your leek to-day? Saint Davy's day is past v 1 2
Daw. Just so much as you may take upon a knife's point and choke a daw withal *Much Ado* ii 3 264
When turtles tread, and rooks, and daws *L. L. Lost* v 2 915
Nightingales answer daws *T. Night* iii 4 39
In these nice sharp quillets of the law, Good faith, I am no wiser than a daw *1 Hen. VI.* ii 4 18
The eagles are gone: crows and daws, crows and daws! *Troi. and Cres.* i 2 265
Then thou dwellest with daws too?—No, I serve not thy master *Coriol.* iv 5 48
I will wear my heart upon my sleeve For daws to peck at *Othello* i 1 65
Dawn. It is almost clear dawn *Meas. for Meas.* iv 2 226
Next day after dawn, Doth rise and help Hyperion to his horse *Hen. V.* iv 1 291
Dawning. As near the dawning, provost, as it is, You shall hear more ere morning *Meas. for Meas.* iv 2 97
Alas, poor Harry of England! he longs not for the dawning as we do *Hen. V.* iii 7 141
But dawning day new comfort hath inspired *T. Andron.* ii 2 10
The bird of dawning singeth all night long: And then, they say, no spirit dare stir abroad *Hamlet* i 1 160
Good dawning to thee, friend: art of this house? *Lear* ii 2 1
Swift, swift, you dragons of the night, that dawning May bear the raven's eye! I lodge in fear *Cymbeline* ii 2 48
Day. There's no harm done.—O, woe the day! *Tempest* i 2 15
What is the time o' the day? i 2 239
After two days I will discharge thee i 2 298
I'll free thee Within two days for this i 2 421
Might I but through my prison once a day Behold this maid i 2 490
Every day some sailor's wife, The masters of some merchant and the merchant Have just our theme of woe ii 1 4
Is not, sir, my doublet as fresh as the first day I wore it? ii 1 103
As I hope For quiet days, fair issue and long life iv 1 24
To take away The edge of that day's celebration iv 1 29
Never till this day Saw I him touch'd with anger so distemper'd iv 1 144
How's the day?—On the sixth hour v 1 3
Were't not affection chains thy tender days *T. G. of Ver.* i 1 3
Of all the fair resort of gentlemen That every day with parle encounter me i 2 5
How this spring of love resembleth The uncertain glory of an April day! i 3 85
When that hour o'erslips me in the day Wherein I sigh not, Julia, for thy sake ii 2 9
Made use and fair advantage of his days ii 4 68
Kept severely from resort of men, That no man hath access by day to her iii 1 109
Unless I look on Silvia in the day, There is no day for me to look upon iii 1 181
Trust me, I think 'tis almost day iv 2 139
Where have you been these two days loitering? iv 4 48
I bruised my shin th' other day with playing at sword and dagger *Mer. Wives* i 1 294
Thine own true knight, By day or night ii 1 16
Youthful still! in your doublet and hose this raw rheumatic day! iii 1 47
And this day we shall have our answer iii 2 60
Heaven knows how I love you; and you shall one day find it iii 3 88
Heaven give you many, many merry days! v 5 254
Within these three days his head to be chopped off *Meas. for Meas.* i 2 69
This day my sister should the cloister enter i 2 182
This news is old enough, yet it is every day's news iii 2 244
And those eyes, the break of day, Lights that do mislead the morn iv 1 3
I have sat here all day iv 1 20
Good morrow; for, as I take it, it is almost day iv 2 109
Drunk many times a day, if not many days entirely drunk iv 2 158
I crave but four days' respite iv 2 170
Within these two days he will be here iv 2 214
He this very day receives letters of strange tenour iv 2 215
He that drinks all night, and is hanged betimes in the morning, may sleep the sounder all the next day iv 3 50
I will not consent to die this day, that's certain iv 3 59
Well, you'll answer this one day iv 3 172
I'll limit thee this day To seek thy life by beneficial help *Com. of Errors* i 1 151
This very day a Syracusian merchant Is apprehended for arrival here i 2 3
Well, I will marry one day, but to try ii 1 42
In the stirring passage of the day, A vulgar comment will be made of it iii 1 99
For locking me out of my doors by day iv 1 18
Have you not heard men say, That Time comes stealing on by night and day? iv 2 60
Hath he not reason to turn back an hour in a day? iv 2 62
O most unhappy day! iv 4 126
This ill day A most outrageous fit of madness took him v 1 138
Beyond imagination is the wrong That she this day hath shameless thrown on me v 1 202
This day, great duke, she shut the doors upon me v 1 204
Ne'er may I look on day, nor sleep on night, But she tells to your highness simple truth! v 1 210
That by this sympathized one day's error Have suffer'd wrong v 1 397
And there live we as merry as the day is long *Much Ado* ii 1 52
I hope to see you one day fitted with a husband ii 1 60
Your grace is too costly to wear every day ii 1 342
When are you married, madam?—Why, every day, to-morrow iii 1 101
O day untowardly turned!—O mischief strangely thwarting! iii 2 134
With grey hairs and bruise of many days, Do challenge thee to trial of a man v 1 65
I'll tell thee how Beatrice praised thy wit the other day v 1 161
The gentle day, Before the wheels of Phœbus, round about Dapples the drowsy east with spots of grey v 3 25
This day to be conjoin'd In the state of honourable marriage v 4 29
And one day in a week to touch no food And but one meal on every day beside *L. L. Lost* i 1 39
To sleep but three hours in the night, And not be seen to wink of all the day i 1 43
And make a dark night too of half the day i 1 45
I'll keep what I have swore And bide the penance of each three years' day i 1 115
Hath this been proclaimed?—Four days ago i 1 122
Affliction may one day smile again; and till then, sit thee down, sorrow! i 1 316
Appertaining to thy young days, which we may nominate tender i 2 15
But a' must fast three days a week i 2 135
What time o' day?—The hour that fools should ask iii 1 122
O heresy in fair, fit for these days! iv 1 22
Here, sweet, put up this: 'twill be thine another day iv 1 109
As fair as day.—Ay, as some days; but then no sun must shine iv 3 90
Day. O, but for my love, day would turn to night! *L. L. Lost* iv 3 233
Her favour turns the fashion of the days iv 3 262
I did converse this quondam day with a companion v 1 7
In the posteriors of this day, which the rude multitude call the afternoon v 1 94
The posterior of the day, most generous sir, is liable v 1 96
Some entertainment of time, some show in the posterior of this day v 1 126
My lady, to the manner of the days, In courtesy gives undeserving praise v 2 365
A twelvemonth and a day I'll mark no words that smooth-faced wooers say v 2 837
It wants a twelvemonth and a day, And then 'twill end v 2 887
Four happy days bring in Another moon *M. N. Dream* i 1 2
Four days will quickly steep themselves in night i 1 7
Upon that day either prepare to die For disobedience to your father's will, Or else to wed Demetrius i 1 86
A proper man, as one shall see in a summer's day i 2 89
In the shape of Corin sat all day, Playing on pipes of corn and versing love ii 1 66
And tarry for the comfort of the day ii 2 38
The sun was not so true unto the day As he to me iii 2 50
For fear lest day should look their shames upon iii 2 385
Make no delay: We may effect this business yet ere day iii 2 395
And here will rest me. Come, thou gentle day! iii 2 418
By day's approach look to be visited iii 2 430
Here will I rest me till the break of day iii 2 446
Since we have the vaward of the day, My love shall hear the music of my hounds iv 1 110
Is not this the day That Hermia should give answer of her choice? iv 1 140
He could not have 'scaped sixpence a day: an the duke had not given him sixpence a day for playing Pyramus, I'll be hanged iv 2 21
Sixpence a day in Pyramus, or nothing iv 2 24
O most courageous day! O most happy hour! iv 2 27
O night with hue so black! O night, which ever art when day is not? v 1 172
Now, until the break of day, Through this house each fairy stray v 1 408
Trip away; make no stay; Meet me all by break of day v 1 429
You shall seek all day ere you find them *Mer. of Venice* i 1 116
You spurn'd me such a day; another time You call'd me dog i 3 128
If you repay me not on such a day i 3 147
If he should break his day, what should I gain By the exaction? i 3 165
My ships come home a month before the day i 3 183
Thy master spoke with me this day, And hath preferr'd thee ii 2 154
Snail-slow in profit, and he sleeps by day More than the wild-cat ii 5 47
Let good Antonio look he keep his day, Or he shall pay for this ii 8 25
A day in April never came so sweet, To show how costly summer was at hand ii 9 93
Such it is As are those dulcet sounds in break of day iii 2 51
I and my friend Have by your wisdom been this day acquitted iv 1 409
We'll away to-night And be a day before our husbands home iv 2 3
My mistress will before the break of day Be here at Belmont v 1 29
Methinks it sounds much sweeter than by day v 1 100
The nightingale, if she should sing by day, When every goose is cackling, would be thought No better a musician than the wren v 1 104
'Tis a day, Such as the day is when the sun is hid v 1 125
We should hold day with the Antipodes, If you would walk in absence of the sun v 1 127
She had rather stay, Or go to bed now, being two hours to day v 1 303
But were the day come, I should wish it dark v 1 304
Many young gentlemen flock to him every day *As Y. Like It* i 1 124
There is not one so young and so villanous this day living i 1 161
You'll be whipped for taxation one of these days i 2 91
Thus men may grow wiser every day i 2 145
Within these ten days if that thou be'st found So near our public court as twenty miles, Thou diest for it i 3 45
He hath been all this day to look you.—And I have been all this day to avoid him ii 5 34
If ever you have look'd on better days ii 7 113
True is it that we have seen better days ii 7 120
I was seven of the nine days out of the wonder before you came iii 2 184
Looks he as freshly as he did the day he wrestled? iii 2 244
What is't o' clock?—You should ask me what time o' day iii 2 318
He [Time] trots hard with a young maid between the contract of her marriage and the day it is solemnized iii 2 332
I set him every day to woo me iii 2 429
Come every day to my cote and woo me iii 2 447
For ever and a day.—Say 'a day,' without the 'ever' iv 1 145
To-morrow is the joyful day, Audrey; to-morrow will we be married v 3 1
Hearing how that every day Men of great worth resorted to this forest v 4 160
That have endured shrewd days and nights with us v 4 179
I do hope good days and long to see *T. of Shrew* i 2 193
My business asketh haste, And every day I cannot come to woo ii 1 116
I'll crave the day When I shall ask the banns and when be married ii 1 180
Now is the day we long have looked for ii 1 335
This is the 'pointed day iii 2 1
I will be married to a wealthy widow, Ere three days pass iv 2 38
He'll have a lusty widow now, That shall be woo'd and wedded in a day iv 2 51
My father is here look'd for every day iv 2 116
And that you look'd for him this day in Padua iv 4 16
I have no more to say, But bid Bianca farewell for ever and a day iv 4 97
To watch the night in storms, the day in cold v 2 150
By our remembrances of days foregone *All's Well* i 3 140
I'ld venture The well-lost life of mine on his grace's cure By such a day and hour i 3 255
Nay, I'll fit you, And not be all day neither ii 1 94
'Twill be two days ere I shall see you, so I leave you to your wisdom ii 5 75
Come, night; end, day! For with the dark, poor thief, I'll steal away iii 2 131
This very day, Great Mars, I put myself into thy file iii 3 8
And writ to me this other day to turn him out o' the band iv 3 227
Since you have made the days and night as one, To wear your gentle limbs in my affairs v 1 3
And water once a day her chamber round With eye-offending brine *T. Night* i 1 29
He hath known you but three days, and already you are no stranger i 4 3
I saw him put down the other day with an ordinary fool i 5 91
O, the twelfth day of December ii 3 90
His eyes do show his days are almost done ii 3 112
And died that day when Viola from her birth Had number'd thirteen years v 1 251
He finished indeed his mortal act That day v 1 255
Keep as true in soul As doth that orbed continent the fire That severs day from night v 1 279

Day. One day shall crown the alliance on 't, so please you . *T. Night* v 1 326
For the rain it raineth every day . v 1 401 ; *Lear* iii 2 77
But that's all one, our play is done, And we'll strive to please you every day . *T. Night* v 1 417
But such a day to-morrow as to-day, And to be boy eternal . *W. Tale* i 2 64
In those unfledged days was my wife a girl . i 2 78
He makes a July's day short as December . i 2 169
My people did expect my hence departure Two days ago . i 2 451
We shall Present our services to a fine new prince One of these days . ii 1 18
Nor night nor day no rest: it is but weakness To bear the matter thus ii 3 1
Twenty three days They have been absent: 'tis good speed . ii 3 198
Once a day I'll visit The chapel where they lie . iii 2 239
The day frowns more and more . iii 3 54
I never saw The heavens so dim by day. A savage clamour! . iii 3 56
'Tis a lucky day, boy, and we'll do good deeds on 't . iii 3 142
It is three days since I saw the prince . iv 2 33
A merry heart goes all the day, Your sad tires in a mile-a . iv 3 134
Lift up your countenance, as it were the day Of celebration of that nuptial which We two have sworn shall come . iv 4 49
Upon This day she was both pantler, butler, cook . iv 4 56
It is my father's will I should take on me The hostess-ship o' the day . iv 4 72
I would I had some flowers o' the spring that might Become your time of day . iv 4 114
In the hottest day prognostication proclaims . iv 4 817
She hath privately twice or thrice a day, ever since the death of Hermione, visited that removed house . v 2 115
You denied to fight with me this other day, because I was no gentleman born . v 2 140
Now blessed be the hour, by night or day, When I was got! . *K. John* i 1 165
Who dares not stir by day must walk by night . i 1 172
This day hath made Much work for tears in many an English mother . ii 1 302
Commander of this hot malicious day . ii 1 314
Fortune shall cull forth Out of one side her happy minion, To whom in favour she shall give the day . ii 1 393
With my vex'd spirits I cannot take a truce, But they will quake and tremble all this day . iii 1 18
And this blessed day Ever in France shall be kept festival . iii 1 75
To solemnize this day the glorious sun Stays in his course . iii 1 77
The yearly course that brings this day about Shall never see it but a holiday . iii 1 81
A wicked day, and not a holy day! . iii 1 83
What hath this day deserved? what hath it done, That it in golden letters should be set Among the high tides in the calendar? . iii 1 84
Rather turn this day out of the week, This day of shame, oppression, perjury . iii 1 87
Let wives with child Pray that their burthens may not fall this day . iii 1 90
On this day let seamen fear no wreck; No bargains break that are not this day made! . iii 1 92
This day, all things begun come to ill end! . iii 1 94
You shall have no cause To curse the fair proceedings of this day . iii 1 97
Let not the hours of this ungodly day Wear out the day in peace . iii 1 110
The sun's o'ercast with blood: fair day, adieu! . iii 1 326
This day grows wondrous hot; Some airy devil hovers in the sky . iii 2 1
The proud day, Attended with the pleasures of the world, Is all too wanton . iii 3 34
In despite of brooded watchful day, I would into thy bosom pour my thoughts . iii 3 52
What have you lost by losing of this day?—All days of glory, joy and happiness . iii 4 116
No scope of nature, no distemper'd day, No common wind . iii 4 154
So I were out of prison and kept sheep, I should be as merry as the day is long . iv 1 18
To choke his days With barbarous ignorance . iv 2 58
The Lady Constance in a frenzy died Three days before . iv 2 123
And on that day at noon, whereon he says I shall yield up my crown, let him be hang'd . iv 2 156
Whose office is this day To feast upon whole thousands of the French . v 2 177
How goes the day with us? O, tell me, Hubert . v 3 1
Faulconbridge, In spite of spite, alone upholds the day . v 4 5
For if the French be lords of this loud day, He means to recompense the pains you take . v 4 14
If Lewis do win the day, He is forsworn, if e'er those eyes of yours Behold another day break in the east . v 4 30
A treacherous fine of all your lives, If Lewis by your assistance win the day . v 4 39
The day shall not be up so soon as I . v 5 21
Many years of happy days befal My gracious sovereign! . *Richard II.* i 1 20
Each day still better other's happiness! . i 1 22
As your lives shall answer it, At Coventry, upon Saint Lambert's day . i 1 199
Shorten my days thou canst with sullen sorrow, And pluck nights from me . i 3 227
Which elder days shall ripen and confirm To more approved service . ii 3 43
We have stay'd ten days, And hardly kept our countrymen together . ii 4 1
Stay yet another day, thou trusty Welshman . ii 4 5
His treasons will sit blushing in his face, Not able to endure the sight of day . iii 2 52
One day too late, I fear me, noble lord, Hath clouded all thy happy days on earth . iii 2 67
To-day, to-day, unhappy day, too late, O'erthrows thy joys, friends, fortune . iii 2 71
The worst is death, and death will have his day . iii 2 103
Like an unseasonable stormy day, Which makes the silver rivers drown their shores . iii 2 106
Men judge by the complexion of the sky The state and inclination of the day . iii 2 195
Let them hence away, From Richard's night to Bolingbroke's fair day . iii 2 218
Thou darest not, coward, live to see that day . iv 1 41
That honourable day shall ne'er be seen . iv 1 91
And send him many years of sunshine days! . iv 1 221
That every day under his household roof Did keep ten thousand men . iv 1 282
The children yet unborn Shall feel this day as sharp to them as thorn . iv 1 323
I'll lay A plot shall show us all a merry day . iv 1 334
She came adorned hither like sweet May, Sent back like Hallowmas or short'st of day . v 1 80
Some bond, that he is enter'd into For gay apparel 'gainst the triumph day . v 2 66
Some two days since I saw the prince, And told him of those triumphs v 3 13
For ever will I walk upon my knees, And never see day that the happy sees . v 3 94
And never show thy head by day nor light . v 6 44

Day. On Holy-rood day, the gallant Hotspur there . 1 *Hen. IV.* i 1 52
Now, Hal, what time of day is it, lad? . i 2 1
What a devil hast thou to do with the time of the day? . i 2 7
I see no reason why thou shouldst be so superfluous to demand the time of the day . i 2 13
Let not us that are squires of the night's body be called thieves of the day's beauty . i 2 28
An old lord of the council rated me the other day in the street about you i 2 95
Well then, once in my days I'll be a madcap . i 2 159
Shall it for shame be spoken in these days? . i 3 170
An it be not four by the day, I'll be hanged . ii 1 2
Let us share, and then to horse before day . ii 2 105
Since the old days of goodman Adam to the pupil age of this present twelve o'clock . ii 4 105
There be four of us here have ta'en a thousand pound this day morning ii 4 176
Let him sleep till day. I'll to the court in the morning . ii 4 594
Nor shall we need his help these fourteen days . iii 1 88
'As true as I live,' and 'as God shall mend me,' and 'as sure as day' . iii 1 255
In the closing of some glorious day . iii 2 133
And that shall be the day, whene'er it lights . iii 2 138
This advertisement is five days old . iii 2 172
Some twelve days hence Our general forces at Bridgenorth shall meet . iii 2 177
And said this other day you ought him a thousand pound . iii 3 152
Doth he keep his bed?—He did, my lord, four days ere I set forth . iv 1 22
He cannot draw his power this fourteen days . iv 1 126
The powers of us may serve so great a day . iv 1 132
I hold as little counsel with weak fear As you, my lord, or any Scot that this day lives . iv 3 12
A day Wherein the fortune of ten thousand men Must bide the touch . iv 4 8
The day looks pale At his distemperature . v 1 2
By his hollow whistling in the leaves Foretells a tempest and a blustering day . v 1 6
I do protest, I have not sought the day of this dislike . v 1 26
Thou owest God a death.—'Tis not due yet; I would be loath to pay him before his day . v 1 128
If he outlive the envy of this day, England did never owe so sweet a hope . v 2 67
A sword, whose temper I intend to stain With the best blood that I can meet withal In the adventure of this perilous day . v 2 96
Up, and away! Our soldiers stand full fairly for the day . v 3 29
Turk Gregory never did such deeds in arms as I have done this day . v 3 47
The trumpet sounds retreat; the day is ours . v 4 163
When he saw The fortune of the day quite turn'd from him . v 5 18
Rebellion in this land shall lose his sway, Meeting the check of such another day . v 5 42
O, such a day, So fought, so follow'd and so fairly won! . 2 *Hen. IV.* i 1 20
God give your lordship good time of day . i 2 107
Your day's service at Shrewsbury hath a little gilded over your night's exploit . i 2 167
Pray, all you that kiss my lady Peace at home, that our armies join not in a hot day . i 2 234
If it be a hot day, and I brandish any thing but a bottle . i 2 236
Fubbed off, and fubbed off, from this day to that day . ii 1 38
I was before Master Tisick, the debuty, t' other day . ii 4 93
Hollow pamper'd jades of Asia, Which cannot go but thirty mile a-day ii 4 179
Then death rock me asleep, abridge my doleful days! . ii 4 211
When wilt thou leave fighting o' days and foining o' nights? . ii 4 251
The very same day did I fight with one Sampson Stockfish . iii 2 35
The mad days that I have spent! . iii 2 37
Jesus, the days that we have seen! . iii 2 233
The dangers of the days but newly gone, Whose memory is written on the earth . iv 1 80
To us all That feel the bruises of the days before . iv 1 100
Let it be booked with the rest of this day's deeds . iv 3 51
He hath a tear for pity and a hand Open as day for melting charity . iv 4 32
As sudden As flaws congealed in the spring of day . iv 4 35
The unguided days And rotten times that you shall look upon . iv 4 59
A summer bird, Which ever in the haunch of winter sings The lifting up of day . iv 4 93
Like a rich armour worn in heat of day, That scalds with safety . iv 5 30
My day is dim . iv 5 101
That action, hence borne out, May waste the memory of the former days iv 5 216
Do you mean to stop any of William's wages, about the sack he lost the other day at Hinckley fair? . v 1 26
No prince nor peer shall have just cause to say, God shorten Harry's happy life one day! . v 2 145
O joyful day! I would not take a knighthood for my fortune . v 3 132
Where is the life that late I led? say they: Why, here it is; welcome these pleasant days! . v 3 148
He would make this a bloody day to somebody . v 4 14
Is at this day in Germany call'd Meisen . *Hen. V.* i 2 53
So do the kings of France unto this day . i 2 90
We understand him well, How he comes o'er us with our wilder days . i 2 267
He'll yield the crow a pudding one of these days . ii 1 92
No awkward claim, Pick'd from the worm-holes of long-vanish'd days . ii 4 86
Between the promise of his greener days And these he masters now . ii 4 136
The day is hot, and the weather, and the wars, and the king, and the dukes . iii 2 113
Our expectation hath this day an end . iii 3 44
A' uttered as prave words at the pridge as you shall see in a summer's day . iii 6 67
Would it were day! . iii 7 2
Will it never be day? . iii 7 86
I'll knock his leek about his pate Upon Saint Davy's day . iv 1 55
Do not you wear your dagger in your cap that day . iv 1 57
We have no great cause to desire the approach of day . iv 1 90
We see yonder the beginning of the day, but I think we shall never see the end of it . iv 1 92
Shall join together at the latter day and cry all 'We died at such a place' iv 1 143
He let him outlive that day to see His greatness and to teach others how they should prepare . iv 1 194
Next day after dawn, Doth rise and help Hyperion to his horse . iv 1 291
Winding up days with toil and nights with sleep . iv 1 296
Who twice a-day their wither'd hands hold up Toward heaven, to pardon blood . iv 1 316
I will go with thee: The day, my friends and all things stay for me . iv 1 325
Come, come, away! The sun is high, and we outwear the day . iv 2 63
This day is call'd the feast of Crispian . iv 3 40
He that outlives this day, and comes safe home, Will stand a tip-toe when this day is named . iv 3 41

Day. He that shall live this day, and see old age, Will yearly on the vigil feast his neighbours . . . *Hen. V.* iv 3 44
Show his scars, And say 'These wounds I had on Crispin's day' . . iv 3 48
But he'll remember with advantages What feats he did that day . . iv 3 51
From this day to the ending of the world . . . iv 3 58
And hold their manhoods cheap whiles any speaks That fought with us upon Saint Crispin's day . . . iv 3 67
And how thou pleasest, God, dispose the day! . . . iv 3 132
I tell thee truly, herald, I know not if the day be ours or no . iv 7 87
The day is yours.—Praised be God, and not our strength, for it! . . iv 7 89
Fought on the day of Crispin Crispianus . . . iv 7 94
Your majesty takes no scorn to wear the leek upon Saint Tavy's day . iv 7 108
As you shall desire in a summer's day . . . iv 8 24
But why wear you your leek to-day? Saint Davy's day is past . v 1 2
I will peat his pate four days . . . v 1 43
So happy be the issue, brother England, Of this good day . . v 2 13
This day Shall change all griefs and quarrels into love . . v 2 19
On which day, My Lord of Burgundy, we'll take your oath . . v 2 398
Hung be the heavens with black, yield day to night! . *1 Hen. VI.* i 1 1
Mars his true moving, even as in the heavens So in the earth, to this day is not known . . . i 2 2
Expect Saint Martin's summer, halcyon days . . . i 2 131
I am come to survey the Tower this day . . . i 3 1
All manner of men assembled here in arms this day . . i 3 75
Even these three days have I watch'd, If I could see them . . i 4 16
This day is ours, as many more shall be . . . i 5 18
Like Adonis' gardens, That one day bloom'd and fruitful were the next i 6 7
'Tis Joan, not we, by whom the day is won . . . i 6 17
Having all day caroused and banqueted . . . ii 1 12
The day begins to break, and night is fled . . . ii 2 1
Like to a pair of loving turtle-doves That could not live asunder day or night . . . ii 2 31
For treason executed in our late king's days . . . ii 4 91
I dare say This quarrel will drink blood another day . . ii 4 134
This day, in argument upon a case, Some words there grew . . ii 5 45
In prison hast thou spent a pilgrimage And like a hermit overpass'd thy days . . . ii 5 117
Doth wish His days may finish ere that hapless time . . iii 1 201
Lost, and recover'd in a day again! . . . iii 2 115
'Tis but the shortening of my life one day . . . iv 6 37
We should have found a bloody day of this . . . iv 7 34
Know who hath obtain'd the glory of the day . . . iv 7 52
By day, by night, waking and in my dreams . . *2 Hen. VI.* i 1 26
A day will come when York shall claim his own . . i 1 239
She vaunted 'mongst her minions t' other day . . . i 3 87
I did correct him for his fault the other day . . . i 3 203
Let these have a day appointed them For single combat . . i 3 211
Let never day nor night unhallow'd pass, But still remember what the Lord hath done . . . ii 1 85
Thou see'st not well.—Yes, master, clear as day . . . ii 1 108
I think, jet did he never see.—But cloaks and gowns, before this day, a many.—Never, before this day, in all his life . . ii 1 115
You made in a day, my lord, whole towns to fly . . . ii 1 164
Do you as I do in these dangerous days . . . ii 2 69
The Earl of Warwick Shall one day make the Duke of York a king . ii 2 79
After three days' open penance done, Live in your country here in banishment . . . ii 3 11
Thus Eleanor's pride dies in her youngest days . . . ii 3 46
This is the day appointed for the combat . . . ii 3 48
Thus sometimes hath the brightest day a cloud . . . ii 4 1
No; dark shall be my light and night my day . . . ii 4 40
These few days' wonder will be quickly worn . . . ii 4 69
In the morn, When every one will give the time of day, He knits his brow iii 1 14
By means whereof the towns each day revolted . . . iii 1 63
These days are dangerous: Virtue is choked with foul ambition . iii 1 142
He'll wrest the sense and hold us here all day . . . iii 1 186
And so break off; the day is almost spent . . . iii 1 325
Within fourteen days At Bristol I expect my soldiers . . iii 1 327
He shall not breathe infection in this air But three days longer . iii 2 288
If, after three days' space, thou here be'st found . . iii 2 295
The gaudy, blabbing and remorseful day Is crept into the bosom of the sea . . . iv 1 1
They have been up these two days.—They have the more need to sleep now iv 2 2
The bricks are alive at this day to testify it; therefore deny it not . iv 2 157
Soldiers, this day have you redeem'd your lives . . . iv 9 15
These five days have I hid me in these woods . . . iv 10 3
I have eat no meat these five days . . . iv 10 41
This day I'll wear aloft my burgonet . . . v 1 204
O, let the vile world end, And the premised flames of the last day Knit earth and heaven together! . . . v 2 41
We will live To see their day and them our fortune give . . v 2 89
This happy day Is not itself, nor have we won one foot . . v 3 5
Now, by my faith, lords, 'twas a glorious day . . . v 3 29
And more such days as these to us befall! . . . v 3 33
The queen this day here holds her parliament . . *3 Hen. VI.* i 1 35
Ah, let me live in prison all my days . . . i 3 43
Ten days ago I drown'd these news in tears . . . ii 1 104
They had no heart to fight, And we in them no hope to win the day . ii 1 136
Ne'er may he live to see a sunshine day, That cries 'Retire' . . ii 1 187
He might have kept that glory to this day . . . ii 2 153
The shepherd, blowing of his nails, Can neither call it perfect day nor night . . . ii 5 4
How many hours bring about the day; How many days will finish up the year . . . ii 5 27
So many days my ewes have been with young . . . ii 5 35
So minutes, hours, days, months, and years, Pass'd over to the end they were created . . . ii 5 38
And thou this day hadst kept thy chair in peace . . . ii 6 20
I'll tell thee what befel me on a day In this self-place . . iii 1 10
That would be ten days' wonder at the least.—That's a day longer than a wonder lasts . . . iii 2 113
I was, I must confess, Great Albion's queen in former golden days . iii 3 7
Often ere this day, When I have heard your king's desert recounted . iii 3 131
To-morrow then belike shall be the day . . . iv 3 7
Warwick may lose, that now hath won the day . . . iv 4 15
I myself will lead a private life And in devotion spend my latter days . iv 6 43
Doubt not of the day, And, that once gotten, doubt not of large pay . iv 7 87
In the midst of this bright-shining day, I spy a black, suspicious, threatening cloud . . . v 3 3
And like the owl by day, If he arise, be mock'd and wonder'd at . v 4 56

Day. Thou keep'st me from the light: But I will sort a pitchy day for thee . . . *3 Hen. VI.* v 6 85
Since I cannot prove a lover, To entertain these fair well-spoken days, I am determined to prove a villain And hate the idle pleasures of these days . . . *Richard III.* i 1 29
This day should Clarence closely be mew'd up, About a prophecy . i 1 38
To the Tower, From whence this present day he is deliver'd . . i 1 69
If I fail not in my deep intent, Clarence hath not another day to live . i 1 150
As all the world is cheered by the sun, So I by that; it is my day, my life . . . i 2 130
Black night o'ershade thy day, and death thy life! . . . i 2 131
That scarce, some two days since, were worth a noble . . i 3 82
In those busy days Which here you urge to prove us enemies . . i 3 145
Long die thy happy days before thy death! . . . i 3 207
Remember this another day, When he shall split thy very heart with sorrow . . . i 3 299
I would not spend another such a night, Though 'twere to buy a world of happy days . . . i 4 6
I every day expect an embassage From my Redeemer to redeem me hence . . . ii 1 3
A happy time of day!—Happy, indeed, as we have spent the day . . ii 1 47
To-morrow, or next day, they will be here . . . ii 4 3
Accursed and unquiet wrangling days, How many of you have mine eyes beheld! . . . ii 4 55
God bless your grace with health and happy days! . . . iii 1 18
Retail'd to all posterity, Even to the general all-ending day . . iii 1 78
This same very day your enemies, The kindred of the queen, must die . iii 2 49
Had no cause to mistrust; But yet, you see, how soon the day o'ercast iii 2 88
What, shall we toward the Tower? the day is spent . . iii 2 91
I tell thee—keep it to thyself—This day those enemies are put to death iii 2 105
In God's name, speak: when is the royal day? . . . iii 4 3
To-morrow, then, I judge a happy day . . . iii 4 6
I myself am not so well provided As else I would be, were the day prolong'd . . . iii 4 47
The subtle traitor This day had plotted, in the council-house To murder me . . . iii 5 38
That it may be this day read o'er in Paul's . . . iii 6 3
He doth entreat your grace To visit him to-morrow or next day . . iii 7 60
Even in the afternoon of her best days . . . iii 7 186
God give your graces both A happy and a joyful time of day! . . iv 1 6
Shall we wear these honours for a day? Or shall they last? . . iv 2 5
Brief abstract and record of tedious days, Rest thy unrest! . . iv 4 28
Forbear to sleep the nights, and fast the days . . . iv 4 118
What! we have many goodly days to see . . . iv 4 320
Day, yield me not thy light; nor, night, thy rest! . . . iv 4 401
This is All-Souls' day, fellows, is it not? . . . v 1 10
All-Souls' day is my body's doomsday . . . v 1 12
This is the day that, in King Edward's time, I wish'd might fall on me v 1 13
This is the day wherein I wish'd to fall By the false faith of him I trusted most . . . v 1 16
This All-Souls' day to my fearful soul Is the determined respite of my wrongs . . . v 1 18
Let's want no discipline, make no delay; For, lords, to-morrow is a busy day . . . v 3 18
By the bright track of his fiery car, Gives signal of a goodly day tomorrow . . . v 3 21
Our wrongs in Richard's bosom Will conquer him! awake, and win the day! . . . v 3 145
Bloody and guilty, guiltily awake, And in a bloody battle end thy days! v 3 147
It is not yet near day. Come, go with me . . . v 3 220
A black day will it be to somebody . . . v 3 280
Rescue, fair lord, or else the day is lost! . . . v 4 6
The day is ours, the bloody dog is dead . . . v 5 2
With smiling plenty and fair prosperous days . . . v 5 34
Abate the edge of traitors, gracious Lord, That would reduce these bloody days again! . . . v 5 36
Each following day Became the next day's master . . *Hen. VIII.* i 1 16
It was usual with him, every day It would infect his speech . . i 2 132
I have this day received a traitor's judgement . . . ii 1 58
I now seal it; And with that blood will make 'em one day groan for t . ii 1 106
Did you not of late days hear A buzzing of a separation? . . ii 1 147
The king will know him one day . . . ii 2 22
Heaven will one day open The king's eyes . . . ii 2 42
'Tis a needful fitness That we adjourn this court till further day . ii 4 232
The third day comes a frost, a killing frost . . . iii 2 355
This day was view'd in open as his queen, Going to chapel . . iii 2 404
They are ever forward—In celebration of this day with shows . . iv 1 10
'Tis the list Of those that claim their offices this day . . iv 1 15
Had their faces Been loose, this day they had been lost . . iv 1 75
Have In them a wilder nature than the business That seeks dispatch by day . . . v 1 16
Indeed this day, Sir, I may tell it you . . . v 1 41
The strangest sight . . . I think your highness saw this many a day . v 2 21
As, of late days, our neighbours, The upper Germany, can dearly witness . . . v 3 29
And there they are like to dance these three days . . . v 4 68
In her days every man shall eat in safety, Under his own vine . . v 5 34
Many days shall see her, And yet no day without a deed to crown it . v 5 58
This day, no man think Has business at his house . . . v 5 75
Helen herself swore th' other day, that Troilus, for a brown favour—for so 'tis, I must confess,—not brown neither . *Troi. and Cres.* i 2 100
She came to him th' other day into the compassed window . . i 2 120
Upon a lazy bed the livelong day Breaks scurril jests . . . i 3 147
Were your days As green as Ajax' and your brain so temper'd . . ii 3 264
I have loved you night and day For many weary months . . iii 2 122
As true as steel, as plantage to the moon, As sun to day . . iii 2 185
Good morrow,—Ay, and good next day too . . . iii 3 69
If to-morrow be a fair day, by eleven o'clock it will go one way or other iii 3 296
A whole week by days, Did haunt you in the field . . . iv 1 9
The busy day, Waked by the lark, hath roused the ribald crows . . iv 2 8
The glory of our Troy doth this day lie On his fair worth and single chivalry . . . iv 4 149
No trumpet answers.—'Tis but early days . . . iv 5 12
Claim it when 'tis due.—Never's my day, and then a kiss of you . . iv 5 52
That old common arbitrator, Time, Will one day end it . . . iv 5 226
You may have every day enough of Hector, If you have stomach . . iv 5 263
And I myself Am like a prophet suddenly enrapt To tell thee that this day is ominous . . . v 3 66
And what one thing, what another, that I shall leave you one o' these days . . . v 3 10

Day. Even with the vail and darking of the sun, To close the day up, Hector's life is done . . . *Troi. and Cres.* v 8 8
'Tis not four days gone Since I heard thence . . . . *Coriolanus* i 2 6
When for a day of kings' entreaties a mother should not sell him an hour from her beholding . . . . i 3 8
As merry as when our nuptial day was done, And tapers burn'd to bedward . . . . i 6 31
In that day's feats, . . . He proved best man i' the field . . ii 2 99
Vagabond exile, flaying, pent to linger But with a grain a day . iii 3 90
Could I meet 'em But once a day, it would unclog my heart Of what lies heavy to't . . . . iv 2 47
The day serves well for them now . . . . iv 3 32
Let me have war, say I; it exceeds peace as far as day does night . iv 5 237
A merrier day did never yet greet Rome . . . . . . v 4 45
A nobler man, a braver warrior, Lives not this day . . *T. Andron.* i 1 26
Outlive thy father's days, And fame's eternal date, for virtue's praise! . i 1 167
For thy favours done To us in our election this day, I give thee thanks i 1 235
The dismall'st day is this that e'er I saw, To be dishonour'd by my sons! i 1 384
Let me alone: I'll find a day to massacre them all . . . i 1 450
This day shall be a love-day, Tamora . . . . . . i 1 491
I have been troubled in my sleep this night, But dawning day new comfort hath inspired . . . . ii 2 10
And in dumb shows Pass the remainder of our hateful days . . iii 1 132
This done, see that you take no longer days . . . . . iv 2 165
God forbid I should be so bold to press to heaven in my young days . iv 3 91
Like stinging bees in hottest summer's day . . . . . v 1 14
I curse the day—and yet, I think, Few come within the compass of my curse—Wherein I did not some notorious ill . . . . v 1 125
Witness the tiring day and heavy night; Witness all sorrow . . v 2 24
And by the waggon-wheel Trot, like a servile footman, all day long . v 2 55
Good morrow, cousin.—Is the day so young?—But new struck nine *Rom. and Jul.* i 1 166
Of all days in the year, Come Lammas-eve at night shall she be fourteen . . . . i 3 16
I never shall forget it,—Of all the days of the year, upon that day . i 3 25
For even the day before, she broke her brow . . . . . i 3 38
Go, girl, seek happy nights to happy days . . . . . . i 3 106
In delay We waste our lights in vain, like lamps by day . . . i 4 45
I have seen the day That I have worn a visor and could tell A whispering tale in a fair lady's ear . . . . i 5 23
For you and I are past our dancing days . . . . . . i 5 33
Flecked darkness like a drunkard reels From forth day's path . . ii 3 4
Ere the sun advance his burning eye, The day to cheer . . . ii 3 6
Let's retire: The day is hot, the Capulets abroad . . . . iii 1 2
For now, these hot days, is the mad blood stirring . . . . iii 1 4
This day's black fate on more days doth depend . . . . iii 1 124
Come, night; come, Romeo; come, thou day in night . . . iii 2 17
So tedious is this day As is the night before some festival To an impatient child . . . . iii 2 28
Either be gone before the watch be set, Or by the break of day disguised from hence . . . . iii 3 168
But, soft! what day is this?—Monday, my lord . . . . iii 4 18
It is not yet near day: It was the nightingale, and not the lark . iii 5 1
Jocund day Stands tiptoe on the misty mountain tops . . . iii 5 9
How is't, my soul? let's talk; it is not day.—It is, it is: hie hence! . iii 5 25
Hunting thee hence with hunt's-up to the day . . . . . iii 5 34
The day is broke; be wary, look about.—Then, window, let day in, and let life out . . . . iii 5 40
I must hear from thee every day in the hour, For in a minute there are many days . . . . iii 5 44
Madam, in happy time, what day is that? . . . . . . iii 5 112
Day, night, hour, tide, time, work, play, Alone, in company . . iii 5 178
Good faith, 'tis day: The county will be here with music straight . iv 4 20
O heavy day!—O me, O me! My child, my only life! . . . iv 5 18
O lamentable day!—O woful time! . . . . iv 5 30
Accursed, unhappy, wretched, hateful day! . . . . . iv 5 43
O woe! O woful, woful, woful day! Most lamentable day, most woful day! . . . . iv 5 49
O day! O day! O day! O hateful day! Never was seen so black a day as this: O woful day, O woful day! . . . . . . iv 5 52
And all this day an unaccustom'd spirit Lifts me above the ground . v 1 4
Bleeding, warm, and newly dead, Who here hath lain these two days buried . . . . v 3 176
What time o' day is't, Apemantus?—Time to be honest . *T. of Athens* i 1 265
I should fear those that dance before me now Would one day stamp upon me . . . . i 2 149
You gave Good words the other day of a bay courser I rode on: it is yours, because you liked it . . . . i 2 217
His days and times are past And my reliances on his fracted dates Have smit my credit . . . . ii 1 21
He hath put me off To the succession of new days this month . . ii 2 20
There will little learning die then, that day thou art hanged . . ii 2 87
How unluckily it happened, that I should purchase the day before for a little part, and undo a great deal of honour! . . . . . iii 2 52
The days are wax'd shorter with him . . . . iii 4 11
'Tis inferr'd to us, His days are foul and his drink dangerous . . iii 5 74
If, after two days' shine, Athens contain thee, Attend our weightier judgement . . . . iii 5 101
I think this honourable lord did but try us this other day . . iii 6 3
I am e'en sick of shame, that, when your lordship this other day sent to me, I was so unfortunate a beggar . . . . iii 6 47
He gave me a jewel th' other day, and now he has beat it out of my hat . . . . iii 6 123
One day he gives us diamonds, next day stones . . . . . iii 6 131
Let's shake our heads, and say, As 'twere a knell unto our master's fortunes, 'We have seen better days' . . . . iv 2 27
This embalms and spices To the April day again . . . . iv 3 41
Where feed'st thou o' days, Apemantus?—Where my stomach finds meat . . . . iv 3 293
When the day serves, before black-corner'd night, Find what thou want'st . . . . v 1 47
Time, with his fairer hand, Offering the fortunes of his former days, The former man may make him . . . . v 1 127
Who once a day with his embossed froth The turbulent surge shall cover . . . . v 1 220
An aged interpreter, though young in days . . . . . . v 3 8
Being mechanical, you ought not walk Upon a labouring day *J. Cæsar* i 1 4
And there have sat The live-long day, with patient expectation . i 1 46
Once, upon a raw and gusty day, The troubled Tiber chafing with her shores . . . . i 2 100

Day. We will shake him, or worse days endure . . . *J. Cæsar* i 2 326
You and I will yet ere day See Brutus at his house . . . . i 3 153
It is after midnight; and ere day We will awake him and be sure of him . . . . i 3 163
I cannot, by the progress of the stars, Give guess how near to day . ii 1 3
It is the bright day that brings forth the adder . . . . ii 1 14
Get you to bed again; it is not day . . . . ii 1 39
Sir, March is wasted fourteen days.—'Tis good . . . . . ii 1 59
O, then by day Where wilt thou find a cavern dark enough To mask thy monstrous visage? . . . . ii 1 79
Here lies the east: doth not the day break here?—No.—O, pardon, sir, it doth . . . . ii 1 101
Yon grey lines That fret the clouds are messengers of day . . ii 1 104
We are two lions litter'd in one day, And I the elder and more terrible ii 2 46
The senate have concluded To give this day a crown to mighty Cæsar . ii 2 94
That we shall die, we know; 'tis but the time And drawing days out, that men stand upon . . . . iii 1 100
That day he overcame the Nervii . . . . iii 2 177
O noble Cæsar!—O woful day!—O traitors, villains! . . . iii 2 204
Octavius, I have seen more days than you . . . . . iv 1 18
From this day forth, I'll use you for my mirth, yea, for my laughter, When you are waspish . . . . iv 3 48
The enemy increaseth every day; We, at the height, are ready to decline . . . . iv 3 216
This is my birth-day; as this very day Was Cassius born . . . v 1 72
That we may, Lovers in peace, lead on our days to age! . . . v 1 95
But this same day Must end that work the ides of March begun . v 1 113
O, that a man might know The end of this day's business ere it come! But it sufficeth that the day will end . . . . v 1 124
This day I breathed first: time is come round, And where I did begin, there shall I end . . . . v 3 23
O setting sun, As in thy red rays thou dost sink to night, So in his red blood Cassius' day is set; The sun of Rome is set! . . . . v 3 62
Our day is gone; Clouds, dews, and dangers come; our deeds are done! v 3 63
I shall have glory by this losing day More than Octavius and Mark Antony . . . . v 5 36
Let's away, To part the glories of this happy day . . . . v 5 81
Sleep shall neither night nor day Hang upon his pent-house lid *Macbeth* i 3 19
So foul and fair a day I have not seen . . . . . . i 3 38
In viewing o'er the rest o' the selfsame day, He finds thee in the stout Norweyan ranks . . . . i 3 94
Come what come may, Time and the hour runs through the roughest day i 3 147
Your pains Are register'd where every day I turn The leaf to read them i 3 151
Shall to all our nights and days to come Give solely sovereign sway and masterdom . . . . i 5 70
When Duncan is asleep—Whereto the rather shall his day's hard journey Soundly invite him . . . . i 7 62
The death of each day's life, sore labour's bath . . . . ii 2 38
By the clock, 'tis day, And yet dark night strangles the travelling lamp: Is't night's predominance, or the day's shame? . . . . ii 4 6
Both grave and prosperous, In this day's council . . . . iii 1 23
Come, seeling night, Scarf up the tender eye of pitiful day . . iii 2 47
Good things of day begin to droop and drowse . . . . . iii 2 52
The west yet glimmers with some streaks of day . . . . iii 3 5
Toad, that under cold stone Days and nights has thirty one Swelter'd venom sleeping got . . . . iv 1 7
It weeps, it bleeds; and each new day a gash Is added to her wounds . iv 3 40
When shalt thou see thy wholesome days again? . . . . . iv 3 105
Oftener upon her knees than on her feet, Died every day she lived . iv 3 111
Receive what cheer you may: The night is long that never finds the day iv 3 240
I hope the days are near at hand That chambers will be safe . . v 4 1
The day almost itself professes yours, And little is to do . . v 7 27
By these I see, So great a day as this is cheaply bought . . . v 8 37
This sweaty haste Doth make the night joint-labourer with the day *Ham.* i 1 78
Doth with his lofty and shrill-sounding throat Awake the god of day . i 1 152
Would I had met my dearest foe in heaven Or ever I had seen that day! i 2 183
To thine own self be true, And it must follow, as the night the day, Thou canst not then be false to any man . . . . i 3 79
Doom'd for a certain term to walk the night, And for the day confined to fast in fires . . . . i 5 11
He closes thus: 'I know the gentleman; I saw him yesterday, or t'other day' . . . . ii 1 56
Being of so young days brought up with him . . . . . ii 2 11
To expostulate . . . what duty is, Why day is day, night night, and time is time, Were nothing but to waste night, day and time . . . ii 2 88
How does your honour for this many a day? . . . . . . iii 1 91
Fain I would beguile The tedious day with sleep . . . . iii 2 237
And do such bitter business as the day Would quake to look on . . iii 2 409
This physic but prolongs thy sickly days . . . . . . iii 3 96
To-morrow is Saint Valentine's day, All in the morning betime . . iv 5 48
It shall as level to your judgement pierce As day does to your eye . iv 5 152
Ere we were two days old at sea . . . . iv 6 15
Of all the days i' the year, I came to't that day that our last king Hamlet overcame Fortinbras . . . . v 1 155
It was the very day that young Hamlet was born . . . . . v 1 160
Let Hercules himself do what he may, The cat will mew and dog will have his day . . . . v 1 315
Now, the next day Was our sea-fight . . . . v 2 53
'Tis the breathing time of day with me . . . . . . v 2 181
Five days we do allot thee, for provision To shield thee from diseases of the world . . . . *Lear* i 1 176
If, on the tenth day following, Thy banish'd trunk be found in our dominions, The moment is thy death . . . . i 1 179
I am thinking, brother, of a prediction I read this other day . . i 2 153
Is it two days ago since I tripped up thy heels? . . . . . ii 2 31
Or well or ill, as this day's battle's fought . . . . . iv 7 98
You have the captives That were the opposites of this day's strife . v 3 42
I have seen the day, with my good biting falchion I would have made them skip . . . . v 3 276
I ran it through, even from my boyish days . . . *Othello* i 3 132
The heavens forbid But that our loves and comforts should increase, Even as our days do grow! . . . . ii 1 197
You have not been a-bed, then?—Why, no; the day had broke Before we parted . . . . iii 1 34
I prithee, name the time, but let it not Exceed three days . . iii 3 63
Within these three days let me hear thee say That Cassio's not alive . iii 3 472
What, keep a week away? seven days and nights? Eight score eight hours? . . . . iii 4 173
Every day thou daffest me with some device . . . . . . iv 2 176
May his pernicious soul Rot half a grain a day! . . . . . v 2 156

Day. I have seen the day, That, with this little arm and this good sword, I have made my way through more impediments Than twenty times your stop *Othello* v 2 261
Who's born that day When I forget to send to Antony, Shall die a beggar . . . . *Ant. and Cleo.* i 5 63
My salad days, When I was green in judgement; cold in blood . i 5 73
Get me ink and paper: He shall have every day a several greeting . i 5 77
Next day I told him of myself; which was as much As to have ask'd him pardon . . . . ii 2 77
We did sleep day out of countenance, and made the night light with drinking . . . . ii 2 181
You'll win two days upon me . . . . . . ii 4 9
Pompey doth this day laugh away his fortune . . . . ii 6 109
I had rather fast from all four days Than drink so much in one . . ii 7 108
She In the habiliments of the goddess Isis That day appear'd . . iii 6 18
To-morrow is the day.—It will determine one way . . . iv 3 1
The gods make this a happy day to Antony! . . . . iv 5 1
Prove this a prosperous day, the three-nook'd world Shall bear the olive freely . . . . iv 6 6
And drink carouses to the next day's fate . . . . iv 8 34
This last day was A shrewd one to's . . . . . iv 9 4
The long day's task is done, And we must sleep . . . iv 14 35
Most heavy day!—Nay, good my fellows, do not please sharp fate To grace it with your sorrows . . . . . . iv 14 134
I must perforce Have shown to thee such a declining day, Or look on thine . . . . v 1 38
The bright day is done, And we are for the dark . . . v 2 193
Within three days You with your children will he send before . v 2 201
Let her languish A drop of blood a day! . . . *Cymbeline* i 1 157
And every day that comes comes to decay A day's work in him . i 5 56
It's almost morning, is't not?—Day, my lord . . . ii 3 11
Quake in the present winter's state and wish That warmer days would come . . . . ii 4 6
If one of mean affairs May plod it in a week, why may not I Glide thither in a day? . . . . iii 2 54
A goodly day not to keep house, with such Whose roof's as low as ours! . . . . iii 3 1
They took thee for their mother, And every day do honour to her grave iii 3 105
Hath Britain all the sun that shines? Day, night, Are they not but in Britain? . . . . iii 4 139
Nor to us hath tender'd The duty of the day . . . . iii 5 32
Her old servant I have not seen these two days . . . iii 5 55
May This night forestall him of the coming day! . . . iii 5 69
I had no mind To hunt this day . . . . . . iv 2 148
The day that she was missing he was here . . . . iv 3 17
It is a day turn'd strangely: or betimes Let's reinforce, or fly . v 2 17
Consider, sir, the chance of war: the day Was yours by accident . v 5 75
Misinterpreting, We might proceed to cancel of your days *Pericles* i 1 113
Forty days longer we do respite you . . . . . . i 1 116
Not an hour, In the day's glorious walk, or peaceful night . . i 2 4
Day serves not light more faithful than I'll be . . . i 2 110
If I had been the sexton, I would have been that day in the belfry . ii 1 41
If it be a day fits you, search out of the calendar, and nobody look after it . . . . ii 1 58
This day I'll rise, or else add ill to ill . . . . . ii 1 172
And on set purpose let his armour rust Until this day, to scorn it in the dust . . . . ii 2 55
And crown you king of this day's happiness . . . . ii 3 11
Call it by what you will, the day is yours . . . . ii 3 13
Your presence glads our days . . . . ii 3 21
Welcome: happy day, my lords . . . . ii 4 22
She'll wed the stranger knight, Or never more to view nor day nor light . . . . ii 5 17
And she is fair too, is she not?—As a fair day in summer, wondrous fair . . . . ii 5 36
When canst thou reach it?—By break of day, if the wind cease . iii 1 77
We every day Expect him here . . . . iv 1 34
Whilst ours was blurted at and held a malkin Not worth the time of day iv 3 35
And ourselves Will in that kingdom spend our following days . v 3 81
Alack (alas) the day! *Mer. Wives* iii 5; iv 2; *L. L. Lost* iv 3; *Mer. of Venice* ii 2; *As Y. Like It* iii 2; *T. Night* ii 1; ii 2; *2 Hen. IV.* ii 1; *Troi. and Cres.* iii 2; *Rom. and Jul.* iii 2; iv 5; *Macbeth* ii 4; *Lear* iv 6; *Othello* iii 4; iv 2
Alack (alas) the heavy day! *Richard II.* iii 3; iv 1; *Othello* iv 2
By this day . . . . *Much Ado* ii 3 254; *Hen. V.* iv 8 66
By this good day . . . . . . *Much Ado* v 4 95; *2 Hen. IV.* iii 2 81
Fair time of day! . . . . . . *L. L. Lost* v 2 339; *Hen. V.* v 2 3
Good time of day! *2 Hen. IV.* i 2; *Richard III.* i 1; i 3; *T. of Athens* iii 6
Good day *T. G. of Ver.* iv 4; *Much Ado* v 1; *As Y. Like It* iv 1; *W. Tale* i 2; *2 Hen. IV.* iv 2; *Richard III.* i 1; *Troi. and Cres.* iii 3; *Coriolanus* i 3

Day and night. Teach me how To name the bigger light, and how the less, That burn by day and night . . . . . . *Tempest* i 2 336
This exceeding posting day and night Must wear your spirits low *All's Well* v 1 1
Both day and night did we keep company . . . . *T. Night* v 1 99
Who studies day and night To answer all the debt he owes to you *1 Hen. IV.* i 3 184
As is the difference betwixt day and night . . . . iii 1 220
And posted day and night To meet you on the way . . . v 1 35
As it were, to ride day and night . . . . *2 Hen. IV.* v 5 21
By day and night, He's traitor to the height . . *Hen. VIII.* i 2 213
It highly us concerns By day and night to attend him carefully *T. Andron.* iv 3 28
O day and night, but this is wondrous strange! . . . *Hamlet* i 5 164
Sport and repose lock from me day and night! . . . iii 2 227
By day and night he wrongs me . . . . . . *Lear* i 3 3

Day-bed. Having come from a day-bed . . . . . *T. Night* ii 5 54
He is not lolling on a lewd day-bed, But on his knees at meditation *Richard III.* iii 7 72

Day by day. 'Tis a chronicle of day by day, Not a relation for a breakfast . . . . *Tempest* v 1 163
The younger of our nature, That surfeit on their ease, will day by day Come here for physic . . . . . . *All's Well* iii 1 18
And day by day I'll do this heavy task . . . *T. Andron.* v 2 58

Days of answer. Procure your sureties for your days of answer *Richard II.* iv 1 159

Day of audience. Rejourn the controversy of three pence to a second day of audience . . . . *Coriolanus* ii 1 80

Day of battle. Take with thee my most heavy curse; Which, in the day of battle, tire thee more Than all the complete armour that thou wear'st! . . . . *Richard III.* iv 4 188

Day of combat. The day of combat shall be the last of the next month *2 Hen. VI.* i 3 224

Day of desolation. If ever I do see the merry days of desolation that I have seen . . . . *L. L. Lost* i 2 164

Day of doom. To change blows with thee for our day of doom *Rich. II.* iii 2 189
And triumph, Henry, in thy day of doom . . . *3 Hen. VI.* v 6 93
This is the day of doom for Bassianus . . . . *T. Andron.* ii 3 42

Day of joy. One who, to put thee from thy heaviness, Hath sorted out a sudden day of joy . . . . . . *Rom. and Jul.* iii 5 110

Day of judgement. Heaven forgive my sins at the day of judgement! *Mer. Wives* iii 3 226

Day of life. Thy eyes' windows fall, Like death, when he shuts up the day of life . . . . *Rom. and Jul.* iv 1 101

Days of love. Joy and fresh days of love Accompany your hearts! *M. N. Dream* v 1 29

Days of marriage. Our day of marriage shall be yours *T. G. of Ver.* v 4 172
Name the day of marriage, and God give thee joy . . *Much Ado* ii 1 312
I will presently go learn their day of marriage . . . . ii 2 57
He'll woo a thousand, 'point the day of marriage, Make feasts *T. of Shrew* iii 2 15

Days of nature. Till the foul crimes done in my days of nature Are burnt and purged away . . . . *Hamlet* i 5 12

Days of quiet. Grating so harshly all his days of quiet With turbulent and dangerous lunacy . . . . iii 1 3

Day of season. I am not a day of season, For thou mayst see a sunshine and a hail In me at once . . . . . *All's Well* v 3 32

Day of success. They met me in the day of success . . *Macbeth* i 5 1

Day o' the world. O thou day o' the world, Chain mine arm'd neck! *Ant. and Cleo.* iv 8 13

Day of trial. Your differences shall all rest under gage Till we assign you to your days of trial . . . . *Richard II.* iv 1 106
Be it your charge To keep him safely till his day of trial . . iv 1 153

Day of triumph. We have not yet set down this day of triumph! *Richard III.* iii 4 44

Day of victory. Let us banquet royally, After this golden day of victory *1 Hen VI.* i 6 31

Day of villany. And what should poor Jack Falstaff do in the days of villany? . . . . *1 Hen. IV.* iii 3 187

Day of wrong. I have seen the day of wrong through the little hole of discretion . . . . *L. L. Lost* v 2 733

Day or two. Please you, deliberate a day or two . *T. G. of Ver.* ii 3 73
I pray you, tarry: pause a day or two Before you hazard *Mer. of Venice* iii 2 1
If I may counsel you, some day or two Your highness shall repose you at the Tower . . . . *Richard III.* iii 1 64
Make pastime with us a day or two, or longer . . . *Cymbeline* iii 1 79

Day's journey. 'Twill be Two long days' journey, lords, or ere we meet *K. John* iv 3 20
You have well saved me a day's journey . . . *Coriolanus* iv 3 12
Now is the sun upon the highmost hill Of this day's journey *Rom. and Jul.* ii 5 10
Marry, sir, half a day's journey . . . . . . *Pericles* ii 1 112

Day's march. From Tamworth thither is but one day's march *Rich. III.* v 2 13

Day's work. Shall witness live in brass of this day's work . *Hen. V.* iv 3 97
Thy heart-blood I will have for this day's work . . *1 Hen. VI.* i 3 83
Now have I done a good day's work . . . . *Richard III.* ii 1 1
Now is my day's work done; I'll take good breath . *Troi. and Cres.* v 8 3
If I should tell thee o'er this thy day's work, Thou'ldst not believe thy deeds . . . . *Coriolanus* i 9 1
Every day that comes comes to decay A day's work in him . *Cymbeline* i 5 57

Day to day. From day to day Visit the speechless sick . . *L. L. Lost* v 2 860
To-morrow, and to-morrow, and to-morrow, Creeps in this petty pace from day to day *Macbeth* v 5 20

Day-wearied. The old, feeble and day-wearied sun . . . *K. John* v 4 35

Day-woman. She is allowed for the day-woman . . . *L. L. Lost* i 2 136

Daylight. We burn daylight: here, read, read . . . *Mer. Wives* ii 1 54
I can see a church by daylight . . . . . . *Much Ado* ii 1 86
Thou shalt buy this dear, If ever I thy face by daylight see *M. N. Dream* iii 2 427
Shine comforts from the east, That I may back to Athens by daylight . iii 2 433
This night methinks is but the daylight sick; It looks a little paler *Mer. of Venice* v 1 124
Daylight and champain discovers not more . . . *T. Night* ii 5 174
Alas the day, how loath you are to offend daylight! . *Troi. and Cres.* iii 2 51
Locks fair daylight out And makes himself an artificial night *R. and J.* i 1 145
Come, we burn daylight, ho!—Nay, that's not so . . . . i 4 43
The brightness of her cheek would shame those stars, As daylight doth a lamp . . . . ii 2 20
Yon light is not day-light, I know it, I: It is some meteor . . iii 5 12
Where have I been? Where am I? Fair daylight? I am mightily abused . . . . *Lear* iv 7 52

Dazzle. I will dazzle all the eyes of France . . . . *Hen V.* i 2 279
Dazzle mine eyes, or do I see three suns? . . . *3 Hen. VI.* ii 1 25
Thy sight is young, And thou shalt read when mine begin to dazzle *T. Andron.* iii 2 85

Dazzled. 'Tis but her picture I have yet beheld, And that hath dazzled my reason's light . . . . *T. G. of Ver.* ii 4 210
More dazzled and drove back his enemies Than mid-day sun . *1 Hen. VI.* i 1 13

Dazzling. Who dazzling so, that eye shall be his heed And give him light that it was blinded by . . . . . . *L. L. Lost* i 1 82

Dead. If he were that which now he's like, that's dead . . *Tempest* ii 1 282
The mistress which I serve quickens what's dead . . . iii 1 6
My love to her is dead . . . . *T. G. of Ver.* ii 6 28
Is Silvia dead?—No, Valentine . . . . . . iii 1 209
I grant, sweet love, that I did love a lady; But she is dead . . iv 2 106
I likewise hear that Valentine is dead.—And so suppose am I . iv 2 113
She is dead, belike?—Not so; I think she lives . . . iv 4 80
Would I might be dead If I in thought felt not her very sorrow! . iv 4 176
I keep but three men and a boy yet, till my mother be dead . *Mer. Wives* i 1 285
By gar, Jack Rugby, he is dead already, if he be come . . . ii 3 8
De herring is no dead so as I vill kill him . . . . ii 3 12
Is he dead, my Ethiopian? is he dead, my Francisco? . . . ii 3 27
Ha! is he dead, bully stale? is he dead? . . . . . ii 3 30
I think, if your husbands were dead, you two would marry . . ii 2 15
Now shall I sin in my wish: I would thy husband were dead . . iii 3 52
So our decrees, Dead to infliction, to themselves are dead *Meas. for Meas.* i 3 28
The law hath not been dead, though it hath slept . . . ii 2 90
Ginger was not much in request, for the old women were all dead . iv 3 9
Enter in And dwell upon your grave when you are dead *Com. of Errors* iii 1 104
How doth the lady?—Dead, I think . . . . . *Much Ado* iv 1 114
Your daughter here the princes left for dead . . . . . iv 1 204

Dead. Let her awhile be secretly kept in, And publish it that she is dead indeed *Much Ado* iv 1 206
Go, comfort your cousin: I must say she is dead iv 1 339
And she is dead, slander'd to death by villains v 1 88
The lady is dead upon mine and my master's false accusation v 1 249
Almost the copy of my child that's dead v 1 298
Graves, yawn and yield your dead, Till death be uttered, Heavily, heavily v 3 19
The former Hero! Hero that is dead! v 4 65
They swore that you were well-nigh dead for me v 4 81
The king your father— Dead, for my life!—Even so *L. L. Lost* v 2 728
On the ground! Dead? or asleep? *M. N. Dream* ii 2 101
So should a murderer look, so dead, so grim iii 2 57
Nor is he dead, for aught that I can tell iii 2 76
See me no more, whether he be dead or no iii 2 81
What, should I hurt her, strike her, kill her dead? iii 2 269
And strike more dead Than common sleep of all these five the sense iv 1 86
Now am I dead, Now am I fled; My soul is in the sky v 1 306
He is but one.—Less than an ace, man; for he is dead; he is nothing v 1 314
Asleep, my love? What, dead, my dove? O Pyramus, arise! v 1 332
Quite dumb? Dead, dead? A tomb Must cover thy sweet eyes v 1 335
Moonshine and Lion are left to bury the dead v 1 356
When the players are all dead, there need none to be blamed v 1 364
Through the house give glimmering light, By the dead and drowsy fire v 1 399
Tell me, is my boy, God rest his soul, alive or dead? *Mer. of Venice* ii 2 75
I would my daughter were dead at my foot, and the jewels in her ear! iii 1 92
O, then be bold to say Bassanio's dead! iii 2 187
Some dear friend dead; else nothing in the world Could turn so much the constitution Of any constant man iii 2 248
If killed, but one dead that is willing to be so *As Y. Like It* i 2 201
Bring him dead or living Within this twelvemonth iii 1 6
It strikes a man more dead than a great reckoning in a little room iii 3 15
The royal disposition of that beast To prey on nothing that doth seem as dead iv 3 119
What's here? one dead, or drunk? See, doth he breathe? *T. of Shrew* Ind. 1 31
My father dead, my fortune lives for me i 2 192
Moderate lamentation is the right of the dead *All's Well* i 1 65
When you are dead, you should be such a one As you are now iv 2 7
He had sworn to marry me When his wife's dead iv 2 72
When you have spoken it, 'tis dead, and I am the grave of it iv 3 16
You must know, I am supposed dead iv 4 11
The nature of his great offence is dead v 3 23
Helen, that's dead, Was a sweet creature v 3 77
Thou didst hate her deadly, And she is dead v 3 118
Upon his many protestations to marry me when his wife was dead v 3 140
Dead though she be, she feels her young one kick: So there's my riddle: one that's dead is quick v 3 303
Is gone.—How! gone!—Is dead.—Apollo's angry *W. Tale* iii 2 146
The queen, the queen, The sweet'st, dear'st creature's dead iii 2 202
I say she's dead; I'll swear't. If word nor oath Prevail not, go and see iii 2 204
I have heard, but not believed, the spirits o' the dead May walk again iii 3 16
One being dead, I shall have more than you can dream of yet iv 4 398
Then stand till he be three quarters and a dram dead iv 4 815
Would I were dead, but that, methinks, already—What was he that did make it? v 3 62
And make't manifest where she has lived, Or how stolen from the dead v 3 115
I saw her, As I thought, dead, and have in vain said many A prayer v 3 140
Or add a royal number to the dead *K. John* ii 1 347
He will awake my mercy which lies dead iv 1 26
The fire is dead with grief, Being create for comfort iv 1 106
Your uncle must not know but you are dead iv 1 128
The suit which you demand is gone and dead iv 2 84
What! mother dead! How wildly then walks my estate in France! iv 2 127
My mother dead! iv 2 181
I had a mighty cause To wish him dead, but thou hadst none to kill him iv 2 206
If thou but frown on me, or stir thy foot, Or teach thy hasty spleen to do me shame, I'll strike thee dead iv 3 98
They found him dead and cast into the streets v 1 39
Conduct me to the king; I doubt he will be dead or ere I come v 6 44
Poison'd,—ill fare—dead, forsook, cast off v 7 35
Lament we may, but not revenge thee dead *Richard II.* i 3 58
Thy word is current with him for my death, But dead, thy kingdom cannot buy my breath i 3 232
Is not Gaunt dead, and doth not Hereford live? ii 1 191
Well, lords, the Duke of Lancaster is dead.—And living too ii 1 224
'Tis thought the king is dead; we will not stay ii 4 7
Our countrymen are gone and fled, As well assured Richard their king is dead ii 4 17
For all the Welshmen, hearing thou wert dead, Are gone to Bolingbroke iii 2 73
Have I not reason to look pale and dead? iii 2 79
Is Bushy, Green, and the Earl of Wiltshire dead?—Ay, all of them iii 2 141
What, are they dead?—They are iii 4 54
Why, bishop, is Norfolk dead?—As surely as I live, my lord iv 1 101
Think I am dead and that even here thou takest, As from my death-bed, thy last living leave v 1 38
Though I did wish him dead, I hate the murderer, love him murdered v 6 39
Was not he proclaim'd By Richard that dead is the next of blood? *1 Hen. IV.* i 3 146
All in England did repute him dead v 1 54
'Tis [honour] insensible, then. Yea, to the dead v 1 140
This earth that bears thee dead Bears not alive so stout a gentleman v 4 92
I am afraid of this gunpowder Percy, though he be dead v 4 124
Did you not tell me this fat man was dead?—I did; I saw him dead v 4 135
And saw thee dead.—Didst thou? Lord, Lord, how this world is given to lying! v 4 147
Let us to the highest of the field, To see what friends are living, who are dead v 4 165
Even such a man, so faint, so spiritless, So dull, so dead in look, so woe-begone *2 Hen. IV.* i 1 71
Ending with 'Brother, son, and all are dead' i 1 81
But, for my lord your son,— Why, he is dead. See what a ready tongue suspicion hath! i 1 83
Yet, for all this, say not that Percy's dead i 1 93
He doth sin that doth belie the dead, Not he which says the dead is not alive i 1 98
I cannot think, my lord, your son is dead i 1 104
The rude scene may end, And darkness be the burier of the dead! i 1 160
How now! whose mare's dead? what's the matter? ii 1 46
I have received A certain instance that Glendower is dead iii 1 103

Dead. To see how many of my old acquaintance are dead! *2 Hen. IV.* iii 2 38
Is old Double of your town living yet?—Dead, sir iii 2 47
Jesu, Jesu, dead! a' drew a good bow; and dead! a' shot a fine shoot iii 2 48
Dead! a' would have clapped i' the clout at twelve score iii 2 51
And is old Double dead? iii 2 58
And noble offices thou mayst effect Of mediation, after I am dead iv 4 25
And bid the merry bells ring to thine ear That thou art crowned, not that I am dead iv 5 113
Thinking you dead, And dead almost, my liege, to think you were iv 5 156
His cares are now all ended.—I hope, not dead v 2 4
I'll to the king my master that is dead v 2 40
I'll bear your cares: Yet weep that Harry's dead v 2 59
What, is the old king dead?—As nail in door v 3 126
The man is dead that you and Pistol beat amongst you v 4 19
Awake remembrance of these valiant dead *Hen. V.* i 2 115
Boy, bristle thy courage up; for Falstaff he is dead ii 3 5
Once more unto the breach, dear friends, once more; Or close the wall up with our English dead iii 1 2
Though we seemed dead, we did but sleep iii 6 126
The organs, though defunct and dead before, Break up their drowsy grave iv 1 21
That being dead, like to the bullet's grazing, Break out into a second course of mischief iv 3 105
That we may wander o'er this bloody field To look our dead iv 7 76
Bring me just notice of the numbers dead On both our parts iv 7 122
Now, herald, are the dead number'd? iv 8 78
There lie dead One hundred twenty six iv 8 87
The names of those their nobles that lie dead iv 8 96
Where is the number of our English dead? iv 8 107
Let there be sung 'Non nobis' and 'Te Deum;' The dead with charity enclosed in clay iv 8 129
News have I, that my Nell is dead i' the spital Of malady of France v 1 86
Henry is dead and never shall revive *1 Hen. VI.* i 1 18
We'll offer up our arms; Since arms avail not now that Henry's dead i 1 47
And none but women left to wail the dead i 1 51
In memory of her when she is dead i 6 23
And the very parings of our nails Shall pitch a field when we are dead iii 1 103
Becomes it thee to taunt his valiant age And twit with cowardice a man half dead? iii 2 55
These eyes, that see thee now well coloured, Shall see thee wither'd, bloody, pale and dead iv 2 38
That, Talbot dead, great York might bear the name iv 4 9
If he be dead, brave Talbot, then adieu! iv 4 45
Fly, to revenge my death when I am dead? iv 6 30
Forbear! for that which we have fled During the life, let us not wrong it dead iv 7 50
I come to know what prisoners thou hast ta'en And to survey the bodies of the dead iv 7 57
O, that I could but call these dead to life! iv 7 81
For Richard, the first son's heir, being dead, The issue of the next son should have reign'd *2 Hen. VI.* ii 2 31
Sleeping or waking, 'tis no matter how, So he be dead iii 1 264
But I would have him dead, my Lord of Suffolk iii 1 273
John Mortimer, which now is dead, In face, in gait, in speech, he doth resemble iii 1 372
Humphrey being dead, as he shall be, And Henry put apart, the next for me iii 1 382
Have you dispatch'd this thing?—Ay, my good lord, he's dead iii 2 7
Dead in his bed, my lord; Gloucester is dead.—Marry, God forfend! iii 2 29
Help, lords! the king is dead.—Rear up his body; wring him by the nose iii 2 33
In the shade of death I shall find joy; In life but double death, now Gloucester's dead iii 2 55
That he is dead, good Warwick, 'tis too true iii 2 130
To survey his dead and earthy image, What were it but to make my sorrow greater? iii 2 147
Who finds the heifer dead and bleeding fresh And sees fast by a butcher with an axe, But will suspect 'twas he that made the slaughter? iii 2 188
Who finds the partridge in the puttock's nest, But may imagine how the bird was dead? iii 2 192
If thou be found by me, thou art but dead iii 2 387
I fear me, love, if that I had been dead, Thou wouldest not have mourn'd so much for me iv 4 23
Oft have I struck Those that I never saw and struck them dead iv 7 87
If I do not leave you all as dead as a door-nail iv 10 43
Sword, I will hallow thee for this thy deed, And hang thee o'er my tomb when I am dead iv 10 73
But is your grace dead, my Lord of Somerset? *3 Hen. VI.* i 1 18
Not till King Henry be dead.—Your right depends not on his life or death i 2 10
How now! is he dead already? or is it fear That makes him close his eyes? i 3 10
And, whilst we breathe, take time to do him dead i 4 108
Would I were dead! if God's good will were so ii 5 19
And wheresoe'er he is, he's surely dead ii 6 41
When Clifford cannot spare his friends an oath. I know by that he's dead ii 6 79
Ay, but he's dead: off with the traitor's head ii 6 85
Why, am I dead? do I not breathe a man? Ah, simple men! iii 1 82
But were he dead, Yet here Prince Edward stands iii 3 72
Come quickly, Montague, or I am dead v 2 39
Either heaven with lightning strike the murderer dead! *Richard III.* i 2 64
Say that I slew them not?—Why, then they are not dead: But dead they are i 2 89
I did not kill your husband.—Why, then he is alive.—Nay, he is dead i 2 92
Thine eyes, sweet lady, have infected mine.—Would they were basilisks, to strike thee dead! i 2 151
If he were dead, what would betide of me? i 3 6
That princely novice was struck dead by thee i 4 228
Who knows not that the noble duke is dead ii 1 79
Who knows not he is dead! who knows he is? ii 1 81
Is Clarence dead? the order was reversed ii 1 86
Tell me, good grandam, is our father dead?—No, boy ii 2 1
Then, grandam, you conclude that he is dead ii 2 12
Edward, my lord, your son, our king, is dead ii 2 40
Hear you the news abroad?—Ay, that the king is dead ii 3 3
His nurse! why, she was dead ere thou wert born ii 4 33
I fear no uncles dead.—Nor none that live, I hope iii 1 146
They smile at me that shortly shall be dead iii 4 109
Hie thee from this slaughter-house, Lest thou increase the number of the dead iv 1 45

Dead. I wish the bastards dead; And I would have it suddenly perform'd . . . *Richard III.* iv 2 18
But didst thou see them dead?—I did, my lord . . . iv 3 27
Edward Plantagenet, why art thou dead? . . . iv 4 19
Thy Edward he is dead, that stabb'd my Edward; Thy other Edward dead, to quit my Edward . . . iv 4 63
Thy Clarence he is dead that kill'd my Edward . . . iv 4 67
Dear God, I pray, That I may live to say, The dog is dead! . . . iv 4 78
O no, my reasons are too deep and dead; Too deep and dead . . . iv 4 362
Is the chair empty? is the sword unsway'd? Is the king dead? . . . iv 4 471
The day is ours, the bloody dog is dead . . . v 5 2
To as much end As give a crutch to the dead . . . *Hen. VIII.* i 1 172
Do no more offices of life to't than The grave does to the dead . . . ii 4 191
The great child of honour, Cardinal Wolsey, Was dead . . . iv 2 7
When I am dead, good wench, Let me be used with honour . . . iv 2 167
Strength should be lord of imbecility, And the rude son should strike his father dead: Force should be right . . . *Troi. and Cres.* i 3 115
There's many a Greek and Trojan dead, Since first I saw yourself and Diomed . . . iv 5 214
As to prenominate in nice conjecture Where thou wilt hit me dead . . . iv 5 251
And all cry, Hector! Hector's dead! O Hector! . . . v 3 87
Hector is slain.—Hector! the gods forbid!—He's dead . . . v 10 4
Hector's dead: There is a word will Priam turn to stone . . . v 10 17
Hector is dead; there is no more to say . . . v 10 22
And waked half dead with nothing . . . *Coriolanus* iv 5 132
Behold the poor remains, alive and dead! . . . *T. Andron.* i 1 81
There greet in silence, as the dead are wont . . . i 1 90
These are their brethren, whom you Goths beheld Alive and dead . . . i 1 123
Dead, if you will; but not to be his wife . . . i 1 297
Brought hither in a most unlucky hour, To find thy brother Bassianus dead.—My brother dead! . . . ii 3 252
You left him all alive; But, out, alas! here have we found him dead . . . ii 3 258
He that wounded her Hath hurt me more than had he kill'd me dead . . . iii 1 92
Thy husband he is dead; and for his death Thy brothers are condemn'd, and dead by this . . . iii 1 108
Let not your sorrow die, though I am dead . . . v 1 140
Even with all my heart Would I were dead, so you did live again! . . . v 3 173
She hath forsworn to love, and in that vow Do I live dead *Rom. and Jul.* i 1 230
Now, by the stock and honour of my kin, To strike him dead I hold it not a sin . . . i 5 61
He heareth not, he stirreth not, he moveth not; The ape is dead . . . ii 1 16
He is already dead; stabbed with a white wench's black eye . . . ii 4 13
But old folks, many feign as they were dead; Unwieldy, slow . . . ii 5 16
O Romeo, Romeo, brave Mercutio's dead! . . . iii 1 121
Why dost thou wring thy hands?—Ah, well-a-day! he's dead, he's dead, he's dead! . . . iii 2 37
Alack the day! he's gone, he's kill'd, he's dead! . . . iii 2 39
Honest gentleman! That ever I should live to see thee dead! . . . iii 2 63
Is Romeo slaughter'd, and is Tybalt dead? . . . iii 2 65
And Tybalt's dead, that would have slain my husband . . . iii 2 106
Tybalt is dead, and Romeo—banished . . . iii 2 112
Why follow'd not, when she said 'Tybalt's dead,' Thy father, or thy mother, nay, or both? . . . iii 2 118
'Romeo is banished,' to speak that word, Is father, mother, Tybalt, Romeo, Juliet, All slain, all dead . . . iii 2 124
Thy Juliet is alive, For whose dear sake thou wast but lately dead . . . iii 3 136
Methinks I see thee, now thou art below, As one dead in the bottom of a tomb . . . iii 5 56
Indeed, I never shall be satisfied With Romeo, till I behold him—dead . . . iii 5 95
Your first is dead; or 'twere as good he were, As living here and you no use of him . . . iii 5 226
When the bridegroom in the morning comes To rouse thee from thy bed, there art thou dead . . . iv 1 108
What if it be a poison, which the friar Subtly hath minister'd to have me dead? . . . iv 3 25
Help, help! my lady's dead! O, well-a-day, that ever I was born! . . . iv 5 14
She's dead, deceased, she's dead; alack the day!—Alack the day, she's dead, she's dead, she's dead! . . . iv 5 23
Dead art thou! Alack! my child is dead; And with my child my joys are buried . . . iv 5 63
I dreamt my lady came and found me dead—Strange dream! . . . v 1 6
That the life-weary taker may fall dead . . . v 1 62
Thy husband in thy bosom there lies dead . . . v 3 155
And Juliet bleeding, warm, and newly dead, Who here hath lain these two days buried . . . v 3 175
Paris slain; And Romeo dead; and Juliet, dead before, Warm and new kill'd . . . v 3 196
Alas, my liege, my wife is dead to-night . . . v 3 210
Romeo, there dead, was husband to that Juliet; And she, there dead, that Romeo's faithful wife . . . v 3 231
Here untimely lay The noble Paris and true Romeo dead . . . v 3 259
All thy living Is 'mongst the dead . . . *T. of Athens* i 2 230
Now all are fled, Save only the gods: now his friends are dead . . . iii 3 37
And thatch your poor thin roofs With burthens of the dead . . . iv 3 145
Would 'twere so! But not till I am dead . . . iv 3 394
Our hope in him is dead . . . v 1 229
Timon is dead, who hath outstretch'd his span . . . v 3 3
Dead, sure; and this his grave. What's on this tomb I cannot read . . . v 3 5
Timon is dead; Entomb'd upon the very hem o' the sea . . . v 4 65
Dead Is noble Timon: of whose memory Hereafter more . . . v 4 79
Woe the while! our fathers' minds are dead . . . *J. Cæsar* i 3 82
Graves have yawn'd, and yielded up their dead . . . ii 2 18
Liberty! Freedom! Tyranny is dead! . . . iii 1 78
Mark Antony shall not lose Cæsar dead So well as Brutus living . . . iii 1 133
Had you rather Cæsar were living and die all slaves, than that Cæsar were dead, to live all free men? . . . iii 2 25
I rather choose To wrong the dead, to wrong myself and you . . . iii 2 131
Portia is dead.—Ha! Portia!—She is dead . . . iv 3 147
Cicero is dead, And by that order of proscription . . . iv 3 179
For certain she is dead, and by strange manner . . . iv 3 189
When you do find him, or alive or dead, He will be found like Brutus . . . v 4 24
Go on, And see whether Brutus be alive or dead . . . v 4 30
Almost dead for breath . . . *Macbeth* i 5 37
Now o'er the one half-world Nature seems dead . . . ii 1 50
The sleeping and the dead Are but as pictures . . . ii 2 53
All is but toys: renown and grace is dead; The wine of life is drawn . . . ii 3 99
Better be with the dead, Whom we, to gain our peace, have sent to peace . . . iii 2 19
The gracious Duncan Was pitied of Macbeth: marry, he was dead . . . iii 6 4
Sirrah, your father's dead: And what will you do now? How will you live? . . . iv 2 30

Dead. My father is not dead, for all your saying.—Yes, he is dead . . . *Macbeth* iv 2 37
If he were dead, you'ld weep for him: if you would not, it were a good sign that I should quickly have a new father . . . iv 2 61
Wherefore was that cry?—The queen, my lord, is dead . . . v 5 16
But like a man he died.—Then he is dead? . . . v 8 43
In the same figure, like the king that's dead . . . *Hamlet* i 1 41
And the sheeted dead Did squeak and gibber in the Roman streets . . . i 1 115
A fault against the dead, a fault to nature, To reason most absurd . . . i 2 102
That it should come to this! But two months dead: nay, not so much, not two . . . i 2 138
A second time I kill my husband dead, When second husband kisses me in bed . . . iii 2 194
No second husband wed; But die thy thoughts when thy first lord is dead . . . iii 2 225
How now! a rat? Dead, for a ducat, dead! . . . iii 4 23
Where is my father?—Dead.—But not by him . . . iv 5 127
How came he dead? I'll not be juggled with . . . iv 5 130
And will he not come again? No, no, he is dead . . . iv 5 192
'Tis for the dead, not for the quick . . . v 1 137
One that was a woman, sir; but, rest her soul, she's dead . . . v 1 147
Imperious Cæsar, dead and turn'd to clay, Might stop a hole to keep the wind away . . . v 1 236
We should profane the service of the dead To sing a requiem and such rest to her As to peace-parted souls . . . v 1 259
Now pile your dust upon the quick and dead . . . v 1 274
I am dead, Horatio. Wretched queen, adieu! . . . v 2 344
Horatio, I am dead; Thou livest; report me and my cause aright . . . v 2 349
The Duke of Cornwall's dead; Slain by his servant . . . *Lear* iv 2 70
Who, thereat enraged, Flew on him, and amongst them fell'd him dead . . . iv 2 76
Therefore I do advise you, take this note: My lord is dead . . . iv 5 30
Alive or dead? Ho, you sir! friend! Hear you, sir! speak! . . . iv 6 45
What, is he dead?—Sit you down, father; rest you . . . iv 6 259
He's dead; I am only sorry He had no other death's-man . . . iv 6 262
O, she's dead!—Who dead? speak, man.—Your lady, sir . . . v 3 224
Produce their bodies, be they alive or dead . . . v 3 230
I know when one is dead, and when one lives; She's dead as earth . . . v 3 260
Your eldest daughters have fordone themselves, And desperately are dead . . . v 3 292
Edmund is dead, my lord.—That's but a trifle here . . . v 3 295
O, my daughter!—Dead?—Ay, to me . . . *Othello* i 3 59
Honest Iago, that look'st dead with grieving, Speak, who began this? . . . ii 3 177
My friend is dead; 'tis done at your request: But let her live . . . iii 3 474
Minion, your dear lies dead, And your unblest fate hies . . . v 1 33
He's almost slain, and Roderigo dead . . . v 1 114
Be thus when thou art dead, and I will kill thee, And love thee after . . . v 2 18
O! my fear interprets: what, is he dead? . . . v 2 73
Not dead? not yet quite dead? I that am cruel am yet merciful; I would not have thee linger in thy pain . . . v 2 85
Yes: 'tis Emilia. By and by. She's dead . . . v 2 91
I am glad thy father's dead: Thy match was mortal to him . . . v 2 204
O Desdemona! Desdemona! dead! Oh! Oh! Oh! . . . v 2 281
Even but now he spake, After long seeming dead . . . v 2 328
Fulvia thy wife is dead.—Where died she? . . . *Ant. and Cleo.* i 2 122
Fulvia is dead.—Sir?—Fulvia is dead.—Fulvia!—Dead . . . i 2 162
Can Fulvia die?—She's dead, my queen . . . i 3 59
His wife that's dead did trespasses to Cæsar . . . ii 1 40
Antonius dead!—If thou say so, villain, Thou kill'st thy mistress . . . ii 5 26
We use To say the dead are well . . . ii 5 33
When Antony found Julius Cæsar dead, He cried almost to roaring . . . iii 2 53
Send him word you are dead . . . iv 13 4
Dead, then?—Dead.—Unarm, Eros; the long day's task is done . . . iv 14 34
How! not dead? not dead? The guard, ho! O, dispatch me! . . . iv 14 103
Let him that loves me strike me dead.—Not I.—Nor I.—Nor any one . . . iv 14 108
She sent you word she was dead; But, fearing since how it might work, hath sent Me to proclaim the truth . . . iv 14 124
How now! is he dead?—His death's upon him, but not dead . . . iv 15 6
O, quietness, lady!—She is dead too, our sovereign . . . iv 15 69
He is dead, Cæsar; Not by a public minister of justice, Nor by a hired knife . . . v 1 19
But keep it till you woo another wife, When Imogen is dead . . . *Cymbeline* i 1 114
Either your unparagoned mistress is dead, or she's outprized by a trifle . . . i 4 88
I'll give but notice you are dead and send him Some bloody sign of it . . . iii 4 127
In my life what comfort, when I am Dead to my husband? . . . iii 4 133
I'll write to my lord she's dead . . . iii 5 104
The bird is dead That we have made so much on . . . iv 2 197
How! a page! Or dead, or sleeping on him! But dead rather . . . iv 2 356
Nature doth abhor to make his bed With the defunct, or sleep upon the dead . . . iv 2 358
Which, being dead many years, shall after revive . . . v 4 142; v 5 439
Thou shalt be then freer than a gaoler; no bolts for the dead . . . v 4 205
He hath been search'd among the dead and living, But no trace of him . . . v 5 11
To sour your happiness, I must report The queen is dead . . . v 5 27
Were't he, I am sure He would have spoke to us.—But we saw him dead . . . v 5 126
Have you ta'en of it?—Most like I did, for I was dead . . . v 5 259
Imogen, Thy mother's dead.—I am sorry for't, my lord . . . v 5 270
By thine own tongue thou art condemn'd, and must Endure our law: thou'rt dead . . . v 5 299
For many years thought dead, are now revived . . . v 5 456
So thou ne'er return Unless thou say 'Prince Pericles is dead' . . . *Pericles* i 1 166
Till Pericles be dead, My heart can lend no succour to my head . . . i 1 170
And give them life whom hunger starved half dead . . . i 4 96
When I am dead, For that I am a man, pray see me buried . . . ii 1 80
Be resolved he lives to govern us, Or dead, gives cause to mourn his funeral . . . ii 4 32
Are letters brought, the tenour these: Antiochus and his daughter dead . . . iii Gower 25
The sea works high, the wind is loud, and will not lie till the ship be cleared of the dead . . . iii 1 49
Your master will be dead ere you return . . . iii 2 7
I heard of an Egyptian That had nine hours lien dead, Who was by good appliance recovered . . . iii 2 85
I'll swear she's dead, And thrown into the sea . . . iv 1 99
The poor Transylvanian is dead, that lay with the little baggage . . . iv 2 24
She is dead. Nurses are not the fates, To foster it, nor ever to preserve . . . iv 3 14
Yet none does know, but you, how she came dead . . . iv 3 29
Let Pericles believe his daughter's dead . . . iv 4 46
She is not dead at Tarsus, as she should have been . . . v 1 217
That Thaisa am I, supposed dead And drown'd . . . v 3 35
My father's dead.—Heavens make a star of him! . . . v 3 78

Dead an ear. You breathe these dead news in as dead an ear *K. John* v 7 65
Dead and buried. Well, the beginning, that is dead and buried *As Y. Like It* i 2 123
Dead and gone. When I am dead and gone, Remember to avenge me on the French . . . . . . 1 *Hen. VI.* i 4 93
When I am dead and gone, May honourable peace attend thy throne 2 *Hen VI.* ii 3 37
He is dead and gone, lady, He is dead and gone . . *Hamlet* iv 5 29
Dead and rotten. The sweet war-man is dead and rotten . *L. L. Lost* v 2 666
If thou 'lt see a thing to talk on when thou art dead and rotten, come hither . . . . *W. Tale.* iii 3 82
He 'll strike, and quickly too: he's dead and rotten . *Lear* v 3 285
Dead blow. Yet we free thee From the dead blow of it *W. Tale* iv 4 445
Dead body. Bring me To the dead bodies of my queen and son . iii 2 236
As the soldiers bore dead bodies by, He call'd them untaught knaves 1 *Hen. IV.* i 3 42
Unloaded all the gibbets and pressed the dead bodies . . . iv 2 41
O, give us leave, great king, To view the field in safety and dispose Of their dead bodies! . . . . . *Hen. V.* iv 7 86
And here is come to do some villanous shame To the dead bodies *Rom. and Jul.* v 3 53
What have you done, my lord, with the dead body? . *Hamlet* iv 2 5
Where the dead body is bestow'd, my lord, We cannot get from him . iv 3 12
Your water is a sore decayer of your whoreson dead body . . v 1 189
He on the ground, my speech of insultment ended on his dead body *Cymbeline* iii 5 145
Dead bones. And mock'd the dead bones that lay scatter'd by *Richard III.* i 4 33
Dead butcher. The cruel ministers Of this dead butcher . *Macbeth* v 8 69
Dead Cæsar. They would go and kiss dead Cæsar's wounds . *J. Cæsar* iii 2 137
I found you as a morsel cold upon Dead Cæsar's trencher *Ant. and Cleo.* iii 13 117
Dead carcasses. Whose loves I prize As the dead carcasses of unburied men . . . . *Coriolanus* iii 3 122
Dead carrion. 'Tis seldom when the bee doth leave her comb In the dead carrion . . . . 2 *Hen. IV.* iv 4 80
Dead Cassius. Look, whether he have not crown'd dead Cassius! *J. Cæsar* v 3 97
Dead chaps. O, now doth Death line his dead chaps with steel *K. John* ii 1 352
Dead cheeks. With dead cheeks advise thee to desist For going on death's net, whom none resist . . . . . *Pericles* i 1 39
Dead coal. Stars, stars, And all eyes else dead coals! . *W. Tale* v 1 68
Your breath first kindled the dead coal of wars . . *K. John* v 2 83
Dead corpse. Upon whose dead corpse there was such misuse 1 *Hen. IV.* i 1 43
To that guileful hole Where the dead corpse of Bassianus lay *T. Andron.* v 1 105
Dead dog. If the sun breed maggots in a dead dog . . *Hamlet* ii 2 181
Dead drunk. Why, he drinks you, with facility, your Dane dead drunk *Othello* ii 3 85
Dead Edward. Drown desperate sorrow in dead Edward's grave *Richard III.* ii 2 99
Dead elm. Answer, thou dead elm, answer . . 2 *Hen. IV.* ii 4 358
Dead father. So is the will of a living daughter curbed by the will of a dead father . . . . *Mer. of Venice* i 2 27
Part of my heritage, Which my dead father did bequeath to me *Pericles* ii 1 130
Dead finger. But chiefly to take thence from her dead finger A precious ring . . . . *Rom. and Jul.* v 3 30
Dead happiness. Compare dead happiness with living woe *Richard III.* iv 4 119
Dead Harry. Here come the heavy issue of dead Harry . 2 *Hen. IV.* v 2 14
Dead Henry. What say'st thou, man, before dead Henry's corse? 1 *Hen. VI.* i 1 62
O, gentlemen, see, see! dead Henry's wounds Open! . *Richard III.* i 2 55
Dead hour. Twice before, and jump at this dead hour . *Hamlet* i 1 65
Dead Indian. When they will not give a doit to relieve a lame beggar, they will lay out ten to see a dead Indian . . *Tempest* ii 2 34
Dead-killing. Else I swoon With this dead-killing news *Richard III.* iv 1 36
Dead king. This dead king to the living king I'll bear . *Richard II.* v 5 118
Dead life. Blind sight, dead life, poor mortal living ghost *Richard III.* iv 4 26
Dead likeness. Her dead likeness, I do well believe, Excels whatever yet you look'd upon . . . . . . *W. Tale* v 3 15
Dead lions. Whose valour plucks dead lions by the beard . *K. John* ii 1 138
Dead lord. Thou that contrivedst to murder our dead lord . 1 *Hen. VI.* i 3 34
Dead love. All this to season A brother's dead love . . *T. Night* i 1 31
Dead man. He's but a dead man . . . . . *Mer. Wives* iv 2 44
With a sense as cold As is a dead man's nose . . *W. Tale* ii 1 152
And this land be call'd The field of Golgotha and dead men's skulls *Richard II.* iv 1 144
The dead men's blood, the pining maidens' groans . . *Hen. V.* ii 4 107
With their drowsy, slow, and flagging wings, Clip dead men's graves 2 *Hen. VI.* iv 1 6
And dead men's cries do fill the empty air . . . . v 2 4
May yet ere night yield both my life and them To some man else, as this dead man doth me . . . . . 3 *Hen. VI.* ii 5 60
Some lay in dead men's skulls . . . . *Richard III.* i 4 29
Which, like a taper in some monument, Doth shine upon the dead man's earthy cheeks . . . . *T. Andron.* ii 3 229
Oft have I digg'd up dead men from their graves, And set them upright at their dear friends' doors . . . . . . v 1 135
O'er-cover'd quite with dead men's rattling bones *Rom. and Jul.* iv 1 82
Bid me go into a new-made grave And hide me with a dead man in his shroud . . . . iv 1 85
Strange dream, that gives a dead man leave to think! . . v 1 7
Poor living corse, closed in a dead man's tomb! . . . v 2 29
Death, lie thou there, by a dead man interr'd . . . v 3 87
With instruments upon them, fit to open These dead men's tombs . v 3 201
I owe more tears To this dead man than you shall see me pay *J. Cæsar* v 3 102
The dead man's knell Is there scarce ask'd for who . *Macbeth* iv 3 170
Our cold maids do dead men's fingers call them . *Hamlet* iv 7 172
Dead masters. And with wild rage Yerk out their armed heels at their dead masters, Killing them twice . . . . . *Hen. V.* iv 7 83
Dead midnight. 'Tis now dead midnight . . . *Meas. for Meas.* iv 2 67
Leave your England, as dead midnight still, Guarded with grandsires *Hen. V.* iii Prol. 19
The lights burn blue. It is now dead midnight . *Richard III.* v 3 180
Dead mistress. I found her trimming up the diadem On her dead mistress . . . . *Ant. and Cleo.* v 2 346
Dead moon-calf. I hid me under the dead moon-calf's gaberdine *Tempest* ii 2 115
Dead news. You breathe these dead news in as dead an ear . *K. John* v 7 65
Dead of darkness. I' the dead of darkness . . . *Tempest* i 2 130
Dead of night. Write loyal cantons of contemned love And sing them loud even in the dead of night . . . . . *T. Night* i 5 290
Drew Priam's curtain in the dead of night . . 2 *Hen. IV.* i 1 72
Dead of sleep. We were dead of sleep . . . *Tempest* v 1 230
Dead or alive. What have we here? a man or a fish? dead or alive? . ii 2 25
Dead queen. Take in your arms this piece Of your dead queen *Pericles* iii 1 18
Will you deliver How this dead queen re-lives? . . . v 3 64
Dead royalty. From forth this morsel of dead royalty, The life, the right and truth of all this realm Is fled to heaven . *K. John* iv 3 143
Dead saint. My other angel husband And that dead saint *Richard III.* iv 1 70
Dead shepherd, now I find thy saw of might . *As Y. Like It* iii 5 82
Dead silence. The night's dead silence Will well become such sweet-complaining grievance . . . . . . *T. G. of Ver.* iii 2 85
Dead temples. This long-usurped royalty From the dead temples of this bloody wretch Have I pluck'd off . . *Richard III.* v 5 5
Dead Thaisa. The voice of dead Thaisa! . . . *Pericles* v 3 34
Dead thing. What think you?—The same dead thing alive . *Cymbeline* v 5 123
Dead time. In that dead time when Gloucester's death was plotted *Richard II.* iv 1 10
Here, at dead time of the night . . . . *T. Andron.* ii 3 99
Dead trunk. And make his dead trunk pillow to our lust . . ii 3 130
Dead vast. In the dead vast and middle of the night . *Hamlet* i 2 198
Dead vomit. And now thou wouldst eat thy dead vomit up . 2 *Hen. IV.* i 3 99
Deadly. Banish'd from her Is self from self: a deadly banishment! *T. G. of Ver.* iii 1 173
I fly not death, to fly his deadly doom . . . . iii 1 185
Sure, it is no sin; Or of the deadly seven it is the least . *Meas. for Meas.* iii 1 111
I know it by their pale and deadly looks . . *Com. of Errors* iv 4 96
Poisons more deadly than a mad dog's tooth . . . . v 1 70
If she did not hate him deadly, she would love him dearly . *Much Ado* v 1 178
'Tis deadly sin to keep that oath, my lord . . *L. L. Lost* ii 1 105
'Twere deadly sickness or else present death . . *T. of Shrew* iv 3 14
Thou didst hate her deadly, And she is dead . . *All's Well* v 3 117
Deadly divorce step between me and you! . . . . v 3 319
With such a suffering, such a deadly life . . . *T. Night* i 5 284
Be yare in thy preparation, for thy assailant is quick, skilful and deadly iii 4 246
And prove a deadly bloodshed but a jest . . . *K. John* iv 3 55
Their love Lies in their purses, and whoso empties them By so much fills their hearts with deadly hate . . . *Richard II.* ii 2 131
Sweet love, I see, changing his property, Turns to the sourest and most deadly hate . . . . iii 2 136
Thy abundant goodness shall excuse This deadly blot in thy digressing son . . . . v 3 66
Never did base and rotten policy Colour her working with such deadly wounds . . . . 1 *Hen. IV.* i 3 109
This is the deadly spite that angers me . . . . iii 1 192
A thousand souls to death and deadly night . . 1 *Hen. VI.* ii 4 127
With full as many signs of deadly hate As lean-faced Envy 2 *Hen. VI.* iii 2 314
But that I hate thee deadly, I should lament thy miserable state 3 *Hen. VI.* i 4 84
What stratagems . . . This deadly quarrel daily doth beget! . . ii 5 91
The air hath got into my deadly wounds . . . . ii 6 27
A deadly groan, like life and death's departing . . . ii 6 43
In deadly hate the one against the other . . *Richard III.* i 1 35
I lay it naked to the deadly stroke . . . . . i 2 178
No sleep close up that deadly eye of thine! . . . . i 3 225
Why strew'st thou sugar on that bottled spider, Whose deadly web ensnareth thee about? . . . . i 3 243
How darkly and how deadly dost thou speak! . . . . i 4 175
Gazed each on other, and look'd deadly pale . . . . iii 7 26
Anointed let me be with deadly venom . . . . . iv 1 62
My anointed body By thee was punched full of deadly holes . . v 3 125
O deadly gall, and theme of all our scorns! . *Troi. and Cres.* iv 5 30
Name her not now, sir; she's a deadly theme . . . iv 5 181
This place is dangerous; The time right deadly . . . v 2 39
Thoas deadly hurt, Patroclus ta'en or slain . . . v 5 12
Yet they lie deadly that tell you you have good faces . *Coriolanus* ii 1 67
Set deadly enmity between two friends . . . *T. Andron.* v 1 131
There's meed for meed, death for a deadly deed! . . . v 3 66
Who, all as hot, turns deadly point to point . *Rom. and Jul.* iii 1 165
O deadly sin! O rude unthankfulness! . . . . . iii 3 24
As if that name, Shot from the deadly level of a gun, Did murder her . iii 3 103
Let's make us medicines of our great revenge, To cure this deadly grief *Macbeth* iv 3 215
Perforce must wither And come to deadly use . . *Lear* iv 2 36
All's cheerless, dark, and deadly . . . . . . v 3 290
Of hair-breadth 'scapes i' the imminent deadly breach . *Othello* i 3 136
It is a deadly sorrow to behold a foul knave uncuckolded *Ant. and Cleo.* i 2 75
Most poisonous compounds, Which are the movers of a languishing death; But though slow, deadly . . . . . *Cymbeline* i 5 10
Deadly-handed. The deadly-handed Clifford slew my steed . 2 *Hen. VI.* v 2 9
Deadly-standing. What signifies my deadly-standing eye? *T. Andron.* ii 3 32
Deaf. You have a quick ear.—Ay, I would I were deaf *T. G. of Ver.* iv 2 64
My dull deaf ears a little use to hear . . *Com. of Errors* v 1 316
What cracker is this same that deafs our ears? . . *K. John* ii 1 147
The sea enraged is not half so deaf, Lions more confident . . ii 1 451
Full of ire, In rage deaf as the sea, hasty as fire . *Richard II.* i 1 19
And bid his ears a little while be deaf, Till I have told this slander . i 1 112
Tell him I am deaf.—You must speak louder; my master is deaf 2 *Hen. IV.* i 2 77
Art thou, like the adder, waxen deaf? . . . 2 *Hen. VI.* iii 2 76
To tell my love unto his dumb deaf trunk . . . . iii 2 144
Wrath makes him deaf . . . . . . 3 *Hen. VI.* i 4 53
Have ears more deaf than adders to the voice Of any true decision *Troi. and Cres.* ii 2 172
The gods are deaf to hot and peevish vows . . . . v 3 16
Peace is a very apoplexy, lethargy; mulled, deaf, sleepy *Coriolanus* iv 5 239
The woods are ruthless, dreadful, deaf, and dull *T. Andron.* ii 1 128
Be not obdurate, open thy deaf ears . . . . . ii 3 160
Were his heart Almost impregnable, his old ears deaf, Yet should both ear and heart obey my tongue . . . . iv 4 98
Why dost not speak? what, deaf? not a word? . . . . v 1 46
The unruly spleen Of Tybalt deaf to peace . . *Rom. and Jul.* iii 1 163
I will be deaf to pleading and excuses . . . . . iii 1 197
O, that men's ears should be To counsel deaf, but not to flattery! *T. of Athens* i 2 257
Come on my right hand, for this ear is deaf . . *J. Cæsar* i 2 213
Infected minds To their deaf pillows will discharge their secrets *Macbeth* v 1 81
Be deaf to my unpitied folly, And all the gods go with you! *Ant. and Cleo.* i 3 98
Deaf'd with the clamours of their own dear groans . *L. L. Lost* v 2 874
Deafened. Make a battery through his deafen'd parts . *Pericles* v 1 47
Deafening. With deafening clamour . . . . 2 *Hen. IV.* iii 1 24
O, still Thy deafening, dreadful thunders! . . . *Pericles* iii 1 5
Deafness. Your tale, sir, would cure deafness . . . *Tempest* i 2 106
I have read the cause of his effects in Galen: it is a kind of deafness 2 *Hen. IV.* i 2 134

Deal. And deal in her command without her power . . . . *Tempest* v 1 271
I will incense Page to deal with poison . . . . *Mer. Wives* i 3 110
Better a little chiding than a great deal of heart-break . . . v 3 11
I will deal in this As secretly and justly as your soul Should with your body . . . . *Much Ado* iv 1 249
Come, 'tis no matter: Do not you meddle; let me deal in this . v 1 101
Gratiano speaks an infinite deal of nothing, more than any man in all Venice . . . . *Mer. of Venice* i 1 114
I will deal in poison with thee, or in bastinado, or in steel *As Y. Like It* v 1 59
That like a father you will deal with him . . . *T. of Shrew* iv 4 44
The fellow has a deal of that too much . . *All's Well* iii 2 92
And for a week escape a great deal of discoveries . . . iii 6 100
Let it be forbid, sir; so should I be a great deal of his act . iv 3 55
But greater a great deal in evil . . . . iv 3 321
O, what a deal of scorn looks beautiful In the contempt and anger of his lip! . . . . *T. Night* iii 1 157
We must deal gently with him . . . . iii 4 106
You pay a great deal too dear for what's given freely . *W. Tale* i 1 18
Such a deal of wonder is broken out within this hour . . . v 2 26
We cannot deal but with the very hand Of stern injustice . *K. John* v 2 22
What a deal of world I wander from the jewels that I love . *Richard II.* i 3 269
Deal mildly with his youth; For young hot colts being raged do rage the more . . . . ii 1 69
What a candy deal of courtesy This fawning greyhound then did proffer me! . . . . 1 *Hen. IV.* i 3 251
A weasel hath not such a deal of spleen As you are toss'd with . ii 3 81
But one half-pennyworth of bread to this intolerable deal of sack! . ii 4 592
Such a deal of skimble-skamble stuff As puts me from my faith . iii 1 154
Out of a great deal of old iron I chose forth . . 1 *Hen. VI.* i 2 101
But God in mercy so deal with my soul, As I in duty love my king and country! . . . . 2 *Hen. VI.* i 3 160
I am never able to deal with my master, he hath learnt so much fence already . . . . ii 3 78
I will deal with him That henceforth he shall trouble us no more . iii 1 323
And doubt not so to deal As all things shall redound unto your good . iv 9 46
And, for I should not deal in her soft laws, She did corrupt frail nature with some bribe . . . . . . 3 *Hen. VI.* iii 2 154
Foes to my rest and my sweet sleep's disturbers Are they that I would have thee deal upon . . . . . *Richard III.* iv 2 75
Men shall deal unadvisedly sometimes . . . . . . iv 4 292
So deal with him as I prove true to you . . . . . iv 4 499
He privily Deals with our cardinal . . . . *Hen. VIII.* i 1 184
A great deal of your wit, too, lies in your sinews . *Troi. and Cres.* ii 1 108
A little proudly, and a great deal misprizing The knight opposed . iv 5 74
A very little thief of occasion will rob you of a great deal of patience *Coriolanus* ii 1 32
To weep with them that weep doth ease some deal . . *T. Andron.* iii 1 245
Show me a murderer, I'll deal with him . . . . . . v 2 93
What a deal of brine Hath wash'd thy sallow cheeks! . *Rom. and Jul.* ii 3 69
Therefore, if you should deal double with her, truly it were an ill thing ii 4 178
Methinks, I could deal kingdoms to my friends, And ne'er be weary *T. of Athens* i 2 226
And undo a great deal of honour . . . . iii 2 53
As rich men deal gifts, Expecting in return twenty for one . . iv 3 516
And uttered such a deal of stinking breath . . *J. Cæsar* i 2 247
But God above Deal between thee and me! . . . . *Macbeth* iv 3 121
Is it a free visitation? Come, deal justly with me . . *Hamlet* ii 2 284
And put upon him such a deal of man, That worthied him . *Lear* ii 2 127
Let us deal justly . . . . iii 6 42
That I am wretched Makes thee the happier: heavens, deal so still! . iv 1 69
Then away she started To deal with grief alone . . . . iv 3 34
To deal plainly, I fear I am not in my perfect mind . . . iv 7 62
Words him, I doubt not, a great deal from the matter . *Cymbeline* i 4 17
You are a great deal abused in too bold a persuasion . . . i 4 124
Live, And deal with others better.—Nobly doom'd! . . . v 5 420
What a man cannot get, he may lawfully deal for—his wife's soul *Pericles* ii 1 121
Have you that a man may deal withal, and defy the surgeon? . iv 6 29
Dealer. Thou didst conclude hairy men plain dealers without wit *Com. of Errors* ii 2 88
Dealest. I do not find that thou dealest justly with me . *Othello* iv 2 173
Dealing. In plain dealing, Pompey, I shall have you whipt *Meas. for Meas.* ii 1 264
If the duke avouch the justice of your dealing . . . . iv 2 201
What these Christians are, Whose own hard dealings teaches them suspect The thoughts of others! . . . . *Mer. of Venice* i 3 163
Were my worth as is my conscience firm, You should find better dealing *T. Night* iii 3 18
There is no honesty in such dealing . . . 2 *Hen. IV.* ii 1 40
Dealing with witches and with conjurers . . 2 *Hen. VI.* ii 1 172
This is close dealing . . . . ii 4 73
The benefit thereof is always granted To those whose dealings have deserved the place . . . . . . *Richard III.* iii 1 49
All will come to nought, When such bad dealing must be seen in thought iii 6 14
Out with it boldly: truth loves open dealing . . *Hen. VIII.* iii 1 39
Lo, Jupiter is yonder, dealing life! . . . . *Troi. and Cres.* iv 5 191
And very weak dealing . . . . *Rom. and Jul.* ii 4 181
Alack, alack, Edmund, I like not this unnatural dealing . *Lear* iii 3 2
And knows all qualities, with a learned spirit, Of human dealings *Othello* iii 3 260
Dealt. I come, to learn how you have dealt for him . . *K. John* v 2 121
I never dealt better since I was a man; all would not do . 1 *Hen. IV.* ii 4 188
Marriage is a matter of more worth Than to be dealt in by attorneyship 1 *Hen. VI.* v 5 56
Urge neither charity nor shame to me: Uncharitably with me have you dealt . . . . *Richard III.* i 3 275
They have dealt with me like thieves of mercy . . *Hamlet* iv 6 20
I protest, I have dealt most directly in thy affair . . *Othello* iv 2 211
Dealt on lieutenantry, and no practice had In the brave squares of war *Ant. and Cleo.* iii 11 39
The nobleman would have dealt with her like a nobleman . *Pericles* iv 6 147
Deanery. At the deanery, where a priest attends, Straight marry her *Mer. Wives* iv 6 31
Take her by the hand, away with her to the deanery . . . v 3 3
She is now with the doctor at the deanery, and there married . v 5 216
Dear, they durst not, So dear the love my people bore me . *Tempest* i 2 140
To one so dear, Of such divine perfection . . . *T. G. of Ver.* ii 7 12
I hold your dainties cheap, sir, and your welcome dear . *Com. of Errors* iii 1 21
You shall buy this sport as dear As all the metal in your shop will answer . . . . iv 1 81
Is it possible that any villany should be so dear? . . *Much Ado* iii 3 118
As prodigal of all dear grace As Nature was in making graces dear *L. L. Lost* ii 1 10

Dear. I never knew man hold vile stuff so dear . . . *L. L. Lost* iv 3 276
And then the king will court thee for his dear . . . . v 2 131
He swore that he did hold me dear As precious eyesight . . . v 2 444
And Lord Biron, I thank him, is my dear . . . . . v 2 457
My lover dear! thy Thisby dear, and lady dear! . . *M. N. Dream* i 2 55
In thy eye that shall appear When thou wakest, it is thy dear . . ii 2 33
For my sake, my dear, Lie further off yet . . . . . . ii 2 43
Odours savours sweet: So hath thy breath, my dearest Thisby dear . iii 1 87
With sighs of love, that costs the fresh blood dear . . . . iii 2 97
Lest, to thy peril, thou aby it dear . . . . iii 2 175
Look, where thy love comes; yonder is thy dear . . . . iii 2 176
Thou shalt buy this dear, If ever I thy face by daylight see . . iii 2 426
How can it be? O dainty duck! O dear! . . . . . . v 1 286
Since lion vile hath here deflower'd my dear . . . . . v 1 297
Your worth is very dear in my regard . . . *Mer. of Venice* i 1 62
Since you are dear bought, I will love you dear . . . . iii 2 315
I am married to a wife Which is as dear to me as life itself . . iv 1 283
As secret and as dear As Anna to the queen of Carthage was *T. of Shrew* i 1 158
Youngling, thou canst not love so dear as I . . . . . ii 1 339
While you, sweet dear, prove mistress of my heart! . . . . iv 2 10
A counsellor, a traitress, and a dear . . . . . *All's Well* i 1 184
He bade me store up, as a triple eye, Safer than mine own two, more dear . . . . ii 1 112
Thy life is dear; for all that life can rate Worth name of life in thee hath estimate . . . . ii 1 182
To buy his will, it would not seem too dear, Howe'er repented after . iii 7 27
Give me that ring.—I'll lend it thee, my dear . . . . . iv 2 40
Time was, I did him a desired office, Dear almost as his life . . iv 4 6
Praising what is lost Makes the remembrance dear . . . . v 3 20
I have been dear to him, lad, some two thousand strong, or so *T. Night* iii 2 58
If I be lapsed in this place, I shall pay dear . . . . . iii 3 37
Whom thou, in terms so bloody and so dear, Hast made thine enemies v 1 74
You pay a great deal too dear for what's given freely . . *W. Tale* i 1 18
Let what is dear in Sicily be cheap . . . . i 2 175
But shall I go mourn for that, my dear? . . . . . . iv 3 15
Golden quoifs and stomachers, For my lads to give their dears . . iv 4 227
Will you buy any tape, Or lace for your cape, My dainty duck, my dear-a? . . . . iv 4 324
Yet sell your face for five pence and 'tis dear . . . *K. John* i 1 153
Thy uncle will As dear be to thee as thy father was . . . iii 3 4
What thy soul holds dear, imagine it To lie that way thou go'st *Richard II.* i 3 286
He loves you, on my life, and holds you dear . . . . . ii 1 143
The cheapest of us is ten groats too dear . . . . . . v 5 68
Here is a dear, a true industrious friend . . . 1 *Hen. IV.* i 1 62
The Lord of Stafford dear to-day hath bought Thy likeness . . . v 3 7
A borrow'd title hast thou bought too dear . . . . . . v 3 23
I had forestall'd this dear and deep rebuke . . . 2 *Hen. IV.* iv 5 141
When flesh is cheap and females dear, And lusty lads roam here and there . . . . v 3 20
God forbid, my dear and faithful lord, That you should . . *Hen. V.* i 2 13
Sell every man his life as dear as mine, And they shall find dear deer of us . . . . 1 *Hen. VI.* iv 2 53
And bought his climbing very dear . . . . . . 2 *Hen. VI.* ii 1 100
If he revenge it not, yet will his friends; So will the queen, that living held him dear . . . . iv 1 147
Ah! sancta majestas, who would not buy thee dear? . . . . v 1 5
He loves me, and he holds me dear: Go you to him from me *Richard III.* i 4 239
Who, as thou know'st, are dear To princely Richard and to Buckingham iii 2 69
I hold my life as dear as you do yours . . . . iii 2 80
So dear I loved the man, that I must weep . . . . . iii 5 24
I know your majesty has always loved her So dear in heart *Hen. VIII.* ii 2 111
She now begs, That little thought, when she set footing here, She should have bought her dignities so dear . . . . iii 1 184
Let heaven Witness, how dear I hold this confirmation . . . . v 3 174
Loss of time, travail, expense, Wounds, friends, and what else dear *Troi. and Cres.* ii 2 5
Every tithe soul, 'mongst many thousand dismes, Hath been as dear as Helen . . . . ii 2 20
Troy holds him very dear . . . . iii 3 19
Nature, what things there are Most abject in regard and dear in use! What things again most dear in the esteem And poor in worth! . iii 3 128
Dear, trouble not yourself: the morn is cold . . . . . iv 2 1
Life every man holds dear; but the brave man Holds honour far more precious-dear than life . . . . v 3 27
They think we are too dear . . . . . . *Coriolanus* i 1 20
Each in my love alike and none less dear . . . . i 3 25
That kiss I carried from thee, dear . . . . v 3 47
If thy sons were ever dear to thee, O, think my son to be as dear to me! *T. Andron.* i 1 107
Purchased at an easy price; And yet dear too, because I bought mine own . . . . iii 1 200
My noble aunt Loves me as dear as e'er my mother did . . . iv 1 23
And that more dear Than hands or tongue, her spotless chastity . v 2 176
Beauty too rich for use, for earth too dear! . . . *Rom. and Jul.* i 5 49
Romeo!—My dear?—At what o'clock to-morrow Shall I send to thee? . ii 2 168
Is Rosaline, whom thou didst love so dear, So soon forsaken? . . ii 3 66
O God's lady dear! Are you so hot? . . . . ii 5 63
As dear to me as are the ruddy drops That visit my sad heart *J. Cæsar* ii 1 289
My thanks are too dear a halfpenny . . . . . *Hamlet* ii 2 282
And by what more dear a better proposer could charge you withal . ii 2 296
For thou dost know, O Damon dear, This realm dismantled was . . iii 2 292
Laertes, was your father dear to you? . . . . iv 7 108
Three of the carriages, in faith, are very dear to fancy . . . v 2 159
When she was dear to us, we did hold her so; But now her price is fall'n *Lear* i 1 199
His breeches cost him but a crown; He held them sixpence all too dear *Othello* ii 3 94
Minion, your dear lies dead, And your unblest fate hies . . . v 1 33
Uncle, I must come forth.—If thou attempt it, it will cost thee dear . v 2 255
The merchandise which thou hast brought from Rome Are all too dear for me . . . . *Ant. and Cleo.* ii 5 105
Welcome to Rome; Nothing more dear to me . . . . . . iii 6 86
Cold-hearted toward me?—Ah, dear, if I be so . . . . . iii 13 158
I dare not, dear—Dear my lord, pardon,—I dare not, Lest I be taken . iv 15 21
But he does buy my injuries, to be friends; Pays dear for my offences *Cymbeline* i 1 106
I will wage against your gold, gold to it: my ring I hold dear as my finger . . . . i 4 145
That's more Than some, whose tailors are as dear as yours, Can justly boast . . . . ii 3 84

Dear. For Imogen's dear life take mine ; and though 'Tis not so dear, yet 'tis a life . . . . *Cymbeline* v 4 22
And yet the end of all is bought thus dear, The breath is gone, and the sore eyes see clear . . . . *Pericles* i 1 98
I have one myself, Who shall not be more dear to my respect Than yours iii 3 33
Whither wilt thou have me?—To take from you the jewel you hold so dear . . . . iv 6 165
A baboon, could he speak, Would own a name too dear . . iv 6 190
Dear boy *L. L. Lost* i 2 ; *K. John* iii 1 ; 1 *Hen. VI.* iv 5
Dear brother *T. Night* iii 4 ; 3 *Hen. VI.* iii 3 ; *Richard III.* ii 1 ; *Hen. VIII.* v 4 ; *J. Cæsar* iv 3 ; *Hamlet* i 2
Dear cousin *Hen. V.* iv 6 ; *Richard III.* ii 2 ; iii 1
Dear daughter . . . . *Lear* ii 4 156 ; iv 6 193
Dear father *Tempest* i 2 ; iii 1 ; *T. of Shrew* v 1 ; *All's Well* ii 1 ; 2 *Hen. IV.* iv 5 ; 2 *Hen. VI.* v 2 ; *T. Andron.* i 1 ; *Rom. and Jul.* iv 1 ; *Hamlet* i 5 ; ii 2 ; iv 5 ; *Lear* ii 4 ; iv 4 ; iv 7
Dear knight . . . . *T. Night* i 3 95 ; ii 3 156
Dear lady *Tempest* i 2 ; *Much Ado* i 1 ; *L. L. Lost* ii 1 ; *Mer. of Venice* iii 2 ; v 1 ; *T. Night* iii 1 ; *Hamlet* ii 2 ; *Ant. and Cleo.* ii 3 ; v 2 ; *Cymbeline* i 1
Dear liege . . . . . . *L. L. Lost* ii 1 34 ; *Hen. V.* i 2 130
Dear lord *Meas. for Meas.* v 1 ; *All's Well* i 3 ; *Richard II.* i 1 ; i 2 ; 2 *Hen. IV.* iii 1 ; *Hen. V.* iv 3 ; 1 *Hen. VI.* iv 7 ; *Richard III.* ii 2 ; iv 1 ; *Troi. and Cres.* ii 3 ; iii 1 ; *T. of Athens* i 1 ; iii 4 ; *Hamlet* ii 2 ; *Lear* ii 4 ; *Othello* i 3 ; *Cymbeline* iii 6
Dear madam *T. G. of Ver.* i 2 ; *Richard III.* iv 1 ; *Ant. and Cleo.* iii 6 ; iv 15
Dear master . . . . . *As Y. Like It* ii 6 1 ; *Ant. and Cleo.* iv 14 89
Dear mother *All's Well* v 3 ; *K. John* v 2 ; *Richard III.* ii 2 ; *Coriolanus* v 3 ; *Hamlet* iv 3
Dear my lord *Much Ado* iv 1 ; *Hen. V.* iv 6 ; *Troi. and Cres.* iii 3 ; *J. Cæsar* ii 1 ; *Hamlet* iii 3 ; *Lear* v 1 ; *Othello* iii 3 ; *A. and C.* iv 15
Dear niece . . . . . . *As Y. Like It* v 4 153 ; *T. Andron.* iii 1 138
Dear princess . . . . . . *L. L. Lost* ii 1 150 ; *Lear* iv 7 29
Dear queen *W. Tale* v 3 ; *Troi. and Cres.* iii 1 ; *Ant. and Cleo.* i 5 ; iii 11 ; v 2
Dear sir *Meas. for Meas.* iii 1 ; *Mer. of Venice* iv 1 ; *All's Well* ii 1 ; *W. Tale* iv 3 ; *K. John* i 1 ; *Troi. and Cres.* v 3 ; *Lear* i 1 ; *Cymbeline* i 6
Dear sister . . . . *Hamlet* i 3 33 ; *Lear* iii 7 13
Dear son *Tempest* v 1 ; *Much Ado* ii 1 ; *All's Well* iii 4 ; *T. Andron.* i 1 ; iii 1 ; *Rom. and Jul.* iii 3 ; *Lear* iv 1 ; *Cymbeline* ii 3
Dear sovereign *As Y. Like It* i 3 ; *All's Well* v 3 ; *T. Andron.* ii 3
Dear uncle . . . . . . *As Y. Like It* i 3 52 ; *Hen. V.* iii 3 54
Dear a loss. Was never widow had so dear a loss ! . . . *Richard III.* ii 2 77
Dear a lover. How dear a lover of my lord your husband *Mer. of Venice* iii 4 7
Dear a show. I should not make so dear a show of zeal . . 1 *Hen. IV.* v 4 95
Dear a trust. Nor did he think it meet To lay so dangerous and dear a trust On any soul removed . . . . iv 1 34
Dear abide. If it be found so, some will dear abide it . . *J. Cæsar* iii 2 119
Dear absence. And I a heavy interim shall support By his dear absence *Othello* i 3 260
Dear account. Claudio shall render me a dear account *Much Ado* iv 1 337
Upon remainder of a dear account . . . . . . *Richard II.* i 1 130
O dear account ! my life is my foe's debt . . . *Rom. and Jul.* i 5 120
Dear actors. And, most dear actors, eat no onions . . *M. N. Dream* iv 2 43
Dear alliance. In love and dear alliance . . . . . *Hen. V.* v 2 373
Dear amity. We swore to you Dear amity . . . . . *K. John* v 4 20
Dear-beloved. To see the nuptial Of these our dear-beloved solemnized *Tempest* v 1 309
Dear blood. With that dear blood which it hath fostered . *Richard II.* i 3 126
I'll empty all these veins, And shed my dear blood drop by drop 1 *Hen. IV.* i 3 134
By Christ's dear blood shed for our grievous sins . . *Richard III.* i 4 195
He slew Mercutio ; Who now the price of his dear blood doth owe? *Rom. and Jul.* iii 1 188
Dear bought. Since you are dear bought, I will love you dear *Mer. of Venice* iii 2 315
With his new bride and England's dear-bought queen . 2 *Hen VI.* i 1 252
Dear Brutus. The fault, dear Brutus, is not in our stars, But in ourselves *J. Cæsar* i 2 140
Dear Cæsar. Hail, Cæsar, and my lord ! hail, most dear Cæsar ! *Ant. and Cleo.* iii 6 39
Dear care. In their dear care And tender preservation of our person *Hen. V.* ii 2 58
Dear cause. Their dear causes Would to the bleeding and the grim alarm Excite the mortified man . . . . *Macbeth* v 2 3
Some dear cause Will in concealment wrap me up awhile . . *Lear* iv 3 53
Dear concernings. Would from a paddock, from a bat, a gib, Such dear concernings hide . . . . *Hamlet* iii 4 191
Dear conjunction. And this dear conjunction Plant neighbourhood and Christian-like accord . . . . *Hen. V.* v 2 380
Dear countryman. Then forth, dear countrymen . . . . ii 2 189
Dear countryman, Bring in thy ranks, but leave without thy rage *T. of Athens* v 4 38
Know we this face or no? Alas, my friend and my dear countryman ! *Othello* v 1 89
Dear creature. Teach me, dear creature, how to think and speak *Com. of Errors* iii 2 33
Dear daughter. Your most dear daughter— No rescue? . . *Lear* iv 6 193
Dear deer. Sell every man his life as dear as mine, And they shall find dear deer of us . . . . 1 *Hen. VI.* iv 2 54
Dear degree. How canst thou urge God's dreadful law to us, When thou hast broke it in so dear degree? . . . . . . *Richard III.* i 4 215
Dear discretion. O dear discretion, how his words are suited ! *Mer. of Venice* iii 5 70
Dear divorce 'Twixt natural son and sire ! . . . . *T. of Athens* iv 3 382
Dear Duff, I prithee, contradict thyself, And say it is not so . *Macbeth* ii 3 94
Dear earth, I do salute thee with my hand . . . *Richard II.* iii 2 6
Dear employment. A ring that I must use In dear employment *Rom. and Jul.* v 3 32
Dear encounter. Let rich music's tongue Unfold the imagined happiness that both Receive in either by this dear encounter . . . ii 6 29
Dear exile. The sly slow hours shall not determinate The dateless limit of thy dear exile . . . . *Richard II.* i 3 151
Dear expedience. Our council did decree In forwarding this dear expedience . . . . 1 *Hen. IV.* i 1 33
Dear expense. If I have thanks, it is a dear expense . *M. N. Dream* i 1 249
Dear faith. Surprise her with discourse of my dear faith . *T. Night* i 4 25
Dear friend. Thy case, dear friend, Shall be my precedent . *Tempest* ii 1 290
There is a gentleman my dear friend . . . . *Mer. Wives* iii 3 129
Dear friend. Hath he not lost much wealth by wreck of sea? Buried some dear friend? . . . . *Com. of Errors* v 1 50
That have gone about To link my dear friend to a common stale *Much Ado* iv 1 66
The death of a dear friend would go near to make a man look sad *M. N. Dream* v 1 293
Some dear friend dead ; else nothing in the world Could turn so much the constitution Of any constant man . . . *Mer. of Venice* iii 2 248
I have engaged myself to a dear friend . . . . . . iii 2 264
Is it your dear friend that is thus in trouble? . . . . . iii 2 293
Even he that did uphold the very life Of my dear friend . . . v 1 215
Arthur ta'en prisoner? divers dear friends slain? . . . *K. John* iii 4 7
Letters came last night To a dear friend of the good Duke of York's *Richard II.* iii 4 70
Once more unto the breach, dear friends, once more . . *Hen. V.* iii 1 1
He is my dear friend, an please you . . . . . . iv 7 174
Shall grow dear friends And interjoin their issues . . *Coriolanus* iv 4 21
Oft have I digg'd up dead men from their graves, And set them upright at their dear friends' doors . . . . . *T. Andron.* v 1 136
Speak, Rome's dear friend, as erst our ancestor . . . . v 3 80
If there be any in this assembly, any dear friend of Cæsar's *J. Cæsar* iii 2 19
I drink to the general joy o' the whole table, And to our dear friend Banquo, whom we miss . . . . *Macbeth* iii 4 90
Sure, dear friends, my thanks are too dear a halfpenny . *Hamlet* ii 2 281
He that lies slain here, Cassio, Was my dear friend . . . *Othello* v 1 102
Dear general, I never gave you cause . . . . v 2 299
Dear gentlewoman, How fares our gracious lady? . . . *W. Tale* ii 2 20
Dear God. Withhold revenge, dear God ! 'tis not my fault 3 *Hen. VI.* ii 2 7
Be satisfied, dear God, with our true blood . . *Richard III.* iii 3 21
Cancel his bond of life, dear God, I pray . . . . . iv 4 77
Dear goddess. Hear, nature, hear ; dear goddess, hear ! . . *Lear* i 4 297
Dear goddess, hear that prayer of the people ! . . *Ant. and Cleo.* i 2 73
Dear good will. Thou art not ignorant what dear good will I bear *T. G. of Ver.* iv 3 14
Dear grace. Be now as prodigal of all dear grace As Nature was in making graces dear . . . . *L. L. Lost* ii 1 9
Dear groans. Deaf'd with the clamours of their own dear groans v 2 874
Dear guiltiness. Your grace is perjured much, Full of dear guiltiness v 2 801
Dear Hamlet. Come hither, my dear Hamlet, sit by me . *Hamlet* iii 2 114
Dear hap. His help to crave, and my dear hap to tell . *Rom. and Jul.* ii 2 190
Dear happiness. Truly, I love none.—A dear happiness to women *Much Ado* i 1 129
Dear Harry. My heart's dear Harry . . . . . 2 *Hen. IV.* ii 3 12
Dear heart. Awake, dear heart, awake ! thou hast slept well *Tempest* i 2 305
Mine eye's clear eye, my dear heart's dearer heart . *Com. of Errors* iii 2 62
Farewell, dear heart, since I must needs be gone . . *T. Night* ii 3 109
What, wilt thou kneel with me? Do, then, dear heart . *T. Andron.* iii 1 211
Dear heart-strings. Though that her jesses were my dear heart-strings, I'll whistle her off . . . . *Othello* iii 3 261
Dear heaven, bless ! Or, ere they meet, in me, O nature, cesse ! *All's Well* v 3 71
Dear highness. I am alone felicitate In your dear highness love *Lear* i 1 78
Dear honour. The heavens hold firm The walls of thy dear honour ! *Cymbeline* ii 1 68
Dear husband. Many a thousand widows Shall this his mock mock out of their dear husbands . . . . *Hen. V.* i 2 285
And I dare think he'll prove to Desdemona A most dear husband *Othello* ii 1 300
A wooer More hateful than the foul expulsion is Of thy dear husband *Cymbeline* ii 1 66
Dear imp. Sadness is one and the self-same thing, dear imp *L. L. Lost* i 2 5
Dear import. The letter was not nice but full of charge Of dear import *Rom. and Jul.* v 2 19
Dear Isabel, I have a motion much imports your good *Meas. for Meas.* v 1 540
Dear judgement. Lear, Lear ! Beat at this gate, that let thy folly in, And thy dear judgement out ! . . . . *Lear* i 4 294
Dear kinsman. O, the blood is spilt Of my dear kinsman ! *R. and J.* iii 1 153
Dear lad. I think not so, my lord.—Dear lad, believe it . . *T. Night* i 4 29
Dear land. This dear dear land, Dear for her reputation through the world . . . . *Richard II.* ii 1 57
Dear Lavinia, dearer than my soul . . . . . *T. Andron.* iii 1 102
Dear life. Bequeath to death your numbness, for from him Dear life redeems you . . . . *W. Tale* v 3 103
Upon whose property and most dear life A damn'd defeat was made *Hamlet* ii 2 597
For Imogen's dear life take mine ; and though 'Tis not so dear, yet 'tis a life . . . . *Cymbeline* v 4 22
Dear loss. Supportable To make the dear loss, have I means much weaker Than you may call to comfort you . . . . *Tempest* v 1 146
Their dear loss, The more of you 'twas felt, the more it shaped Unto my end of stealing them . . . . *Cymbeline* v 5 345
Dear love. Alas ! dear love, I cannot lack thee two hours *As Y. Like It* iv 1 182
From time to time I have acquainted you With the dear love I bear *Mer. Wives* iv 6 9
For whose dear love, They say, she hath abjured the company And sight of men . . . . *T. Night* i 2 39
And out of my dear love I'll give thee more . . . *K. John* ii 1 157
If my heart's dear love— Well, do not swear . . *Rom. and Jul.* ii 2 115
I hear some noise within ; dear love, adieu ! . . . . . ii 2 136
Then plainly know my heart's dear love is set . . . . . ii 3 57
Thy dear love sworn but hollow perjury . . . . . . iii 3 128
My dear dear love To your proceeding bids me tell you this . *J. Cæsar* ii 2 102
No blown ambition doth our arms incite, But love, dear love . . *Lear* iv 4 28
Come, my dear love, The purchase made, the fruits are to ensue *Othello* ii 3 8
Dear-loved. My dear-loved cousin, and my dearer lord . *Rom. and Jul.* iii 2 66
Dear maid. And now, dear maid, be you as free to us . *Meas. for Meas.* v 1 393
O rose of May ! Dear maid, kind sister, sweet Ophelia ! . *Hamlet* iv 5 158
Dear majesty. What might you, Or my dear majesty your queen here, think? . . . . ii 2 135
Dear manakin. This is a dear manakin to you, Sir Toby . *T. Night* iii 2 57
Dear men Of estimation and command in arms . . 1 *Hen. IV.* iv 4 31
Dear mercy. This is dear mercy, and thou seest it not . *Rom. and Jul.* iii 3 28
Dear mistress. O most dear mistress, The sun will set before I shall discharge What I must strive to do . . . . . *Tempest* iii 1 21
Dear morsel. How doth my dear morsel, thy mistress? *Meas. for Meas.* iii 2 56
Dear my brother, Let him that was the cause of this have power *W. Tale* v 3 53
Dear my liege, mine honour let me try . . . *Richard II.* i 1 184
Dear my sweet. In my presence still smile, dear my sweet . *T. Night* ii 5 192
Dear nurse of arts, plenties and joyful births . . . *Hen. V.* v 2 35
We must lose The country, our dear nurse, or else thy person *Coriolanus* v 3 110
What say'st thou, my dear nurse? . . . . . *Rom. and Jul.* ii 4 207
Dear offence. Thou art the issue of my dear offence . . *K. John* i 1 257
God of his mercy give You patience to endure, and true repentance Of all your dear offences ! . . . . *Hen. V.* ii 2 181

Dear one. I have done nothing but in care of thee, Of thee, my dear one *Tempest* i 2 17
Dear particular. Who loved him In a most dear particular *Coriolanus* v 1 3
Dear perfection. Whose dear perfection hearts that scorn'd to serve Humbly call'd mistress *All's Well* v 3 18
So Romeo would, were he not Romeo call'd, Retain that dear perfection *Rom. and Jul.* ii 2 46
Dear peril. And strain what other means is left unto us In our dear peril *T. of Athens* v 1 231
Dear petition. Consort with me in loud and dear petition *Troi. and Cres.* v 3 9
Dear Redeemer. Defaced The precious image of our dear Redeemer *Richard III.* ii 1 123
Dear respect. Out of dear respect *Hen. VIII.* v 3 119
Dear rights. Gave her dear rights To his dog-hearted daughters *Lear* iv 3 46
Dear Romeo. Three words, dear Romeo, and good night indeed *Rom. and Jul.* ii 2 142
Dear saint. O, then, dear saint, let lips do what hands do i 5 105
My name, dear saint, is hateful to myself ii 2 55
Dear sake. For whose dear sake thou didst then rend thy faith *T. G. of Ver.* v 4 47
For whose dear sake thou wast but lately dead *Rom. and Jul.* iii 3 136
Dear self. Am better than thy dear self's better part *Com. of Errors* ii 2 125
Dear services. As recompense of our dear services *W. Tale* ii 3 150
Dear shelter. The gods to their dear shelter take thee, maid! *Lear* i 1 185
Dear sight. With this dear sight Struck pale and bloodless *T. Andron.* iii 1 257
Dear soul. A solemn combination shall be made Of our dear souls *T. Night* v 1 393
This land of such dear souls, this dear dear land *Richard II.* ii 1 57
Since my dear soul was mistress of her choice *Hamlet* iii 2 68
Dear stone. Chide me, dear stone, that I may say indeed Thou art Hermione *W. Tale* v 3 24
Dear thanks. O, a root,—dear thanks! *T. of Athens* iv 3 192
Dear thing. Commend a dear thing to you *Lear* iii 1 19
Dear venom. Thy reason, dear venom, give thy reason *T. Night* iii 2 2
Dear vows. Strangles our dear vows Even in the birth of our own labouring breath *Troi. and Cres.* iv 4 39
Dear wife. Mine own life, My dear wife's estimate *Coriolanus* iii 3 114
O, full of scorpions is my mind, dear wife! *Macbeth* iii 2 36
Deared. Comes dear'd by being lack'd *Ant. and Cleo.* i 4 44
Dearer. I to myself am dearer than a friend *T. G. of Ver.* ii 6 23
Love talks with better knowledge, and knowledge with dearer love *Meas. for Meas.* iii 2 160
Mine eye's clear eye, my dear heart's dearer heart *Com. of Errors* iii 2 62
Whose loves Are dearer than the natural bond of sisters *As Y. Like It* i 2 288
Welcome, count; My son's no dearer *All's Well* i 2 76
Then your blood had been the dearer by I know how much an ounce *W. Tale* iv 4 724
A dearer merit, not so deep a maim *Richard II.* i 3 156
Death hath not struck so fat a deer to-day, Though many dearer *1 Hen. IV.* v 4 108
Had they been ruled by me, You should have won them dearer than you have *2 Hen. IV.* iv 3 73
And that his country's dearer than himself *Coriolanus* i 6 72
I will, sir, flatter my sworn brother, the people, to earn a dearer estimation of them ii 3 103
Dear Lavinia, dearer than my soul *T. Andron.* iii 1 102
He leaves his pledges dearer than his life iii 1 292
My dear-loved cousin, and my dearer lord *Rom. and Jul.* iii 2 66
Shall it not grieve thee dearer than thy death? *J. Cæsar* iii 1 196
A heart Dearer than Plutus' mine, richer than gold iv 3 102
Who yet is no dearer in my account *Lear* i 1 20
Dearer than eye-sight, space, and liberty; Beyond what can be valued i 1 57
I loved him, friend; No father his son dearer iii 4 174
Thou shalt find a dearer father in my love iii 5 26
His meanest garment, That ever hath but clipp'd his body, is dearer In my respect than all the hairs above thee, Were they all made such men *Cymbeline* ii 3 139
Diseases have been sold dearer than physic *Pericles* iv 6 105
Dearest. If by your art, my dearest father, you have Put the wild waters in this roar, allay them *Tempest* i 2 1
The fault's your own.—So is the dear'st o' the loss ii 1 135
Indeed the top of admiration! worth What's dearest to the world! iii 1 39
My mistress, dearest; And I thus humble ever iii 1 86
No, my dear'st love, I would not for the world v 1 172
Now, madam, summon up your dearest spirits *L. L. Lost* ii 1 1
Thine, in the dearest design of industry iv 1 88
Odours savours sweet: So hath thy breath, my dearest Thisby dear *M. N. Dream* iii 1 87
The dearest friend to me, the kindest man *Mer. of Venice* iii 2 294
The dearest ring in Venice will I give you iv 1 435
To have the touches dearest prized *As Y. Like It* iii 2 160
Wherein our dearest friend Prejudicates the business *All's Well* i 2 7
My dearest madam, Let not your hate encounter with my love i 3 213
As the dearest issue of his practice ii 1 109
That from the bloody course of war My dearest master, your dear son, may hie iii 4 9
Which of them both Is dearest to me, I have no skill in sense iii 4 39
And cost me the dearest groans of a mother iv 5 11
My dearest, thou never spokest To better purpose *W. Tale* i 2 88
Sweet villain! Most dear'st! my collop! i 2 137
The sweet'st, dear'st creature's dead, and vengeance for't Not dropp'd down yet iii 2 202
Thou dearest Perdita iv 4 40
And that's the dearest grace it renders you *1 Hen. IV.* iii 1 182
Do I tell thee of my foes, Which art my near'st and dearest enemy? iii 2 123
Bought me lights as good cheap at the dearest chandler's in Europe iii 3 52
We were the first and dearest of your friends v 1 33
Towards York shall bend you with your dearest speed v 5 36
Or else this blow should broach thy dearest blood *1 Hen. VI.* iii 4 40
Thou wouldst have left thy dearest heart-blood there *3 Hen. VI.* i 1 223
Both shall buy this treason Even with the dearest blood your bodies bear v 1 69
And take deep traitors for thy dearest friends! *Richard III.* i 3 224
By that you love the dearest in this world *Hen. VIII.* iv 2 155
For here the Trojans taste our dear'st repute With their finest palate *Troi. and Cres.* i 3 337
Come, my sweet wife, my dearest mother, and My friends *Coriolanus* iv 1 48
Gorged with the dearest morsel of the earth *Rom. and Jul.* v 3 46
I have bred her at my dearest cost In qualities of the best *T. of Athens* i 1 124
My dearest lord, bless'd, to be most accursed iv 2 42
My dearest master!—Away! what art thou? iv 3 478
Dearest. To throw away the dearest thing he owed, As 'twere a careless trifle *Macbeth* i 4 10
This have I thought good to deliver thee, my dearest partner of greatness i 5 12
My dearest love, Duncan comes here to-night i 5 59
Be innocent of the knowledge, dearest chuck iii 2 45
My dearest coz, I pray you, school yourself iv 2 14
With no less nobility of love Than that which dearest father bears his son *Hamlet* i 2 111
Would I had met my dearest foe in heaven Or ever I had seen that day! i 2 182
What says our second daughter, Our dearest Regan? *Lear* i 1 69
The argument of your praise, balm of your age, Most best, most dearest i 1 219
They have used Their dearest action in the tented field *Othello* i 3 85
Now, my dearest queen,— Pray you, stand farther from me *A. and C.* i 3 17
Farewell, my dearest sister, fare thee well iii 2 39
Be ever known to patience: my dear'st sister! iii 6 98
Thou art so leaky, That we must leave thee to thy sinking, for Thy dearest quit thee iii 13 65
My dearest husband, I something fear my father's wrath *Cymbeline* i 1 85
I have enjoyed the dearest bodily part of your mistress i 4 162
O dearest soul! your cause doth strike my heart With pity i 6 118
You, O the dearest of creatures, would even renew me with your eyes iii 2 42
What does he mean? since death of my dear'st mother It did not speak before iv 2 190
His dearest one, sweet Imogen iv 4 61
I will embrace Your offer. Come, dearest madam. O, no tears *Pericles* iii 3 38
My dearest wife was like this maid v 1 108
Dearest-valued. The blood, and dearest-valued blood, of France *K. John* iii 1 343
Dearly. Do you love me, master? no?—Dearly, my delicate Ariel *Temp.* iv 1 49
I something do excuse the thing I hate, For his advantage that I dearly love *Meas. for Meas.* ii 4 120
How dearly would it touch thee to the quick! *Com. of Errors* ii 2 132
An if she did not hate him deadly, she would love him dearly *Much Ado* v 1 179
The pound of flesh, which I demand of him, Is dearly bought *Mer. of Venice* iv 1 100
They are taught their manage, and to that end riders dearly hired *As Y. Like It* i 1 14
The duke my father loved his father dearly.—Doth it therefore ensue that you should love his son dearly? i 3 31
My father hated his father dearly i 3 35
Speakest thou in sober meanings?—By my life, I do; which I tender dearly v 2 77
Did ever in so true a flame of liking Wish chastely and love dearly *All's Well* i 3 218
If I should swear by God's great attributes, I loved you dearly, would you believe my oaths, When I did love you ill? iv 2 26
I'll love her dearly, ever, ever dearly v 3 317
How will this fadge? my master loves her dearly *T. Night* ii 2 34
And whom, by heaven I swear, I tender dearly v 1 129
Most dearly welcome! And your fair princess,—goddess! *W. Tale* v 1 130
Thy voluntary oath Lives in this bosom, dearly cherished *K. John* iii 3 24
Many a soul Shall pay full dearly for this encounter *1 Hen. IV.* v 1 84
Which held thee dearly as his soul's redemption *3 Hen. VI.* ii 1 102
Do you love your children?—Ay, full as dearly as I love myself iii 2 37
Bade me rely on him as on my father, And he would love me dearly as his child *Richard III.* ii 2 26
And a little To love her for her mother's sake, that loved him, Heaven knows how dearly *Hen. VIII.* iv 2 138
Our neighbours, The upper Germany, can dearly witness v 3 30
That man, how dearly ever parted, How much in having *Troi. and Cres.* iii 3 96
Most dearly welcome to the Greeks, sweet lady iv 5 18
He loved his mother dearly *Coriolanus* v 4 15
Will hold thee dearly for thy mother's sake *T. Andron.* v 1 36
Which name I tender As dearly as my own *Rom. and Jul.* iii 1 75
Look you, she loved her kinsman Tybalt dearly iii 4 3
Judge, O you gods, how dearly Cæsar loved him! *J. Cæsar* iii 2 186
Tender yourself more dearly *Hamlet* i 3 107
Which we do tender, as we dearly grieve For that which thou hast done iv 3 43
Wine loved I deeply, dice dearly *Lear* iii 4 94
Ever did, And ever will—though he do shake me off To beggarly divorcement—love him dearly *Othello* iv 2 158
If you did love him dearly, You do not hold the method to enforce The like from him *Ant. and Cleo.* i 3 6
A sister I bequeath you, whom no brother Did ever love so dearly ii 2 153
Nay, but how dearly he adores Mark Antony! iii 2 8
Is in safety And greets your highness dearly *Cymbeline* i 6 13
Rubies unparagon'd, How dearly they do't! ii 2 18
She hath bought the name of whore thus dearly ii 4 128
It kept where I kept, I so dearly loved it *Pericles* ii 1 136
He loved me dearly, And for his sake I wish the having of it ii 1 144
Dearness. He holds you well, and in dearness of heart *Much Ado* iii 2 101
Dearth. Pity the dearth that I have pined in *T. G. of Ver.* ii 7 16
And make a dearth in this revolting land *Richard II.* iii 3 163
Untimely storms make men expect a dearth *Richard III.* ii 3 35
For your wants, Your suffering in this dearth, you may as well Strike at the heaven with your staves *Coriolanus* i 1 69
For the dearth, The gods, not the patricians, make it i 1 74
The dearth is great; The people mutinous i 2 10
And his infusion of such dearth and rareness, as, to make true diction of him, his semblable is his mirror *Hamlet* v 2 123
Death, dearth, dissolutions of ancient amities *Lear* i 2 158
They know, By the height, the lowness, or the mean, if dearth Or foison follow *Ant. and Cleo.* ii 7 22
Death. The wills above be done! but I would fain die a dry death *Temp.* i 1 71
Say, this were death That now hath seized them ii 1 260
I shall laugh myself to death at this puppy-headed monster ii 2 158
Bite him to death, I prithee iii 2 38
Lingering perdition, worse than any death iii 3 77
I shall be pinch'd to death v 1 276
Being destined to a drier death on shore *T. G. of Ver.* i 1 158
Why not death rather than living torment? iii 1 170
I fly not death, to fly his deadly doom iii 1 185
Tarry I here, I but attend on death: But, fly I hence, I fly away from life iii 1 186
I kill'd a man, whose death I much repent iv 1 27
What dangerous action, stood it next to death, Would I not undergo for one calm look! v 4 41
Give back, or else embrace thy death v 4 126
I had rather be set quick i' the earth And bowl'd to death with turnips! *Mer. Wives* iii 4 91

Death. I had been drowned, but that the shore was shelvy and shallow,—a death that I abhor . . . . . *Mer. Wives* iii 5 16
I suffered the pangs of three several deaths . . . iii 5 110
If you find a man there, he shall die a flea's death . . iv 2 158
There is divinity in odd numbers, either in nativity, chance, or death . v 1 5
Let us be keen, and rather cut a little, Than fall, and bruise to death *Meas. for Meas.* ii 1 6
Let mine own judgement pattern out my death . . . ii 1 30
It grieves me for the death of Claudio; But there's no remedy . ii 1 294
Spare him! He's not prepared for death . . . . ii 2 84
Were I under the terms of death, The impression of keen whips I'ld wear as rubies, And strip myself to death . . . ii 4 100
He must not only die the death, But thy unkindness shall his death draw out To lingering sufferance . . . . . . ii 4 165
And fit his mind to death, for his soul's rest . . . ii 4 187
Be absolute for death; either death or life Shall thereby be the sweeter iii 1 5
Thy best of rest is sleep, And that thou oft provokest; yet grossly fear'st Thy death, which is no more . . . . . iii 1 19
Thou bear'st thy heavy riches but a journey, And death unloads thee . iii 1 28
Yet in this life Lie hid moe thousand deaths: yet death we fear, That makes these odds all even . . . . iii 1 40
To sue to live, I find I seek to die; And, seeking death, find life . iii 1 43
That will free your life, But fetter you till death . . . iii 1 67
Darest thou die? The sense of death is most in apprehension . iii 1 78
Be ready, Claudio, for your death to-morrow . . . . iii 1 107
Death is a fearful thing.—And shamed life a hateful . . iii 1 116
Is a paradise To what we fear of death . . . . iii 1 132
I'll pray a thousand prayers for thy death, No word to save thee . iii 1 146
Therefore prepare yourself to death . . . . . iii 1 169
What a merit were it in death to take this poor maid from the world! . iii 1 240
This friar hath been with him, and advised him for the entertainment of death . . . . iii 2 226
Look, here's the warrant, Claudio, for thy death . . . iv 2 66
A man that apprehends death no more dreadfully but as a drunken sleep . . . . iv 2 149
A dangerous courtesy.—Pray, sir, in what?—In the delaying death . iv 2 174
O death's a great disguiser; and you may add to it . . . iv 2 186
It was the desire of the penitent to be so bared before his death . iv 2 189
Perchance of the duke's death; perchance entering into some monastery iv 2 216
You must be so good, sir, to rise and be put to death . . iv 3 29
A creature unprepared, unmeet for death . . . . . iv 3 71
Immediate sentence then and sequent death Is all the grace I beg . v 1 378
Your brother's death, I know, sits at your heart . . . v 1 394
The swift celerity of his death, Which I did think with slower foot came on . . . . v 1 399
That life is better life, past fearing death, Than that which lives to fear v 1 402
An Angelo for Claudio, death for death! . . . . . v 1 414
We do condemn thee to the very block Where Claudio stoop'd to death v 1 420
You do but lose your labour. Away with him to death! . . v 1 434
He dies for Claudio's death . . . . v 1 448
I crave death more willingly than mercy; 'Tis my deserving . . v 1 481
Marrying a punk, my lord, is pressing to death, whipping, and hanging v 1 529
Procure my fall And by the doom of death end woes and all *Com. of Err.* i 1 2
Till my factor's death And the great care of goods at random left . i 1 42
A doubtful warrant of immediate death . . . . . i 1 69
Here must end the story of my life; And happy were I in my timely death . . . . i 1 139
Thou art adjudged to the death . . . . i 1 147
He gains by death that hath such means to die . . . . iii 2 51
Comes this way to the melancholy vale, The place of death . . v 1 121
See where they come: we will behold his death . . . . v 1 128
Unless the fear of death doth make me dote . . . . v 1 195
You are both sure, and will assist me?—To the death, my lord *Much Ado* i 3 72
What life is in that, to be the death of this marriage? . . ii 2 19
She would laugh me Out of myself, press me to death with wit . iii 1 76
A better death than die with mocks, Which is as bad as die with tickling iii 1 79
Death is the fairest cover for her shame That may be wish'd for . iv 1 117
Refuse me, hate me, torture me to death! . . . . . iv 1 186
The supposition of the lady's death Will quench the wonder of her infamy iv 1 240
She is dead, slander'd to death by villains . . . . v 1 88
My heart is sorry for your daughter's death . . . . v 1 103
Her death shall fall heavy on you . . . . . . v 1 150
Which I had rather seal with my death than repeat over to my shame . v 1 248
I thank you, princes, for my daughter's death . . . . v 1 278
Done to death by slanderous tongues Was the Hero that here lies . v 3 3
Death, in guerdon of her wrongs, Gives her fame which never dies . v 3 5
So the life that died with shame Lives in death with glorious fame . v 3 8
Graves, yawn and yield your dead, Till death be uttered, Heavily, heavily . . . . v 3 20
I'll tell you largely of fair Hero's death . . . . . v 4 69
And then grace us in the disgrace of death . . . *L. L. Lost* i 1 3
Will you hear an extemporal epitaph on the death of the deer? . iv 2 51
That the lover, sick to death, Wish himself the heaven's breath . iv 3 107
No, to the death, we will not move a foot . . . . . v 2 146
Raining the tears of lamentation For the remembrance of my father's death . . . . v 2 820
The sudden hand of death close up mine eye! . . . . v 2 825
To move wild laughter in the throat of death? It cannot be . . v 2 865
Either to this gentleman Or to her death, according to our law *M. N. Dream* i 1 44
Either to die the death or to abjure For ever the society of men . i 1 65
Which by no means we may extenuate—To death, or to a vow of single life . . . . i 1 121
If there were a sympathy in choice, War, death, or sickness did lay seige to it . . . . i 1 142
The most lamentable comedy, and most cruel death of Pyramus and Thisby . . . . i 2 12
Either death or you I'll find immediately . . . . . ii 2 156
Whom I do love and will do till my death . . . . . iii 2 167
Which death or absence soon shall remedy . . . . . iii 2 244
With league whose date till death shall never end . . . iii 2 373
To make it the more gracious, I shall sing it at her death . . iv 1 225
The thrice three Muses mourning for the death Of Learning . . v 1 52
'Tide life, 'tide death, I come without delay . . . . v 1 205
The death of a dear friend would go near to make a man look sad . v 1 293
Holy men at their death have good inspirations *Mer. of Venice* i 2 31
A carrion Death, within whose empty eye There is a written scroll! ii 7 63
Made her neighbours believe she wept for the death of a third husband iii 1 11
If I might but see you at my death . . . . . . iii 2 322
I am a tainted wether of the flock, Meetest for death . . . iv 1 115

Death. Have by some surgeon, Shylock, on your charge, To stop his wounds, lest he do bleed to death . . . *Mer. of Venice* iv 1 258
Say how I loved you, speak me fair in death . . . . iv 1 275
To render it, Upon his death, unto the gentleman That lately stole his daughter . . . . iv 1 384
You swore to me, when I did give it you, That you would wear it till your hour of death . . . . v 1 153
A special deed of gift, After his death, of all he dies possess'd of . v 1 293
I faint almost to death . . . . . . *As Y. Like It* ii 4 66
Thy conceit is nearer death than thy powers . . . . . ii 6 8
Hold death awhile at the arm's end . . . . . . ii 6 10
The common executioner, Whose heart the accustom'd sight of death makes hard . . . . iii 5 4
'Tis but one cast away, and so, come, death! Two o'clock is your hour? iv 1 190
Translate thy life into death, thy liberty into bondage . . . v 1 59
Though to have her and death were both one thing . . . v 4 17
Grim death, how foul and loathsome is thine image! . *T. of Shrew* Ind. 1 35
After my death the one half of my lands . . . . . ii 1 122
My master and mistress are almost frozen to death . . . iv 1 40
'Tis death for any one in Mantua To come to Padua . . . iv 2 81
If I should sleep or eat, 'Twere deadly sickness or else present death . iv 3 14
Beat me to death with a bottom of brown thread . . . . iv 3 137
And I in going, madam, weep o'er my father's death anew . *All's Well* i 1 4
Would have made nature immortal, and death should have play for lack of work . . . . i 1 23
I think it would be the death of the king's disease . . . i 1 25
On's bed of death Many receipts he gave me . . . . ii 1 107
Such thanks I give As one near death to those that wish him live . ii 1 134
Thy physic I will try, That ministers thine own death if I die . ii 1 189
Not helping, death's my fee; But, if I help, what do you promise me? ii 1 192
As 'twere, a man assured of a— Uncertain life, and sure death . ii 3 20
Let the white death sit on thy cheek for ever . . . . ii 3 77
And, though I kill him not, I am the cause His death was so effected . iii 2 119
Where death and danger dogs the heels of worth . . . . iii 4 15
He is too good and fair for death and me . . . . . iii 4 16
Which makes her story true, even to the point of her death . . iv 3 67
Her death itself, which could not be her office to say is come, was faithfully confirmed by the rector . . . . iv 3 67
Let me live, or let me see my death! . . . . . . iv 3 345
Let death and honesty Go with your impositions . . . . iv 4 28
It was the death of the most virtuous gentlewoman that ever nature had praise for creating . . . . iv 5 9
Since I heard of the good lady's death . . . . . . iv 5 74
What a plague means my niece, to take the death of her brother thus? *T. Night* i 3 2
Why mournest thou?—Good fool, for my brother's death . . i 5 73
Doth he not mend?—Yes, and shall do till the pangs of death shake him i 5 81
Come away, come away, death, And in sad cypress let me be laid . ii 4 52
My part of death, no one so true Did share it . . . . ii 4 58
Let me boiled to death with melancholy . . . . . ii 5 3
That satisfaction can be none but by pangs of death and sepulchre . iii 4 262
This youth that you see here I snatch'd one half out of the jaws of death iii 4 394
Like to the Egyptian thief at point of death, Kill what I love . . v 1 121
To do you rest, a thousand deaths would die . . . . v 1 136
Three crabbed months had sour'd themselves to death . . *W. Tale* i 2 102
Shall not only be Death to thyself but to thy lewd-tongued wife . ii 3 172
A present death Had been more merciful . . . . . ii 3 184
Thou Shalt feel our justice, in whose easiest passage Look for no less than death . . . . iii 2 92
Look down And see what death is doing . . . . . iii 2 150
Though I with death and with Reward did threaten and encourage him iii 2 164
Nor is't directly laid to thee, the death Of the young prince . . iii 2 195
Upon them shall The causes of their death appear, unto Our shame perpetual . . . . iii 2 238
I do believe Hermione hath suffer'd death . . . . . iii 3 42
It should here be laid, Either for life or death, upon the earth Of its right father . . . . iii 3 45
'Tis a sickness denying thee any thing; a death to grant this . iv 2 3
Help me! pluck but off these rags; and then, death, death! . . iv 3 56
Not yet on summer's death, nor on the birth Of trembling winter . iv 4 80
I will devise a death as cruel for thee As thou art tender to't . iv 4 451
He shall be stoned; but that death is too soft for him . . . iv 4 807
All deaths are too few, the sharpest too easy . . . . iv 4 809
With flies blown to death . . . . iv 4 821
Threatens them With divers deaths in death . . . . . v 1 202
Wrecked the same instant of their master's death . . . . v 2 76
At the relation of the queen's death, with the manner how she came to't v 2 92
Ever since the death of Hermione, visited that removed house . v 2 115
Prepare To see the life as lively mock'd as ever Still sleep mock'd death v 3 20
Bequeath to death your numbness, for from him Dear life redeems you v 3 102
Took it on his death That this my mother's son was none of his *K. John* i 1 110
Madam, I'll follow you unto the death . . . . . . i 1 154
God shall forgive you Cœur-de-lion's death . . . . ii 1 12
Now doth Death line his dead chaps with steel . . . . ii 1 352
Till then, blows, blood and death! . . . . . . ii 1 360
As in a theatre, whence they gape and point At your industrious scenes and acts of death . . . . ii 1 376
No, not Death himself In mortal fury half so peremptory . . . ii 1 453
Here's a stay That shakes the rotten carcass of old Death Out of his rags! ii 1 456
A large mouth, indeed, That spits forth death and mountains, rocks and seas! . . . . ii 1 458
If thou grant my need, Which only lives but by the death of faith, That need must needs infer this principle, That faith would live again by death of need . . . . iii 1 212
Though that my death were adjunct to my act, By heaven, I would do it iii 3 57
He shall not offend your majesty.—Death.—My lord?—A grave . iii 3 65
I defy all counsel, all redress, But that which ends all counsel, true redress, Death, death . . . . iii 4 25
O amiable lovely death! Thou odoriferous stench! sound rottenness! iii 4 25
The foul corruption of a sweet child's death . . . . iv 2 81
We heard how near his death he was Before the child himself felt he was sick . . . . iv 2 87
No certain life achieved by others' death . . . . . iv 2 105
Young Arthur's death is common in their mouths . . . . iv 2 187
Cuts off his tale and talks of Arthur's death . . . . iv 2 202
Why urgest thou so oft young Arthur's death? . . . . iv 2 204
I faintly broke with thee of Arthur's death . . . . . iv 2 227
Civil tumult reigns Between my conscience and my cousin's death . iv 2 248
O death, made proud with pure and princely beauty! . . . iv 3 35
O, he is bold and blushes not at death . . . . . . iv 3 76

Death. If thou didst this deed of death, Art thou damn'd . *K. John* iv 3 118
To win renown Even in the jaws of danger and of death . v 2 116
And in his forehead sits A bare-ribb'd death . v 2 177
Wounded to death . v 4 9
Have I not hideous death within my view, Retaining but a quantity of life? . v 4 22
I do see the cruel pangs of death Right in thine eye . v 4 59
Death, having prey'd upon the outward parts, Leaves them invisible . v 7 15
'Tis strange that death should sing . v 7 20
This pale faint swan, Who chants a doleful hymn to his own death . v 7 22
He did plot the Duke of Gloucester's death . *Richard II.* i 1 100
For Gloucester's death, I slew him not . i 1 132
But my fair name, Despite of death that lives upon my grave, To dark dishonour's use thou shalt not have . i 1 168
Thou dost consent In some large measure to thy father's death . i 2 26
The best way is to venge my Gloucester's death . i 2 36
God's substitute, His deputy anointed in His sight, Hath caused his death . i 2 39
On pain of death, no person be so bold Or daring-hardy . i 3 42
Not sick, although I have to do with death . i 3 65
What is thy sentence then but speechless death? . i 3 172
And blindfold death not let me see my son . i 3 224
Thy word is current with him for my death . i 3 231
My death's sad tale may yet undeaf his ear . ii 1 16
Would the scandal vanish with my life, How happy then were my ensuing death! . ii 1 68
Though death be poor, it ends a mortal woe . ii 1 152
Not Gloucester's death, nor Hereford's banishment . ii 1 165
Even through the hollow eyes of death I spy life peering . ii 1 270
A parasite, a keeper back of death, Who gently would dissolve the bands of life . ii 2 70
These signs forerun the death or fall of kings . ii 4 15
Here in the view of men I will unfold some causes of your deaths . iii 1 7
This and much more, much more than twice all this, Condemns you to the death . iii 1 29
See them deliver'd over To execution and the hand of death . iii 1 30
More welcome is the stroke of death to me Than Bolingbroke to England iii 1 31
Whose double tongue may with a mortal touch Throw death upon thy sovereign's enemies . iii 2 22
The worst is death, and death will have his day . iii 2 103
Those whom you curse Have felt the worst of death's destroying wound iii 2 139
And nothing can we call our own but death And that small model of the barren earth . iii 2 152
Let us sit upon the ground And tell sad stories of the death of kings . iii 2 156
Within the hollow crown That rounds the mortal temples of a king Keeps Death his court . iii 2 162
And fight and die is death destroying death; Where fearing dying pays death servile breath . iii 2 184
O, I am press'd to death through want of speaking . iii 4 72
What thou dost know of noble Gloucester's death, Who wrought it with the king . iv 1 3
In that dead time when Gloucester's death was plotted . iv 1 10
How blest this land would be In this your cousin's death . iv 1 19
There is my gage, the manual seal of death . iv 1 25
Vauntingly thou spakest it, That thou wert cause of noble Gloucester's death . iv 1 37
I am sworn brother, sweet, To grim Necessity, and he and I Will keep a league till death . v 1 22
And hate turns one or both To worthy danger and deserved death . v 1 68
The traitor lives, the true man's put to death . v 3 73
How now! what means death in this rude assault? . v 5 106
His cheek look'd pale, And on my face he turn'd an eye of death 1 *Hen. IV.* i 3 143
For whose death we in the world's wide mouth Live scandalized . i 3 153
Even with the bloody payment of your deaths . i 3 186
Who bears hard His brother's death . i 3 271
It was the death of him . ii 1 14
I doubt not but to die a fair death for this, if I 'scape hanging . ii 2 14
Falstaff sweats to death, And lards the lean earth as he walks along ii 2 115
I know his death will be a march of twelve-score . ii 4 598
I will die a hundred thousand deaths Ere break the smallest parcel of this vow . iii 2 158
I am out of fear Of death or death's hand for this one-half year . iv 2 136
Thou owest God a death.—'Tis not due yet; I would be loath to pay him before his day . v 1 127
Like oxen at a stall, The better cherish'd, still the nearer death . v 2 15
If die, brave death, when princes die with us! . v 2 87
Thou shalt find a king that will revenge Lord Stafford's death . v 3 13
Whose deaths are yet unrevenged . v 3 44
They did me too much injury That ever said I hearken'd for your death v 4 52
I could prophesy, But that the earthy and cold hand of death Lies on my tongue . v 4 84
Death hath not struck so fat a deer to-day, Though many dearer . v 4 107
I'll take it upon my death, I gave him this wound in the thigh . v 4 154
Bear Worcester to the death and Vernon too . v 5 14
Stoop'd his anointed head as low as death . 2 *Hen. IV.* Ind. 32
The king is almost wounded to the death . i 1 14
Where hateful death put on his ugliest mask To fright our party . i 1 66
But Priam found the fire ere he his tongue, And I my Percy's death ere thou report'st it . i 1 75
If he be slain, say so; The tongue offends not that reports his death . i 1 97
His death, whose spirit lent a fire Even to the dullest peasant . i 1 112
I were better to be eaten to death with a rust . i 2 245
Led his powers to death And winking leap'd into destruction . i 3 32
Then death rock me asleep, abridge my doleful days! . ii 4 211
With the hurly, death itself awakes . iii 1 25
Death, as the Psalmist saith, is certain to all; all shall die . iii 2 41
Death is certain. Is old Double of your town living yet? . iii 2 45
By my troth, I care not; a man can die but once: we owe God a death iii 2 251
To end one doubt by death Revives two greater in the heirs of life . iv 1 199
Turning the word to sword and life to death . iv 2 10
The block of death, Treason's true bed and yielder up of breath . iv 2 122
If I do sweat, they are the drops of thy lovers, and they weep for thy death . iv 3 15
My grief Stretches itself beyond the hour of death . iv 4 57
Is he so hasty that he doth suppose My sleep my death . iv 5 62
And at my death Thou hast seal'd up my expectation . iv 5 103
And now my death Changes the mode . iv 5 199
Goodman death, goodman bones! . v 4 32
Till then, I banish thee, on pain of death . v 5 67
The grave doth gape, and doting death is near; Therefore exhale *Hen. V.* ii 1 65

Death. That he should, for a foreign purse, so sell His sovereign's life to death . *Hen. V.* ii 2 11
I repent my fault more than my death . ii 2 152
And from his coffers Received the golden earnest of our death . ii 2 169
Get you therefore hence, Poor miserable wretches, to your death . ii 2 178
Ay'll de gud service, or ay'll lig i' the grund for it; ay, or go to death iii 2 124
He hath stolen a pax, and hanged must a' be: A damned death! . iii 6 43
But Exeter hath given the doom of death For pax of little price . iii 6 46
They purpose not their death, when they purpose their services . iv 1 166
Where they feared the death, they have borne life away . iv 1 181
And dying so, death is to him advantage . iv 1 190
They have said their prayers, and they stay for death . iv 2 56
So espoused to death, with blood he seal'd A testament of noble-ending love . iv 6 26
Here was a royal fellowship of death! . iv 8 106
And be it death proclaimed through our host To boast of this . iv 8 119
Scourge the bad revolting stars That have consented unto Henry's death! 1 *Hen. VI.* i 1 5
Death's dishonourable victory We with our stately presence glorify . i 1 20
The loss of those great towns Will make him burst his lead and rise from death . i 1 64
Him I forgive my death that killeth me When he sees me go back one foot or fly . i 2 20
With Henry's death the English circle ends . i 2 136
Since Henry's death, I fear, there is conveyance . i 3 2
Henceforward, upon pain of death . i 3 79
And craved death Rather than I would be so vile-esteem'd . i 4 32
None durst come near for fear of sudden death . i 4 48
You all consented unto Salisbury's death . i 5 34
The treacherous manner of his mournful death . ii 2 16
I shall as famous be by this exploit As Scythian Tomyris by Cyrus' death ii 3 6
Shall send between the red rose and the white A thousand souls to death . ii 4 127
These grey locks, the pursuivants of death . ii 5 5
The arbitrator of despairs, Just death, kind umpire of men's miseries . ii 5 29
He used his lavish tongue And did upbraid me with my father's death . ii 5 48
If that my fading breath permit And death approach not ere my tale be done . ii 5 62
Thou seest that I no issue have And that my fainting words do warrant death . ii 5 95
Thy humble servant vows obedience And humble service till the point of death . iii 1 168
Break a lance, And run a tilt at death within a chair . iii 2 51
As looks the mother on her lowly babe When death doth close his tender dying eyes . iii 3 48
Whoso draws a sword, 'tis present death . iii 4 39
Not fearing death, nor shrinking for distress, But always resolute . iv 1 37
Henceforth we banish thee, on pain of death . iv 1 47
Thou ominous and fearful owl of death, Our nation's terror! . iv 2 15
On us thou canst not enter but by death . iv 2 18
Death doth front thee with apparent spoil And pale destruction meets thee in the face . iv 2 26
Vexation almost stops my breath, That sunder'd friends greet in the hour of death . iv 3 42
To beat assailing death from his weak legions . iv 4 16
Now thou art come unto a feast of death . iv 5 7
Fly, to revenge my death, if I be slain . iv 5 18
Upon my death the French can little boast; In yours they will . iv 5 24
If death be so apparent, then both fly . iv 5 44
I gave thee life and rescued thee from death . iv 6 5
Fly, to revenge my death when I am dead . iv 6 30
My death's revenge, thy youth, and England's fame . iv 6 39
Triumphant death, smear'd with captivity . iv 7 3
Thou antic death, which laugh'st us here to scorn . iv 7 18
O thou, whose wounds become hard-favour'd death, Speak to thy father! iv 7 23
Brave death by speaking, whether he will or no . iv 7 25
Had death been French, then death had died to-day . iv 7 28
Now it is my chance to find thee out, Must I behold thy timeless cruel death? . v 4 5
This argues what her kind of life hath been, Wicked and vile; and so her death concludes . v 4 16
Murder not then the fruit within my womb, Although ye hale me to a violent death . v 4 64
But darkness and the gloomy shade of death Environ you! . v 4 89
Now, by the death of Him that died for all . 2 *Hen. VI.* i 1 113
Bid him outlive, and die a violent death . i 4 34
Demanding of King Henry's life and death . i 4 175
Richard, his only son, Who after Edward the Third's death reign'd as king . ii 2 20
'Tis that they seek, and they in seeking that Shall find their deaths . ii 2 76
Such as by God's book are adjudged to death . ii 3 4
Welcome is banishment; welcome were my death . ii 3 14
I will take my death, I never meant him any ill . ii 3 90
For by his death we do perceive his guilt . ii 3 104
Nor stir at nothing till the axe of death Hang over thee . ii 4 49
My joy is death; Death, at whose name I oft have been afear'd, Because I wish'd this world's eternity . ii 4 88
Did he not, contrary to form of law, Devise strange deaths for small offences? . iii 1 59
If my death might make this island happy . . . , I would expend it . iii 1 148
That he should die is worthy policy; But yet we want a colour for his death . iii 1 236
We have but trivial argument, More than mistrust, that shows him worthy death . iii 1 242
'Tis York that hath more reason for his death . iii 1 245
So the poor chicken should be sure of death . iii 1 251
Be that thou hopest to be, or what thou art Resign to death . iii 1 334
In the shade of death I shall find joy; In life but double death . iii 2 54
Yet he most Christian-like laments his death . iii 2 58
This get I by his death: ay me, unhappy! . iii 2 70
Myself have calm'd their spleenful mutiny, Until they hear the order of his death . iii 2 129
View his breathless corpse, And comment then upon his sudden death . iii 2 133
With his soul fled all my worldly solace, For seeing him I see my life in death . iii 2 152
Who, in the conflict that it holds with death, Attracts the same for aidance 'gainst the enemy . iii 2 164
Why, Warwick, who should do the duke to death? . iii 2 179
Then you, belike, suspect these noblemen As guilty of Duke Humphrey's timeless death . iii 2 187

Death. Say, if thou darest, proud Lord of Warwickshire, That I am faulty in Duke Humphrey's death . . . *2 Hen. VI.* iii 2 202
Unless Lord Suffolk straight be done to death . . . iii 2 244
Torture him with grievous lingering death . . . iii 2 247
They say, in him they fear your highness' death . . . iii 2 249
That no man should disturb your rest In pain of your dislike or pain of death . . . iii 2 257
He shall not breathe infection in this air But three days longer, on the pain of death . . . iii 2 288
Cardinal Beaufort is at point of death . . . iii 2 369
From thee to die were torture more than death: O, let me stay! . . . iii 2 401
Even as a splitted bark, so sunder we: This way fall I to death . . . iii 2 412
If thou be'st death, I'll give thee England's treasure, Enough to purchase such another island, So thou wilt let me live, and feel no pain . . . iii 3 2
What a sign it is of evil life, Where death's approach is seen so terrible! iii 3 6
See, how the pangs of death do make him grin! . . . iii 3 24
O God, forgive him!—So bad a death argues a monstrous life . . . iii 3 30
What, doth death affright?—Thy name affrights me, in whose sound is death . . . iv 1 32
Thou that smiledst at good Duke Humphrey's death . . . iv 1 76
Come, Suffolk, I must waft thee to thy death . . . iv 1 116
Show what cruelty ye can, That this my death may never be forgot! . . . iv 1 133
How now, madam! Still lamenting and mourning for Suffolk's death? iv 4 22
Sir Humphrey Stafford and his brother's death Hath given them heart iv 4 34
All scholars, lawyers, courtiers, gentlemen, They call false caterpillars and intend their death . . . iv 4 37
Whom have I injured, that ye seek my death? . . . iv 7 107
Yield to mercy while 'tis offer'd you; Or let a rebel lead you to your deaths . . . iv 8 13
Expect your highness' doom, of life or death . . . iv 9 12
I'll yield myself to prison willingly, Or unto death, to do my country good . . . iv 9 43
Are these thy bears? we'll bait thy bears to death . . . v 1 148
I am resolved for death or dignity.—The first I warrant thee . . . v 1 194
Seek thee out some other chase, For I myself must hunt this deer to death . . . v 2 15
Somerset Hath made the wizard famous in his death . . . v 2 69
Three times to-day You have defended me from imminent death . . . v 3 19
Such a messenger As shall revenge his death before I stir . *3 Hen. VI.* i 1 100
Your right depends not on his life or death . . . i 2 11
O, let me pray before I take my death! To thee I pray; sweet Clifford, pity me! . . . i 3 35
They have demean'd themselves Like men born to renown by life or death . . . i 4 8
If thine eyes can water for his death, I give thee this to dry thy cheeks i 4 82
Hath thy fiery heart so parch'd thine entrails That not a tear can fall for Rutland's death? . . . i 4 88
You should not be king Till our King Henry had shook hands with death . . . i 4 102
The adage must be verified, That beggars mounted run their horse to death . . . i 4 127
And every drop cries vengeance for his death . . . i 4 148
Here's for my oath, here's for my father's death . . . i 4 175
I'll venge thy death, Or die renowned by attempting it . . . ii 1 87
Is by the stern Lord Clifford done to death . . . ii 1 103
Who thunders to his captives blood and death . . . ii 1 127
And in that quarrel use it to the death . . . ii 2 65
Smile, gentle heaven! or strike, ungentle death! . . . ii 3 6
And in the very pangs of death he cried, Like to a dismal clangor heard from far, 'Warwick, revenge! brother, revenge my death!' . . . ii 3 17
Never stand still, Till either death hath closed these eyes of mine Or fortune given me measure of revenge . . . ii 3 31
And here's the heart that triumphs in their death . . . ii 4 8
Single out some other chase; For I myself will hunt this wolf to death ii 4 13
O that my death would stay these ruthful deeds! . . . ii 5 95
How will my mother for a father's death Take on with me and ne'er be satisfied! . . . ii 5 103
Was ever son so rued a father's death?—Was ever father so bemoan'd his son? . . . ii 5 109
Away! for death doth hold us in pursuit . . . ii 5 127
I and ten thousand in this luckless realm Had left no mourning widows for our death . . . ii 6 19
A deadly groan, like life and death's departing . . . ii 6 43
Bring forth that fatal screech-owl to our house, That nothing sung but death to us and ours . . . ii 6 57
Now death shall stop his dismal threatening sound . . . ii 6 58
Dark cloudy death o'ershades his beams of life . . . ii 6 62
Such bitter taunts Which in the time of death he gave our father . . . ii 6 67
My love till death, my humble thanks, my prayers . . . iii 2 62
My elder brother, the Lord Aubrey Vere, Was done to death . . . iii 3 103
When nature brought him to the door of death . . . iii 3 105
My father came untimely to his death . . . iii 3 187
Or else you famish; that's a threefold death . . . v 4 32
Here sheathe thy sword, I'll pardon thee my death . . . v 5 70
What scene of death hath Roscius now to act? . . . v 6 10
Wives for their husbands, And orphans for their parents' timeless death v 6 42
See how my sword weeps for the poor king's death! . . . v 6 63
And then, to purge his fear, I'll be thy death . . . v 6 88
More direful hap betide that hated wretch, That makes us wretched by the death of thee! . . . *Richard III.* i 2 18
Let her be made As miserable by the death of him As I am made! . . . i 2 27
O God, which this blood madest, revenge his death! O earth, which this blood drink'st, revenge his death! . . . i 2 62
The causer of the timeless deaths Of these Plantagenets . . . i 2 117
Your beauty, which did haunt me in my sleep To undertake the death of all the world . . . i 2 123
Black night o'ershade thy day, and death thy life! . . . i 2 131
For now they kill me with a living death . . . i 2 153
Like a child, Told the sad story of my father's death . . . i 2 161
And humbly beg the death upon my knee . . . i 2 179
Though I wish thy death, I will not be the executioner . . . i 2 185
To both their deaths thou shalt be accessary . . . i 2 192
Wert thou not banished on pain of death? . . . i 3 167
I do find more pain in banishment Than death can yield me here by my abode . . . i 3 169
Henry's death, my lovely Edward's death, . . . Could all but answer? i 3 192
Long die thy happy days before thy death! . . . i 3 207
Witness my son, now in the shade of death . . . i 3 267
His venom tooth will rankle to the death . . . i 3 291

Death. Sin, death, and hell have set their marks on him . *Richard III.* i 3 293
What ugly sights of death within mine eyes! . . . i 4 23
Had you such leisure in the time of death To gaze upon the secrets of the deep? . . . i 4 34
Who pronounced The bitter sentence of poor Clarence' death? . . . i 4 191
Before I be convict by course of law, To threaten me with death is most unlawful . . . i 4 193
Who shall reward you better for my life Than Edward will for tidings of my death . . . i 4 237
'Tis death to me to be at enmity; I hate it, and desire all good men's love . . . ii 1 60
Have I a tongue to doom my brother's death? . . . ii 1 102
His fault was thought, And yet his punishment was cruel death . . . ii 1 105
Frozen almost to death, how he did lap me Even in his own garments . . . ii 1 115
Look'd pale when they did hear of Clarence' death . . . ii 1 136
I do lament the sickness of the king, As loath to lose him, not your father's death . . . ii 2 10
You cannot guess who caused your father's death . . . ii 2 19
I have bewept a worthy husband's death . . . ii 2 49
But now two mirrors of his princely semblance Are crack'd in pieces by malignant death . . . ii 2 52
But death hath snatch'd my husband from mine arms . . . ii 2 57
You wept not for our father's death; How can we aid you with our kindred tears? . . . ii 2 62
Doth this news hold of good King Edward's death? . . . ii 3 7
Welcome, destruction, death, and massacre! I see, as in a map, the end of all . . . ii 4 53
End thy damned spleen; Or let me die, to look on death no more! . . . ii 4 65
Death makes no conquest of this conqueror . . . iii 1 87
Too late he died that might have kept that title, Which by his death hath lost much majesty . . . iii 1 100
God knows I will not do it, to the death . . . iii 2 55
This day those enemies are put to death, And I in better state than e'er I was . . . iii 2 105
Richard the second here was hack'd to death . . . iii 3 12
Make haste; the hour of death is expiate . . . iii 3 23
Tell me what they deserve That do conspire my death with devilish plots . . . iii 4 62
I say, my lord, they have deserved death . . . iii 4 68
Against the form of law, Proceed thus rashly to the villain's death . . . iii 5 43
Now, fair befall you! he deserved his death . . . iii 5 47
Yet had not we determined he should die, Until your lordship came to see his death . . . iii 5 53
Who haply may Misconstrue us in him and wail his death . . . iii 5 61
Tell them how Edward put to death a citizen . . . iii 5 76
Get thee hence! Death and destruction dog thee at the heels . . . iv 1 40
If thou wilt outstrip death, go cross the seas . . . iv 1 42
O my accursed womb, the bed of death! . . . iv 1 54
As miserable by the life of thee As thou hast made me by my dear lord's death . . . iv 1 77
Know'st thou not any whom corrupting gold Would tempt unto a close exploit of death? . . . iv 2 35
Wept like two children in their deaths' sad stories . . . iv 3 8
Soon at after supper, And thou shalt tell the process of their death . . . iv 3 32
Prosperity begins to mellow And drop into the rotten mouth of death . . . iv 4 2
A hell-hound that doth hunt us all to death . . . iv 4 48
And the dire death of my two sons and brothers . . . iv 4 143
Shame serves thy life and doth thy death attend . . . iv 4 195
My babes were destined to a fairer death . . . iv 4 219
In such a desperate bay of death, Like a poor bark, of sails and tackling reft . . . iv 4 232
My father's death— Thy life hath that dishonour'd . . . iv 4 375
Death, desolation, ruin and decay . . . iv 4 409
Out on you, owls! nothing but songs of death? . . . iv 4 509
I, that was wash'd to death with fulsome wine, Poor Clarence, by thy guile betray'd to death! . . . v 3 133
Let us be lead within thy bosom, Richard, And weigh thee down to ruin, shame, and death! . . . v 3 153
Dream on, dream on, of bloody deeds and death . . . v 3 171
And all on foot he fights, Seeking for Richmond in the throat of death v 4 5
Death! my lord, Their clothes are after such a pagan cut too *Hen. VIII.* i 3 13
I do not think he fears death.—Sure, he does not: He never was so womanish . . . ii 1 37
The law I bear no malice for my death . . . ii 1 62
Nothing but death Shall e'er divorce my dignities . . . iii 1 141
He brings his physic After his patient's death . . . iii 2 41
Which ever has and ever shall be growing, Till death, that winter, kill it . . . iii 2 179
Sick to death! My legs, like loaden branches, bow to the earth . . . iv 2 1
After my death I wish no other herald, No other speaker of my living actions . . . iv 2 69
Tell him, in death I bless'd him, For so I will . . . iv 2 163
Her sufferance made Almost each pang a death . . . v 1 69
Nor none so noble Whose life were ill bestow'd or death unfamed *Troi. and Cres.* ii 2 159
Let thy blood be thy direction till thy death! . . . ii 3 34
A good quarrel to draw emulous factions and bleed to death upon . . . ii 3 80
Death, I fear me, Swooning destruction, or some joy too fine . . . iii 2 23
Press it to death: away! . . . iii 2 218
She hath not given so many good words breath As for her Greeks and Trojans suffer'd death . . . iv 1 74
I knew thou wouldst be his death . . . iv 2 91
'Twill be his death; 'twill be his bane; he cannot bear it . . . iv 2 98
Time, force, and death, Do to this body what extremes you can . . . iv 2 108
I will throw my glove to Death himself, That there's no maculation in thy heart . . . iv 4 65
And bear hence A great addition earned in thy death . . . iv 5 141
To-morrow do I meet thee, fell as death; To-night all friends . . . iv 5 269
I'll take good breath: Rest, sword; thou hast thy fill of blood and death . . . v 8 4
If in his death the gods have us befriended, Great Troy is ours . . . v 9 9
I do not speak of flight, of fear, of death . . . v 10 12
Condemning some to death, and some to exile . . . *Coriolanus* i 6 35
If any think brave death outweighs bad life . . . i 6 71
Well might they fester 'gainst ingratitude, And tent themselves with death . . . i 9 31
Death, that dark spirit, in's nervy arm doth lie . . . ii 1 177
And wish To jump a body with a dangerous physic That's sure of death without it . . . iii 1 155
This deserves death.—Or let us stand to our authority, Or let us lose it iii 1 207

Death. Marcius is worthy Of present death.—Therefore lay hold of him *Coriolanus* iii 1 212
Being angry, does forget that ever He heard the name of death iii 1 260
To eject him hence Were but one danger, and to keep him here Our certain death iii 1 289
What has he done to Rome that's worthy death? iii 1 298
Present me Death on the wheel or at wild horses' heels iii 2 2
For I mock at death With as big heart as thou iii 2 127
Be it either For death, for fine, or banishment iii 3 15
If I say fine, cry 'Fine;' if death, cry 'Death' iii 3 16
Within thine eyes sat twenty thousand deaths, In thy hands clutch'd as many millions iii 3 70
Even this, So criminal and in such capital kind, Deserves the extremest death iii 3 82
Let them pronounce the steep Tarpeian death iii 3 88
If I had fear'd death, of all the men i' the world I would have 'voided thee iv 5 87
Of hanging, or of some death more long in spectatorship, and crueller v 2 71
They'll give him death by inches v 4 42
Sure as death I swore I would not part a bachelor from the priest *T. Andron.* i 1 487
I tell you, lords, you do but plot your deaths By this device ii 1 78
A thousand deaths Would I propose to achieve her whom I love ii 1 79
Vengeance is in my heart, death in my hand ii 3 38
And leave me to this miserable death ii 3 108
'Tis present death I beg; and one thing more ii 3 173
Look down into this den, And see a fearful sight of blood and death ii 3 216
Were there worse end than death, That end upon them should be executed ii 3 302
Unbind my sons, reverse the doom of death iii 1 24
A stone is silent, and offendeth not, And tribunes with their tongues doom men to death iii 1 47
To rescue my two brothers from their death iii 1 49
This way to death my wretched sons are gone iii 1 98
Thy husband he is dead; and for his death Thy brothers are condemn'd iii 1 108
Let it serve To ransom my two nephews from their death iii 1 173
Let me redeem my brothers both from death iii 1 181
Woe is me to think upon thy woes More than remembrance of my father's death iii 1 241
But sorrow flouted at is double death iii 1 246
That ever death should let life bear his name, Where life hath no more interest but to breathe! iii 1 249
A deed of death done on the innocent Becomes not Titus' brother iii 2 56
The emperor, in his rage, will doom her death iv 2 114
And this shall all be buried by my death v 1 67
Wherein I did not some notorious ill, As kill a man, or else devise his death v 1 128
He must not die So sweet a death as hanging presently v 1 146
Confer with me of murder and of death v 2 34
I pray thee, do on them some violent death; They have been violent to me v 2 108
For that vile fault Two of her brothers were condemn'd to death v 2 174
There's meed for meed, death for a deadly deed! v 3 66
Some direful slaughtering death, As punishment for his most wicked life v 3 144
Do with their death bury their parents' strife *Rom. and Jul.* Prol. 8
Turn thee, Benvolio, look upon thy death i 1 74
Once more, on pain of death, all men depart i 1 110
And expire the term Of a despised life closed in my breast By some vile forfeit of untimely death i 4 111
And the place death, considering who thou art, If any of my kinsmen find thee ii 2 64
My life were better ended by their hate, Than death prorogued, wanting of thy love ii 2 78
Full soon the canker death eats up that plant ii 3 30
Sending me about, To catch my death with jaunting up and down! ii 5 53
Then love-devouring death do what he dare; It is enough I may but call her mine ii 6 7
'Zounds, a dog, a rat, a mouse, a cat, to scratch a man to death! iii 1 105
The prince will doom thee death, If thou art taken iii 1 139
With one hand beats Cold death aside, and with the other sends It back iii 1 167
Some word there was, worser than Tybalt's death, That murder'd me iii 2 108
Tybalt's death Was woe enough, if it had ended there iii 2 114
But with a rearward following Tybalt's death, 'Romeo is banished' iii 2 121
'Banished!' There is no end, no limit, measure, bound, In that word's death iii 2 126
Not body's death, but body's banishment iii 3 11
Say 'death;' For exile hath more terror in his look, Much more than death iii 3 12
World's exile is death: then banished, Is death mis-term'd iii 3 20
Calling death banishment, Thou cutt'st my head off with a golden axe iii 3 21
O deadly sin! O rude unthankfulness! Thy fault our law calls death iii 3 25
Hath rush'd aside the law, And turn'd that black word death to banishment iii 3 27
I am banished. And say'st thou yet that exile is not death? iii 3 43
Hadst thou no poison mix'd, no sharp-ground knife, No sudden mean of death? iii 3 45
Well, death's the end of all iii 3 92
The law that threaten'd death becomes thy friend And turns it to exile iii 3 139
Let me be ta'en, let me be put to death; I am content, so thou wilt have it so iii 5 17
I have more care to stay than will to go: Come, death, and welcome! iii 5 24
Evermore weeping for your cousin's death? iii 5 70
Thou weep'st not so much for his death, As that the villain lives which slaughter'd him iii 5 79
Would none but I might venge my cousin's death! iii 5 87
Immoderately she weeps for Tybalt's death iv 1 6
Then is it likely thou wilt undertake A thing like death to chide away this shame, That copest with death himself to 'scape from it iv 1 74
Thy eyes' windows fall, Like death, when he shuts up the day of life iv 1 101
Shall, stiff and stark and cold, appear like death iv 1 103
And in this borrow'd likeness of shrunk death Thou shalt continue two and forty hours iv 1 104
The horrible conceit of death and night iv 3 37
Death lies on her like an untimely frost Upon the sweetest flower of all the field iv 5 28
Death, that hath ta'en her hence to make me wail, Ties up my tongue iv 5 31
O son! the night before thy wedding-day Hath Death lain with thy wife iv 5 36
Death is my son-in-law, Death is my heir; My daughter he hath wedded iv 5 38

Death. I will die, And leave him all; life, living, all is Death's *R. and J.* iv 5 40
One poor and loving child, But one thing to rejoice and solace in, And cruel death hath catch'd it from my sight! iv 5 48
Most detestable death, by thee beguiled, By cruel cruel thee quite overthrown! iv 5 56
O love! O life! not life, but love in death! iv 5 58
Your part in her you could not keep from death, But heaven keeps his part in eternal life iv 5 69
An if a man did need a poison now, Whose sale is present death in Mantua, Here lives a caitiff wretch would sell it him v 1 51
But Mantua's law Is death to any he that utters them v 1 67
Why I descend into this bed of death, Is partly to behold my lady's face v 3 28
Thou detestable maw, thou womb of death! v 3 45
Can vengeance be pursued further than death? v 3 55
Death, lie thou there, by a dead man interr'd v 3 87
How oft when men are at the point of death Have they been merry! v 3 88
A lightning before death: O, how may I Call this a lightning? v 3 90
Death, that hath suck'd the honey of thy breath, Hath had no power yet upon thy beauty v 3 92
Shall I believe That unsubstantial death is amorous? v 3 103
Seal with a righteous kiss A dateless bargain to engrossing death! v 3 115
And fearfully did menace me with death, If I did stay to look on his intents v 3 133
Lady, come from that nest Of death, contagion, and unnatural sleep v 3 152
This sight of death is as a bell, That warns my old age to a sepulchre v 3 206
And then will I be general of your woes, And lead you even to death v 3 220
Whose untimely death Banish'd the new-made bridegroom from this city v 3 234
Which so took effect As I intended, for it wrought on her The form of death v 3 246
I brought my master news of Juliet's death v 3 272
And threaten'd me with death, going in the vault, If I departed not v 3 276
This letter doth make good the friar's words, Their course of love, the tidings of her death v 3 287
A deed thou'lt die for.—Right, if doing nothing be death by the law *T. of Athens* i 1 195
Thou wast whelped a dog, and thou shalt famish a dog's death ii 2 91
Lately Buried his father; by whose death he's stepp'd Into a great estate ii 2 232
And, when he's sick to death, let not that part of nature Which my lord paid for, be of any power To expel sickness, but prolong his hour! iii 1 64
Seeing his reputation touch'd to death, He did oppose his foe iii 5 19
Make thine epitaph, That death in me at others' lives may laugh iv 3 381
Graves only be men's works and death their gain! Sun, hide thy beams! v 1 225
By decimation, and a tithed death—If thy revenges hunger for that food v 4 31
Set honour in one eye and death i' the other, And I will look on both indifferently *J. Cæsar* i 2 86
The gods so speed me as I love The name of honour more than I fear death i 2 89
It must be by his death ii 1 10
Like wrath in death and envy afterwards ii 1 164
The heavens themselves blaze forth the death of princes ii 2 31
Cowards die many times before their deaths; The valiant never taste of death but once ii 2 32
Seeing that death, a necessary end, Will come when it will come ii 2 36
Will crowd a feeble man almost to death ii 4 36
He that cuts off twenty years of life Cuts off so many years of fearing death.—Grant that, and then is death a benefit iii 1 102
So are we Cæsar's friends, that have abridged His time of fearing death iii 1 105
And be resolved How Cæsar hath deserved to lie in death iii 1 132
No place will please me so, no mean of death, As here by Cæsar iii 1 161
Beg not your death of us. Though now we must appear bloody and cruel iii 1 164
If then thy spirit look upon us now, Shall it not grieve thee dearer than thy death? iii 1 196
I will myself into the pulpit first, And show the reason of our Cæsar's death iii 1 237
And public reasons shall be rendered Of Cæsar's death iii 2 8
Joy for his fortune; honour for his valour; and death for his ambition iii 2 30
The question of his death is enrolled in the Capitol iii 2 41
Nor his offences enforced, for which he suffered death iii 2 44
Though he had no hand in his death, shall receive the benefit of his dying iii 2 46
When it shall please my country to need my death iii 2 52
Most noble Cæsar! We'll revenge his death iii 2 248
You shall not come to them.—Nothing but death shall stay me iv 3 128
With her death That tidings came iv 3 154
Have put to death an hundred senators iv 3 175
Even by the rule of that philosophy By which I did blame Cato for the death Which he did give himself v 1 102
Kill Brutus, and be honour'd in his death v 4 14
Brutus only overcame himself, And no man else hath honour by his death v 5 57
Pronounce his present death, And with his former title greet Macbeth *Macbeth* i 2 64
By Sinel's death I know I am thane of Glamis i 3 71
Nothing afeard of what thyself didst make, Strange images of death i 3 97
He died As one that had been studied in his death i 4 9
When in swinish sleep Their drenched natures lie as in a death i 7 68
As we shall make our griefs and clamour roar Upon his death i 7 79
That death and nature do contend about them, Whether they live or die ii 2 7
The death of each day's life, sore labour's bath, Balm of hurt minds ii 2 38
Strange screams of death, And prophesying with accents terrible ii 3 61
Shake off this downy sleep, death's counterfeit, And look on death itself! ii 3 81
Who wear our health but sickly in his life, Which in his death were perfect iii 1 108
With twenty trenched gashes on his head; The least a death to nature iii 4 28
To trade and traffic with Macbeth In riddles and affairs of death iii 5 5
He shall spurn fate, scorn death, and bear His hopes 'bove wisdom, grace and fear iii 5 30
To relate the manner, Were, on the quarry of these murder'd deer, To add the death of you iv 3 207
Death of thy soul! those linen cheeks of thine Are counsellors to fear v 3 16
I will not be afraid of death and bane, Till Birnam forest come to Dunsinane v 3 59

Death. And all our yesterdays have lighted fools The way to dusty death *Macbeth* v 5 23
Those clamorous harbingers of blood and death v 6 10
Had I as many sons as I have hairs, I would not wish them to a fairer death v 8 49
For which, they say, you spirits oft walk in death *Hamlet* i 1 138
Though yet of Hamlet our dear brother's death The memory be green i 2 1
Thinking by our late dear brother's death Our state to be disjoint i 2 19
Whose common theme Is death of fathers i 2 104
Why thy canonized bones, hearsed in death, Have burst their cerements i 4 47
The whole ear of Denmark Is by a forged process of my death Rankly abused i 5 37
What it should be, More than his father's death, that thus hath put him So much from the understanding of himself, I cannot dream of ii 2 8
It is no other but the main; His father's death, and our o'erhasty marriage ii 2 57
The bold winds speechless, and the orb below As hush as death ii 2 508
After your death you were better have a bad epitaph than their ill report while you live ii 2 549
Ay, there's the rub; For in that sleep of death what dreams may come iii 1 66
The dread of something after death, The undiscover'd country iii 1 78
One scene of it comes near the circumstance Which I have told thee of my father's death iii 2 82
O wretched state! O bosom black as death! O limed soul! iii 3 67
I will bestow him, and will answer well The death I gave him iii 4 177
Imports at full, By letters congruing to that effect, The present death of Hamlet iv 3 67
To all that fortune, death and danger dare, Even for an egg-shell iv 4 52
To my shame, I see The imminent death of twenty thousand men iv 4 60
It springs All from her father's death iv 5 77
Thick and unwholesome in their thoughts and whispers, For good Polonius' death iv 5 83
Infect his ear With pestilent speeches of his father's death iv 5 91
This, Like to a murdering-piece, in many places Gives me superfluous death iv 5 96
If you desire to know the certainty Of your dear father's death iv 5 141
I am guiltless of your father's death, And am most sensibly in grief for it iv 5 149
His means of death, his obscure funeral iv 5 213
Repair thou to me with as much speed as thou wouldst fly death iv 6 24
And for his death no wind of blame shall breathe iv 7 67
Can save the thing from death That is but scratch'd withal iv 7 146
That, if I gall him slightly, It may be death iv 7 149
Pull'd the poor wretch from her melodious lay To muddy death iv 7 184
He that is not guilty of his own death shortens not his own life v 1 22
Her death was doubtful v 1 250
He should the bearers put to sudden death, Not shriving-time allow'd v 2 46
Mine and my father's death come not upon thee, Nor thine on me! v 2 341
This fell sergeant, death, Is strict in his arrest v 2 347
O proud death, What feast is toward in thine eternal cell? v 2 375
He never gave commandment for their death v 2 385
Of deaths put on by cunning and forced cause v 2 394
While we Unburthen'd crawl toward death *Lear* i 1 42
If, on the tenth day following, Thy banish'd trunk be found in our dominions, The moment is thy death i 1 181
Death, dearth, dissolutions of ancient amities i 2 158
Life and death! I am ashamed i 4 318
He that conceals him, death ii 1 65
The profits of my death Were very pregnant and potential spurs ii 1 77
'Tis they have put him on the old man's death ii 1 101
Vengeance! plague! death! confusion! ii 4 96
Death on my state! wherefore Should he sit here? ii 4 113
Or at their chamber-door I'll beat the drum Till it cry sleep to death ii 4 120
Death, traitor! nothing could have subdued nature To such a lowness but his unkind daughters iii 4 72
Canst thou blame him? His daughters seek his death iii 4 168
Your brother's evil disposition made him seek his death iii 5 8
I prithee, take him in thy arms; I have o'erheard a plot of death upon him iii 6 96
If she live long, And in the end meet the old course of death, Women will all turn monsters iii 7 101
Conceive, and fare thee well.—Yours in the ranks of death iv 2 25
Is wretchedness deprived that benefit, To end itself by death? iv 6 62
O, untimely death! iv 6 256
For him 'tis well That of thy death and business I can tell iv 6 285
That we the pain of death would hourly die Rather than die at once! v 3 185
Then have we a prescription to die when death is our physician *Othello* i 3 311
Therefore my hopes, not surfeited to death, Stand in bold cure ii 1 50
May the winds blow till they have waken'd death! ii 1 188
What is the matter here?—'Zounds, I bleed still; I am hurt to the death ii 3 164
Tis destiny unshunnable, like death iii 3 275
Death and damnation! O! iii 3 396
To furnish me with some swift means of death For the fair devil iii 3 477
I will show you such a necessity in his death that you shall think yourself bound to put it on him iv 2 247
Nobody come? then shall I bleed to death v 1 45
That death's unnatural that kills for loving v 2 42
'Tis like she comes to speak of Cassio's death v 2 92
A guiltless death I die.—O, who hath done this deed?—Nobody; I myself v 2 122
Did you and he consent in Cassio's death? v 2 297
Imports The death of Cassio to be undertook By Roderigo v 2 311
Who tells me true, though in his tale lie death, I hear him as he flatter'd *Ant. and Cleo.* i 2 102
If they suffer our departure, death's the word i 2 139
I do think there is mettle in death, which commits some loving act upon her i 2 147
The death of Fulvia, with more urgent touches, Do strongly speak to us i 2 187
And that which most with you should safe my going, Is Fulvia's death i 3 56
Now I see, I see, In Fulvia's death, how mine received shall be i 3 65
Now Pleased fortune does of Marcus Crassus' death Make me revenger iii 1 2
So the poor third is up, till death enlarge his confine iii 5 13
Like the token'd pestilence, Where death is sure iii 10 10
Her head's declined, and death will seize her, but Your comfort makes the rescue iii 11 47
The next time I do fight, I'll make death love me iii 13 193
But, like a master Married to your good service, stay till death iv 2 31
Where rather I'll expect victorious life Than death and honour iv 2 44
The hand of death hath raught him iv 9 30

Death. For one death Might have prevented many *Ant. and Cleo.* iv 12 41
Bring me how he takes my death iv 13 10
She hath betray'd me and shall die the death iv 14 26
Death of one person can be paid but once, And that she has discharged iv 14 27
She which by her death our Cæsar tells 'I am conqueror of myself' iv 14 61
There then: thus I do escape the sorrow Of Antony's death iv 14 95
I will be A bridegroom in my death, and run into't As to a lover's bed iv 14 100
Thy death and fortunes bid thy followers fly iv 14 111
Draw thy sword, and give me Sufficing strokes for death iv 14 117
How now! is he dead?—His death's upon him, but not dead iv 15 7
I am dying, Egypt, dying; only I here importune death awhile iv 15 19
Is it sin To rush into the secret house of death, Ere death dare come to us? iv 15 81
Let's do it after the high Roman fashion, And make death proud to take us iv 15 88
The death of Antony Is not a single doom v 1 17
Relieved, but not betray'd.—What, of death too, That rids our dogs of languish? v 2 41
Let the world see His nobleness well acted, which your death Will never let come forth v 2 45
Where art thou, death? Come hither, come! come, come, and take a queen! v 2 46
The stroke of death is as a lover's pinch, Which hurts, and is desired v 2 298
Now boast thee, death, in thy possession lies A lass unparallel'd v 2 318
The manner of their deaths? I do not see them bleed v 2 340
Give me but this I have, And sear up my embracements from a next With bonds of death! *Cymbeline* i 1 117
There cannot be a pinch in death More sharp than this is i 1 130
Most poisonous compounds, Which are the movers of a languishing death i 5 9
There is No danger in what show of death it makes, More than the locking-up the spirits a time i 5 40
It is a thing I made, which hath the king Five times redeem'd from death i 5 63
O sleep, thou ape of death, lie dull upon her! ii 2 31
Though peril to my modesty, not death on't, I would adventure iii 4 155
A lady So tender of rebukes that words are strokes And strokes death to her iii 5 41
Gone she is To death or to dishonour; and my end Can make good use of either iii 5 63
Speak, or thy silence on the instant is Thy condemnation and thy death iii 5 98
At fools I laugh, not fear them.—Die the death iv 2 96
What Cloten's being here to us portends, Or what his death will bring us iv 2 183
What does he mean? since death of my dear'st mother It did not speak before iv 2 190
Newness Of Cloten's death . . . may drive us to a render iv 4 10
Whose answer would be death Drawn on with torture iv 4 13
So I'll die For thee, O Imogen, even for whom my life Is every breath a death v 1 27
Could not find death where I did hear him groan, Nor feel him where he struck v 3 69
For me, my ransom's death; On either side I come to spend my breath v 3 80
He had rather Groan so in perpetuity than be cured By the sure physician, death v 4 7
Come, sir, are you ready for death?—Over-roasted rather; ready long ago. v 4 153
Your death has eyes in's head then; I have not seen him so pictured v 4 184
By medicine life may be prolong'd, yet death Will seize the doctor too v 5 29
There's other work in hand: I see a thing Bitter to me as death v 5 104
Is not this boy revived from death? v 5 120
If this be so, the gods do mean to strike me To death with mortal joy v 5 235
Swore, If I discover'd not which way she was gone, It was my instant death v 5 278
Think death no hazard in this enterprise *Pericles* i 1 5
Death remember'd should be like a mirror, Who tells us life's but breath i 1 45
Thus ready for the way of life or death, I wait the sharpest blow i 1 54
Against the face of death, I sought the purchase of a glorious beauty i 2 71
The shipman's toil, With whom each minute threatens life or death i 3 25
Left me breath Nothing to think on but ensuing death ii 1 7
Here to have death in peace is all he'll crave ii 1 11
It hath been a shield 'Twixt me and death ii 1 133
Whose death indeed's the strongest in our censure ii 4 34
The seaman's whistle Is as a whisper in the ears of death iii 1 9
Tie my treasure up in silken bags, To please the fool and death iii 2 42
Death may usurp on nature many hours, And yet the fire of life kindle again iii 2 82
Here she comes weeping for her only mistress' death iv 1 12
How have I offended, Wherein my death might yield her any profit? iv 1 81
She was of Tyrus the king's daughter, On whom foul death hath made this slaughter iv 4 37
Did you not name a tempest, A birth, and death? v 3 34

Death's black veil. These eyes, that now are dimm'd with death's black veil *3 Hen. VI.* v 2 16

Death's counterfeit. Shake off this downy sleep, death's counterfeit *Macbeth* ii 3 81

Death's dart. Thus smiling, as some fly had tickled slumber, Not as death's dart, being laugh'd at *Cymbeline* iv 2 211

Death's face. A Death's face in a ring *L. L. Lost* v 2 616

Death's fool. Thou art death's fool *Meas. for Meas.* iii 1 11

Death's hand. I am out of fear Of death or death's hand for this one-half year *1 Hen. IV.* iv 1 136

Death's-head. I had rather be married to a death's-head with a bone in his mouth *Mer. of Venice* i 2 55
I make as good use of it as many a man doth of a Death's-head *1 Hen. IV.* iii 3 34
Do not speak like a death's-head; do not bid me remember mine end *2 Hen. IV.* ii 4 255

Death's hour. There is no hour so fit As Cæsar's death's hour *J. Cæsar* iii 1 154

Death's instrument. Thy own hand yields thy death's instrument *Richard II.* v 5 107

Death's net. For going on death's net, whom none resist *Pericles* i 1 40

Death's pale flag is not advanced there *Rom. and Jul.* v 3 96

Death's stamp. His sword, death's stamp, Where it did mark, it took *Coriolanus* ii 2 111

Death-bed. Her grandsire upon his death's-bed—Got deliver to a joyful resurrections! *Mer. Wives* i 1 53
My eye shall be the stream And watery death-bed for him *Mer. of Venice* iii 2 47
Upon his death-bed he by will bequeath'd His lands to me *K. John* i 1 109
Thy death-bed is no lesser than thy land Wherein thou liest in reputation sick *Richard II.* ii 1 95

Death-bed. Think I am dead and that even here thou takest, As from my death-bed, thy last living leave . . . *Richard II.* v 1 39
Wilt thou on thy death-bed play the ruffian? . . . 2 *Hen. VI.* v 1 164
Now old desire doth in his death-bed lie . . . *Rom. and Jul.* ii Prol. 1
No, no, he is dead: Go to thy death-bed: He never will come again *Hamlet* iv 5 193
Sweet soul, take heed, Take heed of perjury; thou art on thy death-bed *Othello* v 2 51
Death-counterfeiting sleep . . . *M. N. Dream* iii 2 364
Death-darting. The death-darting eye of cockatrice . *Rom. and Jul.* iii 2 47
Deathful. Though parting be a fretful corrosive, It is applied to a deathful wound . . . 2 *Hen. VI.* iii 2 404
Death-like. For death-like dragons here affright thee hard *Pericles* i 1 29
Death-marked. The fearful passage of their death-mark'd love *Rom. and Jul.* Prol. 9
Death-practised. The death-practised duke . . . *Lear* iv 6 284
Deathsman. And I should rob the deathsman of his fee . 2 *Hen. VI.* iii 2 217
He's dead; I am only sorry He had no other death's-man . *Lear* iv 6 263
Deathsmen. As, deathsmen, you have rid this sweet young prince! 3 *Hen. VI.* v 5 67
Death-token. He is so plaguy proud that the death-tokens of it Cry 'No recovery' . . . *Troi. and Cres.* ii 3 187
Debase. We do debase ourselves, cousin, do we not? *Richard II.* iii 3 127
You debase your princely knee To make the base earth proud with kissing it . . . iii 3 190
And will she yet debase her eyes on me? . . *Richard III.* i 2 247
Thus we debase The nature of our seats . . *Coriolanus* iii 1 135
Debate. I will debate this matter at more leisure . *Com. of Errors* iv 1 100
Lost in the world's debate . . . *L. L. Lost* v 1 174
This same progeny of evils comes From our debate . *M. N. Dream* ii 1 116
Nature and sickness Debate it at their leisure . . *All's Well* i 2 75
If God doth give successful end To this debate . 2 *Hen. IV.* iv 4 2
Hear him debate of commonwealth affairs . . *Hen. V.* i 1 41
I and my bosom must debate a while, And then I would no other company . . . iv 1 31
We'll debate By what safe means the crown may be recover'd 3 *Hen. VI.* iv 7 51
They had gather'd a wise council to them Of every realm, that did debate this business . . . *Hen. VIII.* ii 4 52
Two thousand souls and twenty thousand ducats Will not debate the question of this straw . . . *Hamlet* iv 4 26
My state Stands on me to defend, not to debate . *Lear* v 1 69
When we debate Our trivial difference loud, we do commit Murder in healing wounds . . . *Ant. and Cleo.* ii 2 20
She is not worth our debate . . . *Cymbeline* i 4 173
Debated. Who accused her Upon the error that you heard debated *Much Ado* v 4 3
Your several suits Have been consider'd and debated on . 1 *Hen. VI.* v 1 35
These quarrels must be quietly debated . . *T. Andron.* v 3 20
Debatement. After much debatement, My sisterly remorse confutes mine honour . . . *Meas. for Meas.* v 1 99
Without debatement further, more or less . . *Hamlet* v 2 45
Debating. In debating which was best, we shall part with neither *Com. of Errors* iii 1 67
I am debating of my present store . . *Mer. of Venice* i 3 54
Early and late, debating to and fro . . . 2 *Hen. VI.* i 1 91
What talk you of debating? . . . 3 *Hen. VI.* i 7 53
Debating A marriage 'twixt the Duke of Orleans and Our daughter Mary *Hen. VIII.* ii 4 173
Debile. In a most weak and debile minister, great power *All's Well* ii 3 39
For that I have not wash'd My nose that bled, or foil'd some debile wretch *Coriolanus* i 9 48
Debility. Did not with unbashful forehead woo The means of weakness and debility . . . *As Y. Like It* ii 3 51
Debitor. Must be be-lee'd and calm'd By debitor and creditor . *Othello* i 1 31
You have no true debitor and creditor but it . *Cymbeline* v 4 171
Debonair. As free, as debonair, unarm'd, As bending angels *Troi. and Cres.* i 3 235
Deborah. Thou art an Amazon And fightest with the sword of Deborah 1 *Hen. VI.* i 2 105
Deboshed. Thou deboshed fish, thou! . . *Tempest* iii 2 29
Debosh'd on every tomb, on every grave A lying trophy . *All's Well* ii 3 145
With all the spots o' the world tax'd and debosh'd . . v 3 206
Men so disorder'd, so debosh'd and bold . . *Lear* i 4 263
Debt. He that dies pays all debts . . . *Tempest* iii 2 140
Go say I sent thee thither. For debt, Pompey? or how? . *M. for M.* iii 2 66
The very debt of your calling . . . iii 2 264
This I wonder at, That he, unknown to me, should be in debt *Com. of Err.* iv 2 48
As if Time were in debt! how fondly dost thou reason! . . iv 2 57
If Time be in debt and theft, and a sergeant in the way . . iv 2 61
If I let him go, The debt he owes will be required of me. . iv 4 121
Knowing how the debt grows, I will pay it . . iv 4 124
As to speak dout, fine, when he should say doubt; det, when he should pronounce debt,—d, e, b, t, not d, e, t . *L. L. Lost* v 1 23
Consciences, that will not die in debt . . . v 2 333
For debt that bankrupt sleep doth sorrow owe . *M. N. Dream* iii 2 85
My chief care Is to come fairly off from the great debts *Mer. of Venice* i 1 128
To unburden all my plots and purposes How to get clear of all the debts I owe . . . i 1 134
You shall have gold To pay the petty debt twenty times over . iii 2 309
All debts are cleared between you and I, if I might but see you at my death . . . iii 2 321
Pray God, Bassanio come To see me pay his debt! . . iii 3 36
Repent but you that you shall lose your friend, And he repents not that he pays your debt . . . iv 1 279
Having come to Padua To gather in some debts . . *T. of Shrew* iv 4 25
Too little payment for so great a debt . . . v 2 154
To pay this debt of love but to a brother . . *T. Night* i 1 34
And yet we should, for perpetuity, Go hence in debt . *W. Tale* i 2 6
My sovereign liege was in my debt Upon remainder of a dear account *Richard II.* i 1 129
This loose behaviour I throw off And pay the debt I never promised 1 *Hen. IV.* i 2 233
Who studies day and night To answer all the debt he owes to you . i 3 185
Bear ourselves as even as we can, The king will always think him in our debt . . . i 3 286
Being no more in debt to years than thou . . . ii 2 103
Pay her the debt you owe her, and unpay the villany you have done her 2 *Hen. IV.* ii 1 129
That were but light payment, to dance out of your debt . . Epil. 21
Some [crying] upon the debts they owe, some upon their children rawly left . . . *Hen. V.* iv 1 146

Debt. Let us our lives, our souls, Our debts, our careful wives, Our children and our sins lay on the king! . . . *Hen. V.* iv 1 248
'Tis call'd ungrateful, With dull unwillingness to repay a debt *Rich. III.* ii 2 92
Much more to be thus opposite with heaven, For it requires the royal debt it lent you . . . ii 2 95
I am in your debt for your last exercise; Come the next Sabbath . iii 2 113
Edward for Edward pays a dying debt . . . iv 4 21
What nearer debt in all humanity Than wife is to the husband? *Troi. and Cres.* ii 2 175
Words pay no debts, give her deeds . . . iii 2 58
I'll pay that doctrine, or else die in debt . . *Rom. and Jul.* i 1 244
Is she a Capulet? O dear account! my life is my foe's debt . . i 5 120
Five talents is his debt, His means most short, his creditors most strait *T. of Athens* i 1 95
A gentleman that well deserves a help: Which he shall have: I'll pay the debt . . . i 1 103
His promises fly so beyond his state That what he speaks is all in debt i 2 204
Demands of date-broke bonds, And the detention of long-since-due debts ii 2 39
I have Prompted you in the ebb of your estate And your great flow of debts . . . ii 2 151
The greatest of your having lacks a half To pay your present debts . ii 2 154
Fawn upon his debts And take down the interest into their gluttonous maws . . . iii 4 51
He should the sooner pay his debts, And make a clear way to the gods . iii 4 76
These debts may well be called desperate ones, for a madman owes 'em iii 4 102
His right arm might purchase his own time And be in debt to none . iii 5 78
In like manner was I in debt to my importunate business . . iii 6 15
Let prisons swallow 'em, Debts wither 'em to nothing . . iv 3 538
Be not affrighted; Fly not; stand still: ambition's debt is paid *J. Cæsar* iii 1 83
Your son, my lord, has paid a soldier's debt . . *Macbeth* v 8 39
Most necessary 'tis that we forget To pay ourselves what to ourselves is debt . . . *Hamlet* iii 2 203
When every case in law is right; No squire in debt, nor no poor knight *Lear* iii 2 86
His steel was in debt; it went o' the backside the town . . *Cymbeline* i 2 13
Paid More pious debts to heaven than in all The fore-end of my time . iii 3 72
Let us bury him, And not protract with admiration what Is now due debt iv 2 233
Praises, which are paid as debts, And not as given . *Pericles* iv Gower 34
Debted. Three odd ducats more Than I stand debted to this gentleman *Com. of Errors* iv 1 31
Debtor. There's my purse; I am yet thy debtor . . *Mer. Wives* ii 2 138
Let me not die your debtor . . . *L. L. Lost* v 2 43
And thankfully rest debtor for the first . . *Mer. of Venice* i 1 152
Yet fortune cannot recompense me better Than to die well and not my master's debtor . . . *As Y. Like It* ii 3 76
I will pay you some and, as most debtors do, promise you infinitely 2 *Hen. IV.* Epil. 17
I am your debtor, claim it when 'tis due.—Never's my day *Tr. and Cr.* iv 5 51
I shall remain your debtor.—I your servant . . *Ant. and Cleo.* v 2 205
I have been debtor to you for courtesies, which I will be ever to pay and yet pay still . . . *Cymbeline* i 4 38
I must die much your debtor . . . ii 4 8
A prison for a debtor, that not dares To stride a limit . . iii 3 34
You are more clement than vile men, Who of their broken debtors take a third, A sixth, a tenth . . . v 4 19
If that ever my low fortune's better, I'll pay your bounties; till then rest your debtor . . . *Pericles* ii 1 149
Debuty. I was before Master Tisick, the debuty, t' other day 2 *Hen. IV.* ii 4 92
Decay. This is enough to be the decay of lust and late-walking through the realm . . . *Mer. Wives* v 5 152
Whilst this muddy vesture of decay Doth grossly close it in *Mer. of Ven.* v 1 64
Infirmity, that decays the wise, doth ever make the better fool *T. Night* i 5 82
Be thou the trumpet of our wrath And sullen presage of your own decay *K. John* i 1 28
The imminent decay of wrested pomp . . . iv 3 154
Cry woe, destruction, ruin and decay; The worst is death *Richard II.* iii 2 102
The which, if you give o'er To stormy passion, must perforce decay 2 *Hen. IV.* i 1 165
With what wings shall his affections fly Towards fronting peril and opposed decay! . . . iv 4 66
For, good King Henry, thy decay I fear . . 2 *Hen. VI.* iii 1 194
Till then fair hope must hinder life's decay . 3 *Hen. VI.* iv 4 16
Death, desolation, ruin and decay . . . *Richard III.* iv 4 409
With a mind That doth renew swifter than blood decays *Troi. and Cres.* iii 2 170
So shall my lungs Coin words till their decay against those measles *Coriolanus* iii 1 78
Is yond despised and ruinous man my lord? Full of decay and failing? *T. of Athens* iv 3 466
When love begins to sicken and decay, It useth an enforced ceremony *J. Cæsar* iv 2 20
That, from your first of difference and decay, Have follow'd your sad steps *Lear* v 3 288
What comfort to this great decay may come Shall be applied . . v 3 297
Whiles we are suitors to their throne, decays The thing we sue for *Ant. and Cleo.* ii 1 4
Every day that comes comes to decay A day's work in him . *Cymbeline* i 5 56
Such strong renown as time shall ne'er decay . . *Pericles* iii 2 48
Decayed. My decayed fair A sunny look of his would soon repair *Com. of Errors* ii 1 98
That takes pity on decayed men and gives them suits of durance . iv 3 26
He looks like a poor, decayed, ingenious, foolish, rascally knave *All's Well* v 2 24
Had not churchmen pray'd, His thread of life had not so soon decay'd 1 *Hen. VI.* i 1 34
Such a decayed dotant as you seem to be . . . *Coriolanus* v 2 47
Decayer. Your water is a sore decayer of your whoreson dead body *Hamlet* v 1 188
Decaying. Kind keepers of my weak decaying age . 1 *Hen. VI.* ii 5 1
Decease. Was cursed instrument of his decease . . . ii 5 58
His advantage following your decease . . 2 *Hen. VI.* iii 1 25
Richard Plantagenet, Enjoy the kingdom after my decease . 3 *Hen. VI.* i 1 175
Deceased. Mourning for the death Of Learning, late deceased in beggary . . . *M. N. Dream* v 1 53
Deceased, or, as you would say in plain terms, gone to heaven *Mer. of Venice* ii 2 67
My father is deceased; And I have thrust myself into this maze *T. of Shrew* i 2 54
And he knew my deceased father well . . . i 2 102
In right and true behalf Of thy deceased brother . . *K. John* i 1 8
With them a bastard of the king's deceased . . . ii 1 65
He tells us Arthur is deceased to-night . . . iv 2 85
There is a history in all men's lives, Figuring the nature of the times deceased . . . 2 *Hen. IV.* iii 1 81

Deceased. Let's not forget The noble Duke of Bedford late deceased 1 *Hen. VI.* iii 2 132
My hope is gone, now Suffolk is deceased . 2 *Hen. VI.* iv 4 56
She's dead, deceased, she's dead ; alack the day ! . . *Rom. and Jul.* iv 5 23
His gentle lady, Big of this gentleman our theme, deceased As he was born *Cymbeline* i 1 39
Deceit. This deceit loses the name of craft, Of disobedience *Mer. Wives* v 5 239
The doubleness of the benefit defends the deceit from reproof *M. for M.* iii 1 269
'Tis no sin, Sith that the justice of your title to him Doth flourish the deceit . . . . iv 1 75
The folded meaning of your words' deceit . . . . *Com. of Errors* iii 2 36
That time and place with this deceit so lawful May prove coherent *All's Well* iii 7 38
I will not practise to deceive, Yet, to avoid deceit, I mean to learn *K. John* i 1 215
What in the world should make me now deceive, Since I must lose the use of all deceit? . . . . v 4 27
What says she, fair one? that the tongues of men are full of deceits?— Oui, dat de tongues of de mans is be full of deceits . . *Hen. V.* v 2 121
Embrace we then this opportunity As fitting best to quittance their deceit . . . . 1 *Hen. VI.* ii 1 14
A man Unsounded yet and full of deep deceit . . . 2 *Hen. VI.* iii 1 57
Who cannot steal a shape that means deceit? . . . . . iii 1 79
That is good deceit Which mates him first that first intends deceit iii 1 264
From deceit bred by necessity . . . . . . 3 *Hen. VI.* iii 3 63
What Clarence but a quicksand of deceit? . . . . . v 4 26
Oh, that deceit should steal such gentle shapes ! . . *Richard III.* ii 2 27
Yet from my dugs he drew not this deceit . . . . . ii 2 30
The untainted virtue of your years Hath not yet dived into the world's deceit . . . . iii 1 8
If that be call'd deceit, I will be honest . . . . *T. Andron.* iii 1 189
O, that deceit should dwell In such a gorgeous palace ! . *Rom. and Jul.* iii 2 84
Who makes the fairest show means most deceit . . . *Pericles* i 4 75
Deceitful. All these are servants to deceitful men . . *T. G. of Ver.* ii 7 72
Talking with the deceiving father of a deceitful son . *T. of Shrew* iv 4 83
Is this thy cunning, thou deceitful dame? . . . 1 *Hen. VI.* ii 1 50
These hands are free from guiltless blood-shedding, This breast from harbouring foul deceitful thoughts . . . . 2 *Hen. VI.* iv 7 109
Deceitful Warwick ! it was thy device . . . . 3 *Hen. VI.* iii 3 141
They fall their crests, and, like deceitful jades, Sink in the trial *J. Cæsar* iv 2 26
Deceitful, Sudden, malicious, smacking of every sin That has a name *Macbeth* iv 3 58
Deceive. If 'twere a substance, you would, sure, deceive it *T. G. of Ver.* iv 2 127
Which, if my augury deceive me not, Witness good bringing up . iv 4 73
By gar, he deceive me too . . . . *Mer. Wives* iii 1 126
Which means she to deceive, father or mother?—Both . . . iv 6 46
Nimble jugglers that deceive the eye, Dark-working sorcerers *Com. of Err.* i 2 98
I see two husbands, or mine eyes deceive me . . . . . v 1 331
Partly by the dark night, which did deceive them . . *Much Ado* iii 3 168
By the heart's still rhetoric disclosed with eyes, Deceive me not now *L. L. Lost* ii 1 230
As the heresies that men do leave Are hated most of those they did deceive . . . . *M. N. Dream* ii 2 140
Here's packing, with a witness, to deceive us all ! . . *T. of Shrew* v 1 121
My project may deceive me, But my intents are fix'd . . *All's Well* i 1 243
I will not practise to deceive, Yet, to avoid deceit, I mean to learn *K. John* i 1 214
What in the world should make me now deceive, Since I must lose the use of all deceit? . . . . v 4 26
Your majestee ave fausse French enough to deceive de most sage demoiselle dat is en France . . . . . *Hen. V.* v 2 234
Deceive more slily than Ulysses could . . . . 3 *Hen. VI.* iii 2 189
Smile in men's faces, smooth, deceive and cog . . . *Richard III.* i 3 48
That which I would I cannot,—With best advantage will deceive the time . . . . v 3 92
Thou dost thyself and all our Troy deceive . . . *Troi. and Cres.* v 3 90
If that be call'd deceit, I will be honest, And never, whilst I live, deceive men so . . . . *T. Andron.* iii 1 190
But I'll deceive you in another sort, And that you'll say . . iii 1 191
There's never a one of you but trusts a knave, That mightily deceives you *T. of Athens* v 1 97
No more that thane of Cawdor shall deceive Our bosom interest *Macbeth* i 2 63
O, she deceives me Past thought ! . . . . . . *Othello* i 1 166
I will rather sue to be despised than to deceive so good a commander . ii 3 279
She did deceive her father, marrying you ; And when she seem'd to shake and fear your looks, She loved them most . . . iii 3 206
The fellow dares not deceive me . . . . . . *Cymbeline* iv 1 27
Deceiveable. There's something in't That is deceiveable . *T. Night* iv 3 21
Whose duty is deceiveable and false . . . . *Richard II.* ii 3 84
Deceived. That hast deceived so many with thy vows *T. G. of Ver.* iv 2 98
I shall be glad if he have deceived me . . . *Mer. Wives* iii 1 13
Boys of art, I have deceived you both . . . . . iii 1 109
O, how have you deceived me ! . . . . iii 3 137
I know not which pleases me better, that my husband is deceived, or Sir John . . . . iii 3 190
O, how much is the good duke deceived ! . . . *Meas. for Meas.* iii 1 197
O, sir, you are deceived.—'Tis not possible . . . . . iii 2 131
I have deceived even your very eyes . . . . . . *Much Ado* v 1 238
Your uncle and the prince and Claudio Have been deceived . . v 4 76
My cousin Margaret and Ursula Are much deceived . . . . v 4 79
I am much deceived but I remember the style . . *L. L. Lost* iv 1 98
So shall your loves Woo contrary, deceived by these removes . . v 2 135
There is five in the first show.—You are deceived ; 'tis not so . v 2 544
Most sweet Jew ! if a Christian did not play the knave and get thee, I am much deceived . . . . *Mer. of Venice* ii 3 13
The world is still deceived with ornament . . . . . iii 2 74
That is the voice, Or I am much deceived . . . . . v 1 111
Pray heaven I be deceived in you ! . . . . . *As Y. Like It* i 2 209
Yet the note was very untuneable.—You are deceived, sir . . v 3 38
For, but I be deceived, Our fine musician groweth amorous *T. of Shrew* iii 1 62
Your worship is deceived ; the gown is made Just as my master had direction . . . . iv 3 116
And but I be deceived Signior Baptista may remember me . . . iv 4 2
Do you think I am so far deceived in him? . . . *All's Well* iii 6 6
This counterfeit module has deceived me, like a double-meaning prophesier . . . . iv 3 114
What a past-saving slave is this !—You're deceived, my lord . . iv 3 160
He will be here to-morrow, or I am deceived . . . . . iv 5 87
I am sure I saw her wear it.—You are deceived, my lord. . . v 3 92
Nor are you therein, by my life, deceived . . . *T. Night* v 1 269
There have been, Or I am much deceived, cuckolds ere now . *W. Tale* i 2 191
We have been Deceived in thy integrity, deceved In that which seems so i 2 240
You have deceived our trust, And made us doff our easy robes of peace . . . . 1 *Hen. IV.* v 1 11
Thou hast deceived me, Lancaster ; I did not think thee lord of such a spirit . . . . v 4 17
You are deceived, my substance is not here . . . 1 *Hen. VI.* ii 3 51
Charles must father it.—You are deceived ; my child is none of his . v 4 72
Deposed he shall be, in despite of all.—Thou art deceived . 3 *Hen. VI.* i 1 155
Our trusty friend, unless I be deceived . . . . . . iv 7 41
But he's deceived ; we are in readiness . . . . . v 4 64
You are deceived, your brother Gloucester hates you . *Richard III.* i 4 238
By the devil's illusions The monk might be deceived . . *Hen. VIII.* i 2 179
Come, you are deceived, I think of no such thing . *Troi. and Cres.* iv 2 40
No, you are deceived ; therefore, back to Rome, and prepare *Coriolanus* v 2 51
You are deceived : for what I mean to do See here . . *T. Andron.* v 2 13
Thou art too much deceived . . . . v 2 156
Thou wouldst else have made thy tale large.—O, thou art deceived *Rom. and Jul.* ii 4 103
Do import Some misadventure.—Tush, thou art deceived . . v 1 29
Be not deceived : if I have veil'd my look, I turn the trouble of my countenance Merely upon myself . . . . . *J. Cæsar* i 2 37
You shall confess that you are both deceived . . . . . ii 1 105
My uncle-father and aunt-mother are deceived . . . *Hamlet* ii 2 394
I loved you not.—I was the more deceived . . . . . iii 1 121
You're much deceived : in nothing am I changed But in my garments *Lear* iv 6 9
Look to her, Moor, if thou hast eyes to see : She has deceived her father, and may thee . . . . *Othello* i 3 294
I am sorry that I am deceived in him . . . . . . iv 1 293
I do not greatly care to be deceived, That have no use for trusting *Ant. and Cleo.* v 2 14
Deceiver. And pardon'd the deceiver . . . . . . *Tempest* Epil. 7
Sigh no more, ladies, sigh no more, Men were deceivers ever . *Much Ado* ii 3 65
Deceivest. Thou deceivest thyself : 'Tis he that sent us . *Richard III.* i 4 249
Deceiveth. If that man should be lewdly given, he deceiveth me 1 *Hen. IV.* ii 4 469
Deceiving. Many deceiving promises of life . . *Meas. for Meas.* iii 2 260
O wicked wall, through whom I see no bliss ! Cursed be thy stones for thus deceiving me ! . . . . *M. N. Dream* v 1 182
'Deceiving me' is Thisby's cue : she is to enter now . . . v 1 185
Talking with the deceiving father of a decitful son . . *T. of Shrew* iv 4 83
Be it lying, note it, The woman's ; flattering, hers ; deceiving, hers *Cymbeline* ii 5 23
December. Exceeds her as much in beauty as the first of May doth the last of December . . . . *Much Ado* i 1 195
Men are April when they woo, December when they wed *As Y. Like It* iv 1 148
O, the twelfth day of December . . . . . . *T. Night* ii 3 90
He makes a July's day short as December . . . *W. Tale* i 2 169
Or wallow naked in December snow By thinking on fantastic summer's heat . . . . *Richard II.* i 3 298
When we shall hear The rain and wind beat dark December . *Cymbeline* iii 3 37
Decent. For honesty and decent carriage, A right good husband *Hen. VIII.* iv 2 145
Deceptious. Doth invert the attest of eyes and ears, As if those organs had deceptious functions . . . . . *Troi. and Cres.* v 2 123
Decern. I would have some confidence with you that decerns you nearly *Much Ado* iii 5 4
Decide. And often at his very loose decides That which long process could not arbitrate . . . . *L. L. Lost* v 2 752
Call the swords Which must decide it . . . . 2 *Hen. IV.* iv 1 182
Betwixt ourselves let us decide it then . . . . 1 *Hen. VI.* iv 1 119
Decimation. By decimation, and a tithed death . . *T. of Athens* v 4 31
Decipher. The white will decipher her well enough . . *Mer. Wives* v 2 10
Which is the natural man, And which the spirit? who deciphers them? *Com. of Errors* v 1 334
Deciphered. I fear we should have seen decipher'd there More rancorous spite . . . . 1 *Hen. VI.* iv 1 184
What's the news?—That you are both decipher'd, that's the news *T. Andron.* iv 2 8
Decision. Whose great decision hath much blood let forth *All's Well* iii 1 3
Ears more deaf than adders to the voice Of any true decision *Tr. and Cr.* ii 2 173
The time approaches That will with due decision make us know *Macbeth* v 4 17
Decius Brutus. Is Decius Brutus and Trebonius there? . *J. Cæsar* i 3 148
This, Decius Brutus.—He is welcome too . . . . . ii 1 95
Decius, well urged : I think it is not meet . . . . . ii 1 155
Here's Decius Brutus, he shall tell them so . . . . . ii 2 57
Tell them so, Decius.—Say he is sick . . . . . . ii 2 64
Decius, go tell them Cæsar will not come . . . . . ii 2 68
Mark well Metellus Cimber : Decius Brutus loves thee not . . ii 3 4
Next, Caius Cassius, do I take your hand ; Now, Decius Brutus, yours iii 1 187
Burn all : some to Decius' house, and some to Casca's . . . iii 3 42
Deck. I boarded the king's ship ; now on the beak, Now in the waist, the deck, in every cabin . . . . *Tempest* i 2 197
He has brave utensils,—for so he calls them,—Which, when he has a house, he'll deck withal . . . . iii 2 105
Sweet ornament that decks a thing divine ! . . . *T. G. of Ver.* ii 1 4
I'll be sure to keep him above deck . . . . *Mer. Wives* ii 1 94
To deck his fortune with his virtuous deeds . . . *T. of Shrew* ii 1 16
The tailor stays thy leisure, To deck thy body with his ruffling treasure iv 3 60
The lining of his coffers shall make coats To deck our soldiers *Richard II.* i 4 62
'Tis your thoughts that now must deck our kings . . *Hen. V.* Prol. 28
And deck my body in gay ornaments . . . . 3 *Hen. VI.* iii 2 149
Whiles he thought to steal the single ten, The king was slily finger'd from the deck ! . . . . v 1 44
Go thou to Juliet, help to deck up her ; I'll not to bed to-night *Rom. and Jul.* iv 2 41
Leak'd is our bark, And we, poor mates, stand on the dying deck *T. of Athens* iv 2 20
He did keep The deck, with glove, or hat, or handkerchief, Still waving *Cymbeline* i 3 11
In your imagination hold This stage the ship, upon whose deck The sea-tost Pericles appears to speak . . . . *Pericles* iii Gower 59
Clasping to the mast, endured a sea That almost burst the deck . iv 1 57
From the deck You may discern the place . . . . . v 1 115
Decked. When I have deck'd the sea with drops full salt *Tempest* i 2 155
If in black my lady's brows be deck'd . . . . *L. L. Lost* iv 3 258
Garnish'd and deck'd in modest complement . . . *Hen. V.* ii 2 134
Deck'd with five flower-de-luces on each side . . 1 *Hen. VI.* i 2 99
Not deck'd with diamonds and Indian stones, Nor to be seen 3 *Hen. VI.* iii 1 63
And see another, as I see thee now, Deck'd in thy rights ! *Richard III.* i 3 206
Disrobe the images, If you do find them deck'd with ceremonies *J. Cæsar* i 1 70

Decked. I thought thy bride-bed to have deck'd, sweet maid . *Hamlet* v 1 268
Decking with liquid pearl the bladed grass . . . *M. N. Dream* i 1 211
Declare. My scutcheon plain declares that I am Alisander . *L. L. Lost* v 2 567
Declare What incidency thou dost guess of harm Is creeping toward me *W. Tale* i 2 402
To know his embassy; Which I could with a ready guess declare *Hen. V.* i 1 96
And now declare, sweet stem from York's great stock . 1 *Hen. VI.* ii 5 41
Declare the cause My father, Earl of Cambridge, lost his head . ii 5 53
Please you to declare, in hearing Of all these ears . . *Hen. VIII.* ii 4 145
Be't so: declare thine office . . . . . . *Ant. and Cleo.* iii 12 10
Read, and declare the meaning . . . . . . *Cymbeline* v 5 434
Declension. Show me now, William, some declensions of your pronouns *Mer. Wives* iv 1 76
Seduced the pitch and height of all his thoughts To base declension *Richard III.* iii 7 189
Thence into a weakness, Thence to a lightness, and, by this declension, Into the madness wherein now he raves . . . . *Hamlet* ii 2 149
Decline. Far more, far more to you do I decline . . *Com. of Errors* iii 2 44
Decline all this, and see what now thou art . . . *Richard III.* iv 4 97
Can thy spirit wonder A great man should decline? . *Hen. VIII.* iii 2 375
O, tell, tell.—I'll decline the whole question . . *Troi. and Cres.* ii 3 55
Hung thy advanced sword i' the air, Not letting it decline on the declined . . . . iv 5 189
And presume to know What's done i' the Capitol; who's like to rise, Who thrives and who declines . . . . . *Coriolanus* i 1 197
Death, that dark spirit, in's nervy arm doth lie; Which, being advanced, declines, and then men die . . . . ii 1 178
Degrees, observances, customs, and laws, Decline to your confounding contraries, And let confusion live! . . . . *T. of Athens* iv 1 20
The enemy increaseth every day; We, at the height, are ready to decline *J. Cæsar* iv 3 217
To decline Upon a wretch whose natural gifts were poor To those of mine! . . . . *Hamlet* i 5 50
Decline your head: this kiss, if it durst speak, Would stretch thy spirits up into the air . . . . *Lear* iv 2 22
Declined. Articles are borrowed of the pronoun, and be thus declined, Singulariter, nominativo, hic, hæc, hoc . . . *Mer. Wives* iv 1 42
He straight declined, droop'd, took it deeply . . . . *W. Tale* ii 3 14
She had one eye declined for the loss of her husband, another elevated . v 2 81
What the declined is He shall as soon read in the eyes of others As feel in his own fall . . . . *Troi. and Cres.* iii 3 76
Hung thy advanced sword i' the air, Not letting it decline on the declined . . . . iv 5 189
I am declined Into the vale of years . . . . . . *Othello* iii 3 265
Her head's declined, and death will seize her . . . *Ant. and Cleo.* iii 11 47
I dare him therefore To lay his gay comparisons apart, And answer me declined, sword against sword . . . . iii 13 27
Declining. Carbuncles, sapphires, declining their rich aspect to the hot breath of Spain . . . . *Com. of Errors* iii 2 138
Tempting kisses, And with declining head into his bosom *T. of Shrew* Ind. 1 119
A royal prince, And many moe Of noble blood in this declining land *Richard II.* ii 1 240
Not one accompanying his declining foot . . . . *T. of Athens* i 1 88
His sword, Which was declining on the milky head Of reverend Priam, seem'd i' the air to stick . . . . *Hamlet* ii 2 500
That, sons at perfect age, and fathers declining, the father should be as ward to the son . . . . *Lear* i 2 78
I must perforce Have shown to thee such a declining day, Or look on thine . . . . *Ant. and Cleo.* v 1 38
Decoct. Can sodden water, A drench for sur-rein'd jades, their barley-broth, Decoct their cold blood to such valiant heat? . *Hen. V.* iii 5 20
Decorum. The baby beats the nurse, and quite athwart Goes all decorum *Meas. for Meas.* i 3 31
Therefore, dear Isis, keep decorum, and fortune him accordingly! *Ant. and Cleo.* i 2 77
Majesty, to keep decorum, must No less beg than a kingdom . . v 2 17
Decrease. If there be no great love in the beginning, yet heaven may decrease it upon better acquaintance . . . . *Mer. Wives* i 1 255
Tyrants' fears Decrease not, but grow faster than the years . *Pericles* i 2 85
Decreased. Heir to all his lands and goods, Which I have better'd rather than decreased . . . . *T. of Shrew* ii 1 119
Decreasing. A white beard? a decreasing leg? an increasing belly? 2 *Hen. IV.* i 2 205
Decree. So our decrees, Dead to infliction, to themselves are dead *Meas. for Meas.* i 3 27
Let me read the same; And to the strict'st decrees I'll write my name *L. L. Lost* i 1 117
We must of force dispense with this decree . . . . . . i 1 148
Young blood doth not obey an old decree . . . . . . iv 3 217
The brain may devise laws for the blood, but a hot temper leaps o'er a cold decree . . . . *Mer. of Venice* i 2 20
If you deny me, fie upon your law! There is no force in the decrees of Venice . . . . iv 1 102
There is no power in Venice Can alter a decree established . . . iv 1 219
As wit and fortune will.—Or as the Destinies decree . *As Y. Like It* i 2 111
On our quick'st decrees The inaudible and noiseless foot of Time Steals ere we can effect them . . . . *All's Well* v 3 40
Let the trumpets sound While we return these dukes what we decree *Richard II.* i 3 122
My acts, decrees, and statutes I deny . . . . iv 1 213
Then let me hear . . . What yesternight our council did decree 1 *Hen. IV.* i 1 32
Some strait decrees That lie too heavy on the commonwealth . . iv 3 79
Pluck down my officers, break my decrees . . . 2 *Hen. IV.* iv 5 118
To have a son set your decrees at nought . . . . . . v 2 85
Coming with a full intent To dash our late decree . . 3 *Hen. VI.* ii 1 118
A man busied about decrees: Condemning some to death, and some to exile . . . . *Coriolanus* i 6 34
Is it your trick to make me ope the door, That so my sad decrees may fly away? . . . . *T. Andron.* v 2 11
How now, wife! Have you deliver'd to her our decree? *Rom. and Jul.* iii 5 139
And turn pre-ordinance and first decree Into the law of children *J. Cæsar* iii 1 38
Decreed. It hath in solemn synods been decreed . . *Com. of Errors* i 1 13
Therefore I have decreed not to sing in my cage . . . *Much Ado* i 3 35
What is decreed must be, and be this so . . . . . *T. Night* i 5 330
It is decreed Hector the great must die . . . *Troi. and Cres.* v 7 8
Therefore it is decreed He dies to-night . . . . *Coriolanus* iii 1 289
Where we decreed to bury Bassianus . . . . . *T. Andron.* ii 3 274
Go, get thee to thy love, as was decreed, Ascend her chamber *R. and J.* iii 3 146
Which read and not expounded, 'tis decreed, As these before thee thou thyself shalt bleed . . . . *Pericles* i 1 57

Decreed. In framing an artist, art hath thus decreed, To make some good, but others to exceed . . . . *Pericles* ii 3 15
Decrepit. Her decrepit, sick and bedrid father . . . *L. L. Lost* i 1 139
Decrepit miser! base ignoble wretch! . . . . . 1 *Hen. VI.* v 4 7
Dedicate. Fasting maids whose minds are dedicate To nothing temporal *Meas. for Meas.* ii 2 154
Seeing how much another man is a fool when he dedicates his behaviours to love . . . . *Much Ado* ii 3 9
Nor doth he dedicate one jot of colour Unto the weary and all-watched night . . . . *Hen. V.* iv Prol. 37
He that is truly dedicate to war Hath no self-love . . 2 *Hen. VI.* v 2 37
This night he dedicates To fair content and you . . . *Hen. VIII.* i 4 2
What folly I commit, I dedicate to you . . . . *Troi. and Cres.* iii 2 110
Ere he can spread his sweet leaves to the air, Or dedicate his beauty to the sun . . . . *Rom. and Jul.* i 1 159
So many As will to greatness dedicate themselves . . . *Macbeth* iv 3 75
I dedicate myself to your sweet pleasure . . . . *Cymbeline* i 6 136
To the face of peril Myself I'll dedicate . . . . v 1 29
Dedicated. All dedicated To closeness and the bettering of my mind *Tempest* i 2 89
And his poor self, A dedicated beggar to the air . . *T. of Athens* iv 2 13
Dedication. And did thereto add My love, without retention or restraint, All his in dedication . . . . *T. Night* v 1 85
A wild dedication of yourselves To unpath'd waters, undream'd shores *W. Tale* iv 4 577
You are rapt, sir, in some work, some dedication To the great lord *T. of Athens* i 1 19
Deed. For which foul deed The powers, delaying, not forgetting, have Incensed the seas and shores . . . . *Tempest* iii 3 72
I will pay thy graces Home both in word and deed . . . . v 1 71
For truth hath better deeds than words to grace it . . *T. G. of Ver.* ii 2 18
When evil deeds have their permissive pass And not the punishment *Meas. for Meas.* i 3 38
If the first that did the edict infringe Had answer'd for his deed . ii 2 93
Nature dispenses with the deed so far That it becomes a virtue . iii 1 135
Would have dark deeds darkly answered . . . . . . iii 2 187
This deed unshapes me quite, makes me unpregnant And dull . iv 4 23
I partly think A due sincerity govern'd his deeds, Till he did look on me . . . . v 1 451
Had you a special warrant for the deed? . . . . . . v 1 464
Ill deeds are doubled with an evil word . . . *Com. of Errors* iii 2 20
Record it with your high and worthy deeds: 'Twas bravely done *M. Ado* v 1 279
One that will do the deed Though Argus were her eunuch and her guard *L. L. Lost* iii 1 200
My deeds upon my head! . . . . *Mer. of Venice* iv 1 206
Send the deed after me, And I will sign it . . . . . iv 1 396
Give him this deed And let him sign it . . . . . . iv 2 1
This deed will be well welcome to Lorenzo . . . . . iv 2 4
How far that little candle throws his beams! So shines a good deed in a naughty world . . . . v 1 91
Thou shouldst have better pleased me with this deed, Hadst thou descended from another house . . . . . *As Y. Like It* i 2 240
I do not know what 'poetical' is: is it honest in deed and word? . iii 3 18
As lively painted as the deed was done . . . *T. of Shrew* Ind. 2 58
To deck his fortune with his virtuous deeds . . . . . i 1 16
Beloved of me; and that my deeds shall prove . . . . . i 2 177
I will compound this strife: 'Tis deeds must win the prize . . ii 1 344
If thou proceed As high as word, my deed shall match thy meed *All's Well* ii 1 213
From lowest place when virtuous things proceed, The place is dignified by the doer's deed . . . . ii 3 133
Do you think he will make no deed at all of this? . . . . iii 6 102
Which, if it speed, Is wicked meaning in a lawful deed . . . iii 7 45
That what in time proceeds May token to the future our past deeds . iv 2 63
For my thoughts, you have them ill to friend Till your deeds gain them v 3 183
'Twere as good a deed as to drink when a man's a-hungry . *T. Night* ii 3 135
One good deed dying tongueless Slaughters a thousand waiting upon that . . . . *W. Tale* i 2 92
My last good deed was to entreat his stay: What was my first? . . i 2 97
To do this deed, Promotion follows . . . . i 2 356
All other circumstances Made up to the deed . . . . . . ii 1 179
Sir, be prosperous In more than this deed does require! . . . ii 3 190
How his piety Does my deeds make the blacker! . . . . . iii 2 173
If there be any of him left, I'll bury it.—That's a good deed . . iii 3 137
'Tis a lucky day, boy, and we'll do good deeds on't . . . iii 3 143
Each your doing, So singular in each particular, Crowns what you are doing in the present deed . . . . iv 4 145
It is my father's music To speak your deeds . . . . . . iv 4 530
I hope your warrant will bear out the deed . . . . *K. John* iv 1 6
I am best pleased to be from such a deed . . . . . . iv 1 86
This is the man should do the bloody deed . . . . . . iv 2 69
How oft the sight of means to do ill deeds Make deeds ill done! . iv 2 219
The deed, which both our tongues held vile to name . . . iv 2 241
The earth had not a hole to hide this deed . . . . . . iv 3 36
Renowned for their deeds as far from home, For Christian service *Richard II.* ii 1 53
That in a Christian climate souls refined Should show so heinous, black, obscene a deed! . . . . iv 1 131
O would the deed were good! For now the devil, that told me I did well, Says that this deed is chronicled in hell . . . . . . v 5 117
From your own mouth, my lord, did I this deed . . . . . v 6 37
An'twere not as good deed as drink, to break the pate on thee 1 *Hen. IV.* ii 1 33
Whose high deeds, Whose hot incursions and great name in arms . . iii 2 107
The time will come, That I shall make this northern youth exchange His glorious deeds for my indignities . . . . iii 2 146
Percy is but my factor, good my lord, To engross up glorious deeds on my behalf . . . . iii 2 148
Is now alive To grace this latter age with noble deeds . . . v 1 92
Turk Gregory never did such deeds in arms as I have done this day . v 3 47
Taught us how to cherish such high deeds Even in the bosom of our adversaries . . . . v 5 30
Stopping my greedy ear with their bold deeds . . . 2 *Hen. IV.* i 1 78
Employ the countenance and grace of heaven, As a false favourite doth his prince's name, In deeds dishonourable . . . . iv 2 26
I beseech your grace, let it be booked with the rest of this day's deeds iv 3 51
If the deed were ill, Be you contented . . . . v 2 83
His few bad words are matched with as few good deeds . *Hen. V.* iii 2 42
And dare not avouch in your deeds any of your words . . . . v 1 77
His deeds exceed all speech: He ne'er lift up his hand but conquered 1 *Hen. VI.* i 1 15
Whose bloody deeds shall make all Europe quake . . . . . i 1 156

Deed. O, let no words, but deeds, revenge this treason! . . 1 *Hen. VI.* iii 2 49
Erects Thy noble deeds as valour's monuments . . . iii 2 120
Thy deeds, thy plainness and thy housekeeping, Hath won the greatest favour of the commons . . . . 2 *Hen. VI.* i 1 191
Cherish Duke Humphrey's deeds, While they do tend the profit of the land . . . . i 1 203
Seeing the deed is meritorious . . . . . . iii 1 270
Say you consent and censure well the deed, And I'll provide his executioner . . . . iii 1 275
Here is my hand, the deed is worthy doing . . . iii 1 278
I will reward you for this venturous deed . . . iii 2 9
Sword, I will hallow thee for this thy deed . . . iv 10 72
Who can be bound by any solemn vow To do a murderous deed, to rob a man? . . . . v 1 185
And die in bands for this unmanly deed! . . . 3 *Hen. VI.* i 1 186
Thy face is, visard-like, unchanging, Made impudent with use of evil deeds . . . . i 4 117
Even my foes will shed fast-falling tears, And say 'Alas, it was a piteous deed!' . . . . i 4 163
Were thy heart as hard as steel, As thou hast shown it flinty by thy deeds, I come to pierce it . . . . ii 1 202
I'll leave my son my virtuous deeds behind . . . ii 2 49
But ere sunset I'll make thee curse the deed . . . ii 2 116
O that my death would stay these ruthful deeds! . . ii 5 95
Thou art fortunate in all thy deeds . . . . . iv 6 25
Were not worthy blame, If this foul deed were by to equal it v 5 55
What black magician conjures up this fiend, To stop devoted charitable deeds? . . . . *Richard III.* i 2 35
If thou delight to view thy heinous deeds, Behold this pattern of thy butcheries . . . . i 2 53
Thy deed, inhuman and unnatural, Provokes this deluge most unnatural i 2 60
God grant me too Thou mayst be damned for that wicked deed! . i 2 103
And God, not we, hath plagued thy bloody deed . . . i 3 181
O, 'twas the foulest deed to slay that babe, And the most merciless! . i 3 183
Remember our reward, when the deed is done . . . i 4 127
The deed you undertake is damnable . . . . . i 4 197
Alas! for whose sake did I that ill deed? . . . . i 4 216
If God will be revenged for this deed, O, know you yet, he doth it publicly i 4 221
He that set you on To do this deed will hate you for the deed . . i 4 262
A bloody deed, and desperately dispatch'd! . . . . i 4 278
The tyrannous and bloody deed is done . . . . iv 3 1
When didst thou sleep when such a deed was done? . . iv 4 24
Shall I go win my daughter to thy will?—And be a happy mother by the deed . . . . iv 4 427
Dream on, dream on, of bloody deeds and death . . . v 3 171
Alas, I rather hate myself For hateful deeds committed by myself! . v 3 190
If it be known to him That I gainsay my deed, how may he wound, And worthily, my falsehood! . . . . . . *Hen. VIII.* ii 4 96
'Tis a kind of good deed to say well: And yet words are no deeds . iii 2 153
And with his deed did crown His word upon you . . . . iii 2 155
Many days shall see her, And yet no day without a deed to crown it v 5 59
And do a deed that fortune never did . . . . *Troi. and Cres.* ii 2 90
She is a theme of honour and renown, A spur to valiant and magnanimous deeds . . . . ii 2 200
Whatever praises itself but in the deed, devours the deed in the praise ii 3 167
And hot thoughts beget hot deeds, and hot deeds is love . . iii 1 142
Is this the generation of love? hot blood, hot thoughts, and hot deeds? iii 1 145
Words pay no debts, give her deeds: but she'll bereave you o' the deeds too . . . . iii 2 58
What, are my deeds forgot? . . . . iii 3 144
Those scraps are good deeds past; which are devour'd As fast as they are made . . . . iii 3 148
Whose glorious deeds, but in these fields of late, Made emulous missions 'mongst the gods themselves . . . . iii 3 188
Matchless, firm of word, Speaking in deeds and deedless in his tongue iv 5 98
I'll endeavour deeds to match these words . . . . iv 5 259
We'll forth and fight, Do deeds worth praise and tell you them at night v 3 93
My love with words and errors still she feeds; But edifies another with her deeds . . . . v 3 112
They have had inkling this fortnight what we intend to do, which now we'll show 'em in deeds . . . . *Coriolanus* i 1 61
If I should tell thee o'er this thy day's work, Thou 'ldst not believe thy deeds . . . . i 9 2
He hath in this action outdone his former deeds doubly . . ii 1 150
Without any further deed to have them at all into their estimation . ii 2 31
The deeds of Coriolanus Should not be utter'd feebly . . ii 2 86
Rewards His deeds with doing them . . . . . ii 2 132
If he show us his wounds and tell us his deeds, we are to put our tongues into those wounds and speak for them . . . . ii 3 6
If he tell us his noble deeds, we must also tell him our noble acceptance ii 3 8
His worthy deeds did claim no less Than what he stood for . . ii 3 194
Let deeds express What's like to be their words . . . iii 1 132
Get you gone: You have done a brave deed . . . . iv 2 38
Thou hast done a deed whereat valour will weep . . . v 6 134
And will with deeds requite thy gentleness . . . *T. Andron.* i 1 237
Agree these deeds with that proud brag of thine . . . i 1 306
Confederates in the deed That hath dishonour'd all our family . i 1 344
My nephew Mutius' deeds do plead for him . . . . i 1 356
Hath express'd himself in all his deeds A father and a friend . . i 1 422
Leave to plead my deeds: 'Tis thou and those that have dishonour'd me i 1 424
O, say thou for her, who hath done this deed? . . . iii 1 87
No, no, they would not do so foul a deed . . . . iii 1 118
Pardon me for reprehending thee, For thou hast done a charitable deed iii 2 70
Till the heavens Reveal the damn'd contriver of this deed . . iv 1 36
What Roman lord it was durst do the deed . . . . iv 1 62
Performers of this heinous, bloody deed . . . . . iv 1 80
Whose high exploits and honourable deeds Ingrateful Rome requites with foul contempt . . . . v 1 11
Acts of black night, abominable deeds, Complots of mischief . . v 1 64
Well, let my deeds be witness of my worth . . . . v 1 103
Art thou not sorry for these heinous deeds? . . . . v 1 123
Was she ravish'd? tell who did the deed . . . . . v 3 53
Die, frantic wretch, for this accursed deed! . . . . v 3 64
There's meed for meed, death for a deadly deed! . . . v 3 66
If one good deed in all my life I did, I do repent it from my very soul . v 3 189
I would forget it fain; But, O, it presses to my memory, Like damned guilty deeds to sinners' minds . . . . . *Rom. and Jul.* iii 2 111
Ere this hand, by thee to Romeo seal'd, Shall be the label to another deed iv 1 57
A deed thou 'lt die for.—Right, if doing nothing be death *T. of Athens* i 1 194
Ceremony was but devised at first To set a gloss on faint deeds . i 2 16

Deed. You undergo too strict a paradox, Striving to make an ugly deed look fair . . . . *T. of Athens* iii 5 25
Mindless of thy worth, Forgetting thy great deeds . . . iv 3 94
O monument And wonder of good deeds evilly bestow'd! . . . iv 3 467
A great observer and he looks Quite through the deeds of men *J. Cæsar* i 2 203
Purchase us a good opinion And buy men's voices to commend our deeds ii 1 146
Let no man abide this deed, But we the doers . . . iii 1 94
Pity to the general wrong of Rome . . . Hath done this deed on Cæsar iii 1 172
All pity choked with custom of fell deeds . . . . iii 1 269
This foul deed shall smell above the earth . . . . iii 1 274
They that have done this deed are honourable . . . iii 2 216
Clouds, dews, and dangers come; our deeds are done! . . v 3 64
Mistrust of my success hath done this deed.—Mistrust of good success hath done this deed . . . . v 3 65
Slaying is the word; It is a deed in fashion . . . . v 5 5
Shall I do such a deed? . . . . v 5 8
As I am his kinsman and his subject, Strong both against the deed *Macbeth* i 7 14
Shall blow the horrid deed in every eye, That tears shall drown the wind i 7 24
Words to the heat of deeds too cold breath gives . . . ii 1 61
The attempt and not the deed Confounds us . . . . ii 2 11
I have done the deed. Didst thou not hear a noise?—I heard the owl scream . . . . ii 2 15
These deeds must not be thought After these ways; so, it will make us mad . . . . ii 2 33
A little water clears us of this deed: How easy is it, then! . . ii 2 67
To know my deed, 'twere best not know myself . . . ii 2 73
'Tis unnatural, Even like the deed that's done . . . ii 4 11
Is't known who did this more than bloody deed? . . . ii 4 22
Are stol'n away and fled; which puts upon them Suspicion of the deed ii 4 27
There shall be done A deed of dreadful note . . . . iii 2 44
Be innocent of the knowledge, dearest chuck, Till thou applaud the deed iii 2 46
We are yet but young in deed . . . . iii 4 144
What is't you do?—A deed without a name . . . . iv 1 49
The flighty purpose never is o'ertook Unless the deed go with it . iv 1 146
No boasting like a fool; This deed I'll do before this purpose cool . iv 1 154
Foul whisperings are abroad: unnatural deeds Do breed unnatural troubles . . . . v 1 79
Foul deeds will rise, Though all the earth o'erwhelm them *Hamlet* i 2 257
As he in his particular act and place May give his saying deed . i 3 27
Is not more ugly to the thing that helps it Than is my deed to my most painted word . . . . iii 1 53
O, what a rash and bloody deed is this!—A bloody deed! . . iii 4 27
O, such a deed As from the body of contraction plucks The very soul . iii 4 45
O heavy deed! It had been so with us, had we been there . . iv 1 12
Alas, how shall this bloody deed be answer'd? It will be laid to us . iv 1 16
This vile deed We must, with all our majesty and skill, Both countenance and excuse . . . . iv 1 30
Hamlet, this deed, for thine especial safety,—Which we do tender, as we dearly grieve For that which thou hast done,—must send thee hence iv 3 42
To show yourself your father's son in deed More than in words . iv 7 126
Whose wicked deed thy most ingenious sense Deprived thee of . . v 1 271
Your large speeches may your deeds approve . . . *Lear* i 1 187
Do deeds to make heaven weep, all earth amazed . . *Othello* iii 3 371
I should make very forges of my cheeks, That would to cinders burn up modesty, Did I but speak thy deeds . . . . iv 2 76
If e'er my will did trespass 'gainst his love, Either in discourse of thought or actual deed . . . . iv 2 153
Wouldst thou do such a deed for all the world?—Why, would not you? iv 3 64
I have no great devotion to the deed . . . . . v 1 8
A guiltless death I die.—O, who hath done this deed?—Nobody; I myself v 2 123
An honest man he is, and hates the slime That sticks on filthy deeds . v 2 149
This deed of thine is no more worthy heaven Than thou wast worthy her v 2 160
O gull! O dolt! As ignorant as dirt! thou hast done a deed . . v 2 164
When you shall these unlucky deeds relate, Speak of me as I am . v 2 341
But I will hope Of better deeds to-morrow . . . *Ant. and Cleo.* i 1 62
Indeed!—Not in deed, madam; for I can do nothing But what indeed is honest to be done . . . . i 5 15
If the great gods be just, they shall assist The deeds of justest men ii 1 2
'Tis a worthy deed, And shall become you well . . . . ii 2 1
Better to leave undone, than by our deed Acquire too high a fame when him we serve's away . . . . iii 1 14
That nature must compel us to lament Our most persisted deeds . v 1 30
It is great To do that thing that ends all other deeds . . . v 2 5
Nay, blush not, Cleopatra; I approve Your wisdom in the deed . v 2 150
What poor an instrument May do a noble deed! . . . . v 2 237
Be our good deed, Though Rome be therefore angry . . . *Cymbeline* iii 1 58
I love thee brotherly, but envy much Thou hast robb'd me of this deed iv 2 159
This is Pisanio's deed, and Cloten's . . . . . . iv 2 329
Such precious deeds in one that promised nought But beggary . . v 5 9
I would not thy good deeds should from my lips Pluck a hard sentence v 5 288
That will prove awful both in deed and word . . . *Pericles* ii Gower 4
To place upon the volume of your deeds, As in a title-page, your worth in arms . . . . ii 3 3
Never did my actions yet commence A deed might gain her love or your displeasure . . . . ii 5 54
My commission Is not to reason of the deed, but do it . . . . iv 1 84
Were I chief lord of all this spacious world, I'ld give it to undo the deed iv 3 6
When fame Had spread their cursed deed . . . . . . v 3 Gower 96

Deed-achieving. By deed-achieving honour newly named . *Coriolanus* ii 1 190

Deedless. Speaking in deeds and deedless in his tongue *Troi. and Cres.* iv 5 98

Deed of charity. We have done deeds of charity . . *Richard III.* ii 1 49
This was but a deed of charity To that which thou shalt hear *T. Andron.* v 1 89

Deed of courage. Who, great and puffed up with this retinue, doth any deed of courage . . . . 2 *Hen. IV.* iv 3 122

Deed of darkness. If she 'ld do the deed of darkness . . . *Pericles* iv 6 32

Deed of death. If thou didst this deed of death, Art thou damn'd *K. John* iv 3 113
A deed of death done on the innocent Becomes not Titus' brother *T. Andron.* iii 2 56

Deed of gift. Clerk, draw a deed of gift . . . *Mer. of Venice* iv 1 394
A special deed of gift, After his death, of all he dies possess'd of . v 1 292

Deed of hospitality. Little recks to find the way to heaven By doing deeds of hospitality . . . . *As Y. Like It* ii 4 82

Deed of kind. In the doing of the deed of kind . . *Mer. of Venice* i 3 86

Deed of love. She names my very deed of love; Only she comes too short *Lear* i 1 73

Deed of malice. Both conjointly bend Your sharpest deeds of malice on this town . . . . *K. John* ii 1 380

Deed of mercy. That same prayer doth teach us all to render The deeds of mercy . . . . *Mer. of Venice* iv 1 202

Deed of policy. O Lord, sir, 'tis a deed of policy . *T. Andron.* iv 2 148
Deed of rage. Rough deeds of rage and stern impatience 1 *Hen. VI.* iv 7 8
Deed of saying. The deed of saying is quite out of use . *T. of Athens* v 1 28
Deed of shame. Quoted and sign'd to do a deed of shame . *K. John* iv 2 222
Deed of slander. Thou hast wrought A deed of slander with thy fatal hand Upon my head . . . . *Richard II.* v 6 35
Deed of war. Shall Henry's conquest, Bedford's vigilance, Your deeds of war and all our counsel die . . . . 2 *Hen. VI.* i 1 97
Deem. As you shall deem yourself lodged in my heart . *L. L. Lost* ii 1 174
To esteem A senseless help when help past sense we deem . *All's Well* ii 1 127
Take those things for bird-bolts that you deem cannon-bullets *T. Night* i 5 100
See, my lord, Would you not deem it breathed? . . . *W. Tale* v 3 64
The souls of men May deem that you are worthily deposed *Richard II.* iv 1 227
What know I how the world may deem of me? . 2 *Hen. VI.* iii 2 65
Sure, in that I deem you an ill husband . . . *Hen. VIII.* iii 2 142
Be thou but true of heart,— I true! how now! what wicked deem is this? *Troi. and Cres.* iv 4 61
In eye of Imogen, that best Could deem his dignity . *Cymbeline* v 4 57
Deemed. In iron walls they deem'd me not secure . . 1 *Hen. VI.* i 4 49
Who deem'd our marriage lawful . . . . *Hen. VIII.* ii 4 53
Deep. Think'st it much to tread the ooze Of the salt deep . *Tempest* i 2 253
The thunder, That deep and dreadful organ-pipe . . . iii 3 98
Huge leviathans Forsake unsounded deeps to dance on sands *T. G. of Ver.* iii 2 81
The anchor is deep . . . . . . *Mer. Wives* i 3 56
And so deep sticks it in my penitent heart . . *Meas. for Meas.* v 1 480
The always wind-obeying deep . . . . *Com. of Errors* i 1 64
Nor shines the silver moon one half so bright Through the transparent bosom of the deep . . . . . . *L. L. Lost* iv 3 31
And they shall fetch thee jewels from the deep . *M. N. Dream* iii 1 161
Being o'er shoes in blood, plunge in the deep, And kill me too . iii 2 48
That thou didst know how many fathom deep I am in love! *As Y. L. It* iv 1 210
That blind rascally boy that abuses every one's eyes because his own are out, let him be judge how deep I am in love . . . iv 1 220
As he that leaves A shallow plash to plunge him in the deep . *T. of Shrew* i 1 23
I leaped from the window of the citadel— How deep?—Thirty fathom *All's Well* iv 1 62
Which to reiterate were sin As deep as that, though true . *W. Tale* i 2 284
Thrust thy hand as deep Into the purse of rich prosperity . *K. John* v 2 60
I'll read you matter deep and dangerous . . . . 1 *Hen. IV.* i 3 190
The bottom of the deep, Where fathom-line could never touch the ground i 3 203
They call drinking deep, dyeing scarlet . . . . ii 4 16
I can call spirits from the vasty deep.—Why, so can I, or so can any man . . . . iii 1 52
To the infernal deep, with Erebus and tortures vile also . 2 *Hen. IV.* ii 4 170
Well, Master Shallow; deep, Master Shallow . . . . iii 2 172
Who hath not heard it spoken How deep you were within the books of God? . . . . iv 2 17
Thus runs the bill.—This would drink deep . . . *Hen. V.* i 1 20
And their wounded steeds Fret fetlock deep in gore . . . iv 7 82
Smooth runs the water where the brook is deep . 2 *Hen. VI.* iii 1 53
That is to see how deep my grave is made . . . . iii 2 150
Reflecting gems, Which woo'd the slimy bottom of the deep *Richard III.* i 4 32
Had you such leisure in the time of death To gaze upon the secrets of the deep? . . . . i 4 35
In this sin he is as deep as I . . . . i 4 220
Deep, hollow, treacherous, and full of guile . . . . ii 1 38
Ready, with every nod, to tumble down Into the fatal bowels of the deep . . . . iii 4 103
My reasons are too deep and dead; Too deep and dead, poor infants . iv 4 362
That trick of state Was a deep envious one . . *Hen. VIII.* ii 1 45
All the commons Hate him perniciously, and, o' my conscience, Wish him ten fathom deep . . . . ii 1 51
Reply not in how many fathoms deep They lie indrench'd *Troi. and Cres.* i 1 50
Light boats sail swift, though greater hulks draw deep . . ii 3 277
Finds bottom in the uncomprehensive deeps . . . . iii 3 198
Would I were as deep under the earth as I am above! . . iv 2 86
Is not my sorrow deep, having no bottom? . *T. Andron.* iii 1 217
Whose loss hath pierced him deep and scarr'd his heart . . iv 4 31
No more deep will I endart mine eye Than your consent gives strength to make it fly . . . . *Rom. and Jul.* i 3 98
Of breaches, ambuscadoes, Spanish blades, Of healths five-fathom deep i 4 85
My bounty is as boundless as the sea, My love as deep . . ii 2 134
'Tis not so deep as a well, nor so wide as a church-door; but 'tis enough iii 1 99
What's yours?—Five thousand mine.—'Tis much deep . *T. of Athens* iii 4 30
To contend Against those honours deep and broad . . *Macbeth* i 6 17
Our fears in Banquo Stick deep . . . . . . iii 1 50
But, in their stead, Curses, not loud but deep, mouth-honour, breath . v 3 27
We'll teach you to drink deep ere you depart . . *Hamlet* i 2 175
Gives me the lie i' the throat, As deep as to the lungs . . ii 2 602
There is a cliff, whose high and bending head Looks fearfully in the confined deep . . . . *Lear* iv 1 77
Humanity must perforce prey on itself, Like monsters of the deep . iv 2 50
To stand against the deep dread-bolted thunder . . . iv 7 33
And wrinkled deep in time . . . . . *Ant. and Cleo.* i 5 29
I swear I love you.—If you but said so, 'twere as deep with me *Cymbeline* ii 3 96
I'll hide my master from the flies, as deep As these poor pickaxes can dig . . . . iv 2 388
Our tongues and sorrows do sound deep Our woes into the air *Pericles* i 4 13
For now the wind begins to blow; Thunder above and deeps below ii Gower 30
Thou, that hast Upon the winds command, bind them in brass, Having call'd them from the deep! . . . . iii 1 4
If fires be hot, knives sharp, or waters deep . . . . iv 2 159
Deep a maim. Not so deep a maim As to be cast forth in the common air *Richard II.* i 3 156
Deep a root. Spring crestless yeomen from so deep a root? . 1 *Hen. VI.* ii 4 85
Deep a sin. Not for all this land Would I be guilty of so deep a sin *Richard III.* iii 1 43
Deep a wound. Ah, that this sight should make so deep a wound! *T. Andron.* iii 1 247
Deep an O. Rise and stand; Why should you fall into so deep an O? *Rom. and Jul.* iii 3 90
Deep as hell. If the bottom were as deep as hell, I should down *Mer. Wives* iii 5 14
His filth within being cast, he would appear A pond as deep as hell *Meas. for Meas.* iii 1 94
Deep bosom. In the deep bosom of the ocean buried . *Richard III.* i 1 4
Deep chat. I myself could make A chough of as deep chat . *Tempest* ii 1 266
Deep chest. From his deep chest laughs out a loud applause *Troi. and Cres.* i 3 163
Deep clerks she dumbs . . . . . . *Pericles* v Gower 5
Deep-contemplative. My lungs began to crow like chanticleer, That fools should be so deep-contemplative . . . . . *As Y. Like I* ii 7 31
Deep contempt. Rewards he my true service With such deep contempt? *Richard III.* iv 2 124
Deep damnation. Will plead like angels, trumpet-tongued, against The deep damnation of his taking-off . . . . . *Macbeth* i 7 20
Deep damned. Thou art more deep damn'd than Prince Lucifer *K. John* iv 3 122
Deep deceit. A man Unsounded yet and full of deep deceit . 2 *Hen. VI.* iii 1 57
Deep defiance. To fill the mouth of deep defiance up . 1 *Hen. IV.* iii 2 116
Deep demeanour. With such a deep demeanour in great sorrow 2 *Hen. IV.* iv 5 85
Deep designs. In deep designs and matters of great moment *Richard III.* iii 7 67
Deep desires. Let not light see my black and deep desires . *Macbeth* i 4 51
Deep despair. Whence springs this deep despair? . . . 3 *Hen. VI.* iii 3 12
Deep disgrace. This deep disgrace in brotherhood Touches me deeper than you can imagine . . . . . . *Richard III.* i 1 111
Deep divines. Meditating with two deep divines . . . . . iii 7 75
Deep-divorcing. And break it with a deep-divorcing vow *Com. of Errors* ii 2 140
Deep-drawing. The deep-drawing barks do there disgorge Their warlike fraughtage . . . . *Troi. and Cres.* Prol. 12
Deep duty. Of thy deep duty more impression show Than that of common sons . . . . *Coriolanus* v 3 51
Deep enemies. Two deep enemies, Foes to my rest . . *Richard III.* iv 2 73
Deep enough. If the Jew do cut but deep enough, I'll pay it presently with all my heart. . . . . *Mer. of Venice* iv 1 280
And the dungeon your place, a place deep enough . 2 *Hen. IV.* iv 3 9
I fear 'tis deepest winter in Lord Timon's purse; That is, one may reach deep enough, and yet find little. . . . . *T. of Athens* iii 4 15
Deep exclaims. Fill'd it with cursing cries and deep exclaims *Rich. III.* i 2 52
Deep experiments. And hold me pace in deep experiments 1 *Hen. IV.* iii 1 49
Deep-fet. Follow'd with a rabble that rejoice To see my tears and hear my deep-fet groans . . . . 2 *Hen. VI.* ii 4 33
Deep glass. A deep glass of rhenish wine . . *Mer. of Venice* i 2 104
Deep grief. O, this is the poison of deep grief . . . *Hamlet* iv 5 76
Deep groans. Sad sighs, deep groans . . . . *T. G. of Ver.* iii 1 230
Deep harmony. They say the tongues of dying men Enforce attention like deep harmony . . . . *Richard II.* ii 1 6
Deep incision. Deep malice makes too deep incision . . . i 1 155
Deep indent. It shall not wind with such a deep indent . 1 *Hen. IV.* iii 1 104
Deep in love. Now the fair goddess, Fortune, Fall deep in love with thee! . . . . *Coriolanus* i 5 22
Deep integrity. His prayers are full of false hypocrisy; Ours of true zeal and deep integrity . . . . . . *Richard II.* v 3 108
Deep intent. If I fail not in my deep intent . . *Richard III.* i 1 149
Deep laments. Good grandsire, leave these bitter deep laments *T. Andron.* iii 2 46
Deep languor. In the dust I write My heart's deep languor . . . iii 1 13
Deep love. On some shallow story of deep love . *T. G. of Ver.* i 1 21
Deep malice makes too deep incision . . . *Richard II.* i 1 155
Deep melancholy. My mind was troubled with deep melancholy 2 *Hen. VI.* v 1 34
Deep midnight. We must starve our sight From lovers' food till morrow deep midnight . . . . *M. N. Dream* i 1 223
Deep-mouthed. Couple Clowder with the deep-mouth'd brach *T. of Shrew* Ind. 1 18
Rattle the welkin's ear And mock the deep-mouth'd thunder *K. John* v 2 173
Whose shouts and claps out-voice the deep-mouth'd sea *Hen. V.* v Prol. 11
Deep-night, dark night, the silent of the night . . 2 *Hen. VI.* i 4 19
Deep nook. In the deep nook, where once Thou call'dst me up at midnight to fetch dew . . . . *Tempest* i 2 227
Deep oaths. Subscribe to your deep oaths, and keep it . *L. L. Lost* i 1 23
Deep of night. There want not many that do fear In deep of night to walk by this Herne's oak . . . . . *Mer. Wives* iv 4 40
The deep of night is crept upon our talk . . *J. Cæsar* iv 3 226
Deep pit. I may be pluck'd into the swallowing womb Of this deep pit *T. Andron.* ii 3 240
Deep plots. Our indiscretion sometimes serves us well, When our deep plots do pall . . . . *Hamlet* v 2 9
Deep prayers. O God! if my deep prayers cannot appease thee *Rich. III.* i 4 69
Deep premeditated. Comest thou with deep premeditated lines? 1 *Hen. VI.* iii 1 1
Deep prophecy. The spirit of deep prophecy she hath . . i 2 55
Deep rebuke. I had forestall'd this dear and deep rebuke 2 *Hen. IV.* iv 5 141
Deep repentance. And set forth A deep repentance . . *Macbeth* i 4 7
Deep-revolving witty Buckingham . . . . *Richard III.* iv 2 42
Deep scars. And took Deep scars to save thy life . *Com. of Errors* v 1 193
And victorious Warwick Received deep scars in France . 2 *Hen. VI.* i 1 87
Deep-searched. Study is like the heaven's glorious sun, That will not be deep-search'd with saucy looks . . . . *L. L. Lost* i 1 85
Deep shame had struck me dumb, made me break off . *K. John* iv 2 235
Give me ample satisfaction For these deep shames . *Com. of Errors* v 1 253
Deep sighs. With tears augmenting the fresh morning's dew, Adding to clouds more clouds with his deep sighs . . . *Rom. and Jul.* i 1 139
Deep sin. O, God defend my soul from such deep sin! . *Richard II.* i 1 187
Deep story. That's a deep story of a deeper love . *T. G. of Ver.* i 1 23
Deep suspicion. Tremble and start at wagging of a straw, Intending deep suspicion . . . . *Richard III.* iii 5 8
I am sorry my integrity should breed, And service to his majesty and you, So deep suspicion . . . . *Hen. VIII.* iii 1 53
Deep-sworn. The latest breath that gave the sound of words Was deep-sworn faith . . . . *K. John* iii 1 231
Deep tragedian. I can counterfeit the deep tragedian . *Richard III.* iii 5 5
Deep traitors. And take deep traitors for thy dearest friends! . i 3 224
Deep trust. Natures of such deep trust we shall much need . *Lear* ii 1 117
Deep-vow. Master Deep-vow, and Master Copper-spur *Meas. for Meas.* iv 3 14
Deep well. Now is this golden crown like a deep well . *Richard II.* iv 1 184
Deeper. I'll seek him deeper than e'er plummet sounded . *Tempest* iii 3 101
Deeper than did ever plummet sound I'll drown my book . . v 1 56
That's a deep story of a deeper love . . . . *T. G. of Ver.* i 1 23
O, sir, the conceit is deeper than you think for . . *T. of Shrew* iv 3 163
Deeper than oblivion we do bury The incensing relics of it . *All's Well* v 3 24
No deeper wrinkles yet? hath sorrow struck So many blows upon this face of mine, And made no deeper wounds? . . . *Richard II.* iv 1 277
Between two dogs, which hath the deeper mouth? . . 1 *Hen. VI.* ii 4 12
Touches me deeper than you can imagine . . . . *Richard III.* i 1 112
But thou art deeper read, and better skill'd . . *T. Andron.* iv 1 33
This avarice Sticks deeper, grows with more pernicious root *Macbeth* iv 3 85
Something deeper, Whereof perchance these are but furnishings *Lear* iii 1 28
Deepest. The private wound is deepest . . . . *T. G. of Ver.* v 4 71
For as a surfeit of the sweetest things The deepest loathing to the stomach brings . . . . *M. N. Dream* ii 2 138

Deepest. With the deepest malice of the war Destroy what lies before 'em *Coriolanus* iv 6 41
I fear 'tis deepest winter in Lord Timon's purse *T. of Athens* iii 4 14
Win us with honest trifles, to betray 's In deepest consequence *Macbeth* i 3 126
Deeply. That most deeply to consider is The beauty of his daughter *Tempest* iii 2 106
And entertain'd 'em deeply in her heart *T. G. of Ver.* v 4 102
Thy beauty sounded, Yet not so deeply as to thee belongs *T. of Shrew* ii 1 194
And she loveth him, Or both dissemble deeply their affections iv 4 42
Now he's deeply in *T. Night* ii 5 47
He straight declined, droop'd, took it deeply *W. Tale* ii 3 14
Not so sound and half so deeply sweet *2 Hen. IV.* iv 5 26
I will deeply put the fashion on And wear it in my heart v 2 52
Are deeply indebted for this piece of pains *2 Hen. VI.* i 4 47
Thou art sworn as deeply to effect what we intend *Richard III.* iii 1 158
She's with the lion deeply still in league *T. Andron.* iv 1 98
Consider it not so deeply *Macbeth* ii 2 30
If she should break it now !—'Tis deeply sworn *Hamlet* iii 2 235
Wine loved I deeply, dice dearly *Lear* iii 4 93
I have spoke this, to know if your affiance Were deeply rooted *Cymb.* i 6 164
Heavens, How deeply you at once do touch me ! iv 3 4
Deer. You have beaten my men, killed my deer *Mer. Wives* i 1 115
Art thou there, my deer? my male deer? v 5 18
I will never take you for my love again ; but I will always count you my deer. v 5 123
When night-dogs run, all sorts of deer are chased v 5 252
Too unruly deer, he breaks the pale And feeds from home *Com. of Errors* ii 1 100
As I for praise alone now seek to spill The poor deer's blood *L. L. Lost* iv 1 35
Well, then, I am the shooter.—And who is your deer? iv 1 116
The deer was, as you know, sanguis, in blood iv 2 3
My haud credo for a deer.—I said the deer was not a haud credo iv 2 20
Will you hear an extemporal epitaph on the death of the deer? iv 2 51
The king he is hunting the deer ; I am coursing myself iv 3 1
'Poor deer,' quoth he, 'thou makest a testament As worldlings do' *As Y. Like It* ii 1 47
Weeping and commenting Upon the sobbing deer ii 1 66
The noblest deer hath them as huge as the rascal iii 3 57
Which is he that killed the deer?—Sir, it was I iv 2 1
Set the deer's horns upon his head, for a branch of victory iv 2 5
What shall he have that kill'd the deer? His leather skin and horns to wear iv 2 11
'Tis thought your deer does hold you at a bay *T. of Shrew* v 2 56
They may joul horns together, like any deer i' the herd *All's Well* i 3 59
And then to sigh, as 'twere The mort o' the deer *W. Tale* i 2 118
Death hath not struck so fat a deer to-day, Though many dearer *1 Hen. IV.* v 4 107
Bounded in a pale, A little herd of England's timorous deer *1 Hen. VI.* iv 2 46
If we be English deer, be then in blood iv 2 48
Sell every man his life as dear as mine, And they shall find dear deer of us iv 2 54
Seek thee out some other chase, For I myself must hunt this deer to death *2 Hen. VI.* v 2 15
Through this laund anon the deer will come ; And in this covert will we make our stand, Culling the principal of all the deer *3 Hen. VI.* iii 1 2
Ay, here's a deer whose skin's a keeper's fee: This is the quondam king iii 1 22
Stand you thus close, to steel the bishop's deer? iv 5 17
Seeking to hide herself, as doth the deer That hath received some unrecuring wound *T. Andron.* iii 1 89
It was my deer ; and he that wounded her Hath hurt me more than had he kill'd me dead iii 1 91
How like a deer, strucken by many princes, Dost thou here lie ! *J. Cæsar* iii 1 209
To relate the manner, Were, on the quarry of these murder'd deer, To add the death of you *Macbeth* iv 3 206
Why, let the stricken deer go weep, The hart ungalled play *Hamlet* iii 2 282
Mice and rats, and such small deer *Lear* iii 4 144
Yield up Their deer to the stand o' the stealer *Cymbeline* ii 3 75
Why hast thou gone so far, To be unbent when thou hast ta'en thy stand, The elected deer before thee? iii 4 112
Déesse. Mon très cher et devin déesse *Hen. V.* v 2 232
Deface. Pay him six thousand, and deface the bond *Mer. of Venice* iii 2 301
And deface The patterns that by God and by French fathers Had twenty years been made *Hen. V.* ii 4 60
How shall we then dispense with that contract, And not deface your honour with reproach? *1 Hen. VI.* v 5 29
Defaced. Look on fertile France, And see the cities and the towns defaced By wasting ruin iii 3 45
My arms torn and defaced, And I proclaim'd a coward ! *2 Hen. VI.* iv 1 42
And defaced The precious image of our dear Redeemer *Richard III.* ii 1 122
Her face defaced with scars of infamy iii 7 126
Defacer. That foul defacer of God's handiwork iv 4 51
Defacers of a public peace *Hen. VIII.* v 3 41
Defacing monuments of conquer'd France *2 Hen. VI.* i 1 102
Defamed. That England was defamed by tyranny *Hen. VIII.* ii 1 123
Default. We that know what 'tis to fast and pray Are penitent for your default to-day *Com. of Errors* i 2 52
I may say in the default, he is a man I know *All's Well* ii 3 242
This was your default *1 Hen. VI.* ii 1 60
And Talbot perisheth by your default iv 4 28
Defeat. And made defeat of her virginity *Much Ado* iv 1 48
My honour's at the stake ; which to defeat, I must produce my power. Here, take her hand *All's Well* ii 3 156
Making defeat on the full power of France *Hen. V.* i 2 107
So may a thousand actions, once afoot, End in one purpose, and be all well borne Without defeat i 2 213
And alleged Many sharp reasons to defeat the law *Hen. VIII.* ii 1 14
Your activity may defeat and quell The source of all erection *T. of Athens* iv 3 163
Therein, ye gods, you tyrants do defeat *J. Cæsar* i 3 92
Upon whose property and most dear life A damn'd defeat was made *Hamlet* ii 2 598
My stronger guilt defeats my strong intent iii 3 40
Their defeat Does by their own insinuation grow v 2 58
Follow thou the wars ; defeat thy favour with an usurped beard *Othello* i 3 346
His unkindness may defeat my life, But never taint my love iv 2 160
Lost, in her greatness, by some mortal stroke She do defeat us *A. and C.* v 1 65
Defeated. Thereby to have defeated you and me *M. N. Dream* iv 1 162
These men have defeated the law and outrun native punishment *Hen. V.* iv 1 175
With a defeated joy,—With an auspicious and a dropping eye *Hamlet* i 2 10
Defeatest. Thou strikest not me, 'tis Cæsar thou defeat'st *A. and C.* iv 14 68
Defeature. Then is he the ground Of my defeatures *Com. of Errors* ii 1 98
Careful hours with time's deformed hand Have written strange defeatures in my face v 1 299
Defect. Some defect in her Did quarrel with the noblest grace she owed *Tempest* iii 1 44
Saying thus, or to the same defect *M. N. Dream* iii 1 40
That is the very defect of the matter, sir *Mer. of Venice* ii 2 152
For those defects I have before rehearsed *T. of Shrew* i 2 124
Oftentimes it doth present harsh rage, Defect of manners *1 Hen. IV.* iii 1 184
So much is my poverty of spirit, So mighty and so many my defects *Richard III.* iii 7 160
The faint defects of age Must be the scene of mirth *Troi. and Cres.* i 3 172
Whether 'twas pride, Which out of daily fortune ever taints The happy man ; whether defect of judgement *Coriolanus* iv 7 39
Being unprepared, Our will became the servant to defect *Macbeth* ii 1 18
These men, Carrying, I say, the stamp of one defect *Hamlet* i 4 31
Now remains That we find out the cause of this effect, Or rather say, the cause of this defect ii 2 102
Our means secure us, and our mere defects Prove our commodities *Lear* iv 1 22
You praise yourself By laying defects of judgement to me *A. and C.* ii 2 55
She spoke, and panted, That she did make defect perfection ii 2 236
Defective. We, poising us in her defective scale, Shall weigh thee to the beam *All's Well* ii 3 161
Defective in their natures, grow to wildness *Hen. V.* v 2 55
Make us think Rather our state's defective for requital *Coriolanus* ii 2 54
Rather say, the cause of this defect, For this effect defective comes by cause *Hamlet* ii 2 102
All which the Moor is defective in *Othello* ii 1 233
Defence. And a thousand other her defences *Mer. Wives* ii 2 259
Muster your wits ; stand in your own defence *L. L. Lost* v 2 85
And by how much defence is better than no skill *As Y. Like It* iii 3 62
Our virginity, though valiant, in the defence yet is weak *All's Well* i 1 127
She is arm'd for him and keeps her guard In honestest defence iii 5 77
That defence thou hast, betake thee to't *T. Night* iii 4 240
Thou art the issue of my dear offence *K. John* i 1 258
By how much unexpected, by so much We must awake endeavour for defence ii 1 81
Nor tempt the danger of my true defence iv 3 84
Let it at least be said They saw we had a purpose of defence v 1 76
O, and there Where honourable rescue and defence Cries out ! v 2 18
He will the rather do it when he sees Ourselves well sinewed to our defence v 7 88
To God, the widow's champion and defence *Richard II.* i 2 43
Who but Rumour, who but only I, Make fearful musters and prepared defence *2 Hen. IV.* Ind. 12
England, being empty of defence, Hath shook and trembled *Hen. V.* i 2 153
And more than carefully it us concerns To answer royally in our defences ii 4 3
Defences, musters, preparations, Should be maintain'd ii 4 18
In cases of defence 'tis best to weigh The enemy more mighty than he seems: So the proportions of defence are fill'd ii 4 43
Will you yield, and this avoid, Or, guilty in defence, be thus destroy'd? iii 3 43
In defence of my lord's worthiness, I crave the benefit of law of arms *1 Hen. VI.* iv 1 99
Now is it manhood, wisdom and defence, To give the enemy way *2 Hen. VI.* v 2 75
Lord Clifford vows to fight in thy defence *3 Hen. VI.* i 1 160
Offering their own lives in their young's defence ii 2 32
Cheer these noble lords And hearten those that fight in your defence ii 2 79
The city being but of small defence, We'll quickly rouse the traitors v 1 64
Alas, I am not coop'd here for defence ! v 1 109
I would not wish a drop of Trojan blood Spent more in her defence *Troi. and Cres.* ii 2 198
For the defence of a town, our general is excellent *Coriolanus* iv 5 178
Desperation Is all the policy, strength and defence, That Rome can make iv 6 127
And thou dismember'd with thine own defence *Rom. and Jul.* iii 3 134
To kill, I grant, is sin's extremest gust ; But, in defence, by mercy, 'tis most just *T. of Athens* iii 5 55
All thy safety were remotion and thy defence absence iv 3 346
Whilst we, lying still, Are full of rest, defence, and nimbleness *J. Cæsar* iv 3 202
Every one did bear Thy praises in his kingdom's great defence *Macbeth* i 3 99
Why then, alas, Do I put up that womanly defence? iv 2 78
Gave you such a masterly report For art and exercise in your defence *Hamlet* iv 7 98
How can that be, unless she drowned herself in her own defence? v 1 7
He is bold in his defence *Lear* v 3 114
O, let the heavens Give him defence against the elements *Othello* ii 1 45
Go put on thy defences *Ant. and Cleo.* iv 4 10
Soft, soft ! we'll no defence ; Obedient as the scabbard *Cymbeline* iii 4 81
Defend. These are devils : O defend me ! *Tempest* ii 2 92
Defend your reputation, or bid farewell to your good life for ever *Mer. Wives* iii 3 126
Heavens defend me from that Welsh fairy ! v 5 85
The doubleness of the benefit defends the deceit from reproof *M. for M.* iii 1 268
God defend the lute should be like the case ! *Much Ado* ii 1 98
O, God defend me ! how am I beset ! iv 1 78
God defend but God should go before such villains ! iv 2 21
God defend me from these two ! *Mer. of Venice* i 2 57
He protests he will not hurt you.—Pray God defend me ! *T. Night* iii 4 331
Drew to defend him when he was beset v 1 88
That for thine own gain shouldst defend mine honour *K. John* i 1 242
But yet I dare defend My innocent life against an emperor iv 3 88
Mean time let this defend my loyalty *Richard II.* i 1 67
Which in myself I boldly will defend i 1 145
O, God defend my soul from such deep sin ! i 1 187
As so defend thee heaven and thy valour ! i 3 15
By my oath—Which God defend a knight should violate ! i 3 18
Both to defend my loyalty and truth To God, my king i 3 19
And as I truly fight, defend me heaven ! i 3 24
Speak like a true knight, so defend thee heaven ! i 3 34
Whom both my oath And duty bids defend ii 3 113
And God defend but still I should stand so *1 Hen. IV.* iv 3 38
I will assay thee : so, defend thyself. v 4 34
Lay down our proportions to defend Against the Scot *Hen. V.* i 2 137
A wall sufficient to defend Our inland from the pilfering borderers i 2 141
The advised head defends itself at home i 2 179
Cannot defend our own doors from the dog i 2 218
To defend the city from the rebels *2 Hen. VI.* iv 5 5
And with their helps only defend ourselves *3 Hen. VI.* iv 1 45
To defend his person from night-foes iv 3 22

Defend. Yield me up the keys ; For Edward will defend the town and thee . . . . 3 *Hen. VI.* iv 7 38
From which no warrant can defend us . . . . . *Richard III.* i 4 114
Whom thou wert sworn to cherish and defend . . . . . i 4 213
Look back, defend thee, here are enemies.—God and our innocency defend and guard us ! . . . . iii 5 19
Which God defend that I should wring from him ! . . . . iii 7 173
Sleeping and waking, O, defend me still ! . . . . . . v 3 117
Upon my wit, to defend my wiles ; upon my secrecy, to defend mine honesty ; my mask, to defend my beauty ; and you, to defend all these . . . . *Troi. and Cres.* i 2 285
And you [merit] as well to keep her, that defend her, Not palating the taste of her dishonour . . . . iv 1 58
What is granted them ?—Five tribunes to defend their vulgar wisdoms *Coriolanus* i 1 219
Defend yourself By calmness or by absence : all's in anger . . . iii 2 94
Defend the justice of my cause with arms . . . . *T. Andron.* i 1 2
The future comes apace : What shall defend the interim ? *T. of Athens* ii 2 158
The mighty gods defend thee ! . . . . *J. Cæsar* ii 3 9
The gods defend him from so great a shame ! . . . . . . v 4 23
Angels and ministers of grace defend us ! Be thou a spirit of health or goblin damn'd . . . . *Hamlet* i 4 39
Why, then the Polack never will defend it.—Yes, it is already garrison'd iv 4 23
O, yet defend me, friends ; I am but hurt . . . . . . v 2 335
Draw ; seem to defend yourself ; now quit you well . . . *Lear* ii 1 32
Defend you From seasons such as these . . . . iii 4 31
If thou shouldst dally half an hour, his life, With thine, and all that offer to defend him, Stand in assured loss . . . . iii 6 101
My state Stands on me to defend, not to debate . . . . . . v 1 69
She fordid herself.—The gods defend her ! . . . . v 3 256
Heaven defend your good souls, that you think I will your serious and great business scant . . . . *Othello* i 3 267
Unless self-charity be sometimes a vice, And to defend ourselves . . ii 3 203
Good heaven, the souls of all my tribe defend From jealousy ! . . . iii 3 175
Hath he seen majesty ? Isis else defend, And serving you so long ! *Ant. and Cleo.* iii 3 46
As the tops of trees, Which fence the roots they grow by and defend them *Pericles* i 2 30
In like necessity—The which the gods protect thee from !—may defend thee ii 1 135
The gods defend me !—If it please the gods to defend you by men, then men must comfort you . . . . iv 2 95
And God defend the right ! *L. L. Lost* i 1 ; *Richard II.* i 3 ; 2 *Hen. VI.* ii 3
Defendant. Indirectly and directly too Thou hast contrived against the very life Of the defendant . . . . . . *Mer. of Venice* iv 1 361
With men of courage and with means defendant . . . *Hen. V.* ii 4 8
And ready are the appellant and defendant . . . . 2 *Hen. VI.* ii 3 49
Defended. If you had pleased to have defended it With any terms of zeal *Mer. of Venice* v 1 204
She hath herself not only well defended But taken and impounded as a stray The King of Scots . . . . *Hen. V.* i 2 159
Three times to-day You have defended me from imminent death 2 *Hen. VI.* v 3 19
Without a heart to dare or sword to draw When Helen is defended *Troi. and Cres.* ii 2 158
Which of your hands hath not defended Rome ? . . *T. Andron.* iii 1 168
Defender. Have the power still To banish your defenders *Coriolanus* iii 3 128
You have pushed out your gates the very defender of them . . . v 2 42
Thou great defender of this Capitol, Stand gracious ! . . *T. Andron.* i 1 77
Defending. I were best to cut my left hand off And swear I lost the ring defending it . . . . *Mer. of Venice* v 1 178
To prove him, in defending of myself, A traitor to my God *Richard II.* i 3 23
Defensible. To abide a field Where nothing but the sound of Hotspur's name Did seem defensible . . . . 2 *Hen. IV.* ii 3 38
Dispose of us and ours ; For we no longer are defensible *Hen. V.* iii 3 50
Defensive. Or as a moat defensive to a house . . . *Richard II.* ii 1 48
Holy Joan was his defensive guard . . . . . . 1 *Hen. VI.* ii 1 49
Defer no time, delays have dangerous ends . . . . iii 2 33
Defer the spoil of the city until night . . . . . 2 *Hen. VI.* iv 7 142
Defiance. Take my defiance ! Die, perish ! . . . *Meas. for Meas.* iii 1 143
Then take my king's defiance from my mouth . . . . . *K. John* i 1 21
Send Defiance to the traitor, and so die . . . . *Richard II.* iii 3 130
To fill the mouth of deep defiance up . . . . . 1 *Hen. IV.* iii 2 116
I have thrown A brave defiance in King Henry's teeth . . . . . v 2 43
Even to the eyes of Richard Gave him defiance . . . 2 *Hen. IV.* iii 1 65
What to him from England ?—Scorn and defiance . . . *Hen. V.* ii 4 117
Let him greet England with our sharp defiance . . . . . . iii 5 37
To this add defiance . . . . iii 6 142
But when I meet you arm'd, as black defiance As heart can think or courage execute . . . . *Troi. and Cres.* iv 1 12
Which, as he breathed defiance to my ears, He swung about his head and cut the winds . . . . *Rom. and Jul.* i 1 117
Defiance, traitors, hurl we in your teeth . . . . . *J. Cæsar* v 1 64
Deficient. I'll look no more ; Lest my brain turn, and the deficient sight Topple down headlong . . . . *Lear* iv 6 23
For nature so preposterously to err, Being not deficient, blind, or lame of sense, Sans witchcraft could not . . . . *Othello* i 3 63
Defied. But as she spit in his face, so she defied him *Meas. for Meas.* ii 1 86
Complexions that liked me and breaths that I defied not *As Y. Like It* Epil. 21
At length they came to the broom-staff to me ; I defied 'em still *Hen. VIII.* v 4 58
Look For fury not to be resisted. Thus defied, I thank thee for myself *Cymbeline* iii 1 68
Defies. She defies me, Like Turk to Christian . . . *As Y. Like It* iv 3 32
Defile. His dove will prove, his gold will hold, And his soft couch defile *Mer. Wives* iii 3 108
I am toiling in a pitch,—pitch that defiles : defile ! a foul word *L. L. Lost* iv 3 3
When saucy trusting of the cozen'd thoughts Defiles the pitchy night *All's Well* iv 4 24
This pitch, as ancient writers do report, doth defile . . 1 *Hen. IV.* ii 4 456
The blind and bloody soldier with foul hand Defile the locks of your shrill-shrieking daughters . . . . *Hen. V.* iii 3 35
And conversed with such As, like to pitch, defile nobility 2 *Hen. VI.* ii 1 196
When false opinion, Whose wrong thought defiles thee, In thy just proof, repeals and reconciles thee . . . . *Lear* iii 6 119
Defiled. I think they that touch pitch will be defiled . *Much Ado* iii 3 60
One Hero died defiled, but I do live, And surely as I live, I am a maid . v 4 63
He is defiled That draws a sword on thee . . . . *M. N. Dream* vi 2 410
He knows himself my bed he hath defiled . . . . . *All's Well* v 3 301
Hath held his current and defiled himself . . . . *Richard II.* v 3 63
Lie in a pitch'd field.—Ay, defiled land, my lord . *T. of Athens* i 2 231
As houses are defiled for want of use . . . . . . *Pericles* i 4 37

Defiler. Thou bright defiler Of Hymen's purest bed ! *T. of Athens* iv 3 383
Defiling. And she an eater of her mother's flesh, By the defiling of her parent's bed . . . . *Pericles* i 1 131
Define, define, well-educated infant . . . . . *L. L. Lost* i 2 99
Behold, as may unworthiness define, A little touch of Harry *Hen. V.* iv Prol. 46
To define true madness, What is 't but to be nothing else but mad ? *Hamlet* ii 2 93
Definement. His definement suffers no perdition in you . . . . v 2 117
Definite. Idiots in this case of favour would Be wisely definite *Cymbeline* i 6 43
Definitive. Never crave him ; we are definitive . . . *Meas. for Meas.* v 1 432
Definitively thus I answer you . . . . *Richard III.* iii 7 153
Deflour. And let my spleenful sons this trull deflour *T. Andron.* ii 3 191
Deflowered. A deflower'd maid ! And by an eminent body that enforced The law against it ! . . . . *Meas. for Meas.* iv 4 24
Since lion vile hath here deflower'd my dear . . . *M. N. Dream* v 1 297
Sure, some Tereus hath deflowered thee . . . . . *T. Andron.* ii 4 26
To slay his daughter with his own right hand, Because she was enforced, stain'd, and deflower'd . . . . v 3 38
There she lies, Flower as she was, deflowered by him *Rom. and Jul.* iv 5 37
Deform. Soul-killing witches that deform the body . . *Com. of Errors* i 2 100
Deformed. You never saw her since she was deformed.—How long hath she been deformed ? . . . . *T. G. of Ver.* ii 1 69
He is deformed, crooked, old and sere, Ill-faced, worse bodied *Com. of Errors* iv 2 19
Careful hours with time's deformed hand Have written strange defeatures in my face . . . . v 1 298
Seest thou not what a deformed thief this fashion is ? *Much Ado* iii 3 131
I know that Deformed ; a' has been a vile thief this seven year . iii 3 133
And one Deformed is one of them : I know him ; a' wears a lock . iii 3 182
You'll be made bring Deformed forth, I warrant you . . . . iii 3 185
And also, the watch heard them talk of one Deformed . . . . v 1 317
O thou monster Ignorance, how deformed dost thou look ! *L. L. Lost* iv 2 24
Your beauty, ladies, Hath much deform'd us . . . . v 2 767
None can be call'd deform'd but the unkind . . . . *T. Night* iii 4 402
An indigested and deformed lump . . . . 3 *Hen. VI.* v 6 51
Deform'd, unfinish'd, sent before my time Into this breathing world *Richard III.* i 1 20
Deformities. What care I What curious eye doth quote deformities ? *Rom. and Jul.* i 4 31
Deformity. Her passing deformity . . . . *T. G. of Ver.* ii 1 82
An envious mountain on my back, Where sits deformity to mock my body . . . . 3 *Hen. VI.* iii 2 158
To spy my shadow in the sun And descant on mine own deformity *Richard III.* i 1 27
Blush, blush, thou lump of foul deformity ! . . . . i 2 57
Proper deformity seems not in the fiend So horrid as in woman . *Lear* iv 2 60
Deftly. Come, high or low ; Thyself and office deftly show ! . *Macbeth* iv 1 68
Defunct. The organs, though defunct and dead before, Break up their drowsy grave and newly move . . . . *Hen. V.* iv 1 21
Nor to comply with heat—the young affects In me defunct . *Othello* i 3 265
Nature doth abhor to make his bed With the defunct . . *Cymbeline* iv 2 358
Defunction. After defunction of King Pharamond . . . *Hen. V.* i 2 58
Defuse. If but as well I other accents borrow, That can my speech defuse *Lear* i 4 2
Defused attire And every thing that seems unnatural . . *Hen. V.* v 2 61
Defused infection of a man . . . . *Richard III.* i 2 78
Defy. He that dies pays all debts : I defy thee . . . . *Tempest* iii 2 140
I defy all angels, in any such sort, as they say, but in the way of honesty *Mer. Wives* ii 2 74
I dare, and do defy thee for a villain . . . . . *Com. of Errors* v 1 32
That for a tricksy word Defy the matter . . . . *Mer. of Venice* iii 5 75
How have you come so early by this lethargy ?—Lechery ! I defy lechery *T. Night* i 5 133
What, man ! defy the devil : consider, he's an enemy to mankind . . iii 4 108
If you offend him, I for him defy you . . . . iii 4 345
Why then defy each other, and pell-mell Make work upon ourselves *K. John* ii 1 406
I defy all counsel, all redress, But that which ends all counsel, true redress, Death, death . . . . iii 4 23
I do defy him, and I spit at him ; Call him a slanderous coward *Rich. II.* i 1 60
All studies here I solemnly defy, Save how to gall and pinch 1 *Hen. IV.* i 3 228
I defy thee : God's light, I was never called so in mine own house before iii 3 71
I cannot flatter ; I do defy The tongues of soothers . . . . . iv 1 6
Defy him by the Lord of Westmoreland . . . . v 2 32
'Couple a gorge !' That is the word. I thee defy again *Hen. V.* ii 1 76
Or like to men proud of destruction Defy us to our worst . . . iii 3 5
Gloucester, I do defy thee . . . . 1 *Hen. VI.* iii 1 27
Give me but the ten meals I have lost, and I'ld defy them all 2 *Hen. VI.* iv 10 67
Defy them then, or else hold close thy lips . . . . 3 *Hen. VI.* ii 2 118
And, in this resolution, I defy thee . . . . ii 2 170
I defy thee, And to my brother turn my blushing cheeks . . . . v 1 98
Is it even so ? then I defy you, stars ! . . . . . *Rom. and Jul.* v 1 24
I do defy thy conjurations, And apprehend thee for a felon here . v 3 68
We defy augury : there's a special providence in the fall of a sparrow *Hamlet* v 2 230
Thy pen from lenders' books, and defy the foul fiend . . . *Lear* iii 4 101
At heel of that, defy him . . . . *Ant. and Cleo.* ii 2 160
Have you that a man may deal withal, and defy the surgeon ? *Pericles* iv 6 29
Defying Those whose great power must try him . . . *Coriolanus* iii 3 79
Degenerate. The more degenerate and base art thou . *T. G. of Ver.* v 4 136
And you degenerate, you ingrate revolts . . . . . . *K. John* v 2 151
A recreant and most degenerate traitor . . . . . *Richard II.* i 1 144
Most degenerate king ! . . . . ii 1 262
To show how much thou art degenerate . . . . . 1 *Hen. IV.* iii 2 128
Oft have I heard that grief softens the mind And makes it fearful and degenerate . . . . 2 *Hen. VI.* iv 4 2
Farewell, faint-hearted and degenerate king . . . . 3 *Hen. VI.* i 1 183
Can it be That so degenerate a strain as this Should once set footing in your generous bosoms ? . . . . *Troi. and Cres.* ii 2 154
Is Lavinia then become so loose, Or Bassianus so degenerate ? *T. Andron.* ii 1 66
Degenerate bastard ! I'll not trouble thee . . . . . . *Lear* i 4 275
A gracious aged man . . . , Most barbarous, most degenerate ! have you madded . . . . iv 2 43
Degraded. Be quite degraded, like a hedge-born swain 1 *Hen. VI.* iv 1 43
Then I degraded you from being king . . . . . 3 *Hen. VI.* iv 3 33
Degree. Come cut and long-tail, under the degree of a squire *Mer. Wives* iii 4 48
Are now to have no successive degrees, But, ere they live, to end *Meas. for Meas.* ii 2 98
He that breaks them in the least degree Stands in attainder of eternal shame . . . . *L. L. Lost* i 1 157
Bear with me, I am sick ; I'll leave it by degrees . . . . . v 2 418
For mine own part, I know not the degree of the Worthy . . . v 2 508

Degree. O, that estates, degrees and offices Were not derived corruptly! *Mer. of Venice* ii 9 41
In these degrees have they made a pair of stairs to marriage *As Y. Like It* v 2 41
Can you nominate in order now the degrees of the lie? v 4 92
I will name you the degrees v 4 96
O my dear niece, welcome thou art to me! Even daughter, welcome, in no less degree v 4 154
That by degrees we mean to look into *T. of Shrew* iii 2 145
She'll not match above her degree, neither in estate, years, nor wit *T. N.* i 3 116
Whatsoever he be, under the degree of my betters i 3 125
Misprision in the highest degree! i 5 61
For he's in the third degree of drink, he's drowned i 5 143
I pity you.—That's a degree to love iii 1 134
Fellow! not Malvolio, nor after my degree, but fellow iii 4 86
I'll requite it in the highest degree iv 2 128
Lest barbarism, making me the precedent, Should a like language use to all degrees *W. Tale* ii 1 85
I'll answer thee in any fair degree *Richard II.* i 1 80
And he our subjects' next degree in hope i 4 36
Even in condition of the worst degree, In gross rebellion iii 3 109
So both the degrees prevent my curses 2 *Hen. IV.* i 2 259
Well, then, Colvile is your name, a knight is your degree iv 3 6
Colvile shall be still your name, a traitor your degree iv 3 8
Art thou aught else but place, degree and form? *Hen. V.* iv 1 263
Quite from the answer of his degree iv 7 143
I will make you to-day a squire of low degree v 1 38
Or flourish to the height of my degree 1 *Hen. VI.* ii 4 111
More than well beseems A man of thy profession and degree iii 1 20
Fester'd members rot but by degree, Till bones and flesh and sinews fall away iii 1 192
Unworthily Thou wast installed in that high degree iv 1 17
Is my Lord of Winchester install'd, And call'd unto a cardinal's degree? v 1 29
How art thou call'd? and what is thy degree? 2 *Hen. VI.* v 1 73
Duke of York: The next degree is England's royal throne 3 *Hen. VI.* ii 1 193
That no man shall have private conference, Of what degree soever *Rich. III.* i 1 87
How canst thou urge God's dreadful law to us, When thou hast broke it in so dear degree? i 4 215
I know not whether to depart in silence, Or bitterly to speak in your reproof, Best fitteth my degree iii 7 143
Perjury, perjury, in the high'st degree; Murder, stern murder, in the direst degree v 3 196
All several sins, all used in each degree, Throng to the bar, crying all, Guilty! guilty! v 3 198
No, nor Hector is not Troilus in some degrees *Troi. and Cres.* i 2 74
Degree being vizarded, The unworthiest shows as fairly in the mask i 3 83
The planets and this centre Observe degree, priority and place i 3 86
O, when degree is shaked, Which is the ladder to all high designs, The enterprise is sick! i 3 101
Degrees in schools and brotherhoods in cities i 3 104
Crowns, sceptres, laurels, But by degree, stand in authentic place i 3 108
Take but degree away, untune that string, And, hark, what discord follows! i 3 109
This chaos, when degree is suffocate, Follows the choking i 3 125
This neglection of degree it is That by a pace goes backward, with a purpose It hath to climb i 3 127
His ascent is not by such easy degrees *Coriolanus* ii 2 29
In the high'st degree He hath abused your powers v 6 85
Degrees, observances, customs, and laws, Decline to your confounding contraries, And let confusion live! *T. of Athens* iv 1 19
The sweet degrees that this brief world affords iv 3 253
Tell Athens, in the sequence of degree From high to low throughout v 1 211
Looks in the clouds, scorning the base degrees By which he did ascend *J. Cæsar* ii 1 26
You know your own degrees; sit down *Macbeth* iii 4 1
Her offence Must be of such unnatural degree, That monsters it *Lear* i 1 222
Any man of quality or degree within the lists of the army v 3 110
Who stands so eminent in the degree of this fortune as Cassio does? *Oth.* ii 1 241
He was a wight of high renown, And thou art but of low degree ii 3 97
What wound did ever heal but by degrees? ii 3 377
Many proposed matches Of her own clime, complexion, and degree iii 3 230
Till by degrees the memory of my womb Lie graveless *A. and C.* iii 13 163
Deifying. All, forsooth, deifying the name of Rosalind *As Y. Like It* iii 2 381
Deign. I fear my Julia would not deign my lines, Receiving them from such a worthless post *T. G. of Ver.* i 1 160
None so dry or thirsty Will deign to sip or touch one drop of it *T. of Shr.* v 2 145
Since thou dost deign to woo her little worth 1 *Hen. VI.* v 3 151
And all those friends that deign to follow me 3 *Hen. VI.* iv 7 39
Nor would we deign him burial of his men *Macbeth* i 2 60
Thy palate then did deign The roughest berry on the rudest hedge *Ant. and Cleo.* i 4 63
Deigned. God's mother deigned to appear to me 1 *Hen. VI.* i 2 78
Deiphobus. What sneaking fellow comes yonder?—Where? yonder?—that's Deiphobus *Troi. and Cres.* i 2 247
Hector, Deiphobus, Helenus, Antenor, and all the gallantry of Troy iii 1 148
There is at hand Paris your brother, and Deiphobus iv 2 63
Deities. The gods themselves, Humbling their deities to love, have taken The shapes of beasts upon them *W. Tale* iv 4 26
More bright in zeal than the devotion which Cold lips blow to their deities *Troi. and Cres.* iv 4 29
For your own gifts, make yourselves praised: but reserve still to give, lest your deities be despised *T. of Athens* iii 6 82
When it pleaseth their deities to take the wife of a man from him, it shows to man the tailors of the earth *Ant. and Cleo.* i 2 168
Deity. I feel not This deity in my bosom *Tempest* ii 1 278
I met her deity Cutting the clouds towards Paphos iv 1 92
The liver-vein, which makes flesh a deity, A green goose a goddess *L. L. L.* iv 3 74
Nor can there be that deity in my nature, Of here and every where *T. Night* v 1 234
Humbly complaining to her deity Got my lord chamberlain his liberty *Richard III.* i 1 76
He leads them like a thing Made by some other deity than nature *Coriol.* iv 6 91
Or we poor ghosts will cry To the shining synod of the rest Against thy deity *Cymbeline* v 4 90
Convey thy deity Aboard our dancing boat! *Pericles* iii 1 12
Déjà. N'avez vous pas déjà oublié ce que je vous ai enseigné? *Hen. V.* iii 4 45
Deject. Reason and respect Make livers pale and lustihood deject *Troi. and Cres.* ii 2 50
Nor once deject the courage of our minds, Because Cassandra's mad ii 2 121
And I, of ladies most deject and wretched, That suck'd the honey of his music vows *Hamlet* iii 1 164

Dejected. You have the start of me; I am dejected *Mer. Wives* v 5 171
There, at the moated grange, resides this dejected Mariana *M. for M.* iii 1 277
Nor the fruitful river in the eye, Nor the dejected 'haviour of the visage *Hamlet* i 2 81
To be worst, The lowest and most dejected thing of fortune, Stands still in esperance, lives not in fear *Lear* iv 1 3
Antony Is valiant, and dejected *Ant. and Cleo.* iv 12 7
From the dejected state wherein he is, He hopes by you his fortunes yet may flourish *Pericles* ii 2 46
Delabreth. Charles Delabreth, high constable of France *Hen. V.* iii 5 40; iv 8 97
Delated. More than the scope Of these delated articles allow *Hamlet* i 2 38
Delation. They are close delations, working from the heart *Othello* iii 3 123
Delay. And lead him on with a fine-baited delay *Mer. Wives* ii 1 99
Forced me to seek delays for them and me *Com. of Errors* i 1 75
Then were you hindered by the sergeant, to tarry for the hoy Delay iv 3 40
Make no delay: We may effect this business yet ere day *M. N. Dream* iii 2 394
'Tide life, 'tide death, I come without delay v 1 205
One inch of delay more is a South-sea of discovery *As Y. Like It* iii 2 207
Let me stay the growth of his beard, if thou delay me not the knowledge of his chin iii 2 222
Whose want, and whose delay, is strew'd with sweets *All's Well* iv 4 45
Now, God delay our rebellion! as we are ourselves, what things are we! iv 3 23
Who of my people hold him in delay? *T. Night* ii 5 112
What's to come is still unsure: In delay there lies no plenty ii 3 51
We make woe wanton with this fond delay: Once more, adieu *Richard II.* v 1 101
Let's away; Advantage feeds him fat, while men delay 1 *Hen. IV.* iii 2 180
Lest that our king Come here himself to question our delay *Hen. V.* ii 4 142
Leave off delays, and let us raise the siege 1 *Hen. VI.* i 2 146
Defer no time, delays have dangerous ends iii 2 33
A plague upon that villain Somerset, That thus delays my promised supply! iv 3 10
Blois, Poictiers, and Tours, are won away, 'Long all of Somerset and his delay iv 3 46
This weighty business will not brook delay 2 *Hen. VI.* i 1 170
I cannot brook delay: May it please your highness to resolve me now 3 *Hen. VI.* iii 2 18
Therefore delay not, give thy hand to Warwick iii 3 246
Nor posted off their suits with slow delays iv 8 40
If we use delay, Cold biting winter mars our hoped-for hay iv 8 60
Be not ta'en tardy by unwise delay *Richard III.* iv 1 52
I have heard that fearful commenting Is leaden servitor to dull delay iv 3 52
Delay leads impotent and snail-paced beggary iv 3 53
Let's want no discipline, make no delay; For, lords, to-morrow is a busy day v 3 17
Compel from each The sixth part of his substance, to be levied Without delay *Hen. VIII.* i 2 59
And that, without delay, their arguments Be now produced and heard ii 4 67
That you not delay the present *Coriolanus* i 6 60
He doth me wrong to feed me with delays *T. Andron.* iv 3 42
In delay We waste our lights in vain, like lamps by day *Rom. and Jul.* i 4 44
The excuse that thou dost make in this delay Is longer than the tale thou dost excuse ii 5 33
O, sweet my mother, cast me not away! Delay this marriage for a month, a week iii 5 201
Delay not, Cæsar; read it instantly *J. Cæsar* iii 1 9
The pangs of despised love, the law's delay, The insolence of office *Hamlet* iii 1 72
Tempt him with speed aboard; Delay it not iv 3 57
Abatements and delays as many As there are tongues, are hands, are accidents iv 7 121
And that without any further delay than this very evening *Lear* i 2 100
What safe and nicely I might well delay v 3 144
Ay, that's the way: Dull not device by coldness and delay *Othello* ii 3 394
That what they do delay, they not deny *Ant. and Cleo.* ii 1 3
Delayed. I am but sorry, not afeard; delay'd, But nothing alter'd *W. Tale* iv 4 474
I would not be delay'd *Othello* iii 4 114
Whom best I love I cross; to make my gift, The more delay'd, delighted *Cymbeline* v 4 102
I do commend her choice; And will no longer have it be delay'd *Pericles* ii 5 22
Delaying. The powers, delaying, not forgetting *Tempest* iii 3 73
A dangerous courtesy.—Pray, sir, in what?—In the delaying death *Meas. for Meas.* iv 2 174
Delectable. Making the hard way sweet and delectable *Richard II.* ii 3 7
Quick, forgetive, full of nimble fiery and delectable shapes 2 *Hen. IV.* iv 3 108
Deliberate. Please you, deliberate a day or two *T. G. of Ver.* i 3 73
Whose settled visage and deliberate word Nips youth i' the head *Meas. for Meas.* iii 1 90
Thus hath the candle singed the moth. O, these deliberate fools *Mer. of Venice* ii 9 80
Not to deliberate, not to remember 2 *Hen. IV.* v 5 22
Your most grave belly was deliberate, Not rash like his accusers *Coriol.* i 1 132
This sudden sending him away must seem Deliberate pause *Hamlet* iv 3 9
Delicate. Thou wast a spirit too delicate To act her earthy and abhorr'd commands *Tempest* i 2 272
Delicate Ariel, I'll set thee free for this i 2 441
Tender and delicate temperance.—Temperance was a delicate wench ii 1 42
Four legs and two voices: a most delicate monster! ii 2 93
Do you love me, master? no?—Dearly, my delicate Ariel iv 1 49
In their rooms Come thronging soft and delicate desires *Much Ado* i 1 305
Delicate fine hats and most courteous feathers *All's Well* iv 5 110
The climate's delicate, the air most sweet, Fertile the isle *W. Tale* iii 1 1
With such delicate burthens of dildos and fadings iv 4 195
As gardeners do with ordure hide those roots That shall first spring and be most delicate *Hen. V.* ii 4 40
Is far beyond a prince's delicates, His viands sparkling in a golden cup 3 *Hen. VI.* ii 5 51
Thou ever young, fresh, loved and delicate wooer! *T. of Athens* iv 3 385
Where they most breed and haunt, I have observed, The air is delicate *Macbeth* i 6 10
Led by a delicate and tender prince *Hamlet* iv 4 48
Very dear to fancy, very responsive to the hilts, most delicate carriages v 2 160
When the mind's free, The body's delicate *Lear* iii 4 12
Now and then an ample tear trill'd down Her delicate cheek iv 3 15
It were a delicate stratagem, to shoe A troop of horse with felt iv 6 188
Abused her delicate youth with drugs or minerals That weaken motion *Oth.* i 2 74
If thou wilt needs damn thyself, do it a more delicate way than drowning i 3 360
Her delicate tenderness will find itself abused ii 1 235
Indeed, she's a most fresh and delicate creature ii 3 20
O curse of marriage, That we can call these delicate creatures ours, And not their appetites! iii 3 269

Delicate. So delicate with her needle: an admirable musician *Othello* iv 1 199
Divers-colour'd fans, whose wind did seem To glow the delicate cheeks which they did cool . . . *Ant. and Cleo.* ii 2 209
Till that the conquering wine hath steep'd our sense In soft and delicate Lethe . . . ii 7 114
Under her breast—Worthy the pressing—lies a mole, right proud Of that most delicate lodging . . . *Cymbeline* ii 4 136
O most delicate fiend! Who is't can read a woman? . . . v 5 47
It smells most sweetly in my sense.—A delicate odour . . . *Pericles* iii 2 61
Delicious. A most delicious banquet by his bed . . . *T. of Shrew* Ind. 1 39
Rotted with delicious feed . . . *T. Andron.* iv 4 93
Now I feed myself With most delicious poison . . . *Ant. and Cleo.* i 5 27
Deliciousness. The sweetest honey Is loathsome in his own deliciousness *Rom. and Jul.* ii 6 12
Delight. There be some sports are painful, and their labour Delight in them sets off . . . *Tempest* iii 1 2
Sounds and sweet airs, that give delight and hurt not . . . iii 2 145
O, flatter me; for love delights in praises . . . *T. G. of Ver.* ii 4 148
I perceive you delight not in music.—Not a whit, when it jars so . . . iv 2 66
At Pentecost, When all our pageants of delight were play'd . . . iv 4 164
Do you think . . . that ever the devil could have made you our delight? *Mer. Wives* v 5 158
'Twas in the Bunch of Grapes, where indeed you have a delight to sit *Meas. for Meas.* ii 1 134
Fortune had left to both of us alike What to delight in, what to sorrow for . . . *Com. of Errors* i 1 107
Hadst thou delight to see a wretched man Do outrage and displeasure to himself? . . . iv 4 118
None but libertines delight in him . . . *Much Ado* ii 1 144
Give not me counsel; Nor let no comforter delight mine ear . . . v 1 6
The grosser manner of these world's delights . . . *L. L. Lost* i 1 29
Stops that hinder study quite And train our intellects to vain delight . . . i 1 71
All delights are vain; but that most vain, Which with pain purchased doth inherit pain . . . i 1 72
You must suffer him to take no delight nor no penance . . . i 2 134
Nor God, nor I, delights in perjured men . . . v 2 346
And cuckoo-buds of yellow hue Do paint the meadows with delight . . . v 2 907
Lull'd in these flowers with dances and delight . . . *M. N. Dream* ii 1 254
When thou wakest, Thou takest True delight In the sight Of thy former lady's eye . . . iii 2 455
How shall we beguile The lazy time, if not with some delight? . . . v 1 41
Our true intent is. All for your delight We are not here . . . v 1 114
I desire no more delight Than to be under sail and gone to-night *Mer. of Venice* ii 6 67
And quicken his embraced heaviness With some delight or other . . . ii 8 53
You will take little delight in it, I can tell you . . . *As Y. Like It* i 2 168
We will begin these rites, As we do trust they'll end, in true delights . . . v 4 204
She taketh most delight In music, instruments and poetry *T. of Shrew* i 1 92
If I can by any means light on a fit man to teach her that wherein she delights . . . i 1 113
Her prayers, whom heaven delights to hear And loves to grant *All's Well* iii 4 27
I delight in masques and revels sometimes altogether . . . *T. Night* i 3 120
I marvel your ladyship takes delight in such a barren rascal . . . i 5 89
A fool that the lady Olivia's father took much delight in . . . ii 4 12
Never to be infected with delight, Nor conversant with ease . . . *K. John* iv 3 69
My legs can keep no measure in delight . . . *Richard II.* iii 4 7
In speech, in gait, In diet, in affections of delight . . . *2 Hen. IV.* ii 3 29
Let us look in; the sight will much delight thee . . . *1 Hen. VI.* i 4 62
Who should study to prefer a peace, If holy churchmen take delight in broils? . . . iii 1 111
She is not so divine, So full-replete with choice of all delights . . . v 5 17
You are all recreants and dastards, and delight to live in slavery to the nobility . . . *2 Hen. VI.* iv 8 29
Now am I seated as my soul delights . . . *3 Hen. VI.* v 7 35
I, in this weak piping time of peace, Have no delight to pass away the time, Unless to spy my shadow in the sun . . . *Richard III.* i 1 25
If thou delight to view thy heinous deeds, Behold this pattern of thy butcheries . . . i 2 53
These should be hours for necessities, Not for delights . . . *Hen. VIII.* v 1 3
You speak Like one besotted on your sweet delights . . . *Troi. and Cres.* ii 2 143
If sanctimony be the gods' delight, If there be rule in unity itself . . . v 2 140
O, had the monster seen those lily hands Tremble, like aspen leaves, upon a lute, And make the silken strings delight to kiss them! *T. Andron.* ii 4 46
O, why should nature build so foul a den, Unless the gods delight in tragedies? . . . iv 1 60
Even such delight Among fresh female buds . . . *Rom. and Jul.* i 2 28
And find delight writ there with beauty's pen . . . i 3 82
I am the drudge and toil in your delight . . . ii 5 77
These violent delights have violent ends And in their triumph die . . . ii 6 9
If sour woe delights in fellowship And needly will be rank'd with other griefs . . . iii 2 116
The labour we delight in physics pain . . . *Macbeth* ii 3 54
Come, sisters, cheer we up his sprites, And show the best of our delights iv 1 128
And delight No less in truth than life . . . iv 3 129
In equal scale weighing delight and dole . . . *Hamlet* i 2 13
Man delights not me: no, nor woman neither, though by your smiling you seem to say so . . . ii 2 321
If you delight not in man, what lenten entertainment the players shall receive from you . . . ii 2 328
What players are they?—Even those you were wont to take delight in . . . ii 2 341
Give him a further edge, And drive his purpose on to these delights . . . iii 1 27
Make after him, poison his delight, Proclaim him in the streets . . . *Othello* i 1 68
Run from her guardage to the sooty bosom Of such a thing as thou, to fear, not to delight . . . i 2 71
Her eye must be fed; and what delight shall she have to look on the devil? . . . ii 1 228
To business that we love we rise betime, And go to't with delight *Ant. and Cleo.* iv 4 21
His delights Were dolphin-like; they show'd his back above The element they lived in . . . v 2 88
To glad the sight, And not so much to feed on as delight . . . *Pericles* i 4 29
Must have inventions to delight the taste . . . i 4 40
Doth give me A more content in course of true delight Than to be thirsty after tottering honour . . . iii 2 39
To see his daughter, all his life's delight . . . iv 4 12
Delighted. And the delighted spirit To bathe in fiery floods . . . *M. for M.* iii 1 121
We are much delighted.—I do adore thy sweet grace's slipper *L. L. Lost* v 2 671
If virtue no delighted beauty lack, Your son-in-law is far more fair than black . . . *Othello* i 3 290

Delighted. Or that mine eyes, mine ears, or any sense, Delighted them in any other form . . . *Othello* iv 2 155
Whom best I love I cross; to make my gift, The more delay'd, delighted *Cymbeline* v 4 102
Delightful. Some delightful ostentation, or show, or pageant . *L. L. Lost* v 1 118
And thy steps no more Than a delightful measure or a dance *Richard II.* i 3 291
Our dreadful marches to delightful measures . . . *Richard III.* i 1 8
O, that delightful engine of her thoughts! . . . *T. Andron.* iii 1 82
A courser, whose delightful steps Shall make the gazer joy . . . *Pericles* ii 1 164
My ears were never better fed With such delightful pleasing harmony . . . ii 5 28
Delinquent. Did he not straight In pious rage the two delinquents tear? *Macbeth* iii 6 12
Deliver. I'll deliver all; And promise you calm seas . . . *Tempest* v 1 313
I am going to deliver them.—Be they of much import? . . . *T. G. of Ver.* iii 1 54
She'll think that it is spoke in hate.—Ay, if his enemy deliver it . . . iii 2 35
I was sent to deliver him as a present . . . iv 4 7
Take this ring with thee, Deliver it to Madam Silvia . . . iv 4 77
My master charged me to deliver a ring . . . v 4 89
Upon his death's-bed—Got deliver to a joyful resurrections! *Mer. Wives* i 1 53
Received and did deliver to our age This tale . . . iv 4 37
I will be revenged, and I will deliver his wife into your hand . . . v 1 31
With a thought that more depends on it than we must yet deliver *Meas. for Meas.* iv 2 128
An express command, under penalty, to deliver his head in the view of Angelo . . . iv 2 177
Deliver us from devices hereafter . . . iv 4 14
These letters at fit time deliver me . . . iv 5 1
Even her very words Didst thou deliver to me on the mart *Com. of Errors* ii 2 166
Here are the angels that you sent for to deliver you . . . iv 3 41
Some blessed power deliver us from hence! . . . iv 3 44
Haply I see a friend will save my life And pay the sum that may deliver me . . . v 1 284
So deliver I up my apes, and away to Saint Peter for the heavens *M. Ado* ii 1 49
If drawing my sword against the humour of affection would deliver me *L. L. Lost* i 2 63
Delivers in such apt and gracious words That aged ears play truant . . . ii 1 73
Deliver this paper into the royal hand of the king . . . iv 2 145
Deliver me the key: Here do I choose, and thrive I as I may! *Mer. of Venice* ii 7 59
I would lose all, ay, sacrifice them all Here to this devil, to deliver you iv 1 287
From all such devils, good Lord deliver us! . . . *T. of Shrew* i 1 66
I have bills for money by exchange From Florence and must here deliver them . . . iv 2 90
And deliver all the intelligence in his power against you . *All's Well* iii 6 32
In fine, delivers me to fill the time, Herself most chastely absent . . . iii 7 33
But I con him no thanks for't, in the nature he delivers it . . . iv 3 175
Pray you, sir, deliver me this paper . . . v 2 16
Sure, you have some hideous matter to deliver . . . *T. Night* i 5 222
I'll deliver thy indignation to him by word of mouth . . . ii 3 140
We shall have a rare letter from him: but you'll not deliver't? . . . iii 2 61
Now will not I deliver his letter . . . iii 4 202
I will deliver his challenge by word of mouth . . . iii 4 209
Look then to be well edified when the fool delivers the madman . . . v 1 299
This you may know And so deliver . . . *W. Tale* iv 4 509
What you as from your father shall deliver, Things known betwixt us three . . . iv 4 570
Heard the old shepherd deliver the manner how he found it . . . v 2 4
He can deliver you more. How goes it now, sir? . . . v 2 29
But from the inward motion to deliver Sweet, sweet, sweet poison *K. John* i 1 212
Your highness should deliver up your crown . . . iv 2 152
Deliver him to safety; and return, For I must use thee . . . iv 2 158
More health and happiness betide my liege Than can my care-tuned tongue deliver him! . . . *Richard II.* iii 2 92
Send the breath of parley Into his ruin'd ears, and thus deliver . . . iii 3 34
Deliver them up without their ransom straight . . . *1 Hen. IV.* i 3 260
Deliver what you will; I'll say 'tis so . . . v 2 26
Deliver up my Lord of Westmoreland . . . v 2 29
Go to the Douglas, and deliver him Up to his pleasure, ransomless and free . . . v 5 27
Deliver to the army This news of peace . . . *2 Hen. IV.* iv 2 69
Health to my sovereign, and new happiness Added to that that I am to deliver! . . . iv 4 82
Such a son, That would deliver up his greatness so Into the hands of justice . . . v 2 111
Deliver them like a man of this world . . . v 3 101
I will deliver her.—There roar'd the sea . . . v 5 41
To her laws We do deliver you . . . *Hen. V.* i 2 177
Let us deliver Our puissance into the hand of God . . . ii 2 189
And bids you, in the bowels of the Lord, Deliver up the crown . . . ii 4 103
So tell your master.—I shall deliver so . . . iii 6 176
That is her ransom; I deliver her . . . *1 Hen. VI.* v 3 157
Deliver up my title in the queen To your most gracious hands *2 Hen. VI.* i 1 13
We may deliver our supplications in the quill . . . i 3 3
I will deliver you, or else lie for you: Meantime, have patience *Rich. III.* i 1 115
I am, in this, commanded to deliver The noble Duke of Clarence to your hands . . . i 4 92
Now he delivers thee From this world's thraldom to the joys of heaven i 4 254
Let me know your mind, What from your grace I shall deliver to him . iv 4 447
My learn'd lord cardinal, Deliver all with charity . . . *Hen. VIII.* i 2 143
Deliver this with modesty to the queen . . . ii 2 137
Pray, do not deliver What here you've heard to her . . . ii 3 106
And to deliver, Like free and honest men, our just opinions And comforts . . . iii 1 59
I most humbly pray you to deliver This to my lord the king . . . iv 2 129
I could not personally deliver to her What you commanded me . . . v 1 62
If entreaties Will render you no remedy, this ring Deliver them . . . v 1 151
Deliver Helen, and all damage else . . . Shall be struck off *Tr. and Cr.* ii 2 3
To deliver her possession up On terms of base compulsion! . . . ii 2 152
It will not in circumvention deliver a fly from a spider . . . ii 3 17
And to his hand when I deliver her, Think it an altar . . . iv 3 7
Here is the lady Which for Antenor we deliver you . . . iv 4 112
But, an't please you, deliver . . . *Coriolanus* i 1 98
All at once cannot See what I do deliver out to each . . . i 1 147
He should Be free as is the wind. Deliver him, Titus . . . i 9 89
Deliver you as most Abated captives to some nation . . . iii 3 131
The sorrow that delivers us thus changed Makes you think so . . . v 3 39
Tell the lords o' the city I am here: Deliver them this paper . . . v 6 2
We'll deliver you Of your great danger . . . v 6 14
We here deliver, Subscribed by the consuls and patricians . . . v 6 81
I'll deliver Myself your loyal servant, or endure Your heaviest censure v 6 141

Deliver. He hath some message to deliver us.—Ay, some mad message *T. Andron.* iv 2 2
I pray you, deliver him this petition ; Tell him, it is for justice and for aid . . . . iv 3 14
Let him deliver the pigeons to the emperor . . . . iv 3 96
Tell me, can you deliver an oration to the emperor with a grace? . . . iv 3 98
Can you with a grace deliver a supplication? . . . . iv 3 107
Deliver up your pigeons, and then look for your reward . . . iv 3 111
Take this letter ; early in the morning See thou deliver it *Rom. and Jul.* v 3 24
Cassius from bondage will deliver Cassius *J. Cæsar* i 3 90
We will deliver you the cause, Why I, that did love Cæsar when I struck him, Have thus proceeded . . . . . iii 1 181
This have I thought good to deliver thee, my dearest partner of greatness . . . . *Macbeth* i 5 11
He delivers Our offices and what we have to do To the direction just . iii 3 2
Till I may deliver, Upon the witness of these gentlemen, This marvel to you . . . . *Hamlet* i 2 193
All this can I Truly deliver.—Let us haste to hear it . . . . v 2 397
Mar a curious tale in telling it, and deliver a plain message bluntly *Lear* i 4 35
From the loathed warmth whereof deliver me . . . . . iv 6 273
I will a round unvarnish'd tale deliver Of my whole course of love *Othello* i 3 90
If . . . Thou dost deliver more or less than truth, Thou art no soldier ii 3 219
The jewels you have had from me to deliver to Desdemona would half have corrupted a votarist . . . . iv 2 189
This is most certain that I shall deliver . *Ant. and Cleo.* ii 1 28
But Your gaoler shall deliver you the keys That lock up your restraint *Cymbeline* i 1 73
Deliver with more openness your answers To my demands . . i 6 88
O, that the gods Would safely deliver me from this place! . *Pericles* iv 6 191
I am great with woe, and shall deliver weeping . . . . . v 1 107
I will believe you by the syllable Of what you shall deliver . . . v 1 170
Will you deliver How this dead queen re-lives? . . . . . v 3 63
Deliverance. O, were it but my life, I'ld throw it down for your deliverance As frankly as a pin . . *Meas. for Meas.* iii 1 105
You shall have your full time of imprisonment and your deliverance with an unpitied whipping . . . . iv 2 13
O happy torment, when my torturer Doth teach me answers for deliverance! . . . . . . *Mer. of Venice* iii 2 38
If seriously I may convey my thoughts In this my light deliverance *All's Well* ii 1 85
You have it from his own deliverance . . . . . . ii 5 4
I do desire deliverance from these officers . . . 2 *Hen. IV.* ii 1 138
At each word's deliverance Stab poniards in our flesh till all were told 3 *Hen. VI.* ii 1 97
We had need pray, And heartily, for our deliverance . *Hen. VIII.* ii 2 46
Ne'er mother Rejoiced deliverance more . . . . *Cymbeline* v 5 370
Delivered. As he most learnedly delivered . . . . *Tempest* ii 1 45
The money and the matter may be both at once delivered *T. G. of Ver.* i 1 138
Deliver'd by a friend that came from him . . . . . . i 3 54
And that letter hath she delivered, and there an end . . . . ii 1 167
Shall be deliver'd Even in the milk-white bosom of thy love . . . iii 1 249
She loved me well deliver'd it to me . . . . . . iv 4 78
I have unadvised Deliver'd you a paper that I should not . . . iv 4 128
My counterfeiting the action of an old woman delivered me *Mer. Wives* iv 5 122
I have deliver'd to Lord Angelo, A man of stricture and firm abstinence, My absolute power and place . . . . *Meas. for Meas.* i 3 11
How came it that the absent duke had not either delivered him to his liberty or executed him? . . . . iv 2 137
In the self-same inn A meaner woman was delivered Of such a burden *Com. of Errors* i 1 55
A purse of ducats?—He came to me and I deliver'd it . . . iv 4 91
And till this present hour My heavy burthen ne'er delivered . . . v 1 402
I have already delivered him letters . . . . . *Much Ado* i 1 20
My Lord Biron, see him deliver'd o'er . . . . *L. L. Lost* i 1 307
Delivered upon the mellowing of occasion . . . . . iv 2 72
See these letters delivered ; put the liveries to making . *Mer. of Venice* ii 2 123
I oft deliver'd from his forfeitures Many that have at times made moan to me . . . . iii 3 22
This she delivered in the most bitter touch of sorrow . *All's Well* i 3 121
You shall know them When back again this ring shall be deliver'd . iv 2 60
You have not given him his mother's letter?—I have delivered it . iv 3 3
O that I served that lady And might not be delivered to the world! *T. Night* i 2 42
If he may be conveniently delivered, I would he were . . . . iv 2 74
It skills not much when they are delivered . . . . . v 1 296
See him deliver'd, Fabian ; bring him hither . . . . . v 1 323
She is something before her time deliver'd . . . . *W. Tale* ii 2 25
This seal'd-up oracle, by the hand deliver'd Of great Apollo's priest iii 2 128
Which I have given already, But not deliver'd . . . . . v 1 371
My reasonable part produces reason How I may be deliver'd of these woes *K. John* iii 4 55
See them deliver'd over To execution and the hand of death *Richard II.* iii 1 29
Take special care my greetings be deliver'd . . . . . iii 1 39
Your daring tongue Scorns to unsay what once it hath deliver'd . . iv 1 9
You Pilates Have here deliver'd me to my sour cross . . . . iv 1 241
Not with such strength denied As is deliver'd to your majesty 1 *Hen. IV.* i 3 26
Two razes of ginger, to be delivered as far as Charing-cross . . . ii 1 27
Althæa dreamed she was delivered of a fire-brand . 2 *Hen. IV.* ii 2 97
There's a letter for you.—Delivered with good respect . . . ii 2 109
Which, delivered o'er to the voice, the tongue, which is the birth, becomes excellent wit . . . . iv 3 109
The constables have delivered her over to me . . . . . v 4 4
A letter was deliver'd to my hands, Writ to your grace . 1 *Hen. VI.* iv 1 11
You shall first receive The sum of money which I promised Should be deliver'd . . . . v 1 53
The county of Maine shall be released and delivered to the king 2 *Hen. VI.* i 1 51
And are the cities, that I got with wounds, Deliver'd up again with peaceful words? . . . . i 1 122
Deliver'd strongly through my fixed teeth . . . . . iii 2 313
At last I well might hear, deliver'd with a groan, 'O, farewell, Warwick!' . . . . 3 *Hen. VI.* v 2 46
The Tower, From whence this present day he is deliver'd *Richard III.* i 1 69
I have not sounded him, nor he deliver'd His gracious pleasure any way iii 4 17
Is the queen deliver'd? Say, ay ; and of a boy . . *Hen. VIII.* v 1 162
A file of boys behind 'em, loose shot, delivered such a shower of pebbles v 4 59
The town is ta'en!—'Twill be deliver'd back on good condition *Coriolanus* i 10 2
I can't say your worships have delivered the matter well . . . ii 1 63
The slave's report is seconded ; and more, More fearful, is deliver'd . iv 6 63
She is deliver'd.—To whom?—I mean, she is brought a-bed *T. Andron.* iv 2 61
The midwife and myself ; And no one else but the deliver'd empress . iv 2 142
Delivered. Demand your hostages, And they shall be immediately deliver'd . . . . *T. Andron.* v 1 161
Behold this child : Of this was Tamora delivered . . . . . v 3 120
How now, wife! Have you deliver'd to her our decree? *Rom. and Jul.* iii 5 139
Where, as they had deliver'd, both in time, Form of the thing, each word made true and good . . . . *Hamlet* i 2 209
A happiness that often madness hits on, which reason and sanity could not so prosperously be delivered of . . . . . . ii 2 215
I will not sleep, my lord, till I have delivered your letter . . *Lear* i 5 7
Deliver'd letters, spite of intermission, Which presently they read . ii 4 33
There are many events in the womb of time which will be delivered *Oth.* i 3 378
My Muse labours, And thus she is deliver'd . . . . . ii 1 129
The which the knight himself With such a graceful courtesy deliver'd *Pericles* ii 2 41
But whether there Deliver'd, by the holy gods, I cannot rightly say . iii 4 7
I was born, As my good nurse Lychorida hath oft Deliver'd weeping . v 1 162
Delivering. Not so much as a ducat for delivering your letter *T. G. of Ver.* i 1 145
I, delivering you, am satisfied And therein do account myself well paid *Mer. of Venice* iv 1 416
In delivering my son from me, I bury a second husband . *All's Well* i 1 1
Delivering o'er to executors pale The lazy yawning drone . *Hen. V.* i 2 203
Delivery. I make a broken delivery of the business . . *W. Tale* v 2 10
Heard ye not what an humble suppliant Lord Hastings was to her for his delivery? . . . . *Richard III.* i 1 75
He hugg'd me in his arms, and swore, with sobs, That he would labour my delivery . . . . i 4 253
The hour prefix'd Of her delivery to this valiant Greek Comes fast upon *Troi. and Cres.* iv 3 2
Delphos. I have dispatch'd in post To sacred Delphos . *W. Tale* ii 1 183
Cleomenes and Dion, Being well arrived from Delphos, are both landed ii 3 196
Cleomenes and Dion have Been both at Delphos . . . . . iii 2 127
Deluded. O, give me leave, I have deluded you . . 1 *Hen. VI.* v 4 76
Deluding. Get thee gone, thou false deluding slave . . *T. of Shrew* iv 3 31
Let loose on me the justice of the state For thus deluding you . *Othello* iv 1 141
Deluge. Thy deed, inhuman and unnatural, Provokes this deluge *Rich. III.* i 2 61
Then must my earth with her continual tears Become a deluge *T. And.* iii 1 230
Delve. And 't shall go hard But I will delve one yard below their mines, And blow them at the moon . . . . *Hamlet* iii 4 208
What's his name and birth?—I cannot delve him to the root *Cymbeline* i 1 28
Delver. Nay, but hear you, goodman delver . . . . *Hamlet* v 1 15
Demand. How now? moody? What is't thou canst demand? *Tempest* i 2 245
I will marry her upon any reasonable demands . . . *Mer. Wives* i 1 233
You will demand of me why I do this? . . . . *Meas. for Meas.* i 3 17
That you might know it, would much better please me Than to demand what 'tis . . . . iii 4 33
Agree with his demands to the point . . . . iii 1 254
I will please you what you will demand . . . *Com. of Errors* iv 4 52
He doth demand to have repaid A hundred thousand crowns ; and not demands, On payment of a hundred thousand crowns, To have his title live . . . . *L. L. Lost* ii 1 143
Where? when? what vizard? why demand you this? . . . . v 2 386
The pound of flesh, which I demand of him, Is dearly bought *Mer. of Ven.* iv 1 99
There is more owing her than is paid ; and more shall be paid her than she'll demand . . . . *All's Well* i 3 109
They say, our French lack language to deny, If they demand . . ii 1 21
Will you see her, For that is her demand, and know her business? . . ii 1 89
Make thy demand.—But will you make it even? . . . . . ii 1 194
It must be an answer of most monstrous size that must fit all demands ii 2 35
Now his important blood will nought deny That she'll demand . . iii 7 22
I perceive, by this demand, you are not altogether in his council . iv 3 52
Demand of him, of what strength they are a-foot . . . . iv 3 180
Where we may leisurely Each one demand and answer to his part *W. Tale* v 3 153
England, impatient of your just demands, Hath put himself in arms *K. John* ii 1 56
From Pope Innocent the legate here, Do in his name religiously demand iii 1 140
This, in our foresaid holy father's name, Pope Innocent, I do demand of thee . . . . iii 1 146
Although my will to give is living, The suit which you demand is gone and dead . . . . iv 2 84
Why may not I demand Of thine affairs, as well as thou of mine? . . v 6 4
Demand of yonder champion The cause of his arrival here in arms *Richard II.* i 3 7
All the number of his fair demands Shall be accomplish'd . . . iii 3 123
Thou hast forgotten to demand that truly which thou wouldst truly know . . . . 1 *Hen. IV.* i 2 5
I see no reason why thou shouldst be so superfluous to demand the time of the day . . . . i 2 12
Of him I did demand what news from Shrewsbury . . 2 *Hen. IV* i 1 40
Wherein It shall appear that your demands are just, You shall enjoy them . . . . iv 1 144
Do not, in grant of all demands at large, Sweeten the bitter mock *Hen. V.* ii 4 121
Let it not disgrace me, If I demand, before this royal view . . v 2 32
You must buy that peace With full accord to all our just demands . v 2 71
Any thing in or out of our demands, And we'll consign thereto . . v 2 89
Leave our cousin Katharine here with us : She is our capital demand . v 2 96
Only he hath not yet subscribed this : Where your majesty demands . v 2 364
I descend To give thee answer of thy just demand . . 1 *Hen. VI.* v 3 144
A proper jest, and never heard before, That Suffolk should demand a whole fifteenth For costs and charges . . . 2 *Hen. VI.* i 1 133
The king hath yielded unto thy demand . . . . v 1 40
Ay, if thou wilt say 'ay' to my request ; No, if thou dost say 'no' to my demand . . . . 3 *Hen. VI.* iii 2 80
His demand Springs not from Edward's well-meant honest love . . iii 3 66
Dreadful war shall answer his demand . . . . iii 3 259
I have not stopp'd mine ears to their demands, Nor posted off their suits iv 8 39
I have consider'd in my mind The late demand that you did sound me in *Richard III.* iv 2 87
What says your highness to my just demand? . . . . . . iv 2 97
Did of me demand What was the speech among the Londoners? *Hen. VIII.* i 2 153
My good lord, Not your demand ; it values not your asking . . . ii 3 52
Why am I a fool?—Make that demand of the prover . *Troi. and Cres.* ii 3 72
What wouldst thou of us, Trojan? make demand . . . . . iii 3 17
Let Patroclus make demands to me, you shall see the pageant of Ajax . iii 3 272
We are the greater poll, and in true fear They gave us our demands *Cor.* iii 1 135
Tush, tush!—A good demand . . . . iii 2 45
I do demand, If you submit you to the people's voices? . . . . iii 3 43
Bid him demand what pledge will please him best . . *T. Andron.* iv 4 106
Willing you to demand your hostages, And they shall be immediately deliver'd . . . . v 1 160
This is my daughter's jointure, for no more Can I demand *Rom. and Jul.* v 3 298

Demand. Put on a most importunate aspect, A visage of demand *T. of Athens* ii 1 29
I am thus encounter'd With clamorous demands of date-broke bonds . ii 2 38
If then that friend demand why Brutus rose against Cæsar, this is my answer . . . . *J. Cæsar* iii 2 21
They mean to warn us at Philippi here, Answering before we do demand v 1 6
Speak.—Demand.—We'll answer . . . . . *Macbeth* iv 1 61
Come you more nearer Than your particular demands will touch it *Hamlet* ii 1 12
Niggard of question ; but, of our demands, Most free in his reply . iii 1 13
He shall with speed to England, For the demand of our neglected tribute iii 1 178
Let him demand his fill . . . . iv 5 129
Acquaint my daughter no further with any thing you know than comes from her demand out of the letter . . . . . *Lear* i 5 3
Demand that demi-devil Why he hath thus ensnared my soul and body? *Othello* v 2 301
Demand me nothing : what you know, you know . . . . v 2 303
I grant him part ; but then, in his Armenia, And other of his conquer'd kingdoms, I Demand the like . . . . *Ant. and Cleo* iii 6 37
Bids thee study on what fair demands Thou mean'st to have him grant thee . . . . v 2 10
If she first meet the curled Antony, He'll make demand of her . . v 2 305
Deliver with more openness your answers To my demands . *Cymbeline* i 6 89
When we have supp'd, We'll mannerly demand thee of thy story . iii 6 92
The bier at door, And a demand who is't shall die, I'ld say 'My father, not this youth' . . . . iv 2 23
I'll give it ; Yea, though thou do demand a prisoner, The noblest ta'en v 5 99
Stand thou by our side ; Make thy demand aloud . . . . v 5 130
What canst thou say When noble Pericles shall demand his child? *Pericles* iv 3 13
Demanded. Well demanded, wench : My tale provokes that question *Temp.* i 2 139
Those prisoners in your highness' name demanded . . . 1 *Hen. IV.* i 3 23
He question'd me ; amongst the rest, demanded My prisoners . . i 3 47
To be demanded of a sponge ! what replication should be made by the son of a king? . . . . *Hamlet* iv 2 12
Methinks our pleasure might have been demanded, Ere you had spoke so far . . . . *Lear* v 3 62
Ere it be demanded—As like enough it will—I'ld have it copied *Othello* iii 4 189
Inform us of thy fortunes, for it seems They crave to be demanded *Cymb.* iv 2 362
With I know not how much more, should be demanded . . . v 5 389
She would never tell Her parentage ; being demanded that, She would sit still and weep . . . . *Pericles* v 1 190
Demandest. Then speak at once what is it thou demand'st *Richard III.* ii 1 98
Demanding. Raising up wicked spirits from under ground, Demanding of King Henry's life and death . . . . 2 *Hen. VI.* ii 1 175
Even but now, demanding after you, Denied me to come in . . *Lear* iii 2 65
Demean. Out of doubt Antipholus is mad, Else would he never so demean himself . . . . *Com. of Errors* iv 3 83
And demean himself Unlike the ruler of a commonweal . . 2 *Hen. VI.* i 1 188
Demeaned. She never reprehended him but mildly, When he demean'd himself rough, rude and wildly . . . *Com. of Errors* v 1 88
If York have ill demean'd himself in France, Then let him be denay'd the regentship . . . . 2 *Hen. VI.* i 3 106
They have demean'd themselves Like men born to renown by life or death 3 *Hen. VI.* i 4 7
Demeanour. Know my aspect And fashion your demeanour to my looks *Com. of Errors* ii 2 33
With such a deep demeanour in great sorrow . . 2 *Hen. IV.* iv 5 85
Blunt-witted lord, ignoble in demeanour ! . . 2 *Hen. VI.* iii 2 210
I perceive But cold demeanour in Octavius' wing . . *J. Cæsar* v 2 4
Demerit. If things go well, Opinion that so sticks on Marcius shall Of his demerits rob Cominius . . . . . . *Coriolanus* i 1 276
Not for their own demerits, but for mine . . . . *Macbeth* iv 3 226
My demerits May speak unbonneted to as proud a fortune . *Othello* i 2 22
Demesne. And the demesnes that there adjacent lie. *Rom. and Jul.* ii 1 20
A gentleman of noble parentage, Of fair demesnes . . . . iii 5 182
This twenty years This rock and these demesnes have been my world *Cymbeline* iii 3 70
Demetrius. Stand forth, Demetrius. My noble lord, This man hath my consent to marry her . . . . . . *M. N. Dream* i 1 24
Consent to marry with Demetrius . . . . i 1 40
Demetrius is a worthy gentleman.—So is Lysander. . . . i 1 52
I beseech your grace that I may know The worst that may befall me in this case, If I refuse to wed Demetrius . . . . . i 1 64
Either prepare to die For disobedience to your father's will, Or else to wed Demetrius . . . . i 1 88
You have her father's love, Demetrius ; Let me have Hermia's . . i 1 93
She is mine, and all my right of her I do estate unto Demetrius . i 1 98
My fortunes every way as fairly rank'd, If not with vantage, as Demetrius' i 1 102
Demetrius, I'll avouch it to his head, Made love to Nedar's daughter . i 1 106
I have heard so much, And with Demetrius thought to have spoke thereof i 1 112
But, Demetrius, come ; And come, Egeus ; you shall go with me . . i 1 114
Demetrius and Egeus, go along : I must employ you in some business . i 1 123
Demetrius loves your fair : O happy fair ! . . . . . . i 1 182
Were the world mine, Demetrius being bated, The rest I'ld give to be to you translated . . . . i 1 190
O, teach me how you look, and with what art You sway the motion of Demetrius' heart . . . . i 1 193
Pray thou for us ; And good luck grant thee thy Demetrius ! . . i 1 221
Adieu : As you on him, Demetrius dote on you ! . . . . i 1 225
I am thought as fair as she. But what of that? Demetrius thinks not so . . . . i 1 228
For ere Demetrius look'd on Hermia's eyne, He hail'd down oaths that he was only mine . . . . i 1 242
Demetrius, The more you beat me, I will fawn on you . . . ii 1 203
Fie, Demetrius ! Your wrongs do set a scandal on my sex . . ii 1 239
Stay, though thou kill me, sweet Demetrius . . . . . ii 2 84
Therefore no marvel though Demetrius Do, as a monster, fly my presence thus . . . . ii 2 96
Where is Demetrius? O, how fit a word Is that vile name to perish on my sword ! . . . . ii 2 106
I did never, no, nor never can, Deserve a sweet look from Demetrius' eye ii 2 127
Lysander? where is he? Ah, good Demetrius, wilt thou give him me? iii 2 63
The noise they make Will cause Demetrius to awake . . . iii 2 117
Demetrius loves her, and he loves not you . . . . . iii 2 136
You are unkind, Demetrius ; be not so . . . . . . iii 2 162
Your other love, Demetrius, Who even but now did spurn me with his foot . . . . iii 2 224
Demetrius, I will keep my word with thee.—I would I had your bond . iii 2 266
In love unto Demetrius, I told him of your stealth unto this wood . iii 2 309
A foolish heart, that I leave here behind.—What, with Lysander?—With Demetrius . . . . iii 2 320
Demetrius. Stir Demetrius up with bitter wrong ; And sometime rail thou like Demetrius . . . . *M. N. Dream* iii 2 361
Where art thou, proud Demetrius? speak thou now . . . iii 2 401
I'll find Demetrius and revenge this spite . . . . . iii 2 420
This Demetrius is ; This Helena, old Nedar's Helena . . . iv 1 134
They would have stolen away ; they would, Demetrius . . . iv 1 161
And I have found Demetrius like a jewel, Mine own, and not mine own iv 1 196
Demetrius, thou dost over-ween in all ; And so in this . *T. Andron.* ii 1 29
Stuprum. Chiron. Demetrius . . . . iv 1 78
Demetrius, here's the son of Lucius ; He hath some message . . iv 2 1
Had he not reason, Lord Demetrius? Did you not use his daughter very friendly? . . . . iv 2 39
Know you these two?—The empress' sons, I take them, Chiron and Demetrius . . . . v 2 155
O villains, Chiron and Demetrius ! . . . . v 2 170
Chiron and Demetrius : They ravish'd her, and cut away her tongue . v 3 56
Cursed Chiron and Demetrius Were they that murdered our emperor's brother . . . . v 3 97
Demi-Atlas. The demi-Atlas of this earth . . . *Ant. and Cleo.* i 5 23
Demi-cannon. What's this? a sleeve? 'tis like a demi-cannon *T. of Shrew* iv 3 88
Demi-devil. This demi-devil—For he's a bastard one . *Tempest* v 1 272
Demand that demi-devil Why he hath thus ensnared my soul and body? *Othello* v 2 301
Demi-god. Thus can the demigod Authority Make us pay down *M. for M.* i 2 124
Like a demigod here sit I in the sky, And wretched fools' secrets heedfully o'er-eye . . . . *L. L. Lost* iv 3 79
What demi-god Hath come so near creation? . . . *Mer. of Venice* iii 2 116
Demi-natured. As had he been incorpsed and demi-natured With the brave beast . . . . *Hamlet* iv 7 88
Demi-paradise. This earth of majesty, this seat of Mars, This other Eden, demi-paradise . . . . *Richard II.* ii 1 42
Demi-puppets that By moonshine do the green sour ringlets make *Tempest* v 1 36
Demise. Tell me what state, what dignity, what honour, Canst thou demise to any child of mine . . . . . *Richard III.* iv 4 247
Demi-wolves. Spaniels, curs, Shoughs, water-rugs and demi-wolves are clept All by the name of dogs . . . . . . *Macbeth* iii 1 94
Demoiselle. Your majestee ave fausse French enough to deceive de most sage demoiselle dat is en France . . . . *Hen. V.* v 2 234
Demon. If that same demon that hath gull'd thee thus Should with his lion gait walk the whole world . . . . ii 2 121
Thy demon, that's thy spirit which keeps thee, is Noble, courageous, high, unmatchable . . . . *Ant. and Cleo.* ii 3 19
Demonstrable. Some unhatch'd practice Made demonstrable here in Cyprus to him Hath puddled his clear spirit . . . *Othello* iii 4 142
Demonstrate. Would demonstrate them now But goers backward *All's Well* i 2 47
To demonstrate the life of such a battle In life so lifeless as it shows itself . . . . *Hen. V.* iv 2 54
Paintings I can show That shall demonstrate these quick blows of Fortune's . . . . *T. of Athens* i 1 91
My outward action doth demonstrate The native act and figure of my heart . . . . *Othello* i 1 61
This may help to thicken other proofs That do demonstrate thinly . iii 3 431
Demonstrated. Have heaven and earth together demonstrated *Hamlet* i 1 124
Demonstrating. Every thing about you demonstrating a careless desolation . . . . *As Y. Like It* iii 2 400
Demonstration. By a familiar demonstration of the working *L. L. Lost* i 2 9
Did your letters pierce the queen to any demonstration of grief? . *Lear* iv 3 12
Demonstrative. He sends you this most memorable line, In every branch truly demonstrative . . . . *Hen. V.* ii 4 89
Demure. After a demure travel of regard . . . . *T. Night* ii 5 59
There's never none of these demure boys come to any proof 2 *Hen. IV.* iv 3 97
With demure confidence This pausingly ensued . . *Hen. VIII.* i 2 167
Demurely. Wear prayer-books in my pocket, look demurely *Mer. of Ven.* ii 2 201
Hark ! the drums Demurely wake the sleepers . . *Ant. and Cleo.* iv 9 31
Demuring. Octavia, with her modest eyes And still conclusion, shall acquire no honour Demuring upon me . . . . iv 15 29
Den. The murkiest den, The most opportune place . . *Tempest* iv 1 25
What art thou then? Food for his rage, repasture for his den *L. L. Lost* iv 1 95
Were I at home, At your den, sirrah, with your lioness . *K. John* ii 1 291
What, shall they seek the lion in his den, And fright him there? . v 1 57
Rouse up revenge from ebon den with fell Alecto's snake 2 *Hen. IV.* v 5 39
To whom do lions cast their gentle looks? Not to the beast that would usurp their den . . . . 3 *Hen. VI.* ii 2 12
Whiles lions war and battle for their dens, Poor harmless lambs abide their enmity . . . . ii 5 74
Look down into this den, And see a fearful sight of blood and death *T. Andron.* ii 3 215
O, why should nature build so foul a den, Unless the gods delight in tragedies? . . . . iv 1 59
The round world Should have shook lions into civil streets, And citizens to their dens . . . . *Ant. and Cleo.* v 1 17
Denay. Say, My love can give no place, bide no denay *T. Night* ii 4 127
Denayed. If York have ill demean'd himself in France, Then let him be denay'd the regentship . . . . . . 2 *Hen. VI.* i 3 107
Denial. Word of denial in thy labras here ! Word of denial *Mer. Wives* i 1 166
Having the truth of honour in her, hath made him that gracious denial *Meas. for Meas.* iii 1 167
Never make denial ; I must and will have Katharine to my wife *T. of Shrew* ii 1 281
Prejudicates the business and would seem To have us make denial *All's Well* i 2 9
He's fortified against any denial . . . . . . *T. Night* i 5 154
In your denial I would find no sense ; I would not understand it . i 5 285
Let us hear your firm resolve.—Your grant, or your denial, shall be mine . . . . 3 *Hen. VI.* iii 3 130
The thing I have forsworn to grant may never Be held by you denials *Coriolanus* v 3 81
Importune him for my moneys ; be not ceased With slight denial *T. of Athens* ii 1 17
Make denials Increase your services . . . . *Cymbeline* ii 3 53
Denied. You hear all these matters denied, gentlemen . . *Mer. Wives* i 1 193
Most manifest, and not denied by himself . . *Meas. for Meas.* iv 2 145
I durst have denied that, before you were so choleric *Com. of Errors* ii 2 67
He did buffet thee and in his blows Denied my house for his, me for his wife . . . . ii 2 161
First he denied you had in him no right . . . . . . iv 2 7
The guilty doors were shut And I denied to enter in my house . iv 4 67
It must not be denied but I am a plain-dealing villain . *Much Ado* i 3 33
I had well hoped thou wouldst have denied Beatrice . . . . v 4 115
Lodged in my heart, Though so denied fair harbour in my house *L. L. L.* ii 1 175

Denied. If it be denied, Will much impeach the justice of his state *Mer. of Venice* iii 3 28
How if the kiss be denied?—Then she puts you to entreaty *As Y. Like It* iv 1 79
He hath arm'd our answer, And Florence is denied before he comes *All's Well* i 2 12
When miracles have by the greatest been denied . . . ii 1 144
Be not denied access, stand at her doors *T. Night* i 4 16
Denied me mine own purse, Which I had recommended to his use . v 1 93
Although 'Twere needful I denied it . *W. Tale* i 2 23
But durst not tempt a minister of honour, Lest she should be denied . ii 2 51
With immodest hatred The child-bed privilege denied . iii 2 104
You denied to fight with me this other day . v 2 139
I am denied to sue my livery here *Richard II.* ii 3 129
I am a subject, And I challenge law: attorneys are denied me . ii 3 134
He prays but faintly and would be denied . v 3 103
Not with such strength denied As is deliver'd to your majesty *1 Hen. IV.* i 3 25
We are denied access unto his person *2 Hen. IV.* iv 1 78
When ever yet was your appeal denied? . iv 1 88
My lungs are wasted so That strength of speech is utterly denied me . iv 5 218
Nor this I have not, brother, so denied, But your request shall make me let it pass *Hen. V.* v 2 371
Thy father, Minos, that denied our course . *3 Hen. VI.* v 6 22
With Free pardon to each man that has denied The force of this commission *Hen. VIII.* i 2 100
Desired my Cressid in right great exchange, Whom Troy hath still denied *Troi. and Cres.* iii 3 22
Have you Ere now denied the asker? and now again Of him that did not ask, but mock, bestow Your sued-for tongues? . *Coriolanus* ii 3 214
It cannot be denied but peace is a great maker of cuckolds . iv 5 243
Who, like a block, hath denied my access to thee . v 2 85
I will not be denied: sweet heart, look back . *T. Andron.* i 1 481
Step aside; I'll know his grievance, or be much denied . *Rom. and Jul.* i 1 163
Nay, urged extremely for't and showed what necessity belonged to't, and yet was denied . *T. of Athens* iii 2 15
Denied that honourable man! there was very little honour showed in't iii 2 19
I should ne'er have denied his occasion so many talents . iii 2 26
Shrunk indeed; And he that's once denied will hardly speed . iii 2 69
They have all been touch'd and found base metal, for They have all denied him . iii 3 7
How! have they denied him? Has Ventidius and Lucullus denied him? iii 3 7
It could not else be, I should prove so base, To sue, and be denied such common grace . iii 5 95
I did send to you For certain sums of gold, which you denied me *J. Cæsar* iv 3 70
I did send To you for gold to pay my legions, Which you denied me iv 3 77
I denied you not.—You did.—I did not . iv 3 82
I, that denied thee gold, will give my heart . iv 3 104
I did repel his letters and denied His access to me . *Hamlet* ii 1 109
Which even but now, demanding after you, Denied me to come in *Lear* iii 2 66
The which you both denied.—Neglected, rather *Ant. and Cleo.* ii 2 89
It cannot be denied what I have done by land.—Nor what I have done by water . ii 6 92
Cæsar, having made use of him in the wars 'gainst Pompey, presently denied him rivality . iii 5 8
Here is a rural fellow That will not be denied your highness' presence v 2 234
O, that's as much as you would be denied Of your fair courtesy *Pericles* ii 3 106
Denier. You will not pay for the glasses you have burst?—No, not a denier *T. of Shrew* Ind. 1 9
Let them coin his cheeks: I'll not pay a denier . *1 Hen. IV.* iii 3 91
My dukedom to a beggarly denier *Richard III.* i 2 252
Denies. Here's a gentlewoman denies all that you have said *M. for M.* v 1 283
Thy fault's thus manifested; Which, though thou wouldst deny, denies thee vantage . v 1 418
Both one and other he denies me now *Com. of Errors* iv 3 86
You say he dined at home; the goldsmith here Denies that saying . v 1 274
Whatsoever a man denies, you are now bound to believe him . v 1 305
She will not add to her damnation A sin of perjury; she not denies it *Much Ado* iv 1 175
A greater power than we denies all this . *K. John* ii 1 368
What merit's in that reason which denies The yielding of her up? *Troi. and Cres.* ii 2 24
And one thing more That womanhood denies my tongue to tell *T. Andron.* ii 3 174
How say'st thou, that Macduff denies his person At our great bidding? *Macbeth* iii 4 128
Then Hamlet does it not, Hamlet denies it . *Hamlet* v 2 247
Now he denies it faintly, and laughs it out . *Othello* iv 1 113
Deniest. If thou deny'st it twenty times, thou liest . *Richard II.* iv 1 38
Since thou deniest the gentle king to speak . *3 Hen. VI.* ii 2 172
Give to dogs What thou deny'st to men; let prisons swallow 'em *T. of Athens* iv 3 537
One whom I will beat into clamorous whining, if thou deniest the least syllable of thy addition . *Lear* ii 2 25
Denis. Saint Denis to Saint Cupid! *L. L. Lost* v 2 87
Saint Denis be my speed! . *Hen. V.* v 2 193
Between Saint Denis and Saint George . v 2 220
No longer on Saint Denis will we cry, But Joan la Pucelle shall be France's saint . *1 Hen. VI.* i 6 28
Saint Denis bless this happy stratagem! . iii 2 18
Denmark. In which the majesty of buried Denmark Did sometimes march *Hamlet* i 1 48
The head is not more native to the heart, The hand more instrumental to the mouth, Than is the throne of Denmark to thy father . i 2 49
Though willingly I came to Denmark, To show my duty in your coronation . i 2 52
Cast thy nighted colour off, And let thine eye look like a friend on Denmark . i 2 69
Why, 'tis a loving and a fair reply: Be as ourself in Denmark . i 2 122
No jocund health that Denmark drinks to-day, But the great cannon to the clouds shall tell . i 2 125
Which is no further Than the main voice of Denmark goes withal . i 3 28
Something is rotten in the state of Denmark . i 4 90
The whole ear of Denmark Is by a forged process of my death Rankly abused . i 5 36
Let not the royal bed of Denmark be A couch for luxury and damned incest . i 5 82
At least I'm sure it may be so in Denmark . i 5 109
There's ne'er a villain dwelling in all Denmark But he's an arrant knave i 5 123
Denmark's a prison.—Then is the world one.—A goodly one . ii 2 249
There are many confines, wards and dungeons, Denmark being one o' the worst . ii 2 252
It is not very strange; for mine uncle is king of Denmark . ii 2 381
Denmark. Thy face is valanced since I saw thee last: comest thou to beard me in Denmark? . *Hamlet* ii 2 443
You have the voice of the king himself for your succession in Denmark iii 2 357
Where is the beauteous majesty of Denmark? . iv 5 21
Upon what ground?—Why, here in Denmark . v 1 176
Larded with many several sorts of reasons Importing Denmark's health and England's too . v 2 21
Your lordship is right welcome back to Denmark . v 2 82
Richer than that which four successive kings In Denmark's crown have worn . v 2 285
Dennis. Holla, Dennis!—Calls your worship? . *As Y. Like It* i 1 92
Denny. Ha! Canterbury?—Ay, my good lord.—'Tis true: where is he, Denny? . *Hen. VIII.* v 1 82
Denote. The better to denote her to the doctor *Mer. Wives* iv 6 39
Thy wild acts denote The unreasonable fury of a beast *Rom. and Jul.* iii 3 110
With all forms, moods, shapes of grief, That can denote me truly *Hamlet* i 2 83
His own courses will denote him so That I may save my speech *Othello* iv 1 290
Denoted. But this denoted a foregone conclusion . iii 3 428
Denotement. He hath devoted and given up himself to the contemplation, mark, and denotement of her parts and graces . ii 3 323
Denounce. I will denounce a curse upon his head *K. John* iii 1 319
Denounced. His curses, then from bitterness of soul Denounced against thee, are all fall'n upon thee *Richard III.* i 3 180
If not denounced against us, why should not we Be there in person? *Ant. and Cleo.* iii 7 5
Denouncing. Tongues of heaven, Plainly denouncing vengeance *K. John* iii 4 159
Denunciation. We do the denunciation lack Of outward order *M. for M.* i 2 152
Deny. Being once perfected how to grant suits, How to deny them *Tempest* i 2 80
To be your fellow You may deny me . iii 1 85
That I can deny by a circumstance *T. G. of Ver.* i 1 84
I not deny, The jury, passing on the prisoner's life, May in the sworn twelve have a thief or two Guiltier than him they try *Meas. for Meas.* ii 1 18
Thy fault's thus manifested; Which, though thou wouldst deny, denies thee vantage . v 1 418
Thou didst deny the gold's receipt *Com. of Errors* ii 2 17
And that I did deny my wife and house . iii 1 9
Why dost thou deny the bag of gold? . iv 4 99
He had the chain of me, Though most dishonestly he doth deny it v 1 3
With circumstance and oaths so to deny This chain which now you wear v 1 16
This chain you had of me; can you deny it? . v 1 22
Who heard me to deny it or forswear it? . v 1 25
Could she here deny The story that is printed in her blood? *Much Ado* iv 1 123
Believe me not; and yet I lie not; I confess nothing, nor I deny nothing iv 1 274
You kill me to deny it. Farewell . iv 1 293
And this is more, masters, than you can deny . iv 2 63
I would not deny you; but, by this good day, I yield upon great persuasion . v 4 94
I deny her virginity . *L. L. Lost* i 1 298
And deny himself for Jove, Turning mortal for thy love . iv 3 119
If you deny to dance, let's hold more chat . v 2 228
You may not deny it: Pompey hath made the challenge . v 2 712
If this thou do deny, let our hands part . v 2 821
If this, or more than this, I would deny . v 2 823
Then by your side no bed-room me deny . *M. N. Dream* ii 2 51
Wherefore doth Lysander Deny your love? . iii 2 229
You must not deny me: I must go with you to Belmont *Mer. of Venice* ii 2 187
And doth impeach the freedom of the state, If they deny him justice . iii 2 281
If law, authority and power deny not, It will go hard with poor Antonio iii 2 291
The duke cannot deny the course of law . iii 3 26
I do desire you Not to deny this imposition . iii 4 33
If you deny it, let the danger light Upon your charter . iv 1 38
'Tis mine and I will have it. If you deny me, fie upon your law! . iv 1 101
Grant me two things, I pray you, Not to deny me, and to pardon me . iv 1 424
I'll take no more; And you in love shall not deny me this . iv 1 429
I could not for my heart deny it him . v 1 165
If I could add a lie unto a fault, I would deny it . v 1 187
I did deny him And suffer'd him to go displeased away . v 1 217
I'll not deny him any thing I have . v 1 227
I confess me much guilty, to deny so fair and excellent ladies *As Y. L. It* i 2 197
Or else by him my love deny, And then I'll study how to die . iv 3 62
If she deny to wed, I'll crave the day When I shall ask the banns *T. of Shr.* ii 1 180
Deny him, forswear him, or else we are all undone . v 1 114
If they deny to come, Swinge me them soundly forth . v 2 103
They say, our French lack language to deny, If they demand *All's Well* ii 1 20
Do all they deny her? An they were sons of mine, I'd have them whipped ii 3 92
Now his important blood will nought deny That she'll demand . iii 7 21
I neither can nor will deny But that I know them . v 3 166
What shall you ask of me that I'll deny? . *T. Night* iii 4 231
There's half my coffer.—Will you deny me now? . iii 4 381
Thou shalt not choose but go: Do not deny . iv 1 62
Husband!—Ay, husband: can he that deny? . v 1 147
Peruse that letter. You must not now deny it is your hand . v 1 339
If I then deny it, 'Tis none of mine . *W. Tale* i 2 266
Which to deny concerns more than avails . iii 2 87
As faithfully as I deny the devil . *K. John* i 1 252
All things that you should use to do me wrong Deny their office . iv 1 119
And deny his youth The rich advantage of good exercise . iv 2 59
I beg cold comfort; and you are so strait And so ingrateful, you deny me that . v 7 43
And deny his offer'd homage . *Richard II.* ii 1 204
With mine own tongue deny my sacred state . iv 1 209
My acts, decrees, and statutes I deny . iv 1 213
My liege, I did deny no prisoners . *1 Hen. IV.* i 3 29
Why, yet he doth deny his prisoners . i 3 77
But that he is, saving your reverence, a whoremaster, that I utterly deny . ii 4 516
I deny your major: if you will deny the sheriff, so . ii 4 544
Thou speak'st as if I would deny my name . v 4 60
If the man were alive and would deny it, 'zounds, I would make him eat a piece of my sword . v 4 156
To marry me and make me my lady thy wife. Canst thou deny it? *2 Hen. IV.* ii 1 101
I put thee now to thy book-oath: deny it, if thou canst . ii 1 112
Do you think I would deny her? . ii 4 192
With all appliances and means to boot, Deny it to a king . iii 1 30
If she deny the appearance of a naked blind boy in her naked seeing self *Hen. V.* v 2 324
How canst thou tell she will deny thy suit? . *1 Hen. VI.* v 3 75
Graceless! wilt thou deny thy parentage? . v 4 14
Deny me not, I prithee, gentle Joan.—Peasant, avaunt! . v 4 20

Deny. Dost thou deny thy father, cursed drab? 1 *Hen. VI.* v 4 32
His son am I; deny it, if you can 2 *Hen. VI.* iv 2 154
And the bricks are alive at this day to testify it; therefore deny it not iv 2 158
Here comes Clifford to deny their bail v 1 123
If thou deny, their blood upon thy head 3 *Hen. VI.* ii 2 129
Which we in justice cannot well deny iii 2 5
It were dishonour to deny it her.—It were no less iii 2 9
How say you, sir? can you deny all this? *Richard III.* i 1 96
You may deny that you were not the cause i 3 90
Help you to many fair preferments, And then deny her aiding hand therein i 3 96
If she deny, Lord Hastings, go with him, And from her jealous arms pluck him perforce iii 1 35
Will he bring his power?—My lord, he doth deny to come v 3 343
Not to deny her that A woman of less place might ask by law *Hen. VIII.* ii 2 111
You charge me That I have blown this coal: I do deny it ii 4 94
Officious lords, I dare and must deny it iii 2 238
I have a suit which you must not deny me v 3 161
Do not deny him: It doth import him much to speak with me *Tr. and Cr.* iv 2 51
Yet dare I never Deny your asking *Coriolanus* i 6 65
Once, if he do require our voices, we ought not to deny him ii 3 2
We may deny him yet.—And will deny him ii 3 217
My young boy Hath an aspect of intercession, which Great nature cries 'Deny not' v 3 33
We have nothing else to ask, but that Which you deny already v 3 89
Does reason our petition with more strength Than thou hast to deny't v 3 177
Which of you all Will now deny to dance? *Rom. and Jul.* i 5 21
Deny thy father and refuse thy name; Or, if thou wilt not, be but sworn my love, And I'll no longer be a Capulet ii 2 34
Fain would I dwell on form, fain, fain deny What I have spoke ii 2 88
Do not deny to him that you love me.—I will confess to you that I love him iv 1 24
He does deny him, in respect of his, What charitable men afford to beggars *T. of Athens* iii 2 81
Raise me this beggar, and deny't that lord iv 3 9
Twould have anger'd any heart alive To hear the men deny't *Macbeth* iii 6 16
I will be satisfied: deny me this, And an eternal curse fall on you! iv 1 104
Which the poor heart would fain deny, and dare not v 3 28
You do, surely, bar the door upon your own liberty, if you deny your griefs to your friend *Hamlet* iii 2 352
I must commune with your grief, Or you deny me right iv 5 203
What I should deny,—As this I would; ay, though thou didst produce My very character *Lear* ii 1 72
Strong and fasten'd villain! Would he deny his letter? ii 1 80
What a brazen-faced varlet art thou, to deny thou knowest me! ii 2 31
Deny to speak with me? They are sick? they are weary? ii 4 89
Is your name Goneril?—She cannot deny it iii 6 53
I wonder in my soul, What you would ask me, that I should deny *Othello* iii 3 69
Let him come when he will; I will deny thee nothing iii 3 76
I will deny thee nothing: Whereon, I do beseech thee, grant me this iii 3 83
Leave me but a little to myself.—Shall I deny you? no: farewell, my lord iii 3 86
To deny each article with oath Cannot remove nor choke the strong conception That I do groan withal v 2 54
Hear me this prayer, though thou deny me a matter of more weight *Ant. and Cleo.* i 2 71
That what they do delay, they not deny ii 1 3
We, ignorant of ourselves, Beg often our own harms, which the wise powers Deny us for our good ii 1 7
Something you can deny for your own safety ii 6 95
You have been a great thief by sea.—And you by land.—There I deny my land service ii 6 98
I will kill thee, if thou dost deny Thou'st made me cuckold.—I'll deny nothing *Cymbeline* ii 4 145
Let his virtue join With my request, which I'll make bold your highness Cannot deny v 5 90
Prithee, valiant youth, Deny't again.—I have spoke it, and I did it v 5 290
I may so.—Who should deny it? *Pericles* iv 2 144
If we should deny, the most just gods For every graff would send a caterpillar v 1 59
Denying. You wrong me much to say so.—You wrong me more, sir, in denying it *Com. of Errors* iv 1 67
How honourable ladies sought my love, Which I denying, they fell sick and died *Mer. of Venice* iii 4 71
His dishonesty appears in leaving his friend here in necessity and denying him *T. Night* iii 4 423
'Tis a sickness denying thee any thing *W. Tale* iv 2 2
Upholding the nice fashion of your country in denying me a kiss *Hen. V.* v 2 300
She may do more, sir, than denying that *Richard III.* i 3 94
Deo. Laus Deo, bene intelligo *L. L. Lost* v 1 30
Depart. I may venture to depart alone *T. G. of Ver.* iv 3 36
At my depart I gave this unto Julia v 4 96
Little have you to say When you depart from him, but, soft and low *Meas. for Meas.* iv 1 69
Hearing how hastily you are to depart, I am come to advise you iv 3 54
Be ruled by me: depart in patience *Com. of Errors* iii 1 94
I will depart in quiet, And, in despite of mirth, mean to be merry iii 1 107
Did not I in rage depart from thence?—In verity you did iv 4 79
Therefore depart and leave him here with me.—I will not v 1 108
Be quiet and depart: thou shalt not have him v 1 112
When you depart from me, sorrow abides and happiness takes his leave *Much Ado* i 1 101
How if the nurse be asleep and will not hear us?—Why, then, depart in peace iii 3 73
I humbly give you leave to depart v 1 334
Wouldst thou come when I called thee?—Yea, signior, and depart when you bid me v 2 44
Foul breath is noisome; therefore I will depart unkissed v 2 54
Which we much rather had depart withal *L. L. Lost* ii 1 147
Sweet hearts, we shall be rich ere we depart v 2 1
And they, well mock'd, depart away with shame v 2 156
I take it, your own business calls on you And you embrace the occasion to depart *Mer. of Venice* i 1 64
Therefore tremble, and depart *As Y. Like It* v 1 63
He is now in some commerce with my lady, and will by and by depart *T. Night* iii 4 192
Depart from me: There's money for thee v 1 19
So you shall pay your fees When you depart, and save your thanks *W Tale* i 2 54
There may be in the cup A spider steep'd, and one may drink, depart, And yet partake no venom ii 1 40

Depart. Those that think it is unlawful business I am about, let them depart *W. Tale* v 3 97
Depart in peace: Be thou as lightning in the eyes of France *K. John* i 1 23
Depart not so; Though this be all, do not so quickly go *Richard. II.* i 2 63
Depart the chamber, leave us here alone 2 *Hen. IV.* iv 5 91
He which hath no stomach to this fight, Let him depart *Hen. V.* iv 3 36
See the coast clear'd, and then we will depart 1 *Hen. VI.* i 3 89
Now, quiet soul, depart when heaven please iii 2 110
Depart to Paris to the king, For there young Henry with his nobles lie iii 2 128
I had in charge at my depart for France 2 *Hen. VI.* i 1 2
If I depart from thee, I cannot live iii 2 388
It is our pleasure one of them depart iv 1 140
Tidings, as swiftly as the posts could run, Were brought me of your loss and his depart 3 *Hen. VI.* ii 1 110
I would your highness would depart the field ii 2 73
At my depart, these were his very words iv 1 92
Tell me if you love Warwick more than me? If it be so, then both depart to him iv 1 138
Let him depart before we need his help v 4 49
Depart and lay no hands on me *Richard III.* i 4 196
I know not whether to depart in silence, Or bitterly to speak in your reproof iii 7 141
Let us depart, I pray you, Lest your displeasure should enlarge itself *Troi. and Cres.* v 2 36
Depart at pleasure; leave us here *T. Andron.* v 2 145
For this time, all the rest depart away *Rom. and Jul.* i 1 105
Once more, on pain of death, all men depart i 1 110
Reason coldly of your grievances, Or else depart iii 1 56
And never from this palace of dim night Depart again v 3 108
Ere we depart, we'll share a bounteous time In different pleasures *T. of Athens* i 1 263
O, thou shalt find— A fool of thee: depart iv 3 232
He shall be satisfied; and, by my honour, Depart untouch'd *J. Cæsar* iii 1 142
With this I depart iii 2 49
Good countrymen, let me depart alone iii 2 60
I do entreat you, not a man depart, Save I alone, till Antony have spoke iii 2 65
Show his eyes, and grieve his heart; Come like shadows, so depart! *Macbeth* iv 1 111
We'll teach you to drink deep ere you depart *Hamlet* i 2 175
'Tis strange that they should so depart from home *Lear* ii 4 1
I will have my revenge ere I depart his house iii 5 1
Should we be taking leave As long a term as yet we have to live, The loathness to depart would grow *Cymbeline* i 1 108
You shall have better cheer Ere you depart iii 6 68
You come in faint for want of meat, depart reeling with too much drink v 4 164
Why, as it were unlicensed of your loves, He would depart *Pericles* i 3 18
Yet, ere you shall depart, this we desire i 3 39
Brief, he must hence depart to Tyre iii Gower 39
Departed. I from thee departed Thy penitent reform'd *W. Tale* i 2 238
John, to stop Arthur's title in the whole, Hath willingly departed with a part *K. John* ii 1 563
How would it fare with your departed souls? 2 *Hen. VI.* iv 7 123
As you wish Christian peace to souls departed *Hen. VIII.* iv 2 156
Threaten'd me with death, going in the vault, If I departed not and left him there *Rom. and Jul.* v 3 277
Let in the maid, that out a maid Never departed more *Hamlet* iv 5 55
Departedest. Say in brief the cause Why thou departed'st from thy native home *Com. of Errors* i 1 30
Departest. That thou depart'st hence safe, Does pay thy labour richly *Ant. and Cleo.* iv 14 36
Departing. Praise in departing *Tempest* iii 3 39
They stay The first departing of the king for Ireland *Richard II.* ii 1 290
His tongue Sounds ever after as a sullen bell, Remember'd tolling a departing friend 2 *Hen. IV.* i 1 103
A deadly groan, like life and death's departing 3 *Hen. VI.* ii 6 43
Departure. My patience, more than thy desert, Is privilege for thy departure hence *T. G. of Ver.* iii 1 160
His Julia gave it him at his departure iv 4 140
I dote on his very absence, and I pray God grant them a fair departure *Mer. of Venice* i 2 121
I am glad of your departure *As Y. Like It* iii 2 311
If the business be of any difficulty, and this morning your departure hence, it requires haste *All's Well* iv 3 108
My people did expect my hence departure Two days ago *W. Tale* i 2 450
You knew of his departure, as you know What you have underta'en to do iii 2 78
I o'erween to think so, which is another spur to my departure iv 2 10
Evils that take leave, On their departure most of all show evil *K. John* iii 4 115
Looking awry upon your lord's departure *Richard II.* ii 2 21
Thrice-gracious queen, More than your lord's departure weep not ii 2 25
We license your departure with your son 1 *Hen. IV.* i 3 123
Break with your wives of your departure hence iii 1 144
At the time of my departure thence He was much fear'd by his physicians iv 1 23
My lady craves To know the cause of your abrupt departure 1 *Hen. VI.* ii 3 30
A warning bell, Sings heavy music to thy timorous soul; And mine shall ring thy dire departure out iv 2 41
Fairest-boding dreams That ever enter'd in a drowsy head, Have I since your departure had *Richard III.* v 3 229
She that's a maid now, and laughs at my departure, Shall not be a maid long *Lear* i 5 55
If they suffer our departure, death's the word *Ant. and Cleo.* i 2 139
Who needs must know of her departure and Dost seem so ignorant *Cymbeline* iv 3 10
Further to question me of your king's departure *Pericles* i 3 12
Depeche. Oui; mette le au mon pocket: depeche, quickly *Mer. Wives* i 4 56
Depend. I find my zenith doth depend upon A most auspicious star *Tempest* i 2 181
More depends on it than we must yet deliver *Meas. for Meas.* iv 2 128
There's more depends on this than on the value *Mer. of Venice* iv 1 434
Tell me whereon the likelihood depends *As Y. Like It* i 3 59
Bidding me depend Upon thy stars, thy fortune and thy strength *K. John* iii 1 125
Your right depends not on his life or death 3 *Hen. VI.* i 2 11
You depend upon him, I mean?—Sir, I do depend upon the lord *Troi. and Cres.* iii 1 4
You depend upon a noble gentleman; I must needs praise him iii 1 6
He that depends Upon your favours swims with fins of lead *Coriolanus* i 1 183

Depend. This day's black fate on more days doth depend *Rom. and Jul.* iii 1 124
Will you be prick'd in number of our friends; Or shall we on, and not depend on you? . . . *J. Cæsar* iii 1 217
On his choice depends The safety and health of this whole state *Hamlet* i 3 20
That spirit upon whose weal depend and rest The lives of many . iii 3 14
And the remainder, that shall still depend, To be such men . *Lear* i 4 271
Wilt thou be fast to my hopes, if I depend on the issue? *Othello* i 3 369
We work by wit, and not by witchcraft; And wit depends on dilatory time . . . . ii 3 379
Which wholly depends on your abode *Ant. and Cleo.* i 2 182
We'll slip you for a season; but our jealousy Does yet depend *Cymbeline* iv 3 23
Poor wretches that depend On greatness' favour . . v 4 127
Look to your little mistress, on whose grace You may depend hereafter *Pericles* iii 3 41
Dependance. 'Tis a cause that hath no mean dependance Upon our joint and several dignities . . . *Troi. and Cres.* ii 2 192
Dependant. I am your free dependant . . *Meas. for Meas.* iv 3 95
Of promise-breach Thereon dependent . . . v 1 411
The best ward of mine honour is rewarding my dependents . *L. L. Lost* iii 1 134
The bone-ache! for that, methinks, is the curse dependant on those that war for a placket . . . *Troi. and Cres.* ii 3 21
All his dependants Which labour'd after him to the mountain's top *T. of Athens* i 1 85
As well in the general dependants as in the duke himself . *Lear* i 4 65
Who, with some other of the lords dependants, Are gone with him . iii 7 18
Depended. When remedies are past, the griefs are ended By seeing the worst, which late on hopes depended. . . . . . *Othello* i 3 203
Dependency. Such a dependency of thing on thing, As e'er I heard in madness . . . . *Meas. for Meas.* v 1 62
Let me report to him Your sweet dependency . *Ant. and Cleo.* v 2 26
On whom there is no more dependency But brats and beggary *Cymbeline* ii 3 123
Depender. To be depender on a thing that leans . . i 5 58
Depending. And not depending on his friendly wish *T. G. of Ver.* i 3 62
Canst thou believe thy living is a life, So stinkingly depending? *Meas. for Meas.* iii 2 28
Unless you may be won by some other sort than your father's imposition depending on the caskets . . *Mer. of Venice* i 2 114
Whereupon our weal, on you depending, Counts it your weal *K. John* iv 2 65
The care on thee depending Hath fed upon the body of my father *2 Hen. IV.* iv 5 159
These bald tribunes? On whom depending, their obedience fails To the greater bench . . . . . *Coriolanus* iii 1 166
Each on one foot standing, nicely Depending on their brands *Cymbeline* ii 4 91
Deplore. Never more Will I my master's tears to you deplore *T. Night* iii 1 174
Deploring. To their instruments Tune a deploring dump *T. G. of Ver.* iii 2 85
Depopulate. Where is this viper That would depopulate the city and Be every man himself? . . . . . *Coriolanus* iii 1 264
Depose. And charges him, my lord, with such a time When I'll depose I had him in mine arms . . . . *Meas. for Meas.* v 1 198
And formally, according to our law, Depose him in the justice of his cause . . . . *Richard II.* i 3 30
Deposing thee before thou wert possess'd, Which art possess'd now to depose thyself . . . . ii 1 108
The breath of worldly men cannot depose The deputy elected by the Lord . . . . iii 2 56
You may my glories and my state depose, But not my griefs . . iv 1 192
Do thou stand for me, and I'll play my father.—Depose me? *1 Hen. IV.* ii 4 478
The duke yet lives, that Henry shall depose . *2 Hen. VI.* i 4 33
Seeing 'twas he that made you to depose, Your oath, my lord, is vain *3 Hen. VI.* i 2 26
Loath to depose the child, your brother's son . *Richard III.* iii 7 209
Deposed. Until our fears, resolved, Be by some certain king purged and deposed . . . . *K. John* ii 1 372
For what can we bequeath Save our deposed bodies to the ground? *Richard II.* iii 2 150
Some have been deposed; some slain in war; Some haunted by the ghosts they have deposed . . . . . iii 2 157
Must he be deposed? The king shall be contented . . iii 3 144
What, think you then the king shall be deposed?—Depress'd he is already, and deposed 'Tis doubt he will be . . . . iii 4 67
Why dost thou say King Richard is deposed? . . . iii 4 77
By confessing them, the souls of men May deem that you are worthily deposed . . . . iv 1 227
Hath Bolingbroke deposed Thine intellect? . . . . v 1 27
From whence he intercepted did return To be deposed . *1 Hen. IV.* i 3 152
In short time after, he deposed the king . . . . iv 3 90
King Pepin, which deposed Childeric . . . *Hen. V.* i 2 65
Henry the Fourth, grandfather to this king, Deposed his nephew Richard . . . . *1 Hen. VI.* ii 5 64
Deposed the rightful king, Sent his poor queen to France *2 Hen. VI.* ii 2 24
Bashful Henry deposed, whose cowardice Hath made us by-words to our enemies . . . . *3 Hen. VI.* i 1 41
Think not that Henry shall be so deposed.—Deposed he shall be . i 1 153
She weeps, and says her Henry is deposed; He smiles, and says his Edward is install'd . . . . iii 1 45
As we think, You are the king King Edward hath deposed . iii 1 69
If not, that, I being queen, you bow like subjects, Yet that, by you deposed, you quake like rebels . . . *Richard III.* i 3 162
He frets That Lepidus of the triumvirate Should be deposed *Ant. and Cleo.* iii 6 29
Deposing thee before thou wert possess'd, Which art possess'd now to depose thyself . . . . . . *Richard II.* ii 1 107
One heinous article, Containing the deposing of a king . . iv 1 234
Some will mourn in ashes, some coal-black, For the deposing of a rightful king . . . . v 1 50
Depositaries. Made you my guardians, my depositaries . . *Lear* ii 4 254
Depravation. Do not give advantage To stubborn critics, apt, without a theme, For depravation . . . *Troi. and Cres.* v 2 132
Deprave. That lie and cog and flout, deprave and slander . *Much Ado* v 1 95
Who lives that's not depraved or depraves? . . *T. of Athens* i 2 145
Depraved. Who lives that's not depraved or depraves? . . . i 2 145
Thou'lt not believe With how depraved a quality—O Regan! . *Lear* ii 4 139
Depress'd he is already, and deposed 'Tis doubt he will be *Richard II.* iii 4 68
Deprive. Which might deprive your sovereignty of reason . *Hamlet* i 4 73
And permit The curiosity of nations to deprive me . . *Lear* i 2 4
Deprived. He deposed the king; Soon after that, deprived him of his life . . . . *1 Hen. IV.* iv 3 91
Deprived of honour and inheritance . . . . *1 Hen. VI.* ii 5 27
Each part, deprived of supple government . . *Rom. and Jul.* iv 1 102
Whose wicked deed thy most ingenious sense Deprived thee of *Hamlet* v 1 272
Deprived. No unchaste action, or dishonour'd step, That hath deprived me of your grace and favour . . . . . *Lear* i 1 232
Is wretchedness deprived that benefit, To end itself by death? . iv 6 61
Depth. To sound the depth of this knavery . . *T. of Shrew* v 1 141
A spirit raised from depth of under-ground . . . . *2 Hen. VI.* i 2 79
To weep is to make less the depth of grief . . *3 Hen. VI.* ii 1 85
In a sea of glory, But far beyond my depth . . *Hen. VIII.* iii 2 361
And sounded all the depths and shoals of honour . . . iii 2 436
I was come to the whole depth of my tale . . *Rom. and Jul.* iii 4 104
Stepp'd into the law, which is past depth To those that, without heed, do plunge into't . . . . *T. of Athens* iii 5 12
I were damn'd beneath all depth in hell, But that I did proceed upon just grounds To this extremity . . . . . . *Othello* v 2 137
Deputation. Given his deputation all the organs Of our own power *Meas. for Meas.* i 1 21
His friends by deputation could not So soon be drawn . *1 Hen. IV.* iv 1 32
All the favourites that the absent king In deputation left behind him . iv 3 87
Thy topless deputation he puts on . . . *Troi. and Cres.* i 3 152
Say to great Cæsar this: in deputation I kiss his conquering hand *Ant. and Cleo.* iii 13 74
Depute. There is especial commission come from Venice to depute Cassio in Othello's place . . . . *Othello* iv 2 226
Deputed. Not the king's crown, nor the deputed sword . *Meas. for Meas.* ii 2 60
Deputies. Hail, you anointed deputies of heaven! . . *K. John* iii 1 136
Deputing. As I think, they do command him home, Deputing Cassio in his government . . . . *Othello* iv 1 248
Deputy. And the new deputy now for the duke . . *Meas. for Meas.* i 2 161
Implore her, in my voice, that she make friends To the strict deputy . i 2 186
This outward-sainted deputy . . . . iii 1 89
And the corrupt deputy scaled . . . . iii 1 265
A strange picklock, which we have sent to the deputy . . . iii 2 19
He must before the deputy, sir; he has given him warning . . iii 2 35
The deputy cannot abide a whoremaster . . . . . iii 2 36
What is the news from this good deputy? . . . . iv 1 27
It is a bitter deputy.—Not so, not so . . . . . iv 2 81
Were you sworn to the duke, or to the deputy? . . . . iv 2 197
Satisfy the deputy with the visage Of Ragozine . . . iv 3 79
Hath yet the deputy sent my brother's pardon? . . . iv 3 118
I went To this pernicious caitiff deputy . . . . . v 1 88
Great deputy, the welkin's vicegerent and sole dominator . *L. L. Lost* i 1 221
In us, that are our own great deputy . . . . *K. John* ii 1 365
God's substitute, His deputy anointed in His sight . *Richard II.* i 2 38
The breath of worldly men cannot depose The deputy elected by the Lord . . . . iii 2 57
Maid Marian may be the deputy's wife of the ward to thee *1 Hen. IV.* iii 3 130
In Henry's royal name, As deputy unto that gracious king *1 Hen. VI.* v 3 161
By His majesty I swear, Whose far unworthy deputy I am *2 Hen. VI.* iii 2 286
His contract with Lady Lucy, And his contract by deputy in France *Richard III.* iii 7 6
Kildare's attainder, Then deputy of Ireland . . . *Hen. VIII.* ii 1 42
Plague of your policy! You sent me deputy for Ireland . . iii 2 260
Deputy-elect. The figure of God's majesty, His captain, steward, deputy-elect . . . . *Richard II.* iv 1 126
Deracinate. The coulter rusts That should deracinate such savagery *Hen. V.* v 2 47
Rend and deracinate The unity and married calm of states *Tr. and Cr.* i 3 99
Derby. Harry of Hereford, Lancaster and Derby Am I . *Richard II.* i 3 35
Dercetas. I am call'd Dercetas; Mark Antony I served *Ant. and Cleo.* v 1 5
Deride. Who cover faults, at last shame them derides . . . *Lear* i 1 284
Derision. Scorn and derision never come in tears . *M. N. Dream* iii 2 123
To conjure tears up in a poor maid's eyes With your derision! . iii 2 159
Have you with these contrived To bait me with this foul derision? . iii 2 197
All this derision Shall seem a dream and fruitless vision . . iii 2 370
I have derision medicinable, To use between your strangeness and his pride . . . . *Troi. and Cres.* iii 3 44
Derivation. Being as good a man as yourself, both in the disciplines of war, and in the derivation of my birth . . . *Hen. V.* iii 2 141
My derivation was from ancestors Who stood equivalent with mighty kings . . . . *Pericles* v 1 91
Derivative. For honour, 'Tis a derivative from me to mine *W. Tale* iii 2 45
Derive. This shame derives itself from unknown loins . *Much Ado* iv 1 137
From women's eyes this doctrine I derive . . *L. L. Lost* iv 3 302
Treason is not inherited, my lord; Or, if we did derive it from our friends, What's that to me? . . . . . *As Y. Like It* i 3 64
She derives her honesty and achieves her goodness . . *All's Well* i 1 52
Honours thrive, When rather from our acts we them derive Than our foregoers . . . . ii 3 143
Things which would derive me ill will to speak of . . . v 3 265
His indignation derives itself out of a very competent injury *T. Night* iii 4 269
Derive a liberty From heartiness, from bounty . . *W. Tale* i 2 112
Derives from heaven his quarrel and his cause. . . . *2 Hen. IV.* i 1 206
This imperial crown, Which, as immediate from thy place and blood, Derives itself to me . . . . iv 5 43
Derive this; come . . . . . . *Troi. and Cres.* ii 3 66
If I might beseech you, gentlemen, to repair some other hour, I should derive much from't . . . . *T. of Athens* iii 4 69
Let the unscarr'd braggarts of the war Derive some pain from you . iv 3 162
Till you can derive from him better testimony of his intent . *Lear* i 2 87
Derived. What says she to my birth?—That you are well derived *T. G. of Ver.* v 2 23
Thou art a gentleman and well derived . . . . . v 4 146
Lend him your kind pains To find out this abuse, whence 'tis derived *Meas. for Meas.* v 1 247
As well derived as he, As well possess'd; my love is more than his *M. N. Dr.* i 1 99
O, that estates, degrees and offices Were not derived corruptly! *Mer. of Venice* ii 9 42
A wretched Florentine, Derived from the ancient Capilet *All's Well* v 3 159
Conceit is still derived From some forefather grief . *Richard II.* ii 2 34
How is this derived? Saw you the field? came you from Shrewsbury? *2 Hen. IV.* i 1 23
The crown and seat of France Derived from Edward . . *Hen. V.* i 1 89
When you find him evenly derived From his most famed of famous ancestors . . . . ii 4 91
By my mother I derived am From Lionel Duke of Clarence . *1 Hen. VI.* ii 5 74
Earl of Cambridge, then derived From famous Edmund Langley, Duke of York . . . . ii 5 84
To tell thee whence thou camest, of whom derived, Were shame enough to shame thee, wert thou not shameless . . . *3 Hen. VI.* i 4 119
What friend of mine That had to him derived your anger did I Continue in my liking? . . . . *Hen. VIII.* ii 4 32

Derived. I do return those talents, Doubled with thanks and service, from whose help I derived liberty . . . *T. of Athens* i 2 8
Soul of Rome! Brave son, derived from honourable loins! . *J. Cæsar* ii 1 322
Dern. By many a dern and painful perch Of Pericles the careful search *Pericles* iii Gower 15
Derogate. From her derogate body never spring A babe to honour her! *Lear* i 4 302
You cannot derogate, my lord.—Not easily, I think . . *Cymbeline* ii 1 48
You are a fool granted; therefore your issues, being foolish, do not derogate . . . . ii 1 51
Derogately. More laugh'd at, that I should Once name you derogately *Ant. and Cleo.* ii 2 34
Derogation. Is it fit I went to look upon him? is there no derogation in't? . . . . *Cymbeline* ii 1 47
Desartless. Who think you the most desartless man to be constable? *Much Ado* iii 3 9
Descant. You are too flat And mar the concord with too harsh a descant *T. G. of Ver.* i 2 94
To spy my shadow in the sun And descant on mine own deformity *Richard III.* i 1 27
On that ground I'll build a holy descant . . . . iii 7 49
Descend. Let her descend, bully, let her descend . *Mer. Wives* iv 5 22
With trial-fire touch me his finger-end: If he be chaste, the flame will back descend . . . . v 5 89
Descend, for you must be my torch-bearer . . *Mer. of Venice* ii 6 40
I'll make the statue move indeed, descend And take you by the hand *W. Tale* v 3 88
'Tis time; descend; be stone no more . . . . v 3 99
We will descend and fold him in our arms . . *Richard II.* iii 3 54
O, pardon me that I descend so low . . . *1 Hen. IV.* i 3 167
To thee it shall descend with better quiet . . *2 Hen. IV.* iv 5 188
Let the inheritance Descend unto the daughter . . *Hen. V.* i 2 100
I descend To give thee answer of thy just demand . *1 Hen. VI.* v 3 143
Descend to darkness and the burning lake! . . *2 Hen. VI.* i 4 42
Descend my throne, And kneel for grace and mercy at my feet *3 Hen. VI.* i 1 74
From these our Henry lineally descends . . . iii 3 87
Say, who art thou that lately didst descend Into this gaping hollow? *T. Andron.* ii 3 248
Farewell, farewell! one kiss, and I'll descend . . *Rom. and Jul.* iii 5 42
Why I descend into this bed of death, Is partly to behold my lady's face . . . . v 3 28
Descend, and open your uncharged ports . . . *T. of Athens* v 4 55
Descend, and keep your words . . . . . v 4 64
Shall I descend? and will you give me leave?—Come down.—Descend *J. Cæsar* iii 2 164
Brother, a word; descend: brother, I say! . . . *Lear* ii 1 21
Descended. And all those oaths Descended into perjury . *T. G. of Ver.* v 4 49
Thou shouldst have better pleased me with this deed, Hadst thou descended from another house . . . *As Y. Like It* i 2 241
Descended Of Blithild, which was daughter to King Clothair *Hen. V.* i 2 66
I am descended of a gentler blood . . . *1 Hen. VI.* v 4 8
Pale and bloodless, Being all descended to the labouring heart *2 Hen. VI.* iii 2 163
My wife descended of the Lacies . . . . . iv 2 47
Jack Cade proclaims himself Lord Mortimer, Descended from the Duke of Clarence' house . . . . iv 4 29
One thus descended, That hath beside well in his person wrought *Coriol.* ii 3 253
Did not you speak?—When?—Now.—As I descended? . *Macbeth* ii 2 17
And fitting for a princess Descended of so many royal kings *A. and C.* v 2 330
He sits 'mongst men like a descended god . . *Cymbeline* i 6 169
This man is better than the man he slew, As well descended as thyself v 5 303
Descending. Ascend his throne, descending now from him *Richard II.* iv 1 111
Thou camest From good descending . . . . *Pericles* v 1 129
Descension. From a God to a bull? a heavy descension! . *2 Hen. IV.* ii 2 193
Descent. Falsehood, cowardice and poor descent, Three things that women highly hold in hate . . . . . *T. G. of Ver.* iii 2 32
A mighty man of such descent, Of such possessions . *T. of Shrew* Ind. 2 15
From son to son, some four or five descents . . *All's Well* iii 7 24
By the glorious worth of my descent, This arm shall do it . *Richard II.* i 1 107
I lay my claim To my inheritance of free descent . . . ii 3 136
The lawful heir Of Edward king, the third of that descent . *1 Hen. VI.* ii 5 66
From whence you spring by lineal descent . . . . iii 1 166
He is near you in descent, And should you fall, he is the next will mount . . . . *2 Hen. VI.* iii 1 21
By reputing of his high descent, As next the king he was successive heir . . . . iii 1 48
And made a preachment of your high descent . . *3 Hen. VI.* i 4 72
If thou be that princely eagle's bird, Show thy descent by gazing 'gainst the sun . . . . ii 1 92
Do me but right, and you must all confess That I was not ignoble of descent . . . . iv 1 70
To bar my master's heirs in true descent, God knows I will not do it *Richard III.* iii 2 54
Not the dreadful spout. . . . Shall dizzy with more clamour Neptune's ear In his descent than shall my prompted sword *Troi. and Cres.* v 2 175
Till we can clear these ambiguities, And know their spring, their head, their true descent . . . . . *Rom. and Jul.* v 3 218
From the extremest upward of thy head To the descent and dust below thy foot . . . . *Lear* v 3 137
How of descent As good as we? . . . . *Cymbeline* v 5 308
My thoughts, That never relish'd of a base descent . . *Pericles* ii 5 60
Describe. I will describe them; and, according to my description, level at my affection . . . . . . *Mer. of Venice* i 2 40
A paltry, insolent fellow!—How he describes himself! *Troi. and Cres.* ii 3 219
Pattern'd by that the poet here describes . . . . *T. Andron.* iv 1 57
Described. Thou hast described A hot friend cooling . *J. Cæsar* iv 2 18
Descried. We are descried; they'll mock us now downright . *L. L. Lost* v 2 389
I kill'd a man and fear I was descried . . . . *T. of Shrew* i 1 237
Who hath descried the number of the foe? . . *Richard III.* v 3 9
The news is true, my lord; he is descried . . *Ant. and Cleo.* iii 7 55
We have descried, upon our neighbouring shore, A portly sail of ships *Pericles* i 4 60
Description. I will description the matter to you, if you be capacity of it . . . . *Mer. Wives* i 1 222
A right description of our sport, my lord . . . *L. L. Lost* v 2 522
I will describe them; and, according to my description, level at my affection . . . . . . *Mer. of Venice* i 2 41
Before a friend of this description Shall lose a hair . . . iii 2 303
If that an eye may profit by a tongue, Then should I know you by description . . . . *As Y. Like It* iv 3 85
I begin to love him for this.—For this description of thine honesty? *All's Well* iv 3 294
Description. Which lames report to follow it and undoes description to do it . . . . *W. Tale* v 2 63
The poet makes a most excellent description of it . . *Hen. V.* iii 6 39
Description cannot suit itself in words To demonstrate the life of such a battle . . . . iv 2 53
Your wondrous rare description, noble earl, Of beauteous Margaret *1 Hen. VI.* v 5 1
Is not this he?—Where?—'Tis his description . . *T. of Athens* iv 3 412
By all description this should be the place . . . . v 3 1
A maid That paragons description and wild fame . . *Othello* ii 1 62
For her own person, It beggar'd all description . *Ant. and Cleo.* ii 2 203
'Tis a strange serpent.—'Tis so. And the tears of it are wet.—Will this description satisfy him? . . . . ii 7 56
The description Of what is in her chamber nothing saves The wager you have laid . . . . *Cymbeline* ii 4 93
This is the very description of their meeting-place . . . iv 1 26
Either our brags Were crack'd of kitchen-trulls, or his description Proved us unspeaking sots . . . . v 5 177
He went to bed to her very description . . . *Pericles* iv 2 109
Descry. What's past and what's to come she can descry . *1 Hen. VI.* i 2 57
But the true ground of all these piteous woes We cannot without circumstance descry . . . . . . *Rom. and Jul.* v 3 181
Moreover, to descry The strength o' the enemy . . . *Lear* iv 5 13
The main descry Stands on the hourly thought . . . iv 6 217
I cannot, 'twixt the heaven and the main, Descry a sail . *Othello* ii 1 4
In Helicanus may you well descry A figure of truth, of faith, of loyalty *Pericles* v 3 Gower 91
Desdemona. For know, Iago, But that I love the gentle Desdemona *Oth.* i 2 25
Fetch Desdemona hither.—Ancient, conduct them . . . i 3 120
This to hear Would Desdemona seriously incline . . . i 3 146
What would you, Desdemona?—That I did love the Moor to live with him . . . . i 3 248
Adieu, brave Moor; use Desdemona well . . . . i 3 292
Honest Iago, My Desdemona must I leave to thee . . . i 3 296
Come, Desdemona; I have but an hour Of love, of worldly matters and direction, To spend with thee . . . . . . i 3 299
It cannot be that Desdemona should long continue her love to the Moor i 3 347
Do omit Their mortal natures, letting go safely by The divine Desdemona ii 1 73
Make love's quick pants in Desdemona's arms . . . ii 1 80
Come, Desdemona, Once more, well met at Cyprus . . . ii 1 213
First, I must tell thee this—Desdemona is directly in love with him ii 1 221
And I dare think he'll prove to Desdemona A most dear husband . ii 1 299
Our general cast us thus early for the love of his Desdemona . ii 3 15
To Desdemona hath to-night caroused Potations pottle-deep . ii 3 55
Come, Desdemona: 'tis the soldiers' life To have their balmy slumbers waked with strife . . . . ii 3 257
In the morning I will beseech the virtuous Desdemona to undertake for me . . . . ii 3 336
For 'tis most easy The inclining Desdemona to subdue In any honest suit . . . . ii 3 346
This honest fool Plies Desdemona to repair his fortunes . . ii 3 360
My suit to her Is, that she will to virtuous Desdemona Procure me some access . . . . iii 1 37
Give me advantage of some brief discourse With Desdemona alone iii 1 56
Not now, sweet Desdemona; some other time . . . iii 3 55
Farewell, my lord.—Farewell, my Desdemona: I'll come to thee straight . . . . iii 3 87
I do not think but Desdemona's honest.—Long live she so! . iii 3 225
Desdemona comes: If she be false, O, then heaven mocks itself! . iii 3 277
What handkerchief! Why, that the Moor first gave to Desdemona . iii 3 308
I heard him say 'Sweet Desdemona, Let us be wary, let us hide our loves' . . . . iii 3 419
How do you, Desdemona?—Well, my good lord . . . iii 4 35
Ply Desdemona well, and you are sure on't . . . iv 1 107
O Desdemona! away! away! away! . . . . iv 2 41
The jewels you have had from me to deliver to Desdemona would half have corrupted a votarist . . . . iv 2 189
I will make myself known to Desdemona . . . . iv 2 200
If thou the next night following enjoy not Desdemona, take me from this world . . . . iv 2 220
Is that true? why, then Othello and Desdemona return again to Venice iv 2 228
He goes into Mauritania and takes away with him the fair Desdemona iv 2 230
O,—Desdemona,— My lord?—Get you to bed on the instant . iv 3 5
He calls me to a restitution large Of gold and jewels that I bobb'd from him, As gifts to Desdemona . . . . . . v 1 17
Who's there? Othello?—Ay, Desdemona . . . . v 2 23
Have you pray'd to-night, Desdemona?—Ay, my lord . . v 2 25
Sweet Desdemona! O sweet mistress, speak!—A guiltless death I die v 2 121
Poor Desdemona! I am glad thy father's dead . . . v 2 204
O Desdemona! Desdemona! dead! Oh! Oh! Oh! . . . v 2 281
Desert. Though this island seem to be desert . . . *Tempest* ii 1 35
Of worth and worthy estimation And not without desert so well reputed *T. G. of Ver.* ii 4 57
My patience, more than thy desert, Is privilege for thy departure hence iii 1 159
Thou hast shown some sign of good desert . . . . iii 2 18
This shadowy desert, unfrequented woods, I better brook than flourishing peopled towns . . . . v 4 2
Dispose of them as thou know'st their deserts . . . v 4 159
Your desert speaks loud . . . . . *Meas. for Meas.* v 1 9
My wife—but, I protest, without desert—Hath oftentimes upbraided me *Com. of Errors* iii 1 112
Come challenge me, challenge me by these deserts . . *L. L. Lost* iv 2 815
And the ill counsel of a desert place . . . *M. N. Dream* ii 1 218
The Hyrcanian deserts and the vasty wilds Of wide Arabia are as throughfares now . . . . *Mer. of Venice* ii 7 41
I will assume desert . . . . ii 9 51
Is that my prize? are my deserts no better? . . . ii 9 60
Being native burghers of this desert city . . . *As Y. Like It* ii 1 23
If that love or gold Can in this desert place buy entertainment . ii 4 72
Thou shalt not die for lack of a dinner, if there live any thing in this desert . . . . ii 6 18
In this desert inaccessible, Under the shade of melancholy boughs . ii 7 110
Why should this a desert be? For it is unpeopled? No . . iii 2 133
As how I came into that desert place . . . . . iv 3 142
Nor would I have him till I do deserve him; Yet never know how that desert should be . . . . *All's Well* i 3 206
That dost in vile misprision shackle up My love and her desert . ii 3 160
Is't possible that my deserts to you Can lack persuasion? . *T. Night* iii 4 382
Bear it To some remote and desert place . . . *W. Tale* ii 3 176
Our ship hath touch'd upon The deserts of Bohemia . . . iii 3 2

Desert. Which elder days shall ripen and confirm To more approved service and desert *Richard II.* ii 3 44
If that the king Have any way your good deserts forgot . 1 *Hen. IV.* iv 3 46
Therefore let me have right, and let desert mount . 2 *Hen. IV.* iv 3 60
Shall forget the office of our hand, Sooner than quittance of desert and merit . . . . *Hen. V.* ii 2 34
Would I were able to load him with his desert ! . . . ii 7 86
And, for these good deserts, We here create you Earl of Shrewsbury 1 *Hen. VI.* iii 4 25
Not of any challenge of desert . . . . . v 4 153
Will, I doubt it not, See you well guerdon'd for these good deserts 2 *Hen. VI.* i 4 49
I have heard your king's desert recounted . 3 *Hen. VI.* iii 3 132
My desert is honour : And to repair my honour lost for him, I here renounce him . . . . . iii 3 192
And lay those honours on your high deserts . *Richard III.* i 3 97
That all without desert have frown'd on me . . ii 1 67
My desert Unmeritable shuns your high request . iii 7 154
Plead what I will be, not what I have been ; Not my deserts, but what I will deserve . . . . . . iv 4 415
The duke by law Found his deserts . . . *Hen VIII.* iii 2 267
We will not name desert before his birth . *Troi. and Cres.* iii 2 101
High birth, vigour of bone, desert in service . . iii 3 172
Tell us what hath brought you to't.—Mine own desert ! . . . . . *Coriolanus* ii 3 71
Let desert in pure election shine . . . *T. Andron.* i 1 16
Andronicus, surnamed Pius For many good and great deserts to Rome . i 1 24
And, as suitors should, Plead your deserts in peace and humbleness . i 1 45
I give thee thanks in part of thy deserts . . . . i 1 236
And when I do forget The least of these unspeakable deserts, Romans, forget your fealty to me . . . . . . i 1 256
O, none of both but are of high desert . . . . iii 1 171
The base o' the mount Is rank'd with all deserts, all kind of natures *T. of Athens* i 1 65
Yet, more to move you, Take my deserts to his, and join 'em both . iii 5 79
Be alive again, And dare me to the desert with thy sword . *Macbeth* iii 4 104
I have words That would be howl'd out in the desert air . . iv 3 194
I will use them according to their desert . . *Hamlet* ii 2 553
Use every man after his desert, and who should 'scape whipping? . ii 2 555
You less know how to value her desert Than she to scant her duty *Lear* ii 4 141
Antres vast and deserts idle, Rough quarries, rocks and hills . *Othello* i 3 140
Whose love is never link'd to the deserver Till his deserts are past *Ant. and Cleo.* i 2 194
I chiefly, That set thee on to this desert, am bound To load thy merit richly . . . . *Cymbeline* i 5 73
Her countless glory, which desert must gain ; And which, without desert, because thine eye Presumes to reach, all thy whole heap must die . . . . *Pericles* i 1 31
It is your grace's pleasure to commend ; Not my desert . . ii 5 30

Deserve. To plead for love deserves more fee than hate . *T. G. of Ver.* i 2 48
A son that well deserves The honour and regard of such a father . ii 4 59
Only deserve my love by loving him . . . . . ii 7 82
And truly she deserves it . . . . . *Mer. Wives* iii 2 125
I know not how I may deserve to be your porter . . iii 2 180
Keep in that mind ; I'll deserve it.—Nay, I must tell you, so you do . iii 3 89
Then let me be your jest ; I deserve it . . . . iii 3 161
Grace and good company !—Who's there? come in : the wish deserves a welcome . . . . . . *Meas. for Meas.* iii 1 45
It deserves, with characters of brass, A forted residence 'gainst the tooth of time . . . . v 1 11
Whipping and hanging.—Slandering a prince deserves it . . v 1 530
Doth not the gentleman Deserve as full as fortunate a bed? . *Much Ado* iii 1 45
He doth deserve As much as may be yielded to a man . . iii 1 47
Others say thou dost deserve, and I Believe it better than reportingly . iii 1 115
How much might the man deserve of me that would right her? . iv 1 263
Margaret, deserve well at my hands by helping me . . . v 2 2
And knows me, and knows me, How pitiful I deserve . . . v 2 29
She deserves well.—To be whipped . . . . *L. L. Lost* i 2 124
Vows for thee broke deserve not punishment . . . . iv 3 63
And you, my liege, and I, Are pick-purses in love, and we deserve to die iv 3 209
When at your hands did I deserve this scorn? . *M. N. Dream* ii 2 124
I did never, no, nor never can, Deserve a sweet look from Demetrius' eye ii 2 127
Who chooseth me shall get as much as he deserves . *Mer. of Venice* ii 7 7
As much as he deserves ! Pause there, Morocco, And weigh thy value . ii 7 24
If thou be'st rated by thy estimation, Thou dost deserve enough . ii 7 27
As much as I deserve ! Why, that's the lady . . . ii 7 31
I do in birth deserve her, and in fortunes, In graces and in qualities of breeding ; But more than these, in love I do deserve . . ii 7 32
Did I deserve no more than a fool's head? Is that my prize? . ii 9 59
Hate him not, for my sake.—Why should I not? doth he not deserve well? . . . . *As Y. Like It* i 3 37
Deserves as well a dark house and a whip as madmen do . . iii 2 421
Do you pity him? no, he deserves no pity . . . . iv 3 66
Your patience and your virtue well deserves it . . . v 4 193
Nor would I have him till I do deserve him ; Yet never know how that desert should be . . . . *All's Well* i 3 205
I have spoken better of you than you have or will to deserve at my hand . . . . ii 5 52
She deserves a lord That twenty such rude boys might tend upon . iii 2 83
Only to seem to deserve well . . . have I run into this danger . iv 3 332
As ever thou wilt deserve well at my hand, help me . *T. Night* iv 2 86
Deserves a name As rank as any flax-wench . . *W. Tale* i 2 276
This her without-door form, Which on my faith deserves high speech . ii 1 70
Whose every word deserves To taste of thy most worst . . iii 2 179
No, nor thou Become thy great birth nor deserve a crown . *K. John* iii 1 50
Did not the one deserve to have an heir? . . *Richard II.* ii 1 193
They well deserve to have, That know the strong'st and surest way to get . . . . iii 3 200
Our house, my sovereign liege, little deserves The scourge of greatness to be used on it . . . . . . 1 *Hen. IV.* i 3 10
I, in my condition, Shall better speak of you than you deserve 2 *Hen. IV.* iv 3 91
And doth deserve a coronet of gold . . . 1 *Hen. VI.* iii 3 89
I accept her, for she well deserves it . . . 3 *Hen. VI.* iii 3 249
For this one speech Lord Hastings well deserves To have the heir of the Lord Hungerford . . . . iv 1 47
To deserve well at my brother's hands, I here proclaim myself thy mortal foe . . . . v 1 93
Bid me farewell.—'Tis more than you deserve . *Richard III.* i 2 223
Deserve not worse than wretched Clarence did . . . ii 1 93
If God sort it so, 'Tis more than we deserve, or I expect . . ii 3 37
Deserve. Tell me what they deserve That do conspire my death? *Richard III.* iii 4 61
Your love deserves my thanks, but my desert Unmeritable shuns your high request . . . . iii 7 154
Plead what I will be, not what I have been ; Not my deserts, but what I will deserve . . . . iv 4 415
Let fall a tear ; The subject will deserve it . . *Hen. VIII.* Prol. 7
Your grace must needs deserve all strangers' loves . . ii 2 102
There's nothing I have done yet, o' my conscience, Deserves a corner . iii 1 31
What he deserves of you and me I know ; What we can do to him, though now the time Gives way to us, I much fear . . . iii 2 14
He will deserve more.—Yes, without all doubt . . . iv 1 113
You are a saucy fellow : Deserve we no more reverence? . . iv 2 101
I hope she will deserve well,—and a little To love her for her mother's sake . . . . iv 2 136
There is not one, I dare avow, And now I should not lie, but will deserve . . . . iv 2 143
And, sweet lady, does Deserve our better wishes . . . v 1 26
This good man,—few of you deserve that title . . . v 3 138
How may I deserve it, That am a poor and humble subject to you? . v 3 165
Who deserves greatness Deserves your hate . . *Coriolanus* i 1 180
Deserve not so honourable a grave as to stuff a botcher's cushion . ii 1 97
Better it is to die, better to starve, Than crave the hire which first we do deserve . . . . ii 3 121
We pray the gods he may deserve your loves . . . ii 3 165
Let me deserve so ill as you, and make me Your fellow tribune . iii 1 51
This kind of service Did not deserve corn gratis . . . iii 1 125
This deserves death . . . . iii 1 207
Even this, So criminal and in such capital kind, Deserves the extremest death . . . . iii 3 82
The people Deserve such pity of him as the wolf Does of the shepherds iv 6 110
Ladies, you deserve To have a temple built you . . . v 3 206
I am as able and as fit as thou To serve, and to deserve my mistress' grace *T. Andron.* ii 1 34
I do know him A gentleman that well deserves a help . *T. of Athens* i 1 102
My estate deserves an heir more raised Than one which holds a trencher i 1 119
We were not all unkind, nor all deserve The common stroke of war . v 4 21
Brave Macbeth—well he deserves that name . . *Macbeth* i 2 16
But under heavy judgement bears that life Which he deserves to lose . i 3 111
I am young ; but something You may deserve of him through me . iv 3 15
The less they deserve, the more merit is in your bounty . *Hamlet* ii 2 557
He which finds him shall deserve our thanks . . . *Lear* ii 1 63
Resolve me, with all modest haste, which way Thou might'st deserve, or they impose, this usage . . . . ii 4 26
He his high authority abused, And did deserve his change *Ant. and Cleo.* iii 6 34
A repulse : though your attempt, as you call it, deserve more ; a punishment too . . . . *Cymbeline* i 4 129
You look on me : what wreck discern you in me Deserves your pity? . i 6 85
The credit that thy lady hath of thee Deserves thy trust . . i 6 158
Nay, many times, Doth ill deserve by doing well . . . iii 3 54
Many dream not to find, neither deserve, And yet are steep'd in favours v 4 130
And he deserves so to be called . . . . *Pericles* ii 1 107
Here take your place : Marshal the rest, as they deserve their grace . ii 3 19

Deserved more than a prison . . . . . . *Tempest* i 2 362
Take thou thy Silvia, for thou hast deserved her . *T. G. of Ver.* v 4 147
Wherein have I so deserved of you, That you extol me thus? *M. for M.* v 1 507
Much deserved on his part and equally remembered . . *Much Ado* i 1 12
He would have deserved it : sixpence a day in Pyramus, or nothing *M. N. Dream* iv 2 23
And know how well I have deserved the ring . *Mer. of Venice* iv 1 446
Gave his ring away Unto the judge that begg'd it and indeed Deserved it too . . . . v 1 181
What, are we cuckolds ere we have deserved it? . . . v 1 265
Sir, you have well deserved . . . . *As Y. Like It* i 2 254
Albeit you have deserved High commendation . . . . i 2 274
Unpitied let me die, And well deserved . . . *All's Well* ii 1 192
I have not, my lord, deserved it.—Yes, good faith, every dram of it . ii 3 232
I know not how I have deserved to run into my lord's displeasure . ii 5 37
His heels have deserved it, in usurping his spurs so long . . iv 3 118
You shall know your mistress Has deserved prison . . *W. Tale* ii 1 120
I have deserved All tongues to talk their bitterest . . . iii 2 216
Very nobly Have you deserved . . . . iv 4 529
What hath this day deserved? what hath it done? . *K. John* iii 1 84
A dearer merit, not so deep a maim As to be cast forth in the common air, Have I deserved . . . . *Richard II.* i 3 158
And hate turns one or both To worthy danger and deserved death . v 1 68
Vary deserved praise on my palfrey . . . . . *Hen. V.* iii 7 35
Richard hath best deserved of all my sons . . 3 *Hen. VI.* i 1 17
Hath he deserved to lose his birthright thus? . . . . i 1 219
At their hands I have deserved no pity . . . . . ii 6 26
And ten times more beloved Than if thou never hadst deserved our hate v 1 104
The benefit thereof is always granted To those whose dealings have deserved the place . . . . *Richard III.* iii 1 49
This prince hath neither claim'd it nor deserved it . . . iii 1 51
I know they do ; and I have well deserved it . . . . iii 2 73
I say, my lord, they have deserved death . . . . iii 4 68
Now, fair befall you ! he deserved his death . . . . iii 5 47
He hath deserved worthily of his country . . . *Coriolanus* ii 2 27
You have deserved nobly of your country, and you have not deserved nobly . . . . ii 3 94
Nor has Coriolanus Deserved this so dishonour'd rub . . . iii 1 60
Renowned Rome, whose gratitude Towards her deserved children is enroll'd . . . . iii 1 292
Give him deserved vexation . . . . iii 3 140
I have deserved no better entertainment . . . . iv 5 10
They charged him even As those should do that had deserved his hate . iv 6 113
If he could burn us all into one coal, We have deserved it . . iv 6 138
You are most welcome home.—I have not deserved it . . . v 6 61
Even to the state's best health, I have Deserved this hearing *T. of Athens* ii 2 207
And be resolved How Cæsar hath deserved to lie in death . *J. Cæsar* iii 1 132
You go to do you know not what : Wherein hath Cæsar thus deserved your loves? . . . . iii 2 241
Would thou hadst less deserved, That the proportion both of thanks and payment Might have been mine ! . . . . . *Macbeth* i 4 18
That hast no less deserved, nor must be known No less to have done so i 4 30
What have you, my good friends, deserved at the hands of fortune? *Hamlet* ii 2 245
An thou hadst been set i' the stocks for that question, thou hadst well deserved it . . . . *Lear* ii 4 66
But his own disorders Deserved much less advancement . . iv 2 203
Devil !—I have not deserved this . . . . . *Othello* iv 1 252

Deserved. Your reproof Were well deserved of rashness . *Ant. and Cleo.* ii 2 124
We had much more monstrous matter of feast, which worthily deserved noting . ii 2 188
You have well deserved ten times as much As I have said you did . ii 6 79
Therefore, he Does pity, as constrained blemishes, Not as deserved . iii 13 60
He has deserved it, were it carbuncled Like holy Phœbus' car . iv 8 28
The king Hath not deserved my service nor your loves . *Cymbeline* iv 4 25
Who deserved So long a breeding as his white beard came to, In doing this for's country . v 3 16
He deserved the praise o' the world . v 4 50
Deservedly. Therefore wast thou Deservedly confined . *Tempest* i 2 361
Deserver. To those fields Where I may wallow in the lily-beds Proposed for the deserver . *Troi. and Cres.* iii 2 14
Signs of nobleness, like stars, shall shine On all deservers . *Macbeth* i 4 42
Whose love is never link'd to the deserver Till his deserts are past *Ant. and Cleo.* i 2 193
Deservest. I love thee; none but thee; and thou deservest it *Mer. Wives* iii 3 81
In most comely truth, thou deservest it . *Much Ado* v 2 8
To speak truth, thou deservest no less . *2 Hen. VI.* v 3 11
Deserving. 'Tis my deserving, and I do entreat it . *Meas. for Meas* v 1 482
He, of all the men that ever my foolish eyes look'd upon, was the best deserving a fair lady . *Mer. of Venice* i 2 131
To be afeard of my deserving Were but a weak disabling of myself . ii 7 29
How much unlike my hopes and my deservings! . ii 9 57
Let his deservings and my love withal Be valued 'gainst your wife's commandment . iv 1 450
We wound our modesty and make foul the clearness of our deservings, when of ourselves we publish them . *All's Well* i 3 7
All her deserving Is a reserved honesty, and that I have not heard examined . iii 5 64
Some of us love you well; and even those some Envy your great deservings and good name . *1 Hen. IV.* iv 3 35
Spoke your deservings like a chronicle, Making you ever better than his praise . v 2 58
It was more of his courtesy than your deserving . *2 Hen. IV.* iv 3 48
Virtue he had, deserving to command . *1 Hen. VI.* i 1 9
What though I know her virtuous And well deserving? . *Hen. VIII.* iii 2 98
You shall not be The grave of your deserving . *Coriolanus* i 9 20
I must love you, and sue to know you better.—Sir, I shall study deserving *Lear* i 1 32
This seems a fair deserving, and must draw me That which my father loses . iii 3 24
All friends shall taste The wages of their virtue, and all foes The cup of their deservings . v 3 304
I confess me knit to thy deserving with cables of perdurable toughness *Othello* i 3 343
But what praise couldst thou bestow on a deserving woman indeed? . ii 1 146
Reputation is an idle and most false imposition; oft got without merit, and lost without deserving . ii 3 270
Vanish, or I shall give thee thy deserving . *Ant. and Cleo.* iv 12 32
Famous in Cæsar's praises, no whit less Than in his feats deserving it *Cymbeline* iii 1 7
Design. Being then appointed Master of this design . *Tempest* i 2 163
His givings-out were of an infinite distance From his true-meant design *Meas. for Meas.* i 4 55
Thine, in the dearest design of industry . *L. L. Lost* iv 1 88
Among other important and most serious designs, and of great import indeed . v 1 105
Only doth backward pull Our slow designs when we ourselves are dull *All's Well* i 1 234
O, for the love of laughter, hinder not the honour of his design . iii 6 44
He has discover'd my design, and I Remain a pinch'd thing . *W. Tale* ii 1 50
Who but to-day hammer'd of this design . ii 2 49
But not prepared For this design . iv 4 513
I'll answer thee in any fair degree, Or chivalrous design . *Richard II.* i 1 81
We shall see Justice design the victor's chivalry . i 1 203
And such officers Appointed to direct these fair designs . i 3 45
His designs crave haste, his haste good hope . ii 2 44
Leave these sad designs To him that hath more cause to be a mourner *Richard III.* i 2 211
I hope, My absence doth neglect no great designs . iii 4 25
In deep designs and matters of great moment . iii 7 67
And be not peevish-fond in great designs . iv 4 417
'Twas dangerous for him To ruminate on this so far, until It forged him some design . *Hen. VIII.* i 2 181
The ample proposition that hope makes In all designs begun on earth *Troi. and Cres.* i 3 4
O, when degree is shaked, Which is the ladder to all high designs, Then enterprise is sick! . i 3 102
In his tent Lies mocking our designs . i 3 146
Why, there you touch'd the life of our design . ii 2 194
Unless, by using means, I lame the foot Of our design . *Coriolanus* iv 7 8
Towards his design Moves like a ghost . *Macbeth* ii 1 55
From this hour The heart of brothers govern in our loves And sway our great designs! . *Ant. and Cleo.* ii 2 151
Thou, my brother, my competitor In top of all design . v 1 43
But my design, To note the chamber: I will write all down . *Cymbeline* ii 2 23
Be a voluntary mute to my design . iii 5 159
Away to Britain Post I in this design . v 5 192
Designed. By the same covenant, And carriage of the article design'd *Hamlet* i 1 94
Designment. Served his designments In mine own person . *Coriolanus* v 6 35
Our wars are done. The desperate tempest hath so bang'd the Turks, That their designment halts . *Othello* ii 1 22
Desire. Dare not offer What I desire to give, and much less take What I shall die to want . *Tempest* iii 1 78
Wherefore waste I time to counsel thee That art a votary to fond desire? *T. G. of Ver.* i 1 52
You must lay lime to tangle her desires By wailful sonnets . iii 2 68
I do desire thy worthy company . iv 3 34
I do desire thee, even from a heart As full of sorrows as the sea of sands iv 3 32
I'll force thee yield to my desire . v 4 59
The council, look you, shall desire to hear the fear of Got . *Mer. Wives* i 1 38
That fery person for all the orld, as just as you will desire . i 1 51
And desire a marriage between Master Abraham and Mistress Anne Page i 1 57
You must speak possitable, if you can carry her your desires towards her i 1 245
My father desires your worships' company . i 1 271
The letter is, to desire and require her to solicit your master's desires . i 2 10
Ay, forsooth; to desire her to— Peace, I pray you . i 4 83
Desire this honest gentlewoman, your maid, to speak a good word . i 4 87
Desire. Would you desire better sympathy? . *Mer. Wives* ii 1 10
Mistress Page would desire you to send her your little page, of all loves ii 2 118
I desire more acquaintance of you . ii 2 168
I had never so good means, as desire, to make myself acquainted with you . ii 2 189
My desires had instance and argument to commend themselves . ii 2 256
I most fehemently desire you you will also look that way . iii 1 8
A cowardly knave as you would desires to be acquainted withal . iii 1 68
I desire you in friendship, and I will one way or other make you amends iii 1 89
I desire you that we may be friends . iii 1 121
As honest a 'omans as I will desires among five thousand, and five hundred too . iii 3 236
She desires you once more to come to her between eight and nine . iii 5 46
Mistress Ford desires you to come suddenly . iv 1 6
Thou art as foolish Christian creatures as I would desires . iv 1 74
The Germans desire to have three of your horses . iv 3 1
Methinks his flesh is punished, he shall have no desires . iv 4 25
Corrupt, corrupt, and tainted in desire! . v 5 94
Lust is but a bloody fire, Kindled with unchaste desire . v 5 100
Serve Got, and leave your desires, and fairies will not pinse you . v 5 137
I will desire thee to laugh at my wife, that now laughs at thee . v 5 181
I shall desire you, sir, to give me leave To have free speech with you *Meas. for Meas.* i 1 77
Why I desire thee To give me secret harbour, hath a purpose . i 3 3
Here is the sister of the man condemn'd Desires access to you . ii 2 19
A vice that most I do abhor, And most desire should meet the blow of justice . ii 2 30
If you should need a pin, You could not with more tame a tongue desire it . ii 2 46
Shall we desire to raze the sanctuary And pitch our evils there? . ii 2 171
Dost thou desire her foully for those things That make her good? . ii 2 174
Do I love her, That I desire to hear her speak again, And feast upon her eyes? . ii 2 178
One Isabel, a sister, desires access to you . ii 4 18
Let me desire you to make your answer before him . iii 2 164
Let me desire to know how you find Claudio prepared . iii 2 253
She comes to do you good.—I do desire the like . iv 1 52
Follow.—I do desire to learn, sir . iv 2 59
Say it was the desire of the penitent to be so bared before his death . iv 2 188
I would desire you to clap into your prayers . iv 3 43
Him I'll desire To meet me at the consecrated fount . iv 3 101
Say, by this token, I desire his company . iv 3 144
In their rooms Come thronging soft and delicate desires . *Much Ado* i 1 305
You have no employment for me?—None, but to desire your good company . ii 1 281
Wake my cousin Beatrice, and desire her to rise . iii 4 2
God send every one their heart's desire! . iii 4 61
His wits are not so blunt as, God help, I would desire they were . iii 5 12
Yea, and I will weep a while longer.—I will not desire that . iv 1 259
And, briefly, I desire nothing but the reward of a villain . v 1 250
I shall desire your help.—My heart is with your liking . v 4 31
And the huge army of the world's desires . *L. L. Lost* i 1 10
At Christmas I no more desire a rose Than wish a snow in May's new-fangled mirth . i 1 105
I would take Desire prisoner, and ransom him to any French courtier for a new-devised courtesy . i 2 64
Sweet health and fair desires consort your grace! . ii 1 178
I desire her name.—She hath but one for herself; to desire that were a shame . ii 1 199
All his behaviours did make their retire To the court of his eye, peeping thorough desire . ii 1 235
Would you desire more? . iii 1 101
But shall we dance, if they desire us to't? . v 2 145
She lingers my desires, Like to a step-dame or a dowager . *M. N. Dream* i 1 4
Question your desires; Know of your youth, examine well your blood . i 1 67
With duty and desire we follow you . i 1 127
And I am to entreat you, request you and desire you . i 2 102
Out of this wood do not desire to go: Thou shalt remain here . iii 1 155
I shall desire you of more acquaintance . iii 1 185
I desire your more acquaintance . iii 1 200
And never did desire to see thee more . iii 2 278
My legs can keep no pace with my desires . iii 2 445
Methinks I have a great desire to a bottle of hay . iv 1 37
Would you desire lime and hair to speak better? . v 1 166
But soft! how many months Do you desire? . *Mer. of Venice* i 3 60
I serve the Jew, and have a desire, as my father shall specify . ii 2 136
I desire no more delight Than to be under sail and gone to-night . ii 6 67
Who chooseth me shall gain what many men desire . ii 7 5
All the world desires her; From the four corners of the earth they come . ii 7 38
What many men desire! that 'many' may be meant By the fool multitude . ii 9 25
I will not choose what many men desire, Because I will not jump with common spirits . ii 9 31
Antonio is at his house and desires to speak with you both . iii 1 78
I do desire you Not to deny this imposition . iii 4 32
Thy desires Are wolvish, bloody, starved and ravenous . iv 1 137
I humbly do desire your grace of pardon . iv 1 402
Your heart's desires be with you! . *As Y. Like It* i 2 211
I shall desire more love and knowledge of you . i 2 297
If with myself I hold intelligence Or have acquaintance with mine own desires . i 3 50
I do not desire you to please me; I do desire you to sing . ii 5 17
I do desire we may be better strangers . iii 2 275
So man hath his desires; and as pigeons bill, so wedlock would be nibbling . iii 3 82
Have I not cause to weep?—As good cause as one would desire . iii 4 5
Can one desire too much of a good thing? . iv 1 123
More new-fangled than an ape, more giddy in my desires than a monkey iv 1 153
When he had a desire to eat a grape, would open his lips . v 1 37
I do desire it with all my heart; and I hope it is no dishonest desire to be a woman of the world . v 3 3
I like him very well.—God 'ild you, sir; I desire you of the like . v 4 56
Since for the great desire I had To see fair Padua . *T. of Shrew* i 1 1
But how did you desire it should be made? . iv 3 120
Madam, I desire your holy wishes . *All's Well* i 1 68
I have a desire to hold my acquaintance with thee . ii 3 240
He desires some private speech with you . ii 5 61
Your daughter, ere she seems as won, Desires this ring . iii 7 32
Stand no more off, But give thyself unto my sick desires . iv 2 35

Desire. You fly them as you swear them lordship, Yet you desire to marry *All's Well* v 3 157
My desires, like fell and cruel hounds, E'er since pursue me *T. Night* i 1 22
I desire better acquaintance i 3 55
A young gentleman much desires to speak with you i 5 108
Desire him not to flatter with his lord, Nor hold him up with hopes i 5 322
If you desire the spleen, and will laugh yourselves into stitches, follow me iii 2 72
My desire, More sharp than filed steel, did spur me forth iii 3 4
Haply your eye shall light upon some toy You have desire to purchase iii 3 45
I will return again into the house and desire some conduct of the lady iii 4 265
Get you on and give him his desire iii 4 271
Do not desire to see this letter.—This is, to give a dog, and in recompense desire my dog again v 1 6
I would not have you to think that my desire of having is the sin of covetousness v 1 50
They that went on crutches ere he was born desire yet their life to see him a man *W. Tale* i 1 45
If there were no other excuse why they should desire to live i 1 48
If the king had no son, they would desire to live on crutches till he had one i 1 50
Though I have for the most part been aired abroad, I desire to lay my bones there iv 2 6
Since my desires Run not before mine honour iv 4 33
No more than were I painted I would wish This youth should say 'twere well and only therefore Desire to breed by me iv 4 103
If I might die within this hour, I have lived To die when I desire iv 4 473
She The fairest I have yet beheld, desires access To your high presence v 1 87
I desire my life Once more to look on him v 1 137
Desires you to attach his son v 1 182
Your honour not o'erthrown by your desires, I am friend to them and you v 1 230
Lest they desire upon this push to trouble Your joys with like relation v 3 129
Now hast thou thy desire *K. John* i 1 176
Faulconbridge Desires your majesty to leave the field v 3 6
With contemplation and devout desires v 4 48
Courageously and with a free desire Attending but the signal to begin *Richard II.* i 3 115
That no man enter till my tale be done.—Have thy desire v 3 38
Such inordinate and low desires 1 *Hen. IV.* iii 2 12
With all speed You shall have your desires with interest iv 3 49
Now trimm'd in thine own desires, Thou, beastly feeder 2 *Hen. IV.* i 3 94
Telling us she had a good dish of prawns; whereby thou didst desire to eat some ii 1 105
Didst thou not, when she was gone down stairs, desire me to be no more so familiarity with such poor people? ii 1 107
I do desire deliverance from these officers ii 1 138
Doth it not show vilely in me to desire small beer? ii 2 7
Your pulsidge beats as extraordinarily as heart would desire ii 4 27
Is it not strange that desire should so many years outlive performance? ii 4 283
And, for mine own part, have a desire to stay with my friends iii 2 241
With grant of our most just and right desires iv 2 40
And sweating with desire to see him v 5 26
You would desire the king were made a prelate *Hen. V.* i 1 40
Desires you let the dukedoms that you claim Hear no more of you i 2 256
I desire Nothing but odds with England ii 4 128
I would desire the duke to use his good pleasure, and put him to execution iii 6 57
And anon Desire them all to my pavilion iv 1 27
We have no great cause to desire the approach of day iv 1 90
I do not desire he should answer for me iv 1 200
Such outward things dwell not in my desires iv 3 27
The constable desires thee thou wilt mind Thy followers of repentance iv 3 84
Look you, as you shall desire in a summer's day iv 8 23
Where that his lords desire him to have borne His bruised helmet v Prol. 17
I will tell him a little piece of my desires v 1 14
At my desires, and my requests, and my petitions v 1 24
I would desire you to eat it v 1 28
I will desire you to live in the mean time, and eat your victuals v 1 34
'Tis thou that must help me: Impatiently I burn with thy desire 1 *Hen. VI.* i 2 108
Swift-winged with desire to get a grave, As witting I no other comfort have ii 5 15
It warm'd thy father's heart with proud desire Of bold-faced victory iv 6 11
I desire no more.—And, to speak truth, thou deservest no less 2 *Hen. VI.* iv 3 10
Whose haughty spirit, winged with desire, Will cost my crown 3 *Hen. VI.* i 1 267
And yet, between my soul's desire and me—The lustful Edward's title buried—Is Clarence, Henry iii 2 128
Mine ear hath tempted judgment to desire iii 3 133
He desires to make atonement *Richard III.* i 3 36
I desire To reconcile me to his friendly peace ii 1 58
'Tis death to me to be at enmity; I hate it, and desire all good men's love ii 1 61
The insatiate greediness of his desires iii 7 7
God he knows, and you may partly see, How far I am from the desire thereof iii 7 236
Meantime, but think how I may do thee good, And be inheritor of thy desire iv 3 34
By the second hour in the morning Desire the earl to see me in my tent v 3 32
I desire you do me right and justice; And to bestow your pity on me *Hen. VIII.* ii 4 13
When was the hour I ever contradicted your desire? ii 4 28
It shall be therefore bootless That longer you desire the court ii 4 62
My endeavours Have ever come too short of my desires iii 2 170
You do desire to know Wherefore I sent for you v 1 89
Your queen Desires your visitation v 1 167
When I am in heaven I shall desire To see what this child does v 5 68
That she was never yet that ever knew Love got so sweet as when desire did sue *Troi. and Cres.* i 2 317
I hope I shall know your honour better.—I do desire it iii 1 14
Fair desires, in all fair measure, fairly guide them! iii 1 47
He desires you, that if the king call for him at supper, you will make his excuse iii 1 83
The desire is boundless and the act a slave to limit iii 2 89
Which his own will shall have desire to drink iii 3 46
I'll send the fool to Ajax and desire him To invite the Trojan lords iii 3 235
Tell him I humbly desire the valiant Ajax to invite the most valorous Hector iii 3 275
May I, sweet lady, beg a kiss of you?—You may.—I do desire it iv 5 48
I would desire My famous cousin to our Grecian tents iv 5 150
Desire them home iv 5 157

Desire. A sick man's appetite, who desires most that Which would increase his evil *Coriolanus* i 1 182
By the suit of the gentry to him And the desire of the nobles ii 1 255
Desire The present consul, and last general In our well-found successes, to report ii 2 46
You must desire them To think upon you ii 3 61
Ay, but not mine own desire.—How not your own desire?—No, sir, 'twas never my desire yet to trouble the poor with begging ii 3 73
Let me desire your company iii 1 335
Let me commend thee first to those that shall Say yea to thy desires iv 5 151
Desire not To allay my rages and revenges with Your colder reasons v 3 84
Made him joint-servant with me; gave him way In all his own desires v 6 33
She will a handmaid be to his desires, A loving nurse *T. Andron.* i 1 331
Though Venus govern your desires, Saturn is dominator over mine ii 3 30
If foul desire had not conducted you ii 3 79
When ye have the honey ye desire, Let not this wasp outlive, us both to sting ii 3 131
Some book there is that she desires to see iv 1 31
There is a messenger from Rome Desires to be admitted v 1 153
Now old desire doth in his death-bed lie, And young affection gapes to be his heir *Rom. and Jul.* ii Prol. 1
If you be he, sir, I desire some confidence with you ii 4 133
Your honourable letter he desires To those have shut him up *T. of Athens* i 1 97
I know thee too; and more than that I know thee, I not desire to know iv 3 58
Thou shouldst desire to die, being miserable iv 3 248
All thy powers Shall make their harbour in our town, till we Have seal'd thy full desire v 4 54
Let me not hinder, Cassius, your desires; I'll leave you *J. Cæsar* i 2 30
'Tis your brother Cassius at the door, Who doth desire to see you ii 1 71
Trebonius doth desire you to o'er-read, At your best leisure, this iii 1 4
Be it so; I do desire no more iii 1 252
Stars, hide your fires; Let not light see my black and deep desires *Macbeth* i 4 51
When I burned in desire to question them further, they made themselves air i 5 4
Art thou afeard To be the same in thine own act and valour As thou art in desire? i 7 41
It provokes the desire, but it takes away the performance ii 3 33
Nought's had, all's spent, Where our desire is got without content iii 2 5
My desire All continent impediments would o'erbear That did oppose my will iv 3 63
Cut off the nobles for their lands, Desire his jewels and this other's house iv 3 80
Whose voices I desire aloud with mine v 8 58
It is most retrograde to our desire *Hamlet* i 2 114
Keep you in the rear of your affection, Out of the shot and danger of desire i 3 35
As if it some impartment did desire To you alone i 4 59
Shake hands and part: You, as your business and desire shall point you i 5 129
Every man has business and desire, Such as it is i 5 130
For your desire to know what is between us, O'ermaster't as you may i 5 139
Most fair return of greetings and desires ii 2 60
She desires to speak with you in her closet, ere you go to bed iii 2 343
If you desire to know the certainty Of your dear father's death iv 5 140
Had my desire, Finger'd their packet v 2 14
The queen desires you to use some gentle entertainment v 2 215
I pray, desire her call her wisdom to her *Lear* iv 5 35
As duteous to the vices of thy mistress As badness would desire iv 6 259
Desire him to go in; trouble him no more Till further settling iv 7 81
So shall you have a shorter journey to your desires *Othello* ii 1 285
'Tis a night of revels: the gallants desire it ii 3 46
The general so likes your music, that he desires you, for love's sake, to make no more noise with it iii 1 13
A housewife that by selling her desires Buys herself bread and clothes iv 1 95
And have not we affections, Desires for sport, and frailty, as men have? iv 3 102
There he dropp'd it for a special purpose Which wrought to his desire v 2 323
Last night you did desire it: speak not to us *Ant. and Cleo.* i 1 55
There's a great spirit gone! Thus did I desire it i 2 126
Make your soonest haste; So your desires are yours iii 4 28
My lord desires you presently: my news I might have told hereafter iii 5 22
The queen Of audience nor desire shall fail, so she From Egypt drive her all-disgraced friend iii 12 21
I spake to you for your comfort; did desire you To burn this night with torches iv 2 40
Confined in all she has, her monument, Of thy intents desires instruction v 1 54
I would not be the party that should desire you to touch him v 2 246
The queen, madam, Desires your highness' company *Cymbeline* i 3 38
I'll move the king To any shape of thy preferment such As thou'lt desire i 5 72
But most miserable Is the desire that's glorious i 6 7
Sluttery to such neat excellence opposed Should make desire vomit emptiness i 6 45
That satiate yet unsatisfied desire, that tub Both fill'd and running i 6 48
Desire My man's abode where I did leave him: he Is strange and peevish i 6 52
Thou art too slow to do thy master's bidding, When I desire it too iii 4 101
Present yourself, desire his service, tell him Wherein you're happy iii 4 176
I desire of you A conduct over-land to Milford-Haven iii 5 7
That's not my desire v 4 21
On my conscience, there are verier knaves desire to live v 4 209
You gods that made me man, and sway in love, That have inflamed desire in my breast *Pericles* i 1 20
Famous princes, like thyself, Drawn by report, adventurous by desire i 1 35
We have no reason to desire it, Commended to our master, not to us i 3 37
Yet, ere you shall depart, this we desire i 3 39
To fulfil his prince' desire, Sends word of all that haps in Tyre ii Gower 21
Were my fortunes equal to my desires, I could wish to make one there ii 1 117
We desire to know of him, Of whence he is, his name and parentage ii 3 73
His queen with child makes her desire—Which who shall cross? iii Gower 40
Welcomed and settled to his own desire iv Gower 2
Well, I will go; But yet I have no desire to it iv 1 44
This is an honourable man.—I desire to find him so iv 6 55
Thy sacred physic shall receive such pay As thy desires can wish v 1 75

Desired. It is a life that I have desired: I will thrive *Mer. Wives* i 3 21
Finding yourself desired of such a person *Meas. for Meas.* ii 4 91
And desired her To try her gracious fortune with Lord Angelo v 1 75
When I desired him to come home to dinner He ask'd me for a thousand marks in gold *Com. of Errors* ii 1 60
Your ladyship's in all desired employment, Biron *L. L. Lost* iv 2 140
This is the pent-house under which Lorenzo Desired us to make stand *Mer. of Venice* ii 6 2
Time was, I did him a desired office *All's Well* iv 4 5

Desired. Not an eye But is a-weary of thy common sight, Save mine, which hath desired to see thee more . . . . 1 *Hen. IV.* iii 2 89
Your grace doo's me as great honours as can be desired . *Hen. V.* iv 7 168
In fine, redeem'd I was as I desired . . . 1 *Hen. VI.* i 4 34
According as your ladyship desired, By message craved . . . ii 3 12
My wife desired some damsons, And made me climb . 2 *Hen. VI.* ii 1 102
Well have we pass'd and now repass'd the seas And brought desired help 3 *Hen. VI.* iv 7 6
The emperor thus desired, That he would please to alter the king's course *Hen. VIII.* i 1 188
Which the duke desired To have brought vivâ voce to his face . ii 1 17
You ever Have wish'd the sleeping of this business ; never desired It to be stirr'd . . . . ii 4 163
And desired your highness Most heartily to pray for her . . v 1 65
He touch'd the ports desired . . . . *Troi. and Cres.* ii 2 76
Desired my Cressid in right great exchange . . . . iii 3 21
He desired their worships to think it was his infirmity . . *J. Cæsar* i 2 273
We should have else desired your good advice . . . *Macbeth* iii 1 21
Be then desired By her, that else will take the thing she begs *Lear* i 4 268
When I desired their leave that I might pity him, they took from me the use of mine own house . . . . iii 3 2
Honey, you shall be well desired in Cyprus . . *Othello* ii 1 206
He partly begs To be desired to give . . . *Ant. and Cleo.* iii 13 67
The stroke of death is as a lover's pinch, Which hurts, and is desired . v 2 299
The queen, That most desired the match . . . . *Cymbeline* i 1 12
She's flown To her desired Posthumus . . . . . iii 5 62
Desired more than constrain'd . . . . . . v 4 15
Desired he might know none of his secrets . . . *Pericles* i 3 6

Desirer. I will counterfeit the bewitchment of some popular man and give it bountiful to the desirers . . . . *Coriolanus* ii 3 109

Desirest. Thy love is far from charity, That in love's grief desirest society *L. L. Lost* iv 3 128
Or say, sweet love, what thou desirest to eat . . *M. N. Dream* iv 1 33
Thou shalt have justice, more than thou desirest . . *Mer. of Venice* iv 1 316
Go to, thou art made, if thou desirest to be so . . *T. Night* ii 5 169 ; iii 4 57
Thou desirest me to stop in my tale against the hair . *Rom. and Jul.* ii 4 99

Desiring. I speak not as desiring more . . . *Meas. for Meas.* i 4 3
Desiring thee to lay aside the sword . . . . . *K. John* i 1 12
Young and old Through casements darted their desiring eyes *Richard II.* v 2 14
In heart desiring still You may behold confusion of your foes 1 *Hen. VI.* i 1 76
Desiring thee that Publius Cimber may Have an immediate freedom of repeal . . . . *J. Cæsar* iii 1 53

Desirous. Where is this young gallant that is so desirous to lie with his mother earth? . . . . *As Y. Like It* i 2 213
Will you encounter the house? my niece is desirous you should enter *T. Night* iii 1 83
I have not been desirous of their wealth . . . 3 *Hen. VI.* iv 8 44
How desirous of our sight they are . . . . *T. Andron.* v 1 4
There are certain ladies most desirous of admittance . *T. of Athens* i 2 122
When you are desirous to be bless'd, I'll blessing beg of you . *Hamlet* iii 4 171

Desist. What do we then but draw anew the model In fewer offices, or at last desist To build at all? . . . . . 2 *Hen. IV.* i 3 47
Desist, and drink . . . . *Ant. and Cleo.* ii 7 86
With dead cheeks advise thee to desist For going on death's net *Pericles* i 1 39
I will desist; But there is something glows upon my cheek . . v 1 95

Desk. In the desk That's cover'd o'er with Turkish tapestry *Com. of Err.* iv 1 103
Here! go; the desk, the purse! sweet, now, make haste . . . iv 2 29
Will you send him, mistress, redemption, the money in his desk? . iv 2 46
What might you, Or my dear majesty your queen here, think, If I had play'd the desk or table-book? . . . . . . *Hamlet* ii 2 136

Desolate. Here, in this most desolate isle . . . . *Tempest* iii 3 80
Alas, poor lady, desolate and left! . . . . . *T. G. of Ver.* iv 4 179
Desolate, desolate, will I hence and die . . . . *Richard II.* i 2 73
Subverts your towns And in a moment makes them desolate 1 *Hen. VI.* ii 3 66
The name of Henry the Fifth hales them to an hundred mischiefs and makes them leave me desolate . . . . . . 2 *Hen. VI.* iv 8 60
Let us seek out some desolate shade, and there Weep our sad bosoms empty . . . . *Macbeth* iv 3 1

Desolation. If ever I do see the merry days of desolation that I have seen *L. L. Lost* i 2 165
You have lived in desolation here, Unseen, unvisited, much to our shame v 2 357
Every thing about you demonstrating a careless desolation *As Y. Like It* iii 2 400
Even till unfenced desolation Leave them as naked as the vulgar air *K. John* ii 1 386
And his whole kingdom into desolation . . . . . *Hen. V.* ii 2 173
All fell feats Enlink'd to waste and desolation . . . . iii 3 18
And where thou art not, desolation . . . . 2 *Hen. VI.* iii 2 364
Death, desolation, ruin and decay . . . . . *Richard III.* iv 4 409
My desolation does begin to make A better life . . *Ant. and Cleo.* v 2 1
O, there were desolation of gaolers and gallowses! . . . *Cymbeline* v 4 213
We have heard your miseries as far as Tyre, And seen the desolation of your streets . . . . *Pericles* i 4 89

Despair. My ending is despair, Unless I be relieved by prayer *Tempest* Epil. 15
To make her heavenly comforts of despair, When it is least expected *Meas. for Meas.* iv 3 114
Moody and dull melancholy, Kinsman to grim and comfortless despair *Com. of Errors* v 1 80
Doubtful thoughts, and rash-embraced despair, And shuddering fear *Mer. of Venice* iii 2 109
'Regia,' presume not, 'celsa senis,' despair not . . *T. of Shrew* iii 1 45
Oft it hits Where hope is coldest and despair most fits . *All's Well* ii 1 147
Our crimes would despair, if they were not cherished by our virtues . iv 3 86
Should all despair That have revolted wives, the tenth of mankind Would hang themselves . . . . *W. Tale* i 2 198
Therefore betake thee To nothing but despair . . . . . iii 2 211
But in despair die under their black weight . . . *K. John* iii 1 297
If thou didst but consent To this most cruel act, do but despair . iv 3 126
Call it not patience, Gaunt; it is despair . . . *Richard II.* i 2 29
And driven into despair an enemy's hope . . . . . . ii 2 47
Despair not, madam.—Who shall hinder me? I will despair . . ii 2 67
Discomfort guides my tongue And bids me speak of nothing but despair iii 2 66
Beshrew thee, cousin, which didst lead me forth Of that sweet way I was in to despair! . . . . iii 2 205
Hope gives not so much warrant as despair . . . 2 *Hen. IV.* i 3 40
The arbitrator of despairs, Just death, kind umpire of men's miseries 1 *Hen. VI.* ii 5 28
Till mischief and despair Drive you to break your necks or hang yourselves v 4 90
God be praised, that to believing souls Gives light in darkness, comfort in despair! . . . . 2 *Hen. VI.* ii 1 67
And from his bosom purge this black despair! . . . . . iii 3 23
Despair. Our hap is loss, our hope but sad despair . . . 3 *Hen. VI.* ii 3 9
Why, say, fair queen, whence springs this deep despair? . . . iii 3 12
How shall poor Henry live, Unless thou rescue him from foul despair? iii 3 215
And I the rather wean me from despair . . . . . . iv 4 17
By such despair, I should accuse myself.—And, by despairing, shouldst thou stand excused . . . . *Richard III.* i 2 85
I'll join with black despair against my soul, And to myself become an enemy . . . . ii 2 36
Despair, therefore, and die! . . . . v 3 120
I shall despair. There is no creature loves me ; And if I die, no soul shall pity me . . . . v 3 200
Dangers, doubts, wringing of the conscience, Fears, and despairs *Hen. VIII.* ii 2 29
Your enemies, with nodding of their plumes, Fan you into despair! *Coriolanus* iii 3 127
Why should he despair that knows to court it With words, fair looks? *T. Andron.* ii 1 91
Too wise, wisely too fair, To merit bliss by making me despair *R. and J.* i 1 228
Let lips do what hands do ; They pray, grant thou, lest faith turn to despair . . . . i 5 106
All swoln and ulcerous, pitiful to the eye, The mere despair of surgery *Macbeth* iv 3 152
Despair thy charm . . . . v 8 13
Why I do trifle thus with his despair Is done to cure it . . . *Lear* iv 6 33
Became his guide, Led him, begg'd for him, saved him from despair . v 3 191
To lay the blame upon her own despair, That she fordid herself . v 3 254
Take the hint Which my despair proclaims . . *Ant. and Cleo.* iii 11 19
Past grace? obedience?—Past hope, and in despair . . *Cymbeline* i 1 137
But for her, Where is she gone? Haply, despair hath seized her . iii 5 60

Despairing. Hope is a lover's staff; walk hence with that And manage it against despairing thoughts . . . . . *T. G. of Ver.* iii 1 247
Despairing of his own arm's fortitude, To join with witches! 1 *Hen. VI.* i 1 17
Base, fearful and despairing Henry! . . . . . 3 *Hen. VI.* i 1 178
And, by despairing, shouldst thou stand excused . . *Richard III.* i 2 86
Fainting, despair ; despairing, yield thy breath! . . . . . v 3 172
Repented The evils she hatch'd were not effected ; so Despairing died *Cymbeline* v 5 61

Desperate. All three of them are desperate . . . . *Tempest* iii 3 104
I am desperate of obtaining her . . . . . . *T. G. of Ver.* iii 2 5
My suit then is desperate ; you'll undertake her no more? *Mer. Wives* iii 5 127
My daughter is sometime afeard she will do a desperate outrage to herself . . . . *Much Ado* ii 3 159
Tutor'd in the rudiments Of many desperate studies *As Y. Like It* v 4 32
I play a merchant's part, And venture madly on a desperate mart *T. of Shrew* ii 1 329
As a desperate offendress against nature . . . . *All's Well* i 1 153
To cure the desperate languishings whereof The king is render'd lost . i 3 235
Thou this to hazard needs must intimate Skill infinite or monstrous desperate . . . . ii 1 187
This is a fond and desperate creature . . . . . . v 3 178
Put your lord into a desperate assurance she will none of him *T. Night* ii 2 8
My state is desperate for my master's love . . . . . ii 2 38
Here in the streets, desperate of shame and state . . . . v 1 67
This is desperate, sir.—So call it : but it does fulfil my vow *W. Tale* iv 4 496
Let belief and life encounter so As doth the fury of two desperate men *K. John* iii 1 32
As dissolute as desperate . . . . *Richard II.* v 3 20
She is desperate here ; a peevish self-will'd harlotry . 1 *Hen. IV.* iii 1 198
Yon island carrions, desperate of their bones . . . . *Hen. V.* iv 2 39
Salisbury is a desperate homicide . . . . . 1 *Hen. VI.* i 2 25
Ne'er heard I of a warlike enterprise More venturous or desperate than this . . . . ii 1 45
Moody-mad and desperate stags, Turn on the bloody hounds with heads of steel . . . . iv 2 50
Talbot Hath sullied all his gloss of former honour By this unheedful, desperate, wild adventure . . . . iv 4 7
Then follow thou thy desperate sire of Crete, Thou Icarus . . iv 6 54
So desperate thieves, all hopeless of their lives, Breathe out invectives 'gainst the officers . . . . 3 *Hen. VI.* i 4 42
Haste is needful in this desperate case . . . . . . iv 1 129
Drown desperate sorrow in dead Edward's grave . . *Richard III.* ii 2 99
Thy school-days frightful, desperate, wild, and furious . . . iv 4 169
And I, in such a desperate bay of death . . . . . . iv 4 232
Desperate ventures and assured destruction . . . . . v 3 319
In desperate manner Daring the event to the teeth . . *Hen. VIII.* i 2 35
Though he be grown so desperate to be honest . . . . . iii 1 86
Are you so desperate grown, to threat your friends? . . *T. Andron.* ii 1 40
Like a forlorn and desperate castaway, Do shameful execution on herself v 3 75
One desperate grief cures with another's languish . *Rom. and Jul.* i 2 49
Hold thy desperate hand : Art thou a man? thy form cries out thou art iii 3 108
I will make a desperate tender Of my child's love : I think she will be ruled . . . . iii 4 12
A kind of hope, Which craves as desperate an execution As that is desperate which we would prevent . . . . iv 1 69
With some great kinsman's bone, As with a club, dash out my desperate brains . . . . iv 3 54
O mischief, thou art swift To enter in the thoughts of desperate men! . v 1 36
Good gentle youth, tempt not a desperate man . . . . . v 3 59
Thou desperate pilot, now at once run on The dashing rocks thy sea-sick weary bark! . . . . v 3 117
And she, too desperate, would not go with me . . . . . v 3 263
These debts may well be called desperate ones, for a madman owes 'em *T. of Athens.* iii 4 103
What an alteration of honour Has desperate want made! . . . iv 3 469
He waxes desperate with imagination . . . . . *Hamlet* i 4 87
Leads the will to desperate undertakings As oft as any passion under heaven . . . . ii 1 104
Diseases desperate grown By desperate appliance are relieved, Or not at all . . . . iv 3 9
A noble father lost ; A sister driven into desperate terms . . . iv 7 26
The corse they follow did with desperate hand Fordo it own life . v 1 243
He is attended with a desperate train . . . . . *Lear* ii 4 308
Go after her : she's desperate ; govern her . . . . . v 3 161
The desperate tempest hath so bang'd the Turks . . . *Othello* ii 1 21
I am desperate of my fortunes if they check me here . . . ii 3 337
Did he live now, This sight would make him do a desperate turn . v 2 207
Quietness, grown sick of rest, would purge By any desperate change *Ant. and Cleo.* i 3 54
My queen Upon a desperate bed . . . . . . *Cymbeline* iv 3 6

Desperately. Insensible of mortality, and desperately mortal *M. for M.* iv 2 152
Desperately he hurried through the street . . . *Com. of Errors* v 1 140

Desperately. Not knowing how to find the open air, But toiling desperately to find it out . . . . . . 3 *Hen. VI.* iii 2 178
A bloody deed, and desperately dispatch'd! . . . *Richard III.* i 4 278
Your eldest daughters have fordone themselves, And desperately are dead *Lear* v 3 292
Desperation. Not a soul But felt a fever of the mad and play'd Some tricks of desperation . . . . . *Tempest* i 2 210
Desperation Is all the policy, strength and defence, That Rome can make against them . . . . *Coriolanus* iv 6 126
The very place puts toys of desperation, Without more motive, into every brain . . . . *Hamlet* i 4 75
To desperation turn my trust and hope! An anchor's cheer in prison be my scope! . . . . iii 2 228
Despise. I despise thee for thy wrongful suit . . *T. G. of Ver.* iv 2 102
I do despise a liar as I do despise one that is false . . *Mer. Wives* i 1 69
Despise me, when I break this oath of mine . . *L. L. Lost* v 2 441
This you should pity rather than despise . . *M. N. Dream* iii 2 235
If he would despise me, I would forgive him . . . *Mer. of Venice* i 2 68
But, being awaked, I do despise my dream . . . 2 *Hen. IV.* v 5 55
You may not, my lord, despise her gentle suit . 1 *Hen. VI.* ii 2 47
How much, methinks, I could despise this man, But that I am bound in charity against it! . . . . . *Hen. VIII.* iii 2 297
The tongues o' the common mouth: I do despise them . *Coriolanus* iii 1 22
Rome will despise her for this foul escape . . . *T. Andron.* iv 2 113
Let not your ears despise my tongue for ever, Which shall possess them with the heaviest sound That ever yet they heard *Macbeth* iv 3 201
Thou didst hold him in thy hate.—Despise me, if I do not . *Othello* i 1 8
One unperfectness shows me another, to make me frankly despise myself ii 3 299
All strange and terrible events are welcome, But comforts we despise *Ant. and Cleo.* iv 15 4
We are gentlemen That neither in our hearts nor outward eyes Envy the great nor do the low despise . *Pericles* ii 3 26
Despise profit where you have most gain . . . iv 2 128
Despised. Since his exile she hath despised me most . *T. G. of Ver.* iii 2 3
His old betrothed but despised . . . . *Meas. for Meas.* iii 2 293
This is he, my master said, Despised the Athenian maid . *M. N. Dream* ii 2 73
Hare lip, nor scar, Nor mark prodigious, such as are Despised in nativity v 1 420
Frighting her pale-faced villages with war And ostentation of despised arms . . . . *Richard II.* ii 3 95
We'll make foul weather with despised tears . . . iii 3 161
Thus ignobly used, Your nephew, late despised Richard, comes 1 *Hen. VI.* ii 5 36
Why didst thou say, of late thou wert despised? . . ii 5 42
Or live in peace abandon'd and despised! . . 3 *Hen. VI.* i 1 188
As you respect the common good, the state Of our despised nobility *Hen. VIII.* iii 2 291
O world! world! world! thus is the poor agent despised! *Troi. and Cres.* v 10 37
Our father's tears despised, and basely cozen'd Of that true hand *T. Andron.* v 3 101
And expire the term Of a despised life closed in my breast *Rom. and Jul.* i 4 110
Despised substance of divinest show! . . . . iii 2 77
Despised, distressed, hated, martyr'd, kill'd! . . . iv 5 59
But reserve still to give, lest your deities be despised *T. of Athens* iii 6 82
In thy rags thou knowest none, but art despised for the contrary iv 3 304
Is yond despised and ruinous man my lord? Full of decay and failing? iv 3 465
The pangs of despised love, the law's delay, The insolence of office *Hamlet* iii 1 72
That art most rich, being poor; Most choice, forsaken; and most loved, despised! . . . . *Lear* i 1 254
A poor, infirm, weak, and despised old man . . . iii 2 20
And what's to come of my despised time Is nought but bitterness *Othello* i 1 162
I will rather sue to be despised than to deceive so good a commander ii 3 278
She hath despised me rejoicingly, and I'll be merry in my revenge *Cymb.* iii 5 149
Despiser. A rude despiser of good manners . . *As Y. Like It* ii 7 92
Despiseth. Why do I pity him That with his very heart despiseth me? *T. G. of Ver.* iv 4 99
Because he loves her, he despiseth me; Because I love him, I must pity him . . . . iv 4 100
Despising many forfeits and subduements . . *Troi. and Cres.* iv 5 187
Despising, For you, the city, thus I turn my back *Coriolanus* iii 3 133
Despite. In despite of the teeth of all rhyme and reason . *Mer. Wives* v 5 132
Grace is grace, despite of all controversy: as, for example, thou thyself art a wicked villain, despite of all grace *Meas. for Meas.* i 2 25
And, in despite of mirth, mean to be merry *Com. of Errors* iii 1 108
Thou wast ever an obstinate heretic in the despite of beauty *Much Ado* i 1 237
In despite of his quick wit and his queasy stomach . . ii 1 398
Only to despite them, I will endeavour any thing . . ii 2 31
In despite of all, dies for him . . . . . . iii 2 68
In despite of his heart, he eats his meat without grudging . iii 4 89
Despite his nice fence and his active practice . . . v 1 75
Not a man of them shall have the grace, Despite of suit, to see a lady's face . . . . *L. L. Lost* v 2 129
Consider then we come but in despite . . . *M. N. Dream* v 1 112
You will try in time, in despite of a fall . . *As Y. Like It* i 3 25
In despite of my invention . . . . ii 5 49
Shall in despite enforce a watery eye . . *T. of Shrew* Ind. 1 128
I will therefore tarry in despite of the flesh and the blood . Ind. 2 129
Let all the world say no, I'll keep mine own, despite of all the world iii 2 144
Full of despite, bloody as the hunter . . . *T. Night* iii 4 243
In despite of brooded watchful day . . . *K. John* iii 3 52
My fair name, Despite of death that lives upon my grave . *Richard II.* i 1 168
On whom, as in despite, the sun looks pale . . . *Hen. V.* iii 5 17
Foul fiend of France, and hag of all despite! . 1 *Hen. VI.* iii 2 52
Despite of fate, To my determined time thou gavest new date . iv 6 8
Winged through the lither sky, In thy despite shall 'scape mortality . iv 7 22
Had his highness in his infancy Crowned in Paris in despite of foes 2 *Hen. VI.* i 1 94
Or thou or I, Somerset, will be protector, Despite Duke Humphrey . i 1 179
In despite of the devils and hell . . . . . iv 8 63
Despite the bear-ward that protects the bear . . . . v 1 210
Deposed he shall be, in despite of all . . 3 *Hen. VI.* i 1 154
'Tis not thy southern power . . . Can set the duke up in despite of me i 1 158
Who crown'd the gracious duke in high despite, Laugh'd in his face . ii 1 59
That I in all despite might rail at him . . . . . ii 6 81
In despite of all that shall withstand you . . . . . iv 1 146
In despite of all mischance, Of thee thyself and all thy complices . iv 3 43
Thou wretch, despite o'erwhelm thee! . . *Coriolanus* iii 1 164
Follow him, As he hath follow'd you, with all despite . . iii 3 139
What, would you bury him in my despite? . *T. Andron.* i 1 361
And, in despite, I'll cram thee with more food! *Rom. and Jul.* v 3 48
In despite of sense and secrecy, Unpeg the basket on the house's top, Let the birds fly . . . . *Hamlet* iii 4 192

Despite. Despite thy victor sword and fire-new fortune . . *Lear* v 3 132
Some good I mean to do, Despite of mine own nature . . v 3 244
Thrown such despite and heavy terms upon her . . *Othello* iv 2 116
Or say they strike us, Or scant our former having in despite . iv 3 92
Whiles he is vaulting variable ramps, In your despite . . *Cymbeline* i 6 135
Yet this imperceiverant thing loves him in my despite . . iv 1 16
Open'd, in despite Of heaven and men, her purposes . . v 5 58
Despiteful. It is my study To seem despiteful and ungentle *As Y. Like It* v 2 86
O despiteful love! unconstant womankind! . . *T. of Shrew* iv 2 14
I, his despiteful Juno, sent him forth . . . *All's Well* iii 4 13
Despiteful tidings! O unpleasing news! . . . *Richard III.* iv 1 37
This is the most despiteful gentle greeting . . *Troi. and Cres.* iv 1 32
Despiteful and intolerable wrongs! Shall I endure this? *T. Andron.* iv 4 50
With which I meant To scourge the ingratitude that despiteful Rome Cast on my noble father . . . . *Ant. and Cleo.* ii 6 22
Despoiled of your honour in your life . . . . 2 *Hen. VI.* ii 3 10
Destined. Being destined to a drier death on shore . . *T. G. of Ver.* i 1 158
Show it now, By putting on the destined livery . *Meas. for Meas.* ii 4 138
My babes were destined to a fairer death, If grace had bless'd thee with a fairer life . . . . *Richard III.* iv 4 219
If thy revenges hunger for that food Which nature loathes—take thou the destined tenth . . . . *T. of Athens* v 4 33
Destinies. According to Fates and Destinies and such odd sayings *Mer. of Venice* ii 2 65
As wit and fortune will.—Or as the Destinies decree *As Y. Like It* i 2 111
Some of those branches by the Destinies cut . . . *Richard II.* i 2 15
A foul mis-shapen stigmatic, Mark'd by the destinies to be avoided 3 *Hen. VI.* ii 2 137
Till the Destinies do cut his thread of life . . . *Pericles* i 2 108
Destiny. Make the rope of his destiny our cable . . *Tempest* i 1 34
By that destiny to perform an act Whereof what's past is prologue . ii 1 252
Destiny, That hath to instrument this lower world And what is in't . iii 3 53
You orphan heirs of fixed destiny, Attend your office . *Mer. Wives* v 5 43
If then true lovers have been ever cross'd, It stands as an edict in destiny *M. N. Dream* i 1 151
The lottery of my destiny Bars me the right of voluntary choosing *Mer. of Venice* ii 1 15
The ancient saying is no heresy, Hanging and wiving goes by destiny . ii 9 83
He brings his destiny with him . . . . *As Y. Like It* iv 1 57
Your marriage comes by destiny, Your cuckoo sings by kind *All's Well* i 3 66
To this I am most constant, Though destiny say no . . *W. Tale* iv 4 46
Think you I bear the shears of destiny? . . . . *K. John* iv 2 91
An't be my destiny, so; an't be not, so . . . 2 *Hen. IV.* iii 2 252
All unavoided is the doom of destiny.—True, when avoided grace makes destiny . . . . *Richard III.* iv 4 217
I have, thou gallant Trojan, seen thee oft Labouring for destiny *Troi. and Cres.* iv 5 184
I would conspire against destiny . . . . . . v 1 69
Alone he enter'd The mortal gate of the city, which he painted With shunless destiny . . . . *Coriolanus* ii 2 116
Thither he Will come to know his destiny: Your vessels and your spells provide . . . . *Macbeth* iii 5 17
'Tis destiny unshunnable, like death . . . . *Othello* iii 3 275
Let determined things to destiny Hold unbewail'd their way *A. and C.* iii 6 84
Destitute. The king himself Of his wings destitute, the army broken *Cymbeline* v 3 5
We are not destitute for want, But weary for the staleness . *Pericles* v 1 57
Destroy. Wherefore did they not That hour destroy us? . . *Tempest* i 2 139
I would my valiant master would destroy thee! . . . iii 2 53
Wilt thou destroy him then?—Ay, on mine honour . . . iii 2 123
Oft our displeasures, to ourselves unjust, Destroy our friends and after weep their dust . . . . *All's Well* v 3 64
Thou, to be endeared to a king, Made it no conscience to destroy a prince *K. John* iv 2 229
Had thy grandsire with a prophet's eye Seen how his son's son should destroy his sons . . . . *Richard II.* ii 1 105
Dost thou teach pardon pardon to destroy? . . . . v 3 120
You mean with obstinate repulse To slay your sovereign and destroy the realm . . . . 1 *Hen. VI.* iii 1 114
Here, purposing the Bastard to destroy, Came in strong rescue . iv 6 25
In which part of his body Shall I destroy him? . *Troi. and Cres.* iv 5 243
Or rudely visit them in parts remote, To fright them, ere destroy *Coriol.* iv 5 149
And with the deepest malice of the war Destroy what lies before 'em . iv 6 42
If it were so that our request did tend To save the Romans, thereby to destroy The Volsces . . . . v 3 133
I'll do this heavy task, So thou destroy Rapine and Murder there *T. Andron.* v 2 59
Approach the chamber, and destroy your sight With a new Gorgon *Macb.* ii 3 76
'Tis safer to be that which we destroy Than by destruction dwell in doubtful joy . . . . iii 2 6
The violence of either grief or joy Their own enactures with themselves destroy . . . . *Hamlet* iii 2 207
Each opposite that blanks the face of joy Meet what I would have well and it destroy! . . . . iii 2 231
The sword is out That must destroy thee . . . . . *Lear* iv 6 234
Husband win, win brother, Prays, and destroys the prayer *Ant. and Cleo.* iii 4 19
And being join'd, I'll thus your hopes destroy . . . *Pericles* ii 5 86
Destroyed. I shall have my music for nothing.—When Prospero is destroyed . . . . *Tempest* iii 2 155
Destroy'd the sweet'st companion that e'er man Bred his hopes out of *W. Tale* v 1 11
They looked as they had heard of a world ransomed, or one destroyed . v 2 17
A partial slander sought I to avoid, And in the sentence my own life destroy'd . . . . *Richard II.* i 3 242
How soon my sorrow hath destroy'd my face . . . . iv 1 291
The shadow of your sorrow hath destroy'd The shadow of your face . iv 1 292
Which many a good tall fellow had destroy'd So cowardly . 1 *Hen. IV.* i 3 62
Will you yield, and this avoid, Or, guilty in defence, be thus destroy'd? *Hen. V.* iii 3 43
King Henry's peers and chief nobility Destroy'd themselves 1 *Hen. VI.* iv 1 147
Destroy'd his country, and his name remains To the ensuing age abhorr'd . . . . *Coriolanus* v 3 147
He hath fought to-day As if a god, in hate of mankind, had Destroy'd in such a shape . . . . *Ant. and Cleo.* iv 8 26
Destroyer. Peace is a very apoplexy . . . ; a getter of more bastard children than war's a destroyer of men . . *Coriolanus* iv 5 241
Detested parasites, Courteous destroyers, affable wolves, meek bears! *T. of Athens* iii 6 105
Destroying. Have felt the worst of death's destroying wound *Richard II.* iii 2 139
And fight and die is death destroying death . . . . iii 2 184

Destroying. I should forge Quarrels unjust against the good and loyal, Destroying them for wealth . . . *Macbeth* iv 3 84
Destruction. We from the west will send destruction Into this city's bosom . . . *K. John* ii 1 409
To push destruction and perpetual shame Out of the weak door of our fainting land . . . v 7 77
Cry woe, destruction, ruin and decay *Richard II.* iii 2 102
Destruction straight shall dog them at the heels . v 3 139
Led his powers to death And winking leap'd into destruction 2 *Hen. IV.* i 3 33
Or like to men proud of destruction Defy us to our worst *Hen. V.* iii 3 4
And pale destruction meets thee in the face 1 *Hen. VI.* iv 2 27
Girdled with a waist of iron And hemm'd about with grim destruction . iv 3 21
Her fume needs no spurs, She'll gallop far enough to her destruction 2 *Hen. VI.* i 3 154
Welcome, destruction, death, and massacre! . *Richard III.* ii 4 53
Get thee hence! Death and destruction dog thee at the heels . iv 1 40
Even for revenge mock my destruction! . . . v 1 9
Desperate ventures and assured destruction . . . v 3 319
You take a precipice for no leap of danger, And woo your own destruction *Hen. VIII.* v 1 140
Swooning destruction, or some joy too fine . *Troi. and Cres.* iii 2 24
Let your brief plagues be mercy, And linger not our sure destructions on! . . . v 10 9
It shall be to him then as our good wills, A sure destruction *Coriolanus* ii 1 259
Bear him to the rock Tarpeian, and from thence Into destruction cast him . . . iii 1 214
Here comes a parcel of our hopeful booty, Which dreads not yet their lives' destruction . . . *T. Andron.* ii 3 50
Writing destruction on the enemy's castle . . . iii 1 170
What is amiss in them, you gods, make suitable for destruction *T. of Athens* iii 6 92
His semblable, yea, himself, Timon disdains: Destruction fang mankind! . . . iv 3 23
Hath in her more destruction than thy sword, For all her cherubin look iv 3 62
Either there is a civil strife in heaven, Or else the world, too saucy with the gods, Incenses them to send destruction *J. Cæsar* i 3 13
Blood and destruction shall be so in use And dreadful objects so familiar . . . iii 1 265
'Tis safer to be that which we destroy Than by destruction dwell in doubtful joy . . . *Macbeth* iii 2 7
Though the treasure Of nature's germens tumble all together, Even till destruction sicken . . . iv 1 60
Destruction on my head, if my bad blame Light on the man! . *Othello* i 3 177
You shall bereave yourself Of my good purposes, and put your children To that destruction which I'll guard them from *Ant. and Cleo.* v 2 132
Virtue preserved from fell destruction's blast, Led on by heaven *Pericles* v 3 Gower 89
Detain. Would that alone, alone he would detain, So he would keep fair quarter with his bed! . *Com. of Errors* ii 1 107
He heartily prays some occasion may detain us longer . *Much Ado* i 1 151
I would detain you here some month or two . *Mer. of Venice* iii 2 9
Give me the letter, sir.—I shall offend, either to detain or give it *Lear* i 2 42
That burning shame Detains him from Cordelia . . . iv 3 49
Not sickness should detain me . . . *Ant. and Cleo.* ii 2 173
That we detain All his revenue . . . iii 6 29
Detain no jot, I charge thee: write to him—I will subscribe—gentle adieus . . . iv 5 13
Detained. Daughter to the banish'd duke, And here detain'd by her usurping uncle . . . *As Y. Like It* i 2 286
What occasion of import Hath all so long detain'd you from your wife? *T. of Shrew* iii 2 105
Your highness' soldiers, The which he hath detain'd for lewd employments . . . *Richard II.* i 1 90
Detain'd me all my flowering youth Within a loathsome dungeon 1 *Hen. VI.* ii 5 56
Detect. I will prevent this, detect my wife, be revenged on Falstaff *Mer. Wives* ii 2 325
Sighing every minute and groaning every hour would detect the lazy foot of Time as well as a clock . . . *As Y. Like It* iii 2 322
To let thy tongue detect thy base-born heart . . . 3 *Hen. VI.* ii 2 143
He cannot lie with his neighbour's wife, but it [conscience] detects him *Richard III.* i 4 141
And, lest thou shouldst detect him, cut thy tongue . *T. Andron.* ii 4 27
All that may men approve or men detect . . . *Pericles* ii 1 55
Detected. To be detected with a jealous rotten bell-wether *Mer. Wives* iii 5 111
I never heard the absent duke much detected for women *Meas. for Meas.* iii 2 130
Detecting. If he steal aught the whilst this play is playing, And 'scape detecting, I will pay the theft . . . *Hamlet* iii 2 94
Detection. Now, could I come to her with any detection in my hand *Mer. Wives* ii 2 255
Detector. O heavens! that this treason were not, or not I the detector! *Lear* iii 5 14
Detention. And the detention of long-since-due debts . *T. of Athens* ii 2 39
Determinate. My determinate voyage is mere extravagancy . *T. Night* ii 1 11
The sly slow hours shall not determinate The dateless limit of thy dear exile . . . *Richard II.* i 3 150
I' the progress of this business, Ere a determinate resolution *Hen. VIII.* ii 4 176
None can be so determinate as the removing of Cassio . *Othello* iv 2 232
Determination. Did she change her determination? *Mer. Wives* iii 5 69
But most willingly humbles himself to the determination of justice *Meas. for Meas.* iii 2 258
They have acquainted me with their determinations . *Mer. of Venice* i 2 111
Would to God You were of our determination! . 1 *Hen. IV.* iv 3 33
The reasons you allege do more conduce To the hot passion of distemper'd blood Than to make up a free determination 'Twixt right and wrong *Troi. and Cres.* ii 2 170
Which for to prevent, I have in quick determination Thus set it down *Hamlet* iii 1 176
Determine. And afterward determine our proceedings . *T. G. of Ver.* iii 2 97
She determines Herself the glory of a creditor, Both thanks and use *Meas. for Meas.* i 1 39
I shall follow it as the flesh and fortune shall better determine . ii 1 268
I will determine this before I stir . . *Com. of Errors* v 1 167
A learned doctor, Whom I have sent for to determine this *Mer. of Ven.* iv 1 106
Determine what we shall do straight . . . *K. John* ii 1 149
To hear and absolutely to determine Of what conditions . 2 *Hen. IV.* iv 1 164
And yet I determine to fight lustily for him . . *Hen. V.* iv 1 201
Long sitting to determine poor men's causes Hath made me full of sickness . . . 2 *Hen. VI.* iv 7 93
And go we to determine Who they shall be that straight shall post to Ludlow . . . *Richard III.* ii 2 141

Determine. The cause why we are met Is, to determine of the coronation *Richard III.* iii 4 2
Till you know How he determines further. . . *Hen. VIII.* i 1 214
Shall I be charged no further than this present? Must all determine here? . . . *Coriolanus* iii 3 43
Determine on some course, More than a wild exposture to each chance iv 1 35
I purpose not to wait on fortune till These wars determine . v 3 120
Let the laws of Rome determine all . . . *T. Andron.* i 1 407
This shall determine that . . . *Rom. and Jul.* iii 1 136
Brief sounds determine of my weal or woe . . . iii 2 51
We shall determine How to cut off some charge in legacies . *J. Cæsar* iv 1 8
You think what now you speak; But what we do determine oft we break *Hamlet* iii 2 197
Let's then determine With the ancient of war on our proceedings *Lear* v 1 31
As we shall find their merits and our safety May equally determine . v 3 45
Be it as you shall privately determine . . . *Othello* i 3 276
The first stone Drop in my neck: as it determines, so Dissolve my life! *Ant. and Cleo.* iii 13 161
To-morrow is the day.—It will determine one way . . . iv 3 2
That he and Cæsar might Determine this great war in single fight! . iv 4 37
She soon shall know of us, by some of ours, How honourable and how kindly we Determine for her . . . v 1 59
Determined. With all the cunning manner of our flight Determined of *T. G. of Ver.* ii 4 181
I know you have determined to bestow her On Thurio . . . iii 1 13
A restraint, Though all the world's vastidity you had, To a determined scope . . . *Meas. for Meas.* iii 1 70
Stir not you till you have well determined Upon these slanderers . . v 1 258
Are you yet determined To-day to marry with my brother's daughter? *Much Ado* v 4 36
Hath drawn him from his own determined aid . . . *K. John* ii 1 584
Where is he that will not stay so long Till his friend sickness hath determined me? . . . 2 *Hen. IV.* iv 5 82
To my determined time thou gavest new date . . 1 *Hen. VI.* iv 6 9
And that succession be determined . . . 3 *Hen. VI.* iv 6 56
I am determined to prove a villain . . . *Richard III.* i 1 30
It is determined, not concluded yet . . . i 3 15
There are two councils held; And that may be determined at the one Which may make you and him to rue at the other . . . iii 2 13
Yet had not we determined he should die, Until your lordship came to see his death . . . iii 5 52
All-Souls' day to my fearful soul Is the determined respite of my wrongs v 1 19
Having determined of the Volsces and To send for Titus Lartius *Coriol.* ii 2 41
How I have govern'd our determined jest . . . *T. Andron.* v 2 139
What are you then determined to do? . . . *J. Cæsar* v 1 100
There comes a fellow crying out for help; And Cassio following him with determined sword . . . *Othello* ii 3 227
Let determined things to destiny Hold unbewail'd their way *A. and C.* iii 6 84
Detest. We detest such vile base practices . *T. G. of Ver.* iv 1 73
I do detest false perjured Proteus . . . v 4 39
But, I detest, an honest maid as ever broke bread . . *Mer. Wives* i 4 160
My wife, sir, whom I detest before heaven and your honour *M. for M.* ii 1 69
Is an honest woman,— Dost thou detest her therefore?—I say, sir, I will detest myself also, as well as she . . . ii 1 74
That I may back to Athens by daylight, From these that my poor company detest . . . *M. N. Dream* iii 2 434
A fashion she detests . . . *T. Night* ii 5 221
A man that more detests, more stirs against, Both in his private conscience and his place . . . *Hen. VIII.* v 3 39
I have lived in such dishonour, that the gods Detest my baseness *Ant. and Cleo.* iv 14 57
I'll write against them, Detest them, curse them . *Cymbeline* ii 5 33
Detestable. And these detestable things put upon me . *W. Tale* iv 3 65
And I will kiss thy detestable bones . . . *K. John* iii 4 29
O detestable villain! call'st thou that trimming? . *T. Andron.* v 1 94
Most detestable death, by thee beguiled! . . *Rom. and Jul.* iv 5 56
Thou detestable maw, thou womb of death! . . . v 3 45
Nothing I'll bear from thee, But nakedness, thou detestable town! *T. of Athens* iv 1 33
Detested. Glory grows guilty of detested crimes . *L. L. Lost* iv 1 31
War is no strife To the dark house and the detested wife *All's Well* ii 3 309
Ay me, detested! how am I beguiled! . . . *T. Night* v 1 142
In gross rebellion and detested treason . . *Richard II.* ii 3 109
Murders, treasons and detested sins . . . iii 2 44
And for his sake wear the detested blot Of murderous subornation 1 *Hen. IV.* i 3 162
Thou rag of honour! thou detested— Margaret.—Richard! *Richard III.* i 3 233
Spotted, detested, and abominable . . . *T. Andron.* ii 3 74
A barren detested vale, you see it is . . . ii 3 93
In this detested, dark, blood-drinking pit . . . ii 3 224
Ah, that this sight should make so deep a wound, And yet detested life not shrink thereat! . . . iii 1 248
Where bloody murder or detested rape Can couch for fear . . v 2 37
Most smiling, smooth, detested parasites, Courteous destroyers! *T. of Athens* iii 6 104
Unnatural, detested, brutish villain! . . . *Lear* i 2 81
Detested kite! thou liest: My train are men of choice and rarest parts i 4 284
Persuade me rather to be slave and sumpter To this detested groom . ii 4 220
Detesting. 'Tis a hard bondage to become the wife Of a detesting lord *All's Well* iii 5 68
Detract. His backward voice is to utter foul speeches and to detract *Tempest* ii 2 96
Shall I, for lucre of the rest unvanquish'd, Detract so much from that prerogative, As to be call'd but viceroy of the whole? 1 *Hen. VI.* v 4 142
Detraction. Happy are they that hear their detractions and can put them to mending . . . *Much Ado* ii 3 238
You might see more detraction at your heels than fortunes before you *T. Night* ii 5 149
Detraction will not suffer it. Therefore I'll none of it . 1 *Hen. IV.* v 1 141
I put myself to thy direction, and Unspeak mine own detraction *Macbeth* iv 3 123
Deucalion. Not hold thee of our blood, no, not our kin, Far than Deucalion off . . . *W. Tale* iv 4 442
In a cheap estimation, is worth all your predecessors since Deucalion *Coriolanus* ii 1 102
Deuce-ace. I am sure, you know how much the gross sum of deuce-ace amounts to . . . *L. L. Lost* i 2 49
Deux. J'ai gagné deux mots d'Anglois vitement . . *Hen. V.* iii 4 14
Gardez ma vie, et je vous donnerai deux cents écus . . iv 4 45
Devesting. Friends all but now, even now, In quarter, and in terms like bride and groom Devesting them for bed . . *Othello* ii 3 181

Device. O excellent device! was there ever heard a better? *T. G. of Ver.* ii 1 145
There is also another device in my prain . . . . . *Mer. Wives* i 1 43
Marry, this is our device . . . . . iv 4 41
Well, husband your device . . . . . iv 6 52
To have a dispatch of complaints, and to deliver us from devices hereafter . . . . . *Meas. for Meas.* iv 4 15
By some device or other The villain is o'er-raught of all my money *Com. of Errors* i 2 95
An excellent device! . . . . . *L. L. Lost* v 1 144
But I will forward with my device . . . . . v 2 669
We shall be dogged with company, and our devices known *M. N. Dream* i 2 107
I have a device to make all well . . . . . iii 1 17
That is an old device . . . . . v 1 50
I'll tell thee all my whole device When I am in my coach *Mer. of Venice* iii 4 81
Entrap thee by some treacherous device . . . . . *As Y. Like It* i 1 157
Full of noble device, of all sorts enchantingly beloved . . . . . i 1 174
This is a letter of your own device . . . . . iv 3 20
That's your device.—It is: may it be done? . . . *T. of Shrew* i 1 198
I may, by this device, at least Have leave and leisure to make love to her . . . . . i 2 135
Excellent! I smell a device.—I have't in my nose too . . *T. Night* ii 3 176
I could marry this wench for this device . . . . . ii 5 200
His very genius hath taken the infection of the device . . . . . iii 4 143
Nay, pursue him now, lest the device take air and taint . . . . . iii 4 144
We will bring the device to the bar and crown thee for a finder of madmen . . . . . iii 4 153
Most freely I confess, myself and Toby Set this device . . . . . v 1 368
And not alone in habit and device . . . . . *K. John* i 1 210
What trick, what device, what starting-hole, canst thou now find out? *1 Hen. IV.* ii 4 290
I blushed to hear his monstrous devices . . . . . ii 4 344
By some odd gimmors or device Their arms are set like clocks *1 Hen. VI.* i 2 41
It was thy device By this alliance to make void my suit *3 Hen. VI.* iii 3 141
O excellent device! make a sop of him . . . *Richard III.* i 4 162
Why, who's so gross, That seeth not this palpable device? . . . iii 6 11
The net has fall'n upon me! I shall perish Under device and practice *Hen. VIII.* i 1 204
Is there no way to cure this? No new device to beat this from his brains? . . . . . iii 2 217
By device, let blockish Ajax draw The sort to fight with Hector *Troi. and Cres.* i 3 375
Whether by device or no, the heavens can tell . . . . *T. Andron.* i 1 395
You do but plot your deaths By this device . . . . . ii 1 79
Let us, that have our tongues, Plot some device of further misery . iii 1 134
I know from whence this same device proceeds: May this be borne? . iv 4 52
Be blithe again, And bury all thy fear in my devices . . . iv 4 112
What says Andronicus to this device? . . . . . v 2 120
And will o'erreach them in their own devices . . . . . v 2 143
And entertain'd me with mine own device . . . . *T. of Athens* i 2 155
Our wills and fates do so contrary run That our devices still are overthrown . . . . . *Hamlet* iii 2 222
I will work him To an exploit, now ripe in my device . . . . . iv 7 65
Dull not device by coldness and delay . . . . . *Othello* ii 3 394
Every day thou daffest me with some device . . . . . iv 2 177
'Tis plate of rare device, and jewels Of rich and exquisite form . *Cymb.* i 6 189
Explain The labour of each knight in his device . . . . *Pericles* ii 2 15
The device he bears upon his shield Is a black Ethiope reaching at the sun . . . . . ii 2 19
The device he bears upon his shield Is an arm'd knight that's conquer'd by a lady . . . . . ii 2 25
And his device, a wreath of chivalry; The word, 'Me pompæ provexit apex' . . . . . ii 2 29
Devil. Hell is empty, And all the devils are here . . . *Tempest* i 2 215
Thou poisonous slave, got by the devil himself Upon thy wicked dam! i 2 319
Have we devils here? Do you put tricks upon's with savages and men of Ind? . . . . . ii 2 59
Where the devil should he learn our language? . . . . . ii 2 69
I should know that voice: it should be—but he is drowned; and these are devils . . . . . ii 2 91
This is a devil, and no monster: I will leave him . . . . . ii 2 102
A murrain on your monster, and the devil take your fingers! . . . iii 2 89
If thou beest a man, show thyself in thy likeness: if thou beest a devil, take't as thou list . . . . . iii 2 138
Some of you there present Are worse than devils . . . . . iii 3 36
A devil, a born devil, on whose nature Nurture can never stick . . . iv 1 188
The devil speaks in him . . . . . v 1 129
He hath a legion of angels.—As many devils entertain *Mer. Wives* i 3 61
The devil himself hath not such a name . . . . . ii 2 314
What spirit, what devil suggests this imagination? . . . . . iii 3 230
Lest the devil that guides him should aid him, I will search impossible places . . . . . iii 5 150
Heaven guide him to thy husband's cudgel, and the devil guide his cudgel! . . . . . iv 2 91
Now shall the devil be shamed . . . . . iv 2 124
If the devil have him not in fee-simple, with fine and recovery . . . iv 2 224
Like three German devils, three Doctor Faustuses . . . . . iv 5 70
The devil take one party and his dam the other! . . . . . iv 5 108
Her husband hath the finest mad devil of jealousy in him . . . . . v 1 19
No man means evil but the devil, and we shall know him by his horns . v 2 15
Where is Nan now and her troop of fairies, and the Welsh devil Hugh? . v 3 13
I think the devil will not have me damned, lest the oil that's in me should set hell on fire . . . . . v 5 38
Do you think . . . that ever the devil could have made you our delight? . . . . . v 5 158
This outward-sainted deputy . . . is yet a devil . . *Meas. for Meas.* iii 1 92
Nay, if the devil have given thee proofs for sin, Thou wilt prove his . iii 2 31
You bid me seek redemption of the devil: Hear me yourself . . . . . v 1 29
Let the devil Be sometime honour'd for his burning throne! . . . . . v 1 294
A devil in an everlasting garment hath him . . *Com. of Errors* iv 2 33
It is the devil.—Nay, she is worse, she is the devil's dam . . . . . iv 3 50
He must have a long spoon that must eat with the devil . . . . . iv 3 65
Some devils ask but the parings of one's nail, A rush, a hair, a drop of blood . . . . . iv 3 72
Be mad, good master: cry 'The devil!' . . . . . iv 4 131
Is there no young squarer now that will make a voyage with him to the devil? . . . . . *Much Ado* i 1 83
Go you into hell?—No, but to the gate; and there will the devil meet me . . . . . ii 1 46
The devil my master knew she was Margaret . . . . . iii 3 165
Love is a devil: there is no evil angel but Love . . . *L. L. Lost* i 2 178

Devil. Devils soonest tempt, resembling spirits of light . . . *L. L. Lost* iv 3 257
No devil will fright thee then so much as she . . . . . iv 3 275
Some tricks, some quillets, how to cheat the devil . . . . . iv 3 288
An angel is not evil; I should have fear'd her had she been a devil . v 2 106
One sees more devils than vast hell can hold, That is, the madman *M. N. Dream* v 1 9
If the devil be within and that temptation without, I know he will choose it . . . . . *Mer. of Venice* i 2 105
If he have the condition of a saint and the complexion of a devil . . . i 2 144
To smell pork; to eat of the habitation which your prophet the Nazarite conjured the devil into . . . . . i 3 36
The devil can cite Scripture for his purpose . . . . . i 3 99
My master, who, God bless the mark, is a kind of devil . . . . . ii 2 25
The fiend, who, saving your reverence, is the devil himself . . . . . ii 2 27
Certainly the Jew is the very devil incarnal . . . . . ii 2 28
Our house is hell, and thou, a merry devil, Didst rob it of some taste of tediousness . . . . . ii 3 2
Let me say 'amen' betimes, lest the devil cross my prayer . . . . . iii 1 23
She is damned for it.—That's certain, if the devil may be her judge . iii 1 35
A third cannot be matched, unless the devil himself turn Jew . . . . . iii 1 81
To do a great right, do a little wrong, And curb this cruel devil of his will . . . . . iv 1 217
I would lose all, ay, sacrifice them all Here to this devil, to deliver you iv 1 287
Why, then the devil give him good of it! I'll stay no longer question . iv 1 345
If thou beest not damned for this, the devil himself will have no shepherds . . . . . *As Y. Like It* iii 2 88
Nay, but the devil take mocking: speak, sad brow and true maid . . . iii 2 226
From all such devils, good Lord, deliver us! . . . . *T. of Shrew* i 1 66
A husband! a devil.—I say, a husband.—I say, a devil . . . . . i 1 125
Why, he's a devil, a devil, a very fiend.—Why, she's a devil, a devil, the devil's dam . . . . . iii 2 157
I am driven on by the flesh; and he must needs go that the devil drives *All's Well* i 3 32
Though the devil lead the measure, such are to be followed . . . . . ii 1 57
The devil it is that's thy master . . . . . ii 3 264
What the devil should move me? . . . . . iv 1 37
The black prince, sir; alias, the prince of darkness; alias, the devil . iv 5 45
Dost thou put upon me at once both the office of God and the devil? . v 2 53
Let him be the devil, an he will, I care not . . . . *T. Night* i 5 136
You are too proud; But, if you were the devil, you are fair . . . . . i 5 270
The devil a puritan that he is, or any thing constantly . . . . . ii 3 159
Follow me.—To the gates of Tartar, thou most excellent devil of wit! . ii 5 227
If all the devils of hell be drawn in little, and Legion himself possessed him . . . . . iii 4 94
What, man! defy the devil: consider, he's an enemy to mankind . . . iii 4 108
La you, an you speak ill of the devil, how he takes it at heart! . . . iii 4 111
He is a devil in private brawl: souls and bodies hath he divorced three iii 4 259
Why, man, he's a very devil; I have not seen such a firago . . . . . iii 4 301
I have persuaded him the youth's a devil . . . . . iii 4 321
The beauteous evil Are empty trunks o'erflourish'd by the devil . . . iii 4 404
I am one of those gentle ones that will use the devil himself with courtesy . . . . . iv 2 37
Who, with dagger of lath, In his rage and his wrath, Cries, ah, ha! to the devil . . . . . iv 2 138
Like a mad lad, Pare thy nails, dad; Adieu, good man devil . . . . . iv 2 141
Of this make no conclusion, lest you say Your queen and I are devils *W. Tale* i 2 82
Though a devil Would have shed water out of fire ere done't . . . . . iii 2 193
As faithfully as I deny the devil . . . . . *K. John* i 1 252
Being as like As rain to water, or devil to his dam . . . . . ii 1 128
What the devil art thou?—One that will play the devil, sir, with you . ii 1 134
That sly devil, That broker, that still breaks the pate of faith . . . ii 1 567
Look to that, devil; lest that France repent . . . . . iii 1 196
The devil tempts thee here In likeness of a new untrimmed bride . . . iii 1 208
Some airy devil hovers in the sky And pours down mischief . . . . . iii 2 2
Thou wert better gall the devil, Salisbury . . . . . iv 3 95
I'll so maul you and your toasting-iron, That you shall think the devil is come from hell . . . . . iv 3 100
That misbegotten devil, Faulconbridge . . . . . v 4 4
The devil take Henry of Lancaster and thee! . . . *Richard II.* v 5 103
The devil, that told me I did well, Says that this deed is chronicled in hell . . . . . v 5 116
What a devil hast thou to do with the time of the day? . . *1 Hen. IV.* i 2 6
Jack! how agrees the devil and thee about thy soul? . . . . . i 2 126
The devil shall have his bargain; for he was never yet a breaker of proverbs . . . . . i 2 131
He will give the devil his due . . . . . i 2 132
Then art thou damned for keeping thy word with the devil . . . . . i 2 135
Else he had been damned for cozening the devil . . . . . i 2 137
He durst as well have met the devil alone As Owen Glendower for an enemy . . . . . i 3 116
An if the devil come and roar for them, I will not send them . . . . . i 3 125
O, the devil take such cozeners! God forgive me! . . . . . i 3 255
As the devil would have it, three misbegotten knaves in Kendal green came at my back . . . . . ii 4 245
And swore the devil his true liegeman upon the cross of a Welsh hook . ii 4 371
That fiend Douglas, that spirit Percy, and that devil Glendower . . . ii 4 405
There is a devil haunts thee in the likeness of an old fat man . . . ii 4 492
Heigh, heigh! the devil rides upon a fiddlestick: what's the matter? . ii 4 534
Why, I can teach you, cousin, to command The devil . . . . . iii 1 56
I can teach thee, coz, to shame the devil By telling truth: tell truth and shame the devil . . . . . iii 1 57
O, while you live, tell truth and shame the devil! . . . . . iii 1 62
He held me last night at least nine hours In reckoning up the several devils' names That were his lackeys . . . . . iii 1 157
Now I perceive the devil understands Welsh . . . . . iii 1 233
If that the devil and mischance look big Upon the maidenhead of our affairs . . . . . iv 1 58
Had as lieve hear the devil as a drum . . . . . iv 2 20
He will foin like any devil . . . . . *2 Hen. IV.* ii 1 18
What the devil hast thou brought there? . . . . . ii 4 1
There is a good angel about him; but the devil outbids him too . . . ii 4 363
And learning a mere hoard of gold kept by a devil . . . . . iv 3 125
Why the devil should we keep knives to cut one another's throats? *Hen. V.* ii 1 95
All other devils that suggest by treasons Do botch and bungle up damnation . . . . . ii 2 114
A' said once, the devil would have him about women . . . . . ii 3 37
And I will take up that with 'Give the devil his due' . . . . . iii 7 127
There stands your friend for the devil: have at the very eye of that proverb with 'A pox of the devil' . . . . . iii 7 129

Devil. They will eat like wolves and fight like devils *Hen. V.* iii 7 162
Thus may we gather honey from the weed, And make a moral of the devil himself . . . iv 1 12
Ten times more valour than this roaring devil i' the old play . . iv 4 75
The devil take order now! I'll to the throng . . . iv 5 22
As good a gentleman as the devil is, as Lucifer and Belzebub himself . iv 7 145
Here, there, and every where, enraged he flew: The French exclaim'd, the devil was in arms . . . . . . *1 Hen. VI.* i 1 125
This cardinal's more haughty than the devil . . . i 3 85
Devil or devil's dam, I'll conjure thee . . . i 5 5
Judge it straight a thing impossible To compass wonders but by help of devils . . . . . . v 4 48
Gold cannot come amiss, were she a devil . . *2 Hen. VI.* i 2 92
This devil here shall be my substitute . . . iii 1 371
There's two of you; the devil make a third! . . . iii 2 303
In despite of the devils and hell . . . . iv 8 63
Let ten thousand devils come against me . . . . iv 10 65
'Good Gloucester' and 'good devil' were alike . *3 Hen. VI.* v 6 4
You are mortal, And mortal eyes cannot endure the devil *Richard III.* i 2 45
Foul devil, for God's sake, hence, and trouble us not . . i 2 50
O wonderful, when devils tell the truth! . . . . i 2 73
I nothing to back my suit at all, But the plain devil and dissembling looks . . . . i 2 237
My pains are quite forgot.—Out, devil! I remember them too well . i 3 118
Whilst some tormenting dream Affrights thee with a hell of ugly devils i 3 227
Dost thou scorn me for my gentle counsel? And soothe the devil that I warn thee from? . . . . . . i 3 298
And seem a saint, when most I play the devil . . . . i 3 338
Take the devil in thy mind, and believe him not . . . i 4 151
My brother's love, the devil, and my rage . . . . i 4 229
'But O! the devil'—there the villain stopp'd . . . iv 3 16
Shall I be tempted of the devil thus?—Ay, if the devil tempt thee to do good . . . . iv 4 418
The devil speed him! no man's pie is freed From his ambitious finger *Hen. VIII.* i 1 52
The devil is a niggard, Or has given all before, and he begins A new hell in himself . . . . i 1 70
Why the devil, Upon this French going out, took he upon him? . . i 1 72
A French song and a fiddle has no fellow.—The devil fiddle 'em! . i 3 42
What cross devil Made me put this main secret in the packet? . . iii 2 214
Whose honesty the devil And his disciples only envy at . . . v 3 111
The devil was amongst 'em, I think, surely . . . . v 4 61
He cares not; an the devil come to him, it's all one *Troi. and Cres.* i 2 228
I'll learn to conjure and raise devils, but I'll see some issue of my spiteful execrations . . . . ii 3 6
Fears make devils of cherubins; they never see truly . . iii 2 74
The devil take Antenor! the young prince will go mad . . iv 2 77
A still and dumb-discoursive devil That tempts most cunningly . iv 4 92
Sometimes we are devils to ourselves . . . . iv 4 97
Wert thou the devil, and worest it on thy horn, It should be challenged v 2 95
A burning devil take them! . . . . . . v 2 197
The devil take thee, coward! . . . . . . v 7 24
He's the devil.—Bolder, though not so subtle . . *Coriolanus* i 10 16
Pray to the devils; the gods have given us over . *T. Andron.* iv 2 48
What hath he sent her?—A devil.—Why, then she is the devil's dam . iv 2 64
This is the incarnate devil That robb'd Andronicus of his good hand . v 1 40
Bring down the devil; for he must not die So sweet a death as hanging v 1 145
If there be devils, would I were a devil, To live and burn in everlasting fire! . . . . v 1 147
Could not all hell afford you such a devil? . . . . v 2 86
It were convenient you had such a devil . . . . v 2 90
This ravenous tiger, this accursed devil . . . . v 3 5
Some devil whisper curses in mine ear, And prompt me! . . v 3 11
Where the devil should this Romeo be? Came he not home to-night? *Rom. and Jul.* ii 4 1
Why the devil came you between us? . . . . iii 1 107
What devil art thou, that dost torment me thus? . . . iii 2 43
The devil knew not what he did when he made man politic *T. of Athens* iii 3 28
They have e'en put my breath from me, the slaves. Creditors? devils! iii 4 105
That would have brook'd The eternal devil to keep his state in Rome As easily as a king . . . . *J. Cæsar* i 2 160
Art thou some god, some angel, or some devil, That makest my blood cold and my hair to stare? . . . . . . iv 3 279
What, can the devil speak true? . . . . *Macbeth* i 3 107
'Tis the eye of childhood That fears a painted devil . . . ii 2 55
A bold one, that dare look on that Which might appal the devil . iii 4 60
Not in the legions Of horrid hell can come a devil more damn'd In evils iv 3 55
At no time broke my faith, would not betray The devil to his fellow iv 3 129
The devil damn thee black, thou cream-faced loon! . . . v 3 11
The devil himself could not pronounce a title More hateful to mine ear v 7 8
The spirit that I have seen May be the devil: and the devil hath power To assume a pleasing shape . . . . . *Hamlet* ii 2 628
With devotion's visage And pious action we do sugar o'er The devil himself . . . . iii 1 49
Nay then, let the devil wear black, for I'll have a suit of sables . iii 2 137
What devil was't That thus hath cozen'd you at hoodman-blind? . iii 4 76
That monster, custom, who all sense doth eat, Of habits devil, is angel yet in this . . . . iii 4 162
Either . . the devil, or throw him out With wondrous potency . iii 4 169
Vows, to the blackest devil! Conscience and grace, to the profoundest pit! . . . . iv 5 131
The devil take thy soul!—Thou pray'st not well . . . v 1 281
Darkness and devils! Saddle my horses; call my train together . *Lear* i 4 273
See thyself, devil! Proper deformity seems not in the fiend So horrid as in woman . . . . iv 2 59
Or else the devil will make a grandsire of you . . . *Othello* i 1 91
You are one of those that will not serve God, if the devil bid you . i 1 109
Wild-cats in your kitchens, Saints in your injuries, devils being offended ii 1 112
Her eye must be fed; and what delight shall she have to look on the devil? . . . . ii 1 229
Thou invisible spirit of wine, if thou hast no name to be known by, let us call thee devil! . . . . ii 3 284
Every inordinate cup is unblessed and the ingredient is a devil . ii 3 312
When devils will the blackest sins put on, They do suggest at first with heavenly shows . . . . ii 3 357
To furnish me with some swift means of death For the fair devil . iii 3 479
For here's a young and sweating devil here, That commonly rebels . iii 4 42
And, like the devil, from his very arm Puff'd his own brother . . iii 4 136
Not mean harm! It is hypocrisy against the devil . . . iv 1 6
They that mean virtuously, and yet do so, The devil their virtue tempts iv 1 8

Devil. Is't possible?—Confess—handkerchief!—O devil! . *Othello* iv 1 44
Let the devil and his dam haunt you! . . . . iv 1 153
I am glad to see you mad.—Why, sweet Othello,— Devil!—I have not deserved this . . . . iv 1 251
O devil, devil! If that the earth could teem with woman's tears, Each drop she falls would prove a crocodile . . . . . iv 1 255
Lest, being like one of heaven, the devils themselves Should fear to seize thee . . . . iv 2 36
O, the more angel she, And you the blacker devil! . . . v 2 131
Thou dost belie her, and thou art a devil . . . . v 2 133
Let heaven and men and devils, let them all, All, all, cry shame against me, yet I'll speak . . . . v 2 221
Whip me, ye devils, From the possession of this heavenly sight! . v 2 277
I look down towards his feet; but that's a fable. If that thou be'st a devil, I cannot kill thee . . . . . . v 2 287
Now, gods and devils! Authority melts from me . *Ant. and Cleo.* iii 13 89
I know the devil himself will not eat a woman . . . v 2 274
I know that a woman is a dish for the gods, if the devil dress her not . v 2 276
These same whoreson devils do the gods great harm in their women; for in every ten that they make, the devils mar five . . . v 2 277
Solicit'st here a lady that disdains Thee and the devil alike *Cymbeline* i 6 147
That such a crafty devil as is his mother Should yield the world this ass! ii 1 57
'His garment!' Now the devil . . . . . . ii 3 142
O, all the devils! This yellow Iachimo, in an hour,—was't not? . ii 5 13
Pray they have their will: The very devils cannot plague them better . ii 5 35
Thou, Conspired with that irregulous devil . . . . iv 2 315
She would make a puritan of the devil, if he should cheapen a kiss of her *Pericles* iv 6 10

Devil drunkenness. It hath pleased the devil drunkenness to give place to the devil wrath . . . . *Othello* ii 3 297

Devil Envy. I have said my prayers and devil Envy say Amen *Tr. and Cr.* ii 3 23

Devil incardinate. We took him for a coward, but he's the very devil incardinate . . . . *T. Night* v 1 184

Devils incarnate. Yes, that a' did; and said they were devils incarnate *Hen V.* ii 3 34

Devil Luxury. How the devil Luxury, with his fat rump and potato-finger, tickles these together! . . . . *Troi. and Cres.* v 2 55

Devil-monk. That devil-monk, Hopkins, that made this mischief *Hen. VIII.* ii 1 21

Devil-porter. I'll devil-porter it no further . . . . *Macbeth* ii 3 19

Devil wrath. It hath pleased the devil drunkenness to give place to the devil wrath . . . . ii 3 298

Devils' additions. They are devils' additions, the names of fiends *Mer. Wives* ii 2 312

Devil's book. Thou thinkest me as far in the devil's book as thou *2 Hen. IV.* ii 2 49

Devil's butcher. Where is that devil's butcher, Hard-favour'd Richard? *3 Hen. VI.* v 5 77

Devil's crest. Let's write good angel on the devil's horn; 'Tis not the devil's crest . . . . *Meas. for Meas.* ii 4 17

Devil's dam. Nay, she is worse, she is the devil's dam . *Com. of Errors* iv 3 51
You may go to the devil's dam: your gifts are so good . . *T. of Shrew* i 1 106
Why, she's a devil, a devil, the devil's dam . . . . iii 2 158
I'll have a bout with thee; Devil or devil's dam, I'll conjure thee *1 Hen. VI.* i 5 5
What hath he sent her?—A devil.—Why, then she is the devil's dam *T. Andron.* iv 2 65

Devil's grace. A goodly prize, fit for the devil's grace! . . *1 Hen. VI.* v 3 33

Devil's horn. Let's write good angel on the devil's horn . *Meas. for Meas.* ii 4 16

Devil's illusions. By the devil's illusions The monk might be deceived *Hen. VIII.* i 2 178

Devil's name. What an unweighed behaviour hath this Flemish drunkard picked—with the devil's name!—out of my conversation? *Mer. Wives* ii 1 24
Why, what, i' devil's name, tailor, call'st thou this? . *T. of Shrew* iv 3 92
Knock, knock! Who's there, in the other devil's name? . *Macbeth* ii 3 9

Devil's teeth. Throw your vile guesses in the devil's teeth, From whence you have them . . . . *Othello* iii 4 184

Devil's writ. Let's see the devil's writ . . . . *2 Hen. VI.* i 4 60

Devilish. There is a devilish mercy in the judge, If you'll implore it *Meas. for Meas.* iii 1 65
For shame, thou hilding of a devilish spirit . . *T. of Shrew* ii 1 26
When, with a most impatient devilish spirit, 'Frets, call you these?' quoth she . . . . ii 1 152
With linstock now the devilish cannon touches . . *Hen. V.* iii Prol. 33
Upon my life, began her devilish practices . . *2 Hen VI.* iii 1 46
By devilish policy art thou grown great . . . . iv 1 83
Unless you be possess'd with devilish spirits, You cannot but forbear . iv 7 80
But dead they are, and, devilish slave, by thee . . *Richard III.* i 2 90
Not to relent is beastly, savage, devilish . . . . i 4 265
Tell me what they deserve That do conspire my death with devilish plots? . . . . iii 4 62
Devilish Macbeth By many of these trains hath sought to win me *Macb.* iv 3 117
A devilish knave. Besides, the knave is handsome, young . *Othello* ii 1 249
Unless thou think'st me devilish—is't not meet That I did amplify my judgement in Other conclusions? . . . . . *Cymbeline* i 5 16

Devilish-holy. O devilish-holy fray! . . . . *M. N. Dream* iii 2 129

Devin. Mon très cher et devin déesse . . . . *Hen. V.* v 2 231

Devise. Then she plots, then she ruminates, then she devises *Mer. Wives* ii 2 321
Devise something: any extremity rather than a mischief . . iv 2 75
Devise but how you'll use him when he comes, And let us two devise to bring him thither . . . . iv 4 26
I will go on the slightest errand now to the Antipodes that you can devise to send me on . . . . *Much Ado* ii 1 274
I'll devise some honest slanders To stain my cousin with . . iii 1 84
I'll devise thee brave punishments for him . . . . v 4 130
He shall endure such public shame as the rest of the court can possibly devise . . . . *L. L. Lost* i 1 133
Devise, wit; write, pen; for I am for whole volumes in folio . . i 2 190
Let us devise Some entertainment for them . . . . iv 3 372
This falls out better than I could devise . . *M. N. Dream* iii 2 35
The brain may devise laws for the blood . . *Mer. of Venice* i 2 19
Be merry.—From henceforth I will, coz, and devise sports *As Y. Like It* i 2 26
Devise with me how we may fly, Whither to go and what to bear with us . . . . i 3 102
Devise the fittest time and safest way To hide us from pursuit . . i 3 137
I shall devise something . . . . i 3 182
I will devise a death as cruel for thee As thou art tender to't *W. Tale* iv 4 451
Thou canst not, cardinal, devise a name So slight, unworthy *K. John* iii 1 149
Out of your grace, devise, ordain, impose Some gentle order . . iii 1 250
Will I make good against thee, arm to arm, What I have spoke, or thou canst worse devise . . . . *Richard II.* i 1 77

Devise. What sport shall we devise here in this garden, To drive away the heavy thought of care? . . . . . *Richard II.* iii 4 1
Also to effect Whatever I shall happen to devise . . . iv 1 330
I will devise matter enough out of this . . . . . 2 *Hen. IV.* v 1 87
Withal devise something to do thyself good . . . . v 3 140
And for his safety there I'll best devise . . . . 1 *Hen. VI.* i 1 172
My lord, where are you? what devise you on? . . . . ii 2 124
Then thus it must be; this doth Joan devise . . . . iii 3 17
Did he not, contrary to form of law, Devise strange deaths for small offences done? . . . . . 2 *Hen. VI.* iii 1 59
You did devise Strange tortures for offenders never heard of . . iii 1 121
We'll devise a mean To reconcile you all unto the king . . . . iv 8 71
Devise excuses for thy faults.—While we devise fell tortures for thy faults . . . . . 3 *Hen. VI.* ii 6 71
Appeased By such invention as I can devise . . . . iv 1 35
Thinking it harder for our mistress to devise imposition enough *Troi. and Cres.* iii 2 85
Did see and hear, devise, instruct, walk, feel . . . . *Coriolanus* i 1 105
He cannot but with measure fit the honours Which we devise him . . ii 2 128
I'll follow thee a month, devise with thee Where thou shalt rest . . iv 1 38
As kill a man, or else devise his death . . . *T. Andron.* v 1 128
Bid her devise Some means to come to shrift this afternoon *Rom. and Jul.* ii 4 191
I never injured thee, But love thee better than thou canst devise . iii 1 72
Bid me devise some mean To rid her from this second marriage . v 3 240
Speak all good you can devise of Cæsar . . . *J. Cæsar* iii 1 246
The rather, if you could devise it so That I might be the organ *Hamlet* iv 7 70
Let her who would be rid of him devise His speedy taking off *Lear* v 1 64
I'll devise a mean to draw the Moor Out of the way . . . *Othello* iii 1 39
For me to devise a lodging and say he lies here or he lies there, were to lie in mine own throat . . . . . iii 4 12
Take me from this world with treachery and devise engines for my life iv 2 221

Devised. They have devised a mean How he her chamber-window will ascend . . . . *T. G. of Ver.* iii 1 38
Will you not eat your word?—With no sauce that can be devised to it *Much Ado* iv 1 281
Who devised this penalty?—Marry, that did I. . . *L. L. Lost* i 1 124
Through Athens' gates have we devised to steal . . *M. N. Dream* i 1 213
Therefore the lottery, that he hath devised in these three chests of gold, silver and lead . . . . . *Mer. of Venice* i 2 32
Thus Rosalind of many parts By heavenly synod was devised *As Y. L. It* iii 2 158
Which is more Than history can pattern, though devised And play'd to take spectators . . . . . . *W. Tale* iii 2 37
Daily new exactions are devised, As blanks, benevolences *Richard II.* ii 1 249
In reproof of many tales devised, Which oft the ear of greatness needs must hear . . . . . 1 *Hen. IV.* iii 2 23
The Salique law Was not devised for the realm of France . *Hen. V.* i 2 55
With written pamphlets studiously devised . . . 1 *Hen. VI.* iii 1 2
The king, provoked by the queen, Devised impeachments to imprison him . . . . *Richard III.* ii 2 22
A thing devised by the enemy . . . . v 3 306
Conscience is but a word that cowards use, Devised at first to keep the strong in awe . . . . v 3 310
They say They are devised by you . . . . *Hen. VIII.* i 2 51
Until we have devised Some never-heard-of torturing pain for them *T. Andron.* ii 3 284
Ceremony was but devised at first To set a gloss on faint deeds *T. of A.* i 2 15
I sat me down, Devised a new commission, wrote it fair . . *Hamlet* v 2 32
I will be hang'd, if . . . Some cogging, cozening slave, to get some office, Have not devised this slander . . . . . *Othello* iv 2 133
There she appeared indeed; or my reporter devised well for her *Ant. and Cleo.* ii 2 194

Devising. His gift is in devising impossible slanders . . *Much Ado* ii 1 143

Devoid. Her life was beast-like, and devoid of pity . . *T. Andron.* v 3 199

Devonshire. In Devonshire, As I by friends am well advertised *Richard III.* iv 4 500

Devote. Or so devote to Aristotle's checks As Ovid be an outcast quite abjured . . . . *T. of Shrew* i 1 32

Devoted. Since the substance of your perfect self Is else devoted *T. G. of Ver.* iv 2 125
Thine, in all compliments of devoted and heart-burning heat of duty *L. L. Lost* i 1 280
This is your devoted friend, sir . . . . . *All's Well* iv 3 264
To stop devoted charitable deeds . . . . *Richard III.* i 2 35
If thy poor devoted suppliant may But beg one favour . . . i 2 207
He hath devoted and given up himself to the contemplation, mark, and denotement of her parts and graces . . . . *Othello* ii 3 321

Devotion. To his image, which methought did promise Most venerable worth, did I devotion . . . . . . *T. Night* iii 4 397
My soul the faithfull'st offerings hath breathed out That e'er devotion tender'd! . . . . v 1 118
In the devotion of a subject's love . . . . . *Richard II.* i 1 31
It shows my earnestness of affection,— It doth so.—My devotion 2 *Hen. IV.* v 5 19
Camest thou here by chance, Or of devotion, to this holy shrine? 2 *Hen. VI.* ii 1 88
On the helmets of our foes Tell our devotion with revengeful arms 3 *Hen. VI.* ii 1 164
In devotion spend my latter days, To sin's rebuke and my Creator's praise . . . . iv 6 43
Pardon us the interruption Of thy devotion . . . *Richard III.* iii 7 103
As I guess, Upon the like devotion as yourselves . . . . . iv 1 9
With pure heart's love Immaculate devotion, holy thoughts . . iv 4 404
More bright in zeal than the devotion which Cold lips blow *Tr. and Cr.* iv 4 28
He seeks their hate with greater devotion than they can render it him *Coriolanus* ii 2 21
Which mannerly devotion shows in this . . . *Rom. and Jul.* i 5 100
God shield I should disturb devotion! . . . . . . iv 1 41
Devotion, patience, courage, fortitude, I have no relish of them *Macbeth* iv 3 94
With devotion's visage And pious action we do sugar o'er The devil himself . . . . *Hamlet* iii 1 47
I have no great devotion to the deed . . . . . *Othello* v 1 8
Now turn The office and devotion of their view Upon a tawny front *Ant. and Cleo.* i 1 5

Devour. Do so much admire That they devour their reason . *Tempest* v 1 155
Greedily devour the treacherous bait . . . . *Much Ado* iii 1 28
And ere a man hath power to say 'Behold!' The jaws of darkness do devour it up . . . . *M. N. Dream* i 1 148
Is a whale to virginity and devours up all the fry it finds *All's Well* iv 3 249
What dangers, by his highness' fail of issue, May drop upon his kingdom and devour Incertain lookers on . . . . *W. Tale* v 1 28
He seem'd in running to devour the way . . . 2 *Hen. IV.* i 1 47

Devour. Whatever praises itself but in the deed, devours the deed in the praise . . . . *Troi. and Cres.* ii 3 167
The present wars devour him: he is grown Too proud to be so valiant *Coriolanus* i 1 263
Who does the wolf love?—The lamb.—Ay, to devour him . . ii 1 10
There cannot be That vulture in you, to devour so many As will to greatness dedicate themselves . . . . . . *Macbeth* iv 3 74
The good-years shall devour them, flesh and fell, Ere they shall make us weep: we'll see 'em starve first . . . . . *Lear* v 3 24
She'ld come again, and with a greedy ear Devour up my discourse *Othello* i 3 150
And at last devours them all at a mouthful . . . *Pericles* ii 1 35

Devoured. That same cowardly, giant-like ox-beef hath devoured many a gentleman of your house . . . . . *M. N. Dream* iii 1 198
I had a sister, Whom the blind waves and surges have devour'd *T. Night* v 1 236
These Lincoln Washes have devoured them . . . *K. John* v 6 41
Were in the Washes all unwarily Devoured by the unexpected flood . v 7 64
Those scraps are good deeds past; which are devour'd As fast as they are made, forgot as soon As done . . . *Troi. and Cres.* iii 3 148
Only that name remains; The cruelty and envy of the people . . . hath devour'd the rest . . . . *Coriolanus* iv 5 82
In sorrow all devour'd, With sighs shot through . . . *Pericles* iv 4 25

Devourer. How happy art thou, then, From these devourers to be banished! . . . . *T. Andron.* iii 1 57

Devouring. A grace it had, devouring . . . . . *Tempest* iii 3 84
Spite of cormorant devouring Time . . . . *L. L. Lost* i 1 4
Devouring pestilence hangs in our air . . . . *Richard II.* i 3 284
So looks the pent-up lion o'er the wretch That trembles under his devouring paws . . . . 3 *Hen. VI.* i 3 13
This fell devouring receptacle . . . . . . *T. Andron.* ii 3 235

Devout. More devout than this in our respects Have we not been *L. L. Lost* v 2 792
A most devout coward, religious in it . . . . *T. Night* iii 4 424
With contemplation and devout desires . . . . *K. John* v 4 48
All the temporal lands which men devout By testament have given to the church . . . . *Hen. V.* i 1 9
When holy and devout religious men Are at their beads . *Richard III.* iii 7 92
What, art thou devout? wast thou in prayer? . *Troi. and Cres.* ii 3 38
When the devout religion of mine eye Maintains such falsehood, then turn tears to fires! . . . . *Rom. and Jul.* i 2 93
Fasting and prayer, Much castigation, exercise devout . . *Othello* iii 4 41

Devoutly. She, sweet lady, dotes, Devoutly dotes, dotes in idolatry *M. N. Dream* i 1 109
And saint-like Cast her fair eyes to heaven and pray'd devoutly *Hen. VIII.* iv 1 84
'Tis a consummation Devoutly to be wish'd . . . *Hamlet* iii 1 64

Dew. Thou call'dst me up at midnight to fetch dew From the still-vex'd Bermoothes . . . . *Tempest* i 2 228
As wicked dew as e'er my mother brush'd With raven's feather from unwholesome fen Drop on you both! . . . . i 2 321
The night of dew that on my cheeks down flows . . . *L. L. Lost* iv 3 29
And I serve the fairy queen, To dew her orbs upon the green *M. N. Dr.* ii 1 9
Bedabbled with the dew and torn with briers, I can no further crawl . iii 2 443
That same dew, which sometime on the buds Was wont to swell like round and orient pearls . . . . iv 1 59
Their heads are hung With ears that sweep away the morning dew . iv 1 126
In such a night Did Thisbe fearfully o'ertrip the dew . *Mer. of Venice* v 1 7
She looks as clear As morning roses newly wash'd with dew *T. of Shrew* ii 1 174
The want of which vain dew Perchance shall dry your pities . *W. Tale* ii 1 109
Before the dew of evening fall . . . . . . *K. John* ii 1 285
Let me wipe off this honourable dew, That silverly doth progress on thy cheeks . . . . v 2 45
Behold, That you in pity may dissolve to dew . . . *Richard II.* v 1 9
O Seigneur Dieu!—O, Signieur Dew should be a gentleman: Perpend my words, O Signieur Dew, and mark; O Signieur Dew *Hen. V.* iv 4 7
Give me thy hand, That I may dew it with my mournful tears 2 *Hen. VI.* iii 2 340
Tears virginal Shall be to me even as the dew to fire . . . . v 2 53
Never yet one hour in his bed Have I enjoy'd the golden dew of sleep *Richard III.* iv 1 84
A hand as fruitful as the land that feeds us; His dews fall every where *Hen. VIII.* i 3 57
You Have blown this coal betwixt my lord and me; Which God's dew quench! . . . . ii 4 80
The dews of heaven fall thick in blessings on her! . . . . iv 2 133
Being three parts melted away with rotten dews . . . *Coriolanus* ii 3 35
He water'd his new plants with dews of flattery, Seducing so my friends v 6 23
As fresh as morning dew distill'd on flowers . . . *T. Andron.* ii 3 201
With tears augmenting the fresh morning's dew . . *Rom. and Jul.* i 1 138
Now, ere the sun advance his burning eye, The day to cheer and night's dank dew to dry . . . . ii 3 6
When the sun sets, the air doth drizzle dew . . . . . iii 5 127
Thy canopy is dust and stones;—Which with sweet water nightly I will dew . . . . v 3 14
Fast asleep? It is no matter; Enjoy the honey-heavy dew of slumber *J. Cæsar* ii 1 230
Our day is gone; Clouds, dews, and dangers come; our deeds are done! v 3 64
To dew the sovereign flower and drown the weeds . . . *Macbeth* v 2 30
As stars with trains of fire and dews of blood, Disasters in the sun *Hamlet* i 1 117
The morn, in russet mantle clad, Walks o'er the dew of yon high eastward hill . . . . i 1 167
O, that this too too solid flesh would melt, Thaw and resolve itself into a dew! . . . . i 2 130
In the morn and liquid dew of youth . . . . i 3 41
Keep up your bright swords, for the dew will rust them . . *Othello* i 2 59
Whiles yet the dew's on ground, gather those flowers . . *Cymbeline* i 5 1
Herbs that have on them cold dew o' the night Are strewings fitt'st for graves . . . . iv 2 284
The benediction of these covering heavens Fall on their heads like dew! v 5 351

Dewberries. Feed him with apricocks and dewberries . *M. N. Dream* iii 1 169

Dewdrop. I must go seek some dewdrops here And hang a pearl in every cowslip's ear . . . . ii 1 14
Like a dew-drop from the lion's mane, Be shook to air . *Troi. and Cres.* iii 3 224

Dew-dropping. Turning his face to the dew-dropping south *R. and J.* i 4 103

Dewlap. Against her lips I bob And on her wither'd dewlap pour the ale *M. N. Dream* ii 1 50

Dew-lapped. Who would believe that there were mountaineers Dewlapp'd like bulls? . . . . *Tempest* iii 3 45
Crook-knee'd, and dew-lapp'd like Thessalian bulls . . *M. N. Dream* iv 1 126

Dewy. I would these dewy tears were from the ground . *Richard III.* v 3 284

Dexter. My mother's blood Runs on the dexter cheek . *Troi. and Cres.* iv 5 128

Dexteriously. Can you do it?—Dexteriously, good madonna . *T. Night* i 5 66

Dexterity. My admirable dexterity of wit . . . . *Mer. Wives* iv 5 121

Dexterity. You carried your guts away as nimbly, with as quick dexterity . . 1 *Hen. IV.* ii 4 286
Dexterity so obeying appetite That what he will he does *Troi. and Cres.* v 5 27
With one hand beats Cold death aside, and with the other sends It back to Tybalt, whose dexterity Retorts it . . *Rom. and Jul.* iii 1 168
O, most wicked speed, to post With such dexterity to incestuous sheets! *Hamlet* i 2 157
Di faciant laudis summa sit ista tuæ! . . . 3 *Hen. VI.* i 3 48
Diable. O diable, diable! vat is in my closet? Villain! larron! *M. Wives* i 4 70
Diable! Jack Rugby,—mine host de Jarteer . . iii 1 93
O diable!—O seigneur! le jour est perdu, tout est perdu! *Hen. V.* iv 5 1
Diablo, ho! The town will rise . . . *Othello* ii 3 161
Diadem. Levied an army, weening to redeem And have install'd me in the diadem . . 1 *Hen. VI.* ii 5 89
Nor wear the diadem upon his head, Whose church-like humours fits not for a crown . . 2 *Hen. VI.* i 1 246
What seest thou there? King Henry's diadem, Enchased with all the honours of the world? . . i 2 7
Kneel'd to me And on my head did set the diadem . i 2 40
A worthless king, Having neither subject, wealth, nor diadem iv 1 82
And will you pale your head in Henry's glory, And rob his temples of the diadem? . . 3 *Hen. VI.* i 4 104
This strong right hand of mine Can pluck the diadem from faint Henry's head . . ii 1 153
Perjured Henry! wilt thou kneel for grace, And set thy diadem upon my head? . . ii 2 82
'Tis my right, And Henry but usurps the diadem iv 7 66
I am his first-born son, that was the last That wore the imperial diadem of Rome . . *T. Andron.* i 1 6
A clout upon that head Where late the diadem stood *Hamlet* ii 2 530
That from a shelf the precious diadem stole, And put it in his pocket . iii 4 100
I found her trimming up the diadem On her dead mistress *Ant. and Cleo.* v 2 345
Dial. By this, I think, the dial points at five *Com. of Errors* v 1 118
And then he drew a dial from his poke . *As Y. Like It* ii 7 20
And I did laugh sans intermission An hour by his dial . ii 7 33
Then my dial goes not true . . *All's Well* ii 5 6
And dials the signs of leaping-houses . 1 *Hen. IV.* i 2 9
To carve out dials quaintly, point by point, Thereby to see the minutes how they run . . 3 *Hen. VI.* ii 5 24
The bawdy hand of the dial is now upon the prick of noon *Rom. and Jul.* ii 4 119
And lovers' absent hours, More tedious than the dial eight score times *Othello* iii 4 175
Dial's centre. As many lines close in the dial's centre . *Hen. V.* i 2 210
Dial's point. Whereto my finger, like a dial's point, Is pointing still *Richard II.* v 5 53
If life did ride upon a dial's point, Still ending at the arrival of an hour 1 *Hen. IV.* v 2 84
Dialect. In her youth There is a prone and speechless dialect, Such as move men . . *Meas. for Meas.* i 2 188
To go out of my dialect, which you discommend so much *Lear* ii 2 115
Dialogue. Fear you not my part of the dialogue . *Much Ado* iii 1 31
Will you hear the dialogue that the two learned men have compiled in praise of the owl and the cuckoo? . . *L. L. Lost* v 2 895
Shall we have this dialogue between the fool and the soldier? *All's Well* iv 3 112
'Tis not that time of moon with me to make one in so skipping a dialogue . . *T. Night* i 5 214
Saving in dialogue of compliment . . *K. John* i 1 201
Doth think it rich To hear the wooden dialogue and sound *Troi. and Cres.* i 3 155
How dost, fool?—Dost dialogue with thy shadow? *T. of Athens* ii 2 52
Diameter. Whose whisper o'er the world's diameter, As level as the cannon to his blank, Transports his poison'd shot . *Hamlet* iv 1 41
Diamond. I see how thine eye would emulate the diamond *Mer. Wives* iii 3 59
Give me the ring of mine you had at dinner, Or, for my diamond, the chain you promised . . *Com. of Errors* iv 3 70
Sir, I must have that diamond from you.—There, take it . v 1 391
A lady wall'd about with diamonds! . . *L. L. Lost* v 2 3
A diamond gone, cost me two thousand ducats! . *Mer. of Venice* iii 1 87
Set this diamond safe In golden palaces, as it becomes . 1 *Hen. VI.* v 3 169
A heart it was, bound in with diamonds . 2 *Hen. VI.* iii 2 107
Not deck'd with diamonds and Indian stones, Nor to be seen 3 *Hen. VI.* iii 1 63
One day he gives us diamonds, next day stones . *T. of Athens* iii 6 131
This diamond he greets your wife withal . *Macbeth* ii 1 15
Which parted thence, As pearls from diamonds dropp'd . *Lear* iv 3 24
This diamond was my mother's: take it, heart; But keep it till you woo another wife . . *Cymbeline* i 1 112
She went before others I have seen, as that diamond of yours outlustres many I have beheld . . i 4 78
I have not seen the most precious diamond that is, nor you the lady . i 4 81
I shall but lend my diamond till your return: let there be covenants drawn between's . . i 4 154
My ten thousand ducats are yours; so is your diamond too . i 4 163
It must be married To that your diamond . . ii 4 98
That diamond upon your finger, say How came it yours? . v 5 137
To me he seems like diamond to glass . *Pericles* ii 3 36
You shall like diamonds sit about his crown . ii 4 53
The diamonds of a most praised water Do appear, to make the world twice rich . . iii 2 102
Dian. You seem to me as Dian in her orb, As chaste as is the bud ere it be blown . . *Much Ado* iv 1 58
Dian's bud o'er Cupid's flower Hath such force and blessed power *M. N. Dream* iv 1 78
Did ever Dian so become a grove As Kate this chamber? *T. of Shrew* ii 1 260
O, be thou Dian, and let her be Kate; And then let Kate be chaste and Dian sportful! . . ii 1 262
Dian no queen of virgins, that would suffer her poor knight surprised *All's Well* i 3 119
Wish chastely and love dearly, that your Dian Was both herself and love . . i 3 218
Now, Dian, from thy altar do I fly, And to imperial Love, that god most high, Do my sighs stream . . ii 3 80
Dian, the count's a fool, and full of gold . iv 3 238
Say a soldier, Dian, told thee this, Men are to mell with, boys are not to kiss . . iv 3 256
Or modest Dian circled with her nymphs . 3 *Hen. VI.* iv 8 21
Chaste as the icicle That's curdied by the frost from purest snow And hangs on Dian's temple . *Coriolanus* v 3 67
Or is it Dian, habited like her, Who hath abandoned her holy groves? *T. Andron.* ii 3 57
Had I the power that some say Dian had, Thy temples should be planted presently With horns, as was Actæon's . . ii 3 61

Dian. She'll not be hit With Cupid's arrow; she hath Dian's wit *Rom. and Jul.* i 1 215
Whose blush doth thaw the consecrated snow That lies on Dian's lap! *T. of Athens* iv 3 387
Her name, that was as fresh As Dian's visage, is now begrimed and black As mine own face . . *Othello* iii 3 387
And the chimney-piece Chaste Dian bathing *Cymbeline* ii 4 82
My mother seem'd The Dian of that time: so doth my wife The non-pareil of this . . ii 5 7
He spake of her, as Dian had hot dreams, And she alone were cold . v 5 180
When She would with rich and constant pen Vail to her mistress Dian *Pericles* iv Gower 29
Celestial Dian, goddess argentine, I will obey thee . v 1 251
In no wise Till he had done his sacrifice, As Dian bade . v 2 278
Pure Dian, bless thee for thy vision! I Will offer night-oblations to thee . . v 3 69
Diana. On Diana's altar to protest For aye austerity and single life *M. N. Dream* i 1 89
If I live to be as old as Sibylla, I will die as chaste as Diana *Mer. of Ven.* i 2 117
Come, ho! and wake Diana with a hymn . . v 1 66
He hath bought a pair of cast lips of Diana . *As Y. Like It* iii 4 17
I will weep for nothing, like Diana in the fountain . iv 1 154
Well, Diana, take heed of this French earl *All's Well* iii 5 11
Beware of them, Diana; their promises, enticements, oaths, tokens iii 5 19
They told me that your name was Fontibell.—No, my good lord, Diana iv 2 2
That is an advertisement to a proper maid in Florence, one Diana . iv 3 241
Will you give me a copy of the sonnet you writ to Diana? . iv 3 355
You, Diana, Under my poor instructions yet must suffer Something in my behalf . . iv 4 26
Diana's lip Is not more smooth and rubious . *T. Night* i 4 31
Let us be Diana's foresters, gentlemen of the shade . 1 *Hen. IV.* i 2 29
By all Diana's waiting-women yond, And by herself, I will not tell you *Troi. and Cres.* v 2 91
Should he make me Live, like Diana's priest, betwixt cold sheets? *Cymb.* i 6 133
'Tis gold Which buys admittance; oft it doth; yea, and makes Diana's rangers false themselves . . ii 3 74
One twelve moons more she'll wear Diana's livery *Pericles* ii 5 10
O dear Diana, Where am I? Where's my lord? What world is this? . iii 2 105
By bright Diana, whom we honour . . iii 3 28
Diana's temple is not distant far, Where you may abide till your date expire . . iii 4 13
His woeful queen we leave at Ephesus, Unto Diana there a votaress iv Gower 4
Diana, aid my purpose!—What have we to do with Diana? . iv 2 161
If you have told Diana's altar true, This is your wife . v 3 17
Recover'd her, and placed her Here in Diana's temple . v 3 25
Diaper. Another bear the ewer, the third a diaper, And say 'Will't please your lordship cool your hands?' *T. of Shrew* Ind. 1 57
Dibble. I'll not put The dibble in earth to set one slip of them *W. Tale* iv 4 100
Dice. Keep a gamester from the dice, and a good student from his book *Mer. Wives* iii 1 38
He won it of me with false dice . *Much Ado* ii 1 290
Well run, dice! . . *L. L. Lost* v 2 233
When he plays at tables, chides the dice In honourable terms v 2 326
If Hercules and Lichas play at dice Which is the better man, the greater throw May turn by fortune from the weaker hand . *Mer. of Venice* ii 1 32
False As dice are to be wish'd by one that fixes No bourn 'twixt his and mine . . *W. Tale* i 2 133
The confident and over-lusty French Do the low-rated English play at dice . . *Hen. V.* iv Prol. 19
Be these the wretches that we play'd at dice for? . iv 5 8
Wine loved I deeply, dice dearly . *Lear* iii 4 93
He hath spoken true: the very dice obey him . *Ant. and Cleo.* ii 3 33
Diced not above seven times a week 1 *Hen. IV.* iii 3 18
Dicers' oaths. Makes marriage-vows As false as dicers' oaths . *Hamlet* iii 4 45
Dich. Much good dich thy good heart, Apemantus! *T. of Athens* i 2 73
Dick. Some trencher-knight, some Dick, That smiles his cheek in years *L. L. Lost* v 2 464
And Dick the shepherd blows his nail And Tom bears logs into the hall v 2 923
Sot, didst see Dick surgeon, sot?—O, he's drunk . *T. Night* v 1 202
Call them all by their christen names, as Tom, Dick, and Francis 1 *Hen. IV.* ii 4 9
And Dick the Butcher,— Then is sin struck down like an ox 2 *Hen. VI.* iv 2 27
Where's Dick, the butcher of Ashford? . iv 3 1
Thou perjured George, And thou mis-shapen Dick . 3 *Hen. VI.* v 5 35
Why in this woolvish toge should I stand here, To beg of Hob and Dick? *Coriolanus* ii 3 123
Dickens. I cannot tell what the dickens his name is *Mer. Wives* iii 2 19
Dickon. Jockey of Norfolk, be not too bold, For Dickon thy master is bought and sold *Richard III.* v 3 305
Dicky your boy, that with his grumbling voice Was wont to cheer his dad in mutinies . 3 *Hen. VI.* i 4 76
Dictator. Our then dictator, Whom with all praise I point at, saw him fight . *Coriolanus* ii 2 93
Diction. To make true diction of him, his semblable is his mirror *Hamlet* v 2 123
Dictynna, goodman Dull; Dictynna, goodman Dull *L. L. Lost* iv 2 37
What is Dictynna?—A title to Phœbe, to Luna, to the moon . iv 2 38
Did. What foul play had we, that we came from thence? Or blessed was't we did? . *Tempest* i 2 61
Sigh To the winds whose pity, sighing back again, Did us but loving wrong . . i 2 151
And did it to minister occasion to these gentlemen . ii 1 173
If it should thunder as it did before, I know not where to hide my head ii 2 23
To take a fault upon me that he did . *T. G. of Ver.* iv 4 16
Ask him what this man did to my wife . *Meas. for Meas.* ii 1 149
And did not she herself revile me there? *Com. of Errors* iv 4 75
Did not her kitchen-maid rail, taunt and scorn me?—Certes, she did . iv 4 78
Did not I in rage depart from thence?—In verity you did . iv 4 80
All Europa shall rejoice at thee, As once Europa did at lusty Jove *Much Ado* v 4 46
Is't not well done?—Excellently done, if God did all . *T. Night* i 5 254
After the last enchantment you did here . iii 1 123
Much more, and much more cause, Did they this Harry. *Hen. V.* v Prol. 35
Into as many gobbets will I cut it As wild Medea young Absyrtus did 2 *Hen. VI.* v 2 59
Suppose, my lords, he did it unconstrain'd 3 *Hen. VI.* i 1 143
Hadst thou but loved him half so well as I, Or felt that pain which I did for him once . . i 1 221
You saw The ceremony?—That I did *Hen. VIII.* iv 1 60
One of which fell with him, Unwilling to outlive the good that did it . iv 2 60
I am still possess'd Of those effects for which I did the murder *Hamlet* iii 3 54

Did. Has banish'd two on's daughters, and did the third a blessing *Lear* i 4 115
His wife that's dead did trespasses to Cæsar *Ant. and Cleo.* ii 1 40
When the best hint was given him, he not took 't, Or did it from his teeth iii 4 10
Or who was he That, otherwise than noble nature did, Hath alter'd that good picture? *Cymbeline* iv 2 364
Didest. That I shall live and tell him to his teeth, 'Thus didest thou' *Hamlet* iv 7 58
Dido. Not since widow Dido's time *Tempest* ii 1 76
How came that widow in? widow Dido! ii 1 78
'Widow Dido' said you? you make me study of that ii 1 81
Bate, I beseech you, widow Dido.—O, widow Dido! ay, widow Dido ii 1 100
In such a night Stood Dido with a willow in her hand *Mer. of Venice* v 1 10
And witch me, As Ascanius did When he to madding Dido would unfold His father's acts 2 *Hen. VI.* iii 2 117
After conflict such as was supposed The wandering prince and Dido once enjoy'd *T. Andron.* ii 3 22
To love-sick Dido's sad attending ear v 3 82
Dido a dowdy; Cleopatra a gipsy *Rom. and Jul.* ii 4 43
'Twas Æneas' tale to Dido; and thereabout of it especially, where he speaks of Priam's slaughter *Hamlet* ii 2 468
Dido and her Æneas shall want troops *Ant. and Cleo.* iv 14 53
Didst. Thou didst promise To bate me a full year *Tempest* i 2 249
Samson! I do excel thee in my rapier as much as thou didst me in carrying gates *L. L. Lost* i 2 79
'Tis very true: thou didst it excellent *T. of Shrew* Ind. 1 89
Die. The wills above be done! but I would fain die a dry death *Tempest* i 1 71
Thou let'st thy fortune sleep—die, rather; wink'st Whiles thou art waking ii 1 216
And sends me forth—For else his project dies—to keep them living ii 1 299
I shall no more to sea, to sea, Here shall I die ashore ii 2 45
Dare not offer What I desire to give, and much less take What I shall die to want iii 1 79
I am your wife, if you will marry me; If not, I'll die your maid iii 1 84
He that dies pays all debts iii 2 140
I'll die on him that says so but yourself *T. G. of Ver.* ii 4 114
To die is to be banish'd from myself; And Silvia is myself iii 1 171
Let him die: sheathe thy impatience *Mer. Wives* ii 3 88
Now let me die, for I have lived long enough: this is the period of my ambition iii 3 46
If you go out in your own semblance, you die, Sir John iv 2 68
If you find a man there, he shall die a flea's death iv 2 158
They are fairies; he that speaks to them shall die v 5 51
A thirsty evil; and when we drink we die *Meas. for Meas.* i 2 134
Sir, he must die.—Be it as your wisdom will ii 1 31
All sects, all ages smack of this vice; and he To die for 't ii 2 7
Is it your will Claudio shall die to-morrow?—Did not I tell thee yea? ii 2 8
Well; the matter?—I have a brother is condemn'd to die ii 2 34
Must he needs die?—Maiden, no remedy ii 2 48
He must die to-morrow.—To-morrow! O, that's sudden! Spare him, spare him! He's not prepared for death ii 2 82
Be satisfied; Your brother dies to-morrow; be content ii 2 105
A young man More fit to do another such offence Than die for this ii 3 15
When must he die?—As I do think, to-morrow ii 3 16
Must die to-morrow! O injurious love, That respites me a life! ii 3 40
Yet may he live awhile; and, it may be, As long as you or I: yet he must die ii 4 36
I'll speak more gross: Your brother is to die ii 4 83
Then must your brother die.—And 'twere the cheaper way ii 4 104
Better it were a brother died at once, Than that a sister, by redeeming him, Should die for ever ii 4 108
Else let my brother die, If not a feodary, but only he Owe and succeed thy weakness ii 4 121
My brother did love Juliet, And you tell me that he shall die for it ii 4 143
Then, Isabel, live chaste, and, brother, die: More than our brother is our chastity ii 4 184
I've hope to live, and am prepared to die iii 1 4
I humbly thank you. To sue to live, I find I seek to die iii 1 42
Darest thou die? The sense of death is most in apprehension iii 1 77
In corporal sufferance finds a pang as great As when a giant dies iii 1 81
If I must die, I will encounter darkness as a bride, And hug it in mine arms iii 1 83
Yes, thou must die: Thou art too noble to conserve a life In base appliances iii 1 87
Ay, but to die, and go we know not where; To lie in cold obstruction iii 1 118
Take my defiance! Die, perish! iii 1 144
To-morrow you must die; go to your knees and make ready iii 1 171
I had rather my brother die by the law than my son should be unlawfully born iii 1 195
Canst thou tell if Claudio die to-morrow or no?—Why should he die, sir? iii 2 180
Claudio must die to-morrow: let him be furnished with divines iii 2 220
Which I by my good leisure have discredited to him, and now is he resolved to die iii 2 262
To-morrow morning are to die Claudio and Barnardine iv 2 8
Have you no countermand for Claudio yet, But he must die to-morrow? iv 2 96
I will not consent to die this day, that's certain iv 3 59
I swear I will not die to-day for any man's persuasion iv 3 62
Unfit to live or die: O gravel heart! After him, fellows iv 3 68
Persuade this rude wretch willingly to die iv 3 85
O Isabel, will you not lend a knee?—He dies for Claudio's death v 1 448
A due sincerity govern'd his deeds, Till he did look on me: since it is so, Let him not die v 1 453
He dies, His goods confiscate to the duke's dispose *Com. of Errors* i 1 20
Therefore by law thou art condemn'd to die i 1 26
Make up the sum, And live; if no, then thou art doom'd to die i 1 155
According to the statute of the town Dies ere the weary sun set in the west i 2 7
I'll weep what's left away, and weeping die ii 1 115
He gains by death that hath such means to die iii 2 51
If any friend will pay the sum for him, He shall not die v 1 132
Is it possible disdain should die while she hath such meet food to feed it? *Much Ado* i 1 121
I will die in it at the stake i 1 235
I shall see thee, ere I die, look pale with love i 1 249
She says she will die, if he love her not, and she will die, ere she make her love known, and she will die, if he woo her ii 3 181
They say too that she will rather die than give any sign of affection ii 3 235
When I said I would die a bachelor, I did not think I should live till I were married ii 3 252
A better death than die with mocks, Which is as bad as die with tickling iii 1 79

Die. Yes, and his ill conditions; and, in despite of all, dies for him *Much Ado* iii 2 69
Did I think thou wouldst not quickly die iv 1 126
Hence from her! let her die.—Hear me a little iv 1 156
Come, lady, die to live: this wedding-day Perhaps is but prolong'd iv 1 255
I cannot be a man with wishing, therefore I will die a woman with grieving iv 1 326
And so dies my revenge v 1 301
If a man do not erect in this age his own tomb ere he dies v 2 80
I will live in thy heart, die in thy lap and be buried in thy eyes v 2 104
Death, in guerdon of her wrongs, Gives her fame which never dies v 3 6
To love, to wealth, to pomp, I pine and die *L. L. Lost* i 1 31
Are pick-purses in love, and we deserve to die iv 3 209
Let me not die your debtor, My red dominical, my golden letter v 2 43
Then die a calf, before your horns do grow.—One word in private with you, ere I die v 2 253
And consciences, that will not die in debt v 2 333
Adding thereto moreover That he would wed me, or else die my lover v 2 447
Die when you will, a smock shall be your shroud v 2 479
And the contents Dies in the zeal of that which it presents v 2 519
Dost thou infamonize me among potentates? thou shalt die v 2 685
Grows, lives and dies in single blessedness *M. N. Dream* i 1 78
So will I grow, so live, so die, my lord, Ere I will yield my virgin patent up i 1 79
Prepare to die For disobedience to your father's will i 1 86
But she, being mortal, of that boy did die ii 1 135
I'll follow thee and make a heaven of hell, To die upon the hand I love so well ii 1 244
Thus die I, thus, thus, thus. Now am I dead v 1 305
Moon, take thy flight: Now die, die, die, die, die.—No die, but an ace, for him v 1 311
If I live to be as old as Sibylla, I will die as chaste as Diana *Mer. of Ven.* i 2 117
Miss that which one unworthier may attain, And die with grieving ii 1 38
If you tickle us, do we not laugh? if you poison us, do we not die iii 1 69
And fancy dies In the cradle where it lies iii 2 68
That he do record a gift, Here in the court, of all he dies possess'd iv 1 389
I'll die for 't but some woman had the ring v 1 208
A special deed of gift, After his death, of all he dies possess'd of v 1 293
And, truly, when he dies, thou shalt be his heir *As Y. Like It* i 2 20
Upon mine honour, And in the greatness of my word, you die i 3 91
Yet fortune cannot recompense me better Than to die well ii 3 76
Dear master, I can go no further: O, I die for food! ii 6 2
If I bring thee not something to eat, I will give thee leave to die ii 6 12
Thou shalt not die for lack of a dinner ii 6 17
He dies that touches any of this fruit Till I and my affairs are answered ii 7 98
An you will not be answered with reason, I must die ii 7 101
I almost die for food; and let me have it.—Sit down and feed ii 7 104
And I to live and die her slave iii 2 162
Will you sterner be Than he that dies and lives by bloody drops? iii 5 7
Then in mine own person I die.—No, faith, die by attorney iv 1 93
Yet he did what he could to die before iv 1 99
Or else by him my love deny, And then I'll study how to die iv 3 63
And here live and die a shepherd v 2 14
That will I, should I die the hour after v 4 12
And if I die to-morrow, this is hers *T. of Shrew* ii 1 363
If you should die before him, where's her dower? ii 1 391
He is old, I young.—And may not young men die, as well as old? ii 1 393
'D sol re,' one clef, two notes have I: 'E la mi,' show pity, or I die iii 1 78
Went they not quickly, I should die with laughing iii 2 243
With many things of worthy memory, which now shall die in oblivion iv 1 85
The hind that would be mated by the lion Must die for love *All's Well* i 1 103
I will stand for 't a little, though therefore I die a virgin i 1 146
And so dies with feeding his own stomach i 1 155
And I His servant live, and will his vassal die i 3 165
But riddle-like lives sweetly where she dies i 3 223
Health shall live free and sickness freely die ii 1 171
Thy physic I will try, That ministers thine own death if I die ii 1 189
Unpitied let me die, And well deserved ii 1 191
Marry that will, I live and die a maid iv 2 74
Not that I am afraid to die; but that, my offences being many, I would repent out the remainder of nature iv 3 271
There is no remedy, sir, but you must die iv 3 338
Therefore you must die. Come, headsman, off with his head iv 3 342
It rejoices me, that I hope I shall see him ere I die iv 5 90
That, surfeiting, The appetite may sicken, and so die *T. Night* i 1 3
But I will never die.—Sir Toby, there you lie ii 3 115
Alas, that they are so; To die, even when they to perfection grow! ii 4 42
I, most jocund, apt and willingly, To do you rest, a thousand deaths would die v 1 136
Would they else be content to die? *W. Tale* i 1 46
Tell me what blessings I have here alive, That I should fear to die? iii 2 109
Pale primroses, That die unmarried iv 4 123
To die upon the bed my father died, To lie close by his honest bones iv 4 466
If I might die within this hour, I have lived To die when I desire iv 4 472
Do not shun her Until you see her die again v 3 106
Rescue those breathing lives to die in beds *K. John* ii 1 419
Teach thou this sorrow how to make me die iii 1 30
As doth the fury of two desperate men Which in the very meeting fall and die iii 1 33
Thou shalt not shake them off, But in despair die under their black weight iii 1 297
There where my fortune lives, there my life dies iii 1 338
O, this will make my mother die with grief! iii 3 5
And so he'll die; and, rising so again, When I shall meet him in the court of heaven I shall not know him iii 4 86
If that young Arthur be not gone already, Even at that news he dies iii 4 164
As good to die and go, as die and stay iv 3 8
Since it is true That I must die here and live hence by truth v 4 29
In that I live and for that will I die *Richard II.* i 1 185
Thou seest thy wretched brother die, Who was the model of thy father's life i 2 27
Desolate, desolate, will I hence and die: The last leave of thee takes my weeping eye i 2 73
However God or fortune cast my lot, There lives or dies i 3 86
I die pronouncing it, Like to a tenement or pelting farm ii 1 59
No, no, men living flatter those that die ii 1 89
Live in thy shame, but die not shame with thee! ii 1 135
Let them die that age and sullens have ii 1 139
And fight and die is death destroying death iii 2 184
Send Defiance to the traitor, and so die iii 3 130

Die. Give Richard leave to live till Richard die *Richard II.* iii 3 174
Mine honour lives when his dishonour dies v 3 70
And, for they cannot, die in their own pride v 5 22
Thy seat is up on high; Whilst my gross flesh sinks downward, here to die v 5 113
So as thou livest in peace, die free from strife v 6 27
With all the rest retold, May reasonably die and never rise *1 Hen. IV.* i 3 74
I doubt not but to die a fair death for all this ii 2 14
Go thy ways, old Jack; die when thou wilt ii 4 141
I will die a hundred thousand deaths Ere break the smallest parcel of this vow iii 2 158
A hundred thousand rebels die in this iii 2 160
Let us take a muster speedily: Doomsday is near; die all, die merrily iv 1 134
If die, brave death, when princes die with us! v 2 87
I am no counterfeit: to die, is to be a counterfeit v 4 116
Now let not Nature's hand Keep the wild flood confined! let order die! *2 Hen. IV.* i 1 154
They that, when Richard lived, would have him die, Are now become enamour'd on his grave i 3 101
Though that be rich, it dies not ii 2 114
Die men like dogs! give crowns like pins! ii 4 188
Would shut the book, and sit him down and die iii 1 56
Death, as the Psalmist saith, is certain to all; all shall die iii 2 42
By my troth, I care not; a man can die but once: we owe God a death iii 2 250
Let it go which way it will, he that dies this year is quit for the next iii 2 254
Thy life did manifest thou lovedst me not, And thou wilt have me die assured of it iv 5 106
If I do feign, O, let me in my present wildness die! iv 5 153
It hath been prophesied to me many years, I should not die but in Jerusalem iv 5 238
I hope to see London once ere I die v 3 64
Under which king, Bezonian? speak, or die v 3 119
I would to God that I might die, that I might have thee hanged v 4 2
A colour that I fear you will die in, Sir John v 5 92
For any thing I know, Falstaff shall die of a sweat Epil. 31
But that his wildness, mortified in him, Seem'd to die *Hen. V.* i 1 27
When the man dies, let the inheritance Descend unto the daughter i 2 99
And by their hands this grace of kings must die ii Prol. 28
Knocks go and come; God's vassals drop and die iii 2 8
Die and be damn'd! and figo for thy friendship! iii 6 60
Methinks I could not die any where so contented as in the king's company iv 1 132
I am afeard there are few die well that die in a battle iv 1 148
If these men do not die well, it will be a black matter for the king that led them iv 1 151
Assailed by robbers and die in many irreconciled iniquities iv 1 160
If they die unprovided, no more is the king guilty of their damnation iv 1 183
'Tis certain, every man that dies ill, the ill upon his own head iv 1 197
If we are mark'd to die, we are enow To do our country loss iv 3 20
We would not die in that man's company That fears his fellowship to die with us iv 3 38
Shame and eternal shame, nothing but shame! Let us die in honour iv 5 11
Base Trojan, thou shalt die.—You say very true v 1 32
Her vine, the merry cheerer of the heart, Unpruned dies v 2 42
If not, to say to thee that I shall die, is true; but for thy love, by the Lord, no v 2 158
Thou shalt not die whiles—He beckons with his hand and smiles on me *1 Hen. VI.* i 4 91
O, would I were to die with Salisbury! i 5 38
My father was attached, not attainted, Condemn'd to die for treason ii 4 97
Here dies the dusky torch of Mortimer, Choked with ambition ii 5 122
Either to get the town again or die iii 2 79
Kings and mightiest potentates must die, For that's the end of human misery iii 2 136
Mad ire and wrathful fury makes me weep, That thus we die iv 3 29
He dies, we lose; I break my warlike word iv 3 31
York set him on to fight and die in shame iv 4 8
But dies, betray'd to fortune by your strife iv 4 39
If we both stay, we both are sure to die iv 5 20
Then both fly.—And leave my followers here to fight and die? iv 5 45
Stay, go, do what you will, the like do I; For live I will not, if my father die iv 5 51
Come, side by side together live and die iv 5 54
If I to-day die not with Frenchmen's rage, To-morrow I shall die with mickle age iv 6 34
In thee thy mother dies, our household's name iv 6 38
Before young Talbot from old Talbot fly, The coward horse that bears me fall and die! iv 6 47
Talk no more of flight, it is no boot; If son to Talbot, die at Talbot's foot iv 6 53
If thou wilt fight, fight by thy father's side; And, commendable proved, let's die in pride iv 6 57
Ah, Joan, sweet daughter Joan, I'll die with thee! v 4 6
Alençon! that notorious Machiavel! It dies, an if it had a thousand lives v 4 75
And shall these labours and these honours die? *2 Hen. VI.* i 1 95
Shall Henry's conquest, Bedford's vigilance, Your deeds of war and all our counsel die? i 1 97
But him outlive, and die a violent death i 4 34
By water shall he die, and take his end i 4 36
Thus Eleanor's pride dies in her youngest days ii 3 46
Here, Robin, an if I die, I give thee my apron ii 3 74
That he should die is worthy policy; But yet we want a colour for his death iii 1 235
So that, by this, you would not have him die iii 1 243
Let him die, in that he is a fox, By nature proved an enemy to the flock iii 1 257
Loather a hundred times to part than die iii 2 355
In thy sight to die, what were it else But like a pleasant slumber in thy lap? iii 2 389
To die by thee were but to die in jest; From thee to die were torture more than death iii 2 400
Died he not in his bed? where should he die? Can I make men live, whether they will or no? iii 3 9
He dies, and makes no sign. O God, forgive him! iii 3 29
Cut both the villains' throats; for die you shall iv 1 20
I lost mine eye in laying the prize aboard, And therefore to revenge it, shalt thou die iv 1 26
A cunning man did calculate my birth And told me that by water I should die iv 1 35
It is impossible that I should die By such a lowly vassal as thyself iv 1 110

Die. Great men oft die by vile bezonians *2 Hen. VI.* iv 1 134
And Suffolk dies by pirates iv 1 138
Unless I find him guilty, he shall not die iv 2 104
The king is merciful, if you revolt.—But angry, wrathful, and inclined to blood, If you go forward; therefore yield, or die iv 2 135
No, my love, I should not mourn, but die for thee iv 4 25
He shall die, an it be but for pleading so well for his life iv 7 112
Die, damned wretch, the curse of her that bare thee iv 10 83
Any thing I have Is his to use, so Somerset may die v 1 53
And, in thy reverence and thy chair-days, thus To die in ruffian battle v 2 49
We'll all assist you: he that flies shall die *3 Hen. VI.* i 1 30
And die in bands for this unmanly deed! i 1 186
Richard, enough; I will be king, or die i 2 35
He shall die.—And I, my lord, will bear him company i 3 5
Hear me speak before I die. I am too mean a subject for thy wrath i 3 18
And when I give occasion of offence, Then let me die i 3 45
No cause! Thy father slew my father; therefore, die i 3 47
I'll venge thy death, Or die renowned by attempting it ii 1 88
Here burns my candle out; ay, here it dies ii 6 1
Let us fly while we may fly: If Warwick take us we are sure to die iv 4 35
So, lie thou there: die thou, and die our fear v 2 1
Live we how we can, yet die we must v 2 28
Die, prophet, in thy speech: For this, amongst the rest, was I ordain'd v 6 57
He cannot live, I hope; and must not die *Richard III.* i 1 145
Would they were basilisks, to strike thee dead!—I would they were, that I might die at once i 2 152
If not by war, by surfeit die your king, As ours by murder! i 3 197
Die in his youth by like untimely violence! i 3 201
Long die thy happy days before thy death! i 3 207
And, after many lengthen'd hours of grief, Die neither mother, wife, nor England's queen! i 3 209
'Zounds, he dies: I had forgot the reward i 4 128
I shall be reconciled to him again.—Never, my lord; therefore prepare to die i 4 185
Make peace with God, for you must die, my lord i 4 256
If you will live, lament; if die, be brief ii 2 43
Make me die a good old man! That is the butt-end of a mother's blessing ii 2 109
End thy damned spleen; Or let me die, to look on death no more! ii 4 65
I'll win our ancient right in France again, Or die a soldier, as I lived a king iii 1 93
The kindred of the queen must die at Pomfret iii 2 50
'Tis a vile thing to die, my gracious lord, When men are unprepared iii 2 64
To-day shalt thou behold a subject die For truth, for duty, and for loyalty iii 3 3
Yet had not we determined he should die, Until your lordship came to see his death iii 5 52
And make me die the thrall of Margaret's curse iv 1 46
And die, ere men can say, God save the queen! iv 1 63
Rumour it abroad That Anne, my wife, is sick and like to die iv 2 52
I say again, give out That Anne my wife is sick and like to die iv 2 58
Thou wilt die, by God's just ordinance, Ere from this war thou turn a conqueror iv 4 183
And must she die for this? O, let her live, And I'll corrupt her manners iv 4 205
Think, how thou stab'dst me in my prime of youth At Tewksbury: despair, therefore, and die! v 3 120
With guilty fear, Let fall thy lance: despair, and die! v 3 143
Think on Buckingham, And die in terror of thy guiltiness! v 3 170
There is no creature loves me; And if I die, no soul shall pity me v 3 201
After the battle let George Stanley die v 3 346
I have set my life upon a cast, And I will stand the hazard of the die v 4 10
If the king Should without issue die, he'll carry it so To make the sceptre his *Hen. VIII.* i 2 134
I have this day received a traitor's judgement, And by that name must die ii 1 59
Killing care and grief of heart Fall asleep, or hearing, die iii 1 14
But as when The bird of wonder dies, the maiden phœnix, Her ashes new create another heir v 5 41
But she must die, She must, the saints must have her v 5 60
I could live and die i' the eyes of Troilus *Troi. and Cres.* i 2 264
And at this sport Sir Valour dies; cries 'O, enough!' i 3 176
These lovers cry Oh! oh! they die! iii 1 131
Do one pluck down another and together Die in the fall iii 3 87
Let him die, With every joint a wound, and that to-morrow! iv 1 28
Some say the Genius so Cries 'come' to him that instantly must die iv 4 53
O heavens! you love me not.—Die I a villain then! iv 4 85
They fly or die, like scaled sculls Before the belching whale v 5 22
It is decreed Hector the great must die v 7 8
You are all resolved rather to die than to famish?—Resolved, resolved *Coriolanus* i 1 4
I had rather had eleven die nobly for their country than one voluptuously surfeit out of action i 3 26
Let the first budger die the other's slave, And the gods doom him after! i 8 5
Death, that dark spirit, in's nervy arm doth lie; Which, being advanced, declines, and then men die ii 1 178
Better it is to die, better to starve, Than crave the hire which first we do deserve ii 3 120
Bear him to the rock.—No, I'll die here iii 1 223
Therefore it is decreed He dies to-night iii 1 290
He that hath a will to die by himself fears it not from another v 2 111
So we will home to Rome, And die among our neighbours v 3 173
Therefore shall he die, And I'll renew me in his fall v 6 48
Let him die for't.—Tear him to pieces. Do it presently v 6 120
And die he must, To appease their groaning shadows that are gone *T. Andron.* i 1 125
I do not flatter thee, But honour thee, and will do till I die i 1 213
And cheer the heart That dies in tempest of thy angry frown i 1 458
This day all quarrels die, Andronicus i 1 465
As any mortal body hearing it Should straight fall mad, or else die suddenly ii 3 104
Agree whose hand shall go along, For fear they die before their pardon come iii 1 176
Now, farewell, flattery: die, Andronicus iii 1 254
And see their blood, or die with this reproach iv 1 94
It shall not live.—It shall not die.—Aaron, it must iv 2 81
He dies upon my scimitar's sharp point That touches this my first-born son! iv 2 91
Let not your sorrow die, though I am dead v 1 140
He must not die So sweet a death as hanging presently v 1 145
Die, die, Lavinia, and thy shame with thee; And, with thy shame, thy father's sorrow die! v 3 46

Die. Die, frantic wretch, for this accursed deed! . . . *T. Andron.* v 3 64
If any one relieves or pities him, For the offence he dies . . . v 3 182
Only poor, That when she dies with beauty dies her store *Rom. and Jul.* i 1 222
I'll pay that doctrine, or else die in debt . . . . . . i 1 244
Take thou some new infection to thy eye, And the rank poison of the old will die . . . . i 2 51
And these, who often drown'd could never die, Transparent heretics, be burnt for liars! . . . . i 2 95
That fair for which love groan'd for and would die . . ii Prol. 3
These violent delights have violent ends And in their triumph die ii 6 10
This is the truth, or let Benvolio die . . . . iii 1 180
When he shall die, Take him and cut him out in little stars . iii 2 21
He made you for a highway to my bed; But I, a maid, die maiden-widowed iii 2 135
Take heed, take heed, for such die miserable . . . . iii 3 145
Well, we were born to die . . . . iii 4 4
I must be gone and live, or stay and die . . . . . iii 5 11
Hang, beg, starve, die in the streets, For, by my soul, I'll ne'er acknowledge thee . . . . iii 5 194
If all else fail, myself have power to die . . . . . iii 5 242
I long to die, If what thou speak'st speak not of remedy . . . iv 1 66
And there die strangled ere my Romeo comes . . . . . iv 3 35
O me! My child, my only life, Revive, look up, or I will die with thee! iv 5 20
I will die, And leave him all; life, living, all is Death's . . . . iv 5 39
She's best married that dies married young . . . . . iv 5 78
Art thou so bare and full of wretchedness, And fear'st to die? . v 1 69
I do apprehend thee: Obey, and go with me; for thou must die . v 3 57
Thus with a kiss I die . . . . v 3 120
I will kiss thy lips; Haply some poison yet doth hang on them, To make me die with a restorative . . . . v 3 166
O happy dagger! This is thy sheath; there rust, and let me die . v 3 170
And therewithal Came to this vault to die, and lie with Juliet . v 3 290
A deed thou'lt die for.—Right, if doing nothing be death *T. of Athens* i 1 194
Who dies, that bears not one spurn to their graves Of their friends' gift? i 2 146
There will little learning die then, that day thou art hanged . . ii 2 86
Thou wast born a bastard, and thou't die a bawd . . . . ii 2 89
The fault's Bloody; 'tis necessary he should die . . . . iii 5 2
He dies.—Hard fate! he might have died in war . . . . iii 5 75
We are for law: he dies; urge it no more, On height of our displeasure iii 5 86
Thou shouldst desire to die, being miserable.—Not by his breath that is more miserable . . . . iv 3 248
Live, and love thy misery.—Long live so, and so die . . . iv 3 397
And by the hazard of the spotted die Let die the spotted . . . v 4 34
If he love Cæsar, all that he can do Is to himself, take thought and die for Cæsar . . . . *J. Cæsar* ii 1 187
There is no fear in him; let him not die; For he will live, and laugh at this hereafter . . . . ii 1 190
When beggars die, there are no comets seen . . . . . ii 2 30
Cowards die many times before their deaths; The valiant never taste of death but once . . . . ii 2 32
That we shall die, we know; 'tis but the time And drawing days out, that men stand upon . . . . iii 1 99
Live a thousand years, I shall not find myself so apt to die . . iii 1 160
Had you rather Cæsar were living and die all slaves, than that Cæsar were dead, to live all free men? . . . . iii 2 24
We'll hear him, we'll follow him, we'll die with him . . . iii 2 213
These many, then, shall die; their names are prick'd . . . iv 1 1
Your brother too must die; consent you? . . . . . . iv 1 2
And took his voice who should be prick'd to die, In our black sentence iv 1 16
We must die, Messala: With meditating that she must die once, I have the patience to endure it now . . . . iv 3 190
Cæsar, thou canst not die by traitors' hands, Unless thou bring'st them with thee . . . . v 1 56
If thou wert the noblest of thy strain, Young man, thou couldst not die more honourable . . . . v 1 60
Yield, or thou diest.—Only I yield to die . . . . . . v 4 12
But I have spoke With one that saw him die . . . *Macbeth* i 4 4
That death and nature do contend about them, Whether they live or die ii 2 8
The time has been, That, when the brains were out, the man would die . iii 4 79
Blow, wind! come, wrack! At least we'll die with harness on our back v 5 52
Why should I play the Roman fool, and die On mine own sword? . v 8 1
All that lives must die, Passing through nature to eternity . *Hamlet* i 2 72
To die: to sleep; No more; and by a sleep to say we end The heart-ache iii 1 60
To die, to sleep; To sleep: perchance to dream: ay, there's the rub iii 1 65
O heavens! die two months ago, and not forgotten yet? . . . iii 2 139
No second husband wed; But die thy thoughts when thy first lord is dead iii 2 225
The cease of majesty Dies not alone . . . . iii 3 16
That inward breaks, and shows no cause without Why the man dies . iv 4 29
For goodness, growing to a plurisy, Dies in his own too much . . iv 7 119
I' faith, if he be not rotten before he die . . . . . . v 1 181
O, I die, Horatio; The potent poison quite o'er-crows my spirit . v 2 363
Keep peace, upon your lives: He dies that strikes again . . *Lear* ii 2 53
Though I die for it, as no less is threatened me, the king my old master must be relieved . . . . iii 3 18
What are you, sir?—Away, and let me die . . . . . . iv 6 48
Henceforth I'll bear Affliction till it do cry out itself 'Enough, enough,' and die . . . . iv 6 77
What was thy cause? Adultery? Thou shalt not die: die for adultery! No . . . . iv 6 113
I will die bravely, like a bridegroom . . . . iv 6 202
Let not my worser spirit tempt me again To die before you please! . iv 6 223
Do you know me?—You are a spirit, I know: when did you die? . . iv 7 49
I should e'en die with pity, To see another thus . . . . iv 7 53
O, our lives' sweetness! That we the pain of death would hourly die Rather than die at once! . . . . v 3 185
Then have we a prescription to die when death is our physician *Othello* i 3 310
If it were now to die, 'Twere now to be most happy . . . . ii 1 191
He that stirs next to carve for his own rage Holds his soul light; he dies upon his motion . . . . ii 3 174
Thy solicitor shall rather die Than give thy cause away . . . iii 3 27
If I do die before thee, prithee, shroud me In one of those same sheets . iv 3 24
'Tis but a man gone. Forth, my sword: he dies . . . . . v 1 10
There stand I in much peril: No, he must die . . . . . v 1 22
Yet she must die, else she'll betray more men . . . . . v 2 6
Thou art on thy death-bed.—Ay, but not yet to die.—Yes, presently . v 2 52
Thou art to die.—Then Lord have mercy on me! . . . . . v 2 56
A guiltless death I die.—O, who hath done this deed?—Nobody; I myself . . . . v 2 122
Hark, canst thou hear me? I will play the swan, And die in music . v 2 248
So come my soul to bliss, as I speak true; So speaking as I think, I die, I die . . . . v 2 251

Die. I'ld have thee live; For, in my sense, 'tis happiness to die *Othello* v 2 290
I kiss'd thee ere I kill'd thee: no way but this; Killing myself, to die upon a kiss . . . . v 2 359
And let her die too, and give him a worse! . . . *Ant. and Cleo.* i 2 67
Under a compelling occasion, let women die . . . . . . i 2 142
Cleopatra, catching but the least noise of this, dies instantly; I have seen her die twenty times upon far poorer moment . . . . i 2 145
Can Fulvia die?—She's dead, my queen . . . . i 3 58
It is reported thou didst eat strange flesh, Which some did die to look on i 4 68
There would he anchor his aspect and die With looking on his life . i 5 33
Who's born that day When I forget to send to Antony, Shall die a beggar i 5 65
What shall we do, Enobarbus?—Think, and die . . . . . iii 13 1
Let the old ruffian know I have many other ways to die . . . iv 1 5
I will go seek Some ditch wherein to die; the foul'st best fits My latter part of life . . . . iv 6 38
The witch shall die: To the young Roman boy she hath sold me, and I fall Under this plot; she dies for't . . . . iv 12 47
Come, then; and, Eros, Thy master dies thy scholar . . . . iv 14 102
Welcome, welcome! die where thou hast lived: Quicken with kissing . iv 15 38
Do now not basely die, Not cowardly put off my helmet to My countryman . . . . iv 15 55
Noblest of men, woo't die? Hast thou no care of me? . . . . iv 15 59
I will speak what you shall please, If you'll employ me to him.—Say, I would die . . . . v 2 70
Those that do die of it do seldom or never recover . . . . . v 2 247
She hath pursued conclusions infinite Of easy ways to die . . . v 2 359
Let her languish A drop of blood a day; and, being aged, Die of this folly! . . . . *Cymbeline* i 1 158
Let it die as it was born, and, I pray you, be better acquainted . . i 4 131
I must die much your debtor . . . . ii 4 8
Dies i' the search, And hath as oft a slanderous epitaph As record of fair act . . . . iii 3 51
I must die; And if I do not by thy hand, thou art No servant of thy master's . . . . iii 4 76
The sweat of industry would dry and die, But for the end it works to . iii 6 31
So sick I am not, yet I am not well; But not so citizen a wanton as To seem to die ere sick . . . . iv 2 9
I'll rob none but myself; and let me die, Stealing so poorly . . iv 2 15
The bier at door, And a demand who is't shall die, I'ld say 'My father, not this youth' . . . . iv 2 23
What thing is it that I never Did see man die! . . . . . iv 4 36
If in your country wars you chance to die, That is my bed too, lads . iv 4 51
So I'll die For thee, O Imogen, even for whom my life Is every breath a death . . . . v 1 25
And cowards living To die with lengthen'd shame . . . . . v 3 13
Our Britain's harts die flying, not our men . . . . . . v 3 24
Those that would die or ere resist are grown The mortal bugs o' the field v 3 50
I am merrier to die than thou art to live . . . . . . v 4 175
There be some of them too that die against their wills; so should I . v 4 210
Briefly die their joys That place them on the truth of girls and boys v 5 106
I had rather thou shouldst live while nature will Than die ere I hear more . . . . v 5 152
Hang there like fruit, my soul, Till the tree die! . . . . . v 5 264
In that he spake too far.—And thou shalt die for't.—We will die all three . . . . v 5 310
So for her many a wight did die, As yon grim looks do testify *Pericles* i Gower 39
To taste the fruit of yon celestial tree, Or die in the adventure . . i 1 22
Because thine eye Presumes to reach, all thy whole heap must die . i 1 33
The earth is throng'd By man's oppression; and the poor worm doth die for't . . . . i 1 102
Instantly this prince must die; For by his fall my honour must keep high . . . . i 1 148
So sharp are hunger's teeth, that man and wife Draw lots who first shall die . . . . i 4 46
Pray see me buried.—Die quoth-a? Now gods forbid! . . . ii 1 82
Here is a thing too young for such a place, Who, if it had conceit, would die, as I Am like to do . . . . iii 1 16
The more my fault To 'scape his hands where I was like to die . . iv 2 80
A curse upon him, die he like a thief, That robs thee of thy goodness! . iv 6 121
The gods preserve you!—And you, sir, to outlive the age I am, And die as I would do . . . . v 1 16
What means the nun? she dies! help, gentlemen! . . . . . v 3 15
Die and drab. With die and drab I purchased this caparison . *W. Tale* iv 3 27
Die the death. He must not only die the death, But thy unkindness shall his death draw out To lingering sufferance . *Meas. for Meas.* ii 4 165
Either to die the death or to abjure For ever the society of men *M. N. Dr.* i 1 65
She hath betray'd me and shall die the death . . *Ant. and Cleo.* iv 14 26
Die the death: When I have slain thee with my proper hand, I'll follow those that even now fled hence . . . . . . *Cymbeline* iv 2 96
Died. A dozen years; within which space she died And left thee *Tempest* i 2 279
I have heard thee say No grief did ever come so near thy heart As when thy lady and thy true love died . . . . . . *T. G. of Ver.* iv 3 20
A man of fourscore pound a year; whose father died at Hallowmas *Meas. for Meas.* ii 1 128
Who is it that hath died for this offence? There's many have committed it . . . . ii 2 88
Better it were a brother died at once, Than that a sister, by redeeming him, Should die for ever . . . . ii 4 106
There died this morning of a cruel fever One Ragozine . . . iv 3 74
My brother had but justice, In that he did the thing for which he died v 1 454
One in the prison, That should by private order else have died, I have reserved alive . . . . v 1 471
This is another prisoner that I saved, Who should have died . . . v 1 493
When he shall hear she died upon his words . . . *Much Ado* iv 1 225
In this very manner refused, and upon the grief of this suddenly died . iv 2 66
Possess the people in Messina here How innocent she died . . . v 1 291
So the life that died with shame Lives in death with glorious fame . v 3 7
One Hero died defiled, but I do live, And surely as I live, I am a maid . v 4 63
She died, my lord, but whiles her slander lived . . . . . v 4 66
He made her melancholy, sad, and heavy; And so she died . *L. L. Lost* v 2 15
She might ha' been a grandam ere she died: And so may you . . v 2 17
And Thisby, tarrying in mulberry shade, His dagger drew, and died *M. N. Dream* v 1 150
How honourable ladies sought my love, Which I denying, they fell sick and died . . . . *Mer. of Venice* iii 4 71
She would have followed her exile, or have died to stay behind her *As Y. Like It* i 1 115
In all this time there was not any man died in his own person . . iv 1 96
Men have died from time to time and worms have eaten them, but not for love . . . . iv 1 107

Died. How long is't, count, Since the physician at your father's died? *All's Well* i 2 70
The daughter of a count That died some twelvemonth since, then leaving her In the protection of his son, her brother, Who shortly also died . . . . *T. Night* i 2 37
But died thy sister of her love, my boy? . . . . ii 4 122
And died that day when Viola from her birth Had number'd thirteen years . . . . v 1 251
Yea, To die upon the bed my father died . . . . *W. Tale* iv 4 466
Not a month 'Fore your queen died, she was more worth such gazes Than what you look on now . . . . v 1 226
This little abstract doth contain that large Which died in Geffrey *K. John* ii 1 102
The first of April died Your noble mother . . . . iv 2 120
An hour before I came, the duchess died . . . . *Richard II.* ii 2 97
Had you first died, and he been thus trod down, He should have found his uncle Gaunt a father . . . . ii 3 126
This house is turned upside down since Robin Ostler died . 1 *Hen. IV.* ii 1 12
Who hath it [honour]? he that died o' Wednesday. Doth he feel it? no v 1 138
Of which disease Our late king, Richard, being infected, died 2 *Hen. IV.* iv 1 58
A little time before That our great-grandsire, Edward, sick'd and died . iv 4 128
For Oldcastle died a martyr, and this is not the man . . . . Epil. 33
The founder of this law; Who died within the year of our redemption *Hen. V.* i 2 60
Shall join together at the latter day and cry all 'We died at such a place' . . . . iv 1 144
Suffolk first died: and York, all haggled over, Comes to him . . . . iv 6 11
For every drop of blood was drawn from him There hath at least five Frenchmen died to-night . . . . 1 *Hen. VI.* ii 2 9
And there died, My Icarus, my blossom, in his pride . . . . iv 7 15
Had death been French, then death had died to-day . . . . iv 7 28
Now, by the death of Him that died for all . . . . 2 *Hen. VI.* i 1 113
Edward the Black Prince died before his father . . . . ii 2 18
But William of Hatfield died without an heir . . . . ii 2 33
Who kept him in captivity till he died . . . . ii 2 42
But how he died God knows, not Henry . . . . iii 2 131
They say, by him the good Duke Humphrey died . . . . iii 2 248
Died he not in his bed? where should he die? Can I make men live? . iii 3 9
Would I had died a maid, And never seen thee, never borne thee son! 3 *Hen. VI.* i 1 216
Say how he died, for I will hear it all . . . . ii 1 49
He, poor soul, by your first order died . . . . *Richard III.* ii 1 87
Too late he died that might have kept that title . . . . iii 1 99
When didst thou sleep when such a deed was done?—When holy Harry died . . . . iv 4 25
Her life is only safest in her birth.—And only in that safety died her brothers . . . . iv 4 214
Let me sit heavy on thy soul to-morrow, Rivers, that died at Pomfret! v 3 140
I died for hope ere I could lend thee aid: But cheer thy heart . v 3 173
Which so grieved him, That he ran mad and died . *Hen. VIII.* ii 2 130
Or died where they were made, or shortly after This world had air'd them . . . . ii 4 192
Tell me how he died: If well, he stepp'd before me, happily For my example . . . . iv 2 9
And, to add greater honours to his age Than man could give him, he died fearing God . . . . iv 2 68
But had he died in the business, madam; how then? . *Coriolanus* i 3 20
That died in honour and Lavinia's cause . . . . *T. Andron.* i 1 377
He lives in fame that died in virtue's cause . . . . i 1 390
'Tis not life that I have begg'd so long; Poor I was slain when Bassianus died . . . . ii 3 171
They died in honour's lofty bed . . . . iii 1 11
As if his traitorous sons, That died by law for murder of our brother, Have by my means been butcher'd wrongfully! . . . . iv 4 54
With which grief, It is supposed, the fair creature died . *Rom. and Jul.* v 3 51
He dies.—Hard fate! he might have died in war *T. of Athens* iii 5 75
She fell distract, And, her attendants absent, swallow'd fire.—And died so? . . . . *J. Cæsar* iv 3 157
Seventy senators that died By their proscriptions, Cicero being one iv 3 177
How died my master, Strato?—I held the sword, and he did run on it . v 5 64
He died As one that had been studied in his death . . . . *Macbeth* i 4 8
Had I but died an hour before this chance, I had lived a blessed time . ii 3 96
Those thoughts which should indeed have died With them they think on iii 2 10
Oftener upon her knees than on her feet, Died every day she lived iv 3 111
I have known those which have walked in their sleep who have died holily in their beds . . . . v 1 67
She should have died hereafter; There would have been a time for such a word . . . . v 5 17
But like a man he died.—Then he is dead? . . . . v 8 43
And who still hath cried, From the first corse till he that died to-day, 'This must be so' . . . . *Hamlet* i 2 105
How cheerfully my mother looks, and my father died within these two hours . . . . iii 2 135
I would give you some violets, but they withered all when my father died . . . . iv 5 185
Alexander died, Alexander was buried, Alexander returneth into dust . v 1 231
She had a song of 'willow;' An old thing 'twas, but it express'd her fortune, And she died singing it . . . . *Othello* iv 3 30
Fulvia thy wife is dead.—Where died she? . *Ant. and Cleo.* i 2 122
See when and where she died . . . . i 3 62
Since Cleopatra died, I have lived in such dishonour, that the gods Detest my baseness . . . . iv 14 55
Rememberest thou any that have died on't?—Very many, men and women . . . . v 2 249
How she died of the biting of it, what pain she felt: truly, she makes a very good report o' the worm . . . . v 2 254
Most probable That so she died . . . . v 2 357
Who in the wars o' the time Died with their swords in hand . *Cymbeline* i 1 36
Know, if you kill me for my fault, I should Have died had I not made it iii 6 58
Took heel to do't, And yet died too! . . . . iv 2 68
I died whilst in the womb he stay'd Attending nature's law . . . . v 4 37
Repented The evils she hatch'd were not effected; so Despairing died v 5 61
One sand another Not more resembles that sweet rosy lad Who died, and was Fidele . . . . v 5 122
And at first meeting loved; Continued so, until we thought he died . v 5 380
This king unto him took a fere, Who died and left a female heir *Per.* i Gower 22
Ay me! poor maid, Born in a tempest, when my mother died . iv 1 19
She died at night; I'll say so. Who can cross it? . . . . iv 3 16
And for an honest attribute cry out 'She died by foul play' . . . . iv 3 19
My mother was the daughter of a king; Who died the minute I was born . . . . v 1 160

Died. At sea in childbed died she, but brought forth A maid-child *Per.* v 3 5
Diedst. Thou diedst, a most rare boy, of melancholy . . *Cymbeline* iv 2 208
Dies. Jove bless thee, master Parson.—Bonos dies, Sir Toby . *T. Night* iv 2 14
Diest. But if thou scorn our courtesy, thou diest . *T. G. of Ver.* iv 1 68
I may not conceal them, sir.—Conceal them, or thou diest *Mer. Wives* iv 5 46
This night's the time That I should do what I abhor to name, Or else thou diest to-morrow . . . . *Meas. for Meas.* iii 1 103
'Tis best that thou diest quickly.—O hear me, Isabella! . . . . iii 1 151
Thou diest and all thy goods are confiscate . *Mer. of Venice* iv 1 332
If that thou be'st found So near our public court as twenty miles, Thou diest for it . . . . *As Y. Like It* i 3 47
If thou diest before I come, thou art a mocker of my labour . . ii 6 13
Thou perishest; or, to thy better understanding, diest . . . . v 1 57
Thou diest in thine unthankfulness, and thine ignorance makes thee away *All's Well* i 1 225
Unless thou tell'st me where thou hadst this ring, Thou diest within this hour . . . . v 3 285
Why, how now, father! Speak ere thou diest . . . . *W. Tale* iv 4 462
O, no! thou diest, though I the sicker be . . . . *Richard II.* ii 1 91
O Signieur Dew, thou diest on point of fox . . . . *Hen. V.* iv 4 9
Who goes there?—Stay, or thou diest!—What are they that fly there? 3 *Hen. VI.* iv 3 26
Farewell, dear Hector! Look, how thou diest! . . . . *Troi. and Cres.* v 3 81
Art thou down? Why, now thou diest as bravely as Titinius *J. Cæsar* v 4 10
Yield, or thou diest.—Only I yield to die . . . . v 4 12
Let go, slave, or thou diest! . . . . *Lear* iv 6 241
I know his gait, 'tis he.—Villain, thou diest! . . . . *Othello* v 1 23
Think on thy sins.—They are loves I bear to you.—Ay, and for that thou diest . . . . v 2 41
If after this command thou fraught the court With thy unworthiness, thou diest . . . . *Cymbeline* i 1 127
Diet. To fast, like one that takes diet . . . . *T. G. of Ver.* ii 1 25
Unless they kept very good diet . . . . *Meas. for Meas.* ii 1 116
I will attend my husband, be his nurse, Diet his sickness *Com. of Errors* v 1 99
You, that have turn'd off a first so noble wife, May justly diet me *All's Well* v 3 221
I will bespeak our diet, Whiles you beguile the time . *T. Night* iii 3 40
For your diet and by-drinkings . . . . 1 *Hen. IV.* iii 3 84
In speech, in gait, In diet, in affections of delight . . 2 *Hen. IV.* ii 3 29
To diet rank minds sick of happiness And purge the obstructions . . iv 1 64
Are they spare in diet, Free from gross passion or of mirth or anger? *Hen. V.* ii 2 131
He hath kept an evil diet long, And overmuch consumed his royal person . . . . *Richard III.* i 1 139
Your diet shall be in all places alike . *T. of Athens* iii 6 74
Bring down rose-cheeked youth To the tub-fast and the diet . iv 3 87
Shark'd up a list of lawless resolutes, For food and diet, to some enterprise That hath a stomach in't . . . . *Hamlet* i 1 99
Your worm is your only emperor for diet: we fat all creatures else to fat us . . . . iv 3 23
Partly led to diet my revenge . . . . *Othello* ii 1 303
Or feed upon such nice and waterish diet . . . . iii 3 15
In their thick breaths, Rank of gross diet, shall we be enclouded *Ant. and Cleo.* v 2 212
Thou art all the comfort The gods will diet me with . *Cymbeline* iii 4 183
Dieted. Not till after midnight; for he is dieted to his hour *All's Well* iv 3 35
They must be dieted like mules And have their provender tied to their mouths . . . . 1 *Hen. VI.* i 2 10
As if I loved my little should be dieted In praises sauced with lies *Coriol.* i 9 52
I'll watch him Till he be dieted to my request . . . . v 1 57
Dieter. And sauced our broths, as Juno had been sick And he her dieter *Cymbeline* iv 2 51
Dieu vous garde, monsieur.—Et vous aussi; votre serviteur *T. Night* iii 1 78
O Seigneur Dieu, je m'en oublie! . . . . *Hen. V.* iii 4 33
Je ne doute point d'apprendre, par la grace de Dieu, et en peu de temps iii 4 44
O Seigneur Dieu! ce sont mots de son mauvais, corruptible, gros . iii 4 55
Let us quit all And give our vineyards to a barbarous people.—O Dieu vivant! . . . . iii 5 5
Dieu de batailles! where have they this mettle? . . . . iii 5 15
O Seigneur Dieu!—O, Signieur Dew should be a gentleman . iv 4 6
O, je vous supplie, pour l'amour de Dieu, me pardonner! . . iv 4 43
O bon Dieu! les langues des hommes sont pleines de tromperies . v 2 118
And are the cities, that I got with wounds, Delivered up again with peaceful words? Mort Dieu! . . . . 2 *Hen. VI.* i 1 123
Differ. Letter for letter, but that the name of Page and Ford differs! *Mer. Wives* ii 1 72
Therein do men from children nothing differ . . . . *Much Ado* v 1 33
Call you that keeping for a gentleman of my birth, that differs not from the stalling of an ox? . . . . *As Y. Like It* i 1 10
There's nothing differs but the outward fame . . *Richard III.* i 4 83
Is't possible the world should so much differ, And we alive that lived? *T. of Athens* iii 1 49
But clay and clay differs in dignity, Whose dust is both alike *Cymbeline* iv 2 4
Difference. If that be all the difference in his love, I'll get me such a colour'd periwig . . . . *T. G. of Ver.* iv 4 195
As long as I have an eye to make difference of men's liking *Mer. Wives* ii 1 57
Let him bear it for a difference between himself and his horse *Much Ado* i 1 69
Thy eyes shall be thy judge, The difference of old Shylock and Bassanio *Mer. of Venice* ii 5 2
There is more difference between thy flesh and hers than between jet and ivory . . . . iii 1 41
Are you acquainted with the difference That holds this present question? . . . . iv 1 171
Thou shalt see the difference of our spirits . . . . iv 1 368
Here feel we but the penalty of Adam, The seasons' difference *As Y. L. It* ii 1 6
'Twas just the difference Betwixt the constant red and mingled damask iii 5 122
Fortune, she said, was no goddess, that had put such difference betwixt their two estates . . . . *All's Well* i 3 116
Strange is it that our bloods, Of colour, weight, and heat, pour'd all together, Would quite confound distinction, yet stand off In differences so mighty . . . . ii 3 128
You shall see, as I have said, great difference . . *W. Tale* i 1 4
To me the difference forges dread . . . . iv 4 17
Mousing the flesh of men, In undetermined differences of kings *K. John* ii 1 355
The difference Is purchase of a heavy curse from Rome . . iii 1 204
Where revenge did paint The fearful difference of incensed kings . iii 1 238
There shall your swords and lances arbitrate The swelling difference of your settled hate . . . . *Richard II.* i 1 201
Your differences shall all rest under gage Till we assign you to your days of trial . . . . iv 1 105

Difference. Making such difference 'twixt wake and sleep As is the difference betwixt day and night — *1 Hen. IV.* iii 1 219
Or to the place of difference call the swords Which must decide it — *2 Hen. IV.* iv 1 181
You'll find a difference, As we his subjects have in wonder found *Hen. V.* ii 4 134
The state takes notice of the private difference Betwixt you and the cardinal — *Hen. VIII.* i 1 101
Or proclaim There's difference in no persons — i 1 139
But to know How you stand minded in the weighty difference — iii 1 58
I am glad thou hast set thy mercy and thy honour At difference in thee — *Coriolanus* v 3 201
The people will remain uncertain whilst 'Twixt you there's difference — v 6 18
'Tis not the difference of a year or two Makes me less gracious or thee more fortunate — *T. Andron.* ii 1 31
Vexed I am Of late with passions of some difference — *J. Cæsar* i 2 40
But it reserved some quantity of choice, To serve in such a difference — *Hamlet* iii 4 76
O, you must wear your rue with a difference — iv 5 183
An absolute gentleman, full of most excellent differences — v 2 112
Come, sir, arise, away! I'll teach you differences — *Lear* i 4 100
Dost thou know the difference, my boy, between a bitter fool and a sweet fool? — i 4 151
Our father he hath writ, so hath our sister, Of differences — ii 1 125
What is your difference? speak.—I am scarce in breath — ii 2 56
O, the difference of man and man! To thee a woman's services are due iv 2 26
That, from your first of difference and decay, Have follow'd your sad steps — v 3 288
As in these cases, where the aim reports, 'Tis oft with difference *Othello* i 3 7
How the fear of us May cement their divisions and bind up The petty difference, we yet not know — *Ant. and Cleo.* ii 1 49
When we debate Our trivial difference loud, we do commit Murder — ii 2 21
Can we, with manners, ask what was the difference?—Safely, I think — *Cymbeline* i 4 57
Where I was taught Of your chaste daughter the wide difference 'Twixt amorous and villanous — v 5 194
You shall have the difference of all complexions — *Pericles* iv 2 85
Differency. There is differency between a grub and a butterfly — *Coriol.* v 4 11
Different. He hath a thousand of these letters, writ with blank space for different names — *Mer. Wives* ii 1 77
Heavy, sour, sad, And much different from the man he was *Com. of Err.* v 1 46
Either it was different in blood — *M. N. Dream* i 1 135
Too well I feel The different plague of each calamity — *K. John* iii 4 60
Patience perforce with wilful choler meeting Makes my flesh tremble in their different greeting — *Rom. and Jul.* i 5 92
Many for many virtues excellent, None but for some and yet all different — ii 3 14
Ere we depart, we'll share a bounteous time In different pleasures — *T. of Athens* i 1 264
Melted down thy youth In different beds of lust — iv 3 257
Haply the seas and countries different With variable objects shall expel This something-settled matter in his heart — *Hamlet* iii 1 179
Else one self mate and mate could not beget Such different issues *Lear* iv 3 37
Differing. Things of like value differing in the owners Are prized by their masters — *T. of Athens* i 1 170
Our conditions So differing in their acts — *Ant. and Cleo.* ii 2 116
Laying by That nothing-gift of differing multitudes — *Cymbeline* iii 6 86
Difficile. Il est trop difficile, madame, comme je pense — *Hen. V.* iii 4 28
Difficult. It shall be full of poise and difficult weight — *Othello* iii 3 82
Difficulties. All difficulties are but easy when they are known — *Meas. for Meas.* iv 2 221
Were I alone to pass the difficulties And had as ample power as I have will — *Troi. and Cres.* ii 2 139
Difficulty. If the business be of any difficulty — *All's Well* iii 3 107
Thinking it harder for our mistress to devise imposition enough than for us to undergo any difficulty imposed — *Troi. and Cres.* iii 2 87
It were a tedious difficulty, I think, To bring them to that prospect — *Othello* iii 3 397
Diffidence. Thou dost shame thy mother And wound her honour with this diffidence — *K. John* i 1 65
We have been guided by thee hitherto And of thy cunning had no diffidence — *1 Hen. VI.* iii 3 10
Needless diffidences, banishment of friends, dissipation of cohorts *Lear* i 2 161
Diffused. Let them from forth a sawpit rush at once With some diffused song — *Mer. Wives* iv 4 54
Diffusest honey-drops, refreshing showers — *Tempest* iv 1 79
Dig. I with my long nails will dig thee pig-nuts — ii 2 172
Then get thee gone and dig my grave thyself — *2 Hen. IV.* iv 5 111
Wilt thou go dig a grave to find out war? — *2 Hen. VI.* v 1 169
For who lived king, but I could dig his grave? — *3 Hen. VI.* v 2 21
Do thou so much as dig the grave for him: Thou know'st our meaning — *T. Andron.* ii 3 270
'Tis you must dig with mattock and with spade, And pierce the inmost centre — iv 3 11
The Scripture says 'Adam digged:' could he dig without arms? *Hamlet* v 1 42
What man dost thou dig it for?—For no man, sir.—What woman, then? v 1 141
As deep As these poor pickaxes can dig — *Cymbeline* iv 2 389
Who digs hills because they do aspire Throws down one mountain to cast up a higher — *Pericles* i 4 5
Digest. I do digest the poison of thy flesh — *Com. of Errors* ii 2 145
It can never be They will digest this harsh indignity — *L. L. Lost* v 2 288
Howsoe'er thou speak'st, 'mong other things I shall digest it — *Mer. of Venice* iii 5 95
Hungry as the sea, And can digest as much — *T. Night* ii 4 104
Our feasts In every mess have folly and the feeders Digest it with a custom — *W. Tale* iv 4 12
And we'll digest The abuse of distance — *Hen. V.* ii Prol. 31
Go cheerfully together and digest Your angry choler on your enemies — *1 Hen. VI.* iv 1 168
Let us sup betimes, that afterwards We may digest our complots in some form — *Richard III.* iii 1 200
Will the king Digest this letter of the cardinal's? — *Hen. VIII.* iii 2 53
Digest things rightly Touching the weal o' the common — *Coriolanus* i 1 154
How shall this bisson multitude digest The senate's courtesy? — iii 1 131
Which gives men stomach to digest his words With better appetite *J. Cæsar* i 2 305
You shall digest the venom of your spleen, Though it do split you — iv 3 47
Cornwall and Albany, With my two daughters' dowers digest this third — *Lear* i 1 130
Digested. My son, in whom my house's name Must be digested *All's Well* v 3 74
When capital crimes, chew'd, swallow'd and digested, Appear before us — *Hen. V.* ii 2 56
Digested. The subjects we have lost, the disgrace we have digested — *Hen. V.* iii 6 136
Starting thence away To what may be digested in a play *Troi. and Cres.* Prol. 29
An excellent play, well digested in the scenes — *Hamlet* ii 2 460
We have cause to be glad that matters are so well digested — *A. and C.* ii 2 179
Digestion. Unquiet meals make ill digestions — *Com. of Errors* v 1 74
Things sweet to taste prove in digestion sour — *Richard II.* i 3 236
A good digestion to you all: and once more I shower a welcome on ye — *Hen. VIII.* i 4 62
Consumed In hot digestion of this cormorant war — *Troi. and Cres.* ii 2 6
Art thou come? why, my cheese, my digestion — ii 3 44
But for your health and your digestion sake, An after-dinner's breath — ii 3 120
Now, good digestion wait on appetite, And health on both! — *Macbeth* iii 4 38
Digged. There lies Two kinsmen digg'd their graves with weeping eyes — *Richard II.* iii 3 169
This villanous salt-petre should be digg'd Out of the bowels of the harmless earth — *1 Hen. IV.* i 3 60
And with my nails digg'd stones out of the ground — *1 Hen. VI.* i 4 45
And if mine arm be heaved in the air, Thy grave is digg'd already in the earth — *2 Hen. VI.* iv 10 55
If I digg'd up thy forefathers' graves And hung their rotten coffins up in chains, It could not slake mine ire — *3 Hen. VI.* i 3 27
Oft have I digg'd up dead men from their graves, And set them upright at their dear friends' doors — *T. Andron.* v 1 135
Root of hemlock digg'd i' the dark — *Macbeth* iv 1 25
The Scripture says 'Adam digged:' could he dig without arms? *Hamlet* v 1 42
Digging. Being loose, unfirm, with digging up of graves — *Rom. and Jul.* v 3 6
Dighton and Forrest, whom I did suborn To do this ruthless piece of butchery — *Richard III.* iv 3 4
'Lo, thus,' quoth Dighton, 'lay those tender babes:' 'Thus, thus,' quoth Forrest — iv 3 9
'But O! the devil'—there the villain stopp'd; Whilst Dighton thus told on — iv 3 17
Dignified. She shall be dignified with this high honour — *T. G. of Ver.* ii 4 158
The place is dignified by the doer's deed — *All's Well* ii 3 133
Virtue itself turns vice, being misapplied; And vice sometimes by action dignified — *Rom. and Jul.* ii 3 22
Thou wert dignified enough, Even to the point of envy — *Cymbeline* ii 3 132
Dignifies. Nor dignifies an impair thought with breath — *Troi. and Cres.* iv 5 103
It is held That valour is the chiefest virtue, and Most dignifies the haver — *Coriolanus* ii 2 89
I can be modest.—That dignifies the renown of a bawd — *Pericles* iv 6 42
Dignify. He leaves his friends to dignify them more — *T. G. of Ver.* i 1 64
Came not till now to dignify the times, Since Cæsar's fortunes *2 Hen. IV.* i 1 22
Dignities. Since their more mature dignities and royal necessities made separation of their society — *W. Tale* i 1 27
Might wear Without corrival all her dignities — *1 Hen. IV.* i 3 207
I will double-charge thee with dignities — *2 Hen. IV.* v 3 131
In spite of pope or dignities of church — *1 Hen. VI.* i 3 50
Nothing but death Shall e'er divorce my dignities — *Hen. VIII.* iii 1 142
She now begs, That little thought, when she set footing here, She should have bought her dignities so dear — iii 1 184
To furnish Rome, and to prepare the ways You have for dignities — iii 2 329
I feel within me A peace above all earthly dignities, A still and quiet conscience — iii 2 379
Tis a cause that hath no mean dependance Upon our joint and several dignities — *Troi. and Cres.* ii 2 193
Special dignities, which vacant lie For thy best use and wearing — *T. of Athens* v 1 145
Your voice shall be as strong as any man's In the disposing of new dignities — *J. Cæsar* iii 1 178
For those of old, And the late dignities heap'd up to them, We rest your hermits — *Macbeth* i 6 19
To throw Pompey the Great and all his dignities Upon his son — *Ant. and Cleo.* i 2 195
And will fit you With dignities becoming your estates — *Cymbeline* v 5 22
Dignity. The prime duke, being so reputed In dignity — *Tempest* i 2 73
Against our laws, Against my crown, my oath, my dignity *Com. of Err.* i 1 144
In her fair cheek, Where several worthies make one dignity *L. L. Lost* iv 3 236
Things base and vile, holding no quantity, Love can transpose to form and dignity — *M. N. Dream* i 1 233
Let none presume To wear an undeserved dignity — *Mer. of Venice* ii 9 40
Forget this new-fall'n dignity And fall into our rustic revelry — *As Y. Like It* v 4 182
The great dignity that his valour hath here acquired for him shall at home be encountered with a shame as ample — *All's Well* iv 3 80
How often said, my dignity would last But till 'twere known! *W. Tale* iv 4 486
Who has—His dignity and duty both cast off—Fled from his father — v 1 183
The dignity of this act was worth the audience of kings and princes — v 2 86
Find liable to our crown and dignity — *K. John* ii 1 490
And bristle up The crest of youth against your dignity — *1 Hen. IV.* i 1 99
My cloud of dignity Is held from falling with so weak a wind That it will quickly drop — *2 Hen. IV.* iv 5 99
Be now the father and propose a son, Hear your own dignity so much profaned — v 2 93
As your wisdoms best Shall see advantageable for our dignity *Hen. V.* v 2 88
Be placed as viceroy under him, And still enjoy thy regal dignity — *1 Hen. VI.* v 4 132
And not a thought but thinks on dignity — *2 Hen. VI.* iii 1 338
Every word you speak in his behalf Is slander to your royal dignity — iii 2 209
Contrary to the king, his crown and dignity, thou hast built a paper-mill — iv 7 40
I am resolved for death or dignity — v 1 194
Take to your royal self This proffer'd benefit of dignity — *Richard III.* iii 7 196
A breath, a bubble, A sign of dignity, a garish flag — iv 4 89
To the dignity and height of honour — iv 4 243
What state, what dignity, what honour, Canst thou demise to any child of mine? — iv 4 246
Call home To high promotions and great dignity — iv 4 314
Not unconsider'd leave your honour, nor The dignity of your office — *Hen. VIII.* i 2 16
By my life And kingly dignity, we are contented — iv 4 227
Why, this hath not a finger's dignity — *Troi. and Cres.* i 3 204
But value dwells not in particular will; It holds his estimate and dignity As well wherein 'tis precious of itself As in the prizer — ii 2 54
Two households, both alike in dignity, In fair Verona — *Rom. and Jul.* Prol. 1
I would not have such a heart in my bosom for the dignity of the whole body — *Macbeth* v 1 62
Whose love was of that dignity That it went hand in hand even with the vow I made to her in marriage — *Hamlet* i 5 48

Dignity. Use them after your own honour and dignity . . *Hamlet* ii 2 557
Immoment toys, things of such dignity As we greet modern friends withal . . . *Ant. and Cleo.* v 2 166
But clay and clay differs in dignity, Whose dust is both alike *Cymbeline* iv 2 4
Or fruitful object be In eye of Imogen, that best Could deem his dignity . . . v 4 57
Digress. I am come to keep my word, Though in some part enforced to digress . *T. of Shrew* iii 2 109
But, soft! methinks I do digress too much, Citing my worthless praise *T. Andron.* v 3 116
Digressing. Thy abundant goodness shall excuse This deadly blot in thy digressing son *Richard II.* v 3 66
But a form of wax, Digressing from the valour of a man *Rom. and Jul.* iii 3 127
Digression. But this is mere digression from my purpose 2 *Hen. IV.* iv 1 140
That I may example my digression by some mighty precedent *L. L. Lost* i 2 121
Digt. Is digt himself four yard under the countermines *Hen. V.* iii 2 66
Dig-you-den. God dig-you-den all! . . . . . *L. L. Lost.* iv 1 42
Dilate. Do me the favour to dilate at full What hath befall'n *Com. of Err.* i 1 123
That I would all my pilgrimage dilate . . . *Othello* i 3 153
Dilated. After them, and take a more dilated farewell *All's Well* ii 1 59
I will not praise thy wisdom, Which, like a bourn, a pale, a shore, confines Thy spacious and dilated parts *Troi. and Cres.* ii 3 261
Dilatory. This dilatory sloth and tricks of Rome *Hen. VIII.* ii 4 237
Thou know'st we work by wit, and not by witchcraft; And wit depends on dilatory time . . . . . *Othello* ii 3 379
Dildos. With such delicate burthens of dildos and fadings *W. Tale* iv 4 195
Dilemma. In perplexity and doubtful dilemma . *Mer. Wives* iv 5 86
I will presently pen down my dilemmas . . . *All's Well* iii 6 80
Diligence. Go, hence with diligence! . . . . *Tempest* i 2 304
Was't well done?—Bravely, my diligence . . . . . v 1 241
With whispering and most guilty diligence, In action all of precept *Meas. for Meas.* iv 1 39
He shall think by our true diligence He is no less than what we say he is *T. of Shrew* Ind. 1 70
This speedy and quick appearance argues proof Of your accustom'd diligence to me . . . . 1 *Hen. VI.* v 3 9
I will receive it, sir, with all diligence of spirit *Hamlet* v 2 94
That which ordinary men are fit for, I am qualified in; and the best of me is diligence . . . . *Lear* i 4 38
If your diligence be not speedy, I shall be there afore you i 5 4
There wants no diligence in seeking him, And will, no doubt, be found *Cymbeline* iv 3 20
With all due diligence That horse and sail and high expense Can stead the quest . . . *Pericles* iii Gower 19
Diligent. The harmony of their tongues hath into bondage Brought my too diligent ear . . . *Tempest* iii 1 42
Thou see'st how diligent I am To dress thy meat myself *T. of Shrew* iv 3 39
I need not tell him that; he knows you are too diligent. *T. of Athens* iii 4 40
Here is the guess of their true strength and forces By diligent discovery *Lear* v 1 53
Thou canst not, in the course of gratitude, but be a diligent follower of mine . . . . . *Cymbeline* iii 5 121
Never master had A page so kind, so duteous, diligent, So tender . v 5 86
'Diluculo surgere,' thou know'st . . *T. Night* ii 3 2
Dim. So doth the greater glory dim the less . . *Mer. of Venice* v 1 93
I never saw The heavens so dim by day . . *W. Tale* iii 3 56
Violets dim, But sweeter than the lids of Juno's eyes . . iv 4 120
He will look as hollow as a ghost, As dim and meagre as an ague's fit *K. John* iii 4 85
The envious clouds are bent To dim his glory . *Richard II.* iii 3 66
My day is dim . . . . 2 *Hen. IV.* iv 5 101
Let not sloth dim your honours new-begot . . 1 *Hen. VI.* i 1 79
These eyes, like lamps whose wasting oil is spent, Wax dim . ii 5 9
May he be suffocate, That dims the honour of this warlike isle! 2 *Hen. VI.* i 1 125
Why are thine eyes fix'd to the sullen earth, Gazing on that which seems to dim thy sight? . . . . . i 2 6
Mine eyes grow dim. Farewell, My lord . *Hen. VIII.* iv 2 164
With our sighs we'll breathe the welkin dim *T. Andron.* iii 1 212
Make the bridal bed In that dim monument where Tybalt lies *Rom. and Jul.* iii 5 203
And never from this palace of dim night Depart again . v 3 107
Not Erebus itself were dim enough To hide thee from prevention *J. Cæsar* ii 1 84
Dimension. Hath not a Jew hands, organs, dimensions, senses? *Mer. of Venice* iii 1 62
In dimension and the shape of nature A gracious person *T. Night* i 5 280
A spirit I am indeed; But am in that dimension grossly clad . . v 1 244
His dimensions to any thick sight were invincible 2 *Hen. IV.* iii 2 336
When my dimensions are as well compact, My mind as generous . *Lear* i 2 7
Diminish. As diminish One dowle that's in my plume *Tempest* iii 3 64
Feed yourselves with questioning; That reason wonder may diminish *As Y. Like It* v 4 145
Diminished. And yond tall anchoring bark, Diminish'd to her cock *Lear* iv 6 19
Diminishing. Without addition or diminishing *Com. of Errors* ii 2 130
Diminution. I see still, A diminution in our captain's brain Restores his heart . . . . . *Ant. and Cleo.* iii 13 198
Till the diminution Of space had pointed him sharp as my needle *Cymb.* i 3 18
Diminutive. With spans and inches so diminutive As fears and reasons *Troi. and Cres.* ii 2 31
The poor world is pestered with such waterflies, diminutives of nature! v 1 38
The poor wren, The most diminutive of birds, will fight, Her young ones in her nest, against the owl . . . . *Macbeth* iv 2 10
Most monster-like, be shown For poor'st diminutives . *Ant. and Cleo.* iv 12 37
Dimmed. Some sudden qualm hath struck me at the heart And dimm'd mine eyes . . . . . . 2 *Hen. VI.* i 1 55
With sad unhelpful tears, and with dimm'd eyes . . iii 1 218
These eyes, that now are dimm'd with death's black vail . 3 *Hen. VI.* v 2 16
Say, that right for right Hath dimm'd your infant morn to aged night *Richard III.* iv 4 16
Is the sun dimm'd, that gnats do fly in it? . . *T. Andron.* iv 4 82
Dimming. Madam, have comfort: all of us have cause To wail the dimming of our shining star . . *Richard III.* ii 2 102
Dimple. The pretty dimples of his chin and cheek, His smiles *W. Tale* ii 3 101
Dimpled. Puts me her white hand to his cloven chin— Juno have mercy! how came it cloven?—Why, you know, 'tis dimpled *Troi. and Cres.* i 2 134
Spare not the babe, Whose dimpled smiles from fools exhaust their mercy . . . . *T. of Athens* iv 3 119
On each side her Stood pretty dimpled boys, like smiling Cupids *Ant. and Cleo.* ii 2 207

Din. Make thee roar That beasts shall tremble at thy din . . *Tempest* i 2 371
O, 'twas a din to fright a monster's ear, To make an earthquake! . ii 1 314
Such a storm That mortal ears might hardly endure the din *T. of Shrew* i 1 178
Think you a little din can daunt mine ears? Have I not in my time heard lions roar? . . . . i 2 200
When, by and by, the din of war gan pierce His ready sense . *Coriol.* ii 2 119
Let them not cease, but with a din confused Enforce the present execution . . . . iii 3 20
Trumpeters, With brazen din blast you the city's ear *Ant. and Cleo.* iv 8 36
No further with your din Express impatience, lest you stir up mine *Cymbeline* v 4 111
Now sleep yslaked hath the rout; No din but snores the house about *Pericles* iii Gower 2
What minstrelsy, and pretty din, The regent made in Mytilene . v 2 272
Dine. Now can I break my fast, dine, sup and sleep, Upon the very naked name of love . . . . *T. G. of Ver.* ii 4 141
We have appointed to dine with Mistress Anne . *Mer. Wives* iii 2 56
I am fain to dine and sup with water and bran *Meas. for Meas.* iv 3 159
Will you walk with me about the town, And then go to my inn and dine with me? . . . . *Com. of Errors* i 2 23
Good sister, let us dine and never fret: A man is master of his liberty ii 1 6
Husband, I'll dine above with you to-day . . . ii 2 209
If any ask you for your master, Say he dines forth and let no creature enter . . . . ii 2 212
Come, come, Antipholus, we dine too late . . . ii 2 221
There will we dine. This woman that I mean . . iii 1 111
Sir, sooth to say, you did not dine at home . . . iv 4 72
Myself, he and my sister To-day did dine together . v 1 208
To the Porpentine, Where Balthazar and I did dine together . v 1 223
Which of you two did dine with me to-day? . . . v 1 369
To study where I well may dine, When I to feast expressly am forbid *L. L. Lost* i 1 61
I do dine to-day at the father's of a certain pupil of mine . . . iv 2 159
If it please you to dine with us.—Yes, to smell pork . *Mer. of Venice* i 3 33
I know you think to dine with me to-day . . . *T. of Shrew* iii 2 187
Dine with my father, drink a health to me; For I must hence . . iii 2 198
He is not there to-day; he dines in London . . . 2 *Hen. IV.* iv 4 51
A thousand men have broke their fasts to-day, That ne'er shall dine unless thou yield the crown . . . . . . 3 *Hen. VI.* ii 2 128
I swear, I will not dine until I see the same . . . *Richard III.* iii 4 79
Where shall we dine? O me! What fray was here? Yet tell me not, for I have heard it all . . . . *Rom. and Jul.* i 1 179
Give me your hand; We must needs dine together . . *T. of Athens* i 1 164
Wilt dine with me, Apemantus?—No; I eat not lords . . . . i 1 206
You must needs dine with me: go not you hence Till I have thank'd you i 1 253
Will you dine with me to-morrow?—Ay, if I be alive and your mind hold and your dinner worth the eating *J. Cæsar* i 2 294
Shall't be to-night at supper?—No, not to-night.—To-morrow dinner, then?—I shall not dine at home . . . . *Othello* iii 3 58
Dined. Why muse you, sir? 'tis dinner-time.—I have dined *T. G. of Ver.* ii 1 177
I have not dined to-day.—Nor to-day here you must not *Com. of Errors* iii 1 40
That is where we dined, Where Dowsabel did claim me for her husband iv 1 109
God doth know you dined at home . . . . . iv 4 68
Dined at home! Thou villain, what sayest thou? . . . iv 4 71
Thus far I witness with him, That he dined not at home . . v 1 255
You say he dined at home; the goldsmith here Denies that saying . v 1 273
What say you?—Sir, he dined with her there, at the Porpentine . v 1 275
All that I will tell you is, that the duke hath dined *M. N. Dream* iv 2 35
What, hast thou dined? The tailor stays thy leisure *T. of Shrew* iv 3 59
The men are not yet cold under water, nor the bear half dined on the gentleman . . . . *W. Tale* iii 3 108
Yet camest thou to a morsel of this feast, Having fully dined before *Coriolanus* i 9 11
He was not taken well; he had not dined . . . . v 1 50
Has he dined, canst thou tell? for I would not speak with him till after dinner . . . . v 2 36
Go thy ways, wench; serve God. What, have you dined at home? *Rom. and Jul.* ii 5 46
Many a time and often I ha' dined with him . *T. of Athens* iii 1 25
When my lust hath dined . . . . . . *Cymbeline* iii 5 146
Diner. C'est assez pour une fois: allons-nous à diner . . *Hen. V.* iii 4 66
Ding. When birds do sing, hey ding a ding, ding: Sweet lovers love the spring . . . . *As Y. Like It* v 3 21
Ding-dong. Hark! now I hear them,—Ding-dong, bell . *Tempest* i 2 404
Let us all ring fancy's knell: I'll begin it,—Ding, dong, bell *Mer. of Ven.* iii 2 71
Dining-chamber. I came no sooner into the dining-chamber but he steps me to her trencher . . . . *T. G. of Ver.* iv 4 9
I must be fain to pawn both my plate and the tapestry of my dining-chambers . . . . . . 2 *Hen. IV.* ii 1 154
Dinner. I must eat my dinner. This island's mine . *Tempest* i 2 330
Dinner is ready, and your father stays.—Well, let us go . *T. G. of Ver.* i 2 131
When you fasted, it was presently after dinner . . . ii 1 30
Come, we have a hot venison pasty to dinner . . . *Mer. Wives* i 1 202
The dinner is on the table; my father desires your worships' company i 1 270
The dinner attends you, sir.—I am not a-hungry, I thank you . i 1 279
I will make an end of my dinner; there's pippins and cheese to come . i 2 12
Have with you. You'll come to dinner, George . . ii 1 162
I beseech you heartily, some of you go home with me to dinner . iii 2 81
Well, I promised you a dinner . . . . . iii 3 239
I pray you home to dinner with me.—I humbly thank you *Meas. for Meas.* ii 1 292
I pray you, jest, sir, as you sit at dinner . . *Com. of Errors* i 2 62
My charge was but to fetch you from the mart Home to your house, the Phœnix, sir, to dinner . . . . i 2 75
She that doth fast till you come home to dinner . . . i 2 89
And prays that you will hie you home to dinner . . . i 2 90
Perhaps some merchant hath invited him And from the mart he's somewhere gone to dinner . . . . . . ii 1 5
When I desired him to come home to dinner, He ask'd me for a thousand marks in gold . . . . ii 1 60
You received no gold? Your mistress sent to have me home to dinner? ii 2 10
Thou didst deny the gold's receipt And told'st me of a mistress and a dinner . . . . ii 2 18
That at dinner they should not drop in his porridge . . ii 2 99
She sent for you by Dromio home to dinner.—By Dromio?—By me? ii 2 156
Go bid the servants spread for dinner . . . . ii 2 189
Tell me wherefore.—Wherefore? for my dinner . . . iii 1 40
Depart in patience, And let us to the Tiger all to dinner . . iii 1 95
To her will we to dinner. Get you home . . . . iii 1 114
Will you go with me? We'll mend our dinner here? . . iv 3 60
Give me the ring of mine you had at dinner . . . . iv 3 69

Dinner. A mad tale he told to-day at dinner, Of his own doors being shut against his entrance . . . *Com. of Errors* iv 3 89
This woman locked me out this day from dinner . . . v 1 218
Our dinner done, and he not coming thither, I went to seek him . . v 1 224
There is a fat friend at your master's house, That kitchen'd me for you to-day at dinner . . . . v 1 415
My lord, will you walk? dinner is ready . . . . *Much Ado* ii 3 218
Let us send her to call him in to dinner . . . . ii 3 227
Against my will I am sent to bid you come in to dinner . . . ii 3 257
Your reasons at dinner have been sharp and sententious . *L. L. Lost* v 1 3
Fare ye well awhile: I'll end my exhortation after dinner *Mer. of Venice* i 1 104
After dinner Your hazard shall be made . . . . . ii 1 44
Bid them prepare for dinner.—That is done, sir; they have all stomachs iii 5 52
Then bid them prepare dinner.—That is done too, sir; only 'cover' is the word . . . . iii 5 56
Cover the table, serve in the meat, and we will come in to dinner . . iii 5 65
For your coming in to dinner, sir, why, let it be as humours and conceits shall govern . . . . iii 5 68
Ask my opinion too of that.—I will anon: first, let us go to dinner . iii 5 91
Sir, I entreat you home with me to dinner . . . . iv 1 401
Hath sent you here this ring, and doth entreat Your company at dinner iv 2 8
Thou shalt not die for lack of a dinner . . . *As Y. Like It* ii 6 18
Dinners and suppers and sleeping-hours excepted . . . . iii 2 102
I must attend the duke at dinner . . . . . . iv 1 184
I would I were as sure of a good dinner . . . *T. of Shrew* i 2 218
We will go walk a little in the orchard, And then to dinner . . ii 1 113
Let us entreat you stay till after dinner.—It may not be . . . iii 2 199
Gentlemen, forward to the bridal dinner . . . . . iii 2 221
A good traveller is something at the latter end of a dinner . *All's Well* ii 5 31
I think there's no man speaks better Welsh. I'll to dinner 1 *Hen. IV.* iii 1 50
He is indited to dinner to the Lubber's-head in Lumbert street 2 *Hen. IV.* ii 1 30
Master Gower, shall I entreat you with me to dinner? . . . ii 1 195
Go in with me to dinner.—Come, I will go drink with you, but I cannot tarry dinner . . . . iii 2 202
Come, let's to dinner: Jesus, the days that we have seen! . . . iii 2 233
Fear no colours: go with me to dinner . . . . . v 5 94
Shall we go send them dinners and fresh suits? . . . *Hen. V.* iv 2 57
Come, let us four to dinner . . . . . 1 *Hen. VI.* ii 4 133
I stay dinner there.—And supper too, although thou know's it not *Richard III.* iii 2 122
Dispatch, my lord; the duke would be at dinner . . . . iii 4 96
Has he dined, canst thou tell? for I would not speak with him till after dinner . . . . *Coriolanus* v 2 37
Will you come to your father's? we'll to dinner, thither *Rom. and Jul.* ii 4 148
Go; I'll to dinner; hie you to the cell . . . . . ii 5 79
Tarry for the mourners, and stay dinner . . . . . iv 5 150
When dinner's done, Show me this piece. I am joyful of your sights *T. of Athens* i 1 254
You had rather be at a breakfast of enemies than a dinner of friends . i 2 79
So soon as dinner's done, we'll forth again . . . . . ii 2 14
Your importunacy cease till after dinner . . . . . ii 2 42
Gentlemen, our dinner will not recompense this long stay . . . iii 6 35
If thou wert the wolf, thy greediness would afflict thee, and oft thou shouldst hazard thy life for thy dinner . . . . . iv 3 338
If I be alive and your mind hold and your dinner worth the eating *J. Cæsar* i 2 296
Prepare for dinner . . . . *Lear* i 3 26
Let me not stay a jot for dinner; go get it ready . . . . i 4 8
If I like thee no worse after dinner, I will not part from thee yet . i 4 44
Dinner, ho, dinner! Where's my knave? my fool? . . . . i 4 45
Shall't be to-night at supper?—No, not to-night.—To-morrow dinner, then?—I shall not dine at home . . . . . *Othello* iii 3 58
Your dinner, and the generous islanders By you invited, do attend your presence . . . . iii 3 280
Mark Antony In Egypt sits at dinner, and will make No wars *Ant. and Cleo.* ii 1 12
I'll stay Till hasty Polydore return, and bring him To dinner presently *Cymbeline* iv 2 166

Dinner-time. Is't near dinner-time?—I would it were . *T. G. of Ver.* i 2 67
Why muse you, sir? 'tis dinner-time . . . . . . ii 1 176
Within this hour it will be dinner-time . . . *Com. of Errors* i 2 11
'Tis dinner-time,' quoth I; 'My gold!' quoth he . . . . i 2 62
Is it dinner-time?—No, sir: I think the meat wants that I have . . ii 2 56
At dinner-time, I pray you, have in mind where we must meet *Mer. of Ven.* i 1 70
Well, we will leave you then till dinner-time . . . . i 1 105
'Tis now some seven o'clock, And well we may come there by dinner-time . . . . *T. of Shrew* iv 3 190
I will, by to-morrow dinner-time, Send him to answer thee . 1 *Hen. IV.* ii 4 564
I have thirty miles to ride yet ere dinner time . . . . . iii 3 222

Dint. By indictment and by dint of sword . . . 2 *Hen. IV.* iv 1 128
O, now you weep; and, I perceive, you feel The dint of pity . *J. Cæsar* iii 2 198

Diomed. As Ulysses and stout Diomede With sleight and manhood stole to Rhesus' tents . . . . 3 *Hen. VI.* iv 2 19
Good Diomed, Furnish you fairly for this interchange . *Troi. and Cres.* iii 3 32
You told how Diomed, a whole week by days, Did haunt you in the field . . . . iv 1 9
The one and other Diomed embraces . . . . . . iv 1 14
Tell me, noble Diomed, faith, tell me true, Even in the soul of sound good-fellowship . . . . iv 1 51
Fair Diomed, you do as chapmen do, Dispraise the thing that you desire to buy . . . . iv 1 75
Welcome, Sir Diomed! here is the lady Which for Antenor we deliver you . . . . iv 4 111
To Diomed You shall be mistress, and command him wholly . . . iv 4 121
I'll tell thee, Diomed, This brave shall oft make thee to hide thy head . iv 4 138
Is not yond Diomed, with Calchas' daughter? . . . . . iv 5 13
Here is Sir Diomed. Go, gentle knight, Stand by our Ajax . . iv 5 88
There's many a Greek and Trojan dead, Since first I saw yourself and Diomed . . . . iv 5 215
At Menelaus' tent, most princely Troilus: There Diomed doth feast . iv 5 280
And you too, Diomed, Keep Hector company an hour or two . . v 1 87
That same Diomed's a false-hearted rogue, a most unjust knave . . v 1 95
The sun borrows of the moon, when Diomed keeps his word . . . v 1 102
What, are you up here, ho? speak.—Who calls?—Diomed . . . v 2 3
Diomed,— No, no, good-night: I'll be your fool no more . . . v 2 31
Here, Diomed, keep this sleeve.—O beauty! where is thy faith? . . v 2 66
I prithee, Diomed, visit me no more.—Now she sharpens . . . v 2 74
You shall not have it, Diomed; faith, you shall not . . . . v 2 85
Thou never shalt mock Diomed again . . . . . . v 2 99
This she? no, this is Diomed's Cressida . . . . . v 2 137
The bits and greasy relics Of her o'er-eaten faith are bound to Diomed . v 2 160
As much as I do Cressid love, So much by weight hate I her Diomed . v 2 168
Diomed. Shall dizzy with more clamour Neptune's ear In his descent than shall my prompted sword Falling on Diomed . *Troi. and Cres.* v 2 176
And, Diomed, Stand fast, and wear a castle on thy head! . . . v 2 186
Would I could meet that rogue Diomed! I would croak like a raven . v 2 190
Proud Diomed, believe, I come to lose my arm, or win my sleeve . . v 3 95
That dissembling abominable varlet, Diomed . . . . . v 4 3
Haste we, Diomed, To reinforcement, or we perish all . . . v 5 15
O traitor Diomed! turn thy false face, thou traitor! . . . . v 6 6
Ha, art thou there?—I'll fight with him alone: stand, Diomed . . v 6 9
Where's Antony?—There, Diomed, there.—Lives he? . *Ant. and Cleo.* iv 14 114
Art thou there, Diomed? Draw thy sword, and give me Sufficing strokes for death . . . . iv 14 116
Too late, good Diomed: call my guard, I prithee . . . . iv 14 128

Diomedes. Let Diomedes bear him, And bring us Cressid hither *Troi. and Cres.* iii 3 30
We must give up to Diomedes' hand The Lady Cressida . . . iv 2 67

Dion. Cleomenes and Dion, whom you know Of stuff'd sufficiency *W. Tale* ii 1 184
Cleomenes and Dion, Being well arrived from Delphos, are both landed ii 3 195
You, Cleomenes and Dion, have Been both at Delphos . . . iii 2 126

Dionyza. My Dionyza, shall we rest us here? . . . . *Pericles* i 4 1
O Dionyza, Who wanteth food, and will not say he wants it? . . i 4 10
Cursed Dionyza hath The pregnant instrument of wrath Prest for this blow . . . . iv Gower 43
The epitaph is for Marina writ By wicked Dionyza . . . . iv 4 33

Dip. It grieves me to see so many dip their meat in one man's blood *T. of Athens* i 2 41
Who can call him His friend that dips in the same dish? . . . iii 2 73
They would go and kiss dead Cæsar's wounds And dip their napkins in his sacred blood . . . . *J. Cæsar* iii 2 138
But dip a knife in it, Where it draws blood no cataplasm so rare *Hamlet* iv 7 143

Dippedst. This cloth thou dip'dst in blood of my sweet boy, And I with tears do wash the blood away . . . . 3 *Hen. VI.* i 4 157

Dipping all his faults in their affection . . . . *Hamlet* iv 7 19

Dire. To bear the extremity of dire mishap . . . *Com. of Errors* i 1 142
Our eyes do hate the dire aspect Of civil wounds . . *Richard II.* i 3 127
The dangerous consorted traitors That sought at Oxford thy dire overthrow . . . . v 6 16
Il me commande de vous dire que vous faites vous prêt . *Hen. V.* iv 4 36
A warning bell, Sings heavy music to thy timorous soul; And mine shall ring thy dire departure out . . . . 1 *Hen. VI.* iv 2 41
A dire induction am I witness to . . . . *Richard III.* iv 4 5
And the dire death of my two sons and brothers . . . . iv 4 143
All this divided York and Lancaster, Divided in their dire division . v 5 28
And cut off All fears attending on so dire a project . . *Troi. and Cres.* ii 2 134
To ruminate strange plots of dire revenge . . . *T. Andron.* v 2 6
This execrable wretch, That hath been breeder of these dire events . v 3 178
I writ to Romeo, That he should hither come as this dire night *Rom. and Jul.* v 3 247
Dire combustion and confused events New hatch'd to the woeful time *Macbeth* ii 3 63
Would create soldiers, make our women fight, To doff their dire distresses . . . . iv 3 188
Thy natural magic and dire property, On wholesome life usurp *Hamlet* iii 2 270
Timorous accent and dire yell . . . . . . *Othello* i 1 75
Here he comes, And brings the dire occasion in his arms *Cymbeline* iv 2 196

Direct. I'll first direct my men what they shall do with the basket *Mer. Wives* iv 2 101
Some god direct my judgement! Let me see . . *Mer. of Venice* ii 7 13
That by direct or indirect attempts He seek the life of any citizen . iv 1 350
And so to the Lie Circumstantial and the Lie Direct . *As Y. Like It* v 4 86
He durst not give me the Lie Direct . . . . . . v 4 90
The seventh, the Lie Direct. All these you may avoid but the Lie Direct v 4 101
Let her in fine consent, As we'll direct her how 'tis best to bear it *All's Well* iii 7 20
Direct thy feet Where thou and I henceforth may never meet *T. Night* v 1 171
Though indirect, Yet indirection thereby grows direct . *K. John* iii 1 276
Command our officers at arms Be ready to direct these home alarms *Richard II.* i 1 205
And such officers Appointed to direct these fair designs . . . i 3 45
Direct not him whose way himself will choose . . . . ii 1 29
No further go in this Than I by letters shall direct your course 1 *Hen. IV.* i 3 293
Direct mine arms I may embrace his neck . . . 1 *Hen. VI.* ii 5 37
I'll direct thee how thou shalt escape By sudden flight . . . iv 5 10
And may direct his course as please himself . . *Richard III.* ii 2 129
There is no English soul More stronger to direct you than yourself *Hen. VIII.* i 1 147
This fault in us I find, The error of our eye directs our mind *Tr. and Cr.* v 2 110
Follow me, and I'll direct you how you shall go . . *Coriolanus* iii 3 51
Direct me, if it be your will, Where great Aufidius lies . . . iv 4 7
But He, that hath the steerage of my course, Direct my sail! *R. and J.* i 4 113
Heaven will direct it . . . . *Hamlet* i 4 91
Be even and direct with me, whether you were sent for, or no . . ii 2 298
If by direct or by collateral hand They find us touch'd . . . iv 5 206
And do't the speedier, that you may direct me To him . . . iv 6 33
Take note, take note, O world, To be direct and honest is not safe *Othello* iii 3 378
May the gods Direct you to the best! . . . . *Cymbeline* iii 4 196
There are none want eyes to direct them the way I am going . . v 4 193
Your rule direct to any; if to me, Day serves not light more faithful than I'll be . . . . *Pericles* i 2 109

Direct answer. Yield me a direct answer . . . . *Meas. for Meas.* iv 2 7

Direct forthright. If you give way, Or hedge aside from the direct forthright . . . . *Troi. and Cres.* iii 3 158

Direct knowledge. In mine own direct knowledge, without any malice *All's Well* iii 6 9

Direct session. To prison, till fit time Of law and course of direct session Call thee to answer . . . . *Othello* i 2 86

Direct villany. There's nothing level in our cursed natures, But direct villany . . . . *T. of Athens* iv 3 20

Direct way. And their consent of one direct way should be at once to all the points o' the compass . . . . . *Coriolanus* ii 3 25

Directed. I have directed you to wrong places . . . . *Mer. Wives* iii 1 110
I am directed by you . . . . *Meas. for Meas.* iv 3 141
But, damosella virgin, was this directed to you? . . *L. L. Lost* iv 2 132
She hath directed How I shall take her from her father's house *Mer. of Ven.* ii 4 30
Happiest of all is that her gentle spirit Commits itself to yours to be directed . . . . iii 2 166
This to my cousin Scroop, and all the rest To whom they are directed 1 *Hen. IV.* iv 4 4
Is altogether directed by an Irishman . . . . *Hen. V.* iii 2 70
Words sweetly placed and modestly directed . . . 1 *Hen. VI.* v 3 179

Directed. They thus directed, we will follow In the main battle
Richard III. v 3 298
More man? plague, plague!—I was directed hither *T. of Athens* iv 3 198
You must either be directed by some that take upon them to know, or
to take upon yourself that which I am sure you do not know *Cymb.* v 4 186
Directed him To seek her on the mountains near to Milford v 5 280
Directing. Who, heavens directing, Is troth-plight to your daughter
W. Tale v 3 150
Direction. I ha' told them over and over; they lack no direction
Mer. Wives iii 3 19
Minister such assistance as I shall give you direction *Much Ado* ii 1 386
Give him direction for this merry bond *Mer. of Venice* i 3 174
I am not solely led By nice direction of a maiden's eyes ii 1 14
The gown is made Just as my master had direction *T. of Shrew* iv 3 117
Embrace but my direction *W. Tale* iv 4 534
From all indifferency, From all direction, purpose, course, intent *K. John* ii 1 580
I do commit his youth To your direction iv 2 68
Then with directions to repair to Ravenspurgh *Richard II.* ii 3 35
Thou variest no more from picking of purses than giving direction doth
from labouring 1 *Hen. IV.* ii 1 56
And humble my intents To your well-practised wise directions 2 *Hen. IV.* v 2 121
I think a' will plow up all, if there is not better directions *Hen. V.* iii 2 68
He has no more directions in the true disciplines of the wars, look you iii 2 76
Upon my particular knowledge of his directions iii 2 84
Touching the direction of the military discipline iii 2 107
Is all things well, According as I gave directions? 2 *Hen. VI.* iii 2 12
I, like a child, will go by thy direction *Richard III.* ii 2 153
Thy head, all indirectly, gave direction iv 4 225
Call for some men of sound direction: Let's want no discipline v 3 16
Why, then 'tis time to arm and give direction v 3 236
What think'st thou, Norfolk?—A good direction, warlike sovereign v 3 302
Let thy blood be thy direction till thy death! *Troi. and Cres.* ii 3 33
By whose direction found'st thou out this place?—By love *Rom. and Jul.* ii 2 79
He needs not our mistrust, since he delivers Our offices and what we have
to do To the direction just *Macbeth* iii 3 4
I put myself to thy direction, and Unspeak mine own detraction iv 3 122
With assays of bias, By indirections find directions out *Hamlet* ii 1 66
I have but an hour Of love, of wordly matters and direction *Othello* i 3 300
Iago hath direction what to do; But, notwithstanding, with my personal
eye Will I look to't ii 3 4
He is a soldier fit to stand by Cæsar And give direction ii 3 128
Direction-giver. Sweet Proteus, my direction-giver *T. G. of Ver.* iii 2 90
Directitude. Whilst he's in directitude.—Directitude! what's that?
Coriolanus iv 5 222
Directive. Limbs are his instruments, In no less working than are
swords and bows Directive by the limbs *Troi. and Cres.* i 3 356
Directly. Not, as you would say, Directly interest *Mer. of Venice* i 3 78
Indirectly and directly too Thou hast contrived againt the very life iv 1 359
This concurs directly with the letter *T. Night* iii 4 73
Nor is't directly laid to thee, the death Of the young prince *W. Tale* iii 2 195
The path which shall directly lead Thy foot to England's throne *K. John* iii 4 129
Answer me Directly unto this question that I ask 1 *Hen. IV.* ii 3 89
Pleaseth your grace to answer them directly 2 *Hen. IV.* iv 2 52
I know no ways to mince it in love, but directly to say 'I love you'
Hen. V. v 2 130
You would swear directly Their very noses had been counsellors *Hen. VIII.* i 3 8
Directly Set me against Aufidius and his Antiates *Coriolanus* i 6 58
He was too hard for him directly iv 5 197
But what trade art thou? answer me directly *J. Cæsar* i 1 12
Stand you directly in Antonius' way, When he doth run his course i 2 3
The high east Stands, as the Capitol, directly here ii 1 111
Are you a married man or a bachelor?—Answer every man directly iii 3 10
Answer every man directly and briefly, wisely and truly iii 3 17
Proceed; directly.—Directly, I am going to Cæsar's funeral iii 3 21
That matter is answered directly iii 3 25
It is a creature that I teach to fight, To wind, to stop, to run directly on iv 1 32
Will she go now to bed?—Directly *Macbeth* v 1 78
Who in want a hollow friend doth try, Directly seasons him his enemy
Hamlet iii 2 219
O, 'tis most sweet, When in one line two crafts directly meet iii 4 210
I must tell thee this—Desdemona is directly in love with him *Othello* ii 1 221
How am I then a villain To counsel Cassio to this parallel course, Directly
to his good? ii 3 356
Strong circumstances, Which lead directly to the door of truth iii 3 407
I protest, I have dealt most directly in thy affair.—It hath not appeared iv 2 212
Give me directly to understand you have prevailed *Cymbeline* i 4 171
I shall flying fight; Rather, directly fly i 6 21
What villany soe'er I bid thee do, to perform it directly and truly iii 5 113
Direful. The direful spectacle of the wreck *Tempest* i 2 26
More direful hap betide that hated wretch, That makes us wretched!
Richard III. i 2 17
The presentation of but what I was; The flattering index of a direful
pageant iv 4 85
To be adjudged some direful slaughtering death *T. Andron* v 3 144
As the time and place Doth make against me, of this direful murder
Rom. and Jul. v 3 225
Shipwrecking storms and direful thunders break *Macbeth* i 2 26
'Tis some mischance; the cry is very direful *Othello* v 1 38
Dire-lamenting. After your dire-lamenting elegies *T. G. of Ver.* iii 2 82
Direness, familiar to my slaughterous thoughts, Cannot once start me
Macbeth v 5 14
Direst. Murder, stern murder, in the direst degree *Richard III.* v 3 197
Fill me from the crown to the toe top-full Of direst cruelty! *Macbeth* i 5 44
Dirge. Our solemn hymns to sullen dirges change *Rom. and Jul.* iv 5 88
With mirth in funeral and with dirge in marriage *Hamlet* i 2 12
Dirt. Out of their saddles into the dirt *T. of Shrew* iv 1 59
How she waded through the dirt iv 1 80
Whose filth and dirt Troubles the silver spring where England drinks
2 *Hen. VI.* iv 1 71
O admirable man! Paris? Paris is dirt to him *Troi. and Cres.* i 2 259
Whose gall coins slanders like a mint, To match us in comparisons with
dirt i 3 194
To have his fine pate full of fine dirt *Hamlet* v 1 116
'Tis a chough; but, as I say, spacious in the possession of dirt v 2 90
Thou borest thy ass on thy back o'er the dirt *Lear* i 4 177
O gull! O dolt! As ignorant as dirt! thou hast done a deed *Othello* v 2 164
All gold and silver rather turn to dirt! As 'tis no better reckon'd, but
of those Who worship dirty gods *Cymbeline* iii 6 54
Dirt-rotten livers, wheezing lungs, bladders full of imposthume *T. and C.* v 1 23
Dirty. On the dank and dirty ground *M. N. Dream* ii 2 75

Dirty. Prizes not quantity of dirty lands *T. Night* ii 4 85
Haled thither By most mechanical and dirty hand 2 *Hen. IV.* v 5 38
To buy a slobbery and a dirty farm In that nook-shotten isle of Albion
Hen. V. iii 5 13
I kiss his dirty shoe, and from heart-string I love the lovely bully iv 1 47
Why does he suffer this rude knave now to knock him about the sconce
with a dirty shovel? *Hamlet* v 1 110
'Tis no better reckon'd, but of those Who worship dirty gods *Cymbeline* iii 6 56
Dis. Since they did plot The means that dusky Dis my daughter got *Temp.* iv 1 89
O Proserpina, For the flowers now, that frighted thou let'st fall From
Dis's waggon! *W. Tale* iv 4 118
Disability. Leave off discourse of disability *T. G. of Ver.* ii 4 109
Disable all the benefits of your own country *As Y. Like It* iv 1 34
Fie, de la Pole! disable not thyself; Hast not a tongue? 1 *Hen. VI.* v 3 67
Disabled. 'Tis not unknown to you, Antonio, How much I have disabled
mine estate *Mer. of Venice* i 1 123
He disabled my judgement *As Y. Like It* v 4 80
Disabling. To be afeard of my deserving Were but a weak disabling of
myself *Mer. of Venice* ii 7 30
Disadvantage. To look upon the hideous god of war In disadvantage
2 *Hen. IV.* ii 3 36
We have at disadvantage fought and did Retire to win our purpose
Coriolanus i 6 49
Disagree. And that within ourselves we disagree 1 *Hen. VI.* iv 1 140
Disallow. What follows if we disallow of this? *K. John* i 1 16
Disanimates his enemies 1 *Hen. VI.* iii 1 183
Disannul. My dignity, Which princes, would they, may not disannul
Com. of Errors i 1 145
Then Warwick disannuls great John of Gaunt 3 *Hen. VI.* iii 3 81
Disappointed. Unhousel'd, disappointed, unaneled *Hamlet* i 5 77
Disarm. I can here disarm thee with this stick *Tempest* i 2 472
Disarm them, and let them question *Mer. Wives* iii 1 78
You shall do more Than all the island kings,—disarm great Hector
Troi. and Cres. iii 1 167
Disaster. His discord dulcet, His faith, his sweet disaster *All's Well* i 1 187
It was a disaster of war that Cæsar himself could not have prevented iii 6 55
To this very instant disaster of his setting i' the stocks iv 3 127
Or sent it us Upon her great disaster v 3 112
Checks and disasters Grow in the veins of actions highest rear'd *T. and C.* i 3 5
So weary with disasters, tugg'd with fortune *Macbeth* iii 1 112
As stars with trains of fire and dews of blood, Disasters in the sun *Hamlet* i 1 118
We make guilty of our disasters the sun, the moon, and the stars *Lear* i 2 131
The holes where eyes should be, which pitifully disaster the cheeks
Ant. and Cleo. ii 7 18
This was a goodly person, Till the disaster that, one mortal night, Drove
him to this *Pericles* v 1 37
Disastrous. Wherein I spake of most disastrous chances *Othello* i 3 134
Disbenched. I hope My words disbench'd you not *Coriolanus* ii 2 75
Disbranch. She that herself will sliver and disbranch From her material
sap, perforce must wither *Lear* iv 2 34
Disburdened. My heart is great; but it must break with silence, Ere't
be disburden'd with a liberal tongue *Richard II.* ii 1 229
Disburse the sum on the receipt thereof *Com. of Errors* iv 1 38
Disbursed. Being but the one half of an entire sum Disbursed by my father
in his wars *L. L. Lost* ii 1 132
Three parts of that receipt I had for Calais Disbursed I duly to his
highness' soldiers *Richard II.* i 1 127
Till he disbursed at Saint Colme's inch Ten thousand dollars *Macbeth* i 2 61
Discandy. Do discandy, melt their sweets On blossoming Cæsar
Ant. and Cleo. iv 12 22
Discandying. My brave Egyptians all, By the discandying of this pelleted
storm, Lie graveless iii 13 165
Discard, bully Hercules; cashier: let them wag *Mer. Wives* i 3 6
Go off; I discard you: let me enjoy my private *T. Night* iii 4 99
By all the gods that Romans bow before, I here discard my sickness!
J. Cæsar ii 1 321
Discarded. These that accuse him in his intent towards our wives are a
yoke of his discarded men *Mer. Wives* ii 1 182
And welcome home again discarded faith *K. John* v 4 12
You are fool'd, discarded and shook off 1 *Hen. IV.* i 3 178
Such as indeed were never soldiers, but discarded unjust serving-men iv 2 30
Is it the fashion, that discarded fathers Should have thus little mercy
on their flesh? *Lear* iii 4 74
The fountain from the which my current runs, Or else dries up; to be
discarded thence! *Othello* iv 2 60
Discase. I will discase me, and myself present As I was sometime Milan
Tempest v 1 85
Discase thee instantly,—thou must think there's a necessity in't *W. Tale* iv 4 648
Discern. If thou mayest discern by that which is left of him what he is,
fetch me to the sight of him iii 3 138
I could discern no part of his face from the window 2 *Hen. IV.* ii 2 86
As far as I could well discern For smoke and dusky vapours of the night
1 *Hen. VI.* ii 2 26
As I discern, It burneth in the Capels' monument *Rom. and Jul.* v 3 126
You should be ruled and led By some discretion, that discerns your state
Better than you yourself *Lear* ii 4 151
What from the cape can you discern at sea?—Nothing at all *Othello* ii 1 1
You look on me: what wreck discern you in me Deserves your pity?
Cymbeline i 6 84
From the deck You may discern the place *Pericles* v 1 116
Discerned. By thrusting out a torch from yonder tower; Which, once
discern'd, shows that her meaning is, No way to that 1 *Hen. VI.* iii 2 24
Discerner. No discerner Durst wag his tongue in censure *Hen. VIII.* i 1 32
Discernest. Indeed! ay, indeed: discern'st thou aught in that? *Othello* iii 3 102
Discerning. Either his notion weakens, his discernings Are lethargied
Lear i 4 248
Who hast not in thy brows an eye discerning Thine honour from thy
suffering iv 2 52
Discharge. After two days I will discharge thee *Tempest* i 2 299
Whereof what's past is prologue, what to come In yours and my discharge ii 1 254
The sun will set before I shall discharge What I must strive to do iii 1 22
There they always use to discharge their birding-pieces *Mer. Wives* iv 2 58
For which I do discharge you of your office *Meas. for Meas.* v 1 466
I will discharge my bond and thank you too *Com. of Errors* iv 1 13
I will discharge thee ere I go from thee iv 4 122
I discharge thee of thy prisoner, and I thank thee *Much Ado* v 1 328
I will discharge it in either your straw-colour beard *M. N. Dream* i 2 95
You have not a man in all Athens able to discharge Pyramus but he iv 2 8
If he had The present money to discharge the Jew, He would not take it
Mer. of Venice iii 2 276

Discharge. Is he not able to discharge the money?—Yes, here I tender it for him . . . . *Mer. of Venice* iv 1 208
Their discharge did stretch his leathern coat Almost to bursting *As Y. Like It* ii 1 37
That power I have, discharge; and let them go To ear the land *Rich. II.* iii 2 211
Discharge my followers: let them hence away . . . iii 2 217
As by discharge of their artillery, And shape of likelihood, the news was told . . . . 1 *Hen. IV.* i 1 57
I charge you with a cup of sack: do you discharge upon mine hostess 2 *Hen. IV.* ii 4 121
I will discharge upon her, Sir John, with two bullets.—She is pistol-proof, sir . . . . . . ii 4 123
I would not have you go off here: discharge yourself of our company, Pistol . . . . . . ii 4 147
A' shall charge you and discharge you with the motion of a pewterer's hammer . . . . . . iii 2 280
Discharge your powers unto their several counties, As we will ours . iv 2 61
We here discharge your grace from being regent . 2 *Hen. VI.* i 1 66
Will keep me here, Without discharge, money, or furniture . i 3 172
Discharge the common sort With pay and thanks . 3 *Hen. VI.* v 5 87
He did discharge a horrible oath . . . *Hen. VIII.* i 2 206
We two, that with so many thousand sighs Did buy each other, must poorly sell ourselves With the rude brevity and discharge of one *Troi. and Cres.* iv 4 43
You have put me now to such a part which never I shall discharge to the life . . . . . . *Coriolanus* iii 2 106
Infected minds To their deaf pillows will discharge their secrets *Macbeth* v 1 81
Thy soldiers, All levied in my name, have in my name Took their discharge . . . . . . *Lear* v 3 105
They do discharge their shot of courtesy: Our friends at least *Othello* ii 1 56
We will discharge our duty . . . *Cymbeline* iii 7 16
Of what's past, is, and to come, the discharge . . v 4 173
Discharged. See him presently discharged, For he is bound to sea and stays but for it . . . *Com. of Errors* iv 1 32
Thus have I, Wall, my part discharged so . . *M. N. Dream* v 1 206
A fine tragedy: and so it is, truly; and very notably discharged . v 1 368
You have discharged this honestly; keep it to yourself . *All's Well* i 3 127
'Tis hoped his sickness is discharged . . *W. Tale* ii 3 11
Go, my lord, And let our army be discharged too 2 *Hen. IV.* iv 2 92
The army is discharged all and gone . . . iv 3 137
Thy office is discharged. Come, Stanley, shall we go? . 2 *Hen. VI.* ii 4 103
Discharged me with these words . . . 3 *Hen. VI.* iv 1 109
Gave notice He was from thence discharged . *Hen. VIII.* ii 4 34
Three times was his nose discharged against me . . v 4 47
The custom of request you have discharged . *Coriolanus* ii 3 150
As the bark, that hath discharged her fraught, Returns with precious lading to the bay . . . . . *T. Andron.* i 1 71
And that the trunk may be discharged of breath . *Rom. and Jul.* v 1 63
Would we were all discharged! . . . *T. of Athens* ii 2 12
Death of one person can be paid but once, And that she has discharged *Ant. and Cleo.* iv 14 28
Discharging. Vowing more than the perfection of ten and discharging less than the tenth part of one . . . *Troi. and Cres.* iii 2 94
Disciple. Whose honesty the devil And his disciples only envy at *Hen. VIII.* v 3 112
Discipled. And was Discipled of the bravest . . *All's Well* i 2 28
Discipline. This discipline shows thou hast been in love . *T. G. of Ver.* iii 2 88
We do admire This virtue and this moral discipline . *T. of Shrew* i 1 30
Call for our chiefest men of discipline . . . *K. John* ii 1 39
Though all these English and their discipline Were harbour'd in their rude circumference . . . . . . ii 1 261
O prudent discipline! . . . . . . ii 1 413
The mines is not according to the disciplines of the war . *Hen. V.* iii 2 63
He has no more directions in the true disciplines of the wars, look you, of the Roman disciplines, than is a puppy-dog . . iii 2 76
In the disciplines of the pristine wars of the Romans . . iii 2 86
As partly touching or concerning the disciplines of the war . . iii 2 103
As touching the direction of the military discipline; that is the point . iii 2 107
Being as good a man as yourself, both in the disciplines of war, and in the derivation of my birth . . . . . . iii 2 141
I will be so bold as to tell you I know the disciplines of war . . iii 2 152
But keeps the bridge most valiantly, with excellent discipline . . iii 6 12
Put him to execution; for discipline ought to be used . . iii 6 58
O, negligent and heedless discipline! . . 1 *Hen. VI.* iv 2 44
Thy acts in Ireland, In bringing them to civil discipline 2 *Hen. VI.* i 1 195
Your discipline in war, wisdom in peace, Your bounty, virtue *Richard III.* iii 7 16
Let's want no discipline, make no delay; For, lords, to-morrow is a busy day . . . . v 3 17
Heaven bless thee from a tutor, and discipline come not near thee *Troi. and Cres.* ii 3 32
Find some occasion to anger Cassio, either by speaking too loud, or tainting his discipline . . . . . *Othello* ii 1 275
Their discipline, Now mingled with their courages, will make known To their approvers . . . . . *Cymbeline* ii 4 23
Disciplined. But he that disciplined thy arms to fight, Let Mars divide eternity in twain, And give him half . . *Troi. and Cres.* iii 3 255
Has he disciplined Aufidius soundly? . . *Coriolanus* ii 1 139
Disclaim. Must these have voices, that can yield them now And straight disclaim their tongues? . . . . . . iii 1 35
Here I disclaim all my paternal care, Propinquity and property of blood . . . . *Lear* i 1 115
You cowardly rascal, nature disclaims in thee: a tailor made thee . ii 2 59
Disclaimed. I have disclaim'd sir Robert and my land . *K. John* i 1 247
Disclaimest. I love thee, Because thou art a woman, and disclaim'st Flinty mankind . . . . . *T. of Athens* iv 3 490
Disclaiming here the kindred of the king . *Richard II.* i 1 70
Let my disclaiming from a purposed evil Free me so far . *Hamlet* v 2 252
Disclose. Come, come, disclose The state of your affection *All's Well* i 3 196
Tell me your counsels, I will not disclose 'em . *J. Cæsar* ii 1 298
I do doubt the hatch and the disclose Will be some danger *Hamlet* iii 1 174
She that could think and ne'er disclose her mind *Othello* ii 1 157
Disclosed. I gave him gentle looks, thereby to find That which thyself hast now disclosed to me . . . . *T. G. of Ver.* iii 1 32
The heart's still rhetoric disclosed with eyes . *L. L. Lost* ii 1 229
To speak that in words which his eye hath disclosed . . ii 1 250
Told our intents before; which once disclosed, The ladies did change favours . . . . v 2 467
For what offence?—The sum of all I can, I have disclosed *Richard III.* i 1 46
Go sit in council, How covert matters may be best disclosed . *J. Cæsar* iv 1 46

Disclosed. Galls the infants of the spring, Too oft before their buttons be disclosed . . . . *Hamlet* i 3 40
As patient as the female dove, When that her golden couplets are disclosed . . . . v 1 310
Discolour. Though it discolours the complexion of my greatness to acknowledge it . . . . . . 2 *Hen. IV.* ii 2 5
We shall your tawny ground with your red blood Discolour . *Hen. V.* iii 6 171
Discoloured. Coldly embracing the discolour'd earth . *K. John* ii 1 306
Or with their blood stain this discolour'd shore . 2 *Hen. VI.* iv 1 11
What mean these masterless and gory swords To lie discolour'd by this place of peace? . . . . . *Rom. and Jul.* v 3 143
Discomfit. Uncurable discomfit Reigns in the hearts of all our present parts . . . . 2 *Hen. VI.* v 2 86
Discomfited. Well, go with me and be not so discomfited *T. of Shrew* ii 1 164
Smooth and welcome news. The Earl of Douglas is discomfited 1 *Hen. IV.* i 1 67
This infant warrior in his enterprizes Discomfited great Douglas . iii 2 114
That monstrous rebel Cade, Who since I heard to be discomfited 2 *Hen. VI.* v 1 63
Discomfiture. Sad tidings bring I to you out of France, Of loss, of slaughter and discomfiture . . . 1 *Hen. VI.* i 1 59
Discomfort guides my tongue And bids me speak of nothing but despair *Richard II.* iii 2 65
I hear his majesty is returned with some discomfort . 2 *Hen. IV.* i 2 118
You do discomfort all the host.—You understand me not *Troi. and Cres.* v 10 10
His funerals shall not be in our camp, Lest it discomfort us . *J. Cæsar* v 3 106
From that spring whence comfort seem'd to come Discomfort swells *Macbeth* i 2 28
Should I stay longer, It would be my disgrace and your discomfort . iv 2 29
Yet, though I distrust, Discomfort you, my lord, it nothing must *Hamlet* iii 2 176
What mean you, sir, To give them this discomfort? Look, they weep *Ant. and Cleo.* iv 2 34
Discomfortable cousin! . . . . . *Richard II.* iii 2 36
Discommend. To go out of my dialect, which you discommend so much *Lear* ii 2 116
Disconsolate. Where did you leave him?—All disconsolate . *J. Cæsar* v 3 55
Discontent. A man of comfort, whose advice Hath often still'd my brawling discontent . . . . . . *Meas. for Meas.* iv 1 9
Can you make no use of your discontent?—I make all use of it, for I use it only . . . . *Much Ado* i 3 40
Content you in my discontent . . . . . *T. of Shrew* i 1 80
'Tis wonderful What may be wrought out of their discontent *K. John* iii 4 179
Whose restraint Doth move the murmuring lips of discontent . iv 2 53
Now powers from home and discontents at home Meet in one line . iv 3 151
I see your brows are full of discontent, Your hearts of sorrow *Rich. II.* iv 1 331
To your quick-conceiving discontents I'll read you matter deep and dangerous . . . . 1 *Hen. IV.* i 3 189
That may please the eye Of fickle changelings and poor discontents v 1 76
For what's more miserable than discontent? 2 *Hen. VI.* iii 1 201
Heart's discontent and sour affliction Be playfellows to keep you company! . . . . iii 2 301
Mine, such as fill my heart with unhoped joys.—Mine, full of sorrow and heart's discontent . . . . . 3 *Hen. VI.* iii 3 173
Now is the winter of our discontent Made glorious summer *Richard III.* i 1 1
Rest on my word, and let not discontent Daunt all your hopes *T. Andron.* i 1 267
Dissemble all your griefs and discontents . . . . i 1 443
My lord leans wondrously to discontent . . . *T. of Athens* iii 4 71
His discontents are unremoveably Coupled to nature . . v 1 227
To the ports The discontents repair . . . *Ant. and Cleo.* i 4 39
So, I leave you, sir, To the worst of discontent . *Cymbeline* ii 3 160
Discontented. O, make a league with me, till I have pleased My discontented peers! . . . . *K. John* iv 2 127
Our discontented counties do revolt; Our people quarrel with obedience v 1 8
As doth the blushing discontented sun . . *Richard II.* iii 3 63
The duke Hath banish'd moody discontented fury . 1 *Hen. VI.* iii 1 123
I know a discontented gentleman, Whose humble means match not his haughty mind . . . . . . *Richard III.* iv 2 36
With a fearful soul Leads discontented steps in foreign soil . iv 4 312
If that your moody discontented souls Do through the clouds behold this present hour, Even for revenge mock my destruction! . . v 1 7
He's discontented.—May be, he hears the king Does whet his anger to him . . . . *Hen. VIII.* iii 2 91
It tauntingly replied To the discontented members . *Coriolanus* i 1 115
As a discontented friend, grief-shot With his unkindness . . v 1 44
I'll cheer up My discontented troops, and lay for hearts *T. of Athens* iii 5 115
Now here's another discontented paper, Found in his pocket too *Othello* v 2 314
Let us know If 'twill tie up thy discontented sword . *Ant. and Cleo.* ii 6 6
Discontenting. Your discontenting father strive to qualify . *W. Tale* iv 4 543
Discontinue. I must discontinue your company . *Much Ado* v 1 192
Discontinued. I have discontinued school Above a twelvemonth *Mer. of Venice* iii 4 75
Discord. Sour-eyed disdain and discord . . . *Tempest* iv 1 20
The enmity and discord which of late Sprung from the rancorous outrage of your duke . . . . . . *Com. of Errors* i 1 5
I never heard So musical a discord, such sweet thunder . *M. N. Dream* iv 1 123
How shall we find the concord of this discord? . . . v 1 60
We shall have shortly discord in the spheres . . *As Y. Like It* ii 7 6
His jarring concord, and his discord dulcet, His faith . *All's Well* i 1 186
Set armed discord 'twixt these perjured kings! . . *K. John* iii 1 111
You two never meet but you fall to some discord . 2 *Hen. IV.* ii 4 61
O, how this discord doth afflict my soul! . . 1 *Hen. VI.* iii 1 106
So will this base and envious discord breed . . . iii 1 194
This jarring discord of nobility, This shouldering of each other . iv 1 188
Let not your private discord keep away The levied succours . . iv 4 22
What is wedlock forced but a hell, An age of discord and continual strife? . . . . v 5 63
And chattering pies in dismal discords sung . . 3 *Hen. VI.* v 6 48
Take but degree away, untune that string, And, hark, what discord follows! . . . . *Troi. and Cres.* i 3 110
An should the empress know This discord's ground, the music would not please . . . . *T. Andron.* ii 1 70
An thou make minstrels of us, look to hear nothing but discords *Rom. and Jul.* iii 1 51
So out of tune, Straining harsh discords and unpleasing sharps . iii 5 28
And I for winking at your discords too Have lost a brace of kinsmen v 3 294
O, come away! My soul is full of discord and dismay *Hamlet* iv 1 45
In cities, mutinies; in countries, discord; in palaces, treason . *Lear* i 2 117
And this, and this, the greatest discords be That e'er our hearts shall make! . . . . *Othello* ii 1 200
Discourse. A kind Of excellent dumb discourse . . *Tempest* iii 3 39
I'll waste With such discourse as, I doubt not, shall make it Go quick away . . . . v 1 303

Discourse. There shall he practise tilts and tournaments, Hear sweet discourse . . . . *T. G. of Ver.* i 3 31
Leave off discourse of disability . . . . . ii 4 109
Now no discourse, except it be of love . . . . . ii 4 140
How likes she my discourse?—Ill, when you talk of war.—But well, when I discourse of love and peace? . . . . . v 2 15
I pray you, stand not to discourse, But mount you presently . v 2 44
I dare be bold With our discourse to make your grace to smile . v 4 163
She discourses, she carves, she gives the leer of invitation *Mer. Wives* i 3 49
You are a gentleman of excellent breeding, admirable discourse . ii 2 235
Would seem in me to affect speech and discourse . *Meas. for Meas.* i 1 4
She hath prosperous art When she will play with reason and discourse i 2 190
Are my discourses dull? barren my wit . . . . *Com. of Errors* ii 1 91
If voluble and sharp discourse be marr'd, Unkindness blunts it more than marble hard . . . . ii 1 92
Of excellent discourse, Pretty and witty, wild and yet, too, gentle . iii 1 109
Of such enchanting presence and discourse . . . . iii 2 166
The body of your discourse is sometime guarded with fragments *M. Ado* i 1 288
Of good discourse, an excellent musician . . . . . ii 3 35
Our whole discourse Is all of her; say that thou overheard'st us . iii 1 5
So sweet and voluble is his discourse . . . . *L. L. Lost* ii 1 76
It is an epilogue or discourse, to make plain Some obscure precedence . iii 1 82
His humour is lofty, his discourse peremptory, his tongue filed . v 1 11
Of this discourse we more will hear anon . . . *M. N. Dream* iv 1 183
I am to discourse wonders: but ask me not what . . . . iv 2 29
Let Lion, Moonshine, Wall, and lovers twain At large discourse . . v 1 152
It is the wittiest partition that ever I heard discourse . . . v 1 169
And discourse grow commendable in none only but parrots *Mer. of Venice* iii 5 50
Surprise her with discourse of my dear faith . . . *T. Night* i 4 25
So far exceed all instance, all discourse . . . . . iv 3 12
Your fair discourse hath been as sugar, Making the hard way sweet *Richard II.* ii 3 6
List his discourse of war, and you shall hear A fearful battle render'd you in music. . . . . *Hen. V.* i 1 43
It is no time to discourse, so Chrish save me: the day is hot, and the weather . . . . iii 2 112
Discourse, I prithee, on this turret's top . . . *1 Hen. VI.* i 4 26
What means this passionate discourse, This peroration with such circumstance? . . . . *2 Hen. VI.* i 1 104
How haps it, in this smooth discourse, You told not how? *3 Hen. VI.* iii 3 88
Left nothing fitting for the purpose Untouch'd, or slightly handled, in discourse . . . . *Richard III.* iii 7 19
Vows of love And ample interchange of sweet discourse . . . v 3 99
Handlest in thy discourse, O, that her hand . . *Troi. and Cres.* i 1 55
Birth, beauty, good shape, discourse, manhood, learning . . . i 2 275
No discourse of reason, Nor fear of bad success in a bad cause . ii 2 116
Imagined worth Holds in his blood such swoln and hot discourse . ii 3 183
O madness of discourse, That cause sets up with and against itself! . v 2 142
And turns up the white o' the eye to his discourse . . *Coriolanus* iv 5 209
When soon I heard The crying babe controll'd with this discourse *T. Andron.* v 1 26
As erst our ancestor, When with his solemn tongue he did discourse To love-sick Dido's sad attending ear . . . . v 3 81
She speaks, yet she says nothing: what of that? Her eye discourses; I will answer it . . . . *Rom. and Jul.* ii 2 13
All these woes shall serve For sweet discourses in our time to come . iii 5 53
According to the which, thou shalt discourse . . . *J. Cæsar* iii 1 295
A beast, that wants discourse of reason, Would have mourn'd longer *Hamlet* i 2 150
Your honesty should admit no discourse to your beauty . . . iii 1 108
Put your discourse into some frame and start not so wildly from my affair . . . . iii 2 320
Give it breath with your mouth, and it will discourse most eloquent music . . . . iii 2 374
Do bend your eye on vacancy And with the incorporal air do hold discourse . . . . iii 4 118
He that made us with such large discourse, Looking before and after . iv 4 36
She'ld come again, and with a greedy ear Devour up my discourse *Othello* i 3 150
Squabble? swagger? swear? and discourse fustian with one's own shadow? . . . . ii 3 282
Give me advantage of some brief discourse . . . . . iii 1 55
If e'er my will did trespass 'gainst his love, Either in discourse of thought or actual deed . . . . iv 2 153
How, In this our pinching cave, shall we discourse The freezing hours away? . . . . *Cymbeline* iii 3 38
Discourse is heavy, fasting . . . . iii 6 91
I'll then discourse our woes, felt several years . . . *Pericles* i 4 18
Discoursed. And hear at large discoursed all our fortunes *Com. of Errors* v 1 395
The manner of their taking may appear At large discoursed in this paper here . . . . *Richard II.* v 6 10
Discourser. The tract of every thing Would by a good discourser lose some life . . . . *Hen. VIII.* i 1 41
Discourtesy. I shall unfold equal discourtesy To your best kindness *Cymbeline* ii 3 101
Discover. Some to discover islands far away . . *T. G. of Ver.* i 3 9
Or fearing else some messenger that might her mind discover . . ii 1 173
That which I would discover The law of friendship bids me to conceal iii 1 4
Frame some feeling line That may discover such integrity . . iii 2 77
I shall discover a thing to you, wherein I must very much lay open mine own imperfection . . . . *Mer. Wives* ii 2 190
He hath some offences in him that thou wouldst discover *Meas. for Meas.* ii 1 195
I will open my lips in vain, or discover his government . . . iii 1 199
Angelo hath seen them both, and will discover the favour . . iv 2 185
Discover how, and thou shalt find me just . . *Com. of Errors* v 1 203
Never counterfeit of passion came so near the life of passion as she discovers it . . . . *Much Ado* ii 3 111
It were good that Benedick knew of it by some other, if she will not discover it . . . . ii 3 161
If there be any impediment, I pray you discover it . . . . iii 2 97
What your wisdoms could not discover, these shallow fools have brought to light . . . . v 1 239
Discover The several caskets to this noble prince . *Mer. of Venice* ii 7 1
I'll Discover that which shall undo the Florentine . . *All's Well* iv 1 80
Daylight and champain discovers not more . . . *T. Night* ii 5 174
When the oracle, Thus by Apollo's great divine seal'd up, Shall the contents discover . . . . *W. Tale* iii 1 20
Any thing that is fitting to be known, discover . . . . iv 4 742
To discover What power the Duke of York had levied there *Richard II.* ii 3 33
And thence discover how with most advantage They may vex us *1 Hen. VI.* i 4 12
Discover more at large what cause that was, For I am ignorant . ii 5 59
Discover thine infirmity, That warranteth by law to be thy privilege . v 4 60
Discover. Your painted gloss discovers, To men that understand you, words and weakness . . . . *Hen. VIII.* v 3 71
Stand where the torch may not discover us . . *Troi. and Cres.* v 2 5
Then you should discover a brace of unmeriting, proud, violent, testy magistrates . . . . *Coriolanus* ii 1 46
Leaves nothing undone that may fully discover him their opposite . ii 2 23
Nourish and bring him up; Or else I will discover nought to thee *T. Andron.* v 1 85
I can discover all The unlucky manage of this fatal brawl *Rom. and Jul.* iii 1 147
I, your glass, Will modestly discover to yourself That of yourself which you yet know not of . . . . *J. Cæsar* i 2 69
Half their faces buried in their cloaks, That by no means I may discover them . . . . ii 1 75
With curst speech I threaten'd to discover him . . . . *Lear* ii 1 68
I think I can discover him, if you please To get good guard . *Othello* i 1 179
Where their appointment we may best discover . . *Ant. and Cleo.* iv 10 8
Yet they are not join'd: where yond pine does stand, I shall discover all iv 12 2
Discover to me What both you spur and stop . . . *Cymbeline* i 6 98
Discover where thy mistress is at once, At the next word . . iii 5 95
What company Discover you abroad? . . . . iv 2 130
Discovered. 'Tis your penance but to hear The story of your loves discovered . . . . *T. G. of Ver.* v 4 171
We discovered Two ships from far making amain to us . *Com. of Errors* i 1 92
The prince discovered to Claudio that he loved my niece . *Much Ado* i 2 12
As,—in love of your brother's honour . . . —that you have discovered thus . . . . ii 2 40
You that have so traitorously discovered the secrets of your army *All's Well* iv 3 339
He has discover'd my design, and I Remain a pinch'd thing . *W. Tale* ii 1 50
Our purposes God justly hath discover'd; And I repent my fault *Hen. V.* ii 2 151
By your espials were discovered Two mightier troops . *1 Hen. VI.* iv 3 6
What good is cover'd with the face of heaven, To be discover'd, that can do me good? . . . . *Richard III.* iv 4 240
Most wisely hath Ulysses here discover'd The fever whereof all our power is sick . . . . *Troi. and Cres.* i 3 138
O wondrous thing! How easily murder is discovered! *T. Andron.* ii 3 287
And here display, at last, What God will have discover'd for revenge . iv 1 74
Pardon me, And not impute this yielding to light love, Which the dark night hath so discovered . . . . . . *Rom. and Jul.* ii 2 106
Thou hast painfully discover'd: are his files As full as thy report? *T. of Athens* v 2 1
I fear our purpose is discovered . . . . . . *J. Cæsar* iii 1 17
And swore, If I discover'd not which way she was gone, It was my instant death . . . . *Cymbeline* v 5 277
Where what is done in action, more, if might, Shall be discover'd *Pericles* v Gower 24
Discoverer. Send discoverers forth To know the numbers of our enemies *2 Hen. IV.* iv 1 3
Discoveries. Pretending in her discoveries of dishonour *Meas. for Meas.* iii 1 236
He will steal himself into a man's favour and for a week escape a great deal of discoveries . . . . *All's Well* iii 6 100
Take and take again such preposterous discoveries! . *Troi. and Cres.* v 1 28
Discovery. That even Ambition cannot pierce a wink beyond, But doubt discovery there . . . . *Tempest* ii 1 243
Do it so cunningly That my discovery be not aimed at . *T. G. of Ver.* iii 1 45
'Tis an office of discovery . . . . . . *Mer. of Venice* ii 6 43
One inch of delay more is a South-sea of discovery . *As Y. Like It* iii 2 207
The heavens have thought well on thee, Lafeu, To bring forth this discovery . . . . *All's Well* v 3 151
For myself, I'll put My fortunes to your service, which are here By this discovery lost . . . . *W. Tale* i 2 441
Never did faithful subject more rejoice At the discovery of most dangerous treason . . . . *Hen. V.* ii 2 162
By the discovery We shall be shorten'd in our aim . . *Coriolanus* i 2 22
So secret and so close, So far from sounding and discovery *Rom. and Jul.* i 1 156
A discovery of the infinite flatteries that follow youth and opulency *T. of Athens* v 1 37
Thereby shall we shadow The numbers of our host and make discovery Err in report of us . . . . *Macbeth* v 4 6
I will tell you why; so shall my anticipation prevent your discovery *Hamlet* ii 2 305
Here is the guess of their true strength and forces By diligent discovery *Lear* v 1 53
Discredit. He will discredit our mystery . . *Meas. for Meas.* iv 2 30
It would not have relished among my other discredits . *W. Tale* v 2 133
As patches set upon a little breach Discredit more in hiding of the fault Than did the fault before it was so patch'd . . *K. John* iv 2 33
To weaken and discredit our exposure . . . *Troi. and Cres.* i 3 195
It would discredit the blest gods, proud man, To answer such a question iv 5 247
Did he not rather Discredit my authority with yours? . *Ant. and Cleo.* ii 2 49
Discredited. Which I by my good leisure have discredited to him *Meas. for Meas.* iii 2 261
Which not to have been blest withal would have discredited your travel *Ant. and Cleo.* i 2 161
Discreet. Nor no railing in a known discreet man . . *T. Night* i 5 103
With such a smooth, discreet and stable bearing . . . . iv 3 19
Breeds no bate with telling of discreet stories . . . *2 Hen. IV.* ii 4 272
You that will be less fearful than discreet . . . *Coriolanus* iii 1 150
A madness most discreet, A choking gall and a preserving sweet *Rom. and Jul.* i 1 199
That then necessity Will call discreet proceeding . . . *Lear* i 4 233
Will she love him still for prating? let not thy discreet heart think it *Othello* ii 1 227
Discreetly. We will afterwards ork upon the cause with as great discreetly as we can . . . . *Mer. Wives* i 1 148
I advise You use your manners discreetly in all kind of companies *T. of Shrew* i 1 247
Discretion. I will not adventure my discretion so weakly . *Tempest* ii 1 188
A youth That can with some discretion do my business . *T. G. of Ver.* iv 4 70
Which peradventure prings goot discretions with it . . *Mer. Wives* i 1 44
It is a fery discretion answer . . . . i 1 261
Old folks, you know, have discretion, as they say, and know the world ii 2 135
'Tis one of the best discretions of a 'oman as ever I did look upon . iv 4 1
Nor do I think the man of safe discretion That does affect it *Meas. for Meas.* i 1 72
Avoids them with great discretion, or undertakes them with a most Christian-like fear . . . . *Much Ado* ii 3 198
Thou halfpenny purse of wit, thou pigeon-egg of discretion . *L. L. Lost* v 1 78
I have seen the day of wrong through the little hole of discretion . . v 2 734
They would have no more discretion but to hang us . . *M. N. Dream* i 2 83
A very fox for his valour.—True; and a goose for his discretion . . v 1 235

Discretion. His valour cannot carry his discretion . . *M. N. Dream* v 1 237
His discretion, I am sure, cannot carry his valour . . . . v 1 241
Leave it to his discretion, and let us listen to the moon . . . v 1 241
It appears, by his small light of discretion, that he is in the wane. . v 1 257
O dear discretion, how his words are suited ! . . . *Mer. of Venice* iii 5 70
Therefore use thy discretion ; I had as lief thou didst break his neck *As Y. Like It* i 1 152
The better part of valour is discretion . . . *1 Hen. IV.* v 4 121
Covering discretion with a coat of folly . . . *Hen. V.* ii 4 38
You do not use me with that affability as in discretion you ought to use me . . . . iii 2 139
Your discretions better can persuade Than I am able to instruct *1 Hen. VI.* iv 1 158
All this was order'd by the good discretion Of the right reverend Cardinal of York . . . . . *Hen. VIII.* i 1 50
Was it discretion, lords, to let this man, This good man,—few of you deserve that title,—This honest man, wait like a lousy footboy At chamber-door? . . . . v 3 137
His valour is crushed into folly, his folly sauced with discretion *Troi. and Cres.* i 2 24
Have you any discretion? have you any eyes? do you know what a man is? . . . . i 2 273
Though abundantly they lack discretion, Yet are they passing cowardly *Coriolanus* i 1 206
Yet so far hath discretion fought with nature . . *Hamlet* i 2 5
It is common for the younger sort To lack discretion . . ii 1 117
Well spoken, with good accent and good discretion . . . ii 2 489
Be not too tame neither, but let your own discretion be your tutor . iii 2 19
You should be ruled and led By some discretion . . *Lear* ii 4 151
Let's teach ourselves that honourable stop, Not to outsport discretion *Othello* ii 3 3
Well, do your discretion . . . . iii 3 34
It raises the greater war between him and his discretion *Ant. and Cleo.* ii 7 11
Well, I perceive he was a wise fellow, and had good discretion *Pericles* i 3 5
Discuss. I will discuss the humour of this love to Page . . *Mer. Wives* i 3 104
Speak, breathe, discuss ; brief, short, quick, snap . . . iv 5 2
Th' athversary, you may discuss unto the duke, look you, is digt himself four yard under the countermines . . . *Hen. V.* iii 2 65
Discuss unto me ; art thou officer? Or art thou base, common? . iv 1 37
Art thou a gentleman? what is thy name? discuss . . . iv 4 5
Discuss the same in French unto him . . . . . . iv 4 30
Disdain. Barren hate, Sour-eyed disdain and discord . . *Tempest* iv 1 20
Trampling contemptuously on thy disdain . . *T. G. of Ver.* i 2 112
Growing proud, Disdain to root the summer-swelling flower . . ii 4 162
I'll knock elsewhere, to see if they'll disdain me . *Com. of Errors* iii 1 121
What, my dear Lady Disdain ! are you yet living? . . *Much Ado* i 1 119
Is it possible disdain should die while she hath such meet food to feed it? . . . . i 1 121
Courtesy itself must convert to disdain, if you come in her presence i 1 123
Disdain and scorn ride sparkling in her eyes, Misprising what they look on . . . . iii 1 51
The red glow of scorn and proud disdain . . *As Y. Like It* iii 4 57
To make a bondmaid and a slave of me ; That I disdain . *T. of Shrew* ii 1 3
Whose apprehensive senses All but new things disdain . . *All's Well* i 2 61
Disdain Rather corrupt me ever ! . . . . ii 3 122
Believe not thy disdain . . . . ii 3 166
Nature might have made me as these are, Therefore I will not disdain *W. Tale* iv 4 774
Pride, haughtiness, opinion and disdain . . *1 Hen. IV.* iii 1 185
Holding in disdain the German women For some dishonest manners of their life . . . . *Hen. V.* i 2 48
It shall be so, disdain they ne'er so much. . . *1 Hen. VI.* v 3 98
The false revolting Normans thorough thee Disdain to call us lord *2 Hen. VI.* iv 1 88
Exempt from envy, but not from disdain . . . *3 Hen. VI.* iii 3 127
These were her words, utter'd with mild disdain . . . . iv 1 98
Who saw the sun to-day?—Not I, my lord.—Then he disdains to shine *Richard III.* v 3 278
The disdain and shame whereof hath ever since kept Hector fasting and waking . . . . *Troi. and Cres.* i 2 35
I do disdain thy courtesy, proud Trojan . . . . . . v 6 15
Disdains the shadow Which he treads on at noon . . *Coriolanus* i 1 264
They do disdain us much beyond our thoughts . . . . . i 4 26
Against those measles, Which we disdain should tetter us . . iii 1 79
Where one part does disdain with cause, the other Insult without all reason . . . . iii 1 143
His semblable, yea, himself, Timon disdains . . *T. of Athens* iv 3 22
What safe and nicely I might well delay By rule of knighthood, I disdain and spurn . . . . *Lear* v 3 145
Solicit'st here a lady that disdains Thee and the devil alike *Cymbeline* i 6 147
Revenges, hers [woman's]; Ambitions, covetings, change of prides, disdain . . . . ii 5 25
The boy disdains me, He leaves me, scorns me . . . . v 5 105
Disdained. It better fits my blood to be disdained of all than to fashion a carriage to rob love from any . . . . *Much Ado* i 3 30
My heart disdained that my tongue Should so profane the word *Richard II.* i 4 12
So proudly as if he disdain'd the ground . . . . . . v 5 83
Revenge the jeering and disdain'd contempt Of this proud king *1 Hen. IV.* i 3 183
Behold yourself so by a son disdain'd . . . *2 Hen. IV.* v 2 95
I disdain'd it, and did scorn to fly . . . . *Richard III.* iii 4 85
The general's disdain'd By him one step below, he by the next *Troi. and Cres.* i 3 129
To assume a semblance That very dogs disdain'd . . . *Lear* v 3 188
You shall find me, wretched man, a thing The most disdain'd of fortune *Cymbeline* iii 4 20
If I should tell my history, it would seem Like lies disdain'd in the reporting . . . . *Pericles* v 1 120
Disdainest. 'Tis only title thou disdain'st in her . . *All's Well* ii 3 124
Disdaineth. And now, like Nilus, it disdaineth bounds . *T. Andron.* iii 1 71
Disdainful. That I was disdainful, and that I had my good wit out of the 'Hundred Merry Tales' . . . . *Much Ado* ii 1 134
She is too disdainful ; I know her spirits are as coy and wild As haggerds . . . . iii 1 34
A sweet Athenian lady is in love With a disdainful youth *M. N. Dream* ii 1 261
You do me wrong, good sooth, you do, In such disdainful manner me to woo . . . . ii 2 130
Praising the proud disdainful shepherdess . . . *As Y. Like It* iii 4 53
I have loved this proud disdainful haggard . . *T. of Shrew* iv 2 39
Abused in disdainful language . . . . *Hen. V.* iii 6 118
Disdainful. Stubborn to justice, apt to accuse it, and Disdainful to be tried by't . . . . *Hen. VIII.* ii 4 123
He makes me angry with him ; for he seems Proud and disdainful *Ant. and Cleo.* iii 13 142
Disdainfully. Either greet him not, Or else disdainfully, which shall shake him more Than if not look'd on . . . *Troi. and Cres.* iii 3 53
Disdaining. Which I disdaining scorn'd and craved death . *1 Hen. VI.* i 4 32
Disdaining duty that to us belongs . . . . *2 Hen. VI.* iii 1 17
Disdaining fortune, with his brandish'd steel, Which smoked with bloody execution, Like valour's minion carved out his passage *Macbeth* i 2 17
Disdaining me and throwing favours on The low Posthumus . *Cymbeline* iii 5 75
Disease. And make him By inch-meal a disease ! . . . *Tempest* ii 2 3
His dissolute disease will scarce obey this medicine . . *Mer. Wives* iii 3 204
I have purchased as many diseases under her roof as come to *M. for M.* i 2 46
Thou art always figuring diseases in me ; but thou art full of error ; I am sound . . . . i 2 53
He will hang upon him like a disease . . . . . *Much Ado* i 1 87
Washes all the air, That rheumatic diseases do abound . *M. N. Dream* ii 1 105
Subject to the same diseases, healed by the same means *Mer. of Venice* iii 1 64
According to the fool's bolt, sir, and such dulcet diseases *As Y. Like It* v 4 68
And that his lady mourns at his disease . . . *T. of Shrew* Ind. 1 62
Though she have as many diseases as two and fifty horses . . i 2 81
I think it would be the death of the king's disease . . . *All's Well* i 1 26
The king's disease—my project may deceive me, But my intents are fix'd i 1 243
Many thousand on's Have the disease, and feel't not . . *W. Tale* i 2 207
I cannot name the disease ; and it is caught Of you that yet are well i 2 386
Before the curing of a strong disease, Even in the instant of repair and health, The fit is strongest . . . . . . *K. John* iii 4 112
A good healthy water ; but, for the party that owed it, he might have more diseases than he knew for . . . . *2 Hen. IV.* i 2 5
It is a kind of deafness.—I think you are fallen into the disease . i 2 136
It is the disease of not listening, the malady of not marking . . i 2 138
Borrowing only lingers and lingers it out, but the disease is incurable . i 2 266
A good wit will make use of any thing : I will turn diseases to commodity . . . . i 2 278
Gluttony and diseases make them ; I make them not . . . ii 4 46
If the cook help to make the gluttony, you help to make the diseases . ii 4 49
What rank diseases grow, And with what danger, near the heart of it . iii 1 39
I am a diseased man.—What disease hast thou?—A whoreson cold . iii 2 192
Of which disease Our late king, Richard, being infected, died . . iv 1 57
This part of his conjoins with my disease, And helps to end me . . iv 5 64
Either wise bearing or ignorant carriage is caught, as men take diseases v 1 85
And, in that ease, I'll tell thee my disease . . . *1 Hen. VI.* ii 5 44
Long sitting to determine poor men's causes Hath made me full of sickness and diseases . . . . *2 Hen. VI.* iv 7 94
That's the appliance only Which your disease requires . . *Hen. VIII.* i 1 125
'Tis time to give 'em physic, their diseases Are grown so catching . . i 3 36
The rotten diseases of the south, the guts-griping, ruptures, catarrhs *Troi. and Cres.* v 1 21
And at that time bequeathe you my diseases . . . . . . v 10 57
As she is now, she will but disease our better mirth . . *Coriolanus* i 3 117
Those cold ways, That seem like prudent helps, are very poisonous Where the disease is violent . . . . iii 1 222
He's a disease that must be cut away.—O, he's a limb that has but a disease . . . . iii 1 295
Thou disease of a friend, and not himself ! . . . *T. of Athens* iii 1 56
O, may diseases only work upon't ! . . . . iii 1 63
A dedicated beggar to the air, With his disease of all-shunn'd poverty . iv 2 14
They love thee not that use thee ; Give them diseases . . . iv 3 84
Be men like blasted woods, And may diseases lick up their false bloods ! iv 3 539
What's the disease he means?—'Tis call'd the evil . . . *Macbeth* iv 3 146
This disease is beyond my practice . . . . v 1 65
Find her disease, And purge it to a sound and pristine health . . v 3 51
Like the owner of a foul disease, To keep it from divulging, let it feed Even on the pith of life . . . . *Hamlet* iv 1 21
Diseases desperate grown By desperate appliance are relieved, Or not at all . . . . iv 3 9
Kill thy physician, and the fee bestow Upon thy foul disease . . *Lear* i 1 167
Five days we do allot thee, for provision To shield thee from diseases of the world . . . . i 1 177
Thou art my flesh, my blood, my daughter ; Or rather a disease that's in my flesh, Which I must needs call mine . . . . . . ii 4 225
We do lance Diseases in our bodies . . . . . *Ant. and Cleo.* v 1 37
Diseases have been sold dearer than physic . . . *Pericles* iv 6 105
Diseased. Be cured Of this diseased opinion, and betimes . *W. Tale* i 2 297
Diseased nature oftentimes breaks forth In strange eruptions *1 Hen. IV.* iii 1 27
I am a diseased man.—What disease hast thou?—A whoreson cold *2 Hen. IV.* iii 2 191
We are all diseased . . . . iv 1 54
Thy flatterers yet wear silk, drink wine, lie soft ; Hug their diseased perfumes . . . . *T. of Athens* iv 3 207
Canst thou not minister to a mind diseased? . . . . *Macbeth* v 3 40
My wit's diseased : but, sir, such answer as I can make, you shall command . . . . *Hamlet* iii 2 334
Diseased ventures That play with all infirmities for gold ! . . *Cymbeline* i 6 123
Disedged. I grieve myself To think, when thou shalt be disedged by her That now thou tirest on . . . . iii 4 96
Disembark. I must unto the road, to disembark Some necessaries *T. G. of Ver.* ii 4 187
Go to the bay and disembark my coffers : Bring thou the master *Othello* ii 1 210
Disfigure. And vows, if he can take you, To scorch your face and to disfigure you . . . . *Com. of Errors* v 1 183
Disfigure not his slop . . . . *L. L. Lost* iv 3 59
You are but as a form in wax By him imprinted and within his power To leave the figure or disfigure it . . . . . *M. N. Dream* i 1 51
And say he comes to disfigure, or to present, the person of Moonshine . iii 1 62
He will throw a figure in her face and so disfigure her with it *T. of Shrew* i 2 114
Disfigured. In this the antique and well noted face Of plain old form is much disfigured . . . . *K. John* iv 2 22
By you unhappied and disfigured clean . . . . *Richard II.* iii 1 10
Disfurnish. My riches are these poor habiliments, Of which if you should here disfurnish me, You take the sum and substance that I have *T. G. of Ver.* iv 1 14
What a wicked beast was I to disfurnish myself against such a good time! *T. of Athens* iii 2 49
Or she'll disfurnish us of all our cavaliers . . . . *Pericles* iv 6 12
Disgestions. Your appetites and your disgestions doo's not agree with it *Hen. V.* v 1 27
Disgorge. Wouldst thou disgorge into the general world . *As Y. Like It* ii 7 69

Disgorge. So, so, thou common dog, didst thou disgorge Thy glutton bosom . . . . *2 Hen. IV.* i 3 97
The deep-drawing barks do there disgorge Their warlike fraughtage *Troi. and Cres.* Prol. 12
The grisled north Disgorges such a tempest forth . . *Pericles* iii Gower 48

Disgrace. There is not only disgrace and dishonour in that, monster, but an infinite loss . . . . *Tempest* iv 1 209
Lest my jealous aim might err And so unworthily disgrace the man *T. G. of Ver.* iii 1 29
Appoint a meeting with this old fat fellow, Where we may take him and disgrace him for it . . . . . . *Mer. Wives* iv 4 16
I will join with thee to disgrace her.—I will disparage her no farther *Much Ado* iii 2 130
To disgrace Hero before the whole assembly, and not marry her . iv 2 56
And then grace us in the disgrace of death . . *L. L. Lost* i 1 3
His disgrace is to be called boy ; but his glory is to subdue men . . i 2 186
Thy grace being gain'd cures all disgrace in me . . . iv 3 67
Like tears that did their own disgrace bewail . *M. N. Dream* iv 1 61
That either you might stay him from his intendment or brook such disgrace well as he shall run into . . *As Y. Like It* i 1 140
If thou dost him any slight disgrace or if he do not mightily grace himself on thee, he will practise against thee by poison . . . i 1 155
To disgrace my man's apparel and to cry like a woman . . . ii 4 4
Well, thou hast a son shall take this disgrace off me . *All's Well* ii 3 249
Disgraces have of late knocked too often at my door . . . v 1 31
To my own disgrace Neglected my sworn duty in that case . *Richard II.* i 1 133
My teeth shall tear The slavish motive of recanting fear, And spit it bleeding in his high disgrace . . . . . . i 1 194
Nor my own disgrace Have ever made me sour my patient cheek . ii 1 168
I will take it as a sweet disgrace . . . *2 Hen. IV.* i 1 89
What a disgrace is it to me to remember thy name ! or to know thy face ! . . . . ii 2 15
Which must proportion . . . the disgrace we have digested . *Hen. V.* iii 6 135
And for our disgrace, his own person, kneeling at our feet, but a weak and worthless satisfaction . . . . iii 6 140
We shall much disgrace With four or five most vile and ragged foils, Right ill-disposed in brawl ridiculous, The name of Agincourt iv Prol. 49
Let it not disgrace me, If I demand, before this royal view . v 2 31
Come, come, 'tis only I that must disgrace thee . . *1 Hen. VI.* i 5 8
I quickly shed Some of his bastard blood ; and in disgrace Bespoke him thus . . . . iv 6 20
A dower, my lords ! disgrace not so your king . . . . v 5 48
From top of honour to disgrace's feet . . . *2 Hen. VI.* i 2 49
Till we have brought Duke Humphrey in disgrace . . . . i 3 99
Causeless have laid disgraces on my head . . . . . iii 1 162
And spread they shall be, to thy foul disgrace And utter ruin *3 Hen. VI.* i 1 253
This deep disgrace in brotherhood Touches me deeper than you can imagine . . . . *Richard III.* i 1 111
Plant some other in the throne, To the disgrace and downfall of your house . . . . iii 7 217
I cannot promise But that you shall sustain moe new disgraces *Hen. VIII.* iii 2 5
How eagerly ye follow my disgraces, As if it fed ye ! . . . iii 2 240
Pray heaven, he sound not my disgrace ! . . . . . v 2 13
Thieves, . . . That in their country did them that disgrace, We fear to warrant in our native place ! . . . . *Troi. and Cres* ii 2 95
Disgrace to your great worths and shame to me . . . . ii 2 151
You must not think to fob off our disgrace with a tale . *Coriolanus* i 1 97
I have forgot my part, and I am out, Even to a full disgrace . . v 3 42
Our empress' shame, and stately Rome's disgrace ! . . *T. Andron.* iv 2 60
I will bite my thumb at them ; which is a disgrace to them *Rom. and Jul.* i 1 49
I hear Macduff lives in disgrace . . . . . . *Macbeth* iii 6 23
Should I stay longer, It would be my disgrace and your discomfort . iv 2 29
No disgrace Shall fall you for refusing him at sea . *Ant. and Cleo.* iii 7 39
Behind me The inevitable prosecution of Disgrace and horror . . iv 14 66
That mine own servant should Parcel the sum of my disgraces by Addition of his envy ! . . . . v 2 163

Disgraced. Your grace is welcome to a man disgraced *T. G. of Ver.* v 4 123
You disgraced her, when you should marry her . . *Much Ado* v 1 245
He hath disgraced me, and hindered me half a million . *Mer. of Venice* iii 1 56
But indeed words are very rascals since bonds disgraced them *T. Night* iii 1 25
And I Play too, but so disgraced a part . . . . *W. Tale* i 2 188
I am disgraced, impeach'd, and baffled here, Pierced to the soul *Rich. II.* i 1 170
Disgraced me in my happy victories, Sought to entrap me *1 Hen. IV.* iv 3 97
Who was shot, who disgraced, what terms the enemy stood on *Hen. V.* iii 6 77
To be disgraced by an inkhorn mate . . . . . *1 Hen. VI.* iii 1 99
When you disgraced me in my embassade, Then I degraded you from being king . . . . *3 Hen. VI.* iv 3 32
Our brother is imprison'd by your means, Myself disgraced *Richard III.* i 3 79
The crown, usurp'd, disgraced his kingly glory . . . . . iv 4 371
If the trial of the law o'ertake ye, You'll part away disgraced *Hen. VIII.* iii 1 97
Has much disgraced me in't ; I'm angry at him . *T. of Athens* iii 3 13

Disgraceful. Away with these disgraceful wailing robes ! . *1 Hen. VI.* i 1 86

Disgracing of these colours that I wear . . . . . . iii 4 29

Disgracious. I have done some offence That seems disgracious in the city's eyes . . . . *Richard III.* iii 7 112
If I be so disgracious in your sight, Let me march on . . . iv 4 177

Disguise. If shame live In a disguise of love . . *T. G. of Ver.* v 4 107
I have a disguise to sound Falstaff . . . . . *Mer. Wives* ii 1 246
How might we disguise him?—Alas the day, I know not! . . . iv 2 70
In which disguise, While other jests are something rank on foot . . iv 6 21
So disguise shall, by the disguised, Pay with falsehood false exacting *Meas. for Meas.* iii 2 294
I will assume thy part in some disguise . . . . . *Much Ado* i 1 323
A fancy that he hath to strange disguises . . . . . . iii 2 33
Disguise us at my lodging and return, All in an hour . *Mer. of Venice* ii 4 2
But one that scorn to live in this disguise . . *T. of Shrew* iv 2 18
When his disguise and he is parted, tell me what a sprat you shall find him . . . . *All's Well* iii 6 112
In this disguise I think't no sin To cozen him that would unjustly win iv 2 75
Be my aid For such disguise as haply shall become The form of my intent . . . . *T. Night* i 2 54
Disguise, I see, thou art a wickedness . . . . ii 2 28
My best Camillo ! We must disguise ourselves . . . *W. Tale* iv 2 61
Ned, where are our disguises ?—Here, hard by : stand close . *1 Hen. IV.* ii 2 78
Disguise fair nature with hard-favour'd rage . . . *Hen. V.* iii 1 8
Disguise the holy strength of their command . . *Troi. and Cres.* ii 3 136
Who in disguise Follow'd his enemy king, and did him service . *Lear* v 3 219
The wild disguise hath almost Antick'd us all . . *Ant. and Cleo.* ii 7 131
But disguise That which, to appear itself, must not yet be But by self-danger . . . . *Cymbeline* iii 4 147

Disguised. You die, Sir John. Unless you go out disguised *Mer. Wives* iv 2 69
Disguised cheaters, prating mountebanks . . . . *Com. of Errors* i 2 101
Known unto these, and to myself disguised ! . . . . . . ii 2 216
Love doth approach disguised, Armed in arguments . . *L. L. Lost* v 2 83
By and by, disguised they will be here . . . . v 2 96
If by me you'll be advised, Let's mock them still, as well known as disguised . . . . v 2 301
What fools were here, Disguised like Muscovites, in shapeless gear . v 2 303
Were not you here but even now disguised ?—Madam, I was . . v 2 433
Orlando hath a disposition to come in disguised against me to try a fall *As Y. Like It* i 1 131
Do me grace, And offer me disguised in sober robes . *T. of Shrew* i 2 132
'Sigeia tellus,' disguised thus to get your love. . . . . . iii 1 33
O, now you look like Hubert ! all this while You were disguised *K. John* iv 1 127
This ship-boy's semblance hath disguised me quite . . . . . iv 3 4
Jove sometime went disguised, and why not I? . *2 Hen. VI.* iv 1 48
Either be gone before the watch be set, Or by the break of day disguised from hence . . . . *Rom. and Jul.* iii 3 168

Disguiser. O, death's a great disguiser ; and you may add to it *M. for M.* iv 2 186

Disguising. I'll give her father notice Of their disguising and pretended flight . . . . *T. G. of Ver.* ii 6 37
Make our faces vizards to our hearts, Disguising what they are *Macbeth* iii 2 35

Dish. Nor scrape trencher, nor wash dish . . . *Tempest* ii 2 187
Three veneys for a dish of stewed prunes . . . . . *Mer. Wives* i 1 296
I was more than half stewed in grease, like a Dutch dish . . . iii 5 121
A fruit-dish, a dish of some three-pence ; your honours have seen such dishes ; they are not China dishes, but very good dishes *M. for M.* ii 1 95
Go to, go to : no matter for the dish, sir.—No, indeed, sir . . ii 1 98
As I said, for prunes ; and having but two in the dish, as I said . ii 1 103
A table full of welcome makes scarce one dainty dish *Com. of Errors* iii 1 23
Here's a dish I love not : I cannot endure my Lady Tongue . *Much Ado* ii 1 283
His words are a very fantastical banquet, just so many strange dishes . ii 3 23
Four woodcocks in a dish ! . . . . . . *L. L. Lost* iv 3 82
I have here a dish of doves that I would bestow upon your worship *Mer. of Venice* ii 2 144
Were to put good meat into an unclean dish . . *As Y. Like It* iii 3 37
A dish that I do love to feed upon . . . . . *T. of Shrew* iv 3 24
Here, take away this dish.—I pray you, let it stand . . . . iv 3 44
Why, this was moulded on a porringer ; A velvet dish : fie, fie ! . iv 3 65
What dish o' poison has she dressed him ! . . . . *T. Night* ii 5 123
For a quart of ale is a dish for a king . . . . . . *W. Tale* iv 3 8
My figured goblets for a dish of wood . . . . . *Richard II.* iii 3 150
For moving such a dish of skim milk with so honourable an action *1 Hen. IV.* ii 3 35
Didst thou never see Titan kiss a dish of butter ? pitiful-hearted Titan ! ii 4 134
A good dish of prawns . . . . *2 Hen. IV.* ii 1 104
The prince once set a dish of apple-johns before him . . . . ii 4 5
With a dish of caraways, and so forth . . . . v 3 3
There's a dish of leather-coats for you . . . . v 3 44
Like fair fruit in an unwholesome dish, Are like to rot untasted *Troi. and Cres.* ii 3 129
From whence, fragment ?—Why, thou full dish of fool, from Troy . . v 1 10
Who can call him His friend that dips in the same dish ? *T. of Athens* iii 2 73
All covered dishes !—Royal cheer, I warrant you.—Doubt not that . iii 6 55
Would poison were obedient and knew my mind !—Where wouldst thou send it ?—To sauce thy dishes . . . . iv 3 299
Let's carve him as a dish fit for the gods, Not hew him as a carcass *J. Cæsar* ii 1 173
Of the chameleon's dish : I eat the air, promise-crammed . *Hamlet* iii 2 99
Your fat king and your lean beggar is but variable service, two dishes, but to one table . . . . iv 3 26
Or feed on nourishing dishes, or keep you warm . . . *Othello* iii 3 78
He will to his Egyptian dish again . . . . . *Ant. and Cleo.* ii 6 134
I know that a woman is a dish for the gods, if the devil dress her not . v 2 275
One bred of alms and foster'd with cold dishes . . . *Cymbeline* iii 3 119
The imperious seas breed monsters, for the dish Poor tributary rivers as sweet fish . . . . iv 2 35
If I prove a good repast to the spectators, the dish pays the shot . . v 4 158
Marry, come up, my dish of chastity with rosemary and bays ! *Pericles* iv 6 160

Dishabited. From their fixed beds of lime Had been dishabited *K. John* ii 1 220

Dishclout. He wore none but a dishclout of Jaquenetta's . *L. L. Lost* v 2 720
O, he's a lovely gentleman ! Romeo's a dishclout to him *Rom. and Jul.* iii 5 221

Dishearten. No man should possess him with any appearance of fear, lest he, by showing it, should dishearten his army . . . *Hen. V.* iv 1 117
It [drink] persuades him, and disheartens him . . . . . *Macbeth* ii 3 37

Dished. For conspiracy, I know not how it tastes ; though it be dish'd For me to try how . . . . *W. Tale* iii 2 73

Dishonest. Hang him, dishonest rascal ! . . . . *Mer. Wives* iii 3 196
Hang him, dishonest varlet ! we cannot misuse him enough . . . iv 2 104
O you beast ! O faithless coward ! O dishonest wretch ! *Meas. for Meas.* iii 1 137
Did not you say you knew that Friar Lodowick to be a dishonest person? . . . . v 1 262
I hope it is no dishonest desire to desire to be a woman of the world *As Y. Like It* v 3 4
You're a dry fool ; I'll no more of you : besides, you grow dishonest *T. Night* i 5 46
Bid the dishonest man mend himself ; if he mend, he is no longer dishonest . . . . i 5 49
A very dishonest paltry boy, and more a coward than a hare . . . iii 4 420
Fie, thou dishonest Satan ! I call thee by the most modest terms . . iv 2 35
Holding in disdain the German women For some dishonest manners of their life . . . . *Hen. V.* i 2 49

Dishonestly. He had the chain of me, Though most dishonestly he doth deny it . . . . *Com. of Errors* v 1 3
He was gentle, but unfortunate ; Dishonestly afflicted, but yet honest *Cymbeline* iv 2 40

Dishonesty. Heaven be my witness you do, if you suspect me in any dishonesty . . . . *Mer. Wives* iv 2 140
Not honestly, my lord ; but so covertly that no dishonesty shall appear *Much Ado* ii 2 10
His dishonesty appears in leaving his friend here in necessity *T. Night* iii 4 421
What, canst not rule her?—From all dishonesty he can . . *W. Tale* ii 3 47

Dishonour. I had rather crack my sinews, break my back, Than you should such dishonour undergo . . . . *Tempest* iii 1 27
There is not only disgrace and dishonour in that, monster, but an infinite loss . . . . iv 1 209
Swallowed his vows whole, pretending in her discoveries of dishonour *Meas. for Meas.* iii 1 236
The cure of it not only saves your brother, but keeps you from dishonour in doing it . . . . iii 1 246

Dishonour. Dishonour not your eye By throwing it on any other object *Meas. for Meas.* v 1 22
I am more amazed at his dishonour Than at the strangeness of it . v 1 385
So shall the prince And all of them that thus dishonour her . *Much Ado* v 1 44
Some dishonour we had in the loss of that drum . *All's Well* iii 6 59
Conceiving the dishonour of his mother, He straight declined, droop'd, took it deeply . . . . *W. Tale* ii 3 13
But my fair name, Despite of death that lives upon my grave, To dark dishonour's use thou shalt not have . *Richard II.* i 1 169
Shall I so much dishonour my fair stars? . . . . . iv 1 21
Mine honour lives when his dishonour dies, Or my shamed life in his dishonour lies . . . . . v 3 70
See riot and dishonour stain the brow Of my young Harry . *1 Hen. IV.* i 1 85
Dishonour not your mothers . . . *Hen. V.* iii 1 22
Lord Talbot, do not so dishonour me . *1 Hen. VI.* iii 2 90
If you love my mother, Dishonour not her honourable name . . iv 5 14
He seems a knight, And will not any way dishonour me . . v 3 102
This dishonour in thine age Will bring thy head with sorrow to the ground! . . . . *2 Hen. VI.* ii 3 18
I rather would have lost my life betimes Than bring a burthen of dishonour home . . . . . iii 1 298
Never yet did base dishonour blur our name, But with our sword we wiped away the blot . . . . iv 1 39
It were dishonour to deny it her.—It were no less . *3 Hen. VI.* iii 2 9
Mischance hath trod my title down, And with dishonour laid me on the ground . . . . . iii 3 9
Look, therefore, Lewis, that by this league and marriage Thou draw not on thy danger and dishonour . . . . iii 3 75
No more my king, for he dishonours me . . . iii 3 184
So good a lady that no tongue could ever Pronounce dishonour of her *Hen. VIII.* ii 3 4
That defend her, Not palating the taste of her dishonour *Troi. and Cres.* iv 1 59
Your dishonour Mangles true judgement . *Coriolanus* iii 1 157
This no more dishonours you at all Than to take in a town with gentle words . . . . . iii 2 58
To beg of thee, it is my more dishonour Than thou of them . iii 2 124
And suffer not dishonour to approach The imperial seat . *T. Andron.* i 1 13
My sons would never so dishonour me . . . i 1 295
Confederates all thus to dishonour me . . . i 1 303
The gods of Rome forfend I should be author to dishonour you! . i 1 435
And withal Thrust these reproachful speeches down his throat That he hath breathed in my dishonour here . . . ii 1 56
Since dishonour traffics with man's nature, He is but outside *T. of Athens* i 1 158
Do what you will, dishonour shall be humour . *J. Cæsar* iv 3 109
Let not my jealousies be your dishonours, But mine own safeties *Macbeth* iv 3 29
And there put on him What forgeries you please; marry, none so rank As may dishonour him . . . *Hamlet* ii 1 21
My lord, that would dishonour him.—Faith, no . . ii 1 27
By looking back what I have left behind 'Stroy'd in dishonour *A. and C.* iii 11 54
I have lived in such dishonour, that the gods Detest my baseness . iv 14 56
Thou art the pandar to her dishonour and equally to me disloyal *Cymb.* iii 4 32
Gone she is To death or to dishonour . . . iii 5 63
Nor boots it me to say I honour him, If he suspect I may dishonour him *Pericles* i 2 21
Dishonourable. Surrey, thou liest.—Dishonourable boy! *Richard II.* iv 1 65
Ten times more dishonourable ragged than an old faced ancient *1 Hen. IV.* iv 2 33
As a false favourite doth his prince's name, In deeds dishonourable *2 Hen. IV.* iv 2 26
Death's dishonourable victory We with our stately presence glorify *1 Hen. VI.* i 1 20
O calm, dishonourable, vile submission! . *Rom. and Jul.* iii 1 76
And peep about To find ourselves dishonourable graves *J. Cæsar* i 2 138
Dishonoured. Have ta'en revenge, By so receiving a dishonour'd life With ransom of such shame . . *Meas. for Meas.* iv 4 34
My wife, That hath abused and dishonour'd me *Com. of Errors* v 1 199
I stand dishonour'd, that have gone about To link my dear friend to a common stale . . . *Much Ado* iv 1 65
A villain, that hath slandered, scorned, dishonoured my kinswoman iv 1 304
He is dishonour'd by a man which ever Profess'd to him *W. Tale* i 2 455
This place commands my patience, Or thou shouldst find thou hast dishonour'd me . . . *1 Hen. VI.* iii 1 9
And give her as a prey to law and shame, That hath dishonour'd Gloucester's honest name . . . *2 Hen VI.* ii 1 199
And Warwick, doing what you gave in charge, Is now dishonoured by this new marriage. . . . *3 Hen. VI.* iv 1 33
By my George, my garter, and my crown,— Profaned, dishonour'd, and the third usurp'd . . . *Richard III.* iv 4 367
My father's death— Thy life hath that dishonour'd . iv 4 375
Nor has Coriolanus Deserved this so dishonour'd rub *Coriolanus* iii 1 60
What is the matter That being pass'd for consul with full voice, I am so dishonour'd? . . . . . iii 3 60
To see your wives dishonour'd to your noses . . iv 6 83
When wert thou wont to walk alone, Dishonour'd thus? . *T. Andron.* i 1 340
Confederates in the deed That hath dishonour'd all our family . i 1 345
The dismall'st day is this that e'er I saw, To be dishonour'd by my sons! i 1 385
'Tis thou and those that have dishonour'd me . . . i 1 425
What, madam! be dishonour'd openly, And basely put it up without revenge? . . . . . . i 1 432
Nor would your noble mother for much more Be so dishonour'd in the court . . . . . . ii 1 52
With the woful fere And father of that chaste dishonour'd dame . iv 1 90
Lest in this marriage he should be dishonour'd . *Rom. and Jul.* iv 3 26
No unchaste action, or dishonour'd step . . . *Lear* i 1 231
Dis-horn the spirit . . . . *Mer. Wives* iv 4 63
Disinherit. My son, Whom I unnaturally shall disinherit *3 Hen. VI.* i 1 193
Father, you cannot disinherit me . . . . i 1 226
Thou, being a king, blest with a goodly son, Didst yield consent to disinherit him . . . . . ii 2 24
Disinherited. And disinherited thine only son . . . i 1 225
Until that act of parliament be repeal'd Whereby my son is disinherited i 1 250
A wizard told him that by G His issue disinherited should be *Richard III.* i 1 57
Disjoin. I may disjoin my hand, but not my faith . *K. John* iii 1 262
The abuse of greatness is, when it disjoins Remorse from power *J. Cæsar* ii 1 18
Disjoined. A whole armado of convicted sail Is scatter'd and disjoin'd from fellowship . . . . *K. John* iii 4 3
Disjoining. And by disjoining hands, hell lose a soul . . iii 1 197
Disjoint. Let the frame of things disjoint, both the worlds suffer *Macbeth* iii 2 16
Or thinking by our late dear brother's death Our state to be disjoint *Ham.* i 2 20
Disjunction. I see, There's no disjunction to be made . *W. Tale* iv 4 540

Dislike. I never heard any soldier dislike it . *Meas. for Meas.* i 2 18
I may neither choose whom I would nor refuse whom I dislike *Mer. of Ven.* i 2 26
I did dislike the cut of a certain courtier's beard . *As Y. Like It* v 4 73
Now you see, sir, how your fooling grows old, and people dislike it *T. Night* i 5 119
Mere dislike Of our proceedings kept the earl from hence *1 Hen. IV.* iv 1 64
I do protest, I have not sought the day of this dislike . . v 1 26
In pain of your dislike or pain of death . . . *2 Hen. VI.* iii 2 257
So your dislike, to whom I would be pleasing, Doth cloud my joys with danger and with sorrow . . . *3 Hen. VI.* iv 1 73
Ever in fear to kindle your dislike . . . . *Hen. VIII.* ii 4 25
No dislike i' the world against the person Of the good queen . ii 4 223
You feed too much on this dislike . . *Troi. and Cres.* ii 3 236
To seem to affect the malice and displeasure of the people is as bad as that which he dislikes, to flatter them . . *Coriolanus* ii 2 25
Art thou not Romeo and a Montague?—Neither, fair saint, if either thee dislike . . . . . . *Rom. and Jul.* ii 2 61
If your mind dislike any thing, obey it . . . *Hamlet* v 2 227
If he dislike it, let him to our sister . . . . *Lear* i 3 14
On every dream, Each buzz, each fancy, each complaint, dislike . i 4 348
What most he should dislike seems pleasant to him; What like, offensive . . . . iv 2 10
I'll do't; but it dislikes me . . . . *Othello* ii 3 49
I do not much dislike the matter, but The manner of his speech *Ant. and Cleo.* ii 2 113
How absolute she's in't, Not minding whether I dislike or no! *Pericles* ii 5 20
Disliken The truth of your own seeming . . *W. Tale* iv 4 666
Dislikest. If she be All that is virtuous, save what thou dislikest, A poor physician's daughter, thou dislikest Of virtue for the name *All's Well* ii 3 129
Dislimn. Even with a thought The rack dislimns . *Ant. and Cleo.* iv 14 10
Dislocate. Apt enough to dislocate and tear Thy flesh and bones *Lear* iv 2 65
Dislodged. The Volscians are dislodged, and Marcius gone *Coriolanus* v 4 44
Disloyal. Thou subtle, perjured, false, disloyal man! *T. G. of Ver.* iv 2 95
The lady is disloyal . . . . . *Much Ado* iii 2 107
Disloyal?—The word is too good to paint out her wickedness . iii 2 111
Summon a session, that we may arraign Our most disloyal lady *W. Tale* ii 3 203
To God, his sovereign and to him disloyal . . *Richard II.* i 3 114
Thou dost suspect That I have been disloyal to thy bed . . v 2 105
Assisted by that most disloyal traitor, The thane of Cawdor . *Macbeth* i 2 52
Such things in a false disloyal knave Are tricks of custom *Othello* iii 3 121
Give me a living reason she's disloyal.—I do not like the office . iii 3 409
O disloyal thing, That shouldst repair my youth, thou heap'st A year's age on me . . . . *Cymbeline* i 1 131
Disloyal! No: She's punish'd for her truth . . . . iii 2 6
Thou art the pandar to her dishonour and equally to me disloyal . iii 4 33
Disloyalty. Look sweet, speak fair, become disloyalty . *Com. of Errors* iii 2 11
Such seeming truth of Hero's disloyalty . . . *Much Ado* iii 2 49
Dismal. I am wrapp'd in dismal thinkings . . . *All's Well* v 3 128
And Bolingbroke my sorrow's dismal heir . . . *Richard II.* ii 2 63
A dismal fight Betwixt the stout Lord Talbot and the French *1 Hen. VI.* i 1 105
A raven's note, Whose dismal tune bereft my vital powers *2 Hen. VI.* iii 2 41
Like to a dismal clangor heard from far . . *3 Hen. VI.* ii 3 18
Now death shall stop his dismal threatening sound . . . ii 6 58
And chattering pies in dismal discords sung . . . v 6 48
So full of dismal terror was the time! . . . *Richard III.* i 4 7
For more slander to thy dismal seat, We give thee up our guiltless blood to drink . . . . iii 3 13
They told me they would bind me here Unto the body of a dismal yew *T. Andron.* ii 3 107
And be this dismal sight The closing up of our most wretched eyes . iii 1 262
A joyless, dismal, black, and sorrowful issue . . . iv 2 66
This torture should be roar'd in dismal hell . . *Rom. and Jul.* iii 2 44
My dismal scene I needs must act alone . . . . iv 3 19
Began a dismal conflict . . . . . *Macbeth* i 2 53
This night I'll spend Unto a dismal and a fatal end . . . iii 5 21
My fell of hair Would at a dismal treatise rouse and stir As life were in't v 5 12
This dread and black complexion smear'd With heraldry more dismal *Hamlet* ii 2 478
The sight is dismal . . . . v 2 378
And now, This ornament Makes me look dismal will I clip to form *Pericles* v 3 74
Dismallest. The dismall'st day is this that e'er I saw . *T. Andron.* i 1 384
With the dismall'st object hurt That ever eye with sight made heart lament! . . . . ii 3 204
Dismantle. Muffle your face, Dismantle you . . *W. Tale* iv 4 666
Commit a thing so monstrous, to dismantle So many folds of favour *Lear* i 1 220
Dismantled. This realm dismantled was Of Jove himself . *Hamlet* iii 2 293
Dismasked. Fair ladies mask'd are roses in their bud; Dismask'd, their damask sweet commixture shown, Are angels vailing clouds, or roses blown . . . . . . *L. L. Lost* v 2 296
Dismay. Brimful of sorrow and dismay . . . *Tempest* v 1 14
She shall not dismay me: I care not for that, but that I am afeard *Mer. Wives* iii 4 27
Come on: in this there can be no dismay . . *Mer. of Venice* i 3 182
With much much more dismay I view the fight than thou that makest the fray . . . . iii 2 61
Dismay not, princes, at this accident . . *1 Hen. VI.* iii 3 1
O, come away! My soul is full of discord and dismay . *Hamlet* iv 1 45
Dismayed. You do look, my son, in a moved sort, As if you were dismay'd *Tempest* iv 1 147
Be not dismayed.—No, she shall not dismay me . *Mer. Wives* ii 4 26
The conqueror is dismay'd. Proceed, good Alexander . *L. L. Lost* v 2 570
And saw the lion's shadow ere himself And ran dismay'd away *Mer. of Ven.* v 1 9
Be not dismay'd, for succour is at hand . . *1 Hen. VI.* i 2 50
Be not dismay'd, fair lady; nor misconstrue The mind of Talbot . ii 3 73
But cheer thy heart, and be thou not dismay'd . *Richard III.* v 3 174
Go, masters, get you home; be not dismay'd . . *Coriolanus* iv 6 150
Dismay'd not this Our captains, Macbeth and Banquo? . . *Macbeth* i 2 33
Do you go back dismay'd? 'tis a lost fear . . . *Othello* v 2 269
Disme. Every tithe soul, 'mongst many thousand dismes, Hath been as dear as Helen . . . . . *Troi. and Cres.* ii 2 19
Dismember. They whirl asunder and dismember me . *K. John* iii 1 330
O, that we then could come by Cæsar's spirit, And not dismember Cæsar! . . . . *J. Cæsar* ii 1 170
Dismembered. Is set afire by thine own ignorance, And thou dismember'd with thine own defence . . . . *Rom. and Jul.* iii 3 134
Dismiss. Use him for the present and dismiss him . *Meas. for Meas.* iv 2 27
O, dismiss this audience, and I shall tell you more . *L. L. Lost* iv 3 210
Upon my power I may dismiss this court . . *Mer. of Venice* iv 1 104
If it be a suit from the count, I am sick, or not at home; what you will, to dismiss it . . . . *T. Night* i 5 117

Dismiss. He hath promised to dismiss the powers Led by the Dauphin — *K. John* v 1 64
Ere the king Dismiss his power, he means to visit us — 1 *Hen. IV.* iv 4 37
Just death, kind umpire of men's miseries, With sweet enlargement doth dismiss me hence — 1 *Hen. VI.* ii 5 30
So, now dismiss your army when ye please; Hang up your ensigns — v 4 173
With thanks and pardon to you all, I do dismiss you — 2 *Hen. VI.* iv 9 21
I do dismiss my powers. Soldiers, I thank you all; disperse yourselves — v 1 44
Please you dismiss me, either with 'ay' or 'no' — 3 *Hen. VI.* iii 2 78
Dismiss the controversy bleeding, the more entangled by your hearing — *Coriolanus* ii 1 85
Will you dismiss the people? — ii 3 162
They Stand in their ancient strength.—Dismiss them home — iv 2 7
Do not bid me Dismiss my soldiers, or capitulate Again with Rome's mechanics — v 3 82
Dismiss your followers and, as suitors should, Plead your deserts in peace and humbleness — *T. Andron.* i 1 44
I will here dismiss my loving friends, And to my fortunes and the people's favour Commit my cause — i 1 53
But life, being weary of these worldly bars, Never lacks power to dismiss itself — *J. Cæsar* i 3 97
Beware the thane of Fife. Dismiss me. Enough — *Macbeth* iv 1 72
Get you to bed on the instant; I will be returned forthwith: dismiss your attendant — *Othello* iv 3 8
He hath commanded me to go to bed, And bade me to dismiss you.—Dismiss me! — iv 3 14
Dismissed. Broom-groves, Whose shadow the dismissed bachelor loves, Being lass-lorn — *Tempest* iv 1 67
I pity those I do not know, Which a dismiss'd offence would after gall — *Meas. for Meas.* ii 2 102
My best train I have from your Sicilian shores dismiss'd — *W. Tale* v 1 164
Show us the hand of God That hath dismiss'd us from our stewardship — *Richard II.* iii 3 78
In rage dismiss'd my father from the court; Broke oath on oath 1 *Hen. IV.* iv 3 100
And, ere they be dismiss'd, let them march by — 2 *Hen. IV.* iv 2 96
We will commit thee thither, Until his army be dismiss'd from him — 2 *Hen. VI.* iv 9 40
Very faintly he said 'Rise;' dismiss'd me Thus, with his speechless hand — *Coriolanus* v 1 66
Return to her, and fifty men dismiss'd? No, rather I abjure all roofs *Lear* ii 4 210
Dismissing. Return and sojourn with my sister, Dismissing half your train — ii 4 207
Dismission. Your dismission Is come from Cæsar — *Ant. and Cleo.* i 1 26
In all obey her, Save when command to your dismission tends *Cymbeline* ii 3 57
Dismount thy tuck, be yare in thy preparation — *T. Night* iii 4 244
I will dismount, and by the waggon-wheel Trot — *T. Andron.* v 2 54
Dismounted. Even as your horse bears your praises; who would trot as well, were some of your brags dismounted — *Hen. V.* iii 7 84
Dismounted from your snow-white goodly steed — *T. Andron.* ii 3 76
Disnatured. Create her child of spleen; that it may live, And be a thwart disnatured torment to her! — *Lear* i 4 305
Disobedience. This deceit loses the name of craft, Of disobedience, or unduteous title — *Mer. Wives* v 5 240
Prepare to die For disobedience to your father's will — *M. N. Dream* i 1 87
Which is most infallible disobedience — *All's Well* i 1 150
Which not to have done I think had been in me Both disobedience and ingratitude — *W. Tale* iii 2 69
Get thee gone; for I do see Danger and disobedience in thine eye 1 *Hen. IV.* i 3 16
How will their grudging stomachs be provoked To wilful disobedience! — 1 *Hen. VI.* iv 1 142
They nourish'd disobedience, fed The ruin of the state — *Coriolanus* iii 1 117
Thou that didst set up My disobedience 'gainst the king my father *Cymb.* iii 4 91
Disobedient. She is peevish, sullen, froward, Proud, disobedient, stubborn — *T. G. of Ver.* iii 1 69
Curb those raging appetites that are Most disobedient *Troi. and Cres.* ii 2 182
Disobedient wretch! I tell thee what: get thee to church *Rom. and Jul.* iii 5 161
Where I have learn'd me to repent the sin Of disobedient opposition To you and your behests — iv 2 18
Disobey. Hail, many-colour'd messenger, that ne'er Dost disobey the wife of Jupiter — *Tempest* iv 1 77
Whom to disobey were against all proportion of subjection — *Hen. V.* iv 1 152
Swear allegiance to his majesty, As thou art knight, never to disobey — 1 *Hen. VI.* v 4 170
By Saint Paul, I'll make a corse of him that disobeys — *Richard III.* i 2 37
Disorbed. And fly like chidden Mercury from Jove, Or like a star disorb'd — *Troi. and Cres.* ii 2 46
Disorder. Though she harbours you as her kinsman, she's nothing allied to your disorders — *T. Night* ii 3 105
I will not keep this form upon my head, When there is such disorder in my wit — *K. John* iii 4 102
Disorder, that hath spoil'd us, friend us now! — *Hen. V.* iv 5 17
Fear frames disorder, and disorder wounds Where it should guard — 2 *Hen. VI.* v 2 32
When the planets In evil mixture to disorder wander, What plagues and what portents! — *Troi. and Cres.* i 3 95
Broke the good meeting, With most admired disorder — *Macbeth* iii 4 110
Treachery, and all ruinous disorders, follow us disquietly to our graves — *Lear* i 2 123
His own disorders Deserved much less advancement — ii 4 203
Friends kill friends, and the disorder's such As war were hoodwink'd — *Cymbeline* v 2 15
Disordered. Nothing impaired, but all disordered — *M. N. Dream* v 1 126
Her fruit-trees all unpruned, her hedges ruin'd, Her knots disorder'd — *Richard II.* iii 4 46
He that hath suffer'd this disorder'd spring Hath now himself met with the fall of leaf — iii 4 48
And here have I the daintiness of ear To check time broke in a disorder'd string — v 5 46
Like prisoners wildly overgrown with hair, Put forth disorder'd twigs — *Hen. V.* v 2 44
Men so disorder'd, so debosh'd and bold — *Lear* i 4 263
Your disorder'd rabble Make servants of their betters — i 4 277
Disorderly. If I know how or which way to order these affairs Thus thrust disorderly into my hands, Never believe me — *Richard II.* ii 2 110
Disparage. I will disparage her no farther till you are my witnesses — *Much Ado* iii 2 131
Disparage not the faith thou dost not know — *M. N. Dream* iii 2 174
Disparagement. If Sir John Falstaff have committed disparagements unto you — *Mer. Wives* i 1 31
But to our honour's great disparagement — *Com. of Errors* i 1 149
Disparagement. I would not for the wealth of all the town Here in my house do him disparagement — *Rom. and Jul.* i 5 72
Dispark'd my parks and fell'd my forest woods — *Richard II.* iii 1 23
Dispatch. With the speediest expedition I will dispatch him *T. G. of Ver.* i 3 38
In lieu thereof, dispatch me hence. Come, answer not, but to it presently! — ii 7 88
Dispatch, sweet gentlemen, and follow me — v 2 48
If he bid you set it down, obey him: quickly, dispatch *Mer. Wives* iv 2 112
Take her by the hand, away with her to the deanery, and dispatch it quickly — v 3 3
At that place call upon me; and dispatch — *Meas. for Meas.* iii 1 278
'Tis an accident that heaven provides! Dispatch it presently — iv 3 82
I am your free dependant.—Quick, dispatch — iv 3 96
To have a dispatch of complaints, and to deliver us from devices — iv 4 14
The hour steals on; I pray you, sir, dispatch — *Com. of Errors* iv 1 52
Serious business, craving quick dispatch — *L. L. Lost* ii 1 31
To-day we shall have our dispatch — iv 1 5
Let them go: Dispatch, I say, and find the forester — *M. N. Dream* iv 1 113
O love, dispatch all business, and be gone! — *Mer. of Venice* iii 2 325
Mistress, dispatch you with your safest haste — *As Y. Like It* i 3 43
Will you dispatch us here under this tree, or shall we go with you to your chapel? — iii 3 66
And, after some dispatch in hand at court, Thither we bend again — *All's Well* iii 2 56
Dispatch the most convenient messenger — iii 4 34
Between these main parcels of dispatch effected many nicer needs — iv 3 104
Take and give back affairs and their dispatch — *T. Night* iv 3 18
Nay, prithee, dispatch; the gentleman is half flayed already — *W. Tale* iv 4 654
Therefore I will be sudden and dispatch — *K. John* iv 1 27
My lord, dispatch; read o'er these articles — *Richard II.* iv 1 243
Some music. Dispatch: the room where they supped is too hot 2 *Hen. IV.* ii 4 14
And now dispatch we toward the court, my lords — iv 3 82
'Twill be two o'clock ere they come from the coronation: dispatch, dispatch — v 5 4
With all swift dispatch, To line and new repair our towns of war *Hen. V.* ii 4 6
Dispatch us with all speed, lest that our king Come here himself to question our delay — ii 4 141
I will dispatch the horsemen straight — 1 *Hen. VI.* iv 4 40
Dispatch: this knave's tongue begins to double — 2 *Hen. VI.* ii 3 94
Nay, never bear me hence, dispatch me here — 3 *Hen. VI.* v 5 69
Nay, now dispatch: 'twas I that stabb'd young Edward. — *Richard III.* i 2 182
Are you now going to dispatch this deed? — i 3 341
I like you, lads; about your business straight; Go, go, dispatch — i 3 356
Dispatch; the limit of your lives is out.—O Pomfret, Pomfret! — iii 3 8
Dispatch, my lord; the duke would be at dinner: Make a short shrift — iii 4 96
Come, come, dispatch; 'tis bootless to exclaim — iii 4 104
A wilder nature than the business That seeks dispatch by day *Hen. VIII.* v 1 16
Let's hence, and hear How the dispatch is made — *Coriolanus* i 1 281
If I do send, dispatch Those centuries to our aid — i 7 2
We are peremptory to dispatch This viperous traitor — iii 1 286
Yet give us our dispatch: I am hush'd until our city be afire — v 3 180
Nurse, give it me; my sword shall soon dispatch it — *T. Andron.* iv 2 86
If you had the strength Of twenty men, it would dispatch you straight — *Rom. and Jul.* v 1 79
I will dispatch you severally; you to Lord Lucius — *T. of Athens* ii 2 196
You shall put This night's great business into my dispatch — *Macbeth* i 5 69
Seyton, send out. Doctor, the thanes fly from me. Come, sir, dispatch — v 3 50
And we here dispatch You, good Cornelius, and you, Voltimand — *Hamlet* i 2 33
I your commission will forthwith dispatch, And he to England shall along — iii 3 3
What needed, then, that terrible dispatch of it into your pocket? — *Lear* i 2 33
Not in this land shall he remain uncaught; And found—dispatch — ii 1 60
The several messengers From hence attend dispatch — ii 1 127
Gone, In pity of his misery, to dispatch His nighted life — iv 5 12
Write from us to him; post-post-haste dispatch — *Othello* i 3 46
Which ever as she could with haste dispatch, She'ld come again — i 3 148
Your mystery, your mystery: nay, dispatch — iv 2 30
Prithee, dispatch.—Shall I go fetch your night-gown?—No, unpin me here — iv 3 33
Ere we put ourselves in arms, dispatch we The business we have talk'd of — *Ant. and Cleo.* ii 2 168
To try thy eloquence, now 'tis time: dispatch — iii 12 26
My queen's a squire More tight at this than thou: dispatch — iv 4 15
How! not dead? not dead? The guard, ho! O, dispatch me! — iv 14 104
We'll dispatch indeed; And, when thou hast done this chare, I'll give thee leave To play till doomsday — v 2 230
Poor venomous fool, Be angry, and dispatch — v 2 309
O, come apace, dispatch! I partly feel thee — v 2 325
Prithee, dispatch: The lamb entreats the butcher — *Cymbeline* iii 4 98
The words of your commission Will tie you to the numbers and the time Of their dispatch — iii 7 16
Save poor me, the weaker.—I am sworn, And will dispatch — *Pericles* iv 1 92
Dispatched. Have you dispatched?—Dispatched! — *Mer. Wives* v 5 189
See this dispatch'd with all the haste thou canst — *T. of Shrew* Ind. 1 129
I have to-night dispatched sixteen businesses — *All's Well* iv 3 98
I have dispatch'd in post To sacred Delphos, to Appolo's temple *W. Tale* ii 1 182
And once dispatch'd him in an embassy To Germany — *K. John* i 1 99
What, are there no posts dispatch'd for Ireland? — *Richard II.* ii 2 103
My Lord Northumberland, see them dispatch'd — iii 1 35
A gentleman of mine I have dispatch'd With letters of your love — iii 1 40
You shall be soon dispatch'd with fair conditions — *Hen. V.* ii 4 144
Whilst a field should be dispatch'd and fought, You are disputing of your generals — 1 *Hen. VI.* i 1 72
Let him know We have dispatched the duke, as he commanded 2 *Hen. VI.* iii 2 2
Now, sirs, have you dispatch'd this thing?—Ay, my good lord, he's dead iii 2 6
A bloody deed, and desperately dispatch'd! — *Richard III.* i 4 278
Now stay your strife: what shall be is dispatch'd — *T. Andron.* i 1 193
Is he dispatch'd?—My lord, his throat is cut; that I did for him *Macbeth* iii 4 15
By a brother's hand Of life, of crown, of queen, at once dispatch'd *Hamlet* i 5 75
They have dispatch'd with Pompey, he is gone — *Ant. and Cleo.* iii 2 2
Those things I bid you do, get them dispatch'd — *Cymbeline* i 3 39
So, They are well dispatch'd; now to my daughter's letter — *Pericles* ii 5 15
Dispensation. Than seek a dispensation for his oath — *L. L. Lost* ii 1 87
And yet a dispensation may be had — 1 *Hen. VI.* v 3 85
Dispense. What is it? dispense with trifles — *Mer. Wives* ii 1 47
Nature dispenses with the deed so far That it becomes a virtue *M. for M.* iii 1 135
Dispense with your leisure, I would by and by have some speech with you iii 1 154
Unfeeling fools can with such wrongs dispense — *Com. of Errors* ii 1 103
We must of force dispense with this decree — *L. L. Lost* i 1 148
How shall we then dispense with that contract? — 1 *Hen. VI.* v 5 28

Dispense. Canst thou dispense with heaven for such an oath? *2 Hen. VI.* v 1 181
Men must learn now with pity to dispense . . . *T. of Athens* iii 2 93
Disperse. Away; disperse: but till 'tis one o'clock . . *Mer. Wives* v 5 78
Therefore we will disperse ourselves . . . *Richard II.* ii 4 4
Glory is like a circle in the water, Which never ceaseth to enlarge itself Till by broad spreading it disperse to nought . . . *1 Hen. VI.* i 2 135
I do dismiss my powers. Soldiers, I thank you all; disperse yourselves *2 Hen. VI.* v 1 45
A little gale will soon disperse that cloud . . . . *3 Hen. VI.* v 3 10
Stop the rumour, and allay those tongues That durst disperse it *Hen. VIII.* ii 1 153
My soul grows sad with troubles; Sing, and disperse 'em, if thou canst iii 1 2
I'll find some cunning practice out of hand, To scatter and disperse the giddy Goths . . . . *T. Andron.* v 2 78
A dram of poison, such soon-speeding gear As will disperse itself through all the veins . . . . *Rom. and Jul.* v 1 61
Friends, disperse yourselves; but all remember What you have said *J. Cæsar* ii 1 222
Dispersed. As thou badest me, In troops I have dispersed them *Tempest* i 2 220
And for the rest o' the fleet Which I dispersed, they all have met again i 2 233
At length the sun, gazing upon the earth, Dispersed those vapours that offended us . . . . *Com. of Errors* i 1 90
He hath forsook the court, Broken his staff of office and dispersed The household of the king . . . . . . *Richard II.* ii 3 27
All the Welshmen, hearing thou wert dead, Are gone to Bolingbroke, dispersed and fled . . . . iii 2 74
The Welshmen are dispersed, and Salisbury Is gone to meet the king . iii 3 2
My lord, our army is dispersed already . . *2 Hen. IV.* iv 2 102
With Henry's death the English circle ends; Dispersed are the glories it included . . . . *1 Hen. VI.* i 2 137
Gather our soldiers, scatter'd and dispersed, And lay new platforms . ii 1 76
Now is Cade driven back, his men dispersed; And now is York in arms to second him . . . . *2 Hen. VI.* iv 9 34
Buckingham's army is dispersed and scatter'd . . *Richard III.* iv 4 513
Good comfort bring I to your grace, The Breton navy is dispersed by tempest . . . . iv 4 523
Dispiteous. How now, foolish rheum! Turning dispiteous torture out of door! . . . . *K. John* iv 1 34
Displace. If it be possible for you to displace it with your little finger *Cor.* v 4 4
Swore, With his own single hand he'd take us in, Displace our heads *Cymbeline* iv 2 122
Displaced. I well might lodge a fear To be again displaced *2 Hen. IV.* iv 5 209
If Gloucester be displaced, he'll be protector . . *2 Hen. VI.* i 1 177
You have displaced the mirth, broke the good meeting . *Macbeth* iii 4 109
Displant. Unless philosophy can make a Juliet, Displant a town *R. and J.* iii 3 59
Displanting. Whose qualifications shall come into no true taste again but by the displanting of Cassio . . . . . . *Othello* ii 1 283
Display. Which . . . they will at once display to the night *Mer. Wives* v 3 17
Our colours do return in those same hands That did display them when we first march'd forth . . . . . . *K. John* ii 1 320
And here display, at last, What God will have discover'd for revenge *T. Andron.* iv 1 73
Displayed. These black masks Proclaim an enshield beauty ten times louder Than beauty could, display'd . . . . *Meas. for Meas.* ii 4 81
We meet, With visages display'd, to talk and greet . *L. L. Lost* v 2 144
For women are as roses, whose fair flower Being once display'd, doth fall that very hour . . . . *T. Night* ii 4 40
The dancing banners of the French, Who are at hand, triumphantly display'd . . . . *K. John* ii 1 309
And to sun's parching heat display'd my cheeks . *1 Hen. VI.* i 2 77
His hands abroad display'd, as one that grasp'd And tugg'd for life *2 Hen. VI.* iii 2 172
And display'd the effects Of disposition gentle . . *Hen. VIII.* ii 4 86
The very fellow that of late Display'd so saucily against your highness *Lear* ii 4 41
By the semblance Of their white flags display'd, they bring us peace *Per.* i 4 72
Displease Her brother's noontide with the Antipodes . *M. N. Dream* iii 2 54
And let it not displease thee, good Bianca, For I will love thee *T. of Shrew* i 1 76
You shall hear in such a kind from me As will displease you *1 Hen. IV.* i 3 122
We must not now displease him . . . . . *Othello* iv 3 17
Displeased. No matter who's displeased when you are gone *T. G. of Ver.* ii 7 66
My mirth it much displeased, but pleased my woe . *Meas. for Meas.* iv 1 13
For which, I hope, thou felt'st I was displeased . *Com. of Errors* ii 2 19
I did deny him And suffer'd him to go displeased away . *Mer. of Venice* v 1 213
There's reason he should be displeased at it . . *2 Hen. VI.* i 1 155
God is much displeased That you take with unthankfulness his doing *Richard III.* ii 2 89
You are not displeased with this?—Not I, my lord . . *T. Andron.* i 1 270
I am gone, Having displeased my father, to Laurence' cell *Rom. and Jul.* iii 5 232
If the tag-rag people did not clap him and hiss him, according as he pleased and displeased them . . . . . . *J. Cæsar* i 2 262
Displeasing. For some displeasing service I have done . *1 Hen. IV.* iii 2 5
I was lately here in the end of a displeasing play . *2 Hen. IV.* Epil. 10
Displeasure. If I should take a displeasure against you, look you *Temp.* iv 1 202
Thou peevish officer? Hast thou delight to see a wretched man Do outrage and displeasure to himself? . . . . *Com. of Errors* iv 4 119
Doing displeasure to the citizens By rushing in their houses . . . v 1 142
This may prove food to my displeasure . . . . *Much Ado* i 3 68
I am sick in displeasure to him . . . . ii 2 6
You would abate the strength of your displeasure . . *Mer. of Venice* v 1 198
This duke Hath ta'en displeasure 'gainst his gentle niece *As Y. Like It* i 2 290
I know not how I have deserved to run into my lord's displeasure *All's Well* ii 5 38
He hath incurred the everlasting displeasure of the king . . . iv 3 11
To stop up the displeasure he hath conceived against your son . iv 5 80
I am now, sir, muddied in fortune's mood, and smell somewhat strong of her strong displeasure . . . . v 2 6
Fortune's displeasure is but sluttish, if it smell so strongly . . . v 2 7
Has fallen into the unclean fishpond of her displeasure . . . v 2 22
Oft our displeasures, to ourselves unjust, Destroy our friends and after weep their dust . . . . v 3 63
Tell me true, I charge you, Not fearing the displeasure of your master v 3 235
On your displeasure's peril and on mine . . . *W. Tale* ii 3 45
Though full of our displeasure, yet we free thee From the dead blow of it iv 4 444
Forage, and run To meet displeasure farther from the doors . *K. John* v 1 60
My fear is, your displeasure; my courtesy, my duty *2 Hen. IV.* Epil. 2
That's a perilous shot out of an elder-gun, that a poor and a private displeasure can do against a monarch! . . . . . *Hen. V.* iv 1 211
His wraths, and his cholers, and his moods, and his displeasures . . iv 7 38
I am sorry that the Duke of Buckingham Is run in your displeasure *Hen. VIII.* i 2 110
What cause Hath my behaviour given to your displeasure? . . . ii 4 20
No, he's settled, Not to come off, in his displeasure . . . . iii 2 23
Displeasure. What news abroad?—The heaviest and the worst Is your displeasure with the king . . . . *Hen. VIII.* iii 2 392
Lest your displeasure should enlarge itself To wrathful terms *Tr. and Cr.* v 2 37
To seem to affect the malice and displeasure of the people is as bad as that which he dislikes, to flatter them for their love . . *Coriolanus* ii 2 24
And witness of the malice and displeasure Which thou shouldst bear me iv 5 78
And urged withal Your high displeasure . . . *Rom. and Jul.* iii 1 160
Urge it no more, On height of our displeasure . . . *T. of Athens* iii 5 87
If aught within that little seeming substance, Or all of it, with our displeasure pieced, And nothing more, may fitly like your grace, She's there . . . . *Lear* i 1 202
Found you no displeasure in him by word or countenance? . . . . i 2 172
Forbear his presence till some little time hath qualified the heat of his displeasure . . . . i 2 177
Which for my part I will not be, though I should win your displeasure to entreat me to't . . . . ii 2 119
He, conjunct, and flattering his displeasure, Tripp'd me behind . . ii 2 125
Charged me, on pain of their perpetual displeasure, neither to speak of him iii 3 5
Pluck out his eyes.—Leave him to my displeasure . . . . . iii 7 6
Her revenge being nigh, Bade her wrong stay and her displeasure fly *Othello* ii 1 154
I am sorry For your displeasure; but all will sure be well . . . iii 1 45
A man that languishes in your displeasure . . . . . . iii 3 43
And stood within the blank of his displeasure For my free speech . iii 4 128
When it appears to you where this begins, Turn your displeasure that way . . . . *Ant. and Cleo.* iii 4 34
I shall incur I know not How much of his displeasure . *Cymbeline* i 1 103
On what cause I know not—Took some displeasure at him . *Pericles* i 3 21
Never did my actions yet commence A deed might gain her love or your displeasure . . . . ii 5 54
Disponge. The poisonous damp of night disponge upon me *Ant. and Cleo.* iv 9 13
Disport. Comes hunting this way to disport himself . *3 Hen. VI.* iv 5 8
We make ourselves fools, to disport ourselves . . . *T. of Athens* i 2 141
That my disports corrupt and taint my business . . *Othello* i 3 272
Dispose. All that is mine I leave at thy dispose . . *T. G. of Ver.* ii 7 86
All the treasure we have got; Which, with ourselves, all rest at thy dispose iv 1 76
Dispose of them as thou know'st their deserts . . . . . v 4 159
Dispose of her To some more fitter place, and that with speed *M. for M.* ii 2 16
His goods confiscate to the duke's dispose . . . *Com. of Errors* i 1 21
I do embrace your offer; and dispose For henceforth of poor Claudio *Much Ado* v 1 303
I beg the ancient privilege of Athens, As she is mine, I may dispose of her . . . . *M. N. Dream* i 1 42
To your own bents dispose you: you'll be found, Be you beneath the sky *W. Tale* i 2 179
Needs must you lay your heart at his dispose . . . *K. John* i 1 263
Somewhat we must do. Come, cousin, I'll Dispose of you *Richard II.* ii 2 117
At my tent The Douglas is; and I beseech your grace I may dispose of him . . . . *1 Hen. IV.* v 5 24
Dispose of us and ours; For we no longer are defensible . *Hen. V.* iii 3 49
How can they charitably dispose of any thing, when blood is their argument? . . . . iv 1 149
And how thou pleasest, God, dispose the day! . . . . . . iv 3 132
To view the field in safety and dispose Of their dead bodies . . . iv 7 85
He doth rely on none, But carries on the stream of his dispose Without observance or respect of any . . . . . *Troi. and Cres.* ii 3 174
There to dispose this treasure in mine arms . . . *T. Andron.* iv 2 173
Come, I'll dispose of thee Among a sisterhood of holy nuns *Rom. and Jul.* v 3 156
There is an idle banquet attends you: Please you to dispose yourselves *T. of Athens* i 2 161
Take thou my soldiers, prisoners, patrimony; Dispose of them, of me *Lear* v 3 76
He hath a person and a smooth dispose To be suspected . . *Othello* i 3 403
We intend so to dispose you as Yourself shall give us counsel *A. and C.* v 2 186
Where I'll hear from thee; And by whose letters I'll dispose myself *Pericles* i 2 117
Disposé. Car ce soldat ici est disposé tout à cette heure de couper votre gorge . . . . *Hen. V.* iv 4 37
Disposed. Of the king's ship The mariners say how thou hast disposed And all the rest o' the fleet . . . . *Tempest* i 2 225
I find not Myself disposed to sleep.—Nor I; my spirits are nimble . ii 1 202
I told you, sir, my daughter is disposed of . . . *Mer. Wives* iii 4 74
The children thus disposed, my wife and I . . . Fasten'd ourselves at either end the mast . . . . *Com. of Errors* i 1 84
Tell me how thou hast disposed thy charge . . . . . . i 2 73
Boyet is disposed.—But to speak that in words which his eye hath disclosed . . . . *L. L. Lost* ii 1 249
And knows the trick To make my lady laugh when she's disposed . v 2 466
I will do that when you are disposed to be merry . *As Y. Like It* iv 1 156
He does well enough if he be disposed, and so do I too . *T. Night* ii 3 88
So hot a speed with such advice disposed . . . . *K. John* iii 4 11
We should on, To see how fortune is disposed to us . *1 Hen. IV.* iv 1 38
Speak low; The king your father is disposed to sleep . *2 Hen. IV.* iv 5 17
He's disposed as the hateful raven . . . . . *2 Hen. VI.* iii 1 76
Yet see, When these so noble benefits shall prove Not well disposed *Hen. VIII.* i 2 116
His blows are well disposed . . . . *Troi. and Cres.* iv 5 116
If You had not show'd them how ye were disposed . . *Coriolanus* iii 2 22
I see, Thy honourable metal may be wrought From that it is disposed *J. C.* i 2 314
If I were disposed to stir Your hearts and minds to mutiny and rage, I should do Brutus wrong . . . . iii 2 126
He was disposed to mirth; but on the sudden A Roman thought hath struck him . . . . *Ant. and Cleo.* i 2 86
You did suspect She had disposed with Cæsar . . . . . . iv 14 123
Is he disposed to mirth? I hope he is.—Exceeding pleasant *Cymbeline* i 6 58
When a gentleman is disposed to swear, it is not for any standers-by to curtail his oaths . . . . ii 1 11
Disposer. I'll lay my life, with my disposer . . . *Troi. and Cres.* iii 1 95
Your poor disposer's sick . . . . iii 1 101
Disposing. And put his cause and quarrel To the disposing of the cardinal *K. John* v 7 92
All was royal; To the disposing of it nought rebell'd . . *Hen. VIII.* i 1 43
To fail in the disposing of those chances Which he was lord of *Coriolanus* iv 7 40
Your voice shall be as strong as any man's In the disposing of new dignities . . . . *J. Cæsar* iii 1 178
Disposition. I would have sworn his disposition would have gone to the truth of his words . . . . *Mer. Wives* iii 1 61
Mercy on me! I have a great dispositions to cry . . . . . iii 1 22
More than the villanous inconstancy of man's disposition is able to bear iv 5 111
I do it not in evil disposition . . . . . . *Meas. for Meas.* i 2 122
To practise his judgement with the disposition of natures . . . iii 1 165
I pray you, sir, of what disposition was the duke? . . . . . iii 2 244

Disposition. He is of a very melancholy disposition . . *Much Ado* ii 1 6
It is the base, though bitter, dispostion of Beatrice that puts the world into her person . . ii 1 215
Hath a disposition to come in disguised against me to try a fall *As Y. L. It* i 1 131
My father's rough and envious disposition Sticks me at heart . . i 2 253
My master is of churlish disposition . . . . ii 4 80
Dost thou think, though I am caparisoned like a man, I have a doublet and hose in my disposition? . . . . iii 2 206
In a more coming-on disposition . . . . iv 1 113
'Tis The royal disposition of that beast . . . . . . iv 3 118
Her dispositions she inherits, which makes fair gifts fairer . *All's Well* i 1 47
This drum sticks sorely in your disposition . . . . . iii 6 47
Be generous, guiltless and of free disposition . . . *T. Night* i 5 99
Unsuitable to her disposition, being addicted to a melancholy as she is ii 5 222
Grace and good disposition Attend your ladyship! . . . . iii 1 146
Since fate against thy better disposition . . . *W. Tale* iii 3 28
Sure this robe of mine Does change my disposition . . . . iv 4 135
Lay aside life-harming heaviness And entertain a cheerful disposition *Richard II.* ii 2 4
Of his own royal disposition, And not provoked by any suitor else *Rich. III.* i 3 63
Of disposition gentle, and of wisdom O'ertopping woman's power *Hen. VIII.* ii 4 87
There is no help; The bitter disposition of the time Will have it so *Troi. and Cres.* iv 1 48
So many so minded, Wave thus, to express his disposition . *Coriolanus* i 6 74
Give your dispositions the reins, and be angry at your pleasures . ii 1 33
Neither to care whether they love or hate him manifests the true knowledge he has in their disposition . . . . ii 2 15
Lesser had been The thwartings of your dispositions . . . iii 2 21
Away, my disposition, and possess me Some harlot's spirit! . . iii 2 111
Tell me, daughter Juliet, How stands your disposition to be married? *Rom. and Jul.* i 3 65
By my holy order, I thought thy disposition better temper'd . . iii 3 115
You make me strange Even to the disposition that I owe . *Macbeth* iii 4 113
But what, in faith, make you from Wittenberg?—A truant disposition, good my lord . . . . *Hamlet* i 2 169
And we fools of nature So horridly to shake our disposition . . . i 4 55
As I perchance hereafter shall think meet To put an antic disposition on i 5 172
It goes so heavily with my disposition that this goodly frame, the earth, seems to me a sterile promontory . . . . ii 2 309
Most like a gentleman.—But with much forcing of his disposition . iii 1 12
If our father carry authority with such dispositions as he bears . *Lear* i 1 309
An admirable evasion of whoremaster man, to lay his goatish disposition to the charge of a star! . . . . i 2 138
Put away These dispositions, that of late transform you . . . i 4 242
Let his disposition have that scope That dotage gives it . . . i 4 314
Whose disposition, all the world well knows, Will not be rubb'd nor stopp'd ii 2 160
It was not altogether your brother's evil disposition made him seek his death . . . . iii 5 7
I fear your disposition . . . . iv 2 31
I crave fit disposition for my wife, Due reference of place . . *Othello* i 3 237
She is of so free, so kind, so apt, so blessed a disposition . . ii 3 326
I know our country disposition well . . . . . . iii 3 201
He was nor sad nor merry.—O well-divided disposition! *Ant. and Cleo.* i 5 53
As they pinch one another by the disposition, he cries out 'No more' . ii 7 8
Dispossess. And fear to kill a woodcock, lest thou dispossess the soul of thy grandam . . . . *T. Night* iv 2 64
Shall then my father's will be of no force To dispossess that child which is not his?—Of no more force to dispossess me, sir, Than was his will to get me . . . . *K. John* i 1 131
I will choose Mine heir from forth the beggars of the world, And dispossess her all . . . . *T. of Athens* i 1 139
Dispossessed. The king hath dispossess'd himself of us . . *K. John* iv 3 23
Dispossessing all my other parts Of necessary fitness . *Meas. for Meas.* ii 4 22
Dispraise. If I can do it By aught that I can speak in his dispraise *T. G. of Ver.* iii 2 47
Which must be done by praising me as much As you in worth dispraise Sir Valentine . . . . iii 2 55
Red, that would avoid dispraise, Paints itself black, to imitate her brow *L. L. Lost* iv 3 264
No abuse.—Not to dispraise me, and call me pantler? . . 2 *Hen. IV.* ii 4 341
You will to her dispraise those parts in me that you love . *Hen. V.* v 2 213
I will not dispraise your sister Cassandra's wit . . *Troi. and Cres.* i 1 46
You do as chapmen do, Dispraise the thing that you desire to buy . iv 1 76
To dispraise my lord with that same tongue Which she hath praised him with above compare So many thousand times . . *Rom. and Jul.* iii 5 237
What, my lord! dispraise?—A mere satiety of commendations *T. of Athens* i 1 165
Dispraised. To praise his faith which I would have dispraised *T. G. of Ver.* iv 4 107
I dispraised him before the wicked, that the wicked might not fall in love with him . . . . 2 *Hen. IV.* ii 4 346
In praising Antony, I have dispraised Cæsar.—Many times, madam *Ant. and Cleo.* ii 5 107
Dispraising. Making you ever better than his praise By still dispraising praise valued with you . . . . 1 *Hen. IV.* v 2 60
Not dispraising whom we praised,—therein He was as calm as virtue *Cymb.* v 5 173
Dispraisingly. So many a time, When I have spoke of you dispraisingly, Hath ta'en your part . . . . *Othello* iii 3 72
Dispropertied. Made them mules, silenced their pleaders and Dispropertied their freedoms . . . . *Coriolanus* ii 1 264
Disproportion. To disproportion me in every part . 3 *Hen. VI.* iii 2 160
One may smell in such a will most rank, Foul disproportion . *Othello* iii 3 233
Disproportioned. He is as disproportion'd in his manners As in his shape *Tempest* v 1 290
There is no composition in these news That gives them credit.—Indeed, they are disproportion'd . . . . *Othello* i 3 2
Disprove. I dare not say I have one friend alive; thou wouldst disprove me . . . . *T. G. of Ver.* v 4 66
That the Lord of Westmoreland shall maintain.—And Warwick shall disprove it . . . . 3 *Hen. VI.* i 1 89
I speak not to disprove what Brutus spoke . . . . *J. Cæsar* iii 2 105
Disprove this villain, if thou be'st a man: He says thou told'st him that his wife was false . . . . *Othello* v 2 172
Disproved. Her shall you hear disproved to her eyes . *Meas. for Meas.* v 1 161
Disprovest. Experience, O, thou disprovest report! . . *Cymbeline* iv 2 34
Dispursed. I dispursed to the garrisons, And never ask'd for restitution 2 *Hen. VI.* iii 1 117
Disputable. He is too disputable for my company . . *As Y. Like It* ii 5 36
Disputation. I understand thy kisses and thou mine, And that's a feeling disputation . . . . 1 *Hen. IV.* iii 1 206
I beseech you now, will you voutsafe me, look you, a few disputations with you . . . . *Hen. V.* iii 2 101

Dispute. Though my soul disputes well with my sense . . *T. Night* iv 3 9
Can he speak? hear? Know man from man? dispute his own estate? *W. Tale* iv 4 411
Whether your grace be worthy, yea or no, Dispute not that 2 *Hen. VI.* i 3 111
Dispute not with her; she is lunatic . . . . *Richard III.* i 3 254
Let me dispute with thee of thy estate.—Thou canst not speak of that thou dost not feel . . . . *Rom. and Jul.* iii 3 63
Dispute it like a man.—I shall do so; But I must also feel it as a man *Macbeth* iv 3 220
Disputed. I'll have't disputed on; 'Tis probable and palpable *Othello* i 2 75
Disputest. Thou disputest like an infant: go, whip thy gig . *L. L. Lost* v 1 69
Disputing. Whilst a field should be dispatch'd and fought, You are disputing of your generals . . . . 1 *Hen. VI.* i 1 73
Disquantity. A little to disquantity your train . . . *Lear* i 4 270
Disquiet. All disquiet, horror and perturbation follows her . *Much Ado* ii 1 268
I pray you, husband, be not so disquiet . . . *T. of Shrew* iv 1 171
I grieving grant Did you too much disquiet . . . *Ant. and Cleo.* ii 2 70
Disquietly. Hollowness, treachery, and all ruinous disorders, follow us disquietly to our graves . . . . *Lear* i 2 124
Disrelish. Her delicate tenderness will find itself abused, begin to heave the gorge, disrelish and abhor . . . . . . *Othello* ii 1 236
Disrobe. O, well did he become that lion's robe That did disrobe the lion of that robe! . . . . *K. John* ii 1 142
Disrobe the images, If you do find them deck'd with ceremonies *J. Cæsar* i 1 69
I'll disrobe me Of these Italian weeds and suit myself As does a Briton peasant . . . . *Cymbeline* v 1 22
Disseat. This push Will cheer me ever, or disseat me now *Macbeth* v 3 21
Dissemble. Tell Whom thou lovest best: see thou dissemble not *T. of Shrew* ii 1 9
Or both dissemble deeply their affections . . . . . iv 4 42
I'll put it on, and I will dissemble myself in't . . *T. Night* iv 2 5
So help me God, as I dissemble not! . . . . 1 *Hen. VI.* iii 1 140
I must dissemble.—York, if thou meanest well, I greet thee well 2 *Hen. VI.* v 1 13
Dissemble not your hatred, swear your love . *Richard III.* ii 1 8
Think you my uncle did dissemble, grandam? . . . . . ii 2 31
I would dissemble with my nature where My fortunes and my friends at stake required I should do so in honour . . *Coriolanus* iii 2 62
Be won at last; Dissemble all your griefs and discontents *T. Andron.* i 1 443
See him dissemble, Know his gross patchery, love him, feed him *T. of A.* v 1 98
O, hardness to dissemble!—How do you, Desdemona? . *Othello* iii 4 34
Soft! here he comes: I must dissemble it . . . *Pericles* ii 5 23
Dissembled. I would I were the first that ever dissembled in such a gown . . . . *T. Night* iv 2 7
Whose fury not dissembled speaks his griefs . . . *T. Andron.* i 1 438
Dissembler. Thou dost wrong me; thou dissembler, thou *Much Ado* v 1 53
Arise, dissembler: though I wish thy death, I will not be the executioner . . . . *Richard III.* i 2 185
There's no trust, No faith, no honesty in men; all perjured, All forsworn, all naught, all dissemblers . . . *Rom. and Jul.* iii 2 87
Dissembling. You dissembling knight! . . . . *Mer. Wives* iii 3 152
Dissembling villain, thou speak'st false in both.—Dissembling harlot, thou art false in all . . . . *Com. of Errors* iv 4 103
What wicked and dissembling glass of mine Made me compare with Hermia's sphery eyne? . . . . *M. N. Dream* ii 2 98
His very hair is of the dissembling colour . . . *As Y. Like It* iii 4 7
O thou dissembling cub! what wilt thou be When time hath sow'd a grizzle on thy case? . . . . *T. Night* v 1 167
Can this be so, That in alliance, amity and oaths, There should be found such false dissembling guile? . . . . 1 *Hen. VI.* iv 1 63
All dissembling set aside, Tell me for truth the measure of his love 3 *Hen. VI.* iii 3 119
Cheated of feature by dissembling nature . . . *Richard III.* i 1 19
And I nothing to back my suit at all, But the plain devil and dissembling looks, And yet to win her! . . . . i 2 237
That dissembling abominable varlet . . . . *Troi. and Cres.* v 4 2
To the dissembling luxurious drab . . . . v 4 8
Good now, play one scene Of excellent dissembling; and let it look Like perfect honour . . . . *Ant. and Cleo.* i 3 79
O Dissembling courtesy! How fine this tyrant Can tickle where she wounds! . . . . *Cymbeline* i 1 84
Dissembly. Is our whole dissembly appeared? . . . *Much Ado* iv 2 1
Dissension. And this same progeny of evils comes From our debate, from our dissension . . . . *M. N. Dream* ii 1 116
Keep you out of prawls, and prabbles, and quarrels, and dissensions *Hen. V.* iv 8 70
And for dissension, who preferreth peace More than I do?—except I be provoked . . . . 1 *Hen. VI.* iii 1 33
Civil dissension is a viperous worm . . . . iii 1 72
This late dissension grown betwixt the peers Burns under feigned ashes of forged love . . . . iii 1 189
Let this dissension first be tried by fight . . . . . . iv 1 116
If they perceive dissension in our looks And that within ourselves we disagree . . . . iv 1 139
I feel such sharp dissension in my breast, Such fierce alarums . . v 5 84
Now join your hands, and with your hands your hearts, That no dissension hinder government . . . . 3 *Hen. VI.* iv 6 40
On a dissension of a doit, break out To bitterest enmity *Coriolanus* iv 4 17
Dissentious. Thy lewd, pestiferous and dissentious pranks 1 *Hen. VI.* iii 1 15
They love his grace but lightly That fill his ears with such dissentious rumours . . . . *Richard III.* i 3 46
What's the matter, you dissentious rogues? . . . *Coriolanus* i 1 168
Dissentious numbers pestering streets . . . . . . iv 6 7
Dissever. Or to dissever so Our great self and our credit . *All's Well* ii 1 125
Dissever your united strengths, And part your mingled colours *K. John* ii 1 388
Dissevered. In this wide gap of time since first We were dissever'd *W. T.* v 3 155
Dissipation. Banishment of friends, dissipation of cohorts . . *Lear* i 2 161
Dissolute. His dissolute disease will scarce obey this medicine *M. Wives* iii 3 204
Takes on the point of honour to support So dissolute a crew *Richard II.* v 3 12
As dissolute as desperate; yet through both I see some sparks of better hope . . . . v 3 20
Dissolutely. That I am freely dissolved, and dissolutely *Mer. Wives* i 1 260
It is a fery discretion answer; save the fall is in the ort 'dissolutely' . i 1 262
A purse of gold most resolutely snatched on Monday night and most dissolutely spent on Tuesday morning . . . 1 *Hen. IV.* i 2 39
Dissolution. A man of continual dissolution and thaw *Mer. Wives* iii 5 118
There is so great a fever on goodness, that the dissolution of it must cure it . . . . *Meas. for Meas.* iii 2 236
Like a broken man.—Reproach and dissolution hangeth over him *Rich. II.* ii 1 258
Dissolutions of ancient amities; divisions in state . . . *Lear* i 2 158

Dissolve. The great globe itself, Yea, all which it inherit, shall dissolve *Tempest* iv 1 154
The charm dissolves apace, And as the morning steals upon the night . v 1 64
Which with an hour's heat Dissolves to water . . . *T. G. of Ver.* iii 2 8
Are now so sure that nothing can dissolve us . . . *Mer. Wives* v 5 237
Would dissolve the bands of life, Which false hope lingers in extremity *Richard II.* ii 2 71
Look up, behold, That you in pity may dissolve to dew . . . . . v 1 9
Lest his ungovern'd rage dissolve the life That wants the means to lead it . . . . *Lear* iv 4 19
I am almost ready to dissolve, Hearing of this . . . . . v 3 203
The first stone Drop in my neck: as it determines, so Dissolve my life! *Ant. and Cleo.* iii 13 162
Dissolve, thick cloud, and rain; that I may say, The gods themselves do weep! . . . . v 2 302
Dissolved. I will marry her; that I am freely dissolved, and dissolutely *Mer. Wives* i 1 259
So he dissolved, and showers of oaths did melt . . *M. N. Dream* i 1 245
Since I nor wax nor honey can bring home, I quickly were dissolved from my hive . . . . *All's Well* i 2 66
As if the world were all dissolved to tears . . . *Richard II.* iii 2 108
The bonds of heaven are slipp'd, dissolved, and loosed . *Troi. and Cres.* v 2 156
What says the other troop?—They are dissolved: hang 'em! *Coriolanus* i 1 208
Dissuade him from her: she is no equal for his birth . *Much Ado* ii 1 171
By underhand means laboured to dissuade him from it . *As Y. Like It* i 1 147
I would fain dissuade him, but he will not be entreated . . i 2 170
Did manifoldly dissuade me from believing . . . . *All's Well* ii 3 215
Cannot for all that dissuade succession . . . . . iii 5 25
Dissuaded. When I dissuaded him from his intent, And found him pight to do it . . . . *Lear* ii 1 66
From the which We were dissuaded by our wicked queen . *Cymbeline* v 5 463
Distaff. It hangs like flax on a distaff . . . . *T. Night* i 3 109
We'll thwack him hence with distaffs . . . . *W. Tale* i 2 37
I must change arms at home, and give the distaff Into my husband's hands . . . . *Lear* iv 2 17
More charming With their own nobleness, which could have turn'd A distaff to a lance . . . . *Cymbeline* v 3 34
Distaff-women manage rusty bills Against thy seat . . *Richard II.* iii 2 118
Distain. You having lands, and blest with beauteous wives, They would restrain the one, distain the other . . *Richard III.* v 3 322
The worthiness of praise distains his worth, If that the praised himself bring the praise forth . . . . . *Troi. and Cres.* i 3 241
She did distain my child, and stood between Her and her fortunes *Pericles* iv 3 31
Distance. And that I hope is an unmeasurable distance . *Mer. Wives* ii 1 109
You stand on distance, your passes, stoccadoes, and I know not what . ii 1 233
To see thee pass thy punto, thy stock, thy reverse, thy distance, thy montant . . . . ii 3 27
His givings-out were of an infinite distance From his true-meant design . . . . *Meas. for Meas.* i 4 54
If there be breadth enough in the world, I will hold a long distance *All's Well* iii 2 27
She knew her distance and did angle for me, Madding my eagerness . v 3 212
To meet his grace just distance 'tween our armies . . 2 *Hen. IV.* iv 1 226
And we'll digest The abuse of distance . . . *Hen. V.* ii Prol. 32
Having brought the queen To a prepared place in the choir, fell off A distance from her . . . . . . *Hen. VIII.* iv 1 65
He fights as you sing prick-song, keeps time, distance, and proportion *Rom. and Jul.* ii 4 22
In such bloody distance, That every minute of his being thrusts Against my near'st of life . . . . *Macbeth* iii 1 116
Advise him to a caution, to hold what distance His wisdom can provide iii 6 44
Noble swelling spirits, That hold their honours in a wary distance *Oth.* ii 3 58
He shall in strangeness stand no further off Than in a politic distance iii 3 13
Yet neither pleasure's art can joy my spirits, Nor yet the other's distance comfort me. . . . . *Pericles* i 2 10
Distant. At that very distant time . . . *Meas. for Meas.* ii 1 94
So far be distant . . . . *M. N. Dream* ii 2 60
Take you, as 'twere, some distant knowledge of him; As thus, 'I know his father and his friends' . . . . *Hamlet* ii 1 13
How far is his court distant from this shore? . . . *Pericles* ii 1 111
Diana's temple is not distant far, Where you may abide . . . iii 4 13
Distaste. How may I avoid, Although my will distaste what it elected, The wife I chose? . . . . . . *Troi. and Cres.* ii 2 66
Her brain-sick raptures Cannot distaste the goodness of a quarrel . ii 2 123
Dangerous conceits are, in their natures, poisons, Which at the first are scarce found to distaste . . . . *Othello* iii 3 327
Distasted. And scants us with a single famish'd kiss, Distasted with the salt of broken tears . . . . *Troi. and Cres.* iv 4 50
Distasteful. After distasteful looks and these hard fractions *T. of Athens* ii 2 220
Distemper. I would not ha' your distemper in this kind . *Mer. Wives* iii 3 231
Thither provoked and instigated by his distemper . . . . iii 5 78
Any madness I ever yet beheld seemed but tameness, civility and patience, to this his distemper . . . . iv 2 28
The malignancy of my fate might perhaps distemper yours . *T. Night* ii 1 5
There is a sickness Which puts some of us in distemper . *W. Tale* i 2 385
If little faults, proceeding on distemper, Shall not be wink'd at *Hen. V.* ii 2 54
He hath found The head and source of all your son's distemper *Hamlet* ii 2 55
Good my lord, what is your cause of distemper? . . . . iii 2 351
Upon the heat and flame of thy distemper Sprinkle cool patience . iii 4 123
If you are sick at sea, Or stomach-qualm'd at land, a dram of this Will drive away distemper . . . . *Cymbeline* iii 4 194
Distemperature. A huge infectious troop Of pale distemperatures and foes to life . . . . *Com. of Errors* v 1 82
Thorough this distemperature we see The seasons alter . *M. N. Dream* ii 1 106
Our grandam earth, having this distemperature, In passion shook 1 *Hen. IV.* iii 1 34
The day looks pale At his distemperature . . . . . v 1 3
Thy earliness doth me assure Thou art up-roused by some distemperature . . . . *Rom. and Jul.* ii 3 40
Upon what ground is his distemperature?—'Twould be too tedious to repeat . . . . *Pericles* v 1 27
Distempered. Never till this day Saw I him touch'd with anger so distemper'd . . . . *Tempest* iv 1 145
This distemper'd messenger of wet, The many-colour'd Iris . *All's Well* i 3 157
And taste with a distempered appetite . . . . . *T. Night* i 5 98
No scope of nature, no distemper'd day . . . . *K. John* iii 4 154
Distemper'd lords! The king by me requests your presence straight . iv 3 21
It is but as a body yet distemper'd; Which to his former strength may be restored . . . . 2 *Hen. IV.* iii 1 41
Distempered. The reasons you allege do more conduce To the hot passion of distemper'd blood . . . . *Troi. and Cres.* ii 2 169
It argues a distemper'd head So soon to bid good morrow to thy bed *Rom. and Jul.* ii 3 33
He cannot buckle his distemper'd cause Within the belt of rule *Macbeth* v 2 15
Is in his retirement marvellous distempered.—With drink, sir? *Hamlet* iii 2 312
Distempering. Being full of supper and distempering draughts *Othello* i 1 99
Distil. Strew'd with sweets, Which they distil now in the curbed time *All's Well* ii 4 46
There is some soul of goodness in things evil, Would men observingly distil it out . . . . *Hen. V.* iv 1 5
O earth, I will befriend thee more with rain, That shall distil from these two ancient urns, Than youthful April shall with all his showers . . . . *T. Andron.* iii 1 17
Hast thou not learn'd me how To make perfumes? distil? preserve? *Cymb.* i 5 13
Distillation. To be stopped in, like a strong distillation . *Mer. Wives* iii 5 115
Distilled. Get you some of this distilled Carduus Benedictus *Much Ado* iii 4 73
But earthlier happy is the rose distill'd . . . *M. N. Dream* i 1 76
Nature presently distill'd Helen's cheek, but not her heart *As Y. Like It* iii 2 152
Balm his foul head in warm distilled waters . . . *T. of Shrew* Ind. 1 48
A man distill'd Out of our virtues . . . . . *Troi. and Cres.* i 3 350
As fresh as morning dew distill'd on flowers . . . *T. Andron.* ii 3 201
This distilled liquor drink thou off . . . . *Rom. and Jul.* iv 1 94
With tears distill'd by moans . . . . v 3 15
Distilled by magic sleights Shall raise such artificial sprites *Macbeth* iii 5 27
Distill'd Almost to jelly with the act of fear, Stand dumb *Hamlet* i 2 204
Distilment. In the porches of my ears did pour The leperous distilment i 5 64
Distinct. To offend, and judge, are distinct offices And of opposed natures . . . . *Mer. of Venice* ii 9 61
With distinct breath and consign'd kisses to them . *Troi. and Cres.* iv 4 47
And make distinct the very breach whereout Hector's great spirit flew iv 5 245
Distinction. Strange is it that our bloods, Of colour, weight, and heat, pour'd all together, Would quite confound distinction, yet stand off In differences so mighty . . . . *All's Well* ii 3 127
I have no skill in sense To make distinction . . . . . iii 4 40
A fool, sir, at a woman's service, and a knave at a man's.—Your distinction? . . . . iv 5 27
On a forgotten matter we can hardly make distinction of our hands *T. N.* ii 3 175
Distinction, with a broad and powerful fan, Puffing at all, winnows the light away . . . . *Troi. and Cres.* i 3 27
And I do fear besides, That I shall lose distinction in my joys . iii 2 28
Meal and bran together He throws without distinction . *Coriolanus* iii 1 323
That Without the which a soldier, and his sword, Grants scarce distinction . . . . *Ant. and Cleo.* iii 1 29
Reverence, That angel of the world, doth make distinction Of place *Cymb.* iv 2 248
This fierce abridgement Hath to it circumstantial branches, which Distinction should be rich in . . . . v 5 384
Distinctly. On the topmast, The yards and bowsprit, would I flame distinctly, Then meet and join . . . . . . *Tempest* i 2 200
Thou dost snore distinctly; There's meaning in thy snores . . . ii 1 217
The office did Distinctly his full function . . . *Hen. VIII.* i 1 45
And bury all, which yet distinctly ranges, In heaps and piles of ruin *Cor.* iii 1 206
The centurions and their charges, distinctly billeted . . . iv 3 48
I remember a mass of things, but nothing distinctly . . *Othello* ii 3 290
I do not in position Distinctly speak of her . . . . . iii 3 235
Distingué. Vaillant, et très distingué seigneur d'Angleterre . *Hen. V.* iv 4 60
Distinguish. Like perspectives, which rightly gazed upon Show nothing but confusion, eyed awry Distinguish form . . *Richard II.* ii 2 20
Sight may distinguish of colours . . . . . 2 *Hen. VI.* ii 1 129
Nor more can you distinguish of a man Than of his outward show *Richard III.* iii 1 9
The valued file Distinguishes the swift, the slow, the subtle, The housekeeper, the hunter . . . . *Macbeth* iii 1 96
Since my dear soul was mistress of her choice And could of men distinguish . . . . *Hamlet* iii 2 69
Every one hears that, Which can distinguish sound . . *Lear* iv 6 215
Since I could distinguish betwixt a benefit and an injury . *Othello* i 3 314
So long As he could make me with this eye or ear Distinguish him *Cymb.* i 3 10
Which can distinguish 'twixt The fiery orbs above and the twinn'd stones Upon the number'd beach . . . . i 6 34
Distinguished. As could not be distinguish'd but by names *Com. of Err.* i 1 53
Nor can we be distinguish'd by our faces For man or master *T. of Shrew* i 1 205
And more he spoke, Which sounded like a clamour in a vault, That mought not be distinguish'd . . . . 3 *Hen. VI.* v 2 45
Distinguishment. And mannerly distinguishment leave out Betwixt the prince and beggar . . . . *W. Tale* ii 1 86
Distract. This news distracts me! . . . . . *Mer. Wives* ii 2 140
The fellow is distract, and so am I . . . . *Com. of Errors* iv 3 42
They say, poor gentleman, he's much distract . . . *T. Night* v 1 287
Mine hair be fix'd on end, as one distract . . . 2 *Hen. VI.* iii 2 318
Is not this a heavy case, To see thy noble uncle thus distract? *T. An.* iv 3 26
She fell distract, And, her attendants absent, swallow'd fire . *J. Cæsar* iv 3 155
She is importunate, indeed distract: Her mood will needs be pitied *Ham.* iv 5 2
Better I were distract: So should my thoughts be sever'd from my griefs . . . . *Lear* iv 6 288
Supply it with one gender of herbs, or distract it with many . *Othello* i 3 327
Distract your army, which doth most consist Of war-mark'd footmen *Ant. and Cleo.* iii 7 44
Distracted. The king, His brother and yours, abide all three distracted *Tempest* v 1 12
In most uneven and distracted manner . . . *Meas. for Meas.* iv 4 3
To fetch my poor distracted husband hence . . . *Com. of Errors* v 1 39
I led them on in this distracted fear . . . . *M. N. Dream* iii 2 31
To the brightest beams Distracted clouds give way . . . *All's Well* v 3 35
She hath been in good case, and the truth is, poverty hath distracted her . . . . 2 *Hen. IV.* ii 1 116
Accept distracted thanks . . . . *Troi. and Cres.* v 2 189
You only speak from your distracted soul . . . *T. of Athens* iii 4 115
Best state, contentless, Hath a distracted and most wretched being . iv 3 246
They stared, and were distracted; no man's life Was to be trusted with them . . . . *Macbeth* ii 3 110
While memory holds a seat In this distracted globe . . . *Hamlet* i 5 97
He does confess he feels himself distracted . . . . . iii 1 5
He's loved of the distracted multitude, Who like not in their judgement, but their eyes . . . . iv 3 4
Silence those whom this vile brawl distracted . . . *Othello* ii 3 256
Distractedly. She did speak in starts distractedly . . . *T. Night* ii 2 22
Distraction. Mine enemies are all knit up In their distractions *Tempest* iii 3 90
In her invention and Ford's wife's distraction, they conveyed me into a buck-basket . . . . *Mer. Wives* iii 5 87

Distraction. In conclusion put strange speech upon me: I know not what 'twas but distraction . . . . . . *T. Night* v 1 71
This savours not much of distraction . . . . . v 1 322
You look As if you held a brow of much distraction . . *W. Tale* i 2 149
With countenance of such distraction that they were to be known by garment, not by favour . . . . v 2 52
This is a mere distraction; You turn the good we offer into envy *Hen. VIII.* iii 1 112
Go off: You flow to great distraction . . . *Troi. and Cres.* v 2 41
Distraction, frenzy and amazement, Like witless antics, one another meet . . . . v 3 85
All his visage wann'd, Tears in his eyes, distraction in's aspect *Hamlet* ii 2 581
You must needs have heard, how I am punish'd With sore distraction . v 2 241
His power went out in such distractions as Beguiled all spies *A. and C.* iii 7 77
Give him no breath, but now Make boot of his distraction . . iv 1 9
Distrained. My father's goods are all distrain'd and sold *Richard II.* ii 3 131
Hath here distrain'd the Tower to his use . . *1 Hen. VI.* i 3 61
Distraught. Then begin again, and stop again, As if thou wert distraught . . . . *Richard III.* iii 5 4
O, if I wake, shall I not be distraught, Environed with all these hideous fears? . . . . *Rom. and Jul.* iv 3 49
Distress. To the nightingale's complaining notes Tune my distresses and record my woes . . . . . . *T. G. of Ver.* v 4 6
I would all of the same strain were in the same distress . *Mer. Wives* iii 3 198
Art thou thus bolden'd, man, by thy distress? . *As Y. Like It* ii 7 91
The thorny point Of bare distress hath ta'en from me the show Of smooth civility . . . . ii 7 95
I do pity his distress in my similes of comfort . . *All's Well* v 2 26
In pity of my hard distress Levied an army . . *1 Hen. VI.* ii 5 87
Not fearing death, nor shrinking for distress, But always resolute . iv 1 37
Entreat for me, As you would beg, were you in my distress *Richard III.* i 4 273
Our fatherless distress was left unmoan'd; Your widow-dolour likewise be unwept! . . . . ii 2 64
If you refuse your aid In this so never-needed help, yet do not Upbraid's with our distress . . . . . *Coriolanus* v 1 35
I tell my sorrows to the stones; Who, though they cannot answer my distress, Yet in some sort they are better than the tribunes *T. An.* iii 1 38
'Tis not amiss we tender our loves to him, in this supposed distress *T. of A.* v 1 15
Make our women fight, To doff their dire distresses . . *Macbeth* iv 3 188
As one incapable of her own distress . . . . . *Hamlet* iv 7 179
Be aidant and remediate In the good man's distress! . . *Lear* iv 4 18
He wrings at some distress.—Would I could free't! . *Cymbeline* iii 6 79
Distressed. Poor distressed soul! . . . . *Com. of Errors* iv 4 62
O, send some succour to the distress'd lord! . . . *1 Hen. VI.* iv 3 30
Thus stands my state, 'twixt Cade and York distress'd *2 Hen. VI.* iv 9 31
How shall Bona be revenged But by thy help to this distressed queen? *3 Hen. VI.* iii 3 213
Alas, you three, on me, threefold distress'd, Pour all your tears! *Rich. III.* ii 2 86
A beauty-waning and distressed widow . . . . . iii 7 185
See what now thou art: For happy wife, a most distressed widow . iv 4 98
Being distress'd, was by that wretch betray'd, And without trial fell *Hen. VIII.* ii 1 110
The eldest son of this distressed queen . . . *T. Andron.* i 1 103
And rather comfort his distressed plight Than prosecute the meanest or the best For these contempts . . . . iv 4 32
Despised, distressed, hated, martyr'd, kill'd! . . . *Rom. and Jul.* iv 5 59
Well, sir, the poor distressed Lear's i' the town . . . *Lear* iv 3 40
This youth, howe'er distress'd, appears he hath had Good ancestors *Cymb.* iv 2 47
O my distressed lord, even such our griefs are. . . . *Pericles* i 4 7
A stranger and distressed gentleman, That never aim'd so high to love your daughter . . . . ii 5 46
Distressful. Gets him to rest, cramm'd with distressful bread *Hen. V.* iv 1 287
To ease your country of distressful war . . . . *1 Hen. VI.* v 4 126
And all the ruins of distressful times Repair'd with double riches of content . . . . *Richard III.* iv 4 318
When I did speak of some distressful stroke That my youth suffer'd *Oth.* i 3 157
Distribute. As much as one sound cudgel of four foot—You see the poor remainder—could distribute, I made no spare, sir . *Hen. VIII.* v 4 20
Not in the presence Of dreaded justice, but on the ministers That do distribute it . . . . *Coriolanus* iii 3 99
Distributed. The spoil got on the Antiates Was ne'er distributed . iii 3 5
Distribution. To be ta'en forth, Before the common distribution . i 9 35
So distribution should undo excess, And each man have enough . *Lear* iv 1 73
Distrust. I am ready to distrust mine eyes . . . *T. Night* iv 3 13
Let not the world see fear and sad distrust Govern the motion of a kingly eye . . . . *K. John* v 1 46
One sudden foil shall never breed distrust . . . *1 Hen. VI.* iii 3 11
So far from cheer and from your former state, That I distrust you *Ham.* iii 2 175
Yet, though I distrust, Discomfort you, my lord, it nothing must . iii 2 175
Make me not offended In your distrust . . . *Ant. and Cleo.* iii 2 34
Distrustful recreants! Fight till the last gasp . . *1 Hen. VI.* i 2 126
Disturb. Not a mouse Shall disturb this hallow'd house . *M. N. Dream* v 1 395
Shall we disturb him, since he keeps no mean? . . *1 Hen. VI.* i 2 121
Are you not ashamed With this immodest clamorous outrage To trouble and disturb the king? . . . . iv 1 127
And charge that no man should disturb your rest . . *2 Hen. VI.* iii 2 256
Disturb him not; let him pass peaceably . . . . . iii 3 25
Here they be that dare and will disturb thee . . . . . iv 8 6
Whom have we here? Buckingham, to disturb me? . . . . v 1 12
Besides, You'll find a most unfit time to disturb him . *Hen. VIII.* ii 2 61
If ever you disturb our streets again, Your lives shall pay the forfeit *Rom. and Jul.* i 1 103
God shield I should disturb devotion! . . . . . iv 1 41
Let none disturb us . . . . *Pericles* i 2 1
Disturbance. I can speak of the disturbances That nature works, and of her cures . . . . iii 2 37
Disturbed. Be not disturb'd with my infirmity . . . *Tempest* iv 1 160
In food, in sport and life-preserving rest To be dirturb'd, would mad or man or beast . . . . *Com. of Errors* v 1 84
Neither disturbed with the effect of wine, Nor heady-rash . . . v 1 215
With thy brawls thou hast disturb'd our sport . . *M. N. Dream* ii 1 87
And o'erswell With course disturb'd even thy confining shores *K. John* ii 1 338
All the courts of France will be disturb'd With chaces . . *Hen. V.* i 2 265
That so the shadows be not unappeased, Nor we disturb'd with prodigies on earth . . . . *T. Andron.* i 1 101
Thee, old Capulet, and Montague, Have thrice disturb'd the quiet of our streets . . . . *Rom. and Jul.* i 1 98
This disturbed sky Is not to walk in . . . . . *J. Cæsar* i 3 39
Disturber. Foes to my rest and my sweet sleep's disturbers *Richard III.* iv 2 74
However these disturbers of our peace Buz in the people's ears *T. An.* iv 4 6

Disturbing. I'ld have beaten him like a dog, but for disturbing the lords within . . . . *Coriolanus* iv 5 57
Disunite. It was a strong composure a fool could disunite *Troi. and Cres.* ii 3 109
Disvalued. Her reputation was disvalued In levity . . *Meas. for Meas.* v 1 221
Disvouched. Every letter he hath writ hath disvouched other . . . iv 4 1
Ditch. Empty it in the muddy ditch close by the Thames side *Mer. Wives* iii 3 16
Behind the ditches of the abbey here . . . . *Com. of Errors* v 1 122
He'll turn your current in a ditch, And make your channel his *Coriol.* iii 1 96
Damn others, and let this damn you, And ditches grave you all! *T. of A.* iv 3 166
Safe in a ditch he bides, With twenty trenched gashes on his head *Macb.* iii 4 27
I will go seek Some ditch wherein to die . . . . *Ant. and Cleo.* iv 6 38
Rather a ditch in Egypt Be gentle grave unto me! . . . . v 2 57
Ditch-delivered. Finger of birth-strangled babe Ditch-deliver'd by a drab *Macbeth* iv 1 31
Ditch-dog. Swallows the old rat and the ditch-dog . . . . *Lear* iii 4 138
Ditch'd, and wall'd with turf . . . . . . *Cymbeline* v 3 14
Ditcher. There is no ancient gentlemen but gardeners, ditchers, and grave-makers . . . . *Hamlet* v 1 34
Dites-moi. Écoutez; dites-moi, si je parle bien . . *Hen. V.* iii 4 17
Dites-moi l'Anglois pour le bras.—De arm, madame . . . iii 4 21
Ditties. Sing no more ditties, sing no moe, Of dumps so dull and heavy *Much Ado* ii 3 72
Thy tongue Makes Welsh as sweet as ditties highly penn'd . *1 Hen. IV.* iii 1 209
Ditty. The ditty does remember my drown'd father . . . *Tempest* i 2 405
This ditty, after me, Sing, and dance it trippingly . . *M. N. Dream* v 1 402
Though there was no great matter in the ditty, yet the note was very untuneable . . . . *As Y. Like It* v 3 36
I framed to the harp Many an English ditty lovely well . *1 Hen. IV.* iii 1 124
Diurnal ring. Ere twice the horses of the sun shall bring Their fiery torcher his diurnal ring . . . . *All's Well* ii 1 165
Dive. To swim, to dive into the fire, to ride On the curl'd clouds *Tempest* i 2 191
To dive like buckets in concealed wells . . . . *K. John* v 2 139
How he did seem to dive into their hearts . . . *Richard II.* i 4 25
Or dive into the bottom of the deep, Where fathom-line could never touch the ground . . . . *1 Hen. IV.* i 3 203
Dive, thoughts, down to my soul: here Clarence comes . *Richard III.* i 1 41
He dives into the king's soul, and there scatters Dangers, doubts *Hen. VIII.* ii 2 27
I'll dive into the burning lake below, And pull her out of Acheron by the heels . . . . *T. Andron.* iv 3 43
O thou wall That girdlest in those wolves, dive in the earth, And fence not Athens! . . . . *T. of Athens* iv 1 2
As a duck for life that dives, So up and down the poor ship drives *Pericles* iii Gower 49
Dived. The untainted virtue of your years Hath not yet dived into the world's deceit . . . . *Richard III.* iii 1 8
Diver. When your diver Did hang a salt-fish on his hook *Ant. and Cleo.* ii 5 16
Divers philosophers hold that the lips is parcel of the mouth *Mer. Wives* i 1 236
There came divers of Antonio's creditors in my company *Mer. of Venice* iii 1 118
Time travels in divers paces with divers persons . . *As Y. Like It* iii 2 326
I will give out divers schedules of my beauty . . . *T. Night* i 5 263
Threatens them With divers deaths in death . . . . *W. Tale* v 1 202
Is not Angiers lost? Arthur ta'en prisoner? divers dear friends slain? *K. John* iii 4 7
For divers reasons Which I shall send you written . . *1 Hen. IV.* i 3 262
And changes fill the cup of alteration With divers liquors *2 Hen. IV.* iii 1 53
Therefore doth heaven divide The state of man in divers functions *Hen. V.* i 2 184
Myself and divers gentlemen beside . . . . . *1 Hen. VI.* iii 1 25
For divers unknown reasons, I beseech you, Grant me this boon *Rich. III.* i 2 218
Confessions Of divers witnesses . . . . . . *Hen. VIII.* ii 1 17
New opinions, Divers and dangerous . . . . v 3 18
Children of divers kind We sucking on her natural bosom find *R. and J.* ii 3 11
To ease ourselves of divers slanderous loads . . . *J. Cæsar* iv 1 20
Divers-coloured. Pretty dimpled boys, like smiling Cupids, With divers-colour'd fans . . . . *Ant. and Cleo.* ii 2 208
Diversely. Our wits are so diversely coloured . . . *Coriolanus* ii 3 22
Diversity. Jingling chains, And moe diversity of sounds . . *Tempest* v 1 234
Divert. With pale policy Seek to divert the English purposes *Hen. V.* ii Prol. 15
As knots, by the conflux of meeting sap, Infect the sound pine and divert his grain . . . . *Troi. and Cres.* i 3 8
Divert and crack, rend and deracinate The unity and married calm of states . . . . i 3 99
Diverted. I rather will subject me to the malice Of a diverted blood and bloody brother . . . . *As Y. Like It* ii 3 37
Had I spoke with her, I could have well diverted her intents *All's Well* iii 4 21
Dives. I never see thy face but I think upon hell-fire and Dives *1 Hen. IV.* iii 3 36
Divest yourself, and lay apart The borrow'd glories . . *Hen. V.* ii 4 78
Now we will divest us, both of rule, Interest of territory, cares of state *Lear* i 1 50
Dividable. Peaceful commerce from dividable shores . *Troi. and Cres.* i 3 105
Dividant. Twinn'd brothers of one womb, Whose procreation, residence, and birth, Scarce is dividant . . . . *T. of Athens* iv 3 5
Divide. Sometime I'ld divide, And burn in many places . . *Tempest* i 2 198
Divide me like a bribe buck, each a haunch . . . *Mer. Wives* v 5 27
He that will divide a minute into a thousand parts . . *As Y. Like It* iv 1 45
O'er and o'er divides him 'Twixt his unkindness and his kindness *W. T.* iv 4 562
Sorrow's eye, glazed with blinding tears, Divides one thing entire to many objects . . . . *Richard II.* ii 2 17
Though he divide the realm and give thee half, It is too little, helping him to all . . . . v 1 60
O, I could divide myself and go to buffets! . . . *1 Hen. IV.* ii 3 34
Shall we divide our right According to our threefold order ta'en? . . iii 1 70
Then this remains, that we divide our power . . . . . v 5 34
That same word, rebellion, did divide The action of their bodies from their souls . . . . *2 Hen. IV.* i 1 194
Into a thousand parts divide one man . . . . . *Hen. V.* Prol. 24
Therefore doth heaven divide The state of man in divers functions . i 2 183
Divide your happy England into four; Whereof take you one quarter . i 2 214
For which I will divide my crown with her . . . *1 Hen. VI.* i 6 18
No more can I be sever'd from your side, Than can yourself yourself in twain divide . . . . iv 5 49
How many years a mortal man may live. When this is known, then to divide the times . . . . *3 Hen. VI.* ii 5 30
So doth valour's show and valour's worth divide In storms of fortune *Troi. and Cres.* i 3 46
Be't of less expect That matter needless, of importless burden, Divide thy lips . . . . i 3 72
Let Mars divide eternity in twain, And give him half . . . ii 3 256
A thing inseparate Divides more wider than the sky and earth . . v 2 149
You shall Divide in all with us . . . . . . *Coriolanus* i 6 87
Whose sore task Does not divide the Sunday from the week . *Hamlet* i 1 76

Divide. To divide him inventorially would dizzy the arithmetic of memory *Hamlet* v 2 118

Love cools, friendship falls off, brothers divide: in cities, mutinies *Lear* i 2 116

My great office will sometimes Divide me from your bosom *Ant. and Cleo.* ii 3 2

I have a ship Laden with gold; take that, divide it iii 11 5

That our stars, Unreconciliable, should divide Our equalness to this v 1 47

And all the fiends of hell Divide themselves between you! *Cymbeline* ii 4 130

Divided. Even in a dream, were we divided from them *Tempest* v 1 239

Beshrew your eyes, They have o'erlook'd me and divided me *Mer. of Ven.* iii 2 15

And she a fair divided excellence, Whose fulness of perfection lies in him *K. John* ii 1 439

And must we be divided? must we part? *Richard II.* v 1 81

The archdeacon hath divided it Into three limits very equally *1 Hen. IV.* iii 1 72

So is the unfirm king In three divided *2 Hen. IV.* i 3 74

The English army, that divided was Into two parties, is now conjoin'd in one *1 Hen. VI.* v 2 11

He little thought of this divided friendship *Richard III.* i 4 244

For we to-morrow hold divided councils iii 1 179

All this divided York and Lancaster, Divided in their dire division v 5 27

Will you the knights Shall to the edge of all extremity Pursue each other, or shall be divided? *Troi. and Cres.* iv 5 69

Pledges the breath of him in a divided draught *T. of Athens* i 2 49

Is it fit, The three-fold world divided, he should stand One of the three to share it? *J. Cæsar* iv 1 14

Poor Ophelia Divided from herself and her fair judgement *Hamlet* iv 5 85

Know that we have divided In three our kingdom *Lear* i 1 38

I do perceive here a divided duty *Othello* i 3 181

The name of Antony; it was divided Between her heart and lips *Ant. and Cleo.* iv 14 32

Divideth. Some say the lark makes sweet division; This doth not so, for she divideth us *Rom. and Jul.* iii 5 30

Divination. Tell thou an earl his divination lies *2 Hen. IV.* i 1 88

Do not these high strains Of divination in our sister work Some touches of remorse? *Troi. and Cres.* ii 2 114

Which portends—Unless my sins abuse my divination—Success *Cymb.* iv 2 351

Divine. How came we ashore?—By Providence divine *Tempest* i 2 159

I might call him A thing divine, for nothing natural I ever saw so noble i 2 418

Sweet ornament that decks a thing divine! *T. G. of Ver.* ii 1 4

She is an earthly paragon.—Call her divine ii 4 147

If not divine, Yet let her be a principality, Sovereign to all the creatures on the earth ii 4 151

One so dear, Of such divine perfection ii 7 13

Let him be furnished with divines *Meas. for Meas.* iii 2 221

I know him for a man divine and holy; Not scurvy v 1 144

I perceive your grace, like power divine, Hath look'd upon my passes v 1 374

Men, more divine, the masters of all these, Lords of the wide world and wild watery seas *Com. of Errors* ii 1 20

Our earth's wonder, more than earth divine iii 2 32

Now, divine air! now is his soul ravished! *Much Ado* ii 3 60

O most divine Kate!—O most profane coxcomb! *L. L. Lost* iv 3 83

Is ebony like her? O wood divine! A wife of such wood were felicity iv 3 248

O Helen, goddess, nymph, perfect, divine! *M. N. Dream* iii 2 137

To call me goddess, nymph, divine and rare, Precious, celestial iii 2 226

It is a good divine that follows his own instructions *Mer. of Venice* i 2 16

With the divine forfeit of his soul upon oath *All's Well* iii 6 33

The oracle, Thus by Apollo's great divine seal'd up *W. Tale* iii 1 19

If powers divine Behold our human actions, as they do iii 2 29

Has not the divine Apollo said, Is't not the tenour of his oracle? v 1 37

Or my divine soul answer it in heaven *Richard II.* i 1 38

Darest thou, thou little better thing than earth, Divine his downfal? iii 4 79

The better sort, As thoughts of things divine, are intermix'd With scruples v 5 12

Your pens to lances, and your tongue divine To a loud trumpet *2 Hen. IV.* iv 1 51

That you should seal this lawless bloody book Of forged rebellion with a seal divine iv 1 92

She is not so divine, So full-replete with choice of all delights *1 Hen. VI.* v 5 16

'Tis government that makes them seem divine *3 Hen. VI.* i 4 132

And this word 'love,' which greybeards call divine v 6 81

Vouchsafe, divine perfection of a woman *Richard III.* i 2 75

By a divine instinct men's minds mistrust Ensuing dangers ii 3 42

To shun the danger that his soul divines iii 2 18

Meditating with two deep divines iii 7 75

An operation more divine Than breath or pen can give expressure to *Troi. and Cres.* iii 3 203

O you gods divine! iv 2 105

With most divine integrity, From heart of very heart iv 5 170

I would they would forget me, like the virtues Which our divines lose by 'em *Coriolanus* ii 3 64

What may be sworn by, both divine and human, Seal what I end withal! iii 1 141

If Jupiter Should from yond cloud speak divine things, And say ''Tis true,' I'ld not believe them iv 5 110

Being a divine, a ghostly confessor, A sin-absolver *Rom. and Jul.* iii 3 49

More needs she the divine than the physician *Macbeth* v 1 82

Whose spirit with divine ambition puff'd *Hamlet* iv 4 49

And all that we are evil in, by a divine thrusting on *Lear* i 2 136

Something from Cyprus, as I may divine *Othello* i 2 39

Do omit Their mortal natures, letting go safely by The divine Desdemona ii 1 73

If I were bound to divine of this unity, I would not prophesy so *A. and C.* ii 6 124

Thou divine Imogen, what thou endurest! *Cymbeline* ii 1 62

Against self-slaughter There is a prohibition so divine That cravens my weak hand iii 4 79

The smile mocking the sigh, that it would fly From so divine a temple iv 2 55

O thou goddess, Thou divine Nature! iv 2 170

Which 'mulier' I divine Is this most constant wife v 5 448

Divinely. Whose protection Is most divinely vow'd *K. John* ii 1 237

With two right reverend fathers, Divinely bent to meditation *Rich. III.* iii 7 62

Divineness. Behold divineness No elder than a boy! *Cymbeline* iii 6 44

Diviner. This drudge, or diviner, laid claim to me *Com. of Errors* iii 2 144

Divinest creature, Astræa's daughter, How shall I honour thee? *1 Hen. VI.* i 6 4

Wolvish-ravening lamb! Despised substance of divinest show! *R. and J.* iii 2 77

Divinest patroness, and midwife gentle To those that cry by night *Per.* iii 1 11

Divining. If secret powers Suggest but truth to my divining thoughts *3 Hen. VI.* iv 6 69

Divinity. There is divinity in odd numbers *Mer. Wives* v 1 4

Trust not my age, My reverence, calling, nor divinity *Much Ado* iv 1 170

To your ears, divinity, to any other's, profanation *T. Night* i 5 233

Give us the place alone: we will hear this divinity i 5 236

Hear him but reason in divinity *Hen. V.* i 1 38

Divinity. There's such divinity doth hedge a king *Hamlet* iv 5 123

There's a divinity that shapes our ends, Rough-hew them how we will v 2 10

'Ay' and 'no' too was no good divinity *Lear* iv 6 101

Divinity of hell! When devils will the blackest sins put on, They do suggest at first with heavenly shows *Othello* ii 3 356

To have divinity preached there! did you ever dream of such a thing? *Pericles* iv 5 4

Division. Rightly reasoned, and in his own division *Much Ado* v 1 230

Or the division of the twentieth part Of one poor scruple *Mer. of Venice* iv 1 329

My having is not much; I'll make division of my present with you *T. Night* iii 4 380

How have you made division of yourself? v 1 229

It will the woefullest division prove That ever fell upon this cursed earth *Richard II.* iv 1 146

Sung by a fair queen in a summer's bower, With ravishing division, to her lute *1 Hen. IV.* iii 1 211

The quality and hair of our attempt Brooks no division iv 1 62

His divisions, as the times do brawl, Are in three heads *2 Hen. IV.* i 3 70

Foretelling this same time's condition And the division of our amity iii 1 79

When envy breeds unkind division; There comes the ruin *1 Hen. VI.* iv 1 193

All this divided York and Lancaster, Divided in their dire division *Richard III.* v 5 28

The spacious breadth of this division Admits no orifex *Troi. and Cres.* v 2 150

And hope to come upon them in the heat of their division *Coriolanus* iv 3 19

Some say the lark makes sweet division *Rom. and Jul.* iii 5 29

Never come such division 'tween our souls! *J. Cæsar* iv 3 235

Abound In the division of each several crime, Acting it many ways *Macb.* iv 3 96

In the division of the kingdom, it appears not which of the dukes he values most *Lear* i 1 4

O, these eclipses do portend these divisions! i 2 149

Divisions in state, menaces and maledictions against king and nobles i 2 159

There is division, Although as yet the face of it be cover'd With mutual cunning iii 1 19

There's a division betwixt the dukes; and a worse matter than that iii 3 9

Nor the division of a battle knows More than a spinster *Othello* i 1 23

Is there division 'twixt my lord and Cassio?—A most unhappy one iv 1 242

How the fear of us May cement their divisions and bind up The petty difference, we yet not know *Ant. and Cleo.* ii 1 48

A more unhappy lady, If this division chance, ne'er stood between iii 4 13

Divorce. So that, in this unjust divorce of us, Fortune had left to both of us alike *Com. of Errors* i 1 105

And quite divorce his memory from his part *L. L. Lost* v 2 150

If it appear not plain and prove untrue, Deadly divorce step between me and you! *All's Well* v 3 319

Mark our contract.—Mark your divorce, young sir *W. Tale* iv 4 428

With your sinful hours Made a divorce betwixt his queen and him *Richard II.* iii 1 12

I would thou wert the man That would divorce this terror from my heart v 4 9

Divorce not wisdom from your honour *2 Hen. IV.* i 1 162

To make divorce of their incorporate league *Hen. V.* v 2 394

I here divorce myself Both from thy table, Henry, and thy bed *3 Hen. VI.* i 1 247

As the long divorce of steel falls on me *Hen. VIII.* ii 1 76

To restore the king, He counsels a divorce ii 2 31

Yet, if that quarrel, fortune, do divorce It from the bearer, 'tis a sufferance panging As soul and body's severing ii 3 14

Nothing but death Shall e'er divorce my dignities iii 1 142

In the divorce his contrary proceedings Are all unfolded iii 2 26

The cardinal did entreat his holiness To stay the judgement o' the divorce iii 2 33

He is return'd in his opinions; which Have satisfied the king for his divorce iii 2 65

O thou sweet king-killer, and dear divorce 'Twixt natural son and sire! *T. of Athens* iv 3 382

If thou shouldst not be glad, I would divorce me from thy mother's tomb *Lear* ii 4 133

The approbation of those that weep this lamentable divorce under her colours are wonderfully to extend him *Cymbeline* i 4 20

That horrid act Of the divorce he'ld make v 1 67

Divorced. Souls and bodies hath he divorced three *T. Night* iii 4 260

Doubly divorced! Bad men, you violate A twofold marriage *Richard II.* v 1 71

This is a sleep That from this golden rigol hath divorced So many English kings *2 Hen. IV.* iv 5 36

By the main assent Of all these learned men she was divorced *Hen. VIII.* iv 1 32

Beguiled, divorced, wronged, spited, slain! *Rom. and Jul.* iv 5 55

Divorcement. Though he do shake me off To beggarly divorcement *Othello* iv 2 158

Divulge Page himself for a secure and wilful Actæon *Mer. Wives* iii 2 43

Divulged. A divulged shame Traduced by odious ballads *All's Well* ii 1 174

In voices well divulged, free, learn'd and valiant *T. Night* i 5 279

That shall be divulged well In characters as red as Mars *Troi. and Cres.* v 2 163

Divulging. But, like the owner of a foul disease, To keep it from divulging, let it feed Even on the pith of life *Hamlet* iv 1 22

Dizy. Then have we here young Dizy, and young Master Deep-vow *Meas. for Meas.* iv 3 13

Dizzy. Shall dizzy with more clamour Neptune's ear *Troi. and Cres.* v 2 174

To divide him inventorially would dizzy the arithmetic of memory *Ham.* v 2 119

How fearful And dizzy 'tis, to cast one's eyes so low! *Lear* iv 6 12

Dizzy-eyed fury and great rage of heart Suddenly made him from my side to start *1 Hen. VI.* iv 7 11

Do. What do you here? Shall we give o'er and drown? *Tempest* i 1 41

Thou attend'st not.—O, good sir, I do i 2 88

To give him annual tribute, do him homage i 2 113

To do me business in the veins o' the earth When it is baked with frost i 2 255

I will be correspondent to command And do my spiriting gently.—Do so i 2 298

What shall I do! say what; what shall I do? i 2 300

But then exactly do All points of my command i 2 499

Do you understand me?—Methinks I do ii 1 268

Let's follow it, and after do our work iii 2 158

There's something else to do: hush, and be mute iv 1 126

Let's alone And do the murder first iv 1 232

Do, do: we steal by line and level, an't like your grace iv 1 239

For a little Follow, and do me service iv 1 267

Are they not lamely writ?—No, boy, but as well as I can do them *T. G. of Ver.* ii 1 98

I seem so.—Seem you that you are not?—Haply I do ii 4 11

Now, tell me, how do all from whence you came? ii 4 122

I cannot leave to love, and yet I do ii 6 17

Provided that you do no outrages On silly women iv 1 71

How do you, man? the music likes you not iv 2 55

How many women would do such a message? iv 4 95

Do. Sir, I thank you; by yea and no, I do . . . *Mer. Wives* i 1 88
Never a woman in Windsor knows more of Anne's mind than I do; nor can do more than I do with her . . . i 4 137
What have you to do whither they bear it? . . . iii 3 164
Nor need you, on mine honour, have to do With any scruple . *M. for M.* i 1 64
What's to do here, Thomas tapster? let's withdraw . i 2 115
Let me not find you before me again . . .; no, not for dwelling where you do . . . ii 1 262
How will you do to content this substitute? . . . iii 1 192
Do with your injuries as seems you best, In any chastisement . v 1 256
Do me the favour to dilate at full What hath befall'n of them *C. of Err.* i 1 123
His company must do his minions grace . . . ii 1 87
To do him all the grace and good I could . . . v 1 164
You could never do him so ill-well . . . *Much Ado* ii 1 122
Do you think I do not know you by your excellent wit? . . ii 1 126
You may do the part of an honest man in it . . . ii 1 172
Do you any embassage to the Pigmies . . . ii 1 277
My daughter is sometime afeard she will do a desperate outrage to herself . . . ii 3 158
Hang mournful epitaphs and do all rites That appertain unto a burial . iv 1 209
What shall become of this? what will this do? . . iv 1 211
I will not have to do with you.—Canst thou so daff me? . . v 1 77
I will bid thee draw, as we do the minstrels . . . v 1 129
You break jests as braggarts do their blades . . . v 1 189
Now, unto thy bones good-night! Yearly will I do this rite . . v 3 23
Strong-jointed Samson! I do excel thee in my rapier . *L. L. Lost* i 2 78
You whoreson loggerhead! you were born to do me shame . iv 3 204
What do you see? you see an ass-head of your own, do you? *M. N. Dr.* iii 1 119
But I will not stir from this place, do what they can . . iii 1 125
Whom I do love and will do till my death . . . iii 2 167
Ay, do, persever, counterfeit sad looks . . . iii 2 237
I love thee; by my life, I do: I swear by that which I will lose for thee iii 2 251
That, he awaking when the other do, May all to Athens back again repair iv 1 71
That curtsy to them, do them reverence . *Mer. of Venice* i 1 13
Then do but say to me what I should do That in your knowledge may by me be done . . . i 1 158
If to do were as easy as to know what were good to do . . i 2 13
But her eyes,—How could he see to do them? . . . iii 2 124
They fell sick and died; I could not do withal . . . iii 4 72
You may see the end; for the best is yet to do . *As Y. Like It* i 2 121
This I must do, or know not what to do: Yet this I will not do, do how I can . . . ii 3 34
I warrant, she is apter to do than to confess she does . . iii 2 408
Good Master What-ye-call't: how do you, sir? . . . iii 3 75
For what had he to do to chide at me? . . . iii 5 129
Now shall my friend Petruchio do me grace . . *T. of Shrew* i 2 131
You mean not her to— Perhaps, him and her, sir: what have you to do? i 2 226
I will be angry: what hast thou to do? Father, be quiet . . iii 2 218
Therefore fire: do thy duty, and have thy duty . . . iv 1 38
I am afraid, sir, Do what you can, yours will not be entreated . v 2 89
My hand is ready; may it do him ease . . . v 2 179
What I can do can do no hurt to try . . . *All's Well* ii 1 137
Damns himself to do and dares better be damned than to do't . iii 6 95
Say it was in stratagem.—'Twould not do. . . . iv 1 56
And will for ever Do thee all rights of service . . . iv 2 17
I saw your niece do more favours to the count's serving-man *T. Night* iii 2 6
What's to do? Shall we go see the reliques of this town? . . iii 3 18
How do you, Malvolio? how is't with you? . . . iii 4 106
And willingly, To do you rest, a thousand deaths would die . . v 1 136
They would do that Which should undo more doing . . *W. Tale* i 2 311
What you do Still betters what is done . . . iv 4 135
What you can make her do, I am content to look on . . . v 3 91
That which thou hast sworn to do amiss Is not amiss when it is truly done . . . *K. John* iii 1 270
How oft the sight of means to do ill deeds Makes deeds ill done! . iv 2 219
How shall we do for money? . . . *Richard II.* ii 2 104
Where kings grow base, To come at traitors' calls and do them grace . iii 3 181
For do we must what force will have us do . . . iii 3 207
Which for sport sake are content to do the profession some grace 1 *Hen. IV.* ii 1 78
I never dealt better since I was a man: all would not do . . ii 4 188
If a lie may do thee grace, I'll gild it with the happiest terms I have . v 4 161
O, it is much that a lie with a slight oath and a jest with a sad brow will do! . . . 2 *Hen. IV.* v 1 93
I will make the king do you grace: I will leer upon him . . v 5 6
When I cannot live any longer, I will do as I may . . *Hen. V.* ii 1 17
Do my good morrow to them, and anon Desire them all to my pavilion iv 1 26
More will I do; Though all that I can do is nothing worth . . iv 1 319
If we are mark'd to die, we are enow To do our country loss . . iv 3 21
Do we all holy rites; Let there be sung 'Non nobis' and 'Te Deum' . iv 8 127
Is removing hence; As princes do their courts, when they are cloy'd 1 *Hen. VI.* ii 5 105
Stay, go, do what you will, the like do I . . . iv 5 50
So we be rid of them, do with 'em what thou wilt . . . iv 7 94
I never had to do with wicked spirits . . . v 4 42
O that it were to do! What have we done? . . 2 *Hen. VI.* ii 2 3
Why, Warwick, who should do the duke to death? . . . iii 2 179
Henceforth I will not have to do with pity . . . iv 2 56
By heaven, I will not do thee so much ease . . 3 *Hen. VI.* v 5 72
Have not to do with him, beware of him . . *Richard III.* i 3 292
If all this will not do, I'll drown you in the malmsey-butt within . i 4 276
And so 'twill do With some men else, who think themselves as safe As thou and I . . . iii 2 67
They account his head upon the bridge.—I know they do . . iii 2 73
Speak suddenly; be brief.—Your grace may do your pleasure . iv 2 21
Lay all the weight ye can upon my patience, I will make as little doubt, as you do conscience In doing daily wrongs . . *Hen. VIII.* v 3 67
What would you have me do?—What should you do, but knock 'em down? . . . v 4 31
If they smile, And say 'twill do, I know, within a while All the best men are ours . . . Epil. 12
May one, that is a herald and a prince, Do a fair message? *Troi. and Cres.* i 3 219
You whoreson cur!—Do, do.—Thou stool for a witch!—Ay, do, do . ii 1 45
Good day, good day.—How do you? how do you? . . . iii 3 63
O heavens, what some men do, While some men leave to do! . . iii 3 132
You bring me to do, and then you flout me too . . . iv 2 27
To do what? let her say what: what have I brought you to do? . iv 2 28
Time, force, and death, Do to this body what extremes you can . iv 2 108
I am half through; The one part suffer'd, the other will I do *Coriolanus* ii 3 131
That, in the official marks invested, you Anon do meet the senate . ii 3 149

Do. I do not flatter thee, But honour thee, and will do till I die *T. Andron.* i 1 213
And resolved withal To do myself this reason and this right . . i 1 279
Or make some sign how I may do thee ease . . . iii 1 121
Thou 'lt do thy message, wilt thou not?—Ay, with my dagger . iv 1 117
Æmilius, do this message honourably . . . iv 4 104
I pray thee, do on them some violent death . . . v 2 108
Henceforward do your messages yourself . . *Rom. and Jul.* ii 5 66
Do as thou wilt, for I have done with thee . . . iii 5 205
The neglecting it May do much danger . . . v 2 20
Now, before the gods, I am not able to do,—the more beast, I say *T. of Athens* iii 2 55
Among the rout of nations, I will make thee Do thy right nature . iv 3 44
What we can do, we'll do, to do you service . . . v 1 78
When Cæsar says 'do this,' it is perform'd . . *J. Cæsar* i 2 10
With a heart new-fired I follow you, To do I know not what . . ii 1 333
Go bid the priests do present sacrifice And bring me their opinions . ii 2 5
I do entreat you, not a man depart, Save I alone . . . iii 2 65
Now lies he there, And none so poor to do him reverence . . iii 2 125
Why, friends, you go to do you know not what . . . iii 2 240
To do you salutation from his master . . . iv 2 5
Do not presume too much upon my love; I may do that I shall be sorry for . . . iv 3 64
And, like a rat without a tail, I'll do, I'll do, and I'll do . *Macbeth* i 3 10
Thus thou must do, if thou have it; And that which rather thou dost fear to do Than wishest should be undone . . . i 5 24
I dare do all that may become a man; Who dares do more is none . i 7 46
And what will you do now? How will you live?—As birds do, mother iv 2 31
The day almost itself professes yours, And little is to do . . v 7 28
In filial obligation for some term To do obsequious sorrow . *Hamlet* i 2 92
I do not set my life at a pin's fee; And for my soul, what can it do to that? . . . i 4 65
There has been much to do on both sides . . . ii 2 369
What do you call the play?—The Mouse-trap . . . iii 2 246
I will do your mother's commandment . . . iii 2 328
What shall I do?—Not this, by no means, that I bid you do . . iii 4 180
This thing's to do; Sith I have cause and will and strength and means To do't . . . iv 4 44
That we would do, We should do when we would; for this 'would' changes . . . iv 7 119
An act hath three branches; it is, to act, to do, and to perform . v 1 12
You shall do small respect, show too bold malice . . *Lear* ii 2 137
'Tis worse than murder, To do upon respect such violent outrage . ii 4 24
Do poor Tom some charity, whom the foul fiend vexes . . iii 4 61
You are my guests: do me no foul play, friends . . . iii 7 31
Do as I bid thee, or rather do thy pleasure; Above the rest, be gone . iv 1 49
And by him do my duties to the senate . . . *Othello* iii 2 2
I will do All my abilities in thy behalf . . . iii 3 1
Well, do your discretion . . . iii 3 34
What will you do with't, that you have been so earnest To have me filch it? . . . iii 3 314
This may do something. The Moor already changes with my poison iii 3 324
So they do nothing, 'tis a venial slip . . . iv 1 9
I would not do such a thing for a joint-ring, nor for measures of lawn . iv 3 72
Beshrew me, if I would do such a wrong For the whole world . . iv 3 78
What is it that they do When they change us for others? Is it sport? iv 3 97
What should I do, I do not?—In each thing give him way *Ant. and Cleo.* i 3 8
Sworest thou not then To do this when I bade thee? . . iv 14 82
Then let it do at once The thing why thou hast drawn it . . iv 14 88
This mortal house I'll ruin, Do Cæsar what he can . . . v 2 52
But something given to lie: as a woman should not do . . v 2 253
He that will believe all that they [women] say, shall never be saved by half that they do . . . v 2 258
You must think this, look you, that the worm will do his kind . v 2 264
What Can it [gold] not do and undo? . . . *Cymbeline* ii 3 78
Caius Lucius Will do's commission throughly . . . iii 4 112
Every good servant does not all commands: No bond but to do just ones v 1 7
If he'll do as he is made to do, I know he'll quickly fly my friendship too . . . v 3 61
Hie thee thither, And do upon mine altar sacrifice . . *Pericles* v 1 242

Do better. Why should I play the Roman fool, and die On mine own sword? whiles I see lives, the gashes Do better upon them *Macbeth* v 8 3
You can do better yet; but this is meetly . . *Ant. and Cleo.* i 3 81

Do bravely. The noble thanes do bravely in the war . *Macbeth* v 7 26
O happy horse, to bear the weight of Antony! Do bravely, horse! *Ant. and Cleo.* i 5 22

Do danger. That at his will he may do danger with . . *J. Cæsar* ii 1 17

Do ease. That may to thee do ease and grace to me . . *Hamlet* i 1 131

Do good. Who can do good on him? . . . *Meas. for Meas.* iv 2 71
Let't not be doubted I shall do good . . . *W. Tale* ii 2 54
One that no persuasion can do good upon . . . 1 *Hen. IV.* iii 1 199
If we mean to thrive and do good, break open the gaols 2 *Hen. VI.* iv 3 17
Where to do harm Is often laudable, to do good sometime Accounted dangerous folly . . . *Macbeth* iv 2 75

Do grace to Cæsar's corpse, and grace his speech . . *J. Cæsar* iii 2 62
Thyself do grace to them, and bring them in . . . *Hamlet* ii 2 53

Do him dead. And, whilst we breathe, take time to do him dead 3 *Hen. VI.* i 4 108

Do ill. You do ill to teach the child such words . . *Mer. Wives* iv 1 67
It does well to those that do ill . . . *Hamlet* v 1 53

Do it. The Duke of Milan And his more braver daughter could control thee, If now 'twere fit to do't . . . *Tempest* i 2 440
I should do it With much more ease . . . iii 1 29
Do it so cunningly That my discovery be not aimed at . *T. G. of Ver.* iii 1 44
If I can do it By aught that I can speak in his dispraise . . iii 2 46
I am glad to see you: much good do it your good heart! . *Mer. Wives* i 1 83
Will it do well?—We will do it . . . ii 3 83
I do it not in evil disposition . . . *Meas. for Meas.* i 2 122
I know thou canst; and therefore see thou do it . *Com. of Errors* ii 2 141
Or if you like elsewhere, do it by stealth . . . iii 2 7
When I do it, I shall do it on a full stomach . . *L. L. Lost* i 2 153
If I do it, let the audience look to their eyes . . *M. N. Dream* i 2 28
You may do it extempore, for it is nothing but roaring . . i 2 70
Anoint his eyes; But do it when the next thing he espies May be the lady . . . ii 1 262
We will do it in action as we will do it before the duke . . iii 1 5
Get thee gone, but do it . . . *Mer. of Venice* iv 1 397
He does it with a better grace, but I do it more natural . *T. Night* ii 3 89
Do't and thou hast the one half of my heart; Do't not, thou split'st thine own.—I'll do't, my lord . . . *W. Tale* i 2 348
My ground to do't Is the obedience to a master . . . i 2 353

Do it. If I could find example Of thousands that had struck anointed kings And flourish'd after, I'ld not do't . . . . *W. Tale* i 2 359
To do't, or no, is certain To me a break-neck . . . . i 2 362
To effect your suits, here is man shall do it . . . . iv 4 829
Which lames report to follow it and undoes description to do it . v 2 63
Sir Robert could not do it: We know his handiwork . *K. John* i 1 237
Though that my death were adjunct to my act, By heaven, I would do it iii 3 58
I have sworn to do it; And with hot irons must I burn them out . iv 1 58
Ah, none but in this iron age would do it! . . . . iv 1 60
You can do it, sir; you can do it: I commend you well . *2 Hen. IV.* iii 2 157
And let us do it with no show of fear . . . *Hen. V.* ii 4 23
Didst thou not hear me swear I would not do it? . . *3 Hen. VI.* v 5 74
With a true heart And brother-love I do it . . . *Hen. VIII.* v 3 173
We do it not alone, sir.—I know you can do very little alone . *Coriolanus* ii 1 37
I must do't: Away, my disposition, and possess me Some harlot's spirit! iii 2 110
I will not do't, Lest I surcease to honour mine own truth . . iii 2 120
Convert o' the instant, green virginity, Do't in your parents' eyes! *T. of Athens* iv 1 8
Now might I do it pat, now he is praying; And now I'll do't *Hamlet* iii 3 73
Do it, England; For like the hectic in my blood he rages . . iv 3 67
They durst not do't; They could not, would not do't; 'tis worse than murder . . . . *Lear* ii 4 22
Look, look, a mouse! Peace, peace; this piece of toasted cheese will do't . . . . iv 6 90
Repair there to me.—Well, my good lord, I'll do't . . *Othello* iii 2 4
I might do't as well i' the dark.—Wouldst thou do such a deed for all the world? . . . . iv 3 67
But if we fail, We then can do't at land . . . *Ant. and Cleo.* iii 7 54
Feast the army; we have store to do't . . . . . iv 1 15
Do it at once; Or thy precedent services are all But accidents unpurposed . . . . iv 14 82
But kiss; one kiss! Rubies unparagon'd, How dearly they do't! *Cymb.* ii 2 18
Must I repent? I cannot do it better than in gyves . . . v 4 14
Do not. O, do not do your cousin such a wrong . . *Much Ado* iii 1 87
Do not be so bitter with me. I evermore did love you *M. N. Dream* iii 2 306
I dare not know, my lord.—How! dare not! do not. Do you know, and dare not? Be intelligent to me . . . *W. Tale* i 2 377
Do not, porpentine, do not: my fingers itch . . *Troi. and Cres.* ii 1 27
It will not speak; then I will follow it.—Do not, my lord . *Hamlet* i 4 64
There's the point.—Which do not be entreated to . *Ant. and Cleo.* ii 6 32
Do outrage. Hast thou delight to see a wretched man Do outrage? *Com. of Errors* iv 4 119
Do reason. At thy request, monster, I will do reason . *Tempest* iii 2 128
I hope, sir, I will do as it shall become one that would do reason *M. W.* i 1 242
Do right unto this princely Duke of York . . . *3 Hen. VI.* i 1 166
Do well. Will it do well?—We will do it . . . *Mer. Wives* ii 3 82
Though it do well, I do not relish well Their loud applause . *M. for M.* i 1 70
But what care I for words? yet words do well . . *As Y. Like It* iii 5 111
It would do well to set the deer's horns upon his head . . iv 2 4
An onion will do well for such a shift . . . *T. of Shrew* Ind. 1 126
Sir Robert could do well: marry, to confess, Could he get me? *K. John* i 1 236
Would not this ill do well? Well, well, I see I talk but idly *Richard II.* iii 3 170
These fellows will do well, Master Shallow . . *2 Hen. IV.* iii 2 307
Fear not, neighbour, you shall do well enough . . *2 Hen. VI.* ii 3 61
You do well, lord: You are a churchman . . . *Hen. VIII.* i 4 87
Farewell, my wife, my mother: I'll do well yet . . *Coriolanus* iv 1 21
Fear not thy sons; they shall do well enough . . *T. Andron.* ii 3 305
It shall do well: but yet do I believe The origin and commencement of his grief Sprung from neglected love . . . . *Hamlet* iii 1 184
Argal, the gallows may do well to thee. To't again . . . v 1 55
I shall do well: The people love me, and the sea is mine *Ant. and Cleo.* ii 1 8
But, since my lord Is Antony again, I will be Cleopatra.—We will yet do well . . . . iii 13 188
Dobbin. Thou hast got more hair on thy chin than Dobbin my fill-horse has on his tail.—It should seem, then, that Dobbin's tail grows backward . . . . *Mer. of Venice* ii 2 100
Dock. He'ld sow't with nettle-seed.—Or docks, or mallows . *Tempest* ii 1 144
Nothing teems But hateful docks, rough thistles, kecksies, burs *Hen. V.* v 2 52
Dock'd in sand, Vailing her high-top lower than her ribs *Mer. of Venice.* i 1 27
Doctor. The French doctor, my master,—I may call him my master *M. Wives* i 4 99
There is a fray to be fought between Sir Hugh the Welsh priest and Caius the French doctor . . . . ii 1 210
Bless thee, bully doctor!—Save you, Master Doctor Caius! . . ii 3 18
Though we are justices and doctors and churchmen . . . ii 3 49
I will bring the doctor about by the fields . . . . ii 3 81
Master Caius, that calls himself doctor of physic . . . iii 1 4
Shall I lose my doctor? no; he gives me the potions and the motions . iii 1 104
I'll to the doctor: he hath my good will, And none but he . . iv 4 84
The doctor is well money'd, and his friends Potent at court . . iv 4 88
She seemingly obedient likewise hath Made promise to the doctor . iv 6 34
The better to denote her to the doctor . . . . . iv 6 39
And when the doctor spies his vantage ripe, To pinch her by the hand . iv 6 43
He will chafe at the doctor's marrying my daughter . . . v 3 9
Tell her Master Slender hath married her daughter.—Doctors doubt that v 5 184
She is now with the doctor at the deanery, and there married . v 5 215
Beaten the maids a-row and bound the doctor . . *Com. of Errors* v 1 170
He is then a giant to an ape; but then is an ape a doctor to such a man *Much Ado* v 1 206
Bellario, a learned doctor, Whom I have sent for to determine this *Mer. of Venice* iv 1 105
Here stays without A messenger with letters from the doctor . iv 1 108
This letter from Bellario doth commend A young and learned doctor . iv 1 144
In loving visitation was with me a young doctor . . . iv 1 153
And here, I take it, is the doctor come . . . . iv 1 168
Let me look upon the bond.—Here 'tis, most reverend doctor . iv 1 226
A civil doctor, Which did refuse three thousand ducats of me . v 1 210
I think you would have begg'd The ring of me to give the worthy doctor v 1 222
Let not that doctor e'er come near my house . . . . v 1 223
By mine honour, which is yet mine own, I'll have that doctor for my bedfellow . . . . v 1 233
Swear to keep this ring.—By heaven, it is the same I gave the doctor! . v 1 257
By this ring, the doctor lay with me . . . . . v 1 259
That same scrubbed boy, the doctor's clerk . . . . v 1 261
There you shall find that Portia was the doctor, Nerissa there her clerk v 1 269
Were you the doctor and I knew you not? . . . . v 1 280
Sweet doctor, you shall be my bedfellow . . . . v 1 284
I should wish it dark, That I were couching with the doctor's clerk . v 1 305
For so your doctors hold it very meet, Seeing too much sadness hath congeal'd your blood . . . . . . *T. of Shrew* Ind. 2 133
Doctor. We thank you, maiden; But may not be so credulous of cure, When our most learned doctors leave us . . . *All's Well* ii 1 119
Our doctors say this is no month to bleed . . . *Richard II.* i 1 157
Sirrah, you giant, what says the doctor to my water? . *2 Hen. IV.* i 2 1
By all the reverend fathers of the land And doctors learn'd *Hen. VIII.* ii 4 206
I thank you, doctor.—What's the disease he means?—'Tis call'd the evil *Macbeth* iv 3 145
I think, but dare not speak.—Good night, good doctor . . v 1 87
How does your patient, doctor?—Not so sick, my lord, As she is troubled . . . . v 3 37
Doctor, the thanes fly from me. Come, sir, dispatch . . v 3 49
If thou couldst, doctor, cast The water of my land, find her disease, And purge it to a sound and pristine health . . . . v 3 50
Your wisdom should show itself more richer to signify this to his doctor *Hamlet* iii 2 317
I wonder, doctor, Thou ask'st me such a question . . *Cymbeline* i 5 10
Doctor, your service for this time is ended; Take your own way . i 5 30
No further service, doctor, Until I send for thee.—I humbly take my leave . . . . i 5 44
By medicine life may be prolong'd, yet death Will seize the doctor too . v 5 30
Master doctor *Mer. Wives* ii 2; ii 3; iii 1; iii 2; iii 4; iv 5; v 3; v 5; *Com. of Errors* iv 4; *Cymbeline* i 5
Doctor Faustuses. Three German devils, three Doctor Faustuses *M. W.* iv 5 71
Doctor Pinch. Good Doctor Pinch, you are a conjurer *Com. of Errors* iv 4 50
Doctor She. What 'her' is this?—Why, Doctor She . *All's Well* ii 1 82
Doctrine. From women's eyes this doctrine I derive . *L. L. Lost* iv 3 302
When the schools, Embowell'd of their doctrine, have left off The danger to itself . . . . *All's Well* i 3 247
A comfortable doctrine, and much may be said of it . . *T. Night* i 5 239
We knew not The doctrine of ill-doing, nor dream'd That any did *W. Tale* i 2 70
In him Sparing would show a worse sin than ill doctrine . *Hen. VIII.* i 3 60
I'll pay that doctrine, or else die in debt . . . *Rom. and Jul.* i 1 244
I hourly learn A doctrine of obedience . . . *Ant. and Cleo.* v 2 31
Document. A document in madness . . . . . *Hamlet* iv 5 178
Do de. Tom's a cold,—O, do de, do de, do de . . . *Lear* iii 4 59
Dodge And palter in the shifts of lowness . . *Ant. and Cleo.* iii 11 62
Doe. Who comes here? my doe? . . . . . *Mer. Wives* v 5 17
Art thou there, my deer? my male deer?—My doe with the black scut! . v 5 20
Whiles, like a doe, I go to find my fawn And give it food *As Y. Like It* ii 7 128
For, O, love's bow Shoots buck and doe . . . *Troi. and Cres.* iii 1 127
Hast not thou full often struck a doe, And borne her cleanly by the keeper's nose? . . . . *T. Andron.* ii 1 93
Single you thither then this dainty doe, And strike her home by force . ii 1 117
We hunt not, we, with horse nor hound, But hope to pluck a dainty doe to ground . . . . ii 2 26
Doer. All great doers in our trade, and are now 'for the Lord's sake' *Meas. for Meas.* iv 3 20
From lowest place when virtuous things proceed, The place is dignified by the doer's deed . . . . . . *All's Well* ii 3 133
Now, justice on the doers! . . . . ii 3 154
Well, Jove, not I, is the doer of this . . . . *T. Night* iii 4 91
We will not stand to prate; Talkers are no good doers . *Richard III.* i 3 352
Let no man abide this deed, But we the doers . . . *J. Cæsar* iii 1 95
You some permit To second ills with ills, each elder worse, And make them dread it, to the doers' thrift . . . . . *Cymbeline* v 1 15
Does. How now, moon-calf! how does thine ague? . . *Tempest* ii 2 139
It would become me As well as it does you . . . . iii 1 29
How does thy honour? Let me lick thy shoe . . . . iii 2 26
But she as far surpasseth Sycorax As great'st does least . . iii 2 111
Great Juno comes; I know her by her gait.—How does my bounteous sister? . . . . iv 1 103
How does your fallow greyhound, sir? . . . *Mer. Wives* i 1 91
What news? how does pretty Mistress Anne? . . . . i 4 146
And, I pray, how does good Mistress Anne? . . . . iii 1 169
How does good Master Fenton? Pray you, a word with you . . iii 4 34
He does it under name of perfect love . . . *T. of Shrew* iv 3 12
O, my knave, how does my old lady? . . . *All's Well* ii 4 19
Our interpreter does it well.—Excellently . . . . iv 3 236
It does indifferent well in a flame-coloured stock . . *T. Night* i 3 143
He does well enough if he be disposed, and so do I too: he does it with a better grace, but I do it more natural . . . . . ii 3 87
These petty brands That calumny doth use—O, I am out—That mercy does . . . . *W. Tale* ii 1 73
The best she shall have; and my favour To him that does best *Hen. VIII.* ii 2 115
Dexterity so obeying appetite That what he will he does, and does so much That proof is call'd impossibility . . . *Troi. and Cres.* v 5 28
Give me mine armour. How does your patient, doctor? . *Macbeth* v 3 37
And then, sir, does he this—he does—what was I about to say? *Hamlet* ii 1 49
Who does me this? Ha! 'Swounds, I should take it . . . ii 2 602
It shall as level to your judgement pierce As day does to your eye . iv 5 152
The gallows does well; but how does it well? it does well to those that do ill . . . . v 1 52
There's none so foul and foolish thereunto, But does foul pranks which fair and wise ones do . . . . *Othello* ii 1 143
Every good servant does not all commands: No bond but to do just ones *Cymbeline* v 1 7
Doff. Fie, doff this habit, shame to your estate! . . *T. of Shrew* iii 2 102
Thou wear a lion's hide! doff it for shame, And hang a calf's-skin on those recreant limbs . . . . *K. John* iii 1 128
And made us doff our easy robes of peace . . . *1 Hen. IV.* v 1 12
Doff thy harness, youth; I am to-day i' the vein of chivalry *Tr. and Cr.* v 3 31
Romeo, doff thy name, And for that name which is no part of thee Take all myself . . . . *Rom. and Jul.* ii 2 47
Make our women fight, To doff their dire distresses . . *Macbeth* iv 3 188
Dog. You bawling, blasphemous, incharitable dog! . . *Tempest* i 1 44
My mistress show'd me thee and thy dog and thy bush . . ii 2 144
You'll lie like dogs and yet say nothing neither . . . iii 2 22
I think Crab my dog be the sourest-natured dog that lives *T. G. of Ver.* ii 3 6
He is a stone, a very pebble stone, and has no more pity in him than a dog ii 3 12
I am the dog: no, the dog is himself, and I am the dog—Oh! the dog is me, and I am myself . . . . ii 3 24
The dog all this while sheds not a tear nor speaks a word . . ii 3 34
What's the unkindest tide?—Why, he that's tied here, Crab, my dog . ii 3 45
Ask my dog: if he say ay, it will; if he say, no, it will . . ii 5 36
Where is Launce?—Gone to seek his dog . . . . iv 2 78
Even as one would say precisely, 'thus I would teach a dog' . . iv 4 7
One that takes upon him to be a dog indeed, to be, as it were, a dog at all things . . . . iv 4 13
Three or four gentlemanlike dogs . . . . . . iv 4 19
'Out with the dog!' says one: 'What cur is that?' says another . iv 4 22

Dog. The fellow that whips the dogs . . . *T. G. of Ver.* iv 4 27
'Friend,' quoth I, 'you mean to whip the dog?' . . . iv 4 28
I carried Mistress Silvia the dog you bade me . . . iv 4 50
Marry, she says your dog was a cur . . . iv 4 52
But she received my dog?—No, indeed, did she not . . . iv 4 55
I offered her mine own, who is a dog as big as ten of yours . . iv 4 62
Go get thee hence, and find my dog again . . . iv 4 64
'Tis your fault; 'tis a good dog.—A cur, sir . . *Mer. Wives* i 1 96
He's a good dog, and a fair dog: can there be more said? . . i 1 98
Why do your dogs bark so? be there bears i' the town? . . i 1 298
By gar, he shall not have a stone to throw at his dog . . i 4 119
Hope is a curtal dog in some affairs . . . ii 1 114
Give them to a dog for a new-year's gift . . . iii 5 8
She had transform'd me to a curtal dog and made me turn i' the wheel
Com. of Errors iii 2 151
I had rather here my dog bark at a crow than a man swear he loves me
Much Ado i 1 132
An he had been a dog that should have howled thus, they would have hanged him . . . ii 3 81
I would not hang a dog by my will, much more a man who hath any honesty in him . . . iii 3 66
The dogs did yell: put L to sore, then sorel jumps from thicket *L. L. Lost* iv 2 60
Than to be used as you use your dog . . *M. N. Dream* ii 1 210
Out, dog! out, cur! thou drivest me past the bounds Of maiden's patience iii 2 65
This man, with lanthorn, dog, and bush of thorn, Presenteth Moonshine v 1 136
This thorn-bush, my thorn-bush; and this dog, my dog . . v 1 264
I am Sir Oracle, And when I ope my lips let no dog bark! *Mer. of Venice* i 1 94
You call me misbeliever, cut-throat dog, And spit upon my Jewish gaberdine . . . i 3 112
Hath a dog money? is it possible A cur can lend three thousand ducats? i 3 122
You spurn'd me such a day; another time You call'd me dog . i 3 129
Thou call'dst me dog before thou hadst a cause; But, since I am a dog, beware my fangs . . . iii 3 6
Like your asses and your dogs and mules, You use in abject and in slavish parts . . . iv 1 91
O, be thou damn'd, inexecrable dog! And for thy life let justice be accused . . . iv 1 128
Get you with him, you old dog.—Is 'old dog' my reward? *As Y. Like It* i 1 85
Not a word?—Not one to throw at a dog . . . i 3 3
I would not lose the dog for twenty pound . . *T. of Shrew* Ind. 1 21
Trust me, I take him for the better dog . . . Ind. 1 25
What dogs are these! Where is the rascal cook? . . iv 1 165
Where death and danger dogs the heels of worth . *All's Well* iii 4 15
I am dog at a catch.—By'r lady, sir, and some dogs will catch well *T. N.* ii 3 64
He is a kind of puritan.—O, if I thought that, I'ld beat him like a dog! ii 3 154
This is, to give a dog, and in recompense desire my dog again . v 1 7
Like a dog that is compell'd to fight, Snatch at his master that doth tarre him on . . . *K. John* iv 1 116
Dogs, easily won to fawn on any man! . . . *Richard II.* iii 2 130
Destruction straight shall dog them at the heels . . . v 3 139
Where no man never comes but that sad dog That brings me food . v 5 70
Peas and beans are as dank here as a dog . . *1 Hen. IV.* ii 1 10
To dog his heels and curtsy at his frowns . . . iii 2 127
I would cudgel him like a dog, if he would say so . . iii 3 101
Slaves as ragged as Lazarus in the painted cloth, where the glutton's dogs licked his sores . . . iv 2 28
I am the fellow with the great belly, and he my dog . *2 Hen. IV.* i 2 165
So, so, thou common dog, didst thou disgorge Thy glutton bosom . i 3 97
I do allow this wen to be as familiar with me as my dog . . ii 2 116
Down, down, dogs! down, faitors! Have we not Hiren here? . ii 4 172
This will grow to a brawl anon.—Die men like dogs! give crowns like pins! ii 4 188
And the wild dog Shall flesh his tooth on every innocent . . iv 5 132
If we, with thrice such powers left at home, Cannot defend our own doors from the dog, Let us be worried . . . *Hen. V.* i 2 218
Pish!—Pish for thee, Iceland dog! thou prick-ear'd cur of Iceland! . ii 1 44
'Solus,' egregious dog? O viper vile! The 'solus' in thy most mervailous face! . . . ii 1 49
Your own reasons turn into your bosoms, As dogs upon their masters . ii 2 83
Men's faiths are wafer-cakes, And hold-fast is the only dog, my duck . ii 3 54
Coward dogs Most spend their mouths when what they seem to threaten Runs far before them . . . ii 4 69
Up to the breach, you dogs! avaunt, you cullions! . . iii 2 21
Let gallows gape for dog; let man go free And let not hemp his windpipe suffocate . . . iii 6 44
Whilst by a slave, no gentler than my dog, His fairest daughter is contaminated . . . iv 5 15
Who ever saw the like? what men have I! Dogs! cowards! dastards!
1 Hen. VI. i 2 23
They call'd us for our fierceness English dogs; Now, like to whelps, we crying run away . . . i 5 25
Between two dogs, which hath the deeper mouth . . ii 4 12
The ancient proverb will be well effected: 'A staff is quickly found to beat a dog' . . . *2 Hen. VI.* iii 1 171
As a bear, encompass'd round with dogs . . *3 Hen. VI.* ii 1 15
Dogs howl'd, and hideous tempest shook down trees . . v 6 46
Which plainly signified That I should snarl and bite and play the dog . v 6 77
So lamely and unfashionable That dogs bark at me as I halt by them
Richard III. i 1 23
Unmanner'd dog! stand thou, when I command . . . i 2 39
Stay, dog, for thou shalt hear me . . . i 3 216
Take heed of yonder dog! Look, when he fawns, he bites . . i 3 289
Death and destruction dog thee at the heels . . . iv 1 40
Although they were flesh'd villains, bloody dogs, Melting with tenderness iv 3 6
That dog, that had his teeth before his eyes, To worry lambs . iv 4 49
I pray, That I may live to say, The dog is dead! . . iv 4 78
The day is ours, the bloody dog is dead . . . v 5 2
Dog!—Then would come some matter from him; I see none now *T. and C.* ii 1 8
You dog!—You scurvy lord!—You cur!—Mars his idiot! . . ii 1 55
A whoreson dog, that shall palter thus with us! Would he were a Trojan! ii 3 244
To be a dog, a mule, a cat, a fitchew, a toad, a lizard, an owl, a puttock v 1 67
I will rather leave to see Hector, than not to dog him . . v 1 103
They set me up, in policy, that mongrel cur, Ajax, against that dog of as bad a kind, Achilles . . . v 4 15
Now, bull! now, dog! 'Loo, Paris, 'loo! now my double-henned sparrow! v 7 10
He's a very dog to the commonalty . . . *Coriolanus* i 1 28
Sigh'd forth proverbs, That hunger broke stone walls, that dogs must eat i 1 210
And that's as easy As to set dogs on sheep . . . i 1 273
Dogs that are as often beat for barking As therefore kept to do so . ii 3 224
I'ld have beaten him like a dog, but for disturbing the lords within . iv 5 57
I have dogs, my lord, Will rouse the proudest panther in the chase *T. An.* ii 2 20

Dog. I have done thy mother.—And therein, hellish dog, thou hast undone
T. Andron. iv 2 77
As true a dog as ever fought at head . . . v 1 102
Canst thou say all this, and never blush?—Ay, like a black dog, as the saying is . . . v 1 122
Away, inhuman dog! unhallow'd slave! . . . v 3 14
A dog of the house of Montague moves me . . *Rom. and Jul.* i 1 9
A dog of that house shall move me to stand . . . i 1 14
Ah, mocker! that's the dog's name . . . ii 4 223
Thou hast quarrelled with a man for coughing in the street, because he hath wakened thy dog . . . iii 1 28
'Zounds, a dog, a rat, a mouse, a cat, to scratch a man to death! . iii 1 104
Every cat and dog And little mouse, every unworthy thing, Live here in heaven and may look on her . . . iii 3 30
When thou art Timon's dog, and these knaves honest . *T. of Athens* i 1 180
You're a dog.—Thy mother's of my generation: what's she, if I be a dog? i 1 203
Away, unpeaceable dog, or I'll spurn thee hence!—I will fly, like a dog, the heels o' the ass . . . i 1 280
Or a harlot, for her weeping; Or a dog, that seems a-sleeping . i 2 68
If I want gold, steal but a beggar's dog, And give it Timon, why, the dog coins gold . . . ii 1 5
Hang him, he'll abuse us.—A plague upon him, dog! . . ii 2 50
Thou wast whelped a dog, and thou shalt famish a dog's death . ii 2 90
Uncover, dogs, and lap.—What does his lordship mean? . . iii 6 95
I do wish thou wert a dog, That I might love thee something . iv 3 54
Men report Thou dost affect my manners, and dost use them.—'Tis, then, because thou dost not keep a dog . . . iv 3 200
Slave, whom Fortune's tender arm With favour never clasp'd; but bred a dog . . . iv 3 251
I understand thee; thou hadst some means to keep a dog . . iv 3 317
I had rather be a beggar's dog than Apemantus . . . iv 3 362
Away, thou issue of a mangy dog! . . . iv 3 371
Give to dogs What thou deny'st to men . . . iv 3 536
You are an alchemist; make gold of that. Out, rascal dogs! . v 1 118
I had rather be a dog, and bay the moon, Than such a Roman *J. Cæsar* iv 3 27
Water-rugs and demi-wolves are clept All by the name of dogs *Macbeth* iii 1 95
Eye of newt and toe of frog, Wool of bat and tongue of dog . iv 1 15
Throw physic to the dogs; I'll none of it . . . v 3 47
If the sun breed maggots in a dead dog, being a god kissing carrion *Ham.* ii 2 182
How cheerfully on the false trail they cry! O, this is counter, you false Danish dogs! . . . iv 5 110
Let Hercules himself do what he may, The cat will mew and dog will have his day . . . v 1 315
You whoreson dog! you slave! you cur!—I am none of these . *Lear* i 4 89
Truth's a dog must to kennel; he must be whipped out . . i 4 124
Knowing nought, like dogs, but following . . . ii 2 86
Why, madam, if I were your father's dog, You should not use me so ii 2 143
Horses are tied by the heads, dogs and bears by the neck . ii 4 8
Hog in sloth, fox in stealth, wolf in greediness, dog in madness . iii 4 96
The little dogs and all, Tray, Blanch, and Sweet-heart, see, they bark at me . . . iii 6 65
For, with throwing thus my head, Dogs leap the hatch, and all are fled . iii 6 76
How now, you dog!—If you did wear a beard upon your chin, I'ld shake it . . . iii 7 75
Ha! Goneril, with a white beard! They flattered me like a dog . iv 6 98
Thou hast seen a farmer's dog bark at a beggar? . . iv 6 158
Behold the great image of authority: a dog's obeyed in office . iv 6 163
Mine enemy's dog, Though he had bit me, should have stood that night Against my fire . . . iv 7 36
To assume a semblance That very dogs disdain'd . . v 3 188
Why should a dog, a horse, a rat, have life, And thou no breath at all? v 3 306
He'll be as full of quarrel and offence As my young mistress' dog. *Oth.* ii 3 53
Even so as one would beat his offenceless dog to affright an imperious lion . . . ii 3 276
Thou hadst been better have been born a dog Than answer my waked wrath! . . . iii 3 362
O, I see that nose of yours, but not that dog I shall throw it to . iv 1 147
O murderous slave! O villain!—O damn'd Iago! O inhuman dog! . v 1 62
I took by the throat the circumcised dog, And smote him, thus . v 2 355
O Spartan dog, More fell than anguish, hunger, or the sea! . v 2 361
Patience is sottish, and impatience does Become a dog that's mad
Ant. and Cleo. iv 15 80
Relieved, but not betray'd.—What, of death too, That rids our dogs of languish? . . . v 2 42
Slave, soulless villain, dog! O rarely base! . . . v 2 157
She'll prove on cats and dogs, Then afterward up higher . *Cymbeline* i 5 38
Whoreson dog! I give him satisfaction? Would he had been one of my rank! . . . ii 1 16
Lay hands on him; a dog! A leg of Rome shall not return to tell What crows have peck'd them here . . . v 3 91
Spit, and throw stones, cast mire upon me, set The dogs o' the street to bay me . . . v 5 223
In killing creatures vile, as cats and dogs, Of no esteem . . v 5 252
Dog-ape. That they call compliment is like the encounter of two dog-apes
As Y. Like It ii 5 27
Dogberry. Well, give them their charge, neighbour Dogberry *Much Ado* iii 3 8
Dog-day. Twenty of the dog-days now reign in's nose . *Hen. VIII.* v 4 43
Dogfish. Pucelle or puzzel, dolphin or dogfish . . *1 Hen. VI.* i 4 107
Dog-fox. That same dog-fox, Ulysses, is not proved worth a blackberry
Troi. and Cres. v 4 12
Dogged. We shall be dogged with company . . *M. N. Dream* i 2 106
I have dogged him, like his murderer . . . *T. Night* iii 2 81
I'll fill these dogged spies with false reports . . *K. John* iv 1 129
Now for the bare-pick'd bone of majesty Doth dogged war bristle his angry crest . . . iv 3 149
That dogg'd the mighty army of the Dauphin . . *1 Hen. VI.* iv 3 2
And dogged York, that reaches at the moon . . *2 Hen. VI.* iii 1 158
Both our honour and our shame in this Are dogg'd with two strange followers . . . *Troi. and Cres.* i 3 365
Such a name, Whose repetition will be dogg'd with curses . *Coriolanus* v 3 144
Dog-hearted. Gave her dear rights To his dog-hearted daughters *Lear* iv 3 47
Dog-hole. France is a dog-hole . . . *All's Well* ii 3 291
Dog Jew. As the dog Jew did utter in the streets . . *Mer. of Venice* ii 8 14
Dogs of war. Cry 'Havoc,' and let slip the dogs of war . . *J. Cæsar* iii 1 273
Dog's death. Thou shalt famish a dog's death . . *T. of Athens* ii 2 91
Dog's-leather. He shall have the skins of our enemies, to make dog's-leather of . . . *2 Hen. VI.* iv 2 26
Dog's tooth. The venom clamours of a jealous woman Poisons more deadly than a mad dog's tooth . . . *Com. of Errors* v 1 70
Dog-weary. I have have watch'd so long That I am dog-weary *T. of Shrew* iv 2 60

Doigt. Les doigts? je pense qu'ils sont appelés de fingres *Hen. V.* iii 4 10
Doing. This is my doing, now *Mer. Wives* iii 4 99
Volumes of report Run with these false and most contrarious guests Upon thy doings *Meas. for Meas.* iv 1 63
I would fain be doing.—I doubt it not *T. of Shrew* ii 1 74
I would it were hell-pains for thy sake, and my poor doing eternal: for doing I am past *All's Well* ii 3 246
It is Jove's doing, and Jove make me thankful! *T. Night* iii 4 83
Among the infinite doings of the world *W. Tale* i 2 253
They would do that Which should undo more doing i 2 312
Each your doing, So singular in each particular, Crowns what you are doing in the present deed iv 4 143
A piece many years in doing and now newly performed v 2 104
Where doing tends to ill, The truth is then most done not doing it *K. John* iii 1 273
And thus still doing, thus he pass'd along *Richard II.* v 2 21
I'll thank myself For doing these fair rites of tenderness 1 *Hen. IV.* v 4 98
Doing is activity; and he will still be doing *Hen. V.* iii 7 107
God is much displeased That you take with unthankfulness his doing *Richard III.* ii 2 90
The precedent was full as long a-doing iii 6 7
Traduced by ignorant tongues, which neither know My faculties nor person, yet will be The chronicles of my doing *Hen. VIII.* i 2 74
This is the cardinal's doing, the king-cardinal ii 2 20
And ever may your highness yoke together, As I will lend you cause, my doing well With my well saying! iii 2 151
Things won are done; joy's soul lies in the doing *Troi. and Cres.* i 2 313
'Twere a concealment Worse than a theft, no less than a traducement, To hide your doings *Coriolanus* i 9 23
And stand upon my common part with those That have beheld the doing i 9 40
Please you That I may pass this doing ii 2 143
Let us seem humbler after it is done Than when it was a-doing iv 2 5
Must my sons be slaughter'd in the streets, For valiant doings in their country's cause? *T. Andron.* i 1 113
Hang his slender gilded wings, And buzz lamenting doings in the air iii 2 62
And slay thy lady too that lives in thee, By doing damned hate upon thyself *Rom. and Jul.* iii 3 118
There is thy gold, worse poison to men's souls, Doing more murders in this loathsome world Than these poor compounds v 1 81
That's a deed thou 'lt die for.—Right, if doing nothing be death by the law *T. of Athens* i 1 195
The service and the loyalty I owe, In doing it, pays itself *Macbeth* i 4 23
Which do but what they should, by doing every thing Safe toward your love and honour i 4 26
To such wondrous doing brought his horse, As had he been incorpsed and demi-natured With the brave beast *Hamlet* iv 7 87
Whose nature is so far from doing harms, That he suspects none *Lear* i 2 196
You have said now.—Ay, and said nothing but what I protest intendment of doing *Othello* iv 2 206
Doing the honour of thy lordliness To one so meek *Ant. and Cleo.* v 2 161
This life Is nobler than attending for a check, Richer than doing nothing for a bauble *Cymbeline* iii 3 23
Nay, many times, Doth ill deserve by doing well iii 3 54
Yet I not doing this, the fool had borne My head as I do his iv 2 116
He, doing so, put forth to seas *Pericles* ii Gower 27
Till fortune, tired with doing bad, Threw him ashore, to give him glad ii Gower 37
Doit. They will not give a doit to relieve a lame beggar *Tempest* ii 2 33
Supply your present wants and take no doit Of usance for my moneys *Mer. of Venice* i 3 141
Little John Doit of Staffordshire 2 *Hen. IV.* iii 2 21
That doit that e'er I wrested from the king 2 *Hen. VI.* iii 1 112
Cushions, leaden spoons, Irons of a doit, doublets *Coriolanus* i 5 7
On a dissension of a doit, break out To bitterest enmity iv 4 17
This morning for ten thousand of your throats I'ld not have given a doit v 4 60
How dost thou like this jewel, Apemantus?—Not so well as plain-dealing, which will not cost a man a doit *T. of Athens* i 1 217
Most monster-like, be shown For poor'st diminutives, for doits *A. and C.* iv 12 37
I cannot be bated one doit of a thousand pieces *Pericles* iv 2 55
Dolabella. Go to him, Dolabella, bid him yield *Ant. and Cleo.* v 1 1
Where's Dolabella, To second Proculeius?—Dolabella! v 1 69
So, Dolabella, It shall content me best: be gentle to her v 2 67
Dolabella, I shall remain your debtor.—I your servant v 2 204
There's Dolabella sent from Cæsar; call him v 2 327
Come, Dolabella, see High order in this great solemnity v 2 368
Dole. What dreadful dole is here! *M. N. Dream* v 1 283
The poor old man, their father, making such pitiful dole over them *As Y. Like It* i 2 139
What great creation and what dole of honour Flies where you bid it *All's Well* ii 3 176
It was your presurmise, That, in the dole of blows, your son might drop 2 *Hen. IV.* i 1 169
In equal scale weighing delight and dole *Hamlet* i 2 13
Omit we all their dole and woe *Pericles* iii Gower 42
Happy man be his dole! *Mer. Wives* iii 4; *T. of Shrew* i 1; *W. Tale* i 2; 1 *Hen. IV.* ii 2
Doleful. I love a ballad but even too well, if it be doleful matter merrily set down *W. Tale* iv 4 189
I love a ballad in print o' life, for then we are sure they are true.—Here's one to a very doleful tune iv 4 265
I am the cygnet to this pale faint swan, Who chants a doleful hymn to his own death *K. John* v 7 22
Then death rock me asleep, abridge my doleful days! 2 *Hen. IV.* ii 4 211
And doleful dumps the mind oppress *Rom. and Jul.* iv 5 129
Dollar. Comes to the entertainer— A dollar.—Dolour comes to him, indeed *Tempest* ii 1 18
Till he disbursed at Saint Colme's inch Ten thousand dollars *Macbeth* i 2 62
Doll Tearsheet. Will you have Doll Tearsheet meet you at supper? 2 *Hen. IV.* ii 1 176
None, my lord, but old Mistress Quickly and Mistress Doll Tearsheet ii 2 167
This Doll Tearsheet should be some road.—I warrant you, as common as the way between Saint Alban's and London ii 2 182
How now, Mistress Doll!—Sick of a calm; yea, good faith ii 4 39
You make fat rascals, Mistress Doll.—I make them! gluttony and diseases make them ii 4 45
You help to make the diseases, Doll: we catch of you, Doll ii 4 49
Hark thee hither, Mistress Doll.—Not I: I tell thee what ii 4 165
The music is come, sir.—Let them play. Play, sirs. Sit on my knee, Doll ii 4 247
Peace, good Doll! do not speak like a death's-head ii 4 254
Kiss me, Doll.—Saturn and Venus this year in conjunction! ii 4 285

Doll Tearsheet. Farewell, hostess; farewell, Doll. You see, my good wenches, how men of merit are sought after 2 *Hen. IV.* ii 4 404
O, run, Doll, run; run, good Doll: come. Yea, will you come, Doll? ii 4 420
Thy Doll, and Helen of thy noble thoughts, Is in base durance v 5 35
For Doll is in. Pistol speaks nought but truth.—I will deliver her v 5 40
Fetch forth the lazar-kite of Cressid's kind, Doll Tearsheet she by name *Hen. V.* ii 1 81
Dolorous. My hearty friends, You take me in too dolorous a sense *Ant. and Cleo.* iv 2 39
Dolour. Comes to the entertainer— A dollar.—Dolour comes to him, indeed *Tempest* ii 1 19
Breathe it in mine ear, As ending anthem of my endless dolour *T. G. of Ver.* iii 1 240
Three thousand dolours a year.—Ay, and more *Meas. for Meas.* i 2 50
From one sign of dolour to another *W. Tale* v 2 95
The tongue's office should be prodigal To breathe the abundant dolour of the heart *Richard II.* i 3 257
How poor Andromache shrills her dolours forth! *Troi. and Cres.* v 3 84
And yell'd out Like syllable of dolour *Macbeth* iv 3 8
Thou shalt have as many dolours for thy daughters as thou canst tell in a year *Lear* ii 4 54
Why hast thou thus adjourn'd The graces for his merits due, Being all to dolours turn'd? *Cymbeline* v 4 80
Dolphin. Once I sat upon a promontory, And heard a mermaid on a dolphin's back *M. N. Dream* ii 1 150
Why, your dolphin is not lustier *All's Well* ii 3 31
Like Arion on the dolphin's back, I saw him hold acquaintance with the waves So long as I could see *T. Night* i 2 15
Great Master of France, the brave Sir Guichard Dolphin *Hen. V.* iv 8 100
Pucelle or puzzel, dolphin or dogfish 1 *Hen. VI.* i 4 107
Dolphin my boy, my boy, sessa! let him trot by *Lear* iii 4 104
Dolphin-chamber. Sitting in my Dolphin-chamber 2 *Hen. IV.* ii 1 94
Dolphin-like. His delights Were dolphin-like *Ant. and Cleo.* v 2 89
Dolt. Asses, fools, dolts! chaff and bran! *Troi. and Cres.* i 2 262
O gull! O dolt! As ignorant as dirt! thou hast done a deed *Othello* v 2 163
Dombledon. What said Master Dombledon about the satin for my short cloak? 2 *Hen. IV.* i 2 33
Domestic broils Clean over-blown *Richard III.* ii 4 60
Your words, Domestics to you, serve your will *Hen. VIII.* ii 4 114
Domestic awe, night-rest, and neighbourhood *T. of Athens* iv 1 17
Domestic fury and fierce civil strife Shall cumber all the parts of Italy *J. Cæsar* iii 1 263
Malice domestic, foreign levy, nothing, Can touch him further *Macbeth* iii 2 25
These domestic and particular broils Are not the question here *Lear* v 1 30
To manage private and domestic quarrel, In night, and on the court and guard of safety! 'Tis monstrous *Othello* ii 3 215
Equality of two domestic powers Breed scrupulous faction *Ant. and Cleo.* i 3 47
Cæsar, that hath more kings his servants than Thyself domestic officers *Cymbeline* iii 1 65
Dominations, royalties and rights Of this oppressed boy *K. John* ii 1 176
Dominator. The welkin's vicegerent and sole dominator *L. L. Lost* i 1 222
Though Venus govern your desires, Saturn is dominator over mine *T. An.* ii 3 31
Magni Dominator poli, Tam lentus audis scelera? tam lentus vides? iv 1 81
Domine. Let me hear a staff, a stanze, a verse; lege, domine *L. L. Lost* iv 2 108
It insinuateth me of insanie: anne intelligis, domine? v 1 28
Domineer. Go to the feast, revel and domineer *T. of Shrew* iii 2 226
Domineering. A domineering pedant o'er the boy *L. L. Lost* iii 1 179
Dominical. My red dominical, my golden letter v 2 44
Dominion. Some remote and desert place quite out Of our dominions *W. T.* ii 3 177
No Italian priest Shall tithe or toll in our dominions *K. John* iii 1 154
Shall not regreet our fair dominions *Richard II.* i 3 142
I am a most poor woman, and a stranger, Born out of your dominions *Hen. VIII.* ii 4 16
Please you to give quiet pass Through your dominions *Hamlet* ii 2 78
If, on the tenth day following, Thy banish'd trunk be found in our dominions, The moment is thy death *Lear* i 1 180
Justice, and your father's wrath, should he take me in his dominion, could not be so cruel to me *Cymbeline* iii 2 41
Domitius. More, Domitius; My lord desires you presently *Ant. and Cleo.* iii 5 21
He will not fight with me, Domitius.—No.—Why should he not? iv 2 1
Don. What should I don this robe, and trouble you? *T. Andron.* i 1 189
Donalbain. Hark! Who lies i' the second chamber?—Donalbain *Macbeth* ii 2 20
Murder and treason! Banquo and Donalbain! Malcolm! awake! ii 3 80
Malcolm and Donalbain, the king's two sons, Are stol'n away and fled ii 4 25
How monstrous It was for Malcolm and for Donalbain To kill their gracious father? damned fact! iii 6 9
Who knows if Donalbain be with his brother? v 2 7
Donation. Some donation freely to estate On the blest lovers *Tempest* iv 1 85
All cause unborn, could never be the motive Of our so frank donation *Coriolanus* iii 1 130
I would have put my wealth into donation *T. of Athens* ii 2 90
It was wise nature's end in the donation, To be his evidence now *Cymb.* v 5 367
Doncaster. And you did swear that oath at Doncaster 1 *Hen. IV.* v 1 42
Forgot your oath to us at Doncaster v 1 58
Done. The wills above be done! *Tempest* i 1 71
Tell your piteous heart There's no harm done i 2 15
I have done nothing but in care of thee i 2 16
I prithee, Remember I have done thee worthy service i 2 247
I prithee, spare.—Well, I have done ii 1 25
Done. The wager?—A laughter.—A match! ii 1 32
Here thought they to have done Some wanton charm iv 1 94
Well done! avoid; no more! iv 1 142
I thank you, gentle servant: 'tis very clerkly done *T. G. of Ver.* ii 1 114
'Twill be this hour ere I have done weeping ii 3 2
You have said, sir.—Ay, sir, and done too, for this time ii 4 30
Have done, have done; here comes the gentleman ii 4 99
When you have done, we look to hear from you ii 4 120
I call to mind your gracious favours Done to me iii 1 7
Your message done, hie home unto my chamber iv 4 93
Let them say 'tis grossly done; so it be fairly done, no matter *M. Wives* ii 2 149
What shall be done with him? what is your plot? ii 1 75
What has he done?—A woman *Meas. for Meas.* i 2 88
What was done to Elbow's wife, that he hath cause to complain of? ii 1 120
What was done to Elbow's wife, once more?—Once, sir? there was nothing done to her once ii 1 144
What shall be done, sir, with the groaning Juliet? ii 2 15
When your words are done, My woes end likewise *Com. of Errors* i 1 27
Come on, sir knave, have done your foolishness i 2 72
Our dinner done, and he not coming thither, I went to seek him v 1 224
God keep him out of my sight when the dance is done! *Much Ado* ii 1 114

Done. If any of the audience hiss, you may cry 'Well done!' *L. L. Lost* v 1 145
If your ladyship would say, 'Thanks, Pompey,' I had done . v 2 559
I believe we must leave the killing out, when all is done *M. N. Dream* iii 1 16
Then do but say to me what I should do That in your knowledge may by me be done *Mer. of Venice* i 1 159
Hie thee, go.—My best endeavours shall be done herein ii 2 182
Excellent piece of work, madam lady: would 'twere done! *T. of Shrew* i 1 259
So said, so done, is well i 2 186
His lecture will be done ere you have tuned iii 1 23
Ha' done with words: To me she's married iii 2 118
My master had direction: Grumio gave order how it should be done iv 3 118
A hundred then.—Content.—A match! 'tis done v 2 74
Seems to undertake this business, which he knows is not to be done *All's W.* iii 6 95
You have won A wife of me, though there my hope be done iv 2 65
What shall be done to him?—Nothing iv 3 194
Our own love waking cries to see what's done v 3 65
The king's a beggar, now the play is done Epil. 1
Is't not well done?—Excellently done, if God did all *T. Night* i 5 253
This is the best fooling, when all is done ii 3 31
His eyes do show his days are almost done ii 3 113
Thou hast, Sebastian, done good feature shame iii 4 400
Thou mightst have done this without thy beard and gown iv 2 69
That's all one, our play is done, And we'll strive to please you every day v 1 416
Unless he take the course that you have done *W. Tale* ii 3 48
What you do Still betters what is done iv 4 136
He so near to Hermione hath done Hermione v 2 109
Excels whatever yet you look'd upon Or hand of man hath done v 3 17
Masterly done: The very life seems warm upon her lip v 3 65
Bedlam, have done.—I have but this to say *K. John* ii 1 183
That which thou hast sworn to do amiss Is not amiss when it is truly done, And being not done, where doing tends to ill, The truth is then most done not doing it iii 1 271
Take honour from me, and my life is done *Richard II.* i 1 183
Shall make their way seem short, as mine hath done ii 3 17
My care is loss of care, by old care done iv 1 196
Such beastly shameless transformation, By those Welshwomen done *1 Hen. IV.* i 1 45
When the fight was done, When I was dry with rage i 3 30
I have done.—Nay, if you have not, to it again; We will stay your leisure.—I have done, i' faith i 3 256
All's done, all's won; here breathless lies the king v 3 16
Our coronation done, we will accite, As I before remember'd, all our state *2 Hen. IV.* v 2 141
O, tish ill done, tish ill done; by my hand, tish ill done! *Hen. V.* iii 2 98
A very little little let us do, And all is done iv 2 34
Well have we done, thrice valiant countrymen: But all's not done iv 6 1
If that my fading breath permit And death approach not ere my tale be done *1 Hen. VI.* ii 5 62
Done like a Frenchman: turn, and turn again! iii 3 85
The life thou gavest me first was lost and done iv 6 7
We thank you all for this great favour done *2 Hen. VI.* i 1 71
Ask what thou wilt. That I had said and done! i 4 31
Have done, for more I hardly can endure i 4 41
After three days' open penance done, Live in your country here in banishment ii 3 11
Your penance done, throw off this sheet ii 4 105
What would your grace have done unto him now? *3 Hen. VI.* i 4 65
Have done with words, my lords, and hear me speak ii 2 117
'Tis better said than done, my gracious lord iii 2 90
And if thou fail us, all our hope is done iii 3 33
If that go forward, Henry's hope is done iii 3 58
Tell him from me that he hath done me wrong iii 3 231
My mourning weeds are done, And I am ready to put armour on iv 1 104
What will your grace have done with Margaret? v 7 37
Have done thy charm, thou hateful wither'd hag! *Richard III.* i 3 215
Have done! for shame, if not for charity i 3 273
Why, so: now have I done a good day's work ii 1 1
There is no more but so: say it is done, And I will love thee iv 2 81
Those wrongs Which thou supposest I have done to thee iv 4 252
Look, what is done cannot be now amended iv 4 291
The early village-cock Hath twice done salutation to the morn v 3 210
How have ye done Since last we saw in France?—I thank your grace, Healthful *Hen. VIII.* i 1 1
Things won are done; joy's soul lies in the doing *Troi. and Cres.* i 2 313
What, blushing still? have you not done talking yet? iii 2 108
To have done is to hang Quite out of fashion, like a rusty mail In monumental mockery iii 3 151
Well, well, 'tis done, 'tis past: and yet it is not; I will not keep my word v 2 97
What he hath done famously, he did it to that end *Coriolanus* i 1 36
My horse to yours, no.—'Tis done.—Agreed i 4 2
As merry as when our nuptial day was done, And tapers burn'd to bedward i 6 31
I have done As you have done; that's what I can i 9 15
I beseech you—In sign of what you are, not to reward What you have done i 9 27
Never shame to hear What you have nobly done ii 2 72
To have my praise for this, perform a part Thou hast not done before iii 2 110
Six of his labours you'ld have done, And saved Your husband so much sweat iv 1 18
Let us seem humbler after it is done Than when it was a-doing iv 2 4
What I have done, as best I may, Answer I must and shall do with my life *T. Andron.* i 1 411
Villain, what hast thou done?—That which thou canst not undo iv 2 73
Thou hast undone our mother.—Villain, I have done thy mother iv 2 76
Have done with woes: Give sentence on this execrable wretch v 3 176
The game was ne'er so fair, and I am done.—Tut, dun's the mouse *R. and J.* i 4 39
The measure done, I'll watch her place of stand i 5 52
Therefore, have done: some grief shows much of love iii 5 73
Do as thou wilt, for I have done with thee iii 5 205
When dinner's done, Show me this piece *T. of Athens* i 1 254
What shall be done? he will not hear, till feel: I must be round with him ii 2 7
So soon as dinner's done, we'll forth again ii 2 14
Sun, hide thy beams! Timon hath done his reign v 1 226
The games are done and Cæsar is returning *J. Cæsar* i 2 178
If he had done or said any thing amiss, he desired their worships to think it was his infirmity i 2 272
I shall unfold to thee, as we are going To whom it must be done ii 1 331
Hath given me some worthy cause to wish Things done, undone iv 2 9
Let no man Come to our tent till we have done our conference iv 2 51
You have done that you should be sorry for iv 3 65
Our deeds are done! Mistrust of my success hath done this deed.—Mistrust of good success hath done this deed v 3 64

Done. Yet let that be, Which the eye fears, when it is done, to see *Macbeth* i 4 53
All our service In every point twice done and then done double i 6 15
If it were done when 'tis done, then 'twere well It were done quickly i 7 1
I go, and it is done; the bell invites me. Hear it not, Duncan ii 1 62
Alack, I am afraid they have awaked, And 'tis not done ii 2 11
Had he not resembled My father as he slept, I had done't ii 2 14
I have done the deed. Didst thou not hear a noise? ii 2 15
I am afraid to think what I have done; Look on't again I dare not ii 2 51
Well, may you see things well done there: adieu! ii 4 37
For't must be done to-night, And something from the palace iii 1 131
Things without all remedy Should be without regard: what's done is done iii 2 12
Why do you make such faces? When all's done, You look but on a stool iii 4 67
And, which is worse, all you have done Hath been but for a wayward son iii 5 10
Well done! I commend your pains; And every one shall share i' the gains iv 1 39
What had he done, to make him fly the land? iv 2 1
I have done no harm. But I remember now I am in this earthly world; where to do harm Is often laudable iv 2 74
Why then, alas, Do I put up that womanly defence, To say I have done no harm? iv 2 79
What's done cannot be undone.—To bed, to bed, to bed! v 1 75
If there be any good thing to be done, That may to thee do ease *Hamlet* i 1 130
So many journeys may the sun and moon Make us again count o'er ere love be done! iii 2 172
Give me your pardon, sir: I've done you wrong v 2 237
What I have done, That might your nature, honour and exception Roughly awake, I here proclaim was madness v 2 241
By the kind gods, 'tis most ignobly done To pluck me by the beard *Lear* iii 7 35
The battle done, and they within our power, Shall never see his pardon v 1 67
We then have done you bold and saucy wrongs *Othello* i 1 129
News, lads! our wars are done ii 1 20
Nor know I aught By me that's said or done amiss this night ii 3 201
If you think fit, or that it may be done, Give me advantage of some brief discourse With Desdemona alone iii 1 54
We have done our course; there's money for your pains iv 2 93
I think I should; and undo't when I had done iv 3 72
Being done, there is no pause.—But while I say one prayer!—It is too late v 2 82
A guiltless death I die.—O, who hath done this deed?—Nobody; I myself v 2 123
I have done the state some service, and they know't. No more of that v 2 339
On: Things that are past are done with me *Ant. and Cleo.* i 2 101
I can do nothing But what indeed is honest to be done i 5 16
Ah, this thou shouldst have done, And not have spoke on't! ii 7 79
Being done unknown, I should have found it afterwards well done; But must condemn it now ii 7 84
I have done enough; a lower place, note well, May make too great an act iii 1 12
Speak not against it; I will not stay behind.—Nay, I have done iii 7 20
Keep whole: provoke not battle, Till we have done at sea iii 8 4
Have you done yet?—Alack, our terrene moon Is now eclipsed iii 13 153
See it done: And feast the army; we have store to do't iv 1 14
What thou wouldst do Is done unto thy hand iv 14 29
I have done my work ill, friends: O, make an end Of what I have begun iv 14 105
What thou hast done thy master Cæsar knows, And he hath sent for thee v 2 65
The bright day is done, And we are for the dark v 2 193
Is this well done?—It is well done, and fitting for a princess v 2 328
O sir, you are too sure an augurer; That you did fear is done v 2 338
You have done Not after our command. Away with her *Cymbeline* i 1 151
So, so: well done, well done i 5 82
A piece of work So bravely done, so rich ii 4 73
What hast thou done?—I am perfect what: cut off one Cloten's head iv 2 117
Would I had done't, So the revenge alone pursued me! iv 2 156
Have done; And do not play in wench-like words with that Which is so serious iv 2 229
We have done our obsequies: come, lay him down iv 2 282
How courtesy would seem to cover sin, When what is done is like an hypocrite! *Pericles* i 1 122
What was first but fear what might be done, Grows elder now and cares it be not done i 2 14
Has done no more than other knights have done ii 3 34
A general praise to her, and care in us At whose expense 'tis done iv 3 46
Done all. For when I am revenged upon my charm, I have done all *Ant. and Cleo.* iv 12 17
Done ill. I have done ill; Of which I do accuse myself so sorely, That I will joy no more iv 6 18
Done nobly. He has done nobly, and cannot go without any honest man's voice *Coriolanus* ii 3 139
Done penance. I have done penance for contemning Love *T. G. of Ver.* ii 4 129
Done to death by slanderous tongues Was the Hero that here lies *Much Ado* v 3 3
Unless Lord Suffolk straight be done to death *2 Hen. VI.* iii 2 244
Is by the stern Lord Clifford done to death *3 Hen. VI.* ii 1 103
My elder brother, the Lord Aubrey Vere, Was done to death iii 3 103
Done well. It works. Come on. Thou hast done well, fine Ariel! *Temp.* i 2 494
That thinks he hath done well in people's eyes *Mer. of Venice* iii 2 143
You have done well, That men must lay their murders on your neck *Oth.* v 2 169
Thanks, gentlemen, to all; all have done well, And you the best *Pericles* ii 3 108
Donne. Sur mes genoux je vous donne mille remercîmens *Hen. V.* iv 4 57
Donned. Then up he rose, and donn'd his clothes *Hamlet* iv 5 52
I did not think This amorous surfeiter would have donn'd his helm For such a petty war *Ant. and Cleo.* ii 1 33
Donner. Pour les écus que vous l'avez promis, il est content de vous donner la liberté *Hen. V.* iv 4 56
Donnerai. Gardez ma vie, et je vous donnerai deux cents écus iv 4 44
Don Worm. If Don Worm, his conscience, find no impediment *Much Ado* v 2 86
Doom. I fly not death, to fly his deadly doom *T. G. of Ver.* iii 1 185
And she hath offer'd to the doom—Which, unreversed, stands in effectual force—A sea of melting pearl iii 1 222
But were you banish'd for so small a fault?—I was, and held me glad of such a doom iv 1 32
That it may stand till the perpetual doom *Mer. Wives* v 5 62
When, after execution, judgement hath Repented o'er his doom *M. for M.* ii 2 11
And by the doom of death end woes and all *Com of Errors* i 1 2
Irrevocable is my doom Which I have pass'd upon her *As Y. Like It* i 3 85
Alter not the doom Forethought by heaven! *K. John* iii 1 311
Norfolk, for thee remains a heavier doom *Richard II.* i 3 148
I come To change blows with thee for our day of doom iii 2 189
To abide Thy kingly doom and sentence of his pride v 6 23
Carlisle, this is your doom: Choose out some secret place v 6 24
In his secret doom, out of my blood He'll breed revengement *1 Hen. IV.* iii 2 6
Exeter hath given the doom of death For pax of little price *Hen. V.* iii 6 46
Stain to thy countrymen, thou hear'st thy doom! *1 Hen. VI.* iv 1 45
What shall we say to this in law?—This doom, my lord, if I may judge *2 Hen. VI.* i 3 208

Doom. This is the law, and this Duke Humphrey's doom . . . 2 *Hen. VI.* i 3 214
It skills not greatly who impugns our doom . . . iii 1 281
Expect your highness' doom, of life or death . . . iv 9 12
Revoke that doom of mercy . . . 3 *Hen. VI.* ii 6 46
By whose injurious doom My elder brother, the Lord Aubrey Vere, Was done to death . . . iii 3 101
I'll throw thy body in another room And triumph, Henry, in thy day of doom . . . v 6 93
Have I a tongue to doom my brother's death? . . . *Richard III.* ii 1 102
Makes me most forward in this noble presence To doom the offenders . iii 4 67
If yet your gentle souls fly in the air And be not fix'd in doom perpetual, Hover about me with your airy wings! . . . iv 4 12
All unavoided is the doom of destiny . . . iv 4 217
Die the other's slave, And the gods doom him after! . . . *Coriolanus* i 8 6
This is the day of doom for Bassianus . . . *T. Andron.* ii 3 42
Unbind my sons, reverse the doom of death . . . iii 1 24
A stone is silent, and offendeth not, And tribunes with their tongues doom men to death . . . iii 1 47
The judges have pronounced My everlasting doom of banishment . . iii 1 51
The emperor, in his rage, will doom her death . . . iv 2 114
If any one relieves or pities him, For the offence he dies. This is our doom . . . v 3 182
The prince will doom thee death, If thou art taken . *Rom. and Jul.* iii 1 139
Then, dreadful trumpet, sound the general doom! . . . iii 2 67
What news? what is the prince's doom? . . . iii 3 4
I bring thee tidings of the prince's doom.—What less than dooms-day is the prince's doom? . . . iii 3 8
Unless philosophy can make a Juliet, Displant a town, reverse a prince's doom, It helps not, it prevails not . . . iii 3 59
Look on death itself! up, up, and see The great doom's image! *Macbeth* ii 3 83
Start, eyes! What, will the line stretch out to the crack of doom? . iv 1 117
With tristful visage, as against the doom, Is thought-sick . *Hamlet* iii 4 50
Reverse thy doom; And, in thy best consideration, check This . *Lear* i 1 151
Revoke thy doom; Or, whilst I can vent clamour from my throat, I'll tell thee thou dost evil . . . i 1 167
From his all-obeying breath I hear The doom of Egypt *Ant. and Cleo.* iii 13 78
The death of Antony Is not a single doom . . . v 1 18
He, obedient to their dooms, Will take the crown . . *Pericles* iii Gower 32
Doomed. If no, then thou art doom'd to die . . . *Com. of Errors* i 1 155
Or, when he doom'd this beauty to a grave, Found it too precious-princely for a grave . . . *K. John* iv 3 39
My condemned lord Is doom'd a prisoner . . . *Richard II.* v 1 4
I am thy father's spirit, Doom'd for a certain term to walk the night *Ham.* i 5 10
Live, And deal with others better.—Nobly doom'd! . . . *Cymbeline* v 5 420
Doomsday. If she lives till doomsday, she'll burn a week longer than the whole world . . . *Com. of Errors* iii 2 101
I'll prove her fair, or talk till doomsday here . . . *L. L. Lost* iv 3 274
Doomsday is near; die all, die merrily . . . 1 *Hen. IV.* iv 1 134
Why, then All-Souls' day is my body's doomsday . . . *Richard III.* v 1 12
What less than dooms-day is the prince's doom? . *Rom. and Jul.* iii 3 9
Their stol'n marriage-day Was Tybalt's dooms-day . . . v 3 234
Stare, cry out and run As it were doomsday . . . *J. Cæsar* iii 1 98
Was sick almost to doomsday with eclipse . . . *Hamlet* i 1 120
The world's grown honest.—Then is doomsday near . . . ii 2 243
A grave-maker: the houses that he makes last till doomsday . . v 1 67
I'll give thee leave To play till doomsday . . . *Ant. and Cleo.* v 2 232
Door. I'll turn my mercy out o' doors . . . *Tempest* iii 2 78
I would resort to her by night.—Ay, but the doors be lock'd *T. G. of V.* iii 1 111
I will peat the door for Master Page. What, hoa! Got pless your house here! . . . *Mer. Wives* i 1 73
I shall turn your head out of my door . . . i 4 132
Here's Mistress Page at the door, sweating and blowing . . . iii 3 93
They took me on their shoulders; met the jealous knave their master in the door . . . iii 5 103
Three of Master Ford's brothers watch the door with pistols . . . iv 2 53
I'll appoint my men to carry the basket again, to meet him at the door iv 2 98
Take the basket again on your shoulders: your master is hard at door . iv 2 111
Out of my door, you witch, you hag, you baggage, you polecat! . . iv 2 194
A little door Which from the vineyard to the garden leads *Meas. for Meas.* iv 1 32
Because their business still lies out o' door . . . *Com. of Errors* ii 1 11
But, soft! my door is lock'd. Go bid them let us in . . . iii 1 30
Either get thee from the door or sit down at the hatch . . . iii 1 33
Who talks within there? ho, open the door! . . . iii 1 38
Master, knock the door hard.—Let him knock till it ache . . . iii 1 58
You'll cry for this, minion, if I beat the door down . . . iii 1 59
Who is that at the door that keeps all this noise? . . . iii 1 61
Your wife, sir knave! go get you from the door . . . iii 1 64
They stand at the door, master; bid them welcome hither . . . iii 1 68
She will well excuse Why at this time the doors are made against you . iii 1 93
Since mine own doors refuse to entertain me, I'll knock elsewhere . iii 1 120
That will I bestow Among my wife and her confederates, For locking me out of my doors . . . iv 1 18
His own doors being shut against his entrance . . . iv 3 90
Driven out of doors with it when I go from home; welcomed home with it . . . iv 4 37
I shall beg with it from door to door . . . iv 4 41
Upon me the guilty doors were shut And I denied to enter in my house iv 4 66
Were not my doors lock'd up and I shut out?—Perdie, your doors were lock'd . . . iv 4 73
She shut the doors upon me, While she with harlots feasted in my house v 1 204
Hang me up at the door of a brothel-house for the sign of blind Cupid *Much Ado* i 1 255
I pray you, watch about Signior Leonato's door . . . iii 3 98
The goose came out of door, And stay'd the odds by adding four *L. L. L.* iii 1 92
I am sent with broom before, To sweep the dust behind the door *M. N. D.* v 1 397
Whiles we shut the gates upon one wooer, another knocks at the door *Mer. of Venice* i 2 147
Hear you me, Jessica: Lock up my doors . . . ii 5 29
Perhaps I will return immediately: Do as I bid you; shut doors after you ii 5 53
I will make fast the doors, and gild myself With some more ducats . ii 6 49
Go one, and call the Jew into the court.—He is ready at the door . iv 1 15
He is here at the door and importunes access to you *As Y. Like It* i 1 96
O unhappy youth! Come not within these doors . . . ii 3 17
Well, push him out of doors . . . iii 1 15
Make the doors upon a woman's wit and it will out at the casement . iv 1 162
Yet would you say ye were beaten out of door . . . *T. of Shrew* Ind. 2 87
The door is open, sir; there lies your way . . . iii 2 212
What, no man at door To hold my stirrup nor to take my horse! . . iv 1 123
Beggars, that come unto my father's door, Upon entreaty have a present alms . . . iv 3 4
Door. Sir, here's the door, this is Lucentio's house . . . *T. of Shrew* v 1 9
His father is come from Pisa and is here at the door . . . v 1 30
Disgraces have of late knocked too often at my door . . . *All's Well* iv 1 32
Address thy gait unto her; Be not denied access, stand at her doors *T. N.* i 4 16
He says, he'll stand at your door like a sheriff's post . . . i 5 157
And bid him turn you out of doors . . . ii 3 78
Let the garden door be shut, and leave me to my hearing . . . iii 1 103
Hence with her, out o' door . . . *W. Tale* ii 3 67
If you did but hear the pedlar at the door, you would never dance again after a tabor and pipe . . . iv 4 182
Let them come in; but quickly now.—Why, they stay at door, sir . iv 4 352
Saint George, that swinged the dragon, and e'er since Sits on his horse back at mine hostess' door . . . *K. John* ii 1 289
How now, foolish rheum! Turning dispiteous torture out of door! . iv 1 34
Forage, and run To meet displeasure farther from the doors . . . v 1 60
That hand which had the strength, even at your door, To cudgel you . v 2 137
Now my soul hath elbow-room; It would not out at windows nor at doors . . . v 7 29
To push destruction and perpetual shame Out of the weak door of our fainting land . . . v 7 78
Open the door, secure, fool-hardy king . . . *Richard II.* v 3 43
Open the door, or I will break it open . . . v 3 45
Pity me, open the door: A beggar begs that never begg'd before . . v 3 77
Sir John, with half-a-dozen more, are at the door . . . 1 *Hen. IV.* ii 4 93
Let them alone awhile, and then open the door . . . ii 4 96
Falstaff and the rest of the thieves are at the door: shall we be merry? ii 4 99
Hostess, clap to the doors: watch to-night, pray to-morrow . . ii 4 305
There is a nobleman of the court at door would speak with you . . ii 4 318
The sheriff with a most monstrous watch is at the door . . . ii 4 530
The sheriff and all the watch are at the door: they are come to search the house . . . ii 4 537
How now, lad! is the wind in that door? . . . iii 3 102
Shut the door; there comes no swaggerers here . . . 2 *Hen. IV.* ii 4 82
Shut the door, I pray you.—Dost thou hear, hostess? . . . ii 4 85
Ne'er tell me: your ancient swaggerer comes not in my doors . . ii 4 91
Have you turned him out o' doors?—Yea, sir. The rascal's drunk . ii 4 229
Who knocks so loud at door? Look to the door there, Francis . . ii 4 381
More knocking at the door! How now! what's the matter? . . . ii 4 399
If God doth give successful end To this debate that bleedeth at our doors iv 4 2
How now! rain within doors, and none abroad! . . . iv 5 9
He is not here.—This door is open; he is gone this way . . . iv 5 56
Look who's at door there, ho! who knocks? . . . v 3 75
What, is the old king dead?—As nail in door . . . v 3 127
If we, with thrice such powers left at home, Cannot defend our own doors from the dog . . . *Hen. V.* i 2 218
For, God before, We'll chide this Dauphin at his father's door . . i 2 308
Even in their wives' and children's sight, Be hang'd up for example at their doors . . . 2 *Hen. VI.* iv 2 190
When nature brought him to the door of death . . . 3 *Hen. VI.* iii 3 105
Let the foul'st contempt Shut door upon me . . . *Hen. VIII.* ii 4 43
They would shame to make me Wait else at door, a fellow-counsellor . v 2 17
Who holds his state at door, 'mongst pursuivants, Pages, and footboys v 2 24
And at the door too, like a post with packets . . . v 2 32
Impossible—Unless we sweep 'em from the door with cannons . . v 4 13
Keep the door close, sirrah.—What would you have me do? . . . v 4 30
Bless me, what a fry of fornication is at door! . . . v 4 37
There is a fellow somewhat near the door, he should be a brazier by his face . . . v 4 41
I stalk about her door, Like a strange soul upon the Stygian banks Staying for waftage . . . *Troi. and Cres.* iii 2 9
Hark! there's one up.—What, 's all the doors open here? . . . iv 2 19
Would he were knock'd i' the head! Who's that at door? good uncle, go and see . . . iv 2 36
Who's there? what's the matter? will you beat down the door? . . iv 2 44
I will not out of doors.—Not out of doors!—She shall, she shall *Coriol.* i 3 78
Turn thy solemness out o' door, and go along with us . . . i 3 120
Here's no place for you: pray, go to the door . . . iv 5 9
With my sword I'll keep this door safe . . . *T. Andron.* i 1 288
Knock at my door, and tell me what he says . . . iv 3 119
Oft have I digg'd up dead men from their graves, And set them upright at their dear friends' doors . . . v 1 136
Is it your trick to make me ope the door, That so my sad decrees may fly away? . . . v 2 10
What's he that now is going out of door? . . . *Rom. and Jul.* i 5 132
O, shut the door! and when thou hast done so, Come weep with me . iv 1 44
Seal'd up the doors, and would not let us forth . . . v 2 11
And, lips, O you The doors of breath, seal with a righteous kiss A dateless bargain to engrossing death! . . . v 3 114
I come to have thee thrust me out of doors . . . *T. of Athens* i 2 25
Men shut their doors against a setting sun . . . i 2 150
Doors, that were ne'er acquainted with their wards Many a bounteous year . . . iii 3 38
What, are my doors opposed against my passage? . . . iii 4 80
'Tis your brother Cassius at the door, Who doth desire to see you *J. C.* ii 1 70
Mark how the blood of Cæsar follow'd it, As rushing out of doors, to be resolved If Brutus so unkindly knock'd, or no . . . iii 2 183
I have no will to wander forth of doors, Yet something leads me forth . iii 3 3
Till we have done our conference. Let Lucius and Titinius guard our door . . . iv 2 52
As his host, Who should against his murderer shut the door . *Macbeth* i 7 15
He is about it: The doors are open; and the surfeited grooms Do mock their charge with snores . . . ii 2 5
This is the door.—I'll make so bold to call . . . ii 3 56
Now go to the door, and stay there till we call . . . iii 1 73
He seem'd to find his way without his eyes; For out o' doors he went without their helps . . . *Hamlet* ii 1 99
Let the doors be shut upon him, that he may play the fool no where but in's own house . . . iii 1 135
You do, surely, bar the door upon your own liberty, if you deny your griefs to your friend . . . iii 2 351
Where are my Switzers? Let them guard the door . . . iv 5 97
The doors are broke.—Where is this king? Sirs, stand you all without iv 5 111
Keep the door. O thou vile king, Give me my father! . . . iv 5 115
O villany! Ho! let the door be lock'd: Treachery! Seek it out . . v 2 321
Leave thy drink and thy whore, And keep in-a-door . . . *Lear* i 4 138
Shut up your doors: He is attended with a desperate train . . . ii 4 307
Shut up your doors, my lord; 'tis a wild night . . . ii 4 311
Court holy-water in a dry house is better than this rain-water out o' door . . . iii 2 11
Though their injunction be to bar my doors . . . iii 4 155

Door. Signior, is all your family within?—Are your doors lock'd?—
Why? wherefore ask you this? . . . *Othello* i 1 85
I have charged thee not to haunt about my doors . . . . . i 1 96
Pictures out of doors, Bells in your parlours, wild-cats in your kitchens ii 1 110
Where are they?—Here at the door; I pray you, call them in . . ii 3 48
Strong circumstances, Which lead directly to the door of truth . iii 3 407
Shut the door; Cough, or cry 'hem,' if any body come . . . iv 2 28
Speak within door.—O, fie upon them! . . . . . . iv 2 144
Come, guard the door without; let him not pass, But kill him rather v 2 241
In Egypt sits at dinner, and will make No wars without doors *A. and C.* ii 1 13
All of her that is out of door most rich! . . . *Cymbeline* i 6 15
Attend you here the door of our stern daughter? Will she not forth? ii 3 42
Her doors lock'd? Not seen of late? Grant, heavens, that which I fear Prove false! . . . . iii 5 51
The bier at door, And a demand who is't shall die, I'ld say 'My father' iv 2 22
If in our youths we could pick up some pretty estate, 'twere not amiss to keep our door hatched . . . . . . *Pericles* iv 2 37
To me The very doors and windows savour vilely . . . . iv 6 117
Would she had never come within my doors! . . . . . iv 6 157
Door-keeper. Avaunt, thou damned door-keeper! . . . . iv 6 126
Thou art the damned doorkeeper to every Coistrel . . . . iv 6 175
Door-nail. If I do not leave you all as dead as a door-nail 2 *Hen. VI.* iv 10 43
Dorcas. Give me those flowers there, Dorcas . . . *W. Tale* iv 4 73
Doreus. Bastard Margarelon Hath Doreus prisoner . *Troi. and Cres.* v 5 8
Doricles. O Doricles, Your praises are too large . . *W. Tale* iv 4 146
With wisdom I might fear, my Doricles, You woo'd me the false way . iv 4 150
They call him Doricles; and boasts himself To have a worthy feeding . iv 4 168
If young Doricles Do light upon her, she shall bring him that Which he not dreams of . . . . iv 4 178
Dormouse. To exasperate you, to awake your dormouse valour *T. Night* iii 2 21
Dorothy. Then to you, Mistress Dorothy; I will charge you 2 *Hen. IV.* ii 4 130
I know you, Mistress Dorothy.—Away, you cut-purse rascal! . . ii 4 136
To Dorothy my woman hie thee presently . . . *Cymbeline* ii 3 143
Dorset. Rivers and Dorset, you were standers by . . *Richard III.* i 3 210
Yourself are not exempt in this, Nor your son Dorset . . . ii 1 19
Dorset, embrace him; Hastings, love lord marquess . . . ii 1 25
Look I so pale, Lord Dorset, as the rest? . . . . . ii 1 83
O Dorset, speak not to me, get thee hence! . . . . . iv 1 39
The Marquis Dorset's fled To Richmond, in those parts beyond the sea iv 2 46
Dorset is fled to Richmond.—I hear that news, my lord . . . iv 2 88
Dorset your son, that with a fearful soul Leads discontented steps in foreign soil . . . . iv 4 311
The king, that calls your beauteous daughter wife, Familiarly shall call thy Dorset brother . . . . iv 4 316
Stirr'd up by Dorset, Buckingham, and Ely, He makes for England iv 4 468
Sir Thomas Lovel and Lord Marquis Dorset, 'Tis said, my liege, in Yorkshire are in arms . . . . iv 4 520
Who's that that bears the sceptre?—Marquess Dorset . *Hen. VIII.* iv 1 38
You shall have two noble partners with you; the old Duchess of Norfolk, and Lady Marquess Dorset . . . . v 3 170
Dorsetshire. Richmond, in Dorsetshire, sent out a boat Unto the shore *Richard III.* iv 4 524
Dost. How now, good woman! how dost thou? . . *Mer. Wives* i 4 142
How dost thou, Charles?—He cannot speak, my lord *As Y. Like It* i 2 231
Why, how dost thou, man? what is the matter with thee? *T. Night* iii 4 26
What dost thou with him That is renown'd for faith? *Rom. and Jul.* iii 5 61
Thou dost ill to say the gallows is built stronger than the church *Ham.* v 1 53
How now, my pretty knave! how dost thou? . . . *Lear* i 4 107
If thou canst cuckold him, thou dost thyself a pleasure, me a sport *Oth.* i 3 376
Dotage. I would she had bestowed this dotage on me . . *Much Ado* ii 3 175
The sport will be, when they hold one an opinion of another's dotage . ii 3 224
Her dotage now I do begin to pity . . . *M. N. Dream* iv 1 52
Banish me! Banish your dotage; banish usury . *T. of Athens* iii 5 99
Let his disposition have that scope That dotage gives it . . *Lear* i 4 315
He may enguard his dotage with their powers, And hold our lives in mercy . . . . i 4 349
All's not offence that indiscretion finds And dotage terms so . . ii 4 200
By their own importunate suit, Or voluntary dotage . . *Othello* iv 1 27
Nay, but this dotage of our general's O'erflows the measure *A. and C.* i 1 1
These strong Egyptian fetters I must break, Or lose myself in dotage . i 2 121
Dotant. Such a decayed dotant as you seem to be . . *Coriolanus* v 2 47
Dotard. I speak not like a dotard nor a fool . . . *Much Ado* v 1 59
Away with the dotard! to the goal with him! . . . *T. of Shrew* v 1 109
Thou dotard! thou art woman-tired, unroosted By thy dame Partlet *W. T.* ii 3 74
To the more mature A glass that feated them, and to the graver A child that guided dotards . . . . *Cymbeline* i 1 50
Dote. What do you mean To dote thus on such luggage? . *Tempest* iv 1 231
Forgive me that I do not dream on thee, Because thou see'st me dote upon my love . . . . *T. G. of Ver.* ii 4 173
How shall I dote on her with more advice, That thus without advice begin to love her! . . . . ii 4 207
You dote on her that cares not for your love . . . . . iv 4 87
I never knew a woman so dote upon a man . . *Mer. Wives* ii 2 106
Sing, siren, for thyself and I will dote . . . *Com. of Errors* iii 2 47
Unless the fear of death doth make me dote . . . . . v 1 195
I see thy age and dangers make thee dote . . . . . . v 1 329
I give away myself for you and dote upon the exchange . *Much Ado* iii 1 320
Most wonderful that she should so dote on Signior Benedick . . ii 3 99
If he do not dote on her upon this, I will never trust my expectation . ii 3 219
For none offend where all alike do dote . . . . *L. L. Lost* iv 3 126
Folly in fools bears not so strong a note As foolery in the wise, when wit doth dote . . . . v 2 76
And she, sweet lady, dotes, Devoutly dotes, dotes in idolatry, Upon this spotted and inconstant man . . . . *M. N. Dream* i 1 109
Helena, adieu: As you on him, Demetrius dote on you! . . . i 1 225
Will make or man or woman madly dote Upon the next live creature . ii 1 171
Which she must dote on in extremity . . . . iii 2 3
O, how I love thee! how I dote on thee! . . . . . . iv 1 50
An idle gawd Which in my childhood I did dote upon . . . iv 1 173
Not one among them but I dote on his very absence *Mer. of Venice* i 2 120
Is there yet another dotes upon rib-breaking? . . *As Y. Like It* i 2 151
Mars dote on you for his novices! what will ye do? . . *All's Well* ii 1 48
And she, mistaken, seems to dote on me . . . . *T. Night* ii 2 36
This duke as much They love and dote on . . . *Hen. VIII.* ii 1 52
The will dotes that is attributive To what infectiously itself affects *Troi. and Cres.* ii 2 58
You are three That Rome should dote on . . . . *Coriolanus* ii 1 204
How now! has sorrow made thee dote already? . . *T. Andron.* iii 2 23
And many more of the same breed that I know the drossy age dotes on *Hamlet* v 2 197
Dote. Not so young, sir, to love a woman for singing, nor so old to dote on her for any thing . . . . *Lear* i 4 41
I prattle out of fashion, and I dote In mine own comforts . *Othello* ii 1 208
O, what damned minutes tells he o'er Who dotes, yet doubts, suspects, yet strongly loves! . . . . iii 3 170
It is a creature That dotes on Cassio . . . . iv 1 97
Doted. All their prayers and love Were set on Hereford, whom they doted on . . . . 2 *Hen. IV.* iv 1 138
Doter. It mourns that painting and usurping hair Should ravish doters with a false aspect . . . . *L. L. Lost* iv 3 260
Doteth. I am afraid my daughter will run mad, So much she doteth on her Mortimer . . . . 1 *Hen. IV.* iii 1 146
Doth. Make the rope of his destiny our cable, for our own doth little advantage . . . . *Tempest* i 1 34
There I'll rest, as after much turmoil A blessed soul doth in Elysium *T. G. of Ver.* ii 7 38
How doth good Mistress Page?—and I thank you always . *Mer. Wives* i 1 84
Heaven doth with us as we with torches do . . *Meas. for Meas.* i 1 33
One doth not know How much an ill word may empoison liking *M. Ado* iii 1 85
How doth the lady?—Dead, I think . . . . iv 1 114
And now tell me, how doth your cousin? . . . . . . iv 2 90
I may speak of thee as the traveller doth of Venice . . *L. L. Lost* iv 2 98
Imitari is nothing: so doth the hound his master . . . . iv 2 130
It doth befall That I, one Snout by name, present a wall *M. N. Dream* v 1 156
I pray you, tell me how my good friend doth . *Mer. of Venice* iii 2 236
How doth thy husband? I love him well; he is an honest man 1 *Hen. IV.* iii 3 107
How doth the prince, and my young son of York? . . *Richard III.* iv 1 14
The brightness of her cheek would shame those stars, As daylight doth a lamp . . . . *Rom. and Jul.* ii 2 20
Where is she? and how doth she? and what says My conceal'd lady? . iii 3 97
Doting. Followed her with a doting observance *Mer. Wives* ii 2 203
Peace, doting wizard, peace! I am not mad . . *Com. of Errors* iv 4 61
As he errs, doting on Hermia's eyes, So I, admiring of his qualities *M. N. Dream* i 1 230
And the old folk, time's doting chronicles, Say it did so 2 *Hen. IV.* iv 4 126
The grave doth gape, and doting death is near; Therefore exhale *Hen. V.* ii 1 65
A grandam's name is little less in love Than is the doting title of a mother . . . . *Richard III.* iv 4 300
That same scurvy doting foolish young knave's sleeve of Troy *Tr. and Cr.* v 4 4
Thou chid'st me oft for loving Rosaline.—For doting, not for loving *Rom. and Jul.* ii 3 82
An hour but married, Tybalt murdered, Doting like me and like me banished . . . . iii 3 67
Doting on his own obsequious bondage, Wears out his time . *Othello* i 1 46
Like a doting mallard, Leaving the fight in height, flies after her *Ant. and Cleo.* iii 10 20
My very hairs do mutiny; for the white Reprove the brown for rashness, and they them For fear and doting . . . . iii 11 15
Double. My jerkin is a doublet.—Well, then, I'll double your folly *T. G. of Ver.* ii 4 21
Double and treble admonition, and still forfeit in the same kind! *M. for M.* iii 2 205
I understand you not: my griefs are double . . . *L. L. Lost* v 2 762
Methinks I see these things with parted eye, When every thing seems double . . . . *M. N. Dream* iv 1 195
Pay him six thousand, and deface the bond; Double six thousand *M. of V.* iii 2 302
As he were double and double a lord . . . . . *All's Well* ii 3 254
Do not shun her Until you see her die again; for then You kill her double . . . . *W. Tale* v 3 107
Your wind short? your chin double? your wit single? . . 2 *Hen. IV.* i 2 207
Rumour doth double, like the voice and echo, The numbers of the fear'd iii 1 97
Is old Double of your town living yet?—Dead, sir . . . . iii 2 45
Dispatch: this knave's tongue begins to double . . 2 *Hen. VI.* ii 3 94
Say untruths; and be ever double Both in his words and meaning *Hen. VIII.* iv 2 38
If you should deal double with her, truly it were an ill thing *R. and J.* ii 4 179
All our service In every point twice done and then done double *Macbeth* i 6 15
Double, double toil and trouble; Fire burn, and cauldron bubble . iv 1 10
Thy fifty yet doth double five-and-twenty, And thou art twice her love *Lear* ii 4 262
And hath in his effect a voice potential As double as the duke's *Othello* i 2 14
A lady So fair, and fasten'd to an empery, Would make the great'st king double . . . . *Cymbeline* i 6 121
Double beer. And here's a pot of good double beer . . 2 *Hen. VI.* ii 3 64
Double blessing. A double blessing is a double grace . . *Hamlet* i 3 53
Double bosoms. Whose double bosoms seem to wear one heart *Coriol.* iv 4 13
Double business. Like a man to double business bound, I stand in pause where I shall first begin . . . . *Hamlet* iii 3 41
Double change. With scarfs and fans and double change of bravery *T. of Shrew* iv 3 57
Double-charge. I will double-charge thee with dignities . 2 *Hen. IV.* v 3 130
Double cherry. Like to a double cherry, seeming parted *M. N. Dream* iii 2 209
Double coronation. Some reasons of this double coronation I have possess'd you with . . . . *K. John* iv 2 40
Double cracks. As cannons overcharged with double cracks, so they Doubly redoubled strokes upon the foe . . . . *Macbeth* i 2 37
Double damned. Therefore be double damn'd . . . *Othello* iv 2 37
Double dealer. I might have cudgelled thee out of thy single life, to make thee a double-dealer . . . . *Much Ado* v 4 116
I will be so much a sinner, to be a double-dealer . . . *T. Night* v 1 38
Double-dealing. It would be double-dealing, sir . . . . v 1 32
Double death. In the shade of death I shall find joy; In life but double death . . . . 2 *Hen. VI.* iii 2 55
But sorrow flouted at is double death . . . . *T. Andron.* iii 1 246
Double ducats. Two sealed bags of ducats, Of double ducats *M. of Ven.* ii 8 19
Double excellency. Is there not a double excellency in this? *M. W.* iii 3 187
Double-fatal. Thy very beadsmen learn to bend their bows Of double-fatal yew against thy state . . . . . . *Richard II.* iii 2 117
Double gain. Advantaging their loan with interest Of ten times double gain of happiness . . . . *Richard III.* iv 4 324
Double gild. England shall double gild his treble guilt 2 *Hen. IV.* iv 5 129
Double gilt. The double gilt of this opportunity you let time wash off *T. Night* iii 2 26
Double grace. A double blessing is a double grace . . . *Hamlet* i 3 53
Double heart. I gave him use for it, a double heart for his single one *Much Ado* ii 1 288
Double-henned. Now my double-henned sparrow! . . *Troi. and Cres.* v 7 11
Double honour. This is a double honour, Burgundy . 1 *Hen. VI.* ii 2 116
Double hunt. The babbling echo mocks the hounds, Replying shrilly to the well-tuned horns, As if a double hunt were heard at once *T. An.* ii 3 19

Double knavery. To get his place and to plume up my will In double knavery . . . . *Othello* i 3 400
Double labour. I do not like that paying back; it is a double labour 1 *Hen. IV.* iii 3 202
Double majesties. Why answer not the double majesties? . *K. John* ii 1 480
Double man. I am not a double man . . . . . 1 *Hen. IV.* v 4 141
Double meaning. There's a double meaning in that . . *Much Ado* ii 3 267
Like a double-meaning prophesier . . . . . *All's Well* iv 3 114
Double occasion. I am courted now with a double occasion . *W. Tale* iv 4 864
Double ones. Will his vouchers vouch him no more of his purchases, and double ones too? . . . . *Hamlet* v 1 118
Double pomp. To be possess'd with double pomp . . . *K. John* iv 2 9
Double power. And gives to every power a double power . *L. L. Lost* iv 3 331
Double recompense. It pays the hearing double recompense *M. N. D.* iii 2 180
Double reign. Nor can one England brook a double reign 1 *Hen. IV.* v 4 66
Double riches. And all the ruins of distressful times Repair'd with double riches of content . . . . *Richard III.* iv 4 319
Double self. Swear by your double self, And there's an oath of credit *Mer. of Venice* v 1 245
Double sense. Be these juggling fiends no more believed, That palter with us in a double sense . . . . . . *Macbeth* v 8 20
Double set. He'll watch the horologe a double set, If drink rock not his cradle . . . . *Othello* ii 3 135
Double shadow. We'll yoke together, like a double shadow 3 *Hen. VI.* iv 6 49
Double spirit. As if he master'd there a double spirit Of teaching and of learning instantly . . . . 1 *Hen. IV.* v 2 64
Double sure. But yet I'll make assurance double sure . *Macbeth* iv 1 83
Double surety. A man Who with a double surety binds his followers 2 *Hen. IV.* i 1 191
Double tongue. There's a double tongue; there's two tongues *Much Ado* v 1 170
You have a double tongue within your mask . *L. L. Lost* v 2 245
You spotted snakes with double tongue . . . *M. N. Dream* ii 2 9
Whose double tongue may with a mortal touch Throw death upon thy sovereign's enemies . . . . *Richard II.* iii 2 21
Double trust. He's here in double trust . . . . *Macbeth* i 7 12
Double varnish. And set a double varnish on the fame The Frenchman gave you . . . . *Hamlet* iv 7 133
Double vigour. Never could the strumpet, With all her double vigour, art and nature, Once stir my temper . . . *Meas. for Meas.* ii 2 184
Double villain. Thy name?—Cloten, thou villain.—Cloten, thou double villain, be thy name . . . . . . *Cymbeline* iv 2 89
Double violation. In double violation Of sacred chastity and of promise breach . . . . *Meas. for Meas.* v 1 409
Double vouchers. His recognizances, his fines, his double vouchers *Ham.* v 1 114
Double worship. This double worship, Where one part does disdain with cause, the other Insult without all reason . *Coriolanus* iii 1 142
Double wrong. 'Tis double wrong, to truant with your bed And let her read it in thy looks at board . . . *Com. of Errors* iii 2 17
You do me double wrong, To strive for that which resteth in my choice *T. of Shrew* iii 1 16
He does me double wrong That wounds me with the flatteries of his tongue . . . . *Richard II.* iii 2 215
Doubled. Ill deeds are doubled with an evil word . *Com. of Errors* iii 2 20
Until it had return'd These terms of treason doubled down his throat *Richard II.* i 1 57
All the virtues that attend the good Shall still be doubled on her *Hen. VIII.* v 5 29
Straight his doubled spirit Re-quicken'd what in flesh was fatigate *Cor.* ii 2 120
I do return those talents, Doubled with thanks and service *T. of Athens* i 2 7
The last of many doubled kisses . . . . *Ant. and Cleo.* i 5 40
Doubleness. The doubleness of the benefit defends the deceit from reproof . . . . *Meas. for Meas.* iii 1 268
Doubler tongue. For with doubler tongue Than thine, thou serpent, never adder stung . . . . *M. N. Dream* iii 2 72
Doublet. Is not, sir, my doublet as fresh as the first day I wore it? *Temp.* ii 1 102
My jerkin is a doublet.—Well, then, I'll double your folly *T. G. of Ver.* ii 4 20
Now will he lie ten nights awake, carving the fashion of a new doublet *Much Ado* ii 3 19
A Spaniard from the hip upward, no doublet . . . . iii 2 37
The fashion of a doublet, or a hat, or a cloak, is nothing to a man . iii 3 125
With your arms crossed on your thin-belly doublet like a rabbit on a spit . . . . *L. L. Lost* iii 1 19
He bought his doublet in Italy, his round hose in France *Mer. of Venice* i 2 80
I have no more doublets than backs . . . *T. of Shrew* Ind. 2 9
A silken doublet! a velvet hose! a scarlet cloak! and a copatain hat! v 1 68
Make thy doublet of changeable taffeta, for thy mind is a very opal *T. N.* ii 4 76
Your white canvas doublet will sully . . . 1 *Hen. IV.* ii 4 84
I am eight times thrust through the doublet, four through the hose . ii 4 185
Unless you should give me your doublet and stuff me out with straw 2 *Hen IV.* v 5 87
Off with your doublet quickly . . . . . 2 *Hen. VI.* ii 1 151
Honester men than thou go in their hose and doublets . . . iv 7 56
Hats, cloaks,—Doublets, I think,—flew up . . *Hen. VIII.* iv 1 74
Doublets that hangmen would Bury with those that wore them *Coriol.* i 5 7
Didst thou not fall out with a tailor for wearing his new doublet before Easter? . . . . *Rom. and Jul.* iii 1 30
He plucked me ope his doublet and offered them his throat to cut *J. C.* i 2 267
With his doublet all unbraced; No hat upon his head . *Hamlet* ii 1 78
I have already fit—'Tis in my cloak-bag—doublet, hat, hose, all *Cymb.* iii 4 172
Doublet and hose. Youthful still! in your doublet and hose this raw rheumatic day! . . . . *Mer. Wives* iii 1 46
This secrecy of thine shall be a tailor to thee and shall make thee a new doublet and hose . . . . iii 3 35
What a pretty thing man is when he goes in his doublet and hose and leaves off his wit! . . . . *Much Ado* v 1 203
Doublet and hose ought to show itself courageous to petticoat *As Y. L. It* ii 4 6
Dost thou think, though I am caparisoned like a man, I have a doublet and hose in my disposition? . . . . iii 2 206
What shall I do with my doublet and hose? . . . . . iii 2 232
We must have your doublet and hose plucked over your head . iv 1 206
Doubling. To instruct for the doubling of files . . . *All's Well* iv 3 303
With joy he will embrace you, for he's honourable And doubling that, most holy . . . . *Cymbeline* iii 4 180
Doubly. In both my eyes he doubly sees himself . . *Mer. of Venice* v 1 244
Will you be mine, now you are doubly won? . . . *All's Well* v 3 315
Let thy blows, doubly redoubled, Fall like amazing thunder *Richard II.* i 3 80
You have engaol'd my tongue, Doubly portcullis'd with my teeth and lips i 3 167
Take leave and part; for you must part forthwith.—Doubly divorced! v 1 71
Appetite, an universal wolf, So doubly seconded with will and power *Troi. and Cres.* i 3 122
He hath in this action outdone his former deeds doubly . . *Coriolanus* ii 1 151

Doubly. So they Doubly redoubled strokes upon the foe . . *Macbeth* i 2 38
Doubt. I not doubt He came alive to land . . . . . *Tempest* ii 1 121
Even Ambition cannot pierce a wink beyond, But doubt discovery there ii 1 243
With such discourse as, I not doubt, shall make it Go quick away . v 1 303
What says she to my valour?—O, sir, she makes no doubt of that *T. G. of Ver.* v 2 20
I doubt he be not well, that he comes not home . . *Mer. Wives* i 4 42
Tell her Master Slender hath married her daughter.—Doctors doubt that v 5 184
Assay the power you have.—My power?—Alas, I doubt . *Meas. for Meas.* i 4 77
Our doubts are traitors And make us lose the good we oft might win . i 4 77
Were you in doubt, sir, that you asked her? . . . . *Much Ado* i 1 106
Had we fought, I doubt we should have been too young for them . v 1 118
As to speak dout, fine, when he should say doubt . . *L. L. Lost* v 1 23
And ever and anon they made a doubt . . . . . . v 2 101
I make no doubt The rest will ne'er come in . . . . . v 2 151
Therefore be out of hope, of question, of doubt . . *M. N. Dream* iii 2 279
I do not doubt but to hear them say, it is a sweet comedy . . iv 2 44
I do not doubt, As I will watch the aim . . . *Mer. of Venice* i 1 149
Still gazing in a doubt Whether those peals of praise be his or no . . iii 2 145
From hence I go, To make these doubts all even . . *As Y. Like It* v 4 25
If any man doubt that, let him put me to my purgation . . . v 4 44
No doubt but he hath got a quiet catch . . . . *T. of Shrew* ii 1 333
I promise you, I should be arguing still upon that doubt . . . iii 1 55
A piece of ice: if thou doubt it, thou mayst slide from my shoulder to my heel . . . . iv 1 14
Then wherefore should I doubt? Hap what hap may, I'll roundly go about her . . . . iv 4 107
Ha' not you seen, Camillo,—But that's past doubt, you have *W. Tale* i 2 268
Past all doubt You'ld call your children yours . . . . . ii 3 80
My letters, by this means being there So soon as you arrive, shall clear that doubt . . . . iv 4 633
Of that I doubt, as all men's children may . . . . *K. John* i 1 63
Ay, who doubts that? a will! a wicked will! . . . . . . ii 1 193
Hang no more in doubt.—Hang nothing but a calf's-skin . . iii 1 219
I would be here, but that I doubt My uncle practises more harm to me iv 1 19
This will break out To all our sorrows, and ere long I doubt . . iv 2 102
Or turn'd an eye of doubt upon my face . . . . . . iv 2 233
Thou shalt find it, Dauphin, do not doubt . . . . . . v 2 180
I doubt he will be dead or ere I come . . . . v 6 44
'Tis doubt, When time shall call him home from banishment *Richard II.* i 4 20
To horse, to horse! urge doubts to them that fear . . . . ii 1 299
Depress'd he is already, and deposed 'Tis doubt he will be . . iii 4 69
But I doubt they will be too hard for us . . . 1 *Hen. IV.* i 2 203
To end one doubt by death Revives two greater in the heirs of life 2 *Hen. IV.* iv 1 199
I do not doubt you.—I am glad of it . . . . iv 2 77
What indeed I should say will, I doubt, prove mine own marring . Epil. 7
Out of doubt and out of question too, and ambiguities *Hen. V.* v 1 47
But answer me one doubt, What pledge have we of thy firm loyalty? 3 *Hen. VI.* iii 3 238
But, ere I go, Hastings and Montague, Resolve my doubt . . iv 1 135
Why, master mayor, why stand you in a doubt? Open the gates . iv 7 27
The doubt is that he will seduce the rest . . . . . . v 8 37
There's no doubt his majesty Will soon recover his accustom'd health *Richard III.* i 3 1
He should be gracious.—Why, madam, so, no doubt, he is.—I hope he is; but yet let mothers doubt . . . . ii 4 21
Doubt you not, right noble princes both, But I'll acquaint our duteous citizens . . . . iii 5 64
You do not doubt my faith, sir?—This secret is so weighty, 'twill require A strong faith to conceal it . . . . . . *Hen. VIII.* ii 1 143
Dangers, doubts, wringing of the conscience, Fears, and despairs . ii 2 28
I committed The daring'st counsel which I had to doubt . . . ii 4 215
A noble spirit, As yours was put into you, ever casts Such doubts, as false coin, from it . . . . iii 1 171
He will deserve more.—Yes, without all doubt . . . . . iv 1 113
I make as little doubt, as you do conscience In doing daily wrongs . v 3 67
Good boy, tell him I come. I doubt he be hurt . . *Troi. and Cres.* i 2 302
But modest doubt is call'd The beacon of the wise . . . . . ii 2 15
Doubt thou not, brave boy, I'll stand to-day for thee and me and Troy v 3 35
We never yet made doubt but Rome was ready To answer us . *Coriolanus* i 2 18
They nothing doubt prevailing and to make it brief wars . . . i 3 111
If any such be here—As it were sin to doubt—that love this painting . i 6 68
This mutiny were better put in hazard, Than stay, past doubt, for greater . . . . ii 3 265
That love the fundamental part of state More than you doubt the change on't . . . . iii 1 152
Where have you lurk'd, that you make doubt of it? . . . . v 4 49
And I will do it without fear or doubt, To live an unstain'd wife *R. and J.* iv 1 88
I'll hide me hereabout: His looks I fear, and his intents I doubt . v 3 44
The worst is filthy; and would not hold taking, I doubt me *T. of Athens* i 2 159
I doubt whether their legs be worth the sums That are given for 'em . i 2 238
But tell me true—For I must ever doubt, though ne'er so sure . iv 3 514
In whose breast Doubt and suspect, alas, are placed too late . . iv 3 519
Unto bad causes swear Such creatures as men doubt . . *J. Cæsar* ii 1 132
I do not doubt But that my noble master will appear . . . iv 2 10
Cabin'd, cribb'd, confined, bound in To saucy doubts and fears *Macbeth* iii 4 25
I doubt some danger does approach you nearly . . . . iv 2 67
I have lost my hopes.—Perchance even there where I did find my doubts iv 3 25
The mind I sway by and the heart I bear Shall never sag with doubt . v 3 10
To doubt the equivocation of the fiend That lies like truth . . v 5 43
My father's spirit in arms! all is not well; I doubt some foul play *Hamlet* i 2 256
Do not sleep, But let me hear from you.—Do you doubt that? . i 3 4
The dram of eale Doth all the noble substance of a doubt To his own scandal . . . . i 4 37
I doubt it is no other but the main; His father's death . . . ii 2 56
Doubt thou the stars are fire; Doubt that the sun doth move; Doubt truth to be a liar; But never doubt I love . . . . . . ii 2 116
And I do doubt the hatch and the disclose Will be some danger . iii 1 174
Where love is great, the littlest doubts are fear . . . . iii 2 181
Speaks things in doubt, That carry but half sense . . . . iv 5 6
Do not doubt, Cassio, But I will have my lord and you again As friendly as you were . . . . *Othello* iii 3 5
My general will forget my love and service.—Do not doubt that . . iii 3 19
O, what damned minutes tells he o'er Who dotes, yet doubts, suspects, yet strongly loves! . . . . iii 3 170
To be once in doubt Is once to be resolved . . . . . iii 3 179
Nor from mine own weak merits will I draw The smallest fear or doubt of her revolt; For she had eyes, and chose me . . . . iii 3 188
I'll see before I doubt; when I doubt, prove . . . . . iii 3 190

Doubt. So prove it, That the probation bear no hinge nor loop To hang a doubt on . . . *Othello* iii 3 366
'Tis a shrewd doubt, though it be but a dream . . . iii 3 429
I do nothing doubt you have store of thieves . . . *Cymbeline* ii 4 106
All other doubts, by time let them be clear'd . . . iv 3 45
A doubt In such a time nothing becoming you, Nor satisfying us . . iv 4 14
And should he doubt it, as no doubt he doth . . . *Pericles* i 2 86
To lop that doubt, he'll fill this land with arms . . . i 2 90
With thousand doubts How I might stop this tempest ere it came . i 2 97
I do not doubt thy faith; But should he wrong my liberties in my absence? . . . . i 2 111
You say she's a virgin?—O, sir, we doubt it not . . . iv 2 46
Truth can never be confirm'd enough, Though doubts did ever sleep . v 1 204
Tell him O'er, point by point, for yet he seems to doubt . . . v 1 227
Doubt it not . . . *T. of Athens* v 1 95; *Ant. and Cleo.* iii 7 1
I doubt it not *Com. of Errors* iv 1; *Much Ado* i 1; *T. of Shrew* ii 1; 2 *Hen. VI.* i 4; *Rom. and Jul.* iii 4; iii 5
No doubt *Tempest* i 2; v 1; *M. N. Dream* iv 1; *Mer. of Venice* i 2; *Hen. V.* i 1; ii 2; iv 3; 3 *Hen. VI.* v 1; *Richard III.* i 1; i 2; ii 3; ii 4; iii 1; iii 7; iv 1; iv 2; iv 4; v 3; *Hen. VIII.* i 3; ii 1; iii 2; v 4; *T. of Athens* i 2; *J. Cæsar* iii 2; *Cymbeline* iv 3; *Pericles* i 2
Out of doubt *Mer. Wives* ii 1; *Com. of Errors* iv 3; *M. N. Dream* iv 2; *Mer. of Venice* i 1; *Hen. V.* iv 1; v 1
We doubt it nothing . . . *Macbeth* v 4 2; *Hamlet* i 2 41
Doubt not. You know the character, I doubt not . . *Meas. for Meas.* iv 2 209
And doubt not, sir, but she will well excuse Why at this time the doors are made against you . . . *Com. of Errors* iii 1 92
I doubt not but to fashion it . . . *Much Ado* ii 1 384
Doubt not but success Will fashion the event in better shape . iv 1 236
Doubt not her care should be To comb your noddle . . *T. of Shrew* i 1 63
Doubt not but heaven Hath brought me up to be your daughter's dower *All's Well* iv 4 18
Your horse now would make him an ass.—Ass, I doubt not . *T. Night* iv 3 185
I doubt not but to do myself much right, or you much shame . v 1 316
I doubt not then but innocence shall make False accusation blush *W. T.* iii 2 31
Though I be old, I doubt not but to ride as fast as York . *Richard II.* v 2 115
I doubt not but to die a fair death for all this . . 1 *Hen. IV.* ii 1 14
Doubt not, my lord, they shall be well opposed . . . iv 4 33
Both which we doubt not but your majesty Shall soon enjoy 2 *Hen. IV.* iv 4 11
We doubt not of a fair and lucky war . . . *Hen. V.* ii 2 184
We doubt not now But every rub is smoothed on our way . . ii 2 187
Let us swear That you are worth your breeding; which I doubt not . iii 1 28
Those bitter injuries, Which Somerset hath offer'd to my house, I doubt not but with honour to redress . . . 1 *Hen. VI.* ii 5 126
You are strong and manly; God on our side, doubt not of victory 2 *Hen. VI.* iv 8 54
Doubt not so to deal As all things shall redound unto your good . iv 9 46
Though the odds be great, I doubt not, uncle, of our victory 3 *Hen. VI.* i 2 73
I doubt not, I, but we shall soon persuade Both him and all his brothers iv 7 33
Doubt not of the day, And, that once gotten, doubt not of large pay iv 7 87
I doubt not but his friends will fly to us . . *Richard III.* v 2 19
O, doubt not that; I speak from certainties . . *Coriolanus* i 2 30
One thing wanting, which I doubt not but Our Rome will cast upon thee ii 1 217
Doubt not The commoners, for whom we stand . . . ii 1 242
Doubt not that, if money and the season can yield it . *T. of Athens* iii 6 57
I doubt not of your wisdom . . . *J. Cæsar* iii 1 183
Be by, good madam, when we do awake him; I doubt not of his temperance . . . . *Lear* iv 7 24
Let me be partaker.—Doubt not, sir; I knew it for my bond . *A. and C.* i 4 83
Words him, I doubt not, a great deal from the matter . *Cymbeline* i 4 16
I doubt not you sustain what you're worthy of by your attempt . i 4 125
I will confirm with oath; which, I doubt not, You'll give me leave to spare . . . . i 4 64
I doubt not but this populous city will Yield many scholars . *Pericles* iv 6 197
I doubt not but I shall find them tractable enough . . . iv 6 210
Doubted. Let it not be doubted but he'll come . . *Mer. Wives* iv 3 43
If ever fearful To do a thing, where I the issue doubted . . *W. Tale* i 2 259
Let't not be doubted I shall do good.—Now be you blest for it! . ii 2 53
If Warwick knew in what estate he stands, 'Tis to be doubted he would waken him . . . 3 *Hen. VI.* iv 3 19
He doubted 'Twould prove the verity of certain words . *Hen. VIII.* i 2 158
And to be doubted that your Moor and you Are singled forth to try experiments . . . *T. Andron.* ii 3 68
Such as he is, full of regard and honour.—He is not doubted . *J. Cæsar* iv 2 13
Our sister's man is certainly miscarried.—'Tis to be doubted . *Lear* iv 2 6
Doubtest. Why doubt'st thou of my forwardness? . . 1 *Hen. VI.* i 1 100
Doubtful. In perplexity and doubtful dilemma . . *Mer. Wives* iv 5 87
A doubtful warrant of immediate death . . . *Com. of Errors* i 1 69
Doubtful thoughts, and rash-embraced despair, And shuddering fear *Mer. of Venice* iii 2 109
Doubtful whether what I see be true, Until confirm'd, sign'd, ratified by you . . . . iii 2 148
But I am doubtful of your modesties . . . *T. of Shrew* Ind. 1 94
That my most jealous and too doubtful soul May live at peace *T. Night* iv 3 27
The little number of your doubtful friends . . . *K. John* iv 1 36
To set so rich a main On the nice hazard of one doubtful hour 1 *Hen. IV.* iv 1 48
His is certain, ours is doubtful . . . . iv 3 4
Let me be umpire in this doubtful strife . . . 1 *Hen. VI.* iv 1 151
By doubtful fear My joy of liberty is half eclipsed . 3 *Hen. VI.* iv 6 62
To the shore Throng many doubtful hollow-hearted friends *Richard III.* iv 4 435
You have no cause to hold my friendship doubtful . . . iv 4 493
Deceive the time, And aid thee in this doubtful shock of arms . v 3 93
Our doubtful hope, our convoy and our bark . . *Troi. and Cres.* i 1 107
Exposed myself, From certain and possess'd conveniences, To doubtful fortunes . . . . iii 3 8
But it is doubtful yet, Whether Cæsar will come forth to-day, or no *J. C.* ii 1 193
Doubtful it stood; As two spent swimmers, that do cling together *Macb.* i 2 7
Safer to be that which we destroy Than by destruction dwell in doubtful joy . . . . iii 2 7
Or by pronouncing of some doubtful phrase . . . *Hamlet* i 5 175
Her death was doubtful . . . . . . v 1 250
Methinks I should know you, and know this man; Yet I am doubtful *Lear* iv 7 65
I am doubtful that you have been conjunct And bosom'd with her . v 1 12
Doubtfully. I writ at random, very doubtfully . . *T. G. of Ver.* ii 1 117
Spake he so doubtfully, thou couldst not feel his meaning? *Com. of Errors* ii 1 50
So doubtfully that I could scarce understand them . . . ii 1 53
Whom the oracle Hath doubtfully pronounced thy throat shall cut *T. of Athens* iv 3 121
Doubting thy birth and lawful progeny . . . 1 *Hen. VI.* iii 3 61
I speak not this as doubting any here . . . . 3 *Hen. VI.* v 4 43
Nothing doubting your present assistance therein.—La, la, la, la! 'nothing doubting,' says he? . . . . *T. of Athens* iii 1 20
Doubting things go ill often hurts more Than to be sure they do *Cymb.* i 6 95
Doubting lest that he had err'd or sinn'd, To show his sorrow, he'ld correct himself . . . . . . *Pericles* i 3 22
Doubtless. Bawd is he doubtless, and of antiquity too . *Meas. for Meas.* iii 2 71
Pretty child, sleep doubtless and secure . . . *K. John* iv 1 130
With as clear excuse As well as I am doubtless I can purge Myself 1 *Hen. IV.* iii 2 20
Doubtless he shrives this woman to her smock . . . 1 *Hen. VI.* i 2 119
Doubtless he would have made a noble knight . . . . iv 7 44
Doubtless Burgundy will yield him help, And we shall have more wars 3 *Hen. VI.* iv 6 90
What is become of Marcius?—Slain, sir, doubtless . . *Coriolanus* i 4 48
Doubtless Sees and knows more, much more, than he unfolds *Othello* iii 3 243
Doubtless With joy he will embrace you, for he's honourable *Cymbeline* iii 4 178
Dough. Our cake's dough on both sides . . . . *T. of Shrew* i 1 110
My cake is dough; but I'll in among the rest, Out of hope of all . v 1 145
Doughty-handed are you, and have fought Not as you served the cause *Ant. and Cleo.* iv 8 5
Doughy. All the unbaked and doughy youth of a nation . . *All's Well* iv 5 3
Douglas. Welcome news. The Earl of Douglas is discomfited 1 *Hen. IV.* i 1 67
Hotspur took Mordake the Earl of Fife, and eldest son To beaten Douglas . . . . i 1 72
Make the Douglas' son your only mean For powers in Scotland . i 3 261
Where you and Douglas and our powers at once, As I will fashion it, shall happily meet . . . . i 3 296
That sprightly Scot of Scots, Douglas . . . . ii 4 377
That fiend Douglas, that spirit Percy, and that devil Glendower . ii 4 404
What never-dying honour hath he got Against renowned Douglas! . iii 2 107
This infant warrior in his enterprizes Discomfited great Douglas . iii 2 114
York, Douglas, Mortimer, Capitulate against us and are up . iii 2 119
Douglas and the English rebels met The eleventh of this month at Shrewsbury . . . . iii 2 165
If speaking truth In this fine age were not thought flattery, Such attribution should the Douglas have . . . . iv 1 3
You speak it out of fear and cold heart.—Do me no slander, Douglas . iv 3 8
You need not fear; There is Douglas and Lord Mortimer . . iv 4 22
The Douglas and the Hotspur both together Are confident against the world . . . . v 1 116
Defy him by the Lord of Westmoreland.—Lord Douglas, go you and tell him so . . . . v 2 33
My name is Douglas; And I do haunt thee in the battle thus Because some tell me that thou art a king . . . . v 3 3
O Douglas, hadst thou fought at Holmedon thus, I never had triumph'd upon a Scot . . . . v 3 14
Here breathless lies the king.—Where?—Here.—This, Douglas? no v 3 19
I am the Douglas, fatal to all those That wear those colours on them . v 4 26
The king himself; who, Douglas, grieves at heart So many of his shadows thou hast met . . . . v 4 29
I might have let alone The insulting hand of Douglas over you . v 4 54
The noble Scot, Lord Douglas, when he saw The fortune of the day quite turn'd from him . . ., fled with the rest. . . v 5 17
At my tent The Douglas is; and I beseech your grace I may dispose of him . . . . v 5 23
Go to the Douglas, and deliver him Up to his pleasure, ransomless and free . . . . v 5 27
The king before the Douglas' rage Stoop'd his anointed head 2 *Hen. IV.* Ind. 31
And both the Blunts Kill'd by the hand of Douglas . . . i 1 17
Your son did thus and thus; Your brother thus: so fought the noble Douglas . . . . i 1 77
Douglas is living, and your brother, yet . . . . i 1 82
The bloody Douglas, whose well-labouring sword Had three times slain the appearance of the king . . . . . . i 1 127
Dout. As to speak dout, fine, when he should say doubt . *L. L. Lost* v 1 22
That their hot blood may spin in English eyes, And dout them with superfluous courage . . . . . *Hen. V.* iv 2 11
I have a speech of fire, that fain would blaze, But that this folly douts it *Hamlet* iv 7 192
Doute. Je ne doute point d'apprendre, par la grace de Dieu . *Hen. V.* iii 4 43
Dove. Falstaff, varlet vile, His dove will prove, his gold will hold *M. Wives* i 3 107
By the simplicity of Venus' doves . . . *M. N. Dream* i 1 171
Aggravate my voice so that I will roar you as gently as any sucking dove i 2 85
The dove pursues the griffin; the mild hind Makes speed to catch the tiger . . . . ii 1 232
Who will not change a raven for a dove? . . . . ii 2 114
Asleep, my love? What, dead, my dove? . . . . v 1 332
I have here a dish of doves that I would bestow upon your worship *Mer. of Venice* ii 2 144
She's not froward, but modest as the dove . . *T. of Shrew* ii 1 295
Tut, she's a lamb, a dove, a fool to him! . . . . iii 2 159
I'll sacrifice the lamb that I do love, To spite a raven's heart within a dove . . . . *T. Night* v 1 134
As valiant as the wrathful dove or most magnanimous mouse 2 *Hen. IV.* iii 2 171
The dove and very blessed spirit of peace . . . . iv 1 46
Was Mahomet inspired with a dove? Thou with an eagle art inspired then . . . . 1 *Hen. VI.* i 2 140
So bees with smoke and doves with noisome stench Are from their hives and houses driven away . . . . i 5 23
As is the sucking lamb or harmless dove . . . . 2 *Hen. VI.* iii 1 71
Seems he a dove? his feathers are but borrow'd . . . iii 1 75
So doves do peck the falcon's piercing talons . . . 3 *Hen. VI.* i 4 41
Doves will peck in safeguard of their brood . . . . ii 2 18
He eats nothing but doves, love, and that breeds hot blood *Tr. and Cr.* iii 1 140
Those doves' eyes, Which can make gods forsworn . . *Coriolanus* v 3 27
So shows a snowy dove trooping with crows . . *Rom. and Jul.* i 5 50
Cry but 'Ay me!' pronounce but 'love' and 'dove' . . . ii 1 10
Therefore do nimble-pinion'd doves draw love . . . . ii 5 7
Fare you well, my dove! . . . . . . *Hamlet* iv 5 167
As patient as the female dove, When that her golden couplets are disclosed . . . . v 1 309
In that mood The dove will peck the estridge . . *Ant. and Cleo.* iii 13 197
So With the dove of Paphos might the crow Vie feathers white *Per.* iv Gower 32
Dove-cote. Like an eagle in a dove-cote, I Flutter'd your Volscians in Corioli . . . . *Coriolanus* v 6 115
Dove-drawn. I met her deity Cutting the clouds towards Paphos and her son Dove-drawn with her . . . . . . *Tempest* iv 1 94
Dove-feather'd raven! wolvish ravening lamb! . . . *Rom. and Jul.* iii 2 76

Dove-house. Sitting in the sun under the dove-house wall *Rom. and Jul.* i 3 27
'Shake,' quoth the dove-house: 'twas no need, I trow, To bid me trudge i 3 33
Dove's down. This hand, As soft as dove's down and as white as it *W. Tale* iv 4 374
Dover. See them guarded And safely brought to Dover . 1 *Hen. VI.* v 1 49
Make your speed to Dover, you shall find Some that will thank you *Lear* iii 1 36
There is a litter ready; lay him in't, And drive towards Dover . iii 6 98
With some other of the lords dependants, Are gone with him towards Dover . iii 7 19
Where hast thou sent the king?—To Dover.—Wherefore to Dover? iii 7 51
Go thrust him out at gates, and let him smell His way to Dover . iii 7 94
Thou wilt o'ertake us, hence a mile or twain, I' the way toward Dover iv 1 45
Know'st thou the way to Dover?—Both stile and gate, horse-way and foot-path . iv 1 57
Dost thou know Dover?—Ay, master . iv 1 74
Dover castle. Nothing there holds out But Dover castle *K. John* v 1 31
Dowager. A dowager Long withering out a young man's revenue *M. N. D.* i 1 5
I have a widow aunt, a dowager Of great revenue . i 1 157
This our marriage with the dowager, Sometimes our brother's wife *Hen. VIII.* ii 4 180
Katharine no more Shall be call'd queen, but princess dowager . iii 2 70
I beseech you, what's become of Katharine, The princess dowager? iv 1 23
Dowdy. Dido a dowdy; Cleopatra a gipsy *Rom. and Jul.* ii 4 43
Dower. By my modesty, The jewel in my dower . *Tempest* iii 1 54
This we came not to, Only for propagation of a dower . *Meas. for Meas.* i 2 154
He of both That can assure my daughter greatest dower Shall have my Bianca's love . *T. of Shrew* ii 1 345
If you should die before him, where's her dower? . ii 1 391
My father is here look'd for every day, To pass assurance of a dower in marriage . iv 2 117
Pass my daughter a sufficient dower, The match is made, and all is done iv 4 45
Virtue and she Is her own dower; honour and wealth from me *All's Well* ii 3 151
Doubt not but heaven Hath brought me up to be your daughter's dower iv 4 19
Choose thou thy husband, and I'll pay thy dower . v 3 328
As liking of the lady's virtuous gifts, Her beauty and the value of her dower . 1 *Hen. VI.* v 1 44
Beside, his wealth doth warrant a liberal dower . v 5 46
A dower, my lords! disgrace not so your king . v 5 48
Mine honesty shall be my dower . 3 *Hen. VI.* iii 2 72
We have this hour a constant will to publish Our daughters' several dowers . *Lear* i 1 45
Let it be so; thy truth, then, be thy dower . i 1 110
With my two daughters' dowers digest this third . i 1 130
What, in the least, Will you require in present dower with her, Or cease your quest of love? . i 1 196
Dower'd with our curse, and stranger'd with our oath . i 1 207
Dowerless. Thy dowerless daughter, king, thrown to my chance, Is queen of us, of ours, and our fair France . i 1 259
The hot-blooded France, that dowerless took Our youngest born . ii 4 215
Dowlas, filthy dowlas: I have given them away to bakers' wives 1 *Hen. IV.* iii 3 79
Dowle. As diminish One dowle that's in my plume . *Tempest* iii 3 65
Down with the topmast! yare! lower, lower! . i 1 37
The sky, it seems, would pour down stinking pitch . i 2 3
Sit down; For thou must now know farther . i 2 32
I'll swear myself thy subject.—Come on then; down, and swear . ii 2 157
Set it down and rest you: when this burns, 'Twill weep for having wearied you . iii 1 18
If you'll sit down, I'll bear your logs the while . iii 1 23
My bosky acres and my unshrubb'd down, Rich scarf to my proud earth iv 1 81
His tears run down his beard, like winter's drops From eaves of reeds v 1 16
Look down, you gods, And on this couple drop a blessed crown! . v 1 201
But twice or thrice was 'Proteus' written down . *T. G. of Ver.* i 2 117
Best to take them up.—Nay, I was taken up for laying them down . i 2 135
If the wind were down, I could drive the boat with my sighs . ii 3 59
A pack of sorrows which would press you down, Being unprevented . iii 1 20
With a corded ladder fetch her down . iii 1 40
She is slow in words.—O villain, that set this down among her vices! . iii 1 337
If there be ten, shrink not, but down with 'em . iv 1 2
And down, down, adown-a . *Mer. Wives* i 4 44
You shall find it a great charge: and to be up early and down late . i 4 108
If the bottom were as deep as hell, I should down . iii 5 14
Thus can the demigod Authority Make us pay down for our offence by weight . *Meas. for Meas.* i 2 125
I will go lose myself And wander up and down to view the city *Com. of Err.* i 2 31
Here's a villain that would face me down . iii 1 6
Pleaseth you walk with me down to his house, I will discharge my bond iv 1 12
There did this perjured goldsmith swear me down That I this day of him received the chain . v 1 227
Here's his dry hand up and down: you are he . *Much Ado* ii 1 124
You have put him down, lady, you have put him down . ii 1 292
As we do trace this alley up and down, Our talk must only be of Benedick iii 1 16
A vile thief this seven year; a' goes up and down like a gentleman . iii 3 135
We have been up and down to seek thee; for we are high-proof melancholy v 1 122
Upon them, lords; Pell-mell, down with them! . *L. L. Lost* iv 3 368
He hail'd down oaths that he was only mine . *M. N. Dream* i 1 243
I will walk up and down here, and I will sing . iii 1 126
Up and down, up and down, I will lead them up and down . iii 2 396
The wall is down that parted their fathers . v 1 359
We have been up and down to seek him . *Mer. of Venice* iii 1 79
Down therefore and beg mercy of the duke . iv 1 363
If I had a thunderbolt in mine eye, I can tell who should down *As Y. L. It* i 2 227
The big round tears Coursed one another down his innocent nose . ii 1 39
Down on your knees, And thank heaven, fasting, for a good man's love iii 5 57
Up and down, carved like an apple-tart . *T. of Shrew* iv 3 89
This hand, As soft as dove's down and as white as it . *W. Tale* iv 4 374
Things known betwixt us three, I'll write you down . iv 4 571
Indeed, paid down More penitence than done trespass . v 1 3
Where is he, That holds in chase mine honour up and down? *K. John* i 1 223
Wild amazement hurries up and down The little number of your doubtful friends . v 1 35
The emptier ever dancing in the air, The other down, unseen and full of water: That bucket down and full of tears am I *Richard II.* iv 1 187
Smooth as oil, soft as young down . 1 *Hen. IV.* i 3 7
Hal, if thou see me down in the battle and bestride me, so . v 1 121
I grant you I was down and out of breath; and so was he . v 4 149
You follow the young prince up and down, like his ill angel 2 *Hen. IV.* i 2 186
She says up and down the town that her eldest son is like you . ii 1 114
Did he suspire, that light and weightless down Perforce must move . iv 5 33
Go down upon him, you have power enough . *Hen. V.* iii 5 53
Here by the cheeks I'll drag thee up and down . 1 *Hen. VI.* i 3 51
Down. Like an angry hive of bees That want their leader, scatter up and down . 2 *Hen. VI.* iii 2 126
Pull down the Savoy; others to the inns of court; down with them all iv 7 1
Up Fish Street! down Saint Magnus' Corner! kill and knock down! . iv 8 1
Nay, then I see that Edward needs must down . 3 *Hen. VI.* iv 3 42
Guess thou the rest; King Edward's friends must down . iv 4 28
'Tis like that Richmond with the rest shall down . iv 6 100
Down, down to hell; and say I sent thee thither . v 6 67
All clinquant, all in gold, like heathen gods, Shone down the English *Hen. VIII.* i 1 20
There have been commissions Sent down among 'em . i 2 21
To whose soft seizure The cygnet's down is harsh . *Troi. and Cres.* i 1 58
Troy, yet upon his basis, had been down . i 3 75
He shall be thrown down the Tarpeian rock With rigorous hands *Coriol.* iii 1 266
That the precipitation might down stretch Below the beam of sight . iii 2 4
We have been down together in my sleep, Unbuckling helms . iv 5 130
He turns away: Down, ladies; let us shame him with our knees . v 3 169
The plebeians have got your fellow-tribune And hale him up and down v 4 40
Up and down she doth resemble thee . *T. Andron.* v 2 107
I'll take him down, an a' were lustier than he is . *Rom. and Jul.* ii 4 159
To catch my death with jaunting up and down! . ii 5 53
Is she not down so late, or up so early? . iii 5 67
What, dress'd! and in your clothes! and down again! . iv 5 12
Thou art early up, To see thy son and heir more early down . v 3 209
In all shapes that man goes up and down in from fourscore to thirteen *T. of Athens* ii 2 120
More fruitful Than their offence can weigh down . v 1 154
Who swore they saw Men all in fire walk up and down the streets *J. Cæsar* i 3 25
Octavius and Mark Antony Come down upon us with a mighty power iv 3 169
O young and noble Cato, art thou down? . v 4 9
How goes the night, boy?—The moon is down; I have not heard the clock.—And she goes down at twelve . *Macbeth* ii 1 2
It will be rain to-night.—Let it come down . iii 3 16
There's but one down; the son is fled . iii 3 19
Well, sit we down, And let us hear Bernardo speak of this . *Hamlet* i 1 33
As he drains his draughts of Rhenish down . i 4 10
And thrice his head thus waving up and down, He raised a sigh so piteous ii 1 93
And bowl the round nave down the hill of heaven, As low as to the fiends! ii 2 518
Run barefoot up and down, threatening the flames With bisson rheum ii 2 528
The observed of all observers, quite, quite down! . iii 1 162
The great man down, you mark his favourite flies . iii 2 214
To be forestalled ere we come to fall, Or pardon'd being down . iii 3 50
To try conclusions, in the basket creep, And break your own neck down iii 4 196
You must sing a-down a-down, An you call him a-down-a . iv 5 170
I dare pawn down my life for him, that he hath wrote this . *Lear* i 2 93
The flinty and steel couch of war My thrice-driven bed of down . *Othello* i 3 232
I'ld whistle her off and let her down the wind, To prey at fortune . iii 3 262
The gold I give thee will I melt and pour Down thy ill-uttering throat *Ant. and Cleo.* ii 5 35
I must go up and down like a cock that nobody can match *Cymbeline* ii 1 23
A woman that Bears all down with her brain . ii 1 59
To beat us down, the which are down already . *Pericles* i 4 68
As a duck for life that dives, So up and down the poor ship drives iii Gower 50
Down on thy knees, thank the holy gods as loud As thunder threatens us v 1 200
Down-bed. How easy?—As easy as a down-bed would afford it *Hen. VIII.* i 4 18
Downfall. Darest thou, thou little better thing than earth, Divine his downfal? . *Richard II.* iii 4 79
Too well given To dream on evil or to work my downfall . 2 *Hen. VI.* iii 1 73
Even in the downfall of his mellow'd years . 3 *Hen. VI.* iii 3 104
O, may such purple tears be always shed From those that wish the downfall of our house! . v 6 65
Ay me, I see the downfall of our house! . *Richard III.* ii 4 49
From Hyperion's rising in the east Until his very downfall in the sea *T. Andron.* v 2 57
Down-fallen. Like good men Bestride our down-fall'n birthdom *Macbeth* iv 3 4
Down-feather. The swan's down-feather, That stands upon the swell at full of tide, And neither way inclines . *Ant. and Cleo.* iii 2 48
Down-gyved. His stockings foul'd, Ungarter'd, and down-gyved *Hamlet* ii 1 80
Down pillow. Weariness Can snore upon the flint, when resty sloth Finds the down pillow hard . *Cymbeline* iii 6 35
Downright. After this downright way of creation . *Meas. for Meas.* iii 2 112
They'll mock us now downright . *L. L. Lost* v 2 389
We shall chide downright, if I longer stay . *M. N. Dream* ii 1 145
You have heard him swear downright . *As Y. Like It* iii 4 31
Threw off his spirit, his appetite, his sleep, And downright languish'd *W. Tale* ii 3 17
Downright oaths, which I never use till urged, nor never break for urging *Hen. V.* v 2 150
And therefore, Peter, have at thee with a downright blow! . 2 *Hen. VI.* ii 3 92
I cleft his beaver with a downright blow . 3 *Hen. VI.* i 1 12
Such mercy as his ruthless arm, With downright payment, show'd . i 4 32
Certainly He flouted us downright.—No, 'tis his kind of speech *Coriolanus* iii 3 168
But for the sunset of my brother's son It rains downright *Rom. and Jul.* iii 5 129
My downright violence and storm of fortunes May trumpet to the world *Othello* i 3 250
Down-roping. The gum down-roping from their pale-dead eyes *Hen. V.* iv 2 48
Downs. Whilst our pinnace anchors in the Downs . 2 *Hen. VI.* iv 1 9
Down sleeves, side sleeves, and skirts . *Much Ado* iii 4 20
Down-stairs. His industry is up-stairs and down-stairs . 1 *Hen. IV.* ii 4 112
Down-trod. I will lift the down-trod Mortimer As high in the air . i 3 135
Down-trodden. For this down-trodden equity, we tread In warlike march these greens before your town . *K. John* ii 1 241
Downward. A German from the waist downward, all slops . *Much Ado* iii 2 35
That downward hath succeeded in his house From son to son *All's Well* iii 7 23
Whilst my gross flesh sinks downward, here to die . *Richard II.* v 5 113
Sit round about some fountain, Looking all downwards . *T. Andron.* iii 1 124
Ravens, crows and kites, Fly o'er our heads and downward look on us *J. Cæsar* v 1 86
Downy. There lies a downy feather which stirs not . 2 *Hen. IV.* iv 5 32
So doth the swan her downy cygnets save . 1 *Hen. VI.* v 3 56
Shake off this downy sleep, death's counterfeit . *Macbeth* ii 3 81
Downy windows, close; And golden Phœbus never be beheld Of eyes again so royal! . *Ant. and Cleo.* v 2 319
Dowries. I never read but England's kings have had Large sums of gold and dowries with their wives . 2 *Hen. VI.* i 1 129
Dowry. Will you, upon good dowry, marry her? . *Mer. Wives* i 1 247
Wrecked at sea, having in that perished vessel the dowry of his sister *Meas. for Meas.* iii 1 226
A dowry for a queen . *L. L. Lost* ii 1 8
Often known To be the dowry of a second head . *Mer. of Venice* iii 2 95

Dowry. That is the dowry of his wife; 'tis none of his own getting *As Y. Like It* iii 3 55
I had as lief take her dowry with this condition, to be whipped at the high cross every morning *T. of Shrew* i 1 136
To woo curst Katharine, Yea, and to marry her, if her dowry please i 2 185
If I get your daughter's love, What dowry shall I have with her to wife? ii 1 121
For that dowry, I'll assure her of Her widowhood, be it that she survive me ii 1 124
Your father hath consented That you shall be my wife; your dowry 'greed on ii 1 272
She is of good esteem, Her dowry wealthy, and of worthy birth iv 5 65
Twenty thousand crowns; Another dowry to another daughter v 2 114
And ask no other dowry with her but such another jest *T. Night* ii 5 202
I would not have him miscarry for the half of my dowry iii 4 70
Make this match; Give with our niece a dowry large enough *K. John* ii 1 469
Her dowry shall weigh equal with a queen ii 1 486
And with her, to dowry, Some petty and unprofitable dukedoms *Hen. V.* iii Prol. 30
Proffers his only daughter to your grace In marriage, with a large and sumptuous dowry *1 Hen. VI.* v 1 20
And she sent over of the King of England's own proper cost and charges, without having any dowry *2 Hen. VI.* i 1 62
Which with her dowry shall be counterpoised *3 Hen. VI.* iii 3 137
If thou dost marry, I'll give thee this plague for thy dowry *Hamlet* iii 1 140
Will you have her? She is herself a dowry *Lear* i 1 244
At whose conception, till Lucina reign'd, Nature this dowry gave *Pericles* i 1 9
Dowsabel. Where Dowsabel did claim me for her husband *Com. of Errors* iv 1 110
Doxy. When daffodils begin to peer, With heigh! the doxy over the dale *W. Tale* iv 3 2
Dozen. Imprison'd thou didst painfully remain A dozen years *Tempest* i 2 279
The dozen white luces in their coat *Mer. Wives* i 1 16
The dozen white louses do become an old coat well i 1 19
Thou never wast where grace was said.—No? a dozen times *Meas. for Meas.* i 2 21
And speak off half a dozen dangerous words *Much Ado* v 1 97
There's half-a-dozen sweets *L. L. Lost* v 2 234
I would esteem him worth a dozen such *T. of Shrew* Ind. 1 27
A dozen of 'em, with delicate fine hats and most courteous feathers *All's W.* iv 5 110
If but a dozen French Were there in arms, they would be as a call *K. John* iii 4 173
A dozen of them here have ta'en the sacrament *Richard II.* v 2 97
Sir John, with half-a-dozen more, are at the door *1 Hen. IV.* ii 4 93
He that kills me some six or seven dozen of Scots at a breakfast ii 4 116
I am a rogue, if I were not at half-sword with a dozen of them two hours ii 4 183
We four set upon some dozen— Sixteen at least, my lord ii 4 193
I bought you a dozen of shirts to your back iii 3 77
A dozen captains, Bare-headed, sweating, knocking at the taverns *2 Hen. IV.* ii 4 387
A dozen captains stay at door for you ii 4 402
Have you provided me here half a dozen sufficient men? iii 2 102
I thank you: I must a dozen mile to-night iii 2 310
I should make four dozen of such bearded hermits' staves v 1 71
You shall have a dozen of cushions again v 4 16
We cannot lodge and board a dozen or fourteen gentlewomen *Hen. V.* ii 1 35
I have half a dozen healths To drink to these fair ladies *Hen. VIII.* i 4 105
Knock 'em down by the dozens v 4 33
Had I a dozen sons, each in my love alike and none less dear than thine and my good Marcius, I had rather had eleven die nobly for their country than one voluptuously surfeit out of action *Coriolanus* i 3 24
Of wounds two dozen odd; battles thrice six I have seen and heard of ii 3 135
We'll have some half a dozen friends, And there an end *Rom. and Jul.* iii 4 27
If there sit twelve women at the table, let a dozen of them be—as they are *T. of Athens* iii 6 88
You could, for a need, study a speech of some dozen or sixteen lines *Ham.* ii 2 566
Thirty dozen moons with borrow'd sheen iii 2 167
The king, sir, hath laid, that in a dozen passes between yourself and him, he shall not exceed you three hits v 2 172
The galleys Have sent a dozen sequent messengers This very night *Othello* i 2 41
I do not think there is any such woman.—Yes, a dozen iv 3 85
Some dozen Romans of us and your lord *Cymbeline* i 6 185
How now! How a dozen of virginities? *Pericles* iv 6 22
Drab. If your worship will take order for the drabs and the knaves *Meas. for Meas.* ii 1 247
With die and drab I purchased this caparison *W. Tale* iv 3 27
Dost thou deny thy father, cursed drab? *1 Hen. VI.* v 4 32
Follow the knave; and take this drab away *2 Hen. VI.* ii 1 156
They say he keeps a Trojan drab *Troi. and Cres.* v 1 104
The parrot will not do more for an almond than he for a commodious drab v 2 195
Back to the dissembling luxurious drab, of a sleeveless errand v 4 9
Ditch-deliver'd by a drab *Macbeth* iv 1 31
Unpack my heart with words, And fall a-cursing, like a very drab *Ham.* ii 2 615
Drabbing. Fencing, swearing, quarrelling, Drabbing ii 1 26
Drachma. That do prize their hours At a crack'd drachma! *Coriolanus* i 5 6
To every Roman citizen he gives, To every several man, seventy five drachmas *J. Cæsar* iii 2 247
I had rather coin my heart, And drop my blood for drachmas iv 3 73
Draff. 'Tis old, but true, Still swine eats all the draff *Mer. Wives* iv 2 109
Lately come from swine-keeping, from eating draff and husks *1 Hen. IV.* iv 2 38
Drag. My affairs Do even drag me homeward *W. Tale* i 2 24
You foresee not what impediments Drag back our expedition *1 Hen. IV.* iv 3 19
Here by the cheeks I'll drag thee up and down *1 Hen. VI.* i 3 51
Away even now, or I will drag thee hence *2 Hen. VI.* iii 2 229
Loud-howling wolves arouse the jades That drag the tragic melancholy night iv 1 4
Hence will I drag thee headlong by the heels Unto a dunghill iv 10 86
Drag hence her husband to some secret hole *T. Andron.* ii 3 129
Drag them from the pit unto the prison: There let them bide ii 3 283
Drag the villain hither by the hair; Nor age nor honour shall shape privilege iv 4 56
Go with Paris to Saint Peter's Church, Or I will drag thee on a hurdle thither *Rom. and Jul.* iii 5 156
Dragged. The bodies shall be dragged at my horse heels *2 Hen. VI.* iv 3 14
And at the murderer's horse's tail, In beastly sort, dragg'd through the shameful field *Troi. and Cres.* v 10 5
Hamlet in madness hath Polonius slain, And from his mother's closet hath he dragg'd him *Hamlet* iv 1 35
Dragon. Night's swift dragons cut the clouds full fast *M. N. Dream* iii 2 379
Fiery voluntaries, With ladies' faces and fierce dragons' spleens *K. John* ii 1 68
Saint George, that swinged the dragon ii 1 288
And of a dragon and a finless fish *1 Hen. IV.* iii 1 151
His arms spread wider than a dragon's wings *1 Hen. VI.* i 1 11
Fair Saint George, Inspire us with the spleen of fiery dragons! *Rich. III.* v 3 350
The dragon wing of night o'erspreads the earth *Troi. and Cres.* v 8 17
Dragon. I go alone, Like to a lonely dragon *Coriolanus* iv 1 30
This Marcius is grown from man to dragon: he has wings v 4 13
Did ever dragon keep so fair a cave? Beautiful tyrant! *Rom. and Jul.* iii 2 74
Go great with tigers, dragons, wolves, and bears *T. of Athens* iv 3 189
Scale of dragon, tooth of wolf, Witches' mummy *Macbeth* iv 1 22
Come not between the dragon and his wrath *Lear* i 1 124
My father compounded with my mother under the dragon's tail i 2 140
Swift, swift, you dragons of the night, that dawning May bear the raven's eye! *Cymbeline* ii 2 48
Death-like dragons here affright thee hard *Pericles* i 1 29
Dragonish. Sometime we see a cloud that's dragonish *Ant. and Cleo.* iv 14 2
Dragon-like. Fights dragon-like, and does achieve as soon As draw his sword *Coriolanus* iv 7 23
Drain. To drain Upon his face an ocean of salt tears *2 Hen. VI.* iii 2 142
How couldst thou drain the life-blood of the child, To bid the father wipe his eyes withal? *3 Hen. VI.* i 4 138
A handkerchief; which, say to her, did drain The purple sap from her sweet brother's body *Richard III.* iv 4 276
I will drain him dry as hay *Macbeth* i 3 18
As he drains his draughts of Rhenish down *Hamlet* i 4 10
Drained. Should by my mortal sword Be drain'd *Troi. and Cres.* iv 5 135
Dram. Void and empty From any dram of mercy *Mer. of Venice* iv 1 6
Every dram of it; and I will not bate thee a scruple *All's Well* ii 3 233
No dram of a scruple, no scruple of a scruple, no obstacle *T. Night* iii 4 87
A lingering dram that should not work Maliciously like poison *W. Tale* i 2 320
Every dram of woman's flesh is false, If she be ii 1 138
Till he be three quarters and a dram dead iv 4 815
Make some dram of a scruple, or indeed a scruple itself *2 Hen. IV.* i 2 148
Shall give him such an unaccustom'd dram, That he shall soon keep Tybalt company *Rom. and Jul.* iii 5 91
Hold, there is forty ducats: let me have A dram of poison v 1 60
Together with a recompense more fruitful Than their offence can weigh down by the dram *T. of Athens* v 1 154
The dram of eale Doth all the noble substance of a doubt To his own scandal *Hamlet* i 4 36
With some dram conjured to this effect, He wrought upon her *Othello* i 3 105
If you buy ladies' flesh at a million a dram, you cannot preserve it from tainting *Cymbeline* i 4 147
A dram of this Will drive away distemper iii 4 193
From whose so many weights of baseness cannot A dram of worth be drawn iii 5 89
We thought he died.—By the queen's dram she swallow'd v 5 381
Drank. I ne'er drank sack in my life *T. of Shrew* Ind. 2 6
I know not Jupiter; I never drank with him in all my life *T. Andron.* iv 3 85
Draught. A morning's draught of sack *Mer. Wives* ii 2 153
One draught above heat makes him a fool; the second mads him *T. Night* i 5 140
A bawbling vessel was he captain of, For shallow draught and bulk unprizable v 1 58
Which draught to me were cordial *W. Tale* i 2 318
I think I have taken my last draught in this world *2 Hen. VI.* ii 3 74
Sweet draught: 'sweet' quoth 'a! sweet sink, sweet sewer *Troi. and Cres.* v 1 82
Pledges the breath of him in a divided draught *T. of Athens* i 2 49
With liquorish draughts And morsels unctuous, greases his pure mind iv 3 194
Hang them or stab them, drown them in a draught, Confound them v 1 105
As he drains his draughts of Rhenish down *Hamlet* i 4 10
In madness, Being full of supper and distempering draughts *Othello* i 1 99
Draught-oxen. Yoke you like draught-oxen and make you plough up the wars *Troi. and Cres.* ii 1 116
Drave. I drave my suitor from his mad humour of love to a living humour of madness *As Y. Like It* iii 2 438
And drave great Mars to faction *Troi. and Cres.* iii 3 190
A troubled mind drave me to walk abroad *Rom. and Jul.* i 1 127
From Italy, Upon the first encounter, drave them *Ant. and Cleo.* i 2 98
Draw thy sword: one stroke Shall free thee *Tempest* ii 1 292
Draw together; And when I rear my hand, do you the like ii 1 294
Let's draw our weapons.—Lead off this ground ii 1 322
My duty pricks me on to utter that Which else no worldly good should draw from me *T. G. of Ver.* iii 1 9
He shall draw, he shall tap *Mer. Wives* i 3 11
It draws something near to the speech we had to such a purpose *Meas. for Meas.* i 2 78
They will draw you, Master Froth, and you will hang them ii 1 215
Hooking both right and wrong to the appetite, To follow as it draws! ii 4 177
To draw with idle spiders' strings Most ponderous and substantial things! iii 2 289
You war against your reputation And draw within the compass of suspect The unviolated honour of your wife *Com. of Errors* iii 1 87
A hound that runs counter and yet draws dry-foot well iv 2 39
I am sorry now that I did draw on him v 1 43
Nor ever didst thou draw thy sword on me v 1 266
Find me a meet hour to draw Don Pedro and the Count Claudio alone *Much Ado* ii 2 33
I have the toothache.—Draw it.—Hang it!—You must hang it first, and draw it afterwards iii 2 22
Wilt thou use thy wit?—It is in my scabbard: shall I draw it? v 1 125
I will bid thee draw, as we do the minstrels; draw, to pleasure us v 1 128
I will draw a bill of properties, such as our play wants *M. N. Dream* i 2 107
You draw me, you hard-hearted adamant; But yet you draw not iron, for my heart Is true as steel: leave you your power to draw, And I shall have no power to follow you ii 1 195
Pyramus must draw a sword to kill himself; which the ladies cannot abide iii 1 11
I'll whip thee with a rod: he is defiled That draws a sword on thee iii 2 411
'Tis to peize the time, To eke it and to draw it out in length *M. of Ven.* iii 2 23
If every ducat in six thousand ducats Were in six parts and every part a ducat, I would not draw them iv 1 87
I am content.—Clerk, draw a deed of gift iv 1 394
Pierce your mistress' ear And draw her home with music v 1 68
You look paler and paler: pray you, draw homewards *As Y. Like It* iv 3 179
Neither do I labour for a greater esteem than may in some little measure draw a belief from you v 2 63
Draw forth thy weapon, we are beset with thieves *T. of Shrew* iii 2 238
I mean to shift my bush; And then pursue me as you draw your bow v 2 47
To see him every hour; to sit and draw His arched brows *All's Well* i 1 104
A man may draw his heart out, ere a' pluck one i 3 93
Would thou mightst never draw sword again *T. Night* i 3 66
I would I might never draw sword again i 3 68
Rouse the night-owl in a catch that will draw three souls out of one weaver ii 3 61
Soon as ever thou seest him, draw; and, as thou drawest, swear horrible iii 4 105

Draw. Therefore draw, for the supportance of his vow . . *T. Night* iii 4 329
Cuff him soundly, but never draw thy sword . . . . iii 4 429
If thou darest tempt me further, draw thy sword . . . iv 1 45
Thy conceit is soaking, will draw in More than the common blocks *W. T.* i 2 224
Draw our throne into a sheep-cote! all deaths are too few . iv 4 808
It draws toward supper in conclusion so . . . *K. John* i 1 204
And the hand of time Shall draw this brief into as huge a volume . ii 1 103
From whom hast thou this great commission, France, To draw my answer from thy articles? . . . . . . ii 1 111
Draws those heaven-moving pearls from his poor eyes . . . ii 1 169
Draw our puissance together. France, I am burn'd up with inflaming wrath . . . . iii 1 339
O, it grieves my soul, That I must draw this metal from my side! . v 2 16
In our country's cradle Draws the sweet infant breath of gentle sleep *Richard II.* i 3 133
This absence of your father's draws a curtain . . . *1 Hen. IV.* iv 1 73
He cannot draw his power this fourteen days . . . iv 1 126
And that no man might draw short breath to-day But I and Harry Monmouth! . . . . v 2 49
And here draw I A sword, whose temper I intend to stain . . v 2 93
When we mean to build, We first survey the plot, then draw the model *2 Hen. IV.* i 3 42
Like one that draws the model of a house Beyond his power to build it i 3 58
Shall we go draw our numbers and set on? . . . . i 3 109
Away, varlets! Draw, Bardolph: cut me off the villain's head . ii 1 50
Go, wash thy face, and draw the action . . . . ii 1 162
You do draw my spirits from me With new lamenting ancient oversights ii 3 46
I pray thee, Jack, I pray thee, do not draw . . . . ii 4 217
I come to draw you out by the ears.—O, the Lord preserve thy good grace! . . . . ii 4 313
Draw no swords but what are sanctified . . . . iv 4 4
Draw the huge bottoms through the furrow'd sea . *Hen. V.* iii Prol. 12
It now draws toward night: Beyond the river we'll encamp ourselves iii 6 179
There the sun shall greet them, And draw their honours reeking up to heaven . . . . iv 3 101
Draw, men, for all this privileged place; Blue coats to tawny coats *1 Hen. VI.* i 3 46
Devil or devil's dam, I'll conjure thee: Blood will I draw on thee . i 5 6
The law of arms is such That whoso draws a sword, 'tis present death iii 4 39
These words of yours draw life-blood from my heart . . iv 6 43
Therefore are we certainly resolved To draw conditions of a friendly peace . . . . v 1 38
And learn this lesson, draw thy sword in right . . *3 Hen. VI.* ii 2 62
I'll draw it as apparent to the crown, And in that quarrel use it to the death . . . . ii 2 64
Draw not on thy danger and dishonour . . . . . iii 3 75
For this I draw in many a tear And stop the rising of blood-sucking sighs . . . . iv 4 21
Nay, rather, wilt thou draw thy forces hence? . . . v 1 25
You do me shameful injury, Falsely to draw me in these vile suspects *Richard III.* i 3 89
To take some privy order, To draw the brats of Clarence out of sight . iii 5 107
In no worldly suit would he be moved, To draw him from his holy exercise . . . . iii 7 64
'Tis hard to draw them thence, So sweet is zealous contemplation iii 7 93
To draw forth your noble ancestry From the corruption of abusing times iii 7 198
I'll draw the form and model of our battle, Limit each leader . v 3 24
Advance your standards, draw your willing swords . . v 3 264
Draw, archers, draw your arrows to the head! . . . v 3 339
Such noble scenes as draw the eye to flow We now present *Hen. VIII.* Prol. 4
They are the poorest, But poverty could never draw 'em from me . iv 2 149
When I might see from far some forty truncheoners draw to her succour v 4 54
I was fain to draw mine honour in . . . . . v 4 60
Trial did draw Bias and thwart, not answering the aim . *Troi. and Cres.* i 3 14
And, by device, let blockish Ajax draw The sort to fight with Hector . i 3 375
Without a heart to dare or sword to draw . . . . ii 2 157
A good quarrel to draw emulous factions and bleed to death upon . ii 3 79
Light boats sail swift, though greater hulks draw deep . . ii 3 277
Come, draw this curtain, and let's see your picture . . iii 2 49
Your silence, Cunning in dumbness, from my weakness draws My very soul of counsel! . . . . iii 2 140
Pardon me this brag; His insolence draws folly from my lips . iv 5 258
O, contain yourself; Your passion draws ears hither . . v 2 181
So, so, we draw together . . . . v 5 44
He has been bred i' the wars Since he could draw a sword *Coriolanus* iii 1 321
Fights dragon-like, and does achieve as soon As draw his sword . iv 7 24
Draw your swords, and sheathe them not Till Saturninus be Rome's emperor . . . . *T. Andron.* i 1 204
So near the emperor's palace dare you draw, And maintain such a quarrel? ii 1 46
Let me see your archery; Look ye draw home enough, and 'tis there straight . . . . iv 3 3
Now, masters, draw. O, well said, Lucius! Good boy, in Virgo's lap . iv 3 63
Draw you near, To shed obsequious tears upon this trunk . . v 3 151
An we be in choler, we'll draw.—Ay, while you live, draw your neck out o' the collar . . . . . . *Rom. and Jul.* i 1 4
Draw thy tool; here comes two of the house of the Montagues . i 1 37
Draw, if you be men. Gregory, remember thy swashing blow . i 1 69
The all-cheering sun Should in the furthest east begin to draw The shady curtains from Aurora's bed . . . . i 1 141
If thou art dun, we'll draw thee from the mire Of this sir-reverence love . . . . i 4 41
I dare draw as soon as another man, if I see occasion in a good quarrel . ii 4 167
Therefore do nimble-pinion'd doves draw love . . . ii 5 7
And by the operation of the second cup draws it on the drawer . iii 1 9
This shall not excuse the injuries That thou hast done me; therefore turn and draw . . . . iii 1 70
Draw, Benvolio; beat down their weapons . . . . iii 1 89
Ere I Could draw to part them, was stout Tybalt slain . . . iii 1 178
O blessed breeding sun, draw from the earth Rotten humidity! *T. of A.* iv 3 1
Assemble all the poor men of your sort; Draw them to Tiber banks *J. C.* i 1 63
No figures nor no fantasies, Which busy care draws in the brains of men ii 1 232
Look you, Brutus, He draws Mark Antony out of the way . . iii 1 26
I draw a sword against conspirators; When think you that the sword goes up again? . . . . v 1 51
I see thee yet, in form as palpable As this which now I draw. *Macbeth* ii 1 41
By the strength of their illusion Shall draw him on to his confusion iii 5 29
Profit again should hardly draw me here . . . . . v 3 62
Might deprive your sovereignty of reason And draw you into madness *Ham.* i 4 74
He falls to such perusal of my face As he would draw it . . ii 1 91
So by your companies To draw him on to pleasures . . . . ii 2 15

Draw. But, like a gulf, doth draw What's near it with it . . *Hamlet* iii 3 16
Come, sir, to draw toward an end with you . . . . iii 4 216
Where is he gone?—To draw apart the body he hath kill'd . . iv 1 24
That, swoopstake, you will draw both friend and foe, Winner and loser iv 5 142
And in this harsh world draw thy breath in pain . . . v 2 359
Of that I shall have also cause to speak, And from his mouth whose voice will draw on more . . . . v 2 403
What can you say to draw A third more opulent than your sisters? *Lear* i 1 87
May not an ass know when the cart draws the horse? . . . i 4 245
In cunning I must draw my sword upon you: Draw; seem to defend yourself . . . . ii 1 31
Draw, you rogue: for, though it be night, yet the moon shines . ii 2 33
Draw, you whoreson cullionly barber-monger, draw . . . ii 2 35
Draw, you rascal: you come with letters against the king . . ii 2 38
Draw, you rogue, or I'll so carbonado your shanks: draw . . ii 2 40
But the great one that goes up the hill, let him draw thee after . ii 4 75
This seems a fair deserving, and must draw me That which my father loses . . . . iii 3 24
That fellow handles his bow like a crow-keeper: draw me a clothier's yard . . . . iv 6 88
I cannot draw a cart, nor eat dried oats; If it be man's work, I'll do't v 3 38
What say'st thou to him?—Draw thy sword . . . . v 3 126
But still the house-affairs would draw her thence . *Othello* i 3 147
And found good means To draw from her a prayer of earnest heart . i 3 152
To mourn a mischief that is past and gone Is the next way to draw new mischief on . . . . i 3 205
I'll set her on; Myself the while to draw the Moor apart . . ii 3 391
I'll devise a mean to draw the Moor Out of the way . . . iii 1 39
Nor from mine own weak merits will I draw The smallest fear or doubt of her revolt . . . . iii 3 187
Think every bearded fellow that's but yoked May draw with you . iv 1 68
Let me the curtains draw. Where art thou? . . . . v 2 104
They have entertained cause enough To draw their swords . *A. and C.* ii 1 47
Her love to both Would, each to other and all loves to both, Draw after her ii 2 139
I did not think to draw my sword 'gainst Pompey . . . ii 2 156
Your way is shorter; My purposes do draw me much about . . ii 4 8
And, as I draw them up, I'll think them every one an Anthony . ii 5 13
Let your best love draw to that point, which seeks Best to preserve it . iii 4 21
Things outward Do draw the inward quality after them, To suffer all alike . . . . iii 13 33
Draw that thy honest sword, which thou hast worn Most useful for thy country . . . . iv 14 79
Draw, and come.—Turn from me, then, that noble countenance . iv 14 84
Draw thy sword, and give me Sufficing strokes for death . . iv 14 116
Help, Iras, help; Help, friends below; let's draw him hither . iv 15 13
Come, come, Antony,—Help me, my women,—we must draw thee up . iv 15 30
To draw upon an exile! . . . . . . *Cymbeline* i 1 166
To apprehend thus, Draws us a profit from all things we see . . iii 3 18
What shall I need to draw my sword? the paper Hath cut her throat already . . . . iii 4 34
I draw the sword myself: take it, and hit The innocent mansion of my love, my heart . . . . iii 4 69
Best draw my sword; and if mine enemy But fear the sword like me, he'll scarcely look on't . . . . iii 6 25
Or hath more ministers than we That draw his knives i' the war . v 3 73
Would draw heaven down, and all the gods, to hearken . *Pericles* i 1 83
If that thy prosperous and artificial feat Can draw him but to answer thee . . . . v 1 73
Draw aside the curtains and discover The several caskets *Mer. of Venice* ii 7 1
Draw back. I'll take this ring from you: Do not draw back your hand iv 1 428
Do not draw back, for we will mourn with thee . *T. Andron.* ii 4 56
Draw backward. An you draw backward, we'll put you i' the fills *Troi. and Cres.* iii 2 47
Draws blood. Where it draws blood no cataplasm so rare . *Hamlet* iv 7 144
Draws breath. One in whom The ancient Roman honour more appears Than any that draws breath in Italy . . *Mer. of Venice* iii 2 298
Draw cuts. We'll draw cuts for the senior . *Com. of Errors* v 1 422
Draw lots. If we draw lots, he speeds . . *Ant. and Cleo.* ii 3 35
We'll feast each other ere we part; an let's Draw lots who shall begin . ii 6 62
That man and wife Draw lots who first shall die to lengthen life *Pericles* i 4 46
Draw near. Pyramus draws near the wall: silence! . *M. N. Dream* v 1 170
Wilt thou draw near the nature of the gods? Draw near them then in being merciful . . . . *T. Andron.* i 1 117
It draws near the season Wherein the spirit held his wont to walk *Ham.* i 4 5
Draw near *Tempest* v 1; *Com. of Errors* v 1; *All's Well* iii 2; *Rich. II.* i 3; *3 Hen. VI.* iii 3; *Coriolanus* iii 3; *T. of Athens* ii 2; iii 6; *Lear* iv 7; *Cymbeline* iii 6
Draw nearer, honest Flaminius. Thy lord's a bountiful gentleman *T. of A.* iii 1 41
Draw nigh, and take your places . . . . *T. Andron.* v 3 24
Draws on. The hour draws on. To the oak, to the oak! *Mer. Wives* v 3 25
Windsor bell hath struck twelve; the minute draws on . . v 5 2
Dispatch it presently; the hour draws on Prefix'd by Angelo *M. for M.* iv 3 82
Our nuptial hour Draws on apace . . . *M. N. Dream* i 1 2
Draw out. Thy unkindness shall his death draw out To lingering sufferance . . . . . . *Meas. for Meas.* ii 4 166
These high wild hills and rough uneven ways Draws out our miles *Richard II.* ii 3 5
Scarce blood enough in all their sickly veins To give each naked curtle-axe a stain, That our French gallants shall to-day draw out *Hen. V.* iv 2 22
Please you to march; And four shall quickly draw out my command *Cor.* i 6 84
Draw the curtains, go. Let all of his complexion choose me so *M. of V.* ii 7 78
Quick, quick, I pray thee; draw the curtain straight . . . ii 9 1
Come, draw the curtain, Nerissa . . . . . . ii 9 84
We will draw the curtain and show you the picture . *T. Night* i 5 251
Do not draw the curtain.—No longer shall you gaze on't *W. Tale* v 3 59
We are mock'd with art.—I'll draw the curtain . . . v 3 68
Shall I draw the curtain?—No, not these twenty years . . v 3 83
Close up his eyes and draw the curtain close . . *2 Hen. VI.* iii 3 32
Let 'em alone, and draw the curtain close: We shall hear more anon *Hen. VIII.* v 2 34
Make no noise, make no noise; draw the curtains . . *Lear* iii 6 89
Draw up. The enemy's in view; draw up your powers . . v 1 51
But, master, I'll go draw up the net . . . *Pericles* ii 1 98
Drawbridge. Look to the drawbridge there!—Hark! a drum *Rich. III.* iii 5 15
Drawer. What's your will? Give us leave, drawer *Mer. Wives* ii 2 165
I am sworn brother to a leash of drawers . . . . *1 Hen. IV.* ii 4 7
Do thou stand in some by-room, while I question my puny drawer . ii 4 33
What cunning match have you made with this jest of the drawer? . ii 4 102
Put on two leathern jerkins and aprons, and wait upon him at his table as drawers . . . . *2 Hen. IV.* ii 2 191

Drawer. Call him up, drawer.—Cheater, call you him? . 2 *Hen. IV.* ii 4 109
I am a gentleman ; thou art a drawer . . . . . ii 4 312
And by the operation of the second cup draws it on the drawer *R. and J.* iii 1 9
Drawest. Draw ; and, as thou drawest, swear horrible . *T. Night* iii 4 196
Thou draw'st a counterfeit Best in all Athens . . *T. of Athens* v 1 83
Draweth from my snow-white pen the ebon-coloured ink . *L. L. Lost* i 1 245
He draweth out the thread of his verbosity finer than the staple of his argument . . . . v 1 18
Drawing. If black, why, Nature, drawing of an antique, Made a foul blot *Much Ado* iii 1 63
If drawing my sword against the humour of affection would deliver me *L. L. Lost* i 2 62
Lusty, young, and cheerly drawing breath . *Richard II.* i 3 66
These eyes, like lamps whose wasting oil is spent, Wax dim, as drawing to their exigent . . . . . . 1 *Hen. VI.* ii 5 9
It will not in circumvention deliver a fly from a spider, without drawing their massy irons and cutting the web . . *Troi. and Cres.* ii 3 18
My love Is as the very centre of the earth, Drawing all things to it . iv 2 111
'Tis but the time And drawing days out, that men stand upon *J. Cæsar* iii 1 100
Drawling. I never heard such a drawling, affecting rogue *Mer. Wives* ii 1 145
Drawn. Thence I have follow'd it, Or it hath drawn me rather *Tempest* i 2 394
Why are you drawn? Wherefore this ghastly looking? . . . ii 1 308
As mine eyes open'd, I saw their weapons drawn . . . ii 1 320
A most poor credulous monster ! Well drawn, monster, in good sooth ! ii 2 150
This pride of hers, Upon advice, hath drawn my love from her *T. G. of V.* iii 1 73
Hath drawn him and the rest of their company from their sport *M. W.* iv 2 34
I never come into any room in a taphouse, but I am drawn in *M. for M.* ii 1 220
Each one with ireful passion, with drawn swords, Met us again *Com. of Er.* v 1 151
O, he hath drawn my picture in his letter !—Any thing like? *L. L. Lost* v 2 38
Where art thou, proud Demetrius? speak thou now.—Here, villain ; drawn and ready . . . . *M. N. Dream* iii 2 402
How many actions most ridiculous Hast thou been drawn to by thy fantasy? . . . . *As Y. Like It* ii 4 31
A lioness, with udders all drawn dry, Lay couching . . . iv 3 115
So workmanly the blood and tears are drawn . . *T. of Shrew* Ind. 2 62
Let specialties be therefore drawn between us, That covenants may be kept . . . . ii 1 127
And there it is in writing, fairly drawn . . . . . iii 1 70
Though our silence be drawn from us with cars, yet peace *T. Night* ii 5 70
Though so much As might have drawn one to a longer voyage . . iii 3 7
If all the devils of hell be drawn in little, and Legion himself possessed him, yet I'll speak to him . . . . iii 4 94
Held my peace until You had drawn oaths from him not to stay *W. Tale* i 2 29
Seest a game play'd home, the rich stake drawn, And takest it all for jest i 2 248
Drawn in the flattering table of her eye . . *K. John* ii 1 503
Hang'd and drawn and quarter'd . . . . . . ii 1 508
Hath drawn him from his own determined aid. . . . . ii 1 584
Where is my mother's care, That such an army could be drawn in France? iv 2 118
I am a scribbled form, drawn with a pen Upon a parchment . . v 7 32
With tears drawn from her eyes by your foul wrongs *Richard II.* iii 1 15
And our indentures tripartite are drawn . . 1 *Hen. IV.* iii 1 80
Within that space you may have drawn together Your tenants . iii 1 89
Are the indentures drawn? shall we be gone? . . . . iii 1 141
By that time will our book, I think, be drawn . . . . iii 1 224
And that his friends by deputation could not So soon be drawn . iv 1 33
But yet the king hath drawn The special head of all the land together . iv 4 27
The condition of the time, Which cannot look more hideously upon me Than I have drawn it in my fantasy . . . . . 2 *Hen. IV.* v 2 13
Thou hast drawn my shoulder out of joint . . . . . v 4 3
O well a day, Lady, if he be not drawn now ! . . . *Hen. V.* ii 1 39
For every drop of blood was drawn from him There hath at least five Frenchmen died to-night . . . . . . 1 *Hen. VI.* ii 2 8
One drop of blood drawn from thy country's bosom Should grieve thee more than streams of foreign gore . . . . iii 3 54
Your wrathful weapons drawn Here in our presence ! 2 *Hen. VI.* iii 2 237
Whose dreadful swords were never drawn in vain . . . iv 1 92
Forthwith shall articles be drawn Touching the jointure 3 *Hen. VI.* iii 3 135
Those eyes of thine from mine have drawn salt tears *Richard III.* i 2 154
My foreward shall be drawn out all in length . . . . v 3 293
'Tis the account Of all that world of wealth I have drawn together For mine own ends . . . . *Hen. VIII.* iii 2 211
Do you note How much her grace is alter'd on the sudden? How long her face is drawn? . . . . iv 2 97
Since the first sword was drawn about this question *Troi. and Cres.* ii 2 18
Nor you, my brother, with your true sword drawn, Opposed to hinder me, should stop my way . . . . v 3 56
When you have drawn your number, Repair to the Capitol . *Coriolanus* ii 3 261
Drawn tuns of blood out of thy country's breast . . . iv 5 105
But wherefore stand'st thou with thy weapon drawn? *T. Andron.* iii 1 48
With this, my weapon drawn, I rush'd upon him, Surprised him suddenly . . . . v 1 37
What, art thou drawn among these heartless hinds? *Rom. and Jul.* i 1 73
What, drawn, and talk of peace ! I hate the word, As I hate hell . i 1 77
Drawn with a team of little atomies Athwart men's noses . . i 4 57
There were drawn Upon a heap a hundred ghastly women *J. Cæsar* i 3 22
The wine of life is drawn, and the mere lees Is left . *Macbeth* ii 3 100
The bow is bent and drawn, make from the shaft . . *Lear* i 1 145
Some blood drawn on me would beget opinion . . . . ii 1 35
Infect her beauty, You fen-suck'd fogs, drawn by the powerful sun ! ii 4 169
Whilst the wheel'd seat Of fortunate Cæsar, drawn before him, branded His baseness that ensued . . . . *Ant. and Cleo.* iv 14 76
My sword is drawn.—Then let it do at once The thing why thou hast drawn it . . . . iv 14 88
You shall see How hardly I was drawn into this war . . v 1 74
Let there be covenants drawn between s . . *Cymbeline* i 4 155
The powers that he already hath in Gallia Will soon be drawn to head . iii 5 25
From whose so many weights of baseness cannot A dram of worth be drawn . . . . iii 5 89
The lines of my body are as well drawn as his ; no less young, more strong . . . . iv 1 10
The Roman legions, all from Gallia drawn, Are landed on your coast . iv 3 24
Whose answer would be death Drawn on with torture . . . iv 4 14
The purse too light, being drawn of heaviness . . . . iv 4 168
Came to me With his sword drawn . . . . . . v 5 276
Famous princes, like thyself, Drawn by report, adventurous by desire *Pericles* i 1 35
I have drawn her picture with my voice . . . . . iv 2 101
Who having drawn to do't, A crew of pirates came and rescued me . v 1 175
Drawn fox. No more truth in thee than in a drawn fox 1 *Hen. IV.* iii 3 129
Drayman. Achilles ! a drayman, a porter, a very camel . *Troi. and Cres.* i 2 270
Draymen. A brace of draymen bid God speed him well . *Richard II.* i 4 32
Dread. Make his bold waves tremble, Yea, his dread trident shake *Temp.* i 2 206
To the dread rattling thunder Have I given fire . . . . v 1 44
O my dread lord, I should be guiltier than my guiltiness *Meas. for Meas.* v 1 371
To fright them hence with that dread penalty . . *L. L. Lost* i 1 128
Dread prince of plackets, king of codpieces . . . . iii 1 186
What judgement shall I dread, doing no wrong? *Mer. of Venice* iv 1 89
The attribute to awe and majesty, Wherein doth sit the dread and fear of kings . . . . iv 1 192
My prisoner? or my guest? by your dread 'Verily,' One of them you shall be . . . . *W. Tale* i 2 55
I cannot Believe this crack to be in my dread mistress . . . i 2 322
He dreads his wife.—So I would you did . . . . . ii 3 79
To me the difference forges dread . . . . . . iv 4 17
If guilty dread have left thee so much strength As to take up mine honour's pawn . . . . *Richard II.* i 1 73
Myself I throw, dread sovereign, at thy foot. My life thou shalt command . . . . i 1 165
That e'er this tongue of mine, That laid the sentence of dread banishment On yon proud man, should take it off again ! . . . . iii 3 134
If he will not yield, Rebuke and dread correction wait on us 1 *Hen. IV.* v 1 111
The sin upon my head, dread sovereign ! . . . . *Hen. V.* i 2 97
Go, my dread lord, to your great-grandsire's tomb . . . i 2 103
Upon his royal face there is no note How dread an army hath enrounded him . . . . iv Prol. 36
As surely as my soul intends to live With that dread King 2 *Hen. VI.* iii 2 154
Dread lord, the commons send you word by me . . . iii 2 243
These dread curses, like the sun 'gainst glass, Or like an overcharged gun, recoil . . . . iii 2 330
A messenger from Henry, our dread liege . . . . . v 1 17
Thou shalt not dread The scatter'd foe that hopes to rise again 3 *Hen. VI.* ii 6 92
Be pitiful, dread lord, and grant it then . . . . . iii 2 32
Did York's dread curse prevail so much with heaven? *Richard III.* i 3 191
Truly, the souls of men are full of dread . . . . . ii 3 38
Well, my dread lord ; so must I call you now . . . . iii 1 97
Bearing a state of mighty moment in't And consequence of dread *Hen. VIII.* ii 4 214
Most dread liege, The good I stand on is my truth and honesty . v 1 122
Dread sovereign, how much are we bound to heaven In daily thanks . v 3 114
Thus far, My most dread sovereign, may it like your grace . . v 3 148
Yet, dread Priam, There is no lady of more softer bowels *Troi. and Cres.* ii 2 10
Weigh you the worth and honour of a king So great as our dread father in a scale Of common ounces? . . . . ii 2 27
Here comes a parcel of our hopeful booty, Which dreads not yet their lives' destruction . . . . *T. Andron.* ii 3 50
Welcome, dread Fury, to my woful house . . . . . v 2 82
Welcome, dread queen ; Welcome, ye warlike Goths . . . v 3 26
Time, thou anticipatest my dread exploits . . . *Macbeth* iv 1 144
What wouldst thou have, Laertes?—My dread lord, Your leave and favour to return to France . . . . *Hamlet* i 2 50
Put your dread pleasures more into command Than to entreaty . ii 2 28
This dread and black complexion smear'd With heraldry more dismal . ii 2 477
The dread of something after death, The undiscover'd country . iii 1 78
Lets go by The important acting of your dread command . . iii 4 108
Think'st thou that duty shall have dread to speak, When power to flattery bows? . . . . *Lear* i 1 149
And, in the fleshment of this dread exploit, Drew on me here again . ii 2 130
Have I fall'n, or no?—From the dread summit of this chalky bourn . iv 6 57
O you mortal engines, whose rude throats The immortal Jove's dread clamours counterfeit ! . . . . *Othello* iii 3 356
Didst thou behold Octavia?—Ay, dread queen . . *Ant. and Cleo.* iii 3 9
And I am come, I dread, too late . . . . . . iv 14 127
You some permit To second ills with ills, each elder worse, And make them dread it, to the doers' thrift . . . . . *Cymbeline* v 1 15
What seest thou in our looks?—An angry brow, dread lord *Pericles* i 2 52
Dread-bolted. To stand against the deep dread-bolted thunder *Lear* iv 7 33
Dreaded. That he should draw his several strengths together And come against us in full puissance, Need not be dreaded . 2 *Hen. IV.* i 3 78
Not in the presence Of dreaded justice . . . *Coriolanus* iii 3 98
And beat the messenger who bids beware Of what is to be dreaded . iv 6 55
This dreaded sight, twice seen of us . . . . *Hamlet* i 1 25
Thyself art coming To see perform'd the dreaded act which thou So sought'st to hinder . . . . *Ant. and Cleo.* v 2 334
Dreadful. Lightnings, the precursors O' the dreadful thunder-claps *Temp.* i 2 202
The thunder, That deep and dreadful organ-pipe . . . . iii 3 98
In a most hideous and dreadful manner . . . *Mer. Wives* iv 4 34
And it in you more dreadful would have seem'd Than in Lord Angelo.—I do fear, too dreadful . . . . *Meas. for Meas.* i 3 33
For my neglect Of his almighty dreadful little might . *L. L. Lost* iii 1 205
Thy eye Jove's lightning bears, thy voice his dreadful thunder . iv 2 119
God shield us !—a lion among ladies, is a most dreadful thing *M. N. Dr.* iii 1 32
What dreadful dole is here ! . . . . v 1 283
Not one vessel 'scape the dreadful touch Of merchant-marring rocks? *Mer. of Venice* iii 2 273
But in such a 'then' I write a 'never.' This is a dreadful sentence *All's Well* iii 2 64
And hath he too Exposed this paragon to the fearful usage, At least ungentle, of the dreadful Neptune? . . . . . . *W. Tale* v 1 154
In dreadful trial of our kingdom's king . . . *K. John* ii 1 286
Like heralds 'twixt two dreadful battles set . . . . iv 2 78
Withhold thy speed, dreadful occasion ! O, make a league with me ! . iv 2 125
With dreadful pomp of stout invasion . . . . . . iv 2 173
Within this bosom never enter'd yet The dreadful motion of a murderous thought . . . . iv 2 255
With harsh-resounding trumpets' dreadful bray . *Richard II.* i 3 135
See your most dreadful laws so loosely slighted . . 2 *Hen. IV.* v 2 94
Advised by good intelligence Of this most dreadful preparation *Hen. V.* ii Prol. 13
With busy hammers closing rivets up, Give dreadful note of preparation . . . . iv Prol. 14
The dreadful judgement-day So dreadful will not be as was his sight 1 *Hen. VI.* i 1 29
This dreadful lord, Retiring from the siege of Orleans . . . i 1 110
Great is the rumour of this dreadful knight . . . . ii 3 7
Or turn our stern upon a dreadful rock . . 2 *Hen. VI.* iii 2 91
A dreadful oath, sworn with a solemn tongue ! . . . . iii 2 158
Whose dreadful swords were never drawn in vain . . . iv 1 92
My soul and body on the action both !—A dreadful lay ! . . v 2 27
In dreadful war mayst thou be overcome, Or live in peace abandon'd ! 3 *Hen. VI.* i 1 187

Dreadful. But what art thou, whose heavy looks foretell Some dreadful story? 3 *Hen. VI.* ii 1 44
To be avoided, As venom toads, or lizards' dreadful stings ii 2 138
But dreadful war shall answer his demand iii 3 259
Our dreadful marches to delightful measures *Richard III.* i 1 8
Avaunt, thou dreadful minister of hell! i 2 46
What pain it was to drown! What dreadful noise of waters in mine ears! i 4 22
How canst thou urge God's dreadful law to us? i 4 214
By the dreadful Pluto *Troi. and Cres.* iv 4 129
Give with thy trumpet a loud note to Troy, Thou dreadful Ajax iv 5 4
Not the dreadful spout Which shipmen do the hurricano call v 2 171
The dreadful Sagittary Appals our numbers v 5 14
Why suffer'st thou thy sons, unburied yet, To hover on the dreadful shore of Styx? *T. Andron.* i 1 88
The woods are ruthless, dreadful, deaf, and dull ii 1 128
I have done a thousand dreadful things As willingly as one would kill a fly v 1 141
I will find them out; And in their ears tell them my dreadful name v 2 39
Then, dreadful trumpet, sound the general doom! *Rom. and Jul.* iii 2 67
When the most mighty gods by tokens send Such dreadful heralds *J. Cæsar* i 3 56
Now could I, Casca, name to thee a man Most like this dreadful night i 3 73
Between the acting of a dreadful thing And the first motion ii 1 63
Blood and destruction shall be so in use And dreadful objects so familiar iii 1 266
I have seen Hours dreadful and things strange *Macbeth* ii 4 3
There shall be done A deed of dreadful note iii 2 44
This to me In dreadful secrecy impart they did *Hamlet* i 2 207
To the dreadful summit of the cliff That beetles o'er his base into the sea i 4 70
Anon the dreadful thunder Doth rend the region ii 2 508
Let the great gods, That keep this dreadful pother o'er our heads, Find out their enemies now *Lear* iii 2 50
Rive your concealing continents, and cry These dreadful summoners grace iii 2 59
Half way down Hangs one that gathers samphire, dreadful trade! iv 6 15
Silence that dreadful bell: it frights the isle From her propriety *Othello* ii 3 175
O, still Thy deafening, dreadful thunders! *Pericles* iii 1 5
Dreadfully. A man that apprehends death no more dreadfully but as a drunken sleep *Meas. for Meas.* iv 2 150
To speak to you like an honest man, I am most dreadfully attended *Ham.* ii 2 276
Dreading the curse that money may buy out *K. John* iii 1 164
I, dreading that her purpose Was of more danger *Cymbeline* v 5 253
Dream. Rather like a dream than an assurance *Tempest* i 2 45
My spirits, as in a dream, are all bound up i 2 486
That, when I waked, I cried to dream again iii 2 152
We are such stuff As dreams are made on iv 1 157
On a trice, so please you, Even in a dream, were we divided from them v 1 239
Forgive me that I do not dream on thee *T. G. of Ver.* ii 4 172
Then never dream on infamy, but go ii 7 64
She dreams on him that has forgot her love; You dote on her that cares not for your love iv 4 86
How like a dream is this I see and hear! v 4 26
I have dreamed to-night; I'll tell you my dream *Mer. Wives* iii 3 172
Hum! ha! is this a vision? is this a dream? do I sleep? iii 5 142
He hath but as offended in a dream! *Meas. for Meas.* ii 2 4
What is't I dream on? O cunning enemy, that, to catch a saint, With saints dost bait thy hook! ii 2 179
Thousand escapes of wit Make thee the father of their idle dreams iv 1 64
What, was I married to her in my dream? Or sleep I now? *Com. of Er.* ii 2 184
If I dream not, thou art Æmilia v 1 346
What I told you then, I hope I shall have leisure to make good; If this be not a dream I see and hear v 1 376
We will hold it as a dream till it appear itself *Much Ado* i 2 21
Are these things spoken, or do I but dream? iv 1 67
But not for that dream I on this strange course iv 1 214
In that each of you have forsworn his book, Can you still dream and pore and thereon look? *L. L. Lost* iv 3 298
Four nights will quickly dream away the time *M. N. Dream* i 1 9
Momentany as a sound, Swift as a shadow, short as any dream i 1 144
Dreams and sighs, Wishes and tears, poor fancy's followers i 1 154
Ay me, for pity! what a dream was here! ii 2 147
All this derision Shall seem a dream and fruitless vision iii 2 371
Think no more of this night's accidents But as the fierce vexation of a dream iv 1 74
It seems to me That yet we sleep, we dream iv 1 199
And by the way let us recount our dreams iv 1 204
I have had a dream, past the wit of man to say what dream it was: man is but an ass, if he go about to expound this dream iv 1 211
Man's hand is not able to taste, his tongue to conceive, nor his heart to report, what my dream was iv 1 220
I will get Peter Quince to write a ballad of this dream: it shall be called Bottom's Dream, because it hath no bottom iv 1 221
From the presence of the sun, Following darkness like a dream v 1 393
And this weak and idle theme, No more yielding but a dream v 1 435
I did dream of money-bags to-night *Mer. of Venice* ii 5 18
If that I do not dream or be not frantic,—As I do trust I am not *As Y. L. It* i 3 51
Even as a flattering dream or worthless fancy *T. of Shrew* Ind. 1 44
Say that he dreams, For he is nothing but a mighty lord Ind. 1 64
Banish hence these abject lowly dreams Ind. 2 34
Do I dream? or have I dream'd till now? I do not sleep Ind. 2 71
These fifteen years you have been in a dream; Or when you waked, so waked as if you slept Ind. 2 81
I would be loath to fall into my dreams again Ind. 2 129
And sits as one new-risen from a dream iv 1 189
That canst not dream, We, poising us in her defective scale, Shall weigh thee to the beam *All's Well* ii 3 160
As 'tis, Poor lady, she were better love a dream *T. Night* ii 2 27
For this night, to bed, and dream on the event ii 3 191
Thou hast put him in such a dream, that when the image of it leaves him he must run mad ii 5 212
Or I am mad, or else this is a dream iv 1 65
If it be thus to dream, still let me sleep! iv 1 67
Dost make possible things not so held, Communicatest with dreams *W. T.* i 2 140
My life stands in the level of your dreams, Which I'll lay down.—Your actions are my dreams iii 2 82
For ne'er was dream So like a waking iii 3 18
Dreams are toys: Yet for this once, yea, superstitiously, I will be squared by this iii 3 39
She shall bring him that Which he not dreams of iv 4 180
I shall have more than you can dream of yet iv 4 399
This dream of mine,—Being now awake, I'll queen it no inch farther, But milk my ewes and weep iv 4 459
Possess'd with rumours, full of idle dreams *K. John* iv 2 145
Dream. Learn, good soul, To think our former state a happy dream *Richard II.* v 1 18
Away, you rascally Althæa's dream, away!—Instruct us, boy; what dream? 2 *Hen. IV.* ii 2 93
But, being awaked, I do despise my dream v 5 55
By interception which they dream not of *Hen. V.* ii 2 7
Thou proud dream, That play'st so subtly with a king's repose iv 1 274
Than is in your knowledge to dream of iv 8 4
By day, by night, waking and in my dreams, In courtly company 2 *Hen. VI.* i 1 26
My troublous dream this night doth make me sad i 2 22
What dream'd my lord? tell me, and I'll requite it With sweet rehearsal of my morning's dream i 2 24
This was my dream: what it doth bode, God knows i 2 31
Are you so choleric With Eleanor, for telling but her dream? Next time I'll keep my dreams unto myself, And not be check'd i 2 52
The duke is virtuous, mild and too well given To dream on evil iii 1 73
I did dream to-night The duke was dumb iii 2 31
Resolved for death or dignity.—The first I warrant thee, if dreams prove true v 1 195
You were best to go to bed and dream again v 1 196
I do but dream on sovereignty 3 *Hen. VI.* iii 2 134
I'll make my heaven to dream upon the crown iii 2 168
By drunken prophecies, libels and dreams *Richard III.* i 1 33
As I can learn, He hearkens after prophecies and dreams i 1 54
Whilst some tormenting dream Affrights thee with a hell of ugly devils i 3 226
I have pass'd a miserable night, So full of ugly sights, of ghastly dreams! i 4 3
What was your dream? I long to hear you tell it i 4 8
My dream was lengthen'd after life; O, then began the tempest to my soul i 4 43
Such terrible impression made the dream i 4 63
And for his dreams, I wonder he is so fond To trust the mockery of unquiet slumbers iii 2 26
Stanley did dream the boar did raze his helm; But I disdain'd it iii 4 84
But have been waked by his timorous dreams iv 1 85
A dream of what thou wert, a breath, a bubble iv 4 88
Dream on thy cousins smother'd in the Tower v 3 151
Dream of success and happy victory! v 3 165
Dream on, dream on, of bloody deeds and death: Fainting, despair! v 3 171
Soft! I did but dream. O coward conscience, how dost thou afflict me! v 3 178
I have dream'd a fearful dream! v 3 212
Fairest-boding dreams That ever enter'd in a drowsy head v 3 227
My soul is very jocund In the remembrance of so fair a dream v 3 233
Let not our babbling dreams affright our souls v 3 308
And then let's dream Who's best in favour *Hen. VIII.* i 4 107
I am most joyful, madam, such good dreams Possess your fancy iv 2 93
You are for dreams and slumbers, brother priest *Troi. and Cres.* ii 2 37
My dreams will, sure, prove ominous to the day v 3 6
If I do dream, would all my wealth would wake me! *T. Andron.* ii 4 13
How stands your disposition to be married?—It is an honour that I dream not of *Rom. and Jul.* i 3 66
I dream'd a dream to-night.—And so did I i 4 50
Dreamers often lie.—In bed asleep, while they do dream things true i 4 52
In this state she gallops night by night Through lovers' brains, and then they dream of love i 4 71
O'er courtiers' knees, that dream on court'sies straight i 4 72
O'er lawyers' fingers, who straight dream on fees, O'er ladies' lips, who straight on kisses dream i 4 73
Sometime she gallops o'er a courtier's nose, And then dreams he of smelling out a suit i 4 78
Tickling a parson's nose as a' lies asleep, Then dreams he of another benefice i 4 81
Sometime she driveth o'er a soldier's neck, And then dreams he of cutting foreign throats i 4 83
True, I talk of dreams, Which are the children of an idle brain i 4 96
All this is but a dream, Too flattering-sweet to be substantial ii 2 140
My dreams presage some joyful news at hand v 1 2
I dreamt my lady came and found me dead—Strange dream, that gives a dead man leave to think! v 1 7
Said he not so? or did I dream it so? Or am I mad? v 3 79
Who would be so mock'd with glory? or to live But in a dream of friendship? *T. of Athens* iv 2 34
All the interim is Like a phantasma, or a hideous dream *J. Cæsar* ii 1 65
Quite from the main opinion he held once Of fantasy, of dreams ii 1 197
This dream is all amiss interpreted; It was a vision fair and fortunate ii 2 83
This by Calpurnia's dream is signified ii 2 90
Break up the senate till another time, When Cæsar's wife shall meet with better dreams ii 2 99
Didst thou dream, Lucius, that thou so criedst out? iv 3 296
Nature seems dead, and wicked dreams abuse The curtain'd sleep *Macbeth* ii 1 50
And sleep In the affliction of these terrible dreams That shake us nightly iii 2 18
Colleagued with the dream of his advantage *Hamlet* i 2 21
What it should be, More than his father's death, that thus hath put him So much from the understanding of himself, I cannot dream of ii 2 10
I could be bounded in a nut-shell and count myself a king of infinite space, were it not that I have bad dreams ii 2 262
Which dreams indeed are ambition, for the very substance of the ambitious is merely the shadow of a dream ii 2 263
A dream itself is but a shadow ii 2 266
In a fiction, in a dream of passion, Could force his soul so to his own conceit ii 2 578
To die, to sleep; To sleep: perchance to dream: ay, there's the rub; For in that sleep of death what dreams may come When we have shuffled off this mortal coil, Must give us pause iii 1 65
That, on every dream, Each buzz, each fancy, each complaint, dislike, He may enguard his dotage *Lear* i 4 347
If ever I did dream of such a matter, Abhor me *Othello* i 1 5
This accident is not unlike my dream i 1 143
If consequence do but approve my dream, My boat sails freely ii 3 64
Nay, this was but his dream.—But this denoted a foregone conclusion iii 3 427
'Tis a shrewd doubt, though it be but a dream iii 3 429
Where have you this? 'tis false.—From Silvius, sir.—He dreams *A. and C.* ii 1 19
May I never To this good purpose, that so fairly shows, Dream of impediment! ii 2 148
That he should dream, Knowing all measures, the full Cæsar will Answer his emptiness! iii 13 34
You laugh when boys or women tell their dreams v 2 74
If she be up, I'll speak with her; if not, Let her lie still and dream *Cymbeline* ii 3 70
These boys know little they are sons to the king; Nor Cymbeline dreams that they are alive iii 3 81

Dream. If sleep charge nature, To break it with a fearful dream of him
And cry myself awake . . . . *Cymbeline* iii 4 45
I hope I dream; For so I thought I was a cave-keeper . . . . iv 2 297
The dream's here still: even when I wake, it is Without me, as within
me; not imagined, felt . . . . iv 2 306
Success to the Roman host.—Dream often so, And never false . . iv 2 352
Poor wretches that depend On greatness' favour dream as I have done,
Wake and find nothing . . . . v 4 128
Many dream not to find, neither deserve, And yet are steep'd in favours v 4 130
'Tis still a dream, or else such stuff as madmen Tongue and brain not . v 4 146
He spake of her, as Dian had hot dreams, And she alone were cold . v 5 180
Did you ever dream of such a thing? . . . . . *Pericles* iv 5 5
This is the rarest dream that e'er dull sleep Did mock sad fools withal . v 1 163
By my silver bow! Awake, and tell thy dream . . . . v 1 250
Dreamed. I have dreamed to-night; I'll tell you my dream *Mer. Wives* iii 3 171
She hath often dreamed of unhappiness and waked herself with laughing
Much Ado ii 1 360
Or do I dream? or have I dream'd till now? I do not sleep *T. of Shr.* Ind. 2 71
They say that I have dream'd And slept above some fifteen year or
more . . . . Ind. 2 114
We knew not The doctrine of ill-doing, nor dream'd That any did *W. Tale* i 2 70
Your actions are my dreams; You had a bastard by Polixenes, And I
but dream'd it . . . . iii 2 85
Althæa dreamed she was delivered of a fire-brand . 2 *Hen. IV.* ii 2 96
I have long dream'd of such a kind of man, So surfeit-swell'd . v 5 53
What dream'd my lord? tell me, and I'll requite it With sweet rehearsal
of my morning's dream . . . . . . 2 *Hen. VI.* i 2 24
O Ratcliff, I have dream'd a fearful dream! . . *Richard III.* v 3 212
We are a queen, or long have dream'd so . . . *Hen. VIII.* ii 4 71
One that ne'er dream'd a joy beyond his pleasure . . . iii 1 135
I have dream'd Of bloody turbulence . . . *Troi. and Cres.* v 3 10
Thy wife hath dream'd; thy mother hath had visions . . . v 3 63
I dream'd a dream to-night.—And so did I . . *Rom. and Jul.* i 4 50
I dream'd there was an Emperor Antony: O, such another sleep!
Ant. and Cleo. v 2 76
Think you there was, or might be, such a man As this I dream'd of? . v 2 94
What have you dream'd of late of this war's purpose? *Cymbeline* iv 2 345
Who dream'd, who thought of such a thing? . . *Pericles* iii Gower 38
I did not think Thou couldst have spoke so well; ne'er dream'd thou
couldst . . . . iv 6 110
Dreamer. Thou idle dreamer, wherefore didst thou so? . *K. John* iv 2 153
Of the dreamer Merlin and his prophecies. . . 1 *Hen. IV.* iii 1 150
Dreamers often lie.—In bed asleep . . . . *Rom. and Jul.* i 4 51
He is a dreamer; let us leave him: pass . . . *J. Cæsar* i 2 24
Dreamest. There are other Trojans that thou dreamest not of 1 *Hen. IV.* ii 1 77
Look, how thou dream'st! . . . . . . *Richard III.* iv 2 57
Dreaming. In dreaming, The clouds methought would open and show
riches . . . . *Tempest* iii 2 149
Thou hast nor youth nor age, But, as it were, an after-dinner's sleep,
Dreaming on both . . . . *Meas. for Meas.* iii 1 34
Those dulcet sounds in break of day That creep into the dreaming bride-
groom's ear And summon him to marriage . . *Mer. of Venice* iii 2 52
Stay we no longer, dreaming of renown . . . 3 *Hen. VI.* ii 1 199
Who, but for dreaming on this fond exploit, For want of means, poor
rats, had hang'd themselves . . . . . . *Richard III.* v 3 330
And dreaming night will hide our joys no longer . *Troi. and Cres.* iv 2 10
This foolish, dreaming, superstitious girl Makes all these bodements v 3 79
It's past the size of dreaming . . . . . *Ant. and Cleo.* v 2 97
Dreamt. I can tell you strange news that you yet dreamt not of *M. Ado* i 2 4
That shows the ignorant a kind of fear Before not dreamt of 1 *Hen. IV.* iv 1 75
Thy bloody mind, Which never dreamt on aught but butcheries *Rich. III.* i 2 100
He dreamt to-night the boar had razed his helm . . . iii 2 11
I have nightly since Dreamt of encounters 'twixt thyself and me *Coriol.* iv 5 129
I dreamt my lady came and found me dead—Strange dream, that gives
a dead man leave to think! . . . . . . *Rom. and Jul.* v 1 6
I dreamt my master and another fought, And that my master slew him v 3 138
Why, this hits right; I dreamt of a silver basin and ewer to-night
T. of Athens iii 1 5
She dreamt to-night she saw my statua . . . *J. Cæsar* ii 2 76
I dreamt to-night that I did feast with Cæsar, And things unluckily
charge my fantasy . . . . iii 3 1
I dreamt last night of the three weird sisters . . . *Macbeth* ii 1 20
There are more things in heaven and earth, Horatio, Than are dreamt
of in your philosophy . . . . *Hamlet* i 5 167
Dreary. To step out of these dreary dumps . . . *T. Andron.* i 1 391
Dreg. I will here shroud till the dregs of the storm be past . *Tempest* ii 2 42
'Faith, some certain dregs of conscience are yet within me *Richard III.* i 4 124
What too curious dreg espies my sweet lady in the fountain of our love?
—More dregs than water . . . . . *Troi. and Cres.* iii 2 70
He, like a puling cuckold, would drink up The lees and dregs of a flat
tamed piece . . . . iv 1 62
The good gods assuage thy wrath, and turn the dregs of it upon this
varlet here . . . . *Coriolanus* v 2 84
Friendship's full of dregs: Methinks, false hearts should never have
sound legs . . . . *T. of Athens* i 2 239
Drench. 'Give my roan horse a drench,' says he . . 1 *Hen. IV.* ii 4 120
Sodden water, A drench for sur-rein'd jades . . . *Hen. V.* iii 5 19
So do our vulgar drench their peasant limbs In blood of princes . iv 7 80
In that sea of blood my boy did drench His over-mounting spirit, and
there died . . . . 1 *Hen. VI.* iv 7 14
Courtiers of beauteous freedom, To drench the Capitol *Ant. and Cleo.* ii 6 18
Drenched in the sea, hold notwithstanding their freshness . *Tempest* ii 1 62
Thus have I shunn'd the fire for fear of burning, And drench'd me in the
sea, where I am drown'd . . . . . . *T. G. of Ver.* i 3 79
When in swinish sleep Their drenched natures lie as in a death *Macbeth* i 7 68
Spout Till you have drench'd our steeples, drown'd the cocks! . *Lear* iii 2 3
Dress. Bake, scour, dress meat and drink, make the beds . *Mer. Wives* i 4 102
We'll come dress you straight . . . . iv 2 84
Let's go dress him like the witch of Brentford . . . . iv 2 100
We'll dress Like urchins . . . . iv 4 48
Dress him in my apparel and make him my waiting-gentlewoman *M. Ado* ii 1 36
Help to dress me, good coz, good Meg, good Ursula . . . iii 4 98
Leave your books And help to dress your sister's chamber up *T. of Shr.* iii 1 83
Thou see'st how diligent I am To dress thy meat myself and bring
it thee . . . . iv 3 40
Thou, old Adam's likeness, set to dress this garden . . *Richard II.* iii 4 73
The glass Wherein the noble youth did dress themselves 2 *Hen. IV.* ii 3 22
Prove that ever I dress myself handsome till thy return . . . ii 4 302
To dress the ugly form Of base and bloody insurrection . . . iv 1 39
Admonishing That we should dress us fairly for our end *Hen. V.* iv 1 10
Dress. To dress the commonwealth, and turn it, and set a new nap
upon it . . . . 2 *Hen. VI.* iv 2 6
If the dull brainless Ajax come safe off, We'll dress him up in voices
Troi. and Cres. i 3 382
Why do you dress me In borrow'd robes? . . . . *Macbeth* i 3 108
Till I shall see you in your soldier's dress, Which will become you both,
farewell . . . . *Ant. and Cleo.* ii 4 4
I know that a woman is a dish for the gods, if the devil dress her not . v 2 276
We'll go dress our hunt . . . . *Cymbeline* iii 6 90
Dressed. Lent him our terror, dress'd him with our love *Meas. for Meas.* i 1 20
With purpose to be dress'd in an opinion Of wisdom, gravity *Mer. of Ven.* i 1 91
And see him dress'd in all suits like a lady . . *T. of Shrew* Ind. 1 106
What dish o' poison has she dressed him! . . . *T. Night* ii 5 123
I'll help you, Sir Toby, because we'll be dressed together . . . v 1 211
O, what pity is it That he had not so trimm'd and dress'd his land As
we this garden! . . . . *Richard II.* iii 4 56
That horse that I so carefully have dress'd . . . . . v 5 80
A certain lord, neat, and trimly dress'd, Fresh as a bridegroom 1 *Hen. IV.* i 3 33
Dress'd myself in such humility That I did pluck allegiance from men's
hearts . . . . iii 2 51
What, dress'd! and in your clothes! and down again! . *Rom. and Jul.* iv 5 12
Was the hope drunk Wherein you dress'd yourself? . . . *Macbeth* i 7 36
Altogether lacks the abilities That Rhodes is dress'd in . . . *Othello* i 3 26
Kind gentlemen, let's go see poor Cassio dress'd . . . . v 1 124
Dresser. How durst you, villains, bring it from the dresser, And serve it
thus to me? . . . . *T. of Shrew* iv 1 166
Dressing. Even so may Angelo, In all his dressings, characts, titles,
forms, Be an arch-villain . . . . . . *Meas. for Meas.* v 1 56
Drest. But man, proud man, Drest in a little brief authority . . ii 2 118
Hem, and stroke thy beard, As he being drest to some oration *T. and C.* i 3 166
Drew. How near the god drew to the complexion of a goose! . *Mer. Wives* v 5 8
The great care of goods at random left Drew me from kind embracements
of my spouse . . . . *Com. of Errors* i 1 44
Some love that drew him oft from home . . . . . v 1 56
And thereupon I drew my sword on you; And then you fled . . . v 1 262
Thisby, tarrying in mulberry shade, His dagger drew, and died *M. N. D.* v 1 150
The poet Did feign that Orpheus drew trees, stones and floods *M. of Ven.* v 1 80
And then he drew a dial from his poke . . . . *As Y. Like It* ii 7 20
He did me kindness, sir, drew on my side . . . . *T. Night* v 1 69
A witchcraft drew me hither . . . . v 1 79
Drew to defend him when he was beset . . . . . . v 1 88
I never hurt you: You drew your sword upon me without cause . . v 1 191
You have been mistook: But nature to her bias drew in that . . v 1 267
Which so drew the rest of the herd to me that all their other senses
stuck in ears . . . . *W. Tale* iv 4 620
Was promised Before I drew this gallant head of war . . *K. John* v 2 113
Such a man . . . Drew Priam's curtain in the dead of night . 2 *Hen. IV.* i 1 72
A' drew a good bow; and dead! a' shot a fine shoot . . . iii 2 48
The ireful bastard Orleans, that drew blood From thee, my boy 1 *Hen. VI.* iv 6 16
Leave off to wonder why I drew you hither . . . 3 *Hen. VI.* iv 5 2
Yet from my dugs he drew not this deceit . . . *Richard III.* ii 2 30
The articles o' the combination drew As himself pleased . . *Hen. VIII.* i 1 169
That in your country's service drew your swords . . *T. Andron.* i 1 175
Drew myself apart And almost broke my heart with extreme laughter . v 1 112
Close fighting ere I did approach: I drew to part them . *Rom. and Jul.* i 1 115
By and by my master drew on him; And then I ran away . . v 3 284
Drew from my heart all love, And added to the gall . . . *Lear* i 4 291
And, in the fleshment of this dread exploit, Drew on me here again . ii 2 131
Having more man than wit about me, drew . . . . . ii 4 42
I think the sun where he was born Drew all such humours from him *Oth.* iii 4 31
From some true reports, That drew their swords with you *Ant. and Cleo.* ii 2 48
When your diver Did hang a salt-fish on his hook, which he With
fervency drew up . . . . ii 5 18
Your son drew on my master.—Ha! No harm, I trust, is done? *Cymb.* i 1 160
Drew sleep out of mine eyes, blood from my cheeks . . . *Pericles* i 2 96
Drewest. And with thy scorns drew'st rivers from his eyes *Richard III.* i 3 176
Dribbling. Believe not that the dribbling dart of love Can pierce a com-
plete bosom . . . . *Meas. for Meas.* i 3 2
Dried. Till I were as crest-fallen as a dried pear . . *Mer. Wives* iv 5 103
Have I laid my brain in the sun and dried it? . . . . . v 5 144
Left her in her tears, and dried not one of them with his comfort
Meas. for Meas. iii 1 234
Time hath not yet so dried this blood of mine . . . *Much Ado* iv 1 195
I had rather have a handful or two of dried peas . . *M. N. Dream* iv 1 42
Thanks, i' faith, for silence is only commendable In a neat's tongue
dried and a maid not vendible . . . . . *Mer. of Venice* i 1 112
I tell thee, Kate, 'twas burnt and dried away . . . *T. of Shrew* iv 1 173
Great seas have dried When miracles have by the greatest been denied
All's Well ii 1 143
Seven fair branches springing from one root: Some of those seven are
dried by nature's course . . . . *Richard II.* i 2 14
You starveling, you elf-skin, you dried neat's tongue . 1 *Hen. IV.* ii 4 271
He lives upon mouldy stewed prunes and dried cakes . 2 *Hen. IV.* ii 4 159
My mercy dried their water-flowing tears . . . . 3 *Hen. VI.* iv 8 43
Here comes Romeo.—Without his roe, like a dried herring *Rom. and Jul.* ii 4 39
I cannot draw a cart, nor eat dried oats; If it be man's work, I'll do't
Lear v 3 38
Which, being dried with grief, will break to powder . *Ant. and Cleo.* iv 9 17
Drier. Being destined to a drier death on shore . . . *T. G. of Ver.* i 1 158
Fetch drier logs: Call Peter, he will show thee where they are *R. and J.* iv 4 15
Dries. It [sherris] ascends me into the brain; dries me there all the
foolish and dull and crudy vapours . . . . . 2 *Hen. IV.* iv 3 105
The blood upon your visage dries; 'tis time It should be look'd to *Coriol.* i 9 93
The fountain from the which my current runs, Or else dries up *Othello* iv 2 60
Drift. They being penitent, The sole drift of my purpose doth extend
Not a frown further . . . . *Tempest* v 1 29
Love, lend me wings to make my purpose swift, As thou hast lent me
wit to plot this drift! . . . . *T. G. of Ver.* ii 6 43
I rather chose To cross my friend in his intended drift . . . iii 1 18
I will so plead That you shall say my cunning drift excels . . iv 2 83
O, understand my drift . . . . *Mer. Wives* ii 2 251
Keep your instruction, And hold you ever to our special drift *M. for M.* iv 5 4
What is the course and drift of your compact? . . *Com. of Errors* ii 2 163
Go in with me, and I will tell you my drift . . . . *Much Ado* ii 1 403
Our thunder from the south Shall rain their drift of bullets . *K. John* ii 1 412
And yet the king not privy to my drift . . . . 3 *Hen. VI.* i 2 46
I do not strain at the position,—It is familiar,—but at the author's drift
Troi. and Cres. iii 3 113
We know your drift: speak what?—There's no more to be said *Coriol.* iii 3 116
Be plain, good son, and homely in thy drift . . *Rom. and Jul.* ii 3 55

Drift. Against thou shalt awake, Shall Romeo by my letters know our drift *Rom. and Jul.* iv 1 114
My free drift Halts not particularly . . . *T. of Athens* i 1 45
Finding By this encompassment and drift of question That they do know my son . . . *Hamlet* ii 1 10
Marry, sir, here's my drift; And, I believe, it is a fetch of wit . . ii 1 37
Can you, by no drift of circumstance, Get from him why he puts on this confusion? . . . iii 1 1
If this should fail, And that our drift look through our bad performance, 'Twere better not assay'd . . . iv 7 152
Drily. Like one of our French withered pears, it looks ill, it eats drily *All's Well* i 1 176
Drink. Sea-water shalt thou drink . . . *Tempest* i 2 462
The poor monster's in drink: an abominable monster! . . ii 2 162
When the butt is out, we will drink water; not a drop before . iii 2 2
Servant-monster, drink to me . . . iii 2 3
When that's gone He shall drink nought but brine . . iii 2 74
I drink the air before me, and return Or ere your pulse twice beat v 1 102
Carry the wine in; we'll drink within . . *Mer. Wives* i 1 196
I hope we shall drink down all unkindness . . i 1 203
That's meat and drink to me, now . . . i 1 306
He was gotten in drink: is not the humour conceited? . . i 3 25
I wash, wring, brew, bake, scour, dress meat and drink . . i 4 102
I will to my honest knight Falstaff, and drink canary with him . ii 2 89
I shall drink in pipe-wine first with him . . iii 2 90
But, whilst I live, forget to drink after thee . *Meas. for Meas.* i 2 40
Like rats that ravin down their proper bane, A thirsty evil; and when we drink we die . . . i 2 134
We shall have all the world drink brown and white bastard . iii 2 3
I drink, I eat, array myself, and live . . . iii 2 26
He that drinks all night, and is hanged betimes in the morning, may sleep the sounder all the next day . . . iv 3 48
Drink some wine ere you go: fare you well . . *Much Ado* iii 5 57
This I think, When they are thirsty, fools would fain have drink *L. L. L.* v 2 372
And sometime make the drink to bear no barm . *M. N. Dream* ii 1 38
And when she drinks, against her lips I bob . . ii 1 49
I will not eat with you, drink with you, nor pray with you *Mer. of Venice* i 3 38
Cover the while; the duke will drink under this tree . *As Y. Like It* ii 5 33
I prithee, take the cork out of thy mouth that I may drink thy tidings iii 2 214
It is meat and drink to me to see a clown . . . v 1 11
It is a figure in rhetoric that drink, being poured out of a cup into a glass, by filling the one doth empty the other . . v 1 45
Will't please your lordship drink a cup of sack? . *T. of Shrew* Ind. 2 2
Do as adversaries do in law, Strive mightily, but eat and drink as friends i 2 279
Dine with my father, drink a health to me; For I must hence . iii 2 198
Thou'rt a tall fellow: hold thee that to drink . . . iv 4 17
You shall not choose but drink before you go . . v 1 12
But I will eat and drink, and sleep as soft As captain shall *All's Well* iv 3 368
These clothes are good enough to drink in; and so be these boots *T. Night* i 3 12
I'll drink to her as long as there is a passage in my throat and drink in Illyria . . . i 3 41
He's a coward and a coystrill that will not drink to my niece . i 3 43
Bring your hand to the buttery-bar and let it drink . . i 3 74
Two faults, madonna, that drink and good counsel will amend . i 5 47
Give the dry fool drink, then is the fool not dry . . i 5 49
He's in the third degree of drink, he's drowned . . i 5 144
Thou'rt a scholar; let us therefore eat and drink . . ii 3 14
'Twere as good a deed as to drink when a man's a-hungry . ii 3 135
If he had not been in drink, he would have tickled you othergates than he did . . . v 1 197
We will give you sleepy drinks . . . *W. Tale* i 1 15
There may be in the cup A spider steep'd, and one may drink . ii 1 40
The iron of itself, though heat red-hot, Approaching near these eyes, would drink my tears . . . *K. John* iv 1 62
If I dare eat, or drink, or breathe, or live, I dare meet Surrey *Rich. II.* iv 1 73
Three times they breathed and three times did they drink . 1 *Hen. IV.* i 3 102
An 'twere not as good deed as drink, to break the pate on thee . ii 1 33
Speak sooner than drink, and drink sooner than pray . . ii 1 86
An 'twere not as good a deed as drink, to turn true man and to leave these rogues . . . ii 2 24
'Tis dangerous to take a cold, to sleep, to drink . . ii 3 9
I can drink with any tinker in his own language during my life . ii 4 20
Why, then, your brown bastard is your only drink . . ii 4 83
I do not speak to thee in drink but in tears, not in pleasure but in passion . . . ii 4 458
Wherein is he good, but to taste sack and drink it? . . ii 4 501
They did fight with queasiness, constrain'd, As men drink potions 2 *Hen. IV.* i 1 197
I'll drink no proofs nor no bullets . . . ii 4 127
I'll drink no more than will do me good, for no man's pleasure, I . ii 4 128
Drinks off candles' ends for flap-dragons, and rides the wild-mare . ii 4 267
Come, I will go drink with you, but I cannot tarry dinner . iii 2 203
Here between the armies Let's drink together friendly and embrace iv 2 63
Will maintain my word: And thereupon I drink unto your grace . iv 2 68
If you knew what pains I have bestow'd to breed this present peace, You would drink freely . . . iv 2 75
Nor a man cannot make him laugh; but that's no marvel, he drinks no wine . . . iv 3 96
Thin drink doth so over-cool their blood . . . iv 3 98
Have you a ruffian that will swear, drink, dance, Revel the night? . iv 5 125
What you want in meat, we'll have in drink: but you must bear . v 3 31
And drink unto the leman mine; And a merry heart lives long-a . v 3 49
I'll drink to Master Bardolph, and to all the cavaleros about London . v 3 61
This would drink deep.—'Twould drink the cup and all . *Hen. V.* i 1 20
I dare say This quarrel will drink blood another day . 1 *Hen. VI.* ii 4 134
I drink to you in a cup of sack . . 2 *Hen. VI.* ii 3 59
Here's a pot of good double beer, neighbour: drink, and fear not your man ii 3 65
I drink to thee: and be not afraid . . . ii 3 68
Drink, and pray for me, I pray you . . . ii 3 72
Poison be their drink! Gall, worse than gall, the daintiest that they taste! . . . iii 2 321
Give me some drink; and bid the apothecary Bring the strong poison iii 3 17
Whose filth and dirt Troubles the silver spring where England drinks . iv 1 72
I will make it felony to drink small beer . . . iv 2 73
There shall be no money; all shall eat and drink on my score . iv 2 79
It hath served me instead of a quart pot to drink in . . iv 10 16
His cold thin drink out of his leather bottle . 3 *Hen. VI.* ii 5 48
For every word I speak, Ye see, I drink the water of mine eyes . v 4 75
Gramercy, fellow: there, drink that for me . *Richard III.* iii 2 108
We give thee up our guiltless blood to drink . . . iii 3 14

Drink. Though we leave it with a root, thus hack'd, The air will drink the sap . . . *Hen. VIII.* i 2 98
I have half a dozen healths To drink to these fair ladies . . i 4 106
How his silence drinks up this applause! . *Troi. and Cres.* iii 3 211
Which his own will shall have desire to drink . . . iii 3 46
He, like a puling cuckold, would drink up The lees and dregs of a flat tamed piece . . . iv 1 61
If the drink you give me touch my palate adversely, I make a crooked face at it . . . *Coriolanus* ii 1 61
We will drink together; and you shall bear A better witness back than words . . . v 3 203
So thou refuse to drink my dear sons blood . . *T. Andron.* iii 1 22
Well I wot Thy napkin cannot drink a tear of mine . . iii 1 140
Come, let's fall to; and, gentle girl, eat this: Here is no drink! . iii 2 35
She says she drinks no other drink but tears, Brew'd with her sorrow iii 2 37
Dry sorrow drinks our blood. . . . *Rom. and Jul.* iii 5 59
Take thou this vial, being then in bed, And this distilled liquor drink thou off . . . iv 1 94
Romeo, I come! this do I drink to thee . . . iv 3 58
Put this in any liquid thing you will, And drink it off . . v 1 78
Make sacred even his stirrup, and through him Drink the free air *T. of A.* i 1 83
If I were a huge man, I should fear to drink at meals . . i 2 51
Great men should drink with harness on their throats . . i 2 53
Mine eyes cannot hold out water, methinks: to forget their faults, I drink to you . . . i 2 112
Thou weepest to make them drink . . . i 2 113
Spend our flatteries, to drink those men Upon whose age we void it up again . . . ii 2 142
He ne'er drinks, But Timon's silver treads upon his lip . . iii 2 77
His days are foul and his drink dangerous . . . iii 5 74
Thy flatterers yet wear silk, drink wine, lie soft . . iv 3 206
How shall I requite you? Can you eat roots, and drink cold water? . v 1 77
Alas, it cried 'Give me some drink, Titinius,' As a sick girl . *J. Cæsar* i 2 127
Fill, Lucius, till the wine o'erswell the cup; I cannot drink too much of Brutus' love . . . iv 3 162
Bid thy mistress, when my drink is ready, She strike upon the bell *Macb.* ii 1 31
Drink, sir, is a great provoker of three things . . ii 3 27
What three things does drink especially provoke? . . ii 3 29
Much drink may be said to be an equivocator with lechery . . ii 3 34
I believe drink gave thee the lie last night . . . ii 3 41
Be large in mirth; anon we'll drink a measure The table round . iii 4 11
Give me some wine; fill full. I drink to the general joy o' the whole table iii 4 89
That were the slaves of drink and thralls of sleep . . . iii 6 13
No jocund health that Denmark drinks to-day, But the great cannon to the clouds shall tell . . . *Hamlet* i 2 125
Is in his retirement marvellous distempered.—With drink, sir? . iii 2 314
Now could I drink hot blood, And do such bitter business . . iii 2 408
And that he calls for drink, I'll have prepared him A chalice for the nonce . . . iv 7 160
Her garments, heavy with their drink, Pull'd the poor wretch from her melodious lay To muddy death . . . iv 7 182
Woo't fast? woo't tear thyself? Woo't drink up eisel? eat a crocodile? v 1 299
The king shall drink to Hamlet's better breath . . v 2 282
Now the king drinks to Hamlet . . . v 2 289
Stay; give me drink. Hamlet, this pearl is thine; Here's to thy health v 2 293
Gertrude, do not drink.—I will, my lord; I pray you, pardon me . v 2 301
I dare not drink yet, madam; by and by . . . v 2 304
The drink, the drink,—O my dear Hamlet,—The drink, the drink! I am poison'd . . . v 2 320
Here, thou incestuous, murderous, damned Dane, Drink off this potion v 2 337
Leave thy drink and thy whore, And keep in-a-door . . *Lear* i 4 137
Drinks the green mantle of the standing pool . . . iii 4 138
Blessed fig's-end! the wine she drinks is made of grapes . *Othello* ii 1 256
A soldier's a man; A life's but a span; Why, then, let a soldier drink . ii 3 75
Your Dane, your German, and your swag-bellied Hollander—Drink, ho!—are nothing to your English . . . ii 3 81
Why, he drinks you, with facility, your Dane dead drunk . . ii 3 84
He'll watch the horologe a double set, If drink rock not his cradle . ii 3 136
A beggar in his drink Could not have laid such terms upon his callat iv 2 120
Wine enough Cleopatra's health to drink . . *Ant. and Cleo.* i 2 12
He fishes, drinks, and wastes The lamps of night in revel . . i 4 4
Thou didst drink The stale of horses, and the gilded puddle Which beasts would cough at . . . i 4 61
Ha, ha! Give me to drink mandragora . . . i 5 4
Lepidus is high-coloured.—They have made him drink alms-drink . ii 7 5
Reconciles them to his entreaty, and himself to the drink . . ii 7 9
Drink thou; increase the reels . . . ii 7 100
I had rather fast from all four days Than drink so much in one . ii 7 109
Shall we dance now the Egyptian Bacchanals, And celebrate our drink? ii 7 111
We all would sup together, And drink carouses to the next day's fate iv 8 34
Sir, I will eat no meat, I'll not drink, sir . . . v 2 49
In their thick breaths, Rank of gross diet, shall we be enclouded, And forced to drink their vapour . . . v 2 213
With mine eyes I'll drink the words you send . . *Cymbeline* i 1 100
You come in faint for want of meat, depart reeling with too much drink v 4 164
Fill to your mistress' lips,—We drink this health to you . *Pericles* ii 3 52
To make his entrance more sweet, Here, say we drink this standing-bowl of wine to him . . . ii 3 65
Drink deep. This would drink deep.—'Twould drink the cup and all *Hen. V.* i 1 20
We'll teach you to drink deep ere you depart . . *Hamlet* i 2 175
Drinkest. What drink'st thou oft, instead of homage sweet, But poison'd flattery? . . . *Hen. V.* iv 1 267
O earth, which this blood drink'st, revenge his death! *Richard III.* i 2 63
Drinking. This can sack and drinking do . . . *Tempest* iii 2 88
They were red-hot with drinking . . . iv 1 171
Drinkings and swearings and starings . . *Mer. Wives* v 5 168
It is impossible to extirp it [lechery] quite, friar, till eating and drinking be put down . . . *Meas. for Meas.* iii 2 110
I have been drinking all night; I am not fitted for't . . iv 3 46
Prove that ever I lose more blood with love than I will get again with drinking, pick out mine eyes . . . *Much Ado* i 1 254
His beard grew thin and hungerly And seem'd to ask him sops as he was drinking . . . *T. of Shrew* iii 2 178
That quaffing and drinking will undo you . . *T. Night* i 3 14
He's drunk nightly in your company.—With drinking healths to my niece . . . i 3 40
I think it [life] rather consists of eating and drinking . . ii 3 12
The task he undertakes Is numbering sands and drinking oceans dry *Richard II.* ii 2 146
Drinking my griefs, whilst you mount up on high . . . iv 1 189

Drinking. Thou art so fat-witted, with drinking of old sack . 1 *Hen. IV.* i 2 2
They call drinking deep, dyeing scarlet . . . . ii 4 16
Glasses, glasses, is the only drinking . . . . 2 *Hen. IV.* ii 1 155
With excellent endeavour of drinking good and good store of fertile sherris . . . . iv 3 131
Come, leave your drinking, and fall to blows . . . . 2 *Hen. VI.* ii 3 80
Drinking, fencing, swearing, quarrelling, Drabbing . . . *Hamlet* ii 1 25
I have very poor and unhappy brains for drinking . . . *Othello* ii 3 35
Is your Englishman so expert in his drinking? . . . . ii 3 83
I had rather heat my liver with drinking . . . . *Ant. and Cleo.* i 2 23
We did sleep day out of countenance, and made the night light with drinking . . . . ii 2 182
For my part, I am sorry it is turned to a drinking . . . . ii 6 109
Drive. I could drive the boat with my sighs . . . *T. G. of Ver.* ii 3 60
Or as one nail by strength drives out another . . . . . ii 4 193
I could drive her then from the ward of her purity . . *Mer. Wives* ii 2 257
What error drives our eyes and ears amiss? . . *Com. of Errors* ii 2 186
Had a rougher task in hand Than to drive liking to the name of love *Much Ado* i 1 302
Here's that shall drive some of them to a noncome . . . iii 5 67
But none can drive him from the envious plea Of forfeiture *Mer. of Ven.* iii 2 284
Which humbleness may drive unto a fine . . . . iv 1 372
He must needs go that the devil drives . . . . . *All's Well* i 3 32
This drives me to entreat you That presently you take your way for home . . . . ii 5 68
And is it I That drive thee from the sportive court? . . . iii 2 109
And with a kind of injunction drives me to these habits . . *T. Night* ii 5 183
And drive the gentleman, as I know his youth will aptly receive it, into a most hideous opinion . . . . iii 4 211
Bell, book, and candle shall not drive me back, When gold and silver becks me to come on . . . . *K. John* iii 3 12
Drive these men away, And I will sit as quiet as a lamb . . . . iv 1 79
To drive away the heavy thought of care . . . . *Richard II.* iii 4 2
Drives him beyond the bounds of patience . . . 1 *Hen. IV.* i 3 200
To drive away the time . . . . ii 4 31
And drive all thy subjects afore thee like a flock of wild-geese . . ii 4 151
Four rogues in buckram let drive at me . . . . ii 4 217
He will drive you out of your revenge and turn all to a merriment 2 *Hen. IV.* ii 4 323
I shall drive you then to confess the wilful abuse . . . . ii 4 338
Raise this tedious siege And drive the English forth . . 1 *Hen. VI.* i 2 54
Drive them from Orleans and be immortalized . . . . . . i 2 148
I will not slay thee, but I'll drive thee back . . . . . . i 3 41
A witch, by fear, not force, like Hannibal, Drives back our troops . i 5 22
Till mischief and despair Drive you to break your necks . . . v 4 91
The sharp thorny points Of my alleged reasons drive this forward *Hen. VIII.* ii 4 225
One fire drives out one fire; one nail, one nail . . . *Coriolanus* iv 7 54
And the hounds Should drive upon thy new-transformed limbs *T. Andron.* ii 3 64
So soon we shall drive back Of Alcibiades the approaches wild *T. of Athens* v 1 166
I'll about, And drive away the vulgar from the streets . . *J. Cæsar* i 1 75
My ancestors did from the streets of Rome The Tarquin drive . . ii 1 54
Pity to the general wrong of Rome—As fire drives out fire, so pity pity —Hath done this deed on Cæsar . . . . iii 1 171
Unequal match'd, Pyrrhus at Priam drives; in rage strikes wide *Hamlet* ii 2 494
Give him a further edge, And drive his purpose on to these delights . iii 1 27
Why do you go about to recover the wind of me, as if you would drive me into a toil? . . . . iii 2 362
Goose, if I had you upon Sarum plain, I'ld drive ye cackling home *Lear* ii 2 90
There is a litter ready; lay him in't, And drive towards Dover . . iii 6 98
Let his shames quickly Drive him to Rome . . . *Ant. and Cleo.* i 4 73
Which drives O'er your content these strong necessities . . . iii 6 82
So she From Egypt drive her all-disgraced friend . . . . iii 12 22
A dram of this Will drive away distemper . . . *Cymbeline* iii 4 194
May drive us to a render Where we have lived . . . . . iv 4 11
Amazement shall drive courage from the state . . . *Pericles* i 2 26
As a duck for life that dives, So up and down the poor ship drives iii Gower 50
If e'er this coffin drive a-land, I, King Pericles, have lost This queen iii 2 69
Drivelling. For this drivelling love is like a great natural, that runs lolling up and down . . . . *Rom. and Jul.* ii 4 95
Driven out of doors with it when I go from home *Com. of Errors* iv 4 37
I know into what straits of fortune she is driven . *As Y. Like It* v 2 71
I am driven on by the flesh . . . . . . *All's Well* i 3 31
And driven into despair an enemy's hope . . . *Richard II.* ii 2 47
So bees with smoke and doves with noisome stench Are from their hives and houses driven away . . . . 1 *Hen. VI.* i 5 24
So am I driven by breath of her renown Either to suffer shipwreck or arrive Where I may have fruition of her love . . . . . v 5 7
But now is Cade driven back, his men dispersed . . 2 *Hen. VI.* iv 9 34
I saw our party to their trenches driven, And then I came away *Coriolanus* i 6 12
Either led or driven, as we point the way . . . . *J. Cæsar* iv 1 23
A sister driven into desperate terms . . . . . . *Hamlet* iv 7 26
Must be driven To find out practices of cunning hell . . *Othello* i 3 101
Reft of ships and men, And after shipwreck driven upon this shore *Per.* ii 3 85
We'll have no more gentlemen driven away . . . . . . iv 6 139
Driven before the winds, he is arrived Here where his daughter dwells v Gower 14
Driven snow. Lawn as white as driven snow . . . . *W. Tale* iv 4 220
Drivest. Thou drivest me past the bounds Of maiden's patience *M. N. Dream* iii 2 65
Driveth. Sometime she driveth o'er a soldier's neck, And then dreams he of cutting foreign throats . . . . . *Rom. and Jul.* i 4 82
Driving. When you and those poor number saved with you Hung on our driving boat . . . . *T. Night* i 2 11
The sun's beams, Driving back shadows over louring hills *R. and J.* ii 5 6
Driving the poor fry before him, and at last devours them all *Pericles* ii 1 34
Drizzle. It drizzles rain . . . . *Much Ado* iii 3 111
When the sun sets, the air doth drizzle dew . . *Rom. and Jul.* iii 5 127
Drizzled. In sap-consuming winter's drizzled snow . . *Com. of Errors* v 1 312
Which drizzled blood upon the Capitol . . . . . *J. Cæsar* ii 2 21
Droit. En vérité, vous prononcez les mots aussi droit que les natifs d'Angleterre . . . . *Hen. V.* iii 4 41
Drollery. What were these?—A living drollery . . . *Tempest* iii 3 21
For thy walls, a pretty slight drollery, or the story of the Prodigal 2 *Hen. IV.* ii 1 156
Dromio. Stay there, Dromio, till I come to thee . . *Com. of Errors* i 2 10
Come, Dromio, come, these jests are out of season . . . . i 2 68
The gold I gave to Dromio is laid up Safe at the Centaur . . . ii 2 1
I could not speak with Dromio since at first I sent him from the mart . ii 2 5
She sent for you by Dromio home to dinner.—By Dromio? . . . ii 2 156
Dromio, thou drone, thou snail, thou slug, thou sot! . . . . ii 2 196
Dromio, keep the gate. Husband, I'll dine above with you to-day . ii 2 208

Dromio. If thou hadst been Dromio to-day in my place, Thou wouldst have changed thy face for a name . . . . . . *Com. of Errors* iii 1 46
Why, how now, Dromio! where runn'st thou so fast? . . . . iii 2 71
Am I Dromio? am I your man? am I myself?—Thou art Dromio . . iii 2 73
Called me Dromio; swore I was assured to her . . . . . iii 2 145
I'll to the mart and there for Dromio stay . . . . . . iii 2 189
I sent you money to redeem you, By Dromio here . . . . iv 4 87
Bind Dromio too, and bear them to my house . . . . . . v 1 35
Is not your name, sir, call'd Antipholus? And is not that your bondman, Dromio? . . . . v 1 287
Now am I Dromio and his man unbound . . . . v 1 290
I, sir, am Dromio: command him away.—I, sir, am Dromio: pray, let me stay . . . . v 1 335
By men of Epidamnum he and I And the twin Dromio all were taken up v 1 350
By and by rude fishermen of Corinth By force took Dromio and my son v 1 352
These two so like, And these two Dromios, one in semblance . . . v 1 358
Drone. Thou drone, thou snail, thou slug, thou sot! . . . . ii 2 196
Drones hive not with me; Therefore I part with him . *Mer. of Venice* ii 5 48
Yea, or the drone of a Lincolnshire bagpipe . . . 1 *Hen. IV.* i 2 85
Delivering o'er to executors pale The lazy yawning drone . . *Hen. V.* i 2 204
Drones suck not eagles' blood but rob bee-hives . . 2 *Hen. VI.* iv 1 109
Not to eat honey like a drone From others' labours . . *Pericles* ii Gower 18
We would purge the land of these drones, that rob the bee of her honey ii 1 51
Droop. A most auspicious star, whose influence If now I court not but omit, my fortunes Will ever after droop . . . . . . *Tempest* i 2 184
O, this is it that makes your servants droop! . . *T. of Shrew* Ind. 2 29
But wherefore do you droop? why look you sad? . . . *K. John* v 1 44
Sick now! droop now! this sickness doth infect The very life-blood of our enterprise . . . . 1 *Hen. IV.* iv 1 28
Like to a wither'd vine That droops his sapless branches . 1 *Hen. VI.* ii 5 12
Why droops my lord, like over-ripen'd corn? . . . 2 *Hen. VI.* i 2 1
Thus droops this lofty pine and hangs his sprays . . . . . ii 3 45
Droop not; adieu. Farewell, my wife, my mother: I'll do well yet *Cor.* iv 1 20
Good things of day begin to droop and drowse . . . *Macbeth* iii 2 52
Drooped. He straight declined, droop'd, took it deeply . . *W. Tale* ii 3 14
Droopeth. Now, France, thy glory droopeth to the dust . 1 *Hen. VI.* v 3 29
Drooping. With drooping fog as black as Acheron . . *M. N. Dream* iii 2 357
Imp out our drooping country's broken wing . . . *Richard II.* ii 1 292
From the orient to the drooping west . . . . . 2 *Hen. IV.* Ind. 3
When sapless age and weak unable limbs Should bring thy father to his drooping chair . . . . 1 *Hen. VI.* iv 5 5
These news, my lords, may cheer our drooping spirits . . . . v 2 1
Cheer'd up the drooping army . . . . 3 *Hen. VI.* i 1 6
Those gracious words revive my drooping thoughts . . . . iii 3 21
Anon, as patient as the female dove, When that her golden couplets are disclosed, His silence will sit drooping . . . . *Hamlet* v 1 311
Who's there?—A Roman, Who had not now been drooping here, if seconds Had answer'd him . . . . *Cymbeline* v 3 90
Drop. He'll be hang'd yet, Though every drop of water swear against it And gape at widest to glut him . . . . *Tempest* i 1 62
When I have deck'd the sea with drops full salt . . . . . i 2 155
As wicked dew as e'er my mother brush'd With raven's feather from unwholesome fen Drop on you both! . . . . i 2 323
I can here disarm thee with this stick And make thy weapon drop . . i 2 473
When the butt is out, we will drink water; not a drop before . . iii 2 2
The clouds methought would open and show riches Ready to drop . . iii 2 151
His tears run down his beard, like winter's drops From eaves of reeds . v 1 16
Mine eyes, even sociable to the show of thine, Fall fellowly drops . . v 1 64
Look down, you gods, And on this couple drop a blessed crown! . . v 1 202
I to the world am like a drop of water That in the ocean seeks another drop . . . . *Com. of Errors* i 2 35
That at dinner they should not drop in his porridge . . . . ii 2 100
As easy mayst thou fall A drop of water in the breaking gulf . . . ii 2 128
Some devils ask but the parings of one's nail, A rush, a hair, a drop of blood . . . . iv 3 73
No true drop of blood in him, to be truly touched with love *Much Ado* iii 2 19
The wide sea Hath drops too few to wash her clean again . . . iv 1 143
So sweet a kiss the golden sun gives not To those fresh morning drops upon the rose . . . . *L. L. Lost* iv 3 27
Thou shinest in every tear that I do weep: No drop but as a coach doth carry thee . . . . iv 3 34
I'll drop the paper: Sweet leaves, shade folly . . . . . . iv 3 43
Having once this juice, I'll watch Titania when she is asleep, And drop the liquor of it in her eyes . . . . *M. N. Dream* ii 1 178
Allay with some cold drops of modesty Thy skipping spirit *Mer. of Ven.* ii 2 195
These foolish drops do something drown my manly spirit . . . ii 3 13
The Jew shall have my flesh, blood, bones and all, Ere thou shalt lose for me one drop of blood . . . . iv 1 113
The weakest kind of fruit Drops earliest to the ground . . . . iv 1 116
If thou dost shed One drop of Christian blood, thy lands and goods Are, by the laws of Venice, confiscate . . . . iv 1 310
Fair ladies, you drop manna in the way Of starved people . . . v 1 294
Wiped our eyes Of drops that sacred pity hath engender'd *As Y. Like It* ii 7 123
It may well be called Jove's tree, when it drops forth such fruit . . iii 2 250
Will you sterner be Than he that dies and lives by bloody drops? . . iii 5 7
Women's gentle brain Could not drop forth such giant-rude invention iv 3 34
None so dry or thirsty Will deign to sip or touch one drop of it *T. of S.* v 2 145
When he swears oaths, bid him drop gold, and take it . . *All's Well* iv 3 252
I will drop in his way some obscure epistles of love . . . *T. Night* ii 3 168
He shall think, by the letters that thou wilt drop, that they come from my niece . . . . ii 3 179
Fortune would not suffer me: she drops booties in my mouth *W. Tale* iv 4 863
What dangers, by his highness' fail of issue, May drop upon his kingdom v 1 28
Now, had I not the dash of my former life in me, would preferment drop on my head . . . . v 2 123
And then we shall repent each drop of blood That hot rash haste so indirectly shed . . . . *K. John* ii 1 48
Thou hast not saved one drop of blood, In this hot trial, more than we ii 1 341
Where but by chance a silver drop hath fallen, Even to that drop ten thousand wiry friends Do glue themselves in sociable grief . . . iii 4 63
I must be brief, lest resolution drop Out at mine eyes . . . . iv 1 35
This effusion of such manly drops, This shower . . . . . . v 2 49
To drop them still upon one place, Till they have fretted us a pair of graves Within the earth . . . . *Richard II.* iii 3 166
Look upon his face; His eyes do drop no tears, his prayers are in jest . v 3 101
Meet and ne'er part till one drop down a corse . . . 1 *Hen. IV.* iv 1 123
It was your presurmise, That, in the dole of blows, your son might drop 2 *Hen. IV.* i 1 169
Doth begin to melt And drop upon our bare unarmed heads . . . ii 4 394
If I do sweat, they are the drops of thy lovers . . . . . iv 3 14

Drop. My cloud of dignity Is held from falling with so weak a wind That it will quickly drop . . . 2 *Hen. IV.* iv 5 101
Let all the tears that should bedew my hearse Be drops of balm . . iv 5 115
Many now in health Shall drop their blood in approbation . *Hen. V.* i 2 19
Whose guiltless drops Are every one a woe . . . . . . i 2 25
Knocks go and come; God's vassals drop and die . . . . iii 2 8
Sweat drops of gallant youth in our rich fields . . . . iii 5 25
He'll drop his heart into the sink of fear . . . . . . iii 5 59
And on it have bestow'd more contrite tears Than from it issued forced drops of blood . . . . iv 1 314
I will fetch thy rim out at thy throat In drops of crimson blood . . iv 4 16
For every drop of blood was drawn from him There hath at least five Frenchmen died to-night . . . . 1 *Hen. VI.* ii 2 8
One drop of blood drawn from thy country's bosom Should grieve thee more than streams of foreign gore . . . . iii 3 54
Drops bloody sweat from his war-wearied limbs . . . . . iv 4 18
I'll have more lives Than drops of blood were in my father's veins 3 *Hen. VI.* i 1 97
And every drop cries vengeance for his death . . . . . . i 4 148
Shamed their aspect with store of childish drops . *Richard III.* i 2 155
Your eyes drop millstones, when fools' eyes drop tears . . . i 3 354
Prosperity begins to mellow And drop into the rotten mouth of death . iv 4 2
The liquid drops of tears that you have shed Shall come again . . iv 4 321
Cold fearful drops stand on my trembling flesh . . . . . v 3 181
So much the more Must pity drop upon her . . . *Hen. VIII.* ii 3 18
My drops of tears I'll turn to sparks of fire . . . . . ii 4 72
I'll prove this truth with my three drops of blood . *Troi. and Cres.* i 3 301
I would not wish a drop of Trojan blood Spent more in her defence . ii 2 197
For every false drop in her bawdy veins A Grecian's life hath sunk . iv 1 69
But the just gods gainsay That any drop thou borrow'dst from thy mother . . ., should by my mortal sword Be drain'd! . . . iv 5 133
The fall of every Phrygian stone will cost A drop of Grecian blood . iv 5 224
The blood I drop is rather physical Than dangerous to me *Coriolanus* i 5 19
A cup of hot wine with not a drop of allaying Tiber in't . . . ii 1 53
Many an heir Of these fair edifices 'fore my wars Have I heard groan and drop . . . . iv 4 4
The extreme dangers and the drops of blood Shed for my thankless country . . . . iv 5 75
I urged our old acquaintance, and the drops That we have bled together v 1 10
At a few drops of women's rheum, which are As cheap as lies . . v 6 46
And given up, For certain drops of salt, your city Rome . . . v 6 93
Be your heart to them As unrelenting flint to drops of rain *T. Andron.* ii 3 141
Rude-growing briers, Upon whose leaves are drops of new-shed blood . ii 3 200
In summer's drought I'll drop upon thee still . . . . . iii 1 19
These sorrowful drops upon thy blood-stain'd face . . . . v 3 154
Like a loving child, Shed yet some small drops from thy tender spring v 3 167
Back, foolish tears . . .; Your tributary drops belong to woe *R. and J.* iii 2 103
O churl! drunk all, and left no friendly drop To help me after? . v 3 163
Even he drops down The knee before him . . . . *T. of Athens* i 1 60
Five thousand crowns, my lord.—Five thousand drops pays that . . iii 4 97
Let high-sighted tyranny range on, Till each man drop by lottery *J. C.* ii 1 119
When every drop of blood That every Roman bears, and nobly bears, Is guilty of a several bastardy . . . . ii 1 136
As dear to me as are the ruddy drops That visit my sad heart . . ii 1 289
I perceive, you feel The dint of pity: these are gracious drops . iii 2 198
I had rather coin my heart, And drop my blood for drachmas . . iv 3 73
If arguing make us sweat, The proof of it will turn to redder drops . v 1 49
My plenteous joys, Wanton in fulness, seek to hide themselves In drops of sorrow . . . . *Macbeth* i 4 35
Certain friends that are both his and mine, Whose loves I may not drop iii 1 122
Upon the corner of the moon There hangs a vaporous drop profound . iii 5 24
And with him pour we in our country's purge Each drop of us . . v 2 29
That drop of blood that's calm proclaims me bastard . . *Hamlet* iv 5 117
Hast stol'n it from her?—No, faith; she let it drop by negligence *Othello* iii 3 311
Each drop she falls would prove a crocodile . . . . . . iv 1 257
I should have found in some place of my soul A drop of patience . iv 2 53
Drop tears as fast as the Arabian trees Their medicinal gum . . v 2 350
In our own filth drop our clear judgements . . *Ant. and Cleo.* iii 13 113
The first stone Drop in my neck: as it determines, so Dissolve my life! iii 13 161
Grace grow where those drops fall! . . . . iv 2 38
Let her languish A drop of blood a day; and, being aged, Die! *Cymbeline* i 1 157
Like the crimson drops I' the bottom of a cowslip . . . . ii 2 38
If there be Yet left in heaven as small a drop of pity As a wren's eye . iv 2 304
That paragon, thy daughter,—For whom my heart drops blood . . v 5 148
Drop by drop. They would melt me out of my fat drop by drop *M. Wives* iv 5 100
And shed my dear blood drop by drop in the dust . 1 *Hen. IV.* iii 2 134
Drop-heir. Young Drop-heir that killed lusty Pudding *Meas. for Meas.* iv 3 16
Droplet. Scorn'dst our brain's flow and those our droplets which From niggard nature fall . . . . *T. of Athens* v 4 76
Dropped. They dropp'd, as by a thunder-stroke . . . *Tempest* ii 1 204
Hast thou not dropp'd from heaven?—Out o' the moon, I do assure thee ii 2 140
I found him under a tree, like a dropped acorn . . *As Y. Like It* iii 2 248
He does obey every point of the letter that I dropped to betray him *T. N.* iii 2 83
The sweet'st, dear'st creature's dead, and vengeance for't Not dropp'd down yet . . . . *W. Tale* iii 2 203
As if an angel dropp'd down from the clouds . . . . 1 *Hen. IV.* iv 1 108
My heart dropp'd love, my power rain'd honour . . *Hen. VIII.* iii 2 185
With terms unsquared, Which, from the tongue of roaring Typhon dropp'd, Would seem hyperboles . . . . . *Troi. and Cres.* i 3 160
The blood he hath lost—Which, I dare vouch, is more than that he hath, By many an ounce—he dropp'd it for his country *Coriolanus* iii 1 301
He would have dropp'd his knife, and fell asleep . . . *T. Andron.* ii 4 50
Such instigations have been often dropp'd . . . . *J. Cæsar* ii 1 49
What guests were in her eyes; which parted thence, As pearls from diamonds dropp'd . . . . *Lear* iv 3 24
There he dropp'd it for a special purpose . . . . . *Othello* v 2 322
Realms and islands were As plates dropp'd from his pocket . *A. and C.* v 2 92
Tremblingly she stood And on the sudden dropp'd . . . . . v 2 347
Droppeth. It [mercy] droppeth as the gentle rain from heaven *M. of Ven.* iv 1 185
Dropping. My strong imagination sees a crown Dropping upon thy head . . . . *Tempest* ii 1 209
Lob down their heads, dropping the hides and hips . . *Hen. V.* iv 2 47
Never till now Did I go through a tempest dropping fire . *J. Cæsar* i 3 10
With an auspicious and a dropping eye . . . . *Hamlet* i 2 11
It doth posset And curd, like eager droppings into milk . . . i 5 69
And with a dropping industry they skip From stem to stern . *Pericles* iv 1 63
Dropsied. Where great additions swell's, and virtue none, It is a dropsied honour . . . . *All's Well* ii 3 135
Dropsies. That swollen parcel of dropsies . . . . . . 1 *Hen. IV.* ii 4 496
Dropsy. The dropsy drown this fool! . . . . *Tempest* iv 1 230

Dross. If aught possess thee from me, it is dross . . *Com. of Errors* ii 2 17
A golden mind stoops not to shows of dross . . . *Mer. of Venice* ii 7 2
And by the merit of vile gold, dross, dust, Purchase corrupted pardon of a man . . . . *K. John* iii 1 165
My love admits no qualifying dross; No more my grief . *Troi. and Cres.* iv 4 9
Drossy. Thus has he—and many more of the same breed that I know the drossy age dotes on . . . . *Hamlet* v 2 197
Drought. In summer's drought I'll drop upon thee still *T. Andron.* iii 1 19
Drouth. And crickets sing at the oven's mouth, E'er the blither for their drouth . . . . *Pericles* iii Gower 8
Drove the grossness of the foppery into a received belief . *Mer. Wives* v 5 131
And in conclusion drove us to seek out This head of safety 1 *Hen. IV.* iv 3 102
More dazzled and drove back his enemies Than mid-day sun 1 *Hen. VI.* i 1 13
And twice by awkward wind from England's bank Drove back 2 *Hen. VI.* iii 2 84
'Twas not your valour, Clifford, drove me thence . 3 *Hen. VI.* ii 2 107
With his Amazonian chin he drove The bristled lips before him *Coriol.* ii 2 95
Mere want of gold, and the falling-from of his friends, drove him into this melancholy . . . . *T. of Athens* iv 3 402
This was a goodly person, Till the disaster that, one mortal night, Drove him to this . . . . *Pericles* v 1 38
Droven. Had we done so at first, we had droven them home *A. and C.* iv 7 5
Drovier. That's spoken like an honest drovier . . . *Much Ado* ii 1 201
Drown. Shall we give o'er and drown? Have you a mind to sink? *Temp.* i 1 42
For my part, the sea cannot drown me . . . . iii 2 15
Even with such-like valour men hang and drown Their proper selves . iii 3 59
The dropsy drown this fool! what do you mean To dote thus? . . iv 1 230
Deeper than did ever plummet sound I'll drown my book . . . v 1 57
I prophesied, if a gallows were on land, This fellow could not drown . v 1 218
O, train me not, sweet mermaid, with thy note, To drown me in thy sister's flood of tears . . . . *Com. of Errors* iii 2 46
The wind doth blow And coughing drowns the parson's saw *L. L. Lost* v 2 932
These foolish drops do something drown my manly spirit *Mer. of Venice* ii 3 14
Make the coming hour o'erflow with joy And pleasure drown the brim *All's Well* ii 4 48
Drown my clothes, and say I was stripped.—Hardly serve . . iv 1 57
How mightily some other times we drown our gain in tears! . . iv 3 79
One draught above heat makes him a fool; the second mads him; and a third drowns him . . . . *T. Night* i 5 141
She is drowned already, sir, with salt water, though I seem to drown her remembrance again with more . . . . ii 1 32
I have That honourable grief lodged here which burns Worse than tears drown . . . . *W. Tale* ii 1 112
Wouldst thou drown thyself, Put but a little water in a spoon *K. John* iv 3 130
Like an unseasonable stormy day, Which makes the silver rivers drown their shores . . . . *Richard II.* iii 2 107
The pretty-vaulting sea refused to drown me . . . 2 *Hen. VI.* iii 2 94
I'll drown more sailors than the mermaid shall . 3 *Hen. VI.* iii 2 186
Lest with my sighs or tears I blast or drown King Edward's fruit . iv 4 23
Lord, Lord! methought, what pain it was to drown! . *Richard III.* i 4 21
If all this will not do, I'll drown you in the malmsey-butt within . i 4 277
What cause have I, Thine being but a moiety of my grief, To overgo thy plaints and drown thy cries! . . . . ii 2 61
That I, being govern'd by the watery moon, May send forth plenteous tears to drown the world! . . . . ii 2 70
Drown desperate sorrow in dead Edward's grave . . . . . ii 2 99
With the clamorous report of war Thus will I drown your exclamations iv 4 153
So in the Lethe of thy angry soul Thou drown the sad remembrance . iv 4 251
One hour's storm will drown the fragrant meads; What will whole months of tears thy father's eyes? . . . . . *T. Andron.* ii 4 54
Drown the lamenting fool in sea-salt tears . . . . . . iii 2 20
Floods of tears will drown my oratory, And break my utterance . . v 3 90
He has a sin that often Drowns him . . . . . *T. of Athens* iii 5 69
'Gainst the stream of virtue they may strive, And drown themselves in riot! . . . . iv 1 28
Hang them or stab them, drown them in a draught, Confound them . v 1 105
Blow the horrid deed in every eye, That tears shall drown the wind *Macb.* i 7 25
To dew the sovereign flower and drown the weeds . . . . v 2 30
He would drown the stage with tears . . . . . . *Hamlet* ii 2 588
If I drown myself wittingly, it argues an act . . . . . v 1 11
If the man go to this water, and drown himself, it is, will he, nill he, he goes,—mark you that; but if the water come to him and drown him, he drowns not himself . . . . v 1 18
And the more pity that great folk should have countenance in this world to drown or hang themselves . . . . v 1 31
I will incontinently drown myself . . . . . . *Othello* i 3 306
Ere I would say, I would drown myself for the love of a guinea-hen . i 3 316
Come, be a man. Drown thyself! drown cats and blind puppies . . i 3 340
Let's to supper, come, And drown consideration . . *Ant. and Cleo.* iv 2 45
Lest this great sea of joys rushing upon me O'erbear the shores of my mortality, And drown me with their sweetness . . . *Pericles* v 1 196
Drowned. We are less afraid to be drowned than thou art . *Tempest* i 1 48
The ditty does remember my drown'd father . . . . . . i 2 405
Will you grant with me That Ferdinand is drown'd?—He's gone . ii 1 244
I should know that voice: it should be—but he is drowned . . ii 2 91
Art thou not drowned, Stephano? I hope now thou art not drowned . ii 2 113
The king and all our company else being drowned, we will inherit . ii 2 179
My man-monster hath drown'd his tongue in sack . . . . . iii 2 14
He is drown'd Whom thus we stray to find . . . . . . iii 3 8
Young Ferdinand, whom they suppose is drown'd . . . . . iii 3 92
The mean is drown'd with your unruly bass . . . *T. G. of Ver.* i 2 96
And drench'd me in the sea, where I am drown'd . . . . . i 3 79
The rogues slighted me into the river with as little remorse as they would have drowned a blind bitch's puppies . . . *Mer. Wives* iii 5 11
I had been drowned, but that the shore was shelvy and shallow . . iii 5 14
What sayest thou to this tune, matter and method? Is't not drowned i' the last rain? . . . . *Meas. for Meas.* iii 2 51
Let Love, being light, be drowned if she sink! . . *Com. of Errors* iii 2 52
The fold stands empty in the drowned field . . . *M. N. Dream* ii 1 96
He is drowned in the brook: look but in, and you shall see him *As Y. L. It* iii 2 305
And being taken with the cramp was drowned . . . . . iv 1 105
My brother he is in Elysium. Perchance he is not drown'd . *T. Night* i 2 5
What's a drunken man like, fool?—Like a drowned man, a fool and a mad man . . . . i 5 139
He's in the third degree of drink, he's drowned . . . . . i 5 144
Some hour before you took me from the breach of the sea was my sister drowned . . . . ii 1 24
She is drowned already, sir, with salt water, though I seem to drown her remembrance again with more . . . . ii 1 31
Thrice-welcome, drowned Viola! . . . . v 1 248
And pluck up drowned honour by the locks . . . 1 *Hen. IV.* i 3 205

Drowned. Lie drown'd and soak'd in mercenary blood *Hen. V.* iv 7 79
Or piteous they will look, like drowned mice *1 Hen. VI.* i 2 12
My heart is drown'd with grief *2 Hen. VI.* iii 1 198
The pretty-vaulting sea refused to drown me, Knowing that thou wouldst have me drown'd on shore iii 2 95
Ten days ago I drown'd these news in tears *3 Hen. VI.* ii 1 104
And stops my tongue, while heart is drown'd in cares iii 3 14
And yet, for all his wings, the fool was drown'd v 6 20
When I do tell thee, there my hopes lie drown'd, Reply not in how many fathoms deep They lie indrench'd *Troi. and Cres.* i 1 49
Thy napkin cannot drink a tear of mine, For thou, poor man, hast drown'd it with thine own *T. Andron.* iii 1 141
Then must my earth with her continual tears Become a deluge, overflow'd and drown'd iii 1 230
Who drown'd their enmity in my true tears, And oped their arms v 3 107
And these, who often drown'd could never die, Transparent heretics, be burnt for liars! *Rom. and Jul.* i 2 95
His wits Are drown'd and lost in his calamities *T. of Athens* iv 3 89
Your sister's drown'd, Laertes.—Drown'd! O, where? *Hamlet* iv 7 165
Alas, then, she is drown'd?—Drown'd, drown'd iv 7 184
Unless she drowned herself in her own defence v 1 7
Argal, she drowned herself wittingly v 1 13
Spout Till you have drench'd our steeples, drown'd the cocks! *Lear* iii 2 3
Seek thou rather to be hanged in compassing thy joy than to be drowned and go without her *Othello* i 3 368
If that the Turkish fleet Be not enshelter'd and embay'd, they are drown'd ii 1 18
News, friends; our wars are done, the Turks are drown'd ii 1 204
In thy fats our cares be drown'd *Ant. and Cleo.* ii 7 122
But tell me now My drown'd queen's name *Pericles* v 1 207
That Thaisa am I, supposed dead And drown'd v 3 36
Drowning. Methinks he hath no drowning mark upon him *Tempest* i 1 31
I'll warrant him for drowning i 1 49
Would thou might'st lie drowning The washing of ten tides! i 1 60
I have not 'scaped drowning to be afeard now of your four legs ii 2 61
A puppy; one that I saved from drowning *T. G. of Ver.* iv 4 4
And then to 'scape drowning thrice, and to be in peril of my life with the edge of a feather-bed *Mer. of Venice* ii 2 172
If thou wilt needs damn thyself, do it a more delicate way than drowning. Make all the money thou canst *Othello* i 3 361
A pox of drowning thyself! it is clean out of the way i 3 366
No more of drowning, do you hear?—I am changed i 3 387
Drowse. Good things of day begin to droop and drowse *Macbeth* iii 2 52
Drowsed. Rather drowsed and hung their eyelids down *1 Hen. IV.* iii 2 81
Drowsily. What, thou speak'st drowsily? Poor knave, I blame thee not *J. Cæsar* iv 3 240
Drowsiness. What a strange drowsiness possesses them!—It is the quality o' the climate *Tempest* ii 1 199
Drowsy. Puts the drowsy and neglected act Freshly on me *Meas. for Meas.* i 2 174
Sleep when I am drowsy and tend on no man's business *Much Ado* i 3 17
Round about Dapples the drowsy east with spots of grey v 3 27
The voice of all the gods Make heaven drowsy with the harmony *L. L. L.* iv 3 345
By the dead and drowsy fire *M. N. Dream* v 1 399
Sound on into the drowsy race of night *K. John* iii 3 39
Life is as tedious as a twice-told tale Vexing the dull ear of a drowsy man iii 4 109
And the third hour of drowsy morning name *Hen. V.* iv Prol. 16
The organs, though defunct and dead before, Break up their drowsy grave iv 1 22
Roused on the sudden from their drowsy beds *1 Hen. VI.* ii 2 23
With their drowsy, slow and flagging wings *2 Hen. VI.* iv 1 5
Fairest-boding dreams That ever enter'd in a drowsy head *Richard III.* v 3 228
Will strike amazement to their drowsy spirits *Troi. and Cres.* ii 2 210
Patroclus' wounds have roused his drowsy blood v 5 32
Through all thy veins shall run A cold and drowsy humour *R. and J.* iv 1 96
The shard-borne beetle with his drowsy hums *Macbeth* iii 2 42
Not poppy, nor mandragora, Nor all the drowsy syrups of the world *Oth.* iii 3 331
Drudge. This drudge, or diviner, laid claim to me *Com. of Errors* iii 2 144
Thou pale and common drudge 'Tween man and man *Mer. of Venice* iii 2 103
You whoreson malt-horse drudge! *T. of Shrew* iv 1 132
If I be his cuckold, he's my drudge *All's Well* i 3 49
O that I were a god, to shoot forth thunder Upon these paltry, servile, abject drudges! *2 Hen. VI.* iv 1 105
Will you credit this base drudge's words? iv 2 159
I am the drudge and toil in your delight *Rom. and Jul.* ii 5 77
Or could this carl, A very drudge of nature's, have subdued me? *Cymb.* v 2 5
Drudgery. My old dame will be undone now for one to do her husbandry and her drudgery *2 Hen. IV.* iii 2 125
Drug. With wholesome syrups, drugs and holy prayers *Com. of Errors* v 1 104
Such mortal drugs I have; but Mantua's law Is death to any he that utters them *Rom. and Jul.* v 1 66
O true apothecary! Thy drugs are quick. Thus with a kiss I die v 3 120
The sweet degrees that this brief world affords To such as may the passive drugs of it Freely command *T. of Athens* iv 3 254
What rhubarb, cyme, or what purgative drug, Would scour these English hence? *Macbeth* v 3 55
Thoughts black, hands apt, drugs fit, and time agreeing *Hamlet* iii 2 266
Abused her delicate youth with drugs or minerals That weaken motion *Othello* i 2 74
What drugs, what charms, What conjuration and what mighty magic i 3 91
If knife, drugs, serpents, have Edge, sting, or operation, I am safe *Ant. and Cleo.* iv 15 25
Now, master doctor, have you brought those drugs? *Cymbeline* i 5 4
And will not trust one of her malice with A drug of such damn'd nature i 5 36
He hath a drug of mine; I pray his absence Proceed by swallowing that iii 5 57
I am sick still; heart-sick. Pisanio, I'll now taste of thy drug iv 2 38
The drug he gave me, which he said was precious And cordial to me, have I not found it Murderous to the senses? iv 2 326
Drug-damned. That drug-damn'd Italy hath out-craftied him iii 4 15
Drugged. I have drugg'd their possets *Macbeth* ii 2 6
Drum. There was no music with him but the drum and the fife *Much Ado* ii 3 14
Adieu, valour! rust, rapier! be still, drum! *L. L. Lost* i 2 188
When you hear the drum And the vile squealing of the wry-neck'd fife, Clamber not you up to the casements *Mer. of Venice* ii 5 29
Whilst I can shake my sword or hear the drum *All's Well* ii 5 96
And I shall prove A lover of thy drum, hater of love iii 3 11
Lose our drum! well.—He's shrewdly vexed iii 5 91
O, for the love of laughter, let him fetch his drum iii 6 37
If you give him not John Drum's entertainment iii 6 41
This drum sticks sorely in your disposition iii 6 46
Drum. 'Tis but a drum.—'But a drum'! is't 'but a drum'? *All's Well* iii 6 49
What the devil should move me to undertake the recovery of this drum? iv 1 38
I would I had any drum of the enemy's: I would swear I recovered it iv 1 66
Faith, sir, has led the drum before the English tragedians iv 3 298
I'll no more drumming; a plague of all drums! iv 3 332
Give me your hand. How does your drum? v 2 44
He's a good drum, my lord, but a naughty orator v 3 253
Good Tom Drum, lend me a handkercher v 3 322
The interruption of their churlish drums Cuts off more circumstance *K. John* ii 1 76
Braying trumpets and loud churlish drums, Clamours of hell iii 1 303
Strike up the drums; and let the tongue of war Plead for our interest v 2 164
Your drums, being beaten, will cry out; And so shall you, being beaten v 2 166
Roused up with boisterous untuned drums *Richard II.* i 3 134
Let's march without the noise of threatening drum iii 3 51
Talk so like a waiting-gentlewoman Of guns and drums and wounds *1 Hen. IV.* i 3 56
O, I could wish this tavern were my drum! iii 3 230
Had as lieve hear the devil as a drum iv 2 20
Cheering a rout of rebels with your drum *2 Hen. IV.* iv 2 9
Strike up our drums, pursue the scatter'd stray iv 2 120
Whilst any trump did sound, or drum struck up, His sword did ne'er leave striking in the field *1 Hen. VI.* i 4 80
By the sound of drum you may perceive Their powers are marching unto Paris-ward iii 3 29
Hark! hark! the Dauphin's drum, a warning bell iv 2 39
Hang up your ensigns, let your drums be still v 4 174
Sound drums and trumpets, and to London all *2 Hen. VI.* v 3 32
Sound drums and trumpets, and the king will fly *3 Hen. VI.* i 1 118
I hear their drums: let's set our men in order i 2 70
Then strike up drums: God and Saint George for us! ii 1 204
Then Clarence is at hand; I hear his drum v 1 11
The drum your honour hears marcheth from Warwick v 1 13
Strike up the drum; cry 'Courage!' and away v 3 24
Sound drums and trumpets! farewell sour annoy! v 7 45
I hear his drum: be copious in exclaims *Richard III.* iv 4 135
A flourish, trumpets! strike alarum, drums! iv 4 148
Strike up the drum.—I prithee, hear me speak iv 4 179
Sound drums and trumpets boldly and cheerfully v 3 269
Hark! I hear their drum. Fight, gentlemen of England! fight, bold yeomen! v 3 337
Hark, hark! what shout is that?—Peace, drums! *Troi. and Cres.* v 9 2
Methinks I hear hither your husband's drum *Coriolanus* i 3 32
He had rather see the swords, and hear a drum, than look upon his schoolmaster i 3 61
Hark! our drums Are bringing forth our youth i 4 15
'Tis not a mile; briefly we heard their drums i 6 16
When drums and trumpets shall I' the field prove flatterers i 9 42
Some certain of your brethren roar'd and ran From the noise of our own drums ii 3 60
My throat of war be turn'd, Which quired with my drum, into a pipe Small as an eunuch! iii 2 113
You shall have the drum struck up this afternoon iv 5 230
Beat thou the drum, that it speak mournfully: Trail your steel pikes v 6 151
Proclaim our honours, lords, with trump and drum *T. Andron.* i 1 275
And then anon Drums in his ear, at which he starts and wakes *R. and J.* i 4 86
Ha! a drum? Thou'rt quick, But yet I'll bury thee *T. of Athens* iv 3 44
Follow thy drum; With man's blood paint the ground, gules, gules iv 3 58
I prithee, beat thy drum, and get thee gone iv 3 96
Strike up the drum towards Athens! Farewell, Timon iv 3 169
The enemies' drum is heard, and fearful scouring Doth choke the air with dust: in, and prepare v 2 15
A drum, a drum! Macbeth doth come *Macbeth* i 3 30
Why does the drum come hither? *Hamlet* v 2 372
Bid them come forth and hear me, Or at their chamber-door I'll beat the drum Till it cry sleep to death *Lear* ii 4 119
Where's thy drum? France spreads his banners in our noiseless land iv 2 55
Give me your hand: Far off, methinks, I hear the beaten drum iv 6 292
Let the drum strike, and prove my title thine v 3 81
The shrill trump, The spirit-stirring drum, the ear-piercing fife *Othello* iii 3 352
But to confound such time, That drums him from his sport *Ant. and Cleo.* i 4 29
Hark! the drums Demurely wake the sleepers iv 9 30
Drumble. Look, how you drumble! *Mer. Wives* iii 3 156
Drummer, strike up, and let us march away *3 Hen. VI.* iv 7 50
Drumming. I'll no more drumming; a plague of all drums! *All's Well* iv 3 331
Drunk. 'Scape being drunk for want of wine *Tempest* ii 1 146
If he have never drunk wine afore, it will go near to remove his fit ii 2 78
Was there ever man a coward that hath drunk so much sack as I to-day? iii 2 31
He is drunk now: where had he wine? v 1 278
I cannot remember what I did when you made me drunk *Mer. Wives* i 1 175
The gentleman had drunk himself out of his five sentences i 1 179
I'll ne'er be drunk whilst I live again, but in honest, civil, godly company i 1 186
If I be drunk, I'll be drunk with those that have the fear of God i 1 188
He would be drunk too; that let me inform you *Meas. for Meas.* iii 2 136
Drunk many times a day, if not many days entirely drunk iv 2 157
Yet my husband Knows not that ever he knew me.—He was drunk then v 1 188
I think you all have drunk of Circe's cup *Com. of Errors* v 1 270
You are to call at all the ale-houses, and bid those that are drunk get them to bed *Much Ado* iii 3 45
Patch grief with proverbs, make misfortune drunk With candle-wasters v 1 17
I have drunk poison whiles he utter'd it v 1 253
He hath not eat paper, as it were; he hath not drunk ink *L. L. Lost* iv 2 27
Most vilely in the afternoon, when he is drunk *Mer. of Venice* i 2 94
What's here? one dead, or drunk? See, doth he breathe? *T. of Shrew* Ind. 1 31
There's one grape yet; I am sure thy father drunk wine *All's Well* ii 3 106
He's drunk nightly in your company *T. Night* i 3 38
By mine honour, half drunk i 5 124
O, he's drunk, Sir Toby, an hour agone v 1 204
Make known How he hath drunk, he cracks his gorge, his sides, With violent hefts *W. Tale* ii 1 44
I have drunk, and seen the spider ii 1 45
I'll swear to the prince thou art a tall fellow of thy hands and that thou wilt not be drunk; but I know thou art no tall fellow of thy hands and that thou wilt be drunk v 2 178
Where hath our intelligence been drunk? Where hath it slept? *K. John* iv 2 116
Is not my teeming date drunk up with time? *Richard II.* v 2 91
What, drunk with choler? stay and pause awhile *1 Hen. IV.* i 3 129
It could not be else; I have drunk medicines ii 2 21
Give me a cup of sack: I am a rogue, if I drunk to-day ii 4 168

Drunk. But the sack that thou hast drunk me would have bought me lights . . . . . . *1 Hen. IV.* iii 3 50
You have drunk too much canaries . . . *2 Hen. IV.* ii 4 29
Have you turned him out o' doors?—Yea, sir. The rascal's drunk . ii 4 230
By the mass, I have drunk too much sack at supper . . v 3 15
Never broke any man's head but his own, and that was against a post when he was drunk . . . . *Hen. V.* iii 2 44
Thy brother's blood the thirsty earth hath drunk *3 Hen. VI.* ii 3 15
England's lawful earth, Unlawfully made drunk with innocents' blood! *Richard III.* iv 4 30
Stands alone.—So do all men, unless they are drunk, sick, or have no legs . . . . . . *Troi. and Cres.* i 2 17
My ears have not yet drunk a hundred words Of that tongue's utterance, yet I know the sound . . *Rom. and Jul.* ii 2 58
There on the ground, with his own tears made drunk . . iii 3 83
O churl! drunk all, and left no friendly drop To help me after? . v 3 163
Was the hope drunk Wherein you dress'd yourself . *Macbeth* i 7 35
That which hath made them drunk hath made me bold . . ii 2 1
When he is drunk asleep, or in his rage . . . *Hamlet* iii 3 89
I have drunk but one cup to-night, and that was craftily qualified *Othello* ii 3 40
If I can fasten but one cup upon him, With that which he hath drunk ii 3 51
Why, he drinks you, with facility, your Dane dead drunk . ii 3 85
Do not think, gentlemen, I am drunk . . . . ii 3 118
I am not drunk now; I can stand well enough, and speak well enough ii 3 119
Why, very well then; you must not think then that I am drunk . ii 3 123
Come, come, you're drunk.—Drunk! . . . . ii 3 156
Drunk? and speak parrot? and squabble? swagger? swear? . ii 3 280
I drunk!—You or any man living may be drunk at a time, man ii 3 317
Fools as gross As ignorance made drunk . . . . iii 3 405
Mine, and most of our fortunes, to-night, shall be—drunk to bed *Ant. and Cleo.* i 2 46
And next morn, Ere the ninth hour, I drunk him to his bed . . ii 5 21
Hast thou drunk well?—No, Pompey, I have kept me from the cup . ii 7 71
A' bears the third part of the world, man; see'st not?—The third part, then, is drunk . . . . ii 7 98
The king my father, sir, has drunk to you.—I thank him *Pericles* ii 3 75
If thou hadst drunk to him, 't had been a kindness Becoming well thy fact . . . . iv 3 11
Drunkard. We are merely cheated of our lives by drunkards . *Tempest* iii 1 59
A most ridiculous monster, to make a wonder of a poor drunkard! . ii 2 170
What a thrice-double ass Was I, to take this drunkard for a god! . v 1 296
What an unweighed behaviour hath this Flemish drunkard picked? *Mer. Wives* ii 1 24
Thou drunkard, thou, what didst thou mean by this? . *Com. of Errors* iii 1 10
I will, like a true drunkard, utter all to thee . . *Much Ado* iii 3 112
One drunkard loves another of the name . . . *L. L. Lost* iv 3 50
Betray themselves to every modern censure worse than drunkards *As Y. Like It* iv 1 7
Conduct him to the drunkard's chamber . . . *T. of Shrew* Ind. 1 107
Such duty to the drunkard let him do . . . . Ind. 1 113
I long to hear him call the drunkard husband . . . . Ind. 1 133
'Rivo!' says the drunkard. Call in ribs, call in tallow . . *1 Hen. IV.* ii 4 124
For why my bowels cannot hide her woes, But like a drunkard must I vomit them . . . . . *T. Andron.* iii 1 232
Flecked darkness like a drunkard reels From forth day's path *R. and J.* ii 3 3
They clepe us drunkards, and with swinish phrase Soil our addition *Ham.* i 4 19
Drunkards, liars, and adulterers, by an enforced obedience of planetary influence . . . . *Lear* i 2 134
I have seen drunkards Do more than this in sport . . . ii 1 36
'Mongst this flock of drunkards, Am I to put our Cassio in some action That may offend the isle . . . . . *Othello* ii 3 61
I will ask him for my place again; he shall tell me I am a drunkard! . ii 3 307
Drunken. By this light, a most perfidious and drunken monster! *Tempest* ii 2 154
A howling monster; a drunken monster! . . . . ii 2 183
Is not this Stephano, my drunken butler? . . . . v 1 277
If I be drunk, I'll be drunk with those that have the fear of God, and not with drunken knaves . . . . *Mer. Wives* i 1 190
Apprehends death no more dreadfully but as a drunken sleep *M. for M.* iv 2 150
Thou drunken slave, I sent thee for a rope . . *Com. of Errors* iv 1 96
I will practise on this drunken man . . . . *T. of Shrew* Ind. 1 36
What's a drunken man like, fool?—Like a drowned man, a fool and a mad man . . . . *T. Night* i 5 138
He's a rogue, and a passy measures panyn: I hate a drunken rogue . v 1 207
You have put me into darkness and given your drunken cousin rule over me . . . . v 1 312
With toss-pots still had drunken heads . . . . . v 1 412
Then let the earth be drunken with our blood . . *3 Hen. VI.* ii 3 23
Plots have I laid, inductions dangerous, By drunken prophecies *Rich. III.* i 1 33
Your carters or your waiting-vassals Have done a drunken slaughter . ii 1 122
Like a drunken sailor on a mast, Ready, with every nod, to tumble down . . . . iii 4 101
When our vaults have wept With drunken spilth of wine *T. of Athens* ii 2 169
So slight, so drunken, and so indiscreet an officer . . *Othello* ii 3 280
Antony Shall be brought drunken forth . . *Ant. and Cleo.* v 2 219
What a drunken knave was the sea to cast thee in our way! . *Pericles* ii 1 61
Drunkenly. And drunkenly caroused . . . . *Richard II.* ii 1 127
Drunkenness is his best virtue, for he will be swine-drunk . *All's Well* iv 3 285
You must amend your drunkenness . . . . . *T. Night* ii 5 81
I hate ingratitude more in a man Than lying, vainness, babbling, drunkenness, Or any taint of vice . . . . . . iii 4 389
It hath pleased the devil drunkenness to give place to the devil wrath *Othello* ii 3 297
Drunkest. Thy lips are scarce wiped since thou drunkest last *1 Hen. IV.* ii 4 171
Dry. So dry he was for sway . . . . . . *Tempest* i 2 112
If the river were dry, I am able to fill it with my tears . *T. G. of Ver.* ii 3 58
Write till your ink be dry, and with your tears Moist it again . . iii 2 75
The duke comes home to-morrow; nay, dry your eyes . *Meas. for Meas.* iv 3 132
This I think, When they are thirsty, fools would fain have drink.—This jest is dry to me . . . . *L. L. Lost* v 2 373
Swearing till my very roof was dry With oaths of love *Mer. of Venice* iii 2 206
His brain, Which is as dry as the remainder biscuit After a voyage *As Y. Like It* ii 7 39
A lioness, with udders all drawn dry, Lay couching . . . . iv 3 115
None so dry or thirsty Will deign to sip or touch one drop of it *T. of Shrew* v 2 144
What's your metaphor?—It's dry, sir.—Why, I think so . *T. Night* i 3 77
I am not such an ass but I can keep my hand dry . . . . i 3 79
Give the dry fool drink, then is the fool not dry . . . . i 5 49
The want of which vain dew Perchance shall dry your pities . *W. Tale* ii 1 110
The statue is but newly fix'd, the colour's Not dry . . . . v 3 48
Dry. Your sorrow was too sore laid on, Which sixteen winters cannot blow away, So many summers dry . . . . . *W. Tale* v 3 51
The task he undertakes Is numbering sands and drinking oceans dry *Richard II.* ii 2 146
Dry your eyes; Tears show their love, but want their remedies . . iii 3 202
When I was dry with rage and extreme toil . . . *1 Hen. IV.* i 3 31
These six dry, round, old, withered knights . . *2 Hen. IV.* ii 4 8
When I have been dry and bravely marching, it hath served me *2 Hen. VI.* iv 10 14
I give thee this to dry thy cheeks withal . . . *3 Hen. VI.* i 4 83
Think but upon the wrong he did us all, And that will quickly dry thy melting tears . . . . ii 4 174
The ruthless queen gave him to dry his cheeks A napkin . . . iii 1 61
And chides the sea that sunders him from thence, Saying, he'll lade it dry . . . . iii 2 139
Now stops thy spring; my sea shall suck them dry . . . iv 8 55
The very beams will dry those vapours up . . . . . v 3 12
And bid her dry her weeping eyes therewith . . *Richard III.* iv 4 278
Thou hast forced me, Out of thy honest truth, to play the woman. Let's dry our eyes . . . . *Hen. VIII.* iii 2 431
Were his brain as barren As banks of Libya,—though, Apollo knows, 'Tis dry enough . . . . *Troi. and Cres.* i 3 329
Force him with praises: pour in, pour in; his ambition is dry . . ii 3 234
Behold our cheeks How they are stain'd, as meadows, yet not dry *T. Andron.* iii 1 125
Patience, dear niece. Good Titus, dry thine eyes . . . . iii 1 138
Now, ere the sun advance his burning eye, The day to cheer and night's dank dew to dry . . . . *Rom. and Jul.* ii 3 6
Wash they his wounds with tears: mine shall be spent, When theirs are dry . . . . iii 2 131
Dry up your tears, and stick your rosemary On this fair corse . . iv 5 79
Dry up thy marrows, vines, and plough-torn leas! . . *T. of Athens* iv 3 193
I will drain him dry as hay . . . . . . *Macbeth* i 3 18
It is but squeezing you, and, sponge, you shall be dry again . *Hamlet* iv 2 22
O heat, dry up my brains! . . . . iv 5 154
When in your motion you are hot and dry . . . . . iv 7 158
Dry up in her the organs of increase . . . . . *Lear* i 4 301
The lion and the belly-pinched wolf Keep their fur dry . . . iii 1 14
Poor Tom, thy horn is dry . . . . iii 6 79
The sweat of industry would dry and die, But for the end it works to *Cymbeline* iii 6 31
Dry antiquity. Under an oak, whose boughs were moss'd with age And high top bald with dry antiquity . . . . *As Y. Like It* iv 3 106
Dry appetite. Let my tears stanch the earth's dry appetite *T. Andron.* iii 1 14
Dry basting. And purchase me another dry basting *Com. of Errors* ii 2 64
Dry-beat. One of your nine lives; that I mean to make bold withal, and, as you shall use me hereafter, dry-beat the rest of the eight *Rom. and Jul.* iii 1 82
I will dry-beat you with an iron wit, and put up my iron dagger . iv 5 126
Dry-beaten. All dry-beaten with pure scoff! . . . *L. L. Lost* v 2 263
Dry cheese. That stale old mouse-eaten dry cheese, Nestor *Troi. and Cres.* v 4 11
Dry convulsions. Grind their joints With dry convulsions *Tempest* iv 1 260
Dry death. I would fain die a dry death . . . . . . i 1 71
Dry fool. Go to, you're a dry fool; I'll no more of you . . *T. Night* i 5 45
Give the dry fool drink, then is the fool not dry . . . . i 5 48
Dry-foot. A hound that runs counter and yet draws dry-foot well *Com. of Errors* iv 2 39
Dry hand. Here's his dry hand up and down . . . *Much Ado* ii 1 123
Have you not a moist eye? a dry hand? a yellow cheek? *2 Hen. IV.* i 2 204
Dry house. Court holy-water in a dry house is better than this rain-water out o' door . . . . *Lear* iii 2 10
Dry jest. But what's your jest?—A dry jest, sir . . . *T. Night* i 3 81
Dry nurse. In the manner of his nurse, or his dry nurse *Mer. Wives* i 2 4
Dry oats. I could munch your good dry oats . . . *M. N. Dream* iv 1 36
Dry serpigo. Now, the dry serpigo on the subject! . . *Troi. and Cres.* ii 3 80
Dry sorrow drinks our blood . . . . . . *Rom. and Jul.* iii 5 59
Dry stubble. This . . . will be his fire To kindle their dry stubble *Cor.* ii 1 274
Dry toasts. As rheumatic as two dry toasts . . . *2 Hen. IV.* ii 4 63
Dry wheel. I had rather hear a brazen canstick turn'd, Or a dry wheel grate on the axle-tree . . . . . . *1 Hen. IV.* iii 1 132
Dryness. Full surfeits, and the dryness of his bones, Call on him for't *Ant. and Cleo.* i 4 27
Dub. Do me right, And dub me knight: Samingo . . *2 Hen. IV.* v 3 78
To dub thee with the name of traitor . . . . . *Hen. V.* ii 2 120
Unsheathe your sword, and dub him presently . . *3 Hen. VI.* ii 2 59
Dubbed with unhatched rapier and on carpet consideration *T. Night* iii 4 257
I am dubb'd! I have it on my shoulder . . . . *K. John* i 1 245
Five hundred were but yesterday dubb'd knights . . *Hen. V.* iv 8 91
Since that our brother dubb'd them gentlewomen, Are mighty gossips in this monarchy . . . . *Richard III.* i 1 82
Ducat. I could perceive nothing at all from her; no, not so much as a ducat for delivering your letter . . . . . *T. G. of Ver.* i 1 145
His use was to put a ducat in her clack-dish . . *Meas. for Meas.* iii 2 134
Which doth amount to three odd ducats more . . *Com. of Errors* iv 1 30
In the desk That's cover'd o'er with Turkish tapestry There is a purse of ducats; let her send it . . . . iv 1 105
A ring he hath of mine worth forty ducats . . . . . iv 3 84
This course I fittest choose; For forty ducats is too much to lose . . iv 3 97
Five hundred ducats, villain, for a rope? . . . . . . iv 4 13
Went'st not thou to her for a purse of ducats? . . . . . iv 4 90
What is the sum he owes?—Two hundred ducats . . . . iv 4 137
I did obey, and sent my peasant home For certain ducats . . . v 1 232
This purse of ducats I received from you . . . . . . v 1 385
These ducats pawn I for my father here . . . . . . v 1 389
And thy fee is a thousand ducats . . . . . . *Much Ado* ii 2 54
I have earned of Don John a thousand ducats . . . . . iii 3 116
Received a thousand ducats of Don John for accusing the Lady Hero . iv 2 50
Three thousand ducats; well.—Ay, sir, for three months *Mer. of Venice* i 3 1
Three thousand ducats for three months and Antonio bound . . . i 3 9
Three thousand ducats; I think I may take his bond . . . . i 3 27
I cannot instantly raise up the gross Of full three thousand ducats . i 3 57
Three thousand ducats; 'tis a good round sum . . . . . i 3 104
Is it possible A cur can lend three thousand ducats? . . . . i 3 123
Give him direction for this merry bond, And I will go and purse the ducats . . . . i 3 175
But fare thee well, there is a ducat for thee . . . . . . ii 3 4
I will make fast the doors, and gild myself With some more ducats . ii 6 50
My daughter! O my ducats! O my daughter! . . . . . . ii 8 15
O my Christian ducats! Justice! the law! my ducats, and my daughter! . . . . ii 8 16

Ducat. A sealed bag, two sealed bags of ducats, Of double ducats, stolen from me! . . . . . . ii 8 18
Find the girl; She hath the stones upon her, and the ducats . . ii 8 22
Why, all the boys in Venice follow him, Crying, his stones, his daughter, and his ducats . . . . . . ii 8 24
A diamond gone, cost me two thousand ducats! . . . . . iii 1 88
Two thousand ducats in that; and other precious, precious jewels . iii 1 91
Would she were hearsed at my foot, and the ducats in her coffin! . iii 1 94
Fourscore ducats at a sitting! fourscore ducats! . . . . iii 1 116
We'll play with them the first boy for a thousand ducats . . . iii 2 217
What sum owes he the Jew?—For me three thousand ducats . . iii 2 300
You'll ask me, why I rather choose to have A weight of carrion flesh than to receive Three thousand ducats . . . . . iv 1 42
What if my house be troubled with a rat And I be pleased to give ten thousand ducats To have it baned? . . . . . iv 1 45
For thy three thousand ducats here is six . . . . . iv 1 84
If every ducat in six thousand ducats Were in six parts and every part a ducat, I would not draw them . . . . . iv 1 85
In lieu whereof, Three thousand ducats, due unto the Jew . . . iv 1 411
A civil doctor, Which did refuse three thousand ducats of me . . v 1 211
Besides two thousand ducats by the year Of fruitful land *T. of Shrew* ii 1 371
He has three thousand ducats a year.—Ay, but he'll have but a year in all these ducats . . . . . . *T. Night* i 3 22
I see that thou art poor: Hold, there is forty ducats *Rom. and Jul.* v 1 59
Give twenty, forty, fifty, an hundred ducats a-piece for his picture *Ham.* ii 2 383
How now! a rat? Dead, for a ducat, dead! . . . . . iii 4 23
To pay five ducats, five, I would not farm it . . . . . iv 4 20
Two thousand souls and twenty thousand ducats Will not debate the question of this straw . . . . iv 4 25
I will lay you ten thousand ducats to your ring . . *Cymbeline* i 4 138
My ten thousand ducats are yours; so is your diamond too . . i 4 163
Ducdame, ducdame, ducdame: Here shall he see Gross fools *As Y. Like It* ii 5 56
What's that 'ducdame'?—'Tis a Greek invocation, to call fools into a circle . . . . ii 5 60
Duchess. I saw the Duchess of Milan's gown that they praise so *M. Ado* iii 4 16
In our interlude before the duke and the duchess . . *M. N. Dream* i 2 6
You would fright the duchess and the ladies, that they would shriek . i 2 77
An hour before I came, the duchess died.—God for his mercy! *Rich. II.* ii 2 97
Hume must make merry with the duchess' gold . . *2 Hen. VI.* i 2 87
Have hired me to undermine the duchess . . . . . . i 2 98
At last Hume's knavery will be the duchess' wreck . . . . i 2 105
The duchess, I tell you, expects performance of your promises . . i 4 1
Ten is the hour that was appointed me To watch the coming of my punish'd duchess . . . . ii 4 7
Whilst I, his forlorn duchess, Was made a wonder and a pointing-stock ii 4 45
And shall I then be used reproachfully?—Like to a duchess . . ii 4 98
The duchess by his subornation, Upon my life, began her devilish practices . . . . iii 1 45
Such high vaunts of his nobility Did instigate the bedlam brain-sick duchess . . . . iii 1 51
He was lately sent From your kind aunt, Duchess of Burgundy *3 Hen. VI.* ii 1 146
What think you of a duchess? have you limbs To bear that load of title?—No, in truth . . . . . *Hen. VIII.* ii 3 38
By this time I know your back will bear a duchess: say, Are you not stronger than you were? . . . . ii 3 99
She that carries up the train Is that old noble lady, Duchess of Norfolk iv 1 52
The old Duchess of Norfolk, and Lady Marquess Dorset . . . v 3 169
Duchies. The duchies of Anjou and Maine shall be released . *2 Hen. VI.* i 1 58
Duchy. The duchy of Anjou and the county of Maine shall be released . i 1 50
Hath given the duchy of Anjou and Maine Unto the poor King Reignier i 1 110
Duck. Swum ashore, man, like a duck: I can swim like a duck, I'll be sworn . . . . *Tempest* ii 2 132
Though thou canst swim like a duck, thou art made like a goose . . ii 2 135
Eyes, do you see? How can it be? O dainty duck! O dear! *M. N. D.* v 1 286
My dainty duck, my dear-a . . . . . . *W. Tale* iv 4 324
And hold-fast is the only dog, my duck . . . . *Hen. V.* ii 3 54
Smooth, deceive and cog, Duck with French nods . *Richard III.* i 3 49
The falcon as the tercel, for all the ducks i' the river *Troi. and Cres.* iii 2 56
Ah, sweet ducks! . . . . iv 4 12
The learned pate Ducks to the golden fool . . *T. of Athens* iv 3 18
Let the labouring bark climb hills of seas Olympus-high and duck again as low As hell's from heaven! . . . . . . *Othello* ii 1 190
As a duck for life that dives, So up and down the poor ship drives *Pericles* iii Gower 49
Ducking. Harbour more craft and more corrupter ends Than twenty silly ducking observants That stretch their duties nicely . . *Lear* ii 2 109
Dudgeon. I see thee still, And on thy blade and dudgeon gouts of blood, Which was not so before . . . . . *Macbeth* ii 1 46
Due. Imprison him: if imprisonment be the due of a bawd *Meas. for Meas.* iii 2 70
I have ta'en a due and wary note upon't . . . . . iv 1 38
So that my errand, due unto my tongue, I thank him, I bare home upon my shoulders . . . . . . *Com. of Errors* ii 1 72
How besides thyself?—Marry, sir, besides myself, I am due to a woman iii 2 81
Since Pentecost the sum is due, And since I have not much importuned you . . . . iv 1 1
How grows it due?—Due for a chain your husband had of him . . iv 4 137
Fair payment for foul words is more than due . . *L. L. Lost* iv 1 19
Pay him the due of honey-tongued Boyet . . . . . v 2 334
With cunning hast thou filch'd my daughter's heart, Turn'd her obedience, which is due to me . . . . . *M. N. Dream* i 1 37
It is a customary cross, As due to love as thoughts and dreams and sighs i 1 154
Like coats in heraldry, Due but to one and crowned with one crest . iii 2 214
To have the due and forfeit of my bond . . . *Mer. of Venice* iv 1 37
The penalty, Which here appeareth due upon the bond . . . iv 1 249
In lieu whereof, Three thousand ducats, due unto the Jew . . . iv 1 411
The great prerogative and rite of love, Which, as your due, time claims, he does acknowledge . . . . *All's Well* ii 4 43
'Tis a saying, sir, not due to me . . . . . *W. Tale* ii 2 59
I'll give thee thy due, thou hast paid all there . . . *1 Hen. IV.* i 2 59
He was never yet a breaker of proverbs: he will give the devil his due i 2 133
'Tis not due yet; I would be loath to pay him before his day . . v 1 128
Look to taste the due Meet for rebellion and such acts as yours *2 Hen. IV.* iv 2 116
Thy due from me Is tears and heavy sorrows of the blood . . . iv 5 37
My due from thee is this imperial crown . . . . . iv 5 41
I will take up that with 'Give the devil his due' . . . *Hen. V.* iii 7 127
The latest glory of thy praise That I, thy enemy, due thee withal *1 Hen. VI.* iv 2 34
Thy honour, state and seat is due to me . . . . *Richard III.* i 3 112
Your state of fortune and your due of birth . . . . . iii 7 120
As my ripe revenue and due by birth . . . . . . iii 7 158
I claim your gift, my due by promise . . . . . . iv 2 91
Due. Woe's scene, world's shame, grave's due by life usurp'd *Rich. III.* iv 4 27
Wrong hath but wrong, and blame the due of blame . . . . v 1 29
Not ever The justice and the truth o' the question carries The due o' the verdict with it . . . . *Hen. VIII.* v 1 131
The primogenitive and due of birth, Prerogative of age *Troi. and Cres.* i 3 106
Nature craves All dues be render'd to their owners . . . . ii 2 174
I am your debtor, claim it when 'tis due . . . . . . iv 5 51
To such as boasting show their scars A mock is due . . . . iv 5 291
My lord, here is a note of certain dues.—Dues! Whence are you? *T. of A.* ii 2 16
'Twas due on forfeiture, my lord, six weeks And past . . . . ii 2 30
What remains will hardly stop the mouth Of present dues . . . ii 2 157
Give't these fellows To whom 'tis instant due . . . . . ii 2 239
A towardly prompt spirit—give thee thy due . . . . . iii 1 37
More is thy due than more than all can pay . . . . *Macbeth* i 4 21
That thou mightst not lose the dues of rejoicing . . . . . i 5 13
The son of Duncan, From whom this tyrant holds the due of birth . iii 6 25
The general cause? or is it a fee-grief Due to some single breast? . iv 3 197
Thou better know'st The offices of nature, bond of childhood, Effects of courtesy, dues of gratitude . . . . *Lear* ii 4 182
To thee a woman's services are due: My fool usurps my body . . iv 2 27
So much I challenge that I may profess Due to the Moor . *Othello* i 3 189
The due of honour in no point omit . . . . . *Cymbeline* iii 5 11
But if you will not, The hazard therefore due fall on me! . . . iv 4 46
Why hast thou thus adjourn'd The graces for his merits due? . . v 4 79
Egregious murderer, thief, any thing That's due to all the villains past, in being, To come! . . . . v 5 212
Due to this heinous capital offence . . . . . . *Pericles* ii 4 5
You have heard Of monstrous lust the due and just reward . . v 3 Gower 86
Due action. I cannot give due action to my words, Except a sword or sceptre balance it . . . . *2 Hen. VI.* v 1 8
Due content. We shall jointly labour with your soul To give it due content . . . . *Hamlet* iv 5 212
Due course. Proceed in justice, which shall have due course . *W. Tale* iii 2 6
So appears this fleet majestical, Holding due course to Harfleur *Hen. V.* iii Prol. 17
Admit the excuse Of time, of numbers and due course of things . v Prol. 4
Steering with due course towards the isle of Rhodes . . *Othello* i 3 34
Due debt. Let us bury him, And not protract with admiration what Is now due debt . . . . *Cymbeline* iv 2 233
Due decision. The time approaches That will with due decision make us know . . . . *Macbeth* v 4 17
Due diligence. With all due diligence . . . . *Pericles* iii Gower 19
Due expedience. With all due expedience . . . *Richard II.* ii 1 287
Due fees. At our enlargement what are thy due fees? . *3 Hen. VI.* iv 6 5
Due functions. But in short time All offices of nature should again Do their due functions . . . . *Cymbeline* v 5 258
Due note. That all the kingdom May have due note of him . . *Lear* ii 1 85
Due observance. With due observance of thy godlike seat *Troi. and Cres.* i 3 31
Due on. Ne'er feels retiring ebb, but keeps due on . . . *Othello* iii 3 455
Due orders. Ere you can take due orders for a priest . *2 Hen. VI.* iii 1 274
Due proportion. Why should we in the compass of a pale Keep law and form and due proportion? . . . . . . *Richard II.* iii 4 41
Due reference. I crave fit disposition for my wife, Due reference of place and exhibition . . . . *Othello* i 3 238
Due resolution. I would unstate myself, to be in a due resolution *Lear* i 2 108
Due reverence. In the due reverence of a sacred vow . . *Othello* iii 3 461
Due sincerity. A due sincerity govern'd his deeds, Till he did look on me *Meas. for Meas.* v 1 451
Due turns. Shall our abode Make with you by due turns . . *Lear* i 1 137
Due west. There lies your way, due west . . . *T. Night* iii 1 145
Duellist. The very butcher of a silk button, a duellist . *Rom. and Jul.* ii 4 24
Duello. The passado he respects not, the duello he regards not *L. L. Lost* i 2 185
He cannot by the duello avoid it . . . . . . *T. Night* iii 4 337
Duer paid. Every third word a lie, duer paid to the hearer than the Turk's tribute . . . . *2 Hen. IV.* iii 2 330
Duff. Dear Duff, I prithee, contradict thyself, And say it is not so *Macbeth* ii 3 94
Dug. I remember the kissing of her batlet and the cow's dugs that her pretty chopt hands had milked . . . . . *As Y. Like It* ii 4 50
Shall thy old dugs once more a traitor rear? . . . *Richard II.* v 3 90
As mild and gentle as the cradle-babe Dying with mother's dug between its lips . . . . *2 Hen. VI.* iii 2 393
Yet from my dugs he drew not this deceit . . . *Richard III.* ii 2 30
I had then laid wormwood to my dug . . . . *Rom. and Jul.* i 3 26
When it did taste the wormwood on the nipple Of my dug and felt it bitter, pretty fool, To see it tetchy and fall out with the dug! . . i 3 31
He did comply with his dug, before he sucked it . . . *Hamlet* v 2 195
Which sleeps, and never palates more the dug . . . *Ant. and Cleo.* v 2 7
Duke. Thy father was the Duke of Milan . . . . . *Tempest* i 2 54
She said thou wast my daughter; and thy father Was Duke of Milan . i 2 58
Prospero the prime duke, being so reputed In dignity . . . . i 2 72
He did believe He was indeed the duke . . . . . . i 2 103
The Duke of Milan And his brave son being twain . . . . i 2 437
The Duke of Milan And his more braver daughter could control thee . i 2 438
Brother, my lord the duke, Stand to and do as we . . . . iii 3 51
Behold, sir king, The wronged Duke of Milan, Prospero . . . v 1 107
I am Prospero and that very duke Which was thrust forth of Milan . v 1 159
A lady, An heir, and near allied unto the duke . . *T. G. of Ver.* iv 1 49
Three or four gentlemanlike dogs, under the duke's table . . . iv 4 20
'Whip him out,' says the third: 'Hang him up,' says the duke . . iv 4 24
Forbear, forbear, I say! it is my lord the duke . . . . . v 4 122
The duke himself will be to-morrow at court, and they are going to meet him . . . . *Mer. Wives* iv 3 2
What duke should that be comes so secretly? . . . . . . iv 3 5
They are gone but to meet the duke . . . . iv 5 72
It is tell-a me dat you make grand preparation for a duke de Jamany . iv 5 88
By my trot, dere is no duke dat the court is know to come . . . iv 5 89
If the duke with the other dukes come not to composition with the King of Hungary, why then all the dukes fall upon the king *Meas. for Meas.* i 2 1
The new deputy now for the duke . . . Awakes me all the enrolled penalties . . . . i 2 161
Send after the duke and appeal to him.—I have done so . . . . i 2 178
The duke is very strangely gone from hence . . . . . . i 4 50
I am the poor duke's constable, and my name is Elbow . . . . ii 1 48
Let not your worship think me the poor duke's officer . . . . ii 1 186
But, O, how much is the good duke deceived in Angelo! . . . . iii 1 197
Do no stain to your own gracious person; and much please the absent duke iii 1 209
What news, friar, of the duke?—I know none . . . . . . iii 2 91
Lord Angelo dukes it well in his absence; he puts transgression to't . iii 2 100
Would the duke that is absent have done this? . . . . . iii 2 123
I never heard the absent duke much detected for women . . . . iii 2 129
You are deceived.—'Tis not possible.—Who, not the duke? . . . iii 2 133

Duke. The duke had crotchets in him. He would be drunk too *Meas. for Meas.* iii 2 135
I was an inward of his. A shy fellow was the duke . . . iii 2 139
The greater file of the subject held the duke to be wise . . . . iii 2 145
If ever the duke return, as our prayers are he may . . . . iii 2 163
My name is Lucio; well known to the duke.—He shall know you better iii 2 170
O, you hope the duke will return no more . . . . iii 2 174
I would the duke we talk of were returned again . . . iii 2 183
The duke yet would have dark deeds darkly answered . . . iii 2 187
The duke, I say to thee again, would eat mutton on Fridays . . iii 2 191
Mistress Kate Keepdown was with child by him in the duke's time . iii 2 212
I pray you, sir, of what disposition was the duke? . . . . iii 2 245
How came it that the absent duke had not either delivered him to his liberty or executed him? . . . . iv 2 136
Were you sworn to the duke, or to the deputy? . . . . . iv 2 196
You have made no offence, if the duke avouch the justice of your dealing iv 2 200
Here is the hand and seal of the duke: you know the character . iv 2 208
The contents of this is the return of the duke . . . . . iv 2 212
Perchance of the duke's death; perchance entering into some monastery iv 2 216
The duke comes home to-morrow; nay, dry your eyes . . . iv 3 132
This letter, then, to Friar Peter give; 'Tis that he sent me of the duke's return . . . . iv 3 143
I'll perfect him withal, and he shall bring you Before the duke . iv 3 147
But they say the duke will be here to-morrow . . . . . iv 3 162
If the old fantastical duke of dark corners had been at home . . iv 3 164
The duke is marvellous little beholding to your reports . . . iv 3 166
Thou knowest not the duke so well as I do . . . . . iv 3 169
I can tell thee pretty tales of the duke . . . . . . iv 3 175
Where you may have such vantage on the duke, He shall not pass you iv 6 11
And very near upon The duke is entering . . . . . iv 6 15
Speak loud and kneel before him.—Justice, O royal duke! . . . v 1 20
O worthy duke, You bid me seek redemption of the devil . . v 1 28
O gracious duke, Harp not on that, nor do not banish reason For inequality . . . . v 1 63
And one that hath spoke most villanous speeches of the duke . . v 1 265
Where is the duke? 'tis he should hear me speak.—The duke's in us v 1 296
Is the duke gone? Then is your cause gone too. The duke's unjust . v 1 301
And then to glance from him To the duke himself, to tax him with injustice? . . . . v 1 312
The duke Dare no more stretch this finger of mine than he Dare rack his own . . . . v 1 315
I met you at the prison, in the absence of the duke . . . v 1 332
Do you remember what you said of the duke?—Most notedly, sir . . v 1 334
Was the duke a fleshmonger, a fool, and a coward, as you then reported? v 1 336
I protest I love the duke as I love myself . . . . . v 1 344
Thou art the first knave that e'er madest a duke . . . . v 1 361
Your highness said even now, I made you a duke . . . . v 1 522
Sprung from the rancorous outrage of your duke To merchants *Com. of Err.* i 1 6
His goods confiscate to the duke's dispose . . . . . i 1 21
And charge you in the duke's name to obey me . . . . iv 1 70
Complain unto the duke of this indignity . . . . . . v 1 113
The duke himself in person Comes this way to the melancholy vale . v 1 119
Kneel to the duke before he pass the abbey . . . . . v 1 129
Justice, most sacred duke, against the abbess! . . . . . v 1 133
Most gracious duke, with thy command Let him be brought forth . v 1 159
Justice, most gracious duke, O, grant me justice! . . . . v 1 190
This day, great duke, she shut the doors upon me . . . . v 1 204
Most mighty duke, vouchsafe me speak a word . . . . . v 1 282
The duke and all that know me in the city Can witness with me that it is not so . . . . v 1 323
Most mighty duke, behold a man much wrong'd . . . . . v 1 330
Renowned duke, vouchsafe to take the pains To go with us into the abbey v 1 393
The duke, my husband and my children both, . . . Go to a gossips' feast v 1 403
But we are the poor duke's officers . . . . . *Much Ado* iii 5 22
Which is the duke's own person?—This, fellow: what wouldst? *L. L. Lost* i 1 182
I have promised to study three years with the duke . . . . i 2 38
Sir, the duke's pleasure is, that you keep Costard safe . . . i 2 132
That are vow-fellows with this virtuous duke . . . . . ii 1 38
Happy be Theseus, our renowned duke! . . . . *M. N. Dream* i 1 20
My gracious duke, This man hath bewitch'd the bosom of my child . i 1 26
And, my gracious duke, Be it so she will not here before your grace Consent to marry . . . . i 1 38
To play in our interlude before the duke and the duchess . . . i 2 6
I will roar, that I will make the duke say 'Let him roar again' . . i 2 74
Adieu.—At the duke's oak we meet . . . . i 2 113
We will do it in action as we will do it before the duke . . . iii 1 6
Do not you think The duke was here, and bid us follow him? . . iv 1 200
I will sing it in the latter end of a play, before the duke . . . iv 1 224
Masters, the duke is coming from the temple . . . . . iv 2 15
An the duke had not given him sixpence a day for playing Pyramus, I'll be hanged . . . . iv 2 21
All that I will tell you is, that the duke hath dined . . . . iv 2 35
The villain Jew with outcries raised the duke . . . *Mer. of Venice* ii 8 4
But there the duke was given to understand That in a gondola were seen together Lorenzo and his amorous Jessica . . . . . . ii 8 7
Antonio certified the duke They were not with Bassanio in his ship . ii 8 10
He plies the duke at morning and at night . . . . . . iii 2 279
Twenty merchants, The duke himself, and the magnificoes Of greatest port, have all persuaded with him . . . . iii 2 282
Since I am a dog, beware my fangs: The duke shall grant me justice . iii 3 8
I am sure the duke Will never grant this forfeiture to hold . . iii 3 24
The duke cannot deny the course of law . . . . . . iii 3 26
The offender's life lies in the mercy Of the duke only . . . iv 1 356
Down therefore and beg mercy of the duke . . . . . iv 1 363
So please my lord the duke and all the court To quit the fine . . iv 1 380
Charles, the duke's wrestler . . . . . *As Y. Like It* i 1 94; i 2 134
The old duke is banished by his younger brother the new duke . . i 1 104
Whose lands and revenues enrich the new duke . . . . . i 1 108
Can you tell if Rosalind, the duke's daughter, be banished with her father?—O, no; for the duke's daughter, her cousin, so loves her . i 1 110
Where will the old duke live?—They say he is already in the forest of Arden . . . . i 1 119
What, you wrestle to-morrow before the new duke? . . . . i 1 127
If my uncle, thy banished father, had banished thy uncle, the duke my father . . . . i 2 11
We will make it our suit to the duke that the wrestling might not go forward . . . . i 2 193
Yet such is now the duke's condition That he misconstrues all . . i 2 276
The duke is humorous; what he is indeed, More suits you to conceive than I to speak of . . . . i 2 278

Duke. Which of the two was daughter of the duke That here was at the wrestling? . . . . *As Y. Like It* i 2 281
The lesser is his daughter: The other is daughter to the banish'd duke i 2 285
Of late this duke Hath ta'en displeasure 'gainst his gentle niece . . i 2 289
From tyrant duke unto a tyrant brother . . . . i 2 300
The duke my father loved his father dearly . . . . . . i 3 30
Look, here comes the duke.—With his eyes full of anger . . . i 3 41
Be cheerful: know'st thou not, the duke Hath banish'd me, his daughter? i 3 96
The bonny priser of the humorous duke . . . . . . ii 3 8
Cover the while; the duke will drink under this tree . . . ii 5 33
I'll go seek the duke: his banquet is prepared . . . . . ii 5 64
I am the duke That loved your father . . . . ii 7 195
He attends here in the forest on the duke your father . . . iii 4 36
I met the duke yesterday and had much question with him . . . iii 4 38
I must attend the duke at dinner: by two o'clock I will be with thee . iv 1 184
Let's present him to the duke, like a Roman conqueror . . . iv 2 3
He led me to the gentle duke, Who gave me fresh array . . . iv 3 143
Thither will I invite the duke and all's contented followers . . v 2 16
They shall be married to-morrow, and I will bid the duke to the nuptial v 2 47
Here come two of the banished duke's pages . . . . . v 3 6
Keep you your word, O duke, to give your daughter; You yours, Orlando v 4 19
Good duke, receive thy daughter: Hymen from heaven brought her . v 4 117
The duke hath put on a religious life . . . . v 4 187
And the duke, For private quarrel 'twixt your duke and him, Hath publish'd and proclaim'd it openly . . . . *T. of Shrew* iv 2 83
Lay hold on him, I charge you, in the duke's name . . . . v 1 92
From below your duke to beneath your constable . . . *All's Well* ii 2 32
The duke will lay upon him all the honour That good convenience claims iii 2 74
With his own hand he slew the duke's brother . . . . . iii 5 7
That is Antonio, the duke's eldest son; That, Escalus . . . . iii 5 79
The duke shall both speak of it, and extend to you what further becomes his greatness . . . . iii 6 72
Where's your master?—He met the duke in the street, sir . . . iv 3 89
The duke hath offered him letters of commendations to the king . . iv 3 91
I have congied with the duke, done my adieu with his nearest . . iv 3 100
Demand of him how many horse the duke is strong . . . . iv 3 149
Demand of him my condition, and what credit I have with the duke . iv 3 197
What is his reputation with the duke?—The duke knows him for no other but a poor officer of mine . . . . iv 3 224
Either it is there, or it is upon a file with the duke's other letters . iv 3 231
That is not the duke's letter, sir; that is an advertisement . . . iv 3 239
You have answered to his reputation with the duke and to his valour . iv 3 278
Who governs here?—A noble duke, in nature as in name . . *T. Night* i 2 25
She will admit no kind of suit, No, not the duke's . . . . . i 2 46
I'll serve this duke: Thou shalt present me as an eunuch to him . . i 2 55
If the duke continue these favours towards you . . . . . i 4 1
By this brave duke came early to his grave . . . . *K. John* ii 1 5
Welcome before the gates of Angiers, duke . . . . . . ii 1 17
Hast thou sounded him, If he appeal the duke on ancient malice? *Rich. II.* i 1 9
Let the trumpets sound While we return these dukes what we decree . i 3 122
The Duke of Lancaster is dead.—And living too; for now his son is duke ii 1 224
Notwithstanding, But by the robbing of the banish'd duke . . . ii 1 261
Alas, poor duke! the task he undertakes Is numbering sands . . ii 2 145
I never in my life did look on him.—Then learn to know him now; this is the duke . . . . ii 3 40
The noble duke hath been too much abused . . . . . . ii 3 137
The noble duke hath sworn his coming is But for his own . . . ii 3 148
Where is the duke my father with his power? . . . . . iii 2 143
Thou, Aumerle, didst send two of thy men To execute the noble duke . iv 1 82
As I said, the duke, great Bolingbroke, Mounted upon a hot and fiery steed . . . . v 2 7
'Twas where the madcap duke his uncle kept, His uncle York 1 *Hen. IV.* i 3 244
I look to be either earl or duke, I can assure you . . . . v 4 146
Be merciful, great duke, to men of mould . . . . *Hen. V.* iii 2 23
Abate thy manly rage, Abate thy rage, great duke! . . . . iii 2 25
To the mines! tell you the duke, it is not so good to come to the mines iii 2 61
For, look you, th' athversary, you may discuss unto the duke, look you iii 2 66
The day is hot, and the weather, and the wars, and the king, and the dukes: it is no time to discourse . . . . iii 2 114
High dukes, great princes, barons, lords and knights . . . . iii 5 46
Therefore, go speak: the duke will hear thy voice . . . . iii 6 48
I would desire the duke to use his good pleasure . . . . . iii 6 57
I can tell your majesty, the duke is a prave man . . . . iii 6 101
For my part, I think the duke hath lost never a man . . . . iii 6 105
Here's Gloucester that would enter.—Have patience, noble duke 1 *Hen. VI.* i 3 18
It is not that offends; It is not that that hath incensed the duke . . iii 1 36
The duke Hath banish'd moody discontented fury . . . . . iii 1 122
Thy noble deeds as valour's monuments.—Thanks, gentle duke . . iii 2 121
Now in the rearward comes the duke and his . . . . . . iii 3 33
Welcome, brave duke! thy friendship makes us fresh . . . . iii 3 86
To Bourdeaux, warlike duke! to Bourdeaux, York! Else, farewell Talbot iv 3 22
'Twas neither Charles nor yet the duke I named, But Reignier . . v 4 77
Suffolk, the new-made duke that rules the roast . . 2 *Hen. VI.* i 1 109
For Suffolk's duke, may he be suffocate, That dims the honour of this warlike isle! . . . . i 1 124
Henry was well pleased To change two dukedoms for a duke's fair daughter . . . . i 1 219
But list to me, my Humphrey, my sweet duke . . . . . . i 2 35
Were I a man, a duke, and next of blood, I would remove these tedious stumbling-blocks . . . . i 2 63
She bears a duke's revenues on her back . . . . i 3 83
The duke yet lives that Henry shall depose; But him outlive . . i 4 33
Injurious duke, that threatest where's no cause . . . . . i 4 51
Father, the duke hath told the truth . . . . ii 2 28
The reverent care I bear unto my lord Made me collect these dangers in the duke . . . . iii 1 35
I will subscribe and say I wrong'd the duke . . . . . . iii 1 38
Well hath your highness seen into this duke . . . . . . iii 1 42
The duke is virtuous mild and too well given To dream on evil . . iii 1 72
He is your prisoner.—Sirs, take away the duke, and guard him sure . iii 1 188
Let him know We have dispatch'd the duke, as he commanded . . iii 2 2
I did dream to-night The duke was dumb and could not speak a word . iii 2 32
Although the duke was enemy to him, Yet he most Christian-like laments his death . . . . iii 2 57
Look pale as primrose with blood-drinking sighs, And all to have the noble duke alive . . . . iii 2 64
We were but hollow friends: It may be judged I made the duke away . iii 2 67
I do believe that violent hands were laid Upon the life of this thrice-famed duke . . . . iii 2 157
Why, Warwick, who should do the duke to death? . . . . . iii 2 179

Duke. And you, forsooth, had the good duke to keep . *2 Hen. VI.* iii 2 183
Muffled up in rags!—Ay, but these rags are no part of the duke . iv 1 47
And make the meanest of you earls and dukes . . . . . iv 8 39
Somerset comes with the queen: Go, bid her hide him quickly from the duke . . . . v 1 84
I have consider'd with myself The title of this most renowned duke . v 1 176
But when the duke is slain, they'll quickly fly . *3 Hen. VI.* i 1 69
'Tis not thy southern power . . . Can set the duke up in despite of me i 1 158
Thou wouldst have left thy dearest heart-blood there, Rather than have made that savage duke thine heir . . . . . . i 1 224
The Earl of Warwick and the duke enforced me.—Enforced thee! art thou king, and wilt be forced? . . . . i 1 229
The duke is made protector of the realm; And yet shalt thou be safe? . i 1 240
Revenged may she be on that hateful duke! . . . . . . i 1 266
For the brat of this accursed duke, Whose father slew my father, he shall die . . . . i 3 4
Who crown'd the gracious duke in high despite, Laugh'd in his face ii 1 59
His name that valiant duke hath left with thee . . . . ii 1 89
Some six miles off the duke is with the soldiers . . . . ii 1 144
He, but a duke, would have his son a king, And raise his issue . ii 2 21
Here is The duke.—The duke! Why, Warwick, when we parted, Thou call'dst me king . . . . iv 3 29
I came to serve a king and not a duke . . . . . iv 7 49
And withal Forbear your conference with the noble duke *Richard III.* i 1 104
Gavest the duke a clout Steep'd in the faultless blood of pretty Rutland i 3 177
It is the queen and her allies That stir the king against the duke . i 3 331
Here are the keys, there sits the duke asleep . . . . . i 4 96
It [conscience] is even now at my elbow, persuading me not to kill the duke . . . . i 4 150
By heavens, the duke shall know how slack thou art! . . . . i 4 282
I repent me that the duke is slain.—So do not I . . . . i 4 285
Hide his body in some hole, Until the duke take order for his burial . i 4 288
And, in good time, here comes the noble duke . . . . . ii 1 45
All without desert have frown'd on me; Dukes, earls, lords, gentlemen ii 1 68
Who knows not that the noble duke is dead? You do him injury to scorn his corse . . . . ii 1 79
Who hath committed them?—The mighty dukes Gloucester and Buckingham . . . . ii 4 44
For the instalment of this noble duke In the seat royal of this famous isle . . . . iii 1 163
Who is most inward with the noble duke?—Your grace, we think . iii 4 8
Now in good time, here comes the duke himself . . . . iii 4 22
Dispatch, my lord; the duke would be at dinner: Make a short shrift iii 4 96
Which well appeared in his lineaments, Being nothing like the noble duke my father . . . . iii 5 92
And his resemblance, being not like the duke . . . . . iii 7 11
Thus saith the duke, thus hath the duke inferr'd . . . . iii 7 32
I dance attendance here; I think the duke will not be spoke withal . iii 7 57
Fly to the duke: Post thou to Salisbury . . . . . . iv 4 443
Dull, unmindful villain, Why stand'st thou still, and go'st not to the duke? . . . . iv 4 445
As the duke said, The will of heaven be done, and the king's pleasure By me obey'd! . . . . *Hen. VIII.* i 1 214
The duke being at the Rose, within the parish Saint Lawrence Poultney i 2 152
Presently the duke Said, 'twas the fear, indeed . . . . i 2 157
Neither the king nor's heirs, Tell you the duke, shall prosper: bid him strive To gain the love o' the commonalty: the duke Shall govern England . . . . i 2 169
If I know you well, You were the duke's surveyor . . . . i 2 172
I told my lord the duke, by the devil's illusions The monk might be deceived . . . . i 2 178
After your highness had reproved the duke About Sir William Blomer . i 2 189
Being my sworn servant, The duke retain'd him his . . . . i 2 192
After 'the duke his father,' with 'the knife,' He stretch'd him . i 2 203
The great duke Came to the bar; where to his accusations He pleaded still not guilty . . . . ii 1 11
Which the duke desired To have brought vivâ voce to his face . ii 1 17
This duke as much They love and dote on; call him bounteous Buckingham . . . . ii 1 51
Prepare there, The duke is coming: see the barge be ready . . ii 1 98
If the duke be guiltless, 'Tis full of woe . . . . . ii 1 139
That may give me Remembrance of my father-in-law, the duke . iii 2 8
The duke by law Found his deserts . . . . . . iii 2 266
Gonzago is the duke's name; his wife, Baptista . . *Hamlet* iii 2 249
It appears not which of the dukes he values most . . . *Lear* i 1 5
Not all the dukes of waterish Burgundy Can buy this unprized precious maid of me . . . . i 1 261
Abatement of kindness appears as well in the general dependants as in the duke himself . . . . i 4 66
The duke be here to-night? The better! best! . . . . ii 1 16
The noble duke my master, My worthy arch and patron, comes to-night ii 1 60
Hark, the duke's trumpets! I know not why he comes. . . . ii 1 81
All ports I'll bar; the villain shall not 'scape; The duke must grant me that . . . . ii 1 83
'Tis the duke's pleasure, Whose disposition, all the world well knows, Will not be rubb'd nor stopp'd . . . . ii 2 159
The duke's to blame in this; 'twill be ill taken . . . . ii 2 166
You know the fiery quality of the duke; How unremoveable and fix'd he is . . . . ii 4 93
Fiery? the fiery duke? Tell the hot duke that—No, but not yet . ii 4 105
This act persuades me That this remotion of the duke and her Is practice only . . . . ii 4 115
Go tell the duke and's wife I'ld speak with them . . . . ii 4 117
What hath been seen, Either in snuffs and packings of the dukes . iii 1 26
There's a division betwixt the dukes; and a worse matter than that . iii 3 9
Go you and maintain talk with the duke . . . . . . iii 3 16
This courtesy, forbid thee, shall the duke Instantly know . . . iii 3 22
Advise the duke, where you are going, to a most festinate preparation . iii 7 9
With this ungracious paper strike the sight Of the death-practised duke iv 6 284
Know of the duke if his last purpose hold . . . . . v 1 1
Fear me not: She and the duke her husband! . . . . . v 1 17
And hath in his effect a voice potential As double as the duke's *Othello* i 2 14
The servants of the duke, and my lieutenant . . . . . i 2 34
The duke does greet you, general, And he requires your haste-post-haste i 2 36
And many of the consuls, raised and met, Are at the duke's already . i 2 44
What if I do obey? How may the duke be therewith satisfied? . . i 2 88
The duke's in council, and your noble self, I am sure, is sent for . i 2 92
How! the duke in council! In this time of the night! . . . . i 2 93
The duke himself, Or any of my brothers of the state, Cannot but feel this wrong as 'twere their own . . . . i 2 95
Duke. Most gracious duke, To my unfolding lend your prosperous ear *Oth.* i 3 244
The duke and senators of Venice greet you . . . . . . iv 1 230
Dukedom. Me, poor man, my library Was dukedom large enough *Tempest* i 2 110
And bend The dukedom yet unbow'd . . . . i 2 115
In lieu o' the premises Of homage and I know not how much tribute, Should presently extirpate me and mine Out of the dukedom . . i 2 126
Volumes that I prize above my dukedom . . . . i 2 168
Thy dukedom I resign and do entreat Thou pardon me my wrongs . v 1 118
I do forgive Thy rankest fault; all of them; and require My dukedom of thee . . . . v 1 133
My dukedom since you have given me again, I will requite you with as good a thing . . . . v 1 168
At least bring forth a wonder, to content ye As much as me my dukedom . . . . v 1 171
Ferdinand, her brother, found a wife Where he himself was lost, Prospero his dukedom In a poor isle . . . . v 1 211
I have my dukedom got And pardon'd the deceiver . . . . . Epil. 6
Thou art thy father's daughter; there's enough.—So was I when your highness took his dukedom . . . . . . *As Y. Like It* i 3 61
A land itself at large, a potent dukedom . . . . . . v 4 175
Your new-fall'n right, The seat of Gaunt, dukedom of Lancaster *1 Hen. IV.* v 1 45
I would you had but the wit: 'twere better than your dukedom *2 Hen. IV.* iv 3 93
Of his true titles to some certain dukedoms . . . *Hen. V.* i 1 87
Ruling in large and ample empery O'er France and all her almost kingly dukedoms . . . . i 2 227
Your highness, lately sending into France, Did claim some certain dukedoms . . . . i 2 247
You cannot revel into dukedoms there . . . . i 2 253
With her, to dowry, Some petty and unprofitable dukedoms . . iii Prol. 31
I will sell my dukedom, To buy a slobbery and a dirty farm . . iii 5 12
Well pleased To change two dukedoms for a duke's fair daughter *2 Hen. VI.* i 1 219
Till Suffolk gave two dukedoms for his daughter . . . . . i 3 90
We'll have the Lord Say's head for selling the dukedom of Maine . iv 2 170
His dukedom and his chair with me is left . . . *3 Hen. VI.* ii 1 90
For chair and dukedom, throne and kingdom say; Either that is thine, or else thou wert not his . . . . ii 1 93
Gloucester's dukedom is too ominous . . . . ii 6 107
What then remains . . . But that we enter, as into our dukedom? . iv 7 9
I challenge nothing but my dukedom, As being well content with that alone . . . . iv 7 23
But we now forget Our title to the crown and only claim Our dukedom iv 7 47
Is not a dukedom, sir, a goodly gift? . . . . v 1 31
My dukedom to a beggarly denier, I do mistake my person *Richard III.* i 2 252
Dulcet. Uttering such dulcet and harmonious breath *M. N. Dream* ii 1 151
Those dulcet sounds in break of day That creep into the dreaming bridegroom's ear And summon him to marriage *Mer. of Venice* iii 2 51
According to the fool's bolt, sir, and such dulcet diseases *As Y. Like It* v 4 68
To make a dulcet and a heavenly sound . . . *T. of Shrew* Ind. 1 51
His jarring concord, and his discord dulcet . . . *All's Well* i 1 186
To hear by the nose, it is dulcet in contagion . . . . *T. Night* ii 3 58
Dull. Makes me unpregnant And dull to all proceedings . *Meas. for Meas.* iv 4 24
When I am dull with care and melancholy . . . *Com. of Errors* i 2 20
Are my discourses dull? barren my wit? . . . . . . ii 1 91
My dull deaf ears a little use to hear . . . . v 1 316
Sing no more ditties, sing no moe, Of dumps so dull and heavy *M. Ado* ii 3 73
Anthony Dull; a man of good repute, carriage, bearing . . *L. L. Lost* i 1 271
Me, an't shall please you; I am Anthony Dull . . . . . i 1 273
Is not lead a metal heavy, dull, and slow? . . . . . . iii 1 60
Dictynna, goodman Dull; Dictynna, goodman Dull . . . . iv 2 37
Via, goodman Dull! thou hast spoken no word all this while . . v 1 156
Most dull, honest Dull! To our sport, away! . . . . . v 1 162
While she was in her dull and sleeping hour . . . *M. N. Dream* iii 2 8
Happier than this, She is not bred so dull but she can learn *M. of Ven.* iii 2 164
The motions of his spirit are dull as night And his affections dark as Erebus . . . . v 1 86
Our natural wits too dull to reason of such goddesses . *As Y. Like It* i 2 56
Doth backward pull Our slow designs when we ourselves are dull *All's W.* i 1 234
And dull unfeeling barren ignorance Is made my gaoler . . *Richard II.* i 3 168
So may you by my dull and heavy eye, My tongue hath but a heavier tale iii 2 196
Their courage with hard labour tame and dull . . . *1 Hen. IV.* iv 3 23
So faint, so spiritless, So dull, so dead in look, so woe-begone *2 Hen. IV.* i 1 71
All the rest Turn'd on themselves, like dull and heavy lead . . . i 1 118
It [sherris] ascends me into the brain; dries me there all the foolish and dull and crudy vapours . . . . iv 3 106
Unless some dull and favourable hand Will whisper music to my weary spirit . . . . iv 5 2
For peace itself should not so dull a kingdom . . . . *Hen. V.* ii 4 16
Is not their climate foggy, raw and dull? . . . . . . iii 5 16
Thou wert not wont to be so dull: Shall I be plain? . . *Richard III.* iv 2 17
My words are dull; O, quicken them with thine! . . . . . iv 4 124
The murderous knife was dull and blunt Till it was whetted on thy stone-hard heart . . . . iv 4 226
Dull, unmindful villain, Why stand'st thou still? . . . . . iv 4 444
When I am forgotten, as I shall be, And sleep in dull cold marble *Hen. VIII.* iii 2 433
In this dull and long-continued truce Is rusty grown . *Troi. and Cres.* i 3 262
If the dull brainless Ajax come safe off, We'll dress him up in voices . i 3 381
I have a roisting challenge sent amongst The dull and factious nobles . ii 2 209
The woods are ruthless, dreadful, deaf, and dull . . . *T. Andron.* ii 1 128
My sight is very dull, whate'er it bodes . . . . ii 3 195
And nature, as it grows again toward earth, Is fashion'd for the journey, dull and heavy . . . . *T. of Athens* ii 2 228
You are dull, Casca, and those sparks of life That should be in a Roman you do want . . . . *J. Cæsar* i 3 57
Do not dull thy palm with entertainment Of each new-hatch'd, unfledged comrade . . . . *Hamlet* i 3 64
And borrowing dulls the edge of husbandry . . . . . . i 3 77
Yet I, A dull and muddy-mettled rascal, peak, Like John-a-dreams . ii 2 594
My spirits grow dull, and fain I would beguile The tedious day with sleep . . . . iii 2 236
You must not think That we are made of stuff so flat and dull . . iv 7 31
Within a dull, stale, tired bed . . . . *Lear* i 2 13
When the blood is made dull with the act of sport . . . . *Othello* ii 1 230
Dull not device by coldness and delay . . . . ii 3 394
Dull of tongue, and dwarfish! What majesty is in her gait? . *A. and C.* iii 3 19
Will stupify and dull the sense awhile . . . . . . *Cymbeline* i 5 37
O sleep, thou ape of death, lie dull upon her! . . . . . ii 2 31

Dull. Sparkles this stone as it was wont? or is't not Too dull for your good wearing? . . . . *Cymbeline* ii 4 41
Dull actor. Like a dull actor now, I have forgot my part . *Coriolanus* v 3 40
Dull ass. Your dull ass will not mend his pace with beating *Hamlet* v 1 64
Dull brain. My dull brain was wrought With things forgotten *Macbeth* i 3 149
Dull-brained. The petty rebel, dull-brain'd Buckingham . *Richard III.* iv 4 332
Dull clouds. Give way, dull clouds, to my quick curses! . i 3 196
Dull conceit. A volume of enticing lines, Able to ravish any dull conceit 1 *Hen. VI.* v 5 15
Dull delay. Fearful commenting Is leaden servitor to dull delay *Richard III.* iv 3 52
Dull ear. Vexing the dull ear of a drowsy man . . . *K. John* iii 4 109
Piercing the night's dull ear . . . . *Hen. V.* iv Prol. 11
Dull earth. She excels each mortal thing Upon the dull earth dwelling *T. G. of Ver.* iv 2 52
Turn back, dull earth, and find thy centre out . *Rom. and Jul.* ii 1 2
Dull elements. The dull elements of earth and water never appear in him . . . . *Hen. V.* iii 7 23
Dull-eyed. I'll not be made a soft and dull-eyed fool . *Mer. of Venice* iii 3 14
The sad companion, dull-eyed melancholy . . *Pericles* i 2 2
Dull fighter. To the latter end of a fray and the beginning of a feast Fits a dull fighter and a keen guest . . . . . 1 *Hen. IV.* iv 2 86
Dull fool. To take this drunkard for a god And worship this dull fool! *Tempest* v 1 297
Why, he is the prince's jester: a very dull fool . . *Much Ado* ii 1 143
Why do you infect yourself with them?—Peace, you dull fool! *As Y. L. It* iii 2 121
Dull god. O thou dull god [sleep], why liest thou with the vile In loathsome beds? . . . . 2 *Hen. IV.* iii 1 15
Dull kindred. May complain of good breeding or comes of a very dull kindred . . . . *As Y. Like It* iii 2 32
Dull lead, with warning all as blunt . . . . *Mer. of Venice* ii 7 8
Dull melancholy. Sweet recreation barr'd, what doth ensue But moody and dull melancholy? . . . . *Com. of Errors* v 1 79
Dull Moor. Fie! Your sword upon a woman?—O thou dull Moor! *Oth.* v 2 225
Dull mouths. In their pale dull mouths the gimmal bit Lies foul with chew'd grass . . . . *Hen. V.* iv 2 49
Dull Octavia. Nor once be chastised with the sober eye Of dull Octavia *Ant. and Cleo.* v 2 55
Dull part. Mark Her eye, and tell me for what dull part in't You chose her . . . . *W. Tale* v 1 64
Dull proceeding. I'll quickly cross By some sly trick blunt Thurio's dull proceeding . . . . . . *T. G. of Ver.* ii 6 41
Dull revenge. How all occasions do inform against me, And spur my dull revenge! . . . . *Hamlet* iv 4 33
Dull sight. This is a dull sight. Are you not Kent? . *Lear* v 3 282
Dull sleep. This is the rarest dream that e'er dull sleep Did mock sad fools withal . . . . *Pericles* v 1 163
Dull thing, I say so; he, that Caliban . . . *Tempest* i 2 285
Dull tribunes. Where the dull tribunes, That, with the fusty plebeians, hate thine honours . . . . . . *Coriolanus* i 9 6
Dull unwillingness. 'Tis call'd ungrateful, With dull unwillingness to repay a debt Which with a bounteous hand was kindly lent *Rich. III.* ii 2 92
Dull watch. At this odd-even and dull watch o' the night . *Othello* i 1 124
Dull woe. I cannot bound a pitch above dull woe . *Rom. and Jul.* i 4 21
Dull workings. Intelligencer Between the grace, the sanctities of heaven And our dull workings. . . . . . 2 *Hen. IV.* iv 2 22
Dull world. Shall I abide In this dull world, which in thy absence is No better than a sty? . . . . . . *Ant. and Cleo.* iv 15 61
Dullard. Thou must make a dullard of the world . . *Lear* ii 1 76
What, makest thou me a dullard in this act? . . *Cymbeline* v 5 265
Dulled. Whom he hath dull'd and cloy'd with gracious favours *Hen. V.* ii 2 9
Duller. I was duller than a great thaw . . . *Much Ado* ii 1 251
He is only an animal, only sensible in the duller parts . *L. L. Lost* iv 2 28
Performance is ever the duller for his act . . . *T. of Athens* v 1 26
And duller shouldst thou be than the fat weed That roots itself in ease on Lethe wharf . . . . *Hamlet* i 5 32
Mine Italian brain 'Gan in your duller Britain operate Most vilely *Cymb.* v 5 197
Dullest. And twice to-day pick'd out the dullest scent *T. of Shrew* Ind. 1 24
A savour that may strike the dullest nostril . . *W. Tale* i 2 421
Whose spirit lent a fire Even to the dullest peasant in his camp 2 *Hen. IV.* i 1 113
Dulling. Attach'd with weariness, To the dulling of my spirits *Tempest* iii 3 6
Dully. Living dully sluggardized at home . . . *T. G. of Ver.* i 1 7
The time shall not go dully by us . . . . *Much Ado* ii 1 379
Dulness. Thou art inclined to sleep; 'tis a good dulness . *Tempest* i 2 185
For always the dulness of the fool is the whetstone of the wits *As Y. L. It* i 2 58
If thou wert the ass, thy dulness would torment thee . *T. of Athens* iv 3 335
Seel with wanton dulness My speculative and officed instruments *Othello* i 3 270
Sauce his appetite; That sleep and feeding may prorogue his honour Even till a Lethe'd dulness! . . . . . *Ant. and Cleo.* ii 1 27
Duly. Let this be duly performed . . . . *Meas. for Meas.* iv 2 127
I duly am inform'd His grace is at Marseilles . . *All's Well* iv 4 8
Three parts of that receipt I had for Calais Disbursed I duly to his highness' soldiers . . . . *Richard II.* i 1 127
As duly, but not as truly, As bird doth sing on bough . *Hen. V.* iii 2 19
In our voiding lobby hast thou stood And duly waited for my coming forth? . . . . 2 *Hen. VI.* iv 1 62
Nor my prayers Are not words duly hallow'd . . . *Hen. VIII.* iii 3 68
That they may have their wages duly paid 'em . . iv 2 150
Crush him together rather than unfold His measure duly . *Cymbeline* i 1 27
Dulzura. Piu por dulzura que por fuerza . . . *Pericles* ii 2 27
Dumain and Longaville Have sworn for three years' term to live with me My fellow-scholars . . . . . . *L. L. Lost* i 1 15
My loving lord, Dumain is mortified . . . . . i 1 28
Dumain, a well-accomplished youth, Of all that virtue love for virtue loved . . . . ii 1 56
I have my wish! Dumain transform'd! four woodcocks in a dish! iv 3 82
O, tell me, good Dumain? And, gentle Longaville, where lies thy pain? iv 3 171
What was sent to you from fair Dumain?—Madam, this glove v 2 47
Dumain was at my service, and his sword: No point, quoth I v 2 276
Dumain is mine, as sure as bark on tree . . . . v 2 285
Demand of him, whether one Captain Dumain be i' the camp *All's Well* iv 3 200
Do you know this Captain Dumain?—I know him . . iv 3 210
Therefore, once more to this Captain Dumain . . . iv 3 277
What's his brother, the other Captain Dumain? . . iv 3 316
Dumb. A kind Of excellent dumb discourse . . . *Tempest* iii 3 39
Alas! this parting strikes poor lovers dumb . . *T. G. of Ver.* ii 2 21
Dumb jewels often in their silent kind More than quick words do move a woman's mind . . . . iii 1 90
My ears are stopt and cannot hear good news . . . —Then in dumb silence will I bury mine . . . . iii 1 207
Dumb. I can be secret as a dumb man; I would have you think so *M. Ado* i 1 212
Hang thou there upon the tomb, Praising her when I am dumb . v 3 10
Speak, speak. Quite dumb? Dead, dead? . . . *M. N. Dream* v 1 334
I must be one of these same dumb wise men . . *Mer. of Venice* i 1 106
By what strange accident I chanced on this letter.—I am dumb . v 1 279
And as oft is dumb Where dust and damn'd oblivion is the tomb Of honour'd bones indeed . . . . *All's Well* ii 3 146
A dumb innocent, that could not say him nay . . . iv 3 213
Deep shame had struck me dumb . . . . . . *K. John* iv 2 235
In dumb significants proclaim your thoughts . . 1 *Hen. VI.* ii 4 26
The duke was dumb and could not speak a word . . 2 *Hen. VI.* iii 2 32
To tell my love unto his dumb deaf trunk . . . iii 2 144
Like dumb statuas or breathing stones, Gazed each on other *Richard III.* iii 7 25
My woe-wearied tongue is mute and dumb . . . iv 4 18
And almost, like the gods, Does thoughts unveil in their dumb cradles *Troi. and Cres.* iii 3 200
The dumb men throng to see him and The blind to hear . *Coriolanus* ii 1 278
In thy dumb action will I be as perfect As begging hermits *T. Andron.* iii 2 40
My scars can witness, dumb although they are, That my report is just . v 3 114
O, why should wrath be mute, and fury dumb? . . v 3 184
Over thy wounds now do I prophesy,—Which, like dumb mouths, do ope their ruby lips . . . . *J. Cæsar* iii 1 260
Show you sweet Cæsar's wounds, poor poor dumb mouths, And bid them speak for me . . . . iii 2 229
Upon my life, This spirit, dumb to us, will speak to him *Hamlet* i 1 171
Whilst they, distill'd Almost to jelly with the act of fear, Stand dumb . i 2 206
Or given my heart a winking, mute and dumb . . . ii 2 137
I have words to speak in thine ear will make thee dumb . iv 6 26
Never saw I figures So likely to report themselves: the cutter Was as another nature, dumb . . . . . . *Cymbeline* ii 4 84
What's dumb in show I'll plain with speech . . *Pericles* iii Gower 14
Deep clerks she dumbs . . . . v Gower 5
Now our sands are almost run: More a little, and then dumb . v 2 267
Dumb-discoursive. A still and dumb-discoursive devil That tempts most cunningly . . . . . . *Troi. and Cres.* iv 4 92
Dumbe. Master Dumbe, our minister, was by then . . 2 *Hen. IV.* ii 4 95
Dumbed. Who neigh'd so high, that what I would have spoke Was beastly dumb'd by him . . . . . *Ant. and Cleo.* i 5 50
Dumbly. And in conclusion dumbly have broke off . . *M. N. Dream* v 1 98
One kiss shall stop our mouths, and dumbly part . . *Richard II.* v 1 95
Dumbness. You should have banged the youth into dumbness *T. Night* iii 2 25
There was speech in their dumbness, language in their very gesture *W. T.* v 2 15
Your silence, Cunning in dumbness . . . . . *Troi. and Cres.* iii 2 140
To the dumbness of the gesture One might interpret . *T. of Athens* i 1 33
Hobbididance, prince of dumbness; Mahu, of stealing . *Lear* iv 1 63
Dumb-show. That's the scene that I would see, which will be merely a dumb-show . . . . *Much Ado* ii 3 226
He is a proper man's picture, but, alas, who can converse with a dumb-show? . . . . *Mer. of Venice* i 2 78
And in dumb shows Pass the remainder of our hateful days *T. Andron.* iii 1 131
Capable of nothing but inexplicable dumb-shows and noise . *Hamlet* iii 2 14
Dump. To their instruments Tune a deploring dump . *T. G. of Ver.* iii 2 85
Sing no more ditties, sing no moe, Of dumps so dull and heavy *M. Ado* ii 3 73
How now, daughter Katharine! in your dumps? . *T. of Shrew* ii 1 286
To step out of these dreary dumps . . . *T. Andron.* i 1 391
O, play me some merry dump, to comfort me.—Not a dump we *R. and J.* iv 5 108
When griping grief the heart doth wound, And doleful dumps the mind oppress, Then music . . . . iv 5 129
Dun's the mouse, the constable's own word . . . i 4 40
If thou art dun, we'll draw thee from the mire Of this sir-reverence love i 4 41
Duncan. The raven himself is hoarse That croaks the fatal entrance of Duncan Under my battlements . . . . . *Macbeth* i 5 40
My dearest love, Duncan comes here to-night.—And when goes hence? i 5 60
This Duncan Hath borne his faculties so meek . . i 7 16
When Duncan is asleep—Whereto the rather shall his day's hard journey Soundly invite him . . . . i 7 61
What cannot you and I perform upon The unguarded Duncan? . i 7 70
The bell invites me. Hear it not, Duncan; for it is a knell That summons thee to heaven or to hell . . . . ii 1 63
Wake Duncan with thy knocking! I would thou couldst! . ii 2 74
Here lay Duncan, His silver skin laced with his golden blood . ii 3 117
Duncan's horses—a thing most strange and certain—Beauteous and swift, the minions of their race, Turn'd wild in nature . ii 4 14
Where is Duncan's body?—Carried to Colmekill, The sacred storehouse of his predecessors . . . . ii 4 32
For them the gracious Duncan have I murder'd . . iii 1 66
Duncan is in his grave; After life's fitful fever he sleeps well . iii 2 22
This is the air-drawn dagger which, you said, Led you to Duncan . iii 4 63
The gracious Duncan Was pitied of Macbeth: marry, he was dead . iii 6 3
Had he Duncan's sons under his key—As, an't please heaven, he shall not—they should find What 'twere to kill a father . . iii 6 18
The son of Duncan, From whom this tyrant holds the due of birth . iii 6 24
Dungeon. Black is the badge of hell, The hue of dungeons . *L. L. Lost* iv 3 255
Let me live, sir, in a dungeon, i' the stocks, or any where, so I may live *All's Well* iv 3 273
Colevile shall be still your name, a traitor your degree, and the dungeon your place . . . . 2 *Hen. IV.* iv 3 8
Detain'd me all my flowering youth Within a loathsome dungeon 1 *Hen. VI.* ii 5 57
And thou unfit for any place but hell.—Yes, one place else, if you will hear me name it.—Some dungeon . . . . *Richard III.* i 2 111
Nor airless dungeon, nor strong links of iron, Can be retentive to the strength of spirit . . . . *J. Cæsar* i 3 94
In which there are many confines, wards and dungeons . . *Hamlet* ii 2 252
I had rather be a toad, And live upon the vapour of a dungeon *Othello* iii 3 271
Lamentable! What, To hide me from the radiant sun and solace I' the dungeon by a snuff? . . . . *Cymbeline* i 6 87
Dunghill. Then did the sun on dunghill shine . . . *Mer. Wives* i 3 70
Thou hast it ad dunghill, at the fingers' ends, as they say . *L. L. Lost* v 1 81
O, I smell false Latin; dunghill for unguem . . . v 1 83
His animals on his dunghills are as much bound to him as I *As Y. Like It* i 1 16
Out, dunghill! darest thou brave a nobleman? . . *K. John* iv 3 87
Shall dunghill curs confront the Helicons? . . . 2 *Hen. IV.* v 3 108
Dying like men, though buried in your dunghills, They shall be famed *Hen. V.* iv 3 99
Shall I be flouted thus by dunghill grooms? . . 1 *Hen. VI.* i 3 14
Base dunghill villain and mechanical . . . . 2 *Hen. VI.* i 3 196
Hence will I drag thee headlong by the heels Unto a dunghill . . iv 10 87
Turn out that eyeless villain; throw this slave Upon the dunghill *Lear* iii 7 97
Chill be plain with you.—Out, dunghill! . . . . . iv 6 249

Dungy. We need no grave to bury honesty : There's not a grain of it the face to sweeten Of the whole dungy earth . . . *W. Tale* ii 1 157
Kingdoms are clay : our dungy earth alike Feeds beast as man *A. and C.* i 1 35
Dunnest. Come, thick night, And pall thee in the dunnest smoke of hell *Macbeth* i 5 52
Dunsinane. Until Great Birnam wood to high Dunsinane hill Shall come iv 1 93
Till Birnam wood remove to Dunsinane, I cannot taint with fear . v 3 2
I will not be afraid of death and bane, Till Birnam forest come to Dunsinane . . . . v 3 60
Were I from Dunsinane away and clear, Profit again should hardly draw me here . . . . v 3 61
The confident tyrant Keeps still in Dunsinane . . . . . v 4 9
'Fear not, till Birnam wood Do come to Dunsinane': and now a wood Comes toward Dunsinane . . . . . . v 5 45
Though Birnam wood be come to Dunsinane, And thou opposed, being of no woman born, Yet I will try the last . . . . . . v 8 30
Dunsmore. How far hence is thy lord, mine honest fellow?—By this at Dunsmore . . . . 3 *Hen. VI.* v 1 3
Dunstable. At Dunstable, six miles off From Ampthill *Hen. VIII.* iv 1 27
Dupped. Then up he rose, and donn'd his clothes, And dupp'd the chamber-door. . . . . *Hamlet* iv 5 53
Durance. Perpetual durance?—Ay, just ; perpetual durance . *M. for M.* iii 1 67
That takes pity on decayed men and gives them suits of durance *C. of E.* iv 3 27
I give thee thy liberty, set thee from durance . . . *L. L. Lost* iii 1 130
He upon some action Is now in durance . . . . *T. Night* v 1 283
Is not a buff jerkin a most sweet robe of durance? . . 1 *Hen. IV.* i 2 49
Is in base durance and contagious prison . . 2 *Hen. IV.* v 5 36
During which time he ne'er saw Syracusa . . *Com. of Errors* v 1 328
I can drink with any tinker in his own language during my life 1 *Hen. IV.* ii 4 21
I shall think the better of myself and thee during my life . . ii 4 302
They are for the town's end, to beg during life . . . . v 3 39
Bred During the time Edward the Third did reign . . 1 *Hen. VI.* i 2 31
During whose reign the Percies of the north . . . Endeavour'd my advancement to the throne . . . . ii 5 67
For that which we have fled During the life, let us not wrong it dead . iv 7 50
During the wars of York and Lancaster That had befall'n us *Richard III.* i 4 15
Bade me enjoy it, with the place and honours, During my life *Hen. VIII.* iii 2 249
Health to you, valiant sir, During all question of the gentle truce *Troi. and Cres.* iv 1 11
Then our office may, During his power, go asleep *Coriolanus* ii 1 239
For us, we will resign, During the life of this old majesty . *Lear* v 3 299
Or receive us For barbarous and unnatural revolts During their use *Cymbeline* iv 4 7
Durst. They durst not, So dear the love my people bore me *Tempest* i 2 140
I durst have denied that, before you were so choleric . *Com. of Errors* ii 2 67
How they might hurt their enemies, if they durst . . *Much Ado* v 1 98
Never durst poet touch a pen to write Until his ink were temper'd with Love's sighs . . . . *L. L. Lost* iv 3 346
Pretty soul ! she durst not lie Near this lack-love . . *M. N. Dream* ii 2 76
Durst thou have look'd upon him being awake, And hast thou kill'd him sleeping? O brave touch ! . . . . iii 2 69
I durst go no further than the Lie Circumstantial, nor he durst not give me the Lie Direct. . . . . . . *As Y. Like It* v 4 89
How durst you, villains, bring it from the dresser? . . *T. of Shrew* iv 1 166
Now, tell me, I pray, You that durst swear . . . . iv 2 12
Write to the king That which I durst not speak . . *All's Well* iii 3 306
Ere my heart Durst make too bold a herald of my tongue . . v 3 46
Durst not tempt a minister of honour, Lest she should be denied *W. Tale* ii 2 50
Were I a tyrant, Where were her life? she durst not call me so . ii 3 123
My face so thin That in mine ear I durst not stick a rose *K. John* i 1 142
Even to the frozen ridges of the Alps, Or any other ground inhabitable, Where ever Englishman durst set his foot . . *Richard II.* i 1 66
He durst as well have met the devil alone . . 1 *Hen. IV.* i 3 116
That even our love durst not come near your sight . . . v 1 63
I had thought weariness durst not have attached one of so high blood 2 *Hen. IV.* ii 2 3
If he durst steal any thing adventurously . . . *Hen. V.* iv 4 78
Hundreds he sent to hell, and none durst stand him . 1 *Hen. VI.* i 1 123
Whom all France . . . Durst not presume to look once in the face . i 1 140
None durst come near for fear of sudden death . . . . i 4 48
He bears him on the place's privilege, Or durst not, for his craven heart, say thus . . . . ii 4 87
Five days have I hid me in these woods, and durst not peep out 2 *Hen. VI.* iv 10 4
He durst not sit there, had your father lived . . . 3 *Hen. VI.* i 1 63
'Twas not your valour, Clifford, drove me thence.—No, nor your manhood that durst make you stay . . . . ii 2 108
Ha ! durst the traitor breathe out so proud words? . . . iv 1 112
And who durst smile when Warwick bent his brow? . . . v 2 22
And no discerner Durst wag his tongue in censure . *Hen. VIII.* i 1 33
To stop the rumour, and allay those tongues That durst disperse it . ii 1 153
Surrey durst better Have burnt that tongue than said so . . iii 2 253
I love you ; And durst commend a secret to your ear . . . v 1 17
There is a mystery—with whom relation Durst never meddle *Tr. and Cr.* iii 3 202
Durst not, look you, sir, show themselves, as we term it, his friends *Cor.* iv 5 220
And durst not once peep out.—Come, what talk you? . . iv 6 46
What Roman lord it was durst do the deed . . *T. Andron.* iv 1 62
For mine own part, I durst not laugh, for fear of opening my lips and receiving the bad air . . . . *J. Cæsar* i 2 251
When Cæsar lived, he durst not thus have moved me.—Peace, peace ! you durst not so have tempted him.—I durst not !—No.—What, durst not tempt him !—For your life you durst not . . . . iv 3 58
So, I am free ; yet would not so have been, Durst I have done my will . v 3 48
When you durst do it, then you were a man . . *Macbeth* i 7 49
Sought to make us break our vow, Which we durst never yet . *Lear* i 1 172
If the matter were good, my lord, I durst swear it were his . . i 2 69
They durst not do't ; They could not, would not do't . . . ii 4 22
This kiss, if it durst speak, Would stretch thy spirits up into the air . iv 2 22
I durst, my lord, to wager she is honest, Lay down my soul at stake *Oth.* iv 2 12
I durst attempt it against any lady in the world *Cymbeline* i 4 122
How durst thy tongue move anger to our face?—How dare the plants look up to heaven? . . . . *Pericles* i 2 54
We have a maid in Mytilene, I durst wager, Would win some words of him . . . . v 1 42
Dusky. They did plot The means that dusky Dis my daughter got *Temp.* iv 1 89
As far as I could well discern For smoke and dusky vapours of the night 1 *Hen. VI.* ii 2 27
Here dies the dusky torch of Mortimer . . . . . . ii 5 122
When the dusky sky began to rob My earnest-gaping sight 2 *Hen. VI.* iii 2 104
And call'd them blind and dusky spectacles . . . . . . iii 2 112

Dusky. Untimely smother'd in their dusky graves . *Richard III.* iv 4 70
Dust. But see how I lay the dust with my tears . . *T. G. of Ver.* ii 3 35
Thou exist'st on many a thousand grains That issue out of dust *M. for M.* iii 1 21
Would it not grieve a woman to be overmastered with a piece of valiant dust? . . . . *Much Ado* ii 1 64
I am sent with broom before, To sweep the dust behind the door *M. N. D.* v 1 397
On every grave A lying trophy, and as oft is dumb Where dust and damn'd oblivion is the tomb Of honour'd bones indeed . *All's Well* ii 3 147
She whom all men praised . . . was in mine eye The dust that did offend it . . . . v 3 55
Oft our displeasures, to ourselves unjust, Destroy our friends and after weep their dust . . . . v 3 64
Wherefore have these gifts a curtain before 'em? are they like to take dust? . . . . *T. Night* i 3 135
And lay me Where no priest shovels in dust . . . *W. Tale* iv 4 469
By the merit of vile gold, dross, dust, Purchase corrupted pardon *K. John* iii 1 165
And stop this gap of breath with fulsome dust . . . . iii 4 32
Shall blow each dust, each straw, each little rub, Out of the path . iii 4 128
A grain, a dust, a gnat, a wandering hair, Any annoyance . . iv 1 93
Her ear Is stopp'd with dust ; the first of April died Your noble mother iv 2 120
So hot a summer in my bosom, That all my bowels crumble up to dust v 7 31
Wipe off the dust that hides our sceptre's gilt . *Richard II.* ii 1 294
Why have those banish'd and forbidden legs Dared once to touch a dust of England's ground? . . . . ii 3 91
Make dust our paper and with rainy eyes Write sorrow on the bosom of the earth . . . . iii 2 146
And lay the summer's dust with showers of blood . . . iii 3 43
Hands from windows' tops Threw dust and rubbish on King Richard's head . . . . v 2 6
But dust was thrown upon his sacred head ; Which with such gentle sorrow he shook off . . . . v 2 30
And shed my dear blood drop by drop in the dust . 1 *Hen. IV.* i 3 134
Thou art dust, And food for— For worms, brave Percy . . v 4 85
Thou, that threw'st dust upon his goodly head . 2 *Hen. IV.* i 3 103
Only compound me with forgotten dust . . . . . iv 5 116
Nor from the dust of old oblivion raked . . . *Hen. V.* ii 4 87
Now, France, thy glory droopeth to the dust . . 1 *Hen. VI.* v 3 29
He hath no eyes, the dust hath blinded them . . 2 *Hen. VI.* iii 3 14
Write in the dust this sentence with thy blood . 3 *Hen. VI.* i 1 56
Lo, now my glory smear'd in dust and blood ! . . . . v 2 23
What is pomp, rule, reign, but earth and dust? . . . . v 2 27
Two tender playfellows for dust . . . . *Richard III.* iv 4 385
Give to dust that is a little gilt More laud than gilt o'er-dusted *Tr. and Cr.* iii 3 178
What custom wills, in all things should we do't, The dust on antique time would lie unswept . . . . . . *Coriolanus* ii 3 126
Let what is meet be said it must be meet, And throw their power i' the dust . . . . iii 1 171
They to dust should grind it And throw't against the wind . . iii 2 103
In the dust I write My heart's deep languor . . *T. Andron.* iii 1 12
I will grind your bones to dust And with your blood and it I'll make a paste . . . . v 2 187
O woe ! thy canopy is dust and stones . . . *Rom. and Jul.* v 3 13
And fearful scouring Doth choke the air with dust . *T. of Athens* v 2 16
That now on Pompey's basis lies along No worthier than the dust *J. Cæsar* iii 1 116
Do not for ever with thy vailed lids Seek for thy noble father in the dust : Thou know'st 'tis common . . . . *Hamlet* i 2 71
And yet, to me, what is this quintessence of dust? . . . . ii 2 321
What have you done, my lord, with the dead body?—Compounded it with dust, whereto 'tis kin . . . . iv 2 6
Why may not imagination trace the noble dust of Alexander, till he find it stopping a bung-hole? . . . . v 1 225
Alexander died, Alexander was buried, Alexander returneth into dust ; the dust is earth ; of earth we make loam . . . . . v 1 232
Now pile your dust upon the quick and dead . . . . v 1 274
You are not worth the dust which the rude wind Blows in your face *Lear* iv 2 30
Use his eyes for garden water-pots, Ay, and laying autumn's dust . iv 6 201
From the extremest upward of thy head To the descent and dust below thy foot, A most toad-spotted traitor . . . . . . v 3 137
The dust Should have ascended to the roof of heaven . *Ant. and Cleo.* iii 6 48
But clay and clay differs in dignity, Whose dust is both alike *Cymbeline* iv 2 5
Though mean and mighty, rotting Together, have one dust . . iv 2 247
Golden lads and girls all must, As chimney-sweepers, come to dust . iv 2 263
The sceptre, learning, physic, must All follow this, and come to dust . iv 2 269
All lovers young, all lovers must Consign to thee, and come to dust . iv 2 275
Vice repeated is like the wandering wind, Blows dust in others' eyes *Per.* i 1 97
On set purpose let his armour rest Until this day, to scour it in the dust ii 2 55
Dusty. Mighty states characterless are grated To dusty nothing *Tr. and Cr.* iii 2 196
And all our yesterdays have lighted fools The way to dusty death *Macbeth* v 5 23
Dutch. I was more than half stewed in grease, like a Dutch dish *M. W.* iii 5 121
German, or Dane, low Dutch, Italian, or French . . *All's Well* iv 1 78
Dutchman. To be a Dutchman to-day, a Frenchman to-morrow *M. Ado* iii 2 33
Veal, quoth the Dutchman. Is not 'veal' a calf? . . *L. L. Lost* v 2 247
Lustig, as the Dutchman says . . . . . . *All's Well* ii 3 47
Where you will hang like an icicle on a Dutchman's beard . *T. Night* iii 2 29
Duteous. Teaching his duteous land Audacious cruelty . 1 *Hen. IV.* iv 3 44
Which my most inward true and duteous spirit Teacheth 2 *Hen. IV.* iv 5 148
But with all duteous love Doth cherish you and yours . *Richard III.* ii 1 33
I entreat true peace of you, Which I will purchase with my duteous service . . . . ii 1 63
I 'll acquaint our duteous citizens With all your just proceedings . . iii 5 65
As duteous to the vices of thy mistress As badness would desire . *Lear* iv 6 258
You shall mark Many a duteous and knee-crooking knave . *Othello* i 1 45
Be but duteous, and true preferment shall tender itself to thee *Cymb.* iii 5 159
So duteous, diligent, So tender over his occasions, true, So feat, so nurse-like . . . . v 5 86
Duties. Only to the plain form of marriage, and you shall recount their particular duties afterwards . . . . *Much Ado* iv 1 3
He gave you all the duties of a man . . . . . 1 *Hen. IV.* v 2 56
Will not go off until they hear you speak.—They know their duties 2 *Hen. IV.* iv 2 101
This makes bold mouths : Tongues spit their duties out . . *Hen. VIII.* i 2 61
Keep your duties, As I have set them down . . *Coriolanus* i 7 1
By all the duties that I owe to Rome. . . . . *T. Andron.* i 1 414
These sorrowful drops upon thy blood-stain'd face, The last true duties of thy noble son ! . . . . v 3 155
Your highness' part Is to receive our duties ; and our duties Are to your throne and state children and servants . . . . *Macbeth* i 4 24
To the which my duties Are with a most indissoluble tie For ever knit . iii 1 16
To all, and him, we thirst, And all to all.—Our duties, and the pledge . iii 4 92
That this great king may kindly say, Our duties did his welcome pay . iv 1 132

Duties. 'Tis sweet and commendable in your nature, Hamlet, To give these mourning duties to your father . . . *Hamlet* i 2 88
You have begot me, bred me, loved me: I Return those duties back as are right fit . . . *Lear* i 1 99
Prescribe not us our duties . . . i 1 279
Than twenty silly ducking observants That stretch their duties nicely ii 2 110
By him do my duties to the senate . . . *Othello* iii 2 2
Say that they slack their duties, And pour our treasures into foreign laps iv 3 88
So seem as if You were inspired to do those duties *Cymbeline* ii 3 55
My friends, The boy hath taught us manly duties . . . iv 2 397
Dutiful. Show men dutiful? Why, so didst thou . . . *Hen. V.* ii 2 127
I must not break my faith. You know me dutiful . . . *Troi. and Cres.* v 3 72
Duty. Unwilling to proceed in But for my duty . . . *T. G. of Ver.* ii 1 113
My duty will I boast of; nothing else . . . ii 4 111
Duty never yet did want his meed . . . ii 4 112
My duty pricks me on to utter that Which else no worldly good should draw from me . . . iii 1 8
For my duty's sake, I rather chose To cross my friend in his intended drift . . . iii 1 17
She is peevish, sullen, froward, Proud, disobedient, stubborn, lacking duty . . . iii 1 69
Mine age Should have been cherish'd by her child-like duty . . . iii 1 75
A charitable duty of my order . . . *Com. of Errors* v 1 107
I owe you all duty.—I thank you . . . *Much Ado* i 1 157
It is my cousin's duty to make curtsy . . . ii 1 55
As my ever-esteemed duty pricks me on . . . *L. L. Lost* i 1 269
In all compliments of devoted and heart-burning heat of duty . . . i 1 280
Stay not thy compliment; I forgive thy duty . . . iv 2 147
Our duty is so rich, so infinite, That we may do it still without accompt v 2 199
With duty and desire we follow you . . . *M. N. Dream* i 1 127
For never any thing can be amiss, When simpleness and duty tender it v 1 83
I love not to see wretchedness o'ercharged And duty in his service perishing . . . v 1 86
What poor duty cannot do, noble respect Takes it in might, not merit . v 1 91
In the modesty of fearful duty I read as much as from the rattling tongue . . . v 1 101
I know my duty.—Yet more quarrelling with occasion! . *Mer. of Venice* iii 5 59
I attend them with all respect and duty . . . *As Y. Like It* i 2 177
The antique world, When service sweat for duty, not for meed . . . ii 3 58
All adoration, duty, and observance, All humbleness, all patience . . . v 2 102
So please your lordship to accept our duty.—With all my heart *T. of S.* Ind. 1 82
Such duty to the drunkard let him do With soft low tongue . . . Ind. 1 113
Wherein your lady and your humble wife May show her duty . . . Ind. 1 117
So shall I no whit be behind in duty . . . i 2 175
What you will command me will I do, So well I know my duty to my elders . . . ii 1 7
Do thy duty, and have thy duty . . . iv 1 38
What, no attendance? no regard? no duty? . . . iv 1 129
Now do your duty throughly, I advise you . . . iv 4 11
What a foolish duty call you this?—I would your duty were as foolish too v 2 125
The wisdom of your duty, fair Bianca, Hath cost me an hundred crowns v 2 127
The more fool you, for laying on my duty . . . v 2 129
Tell these headstrong women What duty they do owe their lords . . . v 2 131
Such duty as the subject owes the prince, Even such a woman oweth to her husband . . . v 2 155
In token of which duty, if he please, My hand is ready . . . v 2 178
My thanks and duty are your majesty's . . . *All's Well* i 2 23
Which I held my duty speedily to acquaint you withal . . . i 3 123
My duty then shall pay me for my pains . . . ii 1 128
That obedient right Which both thy duty owes and our power claims . . . ii 3 168
My duty to you. Your unfortunate son . . . iii 2 27
My mother did but duty . . . iv 2 12
My duty, madam, and most humble service . . . *T. Night* iii 1 106
My lord would speak; my duty hushes me . . . v 1 110
I leave my duty a little unthought of and speak out of my injury . . . v 1 318
His dignity and duty both cast off—Fled from his father . . . *W. Tale* v 1 183
You have broken from his liking Where you were tied in duty . . . v 1 213
Pay that duty which you truly owe To him that owes it . . . *K. John* ii 1 247
Hubert shall be your man, attend on you With all true duty . . . iii 3 73
But to my own disgrace Neglected my sworn duty in that case *Richard II.* i 1 134
My life thou shalt command, but not my shame: The one my duty owes i 1 167
The appellant in all duty greets your highness . . . i 3 52
Swear by the duty that you owe to God . . . i 3 180
Ay, how long Shall tender duty make me suffer wrong? . . . ii 1 164
The one is my sovereign, whom both my oath And duty bids defend . . . ii 2 113
Show me thy humble heart, and not thy knee, Whose duty is deceiveable ii 3 84
Throw away respect, Tradition, form and ceremonious duty . . . iii 2 173
My stooping duty tenderly shall show . . . iii 3 48
How dare thy joints forget To pay their awful duty to our presence? . . . iii 3 76
Stand all apart, And show fair duty to his majesty . . . iii 3 188
They might have lived to bear and he to taste Their fruits of duty . . . iii 4 63
With mine own breath release all duty's rites . . . iv 1 210
Our duty this way lies; for God's sake, come . . . 1 *Hen. IV.* v 4 16
My humble duty remembered, I will not be your suitor . 2 *Hen. IV.* ii 1 137
My fear is, your displeasure; my courtesy, my duty . . . Epil. 3
With hearts create of duty and of zeal . . . *Hen. V.* ii 2 31
A man that I love and honour with my soul, and my heart, and my duty, and my life . . . iii 6 9
Every subject's duty is the king's; but every subject's soul is his own . iv 1 186
I do salute you.—My duty to you both, on equal love . . . v 2 23
Shall this night appear How much in duty I am bound to both 1 *Hen. VI.* ii 1 37
My lord, it were your duty to forbear . . . iii 1 52
In reguerdon of that duty done, I gird thee with the valiant sword of York . . . iii 1 170
And as my duty springs, so perish they That grudge one thought! . . . iii 1 175
I have awhile given truce unto my wars, To do my duty to my sovereign iii 4 4
I owe him little duty, and less love . . . iv 4 34
But God in mercy so deal with my soul, As I in duty love my king and country! . . . 2 *Hen. VI.* i 3 161
Passeth by with stiff unbowed knee, Disdaining duty that to us belongs iii 1 17
In duty bend thy knee to me That bows unto the grave with mickle age v 1 173
Thou art too malapert.—I know my duty; you are all undutiful 3 *Hen. VI.* v 5 33
The duty that I owe unto your majesty I seal upon the lips of this sweet babe . . . v 7 28
I will with all expedient duty see you . . . *Richard III.* i 2 217
Were you well served, you would be taught your duty.—To serve me well, you all should do me duty . . . i 3 250
O, serve me well, and teach yourselves that duty! . . . i 3 253
Our duty, and thy fault, Provoke us hither now . . . i 4 230
Put meekness in thy mind, Love, charity, obedience, and true duty! . ii 2 108
Duty. To-day shalt thou behold a subject die For truth, for duty, and for loyalty . . . *Richard III.* iii 3 4
As he made semblance of his duty . . . *Hen. VIII.* i 2 198
If I but knew him, with my love and duty I would surrender it . i 4 80
Our breach of duty this way Is business of estate . . . ii 2 69
Against mine honour aught, My bond to wedlock, or my love and duty ii 4 40
Notwithstanding that your bond of duty, As 'twere in love's particular iii 2 188
Though all the world should crack their duty to you . . . iii 2 193
Yet my duty, As doth a rock against the chiding flood . . . iii 2 196
It is my duty To attend your highness' pleasure . . . v 1 90
To strengthen That holy duty, out of dear respect . . . v 3 119
What he shall receive of us in duty Gives us more palm in beauty than we have . . . *Troi. and Cres.* iii 1 169
Of thy deep duty more impression show Than that of common sons *Coriol.* v 3 51
And unproperly Show duty, as mistaken all this while Between the child and parent . . . v 3 55
That thou restrain'st from me the duty which To a mother's part belongs . . . v 3 167
Myself, Who had the world as my confectionary, The mouths, the tongues, the eyes and hearts of men At duty . . . *T. of Athens* iv 3 262
That which I show, heaven knows, is merely love, Duty and zeal . . . iv 3 523
I should not urge thy duty past thy might . . . *J. Cæsar* iv 3 261
Acquaint him with it, As needful in our loves, fitting our duty *Hamlet* i 1 173
Farewell, and let your haste commend your duty . . . i 2 39
In that and all things will we show our duty . . . i 2 40
Though willingly I came to Denmark, To show my duty in your coronation, Yet now, I must confess, that duty done, My thoughts and wishes bend again toward France . . . i 2 53
We did think it writ down in our duty To let you know of it . . . i 2 222
Our duty to your honour.—Your loves, as mine to you: farewell . . . i 2 253
I hold my duty, as I hold my soul, Both to my God and to my gracious king . . . ii 2 44
What duty is, Why day is day, night night, and time is time . . . ii 2 87
Who, in her duty and obedience, mark, Hath given me this . . . ii 2 107
If my duty be too bold, my love is too unmannerly . . . iii 2 363
We shall express our duty in his eye . . . iv 4 6
I commend my duty to your lordship . . . v 2 189
That lord whose hand must take my plight shall carry Half my love with him, half my care and duty . . . *Lear* i 1 104
Think'st thou that duty shall have dread to speak, When power to flattery bows? . . . i 1 149
My duty cannot be silent when I think your highness wronged . . . i 4 70
Men of choice and rarest parts, That all particulars of duty know . . . i 4 286
You have shown your father A child-like office.—'Twas my duty, sir . ii 1 108
Ere I was risen from the place that show'd My duty kneeling . . . ii 4 30
You less know how to value her desert Than she to scant her duty . ii 4 142
My duty cannot suffer To obey in all your daughters' hard commands . iii 4 153
My lady charged my duty in this business . . . iv 5 18
Trimm'd in forms and visages of duty . . . *Othello* i 1 50
Not I for love and duty, But seeming so, for my peculiar end . . . i 1 59
Tying her duty, beauty, wit and fortunes In an extravagant and wheeling stranger Of here and every where . . . i 1 136
With his free duty recommends you thus, And prays you to believe him i 3 41
My noble father, I do perceive here a divided duty . . . i 3 181
You are the lord of duty; I am hitherto your daughter . . . i 3 184
Here's my husband, And so much duty as my mother show'd To you, preferring you before her father, So much I challenge . . . i 3 186
A knave teach me my duty! . . . ii 3 151
Have you forgot all sense of place and duty? . . . ii 3 167
Though I am bound to every act of duty, I am not bound to that all slaves are free to . . . iii 3 134
Now I shall have reason To show the love and duty that I bear you . iii 3 194
'Tis a studied, not a present thought, By duty ruminated *Ant. and Cleo.* ii 2 141
Let ill tidings tell Themselves when they be felt.—I have done my duty ii 5 88
Give me grace to lay My duty on your hand . . . iii 13 82
Tend me to-night; May be it is the period of your duty . . . iv 2 25
Always reserved my holy duty . . . *Cymbeline* i 1 87
Nor to us hath tender'd The duty of the day . . . iii 5 32
She looks us like A thing more made of malice than of duty . . . iii 5 33
That duty leave unpaid to you, Which daily she was bound to proffer . iii 5 48
We will discharge our duty . . . iii 7 16
If neglection Should therein make me vile, the common body, By you relieved, would force me to my duty . . . *Pericles* iii 3 22
Dwarf. I had rather, forsooth, go before you like a man than follow him like a dwarf . . . *Mer. Wives* iii 2 6
Get you gone, you dwarf; You minimus . . . *M. N. Dream* iii 2 328
Alas, this is a child, a silly dwarf! . . . 1 *Hen. VI.* ii 3 22
A stirring dwarf we do allowance give Before a sleeping giant *Tr. and Cr.* ii 3 146
Dwarfish. Are you grown so high in his esteem, Because I am so dwarfish and so low? . . . *M. N. Dream* iii 2 295
Is well prepared To whip this dwarfish war, these pigmy arms *K. John* v 2 135
Their dwarfish pages were As cherubins, all gilt . . . *Hen. VIII.* i 1 22
Like a giant's robe Upon a dwarfish thief . . . *Macbeth* v 2 22
Dull of tongue, and dwarfish! What majesty is in her gait? *A. and C.* iii 3 19
Dwell. There's nothing ill can dwell in such a temple . . . *Tempest* i 2 457
If the ill spirit have so fair a house, Good things will strive to dwell with't . . . i 2 459
Queen of Tunis; she that dwells Ten leagues beyond man's life . . . ii 1 246
Let me not . . . dwell In this bare island . . . Epil. 7
As in the sweetest bud The eating canker dwells . . . *T. G. of Ver.* i 1 43
There dwells one Mistress Quickly . . . *Mer. Wives* i 2 2
I myself dwell with Master Doctor Caius . . . i 2 47
She dwells so securely on the excellency of her honour . . . ii 2 251
And dwell upon your grave when you are dead . . . *Com. of Errors* iii 1 104
Here dwells Benedick the married man . . . *Much Ado* v 1 186
O, then, what graces in my love do dwell! . . . *M. N. Dream* i 1 206
I'll rather dwell in my necessity . . . *Mer. of Venice* i 3 156
Can you tell me whether one Launcelot, that dwells with him, dwell with him or no? . . . ii 2 49
Approach; Here dwells my father Jew. Ho! who's within? . . . ii 6 25
Where dwell you, pretty youth?—With this shepherdess, my sister . . . *As Y. Like It* iii 2 352
Are you native of this place?—As the cony that you see dwell where she is kindled . . . iii 2 357
Rich honesty dwells like a miser, sir, in a poor house . . . v 4 62
To other regions France is a stable; we that dwell in't jades *All's Well* ii 3 301
I will tell you a thing, but you shall let it dwell darkly with you . . iv 3 13
The king lies by a beggar, if a beggar dwell near him . . . *T. Night* iii 1 9
Let him not come there, To seek out sorrow that dwells every where . . . *Richard II.* i 2 72

Dwell. I turn me from my country's light, To dwell in solemn shades of endless night . . . . *Richard II.* i 3 177
Such outward things dwell not in my desires *Hen. V.* iv 3 27
Wither, garden ; and be henceforth a burying-place to all that do dwell in this house . . 2 *Hen. VI.* iv 10 68
Where did you dwell when I was King of England? 3 *Hen. VI.* iii 1 74
'Tis thy presence that exhales this blood From cold and empty veins, where no blood dwells *Richard III.* i 2 59
Tear-falling pity dwells not in this eye iv 2 66
Sweet discourse, Which so long sunder'd friends should dwell upon . v 3 100
The leisure and enforcement of the time Forbids to dwell upon . v 3 239
He should still Dwell in his musings *Hen. VIII.* iii 2 133
Farewell The hopes of court! my hopes in heaven do dwell . iii 2 460
So may he ever do! and ever flourish, When I shall dwell with worms! iv 2 126
Yet in the trial much opinion dwells *Troi. and Cres.* i 3 336
What is aught, but as 'tis valued?—But value dwells not in particular will ii 2 53
To be wise and love Exceeds man's might; that dwells with gods above iii 2 164
Fain would I dwell on form, fain, fain deny What I have spoke *R. and J.* ii 2 88
Sleep dwell upon thine eyes, peace in thy breast! . . ii 2 187
O, that deceit should dwell In such a gorgeous palace! . . iii 2 84
I do remember an apothecary,—And hereabouts he dwells . v 1 38
Dwell I but in the suburbs Of your good pleasure? *J. Cæsar* ii 1 285
Whither are you going?—Where do you dwell? . . iii 3 7
Briefly, I dwell by the Capitol . . . . . iii 3 27
'Tis safer to be that which we destroy Than by destruction dwell in doubtful joy. . . . . . . *Macbeth* iii 2 7
Whose easy-borrow'd pride Dwells in the fickle grace of her he follows *Lear* ii 4 189
And, though he in a fertile climate dwell, Plague him with flies *Othello* i 1 70
The fleers, the gibes, and notable scorns, That dwell in every region of his face . . . . iv 1 84
The blest infusions That dwell in vegetives, in metals, stones *Pericles* iii 2 36
The house you dwell in proclaims you to be a creature of sale iv 6 83
Driven before the winds, he is arrived Here where his daughter dwells v Gower 15
Thou seem'st a palace For the crown'd Truth to dwell in . v 1 123
Dwellest. Where dwellest thou?—Under the canopy *Coriolanus* iv 5 40
Then thou dwellest with daws too?—No, I serve not thy master . iv 5 47
Dwelling. She excels each mortal thing Upon the dull earth dwelling *T. G. of Ver.* iv 2 52
Dwelling in a continual 'larum of jealousy *Mer. Wives* iii 5 72
Let me not find you before me again upon any complaint whatsoever; no, not for dwelling where you do . . . . *Meas. for Meas.* ii 1 261
Your accent is something finer than you could purchase in so removed a dwelling.—I have been told so of many . *As Y. Like It* iii 2 360
My name is call'd Vincentio; my dwelling Pisa *T. of Shrew* iv 5 55
The place of your dwelling, your names, your ages . *W. Tale* iv 4 740
You have here a goodly dwelling and a rich . 2 *Hen. IV.* v 3 7
For your dwelling,—briefly.—Briefly, I dwell by the Capitol *J. Cæsar* iii 3 26
Ne'er a villain dwelling in all Denmark But he's an arrant knave *Hamlet* i 5 123
Dwelling-house. His pure brain, Which some suppose the soul's frail dwelling-house . . . . . . *K. John* v 7 3
Dwelling-place. In their assign'd and native dwelling-place *As Y. Like It* ii 1 63
We charge and command you, in his highness' name, to repair to your several dwelling-places . . . . . 1 *Hen. VI.* i 3 77
Dwelt. There dwelt a man in Babylon, lady, lady! . *T. Night* ii 3 84
There was a man . . . Dwelt by a churchyard: I will tell it softly *W. T.* ii 1 30
Dwindle. Am I not fallen away vilely since this last action? do I not bate? do I not dwindle? . . . 1 *Hen. IV.* iii 3 3
Weary se'nnights nine times nine Shall he dwindle, peak and pine *Macb.* i 3 23
Dye. Flower of this purple dye, Hit with Cupid's archery *M. N. Dream* iii 2 102
Meditating that Shall dye your white rose in a bloody red 1 *Hen. VI.* ii 4 61
Dye. That dye is on me Which makes my whitest part black . *Hen. VIII.* i 1 208
Do not believe his vows; for they are brokers, Not of that dye which their investments show *Hamlet* i 3 128
Dyed. Give this napkin Dyed in his blood unto the shepherd *As Y. L. It* iv 3 156
Dyed in the dying slaughter of their foes . . *K. John* ii 1 323
I cannot rest Until the white rose that I wear be dyed Even in the lukewarm blood of Henry's heart . . . . 3 *Hen. VI.* i 2 33
Dyed in mummy which the skilful Conserved of maidens' hearts *Othello* iii 4 74
Dyeing. They call drinking deep, dyeing scarlet . 1 *Hen. IV.* ii 4 16
Dying. A life, whose very comfort Is still a dying horror *Meas. for Meas.* ii 3 42
She dying, as it must be so maintain'd, Upon the instant that she was accused, Shall be lamented . . . *Much Ado* iv 1 216
That strain again! it had a dying fall . . *T. Night* i 1 4
One good deed dying tongueless Slaughters a thousand waiting upon that . . . . *W. Tale* i 2 92
Thou meltest with things dying, I with things new-born iii 3 117
With purpled hands, Dyed in the dying slaughter of their foes *K. John* ii 1 323
The tongues of dying men Enforce attention like deep harmony *Rich. II.* ii 1 5
Should dying men flatter with those that live? . ii 1 88
And fight and die is death destroying death; Where fearing dying pays death servile breath . . . . iii 2 185
The lion dying thrusteth forth his paw, And wounds the earth v 1 29
Die all, die merrily.—Talk not of dying: I am out of fear Of death or death's hand for this one-half year . 1 *Hen. IV.* iv 1 135
To counterfeit dying, when a man thereby liveth, is to be no counterfeit v 4 119
And dying so, death is to him advantage; or not dying, the time was blessedly lost wherein such preparation was gained . *Hen. V.* iv 1 190
Dying like men, though buried in your dunghills, They shall be famed iv 3 99
Hear, hear how dying Salisbury doth groan! 1 *Hen. VI.* i 4 104
Let dying Mortimer here rest himself . . ii 5 2
Undaunted spirit in a dying breast! . . iii 2 99
As looks the mother on her lowly babe When death doth close his tender dying eyes . . . . . . iii 3 48
Dying with mother's dug between its lips 2 *Hen. VI.* iii 2 393
When dying clouds contend with growing light 3 *Hen. VI.* ii 5 2
Edward for Edward pays a dying debt . . *Richard III.* iv 4 21
Whom to leave Is only bitter to him, only dying . *Hen. VIII.* ii 1 74
This from a dying man receive as certain . . ii 1 125
So dying love lives still . . . . *Troi. and Cres.* iii 1 134
A thing of blood, whose every motion Was timed with dying cries *Coriol.* ii 2 114
Leak'd is our bark, And we, poor mates, stand on the dying deck, Hearing the surges threat . . . *T. of Athens* iv 2 20
Horses did neigh, and dying men did groan, And ghosts did shriek *J. C.* ii 2 23
Though he had no hand in his death, shall receive the benefit of his dying . . . . iii 2 47
Dying, mention it within their wills, Bequeathing it as a rich legacy . iii 2 141
And good men's lives Expire before the flowers in their caps, Dying or ere they sicken . . . . . *Macbeth* iv 3 173
He has my dying voice; So tell him, with the occurrents *Hamlet* v 2 367
She, dying, gave it me; And bid me, when my fate would have me wive, To give it her . . . . . *Othello* iii 4 63
She hath such a celerity in dying . . *Ant. and Cleo.* i 2 149
'Tis better playing with a lion's whelp Than with an old one dying . iii 13 95
I will live, Or bathe my dying honour in the blood Shall make it live again . . . . iv 2 6
I am dying, Egypt, dying; only I here importune death awhile . iv 15 18
I am dying, Egypt, dying: Give me some wine, and let me speak a little iv 15 41
Heavens, how they wound! Some slain before; some dying *Cymbeline* v 3 47
How ended she?—With horror, madly dying, like her life . v 5 31
And but she spoke it dying, I would not Believe her lips in opening it v 5 41

E

Each. Divide me like a bribe buck, each a haunch . *Mer. Wives* v 5 27
Good morrow, masters: each his several way . *Much Ado* v 3 29
And bide the penance of each three years' day . *L. L. Lost* i 1 115
Put in practice that Which each to other hath so strongly sworn i 1 309
The king your mote did see; But I a beam do find in each of three iv 3 162
In that each of you have forsworn his book, Can you still dream and pore? . . . . iv 3 297
Nor to their penn'd speech render we no grace, But while 'tis spoke each turn away her face . . . . . . v 2 148
Wink each at other; hold the sweet jest up . *M. N. Dream* iii 2 239
Slow in pursuit, but match'd in mouth like bells, Each under each iv 1 129
Each in his office ready at thy beck . . *T. of Shrew* Ind. 2 36
To each of you one fair and virtuous mistress Fall, when Love please! marry, to each, but one! . . . . . . *All's Well* ii 3 63
Guiltian, Cosmo, Lodowick, Gratii, two hundred and fifty each iv 3 187
And do sigh At each his needless heavings . *W. Tale* ii 3 35
Each your doing, So singular in each particular, Crowns what you are doing . . . . iv 4 143
Like a school broke up, Each hurries toward his home . 2 *Hen. IV.* iv 2 105
Let me see, by ten We shall have each a hundred Englishmen *Hen. V.* iii 7 169
Each hath his place and function to attend: I am left out 1 *Hen. VI.* i 1 173
Each of them had twenty times their power . 2 *Hen. VI.* ii 4 61
Live each of you the subjects to his hate, And he to yours! *Richard III.* i 3 302
Gazed each on other, and look'd deadly pale . . iii 7 26
Which compel from each The sixth part of his substance *Hen. VIII.* i 2 57
Sixth part of each? A trembling contribution! . . i 2 94
'Tis just to each of them; he is himself *Troi. and Cres.* i 2 75
Both merits poised, each weighs nor less nor more . iv 1 65
Though all at once cannot See what I do deliver out to each . *Coriolanus* i 1 147
Each in my love alike and none less dear . . iii 3 24
And tell me, In peace what each of them by the other lose . iii 2 44
And each in either side Give the all-hail to thee . . v 3 138
And men of heart Look'd wondering each at other . . v 6 100
Each wreathed in the other's arms . . *T. Andron.* ii 3 25
Let each take some; Nay, put out all your hands . *T. of Athens* iv 2 27
You seem to understand me, By each at once her choppy finger laying Upon her skinny lips . . . . *Macbeth* i 3 44
Each. Let us speak Our free hearts each to other . *Macbeth* i 3 155
With entertainment Of each new-hatch'd, unfledged comrade. *Hamlet* i 3 65
Ten masts at each make not the altitude Which thou hast perpendicularly fell . . . . *Lear* iv 6 53
Each jealous of the other, as the stung Are of the adder . v 1 56
Whether he kill Cassio, Or Cassio him, or each do kill the other *Othello* v 1 13
Her love to both Would, each to other and all loves to both, Draw after her. . . . . *Ant. and Cleo.* ii 2 138
It had been pity you should have been put together with so mortal a purpose as then each bore . . . . *Cymbeline* i 4 44
Two winking Cupids Of silver, each on one foot standing ii 4 90
If each of you should take this course, how many Must murder wives much better than themselves! . . . . . v 1 3
You some permit To second ills with ills, each elder worse . v 1 14
Each act. We may not think the justness of each act Such and no other than event doth form it . . . *Troi. and Cres.* ii 2 119
Each actor. Then came each actor on his ass . *Hamlet* ii 2 414
Each army. I am with both: each army hath a hand *K. John* iii 1 328
Each article. To deny each article with oath Cannot remove nor choke the strong conception That I do groan withal . . *Othello* v 2 54
Each battle sees the other's umber'd face . . *Hen. V.* iv Prol. 9
Each bound. And like the current flies Each bound it chafes *T. of Athens* i 1 25
Each bush. The thief doth fear each bush an officer . 3 *Hen. VI.* v 6 12
Nature on each bush Lays her full mess before you . *T. of Athens* iv 3 423
Each buzz, each fancy, each complaint, dislike . *Lear* i 4 348
Each calamity. Too well I feel The different plague of each calamity *K. John* iii 4 60
Each chance. Determine on some course, More than a wild exposure to each chance . . . . . . *Coriolanus* iv 1 36
Each circumstance Of place, time, fortune, do cohere *T. Night* v 1 258
Each complaint. Each buzz, each fancy, each complaint, dislike *Lear* i 4 348
Each corporal agent. I am settled, and bend up Each corporal agent to this terrible feat . . . . . . *Macbeth* i 7 80
Each county. Collected choicely, from each county some 2 *Hen. VI.* iii 1 313
Each day still better other's happiness! . . *Richard II.* i 1 22
By means whereof the towns each day revolted 2 *Hen. VI.* iii 1 63
The death of each day's life, sore labour's bath *Macbeth* ii 2 38

Each degree. All several sins, all used in each degree . *Richard III.* v 3 198

Each drop. And then we shall repent each drop of blood That hot rash haste so indirectly shed *K. John* ii 1 48

And with him pour we in our country's purge Each drop of us *Macbeth* v 2 29

Each drop she falls would prove a crocodile . . . . *Othello* iv 1 257

Each dust. Shall blow each dust, each straw, each little rub, Out of the path *K. John* iii 4 128

Each ear. At each ear a hearer *Hamlet* ii 2 400

Each end. And with each end of thy blue bow dost crown My bosky acres . . . . *Tempest* iv 1 80

Each eye. In both my eyes he doubly sees himself; In each eye, one *Mer. of Venice* v 1 245

Each fair instalment, coat, and several crest . *Mer. Wives* v 5 67

Each fairy. Through this house each fairy stray . . *M. N. Dream* v 1 409

Each fancy. Each buzz, each fancy, each complaint, dislike . *Lear* i 4 348

Each following day Became the next day's master . . *Hen. VIII.* i 1 16

Each grace. In each grace of these There lurks a still and dumb-discoursive devil That tempts most cunningly . . *Troi. and Cres.* iv 4 91

Each grain. And proofs as clear as founts in July when We see each grain of gravel *Hen. VIII.* i 1 155

Each groan. His fortunes I will weep and 'twixt each groan Say 'Who's a traitor?' . . . . 2 *Hen. VI.* iii 1 221

Each heart being set On bloody courses . . 2 *Hen. IV.* i 1 158

Each heart in Rome does love and pity you . . *Ant. and Cleo.* iii 6 92

Each hour. Taught thee each hour One thing or other . *Tempest* i 2 354

And each hour's joy wreck'd with a week of teen . *Richard III.* iv 1 97

Each incensed will. This tractable obedience is a slave To each incensed will *Hen. VIII.* i 2 65

Each knight. Explain The labour of each knight in his device *Pericles* ii 2 15

Each leader. Limit each leader to his several charge . *Richard III.* v 3 25

Each letter. Blow not a word away Till I have found each letter in the letter *T. G. of Ver.* i 2 119

Each lord. Achilles shall have word of this intent; So shall each lord of Greece *Troi. and Cres.* i 3 307

Put on A form of strangeness as we pass along: So do each lord . iii 3 52

Each man. Let each man do his best . . . . . 1 *Hen. IV.* v 2 93

No doubt, my liege, if each man do his best . . *Hen. V.* ii 2 19

Come on, my masters, each man take his stand . 3 *Hen. VI.* iv 3 1

Send our letters, with Free pardon to each man . *Hen. VIII.* i 2 100

Each man to his stool, with that spur as he would to the lip of his mistress *T. of Athens* iii 6 73

Lend to each man enough, that one need not lend to another . iii 6 82

Each man apart, all single and alone, Yet an arch-villain keeps him company . . . . v 1 110

So let high-sighted tyranny range on, Till each man drop by lottery *J. C.* ii 1 119

Let each man render me his bloody hand . . . . iii 1 184

Take each man's censure but reserve thy judgement . *Hamlet* i 3 69

So distribution should undo excess, And each man have enough *Lear* iv 1 74

Each man to what sport and revels his addiction leads him . *Othello* ii 2 5

And have fought Not as you served the cause, but as't had been Each man's like mine . . . . . . *Ant. and Cleo.* iv 8 7

Where each man Thinks all is writ he speken can . . *Pericles* ii Gower 11

Each minute teems a new one . . . . . *Macbeth* iv 3 176

With news the time's with labour, and throes forth, Each minute, some *Ant. and Cleo.* iii 7 82

With whom each minute threatens life or death . . . *Pericles* i 3 25

Each mortal thing. She excels each mortal thing . *T. G. of Ver.* iv 2 51

Each naked curtle-axe. Scarce blood enough in all their sickly veins To give each naked curtle-axe a stain . . *Hen. V.* iv 2 21

Each new day a gash Is added to her wounds . . *Macbeth* iv 3 40

Each new morn New widows howl, new orphans cry . . iv 3 4

Each object. Hitting Each object with a joy . . *Cymbeline* v 5 396

Each one, tripping on his toe, Will be here with mop and mow *Tempest* iv 1 46

Each one with ireful passion, with drawn swords, Met us again *C. of Err.* v 1 151

The whole world again Cannot pick out five such, take each one in his vein . . . . *L. L. Lost* v 2 548

To bed with him; And each one to his office when he wakes *T. of Shr.* Ind. 1 73

And therefore for assurance Let's each one send unto his wife . v 2 66

She would to each one sip . . . . . . *W. Tale* iv 4 62

Where we may leisurely Each one demand and answer to his part . v 3 153

Three Judases, each one thrice worse than Judas! . *Richard II.* iii 2 132

Through this grate, I count each one And view the Frenchmen 1 *Hen. VI.* i 4 60

Three glorious suns, each one a perfect sun . . 3 *Hen. VI.* ii 1 26

Each one already blazing by our meeds . . . . . ii 1 36

Circle me about, That I may turn me to each one of you . *T. Andron.* iii 1 278

So, thanks to all at once and to each one, Whom we invite *Macbeth* v 8 74

Ten, chased by one, Are now each one the slaughter-man of twenty *Cymb.* v 3 49

Therefore each one betake him to his rest . . . *Pericles* ii 3 115

Each opposite that blanks the face of joy . . . *Hamlet* iii 2 230

Each other. Has Ford's wife and Page's wife acquainted each other how they love me? . . . . *Mer. Wives* ii 2 114

We still did meet each other's man, And I was ta'en for him, and he for me *Com. of Errors* v 1 386

And from each other look thou lead them thus . . *M. N. Dream* iii 2 363

Consent with both that we may enjoy each other . . *As Y. Like It* v 2 11

Pardon me, sweet one, even for the vows We made each other *T. Night* v 1 222

When that we have dash'd them to the ground, Why then defy each other *K. John* ii 1 406

Austria and France shoot in each other's mouth: I'll stir them to it . ii 1 414

To appeal each other of high treason . . . . *Richard II.* i 1 27

You never shall . . . Embrace each other's love in banishment . i 3 184

Possess'd with fear So strongly that they dare not meet each other 1 *Hen. IV.* ii 2 113

Gentlemen both, you will mistake each other . . *Hen. V.* iii 2 146

The fix'd sentinels almost receive The secret whispers of each other's watch . . . . iv Prol. 7

France and England, whose very shores look pale With envy of each other's happiness . . . . v 2 379

That English may as French, French Englishmen, Receive each other . v 2 396

This shouldering of each other in the court . . 1 *Hen. VI.* iv 1 189

Whiles they each other cross, Lives, honours, lands and all hurry to loss iv 3 52

Ready to catch each other by the throat . . . *Richard III.* i 3 189

And charged us from his soul to love each other . . . i 4 243

Take each other's hand; Dissemble not your hatred . . . ii 1 8

Now cheer each other in each other's love . . . . ii 2 114

We know each other's faces, But for our hearts, he knows no more of mine, Than I of yours . . . . iii 4 10

Four red roses on a stalk, Which in their summer beauty kiss'd each other . . . . iv 3 13

Two curs shall tame each other . . . . *Troi. and Cres.* i 3 391

Each other. But eye to eye opposed Salutes each other with each other's form . . . . *Troi. and Cres.* iii 3 108

We know each other well.—We do; and long to know each other worse iv 1 30

We two, that with so many thousand sighs Did buy each other . . iv 4 42

Will you the knights, Shall to the edge of all extremity Pursue each other? . . . . iv 5 69

Unbuckling helms, fisting each other's throat . . *Coriolanus* iv 5 131

Make war breed peace, make peace stint war, make each Prescribe to other as each other's leech . . . . *T. of Athens* v 4 84

There's one did laugh in's sleep, and one cried 'Murder!' That they did wake each other . . . . . . *Macbeth* ii 2 24

'Tis said they eat each other.—They did so, to the amazement of mine eyes . . . . ii 4 18

Pale as his shirt; his knees knocking each other . . *Hamlet* ii 1 81

And of the Cannibals that each other eat . . . . *Othello* i 3 143

We'll feast each other ere we part; and let's Draw lots . *Ant. and Cleo.* ii 6 61

My heart parted betwixt two friends That do afflict each other! . . iii 6 78

That great face of war, whose several ranges Frighted each other . . iii 13 6

Each pang. Her sufferance made Almost each pang a death *Hen. VIII.* v 1 69

Each part. These your unusual weeds to each part of you Do give a life *W. Tale* iv 4 1

I can see his pride Peep through each part of him . . *Hen. VIII.* i 1 69

For this, being smelt, with that part cheers each part . *Rom. and Jul.* ii 3 25

Each part, deprived of supple government . . . . . . iv 1 102

Each particular. Swear down each particular saint . *Meas. for Meas.* v 1 243

Swear his thought over By each particular star in heaven . *W. Tale* i 2 425

Each your doing, So singular in each particular, Crowns what you are doing in the present deed . . . . iv 4 144

And each particular hair to stand an end . . . . . *Hamlet* i 5 19

Each petty artery. Makes each petty artery in this body As hardy as the Nemean lion's nerve . . . . i 4 82

Each pinch more stinging Than bees that made 'em . . . *Tempest* i 2 329

Each putter-out of five for one will bring us Good warrant of . . iii 3 48

Each royal house. Richmond and Elizabeth, The true succeeders of each royal house . . . . *Richard III.* v 5 30

Each second. Where each second Stood heir to the first . . *Othello* i 1 37

Each several. I'll kiss each several paper for amends *T. G. of Ver.* i 2 108

And each several chamber bless, Through this palace . *M. N. Dream* v 1 424

Each several article herein redress'd . . . . 2 *Hen. IV.* iv 1 170

Abound In the division of each several crime, Acting it many ways *Macb.* iv 3 96

We commit no crime To use one language in each several clime *Pericles* iv 4 6

Each side. My keen-edged sword, Deck'd with five flower-de-luces on each side . . . . 1 *Hen. VI.* i 2 99

What two reverend bishops Were those that went on each side of the queen? . . . . *Hen. VIII.* iv 1 100

On each side her Stood pretty dimpled boys . . . *Ant. and Cleo.* ii 2 206

Each small annexment, petty consequence, Attends the boisterous ruin *Hamlet* iii 3 21

Each soil. Stain'd with the variation of each soil . 1 *Hen. IV.* i 1 64

Each substance of a grief hath twenty shadows . *Richard II.* ii 2 14

Each syllable. I heard Each syllable that breath made up between them *Othello* iv 2 5

Each thing. Be cheerful And think of each thing well . . *Tempest* v 1 251

But like of each thing that in season grows . . *L. L. Lost* i 1 107

Order gave each thing view . . . . . . *Hen. VIII.* i 1 44

Each thing meets In mere oppugnancy . . . . *Troi. and Cres.* i 3 110

Each thing's a thief . . . . *T. of Athens* iv 3 445

In each thing give him way, cross him in nothing . *Ant. and Cleo.* i 3 9

Each toy seems prologue to some great amiss . . . *Hamlet* iv 5 18

Each Trojan that is master of his heart, Let him to field . *Troi. and Cres.* i 1 4

Each true word. For each true word, a blister! . . *T. of Athens* v 1 135

Each way. You are like to do such business.—Not unlike, Each way, to better yours . . . . *Coriolanus* iii 1 49

But float upon a wild and violent sea Each way and move *Macbeth* iv 2 22

Each weary step. Make a pastime of each weary step . *T. G. of Ver.* ii 7 35

Each well-ordered nation. There is a law in each well-order'd nation To curb those raging appetites . . . *Troi. and Cres.* ii 2 180

Each wind. I am a feather for each wind that blows . *W. Tale* ii 3 154

Each word. First, rehearse your song by rote, To each word a warbling note . . . . *M. N. Dream* v 1 405

And at each word's deliverance Stab poniards in our flesh 3 *Hen. VI.* ii 1 97

O Marcius, Marcius! Each word thou hast spoke hath weeded from my heart A root of ancient envy . . . . . *Coriolanus* iv 5 108

Both in time, Form of the thing, each word made true and good *Hamlet* i 2 210

Eager. The bitter clamour of two eager tongues . *Richard II.* i 1 49

With eager feeding food doth choke the feeder . . . ii 1 37

What shrill-voiced suppliant makes this eager cry? . . . v 3 75

They are hare-brain'd slaves, And hunger will enforce them to be more eager . . . . 1 *Hen. VI.* i 2 38

All my followers to the eager foe Turn back and fly . 3 *Hen. VI.* i 4 4

If so thou think'st, vex him with eager words . . . ii 6 68

It is a nipping and an eager air . . . . . *Hamlet* i 4 2

It doth posset And curd, like eager droppings into milk . . i 5 69

Eagerly. How eagerly ye follow my disgraces, As if it fed ye! *Hen. VIII.* iii 2 240

So went to bed; where eagerly his sickness Pursued him still . iv 2 24

Who, having some advantage on Octavius, Took it too eagerly *J. Cæsar* v 3 7

Eagerness. Madding my eagerness with her restraint *All's Well* v 3 213

Eagle. A lover's eyes will gaze an eagle blind . *L. L. Lost* iv 3 334

And like an eagle o'er his aery towers, To souse annoyance *K. John* v 2 149

Behold, his eye, As bright as is the eagle's . . *Richard II.* iii 3 69

When I was about thy years, Hal, I was not an eagle's talon in the waist 1 *Hen. IV.* ii 4 363

Like estridges that with the wind Baited like eagles having lately bathed . . . . iv 1 99

For once the eagle England being in prey, To her unguarded nest the weasel Scot Comes sneaking and so sucks her princely eggs *Hen. V.* i 2 169

Was Mahomet inspired with a dove? Thou with an eagle art inspired then . . . . 1 *Hen. VI.* i 2 141

An empty eagle were set To guard the chicken from a hungry kite 2 *Hen. VI.* iii 1 248

Drones suck not eagles' blood but rob bee-hives . . . iv 1 109

And like an empty eagle Tire on the flesh of me and of my son! 3 *Hen. VI.* i 1 268

Nay, if thou be that princely eagle's bird, Show thy descent by gazing 'gainst the sun . . . . ii 1 91

Thus yields the cedar to the axe's edge, Whose arms gave shelter to the princely eagle . . . . v 2 12

More pity that the eagle should be mew'd, While kites and buzzards prey at liberty . . . . *Richard III.* i 1 132

That wrens make prey where eagles dare not perch . . . i 3 71

Eagle. The eagles are gone: crows and daws, crows and daws! *Tr. and Cr.* i 2 265
Which will in time Break ope the locks o' the senate and bring in The crows to peck the eagles *Coriolanus* iii 1 139
Like an eagle in a dove-cote, I Flutter'd your Volscians in Corioli . v 6 115
The eagle suffers little birds to sing, And is not careful what they mean thereby . . . . *T. Andron.* iv 4 83
An eagle, madam, Hath not so green, so quick, so fair an eye *R. and J.* iii 5 221
Flies an eagle flight, bold and forth on, Leaving no tract behind *T. of A.* i 1 49
These moss'd trees, That have outlived the eagle . . . . iv 3 224
Coming from Sardis, on our former ensign Two mighty eagles fell *J. C.* v 1 81
Dismay'd not this Our captains, Macbeth and Banquo?—Yes; As sparrows eagles, or the hare the lion *Macbeth* i 2 35
This was but as a fly by an eagle . . . . *Ant. and Cleo.* ii 2 186
I chose an eagle, And did avoid a puttock *Cymbeline* i 1 139
We find The sharded beetle in a safer hold Than is the full-wing'd eagle iii 3 21
I saw Jove's bird, the Roman eagle, wing'd From the spongy south iv 2 348
Forthwith they fly Chickens, the way which they stoop'd eagles . v 3 42
Mount, eagle, to my palace crystalline . . . . . iv 4 113
The holy eagle Stoop'd, as to foot us . . . . . v 4 115
As I slept, methought Great Jupiter, upon his eagle back'd, Appear'd v 5 427
The Roman eagle, From south to west on wing soaring aloft, Lessen'd herself . . . . v 5 470
Our princely eagle, The imperial Cæsar . . . . . v 5 473
Thou art like the harpy, Which, to betray, dost, with thine angel's face, Seize with thine eagle's talons . . . . . *Pericles* iv 3 48
Eagle-sighted. What peremptory eagle-sighted eye Dares look upon the heaven of her brow? . . . . . *L. L. Lost* iv 3 226
Eagle-winged. The eagle-winged pride Of sky-aspiring and ambitious thoughts . . . . . . *Richard II.* i 3 129
Eale. The dram of eale Doth all the noble substance of a doubt To his own scandal . . . . . . *Hamlet* i 4 36
Ean. So many days my ewes have been with young; So many weeks ere the poor fools will ean . . . . . 3 *Hen. VI.* ii 5 36
Eaning time. The fulsome ewes, Who then conceiving did in eaning time Fall parti-colour'd lambs . . . *Mer. of Venice* i 3 88
I was shipp'd at sea, I well remember, Even on my eaning time *Pericles* iii 4 6
Eanling. All the eanlings which were streak'd and pied Should fall as Jacob's hire . . . . . . *Mer. of Venice* i 3 80
Ear. The very minute bids thee ope thine ear . . . *Tempest* i 2 37
Set all hearts i' the state To what tune pleased his ear . . . i 2 85
My quaint Ariel, Hark in thine ear.—My lord, it shall be done . i 2 318
You cram these words into mine ears against The stomach of my sense ii 1 106
Didn't not wake you? It struck mine ear most terribly . . . ii 1 313
O, 'twas a din to fright a monster's ear, To make an earthquake! . ii 1 314
The harmony of their tongues hath into bondage Brought my too diligent ear . . . . iii 1 42
Sometimes a thousand twangling instruments Will hum about mine ears iii 2 147
Like unback'd colts, they prick'd their ears, Advanced their eyelids iv 1 176
So I charm'd their ears That calf-like they my lowing follow'd iv 1 178
I will fetch off my bottle, though I be o'er ears for my labour iv 1 214
I long To hear the story of your life, which must Take the ear strangely v 1 313
My ears are stopt and cannot hear good news . . . *T. G. of Ver.* iii 1 205
Breathe it in mine ear, As ending anthem of my endless dolour . iii 1 239
Give some evening music to her ear . . . . . . iv 2 17
You have a quick ear.—Ay, I would I were deaf; it makes me have a slow heart . . . . iv 2 63
He hears with ears . . . . *Mer. Wives* i 1 150
What phrase is this, 'He hears with ear'? why, it is affectations i 1 152
Give ear to his motions, Master Slender . . . . . i 1 221
Notwithstanding,—to tell you in your ear; I would have no words of it i 4 109
Let me tell you in your ear . . . . ii 2 100
Scurvy jack-dog priest! by gar, me vill cut his ears . . . ii 3 66
I pray you, let-a me speak a word with your ear . . . iii 1 82
If it should come to the ear of the court . . . . . iv 5 97
So I have strew'd it in the common ear, And so it is received *M. for M.* i 3 15
If he took you a box o' the ear, you might have your action of slander ii 1 189
Fasten your ear on my advisings . . . . . . iii 1 203
Who hath a story ready for your ear . . . . . . iv 1 56
Lord Angelo hath to the public ear Profess'd the contrary . . iv 2 102
I would commune with you of such things That want no ear but yours iv 3 109
I have stood by, my lord, and I have heard Your royal ear abused v 1 139
But, in foul mouth And in the witness of his proper ear, To call him villain . . . . v 1 310
Whereto if you'll a willing ear incline, What's mine is yours . v 1 542
He's at two hands with me, and that my two ears can witness *C. of Err.* ii 1 46
Know'st thou his mind?—Ay, ay, he told his mind upon mine ear ii 1 48
That never words were music to thine ear, That never object pleasing in thine eye . . . . ii 2 116
What error drives our eyes and ears amiss? . . . . ii 2 186
I'll stop mine ears against the mermaid's song . . . iii 2 169
And teach your ears to list me with more heed . . . iv 1 101
I tell you, 'twill sound harshly in her ears . . . iv 4 7
I am an ass, indeed; you may prove it by my long ears . . iv 4 31
Give me your hand and let me feel your pulse.—There is my hand, and let it feel your ear . . . . iv 4 56
These ears of mine, thou know'st, did hear thee . . . v 1 26
I will be sworn these ears of mine Heard you confess . . v 1 259
My dull deaf ears a little use to hear . . . . . v 1 316
Thus answer I in name of Benedick, But hear these ill news with the ears of Claudio . . . . *Much Ado* ii 1 180
My cousin tells him in his ear that he is in her heart . . ii 1 328
Whisper her ear and tell her, I and Ursula Walk in the orchard . iii 1 4
Then go we near her, that her ear lose nothing Of the false sweet bait . iii 1 32
What fire is in mine ears? Can this be true? . . . iii 1 107
A word in your ear . . . . iv 2 29
Which falls into mine ears as profitless As water in a sieve . . v 1 4
Give not me counsel; Nor let no comforter delight mine ear . . v 1 6
Shall I speak a word in your ear?—God bless me from a challenge! v 1 144
They say he wears a key in his ear and a lock hanging by it . . v 1 318
That aged ears play truant at his tales . . . *L. L. Lost* ii 1 74
Break the neck of the wax, and every one give ear . . . iv 1 59
Hangeth like a jewel in the ear of caelo, the sky, the welkin, the heaven iv 2 5
Who is he comes here? What, Longaville! and reading! listen, ear iv 3 45
A lover's ear will hear the lowest sound . . . . iv 3 335
His lines would ravish savage ears And plant in tyrants mild humility iv 3 348
Our ears vouchsafe it.—But your legs should do it . . . v 2 217
Madam, and pretty mistresses, give ear . . . . . v 2 286
What did you whisper in your lady's ear? . . . . v 2 436
What did the Russian whisper in your ear? . . . . v 2 443
Honest plain words best pierce the ear of grief . . . v 2 763
Ear. A jest's prosperity lies in the ear Of him that hears it . *L. L. Lost* v 2 871
Sickly ears, Deaf'd with the clamours of their own dear groans . v 2 873
Cuckoo, cuckoo: O word of fear, Unpleasing to a married ear! . v 2 912
Your tongue's sweet air More tuneable than lark to shepherd's ear *M. N. Dream* i 1 184
My ear should catch your voice, my eye your eye . . . i 1 188
Go seek some dewdrops here And hang a pearl in every cowslip's ear . ii 1 15
Sing again: Mine ear is much enamour'd of thy note . . iii 1 141
Dark night, that from the eye his function takes, The ear more quick of apprehension makes . . . . iii 2 178
Mine ear, I thank it, brought me to thy sound . . . iii 2 182
Stick musk-roses in thy sleek smooth head, And kiss thy fair large ears iv 1 4
I have a reasonable good ear in music. Let's have the tongs and the bones . . . . iv 1 31
Their heads are hung With ears that sweep away the morning dew . iv 1 126
The eye of man hath not heard, the ear of man hath not seen . iv 1 217
If they should speak, would almost damn those ears . *Mer. of Venice* i 1 98
He borrowed a box of the ear of the Englishman . . . i 2 86
Stop my house's ears, I mean my casements . . . . ii 5 34
I would my daughter were dead at my foot, and the jewels in her ear! iii 1 93
As are those dulcet sounds in break of day That creep into the dreaming bridegroom's ear . . . . iii 2 52
Here will we sit and let the sounds of music Creep in our ears . v 1 56
With sweetest touches pierce your mistress' ear . . . v 1 67
Or any air of music touch their ears, You shall perceive them make a mutual stand . . . . v 1 76
I must tell you friendly in your ear, Sell when you can *As Y. Like It* iii 5 59
To glean the broken ears after the man That the main harvest reaps . iii 5 102
Such a storm That mortal ears might hardly endure the din *T. of Shrew* i 1 178
Think you a little din can daunt mine ears? Have I not in my time heard lions roar? . . . . i 2 200
Let's ha't, good Grumio.—Lend thine ear . . . . iv 1 62
This cuff was but to knock at your ear, and beseech listening . iv 1 67
Your betters have endured me say my mind, And if you cannot, best you stop your ears . . . . iv 3 76
Pitchers have ears . . . . . iv 4 52; *Richard III.* ii 4 37
The Florentines and Senoys are by the ears . . . *All's Well* i 2 1
His plausive words He scatter'd not in ears, but grafted them . i 2 54
He that ears my land spares my team and gives me leave to in the crop i 3 47
Alone she was, and did communicate to herself her own words to her own ears . . . . i 3 113
That pitiful rumour may report my flight, To consolate thine ear . iii 2 131
Know you such a one?—But by the ear . . . . . iii 5 53
Thine, as he vowed to thee in thine ear . . . . . iv 3 260
This man may help me to his majesty's ear, If he would spend his power v 1 7
Whose words all ears took captive . . . . . . v 3 17
She does abuse our ears: to prison with her . . . . v 3 295
It came o'er my ear like the sweet sound, That breathes upon a bank of violets . . . . *T. Night* i 1 5
Speak your office.—It alone concerns your ear . . . . i 5 224
To your ears, divinity, to any other's, profanation . . . i 5 233
Go shake your ears . . . . ii 3 134
My matter hath no voice, lady, but to your own most pregnant and vouchsafed ear . . . . iii 1 100
It is as fat and fulsome to mine ear As howling after music . . v 1 112
Therefore perpend, my princess, and give ear . . . . v 1 308
O'er head and ears a fork'd one! . . . . . . *W. Tale* i 2 186
To have nor eyes nor ears nor thought . . . . . i 2 275
Come on, then, And give't me in mine ear . . . . ii 1 32
He utters them as he had eaten ballads and all men's ears grew to his tunes . . . . iv 4 186
All their other senses stuck in ears . . . . . . iv 4 621
To have an open ear, a quick eye, and a nimble hand, is necessary for a cut-purse . . . . iv 4 685
Then I'ld shriek, that even your ears Should rift to hear me . v 1 65
Bohemia stops his ears, and threatens them With divers deaths in death v 1 201
Though credit be asleep and not an ear open . . . . v 2 68
So much my conscience whispers in your ear . . . *K. John* i 1 42
My face so thin That in mine ear I durst not stick a rose . . i 1 142
What cracker is this same that deafs our ears? . . . ii 1 147
They shoot but calm words folded up in smoke, To make a faithless error in your ears . . . . ii 1 230
He gives the bastinado with his tongue: Our ears are cudgell'd . ii 1 464
Rounded in the ear With that same purpose-changer . . . ii 1 566
If that thou couldst see me without eyes, Hear me without thine ears . iii 3 49
Using conceit alone, Without eyes, ears and harmful sound of words . iii 3 51
Life is as tedious as a twice-told tale Vexing the dull ear of a drowsy man iii 4 109
Her ear Is stopp'd with dust; the first of April died Your noble mother iv 2 119
They shake their heads And whisper one another in the ear . . iv 2 189
And another shall As loud as thine rattle the welkin's ear . . v 2 172
Pardon me, That any accent breaking from thy tongue Should 'scape the true acquaintance of mine ear . . . . v 6 15
You breathe these dead news in as dead an ear . . . . v 7 65
Let my sovereign turn away his face And bid his ears a little while be deaf, Till I have told this slander . . . . . *Richard II.* i 1 112
Impartial are our eyes and ears . . . . i 1 115
Strive not with your breath; For all in vain comes counsel to his ear . ii 1 4
My death's sad tale may yet undeaf his ear . . . . ii 1 16
To whose venom sound The open ear of youth doth always listen . ii 1 20
Where doth the world thrust forth a vanity—So it be new, there's no respect how vile—That is not quickly buzz'd into his ears? . . ii 1 26
Quick is mine ear to hear of good towards him . . . . ii 1 234
Mine ear is open and my heart prepared: The worst is worldly loss . iii 2 93
And let them go To ear the land that hath some hope to grow . iii 2 212
Send the breath of parley Into his ruin'd ears . . . . iii 3 34
Spur thee on with full as many lies As may be holloa'd in thy treacherous ear . . . . iv 1 54
Set thy tongue there; Or in thy piteous heart plant thou thine ear . v 3 126
Here have I the daintiness of ear To check time broke in a disorder'd string . . . . v 5 45
Had not an ear to hear my true time broke . . . . v 5 48
Well, God give thee the spirit of persuasion and him the ears of profiting 1 *Hen. IV.* i 2 171
You start away And lend no ear unto my purposes . . . i 3 217
I will find him when he lies asleep, And in his ear I'll holla 'Mortimer!' i 3 222
This woman's mood, Tying thine ear to no tongue but thine own . i 3 238
Lay thine ear close to the ground and list if thou canst hear the tread of travellers . . . . ii 2 34
Many tales devised, Which oft the ear of greatness needs must hear . iii 2 24
The mailed Mars shall on his altar sit Up to the ears in blood . iv 1 117

Ear. We will not trust our eyes Without our ears . . . 1 *Hen. IV.* v 4 140
Open your ears; for which of you will stop The vent of hearing when loud Rumour speaks? . . 2 *Hen. IV.* Ind. 1
Stuffing the ears of men with false reports . . . Ind. 8
Stopping my greedy ear with their bold deeds . . . i 1 78
In the end, to stop my ear indeed, Thou hast a sigh to blow away this praise . . . i 1 79
To punish you by the heels would amend the attention of your ears . i 2 142
For the box of the ear that the prince gave you, he gave it like a rude prince, and you took it like a sensible lord . . . i 2 218
By this light, I am well spoke on; I can hear it with mine own ears . ii 2 70
Would not this nave of a wheel have his ears cut off? . . . ii 4 279
I come to draw you out by the ears . . . ii 4 314
And bid the merry bells ring to thine ear That thou art crowned . iv 5 112
My voice shall sound as you do prompt mine ear . . . v 2 119
Mute wonder lurketh in men's ears . . . *Hen. V.* i 1 49
Deck'd in modest complement, Not working with the eye without the ear . . . ii 2 135
When the blast of war blows in our ears, Then imitate the action of the tiger . . . iii 1 5
I would fain be about the ears of the English . . . iii 7 91
In high and boastful neighs Piercing the night's dull ear . iv Prol. 11
By this hand, I will take thee a box on the ear . . . iv 1 232
I have sworn to take him a box o' th' ear . . . iv 7 133
The glove which I have given him for a favour May haply purchase him a box o' th' ear . . . iv 7 181
Teach a soldier terms Such as will enter at a lady's ear . . . v 2 100
Which word thou shalt no sooner bless mine ear withal, but I will tell thee aloud 'England is thine' . . . v 2 257
Fain would mine eyes be witness with mine ears . . 1 *Hen. VI.* ii 3 9
Such abominable words as no Christian ear can endure to hear 2 *Hen. VI.* iv 7 44
Give him a box o' the ear and that will make 'em red again . iv 7 91
Northumberland, Whose warlike ears could never brook retreat 3 *Hen. VI.* i 1 5
Though they cannot greatly sting to hurt, Yet look to have them buzz to offend thine ears . . . ii 6 95
Where fame, late entering at his heedful ears, Hath placed thy beauty's image . . . iii 3 63
Mine ear hath tempted judgment to desire . . . iii 3 133
I have not stopp'd mine ears to their demands . . . iv 8 39
Shall we beat the stones about thine ears? . . . v 1 108
My breast can better brook thy dagger's point Than can my ears that tragic history . . . v 6 28
They love his grace but lightly That fill his ears with such dissentious rumours . . . *Richard III* i 3 46
What pain it was to drown! What dreadful noise of waters in mine ears! . . . i 4 22
Environ'd me about, and howled in mine ears Such hideous cries . i 4 59
Lend favourable ears to our request . . . iii 7 101
Rise, and lend thine ear . . . iv 2 80
My tongue should to thy ears not name my boys Till that my nails were anchor'd in thine eyes . . . iv 4 230
Prepare her ears to hear a wooer's tale . . . iv 4 327
Declare, in hearing Of all these ears . . . *Hen. VIII.* ii 4 146
This is yet but young, and may be left To some ears unrecounted . iii 2 48
I think your grace, Out of the pain you suffer'd, gave no ear to't . iv 2 8
I love you; And durst commend a secret to your ear Much weightier . v 1 17
Who hath so far Given ear to our complaint . . . v 1 48
Knit all the Greekish ears To his experienced tongue . *Troi. and Cres.* i 3 67
Having his ear full of his airy fame, Grows dainty of his worth . i 3 144
May one, that is a herald and a prince, Do a fair message to his kingly ears? . . . i 3 219
'Tis for Agamemnon's ears.—He hears nought privately that comes from Troy . . . i 3 248
I bring a trumpet to awake his ear, To set his sense on the attentive bent . . . i 3 251
What modicums of wit he utters! his evasions have ears thus long . ii 1 75
Mine eyes and ears, Two traded pilots 'twixt the dangerous shores Of will and judgement . . . ii 2 63
Pleasure and revenge Have ears more deaf than adders to the voice Of any true decision . . . ii 2 172
One word in your ear.—O plague and madness! . . . v 2 34
So obstinately strong, That doth invert the attest of eyes and ears . v 2 122
Shall dizzy with more clamour Neptune's ear . . . v 2 174
O, contain yourself; Your passion draws ears hither . . . v 2 181
So much ungently temper'd, To stop his ears against admonishment . v 3 2
Were half to half the world by the ears . . . *Coriolanus* i 1 237
And carry with us ears and eyes for the time, But hearts for the event. ii 1 285
Would pluck reproof and rebuke from every ear that heard it . . ii 2 38
Masters o' the people, We do request your kindest ears . . . ii 2 56
He had rather venture all his limbs for honour Than one on's ears to hear it . . . ii 2 85
Let them pull all about mine ears, present me Death on the wheel . iii 2 1
Action is eloquence, and the eyes of the ignorant More learned than the ears . . . iii 2 77
That's worthily As any ear can hear . . . iv 1 54
What is thy name?—A name unmusical to the Volscians' ears . . iv 5 64
He'll go, he says, and sowl the porter of Rome gates by the ears . iv 5 214
He will shake Your Rome about your ears . . . iv 6 99
It is lots to blanks, My name hath touch'd your ears . . . v 2 11
Mine ears against your suits are stronger than Your gates against my force . . . v 2 94
Stopp'd your ears against The general suit of Rome . . . v 3 5
Fresh embassies and suits, Nor from the state nor private friends, hereafter Will I lend ear to . . . v 3 19
Where I, Even in theirs and in the commons' ears, Will vouch the truth of it . . . v 6 4
'Fore your own eyes and ears . . . v 6 120
Like the house of Fame, The palace full of tongues, of eyes, and ears *T. Andron.* ii 1 127
All the bitterest terms That ever ear did hear to such effect . . ii 3 111
Be not obdurate, open thy deaf ears . . . ii 3 160
Sweet varied notes, enchanting every ear! . . . iii 1 86
However these disturbers of our peace Buz in the people's ear . iv 4 7
I can smooth and fill his aged ear With golden promises; that, were his heart Almost impregnable, his old ears deaf, Yet should both ear and heart obey my tongue . . . iv 4 96
And in their ears tell them my dreadful name, Revenge . . v 2 39
Some devil whisper curses in mine ear, And prompt me! . . . v 3 11
He did discourse To love-sick Dido's sad attending ear . . . v 3 82
Tell us what Sinon hath bewitch'd our ears . . . v 3 85

Ear. The which if you with patient ears attend . . *Rom. and Jul.* Prol. 13
Which, as he breathed defiance to my ears, He swung about his head . i 1 117
We'll draw thee from the mire Of this sir-reverence love, wherein thou stick'st Up to the ears . . . i 4 43
And then anon Drums in his ear, at which he starts and wakes . i 4 86
And could tell A whispering tale in a fair lady's ear, Such as would please . . . i 5 25
She hangs upon the cheek of night Like a rich jewel in an Ethiope's ear i 5 48
My ears have not yet drunk a hundred words Of that tongue's utterance ii 2 58
How silver-sweet sound lovers' tongues by night, Like softest music to attending ears! . . . ii 2 167
Thy old groans ring yet in my ancient ears . . . ii 3 74
Shot thorough the ear with a love-song . . . ii 4 15
I will bite thee by the ear for that jest.—Nay, good goose, bite not . ii 4 81
Will you pluck your sword out of his pilcher by the ears? make haste, lest mine be about your ears ere it be out . . . iii 1 84
O, then I see that madmen have no ears.—How should they, when that wise men have no eyes? . . . iii 3 61
The nightingale, and not the lark, That pierced the fearful hollow of thine ear . . . iii 5 3
Lay thee all along, Holding thine ear close to the hollow ground . v 3 4
What fear is this which startles in our ears? . . . v 3 194
Rain sacrificial whisperings in his ear . . . *T. of Athens* i 1 81
Th' ear, Taste, touch and smell, pleased from thy table rise . . i 2 131
O, that men's ears should be To counsel deaf, but not to flattery! . i 2 256
Feast your ears with the music awhile, if they will fare so harshly . iii 6 36
Put armour on thine ears and on thine eyes . . . iv 3 123
Thou gavest thine ears like tapsters that bid welcome To knaves . iv 3 215
And enter in our ears like great triumphers In their applauding gates . v 1 199
Come on my right hand, for this ear is deaf . . . *J. Cæsar* i 2 213
Who's there?—A Roman.—Casca, by your voice.—Your ear is good . i 3 42
Their hats are pluck'd about their ears . . . ii 1 73
Such an exploit have I in hand, Ligarius, Had you a healthful ear to hear of it . . . ii 1 319
Is there no voice more worthy than my own, To sound more sweetly in great Cæsar's ear? . . . iii 1 50
Lend me your ears; I come to bury Cæsar, not to praise him . . iii 2 78
Turn him off, Like to the empty ass, to shake his ears, And graze in commons . . . iv 1 26
I go to meet The noble Brutus, thrusting this report Into his ears . v 3 75
Piercing steel and darts envenomed Shall be as welcome to the ears of Brutus As tidings of this sight . . . v 3 77
Hie thee hither, That I may pour my spirits in thine ear . *Macbeth* i 5 27
The repetition, in a woman's ear, Would murder as it fell . . ii 3 90
Murders have been perform'd Too terrible for the ear . . . iii 4 78
Had I three ears, I ld hear thee.—Be bloody, bold, and resolute . iv 1 78
Let not your ears despise my tongue for ever . . . iv 3 201
The devil himself could not pronounce a title More hateful to mine ear. v 7 9
That keep the word of promise to our ear, And break it to our hope . v 8 21
Let us once again assail your ears, That are so fortified against our story *Hamlet* i 1 31
I would not hear your enemy say so, Nor shall you do mine ear that violence . . . i 2 171
Season your admiration for a while With an attent ear . . . i 2 193
If with too credent ear you list his songs, Or lose your heart . . i 3 30
Give every man thy ear, but few thy voice . . . i 3 68
But this eternal blazon must not be To ears of flesh and blood . . i 5 22
The whole ear of Denmark Is by a forged process of my death Rankly abused . . . i 5 36
In the porches of my ears did pour The leperous distilment . . . i 5 63
And more above, hath his solicitings, As they fell out by time, by means and place, All given to mine ear . . . ii 2 128
Hark you, Guildenstern; and you too: at each ear a hearer . . ii 2 400
Stoops to his base, and with a hideous crash Takes prisoner Pyrrhus ear ii 2 499
Cleave the general ear with horrid speech . . . ii 2 589
And amaze indeed The very faculties of eyes and ears . . . ii 2 592
And I'll be placed, so please you, in the ear Of all their conference . iii 1 192
Tear a passion to tatters, to very rags, to split the ears of the groundlings . . . iii 2 12
Here is your husband; like a mildew'd ear, Blasting his wholesome brother . . . iii 4 64
Feeling without sight, Ears without hands or eyes, smelling sans all . iii 4 79
These words, like daggers, enter in mine ears . . . iii 4 95
A knavish speech sleeps in a foolish ear . . . iv 2 26
And wants not buzzers to infect his ear With pestilent speeches . iv 5 90
Will nothing stick our person to arraign In ear and ear . . . iv 5 94
I have words to speak in thine ear will make thee dumb . . iv 6 25
Sith you have heard, and with a knowing ear . . . iv 7 3
The ears are senseless that should give us hearing . . . v 2 380
Give ear, sir, to my sister . . . *Lear* ii 4 236
What they may incense him to, being apt To have his ear abused, wisdom bids fear . . . ii 4 310
False of heart, light of ear, bloody of hand . . . iii 4 95
Look with thine ears: see how yond justice rails upon yond simple thief iv 6 155
Hark, in thine ear: change places; and, handy-dandy, which is the justice? . . . iv 6 156
Told the most piteous tale of Lear and him That ever ear received . v 3 215
Justly to your grave ears I'll present How I did thrive in this fair lady's love, And she in mine . . . *Othello* i 3 124
She'ld come again, and with a greedy ear Devour up my discourse . i 3 149
I never yet did hear That the bruised heart was pierced through the ear i 3 219
To my unfolding lend your prosperous ear . . . i 3 245
After some time, to abuse Othello's ear That he is too familiar with his wife . . . i 3 401
I'll pour this pestilence into his ear . . . ii 3 362
Thou dost conspire against thy friend, Iago, If thou but think'st him wrong'd and makest his ear A stranger to thy thoughts . . . iii 3 143
Pish! Noses, ears, and lips.—Is't possible?—Confess—handkerchief!—O devil! . . . iv 1 43
Or that mine eyes, mine ears, or any sense, Delighted them in any other form . . . iv 2 154
If an oily palm be not a fruitful prognostication, I cannot scratch mine ear . . . *Ant. and Cleo.* i 2 54
Famous pirates Make the sea serve them, which they ear and wound With keels of every kind . . . i 4 49
His speech sticks in my heart.—Mine ear must pluck it thence . i 5 42
I could have given less matter A better ear . . . ii 1 32
Ram thou thy fruitful tidings in mine ears, That long time have been barren . . . ii 5 24
Pour out the pack of matter to mine ear, The good and bad together . ii 5 54

Ear. Pompey, a word.—Say in mine ear: what is't? . *Ant. and Cleo.* ii 7 42
All take hands. Make battery to our ears with the loud music . . ii 7 115
What, Octavia?—I'll tell you in your ear . . . . . . iii 2 46
Made his will, and read it To public ear . . . . . . iii 4 5
Mark Antony, Hearing that you prepared for war, acquainted My grieved ear withal . . . . iii 6 59
For Antony, I have no ears to his request . . . . . . iii 12 20
Have you no ears? I am Antony yet . . . . iii 13 92
Trumpeters, With brazen din blast you the city's ear . . . iv 8 36
So long As he could make me with this eye or ear Distinguish him *Cymb.* i 3 9
As I have such a heart that both mine ears Must not in haste abuse . i 6 130
Away! I do condemn mine ears that have So long attended thee . i 6 141
To curtail his oaths, ha?—No, my lord; nor crop the ears of them . ii 1 15
If this penetrate, I will consider your music the better: if it do not, it is a vice in her ears . . . . ii 3 33
And will to ears and tongues Be theme and hearing ever . . . iii 1 3
What a strange infection Is fall'n into thy ear! . . . . . iii 2 4
Mine ear, Therein false struck, can take no greater wound . . iii 4 116
Report should render him hourly to your ear As truly as he moves . iii 4 153
Which you'll make him know, If that his head have ear in music . iii 4 178
Have both their eyes And ears so cloy'd importantly as now . . iv 4 19
Mine eyes Were not in fault . . . ; Mine ears, that heard her flattery v 5 64
To glad your ear, and please your eyes . . . . *Pericles* i Gower 4
Heaven forbid That kings should let their ears hear their faults hid! . i 2 62
Her face was to mine eye beyond all wonder; The rest—hark in thine ear—as black as incest . . . . i 2 76
My ears were never better fed With such delightful pleasing harmony . ii 5 27
The seaman's whistle Is as a whisper in the ears of death, Unheard . iii 1 9
Pray; but be not tedious, For the gods are quick of ear . . . iv 1 70
What! do you stop your ears? . . . . iv 2 86
Your ears unto your eyes I'll reconcile . . . . . . iv 4 22
To the choleric fisting of every rogue Thy ear is liable . . . iv 6 178
There is something glows upon my cheek, And whispers in mine ear 'Go not' . . . . v 1 97
Who starves the ears she feeds, and makes them hungry, The more she gives them speech . . . . v 1 113
If he be none of mine, my sanctity Will to my sense bend no licentious ear . . . . v 3 30
Ear-deafening. The ear-deafening voice o' the oracle . . *W. Tale* iii 1 9
Earing. And our ills told us Is as our earing . . *Ant. and Cleo.* i 2 115
Ear-kissing. They are yet but ear-kissing arguments . . . *Lear* ii 1 9
Earl. Yet there has been earls, nay, which is more, pensioners *Mer. Wives* ii 2 78
I shall procure-a you de good guest, de earl, de knight, de lords . iii 3 96
Take heed of this French earl . . . . *All's Well* iii 5 12
A filthy officer he is in those suggestions for the young earl . . iii 5 19
Mere dislike Of our proceedings kept the earl from hence . 1 *Hen. IV.* iv 1 65
A larger dare to our great enterprise Than if the earl were here . . iv 1 79
I look to be either earl or duke, I can assure you . . . . v 4 146
A noble earl and many a creature else Had been alive this hour . . v 5 7
Where is the earl?—What shall I say you are?—Tell thou the earl That the Lord Bardolph doth attend . . . . . . 2 *Hen. IV.* i 1 1
Noble earl, I bring you certain news from Shrewsbury . . . . i 1 11
Tell thou an earl his divination lies, And I will take it as a sweet disgrace i 1 88
Sweet earl, divorce not wisdom from your honour . . . . . i 1 162
Full fifteen earls and fifteen hundred knights . . . . *Hen. V.* i 1 13
Of lusty earls, Grandpré and Roussi, Fauconberg and Foix . . . iv 8 103
But, as the rest, so fell that noble earl And was beheaded . 1 *Hen. VI.* ii 5 90
An earl I am, and Suffolk am I call'd . . . . v 3 53
Welcome, brave earl, into our territories . . . . . . v 3 146
Your wondrous rare description, noble earl, Of beauteous Margaret hath astonish'd me . . . . v 5 1
A poor earl's daughter is unequal odds . . . . v 5 34
Her father is no better than an earl, Although in glorious titles he excel v 5 37
Seven earls, twelve barons and twenty reverend bishops . 2 *Hen. VI.* i 1 8
And make the meanest of you earls and dukes . . . . . iv 8 39
All the northern earls and lords Intend here to besiege you . 3 *Hen. VI.* i 2 49
A goodly gift?—Ay, by my faith, for a poor earl to give . . . v 1 32
All without desert have frown'd on me; Dukes, earls, lords, gentlemen *Richard III.* ii 1 68
By the second hour in the morning Desire the earl to see me in my tent v 3 32
O' Thursday, tell her, She shall be married to this noble earl *R. and J.* iii 4 21
My thanes and kinsmen, Henceforth be earls, the first that ever Scotland In such an honour named . . . . *Macbeth* v 8 63
Where is this daughter?—With the earl, sir, here within . . *Lear* ii 4 59
Let's follow the old earl, and get the Bedlam To lead him where he would . . . . iii 7 103
Earldom. For ever should they be expulsed from France And not have title of an earldom here . . . . 1 *Hen. VI.* iii 3 26
'Twas my inheritance, as the earldom was . . . 3 *Hen. VI.* i 1 78
When I am king, claim thou of me The earldom of Hereford *Richard III.* iii 1 195
The earldom of Hereford and the moveables The which you promised . iv 2 93
My lord, your promise for the earldom . . . . iv 2 105
Earlier. You must come in earlier o' nights . . . . *T. Night* i 3 5
Earliest. The weakest kind of fruit Drops earliest to the ground *M. of V.* iv 1 116
It will be the earliest fruit i' the country . . *As Y. Like It* iii 2 125
To-morrow with your earliest Let me have speech with you . *Othello* ii 3 7
Earliness. Thy earliness doth me assure Thou art up-roused by some distemperature . . . . *Rom. and Jul.* ii 3 39
Early. I am thus early come to know what service It is your pleasure to command me in . . . . *T. G. of Ver.* iv 3 9
To be up early and down late . . . . . . *Mer. Wives* i 4 108
No doubt they rose up early to observe The rite of May . *M. N. Dream* iv 1 137
In the morning early will we both Fly . . . . *Mer. of Venice* iv 1 456
In the morning early They found the bed untreasured of their mistress *As Y. Like It* ii 2 6
With 'Too young' and 'the next year' and ''tis too early' . *All's Well* ii 1 28
How have you come so early by this lethargy? . . *T. Night* i 5 132
To be up after midnight and to go to bed then, is early . . . ii 3 8
Came early to his grave . . . . *K. John* ii 1 5
To-morrow morning, by four o'clock, early at Gadshill! . 1 *Hen. IV.* i 2 139
In the morning early shall my uncle Bring him our purposes . . iv 3 110
As in an early spring We see the appearing buds . . 2 *Hen. IV.* i 3 38
An early stirrer, by the rood! . . . . iii 2 3
Our bad neighbour makes us early stirrers . . . . *Hen. V.* iv 1 6
Sat in the council-house Early and late, debating to and fro 2 *Hen. VI.* i 1 91
You are early stirring: What news, what news? . *Richard III.* iii 2 36
Prepare thy battle early in the morning . . . . v 3 88
The early village-cock Hath twice done salutation to the morn . . v 3 209
Nor could Come pat betwixt too early and too late For any suit *Hen. VIII.* ii 3 84
Early. But Helen was not up.—E'en so: Hector was stirring early *Troi. and Cres.* i 2 52
What business, lord, so early?—I was sent for . . . . . iv 1 34
I knew you not: what news with you so early? . . . . . iv 2 48
'Tis but early days . . . . iv 5 12
Let Titan rise as early as he dare . . . . v 10 25
Somewhat too early for new-married ladies . . . . *T. Andron.* ii 2 15
So early walking did I see your son . . . . . *Rom. and Jul.* i 1 130
And too soon marr'd are those so early made . . . . . . i 2 13
We shall come too late.—I fear, too early . . . . . . i 4 106
Too early seen unknown, and known too late! . . . . . . i 5 141
Good morrow, father.—Benedicite! What early tongue so sweet saluteth me? . . . . ii 3 32
Commend me to your daughter.—I will, and know her mind early to-morrow . . . . iii 4 10
It is so very very late, That we may call it early by and by . . iii 4 35
Is she not down so late, or up so early? . . . . iii 5 67
What day is that?—Marry, my child, early next Thursday morn . . iii 5 113
Juliet, on Thursday early will I rouse ye: Till then, adieu . . iv 1 42
Alack, alack, is it not like that I, So early waking? . . . . iv 3 46
Take this letter; early in the morning See thou deliver it . . . v 3 23
What misadventure is so early up? . . . . v 3 188
Thou art early up, To see thy son and heir more early down . . v 3 208
This letter he early bid me give his father . . . . . . v 3 275
What, Brutus, are you stirr'd so early too? . . . *J. Cæsar* ii 2 110
Early to-morrow will we rise, and hence . . . . iv 3 230
O Cassius, Brutus gave the word too early . . . . v 3 5
A thousand, sir, Early though't be, have on their riveted trim *A. and C.* iv 4 22
I am glad I was up so late; for that's the reason I was up so early *Cymbeline* ii 3 38
Gentlemen, Why do you stir so early? . . . . . *Pericles* iii 2 12
That is the cause we trouble you so early; 'Tis not our husbandry . iii 2 19
Should at these early hours Shake off the golden slumber of repose . iii 2 22
Early in blustering morn this lady was Thrown upon this shore . . v 3 22
Earn. His excellence did earn it, ere he had it . . . *Much Ado* iii 1 99
I earn that I eat, get that I wear . . . . *As Y. Like It* iii 2 77
A barber shall never earn sixpence out of it . . . 2 *Hen. IV.* i 2 29
I will, sir, flatter my sworn brother, the people, to earn a dearer estimation of them . . . . *Coriolanus* ii 3 103
To do the act that might the addition earn Not the world's mass of vanity could make me . . . . *Othello* iv 2 163
And earns a place i' the story . . . . . . *Ant. and Cleo.* iii 13 46
I and my sword will earn our chronicle: There's hope in't yet . . iii 13 175
Earned. I have earned of Don John a thousand ducats . . *Much Ado* iii 3 115
Gives manhood more approbation than ever proof itself would have earned him . . . . *T. Night* iii 4 199
I have spoke to the purpose twice: The one for ever earn'd a royal husband . . . . *W. Tale* i 2 107
Taking their names upon you before you have earned them . 2 *Hen. IV.* ii 4 155
And bear hence A great addition earned in thy death . *Troi. and Cres.* iv 5 141
Half all Cominius' honours are to Marcius, Though Marcius earn'd them not . . . . *Coriolanus* i 1 278
See it done: And feast the army; we have store to do't, And they have earn'd the waste . . . . *Ant. and Cleo.* iv 1 16
That monster envy, oft the wrack Of earned praise . . *Pericles* iv Gower 13
Earnest. Did you perceive her earnest? . . . . *T. G. of Ver.* ii 1 163
After they closed in earnest, they parted very fairly in jest . . ii 5 13
Now your jest is earnest . . . . . . *Com. of Errors* ii 2 24
Mightst thou perceive austerely in his eye That he did plead in earnest? iv 2 3
I will even take sixpence in earnest of the bear-ward . . *Much Ado* ii 1 42
He is in earnest.—In most profound earnest . . . . . . v 1 197
Then you left me—O, the gods forbid!—In earnest, shall I say? *M. N. Dream* iii 2 277
But love no man in good earnest; nor no further in sport *As Y. Like It* i 2 30
But, turning these jests out of service, let us talk in good earnest . i 3 26
By my troth, and in good earnest, and so God mend me . . . . iv 1 192
It was a passion of earnest.—Counterfeit, I assure you . . . . iv 3 172
Are you moved, my lord?—No, in good earnest . . . *W. Tale* i 2 150
Are you in earnest, sir? I smell the trick on't . . . . . iv 4 656
Indeed, I have had earnest; but I cannot with conscience take it . iv 4 659
Pleads he in earnest? look upon his face . . . *Richard II.* v 3 100
'Faith, tell me now in earnest . . . . . . 1 *Hen. IV.* ii 3 334
And from his coffers Received the golden earnest of our death *Hen. V.* ii 2 169
I take thy groat in earnest of revenge . . . . v 1 67
And give it you In earnest of a further benefit . . 1 *Hen. VI.* v 3 16
My tongue should stumble in mine earnest words . 2 *Hen. VI.* iii 2 316
An earnest advocate to plead for him . . . . *Richard III.* i 3 87
Earnest in the service of my God, Neglect the visitation of my friends . iii 7 106
And given in earnest what I begg'd in jest . . . . . . v 1 22
Meanwhile must be an earnest motion Made . . . *Hen. VIII.* ii 4 233
In earnest, it's true; I heard a senator speak it . . . *Coriolanus* i 3 106
How, sir! are you in earnest then, my lord? . . . *T. Andron.* i 1 277
He hath sent me an earnest inviting . . . . . *T. of Athens* iii 6 11
Nay, stay thou out for earnest . . . . iv 3 47
More mischief first; I have given you earnest . . . . . . iv 3 168
For an earnest of a greater honour . . . . . . *Macbeth* i 3 104
Why hath it given me earnest of success, Commencing in a truth? . . i 3 132
An earnest conjuration from the king . . . . . *Hamlet* v 2 38
My friendly knave, I thank thee: there's earnest of thy service . *Lear* i 4 104
And found good means To draw from her a prayer of earnest heart *Othello* i 3 152
What will you do with't, that you have been so earnest To have me filch it? . . . . iii 3 314
It is an earnest of a further good That I mean to thee . . *Cymbeline* i 5 65
If you like her, so; if not, I have lost my earnest . . . *Pericles* iv 2 49
Earnest-gaping. When the dusky sky began to rob My earnest-gaping sight . . . . 2 *Hen. VI.* iii 2 105
Earnestly. Why dost thou whet thy knife so earnestly? . *Mer. of Venice* iv 1 121
He wishes earnestly you never may . . . . . . *W. Tale* iv 1 32
Have earnestly implored a general peace . . . . 1 *Hen. VI.* v 4 98
How earnestly he cast his eyes upon me! . . . . *Hen. VIII.* v 2 12
How earnestly they knock! Pray you, come in . . *Troi. and Cres.* iv 2 41
How earnestly are you set a-work, and how ill requited! . . . . v 10 37
As I earnestly did fix mine eye Upon the wasted building *T. Andron.* v 1 22
Why so earnestly seek you to put up that letter? . . . . *Lear* i 2 28
Earnestness. It shows my earnestness of affection . . 2 *Hen. IV.* v 5 17
All agreeing In earnestness to see him . . . . . *Coriolanus* ii 1 229
The nobles in great earnestness are going All to the senate-house . . iv 6 57
With a solemn earnestness, More than indeed belong'd to such a trifle *Othello* v 2 227
Ear-piercing. The spirit-stirring drum, the ear-piercing fife . . . iii 3 352

Earth. I would have sunk the sea within the earth . . . *Tempest* i 2 11
To do me business in the veins o' the earth When it is baked with frost i 2 255
What, ho! slave! Caliban! Thou earth, thou! speak . . . . . i 2 314
Where should this music be? i' the air or the earth? . . . . . i 2 387
This is no mortal business, nor no sound That the earth owes . . i 2 407
All corners else o' the earth Let liberty make use of . . . . i 2 491
Here lies your brother, No better than the earth he lies upon . . ii 1 281
O heaven, O earth, bear witness to this sound! . . . . . iii 1 68
My bosky acres and my unshrubb'd down, Rich scarf to my proud earth iv 1 82
Earth's increase, foison plenty, Barns and garners never empty . iv 1 110
I'll break my staff, Bury it certain fathoms in the earth . . . v 1 55
No woe to his correction Nor to his service no such joy on earth
T. G. of Ver. ii 4 139
Let her be a principality, Sovereign to all the creatures on the earth . ii 4 153
Lest the base earth Should from her vesture chance to steal a kiss . ii 4 159
His heart as far from fraud as heaven from earth . . . . . ii 7 78
She excels each mortal thing Upon the dull earth dwelling . . . iv 2 52
My love is buried.—Sweet lady, let me rake it from the earth . . iv 2 116
Who by repentance is not satisfied Is nor of heaven nor earth . . v 4 80
For it is as positive as the earth is firm . . . *Mer. Wives* iii 2 49
I had rather be set quick i' the earth And bowl'd to death with turnips! iii 4 91
'Tis set down so in heaven, but not in earth . . *Meas. for Meas.* ii 4 50
At length the sun, gazing upon the earth, Dispersed those vapours that offended us . . . . *Com. of Errors* i 1 89
There's nothing situate under heaven's eye But hath his bound, in earth, in sea, in sky . . . . ii 1 17
Am I in earth, in heaven, or in hell? Sleeping or waking? . . . ii 2 214
Our earth's wonder, more than earth divine . . . . . . iii 2 32
My sweet hope's aim, My sole earth's heaven, and my heaven's claim . iii 2 64
Not till God make men of some other metal than earth . . *Much Ado* ii 1 63
My soul's earth's god, and body's fostering patron . . *L. L. Lost* i 1 223
Like a crab on the face of terra, the soil, the land, the earth . . iv 2 7
Piercing a hogshead! a good lustre of conceit in a turf of earth . . iv 2 90
Thou, fair sun, which on my earth dost shine, Exhalest this vapour-vow iv 3 69
By earth, she is not, corporal, there you lie . . . . . . iv 3 86
All hail, the richest beauties on the earth! . . . . . . v 2 158
Brief as the lightning in the collied night, That, in a spleen, unfolds both heaven and earth . . . . *M. N. Dream* i 1 146
Flying between the cold moon and the earth, Cupid all arm'd . . ii 1 156
I'll put a girdle round about the earth In forty minutes . . . . ii 1 175
I'll believe as soon This whole earth may be bored . . . . . iii 2 53
The poet's eye, in a fine frenzy rolling, Doth glance from heaven to earth, from earth to heaven . . . . v 1 13
Outbrave the heart most daring on the earth . . . *Mer. of Venice* ii 1 28
From the four corners of the earth they come, To kiss this shrine . ii 7 39
A kinder gentleman treads not the earth . . . . ii 8 35
He finds the joys of heaven here on earth; And if on earth he do not mean it, then In reason he should never come to heaven . . . . iii 5 81
Where is this young gallant that is so desirous to lie with his mother earth?—Ready, sir . . . . *As Y. Like It* i 2 213
And fetch shrill echoes from the hollow earth . . *T. of Shrew* Ind. 2 48
That she's in earth, from whence God send her quickly! *All's Well* ii 4 13
A heaven on earth I have won by wooing thee . . . . . . iv 2 66
O, you should not rest Between the elements of air and earth *T. Night* i 5 294
Now heaven walks on earth . . . . v 1 100
Plainly as heaven sees earth and earth sees heaven . . *W. Tale* i 2 315
There's not a grain of it the face to sweeten Of the whole dungy earth ii 1 157
It should here be laid, Either for life or death, upon the earth Of its right father . . . . iii 3 45
I'll not put The dibble in earth to set one slip of them . . . . iv 4 100
And he, and more Than he, and men, the earth, the heavens, and all . iv 4 382
Let nature crush the sides o' the earth together And mar the seeds within! iv 4 489
For all the sun sees or The close earth wombs or the profound seas hide iv 4 501
The most peerless piece of earth, I think, That e'er the sun shone bright on v 1 94
That 'twixt heaven and earth Might thus have stood begetting wonder v 1 132
Welcome hither, As is the spring to the earth . . . . . . v 1 152
Never saw I Wretches so quake: they kneel, they kiss the earth . . v 1 199
She lifted the princess from the earth . . . . v 2 83
Some sins do bear their privilege on earth, And so doth yours *K. John* i 1 261
Thou monstrous slanderer of heaven and earth!—Thou monstrous injurer of heaven and earth! Call not me slanderer . . . . . . ii 1 173
Many a widow's husband grovelling lies, Coldly embracing the discolour'd earth . . . . ii 1 306
By this hand I swear, That sways the earth this climate overlooks . ii 1 344
My grief's so great That no supporter but the huge firm earth Can hold it up . . . . iii 1 72
Plays the alchemist, Turning with splendour of his precious eye The meagre cloddy earth to glittering gold . . . . iii 1 80
O, when the last account 'twixt heaven and earth Is to be made! . . iv 2 216
The earth had not a hole to hide this deed . . . . iv 3 36
My soul shall wait on thee to heaven, As it on earth hath been thy servant v 7 73
Until the heavens, envying earth's good hap, Add an immortal title to your crown . . . . *Richard II.* i 1 23
What I speak My body shall make good upon this earth . . . . i 1 37
Cries, Even from the tongueless caverns of the earth . . . . . i 1 105
Who, when they see the hours ripe on earth, Will rain hot vengeance . i 2 7
For that our kingdom's earth should not be soil'd With that dear blood i 3 125
This scepter'd isle, This earth of majesty, this seat of Mars . . . ii 1 41
This blessed plot, this earth, this realm, this England . . . . ii 1 50
Comfort's in heaven; and we are on the earth . . . . . . ii 2 78
The pale-faced moon looks bloody on the earth . . . . . . ii 4 10
I see thy glory like a shooting star Fall to the base earth from the firmament . . . . ii 4 20
Dear earth, I do salute thee with my hand . . . . iii 2 6
So, weeping, smiling, greet I thee, my earth . . . . iii 2 10
One day too late, I fear me, noble lord, Hath clouded all thy happy days on earth . . . . iii 2 68
Make dust our paper and with rainy eyes Write sorrow on the bosom of the earth . . . . iii 2 147
And that small model of the barren earth Which serves as paste and cover to our bones . . . . iii 2 153
I'll be the yielding water: The rage be his, whilst on the earth I rain My waters; on the earth, and not on him . . . . iii 3 59
Till they have fretted us a pair of graves Within the earth . . . iii 3 168
You debase your princely knee To make the base earth proud with kissing it . . . . iii 3 191
Darest thou, thou little better thing than earth, Divine his downfal? . iii 4 78
I task the earth to the like . . . . iv 1 52
Do lie In earth as quiet as thy father's skull . . . . . . iv 1 69
And there at Venice gave His body to that pleasant country's earth . iv 1 98

Earth. It will the woefullest division prove That ever fell upon this cursed earth . . . . *Richard II.* iv 1 147
Here let us rest, if this rebellious earth Have any resting . . . . v 1 5
The lion dying thrusteth forth his paw, And wounds the earth . . v 1 30
For ever may my knees grow to the earth . . . . v 3 30
I pardon him.—A god on earth thou art . . . . v 3 136
The sovereign'st thing on earth Was parmaceti for an inward bruise
1 Hen. IV. i 3 57
It was great pity, so it was, This villanous salt-petre should be digg'd Out of the bowels of the harmless earth . . . . i 3 61
Falstaff sweats to death, And lards the lean earth as he walks along . ii 2 116
Why dost thou bend thine eyes upon the earth? . . . . . . ii 3 45
If manhood, good manhood, be not forgot upon the face of the earth . ii 4 143
At my birth The frame and huge foundation of the earth Shaked . . iii 1 16
I say the earth did shake when I was born.—And I say the earth was not of my mind, If you suppose as fearing you it shook . . . . iii 1 21
The heavens were all on fire, the earth did tremble.—O, then the earth shook to see the heavens on fire . . . . iii 1 25
Oft the teeming earth Is with a kind of colic pinch'd . . . . iii 1 28
Shakes the old beldam earth and topples down Steeples . . . . iii 1 32
At your birth Our grandam earth, having this distemperature, In passion shook . . . . iii 1 34
For heaven to earth, some of us never shall A second time do such a courtesy . . . . v 2 100
But now two paces of the vilest earth Is room enough . . . . v 4 91
This earth that bears thee dead Bears not alive so stout a gentleman . v 4 92
Still unfold The acts commenced on this ball of earth . *2 Hen. IV.* Ind. 5
Whose swift wrath beat down The never-daunted Percy to the earth . i 1 110
Let heaven kiss earth! now let not Nature's hand Keep the wild flood confined! let order die! . . . . i 1 153
Criest now 'O earth, yield us that king again, And take thou this!' . i 3 106
Whose memory is written on the earth With yet appearing blood . . iv 1 81
For all the soil of the achievement goes With me into the earth . . iv 5 191
Printing their proud hoofs i' the receiving earth . . *Hen. V.* Prol. 27
Your brother kings and monarchs of the earth Do all expect that you should rouse yourself . . . . i 2 122
He bounds from the earth, as if his entrails were hairs . . . . iii 7 13
He trots the air; the earth sings when he touches it . . . . . iii 7 17
The dull elements of earth and water never appear in him . . . iii 7 23
A Jacksauce, as ever his black shoe trod upon God's ground and his earth iv 7 150
Even as in the heavens So in the earth . . . . . *1 Hen. VI.* i 2 25
Bright star of Venus, fall'n down on the earth . . . . . . i 2 144
Night is fled, Whose pitchy mantle over-veil'd the earth . . . . ii 2 2
Even with the earth Shall lay your stately and air-braving towers . iv 2 12
Never so needful on the earth of France . . . . iv 3 18
Ye familiar spirits, that are cull'd Out of the powerful regions under earth v 3 11
Chosen from above, By inspiration of celestial grace, To work exceeding miracles on earth . . . . v 4 41
Why are thine eyes fix'd to the sullen earth? . . . *2 Hen. VI.* i 2 5
Be you prostrate and grovel on the earth . . . . i 4 14
Thy heaven is on earth . . . . ii 1 19
For blessed are the peacemakers on earth . . . . ii 1 35
Blaspheming God and cursing men on earth . . . . iii 2 372
And with the southern clouds contend in tears, Theirs for the earth's increase, mine for my sorrows . . . . iii 2 385
If mine arm be heaved in the air, Thy grave is digg'd already in the earth iv 10 55
Where shall it find a harbour in the earth? . . . . v 1 168
O, let the vile world end, And the premised flames of the last day Knit earth and heaven together! . . . . v 2 42
Join our lights together And over-shine the earth as this the world *3 Hen. VI.* ii 1 38
Thy brother's blood the thirsty earth hath drunk . . . . . . ii 3 15
Let the earth be drunken with our blood . . . . ii 3 23
Ere my knee rise from the earth's cold face . . . . ii 3 35
Take leave until we meet again, Where'er it be, in heaven or in earth . ii 3 43
O Phœbus, hadst thou never given consent That Phaëthon should check thy fiery steeds, Thy burning car never had scorch'd the earth! . . ii 6 13
Since this earth affords no joy to me, But to command . . . . iii 2 165
My blood, my want of strength, my sick heart shows, That I must yield my body to the earth . . . . v 2 9
Why, what is pomp, rule, reign, but earth and dust? . . . . . v 2 27
For thou hast made the happy earth thy hell . . . *Richard III.* i 2 51
O earth, which this blood drink'st, revenge his death! . . . . i 2 63
Earth, gape open wide and eat him quick, As thou dost swallow up this good king's blood! . . . . i 2 65
He was fitter for that place than earth . . . . i 2 108
His better doth not breathe upon the earth . . . . i 2 140
Now in peace my soul shall part to heaven, Since I have set my friends at peace on earth . . . . ii 1 6
The plainest harmless creature That breathed upon this earth a Christian iii 5 26
Rest thy unrest on England's lawful earth, Unlawfully made drunk with innocents' blood! . . . . iv 4 29
Defacer of God's handiwork, That excellent grand tyrant of the earth . iv 4 52
Earth gapes, hell burns, fiends roar, saints pray . . . . . . iv 4 75
Thou camest on earth to make the earth my hell . . . . . . iv 4 166
The high imperial type of this earth's glory . . . . iv 4 244
For me, the ransom of my bold attempt Shall be this cold corpse on the earth's cold face . . . . v 3 266
Take up the rays o' the beneficial sun And keep it from the earth *Hen. VIII.* i 1 57
Would I had never trod this English earth . . . . iii 1 143
His contemplation were above the earth, And fix'd on spiritual object iii 2 131
My legs, like loaden branches, bow to the earth . . . . . . iv 2 2
Give him a little earth for charity! . . . . iv 2 23
Whiles here he lived Upon this naughty earth . . . . v 1 138
In all designs begun on earth below . . . . . *Troi. and Cres.* i 3 4
What raging of the sea! shaking of earth! Commotion in the winds! . i 3 97
As iron to adamant, as earth to the centre . . . . iii 2 186
As false As air, as water, wind, or sandy earth . . . . . . iii 2 199
Would I were as deep under the earth as I am above! . . . . iv 2 86
Is as the very centre of the earth, Drawing all things to it . . . iv 2 110
That spirit of his In aspiration lifts him from the earth . . . iv 5 16
Who neither looks upon the heaven nor earth . . . . iv 5 281
That a thing inseparate Divides more wider than the sky and earth . v 2 149
The dragon wing of night o'erspreads the earth . . . . . . v 8 17
Thou great-sized coward, No space of earth shall sunder our two hates v 10 27
That of all things upon the earth he hated Your person most *Coriolanus* iii 1 14
Those mysteries which heaven Will not have earth to know . . . iv 2 36
I melt, and am not Of stronger earth than others . . . . . v 3 29
Sink, my knee, i' the earth . . . . v 3 50
The man is noble, and his fame folds-in This orb o' the earth . . v 6 127
Nor we disturb'd with prodigies on earth . . . . . *T. Andron.* i 1 101

Earth. At thy feet I kneel, with tears of joy, Shed on the earth, for thy return . . . *T. Andron.* i 1 162
Whose virtues will, I hope, Reflect on Rome as Titan's rays on earth i 1 226
Who art thou that lately didst descend Into this gaping hollow of the earth? . . . ii 3 249
Let my tears stanch the earth's dry appetite . . . iii 1 14
O earth, I will befriend thee more with rain, That shall distil from these two ancient urns, Than youthful April shall . . . iii 1 16
Here I lift this one hand up to heaven, And bow this feeble ruin to the earth . . . iii 1 208
When heaven doth weep, doth not the earth o'erflow? . . . iii 1 222
Hark, how her sighs do blow! She is the weeping welkin, I the earth iii 1 227
Then must my earth with her continual tears Become a deluge . iii 1 229
Enough written upon this earth To stir a mutiny in the mildest thoughts iv 1 84
Dig with mattock and with spade, And pierce the inmost centre of the earth . . . iv 3 12
Sith there's no justice in earth nor hell, We will solicit heaven . iv 3 49
Like to the earth swallow her own increase . . . v 2 192
Set him breast-deep in earth, and famish him . . . v 3 179
This is our doom: Some stay to see him fasten'd in the earth . v 3 183
The earth hath swallow'd all my hopes but she, She is the hopeful lady of my earth . . . *Rom. and Jul.* i 2 15
Beauty too rich for use, for earth too dear! . . . i 5 49
Turn back, dull earth, and find thy centre out . . . ii 1 2
The earth that's nature's mother is her tomb . . . ii 3 9
Nought so vile that on the earth doth live But to the earth some special good doth give . . . ii 3 17
That gallant spirit hath aspired the clouds, Which too untimely here did scorn the earth . . . iii 1 123
Vile earth, to earth resign; end motion here . . . iii 2 59
Where honour may be crown'd Sole monarch of the universal earth . iii 2 94
Why rail'st thou on thy birth, the heaven, and earth? Since birth, and heaven, and earth, all three do meet In thee at once . . iii 3 119
My husband is on earth, my faith in heaven; How shall that faith return again to earth, Unless that husband send it me from heaven By leaving earth? . . . iii 5 207
Where bloody Tybalt, yet but green in earth, Lies festering in his shroud iv 3 42
And shrieks like mandrakes' torn out of the earth . . . iv 3 47
Thou womb of death, Gorged with the dearest morsel of the earth . v 3 46
And nature, as it grows again toward earth, Is fashion'd for the journey, dull and heavy . . . *T. of Athens* ii 2 227
O thou wall, That girdlest in those wolves, dive in the earth! . iv 1 2
O blessed breeding sun, draw from the earth Rotten humidity! . iv 3 1
Earth, yield me roots! Who seeks for better of thee, sauce his palate With thy most operant poison! . . . iv 3 23
Come, damned earth, Thou common whore of mankind, that put'st odds Among the rout of nations . . . iv 3 41
The earth hath roots; Within this mile break forth a hundred springs iv 3 420
The earth's a thief That feeds and breeds by a composture stolen iv 3 443
What viler thing upon the earth than friends Who can bring noblest minds to basest ends! . . . iv 3 470
Why stare you so?—Are not you moved, when all the sway of earth Shakes like a thing unfirm? . . . *J. Cæsar* i 3 3
Who ever knew the heavens menace so?—Those that have known the earth so full of faults . . . i 3 45
Nor heaven nor earth have been at peace to-night . . . ii 2 1
O, pardon me, thou bleeding piece of earth, That I am meek and gentle with these butchers! . . . iii 1 254
This foul deed shall smell above the earth With carrion men . iii 1 274
That look not like the inhabitants o' the earth, And yet are on't *Macbeth* i 3 41
The earth hath bubbles, as the water has, And these are of them . i 3 79
Thou sure and firm-set earth, Hear not my steps, which way they walk ii 1 56
Some say, the earth Was feverous and did shake . . . ii 3 65
Darkness does the face of earth entomb, When living light should kiss it . . . ii 4 9
Avaunt! and quit my sight! let the earth hide thee! . . . iii 4 93
Uproar the universal peace, confound All unity on earth . . iv 3 100
Have heaven and earth together demonstrated Unto our climatures and countrymen . . . *Hamlet* i 1 124
If thou hast uphoarded in thy life Extorted treasure in the womb of earth i 1 137
Whether in sea or fire, in earth or air, The extravagant and erring spirit hies To his confine . . . i 1 153
We pray you, throw to earth This unprevailing woe . . . i 2 106
Heaven and earth! Must I remember? . . . i 2 142
Foul deeds will rise, Though all the earth o'erwhelm them, to men's eyes i 2 258
O all you host of heaven! O earth! what else? And shall I couple hell? i 5 92
Well said, old mole! canst work i' the earth so fast? . . . i 5 162
There are more things in heaven and earth, Horatio, Than are dreamt of in your philosophy . . . i 5 166
How do ye both?—As the indifferent children of the earth . . ii 2 231
This goodly frame, the earth, seems to me a sterile promontory . ii 2 310
What should such fellows as I do crawling between earth and heaven? iii 1 130
Nor earth to me give food, nor heaven light! . . . iii 2 226
Examples gross as earth exhort me . . . iv 4 46
His means of death, his obscure funeral . . . Cry to be heard, as 'twere from heaven to earth . . . iv 5 216
How long will a man lie i' the earth ere he rot? . . . v 1 178
This skull has lain in the earth three and twenty years . . . v 1 190
Dost thou think Alexander looked o' this fashion i' the earth? . v 1 219
Alexander returneth into dust; the dust is earth; of earth we make loam v 1 233
O, that that earth, which kept the world in awe, Should patch a wall to expel the winter's flaw! . . . v 1 238
Lay her i' the earth: And from her fair and unpolluted flesh May violets spring! . . . v 1 261
Hold off the earth awhile, Till I have caught her once more in mine arms v 1 272
The cannons to the heavens, the heavens to earth . . . v 2 288
Heaven and earth! Edmund, seek him out . . . *Lear* i 2 105
I will do such things,—What they are, yet I know not; but they shall be The terrors of the earth . . . ii 4 285
Bids the wind blow the earth into the sea . . . iii 1 5
Mildews the white wheat, and hurts the poor creature of earth . iii 4 124
All you unpublish'd virtues of the earth, Spring with my tears! . iv 4 16
I know when one is dead, and when one lives; She's dead as earth . v 3 261
Do deeds to make heaven weep, all earth amazed . . . *Othello* iii 3 371
If that the earth could teem with woman's tears, Each drop she falls would prove a crocodile . . . iv 1 256
The bawdy wind that kisses all it meets Is hush'd within the hollow mine of earth, And will not hear it . . . iv 2 79
It is the very error of the moon; She comes more nearer earth than she was wont, And makes men mad . . . v 2 110

Earth. Then must thou needs find out new heaven, new earth *Ant. and Cleo.* i 1 17
Kingdoms are clay: our dungy earth alike Feeds beast as man . i 1 35
When it pleaseth their deities to take the wife of a man from him, it shows to man the tailors of the earth . . . i 2 170
The demi-Atlas of this earth, the arm And burgonet of men . . i 5 23
Who now are levying The kings o' the earth for war . . . iii 6 68
We Have used to conquer, standing on the earth, And fighting foot to foot iii 7 66
Let him breathe between the heavens and earth, A private man in Athens . . . iii 12 13
Hark!—Music i' the air.—Under the earth . . . iv 3 13
I am alone the villain of the earth, And feel I am so most . iv 6 30
That heaven and earth may strike their sounds together . . iv 8 38
O, see, my women, The crown o' the earth doth melt . . . iv 15 63
A sun and moon, which kept their course, and lighted The little O, the earth . . . v 2 81
No grave upon the earth shall clip in it A pair so famous . . v 2 362
To seek through the regions of the earth For one his like, there would be something failing In him that should compare . . . *Cymbeline* i 1 20
I am not vexed more at any thing in the earth: a pox on't! . ii 1 20
That all the abhorred things o' the earth amend By being worse than they v 5 216
My riches to the earth from whence they came . . . *Pericles* i 1 52
The earth is throng'd By man's oppression; and the poor worm doth die for't . . . i 1 101
Kings are earth's gods; in vice their law's their will . . i 1 103
We'll mingle our bloods together in the earth, From whence we had our being and our birth . . . i 2 113
These mouths, who but of late, earth, sea, and air, Were all too little to content . . . i 4 34
As chiding a nativity As fire, air, water, earth, and heaven can make . iii 1 33
Our lodgings, standing bleak upon the sea, Shook as the earth did quake iii 2 15
A princess To equal any single crown o' the earth I' the justice of compare! . . . iv 3 8
At her birth, Thetis, being proud, swallow'd some part o' the earth: Therefore the earth, fearing to be o'erflow'd, Hath Thetis' birth-child on the heavens bestow'd . . . iv 4 39
Earth-bound. Who can impress the forest, bid the tree Unfix his earth-bound root? . . . *Macbeth* iv 1 96
Earthed. Who shall be of as little memory When he is earth'd *Tempest* ii 1 234
Earthen pots. Green earthen pots, bladders and musty seeds *R. and J.* v 1 46
Earthlier. But earthlier happy is the rose distill'd . *M. N. Dream* i 1 76
Earthly. The liquor is not earthly . . . *Tempest* ii 2 131
Is she not a heavenly saint?—No; but she is an earthly paragon *T. G. of Ver.* ii 4 146
There were No earthly mean to save him . . . *Meas. for Meas.* ii 4 95
But, for those earthly faults, I quit them all . . . v 1 488
Why, doth not every earthly thing Cry shame upon her? . *Much Ado* iv 1 122
These earthly godfathers of heaven's lights . . . *L. L. Lost* i 1 88
Pardon love this wrong, That sings heaven's praise with such an earthly tongue . . . iv 2 122
My vow was earthly, thou a heavenly love . . . iv 3 66
And on the wager lay two earthly women . . *Mer. of Venice* iii 5 85
Earthly power doth then show likest God's When mercy seasons justice iv 1 196
Then is there mirth in heaven, When earthly things made even Atone together . . . *As Y. Like It* v 4 115
A showing of a heavenly effect in an earthly actor . . . *All's Well* ii 3 28
O thou, the earthly author of my blood . . . *Richard II.* i 3 69
Leaving their earthly parts to choke your clime . . *Hen. V.* iv 3 102
A world of earthly blessings to my soul . . . 2 *Hen VI.* i 1 22
Great is his comfort in this earthly vale . . . ii 1 70
Was ever king that joy'd an earthly throne, And could command no more content than I? . . . iv 9 1
A sceptre, or an earthly sepulchre! . . . 3 *Hen. VI.* i 4 17
Then you lost The view of earthly glory . . . *Hen. VIII.* i 1 14
The queen of earthly queens . . . ii 4 141
You have scarce time To steal from spiritual leisure a brief span To keep your earthly audit . . . iii 2 141
A peace above all earthly dignities, A still and quiet conscience . iii 2 379
And the moon, were she earthly, no nobler . . *Coriolanus* ii 1 108
Upon her wit doth earthly honour wait . . . *T. Andron.* ii 1 10
I am in this earthly world; where to do harm Is often laudable *Macbeth* iv 2 75
The heavens shall bruit again, Re-speaking earthly thunder *Hamlet* i 2 128
Thou art, if thou darest be, the earthly Jove . . *Ant. and Cleo.* ii 7 73
An earthly paragon! Behold divineness No elder than a boy! *Cymbeline* iii 6 44
But, feeling woe, Gripe not at earthly joys as erst they did *Pericles* i 1 49
Earthly man Is but a substance that must yield to you . . i 1 2
Earthquake. O, 'twas a din to fright a monster's ear, To make an earthquake . . . *Tempest* ii 1 315
I look for an earthquake too, then . . . *Much Ado* i 1 275
But mountains may be removed with earthquakes . *As Y. Like It* iii 2 196
An we might have a good woman born but one every blazing star, or at an earthquake, 'twould mend the lottery well . . . *All's Well* i 3 92
Great affections wrestling in thy bosom Doth make an earthquake of nobility . . . *K. John* v 2 42
In fierce tempest is he coming, In thunder and in earthquake . *Hen. V.* ii 4 100
'Tis since the earthquake now eleven years . . *Rom. and Jul* i 3 23
Earth-treading stars that make dark heaven light . . . i 2 25
Earth-vexing. And shielded him From this earth-vexing smart *Cymbeline* v 4 42
Earthy. Thou wast a spirit too delicate To act her earthy and abhorr'd commands . . . *Tempest* i 2 273
What earthy name to interrogatories Can task the free breath of a sacred king? . . . *K. John* iii 1 147
And soon lie Richard in an earthy pit! . . . *Richard II.* iv 1 219
The earthy and cold hand of death Lies on my tongue . 1 *Hen. IV.* v 4 84
Survey his dead and earthy image . . . 2 *Hen. VI.* iii 2 147
Do you note . . . how pale she looks, And of an earthy cold? *Hen. VIII.* iv 2 98
Sacrifice his flesh, Before this earthy prison of their bones . *T. Andron.* i 1 99
Which, like a taper in some monument, Doth shine upon the dead man's earthy cheeks . . . ii 3 229
Earthy-gross. Lay open to my earthy-gross conceit . *Com. of Errors* iii 2 34
Ear-wax. He has not so much brain as ear-wax . *Troi. and Cres.* v 1 58
Ease. I should do it With much more ease; for my good will is to it, And yours it is against . . . *Tempest* iii 1 30
Neither my coat, integrity, nor persuasion can with ease attempt you *Meas. for Meas.* iv 2 205
Is there no play, To ease the anguish of a torturing hour? *M. N. Dream* v 1 37
Leaving his wealth and ease, A stubborn will to please . *As Y. Like It* ii 5 54
I know the more one sickens the worse at ease he is . . . iii 2 25
If he please, My hand is ready; may it do him ease . *T. of Shrew* v 2 179
The younger of our nature, That surfeit on their ease . *All's Well* iii 1 18

Ease. I can with ease translate it to my will; Or if you will, to speak more properly, I will enforce it easily to my love . *K. John* ii 1 513
Never to be infected with delight, Nor conversant with ease and idleness . . . . iv 3 70
He that no more must say is listen'd more Than they whom youth and ease have taught to glose *Richard II.* ii 1 10
And in this thought they find a kind of ease . . . . v 5 28
I will ease my heart, Albeit I make a hazard of my head . 1 *Hen. IV.* i 3 127
We'll walk afoot awhile, and ease our legs . . . ii 2 84
Your money!—Villains!—Got with much ease . . . . ii 2 111
Shall I not take mine ease in mine inn? . . . . . iii 3 93
Vaulted with such ease into his seat, As if an angel dropp'd down from the clouds . . . . iv 1 107
Well, of sufferance comes ease . . . . . 2 *Hen. IV.* v 4 28
Then I will slay myself, For living idly here in pomp and ease 1 *Hen. VI.* i 1 142
Lean thine aged back against mine arm; And, in that ease, I'll tell thee ii 5 44
To ease your country of distressful war . . . . v 4 126
Sorrow would solace and mine age would ease . . . 2 *Hen. VI.* ii 3 21
Here's a vengeful sword, rusted with ease . . . . iii 2 198
It could not slake mine ire, nor ease my heart . . 3 *Hen. VI.* i 3 29
At his ease, Where having nothing, nothing can he lose . . iii 3 151
While he enjoys the honour and his ease . . . . iv 6 52
By heaven, I will not do thee so much ease . . . . v 5 72
Let them have scope: though what they do impart Help not at all, yet do they ease the heart . . . . . *Richard III.* iv 4 131
Reach a chair: So; now, methinks, I feel a little ease . *Hen. VIII.* iv 2 4
At what ease Might corrupt minds procure knaves as corrupt To swear against you? . . . . v 1 131
Some come to take their ease, And sleep an act or two . . . Epil. 2
That holds his honour higher than his ease . . . *Troi. and Cres.* i 3 266
Because thou canst not ease thy smart By friendship nor by speaking . iv 4 20
Till then I'll sweat and seek about for eases . . . v 10 56
He never stood To ease his breast with panting *Coriolanus* ii 2 126
That I might rail at him, to ease my mind! . . *T. Andron.* ii 4 35
We will mourn with thee: O, could our mourning ease thy misery! ii 4 57
Let me kiss thy lips; Or make some sign how I may do thee ease iii 1 121
For losers will have leave To ease their stomachs with their bitter tongues . . . . iii 1 234
To weep with them that weep doth ease some deal . . iii 1 245
I am Revenge; sent from the infernal kingdom, To ease the gnawing vulture of thy mind . . . . v 2 31
They stoop and kneel, And on them shalt thou ease thy angry heart . v 2 119
Who stand so much on the new form, that they cannot sit at ease on the old bench . . . . *Rom. and Jul.* ii 4 36
And tell them that, to ease them of their griefs . *T. of Athens* v 1 201
Now breathless wrong Shall sit and pant in your great chairs of ease v 4 11
Such men as he be never at heart's ease Whiles they behold a greater than themselves . . . . *J. Cæsar* i 2 208
We lay these honours on this man, To ease ourselves of divers slanderous loads . . . . iv 1 20
If there be any good thing to be done, That may to thee do ease and grace to me, Speak to me . . . . . *Hamlet* i 1 131
The fat weed That roots itself in ease on Lethe wharf . . . i 5 33
So that, with ease, Or with a little shuffling, you may choose . . iv 7 137
I beseech you, remember— Nay, good my lord; for mine ease, in good faith . . . . v 2 109
Prithee, go in thyself; seek thine own ease . . . . *Lear* iii 4 23
Neglecting an attempt of ease and gain . . . . . *Othello* i 3 29
I am very ill at ease, Unfit for mine own purposes . . . iii 3 32
Which for more probation I can with ease produce . *Cymbeline* v 5 363
Put forth to seas, Where when men been, there's seldom ease *Per.* ii Gower 28
I leap into the seas, Where's hourly trouble for a minute's ease . ii 4 44
Eased. With nothing shall be pleased, till he be eased With being nothing *Richard II.* v 5 40
So the spirit is eased . . . . *Hen. V.* iv 1 19
Tell thy grief; It shall be eased, if France can yield relief . 3 *Hen VI.* iii 3 20
Easeful. Our glorious sun, Ere he attain his easeful western bed . v 3 6
Easier. That I may pass with a reproof the easier . *Mer. Wives* ii 2 195
You dare easier be friends with me than fight with mine enemy *M. Ado* iv 1 300
Thou art easier swallowed than a flap-dragon . . . *L. L. Lost* v 1 45
I can easier teach twenty what were good to be done *Mer. of Venice* i 2 17
I would your spirit were easier for advice . . . *W. Tale* iv 4 516
Forego the easier.—That's the curse of Rome . . *K. John* iii 1 207
What, is my beaver easier than it was? . . . *Richard III.* v 3 50
Lest our old robes sit easier than our new! . . . *Macbeth* ii 4 38
Do you think I am easier to be played on than a pipe? . . *Hamlet* iii 2 386
Easiest. So thou Shalt feel our justice, in whose easiest passage Look for no less than death . . . . *W. Tale* iii 2 91
Easiliest. Find The ooze, to show what coast thy sluggish crare Might easiliest harbour in . . . . *Cymbeline* iv 2 206
Easily. Which he will break As easily as I do tear his paper *T. G. of Ver.* iv 4 136
Yet I cannot put off my opinion so easily . . . *Mer. Wives* ii 1 243
It is a rupture that you may easily heal . . . *Meas. for Meas.* iii 1 244
Is't possible?—Very easily possible . . . . . *Much Ado* i 1 75
Sir, your wit ambles well; it goes easily . . . . . v 1 159
If they have measured many, The measure then of one is easily told *L. L. Lost* v 2 190
Excuse me so, coming too short of thanks For my great suit so easily obtain'd . . . . v 2 749
Sleeps easily because he cannot study . . . *As Y. Like It* iii 2 339
Truly, madam, if God have lent a man any manners, he may easily put it off at court . . . . *All's Well* ii 2 9
He will bear you easily and reins well . . . . *T. Night* iii 4 358
How came the posterns So easily open? . . . . *W. Tale* ii 1 53
He that perforce robs lions of their hearts May easily win a woman's *K. John* i 1 269
I will enforce it easily to my love . . . . . . ii 1 515
Dogs, easily won to fawn on any man! . . . *Richard II.* iii 2 130
Which, for divers reasons . . . , Will easily be granted . 1 *Hen. IV.* i 3 264
Shall bring this prize in very easily . . . . 2 *Hen. IV.* iii 1 101
A heart unspotted is not easily daunted . . . 2 *Hen. VI.* iii 1 100
But mightier crimes are laid unto your charge, Whereof you cannot easily purge yourself . . . . ii 1 135
And be not easily won to our request: Play the maid's part . *Rich. III.* iii 7 50
The amity that wisdom knits not, folly may easily untie *Troi. and Cres.* ii 3 111
It would have gall'd his surly nature, Which easily endures not article Tying him to aught . . . . *Coriolanus* ii 3 204
O wondrous thing! How easily murder is discovered! . *T. Andron.* ii 3 287
If he care not for't, he will supply us easily . . *T. of Athens* iv 3 407
Would have brook'd The eternal devil to keep his state in Rome As easily as a king . . . . *J. Cæsar* i 2 161
Easily. By and by is easily said . . . . *Hamlet* iii 2 404
O, for a chair, To bear him easily hence! . . . . . *Othello* v 1 83
Of one not easily jealous, but being wrought Perplex'd in the extreme . v 2 345
You see how easily she may be surprised . . . *Ant. and Cleo.* v 2 35
You cannot derogate, my lord.—Not easily, I think . *Cymbeline* ii 1 49
Like egg-shells moved upon their surges, crack'd As easily 'gainst our rocks . . . . iii 1 29
Easiness. If we suffer, Out of our easiness and childish pity To one man's honour, this contagious sickness . . . *Hen. VIII.* v 3 25
Refrain to-night, And that shall lend a kind of easiness To the next abstinence: the next more easy . . . . *Hamlet* iii 4 166
Custom hath made it in him a property of easiness . . . v 1 76
Easing me of the carriage . . . . . . *Mer. Wives* ii 2 179
This 'should' is like a spendthrift sigh, That hurts by easing *Hamlet* iv 7 124
East. They shall be my East and West Indies . . *Mer. Wives* i 3 79
Round about Dapples the drowsy east with spots of grey . *Much Ado* v 3 27
It standeth north-north-east and by east from the west corner *L. L. Lost* i 1 248
At the first opening of the gorgeous east . . . . iv 3 223
By east, west, north, and south, I spread my conquering might . v 2 566
Shine comforts from the east . . . . . . *M. N. Dream* iii 2 432
From the east to western Ind, No jewel is like Rosalind *As Y. Like It* iii 2 93
'Tis powerful, think it, From east, west, north and south *W. Tale* i 2 203
By east and west let France and England mount Their battering cannon *K. John* ii 1 381
If e'er those eyes of yours Behold another day break in the east . v 4 32
Shall see us rising in our throne, the east . . . *Richard II.* iii 2 50
As doth the blushing discontented sun From out the fiery portal of the east . . . . iii 3 64
Send danger from the east unto the west, So honour cross it from the north to south, And let them grapple . . . . 1 *Hen. IV.* i 3 195
England, from Trent and Severn hitherto, By south and east is to my part assign'd . . . . iii 1 75
Before the heavenly-harness'd team Begins his golden progress in the east . . . . iii 1 222
They take their courses East, west, north, south . . 2 *Hen. IV.* iv 2 104
If thou darest, This evening, on the east side of the grove . 2 *Hen. VI.* ii 1 43
Are ye advised? the east side of the grove? . . . . ii 1 47
The silent hours steal on, And flaky darkness breaks within the east *Richard III.* v 3 86
By the book He should have braved the east an hour ago . . v 3 279
Come knights from east to west, And cull their flower . *Troi. and Cres.* ii 3 274
They have press'd a power, but it is not known Whether for east or west *Coriolanus* i 2 10
They would fly east, west, north, south . . . . . ii 3 24
All day long, Even from Hyperion's rising in the east . *T. Andron* v 2 56
An hour before the worshipp'd sun Peer'd forth the golden window of the east . . . . *Rom. and Jul.* i 1 126
Soon as the all-cheering sun Should in the furthest east begin to draw The shady curtains from Aurora's bed . . . . . . i 1 141
What light through yonder window breaks? It is the east, and Juliet is the sun . . . . ii 2 3
Look, love, what envious streaks Do lace the severing clouds in yonder east . . . . iii 5 8
Here lies the east: doth not the day break here? . *J. Cæsar* ii 1 101
The high east Stands, as the Capitol, directly here . . . ii 1 110
And the rich East to boot . . . . . . *Macbeth* iv 3 37
This heavy-headed revel east and west Makes us traduced . *Hamlet* i 4 17
And put in every honest hand a whip To lash the rascals naked through the world Even from the east to the west! . . . *Othello* iv 2 144
All the east, Say thou, shall call her mistress . *Ant. and Cleo.* i 5 46
Though I make this marriage for my peace, I' the east my pleasure lies ii 3 40
I did not think, sir, to have met you here.—The beds i' the east are soft ii 6 51
We must lay his head to the east; My father hath a reason for't *Cymbeline* iv 2 255
I may wander From east to occident, cry out for service . . iv 2 372
Eastcheap. I have bespoke supper to-morrow night in Eastcheap 1 *Hen. IV.* i 2 145
Farewell: you shall find me in Eastcheap.—Farewell, thou latter spring! i 2 176
When I am king of England, I shall command all the good lads in Eastcheap . . . . ii 4 16
Whence come you?—My noble lord, from Eastcheap . . . ii 4 485
I am a poor widow of Eastcheap . . . . . 2 *Hen. IV.* ii 1 76
At the old place, my lord, in Eastcheap . . . . . ii 2 161
Easter. Didst thou not fall out with a tailor for wearing his new doublet before Easter? . . . . *Rom. and Jul.* iii 1 30
Eastern. High Taurus' snow, Fann'd with the eastern wind *M. N. Dr.* iii 2 142
The eastern gate, all fiery-red, Opening on Neptune with fair blessed beams . . . . iii 2 391
He fires the proud tops of the eastern pines . . . *Richard II.* iii 2 42
And whither go they?—Up to the eastern tower . . *Troi. and Cres.* i 2 2
Chequering the eastern clouds with streaks of light *Rom. and Jul.* ii 3 2
O eastern star! . . . . *Ant. and Cleo.* v 2 311
Eastward. But, look, the morn, in russet mantle clad, Walks o'er the dew of yon high eastward hill . . . . *Hamlet* i 1 167
Easy. What impossible matter will he make easy next? . . *Tempest* ii 1 89
You yourself know how easy it is to be such an offender *Mer. Wives* ii 2 196
As easy as a cannon will shoot point-blank twelve score . . iii 2 33
'Tis all as easy Falsely to take away a life true made As to put metal in restrained means To make a false one . *Meas. for Meas.* ii 4 46
As the glasses where they view themselves; Which are as easy broke as they make forms . . . . ii 4 126
All difficulties are but easy when they are known . . . iv 2 221
As easy mayst thou fall A drop of water in the breaking gulf *Com. of Er.* ii 2 127
Any pains that I take for you is as easy as thanks . . *Much Ado* ii 3 271
How easy it is to put 'years' to the word 'three' . . *L. L. Lost* i 2 55
Imagining some fear, How easy is a bush supposed a bear! *M. N. Dream* v 1 22
'Twere as easy For you to laugh and leap and say you are merry, Because you are not sad . . . . *Mer. of Venice* i 1 48
If to do were as easy as to know what were good to do . . i 2 13
It is as easy to count atomies as to resolve the propositions of a lover *As Y. Like It* iii 2 245
You shall as easy Prove that I husbanded her bed in Florence *All's Well* v 3 125
This woman's an easy glove, my lord; she goes off and on at pleasure . v 3 278
How easy is it for the proper-false In women's waxen hearts to set their forms! . . . . *T. Night* ii 2 30
Which is for me less easy to commit Than you to punish . *W. Tale* i 2 58
All deaths are too few, the sharpest too easy . . . . iv 4 809
'Tis as easy To make her speak as move . . . . . v 3 93
And made whole With very easy arguments of love . . *K. John* i 1 36
How easy dost thou take all England up! . . . . . iv 3 142
Have I not here the best cards for the game, To win this easy match? . v 2 106

Easy. This ague fit of fear is over-blown; An easy task it is to win our own . . . . *Richard II.* iii 2 191
An easy leap, To pluck bright honour from the pale-faced moon 1 *Hen. IV.* i 3 201
You have deceived our trust, And made us doff our easy robes of peace v 1 12
Of so easy and so plain a stop . . . . 2 *Hen. IV.* Ind. 17
This new and gorgeous garment, majesty, Sits not so easy on me as you think . . . . v 2 45
Was this easy? May this be wash'd in Lethe, and forgotten? . . . v 2 71
I can never win A soul so easy as that Englishman's . . *Hen. V.* ii 2 125
It is as easy for me, Kate, to conquer the kingdom as to speak so much more French . . . . v 2 195
My lord, these faults are easy, quickly answer'd . 2 *Hen. VI.* iii 1 133
Shall I not hear my task?—An easy task; 'tis but to love a king 3 *Hen. VI.* iii 2 53
Our scouts have found the adventure very easy . . . . iv 2 18
Is it not an easy matter To make William Lord Hastings of our mind? *Richard III.* iii 1 161
They should find easy penance.—Faith, how easy?—As easy as a down-bed would afford it . . . . . *Hen. VIII.* i 4 17
When he thinks, good easy man, full surely His greatness is a-ripening iii 2 356
At last, with easy roads, he came to Leicester . . . . iv 2 17
That's as easy As to set dogs on sheep . . . *Coriolanus* ii 1 272
His ascent is not by such easy degrees . . . . . ii 2 28
O, he's a limb that has but a disease; Mortal, to cut it off; to cure it, easy . . . . iii 1 297
To front his revenges with the easy groans of old women . . v 2 45
What faults he made before the last, I think Might have found easy fines v 6 65
Easy it is Of a cut loaf to steal a shive, we know *T. Andron.* ii 1 86
As for my sons, say I account of them As jewels purchased at an easy price . . . . iii 1 199
A little water clears us of this deed: How easy is it, then! *Macbeth* ii 2 68
To show an unfelt sorrow is an office Which the false man does easy . ii 3 143
As easy mayst thou the intrenchant air With thy keen sword impress . v 8 9
'Tis as easy as lying . . . . *Hamlet* iii 2 372
Refrain to-night, And that shall lend a kind of easiness To the next abstinence: the next more easy . . . . . iii 4 167
On whose foolish honesty My practices ride easy . . . *Lear* i 2 198
'Tis most easy The inclining Desdemona to subdue In any honest suit *Othello* ii 3 345
Those that do teach young babes Do it with gentle means and easy tasks iv 2 112
Which with a snaffle You may pace easy, but not such a wife *A. and C.* ii 2 64
'Tis easy to't; and there I will attend What further comes . . iii 10 32
He makes me angry; And at this time most easy 'tis to do't . . iii 13 144
She hath pursued conclusions infinite Of easy ways to die . . v 2 359
Which else an easy battery might lay flat . . . *Cymbeline* i 4 22
The stone's too hard to come by.—Not a whit, Your lady being so easy ii 4 47

Easy-borrowed. A slave, whose easy-borrow'd pride Dwells in the fickle grace of her he follows . . . . *Lear* ii 4 188

Easy-held. And this her easy-held imprisonment Hath gain'd thy daughter princely liberty . . . . . . 1 *Hen. VI.* v 3 139

Easy-melting. Have wrought the easy-melting king like wax 3 *Hen. VI.* ii 1 171

Easy-yielding. You have, as it appears to me, practised upon the easy-yielding spirit of this woman . . . . . . 2 *Hen. IV.* ii 1 125

Eat. I must eat my dinner. This island's mine . . . *Tempest* i 2 330
It eats and sleeps and hath such senses As we have, such . . . i 2 412
I' faith, I'll eat nothing; I thank you as much as though I did *M. Wives* i 1 290
We stay for you.—I'll eat nothing, I thank you, sir . . . i 1 315
'Tis old, but true, Still swine eats all the draff . . . iv 2 109
Thou shalt eat a posset to-night at my house . . . . v 5 179
From their abominable and beastly touches I drink, I eat *Meas. for Meas.* iii 2 26
The duke, I say to thee again, would eat mutton on Fridays . . iii 2 192
Then 'twill be dry.—If it be, sir, I pray you, eat none of it *Com. of Er.* ii 2 61
He must have a long spoon that must eat with the devil . . iv 3 65
For indeed I promised to eat all of his killing . . . *Much Ado* i 1 45
You had musty victual, and he hath holp to eat it . . . . i 1 51
Eat when I have stomach, and wait for no man's leisure . . . i 3 16
There's a partridge wing saved, for the fool will eat no supper . ii 1 156
In despite of his heart, he eats his meat without grudging . . iii 4 90
Nor age so eat up my invention . . . . iv 1 196
By my sword, Beatrice, thou lovest me.—Do not swear, and eat it . iv 1 277
I will make him eat it that says I love not you . . . . iv 1 279
Will you not eat your word?—With no sauce that can be devised to it . iv 1 280
I would eat his heart in the market-place . . . . . iv 1 309
He hath not eat paper, as it were; he hath not drunk ink . *L. L. Lost* iv 2 26
Methought a serpent eat my heart away, And you sat smiling *M. N. Dream* ii 2 149
Or say, sweet love, what thou desirest to eat . . . . iv 1 34
Eat no onions nor garlic, for we are to utter sweet breath . . iv 2 43
To smell pork; to eat of the habitation which your prophet the Nazarite conjured the devil into . . . . . *Mer. of Venice* i 3 34
I will not eat with you, drink with you, nor pray with you . . i 3 38
Shall I keep your hogs and eat husks with them? . . . *As Y. Like It* i 1 40
Slept together, Rose at an instant, learn'd, play'd, eat together . i 3 76
Seeking the food he eats And pleased with what he gets . . . ii 5 42
If I bring thee not something to eat, I will give thee leave to die . ii 6 12
Forbear, and eat no more.—Why, I have eat none yet . . . ii 7 88
I am a true labourer: I earn that I eat, get that I wear, owe no man hate iii 2 78
When he had a desire to eat a grape, would open his lips when he put it into his mouth; meaning thereby that grapes were made to eat and lips to open . . . . v 1 37
I will not eat my word, now thou art mine . . . . . v 4 155
She eat no meat to-day nor none shall eat . . . *T. of Shrew* iv 1 200
As who should say, if I should sleep or eat, 'Twere deadly sickness . iv 3 13
Eat it up all, Hortensio, if thou lovest me . . . . . iv 3 50
Kate, eat apace . . . . iv 3 52
We sit to chat as well as eat.—Nothing but sit and sit, and eat and eat! v 2 11
Like one of our French withered pears, it looks ill, it eats drily *All's W.* i 1 175
Eat, speak, and move under the influence of the most received star . ii 1 56
O, will you eat no grapes, my royal fox? . . . . . ii 1 73
I think, sir, you can eat none of this homely meat . . . ii 2 48
Please it this matron and this gentle maid To eat with us to-night . iii 5 101
I will henceforth eat no fish of fortune's buttering . . . . v 2 9
Though you are a fool and a knave, you shall eat . . . . v 2 58
And you find so much blood in his liver as will clog the foot of a flea, I'll eat the rest of the anatomy . . . . *T. Night* iii 2 67
She longed to eat adders' heads and toads carbonadoed . *W. Tale* iv 4 268
Sir Robert might have eat his part in me Upon Good-Friday and ne'er broke his fast . . . . *K. John* i 1 234
But now will canker sorrow eat my bud . . . . . . iii 4 82
If I dare eat, or drink, or breathe, or live, I dare meet Surrey *Rich. II.* iv 1 73
That jade hath eat bread from my royal hand . . . . v 5 85

Eat. Shall the blessed sun of heaven prove a micher and eat blackberries? 1 *Hen. IV.* ii 4 450
Wherein neat and cleanly, but to carve a capon and eat it? . . . ii 4 503
I'll give you leave to powder me and eat me too to-morrow . . . v 4 113
'Zounds, I would make him eat a piece of my sword . . . . v 4 157
And now thou wouldst eat thy dead vomit up . . . . 2 *Hen. IV.* i 3 99
She had a good dish of prawns; whereby thou didst desire to eat some ii 1 105
The rest of thy low countries have made a shift to eat up thy holland . ii 2 25
I'll steep this letter in sack and make him eat it.—That's to make him eat twenty of his words . . . . ii 2 149
A' plays at quoits well, and eats conger and fennel . . . ii 4 266
But thou, most fine, most honour'd, most renown'd, Hast eat thy bearer up . . . . iv 5 165
We will eat a last year's pippin of my own graffing . . . . v 3 2
We shall Do nothing but eat, and make good cheer . . . . . v 3 18
Playing the mouse in absence of the cat, To tear and havoc more than she can eat . . . . *Hen. V.* i 2 173
He longs to eat the English.—I think he will eat all he kills . . iii 7 99
That's a valiant flea that dare eat his breakfast on the lip of a lion . iii 7 156
They will eat like wolves and fight like devils . . . . . iii 7 162
They have only stomachs to eat and none to fight . . . . iii 7 166
And prings me pread and salt yesterday, look you, and bid me eat my leek . . . . v 1 10
Eat, look you, this leek: because, look you, you do not love it . . v 1 25
I would desire you to eat it.—Not for Cadwallader and all his goats . v 1 28
There is one goat for you. Will you be so good, scauld knave, as eat it? v 1 31
I will desire you to live in the mean time, and eat your victuals . . v 1 3
I pray you, fall to: if you can mock a leek, you can eat a leek . . v 1 3
I will make him eat some part of my leek, or I will peat his pate four days . . . . v 1 42
I eat and eat, I swear— Eat, I pray you . . . . . v 1 50
Quiet thy cudgel; thou dost see I eat.—Much good do you . . . v 1 54
I have another leek in my pocket, which you shall eat . . . . v 1 66
Whiles thy consuming canker eats his falsehood . . 1 *Hen. VI.* ii 4 71
And caterpillars eat my leaves away . . . . 2 *Hen. VI.* iii 1 90
I climbed into this garden, to see if I can eat grass . . . . iv 10 9
I'll make thee eat iron like an ostrich, and swallow my sword . . iv 10 30
Look on me well: I have eat no meat these five days . . . iv 10 41
I pray God I may never eat grass more . . . . . . iv 10 44
Or earth, gape open wide and eat him quick! . . . *Richard III.* i 2 65
Every man shall eat in safety, Under his own vine, what he plants *Hen. VIII.* v 5 34
If you love an addle egg as well as you love an idle head, you would eat chickens i' the shell . . . . *Troi. and Cres.* i 2 147
Must make perforce an universal prey, And last eat up himself . . i 3 124
He that is proud eats up himself: pride is his own glass . . . ii 3 164
A' should not bear it so, a' should eat swords first . . . . ii 3 227
He eats nothing but doves, love, and that breeds hot blood . . iii 1 140
When we vow to weep seas, live in fire, eat rocks, tame tigers . . iii 2 84
How one man eats into another's pride! . . . . . . iii 3 136
I will go eat with thee and see your knights . . . . . iv 5 158
Yet, in a sort, lechery eats itself . . . . v 4 37
If the wars eat us not up, they will; and there's all the love they bear us *Coriolanus* i 1 87
Sigh'd forth proverbs, That hunger broke stone walls, that dogs must eat i 1 210
So often hast thou beat me, And wouldst do so, I think, should we encounter As often as we eat . . . . i 10 10
Like an unnatural dam Should now eat up her own! . . . . iii 1 294
Look you eat no more Than will preserve just so much strength in us As will revenge these bitter woes of ours . . . *T. Andron.* iii 2 1
Come, let's fall to; and, gentle girl, eat this: Here is no drink! . . iii 2 34
Although the cheer be poor, 'Twill fill your stomachs; please you eat of it . . . . v 3 29
Will't please you eat? will't please your highness feed? . . . v 3 54
Full soon the canker death eats up that plant . . . *Rom. and Jul.* ii 3 30
Wilt dine with me, Apemantus?—No; I eat not lords.—An thou shouldst, thou 'ldst anger ladies.—O, they eat lords . . . *T. of Athens* i 1 207
O you gods, what a number of men eat Timon, and he sees 'em not! . i 2 40
Rich men sin, and I eat root. Much good dich thy good heart, Apemantus! i 2 72
Why then preferr'd you not your sums and bills, When your false masters eat of my lord's meat? . . . . iii 4 50
Here is some gold for thee.—Keep it, I cannot eat it . . . iv 3 100
That the whole life of Athens were in this! Thus would I eat it . . iv 3 282
Where feed'st thou o' days, Apemantus?—Where my stomach finds meat; or, rather, where I eat it . . . . iv 3 295
There's a medlar for thee, eat it.—On what I hate I feed not . . iv 3 305
If thou wert the lamb, the fox would eat thee . . . . . iv 3 332
Moe things like men! Eat, Timon, and abhor them . . . . iv 3 398
Nor on the beasts themselves, the birds, and fishes; You must eat men iv 3 428
How shall I requite you? Can you eat roots and drink cold water? . v 1 77
It will not let you eat, nor talk, nor sleep . . . *J. Cæsar* ii 1 252
'Tis said they eat each other.—They did so, to the amazement of mine eyes That look'd upon't . . . . *Macbeth* ii 4 18
Let the frame of things disjoint, both the worlds suffer, Ere we will eat our meal in fear . . . . iii 2 17
Here let them lie Till famine and the ague eat them up . . . v 5 4
I eat the air, promise-crammed: you cannot feed capons so . *Hamlet* iii 2 99
That monster, custom, who all sense doth eat, Of habits devil . . iii 4 161
At supper! where?—Not where he eats, but where he is eaten . . iv 3 20
A man may fish with the worm that hath eat of a king, and eat of the fish that hath fed of that worm . . . . iv 3 29
The ocean, overpeering of his list, Eats not the flats with more impetuous haste . . . . iv 5 100
Woo't tear thyself? Woo't drink up eisel? eat a crocodile? . . . v 1 299
To fear judgement; to fight when I cannot choose; and to eat no fish *Lear* i 4 18
After I have cut the egg i' the middle, and eat up the meat . . . i 4 174
That eats the swimming frog, the toad, the tadpole, the wall-newt . iii 4 134
In the fury of his heart, when the foul fiend rages, eats cow-dung for sallets . . . . iii 4 137
I cannot draw a cart, nor eat dried oats; If it be man's work, I'll do't . v 3 38
And of the Cannibals that each other eat . . . . . *Othello* i 3 143
They are all but stomachs, and we all but food; They eat us hungerly . iii 4 105
On the Alps It is reported thou didst eat strange flesh *Ant. and Cleo.* i 4 67
And for his ordinary pays his heart For what his eyes eat only . . ii 2 231
When valour preys on reason, It eats the sword it fights with . . iii 13 200
Sir, I will eat no meat, I'll not drink, sir; If idle talk will once be necessary, I'll not sleep neither . . . . v 2 49
Give it nothing, I pray you, for it is not worth the feeding.—Will it eat me?—You must not think I am so simple but I know the devil himself will not eat a woman . . . . v 2 272

Eat. Subtle as the fox for prey, Like warlike as the wolf for what we eat *Cymbeline* iii 3 41
But that it eats our victuals, I should think Here were a fairy . . . iii 6 41
You shall have better cheer Ere you depart; and thanks to stay and eat it . . . . iii 6 68
Care no more to clothe and eat; To thee the reed is as the oak . iv 2 266
Are ready now To eat those little darlings whom they loved . *Pericles* i 4 44
Not to eat honey like a drone From others' labours . . . . ii Gower 18
As men do a-land; the great ones eat up the little ones . . . ii 1 32
All viands that I eat do seem unsavoury, Wishing him my meat . ii 3 31
Eat and drink. Do as adversaries do in law, Strive mightily, but eat and drink as friends . . . . *T. of Shrew* i 2 279
I will eat and drink, and sleep as soft As captain shall . *All's Well* iv 3 368
Thou'rt a scholar; let us therefore eat and drink . . . *T. Night* ii 3 13
There shall be no money; all shall eat and drink on my score 2 *Hen. VI.* iv 2 79
Eaten. As the most forward bud Is eaten by the canker *T. G. of Ver.* i 1 46
Your sorrow hath eaten up my sufferance . . . *Mer. Wives* iv 2 1
This very man, having eaten the rest, as I said, and, as I say, paying for them very honestly . . . . . . *Meas. for Meas.* ii 1 104
She hath eaten up all her beef, and she is herself in the tub . . . iii 2 58
How many hath he killed and eaten in these wars? . . *Much Ado* i 1 43
I marvel thy master hath not eaten thee for a word . . *L. L. Lost* v 1 43
Men have died from time to time and worms have eaten them *As Y. L. It* iv 1 108
Ay, sir, they be ready: the oats have eaten the horses . *T. of Shrew* iii 2 208
I'll go see if the bear be gone from the gentleman and how much he hath eaten . . . . *W. Tale* iii 3 134
He utters them as he had eaten ballads . . . . . . iv 4 185
I were better to be eaten to death with a rust . . . . 2 *Hen. IV.* i 2 245
He hath eaten me out of house and home . . . . . . ii 1 80
There is another indictment upon thee, for suffering flesh to be eaten . ii 4 372
I wish some ravenous wolf had eaten thee! . . . . . 1 *Hen. VI.* v 4 31
An he had been cannibally given, he might have broiled and eaten him *Coriolanus* iv 5 201
Have we eaten on the insane root That takes the reason prisoner? *Macb.* i 3 84
Pour in sow's blood, that hath eaten Her nine farrow . . . iv 1 64
At supper! where?—Not where he eats, but where he is eaten *Hamlet* iv 3 21
I see, sir, you are eaten up with passion . . . . *Othello* iii 3 391
Eater. I am a great eater of beef and I believe that does harm to my wit *T. Night* i 3 90
A knave; a rascal; an eater of broken meats . . . . *Lear* ii 2 15
And she an eater of her mother's flesh . . . . . *Pericles* i 1 130
Eating. As in the sweetest bud The eating canker dwells, so eating love Inhabits in the finest wits of all . . . . . . *T. G. of Ver.* i 1 43
It is impossible to extirp it [lechery] quite, friar, till eating and drinking be put down . . . . *Meas. for Meas.* iii 2 110
I think it [life] rather consists of eating and drinking . *T. Night* ii 3 12
If this be magic, let it be an art Lawful as eating . . *W. Tale* v 3 111
Eating the bitter bread of banishment . . . . *Richard II.* iii 1 21
The weeds which his broad-spreading leaves did shelter, That seem'd in eating him to hold him up . . . . iii 4 51
Prodigals lately come from swine-keeping, from eating draff and husks 1 *Hen. IV.* iv 2 38
Who lined himself with hope, Eating the air on promise of supply 2 *Hen. IV.* i 3 28
His breath stinks with eating toasted cheese . . . . 2 *Hen. VI.* iv 7 13
Eating the flesh that she herself hath bred . . . . *T. Andron.* v 3 62
If I be alive and your mind hold and your dinner worth the eating *J. C.* i 2 296
Eaux. Via! les eaux et la terre.—Rien puis? l'air et le feu *Hen. V.* iv 2 4
Eaves. His tears run down his beard, like winter's drops From eaves of reeds *Tempest* v 1 17
It nothing steads us To chide him from our eaves . . *All's Well* iii 7 42
Eaves-dropper. I'll play the eaves-dropper . . . *Richard III.* v 3 221
Ebb. With mine eyes, never since at ebb, beheld The king . *Tempest* i 2 435
I'll teach you how to flow.—Do so: to ebb Hereditary sloth instruct me ii 1 222
One so strong That could control the moon, make flows and ebbs . . v 1 270
The sea will ebb and flow, heaven show his face . . . *L. L. Lost* iv 3 216
Doth it not flow as hugely as the sea, Till that the weary very means do ebb? . . . . *As Y. Like It* ii 7 73
The fortune of us that are the moon's men doth ebb and flow . 1 *Hen. IV.* i 2 36
In as low an ebb as the foot of the ladder . . . . . . i 2 42
It is a low ebb of linen with thee . . . . . . 2 *Hen. IV.* ii 2 22
The river hath thrice flow'd, no ebb between . . . . . iv 4 125
Now doth it turn and ebb back to the sea . . . . . . v 2 131
And swell so much the higher by their ebb . . . 3 *Hen. VI.* iv 8 56
Yea, watch His pettish lunes, his ebbs, his flows . . *Troi. and Cres.* ii 3 139
Thy eyes, which I may call the sea, Do ebb and flow with tears *R. and J.* iii 5 134
I have Prompted you in the ebb of your estate And your great flow of debts *T. of Athens* ii 2 151
Packs and sects of great ones, That ebb and flow by the moon . *Lear* v 3 19
Like to the Pontic sea, Whose icy current and compulsive course Ne'er feels retiring ebb . . . . *Othello* iii 3 455
Shall ne'er look back, ne'er ebb to humble love . . . . iii 3 458
The higher Nilus swells, The more it promises: as it ebbs, the seedsman Upon the slime and ooze scatters his grain . *Ant. and Cleo.* ii 7 24
Ebbed. Your verse Flow'd with her beauty once: 'tis shrewdly ebb'd *W. Tale* v 1 102
The ebb'd man, ne'er loved till ne'er worth love, Comes dear'd by being lack'd . . . . *Ant. and Cleo.* i 4 43
Ebbing men, indeed, Most often do so near the bottom run *Tempest* ii 1 226
Ye that on the sands with printless foot Do chase the ebbing Neptune . v 1 35
Ebon-coloured. That draweth from my snow-white pen the ebon-coloured ink . . . . *L. L. Lost* i 1 246
Ebon den. Rouse up revenge from ebon den . . . 2 *Hen. IV.* v 5 39
Ebony. By heaven, thy love is black as ebony.—Is ebony like her? O wood divine! . . . . *L. L. Lost* iv 3 247
The clearstores toward the south north are as lustrous as ebony *T. Night* iv 2 42
Ebrew. Or I am a Jew else, an Ebrew Jew . . . 1 *Hen. IV.* ii 4 198
Ecce signum. My sword hacked like a hand-saw—ecce signum! . . ii 4 187
Echapper. Est-il impossible d'échapper la force de ton bras? . *Hen V.* iv 4 17
Eche. Be attent, And time that is so briefly spent With your fine fancies quaintly eche . . . . *Pericles* iii Gower 13
Echo. Mark the musical confusion Of hounds and echo . *M. N. Dream* iv 1 116
If Echo were as fleet, I would esteem him worth a dozen such *T. of Shrew* Ind. 1 26
And fetch shrill echoes from the hollow earth . . . . . Ind. 2 48
With such a clamorous smack That at the parting all the church did echo . . . . iii 2 181
It gives a very echo to the seat Where Love is throned . . *T. Night* ii 4 21
Do but start An echo with the clamour of thy drum . . *K. John* v 2 168
Rumour doth double, like the voice and echo, The numbers 2 *Hen. IV.* iii 1 97
Echo. Ring a hunter's peal, That all the court may echo with the noise *T. Andron.* ii 2 6
Whilst the babbling echo mocks the hounds . . . . . ii 3 17
Else would I tear the cave where Echo lies, And make her airy tongue more hoarse than mine . . . . . . *Rom. and Jul.* ii 2 162
I would applaud thee to the very echo, That should applaud again *Macb.* v 3 53
He echoes me, As if there were some monster in his thought . *Othello* iii 3 106
Eclipse. Born to eclipse thy life this afternoon . . . 1 *Hen. VI.* iv 5 53
Slips of yew Sliver'd in the moon's eclipse . . . . *Macbeth* iv 1 28
Was sick almost to doomsday with eclipse . . . . *Hamlet* i 1 120
These late eclipses in the sun and moon portend no good to us . *Lear* i 2 112
O, these eclipses do portend these divisions! . . . . . . i 2 148
Of a prediction I read this other day, what should follow these eclipses i 2 154
Methinks it should be now a huge eclipse Of sun and moon . *Othello* v 2 99
Eclipsed. By doubtful fear My joy of liberty is half eclipsed 3 *Hen. VI.* iv 6 63
Alack, our terrene moon Is now eclipsed . . . . . *Ant. and Cleo.* iii 13 154
Écolier. Je pense que je suis le bon écolier; j'ai gagné deux mots d'Anglois vitement . . . . *Hen. V.* iii 4 13
Écoutez; dites-moi, si je parle bien . . . . iii 4 17
Écoutez: de hand, de fingres, de nails, de arma, de bilbow . . iii 4 30
Écoutez: comment êtes-vous appelé? . . . . iii 4 26
Ecstasy. Hinder them from what this ecstasy May now provoke them to *Tempest* iii 3 108
Mark how he trembles in his ecstasy! . . . . *Com. of Errors* iv 4 54
The ecstasy hath so much overborne her . . . . *Much Ado* ii 3 157
Be moderate; allay thy ecstasy; In measure rein thy joy *Mer. of Venice* iii 2 112
Attend him in his ecstasy . . . . *T. Andron.* iv 1 125
But if I live, his feigned ecstasies Shall be no shelter to these outrages iv 4 21
Than on the torture of the mind to lie In restless ecstasy . *Macbeth* iii 2 22
Where violent sorrow seems A modern ecstasy . . . . . iv 3 170
This is the very ecstasy of love . . . . *Hamlet* ii 1 102
That unmatch'd form and feature of blown youth Blasted with ecstasy iii 1 168
For madness would not err, Nor sense to ecstasy was ne'er so thrall'd . iii 4 74
This bodiless creation ecstasy Is very cunning in . . . . iii 4 138
Ecstasy! My pulse, as yours, doth temperately keep time . . iii 4 139
I shifted him away, And laid good 'scuse upon your ecstasy . *Othello* iv 1 80
Écus. Gardez ma vie, et je vous donnerai deux cents écus . *Hen. V.* iv 4 45
Pour les écus que vous l'avez promis, il est content de vous donner la liberté, le franchisement . . . . iv 4 55
Eden. This other Eden, demi-paradise . . . . *Richard II.* ii 1 42
Edgar. Legitimate Edgar, I must have your land . . . . *Lear* i 2 16
And live the beloved of your brother, Edgar . . . . . . i 2 57
My son Edgar! Had he a hand to write this? . . . . . . i 2 60
Edgar—and pat he comes like the catastrophe of the old comedy . . i 2 145
Seek your life? He whom my father named? your Edgar? . . . ii 1 94
Poor Turlygod! poor Tom! That's something yet: Edgar I nothing am ii 3 21
Then Edgar was abused. Kind gods, forgive me that, and prosper him! iii 7 91
O dear son Edgar, The food of thy abused father's wrath! . . . iv 1 23
If Edgar live, O, bless him! . . . . iv 6 40
They say Edgar, his banished son, is with the Earl of Kent in Germany iv 7 90
My name is Edgar, and thy father's son . . . . . . v 3 169
Edge. To take away The edge of that day's celebration . *Tempest* iv 1 29
Rebate and blunt his natural edge With profits of the mind . *M. for M.* i 4 60
That honour which shall bate his scythe's keen edge . *L. L. Lost* i 1 6
A sharp wit match'd with too blunt a will; Whose edge hath power to cut . . . . ii 1 50
Hereby, upon the edge of yonder coppice . . . . . . iv 1 9
The tongues of mocking wenches are as keen As is the razor's edge invisible . . . . v 2 257
To be in peril of my life with the edge of a feather-bed . *Mer. of Venice* ii 2 173
She moves me not, or not removes, at least, Affection's edge in me *T. of S.* i 2 73
We'll strive to bear it for your worthy sake To the extreme edge of hazard . . . . *All's Well* iii 3 6
Doth set my pugging tooth on edge . . . . . *W. Tale* iv 3 7
Or cloy the hungry edge of appetite By bare imagination of a feast *Richard II.* i 3 296
The edge of war, like an ill-sheathed knife, No more shall cut his master 1 *Hen. IV.* i 1 17
That would set my teeth nothing on edge, Nothing so much as mincing poetry . . . . iii 1 133
He walk'd o'er perils, on an edge, More likely to fall in than to get o'er 2 *Hen. IV.* i 1 170
The foeman may with as great aim level at the edge of a penknife . iii 2 286
And consecrate commotion's bitter edge . . . . . . iv 1 93
'Gainst him whose wrongs give edge unto the swords . . *Hen. V.* i 2 27
Some say knives have edges. It must be as it may . . . ii 1 25
Let not Bardolph's vital thread be cut With edge of penny cord . . iii 6 50
This news, I think, hath turn'd your weapon's edge . 2 *Hen. VI.* ii 1 180
Steel, if thou turn the edge, or cut not . . . . . . iv 10 60
Though the edge hath something hit ourselves . . . 3 *Hen. VI.* ii 2 166
Thus yields the cedar to the axe's edge . . . . . . v 2 11
Abate the edge of traitors, gracious Lord! . . . *Richard III.* v 5 35
His sword Hath a sharp edge: it's long . . . . *Hen. VIII.* i 1 110
With these your white enchanting fingers touch'd, Shall more obey than to the edge of steel . . . . *Troi. and Cres.* iii 1 165
Shall to the edge of all extremity Pursue each other . . . . iv 5 68
Ripe for his edge, Fall down before him, like the mower's swath . v 5 24
He that retires, I'll take him for a Volsce, And he shall feel mine edge *Coriolanus* i 4 29
Cut me to pieces, Volsces; men and lads, Stain all your edges on me . v 6 113
Thy years want wit, thy wit wants edge, And manners . *T. Andron.* ii 1 26
Give to the edge o' the sword His wife, his babes . . *Macbeth* iv 1 151
Or else my sword with an unbatter'd edge I sheathe again undeeded . v 7 19
And borrowing dulls the edge of husbandry . . . . *Hamlet* i 3 77
Give him a further edge, And drive his purpose on to these delights . iii 1 26
It would cost you a groaning to take off my edge . . . . iii 2 260
If I knew What hoop should hold us stanch, from edge to edge O' the world I would pursue it . . . . . . *Ant. and Cleo.* ii 2 117
To part with unhack'd edges, and bear back Our targes undinted . . ii 6 38
If knife, drugs, serpents, have Edge, sting, or operation, I am safe . iv 15 26
'Tis slander, Whose edge is sharper than the sword . . . *Cymbeline* iii 4 36
We'll bring your grace e'en to the edge o' the shore . . *Pericles* iii 3 35
Edged. With spirit of honour edged More sharper than your swords *Hen. V.* iii 5 38
O, turn thy edged sword another way . . . . 1 *Hen. VI.* iii 3 52
Edgeless. To-morrow in the battle think on me, And fall thy edgeless sword . . . . *Richard III.* v 3 135
Edict. Those many had not dared to do that evil, If the first that did the edict infringe Had answer'd for his deed . . *Meas. for Meas.* ii 2 92
Our late edict shall strongly stand in force . . . *L. L. Lost* i 1 11

Edict. Contrary to thy established proclaimed edict and continent canon *L. L. Lost* i 1 262
It stands as an edict in destiny . . . . . . *M. N. Dream* i 1 151
Takes on him to reform Some certain edicts and some strait decrees *1 Hen. IV.* iv 3 79
Yet, notwithstanding such a strait edict . . . *2 Hen. VI.* iii 2 258
And wilt thou, then, Spurn at his edict and fulfil a man's? *Richard III.* i 4 203
Make edicts for usury, to support usurers . . . *Coriolanus* i 1 84
Make thine own edict for thy pains, which we Will answer as a law *Ant. and Cleo.* iii 12 32
By the tenour of our strict edict, Your exposition misinterpreting *Per.* i 1 111
Edifice. So that I have lost my edifice by mistaking the place where I erected it . . . . *Mer. Wives* ii 2 225
Should I go to church And see the holy edifice of stone, And not bethink me straight of dangerous rocks? *Mer. of Venice* i 1 30
City, 'Tis I that made thy widows: many an heir Of these fair edifices 'fore my wars Have I heard groan and drop . . *Coriolanus* iv 4 3
Edified. Read it.—Look then to be well edified . . *T. Night* v 1 298
I knew you must be edified by the margent ere you had done *Hamlet* v 2 162
Can you inquire him out, and be edified by report? . . *Othello* iii 4 14
Edifies. My love with words and errors still she feeds; But edifies another with her deeds . . . *Troi. and Cres.* v 3 112
Edition. These are of the second edition . . . *Mer. Wives* ii 1 78
Edmund. Commend me to thy brother, Edmund York . *Richard II.* i 2 62
Did King Richard then Proclaim my brother Edmund Mortimer Heir to the crown? . . . . *1 Hen. IV.* i 3 156
These grey locks, the pursuivants of death, . . . Argue the end of Edmund Mortimer . . . . . . *1 Hen. VI.* ii 5 7
The heads of Edmund Duke of Somerset, And William de la Pole *2 Hen. VI.* i 2 29
Philippe, a daughter, Who married Edmund Mortimer, Earl of March: Edmund had issue, Roger Earl of March; Roger had issue, Edmund, Anne and Eleanor . . . . ii 2 36
This Edmund, in the reign of Bolingbroke, As I have read, laid claim unto the crown . . . . ii 2 39
Edmund Mortimer, Earl of March, Married the Duke of Clarence' daughter . . . . iv 2 144
Tell him I'll send Duke Edmund to the Tower . . . . iv 9 38
Do you know this noble gentleman, Edmund?—No, my lord . . *Lear* i 1 25
Our father's love is to the bastard Edmund As to the legitimate . . i 2 17
Edmund the base Shall top the legitimate . . . . . i 2 20
Edmund, how now! what news?—So please your lordship, none . i 2 26
Edmund, seek him out; wind me into him, I pray you . . . i 2 105
Find out this villain, Edmund; it shall lose thee nothing; do it carefully . . . . i 2 125
How now, brother Edmund! what serious contemplation are you in? . i 2 150
Now, Edmund, where's the villain?—Here stood he in the dark . ii 1 39
Edmund, I hear that you have shown your father A child-like office ii 1 107
For you, Edmund, Whose virtue and obedience doth this instant So much commend itself, you shall be ours . . . . . ii 1 114
Alack, alack, Edmund, I like not this unnatural dealing . . iii 3 1
There is some strange thing toward, Edmund; pray you, be careful iii 3 21
Edmund, keep you our sister company . . . . . iii 7 6
Where's my son Edmund? Edmund, enkindle all the sparks of nature, To quit this horrid act . . . . iii 7 85
Back, Edmund, to my brother; Hasten his musters . . . iv 2 15
Lord Edmund spake not with your lord at home?—No, madam . . iv 5 4
Edmund, I think, is gone, In pity of his misery, to dispatch His nighted life . . . . iv 5 11
Why should she write to Edmund? Might not you Transport her purposes? . . . . iv 5 19
She gave strange œillades and most speaking looks To noble Edmund . iv 5 26
Edmund and I have talk'd; And more convenient is he for my hand . iv 5 30
Give the letters which thou find'st about me To Edmund earl of Gloucester . . . . iv 6 255
Edmund, I arrest thee On capital treason . . . . . . v 3 82
If any man of quality or degree within the lists of the army will maintain upon Edmund, supposed Earl of Gloucester, that he is a manifold traitor, let him appear . . . . v 3 112
What's he that speaks for Edmund Earl of Gloucester?—Himself. . v 3 125
Let's exchange charity. I am no less in blood than thou art, Edmund v 3 167
Speak, Edmund, where's the king? and where's Cordelia? . . . v 3 237
Edmund is dead, my lord.—That's but a trifle here . . . v 3 295
Edmundsbury. I will meet him at Saint Edmundsbury . . *K. John* iv 3 11
Upon the altar at Saint Edmundsbury . . . . . . v 4 18
Educate. Do you not educate youth at the charge-house? . *L. L. Lost* v 1 86
Education. Mines my gentility with my education . . *As Y. Like It* i 1 22
My father charged you in his will to give me good education . . i 1 71
By birth a pedlar, by education a cardmaker . . *T. of Shrew* Ind. 2 20
Toward the education of your daughters, I here bestow a simple instrument . . . . ii 1 99
I have those hopes of her good that her education promises . *All's Well* i 1 46
She in beauty, education, blood, Holds hand with any princess . *K. John* ii 1 493
I do perceive here a divided duty: To you I am bound for life and education; My life and education both do learn me How to respect you . . . . *Othello* i 3 182
My name, Pericles; My education been in arts and arms . *Pericles* ii 3 82
Hath gain'd Of education all the grace, Which makes her both the heart and place Of general wonder . . . . iv Gower 9
Edward Bohun. I was lord high constable And Duke of Buckingham; now, poor Edward Bohun . . . . . . *Hen. VIII.* ii 1 103
Edward Confessor's crown, The rod, and bird of peace . . iv 1 88
Is received Of the most pious Edward with such grace . *Macbeth* iii 6 27
Edward Courtney, and the haughty prelate . . *Richard III.* iv 4 502
Edward Duke of Bar . . . . *Hen. V.* iv 8 103
Edward shovel-boards. Two Edward shovel-boards, that cost me two shilling and two pence a-piece . . . . . . *Mer. Wives* i 1 159
Edward (son of Edward IV.) Plant your joys in living Edward's throne *Richard III.* ii 2 100
You say that Edward is your brother's son: So say we too, but not by Edward's wife . . . . iii 7 177
This Edward, whom our manners term the prince . . . . iii 7 191
Young Edward lives: think now what I would say.—Say on, my loving lord . . . . iv 2 10
Ha! am I king? 'tis so: but Edward lives . . . . . iv 2 14
O bitter consequence, That Edward still should live! . . . iv 2 16
Edward Plantagenet, why art thou dead? . . . . . . iv 4 19
Edward for Edward pays a dying debt . . . . . . iv 4 21
Thou hadst an Edward, till a Richard kill'd him . . . . iv 4 42
Thy other Edward dead, to quit my Edward . . . . . iv 4 64
Edward (son of Henry VI.) Gentle son Edward, thou wilt stay with me? —Ay, to be murder'd . . . . *3 Hen. VI.* i 1 259
I, poor Margaret, With this my son, Prince Edward, Henry's heir, Am come to crave thy just and lawful aid . . . . . iii 3 31
Yet here Prince Edward stands, King Henry's son . . . . . iii 3 73
Prince Edward, and Oxford, Vouchsafe, at our request, to stand aside iii 3 109
So link'd in friendship, That young Prince Edward marries Warwick's daughter . . . . iv 1 117
Let me entreat, for I command no more, That Margaret your queen and my son Edward Be sent for . . . . iv 6 60
Is proclamation made, that who finds Edward Shall have a high reward? . . . . v 5 9
And lo, where youthful Edward comes!—Bring forth the gallant . . v 5 11
Edward, what satisfaction canst thou make For bearing arms? . . v 5 14
Poor Anne, Wife to thy Edward, to thy slaughter'd son *Richard III.* i 2 10
The timeless deaths Of these Plantagenets, Henry and Edward . . i 2 118
'Twas I that stabb'd young Edward, But 'twas thy heavenly face that set me on . . . . i 2 182
Hath she forgot already that brave prince, Edward, her lord? . . i 2 241
On me, whose all not equals Edward's moiety? . . . . . i 2 250
Thou slewest my husband Henry in the Tower, And Edward, my poor son . . . . i 3 120
That Henry's death, my lovely Edward's death, Their kingdom's loss . i 3 192
Edward thy son, which now is Prince of Wales, For Edward my son, which was Prince of Wales . . . . i 3 199
Edward for Edward pays a dying debt . . . . iv 4 21
I had an Edward, till a Richard kill'd him . . . . . . iv 4 40
Thy Edward he is dead, that stabb'd my Edward; Thy other Edward dead, to quit my Edward . . . . iv 4 63
Thy Clarence he is dead that kill'd my Edward . . . . . iv 4 67
Holy King Henry, and thy fair son Edward . . . . . . v 1 4
Edward the Black Prince. O, spare me not, my brother Edward's son *Richard II.* ii 1 124
And witness good That thou respect'st not spilling Edward's blood . ii 1 131
Edward the Black Prince, Who on the French ground play'd a tragedy *Hen. V.* i 2 105
And all our princes captived by the hand Of that black name, Edward, Black Prince of Wales . . . . ii 4 56
Your great-uncle Edward the Plack Prince of Wales . . . . iv 7 97
Richard, Edward's son, The first-begotten and the lawful heir Of Edward king, the third of that descent . . . *1 Hen. VI.* ii 5 64
Edward the Third, my lords, had seven sons: The first, Edward the Black Prince, Prince of Wales . . . . . *2 Hen. VI.* ii 2 11
Edward the Black Prince died before his father And left behind him Richard . . . . ii 2 18
Edward the Duke of York, the Earl of Suffolk . . . . *Hen. V.* iv 8 108
While proud ambitious Edward Duke of York Usurps the regal title *3 Hen. VI.* iii 3 27
Edward the Fourth. You, Edward, shall unto my Lord Cobham . . i 2 40
Edward and Richard, you shall stay with me . . . . . . i 2 54
And full as oft came Edward to my side, With purple falchion . . i 4 11
The wanton Edward, and the lusty George . . . . . . i 4 74
When thou fail'st—as God forbid the hour!—Must Edward fall . ii 1 191
King Edward, valiant Richard, Montague, Stay we no longer . . ii 1 198
Edward, kneel down.—Edward Plantagenet, arise a knight . . ii 2 60
Stay, Edward.—No, wrangling woman, we'll no longer stay . . ii 2 175
This world frowns, and Edward's sun is clouded . . . . . ii 3 7
Edward and Richard, like a brace of greyhounds . . ., Are at our backs . . . . ii 5 129
Warwick Is thither gone, to crave the French king's sister To wife for Edward . . . . iii 1 31
She, on his left side, craving aid for Henry, He, on his right, asking a wife for Edward . . . . iii 1 44
She weeps, and says her Henry is deposed; He smiles, and says his Edward is install'd . . . . iii 1 46
And what else, To strengthen and support King Edward's place . . iii 1 52
As we think, You are the king King Edward hath deposed . . iii 1 69
We are true subjects to the king, King Edward.—So would you be again to Henry, If he were seated as King Edward is . . . iii 1 94
Say that King Edward take thee for his queen?—'Tis better said than done . . . . iii 2 89
Ay, Edward will use women honourably . . . . . . iii 2 124
Between my soul's desire and me—The lustful Edward's title buried—Is Clarence, Henry, and his son young Edward . . . . . iii 2 129
Our Earl of Warwick, Edward's greatest friend . . . . . iii 3 45
From worthy Edward, King of Albion, My lord and sovereign . . iii 3 49
His demand Springs not from Edward's well-meant honest love . . iii 3 67
For shame! leave Henry, and call Edward king.—Call him my king? . iii 3 100
Tell me, even upon thy conscience, Is Edward your true king? . . iii 3 114
Our sister shall be Edward's; And now forthwith shall articles be drawn . . . . iii 3 134
Bona shall be wife to the English king.—To Edward, but not to the English king . . . . iii 3 140
If your title to the crown be weak, As may appear by Edward's good success . . . . iii 3 146
This proveth Edward's love and Warwick's honesty . . . . iii 3 180
I am clear from this misdeed of Edward's, No more my king . . iii 3 183
Tell false Edward, thy supposed king, That Lewis of France is sending over masquers To revel it with him . . . . iii 3 223; iv 1 93
With five thousand men Shall cross the seas, and bid false Edward battle . . . . iii 3 235
I long till Edward fall by war's mischance, For mocking marriage with a dame of France . . . . iii 3 254
I came from Edward as ambassador, But I return his sworn and mortal foe . . . . iii 3 256
Not that I pity Henry's misery, But seek revenge on Edward's mockery iii 3 265
I am Edward, Your king and Warwick's, and must have my will . iv 1 15
Edward will be king, And not be tied unto his brother's will . . iv 1 65
What danger or what sorrow can befall thee, So long as Edward is thy constant friend? . . . . iv 1 77
I Stay not for the love of Edward, but the crown . . . . iv 1 126
As he proves true!—And Hastings as he favours Edward's cause! . iv 1 144
I think that Clarence, Edward's brother, Were but a feigned friend . iv 2 10
Beat down Edward's guard And seize himself; I say not, slaughter him iv 2 23
Honour now or never! But follow me, and Edward shall be ours . iv 3 25
Art thou here too? Nay, then I see that Edward needs must down . iv 3 42
Edward will always bear himself as king . . . . . . iv 3 45
Then, for his mind, be Edward England's king . . . . . iv 3 48
See that forthwith Duke Edward be convey'd Unto my brother . . iv 3 52
Are you yet to learn What late misfortune is befall'n King Edward? . iv 4 3

Edward the Fourth. And I the rather wean me from despair For love of Edward's offspring . . . . *3 Hen. VI.* iv 4 18
Lest with my sighs or tears I blast or drown King Edward's fruit . iv 4 24
Guess thou the rest; King Edward's friends must down . . . iv 4 28
Forthwith unto the sanctuary, To save at least the heir of Edward's right . . . . iv 4 32
Now that God and friends Have shaken Edward from the regal seat . iv 6 2
What news, my friend?—That Edward is escaped from your brother . iv 6 78
I like not of this flight of Edward's . . . . iv 6 89
If Edward repossess the crown, 'Tis like that Richmond with the rest shall down . . . . iv 6 99
If Henry be your king, Yet Edward at the least is Duke of York . . iv 7 21
Edward will defend the town and thee, And all those friends . . iv 7 38
Why come you in arms?—To help King Edward in his time of storm . iv 7 43
And now will I be Edward's champion . . . . iv 7 68
Sound trumpet; Edward shall be here proclaim'd . . . . . iv 7 69
Edward the Fourth, by the grace of God, king of England and France . iv 7 71
Whosoe'er gainsays King Edward's right, By this I challenge him . . iv 7 74
Long live Edward the Fourth!—Thanks, brave Montgomery . . . iv 7 76
Edward from Belgia, With hasty Germans and blunt Hollanders, Hath pass'd . . . . iv 8 1
The power that Edward hath in field Should not be able to encounter mine . . . . iv 8 35
Then why should they love Edward more than me? . . . . iv 8 47
O unbid spite! is sportful Edward come? Where slept our scouts? . v 1 18
Speak gentle words and humbly bend thy knee, Call Edward king . v 1 23
Henry is my king, Warwick his subject.—But Warwick's king is Edward's prisoner . . . . v 1 39
Pardon me, Edward, I will make amends: And, Richard, do not frown v 1 100
I will away towards Barnet presently, And bid thee battle, Edward, if thou darest.—Yes, Warwick, Edward dares . . . . . v 1 111
What is Edward but a ruthless sea? What Clarence but a quicksand of deceit? . . . . v 4 25
Prepare you, lords, for Edward is at hand, Ready to fight . . v 4 60
You are all undutiful: Lascivious Edward, and thou perjured George, And thou mis-shapen Dick . . . . v 5 34
The sun that sear'd the wings of my sweet boy Thy brother Edward v 6 24
I will buz abroad such prophecies That Edward shall be fearful of his life v 6 87
If King Edward be as true and just As I am subtle . *Richard III.* i 1 36
A prophecy, which says that G Of Edward's heirs the murderer shall be i 1 40
Whatsoever you will employ me in, Were it to call King Edward's widow sister . . . . i 1 109
God take King Edward to his mercy, And leave the world for me to bustle in! . . . . i 1 151
Clarence still breathes; Edward still lives and reigns . . . i 1 161
Then he is alive.—Nay, he is dead; and slain by Edward's hand . i 2 92
York and Edward wept, To hear the piteous moan that Rutland made . i 2 157
To fight on Edward's party for the crown . . . . . . i 3 138
I would to God my heart were flint, like Edward's; Or Edward's soft and pitiful, like mine . . . . i 3 140
I have done those things, Which now bear evidence against my soul, For Edward's sake; and see how he requites me! . . . . i 4 68
For whose sake did I that ill deed? For Edward, for my brother . i 4 217
Gloucester, Who shall reward you better for my life Than Edward will for tidings of my death . . . . i 4 237
Let us in, To comfort Edward with our company . . . . ii 1 139
Edward, my lord, your son, our king, is dead . . . . . ii 2 40
And pluck'd two crutches from my feeble limbs, Edward and Clarence ii 2 59
Oh for my husband, for my dear lord Edward! . . . . . ii 2 71
Edward and Clarence!—What stay had I but Edward? and he's gone . ii 2 73
She for an Edward weeps, and so do I; I for a Clarence weep, so doth not she . . . . ii 2 82
These babes for Clarence weep, and so do I; I for an Edward weep, so do not they . . . . ii 2 85
Drown desperate sorrow in dead Edward's grave, And plant your joys in living Edward's throne . . . . ii 2 99
Doth this news hold of good King Edward's death? . . . . ii 3 7
And this is Edward's wife, that monstrous witch . . . . iii 4 72
Infer the bastardy of Edward's children: Tell them how Edward put to death a citizen . . . . iii 5 75
When that my mother went with child Of that unsatiate Edward . . iii 5 87
Touch'd you the bastardy of Edward's children? . . . . . iii 7 4
Ah, ha, my lord, this prince is not an Edward! . . . . . iii 7 71
The sons of Edward sleep in Abraham's bosom . . . . . iv 3 38
Thy Edward he is dead, that stabb'd my Edward . . . . iv 4 63
There the little souls of Edward's children Whisper the spirits of thine enemies . . . . iv 4 191
I'll corrupt her manners, stain her beauty; Slander myself as false to Edward's bed . . . . iv 4 207
I will confess she was not Edward's daughter . . . . . iv 4 210
A pair of bleeding hearts; thereon engrave Edward and York . . iv 4 273
Hastings, and Edward's children, Rivers, Grey, Holy King Henry . v 1 3
This is the day that, in King Edward's time, I wish'd might fall on me . v 1 13
Edward's unhappy sons do bid thee flourish . . . . . v 3 158

Edward the Third. Edward's seven sons, whereof thyself art one, Were as seven vials of his sacred blood . . . . *Richard II.* i 2 11
One vial full of Edward's sacred blood . . . Is crack'd . . . i 2 17
Wert thou not brother to great Edward's son . . . . . ii 1 121
O, spare me not, my brother Edward's son, For that I was his father Edward's son . . . . ii 1 124
I am the last of noble Edward's sons . . . . ii 1 171
It did so a little time before That our great-grandsire, Edward, sick'd and died . . . . *2 Hen. IV.* iv 4 128
The crown and seat of France Derived from Edward . . *Hen. V.* i 1 89
To fill King Edward's fame with prisoner kings . . . . . i 2 162
In the right Of your great predecessor, King Edward the Third . i 2 248
Derived From his most famed of famous ancestors, Edward the Third . ii 4 93
A countryman of ours records, England all Olivers and Rowlands bred During the time Edward the Third did reign . . *1 Hen. VI.* i 2 31
Duke of Clarence, Third son to the third Edward King of England . ii 4 84
The lawful heir Of Edward king, the third of that descent . . ii 5 66
Lionel Duke of Clarence, the third son To King Edward the Third . ii 5 76
Edward the Third, my lords, had seven sons . . . *2 Hen. VI.* ii 2 10
Richard, his only son, Who after Edward the Third's death reigned as king . . . . ii 2 20
Edmund Langley, Edward the Third's fifth son . . . . . ii 2 46

Eel. I will praise an eel with the same praise.—What, that an eel is ingenious?—That an eel is quick . . . . *L. L. Lost* i 2 28
Is the adder better than the eel, Because his painted skin contents the eye? . . . . *T. of Shrew* iv 3 179

Eel. Cry to it, nuncle, as the cockney did to the eels when she put 'em i the paste alive . . . . *Lear* ii 4 124
Thunder shall not so awake the beds of eels . . . . *Pericles* iv 2 155

Eel-skin. My arms such eel-skins stuff'd, my face so thin . *K. John* i 1 141
You might have thrust him and all his apparel into an eel-skin *2 Hen. IV.* iii 2 351

Effect. Do not, for one repulse, forego the purpose That you resolved to effect . . . . *Tempest* iii 3 13
And all the fair effects of future hopes . . . . *T. G. of Ver.* i 1 50
Base men, that use them to so base effect! . . . . . . ii 7 73
Thou know'st how willingly I would effect The match . . . iii 2 22
As much as I can do, I will effect . . . . iii 2 66
And what they think in their hearts they may effect, they will break their hearts but they will effect . . . . . . *Mer. Wives* ii 2 322
Or that the resolute acting of your blood Could have attain'd the effect of your own purpose . . . . *Meas. for Meas.* ii 1 13
Thy complexion shifts to strange effects, After the moon . . . iii 1 24
To make you understand this in a manifested effect . . . . iv 2 169
I'll depose I had him in mine arms With all the effect of love . . v 1 199
Light is an effect of fire, and fire will burn . . . *Com. of Errors* iv 3 57
Neither disturbed with the effect of wine, Nor heady-rash . . . v 1 215
What effects of passion shows she? . . . . *Much Ado* ii 3 112
What effects, my lord? She will sit you, you heard my daughter tell you how . . . . ii 3 115
And in dearness of heart hath holp to effect your ensuing marriage . v 2 102
The effect of my intent is to cross theirs . . . . . *L. L. Lost* v 2 138
Effect it with some care that he may prove More fond on her *M. N. Dr.* ii 1 265
Make no delay: We may effect this business yet ere day . . . iii 2 395
Ethiope words, blacker in their effect Than in their countenance *As Y. Like It* iv 3 35
Alack, in me what strange effect Would they work in mild aspect! . iv 3 52
Sorry am I that our good will effects Bianca's grief . . *T. of Shrew* i 1 86
To labour and effect one thing specially.—What's that, I pray? . . i 1 120
While idly I stood looking on, I found the effect of love in idleness . i 1 156
Thou know'st not gold's effect . . . . i 2 93
That we, the poorer born, Whose baser stars do shut us up in wishes, Might with effects of them follow our friends . . . *All's Well* i 1 198
My father left me some prescriptions Of rare and proved effects . . i 3 228
A showing of a heavenly effect in an earthly actor . . . . ii 3 27
On our quick'st decrees The inaudible and noiseless foot of Time Steals ere we can effect them . . . . v 3 42
The effects of his fond jealousies so grieving That he shuts up himself *W. Tale* iv 1 18
If it be in man besides the king to effect your suits, here is man shall do it . . . . iv 4 828
Is it not fair writ?—Too fairly, Hubert, for so foul effect . *K. John* iv 1 38
To this effect, before you were new crown'd, We breathed our counsel . iv 2 35
But also to effect Whatever I shall happen to devise *Richard II.* iv 1 329
I have read the cause of his effects in Galen . . . *2 Hen. IV.* i 2 133
There is not a white hair on your face but should have his effect of gravity.—His effect of gravy, gravy, gravy . . . . . . i 2 183
Answer in the effect of your reputation, and satisfy the poor woman . ii 1 142
And noble offices thou mayst effect Of mediation, after I am dead . . iv 4 24
I did admit it as a motive The sooner to effect what I intended *Hen. V.* ii 2 157
Whose tenours and particular effects You have enscheduled briefly . v 2 72
Notwithstanding the poor and untempering effect of my visage . . v 2 241
The sooner to effect And surer bind this knot of amity . *1 Hen. VI.* v 1 15
Is all our travail turn'd to this effect? . . . . v 4 102
And then to Brittany I'll cross the sea, To effect this marriage *3 Hen. VI.* ii 6 98
Thou art the cause, and most accursed effect.—Your beauty was the cause of that effect . . . . *Richard III.* i 2 120
Whom I will importune With daily prayers all to that effect . . i 2 15
Thou art sworn as deeply to effect what we intend As closely to conceal what we impart . . . . iii 1 158
Good Catesby, go, effect this business soundly . . . . . iii 1 186
To consider further that What his high hatred would effect wants not A minister in his power . . . . *Hen. VIII.* i 1 107
Have stood to charity, and display'd the effects Of disposition gentle . ii 4 86
She was divorced, And the late marriage made of none effect . . iv 1 33
To this effect, Achilles, have I moved you . . *Troi. and Cres.* iii 3 216
They are at hand and ready to effect it . . . . iv 2 70
Mere words, no matter from the heart; The effect doth operate another way . . . . v 3 109
Frown on, you heavens, effect your rage with speed! . . . . v 10 6
All the bitterest terms That ever ear did hear to such effect *T. Andron.* iii 1 111
I have written to effect; There's not a god left unsolicited . . iv 3 59
Bear the faults of Titus' age, The effects of sorrow for his valiant sons . iv 4 30
That so my sad decrees may fly away, And all my study be to no effect v 2 12
Saints do not move, though grant for prayers' sake.—Then move not, while my prayer's effect I take . . . . *Rom. and Jul.* i 5 108
Which so took effect As I intended, for it wrought on her The form of death . . . . v 3 244
Do you dare our anger? 'Tis in few words, but spacious in effect *T. of Athens* iii 5 97
Did Cicero say any thing?—Ay, he spoke Greek.—To what effect? *J. C.* i 2 283
And withal Hoping it was but an effect of humour . . . . . ii 1 250
That no compunctious visitings of nature Shake my fell purpose, nor keep peace between The effect and it . . . . . *Macbeth* i 5 48
To receive at once the benefit of sleep, and do the effects of watching! v 1 12
I shall the effect of this good lesson keep, As watchman to my heart *Ham.* i 3 45
Whose effect Holds such an enmity with blood of man . . . . i 5 64
And now remains That we find out the cause of this effect, Or rather say, the cause of this defect, For this effect defective comes by cause ii 2 101
I am still possess'd Of those effects for which I did the murder . iii 3 54
Do not look upon me; Lest with this piteous action you convert My stern effects . . . . iii 4 129
Which imports at full, By letters congruing to that effect, The present death of Hamlet . . . . iv 3 66
Wilt thou know The effect of what I wrote? . . . . . . v 2 37
Shall I re-deliver you e'en so?—To this effect, sir; after what flourish your nature will . . . . v 2 187
Pre-eminence, and all the large effects That troop with majesty *Lear* i 1 133
May your deeds approve, That good effects may spring from words of love . . . . i 1 188
Though the wisdom of nature can reason it thus and thus, yet nature finds itself scourged by the sequent effects . . . . . i 2 115
I promise you, the effects he writes of succeed unhappily . . . i 2 156
Thou better know'st The offices of nature, bond of childhood, Effects of courtesy . . . . ii 4 182
Have you no more to say?—Few words, but, to effect, more than all yet iii 1 52
Our wishes on the way May prove effects . . . . iv 2 15

Effect. Is much beloved, And hath in his effect a voice potential . *Othello* i 2 13
With some dram conjured to this effect, He wrought upon her . . i 3 105
Opinion, a sovereign mistress of effects . . . . . . i 3 225
If I do find him fit, I'll move your suit And seek to effect it to my uttermost . . . . iii 4 167
Thy thoughts Touch their effects in this . . . *Ant. and Cleo.* v 2 333
And by them gather Their several virtues and effects . . *Cymbeline* i 5 23
The seeing these effects will be Both noisome and infectious . . i 5 25
She is fool'd With a most false effect . . . . . . i 5 43
For the effect of judgement Is oft the cause of fear . . . iv 2 111
Let thy effects So follow, to be most unlike our courtiers, As good as promise . . . . v 4 135
Effected. I am the cause His death was so effected . *All's Well* iii 2 119
And between these main parcels of dispatch effected many nicer needs . iv 3 104
I wish it happily effected . . . . iv 5 84
We'll see these things effected to the full . . . *2 Hen. VI.* i 2 84
The ancient proverb will be well effected . . . . . iii 1 170
He that has but effected his good will Hath overta'en mine act *Coriolanus* i 9 18
Cunningly effected, will beget A very excellent piece of villany *T. And.* ii 3 6
I'll humbly signify what in his name, That magical word of war, we have effected . . . . *Ant. and Cleo.* iii 1 31
Repented The evils she hatch'd were not effected . . *Cymbeline* v 5 60
Effectless. They have served me to effectless use . . *T. Andron.* iii 1 76
Sure, all's effectless; yet nothing we'll omit That bears recovery's name *Pericles* v 1 53
Effectual. Unreversed, stands in effectual force . . *T. G. of Ver.* iii 1 223
More pleasant, pithy and effectual . . . . *T. of Shrew* iii 1 68
Or else conclude my words effectual . . . . *2 Hen. VI.* iii 1 41
A reason mighty, strong, and effectual . . . . *T. Andron.* v 3 43
Effectually. Your bidding shall I do effectually . . . . iv 4 107
Effeminate. Be effeminate, changeable, longing and liking *As Y. Like It* iii 2 430
Young wanton and effeminate boy . . . . . *Richard II.* v 3 10
None do you like but an effeminate prince . . . *1 Hen. VI.* i 1 35
Shall we at last conclude effeminate peace? . . . . . v 4 107
We know your tenderness of heart And gentle, kind, effeminate remorse *Richard III.* iii 7 211
A woman impudent and mannish grown Is not more loathed than an effeminate man . . . . *Troi. and Cres.* iii 3 218
Thy beauty hath made me effeminate . . . . *Rom. and Jul.* iii 1 119
Effigies. Mine eye doth his effigies witness Most truly limn'd and living in your face . . . . *As Y. L. It* ii 7 193
Effuse. And much effuse of blood doth make me faint . . *3 Hen. VI.* ii 6 28
Effused. Whose maiden blood, thus rigorously effused, Will cry for vengeance at the gates of heaven . . . . . . *1 Hen. VI.* v 4 52
Effusion. The mere effusion of thy proper loins, Do curse the gout, serpigo, and the rheum . . . . . . *Meas. for Meas.* iii 1 30
This effusion of such manly drops, This shower . . . *K. John* v 2 49
For the effusion of our blood, the muster of his kingdom too faint a number . . . . *Hen. V.* iii 6 138
The only means To stop effusion of our Christian blood . . *1 Hen. VI.* v 1 9
Eftest. Yea, marry, that's the eftest way . . . . *Much Ado* iv 2 38
Eftsoons I'll tell thee why . . . . *Pericles* v 1 256
Egal. And, for the extent Of egal justice, used in such contempt *T. An.* iv 4 4
Egally. Which we have noted in you to your kin, And egally indeed to all estates . . . . *Richard III.* iii 7 213
Eget. Integer vitæ, scelerisque purus, Non eget Mauri jaculis, nec arcu *T. Andron.* iv 2 21
Egeus. Thanks, good Egeus: what's the news with thee? *M. N. Dream* i 1 21
Come, Egeus; you shall go with me, I have some private schooling for you . . . . i 1 115
Demetrius and Egeus, go along: I must employ you in some business ? i 1 123
But speak, Egeus; is not this the day That Hermia should give answer? iv 1 140
Egeus, I will overbear your will . . . . iv 1 184
Egg. Go brew me a pottle of sack finely.—With eggs, sir *Mer. Wives* iii 5 31
I can suck melancholy out of a song, as a weasel sucks eggs *As Y. L. It* ii 5 14
Truly, thou art damned, like an ill-roasted egg all on one side . iii 2 39
He will steal, sir, an egg out of a cloister . . . *All's Well* iv 3 280
They say we are Almost as like as eggs; women say so . *W. Tale* i 2 130
Mine honest friend, Will you take eggs for money? . . . . i 2 161
Not so much as will serve to be prologue to an egg and butter *1 Hen. IV.* i 2 23
They are up already, and call for eggs and butter . . . . ii 1 65
The weasel Scot Comes sneaking and so sucks her princely eggs *Hen. V.* i 2 171
He esteems her no more than I esteem an addle egg *Troi. and Cres.* i 2 145
If you love an addle egg as well as you love an idle head, you would eat chickens i' the shell . . . . i 2 146
By some chance, Some trick not worth an egg . . . *Coriolanus* iv 4 21
Thy head is as full of quarrels as an egg is full of meat *Rom. and Jul.* iii 1 24
Thy head hath been beaten as addle as an egg for quarrelling . . iii 1 26
Therefore think him as a serpent's egg Which, hatch'd, would, as his kind, grow mischievous . . . . *J. Cæsar* ii 1 32
What, you egg! Young fry of treachery! . . . . *Macbeth* iv 2 83
Give me an egg, nuncle, and I'll give thee two crowns.—What two crowns shall they be?—Why, after I have cut the egg i' the middle, and eat up the meat, the two crowns of the egg . . . . . . *Lear* i 4 170
I'll fetch some flax and whites of eggs To apply to his bleeding face . iii 7 106
So many fathom down precipitating, Thou'dst shiver'd like an egg . iv 6 51
Egg-shell. Exposing what is mortal and unsure To all that fortune, death and danger dare, Even for an egg-shell . . . *Hamlet* iv 4 53
On our terrible seas, Like egg-shells moved upon their surges *Cymbeline* iii 1 28
Eglamour. What think'st thou of the fair Sir Eglamour?—As of a knight well-spoken, neat and fine . . . . . . *T. G. of Ver.* i 2 9
O Eglamour, thou art a gentleman—Think not I flatter . . . iv 3 11
Sir Eglamour, I would to Valentine, To Mantua . . . . iv 3 22
Urge not my father's anger, Eglamour, But think upon my grief . . iv 3 27
Go on, good Eglamour, Out at the postern by the abbey-wall . . v 1 8
Which of you saw Sir Eglamour of late?—Not I.—Nor I . . . v 2 32
She's fled unto that peasant Valentine; And Eglamour is in her company . . . . v 2 36
More to be revenged on Eglamour Than for the love of reckless Silvia . v 2 51
And I will follow, more for Silvia's love Than hate of Eglamour . . v 2 54
Eglantine. Over-canopied with luscious woodbine, With sweet musk-roses, and with eglantine . . . . *M. N. Dream* ii 1 252
The leaf of eglantine, whom not to slander, Out sweeten'd not thy breath *Cymbeline* iv 2 223
Egma. No egma, no riddle, no l'envy; no salve in the mail, sir *L. L. Lost* iii 1 73
Ego et Rex meus . . . . *Hen. VIII.* iii 2 314
Egregious. You give me most egregious indignity . . . *All's Well* ii 3 228
I would have you solus.—'Solus,' egregious dog? O viper vile! *Hen. V.* ii 1 49
Except, O signieur, thou do give to me Egregious ransom . . . iv 4 11
Most credulous fool, Egregious murderer, thief, any thing! . *Cymbeline* v 5 211
Egregiously. Making him egregiously an ass . . . . *Othello* ii 1 318
Egress. Thou shalt have egress and regress . . . . *Mer. Wives* ii 1 225
Egypt. The lover, all as frantic, Sees Helen's beauty in a brow of Egypt *M. N. Dream* v 1 11
If I cannot, I'll rail against all the first-born of Egypt . *As Y. Like It* ii 5 63
There was a lady once, 'tis an old story, That would not be a queen, that would she not, For all the mud in Egypt . . . *Hen. VIII.* ii 3 92
As I am Egypt's queen, Thou blushest, Antony . . *Ant. and Cleo.* i 1 29
I would I had thy inches; thou shouldst know There were a heart in Egypt . . . . i 3 41
Weep for her; Then bid adieu to me, and say the tears Belong to Egypt i 3 78
That, being unseminar'd, thy freer thoughts May not fly forth of Egypt i 5 12
Sovereign of Egypt, hail!—How much unlike art thou Mark Antony! . i 5 34
Say, the firm Roman to great Egypt sends This treasure of an oyster . i 5 43
He was not merry, Which seem'd to tell them his remembrance lay In Egypt . . . . i 5 58
He shall have every day a several greeting, Or I'll unpeople Egypt . i 5 78
Mark Antony In Egypt sits at dinner, and will make No wars without doors . . . . ii 1 12
Since he went from Egypt 'tis A space for further travel . . . ii 1 30
Can from the lap of Egypt's widow pluck The ne'er-lust-wearied Antony ii 1 37
My being in Egypt, Cæsar, What was't to you?—No more than my residing here at Rome Might be to you in Egypt: yet, if you there Did practise on my state, your being in Egypt Might be my question . . . . ii 2 35
Truth is, that Fulvia, To have me out of Egypt, made wars here . . ii 2 95
Welcome from Egypt, sir.—Half the heart of Cæsar, worthy Mecænas! ii 2 174
You stayed well by't in Egypt.—Ay, sir . . . . . . ii 2 180
You do wish yourself in Egypt?—Would I had never come from thence! ii 3 10
But yet Hie you to Egypt again . . . . ii 3 15
I will to Egypt: And though I make this marriage for my peace, I' the east my pleasure lies . . . . ii 3 38
Melt Egypt into Nile! and kindly creatures Turn all to serpents! . ii 5 78
So half my Egypt were submerged and made A cistern for scaled snakes! ii 5 94
I have a health for you.—I shall take it, sir: we have used our throats in Egypt . . . . ii 6 144
Your serpent of Egypt is bred now of your mud by the operation of your sun . . . . ii 7 29
Three in Egypt Cannot make better note . . . . . . iii 3 25
Unto her He gave the stablishment of Egypt . . . . . iii 6 9
You ribaudred nag of Egypt,—Whom leprosy o'ertake! . . . iii 10 10
O, whither hast thou led me, Egypt? . . . . iii 11 51
Egypt, thou knew'st too well My heart was to thy rudder tied by the strings . . . . iii 11 56
Lord of his fortunes he salutes thee, and Requires to live in Egypt . iii 12 12
The queen Of audience nor desire shall fail, so she From Egypt drive her all-disgraced friend . . . . iii 12 22
Tell him, from his all-obeying breath I hear The doom of Egypt . . iii 13 78
He calls me boy; and chides, as he had power To beat me out of Egypt iv 1 2
Betray'd I am: O this false soul of Egypt! . . . . . iv 12 25
I made these wars for Egypt: and the queen,—Whose heart I thought I had, for she had mine . . . . iv 14 15
I am dying, Egypt, dying; only I here importune death awhile . . iv 15 18
I am dying, Egypt, dying: Give me some wine, and let me speak a little iv 15 41
O madam, madam, madam!—Royal Egypt, Empress!—Peace, peace! . iv 15 70
Cæsar sends greeting to the Queen of Egypt . . . . . . v 2 9
If he please To give me conquer'd Egypt for my son, He gives me so much of mine own . . . . v 2 19
Rather a ditch in Egypt Be gentle grave unto me! . . . . v 2 57
Which is the Queen of Egypt?—It is the emperor, madam . . . v 2 112
Arise, you shall not kneel: I pray you, rise; rise, Egypt . . . v 2 115
Now no more The juice of Egypt's grape shall moist this lip . . v 2 285
Egyptian. More puzzled than the Egyptians in their fog . *T. Night* iv 2 48
Like to the Egyptian thief at point of death, Kill what I love . . v 1 121
That handkerchief Did an Egyptian to my mother give; She was a charmer . . . . *Othello* iii 4 56
These strong Egyptian fetters I must break, Or lose myself in dotage *Ant. and Cleo.* i 2 120
And made a gap in nature.—Rare Egyptian! . . . . . ii 2 223
Your fine Egyptian cookery Shall have the fame . . . . ii 6 64
He will to his Egyptian dish again . . . . ii 6 134
Shall we dance now the Egyptian Bacchanals, And celebrate our drink? ii 7 110
Let the Egyptians And the Phœnicians go a-ducking . . . . iii 7 64
The Antoniad, the Egyptian admiral, With all their sixty, fly . . iii 10 2
My brave Egyptians all, By the discandying of this pelleted storm, Lie graveless . . . . iii 13 164
All is lost; This foul Egyptian hath betrayed me: My fleet hath yielded . . . . iv 12 10
Whence are you?—A poor Egyptian yet . . . . v 1 52
Thou, an Egyptian puppet, shalt be shown In Rome, as well as I . . v 2 208
I heard of an Egyptian That had nine hours lien dead, Who was by good appliance recovered . . . . *Pericles* iii 2 84
Eight. Let him be sent for to-morrow, eight o'clock . *Mer. Wives* iii 3 210
She desires you once more to come to her between eight and nine . . iii 5 47
'Twixt eight and nine is the hour, Master Brook.—'Tis past eight already iii 5 132
By eight to-morrow Thou must be made immortal . *Meas. for Meas.* iv 2 67
I have studied eight or nine wise words to speak to you . . *Much Ado* iii 2 74
We will have such a prologue; and it shall be written in eight and six.—No, make it two more; let it be written in eight and eight *M. N. D.* iii 1 25
I'll rhyme you so eight years together . . . . *As Y. Like It* iii 2 101
Here's eight that must take hands To join in Hymen's bands . . v 4 134
His eyes were set at eight i' the morning.—Then he's a rogue *T. Night* v 1 205
With eight tall ships, three thousand men of war . . *Richard II.* ii 1 286
Eight yards of uneven ground is threescore and ten miles afoot *1 Hen. IV.* ii 2 26
How many be there of them?—Some eight or ten . . . . . ii 2 67
One that never spake other English in his life than 'Eight shillings and sixpence' . . . . ii 4 27
I am eight times thrust through the doublet, four through the hose . ii 4 184
As I am a true woman, holland of eight shillings an ell . . . iii 3 83
It is but eight years since This Percy was the man nearest my soul *2 Hen. IV.* iii 1 60
I have served your worship truly, sir, this eight years . . . . v 1 52
Beyond the river Sala, in the year Eight hundred five . . . *Hen. V.* i 2 64
You'll pay me the eight shillings I won of you at betting? . . . ii 1 98
The hour of eight, which he himself Foretold should be his last *Hen. VIII.* iv 2 26
Good king of cats, nothing but one of your nine lives; that I mean to make bold withal, and, as you shall use me hereafter, dry-beat the rest of the eight . . . . *Rom. and Jul.* iii 1 83
What is't o'clock?—Cæsar, 'tis strucken eight . . . *J. Cæsar* ii 2 114
He will last you some eight year or nine year . . . . *Hamlet* v 1 183

Eight. The reason why the seven stars are no more than seven is a pretty reason.—Because they are not eight? . . . *Lear* i 5 40
What, keep a week away? seven days and nights? Eight score eight hours? and lovers absent hours, More tedious than the dial eight score times? O weary reckoning! . . . *Othello* iii 4 174
Eight wild-boars roasted whole at a breakfast . . . *Ant. and Cleo.* ii 2 183
Eighteen. At eighteen years became inquisitive After his brother *C. of Er.* i 1 126
All the treasons for these eighteen years Complotted and contrived *Richard II.* i 1 95
O villain, thou stolest a cup of sack eighteen years ago . . 1 *Hen. IV.* ii 4 346
For eighteen months concluded by consent . . . 2 *Hen. VI.* i 1 42
We here discharge your grace from being regent I' the parts of France, till term of eighteen months . . . i 1 67
Cannot take two from twenty, for his heart, And leave eighteen *Cymb.* ii 1 61
Eighth. By the eighth hour: is that the uttermost? . . . *J. Cæsar* ii 1 213
A seventh! I'll see no more: And yet the eighth appears . *Macbeth* iv 1 119
Eight-penny. A trifle, some eight-penny matter . . 1 *Hen. IV.* iii 3 119
Eighty odd years of sorrow have I seen . . . *Richard III.* iv 1 96
Eight-year-old. He no more remembers his mother now than an eight-year-old horse . . . *Coriolanus* v 4 17
Eisel. Woo't tear thyself? Woo't drink up eisel? eat a crocodile? *Hamlet* v 1 299
Eject. To eject him hence Were but one danger, and to keep him here Our certain death . . . *Coriolanus* iii 1 287
Eke. And I to Ford shall eke unfold . . . *Mer. Wives* i 3 105
Master guest, and Master Page, and eke Cavaleiro Slender . . ii 3 77
Most brisky juvenal and eke most lovely Jew . . *M. N. Dream* iii 1 97
'Tis to peize the time, To eke it and to draw it out in length *Mer. of Ven.* iii 2 23
The little strength that I have, I would it were with you.—And mine, to eke out hers . . . *As Y. Like It* i 2 208
With true observance seek to eke out that . . . *All's Well* ii 5 79
Still be kind, And eke out our performance with your mind *Hen. V.* iii Prol. 35
Elbe. That the land Salique is in Germany, Between the floods of Sala and of Elbe . . . i 2 45
Which Salique, as I said, 'twixt Elbe and Sala, Is at this day in Germany call'd Meisen . . . i 2 52
Elbow. My name is Elbow: I do lean upon justice . *Meas. for Meas.* ii 1 48
Elbow is your name? why dost thou not speak, Elbow?—He cannot, sir; he's out at elbow . . . ii 1 59
As I say, this Mistress Elbow, being, as I say, with child . . ii 1 101
What was done to Elbow's wife, that he hath cause to complain of? ii 1 120
My elbow itched; I thought there would a scab follow . *Much Ado* iii 3 106
One rubb'd his elbow thus, and fleer'd and swore . . *L. L. Lost* v 2 109
The fiend is at mine elbow and tempts me . . *Mer. of Venice* ii 2 3
Thus, leaning on mine elbow, I begin . . . *K. John* i 1 194
Which gape and rub the elbow at the news Of hurlyburly innovation 1 *Hen. IV.* v 1 77
Go, pluck him by the elbow; I must speak with him 2 *Hen. IV.* i 2 81
I care not for his thrust.—No, nor I neither: I'll be at your elbow . ii 1 22
Dites-moi l'Anglois pour le bras.—De arm, madame.—Et le coude?—De elbow . . . *Hen. V.* iii 4 24
De bilbow.—De elbow, madame.—O Seigneur Dieu, je m'en oublie! de elbow . . . iii 4 32
It [conscience] is even now at my elbow, persuading me not to kill the duke . . . *Richard III.* i 4 150
Thou hast no more brain than I have in mine elbows . *Troi. and Cres.* ii 1 49
Let us bathe our hands in Cæsar's blood Up to the elbows . *J. Cæsar* iii 1 107
A sovereign shame so elbows him . . . *Lear* iv 3 44
Fear nothing; I'll be at thy elbow: It makes us, or it mars us *Othello* v 1 3
Elbow-room. Now my soul hath elbow-room . . . *K. John* v 7 28
Eld. The superstitious idle-headed eld . . . *Mer. Wives* iv 4 36
All thy blessed youth Becomes as aged, and doth beg the alms Of palsied eld . . . *Meas. for Meas.* iii 1 36
Virgins and boys, mid-age and wrinkled eld, Soft infancy *Troi. and Cres.* ii 2 104
Elder. What says my Æsculapius? my Galen? my heart of elder? *M. W.* ii 3 30
You are my elder.—That's a question: how shall we try it? *Com. of Er.* v 1 420
You are my elder.—Well followed: Judas was hanged on an elder *L. L. L.* v 2 609
How much more elder art thou than thy looks! . *Mer. of Venice* iv 1 251
Come, elder brother, you are too young in this . *As Y. Like It* i 1 56
Orlando did approach the man And found it was his brother, his elder brother . . . iv 3 121
That is, not to bestow my youngest daughter Before I have a husband for the elder . . . *T. of Shrew* i 1 51
Thus it stands: Her elder sister is so curst and shrewd . . i 1 185
Will not promise her to any man Until the elder sister first be wed . i 2 263
Achieve the elder, set the younger free For our access . . . i 2 268
Well I know my duty to my elders . . . ii 1 7
Let still the woman take An elder than herself . . *T. Night* ii 4 31
My last good deed was to entreat his stay: What was my first? it has an elder sister, Or I mistake you . . . *W. Tale* i 2 98
Is that the elder, and art thou the heir? . . . *K. John* i 1 57
Geffrey was thy elder brother born, And this his son . . . ii 1 104
Son to the elder brother of this man, And king o'er him . . . ii 1 239
Which elder days shall ripen and confirm . . *Richard II.* ii 3 43
I see some sparks of better hope, which elder years May happily bring forth . . . v 3 21
Look, whether the withered elder hath not his poll clawed like a parrot 2 *Hen. IV.* ii 4 281
The elder I wax, the better I shall appear . . . *Hen. V.* v 2 246
If the issue of the elder son Succeed before the younger, I am king 2 *Hen. VI.* ii 2 51
The elder of them, being put to nurse, Was by a beggar-woman stolen . iv 2 150
My elder brother, the Lord Aubrey Vere, Was done to death 3 *Hen. VI.* iii 3 102
Prince Edward marries Warwick's daughter.—Belike the elder . . iv 1 118
Ere a fortnight make me elder, I'll send some packing . *Richard III.* iii 2 62
He is elder.—Pardon me, pardon me.—Th' other's not come to't *T. and C.* i 2 88
See, our best elders . . . *Coriolanus* i 1 230
Therefore, please you, Most reverend and grave elders . . . ii 2 46
Make some meaner choice: Lavinia is thine elder brother's hope *T. An.* ii 1 74
His son is elder, sir; His son is thirty . . . *Rom. and Jul.* i 5 40
I do not always follow lover, elder brother and woman . *T. of Athens* ii 2 130
Our elders say, The barren, touched in this holy chase, Shake off their sterile curse . . . *J. Cæsar* i 2 7
We are two lions litter'd in one day, And I the elder and more terrible . ii 2 47
I said, an elder soldier, not a better: Did I say 'better'? . . . iv 3 56
Some elder masters, of known honour . . . *Hamlet* v 2 259
I have, sir, a son by order of law, some year elder than this . . *Lear* i 1 20
When vantage like a pair of twins appear'd, Both as the same, or rather ours the elder . . . *Ant. and Cleo.* iii 10 13
An earthly paragon! Behold divineness No elder than a boy! *Cymb.* iii 6 45
Let the stinking elder, grief, untwine His perishing root . . . iv 2 60
Elder. You some permit To second ills with ills, each elder worse . *Cymb.* v 1 14
What was first but fear what might be done, Grows elder now and cares it be not done . . . *Pericles* i 2 15
Elder-gun. That's a perilous shot out of an elder-gun . . *Hen. V.* iv 1 210
Elder-tree. Among the nettles at the elder-tree . . *T. Andron.* ii 3 272
This is the pit, and this the elder-tree . . . ii 3 277
Eldest. Your eld'st acquaintance cannot be three hours . . *Tempest* v 1 186
My youngest boy, and yet my eldest care . . *Com. of Errors* i 1 125
The other too like my lady's eldest son, evermore tattling . *Much Ado* ii 1 10
I know you are my eldest brother . . . *As Y. Like It* i 1 47
The eldest of the three wrestled with Charles, the duke's wrestler . i 2 133
This fellow I remember, Since once he play'd a farmer's eldest son *T. of Shrew* Ind. 1 84
By helping Baptista's eldest daughter to a husband we set his youngest free . . . i 1 142
Nor is your firm resolve unknown to me, In the preferment of the eldest sister . . . ii 1 94
That is Antonio, the duke's eldest son . . . *All's Well* iii 5 79
Thou hast spoke for us, madonna, as if thy eldest son should be a fool; whose skull Jove cram with brains! . . . *T. Night* i 5 121
I have three daughters; the eldest is eleven . . *W. Tale* ii 1 144
And eldest son, As I suppose, to Robert Faulconbridge . . *K. John* i 1 51
Philip, good old sir Robert's wife's eldest son . . . i 1 159
This is thy eld'st son's son, Infortunate in nothing but in thee . i 1 177
Mordake the Earl of Fife, and eldest son To beaten Douglas 1 *Hen. IV.* i 1 71
She says up and down the town that her eldest son is like you 2 *Hen. IV.* ii 1 114
Duke of Lancaster, The eldest son and heir of John of Gaunt 2 *Hen. VI.* ii 2 22
His eldest sister, Anne, My mother, being heir unto the crown . ii 2 43
Command my eldest son, nay, all my sons, As pledges of my fealty . v 1 49
I'll join mine eldest daughter and my joy To him forthwith 3 *Hen. VI.* iii 3 242
That blind priest, like the eldest son of fortune, Turns what he list *Hen. VIII.* ii 2 21
The eldest son of this distressed queen . . . *T. Andron.* i 1 103
This suit I make, That you create your emperor's eldest son . . i 1 224
We will establish our estate upon Our eldest, Malcolm . . *Macbeth* i 4 38
It hath the primal eldest curse upon't, A brother's murder *Hamlet* iii 3 37
Your eldest daughters have foredone themselves . . *Lear* v 3 291
The eldest of them at three years old, I' the swathing-clothes the other *Cymbeline* i 1 58
Eldest-born. Goneril, Our eldest-born, speak first . . *Lear* i 1 55
Eleanor. Nay, Eleanor, then must I chide outright; Presumptuous dame, ill-nurtured Eleanor . . . 2 *Hen. VI.* i 2 41
What, my lord! are you so choleric With Eleanor, for telling but her dream? . . . i 2 52
Dame Eleanor gives gold to bring the witch . . . i 2 91
They, knowing Dame Eleanor's aspiring humour, Have hired me to undermine the duchess . . . i 2 97
She shall not strike Dame Eleanor unrevenged . . . i 3 150
I will follow Eleanor, And listen after Humphrey, how he proceeds . i 3 151
Lewdly bent, Under the countenance and confederacy Of Lady Eleanor ii 1 169
Roger had issue, Edmund, Anne and Eleanor . . . ii 2 38
Stand forth, Dame Eleanor Cobham, Gloucester's wife . . . ii 3 1
Eleanor, the law, thou see'st, hath judged thee . . . ii 3 15
Thus Eleanor's pride dies in her youngest days . . . ii 3 46
Elect. Take your oath, That you elect no other king but him 1 *Hen. VI.* iv 1 4
Men Of singular integrity and learning, Yea, the elect o' the land *Hen. VIII.* ii 4 60
Then, if you will elect by my advice, Crown him . . . *T. Andron.* i 1 228
Elected him our absence to supply . . . *Meas. for Meas.* i 1 19
The deputy elected by the Lord . . . *Richard II.* iii 2 57
How may I avoid, Although my will distaste what it elected, The wife I chose? . . . *Troi. and Cres.* ii 2 66
Upon the part o' the people, in whose power We were elected theirs *Cor.* iii 1 211
Why hast thou gone so far, To be unbent when thou hast ta'en thy stand, The elected deer before thee . . . *Cymbeline* iii 4 112
Election. The Prince of Arragon hath ta'en his oath, And comes to his election presently . . . *Mer. of Venice* ii 9 3
'Tis to peize the time, To eke it and to draw it out in length, To stay you from election . . . iii 2 24
Thy frank election make; Thou hast power to choose . *All's Well* ii 3 61
Before we make election, give me leave To show some reason 2 *Hen. VI.* i 3 165
Choice, being mutual act of all our souls, Makes merit her election *Troi. and Cres.* i 3 349
I take to-day a wife, and my election Is led on in the conduct of my will ii 2 61
And on a safer judgement all revoke Your ignorant election *Coriolanus* ii 3 227
We labour'd, No impediment between, but that you must Cast your election on him . . . ii 3 237
Almost all Repent in their election . . . ii 3 263
Let desert in pure election shine . . . *T. Andron.* i 1 16
By common voice, In election for the Roman empery, Chosen Andronicus i 1 22
And name thee in election for the empire . . . i 1 183
For thy favours done To us in our election this day, I give thee thanks i 1 235
Since my dear soul was mistress of her choice And could of men distinguish, her election Hath seal'd thee for herself . *Hamlet* iii 2 69
Popp'd in between the election and my hopes . . . v 2 65
I do prophesy the election lights On Fortinbras: he has my dying voice v 2 366
Election makes not up on such conditions . . . *Lear* i 1 209
Mere prattle, without practice, Is all his soldiership. But he, sir, had the election . . . *Othello* i 1 27
By her election may be truly read What kind of man he is . *Cymbeline* i 1 53
If it be a sin to make a true election, she is damned . . i 2 30
Hath Honour'd with confirmation your great judgement In the election of a sir so rare . . . i 6 175
Leave us to our free election . . . *Pericles* ii 4 33
Elegancy. For the elegancy, facility, and golden cadence of poesy, caret *L. L. Lost* iv 2 126
Elegies. After your dire-lamenting elegies . . . *T. G. of Ver.* iii 2 82
Hangs odes upon hawthorns and elegies on brambles . *As Y. Like It* iii 2 380
Element. If you can command these elements to silence . *Tempest* i 1 24
The elements, Of whom your swords are temper'd, may as well Wound the loud winds . . . iii 3 61
Then to the elements Be free, and fare thou well! . . . v 1 317
Such daubery as this is, beyond our element . . *Mer. Wives* iv 2 186
There's little of the melancholy element in her . . *Much Ado* ii 1 357
With the motion of all elements, Courses as swift as thought *L. L. Lost* iv 3 329
The element itself, till seven years' heat, Shall not behold her face *T. N.* i 1 26
O, you should not rest Between the elements of air and earth, But you should pity me! . . . i 5 294
Does not our life consist of the four elements? . . . ii 3 10
I might say 'element,' but the word is over-worn . . . iii 1 65

Element. You are idle shallow things: I am not of your element *T. N.* iii 4 137
King Richard and myself should meet With no less terror than the elements Of fire and water . . . . . . *Richard II.* iii 3 55
I in the clear sky of fame o'ershine you as much as the full moon doth the cinders of the element . . . *2 Hen. IV.* iv 3 58
The dull elements of earth and water never appear in him . *Hen. V.* iii 7 23
The element shows to him as it doth to me . . . . iv 1 107
One, certes, that promises no element In such a business . *Hen. VIII.* i 1 48
Bounding between the two moist elements, Like Perseus' horse *T. and C.* i 3 41
By the elements, If e'er again I meet him beard to beard, He's mine *Cor.* i 10 10
Whose bare unhoused trunks, To the conflicting elements exposed, Answer mere nature . . . . . *T. of Athens* iv 3 230
The complexion of the element In favour's like the work we have *J. Cæsar* i 3 128
The elements So mix'd in him that Nature might stand up And say to all the world 'This was a man!' . . . . v 5 73
Like a creature native and indued Unto that element . *Hamlet* iv 7 181
Down, thou climbing sorrow, Thy element's below! . . . *Lear* ii 4 58
Where's the king?—Contending with the fretful element . iii 1 4
I tax not you, you elements, with unkindness; I never gave you kingdom . . . . iii 2 16
O, let the heavens Give him defence against the elements! . *Othello* ii 1 45
The very elements of this warlike isle Have I to-night fluster'd . ii 3 59
She's framed as fruitful As the free elements . . . . ii 3 348
You ever-burning lights above, You elements that clip us round about iii 3 464
And the elements once out of it, it transmigrates . *Ant. and Cleo.* ii 7 50
The elements be kind to thee, and make Thy spirits all of comfort! . iii 2 40
His delights Were dolphin-like; they show'd his back above The element they lived in . . . . v 2 90
I am fire and air; my other elements I give to baser life . . v 2 292
No light, no fire: the unfriendly elements Forgot thee utterly *Pericles* iii 1 58

Elephant. In the south suburbs, at the Elephant, Is best to lodge *T. Night* iii 3 39
To the Elephant.—I do remember . . . . iii 3 49
Where's Antonio, then? I could not find him at the Elephant . . iv 3 5
As valiant as the lion, churlish as the bear, slow as the elephant *T. and C.* i 2 22
Shall the elephant Ajax carry it thus? . . . . . . ii 3 2
The elephant hath joints, but none for courtesy: his legs are legs for necessity, not for flexure . . . . ii 3 113
Unicorns may be betray'd with trees, And bears with glasses, elephants with holes, Lions with toils . . . . *J. Cæsar* ii 1 205

Elevated. She had one eye declined for the loss of her husband, another elevated that the oracle was fulfilled . . . *W. Tale* v 2 82

Eleven. Her husband will be absence from his house between ten and eleven.—Ten and eleven? . . . . . . *Mer. Wives* ii 2 87
I say I shall be with her between ten and eleven . . . ii 2 275
Eleven o'clock the hour. I will prevent this . . . . ii 2 324
A bawd of eleven years' continuance . . . *Meas. for Meas.* iii 2 208
Eleven widows and nine maids is a simple coming-in for one man *M. of V.* ii 2 171
How the world wags: 'Tis but an hour ago since it was nine, And after one hour more 'twill be eleven . . . . *As Y. Like It* ii 7 25
Teacheth tricks eleven and twenty long . . . *T. of Shrew* iv 2 57
Hurt him in eleven places: my niece shall take note of it . *T. Night* iii 2 37
The eldest is eleven; The second and the third, nine, and some five *W. T.* ii 1 144
With a thought seven of the eleven I paid.—O monstrous! eleven buckram men grown out of two! . . . . . *1 Hen. IV.* ii 4 242
You shall have a dozen of cushions again; you have but eleven now *2 Hen. IV.* v 4 17
Eleven hours I spent to write it over . . . . *Richard III.* iii 6 5
If to-morrow be a fair day, by eleven o'clock it will go one way or other *Troi. and Cres.* iii 3 296
I had rather had eleven die nobly for their country than one voluptuously surfeit out of action . . . . . . *Coriolanus* i 3 26
'Tis since the earthquake now eleven years . . . *Rom. and Jul.* i 3 23
Since that time it is eleven years; For then she could stand alone . i 3 35
Upon the platform, 'twixt eleven and twelve, I'll visit you *Hamlet* i 2 252
From this present hour of five till the bell have told eleven . *Othello* ii 2 11
I think, I have brought up some eleven— Ay, to eleven . *Pericles* iv 2 16

Eleven-pence. A 'leven-pence farthing better . . *L. L. Lost* iii 1 172

Eleventh. Douglas and the English rebels met The eleventh of this month at Shrewsbury . . . . *1 Hen. IV.* iii 2 166
That self bill is urged, Which in the eleventh year of the last king's reign Was like . . . . *Hen. V.* i 1 2

Elf. Every elf and fairy sprite Hop as light as bird from brier *M. N. Dr.* v 1 400
Blanket my loins; elf all my hair in knots . . . . *Lear* ii 3 10

Elf-lock. And bakes the elf-locks in foul sluttish hairs . *Rom. and Jul.* i 4 90

Elf-skin. You starveling, you elf-skin, you dried neat's tongue! *1 Hen. IV.* ii 4 270

Elizabeth. The Breton Richmond aims At young Elizabeth, my brother's daughter . . . . *Richard III.* iv 3 41
You have a daughter call'd Elizabeth, Virtuous and fair, royal and gracious . . . . iv 4 203
The queen hath heartily consented He shall espouse Elizabeth . . iv 5 18
Richmond and Elizabeth, The true succeeders of each royal house . v 5 29
To the high and mighty princess of England, Elizabeth! . *Hen. VIII.* v 5 4
What is her name?—Elizabeth.—Stand up, lord. With this kiss take my blessing: God protect thee! . . . . v 5 10

Ell. An ell and three quarters will not measure her from hip to hip *Com. of Errors* iii 2 112
As I am a true woman, holland of eight shillings an ell . *1 Hen. IV.* iii 3 83
Here's a wit of cheveril, that stretches from an inch narrow to an ell broad! . . . . *Rom. and Jul.* ii 4 88

Ellen. Your fairest daughter and mine, my god-daughter Ellen *2 Hen. IV.* iii 2 8

Elm. Thou art an elm, my husband, I a vine . *Com. of Errors* ii 2 176
The female ivy so Enrings the barky fingers of the elm . *M. N. Dream* iv 1 49
Answer, thou dead elm, answer . . . . . . *2 Hen. IV.* ii 4 358

Eloquence. And nought esteems my aged eloquence . *T. G. of Ver.* iii 1 83
From the rattling tongue Of saucy and audacious eloquence *M. N. Dream* v 1 103
Thy paleness moves me more than eloquence . . *Mer. of Venice* iii 2 106
Say she be mute and will not speak a word; Then I'll commend her volubility, And say she uttereth piercing eloquence . *T. of Shrew* ii 1 177
His eloquence the parcel of a reckoning . . . *1 Hen. IV.* ii 4 113
I cannot look greenly nor gasp out my eloquence . . *Hen. V.* v 2 149
There is more eloquence in a sugar touch of them than in the tongues of the French council . . . . v 2 302
In such business Action is eloquence . . . . *Coriolanus* iii 2 76
That delightful engine of her thoughts, That blabb'd them with such pleasing eloquence . . . . *T. Andron.* iii 1 83
She brings news; and every tongue that speaks But Romeo's name speaks heavenly eloquence . . . . . . *Rom. and Jul.* iii 2 33
To try thy eloquence, now 'tis time . . . . *Ant. and Cleo.* iii 12 26

Eloquent. It is no matter how witty, so it be eloquent . . *T. Night* iii 2 47
It is a theme as fluent as the sea: turn the sands into eloquent tongues, and my horse is argument for them all . . *Hen. V.* iii 7 37
Be eloquent in my behalf to her . . . . . *Richard III.* iv 4 357
Give it breath with your mouth, and it will discourse most eloquent music. Look you, these are the stops . . . . *Hamlet* iii 2 375

Else. What seest thou else In the dark backward and abysm of time? *Tempest* i 2 49
Thou didst prevent me; I had peopled else This isle with Calibans . i 2 350
And sends me forth—For else his project dies—to keep them living . ii 1 299
I Beyond all limit of what else i' the world Do love, prize, honour you . iii 1 72
And what does else want credit, come to me, And I'll be sworn 'tis true iii 3 25
Which here, in this most desolate isle, else falls Upon your heads . iii 3 80
Of thy success in love and what news else Betideth here *T. G. of Ver.* i 1 58
Or fearing else some messenger that might her mind discover . . ii 1 173
My duty pricks me on to utter that Which else no worldly good should draw from me . . . . iii 1 9
This, or else nothing, will inherit her . . . . . . iii 2 87
Since the substance of your perfect self Is else devoted, I am but a shadow . . . . iv 2 125
We are all frail.—Else let my brother die . . . . *Meas. for Meas.* ii 4 121
Sweet mistress,—what your name is else, I know not *Com. of Errors* iii 2 29
Hath not else his eye Stray'd his affection in unlawful love? . . v 1 50
Else none at all in aught proves excellent . . . *L. L. Lost* iv 3 354
I, one Snug the joiner, am A lion-fell, nor else no lion's dam *M. N. Dr.* v 1 227
But is there any else longs to see this broken music in his sides? *As Y. L. It* i 2 149
Will you give thanks, sweet Kate; or else shall I? *T. of Shrew* iv 1 162
Is this true? or is it else your pleasure, Like pleasant travellers, to break a jest! . . . . iv 5 71
Keeps her guard In honestest defence.—The gods forbid else! *All's Well* iii 5 77
Or will not else thy craft so quickly grow, That thine own trip shall be thine overthrow? . . . . *T. Night* v 1 169
Would they else be content to die?—Yes . . . . *W. Tale* i 1 46
I bring you witnesses, Twice fifteen thousand hearts of England's breed,—Bastards, and else . . . . *K. John* ii 1 276
The fire is dead with grief . . . : see else yourself . . . . iv 1 108
Will her ladyship behold and hear our exorcisms?—Ay, what else? *2 Hen. VI.* i 4 6
Is it upon record, or else reported Successively from age to age? *Rich. III.* iii 1 72
And my favour To him that does best: God forbid else! *Hen. VIII.* ii 2 115
Else would a maiden blush bepaint my cheek . . *Rom. and Jul.* ii 2 86
I'll frown and be perverse and say thee nay, So thou wilt woo; but else, not for the world . . . . ii 2 97
What should I do? Run to the Capitol, and nothing else? And so return to you, and nothing else? . . . . *J. Cæsar* ii 4 11
I know not, gentlemen, what you intend, Who else must be let blood . iii 1 152
We Will fight with him by sea.—By sea! what else? *Ant. and Cleo.* iii 7 29
Comfort him.—Do, most dear queen.—Do! why: what else? . . iii 11 27

Elsewhere. I'll knock elsewhere, to see if they'll disdain me *Com. of Er.* iii 1 121
If you like elsewhere, do it by stealth . . . . . . iii 2 7
If not, elsewhere they meet with charity . . . *T. of Shrew* iv 3 6
Besides I say and will in battle prove, Or here or elsewhere *Richard II.* i 1 93
Thou hast paid all there.—Yea, and elsewhere . . . *1 Hen. IV.* i 2 61
And leave your brothers to go speed elsewhere . . *3 Hen. VI.* iv 1 58
Thus I turn my back: There is a world elsewhere . *Coriolanus* iii 3 135

Elsinore. But what is your affair in Elsinore? . . . . *Hamlet* i 2 174
But, in the beaten way of friendship, what make you at Elsinore? . ii 2 278
Gentlemen, you are welcome to Elsinore . . . . . ii 2 387
My good friends, I'll leave you till night: you are welcome to Elsinore ii 2 573

Eltham. To Eltham will I, where the young king is . . *1 Hen. VI.* i 1 170
The king from Eltham I intend to steal . . . . . i 1 176
You have great reason to do Richard right: Especially for those occasions At Eltham Place . . . . iii 1 156

Elves. Ye elves of hills, brooks, standing lakes and groves . *Tempest* v 1 33
Elves, list your names; silence, you airy toys . . *Mer. Wives* v 5 46
Search Windsor Castle, elves, within and out . . . . v 5 60
Our queen and all her elves come here anon . . *M. N. Dream* ii 1 17
All their elves for fear Creep into acorn-cups and hide them there . ii 1 31
War with rere-mice for their leathern wings, To make my small elves coats . . . . ii 2 5
Nod to him, elves, and do him courtesies . . . . . iii 1 177
And now about the cauldron sing, Like elves and fairies in a ring *Macb.* iv 1 42

Elvish-marked. Thou elvish-mark'd, abortive, rooting hog! *Richard III.* i 3 228

Ely is fled to Richmond; And Buckingham, back'd with the hardy Welshmen, Is in the field . . . . iv 3 46
Ely with Richmond troubles me more near Than Buckingham . . iv 3 49

Ely House. Entreat your majesty to visit him.—Where lies he?—At Ely House . . . . *Richard II.* i 4 58
Bid him repair to us to Ely House To see this business . . . ii 1 216

Elysium. There I'll rest, as after much turmoil A blessed soul doth in Elysium . . . . *T. G. of Ver.* ii 7 38
My brother he is in Elysium. Perchance he is not drown'd *T. Night* i 2 4
Sweats in the eye of Phœbus and all night Sleeps in Elysium *Hen. V.* iv 1 291
And then it lived in sweet Elysium . . . . *2 Hen. VI.* i 2 399
To wear a crown; Within whose circuit is Elysium . . *3 Hen. VI.* i 2 30
Poor shadows of Elysium, hence, and rest . . . . *Cymbeline* v 4 97

Emballing. For little England You'ld venture an emballing *Hen. VIII.* ii 3 47

Embalm me, Then lay me forth . . . . iv 2 170
This embalms and spices To the April day again . *T. of Athens* iv 3 40

Embark. But now he parted hence, to embark for Milan . *T. G. of Ver.* i 1 71
The well-appointed king at Hampton pier Embark his royalty *Hen. V.* iii Prol. 5

Embarked. What stuff of mine hast thou embark'd? . *Com. of Errors* v 1 409
Marking the embarked traders on the flood . . *M. N. Dream* ii 1 127
Methoughts that I had broken from the Tower, And was embark'd to cross to Burgundy . . . . *Richard III.* i 4 10
My necessaries are embark'd: farewell . . . . . *Hamlet* i 3 1
He's embark'd With such loud reason to the Cyprus wars . *Othello* i 1 150
I have a kinsman who Is bound for Italy; he embark'd at Milford *Cymb.* iii 6 62

Embarquements all of fury, shall lift up Their rotten privilege *Coriolanus* i 10 22

Embassade. When you disgraced me in my embassade, Then I degraded you from being king . . . . *3 Hen. VI.* iv 3 32

Embassage. I have almost matter enough in me for such an embassage; and so I commit you . . . . *Much Ado* i 1 282
Do you any embassage to the Pigmies . . . . . . ii 1 277
A pretty knavish page, That well by heart hath conn'd his embassage *L. L. Lost* v 2 98
Doth not thy embassage belong to me, And am I last that knows it? *Richard II.* iii 4 93
I every day expect an embassage From my Redeemer *Richard III.* ii 1 3

Embassy. I have received from her another embassy of meeting *M. W.* iii 5 132
Here comes in embassy The French king's daughter . . *L. L. Lost* i 1 135
To whom he sends, and what's his embassy . . . . . ii 1 3

Embassy. We'll once more hear Orsino's embassy *T. Night* i 5 176
With interchange of gifts, letters, loving embassies *W. Tale* i 1 31
Silence, good mother; hear the embassy *K. John* i 1 6
The farthest limit of my embassy i 1 22
Once dispatch'd him in an embassy To Germany i 1 99
Stay for an answer to your embassy ii 1 44
Then go we in, to know his embassy *Hen. V.* i 1 95
Shall we sparingly show you far off The Dauphin's meaning and our embassy? i 2 240
With what great state he heard their embassy ii 4 32
Fresh embassies and suits, Nor from the state nor private friends, hereafter Will I lend ear to *Coriolanus* v 3 17
I have sent Cloten's clotpoll down the stream, In embassy to his mother *Cymbeline* iv 2 185
Embattailed. Told of a many thousand warlike French That were embattailed *K. John* iv 2 200
Embattle. The night Is shiny; and they say we shall embattle By the second hour i' the morn *Ant. and Cleo.* iv 9 3
Embattled. Too too strongly embattled against me *Mer. Wives* ii 2 260
The English are embattled, you French peers *Hen. V.* iv 2 14
Embayed. If that the Turkish fleet Be not enshelter'd and embay'd, they are drown'd *Othello* ii 1 18
Embellished. All o'er embellished with rubies, carbuncles *Com. of Er.* iii 2 137
Ember. Your speech is passion: But, pray you, stir no embers up *Ant. and Cleo.* ii 2 13
Ember-eves. It hath been sung at festivals, On ember-eves and holy-ales *Pericles* Gower 6
Emblaze. Thou shalt wear it as a herald's coat, To emblaze the honour that thy master got 2 *Hen. VI.* iv 10 76
Emblem. His cicatrice, an emblem of war, here on his sinister cheek *All's Well* ii 1 44
The rod, and bird of peace, and all such emblems *Hen. VIII.* iv 1 89
Embodied. For I by vow am so embodied yours, That she which marries you must marry me *All's Well* v 3 173
Embolden. Nothing emboldens sin so much as mercy *T. of Athens* iii 5 3
Emboldened me to this unseasoned intrusion *Mer. Wives* ii 2 173
With a soul Embolden'd with the glory of her praise *Pericles* i 1 4
Embossed. All the embossed sores and headed evils *As Y. Like It* ii 7 67
Brach Merriman, the poor cur is emboss'd *T. of Shrew* Ind. 1 17
We have almost emboss'd him; you shall see his fall *All's Well* iii 6 107
Thou whoreson, impudent, embossed rascal 1 *Hen. IV.* iii 3 177
Once a day with his embossed froth The turbulent surge shall cover *T. of Athens* v 1 220
A boil, A plague-sore, an embossed carbuncle, In my corrupted blood *Lear* ii 4 227
The boar of Thessaly Was never so emboss'd *Ant. and Cleo.* iv 13 3
Embounded. That sweet breath Which was embounded in this beauteous clay *K. John* iv 3 137
Embowel. If thou embowel me to-day, I'll give you leave to powder me and eat me too to-morrow 1 *Hen. IV.* v 4 111
Embowelled. When the schools, Embowell'd of their doctrine, have left off The danger to itself *All's Well* i 3 247
Embowell'd will I see thee by and by . . .—Embowelled! 1 *Hen. IV.* v 4 109
And makes his trough In your embowell'd bosoms *Richard III.* v 2 10
Embrace. I embrace thy body *Tempest* v 1 109
First, noble friend, Let me embrace thine age v 1 121
Let grief and sorrow still embrace his heart That doth not wish you joy! v 1 214
Now kiss, embrace, contend, do what you will *T. G. of Ver.* i 2 129
Give back, or else embrace thy death v 4 126
Embrace thy brother there; rejoice with him *Com. of Errors* v 1 413
You embrace your charge too willingly *Much Ado* i 1 103
You will say she did embrace me as a husband iv 1 50
Your over-kindness doth wring tears from me! I do embrace your offer v 1 303
O, let us embrace! As true we are as flesh and blood can be *L. L. Lost* iv 3 214
I take it, your own business calls on you And you embrace the occasion to depart *Mer. of Venice* i 1 64
Embrace your own safety and give over this attempt *As Y. Like It* i 2 189
Embrace her for her beauty's sake *T. of Shrew* iv 5 34
Let me embrace with old Vincentio, And wander we to see thy honest son iv 5 68
He is too good and fair for death and me; Whom I myself embrace, to set him free *All's Well* iii 4 17
Thy Fates open their hands; let thy blood and spirit embrace them *T. N.* ii 5 160
Do not embrace me till each circumstance Of place, time, fortune, do cohere v 1 258
Madam, I am most apt to embrace your offer v 1 328
Or hoop his body more with thy embraces *W. Tale* iv 4 450
Embrace but my direction iv 4 534
Then embraces his son-in-law; then again worries he his daughter v 2 57
She embraces him.—She hangs about his neck v 3 111
Embrace him, love him, give him welcome hither *K. John* ii 1 11
We must embrace This gentle offer of the perilous time iv 3 12
And embrace His golden uncontroll'd enfranchisement *Richard II.* i 3 89
You never shall . . . Embrace each other's love in banishment i 3 184
I will embrace him with a soldier's arm 1 *Hen. IV.* v 2 74
Sound all the lofty instruments of war, And by that music let us all embrace v 2 99
I embrace this fortune patiently, Since not to be avoided it falls on me v 5 12
Let's drink together friendly and embrace 2 *Hen. IV.* iv 2 63
Let it be a quarrel between us, if you live.—I embrace it *Hen. V.* iv 1 221
Embrace we then this opportunity As fitting best to quittance their deceit 1 *Hen. VI.* ii 1 13
Direct mine arms I may embrace his neck ii 5 37
And, lords, accept this hearty kind embrace iii 3 82
I do embrace thee, as I would embrace The Christian prince, King Henry v 3 171
Embrace and kiss and take ten thousand leaves 2 *Hen. VI.* iii 2 354
But where's the body that I should embrace? iv 4 6
Who loves the king and will embrace his pardon, Fling up his cap iv 8 14
They join, embrace, and seem to kiss, As if they vow'd some league inviolable 3 *Hen. VI.* ii 1 29
Let me embrace thee in my weary arms: I, that did never weep, now melt with woe ii 3 45
Let me embrace thee, sour adversity, For wise men say it is the wisest course iii 1 24
Dorset, embrace him; Hastings, love lord marquess *Richard III.* ii 1 25
Let us all embrace: And take our leave, until we meet in heaven iii 3 24
Make me no more ado, but all embrace him *Hen. VIII.* v 3 159
I charge you, Embrace and love this man v 3 172
Even such a passion doth embrace my bosom *Troi. and Cres.* iii 2 37
The one and other Diomed embraces. Our bloods are now in calm iv 1 14
What a pair of spectacles is here! Let me embrace too iv 4 15
Embrace. Let me embrace thee, Ajax: By him that thunders, thou hast lusty arms *Troi. and Cres.* iv 5 135
Let an old man embrace thee iv 5 199
Let me embrace thee, good old chronicle iv 5 202
He bears himself more proudlier, Even to my person, than I thought he would When first I did embrace him *Coriolanus* iv 7 10
If one arm's embracement will content thee, I will embrace thee in it *T. Andron.* v 2 69
Who drown'd their enmity in my true tears, And oped their arms to embrace me as a friend v 3 108
Eyes, look your last! Arms, take your last embrace! *Rom. and Jul.* v 3 113
A man, Whom this beneath world doth embrace and hug *T. of Athens* i 1 44
He would embrace no counsel, take no warning by my coming iii 1 27
Brutus is wise, and, were he not in health, He would embrace the means to come by it *J. Cæsar* ii 1 259
Must embrace the fate Of that dark hour *Macbeth* iii 1 137
I embrace it freely; And will this brother's wager frankly play *Hamlet* v 2 263
For me, with sorrow I embrace my fortune v 2 399
Welcome, then, Thou unsubstantial air that I embrace! *Lear* iv 1 7
I must embrace thee; Let sorrow split my heart, if ever I Did hate thee! v 3 176
You embrace not Antony As you did love, but as you fear'd him *A. and C.* iii 13 56
I embrace these conditions; let us have articles betwixt us *Cymbeline* i 4 168
With joy he will embrace you, for he's honourable i 4 179
I will embrace Your offer *Pericles* iii 3 37
I embrace you. Give me my robes. I am wild in my beholding v 1 223
Embrace him, dear Thaisa; this is he v 3 55
Embraced. After we had embraced, kissed, protested *Mer. Wives* iii 5 74
What cannot be eschew'd must be embraced v 5 251
Your brother and his lover have embraced *Meas. for Meas.* i 4 40
Which though myself would gladly have embraced *Com. of Errors* i 1 70
Hugg'd and embraced by the strumpet wind *Mer. of Venice* ii 6 16
Quicken his embraced heaviness With some delight or other ii 8 52
Embraced, as it were, from the ends of opposed winds *W. Tale* i 1 33
The means that heaven yields must be embraced *Richard II.* iii 2 29
You'll see your Rome embraced with fire before You'll speak with Coriolanus *Coriolanus* v 2 7
They met so near with their lips that their breaths embraced together *Othello* ii 1 266
There's the point.—Which do not be entreated to, but weigh What it is worth embraced *Ant. and Cleo.* ii 6 33
And be embraced by a piece of tender air *Cymbeline* v 4 139; v 5 437
Embracement. Drew me from kind embracements of my spouse *C. of Er.* i 1 44
With kind embracements, tempting kisses *T. of Shrew* Ind. 1 118
Assisted with your honour'd friends, Bring them to our embracement *W. T.* v 1 114
Seal thou this league With thy embracements to my wife's allies *Rich. III.* ii 1 30
How they clung In their embracement, as they grew together *Hen. VIII.* i 1 10
The issue is embracement *Troi. and Cres.* iv 5 148
I should freelier rejoice in that absence wherein he won honour than in the embracements of his bed *Coriolanus* i 3 4
If one arm's embracement will content thee, I will embrace thee in it *T. Andron.* v 2 68
Give me but this I have, And sear up my embracements from a next With bonds of death! *Cymbeline* i 1 116
Clothed like a bride, For the embracements even of Jove himself *Pericles* i 1 7
Embracing. And so locks her in embracing, as if she would pin her to her heart *W. Tale* v 2 84
Grovelling lies, Coldly embracing the discolour'd earth *K. John* ii 1 306
Embrasure. Forcibly prevents Our lock'd embrasures *Troi. and Cres.* iv 4 39
Embrewed. Lord Bassianus lies embrewed here, All on a heap *T. Andron.* ii 3 222
Embroidered. Than doth a rich embroider'd canopy To kings 3 *Hen. VI.* ii 5 44
Embroidery. Rich embroidery, Buckled below fair knighthood's bending knee *Mer. Wives* v 5 75
Emerald. In emerald tufts, flowers purple, blue, and white v 5 74
Emilia. Is't lawful, pray you, To see her women? any of them? Emilia? *W. Tale* ii 2 12
Put apart these your attendants, I Shall bring Emilia forth ii 2 15
Do not learn of him, Emilia, though he be thy husband *Othello* ii 1 163
Before Emilia here I give thee warrant of thy place iii 3 19
Where should I lose that handkerchief, Emilia?—I know not, madam iii 4 23
Do not talk to me, Emilia; I cannot weep; nor answer have I none iv 2 102
Therefore, good Emilia, Give me my nightly wearing, and adieu iv 3 15
Dost thou in conscience think,—tell me, Emilia,—That there be women do abuse their husbands In such gross kind? iv 3 61
Emilia, run you to the citadel, And tell my lord and lady v 1 126
My lord, I would speak a word with you!—Yes: 'tis Emilia. By and by v 2 91
I had forgot thee: O, come in, Emilia: Soft; by and by v 2 103
Eminence. Whether the tyranny be in his place, Or in his eminence that fills it up, I stagger in *Meas. for Meas.* i 2 168
A woman's heart; which ever yet Affected eminence, wealth *Hen. VIII.* iii 3 29
In noble eminence enthroned and sphered *Troi. and Cres.* i 3 90
You should not have the eminence of him ii 3 266
Present him eminence, both with eye and tongue *Macbeth* iii 2 31
I protest, Maugre thy strength, youth, place, and eminence *Lear* v 3 131
Eminent. A deflower'd maid! And by an eminent body that enforced The law against it! *Meas. for Meas.* iv 4 25
And bow'd his eminent top to their low ranks *All's Well* i 2 43
Neither allied To eminent assistants *Hen. VIII.* i 1 62
Who stands so eminent in the degree of this fortune as Cassio? *Othello* ii 1 240
There is a Frenchman his companion, one An eminent monsieur *Cymb.* i 6 65
A hilding for a livery, a squire's cloth, A pantler, not so eminent ii 3 129
Emmanuel. What is thy name?—Emmanuel.—They use to write it on the top of letters 2 *Hen. VI.* iv 2 106
Emmew. And follies doth emmew As falcon doth the fowl *M. for M.* iii 1 91
Empale him with your weapons round about *Troi. and Cres.* v 7 5
Emperial. A matter of brawl betwixt my uncle and one of the emperial's men *T. Andron.* iv 3 94
Wouldst thou speak with us?—Yea, forsooth, an your mistership be emperial iv 4 40
Emperor. He's a present for any emperor that ever trod *Tempest* ii 2 72
Youthful Valentine Attends the emperor in his royal court *T. G. of Ver.* i 3 27
With the speediest expedition I will dispatch him to the emperor's court i 3 38
With other gentlemen of good esteem Are journeying to salute the emperor i 3 41
How happily he lives, how well beloved, And daily graced by the emperor i 3 58
Thou shalt spend some time With Valentinus in the emperor's court i 3 67
He is as worthy for an empress' love As meet to be an emperor's counsellor ii 4 77
Thou 'rt an emperor, Cæsar, Keisar, and Pheezar *Mer. Wives* i 3 9
Some say he is with the Emperor of Russia *Meas. for Meas.* iii 2 93

Emperor. The Emperor of Russia was my father: O that he were alive . *W. Tale* iii 2 120
To Germany, there with the emperor To treat of high affairs *K. John* i 1 100
But yet I dare defend My innocent life against an emperor . . iv 3 89
To Charlemain, who was the son To Lewis the emperor . *Hen. V.* i 2 76
Which pillage they with merry march bring home To the tent-royal of their emperor . . . i 2 196
What are you?—As good a gentleman as the emperor . . iv 1 42
The emperor's coming in behalf of France . . v Prol. 38
Have you perused the letters from the pope, The emperor? . 1 *Hen. VI.* v 1 2
Charles the emperor, Under pretence to see the queen his aunt *Hen. VIII.* i 1 176
I am sure the emperor Paid ere he promised . . i 1 185
The emperor thus desired, That he would please to alter the king's course i 1 188
To revenge him on the emperor For not bestowing on him, at his asking, The archbishopric of Toledo . . . ii 1 162
He has crack'd the league Between us and the emperor . . ii 2 26
When you went Ambassador to the emperor . . . iii 2 318
If my sight fail not, You should be lord ambassador from the emperor iv 2 109
And name thee in election for the empire, With these our late-deceased emperor's sons . *T. Andron.* i 1 184
Draw your swords, and sheathe them not Till Saturninus be Rome's emperor . . . i 1 205
This suit I make, That you create your emperor's eldest son, Lord Saturnine . . . i 1 224
Crown him, and say 'Long live our emperor!' . . i 1 229
We create Lord Saturninus Rome's great emperor . . i 1 232
King and commander of our commonweal, The wide world's emperor . i 1 248
Now, madam, are you prisoner to an emperor . . i 1 258
Where is the emperor's guard? Treason, my lord! . . i 1 283
Traitor, restore Lavinia to the emperor.—Dead, if you will . . i 1 296
The emperor needs her not, Nor her, nor thee, nor any of thy stock . i 1 299
Lords, accompany Your noble emperor and his lovely bride . i 1 334
Come, come, sweet emperor; come, Andronicus; Take up this good old man . . . i 1 456
A Roman now adopted happily, And must advise the emperor for his good . . . i 1 464
I have pass'd My word and promise to the emperor . . i 1 469
Trouble us no more.—Nay, nay, sweet emperor, we must all be friends i 1 479
If the emperor's court can feast two brides, You are my guest, Lavinia i 1 489
So near the emperor's palace dare you draw, And maintain such a quarrel? . . . ii 1 46
Though Bassianus be the emperor's brother . . ii 1 88
The emperor's court is like the house of Fame . . ii 1 126
Let us make a bay And wake the emperor and his lovely bride . ii 2 4
Let it be your charge, as it is ours, To attend the emperor's person carefully . . . ii 2 8
High emperor, upon my feeble knee I beg this boon . . ii 3 288
My lord the emperor Sends thee this word . . iii 1 150
O gracious emperor! O gentle Aaron! Did ever raven sing so like a lark? . . . iii 1 157
With all my heart, I'll send the emperor My hand . . iii 1 160
Ill art thou repaid For that good hand thou sent'st the emperor . iii 1 236
Why do the emperor's trumpets flourish thus?—Belike, for joy the emperor hath a son . . . iv 2 49
The emperor, in his rage, will doom her death . . iv 2 114
By this their child shall be advanced, And be received for the emperor's heir . . . iv 2 158
Let the emperor dandle him for his own . . iv 2 161
This wicked emperor may have shipp'd her hence . . iv 3 23
We will afflict the emperor in his pride . . iv 3 62
Let him deliver the pigeons to the emperor from you . . iv 3 97
Can you deliver an oration to the emperor with a grace? . . iv 3 99
Make no more ado, But give your pigeons to the emperor . . iv 3 103
And when thou hast given it the emperor, Knock at my door . iv 3 118
Was ever seen An emperor in Rome thus overborne, Troubled, confronted thus? . . . iv 4 2
Empress I am, but yonder sits the emperor . . iv 4 41
And they have wish'd that Lucius were their emperor . . iv 4 77
Cheer thy spirit: for know, thou emperor, I will enchant the old Andronicus . . . iv 4 88
Say that the emperor requests a parley Of warlike Lucius . iv 4 101
Now, sweet emperor, be blithe again, And bury all thy fear in my devices iv 4 111
Letters from great Rome, Which signify what hate they bear their emperor . . . v 1 3
Had nature lent thee but thy mother's look, Villain, thou mightst have been an emperor . . . v 1 30
The Roman emperor greets you all by me . . v 1 157
Æmilius, let the emperor give his pledges Unto my father . v 1 163
In the emperor's court There is a queen, attended by a Moor . v 2 104
I will bring in the empress and her sons, The emperor himself . v 2 117
Tell him the emperor and the empress too Feast at my house . v 2 127
Bide with him, Whiles I go tell my lord the emperor . . v 2 138
I fear the emperor means no good to us . . v 3 10
The trumpets show the emperor is at hand . . v 3 16
Rome's emperor, and nephew, break the parle . . v 3 19
My lord the emperor, resolve me this . . v 3 35
And bring our emperor gently in thy hand, Lucius our emperor . v 3 138
Lucius, all hail, Rome's royal emperor! . . v 3 141
Some loving friends convey the emperor hence, And give him burial v 3 191
And breathed such life with kisses in my lips, That I revived, and was an emperor . *Rom. and Jul.* v 1 9
Your worm is your only emperor for diet . *Hamlet* iv 3 22
She might lie by an emperor's side and command him tasks . *Othello* iv 1 195
My brave emperor! Shall we dance now the Egyptian Bacchanals? *Ant. and Cleo.* ii 7 109
Nay, I have done. Here comes the emperor . . iii 7 21
O noble emperor, do not fight by sea; Trust not to rotten planks . iii 7 62
Your emperor Continues still a Jove . . . iv 6 28
O my brave emperor, this is fought indeed! . . iv 7 4
My captain, and my emperor, let me say, Before I strike this bloody stroke, farewell . . iv 14 90
What, ho, the emperor's guard! The guard, what, ho! . iv 14 129
I dream'd there was an Emperor Antony: O, such another sleep! . v 2 76
Which is the Queen of Egypt?—It is the emperor, madam . v 2 112
Have mingled sums To buy a present for the emperor . *Cymbeline* i 6 187
My emperor hath wrote, I must from hence . . iii 5 2
Lucius hath wrote already to the emperor How it goes here . iii 5 21
This is the tenour of the emperor's writ . . iii 7 1
The Roman emperor's letters, Sent by a consul to me, should not sooner Than thine own worth prefer thee . . iv 2 384

Empery. There we'll sit, Ruling in large and ample empery . *Hen. V.* i 2 226
Your right of birth, your empery, your own . . *Richard III.* iii 7 136
Ambitiously for rule and empery . . *T. Andron.* i 1 19
In election for the Roman empery, Chosen Andronicus, surnamed Pius i 1 22
Titus, thou shalt obtain and ask the empery . . i 1 201
A lady So fair, and fasten'd to an empery, Would make the great'st king double . . . *Cymbeline* i 6 120

Emphasis. What is he whose grief Bears such an emphasis? . *Hamlet* v 1 278
Be choked with such another emphasis! Say, the brave Antony *Ant. and Cleo.* i 5 68

Empire. Thy blood and virtue Contend for empire in thee! . *All's Well* i 1 72
A maid too virtuous For the contempt of empire . . iii 2 34
Had Henry got an empire by his marriage . 2 *Hen. VI.* i 1 153
Is the king dead? the empire unpossess'd? . . *Richard III.* iv 4 471
And name thee in election for the empire . . *T. Andron.* i 1 183
That proud brag of thine, That said'st I begg'd the empire at thy hands i 1 307
That beasts May have the world in empire! . *T. of Athens* iv 3 393
The moist star Upon whose influence Neptune's empire stands *Hamlet* i 1 119
A vice of kings; A cutpurse of the empire and the rule . . iii 4 99
Let Rome in Tiber melt, and the wide arch Of the ranged empire fall! Here is my space . . *Ant. and Cleo.* i 1 34
Sextus Pompeius Hath given the dare to Cæsar, and commands The empire of the sea . . . i 2 192
He hath given his empire Up to a whore . . iii 6 66
Make as much of me As when mine empire was your fellow too . iv 2 22
My competitor In top of all design, my mate in empire . . v 1 43
We submit to Cæsar, And to the Roman empire . . *Cymbeline* v 5 461
And from their watery empire recollect All that may men approve or men detect! . . . *Pericles* ii 1 54

Empiric. To prostitute our past-cure malady To empirics . *All's Well* ii 1 125

Empiricutic. I will make a lip at the physician: the most sovereign prescription in Galen is but empiricutic . *Coriolanus* ii 1 128

Employ. There's some great matter she'ld employ me in *T. G. of Ver.* iv 3 3
I like thee well And will employ thee in some service presently . iv 4 45
We shall employ thee in a worthier place . *Meas. for Meas.* v 1 537
I must employ him in a letter to my love . . *L. L. Lost* iii 1 6
Stay, slave; I must employ thee . . . iii 1 152
Allons! we will employ thee.—I'll make one in a dance, or so . v 1 159
Go along: I must employ you in some business . *M. N. Dream* i 1 124
Whiles I in this affair do thee employ, I'll to my queen . . iii 2 374
Be merry, and employ your chiefest thoughts To courtship *Mer. of Ven.* ii 8 43
Thy company, which erst was irksome to me, I will endure, and I'll employ thee too . . . *As Y. Like It* iii 5 96
I would not prize them Without her love; for her employ them all *W. T.* iv 4 387
When that my father lived, Your brother did employ my father much *K. John* i 1 96
Employ the countenance and grace of heaven, As a false favourite doth his prince's name, In deeds dishonourable . . 2 *Hen. IV.* iv 2 24
Employ thee then, sweet virgin, for our good . 1 *Hen. VI.* iii 3 16
Whatsoever you will employ me in, Were it to call King Edward's widow sister, I will perform it . . *Richard III.* i 1 108
When I have most need to employ a friend, And most assured that he is a friend . . . ii 1 36
And his commission to employ those soldiers . . *Hamlet* ii 2 74
We must straight employ you Against the general enemy Ottoman *Othello* i 3 48
I will employ thee back again; I find thee Most fit for business *A. and C.* iii 3 39
To Cæsar I will speak what you shall please, If you'll employ me to him v 2 70
Left these notes Of what commands I should be subject to, When't pleased you to employ me . . *Cymbeline* i 1 173
We shall have need To employ you towards this Roman . . ii 3 68

Employed. You shall be employ'd To hasten on his expedition *T. G. of Ver.* i 3 76
Give me pardon, That I, your vassal, have employ'd and pain'd Your unknown sovereignty! . . *Meas. for Meas.* v 1 391
You cannot better be employ'd, Bassanio, Than to live still and write mine epitaph . . *Mer. of Venice* iv 1 117
Be better employed, and be naught awhile . *As Y. Like It* i 1 38
Do not look for further recompense Than thine own gladness that thou art employ'd . . . iii 5 98
That false villain Whom I employ'd was pre-employ'd by him *W. Tale* ii 1 49
Your tale must be how he employ'd my mother . *K. John* i 1 98
Fit for bloody villany, Apt, liable to be employ'd in danger . . iv 2 226
And these and all are all amiss employ'd . . *Richard II.* ii 3 132
You thus employ'd, I will go root away The noisome weeds . . iii 4 37
Your son in Scotland being thus employ'd . . 1 *Hen. IV.* i 3 265
The man, I do assure you, is not here; For I myself at this time have employ'd him . . . ii 4 562
I was employ'd in passing to and fro . . 1 *Hen. VI.* i 1 69
But that I am prevented, I should have begg'd I might have been employ'd . . . iv 1 72
'Tis meet that lucky ruler be employ'd . . 2 *Hen. VI.* iii 1 291
Were glad to be employ'd, To show how quaint an orator you are . . iii 2 273
While you are thus employ'd, what resteth more? . 3 *Hen. VI.* i 2 44
We to-morrow hold divided councils, Wherein thyself shalt highly be employ'd . . . *Richard III.* iii 1 180
How is the king employ'd?—I left him private . *Hen. VIII.* ii 2 15
Have not alone Employ'd you where high profits might come home . iii 2 158
Ajax employ'd plucks down Achilles' plumes . . *Troi. and Cres.* i 3 386
You know a sword employ'd is perilous . . . iii 2 40
Lavinia, thou shalt be employ'd: these arms! . *T. Andron.* iii 1 282
Marry, for Justice, she is so employ'd, He thinks, with Jove in heaven iv 3 39
Tell us, old man, how shall we be employ'd?—Tut, I have work enough v 2 149
Doors, that were ne'er acquainted with their wards Many a bounteous year, must be employ'd Now to guard sure their master *T. of Athens* iii 3 39
Let him alone, for I remember now How he's employed *Ant. and Cleo.* v 1 72

Employer. Troilus the first employer of pandars . . *Much Ado* v 2 31

Employment. Full of good And fit for great employment *T. G. of Ver.* v 4 157
See now how wit may be made a Jack-a-Lent, when 'tis upon ill employment! . . . *Mer. Wives* v 5 135
You have no employment for me? . . . *Much Ado* ii 1 280
Proud of employment, willingly I go . . *L. L. Lost* ii 1 35
Your ladyship's in all desired employment . . iv 2 140
Not much employment for you: you understand me? . *All's Well* ii 2 71
What employment have we here? . . . *T. Night* ii 5 91
His employment between his lord and my niece confirms no less . iii 4 204
At your best command; at your employment; at your service, sir *K. John* i 1 198
The which he hath detain'd for lewd employments . . *Richard II.* i 1 90
What! a young knave, and begging! Is there not wars? is there not employment? . . . 2 *Hen. IV.* i 2 85
Being upon hasty employment in the king's affairs . . ii 1 139
Should famine, sword and fire Crouch for employment . *Hen. V.* Prol. 8

Employment. Whoever the king favours, The cardinal instantly will find employment, And far enough from court too . . *Hen. VIII.* ii 1 48
A precious ring, a ring that I must use In dear employment *Rom. and Jul.* v 3 32
Men At duty, more than I could frame employment *T. of Athens* iv 3 262
The hand of little employment hath the daintier sense . . *Hamlet* v 1 77
They did make love to this employment . . . . . v 2 57
I serve the king; On whose employment I was sent to you . *Lear* ii 2 136
Thy great employment Will not bear question . . . . v 3 32
But to win time To lose so bad employment . . *Cymbeline* iii 4 113
If thou wouldst not be a villain, but do me true service, undergo those employments wherein I should have cause to use thee with a serious industry . . . . iii 5 110
Empoison. One doth not know How much an ill word may empoison liking . . . . *Much Ado* iii 1 86
Empoisoned. As with a man by his own alms empoison'd *Coriolanus* v 6 11
Empress. He is as worthy for an empress' love As meet to be an emperor's counsellor . . . . . *T. G. of Ver.* ii 4 76
I do applaud thy spirit, Valentine, And think thee worthy of an empress' love . . . . v 4 141
O sweet Maria, empress of my love! . . . . *L. L. Lost* iv 3 56
Were now the general of our gracious empress *Hen. V.* v Prol. 30
Avouch the thoughts of your heart with the looks of an empress . v 2 255
More like an empress than Duke Humphrey's wife . . *2 Hen. VI.* i 3 81
Lavinia will I make my empress, Rome's royal mistress . *T. Andron.* i 1 240
I choose thee, Tamora, for my bride, And will create thee empress of Rome i 1 320
Rise, Titus, rise; my empress hath prevail'd . . . i 1 459
Be bright, and shine in pearl and gold, To wait upon this new-made empress . . . . ii 1 20
An should the empress know This discord's ground, the music would not please . . . . ii 1 69
Our empress, with her sacred wit To villany and vengeance consecrate ii 1 120
And so repose, sweet gold, for their unrest That have their alms out of the empress' chest . . . . ii 3 9
The empress of my soul, Which never hopes more heaven than rests in thee ii 3 40
No more, great empress; Bassianus comes: Be cross with him . ii 3 52
Rome's royal empress, Unfurnish'd of her well-beseeming troop? . ii 3 55
Gentle empress, 'Tis thought you have a goodly gift in horning . ii 3 66
And make proud Saturnine and his empress Beg at the gates . iii 1 298
It was a black ill-favour'd fly, Like to the empress' Moor . . iii 2 67
Shalt carry from me to the empress' sons Presents that I intend to send them . . . . iv 1 115
Were our witty empress well afoot, She would applaud Andronicus' conceit . . . . iv 2 29
Our empress' shame, and stately Rome's disgrace! . . . iv 2 60
The empress sends it thee, thy stamp, thy seal, And bids thee christen it iv 2 69
Tell the empress from me, I am of age To keep mine own . . iv 2 104
Aaron, what shall I say unto the empress?—Advise thee, Aaron . iv 2 128
Cornelia the midwife and myself; And no one else but the deliver'd empress . . . . iv 2 142
The empress, the midwife, and yourself: Two may keep counsel when the third's away: Go to the empress, tell her this I said . iv 2 143
And secretly to greet the empress' friends . . . . . iv 2 174
And who should find them but the empress' villain? . . . iv 3 73
Empress I am, but yonder sits the emperor . . . . . iv 4 41
Who, when he knows thou art the empress' babe, Will hold thee dearly v 1 35
This is the pearl that pleased your empress' eye . . . . v 1 42
Save the child, And bear it from me to the empress . . . v 1 54
First know thou, I begot him on the empress . . . . v 1 87
When I told the empress of this sport, She swooned almost at my pleasing tale . . . . v 1 118
Witness all sorrow, that I know thee well For our proud empress . v 2 26
Good Lord, how like the empress' sons they are! And you, the empress! v 2 64
How like the empress and her sons you are! Well are you fitted . v 2 84
For well I wot the empress never wags But in her company there is a Moor . . . . v 2 87
I will bring in the empress and her sons, The emperor himself . . v 2 116
Tell him the emperor and the empress too Feast at my house . v 2 127
Know you these two?—The empress' sons, I take them . . v 2 154
Villains, forbear! we are the empress' sons . . . . v 2 163
Fetter him, Till he be brought unto the empress' face . . v 3 7
Be sure to have all well, To entertain your highness and your empress v 3 32
Royal Egypt, Empress!—Peace, peace, Iras! . . *Ant. and Cleo.* iv 15 71
Most noble empress, you have heard of me?—I cannot tell . . v 2 71
Emptied. Shall our coffers, then, Be emptied to redeem a traitor home? *1 Hen. IV.* i 3 86
Emptier. Like a deep well That owes two buckets, filling one another, The emptier ever dancing in the air . . . *Richard II.* iv 1 186
You are the weaker vessel, as they say, the emptier vessel *2 Hen. IV.* ii 4 66
Empties itself, as doth an inland brook Into the main of waters *Mer. of Ven.* v 1 96
Their love Lies in their purses, and whoso empties them By so much fills their hearts with deadly hate . . . *Richard II.* ii 2 130
Emptiness. His coffers sound With hollow poverty and emptiness *2 Hen. IV.* i 3 75
That he should dream, Knowing all measures, the full Cæsar will Answer his emptiness! . . . . . . *Ant. and Cleo.* iii 13 36
Should make desire vomit emptiness, Not so allured to feed *Cymbeline* i 6 45
Empty. Hell is empty, And all the devils are here . . . *Tempest* i 2 214
Earth's increase, foison plenty, Barns and garners never empty . iv 1 111
Empty it in the muddy ditch close by the Thames side . *Mer. Wives* iii 3 15
Empty the basket, I say!—Why, man, why? . . . . iv 2 149
Heaven hath my empty words . . . . *Meas. for Meas.* ii 4 2
I shall find you empty of that fault . . . . . *L. L. Lost* v 2 878
The fold stands empty in the drowned field . . *M. N. Dream* ii 1 96
What have we here? A carrion Death, within whose empty eye There is a written scroll! . . . . *Mer. of Venice* ii 7 63
Uncapable of pity, void and empty From any dram of mercy . . iv 1 5
In the world I fill up a place, which may be better supplied when I have made it empty . . . . *As Y. Like It* i 2 205
Else a rude despiser of good manners, That in civility thou seem'st so empty . . . . ii 7 93
That drink, being poured out of a cup into a glass, by filling the one doth empty the other . . . . v 1 47
My falcon now is sharp and passing empty . . . *T. of Shrew* iv 1 193
Virtue is beauty, but the beauteous evil Are empty trunks o'erflourish'd by the devil . . . . *T. Night* iii 4 404
An empty casket, where the jewel of life By some damn'd hand was robb'd and ta'en away . . . . *K. John* v 1 40
Grief boundeth where it falls, Not with the empty hollowness, but weight *Richard II.* i 2 59
Empty lodgings and unfurnish'd walls, Unpeopled offices . . i 2 68

Empty. I'll empty all these veins, And shed my dear blood drop by drop *1 Hen. IV.* i 3 133
'When Arthur first in court'—Empty the jordan . . *2 Hen. IV.* ii 4 37
Can a weak empty vessel bear such a huge full hogshead? . . . ii 4 67
Dost thou so hunger for mine empty chair? . . . . iv 5 95
England, being empty of defence, Hath shook and trembled . *Hen. V.* i 2 153
I did never know so full a voice issue from so empty a heart . . iv 4 72
The saying is true, 'The empty vessel makes the greatest sound' . iv 4 73
Were't not all one, an empty eagle were set To guard the chicken from a hungry kite? . . . . *2 Hen. VI.* iii 1 248
And dead men's cries do fill the empty air . . . . v 2 4
And like an empty eagle Tire on the flesh of me and of my son! *3 Hen. VI.* i 1 268
Exhales this blood From cold and empty veins . . *Richard III.* i 2 59
Would not let it forth To seek the empty, vast and wandering air . i 4 39
Is the chair empty? is the sword unsway'd? Is the king dead? . iv 4 470
Nor my wishes More worth than empty vanities . . *Hen. VIII.* ii 3 69
I'm very sorry To sit here at this present, and behold That chair stand empty . . . . v 3 10
Though you bite so sharp at reasons, You are so empty of them *Tr. and Cr.* ii 2 34
Give as soft attachment to thy senses As infants' empty of all thought! iv 2 6
Her chariot is an empty hazel-nut . . . . *Rom. and Jul.* i 4 67
And about his shelves A beggarly account of empty boxes . . v 1 45
More inexorable far Than empty tigers or The roaring sea . . v 3 39
This dagger hath mista'en,—for, lo, his house Is empty . . . v 3 204
What will this come to? He commands us to provide, and give great gifts, And all out of an empty coffer . . . . *T. of Athens* i 2 199
'Faith, nothing but an empty box, sir . . . . . iii 1 16
I hope it remains not unkindly with your lordship that I returned you an empty messenger . . . . iii 6 40
Leave their false vows with him, Like empty purses pick'd . . iv 2 12
Turn him off, Like to the empty ass, to shake his ears . *J. Cæsar* iv 1 26
Let us seek out some desolate shade, and there Weep our sad bosoms empty . . . . *Macbeth* iv 3 2
His purse is empty already; all's golden words are spent *Hamlet* v 2 136
The town is empty; on the brow o' the sea Stand ranks of people *Othello* ii 1 53
When my good stars, that were my former guides, Have empty left their orbs, and shot their fires Into the abysm of hell . *Ant. and Cleo.* iii 13 146
My heart: Fear not; 'tis empty of all things but grief . *Cymbeline* iii 4 71
This Cloten was a fool, an empty purse; There was no money in't . iv 2 113
Purse and brain both empty . . . . v 4 166
Empty Old receptacles, or common shores, of filth . . *Pericles* iv 6 185
Empty-hearted. Nor are those empty-hearted whose low sound Reverbs no hollowness . . . . *Lear* i 1 155
Emptying our bosoms of their counsel sweet . . *M. N. Dream* i 1 216
A few sprays of us, The emptying of our fathers' luxury . *Hen. V.* iii 5 6
It hath been The untimely emptying of the happy throne . *Macbeth* iv 3 68
Emulate. Thine eye would emulate the diamond . . *Mer. Wives* iii 3 58
Prick'd on by a most emulate pride . . . . . *Hamlet* i 1 83
Emulation. The scholar's melancholy, which is emulation *As Y. Like It* iv 1 11
What madness rules in brainsick men, When for so slight and frivolous a cause Such factious emulations shall arise! . . *1 Hen. VI.* iv 1 114
The trust of England's honour, Keep off aloof with worthless emulation iv 4 21
Emulation now, who shall be nearest, Will touch us all too near *Rich. III.* ii 3 25
Grows to an envious fever Of pale and bloodless emulation *Troi. and Cres.* i 3 134
Their great general slept, Whilst emulation in the army crept . ii 2 212
Emulation hath a thousand sons That one by one pursue . . iii 3 156
The obligation of our blood forbids A gory emulation 'twixt us twain . iv 5 123
They threw their caps As they would hang them on the horns o' the moon, Shouting their emulation . . . . . . *Coriolanus* i 1 218
Mine emulation Hath not that honour in't it had . . . . i 10 12
My heart laments that virtue cannot live Out of the teeth of emulation *J. Cæsar* ii 3 14
Emulator. An envious emulator of every man's good parts *As Y. Like It* i 1 150
Emulous. A good quarrel to draw emulous factions . *Troi. and Cres.* ii 3 79
He is not emulous, as Achilles is . . . . . . ii 3 242
Made emulous missions 'mongst the gods themselves . . . iii 3 189
But, in mine emulous honour, let him die . . . . . iv 1 28
Enact. Spirits, which by mine art I have from their confines call'd to enact My present fancies . . . . *Tempest* iv 1 121
The king enacts more wonders than a man . . . *Richard III.* v 4 2
Betray with blushing The close enacts and counsels of the heart *T. Andron.* iv 2 118
What did you enact?—I did enact Julius Cæsar: I was killed i' the Capitol; Brutus killed me . . . . *Hamlet* iii 2 107
Enacted. It is enacted in the laws of Venice . . *Mer. of Venice* iv 1 348
Above human thought Enacted wonders with his sword and lance *1 Hen. VI.* i 1 122
What murder too Hath been enacted through your enmity . . iii 1 116
Charles, and the rest, it is enacted thus . . . . . v 4 123
Enacture. The violence of either grief or joy Their own enactures with themselves destroy . . . . *Hamlet* iii 2 207
Enamelled. He makes sweet music with the enamell'd stones *T. G. of V.* ii 7 28
I see the jewel best enamelled Will lose his beauty . *Com. of Errors* ii 1 109
There the snake throws her enamell'd skin . . *M. N. Dream* ii 1 255
Enamoured. He is enamoured on Hero; I pray you, dissuade him from her . . . . *Much Ado* ii 1 170
Sing again: Mine ear is much enamour'd of thy note . *M. N. Dream* iii 1 141
What visions have I seen! Methought I was enamour'd of an ass . iv 1 82
I think thou art enamoured On his follies . . . *1 Hen. IV.* v 2 70
They that, when Richard lived, would have him die, Are now become enamour'd on his grave . . . . *2 Hen. IV.* i 3 102
Affliction is enamour'd of thy parts . . . . *Rom. and Jul.* iii 3 2
Encamp. Beyond the river we'll encamp ourselves . . *Hen. V.* iii 6 180
Bid him encamp his soldiers where they are . . *T. Andron.* iv 2 126
Two such opposed kings encamp them still In man as well as herbs, grace and rude will . . . . *Rom. and Jul.* ii 3 27
Encamped. What, is the king encamp'd?—He is, Sir John *1 Hen. IV.* iv 2 82
In night's coverture, Thy brother being carelessly encamp'd *3 Hen VI.* iv 2 14
Encave. Do but encave yourself, And mark the fleers, the gibes *Othello* iv 1 82
Enceladus. Not Enceladus, With all his threatening band of Typhon's brood . . . . *T. Andron* iv 2 93
Enchafed. I never did like molestation view On the enchafed flood *Othello* ii 1 17
Yet as rough, Their royal blood enchafed, as the rudest wind *Cymbeline* iv 2 174
Enchant. Now I want Spirits to enforce, art to enchant . . *Tempest* Epil. 14
Speak, Pucelle, and enchant him with thy words . *1 Hen. VI.* iii 3 40
The imaginary relish is so sweet That it enchants my sense *Tr. and Cr.* iii 2 21
I will enchant the old Andronicus With words more sweet *T. Andron.* iv 4 89
He enchants societies into him; Half all men's hearts are his *Cymbeline* i 6 167
Enchanted. Some enchanted trifle to abuse me . . . *Tempest* v 1 112
That all eyes saw his eyes enchanted with gazes . . *L. L. Lost* ii 1 247
In such a night Medea gather'd the enchanted herbs . *Mer. of Venice* v 1 13

Enchanted. Damn'd as thou art, thou hast enchanted her *Othello* i 2 63

Enchanting. Of such enchanting presence and discourse *Com. of Errors* iii 2 166

One whom the music of his own vain tongue Doth ravish like enchanting harmony *L. L. Lost* i 1 168

With these your white enchanting fingers touch'd *Troi. and Cres.* iii 1 164

It sung Sweet varied notes, enchanting every ear! *T. Andron.* iii 1 86

And now about the cauldron sing, Like elves and fairies in a ring, Enchanting all that you put in *Macbeth* iv 1 43

I must from this enchanting queen break off *Ant. and Cleo.* i 2 132

Enchantingly. Of all sorts enchantingly beloved *As Y. Like It* i 1 174

Enchantment. After the last enchantment you did here *T. Night* iii 1 123

And you, enchantment,—Worthy enough a herdsman *W. Tale* iv 4 446

Enchantress. Fell banning hag, enchantress, hold thy tongue! *1 Hen. VI.* v 3 42

Enchased with all the honours of the world *2 Hen. VI.* i 2 8

Encircle. Then let them all encircle him about *Mer. Wives* iv 4 56

Encircled you to hear with reverence Your exposition *2 Hen. IV.* iv 2 6

Enclosed. If therefore you dare trust my honesty, That lies enclosed in this trunk *W. Tale* i 2 435

The dead with charity enclosed in clay *Hen. V.* iv 8 129

Enclosed were they with their enemies *1 Hen. VI.* i 1 136

His soldiers fell to spoil, Whilst we by Antony are all enclosed *J. Cæsar* v 3 8

Titinius is enclosed round about With horsemen v 3 28

And would under-peep her lids, To see the enclosed lights *Cymbeline* ii 2 21

Encloseth. Even so thy breast encloseth my poor heart *Richard III.* i 2 205

Enclosing. Against the Duke of Suffolk, for enclosing the commons of Melford *2 Hen. VI.* i 3 24

Enclouded. In their thick breaths, Rank of gross diet, shall we be enclouded *Ant. and Cleo.* v 2 212

Encompassed. Have I encompassed you? *Mer. Wives* ii 2 159

Was round encompassed and set upon *1 Hen. VI.* i 1 114

Hag of all despite, Encompass'd with thy lustful paramours! iii 2 53

Or as a bear, encompass'd round with dogs *3 Hen. VI.* ii 1 15

Yonder's the head of that arch-enemy That sought to be encompass'd with your crown ii 2 3

When could they say till now, that talk'd of Rome, That her wide walls encompass'd but one man? *J. Cæsar* i 2 155

Encompasseth. Look, how this ring encompasseth thy finger, Even so thy breast encloseth my poor heart *Richard III.* i 2 204

Encompassment. Finding By this encompassment and drift of question That they do know my son *Hamlet* ii 1 10

Encore qu'il est contre son jurement de pardonner aucun prisonnier *Hen. V.* iv 4 53

Encounter. Fair encounter Of two most rare affections! *Tempest* iii 1 74

And these fresh nymphs encounter every one In country footing iv 1 137

These lords At this encounter do so much admire That they devour their reason v 1 154

Of all the fair resort of gentlemen That every day with parle encounter me, In thy opinion which is worthiest love? *T. G. of Ver.* i 2 5

I would prevent The loose encounters of lascivious men ii 7 41

Comes me in the instant of our encounter *Mer. Wives* iii 5 74

If I must die, I will encounter darkness as a bride *Meas. for Meas.* iii 1 84

If the encounter acknowledge itself hereafter, it may compel him to her recompense iii 1 261

The fashion of the world is to avoid cost, and you encounter it *Much Ado* i 1 98

With the force And strong encounter of my amorous tale i 1 327

Saw afar off in the orchard this amiable encounter iii 3 161

Confess'd the vile encounters they have had A thousand times in secret iv 1 94

I did encounter that obscene and most preposterous event *L. L. Lost* i 1 244

Encounters mounted are Against your peace v 2 82

That they call compliment is like the encounter of two dog-apes *As Y. L. It* ii 5 27

Mountains may be removed with earthquakes and so encounter iii 2 196

To give you over at this first encounter *T. of Shrew* i 2 105

That with your strange encounter much amazed me iv 5 54

Let not your hate encounter with my love For loving where you do *All's W.* i 3 214

But that your daughter, ere she seems as won, Desires this ring; appoints him an encounter iii 7 32

Will you encounter the house? my niece is desirous you should enter, if your trade be to her *T. Night* iii 1 82

Their encounters, though not personal, have been royally attorneyed with interchange of gifts *W. Tale* i 1 29

Good time encounter her! ii 1 20

If thou refuse And wilt encounter with my wrath, say so ii 3 138

With what encounter so uncurrent I Have strain'd to appear thus iii 2 50

I never heard of such another encounter, which lames report to follow it v 2 62

Let belief and life encounter so As doth the fury of two desperate men *K. John* iii 1 32

Tell us how near is danger, That we may arm us to encounter it *Rich. II.* v 3 48

Thou dost belie him; He never did encounter with Glendower *1 Hen. IV.* i 3 114

If they 'scape from your encounter, then they light on us ii 2 64

There is many a soul Shall pay full dearly for this encounter v 1 84

And hath sent out A speedy power to encounter you *2 Hen. IV.* i 1 133

If thou encounter any such, apprehend him, an thou dost me love *Hen. V.* iv 7 165

I'll by a sign give notice to our friends, That Charles the Dauphin may encounter them *1 Hen. VI.* iii 2 9

Methinks the power that Edward hath in field Should not be able to encounter mine *3 Hen. VI.* iv 8 36

I spy a black, suspicious, threatening cloud, That will encounter with our glorious sun v 3 5

To leave this keen encounter of our wits *Richard III.* i 2 115

At our last encounter, The Duke of Buckingham came from his trial *Hen. VIII.* iv 1 4

It shall not speak of your pretty encounters *Troi. and Cres.* iii 2 217

And wouldst do so, I think, should we encounter As often as we eat *Cor.* i 10 9

Our very priests must become mockers, if they shall encounter such ridiculous subjects as you are ii 1 94

I am most fortunate, thus accidentally to encounter you iv 3 40

I have nightly since Dreamt of encounters 'twixt thyself and me iv 5 129

In this strange and sad habiliment, I will encounter with Andronicus *T. Andron.* v 2 2

Nor bide the encounter of assailing eyes *Rom. and Jul.* i 1 219

Is he a man to encounter Tybalt?—Why, what is Tybalt? ii 4 17

The imagined happiness that both Receive in either by this dear encounter ii 6 29

Three parts of him Is ours already, and the man entire Upon the next encounter yields him ours *J. Cæsar* i 3 156

They encounter thee with their hearts' thanks *Macbeth* iii 4 9

I'll loose my daughter to him: Be you and I behind an arras then; Mark the encounter *Hamlet* ii 2 164

That, seeing, unseen, We may of their encounter frankly judge iii 1 34

Only got the tune of the time and outward habit of encounter v 2 199

Encounter. Bold in the quarrel's right, roused to the encounter *Lear* ii 1 56

Upon the first encounter, drave them *Ant. and Cleo.* i 2 98

Till which encounter, It is my business too i 4 79

Have charged him, At the sixth hour of morn, at noon, at midnight, To encounter me with orisons *Cymbeline* i 3 32

Fit That all the plagues of hell should at one time Encounter such revolt i 6 112

Found no opposition But what he look'd for should oppose and she Should from encounter guard ii 5 19

Encountered. We were encounter'd by a mighty rock *Com. of Errors* i 1 102

'Shall I,' says she, 'that have so oft encountered him with scorn, write to him that I love him?' *Much Ado* ii 3 132

Men of peace, well encountered *L. L. Lost* v 1 37

Shall at home be encountered with a shame as ample *All's Well* iv 3 81

You are well encounter'd here, my cousin Mowbray *2 Hen. IV.* iv 2 1

Our wars Will turn unto a peaceful comic sport, When ladies crave to be encounter'd with *1 Hen. VI.* ii 2 46

I soon encountered, And interchanging blows I quickly shed Some of his bastard blood iv 6 18

Once I encounter'd him, and thus I said iv 7 37

He shall be encountered with a man as good as himself *2 Hen. VI.* iv 2 124

But match to match I have encounter'd him v 2 10

Here's the Earl of Wiltshire's blood, Whom I encounter'd *3 Hen. VI.* i 1 15

Painted to the hilt In blood of those that had encounter'd him i 4 13

Red as Titan's face Blushing to be encounter'd with a cloud *T. Andron.* ii 4 32

How goes the world, that I am thus encounter'd With clamorous demands of date-broke bonds? *T. of Athens* ii 2 37

Upon that were my thoughts tiring, when we encountered iii 6 5

In the dead vast and middle of the night, Been thus encounter'd *Hamlet* i 2 199

Well encounter'd! 'Tis almost night *Cymbeline* iii 6 66

Encounterer. O, these encounterers, so glib of tongue! *Troi. and Cres.* iv 5 58

Encountering. Like vassalage at unawares encountering The eye of majesty iii 2 40

Both our powers, with smiling fronts encountering *Coriolanus* i 6 8

Encourage. Let us go thank him and encourage him *As Y. Like It* i 2 252

Encourage myself in my certainty *All's Well* ii 6 80

I with death and with Reward did threaten and encourage him *W. Tale* iii 2 165

If thou dost find him tractable to us, Encourage him *Richard III.* iii 1 175

Encouraged. Come on refresh'd, new-added, and encouraged *J. Cæsar* iv 3 209

Encouragement. For the encouragement of the like, which else would stand under grievous imposition *Meas. for Meas.* i 2 192

Lines of fair comfort and encouragement *Richard III.* v 2 6

Encroaching. And lofty proud encroaching tyranny *2 Hen. VI.* iv 1 96

Encumbered. With arms encumber'd thus, or this head-shake *Hamlet* i 5 174

End. I, thus neglecting worldly ends, all dedicated To closeness *Tempest* i 2 89

With colours fairer painted their foul ends i 2 143

Which end o' the beam should bow ii 1 131

The latter end of his commonwealth forgets the beginning ii 1 157

Most poor matters Point to rich ends iii 1 4

And with each end of thy blue bow dost crown My bosky acres iv 1 80

Spring come to you at the farthest In the very end of harvest! iv 1 115

Shortly shall all my labours end, and thou Shalt have the air at freedom iv 1 265

To work mine end upon their senses v 1 53

Muse not that I thus suddenly proceed; For what I will, I will, and there an end *T. G. of Ver.* i 3 65

And that letter hath she delivered, and there an end ii 1 168

I know it well, sir; you always end ere you begin ii 4 31

A slave, that still an end turns me to shame! iv 4 67

Go thou with her to the west end of the wood v 3 9

I'll woo you like a soldier, at arms' end v 4 57

Ha! o' my life, if I were young again, the sword should end it.—It is petter that friends is the sword, and end it *Mer. Wives* i 1 41

We three, to hear it and end it between them i 1 144

I will make an end of my dinner; there's pippins and cheese to come i 2 12

At night, in faith, at the latter end of a sea-coal fire i 4 9

Hard by; at street end; he will be here anon iv 2 40

Hath a purpose More grave and wrinkled than the aims and ends Of burning youth *Meas. for Meas.* i 3 5

But, ere they live, to end ii 2 100

By my troth, I'll go with thee to the lane's end iv 3 188

'Tis a physic That's bitter to sweet end iv 6 8

It is ten times true; for truth is truth To the end of reckoning v 1 46

To procure my fall And by the doom of death end woes and all *C. of Er.* i 1 2

When your words are done, My woes end likewise with the evening sun i 1 28

That the world may witness that my end Was wrought by nature, not by vile offence i 1 34

Fasten'd ourselves at either end the mast i 1 86

But here must end the story of my life i 1 138

But to procrastinate his lifeless end i 1 159

Time himself is bald and therefore to the world's end will have bald followers ii 2 108

Go thou And buy a rope's end iv 1 16

And told thee to what purpose and what end.—You sent me for a rope's end iv 1 97

To what end did I bid thee hie thee home?—To a rope's-end, sir; and to that end am I returned.—And to that end, sir, I will welcome you iv 4 15

'Respice finem,' respect your end; or rather, the prophecy like the parrot, 'beware the rope's-end' iv 4 45

You always end with a jade's trick: I know you of old *Much Ado* i 1 145

Ere you flout old ends any further, examine your conscience i 1 290

Was't not to this end That thou began'st to twist so fine a story? i 1 312

You are he: graces will appear, and there's an end ii 1 129

Will your grace command me any service to the world's end? ii 1 272

To what end? He would make but a sport of it ii 3 162

This is the end of the charge iii 3 78

What is the end of study? let me know *L. L. Lost* i 1 55

Jig off a tune at the tongue's end iii 1 12

Thou hast it ad dunghill, at the fingers' ends, as they say v 1 81

I have acquainted you withal, to the end to crave your assistance v 1 122

He is not so big as the end of his club v 1 139

Therefore I'll darkly end the argument v 2 23

Curtsy, sweet hearts; and so the measure ends v 2 221

And wonder what they were and to what end Their shallow shows v 2 304

Speak for yourselves; my wit is at an end v 2 430

Why dost thou stay?—For the latter end of his name v 2 630

Fashioning our humours Even to the opposed end of our intents v 2 768

At the twelvemonth's end I'll change my black gown for a faithful friend v 2 843

Our wooing doth not end like an old play v 2 884

It wants a twelvemonth and a day, And then 'twill end v 2 888

It should have followed in the end of our show v 2 898

End. Thy love ne'er alter till thy sweet life end! *M. N. Dream* ii 2 61
Amen, to that fair prayer, say I; And then end life when I end loyalty! ii 2 63
With league whose date till death shall never end . . . iii 2 373
I will sing it in the latter end of a play . . . iv 1 223
To show our simple skill, That is the true beginning of our end . v 1 111
She comes; and her passion ends the play . . . v 1 321
And, farewell, friends; Thus Thisby ends . . . v 1 353
Fare ye well awhile: I'll end my exhortation after dinner *Mer. of Venice* i 1 104
The ewes, being rank, In the end of autumn turned to the rams . i 3 82
If thou keep promise, I shall end this strife, Become a Christian . ii 3 20
The end is, he hath lost a ship.—I would it might prove the end of his losses . . . . iii 1 19
Then, if he lose, he makes a swan-like end, Fading in music . . iii 2 44
Tell her the process of Antonio's end; Say how I loved you . . iv 1 274
They are taught their manage, and to that end riders dearly hired *As Y. Like It* i 1 13
I hope I shall see an end of him. . . . . . i 1 171
If it please your ladyships, you may see the end; for the best is yet to do i 2 120
Sing; and you that will not, hold your tongues.—Well, I'll end the song ii 5 32
For my sake be comfortable; hold death awhile at the arm's end . ii 6 10
Last scene of all, That ends this strange eventful history . . ii 7 164
Or at every sentence end, Will I Rosalinda write . . . iii 2 144
Many a man knows no end of his goods . . . . iii 3 53
Many a man has good horns, and knows no end of them . . . iii 3 55
Let us do those ends That here were well begun and well begot . v 4 176
We will begin these rites, As we do trust they'll end, in true delights v 4 204
To what end are all these words? . . . *T. of Shrew* i 2 250
Thus have I politicly begun my reign, And 'tis my hope to end successfully iv 1 192
Straight to him; And bring our horses unto Long-lane end . . iv 3 187
Let's stand aside and see the end of this controversy . . . v 1 64
Let's follow, to see the end of this ado . . . . v 1 147
She will not.—The fouler fortune mine, and there an end . . v 2 98
Why, there't serves well again.—An end, sir; to your business *All's Well* ii 2 66
And to-night, When I should take possession of the bride, End ere I do begin . . . . ii 5 29
A good traveller is something at the latter end of a dinner . . ii 5 31
Come, night; end, day! For with the dark, poor thief, I'll steal away iii 2 131
For which live long to thank both heaven and me! You may so in the end iv 2 68
Till they attain to their abhorred ends . . . . iv 3 28
ALL'S WELL THAT ENDS WELL: still the fine's the crown; Whate'er the course, the end is the renown . . . . . iv 4 35
ALL'S WELL THAT ENDS WELL yet, Though time seem so adverse . . v 1 25
All yet seems well; and if it end so meet, The bitter past, more welcome is the sweet . . . . v 3 333
Are you full of them?—Ay, sir, I have them at my fingers' ends *T. Night* i 3 83
Journeys end in lovers meeting, Every wise man's son doth know . ii 3 44
If thou hast her not i' the end, call me cut . . . ii 3 203
And the end,—what should that alphabetical position portend? . ii 5 130
A should follow, but O does.—And O shall end, I hope . . ii 5 144
This shall end without the perdition of souls . . . iii 4 317
Has hurt me, and there's the end on't . . . . v 1 202
He holds Belzebub at the staves's end as well as a man in his case may do v 1 292
Embraced, as it were, from the ends of opposed winds . *W. Tale* i 1 34
It was my negligence, Not weighing well the end . . . i 2 258
Commend it strangely to some place Where chance may nurse or end it ii 3 183
The violent carriage of it Will clear or end the business . . iii 1 18
But to make an end of the ship, to see how the sea flap-dragoned it . iii 3 99
Now here, At upper end o' the table, now i' the middle . . iv 4 59
Every lane's end, every shop, church, session . . . iv 4 700
This day, all things begun come to ill end! . . *K. John* iii 1 94
Very little pains Will bring this labour to an happy end . . . iii 2 10
I defy all counsel, all redress, But that which ends all counsel, true redress, Death, death . . . . iii 4 24
And pick strong matter of revolt and wrath Out of the bloody fingers' ends of John . . . . iii 4 168
There end thy brave, and turn thy face in peace . . . v 2 159
Let this end where it begun . . . . *Richard II.* i 1 158
Thy sometimes brother's wife With her companion grief must end her life i 2 55
For sorrow ends not when it seemeth done . . . . i 2 61
So I regreet The daintiest last, to make the end most sweet . . i 3 68
Four lagging winters and four wanton springs End in a word . . i 3 215
And in the end, Having my freedom, boast of nothing else But that I was a journeyman to grief . . . . . . i 3 272
More are men's ends mark'd than their lives before . . . ii 1 11
Though death be poor, it ends a mortal woe . . . ii 1 152
Who perform'd The bloody office of his timeless end . . . iv 1 5
Join not with grief, fair woman, do not so, To make my end too sudden v 1 17
My guilt be on my head, and there an end. Take leave and part . v 1 69
While I question my puny drawer to what end he gave me the sugar *1 Hen. IV.* ii 4 33
The end of life cancels all bands . . . . . iii 2 157
Meet me at town's end.—I will, captain . . . . iv 2 10
To the latter end of a fray and the beginning of a feast Fits a dull fighter and a keen guest . . . . iv 2 85
They are for the town's end, to beg during life . . . v 3 39
If not, honour comes unlooked for, and there's an end . . . v 3 65
The hour is come To end the one of us . . . . v 4 69
But in the end, to stop my ear indeed, Thou hast a sigh to blow away this praise . . . . . *2 Hen. IV.* i 1 79
The rude scene may end, And darkness be the burier of the dead! . i 1 159
Let the end try the man . . . . . . ii 2 50
Do not speak like a death's-head; do not bid me remember mine end . ii 4 255
Drinks off candles' ends for flap-dragons . . . . . ii 4 267
Well, hearken at the end . . . . . . ii 4 304
Let time shape, and there an end . . . . . iii 2 358
So the question stands. Briefly to this end . . . . iv 1 54
And either end in peace, which God so frame! Or to the place of difference call the swords Which must decide it . . . iv 1 180
To end one doubt by death Revives two greater in the heirs of life . iv 1 199
If God doth give successful end To this debate that bleedeth at our doors iv 4 1
This apoplexy will certain be his end . . . . iv 4 130
This part of his conjoins with my disease, And helps to end me . iv 5 65
Laud be to God! even there my life must end . . . iv 5 236
I was lately here in the end of a displeasing play . . . Epil. 9
So may a thousand actions, once afoot, End in one purpose *Hen. V.* i 2 212
It will endure cold as another man's sword will: and there's an end ii 1 11
A' made a finer end and went away an it had been any christom child . ii 3 11
And smile upon his fingers' ends . . . . . ii 3 16
To that end, As matching to his youth and vanity . . . ii 4 129
I know the disciplines of war; and there is an end . . . iii 2 153
End. Our expectation hath this day an end . . . *Hen. V.* iii 3 44
Preachers to us all, admonishing That we should dress us fairly for our end . . . . iv 1 10
We see yonder the beginning of the day, but I think we shall never see the end of it . . . . iv 1 92
I shall catch the fly, your cousin, in the latter end and she must be blind too . . . . v 2 341
By magic verses have contrived his end . . *1 Hen. VI.* i 1 27
With Henry's death the English circle ends . . . . i 2 136
These grey locks, the pursuivants of death, Nestor-like aged in an age of care, Argue the end of Edmund Mortimer . . . . ii 5 7
Defer no time, delays have dangerous ends . . . . iii 2 33
Kings and mightiest potentates must die, For that's the end of human misery . . . . iii 2 137
How I will work To bring this matter to the wished end . . . iii 3 28
By water shall he die, and take his end . . *2 Hen. VI.* i 4 36
Here let them end it; and God defend the right! . . . ii 3 55
And, in the end being rescued, I have seen Him caper upright . . iii 1 364
Mine hair be fix'd on end, as one distract. . . . . iii 2 318
Those which fly before the battle ends May, even in their wives' and children's sight, Be hang'd up for example . . . . . iv 2 188
But if thy arms be to no other end, The king hath yielded unto thy demand . . . . v 1 39
O, let the vile world end, And the premised flames of the last day Knit earth and heaven together! . . . . v 2 40
By giving the house of Lancaster leave to breathe, It will outrun you, father, in the end . . . . . *3 Hen. VI.* i 2 14
Here must I stay, and here my life must end . . . . i 4 26
Pass'd over to the end they were created . . . . . ii 5 39
My suit is at an end.—The widow likes him not . . . iii 2 81
To that end I shortly mind to leave you.—Leave me, or tarry . iv 1 64
Take that, to end thy agony.—And there's for twitting me with perjury v 5 39
O, let me make the period to my curse!—'Tis done by me, and ends in 'Margaret' . . . . *Richard III.* i 3 239
False-boding woman, end thy frantic curse . . . . i 3 247
My hair doth stand on end to hear her curses . . . . i 3 304
Thus I clothe my naked villany With old odd ends stolen out of holy writ . . . . i 3 337
Award Either of you to be the other's end . . . . ii 1 15
I see, as in a map, the end of all . . . . . ii 4 54
O, preposterous And frantic outrage, end thy damned spleen! . . ii 4 64
And to that end we wish'd your lordship here. . . . iii 5 67
When mine oratory grew to an end . . . . . iii 7 20
Some followers of mine own, At the lower end of the hall, hurl'd up their caps . . . . iii 7 35
He wonders to what end you have assembled Such troops of citizens . iii 7 84
But at hand, at hand, Ensues his piteous and unpitied end . . iv 4 74
Bloody thou art, bloody will be thy end . . . . iv 4 194
How long shall that title 'ever' last?—Sweetly in force unto her fair life's end . . . . iv 4 351
Bloody and guilty, guiltily awake, And in a bloody battle end thy days! v 3 147
Surely, sir, There's in him stuff that puts him to these ends *Hen. VIII.* i 1 58
To as much end As give a crutch to the dead . . . . i 1 171
What warlike voice, And to what end, is this? . . . . i 4 51
Certainly The cardinal is the end of this . . . . . ii 1 40
Go with me, like good angels, to my end . . . . . ii 1 75
When old time shall lead him to his end, Goodness and he fill up one monument! . . . . ii 1 93
Sir Nicholas Vaux, Who undertakes you to your end . . . ii 1 97
Heaven has an end in all . . . . ii 1 124
All that dare Look into these affairs see this main end . . . ii 2 41
If your grace Could but be brought to know our ends are honest, You'd feel more comfort . . . . iii 1 154
Mine own ends Have been mine so that evermore they pointed To the good of your most sacred person . . . . . . iii 2 171
All that world of wealth I have drawn together For mine own ends . iii 2 212
How innocent I was From any private malice in his end, His noble jury and foul cause can witness . . . . iii 2 268
Let all the ends thou aim'st at be thy country's, Thy God's, and truth's iii 2 447
In great extremity; and fear'd She'll with the labour end . . v 1 20
And the end Was ever, to do well . . . . . v 3 36
I see your end; 'Tis my undoing . . . . . v 3 61
I will leave all as I found it, and there an end . . *Troi. and Cres.* i 1 91
Well, the gods are above; time must friend or end . . . i 2 84
To end a tale of length, Troy in our weakness stands, not in her strength . . . . i 3 136
As near as the extremest ends Of parallels . . . . i 3 167
Let all pitiful goers-between be called to the world's end after my name [Pandarus] . . . . iii 2 209
The end crowns all, And that old common arbitrator, Time, Will one day end it . . . . iv 5 224
Fate, hear me what I say! I reck not though I end my life to-day . v 6 26
I say unto you, what he hath done famously, he did it to that end *Coriolanus* i 1 37
Where great patricians shall attend and shrug, I' the end admire . i 9 5
He cannot temperately transport his honours From where he should begin and end . . . . ii 1 241
For an end, We must suggest the people in what hatred He still hath held them . . . . ii 1 260
And is content To spend the time to end it . . . . ii 2 133
What may be sworn by, both divine and human, Seal what I end withal! . . . . iii 1 142
A brand to the end o' the world . . . . . iii 1 304
Will prove too bloody, and the end of it Unknown to the beginning . iii 1 328
Which, for your best ends, You adopt your policy . . . iii 2 47
What then! He'ld make an end of thy posterity . . . iv 2 26
Set at upper end o' the table . . . . . . iv 5 205
Your soldiers use him as the grace 'fore meat, Their talk at table, and their thanks at end . . . . iv 7 4
Only their ends You have respected . . . . . v 3 4
Rather to show a noble grace to both parts Than seek the end of one . v 3 122
Thou know'st, great son, The end of war's uncertain . . . v 3 141
Down: an end; This is the last: so we will home to Rome . . v 3 171
To this end, He bow'd his nature, never known before But to be rough v 6 24
Holp to reap the fame Which he did end all his . . . v 6 37
But there to end Where he was to begin . . . . v 6 65
By my soul, were there worse end than death, That end upon them should be executed . . . . . *T. Andron.* ii 3 302
Then have I kept it to a worthy end . . . . . iii 1 174
When will this fearful slumber have an end? . . . . iii 1 253

End. You must be hanged.—Hanged! by'r lady, then I have brought up a neck to a fair end *T. Andron.* iv 4 49
The feast is ready, which the careful Titus Hath ordain'd to an honourable end v 3 22
And the continuance of their parents' rage, Which, but their children's end, nought could remove *Rom. and Jul.* Prol. 11
These violent delights have violent ends And in their triumph die ii 6 9
This day's black fate on more days doth depend; This but begins the woe others must end iii 1 125
His fault concludes but what the law should end iii 1 190
Vile earth, to earth resign; end motion here! iii 2 59
There is no end, no limit, measure, bound, In that word's death iii 2 125
Well, death 's the end of all iii 3 92
Therefore we'll have some half a dozen friends, And there an end iii 4 28
Poison, I see, hath been his timeless end v 3 162
I cannot think but, in the end, the villanies of man will set him clear *T. of Athens* iii 3 30
My lord and I have made an end; I have no more to reckon, he to spend iii 4 55
The middle of humanity thou never knewest, but the extremity of both ends iv 3 301
What viler thing upon the earth than friends Who can bring noblest minds to basest ends! iv 3 471
Lips, let sour words go by and language end v 1 223
What can be avoided Whose end is purposed by the mighty gods? *J. C.* ii 2 27
Seeing that death, a necessary end, Will come when it will come ii 2 36
This same day Must end that work the ides of March begun v 1 114
O, that a man might know The end of this day's business ere it come! But it sufficeth that the day will end, And then the end is known v 1 124
Time is come round, And where I did begin, there shall I end v 3 24
The time has been, That, when the brains were out, the man would die, And there an end *Macbeth* iii 4 80
Spiteful and wrathful, who, as others do, Loves for his own ends iii 5 13
This night I'll spend Unto a dismal and a fatal end iii 5 21
O my breast, Thy hope ends here! iv 3 114
Your cause of sorrow Must not be measured by his worth, for then It hath no end v 8 46
And each particular hair to stand an end *Hamlet* i 5 19
It did seem to shatter all his bulk And end his being ii 1 96
To what end, my lord?—That you must teach me ii 2 292
The humorous man shall end his part in peace ii 2 336
Or to take arms against a sea of troubles, And by opposing end them iii 1 60
To die: to sleep; No more; and by a sleep to say we end The heart-ache iii 1 61
For any thing so overdone is from the purpose of playing, whose end, both at the first and now, was and is, to hold, as 'twere, the mirror up to nature iii 2 23
But, orderly to end where I begun iii 2 220
Our thoughts are ours, their ends none of our own iii 2 223
Your pardon and my return shall be the end of my business iii 2 330
Your bedded hair, like life in excrements, Start up, and stand an end iii 4 122
Come, sir, to draw toward an end with you. Good night, mother iii 4 216
Such officers do the king best service in the end iv 2 18
Your fat king and your lean beggar is but variable service, two dishes, but to one table: that's the end iv 3 26
Pretty Ophelia!—Indeed, la, without an oath, I'll make an end on 't iv 5 58
They say he made a good end iv 5 186
When in your motion you are hot and dry—As make your bouts more violent to that end iv 7 159
There's a divinity that shapes our ends, Rough-hew them how we will v 2 10
In this plainness Harbour more craft and more corrupter ends *Lear* ii 2 108
'Tis on such ground, and to such wholesome end, As clears her from all blame ii 4 146
If she live long, And in the end meet the old course of death, Women will all turn monsters iii 7 101
Is wretchedness deprived that benefit, To end itself by death? iv 6 62
If you miscarry, Your business of the world hath so an end v 1 45
Is this the promised end?—Or image of that horror? v 3 263
Not I for love and duty, But seeming so, for my peculiar end *Othello* i 1 60
Here is my journey's end, here is my butt v 2 267
That war had end, and the time's state Made friends of them *A. and C.* i 2 95
So, the gods keep you, And make the hearts of Romans serve your ends! iii 2 37
I was of late as petty to his ends As is the morn-dew on the myrtle-leaf iii 12 8
Whose bosom was my crownet, my chief end iv 12 27
There is left us Ourselves to end ourselves iv 14 22
I have done my work ill, friends: O, make an end Of what I have begun iv 14 105
The miserable change now at my end Lament nor sorrow at iv 15 51
We have no friend But resolution, and the briefest end iv 15 91
It is great To do that thing that ends all other deeds v 2 5
If thou wert honourable, Thou wouldst have told this tale for virtue, not For such an end thou seek'st *Cymbeline* i 6 144
To what end? Why should I write this down, that's riveted, Screw'd to my memory? ii 2 42
Son, let your mother end iii 1 39
Our crows shall fare the better for you; and there's an end iii 1 84
Nay, be brief: I see into thy end, and am almost A man already iii 4 169
Gone she is To death or to dishonour; and my end Can make good use of either iii 5 63
The sweat of industry would dry and die, But for the end it works to iii 6 32
Be not angry, sir.—'Lack, to what end? v 3 56
Which neither here I'll keep nor bear again, But end it by some means v 3 83
Then shall Posthumus end his miseries v 4 144; v 5 441
How you shall speed in your journey's end, I think you'll never return to tell one v 4 190
Failing of her end by his strange absence, Grew shameless-desperate v 5 57
Let me end the story: I slew him there v 5 286
Their dear loss, The more of you 'twas felt, the more it shaped Unto my end v 5 347
It was wise nature's end in the donation, To be his evidence now v 5 367
And yet the end of all is bought thus dear, The breath is gone, and the sore eyes see clear *Pericles* i 1 98
Could I rage and roar As doth the sea she lies in, yet the end Must be as 'tis iii 3 11
The gods revenge it upon me and mine, To the end of generation! iii 3 25
Where a man may serve seven years for the loss of a leg, and have not money enough in the end to buy him a wooden one iv 6 183
But, not to be a troubler of your peace, I will end here v 1 154
Thaisa was my mother, who did end The minute I began v 1 213
End-all. That but this blow Might be the be-all and the end-all here, But here, upon this bank and shoal of time *Macbeth* i 7 5
Endamage. Your slander never can endamage him *T. G. of Ver.* iii 2 43
Endamage. And lay new platforms to endamage them 1 *Hen. VI.* ii 1 77
Endamagement. Have hither march'd to your endamagement *K. John* ii 1 209
Endanger. I hold him but a fool that will endanger His body for a girl that loves him not *T. G. of Ver.* v 4 133
Thinkest thou I'll endanger my soul gratis? *Mer. Wives* ii 2 16
Endart. No more deep will I endart mine eye Than your consent gives strength to make it fly *Rom. and Jul.* i 3 98
Endeared. And thou, to be endeared to a king, Made it no conscience to destroy a prince *K. John* iv 2 228
You broke your word, When you were more endear'd to it than now 2 *Hen. IV.* ii 3 11
So infinitely endear'd *T. of Athens* i 2 233
I am so much endeared to that lord; he's ever sending iii 2 36
Endeavour. All things in common nature should produce Without sweat or endeavour *Tempest* ii 1 160
Only to despite them, I will endeavour any thing *Much Ado* ii 2 31
The endeavour of this present breath may buy That honour *L. L. Lost* i 1 5
I thank you, gracious lords, For all your fair endeavours v 2 740
With all the fierce endeavour of your wit v 2 863
My best endeavours shall be done herein *Mer. of Venice* ii 2 182
Use thou all the endeavour of a man In speed iii 4 48
I wish might be found in the calendar of my past endeavours *All's Well* i 3 5
To my endeavours give consent; Of heaven, not me, make an experiment ii 1 156
Endeavour thyself to sleep, and leave thy vain bibble babble *T. Night* iv 2 104
And, with my best endeavours in your absence, Your discontenting father strive to qualify *W. Tale* iv 4 542
We must awake endeavour for defence *K. John* ii 1 81
With excellent endeavour of drinking 2 *Hen. IV.* iv 3 130
In divers functions, Setting endeavour in continual motion *Hen. V.* i 2 185
I have labour'd, With all my wits, my pains and strong endeavours v 2 25
Promise, Kate, you will endeavour for your French part of such a boy v 2 228
And with your best endeavour have stirr'd up My liefest liege 2 *Hen. VI.* iii 1 163
Every man that means to live well endeavours to trust to himself *Richard III.* i 4 147
Which went Beyond all man's endeavours *Hen. VIII.* iii 2 169
My endeavours Have ever come too short of my desires iii 2 169
I'll endeavour deeds to match these words *Troi. and Cres.* iv 5 259
Why should our endeavour be so loved and the performance so loathed? v 10 39
Their endeavour keeps in the wonted pace *Hamlet* ii 2 353
Some blood drawn on me would beget opinion Of my more fierce endeavour *Lear* ii 1 36
They have put forth the haven . . . Where their appointment we may best discover, And look on their endeavour *Ant. and Cleo.* iv 10 9
We with our travels will endeavour us *Pericles* ii 4 56
Endeavour'd my advancement to the throne 1 *Hen. VI.* ii 5 69
Ended. Our revels now are ended *Tempest* iv 1 148
When you went onward on this ended action *Much Ado* i 1 299
The music ended, We'll fit the kid-fox with a pennyworth ii 3 43
When after that the holy rites are ended, I'll tell you largely v 4 68
Nay, my choler is ended. She is a most sweet lady *L. L. Lost* ii 1 206
The boy's fat l'envoy, the goose that you bought; And he ended the market iii 1 111
Extended With vilest torture let my life be ended *All's Well* ii 1 177
The last was the greatest, but that I have not ended yet iv 3 106
I mean, the business is not ended, as fearing to hear of it hereafter iv 3 110
The play is done: All is well ended, if this suit be won Epil. 336
If the heavens had been pleased, would we had so ended! *T. Night* ii 1 22
Dear queen, that ended when I but began, Give me that hand *W. Tale* v 3 45
This sword hath ended him: so shall it thee 1 *Hen. IV.* v 3 9
Where have you been all this while? When every thing is ended, then you come 2 *Hen. IV.* iv 3 30
His cares are now all ended.—I hope, not dead v 2 3
Our simple supper ended, give me leave In this close walk 2 *Hen. VI.* ii 2 2
Now the battle 's ended, If friend or foe, let him be gently used 3 *Hen. VI.* ii 6 44
Great Troy is ours, and our sharp wars are ended *Troi. and Cres.* v 9 10
Hath been! is it ended, then? Our state thinks not so *Coriolanus* iv 3 16
You have ended my business, and I will merrily accompany you home iv 3 41
My life were better ended by their hate, Than death prorogued, wanting of thy love *Rom. and Jul.* ii 2 77
Tybalt's death Was woe enough, if it had ended there iii 2 115
You shall speak In the same pulpit whereto I am going, After my speech is ended.—Be it so; I do desire no more *J. Cæsar* iii 1 251
Brutus' tongue Hath almost ended his life's history v 5 40
Most welcome home!—This business is well ended *Hamlet* ii 2 85
When remedies are past, the griefs are ended By seeing the worst *Othello* i 3 202
And 'twas I That the mad Brutus ended *Ant. and Cleo.* iii 11 38
Doctor, your service for this time is ended; Take your own way *Cymb.* i 5 30
He on the ground, my speech of insultment ended on his dead body iii 5 145
How ended she?—With horror, madly dying, like her life v 5 30
Ending. My ending is despair, Unless I be relieved by prayer *Tempest* Epil. 15
Breathe it in mine ear, As ending anthem of my endless dolour *T. G. of V.* iii 1 240
The mere effusion of thy proper loins, Do curse the gout, serpigo, and the rheum, For ending thee no sooner *Meas. for Meas.* iii 1 32
Very ominous endings *Much Ado* v 2 40
A good l'envoy, ending in the goose: would you desire more? *L. L. Lost* iii 1 100
Foretell the ending of mortality *K. John* v 7 5
If life did ride upon a dial's point, Still ending at the arrival of an hour 1 *Hen IV.* v 2 85
Thou hast a sigh to blow away this praise, Ending with 'Brother, son, and all are dead' 2 *Hen. IV.* i 1 81
This bitter taste Yield his engrossments to the ending father iv 5 80
The king is not bound to answer the particular endings of his soldiers *Hen. V.* iv 1 164
From this day to the ending of the world iv 3 58
What to ourselves in passion we propose, The passion ending, doth the purpose lose *Hamlet* iii 2 205
Here our play has ending *Pericles* v 3 Gower 101
Endless. As ending anthem of my endless dolour *T. G. of Ver.* iii 1 240
An infinite and endless liar *All's Well* iii 6 11
To dwell in solemn shades of endless night *Richard II.* i 3 177
My oil-dried lamp and time-bewasted light Shall be extinct with age and endless night i 3 222
And all the priests and friars in my realm Shall in procession sing her endless praise 1 *Hen. VI.* i 6 20
Heaven, from thy endless goodness, send prosperous life! *Hen. VIII.* v 5 1
Right and wrong, Between whose endless jar justice resides *Troi. and Cres.* i 3 117
Endow. Even all I have; yea, and myself and all, Will I withal endow a child of thine *Richard III.* iv 4 249
I do not think So fair an outward and such stuff within Endows a man but he.—You speak him far *Cymbeline* i 1 24

Endow'd thy purposes With words that made them known . *Tempest* i 2 357
I would not marry her, though she were endowed with all that Adam had left him before he transgressed *Much Ado* ii 1 259
How shall she be endow'd, If she be mated with an equal husband? *T. of Athens* i 1 139
Thy half o' the kingdom hast thou not forgot, Wherein I thee endow'd *Lear* ii 4 184
Endowment. Base men by his endowments are made great *Richard II.* ii 3 139
Though the catalogue of his endowments had been tabled by his side *Cymbeline* i 4 6
Virtue and cunning were endowments greater Than nobleness and riches *Pericles* iii 2 27
How achieved you these endowments, which You make more rich to owe? . . . . v 1 117
Endue. Now Mercury endue thee with leasing! *T. Night* i 5 105
The tribunes Endue you with the people's voice . *Coriolanus* ii 3 147
Endued. Men endued with worthy qualities . *T. G. of Ver.* v 4 153
Endurance. O, she misused me past the endurance of a block! *Much Ado* ii 1 246
Tell thy story; If thine consider'd prove the thousandth part Of my endurance, thou art a man . . . . . . *Pericles* v 1 137
Endure. Would no more endure This wooden slavery . *Tempest* iii 1 61
O Valentine, this I endure for thee! . . *T. G. of Ver.* v 3 15
I could not endure a husband with a beard on his face *Much Ado* ii 1 32
Here's a dish I love not: I cannot endure my Lady Tongue . ii 1 284
She cannot endure to hear tell of a husband . . ii 1 362
A man loves the meat in his youth that he cannot endure in his age ii 3 248
This wedding-day Perhaps is but prolong'd: have patience and endure iv 1 256
But no man's virtue nor sufficiency To be so moral when he shall endure The like himself . . . . v 1 30
There was never yet philosopher That could endure the toothache patiently . . . . v 1 36
He shall endure such public shame as the rest of the court can possibly devise . . . . *L. L. Lost* i 1 132
I protest, A world of torments though I should endure, I would not yield . . . . v 2 353
Whether, if you yield not to your father's choice, You can endure the livery of a nun . . . . . *M. N. Dream* i 1 70
I will no longer endure it, though yet I know no wise remedy how to avoid it . . . . *As Y. Like It* i 1 25
The spirit of my father grows strong in me, and I will no longer endure it . . . . i 1 74
Thy company, which erst was irksome to me, I will endure . . iii 5 96
It pass your patience and mine to endure her loud alarums *T. of Shrew* i 1 131
That mortal ears might hardly endure the din . . . . i 1 178
I could endure any thing before but a cat, and now he's a cat *All's Well* iv 3 266
'Tis in grain, sir; 'twill endure wind and weather *T. Night* i 5 255
Youth's a stuff will not endure . . . . . ii 3 53
Hardly Will he endure your sight as yet, I fear *W. Tale* iv 4 481
Not able to endure the sight of day . . . *Richard II.* iii 2 52
Majesty might never yet endure The moody frontier of a servant brow 1 *Hen. IV.* i 3 18
What man of good temper would endure this tempest of exclamation? 2 *Hen. IV.* ii 1 87
Thou knowest Sir John cannot endure an apple-john . ii 4 3
I cannot endure such a fustian rascal . . . . ii 4 203
It will endure cold as another man's sword will *Hen. V.* ii 1 10
God of his mercy give You patience to endure! . . ii 2 180
Then they will endure handling, which before would not abide looking on v 2 337
But now the substance shall endure the like . 1 *Hen. VI.* ii 3 38
How I am braved and must perforce endure it! . . iii 4 115
Have done, for more I hardly can endure . . . 2 *Hen. VI.* i 4 41
Uneath may she endure the flinty streets, To tread them . ii 4 8
I am able to endure much.—No question of that . . iv 2 60
Such abominable words as no Christian ear can endure to hear . iv 7 44
Shall I endure the sight of Somerset? False king! . . v 1 90
You are mortal, And mortal eyes cannot endure the devil *Richard III.* i 2 45
These eyes could never endure sweet beauty's wreck . . i 2 127
They do me wrong, and I will not endure it . . . i 3 42
I must have patience to endure the load . . . iii 7 230
Can ye endure to hear this arrogance? And from this fellow? *Hen. VIII.* iii 2 278
I am able now, methinks, Out of a fortitude of soul I feel, To endure more miseries and greater far . . . . . iii 2 389
That no audience, but the tribulation of Tower-hill, or the limbs of Limehouse, their dear brothers, are able to endure . . v 4 67
By the vows We have made to endure friends . *Coriolanus* i 6 58
It would have gall'd his surly nature, Which easily endures not article Tying him to aught . . . . ii 3 204
I'll deliver Myself your loyal servant, or endure Your heaviest censure v 6 142
Why have I patience to endure all this? . *T. Andron.* ii 3 88
The lion moved with pity did endure To have his princely paws pared all away . . . . ii 3 151
Despiteful and intolerable wrongs! Shall I endure this monstrous villany? . . . . iv 4 51
I'll not endure him.—He shall be endured: What, goodman boy! *Rom. and Jul.* i 5 78
Am I the master here, or you? go to. You'll not endure him! . i 5 81
I did endure Not seldom, nor no slight checks . *T. of Athens* ii 2 148
Why do fond men expose themselves to battle, And not endure all threats? . . . . iii 5 43
And we can both Endure the winter's cold as well as he *J. Cæsar* i 2 99
Let Cæsar seat him sure; For we will shake him, or worse days endure i 2 326
But when they should endure the bloody spur, They fall their crests iv 2 25
O ye gods, ye gods! must I endure all this?—All this! ay, more . iv 3 41
With meditating that she must die once, I have the patience to endure it now . . . . iv 3 192
Even so great men great losses should endure . . . iv 3 193
The confident tyrant Keeps still in Dunsinane, and will endure Our setting down before 't . . . . *Macbeth* v 4 9
Liar and slave!—Let me endure your wrath, if't be not so . v 5 36
The terms of our estate may not endure Hazard so near us *Hamlet* iii 3 5
I'll not endure it: His knights grow riotous, and himself upbraids us *Lear* i 3 5
The tyranny of the open night's too rough For nature to endure . iii 4 3
In such a night To shut me out! Pour on; I will endure. In such a night is this! . . . . iii 4 18
I never shall endure her: dear my lord, Be not familiar with her . v 1 15
Men must endure Their going hence, even as their coming hither . v 2 9
The Moor, howbeit that I endure him not, Is of a constant, loving, noble nature . . . . *Othello* ii 1 297
If there be cords, or knives, Poison, or fire, or suffocating streams, I'll not endure it . . . . iii 3 390

Endure. I will indeed no longer endure it, nor am I yet persuaded to put up in peace . . . . *Othello* iv 2 180
The business she hath broached in the state Cannot endure my absence *Ant. and Cleo.* i 2 179
Mine eyes did sicken at the sight, and could not Endure a further view iii 10 18
He that can endure To follow with allegiance a fall'n lord . iii 13 43
Our subjects, sir, Will not endure his yoke . . *Cymbeline* iii 5 5
By thine own tongue thou art condemn'd, and must Endure our law . v 5 299
Endured. Is most tolerable and not to be endured . *Much Ado* iii 3 37
What, to make thee an instrument and play false strains upon thee! not to be endured! . . . . . . *As Y. Like It* iv 3 69
That have endured shrewd days and nights with us . . v 4 179
Your betters have endured me say my mind . . *T. of Shrew* iv 3 75
O vile, Intolerable, not to be endured! . . . . v 2 94
Whose honour and whose honesty till now Endured all weathers *W. Tale* v 1 195
Of such as have before endured the like . . *Richard II.* v 5 30
What wards, what blows, what extremities he endured . 1 *Hen. IV.* i 2 212
I grieve to hear what torments you endured . . 1 *Hen. VI.* i 4 57
By heaven, I will acquaint his majesty With those gross taunts I often have endured . . . . *Richard III.* i 3 106
Of all one pain, save for a night of groans Endured of her . . iv 4 304
I'll not endure him.—He shall be endured: What, goodman boy! *Rom. and Jul.* i 5 78
Such a storm as his bare head In hell-black night endured . *Lear* iii 7 60
Finding Who 'twas that so endured . . . . . v 3 211
The wonder is, he hath endured so long: He but usurp'd his life . v 3 316
But such a night as this, Till now, I ne'er endured . . *Pericles* iii 2 6
Endured a sea That almost burst the deck . . . . . iv 1 56
She speaks, My lord, that, may be, hath endured a grief Might equal yours . . . . v 1 88
Endurest. What thou endurest, Betwixt a father by thy step-dame govern'd, A mother hourly coining plots! . . . . *Cymbeline* ii 1 62
Enduring. He so troubles me, 'Tis past enduring . . . *W. Tale* ii 1 2
Endymion. Peace, ho! the moon sleeps with Endymion And would not be awaked . . . . *Mer. of Venice* v 1 109
Enemies. Bountiful Fortune, Now my dear lady, hath mine enemies Brought to this shore . . . . *Tempest* i 2 179
Mine enemies are all knit up In their distractions . . . iii 3 89
At this hour Lie at my mercy all mine enemies . . . iv 1 264
My friends,— That's not so, sir: we are your enemies . *T. G. of Ver.* iv 1 8
And speak off half a dozen dangerous words, How they might hurt their enemies, if they durst . . . . . . *Much Ado* v 1 98
Stand up. I know you two are rival enemies . *M. N. Dream* iv 1 147
Thwarted my bargains, cooled my friends, heated mine enemies *Mer. of Venice* iii 1 60
You have wrestled well and overthrown More than your enemies *As Y. Like It* i 2 267
To some kind of men Their graces serve them but as enemies . ii 3 11
Such friends are thine enemies, knave . . . *All's Well* i 3 44
I have many enemies in Orsino's court . . . . *T. Night* ii 1 46
'Tis a vulgar proof, That very oft we pity enemies . . . iii 1 136
Whom thou, in terms so bloody and so dear, Hast made thine enemies . v 1 75
You came in arms to spill mine enemies' blood . *K. John* iii 1 102
That the time's enemies may not have this To grace occasions . iv 2 61
O, let me have no subject enemies, When adverse foreigners affright my towns! . . . . iv 2 171
Arm you against your other enemies, I'll make a peace between your soul and you . . . . iv 2 249
Wherein we step after a stranger march Upon her gentle bosom, and fill up Her enemies' ranks . . . . v 2 29
His hands were guilty of no kindred blood, But bloody with the enemies of his kin . . . . *Richard II.* ii 1 183
Yield stinging nettles to mine enemies . . . . . iii 2 18
May with a mortal touch Throw death upon thy sovereign's enemies . iii 2 22
Herein all breathless lies The mightiest of thy greatest enemies . v 6 32
Could the world pick thee out three such enemies? . 1 *Hen. IV.* ii 4 404
Under the hoofs of vaunting enemies, Whose deaths are yet unrevenged v 3 43
Send discoverers forth To know the numbers of our enemies 2 *Hen. IV.* iv 1 4
Every thing set off That might so much as think you enemies . iv 1 146
From enemies heaven keep your majesty! . . . . iv 4 94
Be friends: an thou wilt not, why, then, be enemies with me too *Hen. V.* ii 1 108
Those that were your father's enemies Have steep'd their galls in honey ii 2 29
More dazzled and drove back his enemies Than mid-day sun . 1 *Hen. VI.* i 1 13
We will not fly, but to our enemies' throats . . . . i 1 98
Enclosed were they with their enemies . . . . . i 1 136
I would ne'er have fled, But that they left me 'midst my enemies . i 2 24
It cannot be this weak and writhled shrimp Should strike such terror to his enemies . . . . ii 3 24
The presence of a king engenders love Amongst his subjects and his loyal friends, As it disanimates his enemies . . . . iii 1 183
Depart when heaven please, For I have seen our enemies' overthrow iii 2 111
Go cheerfully together and digest Your angry choler on your enemies . iv 1 168
Boiling choler chokes The hollow passage of my poison'd voice, By sight of these our baleful enemies . . . . v 4 122
Rue my shame, And ban thine enemies, both mine and thine! 2 *Hen. VI.* ii 4 25
Look after him and cannot do him good, So mighty are his vowed enemies iii 1 220
Weaves tedious snares to trap mine enemies. . . . . iii 1 340
He shall have the skins of our enemies, to make dog's-leather of . iv 2 25
Our enemies shall fall before us, inspired with the spirit of putting down kings and princes . . . . iv 2 37
Nay, answer, if you can: the Frenchmen are our enemies . . iv 2 180
Priests pray for enemies, but princes kill . . . . v 2 71
Whose cowardice Hath made us by-words to our enemies . 3 *Hen. VI.* i 1 42
Thou wilt stay with me?—Ay, to be murder'd by his enemies . . i 1 260
So fared our father with his enemies; So fled his enemies my warlike father . . . . ii 1 19
And who shines now but Henry's enemies? . . . . . ii 6 10
Nor how to shroud yourself from enemies . . . . iv 3 40
All these the enemies to our poor bark . . . . . v 4 28
We sit in England's royal throne, Re-purchased with the blood of enemies v 7 2
For they that were your enemies are his . . . . *Richard III.* i 1 130
In those busy days Which here you urge to prove us enemies, We follow'd . . . . i 3 146
This same very day your enemies, The kindred of the queen, must die . iii 2 49
I am no mourner for that news, Because they have been still mine enemies . . . . iii 2 52
Those enemies are put to death, And I in better state than e'er I was . iii 2 105
I now repent I told the pursuivant, As 'twere triumphing at mine enemies . . . . iii 4 91
Look back, defend thee, here are enemies . . . . . iii 5 19

Enemies. Darest thou resolve to kill a friend of mine?—Ay, my lord; But I had rather kill two enemies . . . . *Richard III.* iv 2 72
Two deep enemies, Foes to my rest and my sweet sleep's disturbers . iv 2 73
Stay awhile, And teach me how to curse mine enemies! . . . . iv 4 117
The little souls of Edward's children Whisper the spirits of thine enemies iv 4 192
If not to fight with foreign enemies, Yet to beat down these rebels here iv 4 531
That you have many enemies, that know not Why they are so *Hen. VIII.* ii 4 158
More miseries and greater far Than my weak-hearted enemies dare offer iii 2 390
He would not in mine age Have left me naked to mine enemies . iii 2 457
If they shall fail, I, with mine enemies, Will triumph o'er my person v 1 123
Your enemies are many, and not small . . . . . v 1 128
And know by measure Of their observant toil the enemies' weight *Troi. and Cres.* i 3 203
You slander The helms o' the state, who care for you like fathers, When you curse them as enemies . . . *Coriolanus* i 1 80
Thou madest thine enemies shake, as if the world Were feverous . i 4 60
You have been a scourge to her enemies, you have been a rod to her friends ii 3 98
Stand fast; We have as many friends as enemies . . . iii 1 232
What has he done to Rome that's worthy death? Killing our enemies iii 1 299
I have been consul, and can show for Rome Her enemies' marks upon me iii 3 111
Your enemies, with nodding of their plumes, Fan you into despair! . iii 3 126
Do't! he will do't; for, look you, sir, he has as many friends as enemies iv 5 219
Who is't can blame him? Your enemies and his find something in him iv 6 106
They charged him even As those should do that had deserved his hate, And therein show'd like enemies . . . . . iv 6 114
Chastised with arms Our enemies' pride . . . *T. Andron.* i 1 33
He circumscribed with his sword, And brought to yoke, the enemies of Rome . . . . i 1 69
That noble hand of thine, That hath thrown down so many enemies, Shall not be sent . . . . iii 1 164
Revenge is come to join with him, And work confusion on his enemies v 2 8
Art thou Revenge? and art thou sent to me, To be a torment to mine enemies? . . . . v 2 42
Or, at the least, make them his enemies . . . . v 2 79
Basely cozen'd Of that true hand that fought Rome's quarrel out, And sent her enemies unto the grave . . . . . v 3 103
And turn'd weeping out, To beg relief among Rome's enemies . v 3 106
Rebellious subjects, enemies to peace . . *Rom. and Jul.* i 1 88
Where be these enemies? Capulet! Montague! See, what a scourge is laid upon your hate . . . . . . v 3 291
You had rather be at a breakfast of enemies than a dinner of friends.—So they were bleeding-new, my lord . . *T. of Athens* i 2 79
Would all those flatterers were thine enemies! . . . i 2 84
Happier is he that has no friend to feed Than such that do e'en enemies exceed . . . . i 2 210
He has done fair service, And slain in fight many of your enemies iii 5 64
How rarely does it meet with this time's guise, When man was wish'd to love his enemies! . . . . iv 3 473
The enemies' drum is heard, and fearful scouring Doth choke the air with dust . . . . v 2 15
Those enemies of Timon's and mine own Whom you yourselves shall set out for reproof Fall and no more . . . . . v 4 56
Better than to close In terms of friendship with thine enemies *J. Cæsar* iii 1 203
The enemies of Cæsar shall say this; Then, in a friend, it is cold modesty iii 1 212
We are at the stake, And bay'd about with many enemies . . iv 1 49
Wrong I mine enemies? And, if not so, how should I wrong a brother? iv 2 38
I had rather have Such men my friends than enemies . . v 4 29
Our enemies have beat us to the pit: It is more worthy to leap in ourselves . . . . v 5 23
The poor advanced makes friends of enemies . . *Hamlet* iii 2 215
You will draw both friend and foe, Winner and loser?—None but his enemies . . . . iv 5 144
My life I never held but as a pawn To wage against thy enemies . *Lear* i 1 158
Let the great gods, That keep this dreadful pother o'er our heads, Find out their enemies now . . . . . . iii 2 51
To know our enemies' minds, we'ld rip their hearts . . iv 6 265
With sands that will not bear your enemies' boats . *Cymbeline* iii 1 21

Enemy. Being an enemy To me inveterate . . . *Tempest* i 2 121
I will resist such entertainment till Mine enemy has more power . i 2 466
Valentine I'll hold an enemy, Aiming at Silvia as a sweeter friend *T. G. of V.* ii 6 29
She'll think that it is spoke in hate.—Ay, if his enemy deliver it . iii 2 35
I will not be your friend nor enemy . . . *Mer. Wives* iii 4 93
What is't I dream on? O cunning enemy, that, to catch a saint, With saints dost bait thy hook! . . . *Meas. for Meas.* ii 2 180
You dare easier be friends with me than fight with mine enemy *Much Ado* iv 1 301
For when did friendship take A breed for barren metal of his friend? But lend it rather to thine enemy . . *Mer. of Venice* i 3 136
I have engaged myself to a dear friend, Engaged my friend to his mere enemy . . . . iii 2 265
She would not hold out enemy for ever . . . . iv 1 447
The world esteem'd thy father honourable, But I did find him still mine enemy . . . . . . *As Y. Like It* i 2 239
Within this roof The enemy of all your graces lives . . ii 3 18
Here shall he see No enemy But winter and rough weather . . ii 5 7
I have been politic with my friend, smooth with mine enemy . v 4 47
Excessive grief the enemy to the living.—If the living be enemy to the grief, the excess makes it soon mortal . . *All's Well* i 1 65
Be able for thine enemy Rather in power than use . . . i 1 74
Man is enemy to virginity; how may we barricado it against him? i 1 123
A phœnix, captain and an enemy, A guide, a goddess, and a sovereign i 1 182
Such I will have, whom I am sure he knows not from the enemy . iii 6 25
I would I had any drum of the enemy's: I would swear I recovered it . iv 1 66
I am sure care's an enemy to life . . . . *T. Night* i 3 3
Disguise, I see, thou art a wickedness, Wherein the pregnant enemy does much . . . . ii 2 29
What, man! defy the devil: consider, he's an enemy to mankind . iii 4 108
Thy friend, as thou usest him, and thy sworn enemy . . iii 4 187
Antonio never yet was thief or pirate, Though I confess, on base and ground enough, Orsino's enemy . . . . . v 1 79
Now my sworn friend and then mine enemy . . . *W. Tale* i 2 167
It will let in and out the enemy With bag and baggage . . i 2 205
Mightst bespice a cup, To give mine enemy a lasting wink . . i 2 317
Though Fortune, visible an enemy, Should chase us with my father, power no jot Hath she to change our loves . . . . v 1 216
No further enemy to you Than the constraint of hospitable zeal *K. John* ii 1 243
I may disjoin my hand, but not my faith.—So makest thou faith an enemy to faith . . . . iii 1 263
Your nobles will not hear you, but are gone To offer service to your enemy . . . . v 1 34

Enemy. Let thy blows, doubly redoubled, Fall like amazing thunder on the casque Of thy adverse pernicious enemy . . *Richard II.* i 3 82
I swear.—And I, to keep all this.—Norfolk, so far as to mine enemy . i 3 193
Might have retired his power, And driven into despair an enemy's hope ii 2 47
For us to levy power Proportionable to the enemy Is all impossible . ii 2 125
Where is Green? That they have let the dangerous enemy Measure our confines with such peaceful steps? . . . . . . iii 2 124
Repeal'd he shall be, And, though mine enemy, restored again To all his lands . . . . iv 1 88
Though mine enemy thou hast ever been, High sparks of honour in thee have I seen . . . . v 6 28
I tell thee, He durst as well have met the devil alone As Owen Glendower for an enemy . . . . . . *1 Hen. IV.* i 3 116
Do I tell thee of my foes, Which art my near'st and dearest enemy? . iii 2 123
Not a horse is half the half of himself.—So are the horses of the enemy iv 3 25
Because you are not of our quality, But stand against us like an enemy iv 3 37
I would to God my name were not so terrible to the enemy as it is *2 Hen. IV.* i 2 244
Wilt thou make as many holes in an enemy's battle as thou hast done in a woman's petticoat? . . . . iii 2 165
Give me this man: he presents no mark to the enemy . . iii 2 285
Scarcely off a mile, In goodly form comes on the enemy . . iv 1 20
Nor do I as an enemy to peace Troop in the throngs of military men iv 1 61
Plucking to unfix an enemy, He doth unfasten so and shake a friend iv 1 208
A most furious knight and valorous enemy . . . . iv 3 43
I put it on my head, To try with it, as with an enemy . . iv 5 167
Join'd with an enemy proclaim'd . . . . *Hen. V.* ii 2 168
'Tis best to weigh The enemy more mighty than he seems . . ii 4 44
Who was shot, who disgraced, what terms the enemy stood on . iii 6 78
'Tis no wisdom to confess so much Unto an enemy of craft and vantage iii 6 153
Why, the enemy is loud; you hear him all night . . . iv 1 76
If the enemy is an ass and a fool and a prating coxcomb, is it meet, think you, that we should also, look you, be an ass and a fool? . iv 1 78
It may be his enemy is a gentleman of great sort . . . iv 7 141
He is a friend to Alençon, and an enemy to our person . . iv 7 164
Is it possible dat I sould love de enemy of France?—No; it is not possible you should love the enemy of France . . . . . v 2 178
Arm! arm! the enemy doth make assault! . . . . *1 Hen. VI.* ii 1 38
Thou art a most pernicious usurer, Froward by nature, enemy to peace iii 1 18
Gather we our forces out of hand And set upon our boasting enemy . iii 2 103
When they heard he was thine enemy, They set him free without his ransom . . . . iii 3 71
This is the latest glory of thy praise That I, thy enemy, due thee withal iv 2 34
I here the enemy: Out, some light horsemen, and peruse their wings . iv 2 42
He is mine enemy, Nay, more, an enemy unto you all . . *2 Hen. VI.* i 1 148
O God, have I overcome mine enemy in this presence? . . . ii 3 100
With your best endeavour have stirr'd up My liefest liege to be mine enemy . . . . iii 1 164
Let him die, in that he is a fox, By nature proved an enemy to the flock iii 1 258
Full often, like a shag-hair'd crafty kern, Hath he conversed with the enemy . . . . iii 1 368
The duke was enemy to him, Yet he most Christian-like laments his death . . . . iii 2 57
Who, in the conflict that it holds with death, Attracts the same for aidance 'gainst the enemy . . . . iii 2 165
'Tis like you would not feast him like a friend; And 'tis well seen he found an enemy . . . . iii 2 185
Soft-hearted wretch! Hast thou not spirit to curse thine enemy? . iii 2 308
Can he that speaks with the tongue of an enemy be a good counsellor? iv 2 181
With thy brave bearing should I be in love, But that thou art so fast mine enemy . . . . v 2 21
Now is it manhood, wisdom and defence, To give the enemy way . . v 2 76
I doubt not, uncle, of our victory. Many a battle have I won in France, When as the enemy hath been ten to one . . . . *3 Hen. VI.* i 2 75
We his subjects sworn in all allegiance Will apprehend you as his enemy iii 1 71
King Lewis Becomes your enemy, for mocking him About the marriage iv 1 30
I never sued to friend nor enemy . . . . . *Richard III.* i 2 168
Because I cannot flatter . . . , I must be held a rancorous enemy . i 3 50
I'll join with black despair against my soul, And to myself become an enemy . . . . ii 2 37
One that hath ever been God's enemy: Then, if you fight against God's enemy, God will in justice ward you as his soldiers . . . . v 3 252
A thing devised by the enemy . . . . v 3 306
Which of your friends Have I not strove to love, although I knew He were mine enemy? . . . . *Hen. VIII.* ii 4 31
I do believe, Induced by potent circumstances, that You are mine enemy ii 4 77
Wherein he appears As I would wish mine enemy . . . iii 2 28
What the repining enemy commends, That breath fame blows *T. and C.* i 3 243
You know an enemy intends you harm . . . . . . ii 2 39
As doth a battle, when they charge on heaps The enemy flying . . iii 2 30
As welcome as to one That would be rid of such an enemy . . . iv 5 164
You know Caius Marcius is chief enemy to the people.—We know't *Cor.* i 1 8
Marcius your old enemy, Who is of Rome worse hated than of you . i 2 12
Say, has our general met the enemy?—They lie in view . . i 4 3
Where is the enemy? are you lords o' the field? If not, why cease you? i 6 47
Every gash was an enemy's grave . . . . ii 1 172
When he had no power, But was a petty servant to the state, He was your enemy . . . . ii 3 187
You have found, Scaling his present bearing with his past, That he's your fixed enemy . . . . ii 3 258
I know thou hadst rather Follow thine enemy in a fiery gulf Than flatter him in a bower . . . . iii 2 91
He is banish'd, As enemy to the people and his country . . . iii 3 118
The people's enemy is gone, is gone!—Our enemy is banish'd! he is gone! iii 3 136
Say their great enemy is gone, and they Stand in their ancient strength iv 2 6
A thousand welcomes! And more a friend than e'er an enemy . . iv 5 152
In a violent popular ignorance, given your enemy your shield . . v 2 43
Ah, beastly creature! The blot and enemy to our general name! *T. Andron.* ii 3 183
Rear'd aloft the bloody battle-axe, Writing destruction on the enemy's castle . . . . iii 1 170
This sorrow is an enemy, And would usurp upon my watery eyes . . iii 1 268
I am not Tamora; She is thy enemy, and I thy friend . . v 2 29
And from her bosom took the enemy's point . . . . v 3 111
Romeo, and a Montague; The only son of your great enemy *R. and J.* i 5 139
Prodigious birth of love it is to me, That I must love a loathed enemy . i 5 143
'Tis but thy name that is my enemy; Thou art thyself . . . ii 2 38
My name, dear saint, is hateful to myself, Because it is an enemy to thee ii 2 56
I have been feasting with mine enemy, Where on a sudden one hath wounded me, That's by me wounded . . . . ii 3 49

Enemy. O, what more favour can I do to thee, Than with that hand that cut thy youth in twain To sunder his that was thine enemy? *R. and J.* v 3 100
And must my house Be my retentive enemy, my gaol? . *T. of Athens* iii 4 82
I'll believe him as an enemy, and give over my trade . . . iv 3 459
Cæsar was ne'er so much your enemy As that same ague . *J. Cæsar* ii 2 112
I am going to Cæsar's funeral.—As a friend or an enemy? . . . iii 3 23
'Tis better that the enemy seek us: So shall he waste his means . . iv 3 199
The enemy, marching along by them, By them shall make a fuller number up, Come on refresh'd . . . . iv 3 207
The enemy increaseth every day; We, at the height, are ready to decline iv 3 216
You said the enemy would not come down, But keep the hills . v 1 2
The enemy comes on in gallant show; Their bloody sign of battle is hung out . . . . v 1 13
Myself have to mine own turn'd enemy . . . . v 3 2
That I may rest assured Whether yond troops are friend or enemy . v 3 18
I dare assure thee that no enemy Shall ever take alive the noble Brutus v 4 21
And mine eternal jewel Given to the common enemy of man *Macbeth* iii 1 69
Put that business in your bosoms, Whose execution takes your enemy off . . . . iii 1 105
Both of you Know Banquo was your enemy . . . . . . iii 1 115
You all know, security Is mortals' chiefest enemy . . . . iii 5 33
I would not hear your enemy say so . . . . . *Hamlet* i 2 170
Who in want a hollow friend doth try, Directly seasons him his enemy iii 2 219
His madness is poor Hamlet's enemy . . . . v 2 250
I profess Myself an enemy to all other joys . . . . *Lear* i 1 75
Is gone . . . to descry The strength o' the enemy.—I must needs after iv 5 14
Mine enemy's dog, Though he had bit me, should have stood that night Against my fire . . . . iv 7 36
Why is this reason'd?—Combine together 'gainst the enemy . . v 1 29
The enemy's in view; draw up your powers . . . . . v 1 51
We must straight employ you Against the general enemy Ottoman *Othello* i 3 49
That men should put an enemy in their mouths to steal away their brains! . . . . ii 3 291
That thrust had been mine enemy indeed, But that my coat is better than thou know'st . . . . v 1 24
And false-play'd my glory Unto an enemy's triumph . *Ant. and Cleo.* iv 14 20
The gods withhold me! Shall I do that which all the Parthian darts, Though enemy, lost aim, and could not? . . . . . . iv 14 71
You have prevailed, I am no further your enemy . . *Cymbeline* i 4 172
Upon him Will I first work: he's for his master, And enemy to my son i 5 29
I am to pronounce Augustus Cæsar—Cæsar, that hath more kings his servants than Thyself domestic officers—thine enemy . . . iii 1 65
Thus mine enemy fell, And thus I set my foot on's neck . . . iii 3 91
Am right sorry that I must report ye My master's enemy . . . iii 5 4
Your hand, my lord.—Receive it friendly; but from this time forth I wear it as your enemy . . . . iii 5 14
If mine enemy But fear the sword like me, he'll scarcely look on't . iii 6 25
And though he came our enemy, remember He was paid for that . . iv 2 245
The enemy full-hearted, Lolling the tongue with slaughtering . . v 3 7
He that otherwise accounts of me, This sword shall prove he's honour's enemy . . . . *Pericles* ii 5 64
What canst thou wish thine enemy to be? . . . . . . iv 6 168
Enemy king. Kent; who in disguise Follow'd his enemy king . *Lear* v 3 220
Enemy town. My birth-place hate I, and my love's upon This enemy town . . . . *Coriolanus* iv 4 24
Enfeeble. I have belied a lady, The princess of this country, and the air on't Revengingly enfeebles me . . . . *Cymbeline* v 2 4
Enfeebled. My people are with sickness much enfeebled . *Hen. V.* iii 6 154
This city must be famish'd, Or with light skirmishes enfeebled 1 *Hen. VI.* i 4 69
Enfeoff'd himself to popularity . . . . . . 1 *Hen. IV.* iii 2 69
Enfettered. His soul is so enfetter'd to her love, That she may make, unmake, do what she list . . . . *Othello* ii 3 351
Enfolding. Seest thou not the air of the court in these enfoldings? *W. Tale* iv 4 756
Enforce them to this place, And presently, I prithee . . *Tempest* v 1 100
Now I want Spirits to enforce, art to enchant, And my ending is despair . . . . Epil. 14
Nor how my father would enforce me marry . . . *T. G. of Ver.* iv 3 16
Your scope is as mine own, So to enforce or qualify the laws *M. for M.* i 1 66
Abide here till he come and enforce them against him . . . . v 1 267
Shall I enforce thy love? I could: shall I entreat thy love? I will *L. L. Lost* iv 1 82
To enforce the pained impotent to smile . . . . . . v 2 864
I know you would be prouder of the work Than customary bounty can enforce you . . . . *Mer. of Venice* iii 4 9
Enforce A thievish living on the common road . . *As Y. Like It* ii 3 32
An onion . . . Shall in despite enforce a watery eye . *T. of Shrew* Ind. 1 128
I will no more enforce mine office on you . . . . *All's Well* ii 1 129
The proud control of fierce and bloody war, To enforce these rights *K. John* i 1 18
With swifter spleen than powder can enforce . . . . . ii 1 448
To speak more properly, I will enforce it easily to my love . . ii 1 515
The tongues of dying men Enforce attention like deep harmony *Rich. II.* ii 1 6
When he's return'd, Against Aumerle we will enforce his trial . . iv 1 90
Are you not ashamed to enforce a poor widow to so rough a course to come by her own? . . . . 2 *Hen. IV.* ii 1 89
For competence of life I will allow you, That lack of means enforce you not to evil . . . . v 5 71
His countenance enforces homage . . . . . . *Hen. V.* iii 7 31
Yet they do wink and yield, as love is blind and enforces . . . v 2 328
Hunger will enforce them to be more eager . . . 1 *Hen. VI.* i 2 38
And could it not enforce them to relent? . . . . 2 *Hen. VI.* iv 4 17
Would you enforce me to a world of care? . . . *Richard III.* iii 7 223
Enforce his pride, And his old hate unto you . . . *Coriolanus* ii 3 227
If he evade us there, Enforce him with his envy to the people . . iii 3 3
Let them not cease, but with a din confused Enforce the present execution . . . . iii 3 21
Thus I enforce thy rotten jaws to open . . . *Rom. and Jul.* v 3 47
If wrongs be evils and enforce us kill, What folly 'tis to hazard life for ill! *T. of Athens* iii 5 36
Thou rather shalt enforce it with thy smile Than hew to't with thy sword v 4 45
Sometime with lunatic bans, sometime with prayers, Enforce their charity . . . . *Lear* ii 3 20
He will divorce you; Or put upon you what restraint and grievance The law, with all his might to enforce it on, Will give him cable *Othello* i 2 16
The time, the place, the torture: O, enforce it! . . . . . v 2 369
If you did love him dearly, You do not hold the method to enforce The like from him . . . . *Ant. and Cleo.* i 3 7
Enforce no further The griefs between ye . . . . . . ii 2 99
We will extenuate rather than enforce . . . . v 2 125
We'll enforce it from thee By a sharp torture . . . *Cymbeline* iv 3 11

Enforced. How angerly I taught my brow to frown, When inward joy enforced my heart to smile! . . . . . *T. G. of Ver.* i 2 63
A deflower'd maid! And by an eminent body that enforced The law against it! . . . . *Meas. for Meas.* iv 4 25
Being else by faith enforced To call young Claudio to a reckoning *M. Ado* v 4 8
Weeps every little flower, Lamenting some enforced chastity *M. N. Dr.* iii 1 205
You speak upon the rack, Where men enforced do speak anything *Mer. of Venice* iii 2 33
I was enforced to send it after him . . . . v 1 216
Portia, forgive me this enforced wrong . . . . v 1 240
Come to keep my word, Though in some part enforced to digress *T. of S.* iii 2 109
What Tranio did, myself enforced him to . . . . v 1 132
I must withdraw and weep Upon the spot of this enforced cause *K. John* v 2 30
Call it a travel that thou takest for pleasure.—My heart will sigh when I miscall it so, Which finds it an inforced pilgrimage . *Richard II.* i 3 264
We are inforced to farm our royal realm . . . . . . i 4 45
With nimble wing We were enforced, for safety sake, to fly . 1 *Hen. IV.* v 1 65
Enforced from our most quiet there By the rough torrent of occasion 2 *Hen. IV.* iv 1 71
To the which course if I be enforced . . . . iv 3 55
Th' athversary was have possession of the pridge; but he is enforced to retire . . . . *Hen. V.* iii 6 99
As swift as stones Enforced from the old Assyrian slings . . . iv 7 65
Warwick and the duke enforced me.—Enforced thee! art thou king, and wilt be forced? . . . . 3 *Hen. VI.* i 1 229
Ghastly looks Are at my service, like enforced smiles . *Richard III.* iii 5 9
The peace of England and our persons' safety Enforced us to this execution . . . . iii 5 46
Was it well done of rash Virginius To slay his daughter with his own right hand, Because she was enforced? . . . *T. Andron.* v 3 38
Nor his offences enforced, for which he suffered death . *J. Cæsar* iii 2 43
When love begins to sicken and decay, It useth an enforced ceremony . iv 2 21
Carries anger as the flint bears fire; Who, much enforced, shows a hasty spark . . . . iv 3 112
Liars, and adulterers, by an enforced obedience of planetary influence *Lear* i 2 135
Thy mistress enforced; thy garments cut to pieces . . . *Cymbeline* iv 1 18
My master's garments, Which he enforced from me . . . . v 5 283
Enforcedly. But thou Dost it enforcedly . . . . *T. of Athens* iv 3 241
Enforcement. Let gentleness my strong enforcement be . *As Y. Like It* ii 7 118
By what rough enforcement You got it from her . . . *All's Well* v 3 107
As the thing that's heavy in itself, Upon enforcement flies with greatest speed . . . . 2 *Hen. IV.* i 1 120
And his enforcement of the city wives . . . . . *Richard III.* iii 7 8
Your mere enforcement shall acquittance me From all the impure blots iii 7 233
The leisure and enforcement of the time Forbids to dwell upon . . v 3 238
Enforcest. By virtue, thou enforcest laughter . . . . *L. L. Lost* iii 1 76
Enfranched. He has Hipparchus, my enfranched bondman *A. and C.* iii 13 149
Enfranchise. Silvia, this night I will enfranchise thee . *T. G. of Ver.* iii 1 151
I will enfranchise thee.—O, marry me to one Frances . . *L. L. Lost* iii 1 121
I will perform it to enfranchise you . . . . . *Richard III.* i 1 110
Do this, or this; Take in that kingdom, and enfranchise that *A. and C.* i 1 23
Enfranchised. Belike that now she hath enfranchised them *T. G. of Ver.* ii 4 90
I am trusted with a muzzle and enfranchised with a clog . *Much Ado* i 3 35
By law and process of great nature thence Freed and enfranchised *W. Tale* ii 2 61
From that womb where you imprison'd were He is enfranchised *T. And.* iv 2 125
And being enfranchised, bid him come to me . . . *T. of Athens* i 1 106
Enfranchisement. Heartily request The enfranchisement of Arthur *K. John* iv 2 52
And embrace His golden uncontroll'd enfranchisement . . *Richard II.* i 3 90
To beg Enfranchisement immediate on his knees . . . . . iii 3 114
They'll pawn their swords for my enfranchisement . . 2 *Hen. VI.* v 1 113
As low as to thy foot doth Cassius fall, To beg enfranchisement for Publius Cimber . . . . *J. Cæsar* iii 1 57
Cry out 'Liberty, freedom, and enfranchisement!' . . . . . iii 1 81
Enfreed. There to render him, For the enfreed Antenor, the fair Cressid *Troi. and Cres.* iv 1 38
Enfreedoming. Setting thee at liberty, enfreedoming thy person *L. L. L.* iii 1 125
Engage. This to be true, I do engage my life . . *As Y. Like It* v 4 172
There is my honour's pawn; Engage it to the trial, if thou darest *Richard II.* iv 1 56
I will engage my word to thee . . . . 1 *Hen. IV.* iii 4 563
In the due reverence of a sacred vow I here engage my words *Othello* iii 3 462
Engaged. And I to thee engaged a prince's word . . . *Com. of Errors* v 1 162
Enough, I am engaged; I will challenge him . . . . *Much Ado* iv 1 335
I, that hold it sin To break the vow I am engaged in . . *L. L. Lost* iv 3 178
O spite! too old to be engaged to young . . . . *M. N. Dream* i 1 138
I have engaged myself to a dear friend, Engaged my friend to his mere enemy, To feed my means . . . . . . *Mer. of Venice* iii 2 264
Who hither come engaged by my oath . . . . . *Richard II.* i 3 17
Under whose blessed cross We are impressed and engaged to fight 1 *Hen. IV.* i 1 21
Suffer'd his kinsman March, Who is, if every owner were well placed, Indeed his king, to be engaged in Wales . . . . iv 3 95
I have thrown A brave defiance in King Henry's teeth, And Westmoreland, that was engaged, did bear it . . . . v 2 44
We all that are engaged to this loss Knew that we ventured on such dangerous seas . . . . 2 *Hen. IV.* i 1 180
A quarrel Which hath our several honours all engaged *Troi. and Cres.* ii 2 124
I do stand engaged to many Greeks, Even in the faith of valour . . v 3 68
Let all my land be sold.—'Tis all engaged, some forfeited *T. of Athens* ii 2 155
What other oath Than honesty to honesty engaged, That this shall be? *J. Cæsar* ii 1 127
O limed soul, that, struggling to be free, Art more engaged! . *Hamlet* iii 3 69
Retire, we have engaged ourselves too far . . . *Ant. and Cleo.* iv 7 1
Engagement. All my engagements I will construe to thee . *J. Cæsar* ii 1 307
Engaging and redeeming of himself With such a careless force *Tr. and Cr.* v 5 39
Engaoled. Within my mouth you have engaol'd my tongue . *Richard II.* i 3 166
Engender. And abstinence engenders maladies . . . *L. L. Lost* iv 3 295
It engenders choler, planteth anger . . . . . *T. of Shrew* iv 1 175
And that engenders thunder in his breast . . . . 1 *Hen. VI.* iii 1 39
The presence of a king engenders love Amongst his subjects . . . iii 1 181
For every cloud engenders not a storm . . . . 3 *Hen. VI.* v 3 13
Engenders the black toad and adder blue . . . . *T. of Athens* iv 3 181
If I be so, From my cold heart let heaven engender hail . *Ant. and Cleo.* iii 13 159
Engendered. It is engender'd in the eyes, With gazing fed *Mer. of Venice* iii 2 67
And wiped our eyes Of drops that sacred pity hath engender'd *As Y. L. It* ii 7 123
O error, soon conceived, Thou never comest unto a happy birth, But kill'st the mother that engender'd thee! . . . . . *J. Cæsar* v 3 71
I have't. It is engender'd. Hell and night Must bring this monstrous birth to the world's light . . . . *Othello* i 3 409

Engendering. I do hate a proud man, as I hate the engendering of toads *Troi. and Cres.* ii 3 170
Engild. Fair Helena, who more engilds the night Than all yon fiery oes and eyes of light *M. N. Dream* iii 2 187
Engine. Knife, gun, or need of any engine, Would I not have. *Tempest* ii 1 161
And here an engine fit for my proceeding *T. G. of Ver.* iii 1 138
Promises, enticements, oaths, tokens, and all these engines of lust *All's Well* iii 5 21
So that the ram that batters down the wall, For the great swing and rudeness of his poise, They place before his hand that made the engine *Troi. and Cres.* i 3 208
Let him, like an engine Not portable, lie under this report ii 3 143
When he walks, he moves like an engine *Coriolanus* v 4 19
And she shall file our engines with advice, That will not suffer you to square yourselves *T. Andron.* ii 1 123
O, that delightful engine of her thoughts, That blabb'd them with such pleasing eloquence, Is torn from forth that pretty hollow cage! iii 1 82
Or who hath brought the fatal engine in That gives our Troy, our Rome, the civil wound v 3 86
Like an engine, wrench'd my frame of nature From the fix'd place *Lear* i 4 290
You mortal engines, whose rude throats The immortal Jove's dread clamours counterfeit, Farewell! *Othello* iii 3 355
Take me from this world with treachery and devise engines for my life. iv 2 221
Enginer. Then there's Achilles, a rare enginer! *Troi. and Cres.* ii 3 8
For 'tis the sport to have the enginer Hoist with his own petar *Hamlet* iii 4 206
Engirt. My body round engirt with misery *2 Hen. VI.* iii 1 200
That gold must round engirt these brows of mine v 1 99
England. Were I in England now, as once I was *Tempest* ii 2 29
I shall as soon quarrel at it as any man in England *Mer. Wives* i 1 303
Where England?—I looked for the chalky cliffs *Com. of Errors* iii 2 128
What say you, then, to Falconbridge, the young baron of England? *Mer. of Venice* i 2 72
He hath an argosy bound to Tripolis, . . . a fourth for England i 3 21
They have in England A coin that bears the figure of an angel ii 7 55
What, not one hit? From Tripolis, from Mexico and England? iii 2 271
And there they live like the old Robin Hood of England *As Y. Like It* i 1 123
Although the sheet were big enough for the bed of Ware in England *T. Night* iii 2 51
To the majesty, The borrow'd majesty, of England here *K. John* i 1 4
That England, hedged in with the main, That water-walled bulwark ii 1 26
My Lord Chatillon may from England bring That right in peace ii 1 46
What England says, say briefly, gentle lord; We coldly pause for thee. ii 1 52
England, impatient of your just demands, Hath put himself in arms ii 1 56
Peace be to England, if that war return From France to England ii 1 89
England we love; and for that England's sake With burden of our armour here we sweat ii 1 91
But thou from loving England art so far, That thou hast under-wrought his lawful king ii 1 94
England was Geffrey's right And this is Geffrey's ii 1 105
England and Ireland, Anjou, Touraine, Maine, In right of Arthur do I claim ii 1 152
Who is it that hath warn'd us to the walls?—'Tis France, for England. ii 1 202
We are the king of England's subjects: To him, and in his right, we hold this town ii 1 267
Doth not the crown of England prove the king? ii 1 273
Twice fifteen thousand hearts of England's breed ii 1 275
To enter conquerors and to proclaim Arthur of Bretagne England's king ii 1 311
King John, your king and England's, doth approach ii 1 313
England, thou hast not saved one drop of blood, In this hot trial, more than we of France ii 1 341
Speak, citizens, for England; who's your king?—The king of England. ii 1 362
By east and west let France and England mount Their battering cannon ii 1 381
That daughter there of Spain, the Lady Blanch, Is niece to England ii 1 424
Speak England first, that hath been forward first To speak unto this city ii 1 482
Brother of England, how may we content This widow lady? ii 1 547
O boy, then where art thou? France friend with England, what becomes of me? iii 1 35
Tell him this tale; and from the mouth of England Add thus much more iii 1 152
Brother of England, you blaspheme in this iii 1 161
A heavy curse from Rome, Or the light loss of England for a friend iii 1 206
All form is formless, order orderless, Save what is opposite to England's love iii 1 254
Cousin, away for England! haste before iii 3 6
For England, cousin, go: Hubert shall be your man, attend on you iii 3 71
And bloody England into England gone, O'erbearing interruption iii 4 8
Well could I bear that England had this praise, So we could find some pattern of our shame iii 4 15
To England, if you will.—Bind up your hairs.—Yes, that I will iii 4 68
Shall blow each dust, each straw, each little rub, Out of the path which shall directly lead Thy foot to England's throne iii 4 130
Faulconbridge Is now in England, ransacking the church, Offending charity iii 4 172
For England go: I will whet on the king iii 4 181
How goes all in France?—From France to England iv 2 110
Heaven take my soul, and England keep my bones! iv 3 10
How easy dost thou take all England up! iv 3 142
England now is left To tug and scamble and to part by the teeth iv 3 145
You bloody Neroes, ripping up the womb Of your dear mother England v 2 153
Lead me to the revolts of England here.—When we were happy we had other names v 4 7
What art thou?—Of the part of England.—Whither dost thou go? v 6 2
England never did, nor never shall, Lie at the proud foot of a conqueror v 7 112
Nought shall make us rue, If England to itself do rest but true v 7 118
Save back to England, all the world's my way *Richard II.* i 3 207
Then, England's ground, farewell; sweet soil, adieu! i 3 306
As were our England in reversion his, And he our subjects' next degree in hope i 4 35
This blessed plot, this earth, this realm, this England ii 1 50
England, bound in with the triumphant sea ii 1 61
That England, that was wont to conquer others, Hath made a shameful conquest of itself ii 1 65
For sleeping England long time have I watch'd ii 1 77
Landlord of England art thou now, not king ii 1 113
Not Gaunt's rebukes, nor England's private wrongs ii 1 166
My answer is—to Lancaster; And I am come to seek that name in England ii 3 71
Why have those banish'd and forbidden legs Dared once to touch a dust of England's ground? ii 3 91
If that my cousin king be King of England, It must be granted I am Duke of Lancaster ii 3 123

England. My lords of England, let me tell you this *Richard II.* ii 3 140
More welcome is the stroke of death to me Than Bolingbroke to England iii 1 32
Ten thousand bloody crowns of mothers' sons Shall ill become the flower of England's face iii 3 97
I heard you say that you had rather refuse The offer of an hundred thousand crowns Than Bolingbroke's return to England iv 1 17
An if my word be sterling yet in England, Let it command a mirror hither straight iv 1 264
Shall there be gallows standing in England when thou art king? *1 Hen. IV.* i 2 67
When I am king of England, I shall command all the good lads in Eastcheap ii 4 15
I'll be sworn upon all the books in England, I could find in my heart ii 4 56
There live not three good men unhanged in England ii 4 144
And said he would swear truth out of England ii 4 337
Shall the son of England prove a thief and take purses? ii 4 451
Clipp'd in with the sea That chides the banks of England, Scotland, Wales iii 1 45
England, from Trent and Severn hitherto, By south and east is to my part assign'd iii 1 74
So long in his unlucky Irish wars That all in England did repute him dead v 1 54
If he outlive the envy of this day, England did never owe so sweet a hope v 2 68
Nor can one England brook a double reign v 4 66
An 'twere not for thy humours, there's not a better wench in England *2 Hen. IV.* ii 1 162
Did all the chivalry of England move To do brave acts ii 3 20
It is the foul-mouthed'st rogue in England ii 4 78
Was reputed then In England the most valiant gentleman iv 1 132
Shall hold this quarrel up Whiles England shall have generation iv 2 49
England shall double gild his treble guilt, England shall give him office iv 5 129
What! rate, rebuke, and roughly send to prison The immediate heir of England! v 2 71
Never king of England Had nobles richer and more loyal subjects, Whose hearts have left their bodies here in England *Hen. V.* i 2 126
That England, being empty of defence, Hath shook and trembled at the ill neighbourhood i 2 153
For once the eagle England being in prey, To her unguarded nest the weasel Scot Comes sneaking i 2 169
Divide your happy England into four; Whereof take you one quarter into France, And you withal shall make all Gallia shake i 2 214
We never valued this poor seat of England i 2 269
Now all the youth of England are on fire ii Prol. 1
O England! model to thy inward greatness, Like little body with a mighty heart, What mightst thou do! ii Prol. 16
The signs of war advance: No king of England, if not king of France ii 2 193
For England his approaches makes as fierce As waters to the sucking of a gulf ii 4 9
With no show of fear; No, with no more than if we heard that England Were busied with a Whitsun morris-dance ii 4 24
Ambassadors from Harry King of England Do crave admittance ii 4 65
Bear our full intent Back to our brother England ii 4 115
What to him from England?—Scorn and defiance; slight regard, contempt ii 4 116
I desire Nothing but odds with England ii 4 129
And leave your England, as dead midnight still, Guarded with grandsires iii Prol. 19
And you, good yeomen, Whose limbs were made in England, show us here The mettle of your pasture iii 1 26
And upon this charge Cry 'God for Harry, England, and Saint George!' iii 1 34
Speed him hence: Let him greet England with our sharp defiance iii 5 37
Bar Harry England, that sweeps through our land iii 5 48
Say to England that we send To know what willing ransom he will give iii 5 62
And quickly bring us word of England's fall iii 5 68
Say thou to Harry of England: Though we seemed dead, we did but sleep iii 6 126
England shall repent his folly, see his weakness, and admire our sufferance iii 6 131
Alas, poor Harry of England! he longs not for the dawning as we do iii 7 140
What a wretched and peevish fellow is this king of England! iii 7 143
That island of England breeds very valiant creatures iii 7 150
Go with my brothers to my lords of England iv 1 30
That England shall couch down in fear and yield iv 2 37
O that we now had here But one ten thousand of those men in England That do no work to-day! iv 3 17
No, faith, my coz, wish not a man from England iv 3 30
And gentlemen in England now a-bed Shall think themselves accursed they were not here iv 3 64
Thou dost not wish more help from England, coz? iv 3 73
The most brave, valorous, and thrice-worthy signieur of England iv 4 67
As any is in the universal world, or in France, or in England! iv 8 11
And then to Calais; and to England then iv 8 130
The lamentation of the French Invites the King of England's stay at home v Prol. 37
To England will I steal, and there I'll steal: And patches will I get v 1 92
Right joyous are we to behold your face, Most worthy brother England v 2 10
So happy be the issue, brother England, Of this good day v 2 12
My duty to you both, on equal love, Great Kings of France and England v 2 24
Your majesty shall mock at me; I cannot speak your England v 2 103
Take me by the hand, and say 'Harry of England, I am thine' v 2 256
I will tell thee aloud 'England is thine, Ireland is thine, France is thine, and Henry Plantagenet is thine' v 2 258
They should sooner persuade Harry of England than a general petition v 2 305
We have consented to all terms of reason.—Is't so, my lords of England? v 2 359
That the contending kingdoms Of France and England, whose very shores look pale With envy of each other's happiness, May cease their hatred v 2 378
That never war advance His bleeding sword 'twixt England and fair France v 2 383
Small time, but in that small most greatly lived This star of England. Epil. 6
Henry the Sixth, in infant bands crown'd King Of France and England Epil. 10
That they lost France and made his England bleed. Epil. 12
England ne'er lost a king of so much worth.—England ne'er had a king until his time *1 Hen. VI.* i 1 7
Of England's coat one half is cut away i 1 81
A countryman of ours records, England all Olivers and Rowlands bred i 2 30
Either renew the fight, Or tear the lions out of England's coat i 5 28
Duke of Clarence, Third son to the third Edward King of England ii 4 84

England. We may march in England or in France, Not seeing what is likely to ensue *1 Hen. VI.* iii 1 187
Was not the Duke of Orleans thy foe? And was he not in England prisoner? iii 3 70
Crossing the sea from England into France iv 1 89
The rest After some respite will return to Calais; From thence to England iv 1 171
English John Talbot, captains, calls you forth, Servant in arms to Harry King of England iv 2 4
A little herd of England's timorous deer, Mazed with a yelping kennel of French curs! iv 2 46
God and Saint George, Talbot and England's right, Prosper our colours! iv 2 55
To Bourdeaux, York! Else, farewell Talbot, France, and England's honour iv 3 23
You, his false hopes, the trust of England's honour, Keep off aloof iv 4 20
The fraud of England, not the force of France, Hath now entrapp'd the noble-minded Talbot: Never to England shall he bear his life iv 4 36
In thee thy mother dies, our household's name, My death's revenge, thy youth, and England's fame iv 6 39
Whose life was England's glory, Gallia's wonder iv 7 48
A godly peace concluded of Between the realms of England and of France v 1 6
He doth intend she shall be England's queen v 1 45
Then take my soul, my body, soul and all, Before that England give the French the foil v 3 23
Now the time is come That France must vail her lofty-plumed crest And let her head fall into England's lap v 3 26
Princes should be free.—And so shall you, If happy England's royal king be free v 3 115
I'll over then to England with this news, And make this marriage v 3 167
Give consent That Margaret may be England's royal queen v 5 24
That Lady Margaret do vouchsafe to come To cross the seas to England v 5 90
In sight of England and her lordly peers, Deliver up my title *2 Hen. VI.* i 1 11
Great King of England and my gracious lord i 1 24
Long live Queen Margaret, England's happiness!—We thank you all i 1 37
Marquess of Suffolk, ambassador for Henry King of England i 1 46
And crown her Queen of England ere the thirtieth of May next ensuing i 1 49
And she sent over of the King of England's own proper cost and charges i 1 61
Brave peers of England, pillars of the state i 1 75
O peers of England, shameful is this league! Fatal this marriage i 1 98
I never read but England's kings have had Large sums of gold and dowries with their wives i 1 128
The realms of England, France and Ireland Bear that proportion to my flesh and blood As did the fatal brand Althæa burn'd Unto the prince's heart of Calydon i 1 232
I had hope of France, Even as I have of fertile England's soil i 1 238
With his new bride and England's dear-bought queen i 1 252
Whose bookish rule hath pull'd fair England down i 1 259
Is this the guise, Is this the fashion in the court of England? i 3 46
As I was cause Your highness came to England, so will I In England work your grace's full content i 3 69
Not the least of these But can do more in England than the king.—And he of these that can do most of all Cannot do more in England than the Nevils i 3 74
Not half so bad as thine to England's king i 4 50
Suffolk, England knows thine insolence.—And thy ambition, Gloucester ii 1 31
Craving your opinion of my title, Which is infallible, to England's crown ii 2 5
Long live our sovereign Richard, England's king!—We thank you, lords ii 2 63
To make the Earl of Warwick The greatest man in England but the king ii 2 82
God and King Henry govern England's realm ii 3 30
And Humphrey is no little man in England iii 1 20
I had hope of France As firmly as I hope for fertile England iii 1 88
I have watch'd the night, Ay, night by night, in studying good for England iii 1 111
That England was defamed by tyranny iii 1 123
I will stir up in England some black storm Shall blow ten thousand souls to heaven or hell iii 1 349
And twice by awkward wind from England's bank Drove back again iii 2 83
And bid them blow towards England's blessed shore iii 2 90
And even with this I lost fair England's view iii 2 110
Suffolk straight be done to death, Or banished fair England's territories iii 2 245
If thou be'st death, I'll give thee England's treasure, Enough to purchase such another island, So thou wilt let me live iii 3 2
Whose filth and dirt Troubles the silver spring where England drinks iv 1 72
It was never merry world in England since gentlemen came up iv 2 9
There shall be in England seven halfpenny loaves sold for a penny iv 2 71
For thereby is England mained, and fain to go with a staff iv 2 171
Only that the laws of England may come out of your mouth iv 7 7
My mouth shall be the parliament of England iv 7 17
Spare England, for it is your native coast iv 8 52
Learn to govern better; For yet may England curse my wretched reign iv 9 49
Nay, it shall ne'er be said, while England stands iv 10 45
Burn, bonfires, clear and bright, To entertain great England's lawful king v 1 4
O blood-bespotted Neapolitan, Outcast of Naples, England's bloody scourge! v 1 118
Do repute his grace The rightful heir to England's royal seat v 1 178
Their colours, often borne in France, And now in England to our heart's great sorrow, Shall be my winding-sheet *3 Hen. VI.* i 1 128
What good is this to England and himself! i 1 177
About that which concerns your grace and us; The crown of England, father i 2 9
What! was it you that would be England's king? i 4 70
And when came George from Burgundy to England? ii 1 143
Duke of York: The next degree is England's royal throne; For King of England shalt thou be proclaim'd In every borough as we pass along ii 1 193
To London with triumphant march, There to be crowned England's royal king ii 6 88
Where did you dwell when I was King of England?—Here in this country iii 1 74
Fair Queen of England, worthy Margaret, Sit down with us iii 3 1
Usurps the regal title and the seat Of England's true-anointed lawful king iii 3 29
Grant That virtuous Lady Bona, thy fair sister, To England's king iii 3 57
Then, England's messenger, return in post, And tell false Edward iii 3 222
Tell me some reason why the Lady Grey Should not become my wife and England's queen iv 1 26
Knows not Montague that of itself England is safe, if true within itself? iv 1 40
Then, for his mind, be Edward England's king iv 3 48
Young Henry, earl of Richmond.—Come hither, England's hope iv 6 68

England. Edward the Fourth, by the grace of God, king of England and France *3 Hen. VI.* iv 7 72
Bear him hence; And once again proclaim us king of England iv 8 53
Once more we sit in England's royal throne v 7 1
Small joy have I in being England's queen *Richard III.* i 3 110
Die neither mother, wife, nor England's queen! i 3 209
Thence we look'd toward England, And cited up a thousand fearful times i 4 13
His master's son, as worshipful he terms it, Shall lose the royalty of England's throne iii 4 42
Woe, woe for England! not a whit for me iii 4 82
Miserable England! I prophesy the fearfull'st time to thee iii 4 105
The peace of England and our persons' safety Enforced us to this execution iii 5 45
Cry 'God save Richard, England's royal king!' iii 7 22
Happy were England, would this gracious prince Take on himself the sovereignty thereof iii 7 78
I salute you with this kingly title: Long live Richard, England's royal king! iii 7 240
Nor mother, wife, nor England's counted queen iv 1 47
Rest thy unrest on England's lawful earth! iv 4 29
With my soul I love thy daughter, And mean to make her queen of England iv 4 263
Infer fair England's peace by this alliance iv 4 343
He makes for England, there to claim the crown iv 4 469
And who is England's king but great York's heir? iv 4 473
Awake, awake! Arm, fight, and conquer, for fair England's sake! v 3 150
A base foul stone, made precious by the foil Of England's chair v 3 251
Fight, gentlemen of England! fight, bold yeomen! Draw, archers! v 3 338
England hath long been mad, and scarr'd herself v 5 23
And make poor England weep in streams of blood! v 5 37
Not a man in England Can advise me like you *Hen. VIII.* i 1 134
His fears were, that the interview betwixt England and France might, through their amity, Breed him some prejudice i 1 181
Strive To gain the love o' the commonalty: the duke Shall govern England i 2 171
In faith, for little England You'ld venture an emballing ii 3 46
Proceed.—Say, Henry King of England, come into the court ii 4 6
Say, Katharine Queen of England, come into the court ii 4 10
Your hopes and friends are infinite.—In England But little for my profit iii 1 82
Prosperous life, long, and ever happy, to the high and mighty princess of England, Elizabeth! v 5 3
She shall be, to the happiness of England, An aged princess v 5 57
I'll to England.—To Ireland *Macbeth* ii 3 143
We hear, our bloody cousins are bestow'd In England and in Ireland iii 1 31
Some holy angel Fly to the court of England and unfold His message! iii 6 46
Macduff is fled to England.—Fled to England! iv 1 142
And here from gracious England have I offer Of goodly thousands iv 3 43
A most miraculous work in this good king; Which often, since my here-remain in England, I have seen him do iv 3 148
Gracious England hath Lent us good Siward and ten thousand men iv 3 189
With speed to England, For the demand of our neglected tribute *Hamlet* iii 1 177
To England send him, or confine him where Your wisdom best shall think iii 1 194
I your commission will forthwith dispatch, And he to England shall along with you iii 3 4
I must to England; you know that?—Alack, I had forgot iii 4 200
The associates tend, and every thing is bent For England.—For England! iv 3 48
But, come; for England! Farewell, dear mother.—Thy loving father, Hamlet iv 3 51
And, England, if my love thou hold'st at aught— . . . thou mayst not coldly set Our sovereign process iv 3 60
Do it, England; For like the hectic in my blood he rages, And thou must cure me iv 3 67
It comes from the ambassador that was bound for England iv 6 10
Rosencrantz and Guildenstern hold their course for England iv 6 29
He that is mad, and sent into England.—Ay marry, why was he sent into England?—Why, because he was mad v 1 162
Many several sorts of reasons Importing Denmark's health and England's v 2 21
An earnest conjuration from the king, As England was his faithful tributary v 2 39
It must be shortly known to him from England What is the issue v 2 71
Young Fortinbras, with conquest come from Poland, To the ambassadors of England gives This warlike volley v 2 362
I cannot live to hear the news from England v 2 365
The sight is dismal; And our affairs from England come too late v 2 379
You from the Polack wars, and you from England, Are here arrived v 2 387
An excellent song.—I learned it in England, where, indeed, they are most potent in potting *Othello* ii 3 78
O sweet England! 'King Stephen was a worthy peer' ii 3 91

English. Translated her will out of honesty into English *Mer. Wives* i 3 55
Here will be an old abusing of God's patience and the king's English i 4 6
Here's a fellow frights English out of his wits ii 1 143
Let them keep their limbs whole and hack our English iii 1 80
Let me speak with the gentlemen: they speak English? iv 3 8
I will never mistrust my wife again, till thou art able to woo her in good English v 5 142
Have I lived to stand at the taunt of one that makes fritters of English? v 5 152
I have a poor pennyworth in the English *Mer. of Venice* i 2 77
In the narrow seas that part The French and English ii 8 29
They are bastards to the English; the French ne'er got 'em *All's Well* ii 3 100
Though all these English and their discipline Were harbour'd in their rude circumference *K. John* ii 1 261
Like a jolly troop of huntsmen, come Our lusty English ii 1 322
Fly, noble English, you are bought and sold v 4 10
When English measure backward their own ground In faint retire v 5 3
The language I have learn'd these forty years, My native English, now I must forego *Richard II.* i 3 160
The blood of English shall manure the ground iv 1 137
Forthwith a power of English shall we levy *1 Hen. IV.* i 1 22
Never spake other English in his life than 'Eight shillings and sixpence' ii 4 27
I can speak English, lord, as well as you iii 1 121
My wife can speak no English, I no Welsh iii 1 193
With a great power of English and of Scots *2 Hen. IV.* iv 4 98
O noble English, that could entertain With half their forces the full pride of France! *Hen. V.* i 2 111
Thus comes the English with full power upon us ii 4 1
Left by the fatal and neglected English Upon our fields ii 4 13
Take up the English short, and let them know Of what a monarchy you are the head ii 4 72

English. On, on, you noblest English, Whose blood is fet from fathers of war-proof! . . . . *Hen. V.* iii 1 17
I would fain be about the ears of the English . . . . iii 7 92
The Dauphin longs for morning.—He longs to eat the English . . iii 7 99
The English lie within fifteen hundred paces of your tents . . . iii 7 135
If the English had any apprehension, they would run away . . . iii 7 145
Ay, but these English are shrewdly out of beef . . . . iii 7 163
The confident and over-lusty French Do the low-rated English play at dice . . . . iv Prol. 19
The poor condemned English, Like sacrifices, by their watchful fires Sit iv Prol. 22
The English are embattled, you French peers . . . . . . iv 2 14
Mark then abounding valour in our English . . . . iv 3 104
We are enow yet living in the field To smother up the English . . iv 5 20
You thought, because he could not speak English in the native garb, he could not therefore handle an English cudgel . . . v 1 80
Fairly met: So are you, princes English, every one . . . v 2 11
I am glad thou canst speak no better English . . . . . v 2 127
Dost thou understand thus much English, canst thou love me? . . v 2 205
Compound a boy, half French, half English . . . . . v 2 221
By mine honour, in true English, I love thee . . . . . v 2 237
Thy voice is music and thy English broken; therefore, queen of all, Katharine, break thy mind to me in broken English . . v 2 264
My royal cousin, teach you our princess English?—I would have her learn, my fair cousin, how perfectly I love her; and that is good English . . . . v 2 308
That English may as French, French Englishmen, Receive each other . v 2 395
France is revolted from the English quite, Except some petty towns 1 *Hen. VI.* i 1 90
The famish'd English, like pale ghosts, Faintly besiege us one hour in a month . . . . i 2 7
A holy maid . . . Ordained is to raise this tedious siege And drive the English forth . . . . i 2 54
How Orleans is besieged, And how the English have the suburbs won . i 4 2
The English, in the suburbs close intrench'd . . . . . i 4 9
Rescued is Orleans from the English: Thus Joan la Pucelle hath perform'd her word . . . . i 6 2
There goes the Talbot, with his colours spread, And all the troops of English . . . . iii 3 32
To-day the French, All clinquant, all in gold, like heathen gods, Shone down the English. . . . . *Hen. VIII.* i 1 20
All the good our English Have got by the late voyage is but merely A fit or two o' the face . . . . i 3 5
Because they speak no English, thus they pray'd . . . . i 4 65
A strange tongue makes my cause more strange, suspicious; Pray, speak in English . . . . iii 1 46
The willing'st sin I ever yet committed May be absolved in English . iii 1 50
I thank ye heartily; so shall this lady, When she has so much English v 5 15
What purgative drug Would scour these English hence? . *Macbeth* v 3 56
Your Dane, your German, and your swag-bellied Hollander—Drink, ho!—are nothing to your English . . . . . *Othello* ii 3 81
English army. The English army is grown weak and faint . 1 *Hen. VI.* i 1 158
The English army, that divided was Into two parties, is now conjoin'd in one . . . . v 2 11
English beach. The English beach Pales in the flood with men *Hen. V.* v Prol. 9
English blood. And bedew Her pastures' grass with faithful English blood . . . . *Richard II.* iii 3 100
English bottoms. A braver choice of dauntless spirits Than now the English bottoms have waft o'er Did never float . *K. John* ii 1 73
English breath. And sigh'd my English breath in foreign clouds *Rich. II.* iii 1 20
English circle. With Henry's death the English circle ends 1 *Hen. VI.* i 2 136
English condition. Henceforth let a Welsh correction teach you a good English condition . . . . *Hen. V.* v 1 83
English court. Is not my arm of length, That reacheth from the restful English court As far as Calais, to mine uncle's head? *Richard II.* iv 1 12
To the English court assemble now, From every region, apes of idleness! . . . . 2 *Hen. IV.* iv 5 122
This is the English, not the Turkish court . . . . . v 2 47
The son of Duncan, From whom this tyrant holds the due of birth, Lives in the English court . . . . . *Macbeth* iii 6 26
English courtier. To think an English courtier may be wise, And never see the Louvre . . . . *Hen. VIII.* i 3 22
English crest. There stuck no plume in any English crest That is removed by a staff of France . . . . . . *K. John* ii 1 317
English crown. And heir apparent to the English crown 2 *Hen. VI.* i 1 152
That Richard Duke of York Was rightful heir unto the English crown . i 3 187
Resolve thee, Richard; claim the English crown . 3 *Hen. VI.* i 1 49
Torment myself to catch the English crown . . . . . iii 2 179
But Henry now shall wear the English crown, And be true king indeed iv 3 49
I blast or drown King Edward's fruit, true heir to the English crown . iv 4 24
English cudgel. You thought, because he could not speak English in the native garb, he could not therefore handle an English cudgel *Hen. V.* v 1 81
English dancing-schools. They bid us to the English dancing-schools . iii 5 32
English dead. Once more; Or close the wall up with our English dead iii 1 2
Where is the number of our English dead? . . . . . . iv 8 107
English deer. If we be English deer, be then in blood . 1 *Hen. VI.* iv 2 48
English ditty. I framed to the harp Many an English ditty 1 *Hen. IV.* iii 1 124
English dogs. They call'd us for our fierceness English dogs 1 *Hen. VI.* i 5 25
English earth. Would I had never trod this English earth! *Hen. VIII.* iii 1 143
English epicures. And mingle with the English epicures . *Macbeth* v 3 8
English eye. To the furthest verge That ever was survey'd by English eye . . . . *Richard II.* i 1 94
That their hot blood may spin in English eyes . . . *Hen. V.* iv 2 10
English faces. I will trot to-morrow a mile, and my way shall be paved with English faces . . . . iii 7 88
English feasts. As at English feasts, so I regreet The daintiest last, to make the end most sweet . . . . . . *Richard II.* i 3 67
English fools. You English fools, be friends: we have French quarrels enow . . . . *Hen. V.* iv 1 239
English force. What soldiers, wheyface?—The English force . *Macbeth* v 3 18
English gilt. Iron of Naples hid with English gilt . 3 *Hen. VI.* ii 2 139
English Henry. Now, Salisbury, for thee, and for the right Of English Henry, shall this night appear How much in duty I am bound to both . . . . 1 *Hen. VI.* ii 1 36
As sure as English Henry lives And as his father here was conqueror . iii 2 80
Who then but English Henry will be lord? . . . . . iii 3 66
English John. Thy unnatural uncle, English John . . . *K. John* ii 1 10
English John Talbot, captains, calls you forth . 1 *Hen. VI.* iv 2 3
English kersey. I had as lief be a list of an English kersey *Meas. for Meas.* i 2 34
English king. Now hear our English king . . . . *K. John* v 2 128
This is a sleep That from this golden rigol hath divorced So many English kings . . . . 2 *Hen. IV.* iv 5 37
Be a witness That Bona shall be wife to the English king.—To Edward, but not to the English king . . . . 3 *Hen. VI.* iii 3 139
English legs. I thought upon one pair of English legs Did march three Frenchmen . . . . *Hen. V.* iii 6 158
English lords. The Count Melun is slain; the English lords By his persuasion are again fall'n off . . . . . . *K. John* v 5 10
English Mercuries. With winged heels, as English Mercuries *Hen. V.* ii Prol. 7
English moiety. For my English moiety take the word of a king . . v 2 229
English monsters. See you, my princes and my noble peers, These English monsters! . . . . ii 2 85
English mother. This day hath made Much work for tears in many an English mother . . . . *K. John* ii 1 303
English name. A' has an English name . . . *All's Well* iv 5 41
English nation. It was alway yet the trick of our English nation 2 *Hen. IV.* i 2 241
English nobility. Awake, awake, English nobility! . . 1 *Hen. VI.* i 1 78
English peers. In the balance of great Bolingbroke, Besides himself, are all the English peers . . . . . . *Richard II.* iii 4 88
English power. The English power is near, led on by Malcolm *Macbeth* v 2 1
English princes. You English princes all, I do salute you *Hen. V.* v 2 22
English purposes. The French, advised by good intelligence . . . , Seek to divert the English purposes . . . . ii Prol. 15
English queen. My quarrel and this English queen's are one 3 *Hen. VI.* iii 3 216
English rebels. Douglas and the English rebels met The eleventh of this month at Shrewsbury . . . . . 1 *Hen. IV.* iii 2 165
English scourge. Assign'd am I to be the English scourge 1 *Hen. VI.* i 2 129
English side. Late did he shine upon the English side; Now we are victors . . . . i 2 3
English soul. I say again, there is no English soul More stronger to direct you than yourself . . . . . *Hen. VIII.* i 1 146
English strength. Thou princely leader of our English strength 1 *Hen. VI.* iv 3 17
English tailor. Here's an English tailor come hither, for stealing out of a French hose . . . . *Macbeth* ii 3 15
English Talbot. Ten thousand French have ta'en the sacrament To rive their dangerous artillery Upon no Christian soul but English Talbot 1 *Hen. VI.* iv 2 30
English tongue. Mock-water, in our English tongue, is valour *M. Wives* ii 3 62
Confess it brokenly with your English tongue . . *Hen. V.* v 2 107
English tragedians. Has led the drum before the English tragedians *All's Well* iv 3 299
English treason. It is no English treason to cut French crowns *Hen. V.* iv 1 245
English troops. Our English troops retire, I cannot stay them 1 *Hen. VI.* i 5 2
English weal. The special watchmen of our English weal . . iii 1 66
English woes. These English woes will make me smile in France *Rich. III.* iv 4 115
English yeoman. Yet not so wealthy as an English yeoman 3 *Hen. VI.* i 4 123
English youth. Our mettle is bred out and they will give Their bodies to the lust of English youth . . . . . *Hen. V.* iii 5 30
Englished. The hardest voice of her behaviour, to be Englished rightly, is, 'I am Sir John Falstaff's' . . . . . *Mer. Wives* i 3 52
Englishman. I have as mush mock-vater as de Englishman . . ii 3 65
He borrowed a box of the ear of the Englishman . . *Mer. of Venice* i 2 87
Thinking his voice an armed Englishman . . . *K. John* v 2 145
For that my grandsire was an Englishman, Awakes my conscience to confess all this . . . . v 4 42
Where ever Englishman durst set his foot . . *Richard II.* i 1 66
Boast of this I can, Though banish'd, yet a trueborn Englishman . . i 3 309
Lay the summer's dust with showers of blood Rain'd from the wounds of slaughter'd Englishmen . . . . iii 3 44
I can never win A soul so easy as that Englishman's . . *Hen. V.* ii 2 125
Let me see, by ten We shall have each a hundred Englishmen . . iii 7 169
An Englishman?—An't please your majesty, a rascal . . . iv 7 129
That English may as French, French Englishmen, Receive each other v 2 395
Rebels there are up And put the Englishmen unto the sword 2 *Hen. VI.* iii 1 284
Kerns of Ireland are in arms And temper clay with blood of Englishmen iii 1 311
I do not know that Englishman alive With whom my soul is any jot at odds . . . . *Richard III.* ii 1 69
Can you think, lords, That any Englishman dare give me counsel? *Hen. VIII.* iii 1 84
Is your Englishman so expert in his drinking? . . . *Othello* ii 3 82
Englishwoman. The princess is the better Englishwoman . *Hen. V.* v 2 124
Englut. It engluts and swallows other sorrows And it is still itself *Othello* i 3 57
Englutted. So near the gulf, Thou needs must be englutted . *Hen. V.* iv 3 83
How many prodigal bits have slaves and peasants This night englutted! *T. of Athens* ii 2 175
Engraffed. So lewd and so much engraffed to Falstaff . 2 *Hen. IV.* ii 2 67
Engrave. A pair of bleeding hearts; thereon engrave Edward and York *Richard III.* iv 4 272
Engraved. Who art the table wherein all my thoughts Are visibly character'd and engraved . . . . *T. G. of Ver.* ii 7 4
Upon the which, that every one may read, Shall be engraved the sack of Orleans . . . . 1 *Hen. VI.* ii 2 15
Engross. Percy is but my factor, good my lord, To engross up glorious deeds on my behalf . . . . . . 1 *Hen. IV.* iii 2 148
Not sleeping, to engross his idle body, But praying . *Richard III.* iii 7 76
Engrossed opportunities to meet her . . . . . *Mer. Wives* ii 2 203
Engross'd and piled up The canker'd heaps of strange-achieved gold 2 *Hen. IV.* iv 5 71
Which in a set hand fairly is engross'd . . . *Richard III.* iii 6 2
Engrossest. If thou engrossest all the griefs are thine, Thou robb'st me of a moiety . . . . *All's Well* iii 2 68
Engrossing. Seal with a righteous kiss A dateless bargain to engrossing death! . . . . *Rom. and Jul.* v 3 115
Engrossment. This bitter taste Yield his engrossments to the ending father . . . . 2 *Hen. IV.* iv 5 80
Enguard. He may enguard his dotage with their powers . . *Lear* i 4 349
Enigma. Some enigma, some riddle . . . . . *L. L. Lost* iii 1 72
Your enigma?—You have been a scourge to her enemies, you have been a rod to her friends . . . . *Coriolanus* ii 3 96
Enigmatical. Your answer, sir, is enigmatical . . . . *Much Ado* v 4 27
Enjoin. I would bend under any heavy weight That he'll enjoin me to . v 1 288
We enjoin thee, As thou art liege-man to us . . . *W. Tale* ii 3 173
Enjoined. I would the lightning had Burnt up those logs that you are enjoin'd to pile! . . . . *Tempest* iii 1 17
She enjoined me to write some lines to one she loves . *T. G. of Ver.* ii 1 93
As you enjoin'd me, I have writ your letter . . . . . ii 1 110
It was enjoined him in Rome for want of linen . . *L. L. Lost* v 2 718
I am enjoin'd by oath to observe three things . . *Mer. of Venice* ii 9 9
Of enjoin'd penitents There's four or five . . . . *All's Well* iii 5 97

Enjoined. Most accursed am I To be by oath enjoin'd to this *W. Tale* iii 3 53
And am enjoin'd By holy Laurence to fall prostrate here *Rom. and Jul.* iv 2 19
Enjoineth. And since Lord Helicane enjoineth us, We with our travels will endeavour us *Pericles* ii 4 55
Enjoy. Would it apply well to the vehemency of your affection, that I should win what you would enjoy? *Mer. Wives* ii 2 249
As I am a gentleman, you shall, if you will, enjoy Ford's wife . ii 2 265
What we have we prize not to the worth Whiles we enjoy it *Much Ado* iv 1 221
Out of heart you love her, being out of heart that you cannot enjoy her *L. L. Lost* iii 1 46
And will you persever to enjoy her? . . . . *As Y. Like It* v 2 4
Consent with both that we may enjoy each other . . . . v 2 11
So shall you quietly enjoy your hope . . . *T. of Shrew* iii 2 138
Let me enjoy my private: go off . . . . . *T. Night* iii 4 99
Where you may Enjoy your mistress . . . . *W. Tale* iv 4 539
And as sorry Your choice is not so rich in worth as beauty, That you might well enjoy her . . . . v 1 215
Hadst thou rather be a Faulconbridge And like thy brother, to enjoy thy land? . . . . *K. John* i 1 135
And king o'er him and all that he enjoys . . . . . . ii 1 240
Rich men look sad and ruffians dance and leap, The one in fear to lose what they enjoy, The other to enjoy by rage and war *Richard II.* ii 4 13
He will give you audience; and wherein It shall appear that your demands are just, You shall enjoy them . . 2 *Hen. IV.* iv 1 145
Both which we doubt not but your majesty Shall soon enjoy . iv 4 12
Such are the rich, That have abundance and enjoy it not . iv 4 108
What infinite heart's-ease Must kings neglect, that private men enjoy! *Hen. V.* iv 1 254
The slave, a member of the country's peace, Enjoys it . . iv 1 299
Upon condition I may quietly Enjoy mine own . . 1 *Hen. VI.* v 3 154
Those two counties I will undertake Your grace shall well and quietly enjoy . . . . v 3 159
Thou shalt be placed as viceroy under him, And still enjoy thy regal dignity . . . . v 4 132
Or count them happy that enjoy the sun . . . 2 *Hen. VI.* ii 4 39
Who would live turmoiled in the court, And may enjoy such quiet walks? iv 10 19
Richard Plantagenet, Enjoy the kingdom after my decease . 3 *Hen. VI.* i 1 175
Now you are heir, therefore enjoy it now . . . . . i 2 12
All which secure and sweetly he enjoys . . . . . ii 5 50
My crown is call'd content: A crown it is that seldom kings enjoy . iii 1 65
I speak no more than what my soul intends; And that is, to enjoy thee iii 2 95
In bearing weight of government, While he enjoys the honour and his ease iv 6 52
As little joy, my lord, as you suppose You should enjoy, were you this country's king, As little joy may you suppose in me, That I enjoy, being the queen thereof.—A little joy enjoys the queen thereof *Richard III.* i 3 152
And in record, left them the heirs of shame. Shall these enjoy our lands? v 3 336
Wear it, enjoy it, and make much of it . . . . . v 5 7
With his own hand gave me; Bade me enjoy it . . *Hen. VIII.* iii 2 248
Fortune and I are friends: I do enjoy At ample point all that I did possess, Save these men's looks . . . *Troi. and Cres.* iii 3 88
Thou barr'st us Our prayers to the gods, which is a comfort That all but we enjoy . . . . *Coriolanus* v 3 106
A valiant son-in-law thou shalt enjoy . . . . *T. Andron.* i 1 311
Mistress, now perforce we will enjoy That nice-preserved honesty of yours ii 3 134
Enjoy the honey-heavy dew of slumber . . . *J. Cæsar* ii 1 230
You should enjoy half his revenue . . . . . *Lear* i 2 56
Mean you to enjoy him?—The let-alone lies not in your good will . v 3 78
Thou shalt enjoy her; therefore make money . . *Othello* i 3 365
If thou the next night following enjoy not Desdemona . . iv 2 220
Enjoy thy plainness, It nothing ill becomes thee . . *Ant. and Cleo.* ii 6 80
What do you esteem it at?—More than the world enjoys *Cymbeline* i 4 86
Others do—I was about to say—enjoy your—But It is an office of the gods to venge it . . . . i 6 91
That thou mayst stand, To enjoy thy banish'd lord and this great land! ii 1 70
I'll make a journey twice as far, to enjoy A second night of such sweet shortness . . . . ii 4 43
Enjoyed. He hath enjoyed nothing of Ford's but his buck-basket, his cudgel, and twenty pounds of money . . . *Mer. Wives* v 5 116
All things that are, Are with more spirit chased than enjoy'd *Mer. of Ven.* ii 6 13
And hope to joy is little less in joy Than hope enjoy'd *Richard II.* ii 3 16
My child is none of his: It was Alençon that enjoy'd my love 1 *Hen. VI.* v 4 73
By Him that raised me to this careful height From that contented hap Which I enjoy'd . . . . *Richard III.* i 3 84
Never yet one hour in his bed Have I enjoy'd the golden dew of sleep iv 1 84
After conflict such as was supposed The wandering prince and Dido once enjoy'd . . . . *T. Andron.* ii 3 22
And, though I am sold, Not yet enjoy'd . . . *Rom. and Jul.* iii 2 28
Neither can be enjoy'd, If both remain alive . . . . *Lear* v 1 58
I have enjoyed the dearest bodily part of your mistress . *Cymbeline* i 4 161
They induced to steal it! And by a stranger!—No, he hath enjoy'd her ii 4 126
Enjoying. The conclusion shall be crowned with your enjoying her *Mer. Wives* iii 5 138
As well . . . as for the enjoying of thy life . . *Meas. for Meas.* i 2 194
Mistrust, Which makes me fear the enjoying of my love *Mer. of Venice* iii 2 29
Enjoying but this land, Is it not more than shame to shame it so? *Richard II.* ii 1 111
It is not worth the enjoying . . . . 2 *Hen. VI.* iii 1 334
Enkindle. That trusted home Might yet enkindle you unto the crown *Macbeth* i 3 121
Enkindle all the sparks of nature, To quit this horrid act . . *Lear* iii 7 86
Enkindled. 'Tis far too huge to be blown out With that same weak wind which enkindled it . . . . *K. John* v 2 87
My will enkindled by mine eyes and ears . . . *Troi. and Cres.* ii 2 63
So I did; Fearing to strengthen that impatience Which seem'd too much enkindled . . . . *J. Cæsar* ii 1 249
Enlard. That were to enlard his fat already pride . . *Troi. and Cres.* ii 3 205
Enlarge. He shall enlarge him . . . . *T. Night* v 1 285
And doth enlarge his rising with the blood Of fair King Richard 2 *Hen. IV.* i 1 204
Enlarge the man committed yesterday, That rail'd against our person *Hen. V.* ii 2 40
We'll yet enlarge that man . . . . ii 2 57
Like a circle in the water, Which never ceaseth to enlarge itself 1 *Hen. VI.* i 2 134
Lest your displeasure should enlarge itself To wrathful terms *Tr. and Cr.* v 2 37
Enlarge your griefs, And I will give you audience . . . *J. Cæsar* iv 2 46
So the poor third is up, till death enlarge his confine . *Ant. and Cleo.* iii 5 13
Enlarged him and made a friend of him . . . 1 *Hen. IV.* iii 2 115
Her obsequies have been as far enlarged As we have warranty *Hamlet* v 1 249
Enlargement. Take this key, give enlargement to the swain *L. L. Lost* iii 1 5
Which, for enlargement striving, Shakes the old beldam earth 1 *Hen. IV.* iii 1 31

Enlargement. Just death, kind umpire of men's miseries, With sweet enlargement doth dismiss me hence . . . . . 1 *Hen. VI.* ii 5 30
At our enlargement what are thy due fees? . . 3 *Hen. VI.* iv 6 5
You are curb'd from that enlargement by The consequence o' the crown *Cymbeline* ii 3 125
Enlargeth. She enlargeth her mirth so far that there is shrewd construction made of her . . . . *Mer. Wives* ii 2 231
Enlinked. All fell feats Enlink'd to waste and desolation . *Hen. V.* iii 3 18
Enmesh. And out of her own goodness make the net That shall enmesh them all . . . . *Othello* ii 3 368
Enmities. I know not, Menas, How lesser enmities may give way to greater . . . . *Ant. and Cleo.* ii 1 43
Enmity. He trod the water, Whose enmity he flung aside *Tempest* ii 1 116
The enmity and discord which of late Sprung from the rancorous outrage of your duke . . . . *Com. of Errors* i 1 5
So far from jealousy, To sleep by hate, and fear no enmity? *M. N. Dream* iv 1 150
I will despair, and be at enmity With cozening hope *Richard II.* ii 2 68
While covert enmity Under the smile of safety wounds the world 2 *Hen. IV.* Ind. 9
You see what mischief and what murder too Hath been enacted through your enmity . . . . 1 *Hen. VI.* iii 1 116
Poor harmless lambs abide their enmity . . . . 3 *Hen. VI.* ii 5 75
Till storms be past of civil enmity . . . . iv 6 98
Made peace of enmity, fair love of hate . . . *Richard III.* ii 1 50
'Tis death to me to be at enmity; I hate it, and desire all good men's love ii 1 60
Smile heaven upon this fair conjunction, That long have frown'd upon their enmity! . . . . v 5 21
To stand the push and enmity of those This quarrel would excite *Troi. and Cres.* ii 2 137
On a dissension of a doit, break out To bitterest enmity *Coriolanus* iv 4 18
And to poor we Thine enmity's most capital . . . . . v 3 104
Set deadly enmity between two friends . . . *T. Andron.* v 1 131
Who drown'd their enmity in my true tears . . . . . v 3 107
Look thou but sweet, And I am proof against their enmity *Rom. and Jul.* ii 2 73
As rich shall Romeo's by his lady's lie: Poor sacrifices of our enmity! v 3 304
Whose effect Holds such an enmity with blood of man . *Hamlet* i 5 65
I abjure all roofs, and choose To wage against the enmity o' the air *Lear* ii 4 212
Ennoble. Many fair promotions Are daily given to ennoble those That scarce, some two days since, were worth a noble *Richard III.* i 3 81
Ennobled. Who, so ennobled, Is as 'twere born so . . *All's Well* ii 3 179
Enobarb. Strong Enobarb Is weaker than the wine . . *Ant. and Cleo.* ii 7 129
Enobarbus. How now! Enobarbus!—What's your pleasure, sir? . . i 2 134
Good Enobarbus, 'tis a worthy deed, And shall become you well . ii 2 1
Good Enobarbus, make yourself my guest Whilst you abide here . . ii 2 249
Enobarbus, When Antony found Julius Cæsar dead, He cried . . iii 2 53
What shall we do, Enobarbus?—Think, and die . . . . iii 13 1
Call for Enobarbus, He shall not hear thee; or from Cæsar's camp Say 'I am none of thine' . . . . iv 5 7
Enobarbus, Antony Hath after thee sent all thy treasure, with His bounty iv 6 20
Mock not, Enobarbus. I tell you true: best you safed the bringer . iv 6 25
Be witness to me, O thou blessed moon, When men revolted shall upon record Bear hateful memory, poor Enobarbus did Before thy face repent! . . . . iv 9 9
Enormity. In what enormity is Marcius poor in, that you two have not in abundance? . . . . *Coriolanus* ii 1 18
Enormous. And shall find time From this enormous state . *Lear* ii 2 176
Enough. Blow, till thou burst thy wind, if room enough! . *Tempest* i 1 9
There's wood enough within.—Come forth, I say! . . . . i 2 314
Space enough Have I in such a prison . . . . . . i 2 492
I'll pluck thee berries; I'll fish for thee and get thee wood enough . ii 2 165
Beat him enough: after a little time I'll beat him too . . . iii 2 93
I know that well enough.—What dost thou know? . . *T. G. of Ver.* ii 1 55
Enough; I read your fortune in your eye . . . . . ii 4 143
You, Sir Thurio, are not sharp enough; You must lay lime to tangle her desires . . . . iii 2 67
Currish thanks is good enough for such a present . . . . iv 4 53
If we recover that, we are sure enough . . . . . . v 1 12
Why, now let me die, for I have lived long enough . . *Mer. Wives* iii 3 47
Mistress Ford! I have had ford enough; I was thrown into the ford . iii 5 36
He teaches him to hick and to hack, which they'll do fast enough of themselves . . . . iv 1 69
There is no woman's gown big enough for him . . . . iv 2 72
Hang him, dishonest varlet! we cannot misuse him enough . . iv 2 105
If my wind were but long enough to say my prayers, I would repent . iv 5 105
The white will decipher her well enough . . . . . v 2 11
This is enough to be the decay of lust and late-walking through the realm v 5 152
Have you nuns no farther privileges?—Are not these large enough? *Meas. for Meas.* i 4 2
Having waste ground enough, Shall we desire to raze the sanctuary? . ii 2 170
There is scarce truth enough alive to make societies secure; but security enough to make fellowships accurst . . . . iii 2 240
This news is old enough, yet it is every day's news . . . iii 2 243
If it be too little for your thief, your true man thinks it big enough; if it be too big for your thief, your thief thinks it little enough . . iv 2 48
If they be true; if not true, none were enough . . . . iv 3 178
Sirrah, no more!—Enough, my lord . . . . v 1 215
Is't not enough thou hast suborn'd these women To accuse this worthy man? . . . . v 1 308
Away with him to prison! lay bolts enough upon him . . . . v 1 350
Bear it with you, lest I come not time enough . . *Com. of Errors* iv 1 41
Ay, but not rough enough.—As roughly as my modesty would let me . v 1 58
Even so much that joy could not show itself modest enough *Much Ado* i 1 22
If he have wit enough to keep himself warm . . . . . i 1 68
I have almost matter enough in me for such an embassage . . . i 1 281
With a good leg and a good foot, uncle, and money enough in his purse ii 1 16
The clerk is answered.—I know you well enough . . . . ii 1 116
I am sure you know him well enough.—Not I, believe me . . ii 1 138
What proof shall I make of that?—Proof enough to misuse the prince . ii 2 28
Thou singest well enough for a shift . . . . ii 3 80
May be she doth but counterfeit.—Faith, like enough . . . ii 3 108
If you will follow me, I will show you enough . . . . . iii 2 124
If your husband have stables enough, you'll see he shall lack no barns iii 4 48
Doth not my wit become me rarely?—It is not seen enough . . iii 4 71
There is not chastity enough in language Without offence to utter them iv 1 98
Enough, I am engaged; I will challenge him . . . . . iv 1 335
One that knows the law, go to; and a rich fellow enough, go to . iv 2 87
What though care killed a cat, thou hast mettle enough in thee to kill care v 1 133
Fire enough for a flint, pearl enough for a swine . . *L. L. Lost* iv 2 90
Where will you find men worthy enough to present them? . . . v 1 131
He is not quantity enough for that Worthy's thumb . . . . v 1 138

Enough. And that were enough to hang us all . *M. N. Dream* i 2 78
At the duke's oak we meet.—Enough ; hold or cut bow-strings . i 2 114
Weed wide enough to wrap a fairy in . ii 1 256
Is't not enough, is't not enough, young man, That I did never, no, nor never can? . ii 2 125
If I had wit enough to get out of this wood, I have enough to serve . iii 1 152
Enough, enough, my lord ; you have enough : I beg the law . iv 1 159
It is not enough to speak, but to speak true . v 1 121
You have the grace of God, sir, and he hath enough *Mer. of Venice* ii 2 160
Parts that become thee happily enough . ii 2 191
The patch is kind enough, but a huge feeder ; Snail-slow in profit . ii 5 46
If thou be'st rated by thy estimation, Thou dost deserve enough . ii 7 27
O that I had a title good enough to keep his name company ! . iii 1 15
Can no prayers pierce thee?—No, none that thou hast wit enough to make iv 1 127
The greatness whereof I cannot enough commend . iv 1 159
If the Jew do cut but deep enough, I'll pay it presently with all my heart iv 1 280
Like the mending of highways In summer, where the ways are fair enough v 1 264
My father's love is enough to honour him : enough ! speak no more of him *As Y. Like It* i 2 89
Thou art thy father's daughter ; there's enough . i 3 60
I am in a holiday humour and like enough to consent . iv 1 69
'Tis no matter how it be in tune, so it make noise enough . iv 2 10
The priest was good enough, for all the old gentleman's saying . v 1 3
Marry, I fare well; for here is cheer enough . *T. of Shrew* Ind. 2 103
Would take her with all faults, and money enough . i 1 134
If thou know One rich enough to be Petruchio's wife . i 2 67
Give him gold enough and marry him to a puppet or an aglet-baby . i 2 78
With wealth enough and young and beauteous . i 2 86
Her only fault, and that is faults enough, Is that she is intolerable curst i 2 88
Tell me her father's name and 'tis enough . i 2 94
He was skilful enough to have lived still . *All's Well* i 1 34
And have ability enough to make such knaveries yours . i 3 12
The gift doth stretch itself as 'tis received, And is enough for both . ii 1 5
The rather will I spare my praises towards him ; Knowing him is enough ii 1 107
If there be breadth enough in the world, I will hold a long distance . iii 2 26
Choughs' language, gabble enough, and good enough . iv 1 22
Within these three hours 'twill be time enough to go home . iv 1 28
Enough ; no more : 'Tis not so sweet now as it was before . *T. Night* i 1 7
These clothes are good enough to drink in ; and so be these boots too . i 3 11
It becomes me well enough, does't not?—Excellent: it hangs like flax on a distaff . i 3 106
Not yet old enough for a man, nor young enough for a boy . i 5 165
He does well enough if he be disposed, and so do I too . ii 3 87
Do not think I have wit enough to lie straight in my bed . ii 3 147
I have no exquisite reason for't, but I have reason good enough . ii 3 158
This fellow is wise enough to play the fool . iii 1 67
To one of your receiving Enough is shown . iii 1 132
Although the sheet were big enough for the bed of Ware in England . iii 2 51
Let there be gall enough in thy ink, though thou write with a goose-pen iii 2 52
I am not tall enough to become the function well, nor lean enough to be thought a good student . iv 2 8
Though I confess, on base and ground enough . v 1 78
A gracious innocent soul, More free than he is jealous.—That's enough *W. Tale* ii 3 30
Which is enough, I'll warrant, As this world goes, to pass for honest . ii 3 71
That's true enough ; Though 'tis a saying, sir, not due to me . iii 2 58
Places remote enough are in Bohemia . iii 3 31
Which if I have not enough considered, as too much I cannot . iv 2 19
Your purse is not hot enough to purchase your spice . iv 3 127
I shall have more than you can dream of yet; Enough then for your wonder . iv 4 400
And you, enchantment,—Worthy enough a herdsman . iv 4 446
To unpath'd waters, undream'd shores, most certain To miseries enough iv 4 579
Sir, you have done enough, and have perform'd A saint-like sorrow . v 1 1
Have preserved Myself to see the issue.—There's time enough for that v 3 128
Make this match ; Give with our niece a dowry large enough *K. John* ii 1 469
And it shall be as all the ocean, Enough to stifle such a villain up . iv 3 133
Let hell want pains enough to torture me . iv 3 138
Thou hast said enough. Beshrew thee, cousin ! . *Richard II.* iii 2 203
I am too young to be your father, Though you are old enough to be my heir iii 3 205
That any in this noble presence Were enough noble to be upright judge ! iv 1 118
I'll read enough, When I do see the very book indeed . iv 1 273
What hole in hell were hot enough for him? . *1 Hen. IV.* i 2 120
Time enough to go to bed with a candle, I warrant thee . ii 1 48
The stony-hearted villains know it well enough . ii 2 29
There's enough to make us all.—To be hanged . ii 2 60
You are straight enough in the shoulders, you care not who sees your back ii 4 164
Have done enough To put him quite beside his patience . iii 1 178
Thou that art like enough, through vassal fear . iii 2 124
I was as virtuously given as a gentleman need to be; virtuous enough . iii 3 17
I know you well enough.—No, Sir John ; you do not know me . iii 3 73
They'll find linen enough on every hedge . iv 2 52
I did never see such pitiful rascals.—Tut, tut ; good enough to toss . iv 2 71
I guess their tenour.—Like enough you do . iv 4 7
But now two paces of the vilest earth Is room enough . v 4 92
For this I shall have time enough to mourn . *2 Hen. IV.* i 1 136
To look with forehead bold and big enough . i 3 8
I think we are a body strong enough, Even as we are, to equal with the king . i 3 66
And never shall have length of life enough To rain upon remembrance ii 3 58
I was pricked well enough before, an you could have let me alone . iii 2 122
Thy mother's son ! like enough, and thy father's shadow . iii 2 139
A traitor your degree, and the dungeon your place, a place deep enough iv 3 9
Though thou stand'st more sure than I could do, Thou art not firm enough iv 5 204
I will devise matter enough out of this . v 1 87
And she shall have whipping-cheer enough, I warrant her . v 4 6
Save that there was not time enough to hear . *Hen. V.* i 1 84
I have, and I will hold, the quondam Quickly For the only she ; and—pauca, there's enough . ii 1 83
Go down upon him, you have power enough . iii 5 53
We know enough, if we know we are the king's subjects . iv 1 137
There is not work enough for all our hands ; Scarce blood enough in all their sickly veins To give each naked curtle-axe a stain . iv 2 20
By this day and this light, the fellow has mettle enough in his belly . iv 8 67
Enough, captain : you have astonished him . v 1 40
Have some more sauce to your leek? there is not enough leek to swear by v 1 52
Your majestee ave fausse French enough to deceive de most sage demoiselle dat is en France . v 2 234
How may I reverently worship thee enough? . *1 Hen. VI.* i 2 145
Enough : my soul shall then be satisfied . ii 5 21

Enough. We are well fortified And strong enough to issue out and fight *1 Hen. VI.* iv 2 20
Call these dead to life ! It were enough to fright the realm of France iv 7 82
There is remedy enough, my lord : Consent, and for thy honour give consent . v 3 135
It is enough ; I'll think upon the questions . *2 Hen. VI.* i 2 82
The king is old enough himself To give his censure . i 3 119
If he be old enough, what needs your grace To be protector? . i 3 121
Her fume needs no spurs, She'll gallop far enough to her destruction . i 3 154
And fear not, neighbour, you shall do well enough . ii 3 61
To be used according to your state.—That's bad enough . ii 4 96
Enough, sweet Suffolk ; thou torment'st thyself . iii 2 329
A wilderness is populous enough, So Suffolk had thy heavenly company iii 2 360
I'll give thee England's treasure, Enough to purchase such another island iii 3 3
Is't not enough to break into my garden? . iv 10 35
'Tis not enough our foes are this time fled . v 3 21
You are old enough now, and yet, methinks, you lose . *3 Hen. VI.* i 1 113
Richard, enough ; I will be king, or die . i 2 35
Methinks, 'tis prize enough to be his son . ii 1 20
Why, so I am, in mind ; and that's enough . iii 1 60
Of force enough to bid his brother battle . v 1 77
Give me a cup of wine.—You shall have wine enough, my lord, anon *Richard III.* i 4 168
O, that's the sword to it.—Ay, gentle cousin, were it light enough . iii 1 117
'Tis like enough, for I stay dinner there . iii 2 122
That former fabulous story, Being now seen possible enough *Hen. VIII.* i 1 37
The cardinal instantly will find employment, And far enough from court too . ii 1 49
Heaven's peace be with him ! That's Christian care enough . ii 2 131
Sharp enough, Lord, for thy justice ! . iii 2 92
I have told you enough of this : for my part, I'll not meddle *Troi. and Cres.* i 1 13
Why, Paris hath colour enough.—So he has . i 2 108
He having colour enough, and the other higher, is too flaming a praise i 2 112
O, enough, Patroclus ; Or give me ribs of steel ! . i 3 176
Were his brain as barren As banks of Libya,—though, Apollo knows, 'Tis dry enough . i 3 329
Thinking it harder for our mistress to devise imposition enough than for us to undergo any difficulty imposed . iii 2 86
Princes, enough, so please you.—I am not warm yet . iv 5 117
You may have every day enough of Hector, If you have stomach . iv 5 263
An honest fellow enough, and one that loves quails . v 1 57
He's one honest enough : would all the rest were so! . *Coriolanus* i 1 54
They say there's grain enough ! . i 1 200
You are known well enough too.—I am known to be a humorous patrician . ii 1 49
Follows it that I am known well enough too? what harm can your bisson conspectuities glean out of this character, if I be known well enough too? . ii 1 69
We know you well enough.—You know neither me, yourselves, nor any thing . ii 1 74
Come, enough.—Enough, with over-measure . iii 1 139
Has said enough.—Has spoken like a traitor, and shall answer As traitors do . iii 1 161
You might have been enough the man you are, With striving less to be so iii 2 19
But he was always good enough for him . iv 5 193
Fear not thy sons ; they shall do well enough . *T. Andron.* ii 3 305
There is enough written upon this earth To stir a mutiny in the mildest thoughts . iv 1 84
'Tis sure enough, an you knew how . iv 1 95
Now let me see your archery ; Look ye draw home enough . iv 3 3
I am not mad ; I know thee well enough . v 2 21
How shall we be employ'd?—Tut, I have work enough for you to do . v 2 150
Enough of this ; I pray thee, hold thy peace . *Rom. and Jul.* i 3 49
Love-devouring death do what he dare ; It is enough I may but call her mine . ii 6 8
You shall find me apt enough to that, sir, an you will give me occasion iii 1 44
What, art thou hurt?—Ay, ay, a scratch, a scratch ; marry, 'tis enough iii 1 96
'Tis not so deep as a well, nor so wide as a church-door; but 'tis enough, 'twill serve . iii 1 100
Tybalt's death Was woe enough, if it had ended there . iii 2 115
The tears have got small victory by that; For it was bad enough before iv 1 31
To-morrow?—No, not till Thursday ; there is time enough . iv 2 36
'Tis not enough to help the feeble up, But to support him after *T. of A.* i 1 107
'Tis not enough to give ; Methinks, I could deal kingdoms to my friends i 2 225
Thou knowest well enough, although thou comest to me, that this is no time to lend money . iii 1 43
That is, one may reach deep enough, and yet Find little . iii 4 15
If money were as certain as your waiting, 'Twere sure enough . iii 4 48
No matter what ; he's poor, and that's revenge enough . iii 4 63
If there were no foes, that were enough To overcome him . iii 5 70
Now the gods keep you old enough ; that you may live Only in bone ! . iii 5 104
Lend to each man enough, that one need not lend to another . iii 6 82
Hast thou more?—Enough to make a whore forswear her trade . iv 3 133
Not all the whips of heaven are large enough . v 1 64
Come to me, I'll give you gold enough . v 1 107
Be Alcibiades your plague, you his, And last so long enough ! . v 1 193
Now is it Rome indeed and room enough, When there is in it but one only man . *J. Cæsar* i 2 156
Where wilt thou find a cavern dark enough To mask thy monstrous visage? . ii 1 80
Not Erebus itself were dim enough To hide thee from prevention . ii 1 84
Bear fire enough To kindle cowards and to steel with valour The melting spirits of women . ii 1 120
I will not come ; That is enough to satisfy the senate . ii 2 72
With courtesy and with respect enough ; But not with such familiar instances . iv 2 15
What's the matter?—Have not you love enough to bear with me? . iv 3 119
Fly far off.—This hill is far enough . v 3 12
Where is he?—Safe, Antony ; Brutus is safe enough . v 4 20
Speak Our free hearts each to other.—Very gladly.—Till then, enough *Macbeth* i 3 156
Who committed treason enough for God's sake, yet could not equivocate to heaven . ii 3 11
Macbeth ! beware Macduff ; Beware the thane of Fife. Dismiss me. Enough . iv 1 72
Thou speak'st with all thy wit ; and yet, i' faith, With wit enough for thee iv 2 43
We have willing dames enough . iv 3 73
This push Will cheer me ever, or disseat me now. I have lived long enough . v 3 22
Now near enough : your leavy screens throw down . v 6 1

Enough. Lay on, Macduff, And damn'd be him that first cries 'Hold, enough!' *Macbeth* v 8 34
The chariest maid is prodigal enough, If she unmask her beauty to the moon *Hamlet* i 3 36
Which your modesties have not craft enough to colour ii 2 290
Wise men know well enough what monsters you make of them iii 1 144
I have heard of your paintings too, well enough iii 1 149
Is there not rain enough in the sweet heavens To wash it white as snow? iii 3 45
Which is not tomb enough and continent To hide the slain iv 4 64
But to follow him thither with modesty enough, and likelihood to lead it v 1 230
If thou be as poor for a subject as he is for a king, thou art poor enough *Lear* i 4 23
So distribution should undo excess, And each man have enough iv 1 74
They are apt enough to dislocate and tear Thy flesh and bones iv 2 65
I'll bear Affliction till it do cry out itself 'Enough, enough,' and die iv 6 77
I remember thine eyes well enough. Dost thou squiny at me? iv 6 139
I know thee well enough; thy name is Gloucester iv 6 181
Now let thy friendly hand Put strength enough to't iv 6 235
Nay, it is possible enough to judgement *Othello* i 3 9
Would she give you so much of her lips As of her tongue she oft bestows on me, You'ld have enough ii 1 103
I cannot speak enough of this content; It stops me here; it is too much ii 1 198
I am not drunk now; I can stand well enough, and speak well enough ii 3 120
But you are now well enough: how came you thus recovered? ii 3 295
Poor and content is rich and rich enough iii 3 172
It were enough To put him to ill thinking iii 4 28
Ere it be demanded—As like enough it will—I'ld have it copied iii 4 190
She says enough; yet she's a simple bawd That cannot say as much iv 2 20
Wine enough Cleopatra's health to drink *Ant. and Cleo.* i 2 11
They have entertained cause enough To draw their swords ii 1 46
Therefore Make space enough between you ii 3 23
I have done enough; a lower place, note well, May make too great an act iii 1 12
All may be well enough.—I warrant you, madam iii 3 50
Like enough, high-battled Cæsar will Unstate his happiness! iii 13 29
There are, Of those that served Mark Antony but late, Enough to fetch him in iv 1 14
What have I kept back.—Enough to purchase what you have made known v 2 148
Stand you! You have land enough of your own *Cymbeline* i 2 18
If there were wealth enough for the purchase, or merit for the gift i 4 90
Enough of this: it came in too suddenly; let it die as it was born i 4 130
I have enough: To the trunk again, and shut the spring of it ii 2 46
Thou wert dignified enough, Even to the point of envy ii 3 132
This is not strong enough to be believed Of one persuaded well of ii 4 131
One score 'twixt sun and sun, Madam, 's enough for you: and too much too iii 2 71
Thou then look'dst like a villain; now methinks Thy favour's good enough iii 4 51
She's far enough; and what he learns by this May prove his travel iii 5 102
Though valour Becomes thee well enough iv 2 156
'Tis enough That, Britain, I have kill'd thy mistress v 1 19
Is't enough I am sorry? So children temporal fathers do appease v 4 11
My practice so prevail'd, That I return'd with simular proof enough v 5 200
If Jove stray, who dares say Jove doth ill? It is enough you know *Per.* i 1 105
Say, is it done?—My lord, 'Tis done.—Enough i 1 160
What courage, sir? God save you!—Courage enough iii 1 39
Or that these pirates, Not enough barbarous, had not o'erboard thrown me! iv 2 70
Your honour knows what 'tis to say well enough iv 6 35
Where a man may serve seven years for the loss of a leg, and have not money enough in the end to buy him a wooden one iv 6 183
For truth can never be confirm'd enough, Though doubts did ever sleep v 1 203
Enow. Christians enow before; e'en as many as could well live *M. of V.* iii 5 24
Enow to press a royal merchant down iv 1 29
We have French quarrels enow, if you could tell how to reckon *Hen. V.* iv 1 240
Were enow To purge this field of such a hilding foe iv 2 28
If we are mark'd to die, we are enow To do our country loss iv 3 20
We are enow yet living in the field To smother up the English iv 5 19
Because she is a maid, Spare for no faggots, let there be enow 1 *Hen. VI.* v 4 56
Come in time; have napkins enow about you *Macbeth* ii 3 7
There are liars and swearers enow to beat the honest men and hang up them iv 2 57
I must not think there are Evils enow to darken all his goodness *A. and C.* i 4 11
Enpierced. I am too sore enpierced with his shaft To soar *Rom. and Jul.* i 4 19
Enrage. Let the ruffian Boreas once enrage The gentle Thetis *Tr. and Cr.* i 3 38
Speak not; he grows worse and worse; Question enrages him *Macbeth* iii 4 118
Let grief Convert to anger; blunt not the heart, enrage it iv 3 229
Enraged. Who, all enraged, will banish Valentine *T. G. of Ver.* ii 6 38
She loves him with an enraged affection *Much Ado* ii 3 105
Away went Claudio enraged; swore he would meet her iii 3 170
From the rude sea's enraged and foamy mouth *T. Night* v 1 81
The sea enraged is not half so deaf *K. John* ii 1 451
Those baby eyes That never saw the giant world enraged v 2 57
Even so my limbs, Weaken'd with grief, being now enraged with grief, Are thrice themselves 2 *Hen. IV.* i 1 144
To frown upon the enraged Northumberland i 1 152
Like an offensive wife That hath enraged him on to offer strokes iv 1 211
We may as bootless spend our vain command Upon the enraged soldiers in their spoil *Hen. V.* iii 3 25
Here, there, and every where, enraged he flew 1 *Hen. VI.* i 1 124
Or whether his fall enraged him, or how 'twas, he did so set his teeth and tear it *Coriolanus* i 3 69
Who, thereat enraged, Flew on him, and amongst them fell'd him dead *Lear* iv 2 75
Why is my lord enraged against his love? *Ant. and Cleo.* iv 12 31
Enrank. No leisure had he to enrank his men 1 *Hen. VI.* i 1 115
Enrapt. I myself Am like a prophet suddenly enrapt *Troi. and Cres.* v 3 65
Enrich. Herein mean I to enrich my pain *M. N. Dream* i 1 250
Whose lands and revenues enrich the new duke *As Y. Like It* i 1 108
Henry is able to enrich his queen And not to seek a queen to make him rich: So worthless peasants bargain 1 *Hen. VI.* v 5 51
With what his valour did enrich his wit, His wit set down to make his valour live *Richard III.* iii 1 85
Praying, to enrich his watchful soul iii 7 77
Enrich the time to come with smooth-faced peace, With smiling plenty v 5 33
What lady is that, which doth enrich the hand Of yonder knight? *Rom. and Jul.* i 5 43
He that filches from me my good name Robs me of that which not enriches him And makes me poor indeed *Othello* iii 3 160
Would testify, to enrich mine inventory *Cymbeline* ii 2 30

Enriched. The terms For common justice, you're as pregnant in As art and practice hath enriched any That we remember *Meas. for Meas.* i 1 13
The captive is enriched: on whose side? the beggar's *L. L. Lost* iv 1 76
Such fiery numbers as the prompting eyes Of beauty's tutors have enrich'd you with iv 3 323
Till twice five summers have enrich'd our fields *Richard II.* i 3 141
All my treasury Is yet but unfelt thanks, which more enrich'd Shall be your love and labour's recompense ii 3 61
If thy pocket were enriched with any other injuries but these 1 *Hen. IV.* iii 3 181
Whose chin is but enrich'd With one appearing hair *Hen. V.* iii Prol. 22
Then this land was famously enrich'd With politic grave counsel *Rich. III.* ii 3 19
He likewise enriched poor straggling soldiers *T. of Athens* v 1 6
Her pretty action did outsell her gift, And yet enrich'd it too *Cymbeline* ii 4 103
Enridged. Horns whelk'd and waved like the enridged sea *Lear* iv 6 71
Enring. The female ivy so Enrings the barky fingers of the elm *M. N. Dr.* iv 1 49
Enrobe the roaring waters with my silks *Mer. of Venice* i 1 34
Enrobed. Quaint in green she shall be loose enrobed *Mer. Wives* iv 6 41
Enrolled. This new governor Awakes me all the enrolled penalties *Meas. for Meas.* i 2 170
The which I hope is not enrolled there *L. L. Lost* i 1 41
His oath enrolled in the parliament 3 *Hen. VI.* ii 1 173
This man so complete, Who was enroll'd 'mongst wonders *Hen. VIII.* i 2 119
Renowned Rome, whose gratitude Towards her deserved children is enroll'd In Jove's own book *Coriolanus* iii 1 292
The question of his death is enrolled in the Capitol *J. Cæsar* iii 2 41
Enrooted. His foes are so enrooted with his friends 2 *Hen. IV.* iv 1 207
Enrounded. Upon his royal face there is no note How dread an army hath enrounded him *Hen. V.* iv Prol. 36
Enscheduled. Whose tenours and particular effects You have enscheduled briefly in your hands v 2 73
Ensconce. And yet you, rogue, will ensconce your rags *Mer. Wives* ii 2 27
She shall not see me: I will ensconce me behind the arras iii 3 96
I must get a sconce for my head and insconce it too *Com. of Errors* ii 2 38
Ensconcing ourselves into seeming knowledge *All's Well* ii 3 4
Enseamed. Nay, but to live In the rank sweat of an enseamed bed *Hamlet* iii 4 92
Ensear thy fertile and conceptious womb, Let it no more bring out ingrateful man! *T. of Athens* iv 3 187
Enseigné. N'avez-vous pas déjà oublié ce que je vous ai enseigné *Hen. V.* iii 4 46
Enseignez. Je te prie, m'enseignez; il faut que j'apprenne à parler iii 4 4
Ensemble. Néanmoins, je reciterai une autre fois ma leçon ensemble iii 4 61
Enshield. These black masks Proclaim an enshield beauty *Meas. for Meas.* ii 4 80
Enshrine. Burgundy Enshrines thee in his heart 1 *Hen. VI.* iii 2 119
Ensign. Streaming the ensign of the Christian cross *Richard II.* iv 1 94
Hang up your ensigns, let your drums be still 1 *Hen. VI.* v 4 174
Mine honour's ensigns humbled at thy feet *T. Andron.* i 1 252
Beauty's ensign yet Is crimson in thy lips and in thy cheeks *Rom. and Jul.* v 3 94
On our former ensign Two mighty eagles fell *J. Cæsar* v 1 80
This ensign here of mine was turning back; I slew the coward v 3 3
Let A Roman and a British ensign wave Friendly together *Cymbeline* v 5 480
Enskyed. I hold you as a thing ensky'd and sainted *Meas. for Meas.* i 4 34
Ensnare. Ay, well said, whisper: with as little a web as this will I ensnare as great a fly as Cassio *Othello* ii 1 170
Ensnared. Will you, I pray, demand that demi-devil Why he hath thus ensnared my soul and body? v 2 302
Ensnareth. Whose deadly web ensnareth thee about *Richard III.* i 3 243
Ensteeped. Traitors ensteep'd to clog the guiltless keel *Othello* ii 1 70
Ensue. To bear up Against what should ensue *Tempest* i 2 158
I am almost out at heels.—Why, then, let kibes ensue *Mer. Wives* i 3 35
If we obey them not, this will ensue, They'll suck our breath *Com. of Er.* ii 2 193
Sweet recreation barr'd, what doth ensue But moody and dull melancholy? v 1 78
Of thy misprision must perforce ensue Some true love turn'd *M. N. Dr.* iii 2 90
Doth it therefore ensue that you should love his son dearly? *As Y. Like It* i 3 32
What of her ensues I list not prophesy *W. Tale* iv 1 25
We had a kind of light what would ensue *K. John* iv 3 61
That present medicine must be minister'd, Or overthrow incurable ensues v 1 16
Let not to-morrow then ensue to-day; Be not thyself *Richard II.* ii 1 197
What will ensue hereof, there's none can tell ii 1 212
What perils past, what crosses to ensue 2 *Hen. IV.* iii 1 55
We may march in England or in France, Not seeing what is likely to ensue 1 *Hen. VI.* iii 1 188
But at hand, at hand, Ensues his piteous and unpitied end *Richard III.* iv 4 74
I foretold you then what would ensue *Troi. and Cres.* iv 5 217
The purchase made, the fruits are to ensue; That profit's yet to come *Othello* ii 3 9
Nor here, nor here, Nor what ensues, but have a fog in them *Cymbeline* iii 2 81
What now ensues, to the judgement of your eye I give *Pericles* i Gower 41
And what ensues in this fell storm Shall for itself itself perform iii Gower 53
Ensued. With demure confidence This pausingly ensued *Hen. VIII.* i 2 168
Whilst the wheel'd seat Of fortunate Cæsar, drawn before him, branded His baseness that ensued *Ant. and Cleo.* iv 14 77
Ensuing. Nothing but heart-sorrow And a clear life ensuing *Tempest* iii 3 82
The next ensuing hour some foul mischance Torment me! *T. G. of Ver.* ii 2 11
In dearness of heart hath holp to effect your ensuing marriage *Much Ado* iii 2 102
How happy then were my ensuing death! *Richard II.* ii 1 68
Ere the thirtieth of May next ensuing 2 *Hen. VI.* i 1 50
By a divine instinct men's minds mistrust Ensuing dangers *Richard III.* ii 3 43
This masque Was cried incomparable; and the ensuing night Made it a fool and beggar *Hen. VIII.* i 1 27
Yet I can give you inkling Of an ensuing evil ii 1 141
And his name remains To the ensuing age abhorr'd *Coriolanus* v 3 148
Left me breath Nothing to think on but ensuing death *Pericles* i 1 7
Entail. And cut the entail from all remainders *All's Well* iv 3 313
I here entail The crown to thee and to thine heirs for ever 3 *Hen. VI.* i 1 194
To entail him and his heirs unto the crown, What is it, but to make thy sepulchre And creep into it? i 1 235
Entame. That can entame my spirits to your worship *As Y. Like It* iii 5 48
Entangle. Yea, very force entangles Itself with strength *Ant. and Cleo.* iv 14 48
Entangled. Dismiss the controversy bleeding, the more entangled by your hearing *Coriolanus* ii 1 86
Riotous madness, To be entangled with those mouth-made vows! *A. and C.* i 3 30
Entendre. I cannot tell vat is baiser en Anglish.—To kiss.—Your majesty entendre bettre que moi *Hen. V.* v 2 288
Enter. Terrible To enter human hearing *Tempest* i 2 265
This is the mouth o' the cell: no noise, and enter iv 1 216
What lets but one may enter at her window? *T. G. of Ver.* iii 1 113
This day my sister should the cloister enter *Meas. for Meas.* i 2 182
True prayers That shall be up at heaven and enter there Ere sun-rise ii 2 152
I am bound To enter publicly iv 3 101

Enter. If any ask you for your master, Say he dines forth and let no creature enter . . . *Com. of Errors* ii 2 212
Ay; and let none enter, lest I break your pate . . . ii 2 220
That may with foul intrusion enter in And dwell upon your grave . . iii 1 103
Upon me the guilty doors were shut And I denied to enter in my house iv 4 67
Good people, enter and lay hold on him.—No, not a creature enters . v 1 91
Saw'st thou him enter at the abbey here? . . . . v 1 278
He ought to enter into a quarrel with fear and trembling *Much Ado* ii 3 203
Where honeysuckles, ripen'd by the sun, Forbid the sun to enter . iii 1 9
Before we enter his forbidden gates, To know his pleasure *L. L. Lost* ii 1 26
Than seek a dispensation for his oath, To let you enter his unpeopled house . . . . . . ii 1 88
His enter and exit shall be strangling a snake . . . v 1 141
When you have spoken your speech, enter into that brake *M. N. Dream* iii 1 77
'Deceiving me' is Thisby's cue: she is to enter now, and I am to spy her v 1 186
Let not the sound of shallow foppery enter My sober house *Mer. of Venice* ii 5 35
Let it not enter in your mind of love . . . . ii 8 42
This house is but a butchery: Abhor it, fear it, do not enter it *As Y. L. It* ii 3 28
I am for the house with the narrow gate which I take to be too little for pomp to enter . . . *All's Well* iv 5 54
Nought enters there, Of what validity and pitch soe'er, But falls into abatement and low price . . . *T. Night* i 1 11
I will not open my lips so wide as a bristle may enter . i 5 3
Will you encounter the house? my niece is desirous you should enter . iii 1 83
I mean, to go, sir, to enter.—I will answer you with gait and entrance . iii 1 92
The competitors enter.—Jove bless thee, master Parson . . iv 2 12
You must not enter.—Nay, rather, good my lords, be second to me *W. T.* ii 3 26
To enter conquerors and to proclaim Arthur of Bretagne *K. John* ii 1 310
O, sit my husband's wrongs on Hereford's spear That it may enter butcher Mowbray's breast! . . . *Richard II.* i 2 48
Is Harry Hereford arm'd?—Yea, at all points; and longs to enter in . i 3 2
Steel my lance's point, That it may enter Mowbray's waxen coat . i 3 75
Fare you well; Unless you please to enter in the castle . . ii 3 160
As in a theatre, the eyes of men, After a well-graced actor leaves the stage, Are idly bent on him that enters next . . . v 2 25
Turn the key, That no man enter till my tale be done . . v 3 37
If you will deny the sheriff, so; if not, let him enter . *1 Hen. IV.* ii 4 545
Come, uncle Exeter, Go you and enter Harfleur . . *Hen. V.* iii 3 52
Vouchsafe to teach a soldier terms Such as will enter at a lady's ear . v 2 100
Open the gates; here's Gloucester that would enter . *1 Hen. VI.* i 3 17
Must your bold verdict enter talk with lords? . . . iii 1 63
On us thou canst not enter but by death . . . . iv 2 18
And ready are the appellant and defendant, The armourer and his man, to enter the lists . . . *2 Hen. VI.* ii 3 50
Enter his chamber, view his breathless corpse, And comment then . iii 2 132
Hath stopp'd the passage where thy words should enter *3 Hen. VI.* i 3 22
We enter, as into our dukedom.—The gates made fast! . . iv 7 9
By fair or foul means we must enter in . . . . iv 7 14
The gates are open, let us enter too.—So other foes may set upon our backs . . . . v 1 60
Can curses pierce the clouds and enter heaven? *Richard III.* i 3 195
Kind sister, thanks: we'll enter all together . . . iv 1 11
It is not you I call for: Saw ye none enter since I slept? *Hen. VIII.* iv 2 86
Let him come in.—Your grace may enter now . . . v 3 7
We come to speak with him. Ulysses, enter you . *Troi. and Cres.* ii 3 150
And never suffers matter of the world Enter his thoughts . . ii 3 197
Admits no orifex for a point as subtle As Ariachne's broken woof to enter v 2 152
Following the fliers at the very heels, With them he enters *Coriolanus* i 4 50
How soon confusion May enter 'twixt the gap of both . . iii 1 111
Never more To enter our Rome gates . . . . iii 3 103
I'll enter: if he slay me, He does fair justice . . . iv 4 24
Come, enter with us. Ladies, you deserve To have a temple built you v 3 206
They are near the city?—Almost at point to enter . . . v 4 64
Come, knock and enter; and no sooner in, But every man betake him to his legs . . . . *Rom. and Jul.* i 4 33
When he enters the confines of a tavern claps me his sword upon the table . . . . iii 1 6
O mischief, thou art swift To enter in the thoughts of desperate men! v 1 36
They enter my mistress' house merrily, and go away sadly *T. of Athens* ii 2 107
And enter in our ears like great triumphers In their applauding gates v 1 199
Send thy gentle heart before, To say thou'lt enter friendly . v 4 49
Let 'em enter. They are the faction . . . *J. Cæsar* ii 1 76
We have met with foes That strike beside us.—Enter, sir, the castle *Macb.* v 7 29
Or perchance, 'I saw him enter such a house of sale' *Hamlet* ii 1 60
Let not ever The soul of Nero enter this firm bosom . . iii 2 412
These words, like daggers, enter in mine ears; No more, sweet Hamlet! iii 4 95
Let me alone.—Good my lord, enter here.—Wilt break my heart? *Lear* iii 4 4
Enter the city, clip your wives, your friends . *Ant. and Cleo.* iv 8 8
This sword but shown to Cæsar, with this tidings, Shall enter me with him . . . . iv 14 113
And let instructions enter Where folly now possesses . *Cymbeline* i 5 47
Nay, the secrets of the grave This viperous slander enters . . iii 4 41
Take or lend. Ho! No answer? Then I'll enter . . iii 6 24

Entered. Pricking goss and thorns, Which enter'd their frail shins *Temp.* iv 1 181
I am here enter'd in bond for you . . *Com. of Errors* iv 4 128
Go but with me to-night, you shall see her chamber-window entered *Much Ado* iii 2 116
Forsook his scene and enter'd in a brake . . *M. N. Dream* iii 2 15
I have not yet Enter'd my house . . . *Mer. of Venice* v 1 273
'Tis our hope, sir, After well enter'd soldiers, to return . *All's Well* ii 1 6
Within this bosom never enter'd yet, The dreadful motion of a murderous thought . . . . . . *K. John* iv 2 254
Nothing but some bond, that he is enter'd into For gay apparel *Rich. II.* v 2 65
Have you entered the action?—It is entered . *2 Hen. IV.* ii 1 1
I have entered him and all . . . . . ii 1 10
Since my exion is entered and my case so openly known to the world ii 1 32
They are all girdled with maiden walls that war hath never entered *Hen. V.* v 2 350
Expect Saint Martin's summer, halcyon days, Since I have entered into these wars . . . . . *1 Hen. VI.* i 2 132
Pucelle is enter'd into Orleans, In spite of us or aught that we could do i 5 36
Here enter'd Pucelle and her practisants . . . . iii 2 20
Her meaning is, No way to that, for weakness, which she enter'd . iii 2 25
And stood against them, as the hope of Troy Against the Greeks that would have enter'd Troy . . . *3 Hen. VI.* ii 1 52
Being enter'd, I doubt not, I, but we shall soon persuade Both him and all his brothers unto reason . . . . . iv 7 32
Fairest-boding dreams That ever enter'd in a drowsy head *Richard III.* v 3 228
Enter'd me, Yea, with a splitting power . . *Hen. VIII.* ii 4 182
Like to an enter'd tide, they all rush by And leave you hindmost *Troi. and Cres.* iii 3 159
Entered. So, your opinion is, Aufidius, That they of Rome are enter'd in our counsels, And know how we proceed . . *Coriolanus* i 2 2
Alone he enter'd The mortal gate of the city . . . ii 2 114
The Volsces with two several powers Are enter'd in the Roman territories iv 6 40
Him I accuse The city ports by this hath enter'd . . . v 6 6
Your native town you enter'd like a post, And had no welcomes home . v 6 50
Sith I am enter'd in this cause so far . . . , I will go on . *Othello* iii 3 411
Before I enter'd here, I call'd . . . . *Cymbeline* iii 6 47
The marble pavement closes, he is enter'd His radiant roof . . v 4 120

Entering. Perchance entering into some monastery . . *Meas. for Meas.* iv 2 217
And why should we proclaim it in an hour before his entering? . iv 4 10
And very near upon The duke is entering . . . . iv 6 15
The revellers are entering, brother: make good room . *Much Ado* ii 1 87
Here's the lord of the soil come to seize me for a stray, for entering his fee-simple without leave . . . *2 Hen. VI.* iv 10 27
Fame, late entering at his heedful ears . . *3 Hen. VI.* iii 3 63
I'll take the charge of this: His grace is entering . *Hen. VIII.* i 4 21

Enterprise. She'll take the enterprise upon her, father *Meas. for Meas.* iv 1 66
A manly enterprise, To conjure tears up in a poor maid's eyes! *M. N. Dr.* iii 2 157
And so far blameless proves my enterprise . . . . iii 2 350
Fear of your adventure would counsel you to a more equal enterprise *As Y. Like It* i 2 188
Was converted Both from his enterprise and from the world . . v 4 168
Be magnanimous in the enterprise and go on . . . *All's Well* iii 6 70
Yea, thrust this enterprise into my heart . . *K. John* v 2 90
And hath sent for you To line his enterprize . . *1 Hen. IV.* ii 3 86
This infant warrior in his enterprizes Discomfited great Douglas . iii 2 113
This sickness doth infect The very life-blood of our enterprise . iv 1 29
It lends a lustre and more great opinion, A larger dare to our great enterprise . . . . iv 1 78
Violation of all faith and troth Sworn to us in your younger enterprise v 1 71
This present enterprise set off his head, I do not think a braver gentleman . . . is now alive . . . . v 1 88
Or what hath this bold enterprise brought forth? . *2 Hen. IV.* i 1 178
Ripe for exploits and mighty enterprises . . . *Hen. V.* i 2 121
I do at this hour joy o'er myself, Prevented from a damned enterprise ii 2 164
The enterprise whereof Shall be to you, as us, like glorious . . ii 2 182
Ne'er heard I of a warlike enterprise More venturous or desperate *1 Hen. VI.* ii 1 44
Appear and aid me in this enterprise . . . . v 3 7
To London presently, And whet on Warwick to this enterprise *3 Hen. VI.* i 2 37
So thrive I in my enterprise And dangerous success! . *Richard III.* iv 4 235
And love's full sacrifice He offers in another's enterprise *Troi. and Cres.* i 2 309
O, when degree is shaked, Which is the ladder to all high designs, The enterprise is sick! . . . . i 3 103
So is he now in execution Of any bold or noble enterprise . *J. Cæsar* i 2 302
An enterprise Of honourable-dangerous consequence . . . i 3 123
Do not stain The even virtue of our enterprise . . . ii 1 133
The heavens speed thee in thine enterprise! . . . . ii 4 41
I wish your enterprise to-day may thrive.—What enterprise? . iii 1 13
He wish'd to-day our enterprise might thrive. I fear our purpose is discovered . . . . iii 1 16
What beast was't then, That made you break this enterprise to me? *Macb.* i 7 48
To some enterprise That hath a stomach in't . . . *Hamlet* i 1 99
Please you to give quiet pass Through your dominions for this enterprise ii 2 78
Enterprises of great pitch and moment With this regard their currents turn awry . . . . iii 1 86
Think death no hazard in this enterprise . . . *Pericles* i 1 5
It greets me as an enterprise of kindness Perform'd to your sole daughter iv 3 38

Entertain. Approach, rich Ceres, her to entertain . . . *Tempest* iv 1 75
Sweet lady, entertain him To be my fellow-servant . *T. G. of Ver.* ii 4 104
Sweet lady, entertain him for your servant . . . . ii 4 110
Therefore know thou, for this I entertain thee . . . iv 4 75
I will entertain Bardolph; he shall draw, he shall tap . *Mer. Wives* i 3 10
He hath a legion of angels.—As many devils entertain . . i 3 61
I think the best way were to entertain him with hope . . ii 1 68
I'll entertain myself like one that I am not acquainted withal . ii 1 89
I quake, Lest thou a feverous life shouldst entertain *Meas. for Meas.* iii 1 75
Until I know this sure uncertainty, I'll entertain the offer'd fallacy *Com. of Errors* ii 2 188
Since mine own doors refuse to entertain me, I'll knock elsewhere . iii 1 120
And do a wilful stillness entertain . . . *Mer. of Venice* i 1 90
Then entertain him, then forswear him . . . *As Y. Like It* iii 2 436
And take a lodging fit to entertain Such friends . . *T. of Shrew* i 1 44
I play the noble housewife with the time, To entertain't so merrily with a fool . . . . . . *All's Well* ii 2 63
Address yourself to entertain them sprightly . . *W. Tale* iv 4 53
The misplaced John should entertain an hour, One minute, nay, one quiet breath of rest . . . . *K. John* iii 4 133
Lay aside life-harming heaviness And entertain a cheerful disposition *Richard II.* ii 2 4
Well content To entertain the lag-end of my life With quiet hours *1 Hen. IV.* v 1 24
Entertain no more of it, good brothers, Than a joint burden *2 Hen. IV.* v 2 54
O noble English, that could entertain With half their forces the full pride of France! . . . . *Hen. V.* i 2 111
Now entertain conjecture of a time . . . . . iv Prol. 1
I am sorry that with reverence I did not entertain thee as thou art *1 Hen. VI.* ii 3 72
Let your drums be still, For here we entertain a solemn peace . v 4 175
Then, heaven, set ope thy everlasting gates, To entertain my vows of thanks and praise! . . . . . *2 Hen. VI.* iv 9 14
Burn, bonfires, clear and bright, To entertain great England's lawful king v 1 4
I cannot prove a lover, To entertain these fair well-spoken days *Richard III.* i 1 29
Entertain some score or two of tailors, To study fashions to adorn my body i 2 257
Entertain good comfort, And cheer his grace with quick and merry words i 3 4
Thy conscience flies out.—Let it go; there's few or none will entertain it i 4 135
I would be sure to have all well, To entertain your highness *T. Andron.* v 3 32
Entertain them; give them guide to us . . . *T. of Athens* i 1 252
Entertain me as your steward still . . . . . iv 3 496
All that served Brutus, I will entertain them . . *J. Cæsar* v 5 60
You, sir, I entertain for one of my hundred . . . *Lear* iii 6 83
But entertain it, And, though thou think me poor, I am the man Will give thee all the world . . . *Ant. and Cleo.* ii 7 69
So please you entertain me.—Ay, good youth . . *Cymbeline* iv 2 394
Your entertain shall be As doth befit our honour and your worth *Pericles* i 1 119

Entertained. When every grief is entertain'd that's offer'd, Comes to the entertainer— A dollar.—Dolour comes to him . *Tempest* ii 1 16
You, brother mine, that entertain'd ambition, Expell'd remorse and nature . . . . v 1 75
I have entertained thee, Partly that I have need of such a youth *T. G. of V.* iv 4 68
Thou hast entertain'd A fox to be the shepherd of thy lambs . iv 4 96

Entertained. That gave aim to all thy oaths, And entertain'd 'em deeply in her heart . . . . *T. G. of Ver.* v 4 102
The prince your brother is royally entertained . . . *Much Ado* i 3 45
Being entertained for a perfumer, as I was smoking a musty room . i 3 60
Writ to my lady mother I am returning; entertained my convoy *All's Well* iv 3 103
Yet tell'st thou not how thou wert entertain'd . . . 1 *Hen. VI.* i 4 38
Which entertain'd, limbs are his instruments . . . *Troi. and Cres.* i 3 354
Comes back to Romeo, Who had but newly entertain'd revenge *R. and J.* iii 1 176
And entertain'd me with mine own device . . . *T. of Athens* i 2 155
Let the presents Be worthily entertain'd . . . . . . i 2 191
See them well entertain'd.—Pray, draw near . . . . . ii 2 45
Not entertained with that ceremonious affection as you were wont *Lear* i 4 63
They have entertained cause enough To draw their swords *Ant. and Cleo.* ii 1 46
Let him be so entertained amongst you as suits, with gentlemen of your knowing, to a stranger of his quality . . . . *Cymbeline* i 4 29
Entertainer. When every grief is entertain'd that's offer'd, Comes to the entertainer— A dollar.—Dolour comes to him . . *Tempest* ii 1 17
Entertainest. Thou with mildness entertain'st thy wooers *T. of Shrew* ii 1 252
If thou entertainest my love, let it appear in thy smiling *T. Night* ii 5 190
Entertaining. And add more coals to Cancer when he burns With entertaining great Hyperion . . . . *Troi. and Cres.* ii 3 207
Entertainment. I will resist such entertainment till Mine enemy has more power . . . . *Tempest* i 2 465
I spy entertainment in her . . . . . . *Mer. Wives* i 3 48
Have a care of your entertainments: there is a friend of mine come to town iv 5 77
The stealth of our most mutual entertainment With character too gross is writ on Juliet . . . . . *Meas. for Meas.* i 2 158
Advised him for the entertainment of death . . . . iii 2 225
Let us devise Some entertainment for them . . *L. L. Lost* iv 3 373
Some entertainment of time, some show in the posterior of this day v 1 125
If that love or gold Can in this desert place buy entertainment *As Y. Like It* ii 4 72
He led me to the gentle duke, Who gave me fresh array and entertainment iv 3 144
And, for an entrance to my entertainment, I do present you with a man of mine, Cunning in music . . . . . *T. of Shrew* ii 1 54
Have you so soon forgot the entertainment? . . . . iii 1 2
The owner of no one good quality worthy your lordship's entertainment *All's Well* iii 6 13
If you give him not John Drum's entertainment . . . iii 6 41
He must think us some band of strangers i' the adversary's entertainment iv 1 17
The rudeness that hath appeared in me have I learned from my entertainment . . . . *T. Night* i 5 231
Pardon me, sir, your bad entertainment . . . . . . ii 1 34
Wherein our entertainment shall shame us we will be justified *W. Tale* i 1 9
This entertainment May a free face put on, derive a liberty From heartiness i 2 111
O, that is entertainment My bosom likes not, nor my brows! . . i 2 118
If any rebel or vain spirit of mine Did with the least affection of a welcome Give entertainment to the might of it . . . 2 *Hen. IV.* iv 5 174
We thank you all for this great favour done, In entertainment 2 *Hen. VI.* i 1 72
The centurions and their charges, distinctly billeted, already in the entertainment, and to be on foot . . . *Coriolanus* iv 3 49
I have deserved no better entertainment, In being Coriolanus . . iv 5 10
Guess, but by my entertainment with him, if thou standest not i' the state of hanging . . . . v 2 69
A man, Whom this beneath world doth embrace and hug With amplest entertainment . . . . *T. of Athens* i 1 45
Set a fair fashion on our entertainment, Which was not half so beautiful i 2 152
I prithee, let's be provided to show them entertainment . . i 2 185
Do not dull thy palm with entertainment Of each new-hatch'd, unfledged comrade . . . . *Hamlet* i 3 64
What lenten entertainment the players shall receive from you . ii 2 329
Lest my extent to the players, which, I tell you, must show fairly outward, should more appear like entertainment than yours . . ii 2 392
Use some gentle entertainment to Laertes before you fall to play . . v 2 216
I am now from home, and out of that provision Which shall be needful for your entertainment . . . . *Lear* ii 4 209
Wish courtesy would invent some other custom of entertainment *Othello* ii 3 37
Note, if your lady strain his entertainment With any strong or vehement importunity . . . . iii 3 250
Get thee back to Cæsar, Tell him thy entertainment . *Ant. and Cleo.* iii 13 140
And the rest That fell away have entertainment, but No honourable trust iv 6 17
I have your commendation for my more free entertainment *Cymbeline* i 4 167
Yon knight doth sit too melancholy, As if the entertainment in our court Had not a show might countervail his worth . . *Pericles* ii 3 55
Instruct her what she has to do, that she may not be raw in her entertainment . . . . iv 2 60
Enthralled. Love hath chased sleep from my enthralled eyes *T. G. of Ver.* ii 4 134
O cross! too high to be enthrall'd to low . . . *M. N. Dream* i 1 136
Mine ear is much enamour'd of thy note; So is mine eye enthralled . iii 1 142
But being enthralled as I am, it will also be the bondage of certain ribbons and gloves . . . . *W. Tale* iv 4 234
What though I be enthrall'd? he seems a knight . . 1 *Hen. VI.* v 3 101
Enthroned. It [mercy] is enthroned in the hearts of kings *Mer. of Venice* iv 1 194
After So many courses of the sun enthroned . . . *Hen. VIII.* ii 3 6
Therefore is the glorious planet Sol In noble eminence enthroned *T. and C.* i 3 90
Antony, Enthroned i' the market-place, did sit alone *Ant. and Cleo.* ii 2 220
Cleopatra and himself in chairs of gold Were publicly enthroned . iii 6 5
Entice. Do I entice you? do I speak you fair? . . *M. N. Dream* ii 1 199
By fair persuasions mix'd with sugar'd words We will entice 1 *Hen. VI.* iii 3 19
Bad child; worse father! to entice his own To evil . . *Pericles* i Gower 27
Enticements, oaths, tokens, and all these engines of lust . . *All's Well* iii 5 20
Enticeth. Her face, like heaven, enticeth thee to view . . *Pericles* i 1 30
Enticing. Would make a volume of enticing lines . . 1 *Hen. VI.* v 5 14
A quire of such enticing birds, That she will light to listen to the lays 2 *Hen. VI.* i 3 92
Entire. But the one half of an entire sum Disbursed by my father *L. L. Lost* ii 1 131
I have often heard Of your entire affection to Bianca . . *T. of Shrew* iv 2 23
Sorrow's eye, glazed with blinding tears, Divides one thing entire to many objects . . . . *Richard II.* ii 2 17
Pure fear and entire cowardice . . . . . . 2 *Hen. IV.* ii 4 352
A carbuncle entire, as big as thou art, Were not so rich a jewel *Coriolanus* i 4 55
Three parts of him Is ours already, and the man entire Upon the next encounter yields him ours . . . . *J. Cæsar* i 3 155
Love's not love When it is mingled with regards that stand Aloof from the entire point . . . . *Lear* i 1 243
Such another world Of one entire and perfect chrysolite . . *Othello* v 2 145
Entirely. Drunk many times a day, if not many days entirely drunk *Meas. for Meas.* iv 2 158
But are you sure That Benedick loves Beatrice so entirely? *Much Ado* iii 1 37
Other slow arts entirely keep the brain . . . . *L. L. Lost* iv 3 324
They are entirely welcome . . . . *Mer. of Venice* iii 2 228

Entirely. I know, madam, you love your gentlewoman entirely *All's Well* i 3 104
To his father, that so tenderly and entirely loves him . . . *Lear* i 2 105
Subdue my father Entirely to her love . . . . . *Othello* iii 4 60
Whom I with all the office of my heart Entirely honour . . . iii 4 114
My mistress loved thee, and her fortunes mingled With thine entirely *Ant. and Cleo.* iv 14 25
Entitle. That which we lovers entitle affected . . . *L. L. Lost* ii 1 232
I may entitle thee my loving father . . . . . *T. of Shrew* iv 5 61
That which in mean men we intitle patience Is pale cold cowardice in noble breasts . . . . *Richard II.* i 2 33
Entitling. I am as ignorant in that as you In so entitling me *W. Tale* ii 3 70
Entomb. If thou wouldst not entomb thyself alive . *Troi. and Cres.* iii 3 186
Darkness does the face of earth entomb, When living light should kiss it *Macbeth* ii 4 9
Entombed. To be entombed in an ass's pack-saddle . . *Coriolanus* ii 1 99
Timon is dead; Entomb'd upon the very hem o' the sea *T. of Athens* v 4 66
Entrails. I will rend an oak And peg thee in his knotty entrails *Tempest* i 2 295
Old, cold, withered and of intolerable entrails . . . *Mer. Wives* v 5 162
He bounds from the earth, as if his entrails were hairs . . *Hen. V.* iii 7 14
Hath thy fiery heart so parch'd thine entrails That not a tear can fall? 3 *Hen. VI.* i 4 87
Wilt thou, O God, fly from such gentle lambs, And throw them in the entrails of the wolf? . . . . *Richard III.* iv 4 23
Whetted on thy stone-hard heart, To revel in the entrails of my lambs iv 4 228
Alarbus' limbs are lopp'd, And entrails feed the sacrificing fire *T. Andron.* i 1 144
And shows the ragged entrails of the pit . . . . . . ii 3 230
Plucking the entrails of an offering forth, They could not find a heart within the beast . . . . *J. Cæsar* ii 2 39
Thy spirit walks abroad, and turns our swords In our own proper entrails v 3 96
Round about the cauldron go; In the poison'd entrails throw *Macbeth* iv 1 5
Entrance. Of his own doors being shut against his entrance *Com. of Err.* iv 3 90
They have their exits and their entrances . . . *As Y. Like It* ii 7 141
For an entrance to my entertainment, I do present you . *T. of Shrew* ii 1 54
I will answer you with gait and entrance . . . . *T. Night* iii 1 93
If ever henceforth thou These rural latches to his entrance open *W. Tale* iv 4 449
In peace permit Our just and lineal entrance to our own . *K. John* ii 1 85
The mouth of passage shall we fling wide ope, And give you entrance . ii 1 450
The castle royally is mann'd, my lord, Against thy entrance *Richard II.* iii 3 22
No more the thirsty entrance of this soil Shall daub her lips with her own children's blood . . . . 1 *Hen. IV.* i 1 5
Better far, I guess, That we do make our entrance several ways 1 *Hen. VI.* ii 1 30
If we have entrance, as I hope we shall . . . . . . iii 2 6
A gentleman, sent from the king, to see you.—Admit him entrance *Hen. VIII.* iv 2 107
Achilles stands i' the entrance of his tent . . *Troi. and Cres.* iii 3 38
Has the porter his eyes in his head, that he gives entrance to such companions? Pray, get you out . . . . . *Coriolanus* iv 5 13
Let not young Mutius, then, that was thy joy, Be barr'd his entrance here *T. Andron.* i 1 383
Nor no without-book prologue, faintly spoke After the prompter, for our entrance . . . . *Rom. and Jul.* i 4 8
What blood is this, which stains The stony entrance of this sepulchre? v 3 141
The raven himself is hoarse That croaks the fatal entrance of Duncan *Macbeth* i 5 40
Look'd like a breach in nature For ruin's wasteful entrance . . ii 3 120
Beware Of entrance to a quarrel, but being in, Bear't that the opposed may beware of thee . . . . *Hamlet* i 3 66
To make his entrance more sweet, Here, say we drink this standing-bowl of wine to him . . . . *Pericles* ii 3 64
Entranced. She hath not been entranced Above five hours . . iii 2 94
Entrap. The seeming truth which cunning times put on To entrap the wisest . . . . *Mer. of Venice* iii 2 101
A golden mesh to entrap the hearts of men Faster than gnats in cobwebs iii 2 122
Entrap thee by some treacherous device and never leave thee *As Y. Like It* i 1 157
Sought to entrap me by intelligence . . . . 1 *Hen. IV.* iv 3 98
O, seek not to entrap me, gracious lord, A stranger . . *Pericles* ii 5 45
Entrapped. The fraud of England, not the force of France, Hath now entrapp'd the noble-minded Talbot . . . . 1 *Hen. VI.* iv 4 37
Entreasured. Balm'd and entreasured With full bags of spices! *Pericles* iii 2 65
Entreat. I resign and do entreat Thou pardon me my wrongs *Tempest* v 1 118
Entreat thy company To see the wonders of the world abroad *T. G. of V.* i 1 5
I do entreat your patience To hear me speak . . . . iv 4 116
Give't not o'er so: to him again, entreat him; Kneel down before him *Meas. for Meas.* ii 2 43
Let me entreat you speak the former language . . . . ii 4 140
If for this night he entreat you to his bed, give him promise . . iii 1 274
We shall entreat you to abide here till he come . . . . v 1 266
'Tis my deserving, and I do entreat it . . . . . . v 1 482
They did entreat me to acquaint her of it . . . *Much Ado* iii 1 40
I must entreat your pains, I think . . . . . . v 4 18
Do one thing for me that I shall entreat . . . *L. L. Lost* ii 1 154
Shall I enforce thy love? I could: shall I entreat thy love? I will iv 1 83
And entreat, Out of a new-sad soul . . . . . . v 2 740
I do entreat your grace to pardon me . . . *M. N. Dream* i 1 58
I am to entreat you, request you and desire you . . . . i 2 102
'I would wish you,'—or 'I would request you,'—or 'I would entreat you' iii 1 42
If she cannot entreat, I can compel.—Thou canst compel no more than she entreat . . . . iii 2 248
I would entreat you rather to put on Your boldest suit of mirth *M. of V.* ii 2 210
He did entreat me, past all saying nay, To come with him along . . iii 2 232
I would she were in heaven, so she could Entreat some power to change this currish Jew . . . . iv 1 292
Sir, I entreat you home with me to dinner . . . . . iv 1 401
And doth entreat Your company at dinner . . . . . iv 2 7
You shall not entreat him to a second, that have so mightily persuaded him from a first . . . . *As Y. Like It* i 2 218
I did not then entreat to have her stay . . . . . i 3 71
I will never have her unless thou entreat for her . . . . iv 3 73
Let me entreat of you To pardon me yet for a night or two *T. of Shrew* Ind. 2 120
If you knew my business, You would entreat me rather go than stay . iii 2 194
Let us entreat you stay till after dinner.—It may not be . . . iii 2 199
Let me entreat you.—It cannot be.—Let me entreat you.—I am content iii 2 200
I am content you shall entreat me stay; But yet not stay, entreat me how you can . . . . iii 2 203
Never to marry with her though she would entreat . . . . iv 2 33
I, who never knew how to entreat, Nor never needed that I should entreat iv 3 7
Entreat my wife To come to me forthwith.—O, ho! entreat her! Nay, then she must needs come . . . . v 2 86
This drives me to entreat you That presently you take your way for home; And rather muse than ask why I entreat you *All's Well* ii 5 68

Entreat. I will entreat you, when you see my son, To tell him that his sword can never win The honour that he loses: more I'll entreat you Written to bear along . . . *All's Well* iii 2 95
I could hardly entreat him back . . . *T. Night* iii 4 63
I must entreat of you some of that money . . . iii 4 374
Pursue him, and entreat him to a peace . . . v 1 389
My last good deed was to entreat his stay: What was my first? *W. Tale* i 2 97
Entreat the north To make his bleak winds kiss my parched lips *K. John* v 7 39
And hath sent post haste To entreat your majesty to visit him *Rich. II.* i 4 56
And so let me entreat you leave the house . 1 *Hen. IV.* ii 4 567
But do not use it oft, let me entreat you . . iii 1 176
Shall I entreat you with me to dinner? . . 2 *Hen. IV.* ii 1 194
If my tongue cannot entreat you to acquit me . . Epil. 18
And my speech entreats That I may know the let . *Hen. V.* v 2 64
Entreats, great lord, thou wouldst vouchsafe To visit her poor castle 1 *Hen. VI.* ii 2 40
Cannot my body nor blood-sacrifice Entreat you to your wonted furtherance? . . . v 3 21
Entreat her not the worse in that I pray You use her well . 2 *Hen. VI.* ii 4 81
Had I not been cited so by them, Yet did I purpose as they do entreat iii 2 282
O, let me entreat thee cease. Give me thy hand . . iii 2 339
Entreat him, speak him fair . . . iv 1 120
I'll send some holy bishop to entreat . . . iv 4 9
I'll write unto them and entreat them fair . 3 *Hen. VI.* i 1 271
Let me entreat, for I command no more . . . iv 6 59
Which of you . . . , If two such murderers as yourselves came to you, Would not entreat for life? . . *Richard III.* i 4 269
Entreat for me, As you would beg, were you in my distress . . i 4 272
I entreat true peace of you, Which I will purchase with my duteous service . . . ii 1 62
To your mother, to entreat of her To meet you at the Tower . . iii 1 138
He doth entreat your grace To visit him to-morrow or next day . . iii 7 59
Do, good my lord, your citizens entreat you . . iii 7 201
Here we leave you.—Come, citizens: 'zounds! I'll entreat no more . iii 7 219
I am not made of stones, But penetrable to your kind entreats . . iii 7 225
Entreat me fair, Or with the clamorous report of war Thus will I drown your exclamations . . . iv 4 151
Say that the king, which may command, entreats . . iv 4 345
Entreat An hour of revels with 'em . . . *Hen. VIII.* i 4 71
And did entreat your highness to this course Which you are running here ii 4 216
The cardinal did entreat his holiness To stay the judgement o' the divorce iii 2 32
I humbly do entreat your highness' pardon; My haste made me unmannerly . . . iv 2 104
And heartily entreats you take good comfort . . iv 2 119
And by the way possess thee what she is. Entreat her fair *T. and C.* iv 4 115
The general state, I fear, Can scarce entreat you to be odd with him . iv 5 265
Dost thou entreat me, Hector? To-morrow do I meet thee, fell as death iv 5 268
Afterwards, As Hector's leisure and your bounties shall Concur together, severally entreat him . . . iv 5 274
I cannot Put on the gown, stand naked and entreat them . *Coriolanus* ii 2 141
But entreat of thee To pardon Mutius and to bury him . *T. Andron.* i 1 362
Yield at entreats; and then let me alone . . . i 1 449
For thy sake and thy brother's here, And at my lovely Tamora's entreats i 1 483
Sweet lords, entreat her hear me but a word . . ii 3 138
Do thou entreat her show a woman pity . . ii 3 147
I will entreat the king: Fear not thy sons; they shall do well enough . ii 3 304
Grave tribunes, once more I entreat of you . . iii 1 31
He will not entreat his son for us.—If Tamora entreat him, then he will iv 4 94
Do entreat her eyes To twinkle in their spheres till they return *R. and J.* ii 2 16
My lord, we must entreat the time alone . . . iv 1 40
I must entreat you, honour me so much As to advance this jewel *T. of A.* i 2 175
Lord Lucullus entreats your company to-morrow to hunt with him . i 2 193
Which, in my lord's behalf, I come to entreat your honour to supply . iii 1 17
The senators with one consent of love Entreat thee back to Athens . v 1 144
I would not, so with love I might entreat you, Be any further moved *J. C.* i 2 166
Shall I entreat a word? . . . ii 1 100
I do entreat you, not a man depart, Save I alone, till Antony have spoke iii 2 65
When we can entreat an hour to serve . . *Macbeth* ii 1 22
I entreat you both, That, being of so young days brought up with him *Hamlet* ii 2 10
And he beseech'd me to entreat your majesties To hear and see the matter . . . iii 1 22
Let his queen mother all alone entreat him To show his grief . . iii 1 190
I will not be, though I should win your displeasure to entreat me to 't *Lear* ii 2 120
I'll entreat for thee.—Pray, do not, sir . . ii 2 161
I entreat you To bring but five and twenty . . ii 4 250
My lord, entreat him by no means to stay . . ii 4 302
Neither to speak of him, entreat for him, nor any way sustain him . iii 3 6
Bring some covering for this naked soul, Who I'll entreat to lead me . iv 1 47
Sir, this gentleman Steps in to Cassio, and entreats his pause *Othello* ii 3 229
This broken joint between you and her husband entreat her to splinter ii 3 329
Tell her there's one Cassio entreats her a little favour of speech . iii 1 28
This is not a boon; 'Tis as I should entreat you wear your gloves . iii 3 77
I would I might entreat your honour To scan this thing no further . iii 3 244
Sir, to-night, I do entreat that we may sup together . iv 1 273
Entreat your captain To soft and gentle speech.—I shall entreat him To answer like himself . . *Ant. and Cleo.* ii 2 2
Cæsar entreats, Not to consider in what case thou stand'st . . iii 13 53
Good queen, let us entreat you.—O Cæsar, what a wounding shame is this! . . . v 2 158
I had almost forgot To entreat your grace but in a small request . *Cymb.* i 6 181
Dispatch: The lamb entreats the butcher: where's thy knife? . iii 4 99
This one thing only I will entreat . . . v 5 84
Entreats you pity him; He asks of you, that never used to beg *Pericles* ii 1 65
Let me entreat you to Forbear the absence of your king . . ii 4 45
Once more Let me entreat to know at large the cause Of your king's sorrow . . . v 1 62
Entreated. Therefore the office is indifferent, Being entreated to it by your friend . . . *T. G. of Ver.* iii 2 45
Entreated me to call and know her mind . . iv 3 2
Come on: since the youth will not be entreated, his own peril on his forwardness . . *As Y. Like It* i 2 159
I would fain dissuade him, but he will not be entreated . . i 2 171
I am afraid, sir, Do what you can, yours will not be entreated *T. of Shrew* v 2 89
For God's sake, fairly let her be entreated . *Richard II.* iii 1 37
The Dauphin, whom of succours we entreated, Returns us . *Hen. V.* iii 3 45
I entreated her come forth, And bear this work of heaven *Rom. and Jul.* v 3 260
Am I entreated To speak and strike? . . *J. Cæsar* ii 1 55
I have entreated him along With us to watch the minutes of this night *Hamlet* i 1 26

Entreated. It should be better he became her guest; Which she entreated . . . *Ant. and Cleo.* ii 2 227
Which do not be entreated to, but weigh What it is worth embraced . ii 6 32
Entreating from your royal thoughts A modest one . . *All's Well* ii 1 130
Entreatment. Set your entreatments at a higher rate Than a command to parley . . *Hamlet* i 3 122
Entreaty. It is not my consent, But my entreaty too . *Meas. for Meas.* iv 1 68
I should have given him tears unto entreaties *As Y. Like It* i 2 250
How if the kiss be denied?—Then she puts you to entreaty . iv 1 80
Beggars, that come unto my father's door, Upon entreaty have a present alms . . *T. of Shrew* iv 3 5
How came't, Camillo, That he did stay?—At the good queen's entreaty *W. Tale* i 2 220
To satisfy your highness and the entreaties Of our most gracious mistress.—Satisfy! The entreaties of your mistress! satisfy! . i 2 232
Is too wilful-opposite, And will not temporize with my entreaties *K. John* v 2 125
Use no entreaty, for it is in vain . . . 1 *Hen. VI.* v 4 85
For of that sin My mild entreaty shall not make you guilty 3 *Hen. VI.* iii 1 91
If she be obdurate To mild entreaties *Richard III.* iii 1 40
Would it might please your grace, At our entreaties, to amend that fault! iii 7 115
If entreaties Will render you no remedy, this ring Deliver them *Hen. VIII.* v 1 149
If I might in entreaties find success—As seld I have the chance *T. and C.* iv 5 149
When for a day of kings' entreaties a mother should not sell him an hour from her beholding . . *Coriolanus* i 3 9
The other has half, by the entreaty and grant of the whole table . iv 5 212
Let's hence, And with our fair entreaties haste them on . v 1 74
With letters of entreaty, which imported His fellowship *T. of Athens* v 2 11
Put your dread pleasures more into command Than to entreaty *Hamlet* ii 2 29
With an entreaty, herein further shown, That it might please you ii 2 76
At my entreaty forbear his presence till some little time . *Lear* i 2 175
Reconciles them to his entreaty, and himself to the drink *Ant. and Cleo.* ii 7 9
Entrenched. An emblem of war, here on his sinister cheek; it was this very sword entrenched it . . *All's Well* ii 1 45
Entry. I hear a knocking At the south entry . *Macbeth* ii 2 66
Entwist. So doth the woodbine the sweet honeysuckle Gently entwist *M. N. Dream* iv 1 48
Envelope. The best and wholesomest spirits of the night Envelope you, good Provost! . . *Meas. for Meas.* iv 2 77
His body as a paradise, To envelope and contain celestial spirits *Hen. V.* i 1 31
Envenom. O, what a world is this, when what is comely Envenoms him that bears it! . . *As Y. Like It* ii 3 15
Envenom him with words, or get thee gone And leave those woes *K. John* iii 1 63
This report of his Did Hamlet so envenom with his envy *Hamlet* iv 7 104
Envenomed. With whose envenomed and fatal sting, Your loving uncle, twenty times his worth, They say, is shamefully bereft of life 2 *Hen. VI.* iii 2 267
Piercing steel and darts envenomed Shall be as welcome . *J. Cæsar* v 3 76
The treacherous instrument is in thy hand, Unbated and envenom'd *Ham.* v 2 328
The point envenom'd too! Then, venom, to thy work . . v 2 332
Envied. They will not stick to say you envied him . . *Hen. VIII.* ii 2 127
The discontented members, the mutinous parts That envied his receipt *Coriolanus* i 1 116
He has, As much as in him lies, from time to time Envied against the people . . . iii 3 95
I have seen thee fight, When I have envied thy behaviour *Ant. and Cleo.* ii 6 77
Envies. What louring star now envies thy estate? . 2 *Hen. VI.* iii 1 206
The day is yours; And here, I hope, is none that envies it . *Pericles* ii 3 14
Envious. He shall appear to the envious a scholar . *Meas. for Meas.* iii 2 154
Biron is like an envious sneaping frost . . *L. L. Lost* i 1 100
None can drive him from the envious plea Of forfeiture . *Mer. of Venice* iii 2 284
An envious emulator of every man's good parts . *As Y. Like It* i 1 149
My father's rough and envious disposition Sticks me at heart . i 2 253
Are not these woods More free from peril than the envious court? . ii 1 4
Like envious floods o'er-run her lovely face . *T. of Shrew* Ind. 2 67
Whose rocky shore beats back the envious seige Of watery Neptune *Richard II.* ii 1 62
When he perceives the envious clouds are bent To dim his glory . iii 3 65
Is not quite exempt From envious malice of thy swelling heart 1 *Hen. VI.* iii 1 26
So will this base and envious discord breed . . iii 1 194
As well as you dare patronage The envious barking of your saucy tongue iii 4 33
This fellow here, with envious carping tongue, Upbraided me about the rose . . iv 1 90
The abject people gazing on thy face, With envious looks . 2 *Hen. VI.* ii 4 12
When I start, the envious people laugh And bid me be advised how I tread . . . ii 4 35
Unburthens with his tongue The envious load that lies upon his heart. iii 1 157
To make an envious mountain on my back . 3 *Hen. VI.* iii 2 157
And thyself the sea Whose envious gulf did swallow up his life . v 6 25
Either not believe The envious slanders of her false accusers *Richard III.* i 3 26
But still the envious flood Kept in my soul, and would not let it forth. i 4 37
That trick of state Was a deep envious one . *Hen. VIII.* ii 1 45
Follow your envious courses, men of malice . . iii 2 243
Still in thy right hand carry gentle peace, To silence envious tongues . iii 2 447
Grows to an envious fever Of pale and bloodless emulation . *T. and C.* i 3 133
Love, friendship, charity, are subjects all To envious and calumniating time . . . iii 3 174
When some envious surge Will in his brinish bowels swallow him *T. An.* iii 1 96
As is the bud bit with an envious worm . *Rom. and Jul.* i 1 157
Arise, fair sun, and kill the envious moon, Who is already sick and pale ii 2 4
Be not her maid, since she is envious . . ii 2 7
An envious thrust from Tybalt hit the life Of stout Mercutio . iii 1 173
Can heaven be so envious?—Romeo can, Though heaven cannot . iii 2 40
Look, love, what envious streaks Do lace the severing clouds in yonder east . . . iii 5 7
This shall make Our purpose necessary and not envious . *J. Cæsar* ii 1 178
See what a rent the envious Casca made . . iii 2 179
There, on the pendent boughs her coronet weeds Clambering to hang, an envious sliver broke . . *Hamlet* iv 7 174
Enviously. Hems, and beats her heart; Spurns enviously at straws iv 5 6
Environ. If ever danger do environ thee, Commend thy grievance to my holy prayers . . *T. G. of Ver.* i 1 16
It [sherris] ascends me into the brain; dries me there all the foolish and dull and crudy vapours which environ it . 2 *Hen. IV.* iv 3 106
But darkness and the gloomy shade of death Environ you! . 1 *Hen. VI.* v 4 90
Environed. Shalt thou be safe? such safety finds The trembling lamb environed with wolves . . 3 *Hen. VI.* i 1 242
Environed he was with many foes, And stood against them . . ii 1 50
Bound to revenge, Wert thou environ'd with a brazen wall . . ii 4 4
Methoughts, a legion of foul fiends Environ'd me about . *Richard III.* i 4 59
I stand as one upon a rock Environ'd with a wilderness of sea *T. An.* iii 1 94

Environed. Shall I not be distraught, Environed with all these hideous fears? . . . *Rom. and Jul.* iv 3 50
An hand environed with clouds, Holding out gold . *Pericles* ii 2 36
Envy. Who with age and envy Was grown into a hoop . *Tempest* i 2 258
Lord Angelo is precise; Stands at a guard with envy *Meas. for Meas.* i 3 51
Either this is envy in you, folly, or mistaking . . . iii 2 149
No lawful means can carry me Out of his envy's reach . *Mer. of Venice* iv 1 10
No metal can, No, not the hangman's axe, bear half the keenness Of thy sharp envy . . . . . . iv 1 126
Envy no man's happiness, glad of other men's good . *As Y. Like It* iii 2 78
Is it for him you do envy me so? Nay then you jest . *T. of Shrew* ii 1 18
She bore a mind that envy could not but call fair . . *T. Night* ii 1 30
That very envy and the tongue of loss Cried fame and honour on him v 1 61
I envy at their liberty, And will again commit them to their bonds *K. John* iii 4 73
By envy's hand and murder's bloody axe . . . . *Richard II.* i 2 21
Of sky-aspiring and ambitious thoughts, With rival-hating envy . i 3 131
Or as a moat defensive to a house, Against the envy of less happier lands . . . . ii 1 49
There thou makest me sad and makest me sin In envy . 1 *Hen. IV.* i 1 79
Envy, therefore, or misprision Is guilty of this fault and not my son . i 3 27
Some of us love you well; and even those some Envy your great deservings . . . . iv 3 35
If he outlive the envy of this day, England did never owe so sweet a hope . . . . v 2 67
France and England, whose very shores look pale With envy of each other's happiness . . . . . *Hen. V.* v 2 379
When envy breeds unkind division; There comes the ruin 1 *Hen. VI.* iv 1 193
With full as many signs of deadly hate As lean-faced Envy in her loathsome cave . . . . . 2 *Hen. VI.* iii 2 315
Or gather wealth, I care not, with what envy . . . iv 10 23
Exempt from envy, but not from disdain . . 3 *Hen. VI.* iii 3 127
You envy my advancement and my friends' . *Richard III.* i 3 75
Poor soul, I envy not thy glory; To feed my humour, wish thyself no harm . . . . iv 1 64
Pity, you ancient stones, those tender babes Whom envy hath immured within your walls! . . . . iv 1 100
No black envy Shall mark my grave . . . *Hen. VIII.* ii 1 85
Who can be angry now? what envy reach you? . . ii 2 89
Every eye saw 'em, Envy and base opinion set against 'em . iii 1 36
This is a mere distraction; You turn the good we offer into envy . iii 1 113
Now I feel Of what coarse metal ye are moulded, envy . . iii 2 239
Men that make Envy and crooked malice nourishment Dare bite the best v 3 44
Whose honesty the devil And his disciples only envy at . . v 3 112
Thou art as full of envy at his greatness as Cerberus is at Proserpina's beauty . . . . . . *Troi. and Cres.* ii 1 36
I have said my prayers and devil Envy say Amen . . ii 3 23
What envy can say worst shall be a mock for his truth . iii 2 104
Have the gods envy?—Ay, ay, ay, ay; 'tis too plain a case . iv 4 30
Thou core of envy! Thou crusty batch of nature, what's the news? v 1 4
Why, thou damnable box of envy, thou, what meanest thou to curse thus? v 1 29
Not Afric owns a serpent I abhor More than thy fame and envy *Coriol.* i 8 4
If he evade us there, Enforce him with his envy to the people . iii 3 3
But, as I say, such as become a soldier, Rather than envy you . iii 3 57
The cruelty and envy of the people, Permitted by our dastard nobles iv 5 80
Each word thou hast spoke hath weeded from my heart A root of ancient envy . . . . iv 5 109
Here no envy swells, Here grow no damned grudges . *T. Andron.* i 1 153
Advanced above pale envy's threatening reach . . . ii 1 4
And spend our flatteries, to drink those men Upon whose age we void it up again, With poisonous spite and envy . *T. of Athens* i 2 144
Like wrath in death and envy afterwards . . *J. Cæsar* ii 1 164
All the conspirators save only he Did that they did in envy of great Cæsar . . . . v 5 70
Your sum of parts Did not together pluck such envy from him As did that one . . . . *Hamlet* iv 7 75
This report of his Did Hamlet so envenom with his envy . . iv 7 104
That mine own servant should Parcel the sum of my disgraces by Addition of his envy! . . . *Ant. and Cleo.* v 2 163
Thou wert dignified enough, Even to the point of envy . *Cymbeline* ii 3 133
I love thee brotherly, but envy much Thou hast robb'd me of this deed iv 2 158
We are gentlemen That neither in our hearts nor outward eyes Envy the great nor do the low despise . . . *Pericles* ii 3 26
That monster envy, oft the wrack Of earned praise . . iv Gower 12
Cleon's wife, with envy rare, A present murderer does prepare . iv Gower 37
Envying. Until the heavens, envying earth's good hap, Add an immortal title to your crown . . . . *Richard II.* i 1 23
I sin in envying his nobility . . . . . *Coriolanus* i 1 234
Enwheel. The grace of heaven, Before, behind thee and on every hand, Enwheel thee round! . . . . . *Othello* ii 1 87
Enwombed. And put you in the catalogue of those That were enwombed mine . . . . *All's Well* i 3 150
Enwrap. Though 'tis wonder that enwraps me thus, Yet 'tis not madness . . . . *T. Night* iv 3 3
Ephesian. It is thine host, thine Ephesian, calls . *Mer. Wives* iv 5 19
What company?—Ephesians, my lord, of the old church 2 *Hen. IV.* ii 2 164
Ephesus. Nay, more, If any born at Ephesus be seen At any Syracusian marts and fairs; Again: if any Syracusian born Come to the bay of Ephesus, he dies . . . . *Com. of Errors* i 1 17
And for what cause thou camest to Ephesus . . . . . i 1 31
And, coasting homeward, came to Ephesus . . . . . i 1 135
Try all the friends thou hast in Ephesus . . . . . i 1 153
In Ephesus I am but two hours old . . . . . . ii 2 150
Sir, I shall have law in Ephesus, To your notorious shame . iv 1 83
That I should be attach'd in Ephesus, I tell you, 'twill sound harshly . iv 4 6
Your honour has through Ephesus pour'd forth Your charity *Pericles* iii 2 43
His woeful queen we leave at Ephesus, Unto Diana there a votaress iv Gower 3
My temple stands in Ephesus: hie thee thither . . . v 1 241
Toward Ephesus Turn our blown sails; eftsoons I'll tell thee why . v 1 255
At Ephesus, the temple see, Our king and all his company . v 2 282
Epicure. Fly, false thanes, And mingle with the English epicures *Macb.* v 3 8
Will this description satisfy him?—With the health that Pompey gives him, else he is a very epicure . . *Ant. and Cleo.* ii 7 58
Epicurean. What a damned Epicurean rascal is this! . *Mer. Wives* ii 2 300
Epicurean cooks Sharpen with cloyless sauce his appetite *Ant. and Cleo.* ii 1 24
Epicurism and lust Make it more like a tavern or a brothel Than a graced palace . . . . *Lear* i 4 265
Epicurus. I held Epicurus strong And his opinion . *J. Cæsar* v 1 77
Epidamnum. Prosperous voyages I often made To Epidamnum *C. of Er.* i 1 42
A league from Epidamnum had we sail'd . . . . . i 1 63
Epidamnum. Give out you are of Epidamnum, Lest that your goods too soon be confiscate . . . . . . *Com. of Errors* i 2 1
There is a bark of Epidamnum That stays but till her owner comes aboard iv 1 85
Thou peevish sheep, What ship of Epidamnum stays for me? . v 1 94
By men of Epidamnum he and I And the twin Dromio all were taken up v 1 349
And me they left with those of Epidamnum . . . . v 1 353
Epidaurus. Two ships from far making amain to us, Of Corinth that, of Epidaurus this . . . . i 1 94
Epigram. Dost thou think I care for a satire or an epigram? *Much Ado* v 4 103
Epilepsy. My lord is fall'n into an epilepsy: This is his second fit *Othello* iv 1 51
Epileptic. A plague upon your epileptic visage! . . *Lear* ii 2 87
Epilogue. It is an epilogue or discourse, to make plain Some obscure precedence . . . . *L. L. Lost* iii 1 82
Please you to see the epilogue, or to hear a Bergomask dance? *M. N. Dr.* v 1 360
No epilogue, I pray you; for your play needs no excuse. Never excuse v 1 362
But, come, your Bergomask: let your epilogue alone . . v 1 369
It is not the fashion to see the lady the epilogue . *As Y. Like It* Epil. 2
'Tis true that a good play needs no epilogue . . . . Epil. 5
Good plays prove the better by the help of good epilogues . . Epil. 7
That am neither a good epilogue nor cannot insinuate with you . . Epil. 8
Epistle. I will drop in his way some obscure epistles of love *T. Night* ii 3 169
A madman's epistles are no gospels . . . . . . v 1 294
Epistrophus and Cedius . . . . *Troi. and Cres.* v 5 11
Epitaph. On your family's old monument Hang mournful epitaphs *M. Ado* iv 1 209
Hang her an epitaph upon her tomb And sing it to her bones . v 1 293
Will you hear an extemporal epitaph on the death of the deer? *L. L. Lost* iv 2 51
You cannot better be employ'd, Bassanio, Than to live still and write mine epitaph . . . . *Mer. of Venice* iv 1 118
So in approof lives not his epitaph As in your royal speech *All's Well* i 2 50
Let's talk of graves, of worms and epitaphs . . *Richard II.* iii 2 145
Thy ignominy sleep with thee in the grave, But not remember'd in thy epitaph! . . . . 1 *Hen. IV.* v 4 101
Not worshipp'd with a waxen epitaph . . . . *Hen. V.* i 2 233
Make thine epitaph, That death in me at others' lives may laugh *T. of A.* iv 3 380
I was writing of my epitaph; It will be seen to-morrow . . v 1 188
Better have a bad epitaph than their ill report while you live *Hamlet* ii 2 550
Hath as oft a slanderous epitaph As record of fair act . *Cymbeline* iii 3 52
Her epitaphs In glittering golden characters express A general praise to her, and care in us . . . . . . *Pericles* iv 3 43
Now please you wit The epitaph is for Marina writ . . iv 4 32
Epithet. Suffer love! a good epithet! I do suffer love indeed *Much Ado* v 2 67
The epithets are sweetly varied, like a scholar at the least . *L. L. Lost* iv 2 8
A most singular and choice epithet . . . . . . v 1 17
Your sun-beamed eyes—They will not answer to that epithet . v 2 170
With a bombast circumstance Horribly stuff'd with epithets of war *Othello* i 1 14
Epitheton. Tender juvenal, as a congruent epitheton appertaining to thy young days . . . . *L. L. Lost* i 2 15
Epitome. This is a poor epitome of yours, Which by the interpretation of full time May show like all yourself . . *Coriolanus* v 3 68
Equal. Bestow thy fawning smiles on equal mates . *T. G. of Ver.* iii 1 158
To do't at peril of your soul, Were equal poise of sin and charity *Meas. for Meas.* ii 4 68
Dissuade him from her: she is no equal for his birth . *Much Ado* ii 1 171
And justice always whirls in equal measure . . *L. L. Lost* iv 3 384
An equal pound Of your fair flesh, to be cut off . *Mer. of Venice* i 3 150
Whose souls do bear an equal yoke of love . . . . iii 4 13
Fear of your adventure would counsel you to a more equal enterprise *As Y. Like It* i 2 188
Have fought with equal fortune and continue A braving war *All's Well* i 2 3
Contempt nor bitterness Were in his pride or sharpness; if they were, His equal had awaked them . . . . i 2 38
To eke out that Wherein toward me my homely stars have fail'd To equal my great fortune . . . . ii 5 81
I am as mad as he, If sad and merry madness equal be . *T. Night* iii 4 16
To speak of Perdita, now grown in grace Equal with wondering *W. Tale* iv 1 25
I give my daughter to him, and will make Her portion equal his . . iv 4 397
Back to the stained field, You equal potents, fiery kindled spirits! *K. John* ii 1 358
Her dowry shall weigh equal with a queen . . . . ii 1 486
On equal terms to give him chastisement . . *Richard II.* iv 1 22
My moiety, north from Burton here, In quantity equals not one of yours . . . . 1 *Hen. IV.* iii 1 97
We are a body strong enough, Even as we are, to equal with the king 2 *Hen. IV.* i 3 67
I have in equal balance justly weigh'd What wrongs our arms may do, what wrongs we suffer . . . . iv 1 67
Our state may go In equal rank with the best govern'd nation . v 2 137
My duty to you both, on equal love, Great Kings! . . *Hen. V.* v 2 23
Poor gentleman! his wrong doth equal mine . . 1 *Hen. VI.* ii 5 22
My vows are equal partners with thy vows . . . . iii 2 85
And poise the cause in justice' equal scales . . 2 *Hen. VI.* ii 1 204
To equal him, I will make myself a knight presently . . iv 2 127
Then, York, unloose thy long-imprison'd thoughts, And let thy tongue be equal with thy heart . . . . v 1 89
So is the equal poise of this fell war . . . 3 *Hen. VI.* ii 5 13
Wishing his foot were equal with his eye . . . . iii 2 137
My heart o'erweens too much, Unless my hand and strength could equal them . . . . iii 2 145
Nor were not worthy blame, If this foul deed were by to equal it . v 5 55
On me, whose all not equals Edward's moiety? . *Richard III.* i 2 250
The two kings, Equal in lustre, were now best, now worst *Hen. VIII.* i 1 29
He is equal ravenous As he is subtle . . . . . . i 1 159
Two equal men . . . . ii 2 108
No more assurance Of equal friendship and proceeding . . ii 4 18
He has no equal . . . . *Coriolanus* i 1 257
I thought to crush him in an equal force . . . . . i 10 14
How shall she be endow'd, If she be mated with an equal husband? *T. of A.* i 1 140
Honest water, which ne'er left man i' the mire: This and my food are equals . . . . i 2 61
In equal scale weighing delight and dole . . . *Hamlet* i 2 13
A man that fortune's buffets and rewards Hast ta'en with equal thanks iii 2 73
For our faults Can never be so equal, that your love Can equally move with them . . . . *Ant. and Cleo.* iii 4 35
To tell them that this world did equal theirs Till they had stol'n our jewel . . . . iv 15 77
His taints and honours Waged equal with him . . . v 1 31
'Faith, I shall unfold equal discourtesy To your best kindness *Cymbeline* ii 3 101
Then had my prize Been less, and so more equal ballasting To thee iii 6 78
Were my fortunes equal to my desires, I could wish to make one *Pericles* ii 1 117
A princess To equal any single crown o' the earth I' the justice of compare! . . . . iv 3 8

Equal. She speaks, My lord, that, may be, hath endured a grief Might equal yours . . . *Pericles* v 1 89
My fortunes—parentage—good parentage—To equal mine! . . v 1 99
Thou thought'st thy griefs might equal mine, If both were open'd . v 1 132
Equalities are so weighed, that curiosity in neither can make choice of either's moiety . . . *Lear* i 1 5
Equality. Whose equality By our best eyes cannot be censured *K. John* ii 1 327
Equality of two domestic powers Breed scrupulous faction *Ant. and Cleo.* i 3 47
Equalled. She had not been, Nor was not to be equall'd . *W. Tale* v 1 101
It should seem by the sum, Your master's confidence was above mine; Else, surely, his had equall'd . . *T. of Athens* iii 4 32
Equally. You weigh equally; a feather will turn the scale *M. for M.* iv 2 31
Much deserved on his part and equally remembered . *Much Ado* i 1 12
Let us sit and mock the good housewife Fortune from her wheel, that her gifts may henceforth be bestowed equally *As Y. Like It* i 2 36
The archdeacon hath divided it Into three limits very equally 1 *Hen. IV.* iii 1 73
Consisting equally of horse and foot . *Richard III.* v 3 294
As we shall find their merits and our safety May equally determine *Lear* v 3 45
For our faults Can never be so equal, that your love Can equally move with them . . . *Ant. and Cleo.* iii 4 36
Thou art the pandar to her dishonour and equally to me disloyal *Cymb.* iii 4 32
Equalness. That our stars, Unreconciliable, should divide Our equalness to this . . . . *Ant. and Cleo.* v 1 48
Equinoctial. Of the Vapians passing the equinoctial of Queubus *T. Night* ii 3 24
Equinox. But see his vice; 'Tis to his virtue a just equinox *Othello* ii 3 129
Equity. This down-trodden equity . . . *K. John* ii 1 241
There's no equity stirring . . . 1 *Hen. IV.* ii 2 106
Foul subornation is predominant And equity exiled . 2 *Hen. VI.* iii 1 146
Take thy place; And thou, his yoke-fellow of equity, Bench by his side *Lear* iii 6 39
Equivalent. My derivation was from ancestors Who stood equivalent with mighty kings . . . . *Pericles* v 1 92
Equivocal. What an equivocal companion is this! . . *All's Well* v 3 250
These sentences, to sugar or to gall, Being strong on both sides, are equivocal: But words are words . . *Othello* i 3 217
Equivocate. Committed treason enough for God's sake, yet could not equivocate to heaven . . . *Macbeth* ii 3 12
Equivocates him in a sleep, and, giving him the lie, leaves him . ii 3 39
Equivocation. To doubt the equivocation of the fiend That lies like truth v 5 43
We must speak by the card, or equivocation will undo us . *Hamlet* v 1 149
Equivocator. An equivocator, that could swear in both the scales against either scale . . . . *Macbeth* ii 3 9
O, come in, equivocator. Knock, knock, knock! . . . ii 3 13
Much drink may be said to be an equivocator with lechery . . ii 3 35
Ercles. I could play Ercles rarely, or a part to tear a cat in *M. N. Dream* i 2 31
This is Ercles' vein, a tyrant's vein; a lover is more condoling . i 2 42
Ere. Or ere It should the good ship so have swallow'd . . *Tempest* i 2 11
If thou remember'st aught ere thou camest here . . . i 2 51
Candied be they And melt ere they molest! . . . . ii 1 280
I swam, ere I could recover the shore, five and thirty leagues off and on iii 2 16
I drink the air before me, and return Or ere your pulse twice beat v 1 103
The most forward bud Is eaten by the canker ere it blow *T. G. of Ver.* i 1 46
'Twill be this hour ere I have done weeping . . . . ii 3 1
You always end ere you begin . . . . . . ii 4 31
I'll convey thee through the city-gate; And, ere I part with thee, confer iii 1 253
Unhappy that I am!—Unhappy were you, madam, ere I came . . v 4 29
Inconstancy falls off ere it begins . . . . . . v 4 113
I will find you twenty lascivious turtles ere one chaste man *Mer. Wives* ii 1 83
Take heed, ere summer comes or cuckoo-birds do sing . . ii 1 127
I will be thrown into Etna, as I have been into Thames, ere I will leave her thus . . . . iii 5 129
I'll come no more i' the basket. May I not go out ere he come? . iv 2 51
You might slip away ere he came. But what make you here? . iv 2 54
Find a maid That, ere she sleep, has thrice her prayers said . v 5 54
Why, every fault's condemn'd ere it be done *Meas. for Meas.* ii 2 38
Are now to have no successive degrees, But, ere they live, to end . ii 2 99
And strip myself to death . . . , ere I'ld yield My body up to shame ii 4 103
Correction and instruction must both work Ere this rude beast will profit iii 2 34
Ere he would have hanged a man for the getting a hundred bastards, he would have paid for the nursing a thousand . . . iii 2 124
Ere twice the sun hath made his journal greeting To the under generation iv 3 92
You must, sir, change persons with me, ere you make that my report v 1 340
But ere they came,—O, let me say no more! Gather the sequel *Com. of Err.* i 1 95
Ere the ships could meet by twice five leagues, We were encounter'd by a mighty rock . . . . i 1 101
Dies ere the weary sun set in the west . . . . . i 2 7
Ere I learn love, I'll practise to obey . . . . . ii 1 29
It was two ere I left him, and now the clock strikes one . . iv 2 54
I'll give thee, ere I leave thee, so much money, To warrant thee . iv 4 2
I will discharge thee ere I go from thee . . . . . iv 4 122
It will cost him a thousand pound ere a' be cured . . *Much Ado* i 1 90
Ere you flout old ends any further, examine your conscience . . i 1 290
I liked her ere I went to wars . . . . . . i 1 307
She will die, ere she make her love known . . . . ii 3 182
He hath an excellent good name.—His excellence did earn it, ere he had it . . . . iii 1 99
As chaste as is the bud ere it be blown . . . . iv 1 59
If a man do not erect in this age his own tomb ere he dies . . v 2 80
Let's have a dance ere we are married, that we may lighten our own hearts . . . . v 4 120
Ere you find where light in darkness lies, Your light grows dark *L. L. Lost* i 1 78
Now here is three studied, ere ye'll thrice wink . . . i 2 54
Thou shalt fast for thy offences ere thou be pardoned . . i 2 152
We shall be rich ere we depart, If fairings come thus plentifully in v 2 1
She might ha' been a grandam ere she died . . . . v 2 17
So live, so die, my lord, Ere I will yield my virgin patent up *M. N. Dream* i 1 80
Ere a man hath power to say 'Behold!' . . . . . i 1 147
Ere Demetrius look'd on Hermia's eyne, He hail'd down oaths that he was only mine . . . . i 1 242
And the green corn Hath rotted ere his youth attain'd a beard . ii 1 95
And be thou here again Ere the leviathan can swim a league . . ii 1 174
Ere I take this charm from off her sight, As I can take it . . ii 1 183
Ere he do leave this grove, Thou shalt fly him and he shall seek thy love ii 1 245
And look thou meet me ere the first cock crow . . . ii 1 267
To her, my lord, Was I betroth'd ere I saw Hermia . . . iv 1 177
You shall seek all day ere you find them . . . *Mer. of Venice* i 1 116
I will do any thing, Nerissa, ere I'll be married to a sponge . . i 2 107
You shall look fairer, ere I give or hazard . . . . ii 9 22
Ere I ope his letter, I pray you, tell me how my good friend doth . iii 2 235
Ere. The Jew shall have my flesh, blood, bones and all, Ere thou shalt lose for me one drop of blood . . . *Mer. of Venice* iv 1 113
And saw the lion's shadow ere himself And ran dismay'd away . . v 1 8
What, are we cuckolds ere we have deserved it? . . . . v 1 265
I should have given him tears unto entreaties, Ere he should thus have ventured . . . . . . *As Y. Like It* i 2 251
Ere we have thy youthful wages spent . . . . . ii 3 67
You'll be rotten ere you be half ripe . . . . . iii 2 126
It was a crest ere thou wast born: Thy father's father wore it . . iv 2 15
Play you the whiles; His lecture will be done ere you have tuned *T. of S.* iii 1 23
We will persuade him, be it possible, To put on better ere he go to church . . . . iii 2 128
My heart in my belly, ere I should come by a fire to thaw me . . iv 1 8
I will be married to a wealthy widow, Ere three days pass . . iv 2 38
'Twill be supper-time ere you come there.—It shall be seven ere I go to horse . . . . iv 3 192
It shall be moon, or star, or what I list, Or ere I journey . . iv 5 8
Ere they can hide their levity in honour . . . *All's Well* i 2 35
A man may draw his heart out, ere a' pluck one . . . . i 3 93
Ere twice the horses of the sun shall bring Their fiery torcher his diurnal ring, Ere twice in murk and occidental damp Moist Hesperus hath quench'd his sleepy lamp . . . . . . ii 1 164
To-night, When I should take possession of the bride, End ere I do begin ii 5 29
'Twill be two days ere I shall see you, so I leave you to your wisdom . ii 5 75
We'll make you some sport with the fox ere we case him . . iii 6 111
No more, But that your daughter, ere she seems as won, Desires this ring . . . . iii 7 31
'Fore whose throne 'tis needful, Ere I can perfect mine intents, to kneel iv 4 4
We may pick a thousand salads ere we light on such another herb . iv 5 15
On our quick'st decrees The inaudible and noiseless foot of Time Steals ere we can effect them . . . . v 3 42
Ere my heart Durst make too bold a herald of my tongue . . . v 3 45
O dear heaven, bless! Or, ere they meet, in me, O nature, cesse! . v 3 72
I'ld have seen him damned ere I'ld have challenged him . *T. Night* iii 4 313
Thou shalt hold the opinion of Pythagoras ere I will allow of thy wits iv 2 63
They that went on crutches ere he was born desire yet their life to see him a man . . . . *W. Tale* i 1 44
Ride's With one soft kiss a thousand furlongs ere With spur we heat an acre . . . . i 2 95
Ere I could make thee open thy white hand And clap thyself my love . i 2 103
When you have said 'she's goodly,' come between Ere you can say 'she's honest' . . . . ii 1 76
A devil Would have shed water out of fire ere done't . . . iii 2 194
Ere ancient'st order was Or what is now received . . . iv 1 10
Why, how now, father! Speak ere thou diest . . . . iv 4 462
Be thou as lightning in the eyes of France; For ere thou canst report I will be there, The thunder of my cannon shall be heard . *K. John* i 1 25
And so, ere answer knows what question would . . . . i 1 200
Thou shalt turn To ashes, ere our blood shall quench that fire . . ii 1 345
And, ere our coming, see thou shake the bags Of hoarding abbots . iii 3 7
Ere the next Ascension-day at noon . . . . . . iv 2 151
'Twill be Two long days' journey, lords, or ere we meet . . . iv 3 20
And grapple with him ere he come so nigh . . . . . v 1 61
Conduct me to the king; I doubt he will be dead or ere I come . v 6 44
Ere I move, What my tongue speaks my right drawn sword may prove *Richard II.* i 1 45
But ere I last received the sacrament I did confess it . . . i 1 139
Ere my tongue Shall wound my honour with such feeble wrong . . i 1 190
Confess thy treasons ere thou fly the realm . . . . . i 3 198
Ere the six years that he hath to spend Can change their moons . i 3 219
Ere further leisure yield them further means . . . . i 4 40
It must break with silence, Ere't be disburden'd with a liberal tongue . ii 1 229
Ere her native king Shall falter under foul rebellion's arms . . iii 2 25
Ere the crown he looks for live in peace, Ten thousand bloody crowns . iii 3 95
Fiend, thou torment'st me ere I come to hell! . . . . iv 1 270
Ere thou bid good night, to quit their griefs, Tell thou the lamentable tale . . . . v 1 43
Ere foul sin gathering head Shall break into corruption . . . v 1 58
And beg thy pardon ere he do accuse thee . . . . . v 2 113
My tongue cleave to my roof within my mouth, Unless a pardon ere I rise . . . . v 3 32
My heart is not confederate with my hand.—It was, villain, ere thy hand did set it down . . . . v 3 54
I'll starve ere I'll rob a foot further . . . . 1 *Hen. IV.* ii 2 23
Ere I lead this life long, I'll sew nether stocks and mend them . ii 4 129
I'll see thee damned ere I call thee coward . . . . ii 4 162
I will die a hundred thousand deaths Ere break the smallest parcel of this vow . . . . iii 2 159
Doth he keep his bed?—He did, my lord, four days ere I set forth . iv 1 22
I would the state of time had first been whole Ere he by sickness had been visited . . . . iv 1 26
Ere the king Dismiss his power, he means to visit us . . . iv 4 36
As great as mine!—I'll make it greater ere I part from thee . . v 4 71
But Priam found the fire ere he his tongue . . . 2 *Hen. IV.* i 1 74
But, ere they come, bid them o'er-read these letters . . . iii 1 2
Ere they be dismiss'd, let them march by . . . . . iv 2 96
I had forestall'd this dear and deep rebuke Ere you with grief had spoke iv 5 142
'Twill be two o'clock ere they come from the coronation . . . v 5 3
Ere this year expire, We bear our civil swords and native fire As far as France . . . . v 5 111
This grace of kings must die . . . Ere he take ship for France *Hen. V.* ii Prol. 30
Ere theise eyes of mine take themselves to slomber, ay'll de gud service iii 2 122
You must first go yourself to hazard, ere you have them . . . iii 7 95
To take the tales out of my mouth, ere it is made and finished . iv 7 45
And death approach not ere my tale be done . . . 1 *Hen. VI.* ii 5 62
Ere that we will suffer such a prince . . . To be disgraced . . iii 1 97
I would see his heart out, ere the priest Should ever get that privilege of me . . . . iii 1 120
His days may finish ere that hapless time . . . . . iii 1 201
But, ere we go, regard this dying prince . . . . . iii 2 86
Ere the glass, that now begins to run, Finish the process of his sandy hour . . . . iv 2 35
Speak to thy father ere thou yield thy breath! . . . . iv 7 24
Ere the thirtieth of May next ensuing . . . 2 *Hen. VI.* i 1 49
But I would have him dead, my Lord of Suffolk, Ere you can take due orders for a priest . . . . iii 1 274
She shall pay to me her maidenhead ere they have it . . . iv 7 130
And swallow my sword like a great pin, ere thou and I part . . iv 10 32
Or cut not out the burly-boned clown in chines of beef ere thou sleep . iv 10 61
Ere they will have me go to ward, They'll pawn their swords . . v 1 112

Ere. I would speak blasphemy ere bid you fly: But fly you must 2 *Hen. VI.* v 2 85
Let us pursue him ere the writs go forth . . . . v 3 26
Thy father hath.—But 'twas ere I was born . . . . . 3 *Hen. VI.* i 3 39
Ere my knee rise from the earth's cold face . . . ii 3 35
So many weeks ere the poor fools will ean; So many years ere I shall shear the fleece . . . . ii 5 36
To take their rooms, ere I can place myself . . . iii 2 132
Often ere this day, When I have heard your king's desert recounted . iii 3 131
Will encounter with our glorious sun, Ere he attain his easeful western bed . . . . v 3 6
Ere ye come there, be sure to hear some news . . . . v 5 48
Ere you were queen, yea, or your husband king *Richard III.* i 3 121
'Twas full two years ere I could get a tooth . . . ii 4 29
His nurse! why, she was dead ere thou wert born . . ii 4 33
Shall we hear from you, Catesby, ere we sleep?—You shall, my lord iii 1 188
I'll have this crown of mine cut from my shoulders Ere I will see the crown so foul misplaced . . . . iii 2 44
Ere a fortnight make me elder, I'll send some packing . . . iii 2 62
He will lose his head ere give consent . . . . iii 4 40
And die, ere men can say, God save the queen! . . . iv 1 63
Ere I can repeat this curse again, Even in so short a space . iv 1 78
Ere from this war thou turn a conqueror . . . . iv 4 184
Swear not by time to come; for that thou hast Misused ere used . iv 4 396
I do commend my watchful soul, Ere I let fall the windows of mine eyes v 3 116
I died for hope ere I could lend thee aid . . . . v 3 173
Paid ere he promised; whereby his suit was granted Ere it was ask'd *Hen. VIII.* i 1 186
You have half our power: The other moiety, ere you ask, is given i 2 12
Some of these Should find a running banquet ere they rested . . i 4 12
I' the progress of this business, Ere a determinate resolution . . ii 4 176
Was Hector armed and gone ere ye came to Ilium? *Troi. and Cres.* i 2 49
Whose wit was mouldy ere your grandsires had nails on their toes ii 1 115
I will see you hanged, like clotpoles, ere I come any more . ii 1 129
You must be watched ere you be made tame, must you? . iii 2 46
You shall fight your hearts out ere I part you . . . iii 2 55
Though they be long ere they are wooed, they are constant being won . iii 2 118
Howsoever, he shall pay for me ere he has me . . . iii 3 298
Come, come, you'll do him wrong ere you're ware . . . iv 2 57
Ere the first sacrifice, within this hour, We must give up . . iv 2 66
So glib of tongue, That give accosting welcome ere it comes . . iv 5 59
Were I the general, thou shouldst have my office Ere that correction v 6 5
Let us revenge this with our pikes, ere we become rakes . *Coriolanus* i 1 23
The rabble should have first unroof'd the city, Ere so prevail'd with me i 1 223
I'll lean upon one crutch and fight with t'other, Ere stay behind . i 1 247
Brought to bodily act ere Rome Had circumvention . . . i 2 5
To take in many towns ere almost Rome Should know we were afoot . i 2 24
To our tent; Where, ere we do repose us, we will write To Rome . i 9 74
Ere in our own house I do shade my head, The good patricians must be visited . . . . ii 1 211
If You had not show'd them how ye were disposed Ere they lack'd power to cross you . . . . iii 2 23
Or rudely visit them in parts remote, To fright them, ere destroy . iv 5 149
To be executed ere they wipe their lips . . . . . iv 5 232
All places yield to him ere he sits down . . . . . iv 7 28
Therefore, at your vantage, Ere he express himself . . . v 6 55
And that you'll say, ere half an hour pass . *T. Andron.* iii 1 192
Do me some service, ere I come to thee . . . . . v 2 44
Close fighting ere I did approach . . *Rom. and Jul.* i 1 114
As is the bud bit with an envious worm, Ere he can spread his sweet leaves to the air . . . . i 1 158
Ere we may think her ripe to be a bride . . . . i 2 11
For our judgement sits Five times in that ere once in our five wits . i 4 47
Thou overheard'st, ere I was ware, My true love's passion . . ii 2 103
Now, ere the sun advance his burning eye, The day to cheer . . ii 3 5
I'll tell thee, ere thou ask it me again . . . . . ii 3 48
That is something stale and hoar ere it be spent . . . ii 4 139
A hare that is hoar Is too much for a score, When it hoars ere it be spent ii 4 146
Make haste, lest mine be about your ears ere it be out . . . iii 1 85
Ere I Could draw to part them, was stout Tybalt slain . . iii 1 177
O, by this count I shall be much in years Ere I again behold my Romeo! iii 5 47
That I must wed Ere he, that should be husband, comes to woo . iii 5 120
Ere this hand, by thee to Romeo seal'd, Shall be the label to another deed . . . . iv 1 56
And there die strangled ere my Romeo comes . . . . iv 3 35
Some minute ere the time Of her awaking . . . . . v 3 257
Ere we depart, we'll share a bounteous time In different pleasures *T. of A.* i 1 263
Hollow welcomes, Recanting goodness, sorry ere 'tis shown . . i 2 17
O joy, e'en made away ere't can be born! . . . . . i 2 110
Wherefore ere this time Had you not fully laid my state before me? . ii 2 133
He did behave his anger, ere 'twas spent . . . . . iii 5 22
To let the meat cool ere we can agree upon the first place . . iii 6 76
But let the famish'd flesh slide from the bone, Ere thou relieve the beggar . . . . iv 3 536
Come hither, ere my tree hath felt the axe, And hang himself . . v 1 214
Ere thou hadst power or we had cause of fear . . . . v 4 15
But ere we could arrive the point proposed, Cæsar cried 'Help me!' *J. C.* i 2 110
I would have had thee there, and here again, Ere I can tell thee what thou shouldst do there . . . . ii 4 5
O, that a man might know The end of this day's business ere it come! . v 1 124
When the battle's lost and won.—That will be ere the set of sun *Macbeth* i 1 5
Was it so late, friend, ere you went to bed, That you do lie so late? . ii 3 24
Both the worlds suffer, Ere we will eat our meal in fear . . iii 2 17
Ere the bat hath flown His cloister'd flight, ere to black Hecate's summons The shard-borne beetle . . . . iii 2 40
I' the olden time, Ere humane statute purged the gentle weal . iii 4 76
Which must be acted ere they may be scann'd . . . . iii 4 140
There hangs a vaporous drop profound; I'll catch it ere it come to ground iii 5 25
Fly to the court of England and unfold His message ere he come . iii 6 47
Expire before the flowers in their caps, Dying or ere they sicken . iv 3 173
A little ere the mightiest Julius fell, The graves stood tenantless *Hamlet* i 1 114
A little month, or ere those shoes were old . . . . i 2 147
Ere yet the salt of most unrighteous tears Had left the flushing in her galled eyes, She married . . . . i 2 154
We'll teach you to drink deep ere you depart . . . . i 2 175
So many journeys may the sun and moon Make us again count o'er ere love be done! . . . . iii 2 172
To be forestalled ere we come to fall, Or pardon'd being down . iii 3 49
Ere we were two days old at sea . . . . . . iv 6 14
How long will a man lie i' the earth ere he rot? . . . v 1 179
I knew you must be edified by the margent ere you had done . v 2 163

Ere. And had, indeed, sir, a son for her cradle ere she had a husband *Lear* i 1 15
Ere I was risen from the place that show'd My duty kneeling . . ii 4 29
This heart Shall break into a hundred thousand flaws, Or ere I'll weep . ii 4 289
I will have my revenge ere I depart his house . . . iii 5 1
Fools do those villains pity who are punish'd Ere they have done their mischief . . . . iv 2 55
And told me I had white hairs in my beard ere the black ones were there iv 6 99
The good-years shall devour them, flesh and fell, Ere they shall make us weep . . . . v 3 25
Methinks our pleasure might have been demanded, Ere you had spoke so far . . . . v 3 63
I'll prove it on thy heart, Ere I taste bread . . . . v 3 94
Ere I would say, I would drown myself for the love of a guinea-hen, I would change my humanity with a baboon . . . . . *Othello* i 3 316
He gives your Hollander a vomit, ere the next pottle can be filled . ii 3 87
Ere it be demanded—As like enough it will—I'ld have it copied . iii 4 189
I kiss'd thee ere I kill'd thee . . . . v 2 358
He fell upon me ere admitted . . . . . *Ant. and Cleo.* ii 2 75
Ere we put ourselves in arms, dispatch we The business we have talk'd of ii 2 168
And next morn, Ere the ninth hour, I drunk him to his bed . . ii 5 21
I have a mind to strike thee ere thou speak'st . . . . ii 5 42
We'll feast each other ere we part; and let's Draw lots who shall begin ii 6 61
And The neighs of horse to tell of her approach Long ere she did appear iii 6 46
You were half blasted ere I knew you . . . . . iii 13 105
Is it sin To rush into the secret house of death, Ere death dare come to us? . . . . iv 15 82
Thou shouldst have made him As little as a crow, or less, ere left To after-eye him . . . . *Cymbeline* i 3 15
Ere I could tell him How I would think on him at certain hours . i 3 26
Ere I could Give him that parting kiss . . . . . i 3 33
Did softly press the rushes, ere he waken'd The chastity he wounded . ii 2 13
There be many Cæsars, Ere such another Julius . . . . iii 1 12
Ere wildness Vanquish my staider senses . . . . . iii 4 9
Yet famine, Ere clean it o'erthrow nature, makes it valiant . . iii 6 20
You shall have better cheer Ere you depart . . . . iii 6 68
I am not well; But not so citizen a wanton as To seem to die ere sick . iv 2 9
Those that would die or ere resist are grown The mortal bugs o' the field v 3 50
I had rather thou shouldst live while nature will Than die ere I hear more . . . . v 5 152
Here's my knee; Ere I arise, I will prefer my sons . . . v 5 326
Ere the stroke Of this yet scarce-cold battle . . . . v 5 468
Never was a war did cease, Ere bloody hands were wash'd, with such a peace . . . . v 5 485
Our men be vanquish'd ere they do resist . . . . *Pericles* i 2 27
With thousand doubts How I might stop this tempest ere it came . i 2 98
Yet, ere you shall depart, this we desire . . . . . i 3 39
That all those eyes adored them ere their fall Scorn now their hand should give them burial . . . . ii 4 11
Your master will be dead ere you return . . . . . iii 2 7
Come, give me your flowers, ere the sea mar it . . . iv 1 27
Ere I die *Much Ado* i 1; *L. L. Lost* v 2; *All's Well* iv 5; 2 *Hen. IV.* v 3
Ere I go *Much Ado* v 2; *L. L. Lost* v 2; *M. N. Dream* i 1; 2 *Hen. IV.* ii 4; 3 *Hen. VI.* iv 1; *Lear* iii 2
Ere it be long *Meas. for Meas.* iv 2; 1 *Hen. VI.* iii 2; 3 *Hen. VI.* iii 3; iv 1
Ere long *Tempest* v 1; *Meas. for Meas.* iii 1; *M. N. Dream* v 1; *K. John* iv 2; 2 *Hen. IV.* ii 1; 1 *Hen. VI.* i 3; ii 1; iii 2; iv 1; 2 *Hen. VI.* i 1; iii 1; *Coriolanus* v 1; *Lear* iv 2
Ere now *M. N. Dream* iii 1; *As Y. Like It* ii 4; *All's Well* v 2; *W. Tale* i 2; iv 1; 2 *Hen. IV.* v 3; 1 *Hen. VI.* v 3; *Richard III.* i 3; *Coriolanus* ii 3; *Rom. and Jul.* iv 4; *Macbeth* iii 4
Ere one can say . . . . . . 2 *Hen. IV.* ii 4 31; *Rom. and Jul.* ii 2 120
Ere thou (you) go *Much Ado* iii 5; *T. of Shrew* i 2; 2 *Hen. VI.* ii 3; 3 *Hen. VI.* iii 3; *Coriolanus* iv 3
Ere you go to bed *Rom. and Jul.* iii 4; *Hamlet* iii 2; iii 3
Ere day. We may effect this business yet ere day *M. N. Dream* iii 2 395
You and I will yet ere day See Brutus at his house . . *J. Cæsar* i 3 153
And ere day We will awake him and be sure of him . . . i 3 163
Ere dinner time. I have thirty miles to ride yet ere dinner time 1 *Hen. IV.* iii 3 222
Ere morning. You shall hear more ere morning . *Meas. for Meas.* iv 2 98
My master will be here ere morning . . . *Mer. of Venice* v 1 48
Ere night I will embrace him with a soldier's arm . 1 *Hen. IV.* v 2 73
Ere night They'll be in fresher robes . . . . *Hen. V.* iv 3 116
May yet ere night yield both my life and them To some man else 3 *Hen. VI.* ii 5 59
Must by the roots be hewn up yet ere night . . . . v 4 69
And, Romans, yet ere night We shall try fortune in a second fight *J. C.* v 3 109
Ere noon. Great business must be wrought ere noon . *Macbeth* iii 5 22
Ere sunrise. True prayers That shall be up at heaven and enter there Ere sun-rise . . . . *Meas. for Meas.* ii 2 153
Ere sunset, Set armed discord 'twixt these perjured kings! . *K. John* iii 1 110
But ere sunset I'll make thee curse the deed . . 3 *Hen. VI.* ii 2 116
Ere supper-time must I perform Much business appertaining *Tempest* iii 1 95
Ere this. I have inly wept, Or should have spoke ere this . . v 1 201
Mean to touch our northern shore: Perhaps they had ere this *Rich. II.* ii 1 289
To show in articles; Which long ere this we offer'd to the king 2 *Hen. IV.* iv 1 75
Whose frown hath made thee faint and fly ere this . 3 *Hen. VI.* i 4 48
I thought my mother, and my brother York, Would long ere this have met us on the way . . . . *Richard III.* iii 1 21
Ere this I should have fatted all the region kites With this slave's offal *Hamlet* ii 2 606
Erebus. Dull as night And his affections dark as Erebus . *Mer. of Venice* v 1 87
To the infernal deep, with Erebus and tortures vile also . 2 *Hen. IV.* ii 4 171
Not Erebus itself were dim enough To hide thee from prevention *J. Cæsar* ii 1 84
Erect. If a man do not erect in this age his own tomb ere he dies, he shall live no longer in monument than the bell rings . . *Much Ado* v 2 80
I'll erect A tomb, wherein his corpse shall be interr'd . 1 *Hen. VI.* ii 2 12
Burgundy Enshrines thee in his heart and there erects Thy noble deeds iii 2 119
Erect his statua and worship it . . . . . . 2 *Hen. VI.* iii 2 80
On him erect A second hope . . . . . *Troi. and Cres.* iv 5 108
Erected. So that I have lost my edifice by mistaking the place where I erected it . . . . *Mer. Wives* ii 2 226
These walls of ours Were not erected by their hands from whom You have received your griefs . . . . . . *T. of Athens* v 4 23
Erecting. Thou hast most traitorously corrupted the youth of the realm in erecting a grammar school . . . . . 2 *Hen. VI.* iv 7 36
Erection. They mistook their erection . . . . *Mer. Wives* iii 5 41
Then draw the model; And when we see the figure of the house, Then must we rate the cost of the erection . . . . 2 *Hen. IV.* i 3 44

Erection. Your activity may defeat and quell The source of all erection *T. of Athens* iv 3 164
Erewhile. Else your memory is bad, going o'er it erewhile *L. L. Lost* iv 1 99
I am as fair now as I was erewhile *M. N. Dream* iii 2 274
That young swain that you saw here but erewhile . *As Y. Like It* ii 4 89
Know'st thou the youth that spoke to me erewhile? . . . iii 5 105
Erga. Tanta est erga te mentis integritas, regina serenissima *Hen. VIII.* iii 1 40
Ergo. Light is an effect of fire, and fire will burn; ergo, light wenches will burn . . . . *Com. of Errors* iv 3 57
But I pray you, ergo, old man, ergo, I beseech you . *Mer. of Venice* ii 2 59
Ergo, he that kisses my wife is my friend . . . . *All's Well* i 3 53
Eringoes. Hail kissing-comfits and snow eringoes . *Mer. Wives* v 5 23
Ermengare. Lady Ermengare, Daughter to Charles the foresaid duke of Lorraine . . . . *Hen. V.* i 2 82
Eros. How now, friend Eros!—There's strange news come, sir *A. and C.* iii 5 1
Eros! mine armour, Eros!—Sleep a little.—No, my chuck . iv 4 1
Thou fumblest, Eros; and my queen's a squire More tight at this than thou . . . . iv 4 14
Go, Eros, send his treasure after; do it; Detain no jot, I charge thee . iv 5 12
What, Eros, Eros! Ah, thou spell! Avaunt! . . . . iv 12 30
Eros, ho! The shirt of Nessus is upon me . . . . iv 12 42
Eros, thou yet behold'st me?—Ay, noble lord . . . . iv 14 1
My good knave Eros, now thy captain is Even such a body . . iv 14 12
She, Eros, has Pack'd cards with Cæsar, and false-play'd my glory . iv 14 18
Nay, weep not, gentle Eros; there is left us Ourselves to end ourselves iv 14 21
Unarm, Eros; the long day's task is done, And we must sleep . iv 14 35
Apace, Eros, apace. No more a soldier: bruised pieces, go . iv 14 41
Eros!—I come, my queen:—Eros!—Stay for me . . . iv 14 50
Thou art sworn, Eros, That, when the exigent should come . . on my command, Thou then wouldst kill me: do't; the time is come iv 14 62
Eros, Wouldst thou be window'd in great Rome and see Thy master thus? . . . . iv 14 71
Farewell, great chief. Shall I strike now?—Now, Eros . . iv 14 93
Thrice-nobler than myself! Thou teachest me, O valiant Eros, what I should, and thou couldst not . . . . iv 14 96
My queen and Eros Have by their brave instruction got upon me A nobleness in record . . . . iv 14 97
Come, then; and, Eros, Thy master dies thy scholar . . iv 14 101
Erpingham. Sir Thomas Erpingham, Sir John Ramston . *Richard II.* ii 1 283
Good morrow, old Sir Thomas Erpingham . . . *Hen. V.* iv 1 13
Under what captain serve you?—Under Sir Thomas Erpingham . iv 1 96
Err. Fearing lest my jealous aim might err . . *T. G. of Ver.* iii 1 28
Authority, though it err like others, Hath yet a kind of medicine in itself *Meas. for Meas.* ii 2 134
All these old witnesses—I cannot err—Tell me thou art my son *C. of Er.* v 1 317
He errs, Doting on Hermia's eyes, So I, admiring of his qualities *M. N. D.* i 1 230
As thou lovest her, Thy love's to me religious; else, does err *All's Well* ii 3 190
You cannot, By the good aid that I of you shall borrow, Err in bestowing it . . . . iii 7 12
For worthy Wolsey, Who cannot err, he did it . . . *Hen. VIII.* i 1 174
The error of our eye directs our mind: What error leads must err *Troi. and Cres.* v 2 111
And make discovery Err in report of us . . . . *Macbeth* v 4 7
For madness would not err . . . . . . *Hamlet* iii 4 73
For nature so preposterously to err, Being not deficient, blind, or lame of sense, Sans witchcraft could not . . . . *Othello* i 3 62
That will confess perfection so could err Against all rules of nature . i 3 100
One that truly loves you, That errs in ignorance and not in cunning . iii 3 49
Doth affection breed it? I think it doth: is't frailty that thus errs? It is so too . . . . iv 3 100
In the election of a sir so rare, Which you know cannot err *Cymbeline* i 6 176
These her women Can trip me, if I err . . . . . v 5 35
Whereas reproof, obedient and in order, Fits kings, as they are men, for they may err . . . . *Pericles* i 2 43
Errand. Hear the truth of it: he came of an errand to me *Mer. Wives* i 4 80
Well, I must of another errand to Sir John Falstaff . . iii 4 114
Have I not forbid her my house? She comes of errands, does she? iv 2 182
He were as good go a mile on his errand . *Meas. for Meas.* iii 2 39
So that my errand, due unto my tongue, I thank him, I bare home upon my shoulders . . . . *Com. of Errors* ii 1 72
I will go on the slightest errand now to the Antipodes . *Much Ado* ii 1 273
Look, who comes here.—My errand is to you, fair youth *As Y. Like It* iv 3 6
Tut, fear not me.—But hast thou done thy errand? *T. of Shrew* iv 4 14
There is no lady living So meet for this great errand *W. Tale* ii 2 46
On mine own accord I'll off; But first I'll do my errand . . iii 3 64
Upon which errand I now go toward him; therefore follow me . . v 1 231
To thee, King John, my holy errand is . . . *K. John* iii 1 137
The whiteness in thy cheek Is apter than thy tongue to tell thy errand *2 Hen. IV.* i 1 69
Ay; I know thy errand, I will go with thee . . . *Hen. V.* iv 1 324
Of a sleeveless errand . . . . . *Troi. and Cres.* v 4 9
Now, you companion, I'll say an errand for you *Coriolanus* v 2 65
Let me come in, and you shall know my errand . *Rom. and Jul.* iii 3 79
Stay not to answer me, but get thee gone: Why dost thou stay?—To know my errand . . . . *J. Cæsar* ii 4 3
This is a slight unmeritable man, Meet to be sent on errands . iv 1 13
This Jack of Cæsar's shall Bear us an errand to him *Ant. and Cleo.* iii 13 104
Errant. Divert his grain Tortive and errant from his course of growth *Troi. and Cres.* i 3 9
Erred. Whether you had not sometime in your life Err'd in this point which now you censure him . . . . *Meas. for Meas.* ii 1 15
Nor forward of revenge, though they much err'd . . *3 Hen. VI.* iv 8 46
Doubting lest that he had err'd or sinn'd . . . . *Pericles* i 3 22
Errest. Thou errest: I say, there is no darkness but ignorance *T. Night* iv 2 46
Erring. If I can check my erring love, I will . . *T. G. of Ver.* ii 4 213
How brief the life of man Runs his erring pilgrimage *As Y. Like It* iii 2 138
The extravagant and erring spirit hies To his confine . . *Hamlet* i 1 154
A frail vow betwixt an erring barbarian and a supersubtle Venetian *Oth.* i 3 362
And yet, how nature erring from itself,— Ay, there's the point . iii 3 227
Erroneous. What stratagems, how fell, how butcherly, Erroneous, mutinous and unnatural! . . . . *3 Hen. VI.* ii 5 90
Erroneous vassal! the great King of kings Hath in the tables of his law commanded That thou shalt do no murder . . *Richard III.* i 4 200
Error. That one error Fills him with faults . . *T. G. of Ver.* v 4 111
Thou art full of error; I am sound . . . . *Meas. for Meas.* i 2 54
What error drives our eyes and ears amiss? . . *Com. of Errors* ii 2 186
Smother'd in errors, feeble, shallow, weak . . . . iii 2 35
I was ta'en for him, and he for me, And thereupon these ERRORS are arose . . . . v 1 388
That by this sympathized one day's error Have suffer'd wrong . . v 1 397
Error. And in her eye there hath appear'd a fire, To burn the errors that these princes hold . . . . *Much Ado* iv 1 165
If this sweet lady lie not guiltless here Under some biting error . . iv 1 172
Accused her Upon the error that you heard debated . . . v 4 3
Pardon, sir; error: he is not quantity enough . . *L. L. Lost* v 1 137
To our perjury to add more terror, We are again forsworn, in will and error . . . . v 2 471
Our love being yours, the error that love makes Is likewise yours . . v 2 781
Whose liquor hath this virtuous property, To take from thence all error with his might . . . . *M. N. Dream* iii 2 368
This is the greatest error of all the rest . . . . . v 1 250
In religion, What damned error, but some sober brow Will bless it and approve it with a text? . . . . . *Mer. of Venice* iii 2 78
Many an error by the same example Will rush into the state . . iv 1 221
Error i' the bill, sir; error i' the bill . . . *T. of Shrew* iv 3 146
Religious in mine error, I adore The sun . . . *All's Well* i 3 211
My soul disputes well with my sense, That this may be some error *T. N.* iv 3 10
Both joy and terror Of good and bad, that makes and unfolds error *W. T.* iv 1 2
They shoot but calm words folded up in smoke, To make a faithless error in your ears . . . . *K. John* ii 1 230
Or else was wrangling Somerset in the error? . . *1 Hen. VI.* ii 4 6
And yet thy tongue will not confess thy error . . . . ii 4 67
This fault in us [women] I find, The error of our eye directs our mind: What error leads must err . . . . *Troi. and Cres.* v 2 110
My love with words and errors still she feeds; But edifies another with her deeds . . . . v 3 111
And mountainous error be too highly heapt For truth to o'er-peer *Cor.* ii 3 127
O hateful error, melancholy's child! . . . . *J. Cæsar* v 3 67
O error, soon conceived, Thou never comest unto a happy birth! . v 3 69
Lest more mischance, On plots and errors, happen . . *Hamlet* v 2 406
I do not so secure me in the error, But the main article I do approve *Oth.* i 3 10
When she is sated with his body, she will find the error of her choice . i 3 357
It is the very error of the moon . . . . v 2 109
The wise gods seel our eyes; In our own filth drop our clear judgements; make us Adore our errors . . . . *Ant. and Cleo.* iii 13 114
My boys, There was our error.—This is, sure, Fidele . . *Cymbeline* v 5 260
Death remember'd should be like a mirror, Who tells us life's but breath, to trust it error . . . . *Pericles* i 1 46
Erst. Thy company, which erst was irksome to me, I will endure *As Y. Like It* iii 5 95
The even mead, that erst brought sweetly forth The freckled cowslip *Hen. V.* v 2 48
That erst did follow thy proud chariot-wheels . . . *2 Hen. VI.* ii 4 13
Or slunk not Saturnine, as Tarquin erst? . . . *T. Andron.* iv 1 63
Speak, Rome's dear friend, as erst our ancestor . . . . v 3 80
But, feeling woe, Gripe not at earthly joys as erst they did . *Pericles* i 1 49
Erudition. Famed be thy tutor, and thy parts of nature Thrice famed, beyond all erudition . . . . . . *Troi. and Cres.* ii 3 254
Eruption. The curate and your sweet self are good at such eruptions and sudden breaking out of mirth . . . . . . *L. L. Lost* v 1 121
Diseased nature oftentimes breaks forth In strange eruptions *1 Hen. IV.* iii 1 28
Prodigious grown And fearful, as these strange eruptions are *J. Cæsar* i 3 78
This bodes some strange eruption to our state . . . *Hamlet* i 1 69
Escalus. Old Escalus, Though first in question, is thy secondary *M. for M.* i 1 46
'Tis one thing to be tempted, Escalus, Another thing to fall . . ii 1 17
He hath carried Notice to Escalus and Angelo, Who do prepare to meet him . . . . iv 3 135
Come, Escalus, You must walk by us on our other hand . . v 1 16
You, Lord Escalus, Sit with my cousin; lend him your kind pains . v 1 245
Thanks, good friend Escalus, for thy much goodness . . . v 1 534
That is Antonio, the duke's eldest son; That, Escalus . *All's Well* iii 5 80
Escanes, know this of me, Antiochus from incest lived not free *Pericles* ii 4 1
Old Escanes, whom Helicanus late Advanced in time to great and high estate, Is left to govern . . . . iv 4 13
Escape. For our escape Is much beyond our loss . . *Tempest* ii 1 2
He might put on a hat, a muffler and a kerchief, and so escape *M. Wives* iv 2 74
Thousand escapes of wit Make thee the father of their idle dreams *Meas. for Meas.* iv 1 63
Give him leave to escape hence, he would not . . . . iv 2 157
Anon, I wot not by what strong escape, He broke from those *C. of Err.* v 1 148
He that escapes me without some broken limb shall acquit him well *As Y. Like It* i 1 133
To save my life, Puts my apparel and my countenance on, And I for my escape have put on his . . . . . . *T. of Shrew* i 1 235
And for a week escape a great deal of discoveries . *All's Well* iii 6 99
Mine own escape unfoldeth to my hope . . . *T. Night* i 2 19
Ay, and privy To this their late escape . . . . *W. Tale* ii 1 95
What I do next, shall be to tell the king Of this escape . . . iv 4 677
In him that escapes, it were not sin to think that, making God so free an offer, He let him outlive that day to see His greatness *Hen. V.* iv 1 192
I'll direct thee how thou shalt escape By sudden flight . *1 Hen. VI.* iv 5 10
Had he 'scaped, methinks we should have heard The happy tidings of his good escape . . . . *3 Hen. VI.* ii 1 7
Think you, lords, that Clifford fled with them?—No, 'tis impossible he should escape . . . . ii 6 38
Unsavoury news! but how made he escape? . . . . . iv 6 80
Even he escapes not Language unmannerly . . . *Hen. VIII.* i 2 26
Rome will despise her for this foul escape . . . *T. Andron.* iv 2 113
As chaste as ice, as pure as snow, thou shalt not escape calumny *Hamlet* iii 1 141
If he by chance escape your venom'd stuck, Our purpose may hold there iv 7 162
For thy escape would teach me tyranny, To hang clogs on them *Othello* i 3 197
There then: thus I do escape the sorrow Of Antony's death *A. and C.* iv 14 94
Escaped. I escaped upon a butt of sack . . . *Tempest* ii 2 126
I spoke with some of the sailors that escaped the wreck *Mer. of Venice* iii 1 110
These Lincoln Washes have devoured them; Myself, well mounted, hardly have escaped . . . . *K. John* v 6 42
That hardly we escaped the pride of France . . *1 Hen. VI.* iii 2 40
I wonder how the king escaped our hands . . . *3 Hen. VI.* i 1 1
What news, my friend?—That Edward is escaped from your brother . iv 6 78
By the happy hollow of a tree Escaped the hunt . . . *Lear* ii 3 3
To-morrow, Before the sun shall see's, we'll spill the blood That has to-day escaped . . . . *Ant. and Cleo.* iv 8 4
Escapedst. Swear then how thou escapedst.—Swum ashore, man *Tempest* ii 2 132
Escapen. All perishen of man, of pelf, Ne aught escapen but himself *Pericles* ii Gower 36
Eschewed. What cannot be eschew'd must be embraced . *Mer. Wives* v 5 251
Escoted. What, are they children? who maintains 'em? how are they escoted? . . . . *Hamlet* ii 2 362
Especial. I have, upon especial cause . . . . *1 Hen. VI.* iv 1 55
For thine especial safety,—Which we do tender . . . *Hamlet* iv 3 42

Especial. And gave you such a masterly report For art and exercise in your defence And for your rapier most especial . . *Hamlet* iv 7 99
There is especial commission come from Venice . . . *Othello* iv 2 225
Especially. 'Tis an ill office for a gentleman, Especially against his very friend . . . . *T. G. of Ver.* iii 2 41
Above all other strifes, contended especially to know himself *M. for M.* iii 2 247
I am yours for the walk; and especially when I walk away . *Much Ado* ii 1 93
I would have sworn it had, my lord; especially against Benedick . . ii 3 122
In the heart of the world, and especially of my own people *As Y. Like It* i 1 176
You were born under a charitable star.—Under Mars, I.—I especially think, under Mars . . . . *All's Well* i 1 207
Especially he hath incurred the everlasting displeasure of the king . iv 3 10
Especially for those occasions At Eltham Place . . . 1 *Hen. VI.* iii 1 155
We'll have no bastards live; Especially since Charles must father it . v 4 71
Especially to you, fair queen! fair thoughts be your fair pillow!
Troi. and Cres. iii 1 48
Would you proceed especially against Caius Marcius? . . *Coriolanus* i 1 26
He's poor in no one fault, but stored with all.—Especially in pride . ii 1 22
There is some hope the ladies of Rome, especially his mother, may prevail . . . . v 4 6
This is no time to lend money, especially upon bare friendship *T. of A.* iii 1 45
What three things does drink especially provoke? . . . *Macbeth* ii 3 29
Thereabout of it especially, where he speaks of Priam's slaughter *Hamlet* ii 2 468
The business you have broached here cannot be without you; especially that of Cleopatra's . . . . *Ant. and Cleo.* i 2 181
I prithee tell me, how dost thou find the inclination of the people, especially of the younger sort? . . . . . . *Pericles* iv 2 104
Esperance. O esperance! Bid Butler lead him forth into the park
1 *Hen. IV.* ii 3 74
Now, Esperance! Percy! and set on . . . . . . v 2 97
An esperance so obstinately strong . . . . *Troi. and Cres.* v 2 121
To be worst, The lowest and most dejected thing of fortune, Stands still in esperance, lives not in fear . . . . . *Lear* iv 1 4
Espial. The prince's espials have informed me . . . 1 *Hen. VI.* i 4 8
By your espials were discovered Two mightier troops . . . iv 3 6
Her father and myself, lawful espials . . . . . *Hamlet* iii 1 32
Espied. Now question me no more; we are espied . *T. Andron.* ii 3 48
Straight will I bring you to the loathsome pit Where I espied the panther . . . . ii 3 194
Espies. Anoint his eyes; But do it when the next thing he espies May be the lady . . . . *M. N. Dream* ii 1 262
From whence Lysimachus our Tyrian ship espies . *Pericles* v Gower 18
Espouse. Doll Tearsheet she by name, and her espouse . *Hen. V.* ii 1 81
Henry shall espouse the Lady Margaret, daughter unto Reignier 2 *Hen. VI.* i 1 46
The queen hath heartily consented He shall espouse Elizabeth *Rich. III.* iv 5 18
And in the sacred Pantheon her espouse . . . . *T. Andron.* i 1 242
Espoused. And so espoused to death, with blood he seal'd A testament of noble-ending love . . . . *Hen. V.* iv 6 26
I have perform'd my task and was espoused . . . 2 *Hen. VI.* i 1 9
Till from forth this place I lead espoused my bride along with me *T. An.* i 1 328
Espy. When his love he doth espy, Let her shine as gloriously As the Venus of the sky . . . . *M. N. Dream* iii 2 105
He doth espy Himself love's traitor . . . . . . *K. John* ii 1 506
Securely I espy Virtue with valour couched in thine eye . *Richard II.* i 3 97
Esquire. Robert Shallow, esquire . . *Mer. Wives* i 1 4; 2 *Hen. IV.* iv 3 140
A poor esquire of this county, and one of the king's justices . . iii 2 63
Six thousand and two hundred good esquires . . . *Hen. V.* i 1 14
Of knights, esquires, and gallant gentlemen, Eight thousand and four hundred . . . . iv 8 89
Davy Gam, esquire . . . . iv 8 109
Alexander Iden, an esquire of Kent . . . . 2 *Hen. VI.* iv 10 46
Alexander Iden, that's my name; A poor esquire of Kent . . v 1 75
Essay. He wrote this but as an essay or taste of my virtue . *Lear* i 2 47
Essence. She is my essence, and I leave to be, If I be not by her fair influence Foster'd, illumined, cherish'd, kept alive . *T. G. of Ver.* iii 1 182
His glassy essence, like an angry ape, Plays such fantastic tricks
Meas. for Meas. ii 2 120
Her honour is an essence that's not seen . . . . *Othello* iv 1 16
Essential. And in the essential vesture of creation Does tire the ingener ii 1 64
Essentially. Thou art essentially mad, without seeming so . 1 *Hen. IV.* ii 4 540
He that loves himself Hath not essentially but by circumstance The name of valour . . . . 2 *Hen. VI.* v 2 39
I essentially am not in madness, But mad in craft . . *Hamlet* iii 4 187
Essex. 'Tis not thy southern power, Of Essex, Norfolk, Suffolk, nor of Kent, Which makes thee thus presumptuous . . . 3 *Hen. VI.* i 1 156
Establish him in his true sense again, And I will please you *Com. of Errors* iv 4 51
Not to break peace or any branch of it, But to establish here a peace
2 *Hen. IV.* iv 1 86
Our authority is his consent, And what we do establish he confirms
2 *Hen. VI.* iii 1 317
The senators to-morrow Mean to establish Cæsar as a king . *J. Cæsar* i 3 86
We will establish our estate upon Our eldest, Malcolm . . *Macbeth* i 4 37
Established. Contrary to thy established proclaimed edict . *L. L. Lost* i 1 262
There is no power in Venice Can alter a decree established *Mer. of Venice* iv 1 219
For some dishonest manners of their life, Establish'd then this law
Hen. V. i 2 50
Yet so my fancy may be satisfied, And peace established . 1 *Hen. VI.* v 3 92
One raised in blood, and one in blood establish'd . . *Richard III.* v 3 247
Repeal daily any wholesome act established against the rich . *Coriolanus* i 1 85
By the consent of all, we were establish'd The people's magistrates . iii 1 201
Estate. And some donation freely to estate On the blest lovers *Tempest* iv 1 85
Wounding flouts, Which you on all estates will execute . *L. L. Lost* v 2 855
All my right of her I do estate unto Demetrius . . *M. N. Dream* i 1 98
Nor is my whole estate Upon the fortune of this present year *Mer. of Ven.* i 1 43
I have disabled mine estate, By something showing a more swelling port i 1 123
O, that estates, degrees and offices Were not derived corruptly! . . ii 9 41
His letter there Will show you his estate . . . . . . iii 2 239
My estate is very low, my bond to the Jew is forfeit . . . iii 2 318
I will forget the condition of my estate, to rejoice in yours *As Y. Like It* i 2 17
All the revenue that was old Sir Rowland's will I estate upon you . v 2 13
Fie, doff this habit, shame to your estate, An eye-sore! . *T. of Shrew* iii 2 102
Fortune, she said, was no goddess, that had put such difference betwixt their two estates . . . . *All's Well* i 3 117
Labouring art can never ransom nature From her inaidible estate . . ii 1 122
I promise A counterpoise, if not to thy estate A balance more replete . ii 3 182
Though my estate be fallen, I was well born . . . . . iii 7 4
Till I had made mine own occasion mellow, What my estate is *T. Night* i 2 44
She'll not match above her degree, neither in estate, years, nor wit . i 3 116
Of great estate, of fresh and stainless youth . . . . . . i 5 278
But when I came to man's estate . . . . v 1 402
Is grown into an unspeakable estate . . . . . . *W. Tale* iv 2 46
Can he speak? hear? Know man from man? dispute his own estate? . iv 4 411
Being in so preposterous estate as we are . . . . . . v 2 159
What! mother dead! How wildly then walks my estate in France!
K. John iv 2 128
Showing, as in a model, our firm estate . . . . *Richard II.* iii 4 42
Know our own estate, How able such a work to undergo . 2 *Hen. IV* i 3 53
I pray you, what thinks he of our estate? . . . . *Hen. V.* iv 1 99
Heaven and our Lady gracious hath it pleased To shine on my contemptible estate . . . . 1 *Hen. VI.* i 2 75
What louring star now envies thy estate? . . . 2 *Hen. VI.* iii 1 206
Yet shall you have all kindness at my hand That your estate requires and mine can yield . . . . 3 *Hen. VI.* iii 3 150
If Warwick knew in what estate he stands, 'Tis to be doubted he would waken him . . . . iv 3 18
The estate is green and yet ungovern'd . . . . *Richard III.* ii 2 127
Which we have noted in you to your kin, And egally indeed to all estates . . . . iii 7 213
So sicken'd their estates, that never They shall abound as formerly
Hen. VIII. i 1 82
Our breach of duty this way Is business of estate . . . . ii 2 70
Prithee, to bed; and in thy prayers remember The estate of my poor queen . . . . v 1 74
A letter for me! it gives me an estate of seven years' health . *Coriolanus* ii 1 125
Let me dispute with thee of thy estate.—Thou canst not *Rom. and Jul.* iii 3 63
My estate deserves an heir more raised . . . . *T. of Athens* i 1 119
I have Prompted you in the ebb of your estate And your great flow of debts . . . . ii 2 150
By whose death he's stepp'd Into a great estate . . . . . ii 2 233
Timon's happy hours are done and past, and his estate shrinks from him iii 2 7
Supported his estate; nay, Timon's money Has paid his men their wages iii 2 76
All these Owe their estates unto him . . . . iii 3 5
Suspect still comes where an estate is least . . . . . iv 3 521
We sin against our own estate, When we may profit meet, and come too late . . . . v 1 44
We will establish our estate upon Our eldest, Malcolm . . . *Macbeth* i 4 37
And wish the estate o' the world were now undone . . . . v 5 50
He poisons him i' the garden for's estate . . . . *Hamlet* iii 2 273
The terms of our estate may not endure Hazard so near us . . iii 3 5
'Twas of some estate . . . . v 1 244
Having seen me in my worst estate, Shunn'd my abhorr'd society *Lear* v 3 209
Behold, How pomp is follow'd! mine will now be yours; And, should we shift estates, yours would be mine . . . *Ant. and Cleo.* v 2 152
I dare thereupon pawn the moiety of my estate to your ring *Cymbeline* i 4 119
Would I had put my estate and my neighbour's on the approbation of what I have spoke! . . . . i 4 133
And will fit you With dignities becoming your estates . . . . v 5 22
So think of your estate.—Consider, sir, the chance of war . . . v 5 74
If in our youths we could pick up some pretty estate, 'twere not amiss to keep our door hatched . . . . *Pericles* iv 2 36
Late Advanced in time to great and high estate . . . . . iv 4 14
Esteem. With other gentlemen of good esteem . . . *T. G. of Ver.* i 3 40
For me and my possessions she esteems not . . . . . . iii 1 79
She is nice and coy And nought esteems my aged eloquence . . iii 1 83
Yourself, held precious in the world's esteem . . . *L. L. Lost* ii 1 4
Are you grown so high in his esteem, Because I am so dwarfish?
M. N. Dream iii 2 294
This their jangling I esteem a sport . . . . iii 2 353
Neither do I labour for a greater esteem . . . . *As Y. Like It* v 2 62
I would esteem him worth a dozen such . . . *T. of Shrew* Ind. 1 27
A mighty man of such descent, Of such possessions and so high esteem . . . . Ind. 2 16
She is of good esteem, Her dowry wealthy, and of worthy birth . . iv 5 64
To esteem A senseless help when help past sense we deem . *All's Well* ii 1 126
We lost a jewel of her; and our esteem Was made much poorer by it . v 3 1
We have always truly served you, and beseech you So to esteem of us
W. Tale ii 3 149
The sullen passage of thy weary steps Esteem as foil . . *Richard II.* i 3 266
He esteems himself happy that he hath fallen into the hands of one, as he thinks, the most brave . . . . *Hen. V.* iv 4 64
Five hundred prisoners of esteem . . . . . . 1 *Hen. VI.* iii 4 8
Esteem none friends but such as are his friends . . . . . iv 1 5
Your highness is betroth'd Unto another lady of esteem . . . . v 5 27
From true evidence of good esteem . . . . . . 2 *Hen. VI.* iii 2 21
Nor should thy prowess want praise and esteem, But that 'tis shown ignobly . . . . v 2 22
A man in much esteem with the king, and truly A worthy friend
Hen. VIII. iv 1 109
He esteems her no more than I esteem an addle egg . *Troi. and Cres.* i 2 144
Forestall prescience and esteem no act But that of hand . . . i 3 199
What things again most dear in the esteem And poor in worth! . . iii 3 129
Younger than you, Here in Verona, ladies of esteem, Are made already mothers . . . . *Rom. and Jul.* i 3 70
And live a coward in thine own esteem . . . . . *Macbeth* i 7 43
Macbeth Will seem as pure as snow, and the poor state Esteem him as a lamb . . . . iv 3 54
I hope my noble lord esteems me honest . . . . . *Othello* iv 2 65
What do you esteem it at?—More than the world enjoys . *Cymbeline* i 4 85
In killing creatures vile, as cats and dogs, Of no esteem . . . v 5 253
Esteemed. How is the man esteem'd here in the city? . *Com. of Errors* v 1 4
A man of sovereign parts he is esteem'd; Well fitted in arts . *L. L. Lost* ii 1 44
But, most esteemed greatness, will you hear the dialogue? . . . v 2 894
Life itself, my wife, and all the world, Are not with me esteem'd above thy life . . . . *Mer. of Venice* iv 1 285
The world esteem'd thy father honourable . . . . *As Y. Like It* i 2 238
Esteemed him No better than a poor and loathsome beggar *T. of Shrew* Ind. 1 122
My dear lord and most esteemed friend . . . . *Troi. and Cres.* iii 1 69
Which notwithstanding, thou shalt be no less esteemed . *T. of Athens* ii 2 112
For so this side of our known world esteem'd him . . . *Hamlet* i 1 85
It were pity to cast them [women] away for nothing; though, between them and a great cause, they should be esteemed nothing *A. and C.* i 2 144
Her own price Proclaims how she esteem'd him . . . *Cymbeline* i 1 52
Esteemest. How esteemest thou me? I account of her beauty *T. G. of V.* ii 1 66
Wouldst thou have that Which thou esteem'st the ornament of life, And live a coward in thine own esteem? . . . . . . *Macbeth* i 7 42
Esteemeth. It must with circumstance be spoken By one whom she esteemeth as his friend . . . . *T. G. of Ver.* iii 2 37
Estimable. Is not so estimable, profitable neither, As flesh of muttons
Mer. of Venice i 3 167
I could not with such estimable wonder overfar believe that *T. Night* ii 1 28

Estimate. Thy life is dear; for all that life can rate Worth name of life in thee hath estimate *All's Well* ii 1 183
None else of name and noble estimate *Richard II.* ii 3 56
But value dwells not in particular will; It holds his estimate and dignity As well wherein 'tis precious of itself As in the prizer *Troi. and Cres.* ii 2 54
More holy and profound than mine own life, My dear wife's estimate *Coriolanus* iii 3 114
For the Lord Timon, sir?—If he will touch the estimate *T. of Athens* i 1 14
Estimation. I know the gentleman To be of worth and worthy estimation *T. G. of Ver.* ii 4 56
He cannot plead his estimation with you *Meas. for Meas.* iv 2 28
Against your yet ungalled estimation *Com. of Errors* iii 1 102
Whose estimation do you mightily hold up *Much Ado* ii 2 24
A man of good repute, carriage, bearing, and estimation *L. L. Lost* i 1 272
If thou be'st rated by thy estimation, Thou dost deserve enough *Mer. of Venice* ii 7 26
Let his lack of years be no impediment to let him lack a reverend estimation iv 1 163
If the scale do turn But in the estimation of a hair iv 1 331
Your son, As mad in folly, lack'd the sense to know Her estimation *All's Well* v 3 4
I speak not this in estimation, As what I think might be, but what I know Is ruminated, plotted *1 Hen. IV.* i 3 272
Dear men Of estimation and command in arms iv 4 32
He shall take the odds Of his great name and estimation v 1 98
He is a man of no estimation in the world *Hen. V.* iii 6 16
Beggar the estimation which you prized Richer than sea and land *Troi. and Cres.* ii 2 91
In a cheap estimation, is worth all your predecessors since Deucalion *Coriolanus* ii 1 101
Bonneted, without any further deed to have them at all into their estimation ii 2 31
I will, sir, flatter my sworn brother, the people, to earn a dearer estimation ii 3 103
If thy captain knew I were here, he would use me with estimation v 2 56
You shall know now that I am in estimation v 2 66
Do they hold the same estimation they did when I was in the city? *Ham.* ii 2 348
All indign and base adversities Make head against my estimation! *Othello* i 3 275
Your ring may be stolen too: so your brace of unprizable estimations *Cymbeline* i 4 99
Estime. Je m'estime heureux que je suis tombé entre les mains d'un chevalier *Hen. V.* iv 4 58
Estranged. How comes it, That thou art thus estranged from thyself? *Com. of Errors* ii 2 122
How come you thus estranged? *L. L. Lost* v 2 213
Estridge. All furnish'd, all in arms; All plumed like estridges *1 Hen. IV.* iv 1 98
In that mood The dove will peck the estridge *Ant. and Cleo.* iii 13 197
Et tu, Brute! Then fall, Cæsar! *J. Cæsar* iii 1 77
Etcetera. And are etceteras nothing? *2 Hen. IV.* ii 4 198
O, that she were An open et cætera, thou a poperin pear! *Rom. and Jul.* ii 1 38
Eternal. By penitence the Eternal's wrath's appeased *T. G. of Ver.* v 4 81
If I would but go to hell for an eternal moment or so *Mer. Wives* ii 1 50
That my husband saw this letter! it would give eternal food to his jealousy ii 1 104
Stands in attainder of eternal shame *L. L. Lost* i 1 158
I would it were hell-pains for thy sake, and my poor doing eternal *All's Well* ii 3 246
And sworn to make the 'not' eternal iii 2 24
A contract of eternal bond of love *T. Night* v 1 159
But such a day to-morrow as to-day, And to be boy eternal *W. Tale* i 2 65
A grave unto a soul; Holding the eternal spirit, against her will, In the vile prison of afflicted breath *K. John* iii 4 18
Shame and eternal shame, nothing but shame! *Hen. V.* iv 5 10
I kiss these fingers for eternal peace *1 Hen. VI.* v 3 48
The mortal worm might make the sleep eternal *2 Hen. VI.* iii 2 263
Thou eternal Mover of the heavens, Look with a gentle eye upon this wretch! iii 3 19
His love was an eternal plant *3 Hen. VI.* iii 3 124
In eternal darkness folded up *Richard III.* i 3 269
Into the blind cave of eternal night v 3 62
They promised me eternal happiness; And brought me garlands *Hen. VIII.* iv 2 90
Never did young man fancy With so eternal and so fix'd a soul *T. and C.* v 2 166
Here are no storms, No noise, but silence and eternal sleep *T. Andron.* i 1 155
Outlive thy father's days, And fame's eternal date! i 1 168
If I do wake, some planet strike me down, That I may slumber in eternal sleep! ii 4 15
And keep eternal spring-time on thy face iii 1 21
Your part in her you could not keep from death, But heaven keeps his part in eternal life *Rom. and Jul.* iv 5 70
That would have brook'd The eternal devil to keep his state in Rome As easily as a king *J. Cæsar* i 2 160
Mine eternal jewel Given to the common enemy of man *Macbeth* iii 1 68
Deny me this, And an eternal curse fall on you! iv 1 105
But this eternal blazon must not be To ears of flesh and blood *Hamlet* i 5 21
O proud death, What feast is toward in thine eternal cell? v 2 376
By the worth of man's eternal soul *Othello* iii 3 361
Some eternal villain, Some busy and insinuating rogue iv 2 130
Her life in Rome Would be eternal in our triumph *Ant. and Cleo.* v 1 66
Eternal God. By the eternal God, whose name and power Thou tremblest at *2 Hen. VI.* i 4 28
Eternally. These couples shall eternally be knit *M. N. Dream* iv 1 186
Eterne. But in them nature's copy's not eterne *Macbeth* iii 2 38
Never did the Cyclops' hammers fall On Mars's armour forged for proof eterne With less remorse *Hamlet* ii 2 512
Eternity. And make us heirs of all eternity *L. L. Lost* i 1 7
Who, had he himself eternity and could put breath into his work, would beguile Nature of her custom *W. Tale* v 2 106
I oft have been afear'd, Because I wish'd this world's eternity *2 Hen. VI.* ii 4 90
Let Mars divide eternity in twain, And give him half *Troi. and Cres.* iii 3 256
He wants nothing of a god but eternity and a heaven to throne in *Coriol.* v 4 25
All that lives must die, Passing through nature to eternity *Hamlet* i 2 73
Eternity was in our lips and eyes, Bliss in our brows' bent *Ant. and Cleo.* i 3 35
Eternized. Shall be eternized in all age to come *2 Hen. VI.* v 3 31
Ethiope. And Silvia—witness Heaven, that made her fair!—Shows Julia but a swarthy Ethiope *T. G. of Ver.* ii 6 26
I'll hold my mind, were she an Ethiope *Much Ado* v 4 38
Thou for whom Jove would swear Juno but an Ethiope were *L. L. Lost* iv 3 118
And Ethiopes of their sweet complexion crack iv 3 268
Ethiope. Away, you Ethiope! *M. N. Dream* iii 2 257
Ethiope words, blacker in their effect Than in their countenance *As Y. L. It* iv 3 35
Like a rich jewel in an Ethiope's ear *Rom. and Jul.* i 5 48
Upon his shield Is a black Ethiope reaching at the sun *Pericles* ii 2 20
Ethiopian. Is he dead, my Ethiopian? is he dead? *Mer. Wives* ii 3 28
As soft as dove's down and as white as it, Or Ethiopian's tooth *W. Tale* iv 4 375
Etna. I will be thrown into Etna, as I have been into Thames, ere I will leave her thus *Mer. Wives* iii 5 129
Eton. Steal my Nan away And marry her at Eton iv 4 75
So soon as I came beyond Eton, they threw me off iv 5 68
Away with Slender and with him at Eton Immediately to marry iv 6 24
I came yonder at Eton to marry Mistress Anne Page v 5 194
Eunuch. Though Argus were her eunuch and her guard *L. L. Lost* iii 1 201
The battle with the Centaurs, to be sung By an Athenian eunuch to the harp *M. N. Dream* v 1 45
I would send them to the Turk, to make eunuchs of *All's Well* ii 3 94
Thou shalt present me as an eunuch to him *T. Night* i 2 56
Be you his eunuch, and your mute I'll be i 2 62
Lord Say hath gelded the commonwealth, and made it an eunuch *2 Hen. VI.* iv 2 175
Into a pipe Small as an eunuch *Coriolanus* iii 2 114
An if she do, I would I were an eunuch *T. Andron.* ii 3 128
Thou, eunuch Mardian!—What's your highness' pleasure? *Ant. and Cleo.* i 5 8
I take no pleasure In aught an eunuch has i 5 10
As well a woman with an eunuch play'd As with a woman ii 5 5
'Tis said in Rome That Photinus an eunuch and your maids Manage this war iii 7 15
Hence, saucy eunuch; peace! She hath betray'd me and shall die the death iv 14 25
Nor the voice of unpaved eunuch to boot, can never amend *Cymbeline* iii 3 34
Euphrates. Extended Asia from Euphrates *Ant. and Cleo.* i 2 105
Euriphile, Thou wast their nurse; they took thee for their mother *Cymb.* iii 3 103
Where shall's lay him?—By good Euriphile, our mother iv 2 234
Use like note and words, Save that Euriphile must be Fidele iv 2 238
Their nurse, Euriphile, Whom for the theft I wedded, stole these children v 5 340
Europa. Remember, Jove, thou wast a bull for thy Europa *Mer. Wives* v 5 4
All Europa shall rejoice at thee, As once Europa did at lusty Jove *M. Ado* v 4 45
Europe. That would not bless our Europe with your daughter, But rather lose her to an African *Tempest* ii 1 124
No court in Europe is too good for thee *W. Tale* ii 2 3
Would have bought me lights as good cheap at the dearest chandler's in Europe *1 Hen. IV.* iii 3 52
John with my brothers and sisters, and Sir John with all Europe *2 Hen. IV.* ii 2 146
I were simply the most active fellow in Europe iv 3 24
He'll make your Paris Louvre shake for it, Were it the mistress-court of mighty Europe *Hen. V.* ii 4 133
Let my horse have his due.—It is the best horse of Europe iii 7 5
Whose bloody deeds shall make all Europe quake *1 Hen. VI.* ii 1 156
Thou hast slain The flower of Europe for his chivalry *3 Hen. VI.* ii 1 71
'Shrew me, If I would lose it for a revenue Of any king's in Europe *Cymbeline* ii 3 149
Evade. If he evade us there, Enforce him with his envy to the people *Coriolanus* iii 3 2
Evades them, with a bombast circumstance *Othello* i 1 13
Evans. Tell Master Parson Evans I will do what I can *Mer. Wives* i 4 34
Evasion. No more evasion: We have with a leaven'd and prepared choice Proceeded to you *Meas. for Meas.* i 1 51
His evasions have ears thus long *Troi. and Cres.* ii 1 75
There can be no evasion To blench from this and to stand firm by honour ii 2 67
His evasion, wing'd thus swift with scorn, Cannot outfly our apprehensions ii 3 123
An admirable evasion of whoremaster man, to lay his goatish disposition to the charge of a star! *Lear* i 2 137
Eve. It was Eve's legacy, and cannot be ta'en from her *T. G. of Ver.* iii 1 342
So curses all Eve's daughters, of what complexion soever *Mer. Wives* iv 2 24
Was't not at Hallowmas, Master Froth?—All-hallond eve *Meas. for Meas.* ii 1 130
With a child of our grandmother Eve, a female *L. L. Lost* i 1 267
Had he been Adam, he had tempted Eve v 2 322
Thou wert as witty a piece of Eve's flesh as any in Illyria *T. Night* i 5 30
What Eve, what serpent, hath suggested thee To make a second fall of cursed man? *Richard II.* iii 4 75
Even. That even Ambition cannot pierce a wink beyond *Tempest* ii 1 241
These sweet thoughts do even refresh my labours iii 1 14
Even with such-like valour men hang and drown Their proper selves iii 3 59
Most wicked sir, whom to call brother Would even infect my mouth v 1 131
On a trice, so please you, Even in a dream, were we divided from them v 1 239
Even in the prime And all the fair effects of future hopes *T. G. of Ver.* i 1 49
Even with the speediest expedition I will dispatch him i 3 37
Even that power which gave me first my oath Provokes me to this ii 6 4
Assist me; And even in kind love I do conjure thee ii 7 2
Why even what fashion thou best likest ii 7 52
Even in the milk-white bosom of thy love iii 1 250
And by and by intend to chide myself Even for this time I spend iv 2 104
Even from a heart As full of sorrows as the sea of sands iv 3 32
She did intend confession At Patrick's cell this even v 2 42
So far forth as herself might be her chooser, Even to my wish *M. Wives* iv 6 12
Vile worm, thou wast o'erlook'd even in thy birth v 5 87
Even for our kitchens We kill the fowl of season *Meas. for Meas.* ii 2 84
From thee, even from thy virtue! What's this, what's this? ii 2 161
Yet death we fear That makes these odds all even iii 1 41
His life is parallel'd Even with the stroke and line of his great justice iv 2 83
The law cries out Most audible, even from his proper tongue v 1 413
Even her very words Didst thou deliver to me *Com. of Errors* ii 2 165
Even in the spring of love, thy love-springs rot iii 2 3
She that doth call me husband, even my soul Doth for a wife abhor iii 2 163
Grant me justice! Even for the service that long since I did thee v 1 191
Even for the blood That then I lost for thee, now grant me justice v 1 193
Abused and dishonour'd me Even in the strength and height of injury v 1 200
I will even take sixpence in earnest of the bear-ward *Much Ado* ii 1 42
See her chamber-window entered, even the night before her wedding-day iii 2 117
I have deceived even your very eyes v 1 238
Now the number is even.—True, true; we are four *L. L. Lost* iv 3 211
Fashioning our humours Even to the opposed end of our intents v 2 768
Even that falsehood, in itself a sin, Thus purifies itself v 2 785
O, once tell true, tell true, even for my sake! *M. N. Dream* iii 2 68
Even in the lovely garnish of a boy *Mer. of Venice* ii 6 45
Even in the force and road of casualty ii 9 30

Even. Even at that time I may be married too . . . *Mer. of Venice* iii 2 196
Even from the gallows did his fell soul fleet . . . iv 1 135
I swear to thee, even by thine own fair eyes, Wherein I see myself . . v 1 242
Do choke their service up Even with the having . . *As Y. Like It* ii 3 62
The wise man's folly is anatomized Even by the squandering glances of the fool . . . ii 7 57
Seeking the bubble reputation Even in the cannon's mouth . . . ii 7 153
I have promised to make all this matter even . . . v 4 18
And from hence I go, To make these doubts all even . . v 4 25
When earthly things made even Atone together . . v 4 115
Welcome thou art to me! Even daughter, welcome, in no less degree . v 4 154
The care I have had to even your content . . *All's Well* i 3 3
Make thy demand.—But will you make it even? . . ii 1 194
Even to the world's pleasure and the increase of laughter . . ii 4 37
Who had even tuned his bounty to sing happiness to him . . iv 3 11
Which makes her story true, even to the point of her death . . iv 3 66
What's he?—E'en a crow o' the same nest . . iv 3 319
But falls into abatement and low price Even in a minute . *T. Night* i 1 14
I have unclasp'd To thee the book even of my secret soul . . i 4 14
I am very comptible, even to the least sinister usage . . i 5 187
And sing them loud even in the dead of night . . i 5 290
And cross-gartered, even with the swiftness of putting on . . ii 5 186
The knight is incensed against you, even to a mortal arbitrement . iii 4 287
What shall I do?—Even what it please my lord . . v 1 119
Pardon me, sweet one, even for the vows We made each other but so late ago . v 1 221
Were you a woman, as the rest goes even, I should my tears let fall . v 1 246
My affairs Do even drag me homeward . *W. Tale* i 2 24
And many a man there is, even at this present . . i 2 192
Never Saw I men scour so on their way: I eyed them Even to their ships ii 1 36
This sessions, to our great grief we pronounce, Even pushes 'gainst our heart . iii 2 2
In justice, which shall have due course, Even to the guilt or the purgation iii 2 7
I will even take my leave of you . . iv 3 120
Then I'ld shriek, that even your ears Should rift to hear me . v 1 65
I thought of her, Even in these looks I made . . v 1 228
Thus she stood, Even with such life of majesty . . v 3 35
While they weigh so even, We hold our town for neither, yet for both *K. John* ii 1 332
Made to run even upon even ground . ii 1 576
Even for that name, Which till this time my tongue did ne'er pronounce iii 1 306
Even to that drop ten thousand wiry friends Do glue themselves . iii 4 64
Even in the instant of repair and health, The fit is strongest . iii 4 113
Even the breath of what I mean to speak Shall blow each dust, each straw iii 4 127
If that young Arthur be not gone already, Even at that news he dies . iii 4 164
And quench his fiery indignation Even in the matter of mine innocence iv 1 64
My eyes are out Even with the fierce looks of these bloody men . iv 1 74
My state is braved, Even at my gates, with ranks of foreign powers . iv 2 244
To win renown Even in the jaws of danger and of death . v 2 116
That hand which had the strength, even at your door, To cudgel you . v 2 137
Even at the crying of your nation's crow . v 2 144
Even on that altar where we swore to you Dear amity and everlasting love v 4 19
Even this night, whose black contagious breath Already smokes . v 4 33
And calmly run on in obedience Even to our ocean . v 4 57
Were I tied to run afoot Even to the frozen ridges of the Alps *Richard II.* i 1 64
Cries, Even from the tongueless caverns of the earth, To me for justice i 1 105
Even in the best blood chamber'd in his bosom . i 1 149
Where shame doth harbour, even in Mowbray's face . i 1 195
Furbish new the name of John a Gaunt, Even in the lusty haviour of his son . i 3 77
And make us wade even in our kindred's blood . i 3 138
Even in the glasses of thine eyes I see thy grieved heart . i 3 208
Even through the hollow eyes of death I spy life peering . ii 1 270
Even in condition of the worst degree, In gross rebellion . ii 3 108
Hither come Even at his feet to lay my arms and power . iii 3 39
All must be even in our government . iii 4 36
Rue, even for ruth, here shortly shall be seen . iii 4 106
Trembling even at the name of Mortimer . *1 Hen. IV.* i 3 144
Even with the bloody payment of your deaths . i 3 186
Bear ourselves as even as we can, The king will always think him in our debt . i 3 285
And then he runs straight and even . iii 1 114
Curbs himself even of his natural scope When you come 'cross his humour iii 1 171
Even in the presence of the crowned king . iii 2 54
He shall render every glory up, Yea, even the slightest worship of his time . iii 2 151
'Tis catching hither, even to our camp . iv 1 30
Pages follow'd him Even at the heels in golden multitudes . iv 3 73
Even in thy behalf, I'll thank myself . v 4 97
To cherish such high deeds Even in the bosom of our adversaries . v 5 31
Quenching the flame of bold rebellion Even with the rebels' blood *2 Hen. IV.* Ind. 27
Whose spirit lent a fire Even to the dullest peasant . i 1 113
Yea, for my sake, even to the eyes of Richard Gave him defiance . iii 1 64
Even by those men that most have done us wrong . iv 1 79
That even our corn shall seem as light as chaff . iv 1 195
How smooth and even they do bear themselves! . *Hen. V.* ii 2 3
Even in your hearts, there will he rake for it . ii 4 98
From morn till even fought And sheathed their swords for lack of argument . iii 1 20
By my consent, we'll even let them alone . *1 Hen. VI.* i 2 44
And even these three days have I watch'd . i 4 16
And even with this I lost fair England's view . *2 Hen. VI.* iii 2 110
May, even in their wives' and children's sight, Be hang'd up for example iv 2 189
By these presence, even the presence of Lord Mortimer . iv 7 32
Even to affright thee with the view thereof . v 1 207
Even at this sight My heart is turn'd to stone . v 2 49
Look where the sturdy rebel sits, Even in the chair of state *3 Hen. VI.* i 1 51
Even in the lukewarm blood of Henry's heart . i 2 34
Even my foes will shed fast-falling tears, And say 'Alas!' . i 4 162
Even with those wings Which sometime they have used with fearful flight ii 2 29
Even of pure love, To greet mine own land with my wishful sight . iii 1 13
Even in the downfall of his mellow'd years . iii 3 104
Even with the dearest blood your bodies bear . v 1 69
How he did lap me Even in his own garments . *Richard III.* ii 1 116
As 'twere retail'd to all posterity, Even to the general all-ending day . iii 1 78
If all obstacles were cut away, And that my path were even to the crown iii 7 157
Even in the afternoon of her best days . iii 7 186
Even in so short a space, my woman's heart Grossly grew captive . iv 1 79
As children but one step below, Even of your mettle, of your very blood iv 4 302

Even. This foul swine Lies now even in the centre of this isle *Rich. III.* v 2 11
Whose figure even this instant cloud puts on . *Hen. VIII.* i 1 225
Whither away so fast?—O, God save ye! Even to the hall . ii 1 2
Even of her That, when the greatest stroke of fortune falls, Will bless the king . ii 2 35
Believe me, there's an ill opinion spread then Even of yourself . ii 2 126
Even the billows of the sea Hung their heads . iii 1 10
I know my life so even . iii 1 37
A soul as even as a calm . iii 1 166
And to behold his visage, Even to my full of view . *Troi. and Cres.* iii 3 241
Tell me true, Even in the soul of sound good fellowship . iv 1 52
Strangles our dear vows Even in the birth of our own labouring breath iv 4 40
I charge thee use her well, even for my charge . iv 4 128
You're an odd man; give even, or give none . iv 5 41
One that knows the youth Even to his inches . iv 5 111
Even in the fan and wind of your fair sword, You bid them rise, and live v 3 41
I do stand engaged to many Greeks, Even in the faith of valour . v 3 69
Even with the vail and darking of the sun, To close the day up . v 8 7
Partly proud; which he is, even to the altitude of his virtue *Coriolanus* i 1 40
I send it through the rivers of your blood, Even to the court, the heart i 1 140
Thou wast a soldier Even to Cato's wish . i 4 57
We, Even from this instant, banish him our city . iii 3 101
And you are darken'd in this action, sir, Even by your own . iv 7 6
He bears himself more proudlier, Even to my person, than I thought he would . iv 7 9
A noble servant to them; but he could not Carry his honours even . iv 7 37
Even with the same austerity and garb As he controll'd the war . iv 7 44
I have forgot my part, and I am out, Even to a full disgrace . v 3 42
Where I, Even in theirs and in the commons' ears, Will vouch the truth of it . v 6 4
And With bloody passage led your wars even to The gates of Rome . v 6 76
Even at thy teat thou hadst thy tyranny . *T. Andron.* ii 3 145
Hadst thou in person ne'er offended me, Even for his sake am I pitiless ii 3 162
Till all these mischiefs be return'd again Even in their throats . iii 1 275
Nought hath pass'd, But even with law . iv 4 8
Even by my god I swear to thee I will . v 1 86
Even from Hyperion's rising in the east Until his very downfall in the sea v 2 56
When he is here, even at thy solemn feast, I will bring in the empress v 2 115
Even in the time When it should move you to attend me most . v 3 91
Even with all my heart Would I were dead, so you did live again! . v 3 172
For even the day before, she broke her brow . *Rom. and Jul.* i 3 38
Who, even in pure and vestal modesty, Still blush . iii 3 38
O, he is even in my mistress' case, Just in her case! O woful sympathy! iii 3 84
But thankful even for hate, that is meant love . iii 5 149
Make sacred even his stirrup, and through him Drink the free air *T. of A.* i 1 82
Labour'd after him to the mountain's top Even on their knees and hands i 1 87
O joy, e'en made away ere't can be born! . i 2 110
Happier is he that has no friend to feed Than such that do e'en enemies exceed . i 2 210
She's e'en setting on water to scald such chickens as you are . ii 2 71
Of whom, even to the state's best health, I have Deserved this hearing ii 2 206
They have e'en put my breath from me, the slaves. Creditors? devils! iii 4 104
I am sick of this false world, and will love nought But even the mere necessities upon't . iv 3 377
I did present myself Even in the aim and very flash of it . *J. Cæsar* i 3 52
Some six or seven, who did hide their faces Even from darkness . ii 1 278
And that I am he, Let me a little show it, even in this . iii 1 71
Then walk we forth, even to the market-place . iii 1 108
Muffling up his face, Even at the base of Pompey's statua . iii 2 192
Even by the rule of that philosophy . v 1 101
I will be here again, even with a thought . v 3 19
Thou art revenged, Even with the sword that kill'd thee . v 3 46
Now is that noble vessel full of grief, That it runs over even at his eyes v 5 14
Even for that our love of old, I prithee, Hold thou my sword-hilts . v 5 27
Both sides are even: here I'll sit i' the midst . *Macbeth* iii 4 10
You make me strange Even to the disposition that I owe . iii 4 113
Even the like precurse of fierce events . *Hamlet* i 1 121
Extinct in both, Even in their promise, as it is a-making . i 3 119
Went hand in hand even with the vow I made to her in marriage . i 5 49
Cut off even in the blossoms of my sin . i 5 76
Be even and direct with me . ii 2 298
Even with the very comment of thy soul Observe mine uncle . iii 2 84
'Tis not strange That even our loves should with our fortunes change . iii 2 211
Compell'd, Even to the teeth and forehead of our faults, To give in evidence . iii 3 63
To keep it from divulging, let it feed Even on the pith of life . iv 1 23
To bear all smooth and even . iv 3 7
To all that fortune, death and danger dare, Even for an egg-shell . iv 4 53
But even his mother shall uncharge the practice And call it accident . iv 7 68
How came he mad?—Very strangely, they say.—How strangely?—Faith, e'en with losing his wits . v 1 174
Why, even in that was heaven ordinant . v 2 48
Of all these bounds, even from this line to this . *Lear* i 1 64
Even for want of that for which I am richer . i 1 233
Methinks the ground is even.—Horrible steep . iv 6 3
I should e'en die with pity, To see another thus . iv 7 53
Yet it is danger To make him even o'er the time he has lost . iv 7 80
'Tis hot, it smokes; It came even from the heart of—O, she's dead! . v 3 224
He requires your haste-post-haste appearance, Even on the instant *Othello* i 2 38
Let your sentence Even fall upon my life . i 3 120
Even from my boyish days, To the very moment that he bade me tell it i 3 132
My heart's subdued Even to the very quality of my lord . i 3 252
For even her folly help'd her to an heir . ii 1 138
Even out of that will I cause these of Cyprus to mutiny . ii 1 281
It indues Our other healthful members even to that sense Of pain . iii 4 147
The worser that you give me the addition Whose want even kills me iv 1 106
Strangle her in her bed, even the bed she hath contaminated . iv 1 221
As summer flies are in the shambles, That quicken even with blowing . iv 2 67
To lash the rascals naked through the world Even from the east to the west! . iv 2 144
Even from this instant do build on thee a better opinion than ever before iv 2 208
Even his stubbornness, his checks, his frowns,—Prithee, unpin me,—have grace and favour in them . iv 3 20
For I will contend Even with his pestilent scythe . *Ant. and Cleo.* iii 13 194
That which is now a horse, even with a thought The rack dislimns . iv 14 9
The ingratitude of this Seleucus does Even make me wild . v 2 154
I honour him Even out of your report . *Cymbeline* i 1 55
Rather shunned to go even with what I heard . i 4 47
Make her go back, even to the yielding . i 4 115
Even the very middle of my heart Is warm'd by the rest . i 6 27

Even. Thou wert dignified enough, Even to the point of envy . *Cymbeline* ii 3 133
For even to vice They are not constant, but are changing still . . ii 5 29
You, O the dearest of creatures, would even renew me with your eyes . iii 2 43
There's more to be consider'd; but we'll even All that good time will give us . . . . iii 4 184
I will pursue her Even to Augustus' throne . . . . iii 5 101
Shall find I love my country, Even to the note o' the king . . iv 3 44
Even for whom my life Is every breath a death . . . v 1 26
Clothed like a bride, For the embracements even of Jove himself *Pericles* i 1 7
For riches strew'd herself even in the streets . . . i 4 23
Even in your armours, as you are address'd, Will very well become a soldier's dance . . . . ii 3 94
Even in the height and pride of all his glory . . . ii 4 6
Traitor!—Ay, traitor.—Even in his throat—unless it be the king—That calls me traitor, I return the lie . . . . . . ii 5 56
Patience, good sir, Even for this charge . . . . . iii 1 27
Thou hast a heart That even cracks for woe! . . . . iii 2 77
We'll bring your grace e'en to the edge o' the shore . . . iii 3 35
I well remember, Even on my eaning time . . . . . iii 4 6
Nor let pity, which Even women have cast off, melt thee . . iv 1 7
That even her art sisters the natural roses . . . . v Gower 7
But even now *Tempest* v 1; *L. L. Lost* v 2; *M. of Venice* i 1; *As Y. Like It* ii 7; *W. Tale* iii 3; *K. John* v 3; *Troi. and Cres.* i 3; *Oth.* v 2
Even but now *M. N. Dream* iii 2; *Mer. of Venice* v 1; *Hamlet* i 1; *Lear* i 1; iii 2; *Othello* v 2
Even for that . . . *M. N. Dream* ii 1 202; *Mer. of Venice* ii 1 22
Even now *Tempest* ii 1; v 1; *T. G. of Ver.* iii 2; *Mer. Wives* i 3; iv 5; *Meas. for Meas.* iv 1; v 1; *Com. of Errors* ii 2; iv 1; iv 3; v 1; *Much Ado* iii 1; *Mer. of Venice* iii 2; *T. Night* ii 2; *W. Tale* i 2; iv 2; iv 4; v 1; *K. John* v 7; 1 *Hen. IV.* ii 3; ii 4; 2 *Hen. IV.* ii 2; ii 4; iii 1; *Hen. V.* v Prol.; 2 *Hen. VI.* iii 2; 3 *Hen. VI.* v 2; *Richard III.* i 4; *Hen. VIII.* iv 2; *T. Andron.* v 1; *Rom. and Jul.* i 4; i 5; *Macbeth* i 4; iv 1; iv 3; v 2; *Hamlet* iii 4; *Lear* iv 4; *Othello* i 1; ii 3; iv 1; *Cymbeline* iv 2; v 5; *Pericles* ii 1
Even so *T. G. of Ver.* i 1; *Meas. for Meas.* i 2; i 4; ii 4; v 1; *Much Ado* iii 2; *L. L. Lost* v 2; *Mer. of Venice* iii 2; *As Y. Like It* i 1; iii 3; *All's Well* i 3; *T. Night* ii 3; *K. John* v 1; v 7; *Richard II.* ii 1; v 2; 2 *Hen. IV.* i 1; iv 2; *Hen. V.* iv 1; v 2; 1 *Hen. VI.* ii 2; 3 *Hen. VI.* v 1; *Richard III.* i 1; iv 2; *Troi. and Cres.* i 2; i 3; ii 1; *Coriolanus* i 1; *T. Andron.* iv 4; *Rom. and Jul.* i 5; iii 3; v 1; *T. of Athens* ii 2; v 1; *J. Cæsar* iv 3; v 1; *Macbeth* v 1; *Hamlet* i 1; v 1; *Lear* v 3; *Othello* iii 5; iii 4; v 1
Good even *T. G. of Ver.* ii 1; iv 2; *Mer. Wives* ii 1; *Meas. for Meas.* iii 2; iv 3; *As Y. Like It* ii 4; iii 3; v 1; *Rom. and Jul.* ii 6; *T. of Athens* ii 2; *J. Cæsar* i 3; *Hamlet* i 2
E'en a woman, and commanded By such poor passion as the maid that milks And does the meanest chares . . . *Ant. and Cleo.* iv 15 73
Even all I have; yea, and myself and all, Will I withal endow a child of thine . . . . *Richard III.* iv 4 248
Even already They clap the lubber Ajax on the shoulder *Troi. and Cres.* iii 3 138
Even as I would when I to love begin . . . . *T. G. of Ver.* i 1 10
Even as one heat another heat expels . . . . . ii 4 192
I have taught him, even as one would say precisely . . . iv 4 5
Even as you came in to me, her assistant or go-between parted *M. Wives* ii 2 272
Then music is Even as the flourish when true subjects bow To a new-crowned monarch . . . . . . *Mer. of Venice* iii 2 49
Christians enow before; e'en as many as could well live, one by another iii 5 24
Even as a flattering dream or worthless fancy . . *T. of Shrew* Ind. 1 44
Even as the waving sedges play with wind . . . . Ind. 2 55
And the moon changes even as your mind . . . . iv 5 20
Well, I shall be wiser.—Even as soon as thou canst . . *All's Well* ii 3 236
Even as bad as those That vulgars give bold'st titles . . *W. Tale* ii 1 93
Even as a form of wax Resolveth from his figure 'gainst the fire *K. John* v 4 24
That's even as fair as—at hand, quoth the chamberlain . . 1 *Hen. IV.* ii 1 54
And even as I was then is Percy now . . . . . iii 2 96
I think we are a body strong enough, Even as we are . . 2 *Hen. IV.* i 3 67
Even as your horse bears your praises . . . . *Hen. V.* iii 7 82
Even as men wrecked upon a sand, that look to be washed off the next tide iv 1 100
Mars his true moving, even as in the heavens So in the earth, to this day is not known . . . . 1 *Hen. VI.* i 2 1
For I had hope of France, Even as I have of fertile England's soil 2 *Hen. VI.* i 1 238
And even as willingly at thy feet I leave it . . . . ii 3 35
Even as a splitted bark, so sunder we: This way fall I to death . iii 2 411
Tears virginal Shall be to me even as the dew to fire . . . v 2 53
Let it sink me, Even as the axe falls, if I be not faithful! *Hen. VIII.* ii 1 61
The purpose is perspicuous even as substance . . *Troi. and Cres.* i 3 324
This but done, Even as she speaks, why, their hearts were yours *Coriol.* iii 2 87
Even as an adder when she doth unroll To do some fatal execution *T. Andron.* iii 1 35
What wouldst do then, Apemantus?—E'en as Apemantus does now *T. of A.* i 1 235
E'en as if your lord should wear rich jewels, And send for money for 'em iii 4 23
Thou art e'en as just a man As e'er my conversation coped withal *Hamlet* iii 2 59
Men must endure Their going hence, even as their coming hither . *Lear* v 2 10
The heavens forbid But that our loves and comforts should increase Even as our days do grow! . . . . *Othello* ii 1 197
Even as again they were When you yourself did part them . . ii 3 238
Do what she list, Even as her appetite shall play the god . . ii 3 353
E'en as the o'erflowing Nilus presageth famine . . *Ant. and Cleo.* i 2 49
Did bequeath to me, With this strict charge, even as he left his life *Per.* ii 1 131
Yes, if you love me, sir.—Even as my life my blood that fosters it . ii 5 89
And they with continual action are even as good as rotten . . iv 2 9
Even at hand. How near is our master?—E'en at hand . *T. of Shrew* iv 1 120
Even at hand a drum is ready braced That shall reverberate . *K. John* v 2 169
Even at him. A certain convocation of politic worms are e'en at him *Ham.* iv 3 22
Even at noon-day. And yesterday the bird of night did sit Even at noon-day upon the market-place . . . . *J. Cæsar* i 3 27
Even at the best. My lord, you take us even at the best *T. of Athens* i 2 157
Even at the first Thy loss is more than can thy portage quit . *Pericles* iii 1 34
Even before this truce, but new before . . . *K. John* iii 1 233
My hunger's gone; but even before, I was At point to sink for food *Cymbeline* iii 6 16
Even blest. We are blest in this man, as I may say, even blest *W. Tale* iv 4 859
Even but. Antony Will e'en but kiss Octavia, and we'll follow *A. and C.* ii 4 3
Even Christian. More than their even Christian . . . *Hamlet* v 1 32
Even field. Upon the left hand of the even field . . . *J. Cæsar* v 1 17
Even ground. Made to run even upon even ground . . . *K. John* ii 1 576
Even hand. And weigh thy value with an even hand . *Mer. of Venice* ii 7 25
Even-handed. This even-handed justice . . . . *Macbeth* i 7 10
Even he. Who? the most exquisite Claudio?—Even he . . *Much Ado* i 3 53
Even he that did uphold the very life Of my dear friend *Mer. of Venice* v 1 214

Even he. Is yonder the man?—Even he, madam . . *As Y. Like It* i 2 161
Is't he you mean?—Even he . . . . . *T. of Shrew* i 2 224
I think, Camillo?—Even he, my lord . . . . *W. Tale* iv 4 484
Who dost thou mean shall be her king?—Even he that makes her queen *Richard III.* iv 4 265
Even he escapes not Language unmannerly . . . *Hen. VIII.* i 2 26
Even he, your wife, this lady, and myself, Are suitors to you *Coriolanus* v 3 77
Even he drops down The knee before him . . . *T. of Athens* i 1 60
What, of Venice?—Even he, sir: did you know him? . . *Othello* v 1 92
Even here I will put off my hope and keep it No longer . . *Tempest* iii 3 7
Even here undone! I was not much afeard . . . . *W. Tale* iv 4 452
Even here thou takest, As from my death-bed, thy last living leave *Richard II.* v 1 38
And even here brake off, and came away . . . *Richard III.* iii 7 41
From which even here I slip my weary neck . . . . iv 4 112
Here pitch our tents, even here in Bosworth field . . . v 3 1
I'll sconce me even here. Pray you, be round with him . *Hamlet* iii 4 4
Cries cuckold to my father, brands the harlot Even here . . iv 5 119
No farther, sir; a man may rot even here . . . . *Lear* v 2 8
Fortune and Antony part here; even here Do we shake hands *Ant. and Cleo.* iv 12 19
All goodness that consists in bounty Expect even here . . *Pericles* v 1 71
Even I. Yea, even I alone.—No, not so, villain . . . *Much Ado* v 1 274
What, thou?—I, even I: what think you of it, madam? . *Richard III.* iv 4 267
Even just the sum that I do owe to you Is growing to me *Com. of Errors* iv 1 7
A' parted even just between twelve and one, even at the turning o' the tide *Hen. V.* ii 3 12
Even like an o'ergrown lion in a cave, That goes not out to prey *M. for M.* i 3 22
Even like those that are kin to the king . . . . 2 *Hen. IV.* ii 2 120
Even like a man new haled from the rack . . . . 1 *Hen. VI.* ii 5 3
Even like a fawning greyhound in the leash . . . . *Coriolanus* i 6 38
And thy brother, I, Even like a stony image, cold and numb *T. Andron.* iii 1 259
'Tis unnatural, Even like the deed that's done . . . *Macbeth* ii 4 11
Cold, cold, my girl! Even like thy chastity . . . *Othello* v 2 276
He at Philippi kept His sword e'en like a dancer . . *Ant. and Cleo.* iii 11 36
Even mead. The even mead, that erst brought sweetly forth The freckled cowslip . . . . *Hen. V.* v 2 48
Even mortal. Which to read Would be even mortal to me . *Cymbeline* iii 4 18
Even natural. That thou art even natural in thine art . *T. of Athens* v 1 88
Even of it. That's the even of it . . . . . *Hen. V.* ii 1 128
Even or odd. A fortnight and odd days.—Even or odd, of all days in the year . . . . *Rom. and Jul.* i 3 16
Even play. In plain shock and even play of battle . . . *Hen. V.* iv 8 114
Even-pleached. Her hedges even-pleach'd, Like prisoners wildly over-grown with hair, Put forth disorder'd twigs . . . . v 2 42
Even poor. Beggar that I am, I am even poor in thanks . . *Hamlet* ii 2 280
Even ripe for marriage-rite . . . . . *Pericles* iv Gower 17
Even road. Run smoothly in the even road of a blank verse . *Much Ado* v 2 33
Even she. Hast thou observed that? even she, I mean . *T. G. of Ver.* ii 1 48
Was this the idol that you worship so?—Even she . . . ii 4 145
Who, Hero?—Even she; Leonato's Hero, your Hero . . *Much Ado* iii 2 109
Is this the Lady Cressid?—Even she . . . *Troi. and Cres.* iv 5 17
Why she, even she—O God! a beast, that wants discourse of reason, Would have mourn'd longer . . . . *Hamlet* i 2 149
Even sick. I am e'en sick of shame . . . . *T. of Athens* iii 6 46
Even since. Whose love had spoke, Even since it could speak *W. Tale* iii 2 71
And even since then hath Richard been obscured . . . 1 *Hen. VI.* ii 5 26
Even so as I mine own course have set down . . . *W. Tale* i 2 340
Hast thou read truth?—Ay, my lord; even so As it is here set down . iii 2 139
Even so as one would beat his offenceless dog . . . *Othello* ii 3 275
Even so much that joy could not show itself modest enough . *Much Ado* i 1 21
And not worth The splinter of a lance. Even so much . *Troi. and Cres.* i 3 283
Even so quickly may one catch the plague? . . . *T. Night* i 5 314
Even so remorseless have they borne him hence . . 2 *Hen. VI.* iii 1 213
Even so suspicious is this tragedy . . . . . iii 2 194
Even so void is your false heart of truth . . . *Mer. of Venice* v 1 189
Even sociable. Mine eyes, even sociable to the show of thine, Fall fellowly drops . . . . *Tempest* v 1 63
Even such a husband Hast thou of me as she is for a wife *Mer. of Venice* iii 5 88
Such duty as the subject owes the prince, Even such a woman oweth to her husband . . . . *T. of Shrew* v 2 156
What linsey-woolsey hast thou to speak to us again?—E'en such as you speak to me . . . . *All's Well* iv 1 15
Even such and so In favour was my brother . . . *T. Night* iii 4 415
With a love even such, So and no other, as yourself commanded *W. Tale* iii 2 66
Loose companions, Even such, they say, as stand in narrow lanes *Rich II.* v 3 8
Even such a man, so faint, so spiritless, So dull, so dead in look 2 *Hen. IV.* i 1 70
Even such kin as the parish heifers are to the town bull . . ii 2 171
Even such a passion doth embrace my bosom . . *Troi. and Cres.* iii 2 37
Even such delight Among fresh female buds . . . *Rom. and Jul.* i 2 28
These pencill'd figures are Even such as they give out . *T. of Athens* i 1 160
Even such heaps and sums of love and wealth As shall to thee blot out what wrongs were theirs . . . . v 1 155
Now thy captain is Even such a body . . . . *Ant. and Cleo.* iv 14 13
O my distressed lord, even such our griefs are . . . *Pericles* i 4 7
Even that. What have we here?—E'en that you have there . *All's Well* iii 2 20
What is your grace's pleasure?—Even that, I hope, which pleaseth God above, And all good men . . . . . *Richard III.* iii 7 109
Yorick's skull, the king's jester.—This?—E'en that . . *Hamlet* v 1 201
Even then. Something rare Even then will rush to knowledge *W. Tale* iii 1 21
All the instruments which aided to expose the child were even then lost when it was found . . . . v 2 78
Even then that sunshine brew'd a shower for him . . . 3 *Hen. VI.* ii 2 156
Subtly taints Even then when we sit idly in the sun *Troi. and Cres.* iii 3 233
But even then the morning cock crew loud . . . *Hamlet* i 2 218
Even then this forked plague is fated to us When we do quicken *Othello* iii 3 276
Even then The princely blood flows in his cheek, he sweats *Cymbeline* iii 3 92
Even there where merchants most do congregate . *Mer. of Venice* i 3 50
Even there, his eye being big with tears, Turning his face . . ii 8 46
And even there, methinks, an angel spake . . . *K. John* v 2 64
Laud be to God! even there my life must end . . 2 *Hen. IV.* iv 5 236
Even there, Against the hospitable canon, would I Wash my fierce hand in's heart . . . . *Coriolanus* i 10 25
I have lost my hopes.—Perchance even there where I did find my doubts *Macbeth* iv 3 25
Even there, thou villain Posthumus, will I kill thee . . *Cymbeline* iii 5 135
Even this. My will is even this . . . . . *T. G. of Ver.* iv 2 93
Is this great Agamemnon's tent, I pray you?—Even this *Troi. and Cres.* i 3 217
Even this, So criminal and in such capital kind . . *Coriolanus* iii 3 80
Give me a kiss; Even this repays me . . . *Ant. and Cleo.* iii 11 71

Even those. Some of us love you well; and even those some Envy your great deservings . . . 1 *Hen. IV.* iv 3 34
Even those we love That are misled upon your cousin's part . v 1 104
What players are they?—Even those you were wont to take delight in *Hamlet* ii 2 341
Even thou, that hast A heart so tender o'er it, take it hence . *W. Tale* ii 3 132
Even thou and none but thou. Take it up straight . ii 3 135
Marcus, even thou hast struck upon my crest . . . *T. Andron.* i 1 364
Even thus. Thus I'll visit her.—But thus, I trust, you will not marry her.—Good sooth, even thus . *T. of Shrew* iii 2 118
Even thus—For, look you, I may make the belly smile . *Coriolanus* i 1 112
'Peace, villain, peace!'—even thus he rates the babe . *T. Andron.* v 1 33
Many worthy and chaste dames even thus, All guiltless, meet reproach *Othello* iv 1 47
Even till the eastern gate, all fiery-red, Opening on Neptune *M. N. Dream* iii 2 391
Even till I shrink with cold . . . . *As Y. Like It* ii 1 9
Even till that England, . . Even till that utmost corner of the west Salute thee for her king . . . . *K. John* ii 1 29
Even till unfenced desolation Leave them as naked as the vulgar air . ii 1 386
Nature's germens tumble all together, Even till destruction sicken *Macb.* iv 1 60
May prorogue his honour Even till a Lethe'd dulness! . *Ant. and Cleo.* ii 1 27
Even to death. And lead you even to death . . *Rom. and Jul.* v 3 220
Even to falling. When one so great begins to rage, he's hunted Even to falling . . . . . . *Ant. and Cleo.* iv 1 8
Even to faultiness. Is't long or round?—Round even to faultiness . iii 3 33
Even to it. We'll e'en to't like French falconers . *Hamlet* ii 2 449
Even to loathing. A fire from heaven came and shrivell'd up Their bodies, even to loathing . . . . *Pericles* ii 4 10
Even to madness. Practising upon his peace and quiet Even to madness *Othello* ii 1 320
Even to roaring. I will plague them all, Even to roaring . *Tempest* iv 1 193
Even to the utmost. I know them, yea, And what they weigh, even to the utmost scruple . . . . *Much Ado* v 1 93
Even to the utmost syllable of your worthiness . . *All's Well* iii 6 74
Now he weighs time Even to the utmost grain . . *Hen. V.* ii 4 138
Even to the uttermost. That shall be rack'd even to the uttermost *Mer. of Venice* i 1 181
I will be free Even to the uttermost . . . . *T. of Shrew* iv 3 80
Even too well. I love a ballad but even too well . *W. Tale* iv 4 188
Even truth. To make the even truth in pleasure flow *All's Well* v 3 326
Even virtue. Do not stain The even virtue of our enterprise *J. Cæsar* ii 1 133
Even way. Is there any way to show such friendship?—A very even way, but no such friend . . . . *Much Ado* iv 1 266
Give even way unto my rough affairs . . . 2 *Hen. IV.* ii 3 2
Even weigh. Your vows to her and me, put in two scales, Will even weigh, and both as light as tales . *M. N. Dream* iii 2 133
Even when. To die, even when they to perfection grow . *T. Night* ii 4 42
Even when you please, since you will have it so . *Richard III.* iii 7 243
Even when the navel of the state was touch'd . *Coriolanus* iii 1 123
Even when their sorrows almost were forgot . *T. Andron.* v 1 137
The dream's here still: even when I wake, it is Without me *Cymbeline* iv 2 306
Even where his lustful eye or savage heart, Without control, listed to make his prey . . . . *Richard III.* iii 5 83
Even while men's minds are wild . . . *Hamlet* v 2 405
Even with. Lay this Angiers even with the ground . *K. John* ii 1 399
Even with the earth Shall lay your stately and air-braving towers 1 *Hen. VI.* iv 2 12
He did vow upon his knees he would be even with me . 2 *Hen. VI.* i 3 204
Nay, he nods at us, as who should say, I'll be even with you . iv 7 100
You know 'tis true, That you are odd, and he is even with you *Tr. and Cr.* iv 5 44
Before we reckon with your several loves, And make us even with you *Macbeth* v 8 62
I will be even with thee, doubt it not . *Ant. and Cleo.* iii 7 1
Evened. Nothing can or shall content my soul Till I am even'd with him . . . . . . *Othello* ii 1 308
Evening. And give some evening music to her ear . *T. G. of Ver.* iv 2 17
When will you go?—This evening coming . . . iv 3 42
Lady, a happy evening!—Amen, amen! . . . v 1 7
One, I tell you, that will not miss you morning nor evening prayer *M. W.* ii 2 102
My woes end likewise with the evening sun *Com. of Errors* i 1 28
And about evening come yourself alone . . . iii 1 96
I am at him upon my knees every morning and evening . *Much Ado* ii 1 31
How still the evening is, As hush'd on purpose to grace harmony! . ii 3 40
Say, what abridgement have you for this evening? What masque? *M. N. Dream* v 1 39
You must not now slumber in it.—I'll about it this evening *All's Well* iii 6 79
Before the dew of evening fall . . . *K. John* ii 1 285
And, to conclude, This evening must I leave you . 1 *Hen. IV.* ii 3 109
An if thou darest, This evening, on the east side of the grove 2 *Hen. VI.* ii 1 43
Now Phaëthon hath tumbled from his car, And made an evening at the noontide prick . . . . . 3 *Hen. VI.* i 4 34
I shall fall Like a bright exhalation in the evening . *Hen. VIII.* iii 2 226
Are you at leisure, holy father, now; Or shall I come to you at evening mass?—My leisure serves me . . *Rom. and Jul.* iv 1 38
'Twas on a summer's evening, in his tent . . *J. Cæsar* iii 2 176
Without any further delay than this very evening . . *Lear* i 2 101
I have this present evening from my sister Been well inform'd of them ii 1 103
Evenly. Whatsoever comes athwart his affection ranges evenly with mine . . . . *Much Ado* ii 2 7
And silver Trent shall run In a new channel, fair and evenly 1 *Hen. IV.* iii 1 103
Evenly derived From his most famed of famous ancestors *Hen. V.* ii 4 91
Event. Mark his condition and the event; then tell me If this might be a brother . . . . . . *Tempest* i 2 117
Crown what I profess with kind event If I speak true! . . iii 1 69
These are not natural events; they strengthen From strange to stranger v 1 227
But leave we him to his events . . . . *Meas. for Meas.* iii 2 252
Are they good?—As the event stamps them . . *Much Ado* i 2 7
Doubt not but success Will fashion the event in better shape . iv 1 237
I did encounter that obscene and most preposterous event *L. L. Lost* i 1 245
Yet I am sure you are not satisfied Of these events at full *Mer. of Venice* v 1 297
'Tis I must make conclusion Of these most strange events *As Y. Like It* v 4 133
I'll after him, and see the event of this . . *T. of Shrew* iii 2 129
To the event Of the none-sparing war . . . *All's Well* iii 2 107
For this night, to bed, and dream on the event . *T. Night* iii 3 191
Come, let's see the event.—I dare lay any money 'twill be nothing yet iii 4 431
If the event o' the journey Prove as successful . . *W. Tale* iii 1 11
No distemper'd day, No common wind, no customed event *K. John* iii 4 155
What will ensue hereof, there's none can tell; But by bad courses may be understood That their events can never fall out good *Richard II.* ii 1 214
Heaven hath a hand in these events . . . . . v 2 37

Event. You cast the event of war, my noble lord . . 2 *Hen. IV.* i 1 166
Against ill chances men are ever merry; But heaviness foreruns the good event . . . . iv 2 82
It doth presage some ill event . . . . . 1 *Hen. VI.* iv 1 191
With hope to find the like event in love . . . . v 5 105
You and I must talk of that event . . . . 2 *Hen. VI.* i 1 326
In this the heaven figures some event.—'Tis wondrous strange 3 *Hen. VI.* ii 1 32
O heavy times, begetting such events! . . . . ii 5 63
In desperate manner Daring the event to the teeth . . . *Hen. VIII.* i 2 36
We may not think the justness of each act Such and no other than event doth form it . . . . *Troi. and Cres.* ii 2 120
Carry with us ears and eyes for the time, But hearts for the event *Coriol.* ii 1 286
Execrable wretch, That hath been breeder of these dire events *T. An.* v 3 178
Afterwards, to order well the state, That like events may ne'er it ruinate v 3 204
I'll show you how to observe a strange event . . *T. of Athens* iii 4 17
Dire combustion and confused events New hatch'd to the woeful time *Macbeth* ii 3 63
Let our just censures Attend the true event . . . v 4 15
Like precurse of fierce events, As harbingers preceding still the fates *Ham.* i 1 121
Or some craven scruple Of thinking too precisely on the event . iv 4 41
Makes mouths at the invisible event . . iv 4 50
Nay, then— Well, well; the event . . . . *Lear* i 4 371
There are many events in the womb of time which will be delivered *Othello* i 3 377
All strange and terrible events are welcome . *Ant. and Cleo.* iv 15 3
High events as these Strike those that make them . . . v 2 363
The event Is yet to name the winner . . . *Cymbeline* ii 5 14
The unborn event I do commend to your content . *Pericles* iv Gower 45
Eventful. Last scene of all, That ends this strange eventful history, Is second childishness . . . . *As Y. Like It* ii 7 164
Ever. As wicked dew as e'er my mother brush'd . *Tempest* i 2 321
Now queen.—And the rarest that e'er came there . . ii 1 99
We have lost your son, I fear, for ever . . . ii 1 132
Whom I, with this obedient steel, three inches of it, Can lay to bed for ever . . . . ii 1 284
As proper a man as ever went on four legs . . . ii 2 63
My mistress, dearest; And I thus humble ever . . . iii 1 87
With a heart as willing As bondage e'er of freedom . . . iii 1 89
Was there ever man a coward that hath drunk so much sack as I to-day? iii 2 30
I'll seek him deeper than e'er plummet sounded . . . iii 3 101
Let me live here ever; So rare a wonder'd father and a wife Makes this place Paradise . . . . iv 1 122
Do that good mischief which may make this island Thine own for ever iv 1 217
And deeper than did ever plummet sound I'll drown my book . v 1 56
This is as strange a maze as e'er men trod . . . v 1 242
There is in this business more than nature Was ever conduct of . v 1 244
Home-keeping youth have ever homely wits . . *T. G. of Ver.* i 1 2
If ever danger do environ thee, Commend thy grievance to my holy prayers . . . . i 1 16
It is the unkindest tied that ever any man tied . . . ii 3 42
The key whereof myself have ever kept . . . . iii 1 36
My wrath shall far exceed the love I ever bore my daughter or thyself . iii 1 167
The blackest news that ever thou heardest . . . iii 1 285
It hath been the longest night That e'er I watch'd and the most heaviest iv 2 141
I have heard thee say No grief did ever come so near thy heart . iv 3 19
And she shall thank you for't, if e'er you know her . . iv 4 184
I do as truly suffer As e'er I did commit . . . . v 4 77
Bear witness, Heaven, I have my wish for ever . . . v 4 119
An honest . . . fellow, as ever servant shall come in house withal *M. W.* i 4 11
Honest . . . as ever broke bread . . . i 4 161; *Much Ado* iii 5 42
You're shamed, you're overthown, you're undone for ever! *Mer. Wives* iii 3 103
Defend your reputation, or bid farewell to your good life for ever . iii 3 127
Let me for ever be your table-sport . . . . iv 2 169
'Tis one of the best discretions of a 'oman as ever I did look upon . iv 4 2
One that hath taught me more wit than ever I learned before . iv 5 61
The finest mad devil of jealousy in him . . . that ever governed frenzy v 1 20
Do you think . . . that ever the devil could have made you our delight? v 5 157
The time is yet to come that she was ever respected with man *M. for M.* ii 1 176
If ever I was respected with her, or she with me . . ii 1 184
Better it were a brother died at once, Than that a sister, by redeeming him, Should die for ever . . . . ii 4 108
If ever he return and I can speak to him . . . . iii 1 197
If peradventure he shall ever return to have hearing of this business . iii 1 210
A noble and renowned brother, in his love toward her ever most kind . iii 1 229
If ever the duke return, as our prayers are he may . . . iii 2 163
I have heard it was ever his manner to do so . . . iv 2 138
Keep your instruction, And hold you ever to our special drift . iv 5 4
Yet my husband Knows not that ever he knew me . . . v 1 187
Or else for ever be confixed here, A marble monument! . . . v 1 232
Thou art the first knave that e'er madest a duke . . . v 1 361
Say, wast thou e'er contracted to this woman?—I was, my lord . v 1 380
Was there ever any man thus beaten out of season? . *Com. of Errors* i 2 48
Slander lives upon succession, For ever housed where it gets possession iii 1 106
And ever, as it blazed, they threw on him Great pails of puddled mire v 1 172
Nor ever didst thou draw thy sword on me . . . . v 1 266
O, he's returned; and as pleasant as ever he was . . *Much Ado* i 1 38
As the fashion of his hat; it ever changes with the next block . . i 1 76
Thou wast ever an obstinate heretic in the despite of beauty . . i 1 236
Prove that ever I lose more blood with love than I will get again with drinking . . . . i 1 252
If ever thou dost fall from this faith, thou wilt prove a notable argument i 1 257
If this should ever happen, thou wouldst be horn-mad . . . i 1 271
Men were deceivers ever, One foot in sea and one on shore . . ii 3 65
Whom she hath in all outward behaviours seemed ever to abhor . ii 3 100
Let it be thy part To praise him more than ever man did merit . iii 1 19
As fortunate a bed As ever Beatrice shall couch upon . . . iii 1 46
And seem'd I ever otherwise to you?—Out on thee! Seeming! . iv 1 56
Why ever wast thou lovely in my eyes? . . . . iv 1 132
Then shall he mourn, If ever love had interest in his liver . . iv 1 233
Flat burglary as ever was committed.—Yea, by mass, that it is . iv 2 52
Small have continual plodders ever won . . . *L. L. Lost* i 1 86
If ever I do see the merry days of desolation that I have seen . i 2 164
A woman, that is like a German clock, Still a-repairing, ever out of frame iii 1 193
For all the wealth that ever I did see, I would not have him know so much . . . . iv 3 149
The fairest dames, That ever turn'd their—backs—to mortal views! . v 2 161
That ever turn'd their eyes to mortal views! . . . . v 2 163
Or ever, but in vizards, show their faces . . . . v 2 271
We to ourselves prove false, By being once false for ever to be true . v 2 783
Hence ever then my heart is in thy breast . . . . v 2 826
Either to die the death or to abjure For ever the society of men *M. N. Dr.* i 1 66

Ever. If then true lovers have been ever cross'd, It stands as an edict in destiny . . . *M. N. Dream* i 1 150
By all the vows that ever men have broke, In number more than ever women spoke . . . i 1 175
A stranger Pyramus than e'er played here . . . iii 1 90
If e'er I loved her, all that love is gone . . . iii 2 170
I evermore did love you, Hermia, Did ever keep your counsels . . . iii 2 308
Thou shalt buy this dear, If ever I thy face by daylight see . . . iii 2 427
Fantasies, that apprehend More than cool reason ever comprehends . v 1 6
An the worst fall that ever fell, I hope I shall make shift *Mer. of Venice* i 2 96
He, of all the men that ever my foolish eyes looked upon, was the best i 2 130
If e'er the Jew her father come to heaven, It will be for his gentle daughter's sake . . . ii 4 34
For lovers ever run before the clock . . . ii 6 4
Take what wife you will to bed, I will ever be your head . . ii 9 71
I would she were as lying a gossip in that as ever knapped ginger . iii 1 10
Here are a few of the unpleasant'st words That ever blotted paper ! . iii 2 255
Till I come again, No bed shall e'er be guilty of my stay . . iii 2 328
It is the most impenetrable cur That ever kept with men . . iii 3 19
As I have ever found thee honest-true, So let me find thee still . iii 4 46
She would not hold out enemy for ever . . . iv 1 447
I'll see if I can get my husband's ring, Which I did make him swear to keep for ever . . . iv 2 14
Let not that doctor e'er come near my house . . . v 1 223
Being ever from their cradles bred together . . . *As Y. Like It* i 1 113
If ever he go alone again, I'll never wrestle for prize more . . i 1 167
He had sworn it away before ever he saw those pancakes . . i 2 84
As true a lover As ever sigh'd upon a midnight pillow . . . ii 4 27
If thou remember'st not the slightest folly That ever love did make thee run into, Thou hast not loved . . . ii 4 35
Well then, if ever I thank any man, I'll thank you . . . ii 5 25
If ever you have look'd on better days, If ever been where bells have knoll'd to church, If ever sat at any good man's feast, If ever from your eyelids wiped a tear . . . ii 7 113
Wast ever in court, shepherd ?—No, truly.—Then thou art damned . iii 2 34
Did you ever cure any so ?—Yes, one, and in this manner . . iii 2 426
An excellent colour : your chestnut was ever the only colour . iii 4 13
If ever,—as that ever may be near . . . iii 5 28
For ever and a day.—Say 'a day,' without the 'ever' . . iv 1 146
But kindness, nobler ever than revenge . . . iv 3 129
I will marry you, if ever I marry woman . . . v 2 123
I will satisfy you, if ever I satisfied man . . . v 2 124
Was ever gentleman thus grieved as I? . . . *T. of Shrew* ii 1 37
I love her ten times more than e'er I did . . . ii 1 162
Did ever Dian so become a grove? . . . ii 1 260
Was ever match clapp'd up so suddenly ? . . . ii 1 327
Came you from the church ?—As willingly as e'er I came from school . iii 2 152
Was ever man so beaten ? was ever man so rayed ? was ever man so weary ? iv 1 2
And will repute you ever The patron of my life and liberty . . iv 2 112
If ever I said loose-bodied gown, sew me in the skirts of it . . iv 3 136
Virginity by being once lost may be ten times found ; by being ever kept, it is ever lost . . . *All's Well* i 1 143
Who ever strove To show her merit, that did miss her love ? . . i 1 241
Wilt thou ever be a foul-mouthed and calumnious knave? . . i 3 60
Did ever in so true a flame of liking Wish chastely and love dearly . i 3 217
Thus he his special nothing ever prologues . . . ii 1 95
I see things may serve long, but not serve ever . . . ii 2 61
But, be refused, Let the white death sit on thy cheek for ever . . ii 3 77
And in your bed Find fairer fortune, if you ever wed ! . . ii 3 98
I give Me and my service, ever whilst I live, Into your guiding power . ii 3 110
Disdain Rather corrupt me ever ! . . . ii 3 123
Or I will throw thee from my care for ever . . . ii 3 169
If ever thou be'st bound in thy scarf and beaten, thou shalt find . ii 3 237
Undone, and forfeited to cares for ever ! . . . ii 3 284
You have mistaken him, my lord.—And shall do so ever . . ii 5 45
Madam, my lord is gone, for ever gone.—Do not say so . . iii 2 48
This is the first truth that e'er thine own tongue was guilty of . iv 1 35
And will for ever Do thee all rights of service . . . iv 2 16
Say thou art mine, and ever My love as it begins shall so persever . iv 2 36
Ever a friend whose thoughts more truly labour To recompense your love iv 4 17
The most virtuous gentlewoman that ever nature had praise for creating iv 5 10
The master I speak of ever keeps a good fire . . . iv 5 50
The last that e'er I took her leave at court, I saw upon her finger . v 3 79
I bade her, if her fortunes ever stood Necessitied to help . . v 3 84
If you shall prove This ring was ever hers . . . v 3 125
If ever I knew man, 'twas you . . . v 3 288
I'll love her dearly, ever, ever dearly . . . v 3 317
Infirmity, that decays the wise, doth ever make the better fool *T. Night* i 5 83
If ever thou shalt love, In the sweet pangs of it remember me . ii 4 15
And wished to see thee ever cross-gartered . . . ii 5 167
More favours to the count's serving-man than ever she bestowed upon me . . . iii 2 7
There is no Christian . . . can ever believe such impossible passages . iii 2 76
Thanks, And thanks ; and ever . . . oft good turns Are shuffled off with such uncurrent pay . . . iii 3 15
So soon as ever thou seest him, draw . . . iii 4 195
Gives manhood more approbation than ever proof itself would have earned . . . iii 4 199
I would I were the first that ever dissembled in such a gown . . iv 2 7
As ever thou wilt deserve well at my hand, help me to a candle . iv 2 86
It shall advantage thee more than ever the bearing of letter did . iv 2 120
And, having sworn truth, ever will be true . . . iv 3 33
My soul the faithfull'st offerings hath breathed out That e'er devotion tender'd . . . v 1 118
More than my life, More, by all mores, than e'er I shall love wife . v 1 139
And made the most notorious geck and gull That e'er invention play'd on v 1 352
A gentleman of the greatest promise that ever came into my note *W. Tale* i 1 40
Then didst thou utter, 'I am yours for ever' . . . i 2 105
The one for ever earn'd a royal husband . . . i 2 107
If ever I were wilful-negligent, It was my folly . . . i 2 255
If ever fearful To do a thing, where I the issue doubted . . i 2 258
He is dishonour'd by a man which ever Profess'd to him . . i 2 455
Their familiarity, Which was as gross as ever touch'd conjecture . ii 1 176
For ever Unvenerable be thy hands ! . . . ii 3 76
Which is rotten As ever oak or stone was sound . . . ii 3 90
For the babe Is counted lost for ever, Perdita, I prithee, call't . iii 3 33
This is the chase : I am gone for ever . . . iii 3 58
Of this allow, If ever you have spent time worse ere now . . iv 1 30
O that ever I was born ! . . . iv 3 53
When you speak, sweet, I'ld have you do it ever . . . iv 4 137

Ever. Were I the fairest youth That ever made eye swerve, had force and knowledge More than was ever man's . . . *W. Tale* iv 4 385
If ever henceforth thou These rural latches to his entrance open . iv 4 448
The sweet'st companion that e'er man Bred his hopes out of . . v 1 11
O, that ever I Had squared me to thy counsel ! . . . v 1 51
The most peerless piece of earth, I think, That e'er the sun shone bright on . . . v 1 95
Most true, if ever truth were pregnant by circumstance . . v 2 33
And there was the first gentleman-like tears that ever we shed . v 2 156
Prepare To see the life as lively mock'd as ever Still sleep mock'd death v 3 19
Scarce any joy Did ever so long live . . . v 3 52
Both your pardons, That e'er I put between your holy looks My ill suspicion . . . v 3 148
My bed was ever to thy son as true As thine was to thy husband *K. John* ii 1 124
I'll give thee more Than e'er the coward hand of France can win . ii 1 158
And this blessed day Ever in France shall be kept festival . . iii 1 76
I will pray, If ever I remember to be holy, For your fair safety . iii 3 15
The vilest stroke That ever wall-eyed wrath or staring rage Presented . iv 3 49
The smallest thread That ever spider twisted from her womb . iv 3 128
By all the blood that ever fury breathed, The youth says well . v 2 127
He is forsworn, if e'er those eyes of yours Behold another day break . v 4 31
To the furthest verge That ever was survey'd by English eye *Richard II.* i 1 94
If ever I were traitor, My name be blotted from the book of life ! . i 3 201
Nor my own disgrace Have ever made me sour my patient cheek . ii 1 169
Farewell at once, for once, for all, and ever.—Well, we may meet again ii 2 148
That e'er this tongue of mine, That laid the sentence of dread banishment On yon proud man, should take it off again ! . . . iii 3 133
It will the woefullest division prove That ever fell upon this cursed earth iv 1 147
For ever may my knees grow to the earth, My tongue cleave to my roof v 3 30
For ever will I walk upon my knees, And never see day that the happy sees . . . v 3 93
Did I ever call for thee to pay thy part? . . . *1 Hen. IV.* i 2 57
This is the most omnipotent villain that ever cried 'Stand' to a true man i 2 122
I know them to be as true-bred cowards as ever turned back . . i 2 206
The veriest varlet that ever chewed with a tooth . . . ii 2 25
O, we are undone, both we and ours for ever ! . . . ii 2 92
Argument for a week, laughter for a month and a good jest for ever . ii 2 102
Our plot is a good plot as ever was laid . . . ii 3 18
That ever this fellow should have fewer words than a parrot ! . ii 4 110
A fearful head they are . . As ever offer'd foul play in a state . iii 2 169
I am thrust upon it : well, I cannot last ever . . . *2 Hen. IV.* i 2 240
I love thee better than I love e'er a scurvy young boy of them all . ii 4 295
Prove that ever I dress myself handsome till thy return . . ii 4 302
A' came ever in the rearward of the fashion . . . iii 2 339
A summer bird, Which ever in the haunch of winter sings . . iv 4 92
Let God for ever keep it from my head ! . . . iv 5 175
The very latest counsel That ever I shall breathe . . . iv 5 184
To give a greater sum Than ever at one time the clergy yet Did *Hen. V.* i 1 80
As ever you came of women, come in quickly . . . ii 1 122
Treason and murder ever kept together, As two yoke-devils . . ii 2 105
He's in Arthur's bosom, if ever man went to Arthur's bosom . . ii 3 10
If ever thou darest acknowledge it, I will make it my quarrel . iv 1 224
If ever thou come to me and say, after to-morrow . . . iv 1 229
If ever I live to see it, I will challenge it . . . iv 1 233
Who, if alive and ever dare to challenge this glove . . . iv 7 132
A Jacksauce, as ever his black shoe trod upon God's ground . . iv 7 149
If ever thou beest mine, Kate, as I have a saving faith within me tells me thou shalt . . . v 2 216
Come, officer ; as loud as e'er thou canst : Cry . . *1 Hen. VI.* i 3 72
This pale and angry rose . . . Will I for ever and my faction wear . ii 4 109
Ere the priest Should ever get that privilege of me . . . iii 1 121
I should revive the soldiers' hearts, Because I ever found them as myself iii 2 98
For ever should they be expulsed from France . . . iii 3 25
There is no hope that ever I will stay, If the first hour I shrink . iv 5 30
The greatest miracle that e'er ye wrought . . . v 4 66
The happiest gift that ever marquess gave, The fairest queen that ever king received . . . *2 Hen. VI.* i 1 15
Hang me, if ever I spake the words . . . i 3 200
As willingly do I the same resign As e'er thy father Henry made it mine ii 3 34
Trow'st thou that e'er I'll look upon the world ? . . . ii 4 38
That doit that e'er I wrested from the king . . . iii 1 112
Yet, good Humphrey, is the hour to come That e'er I proved thee false iii 1 205
If ever lady wrong'd her lord so much . . . iii 2 211
The wofull'st cask That ever did contain a thing of worth . . iii 2 410
Was ever feather so lightly blown to and fro as this multitude ? . iv 8 57
Was ever king that joy'd an earthly throne, And could command no more content than I ? . . . iv 9 1
Brave thee ! ay, by the best blood that ever was broached . . iv 10 40
I here entail The crown to thee and to thine heirs for ever . *3 Hen. VI.* i 1 195
The saddest spectacle that e'er I view'd . . . ii 1 67
Didst thou never hear That things ill-got had ever bad success ? . ii 2 46
Was ever son so rued a father's death ?—Was ever father so bemoan'd his son ?—Was ever king so grieved for subjects' woe ? . . ii 5 109
Can Oxford, that did ever fence the right, Now buckler falsehood ? . iii 3 98
But if you ever chance to have a child, Look in his youth to have him so cut off . . . v 5 65
Shall rue the hour that ever thou wast born . . . v 6 43
If ever he have child, abortive be it, Prodigious ! . . *Richard III.* i 2 21
If ever he have wife, let her be made As miserable ! . . . i 2 26
Thou dost confirm his happiness for ever . . . i 2 209
Was ever woman in this humour woo'd ? Was ever woman in this humour won ? . . . i 2 228
To pray for them that have done scathe to us.—So do I ever . . i 3 318
If ever any grudge were lodged between us . . . ii 1 65
I prophesy the fearfull'st time to thee That ever wretched age hath look'd upon . . . iii 4 107
Still live they and for ever may they last ! . . . iv 2 7
What comfortable hour canst thou name, That ever graced me in thy company ? . . . iv 4 174
I intend more good to you and yours Than ever you or yours were by me wrong'd ! . . . iv 4 238
I will love her everlastingly.—But how long shall that title 'ever' last ? iv 4 350
Fairest-boding dreams That ever enter'd in a drowsy head . . v 3 228
Which ever, As ravenous fishes, do a vessel follow . . *Hen. VIII.* i 2 78
Ten times more ugly Than ever they were fair . . . i 2 118
The fairest hand I ever touch'd ! . . . i 4 75
If ever any malice in your heart Were hid against me . . . ii 1 80
All That made me happy at one stroke has taken For ever from the world ii 1 118
It grows again Fresher than e'er it was . . . ii 1 155
But to be commanded For ever by your grace, whose hand has raised me ii 2 120

Ever. So good a lady that no tongue could ever Pronounce dishonour of her . . . *Hen. VIII.* ii 3 3
If your back Cannot vouchsafe this burthen, 'tis too weak Ever to get a boy . . . ii 3 44
Ever in fear to kindle your dislike, Yea, subject to your countenance . ii 4 25
When was the hour I ever contradicted your desire? . . . ii 4 28
Declare . . . whether ever I Did broach this business to your highness ii 4 148
To his music plants and flowers Ever sprung . . . iii 1 7
Nothing but death Shall e'er divorce my dignities . . . iii 1 142
A noble spirit . . . ever casts Such doubts, as false coin, from it . iii 1 170
Matter against him that for ever mars The honey of his language . iii 2 21
Heaven forgive me! Ever God bless your highness! . . . iii 2 136
And ever may your highness yoke together, As I will lend you cause iii 2 150
My endeavours Have ever come too short of my desires . . . iii 2 170
For your highness' good I ever labour'd More than mine own. . iii 2 191
Left me . . . to the mercy Of a rude stream, that must for ever hide me iii 2 364
All my glories In that one woman I have lost for ever . . . iii 2 409
No sun shall ever usher forth mine honours . . . iii 2 410
My prayers For ever and for ever shall be yours . . . iii 2 427
She is the goodliest woman That ever lay by man . . . iv 1 70
And still so rising, That Christendom shall ever speak his virtue . iv 2 63
So may he ever do! and ever flourish, When I shall dwell with worms! iv 2 125
And not ever The justice and the truth o' the question carries The due o' the verdict with it . . . v 1 129
The God of heaven Both now and ever bless her! . . . v 1 165
And the end Was ever, to do well . . . v 3 37
Do my Lord of Canterbury A shrewd turn, and he is your friend for ever v 3 178
All comfort, joy, in this most gracious lady, Heaven ever laid up to make parents happy . . . v 5 8
Patience herself, what goddess e'er she be, Doth lesser blench *Tr. and Cr.* i 1 27
Wiser, fairer, truer, Than ever Greek did compass in his arms . i 3 276
Do not consent That ever Hector and Achilles meet . . . i 3 363
I was won, my lord, With the first glance that ever—pardon me . iii 2 126
If ever you prove false one to another . . . iii 2 206
Welcome ever smiles, And farewell goes out sighing . . . iii 3 168
The man's undone for ever . . . iii 3 259
Make Cressid's name the very crown of falsehood, If ever she leave Troilus! . . . iv 2 107
If e'er thou stand at mercy of my sword, Name Cressid . . . iv 4 116
Than can ever Appear in your impediment . . . *Coriolanus* i 1 73
We have ever your good word . . . i 1 170
Was ever man so proud as is this Marcius? . . . i 1 256
'Tis sworn between us we shall ever strike Till one can do no more . i 2 35
Bear The addition nobly ever! . . . i 9 66
Ever right.—Menenius, ever, ever . . . ii 1 209
And their blaze Shall darken him for ever . . . ii 1 275
He was your enemy, ever spake against Your liberties . . . ii 3 187
And live with such as cannot rule Nor ever will be ruled . . . iii 1 41
Against a graver bench Than ever frown'd . . . iii 1 107
And, being angry, does forget that ever He heard the name of death . iii 1 259
He hath been used Ever to conquer, and to have his worth Of contradiction . . . iii 3 26
And lose advantage, which doth ever cool I' the absence of the needer . iv 1 43
More noble blows than ever thou wise words . . . iv 2 21
To pluck from them their tribunes for ever . . . iv 3 25
Since I have ever follow'd thee with hate . . . iv 5 104
As ever in ambitious strength I did Contend against thy valour . . iv 5 118
A thousand welcomes! And more a friend than e'er an enemy . . iv 5 152
Whether 'twas pride, Which out of daily fortune ever taints The happy man . . . iv 7 38
For I have ever verified my friends . . . v 2 17
'Tis the first time that ever I was forced to scold . . . v 6 105
The most noble corse that ever herald Did follow to his urn . . v 6 145
O cruel, irreligious piety!—Was ever Scythia half so barbarous? *T. And.* i 1 131
If ever Tamora Were gracious in those princely eyes of thine. . i 1 428
And all the bitterest terms That ever ear did hear to such effect . ii 3 111
With the dismall'st object hurt That ever eye with sight made heart lament! . . . ii 3 205
Expecting ever when some envious surge Will in his brinish bowels swallow him . . . iii 1 96
Did ever raven sing so like a lark? . . . iii 1 158
That ever death should let life bear his name! . . . iii 1 249
My noble aunt Loves me as dear as e'er my mother did . . . iv 1 23
By this our mother is for ever shamed . . . iv 2 112
To do As much as ever Coriolanus did . . . iv 4 68
Too like the sire for ever being good . . . v 1 50
As sure a card as ever won the set . . . v 1 100
As true a dog as ever fought at head . . . v 1 102
Women, being the weaker vessels, are ever thrust to the wall *R. and J.* i 1 20
If ever you disturb our streets again, Your lives shall pay the forfeit . i 1 103
Thou wast the prettiest babe that e'er I nursed . . . i 3 60
If e'er thou wast thyself and these woes thine, Thou and these woes were all for Rosaline . . . ii 3 77
O Romeo, Romeo! Who ever would have thought it? Romeo! . . iii 2 42
Honest gentleman! That ever I should live to see thee dead! . . iii 2 63
Did ever dragon keep so fair a cave? Beautiful tyrant! fiend angelical! iii 2 74
Was ever book containing such vile matter So fairly bound? . . iii 2 83
Think'st thou we shall ever meet again?—I doubt it not. . . iii 5 51
Feeling so the loss, I cannot choose but ever weep the friend. . iii 5 78
Pardon, I beseech you! Henceforward I am ever ruled by you . iv 2 22
O, well-a-day, that ever I was born! . . . iv 5 15
Most miserable hour that e'er time saw In lasting labour of his pilgrimage! . . . iv 5 44
Most lamentable day, most woful day, That ever, ever, I did yet behold! iv 5 51
I'll pay the debt, and free him.—Your lordship ever binds him *T. of A.* i 1 104
The noblest mind he carries That ever govern'd man . . . i 1 292
You mistake my love: I gave it freely ever . . . i 2 10
My heart is ever at your service, my lord. . . . i 2 76
We should think ourselves for ever perfect . . . i 2 89
As good a trick as ever hangman served thief . . . ii 2 99
I was the first man That e'er received gift from him . . . iii 3 17
We banish thee for ever.—Banish me! . . . iii 5 98
I'll ever serve his mind with my best will . . . iv 2 49
And have forgot That ever Timon was . . . iv 3 208
I love thee better now than e'er I did.—I hate thee worse . . iv 3 233
Grant I may ever love, and rather woo Those that would mischief me! iv 3 474
But tell me true—For I must ever doubt, though ne'er so sure . iv 3 514
Performance is ever the duller for his act. . . . v 1 26
And write in thee the figures of their love, Ever to read them thine . v 1 158
Therefore it is meet That noble minds keep ever with their likes *J. Cæsar* i 2 315

Ever. You all do know this mantle: I remember The first time ever Cæsar put it on . . . *J. Cæsar* iii 2 175
He hath left them you, And to your heirs for ever . . . iii 2 255
Thou lovedst him better Than ever thou lovedst Cassius . . . iv 3 107
Think not, thou noble Roman, That ever Brutus will go bound to Rome v 1 112
For ever, and for ever, farewell, Cassius! If we do meet again, why, we shall smile . . . v 1 117
For ever, and for ever, farewell, Brutus! If we do meet again, we'll smile indeed . . . v 1 120
It is impossible that ever Rome Should breed thy fellow . . . v 3 100
No enemy Shall ever take alive the noble Brutus . . . v 4 22
Only look up clear; To alter favour ever is to fear . . . *Macbeth* i 5 73
Your servants ever Have theirs, themselves and what is theirs, in compt i 6 25
With a most indissoluble tie For ever knit . . . iii 1 18
Whose heavy hand hath bow'd you to the grave And beggar'd yours for ever . . . iii 1 91
Shall Banquo's issue ever Reign in this kingdom? . . . iv 1 102
More suffer and more sundry ways than ever . . . iv 3 48
Let not your ears despise my tongue for ever . . . iv 3 201
This push Will cheer me ever, or disseat me now . . . v 3 21
Henceforth be earls, the first that ever Scotland In such an honour named . . . v 8 63
Do not for ever with thy vailed lids Seek for thy noble father *Hamlet* i 2 70
Your poor servant ever . . . i 2 162
Would I had met my dearest foe in heaven Or ever I had seen that day! i 2 183
List, list, O, list! If thou didst ever thy dear father love . i 5 23
The time is out of joint: O cursed spite, That ever I was born to set it right! . . . i 5 190
Thou art e'en as just a man As e'er my conversation coped withal. . iii 2 59
Both here and hence pursue me lasting strife, If, once a widow, ever I be wife! . . . iii 2 233
Let not ever The soul of Nero enter this firm bosom . . . iii 2 411
Hath but one part wisdom And ever three parts coward . . . iv 4 43
Was he a gentleman?—A' was the first that ever bore arms . . v 1 37
What is the reason that you use me thus? I loved you ever . . v 1 313
If thou didst ever hold me in thy heart, Absent thee from felicity awhile v 2 357
To thee and thine hereditary ever Remain this ample third . *Lear* i 1 81
And as a stranger to my heart and me Hold thee, from this, for ever . i 1 118
Royal Lear, Whom I have ever honour'd as my king . . . i 1 142
'Tis the infirmity of his age: yet he hath ever but slenderly known himself . . . i 1 297
If our father would sleep till I waked him, you should enjoy half his revenue for ever . . . i 2 56
I'll resume the shape which thou dost think I have cast off for ever . i 4 332
The basest and most poorest shape That ever penury, in contempt of man, Brought near to beast . . . ii 3 8
Who is't can say 'I am at the worst'? I am worse than e'er I was . iv 1 28
Take my purse; If ever thou wilt thrive, bury my body. . . iv 6 253
If e'er your grace had speech with man so poor, Hear me one word . v 1 38
If ever I return to you again, I'll bring you comfort . . . v 2 3
This sword of mine shall give them instant way, Where they shall rest for ever . . . v 3 150
Let sorrow split my heart, if ever I Did hate thee or thy father! . v 3 177
Told the most piteous tale of Lear and him That ever ear received . v 3 215
She's gone for ever! I know when one is dead, and when one lives . v 3 259
She lives! if it be so, It is a chance which does redeem all sorrows That ever I have felt . . . v 3 267
Traitors all! I might have saved her; now she's gone for ever! . . v 3 270
If ever I did dream of such a matter, Abhor me . . . *Othello* i 1 5
If it prove lawful prize, he's made for ever . . . i 2 51
Which ever as she could with haste dispatch, She'ld come again . i 3 148
Thus do I ever make my fool my purse . . . i 3 389
She was a wight, if ever such wight were . . . ii 1 159
And this, and this, the greatest discords be That e'er our hearts shall make! . . . ii 1 201
Hold! You will be shamed for ever . . . ii 3 163
What wound did ever heal but by degrees? . . . ii 3 377
I am bound to thee for ever . . . iii 3 213
She so loves the token, For he conjured her she should ever keep it . iii 3 294
Shall ever medicine thee to that sweet sleep Which thou owedst yesterday iii 3 332
O, now, for ever Farewell the tranquil mind! farewell content! . iii 3 347
Damn them then, If ever mortal eyes do see them bolster! . . iii 3 399
And to obey shall be in me remorse, What bloody business ever . . iii 3 469
Now art thou my lieutenant.—I am your own for ever . . . iii 3 480
If e'er my will did trespass 'gainst his love . . . iv 2 152
Which I have greater reason to believe now than ever . . . iv 2 218
I am maim'd for ever. Help, ho! murder! murder! . . . v 1 27
Thou hast kill'd the sweetest innocent That e'er did lift up eye . v 2 200
Did I, Charmian, Ever love Cæsar so? . . . *Ant. and Cleo.* i 5 67
A sister I bequeath you, whom no brother Did ever love so dearly . ii 2 153
And his quails ever Beat mine, inhoop'd, at odds . . . ii 3 37
Cæsar and he are greater friends than ever . . . ii 5 48
Let him for ever go:—let him not . . . ii 5 115
Then is Cæsar and he for ever knit together . . . ii 6 122
I have ever held my cap off to thy fortunes . . . ii 7 63
Repent that e'er thy tongue Hath so betray'd thine act . . . ii 7 83
Cæsar and Antony have ever won More in their officer than person . iii 1 16
What majesty is in her gait? Remember, If e'er thou look'dst on majesty iii 3 21
That ever I should call thee castaway!—You have not call'd me so . iii 6 40
I am so lated in the world, that I Have lost my way for ever . . iii 11 4
You have been a boggler ever . . . iii 13 110
I will remain The loyal'st husband that did e'er plight troth. *Cymbeline* i 1 96
Debtor to you for courtesies, which I will be ever to pay and yet pay still i 4 39
A lady to the worthiest sir that ever Country call'd his! . . . i 6 160
Was there ever man had such luck! . . . ii 1 1
Here's a voucher, Stronger than ever law could make . . . ii 2 40
The most coldest that ever turned up ace. . . . ii 3 2
His meanest garment, That ever hath but clipp'd his body, is dearer . ii 3 139
Lives in men's eyes and will to ears and tongues Be theme and hearing ever iii 1 4
And, to kill the marvel, Shall be so ever . . . iii 1 11
With shame—The first that ever touch'd him . . . iii 1 25
Why should excuse be born or e'er begot? . . . iii 2 67
Plenty and peace breeds cowards: hardness ever Of hardiness is mother iii 6 21
Well or ill, I am bound to you.—And shalt be ever . . . iv 2 46
Give me The penitent instrument to pick that bolt, Then, free for ever! v 4 11
Hath More of thee merited than a band of Clotens Had ever scar for . v 5 305
Did you e'er meet?—Ay, my good lord.—And at first meeting loved . v 5 378
Thou art my brother; so we'll hold thee ever . . . v 5 399
The bracelet of the truest princess That ever swore her faith . . v 5 417
As from thence Sorrow were ever razed . . . *Pericles* i 1 17

Ever. And if that ever my low fortune's better, I'll pay your bounties *Pericles* ii 1 148
When peers thus knit, a kingdom ever stands ii 4 58
I hold it ever, Virtue and cunning were endowments greater Than nobleness and riches iii 2 26
A delicate odour.—As ever hit my nostril iii 2 62
Here I give to understand, If e'er this coffin drive a-land iii 2 69
The heavens, Through you, increase our wonder and set up Your fame for ever iii 2 98
It is said For certain in our story, she Would ever with Marina be iv Gower 20
Nurses are not the fates, To foster it, nor ever to preserve iv 3 15
To such proceeding Who ever but his approbation added iv 3 26
But to have divinity preached there! did you ever dream of such a thing? iv 5 5
But I am out of the road of rutting for ever iv 5 10
Marry, hang her up for ever! iv 6 146
This is the rarest dream that e'er dull sleep Did mock sad fools withal v 1 163
For truth can never be confirm'd enough, Though doubts did ever sleep v 1 204
Ever a son. Has the old man e'er a son, sir? *W. Tale* iv 4 810
Ever after. Whose influence If now I court not but omit, my fortunes Will ever after droop *Tempest* i 2 184
But when you find him out, you have him ever after *All's Well* iii 6 101
And his tongue Sounds ever after as a sullen bell 2 *Hen. IV.* i 1 102
Ever again. If e'er again I meet him beard to beard, He's mine, or I am his *Coriolanus* i 10 11
Ever among. So merrily, And ever among so merrily 2 *Hen. IV.* v 3 23
Ever and a day. For ever and a day.—Say 'a day,' without the 'ever' *As Y. Like It* iv 1 145
I have no more to say, But bid Bianca farewell for ever and a day *T. of S.* iv 4 97
Ever and anon they made a doubt *L. L. Lost* v 2 101
A pouncet-box, which ever and anon He gave his nose 1 *Hen. IV.* i 3 38
Ever angry. Penetrate the breasts Of ever angry bears *Tempest* i 2 289
'Ira furor brevis est;' but yond man is ever angry *T. of Athens* i 2 29
Ever art. O night, which ever art when day is not! *M. N. Dream* v 1 172
Ever at the best. How fare you?—Ever at the best, hearing well of your lordship *T. of Athens* iii 6 29
Ever been. Have you ever been at Pisa?—Ay, sir *T. of Shrew* iv 2 93
As you have ever been my father's honour'd friend *W. Tale* iv 4 504
For though mine enemy thou hast ever been, High sparks of honour in thee have I seen *Richard II.* v 6 28
One that hath ever been God's enemy *Richard III.* v 3 252
Whose friend in justice thou hast ever been *T. Andron.* i 1 180
Ever before. I see there's mettle in thee, and even from this instant do build on thee a better opinion than ever before *Othello* iv 2 209
Ever beloved and loving may his rule be! *Hen. VIII.* ii 1 92
Ever better. Making you ever better than his praise 1 *Hen. IV.* v 2 59
Ever-burning. And be my heart an ever-burning hell! *T. Andron.* iii 1 243
Witness, you ever-burning lights above, You elements *Othello* iii 3 463
Ever common. 'Tis ever common That men are merriest when they are from home *Hen. V.* i 2 271
Ever dancing. The emptier ever dancing in the air *Richard II.* iv 1 186
Ever dear. If thy sons were ever dear to thee, O, think my son to be as dear to me! *T. Andron.* i 1 107
Ever did. Thus ever did rebellion find rebuke 1 *Hen. IV.* v 5 1
Nor ever heard, nor ever did suspect *Othello* iv 2 2
Or that I do not yet, and ever did, And ever will—though he do shake me off To beggarly divorcement—love him dearly iv 2 156
Ever do. That you might ever do Nothing but that *W. Tale* iv 4 141
How does his highness?—Madam, in good health.—So may he ever do! *Hen. VIII.* iv 2 125
Ever double. And be ever double Both in his words and meaning iv 2 38
Ever-esteemed. As my ever-esteemed duty pricks me on *L. L. Lost* i 1 268
Ever fair. But grace, being the soul of your complexion, shall keep the body of it ever fair *Meas. for Meas.* iii 1 188
She that was ever fair and never proud *Othello* ii 1 149
Ever-fixed. And quench the guards of the ever-fixed pole ii 1 15
Ever fools. Yet come a little,—Wishers were ever fools *Ant. and Cleo.* iv 15 37
Ever forward—In celebration of this day with shows *Hen. VIII.* iv 1 9
Ever free. Have I been ever free, and must my house Be my retentive enemy, my gaol? *T. of Athens* iii 4 81
Ever 'gainst that season comes Wherein our Saviour's birth is celebrated, The bird of dawning singeth all night long *Hamlet* i 1 158
Ever-gentle. My ever-gentle cousin, welcome hither *Macbeth* iv 3 161
You ever-gentle gods, take my breath from me *Lear* iv 6 221
Ever good. You were ever good at sudden commendations *Hen. VIII.* v 3 122
Ever had. Nor ever had one penny bribe from France 2 *Hen. VI.* iii 1 109
Ever happy. Send prosperous life, long, and ever happy! *Hen. VIII.* v 5 2
Ever-harmless. Sedged crowns and ever-harmless looks *Tempest* iv 1 129
Ever has. My loyalty, Which ever has and ever shall be growing *Hen. VIII.* iii 2 178
Ever have. Because we ever have been near the king *Richard II.* ii 2 134
Good wishes, praise and prayers Shall Suffolk ever have of Margaret 1 *Hen. VI.* v 3 174
Or ever Have to you . . . spake one the least word *Hen. VIII.* ii 4 151
You ever Have wish'd the sleeping of this business ii 4 162
What ever have been thought on in this state, That could be brought to bodily act ere Rome Had circumvention? *Coriolanus* i 2 5
No man that's born of woman Shall e'er have power upon thee *Macbeth* v 3 7
Would ever have, to incur a general mock, Run from her guardage *Othello* i 2 69
'Tis known, I ever Have studied physic *Pericles* iii 2 31
Ever hear. Did you ever hear the like? *Mer. Wives* ii 1 70; *Pericles* iv 5 1
What vane? what weathercock? did you ever hear better? *L. L. Lost* iv 1 97
For aught that I could ever read, Could ever hear by tale or history *M. N. Dream* i 1 133
Did you ever hear such railing? *As Y. Like It* iv 3 46
What have we done? Didst ever hear a man so penitent? 2 *Hen. VI.* iii 2 4
Ever heard. O, excellent device! was there ever heard a better? *T. G. of Ver.* ii 1 145
Was ever heard the like? *T. Andron.* ii 3 276
You have seen nothing then?—Nor ever heard, nor ever did suspect *Oth.* iv 2 2
Ever I heard. Such a dependency of thing on thing, As e'er I heard in madness *Meas. for Meas.* v 1 63
Not so well as I looked for, but the best that ever I heard *L. L. Lost* i 1 283
It is the wittiest partition that ever I heard discourse *M. N. Dream* v 1 168
It is the first time that ever I heard breaking of ribs was sport for ladies.—Or I, I promise thee *As Y. Like It* i 2 146
In the most bitter touch of sorrow that e'er I heard *All's Well* i 3 122
Here is the strangest controversy . . . That e'er I heard *K. John* i 1 46
And still run and roared, as ever I heard bull-calf 1 *Hen. IV.* ii 4 287
This is the strangest tale that ever I heard v 4 158
The most complete champion that ever I heard! 2 *Hen. VI.* iv 10 59
The noblest hateful love that e'er I heard of *Troi. and Cres.* iv 1 33
Ever I looked on. This is a strange thing as e'er I look'd on *Tempest* v 1 289
In mine eye she is the sweetest lady that ever I looked on *Much Ado* i 1 190
What fellow's this?—A strange one as ever I looked on *Coriolanus* iv 5 21
Ever I saw. This Is the third man that e'er I saw, the first That e'er I sigh'd for *Tempest* i 2 445
The very best at a beast, my lord, that e'er I saw *M. N. Dream* v 1 233
Fairer than ever I saw her look, or any woman else *Troi. and Cres.* i 1 33
The dismall'st day is this that e'er I saw *T. Andron.* i 1 384
Ever I see. As like one of these harlotry players as ever I see! 1 *Hen. IV.* ii 4 437
Ever jealous. They are not ever jealous for the cause, But jealous for they are jealous *Othello* iii 4 160
Ever knew. That she was never yet that ever knew Love got so sweet as when desire did sue *Troi. and Cres.* i 2 316
Who ever knew the heavens menace so? *J. Cæsar* i 3 44
Ever know. If I may ever know thou dost but sigh *W. Tale* iv 4 438
What man didst thou ever know unthrift that was beloved after his means?—Who, without those means thou talkest of, didst thou ever know beloved? *T. of Athens* iv 3 311
Ever known. Was ever known so great and little loss? *Hen. V.* iv 8 115
Welcome: pray you, Be ever known to patience *Ant. and Cleo.* iii 6 98
Ever like. But if thy love were ever like to mine *As Y. Like It* ii 4 28
Ever lived. The covert'st shelter'd traitor That ever lived *Richard III.* iii 5 34
The wofull'st man that ever lived in Rome *T. Andron.* iii 1 290
The noblest man That ever lived in the tide of times *J. Cæsar* iii 1 257
Ever living. That ever living man of memory 1 *Hen. VI.* iv 3 51
Ever looked on. The sweetest face I ever look'd on *Hen. VIII.* iv 1 43
I never Did see man die! scarce ever look'd on blood! *Cymbeline* iv 4 36
Ever loved. I have ever loved the life removed *Meas. for Meas.* i 3 8
Who ever loved that loved not at first sight? *As Y. Like It* iii 5 83
As much as child e'er loved, or father found *Lear* i 1 60
Ever May. Love, whose month is ever May *L. L. Lost* iv 3 102
Ever merry. Against ill chances men are ever merry 2 *Hen. IV.* iv 2 81
Ever more. Nor ever more Upon this business my appearance make *Hen. VIII.* ii 4 131
Ever near. Who's gone this morning?—Who! One ever near thee *Ant. and Cleo.* iv 5 7
Ever note, Lucilius, When love begins to sicken and decay, It useth an enforced ceremony *J. Cæsar* iv 2 19
Ever parted. That man, how dearly ever parted, How much in having, or without or in, Cannot make boast to have that which he hath *Troi. and Cres.* iii 3 96
Ever precise. He was ever precise in promise-keeping *Meas. for Meas.* i 2 76
Ever-preserved. By the obligation of our ever-preserved love *Hamlet* ii 2 296
Ever ranking Himself with princes *Hen. VIII.* iv 2 34
Ever right.—Menenius ever, ever *Coriolanus* ii 1 208
Ever royal. The king, my ever royal master *Hen. VIII.* iii 2 273
Ever running. And follows so the ever-running year *Hen. V.* iv 1 293
Ever sad. She is never sad but when she sleeps, and not ever sad then *Much Ado* ii 1 359
Ever said. Have I not ever said How that ambitious Constance would not cease? *K. John* i 1 31
O God! they did me too much injury That ever said I hearken'd for your death 1 *Hen. IV.* v 4 52
I ever said we were i' the wrong when we banished him *Coriolanus* iv 6 155
Ever saw. A thing divine, for nothing natural I ever saw so noble *Tempest* i 2 419
The first time that I ever saw him Methought he was a brother *As Y. L. It* v 4 28
Such . . . men as these Which never were nor no man ever saw *T. of S.* Ind. 2 98
Who ever saw the like? what men have I! 1 *Hen. VI.* i 2 22
Do you know a man if you see him?—Ay, if I ever saw him before and knew him *Troi. and Cres.* i 2 68
Ever see. Would I might But ever see that man! *Tempest* i 2 169
Didst thou ever see me do such a trick? *T. G. of Ver.* iv 4 42
Didst ever see the like?—He kills her in her own humour *T. of Shrew* iv 1 182
Whether I shall ever see thee again or no, there is nobody cares 2 *Hen. IV.* ii 4 72
We Have no such daughter, nor shall ever see That face of hers again *Lear* i 1 266
Ever seen. Was ever seen An emperor in Rome thus overborne? *T. An.* iv 4 1
Ever sending. He's ever sending: how shall I thank him? *T. of Athens* iii 2 36
Ever shall. The issue there create Ever shall be fortunate *M. N. Dream* v 1 413
And the owner of it blest Ever shall in safety rest v 1 427
And ever shall With true observance seek to eke out that *All's Well* ii 5 78
My loyalty, Which ever has and ever shall be growing *Hen. VIII.* iii 2 178
Not the imperious show Of the full-fortuned Cæsar ever shall Be brooch'd with me *Ant. and Cleo.* iv 15 24
Ever since. How long hath she been deformed?—Ever since you loved her.—I have loved her ever since I saw her *T. G. of Ver.* ii 1 71
How long have you professed apprehension?—Ever since you left it *M. Ado* iii 4 69
I have brought him up ever since he was three years old *T. of Shrew* v 1 85
My desires, like fell and cruel hounds, E'er since pursue me *T. Night* i 1 23
Twice or thrice a day, ever since the death of Hermione *W. Tale* v 2 115
And e'er since Sits on his horse back at mine hostess' door *K. John* ii 1 288
And ever since thou hast blushed extempore 1 *Hen. IV* ii 4 347
Which ever since hath kept my eyes from rest *Richard III.* iv 1 82
And ever since a fresh admirer Of what I saw there *Hen. VIII.* i 1 3
Shame whereof hath ever since kept Hector fasting and waking *Tr. and Cr.* i 2 36
And my true lip Hath virgin'd it e'er since *Coriolanus* v 3 48
Ever since thou madest thy daughters thy mother *Lear* i 4 187
I have served you ever since I was a child iii 7 73
Ever so. The fraud of men was ever so, Since summer first was leavy *Much Ado* ii 3 74
Ever soft. Her voice was ever soft, Gentle, and low *Lear* v 3 272
Ever strong. Her mother, ever strong against that match *Mer. Wives* iv 6 27
Thou ever strong upon the stronger side! *K. John* iii 1 117
Ever suppose. Who would e'er suppose They had such courage? 1 *Hen. VI.* i 2 35
Ever tell. But did you ever tell him she was false?—I did.—You told a lie *Othello* v 2 178
Ever till now, When men were fond, I smiled and wonder'd how *M. for M.* ii 2 186
Ever thick. My sight was ever thick *J. Cæsar* v 3 21
Ever thus. Will it be ever thus? Ungracious wretch! *T. Night* iv 1 51
Ever too hard. He was ever too hard for him *Coriolanus* iv 5 195
Ever trod. For any emperor that ever trod on neat's-leather *Tempest* ii 2 73
As proper men as ever trod upon neat's leather *J. Cæsar* i 1 29
Ever true. So shall all the couples three Ever true in loving be *M. N. D.* v 1 415
Ever-valiant. Archibald, That ever-valiant and approved Scot 1 *Hen. IV.* i 1 54
Ever virtuous. Your father was ever virtuous *Mer. of Venice* i 2 30
Ever was. Cyprus black as e'er was crow *W. Tale* iv 4 221
A statelier pyramis to her I'll rear Than Rhodope's or Memphis' ever was: In memory of her when she is dead 1 *Hen. VI.* i 6 22
The rudeliest welcome to this world That ever was prince's child *Pericles* iii 1 31
Ever was heard. The great'st infection That e'er was heard or read! *W. T.* i 2 424
And the most merciless that e'er was heard of! *Richard III.* i 3 184

Ever was known. The most dangerous piece of lechery that ever was known *Much Ado* iii 3 180
Ever welcome. Best of comfort; And ever welcome to us *Ant. and Cleo.* iii 6 90
Ever were. But, if there be, or ever were, one such, It's past the size of dreaming v 2 96
Good phrases are surely, and ever were, very commendable 2 *Hen. IV.* iii 2 77
Ever witness for him Those twins of learning that he raised! *Hen. VIII.* iv 2 57
Ever yet. A rashness that I ever yet have shunn'd *T. G. of Ver.* iii 1 30
Any madness I ever yet beheld seemed but tameness, civility and patience, to this his distemper *Mer. Wives* iv 2 27
What fine chisel Could ever yet cut breath? *W. Tale* v 3 79
When ever yet was your appeal denied? 2 *Hen. IV.* iv 1 88
The most arch act of piteous massacre That ever yet this land was guilty of *Richard III.* iv 3 3
A woman's heart; which ever yet Affected eminence, wealth *Hen. VIII.* ii 3 28
You speak not like yourself; who ever yet Have stood to charity ii 4 85
The willing'st sin I ever yet committed May be absolved in English iii 1 49
Ten thousand worse than ever yet I did Would I perform *T. Andron.* v 3 187
O melancholy! Who ever yet could sound thy bottom? *Cymbeline* iv 2 204
Ever you saw. Is at most odds with his own gravity and patience that ever you saw *Mer. Wives* iii 1 55
Ever young, fresh, loved and delicate wooer [gold] *T. of Athens* iv 3 385
Everlasting. Hath threatened to put me into everlasting liberty *M. Wives* iii 3 31
Where you shall be an everlasting leiger *Meas. for Meas.* iii 1 59
A devil in an everlasting garment hath him *Com. of Errors* iv 2 33
Thou wilt be condemned into everlasting redemption for this *Much Ado* iv 2 59
For everlasting bond of fellowship *M. N. Dream* i 1 85
He hath incurred the everlasting displeasure of the king *All's Well* iv 3 11
To their everlasting residence *K. John* ii 1 284
On that altar where we swore to you Dear amity and everlasting love v 4 20
Thou art a perpetual triumph, an everlasting bonfire-light! 1 *Hen. IV.* iii 3 47
Reproach and everlasting shame Sits mocking in our plumes *Hen. V.* iv 5 4
To heaven?—The treasury of everlasting joy 2 *Hen. VI.* ii 1 18
Then, heaven, set ope thy everlasting gates, To entertain my vows! iv 9 13
By all the everlasting gods, I'll go! *Troi. and Cres.* v 3 5
The judges have pronounced My everlasting doom of banishment *T. An.* iii 1 51
Would I were a devil, To live and burn in everlasting fire! v 1 148
O, so light a foot Will ne'er wear out the everlasting flint *Rom. and Jul.* ii 6 17
Here Will I set up my everlasting rest v 3 110
Timon hath made his everlasting mansion Upon the beached verge of the salt flood *T. of Athens* v 1 218
And whether we shall meet again I know not. Therefore our everlasting farewell take *J. Cæsar* v 1 116
That go the primrose way to the everlasting bonfire *Macbeth* ii 3 22
That the Everlasting had not fix'd His canon 'gainst self-slaughter! *Ham.* i 2 131
Everlastingly. And make rough winter everlastingly *T. G. of Ver.* ii 4 163
I do bequeath my faithful services And true subjection everlastingly *K. John* v 7 105
I'll hate him everlastingly That bids me be of comfort any more *Richard II.* iii 2 207
Say, I will love her everlastingly.—But how long shall that title 'ever' last? *Richard III.* iv 4 349
Evermore. So shall I evermore be bound to thee *Mer. Wives* iv 6 54
With loyal blazon, evermore be blest! v 5 68
He hath evermore had the liberty of the prison *Meas. for Meas.* iv 2 155
Evermore tattling *Much Ado* ii 1 11
So study evermore is overshot *L. L. Lost* i 1 143
I evermore did love you, Hermia, Did ever keep your counsels *M. N. Dr.* iii 2 307
Nor do I wish it, love it, long for it, And will for evermore be true to it iv 1 181
Evermore peep through their eyes And laugh like parrots *Mer. of Venice* i 1 52
And stand indebted, over and above, In love and service to you evermore iv 1 414
Evermore cross'd and cross'd; nothing but cross'd! *T. of Shrew* iv 5 10
To whom I am now in ward, evermore in subjection *All's Well* i 1 6
To rest without a spot for evermore *K. John* v 7 107
Evermore thanks, the exchequer of the poor *Richard II.* ii 3 65
After summer evermore succeeds Barren winter 2 *Hen. VI.* ii 4 2
Evermore they pointed To the good of your most sacred person *Hen. VIII.* iii 2 172
Paris and I kiss evermore for him.—I'll have my kiss, sir *Troi. and Cres.* iv 5 34
Now help, or woe betide thee evermore! *T. Andron.* iv 2 56
Evermore weeping for your cousin's death? *Rom. and Jul.* iii 5 70
What, still in tears? Evermore showering? iii 5 131
Thine evermore, most dear lady, whilst this machine is to him *Hamlet* ii 2 123
'Tis evermore the prologue to his sleep *Othello* iii 3 134
She reserves it evermore about her To kiss and talk to iii 3 295
So, on your patience evermore attending, New joy wait on you! *Per.* v 3 Gower 100
Every. I'll show thee every fertile inch o' th' island *Tempest* ii 2 152
Of every These happen'd accidents v 1 249
Where Every third thought shall be my grave v 1 311
Engross'd opportunities to meet her; fee'd every slight occasion *M. Wives* ii 2 204
Strew good luck, ouphes, on every sacred room v 5 61
Look you scour With juice of balm and every precious flower v 5 66
Every pelting, petty officer Would use his heaven for thunder *M. for M.* ii 2 112
Every true man's apparel fits your thief iv 2 46
We must follow the leaders.—In every good thing *Much Ado* ii 1 158
Why, doth not every earthly thing Cry shame upon her? iv 1 122
Every lovely organ of her life Shall come apparell'd in more precious habit iv 1 228
That give a name to every fixed star *L. L. Lost* i 1 89
As the eye doth roll To every varied object in his glance v 2 775
Have every pelting river made so proud *M. N. Dream* ii 1 91
And when she weeps, weeps every little flower iii 1 204
Abominable fellows and betray themselves to every modern censure *As Y. Like It* iv 1 6
Every of this happy number v 4 178
An we might have a good woman born but one every blazing star *All's W.* i 3 91
Journeys end in lovers meeting, Every wise man's son doth know *T. N.* ii 3 45
As every present time doth boast itself Above a better gone *W. Tale* v 1 96
Every tedious stride I make Will but remember me *Richard II.* i 3 268
And darts his light through every guilty hole iii 2 43
And stand the push Of every beardless vain comparative 1 *Hen. IV.* iii 2 67
And every third word a lie, duer paid to the hearer 2 *Hen. IV.* iii 2 329
Every slight and false-derived cause, Yea, every idle, nice and wanton reason Shall to the king taste of this action iv 1 190
Was in the mouth of every sucking babe 1 *Hen. VI.* iii 1 197
And a pointing-stock To every idle rascal follower 2 *Hen. VI.* ii 4 47
For where thou art, there is the world itself, With every several pleasure iii 2 363
As every loyal subject ought to do 3 *Hen. VI.* iv 7 44
A garish flag, To be the aim of every dangerous shot *Richard III.* iv 4 90
That honour every good tongue blesses *Hen. VIII.* iii 1 55
Every. Every tithe soul, 'mongst many thousand dismes *T. and C.* ii 2 19
And wide unclasp the tables of their thoughts To every ticklish reader! iv 5 61
The fall of every Phrygian stone will cost A drop of Grecian blood iv 5 223
I know the sound of Marcius' tongue From every meaner man *Coriolanus* i 6 27
Let every feeble rumour shake your hearts! iii 3 125
Examine every married lineament *Rom. and Jul.* i 3 83
Signify from time to time Every good hap to you that chances here iii 3 171
To stale with ordinary oaths my love To every new protester *J. Cæsar* i 2 74
Every one doth wish You had but that opinion of yourself Which every noble Roman bears of you ii 1 93
To every Roman citizen he gives, To every several man, seventy five drachmas iii 2 246
It is not meet That every nice offence should bear his comment iv 3 8
Every inordinate cup is unblessed and the ingredient is a devil *Othello* ii 3 310
Think every bearded fellow that's but yoked May draw with you iv 1 67
And put in every honest hand a whip To lash the rascals iv 2 142
I am not valiant neither, But every puny whipster gets my sword v 2 244
If every of your wishes had a womb, And fertile every wish *Ant. and Cleo.* i 2 38
Every good servant does not all commands *Cymbeline* v 1 6
Every acre. Search every acre in the high-grown field *Lear* iv 4 7
Every act. Though I am bound to every act of duty, I am not bound to that all slaves are free to *Othello* iii 3 134
Every action that hath gone before, Whereof we have record, trial did draw Bias and thwart *Troi. and Cres.* i 3 13
In my every action to be guided by others' experiences *Cymbeline* i 4 48
Every article. Hast thou, spirit, Perform'd to point the tempest that I bade thee?—To every article *Tempest* i 2 195
The king hath granted every article: His daughter first *Hen. V.* v 2 360
Every bondman. So every bondman in his own hand bears The power to cancel his captivity *J. Cæsar* i 3 101
Every borough. Proclaim'd In every borough as we pass along 3 *Hen. VI.* ii 1 195
Every braggart shall be found an ass *All's Well* iv 3 372
Every brain. The very place puts toys of desperation, Without more motive, into every brain *Hamlet* i 4 76
Every branch. In every branch truly demonstrative *Hen. V.* ii 4 89
Every breath. Even for whom my life Is every breath a death *Cymbeline* v 1 27
Every bush. The bird that hath been limed in a bush, With trembling wings misdoubteth every bush 3 *Hen. VI.* v 6 14
The birds chant melody on every bush *T. Andron.* ii 3 12
Every cabin. In every cabin I flamed amazement *Tempest* i 2 197
Every case. When every case in law is right; No squire in debt *Lear* iii 2 85
Every cat and dog And little mouse, every unworthy thing *Rom. and Jul.* iii 3 30
Every churl. Good meat, sir, is common; that every churl affords *Com. of Errors* iii 1 24
Every circumstance. If your grace mark every circumstance 1 *Hen. VI.* iii 1 153
Every cloud. For every cloud engenders not a storm 3 *Hen. VI.* v 3 13
Every coast. The four winds blow in from every coast Renowned suitors *Mer. of Venice* i 1 168
Every coistrel. Thou art the damned doorkeeper to every Coistrel *Per.* iv 6 175
Every companion. It is not fit your lordship should undertake every companion that you give offence to *Cymbeline* ii 1 29
Every corner. And at every corner have them kiss 2 *Hen. VI.* iv 7 145
Every country. Have I sought every country far and near? 1 *Hen. VI.* v 4 3
Every county. Our strength will be augmented In every county as we go along 3 *Hen. VI.* v 3 23
To every county Where this is question'd send our letters *Hen. VIII.* i 2 98
Every course. Here at more leisure may your highness read, With every course in his particular 2 *Hen. IV.* iv 4 90
Every cowslip. And hang a pearl in every cowslip's ear *M. N. Dream* ii 1 15
Every creature. Created Of every creature's best *Tempest* iii 1 48
Every cubit. A space whose every cubit Seems to cry out ii 1 257
Every danger. Daring an opposite to every danger *Richard III.* iv 4 3
Every day some sailor's wife, The masters of some merchant and the merchant Have just our theme of woe *Tempest* ii 1 4
Gentlemen That every day with parle encounter me *T. G. of Ver.* i 2 5
This news is old enough, yet it is every day's news *Meas. for Meas.* iii 2 244
Your grace is too costly to wear every day *Much Ado* ii 1 342
When are you married, madam?—Why, every day, to-morrow iii 1 101
And one day in a week to touch no food And but one meal on every day beside *L. L. Lost* i 1 40
Many young gentlemen flock to him every day *As Y. Like It* i 1 124
Thus men may grow wiser every day i 2 145
And I set him every day to woo me iii 2 429
Call me Rosalind and come every day to my cote and woo me iii 2 447
Hearing how that every day Men of great worth resorted to this forest v 4 160
My business asketh haste, And every day I cannot come to woo *T. of Shr.* ii 1 116
My father is here look'd for every day iv 2 116
For the rain it raineth every day *T. Night* v 1 401; *Lear* iii 2 77
That's all one, our play is done, And we'll strive to please you every day *T. Night* v 1 417
That every day under his household roof Did keep ten thousand men *Richard II.* iv 1 282
I every day expect an embassage From my Redeemer to redeem me *Richard III.* ii 1 3
Every day It would infect his speech *Hen. VIII.* i 2 132
You may have every day enough of Hector *Troi. and Cres.* iv 5 263
I must hear from thee every day in the hour *Rom. and Jul.* iii 5 44
The enemy increaseth every day *J. Cæsar* iv 3 216
Your pains Are register'd where every day I turn The leaf to read them *Macbeth* i 3 151
Oftener upon her knees than on her feet, Died every day she lived iv 3 111
Every day thou daffest me with some device *Othello* iv 2 176
He shall have every day a several greeting *Ant. and Cleo.* i 5 77
And every day that comes comes to decay A day's work in him *Cymbeline* i 5 56
They took thee for their mother, And every day do honour to her grave iii 3 105
We every day Expect him here *Pericles* iii 1 34
Every dram. I have not, my lord, deserved it.—Yes, good faith, every dram of it *All's Well* ii 3 233
Ay, every dram of woman's flesh is false, If she be *W. Tale* ii 1 138
Every dream. On every dream, Each buzz, each fancy *Lear* i 4 347
Every drop. He'll be hanged yet, Though every drop of water swear against it *Tempest* i 1 62
For every drop of blood was drawn from him There hath at least five Frenchmen died to-night 1 *Hen. VI.* ii 2 8
And every drop cries vengeance for his death 3 *Hen. VI.* i 4 148
When every drop of blood That every Roman bears, and nobly bears, Is guilty of a several bastardy *J. Cæsar* ii 1 136
Every ducat. If every ducat in six thousand ducats Were in six parts and every part a ducat, I would not draw them *Mer. of Venice* iv 1 85
Every ear. Would pluck reproof and rebuke from every ear *Coriolanus* ii 2 38

Every ear. Sweet varied notes, enchanting every ear! *T. Andron.* iii 1 86
Every elf and fairy sprite Hop as light as bird from brier *M. N. Dream* v 1 400
Every exercise. In eye of every exercise Worthy his youth *T. G. of Ver.* i 3 32
Every eye. Let every eye negotiate for itself And trust no agent *M. Ado* ii 1 185
My thoughts I'll character; That every eye which in this forest looks
Shall see thy virtue witness'd every where *As Y. Like It* iii 2 7
If my actions Were tried by every tongue, every eye saw 'em *Hen. VIII.* iii 1 35
Shall blow the horrid deed in every eye *Macbeth* i 7 24
Every eyeball. Invisible To every eyeball else *Tempest* i 2 303
Every fairy. With this field-dew consecrate, Every fairy take his gait
M. N. Dream v 1 423
Every fault. Why, every fault's condemn'd ere it be done *Meas. for Meas.* ii 2 38
Every feather. You boggle shrewdly, every feather starts you *All's Well* v 3 232
Like the haggard, check at every feather That comes before his eye *T. N.* iii 1 71
When every feather sticks in his own wing, Lord Timon will be left a
naked gull, Which flashes now a phœnix *T. of Athens* ii 1 30
Every figure. Our captain hath in every figure skill v 3 7
Every finger. You may tell every finger I have with my ribs *Mer. of Ven.* ii 2 114
Every flatterer. And just of the same piece Is every flatterer's spirit
T. of Athens iii 2 72
Every flaw. Standing every flaw, And saving those that eye thee *Coriol.* v 3 75
Every flower. Culling from every flower The virtuous sweets 2 *Hen. IV.* iv 5 75
Where every flower Did, as a prophet, weep what it foresaw *Tr. and Cr.* i 2 9
Every fool. How every fool can play upon the word! *Mer. of Venice* iii 5 48
Subject to the breath Of every fool *Hen. V.* iv 1 252
Cannot you tell that? every fool can tell that *Hamlet* v 1 159
Every foot. I would give it every foot to have this face *K. John* i 1 146
By the good gods, I'ld with thee every foot *Coriolanus* iv 1 57
Every function. Your brain, and every function of your power *Hen. VIII.* iii 2 187
Every gale. And turn their halcyon beaks With every gale and vary of
their masters *Lear* ii 2 85
Every gash. Every gash was an enemy's grave *Coriolanus* ii 1 171
Thou lay'st in every gash that love hath given me The knife *Tr. and Cr.* i 1 62
Every god. Where every god did seem to set his seal *Hamlet* iii 4 61
Every godfather can give a name *L. L. Lost* i 1 93
Every good. Thou art as opposite to every good As the Antipodes are
unto us 3 *Hen. VI.* i 4 134
Every goose. The nightingale, if she should sing by day, When every
goose is cackling *Mer. of Venice* v 1 105
Every graff. For every graff would send a caterpillar *Pericles* v 1 60
Every grain. Knows almost every grain of Plutus' gold *Troi. and Cres.* iii 3 197
Every grave. On every grave A lying trophy *All's Well* ii 3 145
Every Greek of mettle, let him know, What Troy means fairly *Tr. and Cr.* i 3 258
Every grief. When every grief is entertain'd that's offer'd *Tempest* ii 1 16
Every grise of fortune Is smooth'd by that below *T. of Athens* iv 3 16
Every hair. By my old beard, And every hair that's on't *All's Well* v 3 77
Every hand. If promises be kept on every hand 1 *Hen. IV.* iii 2 168
Before, behind thee and on every hand, Enwheel thee round! *Othello* ii 1 86
Every hearer. Lamented, pitied and excused Of every hearer *Much Ado* iv 1 219
Every hedge. They'll find linen enough on every hedge 1 *Hen. IV.* iv 2 52
Every honour. For every honour sitting on his helm, Would they were
multitudes! iii 2 142
Every horse. Where every horse bears his commanding rein *Richard III.* ii 2 128
Every hour. Sighing every minute and groaning every hour *As Y. L. It* iii 2 321
'Twas pretty, though a plague, To see him every hour *All's Well* i 1 104
And every hour more competitors Flock to their aid *Richard III.* iv 4 506
I should be glad to hear such news as this Once every hour *Hen. VIII.* iii 2 25
Thou grumblest and railest every hour *Troi. and Cres.* ii 1 35
Every hour He flashes into one gross crime or other *Lear* i 3 3
Every hour, Most noble Cæsar, shalt thou have report How 'tis *A. and C.* i 4 34
Mark Antony is every hour in Rome Expected ii 1 29
Every house. At every house I'll call; I may command at most *Othello* ii 1 181
Every inch. For every inch of woman in the world, Ay, every dram of
woman's flesh is false *W. Tale* ii 1 137
Is't not the king?—Ay, every inch a king *Lear* iv 6 109
Every innocent. And the wild dog Shall flesh his tooth on every innocent
2 *Hen. IV.* iv 5 133
Every Jack. Since every Jack became a gentleman, There's many a gentle
person made a Jack *Richard III.* i 3 72
Every Jack-slave hath his bellyful of fighting *Cymbeline* ii 1 22
Every jest. Not a word with him but a jest.—And every jest but a word
L. L. Lost ii 1 216
Every joint. Ay, every joint should seem to curse and ban 2 *Hen. VI.* iii 2 319
Let him die, With every joint a wound, and that to-morrow! *Tr. and Cr.* iv 1 29
Her wanton spirits look out At every joint and motive of her body iv 5 57
Every kennel. Go, hop me over every kennel home *T. of Shrew* iv 3 98
Every kind. With keels of every kind *Ant. and Cleo.* i 4 50
Every knave. Unless a woman should be made an ass and a beast, to
bear every knave's wrong 2 *Hen. IV.* ii 1 41
And suffer every knave to use me at his pleasure? *Rom. and Jul.* ii 4 163
Every lane's end, every shop, church, session, hanging, yields a careful
man work *W. Tale* iv 4 700
Every language. Upon my [Rumour's] tongues continual slanders ride,
The which in every language I pronounce 2 *Hen. IV.* Ind. 7
Every leader to his charge 1 *Hen. IV.* iv 1 118
Every letter he hath writ hath disvouched other *Meas. for Meas.* iv 4 1
Every 'leven. Let me see: every 'leven wether tods; every tod yields
pound and odd shilling *W. Tale* iv 3 33
Every like. That every like is not the same, O Cæsar, The heart of
Brutus yearns to think upon! *J. Cæsar* ii 2 128
Every line. Heart too capable Of every line and trick of his sweet favour
All's Well i 1 107
Every lineament. In every lineament, branch, shape, and form *M. Ado* v 1 14
Every loop. Stop all sight-holes, every loop from whence The eye of
reason may pry in upon us 1 *Hen. IV.* iv 1 71
Every man shift for all the rest *Tempest* v 1 256
So turns she every man the wrong side out *Much Ado* iii 1 68
Even she; Leonato's Hero, your Hero, every man's Hero iii 2 110
For every man with his affects is born, Not by might master'd *L. L. Lost* i 1 152
Peace!—Be to me and every man that dares not fight! v 1 229
Then homeward every man attach the hand Of his fair mistress iv 3 375
Here is the scroll of every man's name, which is thought fit *M. N. Dream* i 2 4
And the country proverb known, That every man should take his own iii 2 459
Meet presently at the palace; every man look o'er his part iv 2 38
A stage where every man must play a part, And mine a sad one *M. of Ven.* i 1 78
He is every man in no man i 2 64
An envious emulator of every man's good parts *As Y. Like It* i 1 150
Thou art a general offence, and every man should beat thee *All's Well* ii 3 270
There's place and means for every man alive iv 3 375
Most courteous feathers, which bow the head and nod at every man iv 5 112
Every man. Every man that Bolingbroke hath press'd To lift shrewd
steel *Richard II.* iii 2 58
Happy man be his dole, say I: every man to his business 1 *Hen. IV.* ii 2 81
You rogue, they were bound, every man of them ii 4 197
The soul of every man Prophetically doth forethink thy fall iii 2 37
Yea, every man Shall be my friend again and I'll be his v 1 107
Counsel every man The aptest way for safety and revenge 2 *Hen. IV.* i 1 212
It would be every man's thought; and thou art a blessed fellow to think
as every man thinks ii 2 60
Every man must know that, as oft as he has occasion to name himself ii 2 118
Let every man now task his thought *Hen. V.* i 2 309
And honour's thought Reigns solely in the breast of every man ii Prol. 4
Every man that dies ill, the ill upon his own head iv 1 197
Sell every man his life as dear as mine, And they shall find dear deer of
us, my friends 1 *Hen. VI.* iv 2 53
Every man that means to live well endeavours to trust to himself
Richard III. i 4 147
Every man's conscience is a thousand swords v 2 17
Go, gentlemen, every man unto his charge v 3 307
Every man that stood Show'd like a mine *Hen. VIII.* i 1 21
Every man, After the hideous storm that follow'd, was A thing inspired i 1 89
In her days every man shall eat in safety, Under his own vine v 5 34
An odd man, lady! every man is odd *Troi. and Cres.* iv 5 42
Life every man holds dear; but the brave man Holds honour far more
precious-dear than life v 3 27
That would depopulate the city and Be every man himself *Coriolanus* iii 1 265
Enter; and no sooner in, But every man betake him to his legs *R. and J.* i 4 34
Every man has his fault, and honesty is his *T. of Athens* iii 1 29
I am sick of that grief too, as I understand how all things go.—Every
man here's so iii 6 21
Yes, every man of them, and no man here But honours you *J. Cæsar* ii 1 90
Break off betimes, And every man hence to his idle bed ii 1 117
An effect of humour, Which sometime hath his hour with every man ii 1 251
What, shall we forth?—Ay, every man away: Brutus shall lead ii 1 119
Answer every man directly.—Ay, and briefly iii 3 10
Then, to answer every man directly and briefly, wisely and truly iii 3 16
Let every man be master of his time Till seven at night *Macbeth* iii 1 41
Give every man thy ear, but few thy voice *Hamlet* i 3 68
For every man has business and desire, Such as it is i 5 130
Use every man after his desert, and who should 'scape whipping? ii 2 555
Every man put himself into triumph; some to dance *Othello* ii 2 4
The boy shall sing; The holding every man shall bear as loud As his
strong sides can volley *Ant. and Cleo.* ii 7 117
It would make any man cold to lose.—But not every man patient *Cymb.* ii 3 5
Every market-town. Let them be whipped through every market-town
2 *Hen. VI.* ii 1 158
Every measure. My life will be too short, And every measure fail me *Lear* iv 7 3
Every mess. Our feasts In every mess have folly *W. Tale* iv 4 11
Every minute. Sighing every minute and groaning every hour
As Y. Like It iii 2 321
Every minute now Should be the father of some stratagem 2 *Hen. IV.* i 1 7
The examples Of every minute's instance, present now iv 1 83
Wherefore a guard of chosen shot I had That walk'd about me every
minute while 1 *Hen. VI.* i 4 54
His confessor; who fed him every minute With words of sovereignty
Hen. VIII. i 2 149
Trust ye? With every minute you do change a mind *Coriolanus* i 1 186
That every minute of his being thrusts Against my near'st of life *Macbeth* iii 1 117
For every minute is expectancy Of more arrivance *Othello* ii 1 41
Every month. He hath every month a new sworn brother *Much Ado* i 1 72
Every morning. For the which blessing I am at him upon my knees
every morning and evening ii 1 31
To be whipped at the high cross every morning *T. of Shrew* i 1 137
Every mote. Wash every mote out of his conscience *Hen. V.* iv 1 189
Every mother breeds not sons alike *T. Andron.* ii 3 146
Every mother's son. That would hang us, every mother's son *M. N. Dr.* i 2 80
Come, sit down, every mother's son, and rehearse your parts iii 1 75
Every motion. Whose every motion Was timed with dying cries *Coriol.* ii 2 113
Every nation. If we had of every nation a traveller, we should lodge
them with this sign *Pericles* iv 2 123
Every night he comes With musics of all sorts *All's Well* iii 7 39
Every nod. Ready, with every nod, to tumble down *Richard III.* iii 4 102
Every noise. Bid every noise be still: peace yet again! *J. Cæsar* i 2 14
How is't with me, when every noise appals me? *Macbeth* ii 2 58
Every object. For every object that the one doth catch The other turns
to a mirth-moving jest *L. L. Lost* ii 1 70
Every object that might make me fear Misfortune to my ventures
Mer. of Venice i 1 20
Every offence is not a hate at first iv 1 68
Every office. A cold world, Curtis, in every office but thine *T. of Shrew* iv 1 37
Every officer. And every officer his wedding-garment on iv 1 50
Every old man. Care keeps his watch in every old man's eye *R. and J.* ii 3 35
Every one. And these fresh nymphs encounter every one *Tempest* iv 1 137
Every one go home, And laugh this sport o'er by a country fire *M. Wives* v 5 255
If every one knows us and we know none, 'Tis time, I think, to trudge,
pack and be gone *Com. of Errors* iii 2 157
And every one doth call me by my name iv 3 3
Thus goes every one to the world but I, and I am sunburnt *Much Ado* ii 1 331
Every one can master a grief but he that has it iii 2 28
God send every one their heart's desire! iii 4 60
Are they all in love, That every one her own hath garnished? *L. L. Lost* ii 1 78
Break the neck of the wax, and every one give ear iv 1 59
Every one his love-feat will advance Unto his several mistress v 2 123
The gallants shall be task'd; For, ladies, we will every one be mask'd v 2 127
This is the flower that smiles on every one, To show his teeth v 2 331
It is vara fine, For every one pursents three v 2 488
And so every one according to his cue *M. N. Dream* iii 1 78
Every one lets forth his sprite, In the church-way paths to glide v 1 388
To these injunctions every one doth swear That comes to hazard
Mer. of Venice ii 9 17
Every one fault seeming monstrous till his fellow-fault came *As Y. L. It* iii 2 372
That blind rascally boy that abuses every one's eyes iv 1 219
Give them friendly welcome every one *T. of Shrew* Ind. 1 103
Therefore we must every one be a man of his own fancy *All's Well* iv 1 19
Every one of these letters are in my name *T. Night* ii 5 153
Negligent, foolish and fearful; In every one of these no man is free
W. Tale i 2 251
You precious winners all; your exultation Partake to every one v 3 132
They'll talk of state; for every one doth so Against a change *Richard II.* iii 4 27
You will find it so; I speak no more than every one doth know iii 4 91

Every one. Knocking at the taverns, And asking every one for Sir John Falstaff . . . . *2 Hen. IV.* ii 4 389
Whose guiltless drops Are every one a woe, a sore complaint *Hen. V.* i 2 26
A largess universal like the sun His liberal eye doth give to every one . . . . iv Prol. 44
That every one may pare his nails with a wooden dagger . . . iv 4 76
Fairly met: So are you, princes English, every one . . . v 2 11
Upon the which, that every one may read, Shall be engraved *1 Hen. VI.* ii 2 14
You fled for vantage, every one will swear . . . . . iv 5 28
And, as you please, So let them have their answers every one . v 1 25
Be it in the morn, When every one will give the time of day *2 Hen. VI.* iii 1 14
Every one did threat To-morrow's vengeance on the head of Richard *Richard III.* v 3 205
Lead in your ladies, every one . . . . . . *Hen. VIII.* i 4 103
'Tis thought of every one Coriolanus will carry it . . . *Coriolanus* ii 2 4
Wherein every one of us has a single honour . . . . . ii 3 48
My foes I do repute you every one . . . . . *T. Andron.* i 1 366
Come, come, be every one officious To make this banquet . . . v 2 202
Every one prepare To follow this fair corse unto her grave *Rom. and Jul.* iv 5 92
Every one doth wish You had but that opinion of yourself . *J. Cæsar* ii 1 91
And so good morrow to you every one . . . . . . ii 1 228
The skies are painted with unnumber'd sparks, They are all fire and every one doth shine . . . . iii 1 64
Farewell, every one. Give me the gown . . . . . iv 3 238
And every one did bear Thy praises in his kingdom's great defence *Macb.* i 3 98
Every one According to the gift which bounteous nature Hath in him closed . . . . iii 1 97
I commend your pains; And every one shall share i' the gains . iv 1 40
Every one that does so is a traitor, and must be hanged . . iv 2 49
His liberty is full of threats to all; To you yourself, to us, to every one *Hamlet* iv 1 15
Every one hears that, Which can distinguish sound . . *Lear* iv 6 214
Let it be so. Good night to every one . . . . *Othello* i 3 289
As I draw them up, I'll think them every one an Antony *Ant. and Cleo.* ii 5 14
From every one The best she hath, and she, of all compounded, Outsells them all . . . . *Cymbeline* iii 5 72
Like gods above, Who freely give to every one that comes *Pericles* ii 3 60
And every one with claps can sound, 'Our heir-apparent is a king!' iii Gower 36
Every other. Which warp'd the line of every other favour . *All's Well* v 3 49
Every owner. Who is, if every owner were well placed, Indeed his king *1 Hen. IV.* iv 3 94
Every part. My lips on thy foot, my eyes on thy picture, and my heart on thy every part . . . . *L. L. Lost* iv 1 87
If every ducat in six thousand ducats Were in six parts and every part a ducat, I would not draw them . . . . *Mer. of Venice* iv 1 86
Since all and every part of what we would Doth make a stand *K. John* iv 2 38
And every part about you blasted with antiquity *2 Hen. IV.* i 2 207
'Tis all in every part.—'Tis so, indeed . . . . . . v 5 31
I am so vexed, that every part about me quivers . . *Rom. and Jul.* ii 4 171
Every particle and utensil labelled to my will . . *T. Night* i 5 264
Every passion. For every passion something and for no passion truly any thing . . . . *As Y. Like It* iii 2 433
Smooth every passion That in the natures of their lords rebel . *Lear* ii 2 81
Whose every passion fully strives To make itself, in thee, fair! *A. and C.* i 1 50
Every place. Thy own wish wish I thee in every place! . . *L. L. Lost* ii 1 179
Thou runn'st before me, shifting every place . . *M. N. Dream* iii 2 423
She was here even now; she haunts me in every place . . *Othello* iv 1 137
Every point. He does obey every point of the letter . . *T. Night* iii 2 82
All our service In every point twice done and then done double *Macbeth* i 6 15
Every post. Myself on every post Proclaimed a strumpet . *W. Tale* iii 2 102
Every power. Courses as swift as thought in every power, And gives to every power a double power . . . . . . *L. L. Lost* iv 3 330
Observe how Antony becomes his flaw, And what thou think'st his very action speaks In every power that moves . . *Ant. and Cleo.* iii 12 36
Every prince. So I bequeath a happy peace to you And all good men, as every prince should do . . . . *Pericles* i 1 51
Every purpose. But vows to every purpose must not hold *Troi. and Cres.* v 3 24
That speak'st with every tongue, To every purpose! . . *T. of Athens* iv 3 390
Every putting-by. At every putting-by mine honest neighbours shouted *J. Cæsar* i 2 231
Every realm. They had gather'd a wise council to them Of every realm *Hen. VIII.* ii 4 52
Every reason excites to this, that my lady loves me . . . *T. Night* ii 5 179
Every region near Seem'd all one mutual cry . . *M. N. Dream* iv 1 121
To the English court assemble now, From every region . *2 Hen. IV.* iv 5 123
Notable scorns, That dwell in every region of his face . . *Othello* iv 1 84
Every room Hath blazed with lights and bray'd with minstrelsy *T. of A.* ii 2 169
Every rub. We doubt not now But every rub is smoothed on our way *Hen. V.* ii 2 188
Every sail. I would thou grew'st unto the shores o' the haven, And question'dst every sail . . . . *Cymbeline* i 3 2
Every scope by the immoderate use Turns to restraint . *Meas. for Meas.* i 2 131
Every scruple. For every scruple Of her contaminated carrion weight, A Trojan hath been slain . . . . *Troi. and Cres.* iv 1 70
Every sedge. Giving a gentle kiss to every sedge . . *T. G. of Ver.* ii 7 29
Every sense. A father's curse Pierce every sense about thee! . . *Lear* i 4 323
Every sentence. At every sentence end, Will I Rosalinda write *As Y. Like It* iii 2 144
Every shire. Let there be letters writ to every shire . . *Hen. VIII.* i 2 103
Every side. And stablish quietness on every side . . *1 Hen. VI.* v 1 10
Pry on every side, Tremble and start at wagging of a straw *Richard III.* iii 5 6
Every sin. Smacking of every sin That has a name . . . *Macbeth* iv 3 59
Every sitting. I'll write you down: The which shall point you forth at every sitting What you must say . . . . . *W. Tale* iv 4 572
Every soldier in the wars do as every sick man in his bed . *Hen V.* iv 1 187
Then every soldier kill his prisoners; Give the word through . . iv 6 37
Most worthily, hath caused every soldier to cut his prisoner's throat . iv 7 10
Let every soldier hew him down a bough And bear't before him *Macbeth* v 4 4
Every something, being blent together, Turns to a wild of nothing *Mer. of Venice* iii 2 183
Every sort. With voices and applause of every sort . . *T. Andron.* i 1 230
Every spirit. And bend up every spirit To his full height . *Hen. V.* iii 1 16
So help me every spirit sanctified! . . . . . *Othello* iii 4 126
Every sprite. The quintessence of every sprite . *As Y. Like It* iii 2 147
Every stage. Supplying every stage With an augmented greeting *Ant. and Cleo.* iii 6 54
Every stale. To cast thy wandering eyes on every stale . *T. of Shrew* iii 1 90
Every stamp. 'Tween man and man they weigh not every stamp *Cymb.* v 4 24
Every step. So every step Exampled by the first pace that is sick Of his superior, grows to an envious fever . . . *Troi. and Cres.* i 3 131

Every storm. Left me open, bare For every storm that blows *T. of Athens* iv 3 266
Every strain. And let it answer every strain for strain . *Much Ado* v 1 12
Every street. Our windows are broke down in every street *1 Hen. VI.* iii 1 84
Every stride he makes upon my land Is dangerous treason *Richard II.* iii 3 92
Every subject's duty is the king's; but every subject's soul is his own *Hen. V.* iv 1 186
Every syllable. By every syllable a faithful verity . *Meas. for Meas.* iv 3 131
To make a recordation to my soul Of every syllable . *Troi. and Cres.* v 2 117
Every tale. And every tongue brings in a several tale, And every tale condemns me for a villain . . . . . . *Richard III.* v 3 195
Every tear. Thou shinest in every tear that I do weep . . *L. L. Lost* iv 3 33
Every tempest. If after every tempest come such calms, May the winds blow till they have waken'd death! . . . . . *Othello* ii 1 187
Every ten. In every ten that they make, the devils mar five *Ant. and Cleo.* v 2 278
Every thing. Here is every thing advantageous to life . . *Tempest* ii 1 49
Like a child, That longs for every thing that he can come by *T. G. of Ver.* iii 1 125
Tell him there is measure in every thing . . . . *Much Ado* ii 1 75
She is exceeding wise.—In every thing but in loving Benedick . . ii 3 168
One that hath two gowns and every thing handsome about him . iv 2 88
I see these things with parted eye, When every thing seems double *M. N. Dream* iv 1 195
I will tell you every thing, right as it fell out . . . . . . v 2 31
Sermons in stones and good in every thing . . *As Y. Like It* ii 1 17
Sans teeth, sans eyes, sans taste, sans every thing . . . . ii 7 166
And every thing about you demonstrating a careless desolation . iii 2 399
Every thing I look on seemeth green . . . *T. of Shrew* iv 5 47
In every thing I wait upon his will.—I shall report it so . *All's Well* ii 4 55
Nor believe he can have every thing in him by wearing his apparel neatly iv 3 167
He has every thing that an honest man should not have . . . iv 3 290
Their business might be every thing and their intent every where *T. N.* ii 4 79
I will do everything that thou wilt have me . . . . . . ii 5 195
By maidhood, honour, truth and every thing . . . . . iii 1 162
Why, every thing adheres together . . . . iii 4 86
All is uneven, And every thing is left at six and seven . *Richard II.* ii 2 122
For in every thing the purpose must weigh with the folly . *2 Hen. IV.* ii 2 195
Every thing set off That might so much as think you enemies . iv 1 145
When every thing is ended, then you come . . . . . iv 3 30
And every thing lies level to our wish . . . . . . iv 4 7
Defused attire And every thing that seems unnatural . . *Hen. V.* v 2 62
You shall have pay and every thing you wish . . *2 Hen. VI.* v 1 47
If that be right which Warwick says is right, There is no wrong, but every thing is right . . . . *3 Hen. VI.* ii 2 132
The tract of every thing Would by a good discourser lose some life *Hen. VIII.* i 1 40
Every thing that heard him play, Even the billows of the sea, Hung their heads . . . . iii 1 9
How sleek and wanton Ye appear in every thing may bring my ruin! . iii 2 242
He hath the joints of every thing, but every thing so out of joint that he is a gouty Briareus . . . . *Troi. and Cres.* i 2 28
Every thing includes itself in power, Power into will, will into appetite i 3 119
Bastard in mind, bastard in valour, in every thing illegitimate . v 7 18
Good madam; I will obey you in every thing hereafter . *Coriolanus* i 3 115
Every thing In readiness for Hymenæus stand . . . *T. Andron.* i 1 324
Wherefore look'st thou sad, When every thing doth make a gleeful boast? . . . . ii 3 11
The nurse cursed in the pantry, and every thing in extremity *R. and J.* i 3 102
Every thing is well.—Good night, my lord . . . *J. Cæsar* iv 3 236
Alas, thou hast misconstrued every thing! . . . . . . v 3 84
Bring us word unto Octavius' tent How every thing is chanced . v 4 32
By doing every thing Safe toward your love and honour . *Macbeth* i 4 26
Your vessels and your spells provide, Your charms and every thing beside . . . . iii 5 19
And every thing is bent For England . . . . . *Hamlet* iv 3 47
I'll have him hence to-night: Away! for every thing is seal'd and done iv 3 58
To say 'ay' and 'no' to every thing that I said! . . . *Lear* iv 6 100
They told me I was every thing: 'tis a lie, I am not ague-proof . iv 6 106
In spite of nature, Of years, of country, credit, every thing . *Othello* i 3 97
I'll intermingle every thing he does With Cassio's suit . . . iii 3 25
Whom every thing becomes, to chide, to laugh, To weep *Ant. and Cleo.* i 1 49
With every thing that pretty is, My lady sweet, arise . *Cymbeline* ii 3 28
Every time. He put it by thrice, every time gentler than other *J. Cæsar* i 2 230
Every time Serves for the matter that is then born in't . *Ant. and Cleo.* ii 2 9
Every tomb. The mere word's a slave Debosh'd on every tomb *All's Well* ii 3 145
Every tongue brings in a several tale, And every tale condemns me *Richard III.* v 3 194
These news are every where; every tongue speaks 'em *Hen. VIII.* ii 2 39
If my actions Were tried by every tongue, every eye saw 'em . iii 1 35
She brings news; and every tongue that speaks But Romeo's name speaks heavenly eloquence . . . . . . *Rom. and Jul.* iii 2 32
That speak'st with every tongue, To every purpose! . *T. of Athens* iv 3 389
Every touch. Whose touch, Whose every touch, would force the feeler's soul To the oath of loyalty . . . . *Cymbeline* i 6 101
Every town. 'Tis Hymen peoples every town; High wedlock then be honoured: Honour, high honour and renown, To Hymen, god of every town! . . . . *As Y. Like It* v 4 149
Hearing thy mildness praised in every town, Thy virtues spoke of *T. of Shrew* ii 1 192
Throughout every town Proclaim them traitors . . *2 Hen. VI.* iv 2 186
Every trade. If there be not a conscience to be used in every trade, we shall never prosper . . . . *Pericles* iv 2 12
Every tree. The cuckoo then, on every tree, Mocks married men *L. L. L.* v 2 908
Carve on every tree The fair, the chaste and unexpressive she *As Y. Like It* iii 2 9
Tongues I'll hang on every tree, That shall civil sayings show . . iii 2 135
Why, we take From every tree lop, bark, and part o' the timber *Hen. VIII.* i 2 96
Every trifle. For every trifle are they set upon me . . *Tempest* ii 2 8
His knights grow riotous, and himself upbraids us On every trifle *Lear* i 3 7
Every villain Be call'd Posthumus Leonatus! . . . . *Cymbeline* v 5 223
Every virtue. And her thoughts the king Of every virtue gives renown to men! . . . . *Pericles* i 1 14
Every way; old Windsor way, and every way but the town way *M. Wives* iii 1 6
If he be amazed, he will every way be mock'd . . . . . . v 3 20
If I can cross him any way, I bless myself every way . . *Much Ado* i 3 70
My fortunes every way as fairly rank'd, If not with vantage *M. N. Dream* i 1 101
Such as she is, in beauty, virtue, birth, Is the young Dauphin every way complete . . . . *K. John* ii 1 433
Princely shall be thy usage every way. Rest on my word . *T. Andron.* i 1 266
You wrong me every way; you wrong me, Brutus . . . *J. Cæsar* iv 3 55
Now, whether he kill Cassio, Or Cassio him, or each do kill the other, Every way makes my gain . . . . *Othello* v 1 14

Every where. Ill-faced, worse bodied, shapeless every where . *C. of Er.* iv 2 20
So the boy Love is perjured every where . *M. N. Dream* i 1 241
Thorough flood, thorough fire, I do wander every where . ii 1 6
His bonnet in Germany and his behaviour every where . *Mer. of Venice* i 2 82
My thoughts I'll character; That every eye which in this forest looks Shall see thy virtue witness'd every where . . *As Y. Like It* iii 2 8
Their business might be every thing and their intent every where *T. N.* ii 4 80
Foolery, sir, does walk about the orb like the sun, it shines every where iii 1 44
Nor can there be that deity in my nature, Of here and every where . v 1 235
Let him not come there, To seek out sorrow that dwells every where *Richard II.* i 2 72
But Peace puts forth her olive every where . . . *2 Hen. IV.* iv 4 87
Here, there, and every where, enraged he flew . . *1 Hen. VI.* i 1 124
His dews fall every where.—No doubt he's noble . *Hen. VIII.* i 3 57
'Tis most true These news are every where; every tongue speaks 'em . ii 2 39
I'll kill thee every where, yea, o'er and o'er . *Troi. and Cres.* iv 5 256
Here, there, and every where, he leaves and takes . . v 5 26
Follows me every where, I know not why . . *T. Andron.* iv 1 2
Libelling against the senate, And blazoning our injustice every where . iv 4 18
An extravagant and wheeling stranger Of here and every where . *Othello* i 1 138
Every why. For they say every why hath a wherefore . *Com. of Errors* ii 2 45
Every wind. And flies Of every wind that blows . . *W. Tale* iv 4 552
Every wink of an eye some new grace will be born . . v 2 119
Every wish. If every of your wishes had a womb, And fertile every wish *Ant. and Cleo.* i 2 39
Every word. Who, every word by all my wit being scann'd, Want wit in all one word to understand . . *Com. of Errors* ii 2 152
She speaks poniards, and every word stabs . . *Much Ado* ii 1 255
Here is a letter, lady; The paper as the body of my friend, And every word in it a gaping wound . . *Mer. of Venice* iii 2 268
Let every word weigh heavy of her worth . . *All's Well* iii 4 31
Whose every word deserves To taste of thy most worst . *W. Tale* iii 2 179
I will tell the king all, every word, yea, and his son's pranks too . iv 4 717
Every word you speak in his behalf Is slander to your royal dignity *2 Hen. VI.* iii 2 208
For every word I speak, Ye see, I drink the water of mine eyes *3 Hen. VI.* v 4 74
What he speaks is all in debt; he owes For every word . *T. of Athens* i 2 205
The ratifiers and props of every word . . . *Hamlet* iv 5 105
Every worth. Since every worth in show commends itself . *Pericles* ii 3 6
Every wound. And put a tongue In every wound of Cæsar . *J. Cæsar* iii 2 233
Every wretch, pining and pale before, Beholding him, plucks comfort from his looks . . . . . . *Hen. V.* iv Prol. 41
Evidence. Comes not that blood as modest evidence To witness simple virtue? . . . . *Much Ado* iv 1 38
Thou art too fine in thy evidence; therefore stand aside . *All's Well* v 3 270
And many other evidences proclaim her with all certainty . *W. Tale* v 2 41
From true evidence of good esteem . . *2 Hen. VI.* iii 2 21
I have done those things, Which now bear evidence against my soul *Richard III.* i 4 67
What is my offence? Where are the evidence that do accuse me? . i 4 188
So his peers, upon this evidence, Have found him guilty . *Hen. VIII.* ii 1 26
And we ourselves compell'd, Even to the teeth and forehead of our faults, To give in evidence . . . . . *Hamlet* iii 3 64
Bring in the evidence. Thou robed man of justice, take thy place *Lear* iii 6 37
Forbear; And give true evidence to his love . . *Ant. and Cleo.* i 3 74
It was wise nature's end in the donation, To be his evidence now *Cymb.* v 5 368
Evident. Why, this is evident to any formal capacity . *T. Night* ii 5 128
Your honour and your goodness is so evident . . *W. Tale* ii 2 43
So evident That it will glimmer through a blind man's eye . *1 Hen. VI.* ii 4 23
Hath not a tomb so evident as a chair To extol what it hath done *Coriol.* iv 7 52
We must find An evident calamity, though we had Our wish . . v 3 112
Render to me some corporal sign about her, More evident than this *Cymbeline* ii 4 120
Evil. What I have suffered to bring this woman to evil for your good *Mer. Wives* iii 5 97
No man means evil but the devil, and we shall know him by his horns . v 2 15
Like rats that ravin down their proper bane, A thirsty evil *Meas. for Meas.* i 2 134
Those many had not dared to do that evil, If the first that did the edict infringe Had answer'd for his deed . . . . ii 2 91
And, like a prophet, Looks in a glass, that shows what future evils . ii 2 95
Shall we desire to raze the sanctuary And pitch our evils there? . ii 2 172
I do repent me, as it is an evil, And take the shame with joy . ii 3 35
And in my heart the strong and swelling evil Of my conception . ii 4 6
The evil that thou causest to be done, That is thy means to live . iii 2 21
Keep me in patience, and with ripen'd time Unfold the evil . . v 1 117
Well, Angelo, your evil quits you well . . . . v 1 501
No evil lost is wail'd when it is gone . *Com. of Errors* iv 2 24
So politic a state of evil that they will not admit any good part *M. Ado* v 2 63
Some flattery for this evil.—O, some authority how to proceed *L. L. Lost* iv 3 286
An angel is not evil; I should have fear'd her had she been a devil . v 2 105
This same progeny of evils comes From our debate . . *M. N. Dream* ii 1 115
Being season'd with a gracious voice, Obscures the show of evil *M. of V.* iii 2 77
All the embossed sores and headed evils . . *As Y. Like It* ii 7 67
Oppress'd with two weak evils, age and hunger . . . ii 7 132
Can you remember any of the principal evils that he laid to the charge of women?—There were none principal . . . . iii 2 370
These fix'd evils sit so fit in him . . . . *All's Well* i 1 113
But we must do good against evil . . . . . ii 5 53
Not altogether so great as the first in goodness, but greater a great deal in evil . . . . iv 3 321
I shall crave of you your leave that I may bear my evils alone *T. Night* ii 1 6
But the beauteous evil Are empty trunks o'erflourish'd by the devil . iii 4 403
With thine eyes at once see good and evil, Inclining to them both *W. Tale* i 2 303
Your most obedient counsellor, yet that dare Less appear so in comforting your evils . . . . ii 3 56
Do as the heavens have done, forget your evil; With them forgive yourself . . . . v 1 5
There's magic in thy majesty, which has My evils conjured to remembrance . . . . v 3 40
Evils that take leave, On their departure most of all show evil *K. John* iii 4 114
I left him almost speechless; and broke out To acquaint you with this evil . . . . v 6 25
Turning past evils to advantages . . *2 Hen. IV.* iv 4 78
For competence of life I will allow you, That lack of means enforce you not to evil . . . . v 5 71
One spark of evil That might annoy my finger . . . *Hen. V.* ii 2 101
There is some soul of goodness in things evil, Would men observingly distil it out . . . . iv 1 4
Mild and too well given To dream on evil or to work my downfall *2 Hen. VI.* iii 1 73

Evil. How evil it beseems thee, To flatter Henry and forsake thy brother! *3 Hen. VI.* iv 7 84
Vouchsafe, divine perfection of a woman, Of these supposed evils, to give me leave, By circumstance, but to acquit myself *Richard III.* i 2 76
Vouchsafe, defused infection of a man, For these known evils, but to give me leave, By circumstance, to curse thy cursed self . . i 2 79
Tell them that God bids us do good for evil . . . i 3 335
Nor build their evils on the graves of great men . *Hen. VIII.* ii 1 67
Yet I can give you inkling Of an ensuing evil, if it fall, Greater than this ii 1 141
Whose medicinable eye Corrects the ill aspects of planets evil *Troi. and Cres.* i 3 92
Or, shedding, breed a nursery of like evil, To overbulk us all . . i 3 319
Your affections are A sick man's appetite, who desires most that Which would increase his evil . . . *Coriolanus* i 1 183
I am no baby, I, that with base prayers I should repent the evils I have done . . . . . . *T. Andron.* v 3 186
If wrongs be evils and enforce us kill, What folly 'tis to hazard life for ill! . . . . *T. of Athens* iii 5 36
O conspiracy, Shamest thou to show thy dangerous brow by night, When evils are most free? . . . *J. Cæsar* ii 1 79
For warnings, and portents, And evils imminent . . . ii 2 81
The evil that men do lives after them; The good is oft interred with their bones . . . . iii 2 80
Of your philosophy you make no use, If you give place to accidental evils . . . . iv 3 146
Not in the legions Of horrid hell can come a devil more damn'd In evils to top Macbeth . . . . . *Macbeth* iv 3 57
These evils thou repeat'st upon thyself Have banish'd me from Scotland iv 3 112
What's the disease he means?—'Tis call'd the evil: A most miraculous work . . . . iv 3 146
To let this canker of our nature come In further evil . . *Hamlet* v 2 70
Let my disclaiming from a purposed evil Free me so far . . . v 2 252
Whilst I can vent clamour from my throat, I'll tell thee thou dost evil *Lear* i 1 169
And all that we are evil in, by a divine thrusting on . . . i 2 136
Thou worse than any name, read thine own evil . . . v 3 156
It is too true an evil: gone she is . . . . *Othello* i 1 161
Prizes the virtue that appears in Cassio, And looks not on his evils . ii 3 140
I do love Cassio well; and would do much To cure him of this evil . ii 3 149
Are you of good or evil?—As you shall prove us, praise us . v 1 65
I must not think there are Evils enow to darken all his goodness *Ant. and Cleo.* i 4 11
Repented The evils she hatch'd were not effected; so Despairing died *Cymbeline* v 5 60
Bad child; worse father! to entice his own To evil should be done by none . . . . *Pericles* i Gower 28
Be it our wives, our children, or ourselves, The curse of heaven and men succeed their evils! . . . . i 4 104
Evil angel. He that came behind you, sir, like an evil angel *Com. of Err.* iv 3 20
Love is a devil: there is no evil angel but Love . *L. L. Lost* i 2 178
Evil deeds. When evil deeds have their permissive pass . *Meas. for Meas.* i 3 38
But that thy face is, visard-like, unchanging, Made impudent with use of evil deeds . . . . *3 Hen. VI.* i 4 117
Evil diet. He hath kept an evil diet long . . . . *Richard III.* i 1 139
Evil disposition. I do it not in evil disposition . . *Meas. for Meas.* i 2 122
Your brother's evil disposition made him seek his death . *Lear* iii 5 7
Evil-eyed. You shall not find me, daughter, After the slander of most stepmothers, Evil-eyed unto you . . . . . *Cymbeline* i 1 72
Evil life. Ah, what a sign it is of evil life, Where death's approach is seen so terrible! . . . . . . *2 Hen. VI.* iii 3 5
Evil manners. Men's evil manners live in brass; their virtues We write in water . . . . *Hen. VIII.* iv 2 45
Evil mixture. But when the planets In evil mixture to disorder wander, What plagues and what portents! . . . *Troi. and Cres.* i 3 95
Evil nature. In my false brother Awaked an evil nature . *Tempest* i 2 93
Evil sign. The owl shriek'd at thy birth,—an evil sign . *3 Hen. VI.* v 6 44
Evil soul. An evil soul producing holy witness Is like a villain with a smiling cheek . . . . *Mer. of Venice* i 3 100
Evil spirit. Speak to me what thou art.—Thy evil spirit . . *J. Cæsar* iv 3 282
Evil used. Were he evil used, he would outgo His father . *Hen. VIII.* i 2 207
Evil word. Ill deeds are doubled with an evil word . *Com. of Errors* iii 2 20
Evilly. This act so evilly born shall cool the hearts Of all his people *K. John* iii 4 149
O monument And wonder of good deeds evilly bestow'd! *T. of Athens* iv 3 467
Evitate. Since therein she doth evitate and shun A thousand irreligious cursed hours . . . . *Mer. Wives* v 5 241
Ewe. You demi-puppets that By moonshine do the green sour ringlets make, Whereof the ewe not bites . . . . . *Tempest* v 1 38
The ewe that will not hear her lamb when it baes . . *Much Ado* iii 3 74
The ewes, being rank, In the end of autumn turned to the rams *M. of Ven.* i 3 81
He stuck them up before the fulsome ewes . . . . i 3 87
Is your gold and silver ewes and rams?—I cannot tell . . . i 3 96
You may as well use question with the wolf Why he hath made the ewe bleat for the lamb . . . . iv 1 74
We are still handling our ewes, and their fells, you know, are greasy *As Y. Like It* iii 2 54
The greatest of my pride is to see my ewes graze and my lambs suck . iii 2 81
Another simple sin in you, to bring the ewes and the rams together . iii 2 83
I'll queen it no inch farther, But milk my ewes and weep . *W. Tale* iv 4 461
How a score of ewes now?—Thereafter as they be: a score of good ewes may be worth ten pounds . . . . . *2 Hen. IV.* iii 2 55
So many days my ewes have been with young . . *3 Hen. VI.* ii 5 35
An old black ram Is tupping your white ewe . . . *Othello* i 1 89
Ewer. Another bear the ewer, the third a diaper . . *T. of Shrew* Ind. 1 57
Basins and ewers to lave her dainty hands . . . ii 1 350
This hits right; I dreamt of a silver basin and ewer to-night *T. of Athens* iii 1 6
Exact. Thus lorded, Not only with what my revenue yielded, But what my power might else exact . . . . . *Tempest* i 2 99
If he break, thou mayst with better face Exact the penalty *Mer. of Venice* i 3 138
The merit of service is seldom attributed to the true and exact performer *All's Well* iii 6 65
To set the exact wealth of all our states All at one cast . *1 Hen. IV.* iv 1 46
Gifts, natures, shapes, Severals and generals of grace exact *Troi. and Cres.* i 3 180
I have fed mine eyes on thee; I have with exact view perused thee . iv 5 232
An exact command, Larded with many several sorts of reasons *Hamlet* v 2 19
In the most exact regard support The worships of their name . *Lear* i 4 287
Exacted. When have I aught exacted at your hands? *2 Hen. VI.* iv 7 74
Exactest. Where thou now exact'st the penalty . *Mer. of Venice* iv 1 22
Call me before the exactest auditors And set me on the proof *T. of Athens* ii 2 165
Exacting. Pay with falsehood false exacting . . *Meas. for Meas.* iii 2 295

Exaction. What should I gain By the exaction of the forfeiture? *Mer. of Venice* i 3 165
Daily new exactions are devised, As blanks, benevolences *Richard II.* ii 1 249
Lord cardinal, they vent reproaches Most bitterly on you, as putter on Of these exactions *Hen. VIII.* i 2 25
These exactions, Whereof my sovereign would have note, they are Most pestilent to the hearing i 2 47
Still exaction! The nature of it? in what kind, let's know, Is this exaction? i 2 52
Exactly. Thy charge Exactly is perform'd *Tempest* i 2 238
Exactly do All points of my command i 2 499
I did confess it, and exactly begg'd Your grace's pardon *Richard II.* i 1 140
A figure like your father, Armed at point exactly, cap-a-pe *Hamlet* i 2 200
'Tis exactly valued; Not petty things admitted *Ant. and Cleo.* v 2 139
Which I wonder'd Could be so rarely and exactly wrought *Cymbeline* ii 4 75
Exalt. Not so hot: In his own grace he doth exalt himself, More than in your addition *Lear* v 3 67
Exalted. She uses me with a more exalted respect than any one else *T. N.* ii 5 31
Till the lowest stream Do kiss the most exalted shores of all *J. Cæsar* i 1 65
I have seen The ambitious ocean swell and rage and foam, To be exalted with the threatening clouds i 3 8
Examination. Take their examination yourself and bring it me *M. Ado* iii 5 53
We are now to examination these men iii 5 64
I will go before and show him their examination iv 2 68
Be but your lordship present at his examination *All's Well* iii 6 29
Where's his examination?—Here, so please you *Hen. VIII.* i 1 116
The king's attorney on the contrary Urged on the examinations ii 1 16
Examine. Ere you flout old ends any further, examine your conscience *Much Ado* i 1 291
I could wish he would modestly examine himself ii 3 214
We have the exhibition to examine iv 2 6
Master constable, you go not the way to examine iv 2 36
Pray you, examine him upon that point v 1 322
Know of your youth, examine well your blood *M. N. Dream* i 1 68
Well, Time is the old justice that examines all such offenders *As Y. L. It* iv 1 203
Examine me upon the particulars of my life *1 Hen. IV.* ii 4 413
Take the pains but to examine the wars of Pompey the Great *Hen. V.* iv 1 69
Come hither, sirrah, I must examine thee: what is thy name? *2 Hen. VI.* iv 2 105
Examine Their counsels and their cares, digest things rightly *Coriolanus* i 1 153
Examine other beauties.—'Tis the way To call hers exquisite *R. and J.* i 1 234
Examine every married lineament And see how one another lends content i 3 83
Examined my parts with most judicious œillades *Mer. Wives* i 3 67
Our watch, sir, have indeed comprehended two aspicious persons, and we would have them this morning examined *Much Ado* iii 5 51
Which are the offenders that are to be examined? iv 2 8
All her deserving Is a reserved honesty, and that I have not heard examined *All's Well* iii 5 66
Mine eye hath well examined his parts *K. John* i 1 89
Example. For example, thou thyself art a wicked villain *Meas. for Meas.* i 2 26
Follows close the rigour of the statute, To make him an example i 4 68
But that frailty hath examples for his falling, I should wonder iii 1 191
No such example have we iv 2 100
I beseech your worship to correct yourself, for the example of others *M. Ado* v 1 332
I may example my digression by some mighty precedent *L. L. Lost* i 2 121
Some obscure precedence that hath tofore been sain. I will example it iii 1 84
Ill, to example ill, Would from my forehead wipe a perjured note iv 3 124
What should his sufferance be by Christian example? Why, revenge *Mer. of Venice* iii 1 74
Many an error by the same example Will rush into the state iv 1 221
And the misery is, example, that so terrible shows in the wreck of maidenhood *All's Well* iii 5 23
Peace, peace!—There is example for't *T. Night* ii 5 44
If I could find example Of thousands that had struck anointed kings And flourish'd after, I'ld not do't *W. Tale* i 2 357
Hang him, he'll be made an example iv 4 847
Such temperate order in so fierce a cause Doth want example *K. John* iii 4 13
Grow great by your example and put on The dauntless spirit of resolution v 1 52
The examples Of every minute's instance, present now *2 Hen. IV.* iv 1 82
Lest example Breed, by his sufferance, more of such a kind *Hen. V.* ii 2 45
It fits us then to be as provident As fear may teach us out of late examples ii 4 12
'Tis good for men to love their present pains Upon example iv 1 19
Even in their wives' and children's sight, Be hang'd up for example *2 Hen. VI.* iv 2 190
And work in their shirt too; as myself, for example, that am a butcher iv 7 58
Things done without example, in their issue Are to be fear'd *Hen. VIII.* i 2 90
Men of his way should be most liberal; They are set here for examples i 3 62
Tell me how he died: If well, he stepp'd before me, happily For my example iv 2 11
Of his own body he was ill, and gave The clergy ill example iv 2 44
By his rare example made the coward Turn terror into sport *Coriolanus* ii 2 108
Three examples of the like have been Within my age iv 6 50
There's much example for't *T. of Athens* i 2 47
I'll example you with thievery: The sun's a thief iv 3 438
Examples gross as earth exhort me *Hamlet* iv 4 46
I'll make thee an example *Othello* ii 3 251
They say, the wars must make examples Out of their best iii 3 65
O, he has given example for our flight, Most grossly, by his own! *Ant. and Cleo.* iii 10 28
Some, turn'd coward But by example—O, a sin in war! *Cymbeline* v 3 36
Exampled. And prove a deadly bloodshed but a jest, Exampled by this heinous spectacle *K. John* iv 3 56
For hear her but exampled by herself *Hen. V.* i 2 156
So every step, Exampled by the first pace that is sick Of his superior, grows to an envious fever *Troi. and Cres.* i 3 132
Exasperate. To exasperate you, to awake your dormouse valour *T. Night* iii 2 20
No! why art thou then exasperate? *Troi. and Cres.* v 1 34
This report Hath so exasperate the king that he Prepares for some attempt of war *Macbeth* iii 6 38
To take the widow Exasperates, makes mad her sister Goneril *Lear* v 1 60
Exceed. My wrath shall far exceed the love I ever bore *T. G. of Ver.* iii 1 166
Your own science Exceeds, in that, the lists of all advice *Meas. for Meas.* i 1 6
An she were not possessed with a fury, exceeds her as much in beauty as the first of May doth the last of December *Much Ado* i 1 193
I saw the Duchess of Milan's gown that they praise so.—O, that exceeds iii 4 17
Might in virtues, beauties, livings, friends, Exceed account *Mer. of Ven.* iii 2 159
So far exceed all instance *T. Night* iv 3 12
His deeds exceed all speech *1 Hen. VI.* i 1 15
And thou shalt find that I exceed my sex i 2 90
Master sheriff, Let not her penance exceed the king's commission *2 Hen. VI.* ii 4 75

Exceed. My mind exceeds the compass of her [fortune's] wheel *3 Hen. VI.* iv 3 47
For to be wise and love Exceeds man's might *Troi. and Cres.* iii 2 164
Your son Will or exceed the common or be caught *Coriolanus* iv 1 32
As far as doth the Capitol exceed The meanest house in Rome iv 2 39
This lady's husband here, this, do you see—Whom you have banish'd, does exceed you all iv 2 42
Let me have war, say I; it exceeds peace as far as day does night iv 5 236
Happier is he that has no friend to feed Than such that do e'en enemies exceed *T. of Athens* i 2 210
That in a dozen passes between yourself and him, he shall not exceed you three hits *Hamlet* v 2 173
I prithee, name the time, but let it not Exceed three days *Othello* iii 3 63
Do not exceed The prescript of this scroll *Ant. and Cleo.* iii 8 4
Cæsar himself has work, and our oppression Exceeds what we expected iv 7 3
Exceeds in goodness the hugeness of your unworthy thinking *Cymbeline* i 4 156
If that thy gentry, Britain, go before This lout as he exceeds our lords v 2 9
In framing an artist, art hath thus decreed, To make some good, but others to exceed *Pericles* ii 3 16
Exceeded. You have exceeded all promise *As Y. Like It* i 2 256
Thy cruelty in execution Upon offenders hath exceeded law *2 Hen. VI.* i 3 136
Exceedeth. The number of the king exceedeth ours *1 Hen. IV.* iv 3 28
Exceeding. O excellent motion! O exceeding puppet! *T. G. of Ver.* ii 1 100
Those, for their parents were exceeding poor, I bought *Com. of Errors* i 1 57
Out of all suspicion, she is virtuous.—And she is exceeding wise *M. Ado* ii 3 167
My heart is exceeding heavy iii 4 25
By my troth, I am exceeding ill: heigh-ho! iii 4 53
If my cousin do not look exceeding narrowly to thee v 4 118
I protest, the schoolmaster is exceeding fantastical *L. L. Lost* v 2 532
When shall we laugh? say, when? You grow exceeding strange *M. of V.* i 1 67
Is an honest exceeding poor man ii 2 54
This exceeding posting day and night Must wear your spirits low *All's W.* v 1 1
Which we will pay, With strife to please you, day exceeding day Epil. 338
Very brief, and to exceeding good sense—less *T. Night* iii 4 174
They are exceeding poor and bare, too beggarly *1 Hen. IV.* iv 2 75
Before God, I am exceeding weary *2 Hen. IV.* ii 2 1
A word of exceeding good command iii 2 84
Very good, exceeding good iii 2 293
How doth the king?—Exceeding ill iv 5 11
How doth the king?—Exceeding well; his cares are now all ended v 2 3
The spirit of deep prophecy she hath, Exceeding the nine sibyls of old Rome *1 Hen. VI.* i 2 56
By inspiration of celestial grace, To work exceeding miracles on earth v 4 41
O, let me view his visage, being dead, That living wrought me such exceeding trouble *2 Hen. VI.* v 1 70
If heaven have any grievous plague in store Exceeding those that I can wish upon thee *Richard III.* i 3 218
O, very mad, exceeding mad, in love too *Hen. VIII.* i 4 28
A scholar, and a ripe and good one; Exceeding wise, fair-spoken iv 2 52
No gift to him, But breeds the giver a return exceeding All use of quittance *T. of Athens* i 1 290
This fellow's of exceeding honesty, And knows all qualities *Othello* iii 3 258
Is he disposed to mirth? I hope he is.—Exceeding pleasant *Cymbeline* i 6 59
Exceedingly well met *L. L. Lost* iii 1 144
In faith, it is exceedingly well aim'd *1 Hen. IV.* i 3 282
Exceedingly well read, and profited In strange concealments iii 1 166
It is very sultry and hot for my complexion.—Exceedingly, my lord *Ham.* v 2 103
I have been to-night exceedingly well cudgelled *Othello* ii 3 372
Excel. I would with such perfection govern, sir, To excel the golden age *Tempest* ii 1 168
She excels each mortal thing Upon the dull earth dwelling *T. G. of Ver.* iv 2 51
I will so plead That you shall say my cunning drift excels iv 2 83
Samson! I do excel thee in my rapier as much as thou didst me in carrying gates *L. L. Lost* i 2 78
How far dost thou excel, No thought can think, nor tongue of mortal tell iv 3 41
He excels his brother for a coward, yet his brother is reputed one of the best that is *All's Well* iv 3 321
Excels whatever yet you look'd upon Or hand of man hath done *W. Tale* v 3 16
No better than an earl, Although in glorious titles he excel *1 Hen. VI.* v 5 38
Valour and pride excel themselves in Hector *Troi. and Cres.* iv 5 79
Though his face be better than any man's, yet his leg excels all men's *Rom. and Jul.* ii 5 41
I think you are happy in this second match, For it excels your first iii 5 225
One that excels the quirks of blazoning pens *Othello* ii 1 63
Excelled. I could not but believe she excelled many *Cymbeline* i 4 80
Excellence. Nature never lends The smallest scruple of her excellence *Meas. for Meas.* i 1 38
His excellence did earn it, ere he had it *Much Ado* iii 1 99
Have found the ground of study's excellence *L. L. Lost* iv 3 300
What is thy excellence in a galliard, knight? *T. Night* i 3 127
So crammed, as he thinks, with excellencies ii 3 163
So much the more our carver's excellence *W. Tale* v 3 30
She a fair divided excellence, Whose fulness of perfection lies in him *K. John* ii 1 439
Breathing to his breathless excellence The incense of a vow iv 3 66
Hath got the voice in hell for excellence *Hen. V.* ii 2 113
They humbly sue unto your excellence To have a godly peace *1 Hen. VI.* v 1 4
I do greet your excellence With letters of commission from the king v 4 94
As procurator to your excellence *2 Hen. VI.* i 1 3
Crying with loud voice, 'Jesu maintain your royal excellence!' i 1 161
What needs your grace To be protector of his excellence? i 3 122
Loves him with that excellence That angels love good men with *Hen. VIII.* ii 2 34
We'll put on those shall praise your excellence *Hamlet* iv 7 132
You are not ignorant of what excellence Laertes is v 2 143
I dare not confess that, lest I should compare with him in excellence v 2 146
Sluttery to such neat excellence opposed Should make desire vomit emptiness, Not so allured to feed *Cymbeline* i 6 44
Excellency. She dwells so securely on the excellency of her honour, that the folly of my soul dares not present itself *Mer. Wives* ii 2 252
Is there not a double excellency in this? iii 3 187
It is the witness still of excellency To put a strange face on his own perfection *Much Ado* ii 3 48
Excellent. Dost thou like the plot, Trinculo?—Excellent *Tempest* iii 2 118
A kind Of excellent dumb discourse iii 3 39
'Steal by line and level' is an excellent pass of pate iv 1 244
O excellent motion! O exceeding puppet! *T. G. of Ver.* ii 1 100
O excellent device! was there ever heard a better? ii 1 145
A gentleman of excellent breeding, admirable discourse *Mer. Wives* ii 2 234
Ay, dat is very good; excellent.—Peace, I say! iii 1 101
The firm fixture of thy foot would give an excellent motion to thy gait iii 3 67
That will be excellent. I'll go buy them vizards iv 4 69

Excellent. O, it is excellent To have a giant's strength; but it is tyrannous To use it like a giant . . . *Meas. for Meas.* ii 2 107
I know a wench of excellent discourse, Pretty and witty *Com. of Errors* iii 1 109
He is a very valiant trencher-man; he hath an excellent stomach *M. Ado* i 1 52
He were an excellent man that were made just in the midway between him and Benedick . . . . ii 1 7
Do you think I do not know you by your excellent wit? . . . ii 1 127
Your father got excellent husbands, if a maid could come by them . ii 1 337
She were an excellent wife for Benedick . . . . . . ii 1 366
An excellent musician, and her hair shall be of what colour it please God ii 3 36
I pray thee, get us some excellent music . . . . . . ii 3 87
She's an excellent sweet lady; and, out of all suspicion, she is virtuous ii 3 165
Having so swift and excellent a wit . . . . iii 1 89
He hath an excellent good name . . . . iii 1 98
For a fine, quaint, graceful and excellent fashion, yours is worth ten on't iii 4 23
These gloves the count sent me; they are an excellent perfume . iii 4 63
Yet was Samson so tempted, and he had an excellent strength *L. L. Lost* i 2 179
Else none at all in aught proves excellent . . . . . iv 3 354
I will have an apology for that purpose.—An excellent device! . v 1 144
O excellent!—Sweet, do not scorn her so . . . *M. N. Dream* iii 2 247
If we imagine no worse of them than they of themselves, they may pass for excellent men . . . . v 1 219
O excellent young man! . . *Mer. of Venice* iv 1 246; *As Y. Like It* i 2 225
Three proper young men, of excellent growth and presence . . i 2 129
I confess me much guilty, to deny so fair and excellent ladies any thing i 2 197
An excellent colour: your chestnut was ever the only colour . iii 4 12
'So so' is good, very good, very excellent good; and yet it is not . v 1 29
It will be pastime passing excellent . . . *T. of Shrew* Ind. 1 67
Thou didst it excellent. Well, you are come to me in happy time Ind. 1 89
'Tis a very excellent piece of work, madam lady: would 'twere done! . i 1 258
O excellent motion! Fellows, let's be gone.—The motion's good indeed i 2 280
He was excellent indeed, madam . . . . . *All's Well* i 1 32
Excellent command,—to charge in with our horse upon our own wings! iii 6 51
Then hadst thou had an excellent head of hair . . *T. Night* i 3 100
It becomes me well enough, does't not?—Excellent . . . i 3 108
The excellent constitution of thy leg . . . . . . i 3 141
Let me see thee caper: ha! higher: ha, ha! excellent! . . . i 3 151
I perceive in you so excellent a touch of modesty . . . ii 1 13
By my troth, the fool has an excellent breast . . . . ii 3 19
Excellent! why, this is the best fooling, when all is done . . ii 3 30
Excellent good, i' faith . . . . ii 3 46
Excellent! I smell a device.—I have't in my nose too . . ii 3 176
A fustian riddle!—Excellent wench, say I . . . . . ii 5 120
The cur is excellent at faults . . . . ii 5 140
Follow me.—To the gates of Tartar, thou most excellent devil of wit! ii 5 227
Most excellent accomplished lady, the heavens rain odours on you! . iii 1 95
With some excellent jests, fire-new from the mint . . . . iii 2 23
Why, this is excellent.—By my troth, sir, no . . . . v 1 27
And thou, fresh piece Of excellent witchcraft . . . *W. Tale* iv 4 434
An excellent plot, very good friends . . . . . 1 *Hen. IV.* ii 3 20
O Jesu, this is excellent sport, i' faith! . . . . . ii 4 430
Shall I tell thee one thing, Poins?—Yes, faith; and let it be an excellent good thing . . . . 2 *Hen. IV.* ii 2 36
Here will be old Utis: it will be an excellent stratagem . . ii 4 22
Methinks now you are in an excellent good temperality. . . ii 4 25
'Occupy;' which was an excellent good word before it was ill sorted . ii 4 161
Which is an excellent thing.—It is very just . . . . iii 2 88
Most excellent, i' faith! things that are mouldy lack use . . iii 2 118
The tongue, which is the birth, becomes excellent wit . . . iv 3 110
The second property of your excellent sherris is, the warming of the blood iv 3 111
Husbanded and tilled with excellent endeavour of drinking . . iv 3 130
Excellent, madame!—C'est assez pour une fois . . *Hen. V.* iii 4 64
There is very excellent services committed at the bridge . . iii 6 3
But keeps the bridge most valiantly, with excellent discipline . iii 6 12
In good truth, the poet makes a most excellent description of it: Fortune is an excellent moral . . . . iii 6 39
You have an excellent armour: but let my horse have his due . . iii 7 3
It is a most absolute and excellent horse . . . . . iii 7 28
Excellent Pucelle, if thy name be so. . . . 1 *Hen. VI.* i 2 110
Doth sting a child That for the beauty thinks it excellent 2 *Hen. VI.* iii 1 230
O excellent device! make a sop of him . . . *Richard III.* i 4 162
That excellent grand tyrant of the earth . . . . . iv 4 52
Of an excellent And unmatch'd wit and judgement . *Hen. VIII.* ii 4 46
So famous, So excellent in art, and still so rising . . . iv 2 62
Here's an excellent place; here we may see most bravely *Troi. and Cres.* i 2 197
From his deep chest laughs out a loud applause; Cries 'Excellent!' . i 3 164
Yet god Achilles still cries 'Excellent! 'Tis Nestor right' . . i 3 169
Go with me; and I'll tell you excellent news of your husband . *Coriol.* i 3 101
For the defence of a town, our general is excellent . . . iv 5 179
Cunningly effected, will beget A very excellent piece of villany *T. An.* ii 3 7
Your plaintain-leaf is excellent for that.—For what, I pray thee?—For your broken shin . . . . *Rom. and Jul.* i 2 52
Many for many virtues excellent, None but for some and yet all different ii 3 13
This comes off well and excellent . . . . *T. of Athens* i 1 29
Excellent! Your lordship's a goodly villain . . . . . iii 3 27
Praise his most vicious strain, And call it excellent . . . iv 3 214
Only I will promise him an excellent piece . . . . . v 1 21
Excellent workman! thou canst not paint a man so bad as is thyself . v 1 32
So excellent a king; that was, to this, Hyperion to a satyr . *Hamlet* i 2 139
But you shall hear. Thus: 'In her excellent white bosom, these, etc.' ii 2 113
Do you know me, my lord?—Excellent well; you are a fishmonger . ii 2 174
My excellent good friends! How dost thou, Guildenstern? Ah, Rosencrantz! . . . . ii 2 228
This most excellent canopy, the air . . . . ii 2 311
An excellent play, well digested in the scenes . . . . ii 2 460
How fares our cousin Hamlet?—Excellent, i' faith . . . . iii 2 98
There is much music, excellent voice, in this little organ . . iii 2 384
A fellow of infinite jest, of most excellent fancy . . . . v 1 204
An absolute gentleman, full of most excellent differences . . . v 2 102
This is the excellent foppery of the world . . . *Lear* i 2 128
Her voice was ever soft, Gentle, and low, an excellent thing in woman v 3 273
Very good; well kissed! an excellent courtesy! 'tis so, indeed *Othello* ii 1 176
An excellent song.—I learned it in England . . . . ii 3 77
I can . . . speak well enough.—Excellent well.—Why, very well then . ii 3 121
Excellent wretch! Perdition catch my soul, But I do love thee! . iii 3 90
You shall hear more by midnight.—Excellent good . . . iv 1 226
Excellent falsehood! Why did he marry Fulvia, and not love her? *Ant. and Cleo.* i 1 40
Nay, hear him.—Good now, some excellent fortune! . . . . i 2 25
O excellent! I love long life better than figs . . . . i 2 32

Excellent. Good now, play one scene Of excellent dissembling *A. and C.* i 3 79
Indeed, he plied them both with excellent praises . . . . iii 2 14
The fellow has good judgement.—Excellent . . . . . iii 3 28
A very excellent good-conceited thing . . . . . *Cymbeline* ii 3 18
Mine Italian brain 'Gan in your duller Britain operate Most vilely; for my vantage, excellent . . . . v 5 198
I have heard, you knights of Tyre Are excellent in making ladies trip; And that their measures are as excellent . . . *Pericles* ii 3 103
Walk, and be cheerful once again; reserve That excellent complexion . iv 1 41
She has a good face, speaks well, and has excellent good clothes . iv 2 52
Excellently. I like the new tire within excellently . . *Much Ado* iii 4 13
Our interpreter does it well.—Excellently . . . *All's Well* iv 3 237
It is excellently well penned . . . . . . *T. Night* i 5 185
Is't not well done?—Excellently done, if God did all . . . i 5 254
This letter, being so excellently ignorant, will breed no terror in the youth . . . . iii 4 206
No man alive can love in such a sort The thing he means to kill more excellently . . . . *Troi. and Cres.* iv 1 24
Excelling. To Silvia let us sing, That Silvia is excelling . *T. G. of Ver.* iv 2 50
Thou cunning'st pattern of excelling nature . . . . *Othello* v 2 11
Except. Blow not a word away Till I have found each letter in the letter, Except mine own name . . . . . . *T. G. of Ver.* i 2 120
Did you perceive her earnest?—She gave me none, except an angry word ii 1 164
Now no discourse, except it be of love . . . . . . ii 4 140
Except my mistress.—Sweet, except not any; Except thou wilt except against my love . . . . ii 4 155
Except I be by Silvia in the night, There is no music in the nightingale iii 1 178
Which of these sorrows is he subject to?—To none of these, except it be the last . . . . *Com. of Errors* v 1 55
I would not change this hue, Except to steal your thoughts *Mer. of Venice* ii 1 12
Why, let her except, before excepted . . . . . *T. Night* i 3 7
Why, being younger born, Doth he lay claim to thine inheritance?—I know not why, except to get the land . . . . . *K. John* i 1 73
Except this city now by us besieged . . . . . . ii 1 489
Which fear, not reverence, makes thee to except . . *Richard II.* i 1 72
Except the marshal and such officers Appointed to direct . . . i 3 44
Faith, none for me; except the north-east wind, Which then blew bitterly i 4 6
For little office The hateful commons will perform for us, Except like curs to tear us all to pieces . . . . ii 2 139
Thou diest on point of fox, Except, O signieur, thou do give to me Egregious ransom . . . . *Hen. V.* iv 4 10
And ne'er throughout the year to church thou go'st Except it be to pray against thy foes . . . . 1 *Hen. VI.* i 1 43
France is revolted from the English quite, Except some petty towns . i 1 91
Mourn not, except thou sorrow for my good . . . . . ii 5 111
Who preferreth peace More than I do?—except I be provoked . . iii 1 34
Except you mean with obstinate repulse To slay your sovereign . . iii 1 113
Then be at peace, except ye thirst for blood . . . . . iii 1 117
'Tis resolutely spoke.—Not resolute, except so much were done 2 *Hen. VI.* iii 1 267
I cannot give due action to my words, Except a sword or sceptre balance it v 1 9
But you will take exceptions to my boon.—No, gracious lord, except I cannot do it . . . . 3 *Hen. VI.* iii 2 47
Richard except, those whom we fight against Had rather have us win *Richard III.* v 3 243
Many of the best respect in Rome, Except immortal Cæsar . *J. Cæsar* i 2 60
Except they meant to bathe in reeking wounds, Or memorize another Golgotha, I cannot tell . . . . *Macbeth* i 2 39
Except my life, except my life, except my life . . . . *Hamlet* ii 2 221
She after, Except she bend her humour, shall be assured To taste of *Cymbeline* i 5 81
Excepted. Hath he excepted most against my love . . *T. G. of Ver.* i 3 83
It is certain I am loved of all ladies, only you excepted . . *Much Ado* i 1 126
He is the only man of Italy, Always excepted my dear Claudio . . iii 1 93
Dinners and suppers and sleeping-hours excepted . . *As Y. Like It* iii 2 103
Why, let her except, before excepted . . . . . *T. Night* i 3 7
Is it excepted I should know no secrets That appertain to you? *J. Cæsar* ii 1 281
Excepting. Our watch to-night, excepting your worship's presence, ha' ta'en a couple of as arrant knaves as any in Messina . *Much Ado* iii 5 33
Excepting one, I would he were the best In all this presence that hath moved me so . . . . *Richard II.* iv 1 31
Hath won the greatest favour of the commons, Excepting none but good Duke Humphrey . . . . 2 *Hen. VI.* i 1 193
He that doth naught with her, excepting one, Were best he do it secretly, alone . . . . *Richard III.* i 1 99
Exception. Lest he should take exceptions to my love . *T. G. of Ver.* i 3 81
Milder than she was; And yet she takes exceptions at your person . v 2 3
Knew the true minute when Exception bid him speak . *All's Well* i 2 40
Your cousin, my lady, takes great exceptions to your ill hours *T. Night* i 3 6
But with proviso and exception . . . . . . 1 *Hen. IV.* i 3 78
How modest in exception, and withal How terrible . . *Hen. V.* ii 4 34
'Tis positive 'gainst all exceptions . . . . . . iv 2 25
And he first took exceptions at this badge . . . . 1 *Hen. VI.* iv 1 105
But you will take exceptions to my boon . . . . 3 *Hen. VI.* iii 2 46
What I have done, That might your nature, honour and exception Roughly awake, I here proclaim was madness . . . . *Hamlet* v 2 242
Thou hast taken against me a most just exception . . . *Othello* iv 2 211
Exceptless. Forgive my general and exceptless rashness *T. of Athens* iv 3 502
Excess. I have fed upon this woe already, And now excess of it will make me surfeit . . . . *T. G. of Ver.* iii 1 220
The blood of youth burns not with such excess As gravity's revolt *L. L. Lost* v 2 73
I neither lend nor borrow By taking nor by giving of excess *Mer. of Venice* i 3 63
In measure rein thy joy; scant this excess . . . . . iii 2 113
If the living be enemy to the grief, the excess makes it soon mortal *All's Well* i 1 67
If music be the food of love, play on; Give me excess of it *T. Night* i 1 2
With taper-light To seek the beauteous eye of heaven to garnish, Is wasteful and ridiculous excess . . . . *K. John* iv 2 16
We consider It was excess of wine that set him on . . . *Hen. V.* ii 2 42
My true love is grown to such excess . . . . *Rom. and Jul.* ii 6 33
Shame that they wanted cunning, in excess Hath broke their hearts *T. of Athens* v 4 28
So distribution should undo excess, And each man have enough *Lear* iv 1 73
He, when he hears of her, cannot refrain From the excess of laughter *Oth.* iv 1 100
Excessive. Moderate lamentation is the right of the dead, excessive grief the enemy to the living . . . . *All's Well* i 1 65
Exchange. Keep this remembrance for thy Julia's sake.—Why, then, we'll make exchange . . . . *T. G. of Ver.* ii 2 6
And he wants wit that wants resolved will To learn his wit to exchange the bad for better . . . . ii 6 13

Exchange. Spend all I have; only give me so much of your time in exchange . . . . Mer. Wives ii 2 243
I give away myself for you and dote upon the exchange . . Much Ado ii 1 320
What shalt thou exchange for rags? robes; for tittles? titles L. L. Lost iv 1 84
The allusion holds in the exchange.—'Tis true indeed; the collusion holds in the exchange . . . . iv 2 42
I say, the allusion holds in the exchange.—And I say, the pollusion holds in the exchange . . . . iv 2 45
I am much ashamed of my exchange . . . . Mer. of Venice ii 6 35
I have bills for money by exchange From Florence . . T. of Shrew iv 2 89
Bianca's love Made me exchange my state with Tranio . . . . v 1 128
Was turned into a cold fish for she would not exchange flesh with one that loved her . . . . W. Tale iv 4 284
Yet for the outside of thy poverty we must make an exchange . iv 4 647
What an exchange had this been without boot! What a boot is here with this exchange! . . . . iv 4 688
I shall make this northern youth exchange His glorious deeds for my indignities . . . . 1 Hen. IV. iii 2 145
In exchange of a hundred and fifty soldiers, three hundred and odd pounds . . . . iv 2 14
Oft have you . . . Desired my Cressid in right great exchange T. and C. iii 3 21
What satisfaction canst thou have to-night?—The exchange of thy love's faithful vow for mine . . . . Rom. and Jul. ii 2 127
When and where and how We met, we woo'd and made exchange of vow ii 3 62
It cannot countervail the exchange of joy That one short minute gives me in her sight . . . . ii 6 4
For any benefit that points to me, Either in hope or present, I'ld exchange For this one wish . . . . T. of Athens iv 3 527
If Hamlet give the first or second hit, Or quit in answer of the third exchange . . . . Hamlet v 2 280
Exchange forgiveness with me, noble Hamlet . . . . . . v 2 340
A plot upon her virtuous husband's life; And the exchange my brother! Lear iv 6 280
There is my pledge . . .—There's my exchange . . . . . v 3 97
Let's exchange charity. I am no less in blood than thou art . . v 3 166
Exchange me for a goat . . . . Othello iii 3 180
As I my poor self did exchange for you, To your so infinite loss Cymb. i 1 119
To shift his being Is to exchange one misery with another . . . i 5 55
Exchanged. O that it could be proved That some night-tripping fairy had exchanged In cradle-clothes our children! . . 1 Hen. IV. i 1 87
For him was I exchanged and ransomed . . . . 1 Hen. VI. i 4 29
Exchequer. You have an exchequer of words . . T. G. of Ver. ii 4 43
I will be cheater to them both, and they shall be exchequers to me M. W. i 3 78
Evermore thanks, the exchequer of the poor . . . Richard II. ii 3 65
For all the coin in thy father's exchequer . . . 1 Hen. IV. ii 2 39
There's money of the king's coming down the hill; 'tis going to the king's exchequer . . . . ii 2 57
Rob me the exchequer the first thing thou doest . . . . iii 3 205
For our losses, his exchequer is too poor . . . Hen. V. iii 6 137
Excite. Every reason excites to this, that my lady loves me . T. Night ii 5 179
To stand the push and enmity of those This quarrel would excite Troi. and Cres. ii 2 138
Would to the bleeding and the grim alarm Excite the mortified man Macb. v 2 5
Excited. Beaten for loyalty Excited me to treason . . . Cymbeline v 5 345
Excitements to the field, or speech for truce . . Troi. and Cres. i 3 182
Excitements of my reason and my blood . . . . Hamlet iv 4 58
Exclaim. Let it presage the ruin of your love And be my vantage to exclaim on you . . . . Mer. of Venice iii 2 176
The most bitter touch of sorrow that e'er I heard virgin exclaim in All's W. i 3 123
Alas, the part I had in Woodstock's blood Doth more solicit me than your exclaims! . . . . Richard II. i 2 2
All French and France exclaims on thee . . . 1 Hen. VI. iii 3 60
Say, gentlemen, what makes you thus exclaim? . . . . iv 1 83
York should have sent him aid.—And York as fast upon you grace exclaims iv 4 30
I am a soldier and unapt to weep Or to exclaim on fortune's fickleness . v 3 134
Is Cade the son of Henry the Fifth, That thus you do exclaim you'll go with him? . . . . 2 Hen. VI. iv 8 37
Thou hast made the happy earth thy hell, Fill'd it with cursing cries and deep exclaims . . . . Richard III. i 2 52
Come, come, dispatch; 'tis bootless to exclaim . . . . iii 4 104
Be copious in exclaims . . . . iv 4 135
You are amazed, my liege, at her exclaim . . . . Troi. and Cres. v 3 91
And arm the minds of infants to exclaims . . . . T. Andron. iv 1 86
Do them wrong, to make them exclaim against their own succession Ham. ii 2 367
Exclaim no more against it . . . . . . Othello ii 3 314
Exclaimed. The French exclaim'd, the devil was in arms . 1 Hen. VI. i 1 125
Exclamation. I hear as good exclamation on your worship as of any man in the city . . . . Much Ado iii 5 28
In some measure satisfy her so That we shall stop her exclamation K. John ii 1 558
What man of good temper would endure this tempest of exclamation? Are you not ashamed? . . . . . 2 Hen. IV. ii 1 88
Entreat me fair, Or with the clamorous report of war Thus will I drown your exclamations . . . . Richard III. iv 4 153
Or else you suffer Too hard an exclamation . . . . Hen. VIII. i 2 52
Excludes all pity from our threatening looks . . Com. of Errors i 1 10
Excommunicate. Thou shalt stand cursed and excommunicate K. John iii 1 173
Excommunication. Only get the learned writer to set down our excommunication . . . . Much Ado iii 5 69
Excrement. Why is Time such a niggard of hair, being, as it is, so plentiful an excrement? . . . . . . Com. of Errors ii 2 79
Dally with my excrement, with my mustachio . . L. L. Lost v 1 109
These assume but valour's excrement To render them redoubted! Mer. of Venice iii 2 87
Let me pocket up my pedlar's excrement . . . W. Tale iv 4 734
The earth's a thief, That feeds and breeds by a composture stolen From general excrement . . . . . . T. of Athens iv 3 445
Your bedded hair, like life in excrements, Start up . . Hamlet iii 4 121
Excusable. Not only that,—That were excusable . . Ant. and Cleo. iii 4 2
Excuse it not, for I am peremptory . . . . T. G. of Ver. i 3 71
With the vantage of mine own excuse Hath he excepted most against my love . . . . i 3 82
If thou hast sinn'd, Teach me, thy tempted subject, to excuse it! . . ii 6 8
I will not hear thy vain excuse . . . . iii 1 168
I pray you all go with me.—I must excuse myself, Master Ford M. W. iii 2 54
To him, and excuse his throwing into the water . . . . iii 3 206
I something do excuse the thing I hate, For his advantage that I dearly love . . . . Meas. for Meas. ii 4 119
Let me excuse me, and believe me so, My mirth it much displeased . iv 1 12
You must excuse us all; My wife is shrewish when I keep not hours Com. of Errors iii 1 1
Excuse. But she will well excuse Why at this time the doors are made against you . . . . Com. of Errors iii 1 92
You use this dalliance to excuse Your breach of promise . . . iv 1 48
She not denies it: Why seek'st thou then to cover with excuse That which appears in proper nakedness? . . . . . Much Ado iv 1 176
Your own good thoughts excuse me, and farewell . . L. L. Lost ii 1 176
Teach us, sweet madam, for our rude transgression Some fair excuse . v 2 432
In your rich wisdom to excuse or hide The liberal opposition of our spirits v 2 742
Excuse me so, coming too short of thanks For my great suit . . v 2 748
Hear my excuse: My love, my life, my soul, fair Helena! M. N. Dream iii 2 245
No epilogue, I pray you; for your play needs no excuse. Never excuse v 1 363
And never dare misfortune cross her foot, Unless she do it under this excuse, That she is issue to a faithless Jew . . Mer. of Venice ii 4 37
This is no answer thou unfeeling man, To excuse the current of thy cruelty . . . . iv 1 64
And not being well married, it will be a good excuse for me hereafter to leave my wife . . . . . . As Y. Like It iii 3 94
And what wit could wit have to excuse that? . . . . . iv 1 172
That you might excuse His broken promise . . . . . iv 3 154
I must bear answer back How you excuse my brother . . . iv 3 181
I hope this reason stands for my excuse . . . . T. of Shrew Ind. 2 126
I will so excuse As you shall well be satisfied withal . . . iii 2 110
I will not open my lips so wide as a bristle may enter in way of thy excuse . . . . T. Night i 5 3
Make your excuse wisely, you were best . . . . . . i 5 33
Would they else be content to die?—Yes; if there were no other excuse why they should desire to live . . . . . W. Tale i 1 47
Thou dost usurp authority.—Excuse; it is to beat usurping down K. John ii 1 119
Oftentimes excusing of a fault Doth make the fault the worse by the excuse . . . . iv 2 31
And thy abundant goodness shall excuse This deadly blot in thy digressing son . . . . Richard II. v 3 65
I would I could Quit all offences with as clear excuse . 1 Hen. IV. iii 2 19
It hath the excuse of youth and heat of blood . . . . . v 2 17
And thou mightst win the more thy father's love, Pleading so wisely in excuse of it . . . . 2 Hen. IV. iv 5 181
You must excuse me, Master Robert Shallow.—I will not excuse you; you shall not be excused; excuses shall not be admitted; there is no excuse shall serve . . . . v 1 3
Admit the excuse Of time, of numbers and due course of things Hen. V. v Prol. 3
It will excuse This sudden execution of my will . . 1 Hen. VI. v 5 98
Pray God the Duke of York excuse himself! . . . 2 Hen. VI. i 3 181
Devise excuses for thy faults . . . . . . 3 Hen. VI. ii 6 71
Excuse me to the king my brother; I'll hence to London . . . v 5 46
Let me have Some patient leisure to excuse myself . . Richard III. i 2 82
Thou canst make No excuse current, but to hang thyself . . . i 2 84
My lord, you'll bear us company?—Excuse me . . . Hen. VIII. ii 2 59
I do excuse you; yea, upon mine honour, I free you from't . . ii 4 156
May it like your grace To let my tongue excuse all . . . . v 3 149
Excuse me.—He is elder.—Pardon me, pardon me . . Troi. and Cres. i 2 87
What's his excuse?—He doth rely on none . . . . . ii 3 173
If the king call for him at supper, you will make his excuse . . iii 1 85
Your disposer is sick.—Well, I'll make excuse . . . . iii 1 99
You'll remember your brother's excuse?—To a hair . . . iii 1 156
And so, I pray, go with us.—Give me excuse, good madam . Coriolanus i 3 114
I must excuse What cannot be amended . . . . . . iv 7 11
This admits no excuse . . . . v 6 69
I am of age To keep mine own, excuse it how she can . T. Andron. iv 2 105
Shall this speech be spoke for our excuse? Or shall we on? Rom. and Jul. i 4 1
The excuse that thou dost make in this delay Is longer than the tale thou dost excuse . . . . ii 5 33
The reason that I have to love thee Doth much excuse the appertaining rage . . . . iii 1 66
Boy this shall not excuse the injuries That thou hast done me . . iii 1 69
I will be deaf to pleading and excuses . . . . . . iii 1 197
And that unaptness made your minister, Thus to excuse yourself T. of A. ii 2 141
In like manner was I in debt to my importunate business, but he would not hear my excuse . . . . iii 6 17
This vile deed We must . . Both countenance and excuse . Hamlet iv 1 32
These bloody accidents must excuse my manners . . . Othello v 1 94
Yet must Antony No way excuse his soils . . . . Ant. and Cleo. i 4 24
But You patch'd up your excuses.—Not so, not so . . . . ii 2 56
The luck of Cæsar, which the gods give men To excuse their after wrath v 2 290
For the gap That we shall make in time, from our hence-going And our return, to excuse . . . . Cymbeline iii 2 66
Why should excuse be born or e'er begot? We'll talk of that hereafter iii 2 67
When last I went to visit her, She pray'd me to excuse her keeping close iii 5 46
I will not have excuse, with saying this Loud music is too harsh Pericles ii 3 96
Excused. We cite our faults, That they may hold excused our lawless lives T. G. of Ver. iv 1 54
Shall be lamented, pitied and excused Of every hearer . . Much Ado iv 1 218
Well excused: That thou didst love her, strikes some scores away All's W. v 3 55
All murders past do stand excused in this . . . . K. John iv 3 51
There is no excuse shall serve; you shall not be excused . 2 Hen. IV. v 1 7
They are then excused, my lord, when they see not what they do Hen. V. v 2 329
And, by despairing, shouldst thou stand excused . . Richard III. i 2 86
You're excused: But will you be more justified? . . . Hen. VIII. ii 4 161
Here I stand, both to impeach and purge Myself condemned and myself excused . . . . Rom. and Jul. v 3 227
Excusez-moi, Alice; écoutez: de hand, de fingres, de nails . Hen. V iii 4 30
Excusez-moi, je vous supplie, mon très-puissant seigneur . . . v 2 276
Excusing. And oftentimes excusing of a fault Doth make the fault the worse by the excuse . . . . K. John iv 2 30
Execrable. Give sentence on this execrable wretch . . T. Andron. v 3 177
Execration. Cease, gentle queen, these execrations . . 2 Hen. VI. iii 2 305
But I'll see some issue of my spiteful execrations . . Troi. and Cres. ii 3 7
Execute. I' the commonwealth I would by contraries Execute all things Tempest ii 1 148
Claudio, whom here you have warrant to execute . . Meas. for Meas. iv 2 167
Wounding flouts, Which you on all estates will execute . . L. L. Lost v 2 855
The villany you teach me, I will execute . . . . Mer. of Venice iii 1 75
One thing more rests, that thyself execute . . . . T. of Shrew i 1 251
Having made me businesses which none without thee can sufficiently manage, must either stay to execute them thyself . . . W. Tale iv 2 17
We have cross'd, To execute the charge my father gave me . . . . v 1 162
Didst send two of thy men To execute the noble duke at Calais Rich. II. iv 1 82
I have a jest to execute that I cannot manage alone . . 1 Hen. IV. i 2 180
A business that this night may execute . . . . . . iii 1 82
Whom with my bare fists I would execute . . . . 1 Hen. VI. i 4 36
More can I bear than you dare execute . . . . . 2 Hen. VI. iv 1 130

Execute. And cheers these hands that slew thy sire and brother To execute the like upon thyself — 3 *Hen. VI.* ii 4 10
Work thou the way,—and thou shalt execute — v 7 25
Yet execute thy wrath in me alone, O, spare my guiltless wife! *Rich. III.* i 4 71
Your office, sergeant; execute it — *Hen. VIII.* i 1 198
We'll execute your purpose, and put on A form of strangeness *Tr. and Cr.* iii 3 50
As black defiance As heart can think or courage execute — iv 1 13
In fellest manner execute your aims — v 7 6
Cassio following him with determined sword, To execute upon him *Oth.* ii 3 228
To vex her I will execute in the clothes that she so praised *Cymbeline* iii 5 147
Or the common hangman shall execute it — *Pericles* iv 6 137
Executed. I have sat in the stocks for puddings he hath stolen, otherwise he had been executed — *T. G. of Ver.* iv 4 35
See that Claudio Be executed by nine to-morrow morning *M. for M.* ii 1 34
Let Claudio be executed by four of the clock — iv 2 124
What is that Barnardine who is to be executed in the afternoon? iv 2 133
How came it that the absent duke had not either delivered him to his liberty or executed him? — iv 2 137
Let this Barnardine be this morning executed, and his head borne to Angelo — iv 2 182
Awake till you are executed, and sleep afterwards — iv 3 35
Take him to prison; And see our pleasure herein executed — v 1 527
It did come to his hands, and commands shall be executed *T. Night* iii 4 30
One that is like to be executed for robbing a church *Hen. V.* iii 6 106
His nose is executed, and his fire's out — iii 6 111
For treason executed in our late king's days 1 *Hen. VI.* ii 4 91
Being accused a crafty murderer, His guilt should be but idly posted over, Because his purpose is not executed 2 *Hen. VI.* iii 1 256
But on thy side I may not be too forward, Lest, being seen, thy brother, tender George, Be executed in his father's sight *Richard III.* v 3 96
And to be executed ere they wipe their lips *Coriolanus* iv 5 232
Had you not by wondrous fortune come This vengeance on me had they executed *T. Andron.* ii 3 113
Were there worse end than death, That end upon them should be executed — ii 3 303
In bloody lines I have set down; And what is written shall be executed v 2 15
And, not to swell our spirit, He shall be executed presently *T. of Athens* iii 5 103
Executing the outward face of royalty, With all prerogative *Tempest* i 2 104
If murdering innocents be executing, Why, then thou art an executioner 3 *Hen. VI.* v 6 32
Execution. That thou mayst perceive how well I like it The execution of it shall make known *T. G. of Ver.* i 3 36
As wretches have o'ernight That wait for execution in the morn iv 2 134
To the hopeful execution do I leave you Of your commissions *M. for M.* i 1 60
The provost hath A warrant for his execution — i 4 74
I have seen, When, after execution, judgement hath Repented o'er his doom — ii 2 11
Here's a fellow will help you to-morrow in your execution iv 2 24
We have very oft awaked him, as if to carry him to execution iv 2 159
The place of death and sorry execution *Com. of Errors* v 1 121
Whereof the execution did cry out Against the non-performance *W. Tale* i 2 260
Condemn'd by the king's own mouth, thereon His execution sworn i 2 446
Be swift like lightning in the execution *Richard II.* i 3 79
See them deliver'd over To execution and the hand of death iii 1 30
By a true substantial form And present execution of our wills 2 *Hen. IV.* iv 1 174
Hangs resolved correction in the arm That was uprear'd to execution iv 1 214
Retreat is made and execution stay'd — iv 3 78
Send Colevile with his confederates To York, to present execution iv 3 80
Doing the execution and the act For which we have in head assembled them *Hen. V.* ii 2 17
I would desire the duke to use his good pleasure, and put him to execution — iii 6 58
My father's execution Was nothing less than bloody tyranny 1 *Hen. VI.* ii 5 99
Enter, and cry 'The Dauphin!' presently, And then do execution on the watch — iii 2 35
Ay, ay: away with her to execution! — v 4 54
It will excuse This sudden execution of my will — v 5 99
Thy cruelty in execution Upon offenders hath exceeded law 2 *Hen. VI.* i 3 135
From hence to prison back again; From thence unto the place of execution — ii 3 6
For scarce I can refrain The execution of my big-swoln heart 3 *Hen. VI.* ii 2 111
Be sudden in the execution, Withal obdurate *Richard III.* i 3 346
The peace of England and our persons' safety Enforced us to this execution — iii 5 46
That comfort comes too late; 'Tis like a pardon after execution *Hen. VIII.* iv 2 121
With the fineness of their souls By reason guide his execution *Tr. and Cr.* i 3 210
The will is infinite and the execution confined — iii 2 89
Who hath done to-day Mad and fantastic execution — v 5 38
I wish no better Than have him hold that purpose and to put it In execution.—'Tis most like he will *Coriolanus* ii 1 257
Let them not cease, but with a din confused Enforce the present execution — iii 3 21
Back to Rome, and prepare for your execution — v 2 52
Our throats are sentenced and stay upon execution — v 4 8
As an adder when she doth unroll To do some fatal execution *T. Andron.* ii 3 36
Let no man but I Do execution on my flesh and blood — iv 2 84
Like a forlorn and desperate castaway, Do shameful execution on herself — v 3 76
A kind of hope, Which craves as desperate an execution As that is desperate which we would prevent *Rom. and Jul.* iv 1 69
So is he now in execution Of any bold or noble enterprise *J. Cæsar* i 2 301
His brandish'd steel, Which smoked with bloody execution *Macbeth* i 2 18
Is execution done on Cawdor? — i 4 1
Put that business in your bosoms, Whose execution takes your enemy off iii 1 105
The sway, revenue, execution of the rest, Beloved sons, be yours *Lear* i 1 139
Witness that here Iago doth give up The execution of his wit, hands, heart, To wrong'd Othello's service! *Othello* iii 3 466
Why, one that rode to's execution, man, Could never go so slow *Cymb.* iii 2 72
Executioner. A common executioner, who in his office lacks a helper *Meas. for Meas.* iv 2 9
Call your executioner, and off with Barnardine's head iv 2 222
The common executioner, Whose heart the accustom'd sight of death makes hard, Falls not the axe *As Y. Like It* iii 5 3
I would not be thy executioner: I fly thee, for I would not injure thee iii 5 8
Like an executioner, Cut off the heads of too fast growing sprays *Richard II.* iii 4 33
Consent and censure well the deed, And I'll provide his executioner 2 *Hen. VI.* iii 1 276
Therefore be still.—Then, executioner, unsheathe thy sword 3 *Hen. VI.* ii 2 123
Executioner. Think'st thou I am an executioner? 3 *Hen. VI.* v 6 30
If murdering innocents be executing, Why, then thou art an executioner v 6 33
Is not the causer of the timeless deaths Of these Plantagenets, Henry and Edward, As blameful as the executioner? *Richard III.* i 2 119
Though I wish thy death, I will not be the executioner — i 2 186
Here come my executioners. How now, my hardy, stout resolved mates! — i 3 339
Why should we be tender To let an arrogant piece of flesh threat us, Play judge and executioner all himself? *Cymbeline* iv 2 128
Executor. Such baseness Had never like executor *Tempest* iii 1 13
Let's choose executors and talk of wills: And yet not so *Richard II.* iii 2 148
Delivering o'er to executors pale The lazy yawning drone *Hen. V.* i 2 203
Their executors, the knavish crows, Fly o'er them, all impatient for their hour — iv 2 51
Exempt. Be it my wrong you are from me exempt *Com. of Errors* ii 2 173
This our life exempt from public haunt Finds tongues in trees *As Y. L. It* ii 1 15
Exempt from ancient gentry — 1 *Hen. VI.* ii 4 93
The king, thy sovereign, is not quite exempt From envious malice iii 1 25
True nobility is exempt from fear 2 *Hen. VI.* iv 1 129
Exempt from envy, but not from disdain 3 *Hen. VI.* iii 3 127
Madam, yourself are not exempt in this *Richard III.* ii 1 18
Things done well, And with a care, exempt themselves from fear *Hen. VIII.* i 2 89
Who would not wish to be from wealth exempt? *T. of Athens* iv 2 31
Exempted be from me the arrogance To choose from forth the royal blood of France — *All's Well* ii 1 198
Exequies. But see his exequies fulfill'd 1 *Hen. VI.* iii 2 133
Exercise. Urchins Shall, for that vast of night that they may work, All exercise on thee *Tempest* i 2 328
For any or for all these exercises He said that Proteus your son was meet *T. G. of Ver.* i 3 11
Be in eye of every exercise Worthy his youth and nobleness of birth i 3 32
Allow me such exercises as may become a gentleman *As Y. Like It* i 1 75
He's all my exercise, my mirth, my matter *W. Tale* i 2 166
So long as nature Will bear up with this exercise, so long I daily vow to use it — iii 2 242
Is less frequent to his princely exercises than formerly — iv 2 37
And deny his youth The rich advantage of good exercise *K. John* iv 2 60
To gentle exercise and proof of arms 1 *Hen. IV.* v 2 55
For this they have been thoughtful to invest Their sons with arts and martial exercises 2 *Hen. IV.* iv 5 74
Hunting was his daily exercise 3 *Hen. VI.* iv 6 85
I am in your debt for your last exercise; Come the next Sabbath *Richard III.* iii 2 112
In no worldly suit would he be moved, To draw him from his holy exercise — iii 7 64
Flowing and swelling o'er with arts and exercise *Troi. and Cres.* iv 4 80
Worthy sir, thou bleed'st; Thy exercise hath been too violent *Coriolanus* i 5 16
Whose hours, whose bed, whose meal, and exercise, Are still together iv 4 14
Lost all my mirth, forgone all custom of exercises *Hamlet* ii 2 308
Read on this book; That show of such an exercise may colour Your loneliness — iii 1 45
Gave you such a masterly report For art and exercise in your defence iv 7 98
Hard at hand comes the master and main exercise *Othello* ii 1 269
Fasting and prayer, Much castigation, exercise devout iii 4 41
I' the common show-place, where they exercise *Ant. and Cleo.* iii 6 12
No longer exercise Upon a valiant race thy harsh And potent injuries *Cymbeline* v 4 82
They are now starved for want of exercise *Pericles* i 4 38
Exeter. That late broke from the Duke of Exeter *Richard II.* ii 1 281
Uncle of Exeter, Enlarge the man committed yesterday *Hen. V.* ii 2 39
My Lord of Westmoreland, and uncle Exeter, We will aboard to-night ii 2 70
Come, uncle Exeter, Go you and enter Harfleur — iii 3 51
Is the Duke of Exeter safe?—The Duke of Exeter is as magnanimous as Agamemnon — iii 6 5
The Duke of Exeter doth love thee well.—Ay, I praise God iii 6 23
But Exeter hath given the doom of death For pax of little price iii 6 46
The Duke of Exeter has very gallantly maintained the pridge iii 6 95
My good Lord Exeter, And my kind kinsman, warriors all, adieu! iv 3 9
Harry the king, Bedford and Exeter, Warwick and Talbot iv 3 53
Here, uncle Exeter, fill this glove with crowns, And give it to this fellow — iv 8 61
That Exeter doth wish His days may finish ere that hapless time 1 *Hen. VI.* iii 1 200
Cousin of Exeter, frowns, words and threats Shall be the war that Henry means to use 3 *Hen VI.* i 1 72
Exeter, thou art a traitor to the crown In following this usurping Henry — i 1 80
Art thou against us, Duke of Exeter?—His is the right, and therefore pardon — i 1 147
Ah, Exeter!—Why should you sigh, my lord?—Not for myself i 1 191
I'll steal away.—Exeter, so will I.—Nay, go not from me i 1 212
Nay, take me with thee, good sweet Exeter: Not that I fear to stay ii 5 137
Cousin of Exeter, what thinks your lordship? — iv 8 34
When last I was at Exeter, The mayor in courtesy show'd me the castle, And call'd it Rougemont *Richard III.* iv 2 106
Sir Edward Courtney, and the haughty prelate Bishop of Exeter, his brother — iv 4 503
Exhalation. No natural exhalation in the sky, No scope of nature *K. John* iii 4 153
Do you see these meteors? do you behold these exhalations? 1 *Hen. IV.* ii 4 352
I shall fall Like a bright exhalation in the evening 1 *Hen. VIII.* iii 2 226
The exhalations whizzing in the air Give so much light that I may read by them *J. Cæsar* ii 1 44
Exhale. The grave doth gape, and doting death is near; Therefore exhale *Hen. V.* ii 1 66
'Tis thy presence that exhales this blood From cold and empty veins, where no blood dwells *Richard III.* i 2 58
And what these sorrows could not thence exhale, Thy beauty hath i 2 166
It is some meteor that the sun exhales *Rom. and Jul.* iii 5 13
Exhaled. And be no more an exhaled meteor, A prodigy of fear 1 *Hen. IV.* v 1 19
Exhalest. Then thou, fair sun, which on my earth dost shine, Exhalest this vapour-vow *L. L. Lost* iv 3 70
Exhaust. Spare not the babe, Whose dimpled smiles from fools exhaust their mercy — *T. of Athens* iv 3 119
Exhibit. I'll exhibit a bill in the parliament for the putting down of men *Mer. Wives* ii 1 29
They should exhibit their petitions in the street *Meas. for Meas.* iv 4 11
Tears exhibit my tongue — *Mer. of Venice* ii 3 10
In the right of Richard Plantagenet We do exhibit to your majesty 1 *Hen. VI.* iii 1 151

Exhibiter. Rather swaying more upon our part Than cherishing the exhibiters against us . . . *Hen. V.* i 1 74

Exhibition. Like exhibition thou shalt have from me . . . *T. G. of Ver.* i 3 69
We have the exhibition to examine . . . *Much Ado* iv 2 5
The king gone to-night! subscribed his power! Confined to exhibition! *Lear* i 2 25
Bending to your state, I crave fit disposition for my wife, Due reference of place and exhibition . . . *Othello* i 3 238
Nor for gowns, petticoats, nor caps, nor any petty exhibition . iv 3 75

Exhort all the world to be cowards . . . *2 Hen. VI.* iv 10 79
Examples gross as earth exhort me . . . *Hamlet* iv 4 46

Exhortation. I'll end my exhortation after dinner . . *Mer. of Venice* i 1 104

Exigent. These eyes, like lamps whose wasting oil is spent, Wax dim, as drawing to their exigent . . . *1 Hen. VI.* ii 5 9
Why do you cross me in this exigent?—I do not cross you . *J. Cæsar* v 1 19
That, when the exigent should come, which now Is come indeed *Ant. and Cleo.* iv 14 63

Exile. Since his exile she hath despised me most . . *T. G. of Ver.* iii 2 3
Let them be recall'd from their exile: They are reformed . . v 4 155
They wilfully themselves exile from light . . *M. N. Dream* iii 2 386
Three or four loving lords have put themselves into voluntary exile with him . . . *As Y. Like It* i 1 107
She would have followed her exile, or have died to stay behind her . i 1 115
Now, my co-mates and brothers in exile . . . ii 1 1
The sly slow hours shall not determinate The dateless limit of thy dear exile; The hopeless word of 'never to return' Breathe I *Richard II.* i 3 151
In regard of me He shortens four years of my son's exile . . i 3 217
But wherefore grieve I at an hour's poor loss, Omitting Suffolk's exile? *2 Hen. VI.* iii 2 382
Condemning some to death, and some to exile . *Coriolanus* i 6 35
Let them pronounce the steep Tarpeian death, Vagabond exile . iii 3 89
You cast Your stinking greasy caps in hooting at Coriolanus' exile . iv 6 132
O, a kiss Long as my exile, sweet as my revenge! . . v 3 45
Would bewray what life We have led since thy exile . . v 3 96
Thou art an exile, and thou must not stay . . *T. Andron.* iii 1 285
And for that offence Immediately we do exile him hence *Rom. and Jul.* iii 1 192
Be merciful, say 'death;' For exile hath more terror in his look . iii 3 13
Hence-banished is banish'd from the world, And world's exile is death . iii 3 20
And say'st thou yet that exile is not death? . . iii 3 43
The law that threaten'd death becomes thy friend And turns it to exile iii 3 140
My wife is dead to-night; Grief of my son's exile hath stopp'd her breath v 3 211
To draw upon an exile! O brave sir! . . *Cymbeline* i 1 166
The exile of her minion is too new; She hath not yet forgot him . ii 3 46
Since the exile of Posthumus, most retired Hath her life been . iii 5 36
Who find in my exile the want of breeding, The certainty of this hard life iv 4 26

Exiled. And all their lands restored to them again That were with him exiled . . . *As Y. Like It* v 4 171
Say I sent thee forth to purchase honour, And not the king exiled thee *Richard II.* i 3 283
Foul subornation is predominant And equity exiled . *2 Hen. VI.* iii 1 146
You are beguiled, Both you and I; for Romeo is exiled . *Rom. and Jul.* iii 2 133
As calling home our exiled friends abroad . . *Macbeth* v 8 66
With marriage wherefore was he mock'd, To be exiled? . *Cymbeline* v 4 59

Exion. Since my exion is entered and my case so openly known *2 Hen. IV.* ii 1 32

Exist. The orbs From whom we do exist, and cease to be . . *Lear* i 1 114
I do beseech you That by your virtuous means I may again Exist *Othello* iii 4 112

Existest. Thou [life] exist'st on many a thousand grains That issue out of dust . . . *Meas. for Meas.* iii 1 20

Exit. His enter and exit shall be strangling a snake . . *L. L. Lost* v 1 141
Ergo I come with this apology. Keep some state in thy exit, and vanish v 2 598
They have their exits and their entrances . . *As Y. Like It* ii 7 141

Exorciser. No exorciser harm thee!—Nor no witchcraft charm thee! *Cymbeline* iv 2 276

Exorcism. Will her ladyship behold and hear our exorcisms? *2 Hen. VI.* i 4 5

Exorcist. Is there no exorcist Beguiles the truer office of mine eyes? Is't real that I see? . . . *All's Well* v 3 305
Thou, like an exorcist, hast conjured up My mortified spirit . *J. Cæsar* ii 1 323

Expect. It is my promise, And they expect it from me . . *Tempest* iv 1 42
My father at the road Expects my coming . . *T. G. of Ver.* i 1 54
Expect spoon-meat; or bespeak a long spoon . *Com. of Errors* iv 3 61
He hath indeed better bettered expectation than you must expect of me to tell you how . . . *Much Ado* i 1 17
To-morrow then I will expect your coming . . . v 1 305
I do expect return Of thrice three times the value of this bond *M. of V.* i 3 160
I beseech you, sir, go: my young master doth expect your reproach . ii 5 20
We all expect a gentle answer, Jew . . . iv 1 34
Sweet soul, let's in, and there expect their coming . . v 1 49
I have better news in store for you Than you expect . . v 1 275
Expect they are busied about a counterfeit assurance . *T. of Shrew* iv 4 91
My people did expect my hence departure Two days ago . *W. Tale* i 2 450
Your brother kings and monarchs of the earth Do all expect that you should rouse yourself . . . *Hen. V.* i 2 123
Expect Saint Martin's summer, halcyon days . . *1 Hen. VI.* i 2 131
Renowned Talbot doth expect my aid, And I am lowted by a traitor villain . . . iv 3 12
And here I will expect thy coming . . . v 3 145
The duchess, I tell you, expects performance of your promises *2 Hen. VI.* i 4 2
Within fourteen days At Bristol I expect my soldiers . . iii 1 328
With halters on their necks, Expect your highness' doom . . iv 9 12
And do expect him here some two hours hence . . *3 Hen. VI.* v 1 10
I every day expect an embassage From my Redeemer . *Richard III.* ii 1 3
God punish me With hate in those where I expect most love! . . ii 1 35
Untimely storms make men expect a dearth . . . ii 3 35
But, if God sort it so, 'Tis more than we deserve, or I expect . . ii 3 37
If my weak oratory Can from his mother win the Duke of York, Anon expect him here . . . iii 1 39
What other Would you expect? you are strangely troublesome *Hen. VIII.* v 3 94
And be't of less expect That matter needless, of importless burden, Divide thy lips . . . *Troi. and Cres.* i 3 70
Save the thanks this prince expects . . . iv 4 119
No talk of Timon, nothing of him expect . . *T. of Athens* v 2 14
Ay, if I be alive and your mind hold and your dinner worth the eating.—Good: I will expect you . . . *J. Cæsar* i 2 297
Where rather I'll expect victorious life Than death and honour *A. and C.* iv 2 43
Early though't be, have on their riveted trim, And at the port expect you iv 4 23
What shalt thou expect, To be depender on a thing that leans? *Cymbeline* i 5 57
From proof as strong as my grief and as certain as I expect my revenge iii 4 25
When expect you them?—With the next benefit o' the wind . . iv 2 341
Comfort is too far for us to expect . . . *Pericles* i 4 59
Were more than you expect, or more than's fit . . ii 3 5
We every day Expect him here . . . . *Pericles* iv 1 35
All goodness that consists in bounty Expect even here . . . v 1 71

Expectance. There is expectance here from both the sides *Troi. and Cres.* iv 5 146

Expectancy. The expectancy and rose of the fair state . . *Hamlet* iii 1 160
For every minute is expectancy Of more arrivance . . . *Othello* ii 1 41

Expectation. He hath indeed better bettered expectation . . *Much Ado* i 1 16
If he do not dote on her upon this, I will never trust my expectation . ii 3 220
Oft expectation fails and most oft there Where most it promises *All's W.* ii 1 145
Fresh expectation troubled not the land With any long'd-for change *K. John* iv 2 7
A good plot, good friends, and full of expectation . . *1 Hen. IV.* ii 3 20
The hope and expectation of thy time Is ruin'd . . . iii 2 36
Expectation and surmise Of aids incertain should not be admitted *2 Hen. IV.* i 3 23
That we now possess'd The utmost man of expectation . . . i 3 65
And at my death Thou hast seal'd up my expectation . . . iv 5 104
You stand in coldest expectation: I am the sorrier . . . v 2 31
Sadly I survive, To mock the expectation of the world . . . v 2 126
For now sits Expectation in the air, And hides a sword . *Hen. V.* ii Prol. 8
Assembled and collected, As were a war in expectation . . . ii 4 20
Our expectation hath this day an end . . . . iii 3 44
Now expectation, tickling skittish spirits, On one and other side *Troi. and Cres.* Prol. 20
I am giddy; expectation whirls me round . . . iii 2 19
Promising is the very air o' the time: it opens the eyes of expectation: performance is ever the duller for his act . . *T. of Athens* v 1 25
There have sat The live-long day, with patient expectation . *J. Cæsar* i 1 46
Here's a farmer, that hanged himself on the expectation of plenty *Macb.* ii 3 5
The rest That are within the note of expectation Already are i' the court iii 3 10
'Tis known before; our preparation stands In expectation of them *Lear* iv 4 23
Without the which there were no expectation of our prosperity *Othello* ii 1 287
Expectations and comforts of sudden respect and acquaintance . iv 2 191
Expectation fainted, Longing for what it had not . . *Ant. and Cleo.* iii 6 47
Our expectation that it would be thus Hath made us forward *Cymbeline* iii 5 28

Expected. To make her heavenly comforts of despair, When it is least expected . . . *Meas. for Meas.* iv 3 115
The great supply That was expected by the Dauphin here, Are wreck'd three nights ago . . . *K. John* v 3 10
All the expected good we're like to hear . . . *Hen. VIII.* Epil. 8
When that the general is not like the hive To whom the foragers shall all repair, What honey is expected? . . *Troi. and Cres.* i 3 83
I would have been much more a fresher man, Had I expected thee . v 6 21
I minded him how royal 'twas to pardon When it was less expected *Cor.* v 1 19
Mark Antony is every hour in Rome Expected . . *Ant. and Cleo.* ii 1 30
Cæsar himself has work, and our oppression Exceeds what we expected iv 7 3
Expected to prove so worthy as since he hath been allowed the name of *Cymbeline* i 4 2
He was expected then, But not approach'd . . . ii 4 38

Expecter. And signify this loving interview To the expecters of our Trojan part . . . *Troi. and Cres.* iv 5 156

Expectest. A sudden day of joy, That thou expect'st not *Rom. and Jul.* iii 5 111

Expecting thy reply, I profane my lips on thy foot . *L. L. Lost* iv 1 85
The solemn feast Shall more attend upon the coming space, Expecting absent friends . . . *All's Well* ii 3 189
There they hull, expecting but the aid Of Buckingham . *Richard III.* iv 4 438
Expecting ever when some envious surge Will in his brinish bowels swallow him . . . *T. Andron.* iii 1 96
As rich men deal gifts, Expecting in return twenty for one *T. of Athens* iv 3 517
You happily may think Are like the Trojan horse was stuff'd within With bloody veins, expecting overthrow . . *Pericles* i 4 94

Expedience. Are making hither with all due expedience *Richard II.* ii 1 287
In forwarding this dear expedience . . . *1 Hen. IV.* i 1 33
And will with all expedience charge on us . . . *Hen. V.* iv 3 70
I shall break The cause of our expedience to the queen *Ant. and Cleo.* i 2 185

Expedient. Therefore is it most expedient for the wise . *Much Ado* v 2 85
Whose ceremony Shall seem expedient on the now-born brief *All's Well* ii 3 186
His marches are expedient to this town, His forces strong . *K. John* ii 1 60
Who painfully with much expedient march Have brought a countercheck ii 1 223
To my closet bring The angry lords with all expedient haste . iv 2 268
Expedient manage must be made, my liege, Ere further leisure *Richard II.* i 4 39
A breach that craves a quick expedient stop! . . *2 Hen. VI.* iii 1 288
I will with all expedient duty see you . . . *Richard III.* i 2 217

Expediently. Do this expediently and turn him going . *As Y. Like It* iii 1 18

Expedition. With the speediest expedition I will dispatch him *T. G. of V.* i 3 37
You shall be employ'd To hasten on his expedition . . . i 3 77
Longer than swiftest expedition Will give thee time to leave . . iii 1 164
So much they spur their expedition . . . . v 1 6
Why, sir, I brought you word an hour since that the bark Expedition put forth to-night . . . *Com. of Errors* iv 3 38
Good expedition be my friend! . . . *W. Tale* i 2 458
Our abbeys and our priories shall pay This expedition's charge *K. John* i 1 49
How much unlook'd for is this expedition! . . . ii 1 79
The unhappy king,—Whose wrongs in us God pardon!—did set forth Upon his Irish expedition . . . *1 Hen. IV.* i 3 150
You foresee not what impediments Drag back our expedition . iv 3 19
I sent for you before your expedition to Shrewsbury . *2 Hen. IV.* ii 2 116
Be honest; and God bless your expedition! . . . i 2 249
Have I, in my poor and old motion, the expedition of thought? . iv 3 37
Omit no happy hour That may give furtherance to our expedition *Hen. V.* i 2 301
Deliver Our puissance into the hand of God, Putting it straight in expedition . . . ii 2 191
Of great expedition and knowledge in th' aunchient wars . . iii 2 82
This expedition was by York and Talbot Too rashly plotted *1 Hen. VI.* iv 4 2
Swearing that you withhold his levied host, Collected for this expedition iv 4 32
Then fiery expedition be my wing, Jove's Mercury! . *Richard III.* iv 3 54
Who intercepts my expedition?—O, she that might have intercepted thee! . . . iv 4 136
He had, before this last expedition, twenty-five wounds upon him *Coriolanus* ii 1 169
His expedition promises Present approach . . *T. of Athens* v 2 3
A mighty power, Bending their expedition toward Philippi *J. Cæsar* iv 3 170
The expedition of my violent love Outrun the pauser, reason *Macbeth* ii 3 116
Be content to slubber the gloss of your new fortunes with this more stubborn and boisterous expedition . . . *Othello* i 3 229

Expeditious. Calm seas, auspicious gales And sail so expeditious *Temp.* v 1 315

Expel. Even as one heat another heat expels . *T. G. of Ver.* ii 4 192
Why gentle Peace Should not expel these inconveniences . *Hen. V.* v 2 66
Their people Will be as rash in the repeal, as hasty To expel him *Coriolanus* iv 7 33
Let not that part of nature Which my lord paid for, be of any power To expel sickness, but prolong his hour! . . *T. of Athens* iii 1 66

Expel. Variable objects shall expel This something-settled matter in his heart . . . . *Hamlet* iii 1 180
Should patch a wall to expel the winter's flaw! . . . . v 1 239
Expelled. You, brother mine, that entertain'd ambition, Expell'd remorse and nature . . . . . *Tempest* v 1 76
Expend. I would expend it with all willingness . . . *2 Hen. VI.* iii 1 150
Expend your time with us awhile . . . . . *Hamlet* ii 2 23
If I would time expend with such a snipe, But for my sport . . *Othello* i 3 391
Careless heirs May the two latter darken and expend . . *Pericles* iii 2 29
Expense. Wilt thou, after the expense of so much money, be now a gainer? *Mer. Wives* ii 2 147
My state being gall'd with my expense, I seek to heal it only by his wealth . . . . iii 4 5
This jest shall cost me some expense . . . *Com. of Errors* iii 1 123
I implore so much expense of thy royal sweet breath as will utter a brace of words . . . . . . *L. L. Lost* v 2 523
If I have thanks, it is a dear expense . . . *M. N. Dream* i 1 249
Hold, there's expenses for thee . . . . . . *T. Night* iii 1 49
A third thinks, without expense at all, By guileful fair words peace may be obtain'd . . . . . . *1 Hen. VI.* i 1 76
For your expenses and sufficient charge, Among the people gather up a tenth . . . . v 5 92
What expense by the hour Seems to flow from him! . . *Hen. VIII.* iii 2 108
As honour, loss of time, travail, expense, Wounds, friends *Troi. and Cres.* ii 2 4
No care, no stop! so senseless of expense . . . *T. of Athens* ii 2 1
That I might so have rated my expense, As I had leave of means . . ii 2 135
We shall not spend a large expense of time Before we reckon . *Macbeth* v 8 60
What means, and where they keep, What company, at what expense *Hamlet* ii 1 9
To have the expense and waste of his revenues . . . *Lear* ii 1 102
The careful search . . . Is made with all due diligence That horse and sail and high expense Can stead the quest . . . *Pericles* iii Gower 20
Her epitaphs In glittering golden characters express A general praise to her, and care in us At whose expense 'tis done . . . . iv 3 46
His banners sable, trimm'd with rich expense . . . . . v Gower 19
Experience is by industry achieved . . . . *T. G. of Ver.* i 3 22
His years but young, but his experience old; His head unmellow'd . ii 4 69
Unless experience be a jewel that I have purchased at an infinite rate *Mer. Wives* ii 2 212
Your long experience of her wisdom, Her sober virtue . *Com. of Errors* iii 1 89
How hast thou purchased this experience?—By my penny of observation *L. L. Lost* iii 1 27
Yes, I have gained my experience.—And your experience makes you sad: I had rather have a fool to make me merry than experience to make me sad . . . . *As Y. Like It* iv 1 26
Scatters young men through the world To seek their fortunes farther than at home, Where small experience grows . . *T. of Shrew* i 2 52
Such as his reading And manifest experience had collected . *All's Well* i 3 229
The dearest issue of his practice, And of his old experience the only darling . . . . ii 1 110
I have then sinned against his experience . . . . . ii 5 10
Why art thou old, and want'st experience? . . . *2 Hen. VI.* v 1 171
Make bold her bashful years with your experience . *Richard III.* iv 4 326
Frosty signs and chaps of age, Grave witnesses of true experience *T. An.* v 3 78
The issue will be, I shall have so much experience for my pains *Othello* ii 3 373
Pawn their experience to their present pleasure . *Ant. and Cleo.* i 4 32
Experience, manhood, honour, ne'er before Did violate so itself . . iii 10 23
Than in my every action to be guided by others' experiences . *Cymbeline* i 4 49
Experience, O, thou disprovest report! . . . . . iv 2 34
Peace, peace, and give experience tongue . . . . *Pericles* i 2 37
Experienced. A gentleman, thereto Clerk-like experienced . *W. Tale* i 2 392
Knit all the Greekish ears To his experienced tongue . *Troi. and Cres.* i 3 68
And set down—As best thou art experienced . . *Coriolanus* iv 5 145
Experiment. To make another experiment of his suspicion *Mer. Wives* iv 2 36
Of heaven, not me, make an experiment . . . *All's Well* ii 1 157
And hold me pace in deep experiments . . . *1 Hen. IV.* iii 1 49
Your Moor and you Are singled forth to try experiments *T. Andron.* ii 3 69
Experimental. Which with experimental seal doth warrant The tenour of my book . . . . *Much Ado* iv 1 168
Expert. A valiant and most expert gentleman . . . *Hen. V.* iii 7 139
Take some order in the town, Placing therein some expert officers *1 Hen. VI.* iii 2 127
And his pilot Of very expert and approved allowance . . *Othello* ii 1 49
Is your Englishman so expert in his drinking? . . . . ii 3 82
Expertness. What his valour, honesty, and expertness in wars *All's Well* iv 3 202
What say you to his expertness in war? . . . . . iv 3 296
Expiate. Make haste; the hour of death is expiate . *Richard III.* iii 3 23
Expiration. At the expiration of the year, Come challenge me *L. L. Lost* v 2 814
And here art come Before the expiration of thy time *Richard II.* ii 3 111
If, till the expiration of your month, You will return . . *Lear* ii 4 205
Expire. That's a month before This bond expires . . *Mer. of Venice* i 3 160
Garments; whose constancies Expire before their fashions . *All's Well* i 2 63
Even this ill night, your breathing shall expire . . . *K. John* v 4 36
I will lay odds that, ere this year expire, We bear our civil swords and native fire As far as France . . . . *2 Hen. IV.* v 5 111
And expire the term Of a despised life closed in my breast *Rom. and Jul.* i 4 109
And good men's lives Expire before the flowers in their caps . *Macbeth* iv 3 172
Where you may abide till your date expire . . . *Pericles* iii 4 14
Expired. I would his troubles likewise were expired . . *1 Hen. VI.* ii 5 31
Till term of eighteen months Be full expired . . . *2 Hen. VI.* i 1 68
Your time's expired: Either expound now, or receive your sentence *Per.* i 1 89
If in which time expired, he not return . . . . . . ii 4 47
I must needs be gone; My twelve months are expired . . . iii 3 2
Expiring. Methinks I am a prophet new inspired And thus expiring do foretell of him . . . . *Richard II.* ii 1 32
Explain The labour of each knight in his device . . . *Pericles* ii 2 14
Explication. Most barbarous intimation! yet a kind of insinuation, as it were, in via, in way, of explication . . . . . *L. L. Lost* iv 2 14
Exploit. He that sets up his rest to do more exploits with his mace than a morris-pike . . . . *Com. of Errors* iv 3 27
A trim exploit, a manly enterprise, To conjure tears up in a poor maid's eyes With your derision! . . . . . . *M. N. Dream* iii 2 157
With bleared visages, come forth to view The issue of the exploit *Mer. of Venice* iii 2 60
A nursery to our gentry, who are sick For breathing and exploit *All's W.* i 2 17
I will grace the attempt for a worthy exploit . . . . iii 6 72
I must give myself some hurts, and say I got them in exploit . . iv 1 41
And then will they adventure upon the exploit themselves . *1 Hen. IV.* i 2 192
Imagination of some great exploit Drives him beyond the bounds of patience . . . . i 3 199
Exploit. Your day's service at Shrewsbury hath a little gilded over your night's exploit on Gad's-hill . . . . . . *2 Hen. IV.* i 2 169
In the very May-morn of his youth, Ripe for exploits . . *Hen. V.* i 2 121
Of all exploits since first I follow'd arms, Ne'er heard I of a warlike enterprise More venturous or desperate than this . . *1 Hen. VI.* ii 1 43
I shall as famous be by this exploit As Scythian Tomyris by Cyrus' death . . . . ii 3 5
Flight cannot stain the honour you have won; But mine it will, that no exploit have done . . . . iv 5 27
Thy late exploits done in the heart of France . . . *2 Hen. VI.* i 1 196
Know'st thou not any whom corrupting gold Would tempt unto a close exploit of death? . . . . *Richard III.* iv 2 35
Who, but for dreaming on this fond exploit, For want of means, poor rats, had hang'd themselves . . . . v 3 330
What exploit's in hand? where sups he to-night? . *Troi. and Cres.* iii 1 89
Whose high exploits and honourable deeds Ingrateful Rome requites with foul contempt . . . . *T. Andron.* v 1 11
If Brutus have in hand Any exploit worthy the name of honour.—Such an exploit have I in hand . . . . . . *J. Cæsar* ii 1 317
Time, thou anticipatest my dread exploits . . . *Macbeth* iv 1 144
I will work him To an exploit, now ripe in my device . *Hamlet* iv 7 65
And, in the fleshment of this dread exploit, Drew on me here again *Lear* ii 2 130
Expose. And expose Those tender limbs of thine to the event Of the none-sparing war . . . . *All's Well* iii 2 106
For his sake Did I expose myself, pure for his love . . . *T. Night* v 1 86
All the instruments which aided to expose the child were even then lost when it was found . . . . *W. Tale* v 2 78
Why do fond men expose themselves to battle? . *T. of Athens* iii 5 42
Take physic, pomp; Expose thyself to feel what wretches feel . *Lear* iii 4 34
Exposed unto the sea, which hath requit it . . . *Tempest* iii 3 71
Poor wretch, That for thy mother's fault art thus exposed To loss! *W. T.* iii 3 50
And hath he too Exposed this paragon? . . . . . . v 1 153
Incurr'd a traitor's name; exposed myself, From certain and possess'd conveniences, To doubtful fortunes . . . *Troi. and Cres.* iii 3 6
O, you shall be exposed, my lord, to dangers As infinite as imminent! iv 4 70
Whose bare unhoused trunks, To the conflicting elements exposed *T. of Athens* iv 3 230
Exposing what is mortal and unsure To all that fortune, death and danger dare, Even for an egg-shell . . . . *Hamlet* iv 4 51
Exposing it . . . to the greedy touch Of common-kissing Titan *Cymb.* iii 4 164
Exposition. I have an exposition of sleep come upon me. *M. N. Dream* iv 1 43
You know the law, your exposition Hath been most sound *Mer. of Ven.* iv 1 237
To hear with reverence Your exposition on the holy text . *2 Hen. IV.* iv 2 7
A most courteous exposition . . . . . . *Rom. and Jul.* ii 4 60
Your exposition misinterpreting, We might proceed to cancel of your days . . . . *Pericles* i 1 112
Expositor. His fair tongue, conceit's expositor . . . *L. L. Lost* ii 1 72
Expostulate. The time now serves not to expostulate . *T. G. of Ver.* iii 1 251
Stay not to expostulate, make speed . . . . . *3 Hen. VI.* ii 5 135
Bitterly could I expostulate, Save that, for reverence to some alive *Richard III.* iii 7 192
To expostulate What majesty should be, what duty is, Why day is day, night night . . . . *Hamlet* ii 2 86
I'll not expostulate with her, lest her body and beauty unprovide my mind again . . . . *Othello* iv 1 217
Expostulation. We must use expostulation kindly, For it is parting from us . . . . *Troi. and Cres.* iv 4 62
Exposture. Determine on some course, More than a wild exposture to each chance . . . . *Coriolanus* iv 1 36
Exposure. To weaken and discredit our exposure . *Troi. and Cres.* i 3 195
When we have our naked frailties hid, That suffer in exposure *Macbeth* ii 3 133
Expound. Man is but an ass, if he go about to expound this dream *M. N. Dream* iv 1 212
Left me here behind, to expound the meaning or moral of his signs *T. of Shrew* iv 4 79
Expound unto me, boy . . . . *Hen. V.* iv 4 62
And to expound His beastly mind to us . . . . *Cymbeline* i 6 152
Your time's expired: Either expound now, or receive your sentence *Per.* i 1 90
Expounded. This by Calpurnia's dream is signified.—And this way have you well expounded it . . . . *J. Cæsar* ii 2 91
Which read and not expounded, 'tis decreed . . . *Pericles* i 1 57
Express. On mine honour, My words express my purpose *Meas. for Meas.* ii 4 148
An express command, under penalty, to deliver his head . . iv 2 176
That shall express my true love's fasting pain . . . *L. L. Lost* iv 3 122
Neither rhyme nor reason can express how much . . *As Y. Like It* iii 2 418
To express the like kindness, myself, that have been more kindly beholding to you than any . . . . *T. of Shrew* ii 1 77
You ne'er oppress'd me with a mother's groan, Yet I express to you a mother's care . . . . *All's Well* i 3 154
All the progress, more and less, Resolvedly more leisure shall express . v 3 332
All is well ended, if this suit be won, That you express content . . Epil. 337
Therefore it charges me in manners the rather to express myself *T. Night* ii 1 16
To the contrary I have express commandment . . . *W. Tale* ii 2 8
Mine integrity Being counted falsehood, shall, as I express it, Be so received . . . . iii 2 28
Ballad-makers cannot be able to express it . . . . . v 2 27
How I have sped among the clergymen, The sums I have collected shall express . . . . *K. John* iv 2 142
Bid me tell my tale in express words . . . . . . iv 2 234
We give express charge, . . . there be nothing compelled . *Hen. V.* iii 6 114
I have express commandment That thou nor none of thine shall be let in *1 Hen. VI.* i 3 20
Let me have your express opinions . . . . . . i 4 64
I can express no kinder sign of love Than this kind kiss . *2 Hen. VI.* i 1 18
As I in justice and true right express it . . . . . . v 2 25
May worthy Troilus be half attach'd With that which here his passion doth express? . . . . *Troi. and Cres.* v 2 162
Daughter, sing; or express yourself in a more comfortable sort *Coriolanus* i 3 1
Let him alone, or so many so minded, Wave thus, to express his disposition . . . . i 6 74
Let deeds express What's like to be their words . . . . iii 1 132
Ere he express himself, or move the people With what he would say . v 6 55
That you would once use our hearts, whereby we might express some part of our zeals . . . . *T. of Athens* i 2 88
These well express in thee thy latter spirits . . . . . v 4 74
What so poor a man as Hamlet is May do, to express his love *Hamlet* i 5 186
How infinite in faculty! in form and moving how express and admirable! ii 2 317
We shall express our duty in his eye . . . . . . iv 4 6
Meantime we shall express our darker purpose . . . . *Lear* i 1 37
Patience and sorrow strove Who should express her goodliest . . iv 3 19

Express. As the fits and stirs of's mind Could best express how slow his soul sail'd on, How swift his ship *Cymbeline* i 3 13
No further with your din Express impatience, lest you stir up mine v 4 112
It pleaseth you, my royal father, to express My commendations great *Pericles* ii 2 8
Her epitaphs In glittering golden characters express A general praise to her iv 3 44
Expressed. As you are well express'd By all external warrants *M. for M.* ii 4 136
Proud with his form, in his eye pride express'd *L. L. Lost* ii 1 237
My wooing mind shall be express'd In russet yeas and honest kersey noes v 2 412
Such sum or sums as are Express'd in the condition *Mer. of Venice* i 3 149
Turns to a wild of nothing, save of joy, Express'd and not express'd iii 2 185
It is not so express'd: but what of that? iv 1 260
Scorn'd a fair colour, or express'd it stolen *All's Well* v 3 50
Express'd himself in all his deeds A father and a friend to thee *T. Andron.* i 1 422
Would be well express'd In our condition *T. of Athens* i 1 76
Costly thy habit as thy purse can buy, But not express'd in fancy *Hamlet* i 3 71
An old thing 'twas, but it express'd her fortune *Othello* iv 3 29
Expresseth. So her plenteous womb Expresseth his full tilth *M. for M.* i 4 44
Expressing. Such gesture and such sound, expressing, Although they want the use of tongue, a kind Of excellent dumb discourse *Tempest* iii 3 37
Past all expressing *Mer. of Venice* iii 5 78
Expressive. Be more expressive to them *All's Well* ii 1 54
Expressly. When I to feast expressly am forbid *L. L. Lost* ii 1 62
The words expressly are 'a pound of flesh' *Mer. of Venice* iv 1 307
Your physicians have expressly charged *T. of Shrew* Ind. 2 123
And I expressly am forbid to touch it iv 1 174
To whom expressly I bring greeting too *Hen. V.* ii 4 112
'Tis expressly against the law of arms iv 7 1
Who dare cross 'em, Bearing the king's will from his mouth expressly? *Hen. VIII.* iii 2 235
Expressly proves That no man is the lord of any thing *Troi. and Cres.* iii 3 114
The prince expressly hath Forbidden bandying in Verona streets *R. and J.* iii 1 91
I am sent expressly to your lordship.—Give me breath *T. of Athens* ii 2 33
Expressure. The expressure that it bears, green let it be *Mer. Wives* v 5 71
The expressure of his eye, forehead, and complexion *T. Night* ii 3 171
An operation more divine Than breath or pen can give expressure to *Troi. and Cres.* iii 3 204
Expulsed. For ever should they be expulsed from France *1 Hen. VI.* iii 3 25
Expulsion. A merrier day did never yet greet Rome, No, not the expulsion of the Tarquins *Coriolanus* v 4 46
A wooer More hateful than the foul expulsion is Of thy dear husband *Cymbeline* ii 1 65
Exquisite. Her beauty is exquisite, but her favour infinite *T. G. of Ver.* ii 1 59
Who? the most exquisite Claudio?—Even he *Much Ado* i 3 52
Most radiant, exquisite and unmatchable beauty *T. Night* i 5 181
Thy exquisite reason, dear knight?—I have no exquisite reason for't ii 3 155
My most exquisite Sir Topas!—Nay, I am for all waters iv 2 67
Examine other beauties.—'Tis the way To call hers exquisite *R. and J.* i 1 235
Thy honourable virtuous lord, my very exquisite friend *T. of Athens* iii 2 32
She's a most exquisite lady.—And, I'll warrant her, full of game *Othello* ii 3 18
Why, this is a more exquisite song than the other ii 3 101
Jewels Of rich and exquisite form *Cymbeline* i 6 190
She hath all courtly parts more exquisite Than lady, ladies, woman iii 5 71
Exsufflicate. To such exsufflicate and blown surmises *Othello* iii 3 182
Extant. Both the proofs are extant *Mer. Wives* v 5 127
Is there no virtue extant? *1 Hen. IV.* ii 4 132
But in this extant moment *Troi. and Cres.* iv 5 168
The story is extant, and writ in choice Italian *Hamlet* iii 2 273
Extemporal. Assist me, some extemporal god of rhyme *L. L. Lost* i 2 189
Will you hear an extemporal epitaph on the death of the deer? iv 2 50
I with sudden and extemporal speech Purpose to answer *1 Hen. VI.* iii 1 6
Extemporally. The quick comedians Extemporally will stage us *A. and C.* v 2 217
Extempore. I am slow of study.—You may do it extempore, for it is nothing but roaring *M. N. Dream* i 2 70
It is extempore, from my mother-wit *T. of Shrew* ii 1 265
Sure the gods do this year connive at us, and we may do any thing extempore *W. Tale* iv 4 692
Shall we have a play extempore?—Content *1 Hen. IV.* ii 4 309
And ever since thou hast blushed extempore ii 4 347
Extend. My purpose doth extend Not a frown further *Tempest* v 1 29
To buy his favour, I extend this friendship *Mer. of Venice* i 3 169
Thou dost deserve enough; and yet enough May not extend so far ii 7 28
That would not extend his might, only where qualities were level *All's W.* i 3 118
The duke shall both speak of it, and extend to you what further becomes iii 6 73
I extend my hand to him thus *T. Night* ii 5 72
You do lack That mercy which fierce fire and iron extends *K. John* iv 1 120
It reaches far, and where 'twill not extend, Thither he darts it *Hen. VIII.* i 1 111
To Lacedæmon did my land extend *T. of Athens* ii 2 160
If much you note him, You shall offend him and extend his passion *Macbeth* iii 4 57
Which of you shall we say doth love us most? That we our largest bounty may extend *Lear* i 1 53
Let it not gall your patience, good Iago, That I extend my manners *Oth.* ii 1 99
You do extend These thoughts of horror further than you shall Find cause in Cæsar *Ant. and Cleo.* v 2 62
You speak him far.—I do extend him, sir, within himself *Cymbeline* i 1 25
The approbation of those that weep this lamentable divorce under her colours are wonderfully to extend him i 4 21
Towards himself, his goodness forespent on us, We must extend our notice ii 3 65
Extended. When vice makes mercy, mercy's so extended *M. for M.* iv 2 115
Extended With vilest torture let my life be ended *All's Well* ii 1 176
Extended or contracted all proportions To a most hideous object v 3 51
The report of her is extended more than can be thought to begin from such a cottage *W. Tale* iv 2 49
Form'd in the applause Where they're extended *Troi. and Cres.* iii 3 120
Hath, with his Parthian force, Extended Asia from Euphrates *A. and C.* i 2 105
Extent. Make an extent upon his house and lands *As Y. Like It* iii 1 17
In this uncivil and unjust extent Against thy peace *T. Night* iv 1 57
And, for the extent Of egal justice, used in such contempt *T. Andron.* iv 4 3
Lest my extent to the players, which, I tell you, must show fairly outward, should more appear like entertainment than yours *Hamlet* ii 2 390
The very head and front of my offending Hath this extent, no more *Oth.* i 3 81
Extenuate. You may not so extenuate his offence *Meas. for Meas.* ii 1 27
And so extenuate the 'forehand sin *Much Ado* iv 1 51
Which by no means we may extenuate *M. N. Dream* i 1 120
To persist In doing wrong extenuates not wrong *Troi. and Cres.* ii 2 187
Speak of me as I am; nothing extenuate *Othello* v 2 342
We will extenuate rather than enforce *Ant. and Cleo.* v 2 125
Extenuated. His glory not extenuated, wherein he was worthy *J. Cæsar* iii 2 42
Extenuation. Yet such extenuation let me beg *1 Hen. IV.* iii 2 22
Exterior. She did so course o'er my exteriors *Mer. Wives* i 3 72
Would you not swear, All you that see her, that she were a maid, By these exterior shows? *Much Ado* iv 1 41
And not alone in habit and device, Exterior form *K. John* i 1 211
This prostrate and exterior bending *2 Hen. IV.* iv 5 149
Sith nor the exterior nor the inward man Resembles that it was *Hamlet* ii 2 6
Exteriorly. Which, howsoever rude exteriorly, Is yet the cover of a fairer mind *K. John* iv 2 257
Extermined. If you do sorrow at my grief in love, By giving love your sorrow and my grief Were both extermined *As Y. Like It* iii 5 89
Extern. My outward action doth demonstrate The native act and figure of my heart In compliment extern *Othello* i 1 63
External. As you are well express'd By all external warrants *Meas. for Meas.* ii 4 137
But that our soft conditions and our hearts Should well agree with our external parts *T. of Shrew* v 2 168
Having no external thing to lose But the word 'maid' *K. John* ii 1 571
These external manners of laments Are merely shadows to the unseen grief That swells with silence *Richard II.* iv 1 296
Her virtues graced with external gifts *1 Hen. VI.* v 5 3
If they had swallow'd poison, 'twould appear By external swelling *Ant. and Cleo.* v 2 349
Extinct. My oil-dried lamp and time-bewasted light Shall be extinct with age and endless night *Richard II.* i 3 222
Giving more light than heat, extinct in both, Even in their promise *Ham.* i 3 118
Extincted. Give renew'd fire to our extincted spirits! *Othello* ii 1 81
Extinguish. Natural graces that extinguish art *1 Hen. VI.* v 3 192
Extinguit. Quod me alit, me extinguit *Pericles* ii 2 33
Extirp. It is impossible to extirp it [lechery] quite *Meas. for Meas.* iii 2 110
Extirpate. Should presently extirpate me and mine *Tempest* i 2 125
Extirped. But be extirped from our provinces *1 Hen. VI.* iii 3 24
Extol. Flatter and praise, commend, extol their graces *T. G. of Ver.* iii 1 102
Wherein have I so deserved of you, That you extol me thus? *M. for M.* v 1 508
My mother, Who has a charter to extol her blood *Coriolanus* i 9 14
Hath not a tomb so evident as a chair To extol what it hath done iv 7 53
Extolled. If I should pay you for't as 'tis extoll'd, It would unclew me quite *T. of Athens* i 1 167
Extolment. But, in the verity of extolment, I take him to be a soul of great article *Hamlet* v 2 121
Exton. Sir Pierce of Exton, who lately came from the king *Richard II.* v 5 100
Exton, thy fierce hand Hath with the king's blood stain'd the king's own land v 5 110
Exton, I thank thee not; for thou hast wrought A deed of slander v 6 34
Extort. None of noble sort Would so offend a virgin and extort A poor soul's patience *M. N. Dream* iii 2 160
You will not extort from me what I am willing to keep in *T. Night* ii 1 14
Do not extort thy reasons from this clause iii 1 165
Till the injurious Romans did extort This tribute from us *Cymbeline* iii 1 48
Extort from's that Which we have done, whose answer would be death iv 4 12
Extorted. Are my chests fill'd up with extorted gold? *2 Hen. VI.* iv 7 105
Or if thou hast uphoarded in thy life Extorted treasure *Hamlet* i 1 137
Extortion. The clergy's bags Are lank and lean with thy extortions *2 Hen. VI.* i 3 132
That goodness Of gleaning all the land's wealth into one, Into your own hands, cardinal, by extortion *Hen. VIII.* iii 2 285
Extract. May it be possible, that foreign hire Could out of thee extract one spark of evil? *Hen. V.* ii 2 101
Extracted. Compounded of many simples, extracted from many objects *As Y. Like It* iv 1 17
Extracting. A most extracting frenzy of mine own *T. Night* v 1 288
For putting the hand in the pocket and extracting it clutched *M. for M.* iii 2 49
Extraordinary. There's something extraordinary in thee *Mer. Wives* iii 3 75
You must not learn me how to remember any extraordinary pleasure *As Y. Like It* i 2 7
By some severals Of head-piece extraordinary *W. Tale* i 2 227
These signs have mark'd me extraordinary *1 Hen. IV.* iii 1 41
Such eyes As, sick and blunted with community, Afford no extraordinary gaze iii 2 78
Extraordinarily. I mean not to sweat extraordinarily *2 Hen. IV.* i 2 235
Your pulsidge beats as extraordinarily as heart would desire ii 4 26
Extraught. Shamest thou not, knowing whence thou art extraught, To let thy tongue detect thy base-born heart? *3 Hen. VI.* ii 2 142
Extravagancy. My determinate voyage is mere extravagancy *T. Night* ii 1 12
Extravagant. A foolish extravagant spirit, full of forms, figures *L. L. Lost* iv 2 68
The extravagant and erring spirit hies To his confine *Hamlet* i 1 154
An extravagant and wheeling stranger Of here and every where *Othello* i 1 137
Extreme. But qualify the fire's extreme rage *T. G. of Ver.* ii 7 22
Be not as extreme in submission As in offence *Mer. Wives* iv 4 11
The extreme parts of time extremely forms All causes to the purpose of his speed *L. L. Lost* v 2 750
My presence May well abate the over-merry spleen Which otherwise would grow into extremes *T. of Shrew* Ind. 1 138
Though little fire grows great with little wind, Yet extreme gusts will blow out fire and all ii 1 136
I have caught extreme cold iv 1 47
To the extreme edge of hazard *All's Well* iii 3 6
To chide at your extremes it not becomes me *W. Tale* iv 4 6
The fire is dead with grief, Being create for comfort, to be used In undeserved extremes *K. John* iv 1 108
Fierce extremes In their continuance will not feel themselves v 7 13
When I was dry with rage and extreme toil, Breathless and faint *1 Hen. IV.* i 3 31
And makes it course from the inwards to the parts extreme *2 Hen. IV.* iv 3 116
Nor shrinking for distress, But always resolute in most extremes *1 Hen. VI.* iv 1 38
Who can be patient in such extremes? Ah, wretched man! *3 Hen. VI.* i 1 215
By so much is the wonder in extremes ii 2 115
The extreme peril of the case *Richard III.* iii 5 44
I with grief and extreme age shall perish And never look upon thy face iv 4 185
Time, force, and death, Do to this body what extremes you can *Tr. and Cr.* iv 2 108
The painful service, The extreme dangers *Coriolanus* iv 5 75
Speak with possibilities, And do not break into these deep extremes *T. Andron.* iii 1 216
Almost broke my heart with extreme laughter v 1 113
Tempering extremities with extreme sweet *Rom. and Jul.* ii Prol. 14
'Twixt my extremes and me this bloody knife Shall play the umpire iv 1 62
You are now within a foot Of the extreme verge *Lear* iv 6 26
'Twixt two extremes of passion, joy and grief v 3 198
Not easily jealous, but being wrought Perplex'd in the extreme *Othello* v 2 346

Extreme. Like to the time o' the year between the extremes Of hot and cold . . . . *Ant. and Cleo.* i 5 51
Prays, and destroys the prayer ; no midway 'Twixt these extremes at all iii 4 20
Extremely. The extreme parts of time extremely forms All causes to the purpose of his speed . . . . . *L. L. Lost* v 2 750
Extremely stretch'd and conn'd with cruel pain . *M. N. Dream* v 1 80
He was stirr'd With such an agony, he sweat extremely *Hen. VIII.* ii 1 33
Others, to hear the city Abused extremely, and to cry 'That's witty!' Epil. 6
Urged extremely for't and showed what necessity belonged to't *T. of A.* iii 2 14
Extremest. To the extremest shore of my modesty . *Meas. for Meas.* iii 2 266
My extremest means Lie all unlock'd to your occasions *Mer. of Venice* i 1 138
Stood on the extremest verge of the swift brook . . *As Y. Like It* ii 1 42
To the extremest point Of mortal breathing . . *Richard II.* iv 1 47
I have speeded hither with the very extremest inch of possibility *2 Hen. IV.* iv 3 38
To take her in her heart's extremest hate, With curses in her mouth *Richard III.* i 2 232
As near as the extremest ends Of parallels . . . *Troi. and Cres.* i 3 167
Deserves the extremest death . . . . *Coriolanus* iii 3 82
To kill, I grant, is sin's extremest gust . . *T. of Athens* iii 5 54
From the extremest upward of thy head To the descent and dust below thy foot, A most toad-spotted traitor . . . . *Lear* v 3 136
Extremities. What blows, what extremities he endured . . . *1 Hen. IV.* i 2 213
You are too absolute ; Though therein you can never be too noble, But when extremities speak . . . . *Coriolanus* iii 2 41
Tempering extremities with extreme sweet . . *Rom. and Jul.* ii Prol. 14
What he is, augmented, Would run to these and these extremities *J. Cæsar* ii 1 31
Extremity. Any extremity rather than a mischief . . *Mer. Wives* iv 2 75
If I find not what I seek, show no colour for my extremity . iv 2 169
Whom the fates have mark'd To bear the extremity of dire mishap! *C. of Er.* i 1 142
Till this afternoon his passion Ne'er brake into extremity of rage . . v 1 48
O time's extremity, Hast thou so crack'd and splitted my poor tongue? v 1 307
Which she must dote on in extremity . . *M. N. Dream* iii 2 3
Those that are in extremity of either are abominable fellows *As Y. L. It* iv 1 5
You are a fool And turn'd into the extremity of love . . iv 3 23
To save your life in this extremity, This favour will I do you *T. of S.* iv 2 102
Could not say if the importance were joy or sorrow ; but in the extremity of the one, it must needs be . . . . *W. Tale* v 2 20
Extremity of weather continuing, this mystery remained undiscovered v 2 129
Dissolve the bands of life, Which false hope lingers in extremity *Rich. II.* ii 2 72
'Tis she That tempers him to this extremity . . *Richard III.* i 1 65
The queen's in labour, They say, in great extremity . *Hen. VIII.* v 1 19
Shall to the edge of all extremity Pursue each other . *Troi. and Cres.* iv 5 68
In the extremity of great and little, Valour and pride excel themselves in Hector . . . . iv 5 78
You were used To say extremity was the trier of spirits *Coriolanus* iv 1 4
Now this extremity Hath brought me to thy hearth . . iv 5 84
I have heard my grandsire say full oft, Extremity of griefs would make men mad . . . . *T. Andron.* iv 1 19
The nurse cursed in the pantry, and every thing in extremity *R. and J.* i 3 103
The middle of humanity thou never knewest, but the extremity of both ends . . . . *T. of Athens* iv 3 301
In my youth I suffered much extremity for love ; very near this *Hamlet* ii 2 192
Women's fear and love holds quantity ; In neither aught, or in extremity iii 2 178
Thou wert better in thy grave than to answer with thy uncovered body this extremity of the skies . . . . *Lear* iii 4 106
To amplify too much, would make much more, And top extremity . v 3 207
I did proceed upon just grounds To this extremity . . *Othello* v 2 139
Speak, man : thy tongue May take off some extremity . . *Cymbeline* iii 4 17
Smiling Extremity out of act . . . . . . *Pericles* v 1 140
Exult. Who might be your mother, That you insult, exult, and all at once, Over the wretched? . . . . . *As Y. Like It* iii 5 36
I would exult, man : you know, he brought me out o' favour *T. Night* ii 5 8
Exultation. Your exultation Partake to every one . *W. Tale* v 3 131
Eyases. An aery of children, little eyases . . . . *Hamlet* ii 2 355
Eyas-musket. How now, my eyas-musket! . . . *Mer. Wives* iii 3 22
Eye. Wipe thou thine eyes ; have comfort . . . *Tempest* i 2 25
It is a hint That wrings mine eyes to't . . . . . . i 2 135
Of his bones are coral made ; Those are pearls that were his eyes . i 2 398
The fringed curtains of thine eye advance And say what thou seest yond i 2 408
Who with mine eyes, never since at ebb, beheld The king my father wreck'd . . . . i 2 435
At the first sight They have changed eyes . . . . . i 2 441
The ground indeed is tawny.—With an eye of green in't . . ii 1 55
She at least is banish'd from your eye, Who hath cause to wet the grief on't . . . . ii 1 126
I wish mine eyes Would, with themselves, shut up my thoughts . ii 1 191
This is a strange repose, to be asleep With eyes wide open . . ii 1 214
The setting of thine eye and cheek proclaim A matter from thee . . ii 1 229
As mine eyes open'd, I saw their weapons drawn . . . . ii 1 319
Thy eyes are almost set in thy head . . . . iii 2 10
I must Bestow upon the eyes of this young couple Some vanity of mine iv 1 40
Appear, and pertly! No tongue! all eyes! be silent . . . iv 1 59
Mine eyes, even sociable to the show of thine, Fall fellowly drops . v 1 63
They devour their reason and scarce think Their eyes do offices of truth v 1 156
Our royal, good and gallant ship, our master Capering to eye her . v 1 238
In eye of every exercise Worthy his youth and nobleness of birth *T. G. of V.* i 3 32
Not an eye that sees you but is a physician to comment on your malady ii 1 41
O, that you had mine eyes ; or your own eyes had the lights they were wont to have! . . . . ii 1 77
My grandam, having no eyes, look you, wept herself blind at my parting ii 3 14
His mistress Did hold his eyes lock'd in her crystal looks . . ii 4 89
Love hath twenty pair of eyes.—They say that Love hath not an eye at all ii 4 95
Love hath chased sleep from my enthralled eyes . . . . ii 4 134
I read your fortune in your eye. Was this the idol that you worship so? ii 4 143
Which way I may bestow myself To be regarded in her sun-bright eye . iii 1 88
Love doth to her eyes repair, To help him of his blindness . . iv 2 46
Her eyes are grey as glass, and so are mine: Ay, but her forehead's low iv 4 197
By Jove I vow, I should have scratch'd out your unseeing eyes . iv 4 209
The old saying is, Black men are pearls in beauteous ladies' eyes.—'Tis true ; such pearls as put out ladies' eyes . . . . . . v 2 12
Nought but mine eye Could have persuaded me . . . . . v 4 64
What is in Silvia's face, but I may spy More fresh in Julia's with a constant eye? . . . . v 4 115
Who even now gave me good eyes too . . . . *Mer. Wives* i 3 67
The appetite of her eye did seem to scorch me up like a burning-glass! i 3 74
Have not your worship a wart above your eye? . . . . . i 4 157
As long as I have an eye to make difference of men's liking . . ii 1 57
Take heed, have open eye, for thieves do foot by night . . . ii 1 126
Eye. As you have one eye upon my follies, as you hear them unfolded, turn another into the register of your own . . . *Mer. Wives* ii 2 192
Had you rather lead mine eyes, or eye your master's heels? . . . iii 2 4
Hath he any eyes? hath he any thinking? . . . . . . iii 2 31
He capers, he dances, he has eyes of youth, he writes verses . . . iii 2 68
I see how thine eye would emulate the diamond . . . . iii 3 58
I'll wink and couch : no man their works must eye . . . v 5 52
I love the people, But do not like to stage me to their eyes *Meas. for Meas.* i 1 69
You that have worn your eyes almost out in the service . . . i 2 113
Do I love her, That I desire to hear her speak again, And feast upon her eyes? . . . . ii 2 179
And those eyes, the break of day, Lights that do mislead the morn . iv 1 3
O place and greatness! millions of false eyes Are stuck upon thee! . iv 1 60
O, I will to him and pluck out his eyes! . . . . iv 3 124
The duke comes home to-morrow ; nay, dry your eyes . . . iv 3 132
Command these fretting waters from your eyes With a light heart . iv 3 151
I am pale at mine heart to see thine eyes so red : thou must be patient iv 3 158
Dishonour not your eye By throwing it on any other object . . . v 1 22
Her shall you hear disproved to her eyes, Till she herself confess it . v 1 161
Methinks I see a quickening in his eye . . . . v 1 500
Fixing our eyes on whom our care was fix'd . . *Com. of Errors* i 1 85
Nimble jugglers that deceive the eye, Dark-working sorcerers . . i 2 98
There's nothing situate under heaven's eye But hath his bound . . ii 1 16
I know his eye doth homage otherwhere . . . . ii 1 104
Since that my beauty cannot please his eye, I'll weep what's left away ii 1 114
Never object pleasing in thine eye . . . Unless I spake, or look'd . ii 2 117
What error drives our eyes and ears amiss? . . . . . . ii 2 186
No longer will I be a fool, To put the finger in the eye and weep . ii 2 206
Muffle your false love . . . : Let not my sister read it in your eye . iii 2 9
It is a fault that springeth from your eye . . . . . . iii 2 55
Mine eye's clear eye, my dear heart's dearer heart, My food, my fortune iii 2 62
Mightst thou perceive austerely in his eye That he did plead in earnest? iv 2 2
I think him better than I say, And yet would herein others' eyes were worse . . . . iv 2 26
I'll pluck out these false eyes That would behold in me this shameful sport . . . . iv 4 107
Hath not else his eye Stray'd his affection in unlawful love? . . . v 1 50
A sin prevailing much in youthful men, Who give their eyes the liberty of gazing . . . . v 1 53
Gazing in mine eyes, feeling my pulse . . . . v 1 243
I see two husbands, or mine eyes deceive me . . . . . . v 1 331
In mine eye she is the sweetest lady that ever I looked on . *Much Ado* i 1 189
Pick out mine eyes with a ballad-maker's pen . . . . . . i 1 254
I look'd upon her with a soldier's eye, That liked . . . . . i 1 300
I have a good eye, uncle ; I can see a church by daylight . . . ii 1 85
Let every eye negotiate for itself And trust no agent . . . . ii 1 185
May I be so converted and see with these eyes? I cannot tell . . ii 3 24
Disdain and scorn ride sparkling in her eyes, Misprising what they look on iii 1 51
Methinks you look with your eyes as other women do . . . . iii 4 92
Are our eyes our own?—All this is so . . . . iv 1 72
Do not live, Hero ; do not ope thine eyes . . . . . . iv 1 125
Why ever wast thou lovely in my eyes? . . . . iv 1 132
And in her eye there hath appear'd a fire, To burn the errors . . iv 1 164
Into the eye and prospect of his soul . . . . iv 1 231
In some reclusive and religious life, Out of all eyes, tongues, minds . iv 1 245
I have deceived even your very eyes . . . . v 1 239
Let me see his eyes, That, when I note another man like him, I may avoid him . . . . v 1 269
I will live in thy heart, die in thy lap and be buried in thy eyes . . v 2 105
Your niece regards me with an eye of favour.—That eye my daughter lent her . . . . v 4 22
And I do with an eye of love requite her . . . . v 4 24
Your light grows dark by losing of your eyes . . . . *L. L. Lost* i 1 79
Study me how to please the eye indeed By fixing it upon a fairer eye, Who dazzling so, that eye shall be his heed And give him light that it was blinded by . . . . i 1 80
Beauty is bought by judgement of the eye . . . . ii 1 15
His eye begets occasion for his wit . . . . ii 1 69
By the heart's still rhetoric disclosed with eyes, Deceive me not now . ii 1 229
All his behaviours did make their retire To the court of his eye . . ii 1 235
Proud with his form, in his eye pride express'd . . . . . ii 1 237
Methought all his senses were lock'd in his eye, As jewels in crystal . ii 1 242
That all eyes saw his eyes enchanted with gazes . . . . . ii 1 247
To speak that in words which his eye hath disclosed . . . . ii 1 250
I only have made a mouth of his eye, By adding a tongue . . . ii 1 251
With your hat penthouse-like o'er the shop of your eyes . . . iii 1 18
With a velvet brow, With two pitch-balls stuck in her face for eyes . iii 1 199
King Cophetua set eye upon the pernicious and indubitate beggar Zenelophon . . . . iv 1 66
I profane my lips on thy foot, my eyes on thy picture . . . . iv 1 86
Study his bias leaves and makes his book thine eyes . . . . iv 2 113
Thy eye Jove's lightning bears, thy voice his dreadful thunder . . iv 2 119
O, but her eye,—by this light, but for her eye, I would not love her ; yes, for her two eyes . . . . iv 3 10
The heavenly rhetoric of thine eye, 'Gainst whom the world cannot hold argument . . . . iv 3 60
By heaven, the wonder in a mortal eye!—By earth, she is not, corporal iv 3 85
One, her hairs were gold, crystal the other's eyes . . . . . iv 3 142
Your eyes do make no coaches ; in your tears There is no certain princess iv 3 155
When shall you hear that I Will praise a hand, a foot, a face, an eye? . iv 3 184
What peremptory eagle-sighted eye, Dares look upon the heaven of her brow, That is not blinded? . . . . iv 3 226
My eyes are then no eyes, nor I Biron . . . . iv 3 232
A wither'd hermit, five-score winters worn, Might shake off fifty, looking in her eye . . . . iv 3 243
Beauty doth beauty lack, If that she learn not of her eye to look . . iv 3 252
O, if the streets were paved with thine eyes, Her feet were much too dainty for such tread! . . . . iv 3 278
From women's eyes this doctrine I derive: They are the ground, the books iv 3 302
For not looking on a woman's face, You have in that forsworn the use of eyes . . . . iv 3 310
Where is any author in the world Teaches such beauty as a woman's eye? iv 3 313
Then when ourselves we see in ladies' eyes, Do we not likewise see our learning there? . . . . iv 3 316
As the prompting eyes Of beauty's tutors have enrich'd you with . iv 3 322
Love, first learned in a lady's eyes, Lives not alone immured in the brain iv 3 327
It [love] adds a precious seeing to the eye ; A lover's eyes will gaze an eagle blind . . . . iv 3 333
From women's eyes this doctrine I derive : They sparkle still the right Promethean fire . . . . iv 3 350

Eye. His eye ambitious, his gait majestical, and his general behaviour vain *L. L. Lost* v 1 12
I thought to close mine eyes some half an hour v 2 90
That ever turn'd their—backs—to mortal views!—Their eyes, villain, their eyes.—That ever turn'd their eyes to mortal views! v 2 162
Once to behold with your sun-beamed eyes,—with your sun-beamed eyes v 2 168
You were best call it 'daughter-beamed eyes' v 2 171
The virtue of your eye must break my oath v 2 348
When we greet, With eyes best seeing heaven's fiery eye v 2 375
This proves you wise and rich, for in my eye,— I am a fool v 2 379
They have the plague, and caught it of your eyes v 2 421
Know my lady's foot by the squier, And laugh upon the apple of her eye v 2 475
You leer upon me, do you? there's an eye Wounds like a leaden sword v 2 480
Form'd by the eye and therefore, like the eye, Full of strange shapes v 2 772
Varying in subjects as the eye doth roll To every varied object v 2 774
If, in your heavenly eyes, Have misbecomed our oaths and gravities, Those heavenly eyes, that look into these faults, Suggested us to make v 2 777
The sudden hand of death close up mine eye! v 2 825
Mistress, look on me; Behold the window of my heart, mine eye v 2 848
I would my father look'd but with my eyes.—Rather your eyes must with his judgement look *M. N. Dream* i 1 56
I could well Beteem them from the tempest of my eyes i 1 131
O hell! to choose love by another's eyes i 1 140
O happy fair! Your eyes are lode-stars i 1 183
My ear should catch your voice, my eye your eye i 1 188
And thence from Athens turn away our eyes i 1 218
And as he errs, doting on Hermia's eyes, So I, admiring of his qualities i 1 230
Love looks not with the eyes, but with the mind; And therefore is wing'd Cupid painted blind i 1 234
Wings and no eyes figure unheedy haste i 1 237
If I do it, let the audience look to their eyes; I will move storms i 2 29
I'll watch Titania when she is asleep, And drop the liquor of it in her eyes ii 1 178
I'll streak her eyes, And make her full of hateful fantasies ii 1 257
Anoint his eyes; But do it when the next thing he espies May be the lady ii 1 261
In thy eye that shall appear When thou wakest, it is thy dear ii 2 32
With half that wish the wisher's eyes be press'd! ii 2 65
On whose eyes I might approve This flower's force in stirring love ii 2 68
Upon thy eyes I throw All the power this charm doth owe ii 2 78
She hath blessed and attractive eyes. How came her eyes so bright? Not with salt tears: If so, my eyes are oftener wash'd than hers ii 2 91
Reason becomes the marshal to my will And leads me to your eyes ii 2 121
I did never, no, nor never can, Deserve a sweet look from Demetrius' eye ii 2 127
Mine ear is much enamour'd of thy note; So is mine eye enthralled iii 1 142
Hop in his walks and gambol in his eyes; Feed him with apricocks iii 1 168
Light them at the fiery glow-worm's eyes iii 1 173
Wings from painted butterflies To fan the moonbeams from his sleeping eyes iii 1 176
I promise you your kindred hath made my eyes water ere now iii 1 200
The moon methinks looks with a watery eye iii 1 203
What it was that next came in her eye, Which she must dote on iii 2 2
They him spy, As wild geese that the creeping fowler eye iii 2 20
But hast thou yet latch'd the Athenians eyes With the love-juice? iii 2 36
I'll charm his eyes against she do appear iii 2 99
Flower of this purple dye Hit with Cupid's archery, Sink in apple of his eye iii 2 104
A manly enterprise, To conjure tears up in a poor maid's eyes! iii 2 158
Dark night, that from the eye his function takes iii 2 177
Thou art not by mine eye, Lysander, found iii 2 181
Who more engilds the night Than all yon fiery oes and eyes of light iii 2 188
Have you not set Lysander, as in scorn, To follow me and praise my eyes? iii 2 223
I am not yet so low But that my nails can reach unto thine eyes iii 2 298
That I have 'nointed an Athenian's eyes iii 2 351
Then crush this herb into Lysander's eye iii 2 366
I will her charmed eye release From monster's view iii 2 376
Sleep, that sometimes shuts up sorrow's eye iii 2 435
I'll apply To your eye, Gentle lover, remedy iii 2 451
True delight In the sight Of thy former lady's eye iii 2 457
Stood now within the pretty flowerets' eyes Like tears that did their own disgrace bewail iv 1 60
I will undo This hateful imperfection of her eyes iv 1 68
O, how mine eyes do loathe his visage now! iv 1 84
When thou wakest, with thine own fool's eyes peep iv 1 89
The object and the pleasure of mine eye Is only Helena iv 1 175
Methinks I see these things with parted eye iv 1 194
The eye of man hath not heard, the ear of man hath not seen iv 1 216
The poet's eye, in a fine frenzy rolling, Doth glance from heaven to earth v 1 12
Made mine eyes water; but more merry tears The passion of loud laughter never shed v 1 69
What dreadful dole is here! Eyes, do you see? How can it be? v 1 284
She hath spied him already with those sweet eyes v 1 329
Dead, dead? A tomb Must cover thy sweet eyes v 1 336
Lovers, make moan: His eyes were green as leeks v 1 342
Evermore peep through their eyes And laugh like parrots *Mer. of Venice* i 1 52
If it stand, as you yourself still do, Within the eye of honour i 1 137
Sometimes from her eyes I did receive fair speechless messages i 1 163
He, of all the men that ever my foolish eyes looked upon, was the best i 2 130
I am not solely led By nice direction of a maiden's eyes ii 1 14
I would outstare the sternest eyes that look ii 1 27
If you had your eyes, you might fail of the knowing me ii 2 79
I'll take my leave of the Jew in the twinkling of an eye ii 2 177
Become thee happily enough And in such eyes as ours appear not faults ii 2 192
While grace is saying, hood mine eyes Thus with my hat, and sigh ii 2 202
Thou shalt see, thy eyes shall be thy judge ii 5 1
There will come a Christian by, Will be worth a Jewess' eye ii 5 43
Fair she is, if that mine eyes be true, And true she is, as she hath proved ii 6 54
A carrion Death, within whose empty eye There is a written scroll! ii 7 63
His eye being big with tears, Turning his face, he put his hand behind him ii 8 46
That choose by show, Not learning more than the fond eye doth teach ii 9 27
Hath not a Jew eyes? hath not a Jew hands, organs, dimensions, senses? iii 1 61
Beshrew your eyes, They have o'erlook'd me and divided me iii 2 14
My eye shall be the stream And watery death-bed for him iii 2 46
It is engender'd in the eyes, With gazing fed iii 2 67
Move these eyes? Or whether, riding on the balls of mine, Seem they in motion? iii 2 117
But her eyes,—How could he see to do them? iii 2 123
That thinks he hath done well in people's eyes, Hearing applause iii 2 143
My eyes, my lord, can look as swift as yours iii 2 199
Glancing an eye of pity on his losses iv 1 27
To view with hollow eye and wrinkled brow An age of poverty iv 1 270
Their savage eyes turn'd to a modest gaze By the sweet power of music v 1 78

Eye. I swear to thee, even by thine own fair eyes, Wherein I see myself *Mer. of Venice* v 1 242
In both my eyes he doubly sees himself; In each eye, one v 1 244
If you saw yourself with your eyes or knew yourself *As Y. Like It* i 2 186
Let your fair eyes and gentle wishes go with me to my trial i 2 198
If I had a thunderbolt in mine eye, I can tell who should down i 2 226
Look, here comes the duke.—With his eyes full of anger i 3 42
Looking on it with lack-lustre eye, Says very wisely, 'It is ten o'clock' ii 7 21
And wiped our eyes Of drops that sacred pity hath engender'd ii 7 122
With eyes severe and beard of formal cut, Full of wise saws ii 7 155
Second childishness and mere oblivion, Sans teeth, sans eyes, sans taste ii 7 166
As mine eye doth his effigies witness Most truly limn'd and living ii 7 193
Queen of night, survey With thy chaste eye, from thy pale sphere above iii 2 3
Every eye which in this forest looks Shall see thy virtue witness'd iii 2 7
By heavenly synod was devised, Of many faces, eyes and hearts iii 2 159
A lean cheek, which you have not, a blue eye and sunken iii 2 393
Thou tell'st me there is murder in mine eye: 'Tis pretty, sure, and very probable, That eyes, that are the frail'st and softest things, Who shut their coward gates on atomies, Should be call'd tyrants, butchers, murderers! iii 5 10
If mine eyes can wound, now let them kill thee iii 5 16
For shame, Lie not, to say mine eyes are murderers! iii 5 19
Now show the wound mine eye hath made in thee iii 5 20
But now mine eyes, Which I have darted at thee, hurt thee not, Nor, I am sure, there is no force in eyes That can do hurt iii 5 24
'Od's my little life, I think she means to tangle my eyes too! iii 5 44
And faster than his tongue Did make offence his eye did heal it up iii 5 117
He said mine eyes were black and my hair black iii 5 130
To have seen much and to have nothing, is to have rich eyes and poor hands iv 1 24
That blind rascally boy that abuses every one's eyes because his own are out iv 1 219
Whiles the eye of man did woo me, That could do no vengeance to me iv 3 47
If that an eye may profit by a tongue, Then should I know you iv 3 84
He threw his eye aside, And mark what object did present itself iv 3 103
Wounded it is, but with the eyes of a lady v 2 27
How bitter a thing it is to look into happiness through another man's eyes! v 2 49
To set her before your eyes to-morrow human as she is v 2 73
An onion . . . Shall in despite enforce a watery eye *T. of Shrew* Ind. 1 128
A pretty peat! it is best Put finger in the eye, an she knew why i 1 79
Whose sudden sight hath thrall'd my wounded eye i 1 225
She shall have no more eyes to see withal than a cat i 2 115
To make mine eye the witness Of that report which I so oft have heard ii 1 52
'Tis age that nourisheth.—But youth in ladies' eyes that flourisheth ii 1 342
Be so humble To cast thy wandering eyes on every stale iii 1 90
And since mine eyes are witness of her lightness, I will with you iv 2 24
Is the adder better than the eel, Because his painted skin contents the eye? iv 3 180
What stars do spangle heaven with such beauty, As those two eyes? iv 5 32
My mistaking eyes, That have been so bedazzled with the sun iv 5 45
And dart not scornful glances from those eyes v 2 137
To sit and draw His arched brows, his hawking eye *All's Well* i 1 105
Her eye is sick on't: I observe her now i 3 142
This distemper'd messenger of wet, The many-colour'd Iris, rounds thine eye i 3 158
Thine eyes See it so grossly shown in thy behaviours That in their kind they speak it i 3 183
He bade me store up, as a triple eye, Safer than mine own two, more dear ii 1 111
Send forth thine eye: this youthful parcel Of noble bachelors stand at my bestowing ii 3 58
The honour, sir, that flames in your fair eyes, Before I speak, too threateningly replies ii 3 86
In such a business give me leave to use The help of mine own eyes ii 3 115
Pardon, my gracious lord; for I submit My fancy to your eyes ii 3 175
From the sportive court, where thou Wast shot at with fair eyes iii 2 110
O, ransom, ransom! do not hide mine eyes iv 1 74
Whose beauty did astonish the survey Of richest eyes v 3 17
Where the impression of mine eye infixing, Contempt his scornful perspective did lend me v 3 47
Was in mine eye The dust that did offend it v 3 54
Let me see it; for mine eye, While I was speaking, oft was fasten'd to't v 3 81
Which nothing, but to close Her eyes myself, could win me to believe v 3 119
Is there no exorcist Beguiles the truer office of mine eyes? v 3 306
Mine eyes smell onions; I shall weep anon v 3 321
When mine eyes did see Olivia first, Methought she purged the air *T. Night* i 1 19
When my tongue blabs, then let mine eyes not see i 2 63
Item, two lips, indifferent red; item, two grey eyes, with lids to them i 5 266
With an invisible and subtle stealth To creep in at mine eyes i 5 317
And fear to find Mine eye too great a flatterer for my mind i 5 328
That upon the least occasion more mine eyes will tell tales of me ii 1 43
If it be worth stooping for, there it lies in your eye ii 2 16
Methought her eyes had lost her tongue, For she did speak in starts ii 2 21
His eyes do show his days are almost done ii 3 112
The shape of his leg, the manner of his gait, the expressure of his eye ii 3 171
Thine eye Hath stay'd upon some favour that it loves ii 4 24
O, for a stone-bow, to hit him in the eye! ii 5 52
An you had any eye behind you, you might see more detraction at your heels ii 5 148
And, like the haggard, check at every feather That comes before his eye iii 1 72
Let us satisfy our eyes With the memorials and the things of fame iii 3 22
Haply your eye shall light upon some toy You have desire to purchase iii 3 44
If it please the eye of one, it is with me as the very true sonnet is iii 4 23
I am ready to distrust mine eyes And wrangle with my reason iv 3 13
Him will I tear out of that cruel eye, Where he sits crowned v 1 130
After him I love More than I love these eyes, more than my life v 1 138
His eyes were set at eight i' the morning v 1 205
Your precious self had then not cross'd the eyes Of my young play-fellow *W. Tale* i 2 79
Come, sir page, Look on me with your welkin eye: sweet villain! i 2 136
Or else be impudently negative, To have nor eyes nor ears nor thought i 2 275
And all eyes Blind with the pin and web but theirs, theirs only i 2 290
Canst with thine eyes at once see good and evil, Inclining to them both i 2 303
That bare eyes To see alike mine honour as their profits i 2 309
Wafting his eyes to the contrary and falling A lip of much contempt i 2 372
But if one present The abhorr'd ingredient to his eye ii 1 43
The queen is spotless I' the eyes of heaven and to you ii 1 132
Let him that makes but trifles of his eyes First hand me ii 3 62
The whole matter And copy of the father, eye, nose, lip ii 3 99
That he did but see The flatness of my misery, yet with eyes Of pity, not revenge! iii 2 123

Eye. If you can bring Tincture or lustre in her lip, her eye, Heat outwardly *W. Tale* iii 2 206
Gasping to begin some speech, her eyes Became two spouts iii 3 25
I have eyes under my service which look upon his removedness iv 2 40
Violets dim, But sweeter than the lids of Juno's eyes iv 4 121
Never gazed the moon Upon the water as he'll stand and read As 'twere my daughter's eyes iv 4 174
Were I the fairest youth That ever made eye swerve iv 4 385
That you may—For I do fear eyes over—to shipboard Get undescried iv 4 668
An open ear, a quick eye, and a nimble hand, is necessary for a cut-purse iv 4 685
The sun looking with a southward eye upon him iv 4 819
I might have look'd upon my queen's full eyes v 1 53
Mark Her eye, and tell me for what dull part in't You chose her v 1 64
Stars, stars, And all eyes else dead coals! v 1 68
Unless another, As like Hermione as is her picture, Affront his eye v 1 75
When she has obtain'd your eye, Will have your tongue too v 1 105
Your eye hath too much youth in't v 1 225
Seemed almost, with staring on one another, to tear the cases of their eyes v 2 14
There was casting up of eyes, holding up of hands v 2 51
She had one eye declined for the loss of her husband v 2 81
One of the prettiest touches of all and that which angled for mine eyes v 2 90
Every wink of an eye some new grace will be born v 2 119
The fixure of her eye has motion in't, As we are mock'd with art v 3 67
Be thou as lightning in the eyes of France *K. John* i 1 24
Mine eye hath well examined his parts i 1 89
These eyes, these brows, were moulded out of his ii 1 100
Draws those heaven-moving pearls from his poor eyes ii 1 169
Before the eye and prospect of your town ii 1 208
Your city's eyes, your winking gates ii 1 215
Whose equality By our best eyes cannot be censured ii 1 328
In her eye I find A wonder, or a wondrous miracle ii 1 496
I beheld myself Drawn in the flattering table of her eye.—Drawn in the flattering table of her eye! ii 1 503
This all-changing word, Clapp'd on the outward eye of fickle France ii 1 583
Why holds thine eye that lamentable rheum? iii 1 22
Turning with splendour of his precious eye The meagre cloddy earth to glittering gold iii 1 79
Making that idiot, laughter, keep men's eyes And strain their cheeks iii 3 45
If that thou couldst see me without eyes, Hear me without thine ears iii 3 49
Using conceit alone, Without eyes, ears and harmful sound of words iii 3 51
Hubert, throw thine eye On yon young boy iii 3 59
When Fortune means to men most good, She looks upon them with a threatening eye iii 4 120
I must be brief, lest resolution drop Out at mine eyes iv 1 36
Must you with hot irons burn out both mine eyes? iv 1 39
Will you put out mine eyes? These eyes that never did nor never shall So much as frown on you iv 1 56
The iron of itself, though heat red-hot, Approaching near these eyes, would drink my tears iv 1 62
After that, consume away in rust, But for containing fire to harm mine eye iv 1 66
If an angel should have come to me And told me Hubert should put out mine eyes, I would not have believed him,—no tongue but Hubert's iv 1 69
Save me! my eyes are out Even with the fierce looks of these bloody men iv 1 73
Prepare yourself.—Is there no remedy?—None, but to lose your eyes iv 1 91
A brace of tongues Must needs want pleading for a pair of eyes iv 1 99
Cut out my tongue, So I may keep mine eyes: O, spare mine eyes! iv 1 102
Nay, it perchance will sparkle in your eyes iv 1 115
I will not touch thine eye For all the treasure that thine uncle owes iv 1 122
Once again crown'd, And look'd upon, I hope, with cheerful eyes iv 2 2
With taper-light To seek the beauteous eye of heaven to garnish, Is wasteful iv 2 15
The image of a wicked heinous fault Lives in his eye iv 2 72
A fearful eye thou hast iv 2 106
With eyes as red as new-enkindled fire iv 2 163
With wrinkled brows, with nods, with rolling eyes iv 2 192
Or turn'd an eye of doubt upon my face iv 2 233
Foul imaginary eyes of blood Presented thee more hideous than thou art iv 2 265
Trust not those cunning waters of his eyes iv 3 107
Doth dogged war bristle his angry crest And snarleth in the gentle eyes of peace iv 3 150
Let not the world see fear and sad distrust Govern the motion of a kingly eye v 1 47
Inferior eyes, That borrow their behaviours from the great v 1 50
This shower, blown up by tempest of the soul, Startles mine eyes v 2 51
Those baby eyes That never saw the giant world enraged v 2 56
Unthread the rude eye of rebellion And welcome home again discarded faith v 4 11
He is forsworn, if e'er those eyes of yours Behold another day break v 4 31
I do see the cruel pangs of death Right in thine eye v 4 60
O cousin, thou art come to set mine eye v 7 51
To the furthest verge That ever was survey'd by English eye *Richard II.* i 1 94
Impartial are our eyes and ears i 1 115
The last leave of thee takes my weeping eye i 2 74
O, let no noble eye profane a tear For me i 3 59
Securely I espy Virtue with valour couched in thine eye i 3 98
Our eyes do hate the dire aspect Of civil wounds i 3 127
Even in the glasses of thine eyes I see thy grieved heart i 3 208
All places that the eye of heaven visits Are to a wise man ports i 3 275
Had thy grandsire with a prophet's eye Seen ii 1 104
Even through the hollow eyes of death I spy life peering ii 1 270
Sorrow's eye, glazed with blinding tears, Divides one thing entire to many objects ii 2 16
'Tis with false sorrow's eye, Which for things true weeps things imaginary ii 2 26
I beseech your grace, Look on my wrongs with an indifferent eye ii 3 116
With the eyes of heavy mind ii 4 18
With tears drawn from her eyes by your foul wrongs iii 1 15
When the searching eye of heaven is hid, Behind the globe, that lights the lower world iii 2 37
And with rainy eyes Write sorrow on the bosom of the earth iii 2 146
Men judge by the complexion of the sky The state and inclination of the day: So may you by my dull and heavy eye iii 2 196
His eye, As bright as is the eagle's, lightens forth Controlling majesty iii 3 68
There lies Two kinsmen digg'd their graves with weeping eyes iii 3 169
Me rather had my heart might feel your love Than my unpleased eye see your courtesy iii 3 193
Nay, dry your eyes; Tears show their love, but want their remedies iii 3 202
Mine eyes are full of tears, I cannot see iv 1 244
Nay, if I turn mine eyes upon myself, I find myself a traitor with the rest iv 1 247
I see your brows are full of discontent, Your hearts of sorrow and your eyes of tears iv 1 332

Eye. Young and old Through casements darted their desiring eyes *Richard II.* v 2 14
As in a theatre, the eyes of men, After a well-graced actor leaves the stage, Are idly bent on him that enters next v 2 23
With much more contempt men's eyes Did scowl on gentle Richard v 2 27
Look upon his face; His eyes do drop no tears, his prayers are in jest v 3 101
Thine eye begins to speak; set thy tongue there v 3 125
As for a camel To thread the postern of a small needle's eye v 5 17
My thoughts are minutes; and with sighs they jar Their watches on unto mine eyes v 5 52
Those opposed eyes, Which, like the meteors of a troubled heaven, All of one nature *1 Hen. IV.* i 1 9
And attract more eyes Than that which hath no foil to set it off i 2 238
I do see Danger and disobedience in thine eye i 3 16
Then his cheek look'd pale, And on my face he turn'd an eye of death i 3 143
Hast thou never an eye in thy head? canst not hear? ii 1 31
Why dost thou bend thine eyes upon the earth, And start so often? ii 3 45
Give me a cup of sack to make my eyes look red ii 4 423
Tears do stop the flood-gates of her eyes ii 4 435
A villanous trick of thine eye and a foolish hanging of thy nether lip ii 4 446
A cheerful look, a pleasing eye and a most noble carriage ii 4 465
So common-hackney'd in the eyes of men, So stale and cheap iii 2 40
That, being daily swallow'd by men's eyes, They surfeited with honey iii 2 70
Such eyes As, sick and blunted with community, Afford no extraordinary gaze iii 2 76
Such as is bent on sun-like majesty When it shines seldom in admiring eyes iii 2 80
Not an eye But is a-weary of thy common sight, Save mine iii 2 87
Stop all sight-holes, every loop from whence The eye of reason may pry in iv 1 72
No eye hath seen such scarecrows iv 2 41
With some fine colour that may please the eye Of fickle changelings v 1 75
Suspicion all our lives shall be stuck full of eyes v 2 8
Nothing confutes me but eyes, and nobody sees me v 4 129
We will not trust our eyes Without our ears v 4 139
He that but fears the thing he would not know Hath by instinct knowledge from others' eyes That what he fear'd is chanced *2 Hen. IV.* i 1 86
I see a strange confession in thine eye i 1 94
These mine eyes saw him in bloody state, Rendering faint quittance i 1 107
Have you not a moist eye? a dry hand? a yellow cheek? a white beard? i 2 204
I spied his eyes, and methought he had made two holes in the ale-wife's new petticoat and so peeped through ii 2 87
To rain upon remembrance with mine eyes ii 3 59
Wilt thou upon the high and giddy mast Seal up the ship-boy's eyes? iii 1 19
Yea, for my sake, even to the eyes of Richard Gave him defiance iii 1 64
Richard, with his eye brimful of tears, Then check'd and rated iii 1 67
Their eyes of fire sparkling through sights of steel iv 1 121
Whose dangerous eyes may well be charm'd asleep iv 2 39
That all their eyes may bear those tokens home Of our restored love iv 2 64
His eye is hollow, and he changes much iv 5 6
That I will dazzle all the eyes of France *Hen. V.* i 2 279
How shall we stretch our eye When capital crimes, chew'd, swallow'd and digested, Appear before us? ii 2 55
Though the truth of it stands off as gross As black and white, my eye will scarcely see it ii 2 104
Deck'd in modest complement, Not working with the eye without the ear ii 2 135
Lend the eye a terrible aspect; Let it pry though the portage of the head iii 1 9
None of you so mean and base, That hath not noble lustre in your eyes iii 1 30
Ere theise eyes of mine take themselves to slomber, ay'll de gud service iii 2 122
Fortune is painted blind, with a muffler afore her eyes iii 6 34
Have at the very eye of that proverb with 'A pox of the devil' iii 7 129
A largess universal like the sun His liberal eye doth give to every one iv Prol. 44
Sweats in the eye of Phœbus and all night sleeps in Elysium iv 1 290
Make incision in their hides, That their hot blood may spin in English eyes iv 2 10
The gum down-roping from their pale-dead eyes iv 2 48
All my mother came into mine eyes And gave me up to tears iv 6 31
I must perforce compound With mistful eyes, or they will issue too iv 6 34
His eyes are humbler than they used to be iv 7 70
Then brook abridgement, and your eyes advance, After your thoughts v Prol. 44
As we are now glad to behold your eyes; Your eyes, which hitherto have borne in them . . . The fatal balls of murdering basilisks v 2 14
I have but with a cursorary eye O'erglanced the articles v 2 77
Let thine eye be thy cook v 2 155
A fair face will wither; a full eye will wax hollow v 2 170
Like flies at Bartholomew-tide, blind, though they have their eyes v 2 337
His sparkling eyes, replete with wrathful fire *1 Hen. VI.* i 1 12
When at their mothers' moist eyes babes shall suck i 1 49
Wounds will I lend the French instead of eyes, To weep their intermissive miseries i 1 87
One of thy eyes and thy cheek's side struck off! i 4 75
One eye thou hast, to look to heaven for grace: The sun with one eye vieweth all the world i 4 83
Fain would mine eyes be witness with mine ears, To give their censure ii 3 9
Between two girls, which hath the merriest eye ii 4 15
The truth appears so naked on my side That any purblind eye may find it ii 4 21
So evident That it will glimmer through a blind man's eye ii 4 24
These eyes, like lamps whose wasting oil is spent, Wax dim ii 5 8
As looks the mother on her lowly babe When death doth close his tender dying eyes iii 3 48
These eyes, that see thee now well coloured, Shall see thee wither'd, bloody iv 2 37
No shape but his can please your dainty eye v 3 38
So seems this gorgeous beauty to mine eyes v 3 64
Some sudden qualm hath struck me at the heart And dimm'd mine eyes, that I can read no further *2 Hen. VI.* i 1 55
My sword should shed hot blood, mine eyes no tears i 1 118
Why are thine eyes fix'd to the sullen earth, Gazing on that which seems to dim thy sight? i 2 5
Thine eyes and thoughts Beat on a crown, the treasure of thy heart ii 1 19
Let me see thine eyes: wink now: now open them ii 1 105
Mine eyes are full of tears, my heart of grief ii 3 17
I'll prepare My tear-stain'd eyes to see her miseries ii 4 16
See how the giddy multitude do point, And nod their heads, and throw their eyes on thee! ii 4 22
He knits his brow and shows an angry eye iii 1 15
Beaufort's red sparkling eyes blab his heart's malice iii 1 154
My heart is drown'd with grief, Whose flood begins to flow within mine eyes iii 1 199
With sad unhelpful tears, and with dimm'd eyes iii 1 218
O Henry, ope thine eyes!—He doth revive again: madam, be patient iii 2 35
Look not upon me, for thine eyes are wounding iii 2 51

Eye. And bid mine eyes be packing with my heart And call'd them blind and dusky spectacles . . . . 2 *Hen. VI.* iii 2 111
Mine eyes should sparkle like the beaten flint; Mine hair be fix'd on end iii 2 317
I should be raging mad And cry out for thee to close up mine eyes . iii 2 395
He hath no eyes, the dust hath blinded them . . . . . . iii 3 14
Eternal Mover of the heavens, Look with a gentle eye upon this wretch! iii 3 20
Close up his eyes and draw the curtain close; And let us all to meditation iii 3 32
I lost mine eye in laying the prize abroad . . . . . iv 1 25
The sight of me is odious in their eyes . . . . iv 4 46
Oppose thy steadfast-gazing eyes to mine, See if thou canst outface me iv 10 48
I vow by heaven these eyes shall never close . . . . 3 *Hen. VI.* i 1 24
Is he dead already? or is it fear That makes him close his eyes? . . i 3 11
In that hope I throw mine eyes to heaven . . . . . . i 4 37
If thine eyes can water for his death, I give thee this to dry thy cheeks i 4 82
How couldst thou drain the life-blood of the child, To bid the father wipe his eyes withal? . . . . i 4 139
His passion moves me so That hardly can I check my eyes from tears . i 4 151
Dazzle mine eyes, or do I see three suns?—Three glorious suns . . ii 1 25
Though man's face be fearful to their eyes . . . . . . ii 2 27
Never stand still, Till either death hath closed these eyes of mine . ii 3 31
I throw my hands, mine eyes, my heart to thee . . . . . ii 3 36
Let our hearts and eyes, like civil war, Be blind with tears . . . ii 5 77
Throw up thine eye! see, see what showers arise, Blown with the windy tempest of my heart, Upon thy wounds, that kill mine eye and heart! . . . . ii 5 85
With fiery eyes sparkling for very wrath . . . . ii 5 131
Wishing his foot were equal with his eye . . . . iii 2 137
My eye's too quick, my heart o'erweens too much . . . . . iii 2 144
Such a cause as fills mine eyes with tears And stops my tongue . . iii 3 13
But is he gracious in the people's eye? . . . . iii 3 117
These eyes, that now are dimm'd with death's black veil, Have been as piercing as the mid-day sun. . . . . v 2 16
With tearful eyes add water to the sea . . . . v 4 8
For every word I speak, Ye see, I drink the water of mine eyes . . v 4 75
Have now the fatal object in my eye Where my poor young was limed . v 6 16
Many a widow's And many an orphan's water-standing eye . . . v 6 40
A cherry lip, a bonny eye, a passing pleasing tongue . *Richard III.* i 1 94
I pour the helpless balm of my poor eyes . . . . . . i 2 13
You are mortal, And mortal eyes cannot endure the devil . . . . i 2 45
These eyes could never endure sweet beauty's wreck . . . . i 2 127
Out of my sight! thou dost infect my eyes . . . . . . i 2 149
Thine eyes, sweet lady, have infected mine.—Would they were basilisks! i 2 150
Those eyes of thine from mine have drawn salt tears . . . . i 2 154
These eyes, which never shed remorseful tear . . . . . . i 2 156
In that sad time My manly eyes did scorn an humble tear . . . i 2 165
With curses in her mouth, tears in her eyes . . . . . . i 2 233
And will she yet debase her eyes on me? . . . . i 2 247
And with thy scorns drew'st rivers from his eyes . . . . . i 3 176
No sleep close up that deadly eye of thine! . . . . . . i 3 225
Your eyes drop millstones, when fools' eyes drop tears . . . . i 3 354
What ugly sights of death within mine eyes! . . . . . . i 4 23
In those holes Where eyes did once inhabit, there were crept, As 'twere in scorn of eyes, reflecting gems . . . . i 4 30
How darkly and how deadly dost thou speak! Your eyes do menace me i 4 175
O, if thine eye be not a flatterer, Come thou on my side, and entreat for me i 4 271
All springs reduce their currents to mine eyes . . . . . . ii 2 68
Unquiet wrangling days, How many of you have mine eyes beheld! . ii 4 56
Be your eyes the witness of this ill: See how I am bewitch'd . . iii 4 69
Even where his lustful eye or savage heart, Without control, listed to make his prey . . . . iii 5 83
I have done some offence That seems disgracious in the city's eyes . iii 7 112
Made prize and purchase of his lustful eye . . . . iii 7 187
A cockatrice hast thou hatch'd to the world, Whose unavoided eye is murderous . . . . iv 1 56
Which ever since hath kept my eyes from rest . . . . . . iv 1 82
None are for me That look into me with considerate eyes . . . iv 2 30
Tear-falling pity dwells not in this eye . . . . iv 2 66
That dog, that had his teeth before his eyes, To worry lambs . . iv 4 49
Grand tyrant of the earth, That reigns in galled eyes of weeping souls . iv 4 53
Till that my nails were anchor'd in thine eyes . . . . . . iv 4 231
And bid her dry her weeping eyes therewith . . . . . . iv 4 278
O Thou, whose captain I account myself, Look on my forces with a gracious eye! . . . . v 3 109
To thee I do commend my watchful soul, Ere I let fall the windows of mine eyes . . . . v 3 116
Such noble scenes as draw the eye to flow, We now present *Hen. VIII.* Prol. 4
Him in eye, Still him in praise . . . . i 1 30
Let some graver eye Pierce into that . . . . i 1 67
I read in 's looks Matter against me; and his eye reviled Me . . . i 1 126
Mounting his eyes, He did discharge a horrible oath . . . . . i 2 205
Eyes, that so long have slept upon This bold bad man . . . . ii 2 43
If my actions Were tried by every tongue, every eye saw 'em . . . iii 1 35
The cardinal's letters to the pope miscarried, And came to the eye o' the king . . . . iii 2 31
And anon he casts His eye against the moon . . . . . . iii 2 118
Some spirit put this paper in the packet, To bless your eye withal . iii 2 130
He parted frowning from me, as if ruin Leap'd from his eyes . . . iii 2 206
Thou hast forced me, Out of thy honest truth, to play the woman. Let's dry our eyes . . . . iii 2 431
And saint-like Cast her fair eyes to heaven and pray'd devoutly . . iv 1 84
Mark her eyes!—She is going, wench: pray, pray . . . . . iv 2 98
Mine eyes grow dim. Farewell, My lord. Griffith, farewell . . . iv 2 164
As he pass'd along, How earnestly he cast his eyes upon me! . . v 2 12
Pour'st in the open ulcer of my heart Her eyes, her hair, her cheek, her gait, her voice . . . . *Troi. and Cres.* i 1 54
Purblind Argus, all eyes and no sight . . . . i 2 31
Queen Hecuba laughed that her eyes ran o'er . . . . . . i 2 157
But there was more temperate fire under the pot of her eyes: did her eyes run o'er too? . . . . i 2 161
I warrant, Helen, to change, would give an eye to boot . . . . i 2 260
Porridge after meat! I could live and die i' the eyes of Troilus . . i 2 264
Have you any discretion? have you any eyes? do you know what a man is? . . . . i 2 274
Though my heart's content firm love doth bear, Nothing of that shall from mine eyes appear . . . . i 2 321
Whose medicinable eye Corrects the ill aspects of planets evil . . i 3 91
How may A stranger to those most imperial looks Know them from eyes of other mortals? . . . . i 3 225
Modest as morning when she coldly eyes The youthful Phœbus . . i 3 229
I see them not with my old eyes: what are they? . . . . . i 3 366

Eye. We were better parch in Afric sun Than in the pride and salt scorn of his eyes . . . . *Troi. and Cres.* i 3 371
Has not so much wit— Nay, I must hold you.—As will stop the eye of Helen's needle . . . . ii 1 87
My will enkindled by mine eyes and ears . . . . ii 2 63
Lend me ten thousand eyes, And I will fill them with prophetic tears . ii 2 101
Cry, Trojans, cry! practise your eyes with tears! . . . . . ii 2 108
Yet all his virtues . . . Do in our eyes begin to lose their gloss . ii 3 128
Like vassalage at unawares encountering The eye of majesty . . . iii 2 41
More dregs than water, if my fears have eyes . . . . . . iii 2 73
'Tis like he'll question me Why such unplausive eyes are bent on him . iii 3 43
What the declined is He shall as soon read in the eyes of others As feel in his own fall . . . . iii 3 77
The beauty that is borne here in the face The bearer knows not, but commends itself To others' eyes . . . . iii 3 105
Nor doth the eye itself, That most pure spirit of sense, behold itself, Not going from itself . . . . iii 3 105
How some men creep in skittish fortune's hall, Whiles others play the idiots in her eyes! . . . . iii 3 135
The present eye praises the present object . . . . . . iii 3 180
Since things in motion sooner catch the eye Than what not stirs . . iii 3 183
To bed, to bed: sleep kill those pretty eyes! . . . . . . iv 2 4
The lustre in your eye, heaven in your cheek, Pleads your fair uasge . iv 4 120
Come, stretch thy chest, and let thy eyes spout blood . . . . iv 5 10
There's language in her eye, her cheek, her lip, Nay, her foot speaks . iv 5 55
Mine own searching eyes Shall find him by his large and portly size . iv 5 161
I have fed mine eyes on thee; I have with exact view perused thee . iv 5 231
Why dost thou so oppress me with thine eye? . . . . . . iv 5 241
Cold palsies, raw eyes, dirt-rotten livers, wheezing lungs . . . v 1 23
Thou green sarcenet flap for a sore eye, thou tassel of a prodigal's purse v 1 36
One eye yet looks on thee; But with my heart the other eye doth see . v 2 108
This fault in us I find, The error of our eye directs our mind . . . v 2 110
O, then conclude Minds sway'd by eyes are full of turpitude . . . v 2 112
So obstinately strong, That doth invert the attest of eyes and ears . v 2 122
Will he swagger himself out on's own eyes? . . . . . . v 2 136
Their eyes o'ergalled with recourse of tears . . . . . . v 3 55
Look, how thou diest! look, how thy eye turns pale! . . . . . v 3 81
I have a rheum in mine eyes too, and such an ache in my bones . . v 3 105
Follow me, sirs, and my proceedings eye . . . . v 7 7
Your eyes, half out, weep out at Pandar's fall . . . . . . v 10 49
The vigilant eye, The counsellor heart, the arm our soldier *Coriolanus* i 1 119
Mark'd you his lip and eyes?—Nay, but his taunts . . . . . i 1 259
O that you could turn your eyes toward the napes of your necks! . ii 1 42
Whither do you follow your eyes so fast? . . . . ii 1 109
Such eyes the widows in Corioli wear, And mothers that lack sons . ii 1 195
Clambering the walls to eye him: stalls, bulks, windows, Are smother'd up ii 1 226
And carry with us ears and eyes for the time, But hearts for the event. ii 1 285
Planted his honours in their eyes, and his actions in their hearts . ii 2 33
Action is eloquence, and the eyes of the ignorant More learned than the ears. . . . . iii 2 76
Within thine eyes sat twenty thousand deaths . . . . . . iii 3 70
Thy tears are salter than a younger man's, And venomous to thine eyes iv 1 23
Has the porter his eyes in his head, that he gives entrance to such companions? . . . . iv 5 13
And turns up the white o' the eye to his discourse . . . . . iv 5 209
Go whip him 'fore the people's eyes:—his raising; Nothing but his report iv 6 60
So he thinks, and is no less apparent To the vulgar eye . . . . iv 7 21
I tell you, he does sit in gold, his eye Red as 'twould burn Rome . . v 1 63
Those doves' eyes, Which can make gods forsworn . . . . . v 3 27
These eyes are not the same I wore in Rome . . . . . . v 3 38
Like a great sea-mark, standing every flaw, And saving those that eye thee! . . . . v 3 75
Which should Make our eyes flow with joy, hearts dance with comforts v 3 99
It is no little thing to make Mine eyes to sweat compassion . . . v 3 196
He is able to pierce a corslet with his eye; talks like a knell . . . v 4 21
'Fore your own eyes and ears . . . . v 6 120
If ever Bassianus . . . Were gracious in the eyes of royal Rome *T. An.* i 1 11
My beloved brother, Gracious triumpher in the eyes of Rome! . . i 1 170
If ever Tamora Were gracious in those princely eyes of thine, Then hear me speak . . . . i 1 429
Faster bound to Aaron's charming eyes Than is Prometheus tied to Caucasus . . . . ii 1 16
Like the house of Fame, The palace full of tongues, of eyes, and ears . ii 1 127
There serve your lusts, shadow'd from heaven's eye . . . . . ii 1 130
What signifies my deadly-standing eye, My silence? . . . . . ii 3 32
Into some loathsome pit, Where never man's eye may behold my body. ii 3 177
With the dismall'st object hurt That ever eye with sight made heart lament! . . . . ii 3 205
My heart suspects more than mine eye can see . . . . . . ii 3 213
My compassionate heart Will not permit mine eyes once to behold The thing whereat it trembles by surmise. . . . . ii 3 218
For such a sight will blind a father's eye . . . . ii 4 53
One hour's storm will drown the fragrant meads; What will whole months of tears thy father's eyes? . . . . ii 4 55
Prepare thy aged eyes to weep; Or, if not so, thy noble heart to break iii 1 59
Patience, dear niece. Good Titus, dry thine eyes . . . . . iii 1 138
And be this dismal sight The closing up of our most wretched eyes . iii 1 263
This sorrow is an enemy, And would usurp upon my watery eyes . . iii 1 269
That all the tears that thy poor eyes let fall May run into that sink . iii 2 18
Mine eyes are cloy'd with view of tyranny . . . . iii 2 55
That which I would hide from heaven's eye . . . . iv 2 59
I earnestly did fix mine eye Upon the wasted building . . . . v 1 22
This is the pearl that pleased your empress' eye . . . . . . v 1 42
And laugh'd so heartily, That both mine eyes were rainy like to his . v 1 117
We worldly men Have miserable, mad, mistaking eyes . . . . . v 2 66
Can the son's eye behold his father bleed? There's meed for meed! . v 3 65
Alas, that love, whose view is muffled still, Should, without eyes, see pathways to his will! . . . . *Rom. and Jul.* i 1 178
Love is a smoke raised with the fume of sighs; Being purged, a fire sparkling in lovers' eyes . . . . i 1 197
She will not stay the siege of loving terms, Nor bide the encounter of assailing eyes . . . . i 1 219
Teach me how I should forget to think.—By giving liberty unto thine eyes . . . . i 1 233
Take thou some new infection to thy eye . . . . i 2 50
With unattainted eye, Compare her face with some that I shall show . i 2 90
When the devout religion of mine eye Maintains such falsehood, then turn tears to fires! . . . . i 2 93
You saw her fair, none else being by, Herself poised with herself in either eye . . . . i 2 100

Eyne. Dissembling glass of mine Made me compare with Hermia's sphery eyne . . . . *M. N. Dream* ii 2 99
To what, my love, shall I compare thine eyne? Crystal is muddy . iii 2 138
Show me thy chink, to blink through with mine eyne! . . . . v 1 178
If the scorn of your bright eyne Have power to raise such love in mine *As Y. Like It* iv 3 50

Eyne. By marriage made thy daughter mine, While counterfeit supposes blear'd thine eyne . . . . . . *T. of Shrew* v 1 120
Come, thou monarch of the vine, Plumpy Bacchus with pink eyne *Ant. and Cleo.* ii 7 121
The cat, with eyne of burning coal, Now couches fore the mouse's hole *Pericles* iii Gower 5

F

Fa. Ut, re, sol, la, mi, fa. Under pardon, sir . . . . *L. L. Lost* iv 2 102
I'll try how you can sol, fa, and sing it . . . . . *T. of Shrew* i 2 17
Take him for thy lord, 'C fa ut,' that loves with all affection . iii 1 76
I'll re you, I'll fa you; do you note me?—An you re us and fa us, you note us . . . . *Rom. and Jul.* iv 5 121
O, these eclipses do portend these divisions! fa, sol, la, mi . . *Lear* i 2 149

Fabian. Come thy ways, Signior Fabian.—Nay, I'll come . *T. Night* ii 5 1
Signior Fabian, stay you by this gentleman till my return . . . iii 4 281
But he will not now be pacified: Fabian can scarce hold him yonder . iii 4 310
And for his cowardship, ask Fabian.—A coward, a most devout coward iii 4 423
Good Master Fabian, grant me another request.—Any thing . . . v 1 3

Fable. Sans fable, she herself reviled you there . . *Com. of Errors* iv 4 76
By the world, I recount no fable . . . . . . *L. L. Lost* v 1 111
I never may believe These antique fables, nor these fairy toys *M. N. Dr.* v 1 3
He fables not; I hear the enemy . . . . . . 1 *Hen. VI.* iv 2 42
Let Æsop fable in a winter's night . . . . . . 3 *Hen. VI.* v 5 25
I look down towards his feet; but that's a fable. If that thou be'st a devil, I cannot kill thee . . . . *Othello* v 2 286

Fabric. Like the baseless fabric of this vision . . . . *Tempest* iv 1 151
By oath remove or counsel shake The fabric of his folly . . *W. Tale* i 2 429
With other muniments and petty helps In this our fabric . *Coriolanus* i 1 123
And manhood is call'd foolery, when it stands Against a falling fabric . iii 1 247

Fabulous. I see report is fabulous and false . . . . 1 *Hen. VI.* ii 3 18
That former fabulous story, Being now seen possible enough, got credit, That Bevis was believed . . . . *Hen. VIII.* i 1 36

Face. Executing the outward face of royalty, With all prerogative *Tempest* i 2 104
And yet methinks I see it in thy face, What thou shouldst be . . ii 1 206
No woman's face remember, Save, from my glass, mine own . . . iii 1 49
So full of valour that they smote the air For breathing in their faces . iv 1 173
O jest unseen, inscrutable, invisible, As a nose on a man's face! *T. G. of V.* ii 1 142
Extol their graces; Though ne'er so black, say they have angels' faces . iii 1 103
But chiefly for thy face and thy behaviour, Which, if my augury deceive me not, Witness good bringing up . . . . iv 4 72
The air hath starved the roses in her cheeks And pinch'd the lily-tincture of her face . . . . iv 4 160
If I had such a tire, this face of mine Were full as lovely as is this of hers . . . . iv 4 190
What says she to my face?—She says it is a fair one.—Nay then, the wanton lies; my face is black . . . . v 2 8
What is in Silvia's face, but I may spy More fresh in Julia's? . . v 4 114
By this hat, then, he in the red face had it . . . *Mer. Wives* i 1 173
A little wee face, with a little yellow beard, a Cain-coloured beard . i 4 23
He is de coward Jack priest of de vorld; he is not show his face . . ii 3 33
If you speak, you must not show your face, Or, if you show your face, you must not speak . . . . *Meas. for Meas.* i 4 12
But as she spit in his face, so she defied him . . . . . . ii 1 86
I beseech you, sir, look in this gentleman's face . . . . . ii 1 154
Doth your honour mark his face?—Ay, sir, very well . . . . ii 1 156
Doth your honour see any harm in his face?—Why, no . . . . ii 1 160
His face is the worst thing about him . . . . ii 1 162
First, let her show her face, and after speak.—Pardon, my lord; I will not show my face . . . . v 1 168
This is a strange abuse. Let's see thy face . . . . . . v 1 205
This is that face, thou cruel Angelo, Which once thou sworest was worth the looking on . . . . v 1 207
Show your sheep-biting face, and be hanged an hour! . . . . v 1 359
What, wilt thou flout me thus unto my face, Being forbid? *C. of Errors* i 2 91
Fie, how impatience loureth in your face! . . . . ii 1 86
Spurn at me And hurl the name of husband in my face . . . . ii 2 137
But here's a villain that would face me down He met me on the mart . iii 1 6
Thou wouldst have changed thy face for a name or thy name for an ass iii 1 47
Words are but wind, Ay, and break it in your face, so he break it not behind . . . . iii 1 76
Swart, like my shoe, but her face nothing like so clean kept . . . iii 2 104
What observation madest thou in this case Of his heart's meteors tilting in his face? . . . . iv 2 6
He cries for you and vows, if he can take you, To scorch your face . v 1 183
And with no face, as 'twere, outfacing me . . . . . . v 1 244
Careful hours with time's deformed hand Have written strange defeatures in my face . . . . v 1 299
This grained face of mine be hid In sap-consuming winter's drizzled snow . . . . v 1 311
There are no faces truer than those that are so washed . . *Much Ado* i 1 27
Some gentleman or other shall 'scape a predestinate scratched face . i 1 136
Scratching could not make it worse, an 'twere such a face as yours were i 1 138
And half Count John's melancholy in Signior Benedick's face . . ii 1 14
I could not endure a husband with a beard on his face . . . ii 1 32
It is the witness still of excellency To put a strange face on his own perfection . . . . ii 3 49
And when was he wont to wash his face? . . . . iii 2 57
She shall be buried with her face upwards . . . . . . iii 2 70
Is this face Hero's? are our eyes our own? . . . . . . iv 1 72
I have mark'd A thousand blushing apparitions To start into her face . iv 1 162
You have such a February face, So full of frost, of storm and cloudiness v 4 41
Sweet, let me see your face.—No, that you shall not . . . . v 4 55
I will tell thee wonders.—With that face? . . . . *L. L. Lost* i 2 145
Now fair befall your mask!—Fair fall the face it covers! . . . ii 1 125
His face's own margent did quote such amazes . . . . . . ii 1 246
I must sigh in thy face: Most rude melancholy, valour gives thee place iii 1 68
A wightly wanton with a velvet brow, With two pitch-balls stuck in her face for eyes . . . . iii 1 199

Face. Anon falleth like a crab on the face of terra, the soil, the land, the earth . . . . *L. L. Lost* iv 2 7
As doth thy face through tears of mine give light . . . . . iv 3 32
When shall you hear that I Will praise a hand, a foot, a face, an eye? . iv 3 184
The sea will ebb and flow, heaven show his face . . . . . iv 3 216
No face is fair that is not full so black.—O paradox! . . . . iv 3 253
To tell you plain, I'll find a fairer face not wash'd to-day . . . iv 3 273
Look, here's thy love: my foot and her face see . . . . . iv 3 277
When would you . . . Have found the ground of study's excellence Without the beauty of a woman's face? . . . . iv 3 301
For not looking on a woman's face, You have in that forsworn the use of eyes . . . . iv 3 309
An if my face were but as fair as yours, My favour were as great . . v 2 32
O that your face were not so full of O's! . . . . v 2 45
Here comes Boyet, and mirth is in his face . . . . . . v 2 79
Not a man of them shall have the grace, Despite of suit, to see a lady's face . . . . v 2 129
But while 'tis spoke each turn away her face . . . . . . v 2 148
Show the sunshine of your face, That we, like savages, may worship it v 2 201
My face is but a moon, and clouded too.—Blessed are clouds, to do as such clouds do! . . . . v 2 203
Or ever, but in vizards, show their faces . . . . v 2 271
That superfluous case That hid the worse and show'd the better face . v 2 388
Can any face of brass hold longer out? . . . . v 2 395
I will not be put out of countenance.—Because thou hast no face . . v 2 612
The head of a bodkin.—A Death's face in a ring . . . . . v 2 616
The face of an old Roman coin, scarce seen . . . . . . v 2 617
The carved-bone face on a flask . . . . v 2 619
You have put me out of countenance.—False; we have given thee faces v 2 625
He's a god or a painter; for he makes faces . . . . . . v 2 649
Take comfort: he no more shall see my face . . . *M. N. Dream* i 1 202
An I may hide my face, let me play Thisby too . . . . . i 2 53
It is not night when I do see your face . . . . ii 1 221
Name his name, and half his face must be seen through the lion's neck iii 1 38
Have you not set Lysander, as in scorn, To follow me and praise my eyes and face? . . . . iii 2 223
And darest not stand, nor look me in the face . . . . . . iii 2 424
Thou shalt buy this dear, If ever I thy face by daylight see . . . iii 2 427
Methinks I am marvellous hairy about the face . . . . . . iv 1 27
Now will I to the chink, To spy an I can hear my Thisby's face . . v 1 195
Lend it rather to thine enemy, Who, if he break, thou mayst with better face Exact the penalty . . . . *Mer. of Venice* i 3 137
He had more hair of his tail than I have of my face when I last saw him ii 2 104
To gaze on Christian fools with varnish'd faces . . . . . ii 5 33
Whose ambitious head Spits in the face of heaven . . . . . ii 7 45
His eye being big with tears, Turning his face, he put his hand behind him . . . . ii 8 47
Make room, and let him stand before our face . . . . . . iv 1 16
The clerk will ne'er wear hair on's face that had it . . . . . v 1 158
And with a kind of umber smirch my face . . . . *As Y. Like It* i 3 114
Then the whining school-boy, with his satchel And shining morning face ii 7 146
Mine eye doth his effigies witness Most truly limn'd and living in your face . . . . ii 7 194
Of many faces, eyes and hearts, To have the touches dearest prized . iii 2 159
As many as have good beards or good faces or sweet breaths . . . Epil. 22
Till the tears that she hath shed for thee Like envious floods o'er-run her lovely face . . . . *T. of Shrew* Ind. 2 67
And paint your face and use you like a fool . . . . . . i 1 65
I saw sweet beauty in her face, Such as the daughter of Agenor had . i 1 172
Nor can we be distinguish'd by our faces For man or master . . . i 1 205
He will throw a figure in her face and so disfigure her with it . . i 2 114
Of all the men alive I never yet beheld that special face Which I could fancy more than any other . . . . ii 1 11
Show it me.—Had I a glass, I would.—What, you mean my face? . . ii 1 235
That thinks with oaths to face the matter out . . . . . . ii 1 291
Quaff'd off the muscadel And threw the sops all in the sexton's face . iii 2 175
Why, she hath a face of her own.—Who knows not that? . . . iv 1 102
Thou hast faced many things.—I have.—Face not me . . . . iv 3 125
What stars do spangle heaven with such beauty, As those two eyes become that heavenly face? . . . . iv 5 32
Youth, thou bear'st thy father's face . . . . . . *All's Well* i 2 19
Was this fair face the cause, quoth she, Why the Grecians sacked Troy? i 3 74
I have felt so many quirks of joy and grief, That the first face of neither, on the start, Can woman me unto't . . . . iii 2 52
His face I know not.—Whatsome'er he is, He's bravely taken here . iii 5 54
It shall be read to his face . . . . iv 3 131
Yonder's my lord your son with a patch of velvet on's face . . . iv 5 100
But it is your carbonadoed face . . . . iv 5 107
The element itself, till seven years' heat, Shall not behold her face at ample view . . . . *T. Night* i 1 27
Give me my veil: come, throw it o'er my face . . . . . . i 5 175
Good madam, let me see your face . . . . i 5 248
Have you any commission from your lord to negotiate with my face? . i 5 250
Thy face, thy limbs, actions and spirit, Do give thee five-fold blazon . i 5 311
He does smile his face into more lines than is in the new map . . iii 2 84
A sad face, a reverend carriage, a slow tongue . . . . . . iii 4 80
And do all they can to face me out of my wits . . . . . . iv 2 101
That face of his I do remember well . . . . v 1 54
Taught him to face me out of his acquaintance . . . . . . v 1 91
One face, one voice, one habit, and two persons . . . . . v 1 223
This entertainment May a free face put on . . . . . *W. Tale* i 2 112

Face. Looking on the lines Of my boy's face, methoughts I did recoil Twenty-three years, and saw myself unbreech'd . . . *W. Tale* i 2 154
I saw his heart in 's face . . . . i 2 447
Who taught you this?—I learnt it out of women's faces . . . . ii 1 12
There's not a grain of it the face to sweeten Of the whole dungy earth . ii 1 156
Her face o' fire With labour and the thing she took to quench it . . iv 4 60
Gloves as sweet as damask roses; Masks for faces and for noses . iv 4 223
Will they wear their plackets where they should bear their faces? . iv 4 246
Take your sweetheart's hat And pluck it o'er your brows, muffle your face . . . . iv 4 665
Compare our faces and be judge yourself . . . . . . *K. John* i 1 79
He hath a trick of Cœur-de-lion's face . . . . i 1 85
My face so thin That in mine ear I durst not stick a rose . . . i 1 141
Would I might never stir from off this place, I would give it every foot to have this face . . . . i 1 146
Your face hath got five hundred pound a year, Yet sell your face for five pence and 'tis dear . . . . i 1 153
Inconsiderate, fiery voluntaries, With ladies' faces . . . . . ii 1 68
Look here upon thy brother Geffrey's face; These eyes, these brows . ii 1 99
Some bastards too.—Stand in his face to contradict his claim . . ii 1 280
What say'st thou, boy? look in the lady's face . . . . . ii 1 495
In this the antique and well noted face Of plain old form is much disfigured . . . . iv 2 21
Or turn'd an eye of doubt upon my face . . . . iv 2 233
You taught me how to know the face of right . . . . . . v 2 88
Turn thy face in peace; We grant thou canst outscold us . . . v 2 159
O, let my sovereign turn away his face And bid his ears a little while be deaf, Till I have told this slander . . . . . *Richard II.* i 1 111
Where shame doth harbour, even in Mowbray's face . . . . i 1 195
Nor never look upon each other's face; Nor never write . . . i 3 185
Except the north-east wind, Which then blew bitterly against our faces i 4 7
His face thou hast, for even so look'd he . . . . ii 1 176
His treasons will sit blushing in his face . . . . iii 2 51
But now the blood of twenty thousand men Did triumph in my face . iii 2 77
Ten thousand bloody crowns of mothers' sons Shall ill become the flower of England's face . . . . iii 3 97
Command a mirror hither straight, That it may show me what a face I have . . . . iv 1 266
Hath sorrow struck So many blows upon this face of mine, And made no deeper wounds? . . . . iv 1 278
Was this face the face That every day under his household roof Did keep ten thousand men? . . . . iv 1 281
Was this the face That, like the sun, did make beholders wink? . . iv 1 283
Was this the face that faced so many follies, And was at last out-faced by Bolingbroke? . . . . iv 1 285
A brittle glory shineth in this face: As brittle as the glory is the face . iv 1 287
How soon my sorrow hath destroy'd my face . . . . iv 1 291
The shadow of your sorrow hath destroy'd The shadow of your face . iv 1 293
His face still combating with tears and smiles . . . . . . v 2 32
Shall I for love speak treason to thy face? . . . . v 3 44
Look upon his face; His eyes do drop no tears, his prayers are in jest . v 3 100
At length have gotten leave To look upon my sometimes royal master's face . . . . v 5 75
And on my face he turn'd an eye of death . . . . . *1 Hen. IV.* i 3 143
Only stays but to behold the face Of that occasion that shall bring it on i 3 275
In thy face strange motions have appear'd, Such as we see when men restrain their breath . . . . ii 3 63
If manhood, good manhood, be not forgot upon the face of the earth . ii 4 142
I'll never wear hair on my face more . . . . ii 4 153
A plague upon such backing! give me them that will face me . . ii 4 167
If I tell thee a lie, spit in my face, call me horse . . . . . ii 4 214
Now, my masters, for a true face and good conscience . . . . ii 4 551
But rather drowsed and hung their eyelids down, Slept in his face . iii 2 82
Do thou amend thy face, and I'll amend my life . . . . . iii 3 27
My face does you no harm.—No, I'll be sworn . . . . . . iii 3 31
I never see thy face but I think upon hell-fire and Dives that lived in purple . . . . iii 3 35
If thou wert any way given to virtue, I would swear by thy face . . iii 3 39
'Sblood, I would my face were in your belly! . . . . iii 3 56
He hath nothing.—How! poor? look upon his face; what call you rich? iii 3 89
By this face, This seeming brow of justice, did he win The hearts of all iv 3 82
Read in churches, To face the garment of rebellion With some fine colour . . . . v 1 74
I know this face full well: A gallant knight he was . . . . . v 3 19
But let my favours hide thy mangled face . . . . v 4 96
He will not stick to say his face is a face-royal . . . *2 Hen. IV.* i 2 26
There is not a white hair on your face but should have his effect of gravity . . . . i 2 183
Go, wash thy face, and draw the action . . . . ii 1 162
What a disgrace is it to me to remember thy name! or to know thy face to-morrow! . . . . ii 2 16
I could discern no part of his face from the window . . . . . ii 2 87
Alas, poor ape, how thou sweatest! come, let me wipe thy face . . ii 4 235
Now, the Lord bless that sweet face of thine! . . . . ii 4 317
His face is Lucifer's privy-kitchen, where he doth nothing but roast malt-worms . . . . ii 4 360
Let us sway on and face them in the field . . . . iv 1 24
It illumineth the face, which as a beacon gives warning . . . . iv 3 116
As with an enemy That had before my face murder'd my father . . iv 5 168
You shall see him laugh till his face be like a wet cloak ill laid up! . v 1 95
I dare swear you borrow not that face Of seeming sorrow, it is sure your own . . . . v 2 28
Good Bardolph, put thy face between his sheets, and do the office of a warming-pan . . . . *Hen. V.* ii 1 87
By the means whereof a' faces it out, but fights not . . . . . iii 2 35
His face is all bubukles, and whelks, and knobs, and flames o' fire . iii 6 108
I will trot to-morrow a mile, and my way shall be paved with English faces . . . . iii 7 88
Through their paly flames Each battle sees the other's umber'd face iv Prol. 9
Upon his royal face there is no note How dread an army hath enrounded him . . . . iv Prol. 35
You may as well go about to turn the sun to ice with fanning in his face iv 1 213
Kisses the gashes That bloodily did yawn upon his face . . . . iv 6 14
He smiled me in the face, raught me his hand . . . . . . iv 6 21
Right joyous are we to behold your face . . . . v 2 9
Whose face is not worth sun-burning, that never looks in his glass for love of any thing he sees there . . . . v 2 153
A curled pate will grow bald; a fair face will wither . . . . v 2 169
Old age, that ill layer up of beauty, can do no more spoil upon my face v 2 249
Though I speak it before his face . . . . v 2 260

Face. His sparkling eyes, replete with wrathful fire, More dazzled and drove back his enemies Than mid-day sun fierce bent against their faces . . . . *1 Hen. VI.* i 1 14
Durst not presume to look once in the face . . . . i 1 140
I beard thee to thy face.—What! am I dared and bearded to my face? . i 3 44
Because till now we never saw your face . . . . iii 4 24
And pale destruction meets thee in the face . . . . iv 2 27
O, were mine eye-balls into bullets turn'd, That I in rage might shoot them at your faces! . . . . iv 7 80
Fair Margaret knows That Suffolk doth not flatter, face, or feign . v 3 142
Thou hast given me in this beauteous face A world of earthly blessings to my soul . . . . *2 Hen. VI.* i 1 21
Rancour will out: proud prelate, in thy face I see thy fury . . . i 1 142
Gaze on, and grovel on thy face, Until thy head be circled with the same i 2 9
Could I come near your beauty with my nails, I'ld set my ten commandments in your face . . . . i 3 145
Ill can thy noble mind abrook The abject people gazing on thy face . ii 4 11
In thy face I see The map of honour, truth and loyalty . . . . iii 1 202
In face, in gait, in speech, he doth resemble . . . . . . iii 1 373
What, dost thou turn away and hide thy face? I am no loathsome leper . . . . iii 2 74
To drain Upon his face an ocean of salt tears, To tell my love . . iii 2 143
See how the blood is settled in his face . . . . iii 2 160
His face is black and full of blood, His eye-balls further out than when he lived . . . . iii 2 168
Hath this lovely face Ruled, like a wandering planet, over me? . . iv 4 15
It will be proved to thy face . . . . iv 7 42
Ravish your wives and daughters before your faces . . . . . iv 8 32
He shall not hide his head, But boldly stand and front him to his face v 1 86
If thou canst for blushing, view this face, And bite thy tongue *3 Hen. VI.* i 4 46
Thy face is, visard-like, unchanging, Made impudent with use of evil deeds . . . . i 4 116
And yet be seen to bear a woman's face? Women are soft, mild, pitiful i 4 140
That face of his the hungry cannibals Would not have touch'd . . i 4 152
Laugh'd in his face . . . . ii 1 60
Whose hand is that the forest bear doth lick? Not his that spoils her young before her face . . . . ii 2 14
Though man's face be fearful to their eyes . . . . ii 2 27
Let his manly face, which promiseth Successful fortune, steel thy melting heart To hold thine own . . . . ii 2 40
Ere my knee rise from the earth's cold face . . . . ii 3 35
O God! it is my father's face, Whom in this conflict I unwares have kill'd . . . . ii 5 61
Is this our foeman's face? Ah, no, no, no, it is mine only son! . . ii 5 82
The red rose and the white are on his face . . . . ii 5 97
Though before his face I speak the words . . . . ii 6 39
As I blow this feather from my face, And as the air blows it to me again iii 1 84
And wet my cheeks with artificial tears, And frame my face to all occasions . . . . iii 2 185
I had rather chop this hand off at a blow, And with the other fling it at thy face . . . . v 1 51
'Twas I that stabb'd young Edward, But 'twas thy heavenly face that set me on . . . . *Richard III.* i 2 183
Because I cannot flatter and speak fair, Smile in men's faces . . . i 3 48
We know each other's faces, But for our hearts, he knows no more of mine, Than I of yours . . . . iii 4 10
For by his face straight shall you know his heart.—What of his heart perceive you in his face By any likelihood he show'd to-day? . . . iii 4 55
Her face defaced with scars of infamy . . . . iii 7 126
O, when, I say, I look'd on Richard's face, This was my wish . . iv 1 71
Or I with grief and extreme age shall perish And never look upon thy face again . . . . iv 4 186
What good is cover'd with the face of heaven, To be discover'd? . . iv 4 239
The prayers of holy saints and wronged souls, Like high-rear'd bulwarks, stand before our faces . . . . v 3 242
For me, the ransom of my bold attempt Shall be this cold corpse on the earth's cold face . . . . v 3 266
All the good our English Have got by the late voyage is but merely A fit or two o' the face . . . . *Hen. VIII.* i 3 7
Which the duke desired To have brought vivâ voce to his face . . ii 1 18
Ye have angels' faces, but heaven knows your hearts . . . . iii 1 145
Thou hast the sweetest face I ever look'd on . . . . iv 1 43
Had their faces Been loose, this day they had been lost . . . . iv 1 74
Whose bright faces Cast thousand beams upon me, like the sun . . iv 2 88
How long her face is drawn? how pale she looks, And of an earthy cold? . . . . iv 2 97
He should be a brazier by his face . . . . v 4 42
If I go to him, with my armed fist I'll pash him o'er the face *Tr. and Cr.* ii 3 213
Here is a man—but 'tis before his face; I will be silent . . . . ii 3 240
The beauty that is borne here in the face The bearer knows not . . iii 3 103
Thou shalt hunt a lion, that will fly With his face backward . . . iv 1 20
Come, come, thou boy-queller, show thy face . . . . . . v 5 45
Turn thy false face, thou traitor, And pay thy life thou owest me for my horse! . . . . v 6 6
Thou Shalt see me once more strike at Tullus' face . . . *Coriolanus* i 1 244
All hurt behind; backs red, and faces pale With flight and agued fear! i 4 37
I will go wash; And when my face is fair, you shall perceive Whether I blush . . . . i 9 69
If the drink you give me touch my palate adversely, I make a crooked face at it . . . . ii 1 62
They lie deadly that tell you you have good faces . . . . . ii 1 68
If you chance to be pinched with the colic, you make faces like mummers . . . . ii 1 83
From face to foot He was a thing of blood . . . . ii 2 112
Bid them wash their faces And keep their teeth clean . . . . iii 3 66
Thou hast a grim appearance, and thy face Bears a command in't . iv 5 66
I knew by his face that there was something in him . . . . iv 5 162
He had, sir, a kind of face, methought,—I cannot tell how to term it . iv 5 163
I have not the face To say 'Beseech you, cease' . . . . . iv 6 116
Not of a woman's tenderness to be, Requires nor child nor woman's face to see . . . . v 3 130
The tartness of his face sours ripe grapes . . . . v 4 18
O Tamora! thou bear'st a woman's face . . . . . *T. Andron.* ii 3 136
And wonder greatly that man's face can fold In pleasing smiles such murderous tyranny . . . . ii 3 266
Ah, now thou turn'st away thy face for shame! . . . . . . ii 4 28
Thy cheeks look red as Titan's face Blushing to be encounter'd with a cloud . . . . ii 4 31
In winter with warm tears I'll melt the snow, And keep eternal spring-time on thy face . . . . iii 1 21

Fain. There was not time enough to hear, As I perceived his grace would fain have done *Hen. V.* i 1 85
I wad full fain hear some question 'tween you tway iii 2 127
I would fain be about the ears of the English iii 7 91
I would fain see the man, that has but two legs iv 7 169
I would fain see it once, an please God of his grace that I might see iv 7 171
Fain would mine eyes be witness with mine ears 1 *Hen. VI.* ii 3 9
They that of late were daring with their scoffs Are glad and fain by flight to save themselves iii 2 114
Fain would I woo her, yet I dare not speak v 3 65
Yea, man and birds are fain of climbing high 2 *Hen. VI.* ii 1 8
No man alive so fain as I! iii 1 244
Fain would I go to chafe his paly lips With twenty thousand kisses iii 2 141
Thereby is England mained, and fain to go with a staff iv 2 172
The good old man would fain that all were well 3 *Hen. VI.* iv 7 31
My soul is heavy, and I fain would sleep *Richard III.* i 4 74
How fain, like Pilate, would I wash my hands Of this most grievous guilty murder done! i 4 279
The tender prince Would fain have come with me to meet your grace iii 1 29
Which he fain Would have flung from him, but, indeed, he could not *Hen. VIII.* ii 1 24
I was fain to draw mine honour in v 4 60
I would fain have armed to-day, but my Nell would not have it so *Troi. and Cres.* iii 1 149
I would fain see them meet v 4 5
Fain would I dwell on form, fain, fain deny What I have spoke *R. and J.* ii 2 88
One Paris, that would fain lay knife aboard ii 4 214
I would forget it fain iii 2 109
How fain would I have hated all mankind! *T. of Athens* iv 3 506
To my thinking, he would fain have had it *J. Cæsar* i 2 240
Which the poor heart would fain deny, and dare not *Macbeth* v 3 28
A man faithful and honourable.—I would fain prove so *Hamlet* ii 2 131
Hath there been such a time—I'd fain know that? ii 2 153
My spirits grow dull, and fain I would beguile The tedious day with sleep iii 2 236
I have a speech of fire, that fain would blaze, But that this folly douts it iv 7 191
In respect of that, I would fain think it were not *Lear* i 2 70
You have that in your countenance which I would fain call master i 4 30
I would fain learn to lie.—An you lie, sirrah, we'll have you whipped i 4 196
And wast thou fain, poor father, To hovel thee with swine, and rogues forlorn? iv 7 38
A brace of Cyprus gallants that would fain have a measure *Othello* ii 3 32
I would very fain speak with you.—Prithee, come iv 1 175

Faint. What strength I have's mine own, Which is most faint *Tempest* Epil. 3
Chanting faint hymns to the cold fruitless moon *M. N. Dream* i 1 73
Where often you and I Upon faint primrose-beds were wont to lie i 1 215
Fair love, you faint with wandering in the wood ii 2 35
A more swelling port Than my faint means would grant continuance *Mer. of Venice* i 1 125
One of you question yond man If he for gold will give us any food: I faint almost to death *As Y. Like It* ii 4 66
Here's a young maid with travel much oppress'd And faints for succour ii 4 75
To my litter straight; Weakness possesseth me, and I am faint *K. John* v 3 17
When English measure backward their own ground In faint retire v 5 4
I am the cygnet to this pale faint swan v 7 21
But if you faint, as fearing to do so, Stay and be secret *Richard II.* ii 1 297
As, though on thinking on no thought I think, Makes me with heavy nothing faint and shrink ii 2 32
When I was dry with rage and extreme toil, Breathless and faint 1 *Hen. IV.* i 3 32
In thy faint slumbers I by thee have watch'd ii 3 50
Even such a man, so faint, so spiritless, So dull, so dead in look 2 *Hen. IV.* i 1 70
But these mine eyes saw him in bloody state, Rendering faint quittance i 1 108
To relief of lazars and weak age, Of indigent faint souls *Hen. V.* i 1 16
For the effusion of our blood, the muster of his kingdom too faint a number iii 6 139
The English army is grown weak and faint 1 *Hen. VI.* i 1 158
Why faint you, lords? My title's good, and better far than his 3 *Hen. VI.* i 1 129
I am faint and cannot fly their fury: And were I strong, I would not i 4 23
This strong right hand of mine Can pluck the diadem from faint Henry's head ii 1 153
This soft courage makes your followers faint ii 2 57
And much effuse of blood doth make me faint ii 6 28
Women and children of so high a courage, And warriors faint! v 4 51
It faints me, To think what follows *Hen. VIII.* ii 3 103
Forsooth, the faint defects of age Must be the scene of mirth *Tr. and Cr.* i 3 172
Paris should ne'er retract what he hath done, Nor faint in the pursuit ii 2 142
Help me with thy fainting hand—If fear hath made thee faint *T. Andron.* ii 3 234
Come between us, good Benvolio; my wits faint *Rom. and Jul.* ii 4 72
Help me into some house, Benvolio, Or I shall faint iii 1 111
I have a faint cold fear thrills through my veins iv 3 15
Ceremony was but devised at first To set a gloss on faint deeds *T. of Athens* i 2 16
Has friendship such a faint and milky heart, It turns in less than two nights? iii 1 57
Return, And with their faint reply this answer join iii 3 25
O, I grow faint. Run, Lucius, and commend me to my lord *J. Cæsar* ii 4 43
I am faint, my gashes cry for help *Macbeth* i 2 42
I have perceived a most faint neglect of late *Lear* i 4 73
Look there, look there!—He faints! My lord, my lord! v 3 311
O, for a chair, To bear him easily hence!—Alas, he faints! *Othello* v 1 84
And in our sports my better cunning faints Under his chance *Ant. and Cleo.* ii 3 34
Lead me from hence; I faint: O Iras, Charmian! 'tis no matter ii 5 110
I cannot find those runagates; that villain Hath mock'd me. I am faint *Cymbeline* iv 2 63
You come in faint for want of meat, depart reeling with too much drink v 4 163
My false spirits Quail to remember—Give me leave; I faint v 5 149

Fainted. He fainted And cried, in fainting, upon Rosalind *As Y. Like It* iv 3 149
Expectation fainted, Longing for what it had not *Ant. and Cleo.* iii 6 47

Fainter. Not like me—yet long'st, But in a fainter kind *Cymbeline* iii 2 57

Faint-hearted Woodvile, prizest him 'fore me? 1 *Hen. VI.* i 3 22
Farewell, faint-hearted and degenerate king 3 *Hen. VI.* i 1 183
Faint-hearted boy, arise, and look upon her *T. Andron.* iii 1 65

Fainting under The pleasing punishment that women bear *Com. of Errors* i 1 46
And now he fainted And cried, in fainting, upon Rosalind *As Y. Like It* iv 3 150
Out of the weak door of our fainting land *K. John* v 7 78
That I may kindly give one fainting kiss 1 *Hen. VI.* i 5 40
My fainting words do warrant death ii 5 95
Dream on, dream on, of bloody deeds and death: Fainting, despair! *Richard III.* v 3 172
Help me with thy fainting hand—If fear hath made thee faint *T. An.* ii 3 233

Faintly. I faintly broke with thee of Arthur's death *K. John* iv 2 227
Woe doth the heavier sit, Where it perceives it is but faintly borne *Rich. II.* i 3 281
He prays but faintly and would be denied v 3 103
Big Mars seems bankrupt in their beggar'd host And faintly through a rusty beaver peeps *Hen. V.* iv 2 44
Like pale ghosts, Faintly besiege us one hour in a month 1 *Hen. VI.* i 2 8
I kneel'd before him; 'Twas very faintly he said 'Rise' *Coriolanus* v 1 66
Without-book prologue, faintly spoke After the prompter *Rom. and Jul.* i 4 7
But faintly, nothing like the image and horror of it *Lear* i 2 191
Why do you speak so faintly? Are you not well? *Othello* iii 3 282
Now he denies it faintly, and laughs it out iv 1 113

Faintness constraineth me To measure out my length on this cold bed *M. N. Dream* iii 2 428
Pronouncing that the paleness of this flower Bewray'd the faintness of my master's heart 1 *Hen. VI.* iv 1 107

Fair. Not so fair, boy, as well-favoured *T. G. of Ver.* ii 1 54
What dost thou know?—That she is not so fair as, of you, well favoured ii 1 57
So painted, to make her fair, that no man counts of her beauty ii 1 65
She is fair; and so is Julia that I love—That I did love ii 4 199
And Silvia—witness Heaven, that made her fair!—Shows Julia but a swarthy Ethiope ii 6 25
Silvia is too fair, too true, too holy, To be corrupted with my worthless gifts iv 2 5
Holy, fair and wise is she; The heaven such grace did lend her iv 2 41
Is she kind as she is fair? For beauty lives with kindness iv 2 44
Is she not passing fair?—She hath been fairer, madam, than she is iv 4 153
When she did think my master loved her well, She, in my judgement, was as fair as you iv 4 156
My face is black.—But pearls are fair v 2 11
What is 'fair,' William?—Pulcher *Mer Wives* iv 1 26
Gentle and fair, your brother kindly greets you *Meas. for Meas.* i 4 24
Heaven shield my mother play'd my father fair iii 1 141
The hand that hath made you fair hath made you good iii 1 184
Grace, being the soul of your complexion, shall keep the body of it ever fair iii 1 188
Good morning to you, fair and gracious daughter iv 3 116
If any born at Ephesus be seen At any Syracusian marts and fairs *C. of Er.* i 1 18
My decayed fair A sunny look of his would soon repair ii 1 98
Look sweet, speak fair, become disloyalty iii 2 11
That would refuse so fair an offer'd chain iii 2 186
The merry wind Blows fair from land iv 1 91
First he did praise my beauty, then my speech.—Didst speak him fair? iv 2 16
They will surely do us no harm: you saw they speak us fair iv 4 157
Soft and delicate desires, All prompting me how fair young Hero is *M. Ado* i 1 306
One woman is fair, yet I am well; another is wise, yet I am well ii 3 28
Fair, or I'll never look on her; mild, or come not near me ii 3 33
They say the lady is fair; 'tis a truth, I can bear them witness ii 3 239
Most foul, most fair! farewell, Thou pure impiety and impious purity! iv 1 104
All senses to that sense did make their repair, To feel only looking on fairest of fair *L. L. Lost* ii 1 241
I thank my beauty, I am fair that shoot iv 1 11
O short-lived pride! Not fair? alack for woe!—Yes, madam, fair iv 1 15
Where fair is not, praise cannot mend the brow iv 1 17
Nothing but fair is that which you inherit iv 1 20
My beauty will be saved by merit! O heresy in fair, fit for these days! iv 1 22
By heaven, that thou art fair, is most infallible iv 1 60
More fairer than fair, beautiful than beauteous iv 1 63
Spied a blossom passing fair Playing in the wanton air iv 3 103
Of all complexions the cull'd sovereignty Do meet, as at a fair, in her fair cheek, Where several worthies make one dignity iv 3 235
No face is fair that is not full so black.—O paradox! iv 3 253
And therefore is she born to make black fair iv 3 261
I'll prove her fair, or talk till doomsday here iv 3 274
An if my face were but as fair as yours, My favour were as great v 2 32
I am compared to twenty thousand fairs v 2 37
Beauteous as ink; a good conclusion.—Fair as a text B in a copy-book v 2 42
And retails his wares At wakes and wassails, meetings, markets, fairs v 2 318
All hail, sweet madam, and fair time of day!—'Fair' in 'all hail' is foul, as I conceive v 2 339
That is all one, my fair, sweet, honey monarch v 2 530
Call you me fair? that fair again unsay. Demetrius loves your fair: O happy fair! *M. N. Dream* i 1 181
Through Athens I am thought as fair as she i 1 227
Do I entice you? do I speak you fair? ii 1 199
If I were fair, Thisby, I were only thine iii 1 106
I am as fair now as I was erewhile. Since night you loved me iii 2 274
Opening on Neptune with fair blessed beams iii 2 392
She is fair and, fairer than that word, Of wondrous virtues *Mer. of Venice* i 1 162
Sometimes from her eyes I did receive fair speechless messages i 1 164
Rest you fair, good signior i 3 60
Stood as fair As any comer I have look'd on yet For my affection ii 1 20
Fair she is, if that mine eyes be true, And true she is, as she hath proved ii 6 54
Like herself, wise, fair and true, Shall she be placed in my constant soul ii 6 56
You that choose not by the view, Chance as fair and choose as true! iii 2 133
A thousand times more fair, ten thousand times More rich iii 2 155
Say how I loved you, speak me fair in death iv 1 275
His horses are bred better; for, besides that they are fair with their feeding, they are taught their manage. *As Y. Like It* i 1 12
Those that she makes fair she scarce makes honest i 2 40
I confess me much guilty, to deny so fair and excellent ladies any thing i 2 197
If ladies be but young and fair, They have the gift to know it ii 7 37
And then the justice, In fair round belly with good capon lined ii 7 154
Carve on every tree The fair, the chaste and unexpressive she iii 2 10
Let no fair be kept in mind But the fair of Rosalind iii 2 99
Well, I am not fair; and therefore I pray the gods make me honest iii 3 33
She says I am not fair, that I lack manners; She calls me proud iv 3 15
The boy is fair, Of female favour, and bestows himself Like a ripe sister iv 3 86
If you speak me fair, I'll tell you news indifferent good for either *T. of Shrew* i 2 180
You will have Gremio to keep you fair ii 1 17
Have you not a daughter Call'd Katharina, fair and virtuous? ii 1 43
A suitor to your daughter, Unto Bianca, fair and virtuous ii 1 92
Be the jacks fair within, the jills fair without? iv 1 51
Fair lovely maid, once more good day to thee iv 5 33
Young budding virgin, fair and fresh and sweet, Whither away? iv 5 37
To each of you one fair and virtuous mistress Fall! *All's Well* ii 3 63
She is young, wise, fair; In these to nature she's immediate heir ii 3 138
He is too good and fair for death and me iii 4 16
Distracted clouds give way; so stand thou forth; The time is fair again v 3 36
I will buy me a son-in-law in a fair, and toll for this v 3 148

Fair. Thou hast a mind that suits With this thy fair and outward character . . . . *T. Night* i 2 51
You are too proud; But, if you were the devil, you are fair . i 5 270
She bore a mind that envy could not but call fair . . . ii 1 31
I am slain by a fair cruel maid . . . . . . ii 4 55
I bespake you fair, and hurt you not . . . . . v 1 192
He haunts wakes, fairs and bear-baitings . *W. Tale* iv 3 109
I'll be thine, my fair, Or not my father's . . . . iv 4 42
How prettily the young swain seems to wash The hand was fair before! iv 4 378
Happy be you! All that you speak shows fair . . . iv 4 636
She a fair divided excellence, Whose fulness of perfection lies in him *K. John* ii 1 439
But thou art fair, and at thy birth, dear boy, Nature and Fortune join'd to make thee great . . . . . . iii 1 51
Since the more fair and crystal is the sky, The uglier seem the clouds that in it fly . . . . . . *Richard II.* i 1 41
The wind sits fair for news to go to Ireland . . . ii 2 123
The news is very fair and good, my lord . . . . iii 3 5
We do debase ourselves, cousin, do we not, To look so poorly and to speak so fair? . . . . iii 3 128
A fair hot wench in flame-coloured taffeta . . . . 1 *Hen. IV.* i 2 10
By Phœbus, he, 'that wandering knight so fair' . . . i 2 17
That's even as fair as—at hand, quoth the chamberlain . ii 1 54
Now, sirs: by'r lady, you fought fair; so did you, Peto . . ii 4 329
These promises are fair, the parties sure . . . . iii 1 1
Silver Trent shall run In a new channel, fair and evenly . . iii 1 103
The moon shines fair; you may away by night . . . iii 1 142
Move in that obedient orb again Where you did give a fair and natural light . . . . v 1 18
We will not now be troubled with reply: We offer fair; take it advisedly v 1 114
The arms are fair, When the intent of bearing them is just . . v 2 88
Since this business so fair is done, Let us not leave till all our own be won v 5 43
The right fencing grace, my lord; tap for tap, and so part fair 2 *Hen. IV.* ii 1 207
How a good yoke of bullocks at Stamford fair? . . . iii 2 43
About the sack he lost the other day at Hinckley fair . . v 1 26
Well, you must now speak Sir John Falstaff fair . . v 2 33
Now sits the wind fair, and we will aboard . . *Hen. V.* ii 2 12
We doubt not of a fair and lucky war . . . . . ii 2 184
Joy and good wishes To our most fair and princely cousin! . v 2 4
What sayest thou then to my love? speak, my fair, and fairly, I pray thee v 2 177
Fair be all thy hopes! . . . . . . 1 *Hen. VI.* ii 5 113
Have you laid fair the bed? Is all things well? . 2 *Hen. VI.* iii 2 11
My gracious lord, entreat him, speak him fair . . . iv 1 120
I'll write unto them and entreat them fair . . . 3 *Hen. VI.* i 1 271
Son Edward, she is fair and virtuous, Therefore delay not . . iii 3 245
As good to chide the waves as speak them fair . . . v 4 24
Since I cannot prove a lover, To entertain these fair well-spoken days, I am determined to prove a villain . . . . *Richard III.* i 1 29
His noble queen Well struck in years, fair, and not jealous . i 1 92
Because I cannot flatter and speak fair, Smile in men's faces . i 3 47
Entreat me fair, Or with the clamorous report of war Thus will I drown your exclamations . . . . iv 4 151
You have a daughter call'd Elizabeth, virtuous and fair . . iv 4 204
With smiling plenty and fair prosperous days . . . v 5 34
Ten times more ugly Than ever they were fair . . *Hen. VIII.* i 2 118
From all parts they are coming, As if we kept a fair here! . v 4 73
I tell thee I am mad In Cressid's love: thou answer'st 'she is fair' *Troi. and Cres.* i 1 52
Let her be as she is: if she be fair, 'tis the better for her . i 1 67
Because she's kin to me, therefore she's not so fair as Helen: an she were not kin to me, she would be as fair on Friday as Helen is on Sunday . . . . i 1 77
Say I she is not fair?—I do not care whether you do or no . i 1 81
Helen must needs be fair, When with your blood you daily paint her thus i 1 93
Fair be to you, my lord, and to all this fair company . . iii 1 46
And by the way possess thee what she is. Entreat her fair . . iv 4 115
Here art thou in appointment fresh and fair . . . . iv 5 1
Stand fair, I pray thee: let me look on thee . . . . iv 5 235
Farewell, revolted fair! and, Diomed, Stand fast, and wear a castle on thy head! . . . . v 2 186
Most putrefied core, so fair without, Thy goodly armour thus hath cost thy life . . . . v 8 1
And when my face is fair, you shall perceive Whether I blush or no *Cor.* i 9 69
How now, my as fair as noble ladies? . . . . . ii 1 107
What the vengeance! Could he not speak 'em fair? . . . iii 1 263
Speak fair: you may salve so, Not what is dangerous present, but the loss Of what is past . . . . iii 2 70
You have made fair hands, You and your crafts! you have crafted fair! iv 6 118
How fair the tribune speaks to calm my thoughts! . *T. Andron.* i 1 46
His child is like to her, fair as you are . . . . iv 2 154
Smooth and speak him fair, And tarry with him till I turn again . v 2 140
And she's fair I love.—A right fair mark, fair coz, is soonest hit *R. and J.* i 1 212
She is too fair, too wise, wisely too fair, To merit bliss by making me despair . . . . i 1 227
These happy masks that kiss fair ladies' brows Being black put us in mind they hide the fair . . . . i 1 236
Show me a mistress that is passing fair, What doth her beauty serve, but as a note Where I may read who pass'd that passing fair? . i 1 240
Within her scope of choice Lies my consent and fair according voice . i 2 19
Tut, you saw her fair, none else being by, Herself poised with herself . i 2 99
The fish lives in the sea, and 'tis much pride For fair without the fair within to hide . . . . i 3 90
The game was ne'er so fair, and I am done.—Tut, dun's the mouse . i 4 39
That fair for which love groan'd for and would die, With tender Juliet match'd, is now not fair . . . . ii Prol. 3
That were some spite: my invocation Is fair and honest . . ii 1 28
Sick and pale with grief, That thou her maid art far more fair than she ii 2 6
Romeo that spoke him fair, bade him bethink How nice the quarrel was iii 1 158
Ah, dear Juliet, Why art thou yet so fair? . . . . v 3 102
The maid is fair, o' the youngest for a bride . *T. of Athens* i 1 123
Faults that are rich are fair . . . . i 2 13
You undergo too strict a paradox, Striving to make an ugly deed look fair iii 5 25
Thus much of this [gold] will make black white, foul fair, Wrong right iv 3 28
This dream is all amiss interpreted; It was a vision fair and fortunate *J. Cæsar* ii 2 84
Fair is foul, and foul is fair: Hover through the fog and filthy air *Macbeth* i 1 11
Why do you start; and seem to fear Things that do sound so fair? . i 3 52
Fair and noble hostess, We are your guest to-night . . . i 6 24
That fair and warlike form In which the majesty of buried Denmark Did sometimes march . . . . *Hamlet* i 1 47

Fair. Ha, ha! are you honest?—My lord?—Are you fair?—What means your lordship?—That if you be honest and fair, your honesty should admit no discourse to your beauty . . . . *Hamlet* iii 1 105
That to the use of actions fair and good He likewise gives a frock or livery . . . . iii 4 163
For who, that's but a queen, fair, sober, wise . . . . iii 4 189
Go seek him out; speak fair, and bring the body Into the chapel . iv 1 36
And from her fair and unpolluted flesh May violets spring! . . v 1 262
I sat me down, Devised a new commission, wrote it fair: I once did hold it, as our statists do, A baseness to write fair . . . . v 2 32
Though this knave came something saucily into the world before he was sent for, yet was his mother fair . . . . . *Lear* i 1 23
March to wakes and fairs and market-towns. Poor Tom, thy horn is dry iii 6 78
Since thy outside looks so fair and warlike . . . . v 3 142
A maid so tender, fair and happy, So opposite to marriage . *Othello* i 2 66
If virtue no delighted beauty lack, Your son-in-law is far more fair than black . . . . i 3 291
If she be fair and wise, fairness and wit, The one's for use, the other useth it . . . . ii 1 130
How if fair and foolish?—She never yet was foolish that was fair . ii 1 136
There's none so foul and foolish thereunto, But does foul pranks which fair and wise ones do . . . . ii 1 143
She that was ever fair and never proud . . . . . ii 1 149
Though other things grow fair against the sun, Yet fruits that blossom first will first be ripe . . . . ii 3 382
'Tis not to make me jealous To say my wife is fair, feeds well, loves company . . . . iii 3 184
O thou weed, Who art so lovely fair and smell'st so sweet! . . iv 2 68
Every passion fully strives To make itself, in thee, fair and admired! *Ant. and Cleo.* i 1 51
The morn is fair. Good morrow, general . . . . . iv 4 24
His to be more fair, virtuous, wise, chaste, constant-qualified *Cymbeline* i 4 64
As fair and as good—a kind of hand-in-hand comparison—had been something too fair and too good for any lady in Britain . . . i 4 75
Can we not Partition make with spectacles so precious 'Twixt fair and foul? . . . . i 6 38
A lady So fair, and fasten'd to an empery, Would make the great'st king double . . . . i 6 120
I love and hate her: for she's fair and royal . . . . iii 5 70
This forwardness Makes our hopes fair . . . . . iv 2 343
Great nature, like his ancestry, Moulded the stuff so fair . . v 4 49
She is fair too, is she not?—As a fair day in summer, wondrous fair *Per.* ii 5 35
As you are as virtuous as fair, Resolve your angry father . . ii 5 67
Fair a cave. Did ever dragon keep so fair a cave? . . *Rom. and Jul.* iii 2 74
Fair a child. Happy the parents of so fair a child! . . *T. of Shrew* iv 5 39
Fair a dame. I unworthy am To woo so fair a dame . . 1 *Hen. VI.* v 3 124
Fair a day. So foul and fair a day I have not seen . . . *Macbeth* i 3 38
Fair a dream. My soul is very jocund In the remembrance of so fair a dream . . . . *Richard III.* v 3 233
Fair a house. If the ill spirit have so fair a house, Good things will strive to dwell with't . . . . *Tempest* i 2 458
Fair a name. Write them together, yours is as fair a name *J. Cæsar* i 2 144
Fair a show. Alack, alack, for woe, That any harm should stain so fair a show! . . . . *Richard II.* iii 3 71
Fair a tree. Yet hope, succeeding from so fair a tree As your fair self, doth tune us otherwise . . . . *Pericles* i 1 114
Fair a troop. Would it not shame thee in so fair a troop To read a lecture of them? . . . . *Richard II.* iv 1 231
Fair act. As oft a slanderous epitaph As record of fair act *Cymbeline* iii 3 53
Fair action. Let every man now task his thought, That this fair action may on foot be brought . . . . . . *Hen. V.* i 2 310
Fair advantage. Made use and fair advantage of his days *T. G. of Ver.* ii 4 68
Men that hazard all Do it in hope of fair advantages *Mer. of Venice* ii 7 19
And from this swarm of fair advantages You took occasion to be quickly woo'd To gripe the general sway . . . . 1 *Hen. IV.* v 1 55
Fair adventure. To try the fair adventure of to-morrow *K. John* v 5 22
Fair Ægle. And make him with fair Ægle break his faith *M. N. Dream* ii 1 79
Fair affliction. O fair affliction, peace!—No, no, I will not *K. John* iii 4 36
Fair alliance. This fair alliance quickly shall call home To high promotions and great dignity . . . . . *Richard III.* iv 4 313
Fair an eye. An eagle, madam, Hath not so green, so quick, so fair an eye As Paris hath . . . . . . *Rom. and Jul.* iii 5 222
Fair an outward. I do not think So fair an outward and such stuff within Endows a man but he . . . . . . *Cymbeline* i 1 23
Fair angels. Not that I have the power to clutch my hand, When his fair angels would salute my palm . . . . *K. John* ii 1 590
Fair appointments. From this castle's tatter'd battlements Our fair appointments may be well perused . . . . *Rich. II.* iii 3 53
Fair approach. Navarre had notice of your fair approach *L. L. Lost* ii 1 81
Fair as day. As fair as day.—Ay, as some days; but then no sun must shine . . . . iv 3 90
Fair assembly. Good morrow to this fair assembly . . *Much Ado* v 4 34
That bring these tidings to this fair assembly . . *As Y. Like It* v 4 159
Having heard by fame Of this so noble and so fair assembly . *Hen. VIII.* i 4 67
You hold a fair assembly; you do well, lord . . . . i 4 87
A fair assembly: whither should they come? . . *Rom. and Jul.* i 2 75
Fair Athens. But if he sack fair Athens, And take our goodly aged men by the beards . . . . *T. of Athens* v 1 174
Fair Beatrice, I thank you for your pains . . . *Much Ado* ii 3 258
Fair befall your mask!—Fair fall the face it covers! . . *L. L. Lost* ii 1 124
Now, fair befall thee, good Petruchio! The wager thou hast won *T. of S.* v 2 111
Plain well-meaning soul, Whom fair befal in heaven! . *Richard II.* ii 1 129
Now fair befal thee and thy noble house! . . . *Richard III.* i 3 282
Now, fair befall you! he deserved his death . . . . iii 5 47
Fair behaviour. There is a fair behaviour in thee, captain *T. Night* i 2 47
Fair beholders. To tell you, fair beholders, that our play Leaps o'er the vaunt and firstlings of those broils . . . *Troi. and Cres.* Prol. 26
Fair beloved. Will I break my oath To this my fair beloved *W. Tale* iv 4 503
Fair-betrothed. The fair-betrothed of your daughter . . *Pericles* v 3 71
Fair birth. Grant that our hopes, yet likely of fair birth, Should be still-born . . . . 2 *Hen. IV.* i 3 63
Fair Bohemia. Imagine me, Gentle spectators, that I now may be In fair Bohemia . . . . *W. Tale* iv 1 21
Fair boy. Till then, fair boy, Will I not think of home . . *K. John* ii 1 30
Fair branches. Seven fair branches springing from one root . *Richard II.* i 2 13
Fair buds. Confounds thy fame as whirlwinds shake fair buds *T. of S.* v 2 140
Fair Calipolis. Then feed, and be fat, my fair Calipolis . 2 *Hen. IV.* ii 4 193
Fair cheek. Of all complexions the cull'd sovereignty Do meet, as at a fair, in her fair cheek . . . . *L. L. Lost* iv 3 235
The red wine first must rise In their fair cheeks . . . *Hen. VIII.* i 4 44

Fair colour. Scorn'd a fair colour, or express'd it stolen . *All's Well* v 3 50
Fair comfort. Lines of fair comfort and encouragement . *Richard III.* v 2 6
Fair commands. I shall obey you in all fair commands . *Mer. of Venice* iii 4 36
Fair company. The very thought of this fair company Clapp'd wings to me *Hen. VIII.* i 4 8
Fair be to you, my lord, and to all this fair company . *Troi. and Cres.* iii 1 47
Fair conceit. Lady, I shall not fail to approve the fair conceit The king hath of you . *Hen. VIII.* ii 3 74
Fair conditions. You shall be soon dispatch'd with fair conditions *Hen. V.* ii 4 144
Fair conduct. Under your fair conduct . . . . *Hen. VIII.* i 4 70
Fair conjunction. Smile heaven upon this fair conjunction ! *Richard III.* v 5 20
Fair consent. We carry not a heart with us from hence That grows not in a fair consent with ours . . . . . *Hen. V.* ii 2 22
Fair content. This night he dedicates To fair content and you *Hen. VIII.* i 4 3
Fair corse. If she that lays thee out says thou art a fair corse *T. and C.* ii 3 35
Dry up your tears, and stick your rosemary On this fair corse *R. and J.* iv 5 80
Every one prepare To follow this fair corse unto her grave . . iv 5 93
Fair couple. In the chase, it seems, Of this fair couple . *W. Tale* v 1 190
Fair course. When his fair course is not hindered . . *T. G. of Ver.* ii 7 27
Fair courtesy. O, that's as much as you would be denied Of your fair courtesy . . . . *Pericles* ii 3 107
Fair cousin. I do believe your fair cousin is wronged . *Much Ado* iv 1 261
Fair cousin, you debase your princely knee . . . *Richard II.* iii 3 190
Name it, fair cousin.—'Fair cousin'? I am greater than a king . iv 1 304
Now are we well prepared to know the pleasure Of our fair cousin *Hen. V.* i 2 235
My fair cousin : If we are mark'd to die, we are enow . . . iv 3 19
I would have her learn, my fair cousin, how perfectly I love her . v 2 309
And therefore is he idle ?—O, my fair cousin, I must not say so *Rich. III.* iii 1 106
Fair creature. When Nature hath made a fair creature, may she not by Fortune fall into the fire ? . . . . . . *As Y. Like It* i 2 46
She's a fair creature : Will you go see her ? . . . *All's Well* iii 6 124
Curse not thyself, fair creature . . . . . . *Richard III.* i 2 132
With which grief, It is supposed, the fair creature died . *Rom. and Jul.* v 3 51
Live, And make us weep to hear your fate, fair creature . *Pericles* iii 2 104
Is she not a fair creature ?—'Faith, she would serve after a long voyage iv 6 47
Fair Cressid. And when fair Cressid comes into my thoughts,—So, traitor ! 'When she comes !' When is she thence? *Troi. and Cres.* i 1 30
But gives all gaze and bent of amorous view On the fair Cressid . iv 5 283
Fair cruelty. Farewell, fair cruelty . . . . . *T. Night* i 5 307
Fair dame. Plead you to me, fair dame? I know you not *Com. of Errors* ii 2 149
Bless you, fair dame ! I am not to you known . . . *Macbeth* iv 2 65
Fair daughter. At the marriage of the king's fair daughter Claribel *Temp.* ii 1 70
Beseeming such a wife as your fair daughter . . *T. G. of Ver.* iii 1 66
He that has the two fair daughters : is't he you mean? . *T. of Shrew* i 2 222
Here is my throne, bid kings come bow to it.—'Tis true, fair daughter *K. John* iii 1 75
Fair daughter, you do draw my spirits from me . . *2 Hen. IV.* ii 3 46
Well pleased To change two dukedoms for a duke's fair daughter *2 Hen. VI.* i 1 219
My heart's dear love is set On the fair daughter of rich Capulet *R. and J.* ii 3 58
One fair daughter, and no more, The which he loved passing well *Hamlet* ii 2 426
Your fair daughter, At this odd-even and dull watch o' the night *Othello* i 1 123
He hath a fair daughter, and to-morrow is her birth-day . *Pericles* ii 1 113
Fair day. The sun's o'ercast with blood : fair day, adieu ! *K. John* iii 1 326
Hence away, From Richard's night to Bolingbroke's fair day *Richard II.* iii 2 218
If to-morrow be a fair day, by eleven o'clock it will go one way or other : howsoever, he shall pay for me . . . . *Troi. and Cres.* iii 3 296
She is fair too, is she not?—As a fair day in summer, wondrous fair *Per.* ii 5 36
Fair daylight. Shuts up his windows, locks fair daylight out *R. and J.* i 1 145
Where have I been? Where am I? Fair daylight? I am mightily abused . . . . *Lear* iv 7 52
Fair death. I doubt not but to die a fair death for all this . *1 Hen. IV.* ii 2 14
Fair degree. I'll answer thee in any fair degree . . *Richard II.* i 1 80
Fair demands. All the number of his fair demands Shall be accomplish'd iii 3 123
And bids thee study on what fair demands Thou mean'st to have him grant thee . . . . *Ant. and Cleo.* v 2 10
Fair demesnes. Of noble parentage, Of fair demesnes . *Rom. and Jul.* iii 5 182
Fair departure. I pray God grant them a fair departure. *Mer. of Venice* i 2 121
Fair Desdemona. He goes into Mauritania and takes away with him the fair Desdemona . . . . *Othello* iv 2 230
Fair deserving. This seems a fair deserving . . . *Lear* iii 3 24
Fair designs. Officers Appointed to direct these fair designs . *Richard II.* i 3 45
Fair desires. Sweet health and fair desires consort your grace ! *L. L. Lost* ii 1 178
Fair desires, in all fair measure, fairly guide them ! . *Troi. and C* . iii 1 47
Fair devil. I will withdraw, To furnish me with some swift means of death For the fair devil . . . . *Othello* iii 3 479
Fair discourse. Your fair discourse hath been as sugar, Making the hard way sweet . . . . *Richard II.* ii 3 6
Fair dog. He's a good dog, and a fair dog : can there be more said? he is good and fair . . . . *Mer. Wives* i 1 98
Fair dominions. Shall not regreet our fair dominions . *Richard II.* i 3 142
Fair duty. Stand all apart, And show fair duty to his majesty . iii 3 188
Fair edifices. Many an heir Of these fair edifices 'fore my wars Have I heard groan and drop . . . . *Coriolanus* iv 4 3
Fair effects. Even in the prime And all the fair effects of future hopes *T. G. of Ver.* i 1 50
Fair encounter Of two most rare affections ! . . . . *Tempest* iii 1 74
Fair end. Hanged ! by'r lady, then I have brought up a neck to a fair end *T. Andron.* iv 4 49
Fair endeavours. I thank you, gracious lords, For all your fair endeavours *L. L. Lost* v 2 740
Fair England. Whose bookish rule hath pull'd fair England down *2 Hen. VI.* i 1 259
I lost fair England's view And bid mine eyes be packing with my heart iii 2 110
Be done to death, Or banished fair England's territories . . iii 2 245
Infer fair England's peace by this alliance . . . *Richard III.* iv 4 343
Awake! Arm, fight, and conquer, for fair England's sake ! . . v 3 150
Fair enough. Like the mending of highways In summer, where the ways are fair enough . . . . *Mer. of Venice* v 1 264
Fair entreaties. And with our fair entreaties haste them on *Coriolanus* v 1 74
Fair excuse. Teach us, sweet madam, for our rude transgression Some fair excuse . . . . *L. L. Lost* v 2 432
Fair eyes. I swear to thee, even by thine own fair eyes . *Mer. of Venice* v 1 242
Let your fair eyes and gentle wishes go with me to my trial *As Y. Like It* i 2 198
The honour, sir, that flames in your fair eyes, Before I speak, too threateningly replies . . . . *All's Well* ii 3 86
Drive thee from the sportive court, where thou Wast shot at with fair eyes . . . . iii 2 110
She kneel'd, and saintlike Cast her fair eyes to heaven . *Hen. VIII.* iv 1 84
Fair face. Was this fair face the cause, quoth she, Why the Grecians sacked Troy? . . . . *All's Well* i 3 74
A fair face will wither ; a full eye will wax hollow . . . *Hen. V.* v 2 169
Fair-faced. If fair-faced, She would swear the gentleman should be her sister . . . . *Much Ado* iii 1 61
I shall show you peace and fair-faced league . . . *K. John* ii 1 417
Fair faith. Few words to fair faith . . . *Troi. and Cres.* iii 2 103
Fair fall. Fair befall your mask !—Fair fall the face it covers ! *L. L. Lost* ii 1 125
Fair fall the bones that took the pains for me ! . . . *K. John* i 1 78
Fair five hundred pound a year . . . . i 1 69
Fair flesh. For an equal pound Of your fair flesh . *Mer. of Venice* i 3 151
Fair flower. Women are as roses, whose fair flower Being once display'd, doth fall that very hour . . . . . *T. Night* ii 4 39
Fair flower-de-luce. What sayest thou, my fair flower-de-luce? *Hen. V.* v 2 224
Fair forehead. Calls virtue hypocrite, takes off the rose From the fair forehead of an innocent love . . . . . *Hamlet* iii 4 43
Fair France. That never war advance His bleeding sword 'twixt England and fair France . . . . *Hen. V.* v 2 383
Queen of us, of ours, and our fair France . . . . *Lear* i 1 260
Fair fray. Welcome, pure wit ! thou partest a fair fray . . *L. L. Lost* v 2 484
Fair French city. Who cannot see many a fair French city for one fair French maid . . . . *Hen. V.* v 2 345
Fair friendship. And hold fair friendship with his majesty . *L. L. Lost* ii 1 141
Fair fruit. Like fair fruit in an unwholesome dish . . *Troi. and Cres.* ii 3 129
Fair gentleman. Fair you well, fair gentleman . . *As Y. Like It* i 2 260
Fair gentle sweet, Your wit makes wise things foolish . . *L. L. Lost* v 2 373
Fair gentlewoman. This fair gentlewoman, her sister here, Did call me brother . . . . *Com. of Errors* v 1 373
God ye good den, fair gentlewoman . . . . *Rom. and Jul.* ii 4 116
Your name, fair gentlewoman? . . . . *Lear* i 4 257
Fair gifts. Her dispositions she inherits, which makes fair gifts fairer *All's Well* i 1 47
Fair glass of light, I loved you, and could still . . . . *Pericles* i 1 76
Fair goddess. Now the fair goddess, Fortune, Fall deep in love with thee ! *Coriolanus* i 5 21
Fair grace. Vanquish'd thereto by the fair grace and speech Of the poor suppliant . . . . *All's Well* v 3 133
Fair greeting. Health and fair greeting from our general *2 Hen. IV.* iv 1 27
Fair ground. On fair ground I could beat forty of them . *Coriolanus* iii 1 242
Fair guests. You're welcome, my fair guests . . . *Hen. VIII.* i 4 35
Fair hand. 'Tis a fair hand ; And whiter than the paper it writ on Is the fair hand that writ . . . . . *Mer. of Venice* ii 4 12
You have made fair hands, You and your crafts ! . . *Coriolanus* iv 6 117
Fair harbour. Though so denied fair harbour in my house . *L. L. Lost* ii 1 175
Fair health. A beard, fair health, and honesty . . . . v 2 834
Fair heaven. Hail, thou fair heaven ! We house i' the rock, yet use thee not so hardly As prouder livers do . . . . *Cymbeline* iii 3 7
Fair Helen told me of their stealth . . . . *M. N. Dream* iv 1 165
Who, in your thoughts, merits fair Helen best, Myself or Menelaus? *Troi. and Cres.* iv 1 53
Fair Helena. Here comes Helena.—God speed fair Helena ! *M. N. Dream* i 1 180
Fair Helena, who more engilds the night Than all yon fiery oes and eyes of light . . . . iii 2 187
Hear my excuse : My love, my life, my soul, fair Helena ! . . . iii 2 246
Fair Helena in fancy following me . . . . iv 1 168
Fair Hermia. Therefore, fair Hermia, question your desires . . . i 1 67
For you, fair Hermia, look you arm yourself . . . . . i 1 117
Sickness is catching : O, were favour so, Yours would I catch, fair Hermia i 1 187
I will go tell him of fair Hermia's flight: Then to the wood will he i 1 246
Fair Hero. If thou dost love fair Hero, cherish it . . *Much Ado* i 1 310
Tell fair Hero I am Claudio, And in her bosom I'll unclasp my heart . i 1 324
Here, Claudio, I have wooed in thy name, and fair Hero is won . ii 1 310
After that the holy rites are ended, I'll tell you largely of fair Hero's death . . . . v 4 69
Fair Hesperides. Before thee stands this fair Hesperides . *Pericles* i 1 27
Fair Hippolyta, our nuptial hour Draws on apace . *M. N. Dream* i 1 1
Fair honours. To dress the ugly form Of base and bloody insurrection With your fair honours . . . . *2 Hen. IV.* iv 1 41
Fair hope. Till then fair hope must hinder life's decay . *3 Hen. VI.* iv 4 16
Fair hour. Take thy fair hour, Laertes ; time be thine ! . . *Hamlet* i 2 62
Fair house. Like a fair house built on another man's ground . *Mer. Wives* ii 2 224
Fair humility. Your bounty, virtue, fair humility . *Richard III.* iii 7 17
Fair influence. If I be not by her fair influence Foster'd *T. G. of Ver.* iii 1 183
Fair in hand. She bears me fair in hand . . . *T. of. Shrew* iv 2 3
Fair instalment. Each fair instalment, coat, and several crest *Mer. Wives* v 5 67
Fair island. Plantagenet lays most lawful claim To this fair island *K. John* i 1 10
Say So to the Moor.—Not I, for this fair island . . *Othello* ii 3 147
Fair issue. As I hope For quiet days, fair issue and long life *Tempest* iv 1 24
I had rather glib myself than they Should not produce fair issue *W. Tale* ii 1 150
Fair Jessica. Was not that letter from fair Jessica? . *Mer. of Venice* ii 4 29
Peruse this as thou goest : Fair Jessica shall be my torch-bearer . ii 4 40
Fair judgement. Divided from herself and her fair judgement *Hamlet* iv 5 85
Fair Juliet. Within this three hours will fair Juliet wake *Rom. and Jul.* v 2 24
Fair justice. I'll enter : if he slay me, He does fair justice *Coriolanus* iv 4 25
Fair Katharine, and most fair, Will you vouchsafe to teach a soldier terms Such as will enter at a lady's ear? . . . . . *Hen. V.* v 2 98
O fair Katharine, if you will love me soundly with your French heart . v 2 104
Therefore tell me, most fair Katharine, will you have me? . . . v 2 252
Fair kindness. For the fair kindness you have show'd me here *T. Night* iii 4 376
Fair kingdom. This ample third of our fair kingdom . . . *Lear* i 1 82
Fair King Richard. Should bedrench The fresh green lap of fair King Richard's land . . . . *Richard II.* iii 3 47
And doth enlarge his rising with the blood Of fair King Richard *2 Hen. IV.* i 1 205
Fair knighthood. Buckled below fair knighthood's bending knee *M. W.* v 5 76
Fair lady. She's a fair lady : I do spy some marks of love in her *M. Ado* ii 3 254
Will you vouchsafe with me to change a word ?—Name it.—Fair lady,— Say you so? Fair lord,—Take that for your fair lady . *L. L. Lost* v 2 239
A calf, fair lady !—No, a fair lord calf . . . . v 2 248
Fair ladies mask'd are roses in their bud . . . . . . v 2 295
We to ourselves prove false, By being once false for ever to be true To those that make us both,—fair ladies, you . . . . . . v 2 784
'Fair ladies,—I would wish you,'—or 'I would request you' *M. N. Dream* iii 1 40
Was the best deserving a fair lady . . . . . *Mer. of Venice* i 2 131
Fair lady, by your leave ; I come by note, to give and to receive . . iii 2 140
Fair ladies, you drop manna in the way Of starved people . . . v 1 294
Fair lady, do you think you have fools in hand? . . . *T. Night* i 3 68
The singing birds musicians, The grass whereon thou tread'st the presence strew'd, The flowers fair ladies . . . . . *Richard II.* i 3 290
Be not dismay'd, fair lady ; nor misconstrue The mind of Talbot *1 Hen. VI.* ii 3 73
So, now you're fairly seated. Gentlemen, The penance lies on you, if these fair ladies Pass away frowning . . . . . *Hen. VIII.* i 4 32

Fair lady. Prithee, come hither: what fair lady's that? . *Hen. VIII.* i 4 91
I have half a dozen healths To drink to these fair ladies . . i 4 106
That you may, fair lady, Perceive I speak sincerely. . ii 3 58
The king already Hath married the fair lady . . . iii 2 42
Fair Lady Cressid, So please you, save the thanks . *Troi. and Cres.* iv 4 118
I'll take that winter from your lips, fair lady . . . iv 5 24
These happy masks that kiss fair ladies' brows . *Rom. and Jul.* i 1 236
And could tell A whispering tale in a fair lady's ear . . i 5 25
You have done our pleasures much grace, fair ladies . *T. of Athens* i 2 151
I'll present How I did thrive in this fair lady's love, And she in mine *Othello* i 3 125
Am I that name, Iago?—What name, fair lady?—Such as she says iv 2 118
Fair land. Let them not live to taste this land's increase That would with treason wound this fair land's peace! *Richard III.* v 5 39
Fair league. Keep then fair league and truce with thy true bed *C. of Er.* ii 2 147
Fair leave and large security . . . . . *Troi. and Cres.* i 3 223
Fair Leda's daughter had a thousand wooers . . *T. of Shrew* i 2 244
Fair life. Sweetly in force unto her fair life's end . . *Richard III.* iv 4 351
Fair look. Vouchsafe me, for my meed, but one fair look . *T. G. of Ver.* v 4 23
Craves no other tribute at thy hands But love, fair looks . *T. of Shrew* v 2 153
Then why should he despair that knows to court it With words, fair looks and liberality? . . . . *T. Andron.* ii 1 92
Fair lord. Fair lady,— Say you so? Fair lord,—Take that for your fair lady . . . . *L. L. Lost* v 2 239
A calf, fair lady!—No, a fair lord calf . . . . v 2 248
How now, fair lords! What fare? what news abroad? . *3 Hen. VI.* ii 1 95
Fair lords, take leave and stand not to reply . . . iv 8 23
Rescue, fair lord, or else the day is lost! . . . *Richard III.* v 4 6
Fair Lord Æneas, let me touch your hand . . *Troi. and Cres.* i 3 304
Fair lords, your fortunes are alike in all . . . *T. Andron.* i 1 174
Fair love. Revels, dances, masks and merry hours Forerun fair Love *L. L. L.* iv 3 380
Fair love, you faint with wandering in the wood . *M. N. Dream* ii 2 35
Made peace of enmity, fair love of hate . . . *Richard III.* ii 1 50
A token from her daughter, my fair love . . *Troi. and Cres.* v 1 45
Fair lovers, you are fortunately met . . . *M. N. Dream* iv 1 182
Fair madam. Not for the world, fair madam, by my will . *L. L. Lost* ii 1 99
And were you well advised?—I was, fair madam . . . v 2 435
Please you to interpose, fair madam . . . . *W. Tale* v 3 119
Listen, fair madam: let it be your glory To see her tears . *T. Andron.* ii 3 139
Fair maid. Be you content, fair maid; It is the law, not I condemn your brother . . . . *Meas. for Meas.* ii 2 79
How now, fair maid?—I am come to know your pleasure . . ii 4 30
Be advised, fair maid: To you your father should be as a god *M. N. Dr.* i 1 46
Fair maid, send forth thine eye . . . . *All's Well* ii 3 58
Fair maid, is't thou wilt do these wondrous feats? . *1 Hen. VI.* i 2 64
Heaven and yourself Had part in this fair maid . . *Rom. and Jul.* iv 5 67
Fair mansion. But now I was the lord Of this fair mansion *Mer. of Ven.* iii 2 170
Fair Margaret knows That Suffolk doth not flatter . . *1 Hen. VI.* v 3 141
If with a lady of so high resolve As is fair Margaret he be link'd . v 5 76
Fair mark. A right fair mark, fair coz, is soonest hit . *Rom. and Jul.* i 1 213
Fair meanings. I have fair meanings, sir.—And fair words to them *Ant. and Cleo.* ii 6 67
Fair measure. Fair desires, in all fair measure, fairly guide them *Troi. and Cres.* iii 1 47
Fair men. Let fools do good, and fair men call for grace . *T. Andron.* iii 1 205
Fair message. May one, that is a herald and a prince, Do a fair message to his kingly ears? . . . . *Troi. and Cres.* i 3 219
Fair Milan. And confer fair Milan With all the honours on my brother *Tempest* i 2 126
I Pandulph, of fair Milan cardinal . . . . *K. John* iii 1 138
Fair mind. In your fair minds let this acceptance take . *Hen. V.* Epil. 14
Keep unshaked That temple, thy fair mind! . . . *Cymbeline* ii 1 69
Fair mistress. Homeward every man attach the hand Of his fair mistress *L. L. Lost* iv 3 376
With five times so much conversation, I should get ground of your fair mistress, make her go back . . . . *Cymbeline* i 4 114
Fair Montague. In truth, fair Montague, I am too fond . *Rom. and Jul.* ii 2 98
Fair mountain. Could you on this fair mountain leave to feed, And batten on this moor? . . . . *Hamlet* iii 4 66
Fair multitude. O, what love I note In the fair multitude of those her hairs! . . . . *K. John* iii 4 62
Fair name. Is thy name William?—William, sir.—A fair name *As Y. L. It* v 1 24
But my fair name, Despite of death that lives upon my grave, To dark dishonour's use thou shalt not have . . . *Richard II.* i 1 167
Fair nature. Disguise fair nature with hard-favour'd rage . *Hen. V.* iii 1 8
Fair nephew. That cause, fair nephew, that imprison'd me . *1 Hen. VI.* ii 5 55
Fair occasion. But I do love the favour and the form Of this most fair occasion . . . . *K. John* v 4 51
Fair one. What says she to my face?—She says it is a fair one *T. G. of V.* v 2 9
Repent you, fair one, of the sin you carry? . . *Meas. for Meas.* ii 3 19
I got a promise of this fair one here To have her love . *Mer. of Venice* iii 2 208
Here comes more company.—Good morrow, fair ones . *As Y. Like It* iv 3 76
Now, fair one, does your business follow us? . . . *All's Well* ii 1 102
Fair one, I think not so . . . . ii 3 100
Shepherdess,—A fair one are you—well you fit our ages . *W. Tale* iv 4 78
What says she, fair one? that the tongues of men are full of deceits? *Hen. V.* v 2 120
By my life, They are a sweet society of fair ones . . *Hen. VIII.* i 4 14
Welcome, fair one! Is't not a goodly presence? . . . *Pericles* v 1 65
Fair one, all goodness that consists in bounty Expect even here . . v 1 70
Fair Ophelia. Soft you now! The fair Ophelia! . . . *Hamlet* iii 1 89
What, the fair Ophelia!—Sweets to the sweet: farewell . . . v 1 265
Fair order. Having our fair order written down . . . *K. John* v 2 4
Fair ordinance. By God's fair ordinance conjoin together! *Richard III.* v 5 31
Fair or foul. By fair or foul means we must enter in . *3 Hen. VI.* iv 7 14
Fair ornament. Hiding the grossness with fair ornament *Mer. of Venice* iii 2 80
Fair ostents. Such fair ostents of love As shall conveniently become you ii 8 44
Fair Padua. The great desire I had To see fair Padua . . *T. of Shrew* i 1 2
Fair pair. Show it a fair pair of heels and run from it . *1 Hen. IV.* ii 4 53
Fair paper. Was this fair paper, this most goodly book, Made to write 'whore' upon? . . . . *Othello* iv 2 71
Fair parts. You, that have so fair parts of woman on you, Have too a woman's heart . . . . *Hen. VIII.* ii 3 27
Fair payment for foul words is more than due . . *L. L. Lost* iv 1 19
Fair peace. Might from our quiet confines fright fair peace . *Richard II.* i 3 137
Fair persuasions mix'd with sugar'd words . . *1 Hen. VI.* iii 3 18
Fair Philomela, she but lost her tongue . . . *T. Andron.* ii 4 38
Fair pillow. Fair thoughts be your fair pillow! . . *Troi. and Cres.* iii 1 49
Fair play. For a score of kingdoms you should wrangle, And I would call it fair play . . . . *Tempest* v 1 175
Fair play. Shall we, upon the footing of our land, Send fair-play orders? *K. John* v 1 67
According to the fair play of the world, Let me have audience . . v 2 118
Simony was fair-play; His own opinion was his law . *Hen. VIII.* iv 2 36
O, 'tis fair play.—Fool's play, by heaven . . *Troi. and Cres.* v 3 43
Fair pleasure. You speak your fair pleasure, sweet queen . . iii 1 51
Fair Portia. To furnish thee to Belmont, to fair Portia . *Mer. of Venice* i 1 182
Are as throughfares now For princes to come view fair Portia . . ii 7 43
But they come, As o'er a brook, to see fair Portia . . . ii 7 47
What find I here? Fair Portia's counterfeit! . . . . iii 2 116
Fair posterity. The father, all whose joy is nothing else But fair posterity . . . . *W. Tale* iv 4 420
Fair praise. Too brown for a fair praise . . . *Much Ado* i 1 174
A giving hand, though foul, shall have fair praise . . *L. L. Lost* iv 1 23
Fair prayer. Unless you have the grace by your fair prayer . *M. for M.* i 4 69
Amen, amen, to that fair prayer, say I! . . . *M. N. Dream* ii 2 62
Fair preferments. She may help you to many fair preferments *Rich. III.* i 3 95
Fair presence. Bear a fair presence, though your heart be tainted *Com. of Errors* iii 2 13
Show a fair presence and put off these frowns . . *Rom. and Jul.* i 5 75
Fair prince, here is good broken music.—You have broke it *Tr. and Cr.* iii 1 52
So now, fair Prince of Troy, I bid good night . . . . v 1 78
Fair princess, welcome to the court of Navarre.—'Fair' I give you back again . . . . *L. L. Lost* ii 1 90
You may not come, fair princess, in my gates . . . . ii 1 172
Fair princess, you have lost much good sport . . *As Y. Like It* i 2 105
And there present yourself and your fair princess . *W. Tale* iv 4 555
Most dearly welcome! And your fair princess,—goddess! . . v 1 131
Fair proceeding. You shall have no cause To curse the fair proceedings of this day . . . . *K. John* iii 1 97
I like this fair proceeding of the king's . . . *2 Hen. IV.* v 5 103
Fair promotions. Whilst many fair promotions Are daily given *Rich. III.* i 3 80
Fair proportion. I, that am curtail'd of this fair proportion . . i 1 18
Fair prosperity. And bless it to all fair prosperity . . *M. N. Dream* iv 1 95
Fair purgation. For his trial, And fair purgation to the world *Hen. VIII.* v 3 152
Fair quarter. So he would keep fair quarter with his bed *Com. of Errors* ii 1 108
Fair queen. We will, fair queen, up to the mountain's top *M. N. Dream* iv 1 114
Save you, fair queen!—And you, monarch! . . . *All's Well* i 1 117
And stain'd the beauty of a fair queen's cheeks . . *Richard II.* iii 1 14
Sung by a fair queen in a summer's bower . . . *1 Hen. IV.* iii 1 210
Fair Queen of England, worthy Margaret, Sit down with us *3 Hen. VI.* iii 3 1
Why, say, fair queen, whence springs this deep despair? . . iii 3 12
I like it well that our fair queen and mistress Smiles at her news . iii 3 167
As mother, And reverend looker on, of two fair queens *Richard III.* iv 1 31
Especially to you, fair queen! fair thoughts be your fair pillow! *Troi. and Cres.* iii 1 48
Clear up, fair queen, that cloudy countenance . . *T. Andron.* i 1 263
Ascend, fair queen, Pantheon . . . . i 1 333
Fair question. Such fair question As soul to soul affordeth . *Othello* i 3 113
Fair rape. I would have the soil of her fair rape Wiped off *Troi. and Cres.* ii 2 148
Fair regard. The king is full of grace and fair regard . . *Hen. V.* i 1 22
Fair reply. Why, 'tis a loving and a fair reply . . . *Hamlet* i 2 121
Fair request. Why will he not upon our fair request Untent his person? *Troi. and Cres.* ii 3 177
Fair rescue. Thou makest some tender of my life, In this fair rescue thou hast brought to me . . . . *1 Hen. IV.* v 4 50
Fair resort. Of all the fair resort of gentlemen That every day with parle encounter me . . . . *T. G. of Ver.* i 2 4
Fair respect. To tread down fair respect of sovereignty . *K. John* iii 1 58
Fair return. O fair return of banish'd majesty! . . . . v 1 321
If my father render fair return, It is against my will . . *Hen. V.* ii 4 127
Most fair return of greetings and desires . . . *Hamlet* ii 2 60
Fair reverence. The fair reverence of your highness curbs me From giving reins and spurs to my free speech . . . *Richard II.* i 1 54
Fair reward. Let them be received, Not without fair reward *T. of Athens* i 2 197
Fair rites. I'll thank myself For doing these fair rites of tenderness *1 Hen. IV.* v 4 98
Fair Rosaline. At this same ancient feast of Capulet's Sups the fair Rosaline . . . . *Rom. and Jul.* i 2 88
Fair rose. But see, or rather do not see, My fair rose wither *Richard II.* v 1 8
Fair safety. I will pray, If ever I remember to be holy, For your fair safety . . . . *K. John* iii 3 16
Fair saint. Art thou not Romeo and a Montague?—Neither, fair saint, if either thee dislike . . . . . . *Rom. and Jul.* ii 2 61
Fair Saint George. Our ancient word of courage, fair Saint George, Inspire us! . . . . *Richard III.* v 3 349
Fair sakes. For your fair sakes have we neglected time . *L. L. Lost* v 2 765
Fair self. Your fair self should make A yielding 'gainst some reason in my breast . . . . ii 1 151
Fair sequence. How art thou a king But by fair sequence? *Richard II.* ii 1 199
Fair service. I say, my lord, he has done fair service . *T. of Athens* iii 5 63
Fair shepherd! Your heart is full of something that does take Your mind from feasting . . . . *W. Tale* iv 4 355
Fair-shining. Henceforward will I bear Upon my target three fair-shining suns . . . . *3 Hen. VI.* ii 1 40
Fair show. Your fair show shall suck away their souls . *Hen. V.* iv 2 17
Fair shrew. Bless you, fair shrew.—And you too, sir . . *T. Night* i 3 50
Fair Silvia. To love fair Silvia, shall I be forsworn . *T. G. of Ver.* ii 6 2
Fair sir, God save you! . . . . . . *L. L. Lost* v 2 310
Fair sir, you spit on me on Wednesday last . . *Mer. of Venice* i 3 127
Fair sir, you are well o'erta'en . . . . . . iv 2 5
Fair sir, I pity her, And wish, for her sake . . *As Y. Like It* ii 4 75
Fair sir, and you my merry mistress . . . . *T. of Shrew* iv 5 53
Fair sister. The fair sister To her unhappy brother . *Meas. for Meas.* i 4 19
But her fair sister, Possess'd with such a gentle sovereign grace *C. of Er.* iii 2 164
God save you, brother.—And you, fair sister . . *As Y. Like It* v 2 21
Will you, fair sister, Go with the princes, or stay here with us? *Hen. V.* v 2 90
That virtuous Lady Bona, thy fair sister . . . *3 Hen. VI.* iii 3 56
For your claim, fair sister, I bar it in the interest of my wife . . *Lear* v 3 84
Fair slips. Thy sons, fair slips of such a stock . . *2 Hen. VI.* ii 2 58
Fair solicitor. We single you As our best-moving fair solicitor *L. L. Lost* ii 1 29
Fair son. Æmilia That bore thee at a burden two fair sons *Com. of Errors* v 1 343
My boy, my Arthur, my fair son! My life, my joy, my food! *K. John* iii 4 103
And wilt thou pluck my fair son from mine age? . . *Richard II.* v 2 92
Take her, fair son, and from her blood raise up Issue to me . . *Hen. V.* v 2 376
Then here I take my leave of thee, fair son . . . *1 Hen. VI.* iv 5 52
Fair soul. And the fair soul herself Weigh'd between loathness and obedience . . . . *Tempest* ii 1 129
But, fair soul, In your fine frame hath love no quality? . . *All's Well* iv 2 3
Fair speech. All's in anger.—Only fair speech . . . *Coriolanus* iii 2 96

Fair spirit. With a noble fury and fair spirit . . . *T. of Athens* iii 5 18
Fair-spoken. Exceeding wise, fair-spoken, and persuading *Hen. VIII.* iv 2 52
Fair stars. Shall I so much dishonour my fair stars? *Richard II.* iv 1 21
Fair state. The expectancy and rose of the fair state . *Hamlet* iii 1 160
Fair steed. Present the fair steed to my lady Cressid *Troi. and Cres.* v 5 2
Fair sun. It is a fault that springeth from your eye.—For gazing on your beams, fair sun, being by *Com. of Errors* iii 2 56
Thou, fair sun, which on my earth dost shine . . *L. L. Lost* iv 3 69
By that fair sun which shows me where thou stand'st *Richard II.* iv 1 35
Shine out, fair sun, till I have bought a glass, That I may see my shadow as I pass . . . . *Richard III.* i 2 263
Arise, fair sun, and kill the envious moon . . . *Rom. and Jul.* ii 2 4
Fair sword. Even in the fan and wind of your fair sword *Troi. and Cres.* v 3 41
Fair terms. I like not fair terms and a villain's mind *Mer. of Venice* i 3 181
I will scour you with my rapier, as I may, in fair terms . . *Hen. V.* ii 1 60
I will cut thy throat, one time or other, in fair terms . . ii 1 74
Fair thoughts and happy hours attend on you! *Mer. of Venice* iii 4 41
Fair thoughts be your fair pillow! . . . . . *Troi. and Cres.* iii 1 49
That's a fair thought to lie between maid's legs . . . *Hamlet* iii 2 125
Fair time of day. All hail, sweet madam, and fair time of day!—'Fair' in 'all hail' is foul, as I conceive . . . *L. L. Lost* v 2 339
And to our sister Health and fair time of day! . . *Hen. V.* v 2 3
Fair tongue. His fair tongue, conceit's expositor . . *L. L. Lost* ii 1 72
Fair town. And this rich fair town We make him lord of . *K. John* ii 1 552
Fair usage. The lustre in your eye, heaven in your cheek, Pleads your fair usage . . . . *Troi. and Cres.* iv 4 121
Fair use. Nor aught so good but strain'd from that fair use Revolts from true birth . . . . *Rom. and Jul.* ii 3 19
Fair Verona. Two households, both alike in dignity, In fair Verona . Prol. 2
Go, sirrah, trudge about Through fair Verona; find those persons out . i 2 35
Fair vestal. A certain aim he took At a fair vestal . *M. N. Dream* ii 1 158
Fair victory. Our advantage serves For a fair victory . *Ant. and Cleo.* iv 7 12
Fair viol. You are a fair viol, and your sense the strings . *Pericles* i 1 81
Fair virtue. The only soil of his fair virtue's gloss . *L. L. Lost* ii 1 47
Thy fair virtue's force perforce doth move me On the first view to say, to swear, I love thee. . . . . . *M. N. Dream* iii 1 143
Saba was never More covetous of wisdom and fair virtue *Hen. VIII.* v 5 25
Fair virtues all, To which the Grecians are most prompt *Troi. and Cres.* iv 4 89
Fair visage. There's more in't than fair visage . . *Hen. VIII.* iii 2 88
Fair volume. And what obscured in this fair volume lies Find written in the margent of his eyes . . . . *Rom. and Jul.* i 3 85
Fair warning. I think he hath a very fair warning . *2 Hen. VI.* iv 6 11
Fair warrior. O my fair warrior!—My dear Othello! *Othello* ii 1 184
Fair way. Let all the number of the stars give light To thy fair way!—Farewell, farewell! . . . . *Ant. and Cleo.* iii 2 66
Fair weather. It is impossible you should take true root but by the fair weather that you make yourself . . . . *Much Ado* i 3 25
And so, farewell.—Fair weather after you! . . *L. L. Lost* i 2 149
And make fair weather in your blustering land . . *K. John* v 1 21
But I must make fair weather yet a while . . . *2 Hen. VI.* v 1 30
Fair wife. A fellow almost damn'd in a fair wife . . *Othello* i 1 21
Fair woman. A word or two?—Two thousand, fair woman *Mer. Wives* ii 2 43
Join not with grief, fair woman, do not so, To make my end too sudden *Richard II.* v 1 16
There was never yet fair woman but she made mouths in a glass *Lear* iii 2 35
A fine woman! a fair woman! a sweet woman! . . *Othello* iv 1 189
There is never a fair woman has a true face.—No slander *Ant. and Cleo.* ii 6 104
Fair word. Will Fortune never come with both hands full, But write her fair words still in foulest letters? . . . . *2 Hen. IV.* iv 4 104
Without expense at all, By guileful fair words peace may be obtained *1 Hen. VI.* i 1 77
You are full of fair words.—You speak your fair pleasure *Troi. and Cres.* iii 1 50
I would not buy Their mercy at the price of one fair word *Coriolanus* iii 3 91
Speak to my gossip Venus one fair word . . *Rom. and Jul.* ii 1 11
I have fair meanings, sir.—And fair words to them . *Ant. and Cleo.* ii 6 67
Fair work. Here's a good world! Knew you of this fair work? *K. John* iv 3 116
You have made fair work!—But is this true, sir? . *Coriolanus* iv 6 100
Fair world. And thou shalt live in this fair world behind, Honour'd, beloved . . . . *Hamlet* iii 2 185
Fair worth. The glory of our Troy doth this day lie On his fair worth and single chivalry . . . . . . *Troi. and Cres.* iv 4 150
Fair writ. Can you not read it? is it not fair writ?—Too fairly *K. John* iv 1 37
Fair year. He would have lived many a fair year . *As Y. Like It* iv 1 101
Fair yokes. Do not these fair yokes Become the forest better than the town? . . . . *Mer. Wives* v 5 111
Fair young maid. A fair young maid that yet wants baptism *Hen. VIII.* v 3 162
Fair young man. 'Tis a fair young man, and well attended . *T. Night* i 5 110
Fair youth, I would I could make thee believe I love *As Y. Like It* iii 2 404
My errand is to you, fair youth . . . . iv 3 6
Fair youth, Think us no churls . . . . *Cymbeline* iii 6 64
Fair youth, come in: Discourse is heavy, fasting . . . iii 6 90
Fairer. With colours fairer painted their foul ends . . *Tempest* i 2 143
Is she not passing fair?—She hath been fairer, madam . *T. G. of Ver.* iv 4 154
Pulcher.—Polecats! there are fairer things than polecats, sure *M. Wives* iv 1 29
Your company is fairer than honest . . . . *Meas. for Meas.* iv 3 185
Study me how to please the eye indeed By fixing it upon a fairer eye *L. L. Lost* i 1 81
Remuneration! why, it is a fairer name than French crown . . iii 1 142
More fairer than fair, beautiful than beauteous, truer than truth itself iv 1 62
To tell you plain, I'll find a fairer face not wash'd to-day . . iv 3 273
And she is fair and, fairer than that word, Of wondrous virtues *M. of V.* i 1 162
If any man in Italy have a fairer table which doth offer to swear upon a book . . . . ii 2 167
You shall look fairer, ere I give or hazard . . . . ii 9 22
Were his daughter fairer than she is, She may more suitors have *T. of S.* i 2 242
Her dispositions she inherits, which makes fair gifts fairer . *All's Well* i 1 48
And in your bed Find fairer fortune, if you ever wed! . . . ii 3 98
Fairer prove your honour Than in my thought it lies . . . v 3 183
If lusty love should go in quest of beauty, Where should he find it fairer than in Blanch? . . . . *K. John* ii 1 427
Is yet the cover of a fairer mind Than to be butcher of an innocent child iv 2 258
What in me was purchased, Falls upon thee in a more fairer sort *2 Hen. IV.* iv 5 201
Helen of Greece was fairer far than thou . . . *3 Hen. VI.* ii 2 146
Fairer than tongue can name thee . . . . . *Richard III.* i 2 81
Think that thy babes were fairer than they were, And he that slew them fouler than he is . . . . iv 4 120
My babes were destined to a fairer death, If grace had bless'd thee with a fairer life . . . . iv 4 219
So much fairer And spotless shall mine innocence arise . *Hen. VIII.* iii 2 300

Fairer. She looked yesternight fairer than ever I saw her look, or any woman else . . . . *Trio. and Cres.* i 1 32
He hath a lady, wiser, fairer, truer, Than ever Greek did compass in his arms . . . . i 3 275
Tell him that my lady Was fairer than his grandam and as chaste As may be in the world . . . . i 3 299
Your mind is the clearer, Ajax, and your virtues the fairer . . ii 3 164
One fairer than my love! the all-seeing sun Ne'er saw her match *R. and J.* i 2 97
My fan, Peter.—Good Peter, to hide her face; for her fan's the fairer face ii 4 114
Time, with his fairer hand, Offering the fortunes of his former days, The former man may make him . . . . . . *T. of Athens* v 1 126
Had I as many sons as I have hairs, I would not wish them to a fairer death . . . . *Macbeth* v 8 49
You shall be yet far fairer than you are.—He means in flesh *Ant. and Cleo.* i 2 16
You have seen and proved a fairer former fortune Than that which is to approach . . . . i 2 33
With faces fit for masks, or rather fairer Than those for preservation cased, or shame . . . . *Cymbeline* v 3 21
Fairest. The fairest, that would have won any woman's heart *Mer. Wives* ii 2 70
I'll rent the fairest house in it after three-pence a bay *Meas. for Meas.* ii 1 255
The fairest grant is the necessity . . . . . *Much Ado* i 1 319
Death is the fairest cover for her shame That may be wish'd for . iv 1 117
All senses to that sense did make their repair, To feel only looking on fairest of fair . . . . *L. L. Lost* ii 1 241
A stand where you may make the fairest shoot . . . iv 1 10
I were the fairest goddess on the ground . . . . v 2 36
A holy parcel of the fairest dames, That ever turn'd their—backs—to mortal views! . . . . v 2 160
Some fair excuse.—The fairest is confession . . . . v 2 432
Which is—no, no—which was the fairest dame That lived, that loved *M. N. Dream* v 1 298
Bring me the fairest creature northward born . *Mer. of Venice* ii 1 4
All the pictures fairest lined Are but black to Rosalind . *As Y. Like It* iii 2 97
But upon the fairest boughs, Or at every sentence end, Will I Rosalinda write . . . . iii 2 143
Carry him gently to my fairest chamber . . *T. of Shrew* Ind. 1 46
She was the fairest creature in the world; And yet she is inferior to none . . . . Ind. 2 68
The fairest flowers o' the season Are our carnations . *W. Tale* iv 4 81
Now, my fair'st friend, I would I had some flowers o' the spring . iv 4 112
Were I the fairest youth That ever made eye swerve . . iv 4 384
His princess, she The fairest I have yet beheld . . . v 1 87
The whole land Is full of weeds, her fairest flowers choked up *Richard II.* iii 4 44
Your fairest daughter and mine, my god-daughter Ellen? *2 Hen. IV.* iii 2 7
His fairest daughter is contaminated . . . . *Hen. V.* iv 5 16
O fairest beauty, do not fear nor fly! . . . *1 Hen VI.* v 3 46
The fairest queen that ever king received . . . *2 Hen. VI.* i 1 16
The fairest hand I ever touch'd! . . . . . *Hen. VIII.* i 4 75
If there be one among the fair'st of Greece That holds his honour higher than his ease . . . . *Troi. and Cres.* i 3 265
As loathsome as a toad Amongst the fairest breeders of our clime *T. An.* iv 2 68
Two of the fairest stars in all the heaven, Having some business, do entreat her eyes To twinkle in their spheres . . *Rom. and Jul.* ii 2 15
I hope his honour will conceive the fairest of me . . *T. of Athens* iii 2 60
Away, and mock the time with fairest show . . . *Macbeth* i 7 81
Fairest Cordelia, that art most rich, being poor! . . . *Lear* i 1 253
Sweetest, fairest, As I my poor self did exchange for you *Cymbeline* i 1 118
It is a manacle of love; I'll place it Upon this fairest prisoner . i 1 123
Thanks, fairest lady. What, are men mad? . . . . . i 6 31
Good morrow, fairest: sister, your sweet hand . . . . ii 3 91
One of the fairest that I have look'd upon.—And therewithal the best . ii 4 32
O sweetest, fairest lily! My brother wears thee not the one half so well As when thou grew'st thyself . . . . iv 2 201
With fairest flowers Whilst summer lasts and I live here, Fidele, I'll sweeten thy sad grave . . . . iv 2 218
Built up, this city, for his chiefest seat; The fairest in all Syria *Per.* i Gower 19
Who makes the fairest show means most deceit . . . . i 4 75
The fairest, sweet'st, and best lies here, Who wither'd in her spring of year . . . . iv 4 34
She is all happy as the fairest of all . . . . . . v 1 49
Fairest-boding dreams That ever enter'd in a drowsy head *Richard III.* v 3 227
Fairing. We shall be rich ere we depart, If fairings come thus plentifully in *L. L. Lost* v 2 2
Fairly spoke. Sit then and talk with her . . . . *Tempest* iv 1 31
After they closed in earnest, they parted very fairly in jest *T. G. of Ver.* ii 5 14
Let them say 'tis grossly done; so it be fairly done, no matter *M. Wives* ii 2 149
Fairly met! Our old and faithful friend, we are glad to see you *M. for M.* v 1 1
Fairly I bespoke the officer To go in person with me to my house *C. of Er.* v 1 233
My love is more than his; My fortunes every way as fairly rank'd *M. N. Dream* i 1 101
My chief care Is to come fairly off from the great debts *Mer. of Venice* i 1 128
As, after some oration fairly spoke By a beloved prince . . . iii 2 180
Thou offer'st fairly to thy brothers' wedding . . *As Y. Like It* v 4 173
We may blow our nails together, and fast it fairly out . *T. of Shrew* i 1 109
I'll have them very fairly bound: All books of love . . . i 2 146
And there it is in writing, fairly drawn . . . . . iii 1 70
Which hath two letters for her name fairly set down in studs . iii 2 62
To be said an honest man and a good housekeeper goes as fairly as to say a careful man and a great scholar . . . . . *T. Night* iv 2 11
And heavens so shine, That they may fairly note this act of mine! . iv 3 35
Your youth, And the true blood which peepeth fairly through't *W. Tale* iv 4 148
Fairly offer'd.—This shows a sound affection . . . . iv 4 389
Is it not fair writ?—Too fairly, Hubert, for so foul effect *K. John* iv 1 38
For God's sake, fairly let her be entreated . . *Richard II.* iii 1 37
Our soldiers stand full fairly for the day . . . . *1 Hen. IV.* v 3 29
O, such a day, So fought, so follow'd and so fairly won! . *2 Hen. IV.* i 1 21
Thou dost thy office fairly . . . . *Hen. V.* iii 6 148
Admonishing That we should dress us fairly for our end . . iv 1 10
Fairly met: So are you, princes English, every one . . . v 2 10
The venom of such looks, we fairly hope, Have lost their quality . v 2 18
Speak, my fair, and fairly, I pray thee . . . . . v 2 177
Which in a set hand fairly is engross'd . . . *Richard III.* iii 6 2
But how long fairly shall her sweet life last? . . . . iv 4 352
Well said, my lord. So, now you're fairly seated *Hen. VIII.* i 4 31
Fairly answer'd; A loyal and obedient subject is Therein illustrated . iii 2 179
How much more is his life in value with him? Would I were fairly out on't! . . . . v 3 109
Degree being vizarded, The unworthiest shows as fairly in the mask *Troi. and Cres.* i 3 84
Let him know, What Troy means fairly shall be spoke aloud . . . i 3 259

Fairly. Fair desires, in all fair measure, fairly guide them! *Tr. and Cr.* iii 1 48
Furnish you fairly for this interchange . . . iii 3 33
And on him erect A second hope, as fairly built as Hector . iv 5 109
No less apparent To the vulgar eye, that he bears all things fairly *Coriol.* iv 7 21
You gave us the counterfeit fairly last night . *Rom. and Jul.* ii 4 48
Was ever book containing such vile matter So fairly bound? . iii 2 84
They are fairly welcome . . . . . . *T. of Athens* i 2 182
I shall accept them fairly; let the presents Be worthily entertain'd . i 2 190
How fairly this lord strives to appear foul! . . . iii 3 31
Which, I tell you, must show fairly outward . . . *Hamlet* ii 2 391
May I never To this good purpose, that so fairly shows, Dream of impediment! . . . . . . *Ant. and Cleo.* ii 2 147
I pray ye, greet them fairly . . . . . *Pericles* v 1 10

Fairness. Golden locks Which make such wanton gambols with the wind, Upon supposed fairness . . . . . *Mer. of Venice* iii 2 94
To undercrest your good addition To the fairness of my power *Coriolanus* i 9 73
If she be fair and wise, fairness and wit, The one's for use, the other useth it.—Well praised! . . . . . *Othello* ii 1 130
Besides that hook of wiving, Fairness which strikes the eye . *Cymbeline* v 5 168

Fairy. Monster, your fairy, which you say is a harmless fairy, has done little better than played the Jack with us . . . *Tempest* iv 1 196
Yet this is your harmless fairy, monster . . . . iv 1 212
We'll dress Like urchins, ouphes and fairies . . *Mer. Wives* iv 4 49
Ask him why, that hour of fairy revel, In their so sacred paths he dares to tread In shape profane . . . . . . iv 4 58
Let the supposed fairies pinch him sound . . . . iv 4 61
My Nan shall be the queen of all the fairies, Finely attired in a robe of white . . . . iv 4 71
Go get us properties And tricking for our fairies . . . iv 4 79
We'll couch i' the castle-ditch till we see the light of our fairies . v 2 2
Where is Nan now and her troop of fairies? . . . . v 3 13
Trib, trib, fairies; come; and remember your parts . . . v 4 1
Fairies, black, grey, green, and white, You moonshine revellers . v 5 41
Crier Hobgoblin, make the fairy oyes.—Elves, list your names . v 5 45
They are fairies; he that speaks to them shall die . . . v 5 51
Fairies use flowers for their charactery . . . . . v 5 77
Heavens defend me from that Welsh fairy, lest he transform me to a piece of cheese! . . . . v 5 86
About him, fairies; sing a scornful rhyme . . . . v 5 95
Pinch him, fairies, mutually; Pinch him for his villany . . v 5 103
And these are not fairies? I was three or four times in the thought they were not fairies . . . . v 5 128
Leave your desires, and fairies will not pinse you.—Well said, fairy Hugh . . . . v 5 137
Those be rubies, fairy favours, In those freckles live their savours *M. N. Dream* ii 1 12
Give me that boy, and I will go with thee.—Not for thy fairy kingdom. Fairies, away! We shall chide downright, if I longer stay . ii 1 144
The snake throws her enamell'd skin, Weed wide enough to wrap a fairy in . . . . ii 1 256
Come, now a roundel and a fairy song . . . . . ii 2 1
Go with me; I'll give thee fairies to attend on thee . . . iii 1 160
Captain of our fairy band . . . . iii 2 110
My fairy lord, this must be done with haste . . . . iii 2 378
I have a venturous fairy that shall seek The squirrel's hoard . . iv 1 39
Fairies, be gone, and be all ways away . . . . . iv 1 46
And her fairy sent To bear him to my bower in fairy land . . iv 1 65
Fairy king, attend, and mark: I do hear the morning lark . . iv 1 98
I never may believe These antique fables, nor these fairy toys . v 1 3
The iron tongue of midnight hath told twelve: Lovers, to bed; 'tis almost fairy time . . . . v 1 371
And we fairies, that do run By the triple Hecate's team . . . v 1 390
Every elf and fairy sprite Hop as light as bird from brier . . v 1 400
Hand in hand, with fairy grace, Will we sing, and bless this place . v 1 406
Now, until the break of day, Through this house each fairy stray . v 1 409
With this field-dew consecrate, Every fairy take his gait . . v 1 423
It was told me I should be rich by the fairies . . *W. Tale* iii 3 121
This is fairy gold, boy, and 'twill prove so . . . . iii 3 127
O that it could be proved That some night-tripping fairy had exchanged In cradle-clothes our children where they lay! . . . *1 Hen. IV.* i 1 87
Queen Mab hath been with you. She is the fairies' midwife, and she comes In shape no bigger than an agate-stone . . *Rom. and Jul.* i 4 55
The joiner squirrel or old grub, Time out o' mind the fairies' coachmakers i 4 69
And now about the cauldron sing, Like elves and fairies in a ring *Macb.* iv 1 42
Then no planets strike, No fairy takes, nor witch hath power *Hamlet* i 1 163
Fairies and gods Prosper it with thee! . . . . *Lear* iv 6 29
To this great fairy I'll commend thy acts . . *Ant. and Cleo.* iv 8 12
From fairies and the tempters of the night Guard me, beseech ye *Cymb.* ii 2 9
But that it eats our victuals, I should think Here were a fairy . iii 6 42
With female fairies will his tomb be haunted . . . . iv 2 217
What fairies haunt this ground? A book? O rare one! . . v 4 133
Are you flesh and blood? Have you a working pulse? and are no fairy? *Pericles* v 1 155

Fairy land. This is the fairy land: O spite of spites! We talk with goblins, owls and sprites . . . . . *Com. of Errors* ii 2 191
But I know When thou hast stolen away from fairy land *M. N. Dream* ii 1 65
The fairy land buys not the child of me . . . . . ii 1 122
And her fairy sent To bear him to my bower in fairy land . . iv 1 66

Fairy-like. Then let them all encircle him about And, fairy-like, to pinch the unclean knight . . . . . . *Mer. Wives* iv 4 57

Fairy Queen. Just 'twixt twelve and one, Must my sweet Nan present the Fairy Queen . . . . iv 6 20
And I serve the fairy queen, To dew her orbs upon the green *M. N. Dr.* ii 1 8
Newts and blind-worms, do no wrong, Come not near our fairy queen . ii 2 12
What hempen home-spuns have we swaggering here, So near the cradle of the fairy queen? . . . . iii 1 80
But first I will release the fairy queen. Be as thou wast wont to be . iv 1 75

Faith. I have been forsworn In breaking faith with Julia *T. G. of Ver.* iv 2 11
I do desire thy worthy company, Upon whose faith and honour I repose iv 3 26
To praise his faith which I would have dispraised . . . iv 4 107
For whose dear sake thou didst then rend thy faith Into a thousand oaths . . . . v 4 47
Thou hast no faith left now, unless thou'dst two; And that's far worse than none; better have none Than plural faith . . . v 4 50
Thou common friend, that's without faith or love, For such is a friend now . . . . v 4 62
Now doth thy honour stand, In him that was of late an heretic, As firm as faith . . . . *Mer. Wives* iv 4 10
I never spake with her, saw her, nor heard from her, Upon my faith and honour . . . . *Meas. for Meas.* v 1 224

Faith. If my breast had not been made of faith and my heart of steel *Com. of Errors* iii 2 150
He wears his faith but as the fashion of his hat . . *Much Ado* i 1 75
And, by my two faiths and troths, my lord, I spoke mine . . i 1 228
If ever thou dost fall from this faith, thou wilt prove a notable argument i 1 258
Beauty is a witch Against whose charms faith melteth into blood . ii 1 187
Being else by faith enforced To call young Claudio to a reckoning . v 4 8
If I break faith, this word shall speak for me . . *L. L. Lost* i 1 154
Ah, never faith could hold, if not to beauty vow'd . . . iv 2 110
You would for paradise break faith and troth . . . . iv 3 143
What will Biron say when that he shall hear Faith so infringed, which such zeal did swear? . . . . iv 3 146
Now prove Our loving lawful, and our faith not torn . . . iv 3 285
And quick Biron hath plighted faith to me . . . . . v 2 283
My faith and this the princess I did give . . . . . v 2 454
And make him with fair Ægle break his faith, With Ariadne *M. N. Dream* ii 1 79
Bearing the badge of faith, to prove them true . . . . iii 2 127
Disparage not the faith thou dost not know . . . . iii 2 174
All the faith, the virtue of my heart, The object and the pleasure of mine eye, Is only Helena . . . . iv 1 174
They are wont To keep obliged faith unforfeited . . *Mer. of Venice* ii 6 7
To solemnize The bargain of your faith . . . . . . iii 2 195
And do you, Gratiano, mean good faith?—Yes, faith, my lord . iii 2 212
Thou almost makest me waver in my faith To hold opinion with Pythagoras . . . . iv 1 130
Stealing her soul with many vows of faith And ne'er a true one . v 1 19
A thing stuck on with oaths upon your finger And so riveted with faith unto your flesh . . . . v 1 169
Your lord Will never more break faith advisedly . . . . v 1 253
Now, by the faith of my love, I will . . . . *As Y. Like It* iii 2 449
It [to love] is to be all made of faith and service . . . . v 2 95
Thy faith my fancy to thee doth combine . . . . . v 4 156
You to a love that your true faith doth merit: You to your land . v 4 194
His jarring concord, and his discord dulcet, His faith . . *All's Well* i 1 187
Betake thee to thy faith, for seventeen poniards are at thy bosom . iv 1 83
Surprise her with discourse of my dear faith . . . *T. Night* i 4 25
Let him be the devil, an he will, I care not: give me faith, say I . i 5 137
It is his grounds of faith that all that look on him love him . . ii 3 164
Plight me the full assurance of your faith . . . . . iv 3 26
But hear me this: Since you to non-regardance cast my faith . . v 1 124
O, do not swear! Hold little faith, though thou hast too much fear . v 1 174
Whose foundation Is piled upon his faith . . . . *W. Tale* i 2 430
Which on my faith deserves high speech . . . . . ii 1 70
Contrary to the faith and allegiance of a true subject . . . iii 2 20
Since my desires Run not before mine honour, nor my lusts Burn hotter than my faith . . . . iv 4 35
O cursed wretch, That knew'st this was the prince, and wouldst adventure To mingle faith with him! . . . . iv 4 471
It cannot fail but by The violation of my faith . . . . iv 4 488
It is required You do awake your faith . . . . . v 3 95
That sly devil, That broker, that still breaks the pate of faith *K. John* ii 1 568
Since kings break faith upon commodity, Gain, be my lord . . ii 1 597
All things begun come to ill end, Yea, faith itself to hollow falsehood change! . . . . iii 1 95
The Lady Constance speaks not from her faith, But from her need . iii 1 210
O, if thou grant my need, Which only lives but by the death of faith, That need must needs infer this principle, That faith would live again by death of need. O then, tread down my need, and faith mounts up; Keep my need up, and faith is trodden down! . . iii 1 212
The latest breath that gave the sound of words Was deep-sworn faith . iii 1 231
Play fast and loose with faith? so jest with heaven? . . . iii 1 242
To snatch our palm from palm, Unswear faith sworn . . . iii 1 245
I may disjoin my hand, but not my faith.—So makest thou faith an enemy to faith . . . . iii 1 262
And that high royalty was ne'er pluck'd off, The faiths of men ne'er stained with revolt . . . . iv 2 6
Wherefore we took the sacrament And keep our faiths firm and inviolable . . . . v 2 7
We swear A voluntary zeal and an unurged faith To your proceedings . v 2 10
Unthread the rude eye of rebellion And welcome home again discarded faith . . . . v 4 12
Show now your mended faiths, And instantly return with me again . v 7 75
They break their faith to God as well as us . . . *Richard II.* iii 2 101
And sends allegiance and true faith of heart To his most royal person . iii 3 37
There is my bond of faith, To tie thee to my strong correction . . v 1 76
Come, and be hanged! hast no faith in thee? . . . *1 Hen. IV.* ii 1 35
Such a deal of skimble-skamble stuff As puts me from my faith . . iii 1 155
There's neither faith, truth, nor womanhood in me else . . . iii 3 125
There's no more faith in thee than in a stewed prune . . . iii 3 127
There's no room for faith, truth, nor honesty in this bosom of thine . iii 3 174
And violation of all faith and troth Sworn to us . . . . v 1 70
That, were our royal faiths martyrs in love, We shall be winnow'd *2 Hen. IV.* iv 1 193
Will you thus break your faith?—I pawn'd thee none . . . iv 2 112
As if allegiance in their bosoms sat, Crowned with faith . . *Hen. V.* ii 2 5
For oaths are straws, men's faiths are wafer-cakes . . . ii 3 53
By faith and honour, Our madams mock at us . . . . iii 5 27
I love you: then if you urge me farther than to say 'do you in faith?' I wear out my suit . . . . v 2 132
I have a saving faith within me . . . . v 2 217
It was both impious and unnatural That such immanity and bloody strife Should reign among professors of one faith . . *1 Hen. VI.* v 1 14
Give thee her hand, for sign of plighted faith . . . . v 3 162
And yet, good Humphrey, is the hour to come That e'er I proved thee false or fear'd thy faith . . . . . . *2 Hen. VI.* iii 1 205
Why hast thou broken faith with me, Knowing how hardly I can brook abuse? . . . . v 1 91
O, where is faith? O, where is loyalty? If it be banish'd from the frosty head . . . . v 1 166
And, with thy hand, thy faith irrevocable . . . *3 Hen. VI.* iii 3 247
Trust not him that hath once broken faith . . . . . iv 4 30
For which your honour and your faith is pawn'd . . *Richard III.* iv 2 92
Which now . . Thy broken faith hath made a prey for worms . iv 4 386
Look your faith be firm, Or else his head's assurance is but frail . iv 4 497
The day wherein I wish'd to fall By the false faith of him I trusted most . . . . v 1 17
Renouncing clean The faith they have in tennis, and tall stockings *Hen. VIII.* i 3 30
You do not doubt my faith, sir?—This secret is so weighty, 'twill require A strong faith to conceal it . . . . ii 1 143

Faith. So deep suspicion, where all faith was meant . *Hen. VIII.* iii 1 53
His imprisonment was rather, If there be faith in men, meant for his trial . . . . v 3 151
Few words to fair faith . . . *Troi. and Cres.* iii 2 103
Your uncle's word and my firm faith . . . . iii 2 116
In this I do not call your faith in question So mainly as my merit . iv 4 86
Faith and troth, Strain'd purely from all hollow bias-drawing . . iv 5 168
O beauty! where is thy faith? . . . . . . v 2 67
The fractions of her faith, orts of her love . . . . v 2 158
The fragments, scraps, the bits and greasy relics Of her o'er-eaten faith v 2 160
I do stand engaged to many Greeks, Even in the faith of valour . v 3 69
I must not break my faith. You know me dutiful . . . v 3 71
By the faith of men, We have some old crab-trees here at home *Coriol.* ii 1 204
They pray, grant thou, lest faith turn to despair . *Rom. and Jul.* i 5 106
There's no trust, No faith, no honesty in men; all perjured . iii 2 86
If thou art fickle, what dost thou with him That is renown'd for faith? iii 5 62
My husband is on earth, my faith in heaven; How shall that faith return again to earth, Unless that husband send it me from heaven? iii 5 207
What will you give us?—No money, on my faith, but the gleek . iv 5 115
Thorough the hazards of this untrod state With all true faith *J. Cæsar* iii 1 137
There are no tricks in plain and simple faith . . . iv 2 22
At no time broke my faith, would not betray The devil to his fellow *Macbeth* iv 3 128
A faith that reason without miracle Could never plant in me . *Lear* i 1 225
By the faith of man, I know my price, I am worth no worse a place *Oth.* i 1 10
She has deceived her father, and may thee.—My life upon her faith! i 3 295
Thou hast served me with much faith. What's else to say? *A. and C.* ii 7 64
The loyalty well held to fools does make Our faith mere folly . iii 13 43
If thy faith be not tainted with the breach of hers . . *Cymbeline* iii 4 27
All turn'd to heresy? Away, away, Corrupters of my faith! . . iii 4 85
Thy name well fits thy faith, thy faith thy name . . . iv 2 381
And here the bracelet of the truest princess That ever swore her faith . v 5 417
I do not doubt thy faith; But should he wrong my liberties? *Pericles* i 2 111
I'll take thy word for faith, not ask thine oath: Who shuns not to break one will sure crack both . . . . . . i 2 120
A figure of truth, of faith, of loyalty . . . . . v 3 Gower 92
By my faith *Much Ado* ii 1; *As Y. Like It* iii 5; iv 1; v 4; *All's Well* ii 1; *K. John* ii 1; 1 *Hen. IV.* i 2; iv 1; v 4; *Hen. V.* iii 7; 2 *Hen. VI.* iv 2; v 3; 3 *Hen. VI.* v 1; *Hen. VIII.* i 4; *Pericles* iv 2
Faith (prefix) *Tempest* iii 3; *Mer. Wives* ii 1; *Meas. for Meas.* ii 1; v 1; *Com. of Errors* iii 1; iii 2; *Much Ado* i 1; ii 3; *As Y. Like It* v 1; v 4; *T. of Shrew* i 1; *All's Well* i 3; *T. Night* ii 3; 1 *Hen. VI.* ii 4; 2 *Hen. VI.* ii 1; *Richard III.* i 4; iv 4
Good faith *Mer. Wives* i 4; *As Y. Like It* iii 2; *All's Well* ii 1; iii 3; 1 *Hen. VI.* ii 4; 3 *Hen. VI.* iii 2; *Richard III.* ii 4; iii 2; *Troi. and Cres.* iii 2; *Coriolanus* v 1; *Rom. and Jul.* iv 4; *Othello* ii 3; *Cymbeline* iv 2; *Pericles* v 1
In faith *Mer. Wives* i 1; i 4; *Much Ado* i 1; ii 1; iii 4; iii 5; iv 1; v 1; *L. L. Lost* iv 1; iv 3; v 2; *Mer. of Venice* i 3; ii 4; v 1; *As Y. Like It* iii 4; iv 3; v 3; *T. of Shrew* Ind. 1; i 1; ii 1; *T. Night* ii 3; ii 4; *W. Tale* iv 4; *K. John* ii 1; 1 *Hen. IV.* ii 3; iii 1; v 4; 2 *Hen. IV.* iii 2; *Hen. V.* v 2; *Hen. VIII.* ii 3; *Troi. and Cres.* v 2; *Rom. and Jul.* i 3; v 3; *Hamlet* i 2; i 5; v 2; *Othello* i 3; ii 1
In good faith *L. L. Lost* v 2; *All's Well* ii 2; *T. Night* i 5; *Coriolanus* i 3; *Hamlet* v 1; v 2; *Othello* iv 2

Faith-breach. Now minutely revolts upbraid his faith-breach *Macbeth* v 2 18

Faithed. Would the reposal Of any trust, virtue, or worth in thee Make thy words faith'd? . . . . . . *Lear* ii 1 72

Faithful. Which you shall find By every syllable a faithful verity *Meas. for Meas.* iv 3 131
Our old and faithful friend, we are glad to see you . . . v 1 2
Though to myself forsworn, to thee I'll faithful prove . *L. L. Lost* iv 2 111
Some thousand verses of a faithful lover, A huge translation of hypocrisy v 2 50
At the twelvemonth's end I'll change my black gown for a faithful friend . . . . v 2 844
There shall the pairs of faithful lovers be Wedded . *M. N. Dream* iv 1 96
I will your very faithful feeder be . . *As Y. Like It* ii 4 99
Whether that thy youth and kind Will the faithful offer take Of me iv 3 60
You are there followed by a faithful shepherd . . . v 2 87
But if you do refuse to marry me, You'll give yourself to this most faithful shepherd? . . . . v 4 14
What men are you?—Your faithful subject I, a gentleman *K. John* i 1 50
Like true, inseparable, faithful loves, Sticking together in calamity . iii 4 66
I do bequeath my faithful services And true subjection everlastingly v 7 104
And bedew Her pastures' grass with faithful English blood *Richard II.* iii 3 100
And his heart To faithful service of your majesty . . . iii 3 118
God forbid, my dear and faithful lord, That you should fashion, wrest, or bow your reading . . . . . *Hen. V.* i 2 13
Never did faithful subject more rejoice At the discovery of most dangerous treason Than I do . . . . . . ii 2 161
Long since we were resolved of your truth, Your faithful service 1 *Hen. VI.* iii 4 21
And be crown'd King Henry's faithful and anointed queen . v 5 91
As I am a Christian faithful man . . . *Richard III.* i 4 4
This suit of yours, So season'd with your faithful love to me . iii 7 149
And if I have a conscience, let it sink me, Even as the axe falls, if I be not faithful! . . . . . . *Hen. VIII.* ii 1 61
Are all these Your faithful friends o' the suburbs? . . . v 4 76
Approved warriors, and my faithful friends . . *T. Andron.* v 1 1
What satisfaction canst thou have to-night?—The exchange of thy love's faithful vow for mine . . . *Rom. and Jul.* ii 2 127
And she, there dead, that Romeo's faithful wife . . . v 3 232
There shall no figure at such rate be set As that of true and faithful Juliet . . . . v 3 302
He was my friend, faithful and just to me . . *J. Cæsar* iii 2 90
Do faithful homage and receive free honours . . *Macbeth* iii 6 36
Good madam, stay awhile; I will be faithful . . *Hamlet* ii 2 115
What do you think of me?—As of a man faithful and honourable . ii 2 130
As England was his faithful tributary . . . . . v 2 39
This hath been Your faithful servant . . . *Cymbeline* i 1 174
Day serves not light more faithful than I'll be . . *Pericles* i 2 110

Faithfullest. My soul the faithfull'st offerings hath breathed out That e'er devotion tender'd! . . . . . . *T. Night* v 1 117

Faithfully. In so unseeming to confess receipt Of that which hath so faithfully been paid . . . . . *L. L. Lost* ii 1 157
I'll serve thee true and faithfully till then . . . . v 2 841
And we will answer all things faithfully . . *Mer. of Venice* v 1 299
As you have whisper'd faithfully you were . . *As Y. Like It* ii 7 192
But wilt thou faithfully?—If I do not, damn me . . *All's Well* iv 1 95
Was faithfully confirmed by the rector of the place . . iv 3 68

Faithfully. As faithfully as I deny the devil . . . *K. John* i 1 252
Yet their own authors faithfully affirm . . . . *Hen. V.* i 2 43
Have some pity Upon my wretched women, that so long Have follow'd both my fortunes faithfully . . . . *Hen. VIII.* iv 2 141
O gentle Romeo, If thou dost love, pronounce it faithfully *Rom. and Jul.* ii 2 94
If his occasion were not virtuous, I should not urge it half so faithfully.—Dost thou speak seriously? . . . *T. of Athens* iii 2 46

Faithfulness. I assume the lists, Nor ask advice of any other thought But faithfulness and courage . . . . . *Pericles* i 1 63
And for your faithfulness we will advance you . . . . i 1 154

Faithless. O faithless coward! O dishonest wretch! *Meas. for Meas.* iii 1 137
Never dare misfortune cross her foot, Unless she do it under this excuse, That she is issue to a faithless Jew . . *Mer. of Venice* ii 4 38
They shoot but calm words folded up in smoke, To make a faithless error in your ears. . . . . . . *K. John* ii 1 230
Both Fell by our servants, by those men we loved most, A most unnatural and faithless service! . . . . . *Hen. VIII.* ii 1 123

Faitor. Down, dogs! down, faitors! Have we not Hiren here? 2 *Hen. IV.* ii 4 173

Falchion. With purple falchion, painted to the hilt In blood of those that had encounter'd him . . . . . 3 *Hen. VI.* i 4 12
Queen Margaret saw Thy murderous falchion smoking in his blood *Rich. III.* i 2 94
With my good biting falchion I would have made them skip . . *Lear* v 3 276

Falcon. And follies doth emmew As falcon doth the fowl *Meas. for Meas.* iii 1 92
As the ox hath his bow, sir, the horse his curb and the falcon her bells, so man hath his desires . . . . . *As Y. Like It* iii 3 81
My falcon now is sharp and passing empty . . *T. of Shrew* iv 1 193
I bless the time When my good falcon made her flight across Thy father's ground . . . . *W. Tale* iv 4 15
As confident as is the falcon's flight Against a bird . . *Richard II.* i 3 61
But what a point, my lord, your falcon made, And what a pitch she flew above the rest! . . . . 2 *Hen. VI.* ii 1 5
Their master loves to be aloft And bears his thoughts above his falcon's pitch . . . . ii 1 12
So doves do peck the falcon's piercing talons . . 3 *Hen. VI.* i 4 41
The falcon as the tercel, for all the ducks i' the river . *Troi. and Cres.* iii 2 55
A falcon, towering in her pride of place, Was by a mousing owl hawk'd at and kill'd . . . . *Macbeth* ii 4 12

Falconbridge. The beauteous heir Of Jaques Falconbridge . *L. L. Lost* ii 1 42
Good sir, be not offended. She is an heir of Falconbridge . . ii 1 205
What say you, then, to Falconbridge, the young baron of England? *Mer. of Venice* i 2 71
Eldest son, As I suppose, to Robert Faulconbridge . . *K. John* i 1 52
What art thou?—The son and heir to that same Faulconbridge . . i 1 56
Hadst thou rather be a Faulconbridge And like thy brother? . . i 1 134
Go, Faulconbridge: now hast thou thy desire . . . . i 1 176
Hast thou denied thyself a Faulconbridge?—As faithfully as I deny the devil . . . . i 1 251
The bastard Faulconbridge Is now in England, ransacking the church . iii 4 171
Stand by, or I shall gall you, Faulconbridge.—Thou wert better gall the devil . . . . iv 3 94
What wilt thou do, renowned Faulconbridge? Second a villain and a murderer? . . . . iv 3 101
Faulconbridge Desires your majesty to leave the field . . . v 3 5
That misbegotten devil, Faulconbridge . . . . . v 4 4
The thrice-victorious Lord of Falconbridge . . . 1 *Hen. VI.* iv 7 67
Stern Falconbridge commands the narrow seas . . . 3 *Hen. VI.* i 1 239

Falconer. Hist! Romeo, hist! O, for a falconer's voice, To lure this tassel-gentle back again! . . . . . *Rom. and Jul.* ii 2 159
We'll e'en to't like French falconers, fly at any thing we see *Hamlet* ii 2 450

Fall. When I rear my hand, do you the like, To fall it on Gonzalo *Tempest* ii 1 296
All the infections that the sun sucks up From bogs, fens, flats, on Prosper fall! . . . . ii 2 2
Yond same cloud cannot choose but fall by pailfuls . . . ii 2 24
Whose wraths to guard you from—Which here, in this most desolate isle, else falls Upon your heads . . . . iii 3 80
No sweet aspersion shall the heavens let fall To make this contract grow iv 1 18
Tread softly, that the blind mole may not Hear a foot fall . . iv 1 195
Mine eyes, even sociable to the show of thine, Fall fellowly drops . v 1 64
Why didst thou stoop, then?—To take a paper up that I let fall *T. G. of V.* i 2 73
Leave not the mansion so long tenantless, Lest, growing ruinous, the building fall And leave no memory of what it was! . . . . v 4 9
A fery discretion answer; save the fall is in the ort 'dissolutely' *M. W.* i 1 262
To shallow rivers, to whose falls Melodious birds sings madrigals . . iii 1 17
Why then all the dukes fall upon the king . . *Meas. for Meas.* i 2 3
Under whose heavy sense your brother's life Falls into forfeit . . i 4 66
Let us be keen, and rather cut a little, Than fall, and bruise to death . ii 1 6
'Tis one thing to be tempted, Escalus, Another thing to fall . . ii 1 18
And forgive us all! Some rise by sin, and some by virtue fall . . ii 1 38
If any thing fall to you upon this, more than thanks and good fortune . iv 2 190
Shall we thus permit A blasting and a scandalous breath to fall On him? v 1 122
Procure my fall And by the doom of death end woes and all *Com. of Er.* i 1 1
The capon burns, the pig falls from the spit . . . . i 2 44
As easy mayst thou fall A drop of water in the breaking gulf . . ii 2 127
If ever thou dost fall from this faith, thou wilt prove a notable argument.—If I do, hang me in a bottle . . . . . *Much Ado* i 1 257
Falls into the cinque pace faster and faster, till he sink into his grave . ii 1 82
Then down upon her knees she falls, weeps, sobs, beats her heart . . ii 3 152
Cease thy counsel, Which falls into mine ears as profitless As water in a sieve . . . . v 1 4
You have killed a sweet lady, and her death shall fall heavy on you . v 1 150
Now fair befall your mask!—Fair fall the face it covers! . *L. L. Lost* ii 1 125
Submissive fall his princely feet before . . . . . iv 1 92
Down topples she, And 'tailor' cries, and falls into a cough *M. N. Dream* ii 1 54
Hoary-headed frosts Fall in the fresh lap of the crimson rose . . ii 1 108
And, at our stamp, here o'er and o'er one falls . . . . iii 2 25
And, as she fled, her mantle she did fall . . . . . v 1 143
If a throstle sing, he falls straight a capering . . *Mer. of Venice* i 2 65
An the worst fall that ever fell, I hope I shall make shift to go without him i 2 96
That all the eanlings which were streak'd and pied Should fall as Jacob's hire . . . . i 3 81
Who then conceiving did in eaning time Fall parti-colour'd lambs . i 3 89
Since this fortune falls to you, Be content and seek no new . . . iii 2 134
Your fortune stood upon the casket there, And so did mine too, as the matter falls . . . . iii 2 204
When I shun Scylla, your father, I fall into Charybdis, your mother . iii 5 19
Repair thy wit, good youth, or it will fall To cureless ruin . . iv 1 141
Orlando hath a disposition to come in disguised against me to try a fall *As Y. Like It* i 1 132
When Nature hath made a fair creature, may she not by Fortune fall into the fire? . . . . i 2 47

Fall. You shall try but one fall.—No, I warrant your grace, you shall not entreat him to a second . . . . *As Y. Like It* i 2 216
You will try in time, in despite of a fall . . . . i 3 25
Is it possible, on such a sudden, you should fall into so strong a liking? i 3 27
Though he go as softly as foot can fall, he thinks himself too soon there iii 2 346
The common executioner, Whose heart the accustom'd sight of death makes hard, Falls not the axe upon the humbled neck But first begs pardon . . . . iii 5 5
Meantime, forget this new-fall'n dignity And fall into our rustic revelry v 4 183
With measure heap'd in joy, to the measures fall . . . . v 4 185
But I would be loath to fall into my dreams again . . *T. of Shrew* Ind. 2 128
Swore so loud, That, all-amazed, the priest let fall the book . . . iii 2 163
You whoreson villain! will you let it fall? . . . . . iv 1 158
What heaven more will, That thee may furnish and my prayers pluck down, Fall on thy head! . . . . *All's Well* i 1 79
Higher Italy,—Those bated that inherit but the fall Of the last monarchy ii 1 13
To each of you one fair and virtuous mistress Fall, when Love please! . ii 3 64
You know your places well; When better fall, for your avails they fell iii 1 22
We have almost embossed him; you shall see his fall to-night . . iii 6 108
I know his brains are forfeit to the next tile that falls . . . iv 3 217
You shall find yourself to be well thank'd Whate'er falls more . v 1 37
My fore-past proofs, howe'er the matter fall, Shall tax my fears . v 3 121
That strain again! it had a dying fall . . . . . *T. Night* i 1 4
But falls into abatement and low price, Even in a minute . . . i 1 13
If both break, your gaskins fall . . . . i 5 27
For women are as roses, whose fair flower Being once display'd, doth fall that very hour . . . . ii 4 40
If this fall into thy hand, revolve . . . . ii 5 155
How much the better To fall before the lion than the wolf! . . . iii 1 140
I should my tears let fall upon your cheek, And say, 'Thrice-welcome!' v 1 247
O Proserpina, For the flowers now, that frighted thou let'st fall From Dis's waggon! . . . . *W. Tale* iv 4 117
Fair fall the bones that took the pains for me! . . . *K. John* i 1 78
Before the dew of evening fall . . . . ii 1 285
As doth the fury of two desperate men Which in the very meeting fall and die . . . . iii 1 33
Let wives with child Pray that their burthens may not fall this day . iii 1 90
England, I will fall from thee.—O fair return of banish'd majesty! . iii 1 320
But what shall I gain by young Arthur's fall? . . . . . iii 4 141
But if you be afeard to hear the worst, Then let the worst unheard fall on your head . . . . iv 2 136
Seek out King John and fall before his feet . . . . . v 4 13
Yet one word more: grief boundeth where it falls, Not with the empty hollowness, but weight . . . . *Richard II.* i 2 58
Let thy blows, doubly redoubled, Fall like amazing thunder . . . i 3 81
The ripest fruit first falls, and so doth he; His time is spent . . . ii 1 153
These signs forerun the death or fall of kings . . . . . ii 4 15
I see thy glory like a shooting star Fall to the base earth from the firmament . . . . ii 4 20
If angels fight, Weak men must fall, for heaven still guards the right iii 2 62
He that hath suffer'd this disorder'd spring Hath now himself met with the fall of leaf . . . . iii 4 49
What Eve, what serpent, hath suggested thee To make a second fall of cursed man? . . . . iii 4 76
Here did she fall a tear; here in this place I'll set a bank of rue . . iii 4 104
Conveyers are you all, That rise thus nimbly by a true king's fall . . iv 1 318
Would he not fall down, Since pride must have a fall? . . . . v 5 88
The soul of every man Prophetically doth forethink thy fall 1 *Hen. IV.* iii 2 38
An I do, I pray God my girdle break.—O, if it should, how would thy guts fall about thy knees! . . . . iii 3 173
I embrace this fortune patiently, Since not to be avoided it falls on me v 5 13
You two never meet but you fall to some discord . . 2 *Hen. IV.* ii 4 61
Making many fish-meals, that they fall into a kind of male green-sickness iv 3 100
And, when they stand against you, may they fall As those that I am come to tell you of! . . . . iv 4 95
How quickly nature falls into revolt When gold becomes her object! . iv 5 66
For what in me was purchased, Falls upon thee in a more fairer sort . iv 5 201
I know thee not, old man: fall to thy prayers . . . . . v 5 51
Never two such kingdoms did contend Without much fall of blood *Hen. V.* i 2 25
And thus thy fall hath left a kind of blot, To mark the full-fraught man ii 2 138
This revolt of thine, methinks, is like Another fall of man . . . ii 2 142
Your pure maidens fall into the hand Of hot and forcing violation . iii 3 20
And quickly bring us word of England's fall . . . . . iii 5 68
They that ride so and ride not warily, fall into foul bogs . . . iii 7 61
Stars, my lord.—Some of them will fall to-morrow, I hope . . . iii 7 77
A good leg will fall; a straight back will stoop . . . . . v 2 167
And fall on my side so, against your will . . . . 1 *Hen. VI.* ii 4 51
And so thrive Richard as thy foes may fall! . . . . . . iii 1 174
Now shine it like a comet of revenge, A prophet to the fall of all our foes! . . . . iii 2 32
Lets fall his sword before your highness' feet . . . . . iii 4 9
Before young Talbot from old Talbot fly, The coward horse that bears me fall and die! . . . . iv 6 47
France must vail her lofty-plumed crest And let her head fall into England's lap . . . . v 3 26
Makes me from wondering fall to weeping joys . . . 2 *Hen. VI.* i 1 34
Hume's knavery will be the duchess' wreck, And her attainture will be Humphrey's fall . . . . i 2 106
How camest thou so?—A fall off of a tree.—A plum-tree, master . . ii 1 96
He is near you in descent, And should you fall, he is the next will mount iii 1 22
By wicked means to frame our sovereign's fall . . . . . iii 1 52
Even as a splitted bark, so sunder we: This way fall I to death . . iii 2 412
For our enemies shall fall before us . . . . iv 2 37
What, hath thy fiery heart so parch'd thine entrails That not a tear can fall for Rutland's death? . . . . 3 *Hen. VI.* i 4 88
And when thou fail'st—as God forbid the hour!—Must Edward fall . ii 1 191
And, now I fall, thy tough commixture melts . . . . . ii 6 6
I fear her not, unless she chance to fall . . . . . . iii 2 24
My letters tell me, He's very likely now to fall from him . . . iii 3 209
I long till Edward fall by war's mischance . . . . . . iii 3 254
My sick heart shows That I must yield my body to the earth And, by my fall, the conquest to my foe . . . . v 2 10
Obsequiously lament The untimely fall of virtuous Lancaster *Richard III.* i 2 4
Leave this keen encounter of our wits, And fall somewhat into a slower method . . . . i 2 116
And if they fall, they dash themselves to pieces . . . . . i 3 260
When great leaves fall, the winter is at hand . . . . . ii 3 33
Two props of virtue for a Christian prince, To stay him from the fall of vanity . . . . iii 7 97
By sudden floods and fall of waters, Buckingham's army is dispersed . iv 4 512

Fall. This is the day that, in King Edward's time, I wish'd might fall on me . . . . *Richard III.* v 1 14
The day wherein I wish'd to fall By the false faith of him I trusted most v 1 16
Lest his son George fall Into the blind cave of eternal night . . v 3 61
Crush down with a heavy fall The usurping helmets of our adversaries! v 3 111
To thee I do commend my watchful soul, Ere I let fall the windows of mine eyes . . . . v 3 116
To-morrow in the battle think on me, And fall thy edgeless sword . v 3 135
With guilty fear, Let fall thy lance: despair, and die! . . . v 3 143
And Richard falls in height of all his pride . . . . . v 3 176
Here May, if they think it well, let fall a tear . . . *Hen. VIII.* Prol. 6
A hand as fruitful as the land that feeds us; His dews fall every where i 3 57
Let it [conscience] sink me, Even as the axe falls, if I be not faithful! ii 1 61
As the long divorce of steel falls on me . . . . . . ii 1 76
Yet I can give you inkling Of an ensuing evil, if it fall, Greater than this ii 1 141
The cardinal Will have his will, and she must fall . . . . ii 1 167
Of her That, when the greatest stroke of fortune falls, Will bless the king ii 2 36
Take heed, lest at once The burthen of my sorrows fall upon ye . . iii 1 111
I persuade me, from her Will fall some blessing to this land . . iii 2 51
O negligence! Fit for a fool to fall by . . . . . . iii 2 214
I shall fall Like a bright exhalation in the evening . . . . iii 2 225
Fall into the compass of a præmunire . . . . iii 2 340
Nips his root, And then he falls, as I do . . . . . . iii 2 358
And when he falls, he falls like Lucifer, Never to hope again . . iii 2 371
Mark but my fall, and that that ruin'd me. Cromwell, I charge thee, fling away ambition . . . . iii 2 439
The dews of heaven fall thick in blessings on her! . . . . iv 2 133
God and your majesty Protect mine innocence, or I fall into The trap! v 1 141
Thus pray: All comfort, joy, in this most gracious lady, Heaven ever laid up to make parents happy, May hourly fall upon ye! . . . v 5 9
And make him fall His crest that prouder than blue Iris bends *T. and C.* i 3 379
The walls will stand till they fall of themselves . . . . . ii 3 10
What the declined is He shall as soon read in the eyes of others As feel in his own fall . . . . iii 3 78
Which when they fall, as being slippery standers, The love that lean'd on them as slippery too, Do one pluck down another and together Die in the fall . . . . iii 3 84
Hector would have them fall upon him thus . . . . . iv 5 137
The fall of every Phrygian stone will cost A drop of Grecian blood . iv 5 223
I will not break it: Fall Greeks; fail fame; honour or go or stay . v 1 48
When many times the captive Grecian falls, Even in the fan and wind of your fair sword, You bid them rise, and live . . . . . v 3 40
Now if thou lose thy stay, Thou on him leaning, and all Troy on thee, Fall all together . . . . v 3 62
So, Ilion, fall thou next! now, Troy, sink down! . . . . . v 8 11
Your eyes, half out, weep out at Pandar's fall . . . . . v 10 49
Or whether his fall enraged him, or how 'twas, he did so set his teeth and tear it . . . . *Coriolanus* i 3 69
Now the fair goddess, Fortune, Fall deep in love with thee! . . i 5 22
If, as his nature is, he fall in rage With their refusal . . . ii 3 266
Stop, Or all will fall in broil . . . . iii 1 33
But the fall of either Makes the survivor heir of all . . . v 6 18
Therefore shall he die, And I'll renew me in his fall . . . v 6 49
Speak, brother, hast thou hurt thee with the fall? . . *T. Andron.* ii 3 205
Like to a bubbling fountain stirr'd with wind, Doth rise and fall . ii 4 24
Just against thy heart make thou a hole; That all the tears that thy poor eyes let fall May run into that sink . . . . . . iii 2 18
'Yea,' quoth he, 'dost thou fall upon thy face? Thou wilt fall backward when thou hast more wit' . . . . . . *Rom. and Jul.* i 3 41
Women may fall, when there's no strength in men . . . . ii 3 80
What a head have I! It beats as it would fall in twenty pieces . . ii 5 50
A lover may bestride the gossamer That idles in the wanton summer air, And yet not fall; so light is vanity . . . . ii 6 20
Fall upon the ground, as I do now, Taking the measure of an unmade grave . . . . iii 3 69
Rise and stand; Why should you fall into so deep an O? . . . iii 3 90
And now falls on her bed; and then starts up, And Tybalt calls; and then on Romeo cries, And then down falls again . . . . iii 3 100
Thy eyes' windows fall, Like death, when he shuts up the day of life iv 1 100
Humbly I thank your lordship: never may That state or fortune fall into my keeping, Which is not owed to you! . . . *T. of Athens* i 1 150
That now they are at fall, want treasure, cannot Do what they would ii 2 214
Tear me, take me, and the gods fall upon you! . . . . . iii 4 100
Wouldst thou have thyself fall in the confusion of men, and remain a beast with the beasts? . . . . iv 3 325
In, and prepare: Ours is the fall, I fear; our foes the snare . . v 2 17
Before proud Athens he's set down by this, Whose fall the mark of his ambition is . . . . v 3 10
That these great towers, trophies and schools should fall For private faults v 4 25
Spare thy Athenian cradle and those kin Which in the bluster of thy wrath must fall With those that have offended . . . . . . v 4 41
Those enemies of Timon's and mine own Whom you yourselves shall set out for reproof Fall and no more . . . . v 4 58
And those our droplets which From niggard nature fall . . . . v 4 77
Run to your houses, fall upon your knees, Pray to the gods . *J. Cæsar* i 1 58
What other oath Than honesty to honesty engaged, That this shall be, or we will fall for it? . . . . ii 1 128
Let Antony and Cæsar fall together.—Our course will seem too bloody ii 1 161
As low as to thy foot doth Cassius fall . . . . iii 1 56
Et tu, Brute! Then fall, Cæsar!—Liberty! Freedom! Tyranny is dead! iii 1 77
And my misgiving still Falls shrewdly to the purpose . . . . iii 1 146
Here wast thou bay'd, brave hart; Here didst thou fall . . . iii 1 205
I know not what may fall; I like it not . . . . . . iii 1 243
Great Cæsar fell. O, what a fall was there, my countrymen! . . iii 2 194
They fall their crests, and, like deceitful jades, Sink in the trial . iv 2 26
I do find it cowardly and vile, For fear of what might fall, so to prevent The time of life . . . . v 1 105
Vaulting ambition, which o'erleaps itself And falls on the other *Macbeth* i 7 28
Then 'tis most like The sovereignty will fall upon Macbeth . . . ii 4 30
But wail his fall Who I myself struck down . . . . . . iii 1 122
Deny me this, And an eternal curse fall on you! . . . . . iv 1 105
It hath been The untimely emptying of the happy throne And fall of many kings . . . . iv 3 69
Let fall thy blade on vulnerable crests; I bear a charmed life . . v 8 11
He falls to such perusal of my face As he would draw it . . . *Hamlet* ii 1 90
His antique sword, Rebellious to his arm, lies where it falls . . ii 2 492
But with the whiff and wind of his fell sword The unnerved father falls ii 2 496
And never did the Cyclops' hammers fall On Mars's armour forged for proof eterne With less remorse than Pyrrhus' bleeding sword Now falls on Priam . . . . ii 2 511

Fall. Like fruit unripe, sticks on the tree; But fall, unshaken, when they mellow be . . . . *Hamlet* iii 2 201
Which, when it falls, Each small annexment, petty consequence, Attends the boisterous ruin . . . . iii 3 20
What's in prayer but this two-fold force, To be forestalled ere we come to fall, Or pardon'd being down? . . . iii 3 49
And where the offence is let the great axe fall . . . . iv 5 218
Under the which he shall not choose but fall . . . . iv 7 66
It falls right. You have been talk'd of since your travel much . . iv 7 71
O, treble woe Fall ten times treble on that cursed head! . . v 1 270
There's a special providence in the fall of a sparrow . . v 2 231
Let it fall rather, though the fork invade The region of my heart . *Lear* i 1 146
The king falls from bias of nature; there's father against child . i 2 120
All the stored vengeances of heaven fall On her ingrateful top! . . ii 4 164
Infect her beauty, You fen-suck'd fogs, drawn by the powerful sun, To fall and blast her pride! . . . . ii 4 170
Then let fall Your horrible pleasure; here I stand, your slave . iii 2 18
The younger rises when the old doth fall . . . . . iii 3 26
Preferment falls on him that cuts him off . . . . . iv 5 38
Fall, and cease!—This feather stirs: she lives! . . . . v 3 264
The trust, the office I do hold of you, Not only take away, but let your sentence Even fall upon my life . . . . *Othello* i 3 120
Lest by his clamour—as it so fell out—The town might fall in fright . ii 3 232
I heard the clink and fall of swords, And Cassio high in oath . ii 3 234
My speech should fall into such vile success As my thoughts aim not at iii 3 222
Her will, recoiling to her better judgement, May fall to match you . iii 3 237
Thither comes the bauble, and, by this hand, she falls me thus about my neck . . . . iv 1 139
If that the earth could teem with woman's tears, Each drop she falls would prove a crocodile . . . . iv 1 257
I will be near to second your attempt, and he shall fall between us . iv 2 245
But I do think it is their husband's faults If wives do fall . . iv 3 88
The woman falls; sure, he hath kill'd his wife . . . . v 2 236
And the wide arch Of the ranged empire fall! . . . *Ant. and Cleo.* i 1 34
Help me away, dear Charmian; I shall fall . . . . i 3 15
Let me cut the cable; And, when we are put off, fall to their throats . ii 7 78
Take heed you fall not. Menas, I'll not on shore . . . ii 7 136
No disgrace Shall fall you for refusing him at sea, Being prepared for land iii 7 40
Fall not a tear, I say; one of them rates All that is won and lost . iii 11 69
Our terrene moon Is now eclipsed; and it portends alone The fall of Antony! . . . . iii 13 155
Grace grow where those drops fall! . . . . . . iv 2 38
To the young Roman boy she hath sold me, and I fall Under this plot iv 12 48
The gods! it smites me Beneath the fall I have . . . v 2 172
And, when we fall, We answer others' merits in our name, Are therefore to be pitied . . . . v 2 177
Have I the aspic in my lips? Dost fall? . . . . . v 2 296
Would there had been some hurt done!—I wish not so; unless it had been the fall of an ass . . . . . . *Cymbeline* i 2 39
If you fall in the adventure, our crows shall fare the better for you . iii 1 82
Be sprightly, for you fall 'mongst friends . . . . . iii 6 75
Some falls are means the happier to arise . . . . . iv 2 403
These present wars shall find I love my country, Even to the note o' the king, or I'll fall in them . . . . iv 3 44
But if you will not, The hazard therefore due fall on me! . . iv 4 46
But, alack, You snatch some hence for little faults; that's love, To have them fall no more . . . . v 1 13
My tears that fall Prove holy water on thee! . . . . v 5 268
The benediction of these covering heavens Fall on their heads like dew! v 5 351
This prince must die; For by his fall my honour must keep high *Pericles* i 1 149
Here many sink, yet those which see them fall Have scarce strength left to give them burial . . . . i 4 48
That all those eyes adored them ere their fall Scorn now their hand should give them burial . . . . ii 4 11
The lady shrieks, and well-a-near Does fall in travail with her fear iii Gower 52
For which the people's prayers still fall upon you . . . iii 3 19
Fall a-cursing, like a very drab, A scullion! . . . *Hamlet* ii 2 615
Fall a-hooting. The people fall a-hooting . . . *L. L. Lost* iv 2 61
Fall asleep. In sweet music is such art, Killing care and grief of heart Fall asleep, or hearing, die . . . . . *Hen. VIII.* iii 1 14
Fall away. Till bones and flesh and sinews fall away 1 *Hen. VI.* iii 1 193
When they once perceive The least rub in your fortunes, fall away Like water from ye . . . . *Hen. VIII.* ii 1 129
Fall back. Unto the white-upturned wondering eyes Of mortals that fall back to gaze on him . . . . . . *Rom. and Jul.* ii 2 30
Fall backward. Thou wilt fall backward when thou hast more wit . i 3 42
Fall dead. That the life-weary taker may fall dead . . . v 1 62
Fall down. Now counterfeit to swoon; why now fall down *As Y. Like It* iii 5 17
Would he not fall down, Since pride must have a fall? . . *Richard II.* v 5 87
Though we here fall down, We have supplies to second our attempt 2 *Hen. IV.* iv 2 44
Not rascal-like, to fall down with a pinch . . 1 *Hen. VI.* iv 2 49
Fall down before him, like the mower's swath . . *Troi. and Cres.* v 5 25
A mile before his tent fall down, and knee The way into his mercy *Cor.* v 1 5
My master bid me kneel; Thus did Mark Antony bid me fall down *J. C.* iii 1 124
That is a step On which I must fall down, or else o'erleap *Macbeth* i 4 49
Fall flat. I'll fall flat; Perchance he will not mind me . *Tempest* ii 2 16
Fall foul. Let the welkin roar. Shall we fall foul for toys? 2 *Hen. IV.* ii 4 183
Fall in. If he fall in, good night! or sink or swim . 1 *Hen. IV.* i 3 194
You knew he walk'd o'er perils, on an edge, More likely to fall in than to get o'er . . . . 2 *Hen. IV.* i 1 171
Come, come, let's fall in with them . . . . 2 *Hen. VI.* iv 2 32
Fall in love. Wouldst thou then counsel me to fall in love? *T. G. of Ver.* i 2 2
I will teach you how to humour your cousin, that she shall fall in love with Benedick . . . . *Much Ado* ii 1 396
That, in despite of his quick wit and his queasy stomach, he shall fall in love with Beatrice . . . . ii 1 399
For which of my bad parts didst thou first fall in love with me? . v 2 61
He's fallen in love with your foulness and she'll fall in love with my anger . . . . *As Y. Like It* iii 5 66
Do not fall in love with me, For I am falser than vows made in wine . iii 5 72
Would have gone near To fall in love with him . . . . iii 5 126
I dispraised him before the wicked, that the wicked might not fall in love with him . . . . 2 *Hen. IV.* ii 4 347
To fall in love with what she fear'd to look on! . . . *Othello* i 3 98
Fall mad. As any mortal body hearing it Should straight fall mad *T. An.* ii 3 104
Fall off. Inconstancy falls off ere it begins . . *T. G. of Ver.* v 4 113
He never did fall off, my sovereign liege, But by the chance of war 1 *Hen. IV.* i 3 94
Love cools, friendship falls off, brothers divide: in cities, mutinies *Lear* i 2 116

Fall out. It oft falls out, To have what we would have, we speak not what we mean . . . . *Meas. for Meas.* ii 4 117
For it so falls out That what we have we prize not to the worth Whiles we enjoy it . . . . *Much Ado* iv 1 219
This falls out better than I could devise . . . *M. N. Dream* iii 2 35
I did upbraid her and fall out with her . . . . . iv 1 55
I tell thee so before, because I would not fall out with thee *All's Well* iv 5 61
Foreknowing that the truth will fall out so . . . *K. John* iv 2 154
None can tell; But by bad courses may be understood That their events can never fall out good . . . . . . *Richard II.* ii 1 214
If all things fall out right, I shall as famous be by this exploit 1 *Hen. VI.* ii 3 4
Hear me, you wrangling pirates, that fall out In sharing that which you have pill'd from me! . . . . *Richard III.* i 3 158
O monstrous, monstrous! and so falls it out With Rivers, Vaughan, Grey iii 2 66
My cousin will fall out with you . . . . . *Troi. and Cres.* iii 1 93
Greatness, once fall'n out with fortune, Must fall out with men too . iii 3 76
So it must fall out To him or our authorities . . . *Coriolanus* ii 1 259
Pretty fool, To see it tetchy and fall out with the dug! *Rom. and Jul.* i 3 32
Didst thou not fall out with a tailor for wearing his new doublet before Easter? . . . . iii 1 29
Which I will fashion to fall out between twelve and one . *Othello* iv 2 242
With Mars fall out, with Juno chide . . . . . *Cymbeline* v 4 32
Sails are fill'd, And wishes fall out as they're will'd . *Pericles* v 2 281
Fall over. And dost thou now fall over to my foes? . . *K. John* iii 1 127
Fall pat. You shall see, it will fall pat as I told you . *M. N. Dream* v 1 188
Fall prostrate. I will fall prostrate at his feet And never rise until my tears and prayers Have won his grace . . . *Com. of Errors* v 1 114
And am enjoin'd By holy Laurence to fall prostrate here *Rom. and Jul.* iv 2 20
Fall to. Welcome; fall to: I will not trouble you As yet *As Y. Like It* ii 7 171
Fall to them as you find your stomach serves you . . *T. of Shrew* i 1 38
Will't please you to fall to?—Taste of it first, as thou art wont *Rich. II.* v 5 98
I pray you, fall to: if you can mock a leek, you can eat a leek *Hen. V.* v 1 38
Come, let's fall to; and, gentle girl, eat this: Here is no drink! *T. An.* iii 2 34
Fall to blows. Come, leave your drinking, and fall to blows 2 *Hen. VI.* ii 3 80
Fall to't, yarely, or we run ourselves aground . . . *Tempest* i 1 3
Nay, if we be forbidden stones, we'll fall to it with our teeth 1 *Hen. VI.* iii 1 90
So fall to't: Rich men sin, and I eat root . . . *T. of Athens* i 2 71
Fall to play. Before you fall to play . . . . . *Hamlet* v 2 216
Fall to quarrel. If I could bear it longer, and not fall To quarrel with your great opposeless wills . . . . *Lear* iv 6 37
Fall to reprobation. Curse his better angel from his side, And fall to reprobation . . . . *Othello* v 2 209
Fall to ruin. Like goodly buildings left without a roof Soon fall to ruin *Pericles* ii 4 37

Fallacy. Until I know this sure uncertainty, I'll entertain the offer'd fallacy . . . . *Com. of Errors* ii 2 188
Fallen. What a blow was there given!—An it had not fallen flat-long *Tempest* ii 1 181
Though he hath fall'n by prompture of the blood . . *Meas. for Meas.* ii 4 178
Why, she, O, she is fallen Into a pit of ink! . . . *Much Ado* iv 1 141
Fallen am I in dark uneven way, And here will rest me *M. N. Dream* iii 2 417
Grieve not that I am fallen to this for you . . . *Mer. of Venice* iv 1 266
He's fallen in love with your foulness . . . . *As Y. Like It* iii 5 66
My horse is tired; my master and mistress fallen out . *T. of Shrew* iv 1 57
I do presume, sir, that you are not fallen From the report that goes upon your goodness . . . . *All's Well* v 1 12
Has fallen into the unclean fishpond of her displeasure . . . v 2 21
Where but by chance a silver drop hath fallen . . . *K. John* iii 4 63
The English lords By his persuasion are again fall'n off . . . v 5 11
Am I not fallen away vilely since this last action? . . 1 *Hen. IV.* iii 3 1
His highness is fallen into this same whoreson apoplexy . 2 *Hen. IV.* i 2 123
It is a kind of deafness.—I think you are fallen into the disease . i 2 135
He esteems himself happy that he hath fallen into the hands of one, as he thinks, the most brave . . . . *Hen. V.* iv 4 65
Bright star of Venus, fall'n down on the earth . . 1 *Hen. VI.* i 2 144
Had your watch been good, This sudden mischief never could have fall'n . . . . ii 1 59
And Humphrey with the peers be fall'n at jars . . 2 *Hen. VI.* i 1 253
His curses, then from bitterness of soul Denounced against thee, are all fall'n upon thee . . . . *Richard III.* i 3 180
Now Margaret's curse is fallen upon our (my) head . . iii 3 15; v 1 25
The net has fall'n upon me! I shall perish Under device . *Hen. VIII.* i 1 203
What can be their business With me, a poor weak woman, fall'n from favour? . . . . iii 1 20
Nay, an you weep, I am fall'n indeed . . . . . iii 2 376
I am a poor fall'n man, unworthy now To be thy lord and master . . iii 2 413
'Tis certain, greatness, once fall'n out with fortune, Must fall out with men too . . . . *Troi. and Cres.* iii 3 75
Or, like a gallant horse fall'n in first rank, Lie there for pavement . iii 3 161
I have heard it said, the fittest time to corrupt a man's wife is when she's fallen out with her husband . . . . *Coriolanus* iv 3 34
What, art thou fall'n? What subtle hole is this? . . *T. Andron.* ii 3 198
Things have fall'n out, sir, so unluckily, That we have had no time to move our daughter . . . . *Rom. and Jul.* iii 4 1
Such a house broke! So noble a master fall'n! . . . *T. of Athens* iv 2 6
Hearing you were retired, your friends fall'n off . . . . v 1 62
My way of life Is fall'n into the sear, the yellow leaf . *Macbeth* v 3 23
If he love her not And be not from his reason fall'n thereon, Let me be no assistant for a state . . . . *Hamlet* ii 2 165
And, in this upshot, purposes mistook Fall'n on the inventors' heads . v 2 396
When she was dear to us, we did hold her so; But now her price is fall'n . . . . *Lear* i 1 200
Your fore-vouch'd affection Fall'n into taint . . . . . i 1 224
I'll forbear; And am fall'n out with my more headier will . . ii 4 111
But have I fall'n, or no?—From the dread summit of this chalky bourn iv 6 56
What's the matter?—My lord is fall'n into an epilepsy . . *Othello* iv 1 51
There's fall'n between him and my lord An unkind breach . . iv 1 237
O thou Othello, that wert once so good, Fall'n in the practice of a damned slave, What shall be said to thee? . . . . . . v 2 292
Yet he that can endure To follow with allegiance a fall'n lord Does conquer him that did his master conquer . . *Ant. and Cleo.* iii 13 44
The star is fall'n.—And time is at his period . . . . iv 14 106
O, wither'd is the garland of the war, The soldier's pole is fall'n . iv 15 65
Be of good cheer; You're fall'n into a princely hand, fear nothing . v 2 22
By such two that would by all likelihood have confounded one the other, or have fallen both . . . . . . *Cymbeline* i 4 55
What a strange infection Is fall'n into thy ear! . . . . iii 2 4
Almost spent with hunger, I am fall'n in this offence . . iii 6 64
Fallen-off. The legions now in Gallia are Full weak to undertake our wars against The fall'n-off Britons . . . . . . iii 7 6

Fallest. But, seeing thou fall'st on me so luckily, I will assay thee 1 *Hen. IV.* v 4 33
Then if thou fall'st, O Cromwell, Thou fall'st a blessed martyr! *Hen. VIII.* iii 2 448
'Yea,' quoth my husband, 'fall'st upon thy face?' . *Rom. and Jul.* i 3 55
Falleth. And anon falleth like a crab on the face of terra . *L. L. Lost* iv 2 6
Fallible. Do not satisfy your resolution with hopes that are fallible *Meas. for Meas.* iii 1 170
This is most fallible, the worm's an odd worm . . *Ant. and Cleo.* v 2 258
Falling in the flaws of her own youth, Hath blister'd her report *M. for M.* ii 3 11
But that frailty hath examples for his falling, I should wonder . iii 1 191
A drop of water That in the ocean seeks another drop, Who, falling there to find his fellow forth, Unseen, inquisitive, confounds himself . . . . *Com. of Errors* i 2 37
Become the argument of his own scorn by falling in love . *Much Ado* ii 3 12
Contagious fogs; which falling in the land Have every pelting river made so proud . . . . . . *M. N. Dream* ii 1 90
Falling out that year on Ash-Wednesday was four year *Mer. of Venice* ii 5 26
Let me see; what think you of falling in love? . . *As Y. Like It* i 2 27
Falling A lip of much contempt . . . . *W. Tale* i 2 372
Falling from a hill, he was so bruised That the pursuers took him 1 *Hen. IV.* v 5 21
Stay but a little; for my cloud of dignity Is held from falling with so weak a wind That it will quickly drop . . . 2 *Hen. IV.* iv 5 100
Gloucester stumbled; and, in falling, Struck me . *Richard III.* i 4 18
Press not a falling man too far! 'tis virtue: His faults lie open *Hen. VIII.* iii 2 333
These are stars indeed; And sometimes falling ones . . . . iv 1 55
'Tis a cruelty To load a falling man . . . . . . v 3 77
She'll none of him; they two are twain.—Falling in, after falling out, may make them three . . . . *Troi. and Cres.* iii 1 112
Shall dizzy with more clamour Neptune's ear In his descent than shall my prompted sword Falling on Diomed . . . . . v 2 176
Manhood is call'd foolery, when it stands Against a falling fabric *Coriol.* iii 1 247
He hath the falling sickness.—No, Cæsar hath it not; but you and I And honest Casca, we have the falling sickness . . *J. Cæsar* i 2 256
There o'ertook in's rouse; There falling out at tennis . *Hamlet* ii 1 59
When one so great begins to rage, he's hunted Even to falling *A. and C.* iv 1 8
Whose top to climb Is certain falling, or so slippery that The fear's as bad as falling . . . . *Cymbeline* iii 3 48
Struck down Some mortally, some slightly touch'd, some falling Merely through fear . . . . v 3 10
Falling-from. Mere want of gold, and the falling-from of his friends, drove him into this melancholy . . . *T. of Athens* iv 3 401
Falling-off. O Hamlet, what a falling-off was there! . . *Hamlet* i 5 47
Fallow. How does your fallow greyhound, sir? . . *Mer. Wives* i 1 91
That from the seedness the bare fallow brings To teeming foison *M. for M.* i 4 42
Her fallow leas The darnel, hemlock and rank fumitory Doth root upon . . . . *Hen. V.* v 2 44
As our vineyards, fallows, meads and hedges, Defective in their natures, grow to wildness . . . . v 2 54
Falorous. A marvellous falorous gentleman, that is certain . . iii 2 81
False. Sweet lord, you play me false.—No, my dear'st love . *Tempest* v 1 172
Already have I been false to Valentine And now I must be as unjust to Thurio . . . . *T. G. of Ver.* iv 2 1
He plays false, father.—How? out of tune on the strings?—Not so; but yet so false that he grieves my very heart-strings . . . iv 2 59
Hie you home to bed. Thou subtle, perjured, false, disloyal man! . iv 2 95
But she is dead.—'Twere false, if I should speak it . . . . iv 2 107
I do despise a liar as I do despise one that is false, or as I despise one that is not true . . . . *Mer. Wives* i 1 70
Is this true, Pistol?—No; it is false, if it is a pick-purse . . i 1 163
As for you, Say what you can, my false o'erweighs your true *M. for M.* ii 4 170
Volumes of report Run with these false and most contrarious quests . iv 1 62
Let your reason serve To make the truth appear where it seems hid, And hide the false seems true . . . . v 1 67
To speak, as from his mouth, what he doth know Is true and false v 1 156
My blood is mingled with the crime of lust: For if we two be one and thou play false, I do digest the poison of thy flesh *Com. of Errors* ii 2 144
Dissembling villain, thou speak'st false in both.—Dissembling harlot, thou art false in all . . . . iv 4 103
Thy master and his man are here, And that is false thou dost report to us v 1 179
So befall my soul As this is false he burthens me withal! . . v 1 209
So help me Heaven! And this is false you burden me withal . . v 1 268
I'll be sworn, if he be so, his conceit is false . . . *Much Ado* ii 1 309
Go we near her, that her ear lose nothing Of the false sweet bait . iii 1 33
But if all aim but this be levell'd false . . . . . iv 1 239
False; we have given thee faces.—But you have out-faced them all *L. L. Lost* v 2 625
We to ourselves prove false, By being once false for ever to be true . v 2 782
Of thy misprision must perforce ensue Some true love turn'd and not a false turn'd true . . . . *M. N. Dream* iii 2 91
I swear by that which I will lose for thee, To prove him false that says I love thee not . . . . iii 2 253
I am much afeard my lady his mother played false with a smith *M. of V.* i 2 48
How many cowards, whose hearts are all as false As stairs of sand! . iii 2 83
Go, get thee gone, thou false deluding slave . . . *T. of Shrew* iv 3 31
The story then goes false . . . . . . *All's Well* v 3 229
Words are grown so false, I am loath to prove reason with them *T. N.* iii 1 28
Were they false As o'er-dyed blacks, as wind, as waters, false As dice *W. T.* i 2 131
Every dram of woman's flesh is false, If she be . . . ii 1 138
I am false of heart that way . . . . iv 3 116
How if it be false, son?—If it be ne'er so false, a true gentleman may swear it in the behalf of his friend . . . . . v 2 174
If she did play false, the fault was hers . . . *K. John* i 1 118
As true as I believe you think them false . . . . iii 1 27
But this from rumour's tongue I idly heard; if true or false I know not iv 2 124
Whose tongue soe'er speaks false, Not truly speaks; who speaks not truly, lies . . . . iv 3 91
Why should I then be false, since it is true That I must die here and live hence by truth? . . . . v 4 28
On pain to be found false and recreant . . . *Richard II.* i 3 106
Show me thy humble heart, and not thy knee, Whose duty is deceiveable and false . . . . ii 3 84
I say, thou liest, And will maintain what thou hast said is false . iv 1 27
As false, by heaven, as heaven itself is true . . . . iv 1 64
I'll be a brave judge.—Thou judgest false already . 1 *Hen. IV.* i 2 74
The complaints I hear of thee are grievous.—'Sblood, my lord, they are false . . . . ii 4 488
They bring smooth comforts false, worse than true wrongs 2 *Hen. IV.* Ind. 40
King Richard might create a perfect guess That great Northumberland, then false to him, Would of that seed grow to a greater falseness . iii 1 89
False. No prophet will I trust, if she prove false . . . 1 *Hen. VI.* i 2 150
I see report is fabulous and false . . . . ii 3 18
Unless my study and my books be false, The argument you held was wrong . . . . ii 4 56
Can this be so, That in alliance, amity and oaths, There should be found such false dissembling guile? . . . . iv 1 63
I lose, indeed; Beshrew the winners, for they play'd me false! 2 *Hen. VI.* iii 1 184
Ah, that my fear were false! ah, that it were! . . . . iii 1 193
Is the hour to come That e'er I proved thee false or fear'd thy faith . iii 1 205
Am I not witch'd like her? or thou not false like him? . . . iii 2 119
If my suspect be false, forgive me, God . . . . . iii 2 139
I would, false murderous coward, on thy knee Make thee beg pardon . iii 2 220
The false revolting Normans thorough thee Disdain to call us lord . iv 1 87
By her he had two children at one birth.—That's false . . iv 2 148
If King Edward be as true and just As I am subtle, false *Richard III.* i 1 37
I fear me both are false.—Then never man was true . . . i 2 195
False, fleeting, perjured Clarence, That stabb'd me in the field by Tewksbury . . . . i 4 55
Slander myself as false to Edward's bed . . . . . iv 4 207
You have no cause to hold my friendship doubtful: I never was nor never will be false . . . . iv 4 494
False to his children or his wife's allies . . . . . v 1 15
My surveyor is false; the o'er-great cardinal Hath show'd him gold *Hen. VIII.* i 1 222
Let him in nought be trusted, For speaking false in that . . ii 4 136
This, and all else This talking lord can lay upon my credit, I answer is most false . . . . iii 2 266
Prophet may you be! If I be false, or swerve a hair from truth *T. and C.* iii 2 191
Yet let memory, From false to false, among false maids in love, Upbraid my falsehood! . . . . iii 2 197
As false As air, as water, wind, or sandy earth, As fox to lamb . iii 2 198
'Yea,' let them say, to stick the heart of falsehood, 'As false as Cressid' iii 2 203
If ever you prove false one to another . . . . . iii 2 206
You'll be so true to him, to be false to him . . . . iv 2 58
Would you have me False to my nature? . . . . *Coriolanus* iii 2 15
Yet, if thou swear'st, Thou mayst prove false . . . *Rom. and Jul.* ii 2 92
He is a kinsman to the Montague; Affection makes him false; he speaks not true . . . . iii 1 182
For each true word, a blister! and each false Be as a cauterizing to the root o' the tongue, Consuming it with speaking! . *T. of Athens* v 1 135
Cannot, is false, and that I dare not, falser . . . *J. Cæsar* ii 2 63
The strings, my lord, are false.—He thinks he still is at his instrument iv 3 292
Wouldst not play false, And yet wouldst wrongly win . *Macbeth* i 5 22
I grant him bloody, Luxurious, avaricious, false, deceitful . iv 3 58
If thou speak'st false, Upon the next tree shalt thou hang alive . v 5 38
To thine own self be true, And it must follow, as the night the day, Thou canst not then be false to any man . . . *Hamlet* i 3 80
Makes marriage-vows As false as dicers' oaths . . . . iii 4 45
False of heart, light of ear, bloody of hand; hog in sloth . *Lear* iii 4 95
True or false, it hath made thee earl of Gloucester . . . . iii 5 18
Cunning.—And false.—Where hast thou sent the king? . . . iii 7 49
False to thy gods, thy brother, and thy father . . . . v 3 134
He hath a person and a smooth dispose To be suspected, framed to make women false . . . . *Othello* i 3 404
Such things in a false disloyal knave Are tricks of custom . . iii 3 121
Utter my thoughts? Why, say they are vile and false? . . . iii 3 136
If she be false, O, then heaven mocks itself! I'll not believe't . iii 3 278
Ha! ha! false to me?—Why, how now, general! no more of that . iii 3 333
Swear thou art honest.—Heaven doth truly know it.—Heaven truly knows that thou art false as hell.—To whom, my lord? with whom? how am I false?—O Desdemona! away! away! . . . . iv 2 39
She was false as water.—Thou art rash as fire, to say That she was false v 2 134
That she was false to wedlock?—Ay, with Cassio . . . . v 2 142
My husband say that she was false!—He, woman; I say thy husband . v 2 152
He says thou told'st him that his wife was false: I know thou didst not v 2 173
But did you ever tell him she was false?—I did.—You told a lie . v 2 178
She false with Cassio!—did you say with Cassio?—With Cassio, mistress v 2 182
Why should I think you can be mine and true, Though you in swearing shake the throned gods, Who have been false to Fulvia? *A. and C.* i 3 29
A mighty strength they carry.—Where have you this? 'tis false . ii 1 18
Ah, let be, let be! thou art The armourer of my heart: false, false; this, this . . . . iv 4 7
And I the truer, So to be false with her . . . . *Cymbeline* i 5 44
A father cruel, and a step-dame false; A foolish suitor to a wedded lady i 6 1
'Tis gold Which buys admittance; oft it doth; yea, and makes Diana's rangers false themselves . . . . ii 3 74
O, above measure false! . . . . ii 4 113
False to his bed! What is it to be false? To lie in watch there and to think on him? . . . that's false to's bed, is it? . . . . iii 4 42
True honest men being heard, like false Æneas, Were in his time thought false . . . . iii 4 61
Wilt lay the leaven on all proper men; Goodly and gallant shall be false and perjured From thy great fail . . . . . . iii 4 65
Grant, heavens, that which I fear Prove false! . . . . iii 5 53
For true to thee Were to prove false, which I will never be, To him that is most true . . . . iii 5 164
I'ld change my sex to be companion with them, Since Leonatus's false iii 6 89
Dream often so, And never false . . . . iv 2 353
Wherein I am false I am honest; not true, to be true . . . iv 3 42
If it be true that I interpret false, Then were it certain . . *Pericles* i 1 124
False accusation. The lady is dead upon mine and my master's false accusation . . . . *Much Ado* v 1 249
I doubt not then but innocence shall make False accusation blush *W. Tale* iii 2 32
False accuse. By false accuse doth level at my life . 2 *Hen. VI.* iii 1 160
False accusers. The envious slanders of her false accusers *Richard III.* i 3 26
False Æneas. True honest men being heard, like false Æneas, Were in his time thought false . . . . *Cymbeline* iii 4 60
False aim. O you leaden messengers, That ride upon the violent speed of fire, Fly with false aim . . . . *All's Well* iii 2 113
False allegations to o'erthrow his state . . . . 2 *Hen. VI.* iii 1 181
False aspect. It mourns that painting and usurping hair Should ravish doters with a false aspect . . . . *L. L. Lost* iv 3 260
False blood to false blood join'd! gone to be friends! . *K. John* iii 1 2
Be men like blasted woods, And may diseases lick up their false bloods! And so farewell and thrive . . . . *T. of Athens* iv 3 539
False-boding woman, end thy frantic curse . . . *Richard III.* i 3 247
False brother. In my false brother Awaked an evil nature . . *Tempest* i 2 92
False caterpillars. All scholars, lawyers, courtiers, gentlemen, They call false caterpillars . . . . 2 *Hen. VI.* iv 4 37

False Clarence. What scourge for perjury Can this dark monarchy afford false Clarence? . . . . *Richard III.* i 4 51
False coin. A noble spirit, As yours was put into you, ever casts Such doubts, as false coin, from it . . . . . *Hen. VIII.* iii 1 171
False conclusion. A false conclusion: I hate it as an unfilled can *T. N.* ii 3 6
False confederates. Joan of Arc, Nor any of his false confederates 1 *Hen. VI.* ii 2 21
False creation. A dagger of the mind, a false creation . *Macbeth* ii 1 38
False Cressid. O false Cressid! false, false, false! Let all untruths stand by thy stained name . . . . . . *Troi. and Cres.* v 2 178
False cunning. His false cunning, Not meaning to partake with me in danger, Taught him to face me out . . . . *T. Night* v 1 89
False Danish dogs. O, this is counter, you false Danish dogs! *Hamlet* iv 5 110
False-derived. Every slight and false-derived cause, Yea, every idle, nice and wanton reason . . . . 2 *Hen. IV.* iv 1 190
False dice. Once before he won it of me with false dice . *Much Ado* ii 1 290
False drop. For every false drop in her bawdy veins A Grecian's life hath sunk . . . . *Troi. and Cres.* iv 1 69
False Duke. But now return we to the false Duke Humphrey 2 *Hen. VI.* iii 1 322
False Edward. Tell false Edward, thy supposed king, That Lewis of France is sending over masquers . . . . 3 *Hen. VI.* iii 3 223
Thou and Oxford, with five thousand men, Shall cross the seas, and bid false Edward battle . . . . iii 3 235
False effect. She is fool'd With a most false effect; and I the truer, So to be false with her . . . . . . *Cymbeline* i 5 43
False exacting. So disguise shall, by the disguised, Pay with falsehood false exacting . . . . . . *Meas. for Meas.* iii 2 295
False eyes. O place and greatness! millions of false eyes Are stuck upon thee . . . . iv 1 60
But with these nails I'll pluck out these false eyes . *Com. of Errors* iv 4 107
False face. Turn thy false face, thou traitor! . . . *Troi. and Cres.* v 6 6
False face must hide what the false heart doth know . *Macbeth* i 7 82
False-faced. Let courts and cities he Made all of false-faced soothing! *Coriolanus* i 9 44
False faith. This is the day wherein I wish'd to fall By the false faith of him I trusted most . . . . . . *Richard III.* v 1 17
False favourite. Employ the countenance and grace of heaven, As a false favourite doth his prince's name, In deeds dishonourable 2 *Hen. IV.* iv 2 25
False fiend. Descend to darkness and the burning lake! False fiend, avoid! . . . . 2 *Hen. VI.* i 4 43
False finger. Though his false finger have profaned the ring *T. G. of V.* iv 4 141
False fire. The king rises.—What, frighted with false fire! . *Hamlet* iii 2 277
False forswearing. And that same vengeance doth he hurl on thee, For false forswearing and for murder too . . *Richard III.* i 4 207
False fortune. Myself could else out-frown false fortune's frown . *Lear* v 3 6
False French. Now, fie upon my false French! By mine honour, in true English, I love thee . . . . *Hen. V.* v 2 236
False Frenchwoman. 'Gainst thee, fell Clifford, and thee, false French-woman . . . . 3 *Hen. VI.* i 4 149
False friends. God keep you from them, and from such false friends!—God keep me from false friends! but they were none *Richard III.* iii 1 15
False gallop. This is the very false gallop of verses . *As Y. Like It* iii 2 119
What pace is this that thy tongue keeps?—Not a false gallop *M. Ado* iii 4 94
False gaze. 'Tis a pageant, To keep us in false gaze . . *Othello* i 3 19
False generations. Fourteen they shall not see, To bring false genera-tions . . . . *W. Tale* ii 1 148
False glass. And I for comfort have but one false glass . *Richard III.* ii 2 53
False hand. And from my false hand cut the wedding-ring *Com. of Er.* ii 2 139
False heart. Even so void is your false heart of truth . *Mer. of Venice* v 1 189
I am thy king, and thou a false-heart traitor . . . 2 *Hen. VI.* v 1 143
Methinks, false hearts should never have sound legs . *T. of Athens* i 2 240
False face must hide what the false heart doth know . *Macbeth* i 7 82
Let her beauty Look through a casement to allure false hearts And be false with them . . . . *Cymbeline* ii 4 34
False-hearted. Diomed's a false-hearted rogue . . *Troi. and Cres.* v 1 95
False hope. Who gently would dissolve the bands of life, Which false hope lingers in extremity . . . . . *Richard II.* ii 2 72
You, his false hopes, the trust of England's honour 1 *Hen. IV.* iv 4 20
False hound! If you have writ your annals true, 'tis there . *Coriolanus* v 6 113
False housewife. The false housewife Fortune . . *Ant. and Cleo.* iv 15 44
False hypocrisy. His prayers are full of false hypocrisy *Richard II.* v 3 107
False imposition. Reputation is an idle and most false imposition *Othello* ii 3 269
False intelligence. By false intelligence, or wrong surmise *Richard III.* ii 1 54
False interpreter. It will not lie where it concerns, Unless it have a false interpreter . . . . *T. G. of Ver.* i 2 78
False Italian. What false Italian, As poisonous-tongued as handed, hath prevail'd On thy too ready hearing? . . . *Cymbeline* iii 2 4
False justicer, why hast thou let her 'scape? . . . *Lear* iii 6 59
False king! why hast thou broken faith with me? . . 2 *Hen. VI.* v 1 91
False knaves. It is proved already that you are little better than false knaves . . . . *Much Ado* iv 2 24
I say to you, it is thought you are false knaves . . . . . iv 2 30
False Latin. O, I smell false Latin; dunghill for unguem . *L. L. Lost* v 1 83
False love. Muffle your false love with some show of blindness *C. of Er.* iii 2 8
Thy sly conveyance and thy lord's false love . . 3 *Hen. VI.* iii 3 160
I call'd my love false love; but what said he then? . . *Othello* iv 3 55
O most false love! Where be the sacred vials thou shouldst fill With sorrowful water? . . . . *Ant. and Cleo.* i 3 62
False maids. Yet let memory, From false to false, among false maids in love, Upbraid my falsehood! . . . . . *Troi. and Cres.* iii 2 197
False man. To show an unfelt sorrow is an office Which the false man does easy . . . . *Macbeth* ii 3 143
False masters. When your false masters eat of my lord's meat *T. of A.* iii 4 50
False Mowbray. Fetch from false Mowbray their first head *Richard II.* i 1 97
False oaths. Two villains whose false oaths prevail'd Before my perfect honour . . . . *Cymbeline* iii 3 66
False objections. As for your spiteful false objections, Prove them 2 *Hen. VI.* i 3 158
False one. 'Tis all as easy Falsely to take away a life true made As to put metal in restrained means To make a false one . *Meas. for Meas.* ii 4 49
My dear lord! Thou art one o' the false ones . . . *Cymbeline* iii 6 15
False opinion. When false opinion, whose wrong thought defiles thee, In thy just proof, repeals and reconciles thee . . . *Lear* iii 6 119
False passage. Through the false passage of thy throat, thou liest *Richard II.* i 1 125
False peer. Back'd by the power of Warwick, that false peer 3 *Hen. VI.* i 1 52
False perjury. Persuade my heart to this false perjury . . *L. L. Lost* iv 3 62
False persuaded. I should be false persuaded I had daughters *Lear* i 4 254
False Plantagenet. Where false Plantagenet dare not be seen 1 *Hen. VI.* i 4 74
False-played. She, Eros, has Pack'd cards with Cæsar, and false-play'd my glory . . . . *Ant. and Cleo.* iv 14 19
False priest. Impious Beaufort, that false priest . . . 2 *Hen. VI.* ii 4 53
False prints. And credulous to false prints . . . *Meas. for Meas.* ii 4 130
False professors. Woe upon ye And all such false professors! *Hen. VIII.* iii 1 115
False Proteus. I would have been a breakfast to the beast, Rather than have false Proteus rescue me . . . . . *T. G. of Ver.* v 4 35
I do detest false perjured Proteus . . . . v 4 39
False quarrel. In a false quarrel there is no true valour . . *Much Ado* v 1 120
False reckonings. The oath of a lover is no stronger than the word of a tapster; they are both the confirmer of false reckonings *As Y. L. It* iii 4 35
False report. They have committed false report . . . *Much Ado* v 1 219
I'll fill these dogged spies with false reports . . . *K. John* iv 1 129
Stuffing the ears of men with false reports . . . 2 *Hen. IV.* Ind. 8
And yet my mind gave me his clothes made a false report of him *Coriol.* iv 5 157
I have adventured To try your taking of a false report . . *Cymbeline* i 6 173
False seeming. And tie the wiser souls To thy false seeming! *M. for M.* ii 4 15
False shadows. He takes false shadows for true substances *T. Andron.* iii 2 80
False shapes. Your falsehood shall become you well To worship shadows and adore false shapes . . . . *T. G. of Ver.* iv 2 131
False sorrow. More's not seen; Or if it be, 'tis with false sorrow's eye *Richard II.* ii 2 26
False soul. O this false soul of Egypt! this grave charm *Ant. and Cleo.* iv 12 25
False speaking. My first false speaking Was this upon myself *Macbeth* iv 3 130
False spirits. My false spirits Quail to remember . . . *Cymbeline* v 5 148
False sport. They have conjoin'd all three To fashion this false sport, in spite of me . . . . *M. N. Dream* iii 2 194
False steward. The false steward, that stole his master's daughter *Ham.* iv 5 172
False strains. Wilt thou love such a woman? What, to make thee an instrument and play false strains upon thee! . . *As Y. Like It* iv 3 68
False struck. And mine ear, Therein false struck, can take no greater wound, Nor tent to bottom that . . . . . *Cymbeline* iii 4 117
False Suffolk. What dares not Warwick, if false Suffolk dare him? 2 *Hen. VI.* iii 2 203
From such fell serpents as false Suffolk is . . . . . . iii 2 266
False teachers. Thus may poor fools Believe false teachers . *Cymbeline* iii 4 87
False thanes. Then fly, false thanes, And mingle with the English epicures . . . . *Macbeth* v 3 7
False thief. The true prince may, for recreation sake, prove a false thief 1 *Hen. IV.* i 2 174
Nay, rather let me have it, as you are a false thief . . . . ii 1 103
False times. You should have fear'd false times when you did feast *T. of Athens* iv 3 520
False title. Crack the lawyer's voice, That he may never more false title plead . . . . iv 3 154
False trail. How cheerfully on the false trail they cry! . . *Hamlet* iv 5 109
False traitor. Unless I prove false traitor to myself *T. G. of Ver.* iv 4 110
Like a false traitor and injurious villain . . . *Richard II.* i 1 91
To warn false traitors from the like attempts . . *Richard III.* iii 5 49
False transgression. Her true perfection, or my false transgression *T. G. of Ver.* ii 4 197
False Troyan. When the false Troyan under sail was seen *M. N. Dream* i 1 174
False uncle. Thy false uncle—Dost thou attend me? . . *Tempest* i 2 77
False vantage. I slew him manfully in fight, Without false vantage or base treachery . . . . *T. G. of Ver.* iv 1 29
False villain. That false villain Whom I employ'd was pre-employ'd by him *W. Tale* ii 1 48
False vows. Slink all away, leave their false vows with him, Like empty purses pick'd . . . . *T. of Athens* iv 2 11
False way. With wisdom I might fear, my Doricles, You woo'd me the false way . . . . *W. Tale* iv 4 151
I am well acquainted with your manner of wrenching the true cause the false way . . . . 2 *Hen. IV.* ii 1 121
False wench. He loved me—O false wench!—Give't me again *T. and C.* v 2 70
False witness. I shall not want false witness to condemn me 2 *Hen. VI.* iii 1 168
False woman. See the hell of having a false woman! . *Mer. Wives* ii 2 305
And ne'er was Agamemnon's brother wrong'd By that false woman, as this king by thee . . . . 3 *Hen. VI.* ii 2 149
Let all constant men be Troiluses, all false women Cressids *Tr. and Cr.* iii 2 211
False world. I am sick of this false world . . *T. of Athens* iv 3 376
Falsehood. A falsehood in its contrary as great As my trust was *Tempest* i 2 95
Falsehood, cowardice and poor descent, Three things that women highly hold in hate . . . . *T. G. of Ver.* iii 2 32
When I protest true loyalty to her, She twits me with my falsehood to my friend . . . . iv 2 8
Your falsehood shall become you well To worship shadows . . iv 2 130
So disguise shall, by the disguised, Pay with falsehood false exacting *Meas. for Meas.* iii 2 295
No man that hath a name, By falsehood and corruption doth it shame *Com. of Errors* iii 1 113
I shall be forsworn, which is a great argument of falsehood, if I love *L. L. Lost* i 2 175
Even that falsehood, in itself a sin, Thus purifies itself and turns to grace v 2 785
O, what a goodly outside falsehood hath! . . *Mer. of Venice* i 3 103
Mine integrity Being counted falsehood . . . . . *W. Tale* iii 2 28
There is no truth at all i' the oracle: The sessions shall proceed: this is mere falsehood . . . . iii 2 142
This day, all things begun come to ill end, Yea, faith itself to hollow falsehood change! . . . . *K. John* iii 1 95
Falsehood falsehood cures, as fire cools fire . . . . . iii 1 277
I will turn thy falsehood to thy heart, Where it was forged *Richard II.* iv 1 39
As truly as a man of falsehood may . . . . . 1 *Hen. IV.* ii 1 71
Whiles thy consuming canker eats his falsehood . . 1 *Hen. VI.* ii 4 71
Have we not lost most part of all the towns, By treason, falsehood? . v 4 109
Can Oxford, that did ever fence the right, Now buckler falsehood with a pedigree? . . . . 3 *Hen. VI.* iii 3 99
Either betray'd by falsehood of his guard Or by his foe surprised . iv 4 8
Dally not before your king; Lest he that is the supreme King of kings Confound your hidden falsehood . . . . . *Richard III.* ii 1 14
If it be known to him That I gainsay my deed, how may he wound, And worthily, my falsehood! . . . . *Hen. VIII.* ii 4 97
Yet let memory, From false to false, among false maids in love, Upbraid my falsehood! . . . . *Troi. and Cres.* iii 2 198
'Yea,' let them say, to stick the heart of falsehood, 'As false as Cressid' iii 2 202
Make Cressid's name the very crown of falsehood, If ever she leave Troilus! . . . . iv 2 106
When the devout religion of mine eye Maintains such falsehood, then turn tears to fires! . . . . *Rom. and Jul.* i 2 94
If you suspect my husbandry or falsehood, Call me before the exactest auditors And set me on the proof . . . . *T. of Athens* ii 2 164

Falsehood. Your bait of falsehood takes this carp of truth . *Hamlet* ii 1 63
Excellent falsehood! Why did he marry Fulvia, and not love her? *Ant. and Cleo.* i 1 40
Join gripes with hands Made hard with hourly falsehood—falsehood, as With labour . *Cymbeline* i 6 107
Falsehood Is worse in kings than beggars . . . . iii 6 13
Bitter torture shall Winnow the truth from falsehood . . v 5 134
Falsely. Ay, or very falsely pocket up his report . *Tempest* ii 1 67
'Tis all as easy Falsely to take away a life true made As to put metal in restrained means To make a false one . *Meas. for Meas.* ii 4 47
It is proved my Lady Hero hath been falsely accused . *Much Ado* v 2 99
While truth the while Doth falsely blind the eyesight of his look *L. L. L.* i 1 76
How can that be true love which is falsely attempted? . . . i 2 177
Thou speak'st it falsely, as I love mine honour *All's Well* v 3 113
Standing on slippers, which his nimble haste Had falsely thrust upon contrary feet . *K. John* iv 2 198
Most falsely doth he lie . *Richard II.* i 1 68
God is my witness, I am falsely accused by the villain . 2 *Hen. VI.* i 3 192
You do me shameful injury, Falsely to draw me in these vile suspects *Richard III.* i 3 89
A base foul stone, made precious by the foil Of England's chair, where he is falsely set . v 3 251
Laid falsely I' the plain way of his merit . *Coriolanus* iii 1 60
That so his sickness, age and impotence Was falsely borne in hand *Ham.* ii 2 67
Now I find I had suborn'd the witness, And he's indicted falsely *Oth.* iii 4 154
O, falsely, falsely murder'd!—Alas, what cry is that? . v 2 117
Falseness. Would of that seed grow to a greater falseness . 2 *Hen. IV.* iii 1 90
Falseness cannot come from thee; for thou look'st Modest as Justice *Per.* v 1 121
Falser. I am falser than vows made in wine . *As Y. Like It* iii 5 73
Cannot, is false, and that I dare not, falser: I will not come to-day *J. C.* ii 2 63
Falsify. By how much better than my word I am, By so much shall I falsify men's hopes . 1 *Hen. IV.* i 2 235
Falsing. Nay, not sure, in a thing falsing . *Com. of Errors* ii 2 95
Falstaff. If he were twenty Sir John Falstaffs, he shall not abuse Robert Shallow . *Mer. Wives* i 1 3
If Sir John Falstaff have committed disparagements unto you, I am of the church, and will be glad to do my benevolence . i 1 31
And the hardest voice of her behaviour, to be Englished rightly, is, 'I am Sir John Falstaff's' . i 3 53
Falstaff will learn the humour of the age . i 3 92
And I to Ford shall eke unfold How Falstaff, varlet vile, His dove will prove . i 3 106
Thine own true knight, By day or night, Or any kind of light, With all his might For thee to fight, JOHN FALSTAFF . ii 1 19
My name is Nym and Falstaff loves your wife . ii 1 139
I will look further into't: and I have a disguise to sound Falstaff . ii 1 246
I will prevent this, detect my wife, be revenged on Falstaff . ii 2 326
What do you call your knight's name, sirrah?—Sir John Falstaff . iii 2 22
And now she's going to my wife, and Falstaff's boy with her . iii 2 37
And my assurance bids me search: there I shall find Falstaff . iii 2 47
For it is as positive as the earth is firm that Falstaff is there . iii 2 50
I will to my honest knight Falstaff, and drink canary with him . iii 2 89
What, Sir John Falstaff! Are these your letters, knight? . iii 3 147
My husband hath some special suspicion of Falstaff's being here . iii 3 200
We will yet have more tricks with Falstaff . iii 3 203
I must of another errand to Sir John Falstaff from my two mistresses . iii 4 114
This is our device; That Falstaff at that oak shall meet with us . iv 4 42
Upon a sudden, As Falstaff, she and I, are newly met . iv 4 52
I come to speak with Sir John Falstaff from Master Slender . iv 5 5
Fat Falstaff Hath a great scene: the image of the jest I'll show you here iv 6 16
My husband will not rejoice so much at the abuse of Falstaff as he will chafe at the doctor's marrying my daughter . v 3 9
Obscured lights; which, at the very instant of Falstaff's and our meeting, they will at once display to the night . v 3 16
Falstaff's a knave, a cuckoldly knave; here are his horns . v 5 114
Falstaff, serve Got, and leave your desires, and fairies will not pinse you v 5 136
Falstaff, Bardolph, Peto and Gadshill shall rob those men . 1 *Hen. IV.* i 2 181
I have removed Falstaff's horse, and he frets like a gummed velvet . ii 2 2
Falstaff sweats to death, And lards the lean earth as he walks along . ii 2 115
I am no proud Jack, like Falstaff, but a Corinthian, a lad of mettle . ii 4 12
To drive away the time till Falstaff come . ii 4 31
Falstaff and the rest of the thieves are at the door . ii 4 98
Call in Falstaff: I'll play Percy, and that damned brawn shall play Dame Mortimer his wife . ii 4 122
And, Falstaff, you carried your guts away as nimbly . ii 4 285
How came Falstaff's sword so hack'd?—Why, he hacked it with his dagger . ii 4 335
Now I remember me, his name is Falstaff . ii 4 468
There is virtue in that Falstaff: him keep with, the rest banish . ii 4 473
Abominable misleader of youth, Falstaff, that old white-bearded Satan ii 4 509
But for sweet Jack Falstaff, kind Jack Falstaff, true Jack Falstaff, valiant Jack Falstaff, and therefore more valiant, being, as he is, old Jack Falstaff . ii 4 522
I have much to say in the behalf of that Falstaff . ii 4 532
Falstaff!—Fast asleep behind the arras, and snorting like a horse . ii 4 577
And what should poor Jack Falstaff do in the days of villany? . iii 3 187
If I be not Jack Falstaff, then am I a Jack . v 4 142
What's he that goes there?—Falstaff an't please your lordship 2 *Hen. IV.* i 2 67
Sir John Falstaff!—Boy, tell him I am deaf . i 2 76
My lord would speak with you.—Sir John Falstaff, a word with you . i 2 105
Snare, we must arrest Sir John Falstaff.—Yea, good Master Snare . ii 1 9
Thou thinkest me as far in the devil's book as thou and Falstaff . ii 2 49
You have been so lewd and so much engraffed to Falstaff . ii 2 67
Here comes Bardolph.—And the boy that I gave Falstaff . ii 2 75
Look you how he writes.—'John Falstaff, knight' . ii 2 118
JACK FALSTAFF with my familiars, JOHN with my brothers and sisters . ii 2 143
How might we see Falstaff bestow himself to-night in his true colours? ii 2 186
Knocking at the taverns, And asking every one for Sir John Falstaff . ii 4 389
Give me my sword and cloak. Falstaff, good night . ii 4 395
Then was Jack Falstaff, now Sir John, a boy, and page to Thomas Mowbray . iii 2 28
Here come two of Sir John Falstaff's men, as I think . iii 2 59
Sir John Falstaff, a tall gentleman, by heaven, and a most gallant leader . iii 2 67
Are not you Sir John Falstaff?—As good a man as he, sir, whoe'er I am iv 3 11
I think you are Sir John Falstaff, and in that thought yield me . iv 3 18
Now, Falstaff, where have you been all this while? . iv 3 29
You must now speak Sir John Falstaff fair; Which swims against your stream of quality . v 2 33
Go, carry Sir John Falstaff to the Fleet: Take all his company along . v 5 97
Falstaff. Where, for any thing I know, Falstaff shall die of a sweat 2 *Hen. IV.* Epil. 31
For Falstaff he is dead, And we must yearn therefore . *Hen. V.* ii 3 5
He was full of jests, and gipes, and knaveries, and mocks; I have forgot his name.—Sir John Falstaff . iv 7 54
Falter under foul rebellion's arms . *Richard II.* ii 2 26
Fame. Shame hath a bastard fame, well managed . *Com. of Errors* iii 2 19
I have played the part of Lady Fame . *Much Ado* ii 1 221
Death, in guerdon of her wrongs, Gives her fame which never dies . v 3 6
So the life that died with shame Lives in death with glorious fame . v 3 8
Let fame, that all hunt after in their lives, Live register'd upon our brazen tombs . *L. L Lost* i 1 1
Too much to know is to know nought but fame . i 1 92
You are not ignorant, all-telling fame Doth noise abroad . ii 1 21
For fame's sake, for praise, an outward part, We bend to that the working of the heart . iv 1 32
Confounds thy fame as whirlwinds shake fair buds . *T. of Shrew* v 2 140
Find what you seek, That fame may cry you loud . *All's Well* ii 1 17
I have letters sent me That set him high in fame . v 3 31
Let us satisfy our eyes With the memorials and the things of fame That do renown this city . *T. Night* iii 3 23
That very envy and the tongue of loss Cried fame and honour on him . v 1 62
I am in good name and fame with the very best . 2 *Hen. IV.* ii 4 82
I in the clear sky of fame o'ershine you . iv 3 56
The heavens thee guard and keep, most royal imp of fame! . v 5 46
To fill King Edward's fame with prisoner kings . *Hen. V.* i 2 162
Sword and shield, In bloody field, Doth win immortal fame . iii 2 11
I would give all my fame for a pot of ale and safety . iii 2 13
The king's a bawcock, and a heart of gold, A lad of life, an imp of fame iv 1 45
How much he wrongs his fame, Despairing of his own arm's fortitude! 1 *Hen. VI.* ii 1 16
Pardon my abuse: I find thou art no less than fame hath bruited . ii 3 68
Or else reproach be Talbot's greatest fame! . iii 2 76
His fame lives in the world, his shame in you . iv 4 46
My death's revenge, thy youth, and England's fame . iv 6 39
To save a paltry life and slay bright fame . iv 6 45
Shameful is this league! Fatal this marriage, cancelling your fame! 2 *Hen. VI.* i 1 99
In cruelty will I seek out my fame . v 2 60
Fame, late entering at his heedful ears . 3 *Hen. VI.* iii 3 63
My meed hath got me fame . iv 8 38
So that, betwixt their titles and low names, There's nothing differs but the outward fame . *Richard III.* i 4 83
I say, without characters, fame lives long . iii 1 81
Death makes no conquest of this conqueror; For now he lives in fame . iii 1 88
And many moe of noble fame and worth . iv 5 13
Having heard by fame Of this so noble and so fair assembly *Hen. VIII.* i 4 66
Shall star-like rise, as great in fame as she was, And so stand fix'd . v 5 47
Having his ear full of his airy fame, Grows dainty of his worth *T. and C.* i 3 144
As free, as debonair, unarm'd, As bending angels; that's their fame in peace . i 3 236
But what the repining enemy commends, That breath fame blows . i 3 244
And fame in time to come canonize us . ii 2 202
When fame shall in our islands sound her trump . iii 3 210
I see my reputation is at stake; My fame is shrewdly gored . iii 3 228
On whose bright crest Fame with her loud'st Oyes Cries 'This is he' . iv 5 143
Fail fame; honour or go or stay; My major vow lies here, this I'll obey v 1 48
Fame, at the which he aims, In whom already he's well graced, can not Better be held nor more attain'd than by A place below the first *Cor.* i 1 267
Was pleased to let him seek danger where he was like to find fame . i 3 14
Not Afric owns a serpent I abhor More than thy fame and envy . i 8 4
Within Corioli gates: where he hath won, With fame, a name to Caius Marcius . ii 1 181
The book of his good acts, whence men have read His fame unparallel'd v 2 16
Holp to reap the fame Which he did end all his . v 6 36
The man is noble and his fame folds-in This orb o' the earth . v 6 126
My noble lord and father, live in fame! . *T. Andron.* i 1 158
Outlive thy father's days, And fame's eternal date, for virtue's praise! i 1 168
Welcome, nephews, from successful wars, You that survive, and you that sleep in fame! . i 1 173
Here none but soldiers and Rome's servitors Repose in fame . i 1 353
He lives in fame that died in virtue's cause . i 1 390
The emperor's court is like the house of Fame, The palace full of tongues, of eyes, and ears . ii 1 126
For a fantasy and trick of fame, Go to their graves like beds . *Hamlet* iv 4 61
Set a double varnish on the fame The Frenchman gave you . iv 7 133
A maid That paragons description and wild fame . *Othello* ii 1 62
He you hurt is of great fame in Cyprus And great affinity . iii 1 48
So is the fame . *Ant. and Cleo.* ii 2 166
First Or last, your fine Egyptian cookery Shall have the fame . ii 6 65
Better to leave undone, than by our deed Acquire too high a fame when him we serve's away . iii 1 15
Besides what hotter hours, Unregister'd in vulgar fame . iii 13 119
The toil o' the war, A pain that only seems to seek out danger I' the name of fame and honour . *Cymbeline* iii 3 51
Fame answering the most strange inquire . *Pericles* iii Gower 22
The heavens, Through you, increase our wonder and set up Your fame for ever . iii 2 98
When fame Had spread their cursed deed . v 3 Gower 95
Famed. He was much famed . *All's Well* i 2 71
Evenly derived From his most famed of famous ancestors . *Hen. V.* ii 4 92
Though buried in your dunghills, They shall be famed . iv 3 100
As famous and as bold in war As he is famed for mildness, peace, and prayer . 3 *Hen. VI.* ii 1 156
Your grace hath still been famed for virtuous; And now may seem as wise . iv 6 26
Famed be thy tutor, and thy parts of nature Thrice famed *Troi. and Cres.* ii 3 253
When went there by an age, since the great flood, But it was famed with more than with one man? . *J. Cæsar* i 2 153
The famed Cassibelan, who was once at point—O giglot fortune!—to master Cæsar's sword . *Cymbeline* iii 1 30
Familiar. It is a familiar beast to man, and signifies love . *Mer. Wives* i 1 21
I can construe the action of her familiar style . i 3 51
'Tis my familiar sin With maids to seem the lapwing and to jest *M. for M.* i 4 31
Meantime let wonder seem familiar . *Much Ado* v 4 70
By a familiar demonstration of the working, my tough senior *L. L. Lost* i 2 9
Love is a familiar; Love is a devil: there is no evil angel but Love . i 2 177
The king is a noble gentleman, and my familiar . v 1 101
To make modern and familiar, things supernatural and causeless *All's W.* ii 3 2
Quenching my familiar smile with an austere regard of control *T. Night* ii 5 73

Familiar. To dive into their hearts With humble and familiar courtesy *Richard II.* i 4 26
As familiar with me as my dog; and he holds his place . . 2 *Hen. IV.* ii 2 115
JACK FALSTAFF with my familiars, JOHN with my brothers and sisters ii 2 144
May be As things acquainted and familiar to us . . . . v 2 139
The Gordian knot of it he will unloose, Familiar as his garter *Hen. V.* i 1 47
He is bred out of that bloody strain That haunted us in our familiar paths . . . . ii 4 52
As familiar with men's pockets as their gloves or their handkerchers . iii 2 51
And for the world, familiar to us and unknown . . . . iii 7 40
Our names, Familiar in his mouth as household words . . . iv 3 52
I think her old familiar is asleep . . . . . . 1 *Hen. VI.* iii 2 122
Now, ye familiar spirits, that are cull'd Out of the powerful regions under earth, Help me this once . . . . . v 3 10
Away with him! he has a familiar under his tongue . 2 *Hen. VI.* iv 7 114
Made tame and most familiar to my nature . . *Troi. and Cres.* iii 3 10
I do not strain at the position,—It is familiar,—but at the author's drift iii 3 113
Yea, so familiar!—She will sing any man at first sight . . . v 2 8
That we have been familiar, Ingrate forgetfulness shall poison *Coriolanus* v 2 91
Too familiar Is my dear son with such sour company *Rom. and Jul.* iii 3 6
So his familiars to his buried fortunes Slink all away . *T. of Athens* iv 2 10
Blood and destruction shall be so in use And dreadful objects so familiar That mothers shall but smile . . . . . *J. Cæsar* iii 1 266
Not with such familiar instances, Not with such free and friendly conference . . . . iv 2 16
Direness, familiar to my slaughterous thoughts, Cannot once start me *Macbeth* v 5 14
Be thou familiar, but by no means vulgar . . . . *Hamlet* i 3 61
I never shall endure her: dear my lord, Be not familiar with her *Lear* v 1 16
To abuse Othello's ear That he is too familiar with his wife . . *Othello* i 3 402
Good wine is a good familiar creature, if it be well used . . . ii 3 313
To let a fellow that will take rewards And say 'God quit you!' be familiar with My playfellow, your hand! . . . *Ant. and Cleo.* iii 13 124
I thank him, makes no stranger of me; we are familiar at first *Cymbeline* i 4 112
I have surely seen him: His favour is familiar to me . . . v 5 93
Made familiar To me and to my aid the blest infusions That dwell in vegetives, in metals, stones . . . . . . *Pericles* iii 2 34
Familiarity. I hope, upon familiarity will grow more contempt *M. Wives* i 1 257
When I have held familiarity with fresher clothes . . *All's Well* v 2 3
Their familiarity, Which was as gross as ever touch'd conjecture *W. Tale* ii 1 175
To be no more so familiarity with such poor people . . 2 *Hen. IV.* ii 1 108
Familiarly. I familiarly sometimes Do use you for my fool *Com. of Errors* ii 2 26
Here's a large mouth, indeed, That . . . Talks as familiarly of roaring lions As maids of thirteen do of puppy-dogs! . . . *K. John* ii 1 459
And talks as familiarly of John a Gaunt as if he had been sworn brother to him . . . . 2 *Hen. IV.* iii 2 344
The king, that calls your beauteous daughter wife, Familiarly shall call thy Dorset brother . . . . . . *Richard III.* iv 4 316
Family. On your family's old monument Hang mournful epitaphs *M. Ado* iv 1 208
Come they of noble family? Why, so didst thou . . *Hen. V.* ii 2 129
Here in the parliament Let us assail the family of York . 3 *Hen. VI.* i 1 65
To advance Thy name and honourable family . . . *T. Andron.* i 1 239
Confederates in the deed That hath dishonour'd all our family . . i 1 345
I'll find a day to massacre them all And raze their faction and their family . . . . i 1 451
Signior, is all your family within?—Are your doors lock'd? . *Othello* i 1 84
Famine. A' was the very genius of famine . . 2 *Hen. IV.* iii 2 337
Should famine, sword and fire Crouch for employment . *Hen. V.* Prol. 7
My three attendants, Lean famine, quartering steel, and climbing fire 1 *Hen. VI.* iv 2 11
O, I am slain! famine and no other hath slain me . 2 *Hen. VI.* iv 10 64
I, that never feared any, am vanquished by famine, not by valour . iv 10 81
Famine is in thy cheeks, Need and oppression starveth in thine eyes, Contempt and beggary hangs upon thy back . *Rom. and Jul.* v 1 69
Here let them lie Till famine and the ague eat them up . *Macbeth* v 5 4
Upon the next tree shalt thou hang alive, Till famine cling thee . v 5 40
E'en as the o'erflowing Nilus presageth famine . *Ant. and Cleo.* i 2 50
Where thou slew'st Hirtius and Pansa, consuls, at thy heel Did famine follow . . . . i 4 59
Yet famine, Ere clean it o'erthrow nature, makes it valiant *Cymbeline* iii 6 19
Famish. What, did he marry me to famish me? . *T. of Shrew* iv 3 3
Fie on myself, that have a sword, and yet am ready to famish! 2 *Hen. VI.* iv 10 2
The tide will wash you off, Or else you famish . . 3 *Hen. VI.* v 4 32
You are all resolved rather to die than to famish?—Resolved, resolved *Coriolanus* i 1 5
Suffer us to famish, and their store-houses crammed with grain . i 1 82
Some say that ravens foster forlorn children, The whilst their own birds famish in their nests . . . . *T. Andron.* ii 3 154
Set him breast-deep in earth, and famish him . . . . v 3 179
Thou wast whelped a dog, and thou shalt famish a dog's death *T. of A.* ii 2 91
Who wanteth food, and will not say he wants it, Or can conceal his hunger till he famish? . . . . *Pericles* i 4 12
Famished. I am famished in his service; you may tell every finger I have with my ribs . . . . . . *Mer. of Venice* ii 2 113
You blue-bottle rogue, you filthy famished correctioner . 2 *Hen. IV.* v 4 22
Sorry am I his numbers are so few, His soldiers sick and famish'd *Hen. V.* iii 5 57
Otherwhiles the famish'd English, like pale ghosts, Faintly besiege us one hour in a month . . . . 1 *Hen. VI.* i 2 7
For aught I see, this city must be famish'd . . . . . i 4 68
Till Paris was besieged, famish'd, and lost . . 2 *Hen. VI.* i 3 175
Took odds to combat a poor famish'd man . . . . . iv 10 47
These overweening rags of France, These famish'd beggars *Richard III.* v 3 329
And scants us with a single famish'd kiss . *Troi. and Cres.* iv 4 49
Show charity to none, But let the famish'd flesh slide from the bone, Ere thou relieve the beggar . . . . . *T. of Athens* iv 3 535
Famous. Daughter to this famous Duke of Milan . . *Tempest* v 1 192
Brought to this town by that most famous warrior, Duke Menaphon *Com. of Errors* v 1 367
He hath two, The one as famous for a scolding tongue As is the other for beauteous modesty . . . . . *T. of Shrew* i 2 254
He was famous, sir, in his profession, and it was his great right *All's Well* i 1 29
This place is famous for the creatures Of prey that keep upon't *W. Tale* iii 3 12
Fear'd by their breed and famous by their birth *Richard II.* ii 1 52
Thou hast wrought A deed of slander with thy fatal hand Upon my head and all this famous land . . . . v 6 36
Is thy name Colevile?—It is, my lord.—A famous rebel art thou, Colevile.—And a famous true subject took him . 2 *Hen. IV.* iv 3 69
Derived From his most famed of famous ancestors . *Hen. V.* ii 4 92
Your grandfather of famous memory . . . . . . iv 7 95
King Henry the Fifth, too famous to live long! . . . 1 *Hen. VI.* i 1 6

Famous. I shall as famous be by this exploit As Scythian Tomyris by Cyrus' death . . . . 1 *Hen. VI.* ii 3 5
Derived From famous Edmund Langley, Duke of York . . . . ii 5 85
We will make thee famous through the world . . . . iii 3 13
In the famous ancient city Tours . . . . . 2 *Hen. VI.* i 1 5
Somerset Hath made the wizard famous in his death . . . v 2 69
Saint Alban's battle won by famous York Shall be eternized in all age . v 3 30
Were he as famous and as bold in war As he is famed for mildness 3 *Hen. VI.* ii 1 155
Thy famous grandfather Doth live again in thee . . . . v 4 52
That Julius Cæsar was a famous man . . . *Richard III.* iii 1 84
In the seat royal of this famous isle . . . . . . iii 1 164
Famous Plantagenet, most gracious prince, Lend favourable ears . iii 7 100
With all famous colleges Almost in Christendom . . *Hen. VIII.* iii 2 66
So famous, So excellent in art, and still so rising . . . iv 2 61
I would desire My famous cousin to our Grecian tents . *Troi. and Cres.* iv 5 151
Like the famous ape, To try conclusions, in the basket creep *Hamlet* iii 4 194
Menecrates and Menas, famous pirates . . . *Ant. and Cleo.* i 4 48
No grave upon the earth shall clip in it A pair so famous . . v 2 363
Cassibelan, thine uncle,—Famous in Cæsar's praises . . *Cymbeline* iii 1 6
Yon sometimes famous princes, like thyself, Drawn by report *Pericles* i 1 34
Famously. For then this land was famously enrich'd With politic grave counsel . . . . *Richard III.* ii 3 19
I say unto you, what he hath done famously, he did it to that end *Coriol.* i 1 37
Fan. When Mistress Bridget lost the handle of her fan *Mer. Wives* ii 2 12
O, a most dainty man! To see him walk before a lady and to bear her fan! To see him kiss his hand! . . . . . *L. L. Lost* iv 1 147
And pluck the wings from painted butterflies To fan the moonbeams from his sleeping eyes . . . . . *M. N. Dream* iii 1 176
With scarfs and fans and double change of bravery . *T. of Shrew* iv 3 57
Although The air of paradise did fan the house . . *All's Well* iii 2 128
An I were now by this rascal, I could brain him with his lady's fan 1 *Hen. IV.* ii 3 25
Give me my fan: what, minion! can ye not? . . 2 *Hen. VI.* i 3 141
Distinction, with a broad and powerful fan, Puffing at all, winnows the light away . . . . *Troi. and Cres.* i 3 27
Even in the fan and wind of your fair sword . . . . v 3 41
Your enemies, with nodding of their plumes, Fan you into despair! *Cor.* iii 3 127
Peter!—Anon!—My fan, Peter.—Good Peter, to hide her face; for her fan's the fairer face . . . . . . *Rom. and Jul.* ii 4 112
Peter, take my fan, and go before, and apace . . . . ii 4 232
Where the Norweyan banners flout the sky And fan our people cold *Macb.* i 2 50
To fetch her fan, her gloves, her mask, nor nothing? . . *Othello* iv 2 9
And is become the bellows and the fan To cool a gipsy's lust *A. and C.* i 1 9
Pretty dimpled boys, like smiling Cupids, With divers-colour'd fans . ii 2 208
The love I bear him Made me to fan you thus . . . *Cymbeline* i 6 177
Fanatical. I abhor such fanatical phantasimes . . . *L. L. Lost* v 1 20
Fancy. Spirits, which by mine art I have from their confines call'd to enact My present fancies . . . . *Tempest* iv 1 122
A solemn air and the best comforter To an unsettled fancy . . v 1 59
Cannot your Grace win her to fancy him? . . . *T. G. of Ver.* iii 1 67
Stones whose rates are either rich or poor As fancy values them *Meas. for Meas.* ii 2 151
Thousand escapes of wit Make thee the father of their idle dreams And rack thee in their fancies . . . . iv 1 65
Be not angry with me, madam, Speaking my fancy . . *Much Ado* iii 1 95
There is no appearance of fancy in him, unless it be a fancy that he hath to strange disguises . . . . iii 2 31
Unless he have a fancy to this foolery, as it appears he hath, he is no fool for fancy, as you would have it appear he is . . . . iii 2 37
This child of fancy that Armado hight . . . . *L. L. Lost* i 1 171
Smelling out the odoriferous flowers of fancy, the jerks of invention . iv 2 129
Look you arm yourself To fit your fancies to your father's will *M. N. Dr.* i 1 118
Dreams and sighs, Wishes and tears, poor fancy's followers . . . i 1 155
I in fury hither follow'd them, Fair Helena in fancy following me . iv 1 168
More witnesseth than fancy's images . . . . . . v 1 25
Tell me where is fancy bred, Or in the heart or in the head? *M. of Ven.* iii 2 63
Fancy dies In the cradle where it lies. Let us all ring fancy's knell . iii 2 68
If ever,—as that ever may be near,—You meet in some fresh cheek the power of fancy . . . . *As Y. Like It* iii 5 29
Pacing through the forest, Chewing the food of sweet and bitter fancy iv 3 102
Thy faith my fancy to thee doth combine . . . . . v 4 156
Even as a flattering dream or worthless fancy . . *T. of Shrew* Ind. 1 44
I never yet beheld that special face Which I could fancy more than any other . . . . ii 1 12
O then, belike, you fancy riches more . . . . . . ii 1 16
An old hat and 'the humour of forty fancies' pricked in't . . . iii 2 70
Is't possible, friend Licio, that Mistress Bianca Doth fancy any other? iv 2 2
He's gone, and my idolatrous fancy Must sanctify his reliques *All's Well* i 1 108
Pardon, my gracious lord; for I submit My fancy to your eyes . . ii 3 175
We must every one be a man of his own fancy, not to know what we speak . . . . iv 1 20
As all impediments in fancy's course Are motives of more fancy . . v 3 214
So full of shapes is fancy That it alone is high fantastical . *T. Night* i 1 14
Our fancies are more giddy and unfirm, More longing, wavering, sooner lost and worn, Than women's are . . . . ii 4 34
Should she fancy, it should be one of my complexion . . . . ii 5 29
I am mad, or else this is a dream: Let fancy still my sense in Lethe steep! . . . . iv 1 66
Orsino's mistress and his fancy's queen . . . . . . v 1 397
This most cruel usage of your queen, Not able to produce more accusation Than your own weak-hinged fancy . . . . *W. Tale* ii 3 119
Fancies too weak for boys, too green and idle For girls of nine . . iii 2 182
Be advised.—I am, and by my fancy . . . . iv 4 493
No longer shall you gaze on't, lest your fancy May think anon it moves v 3 60
And sware they were his fancies or his good-nights . 2 *Hen. IV.* iii 2 342
Play with your fancies . . . . *Hen. V.* iii Prol. 7
Tush, that was but his fancy, blame him not . . 1 *Hen. VI.* iv 1 178
Yet so my fancy may be satisfied . . . . v 3 91
Although we fancy not the cardinal, Yet must we join with him 2 *Hen. VI.* i 3 97
Make yourself mirth with your particular fancy, And leave me out *Hen. VIII.* ii 3 101
I am most joyful, madam, such good dreams Possess your fancy . iv 2 94
I did never win of you before.—But little, Charles; Nor shall not, when my fancy's on my play . . . . v 1 60
The bless'd gods, as angry with my fancy, . . . take thee from me *Troi. and Cres.* iv 4 27
Never did young man fancy With so eternal and so fix'd a soul . . v 2 165
I have lived To see inherited my very wishes And the buildings of my fancy: only There's one thing wanting . . . *Coriolanus* ii 1 216

Fancy. Why do you keep alone, Of sorriest fancies your companions making? *Macbeth* iii 2 9
She is troubled with thick-coming fancies, That keep her from her rest v 3 38
Costly thy habit as thy purse can buy, But not express'd in fancy *Ham.* i 3 71
I knew him, Horatio: a fellow of infinite jest, of most excellent fancy . v 1 204
Three of the carriages, in faith, are very dear to fancy v 2 159
On every dream, Each buzz, each fancy, each complaint, dislike, He may enguard his dotage *Lear* i 4 348
May all the building in my fancy pluck Upon my hateful life iv 2 86
Be as your fancies teach you; Whate'er you be, I am obedient *Othello* iii 3 88
My father's eye Should hold her loathed and his spirits should hunt After new fancies iii 4 63
Let me see your eyes; Look in my face.—What horrible fancy's this iv 2 26
O'er-picturing that Venus where we see The fancy outwork nature *A. and C.* ii 2 206
Nature wants stuff To vie strange forms with fancy; yet, to imagine An Antony, were nature's piece 'gainst fancy, Condemning shadows quite v 2 98
Time that is so briefly spent With your fine fancies quaintly eche *Pericles* iii Gower 13
That he can hither come so soon, Is by your fancy's thankful doom v 2 285
Fancy-free. In maiden meditation, fancy-free *M. N. Dream* ii 1 164
Fancy-monger. If I could meet that fancy-monger, I would give him some good counsel *As Y. Like It* iii 2 382
Fancy-sick. All fancy-sick she is and pale of cheer *M. N. Dream* iii 2 96
Fane. Nor fane nor Capitol, The prayers of priests nor times of sacrifice, Embarquements all of fury *Coriolanus* i 10 20
I'll weep, and word it with thee; For notes of sorrow out of tune are worse Than priests and fanes that lie *Cymbeline* iv 2 242
Fang. Since I am a dog, beware my fangs *Mer. of Venice* iii 3 7
The icy fang And churlish chiding of the winter's wind *As Y. Like It* ii 1 6
By the very fangs of malice I swear, I am not that I play *T. Night* i 5 196
The swords of soldiers are his teeth, his fangs *K. John* ii 1 353
Master Fang, have you entered the action? 2 *Hen. IV.* ii 1 1
Good Master Fang, hold him sure: good Master Snare, let him not 'scape ii 1 27
Master Fang and Master Snare, do me, do me, do me your offices ii 1 44
Destruction fang mankind! *T. of Athens* iv 3 23
In his anointed flesh stick boarish fangs *Lear* iii 7 58
Fanged. My two schoolfellows, Whom I will trust as I will adders fang'd *Hamlet* iii 4 203
Fangled. Be not, as is our fangled world, a garment Nobler than that it covers *Cymbeline* v 4 134
Fangless. His power, like to a fangless lion, May offer, but not hold 2 *Hen. IV.* iv 1 218
Fanned. High Taurus' snow, Fann'd with the eastern wind *M. N. Dream* iii 2 142
Or the fann'd snow that's bolted By the northern blasts twice o'er *W. T.* iv 4 375
Fanning. With silken streamers the young Phœbus fanning *Hen. V.* iii Prol. 6
To turn the sun to ice with fanning in his face with a peacock's feather iv 1 212
Fantasied. I find the people strangely fantasied *K. John* iv 2 144
Fantastic. To be fantastic may become a youth Of greater time than I shall show to be *T. G. of Ver.* ii 7 47
But man, proud man, . . . Plays such fantastic tricks before high heaven As make the angels weep *Meas. for Meas.* ii 2 121
Or wallow naked in December snow By thinking on fantastic summer's heat *Richard II.* i 3 299
Who hath done to-day Mad and fantastic execution *Troi. and Cres.* v 5 38
There with fantastic garlands did she come Of crow-flowers, nettles *Ham.* iv 7 169
Fantastical. This is fery fantastical humours and jealousies *Mer. Wives* iii 3 181
It was a mad fantastical trick *Meas. for Meas.* iii 2 98
The old fantastical duke of dark corners iv 3 164
Hot and hasty, like a Scotch jig, and full as fantastical *Much Ado* ii 1 79
His words are a very fantastical banquet, just so many strange dishes ii 3 22
The schoolmaster is exceeding fantastical; too too vain *L. L. Lost* v 2 532
Fantastical, apish, shallow, inconstant *As Y. Like It* iii 2 431
Ne'er a fantastical knave of them all shall flout me out of my calling iii 3 108
So full of shapes is fancy That it alone is high fantastical *T. Night* i 1 15
He seems to be the more noble in being fantastical *W. Tale* iv 4 779
Are ye fantastical, or that indeed Which outwardly ye show? *Macbeth* i 3 53
My thought, whose murder yet is but fantastical, Shakes so my single state of man i 3 139
Bragging and telling her fantastical lies *Othello* ii 1 226
Fantastically. Like a forked radish, with a head fantastically carved upon it with a knife 2 *Hen. IV.* iii 2 334
She is so idly king'd, Her sceptre so fantastically borne By a vain, giddy, shallow, humorous youth *Hen. V.* ii 4 27
Fantasticoes. Such antic, lisping, affecting fantasticoes *Rom. and Jul.* ii 4 30
Fantasy. Raise up the organs of her fantasy *Mer. Wives* v 5 55
Fie on sinful fantasy! Fie on lust and luxury! v 5 97
Stolen the impression of her fantasy With bracelets of thy hair *M. N. Dr.* i 1 32
And make her full of hateful fantasies ii 1 258
Lovers and madmen have such seething brains, Such shaping fantasies v 1 5
How many actions most ridiculous Hast thou been drawn to by thy fantasy?—Into a thousand *As Y. Like It* ii 4 31
It [to love] is to be all made of fantasy, All made of passion v 2 100
His siege is now Against the mind, the which he pricks and wounds With many legions of strange fantasies *K. John* v 7 18
Art thou alive? Or is it fantasy that plays upon our eyesight? 1 *Hen. IV.* v 4 138
The condition of the time, Which cannot look more hideously upon me Than I have drawn it in my fantasy 2 *Hen. IV.* v 2 13
Children of an idle brain, Begot of nothing but vain fantasy *Rom. and Jul.* i 4 98
Quite from the main opinion he held once Of fantasy, of dreams *J. Cæsar* ii 1 197
Thou hast no figures nor no fantasies, Which busy care draws in the brains of men; Therefore thou sleep'st so sound ii 1 231
Things unluckily charge my fantasy: I have no will to wander forth of doors iii 3 2
Horatio says 'tis but our fantasy, And will not let belief take hold of him Touching this dreaded sight *Hamlet* i 1 23
You tremble and look pale: Is not this something more than fantasy? i 1 54
For a fantasy and trick of fame, Go to their graves like beds iv 4 61
What he will do with it Heaven knows, not I; I nothing but to please his fantasy *Othello* iii 3 299
Fap. And being fap, sir, was, as they say, cashiered *Mer. Wives* i 1 183
Far. Who is so far from Italy removed I ne'er again shall see her *Tempest* ii 1 110
His heart as far from fraud as heaven from earth *T. G. of Ver.* ii 7 78
Her chamber is aloft, far from the ground iii 1 114
I am so far from granting thy request That I despise thee for thy wrongful suit iv 2 101
He's as far from jealousy as I am from giving him cause *Mer. Wives* ii 1 107
She enlargeth her mirth so far that there is shrewd construction made of her ii 2 232
Far. To jest, Tongue far from heart *Meas. for Meas.* i 4 33
Nature dispenses with the deed so far That it becomes a virtue iii 1 135
We discovered Two ships from far making amain to us *Com. of Errors* i 1 93
Far from her nest the lapwing cries away iv 2 27
In truth, thus far I witness with him v 1 254
Thus far can I praise him; he is of a noble strain *Much Ado* ii 1 393
Were not his requests so far From reason's yielding *L. L. Lost* ii 1 150
How far dost thou excel, No thought can think, nor tongue of mortal tell iv 3 41
Thy love is far from charity, That in love's grief desirest society iv 3 127
And Phibbus' car Shall shine from far *M. N. Dream* i 2 38
Such separation as may well be said Becomes a virtuous bachelor and a maid, So far be distant ii 2 60
So far blameless proves my enterprise, That I have nointed an Athenian's eyes iii 2 350
And so far am I glad it so did sort As this their jangling I esteem a sport iii 2 352
That hatred is so far from jealousy, To sleep by hate, and fear no enmity iv 1 149
If I serve not him, I will run as far as God has any ground *Mer. of Venice* ii 2 117
Dost deserve enough; and yet enough May not extend so far as to the lady ii 7 28
How far The substance of my praise doth wrong this shadow In underprizing it, so far this shadow Doth limp behind the substance iii 2 129
You press me far, and therefore I will yield iv 1 425
And with an unthrift love did run from Venice As far as Belmont v 1 17
How far that little candle throws his beams! So shines a good deed v 1 90
Alas, what danger will it be to us, Maids as we are, to travel forth so far! Beauty provoketh thieves sooner than gold *As Y. Like It* i 3 111
Since we are stepp'd thus far in, I will continue *T. of Shrew* i 2 83
That never read so far To know the cause why music was ordain'd! iii 1 9
But then up farther, and as far as Rome; And so to Tripoli iv 2 75
Forward, I pray, since we have come so far, And be it moon, or sun iv 5 12
Whose skill was almost as great as his honesty; had it stretched so far, would have made nature immortal *All's Well* i 1 22
He did look far Into the service of the time i 2 26
Do not plunge thyself too far in anger ii 3 222
Bless him at home in peace, whilst I from far His name with zealous fervour sanctify iii 4 10
Do you think I am so far deceived in him? iii 6 6
Reposing too far in his virtue, which he hath not iii 6 15
Let me buy your friendly help thus far, Which I will over-pay and pay again iii 7 15
He hath out-villained villany so far, that the rarity redeems him iv 3 306
My suit, as I do understand, you know, And therefore know how far I may be pitied v 3 161
Yet thus far I will boldly publish her *T. Night* ii 1 29
I am now so far in offence with my niece iv 2 75
Too hot! too hot! To mingle friendship far is mingling bloods *W. Tale* i 2 109
Make your best haste, and go not Too far i' the land iii 3 11
So far that I have eyes under my service which look upon his removedness iv 2 40
Not hold thee of our blood, no, not our kin, Far than Deucalion off iv 4 442
Let him call me rogue for being so far officious iv 4 871
My lord's almost so far transported that He'll think anon it lives v 3 69
I am sorry, sir, I have thus far stirr'd you v 3 74
I'll not seek far—For him, I partly know his mind—to find thee An honourable husband v 3 141
But thou from loving England art so far, That thou hast under-wrought his lawful king *K. John* ii 1 94
Norfolk, so far as to mine enemy *Richard II.* i 3 193
Since thou hast far to go, bear not along The clogging burthen of a guilty soul i 3 199
I will ride, As far as land will let me, by your side i 3 252
How far brought you high Hereford on his way? i 4 2
Renowned for their deeds as far from home, For Christian service ii 1 53
How far is it, my lord, to Berkeley now? ii 3 1
Richard not far from hence hath hid his head iii 3 6
Your own is yours, and I am yours, and all.—So far be mine iii 3 198
Is not my arm of length, That reacheth from the restful English court As far as Calais? iv 1 13
As far as to the sepulchre of Christ 1 *Hen. IV.* i 1 19
Thou hast paid all there.—Yea, and elsewhere, so far as my coin would stretch i 2 61
Two razes of ginger, to be delivered as far as Charing-cross ii 1 27
I'll not bear mine own flesh so far afoot again for all the coin in thy father's exchequer ii 2 38
But if you go,— So far afoot, I shall be weary, love ii 3 87
And so far will I trust thee, gentle Kate.—How! so far? ii 3 115
I had rather live With cheese and garlic in a windmill, far, Than feed on cates iii 1 162
You strain too far iv 1 75
We should not step too far Till we had his assistance by the hand 2 *Hen. IV.* i 3 20
Thou thinkest me as far in the devil's book as thou and Falstaff ii 2 49
Ere you with grief had spoke and I had heard The course of it so far iv 5 143
We bear our civil swords and native fire As far as France v 5 113
So far my king and master; so much my office *Hen. V.* iii 6 144
To mope with his fat-brained followers so far out of his knowledge! iii 7 144
Since then my office hath so far prevail'd v 2 29
Thus far, with rough and all-unable pen, Our bending author hath pursued the story Epil. 1
But with a baser man of arms by far Once in contempt they would have barter'd me 1 *Hen. VI.* i 4 30
Better far, I guess, That we do make our entrance several ways ii 1 29
As far as I could well discern For smoke and dusky vapours of the night ii 2 26
As far as I could ken thy chalky cliffs 2 *Hen. VI.* iii 2 101
Far be it we should honour such as these With humble suit iv 1 123
Far be the thought of this from Henry's heart! 3 *Hen. VI.* i 1 70
Why faint you, lords? My title's good, and better far than his i 1 130
Helen of Greece was fairer far than thou ii 2 146
He cried, Like to a dismal clangor heard from far ii 3 18
Alas, you know, 'tis far from hence to France iv 1 4
Yet thus far fortune maketh us amends iv 7 2
Thus far our fortune keeps an upward course v 3 1
I had rather be a pedlar: Far be it from my heart, the thought of it! *Richard III.* i 3 150
The prince my brother hath outgrown me far.—He hath, my lord ii 1 104
Nay, for a need, thus far come near my person iii 5 85
For God he knows, and you may partly see, How far I am from the desire iii 7 236
I am in So far in blood that sin will pluck on sin iv 2 65

Far. Thus far into the bowels of the land Have we march'd on without impediment *Richard III.* v 2 3
How far into the morning is it? v 3 234
O, you go far *Hen. VIII.* i 1 38
His sword Hath a sharp edge: it's long and, 't may be said, It reaches far i 1 111
'Twas dangerous for him To ruminate on this so far i 2 180
As far as I see, all the good our English Have got by the late voyage i 3 5
You that thus far have come to pity me, Hear what I say ii 1 56
Yet thus far we are one in fortunes ii 1 121
How far I have proceeded, Or how far further shall, is warranted ii 4 91
I speak my good lord cardinal to this point, And thus far clear him ii 4 167
Be pleased yourself to say How far you satisfied me ii 4 211
Your late censure Both of his truth and him, which was too far iii 1 65
Far from his succour, from the king, from all That might have mercy iii 2 261
Press not a falling man too far! 'tis virtue: His faults lie open to the laws iii 2 333
More miseries and greater far Than my weak-hearted enemies dare offer iii 2 389
Let's dry our eyes: and thus far hear me, Cromwell iii 2 431
Yet thus far, Griffith, give me leave to speak him, And yet with charity iv 2 32
Have broken with the king; who hath so far Given ear to our complaint v 1 47
Did my commission Bid ye so far forget yourselves? v 3 142
Thus far, My most dread sovereign, may it like your grace To let my tongue excuse all v 3 147
When I might see from far some forty truncheoners v 4 54
That we come short of our suppose so far *Troi. and Cres.* i 3 11
No man lesser fears the Greeks than I As far as toucheth my particular ii 2 9
She is as far high-soaring o'er thy praises iv 4 126
Go to them, with this bonnet in thy hand; And thus far having stretch'd it—here be with them—Thy knee bussing the stones *Coriolanus* iii 2 74
So far As thou hast power and person iii 2 85
As far as doth the Capitol exceed The meanest house in Rome, so far my son . . . does exceed you all iv 2 39
Let me have war, say I; it exceeds peace as far as day does night iv 5 237
He hath spices of them all, not all, For I dare so far free him iv 7 47
Is she not then beholding to the man That brought her for this high good turn so far? *T. Andron.* i 1 397
O, what a sympathy of woe is this, As far from help as Limbo is from bliss! iii 1 149
Not far, one Muli lives, my countryman iv 2 152
So secret and so close, So far from sounding and discovery *Rom. and Jul.* i 1 156
Wert thou as far As that vast shore wash'd with the farthest sea, I would adventure for such merchandise ii 2 82
More fierce and more inexorable far Than empty tigers or the roaring sea v 3 38
And thus far I confirm you *T. of Athens* i 2 98
I am so far already in your gifts,— So are we all i 2 177
Will you befriend me so far, as to use mine own words to him? iii 2 64
As I took note of the place, it cannot be far where he abides v 1 2
And I will set this foot of mine as far As who goes farthest *J. Cæsar* i 3 119
His means, If he improve them, may well stretch so far As to annoy us all ii 1 159
Shall Cæsar send a lie? Have I in conquest stretch'd mine arm so far? ii 2 66
Far from this country Pindarus shall run, Where never Roman shall take note of him v 3 49
How far is't call'd to Forres? What are these So wither'd? *Macbeth* i 3 39
Is't far you ride?—As far, my lord, as will fill up the time 'Twixt this and supper iii 1 24
I am in blood Stepp'd in so far that, should I wade no more, Returning were as tedious as go o'er iii 4 137
Yet so far hath discretion fought with nature *Hamlet* i 2 5
If he says he loves you, It fits your wisdom so far to believe it As he in his particular act and place May give his saying deed i 3 25
Drinking, fencing, swearing, quarrelling, Drabbing: you may go so far ii 1 26
But, woe is me, you are so sick of late, So far from cheer iii 2 174
And for my means, I'll husband them so well, They shall go far with little iv 5 139
So far he topp'd my thought, That I, in forgery of shapes and tricks, Come short of what he did iv 7 89
Her obsequies have been as far enlarged As we have warranty v 1 249
Let my disclaiming from a purposed evil Free me so far v 2 253
Whose nature is so far from doing harms, That he suspects none *Lear* i 2 196
Well, you may fear too far.—Safer than trust too far i 4 351
How far your eyes may pierce I cannot tell: Striving to better, oft we mar what's well i 4 368
Let him fly far: Not in this land shall he remain uncaught ii 1 58
If on my credit you dare build so far ii 1 35
The Marshal of France, Monsieur La Far iv 3 10
The shrill-gorged lark so far Cannot be seen or heard iv 6 58
I am doubtful that you have been conjunct And bosom'd with her, as far as we call hers v 1 13
Methinks our pleasure might have been demanded, Ere you had spoke so far v 3 63
I'll not be far from you: do you find some occasion to anger Cassio *Oth.* ii 1 273
But, sith I am enter'd in this cause so far, . . . I will go on iii 3 411
I'll set a bourn how far to be beloved *Ant. and Cleo.* i 1 16
Tempt him not so far; I wish, forbear i 3 11
For which myself, the ignorant motive, do So far ask pardon ii 2 97
Follow the noise so far as we have quarter iv 3 22
Retire, we have engaged ourselves too far iv 7 1
You speak him far *Cymbeline* i 1 24
You must not so far prefer her 'fore ours of Italy.—Being so far provoked as I was in France, I would abate her nothing i 4 70
Only, thus far you shall answer i 4 169
Having thus far proceeded,—Unless thou think'st me devilish i 5 15
So far I read aloud: But even the very middle of my heart Is warm'd by the rest, and takes it thankfully i 6 26
A gentleman, who is as far From thy report as thou from honour i 6 145
I'll make a journey twice as far, to enjoy A second night of such sweet shortness which Was mine in Britain ii 4 43
Read, and tell me How far 'tis thither iii 2 52
How far it is To this same blessed Milford iii 2 60
Why hast thou gone so far, To be unbent when thou hast ta'en thy stand, The elected deer before thee? iii 4 110
Thus far; and so farewell.—Thanks, royal sir iii 5 1
We'll mannerly demand thee of thy story, So far as thou wilt speak it iii 6 93
Not frenzy, not Absolute madness could so far have raved iv 2 135
Pray, how far thither? 'Ods pittikins! can it be six mile yet? iv 2 292
In that he spake too far.—And thou shalt die for't v 5 309
For comfort is too far for us to expect *Pericles* i 4 59
We have heard your miseries as far as Tyre i 4 88
How far is his court distant from this shore? ii 1 111
Diana's temple is not distant far, Where you may abide till your date expire iii 4 13
But, since your kindness We have stretch'd thus far, let us beseech you v 1 55

Far and near. Have I sought every country far and near? 1 *Hen. VI.* v 4 3
His picture I will send far and near, that all the kingdom May have due note of him *Lear* ii 1 84
Far and wide. Proves thee far and wide a broad goose *Rom. and Jul.* ii 4 90
Far away. Some to discover islands far away *T. G. of Ver.* i 3 9
Far before. For coward dogs Most spend their mouths when what they seem to threaten Runs far before them *Hen. V.* ii 4 71
To make thy sepulchre And creep into it far before thy time 3 *Hen. VI.* i 1 237
Thou art so far before That swiftest wing of recompense is slow To overtake thee *Macbeth* i 4 16
Far behind his worth Comes all the praises that I now bestow *T. G. of Ver.* ii 4 71
And there's Troilus will not come far behind him *Troi. and Cres.* i 2 59
Far beneath. So far beneath your soft and tender breeding *T. Night* v 1 331
Far better. I am far better born than is the king 2 *Hen. VI.* v 1 28
Far beyond. Is far beyond a prince's delicates 3 *Hen. VI.* ii 5 51
In a sea of glory, But far beyond my depth *Hen. VIII.* iii 2 361
If it be so far beyond his health, Methinks he should the sooner pay his debts, And make a clear way to the gods *T. of Athens* iii 4 75
Far enough. She'll gallop far enough to her destruction 2 *Hen. VI.* i 3 154
Whoever the king favours, The cardinal instantly will find employment, And far enough from court too *Hen. VIII.* ii 1 49
Fly far off.—This hill is far enough *J. Cæsar* v 3 12
Far exceed. My wrath shall far exceed the love I ever bore *T. G. of Ver.* iii 1 166
This accident and flood of fortune So far exceed all instance *T. Night* iv 3 12
Far fairer. You shall be yet far fairer than you are *Ant. and Cleo.* i 2 16
Far-fet. With all his far-fet policy 2 *Hen. VI.* iii 1 293
Far forth. Know thus far forth *Tempest* i 2 177
Answer'd my affection, So far forth as herself might be her chooser *M. W.* iv 6 11
Since this bar in law makes us friends, it shall be so far forth friendly maintained *T. of Shrew* i 2 140
Answer them directly How far forth you do like their articles 2 *Hen. IV.* iv 2 53
Far gone. 'Tis far gone, When I shall gust it last *W. Tale* i 2 218
Is it not too far gone? 'Tis time to part them iv 4 354
York is too far gone with grief *Richard II.* ii 1 184
He knew me not at first; he said I was a fishmonger: he is far gone, far gone *Hamlet* ii 2 190
Far hence. How far hence is thy lord, mine honest fellow? 3 *Hen. VI.* v 1 2
They are, as all my other comforts, far hence In mine own country *Hen. VIII.* iii 1 90
Far in years. Too far in years to be a pupil now *Richard II.* i 3 171
Far more, far more to you do I decline *Com. of Errors* iii 2 44
A lady far more beautiful Than any woman in this waning age *T. of S.* Ind. 2 64
A far more glorious star thy soul will make Than Julius Cæsar 1 *Hen. VI.* i 1 55
Though far more cause, yet much less spirit to curse Abides in me *Richard III.* iv 4 196
But the brave man Holds honour far more precious-dear than life *Troi. and Cres.* v 3 28
Thou her maid art far more fair than she *Rom. and Jul.* ii 2 6
Your son-in-law is far more fair than black *Othello* i 3 291
Far off. 'Tis far off And rather like a dream than an assurance *Tempest* i 2 44
And sail so expeditious that shall catch Your royal fleet far off v 1 316
Like far-off mountains turned into clouds *M. N. Dream* iv 1 193
Near or far off, well won is still well shot *K. John* i 1 174
Your husband, he is gone to save far off, Whilst others come to make him lose at home *Richard II.* ii 2 80
How far off lies your power?—Nor near nor farther off, my gracious lord, Than this weak arm iii 2 63
The which, how far off from the mind of Bolingbroke It is iii 3 45
Better far off than near, be ne'er the near v 1 88
Or shall we sparingly show you far off The Dauphin's meaning? *Hen. V.* i 2 239
He was mild and affable, And if we did but glance a far-off look, Immediately he was upon his knee 2 *Hen. VI.* iii 1 10
Like one that stands upon a promontory, And spies a far-off shore 3 *Hen. VI.* iii 2 136
So do I wish the crown, being so far off iii 2 140
How far off is our brother Montague? v 1 4
Go, gentle Catesby, And, as it were far off, sound thou Lord Hastings *Richard III.* iii 1 170
But touch this sparingly, as 'twere far off iii 5 93
How far off lie these armies?—Within this mile and half *Coriolanus* i 4 8
Hark you, far off! There is Aufidius; list, what work he makes i 4 19
Nay, press not so upon me; stand far off.—Stand back; room *J. Cæsar* iii 2 171
Fly, therefore, noble Cassius, fly far off.—This hill is far enough v 3 11
Far off, methinks, I hear the beaten drum *Lear* iv 6 292
My music playing far off, I will betray Tawny-finn'd fishes *Ant. and Cleo.* ii 5 11
When a soldier was the theme, my name Was not far off *Cymbeline* iii 3 60
Far on. Travel you far on, or are you at the farthest? *T. of Shrew* iv 2 73
Far poorer. I have seen her die twenty times upon far poorer moment *Ant. and Cleo.* i 2 146
Far surmounts. Your presence makes us rich, most noble lord.—And far surmounts our labour to attain it *Richard II.* ii 3 64
Far surmounted. This Hector far surmounted Hannibal *L. L. Lost* v 2 677
Far surpasseth. But she as far surpasseth Sycorax As great'st does least *Tempest* iii 2 110
Far the lesser. Set limb to limb, and thou art far the lesser 2 *Hen. VI.* iv 10 50
Far too huge. And now 'tis far too huge to be blown out With that same weak wind which enkindled it *K. John* v 2 86
Far too short. Whose arm seems far too short to hit me here *Pericles* i 2 8
Far truer spoke than meant 2 *Hen. VI.* iii 1 183
That hand, which, for thy love, did kill thy love, Shall, for thy love, kill a far truer love *Richard III.* i 2 191
Far unfit. I am a subject fit to jest withal, But far unfit to be a sovereign 3 *Hen. VI.* iii 2 92
Far unworthy. By His majesty I swear, Whose far unworthy deputy I am 2 *Hen. VI.* iii 2 286
Far wide. Still, still, far wide!—He's scarce awake *Lear* iv 7 50
Far worse. Thou hast no faith left now, unless thou'dst two; And that's far worse than none *T. G. of Ver.* v 4 51
Far worser. Were my state far worser than it is, I would not wed her for a mine of gold *T. of Shrew* i 2 91
Farced. The farced title running 'fore the king *Hen. V.* iv 1 280
Fardel. There is that in this fardel will make him scratch his beard *W. Tale* iv 4 728
The condition of that fardel, the place of your dwelling, your names iv 4 739
The fardel there? what's i' the fardel? iv 4 781
There lies such secrets in this fardel and box, which none must know iv 4 783
I was by at the opening of the fardel v 2 4
I heard them talk of a fardel and I know not what v 2 125
Who would fardels bear, To grunt and sweat under a weary life? *Hamlet* iii 1 76
Fardingale. With ruffs and cuffs and fardingales *T. of Shrew* iv 3 56

Fare. Say, my spirit, How fares the king and 's followers? *Tempest* v 1 7
Untie the spell. How fares my gracious sir? v 1 253
Then to the elements Be free, and fare thou well! v 1 318
But fare thee well, most foul, most fair! farewell, Thou pure impiety! *Much Ado* iv 1 104
So will it fare with Claudio: When he shall hear she died upon his words iv 1 224
How fares your majesty?—Boyet, prepare; I will away to-night *L. L. L.* v 2 736
Give me your hand, Bassanio: fare you well! Grieve not *Mer. of Ven.* iv 1 265
How fares my noble lord?—Marry, I fare well; for here is cheer enough. Where is my wife? *T. of Shrew* Ind. 2 102
How fares my Kate? What, sweeting, all amort? iv 3 36
I must not hear thee; fare thee well, kind maid *All's Well* ii 1 148
Fare ye well at once: my bosom is full of kindness *T. Night* ii 1 40
Dear gentlewoman, How fares our gracious lady? *W. Tale* ii 2 21
How fares your majesty?—This fever, that hath troubled me so long, Lies heavy on me *K. John* v 3 2
How fares your majesty?—Poison'd,—ill fare—dead, forsook, cast off v 7 34
How fares our noble uncle, Lancaster?—What comfort, man? *Rich. II.* ii 1 71
Harry, how fares your uncle?—I had thought, my lord, to have learn'd his health of you ii 3 23
Cheerly, my lord: how fares your grace? *1 Hen. IV.* v 4 44
And food for— For worms, brave Percy: fare thee well, great heart! v 4 87
How fares your grace?—Why did you leave me here alone? *2 Hen. IV.* iv 5 50
Even like a man new haled from the rack, So fare my limbs with long imprisonment *1 Hen. VI.* ii 5 4
Art thou not weary, John? how dost thou fare? iv 6 27
Farewell, and better than I fare *2 Hen. VI.* ii 4 100
How fares my lord? Help, lords! the king is dead iii 2 33
How fares my gracious lord?—Comfort, my sovereign! iii 2 37
How fares my lord? speak, Beaufort, to thy sovereign iii 3 1
If when you make your prayers, God should be so obdurate as yourselves, How would it fare with your departed souls? iv 7 123
How fares my brother? why is he so sad? *3 Hen. VI.* ii 1 8
How now, fair lords! What fare? what news abroad? ii 1 95
This battle fares like to the morning's war ii 5 1
Let's away to London And see our gentle queen how well she fares v 5 89
How fares the prince?—Well, madam, and in health *Richard III.* ii 4 40
How fares our loving brother?—Well, my dread lord iii 1 96
How fares our cousin, noble Lord of York?—I thank you, gentle uncle iii 1 101
Mother, how fares your grace?—O Dorset, speak not to me! iv 1 38
How fares our loving mother?—I, by attorney, bless thee from thy mother v 3 82
So fare you well, my little good lord cardinal.—So farewell to the little good you bear me *Hen. VIII.* iii 2 349
Is my father well? How fares my Juliet? that I ask again *Rom. and Jul.* v 1 15
Well fare you, gentleman: give me your hand *T. of Athens* i 1 163
Fare thee well, fare thee well.—Thou art a fool to bid me farewell twice i 1 272
How fare you?—Ever at the best, hearing well of your lordship iii 6 28
Feast your ears with the music awhile, if they will fare so harshly iii 6 37
The last of all the Romans, fare thee well! *J. Cæsar* v 3 99
Fare thee well at once! The glow-worm shows the matin to be near *Hamlet* i 5 88
How fares our cousin Hamlet?—Excellent, i' faith iii 2 97
How fares my lord?—Give o'er the play.—Give me some light iii 2 278
How fares your grace?—What's he?—Who's there? *Lear* iii 4 130
Conceive, and fare thee well.—Yours in the ranks of death iv 2 24
How fares your majesty?—You do me wrong to take me out o' the grave iv 7 44
Farewell, my dearest sister, fare thee well: The elements be kind to thee, and make Thy spirits all of comfort! fare thee well *A. and C.* iii 2 39
Fare thee well, dame, whate'er becomes of me: This is a soldier's kiss iv 4 29
If you fall in the adventure, our crows shall fare the better *Cymbeline* iii 1 83
How fares my mistress?—O, get thee from my sight v 5 235
You shall fare well; you shall have the difference of all complexions *Pericles* iv 2 84

Fare thee (you) well. *Repeated often.*

Fared. So fared our father with his enemies *3 Hen. VI.* ii 1 18
Farest. How farest thou, mirror of all martial men? *1 Hen. VI.* i 4 74
How farest thou, soldier?—Well; And well am like to do *Ant. and Cleo.* ii 6 72
Farewell my wife and children!—Farewell, brother! *Tempest* i 1 64
Farewell, master; farewell, farewell!—A howling monster! ii 2 182
And now farewell Till half an hour hence iii 1 90
Julia, farewell! What, gone without a word? *T. G. of Ver.* ii 2 16
Well, farewell; I am in great haste now.—Farewell to your worship *Mer. Wives* i 4 174
Farewell, my hearts: I will to my honest knight Falstaff, and drink canary with him iii 2 88
Defend your reputation, or bid farewell to your good life for ever iii 3 127
Till then farewell, sir: she must needs go in; Her father will be angry. —Farewell, gentle mistress: farewell, Nan iii 4 96
Farewell till then: I will go lose myself And wander up and down *Com. of Errors* i 2 30
Stand I condemn'd for pride and scorn so much? Contempt, farewell! *Much Ado* iii 1 109
Farewell, Thou pure impiety and impious purity! iv 1 104
Your own good thoughts excuse me, and farewell *L. L. Lost* ii 1 176
Farewell to me, sir, and welcome to you ii 1 214
Farewell, mad wenches; you have simple wits v 2 264
Farewell, worthy lord! A heavy heart bears not a nimble tongue v 2 746
Farewell, sweet playfellow: pray thou for us *M. N. Dream* i 1 220
Farewell, thou lob of spirits; I'll be gone ii 1 16
And, farewell, friends; Thus Thisby ends: Adieu, adieu, adieu v 1 352
If I could bid the fifth welcome with so good a heart as I can bid the other four farewell, I should be glad *Mer. of Venice* i 2 141
His words were 'Farewell mistress;' nothing else ii 5 45
Cold, indeed; and labour lost: Then, farewell, heat, and welcome, frost! ii 7 75
I'll tarry no longer with you: farewell, good Signior Love *As Y. Like It* iii 2 309
Farewell, Monsieur Traveller: look you lisp and wear strange suits iv 1 33
When I make curtsy, bid me farewell Epil. 24
Farewell, sweet masters both; I must be gone *T. of Shrew* iii 1 85
Drink a health to me; For I must hence; and farewell to you all iii 2 199
I have no more to say, But bid Bianca farewell for ever and a day iv 4 97
Farewell, pretty lady: you must hold the credit of your father *All's W.* i 1 88
Little Helen, farewell: if I can remember thee, I will think of thee at court i 1 202
Farewell, young lords; these warlike principles Do not throw from you: and you, my lords, farewell ii 1 1
After them, and take a more dilated farewell ii 1 59
Farewell, fair cruelty *T. Night* i 5 307
Farewell. Farewell, dear heart, since I must needs be gone *T. Night* ii 3 109
Farewell, and take her; but direct thy feet Where thou and I henceforth may never meet v 1 171
My stay To you a charge and trouble: to save both, Farewell *W. T.* i 2 27
Let us take a ceremonious leave And loving farewell *Richard II.* i 3 51
Cousin, farewell; and, uncle, bid him so i 3 247
Farewell: what presence must not know, From where you do remain let paper show i 3 249
Then, England's ground, farewell; sweet soil, adieu! i 3 306
Would the word 'farewell' have lengthen'd hours And added years to his short banishment, He should have had a volume of farewells i 4 16
I know no cause Why I should welcome such a guest as grief, Save bidding farewell to so sweet a guest ii 2 8
Farewell: if heart's presages be not vain, We three here part that ne'er shall meet again ii 2 142
Farewell at once, for once, for all, and ever.—Well, we may meet again ii 2 148
And with a little pin Bores through his castle wall, and farewell king! iii 2 170
Farewell, thou latter spring! farewell, All-hallown summer! *1 Hen. IV.* i 2 177
Farewell, you muddy knave ii 1 106
Farewell, and stand fast ii 2 75
Say thy prayers, and farewell v 1 124
Poor Jack, farewell! I could have better spared a better man v 4 103
Pay the musicians, sirrah. Farewell, hostess; farewell, Doll *2 Hen. IV.* ii 4 404
Farewell, hostess.—I cannot kiss, that is the humour of it; but, adieu *Hen. V.* ii 3 62
Talbot, farewell; thy hour is not yet come *1 Hen. VI.* i 5 13
If he miscarry, farewell wars in France iv 3 16
Else, farewell Talbot, France, and England's honour iv 3 23
Farewell, my lord: good wishes, praise and prayers Shall Suffolk ever have of Margaret.—Farewell, sweet madam v 3 173
Lordings, farewell; and say, when I am gone, I prophesied France will be lost ere long *2 Hen. VI.* i 1 145
Farewell, good king: when I am dead and gone, May honourable peace attend thy throne! ii 3 37
And so, Sir John, farewell!—What, gone, my lord, and bid me not farewell! ii 4 84
Sheriff, farewell, and better than I fare ii 4 100
Yet now farewell; and farewell life with thee! iii 2 356
Farewell, faint-hearted and degenerate king *3 Hen. VI.* i 1 183
See how the morning opes her golden gates, And takes her farewell of the glorious sun! ii 1 22
Away, away! Once more, sweet lords, farewell ii 3 48
Now, brother king, farewell, and sit you fast iv 1 119
Now, for a while farewell iv 3 57
Farewell, my sovereign.—Farewell, my Hector, and my Troy's true hope iv 8 24
And all at once, once more a happy farewell.—Farewell, sweet lords iv 8 31
With a groan, 'O, farewell, Warwick!' v 2 47
Save yourselves; For Warwick bids you all farewell, to meet in heaven v 2 49
Farewell sour annoy! For here, I hope, begins our lasting joy v 7 45
Bid me farewell.—'Tis more than you deserve; But since you teach me how to flatter you, Imagine I have said farewell already *Richard III.* i 2 223
And so, my good lord mayor, we bid farewell iii 5 71
Farewell, good cousin; farewell, gentle friends iii 7 247
Farewell, thou woful welcomer of glory! iv 1 90
Use my babies well! So foolish sorrow bids your stones farewell iv 1 104
Be inheritor of thy desire. Farewell till soon iv 3 35
Farewell, York's wife, and queen of sad mischance iv 4 114
Farewell! I have touch'd the highest point of all my greatness *Hen. VIII.* iii 2 222
If we live thus tamely, To be thus jaded by a piece of scarlet, Farewell nobility; let his grace go forward iii 2 281
So farewell to the little good you bear me. Farewell! a long farewell, to all my greatness! iii 2 350
Farewell The hopes of court! my hopes in heaven do dwell iii 2 458
Mine eyes grow dim. Farewell, My lord. Griffith, farewell iv 2 164
If we suffer, Out of our easiness and childish pity To one man's honour, this contagious sickness, Farewell all physic v 3 27
Farewell, sweet queen.—Commend me to your niece *Troi. and Cres.* iii 1 158
Welcome ever smiles, And farewell goes out sighing iii 3 169
As many farewells as be stars in heaven iv 4 46
I will not keep my word.—Why, then, farewell v 2 98
Do come:—I shall be plagued.—Farewell till then v 2 106
Farewell, revolted fair! and, Diomed, Stand fast! v 2 186
O, farewell, dear Hector! Look, how thou diest! look, how thy eye turns pale! v 3 80
Farewell: the gods with safety stand about thee! v 3 94
A brief farewell: the beast With many heads butts me away *Coriolanus* iv 1 1
Farewell, my wife, my mother: I'll do well yet iv 1 20
When I am forth, Bid me farewell, and smile iv 1 50
And let Andronicus Make this his latest farewell to their souls *T. Andron.* i 1 149
Farewell, my sons: see that you make her sure ii 3 187
Now, farewell, flattery: die, Andronicus iii 1 254
Farewell, Andronicus, my noble father, The woful'st man that ever lived iii 1 289
Farewell, proud Rome; till Lucius come again, He leaves his pledges dearer than his life iii 1 291
Farewell, Lavinia, my noble sister; O, would thou wert as thou tofore hast been! iii 1 293
Bid him farewell; commit him to the grave v 3 170
Farewell, my coz.—Soft! I will go along *Rom. and Jul.* i 1 201
Farewell: thou canst not teach me to forget i 1 243
But farewell compliment! Dost thou love me? I know thou wilt say 'Ay' ii 2 89
Farewell, ancient lady; farewell, 'lady, lady, lady'.—Marry, farewell! ii 4 150
Farewell; be trusty, and I'll quit thy pains: Farewell; commend me to thy mistress ii 4 204
Hie to high fortune! Honest nurse, farewell ii 5 80
Villain am I none; Therefore farewell; I see thou know'st me not iii 1 68
Give this ring to my true knight, And bid him come to take his last farewell iii 2 143
Farewell, farewell! one kiss, and I'll descend iii 5 42
Farewell! God knows when we shall meet again iv 3 14
Live, and be prosperous: and farewell, good fellow v 3 42
Thou art a fool to bid me farewell twice.—Why, Apemantus?—Shouldst have kept one to thyself, for I mean to give thee none *T. of Athens* i 1 273
Farewell; and come with better music i 2 252
Why, farewell, Portia. We must die, Messala *J. Cæsar* iv 3 190
And whether we shall meet again I know not. Therefore our everlasting farewell take v 1 116
For ever, and for ever, farewell, Cassius! If we do meet again, why, we shall smile; If not, why then, this parting was well made v 1 117

Farewell. For ever, and for ever, farewell, Brutus! If we do meet again, we'll smile indeed *J. Cæsar* v 1 120
Farewell to you; and you; and you, Volumnius v 5 31
Fare you well, my lord.—Farewell, good Strato. Cæsar, now be still v 5 50
Ne'er shook hands, nor bade farewell to him, Till he unseam'd him from the nave to the chaps *Macbeth* i 2 21
Lay it to thy heart, and farewell i 5 15
Farewell, father.—God's benison go with you! ii 4 39
O, farewell, honest soldier: Who hath relieved you? *Hamlet* i 1 16
Farewell, and let your haste commend your duty i 2 39
We doubt it nothing: heartily farewell i 2 41
Farewell: my blessing season this in thee! i 3 81
Farewell, Ophelia; and remember well What I have said to you i 3 84
A foolish figure; But farewell it, for I will use no art ii 2 99
Get thee to a nunnery, go: farewell iii 1 142
Thou wretched, rash, intruding fool, farewell! iii 4 31
But, come; for England! Farewell, dear mother iv 3 51
Sweets to the sweet: farewell! v 1 266
Bid them farewell, Cordelia, though unkind: Thou losest here, a better where to find *Lear* i 1 263
Bid farewell to your sisters i 1 270
I will not trouble thee, my child; farewell: We'll no more meet ii 4 222
Go thou farther off; Bid me farewell, and let me hear thee going iv 6 31
Farewell; for I must leave you *Othello* i 1 145
Farewell, farewell: If more thou dost perceive, let me know more iii 3 238
O, now, for ever Farewell the tranquil mind! farewell content! iii 3 348
Farewell the plumed troop, and the big wars, That make ambition virtue! iii 3 349
Farewell the neighing steed, and the shrill trump, The spirit-stirring drum! iii 3 351
Farewell! Othello's occupation's gone! iii 3 357
Seek no colour for your going, But bid farewell, and go *Ant. and Cleo.* i 3 33
Let Neptune hear we bid a loud farewell To these great fellows ii 7 139
Good fortune, worthy soldier; and farewell iii 2 22
Farewell, my dearest sister, fare thee well: The elements be kind to thee! iii 2 39
Let all the number of the stars give light To thy fair way!—Farewell, farewell! iii 2 66
My emperor, let me say, Before I strike this bloody stroke, farewell.—'Tis said, man; and farewell.—Farewell, great chief iv 14 91
Farewell, kind Charmian; Iras, long farewell v 2 295
We must take a short farewell, Lest, being miss'd, I be suspected *Cymb.* iii 4 188
Farewell; you're angry.—Still going? v 3 63
Loath to bid farewell, we take our leaves *Pericles* ii 5 13
Lay the babe Upon the pillow: hie thee, whiles I say A priestly farewell iii 1 70
Farewell *T. G. of Ver.* iv 2; iv 4; *M. Wives* ii 1; iv 1; *M. for M.* ii 1; iii 1; iii 2; *Much Ado* ii 3; iv 1; v 1; *Mer. of Venice* i 1; ii 3; ii 5; *As Y. Like It* i 1; ii 6; iii 3; *T. of Shrew* i 1; *All's Well* i 1; ii 1; ii 5; iii 6; *T. N.* ii 1; ii 3; ii 4; ii 5; *W. T.* ii 3; iii 3; iv 4; *K. John* i 1; iii 3; *Richard II.* i 2; i 3; ii 1; ii 4; iii 1; v 3; 1 *Hen. IV.* i 2; i 3; iv 2; *Hen. V.* ii 3; iv 3; 1 *Hen. VI.* i 1; i 3; 2 *Hen. VI.* iv 4; iv 10; *Rich. III.* i 1; ii 4; iv 5; v 3; *Hen. VIII.* i 1; ii 1; *T. and C.* ii 1; iv 5; v 7; *Coriol.* i 2; i 3; iv 4; iv 6; *T. And.* v 2; *R. and J.* iii 3; iii 4; iii 5; iv 1; v 1; *T. of Athens* iv 3; *J. Cæsar* i 2; i 3; iv 3; v 5; *Macbeth* iii 1; *Hamlet* i 2; i 3; ii 1; iii 1; iv 6; *Lear* iii 7; iv 6; *Othello* i 3; ii 1; iii 3; v 2; *Ant. and Cleo.* i 4; ii 4; iii 2; v 2; *Cymbeline* iv 2; *Pericles* i 1
And (so) farewell *T. G. of Ver.* i 1; *Much Ado* iv 1; *L. L. Lost* i 2; *Mer. of Venice* ii 3; iii 4; *T. of Shrew* i 1; ii 1; iv 2; *All's Well* i 1; *K. John* iv 2; 1 *Hen. IV.* ii 4; iv 3; iv 4; 2 *Hen. IV.* ii 2; 1 *Hen. VI.* ii 4; ii 5; iii 3; v 3; 2 *Hen. VI.* ii 4; iv 5; *Richard III.* iv 4; *Coriolanus* i 5; *T. of Athens* iv 3; *Lear* i 1; ii 1; *Othello* i 1; *Cymb.* iii 5; *Pericles* i 1

Farm. At my farm I have a hundred milch-kine to the pail *T. of Shrew* ii 1 358
We are inforced to farm our royal realm *Richard II.* i 4 45
Like to a tenement or pelting farm ii 1 60
The Earl of Wiltshire hath the realm in farm ii 1 256
I will sell my dukedom, To buy a slobbery and a dirty farm In that nook-shotten isle of Albion *Hen. V.* iii 5 13
Thou wouldst think I had sold my farm to buy my crown v 2 129
Let me be no assistant for a state, But keep a farm and carters *Hamlet* ii 2 167
To pay five ducats, five, I would not farm it iv 4 20
Low farms, Poor pelting villages, sheep-cotes, and mills *Lear* ii 3 17

Farmer. This fellow I remember, Since once he play'd a farmer's eldest son *T. of Shrew* Ind. 1 84
Not half so great a blow to hear As will a chestnut in a farmer's fire i 2 210
Here's a farmer, that hanged himself on the expectation of plenty *Macb.* ii 3 5
Thou hast seen a farmer's dog bark at a beggar? *Lear* iv 6 158

Farm-house. I will bring thee where Mistress Anne Page is, at a farm-house a-feasting *Mer. Wives* ii 3 91

Farrow. Pour in sow's blood, that hath eaten Her nine farrow *Macbeth* iv 1 65

Farther. 'Tis time I should inform thee farther *Tempest* i 2 23
Sit down; For thou must now know farther i 2 33
And have you nuns no farther privileges? *Meas. for Meas.* i 4 1
Let me hear you speak farther iii 1 212
I will disparage her no farther till you are my witnesses *Much Ado* iii 2 131
Let me go no farther to mine answer: do you hear me v 1 236
Importune me no farther, For how I firmly am resolved you know *T. of S.* i 1 48
Such wind as scatters young men through the world To seek their fortunes farther than at home i 2 51
But then up farther, and as far as Rome; And so to Tripoli, if God lend me life iv 2 75
Than when I feel and see her no farther trust her *W. Tale* ii 1 136
I'll queen it no inch farther, But milk my ewes and weep iv 4 460
I have thus far stirr'd you: but I could afflict you farther v 3 75
Forage, and run To meet displeasure farther from the doors *K. John* v 1 60
I know you wise, but yet no farther wise Than Harry Percy's wife 1 *Hen. IV.* ii 3 110
The scambling and unquiet time Did push it out of farther question *Hen. V.* i 1 5
I love you: then if you urge me farther than to say 'do you in faith?' I wear out my suit v 2 131
Whither away?—No farther than the Tower *Richard III.* iv 1 8
Have mind upon your health, tempt me no farther *J. Cæsar* iv 3 36
Come on.—No farther, sir; a man may rot even here *Lear* v 2 8
Pray you, stand farther from me.—What's the matter? *Ant. and Cleo.* i 3 18
Since the torch is out, Lie down, and stray no farther iv 14 47

Farther means. Use no farther means, But with all brief and plain conveniency Let me have judgement *Mer. of Venice* iv 1 81

Farther off. Why, what did I? I did nothing. I'll go farther off *Temp.* iii 2 81
Now, forward with your tale. Prithee, stand farther off iii 2 92
How far off lies your power?—Nor near nor farther off, my gracious lord, Than this weak arm *Richard II.* iii 2 64

Farther off. Can I do this, and cannot get a crown? Tut, were it farther off, I'll pluck it down 3 *Hen. VI.* iii 2 195
Go thou farther off; Bid me farewell, and let me hear thee going *Lear* iv 6 30

Farthest. Spring come to you at the farthest In the very end of harvest! *Tempest* iv 1 114
Why art thou here, Come from the farthest steppe of India? *M. N. Dream* ii 1 69
That supper be ready at the farthest by five of the clock *Mer. of Venice* ii 2 122
Travel you far on, or are you at the farthest?—Sir, at the farthest for a week or two: But then up farther *T. of Shrew* iv 2 73
Brother-in-law was the farthest off you could have been to him *W. Tale* iv 4 722
Take my king's defiance from my mouth, The farthest limit of my embassy *K. John* i 1 22
Wert thou as far As that vast shore wash'd with the farthest sea *R. and J.* ii 2 83
And I will set this foot of mine as far As who goes farthest *J. Cæsar* i 3 120
Prove such a wife As my thoughts make thee, and as my farthest band Shall pass on thy approof *Ant. and Cleo.* iii 2 26

Farthing. Remuneration! O, that's the Latin word for three farthings *L. L. Lost* iii 1 138
What is a remuneration?—Marry, sir, halfpenny farthing iii 1 149
Better than remuneration, a 'leven-pence farthing better iii 1 172
Lest men should say 'Look, where three-farthings goes!' *K. John* i 1 143

Farthingale. What compass will you wear your farthingale? *T. G. of Ver.* ii 7 51
And make water against a gentlewoman's farthingale iv 4 42
In a semi-circled farthingale *Mer. Wives* iii 3 69

Fartuous. She's as fartuous a civil modest wife ii 2 100

Fas. Sit fas aut nefas, till I find the stream To cool this heat *T. Andron.* ii 1 133

Fashion. In the same fashion as you gave in charge *Tempest* v 1 8
What fashion, madam, shall I make your breeches?— ... Why even what fashion thou best likest *T. G. of Ver.* ii 7 49
I have forgot to court; Besides, the fashion of the time is changed iii 1 86
How shall I fashion me to wear a cloak? iii 1 135
Let go that rude uncivil touch, Thou friend of an ill fashion! v 4 61
'Tis no the fashion of France; it is not jealous in France *Mer. Wives* iii 3 183
I love your daughter In such a righteous fashion iii 4 83
The pretty babes, That mourn'd for fashion, ignorant what to fear *Com. of Errors* i 1 74
Know my aspect And fashion your demeanour to my looks ii 2 33
The fineness of the gold and chargeful fashion iv 1 29
He wears his faith but as the fashion of his hat *Much Ado* i 1 76
The fashion of the world is to avoid cost, and you encounter it i 1 97
It better fits my blood to be disdained of all than to fashion a carriage to rob love from any i 3 30
What fashion will you wear the garland of? ii 1 195
I would fain have it a match, and I doubt not but to fashion it ii 1 384
In the mean time I will so fashion the matter that Hero shall be absent ii 2 47
Lie ten nights awake, carving the fashion of a new doublet ii 3 18
To be so odd and from all fashions As Beatrice is, cannot be commendable iii 1 72
Thou knowest that the fashion of a doublet, or a hat, or a cloak, is nothing to a man.—Yes, it is apparel.—I mean, the fashion.—Yes, the fashion is the fashion iii 3 125
But seest thou not what a deformed thief this fashion is? iii 3 132
I see that the fashion wears out more apparel than the man iii 3 148
Art not thou thyself giddy with the fashion too, that thou hast shifted out of thy tale into telling me of the fashion? iii 3 150
Your gown's a most rare fashion, i' faith iii 4 15
For a fine, quaint, graceful and excellent fashion, yours is worth ten on't iii 4 23
Doubt not but success Will fashion the event in better shape iv 1 237
A man in all the world's new fashion planted *L. L. Lost* i 1 165
A most illustrious wight, A man of fire-new words, fashion's own knight i 1 179
Untrained, or rather, unlettered, or ratherest, unconfirmed fashion iv 2 19
I heard your guilty rhymes, observed your fashion iv 3 139
Her favour turns the fashion of the days, For native blood is counted painting now iv 3 262
And therefore met your loves In their own fashion, like a merriment v 2 794
They have conjoin'd all three To fashion this false sport *M. N. Dream* iii 2 194
This reasoning is not in the fashion to choose me a husband *Mer. of Ven.* i 2 23
Thou but lead'st this fashion of thy malice To the last hour of act iv 1 18
As I remember, Adam, it was upon this fashion *As Y. Like It* i 1 2
'Tis just the fashion ii 1 56
Thou art not for the fashion of these times, Where none will sweat but for promotion ii 3 59
This shepherd's passion Is much upon my fashion ii 4 62
But yet, for fashion sake, I thank you too for your society iii 2 271
It is not the fashion to see the lady the epilogue Epil. 1
You must not look so sour.—It is my fashion, when I see a crab *T. of S.* ii 1 230
I like it not: Old fashions please me best iii 1 80
Infected with the fashions, full of windgalls, sped with spavins iii 2 53
'Tis some odd humour pricks him to this fashion iii 2 74
You bid me make it orderly and well, According to the fashion and the time iv 3 95
Here is the note of the fashion to testify iv 3 130
Virginity, like an old courtier, wears her cap out of fashion *All's Well* i 1 170
Whose constancies Expire before their fashions i 2 63
Why dost thou garter up thy arms o' this fashion? ii 3 265
A fashion she detests *T. Night* ii 5 220
And he went Still in this fashion, colour, ornament, For him I imitate iii 4 417
The child-bed privilege denied, which 'longs To women of all fashion *W. Tale* iii 2 105
Report of fashions in proud Italy *Richard II.* ii 1 21
Where you and Douglas and our powers at once, As I will fashion it, shall happily meet 1 *Hen. IV.* i 3 297
Yea, two and two, Newgate fashion iii 3 104
By my troth, this is the old fashion; you two never meet but you fall to some discord 2 *Hen. IV.* ii 4 60
A' came ever in the rearward of the fashion iii 2 340
In continual laughter the wearing out of six fashions, which is four terms v 1 89
I will deeply put the fashion on And wear it in my heart v 2 52
God forbid, my dear and faithful lord, That you should fashion, wrest, or bow your reading *Hen. V.* i 2 14
Though it appear a little out of fashion, There is much care and valour iv 1 85
Dat it is not be de fashion pour les ladies of France v 2 284
It is not a fashion for the maids in France to kiss before they are married v 2 289
You and I cannot be confined within the weak list of a country's fashion v 2 296
For upholding the nice fashion of your country in denying me a kiss v 2 299
I scorn thee and thy fashion, peevish boy 1 *Hen. VI.* ii 4 76
Is this the guise, Is this the fashion in the court of England? 2 *Hen. VI.* i 3 46
I'll be at charges for a looking-glass, And entertain some score or two of tailors, To study fashions to adorn my body *Richard III.* i 2 258
By heaven, I will, Or let me lose the fashion of a man! *Hen. VIII.* iv 2 159
In this fashion, All our abilities, gifts, natures, shapes *Troi. and Cres.* i 3 178

Fashion. An all men were o' my mind,— Wit would be out of fashion *Troi. and Cres.* ii 3 226
Quite out of fashion, like a rusty mail In monumental mockery . . iii 3 152
'Be thou true,' say I, to fashion in My sequent protestation . . . iv 4 67
Still, wars and lechery; nothing else holds fashion . . . . v 2 196
Let's hence, and hear How the dispatch is made, and in what fashion, More than his singularity, he goes Upon this present action *Coriol.* i 1 281
Gibingly, ungravely, he did fashion After the inveterate hate he bears you ii 3 233
Set a fair fashion on our entertainment . . . . *T. of Athens* i 2 152
He will, after his sour fashion, tell you What hath proceeded *J. Cæsar* i 2 180
Men may construe things after their fashion, Clean from the purpose of the things themselves . . . . i 3 34
Since the quarrel Will bear no colour for the thing he is, Fashion it thus ii 1 30
Send him but hither, and I'll fashion him . . . . ii 1 220
Imitations, Which, out of use and staled by other men, Begin his fashion iv 1 39
Saucy fellow, hence!—Bear with him, Brutus; 'tis his fashion . . iv 3 135
Slaying is the word; It is a deed in fashion . . . . . . v 5 5
Hold it a fashion and a toy in blood . . . . *Hamlet* i 3 6
He hath importuned me with love In honourable fashion.—Ay, fashion you may call it; go to, go to . . . . i 3 111
These are now the fashion, and so berattle the common stages . . ii 2 357
The appurtenance of welcome is fashion and ceremony . . . . . ii 2 389
The glass of fashion and the mould of form, The observed of all observers iii 1 161
Whereon his brains still beating puts him thus From fashion of himself iii 1 183
Dost thou think Alexander looked o' this fashion i' the earth? . . v 1 219
All with me's meet that I can fashion fit . . . . . . *Lear* i 2 200
Is it the fashion, that discarded fathers Should have thus little mercy on their flesh? Judicious punishment! . . . . iii 4 74
I do not like the fashion of your garments . . . . . . iii 6 84
I prattle out of fashion, and I dote In mine own comforts *Othello* ii 1 208
Which I will fashion to fall out between twelve and one . . . iv 2 242
Let's do it after the high Roman fashion . . . . *Ant. and Cleo.* iv 15 87
Poor I am stale, a garment out of fashion . . . . *Cymbeline* iii 4 53
I will begin The fashion, less without and more within . . . v 1 33
Yes, indeed shall you, and taste gentlemen of all fashions . *Pericles* iv 2 84
Fashionable. Time is like a fashionable host That slightly shakes his parting guest by the hand . . . . *Troi. and Cres.* iii 3 165
To promise is most courtly and fashionable . . . *T. of Athens* v 1 29
Fashioned. Here's a paper written in his hand, A halting sonnet of his own pure brain, Fashion'd to Beatrice . . . . *Much Ado* v 4 88
Sway'd and fashion'd by the hand of heaven . . . *Mer. of Venice* i 3 94
For putting on so new a fashion'd robe . . . . . *K. John* iv 2 27
That metal, that self mould, that fashion'd thee Made him a man *Rich. II.* i 2 23
He was the mark and glass, copy and book, That fashion'd others *2 Hen. IV.* ii 3 32
And fashion'd thee that instrument of ill . . . . *1 Hen. VI.* iii 3 65
All men's honours Lie like one lump before him, to be fashion'd Into what pitch he please . . . . *Hen. VIII.* ii 2 49
Undoubtedly Was fashion'd to much honour from his cradle . . . iv 2 50
And nature, as it grows again toward earth, Is fashion'd for the journey, dull and heavy . . . . *T. of Athens* ii 2 228
Fashioning them like Pharaoh's soldiers in the reechy painting *Much Ado* iii 3 142
Fashioning our humours Even to the opposed end of our intents *L. L. Lost* v 2 767
Fashion-monger. These fashion-mongers, these perdona-mi's, who stand so much on the new form . . . . *Rom. and Jul.* ii 4 34
Fashion-monging. Scambling, out-facing, fashion-monging boys *M. Ado* v 1 94
Fast. Stand fast, good Fate, to his hanging . . . . *Tempest* i 1 32
Where thou didst vent thy groans As fast as mill-wheels strike . . i 2 281
To fast, like one that takes diet . . . . . *T. G. of Ver.* ii 1 25
Have punish'd me With bitter fasts, with penitential groans . . . ii 4 131
Now can I break my fast, dine, sup and sleep, Upon the very naked name of love . . . . ii 4 141
Sir Valentine, whither away so fast? . . . . iii 1 51
Fellows, stand fast; I see a passenger . . . . iv 1 1
Surfeit is the father of much fast . . . . *Meas. for Meas.* i 2 130
You know the lady; she is fast my wife . . . . i 2 151
With profits of the mind, study and fast . . . . i 4 61
As fast lock'd up in sleep as guiltless labour . . . . . . iv 2 69
You have no stomach having broke your fast . . *Com. of Errors* i 2 50
We that know what 'tis to fast and pray Are penitent for your default . i 2 51
She that doth fast till you come home to dinner . . . . . i 2 89
Why, how now, Dromio! where runn'st thou so fast? . . . . iii 2 72
How hast thou lost thy breath?—By running fast . . . . . iv 2 30
Bind him fast And bear him home for his recovery . . . . . v 1 40
'Tis but a three years' fast: The mind shall banquet, though the body pine . . . . *L. L. Lost* i 1 24
Barren tasks, too hard to keep, Not to see ladies, study, fast, not sleep! i 1 48
I will pronounce your sentence: you shall fast a week with bran and water . . . . i 1 303
You must suffer him to take no delight nor no penance; but a' must fast three days a week . . . . i 2 134
Villain, thou shalt fast for thy offences ere thou be pardoned . . i 2 151
Let me not be pent up, sir: I will fast, being loose.—No, sir; that were fast and loose . . . . i 2 160
Your wit's too hot, it speeds too fast, 'twill tire . . . . . ii 1 120
Whither away so fast? A true man or a thief that gallops so? . . iv 3 186
What you first did swear unto, To fast, to study, and to see no woman iv 3 292
Say, can you fast? your stomachs are too young . . . . . iv 3 294
If frosts and fasts, hard lodging and thin weeds Nip not the gaudy blossoms of your love . . . . v 2 811
Why is your cheek so pale? How chance the roses there do fade so fast?—Belike for want of rain . . . . . *M. N. Dream* i 1 129
Night's swift dragons cut the clouds full fast . . . . . . iii 2 379
The villain is much lighter-heel'd than I: I follow'd fast, but faster he did fly . . . . iii 2 416
Or is your gold and silver ewes and rams?—I cannot tell; I make it breed as fast . . . . *Mer. of Venice* i 3 97
I will make fast the doors, and gild myself With some more ducats . ii 6 49
Who comes so fast in silence of the night?—A friend . . . . v 1 25
Fast as she answers thee with frowning looks, I'll sauce her *As Y. Like It* iii 5 68
Ay, but when?—Why now; as fast as she can marry us . . . iv 1 134
As fast as you pour affection in, it runs out . . . . . . iv 1 214
We may blow our nails together, and fast it fairly out . *T. of Shrew* i 1 109
And kiss on kiss She vied so fast, protesting oath on oath . . ii 1 311
And better 'twere that both of us did fast, Since, of ourselves, ourselves are choleric . . . . iv 1 176
To-morrow 't shall be mended, And, for this night, we'll fast for company iv 1 180
Not too fast: soft, soft! . . . . *T. Night* i 5 312
Sir Robert might have eat his part in me Upon Good-Friday and ne'er broke his fast . . . . *K. John* i 1 235
Fast. Stand fast! the devil tempts thee here In likeness of a new untrimmed bride . . . . *K. John* iii 1 208
Bind the boy which you shall find with me Fast to the chair . . iv 1 5
I conjure thee but slowly; run more fast . . . . iv 2 269
He tires betimes that spurs too fast betimes . . . *Richard II.* ii 1 36
Within me grief hath kept a tedious fast . . . . ii 1 75
The pleasure that some fathers feed upon, Is my strict fast . . . ii 1 80
Though I be old, I doubt not but to ride as fast as York . . . v 2 115
Farewell, and stand fast.—Now cannot I strike him . . *1 Hen. IV.* ii 2 75
I would give a thousand pound I could run as fast as thou canst . . ii 4 163
Do pelt so fast at one another's pate . . . . *1 Hen. VI.* iii 1 82
I think the Duke of Burgundy will fast Before he'll buy again at such a rate . . . . iii 2 42
And York as fast upon your grace exclaims . . . . . . iv 4 30
I think I have you fast . . . . v 3 30
Whom we raise, We will make fast within a hallow'd verge . *2 Hen. VI.* i 4 25
Thither go these news, as fast as horse can carry them . . . . i 4 78
Whither goes Vaux so fast? what news, I prithee? . . . . . iii 2 367
With thy brave bearing should I be in love, But that thou art so fast mine enemy . . . . v 2 21
A thousand men have broke their fasts to-day, That ne'er shall dine unless thou yield the crown . . . . . *3 Hen. VI.* ii 2 127
Now, brother king, farewell, and sit you fast . . . . . iv 1 119
The gates made fast! Brother, I like not this . . . . . iv 7 10
This hand, fast wound about thy coal-black hair . . . . . v 1 54
For Warwick was a bug that fear'd us all. Now, Montague, sit fast . v 2 3
It is his policy To haste thus fast, to find us unprovided . . . v 4 63
Neighbour, well met: whither away so fast? . . . *Richard III.* ii 3 1
I would not grow so fast, Because sweet flowers are slow . . . ii 4 14
They say my uncle grew so fast That he could gnaw a crust at two hours old . . . . ii 4 27
You said that idle weeds are fast in growth: The prince my brother hath outgrown me far . . . . iii 1 103
Forbear to sleep the nights, and fast the days . . . . . . iv 4 118
Whither away so fast?—O, God save ye! . . . . . *Hen. VIII.* ii 1 1
All fast? what means this? Ho! Who waits there? Sure, you know me? v 2 3
To-morrow We must with all our main of power stand fast *Tr. and Cr.* ii 3 273
Devour'd As fast as they are made, forgot as soon As done . . . iii 3 149
And, Diomed, Stand fast, and wear a castle on thy head! . . . v 2 187
Lay hold upon him, Priam, hold him fast: He is thy crutch . . . v 3 59
If you'll stand fast, we'll beat them to their wives . . . *Coriolanus* i 4 41
Whither do you follow your eyes so fast? . . . . ii 1 109
Stand fast; We have as many friends as enemies . . . . . iii 1 231
With wine and feeding, we have suppler souls Than in our priest-like fasts . . . . v 1 56
Who is this? my niece, that flies away so fast! . . . *T. Andron.* ii 4 11
Is he sure bound? look that you bind them fast . . . . . v 2 166
Sad hours seem long. Was that my father that went hence so fast? *Rom. and Jul.* i 1 168
I stand on sudden haste.—Wisely and slow; they stumble that run fast ii 3 94
Mistress! what, mistress! Juliet! fast, I warrant her, she . . . iv 5 1
Bankrupts, hold fast; Rather than render back, out with your knives! *T. of Athens* iv 1 8
Stand fast together, lest some friend of Cæsar's Should chance *J. Cæsar* iii 1 87
Had I as many eyes as thou hast wounds, Weeping as fast as they . . iii 1 201
Stand fast, Titinius: we must out and talk . . . . v 1 22
Let us rather Hold fast the mortal sword . . . . . . *Macbeth* iv 3 3
Doom'd for a certain term to walk the night, And for the day confined to fast in fires . . . . *Hamlet* i 5 11
Well said, old mole! canst work i' the earth so fast? A worthy pioner! i 5 162
Fell into a sadness, then into a fast, Thence to a watch . . . . ii 2 147
One woe doth tread upon another's heel, So fast they follow . . . iv 7 165
Woo't weep? woo't fight? woo't fast? woo't tear thyself? . . . v 1 298
Ingrateful fox! 'tis he.—Bind fast his corky arms . . . . *Lear* iii 7 29
Wilt thou be fast to my hopes, if I depend on the issue? . . *Othello* i 3 369
Drop tears as fast as the Arabian trees Their medicinal gum . . . v 2 350
I had rather fast from all four days Than drink so much in one *Ant. and Cleo.* ii 7 108
Which he took, As we do air, fast as 'twas minister'd . . *Cymbeline* i 1 45
And will continue fast to your affection, Still close as sure . . . i 6 138
Last night the very gods show'd me a vision—I fast and pray'd for their intelligence . . . . iv 2 347
Fast and loose. I will fast, being loose.—No, sir; that were fast and loose *L. L. Lost* i 2 162
To sell a bargain well is as cunning as fast and loose . . . . iii 1 104
Play fast and loose with faith . . . . *K. John* iii 1 242
Like a right gipsy, hath, at fast and loose, Beguiled me *Ant. and Cleo.* iv 12 28
Fast asleep. Standing, speaking, moving, And yet so fast asleep *Tempest* ii 1 215
This love of theirs myself have often seen, Haply when they have judged me fast asleep . . . . *T. G. of Ver.* iii 1 25
By my halidom, I was fast asleep . . . . iv 2 136
Falstaff!—Fast asleep behind the arras, and snorting like a horse *1 Hen. IV.* ii 4 577
To the loathsome pit Where I espied the panther fast asleep *T. Andron.* ii 3 194
Fast asleep? It is no matter; Enjoy the honey-heavy dew of slumber *J. Cæsar* ii 1 229
This is her very guise; and, upon my life, fast asleep . . . *Macbeth* v 1 23
Fast belocked. This is the hand which, with a vow'd contract, Was fast belock'd in thine . . . . *Meas. for Meas.* v 1 210
Fast bind, fast find; A proverb never stale in thrifty mind *Mer. of Ven.* ii 5 54
Fast by. Who finds the heifer dead and bleeding fresh And sees fast by a butcher with an axe, But will suspect 'twas he that made the slaughter? . . . . *2 Hen. VI.* iii 2 189
Fast-closed. This union shall do more than battery can To our fast-closed gates . . . . *K. John* ii 1 447
Fast enough. He teaches him to hick and to hack, which they'll do fast enough of themselves . . . . *Mer. Wives* iv 1 69
Fast-falling. Even my foes will shed fast-falling tears . *3 Hen. VI.* i 4 162
Fast foe to the plebeii . . . . *Coriolanus* ii 3 192
Fast gait. Springs out into fast gait; then stops again . *Hen. VIII.* iii 2 116
Fast-growing. Cut off the heads of two fast-growing sprays *Richard II.* iii 4 34
Whom our fast-growing scene must find At Tarsus . . *Pericles* iv Gower 6
Fast intent. 'Tis our fast intent To shake all cares and business from our age . . . . *Lear* i 1 39
Fast married. But, I pray you, sir, Are you fast married? . . *Othello* i 2 11
Fast sleep. Yet all this while in a most fast sleep . . . *Macbeth* v 1 9
Fast sworn. Friends now fast sworn . . . . . . *Coriolanus* iv 4 12
Fast upon. It is great morning, and the hour prefix'd Of her delivery to this valiant Greek Comes fast upon . . . . *Troi. and Cres.* iv 3 3
Fasted. When you fasted, it was presently after dinner . *T. G. of Ver.* ii 1 29

Father. What heinous sin is it in me To be ashamed to be my father's child! *Mer. of Venice* ii 3 17
She hath directed How I shall take her from her father's house ii 4 31
If e'er the Jew her father come to heaven, It will be for his gentle daughter's sake ii 4 34
Farewell; and if my fortune be not crost, I have a father, you a daughter, lost ii 5 57
The sins of the father are to be laid upon the children iii 5 2
You may partly hope that your father got you not iii 5 12
Truly then I fear you are damned both by father and mother iii 5 18
Thus when I shun Scylla, your father, I fall into Charybdis, your mother iii 5 19
The spirit of my father, which I think is within me, begins to mutiny against this servitude *As Y. Like It* i 1 23
I have as much of my father in me as you i 1 53
He was my father, and he is thrice a villain that says such a father begot villains i 1 60
Sweet masters, be patient: for your father's remembrance, be at accord i 1 67
My father charged you in his will to give me good education i 1 70
The spirit of my father grows strong in me, and I will no longer endure it i 1 73
Give me the poor allottery my father left me by testament i 1 77
Can you tell if Rosalind, the duke's daughter, be banished with her father? i 1 111
Unless you could teach me to forget a banished father i 2 6
If my uncle, thy banished father, had banished thy uncle, the duke my father, so thou hadst been still with me, I could have taught my love to take thy father for mine i 2 10
You know my father hath no child but I, nor none is like to have i 2 18
Mistress, you must come away to your father i 2 61
One that old Frederick, your father, loves.—My father's love is enough to honour him: enough! speak no more of him i 2 87
The poor old man, their father, making such pitiful dole over them i 2 138
The world esteem'd thy father honourable, But I did find him still mine enemy i 2 238
I would thou hadst told me of another father.—Were I my father, coz, would I do this? i 2 243
My father loved Sir Rowland as his soul, And all the world was of my father's mind i 2 247
My father's rough and envious disposition Sticks me at heart i 2 253
Praise her for her virtues And pity her for her good father's sake i 2 293
Is all this for your father?—No, some of it is for my child's father i 3 10
The duke my father loved his father dearly i 3 30
I should hate him, for my father hated his father dearly i 3 34
Thou art thy father's daughter; there's enough i 3 60
What's that to me? my father was no traitor i 3 65
We stay'd her for your sake, Else had she with her father ranged along i 3 70
Whither wilt thou go? Wilt thou change fathers? i 3 93
Let my father seek another heir i 3 101
What if we assay'd to steal The clownish fool out of your father's court? i 3 132
I will not call him son Of him I was about to call his father ii 3 21
I have five hundred crowns, The thrifty hire I saved under your father ii 3 39
I am the duke That loved your father ii 7 196
He attends here in the forest on the duke your father iii 4 37
But what talk we of fathers, when there is such a man as Orlando? iii 4 42
Thy father's father wore it, And thy father bore it iv 2 16
My father's house and all the revenue that was old Sir Rowland's will I estate upon you v 2 12
I'll have no father, if you be not he: I'll have no husband, if you be not he v 4 128
By my father's love and leave am arm'd With his good will *T. of Shrew* i 1 5
Pisa renowned for grave citizens Gave me my being and my father first i 1 11
I will wish him to her father i 1 114
Though her father be very rich, any man is so very a fool to be married to hell i 1 128
Till the father rid his hands of her i 1 186
What a cruel father's he! i 1 190
Your father charged me at our parting, 'Be serviceable to my son,' quoth he i 1 218
My father is deceased; And I have thrust myself into this maze i 2 54
Tell me her father's name and 'tis enough i 2 94
I know her father, though I know not her; And he knew my deceased father well i 2 101
My father dead, my fortune lives for me i 2 192
A noble gentleman, To whom my father is not all unknown i 2 241
The youngest daughter . . . Her father keeps from all access of suitors i 2 261
You knew my father well, and in him me, Left solely heir to all his lands ii 1 117
I tell you, father, I am as peremptory as she proud-minded ii 1 131
Your father hath consented That you shall be my wife ii 1 271
Here comes your father: never make denial ii 1 281
Provide the feast, father, and bid the guests ii 1 318
Father, and wife, and gentlemen, adieu; I will to Venice ii 1 323
List to me: I am my father's heir and only son ii 1 366
'Tis known my father hath no less Than three great argosies ii 1 379
And, let your father make her the assurance, She is your own ii 1 389
Your father were a fool To give thee all, and in his waning age Set foot under thy table ii 1 402
Supposed Lucentio Must get a father, call'd 'supposed Vincentio' ii 1 410
Fathers commonly Do get their children ii 1 411
Your father prays you leave your books And help to dress your sister's chamber up iii 1 82
But where is Kate? where is my lovely bride? How does my father? iii 2 95
But to her love concerneth us to add Her father's liking iii 2 131
We'll over-reach the greybeard, Gremio, The narrow-prying father, Minola iii 2 148
Dine with my father, drink a health to me; For I must hence iii 2 198
Father, be quiet: he shall stay my leisure iii 2 219
Formal in apparel, In gait and countenance surely like a father iv 2 65
He is my father, sir; and, sooth to say, In countenance somewhat doth resemble you iv 2 99
My father is here look'd for every day iv 2 116
Beggars, that come unto my father's door, Upon entreaty have a present alms iv 3 4
And now, my honey love, Will we return unto thy father's house iv 3 53
We will unto your father's Even in these honest mean habiliments iv 3 171
We will hence forthwith, To feast and sport us at thy father's house iv 3 185
With such austerity as 'longeth to a father iv 4 7
I pray you, stand good father to me now iv 4 21
I am content, in a good father's care, To have him match'd iv 4 31
If you say no more than this, That like a father you will deal with him iv 4 44
Then at my lodging, an it like you: There doth my father lie iv 4 56
Baptista is safe, talking with the deceiving father of a deceitful son iv 4 83

Father. Come on, i' God's name; once more toward our father's *T. of S.* iv 5 1
It shall be moon, or star, or what I list, Or ere I journey to your father's house iv 5 8
Pardon, old father, my mistaking eyes, That have been so bedazzled iv 5 45
Now I perceive thou art a reverend father; Pardon, I pray thee, for my mad mistaking iv 5 48
By law, as well as reverend age, I may entitle thee my loving father iv 5 61
I do assure thee, father, so it is iv 5 74
This is Lucentio's house: My father's bears more toward the market-place v 1 10
Tell Signior Lucentio that his father is come from Pisa v 1 29
Thou liest: his father is come from Padua v 1 31
Art thou his father?—Ay, sir; so his mother says, if I may believe her v 1 33
You notorious villain, didst thou never see thy master's father, Vincentio? v 1 55
What 'cerns it you if I wear pearl and gold? I thank my good father, I am able to maintain it v 1 78
Thy father! O villain! he is a sail-maker in Bergamo v 1 80
Pardon, sweet father.—Lives my sweet son?—Pardon, dear father v 1 115
Myself enforced him to; Then pardon him, sweet father, for my sake v 1 133
Look not pale, Bianca; thy father will not frown v 1 143
Bid my father welcome, While I with self-same kindness welcome thine v 2 4
And I in going, madam, weep o'er my father's death anew *All's Well* i 1 4
You shall find of the king a husband, madam; you, sir, a father i 1 8
This young gentlewoman had a father,—O, that 'had'! i 1 19
The remembrance of her father never approaches her heart i 1 56
Succeed thy father In manners, as in shape! i 1 70
Farewell, pretty lady: you must hold the credit of your father i 1 89
O, were that all! I think not on my father i 1 90
Youth, thou bear'st thy father's face i 2 19
Thy father's moral parts Mayst thou inherit too! i 2 21
I would I had that corporal soundness now, As when thy father and myself in friendship First tried our soldiership! i 2 25
It much repairs me To talk of your good father i 2 31
Whose judgements are Mere fathers of their garments i 2 62
How long is't, count, Since the physician at your father's died? i 2 70
My father left me some prescriptions Of rare and proved effects i 3 227
There's something in't, More than my father's skill i 3 249
Gerard de Narbon was my father; In what he did profess, well found ii 1 104
Wherein the honour Of my dear father's gift stands chief in power ii 1 115
O'er whom both sovereign power and father's voice I have to use ii 3 60
Not one of those but had a noble father ii 3 68
I am sure thy father drunk wine ii 3 106
I know her well: She had her breeding at my father's charge ii 3 121
Show me a child begotten of thy body that I am father to iii 2 61
Some four or five descents Since the first father wore it iii 7 25
I have heard my father name him *T. Night* i 2 28
My father was that Sebastian of Messaline, whom I know you have heard of ii 1 18
A fool that the lady Olivia's father took much delight in ii 4 12
My father had a daughter loved a man, As it might be, perhaps, were I a woman, I should your lordship ii 4 110
I am all the daughters of my father's house, And all the brothers too ii 4 123
Then lead the way, good father iv 3 34
O, welcome, father! Father, I charge thee, by thy reverence, Here to unfold v 1 153
Sebastian was my father; Such a Sebastian was my brother too v 1 239
My father had a mole upon his brow.—And so had mine v 1 249
I will respect thee as a father if Thou bear'st my life off hence *W. Tale* i 2 461
The whole matter And copy of the father, eye, nose, lip ii 3 99
Shall I live on to see this bastard kneel And call me father? ii 3 156
Thy brat hath been cast out, like to itself, No father owning it iii 2 89
The Emperor of Russia was my father: O that he were alive! iii 2 120
Here be laid, Either for life or death, upon the earth Of its right father iii 3 46
My father named me Autolycus iv 3 24
My father hath made her mistress of the feast, and she lays it on iv 3 42
I bless the time When my good falcon made her flight across Thy father's ground iv 4 16
I tremble To think your father, by some accident, Should pass this way iv 4 19
I'll be thine, my fair, Or not my father's iv 4 43
It is my father's will I should take on me The hostess-ship o' the day iv 4 71
My father and the gentlemen are in sad talk, and we'll not trouble them iv 4 316
O, father, you'll know more of that hereafter iv 4 353
Have you a father?—I have: but what of him? iv 4 403
A father Is at the nuptial of his son a guest That best becomes the table iv 4 405
Is not your father grown incapable Of reasonable affairs? iv 4 408
Reason my son Should choose himself a wife, but as good reason The father, all whose joy is nothing else But fair posterity, should hold some counsel In such a business iv 4 419
But for some other reasons . . . I not acquaint My father of this business iv 4 424
Why, how now, father! Speak ere thou diest iv 4 461
To die upon the bed my father died iv 4 466
You know your father's temper: at this time He will allow no speech iv 4 478
From my succession wipe me, father; I Am heir to my affection iv 4 491
I pray you, As you have ever been my father's honour'd friend iv 4 504
You have heard of my poor services, i' the love That I have borne your father? iv 4 528
It is my father's music To speak your deeds iv 4 529
Your discontenting father strive to qualify And bring him up to liking iv 4 543
Asks thee the son forgiveness, As 'twere i' the father's person iv 4 561
Sent by the king your father To greet him and to give him comforts iv 4 567
What you as from your father shall deliver iv 4 570
He shall not perceive But that you have your father's bosom there iv 4 574
There shall not at your father's house these seven years Be born another such iv 4 589
Preserver of my father, now of me, The medicine of our house iv 4 597
And those that you'll procure from King Leontes— Shall satisfy your father iv 4 635
Should I now meet my father, He would not call me son iv 4 671
Stealing away from his father with his clog at his heels iv 4 693
I may say, is no honest man, neither to his father nor to me iv 4 719
He comes not Like to his father's greatness v 1 89
She did print your royal father off, Conceiving you v 1 125
Your father's image is so hit in you, His very air v 1 127
I lost—All mine own folly—the society, Amity too, of your brave father v 1 136
We have cross'd, To execute the charge my father gave me v 1 162
You have a holy father, A graceful gentleman v 1 170
And your father's blest, As he from heaven merits it, with you v 1 174
Fled from his father, from his hopes, and with A shepherd's daughter v 1 184
Meets he on the way The father of this seeming lady v 1 191

Father. O my poor father! The heaven sets spies upon us *W. Tale* v 1 202
When once she is my wife.—That 'once,' I see by your good father's speed, Will come on very slowly v 1 210
Though Fortune, visible an enemy, Should chase us with my father, power no jot Hath she to change our loves v 1 217
At your request My father will grant precious things as trifles v 1 222
But your petition Is yet unanswer'd. I will to your father v 1 229
I was a gentleman born before my father v 2 151
And then the two kings called my father brother v 2 153
Then the prince my brother and the princess my sister called my father father v 2 155
Where hast thou been preserved? where lived? how found Thy father's court? v 3 125
Most certain of one mother, mighty king; That is well known; and, as I think, one father *K. John* i 1 60
If old sir Robert did beget us both And were our father and this son like him, O old sir Robert, father, on my knee I give heaven thanks I was not like to thee! i 1 82
He hath a half-face, like my father i 1 92
When that my father lived, Your brother did employ my father much i 1 95
The advantage of his absence took the king And in the mean time sojourn'd at my father's i 1 103
Large lengths of seas and shores Between my father and my mother lay, As I have heard my father speak himself i 1 106
Let me have what is mine, My father's land, as was my father's will i 1 115
Your brother is legitimate; Your father's wife did after wedlock bear him i 1 117
Tell me, how if my brother, Who, as you say, took pains to get this son, Had of your father claim'd this son for his? i 1 122
Your father might have kept This calf bred from his cow from all the world i 1 123
My brother might not claim him; nor your father, Being none of his, refuse him i 1 126
My mother's son did get your father's heir; Your father's heir must have your father's land i 1 128
Shall then my father's will be of no force To dispossess that child which is not his? i 1 130
Give me your hand: My father gave me honour, yours gave land i 1 164
Let me know my father; Some proper man, I hope: who was it, mother? i 1 249
King Richard Cœur-de-lion was thy father i 1 253
Were I to get again, Madam, I would not wish a better father i 1 260
Ay, my mother, With all my heart I thank thee for my father! i 1 270
Liker in feature to his father Geffrey Than thou and John in manners ii 1 126
His father never was so true begot: It cannot be, and if thou wert his mother ii 1 130
There's a good mother, boy, that blots thy father ii 1 132
Since I first call'd my brother's father dad ii 1 467
This, in our foresaid holy father's name, Pope Innocent, I do demand iii 1 145
Good reverend father, make my person yours iii 1 224
O, holy sir, My reverend father, let it not be so! iii 1 249
Father, to arms!—Upon thy wedding-day? iii 1 300
Father, I may not wish the fortune thine iii 1 333
Thy uncle will As dear be to thee as thy father was iii 3 4
Other princes that may best be spared Shall wait upon your father's funeral v 7 98
My noble Lord of Lancaster, The honourable father to my foe *Richard II.* i 1 136
Shall I seem crest-fall'n in my father's sight? i 1 188
Thou dost consent In some large measure to thy father's death, In that thou seest thy wretched brother die, Who was the model of thy father's life i 2 26
I had rather You would have bid me argue like a father i 3 238
The pleasure that some fathers feed upon, Is my strict fast ii 1 79
O, spare me not, my brother Edward's son, For that I was his father Edward's son ii 1 125
The last of noble Edward's sons, Of whom thy father, Prince of Wales, was first ii 1 172
His noble hand Did win what he did spend and spent not that Which his triumphant father's hand had won ii 1 181
As when brave Gaunt, thy father, and myself Rescued the Black Prince ii 3 100
You are my father, for methinks in you I see old Gaunt alive; O, then, my father, Will you permit that I shall stand condemn'd A wandering vagabond? ii 3 117
Where is the duke my father with his power? iii 2 143
My father hath a power; inquire of him, And learn to make a body of a limb iii 2 186
I am too young to be your father, Though you are old enough to be my heir iii 3 204
Till thou the lie-giver and that lie do lie In earth as quiet as thy father's skull iv 1 69
O loyal father of a treacherous son! v 3 60
He shall spend mine honour with his shame, As thriftless sons their scraping father's gold v 3 69
My brain I'll prove the female to my soul, My soul the father v 5 7
And makest me sin In envy that my Lord Northumberland Should be the father to so blest a son *1 Hen. IV.* i 1 80
I think his father loves him not And would be glad he met with some mischance i 3 231
For all the coin in thy father's exchequer ii 2 38
Is there not my father, my uncle and myself? ii 3 25
These lies are like their father that begets them; gross as a mountain ii 4 249
He says he comes from your father ii 4 319
Here was Sir John Bracy from your father; you must to the court ii 4 368
Thy father's beard is turned white with the news ii 4 393
Thou wilt be horribly chid to-morrow when thou comest to thy father ii 4 411
Stand for my father, and examine me upon the particulars of my life ii 4 413
O, the father, how he holds his countenance! ii 4 432
Dost thou speak like a king? Do thou stand for me, and I'll play my father ii 4 477
My good Lord of Worcester will set forth To meet your father iii 1 85
My father Glendower is not ready yet, Nor shall we need his help iii 1 87
Fie, cousin Percy! how you cross my father!—I cannot choose iii 1 147
Good father, tell her that she and my aunt Percy Shall follow iii 1 196
Dost thou think I'll fear thee as I fear thy father? iii 3 171
I am good friends with my father and may do any thing iii 3 203
These letters come from your father.—Letters from him! iv 1 14
Your father's sickness is a maim to us.—A perilous gash iv 1 42
But yet I would your father had been here iv 1 60
This absence of your father's draws a curtain, That shows the ignorant a kind of fear Before not dreamt of iv 1 73

Father. My father and Glendower being both away, The powers of us may serve *1 Hen. IV.* iv 1 131
My father and my uncle and myself Did give him that same royalty iv 3 54
A poor unminded outlaw sneaking home, My father gave him welcome iv 3 59
My father, in kind heart and pity moved, Swore him assistance iv 3 64
Steps me a little higher than his vow Made to my father iv 3 76
In rage dismiss'd my father from the court; Broke oath on oath iv 3 100
This before my father's majesty—I am content that he shall take the odds v 1 96
All his offences live upon my head And on his father's v 2 21
If your father will do me any honour, so; if not, let him kill the next Percy v 4 144
Where Hotspur's father, old Northumberland, Lies crafty-sick *2 Hen. IV.* Ind. 36
Every minute now Should be the father of some stratagem i 1 8
As if he had writ man ever since his father was a bachelor i 2 31
When the prince broke thy head for liking his father to a singing-man ii 1 97
How many good young princes would do so, their fathers being so sick? ii 2 34
But I tell thee, my heart bleeds inwardly that my father is so sick ii 2 52
To the son of the king, nearest his father, Harry Prince of Wales ii 2 130
The time was, father, that you broke your word ii 3 10
When my heart's dear Harry Threw many a northward look to see his father ii 3 13
I have done the part of a careful friend and a true subject, and thy father is to give me thanks for it ii 4 349
What news?—The king your father is at Westminster ii 4 384
Thy mother's son! like enough, and thy father's shadow: so the son of the female is the shadow of the male: it is often so, indeed; but much of the father's substance! iii 2 140
You, reverend father, and these noble lords Had not been here iv 1 38
Your noble and right well remember'd father's iv 1 112
What thing, in honour, had my father lost, That need to be revived and breathed in me? iv 1 113
Nothing could have stay'd My father from the breast of Bolingbroke iv 1 124
If your father had been victor there, He ne'er had borne it out of Coventry iv 1 134
A full commission, In very ample virtue of his father iv 1 163
You have ta'en up, Under the counterfeited zeal of God, The subjects of his substitute, my father iv 2 28
I am not here against your father's peace iv 2 31
By the honour of my blood, My father's purposes have been mistook iv 2 56
I hear the king my father is sore sick iv 3 83
The cold blood he did naturally inherit of his father iv 3 128
What would my lord and father.—Nothing but well to thee iv 4 18
Comfort, your majesty!—O my royal father!—My sovereign lord, cheer up iv 4 112
Speak low; The king your father is disposed to sleep iv 5 17
My gracious lord! my father! This sleep is sound indeed iv 5 34
Love, and filial tenderness, Shall, O dear father, pay the plenteously iv 5 40
The foolish over-careful fathers Have broke their sleep with thoughts iv 5 68
This bitter taste Yield his engrossments to the ending father iv 5 80
Thy wish was father, Harry, to that thought iv 5 93
The care on thee depending Hath fed upon the body of my father iv 5 160
As with an enemy That had before my face murder'd my father iv 5 168
That thou mightst win the more thy father's love, Pleading so wisely iv 5 180
Health, peace, and happiness to my royal father! iv 5 227
I'll be your father and your brother too v 2 57
I then did use the person of your father; The image of his power lay then in me v 2 73
As an offender to your father, I gave bold way to my authority v 2 81
Make the case yours; Be now the father and propose a son v 2 92
So shall I live to speak my father's words v 2 107
There is my hand. You shall be as a father to my youth v 2 118
My father is gone wild into his grave, For in his tomb lie my affections v 2 123
In which you, father, shall have foremost hand v 2 140
The breath no sooner left his father's body, But that his wildness, mortified in him, Seem'd to die too *Hen. V.* i 1 25
His most mighty father on a hill Stood smiling to behold his lion's whelp i 2 108
By God's grace, play a set Shall strike his father's crown into the hazard i 2 263
For, God before, We'll chide this Dauphin at his father's door i 2 308
Those that were your father's enemies Have steep'd their galls in honey ii 2 29
My most redoubted father, It is most meet we arm us 'gainst the foe ii 4 14
And deface The patterns that by God and by French fathers Had twenty years been made ii 4 61
The pining maidens' groans, For husbands, fathers and betrothed lovers ii 4 108
If your father's highness Do not, in grant of all demands at large, Sweeten the bitter mock you sent his majesty ii 4 120
Say, if my father render fair return, It is against my will ii 4 127
Whose blood is fet from fathers of war-proof! Fathers that, like so many Alexanders, Have in these parts from morn till even fought iii 1 19
Now attest That those whom you call'd fathers did beget you iii 1 23
By my hand, I swear, and my father's soul, the work ish ill done iii 2 95
Your fathers taken by the silver beards, And their most reverend heads dash'd to the walls iii 3 36
A few sprays of us, The emptying of our fathers' luxury iii 5 6
So, if a son that is by his father sent about merchandise do sinfully miscarry upon the sea, the imputation of his wickedness, by your rule, should be imposed upon his father iv 1 154
The king is not bound to answer the particular endings of his soldiers, the father of his son iv 1 164
Think not upon the fault My father made in compassing the crown! iv 1 311
His father was called Philip of Macedon, as I take it iv 7 21
Beshrew my father's ambition! he was thinking of civil wars when he got me v 2 242
Father, I know; and oft have shot at them *1 Hen. VI.* i 4 3
Father, I warrant you; take you no care; I'll never trouble you i 4 21
Was not thy father, Richard Earl of Cambridge, For treason executed? ii 4 90
My father was attached, not attainted ii 4 96
He used his lavish tongue, And did upbraid me with my father's death ii 5 48
For my father's sake, In honour of a true Plantagenet, And for alliance sake, declare the cause My father, Earl of Cambridge, lost his head ii 5 51
My father's execution Was nothing less than bloody tyranny ii 5 99
So kind a father of the commonweal, To be disgraced by an inkhorn mate iii 1 98
So shall his father's wrongs be recompensed iii 1 161
As sure as English Henry lives And as his father here was conqueror iii 2 81
My father said A stouter champion never handled sword iii 4 18
O, think upon the conquest of my father! iv 1 148

Father. I am guiltless of your father's death, And am most sensibly in grief for it . . . . *Hamlet* iv 5 149
I would give you some violets, but they withered all when my father died . . . . iv 5 185
He which hath your noble father slain Pursued my life . . . . iv 7 4
And so have I a noble father lost; A sister driven into desperate terms iv 7 25
I loved your father, and we love ourself; And that, I hope, will teach you to imagine . . . . iv 7 34
Was your father dear to you? Or are you like the painting of a sorrow? iv 7 108
Why ask you this?—Not that I think you did not love your father . iv 7 111
Show yourself your father's son in deed More than in words . . iv 7 126
Choose A sword unbated, and in a pass of practice Requite him for your father . . . . iv 7 140
I had my father's signet in my purse . . . . v 2 49
Mine and my father's death come not upon thee, Nor thine on me! . v 2 341
As much as child e'er loved, or father found . . . . . . *Lear* i 1 60
Sure, I shall never marry like my sisters, To love my father all . i 1 106
So be my grave my peace, as here I give Her father's heart from her! . i 1 128
Royal Lear, Whom I have ever honour'd as my king, Loved as my father . . . . i 1 143
I am sorry, then, you have so lost a father That you must lose a husband . . . . i 1 249
The jewels of our father, with wash'd eyes, Cordelia leaves you . i 1 271
Use well our father: To your professed bosoms I commit him . . i 1 274
I think our father will hence to-night . . . . i 1 288
If our father carry authority with such dispositions as he bears . i 1 308
Our father's love is to the bastard Edmund As to the legitimate . i 2 17
If our father would sleep till I waked him, you should enjoy half his revenue . . . . i 2 55
That, sons at perfect age, and fathers declining, the father should be as ward to the son . . . . i 2 78
To his father, that so tenderly and entirely loves him . . . . i 2 104
In palaces, treason; and the bond cracked 'twixt son and father . . i 2 118
This villain of mine comes under the prediction; there's son against father . . . . i 2 120
The king falls from bias of nature; there's father against child . i 2 121
My father compounded with my mother under the dragon's tail . . i 2 139
When saw you my father last?—Why, the night gone by . . . i 2 166
A credulous father! and a brother noble! . . . . . . i 2 195
Did my father strike my gentleman for chiding of his fool? . . . i 3 1
Who am I, sir?—My lady's father.—'My lady's father'! my lord's knave i 4 87
I should be false persuaded I had daughters.—Which they will make an obedient father . . . . i 4 256
The untented woundings of a father's curse Pierce every sense about thee! . . . . i 4 322
I will forget my nature. So kind a father! . . . . . . i 5 36
I have been with your father, and given him notice . . . . ii 1 3
My father hath set guard to take my brother . . . . . . ii 1 18
Brother, I say! My father watches: O sir, fly this place . . . ii 1 22
I hear my father coming: pardon me . . . . ii 1 30
Father, father! Stop, stop! No help? . . . . ii 1 37
With how manifold and strong a bond The child was bound to the father . . . . ii 1 50
What, did my father's godson seek your life? He whom my father named? . . . . ii 1 93
Was he not companion with the riotous knights That tend upon my father? . . . . ii 1 97
I hear that you have shown your father A child-like office . . . ii 1 107
Our father he hath writ, so hath our sister . . . . . . ii 1 124
And take vanity the puppet's part against the royalty of her father . ii 2 40
If I were your father's dog, You should not use me so . . . . ii 2 143
Fathers that wear rags Do make their children blind; But fathers that bear bags Shall see their children kind . . . . ii 4 48
The dear father Would with his daughter speak, commands her service ii 4 102
I pray you, father, being weak, seem so . . . . ii 4 204
If it be you that stir these daughters' hearts Against their father . . ii 4 278
This seems a fair deserving, and must draw me That which my father loses . . . . iii 3 25
Your old kind father, whose frank heart gave all,—O, that way madness lies . . . . iii 4 20
Is it the fashion, that discarded fathers Should have thus little mercy on their flesh? Judicious punishment! . . . . iii 4 74
I loved him, friend; No father his son dearer: truth to tell thee, The grief hath crazed my wits . . . . iii 4 174
Seek out where thy father is, that he may be ready for our apprehension . . . . iii 5 19
I will lay trust upon thee; and thou shalt find a dearer father in my love iii 5 26
I here take my oath before this honourable assembly, she kicked the poor king her father . . . . iii 6 50
The revenges we are bound to take upon your traitorous father are not fit for your beholding . . . . iii 7 8
But who comes here? My father, poorly led? World, world, O world! iv 1 10
I have been your tenant, and your father's tenant, these fourscore years iv 1 14
O dear son Edgar, The food of thy abused father's wrath! . . . iv 1 24
A father, and a gracious aged man . . . . iv 2 41
Once or twice she heaved the name of 'father' Pantingly forth . . iv 3 27
Cried 'Sisters! sisters! Shame of ladies! sisters! Kent! father! sisters!' . . . . iv 3 30
O dear father, It is thy business that I go about . . . . . iv 4 23
No blown ambition doth our arms incite, But love, dear love, and our aged father's right . . . . iv 4 28
Therefore, thou happy father, Think that the clearest gods, who make them honours Of men's impossibilities, have preserved thee . . iv 6 72
Gloucester's bastard son Was kinder to his father than my daughters . iv 6 117
Sit you down, father; rest you . . . . iv 6 260
Come, father, I'll bestow you with a friend . . . . . . iv 6 293
The untuned and jarring senses, O, wind up Of this child-changed father! . . . . iv 7 17
O my dear father! Restoration hang Thy medicine on my lips! . . iv 7 26
Had you not been their father, these white flakes Had challenged pity of them . . . . iv 7 30
Wast thou fain, poor father, To hovel thee with swine, and rogues forlorn? . . . . iv 7 38
Here, father, take the shadow of this tree For your good host . . v 2 1
The question of Cordelia and her father Requires a fitter place . . v 3 58
False to thy gods, thy brother, and thy father . . . . . v 3 134
My name is Edgar, and thy father's son . . . . v 3 169
Let sorrow split my heart, if ever I Did hate thee or thy father! . . v 3 178
How have you known the miseries of your father?—By nursing them . v 3 180
In this habit Met I my father with his bleeding rings . . . . v 3 189

Father. He fasten'd on my neck, and bellow'd out As he'ld burst heaven; threw him on my father . . . . *Lear* v 3 213
Call up her father, Rouse him: make after him . . . . *Othello* i 1 67
Here is her father's house; I'll call aloud . . . . . . i 1 74
Who would be a father! How didst thou know 'twas she? . . . i 1 165
Fathers, from hence trust not your daughters' minds By what you see them act . . . . i 1 171
What lights come yond?—Those are the raised father and his friends . i 2 29
Send for the lady to the Sagittary, And let her speak of me before her father . . . . i 3 116
Her father loved me; oft invited me; Still question'd me the story of my life . . . . i 3 128
My noble father, I do perceive here a divided duty . . . . . i 3 180
Here's my husband, And so much duty as my mother show'd To you, preferring you before her father, So much I challenge that I may profess . . . . i 3 187
If you please, Be't at her father's.—I'll not have it so.—Nor I.—Nor I i 3 241
I would not there reside, To put my father in impatient thoughts . i 3 243
Look to her, Moor, if thou hast eyes to see: She has deceived her father, and may thee . . . . i 3 294
She did deceive her father, marrying you . . . . iii 3 206
She that, so young, could give out such a seeming, To seel her father's eyes up close as oak . . . . iii 3 210
She told her, while she kept it, 'Twould make her amiable and subdue my father Entirely to her love, but if she lost it Or made a gift of it, my father's eye Should hold her loathed . . . . . . iii 4 59
If haply you my father do suspect An instrument of this your calling back, Lay not your blame on me . . . . iv 2 44
Hath she forsook so many noble matches, Her father and her country? iv 2 126
I am glad thy father's dead: Thy match was mortal to him . . . v 2 204
It was a handkerchief, an antique token My father gave my mother . v 2 217
Rich in his father's honour . . . . *Ant. and Cleo.* i 3 50
I do not know Wherefore my father should revengers want, Having a son . . . . ii 6 11
To scourge the ingratitude that despiteful Rome Cast on my noble father . . . . ii 6 23
At land, indeed, Thou dost o'er-count me of my father's house . . ii 6 27
Thy father, Pompey, would ne'er have made this treaty . . . . ii 6 84
O Antony, You have my father's house . . . . ii 7 135
Cæsarion, whom they call my father's son . . . . . . iii 6 6
Cæsar's father oft, When he hath mused of taking kingdoms in, Bestow'd his lips on that unworthy place, As it rain'd kisses . . . . iii 13 82
If that thy father live, let him repent Thou wast not made his daughter iii 13 134
I cannot delve him to the root: his father Was called Sicilius *Cymbeline* i 1 28
Their father, Then old and fond of issue, took such sorrow That he quit being . . . . i 1 36
I something fear my father's wrath; but nothing—Always reserved my holy duty—what His rage can do on me . . . . i 1 86
Who to my father was a friend, to me Known but by letter . . . i 1 98
Your son's my father's friend; he takes his part. To draw upon an exile! . . . . i 1 165
Comes in my father And like the tyrannous breathing of the north Shakes all our buds from growing . . . . i 3 35
His father and I were soldiers together; to whom I have been often bound . . . . i 4 26
A father cruel, and a step-dame false; A foolish suitor to a wedded lady i 6 1
The king my father shall be made acquainted Of thy assault . . . i 6 149
Betwixt a father by thy step-dame govern'd, A mother hourly coining plots . . . . ii 1 63
You sin against Obedience, which you owe your father . . . . ii 3 117
I will inform your father.—Your mother too . . . . . . ii 3 157
I will go there and do't, i' the court, before Her father . . . ii 4 149
That most venerable man which I Did call my father, was I know not where When I was stamp'd . . . . ii 5 4
Justice, and your father's wrath, should he take me in his dominion, could not be so cruel to me, as you . . . . iii 2 40
Go bid my woman feign a sickness; say She'll home to her father . iii 2 77
Myself, Belarius, that am Morgan call'd, They take for natural father . iii 3 107
Thou that didst set up My disobedience 'gainst the king my father . iii 4 91
No court, no father; nor no more ado With that harsh, noble, simple nothing . . . . iii 4 134
Would it had been so, that they Had been my father's sons! . . . iii 6 77
And all this done, spurn her home to her father . . . . . iv 1 21
I love thee; I have spoke it: How much the quantity, the weight as much, As I do love my father . . . . iv 2 18
The bier at door, And a demand who is't shall die, I'ld say 'My father, not this youth' . . . . iv 2 24
Cowards father cowards and base things sire base . . . . . iv 2 26
I'm not their father; yet who this should be, Doth miracle itself, loved before me . . . . iv 2 28
We are all undone.—Why, worthy father, what have we to lose? . . iv 2 124
Those rich-left heirs that let their fathers lie Without a monument . iv 2 226
We must lay his head to the east; My father hath a reason for't . . iv 2 256
Entertain me.—Ay, good youth; And rather father thee than master thee . . . . iv 2 395
Is't enough I am sorry? So children temporal fathers do appease . v 4 12
Whose father then, as men report Thou orphans' father art . . . v 4 39
Sleep, thou hast been a grandsire, and begot A father to me . . . v 4 124
I will prefer my sons; Then spare not the old father . . . . v 5 327
These two young gentlemen, that call me father And think they are my sons, are none of mine . . . . v 5 328
How! my issue!—So sure as you your father's . . . . . . v 5 332
You are my father too, and did relieve me, To see this gracious season . v 5 400
With whom the father liking took, And her to incest did provoke: Bad child; worse father! to entice his own To evil . . . *Pericles* i Gower 25
I sought a husband, in which labour I found that kindness in a father . i 1 67
He's father, son, and husband mild; I mother, wife, and yet his child i 1 68
Where now you're both a father and a son . . . . i 1 127
Which pleasure fits an husband, not a father . . . . . . i 1 129
By my knowledge found, the sinful father Seem'd not to strike, but smooth . . . . i 2 77
Part of my heritage, Which my dead father did bequeath to me . . ii 1 130
My shipwreck now's no ill, Since I have here my father's gift in's will ii 1 140
It pleaseth you, my royal father, to express My commendations great . ii 2 8
Who is the first . . . ?—A night of Sparta, my renowned father . . ii 2 18
Yon king's to me like to my father's picture, Which tells me in that glory once he was . . . . ii 3 37
What is it To me, my father?—O, attend, my daughter . . . . ii 3 58
Alas, my father, it befits not me Unto a stranger knight to be so bold . ii 3 66
Resolve your angry father, if my tongue Did e'er solicit . . . . ii 5 68

Father. I love the king your father, and yourself . . . *Pericles* iv 1 33
My father, as nurse said, did never fear . . . . . iv 1 53
They listened to me as they would have hearkened to their father's testament . . . . . iv 2 107
The name Was given me by one that had some power, My father, and a king . . . . . v 1 151
Where were you bred?—The king my father did in Tarsus leave me . v 1 172
The heir of kingdoms and another like To Pericles thy father . v 1 210
The king my father gave you such a ring.—This, this: no more . v 3 39
My father's dead.—Heavens make a star of him! . . . . v 3 78
Father abbot. O, father abbot, An old man, broken with the storms of state, Is come to lay his weary bones among ye . *Hen. VIII.* iv 2 20
Father Abram. O father Abram, what these Christians are! *Mer. of Ven.* i 3 162
Father antic. With the rusty curb of old father antic the law 1 *Hen. IV.* i 2 69
Father cardinal, cry thou amen To my keen curses . . *K. John* iii 1 181
And, father cardinal, I have heard you say That we shall see and know our friends in heaven . . . . . iii 4 76
Father friar. 'Bless you, good father friar . . *Meas. for Meas.* iii 2 13
Father Jew. Approach; Here dwells my father Jew . *Mer. of Venice* ii 6 25
Father ruffian. That grey iniquity, that father ruffian . 1 *Hen. IV.* ii 4 500
Father Time. A rule as plain as the plain bald pate of father Time himself *Com. of Errors* ii 2 71
Fathered. Think you I am no stronger than my sex, Being so father'd and so husbanded? . . . . . *J. Cæsar* ii 1 297
Father'd he is, and yet he's fatherless . . . *Macbeth* iv 2 27
That which makes me bend makes the king bow, He childed as I father'd! . . . . . *Lear* iii 6 117
Father-in-law. The first that there did greet my stranger soul Was my great father-in-law . . . . . *Richard III.* i 4 49
Noble father-in-law! Tell me, how fares our loving mother? . . v 3 81
I am joyful To meet the least occasion that may give me Remembrance of my father-in-law . . . . . *Hen. VIII.* iii 2 8
Robb'd this bewailing land Of noble Buckingham, my father-in-law . iii 2 256
Fatherless. Our fatherless distress was left unmoan'd . *Richard III.* ii 2 64
Father'd he is, and yet he's fatherless . . . *Macbeth* iv 2 27
Fatherly. And, by that fatherly and kindly power That you have in her, bid her answer truly . . . . . *Much Ado* iv 1 75
You have show'd a tender fatherly regard . . . *T. of Shrew* ii 1 288
He cannot choose but take this service I have done fatherly . *Cymbeline* iii 3 39
Fathom. Full fathom five thy father lies . . . *Tempest* i 2 396
I'll break my staff, Bury it certain fathoms in the earth . . v 1 55
That thou didst know how many fathom deep I am in love! *As Y. L. It* iv 1 210
How deep?—Thirty fathom.—Three great oaths would scarce make that be believed . . . . . *All's Well* iv 1 63
The fourscore of April, forty thousand fathom above water . *W. Tale* iv 4 281
For all the sun sees or The close earth wombs or the profound seas hide In unknown fathoms . . . . . iv 4 502
All the commons Hate him perniciously, and, o' my conscience, Wish him ten fathom deep . . . . . *Hen. VIII.* ii 1 51
When I do tell thee, there my hopes lie drown'd, Reply not in how many fathoms deep They lie indrench'd . . . *Troi. and Cres.* i 1 50
Of healths five-fathom deep . . . . *Rom. and Jul.* i 4 85
The very place puts toys of desperation, Without more motive, into every brain That looks so many fathoms to the sea . . *Hamlet* i 4 77
Fathom and half, fathom and half! Poor Tom!—Come not in here *Lear* iii 4 37
Hadst thou been aught but gossamer, feathers, air, So many fathom down precipitating, Thou'dst shiver'd like an egg . . . iv 6 50
Another of his fathom they have none, To lead their business . *Othello* i 1 153
Fathomless. And buckle in a waist most fathomless With spans and inches so diminutive As fears and reasons . . *Troi. and Cres.* ii 2 30
Fathom-line. Or dive into the bottom of the deep, Where fathom-line could never touch the ground . . . . 1 *Hen. IV.* i 3 204
Fatigate. Then straight his doubled spirit Re-quicken'd what in flesh was fatigate . . . . . *Coriolanus* ii 2 121
Fat-kidneyed. Peace, ye fat-kidneyed rascal! . . . 1 *Hen. IV.* ii 2 5
Fatness. In the fatness of these pursy times . . *Hamlet* iii 4 153
Fatted. And crows are fatted with the murrion flock . *M. N. Dream* ii 1 97
I should have fatted all the region kites With this slave's offal *Hamlet* ii 2 607
Fatter. Would he were fatter! But I fear him not . *J. Cæsar* i 2 198
Fattest. A Windsor stag; and the fattest, I think, i' the forest *M. Wives* v 5 14
Most subject is the fattest soil to weeds . . 2 *Hen. IV.* iv 4 54
Fatting. He is frank'd up to fatting for his pains . *Richard III.* i 3 314
Fat-witted. Thou art so fat-witted, with drinking of old sack 1 *Hen. IV.* i 2 2
Fauconberg. Beaumont, Grandpré, Roussi, and Fauconberg . *Hen. V.* iii 5 44
Of lusty earls, Grandpré and Roussi, Fauconberg and Foix . iv 8 104
Faulconbridge. (*See* Falconbridge.)
Fault. The fault's your own.—So is the dear'st o' the loss *Tempest* ii 1 135
I do forgive Thy rankest fault; all of them . . . . v 1 132
Unless I be relieved by prayer, Which pierces so that it assaults Mercy itself and frees all faults . . . . . Epil. 18
Did in your name receive it: pardon the fault, I pray . *T. G. of Ver.* i 2 40
It were a shame to call her back again And pray her to a fault for which I chid her . . . . . i 2 52
Ere I have done weeping; all the kind of the Launces have this very fault . . . . . ii 3 3
That fault may be mended with a breakfast . . . . iii 1 328
She hath more hair than wit, and more faults than hairs . . iii 1 362
'More wealth than faults.'—Why, that word makes the faults gracious iii 1 376
But were you banish'd for so small a fault?—I was, and held me glad iv 1 31
We cite our faults, That they may hold excused our lawless lives . iv 1 53
If I had not had more wit than he, to take a fault upon me that he did iv 4 15
Were man But constant, he were perfect. That one error Fills him with faults . . . . . v 4 112
'Tis your fault, 'tis your fault; 'tis a good dog . . *Mer. Wives* i 1 95
His worst fault is, that he is given to prayer; he is something peevish that way: but nobody but has his fault . . . . i 4 13
For fault of a better . . . . . i 4 17; 2 *Hen. IV.* ii 2 45
'Tis my fault, Master Page: I suffer for it . . *Mer. Wives* iii 3 233
O, what a world of vile ill-favour'd faults Looks handsome in three hundred pounds a-year! . . . . . iii 4 32
Alas the day! good heart, that was not her fault . . . iii 5 40
A fault done first in the form of a beast. O Jove, a beastly fault! v 5 9
Another fault in the semblance of a fowl; think on't, Jove; a foul fault! . . . . . v 5 11
Whether it be the fault and glimpse of newness *Meas. for Meas.* i 2 162
Sith 'twas my fault to give the people scope, 'Twould be my tyranny to strike and gall them . . . . . i 3 35
You may not so extenuate his offence For I have had such faults . ii 1 28
Some run from brakes of ice, and answer none: And some condemned for a fault alone . . . . . ii 1 40

Fault. I do beseech you, let it be his fault, And not my brother *M. for M.* ii 2 35
Condemn the fault, and not the actor of it? Why, every fault's condemn'd ere it be done . . . . . ii 2 37
Mine were the very cipher of a function, To fine the faults whose fine stands in record, And let go by the actor . . . . ii 2 40
Ask your heart what it doth know That's like my brother's fault . ii 2 138
Is this her fault or mine? The tempter or the tempted, who sins most? ii 2 162
I'll make it my morn prayer To have it added to the faults of mine . ii 4 72
We are made to be no stronger Than faults may shake our frames . ii 4 133
That we were all, as some would seem to be, From our faults, as faults from seeming, free! . . . . . iii 2 41
Shame to him whose cruel striking Kills for faults of his own liking! . iii 2 282
When vice makes mercy, mercy's so extended, That for the fault's love is the offender friended . . . . . iv 2 116
That with such vehemency he should pursue Faults proper to himself . v 1 110
Laws for all faults, But faults so countenanced, that the strong statutes Stand like the forfeits in a barber's shop . . . v 1 321
Then, Angelo, thy fault's thus manifested . . . . v 1 417
They say, best men are moulded out of faults . . . . v 1 444
I have bethought me of another fault . . . . . v 1 461
I thought it was a fault, but knew it not; Yet did repent me . v 1 468
Thou'rt condemn'd: But, for those earthly faults, I quit them all . v 1 488
She will score your fault upon my pate . . *Com. of Errors* i 2 65
Do their gay vestments his affections bait? That's not my fault . ii 1 95
It is a fault that springeth from your eye . . . . iii 2 55
That's a fault that water will mend.—No, sir, 'tis in grain . iii 2 107
A grievous fault! Say, woman, didst thou so? . . . . v 1 206
The fault will be in the music, cousin, if you be not wooed . *Much Ado* ii 1 72
What's his fault?—The flat transgression of a school-boy . . ii 1 228
Margaret was in some fault for this, Although against her will . v 4 4
If she be made of white and red, Her faults will ne'er be known *L. L. Lost* i 2 105
Blushing cheeks by faults are bred And fears by pale white shown . i 2 106
If broken then, it is no fault of mine . . . . . iv 3 71
It were a fault to snatch words from my tongue . . . v 2 382
I hope I was perfect: I made a little fault in 'Great' . . . v 2 562
Those heavenly eyes, that look into these faults . . . v 2 779
Your sins are rack'd, You are attaint with faults and perjury . v 2 829
Continue then, And I will have you and that fault withal . . v 2 876
I shall find you empty of that fault, Right joyful of your reformation . v 2 878
His folly, Helena, is no fault of mine.—None, but your beauty: would that fault were mine! . . . . . *M. N. Dream* i 1 200
'Tis partly my own fault; Which death or absence soon shall remedy . iii 2 243
And in such eyes as ours appear not faults . . *Mer. of Venice* ii 2 192
Treble that, Before a friend of this description Shall lose a hair through Bassanio's fault . . . . . iii 2 304
If I could add a lie unto a fault, I would deny it . . . v 1 186
Pardon this fault, and by my soul I swear I never more will break an oath v 1 247
Let me the knowledge of my fault bear with me . . *As Y. Like It* i 3 48
I will chide no breather in the world but myself, against whom I know most faults . . . . . iii 2 298
The worst fault you have is to be in love.—'Tis a fault I will not change for your best virtue . . . . . iii 2 299
Every one fault seeming monstrous till his fellow-fault came to match it iii 2 373
O, that woman that cannot make her fault her husband's occasion! . iv 1 177
Silver made it good At the hedge-corner, in the coldest fault *T. of S.* Ind. 1 20
Would take her with all faults, and money enough . . . i 1 134
Her only fault, and that is faults enough, Is that she is intolerable curst i 2 88
Have you told him all her faults? . . . . . i 2 187
Patience, I pray you; 'twas a fault unwilling . . . iv 1 159
Some undeserved fault I'll find about the making of the bed . . iv 1 202
We'ld find no fault with the tithe-woman, if I were the parson *All's Well* i 3 89
Such were our faults, or then we thought them none . . . i 3 141
You will stay behind us!—'Tis not his fault, the spark . . ii 1 25
That barefoot plod I the cold ground upon, With sainted vow my faults to have amended . . . . . iii 4 7
But you say she's honest.—That's all the fault . . . iii 6 120
Our virtues would be proud, if our faults whipped them not . . iv 3 85
Our rash faults Make trivial price of serious things we have . v 3 60
Two faults, madonna, that drink and good counsel will amend *T. Night* i 5 47
Did not I say he would work it out? the cur is excellent at faults . ii 5 140
There's something in me that reproves my fault . . . iii 4 223
Such a headstrong potent fault it is, That it but mocks reproof . iii 4 224
If this young gentleman Have done offence, I take the fault on me . iii 4 344
If you first sinn'd with us and that with us You did continue fault *W. T.* i 2 85
These proclamations, So forcing faults upon Hermione, I little like . iii 1 16
More than mistress of Which comes to me in name of fault, I must not At all acknowledge . . . . . iii 2 61
You have made fault I' the boldness of your speech . . . iii 2 218
All faults I make, when I shall come to know them, I do repent . iii 2 220
Poor wretch, That for thy mother's fault art thus exposed To loss! . iii 3 50
No fault could you make, Which you have not redeem'd . . . v 1 2
Pardon me all the faults I have committed to your worship . . v 2 161
If she did play false, the fault was hers; Which fault lies on the hazards of all husbands That marry wives . . . *K. John* i 1 119
Your fault was not your folly: Needs must you lay your heart at his dispose . . . . . i 1 262
Is it my fault that I was Geffrey's son? No, indeed, is't not . iv 1 22
Oftentimes excusing of a fault Doth make the fault the worse by the excuse . . . . . iv 2 30
As patches set upon a little breach Discredit more in hiding of the fault Than did the fault before it was so patch'd . . . . iv 2 33
The image of a wicked heinous fault Lives in his eye . . . iv 2 71
This is my fault: as for the rest appeal'd, It issues from the rancour of a villain, A recreant . . . . . *Richard II.* i 1 142
Correction lieth in those hands Which made the fault that we cannot correct . . . . . i 2 5
To smooth his fault I should have been more mild . . . i 3 240
Let me know my fault; On what condition stands it and wherein? . ii 3 106
Intended or committed was this fault? . . . . . v 3 33
My reformation, glittering o'er my fault, Shall show more goodly 1 *Hen. IV.* i 2 237
Either envy, therefore, or misprision Is guilty of this fault and not my son . . . . . i 3 28
If sack and sugar be a fault, God help the wicked! . . . ii 4 517
You must needs learn, lord, to amend this fault . . . iii 1 180
Then be still.—Neither; 'tis a woman's fault . . . . iii 1 245
And find a time To punish this offence in other faults . . . v 2 7
The midwives say the children are not in the fault . . 2 *Hen. IV.* ii 2 29
Chide him for faults, and do it reverently . . . . iv 4 37
Never came reformation in a flood, With such a heady currance, scouring faults, . . . As in this king . . . . . *Hen. V.* i 1 34

Fault. But see thy fault! France hath in thee found out A nest of hollow bosoms . . . *Hen. V.* ii Prol. 20
If little faults, proceeding on distemper, Shall not be wink'd at . ii 2 54
I do confess my fault; And do submit me to your highness' mercy . ii 2 76
Their faults are open; Arrest them to the answer of the law . ii 2 142
I repent my fault more than my death . . . ii 2 152
My fault, but not my body, pardon, sovereign. . . ii 2 165
You will mistake each other.—A! that's a foul fault . iii 2 148
Not to-day, O Lord, O, not to-day, think not upon the fault My father made! . . . . . . iv 1 310
I beseech you take it for your own fault and not mine . iv 8 57
Sleeping or waking must I still prevail, Or will you blame and lay the fault on me? Improvident soldiers! . . . *1 Hen. VI.* ii 1 57
I did correct him for his fault the other day . . *2 Hen. VI.* i 3 202
If he were not privy to those faults, Yet, by reputing of his high descent iii 1 47
These are petty faults to faults unknown, Which time will bring to light iii 1 64
Pity was all the fault that was in me; For I should melt at an offender's tears, And lowly words were ransom for their fault . . iii 1 125
These faults are easy, quickly answer'd . . . iii 1 133
O, 'tis a fault too too unpardonable!. . . . *3 Hen. VI.* i 4 106
And he that throws not up his cap for joy Shall for the fault make forfeit of his head . . . . . ii 1 197
'Tis not my fault, Nor wittingly have I infringed my vow . . ii 2 7
Pity that this goodly boy Should lose his birthright by his father's fault ii 2 35
Devise excuses for thy faults.—While we devise fell tortures for thy faults ii 6 71
O monstrous fault, to harbour such a thought! . . . iii 2 164
I forgive and quite forget old faults . . . . iii 3 200
Do not frown upon my faults, For I will henceforth be no more unconstant v 1 101
Ah, what a shame! ah, what a fault were this! . . . v 4 12
Upon what cause?—Because my name is George.—Alack, my lord, that fault is none of yours . . . *Richard III.* i 1 47
Thy brother's love, our duty, and thy fault, Provoke us hither now . i 4 230
His fault was thought, And yet his punishment was cruel death . ii 1 104
Would it might please your grace, At our entreaties, to amend that fault! iii 7 115
It is your fault that you resign The supreme seat, the throne majestical iii 7 117
Ladies, you are not merry: gentlemen, Whose fault is this? . *Hen. VIII.* i 4 43
Nor will I sue, although the king have mercies More than I dare make faults . . . . ii 1 71
Far . . . from all That might have mercy on the fault thou gavest him iii 2 262
His faults lie open to the laws; let them, Not you, correct him . iii 2 334
So may he rest; his faults lie gently on him! . . . iv 2 31
Like or find fault; do as your pleasures are . . *Troi. and Cres.* Prol. 30
Will you be true?—Who, I? alas, it is my vice, my fault . iv 4 104
'Tis Troilus' fault: come, come, to field with him . . iv 4 145
This fault in us I find, The error of our eye directs our mind . . v 2 109
He hath faults, with surplus, to tire in repetition . . *Coriolanus* i 1 46
What miscarries Shall be the general's fault, though he perform To the utmost . . . . i 1 271
And all his faults To Marcius shall be honours, though indeed In aught he merit not . . . . i 1 278
He's poor in no one fault, but stored with all.—Especially in pride ii 1 20
We call a nettle but a nettle and The faults of fools but folly. . ii 1 208
Lay A fault on us, your tribunes; that we labour'd . . ii 3 235
Lay the fault on us.—Ay, spare us not. Say we read lectures to you . ii 3 242
As I do know the consul's worthiness, So can I name his faults . iii 1 279
To suffer lawful censure for such faults As shall be proved upon you . iii 3 46
What faults he made before the last, I think Might have found easy fines v 6 64
I do remit these young men's heinous faults: Stand up . . *T. Andron.* i 1 484
This fell fault of my accursed sons, Accursed, if the fault be proved in them . . . . ii 3 290
And that shall be the ransom for their fault . . . iii 1 156
Commander of my thoughts, Calm thee, and bear the faults of Titus' age iv 4 29
You kill'd her husband, and for that vile fault Two of her brothers were condemn'd to death . . . . v 2 173
For their fell faults our brothers were beheaded . . . v 3 100
I am the youngest of that name, for fault of a worse . *Rom. and Jul.* ii 4 129
His fault concludes but what the law should end . . . iii 1 190
O deadly sin! O rude unthankfulness! Thy fault our law calls death iii 3 25
If aught in this Miscarried by my fault, let my old life Be sacrificed . v 3 267
Faults that are rich are fair . . . . *T. of Athens* i 2 13
Mine eyes cannot hold out water, methinks: to forget their faults, I drink to you . . . . i 2 112
Every man has his fault, and honesty is his . . . . iii 1 29
You have my voice to it; the fault's Bloody; 'tis necessary he should die iii 5 1
Nor did he soil the fact with cowardice—An honour in him which buys out his fault . . . . iii 5 17
Wilt thou whip thine own faults in other men? . . . v 1 41
My honest-natured friends, I must needs say you have a little fault . v 1 90
That these great towers, trophies and schools should fall For private faults . . . . v 4 26
To make vast Neptune weep for aye On thy low grave, on faults forgiven . . . . v 4 79
And, for this fault, Assemble all the poor men of your sort . *J. Cæsar* i 1 61
The fault, dear Brutus, is not in our stars, But in ourselves . . i 2 140
Who ever knew the heavens menace so?—Those that have known the earth so full of faults . . . . i 3 45
I would it were my fault to sleep so soundly . . . ii 1 4
It was a grievous fault, And grievously hath Cæsar answer'd it . . iii 2 84
I do not like your faults.—A friendly eye could never see such faults . iv 3 89
All his faults observed, Set in a note-book, learn'd, and conn'd by rote . iv 3 97
'Tis a fault to heaven, A fault against the dead, a fault to nature *Hamlet* i 2 101
Shall in the general censure take corruption From that particular fault i 4 36
But breathe his faults so quaintly That they may seem the taints of liberty . . . . ii 1 31
Then I'll look up; My fault is past . . . . . iii 3 51
Compell'd, Even to the teeth and forehead of our faults, To give in evidence . . . . iii 3 63
Dipping all his faults in their affection . . . . iv 7 19
Do you smell a fault?—I cannot wish the fault undone . . *Lear* i 1 16
Like a sister am most loath to call Your faults as they are named . i 1 274
Who cover faults, at last shame them derides . . . . i 1 284
If you come slack of former services, You shall do well; the fault of it I'll answer . . . . i 3 10
The fault Would not 'scape censure, nor the redresses sleep . . i 4 228
O most small fault, How ugly didst thou in Cordelia show! . . i 4 288
His fault is much, and the good king his master Will check him for't . ii 2 148
All the plagues that in the pendulous air Hang fated o'er men's faults . iii 4 70
Never,—O fault!—reveal'd myself unto him, Until some half-hour past . v 3 192
Is not almost a fault To incur a private check . . *Othello* iii 3 66
Oft my jealousy Shapes faults that are not . . . . iii 3 148

Fault. I have it not about me.—Not?—No, indeed, my lord.—That is a fault . . . . *Othello* iii 4 54
Or did the letters work upon his blood, And new-create this fault? . iv 1 287
But I do think it is their husbands' faults If wives do fall . . iv 3 87
You shall close prisoner rest, Till that the nature of your fault be known v 2 336
And taunt my faults With such full license as both truth and malice Have power to utter . . . . *Ant. and Cleo.* i 2 111
A man who is the abstract of all faults That all men follow . . i 4 9
His faults in him seem as the spots of heaven, More fiery by night's blackness . . . . i 4 12
What mean you, madam? I have made no fault . . . ii 5 74
O, that his fault should make a knave of thee! . . . ii 5 102
Our faults Can never be so equal, that your love Can equally move with them . . . . iii 4 34
Is Antony or we in fault for this?—Antony only . . . iii 13 2
Throw my heart Against the flint and hardness of my fault . . iv 9 16
But you, gods, will give us Some faults to make us men . . . v 1 33
Sir, It is your fault that I have loved Posthumus . . *Cymbeline* i 1 144
He comes on angry purpose now; But that's no fault of his . . i 3 62
All faults that may be named, nay, that hell knows, Why, hers [woman's], in part or all; but rather, all . . . ii 5 27
My fault being nothing—as I have told you oft . . . iii 3 65
Know, if you kill me for my fault, I should Have died had I not made it iii 6 57
If it be sin to say so, sir, I yoke me In my good brother's fault . iv 2 20
Gods! if you Should have ta'en vengeance on my faults, I never Had lived to put on this . . . . v 1 8
You snatch some hence for little faults; that's love, To have them fall no more . . . . v 1 12
Mine eyes Were not in fault, for she was beautiful . . . v 5 63
Heaven forbid That kings should let their ears hear their faults hid! *Per.* i 2 62
The more my fault To scape his hands where I was like to die . . iv 2 79
Of all the faults beneath the heavens, the gods Do like this worst . iv 6 20
Faultiness. Is't long or round?—Round even to faultiness *Ant. and Cleo.* iii 3 33
Faultless. See here the tainture of thy nest, And look thyself be faultless, thou wert best . . . . *2 Hen. VI.* ii 1 189
God forbid any malice should prevail, That faultless may condemn a nobleman! . . . . iii 2 24
A clout Steep'd in the faultless blood of pretty Rutland . *Richard III.* i 3 178
Faulty. Wherein my youth Hath faulty wander'd . . *1 Hen. IV.* iii 2 27
Say, if thou darest, proud Lord of Warwickshire, That I am faulty in Duke Humphrey's death . . . . *2 Hen VI.* iii 2 202
Men so noble, However faulty, yet should find respect For what they have been: 'tis a cruelty To load a falling man . . . *Hen. VIII.* v 3 75
Fauste, precor gelida quando pecus omne sub umbra Ruminat . *L. L. Lost* iv 2 95
Faustuses. Like three German devils, three Doctor Faustuses *Mer. Wives* iv 5 71
Favour. Good my lord, give me thy favour still . . . *Tempest* iv 1 204
I mean that her beauty is exquisite, but her favour infinite *T. G. of Ver.* ii 1 60
I beseech you, Confirm his welcome with some special favour . . ii 4 101
And, of so great a favour growing proud . . . . . ii 4 161
When I call to mind your gracious favours Done to me, undeserving as I am . . . . iii 1 6
Thank me for this more than for all the favours Which all too much I have bestow'd on thee . . . . iii 1 161
By your good favour,—for surely, sir, a good favour you have, but that you have a hanging look . . . *Meas. for Meas.* iv 2 33
Angelo hath seen them both, and will discover the favour . . iv 2 185
Outward courtesies would fain proclaim Favours that keep within . v 1 16
Do me the favour to dilate at full What hath befall'n of them *Com. of Er.* i 1 123
Yet I will favour thee in what I can . . . . . i 1 150
And when please you to say so?—When I like your favour . *Much Ado* ii 1 97
I am in the favour of Margaret, the waiting gentlewoman . . ii 2 13
For your favour, sir, why, give God thanks, and make no boast of it . iii 3 19
Truth it is, good signior, Your niece regards me with an eye of favour . v 4 22
By thy favour, sweet welkin, I must sigh in thy face . . *L. L. Lost* iii 1 68
As thou wilt win my favour, good my knave, Do one thing for me . iii 1 153
Her favour turns the fashion of the days, For native blood is counted painting now . . . . iv 3 262
You have a favour too: Who sent it? and what is it? . . . v 2 30
An if my face were but as fair as yours, My favour were as great . v 2 33
They'll know By favours several which they did bestow . . v 2 125
This favour thou shalt wear, And then the king will court thee for his dear. . . . . v 2 130
So shall Biron take me for Rosaline. And change you favours too . v 2 134
Come on, then; wear the favours most in sight . . . v 2 136
Out of your favours, heavenly spirits, vouchsafe Not to behold . v 2 166
Change favours; and, when they repair, Blow like sweet roses . v 2 292
Told our intents before; which once disclosed, The ladies did change favours . . . . v 2 468
And that a' wears next his heart for a favour . . . . v 2 722
Received your letters full of love; Your favours, the ambassadors of love . . . . v 2 788
If you my favour mean to get, A twelvemonth shall you spend . v 2 830
Sickness is catching: O, were favour so, Yours would I catch *M. N. Dr.* i 1 186
Those be rubies, fairy favours . . . . . . ii 1 12
Seeking sweet favours for this hateful fool, I did upbraid her . iv 1 54
To buy his favour, I extend this friendship . . *Mer. of Venice* i 3 169
That, for this favour, He presently become a Christian . . iv 1 386
The boy is fair, Of female favour . . . . *As Y. Like It* iv 3 87
In this shepherd boy Some lively touches of my daughter's favour . v 4 27
I may have welcome 'mongst the rest that woo And free access and favour as the rest . . . . . . *T. of Shrew* ii 1 98
Do forswear her, As one unworthy all the former favours . . iv 2 30
My imagination Carries no favour in't but Bertram's . . *All's Well* i 1 94
Heart too capable Of every line and trick of his sweet favour . . i 1 107
Good fortune and the favour of the king Smile upon this contract . ii 3 184
Rash and unbridled boy, To fly the favours of so good a king . . iii 2 31
Certain it is, that he will steal himself into a man's favour . . iii 6 99
Nay, I'll read it first, by your favour . . . . . iv 3 245
Contempt his scornful perspective did lend me, Which warp'd the line of every other favour . . . . v 3 49
Give a favour from you To sparkle in the spirits of my daughter . v 3 74
If the duke continue these favours towards you, Cesario, you are like to be much advanced . . . . *T. Night* i 4 1
Is he inconstant, sir, in his favours? . . . . . i 4 7
If you prized my lady's favour at any thing more than contempt . ii 3 131
Young though thou art, thine eye Hath stay'd upon some favour that it loves: Hath it not, boy?—A little, by your favour . . . ii 4 25
He brought me out o' favour with my lady about a bear-baiting here . ii 5 9
I saw your niece do more favours to the count's serving-man . . iii 2 7
She did show favour to the youth in your sight only to exasperate you iii 2 19

Favour. My lady will strike him: if she do, he'll smile and take 't for a great favour . . . . *T. Night* iii 2 89
I know your favour well, Though now you have no sea-cap on your head iii 4 363
Even such and so In favour was my brother . . . . . iii 4 416
The instrument That screws me from my true place in your favour . v 1 126
Tell me . . . Why you have given me such clear lights of favour . . v 1 344
Methinks My favour here begins to warp . . . . *W. Tale* i 2 365
Leave it, Without more mercy, to it own protection And favour of the climate . . . . ii 3 179
The crown and comfort of my life, your favour, I do give lost . . iii 2 95
They were to be known by garment, not by favour . . . . v 2 53
To whom in favour she shall give the day. . . . . *K. John* ii 1 393
Speak on with favour; we are bent to hear . . . . . ii 1 422
I do love the favour and the form Of this most fair occasion . . . v 4 50
Greet I thee, my earth, And do thee favours with my royal hands *Richard II.* iii 2 11
I well remember The favours of these men: were they not mine? . . iv 1 168
And from the common'st creature pluck a glove, And wear it as a favour v 3 18
The guilt of conscience take thou for thy labour, But neither my good word nor princely favour . . . . v 6 42
And stain my favours in a bloody mask . . . . 1 *Hen. IV.* iii 2 136
It pleased your majesty to turn your looks Of favour from myself . . v 1 31
Let my favours hide thy mangled face . . . . . . v 4 96
For he misuses thy favours so much, that he swears thou art to marry his sister . . . . 2 *Hen. IV.* ii 2 138
And ripens in the sunshine of his favour . . . . . . iv 2 12
Whom he hath dull'd and cloy'd with gracious favours . . *Hen. V.* ii 2 9
Captain, I thee beseech to do me favours . . . . . . iii 6 22
Wear thou this favour for me and stick it in thy cap . . . . iv 7 160
The glove which I have given him for a favour May haply purchase him a box o' th' ear . . . . iv 7 180
Which to reduce into our former favour You are assembled . . . v 2 63
If I might buffet for my love, or bound my horse for her favours . v 2 147
Fellows of infinite tongue, that can rhyme themselves into ladies' favours v 2 165
A fiend of hell.—If not of hell, the heavens, sure, favour him 1 *Hen. VI.* ii 1 47
Fortune in favour makes him lag behind . . . . . . iii 3 34
I charge you, as you love our favour, Quite to forget this quarrel . iv 1 135
We thank you all for this great favour done, In entertainment 2 *Hen. VI.* i 1 71
What though the common people favour him . . . . . i 1 158
Thy housekeeping Hath won the greatest favour of the commons . . i 1 192
Knit his brows, As frowning at the favours of the world . . . i 2 4
Go, and take me hence; I care not whither, for I beg no favour . . ii 4 92
Used to command, untaught to plead for favour . . . . . iv 1 122
Justice with favour have I always done . . . . . . iv 7 72
Ah, know you not the city favours them? . . . . 3 *Hen. VI.* i 1 67
I am commanded, with your leave and favour, Humbly to kiss your hand iii 3 60
So God help Montague as he proves true!—And Hastings as he favours Edward's cause! . . . . iv 1 144
I think it is our way, If we will keep in favour with the king *Richard III.* i 1 79
If thy poor devoted suppliant may But beg one favour at thy gracious hand . . . . i 2 208
Since I am crept in favour with myself, I will maintain it . . . i 2 259
And I myself secure in grace and favour . . . . . . iii 4 93
Pray, give me favour, sir . . . . *Hen. VIII.* i 1 168
And then let's dream Who's best in favour . . . . . . i 4 108
Whoever the king favours, The cardinal instantly will find employment ii 1 47
The Spaniard, tied by blood and favour to her, Must now confess . . ii 2 90
Ay, and the best she shall have; and my favour To him that does best ii 2 114
Give me your hand: much joy and favour to you . . . . . ii 3 118
You have, by fortune and his highness' favours, Gone slightly o'er low steps . . . . ii 4 111
What can be their business With me, a poor weak woman, fall'n from favour? . . . . iii 1 20
One Hath crawl'd into the favour of the king, And is his oracle . . iii 2 103
O, how wretched Is that poor man that hangs on princes' favours! . iii 2 367
May he continue Long in his highness' favour, and do justice For truth's sake! . . . . iii 2 396
A man of his place, and so near our favour . . . . . . v 2 30
You are a little, By your good favour, too sharp . . . . . v 3 74
For a brown favour—for so 'tis, I must confess . . *Troi. and Cres.* i 2 101
You may call it melancholy, if you will favour the man . . . ii 3 94
As place, riches, favour, Prizes of accident as oft as merit . . . iii 3 82
I know your favour, Lord Ulysses, well . . . . . . iv 5 213
He that depends Upon your favours swims with fins of lead *Coriolanus* i 1 184
Your favour is well approved by your tongue . . . . . . iv 3 9
And to my fortunes and the people's favour Commit my cause *T. Andron.* i 1 54
And to the love and favour of my country Commit myself, my person . i 1 58
For thy favours done To us in our election this day, I give thee thanks i 1 234
But the citizens favour Lucius, And will revolt from me to succour him iv 4 79
In love?—Out— Of love?—Out of her favour, where I am in love *R. and J.* i 1 174
O, what more favour can I do to thee, Than with that hand that cut thy youth in twain To sunder his that was thine enemy? . . . . v 3 98
Then, under favour, pardon me, If I speak like a captain *T. of Athens* iii 5 40
Whom Fortune's tender arm With favour never clasp'd . . . . iv 3 251
I know that virtue to be in you, Brutus, As well as I do know your outward favour . . . . *J. Cæsar* i 2 91
The complexion of the element In favour's like the work we have in hand . . . . i 3 129
Half their faces buried in their cloaks, That by no means I may discover them By any mark of favour . . . . ii 1 76
To me, who neither beg nor fear Your favours nor your hate . *Macbeth* i 3 61
Give me your favour: my dull brain was wrought With things forgotten i 3 149
Look up clear; To alter favour ever is to fear: Leave all the rest to me i 5 73
My dread lord, Your leave and favour to return to France . *Hamlet* i 2 51
For Hamlet and the trifling of his favour, Hold it a fashion and a toy in blood . . . . i 3 5
Then you live about her waist, or in the middle of her favours? . . ii 2 237
Affliction, passion, hell itself, She turns to favour and to prettiness . iv 5 189
Let her paint an inch thick, to this favour she must come . . . v 1 214
I'll court his favours . . . . v 2 78
A thing so monstrous, to dismantle So many folds of favour . . *Lear* i 1 221
Make known It is . . . No unchaste action, or dishonour'd step, That hath deprived me of your grace and favour . . . . . . i 1 232
Take my coxcomb.—Why, fool?—Why, for taking one's part that's out of favour . . . . i 4 112
With robbers' hands my hospitable favours You should not ruffle thus . iii 7 40
But, by your favour, How near's the other army? . . . . . iv 6 215
Which, as a grise or step, may help these lovers Into your favour *Othello* i 3 201
Defeat thy favour with an usurped beard; I say, put money in thy purse i 3 346
Loveliness in favour, sympathy in years, manners and beauties . . ii 1 232

Favour. Tell her there's one Cassio entreats her a little favour of speech *Othello* iii 1 28
My lord is not my lord; nor should I know him, Were he in favour as in humour alter'd . . . . iii 4 125
Even his stubbornness, his checks, his frowns,—Prithee, unpin me,—have grace and favour in them . . . . iv 3 21
So tart a favour To trumpet such good tidings! . . *Ant. and Cleo.* ii 5 38
His lieutenant, For quick accumulation of renown, Which he achieved by the minute, lost his favour . . . . iii 1 20
Favours, by Jove that thunders! What art thou, fellow? . . . iii 13 85
Cried he? and begg'd a' pardon?—He did ask favour . . . . iii 13 133
Idiots in this case of favour would Be wisely definite . . . *Cymbeline* i 6 42
And left me bare to weather.—Uncertain favour! . . . . . iii 3 64
Thou then look'dst like a villain; now methinks Thy favour's good enough . . . . iii 4 51
Disdaining me and throwing favours on The low Posthumus . . . iii 5 75
Time hath nothing blurr'd those lines of favour Which then he wore . iv 2 104
Poor wretches that depend On greatness' favour dream as I have done . v 4 128
Many dream not to find, neither deserve, And yet are steep'd in favours v 4 131
I have surely seen him: His favour is familiar to me . . . . v 5 93
Imperial Cæsar should again unite His favour with the radiant Cymbeline . . . . v 5 475
How your favour's changed With this unprofitable woe! . . *Pericles* iv 1 25
Voice and favour! You are, you are—O royal Pericles! . . . . v 3 13
Favourable. Happier the man, whom favourable stars Allot thee for his lovely bed-fellow! . . . . *T. of Shrew* iv 5 40
Be patient till the heavens look With an aspect more favourable *W. Tale* ii 1 107
Unless some dull and favourable hand Will whisper music 2 *Hen. IV.* iv 5 2
Lend favourable ears to our request . . . . . *Richard III.* iii 7 101
Has had most favourable and happy speed . . . . . *Othello* ii 1 67
Favourably. Which the time shall more favourably minister . . . ii 1 277
Favoured. What dost thou know?—That she is not so fair as, of you, well favoured . . . . *T. G. of Ver.* ii 1 58
With old Menenius, and those senators That always favour'd him *Coriol.* iii 3 8
Well favour'd, and your looks foreshow You have a gentle heart *Pericles* iv 1 86
Favourer. Do not I know you for a favourer Of this new sect? *Hen. VIII.* v 3 80
Romans, friends, followers, favourers of my right . . *T. Andron.* i 1 9
For being now a favourer to the Briton, No more a Briton . *Cymbeline* v 3 74
They bring us peace, And come to us as favourers, not as foes *Pericles* i 4 73
Favouring. Something imperfect in favouring the first complaint *Coriol.* ii 1 54
Commend unto his lips thy favouring hand: Kiss it, my warrior *Ant. and Cleo.* iv 8 23
Favourite. Like favourites, Made proud by princes, that advance their pride Against that power that bred it . . . . . *Much Ado* iii 1 9
Look not to the ground, Ye favourites of a king: are we not high? *Richard II.* iii 2 88
Cut me off the heads Of all the favourites that the absent king In deputation left behind him here . . . . . . 1 *Hen. IV.* iv 3 86
Employ the countenance and grace of heaven, As a false favourite doth his prince's name, In deeds dishonourable . . . 2 *Hen. IV.* iv 2 25
This factious bandying of their favourites . . . . 1 *Hen. VI.* iv 1 190
You both have vow'd revenge On him, his sons, his favourites 3 *Hen. VI.* i 1 56
The great man down, you mark his favourite flies . . . *Hamlet* iii 2 214
Fawn. How I would make him fawn and beg and seek . . *L. L. Lost* v 2 62
The more you beat me, I will fawn on you . . . *M. N. Dream* ii 1 204
Whiles, like a doe, I go to find my fawn And give it food *As Y. Like It* ii 7 128
I am too old to fawn upon a nurse, Too far in years to be a pupil *Rich. II.* i 3 170
Dogs, easily won to fawn on any man! . . . . iii 2 130
Kiss the rod, And fawn on rage with base humility . . . . v 1 33
And take foul scorn to fawn on him by sending . . . 1 *Hen. VI.* iv 4 35
My love, forbear to fawn upon their frowns . . . . 3 *Hen. VI.* iv 1 75
When the lion fawns upon the lamb, The lamb will never cease to follow him . . . . iv 8 49
Take heed of yonder dog! Look, when he fawns, he bites *Richard III.* i 3 290
And you will rather show our general louts How you can frown than spend a fawn upon 'em . . . . *Coriolanus* iii 2 67
Then they could smile and fawn upon his debts . . *T. of Athens* iv 2 51 [sic: iv 4 51]
If you know That I do fawn on men and hug them hard . . *J. Cæsar* i 2 75
If thou dost bend and pray and fawn for him, I spurn thee like a cur . iii 1 45
Fawn'd like hounds, And bow'd like bondmen, kissing Cæsar's feet . . v 1 41
Fawneth. The more she spurns my love, The more it grows and fawneth on her still . . . . *T. G. of Ver.* iv 2 15
Fawning. Bestow thy fawning smiles on equal mates . . . . iii 1 158
How like a fawning publican he looks! I hate him . *Mer. of Venice* i 3 42
You say true: Why, what a candy deal of courtesy This fawning greyhound then did proffer me! . . . . 1 *Hen. IV.* i 3 252
Even like a fawning greyhound in the leash . . . . *Coriolanus* i 6 38
Let the candied tongue lick absurd pomp, And crook the pregnant hinges of the knee Where thrift may follow fawning . . *Hamlet* iii 2 67
Fay. By my fay, a goodly nap . . . . . . *T. of Shrew* Ind. 2 83
Let's to bed. Ah, sirrah, by my fay, it waxes late . *Rom. and Jul.* i 5 128
By my fay, I cannot reason . . . . *Hamlet* ii 2 271
Fealty. Belike that now she hath enfranchised them Upon some other pawn for fealty . . . . *T. G. of Ver.* ii 4 91
Pledge for his truth And lasting fealty to the new made king *Richard II.* v 2 45
Command my eldest son, nay, all my sons, As pledges of my fealty 2 *Hen. VI.* v 1 50
And when I do forget The least of these unspeakable deserts, Romans, forget your fealty to me . . . . *T. Andron.* i 1 257
Fear. I fear you have done yourself some wrong: a word . . *Tempest* i 2 443
We have lost your son, I fear, for ever . . . . ii 1 132
Ebbing men, indeed, Most often do so near the bottom run By their own fear or sloth . . . . ii 1 228
I hid me under the dead moon-calf's gaberdine for fear of the storm . ii 2 117
Will't please you taste of what is here?—Not I.—Faith, sir, you need not fear . . . . iii 3 43
The affliction of my mind amends, with which, I fear, a madness held me v 1 116
I shall not fear fly-blowing . . . . v 1 284
You call me fool.—So, by your circumstance, I fear you'll prove *T. G. of Ver.* i 1 37
I fear she'll prove as hard to you in telling your mind . . . i 1 147
I fear my Julia would not deign my lines . . . . . . i 1 160
I shunn'd the fire for fear of burning, And drench'd me in the sea . . i 3 78
To fast, like one that takes diet; to watch, like one that fears robbing . ii 1 26
Why dost thou stop my mouth?—For fear thou shouldst lose thy tongue ii 3 52
That is the least, Lucetta, of my fear . . . . ii 7 68
Fear not but that she will love you . . . . iii 2 1
These are the villains That all the travellers do fear so much . . . iv 1 6
Fear not you: I will so plead That you shall say my cunning drift excels iv 2 82
I fear I am attended by some spies.—Fear not . . . . . . v 1 10

Fear. Fear not; he bears an honourable mind, And will not use a woman lawlessly . . . . *T. G. of Ver.* v 3 13
There is no fear of Got in a riot . . . . *Mer. Wives* i 1 37
The council, look you, shall desire to hear the fear of Got . . i 1 38
If I be drunk, I'll be drunk with those that have the fear of God . i 1 189
Leaving the fear of God on the left hand . . . . . ii 2 24
Do not betray me, sir. I fear you love Mistress Page . . . iii 3 82
I fear not mine own shame so much as his peril . . . . iii 3 129
I quaked for fear . . . . iii 5 104
Many that do fear In deep of night to walk by this Herne's oak . iv 4 39
Sure, he'll come.—Fear not you that . . . . . . iv 4 78
I fear not Goliath with a weaver's beam . . . . . v 1 23
What shall become of me?—Come; fear not you . . *Meas. for Meas.* i 2 109
I do fear, too dreadful: Sith 'twas my fault . . . . . i 3 34
To give fear to use and liberty . . . . i 4 62
Make a scarecrow of the law, Setting it up to fear the birds of prey ii 1 2
You need not to fear the bawds . . . . ii 1 248
Showing we would not spare heaven as we love it, But as we stand in fear ii 3 34
Thou'rt by no means valiant; For thou dost fear the soft and tender fork Of a poor worm . . . . iii 1 16
Yet death we fear, That makes these odds all even . . . . iii 1 40
Let me know the point.—O, I do fear thee . . . . . iii 1 74
Is a paradise To what we fear of death . . . . . . iii 1 132
He shall know you better, sir, if I may live to report you.—I fear you not iii 2 173
Fear me not.—Nor, gentle daughter, fear you not at all . . . iv 1 70
I will go further than I meant, to pluck all fears out of you . iv 2 207
That life is better life, past fearing death, Than that which lives to fear v 1 403
The pretty babes, That mourn'd for fashion, ignorant what to fear *Com. of Errors* i 1 74
I greatly fear my money is not safe . . . . i 2 105
Receive the money now, For fear you ne'er see chain nor money more . iii 2 182
If any hour meet a sergeant, a' turns back for very fear . . . iv 2 56
Fear me not, man; I will not break away . . . . . iv 4 1
Come, stand by me; fear nothing. Guard with halberds! . . . v 1 185
Unless the fear of death doth make me dote . . . . . v 1 195
Undertakes them with a most Christian-like fear . . . *Much Ado* ii 3 200
If he do fear God, a' must necessarily keep peace . . . . ii 3 201
He ought to enter into a quarrel with fear and trembling . . . ii 3 203
The man doth fear God, howsoever it seems not in him . . . ii 3 205
Fear you not my part of the dialogue . . . . . . iii 1 31
Nay, never lay thy hand upon thy sword; I fear thee not . . . v 1 55
Beshrew my hand, If it should give your age such cause of fear . . v 1 56
Tush, fear not, man; we'll tip thy horns with gold . . . v 4 44
Blushing cheeks by faults are bred And fears by pale white shown *L. L. Lost* i 2 107
Then if she fear, or be to blame, By this you shall not know . . i 2 108
You have done this in the fear of God, very religiously . . . iv 2 152
I do fear colourable colours . . . . iv 2 155
I fear these stubborn lines lack power to move . . . . iv 3 55
A toy, my liege, a toy: your grace needs not fear it . . . iv 3 201
Your mistresses dare never come in rain, For fear their colours should be wash'd away . . . . iv 3 271
An angel shalt thou see; Yet fear not thou, but speak audaciously . v 2 104
Cuckoo, cuckoo: O word of fear, Unpleasing to a married ear! . . v 2 911
All their elves for fear Creep into acorn-cups . . . *M. N. Dream* ii 1 30
Fear not, my lord, your servant shall do so . . . . . ii 1 268
I am as ugly as a bear; For beasts that meet me run away for fear . ii 2 95
Look how I do quake with fear . . . . ii 2 148
Speak, of all loves! I swoon almost with fear . . . . . ii 2 154
A parlous fear.—I believe we must leave the killing out . . . iii 1 14
This will put them out of fear . . . . iii 1 23
Will not the ladies be afeard of the lion?—I fear it, I promise you . iii 1 29
I would entreat you,—not to fear, not to tremble: my life for yours . iii 1 42
Their sense thus weak, lost with their fears thus strong . . . iii 2 27
I led them on in this distracted fear . . . . iii 2 31
For thou, I fear, hast given me cause to curse . . . . . iii 2 46
For fear lest day should look their shames upon . . . . iii 2 385
To sleep by hate, and fear no enmity . . . . . . iv 1 150
In the night, imagining some fear, How easy is a bush supposed a bear! v 1 21
Throttle their practised accent in their fears . . . . . v 1 97
Alack, alack, I fear my Thisby's promise is forgot! . . . . v 1 174
You, ladies, you, whose gentle hearts do fear The smallest monstrous mouse . . . . v 1 222
I fear we shall out-sleep the coming morn . . . . . v 1 372
Every object that might make me fear Misfortune to my ventures, out of doubt Would make me sad . . . . . *Mer. of Venice* i 1 20
I fear he will prove the weeping philosopher when he grows old . . i 2 52
For fear of the worst, I pray thee . . . . i 2 103
You need not fear, lady, the having any of these lords . . . i 2 109
Why, fear not, man; I will not forfeit it . . . . . . i 3 158
None but that ugly treason of mistrust, Which makes me fear . . iii 2 29
I fear you speak upon the rack, Where men enforced do speak anything iii 2 32
Rash-embraced despair, And shuddering fear, and green-eyed jealousy . iii 2 110
I feel too much thy blessing: make it less, For fear I surfeit . . iii 2 115
Therefore, I promise ye, I fear you. I was always plain with you . . iii 5 3
Truly then I fear you are damned both by father and mother . . iii 5 17
If you thus get my wife into corners.—Nay, you need not fear us . . iii 5 33
Wherein doth sit the dread and fear of kings . . . . . iv 1 192
We are no tell-tales, madam; fear you not . . . . . v 1 123
I'll fear no other thing So sore as keeping safe Nerissa's ring . . v 1 306
If you saw yourself with your eyes . . . , the fear of your adventure would counsel you to a more equal enterprise . . . *As Y. L. It* i 2 187
In my heart Lie there what hidden woman's fear there will . . i 3 121
This house is but a butchery: Abhor it, fear it, do not enter it . . ii 3 28
I fear you have sold your own lands to see other men's . . . iv 1 22
As those that fear they hope, and know they fear . . . . v 4 4
Fear not, my lord: we can contain ourselves . . . *T. of Shrew* Ind. 1 100
I' faith, sir, you shall never need to fear . . . . . i 1 61
I kill'd a man and fear I was descried . . . . . . i 1 237
Tush, tush! fear boys with bugs.—For he fears none . . . i 2 211
Why dost thou look so pale?—For fear, I promise you, if I look pale ii 1 144
I fear thee not: Sirrah young gamester, your father were a fool . ii 1 401
Fear not, sweet wench, they shall not touch thee . . . . iii 2 240
I fear it is too choleric a meat. How say you to a fat tripe finely broil'd? iv 3 19
'Twere good he were school'd.—Fear you not him . . . . iv 4 10
Tut, fear not me.—But has thou done thy errand? . . . . iv 4 13
Fear not, Baptista; we will content you, go to . . . . v 1 138
Hortensio fears his widow.—Then never trust me, if I be afeared . v 2 16
You go so much backward when you fight.—That's for advantage.—So is running away, when fear proposes the safety . . *All's Well* i 1 216

Fear. The composition that your valour and fear makes in you is a virtue of a good wing . . . . *All's Well* i 1 218
If men could be contented to be what they are, there were no fear in marriage . . . . i 3 55
My fear hath catch'd your fondness . . . . i 3 176
But such traitors His majesty seldom fears . . . . . ii 1 100
Ensconcing ourselves into seeming knowledge, when we should submit ourselves to an unknown fear . . . . ii 3 6
You shall not need to fear me.—I hope so . . . . . iii 5 31
In the highest compulsion of base fear . . . . . . iii 6 31
My tongue is too foolhardy; but my heart hath the fear of Mars before it . . . . iv 1 33
Who knows himself a braggart, Let him fear this . . . . iv 3 371
Makest conjectural fears to come into me, Which I would fain shut out v 3 114
Shall tax my fears of little vanity, Having vainly fear'd too little . v 3 122
You either fear his humour or my negligence . . . . *T. Night* i 4 5
He that is well hanged in this world needs to fear no colours.—Make that good.—He shall see none to fear . . . . i 5 6
I can tell thee where that saying was born, of 'I fear no colours' . i 5 10
And fear to find Mine eye too great a flatterer for my mind . . i 5 327
The rather by these arguments of fear, Set forth in your pursuit . . iii 3 12
Fear to kill a woodcock, lest thou dispossess the soul of thy grandam . iv 2 63
It is the baseness of thy fear That makes thee strangle thy propriety . v 1 149
Fear not, Cesario; take thy fortunes up; Be that thou know'st thou art . . . . v 1 151
O, do not swear! Hold little faith, though thou hast too much fear . v 1 174
I am question'd by my fears, of what may chance . . . . *W. Tale* i 2 11
No man is free, But that his negligence, his folly, fear, Among the infinite doings of the world, Sometime puts forth . . . . i 2 252
'Twas a fear Which oft infects the wisest . . . . . . i 2 261
Fear o'ershades me: Good expedition be my friend! . . . . i 2 457
What I shall incur to pass it, Having no warrant.—You need not fear it ii 2 58
Do not you fear: upon mine honour, I Will stand betwixt you and danger . . . . ii 2 65
Fear you his tyrannous passion more, alas, Than the queen's life? . ii 3 28
Tell me what blessings I have here alive, That I should fear to die? . iii 2 109
Your son, with mere conceit and fear Of the queen's speed, is gone . iii 2 145
Ay, my lord; and fear We have landed in ill time . . . . iii 3 2
Two of my best sheep, which I fear the wolf will sooner find than the master . . . . iii 3 67
But, I fear, the angle that plucks our son thither . . . . iv 2 52
I fear, sir, my shoulder-blade is out . . . . iv 3 76
Your greatness Hath not been used to fear . . . . . . iv 4 18
With wisdom I might fear, my Doricles, You woo'd me the false way . iv 4 150
You have As little skill to fear as I have purpose To put you to't . . iv 4 152
Fear not thou, man, thou shalt lose nothing here . . . . iv 4 258
And as hardly Will he endure your sight as yet, I fear . . . iv 4 481
Fear none of this: I think you know my fortunes Do all lie there . . iv 4 601
Fear not, man; here's no harm intended to thee . . . . iv 4 642
That you may—For I do fear eyes over—to shipboard Get undescried . iv 4 668
Fear thou no wife; I'll have no wife . . . . v 1 68
King'd of our fears, until our fears, resolved, Be by some certain king purged and deposed . . . . *K. John* ii 1 371
Sick and capable of fears, Oppress'd with wrongs and therefore full of fears . . . . iii 1 12
A widow, husbandless, subject to fears, A woman, naturally born to fears . . . . iii 1 14
But on this day let seamen fear no wreck; No bargains break! . . iii 1 92
My mother is assailed in our tent, And ta'en, I fear.—My lord, I rescued her; Her highness is in safety, fear you not . . . . iii 2 7
I fear some outrage, and I'll follow her . . . . . . iii 4 106
I hope your warrant will bear out the deed.—Uncleanly scruples! fear not you . . . . iv 1 7
And more, more strong, then lesser is my fear, I shall indue you with . iv 2 42
Your fears, which, as they say, attend The steps of wrong . . . iv 2 56
I fear will issue thence The foul corruption of a sweet child's death . iv 2 80
Full of idle dreams, Not knowing what they fear, but full of fear . . iv 2 146
Why seek'st thou to possess me with these fears? . . . . iv 2 203
Those thy fears might have wrought fears in me . . . . iv 2 236
Let not the world see fear and sad distrust Govern the motion of a kingly eye: Be stirring as the time . . . . v 1 46
How goes the day with us? O, tell me, Hubert.—Badly, I fear . . v 3 2
The king, I fear, is poison'd by a monk . . . . . . v 6 23
Which fear, not reverence, makes thee to except . . . *Richard II.* i 1 72
My teeth shall tear The slavish motive of recanting fear . . . i 1 193
And all too soon, I fear, the king shall rue . . . . . i 3 205
To horse, to horse! urge doubts to them that fear . . . . ii 1 299
The commons they are cold, And will, I fear, revolt . . . . ii 2 89
The one in fear to lose what they enjoy, The other to enjoy by rage and war . . . . ii 4 13
Fear not, my lord: that Power that made you king Hath power to keep you king . . . . iii 2 27
To fear the foe, since fear oppresseth strength, Gives in your weakness strength unto your foe . . . . iii 2 180
Fear, and be slain: no worse can come to fight . . . . . iii 2 183
This ague fit of fear is over-blown; An easy task it is to win our own . iii 2 190
Disorder, horror, fear, and mutiny Shall here inhabit . . . . iv 1 142
The love of wicked men converts to fear; That fear to hate . . . v 1 67
I fear, I fear,— What should you fear? 'Tis nothing but some bond . v 2 64
Stay thy revengeful hand; thou has no cause to fear . . . . v 3 42
Fear, and not love, begets his penitence; Forget to pity him . . v 3 56
Yet am I sick for fear: speak it again . . . . . . v 3 133
Have I no friend will rid me of this living fear? . . . . v 4 2
Great king, within this coffin I present Thy buried fear . . . v 6 31
Shall we buy treason? and indent with fears, When they have lost and forfeited themselves? . . . . *1 Hen. IV.* i 3 87
The thieves are all scatter'd and possess'd with fear . . . . ii 2 112
Now in very sincerity of fear and cold heart, will he to the king . . ii 3 33
I fear my brother Mortimer doth stir About his title . . . . ii 3 84
The earth shook to see the heavens on fire, And not in fear of your nativity . . . . iii 1 26
Through vassal fear, Base inclination and the start of spleen . . iii 2 124
I fear thee as I fear the roaring of the lion's whelp . . . . iii 3 167
Dost thou think I'll fear thee as I fear thy father? . . . . iii 3 170
That shows the ignorant a kind of fear Before not dreamt of . . iv 1 74
There is not such a word Spoke of in Scotland as this term of fear . iv 1 85
Talk not of dying: I am out of fear Of death or death's hand . . iv 1 135
Such as fear the report of a caliver worse than a struck fowl . . iv 2 20
Tut, never fear me: I am as vigilant as a cat to steal cream . . iv 2 64
I fear we shall stay too long . . . . iv 2 83

Fear. You do not counsel well: You speak it out of fear and cold heart *1 Hen. IV.* iv 3 7
If well-respected honour bid me on, I hold as little counsel with weak fear As you iv 3 11
Let it be seen to-morrow in the battle Which of us fears iv 3 14
I fear, Sir Michael, What with the sickness of Northumberland iv 4 13
You need not fear; There is Douglas and Lord Mortimer iv 4 21
I hope no less, yet needful 'tis to fear iv 4 34
And be no more an exhaled meteor, A prodigy of fear v 1 20
Even our love durst not come near your sight For fear of swallowing v 1 64
Though I could 'scape shot-free at London, I fear the shot here v 3 31
I fear thou art another counterfeit v 4 35
All his men Upon the foot of fear, fled with the rest v 5 20
He that but fears the thing he would not know Hath by instinct knowledge from others' eyes That what he fear'd is chanced *2 Hen. IV.* i 1 85
Your spirit is too true, your fears too certain i 1 92
Thou shakest thy head and hold'st it fear or sin To speak a truth i 1 95
Such lightness with their fear That arrows fled not swifter i 1 122
And in his flight, Stumbling in fear, was took i 1 131
If he should do so, He leaves his back unarm'd . . : never fear that i 3 80
Fear we broadsides? no, let the fiend give fire ii 4 196
See now, whether pure fear and entire cowardice doth not make thee wrong this virtuous gentlewoman ii 4 352
This offer comes from mercy, not from fear iv 1 150
All too confident To give admittance to a thought of fear iv 1 153
No conditions of our peace can stand.—Fear you not that iv 1 185
Rouse up fear and trembling, and do observance to my mercy iv 3 16
The people fear me; for they do observe Unfather'd heirs iv 4 121
All these bold fears Thou see'st with peril I have answered iv 5 196
By whose power I well might lodge a fear To be again displaced iv 5 208
O God, I fear all will be overturn'd! v 2 19
Brothers, you mix your sadness with some fear v 2 46
Fear not your advancements v 5 84
A colour that I fear you will die in, Sir John.—Fear no colours v 5 92
First my fear; then my courtesy; last my speech Epil. 1
My fear is, your displeasure; my courtesy, my duty Epil. 2
But fear the main intendment of the Scot *Hen. V.* i 2 144
Shake in their fear and with pale policy Seek to divert the English purposes ii Prol. 14
It fits us then to be as provident As fear may teach us out of late examples ii 4 12
And let us do it with no show of fear ii 4 23
Her sceptre so fantastically borne By a vain, giddy, shallow, humorous youth, That fear attends her not ii 4 29
And let us fear The native mightiness and fate of him ii 4 63
He'll drop his heart into the sink of fear iii 5 59
I will not say so, for fear I should be faced out of my way iii 7 89
His liberal eye doth give to every one, Thawing cold fear iv Prol. 45
When he sees reason of fears, as we do, his fears, out of doubt, be of the same relish as ours are iv 1 113
No man should possess him with any appearance of fear iv 1 116
Creating awe and fear in other men iv 1 264
Steel my soldiers' hearts; Possess them not with fear iv 1 307
For our approach shall so much dare the field That England shall couch down in fear and yield iv 2 37
We would not die in that man's company That fears his fellowship to die with us iv 3 39
I fear thou'lt once more come again for ransom iv 3 128
Why live we idly here? Talbot is taken, whom we wont to fear *1 Hen. VI.* i 2 14
Then come, o' God's name; I fear no woman i 2 102
Since Henry's death, I fear, there is conveyance i 3 2
None durst come near for fear of sudden death i 4 48
So great fear of my name 'mongst them was spread That they supposed I could rend bars of steel i 4 50
A witch, by fear, not force, like Hannibal, Drives back our troops i 5 21
Your cheeks do counterfeit our roses; For pale they look with fear ii 4 63
'Tis not for fear but anger that thy cheeks Blush for pure shame ii 4 65
And we for fear compell'd to shut our shops iii 1 85
Now I fear that fatal prophecy iv 1 195
I fear we should have seen decipher'd there More rancorous spite iv 1 184
But, if I bow, they'll say it was for fear iv 5 29
Now he is gone, my lord, you need not fear v 2 17
Of all base passions, fear is most accursed v 2 18
O fairest beauty, do not fear nor fly! v 3 46
Such fierce alarums both of hope and fear, As I am sick v 5 85
Nay, fear not, man, We are alone; here's none but thee and I *2 Hen. VI.* i 2 68
I fear, at last Hume's knavery will be the duchess' wreck i 2 104
Fear you not her courage i 4 6
Madam, sit you and fear not: whom we raise, We will make fast i 4 24
And fear not, neighbour, you shall do well enough ii 3 60
Here's a pot of good double beer, neighbour: drink, and fear not your man ii 3 65
Fear not thy master: fight for credit of the 'prentices ii 3 70
But fear not thou, until thy foot be snared ii 4 56
If it be fond, call it a woman's fear; Which fear if better reasons can supplant, I will subscribe iii 1 36
Ah, that my fear were false! ah, that it were! For, good King Henry, thy decay I fear iii 1 193
Gloucester should be quickly rid the world, To rid us from the fear we have of him iii 1 234
Let pale-faced fear keep with the mean-born man iii 1 335
They say, in him they fear your highness' death iii 2 249
It is thee I fear.—Thou shalt have cause to fear before I leave thee iv 1 118
True nobility is exempt from fear iv 1 129
I fear neither sword nor fire.—He need not fear the sword iv 2 63
He should stand in fear of fire, being burnt i' the hand for stealing of sheep iv 2 67
Fear not that, I warrant thee iv 3 19
Trust nobody, for fear you be betray'd iv 4 58
Why dost thou quiver, man?—The palsy, and not fear, provokes me iv 7 98
Fear frames disorder, and disorder wounds Where it should guard v 2 32
What! think'st thou that we fear them? *3 Hen. VI.* i 2 53
Brother, I go; I'll win them, fear it not i 2 60
A woman's general; what should we fear? i 2 69
Is he dead already? or is it fear That makes him close his eyes? i 3 10
Why come you not? what! multitudes, and fear? i 4 39
Or more than common fear of Clifford's rigour ii 1 126
Doth not the object cheer your heart, my lord?—Ay, as the rocks cheer them that fear their wreck ii 2 5
Gives not the hawthorn-bush a sweeter shade . . . Than doth a rich embroider'd canopy To kings that fear their subjects' treachery? ii 5 45
Not that I fear to stay, but love to go Whither the queen intends ii 5 138

Fear. I fear thy overthrow More than my body's parting with my soul! *3 Hen. VI.* ii 6 3
My love and fear glued many friends to thee ii 6 5
I fear her not, unless she chance to fall iii 2 24
Thou seest what's past, go fear thy king withal iii 3 226
Are we all friends?—Fear not that, my lord iv 2 5
And turn'd my captive state to liberty, My fear to hope iv 6 4
By doubtful fear My joy of liberty is half eclipsed iv 6 62
What! fear not, man, but yield me up the keys iv 7 37
The doubt is that he will seduce the rest.—That's not my fear iv 8 38
So, lie thou there: die thou, and die our fear v 2 1
What cannot be avoided 'Twere childish weakness to lament or fear v 4 38
The thief doth fear each bush an officer v 6 12
Many a thousand, Which now mistrust no parcel of my fear v 6 38
To hell; and say I sent thee thither: I, that have neither pity, love, nor fear v 6 68
To purge his fear, I'll be thy death v 6 88
His physicians fear him mightily *Richard III.* i 1 137
I fear our happiness is at the highest i 3 41
O God, I fear thy justice will take hold On me, and you, and mine! ii 1 131
The fear of harm, as harm apparent, In my opinion, ought to be prevented ii 2 130
I fear, I fear 'twill prove a troublous world ii 3 5
Come, come, we fear the worst; all shall be well ii 3 31
Ye cannot reason almost with a man That looks not heavily and full of fear ii 3 40
Why, what should you fear?—Marry, my uncle Clarence' angry ghost iii 1 143
I fear no uncles dead.—Nor none that live, I hope.—An if they live, I hope I need not fear iii 1 146
Bid him not fear the separated councils iii 2 20
Tell him his fears are shallow, wanting instance iii 2 25
Fear you the boar, and go so unprovided? iii 2 75
Intend some fear; Be not you spoke with, but by mighty suit iii 7 45
I fear, we shall ne'er win him to it.—Marry, God forbid his grace should say us nay!—I fear he will iii 7 80
He fears you mean no good to him.—Sorry I am my noble cousin should Suspect me iii 7 87
The boy is foolish, and I fear not him. Look, how thou dream'st! iv 2 56
Soon I'll rid you from the fear of them.—Thou sing'st sweet music iv 2 78
The Welshman comes. Thou wilt revolt, and fly to him, I fear iv 4 478
If I revolt, off goes young George's head; The fear of that withholds my present aid iv 5 5
He hath no friends but who are friends for fear v 2 20
With guilty fear, Let fall thy lance v 3 142
Cold fearful drops stand on my trembling flesh. What do I fear? myself? v 3 182
O Ratcliff, I fear, I fear,— Nay, good my lord, be not afraid of shadows v 3 214
His fears were, that the interview betwixt England and France might, through their amity, Breed him some prejudice *Hen. VIII.* i 1 80
We must not stint Our necessary actions, in the fear To cope malicious censurers; which ever, As ravenous fishes, do a vessel follow i 2 77
If we shall stand still, In fear our motion will be mock'd or carp'd at, We should take root here i 2 86
Things done well, And with a care, exempt themselves from fear i 2 89
Presently the duke Said, 'twas the fear, indeed i 2 158
Nay, ladies, fear not; By all the laws of war you're privileged i 4 51
Your grace, I fear, with dancing is a little heated.—I fear, too much i 4 100
I do not think he fears death.—Sure, he does not ii 1 37
It calls, I fear, too many curses on their heads That were the authors ii 1 138
I fear he will indeed: well, let him have them: He will have all ii 2 11
Dangers, doubts, wringing of the conscience, Fears, and despairs ii 2 29
I love him not, nor fear him; there's my creed ii 2 51
Ever in fear to kindle your dislike, Yea, subject to your countenance ii 4 25
In such a point of weight, so near mine honour,—More near my life, I fear iii 1 72
Madam, you wrong the king's love with these fears iii 1 81
But cardinal sins and hollow hearts I fear ye iii 1 104
All your studies Make me a curse like this.—Your fears are worse iii 1 124
You wrong your virtues With these weak women's fears iii 1 169
What we can do to him, though now the time Gives way to us, I much fear iii 2 16
O, fear him not; His spell in that is out iii 2 19
I must read this paper; I fear, the story of his anger iii 2 209
More pangs and fears than wars or women have iii 2 370
Be just, and fear not iii 2 446
Let's sit down quiet, For fear we wake her iv 2 82
I fear nothing What can be said against me v 1 125
Many dare accuse you boldly, More than, I fear, you are provided for v 3 57
Would you were half so honest! Men's prayers then would seek you, not their fears.—I shall remember this v 3 83
But those, we fear, We have frighted with our trumpets Epil. 3
I fear, All the expected good we're like to hear For this play Epil. 7
That seeks his praise more than he fears his peril, That knows his valour, and knows not his fear *Troi. and Cres.* i 3 267
Though no man lesser fears the Greeks than I ii 2 8
No lady of more softer bowels, More spongy to suck in the sense of fear ii 2 12
With spans and inches so diminutive As fears and reasons ii 2 32
O, theft most base, That we have stol'n what we do fear to keep! ii 2 93
We fear to warrant in our native place ii 2 96
Nor fear of bad success in a bad cause, Can qualify the same ii 2 117
Your full consent Gave wings to my propension and cut off All fears ii 2 134
I fear it much; and I do fear besides, That I shall lose distinction in my joys iii 2 27
More dregs than water, if my fears have eyes iii 2 72
Fears make devils of cherubins; they never see truly iii 2 74
Blind fear, that seeing reason leads, finds safer footing than blind reason stumbling without fear iii 2 76
To fear the worst oft cures the worse iii 2 78
O, let my lady apprehend no fear iii 2 80
I fear We shall be much unwelcome.—That I assure you iv 1 44
Fear not my truth: the moral of my wit Is 'plain and true' iv 4 109
The general state, I fear, Can scarce entreat you to be odd with him iv 5 264
You have sworn patience.—Fear me not, sweet lord v 2 62
I do not speak of flight, of fear, of death, But dare all imminence v 10 12
My fear is this, Some galled goose of Winchester would hiss v 10 54
You cowards! you were got in fear, Though you were born in Rome *Coriol.* i 3 36
Nor a man that fears you less than he, That's lesser than a little i 4 14
They fear us not, but issue forth their city i 4 23
Backs red, and faces pale With flight and agued fear! i 4 38
If any fear Lesser his person than an ill report i 6 69
We cannot keep the town.—Fear not our care i 7 5
We are the greater poll, and in true fear They gave us our demands iii 1 134
We debase The nature of our seats and make the rabble Call our cares fears iii 1 137
Let thy mother rather feel thy pride than fear Thy dangerous stoutness iii 2 126

Fear. We hear not of him, neither need we fear him . . . *Coriolanus* iv 6 1
Who did hoot him out o' the city.—But I fear They'll roar him in again iv 6 123
That would be glad to have This true which they so seem to fear . . iv 6 152
Go home, And show no sign of fear . . . . . . iv 6 153
He that hath a will to die by himself fears it not from another . . v 2 111
Constrains them weep and shake with fear and sorrow . . . . v 3 100
Fear not, lords, and you, Lavinia . . . . . *T. Andron.* i 1 471
I am surprised with an uncouth fear: A chilling sweat o'er-runs my trembling joints . . . . ii 3 211
Tell me how it is; for ne'er till now Was I a child to fear I know not what ii 3 221
Help me with thy fainting hand—If fear hath made thee faint . ii 3 234
Fear not thy sons; they shall do well enough . . . . ii 3 305
Agree whose hand shall go along, For fear they die before their pardon come . . . . iii 1 176
Do not fear thine aunt.—She loves thee, boy, too well to do thee harm iv 1 5
Fear her not, Lucius: somewhat doth she mean . . . . iv 1 9
I have read that Hecuba of Troy Ran mad for sorrow: that made me to fear . . . . iv 1 21
And rape, I fear, was root of thine annoy . . . . . iv 1 49
Why should you fear? is not your city strong? . . . . iv 4 78
Be blithe again, And bury all thy fear in my devices . . . iv 4 112
Where bloody murder or detested rape Can couch for fear . . . v 2 38
I fear the emperor means no good to us . . . . . v 3 10
Fear me not.—No, marry; I fear thee! . . . *Rom. and Jul.* i 1 42
Supper is done, and we shall come too late.—I fear, too early . . i 4 106
The sport is at the best.—Ay, so I fear; the more is my unrest . . i 5 122
We will have vengeance for it, fear thou not: Then weep no more . iii 5 88
And I will do it without fear or doubt, To live an unstain'd wife . iv 1 87
If no inconstant toy, nor womanish fear, Abate thy valour . . iv 1 119
Give me, give me! O, tell not me of fear! . . . . . iv 1 121
I have a faint cold fear thrills through my veins, That almost freezes up iv 3 15
I fear it is: and yet, methinks, it should not . . . . . iv 3 28
If I wake, shall I not be distraught, Environed with all these hideous fears? iv 3 50
His looks I fear, and his intents I doubt . . . . . v 3 44
For fear of that, I still will stay with thee . . . . . v 3 106
Fear comes upon me: O, much I fear some ill unlucky thing . . v 3 135
What fear is this which startles in our ears? . . . . . v 3 194
If I were a huge man, I should fear to drink at meals . *T. of Athens* i 2 51
I should fear those that dance before me now Would one day stamp upon me . . . . i 2 148
I do fear, When every feather sticks in his own wing, Lord Timon will be left a naked gull . . . . ii 1 29
Would we were all discharged!—I fear it . . . . . ii 2 12
I fear 'tis deepest winter in Lord Timon's purse . . . . iii 4 14
I am of your fear for that . . . . iii 4 16
Piety, and fear, Religion to the gods, peace, justice, truth . . iv 1 15
The plague of company light upon thee! I will fear to catch it and give way . . . . iv 3 357
To ease them of their griefs, Their fears of hostile strokes . . v 1 202
In, and prepare: Ours is the fall, I fear; our foes the snare . . v 2 17
Pursy insolence shall break his wind With fear and horrid flight . v 4 13
Ere thou hadst power or we had cause of fear, We sent to thee . . v 4 15
To atone your fears With my more noble meaning, not a man Shall pass v 4 58
I do fear, the people Choose Cæsar for their king.—Ay, do you fear it? Then must I think you would not have it so . . . *J. Cæsar* i 2 79
I love The name of honour more than I fear death . . . . i 2 89
Fear him not, Cæsar; he's not dangerous; He is a noble Roman . i 2 196
I fear him not: Yet if my name were liable to fear, I do not know the man I should avoid So soon . . . . i 2 198
I rather tell thee what is to be fear'd Than what I fear . . . i 2 212
I durst not laugh, for fear of opening my lips and receiving the bad air i 2 251
Upon a heap a hundred ghastly women, Transformed with their fear . i 3 24
It is the part of men to fear and tremble, When the most mighty gods by tokens send Such dreadful heralds . . . . . . i 3 54
You look pale and gaze And put on fear and cast yourself in wonder . i 3 60
To make them instruments of fear and warning Unto some monstrous state i 3 70
Yet I fear him; For in the ingrafted love he bears to Cæsar . . ii 1 183
There is no fear in him; let him not die: For he will live, and laugh at this ii 1 190
Never fear that; if he be so resolved, I can o'ersway him . . ii 1 202
These things are beyond all use, And I do fear them . . . ii 2 26
It seems to me most strange that men should fear; Seeing that death, a necessary end, Will come when it will come . . . . . ii 2 35
Cæsar should be a beast without a heart, If he should stay at home to-day for fear. No, Cæsar shall not . . . . ii 2 43
Call it my fear That keeps you in the house, and not your own . . ii 2 50
How foolish do your fears seem now, Calpurnia! I am ashamed I did yield to them . . . . ii 2 105
None that I know will be, much that I fear may chance . . . ii 4 32
I fear our purpose is discovered . . . . iii 1 17
Casca, be sudden, for we fear prevention. Brutus, what shall be done? iii 1 19
Yet have I a mind That fears him much; and my misgiving still Falls shrewdly . . . . iii 1 145
Be patient till we have appeased The multitude, beside themselves with fear . . . . iii 1 180
I fear I wrong the honourable men Whose daggers have stabb'd Cæsar; I do fear it . . . . iii 2 156
You'll bear me a bang for that, I fear . . . . . . iii 3 21
Some that smile have in their hearts, I fear, Millions of mischiefs . iv 1 50
But I do find it cowardly and vile, For fear of what might fall, so to prevent The time of life . . . . v 1 105
Why do you start; and seem to fear Things that do sound so fair? *Macb.* i 3 51
Speak then to me, who neither beg nor fear Your favours nor your hate i 3 60
Present fears Are less than horrible imaginings . . . . . i 3 137
Yet let that be, Which the eye fears, when it is done, to see . . i 4 53
Yet do I fear thy nature; It is too full o' the milk of human kindness . i 5 17
That which rather thou dost fear to do Than wishest should be undone i 5 25
Only look up clear; To alter favour ever is to fear . . . . i 5 73
Hear not my steps, which way they walk, for fear Thy very stones prate ii 1 57
Listening their fear, I could not say 'Amen' . . . . . ii 2 29
'Tis the eye of childhood That fears a painted devil . . . . ii 2 55
Fears and scruples shake us: In the great hand of God I stand . ii 3 135
I fear, Thou play'dst most foully for't . . . . . . iii 1 2
Our fears in Banquo Stick deep; and in his royalty of nature Reigns that which would be fear'd . . . . iii 1 49
There is none but he Whose being I do fear . . . . . iii 1 55
Both the worlds suffer, Ere we will eat our meal in fear . . . iii 2 17
I am cabin'd, cribb'd, confined, bound in To saucy doubts and fears . iii 4 25
O proper stuff! This is the very painting of your fear . . . iii 4 61
O, these flaws and starts, Impostors to true fear . . . . iii 4 64
And keep the natural ruby of your cheeks, When mine is blanch'd with fear iii 4 116

Fear. My strange and self-abuse Is the initiate fear that wants hard use *Macbeth* iii 4 143
Spurn fate, scorn death, and bear His hopes 'bove wisdom, grace and fear iii 5 31
For thy good caution, thanks; Thou hast harp'd my fear aright . iv 1 74
Then live, Macduff: what need I fear of thee? . . . . . iv 1 82
That I may tell pale-hearted fear it lies, And sleep in spite of thunder iv 1 85
When our actions do not, Our fears do make us traitors . . . iv 2 4
You know not Whether it was his wisdom or his fear . . . . iv 2 5
All is the fear and nothing is the love; As little is the wisdom . . iv 2 12
When we hold rumour From what we fear, yet know not what we fear iv 2 20
Poor bird! thou'ldst never fear the net nor lime, The pitfall nor the gin iv 2 34
Be not offended: I speak not as in absolute fear of you . . . iv 3 38
But fear not yet To take upon you what is yours . . . . iv 3 69
Yet do not fear; Scotland hath foisons to fill up your will . . iv 3 87
What need we fear who knows it, when none can call our power to account? v 1 42
Till Birnam wood remove to Dunsinane, I cannot taint with fear . . v 3 3
Fear not, Macbeth; no man that's born of woman Shall e'er have power upon thee . . . . v 3 6
The heart I bear Shall never sag with doubt nor shake with fear . . v 3 10
Go prick thy face, and over-red thy fear, Thou lily-liver'd boy . . v 3 14
Those linen cheeks of thine Are counsellors to fear . . . . v 3 17
Skirr the country round; Hang those that talk of fear . . . v 3 36
I have almost forgot the taste of fears . . . . . . v 5 9
Fear not, till Birnam wood Do come to Dunsinane . . . . v 5 44
Such a one Am I to fear, or none . . . . v 7 4
It harrows me with fear and wonder . . . . . . *Hamlet* i 1 44
Distill'd Almost to jelly with the act of fear, Stand dumb and speak not i 2 205
But you must fear, His greatness weigh'd, his will is not his own . i 3 16
Fear it, Ophelia, fear it, my dear sister, And keep you in the rear of your affection, Out of the shot and danger of desire . . . . . i 3 33
Be wary then; best safety lies in fear . . . . . . i 3 43
My brother, Do not, as some ungracious pastors do, . . . —O, fear me not i 3 51
Why, what should be the fear? I do not set my life at a pin's fee . i 4 64
Mad for thy love?—My lord, I do not know; But truly, I do fear it . ii 1 86
A blanket, in the alarm of fear caught up . . . . . . ii 2 532
Women's fear and love holds quantity; In neither aught, or in extremity iii 2 177
What my love is, proof hath made you know; And as my love is sized, my fear is so . . . . iii 2 180
Where love is great, the littlest doubts are fear; Where little fears grow great, great love grows there . . . . iii 2 181
Most holy and religious fear it is To keep those many many bodies safe iii 3 8
We will fetters put upon this fear, Which now goes too free-footed . iii 3 25
Be round with him.— . . . I'll warrant you, Fear me not . . . iii 4 7
Let him go, Gertrude; do not fear our person . . . . . iv 5 122
Much I had to do to calm his rage! Now fear I this will give it start again iv 7 194
Yet have I something in me dangerous, Which let thy wiseness fear . v 1 286
Making so bold, My fears forgetting manners . . . . . v 2 17
Your grace hath laid the odds o' the weaker side.—I do not fear it . v 2 273
My life I never held but as a pawn To wage against thy enemies; nor fear to lose it, Thy safety being the motive . . . . . *Lear* i 1 158
Some villain hath done me wrong.—That's my fear . . . . i 2 181
To fear judgement; to fight when I cannot choose; and to eat no fish . i 4 17
Well, you may fear too far.—Safer than trust too far . . . i 4 351
Let me still take away the harms I fear, Not fear still to be taken . i 4 352
Away to horse: Inform her full of my particular fear . . . . i 4 360
And what they may incense him to, being apt To have his ear abused, wisdom bids fear . . . . ii 4 310
If you shall see Cordelia,—As fear not but you shall,—show her this ring iii 1 47
Man's nature cannot carry The affliction nor the fear . . . . iii 2 49
That nature thus gives way to loyalty, something fears me to think of . iii 5 4
To be worst, The lowest and most dejected thing of fortune, Stands still in esperance, lives not in fear . . . . iv 1 4
I fear your disposition . . . . iv 2 31
Which imports to the kingdom so much fear and danger . . . iv 3 5
And, to deal plainly, I fear I am not in my perfect mind . . . iv 7 63
Dear my lord, Be not familiar with her.—Fear me not . . . . v 1 16
With others, whom, I fear, Most just and heavy causes make oppose . v 1 26
Run from her guardage to the sooty bosom Of such a thing as thou, to fear, not to delight . . . . *Othello* i 2 71
Nor know I aught But that he's well and will be shortly here.—O, but I fear . . . . ii 1 91
I fear, My soul hath her content so absolute . . . . . ii 1 192
For I fear Cassio with my night-cap too . . . . . . ii 1 316
I fear the trust Othello puts him in, On some odd time of his infirmity, Will shake this island . . . . ii 3 131
In a town of war, Yet wild, the people's hearts brimful of fear . . ii 3 214
Riches fineless is as poor as winter To him that ever fears he shall be poor iii 3 174
Nor from mine own weak merits will I draw The smallest fear or doubt of her revolt; For she had eyes, and chose me . . . . . iii 3 188
And when she seem'd to shake and fear your looks, She loved them most iii 3 207
A little dash'd your spirits.—Not a jot, not a jot.—I' faith, I fear it has iii 3 215
Though I may fear Her will, recoiling to her better judgement . . iii 3 235
Let me be thought too busy in my fears—As worthy cause I have to fear I am—And hold her free . . . . iii 3 253
Fear not my government . . . . iii 3 256
The devils themselves Should fear to seize thee . . . . . iv 2 37
Quick, quick; fear nothing; I'll be at thy elbow . . . . v 1 3
Yet I fear you; for you are fatal then When your eyes roll so . . v 2 37
Why I should fear I know not, Since guiltiness I know not; but yet I feel I fear . . . . v 2 38
O! my fear interprets: what, is he dead? . . . . . . v 2 73
Do you go back dismay'd? 'tis a lost fear . . . . . . v 2 269
This did I fear, but thought he had no weapon; For he was great of heart . . . . v 2 360
In time we hate that which we often fear . . . *Ant. and Cleo.* i 3 12
How the fear of us May cement their divisions . . . . . ii 1 47
All great fears, which now import their dangers, Would then be nothing ii 2 135
Near him, thy angel Becomes a fear, as being o'erpower'd . . . ii 3 22
Thou canst not fear us, Pompey, with thy sails . . . . . ii 6 24
You shall not find, Though you be therein curious, the least cause For what you seem to fear . . . . iii 2 36
My very hairs do mutiny; for the white Reprove the brown for rashness, and they them For fear and doting . . . . iii 11 15
To be furious, Is to be frighted out of fear . . . . . . iii 13 196
By starts, His fretted fortunes give him hope, and fear . . . iv 12 8
She had a prophesying fear Of what hath come to pass . . . iv 14 120
Be of good cheer; You're fall'n into a princely hand, fear nothing . v 2 22
O sir, you are too sure an augurer; That you did fear is done . . v 2 338
I something fear my father's wrath; but nothing—Always reserved my holy duty—what His rage can do on me . . . . *Cymbeline* i 1 86

Fear. A touch more rare Subdues all pangs, all fears . . *Cymbeline* i 1 136
Notwithstanding, I fear not my ring . . . . . . i 4 107
I see you have some religion in you, that you fear . . . . i 4 149
My lord, I fear, Has forgot Britain . . . . . . i 6 112
I lodge in fear; Though this a heavenly angel, hell is here . . . ii 2 49
Fear it not, sir: I would I were so sure To win the king . . ii 4 1
So slippery that The fear's as bad as falling . . . . iii 3 49
We will fear no poison, which attends In place of greater state . iii 3 77
Put thyself Into a haviour of less fear, ere wildness Vanquish my staider senses. What's the matter? . . . . iii 4 9
If thou fear to strike and to make me certain it is done, thou art the pandar to her dishonour . . . . iii 4 30
Hit . . . my heart: Fear not; 'tis empty of all things but grief . iii 4 71
Fear and niceness—The handmaids of all women . . . . iii 4 158
Grant, heavens, that which I fear Prove false! . . . . iii 5 52
If mine enemy But fear the sword like me, he'll scarcely look on't . iii 6 26
I fear some ambush. I saw him not these many years, and yet I know 'tis he . . . . iv 2 65
To thy further fear, Nay, to thy mere confusion, thou shalt know . iv 2 91
Those that I reverence those I fear, the wise: At fools I laugh, not fear them . . . . iv 2 95
The effect of judgement Is oft the cause of fear . . . . iv 2 112
The law Protects not us: then why should we be tender To let an arrogant piece of flesh threat us, . . . For we do fear the law? . iv 2 129
Then on good ground we fear, If we do fear this body hath a tail More perilous than the head . . . . iv 2 143
I fear 'twill be revenged: Would, Polydore, thou hadst not done't! . iv 2 154
Fear no more the heat o' the sun, Nor the furious winter's rages . iv 2 258
Fear no more the frown o' the great; Thou art past the tyrant's stroke iv 2 264
Fear no more the lightning flash,—Nor the all-dreaded thunder-stone . iv 2 270
Fear not slander, censure rash;—Thou hast finish'd joy and moan . iv 2 272
Good faith, I tremble still with fear . . . . . . iv 2 303
We fear not What can from Italy annoy us; but We grieve at chances here iv 3 33
Nothing routs us but The villany of our fears . . . . v 2 13
Some mortally, some slightly touch'd, some falling Merely through fear v 3 11
You shall be called to no more payments, fear no more tavern-bills . v 4 161
My lord, Now fear is from me, I'll speak troth . . . . v 5 274
By flight I'll shun the danger which I fear . . . *Pericles* i 1 142
What was first but fear what might be done, Grows elder now and cares it be not done . . . . i 2 14
But thou know'st this 'Tis time to fear when tyrants seem to kiss . i 2 79
Which fear so grew in me, I hither fled, Under the covering of a careful night . . . . i 2 80
And tyrants' fears Decrease not, but grow faster than the years . . i 2 84
Antiochus you fear, And justly too, I think, you fear the tyrant . . i 2 102
That's the least fear . . . . i 4 71
But bring they what they will and what they can, What need we fear? i 4 77
The lady shrieks, and well-a-near Does fall in travail with her fear iii Gower 52
Courage enough: I do not fear the flaw; It hath done to me the worst iii 1 39
Pure surprise and fear Made me to quit the house . . . . iii 2 17
Fear not, my lord, but think Your grace . . . Must in your child be thought on . . . . iii 3 17
My father, as nurse said, did never fear . . . . . iv 1 53
I fear me *Tempest* v 1; *T. G. of Ver.* ii 7; *Meas. for Meas.* v 1; *T. Night* iii 1; *Richard II.* ii 2; iii 2; 1 *Hen. VI.* iii 1; v 5; 2 *Hen. VI.* i 1; iii 1; iv 4; 3 *Hen. VI.* iii 2; *Richard III.* i 2; *Troi. and Cres.* iii 2; *Coriolanus* iv 6; *T. of Athens* i 2; *Ant. and Cleo.* ii 7
Feared. But I fear'd Lest I might anger thee . . . *Tempest* iv 1 168
I fear'd to show my father Julia's letter . . *T. G. of Ver.* i 3 80
In time the rod Becomes more mock'd than fear'd . *Meas. for Meas.* i 3 27
Is like a good thing, being often read, Grown fear'd and tedious . ii 4 9
An angel is not evil; I should have fear'd her had she been a devil *L. L. Lost* v 2 106
I will lead them up and down: I am fear'd in field and town *M. N. Dr.* iii 2 398
This aspect of mine Hath fear'd the valiant . . *Mer. of Venice* ii 1 9
Shall tax my fears of little vanity, Having vainly fear'd too little *All's W.* v 3 123
That noble honour'd lord is fear'd and loved . . . *W. Tale* v 1 158
And I do fearfully believe 'tis done, What we so fear'd . *K. John* iv 2 75
Indeed we fear'd his sickness was past cure . . . . iv 2 86
Fear'd by their breed and famous by their birth . . *Richard II.* ii 1 52
To monarchize, be fear'd and kill with looks . . . . iii 2 165
I will from henceforth rather be myself, Mighty and to be fear'd, than my condition . . . . 1 *Hen. IV.* i 3 6
The king himself is to be feared as the lion . . . . iii 3 169
He was much fear'd by his physicians . . . . . . iv 1 24
He that but fears the thing he would not know Hath by instinct knowledge from others' eyes That what he fear'd is chanced 2 *Hen. IV.* i 1 87
We ventured, for the gain proposed Choked the respect of likely peril fear'd . . . . i 1 184
Rumour doth double, like the voice and echo, The numbers of the fear'd iii 1 98
She hath been then more fear'd than harm'd . . . *Hen. V.* i 2 155
Never was monarch better fear'd and loved Than is your majesty . . ii 2 25
Where they feared the death, they have borne life away . . iv 1 181
Wherein thou art less happy being fear'd Than they in fearing . iv 1 265
Is this the Talbot, so much fear'd abroad That with his name the mothers still their babes? . . . . 1 *Hen. VI.* ii 3 16
Have made thee fear'd and honour'd of the people . . 2 *Hen. VI.* i 1 198
'Tis to be fear'd they all will follow him . . . . . iii 1 30
Is the hour to come That e'er I proved thee false or fear'd thy faith . iii 1 205
For I, that never feared any, am vanquished by famine, not by valour iv 10 80
Warwick was a bug that fear'd us all . . . . 3 *Hen. VI.* v 2 2
For one being fear'd of all, now fearing one . . . *Richard III.* iv 4 103
If thou hadst fear'd to break an oath by Him, The unity the king thy brother made Had not been broken . . . . iv 4 378
Things done without example, in their issue Are to be fear'd *Hen. VIII.* i 2 91
Men fear'd the French would prove perfidious, To the king's danger . i 2 156
In great extremity; and fear'd She'll with the labour end . . v 1 19
She shall be loved and fear'd: her own shall bless her . . . v 5 31
I go alone, Like to a lonely dragon, that his fen Makes fear'd and talk'd of more than seen . . . . *Coriolanus* iv 1 31
If I had fear'd death, of all the men i' the world I would have 'voided thee iv 5 87
Made him fear'd, So hated, and so banish'd . . . . . iv 7 47
You should have fear'd false times when you did feast . *T. of Athens* iv 3 520
I rather tell thee what is to be fear'd Than what I fear . . *J. Cæsar* i 2 211
Say I fear'd Cæsar, honour'd him and loved him . . . . iii 1 129
In his royalty of nature Reigns that which would be fear'd . *Macbeth* iii 1 51
I fear'd he did but trifle, And meant to wreck thee . . . *Hamlet* ii 1 112
If he be taken, he shall never more Be fear'd of doing harm . . *Lear* ii 1 113
To fall in love with what she fear'd to look on! . . . *Othello* i 3 98
It appears he is beloved of those That only have fear'd Cæsar *A. and C.* i 4 38
Feared. That you embrace not Antony As you did love, but as you fear'd him . . . . *Ant. and Cleo.* iii 13 57
But if there be Yet left in heaven as small a drop of pity As a wren's eye, fear'd gods, a part of it! . . . . *Cymbeline* iv 2 305
Danger, which I fear'd, is at Antioch . . . . . *Pericles* i 2 7
Fearest. Thy best of rest is sleep, And that thou oft provokest; yet grossly fear'st Thy death, which is no more . . *Meas. for Meas.* iii 1 18
Take thy fortunes up; Be that thou know'st thou art, and then thou art As great as that thou fear'st . . . . *T. Night* v 1 153
Sebastian are you?—Fear'st thou that, Antonio? . . . . v 1 228
Art thou so bare and full of wretchedness, And fear'st to die? *R. and J.* v 1 69
Fearful. Make not too rash a trial of him, for He's gentle and not fearful *Tempest* i 2 468
Some heavenly power guide us Out of this fearful country! . . v 1 106
Death is a fearful thing.—And shamed life a hateful . *Meas. for Meas.* iii 1 116
Virtue is bold, and goodness never fearful . . . . . iii 1 216
Since I see you fearful, that neither my coat, integrity, nor persuasion can with ease attempt you . . . . iv 2 204
Unto our fearful minds A doubtful warrant of immediate death *C. of Er.* i 1 68
There is not a more fearful wild-fowl than your lion living *M. N. Dream* iii 1 33
In the modesty of fearful duty I read as much as from the rattling tongue . . . . v 1 101
And this the cranny is, right and sinister, Through which the fearful lovers are to whisper . . . . v 1 165
See to my house, left in the fearful guard Of an unthrifty knave *M. of V.* i 3 176
A man may, if he were of a fearful heart, stagger in this attempt *As Y. L. It* iii 3 49
Holy seems the quarrel Upon your grace's part; black and fearful On the opposer . . . . *All's Well* iii 1 5
Sure, you have some hideous matter to deliver, when the courtesy of it is so fearful . . . . *T. Night* i 5 222
I may be negligent, foolish and fearful . . . . *W. Tale* i 2 250
If ever fearful To do a thing, where I the issue doubted . . . . i 2 258
To the fearful usage, At least ungentle, of the dreadful Neptune . . v 1 153
The manage of two kingdoms must With fearful bloody issue arbitrate *K. John* i 1 38
Where revenge did paint The fearful difference of incensed kings . . iii 1 238
A fearful eye thou hast . . . . iv 2 106
Whilst he that hears makes fearful action, With wrinkled brows . . iv 2 191
News fitting to the night, Black, fearful, comfortless and horrible . v 6 20
We hear this fearful tempest sing, Yet seek no shelter . *Richard II.* ii 1 263
And lean-look'd prophets whisper fearful change . . . . ii 4 11
Covering your fearful land With hard bright steel and hearts harder . iii 2 110
Thus long have we stood To watch the fearful bending of thy knee . iii 3 73
A mighty and a fearful head they are, If promises be kept 1 *Hen. IV.* iii 2 167
Think how such an apprehension May turn the tide of fearful faction . iv 1 67
Who but Rumour, who but only I, Make fearful musters? 2 *Hen. IV.* Ind. 12
That your attempts may overlive the hazard And fearful meeting . iv 1 16
Rather show awhile like fearful war, To diet rank minds sick of happiness iv 1 63
And you shall hear A fearful battle render'd you in music . *Hen. V.* i 1 44
O guilt indeed!—Confirm'd conspiracy with fearful France . . ii Prol. 27
God's arm strike with us! 'tis a fearful odds . . . . . iv 3 5
Thou ominous and fearful owl of death, Our nation's terror! 1 *Hen. VI.* iv 2 15
Steel thy fearful thoughts, And change misdoubt to resolution 2 *Hen. VI.* iii 1 331
And after all this fearful homage done, Give thee thy hire and send thy soul to hell . . . . iii 2 224
Oft have I heard that grief softens the mind And makes it fearful . iv 4 2
The fearful French, whom you late vanquished, Should make a start . iv 8 44
This is the palace of the fearful king . . . . . 3 *Hen. VI.* i 1 25
Base, fearful and despairing Henry! . . . . i 1 178
Though man's face be fearful to their eyes . . . . . . ii 2 27
Even with those wings Which sometime they have used with fearful flight, Make war with him . . . . ii 2 30
Like a brace of greyhounds Having the fearful flying hare in sight . ii 5 130
And like a fearful lad With tearful eyes add water to the sea . . v 4 7
Did I but suspect a fearful man, He should have leave to go away betimes v 4 44
I will buz abroad such prophecies That Edward shall be fearful of his life v 6 87
To fright the souls of fearful adversaries . . . . *Richard III.* i 1 11
We look'd toward England, And cited up a thousand fearful times . i 4 14
Methought I saw a thousand fearful wrecks . . . . . . i 4 24
O, let me think on Hastings, and be gone To Brecknock, while my fearful head is on! . . . . iv 2 126
I have heard that fearful commenting Is leaden servitor to dull delay . iv 3 51
Your son, that with a fearful soul Leads discontented steps in foreign soil iv 4 311
All-Souls' day to my fearful soul Is the determined respite of my wrongs v 1 18
The leisure and the fearful time Cuts off the ceremonious vows of love v 3 97
Cold fearful drops stand on my trembling flesh. What do I fear? myself? v 3 181
I have dream'd a fearful dream! . . . . v 3 212
I am fearful: wherefore frowns he thus? . . . . . *Hen. VIII.* v 1 87
You that will be less fearful than discreet . . . *Coriolanus* iii 1 150
And more, More fearful, is deliver'd.—What more fearful? . . . iv 6 63
A fearful army, led by Caius Marcius Associated with Aufidius, rages . iv 6 75
As many urchins, Would make such fearful and confused cries *T. An.* ii 3 102
Look down into this den, And see a fearful sight of blood and death . ii 3 216
When will this fearful slumber have an end? . . . . . iii 1 253
Let them not speak to me; But let them hear what fearful words I utter v 2 169
The fearful passage of their death-mark'd love . . *Rom. and Jul.* Prol. 9
Some consequence yet hanging in the stars Shall bitterly begin his fearful date With this night's revels . . . . i 4 108
And she steal love's sweet bait from fearful hooks . . . . ii Prol. 8
Romeo, come forth; come forth, thou fearful man . . . . iii 3 1
The nightingale, and not the lark, That pierced the fearful hollow of thine ear . . . . iii 5 3
There's a fearful point! . . . . iv 3 32
So fearful were they of infection . . . . v 2 16
And fearful scouring Doth choke the air with dust . . *T. of Athens* v 2 15
Prodigious grown And fearful, as these strange eruptions are *J. Cæsar* i 3 78
What a fearful night is this! There's two or three of us have seen strange sights . . . . i 3 137
Come down With fearful bravery, thinking by this face To fasten in our thoughts that they have courage . . . . v 1 10
The devil himself could not pronounce a title More hateful to mine ear. —No, nor more fearful . . . . *Macbeth* v 7 9
And then it started like a guilty thing Upon a fearful summons . *Hamlet* i 1 149
But now grow fearful, By what yourself too late have spoke and done *Lear* i 4 225
How fearful And dizzy 'tis, to cast one's eyes so low! . . . iv 6 11
But the main article I do approve In fearful sense . . . *Othello* i 3 12
It shall be full of poise and difficult weight And fearful to be granted . iii 3 83
O my lord, my lord, Forgive my fearful sails! . . *Ant. and Cleo.* iii 11 55
If sleep charge nature, To break it with a fearful dream of him *Cymb.* iv 4 45
That Cloten, whose love-suit hath been to me As fearful as a siege . iii 4 137

Fearful. In a time When fearful wars point at me . . . . *Cymbeline* iv 3 7
And by those fearful objects to prepare This body, like to them, to what I must . . . . . . *Pericles* i 1 43
Fearful-hanging. That some whirlwind bear Unto a ragged fearful-hanging rock! . . . . . *T. G. of Ver.* i 2 121
Fearfullest. I prophesy the fearfull'st time to thee That ever wretched age hath look'd upon . . . . *Richard III.* iii 4 106
Fearfully. Did Thisbe fearfully o'ertrip the dew . . *Mer. of Venice* v 1 7
I do fearfully believe 'tis done, What we so fear'd . . *K. John* iv 2 74
Ran fearfully among the trembling reeds . . . . 1 *Hen. IV.* i 3 105
As fearfully as doth a galled rock O'erhang . . . *Hen. V.* iii 1 12
Fearfully did menace me with death, If I did stay . *Rom. and Jul.* v 3 133
There is a cliff, whose high and bending head Looks fearfully in the confined deep . . . . . . *Lear* iv 1 77
You must seem to do that fearfully which you commit willingly *Pericles* iv 2 127
Fearfulness. And keep us all in servile fearfulness . . . *J. Cæsar* i 1 80
Fearing else some messenger that might her mind discover *T. G. of Ver.* ii 1 173
Fearing lest my jealous aim might err And so unworthily disgrace the man . . . . iii 1 28
Nor fearing me as if I were her father . . . . . iii 1 71
Make us lose the good we oft might win By fearing to attempt *M. for M.* i 4 79
That life is better life, past fearing death, Than that which lives to fear v 1 402
First were we sad, fearing you would not come; Now sadder *T. of Shrew* iii 2 100
The business is not ended, as fearing to hear of it hereafter *All's Well* iv 3 111
Tell me true, I charge you, Not fearing the displeasure of your master v 3 235
But if you faint, as fearing to do so, Stay and be secret . *Richard II.* ii 1 297
Where fearing dying pays death servile breath . . . . iii 2 185
The earth was not of my mind, If you suppose as fearing you it shook 1 *Hen. IV.* iii 1 23
Wherein thou art less happy being fear'd Than they in fearing *Hen. V.* iv 1 266
Not fearing death, nor shrinking for distress, But always resolute in most extremes . . . . . 1 *Hen. VI.* iv 1 37
For one being fear'd of all, now fearing one . . . *Richard III.* iv 4 103
Fearing he would rise, he was so virtuous, Kept him a foreign man *Hen. VIII.* ii 2 128
And, to add greater honours to his age Than man could give him, he died fearing God . . . . iv 2 68
I speak not 'be thou true,' as fearing thee . . *Troi. and Cres.* iv 4 64
As for my country I have shed my blood, Not fearing outward force *Coriolanus* iii 1 77
So I did; Fearing to strengthen that impatience . . *J. Cæsar* i 2 248
He that cuts off twenty years of life Cuts off so many years of fearing death . . . . iii 1 102
So are we Cæsar's friends, that have abridged His time of fearing death iii 1 105
So full of artless jealousy is guilt, It spills itself in fearing to be spilt *Hamlet* iv 5 20
She sent you word she was dead; But, fearing since how it might work, hath sent Me to proclaim the truth . . . *Ant. and Cleo.* iv 14 125
The earth, fearing to be o'erflow'd . . . . *Pericles* iv 1 40
Fearless. Careless, reckless, and fearless of what's past, present, or to come; insensible of mortality . . . *Meas. for Meas.* iv 2 151
Free speech and fearless I to thee allow . . . *Richard II.* i 1 123
Fearless minds climb soonest unto crowns . . . 3 *Hen. VI.* iv 7 62
Fear-surprised. Thrice he walk'd By their oppress'd and fear-surprised eyes, Within his truncheon's length . . . . *Hamlet* i 2 203
Feast. One feast, one house, one mutual happiness . *T. G. of Ver.* v 4 173
Thy bones are hollow; impiety has made a feast of thee *Meas. for Meas.* i 2 57
Feast upon her eyes . . . . ii 2 179
Small cheer and great welcome makes a merry feast *Com. of Errors* iii 1 26
Did this companion with the saffron face Revel and feast it at my house? iv 4 65
Go to a gossips' feast, and go with me; After so long grief, such festivity! . . . . v 1 405
With all my heart, I'll gossip at this feast . . . . v 1 407
What, a feast, a feast? . . . . . . *Much Ado* v 1 154
Study where I well may dine, When I to feast expressly am forbid *L. L. L.* i 1 62
They have been at a great feast of languages, and stolen the scraps v 1 40
Three and three, We'll hold a feast in great solemnity . *M. N. Dream* iv 1 190
I do feast to-night My best-esteem'd acquaintance . . *Mer. of Venice* ii 2 180
Who riseth from a feast With that keen appetite that he sits down? ii 6 8
We are stay'd for at Bassanio's feast . . . . . ii 6 48
Our feast shall be much honour'd in your marriage . . . iii 2 214
If ever sat at any good man's feast . . . . *As Y. Like It* ii 7 115
Provide the feast, father, and bid the guests . . *T. of Shrew* ii 1 318
Obey the bride, you that attend on her; Go to the feast, revel and domineer . . . . iii 2 226
You know there wants no junkets at the feast . . . . iii 2 250
We will hence forthwith, To feast and sport us at thy father's house iv 3 185
I'll in among the rest, Out of hope of all, but my share of the feast . v 1 146
Feast with the best, and welcome to my house . . . . v 2 8
The solemn feast Shall more attend upon the coming space, Expecting absent friends . . . . *All's Well* ii 3 187
He says he'll come; How shall I feast him? what bestow of him? *T. N.* iii 4 2
With a countenance as clear As friendship wears at feasts . *W. Tale* i 2 344
Let me see; what am I to buy for our sheep-shearing feast? . iv 3 40
My father hath made her mistress of the feast, and she lays it on . iv 3 43
Our feasts In every mess have folly and the feeders Digest it with a custom . . . . iv 4 10
With these forced thoughts, I prithee, darken not The mirth o' the feast iv 4 42
Present yourself That which you are, mistress o' the feast . . iv 4 68
I was promised them against the feast; but they come not too late now iv 4 237
And now he feasts, mousing the flesh of men . . . *K. John* ii 1 354
What, shall our feast be kept with slaughter'd men? . . . iii 1 302
Nor met with fortune other than at feasts, Full of warm blood, of mirth v 2 58
A bare-ribb'd death, whose office is this day To feast upon whole thousands of the French . . . . v 2 178
Lo, as at English feasts, so I regreet The daintiest last, to make the end most sweet . . . . *Richard II.* i 3 67
Or cloy the hungry edge of appetite By bare imagination of a feast . i 3 297
And so my state, Seldom but sumptuous, showed like a feast 1 *Hen. IV.* iii 2 58
To the latter end of a fray and the beginning of a feast Fits a dull fighter and a keen guest . . . . iv 2 85
Did feast together, and in two years after Were they at wars 2 *Hen. IV.* iii 1 59
Or else a feast And takes away the stomach; such are the rich . iv 4 106
Will yearly on the vigil feast his neighbours . . . *Hen. V.* iv 3 45
Bonfires in France forthwith I am to make, To keep our great Saint George's feast withal . . . . . . 1 *Hen. VI.* i 1 154
Make bonfires And feast and banquet in the open streets . . i 6 13
And think me honoured To feast so great a warrior in my house . ii 3 82
'Tis like you would not feast him like a friend . . 2 *Hen. VI.* iii 2 184
Paced back again To York-place, where the feast is held . *Hen. VIII.* iv 1 94
Feast. Make factious feasts; rails on our state of war . *Troi. and Cres.* i 3 191
Yourself shall feast with us before you go . . . . . i 3 308
I beseech you next To feast with me . . . . . . iv 5 229
There Diomed doth feast with him to-night . . . . . iv 5 280
Let us feast him to the height . . . . v 1 3
Camest thou to a morsel of this feast, Having fully dined before *Coriol.* i 9 10
Is he in Antium?—He is, and feasts the nobles of the state At his house iv 4 9
The feast smells well; but I Appear not like a guest . . . iv 5 5
A parcel of their feast, and to be executed ere they wipe their lips . iv 5 231
If the emperor's court can feast two brides, You are my guest *T. Andron.* i 1 489
Even at thy solemn feast, I will bring in the empress and her sons v 2 115
Tell him the emperor and the empress too Feast at my house, and he shall feast with them . . . . v 2 128
You know your mother means to feast with me . . . . v 2 185
This is the feast that I have bid her to, And this the banquet . . v 2 193
May prove More stern and bloody than the Centaurs' feast . . v 2 204
The feast is ready, which the careful Titus Hath ordain'd to an honourable end . . . . v 3 21
This night I hold an old accustom'd feast . . . *Rom. and Jul.* i 2 20
At this same ancient feast of Capulet's Sups the fair Rosaline . . i 2 87
Against some other maid That I will show you shining at this feast . i 2 103
Can you love the gentleman? This night you shall behold him at our feast . . . . i 3 80
Put off these frowns, An ill-beseeming semblance for a feast . . i 5 76
Our wedding cheer to a sad burial feast . . . . . iv 5 87
Going to Lord Timon's feast?—Ay, to see meat fill knaves *T. of Athens* i 1 270
Feasts are too proud to give thanks to the gods . . . . i 2 62
There's no meat like 'em: I could wish my best friend at such a feast . i 2 82
They only now come but to feast thine eyes . . . . . i 2 133
What need these feasts, pomps and vain-glories? . . . . i 2 248
All, sirrah, all: I'll once more feast the rascals . . . . iii 4 114
Feast your ears with the music awhile . . . . . . iii 6 36
Here's a noble feast toward.—This is the old man still . . . iii 6 68
Make not a city feast of it, to let the meat cool ere we can agree upon the first place: sit, sit . . . . iii 6 76
May you a better feast never behold! . . . . . . iii 6 98
Henceforth be no feast, Whereat a villain's not a welcome guest . iii 6 112
Therefore, be abhorr'd All feasts, societies, and throngs of men! . iv 3 21
I will mend thy feast.—First mend my company, take away thyself . iv 3 282
You should have fear'd false times when you did feast . . . iv 3 520
I dreamt to-night that I did feast with Cæsar . . *J. Cæsar* iii 3 1
Great nature's second course, Chief nourisher in life's feast . *Macbeth* ii 2 40
If he had been forgotten, It had been as a gap in our great feast . iii 1 12
Fail not our feast.—My lord, I will not . . . . . iii 1 28
The feast is sold That is not often vouch'd, while 'tis a-making, 'Tis given with welcome . . . . iii 4 33
From broad words and 'cause he fail'd His presence at the tyrant's feast iii 6 22
Free from our feasts and banquets bloody knives . . . . iii 6 35
My news shall be the fruit to that great feast . . . *Hamlet* ii 2 52
Go to your rest; at night we'll feast together . . . . ii 2 84
O proud death, What feast is toward in thine eternal cell? . . v 2 376
Tie up the libertine in a field of feasts, Keep his brain fuming *A. and C.* ii 1 23
We had much more monstrous matter of feast . . . . ii 2 187
Being barber'd ten times o'er, goes to the feast . . . . ii 2 229
We'll feast each other ere we part; and let's Draw lots who shall begin ii 6 61
How farest thou, soldier?—Well; And well am like to do; for, I perceive, Four feasts are toward . . . . ii 6 75
This is not yet an Alexandrian feast.—It ripens towards it . . ii 7 102
Cæsar is sad; and Lepidus, Since Pompey's feast . . . . iii 2 5
Feast the army; we have store to do't, And they have earn'd the waste iv 1 15
He that strikes The venison first shall be the lord o' the feast *Cymbeline* iii 3 75
You, Polydore, have proved best woodman and Are master of the feast iii 6 29
'Twas at a feast,—O, would Our viands had been poison'd! . . . v 5 155
Our peace we'll ratify; seal it with feasts . . . . . v 5 483
This we desire, As friends to Antioch, we may feast in Tyre . *Pericles* i 3 40
Feast here awhile, Until our stars that frown lend us a smile . . i 4 107
Prepare for mirth, for mirth becomes a feast . . . . . ii 3 7
Come, queen o' the feast,—For, daughter, so you are,—here take your place . . . . ii 3 17
The city strived God Neptune's annual feast to keep . . . v Gower 17
Feast of battle. My dancing soul doth celebrate This feast of battle with mine adversary . . . . *Richard II.* i 3 92
Feast of Crispian. This day is call'd the feast of Crispian . *Hen. V.* iv 3 40
Feast of death. Now thou art come unto a feast of death 1 *Hen. VI.* iv 5 7
Feast of Lupercal. You know it is the feast of Lupercal . *J. Cæsar* i 1 72
Feasted. She shut the doors upon me, While she with harlots feasted in my house . . . . *Com. of Errors* v 1 205
You are retired, As if you were a feasted one and not The hostess *W. T.* iv 4 63
Fed from my trencher, kneel'd down at the board, When I had feasted with Queen Margaret . . . . 2 *Hen. VI.* iv 1 58
The place which I have feasted, does it now, Like all mankind, show me an iron heart? . . . . *T. of Athens* iii 4 83
Three kings I had newly feasted, and did want Of what I was i' the morning: but next day I told him of myself . *Ant. and Cleo.* ii 2 76
Feasting. At a farm-house a-feasting . . . . *Mer. Wives* ii 3 92
I have no mind of feasting forth to-night: But I will go *Mer. of Venice* ii 5 37
How now, fair shepherd! Your heart is full of something that does take Your mind from feasting . . . . . . *W. Tale* iv 4 358
I have been feasting with mine enemy . . . . *Rom. and Jul.* ii 3 49
Her beauty makes This vault a feasting presence full of light . v 3 86
It should not be, by the persuasion of his new feasting *T. of Athens* iii 6 9
There is full liberty of feasting from this present hour of five till the bell have told eleven . . . . *Othello* ii 2 10
I have heard that Julius Cæsar Grew fat with feasting there *Ant. and Cleo* ii 6 66
Feast-won, fast-lost; one cloud of winter showers, These flies are couch'd *T. of Athens* ii 2 180
Feat. Doing, in the figure of a lamb, the feats of a lion . . *Much Ado* i 1 15
And got a calf in that same noble feat Much like to you . . . v 4 50
If you break the ice and do this feat . . . . . *T. of Shrew* i 2 267
Hang all the husbands That cannot do that feat, you'll leave yourself Hardly one subject . . . . *W. Tale* ii 3 111
This same starved justice hath done nothing but prate to me of the wildness of his youth, and the feats he hath done . 2 *Hen. IV.* iii 2 328
Awake remembrance of these valiant dead And with your puissant arm renew their feats . . . . *Hen. V.* i 2 116
All fell feats Enlink'd to waste and desolation . . . . iii 3 17
But he'll remember with advantages What feats he did that day . iv 3 51
Fair maid, is't thou wilt do these wondrous feats? . . 1 *Hen. VI.* i 2 64
For high feats done to the crown . . . . . . *Hen. VIII.* i 1 61
In that day's feats, When he might act the woman in the scene *Coriol.* ii 2 99

Feat. I am settled, and bend up Each corporal agent to this terrible feat *Macbeth* i 7 80
Tell me Why you proceeded not against these feats, So crimeful *Hamlet* iv 7 6
And little of this great world can I speak, More than pertains to feats of broil and battle . . . . *Othello* i 3 87
Clip your wives, your friends, Tell them your feats . *Ant. and Cleo.* iv 8 9
Famous in Cæsar's praises, no whit less Than in his feats deserving *Cymb.* iii 1 7
When on my three-foot stool I sit and tell The warlike feats I have done iii 3 90
So tender over his occasions, true, So feat, so nurse-like . . . v 5 88
If that thy prosperous and artificial feat Can draw him but to answer thee in aught . . . . *Pericles* v 1 72
What feats, what shows, What minstrelsy, and pretty din, The regent made . . . . v 2 271
Feated. To the more mature A glass that feated them . . *Cymbeline* i 1 49
Feater. Look how well my garments sit upon me; Much feater than before *Tempest* ii 1 273
Feather. As wicked dew as e'er my mother brush'd With raven's feather from unwholesome fen . . . . i 2 322
You weigh equally; a feather will turn the scale . *Meas. for Meas.* iv 2 31
When fowls have no feathers and fish have no fin . *Com. of Errors* iii 1 79
A crow without feather? Master, mean you so? . . . . iii 1 81
For a fish without a fin, there's a fowl without a feather . . iii 1 82
What plume of feathers is he that indited this letter? . *L. L. Lost* iv 1 96
An old hat and 'the humour of forty fancies' prick'd in't for a feather: a monster, a very monster in apparel . . . *T. of Shrew* iii 2 71
What is the jay more precious than the lark, Because his feathers are more beautiful? . . . . iv 3 178
With delicate fine hats and most courteous feathers . *All's Well* iv 5 111
You boggle shrewdly, every feather starts you . . . v 3 232
Like the haggard, check at every feather That comes before his eye *T. Night* iii 1 71
I am a feather for each wind that blows . . . *W. Tale* ii 3 154
Be Mercury, set feathers to thy heels, And fly like thought . *K. John* iv 2 174
He'll not swagger with a Barbary hen, if her feathers turn back *2 Hen. IV.* ii 4 108
By his gates of breath There lies a downy feather which stirs not . iv 5 32
And all things thought upon That may with reasonable swiftness add More feathers to our wings . . . . *Hen. V.* i 2 307
To turn the sun to ice with fanning in his face with a peacock's feather iv 1 213
There's not a piece of feather in our host—Good argument, I hope, we will not fly . . . . iv 3 112
Seems he a dove? his feathers are but borrow'd . *2 Hen. VI.* iii 1 75
Was ever feather so lightly blown to and fro as this multitude? . iv 8 57
And of their feather many moe proud birds . . *3 Hen. VI.* ii 1 170
As I blow this feather from my face, And as the air blows it to me again iii 1 84
For both of you are birds of selfsame feather . . . . iii 3 161
Leave those remnants Of fool and feather . . . *Hen. VIII.* i 3 25
Feather of lead, bright smoke, cold fire, sick health! . *Rom. and Jul.* i 1 186
I am too sore enpierced with his shaft To soar with his light feathers . i 4 20
I am not of that feather to shake off My friend when he must need me *T. of Athens* i 1 100
I do fear, When every feather sticks in his own wing, Lord Timon will be left a naked gull . . . . ii 1 30
These growing feathers pluck'd from Cæsar's wing Will make him fly an ordinary pitch . . . . *J. Cæsar* i 1 77
And your secrecy to the king and queen moult no feather . *Hamlet* ii 2 306
And a forest of feathers . . . . iii 2 286
Hadst thou been aught but gossamer, feathers, air, So many fathom down precipitating, Thou'dst shiver'd like an egg . . . *Lear* iv 6 49
This feather stirs: she lives! . . . . v 3 265
Some dozen Romans of us and your lord—The best feather of our wing *Cymbeline* i 6 186
So With the dove of Paphos might the crow Vie feathers white *Per.* iv Gower 33
Feather-bed. In peril of my life with the edge of a feather-bed *M. of Ven.* ii 2 174
Feathered. Rise from the ground like feather'd Mercury . *1 Hen. IV.* iv 1 106
Light-wing'd toys Of feather'd Cupid . . . . . *Othello* i 3 270
In feather'd briefness sails are fill'd . . . . . *Pericles* v 2 280
Featly. Foot it featly here and there . . . . . *Tempest* i 2 380
She dances featly.—So she does any thing . . . *W. Tale* iv 4 176
Feature. How features are abroad, I am skilless of . . *Tempest* iii 1 52
He is complete in feature and in mind . . . *T. G. of Ver.* ii 4 73
Am I the man yet? doth my simple feature content you?—Your features! Lord warrant us! what features? . . . . *As Y. Like It* iii 3 3
Nor know I you by voice or any feature . . . *T. Night* iii 4 387
Thou hast, Sebastian, done good feature shame . . . . iii 4 400
Liker in feature to his father Geffrey Than thou and John in manners *K. John* ii 1 126
Forgive the comment that my passion made Upon thy feature . . iv 2 264
Her peerless feature, joined with her birth, Approves her fit for none but for a king . . . . *1 Hen. VI.* v 5 68
Cheated of feature by dissembling nature, Deform'd, unfinish'd *Rich. III.* i 1 19
She is a gallant creature, and complete In mind and feature *Hen. VIII.* i 2 50
That unmatch'd form and feature of blown youth Blasted with ecstasy *Hamlet* iii 1 167
To show virtue her own feature, scorn her own image . . . iii 2 25
Self-cover'd thing, for shame, Be-monster not thy feature . . *Lear* iv 2 63
Bid him Report the feature of Octavia, her years, Her inclination *Ant. and Cleo.* ii 5 112
For feature, laming The shrine of Venus, or straight-pight Minerva *Cymbeline* v 5 163
Featured. How wise, how noble, young, how rarely featured *Much Ado* iii 1 60
February. You have such a February face, So full of frost, of storm . v 4 41
Fecks. Art thou my boy?—Ay, my good lord.—I' fecks! . *W. Tale* i 2 120
Fed. I have fed upon this woe already, And now excess of it will make me surfeit . . . . *T. G. of Ver.* iii 1 219
Lust is but a bloody fire, Kindled with unchaste desire, Fed in heart *Mer. Wives* v 5 101
At board he fed not for my urging it . . . . *Com. of Errors* v 1 64
He hath never fed of the dainties that are bred in a book . *L. L. Lost* iv 2 25
Fed with the same food, hurt with the same weapons . *Mer. of Venice* iii 1 63
It [fancy] is engender'd in the eyes, With gazing fed . . . iii 2 68
With oaths kept waking and with brawling fed . . *T. of Shrew* iv 3 10
I will show myself highly fed and lowly taught . . *All's Well* ii 2 3
A good knave, i' faith, and well fed . . . . iv 4 39
The fat ribs of peace Must by the hungry now be fed upon . *K. John* iii 3 10
You have fed upon my signories, Dispark'd my parks . *Richard II.* iii 1 22
And being fed by us you used us so As that ungentle gull, the cuckoo's bird, Useth the sparrow . . . . *1 Hen. IV.* v 1 59
The care on thee depending Hath fed upon the body of my father *2 Hen. IV.* iv 5 160
Fed from my trencher, kneel'd down at the board . . *2 Hen. VI.* iv 1 57
Who fed him every minute With words of sovereignty . . *Hen. VIII.* i 2 149
That was he That fed him with his prophecies?—The same . . . ii 1 23
How eagerly ye follow my disgraces, As if it fed ye! . . . . iii 2 241
I have fed mine eyes on thee . . . . . *Troi. and Cres.* iv 5 231
My half-supp'd sword, that frankly would have fed, Pleased with this dainty bait, thus goes to bed . . . . v 8 19
They nourish'd disobedience, fed The ruin of the state . *Coriolanus* iii 1 117
He is your brother, lords, sensibly fed Of that self-blood that first gave life to you . . . . *T. Andron.* iv 2 122
They are both baked in that pie; Whereof their mother daintily hath fed . . . . v 3 61
We both have fed as well, and we can both Endure the winter's cold as well as he . . . . *J. Cæsar* i 2 98
In his commendations I am fed; It is a banquet to me . . *Macbeth* i 4 55
As if increase of appetite had grown By what it fed on . . *Hamlet* i 2 145
A man may fish with the worm that hath eat of a king, and eat of the fish that hath fed of that worm . . . . iv 3 30
The hedge-sparrow fed the cuckoo so long, That it had it head bit off by it young. So, out went the candle . . . . *Lear* i 4 235
Let not thy discreet heart think it. Her eye must be fed . *Othello* ii 1 228
Unlustrous as the smoky light That's fed with stinking tallow . *Cymb.* i 6 110
My ears were never better fed With such delightful pleasing harmony *Pericles* ii 5 27
Your grace, that fed my country with your corn . . . . iii 3 18
Federary. She's a traitor and Camillo is A federary with her . *W. Tale* ii 1 90
Fee. To plead for love deserves more fee than hate . . *T. G. of Ver.* i 2 48
Here is thy fee; arrest him, officer. I would not spare my brother *Com. of Errors* iv 1 76
Be cunning in the working this, and thy fee is a thousand ducats *M. Ado* ii 2 54
Pleading for a lover's fee . . . . . . *M. N. Dream* iii 2 113
Fee me an officer; bespeak him a fortnight before . . *Mer. of Venice* iii 1 131
Take some remembrance of us, as a tribute, Not as a fee . . . iv 1 423
A prating boy, that begg'd it as a fee . . . . . . v 1 164
Ay, and I'll give them him without a fee . . . . . . v 1 290
I'll fee thee to stand up . . . . *All's Well* ii 1 64
Not helping, death's my fee . . . . ii 1 192
You shall pay your fees When you depart, and save your thanks *W. Tale* i 2 53
Which heaven shall take in nature of a fee . . . *K. John* ii 1 170
And I should rob the deathsman of his fee . . . *2 Hen. VI.* iii 2 217
Here's a deer whose skin's a keeper's fee . . . *3 Hen. VI.* iii 1 22
At our enlargement what are thy due fees? . . . . . iv 6 5
But, now thy beauty is proposed my fee, My proud heart sues *Rich. III.* i 2 170
Take thou the fee, and tell him what I say . . . . . i 4 284
As if the golden fee for which I plead Were for myself . . . . iii 5 96
To gain the popedom, And fee my friends in Rome . . *Hen. VIII.* iii 2 213
Supple knees Feed arrogance and are the proud man's fees *Troi. and Cres.* iii 3 49
So should I rob my sweet sons of their fee . . . *T. Andron.* ii 3 179
O'er lawyers' fingers, who straight dream on fees, O'er ladies' lips *Rom. and Jul.* i 4 73
The rest of your fees, O gods—the senators of Athens, together with the common lag of people—what is amiss in them, you gods, make suitable for destruction . . . . *T. of Athens* iii 6 89
Why, what should be the fear? I do not set my life at a pin's fee *Hamlet* i 4 65
Overcome with joy, Gives him three thousand crowns in annual fee . ii 2 73
I would not farm it; Nor will it yield to Norway or the Pole A ranker rate, should it be sold in fee . . . . iv 4 22
Kill thy physician, and the fee bestow Upon thy foul disease . . *Lear* i 1 166
Besides this treasure for a fee, The gods requite his charity! . *Pericles* iii 2 74
Feeble. A true-devoted pilgrim is not weary To measure kingdoms with his feeble steps . . . . *T. G. of Ver.* ii 7 10
Smother'd in errors, feeble, shallow, weak . . *Com. of Errors* ii 2 35
My only son Knows not my feeble key of untuned cares . . . v 1 310
That fell anatomy Which cannot hear a lady's feeble voice . *K. John* iii 4 41
The old, feeble and day-wearied sun . . . . v 4 35
Ere my tongue Shall wound my honour with such feeble wrong *Rich. II.* i 1 191
But if without him we be thought too feeble, My judgement is, we should not step too far . . . . *2 Hen. IV.* i 3 19
Francis Feeble!—Here, sir.—What trade art thou, Feeble?—A woman's tailor . . . . iii 2 158
Well said, courageous Feeble! thou wilt be as valiant as the wrathful dove . . . . iii 2 170
Let that suffice, most forcible Feeble . . . . iii 2 179
I am bound to thee, reverend Feeble . . . . iii 2 181
And for a retreat; how swiftly will this Feeble the woman's tailor run off! . . . . iii 2 287
'Tis meet we all go forth To view the sick and feeble parts of France *Hen. V.* ii 4 22
Raught me his hand, And, with a feeble gripe, says 'Dear my lord' . iv 6 22
And pluck the crown from feeble Henry's head . . *2 Hen. VI.* v 1 2
Like rich hangings in a homely house, So was his will in his old feeble body . . . . v 3 13
Pluck'd two crutches from my feeble limbs, Edward and Clarence *Richard III.* ii 2 58
Let every feeble rumour shake your hearts! . . . *Coriolanus* iii 3 125
Upon my feeble knee I beg this boon, with tears not lightly shed *T. An.* ii 3 288
I lift this one hand up to heaven, And bow this feeble ruin to the earth iii 1 208
'Tis not enough to help the feeble up, But to support him after *T. of A.* i 1 107
Ye gods, it doth amaze me A man of such a feeble temper should So get the start of the majestic world And bear the palm alone *J. Cæsar* i 2 129
Old feeble carrions and such suffering souls That welcome wrongs . ii 1 130
Vouchsafe good morrow from a feeble tongue . . . . . ii 1 313
Will crowd a feeble man almost to death . . . . . . ii 4 36
Feebled. Shall that victorious hand be feebled here? . . *K. John* v 2 146
Feebleness. A better head her glorious body fits Than his that shakes for age and feebleness . . . . *T. Andron.* i 1 188
Feebling. Making parties strong And feebling such as stand not in their liking Below their cobbled shoes . . . . . *Coriolanus* i 1 199
Feebly. The deeds of Coriolanus Should not be utter'd feebly . . ii 2 87
Feed. All abundance, To feed my innocent people . . . *Tempest* ii 1 164
I will stand to and feed, Although my last . . . . . iii 3 49
Injurious wasps, to feed on such sweet honey And kill the bees! *T. G. of Ver.* i 2 106
Though the chameleon Love can feed on the air, I am one that am nourished by my victuals . . . . ii 1 179
A kind of chameleon.—That hath more mind to feed on your blood than live in your air . . . . ii 4 27
To think that she is by And feed upon the shadow of perfection . iii 1 177
As those that feed grow full . . . . . *Meas. for Meas.* i 4 41
Too unruly deer, he breaks the pale And feeds from home *Com. of Errors* ii 1 101

Feed. Is it possible disdain should die while she hath such meet food to feed it as Signior Benedick? *Much Ado* i 1 122
Unless we feed on your lips *L. L. Lost* ii 1 220
Feed him with apricocks and dewberries, With purple grapes *M. N. Dr.* iii 1 169
I will feed fat the ancient grudge I bear him *Mer. of Venice* i 3 48
But yet I'll go in hate, to feed upon The prodigal Christian ii 5 14
If it will feed nothing else, it will feed my revenge iii 1 55
To feed my means iii 2 266
He lets me feed with his hinds, bars me the place of a brother *As Y. L. It* i 1 20
His mouth full of news.—Which he will put on us, as pigeons feed their young i 2 99
He that doth the ravens feed, Yea, providently caters for the sparrow ii 3 43
Bring us where we may rest ourselves and feed ii 4 73
His flocks and bounds of feed Are now on sale ii 4 83
By reason of his absence, there is nothing That you will feed on ii 4 86
Sit down and feed, and welcome to our table ii 7 105
Set down your venerable burden, And let him feed ii 7 168
Feed yourselves with questioning v 4 144
And where two raging fires meet together They do consume the thing that feeds their fury *T. of Shrew* ii 1 134
And better 'twere that both of us did fast, Since, of ourselves, ourselves are choleric, Than feed it with such over-roasted flesh iv 1 178
A dish that I do love to feed upon iv 3 24
That makes me see, and cannot feed mine eye *All's Well* i 1 236
Let concealment, like a worm i' the bud, Feed on her damask cheek *T. Night* ii 4 115
I will bespeak our diet, Whiles you beguile the time and feed your knowledge iii 3 41
And brought in matter that should feed this fire *K. John* v 2 85
The pleasure that some fathers feed upon, Is my strict fast *Richard II.* ii 1 79
Feed not thy sovereign's foe, my gentle earth iii 2 12
I had rather live With cheese and garlic in a windmill, far, Than feed on cates and have him talk to me 1 *Hen. IV.* iii 1 163
Let's away; Advantage feeds him fat, while men delay iii 2 180
We shall feed like oxen at a stall v 2 14
Let order die! And let this world no longer be a stage To feed contention in a lingering act 2 *Hen. IV.* i 1 156
Where sups he? doth the old boar feed in the old frank? ii 2 160
Then feed, and be fat, my fair Calipolis ii 4 193
I am not covetous for gold, Nor care I who doth feed upon my cost *Hen. V.* iv 3 25
With the pitiful complaints Of such as your oppression feeds upon 1 *Hen. VI.* iv 1 58
While the vulture of sedition Feeds in the bosom of such great commanders iv 3 48
Where I was wont to feed you with my blood, I'll lop a member off v 3 14
Nay, then, this spark will prove a raging fire, If wind and fuel be brought to feed it with 2 *Hen. VI.* iii 1 303
Now the word 'sallet' must serve me to feed on iv 10 17
Leaving thy trunk for crows to feed upon iv 10 90
Unreasonable creatures feed their young 3 *Hen. VI.* ii 2 26
I envy not thy glory; To feed my humour, wish thyself no harm *Richard III.* iv 1 65
A hand as fruitful as the land that feeds us *Hen. VIII.* i 3 56
You feed too much on this dislike *Troi. and Cres.* ii 3 235
To feed for aye her lamp and flames of love iii 2 167
Supple knees Feed arrogance and are the proud man's fees iii 3 49
My love with words and errors still she feeds v 3 111
The noble senate, who, Under the gods, keep you in awe, which else Would feed on one another *Coriolanus* i 1 192
And entrails feed the sacrificing fire *T. Andron.* i 1 144
I'll make you feed on berries and on roots, And feed on curds and whey iv 2 177
Feed his humour kindly as we may, Till time beget some careful remedy iv 3 29
He doth me wrong to feed me with delays iv 3 42
The one is wounded with the bait, The other rotted with delicious feed iv 4 93
Whate'er I forge to feed his brain-sick fits, Do you uphold and maintain v 2 71
Will't please you eat? will't please your highness feed? v 3 54
I feed Most hungerly on your sight.—Right welcome, sir! *T. of Athens* i 1 261
Happier is he that has no friend to feed Than such that do e'en enemies exceed i 2 209
Common mother, thou, Whose womb unmeasurable, and infinite breast, Teems, and feeds all iv 3 179
There's a medlar for thee, eat it.—On what I hate I feed not iv 3 306
The earth's a thief, That feeds and breeds by a composture stolen iv 3 444
What a god's gold, That he is worshipp'd in a baser temple Than where swine feed! v 1 52
See him dissemble, Know his gross patchery, love him, feed him v 1 99
Now, in the names of all the gods at once, Upon what meat doth this our Cæsar feed, That he is grown so great? *J. Cæsar* i 2 149
A barren-spirited fellow; one that feeds On abjects, orts and imitations iv 1 36
To feed were best at home; From thence the sauce to meat is ceremony *Macbeth* iii 4 35
Feed, and regard him not iii 4 58
That no revenue hast but thy good spirits, To feed and clothe thee *Ham.* iii 2 64
I eat the air, promise-crammed: you cannot feed capons so iii 2 100
That live and feed upon your majesty iii 3 10
Could you on this fair mountain leave to feed, And batten on this moor? iii 4 66
But, like the owner of a foul disease, To keep it from divulging, let it feed Even on the pith of life iv 1 22
What is a man, If his chief good and market of his time Be but to sleep and feed? a beast, no more iv 4 35
Feeds on his wonder, keeps himself in clouds iv 5 89
Or feed upon such nice and waterish diet *Othello* iii 3 15
'Tis as I should entreat you wear your gloves, Or feed on nourishing dishes iii 3 78
It [jealousy] is the green-eyed monster which doth mock The meat it feeds on iii 3 167
'Tis not to make me jealous To say my wife is fair, feeds well, loves company iii 3 184
Kingdoms are clay: our dungy earth alike Feeds beast as man *Ant. and Cleo.* i 1 36
Now I feed myself With most delicious poison i 5 26
Other women cloy The appetites they feed; but she makes hungry ii 2 242
Feed, and sleep: Our care and pity is so much upon you v 2 187
Sluttery to such neat excellence opposed Should make desire vomit emptiness, Not so allured to feed *Cymbeline* i 6 46
It gave me present hunger To feed again, though full ii 4 138
Should by the minute feed on life and lingering By inches waste you v 5 51
I am no viper, yet I feed On mother's flesh which did me breed *Pericles* i 1 64
Who though they feed On sweetest flowers, yet they poison breed i 1 132

Feed. Their tables were stored full, to glad the sight, And not so much to feed on as delight *Pericles* i 4 29
Men must comfort you, men must feed you, men must stir you up iv 2 97
Who starves the ears she feeds, and makes them hungry, The more she gives them speech v 1 113
Fee'd. Engrossed opportunities to meet her; fee'd every slight occasion that could but niggardly give me sight of her *Mer. Wives* ii 2 204
I am no fee'd post, lady *T. Night* i 5 303
Thou wouldst be fee'd, I see, to make me sport 3 *Hen. VI.* i 4 92
In his house I keep a servant fee'd *Macbeth* iii 4 132
Feeder. The patch is kind enough, but a huge feeder *Mer. of Venice* ii 5 46
I will your very faithful feeder be *As Y. Like It* ii 4 99
Our feasts In every mess have folly and the feeders Digest it *W. Tale* iv 4 11
With eager feeding food doth choke the feeder *Richard II.* ii 1 37
Thou, beastly feeder, art so full of him, That thou provokest thyself to cast him up. So, so, thou common dog 2 *Hen. IV.* i 3 95
The tutor and the feeder of my riots v 5 66
When all our offices have been oppress'd With riotous feeders *T. of Athens* ii 2 168
To be abused By one that looks on feeders *Ant. and Cleo.* iii 13 109
Feedest. Thou false deluding slave, That feed'st me with the very name of meat *T. of Shrew* iv 3 32
Where feed'st thou o' days, Apemantus?—Where my stomach finds meat; or, rather, where I eat it *T. of Athens* iv 3 293
Feedeth. The sight of lovers feedeth those in love *As Y. Like It* iii 4 60
Feeding. For, besides that they are fair with their feeding, they are taught their manage i 1 12
And so dies with feeding his own stomach *All's Well* i 1 155
Boasts himself To have a worthy feeding *W. Tale* iv 4 169
With eager feeding food doth choke the feeder *Richard II.* ii 1 37
Grew by our feeding to so great a bulk That even our love durst not come near your sight For fear of swallowing 1 *Hen. IV.* v 1 62
Contention, like a horse Full of high feeding, madly hath broke loose 2 *Hen. IV.* i 1 10
Anger's my meat; I sup upon myself, And so shall starve with feeding *Coriolanus* iv 2 51
With wine and feeding, we have suppler souls Than in our priest-like fasts v 1 55
And they have nursed this woe, in feeding life *T. Andron.* iii 1 74
There they perch'd, Gorging and feeding from our soldiers' hands *J. C.* v 1 82
Sauce his appetite; That sleep and feeding may prorogue his honour Even till a Lethe'd dulness! *Ant. and Cleo.* ii 1 26
But please your thoughts In feeding them with those my former fortunes iv 15 53
Give it nothing, I pray you, for it is not worth the feeding.—Will it eat me? v 2 271
Fee-farm. A kiss in fee-farm! build there, carpenter *Troi. and Cres.* iii 2 53
Fee-grief. Or is it a fee-grief Due to some single breast? *Macbeth* iv 3 196
Feel. My father's loss, the weakness which I feel *Tempest* i 2 487
But I feel not This deity in my bosom ii 1 277
No matter, since I feel The best is past iii 3 50
I pray thee, let me feel thy cloak upon me *T. G. of Ver.* iii 1 136
That it may know He can command, lets it straight feel the spur *Meas. for Meas.* i 2 166
One who never feels The wanton stings and motions of the sense i 4 58
Spake he so doubtfully, thou couldst not feel his meaning?—Nay, he struck so plainly, I could too well feel his blows *Com. of Errors* ii 1 51
I would I were senseless, sir, that I might not feel your blows iv 4 27
Give me your hand and let me feel your pulse.—There is my hand, and let it feel your ear iv 4 55
That I love her, I feel.—That she is worthy, I know *Much Ado* i 1 230
I neither feel how she should be loved nor know how she should be worthy i 1 232
Men Can counsel and speak comfort to that grief Which they themselves not feel; but, tasting it, Their counsel turns to passion v 1 22
All senses to that sense did make their repair, To feel only looking on fairest of fair *L. L. Lost* ii 1 241
Though I alone do feel the injury *M. N. Dream* iii 2 219
I feel too much thy blessing: make it less, For fear I surfeit *M. of Ven.* iii 2 114
Here feel we but the penalty of Adam, The seasons' difference *As Y. L. It* ii 1 5
Our hands are hard.—Your lips will feel them the sooner iii 2 61
Lives merrily because he feels no pain iii 2 340
I smell sweet savours and I feel soft things *T. of Shrew* Ind. 2 73
Thou shalt soon feel, to thy cold comfort, for being slow in thy hot office iv 1 33
This is to feel a tale, not to hear a tale iv 1 65
My greatest grief, Though little he do feel it, set down sharply *All's Well* iii 4 33
Dead though she be, she feels her young one kick v 3 303
I feel this youth's perfections With an invisible and subtle stealth *T. Night* i 5 315
That is the glorious sun; This pearl she gave me, I do feel't and see't iv 3 2
Many thousand on's Have the disease, and feel't not *W. Tale* i 2 207
But I do see't and feel't, As you feel doing thus; and see withal The instruments that feel ii 1 152
So thou Shalt feel our justice iii 2 91
Your favour I do give lost; for I do feel it gone, But know not how it went iii 2 96
The tortures he shall feel will break the back of man, the heart of monster iv 4 797
Too well, too well I feel The different plague of each calamity *K. John* iii 4 59
Fierce extremes In their continuance will not feel themselves v 7 14
I live with bread like you, feel want, Taste grief, need friends *Rich. II.* iii 2 175
Me rather had my heart might feel your love Than my unpleased eye see your courtesy iii 3 192
The children yet unborn Shall feel this day as sharp to them as thorn iv 1 323
Doth he feel it [honour]? no. Doth he hear it? no. 'Tis insensible, then 1 *Hen. IV.* v 1 139
Feel, masters, how I shake; look you, I warrant you 2 *Hen. IV.* ii 4 113
I feel me much to blame, So idly to profane the precious time ii 4 390
To us all That feel the bruises of the days before iv 1 100
You speak this to feel other men's minds *Hen. V.* iv 1 131
Whose sense no more can feel But his own wringing iv 1 252
I feel such sharp dissension in my breast, Such fierce alarums 1 *Hen. VI.* v 5 84
And with my fingers feel his hand unfeeling 2 *Hen. VI.* iii 2 145
So thou will let me live, and feel no pain iii 3 4
And they shall feel the vengeance of my wrath 3 *Hen. VI.* iv 1 82
For unfelt imagination, They often feel a world of restless cares *Rich. III.* i 4 81
How dost thou feel thyself now? i 4 123
Whereof We cannot feel too little, hear too much *Hen. VIII.* i 2 128
But is't not cruel That she should feel the smart of this? ii 1 166
I meant to rectify my conscience,—which I then did feel full sick ii 4 204
I feel The last fit of my greatness iii 1 77

Feel. If your grace Could but be brought to know our ends are honest, You'ld feel more comfort . . . *Hen. VIII.* iii 1 155
Now I feel Of what coarse metal ye are moulded, envy . . iii 2 238
Your long coat, priest, protects you; thou shouldst feel My sword i' the life-blood of thee else . . . iii 2 276
Vain pomp and glory of this world, I hate ye: I feel my heart new open'd . . . iii 2 366
I know myself now; and I feel within me A peace above all earthly dignities, A still and quiet conscience . . iii 2 378
I am able now, methinks, Out of a fortitude of soul I feel, To endure more miseries and greater far . . iii 2 388
Reach a chair: So; now, methinks, I feel a little ease . iv 2 4
Garlands, Griffith, which I feel I am not worthy yet to wear . iv 2 91
Thou bitch-wolf's son, canst thou not hear? Feel, then *Troi. and Cres.* ii 1 12
He shall as soon read in the eyes of others As feel in his own fall . iii 3 78
Nor feels not what he owes, but by reflection . iii 3 99
I will not be myself, nor have cognition Of what I feel . v 2 64
The other instruments Did see and hear, devise, instruct, walk, feel *Cor.* i 1 105
He that retires, I'll take him for a Volsce, And he shall feel mine edge i 4 29
Let Thy mother rather feel thy pride than fear Thy dangerous stoutness . iii 2 126
Your ignorance, which finds not till it feels . iii 3 129
Ere he express himself, or move the people With what he would say, let him feel your sword . v 6 56
They must take it in sense that feel it.—Me they shall feel while I am able to stand . *Rom. and Jul.* i 1 32
This love feel I, that feel no love in this . i 1 188
Such comfort as do lusty young men feel . i 2 26
Thou canst not speak of that thou dost not feel . iii 3 64
So shall you feel the loss, but not the friend Which you weep for iii 5 76
What shall be done? he will not hear, till feel. *T. of Athens* ii 2 7
O you gods, I feel my master's passion! . iii 1 59
I feel't upon my bones . iii 6 130
O, now you weep; and, I perceive, you feel The dint of pity *J. Cæsar* iii 2 197
I feel now The future in the instant . *Macbeth* i 5 58
Dispute it like a man.—I shall do so; But I must also feel it as a man . iv 3 221
Now does he feel His secret murders sticking on his hands . v 2 16
Now does he feel his title Hang loose about him . v 2 20
Senseless Ilium, Seeming to feel this blow, with flaming top Stoops *Ham.* ii 2 497
He does confess he feels himself distracted . iii 1 5
He hath wrote this to feel my affection to your honour . *Lear* i 2 94
That she may feel How sharper than a serpent's tooth it is To have a thankless child! . i 4 309
Take physic, pomp; Expose thyself to feel what wretches feel . iii 4 34
Let the superfluous and lust-dieted man, That slaves your ordinance, that will not see Because he doth not feel, feel your power quickly iv 1 72
He'll not feel wrongs Which tie him to an answer . iv 2 13
How is't? Feel you your legs? You stand . iv 6 65
I will not swear these are my hands: let's see; I feel this pin prick . iv 7 56
The best quarrels, in the heat, are cursed By those that feel their sharpness . v 3 57
Speak what we feel, not what we ought to say . v 3 324
Cannot but feel this wrong as 'twere their own . *Othello* i 2 97
Whose icy current and compulsive course Ne'er feels retiring ebb iii 3 455
To the felt absence now I feel a cause: Is't come to this? Well, well . iii 4 182
Why I should fear I know not, Since guiltiness I know not; but yet I feel I fear . v 2 39
I am alone the villain of the earth, And feel I am so most *Ant. and Cleo.* iv 6 31
If swift thought break it not, a swifter mean Shall outstrike thought: but thought will do't, I feel . iv 6 36
I do feel, By the rebound of yours, a grief that smites My very heart at root . v 2 103
O, come apace, dispatch! I partly feel thee . v 2 325
Those that are betray'd Do feel the treason sharply, yet the traitor Stands in worse case of woe . *Cymbeline* iii 4 88
Could not find death where I did hear him groan, Nor feel him where he struck . v 3 70
Indeed, sir, he that sleeps feels not the tooth-ache . v 4 177
Must feel war's blow, who spares not innocence . *Pericles* i 2 93
Feeler. This hand, whose touch, Whose every touch, would force the feeler's soul To the oath of loyalty . *Cymbeline* i 6 101
Feeling. Hast thou, which art but air, a touch, a feeling Of their afflictions? . *Tempest* v 1 21
With your tears Moist it again, and frame some feeling line *T. G. of Ver.* iii 2 76
With most painful feeling of thy speech . *Meas. for Meas.* i 2 38
He had some feeling of the sport . iii 2 127
Gazing in mine eyes, feeling my pulse . *Com. of Errors* v 1 243
I will tell you sensibly.—Thou hast no feeling of it. *L. L. Lost* iii 1 115
That we thankful should be, Which we of taste and feeling are . iv 2 30
Love's feeling is more soft and sensible Than are the tender horns of cockled snails . iv 3 337
To whose feeling sorrows I might be some allay . *W. Tale* iv 2 8
No hearing, no feeling, but my sir's song, and admiring the nothing of it iv 4 625
Feeling what small things are boisterous there . *K. John* iv 1 95
Apprehension of the good Gives but the greater feeling to the worse *Richard II.* i 3 301
I have had feeling of my cousin's wrongs And laboured all I could ii 3 141
This earth shall have a feeling and these stones Prove armed soldiers . iii 2 24
I understand thy kisses and thou mine, And that's a feeling disputation: But I will never be a truant, love . *1 Hen. IV.* iii 1 206
Hast thou that holy feeling in thy soul, To counsel me to make my peace with God, And art thou yet to thy own soul so blind? *Richard III.* i 4 257
With lines, That wound, beyond their feeling, to the quick *T. Andron.* iv 2 28
Yet let me weep for such a feeling loss.—So shall you feel the loss, but not the friend Which you weep for . *Rom. and Jul.* iii 5 75
Feeling so the loss, I cannot choose but ever weep the friend . iii 5 77
Feeling in itself A lack of Timon's aid, hath sense withal Of it own fail, restraining aid to Timon . *T. of Athens* v 1 149
Art thou not, fatal vision, sensible To feeling as to sight? *Macbeth* ii 1 37
Eyes without feeling, feeling without sight . *Hamlet* iii 4 78
Has this fellow no feeling of his business, that he sings at grave-making? v 1 73
The tempest in my mind Doth from my senses take all feeling else *Lear* iii 4 13
Who, by the art of known and feeling sorrows, Am pregnant to good pity iv 6 226
I stand up, and have ingenious feeling Of my huge sorrows . iv 6 287
That it was folly in me, thou mayst say, And prove it in thy feeling *Cymb.* v 5 68
But, feeling woe, Gripe not at earthly joys as erst they did . *Pericles* i 1 48
Feelingly. Do I speak feelingly now?—I think thou dost *Meas. for Meas.* i 2 36
These are counsellors That feelingly persuade me what I am *As Y. Like It* ii 1 11
He shall find himself most feelingly personated . *T. Night* ii 3 172
To speak feelingly of him, he is the card or calendar of gentry *Hamlet* v 2 113
Feelingly. Yet you see how this world goes.—I see it feelingly . *Lear* iv 6 152
Fee-simple. If the devil have him not in fee-simple . . *Mer. Wives* iv 2 225
For a quart d'écu he will sell the fee-simple of his salvation . *All's Well* iv 3 312
Here's the lord of the soil come to seize me for a stray, for entering his fee-simple without leave . *2 Hen. VI.* iv 10 27
The rivelled fee-simple of the tetter . *Troi. and Cres.* v 1 26
An I were so apt to quarrel as thou art, any man should buy the fee-simple of my life for an hour and a quarter.—The fee-simple! O simple! . *Rom. and Jul.* iii 1 35
Feet. I'll manacle thy neck and feet together . *Tempest* i 2 461
Beat the ground For kissing of their feet . iv 1 174
The foul lake O'erstunk their feet . iv 1 184
Those at her father's churlish feet she tender'd . *T. G. of Ver.* iii 1 225
Let him walk from whence he came, lest he catch cold on's feet *C. of Er.* iii 1 37
I will fall prostrate at his feet And never rise . v 1 114
Canary to it with your feet, humour it with turning up your eyelids *L. L. Lost* iii 1 13
Submissive fall his princely feet before . iv 1 92
O, if the streets were paved with thine eyes, Her feet were much too dainty for such tread! . iv 3 279
The stairs, as he treads on them, kiss his feet . v 2 330
Some of them had in them more feet than the verses would bear *As Y. L. It* iii 2 174
The feet might bear the verses.—Ay, but the feet were lame and could not bear themselves . iii 2 176
No more shoes than feet; nay, sometime more feet than shoes *T. of S.* Ind. 2 11
He pays you as surely as your feet hit the ground they step on *T. Night* iii 4 306
Direct thy feet Where thou and I henceforth may never meet . v 1 171
Standing on slippers, which his nimble haste Had falsely thrust upon contrary feet . *K. John* iv 2 198
Seek out King John and fall before his feet . v 4 13
Heavy-gaited toads lie in their way, Doing annoyance to the treacherous feet Which with usurping steps do trample thee . *Richard II.* iii 2 16
Hither come Even at his feet to lay my arms and power. . iii 3 39
Where subjects' feet May hourly trample on their sovereign's head . iii 3 156
In those holy fields Over whose acres walk'd those blessed feet *1 Hen. IV.* i 1 25
So a' bade me lay more clothes on his feet . *Hen. V.* ii 3 24
And for our disgrace, his own person, kneeling at our feet . iii 6 141
Under my feet I stamp thy cardinal's hat. . *1 Hen. VI.* i 3 49
Feet, whose strengthless stay is numb, Unable to support this lump of clay . ii 5 13
Lets fall his sword before your highness' feet . iii 4 9
Stinking and fly-blown lies here at our feet . iv 7 76
Kneel at Henry's feet, Thou mayst bereave him of his wits with wonder v 3 194
From top of honour to disgrace's feet . *2 Hen. VI.* i 2 49
God shall be my hope, My stay, my guide and lantern to my feet . ii 3 25
Uneath may she endure the flinty streets, To tread them with her tender-feeling feet . ii 4 9
The ruthless flint doth cut my tender feet . ii 4 34
Kneel for grace and mercy at my feet; I am thy sovereign . *3 Hen. VI.* i 1 75
Who, in my rage, Kneel'd at my feet, and bade me be advised? *Rich. III.* ii 1 107
Yonder walls, that pertly front your town, Yond towers, whose wanton tops do buss the clouds, Must kiss their own feet . *Troi. and Cres.* iv 5 221
At thy feet I kneel, with tears of joy . *T. Andron.* i 1 161
The tribute that I owe, Mine honour's ensigns humbled at thy feet . i 1 252
And fell asleep, As Cerberus at the Thracian poet's feet . ii 4 51
When I do weep, they humbly at my feet Receive my tears . iii 1 41
How oft to-night Have my old feet stumbled at graves! . *Rom. and Jul.* v 3 122
Fawn'd like hounds, And bow'd like bondmen, kissing Cæsar's feet *J. C.* v 1 42
Oftener upon her knees than on her feet, Died every day she lived *Macb.* iv 3 110
I will not yield, To kiss the ground before young Malcolm's feet . v 8 28
In the full bent To lay our service freely at your feet . *Hamlet* ii 2 31
Wise in our negligence, have secret feet In some of our best ports *Lear* iii 1 32
Then comes the time, who lives to see't, That going shall be used with feet iii 2 94
I look down towards his feet; but that's a fable. If that thou be'st a devil, I cannot kill thee . *Othello* v 2 286
And smooth success Be strew'd before your feet! . *Ant. and Cleo.* i 3 101
At the feet sat Cæsarion, whom they call my father's son . iii 6 5
Tell him, I am prompt To lay my crown at's feet, and there to kneel . iii 13 76
I thought he slept, and put My clouted brogues from off my feet *Cymb.* iv 2 214
Only I carry winged time Post on the lame feet of my rhyme *Per.* iv Gower 48
Fehemently. I most fehemently desire you . *Mer. Wives* iii 1 8
Feign. Therefore the poet Did feign that Orpheus drew trees *Mer. of Ven.* v 1 80
What they swear in poetry may be said as lovers they do feign *As Y. L. It* iii 3 22
If thou wert a poet, I might have some hope thou didst feign . iii 3 27
If I do feign, you witnesses above Punish my life! . *T. Night* v 1 140
If I do feign, O, let me in my present wildness die! . *2 Hen. IV.* iv 5 152
Fair Margaret knows That Suffolk doth not flatter, face, or feign *1 Hen. VI.* v 3 142
And all that poets feign of bliss and joy . *3 Hen. VI.* i 2 31
But old folks, many feign as they were dead; Unwieldy, slow *R. and J.* ii 5 16
But this is foolery; Go bid my woman feign a sickness . *Cymbeline* iii 2 76
Feigned. 'Tis poetical.—It is the more like to be feigned . *T. Night* i 5 208
Burns under feigned ashes of forged love . *1 Hen. VI.* iii 1 190
Were but a feigned friend to our proceedings . *3 Hen. VI.* iv 2 11
Hath turn'd my feigned prayer on my head . *Richard III.* v 1 21
His feigned ecstasies Shall be no shelter to these outrages *T. Andron.* iv 4 21
Upon a high and pleasant hill Feign'd Fortune to be throned *T. of Athens* i 1 64
Thou hast feigned him a worthy fellow . i 1 229
I had a feigned letter of my master's Then in my pocket . *Cymbeline* v 5 279
Feigning. Sung With feigning voice verses of feigning love *M. N. Dream* i 1 31
Most friendship is feigning, most loving mere folly . *As Y. Like It* ii 7 181
The truest poetry is the most feigning . iii 3 20
'Twas never merry world Since lowly feigning was call'd compliment *T. Night* iii 1 110
Felicitate. I am alone felicitate In your dear highness' love . *Lear* i 1 77
Felicity. O wood divine! A wife of such wood were felicity . *L. L. Lost* iv 3 249
Absent thee from felicity awhile . *Hamlet* v 2 358
Fell. They fell together all, as by consent; They dropp'd . *Tempest* ii 1 203
Then all together They fell upon me, bound me . *Com. of Errors* v 1 246
Fell over the threshold, and broke my shin . *L. L. Lost* iii 1 118
The fourth turn'd on the toe, and down he fell . v 2 114
Oberon is passing fell and wrath . *M. N. Dream* ii 1 20
Yet mark'd I where the bolt of Cupid fell: It fell upon a little western flower . ii 1 166
Approach, ye Furies fell! O Fates, come, come, Cut thread and thrum v 1 289
An the worst fall that ever fell, I hope I shall make shift *Mer. of Venice* i 2 97
The curse never fell upon our nation till now . iii 1 89
My pride fell with my fortunes; I'll ask him what he would *As Y. Like It* i 2 264
We are still handling our ewes, and their fells, you know, are greasy . iii 2 55
Nature, stronger than his just occasion, Made him give battle to the lioness, Who quickly fell before him . iv 3 132

Fell. That down fell priest and book and book and priest *T. of Shrew* iii 2 166
Thou shouldst have heard how her horse fell and she under her horse . iv 1 76
When better fall, for your avails they fell . . *All's Well* iii 1 22
And my desires, like fell and cruel hounds, E'er since pursue me *T. Night* i 1 22
Alas, sir, how fell you besides your five wits? . . . . iv 2 92
It will the woefullest division prove That ever fell upon this cursed earth . . . . . . *Richard II.* iv 1 147
Their points being broken,— Down fell their hose . 1 *Hen. IV.* ii 4 239
Thou knowest in the state of innocency Adam fell . . . . iii 3 186
And such a flood of greatness fell on you . . . . v 1 48
Harry Monmouth fell Under the wrath of noble Hotspur's sword 2 *Hen. IV.* Ind. 29
But, as the rest, so fell that noble earl And was beheaded . 1 *Hen. VI.* ii 5 90
Fell banning hag, enchantress, hold thy tongue! . . . v 3 42
Villain, stand, or I'll fell thee down . . . . 2 *Hen. VI.* iv 2 123
They fell before thee like sheep and oxen . . . . iv 3 4
And many strokes, though with a little axe, Hew down and fell the hardest-timber'd oak . . . . . 3 *Hen. VI.* ii 1 55
Or like an idle thresher with a flail, Fell gently down . . ii 1 132
What stratagems, how fell, how butcherly! . . . . ii 5 89
But he fell to himself again, and sweetly In all the rest show'd a most noble patience . . . . *Hen. VIII.* ii 1 35
And without trial fell; God's peace be with him! . . . ii 1 111
Both Fell by our servants, by those men we loved most . . ii 1 122
And when you would say something that is sad, Speak how I fell . ii 1 136
I charge thee, fling away ambition: By that sin fell the angels . . iii 2 441
For, since the cardinal fell, that title's lost . . . . iv 1 96
One of which fell with him, Unwilling to outlive the good that did it . iv 2 59
Fell so roundly to a large confession, To angle for your thoughts *Troi. and Cres.* iii 2 161
To-morrow do I meet thee, fell as death; To-night all friends . . iv 5 269
As weeds before A vessel under sail, so men obey'd And fell below his stem: his sword, death's stamp . . . . *Coriolanus* ii 2 111
Gave Aries such a knock That down fell both the Ram's horns *T. An.* iv 3 72
As he fell, did Romeo turn and fly. This is the truth *Rom. and Jul.* iii 1 179
Have with one winter's brush Fell from their boughs *T. of Athens* iv 3 265
Thou redeem'st thyself: but all, save thee, I fell with curses . iv 3 508
That mine own use invites me to cut down, And shortly must I fell it . v 1 210
Great Cæsar fell. O, what a fall was there, my countrymen! *J. Cæsar* iii 2 193
On our former ensign Two mighty eagles fell, and there they perch'd . v 1 81
His soldiers fell to spoil, Whilst we by Antony are all enclosed . . v 3 7
And, to conclude, The victory fell on us . . . . . *Macbeth* i 2 58
The repetition, in a woman's ear, Would murder as it fell . . . ii 3 91
Angels are bright still, though the brightest fell . . . iv 3 22
Not for their own demerits, but for mine, Fell slaughter on their souls iv 3 227
My fell of hair Would at a dismal treatise rouse and stir As life were in't v 5 11
A little ere the mightiest Julius fell, The graves stood tenantless *Hamlet* i 1 114
Fell into a sadness, then into a fast, Thence to a watch . . . ii 2 147
When down her weedy trophies and herself Fell in the weeping brook . iv 7 176
What, art thou mad, old fellow?—How fell you out? say that *Lear* ii 2 92
Ten masts at each make not the altitude Which thou hast perpendicularly fell . . . . iv 6 54
The good-years shall devour them, flesh and fell, Ere they shall make us weep . . . . v 3 24
Her salt tears fell from her, and soften'd the stones . *Othello* iv 3 47
O Spartan dog, More fell than anguish, hunger, or the sea! . . v 2 362
Sir, He fell upon me ere admitted . . . . *Ant. and Cleo.* ii 2 75
Where each of us fell in praise of our country mistresses . *Cymbeline* i 4 61
Thus mine enemy fell, And thus I set my foot on's neck . . . iii 3 91
I wish my brother make good time with him, You say he is so fell . iv 2 109
That striking in our country's cause Fell bravely and were slain . v 4 72
Fell a-bleeding. It was not for nothing that my nose fell a-bleeding on Black-Monday last . . . . . *Mer. of Venice* ii 5 24
Fell Alecto. Rouse up revenge from ebon den with fell Alecto's snake 2 *Hen. IV.* v 5 39
Fell anatomy. And rouse from sleep that fell anatomy Which cannot hear a lady's feeble voice . . . . . *K. John* iii 4 40
Fell a-shouting. And then the people fell a-shouting *J. Cæsar* i 2 222
Fell asleep. I fell asleep here behind the arras 1 *Hen. IV.* iii 3 112
He would have dropp'd his knife, and fell asleep *T. Andron.* iii 4 50
Fell Aufidius. Heavens bless my lord from fell Aufidius! *Coriolanus* i 3 48
Fell away. Canidius and the rest That fell away have entertainment, but No honourable trust . . . . *Ant. and Cleo.* iv 6 17
Fell Clifford. And every drop cries vengeance for his death, 'Gainst thee, fell Clifford . . . . . . 3 *Hen. VI.* i 4 149
Fell cruelty. To do worse to you were fell cruelty . *Macbeth* iv 2 71
Fell curs. Two of thy whelps, fell curs of bloody kind *T. Andron.* ii 3 281
Fell deeds. All pity choked with custom of fell deeds *J. Cæsar* iii 1 269
Fell destruction. Virtue preserved from fell destruction's blast *Per.* v 3 Gower 89
Fell devouring. Out of this fell devouring receptacle *T. Andron.* ii 3 235
Fell distract. With this she fell distract . . . *J. Cæsar* iv 3 155
Fell down. He swounded and fell down at it . . . . . i 2 250
He fell down in the market-place, and foamed at mouth, and was speechless . . . . i 2 254
I know not what you mean by that; but, I am sure, Cæsar fell down . i 2 260
Then I, and you, and all of us fell down, Whilst bloody treason flourish'd . . . . iii 2 195
Fell fault. This fell fault of my accursed sons . *T. Andron.* ii 3 290
For their fell faults our brothers were beheaded . . . . v 3 100
Fell feats. All fell feats Enlink'd to waste and desolation *Hen. V.* iii 3 17
Fell in. I never looked for better at his hands, After he once fell in with Mistress Shore . . . . . . *Richard III.* iii 5 51
Fell incensed. Between the pass and fell incensed points Of mighty opposites . . . . *Hamlet* v 2 61
Fell in love. One that knew courtship too well, for there he fell in love *As Y. Like It* iii 2 364
Fell jealousy, Which troubles oft the bed of blessed marriage . *Hen. V.* v 2 391
Fell-lurking. Astonish these fell-lurking curs . 2 *Hen. VI.* v 1 146
Fell mischiefs. Foreseeing those fell mischiefs . . *Hen. VIII.* v 1 49
Fell motion. In fell motion, With his prepared sword . *Lear* ii 1 52
Fell Mowbray. Our cousin Hereford and fell Mowbray fight *Richard II.* i 2 46
Fell off A distance from her; while her grace sat down . *Hen. VIII.* iv 1 64
Railed upon me till her pinked porringer fell off her head . . v 4 50
Fell on. They fell on; I made good my place . . . . v 4 56
Fell out. I will tell you every thing, right as it fell out *M. N. Dream* iv 2 32
And more above, hath his solicitings, As they fell out by time, by means and place, All given to mine ear . . . *Hamlet* ii 2 127
It so fell out, that certain players We o'er-raught on the way . iii 1 16
Lest by his clamour—as it so fell out—The town might fall in fright *Othello* ii 3 231
Fell out. It was much like an argument that fell out last night *Cymbeline* i 4 61
Fell paw. Being suffer'd with the bear's fell paw . . 2 *Hen. VI.* v 1 153
Fell poison. It would allay the burning quality Of that fell poison *K. John* v 7 9
Fell purpose. That no compunctious visitings of nature Shake my fell purpose . . . . *Macbeth* i 5 47
Fell sergeant. This fell sergeant, death, Is strict in his arrest *Hamlet* v 2 347
Fell serpents. Such fell serpents as false Suffolk is . . 2 *Hen. VI.* iii 2 266
Fell sick. How honourable ladies sought my love, Which I denying, they fell sick and died . . . . *Mer. of Venice* iii 4 71
He fell sick suddenly, and grew so ill He could not sit his mule *Hen. VIII.* iv 2 15
Fell sorrow's tooth doth never rankle more Than when he bites, but lanceth not the sore . . . . *Richard II.* i 3 302
Fell soul. Even from the gallows did his fell soul fleet . *Mer. of Venice* iv 1 135
Fell storm. And what ensues in this fell storm . *Pericles* iii Gower 53
Fell swoop. What, all my pretty chickens and their dam At one fell swoop? . . . . *Macbeth* iv 3 219
Fell sword. With the whiff and wind of his fell sword The unnerved father falls . . . . *Hamlet* ii 2 495
Fell tempest. This fell tempest shall not cease to rage 2 *Hen. VI.* iii 1 351
Fell tortures. While we devise fell tortures for thy faults 3 *Hen. VI.* ii 6 72
Fell war. So is the equal poise of this fell war . . . . ii 5 13
Fell Warwick. The Bishop of York, Fell Warwick's brother . . iv 4 12
Fell whore. This fell whore of thine Hath in her more destruction than thy sword . . . . *T. of Athens* iv 3 61
Fell working. By whose fell working I was first advanced 2 *Hen. IV.* iv 5 207
Felled. Dispark'd my parks and fell'd my forest woods . *Richard II.* iii 1 23
Flew on him, and amongst them fell'd him dead . . . *Lear* iv 2 76
Fellest. In fellest manner execute your aims . *Troi. and Cres.* v 7 6
Fellest foes, Whose passions and whose plots have broke their sleep *Coriolanus* iv 4 18
Better 'twere Thou fell'st into my fury . . . *Ant. and Cleo.* iv 12 41
Fellies. Break all the spokes and fellies from her wheel . *Hamlet* ii 2 517
Fellow. I have great comfort from this fellow . . . *Tempest* i 1 30
He hath lost his fellows And strays about to find 'em . . . i 2 416
My brother's servants Were then my fellows; now they are my men ii 1 274
To be your fellow You may deny me; but I'll be your servant . iii 1 84
I and my fellows Are ministers of Fate . . . . . . iii 3 60
Thou and thy meaner fellows your last service Did worthily perform . iv 1 35
I prophesied, if a gallows were on land, This fellow could not drown v 1 218
Two of these fellows you Must know and own . . . . v 1 274
Fellows, stand fast; I see a passenger . . . *T. G. of Ver.* iv 1 1
This fellow were a king for our wild faction! . . . . iv 1 37
Knew it was Crab, and goes me to the fellow that whips the dogs . iv 4 26
An honest, willing, kind fellow, as ever servant shall come in house *M. W.* i 4 11
Here's a fellow frights English out of his wits . . . . ii 1 143
A true man.—'Twas a good sensible fellow . . . . . ii 1 151
I would have made you four tall fellows skip like rats . . . ii 1 237
Swearing to gentlemen my friends, you were good soldiers and tall fellows . . . . ii 2 11
To make us public sport, Appoint a meeting with this old fat fellow . iv 4 15
I will keep my sides to myself, my shoulders for the fellow of this walk v 5 29
Fellow, why dost thou show me thus to the world? . *Meas. for Meas.* i 2 120
The house is a respected house; next, this is a respected fellow . . ii 1 170
Truly, sir, I am a poor fellow that would live . . . . ii 1 234
I was an inward of his. A shy fellow was the duke . . . iii 2 139
A very superficial, ignorant, unweighing fellow . . . . iii 2 148
That fellow is a fellow of much license . . . . . . iii 2 216
Here's a fellow will help you to-morrow in your execution . . iv 2 23
O gravel heart! After him, fellows; bring him to the block . . iv 3 69
A saucy friar, A very scurvy fellow . . . . . . v 1 136
Silence that fellow: I would he had some cause To prattle for himself . v 1 181
We shall find this friar a notable fellow . . . . . v 1 268
O thou damnable fellow! Did not I pluck thee by the nose for thy speeches? . . . . v 1 342
Such a fellow is not to be talked withal . . . . . v 1 348
What muffled fellow's that?—This is another prisoner that I saved . v 1 491
Is any woman wrong'd by this lewd fellow, . . . let her appear . v 1 515
A drop of water That in the ocean seeks another drop, Who, falling there to find his fellow forth, Unseen, inquisitive, confounds himself *Com. of Errors* i 2 37
Arrest me, foolish fellow, if thou darest . . . . . . iv 1 75
A wolf, nay, worse, a fellow all in buff . . . . . . iv 2 36
The fellow is distract, and so am I; And here we wander in illusions . iv 3 42
The fellow finds his vein And yielding to him humours well his frenzy . iv 4 83
Hath the fellow any wit that told you this?—A good sharp fellow *M. Ado* i 2 17
But yet for all that, cousin, let him be a handsome fellow . . ii 1 58
I should think this a gull, but that the white-bearded fellow speaks it . ii 3 124
Keep your fellows' counsels and your own . . . . . iii 3 92
A marvellous witty fellow, I assure you . . . . . . iv 2 27
Pray thee, fellow, peace: I do not like thy look, I promise thee . . iv 2 46
I am a wise fellow, and, which is more, an officer . . . . iv 2 83
One that knows the law, go to; and a rich fellow enough, go to . . iv 2 86
A fellow that hath had losses, and one that hath two gowns . . iv 2 87
Bring you these fellows on. We'll talk with Margaret, How her acquaintance grew with this lewd fellow . . . . v 1 341
Which is the duke's own person?—This, fellow: what wouldst? *L. L. Lost* i 1 183
I am more bound to you than your fellows . . . . . . i 2 156
Which is the head lady?—Thou shalt know her, fellow, by the rest that have no heads . . . . iv 1 44
Thou fellow, a word: Who gave thee this letter? . . . . iv 1 102
This fellow pecks up wit as pigeons pease, And utters it again . . v 2 315
So, at his sight, away his fellows fly . . . . *M. N. Dream* iii 2 24
Good hay, sweet hay, hath no fellow . . . . iv 1 38
This fellow doth not stand upon points . . . . v 1 118
Nature hath framed strange fellows in her time . . *Mer. of Venice* i 1 51
I shot his fellow of the self-same flight The self-same way . . . i 1 141
Give him a livery More guarded than his fellows' . . . . ii 2 164
When we are both accoutred like young men, I'll prove the prettier fellow iii 4 64
Go to thy fellows; bid them cover the table, serve in the meat . . iii 5 63
The poor rude world Hath not her fellow . . . . . . iii 5 88
It is the stubbornest young fellow of France . . . *As Y. Like It* i 1 149
I would I were invisible, to catch the strong fellow by the leg . . i 2 224
This fellow will but join you together as they join wainscot . . iii 3 87
They say you are a melancholy fellow.—I am so . . . . iv 1 3
Those that are in extremity of either are abominable fellows . . . iv 1 6
Good my lord, like this fellow.—I like him very well . . . v 4 54
Is not this a rare fellow, my lord? he's as good at any thing and yet a fool . . . . v 4 109
Now, fellows, you are welcome.—We thank your honour *T. of Shrew* Ind. 1 79

Fellow. This fellow I remember, Since once he play'd a farmer's eldest son *T. of Shrew* Ind. 1 83
There be good fellows in the world, an a man could light on them . i 1 132
O excellent motion! Fellows, let's be gone . i 2 280
Welcome, you;—how now, you;—what, you;—fellow, you . iv 1 115
Thou 'rt a tall fellow: hold thee that to drink . iv 4 17
'Tis not unknown to you, madam, I am a poor fellow . *All's Well* i 3 15
Worthy fellows; and like to prove most sinewy sword-men . ii 1 61
And indeed such a fellow, to say precisely, were not for the court . ii 2 12
All the learned and authentic fellows . ii 3 14
I did think thee, for two ordinaries, to be a pretty wise fellow . ii 3 212
Shall furnish me to those Italian fields, Where noble fellows strike . ii 3 308
A very tainted fellow, and full of wickedness . iii 2 89
The fellow has a deal of that too much, Which holds him much to have iii 2 92
'Tis a most gallant fellow. I would he loved his wife . iii 5 81
A strange fellow, my lord, that so confidently seems to undertake this iii 6 93
No, no, no, your son was misled with a snipt-taffeta fellow there . iv 5 2
I am a woodland fellow, sir, that always loved a great fire . iv 5 49
I am a fellow o' the strangest mind i' the world *T. Night* i 3 120
Take the fool away.—Do you not hear, fellows? Take away the lady . i 5 43
Madam, yond young fellow swears he will speak with you . i 5 147
O, fellow, come, the song we had last night . ii 4 43
Shall this fellow live? . ii 5 69
The fellow of servants, and not worthy to touch Fortune's fingers . ii 5 170
I warrant thou art a merry fellow and carest for nothing . iii 1 30
This fellow is wise enough to play the fool . iii 1 67
Let this fellow be looked to . iii 4 67
Fellow! not Malvolio, nor after my degree, but fellow . iii 4 85
Youth, whatsoever thou art, thou art but a scurvy fellow . iii 4 163
Go to, thou art a foolish fellow: Let me be clear of thee . iv 1 3
Maintain no words with him, good fellow . iv 2 107
I know thee well: how dost thou, my good fellow? . v 1 12
But for thee, fellow; fellow, thy words are madness . v 1 101
These lords, my noble fellows, if they please, Can clear me . *W. Tale* ii 3 142
Behold me A fellow of the royal bed . iii 2 39
What manner of fellow was he that robbed you? . iv 3 89
A fellow, sir, that I have known to go about with troll-my-dames . iv 3 91
A brave fellow.—Believe me, thou talkest of an admirable conceited fellow . iv 4 202
How now, good fellow! why shakest thou so? Fear not, man . iv 4 641
I am a poor fellow, sir.—Why, be so still; here's nobody will steal that iv 4 644
We are but plain fellows, sir.—A lie; you are rough and hairy . iv 4 743
To bless the bed of majesty again With a sweet fellow to't . v 1 34
Thou art as honest a true fellow as any is in Bohemia . v 2 169
I'll swear to the prince thou art a tall fellow of thy hands and that thou wilt not be drunk; but I know thou art no tall fellow of thy hands . v 2 177
I would thou wouldst be a tall fellow of thy hands . v 2 181
By any means prove a tall fellow: if I do not wonder how thou darest venture to be drunk, not being a tall fellow, trust me not . v 2 183
A good blunt fellow . *K. John* i 1 71
'Good den, sir Richard!'—'God-a-mercy, fellow!'—And if his name be George, I'll call him Peter . i 1 185
What becomes of me? Fellow, be gone: I cannot brook thy sight . iii 1 36
Tell me, thou fellow, is not France forsworn? . iii 1 62
A fellow by the hand of nature mark'd, Quoted and sign'd to do a deed of shame . iv 2 221
Go, fellow, get thee home, provide some carts . *Richard II.* ii 2 106
If he serve God, We'll serve Him too and be his fellow so . iii 2 99
Fellow, give place; here is no longer stay . v 5 95
Which many a good tall fellow had destroy'd So cowardly . *1 Hen. IV.* i 3 62
Poor fellow, never joyed since the price of oats rose . ii 1 13
Each takes his fellow for an officer . ii 2 114
That ever this fellow should have fewer words than a parrot! . ii 4 110
That same mad fellow of the north, Percy . ii 4 369
A fellow of no mark nor likelihood . iii 2 45
A mad fellow met me on the way and told me I had unloaded all the gibbets . iv 2 39
Whose fellows are these that come after?—Mine, Hal, mine . iv 2 68
And, fellows, soldiers, friends, Better consider what you have to do . v 2 76
This is the strangest tale that ever I heard.—This is the strangest fellow v 4 159
He was some hilding fellow that had stolen The horse he rode on *2 Hen. IV.* i 1 57
I am the fellow with the great belly . i 2 165
Stand from him, fellow: wherefore hang'st upon him? . ii 1 74
Thou art a blessed fellow to think as every man thinks . ii 2 61
That I am a second brother and that I am a proper fellow of my hands ii 2 72
A good shallow young fellow: a' would have made a good pantler . ii 4 257
A good-limbed fellow; young, strong, and of good friends . iii 2 114
Peace, fellow, peace; stand aside: know you where you are? . iii 2 130
'Fore God, a likely fellow! Come, prick me Bullcalf till he roar again iii 2 186
Well said; thou'rt a good fellow.—Faith, I'll bear no base mind . iii 2 256
And this same half-faced fellow, Shadow; give me this man . iii 2 283
There was a little quiver fellow, and a' would manage you his piece thus iii 2 301
I shall ne'er see such a fellow.—These fellows will do well . iii 2 306
An I had but a belly of any indifferency, I were simply the most active fellow in Europe . iv 3 24
Say, with the hook-nosed fellow of Rome, 'I came, saw, and overcame' iv 3 45
But thou, like a kind fellow, gavest thyself away gratis . iv 3 75
And welcome, my tall fellow . v 1 65
A fellow that never had the ache in his shoulders . v 1 93
Such fellows are perfect in the great commanders' names . *Hen. V.* iii 6 73
What a wretched and peevish fellow is this king of England! . iii 7 142
Good God! why should they mock poor fellows thus? . iv 3 92
Call yonder fellow hither.—Soldier, you must come to the king . iv 7 123
Keep thy vow, sirrah, when thou meetest the fellow.—So I will, my liege . iv 7 152
This was my glove; here is the fellow of it . iv 8 30
Fill this glove with crowns, And give it to this fellow. Keep it, fellow iv 8 62
The fellow has mettle enough in his belly . iv 8 66
All the world know to be no petter than a fellow, look you now, of no merits . v 1 8
If thou canst love a fellow of this temper, Kate . v 2 153
Take a fellow of plain and uncoined constancy . v 2 160
These fellows of infinite tongue, that can rhyme themselves into ladies' favours, they do always reason themselves out again . v 2 163
If he be not fellow with the best king, thou shalt find the best king of good fellows . v 2 261
This fellow here, with envious carping tongue, Upbraideth me *1 Hen. VI.* iv 1 90
How now, fellow! wouldst any thing with me? . *2 Hen. VI.* i 3 11

Fellow. What means this noise? Fellow, what miracle dost thou proclaim? . *2 Hen. VI.* ii 1 60
I never saw a fellow worse bested, Or more afraid to fight . ii 3 56
Fellow, thank God, and the good wine in thy master's way . ii 3 98
God in justice hath reveal'd to us The truth and innocence of this poor fellow . ii 3 106
Come, fellow, follow us for thy reward . ii 3 108
Where's our general?—Here I am, thou particular fellow . iv 2 119
If this fellow be wise, he'll never call ye Jack Cade more . iv 6 10
When I have fought with Pembroke and his fellows, I'll follow you *3 Hen. VI.* iv 3 54
How far hence is thy lord, mine honest fellow? . v 1 2
Mistress Shore! I tell thee, fellow, He that doth naught with her, excepting one, Were best he do it secretly, alone *Richard III.* i 1 98
I'll turn yon fellow in his grave; And then return lamenting to my love i 2 261
Spoke like a tall fellow that respects his reputation . i 4 156
Go, fellow, go, return unto thy lord; Bid him not fear the separated councils . iii 2 19
I'll talk with this good fellow. How now, sirrah! how goes the world with thee? . iii 2 97
Gramercy, fellow: there, drink that for me . iii 2 108
This is All-Souls' day, fellows, is it not?—It is, my lord . v 1 10
Fellows in arms, and my most loving friends . v 2 1
A paltry fellow, Long kept in Bretagne at our mother's cost . v 3 323
To see a fellow In a long motley coat guarded with yellow *Hen. VIII.* Prol. 15
And from a mouth of honour quite cry down This Ipswich fellow's insolence . i 1 138
This top-proud fellow, Whom from the flow of gall I name not . i 1 151
A French song and a fiddle has no fellow . i 3 41
His noble friends and fellows, whom to leave Is only bitter to him, only dying . ii 1 73
My new secretary: I find him a fit fellow . ii 2 117
That good fellow, If I command him, follows my appointment . ii 2 133
Like to village-curs, Bark when their fellows do . ii 4 160
A worthy fellow, and hath ta'en much pain In the king's business . iii 2 72
Can ye endure to hear this arrogance? And from this fellow? . iii 2 279
You are a saucy fellow: Deserve we no more reverence? . iv 2 100
But this fellow Let me ne'er see again . iv 2 107
A fellow somewhat near the door, he should be a brazier by his face . v 4 41
Ye have made a fine hand, fellows: There's a trim rabble let in . v 4 74
You great fellow, Stand close up, or I'll make your head ache . v 4 91
That's Hector, that, that, look you, that; there's a fellow! *Tr. and Cr.* i 2 216
What sneaking fellow comes yonder?—Where? yonder? that's Deiphobus i 2 246
A paltry insolent fellow!—How he describes himself! . ii 3 218
It should seem, fellow, that thou hast not seen the Lady Cressida . iii 1 39
What mean these fellows? Know they not Achilles? . iii 3 70
A strange fellow here Writes me . iii 3 95
An honest fellow enough, and one that loves quails . v 1 57
Fellow, commend my service to her beauty . v 5 3
Strike, fellows, strike; this is the man I seek . v 8 10
What then? 'Fore me, this fellow speaks! What then? what then? *Coriolanus* i 1 124
Come on, my fellows: He that retires, I'll take him for a Volsce . i 4 27
O noble fellow! Who sensibly outdares his senseless sword . i 4 52
March on, my fellows: Make good this ostentation . i 6 85
That's a brave fellow; but he's vengeance proud . ii 2 5
Wine, wine! What service is here! I think our fellows are asleep . iv 5 2
What fellow's this?—A strange one as ever I looked on . iv 5 20
What have you to do here, fellow? Pray you, avoid the house . iv 5 25
Where is this fellow?—Here, sir: I'ld have beaten him like a dog . iv 5 55
Come, we are fellows and friends: he was ever too hard for him . iv 5 194
This is a happier and more comely time Than when these fellows ran about the streets, Crying confusion . iv 6 28
But reason with the fellow, Before you punish him . iv 6 51
His mother, wife, his child, And this brave fellow too . v 1 30
I tell thee, fellow, Thy general is my lover . v 2 13
Therefore, fellow, I must have leave to pass . v 2 22
Prithee, fellow, remember my name . v 2 29
Nay, but, fellow, fellow,— What's the matter? . v 2 63
A noble fellow, I warrant him.—The worthy fellow is our general . v 2 115
Come, let us go: This fellow had a Volscian to his mother . v 3 178
How now, good fellow! wouldst thou speak with us? . *T. Andron.* iv 4 39
God-den, good fellow.—God gi' god-den . *Rom. and Jul.* i 2 57
So shows a snowy dove trooping with crows, As yonder lady o'er her fellows shows . i 5 51
One of those fellows that when he enters the confines of a tavern claps me his sword upon the table . iii 1 5
Am I like such a fellow? . iii 1 11
Now, fellow, What's there?—Things for the cook, sir . iv 4 13
Honest good fellows, ah, put up, put up . iv 5 98
Live, and be prosperous: and farewell, good fellow . v 3 42
All those which were his fellows but of late . *T. of Athens* i 1 78
This fellow here, Lord Timon, this thy creature, By night frequents my house . i 1 116
Thou hast feigned him a worthy fellow.—That's not feigned; he is so . i 1 229
The fellow that sits next him now, parts bread with him . i 2 47
A brave fellow! he keeps his tides well . i 2 56
These old fellows Have their ingratitude in them hereditary . ii 2 223
Those five talents. That had, give't these fellows To whom 'tis instant due ii 2 238
Nothing remaining?—Alack, my fellows, what should I say to you? Let me be recorded by the righteous gods, I am as poor as you . iv 2 3
More of our fellows.—All broken implements of a ruin'd house . iv 2 15
We are fellows still, Serving alike in sorrow . iv 2 18
Good fellows all, The latest of my wealth I'll share amongst you . iv 2 22
Wherever we shall meet, for Timon's sake, Let's yet be fellows . iv 2 25
Mend me, thou saucy fellow!—Why, sir, cobble you . *J. Cæsar* i 1 21
Let me see his face.—Fellow, come from the throng . i 2 21
What a blunt fellow is this grown to be! . i 2 299
Come hither, fellow: which way hast thou been? . ii 4 21
Delay not, Cæsar; read it instantly.—What, is the fellow mad? . iii 1 10
Of whose true-fixed and resting quality There is no fellow in the firmament iii 1 62
How now, fellow!—Sir, Octavius is already come to Rome . iii 2 266
A barren-spirited fellow; one that feeds On abjects, orts and imitations iv 1 36
Saucy fellow, hence!—Bear with him, Brutus: 'tis his fashion . iv 3 134
Fellow thou, awake!—My lord?—My lord?—Why did you so cry out, sirs? . iv 3 301
It is impossible that ever Rome Should breed thy fellow . v 3 101
Thou art a fellow of a good respect . v 5 45
Fellow, wilt thou bestow thy time with me? . v 5 61
One of my fellows had the speed of him . *Macbeth* i 5 36

Fellow. My young remembrance cannot parallel A fellow to it *Macbeth* ii 3 68
At no time broke my faith, would not betray The devil to his fellow iv 3 129
There ran a rumour Of many worthy fellows that were out iv 3 183
Come on—you hear this fellow in the cellarage *Hamlet* i 5 151
What should such fellows as I do crawling between earth and heaven? iii 1 130
To hear a robustious periwig-pated fellow tear a passion to tatters iii 2 11
I would have such a fellow whipped for o'erdoing Termagant iii 2 15
We shall know by this fellow: the players cannot keep counsel iii 2 151
Give these fellows some means to the king iv 6 13
These good fellows will bring thee where I am iv 6 27
Has this fellow no feeling of his business, that he sings at grave-making? v 1 73
This fellow might be in's time a great buyer of land v 1 112
I will speak to this fellow. Whose grave's this, sirrah? v 1 126
Whose was it?—A whoreson mad fellow's it was v 1 193
I knew him, Horatio: a fellow of infinite jest, of most excellent fancy v 1 204
I cannot conceive you.—Sir, this young fellow's mother could *Lear* i 1 13
Put on what weary negligence you please, You and your fellows i 3 13
What grows of it, no matter; advise your fellows so i 3 23
A very honest-hearted fellow, and as poor as the king i 4 20
Who wouldst thou serve?—You.—Dost thou know me, fellow? i 4 28
What says the fellow there? Call the clotpoll back i 4 50
I thank thee, fellow; thou servest me, and I'll love thee i 4 97
This fellow has banished two on's daughters, and did the third a blessing i 4 114
Thou wast a pretty fellow when thou hadst no need to care for her frowning i 4 210
Fellow, I know thee.—What dost thou know me for? ii 2 13
Why, what a monstrous fellow art thou, thus to rail! ii 2 27
A tailor made thee.—Thou art a strange fellow: a tailor make a man? ii 2 61
What, art thou mad, old fellow?—How fell you out? ii 2 91
This is some fellow, Who, having been praised for bluntness, doth affect A saucy roughness ii 2 101
This is a fellow of the self-same colour Our sister speaks of ii 2 145
The very fellow that of late Display'd so saucily against your highness ii 4 40
She will tell you who your fellow is That yet you do not know iii 1 48
I am cold myself. Where is this straw, my fellow? iii 2 69
Tom's a-cold.—In, fellow, there, into the hovel: keep thee warm iii 4 179
Good my lord, soothe him; let him take the fellow iii 4 182
Fellows, hold the chair. Upon these eyes of thine I'll set my foot iii 7 67
Fellow, where goest?—Is it a beggar-man?—Madman and beggar too iv 1 31
I' the last night's storm I such a fellow saw; Which made me think a man a worm iv 1 34
Bless thee, master!—Is that the naked fellow?—Ay, my lord iv 1 42
Sirrah, naked fellow,— Poor Tom's a-cold. I cannot daub it further iv 1 53
Now, fellow, fare thee well.—Gone, sir: farewell iv 6 41
That fellow handles his bow like a crow-keeper: draw me a clothier's yard iv 6 87
Lies not in your good will.—Nor in thine, lord.—Half-blooded fellow, yes v 3 80
I kill'd the slave that was a-hanging thee.—'Tis true, my lords, he did.—Did I not, fellow? v 3 275
He's a good fellow, I can tell you that; He'll strike, and quickly too v 3 284
A fellow almost damn'd in a fair wife *Othello* i 1 21
These fellows have some soul; And such a one do I profess myself i 1 54
You see this fellow that is gone before; He is a soldier fit to stand by Cæsar ii 3 126
There comes a fellow crying out for help; And Cassio following him ii 3 226
Myself the crying fellow did pursue ii 3 230
It grieves my husband As if the case were his.—O, that's an honest fellow iii 3 5
This fellow's of exceeding honesty, And knows all qualities iii 3 258
Think every bearded fellow that's but yoked May draw with you iv 1 67
Some most villanous knave, Some base notorious knave, some scurvy fellow iv 2 140
This is Othello's ancient, as I take it.—The same indeed; a very valiant fellow v 1 52
Set on in the dark By Roderigo and fellows that are scaped v 1 113
Let this fellow Be nothing of our strife *Ant. and Cleo.* ii 2 79
Go to the fellow, good Alexas; bid him Report the feature of Octavia ii 5 111
There's a strong fellow, Menas.—Why?—A' bears the third part of the world ii 7 94
Let Neptune hear we bid a loud farewell To these great fellows ii 7 140
Where is the fellow?—Half afeard to come iii 3 1
There's nothing in her yet: The fellow has good judgement.—Excellent iii 3 28
What art thou, fellow?—One that but performs The bidding of the fullest man iii 13 86
Whip him, fellows, Till, like a boy, you see him cringe his face iii 13 99
To let a fellow that will take rewards And say 'God quit you!' be familiar with My playfellow, your hand! iii 13 123
You have served me well, And kings have been your fellows iv 2 13
Well, my good fellows, wait on me to-night: Scant not my cups; and make as much of me As when mine empire was your fellow too iv 2 20
Mine armour, Eros! Come, good fellow, put mine iron on iv 4 3
We shall thrive now. Seest thou, my good fellow? Go put on thy defences iv 4 9
Good my fellows, do not please sharp fate To grace it with your sorrows iv 14 135
Here is a rural fellow, That will not be denied your highness' presence v 2 233
And that she should love this fellow and refuse me! *Cymbeline* i 2 27
He's a strange fellow himself, and knows it not ii 1 38
A worthy fellow, Albeit he comes on angry purpose now ii 3 60
Profane fellow! Wert thou the son of Jupiter and no more But what thou art besides, thou wert too base To be his groom ii 3 129
Come, fellow, be thou honest: Do thou thy master's bidding iii 4 66
And make me put into contempt the suits Of princely fellows iii 4 93
Why, good fellow, What shall I do the while? where bide? how live? iii 4 130
And the fellow dares not deceive me iv 1 27
But for thee, fellow, Who needs must know of her departure and Dost seem so ignorant, we'll enforce it from thee iv 3 9
You know not which way you shall go.—Yes, indeed do I, fellow v 4 183
I tell thee, fellow, there are none want eyes to direct them the way I am going v 4 192
Dangerous fellow, hence! Breathe not where princes are v 5 237
I perceive he was a wise fellow, and had good discretion *Pericles* i 3 4
Honest! good fellow, what's that? ii 1 57
Now, afore me, a handsome fellow! Come, thou shalt go home ii 1 84
Fellow-counsellor. A fellow-counsellor, 'Mong boys, grooms, and lackeys *Hen. VIII.* v 2 17
Fellow Curtis. It hath tamed my old master and my new mistress and myself, fellow Curtis *T. of Shrew* iv 1 26
Fellow-fault. Every one fault seeming monstrous till his fellow-fault came to match it *As Y. Like It* iii 2 373
Fellow Grumio!—How now, old lad? *T. of Shrew* iv 1 112
Fellow Hector. The party is gone, fellow Hector, she is gone *L. L. Lost* v 2 678
Fellow kings. I tell you that that Lord Say hath gelded the commonwealth, and made it an eunuch *2 Hen. VI.* iv 2 173
Fellow maids. With her fellow maids *Pericles* v 1 50
Fellow-minister. My fellow-ministers Are like invulnerable *Tempest* iii 3 65
Fellow partner. I would be glad to receive some instruction from my fellow partner *Meas. for Meas.* iv 2 19
Fellow peers. You shall not need, my fellow peers of Tyre, Further to question me *Pericles* i 3 11
Fellow-scholar. Live with me My fellow-scholars *L. L. Lost* i 1 17
Fellow-schoolmaster. My fellow-schoolmaster Doth watch Bianca's steps so narrowly *T. of Shrew* iii 2 140
Fellow-servant. Entertain him To be my fellow-servant *T. G. of Ver.* ii 4 105
Fellow-soldier, make thou proclamation *3 Hen. VI.* iv 7 70
Fellow-student. I pray thee, do not mock me, fellow-student *Hamlet* i 2 177
Fellow Tranio. Has my fellow Tranio stolen your clothes? *T. of Shrew* i 1 228
Your fellow Tranio here, to save my life, Puts my apparel and my countenance on i 1 233
Fellow tribune. Let me deserve so ill as you, and make me Your fellow tribune *Coriolanus* iii 1 52
The plebeians have got your fellow-tribune And hale him up and down v 4 39
Fellow Trinculo, we'll fill him by and by again *Tempest* ii 2 180
Fellowest. With what's unreal thou coactive art, And fellow'st nothing *W. Tale* i 2 142
Fellowly. Mine eyes, even sociable to the show of thine, Fall fellowly drops *Tempest* v 1 64
Fellowship. Security enough to make fellowships accurst *Meas. for Meas.* iii 2 241
Sweet fellowship in shame!—One drunkard loves another *L. L. Lost* iv 3 49
By the next new moon—The sealing-day betwixt my love and me, For everlasting bond of fellowship *M. N. Dream* i 1 85
By a roaring tempest on the flood, A whole armado of convicted sail Is scatter'd and disjoin'd from fellowship *K. John* iii 4 3
There's neither honesty, manhood, nor good fellowship in thee *1 Hen. IV.* i 2 156
But out upon this half-faced fellowship! i 3 208
Lads, boys, hearts of gold, all the titles of good fellowship come to you! ii 4 307
We would not die in that man's company That fears his fellowship to die with us *Hen. V.* iv 3 39
Here was a royal fellowship of death! iv 8 106
All the fellowship I hold now with him Is only my obedience *Hen. VIII.* iii 1 121
This boy, that cannot tell what he would have, But kneels and holds up hands for fellowship *Coriolanus* v 3 175
If sour woe delights in fellowship *Rom. and Jul.* iii 2 116
Letters of entreaty, which imported His fellowship i' the cause *T. of A.* v 2 12
By the rights of our fellowship, by the consonancy of our youth *Hamlet* ii 2 294
Would not this . . . get me a fellowship in a cry of players, sir? iii 2 289
The mind much sufferance doth o'erskip, When grief hath mates, and bearing fellowship *Lear* iii 6 114
The great contention of the sea and skies Parted our fellowship *Othello* ii 1 93
This it is to have a name in great men's fellowship *Ant. and Cleo.* ii 7 13
Felon. Murder indeed, that bloody sin, I tortured Above the felon *2 Hen. VI.* iii 1 132
I do defy thy conjurations, And apprehend thee for a felon *Rom. and Jul.* v 3 69
The felon Loaden with irons wiser than the judge *T. of Athens* iii 5 49
Felonious. Foul felonious thief that fleeced poor passengers *2 Hen. VI.* iii 1 129
Felony. Treason, felony, Sword, pike, knife, gun, or need of any engine, Would I not have *Tempest* ii 1 160
I will make it felony to drink small beer *2 Hen. VI.* iv 2 73
Felt. Not a soul But felt a fever of the mad *Tempest* i 2 209
Would I might be dead If I in thought felt not her very sorrow! *T. G. of V.* iv 4 177
Faith, I saw it not; but I felt it hot in her breath *Com. of Errors* iii 2 134
My bones bear witness, That since have felt the vigour of his rage iv 4 81
And when this hail some heat from Hermia felt, So he dissolved *M. N. Dream* i 1 244
The curse never fell upon our nation till now; I never felt it till now *Mer. of Venice* iii 1 90
That wishing well had not a body in't, Which might be felt *All's Well* i 1 196
I have felt so many quirks of joy and grief iii 2 51
Indeed we heard how near his death he was Before the child himself felt he was sick *K. John* iv 2 88
Have felt the worst of death's destroying wound And lie full low *Richard II.* iii 2 139
Then I felt to his knees, and they were as cold as any stone *Hen. V.* ii 3 26
Hadst thou but loved him half so well as I, Or felt that pain which I did for him once *3 Hen. VI.* ii 1 221
Thy mother felt more than a mother's pain v 6 49
The first was I that help'd thee to the crown; The last was I that felt thy tyranny *Richard III.* v 3 168
One that never in his life Felt so much cold as over shoes in snow v 3 326
Would I had never trod this English earth, Or felt the flatteries that grow upon it! *Hen. VIII.* iii 1 144
Not till then, he felt himself, And found the blessedness of being little iv 2 65
When it did taste the wormwood on the nipple Of my dug and felt it bitter, pretty fool, To see it tetchy! *Rom. and Jul.* i 3 31
He jests at scars that never felt a wound ii 2 1
He and myself Have travail'd in the great shower of your gifts, And sweetly felt it *T. of Athens* v 1 74
Come hither, ere my tree hath felt the axe v 1 214
New sorrows Strike heaven on the face, that it resounds As if it felt with Scotland and yell'd out Like syllable of dolour *Macbeth* iv 3 7
Where the greater malady is fix'd, The lesser is scarce felt *Lear* iii 4 9
It were a delicate stratagem, to shoe A troop of horse with felt iv 6 189
It is a chance which does redeem all sorrows That ever I have felt v 3 267
This hand is moist, my lady.—It yet hath felt no age *Othello* iii 4 37
To the felt absence now I feel a cause: Is't come to this? iii 4 182
Let ill tidings tell Themselves when they be felt *Ant. and Cleo.* ii 5 88
How she died of the biting of it, what pain she felt v 2 255
I hate you; which I had rather You felt than make't my boast *Cymbeline* ii 3 116
Did you but know the city's usuries And felt them knowingly iii 3 46
The dream's here still: even when I wake, it is Without me, as within me; not imagined, felt iv 2 307
Their dear loss, The more of you 'twas felt, the more it shaped Unto my end v 5 346
Here they're but felt, and seen with mischief's eyes *Pericles* i 4 8
I'll then discourse our woes, felt several years i 4 18
Feltest. I hope, thou felt'st I was displeased *Com. of Errors* ii 2 19
Female. Men . . . Are masters to their females, and their lords ii 1 24
A female; or, for thy more sweet understanding, a woman *L. L. Lost* i 1 267
Cupid is a knavish lad, Thus to make poor females mad *M. N. Dream* iii 2 441
The female ivy so Enrings the barky fingers of the elm iv 1 48
Of female favour, and bestows himself Like a ripe sister *As Y. Like It* iv 3 87
This female,—which in the common is woman v 1 54
Abandon the society of this female, or, clown, thou perishest v 1 56
Carry This female bastard hence *W. Tale* ii 3 175

Female. And clap their female joints In stiff unwieldy arms *Richard II.* iii 2 114
My brain I'll prove the female to my soul, My soul the father . v 5 6
So the son of the female is the shadow of the male: it is often so
2 Hen. IV. iii 2 140
When flesh is cheap and females dear, And lusty lads roam here and there v 3 20
Pharamond The founder of this law and female bar . . . *Hen. V.* i 2 42
No female Should be inheritrix in Salique land . . . . i 2 50
All appear To hold in right and title of the female . . . . i 2 89
Hold up this Salique law To bar your highness claiming from the female i 2 92
Even such delight Among fresh female buds shall you this night Inherit at my house . . . . *Rom. and Jul.* i 2 29
Anon, as patient as the female dove . . . . *Hamlet* v 1 309
With female fairies will his tomb be haunted . *Cymbeline* iv 2 217
This king unto him took a fere, Who died and left a female heir *Per.* 1 Gower 22
Feminine. A soul feminine saluteth us . *L. L. Lost* iv 2 83
Fen. As wicked dew as e'er my mother brush'd With raven's feather from unwholesome fen Drop on you! . . . . . . *Tempest* i 2 322
Or as 'twere perfumed by a fen . . . . . . ii 1 48
All the infections that the sun sucks up From bogs, fens, flats, on Prosper fall! . . . . ii 2 2
Common cry of curs! whose breath I hate As reek o' the rotten fens
Coriolanus iii 3 121
A lonely dragon, that his fen Makes fear'd and talk'd of more than seen iv 1 30
Fence. Playing at sword and dagger with a master of fence *Mer. Wives* i 1 295
Alas, sir, I cannot fence.—Villany, take your rapier . . . ii 3 15
Despite his nice fence and his active practice, His May of youth *M. Ado* v 1 75
I'll whip you from your foining fence; Nay, as I am a gentleman, I will v 1 84
He will fence with his own shadow . . . *Mer. of Venice* i 2 66
An I thought he had been valiant and so cunning in fence *T. Night* iii 4 312
Saint George, that swinged the dragon, . . . Teach us some fence! *K. John* ii 1 290
Priest, I'll shave your crown for this, Or all my fence shall fail *2 Hen. VI.* ii 1 52
I am never able to deal with my master, he hath learnt so much fence already . . . . ii 3 79
Where's Captain Margaret, to fence you now? . . *3 Hen. VI.* ii 6 75
Can Oxford, that did ever fence the right, Now buckler falsehood with a pedigree? For shame! . . . . iii 3 98
Back'd with God and with the seas Which He hath given for fence impregnable . . . . iv 1 44
O thou wall, That girdlest in those wolves, dive in the earth, And fence not Athens! . . . . . . *T. of Athens* iv 1 3
As the tops of trees, Which fence the roots they grow by . *Pericles* i 2 30
Fenced. A sheep-cote fenced about with olive trees . *As Y. Like It* iv 3 78
Fencer. Blunt as the fencer's foils, which hit, but hurt not *Much Ado* v 2 13
They say he has been fencer to the Sophy . . *T. Night* iii 4 307
Fencing. I would I had bestowed that time in the tongues that I have in fencing, dancing . . . . i 3 98
The right fencing grace, my lord; tap for tap, and so part fair *2 Hen. IV.* ii 1 206
As gaming, my lord.—Ay, or drinking, fencing, swearing *Hamlet* ii 1 25
Without any more virginal fencing . . . . . *Pericles* iv 6 63
Fennel. Eats conger and fennel . . . . . *2 Hen. IV.* ii 4 267
There's fennel for you, and columbines: there's rue for you . *Hamlet* iv 5 180
Fenny. Fillet of a fenny snake, In the cauldron boil and bake *Macbeth* iv 1 12
Fen-sucked. Infect her beauty, You fen-suck'd fogs, drawn by the powerful sun! . . . . *Lear* ii 4 169
Fenton. Master Fenton, I'll be sworn on a book, she loves you *Mer. Wives* i 4 155
What say you to young Master Fenton? he capers, he dances . iii 2 67
Gentle Master Fenton, Yet seek my father's love; still seek it, sir . iii 4 18
And how does good Master Fenton? Pray you, a word with you . iii 4 34
What does Master Fenton here? You wrong me, sir, thus still to haunt my house . . . . iii 4 72
Good Master Fenton, come not to my child.—She is no match for you . iii 4 76
Sir, will you hear me?—No, good Master Fenton . . . iii 4 78
Knowing my mind, you wrong me, Master Fenton . . . iii 4 80
Good Master Fenton, I will not be your friend nor enemy . . iii 4 92
Will you cast away your child on a fool, and a physician? Look on Master Fenton . . . . iii 4 101
I would Master Slender had her; or, in sooth, I would Master Fenton had her . . . . iii 4 110
And I'll be as good as my word; but speciously for Master Fenton . iii 4 113
Master Fenton, talk not to me; my mind is heavy: I will give over all iv 6 1
I will hear you, Master Fenton; and I will at the least keep your counsel . . . . iv 6 6
My heart misgives me: here comes Master Fenton. How now, Master Fenton! . . . . v 5 227
Fenton, heaven give thee joy! What cannot be eschew'd must be embraced . . . . v 5 250
Master Fenton, Heaven give you many, many merry days! . . v 5 253
Feodary. Let my brother die, If not a feodary, but only he Owe and succeed thy weakness . . . . . . *Meas. for Meas.* ii 4 122
Art thou a feodary for this act, and look'st So virgin-like? . *Cymbeline* iii 2 21
Fer. Master Fer! I'll fer him, and firk him, and ferret him . *Hen. V.* iv 4 29
I do not know the French for fer, and ferret, and firk . . iv 4 32
Ferdinand. The king's son, Ferdinand, With hair up-staring,—then like reeds, not hair,—Was the first man that leap'd . . *Tempest* i 2 212
Will you grant with me That Ferdinand is drown'd? . . . ii 1 244
In these fits I leave them, while I visit Young Ferdinand . . iii 3 92
O Ferdinand, Do not smile at me that I boast her off . . iv 1 8
How sharp the point of this remembrance is!—My dear son Ferdinand v 1 139
And Ferdinand, her brother, found a wife Where he himself was lost . v 1 210
Get you hence, And bid my cousin Ferdinand come hither *T. of Shrew* iv 1 154
Ferdinand, My father, king of Spain, was reckon'd one The wisest prince that there had reign'd . . . . . . *Hen. VIII.* ii 4 47
Fere. The woful fere And father of that chaste dishonour'd dame *T. An.* iv 1 89
This king unto him took a fere, Who died and left a female heir *Per.* i Gower 21
Fern-seed. We have the receipt of fern-seed, we walk invisible *1 Hen. IV.* ii 1 96
You are more beholding to the night than to fern-seed for your walking invisible . . . . ii 1 98
Ferrara. A league between his highness and Ferrara . *Hen. VIII.* iii 2 323
Ferrers. Walter Lord Ferrers, Sir Robert Brakenbury *Richard III.* v 5 13
Ferret. I'll fer him, and firk him, and ferret him: discuss the same in French unto him.—I do not know the French for fer, and ferret, and firk . . . . *Hen. V.* iv 4 30
Cicero Looks with such ferret and such fiery eyes . . *J. Cæsar* i 2 186
Ferry. With imagined speed Unto the tranect, to the common ferry Which trades to Venice . . . . . *Mer. of Venice* iii 4 53
Ferryman. That grim ferryman which poets write of . *Richard III.* i 4 46
Fertile. The fresh springs, brine-pits, barren place and fertile *Tempest* i 2 338
I'll show thee every fertile inch o' th' island . . . . ii 2 152
With adorations, fertile tears, With groans that thunder love *T. Night* i 5 274
Derive a liberty From heartiness, from bounty, fertile bosom *W. Tale* i 2 113
Fertile. The climate's delicate, the air most sweet, Fertile the isle
W. Tale iii 1 2
And all the fertile land within that bound . . *1 Hen. IV.* iii 1 77
Good store of fertile sherris . . . . . *2 Hen. IV.* iv 3 131
This best garden of the world, Our fertile France . . *Hen. V.* v 2 37
Look on thy country, look on fertile France . . *Hen. VI.* iii 3 44
I had hope of France, Even as I have of fertile England's soil *2 Hen. VI.* i 1 238
I had hope of France As firmly as I hope for fertile England . . . iii 1 88
Ensear thy fertile and conceptious womb, Let it no more bring out ingrateful man! Go great with tigers, dragons *T. of Athens* iv 3 187
He hath much land, and fertile . . . . . . *Hamlet* v 2 88
Though he in a fertile climate dwell, Plague him with flies . *Othello* i 1 70
How many boys and wenches must I have?—If every of your wishes had a womb, And fertile every wish, a million . *Ant. and Cleo.* i 2 39
Fertile-fresh. More fertile-fresh than all the field to see . *Mer. Wives* v 5 72
Fertility. The noisome weeds, which without profit suck The soil's fertility from wholesome flowers . . . . . *Richard II.* iii 4 39
All her husbandry doth lie on heaps, Corrupting in it own fertility
Hen. V. v 2 40
Fervency. When your diver Did hang a salt-fish on his hook, which he With fervency drew up . . . . . *Ant. and Cleo.* ii 5 18
Fervour. Whilst I from far His name with zealous fervour sanctify
All's Well iii 4 11
Let your fervour, like my master's, be Placed in contempt! . *T. Night* i 5 306
Or, wing'd with fervour of her love, she's flown . *Cymbeline* iii 5 61
Feste. Who was it?—Feste, the jester, my lord . *T. Night* ii 4 11
Fester. Where, wretches, their poor bodies Must lie and fester *Hen. V.* iv 3 88
Should they not, Well might they fester 'gainst ingratitude . *Coriolanus* i 9 30
Festered. This fester'd joint cut off, the rest rest sound . *Richard II.* v 3 85
As fester'd members rot but by degree . . . *1 Hen. VI.* iii 1 192
Festering. Where bloody Tybalt, yet but green in earth, Lies festering in his shroud . . . . *Rom and Jul.* iv 3 43
Festinate. Advise the duke, where you are going, to a most festinate preparation . . . . *Lear* iii 7 10
Festinately. Bring him festinately hither . . *L. L. Lost* iii 1 6
Festival. I cannot woo in festival terms . . . *Much Ado* v 2 41
An eye-sore to our solemn festival! . . . *T. of Shrew* iii 2 103
I picked and cut most of their festival purses . *W. Tale* iv 4 627
This blessed day Ever in France shall be kept festival . *K. John* iii 1 76
At high festivals Before the kings and queens of France . *1 Hen. VI.* i 6 26
So tedious is this day As is the night before some festival To an impatient child that hath new robes . . . . *Rom. and Jul.* iii 2 29
All things that we ordained festival, Turn from their office to black funeral . . . . iv 5 84
It hath been sung at festivals, On ember-eves and holy-ales *Pericles* i Gower 5
Festivity. After so long grief, such festivity! . *Com. of Errors* v 1 406
Fet. On, on, you noblest English, Whose blood is fet from fathers of war-proof! . . . . *Hen. V.* iii 1 18
Fetch. To fetch dew From the still-vex'd Bermoothes . *Tempest* i 2 228
He does make our fire, Fetch in our wood and serves in offices . i 2 312
Hag-seed, hence! Fetch us in fuel; and be quick . . . i 2 366
No more dams I'll make for fish; Nor fetch in firing At requiring . ii 2 185
I will fetch off my bottle, though I be o'er ears for my labour . iv 1 213
Go release them, Ariel . . . —I'll fetch them, sir . . . v 1 32
Fetch me the hat and rapier in my cell . . . . . v 1 84
And with a corded ladder fetch her down . . *T. G. of Ver.* iii 1 40
She can fetch and carry. Why, a horse can do no more: nay, a horse cannot fetch, but only carry . . . . iii 1 274
Do intend vat I speak? a green-a box.—Ay, forsooth; I'll fetch it you
Mer. Wives i 4 49
I am come to fetch you home. I am sworn of the peace . . ii 3 54
Go fetch me a quart of sack; put a toast in't . . . . iii 5 3
Whose credit with the judge, or own great place, Could fetch your brother from the manacles Of the all-building law . *Meas. for Meas.* ii 4 93
Think you I can a resolution fetch From flowery tenderness? . . iii 1 82
Go in to him, and fetch him out.—He is coming, sir . . iv 3 36
Your provost knows the place where he abides And he may fetch him . v 1 253
Go fetch him hither; let me look upon him . . . . v 1 474
My charge was but to fetch you from the mart *Com. of Errors* i 2 74
Go back again, thou slave, and fetch him home . . . ii 1 75
Hence, prating peasant! fetch thy master home . . . ii 1 81
Go fetch me something: I'll break ope the gate . . . iii 1 73
Go get thee gone; fetch me an iron crow . . . . iii 1 84
Get you home And fetch the chain . . . . . . iii 1 115
Hold you still: I'll fetch my sister, to get her good will . . iii 2 70
The chain!—Why, give it to my wife and fetch your money . iv 1 54
Will you send him, mistress, redemption, the money in his desk?—Go fetch it . . . . iv 2 47
Come to the Centaur; fetch our stuff from thence . . . iv 4 153
Wherefore throng you hither?—To fetch my poor distracted husband hence . . . . v 1 39
The abbess shuts the gates on us And will not suffer us to fetch him out v 1 157
Who parted with me to go fetch a chain . . . . v 1 221
Master, shall I fetch your stuff from shipboard? . . . v 1 408
You speak this to fetch me in, my lord . . . *Much Ado* i 1 225
I will fetch you a tooth-picker now from the furthest inch of Asia . ii 1 274
Fetch you a hair off the great Cham's beard . . . . ii 1 276
All the gallants of the town are come to fetch you to church . . iii 4 97
To fetch hither the swain: he must carry me a letter . *L. L. Lost* iii 1 50
To fetch me trifles, and return again . . . *M. N. Dream* ii 1 133
Fetch me that flower; the herb I shew'd thee once . . . ii 1 169
Fetch me this herb; and be thou here again Ere the leviathan can swim a league . . . . ii 1 173
And they shall fetch thee jewels from the deep . . . . iii 1 161
Shall seek The squirrel's hoard, and fetch thee new nuts . . iv 1 40
Fetch that gallant hither; If he be absent, bring his brother *As Y. L. It* ii 2 17
I will fetch up your goats, Audrey . . . . . . iii 3 2
I know my remedy; I must go fetch the third-borough *T. of Shrew* Ind. 1 11
And fetch shrill echoes from the hollow earth . . . Ind. 2 48
We will fetch thee straight Adonis painted by a running brook . Ind. 2 51
Go, rascals, go, and fetch my supper in . . . . . iv 1 142
I like it well: good Grumio, fetch it me . . . . . iv 3 21
My boy shall fetch the scrivener presently . . . . iv 4 59
Go on, and fetch our horses back again . . . . . iv 5 9
Go, fetch them hither: if they deny to come, Swinge me them soundly v 2 103
None better than to let him fetch off his drum . . *All's Well* iii 6 20
Let him fetch off his drum in any hand . . . . . iii 6 45
To prison with her.—Good mother, fetch my bail . . . v 3 296
Fetch him off, I pray you; he speaks nothing but madman . *T. Night* i 5 114
I will fetch you light and paper and ink . . . . . . iv 2 126

Fetch. He shall enlarge him : fetch Malvolio hither . . . *T. Night* v 1 285
I must believe you, sir : I do ; and will fetch off Bohemia for't *W. Tale* i 2 334
Fetch me to the sight of him . . . . . iii 3 139
It makes the course of thoughts to fetch about . . *K. John* iv 2 24
Since last I went to France to fetch his queen . . *Richard II.* i 1 131
Fetch hither Richard, that in common view He may surrender . . iv 1 155
Go some of you and fetch a looking-glass . . . iv 1 268
Hark, how hard he fetches breath. Search his pockets . 1 *Hen. IV.* ii 4 579
Didst thou not kiss me and bid me fetch thee thirty shillings? 2 *Hen. IV.* ii 1 110
They will be kin to us, or they will fetch it from Japhet . ii 2 128
As I return, I will fetch off these justices . . . iii 2 324
Fetch forth the lazar kite of Cressid's kind . . *Hen. V.* ii 1 80
Or I will fetch thy rim out at thy throat In drops of crimson blood . iv 4 15
Go seek him, and bring him to my tent.—I will fetch him . . iv 7 177
Go forth and fetch their conquering Cæsar in . . . v Prol. 28
Go fetch the beadle hither straight.—Now fetch me a stool . 2 *Hen. VI.* ii 1 140
From off the gates of York fetch down the head, Your father's head 3 *Hen. VI.* ii 6 52
It is meet so few should fetch the prince . . . *Richard III.* ii 2 139
The honourable board of council out, Must fetch him in he papers *Hen. VIII.* i 1 80
Fetch me a dozen crab-tree staves, and strong ones . . v 4 7
She does so blush, and fetches her wind so short . *Troi. and Cres.* iii 2 33
I'll fetch her. It is the prettiest villain : she fetches her breath as short as a new-ta'en sparrow . . . iii 2 34
Do not you know of him, but yet go fetch him hither . . iv 2 59
Give me some token for the surety of it.—I'll fetch you one . v 2 61
Let's fetch him off, or make remain alike . . *Coriolanus* i 4 62
I'll go fetch thy sons To back thy quarrels, whatsoe'er they be *T. An.* ii 3 53
Now will I fetch the king to find them here . . . ii 3 206
Then I'll go fetch an axe.—But I will use the axe . . iii 1 185
Go fetch them hither to us presently.—Why, there they are . . v 3 59
Fetch me my rapier, boy. What dares the slave Come hither? *R. and J.* i 5 57
I must another way, To fetch a ladder . . . . ii 5 75
Fetch a surgeon.—Courage, man ; the hurt cannot be much . . iii 1 97
What hast thou there? the cords That Romeo bid thee fetch? . iii 2 34
Let me see the county ; Ay, marry, go, I say, and fetch him hither . iv 2 30
Hold, take these keys, and fetch more spices, nurse . . . iv 4 1
Fetch drier logs : Call Peter, he will show thee where they are . iv 4 15
Nay, we will all of us be there to fetch him . . *J. Cæsar* ii 1 212
Worthy Cæsar : I come to fetch you to the senate-house . . ii 2 59
I will go. And look where Publius is come to fetch me . . ii 2 108
I'll fetch him presently.—I know that we shall have him well to friend iii 1 142
Go fetch fire.—Pluck down benches.—Pluck down forms, windows, any thing . . . . . . iii 2 262
Go you to Cæsar's house ; Fetch the will hither . . . iv 1 8
Here's my drift ; And, I believe, it is a fetch of wit . *Hamlet* ii 1 38
Go, get thee to Yaughan : fetch me a stoup of liquor . . v 1 68
Fetch forth the stocks ! . . . . . *Lear* ii 2 132
Mere fetches ; The images of revolt and flying off. Fetch me a better answer . . . . ii 4 90
I'll fetch some flax and whites of eggs To apply to his bleeding face . iii 7 106
I fetch my life and being From men of royal siege . . *Othello* i 2 21
Fetch Desdemona hither.—Ancient, conduct them ; you best know the place . . . . i 3 120
Meet me by and by at the citadel : I must fetch his necessaries ashore ii 1 292
Fetch't, let me see't.—Why, so I can, sir, but I will not now . iii 4 85
Fetch me the handkerchief : my mind misgives . . . iii 4 89
To fetch her fan, her gloves, her mask, nor nothing? . . iv 2 9
Shall I go fetch your night-gown?—No, unpin me here . . iv 3 34
Bear him carefully from hence ; I'll fetch the general's surgeon . v 1 100
Within our files there are, Of those that served Mark Antony but late, Enough to fetch him in . . . *Ant. and Cleo.* iv 1 14
Had I great Juno's power, The strong-wing'd Mercury should fetch thee up iv 15 35
Show me, my women, like a queen : go fetch My best attires . v 2 227
I'll fetch a turn about the garden . . . *Cymbeline* i 1 81
I will fetch my gold and have our two wagers recorded . . i 4 180
The first service thou dost me, fetch that suit hither . . iii 5 130
As it is like him—might break out, and swear He'ld fetch us in . iv 2 141
Pray you, fetch him hither. Thersites' body is as good as Ajax' . iv 2 251
If you'll go fetch him, We'll say our song the whilst . . iv 2 253
Our eyes do weep, Till tongues fetch breath that may proclaim them *Per.* i 4 15
Look how thou stirrest now! come away, or I'll fetch thee with a wanion ii 1 17
Fetch hither all my boxes in my closet . . . . iii 2 81
To fetch his daughter home, who first is gone . . . iv 4 20
Fetched. With patches, colours, and with forms being fetch'd From glistering semblances of piety . . . *Hen. V.* ii 2 116
Forthwith from Ludlow the young prince be fetch'd Hither *Richard III.* ii 2 121
Fetching mad bounds, bellowing and neighing loud . *Mer. of Venice* v 1 73
Fetlock. And their wounded steeds Fret fetlock deep in gore *Hen. V.* iv 7 82
That stain'd their fetlocks in his smoking blood . . 3 *Hen. VI.* ii 3 21
Fetter. Will free your life, But fetter you till death *Meas. for Meas.* iii 1 67
Fetter strong madness in a silken thread, Charm ache with air *Much Ado* v 1 25
But rather reason thus with reason fetter, Love sought is good *T. Night* iii 1 167
Fetter him, Till he be brought unto the empress' face . *T. Andron.* v 3 6
We will fetters put upon this fear, Which now goes too free-footed *Hamlet* iii 3 25
These strong Egyptian fetters I must break, Or lose myself *Ant. and Cleo.* i 2 120
Fettered. A Christian king ; Unto whose grace our passion is as subject As are our wretches fetter'd in our prisons . . *Hen. V.* i 2 243
Warwick and Montague, That in their chains fetter'd the kingly lion 3 *Hen. VI.* v 7 11
Fetter'd in amorous chains . . . . *T. Andron.* ii 1 15
My conscience, thou art fetter'd More than my shanks and wrists *Cymb.* v 4 8
Fettering. I must be patient ; there is no fettering of authority *All's Well* ii 3 251
Fettle. But fettle your fine joints 'gainst Thursday next . *Rom. and Jul.* iii 5 154
Feu. Le cheval volant, the Pegasus, chez les narines de feu ! . *Hen. V.* iii 7 15
Via ! les eaux et la terre.—Rien puis? l'air et le feu . . iv 2 5
Feud. Thou shouldst not bear from me a Greekish member Wherein my sword had not impressure made Of our rank feud . *Troi. and Cres.* iv 5 132
Fever. Not a soul But felt a fever of the mad . . *Tempest* i 2 209
There is so great a fever on goodness, that the dissolution of it must cure it : novelty is only in request . . *Meas. for Meas.* iii 2 235
There died this morning of a cruel fever One Ragozine . . iv 3 74
He is sick, my lord, Of a strange fever . . . . v 1 152
Unquiet meals make ill digestions ; Thereof the raging fire of fever bred ; And what's a fever but a fit of madness? . . *Com. of Errors* v 1 76
A fever she Reigns in my blood and will remember'd be.—A fever in your blood ! why, then incision Would let her out in saucers . *L. L. Lost* iv 3 95
Bullets wrapp'd in fire, To make a shaking fever in your walls *K. John* ii 1 228
This fever, that hath troubled me so long, Lies heavy on me . . v 3 3
Fever. Ay me ! this tyrant fever burns me up . . . *K. John* v 3 14
Wanton hours Have brought ourselves into a burning fever 2 *Hen. IV.* iv 1 56
Think'st thou the fiery fever will go out With titles blown from adulation? Will it give place to flexure? . . . . . *Hen. V.* iv 1 270
Grows to an envious fever Of pale and bloodless emulation *Troi. and Cres.* i 3 133
And 'tis this fever that keeps Troy on foot, Not her own sinews . i 3 135
Wisely hath Ulysses here discover'd The fever whereof all our power is sick . . . . i 3 139
Your potent and infectious fevers heap On Athens ! . . *T. of Athens* iv 1 22
Go, suck the subtle blood o' the grape, Till the high fever seethe your blood to froth, And so 'scape hanging . . . . . iv 3 433
He had a fever when he was in Spain . . . *J. Cæsar* i 2 119
After life's fitful fever he sleeps well ; Treason has done his worst *Macb.* iii 2 23
Henceforth The white hand of a lady fever thee . *Ant. and Cleo.* iii 13 138
A fever with the absence of her son . . . *Cymbeline* iv 3 2
Feverous. I quake, Lest thou a feverous life shouldst entertain *M. for M.* iii 1 75
My heart beats thicker than a feverous pulse . *Troi. and Cres.* iii 2 38
Thou madest thine enemies shake, as if the world Were feverous *Coriolanus* i 4 61
Some say, the earth Was feverous and did shake . . *Macbeth* ii 3 66
Fever-weakened. Whose fever-weaken'd joints, Like strengthless hinges, buckle under life . . . . . . 2 *Hen. IV.* i 1 140
Few. In few, they hurried us aboard a bark . . . . *Tempest* i 2 144
Few in millions Can speak like us . . . . . ii 1 7
Here have I few attendants And subjects none abroad . . . v 1 166
There are yet missing of your company Some few odd lads . . v 1 255
Faith, sir, few of any wit in such matters . . *Meas. for Meas.* ii 1 282
In few, bestowed her on her own lamentation . . . iii 1 237
But few of any sort, and none of name . . . . *Much Ado* i 1 7
The wide sea Hath drops too few to wash her clean again . . iv 1 143
That is the way to make an offence gracious, though few have the grace to do it . . . . *L. L. Lost* v 1 147
The time is long.—The liker you ; few taller are so young . . v 2 846
A few of the unpleasant'st words That ever blotted paper ! *Mer. of Venice* iii 2 254
But in a few, Signior Hortensio, thus it stands with me . *T. of Shrew* i 2 52
Love all, trust a few, Do wrong to none . . . *All's Well* i 1 73
All deaths are too few, the sharpest too easy . . *W. Tale* iv 4 809
What train?—But few, And those but mean . . . . v 1 92
Be pitiful and hurt me not ! There's few or none do know me *K. John* iv 3 3
To what purpose dost thou hoard thy words, That thou return'st no greeting to thy friends?—I have too few to take my leave of you *Richard II.* i 3 255
Is gone to meet the king, who lately landed With some few private friends iii 3 4
Nothing but himself, And some few vanities that make him light . iii 4 86
Tom, beat Cut's saddle, put a few flocks in the point . 1 *Hen. IV.* ii 1 7
In few, his death, whose spirit lent a fire Even to the dullest peasant in his camp, Being bruited once, took fire and heat away . 2 *Hen. IV.* i 1 112
Make friends with speed : Never so few, and never yet more need . i 1 215
Thou hast stolen that which after some few hours Were thine without offence . . . . iv 5 102
Tell us the Dauphin's mind.—Thus, then, in few . . *Hen. V.* i 2 245
And this man Hath, for a few light crowns, lightly conspired . . ii 2 89
His few bad words are matched with as few good deeds . . . iii 2 41
Voutsafe me, look you, a few disputations with you . . . iii 2 101
A few sprays of us, The emptying of our father's luxury . . iii 5 5
Sorry am I his numbers are so few, His soldiers sick and famish'd . iii 5 56
Those few I have Almost no better than so many French . . iii 6 155
I am afeard there are few die well that die in a battle . . iv 1 148
We few, we happy few, we band of brothers . . . . iv 3 60
And hardly keeps his men from mutiny, Since they, so few, watch such a multitude . . . . 1 *Hen. VI.* i 1 161
These few days' wonder will be quickly worn . . . 2 *Hen. VI.* ii 4 69
Having pinch'd a few and made them cry, The rest stand all aloof 3 *Hen. VI.* ii 1 16
Vouchsafe to furnish us With some few bands of chosen soldiers . . iii 3 204
For few men rightly temper with the stars . . . . iv 6 29
Let it [conscience] go ; there's few or none will entertain it *Richard III.* i 4 134
It is meet so few should fetch the prince . . . . ii 2 139
And thus I took the vantage of those few . . . . iii 7 37
I am solicited, not by a few, And those of true condition *Hen. VIII.* i 2 18
Set here for examples.—True, they are so ; But few now give so great ones i 3 63
You few that loved me, And dare be bold to weep for Buckingham . ii 1 71
But we all are men, In our own natures frail, and capable Of our flesh ; few are angels . . . . v 3 12
This good man,—few of you deserve that title . . . . v 3 138
Few now living can behold that goodness—A pattern to all princes living v 5 22
At a few drops of women's rheum, which are As cheap as lies *Coriolanus* v 6 46
I curse the day—and yet, I think, Few come within the compass of my curse—Wherein I did not some notorious ill . . *T. Andron.* v 1 126
That few things loves better Than to abhor himself . . *T. of Athens* i 1 59
These few precepts in thy memory See thou character . . *Hamlet* i 3 58
Give every man thy ear, but few thy voice . . . . i 3 68
In few, Ophelia, Do not believe his vows . . . . . i 3 126
Here's a few flowers ; but 'bout midnight, more . . *Cymbeline* iv 2 283
Few love to hear the sins they love to act . . . *Pericles* i 1 92
Few words. Which is the way? Is it sad, and few words? or how? *Meas. for Meas.* iii 2 54
'Twixt such friends as we Few words suffice . . . *T. of Shrew* i 2 66
He hath heard that men of few words are the best men . . *Hen. V.* iii 2 39
No letters ; and few words, But such as I, without your special pardon, Dare not relate . . . . 3 *Hen. VI.* iv 1 86
In few words, If you'll not here proclaim yourself our king, I'll leave you . . . . iv 7 53
Few words to fair faith . . . . . *Troi. and Cres.* iii 2 102
'Tis in few words, but spacious in effect ; We banish thee *T. of Athens* iii 5 97
Say to the king, I would attend his leisure For a few words . *Macbeth* iii 2 4
Have you no more to say?—Few words, but, to effect, more than all yet *Lear* iii 1 52
Fewer. That ever this fellow should have fewer words than a parrot, and yet the son of a woman ! . . . . . . 1 *Hen. IV.* ii 4 111
What do we then but draw anew the model In fewer offices? . 2 *Hen. IV.* i 3 47
The fewer men, the greater share of honour . . . *Hen. V.* iv 3 22
Fewest. He upon whose side The fewest roses are cropp'd from the tree Shall yield the other in the right opinion . . . . 1 *Hen. VI.* ii 4 41
It is well objected : If I have fewest, I subscribe in silence . . ii 4 44
Fewness and truth, 'tis thus . . . . . *Meas. for Meas.* i 4 39
Fickle. Clapp'd on the outward eye of fickle France . . *K. John* ii 1 583
Some fine colour that may please the eye Of fickle changelings 1 *Hen. IV.* v 1 76
By cruel fate, And giddy Fortune's furious fickle wheel . . *Hen. V.* iii 6 29
In France, amongst a fickle wavering nation . . 1 *Hen. VI.* iv 1 138

Fickle. O fortune, fortune! all men call thee fickle: If thou art fickle, what dost thou with him That is renown'd for faith? *Rom. and Jul.* iii 5 60
Be fickle, fortune; For then, I hope, thou wilt not keep him long iii 5 62
Whose easy-borrow'd pride Dwells in the fickle grace of her he follows *Lear* ii 4 189
Fickleness. I am a soldier and unapt to weep Or to exclaim on fortune's fickleness . . . . 1 *Hen. VI.* v 3 134
Fico. 'Steal!' foh! a fico for the phrase! . . . . *Mer. Wives* i 3 33
Fiction. I could condemn it as an improbable fiction . *T. Night* iii 4 141
And, for thy fiction, Why, thy verse swells with stuff so fine and smooth That thou art even natural in thine art . . *T. of Athens* v 1 86
In a fiction, in a dream of passion, Could force his soul so to his own conceit That from her working all his visage wann'd . *Hamlet* ii 2 578
Fiddle. A French song and a fiddle has no fellow.—The devil fiddle 'em! *Hen. VIII.* i 3 41
Fiddler. She did call me rascal fiddler And twangling Jack *T. of Shrew* ii 1 158
Fiddler, forbear; you grow too forward . . . . . iii 1 1
Unless the fiddler Apollo get his sinews to make catlings on *Tr. and Cr.* iii 3 305
Fiddlestick. Heigh! the devil rides upon a fiddlestick . 1 *Hen. IV.* ii 4 535
Here's my fiddlestick; here's that shall make you dance *Rom. and Jul.* iii 1 51
Fidele. What's your name?—Fidele, sir . . . *Cymbeline* iii 6 61
The boy Fidele's sickness Did make my way long forth . . iv 2 148
You and Fidele play the cooks . . . . . . iv 2 164
Poor sick Fidele! I'll willingly to him . . . . iv 2 166
Whilst summer lasts and I live here, Fidele, I'll sweeten thy sad grave iv 2 219
Use like note and words, Save that Euriphile must be Fidele . iv 2 238
Thy name?—Fidele, sir.—Thou dost approve thyself the very same . iv 2 379
One sand another Not more resembles that sweet rosy lad Who died, and was Fidele. What think you? . . . . . v 5 122
My boys, There was our error.—This is, sure, Fidele . . v 5 260
Fidelicet. That is, Master Page, fidelicet Master Page; and there is myself, fidelicet myself . . . . . *Mer. Wives* i 1 140
Fidelity. By my fidelity, this is not well . . . . iv 2 160
Fides. The motto thus, 'Sic spectanda fides' . . . *Pericles* ii 2 38
Fidiused. I would not have been so fidiused for all the chests in Corioli, and the gold that's in them . . . . *Coriolanus* ii 1 144
Fie, fie, how wayward is this foolish love! . . . *T. G. of Ver.* i 2 57
Fie, Fie, unreverend tongue! to call her bad . . . . ii 6 14
Fie on thee, jolt-head! thou canst not read . . . . iii 1 290
It is his five senses: fie, what the ignorance is! . . *Mer. Wives* i 1 181
Fie, fie, fie! cuckold! cuckold! cuckold! . . . . ii 2 328
Vengeance of Jenny's case! fie on her! never name her, child . iv 1 64
Fie, fie! he'll never come . . . . iv 4 19
My chambers are honourable: fie! privacy? fie! . . . iv 5 24
Fie on sinful fantasy! Fie on lust and luxury! . . . v 5 97
O, fie, fie, fie! What dost thou, or what art thou, Angelo? . *M. for M.* ii 2 172
O, fie, fie, fie! Thy sin's not accidental, but a trade . . iii 1 148
Fie, how impatience loureth in your face! . . *Com. of Errors* ii 1 86
Self-harming jealousy! fie, beat it hence! . . . . ii 1 102
Fie, brother! how the world is changed with you! . . . ii 2 154
Fie, now you run this humour out of breath . . . . iv 1 57
Fie on thee, wretch! 'tis pity that thou livest To walk . . iv 1 27
Fie upon thee! art not ashamed?—Of what, lady? . . *Much Ado* iii 4 28
Fie, fie! they are not to be named, my lord, Not to be spoke of . iv 1 96
Fie, fie! you counterfeit, you puppet, you! . . *M. N. Dream* iii 2 288
Why, then you are in love.—Fie, fie!—Not in love neither? *Mer. of Venice* i 1 46
If you deny me, fie upon your law! . . . . . iv 1 101
Fie, fie on all tired jades, on all mad masters! . . *T. of Shrew* iv 1 1
Fie, fie! no thought of him . . . . . *W. Tale* ii 3 18
Fie, Joan, that thou wilt be so obstacle! . . . 1 *Hen. VI.* v 4 17
Fie on ambition! fie on myself, that have a sword, and yet am ready to famish! . . . . 2 *Hen. VI.* iv 10 1
Fie on this storm! I will go seek the king . . . *Lear* iii 1 49
Fie, foh, and fum, I smell the blood of a British man . . iii 4 188
Field. I will bring the doctor about by the fields . . *Mer. Wives* ii 3 81
Go about the fields with me through Frogmore . . . ii 3 90
Green let it be, More fertile-fresh than all the field to see . v 5 72
Against my soul's pure truth why labour you To make it wander in an unknown field? . . . . . *Com. of Errors* iii 2 38
He rather means to lodge you in the field . . *L. L. Lost* ii 1 85
And welcome to the wide fields too base to be mine . . ii 1 94
And I to be a corporal of his field, And wear his colours! . . iii 1 189
Saint Cupid, then! and, soldiers, to the field! . . . iv 3 366
This field shall hold me; and so hold your vow . . . v 2 345
That oft in field, with targe and shield, did make my foe to sweat . v 2 556
The fold stands empty in the drowned field . . *M. N. Dream* ii 1 96
In the temple, in the town, the field, You do me mischief . . ii 1 238
I am fear'd in field and town: Goblin, lead them up and down . iii 2 398
That won three fields of Sultan Solyman . . *Mer. of Venice* ii 1 26
In respect it is in the fields, it pleaseth me well . *As Y. L. It* iii 2 18
Have I not heard great ordnance in the field? . . *T. of Shrew* i 2 204
She is my house, My household stuff, my field, my barn . . iii 2 233
Go thy ways; the field is won . . . . . . iv 5 23
Shall furnish me to those Italian fields, Where noble fellows strike *All's Well* ii 3 307
When better fall, for your avails they fell: To-morrow to the field . iii 1 23
To challenge him the field, and then to break promise with him *T. Night* ii 3 137
By the honour-giving hand Of Cœur-de-lion knighted in the field *K. John* i 1 54
Speed then, to take advantage of the field.—It shall be so . . ii 1 297
Back to the stained field, You equal potents, fiery kindled spirits! . ii 1 357
Rescue those breathing lives to die in beds, That here come sacrifices for the field . . . . ii 1 420
Whom zeal and charity brought to the field . . . . ii 1 565
Away, and glister like the god of war, When he intendeth to become the field . . . . v 1 55
Shall a beardless boy, A cocker'd silken wanton, brave our fields? . v 1 70
Faulconbridge Desires your majesty to leave the field . . . v 3 6
They say King John sore sick hath left the field . . . v 4 6
Bear me hence From forth the noise and rumour of the field . . v 4 45
Last in the field, and almost lords of it! . . . . . v 5 8
Till twice five summers have enrich'd our fields . . *Richard II.* i 3 141
Fought For Jesu Christ in glorious Christian field . . . iv 1 93
And this land be call'd The field of Golgotha and dead men's skulls . iv 1 144
No more shall trenching war channel her fields . . 1 *Hen. IV.* i 1 7
In those holy fields Over whose acres walk'd those blessed feet . i 1 24
Let the hours be short Till fields and blows and groans applaud our sport! . . . . i 3 302
Speak terms of manage to thy bounding steed; Cry 'Courage! to the field!' . . . . ii 3 53
And the herds Were strangely clamorous to the frighted fields . . iii 1 40
Field. He doth fill fields with harness in the realm . . 1 *Hen. IV.* iii 2 101
But, sirrah, make haste: Percy is already in the field . . . iv 2 81
God forbid a shallow scratch should drive The Prince of Wales from such a field as this! . . . . v 4 12
I have two boys Seek Percy and thyself about the field . . . v 4 32
Let us to the highest of the field, To see what friends are living, who are dead . . . . v 4 164
How goes the field? . . . . v 5 16
In a bloody field by Shrewsbury . . . . 2 *Hen. IV.* Ind. 24
Young Prince John And Westmoreland and Stafford fled the field . i 1 18
How is this derived? Saw you the field? came you from Shrewsbury? i 1 24
That arrows fled not swifter toward their aim Than did our soldiers, aiming at their safety, Fly from the field . . . . . i 1 125
A field Where nothing but the sound of Hotspur's name Did seem defensible . . . . ii 3 36
Since we lay all night in the windmill in Saint George's field . . iii 2 207
Let us sway on and face them in the field . . . . iv 1 24
We will our youth lead on to higher fields . . . . iv 4 3
Can this cockpit hold The vasty fields of France? . . *Hen. V.* Prol. 12
Whose hearts have left their bodies here in England And lie pavilion'd in the fields of France . . . . i 2 129
His nose was as sharp as a pen, and a' babbled of green fields . ii 3 18
Of late examples Left by the fatal and neglected English Upon our fields . . . . ii 4 14
And sword and shield, In bloody field, Doth win immortal fame . iii 2 10
Whiles a more frosty people Sweat drops of gallant youth in our rich fields . . . . iii 5 25
Up, princes! and, with spirit of honour edged More sharper than your swords, hie to the field . . . . iii 5 39
Our peasants . . . were enow To purge this field of such a hilding foe . iv 2 29
For our approach shall so much dare the field That England shall couch down in fear and yield . . . . iv 2 36
Yon island carrions, desperate of their bones, Ill-favouredly become the morning field . . . . iv 2 40
I stay but for my guidon: to the field! . . . . . iv 2 60
That their souls May make a peaceful and a sweet retire From off these fields . . . . iv 3 87
Our gayness and our gilt are all besmirch'd With rainy marching in the painful field . . . . iv 3 111
We are enow yet living in the field To smother up the English . iv 5 19
But all's not done; yet keep the French the field . . . iv 6 2
As in this glorious and well-foughten field We kept together in our chivalry . . . . iv 6 18
If they will fight with us, bid them come down, Or void the field . iv 7 62
That we may wander o'er this bloody field To look our dead . . iv 7 75
O, give us leave, great king, To view the field in safety! . . iv 7 85
For yet a many of your horsemen peer And gallop o'er the field . iv 7 89
Then call we this the field of Agincourt . . . . iv 7 93
This note doth tell me of ten thousand French That in the field lie slain iv 8 86
And whilst a field should be dispatch'd and fought, You are disputing of your generals . . . . 1 *Hen. VI.* i 1 72
His sword did ne'er leave striking in the field . . . . i 4 81
Amongst the troops of armed men Leap o'er the walls for refuge in the field . . . . ii 2 25
The very parings of our nails Shall pitch a field when we are dead . iii 1 103
Dare ye come forth and meet us in the field? . . . . iii 2 61
I read That stout Pendragon in his litter sick Came to the field . . iii 2 96
But where's the great Alcides of the field? . . . . iv 7 60
Help me this once, that France may get the field . . . v 3 12
Did he so often lodge in open field, In winter's cold and summer's parching heat, To conquer France? . . . . 2 *Hen. VI.* i 1 80
Let thy betters speak.—The cardinal's not my better in the field . i 3 113
Ay, by my faith, the field is honourable; and there was he born . iv 2 54
Tut, when struck'st thou one blow in the field? . . . iv 7 85
Disperse yourselves; Meet me to-morrow in Saint George's field . v 1 46
Go to bed and dream again, To keep thee from the tempest of the field v 1 197
You forget That we are those which chased you from the field 3 *Hen. VI.* i 1 90
Will you we show our title to the crown? If not, our swords shall plead it in the field . . . . i 1 103
When I return with victory from the field I'll see your grace . i 1 261
We'll meet her in the field.—What, with five thousand men? . i 2 65
The army of the queen hath got the field . . . . . i 4 1
I think it cites us, brother, to the field . . . . ii 1 34
I would your highness would depart the field . . . . ii 2 73
Wilt thou kneel for grace, And set thy diadem upon my head; Or bide the mortal fortune of the field? . . . . ii 2 83
At Saint Alban's field This lady's husband, Sir Richard Grey, was slain iii 2 1
But why commands the king That his chief followers lodge in towns about him, While he himself keeps in the cold field? . . . iv 3 14
Methinks the power that Edward hath in field Should not be able to encounter mine . . . . iv 8 35
Lords, to the field; Saint George and victory! . . . . v 1 113
We, having now the best at Barnet field, Will thither straight . v 3 20
Clarence, That stabb'd me in the field by Tewksbury *Richard III.* i 4 56
Who told me, in the field by Tewksbury, When Oxford had me down . ii 1 111
Who told me, when we both lay in the field Frozen almost to death . ii 1 114
Buckingham, back'd with the hardy Welshmen, Is in the field . iv 3 48
We must be brief when traitors brave the field . . . . iv 3 57
The wretched, bloody, and usurping boar, That spoil'd your summer fields . . . . v 2 8
Here pitch our tents, even here in Bosworth field . . . . v 3 1
Let us survey the vantage of the field . . . . . v 3 15
Saddle white Surrey for the field to-morrow . . . . v 3 64
Arm, arm, my lord; the foe vaunts in the field.—Come, bustle, bustle v 3 288
I think there be six Richmonds in the field; Five have I slain to-day . v 4 11
Like the lily, That once was mistress of the field and flourish'd *Hen. VIII.* iii 1 152
Her own shall bless her; Her foes shake like a field of beaten corn . v 5 32
Each Trojan that is master of his heart, Let him to field *Troi. and Cres.* i 1 5
What news, Æneas, from the field to-day?—That Paris is returned home i 1 111
To the field goes he; where every flower Did, as a prophet, weep what it foresaw In Hector's wrath . . . . i 2 9
They are coming from the field: shall we stand up here? . . . i 2 192
Achievements, plots, orders, preventions, Excitements to the field . i 3 182
Achilles will not to the field to-morrow.—What's his excuse? . . ii 3 172
They're come from field: let us to Priam's hall, To greet the warriors iii 1 161
O, be thou my Charon, And give me swift transportance to those fields Where I may wallow in the lily-beds! . . . . . . iii 2 12
Whose glorious deeds, but in these fields of late, Made emulous missions 'mongst the gods themselves . . . . iii 3 188
Ajax goes up and down the field, asking for himself . . . . iii 3 244

Field. You told how Diomed, a whole week by days, Did haunt you in the field . . . . *Troi. and Cres.* iv 1 10
The prince must think me tardy and remiss, That swore to ride before him to the field . . . . iv 4 144
Come, come, to field with him . . . . . . iv 4 145
Will you the knights Shall to the edge of all extremity Pursue each other, or shall be divided By any voice or order of the field? . . . iv 5 70
I pray you, let us see you in the field . . . . iv 5 266
I beseech you, In what place of the field doth Calchas keep? . iv 5 278
There is a thousand Hectors in the field . . . . v 5 19
Tie his body to my horse's tail; Along the field I will the Trojan trail . v 8 22
Stand, ho! yet are we masters of the field: Never go home . . v 10 1
He's dead; and at the murderer's horse's tail, In beastly sort, dragg'd through the shameful field . . . . v 10 5
Our army's in the field: We never yet made doubt but Rome was ready To answer us . . . . . . *Coriolanus* i 2 17
Are you lords o' the field? If not, why cease you till you are so? . i 6 47
If we lose the field, We cannot keep the town . . . . i 7 4
Of all The treasure in this field achieved and city, We render you the tenth . . . . i 9 33
When drums and trumpets shall I' the field prove flatterers . . i 9 43
He proved best man i' the field . . . . . . ii 2 101
Till we call'd Both field and city ours, he never stood To ease his breast ii 2 125
Bearing his valiant sons In coffins from the field . . . *T. Andron.* i 1 35
And buried one and twenty valiant sons, Knighted in field . . . i 1 196
The morn is bright and grey, The fields are fragrant . . . ii 2 2
The fields are near, and you are gallant grooms . . . . iv 2 164
Like stinging bees in hottest summer's day Led by their master to the flowered fields . . . . v 1 15
Marry, go before to field, he'll be your follower . *Rom. and Jul.* iii 1 61
Like an untimely frost Upon the sweetest flower of all the field . . iv 5 29
Your heart's in the field now.—My heart is ever at your service *T. of A.* i 2 75
And all the lands thou hast Lie in a pitch'd field . . . . i 2 231
Lead your battle softly on, Upon the left hand of the even field *J. Cæsar* v 1 17
If you dare fight to-day, come to the field; If not, when you have stomachs . . . . v 1 65
Regard Titinius, And tell me what thou notest about the field . . v 3 22
And come, young Cato; let us to the field . . . . . v 3 107
Who will go with me? I will proclaim my name about the field . . v 4 3
The ghost of Cæsar hath appear'd to me Two several times by night; at Sardis once, And, this last night, here in Philippi fields . . . v 5 19
So call the field to rest; and let's away, To part the glories of this happy day . . . . v 5 80
Since his majesty went into the field, I have seen her rise . *Macbeth* v 1 4
Then he is dead?—Ay, and brought off the field . . . . v 8 44
Such a sight as this Becomes the field, but here shows much amiss *Ham.* v 2 413
When usurers tell their gold i' the field . . . . . *Lear* iii 2 89
Now a little fire in a wild field were like an old lecher's heart . . iii 4 117
Search every acre in the high-grown field, And bring him to our eye . iv 4 7
That never set a squadron in the field . . . . . *Othello* i 1 22
They have used Their dearest action in the tented field . . . i 3 85
Of moving accidents by flood and field, Of hair-breadth scapes . . i 3 135
Fulvia thy wife first came into the field . . . . *Ant. and Cleo.* i 2 92
'Tis time we twain Did show ourselves i' the field . . . . i 4 74
Cæsar and Lepidus Are in the field: a mighty strength they carry . . ii 1 17
Tie up the libertine in a field of feasts, Keep his brain fuming . . ii 1 23
The ne'er-yet-beaten horse of Parthia We have jaded out o' the field . iii 1 34
If from the field I shall return once more To kiss these lips . . . iii 13 173
Antony Is come into the field . . . . iv 6 8
To the field, to the field! We'll leave you for this time . *Cymbeline* iv 2 42
Those that would die or ere resist are grown The mortal bugs o' the field v 3 51
O noble misery, To be i' the field, and ask 'what news?' of me! . . v 3 65
His ascension is More sweet than our blest fields . . . . v 4 117
Without covering, save yon field of stars . . . . . *Pericles* i 1 37
Field-bed. This field-bed is too cold for me to sleep . . *Rom. and Jul.* ii 1 40
Field-dew. With this field-dew consecrate, Every fairy take his gait *M. N. D.* v 1 422
Fielded. To help our fielded friends . . . . . *Coriolanus* i 4 12
Fiend. But one fiend at a time, I'll fight their legions o'er . *Tempest* iii 3 102
They are devils' additions, the names of fiends . . *Mer. Wives* ii 2 313
A fiend, a fury, pitiless and rough . . . . *Com. of Errors* iv 2 35
Avoid then, fiend! what tell'st thou me of supping? . . . iv 3 66
The fiend is strong within him . . . . iv 4 110
The fiend is at mine elbow and tempts me . . . *Mer. of Venice* ii 2 2
The most courageous fiend bids me pack: 'Via!' says the fiend; 'away!' says the fiend; 'for the heavens, rouse up a brave mind,' says the fiend, 'and run' . . . . ii 2 10
'Budge,' says the fiend. 'Budge not,' says my conscience. 'Conscience,' say I, 'you counsel well;' 'Fiend,' say I, 'you counsel well' ii 2 20
To run away from the Jew, I should be ruled by the fiend . . . ii 2 27
The fiend gives the more friendly counsel: I will run, fiend . . . ii 2 31
Why will you mew her up, Signior Baptista, for this fiend of hell? *T. of S.* i 1 88
Why, he's a devil, a devil, a very fiend . . . . . . iii 2 157
How hollow the fiend speaks within him! . . . . *T. Night* iii 4 101
Gently: the fiend is rough, and will not be roughly used . . . iii 4 124
Fare thee well: A fiend like thee might bear my soul to hell . . iii 4 237
Out, hyperbolical fiend! how vexest thou this man! . . . . iv 2 29
There is not yet so ugly a fiend of hell As thou shalt be . . *K. John* iv 3 123
A fiend confined to tyrannize On unreprievable condemned blood . . v 7 47
Fiend, thou torment'st me ere I come to hell! . . . *Richard II.* iv 1 270
That fiend Douglas, that spirit Percy, and that devil Glendower 1 *Hen. IV.* ii 4 404
Fear we broadsides? no, let the fiend give fire . . . 2 *Hen. IV.* ii 4 196
The fiend hath pricked down Bardolph irrecoverable . . . . ii 4 359
Let floods o'erswell, and fiends for food howl on! . . . *Hen. V.* ii 1 97
Whatsoever cunning fiend it was That wrought upon thee so preposterously Hath got the voice in hell for excellence . . . . . . ii 2 111
Array'd in flames like to the prince of fiends . . . . . iii 3 16
I think this Talbot be a fiend of hell . . . . . 1 *Hen. VI.* ii 1 46
Scoff on, vile fiend and shameless courtezan! . . . . . iii 2 45
Foul fiend of France, and hag of all despite! . . . . . iii 2 52
Descend to darkness and the burning lake! False fiend, avoid! 2 *Hen. VI.* i 4 43
O, beat away the busy meddling fiend That lays strong siege unto this wretch's soul! . . . . iii 3 21
What black magician conjures up this fiend? . . . *Richard III.* i 2 34
Methoughts, a legion of foul fiends Environ'd me about . . . . i 4 58
Earth gapes, hell burns, fiends roar, saints pray . . . . iv 4 75
For I will fight Against my canker'd country with the spleen Of all the under fiends . . . . *Coriolanus* iv 5 98
A thousand fiends, a thousand hissing snakes . . . *T. Andron.* ii 3 100
Accursed the offspring of so foul a fiend! . . . . . . iv 2 79
Beautiful tyrant! fiend angelical! Dove-feather'd raven! *Rom. and Jul.* iii 2 75

Fiend. O nature, what hadst thou to do in hell, When thou didst bower the spirit of a fiend In mortal paradise of such sweet flesh? *R. and J.* iii 2 81
Ancient damnation! O most wicked fiend! . . . . . . iii 5 235
Front to front Bring thou this fiend of Scotland and myself *Macbeth* iv 3 233
And begin To doubt the equivocation of the fiend That lies like truth . v 5 44
And be these juggling fiends no more believed, That palter with us in a double sense . . . . v 8 19
Bowl the round nave down the hill of heaven, As low as to the fiends! *Hamlet* ii 2 519
Ingratitude, thou marble-hearted fiend! . . . . . . *Lear* i 4 281
What art thou that dost grumble there i' the straw? Come forth.— Away! the foul fiend follows me! . . . . iii 4 46
Whom the foul fiend hath led through fire and through flame . . iii 4 52
Do poor Tom some charity, whom the foul fiend vexes . . . iii 4 62
Take heed o' the foul fiend: obey thy parents; keep thy word justly . iii 4 82
Keep thy foot out of brothels, thy hand out of plackets, thy pen from lenders' books, and defy the foul fiend . . . . iii 4 101
This is the foul fiend Flibbertigibbet: he begins at curfew . . . iii 4 120
In the fury of his heart, when the foul fiend rages, eats cow-dung for sallets . . . . iii 4 137
Beware my follower. Peace, Smulkin; peace, thou fiend! . . . iii 4 146
What is your study?—How to prevent the fiend, and to kill vermin . iii 4 164
Pray, innocent, and beware the foul fiend . . . . . . iii 6 9
The foul fiend bites my back . . . . iii 6 18
The foul fiend haunts poor Tom in the voice of a nightingale . . iii 6 31
Bless thee, good man's son, from the foul fiend! . . . . . iv 1 61
Five fiends have been in poor Tom at once . . . . . . iv 1 61
Proper deformity seems not in the fiend So horrid as in woman . . iv 2 60
Howe'er thou art a fiend, A woman's shape doth shield thee . . . iv 2 66
He had a thousand noses, Horns whelk'd and waved like the enridged sea: It was some fiend . . . . iv 6 72
I took it for a man; often 'twould say 'The fiend, the fiend' . . iv 6 79
But to the girdle do the gods inherit, Beneath is all the fiends' . . iv 6 129
O, 'tis the spite of hell, the fiend's arch-mock! . . . . *Othello* iv 1 71
When we shall meet at compt, This look of thine will hurl my soul from heaven, And fiends will snatch at it . . . . v 2 275
All the fiends of hell Divide themselves between you! . . *Cymbeline* ii 4 129
Where is thy lady? In a word; or else Thou art straightway with the fiends . . . . iii 5 83
O most delicate fiend! Who is't can read a woman? . . . . v 5 47
Italian fiend! Ay me, most credulous fool, Egregious murderer! . . v 5 210
Thou hold'st a place, for which the pained'st fiend Of hell would not in reputation change . . . . *Pericles* iv 6 173
Fiend-like. This growing image of thy fiend-like face . . *T. Andron.* v 1 45
This dead butcher and his fiend-like queen . . . . *Macbeth* v 8 69
Fierce. With all the fierce endeavour of your wit . . . *L. L. Lost* v 2 863
There is no following her in this fierce vein . . . *M. N. Dream* iii 2 82
Though she be but little, she is fierce . . . . . . iii 2 325
But as the fierce vexation of a dream . . . . iv 1 74
The proud control of fierce and bloody war . . . . . *K. John* i 1 17
Fiery voluntaries, With ladies' faces and fierce dragons' spleens . . ii 1 68
Such temperate order in so fierce a cause Doth want example . . iii 4 12
My eyes are out Even with the fierce looks of these bloody men . . iv 1 74
You do lack That mercy which fierce fire and iron extends . . . iv 1 120
Their needles to lances, and their gentle hearts To fierce and bloody inclination . . . . v 2 158
Fierce extremes In their continuance will not feel themselves . . v 7 13
His rash fierce blaze of riot cannot last . . . . *Richard II.* ii 1 33
In war was never lion raged more fierce . . . . . . ii 1 173
Thy fierce hand Hath with the king's blood stain'd the king's own land v 5 110
His approaches makes as fierce As waters to the sucking of a gulf *Hen. V.* ii 4 9
In fierce tempest is he coming, In thunder and in earthquake, like a Jove ii 4 99
What rein can hold licentious wickedness When down the hill he holds his fierce career? . . . . iii 3 23
Than mid-day sun fierce bent against their faces . . . 1 *Hen. VI.* i 1 14
Sharp dissension in my breast, Such fierce alarums both of hope and fear v 5 85
He is fierce and cannot brook hard language . . . 2 *Hen. VI.* iv 9 45
No beast so fierce but knows some touch of pity . . *Richard III.* i 2 71
What had he To do in these fierce vanities? . . . . *Hen. VIII.* i 1 54
The Greeks are strong and skilful to their strength, Fierce to their skill and to their fierceness valiant . . . . . *Troi. and Cres.* i 1 8
Not fierce and terrible Only in strokes . . . . . *Coriolanus* i 4 57
Against the hospitable canon, would I Wash my fierce hand in 's heart . i 10 27
But fierce Andronicus would not relent . . . . . *T. Andron.* ii 3 165
More fierce and more inexorable far Than empty tigers . *Rom. and Jul.* v 3 38
O, the fierce wretchedness that glory brings us! . . . *T. of Athens* iv 2 30
Fierce fiery warriors fought upon the clouds . . . . . *J. Cæsar* ii 2 19
Domestic fury and fierce civil strife Shall cumber all the parts of Italy iii 1 263
The like precurse of fierce events . . . . *Hamlet* i 1 121
More composition and fierce quality . . . . *Lear* i 2 12
Would beget opinion Of my more fierce endeavour . . . . . ii 1 36
Her eyes are fierce; but thine Do comfort and not burn . . . . ii 4 175
Nor thy fierce sister In his anointed flesh stick boarish fangs . . . iii 7 57
Yet have I fierce affections, and think What Venus did with Mars *Ant. and Cleo.* i 5 17
This fierce abridgement Hath to it circumstantial branches . *Cymbeline* v 5 382
Although assail'd with fortune fierce and keen . . . . *Pericles* v 3 Gower 88
Fiercely. And both sides fiercely fought . . . . . 3 *Hen. VI.* i 1 121
Fierceness. My name is Pistol call'd.—It sorts well with your fierceness *Hen. V.* iv 1 63
They call'd us for our fierceness English dogs . . . . 1 *Hen. VI.* i 5 25
Fierce to their skill and to their fierceness valiant . . *Troi. and Cres.* i 1 8
Fiery. And the delighted spirit To bathe in fiery floods . *Meas. for Meas.* iii 1 122
How fiery and how sharp he looks! . . . . . *Com. of Errors* iv 4 53
Such fiery numbers as the prompting eyes Of beauty's tutors have enrich'd you with . . . . *L. L. Lost* iv 3 322
When we greet, With eyes best seeing, heaven's fiery eye . . . v 2 375
But I might see young Cupid's fiery shaft Quench'd in the chaste beams of the watery moon . . . . *M. N. Dream* ii 1 161
Light them at the fiery glow-worm's eyes . . . . iii 1 173
Who more engilds the night Than all yon fiery oes and eyes of light . iii 2 188
How fiery and forward our pedant is! . . . . . . *T. of Shrew* iii 1 48
Ere twice the horses of the sun shall bring Their fiery torcher *All's Well* ii 1 165
And high curvet Of Mars's fiery steed . . . . ii 3 300
Fiery voluntaries, With ladies' faces and fierce dragons' spleens *K. John* ii 1 67
Would drink my tears And quench his fiery indignation . . . . iv 1 63
Before I drew this gallant head of war, And cull'd these fiery spirits . v 2 114
From out the fiery portal of the east . . . . . *Richard II.* iii 3 64
Mounted upon a hot and fiery steed Which his aspiring rider seem'd to know . . . . v 2 8

Fiery. At my nativity The front of heaven was full of fiery shapes *1 Hen. IV.* iii 1 14
As if an angel dropp'd down from the clouds, To turn and wind a fiery Pegasus . . . . . iv 1 109
The fiery Trigon, his man . . . *2 Hen. IV.* ii 4 288
Apprehensive, quick, forgetive, full of nimble fiery and delectable shapes iv 3 108
Think'st thou the fiery fever will go out? . . . *Hen. V.* iv 1 270
What, hath thy fiery heart so parch'd thine entrails? . . *3 Hen. VI.* i 4 87
Having the fearful flying hare in sight, With fiery eyes . . . ii 5 131
O Phœbus, hadst thou never given consent That Phaëthon should check thy fiery steeds! . . . . ii 6 12
Then fiery expedition be my wing, Jove's Mercury! *Richard III.* iv 3 54
By the bright track of his fiery car, Gives signal of a goodly day . v 3 20
Fair Saint George Inspire us with the spleen of fiery dragons! . . v 3 350
Nor the hand of Mars Beckoning with fiery truncheon my retire *T. and C.* v 3 53
I know thou hadst rather Follow thine enemy in a fiery gulf Than flatter him in a bower . . . *Coriolanus* iii 2 91
Then let the mutinous winds Strike the proud cedars 'gainst the fiery sun v 3 60
In the instant came The fiery Tybalt, with his sword prepared *R. and J.* i 1 116
And flecked darkness like a drunkard reels From forth day's path and Titan's fiery wheels . . . . ii 3 4
Cicero Looks with such ferret and such fiery eyes *J. Cæsar* i 2 186
Like the work we have in hand, Most bloody, fiery, and most terrible . i 3 130
Fierce fiery warriors fought upon the clouds, In ranks and squadrons . ii 2 19
The flash and outbreak of a fiery mind *Hamlet* ii 1 33
Must send thee hence With fiery quickness: therefore prepare thyself . iv 3 45
In mine ignorance Your skill shall, like a star i' the darkest night, Stick fiery off indeed . . . . v 2 268
You know the fiery quality of the duke; How unremoveable and fix'd *Lear* ii 4 93
Fiery? what quality? Why, Gloucester, Gloucester, I'ld speak with the Duke of Cornwall and his wife . . . ii 4 97
Fiery? the fiery duke? Tell the hot duke that—No, but not yet: may be he is not well . . . . ii 4 105
Seem as the spots of heaven, More fiery by night's blackness *A. and C.* i 4 13
Which can distinguish 'twixt The fiery orbs above and the twinn'd stones Upon the number'd beach . . *Cymbeline* i 6 35
Fiery-footed. Gallop apace, you fiery-footed steeds, Towards Phœbus' lodging . . . *Rom. and Jul.* iii 2 1
Fiery kindled. You equal potents, fiery kindled spirits! *K. John* ii 1 358
Fiery-red. The eastern gate, all fiery-red . . *M. N. Dream* iii 2 391
Bloody with spurring, fiery-red with haste *Richard II.* ii 3 58
Fife. There was no music with him but the drum and the fife *Much Ado* ii 3 14
And the vile squealing of the wry-neck'd fife . *Mer. of Venice* ii 5 30
Of prisoners, Hotspur took Mordake the Earl of Fife *1 Hen. IV.* i 1 71
And sends me word, I shall have none but Mordake Earl of Fife . i 1 95
Psalteries and fifes, Tabors and cymbals and the shouting Romans, Make the sun dance . . . *Coriolanus* v 4 52
Whence camest thou, worthy thane?—From Fife, great king . *Macbeth* i 2 48
Will you to Scone?—No, cousin, I'll to Fife . . . ii 4 36
Macbeth! Macbeth! Macbeth! beware Macduff; Beware the thane of Fife . . . . iv 1 72
The castle of Macduff I will surprise; Seize upon Fife . . iv 1 151
The thane of Fife had a wife: where is she now? . . . v 1 47
The spirit-stirring drum, the ear-piercing fife, The royal banner *Othello* iii 3 352
Fifteen. Didst not thou share? hadst thou not fifteen pence? *Mer. Wives* ii 2 14
With as little remorse as they would have drowned a blind bitch's puppies, fifteen i' the litter . . . . . . iii 5 11
A small trifle of wives; alas, fifteen wives is nothing! . *Mer. of Venice* iii 2 170
These fifteen years you have been in a dream . *T. of Shrew* Ind. 2 81
These fifteen years! by my fay, a goodly nap . . Ind. 2 83
They say that I have dream'd And slept above some fifteen year or more Ind. 2 115
Upon my life, amounts not to fifteen thousand poll . *All's Well* iv 3 190
It is fifteen years since I saw my country . . . *W. Tale* iv 2 4
Fifteen hundred shorn, what comes the wool to? . . . iv 3 34
Witnesses, Twice fifteen thousand hearts of England's . *K. John* ii 1 275
Fifteen hundred foot, five hundred horse, Are march'd up . *2 Hen. IV.* ii 1 186
Full fifteen earls and fifteen hundred knights . . *Hen. V.* i 1 13
The English lie within fifteen hundred paces of your tents . iii 7 136
Knights and squires, Full fifteen hundred, besides common men iv 8 84
Made us pay one and twenty fifteens, and one shilling to the pound *2 Hen. VI.* iv 7 24
Fifteenth. A proper jest, and never heard before, That Suffolk should demand a whole fifteenth! . . . . . . i 1 133
Fifth. The third of the five vowels, if you repeat them; or the fifth, if I.—I will repeat them . . . *L. L. Lost* v 1 57
There is a forerunner come from a fifth, the Prince of Morocco *M. of Ven.* i 2 137
If I could bid the fifth welcome with so good a heart as I can bid the other four farewell, I should be glad . . . . i 2 140
The fifth, the Countercheck Quarrelsome . . *As Y. Like It* v 4 99
Third, or fourth, or fifth borough, I'll answer him by law *T. of Shrew* Ind. 1 13
They say five moons were seen to-night; Four fixed, and the fifth did whirl about The other four . . . *K. John* iv 2 183
For the fifth Harry from curb'd license plucks The muzzle of restraint *2 Hen. IV.* iv 5 131
By the fifth hour of the sun . . *Troi. and Cres.* ii 1 134
The fifth, an hand environed with clouds . . . *Pericles* ii 2 36
Fifty. A hundred and fifty pounds jointure . *Mer. Wives* iii 4 49
Who, not the duke? yes, your beggar of fifty *Meas. for Meas.* iii 2 134
If sore be sore, then L to sore makes fifty sores one sorel *L. L. Lost* iv 2 62
A wither'd hermit, five-score winters worn, Might shake off fifty, looking in her eye . . . . iv 3 243
I will kill thee a hundred and fifty ways . *As Y. Like It* v 1 63
Though she have as many diseases as two and fifty horses *T. of Shrew* i 2 81
Spurio, a hundred and fifty; . . . Vaumond, Bentii, two hundred and fifty each . . . . . . *All's Well* iv 3 184
But those that are germane to him, though removed fifty times, shall all come under the hangman . . . *W. Tale* iv 4 802
But if I fought not with fifty of them, I am a bunch of radish: if there were not two or three and fifty upon poor old Jack, then am I no two-legged creature . . . . . *1 Hen. IV.* ii 4 205
As I think, his age some fifty, or, by'r lady, inclining to three score . ii 4 467
I have got, in exchange of a hundred and fifty soldiers, three hundred and odd pounds . . . . iv 2 15
You would think that I had a hundred and fifty tattered prodigals . iv 2 37
There's not three of my hundred and fifty left alive . . v 3 38
They say the bishop and Northumberland Are fifty thousand strong *2 Hen. IV.* iii 1 96
Hath reclaim'd To your obedience fifty fortresses . *1 Hen. VI.* iii 4 6
The Turk, that two and fifty kingdoms hath, Writes not so tedious a style . . . . iv 7 73
Fifty. Here's but two and fifty hairs on your chin, and one of them is white . . . . *Troi. and Cres.* i 2 171
'Two and fifty hairs,' quoth he, 'and one white' . . . i 2 175
Let the request be fifty talents.—As you have said, my lord *T. of Athens* ii 2 201
Having great and instant occasion to use fifty talents . . iii 1 19
Cut my heart in sums.—Mine, fifty talents.—Tell out my blood . iii 4 94
Give twenty, forty, fifty, an hundred ducats a-piece for his picture *Ham.* ii 2 383
What, fifty of my followers at a clap! Within a fortnight! . . *Lear* i 4 316
Return to her, and fifty men dismiss'd? . . . ii 4 210
What, fifty followers? Is it not well? What should you need of more? ii 4 240
Thy fifty yet doth double five-and-twenty, And thou art twice her love ii 4 262
Let me have a child at fifty . . . . *Ant. and Cleo.* i 2 27
Fifty-five. That's fifty five year ago . . . *2 Hen. IV.* iii 2 224
He cannot want fifty five hundred talents . . *T. of Athens* iii 2 43
Fifty-fold a cuckold! . . . . . . *Ant. and Cleo.* i 2 69
Fig. With purple grapes, green figs, and mulberries . *M. N. Dream* iii 1 170
It grandam will Give it a plum, a cherry, and a fig . . *K. John* ii 1 162
When Pistol lies, do this; and fig me, like The bragging Spaniard *2 Hen. IV.* v 3 124
Figo for thy friendship!—It is well.—The fig of Spain! . *Hen. V.* iii 6 62
A fig for Peter! . . . . . . *2 Hen. VI.* ii 3 67
Virtue! a fig! 'tis in ourselves that we are thus or thus . . *Othello* i 3 322
O excellent! I love long life better than figs . . *Ant. and Cleo.* i 2 32
Here is a rural fellow That will not be denied your highness' presence: He brings you figs . . . . v 2 235
A simple countryman, that brought her figs: This was his basket . v 2 342
Fight. But one fiend at a time, I'll fight their legions o'er . *Tempest* iii 3 103
I slew him manfully in fight . . . . *T. G. of Ver.* iv 1 28
With all his might For thee to fight . . . . *Mer. Wives* iii 1 19
I had rather hear them scold than fight . . . . ii 1 240
Up with your fights: Give fire . . . . . ii 2 142
To see thee fight, to see thee foin, to see thee traverse . . ii 3 24
If you should fight, you go against the hair of your professions . ii 3 41
I warrant you, he's the man should fight with him . . . iii 1 71
And yet my nature never in the fight To do in slander *Meas. for Meas.* i 3 42
Counsel him to fight against his passion . . . *Much Ado* iii 1 83
You dare easier be friends with me than fight with mine enemy . iv 1 301
Peace!—Be to me and every man that dares not fight! . *L. L. Lost* i 1 230
A man so breathed, that certain he would fight; yea From morn till night . . . . v 2 659
I will not fight with a pole, like a northern man . . . v 2 700
We cannot fight for love, as men may do . . *M. N. Dream* ii 1 241
Thou see'st these lovers seek a place to fight . . . iii 2 354
Live thou, I live: with much much more dismay I view the fight than thou that makest the fray . . . *Mer. of Venice* iii 2 62
There was never any thing so sudden but the fight of two rams *As Y. L. It* v 2 33
You go so much backward when you fight . . . *All's Well* i 1 214
Challenge me the count's youth to fight with him . . *T. Night* iii 2 37
There's no remedy, sir; he will fight with you for's oath sake . iii 4 326
No, my lord, I'll fight.—You will! why, happy man be's dole! *W. Tale* i 2 162
Blessing Against this cruelty fight on thy side, Poor thing, condemn'd to loss! . . . . ii 3 191
You denied to fight with me this other day, because I was no gentleman born . . . . v 2 140
Against whose fury and unmatched force The aweless lion could not wage the fight . . . . . . *K. John* i 1 266
They are at hand, To parley or to fight; therefore prepare . . ii 1 78
Then after fight who shall be king? . . . . . ii 1 400
That dost never fight But when her humorous ladyship is by . iii 1 118
Like a dog that is compell'd to fight, Snatch at his master . . iv 1 116
The French fight coldly, and retire themselves . . . v 3 13
Alive may I not light, If I be traitor or unjustly fight! . *Richard II.* i 1 83
To Coventry, there to behold Our cousin Hereford and fell Mowbray fight . . . . i 2 46
And as I truly fight, defend me heaven! . . . . i 3 41
As thy cause is right, So be thy fortune in this royal fight! . . i 3 56
As confident as is the falcon's flight Against a bird, do I with Mowbray fight . . . . i 3 62
As gentle and as jocund as to jest Go I to fight . . . i 3 96
And dares him to set forward to the fight . . . . i 3 109
Where one on his side fights, thousands will fly . . . ii 2 147
Come, lords, away, To fight with Glendower and his complices . iii 1 43
Then, if angels fight, Weak men must fall, for heaven still guards the right . . . . iii 2 61
And so your follies fight against yourself . . . . iii 2 182
Fear, and be slain; no worse can come to fight: And fight and die is death destroying death . . . . iii 2 183
Let's fight with gentle words Till time lend friends . . iii 3 131
Under whose blessed cross We are impressed and engaged to fight *1 Hen. IV.* i 1 21
To fight Against the irregular and wild Glendower . . . i 1 39
If he fight longer than he sees reason, I'll forswear arms . . i 2 207
When the fight was done, When I was dry with rage and extreme toil . i 3 30
Hath wilfully betray'd The lives of those that he did lead to fight . i 3 82
And all the currents of a heady fight . . . . . ii 3 58
To hack thy sword as thou hast done, and then say it was in fight! . ii 4 289
He would make you believe it was done in fight . . . ii 4 338
Thou that art like enough . . . To fight against me under Percy's pay . iii 2 126
We'll fight with him to-night.—It may not be . . . iv 3 1
To save the blood on either side, Try fortune with him in a single fight v 1 100
The Prince of Wales stepp'd forth before the king, And, nephew, challenged you to single fight . . . . v 2 47
Myself and you, son Harry, will towards Wales, To fight with Glendower v 5 40
Had only but the corpse, But shadows and the shows of men, to fight *2 Hen. IV.* i 1 193
They did fight with queasiness, constrain'd, As men drink potions . i 1 196
The very same day did I fight with one Sampson Stockfish, a fruiterer . iii 2 35
The manner and true order of the fight This packet, please it you, contains . . . . iv 4 100
While that the armed hand doth fight abroad, The advised head defends itself at home . . . . *Hen. V.* i 2 178
I dare not fight; but I will wink and hold out mine iron . . ii 1 7
By the means whereof a' faces it out, but fights not . . iii 2 35
They will eat like wolves and fight like devils . . . iii 7 162
They have only stomachs to eat and none to fight . . . iii 7 166
And yet I determine to fight lustily for him . . . iv 1 201
Ay, he said so, to make us fight cheerfully . . . iv 1 204
Give their fasting horses provender, And after fight with them . iv 2 59
Fight valiantly to-day: And yet I do thee wrong to mind thee of it . iv 3 12
He which hath no stomach to this fight, Let him depart . . iv 3 35

Fight. Would you and I alone, Without more help, could fight this royal battle! . . . . *Hen. V.* iv 3 75
If they will fight with us, bid them come down, Or void the field . . iv 7 61
'Tis the gage of one that I should fight withal, if he be alive . . iv 7 128
Give me my steeled coat. I'll fight for France . . 1 *Hen. VI.* i 1 85
If thou be slack, I'll fight it out.—Gloucester, why doubt'st thou? . . i 1 99
I must inform you of a dismal fight . . . . i 1 105
More than three hours the fight continued . . . . . i 1 120
Distrustful recreants! Fight till the last gasp . . . . i 2 127
We'll fight it out . . . . i 2 128
I myself fight not once in forty year . . . . i 3 91
Either renew the fight, Or tear the lions out of England's coat . . i 5 27
When the fight began, Roused on the sudden from their drowsy beds . ii 2 22
Leave this peevish broil And set this unaccustom'd fight aside . . iii 1 93
We and our wives and children all will fight . . . . . iii 1 100
Will ye, like soldiers, come and fight it out? . . . . . iii 2 66
Let this dissension first be tried by fight . . . . . . iv 1 116
We are well fortified And strong enough to issue out and fight . . iv 2 20
Prosper our colours in this dangerous fight! . . . . . . iv 2 56
He is march'd to Bourdeaux with his power, To fight with Talbot . iv 3 5
York set him on to fight and die in shame . . . . . . iv 4 8
Upon my blessing, I command thee go.—To fight I will, but not to fly the foe . . . . iv 5 37
Then both fly.—And leave my followers here to fight and die? . . iv 5 45
Saint George and victory! fight, soldiers, fight . . . . . iv 6 1
And had the maidenhood Of thy first fight . . . . . . iv 6 18
If thou wilt fight, fight by thy father's side . . . . . iv 6 56
Rushing in the bowels of the French, He left me proudly, as unworthy fight . . . . iv 7 43
I cannot fight; for God's sake, pity my case . . 2 *Hen. VI.* i 3 217
O Lord, have mercy upon me! I shall never be able to fight a blow . i 3 220
Sirrah, or you must fight, or else be hang'd . . . . . . i 3 222
So please your highness to behold the fight . . . . . . ii 3 51
I never saw a fellow worse bested, Or more afraid to fight . . . ii 3 57
Fear not thy master: fight for credit of the 'prentices . . . ii 3 71
The lives of those which we have lost in fight Be counterpoised with such a petty sum! . . . . iv 1 21
Fight for your king, your country and your lives . . . . . iv 5 12
Let's go fight with them: but first, go and set London bridge on fire . iv 6 15
My foot shall fight with all the strength thou hast . . . . iv 10 53
O, I could hew up rocks and fight with flint, I am so angry . . . v 1 24
And fight against that monstrous rebel Cade . . . . . . v 1 62
Clifford, I say, come forth and fight with me . . . . . . v 2 5
What are you made of? you'll nor fight nor fly . . . . . v 2 74
Let's fight it out and not stand cavilling thus . . 3 *Hen. VI.* i 1 117
Be thy title right or wrong, Lord Clifford vows to fight in thy defence . i 1 160
And thrice cried 'Courage, father! fight it out!' . . . . . i 4 10
So cowards fight when they can fly no further . . . . . . i 4 40
They had no heart to fight, And we in them no hope to win the day . ii 1 135
We heard you were Making another head to fight again . . . ii 1 141
I'll stay.—Be it with resolution then to fight . . . . . . ii 2 77
Cheer these noble lords And hearten those that fight in your defence . ii 2 79
For God's sake, lords, give signal to the fight . . . . . . ii 2 100
This man, whom hand to hand I slew in fight, May be possessed with some store of crowns . . . . ii 5 56
Let them fight that will, For I have murdered where I should not kill . ii 5 121
Fight closer, or, good faith, you'll catch a blow . . . . . iii 2 23
Why shall we fight, if you pretend no title? . . . . . . iv 7 57
By this I challenge him to single fight . . . . iv 7 75
What, Warwick, wilt thou leave the town and fight? . . . . . v 1 107
Have arrived our coast, And, as we hear, march on to fight with us . v 3 9
He that will not fight for such a hope, Go home to bed . . . . v 4 55
Edward is at hand, Ready to fight; therefore be resolute . . . v 4 61
Give signal to the fight, and to it, lords! . . . . v 4 72
You fight in justice: then, in God's name, lords, Be valiant and give signal to the fight . . . . v 4 81
Forswore himself . . . To fight on Edward's party for the crown *Richard III.* i 3 138
Thou didst receive the holy sacrament, To fight in quarrel of the house of Lancaster . . . . i 4 209
Who told me how the poor soul did forsake The mighty Warwick, and did fight for me? . . . . ii 1 110
My prayers on the adverse party fight . . . . iv 4 190
If not to fight with foreign enemies, Yet to beat down these rebels here iv 4 531
Every man's conscience is a thousand swords, To fight against that bloody homicide . . . . v 2 18
The wronged souls Of butcher'd princes fight in thy behalf . . . v 3 122
Awake, awake! Arm, fight, and conquer, for fair England's sake! . . v 3 150
God and good angels fight on Richmond's side . . . . . . v 3 175
Yet remember this, God and our good cause fight upon our side . . v 3 240
Richard except, those whom we fight against Had rather have us win . v 3 243
Then, if you fight against God's enemy, God will in justice ward you . v 3 253
If you do fight against your country's foes, Your country's fat shall pay your pains the hire . . . . v 3 257
If you do fight in safeguard of your wives, Your wives shall welcome home the conquerors . . . . v 3 259
Fight, gentlemen of England! fight, bold yeomen! Draw, archers! . v 3 338
His horse is slain, and all on foot he fights, Seeking for Richmond . v 4 4
To rank our chosen truth with such a show As fool and fight is *Hen. VIII.* Prol. 19
Those remnants Of fool and feather that they got in France, With all their honourable points of ignorance Pertaining thereunto, as fights and fireworks . . . . i 3 27
Youths that thunder at a playhouse, and fight for bitten apples . . v 4 64
I cannot fight upon this argument . . . . *Troi. and Cres.* i 1 95
Can Helenus fight, uncle?—Helenus? no. Yes, he'll fight indifferent well . . . . i 2 241
Let blockish Ajax draw The sort to fight with Hector . . . . i 3 376
Has not so much wit . . . As will stop the eye of Helen's needle, for whom he comes to fight . . . . ii 1 88
Such things as might offend the weakest spleen To fight for and maintain . . . . ii 2 129
Then, I say, Well may we fight for her whom, we know well, The world's large spaces cannot parallel . . . . ii 2 161
You must prepare to fight without Achilles . . . . . . ii 3 238
But he that disciplined thy arms to fight, Let Mars divide eternity in twain, And give him half . . . . ii 3 255
Nay, you shall fight your hearts out ere I part you . . . . iii 2 54
O virtuous fight, When right with right wars who shall be most right! iii 2 178
You know my mind, I'll fight no more 'gainst Troy . . . . iii 3 56
Fight. Shall Ajax fight with Hector?—Ay, and perhaps receive much honour by him . . . . *Troi. and Cres.* iii 3 225
He must fight singly to-morrow with Hector . . . . . . iii 3 247
Consent upon the order of their fight, So be it . . . . . iv 5 90
I am not warm yet; let us fight again.—As Hector pleases . . iv 5 118
By this white beard, I'ld fight with thee to-morrow . . . . iv 5 209
Within my soul there doth conduce a fight Of this strange nature . v 2 147
Unarm, unarm, and do not fight to-day . . . . v 3 3
How now, young man! mean'st thou to fight to-day? . . . . v 3 29
Troilus, I would not have you fight to-day . . . . . . v 3 50
We'll forth and fight, Do deeds worth praise and tell you them at night v 3 92
Now here he fights on Galathe his horse, And there lacks work . . v 5 20
Art thou there?—I'll fight with him alone . . . . v 6 9
Turn, slave, and fight.—What art thou? . . . . v 7 13
If the son of a whore fight for a whore, he tempts judgement . . v 7 22
I'll lean upon one crutch and fight with t'other, Ere stay behind . *Cor.* i 1 246
And fight With hearts more proof than shields . . . . . . i 4 24
Ere yet the fight be done, pack up: down with them! . . . . i 5 9
Thy exercise hath been too violent For a second course of fight . . i 5 17
To Aufidius thus I will appear, and fight . . . . i 5 21
The rest Shall bear the business in some other fight . . . . i 6 82
I'll fight with none but thee; for I do hate thee Worse than a promise-breaker . . . . i 8 1
Know, Rome, that all alone Marcius did fight Within Corioli gates . ii 1 179
Our then dictator Whom with all praise I point at, saw him fight . ii 2 94
For I will fight Against my canker'd country with the spleen Of all the under fiends . . . . iv 5 96
Fights dragon-like, and does achieve as soon As draw his sword . . iv 7 23
I'll run away till I am bigger, but then I'll fight . . . . . v 3 128
And, Romans, fight for freedom in your choice . . . *T. Andron.* i 1 17
Rome's best champion, Successful in the battles that he fights . . i 1 66
If to fight for king and commonweal Were piety in thine, it is in these . i 1 114
He fights as you sing prick-song, keeps time, distance *Rom. and Jul.* ii 4 21
A braggart, a rogue, a villain, that fights by the book of arithmetic . iii 1 106
O Lord, they fight! I will go call the watch . . . . . . v 3 71
Has done fair service, And slain in fight many of your enemies *T. of A.* iii 5 64
It is a creature that I teach to fight, To wind, to stop . . *J. Cæsar* iv 1 31
If you dare fight to-day, come to the field; If not, when you have stomachs . . . . v 1 65
And, Romans, yet ere night We shall try fortune in a second fight . v 3 110
When he reads Thy personal venture in the rebels' fight, His wonders and his praises do contend . . . . *Macbeth* i 3 91
Against the undivulged pretence I fight Of treasonous malice . . ii 3 137
Though you untie the winds and let them fight Against the churches . iv 1 52
The poor wren, The most diminutive of birds, will fight . . . . iv 2 10
Your eye in Scotland Would create soldiers, make our women fight . iv 3 187
I'll fight till from my bones my flesh be hack'd . . . . . v 3 32
Let us be beaten, if we cannot fight . . . . v 6 8
I cannot fly, But, bear-like, I must fight the course . . . . v 7 2
The castle's gently render'd: The tyrant's people on both sides do fight . . . . v 7 25
I'll not fight with thee.—Then yield thee, coward . . . . . v 8 22
Fight for a plot Whereon the numbers cannot try the cause . *Hamlet* iv 4 62
I will fight with him upon this theme Until my eyelids will no longer wag . . . . v 1 289
Woo't weep? woo't fight? woo't fast? woo't tear thyself? Woo't drink up eisel? . . . . v 1 298
To fear judgement; to fight when I cannot choose; and to eat no fish *Lear* i 4 18
Before you fight the battle, ope this letter . . . . . . v 1 40
Were it my cue to fight, I should have known it Without a prompter *Oth.* i 2 83
His captain's heart, Which in the scuffles of great fights hath burst The buckles on his breast . . . . *Ant. and Cleo.* i 1 7
Were we before our armies, and to fight, I should do thus . . . ii 2 26
Your hostages I have, so have you mine; And we shall talk before we fight . . . . ii 6 2
I have seen thee fight, When I have envied thy behaviour . . . ii 6 76
We came hither to fight with you.—For my part, I am sorry it is turned to a drinking . . . . ii 6 107
We Will fight with him by sea.—By sea! what else? . . . . iii 7 29
For that he dares us to't.—So hath my lord dared him to single fight . iii 7 31
I'll fight at sea.—I have sixty sails, Cæsar none better . . . iii 7 49
O noble emperor, do not fight by sea; Trust not to rotten planks . iii 7 62
How appears the fight?—On our side like the token'd pestilence . iii 10 8
I' the midst o' the fight, When vantage like a pair of twins appeared . iii 10 11
And, like a doting mallard, Leaving the fight in height, flies after her . iii 10 21
I will be treble-sinew'd, hearted, breathed, And fight maliciously . iii 13 179
The next time I do fight, I'll make death love me . . . . iii 13 192
When valour preys on reason, It eats the sword it fights with . . iii 13 200
Know, that to-morrow the last of many battles We mean to fight . . iv 1 12
He will not fight with me, Domitius.—No.—Why should he not? . . iv 2 1
To-morrow, soldier, By sea and land I'll fight . . . . . . iv 2 5
Woo't thou fight well?—I'll strike, and cry 'Take all' . . . . iv 2 7
You that will fight, Follow me close; I'll bring you to't . . . iv 4 33
That he and Cæsar might Determine this great war in single fight! . iv 4 37
Would thou and those thy scars had once prevail'd To make me fight at land! . . . . iv 5 3
Begin the fight: Our will is Antony be took alive; Make it so known . iv 6 1
I fight against thee! No: I will go seek Some ditch wherein to die . iv 6 37
I would they'ld fight i' the fire or i' the air; We'ld fight there too . iv 10 3
Or, like the Parthian, I shall flying fight; Rather, directly fly *Cymbeline* i 6 20
They dare not fight with me, because of the queen my mother . . ii 1 21
I am brought hither . . . to fight Against my lady's kingdom . . v 1 18
So I'll fight Against the part I come with . . . . v 1 24
Stand, stand, and fight!—Away, boy, from the troops, and save thyself v 2 13
Fight I will no more, But yield me to the veriest hind that shall Once touch my shoulder . . . . v 3 76
Fighter. You have yourself been a great fighter, thou now a man of peace . . . . *Mer. Wives* ii 3 44
I am no fighter. I have heard of some kind of men that put quarrels purposely on others, to taste their valour . . . *T. Night* iii 4 265
I am no fighter: I am false of heart that way . . . *W. Tale* iv 3 116
To the latter end of a fray and the beginning of a feast Fits a dull fighter and a keen guest . . . . 1 *Hen. IV.* iv 2 86
Fightest. Thou art an Amazon And fightest with sword of Deborah 1 *Hen. VI.* i 2 105
See, then, thou fight'st against thy countrymen . . . . . iii 3 74
Then, nobly, York; 'tis for a crown thou fight'st . . 2 *Hen. VI.* v 2 16
Fighteth. He fighteth as one weary of his life . . 1 *Hen. VI.* i 2 26
Fighting. Wronging the ancientry, stealing, fighting . *W. Tale* iii 3 63
When wilt thou leave fighting o' days and foining o' nights? . 2 *Hen. IV.* ii 4 251

Fighting. Thrice within this hour I saw him down; thrice up again, and fighting . . . . *Hen. V.* iv 6 5
Some among you have beheld me fighting: Come, try upon yourselves what you have seen me . . . . *Coriolanus* iii 1 224
The servants of your adversary, And yours, close fighting *Rom. and Jul.* i 1 114
O, step between her and her fighting soul . . . *Hamlet* iii 4 113
In my heart there was a kind of fighting, That would not let me sleep . v 2 4
Used to conquer, standing on the earth, And fighting foot to foot *Ant. and Cleo.* iii 7 67
Every jack-slave hath his bellyful of fighting . . . *Cymbeline* ii 1 23
Fighting men. Thou shalt have twelve thousand fighting men! *Rich. II.* iii 2 70
Of fighting men they have full three score thousand . . *Hen. V.* iv 3 3
Fig-leaves. These fig-leaves Have slime upon them, such as the aspic leaves Upon the caves of Nile . . . . *Ant. and Cleo.* v 2 354
Figo. Die and be damn'd! and figo for thy friendship! . . *Hen. V.* iii 6 60
Art thou his friend?—And his kinsman too.—The figo for thee, then! . iv 1 60
Fig's-end. She's full of most blessed condition.—Blessed fig's-end! *Oth.* ii 1 256
Figure. Bravely the figure of this harpy hast thou Perform'd, my Ariel *Tempest* iii 3 83
She wooes you by a figure.—What figure?—By a letter, I should say *T. G. of Ver.* ii 1 154
This weak impress of love is as a figure Trenched in ice . . . . iii 2 6
She works by charms, by spells, by the figure, and such daubery *M. W.* iv 2 185
If it be but to scrape the figures out of your husband's brains . . iv 2 231
What figure of us think you he will bear? . . *Meas. for Meas.* i 1 17
Let there be some more test made of my metal, Before so noble and so great a figure Be stamp'd upon it . . . . i 1 50
Doing, in the figure of a lamb, the feats of a lion . . . *Much Ado* i 1 15
A most fine figure!—To prove you a cipher . . . *L. L. Lost* i 2 58
A foolish extravagant spirit, full of forms, figures, shapes, objects . iv 2 68
What is the figure? what is the figure?—Horns . . . . . v 1 67
Three-piled hyperboles, spruce affectation, Figures pedantical . . v 2 408
Within his power To leave the figure or disfigure it . . *M. N. Dream* i 1 51
Wings and no eyes figure unheedy haste . . . . . . i 1 237
A coin that bears the figure of an angel Stamped in gold *Mer. of Venice* ii 7 56
In the brook: look but in, and you shall see him.—There I shall see mine own figure.—Which I take to be either a fool or a cipher *As Y. Like It* iii 2 307
It is a figure in rhetoric . . . . v 1 45
He will throw a figure in her face and so disfigure her with it *T. of Shrew* i 2 114
That the great figure of a council frames By self-unable motion *All's Well* iii 1 12
Even as a form of wax Resolveth from his figure 'gainst the fire *K. John* v 4 25
The figure of God's majesty . . . . . . *Richard II.* iv 1 125
He apprehends a world of figures here, But not the form . 1 *Hen. IV.* i 3 209
When we see the figure of the house, Then must we rate the cost 2 *Hen. IV.* i 3 43
We fortify in paper and in figures, Using the names of men instead of men . . . . i 3 56
Whose white investments figure innocence . . . . . iv 1 45
A crooked figure may Attest in little place a million . . *Hen. V.* Prol. 15
For there is figures in all things . . . . iv 7 35
I speak but in the figures and comparisons of it . . . . iv 7 46
In this the heaven figures some event . . . . 3 *Hen. VI.* ii 1 32
Poor key-cold figure of a holy king! . . . . . *Richard III.* i 2 5
Whose figure even this instant cloud puts on . . . *Hen. VIII.* i 1 225
That unbodied figure of the thought That gave't surmised shape *T. and C.* i 3 16
The baby figure of the giant mass Of things to come at large . . i 3 345
Like a gate of steel Fronting the sun, receives and renders back His figure and his heat . . . . iii 3 123
While Verona by that name is known, There shall no figure at such rate be set As that of true and faithful Juliet . . . *Rom. and Jul.* v 3 301
These pencill'd figures are Even such as they give out . *T. of Athens* i 1 159
And write in thee the figures of their love, Ever to read them thine . v 1 157
Our captain hath in every figure skill, An aged interpreter, though young . . . . v 3 7
Thou hast no figures nor no fantasies, Which busy care draws in the brains of men; Therefore thou sleep'st so sound . . *J. Cæsar* ii 1 231
In the same figure, like the king that's dead . . . *Hamlet* i 1 41
This portentous figure Comes armed through our watch . . . i 1 109
A figure like your father, Armed at point exactly, cap-a-pe . . . i 2 199
A foolish figure; But farewell it, for I will use no art . . . ii 2 98
What would your gracious figure? . . . . iii 4 104
Now thou art an O without a figure: I am better than thou art now *Lear* i 4 212
My outward action doth demonstrate The native act and figure of my heart In compliment extern . . . . *Othello* i 1 62
A fixed figure for the time of scorn To point his slow unmoving finger at! iv 2 54
Ho! hearts, tongues, figures, scribes, bards, poets, cannot Think, speak, cast, write, sing, number, ho! His love to Antony . *Ant. and Cleo.* iii 2 16
Figures, Why, such and such; and the contents o' the story *Cymbeline* ii 2 26
Never saw I figures So likely to report themselves . . . . ii 4 82
In as like a figure . . . . iii 3 96
'Tween man and man they weigh not every stamp; Though light, take pieces for the figure's sake . . . . v 4 25
A figure of truth, of faith, of loyalty . . . . *Pericles* v 3 Gower 92
Figured. My figured goblets for a dish of wood . . *Richard II.* iii 3 150
The vaulty top of heaven Figured quite o'er with burning meteors *K. John* v 2 53
I would I knew thy heart.—'Tis figured in my tongue . *Richard III.* i 2 194
Figuring. Thou art always figuring diseases in me . . *Meas. for Meas.* i 2 53
There is a history in all men's lives, Figuring the nature of the times deceased . . . . 2 *Hen. IV.* iii 1 81
Filbert. I'll bring thee To clustering filberts . . . . *Tempest* ii 2 175
Filch. He that filches from me my good name Robs me of that which not enriches him, And makes me poor indeed . . . . *Othello* iii 3 159
What will you do with't, that you have been so earnest To have me filch it? . . . . iii 3 315
Filched. With cunning hast thou filch'd my daughter's heart *M. N. Dream* i 1 36
Filching. His filching was like an unskilful singer . . *Mer. Wives* i 3 28
Nym and Bardolph are sworn brothers in filching . . . *Hen. V.* iii 2 48
File. The greater file of the subject held the duke to be wise *M. for M.* iii 2 144
Great Mars, I put myself into thy file . . . . . *All's Well* iii 3 9
It is upon a file with the duke's other letters . . . . . . iv 3 231
To instruct for the doubling of files . . . . iv 3 303
Our present musters grow upon the file . . . 2 *Hen. IV.* i 3 10
He makes up the file Of all the gentry . . . . . *Hen. VIII.* i 1 75
And front but in that file Where others tell steps with me . . . i 2 42
A file of boys behind 'em, loose shot, delivered such a shower of pebbles v 4 59
The common file—a plague! tribunes for them! . . . *Coriolanus* i 6 43
How you are censured here in the city, I mean of us o' the right-hand file ii 1 26
Choose Out of my files, his projects to accomplish, My best and freshest men . . . . v 6 34
File. And she shall file our engines with advice, That will not suffer you to square yourselves . . . . *T. Andron.* ii 1 123
Are his files As full as thy report? . . . . . . *T. of Athens* v 2 1
The valued file Distinguishes the swift, the slow, the subtle *Macbeth* iii 1 95
If you have a station in the file, Not i' the worst rank of manhood, say't iii 1 102
I have a file Of all the gentry . . . . v 2 8
Those his goodly eyes, That o'er the files and musters of the war Have glow'd like plated Mars . . . . *Ant. and Cleo.* i 1 3
Within our files there are, Of those that served Mark Antony but late, Enough to fetch him in . . . . iv 1 12
For three performers are the file when all The rest do nothing *Cymbeline* v 3 30
Filed. His tongue filed, his eye ambitious . . . . . *L. L. Lost* v 1 12
My desire, More sharp than filed steel . . . . . *T. Night* iii 3 5
I could have filed keys off that hung in chains . . . . *W. Tale* iv 4 624
My endeavours Have ever come too short of my desires, Yet filed with my abilities . . . . *Hen. VIII.* iii 2 171
For Banquo's issue have I filed my mind . . . . *Macbeth* iii 1 65
Filial. Love and filial tenderness Shall, O dear father, pay thee plenteously 2 *Hen. IV.* iv 5 39
Bound In filial obligation for some term To do obsequious sorrow *Hamlet* i 2 91
Filial ingratitude! Is it not as this mouth should tear this hand For lifting food to't? . . . . *Lear* iii 4 14
Filius. Præclarissimus filius noster Henricus . . . . *Hen. V.* v 2 369
Fill. I'll rack thee with old cramps, Fill all thy bones with aches *Tempest* i 2 370
Bear my bottle: fellow Trinculo, we'll fill him by and by again . . ii 2 181
From toe to crown he'll fill our skins with pinches, Make us strange stuff . . . . iv 1 233
The approaching tide Will shortly fill the reasonable shore . . . v 1 81
Gentle breath of yours my sails Must fill, or else my project fails . . Epil. 12
There wanteth but a mean to fill your song . . . *T. G. of Ver.* i 2 95
If the river were dry, I am able to fill it with my tears . . . . ii 3 58
That one error Fills him with faults . . . . v 4 112
Whether the tyranny be in his place, Or in his eminence that fills it up, I stagger in . . . . *Meas. for Meas.* i 2 168
I dare not for my head fill my belly; one fruitful meal would set me to't . . . . iv 3 160
The princess bids you tell How many inches doth fill up one mile *L. L. Lost* v 2 193
Comes with him, at my importunity, to fill up your grace's request *Mer. of Venice* iv 1 160
Only in the world I fill up a place, which may be better supplied when I have made it empty . . . . *As Y. Like It* i 2 204
Mum! and gaze your fill . . . . *T. of Shrew* i 1 73
You are loved, sir; They that least lend it you shall lack you first.—I fill a place, I know't . . . . *All's Well* i 2 69
In fine, delivers me to fill the time, Herself most chastely absent . . iii 7 33
O sir! You have undone a man of fourscore three, That thought to fill his grave in quiet . . . . *W. Tale* iv 4 465
Come, I'll fill your grave up: stir, nay, come away . . . . v 3 101
If not fill up the measure of her will, Yet in some measure satisfy her *K. John* ii 1 556
Grief fills the room up of my absent child, Lies in his bed . . . iii 4 93
I'll fill these dogged spies with false reports . . . . . . iv 1 129
Wherein we step after a stranger march Upon her gentle bosom, and fill up Her enemies' rank . . . . v 2 28
Whoso empties them By so much fills their hearts with deadly hate *Richard II.* ii 2 131
Go thou, and fill another room in hell . . . . v 5 108
Or fill up chronicles in time to come . . . . . 1 *Hen. IV.* i 3 171
He doth fill fields with harness in the realm . . . . . . iii 2 101
Enlarged him and made a friend of him, To fill the mouth of deep defiance up . . . . iii 2 116
Get thee before to Coventry; fill me a bottle of sack . . . . iv 2 2
Such have I, to fill up the rooms of them that have bought out their services . . . . iv 2 35
Food for powder; they'll fill a pit as well as better . . . . iv 2 72
How chances mock, And changes fill the cup of alteration! 2 *Hen. IV.* iii 1 52
We have a number of shadows to fill up the muster-book . . . iii 2 145
Fill the cup, and let it come; I'll pledge you a mile to the bottom . v 3 56
To fill King Edward's fame with prisoner kings . . . *Hen. V.* i 2 162
A nest of hollow bosoms, which he fills With treacherous crowns . ii Prol. 21
Creeping murmur and the poring dark Fills the wide vessel of the universe . . . . iv Prol. 3
Fill this glove with crowns, And give it to this fellow . . . . iv 8 61
She hath beheld the man Whose glory fills the world with loud report 1 *Hen. VI.* ii 2 43
She hath lived too long, To fill the world with vicious qualities . . v 4 35
And dead men's cries do fill the empty air . . . . 2 *Hen. VI.* v 2 4
Or I will fill the house with armed men . . . . 3 *Hen. VI.* i 1 167
And no more words till they have flow'd their fill . . . . . ii 5 72
I'll bear thee hence, where I may weep my fill . . . . . . ii 5 113
Such a cause as fills mine eyes with tears And stops my tongue . . iii 3 13
Mine, such as fill my heart with unhoped joys.—Mine, full of sorrow . iii 3 172
Why should she live, to fill the world with words? . . . . . v 5 44
That fill his ears with such dissentious rumours . . . *Richard III.* i 3 46
It [conscience] fills one full of obstacles: it made me once restore a purse . . . . i 4 143
A queen in jest, only to fill the scene . . . . iv 4 91
Fill me a bowl of wine. Give me a watch . . . . v 3 63
Now fills thy sleep with perturbations . . . . v 3 161
Our travell'd gallants, That fill the court with quarrels, talk *Hen. VIII.* i 3 20
Goodness and he fill up one monument! . . . . ii 1 94
Cry, Trojans, cry! lend me ten thousand eyes, And I will fill them with prophetic tears . . . . *Troi. and Cres.* ii 2 102
An you draw backward, we'll put you i' the fills . . . . . iii 2 48
Stand fair, I pray thee: let me look on thee.—Behold thy fill . . iv 5 236
I'll take good breath: Rest, sword; thou hast thy fill of blood and death . . . . v 8 4
Yet, they say, all the yarn she spun in Ulysses' absence did but fill Ithaca full of moths . . . . *Coriolanus* i 3 94
I can smooth and fill his aged ear With golden promises *T. Andron.* iv 4 96
Although the cheer be poor, 'Twill fill your stomachs . . . . v 3 29
His lobbies fill with tendance . . . . . . *T. of Athens* i 1 80
To see meat fill knaves and wine heat fools . . . . . . i 1 271
You are very respectively welcome, sir. Fill me some wine . . . iii 1 8
Pass by and curse thy fill, but pass and stay not here thy gait . . v 4 73
Whose ransoms did the general coffers fill . . . . *J. Cæsar* iii 2 94
Fill, Lucius, till the wine o'erswell the cup . . . . . . iv 3 161
And fill me from the crown to the toe top-full Of direst cruelty! *Macbeth* i 5 43
As far, my lord, as will fill up the time 'Twixt this and supper . . iii 1 25

Fill. Give me some wine; fill full. I drink to the general joy o' the whole table . . . . *Macbeth* iii 4 88
Your matrons and your maids could not fill up The cistern of my lust . iv 3 62
Foisons to fill up your will, Of your mere own . . . . . iv 3 88
Let him demand his fill.—How came he dead? . . . *Hamlet* iv 5 129
Fill thy purse with money . . . . *Othello* i 3 353
I do follow here in the chase, not like a hound that hunts, but one that fills up the cry . . . . ii 3 370
It be fit that Cassio have his place, For, sure, he fills it up with great ability . . . . iii 3 247
O most false love! Where be the sacred vials thou shouldst fill With sorrowful water? . . . . . . *Ant. and Cleo.* i 3 63
Fill till the cup be hid . . . . ii 7 93
And he will fill thy wishes to the brim With principalities . . iii 13 18
Fill our bowls once more; Let's mock the midnight bell . . . iii 13 184
Say, and speak thick; Love's counsellor should fill the bores of hearing, To the smothering of the sense . . . *Cymbeline* iii 2 59
To lop that doubt, he'll fill this land with arms . . *Pericles* i 2 90
Here, with a cup that's stored unto the brim,—As you do love, fill to your mistress' lips . . . . ii 3 51
Filled. The nine men's morris is fill'd up with mud . *M. N. Dream* ii 1 98
That one body should be fill'd With all graces wide-enlarged *As Y. L. It* iii 2 150
And fill'd Her sweet perfections with one self king . . *T. Night* i 1 38
For his thoughts, Would they were blanks, rather than fill'd with me! iii 1 115
Time as long again Would be fill'd up, my brother, with our thanks *W. Tale* i 2 4
Humane And fill'd with honour, to my kingly guest Unclasp'd my practice . . . . iii 2 167
I never saw a vessel of like sorrow, So fill'd and so becoming . . iii 3 22
It is all filled up with guts and midriff . . . *1 Hen. IV.* iii 3 175
His hours fill'd up with riots, banquets, sports . . *Hen. V.* i 1 56
So the proportions of defence are fill'd . . . . . ii 4 45
Who with a body fill'd and vacant mind Gets him to rest . . iv 1 286
Have fill'd their pockets full of pebble stones . . *1 Hen. VI.* iii 1 80
And princes' courts be fill'd with my reproach . . *2 Hen. VI.* iii 2 69
Speak. Are my chests fill'd up with extorted gold? . . . iv 7 105
As doth a sail, fill'd with a fretting gust, Command an argosy *3 Hen. VI.* ii 6 35
Thy place is fill'd, thy sceptre wrung from thee, Thy balm wash'd off . iii 1 16
The wrinkles in my brows, now fill'd with blood, Were liken'd oft to kingly sepulchres . . . . v 2 19
Made the happy earth thy hell, Fill'd it with cursing cries *Richard III.* i 2 52
Have your mouth fill'd up Before you open it . . . *Hen. VIII.* ii 3 87
Windows Are smother'd up, leads fill'd, and ridges horsed . *Coriolanus* ii 1 227
And fill'd the time With all licentious measure . . *T. of Athens* v 4 3
He gives your Hollander a vomit, ere the next pottle can be fill'd *Othello* ii 3 87
If he fill'd His vacancy with his voluptuousness . . *Ant. and Cleo.* i 4 25
That satiate yet unsatisfied desire, that tub Both fill'd and running *Cymb.* i 6 49
In feather'd briefness sails are fill'd . . . . *Pericles* v 2 280
Fillet of a fenny snake, In the cauldron boil and bake . *Macbeth* iv 1 12
Fill-horse. Thou hast got more hair on thy chin than Dobbin my fill-horse has on his tail . . . . . . *Mer. of Venice* ii 2 100
Filling. Why should he die, sir?—Why? For filling a bottle with a tun-dish . . . . *Meas. for Meas.* iii 2 182
Drink, being poured out of a cup into a glass, by filling the one doth empty the other . . . . . . *As Y. Like It* v 1 46
Like a deep well That owes two buckets, filling one another *Richard II.* iv 1 185
In filling The whole realm, by your teaching and your chaplains *Hen. VIII.* v 3 15
Filling the air with swords advanced and darts . . *Coriolanus* i 6 61
For these bitter tears, which now you see Filling the aged wrinkles in my cheeks; Be pitiful . . . . . . *T. Andron.* iii 1 7
The one is filling still, never complete; The other, at high wish *T. of A.* iv 3 244
Filling their hearers With strange invention . . . *Macbeth* iii 1 32
Fillip. If I do, fillip me with a three-man beetle . *2 Hen. IV.* i 2 255
You fillip me o' the head . . . . . . *Troi. and Cres.* iv 5 45
Then let the pebbles on the hungry beach Fillip the stars . *Coriolanus* v 3 59
Filly foal. Neighing in likeness of a filly foal . . *M. N. Dream* ii 1 46
Film. Her whip of cricket's bone, the lash of film . . *Rom. and Jul.* i 4 63
It will but skin and film the ulcerous place . . . *Hamlet* iii 4 147
Fils. Notre très-cher fils Henri, Roi d'Angleterre . . *Hen. V.* v 2 368
Filth. I have used thee, Filth as thou art, with human care . *Tempest* i 2 346
His filth within being cast, he would appear A pond as deep as hell *Meas. for Meas.* iii 1 93
Whose filth and dirt Troubles the silver spring where England drinks *2 Hen. VI.* iv 1 71
Rebellious hinds, the filth and scum of Kent . . . . . iv 2 130
I am the besom that must sweep the court clean of such filth as thou art . . . . iv 7 35
To general filths Convert o' the instant, green virginity! *T. of Athens* iv 1 6
My face I'll grime with filth; Blanket my loins . . . *Lear* ii 3 9
Wisdom and goodness to the vile seem vile: Filths savour but themselves . . . . iv 2 39
Filth, thou liest! . . . . *Othello* v 2 231
In our own filth drop our clear judgements . . *Ant. and Cleo.* iii 13 113
Empty Old receptacles, or common shores, of filth . . *Pericles* iv 6 186
Filthy. Ha! fie, these filthy vices! . . . . *Meas. for Meas.* ii 4 42
But think What 'tis to cram a maw or clothe a back From such a filthy vice . . . . iii 2 24
'Tis lewd and filthy: Why, 'tis a cockle or a walnut-shell *T. of Shrew* iv 3 65
Scurvy, old, filthy, scurvy lord! Well, I must be patient *All's Well* iii 3 250
A filthy officer he is in those suggestions for the young earl . . iii 5 18
An I have not ballads made on you all and sung to filthy tunes *1 Hen. IV.* ii 2 49
Dowlas, filthy dowlas: I have given them away to bakers' wives . . iii 3 79
Away, you cut-purse rascal! you filthy bung, away! . *2 Hen. IV.* ii 4 137
You blue-bottle rogue, you filthy famished correctioner . . . v 4 22
Whiles yet the cool and temperate wind of grace O'erblows the filthy and contagious clouds Of heady murder . . . . *Hen. V.* iii 3 31
I am a rascal; a scurvy railing knave; a very filthy rogue *Troi. and Cres.* v 4 31
And yet he's but a filthy piece of work . . . *T. of Athens* i 1 202
You take us even at the best.—'Faith, for the worst is filthy . . i 2 158
Fair is foul, and foul is fair: Hover through the fog and filthy air *Macb.* i 1 12
Go get some water, And wash this filthy witness from your hand . . ii 2 47
Filthy hags! Why do you show me this? A fourth! Start, eyes! . iv 1 115
Hundred-pound, filthy, worsted-stocking knave . . . *Lear* ii 2 17
O filthy traitor!—Unmerciful lady as you are, I'm none. . . iii 7 32
An honest man he is, and hates the slime That sticks on filthy deeds *Othello* v 2 149
He lies to the heart: She was too fond of her most filthy bargain . . v 2 157
Filthy-mantled pool . . . . *Tempest* iv 1 182

Fin. Legged like a man! and his fins like arms! . . . *Tempest* ii 2 35
When fowls have no feathers and fish have no fin . *Com. of Errors* iii 1 79
For a fish without a fin, there's a fowl without a feather . . . iii 1 82
La fin couronne les œuvres . . . . . . *2 Hen. VI.* v 2 28
He that depends Upon your favours swims with fins of lead . *Coriolanus* i 1 184
Finally. Lastly and finally . . . . . . *Mer. Wives* i 1 142
Finch. The finch, the sparrow and the lark . . . *M. N. Dream* iii 1 133
Finch-egg. Out, gall!—Finch-egg! . . . . *Troi. and Cres.* v 1 41
Find. I find my zenith doth depend upon A most auspicious star *Tempest* i 2 181
Thou best know'st What torment I did find thee in . . . . i 2 287
He hath lost his fellows And strays about to find 'em . . . i 2 417
I wish mine eyes Would, with themselves, shut up my thoughts: I find They are inclined to do so . . . . ii 1 192
I find not Myself disposed to sleep . . . . ii 1 201
I could find in my heart to beat him . . . . ii 2 160
He is drown'd Whom thus we stray to find . . . . . . iii 3 9
Their manners are more gentle-kind than of Our human generation you shall find Many, nay, almost any . . . . iii 3 33
We find Each putter-out of five for one will bring us Good warrant of . iii 3 47
Thou shalt find she will outstrip all praise And make it halt behind her iv 1 10
There shalt thou find the mariners asleep Under the hatches . . . v 1 98
In one voyage Did Claribel her husband find at Tunis . . . v 1 209
Where should they Find this grand liquor that hath gilded 'em? . . v 1 280
If I lose them, thus find I by their loss For Valentine myself *T. G. of Ver.* ii 6 21
I gave him gentle looks, thereby to find That which thyself hast now disclosed . . . . iii 1 31
What seest thou?—Him we go to find . . . . iii 1 191
Find my dog again, Or ne'er return again into my sight . . . iv 4 64
Hie home unto my chamber, Where thou shalt find me, sad and solitary iv 4 94
I find her milder than she was; And yet she takes exceptions at your person . . . . v 2 2
It is the lesser blot, modesty finds, Women to change their shapes than men their minds . . . . v 4 108
You shall find me reasonable . . . . . . *Mer. Wives* i 1 217
If he do, i' faith, and find any body in the house . . . . i 4 4
Ay me, he'll find the young man there, and be mad! . . . . i 4 68
You shall find it a great charge: and to be up early and down late . i 4 107
I will find you twenty lascivious turtles ere one chaste man . . ii 1 82
I will be patient; I will find out this . . . . . . ii 1 130
If I do find it: well.—I will not believe such a Cataian . . . ii 1 147
If I find her honest, I lose not my labour . . . . . . ii 1 246
My assurance bids me search: there I shall find Falstaff . . . iii 2 47
Heaven knows how I love you; and you shall one day find it . . iii 3 88
Search, seek, find out: I'll warrant we'll unkennel the fox . . iii 3 173
I cannot find him: may be the knave bragged of that he could not compass . . . . iii 3 211
My daughter will I question how she loves you, And as I find her, so am I . . . . iii 4 95
And did he search for you, and could not find you? . . . . iii 5 83
Let the clothes alone.—I shall find you anon . . . . . iv 2 146
If you find a man there, he shall die a flea's death . . . iv 2 157
If I find not what I seek, show no colour for my extremity . . iv 2 168
If they can find in their hearts the poor unvirtuous fat knight shall be any further afflicted . . . . iv 2 232
Find a maid That, ere she sleep, has thrice her prayers said . . v 5 53
The jewel that we find, we stoop and take't Because we see it *M. for M.* ii 1 24
Hoping you'll find good cause to whip them all . . . . ii 1 142
Let me not find you before me again upon any complaint whatsoever . ii 1 260
To sue to live, I find I seek to die; And, seeking death, find life . iii 1 42
In corporal sufferance finds a pang as great As when a giant dies . iii 1 80
And let me desire to know how you find Claudio prepared . . iii 2 254
But shall you on your knowledge find this way? . . . . iv 1 37
I do find your hangman is a more penitent trade than your bawd . . iv 2 52
If you have occasion to use me for your own turn, you shall find me yare . . . . iv 2 61
You shall find, within these two days he will be here . . . iv 2 213
Now, sir, how do you find the prisoner?—A creature unprepared . iv 3 70
You shall find Your safety manifested . . . . . . iv 3 93
Which you shall find By every syllable a faithful verity . . . iv 3 130
Let me have way, my lord, To find this practice out . . . v 1 239
Lend him your kind pains To find out this abuse . . . . v 1 247
We shall find this friar a notable fellow . . . . . . v 1 268
I find an apt remission in myself . . . . v 1 503
Hopeless to find, yet loath to leave unsought . *Com. of Errors* i 1 136
Falling there to find his fellow forth, Unseen, inquisitive, confounds himself . . . . i 2 37
So I, to find a mother and a brother, In quest of them, unhappy, lose myself . . . . i 2 39
She is spherical, like a globe; I could find out countries in her . iii 2 117
I looked for the chalky cliffs, but I could find no whiteness in them . iii 2 130
The fellow finds his vein And yielding to him humours well his frenzy iv 4 83
I could find in my heart to stay here still and turn witch . . iv 4 159
Discover how, and thou shalt find me just . . . . . . v 1 203
I would I could find in my heart that I had not a hard heart *Much Ado* i 1 127
Talk not of her: you shall find her the infernal Ate in good apparel . ii 1 263
Find me a meet hour to draw Don Pedro and the Count Claudio alone . ii 2 33
Run thee to the parlour; There shalt thou find my cousin Beatrice . iii 1 2
I could find it in my heart to bestow it all of your worship . . iii 5 24
But they shall find, awaked in such a kind, Both strength of limb and policy of mind . . . . iv 1 199
Then we find The virtue that possession would not show us . . . iv 1 222
Shall I not find a woodcock too? . . . . v 1 158
I can find out no rhyme to 'lady' but 'baby,' an innocent rhyme . . v 2 37
If Don Worm, his conscience, find no impediment to the contrary . v 2 86
Ere you find where light in darkness lies, Your light grows dark *L. L. L.* i 1 78
You find not the apostraphas, and so miss the accent . . . iv 2 123
Through the velvet leaves the wind, All unseen, can passage find . . iv 3 106
The king your mote did see; But I a beam do find in each of three . iv 3 162
To tell you plain, I'll find a fairer face not wash'd to-day . . iv 3 273
Let us once lose our oaths to find ourselves, Or else we lose ourselves to keep our oaths . . . . iv 3 361
We need more light to find your meaning out . . . . . v 2 21
Throw away that spirit, And I shall find you empty of that fault . . v 2 878
Find you out a bed; For I upon this bank will rest my head *M. N. Dream* ii 2 39
Either death or you I'll find immediately . . . . . . ii 2 156
A calendar! look in the almanac; find out moonshine . . . . iii 1 55
Go swifter than the wind, And Helena of Athens look thou find . . iii 2 95
If but once thou show me thy grey light, I'll find Demetrius . . iii 2 420
Find out the forester; For now our observation is perform'd . . iv 1 108
Nothing in the world; Unless you can find sport in their intents . . v 1 79

Find. Comes Pyramus, sweet youth and tall, And finds his trusty Thisby's mantle *M. N. Dream* v 1 146
How chance Moonshine is gone before Thisbe comes back and finds her lover?—She will find him by starlight v 1 319
You shall seek all day ere you find them, and when you have them, they are not worth the search *Mer. of Venice* i 1 117
I shot his fellow of the self-same flight The self-same way with more advised watch, To find the other forth i 1 143
To find both Or bring your latter hazard back again i 1 150
Fast bind, fast find; A proverb never stale in thrifty mind ii 5 54
Justice! find the girl; She hath the stones upon her, and the ducats ii 8 21
Find him out And quicken his embraced heaviness With some delight ii 8 51
Too long a pause for that which you find there ii 9 53
I often came where I did hear of her, but cannot find her iii 1 86
The thief gone with so much, and so much to find the thief iii 1 97
If you do love me, you will find me out iii 2 41
What find I here? Fair Portia's counterfeit! iii 2 115
As I have ever found thee honest-true, So let me find thee still iii 4 47
He finds the joys of heaven here on earth iii 5 81
Do so much for charity.—I cannot find it; 'tis not in the bond iv 1 262
The dearest ring in Venice will I give you, And find it out by proclamation iv 1 436
There you shall find that Portia was the doctor, Nerissa there her clerk v 1 269
There you shall find three of your argosies Are richly come to harbour v 1 276
Which thou shalt find I will most kindly requite *As Y. Like It* i 1 144
The world esteem'd thy father honourable, But I did find him still mine enemy i 2 239
Finds tongues in trees, books in the running brooks, Sermons in stones ii 1 16
If he be absent, bring his brother to me; I'll make him find him ii 2 19
I could find in my heart to disgrace my man's apparel ii 4 4
And little recks to find the way to heaven By doing deeds of hospitality ii 4 81
I think he be transform'd into a beast; For I can no where find him like a man ii 7 2
Like a doe, I go to find my fawn And give it food ii 7 128
Go find him out, And we will nothing waste till you return ii 7 133
Find out thy brother, wheresoe'er he is; Seek him with candle iii 1 5
He that sweetest rose will find Must find love's prick and Rosalind iii 2 117
Now I find thy saw of might, 'Who ever loved that loved not at first sight?' iii 5 82
I'll go find a shadow and sigh till he come iv 1 222
We shall find a time, Audrey; patience, gentle Audrey v 1 1
How did you find the quarrel on the seventh cause? v 4 70
Fall to them as you find your stomach serves you *T. of Shrew* i 1 38
I will go sit and weep Till I can find occasion of revenge ii 1 36
Mistake me not; I speak but as I find ii 1 66
Ay, if the fool could find it where it lies ii 1 213
Let me go.—No, not a whit: I find you passing gentle ii 1 244
And now I find report a very liar ii 1 246
If once I find thee ranging, Hortensio will be quit with thee by changing iii 1 91
A groom indeed, A grumbling groom, and that the girl shall find iii 2 155
And that thou and the proudest of you all shall find when he comes home iv 1 90
Some undeserved fault I'll find about the making of the bed iv 1 203
Upon some agreement Me shall you find ready and willing iv 4 34
You shall find of the king a husband, madam *All's Well* i 1 7
And finds no other advantage in the process but only the losing of hope i 1 17
For I the ballad will repeat, Which men full true shall find i 3 65
We'ld find no fault with the tithe-woman, if I were the parson i 3 88
May lawfully make title to as much love as she finds i 3 108
Now I see The mystery of your loneliness, and find Your salt tears' head i 3 177
That seeks not to find that her search implies i 3 222
'Tis our hope, sir, After well enter'd soldiers, to return And find your grace in health ii 1 7
When The bravest questant shrinks, find what you seek ii 1 16
You shall find in the regiment of the Spinii one Captain Spurio ii 1 42
And in your bed Find fairer fortune, if you ever wed! ii 3 98
I find that she, which late Was in my nobler thoughts most base, is now The praised of the king ii 3 177
Thou shalt find what it is to be proud of thy bondage ii 3 239
Did you find me in yourself, sir? or were you taught to find me? ii 4 34
And much fool may you find in you, even to the world's pleasure ii 4 36
I cannot yet find in my heart to repent ii 5 13
Find you that there?—Ay, madam iii 2 78
If your lordship find him not a hilding, hold me no more in your respect iii 6 3
But when you find him out, you have him ever after iii 6 100
When his disguise and he is parted, tell me what a sprat you shall find him iii 6 113
I find my tongue is too foolhardy iv 1 32
Who is a whale to virginity and devours up all the fry it finds iv 3 250
If you could find out a country where but women were that had received so much shame iv 3 361
And you shall find yourself to be well thank'd, Whate'er falls more v 1 36
I saw the man to-day, if man he be.—Find him, and bring him hither v 3 204
Where did you find it, then?—I found it not v 3 275
In your denial I would find no sense; I would not understand it *T. Night* i 5 285
And fear to find Mine eye too great a flatterer for my mind i 5 327
There it lies in your eye; if not, be it his that finds it ii 2 17
And on that vice in him will my revenge find notable cause to work ii 3 166
He shall find himself most feelingly personated ii 3 172
I will plant you two . . . where he shall find the letter ii 3 189
Lay me, O, where Sad true lover never find my grave, To weep there! ii 4 66
Where shall I find you?—We'll call thee at the cubiculo iii 2 55
And you find so much blood in his liver as will clog the foot of a flea iii 2 65
Were my worth as is my conscience firm, You should find better dealing iii 3 18
He will find it comes from a clodpole iii 4 208
You'll find it otherwise, I assure you iii 4 251
Nothing of that wonderful promise, to read him by his form, as you are like to find him in the proof iii 4 291
And he finds that now scarce to be worth talking of iii 4 328
I could not find him at the Elephant: Yet there he was iv 3 5
I find it, And that to the infection of my brains *W. Tale* i 2 144
Which I fear the wolf will sooner find than the master iii 3 67
Care not for issue; The crown will find an heir v 1 47
I'll not seek far . . . to find thee An honourable husband v 3 142
Mine eye hath well examined his parts And finds them perfect *K. John* i 1 90
If lusty love should go in quest of beauty, Where should he find it fairer? ii 1 427
And all that we upon this side the sea . . . Find liable to our crown ii 1 490
And in her eye I find A wonder, or a wondrous miracle ii 1 496
Nothing do I see in you . . . That I can find should merit any hate ii 1 520
Well could I bear that England had this praise, So we could find some pattern of our shame iii 4 16
For he that steeps his safety in true blood Shall find but bloody safety iii 4 148
Rush forth, And bind the boy which you shall find with me iv 1 4

Find. I'll go with thee, And find the inheritance of this poor child *K. John* iv 2 97
I find the people strangely fantasied; Possess'd with rumours iv 2 144
I'll find a thousand shifts to get away iv 3 7
Mocking the air with colours idly spread, And find no check v 1 73
Strike up our drums, to find this danger out.—And thou shalt find it v 2 179
Why, here walk I in the black brow of night, To find you out v 6 18
Finds brotherhood in thee no sharper spur? *Richard II.* i 2 9
My heart will sigh when I miscall it so, Which finds it an inforced pilgrimage i 3 264
Find shapes of grief, more than himself, to wail ii 2 22
And I must find that title in your tongue, Before I make reply to aught ii 3 72
To find out right with wrong, it may not be ii 3 145
You will find it so; I speak no more than every one doth know iii 4 90
If thou wouldst, There shouldst thou find one heinous article iv 1 233
Nay, if I turn mine eyes upon myself, I find myself a traitor with the rest iv 1 248
And in this thought they find a kind of ease v 5 28
Find we a time for frighted peace to pant *1 Hen. IV.* i 1 2
Farewell: you shall find me in Eastcheap i 2 176
But I will find him when he lies asleep, And in his ear I'll holla i 3 221
When thou needest him, there thou shalt find him ii 2 75
I'll be sworn upon all the books in England, I could find in my heart ii 4 56
What starting-hole canst thou now find out to hide thee? ii 4 291
Find pardon on my true submission iii 2 28
Do not think so; you shall not find it so iii 2 129
Thou shalt find me tractable to any honest reason iii 3 194
Where shall I find one that can steal well? iii 3 211
His present want Seems more than we shall find it iv 1 45
They'll find linen enough on every hedge iv 2 52
To pry Into his title, the which we find Too indirect for long continuance iv 3 104
And find a time To punish this offence in other faults v 2 6
And thou shalt find a king that will revenge Lord Stafford's death v 3 12
Nay, you shall find no boy's play here, I can tell you v 4 76
Thus ever did rebellion find rebuke v 5 1
About it: you know where to find me *2 Hen. IV.* i 2 272
If we find outweighs ability, What do we then but draw anew the model? i 3 45
And now thou wouldst eat thy dead vomit up, And howl'st to find it i 3 100
Or it will seek me in another place And find me worse provided ii 3 50
Set them down: and see if thou canst find out Sneak's noise ii 4 12
Which should not find a ground to root upon, Unless on you iii 1 91
And find our griefs heavier than our offences iv 1 69
Our corn shall seem as light as chaff And good from bad find no partition iv 1 196
Find him, my Lord of Warwick; chide him hither iv 5 63
Though no man be assured what grace to find, You stand in coldest expectation v 2 30
To find his title with some shows of truth *Hen V.* i 2 72
And you shall find his vanities forespent Were but the outside ii 4 36
When you find him evenly derived From his most famed of famous ancestors ii 4 91
And, be assured, you'll find a difference ii 4 134
If I find a hole in his coat, I will tell him my mind iii 6 88
Then shall we find to-morrow they have only stomachs to eat and none to fight iii 7 165
You shall find, I warrant you, that there is no tiddle taddle iv 1 70
You shall find the ceremonies of the wars, and the cares of it iv 1 72
No, thou proud dream, That play'st so subtly with a king's repose; I am a king that find thee iv 1 276
Your nobles, jealous of your absence, Seek through your camp to find you iv 1 303
A many of our bodies shall no doubt Find native graves iv 3 96
You sall find, in the comparisons between Macedon and Monmouth iv 7 25
I would fain see the man, that has but two legs, that shall find himself aggriefed at this glove iv 7 170
You find it otherwise v 1 82
If thou couldst, thou wouldst find me such a plain king v 2 128
Thou shalt find the best king of good fellows v 2 261
And thou shalt find that I exceed my sex *1 Hen. VI.* i 2 90
Bring me word; And thou shalt find me at the governor's i 4 20
I find thou art no less than fame hath bruited ii 3 68
The truth appears so naked on my side That any purblind eye may find it out ii 4 21
I'll find friends to wear my bleeding roses ii 4 72
Ah, thou shalt find us ready for thee still ii 4 104
Or thou shouldst find thou hast dishonour'd me iii 1 9
And that we find the slothful watch but weak, I'll by a sign give notice iii 2 7
Sell every man his life as dear as mine, And they shall find dear deer of us iv 2 54
Now it is my chance to find thee out, Must I behold thy timeless cruel death? v 4 4
Ten to one We shall not find like opportunity v 4 158
With hope to find the like event in love v 5 105
I dare not say, from the rich cardinal . . ., Yet I do find it so *2 Hen. VI.* i 2 96
Well, sir, we must have you find your legs ii 1 147
'Tis that they seek, and they in seeking that Shall find their deaths ii 2 76
Let pale-faced fear keep with the mean-born man, And find no harbour in a royal heart iii 1 336
For in the shade of death I shall find joy iii 2 54
Who finds the heifer dead and bleeding fresh And sees fast by a butcher with an axe, But will suspect 'twas he that made the slaughter? iii 2 188
Who finds the partridge in the puttock's nest, But may imagine how the bird was dead? iii 2 191
Wheresoe'er thou art in this world's globe, I'll have an Iris that shall find thee out iii 2 407
Unless I find him guilty, he shall not die iv 2 103
If it be banish'd from the frosty head, Where shall it find a harbour? v 1 168
Wilt thou go dig a grave to find out war? v 1 169
Such safety finds The trembling lamb environed with wolves. *3 Hen. VI.* i 1 241
Not knowing how to find the open air, But toiling desperately to find it out iii 2 177
He shall here find his friends with horse and men iv 5 12
But when the fox hath once got in his nose, He'll soon find means to make the body follow iv 7 26
Shalt find Men well inclined to hear what thou command'st iv 8 15
It is his policy To haste thus fast, to find us unprovided v 4 63
Who finds Edward Shall have a high reward, and he his life v 5 9
She finds, although I cannot, Myself to be a marvellous proper man *Richard III.* i 2 254
I do find more pain in banishment Than death can yield me here i 3 168
If thou dost find him tractable to us, Encourage him iii 1 174
At Crosby Place, there shall you find us both iii 1 190
And hopes to find you forward Upon his party for the gain thereof iii 2 46
Finds the testy gentleman so hot, As he will lose his head ere give consent iii 4 39
You shall find me well accompanied With reverend fathers iii 5 99
Since that I myself Find in myself no pity to myself v 3 203

Find. Such as give Their money out of hope they may believe, May here find truth too *Hen. VIII.* Prol. 9
Bosom up my counsel, You 'll find it wholesome i 1 113
Almost with ravish'd listening, could not find His hour of speech a minute i 2 120
Call him to present trial: if he may Find mercy in the law, 'tis his i 2 212
Some of these Should find a running banquet ere they rested i 4 12
They should find easy penance.—Faith, how easy? i 4 17
Which they would have your grace Find out, and he will take it i 4 84
The cardinal instantly will find employment, And far enough from court too ii 1 48
Besides, You'll find a most unfit time to disturb him ii 2 61
Call Gardiner to me, my new secretary: I find him a fit fellow ii 2 117
Your graces find me here part of a housewife, I would be all iii 1 24
Let me speak myself, Since virtue finds no friends—a wife, a true one iii 1 126
Peace-makers, friends, and servants.—Madam, you'll find it so iii 1 168
Which I find at such proud rate, that it out-speaks Possession of a subject iii 2 127
Till I find more than will or words to do it iii 2 236
And, no doubt, In time will find their fit rewards iii 2 245
When it comes, Cranmer will find a friend will not shrink from him iv 1 107
I pray for heartily, that it may find Good time, and live v 1 21
Pray heaven, the king may never find a heart With less allegiance in it! v 3 42
I shall both find your lordship judge and juror, You are so merciful v 3 60
Men so noble, However faulty, yet should find respect For what they have been v 3 75
I had thought I had had men of some understanding And wisdom of my council; but I find none v 3 136
Go, break among the press, and find a way out To let the troop pass fairly; or I'll find A Marshalsea shall hold ye play these two months v 4 88
And the words I utter Let none think flattery, for they'll find 'em truth v 5 17
I have received much honour by your presence, And ye shall find me thankful v 5 73
Why should I war without the walls of Troy, That find such cruel battle here within? *Troi. and Cres.* i 1 3
The protractive trials of great Jove To find persistive constancy in men i 3 21
Feast with us before you go And find the welcome of a noble foe i 3 309
Will . . . find Hector's purpose Pointing on him i 3 330
Could you not find out that by her attributes? iii 1 37
Blind fear, that seeing reason leads, finds safer footing iii 2 77
Who do, methinks, find out Something not worth in me such rich beholding iii 3 90
Finds bottom in the uncomprehensive deeps, Keeps place with thought iii 3 198
We met by chance; you did not find me here iv 2 73
If I might in entreaties find success—As seld I have the chance iv 5 149
Mine own searching eyes Shall find him by his large and portly size iv 5 162
This fault in us I find, The error of our eye directs our mind v 2 109
Touching the weal o' the common, you shall find No public benefit which you receive But it proceeds or comes from them *Coriolanus* i 1 155
He that trusts to you, Where he should find you lions, finds you hares i 1 175
But, I think, you'll find They've not prepared for us i 2 29
Was pleased to let him seek danger where he was like to find fame i 3 14
What good condition can a treaty find I' the part that is at mercy? i 10 6
Where I find him, were it At home, upon my brother's guard, even there i 10 24
I find the ass in compound with the major part of your syllables ii 1 63
We hope to find you our friend; and therefore give you our voices heartily ii 3 111
This tiger-footed rage, when it shall find The harm of unscann'd swiftness, will too late Tie leaden pounds to's heels iii 1 312
Your ignorance, which finds not till it feels iii 3 129
I have a note from the Volscian state, to find you out there iv 3 11
Is this true, sir?—Ay; and you'll look pale Before you find it other iv 6 102
Who is't can blame him? Your enemies and his find something in him iv 6 106
We must find An evident calamity, though we had Our wish v 3 111
There is no more mercy in him than there is milk in a male tiger; that shall our poor city find v 4 31
We must proceed as we do find the people v 6 16
I'll find a day to massacre them all *T. Andron.* i 1 450
Sit fas aut nefas, till I find the stream To cool this heat ii 1 133
Yet have I heard,—O, could I find it now! ii 3 150
Now will I fetch the king to find them here ii 3 206
Brought hither in a most unlucky hour, To find thy brother Bassianus dead ii 3 252
Look, sirs, if you can find the huntsman out ii 3 278
Then which way shall I find Revenge's cave? iii 1 271
See how busily she turns the leaves! What would she find? iv 1 46
Jove, or Mercury, Inspire me, that I may this treason find! iv 1 67
And who should find them but the empress' villain? iv 3 73
I will find them out; And in their ears tell them my dreadful name v 2 38
Swift away, And find out murderers in their guilty caves v 2 52
I'll find some cunning practice out of hand v 2 77
When it is thy hap To find another that is like to thee, Good Rapine, stab him v 2 102
Oft have you heard me wish for such an hour, And now I find it v 2 161
Find those persons out Whose names are written there *Rom. and Jul.* i 2 35
I am sent to find those persons whose names are here writ, and can never find what names the writing person hath here writ i 2 42
Read o'er the volume of young Paris' face And find delight writ there i 3 82
And what obscured in this fair volume lies Find written in the margent of his eyes i 3 86
Turn back, dull earth, and find thy centre out ii 1 2
And the place death, considering who thou art, If any of my kinsmen find thee ii 2 65
And but thou love me, let them find me here ii 2 76
From her womb children of divers kind We sucking on her natural bosom find ii 3 12
Riddling confession finds but riddling shrift ii 3 56
Can any of you tell me where I may find the young Romeo? ii 4 125
And if I cannot, I'll find those that shall ii 4 161
You shall find me apt enough to that, sir, an you will give me occasion iii 1 44
Ask for me to-morrow, and you shall find me a grave man iii 1 102
O, find him! give this ring to my true knight iii 2 142
Till we can find a time To blaze your marriage iii 3 150
I'll find out your man, And he shall signify from time to time Every good hap iii 3 169
If you could find out but a man To bear a poison, I would temper it iii 5 97
Find thou the means, and I'll find such a man iii 5 104
I have a head, sir, that will find out logs iv 4 17
Going to find a bare-foot brother out, One of our order v 2 5
Go, some of you, whoe'er you find attach v 3 173
That heaven finds means to kill your joys with love v 3 293
I like your work; And you shall find I like it *T. of Athens* i 1 161
My relief Must not be toss'd and turn'd to me in words, But find supply ii 1 27

Find. That is, one may reach deep enough, and yet Find little *T. of Athens* iii 4 16
Where he shall find The unkindest beast more kinder than mankind iv 1 35
Thou spokest well of me.—Call'st thou that harm?—Men daily find it iv 3 174
Bid them flatter thee; O, thou shalt find— A fool of thee iv 3 232
Where feed'st thou o' days, Apemantus?—Where my stomach finds meat iv 3 294
Before black-corner'd night, Find what thou want'st by free and offer'd light v 1 48
Trouble him no further; thus you still shall find him v 1 216
Disrobe the images, If you do find them deck'd with ceremonies *J. Cæsar* i 1 70
And peep about To find ourselves dishonourable graves i 2 138
And find a time Both meet to hear and answer such high things i 2 169
You shall find That heaven hath infused them with these spirits i 3 68
Where haste you so?—To find out you i 3 134
Lay it in the prætor's chair, Where Brutus may but find it i 3 144
All this done, Repair to Pompey's porch, where you shall find us i 3 147
Where wilt thou find a cavern dark enough To mask thy monstrous visage? ii 1 80
They could not find a heart within the beast ii 2 40
Live a thousand years, I shall not find myself so apt to die iii 1 160
What, shall I find you here?—Or here, or at the Capitol iv 1 10
I do find it cowardly and vile, For fear of what might fall, so to prevent The time of life v 1 104
Come, Cassius' sword, and find Titinius' heart v 3 90
I shall find time, Cassius, I shall find time v 3 103
When you do find him, or alive or dead, He will be found like Brutus v 4 24
There's no art To find the mind's construction in the face *Macbeth* i 4 12
Do you find Your patience so predominant in your nature That you can let this go? iii 1 86
Thy soul's flight, If it find heaven, must find it out to-night iii 1 142
They should find What 'twere to kill a father iii 6 19
I hope, in no place so unsanctified Where such as thou mayst find him iv 2 82
What I can redress, As I shall find the time to friend, I will iv 3 10
I have lost my hopes.—Perchance even there where I did find my doubts iv 3 25
Receive what cheer you may: The night is long that never finds the day iv 3 240
If thou couldst, doctor, cast The water of my land, find her disease v 3 51
Do we but find the tyrant's power to-night, Let us be beaten, if we cannot fight v 6 7
Let me find him, fortune! And more I beg not v 7 22
I this morning know Where we shall find him most conveniently *Hamlet* i 1 175
I find thee apt i 5 31
With windlasses and with assays of bias, By indirections find directions out ii 1 66
He seem'd to find his way without his eyes ii 1 98
And now remains That we find out the cause of this effect ii 2 101
If circumstances lead me, I will find Where truth is hid ii 2 157
Anon he finds him Striking too short at Greeks ii 2 490
He will by no means speak.—Nor do we find him forward to be sounded iii 1 7
If she find him not, To England send him iii 1 193
I have sent to seek him, and to find the body iv 3 1
If your messenger find him not there, seek him i' the other place yourself iv 3 36
If you find him not within this month, you shall nose him as you go up the stairs into the lobby iv 3 37
But greatly to find quarrel in a straw When honour's at the stake iv 4 55
If by direct or by collateral hand They find us touch'd iv 5 207
The crowner hath sat on her, and finds it Christian burial v 1 5
Why may not imagination trace the noble dust of Alexander, till he find it stopping a bung-hole? v 1 225
In the dark Groped I to find out them v 2 14
You shall find in him the continent of what part a gentleman would see v 2 115
I find she names my very deed of love; Only she comes too short *Lear* i 1 73
And find I am alone felicitate In your dear highness' love i 1 77
Thou losest here, a better where to find i 1 264
For so much as I have perused, I find it not fit for your o'er-looking i 2 39
I begin to find an idle and fond bondage in the oppression of aged tyranny i 2 51
Convey the business as I shall find means, and acquaint you withal i 2 110
Yet nature finds itself scourged by the sequent effects i 2 114
Find out this villain, Edmund; it shall lose thee nothing i 2 124
So may it come, thy master, whom thou lovest, Shall find thee full of labours i 4 7
If I speak like myself in this, let him be whipped that first finds it so i 4 180
Thou shalt find That I'll resume the shape which thou dost think I have cast off for ever i 4 330
He which finds him shall deserve our thanks ii 1 63
And shall find time From this enormous state ii 2 175
All's not offence that indiscretion finds And dotage terms so ii 4 199
You shall find Some that will thank you iii 1 36
Let the great gods, That keep this dreadful pother o'er our heads, Find out their enemies now iii 2 51
If I find him comforting the king, it will stuff his suspicion more fully iii 5 21
And thou shalt find a dearer father in my love iii 5 26
To this chair bind him. Villain, thou shalt find iii 7 34
If you do find him, pray you, give him this iv 5 33
So to use them As we shall find their merits and our safety v 3 44
If't be your pleasure and most wise consent, As partly I find it is *Othello* i 1 123
That you shall surely find him, Lead to the Sagittary the raised search i 1 158
And must be driven To find out practices of cunning hell i 3 102
If you do find me foul in her report i 3 117
I do agnize A natural and prompt alacrity I find in hardness i 3 234
Let me find a charter in your voice, To assist my simpleness i 3 246
She will find the error of her choice: she must have change i 3 357
She has no speech.—In faith, too much; I find it still, when I have list to sleep ii 1 105
If she be black, and thereto have a wit, She'll find a white that shall her blackness fit ii 1 134
Her delicate tenderness will find itself abused ii 1 235
Do you find some occasion to anger Cassio ii 1 274
And bring him jump when he may Cassio find Soliciting his wife ii 3 392
I will in Cassio's lodging lose this napkin, And let him find it iii 3 322
But now I find I had suborn'd the witness, And he's indicted falsely iii 4 153
If I do find him fit, I'll move your suit And seek to effect it iii 4 166
A likely piece of work, that you should find it in your chamber! iv 1 157
I do not find that thou dealest justly with me.—What in the contrary? iv 2 173
And returned me expectations and comforts of sudden respect and acquaintance, but I find none iv 2 193
I think it is scurvy, and begin to find myself fopped in it iv 2 197
I am sorry to find you thus: I have been to seek you v 1 81
Then must thou needs find out new heaven, new earth *Ant. and Cleo.* i 1 17
Find me to marry me with Octavius Cæsar i 2 28
If you find him sad, Say I am dancing; if in mirth, report That I am sudden sick i 3 3

Find. You shall find there A man who is the abstract of all faults *A. and C.* i 4 8
So find we profit By losing of our prayers . . . ii 1 7
Your mother came to Sicily and did find Her welcome friendly . . ii 6 46
You shall find, the band that seems to tie their friendship together will be the very strangler of their amity . . . . ii 6 128
Who seeks, and will not take when once 'tis offer'd, Shall never find it more . . . . ii 7 90
You shall not find, Though you be therein curious, the least cause For what you seem to fear . . . . . . iii 2 34
I will employ thee back again; I find thee Most fit for business . iii 3 39
Should I find them So saucy with the hand of she here,—what's her name? . . . . iii 13 97
Say that I wish he never find more cause To change a master . iv 5 15
With your speediest bring us what she says, And how you find of her . v 1 68
You shall find A conqueror that will pray in aid for kindness . . v 2 26
You do extend These thoughts of horror further than you shall Find cause . . . . v 2 64
You shall find A benefit in this change . . . . . v 2 127
You shall not find me, daughter, After the slander of most stepmothers, Evil-eyed unto you . . . . . . *Cymbeline* i 1 70
As welcome, worthy sir, as I Have words to bid you, and shall find it so i 6 30
You'll give me leave to spare, when you shall find You need it not . ii 4 65
Could I find out The woman's part in me! . . . . ii 5 19
Would show the Britons cold: So Cæsar shall not find them . . . iii 1 77
You shall find us in our salt-water girdle . . . . . iii 1 80
We find The sharded beetle in a safer hold Than is the full-wing'd eagle iii 3 19
You shall find me, wretched man, a thing The most disdain'd of fortune iii 4 19
Shalt hereafter find It is no act of common passage, but A strain of rareness . . . . iii 4 93
I'll have this secret from thy heart, or rip Thy heart to find it . . iii 5 87
To Milford go, And find not her whom thou pursuest . . . iii 5 166
When resty sloth Finds the down pillow hard . . . . . iii 6 35
I cannot find those runagates; that villain Hath mock'd me . . iv 2 62
O melancholy! Who ever yet could sound thy bottom? find The ooze? iv 2 204
That we the horrider may seem to those Which chance to find us . . iv 2 332
Let us Find out the prettiest daisied plot we can . . . . iv 2 398
These present wars shall find I love my country . . . . iv 3 43
What pleasure, sir, find we in life, to lock it From action and adventure? iv 4 2
Who find in my exile the want of breeding, The certainty of this hard life . . . . iv 4 26
I, in mine own woe charm'd, Could not find death where I did hear him groan. . . . Well, I will find him . . . . . v 3 69
So graze as you find pasture.—Ay, or a stomach . . . v 4 2
Poor wretches that depend On greatness' favour dream as I have done, Wake and find nothing . . . . v 4 129
Shall, to himself unknown, without seeking find . . v 4 139; v 5 436
He shall be happy that can find him, if Our grace can make him so . v 5 6
He, true knight, No lesser of her honour confident Than I did truly find her, stakes this ring . . . . v 5 188
If in the world he live, we'll seek him out; If in his grave he rest, we'll find him there . . . . *Pericles* ii 4 30
Thy loss is more than can thy portage quit, With all thou canst find here . . . . iii 1 36
Who finds her, give her burying; She was the daughter of a king . iii 2 72
Whom our fast-growing scene must find At Tarsus . . . iv Gower 6
When he shall come and find Our paragon to all reports thus blasted . iv 1 35
Tell me, how dost thou find the inclination of the people? . . . iv 2 104
Yet I find It greets me as an enterprise of kindness . . . . iv 3 37
This is an honourable man.—I desire to find him so . . . iv 6 55
I doubt not but I shall find them tractable enough . . . . iv 6 211
Finder. And crown thee for a finder of madmen . . . *T. Night* iii 4 154
A slipper and subtle knave, a finder of occasions . . *Othello* ii 1 246
Finder out. Had I been the finder out of this secret . *W. Tale* v 2 131
Findest. Where fires thou find'st unraked and hearths unswept *M. Wives* v 5 48
To him in thine own voice, and bring me word how thou findest him *T. Night* iv 2 72
When thou find'st a man that's like thyself, Good Murder, stab him *T. An.* v 2 99
Take thy fortune; Thou find'st to be too busy is some danger *Hamlet* iii 4 33
Give the letters which thou find'st about me To Edmund . . *Lear* iv 6 254
Find-faults. The liberty that follows our places stops the mouth of all find-faults . . . . *Hen. V.* v 2 298
Like or find fault; do as your pleasures are . . *Troi. and Cres.* Prol. 30
Finding yourself desired of such a person . . *Meas. for Meas.* ii 4 91
Who, being overjoyed with finding a birds' nest, shows it his companion, and he steals it . . . . . . *Much Ado* ii 1 230
Finding barren practisers, Scarce show a harvest of their heavy toil *L. L. Lost* iv 3 325
But take a taste of my finding him, and relish it . *As Y. Like It* iii 2 247
I must be A party in this alteration, finding Myself thus alter'd with't *W. Tale* i 2 383
Go you the next way with your findings . . . . . iii 3 132
Finding thee fit for bloody villany, Apt, liable to be employ'd *K. John* iv 2 225
Finding his usurpation most unjust, Endeavour'd my advancement *1 Hen. VI.* ii 5 68
There cannot be That vulture in you, to devour so many As will to greatness dedicate themselves, Finding it so inclined . *Macbeth* iv 3 76
And finding By this encompassment and drift of question That they do know my son . . . . *Hamlet* ii 1 9
Finding ourselves too slow of sail, we put on a compelled valour . iv 6 16
Finding Who 'twas that so endured, with his strong arms He fasten'd on my neck, and bellow'd out . . . . . *Lear* v 3 210
And finding little comfort to relieve them, I thought it princely charity to grieve them . . . . *Pericles* i 2 99
Fine. How fine my master is! . . . . . . *Tempest* v 1 262
A knight well-spoken, neat and fine . . . *T. G. of Ver.* i 2 10
If the devil have him not in fee-simple, with fine and recovery *M. Wives* iv 2 225
Mine were the very cipher of a function, To fine the faults whose fine stands in record, And let go by the actor . . *Meas. for Meas.* ii 2 40
May he not do it by fine and recovery?—Yes, to pay a fine for a periwig and recover the lost hair of another man . . *Com. of Errors* ii 2 75
The fine is, for the which I may go the finer, I will live a bachelor *M. Ado* i 1 247
For a fine, quaint, graceful and excellent fashion, yours is worth ten on't . . . . iii 4 22
Or study where to meet some mistress fine . . . *L. L. Lost* i 1 63
Such rackers of orthography, as to speak dout, fine, when he should say doubt . . . . v 1 22
Are there but three?—No, sir; but it is vara fine, For every one pursents three . . . . v 2 487
Fine, i' faith! Have you no modesty, no maiden shame? *M. N. Dream* iii 2 284
Speak of frays Like a fine bragging youth, and tell quaint lies *M. of Ven.* iii 4 69

Fine. Which humbleness may drive unto a fine . *Mer. of Venice* iv 1 372
To quit the fine for one half of his goods, I am content 381
I will be sure my Katharine shall be fine . . . *T. of Shrew* ii 1 319
There were none fine but Adam, Ralph, and Gregory . . . iv 1 139
Let her in fine consent, As we'll direct her . . . *All's Well* iii 7 19
In fine, delivers me to fill the time, Herself most chastely absent . . iii 7 33
In fine, made a groan of her last breath . . . . . iv 3 62
Still the fine's the crown; Whate'er the course, the end is the renown . iv 4 35
In fine, Her infinite cunning, with her modern grace, Subdued me to her rate . . . . v 3 215
Thou art too fine in thy evidence; therefore stand aside . . . v 3 270
We shall Present our services to a fine new prince One of these days *W. Tale* ii 1 17
Your breathing shall expire, Paying the fine of rated treachery Even with a treacherous fine of all your lives . . . *K. John* v 4 37
Therefore, thou best of gold art worst of gold: Other, less fine in carat, is more precious . . . . *2 Hen. IV.* iv 5 162
But thou, most fine, most honour'd, most renown'd, Hast eat thy bearer up . . . . iv 5 164
A cup of wine, sir?—A cup of wine that's brisk and fine . . v 3 48
O'ercharging your free purses with large fines . . . *1 Hen. VI.* i 3 64
In fine, redeem'd I was as I desired . . . . . . i 4 34
And on your heads Clap round fines for neglect . . . *Hen. VIII.* v 4 84
Some joy too fine, Too subtle-potent, tuned too sharp in sweetness *Troi. and Cres.* iii 2 24
The grief is fine, full, perfect, that I taste . . . . iv 4 3
Be it either For death, for fine, or banishment, then let them, If I say fine, cry 'Fine;' if death, cry 'Death' . . . *Coriolanus* iii 3 15
What faults he made before the last, I think Might have found easy fines v 6 65
If I profane with my unworthiest hand This holy shrine, the gentle fine is this . . . . *Rom. and Jul.* i 5 96
But I'll amerce you with so strong a fine That you shall all repent . iii 1 195
And he will make the face of heaven so fine That all the world will be in love with night . . . . iii 2 23
Thy verse swells with stuff so fine and smooth . . *T. of Athens* v 1 87
In fine Makes vow before his uncle never more To give the assay *Hamlet* ii 2 69
As wholesome as sweet, and by very much more handsome than fine . ii 2 467
Nature is fine in love, and where 'tis fine, It sends some precious instance of itself After the thing it loves . . . . . . iv 5 161
Bring you in fine together And wager on your heads . . . iv 7 134
Is this the fine of his fines, and the recovery of his recoveries? . . v 1 115
And in fine withdrew To mine own room again . . . . v 2 15
First Or last, your fine Egyptian cookery Shall have the fame *A. and C.* ii 6 64
How fine this tyrant Can tickle where she wounds! . *Cymbeline* i 1 84
Such gain the cap of him that makes 'em fine, Yet keeps his book uncross'd . . . . iii 3 25
Fine a story. Was't not to this end That thou began'st to twist so fine a story? . . . . *Much Ado* i 1 313
Fine age. If speaking truth In this fine age were not thought flattery *1 Hen. IV.* iv 1 2
Fine apparition! My quaint Ariel, Hark in thine ear . *Tempest* i 2 317
Fine Ariel. It works. Come on. Thou hast done well, fine Ariel! . i 2 494
Fine array. We will have rings and things and fine array *T. of Shrew* ii 1 325
Fine-baited. Lead him on with a fine-baited delay . *Mer. Wives* ii 1 99
Fine change. Hark, what fine change is in the music! *T. G. of Ver.* iv 2 68
Fine chisel. What fine chisel Could ever yet cut breath? *W. Tale* v 3 78
Fine colour. With some fine colour that may please the eye *1 Hen. IV* v 1 75
Fine dirt. To have his fine pate full of fine dirt . . *Hamlet* v 1 116
Fine fancies. Be attent, And time that is so briefly spent With your fine fancies quaintly eche . . . . . *Pericles* iii Gower 13
Fine figure. A most fine figure! . . . . . *L. L. Lost* i 2 58
Fine fool. I was a fine fool to take it . . . . *Othello* iv 1 155
Fine foot. By her fine foot, straight leg . . . *Rom. and Jul.* ii 1 19
Fine forehead. Sweet lord, thou hast a fine forehead *Troi. and Cres.* iii 1 117
Fine frame. In your fine frame hath love no quality? *All's Well* iv 2 4
O, she that hath a heart of that fine frame To pay this debt of love but to a brother, How will she love! . . . . *T. Night* i 1 33
Fine frenzy. The poet's eye, in a fine frenzy rolling . *M. N. Dream* v 1 12
Fine hand. Ye have made a fine hand, fellows . . *Hen. VIII.* v 4 74
Fine hats. With delicate fine hats and most courteous feathers *All's W.* iv 5 111
Fine hawk. I have a fine hawk for the bush . . *Mer. Wives* iii 3 247
Fine issues. Spirits are not finely touch'd But to fine issues *M. for M.* i 1 37
Fine joints. Fettle your fine joints 'gainst Thursday next *Rom. and Jul.* iii 5 154
Fine linen, Turkey cushions boss'd with pearl . *T. of Shrew* ii 1 355
Fine musician. A fine musician to instruct our mistress . . i 2 174
For, but I be deceived, Our fine musician groweth amorous . . iii 1 63
Fine one. 'Tis a noble Lepidus.—A very fine one . *Ant. and Cleo.* iii 2 7
Fine pate. To have his fine pate full of fine dirt . . *Hamlet* v 1 116
Fine revolution. Here's fine revolution, an we had the trick to see't . v 1 98
Fine shoot. A' shot a fine shoot . . . . *2 Hen. IV.* iii 2 49
Fine spirit! I'll free thee Within two days for this . *Tempest* i 2 420
Fine spot. What are you sewing here? A fine spot, in good faith *Coriol.* i 3 56
Fine strains. Thou hast affected the fine strains of honour . . v 3 149
Fine thief. O for a fine thief, of the age of two and twenty! *1 Hen. IV.* iii 3 211
Fine things. These be fine things, an if they be not sprites *Tempest* ii 2 121
Fine tragedy. It would have been a fine tragedy: and so it is *M. N. D.* v 1 367
Fine villain. O fine villain! A silken doublet! a velvet hose! *T. of Shrew* v 1 68
Fine volley. A fine volley of words, gentlemen . *T. G. of Ver.* ii 4 33
Fine wit. I warrant they would whip me with their fine wits *Mer. Wives* iv 5 102
I said, thou hadst a fine wit: 'True,' said she, 'a fine little one' *M. Ado* v 1 161
Fine woman. A fine woman! a fair woman! a sweet woman! *Othello* iv 1 189
Fine word,—legitimate! . . . . *Lear* i 2 18
Fine workman. In respect of a fine workman, I am but, as you would say, a cobbler . . . . *J. Cæsar* i 1 10
Fined. Why would he for the momentary trick Be perdurably fined? *Meas. for Meas.* iii 1 115
The nobles hath he fined For ancient quarrels . . *Richard II.* ii 1 247
Know'st thou not That I have fined these bones of mine for ransom? *Hen. V.* iv 7 72
Fineless. Riches fineless is as poor as winter To him that ever fears he shall be poor . . . . *Othello* iii 3 173
Finely. Go brew me a pottle of sack finely.—With eggs, sir? *Mer. Wives* iii 5 30
My Nan shall be the queen of all the fairies, Finely attired in a robe of white . . . . iv 4 72
We'll betray him finely . . . . v 3 22
Spirits are not finely touch'd But to fine issues . *Meas. for Meas.* i 1 36
Finely put off! . . . . *L. L. Lost* iv 1 118
Finely put on, indeed! . . . . iv 1 118
We will turn it finely off, sir . . . . . . v 2 511
How say you to a fat tripe finely broil'd? . . . *T. of Shrew* iv 3 20

Finely. Such and so finely bolted didst thou seem . . . *Hen. V.* ii 2 137
Fineness. Here's the note How much your chain weighs to the utmost carat, The fineness of the gold . . *Com. of Errors* iv 1 29
The fineness of which metal is not found In fortune's love *Troi. and Cres.* i 3 22
Or those that with the fineness of their souls By reason guide . . i 3 209
Finer. And the fine is, for the which I may go the finer, I will live a bachelor . . . . *Much Ado* i 1 248
He draweth out the thread of his verbosity finer than the staple of his argument . . . . *L. L. Lost* v 1 19
Your accent is something finer than you could purchase in so removed a dwelling . . . . *As Y. Like It* iii 2 359
I'll confine myself no finer than I am . . . . *T. Night* i 3 10
Not noted, is't, But of the finer natures? . . . . *W. Tale* i 2 226
A' made a finer end and went away an it had been any christom child *Hen. V.* ii 3 11
Finest. So eating love Inhabits in the finest wits of all . *T. G. of Ver.* i 1 44
Her husband hath the finest mad devil of jealousy in him *Mer. Wives* v 1 19
Any toys for your head, Of the new'st and finest, finest wear-a? *W. Tale* iv 4 327
The Trojans taste our dear'st repute With their finest palate *T. and C.* i 3 338
Her passions are made of nothing but the finest part of pure love *A. and C.* i 2 152
Finger. And the devil take your fingers! . . . . . *Tempest* iii 2 89
Come, put some lime upon your fingers . . . . . . iv 1 247
Lay-to your fingers: help to bear this away . . . . . iv 1 251
Though his false finger have profaned the ring . . *T. G. of Ver.* iv 4 141
But I'll ne'er put my finger in the fire, and need not . . *Mer. Wives* i 4 91
If I see a sword out, my finger itches to make one . . . . ii 3 48
He shall not knit a knot in his fortunes with the finger of my substance iii 2 76
The duke Dare no more stretch this finger of mine than he Dare rack his own: his subject am I not . . . . . *Meas. for Meas.* v 1 316
No longer will I be a fool, To put the finger in the eye and weep *C. of E.* ii 2 206
And took away my ring—The ring I saw upon his finger now . . iv 4 142
He did, and from my finger snatch'd that ring . . . . . . v 1 276
And with his royal finger, thus, dally with my excrement . *L. L. Lost* v 1 109
With his finger and his thumb, Cried, 'Via! we will do't, come what will' v 2 111
I will kiss thy royal finger, and take leave . . . . . . v 2 891
Let him hold his fingers thus, and through that cranny shall Pyramus and Thisby whisper . . . . *M. N. Dream* iii 1 72
Good Master Cobweb: if I cut my finger, I shall make bold with you . . iii 1 186
The female ivy so Enrings the barky fingers of the elm . . . iv 1 49
You may tell every finger I have with my ribs . . *Mer. of Venice* ii 2 114
When this ring Parts from this finger, then parts life from hence . . iii 2 186
A thing stuck on with oaths upon your finger . . . . . . v 1 168
Nor pluck it from his finger, for the wealth That the world masters . v 1 173
But you see my finger Hath not the ring upon it; it is gone . . . v 1 187
I had as lief thou didst break his neck as his finger . *As Y. Like It* i 1 153
Wrapp'd in sweet clothes, rings put upon his fingers . *T. of Shrew* Ind. 1 38
A pretty peat! it is best Put finger in the eye, an she knew why . . i 1 79
That I'll prove upon thee, though thy little finger be armed in a thimble iv 3 149
Here's my passport. 'When thou canst get the ring upon my finger which never shall come off' . . . . *All's Well* iii 2 60
And on your finger in the night I'll put Another ring . . . . iv 2 61
Such a ring as this, The last that e'er I took her leave at court, I saw upon her finger . . . . v 3 80
She call'd the saints to surety That she would never put it from her finger, Unless she gave it to yourself in bed . . . . . . v 3 109
What ring was yours, I pray you?—Sir, much like The same upon your finger . . . . v 3 226
And not worthy to touch Fortune's fingers . . . . . *T. Night* ii 5 171
But to be paddling palms and pinching fingers . . . . *W. Tale* i 2 115
His smiles, The very mould and frame of hand, nail, finger . . . ii 3 103
And ring these fingers with thy household worms . . . *K. John* iii 4 31
None of you will bid the winter come, To thrust his icy fingers in my maw v 7 37
Whereto my finger, like a dial's point, Is pointing still . . *Richard II.* v 5 53
And 'twixt his finger and his thumb he held A pouncet-box . 1 *Hen. IV.* i 3 37
I'll break thy little finger, Harry, An if thou wilt not tell me . . ii 3 90
Unless you call three fingers on the ribs bare . . . . . . iv 2 80
They never prick their finger but they say, 'There's some of the king's blood spilt' . . . . 2 *Hen. IV.* ii 2 121
I have him already tempering between my finger and my thumb . iv 3 141
One spark of evil That might annoy my finger . . . . *Hen. V.* ii 2 102
'Tis all one, 'tis alike as my fingers is to my fingers . . . . iv 7 32
Prick not your finger as you pluck it off . . . . 1 *Hen. VI.* ii 4 49
I kiss these fingers for eternal peace . . . . v 3 48
And with my fingers feel his hand unfeeling . . . 2 *Hen. VI.* iii 2 145
Thou art far the lesser; Thy hand is but a finger to my fist . . . iv 10 51
Hold, Clifford! do not honour him so much To prick thy finger, though to wound his heart . . . . 3 *Hen. VI.* i 4 55
Look, how this ring encompasseth thy finger, Even so thy breast encloseth my poor heart . . . . *Richard III.* i 2 204
No man's pie is freed From his ambitious finger . . . *Hen. VIII.* i 1 53
Stops on a sudden, looks upon the ground, Then lays his finger on his temple . . . . iii 2 115
Where a finger Could not be wedged in more . . . . . . v 4 37
Do you think, my lords, The king will suffer but the little finger Of this man to be vex'd? . . . . v 3 106
Now let me see the proudest He, that dares most, but wag his finger at thee v 3 131
Why, this hath not a finger's dignity . . . . *Troi. and Cres.* i 3 204
Peace, Trojan; lay thy finger on thy lips! . . . . iv 5 240
Do not, porpentine, do not: my fingers itch . . . . . . ii 1 27
His stubborn buckles, With these your white enchanting fingers touch'd iii 1 164
I would your cambric were sensible as your finger . . . *Coriolanus* i 3 95
He turned me about with his finger and his thumb, as one would set up a top . . . . iv 5 160
If it be possible for you to displace it with your little finger . . . v 4 5
Upon his bloody finger he doth wear A precious ring . . *T. Andron.* ii 3 226
And he hath cut those pretty fingers off, That could have better sew'd than Philomel . . . . ii 4 42
A round little worm Prick'd from the lazy finger of a maid *Rom. and Jul.* i 4 66
O'er lawyers' fingers, who straight dream on fees, O'er ladies' lips . . i 4 73
Speak not, reply not, do not answer me; My fingers itch . . . . iii 5 165
You shall have none ill, sir; for I'll try if they can lick their fingers iv 2 4
Marry, sir, 'tis an ill cook that cannot lick his own fingers: therefore he that cannot lick his fingers goes not with me . . . . iv 2 7
To take thence from her dead finger A precious ring . . . . . v 3 30
But must not break my back to heal his finger . . *T. of Athens* ii 2 24
To my thinking, he was very loath to lay his fingers off it . *J. Cæsar* i 2 243
To see thy Antony making his peace, Shaking the bloody fingers of thy foes iii 1 198
Shall we now Contaminate our fingers with base bribes? . . . . iv 3 24
You seem to understand me, By each at once her choppy finger laying Upon her skinny lips . . . . *Macbeth* i 3 44
Finger. Finger of birth-strangled babe Ditch-deliver'd by a drab *Macbeth* iv 1 30
Still your fingers on your lips, I pray . . . . . *Hamlet* i 5 188
They are not a pipe for fortune's finger To sound what stop she please iii 2 75
Govern these ventages with your fingers and thumb, give it breath . iii 2 373
For a pair of reechy kisses, Or paddling in your neck with his damn'd fingers . . . . iii 4 185
Our cold maids do dead men's fingers call them . . . . . . iv 7 172
I prithee, take thy fingers from my throat . . . . v 1 283
It had been better you had not kissed your three fingers so oft *Othello* ii 1 174
Yet again your fingers to your lips? would they were clyster-pipes! . ii 1 177
Lay thy finger thus, and let thy soul be instructed . . . . . ii 1 223
Let our finger ache, and it indues Our other healthful members even to that sense Of pain . . . . iii 4 146
A fixed figure for the time of scorn To point his slow unmoving finger at! iv 2 55
My ring I hold dear as my finger; 'tis part of it . . . *Cymbeline* i 4 145
That diamond upon your finger, say How came it yours? . . . . v 5 137
Wager'd with him Pieces of gold 'gainst this which then he wore Upon his honour'd finger . . . . v 5 184
The fingers of the powers above do tune The harmony of this peace . v 5 466
She weaved the sleided silk With fingers long, small, white as milk *Pericles* iv Gower 22
Finger end. With trial-fire touch me his finger-end . . *Mer. Wives* v 5 88
Thou hast it ad dunghill, at the fingers' ends, as they say.—O, I smell false Latin . . . . *L. L. Lost* v 1 81
Ay, sir, I have them at my fingers' ends: marry, now I let go your hand, I am barren . . . . *T. Night* i 3 83
And pick strong matter of revolt and wrath Out of the bloody fingers' ends of John . . . . *K. John* iii 4 168
I saw him fumble with the sheets and play with flowers and smile upon his fingers' ends . . . . *Hen. V.* ii 3 16
Fingered. The king was slily finger'd from the deck . . 3 *Hen. VI.* v 1 44
Finger'd their packet, and in fine withdrew To mine own room *Hamlet* v 2 15
Who, finger'd to make man his lawful music, Would draw heaven down, and all the gods, to hearken . . . . *Pericles* i 1 82
Fingering. Go get you gone, and let the papers lie: You would be fingering them, to anger me . . . . *T. G. of Ver.* i 2 101
And bow'd her hand to teach her fingering . . . . *T. of Shrew* ii 1 151
To learn the order of my fingering, I must begin with rudiments of art iii 1 65
Come on; tune: if you can penetrate her with your fingering, so *Cymb.* ii 3 16
Fingre. Les doigts? je pense qu'ils sont appelés de fingres; oui, de fingres *Hen. V.* iii 4 11
Dites-moi, si je parle bien: de hand, de fingres, et de nails . . . iii 4 18
Finical. Superserviceable, finical rogue . . . . *Lear* ii 2 19
Finish. You sheep, and I pasture: shall that finish the jest? *L. L. Lost* ii 1 221
Feed yourselves with questioning; That reason wonder may diminish, How thus we met, and these things finish . . . . . *As Y. Like It* v 4 146
God may finish it when he will, 'tis not a hair amiss yet . 2 *Hen. IV.* i 2 27
His days may finish ere that hapless time . . . . 1 *Hen. VI.* iii 1 201
Ere the glass, that now begins to run, Finish the process of his sandy hour iv 2 36
How many days will finish up the year . . . . . 3 *Hen. VI.* ii 5 28
Which, being dried with grief, will break to powder, And finish all foul thoughts . . . . *Ant. and Cleo.* iv 9 18
Finish, good lady; the bright day is done, And we are for the dark . v 2 193
I had you down and might Have made you finish . . . *Cymbeline* v 5 412
Finished. The nuptial finish'd, Let him be whipt and hang'd *M. for M.* v 1 518
I took him sleeping,—that is finish'd too . . . . *M. N. Dream* iii 2 38
He finished indeed his mortal act That day . . . . . *T. Night* v 1 254
The half part of a blessed man, Left to be finished by such as she *K. John* ii 1 438
It is not well done, mark you now, to take the tales out of my mouth, ere it is made and finished . . . . *Hen. V.* iv 7 46
What he bids be done is finished with his bidding . . . *Coriolanus* v 4 24
Fear not slander, censure rash;—Thou hast finish'd joy and moan *Cymb.* iv 2 273
Who with wet cheeks Were present when she finish'd . . . . . v 5 36
Her monument Is almost finish'd . . . . *Pericles* iv 3 43
Finisher. He that of greatest works is finisher Oft does them by the weakest minister . . . . *All's Well* ii 1 139
Finless. A dragon and a finless fish . . . . . . 1 *Hen. IV.* iii 1 151
Finny. How from the finny subject of the sea These fishers tell the infirmities of men! . . . . *Pericles* ii 1 52
Finsbury. As if thou never walk'st further than Finsbury 1 *Hen. IV.* iii 1 257
Firago. He's a very devil; I have not seen such a firago . *T. Night* iii 4 302
Fire. The sea, mounting to the welkin's cheek, Dashes the fire out *Tempest* i 2 5
To fly, To swim, to dive into the fire . . . . i 2 191
The fire and cracks Of sulphurous roaring the most mighty Neptune Seem to besiege and make his bold waves tremble . . . . i 2 203
He does make our fire, Fetch in our wood and serves in offices . . i 2 311
The strongest oaths are straw To the fire i' the blood . . . . iv 1 53
To the dread rattling thunder Have I given fire . . . . . . v 1 45
Fire that's closest kept burns most of all . . . . *T. G. of Ver.* i 2 30
I shunn'd the fire for fear of burning, And drench'd me in the sea . . i 3 78
Yourself, sweet lady; for you gave the fire . . . . ii 4 38
Like a waxen image 'gainst a fire, Bears no impression of thing it was . ii 4 201
Thou wouldst as soon go kindle fire with snow As seek to quench the fire of love with words . . . . ii 7 19
I do not seek to quench your love's hot fire, But qualify the fire's extreme rage, Lest it should burn above the bounds of reason . . . . ii 7 21
At the latter end of a sea-coal fire . . . . *Mer. Wives* i 4 10
But I'll ne'er put my finger in the fire, and need not . . . . . i 4 91
Up with your fights: Give fire: she is my prize, or ocean whelm them all! ii 2 143
I think the devil will not have me damned, lest the oil that's in me should set hell on fire . . . . v 5 40
Where fires thou find'st unraked and hearths unswept, There pinch the maids . . . . v 5 48
Come, will this wood take fire? . . . . v 5 92
Lust is but a bloody fire, Kindled with unchaste desire . . . . . v 5 99
Let us every one go home, And laugh this sport o'er by a country fire . v 5 256
They appear to men like angels of light: light is an effect of fire, and fire will burn; ergo, light wenches will burn . . *Com. of Errors* iv 3 57
Unquiet meals make ill digestions; Thereof the raging fire of fever bred v 1 75
Whose beard they have singed off with brands of fire . . . . . v 1 171
Is the opinion that fire cannot melt out of me . . . . *Much Ado* i 1 234
She would have made Hercules have turned spit, yea, and have cleft his club to make the fire too . . . . ii 1 262
Like cover'd fire, Consume away in sighs, waste inwardly . . . . iii 1 77
What fire is in mine ears? Can this be true? . . . . iii 1 107
And in her eye there hath appear'd a fire, To burn the errors . . . iv 1 164
'Tis won as towns with fire, so won, so lost . . . . *L. L. Lost* i 1 147
Fire enough for a flint, pearl enough for a swine: 'tis pretty; it is well iv 2 90
Which, not to anger bent, is music and sweet fire . . . . . . iv 2 120
The academes From whence doth spring the true Promethean fire . iv 3 304

Fire. From women's eyes this doctrine I derive: They sparkle still the right Promethean fire . . . *L. L. Lost* iv 3 351
And stand between her back, sir, and the fire, Holding a trencher . v 2 476
By that fire which burn'd the Carthage queen . . . *M. N. Dream* i 1 173
Thorough flood, thorough fire, I do wander every where . . ii 1 5
And run through fire I will for thy sweet sake . . . ii 2 103
Sometime a horse I'll be, sometime a hound, A hog, a headless bear, sometime a fire; And neigh, and bark, and grunt, and roar, and burn, Like horse, hound, hog, bear, fire, at every turn . . iii 1 112
Through the house give glimmering light, By the dead and drowsy fire v 1 399
Where Phœbus' fire scarce thaws the icicles . . *Mer. of Venice* ii 1 5
Where is the horse that doth untread again His tedious measures with the unbated fire That he did pace them first? . . . . . ii 6 11
The fire seven times tried this . . . . ii 9 63
There may as well be amity and life 'Tween snow and fire . . iii 2 31
When Nature hath made a fair creature, may she not by Fortune fall into the fire? . . . . *As Y. Like It* i 2 47
That the property of rain is to wet and fire to burn . . . iii 2 28
A woman's tongue, That gives not half so great a blow to hear As will a chestnut in a farmer's fire . . . . . *T. of Shrew* i 2 210
Where two raging fires meet together They do consume the thing that feeds their fury . . . . ii 1 133
Though little fire grows great with little wind, Yet extreme gusts will blow out fire and all . . . . ii 1 135
I am sent before to make a fire, and they are coming after to warm them iv 1 4
My heart in my belly, ere I should come by a fire to thaw me: but I, with blowing the fire, shall warm myself . . . . . iv 1 9
And therefore fire, fire; cast on no water . . . . . iv 1 20
Wilt thou make a fire, or shall I complain on thee to our mistress? . iv 1 31
And therefore fire: do thy duty, and have thy duty . . . iv 1 38
There's fire ready; and therefore, good Grumio, the news . . iv 1 41
Why, therefore fire; for I have caught extreme cold . . . iv 1 46
They sit conferring by the parlour fire . . . . . . v 2 102
And make you dance canary With spritely fire and motion . *All's Well* ii 1 78
O you leaden messengers, That ride upon the violent speed of fire . iii 2 112
Yet in his idle fire, To buy his will, it would not seem too dear . iii 7 26
I am a woodland fellow, sir, that always loved a great fire; and the master I speak of ever keeps a good fire . . . . . iv 5 50
The flowery way that leads to the broad gate and the great fire . iv 5 58
I' the blaze of youth; When oil and fire, too strong for reason's force, O'erbears it and burns on . . . . v 3 7
With groans that thunder love, with sighs of fire . . *T. Night* i 5 275
To put fire in your heart, and brimstone in your liver . . iii 2 21
As doth that orbed continent the fire That severs day from night . . v 1 278
Say that she were gone, Given to the fire, a moiety of my rest Might come to me again . . . . *W. Tale* ii 3 8
Hence with it, and together with the dam Commit them to the fire! . ii 3 95
It is an heretic that makes the fire, Not she which burns in't . . ii 3 115
Take it hence And see it instantly consumed with fire . . . ii 3 134
Go, take it to the fire; For thou set'st on thy wife . . . . ii 3 140
What wheels? racks? fires? what flaying? boiling? In leads or oils? . iii 2 177
Though a devil Would have shed water out of fire ere done't . . iii 2 194
Her face o' fire With labour and the thing she took to quench it . iv 4 60
Bullets wrapp'd in fire, To make a shaking fever in your walls *K. John* ii 1 227
How high thy glory towers, When the rich blood of kings is set on fire! ii 1 351
He speaks plain cannon fire, and smoke and bounce . . . ii 1 462
Falsehood falsehood cures, as fire cools fire . . . . . iii 1 277
Thou shalt turn To ashes, ere our blood shall quench that fire . . iii 1 345
Consume away in rust, But for containing fire to harm mine eye . iv 1 66
The fire is dead with grief, Being create for comfort . . . iv 1 106
Only you do lack That mercy which fierce fire and iron extends . iv 1 120
With eyes as red as new-enkindled fire . . . . . . iv 2 163
Be stirring as the time; be fire with fire; Threaten the threatener . v 1 48
And brought in matter that should feed this fire . . . . v 2 85
Even as a form of wax Resolveth from his figure 'gainst the fire . v 4 25
I am a scribbled form, drawn with a pen Upon a parchment, and against this fire Do I shrink up . . . . v 7 33
Full of ire, In rage deaf as the sea, hasty as fire . . *Richard II.* i 1 19
Hath love in thy old blood no living fire? . . . . . i 2 10
O, who can hold a fire in his hand By thinking on the frosty Caucasus? i 3 294
For violent fires soon burn out themselves . . . . . ii 1 34
From under this terrestrial ball He fires the proud tops of the eastern pines iii 2 42
Be he the fire, I'll be the yielding water . . . . . iii 3 58
In winter's tedious nights sit by the fire With good old folks . . v 1 40
The senseless brands will sympathize The heavy accent of thy moving tongue And in compassion weep the fire out . . . . . v 1 48
That hand shall burn in never-quenching fire . . . . . v 5 109
The rebels have consumed with fire Our town of Cicester . . . v 6 2
The heavens were all on fire, the earth did tremble . *1 Hen. IV.* iii 1 24
You are as slow As hot Lord Percy is on fire to go . . . . iii 1 269
My oath should be 'By this fire, that's God's angel' . . . iii 3 39
I have maintained that salamander of yours with fire . . . iii 3 53
I am on fire To hear this rich reprisal is so nigh And yet not ours . iv 1 117
But Priam found the fire ere he his tongue . . . *2 Hen. IV.* i 1 74
Whose spirit lent a fire Even to the dullest peasant in his camp . . i 1 112
Took fire and heat away From the best-temper'd courage in his troops . i 1 114
Impatient of his fit, breaks like a fire Out of his keeper's arms . . i 1 142
Sitting in my Dolphin-chamber, at the round table, by a sea-coal fire . ii 1 96
Fear we broadsides? no, let the fiend give fire . . . . ii 4 196
Their eyes of fire sparkling through sights of steel . . . . iv 1 121
Ere this year expire, We bear our civil swords and native fire As far as France . . . . v 5 112
O for a Muse of fire, that would ascend The brightest heaven of invention, A kingdom for a stage! . . . . . . *Hen. V.* Prol. 1
And at his heels, Leash'd in like hounds, should famine, sword and fire Crouch for employment . . . . Prol. 7
With blood and sword and fire to win your right . . . . i 2 131
Now all the youth of England are on fire . . . . . ii Prol. 1
For I can take, and Pistol's cock is up, And flashing fire will follow . ii 1 56
The fuel is gone that maintained that fire . . . . . ii 3 46
His face is all bubukles, and whelks, and knobs, and flames o' fire: and his lips blows at his nose, and it is like a coal of fire . . . iii 6 109
It is a beast for Perseus: he is pure air and fire . . . . iii 7 22
Fire answers fire, and through their paly flames Each battle sees the other's umber'd face . . . . iv Prol. 8
Like sacrifices, by their watchful fires Sit patiently and inly ruminate iv Prol. 23
His sparkling eyes, replete with wrathful fire . . . *1 Hen. VI.* i 1 12
My three attendants, Lean famine, quartering steel, and climbing fire . iv 2 11
When from the Dauphin's crest thy sword struck fire, It warm'd thy father's heart with proud desire . . . . iv 6 10

Fire. The time of night when Troy was set on fire . . *2 Hen. VI.* i 4 20
This spark will prove a raging fire, If wind and fuel be brought to feed it iii 1 302
And now the house of York, thrust from the crown, . . . Burns with revenging fire . . . . iv 1 97
I fear neither sword nor fire . . . . iv 2 63
He should stand in fear of fire, being burnt i' the hand for stealing of sheep . . . . iv 2 67
Set London bridge on fire; and, if you can, burn down the Tower too . iv 6 16
Tears virginal Shall be to me even as the dew to fire . . . v 2 53
That fires all my breast, And burns me up with flames . . *3 Hen. VI.* ii 1 83
As red as fire! . . . . iii 2 51
A little fire is quickly trodden out; Which, being suffer'd, rivers cannot quench . . . . iv 8 7
I need not add more fuel to your fire, For well I wot ye blaze to burn them out . . . . v 4 70
Know you not, The fire that mounts the liquor till't run o'er, In seeming to augment it wastes it? . . . . *Hen. VIII.* i 1 144
My drops of tears I'll turn to sparks of fire . . . . . ii 4 73
Ye blew the fire that burns ye: now have at ye! . . . . v 3 113
There was more temperate fire under the pot of her eyes *Troi. and Cres.* i 2 160
If there be not in our Grecian host One noble man that hath one spark of fire . . . . i 3 294
Come in, come in: I'll go get a fire . . . . . . iii 2 63
When we vow to weep seas, live in fire, eat rocks, tame tigers . . iii 2 84
It lies as coldly in him as fire in a flint . . . . . iii 3 257
Hoy-day! spirits and fires! . . . . v 1 72
You are no surer, no, Than is the coal of fire upon the ice . *Coriolanus* i 1 177
They'll sit by the fire, and presume to know What's done i' the Capitol i 1 195
Or, by the fires of heaven, I'll leave the foe And make my wars on you i 4 39
This . . . will be his fire To kindle their dry stubble . . . ii 1 273
The fires i' the lowest hell fold-in the people! Call me their traitor! . iii 3 68
O'erborne their way, consumed with fire, and took What lay before them iv 6 78
One fire drives out one fire; one nail, one nail; Rights by rights falter iv 7 54
Titleless, Till he had forged himself a name o' the fire Of burning Rome v 1 14
You'll see your Rome embraced with fire before You'll speak with Coriolanus . . . . v 2 7
Can you think to blow out the intended fire your city is ready to flame in, with such weak breath as this? . . . . v 2 49
My son! thou art preparing fire for us; look thee, here's water to quench it . . . . v 2 77
Is it most certain?—As certain as I know the sun is fire . . . v 4 48
Praise the gods, And make triumphant fires . . . . . v 5 3
Away with him! and make a fire straight . . . . *T. Andron.* i 1 127
And entrails feed the sacrificing fire . . . . i 1 144
Set fire on barns and hay-stacks in the night, And bid the owners quench them with their tears . . . . v 1 133
Would I were a devil, To live and burn in everlasting fire! . . . v 1 148
Quench the fire of your pernicious rage With purple fountains *R. and J.* i 1 91
Feather of lead, bright smoke, cold fire, sick health! Still-waking sleep! i 1 186
Love is a smoke raised with the fume of sighs; Being purged, a fire sparkling in lovers' eyes . . . . i 1 197
One fire burns out another's burning . . . . i 2 46
When the devout religion of mine eye Maintains such falsehood, then turn tears to fires! . . . . i 2 94
Quench the fire, the room is grown too hot . . . . . . i 5 30
In their triumph die, like fire and powder, Which as they kiss consume ii 6 10
The fire i' the flint Shows not till it be struck . . . *T. of Athens* i 1 22
Like those that under hot ardent zeal would set whole realms on fire . iii 3 34
Let your close fire predominate his smoke, And be no turncoats . . iv 3 142
Whereon Hyperion's quickening fire doth shine . . . . . iv 3 184
The moon's an arrant thief, And her pale fire she snatches from the sun iv 3 441
I am glad that my weak words Have struck but thus much show of fire from Brutus . . . . *J. Cæsar* i 2 177
Never till to-night, never till now, Did I go through a tempest dropping fire . . . . i 3 10
And yet his hand, Not sensible of fire, remain'd unscorch'd . . . i 3 18
Who swore they saw Men all in fire walk up and down the streets . . i 3 25
Why all these fires, why all these gliding ghosts . . . . . i 3 63
Those that with haste will make a mighty fire Begin it with weak straws i 3 107
Two months hence up higher toward the north He first presents his fire ii 1 110
Fire enough To kindle cowards and to steel with valour The melting spirits of women . . . . ii 1 120
These lowly courtesies Might fire the blood of ordinary men . . iii 1 37
The skies are painted with unnumber'd sparks, They are all fire . . iii 1 64
As fire drives out fire, so pity pity . . . . iii 1 171
Poor soul! his eyes are red as fire with weeping . . . . iii 2 120
We'll burn his body in the holy place, And with the brands fire the traitors' houses . . . . iii 2 260
Go fetch fire.—Pluck down benches.—Pluck down forms . . . iii 2 262
You are yoked with a lamb That carries anger as the flint bears fire . iv 3 111
With this she fell distract, And, her attendants absent, swallow'd fire . iv 3 156
Are those my tents where I perceive the fire? . . . . . v 3 13
The conquerors can but make a fire of him . . . . . . v 5 55
Stars, hide your fires; Let not light see my black and deep desires *Macb.* i 4 50
What hath quench'd them hath given me fire . . . . . ii 2 2
A woman's story at a winter's fire, Authorized by her grandam . . iii 4 65
Double, double toil and trouble; Fire burn, and cauldron bubble . iv 1 11
As stars with trains of fire and dews of blood, Disasters in the sun *Ham.* i 1 117
Whether in sea or fire, in earth or air, The extravagant and erring spirit hies To his confine . . . . i 1 153
These blazes, daughter, . . . You must not take for fire . . . i 3 120
And for the day confined to fast in fires . . . . . . i 5 11
The glow-worm shows the matin to be near, And 'gins to pale his uneffectual fire . . . . i 5 90
Doubt thou the stars are fire; Doubt that the sun doth move . . ii 2 116
This majestical roof fretted with golden fire . . . . . ii 2 313
Roasted in wrath and fire, And thus o'ersized with coagulate gore . ii 2 483
What, frighted with false fire! . . . . iii 2 277
Let virtue be as wax, And melt in her own fire . . . . iii 4 85
In passages of proof, Time qualifies the spark and fire of it . . iv 7 114
I have a speech of fire, that fain would blaze, But that this folly douts it iv 7 191
Let all the battlements their ordnance fire . . . . . v 2 281
He must be whipped out, when Lady the brach may stand by the fire *Lear* i 4 126
Bring oil to fire, snow to their colder moods . . . . . ii 2 83
Like the wreath of radiant fire On flickering Phœbus' front . . ii 2 113
Thought-executing fires, Vaunt-couriers to oak-cleaving thunderbolts . iii 2 4
Rumble thy bellyful! Spit, fire! spout, rain! . . . . . iii 2 14
Nor rain, wind, thunder, fire, are my daughters: I tax not you, you elements . . . . iii 2 15
Such sheets of fire, such bursts of horrid thunder . . . . iii 2 46

Fire. Through fire and through flame, and through ford and whirlpool *Lear* iii 4 52
Now a little fire in a wild field were like an old lecher's heart . iii 4 116
Look, here comes a walking fire . . . . iii 4 119
And bring you where both fire and food is ready . . . iii 4 158
Stop her there! Arms, arms, sword, fire! Corruption in the place! iii 6 58
The sea . . . would have buoy'd up, And quench'd the stelled fires iii 7 61
Mine enemy's dog, Though he had bit me, should have stood that night Against my fire . . . . iv 7 38
Thou art a soul in bliss; but I am bound Upon a wheel of fire iv 7 47
He that parts us shall bring a brand from heaven, And fire us hence like foxes . . . . v 3 23
As when, by night and negligence, the fire Is spied in populous cities *Othello* i 1 76
Give renew'd fire to our extincted spirits, And bring all Cyprus comfort! ii 1 81
If there be cords, or knives, Poison, or fire, or suffocating streams, I'll not endure it . . . . iii 3 389
Thou art rash as fire, to say That she was false: O, she was heavenly true! . . . . v 2 134
Roast me in sulphur! Wash me in steep-down gulfs of liquid fire! v 2 280
By the fire That quickens Nilus' slime . . . *Ant. and Cleo.* i 3 68
Then shall the sighs of Octavia blow the fire up in Cæsar . ii 6 136
And shot their fires Into the abysm of hell . . . iii 13 146
I would they'ld fight i' the fire or i' the air; We'ld fight there too . iv 10 3
I am fire and air; my other elements I give to baser life . . v 2 292
Made Lud's town with rejoicing fires bright . . *Cymbeline* iii 1 32
When they hear the Roman horses neigh, Behold their quarter'd fires . iv 4 18
I stand on fire: Come to the matter.—All too soon I shall . v 5 168
That were to blow at fire in hope to quench it . . *Pericles* i 4 4
Like a glow-worm in the night, The which hath fire in darkness, none in light . . . . ii 3 44
A fire from heaven came and shrivell'd up Their bodies, even to loathing ii 4 9
Thou hast as chiding a nativity As fire, air, water, earth, and heaven can make . . . . iii 1 33
No light, no fire: the unfriendly elements Forgot thee utterly . iii 1 58
Get fire and meat for these poor men: 'T has been a turbulent and stormy night . . . . iii 2 3
Make a fire within: Fetch hither all my boxes in my closet . . iii 2 80
If fires be hot, knives sharp, or waters deep . . . iv 2 159
Fire and brimstone!—O, peace, peace! . . . . *T. Night* ii 5 56
Fire and brimstone!—My lord?—Are you wise? . . *Othello* iv 1 245
Fire and sword. Thou hadst fire and sword on thy side, and yet thou rannest away . . . . *1 Hen. IV.* ii 4 348
Fire and water. A woman would run through fire and water for such a kind heart . . . . *Mer. Wives* iii 4 107
With no less terror than the elements Of fire and water, when their thundering shock At meeting tears the cloudy cheeks of heaven *Richard II.* iii 3 56
Fire of grace. An the fire of grace be not quite out of thee, now shalt thou be moved . . . . *1 Hen. IV.* ii 4 421
Fire of injuries. Burns With an incensed fire of injuries 2 *Hen. IV.* i 3 14
Fire of life. Death may usurp on nature many hours, And yet the fire of life kindle again The o'erpress'd spirits . . *Pericles* iii 2 83
Fire of love. As soon go kindle fire with snow As seek to quench the fire of love with words . . . . . . *T. G. of Ver.* ii 7 20
My riches to the earth from whence they came; But my unspotted fire of love to you . . . . *Pericles* i 1 53
Fire of lust. Till the wicked fire of lust have melted him in his own grease *Mer. Wives* ii 1 68
Fire of passion. If with the sap of reason you would quench, Or but allay, the fire of passion . . . . . . *Hen. VIII.* i 1 149
Fire of rage. The fire of rage is in him, and 'twere good You lean'd unto his sentence . . . . *Cymbeline* i 1 77
Fire of youth. If the quick fire of youth light not your mind, You are no maiden, but a monument . . . . . *All's Well* iv 2 5
Firebrand. Lead me, like a firebrand, in the dark Out of my way *Tempest* ii 2 6
Althæa dreamed she was delivered of a fire-brand . 2 *Hen. IV.* ii 2 97
Our firebrand brother, Paris, burns us all . *Troi. and Cres.* ii 2 110
Ho! fire-brands: to Brutus', to Cassius'; burn all . *J. Cæsar* iii 3 41
Fired. Is that lead slow which is fired from a gun? . *L. L. Lost* iii 1 63
As hasty powder fired Doth hurry from the fatal cannon's womb *R. and J.* v 1 64
Be like a beacon fired to amaze your eyes . . . *Pericles* i 4 87
Fire-drake. That fire-drake did I hit three times on the head *Hen. VIII.* v 4 45
Fire-eyed maid of smoky war . . . . . *1 Hen. IV.* iv 1 114
And fire-eyed fury be my conduct now! . . *Rom. and Jul.* iii 1 129
Fire-new. A man of fire-new words, fashion's own knight *L. L. Lost* i 1 179
Some excellent jests, fire-new from the mint . . *T. Night* iii 2 23
Your fire-new stamp of honour is scarce current . *Richard III.* i 3 256
Despite thy victor sword and fire-new fortune, Thy valour . *Lear* v 3 132
Fire-robed. The fire-robed god, Golden Apollo . . *W. Tale* iv 4 29
Fire-shovel. They stole a fire-shovel: I knew by that piece of service the men would carry coals . . . . *Hen. V.* iii 2 48
Firework. Some delightful ostentation, or show, or pageant, or antique, or firework . . . . *L. L. Lost* v 1 119
Those remnants Of fool and feather that they got in France, With all their honourable points of ignorance Pertaining thereunto, as fights and fireworks . . . . *Hen. VIII.* i 3 27
Firing. Nor fetch in firing At requiring; Nor scrape trencher *Tempest* ii 2 185
Firk. I'll fer him, and firk him, and ferret him . . *Hen. V.* iv 4 29
I do not know the French for fer, and ferret, and firk . iv 4 33
Firm. Who was so firm, so constant, that this coil Would not infect his reason? . . . . *Tempest* i 2 207
You are already Love's firm votary And cannot soon revolt *T. G. of Ver.* iii 2 58
For it is as positive as the earth is firm that Falstaff is there *M. Wives* iii 2 49
The firm fixture of thy foot would give an excellent motion to thy gait in a semi-circled farthingale . . . . iii 3 67
As firm as faith . . . . iv 4 10
Her mother, ever strong against that match And firm for Doctor Caius iv 6 28
A man of stricture and firm abstinence . . . *Meas. for Meas.* i 3 12
Her wits, I fear me, are not firm . . . . v 1 33
As there is no firm reason to be render'd, Why he cannot abide a gaping pig; Why he, a harmless necessary cat . . *Mer. of Venice* iv 1 53
Firm and irrevocable is my doom . . . . *As Y. Like It* i 3 85
Nor is your firm resolve unknown to me . . . *T. of Shrew* ii 1 93
The maid is mine from all the world, By your firm promise . ii 1 387
Were my worth as is my conscience firm . . *T. Night* iii 3 17
My grief's so great That no supporter but the huge firm earth Can hold it up: here I and sorrows sit . . . . . *K. John* iii 1 72
Wherefore we took the sacrament And keep our faiths firm and inviolable v 2 7
Showing, as in a model, our firm estate . . . *Richard II.* iii 4 42

Firm. Our peace shall stand as firm as rocky mountains . 2 *Hen. IV.* iv 1 188
Thou art not firm enough, since griefs are green . . . iv 5 204
A soldier, firm and sound of heart, And of buxom valour . *Hen. V.* iii 6 25
Thou art framed of the firm truth of valour . . . . . iv 3 14
And then in sequel all, According to their firm proposed natures . v 2 362
Throws away his crutch Before his legs be firm . 2 *Hen. VI.* ii 1 190
Let us hear your firm resolve . . . . 3 *Hen. VI.* iii 3 129
But answer me one doubt, What pledge have we of thy firm loyalty? . iii 3 239
The compact is firm and true in me . . . . *Richard III.* ii 2 133
Look your faith be firm, Or else his head's assurance is but frail . iv 4 497
Then though my heart's content firm love doth bear, Nothing of that shall from mine eyes appear . . . *Troi. and Cres.* i 2 320
There can be no evasion To blench from this and to stand firm by honour ii 2 68
You know now your hostages; your uncle's word and my firm faith . iv 1 116
Firm of word, Speaking in deeds and deedless in his tongue . . iv 5 97
For who so firm that cannot be seduced? . . . *J. Cæsar* i 2 316
Take any shape but that, and my firm nerves Shall never tremble *Macb.* iii 4 102
Cool it with a baboon's blood, Then the charm is firm and good . iv 1 38
Let not ever The soul of Nero enter this firm bosom . *Hamlet* iii 2 412
Nothing: I have sworn; I am firm . . . . . *Lear* i 1 248
Think on that, And fix most firm thy resolution . . *Othello* v 1 5
Say, the firm Roman to great Egypt sends This treasure *Ant. and Cleo.* i 5 43
And Give up yourself merely to chance and hazard, From firm security iii 7 49
Very many there could behold the sun with as firm eyes as he *Cymbeline* i 4 13
The heavens hold firm The walls of thy dear honour! . . . ii 1 67
Firmament. I am not to say it is a sea, for it is now the sky: betwixt the firmament and it you cannot thrust a bodkin's point . *W. Tale* iii 3 86
I see thy glory like a shooting star Fall to the base earth from the firmament. Thy sun sets weeping . . . *Richard II.* ii 4 20
Hath the firmament more suns than one?—What boots it thee? *T. Andron.* v 3 17
The northern star, Of whose true-fix'd and resting quality There is no fellow in the firmament . . . . *J. Cæsar* iii 1 62
This brave o'erhanging firmament, this majestical roof . . *Hamlet* ii 2 312
I should have been that I am, had the maidenliest star in the firmament twinkled on my bastardizing . . . . *Lear* i 2 144
Firmly. A secure fool, and stands so firmly on his wife's frailty *M. Wives* ii 1 242
How I firmly am resolved you know . . . . *T. of Shrew* i 1 49
As firmly as yourself were still in place . . . . . i 2 157
I firmly vow Never to woo her more . . . . . . iv 2 28
I had hope of France As firmly as I hope for fertile England 2 *Hen. VI.* i 1 88
At last I firmly am resolved . . . . . 3 *Hen. VI.* iii 3 219
Now he firmly takes me for Revenge . . . . *T. Andron.* v 2 73
I will maintain My truth and honour firmly . . . *Lear* v 3 101
Firmness. Nor partialize The unstooping firmness of my upright soul *Richard II.* i 1 121
Make mountains level, and the continent, Weary of solid firmness, melt itself Into the sea! . . . . 2 *Hen. IV.* iii 1 48
Firm-set. Thou sure and firm-set earth, Hear not my steps . *Macbeth* ii 1 56
First. At that time Through all the signories it was the first *Tempest* i 2 71
When thou camest first, Thou strokedst me . . . . . i 2 332
For I am all the subjects that you have, Which first was mine own king i 2 342
This Is the third man that e'er I saw, the first That e'er I sigh'd for . i 2 445
Which, of he or Adrian, for a good wager, first begins to crow? . ii 1 29
Our garments are now as fresh as when we put them on first in Afric ii 1 69
There thou mayst brain him, Having first seized his books . . iii 2 97
Remember First to possess his books; for without them He's but a sot iii 2 100
Let's alone And do the murder first . . . . . . iv 1 232
I did say so, When first I raised the tempest . . . . v 1 6
Tight and yare and bravely rigg'd as when We first put out to sea . v 1 225
First, you have learned, like Sir Proteus, to wreathe your arms *T. G. of V.* ii 1 18
That power which gave me first my oath Provokes me to this threefold perjury . . . . ii 6 4
At first I did adore a twinkling star, But now I worship a celestial sun ii 6 9
For scorn at first makes after-love the more . . . . iii 1 95
Thy first best love, For whose dear sake thou didst then rend thy faith v 4 46
Mistress Anne, yourself shall go first.—Not I, sir . *Mer. Wives* i 1 320
Truly, I will not go first; truly, la! I will not do you that wrong . i 1 322
Here's the twin-brother of thy letter: but let thine inherit first . ii 1 75
I will first make bold with your money . . . . . ii 2 262
I think I shall drink in pipe-wine first with him . . . iii 2 91
I suffered the pangs of three several deaths; first, an intolerable fright iii 5 110
I'll first direct my men what they shall do with the basket . iv 2 101
A fault done first in the form of a beast . . . . . v 5 9
First, an it like you, the house is a respected house . *Meas. for Meas.* ii 1 169
Those many had not dared to do that evil, If the first that did the edict infringe Had answer'd for his deed . . . . ii 2 92
So you must be the first that gives this sentence, And he, that suffers . ii 2 106
Refer yourself to this advantage, first, that your stay with him may not be long . . . . iii 1 255
You'll forswear this again.—I'll be hanged first . . . iii 2 178
First, here's young Master Rash . . . . iv 3 4
First, his integrity Stands without blemish . . . . . v 1 107
First, hath this woman Most wrongfully accused your substitute . v 1 139
First, let her show her face, and after speak . . . . v 1 168
First, provost, let me bail these gentle three . . . . v 1 362
Whipt first, sir, and hanged after . . . . v 1 513
I could not speak with Dromio since at first I sent him . *Com. of Errors* ii 2 5
Every why hath a wherefore.—Why, first,—for flouting me; and then, wherefore,—For urging it the second time to me . . . . ii 2 46
But, like a shrew, you first begin to brawl . . . . iv 1 51
First he denied you had in him no right . . . . . iv 2 7
First he did praise my beauty, then my speech . . . . iv 2 15
Heard you confess you had the chain of him After you first forswore it v 1 261
Antipholus, thou camest from Corinth first? . . . . . v 1 362
We'll draw cuts for the senior: till then lead thou first . . v 1 422
The fraud of men was ever so, Since summer first was leavy . *Much Ado* ii 3 75
That's impossible: she may wear her heart out first . . . ii 3 210
You must hang it first, and draw it afterwards . . . . iii 2 24
First, who think you the most desartless man to be constable? . iii 3 9
I tell this tale vilely:—I should first tell thee . . . . iii 3 158
Partly by his oaths, which first possessed them . . . . iii 3 166
In faith, I will go.—We'll be friends first . . . . . iv 1 299
Write down, that they hope they serve God: and write God first . iv 2 21
He shall kill two of us, and men indeed: But that's no matter; let him kill one first . . . . v 1 81
First, I ask thee what they have done; thirdly, I ask thee what's their offence . . . . v 1 225
Now thy image doth appear In the rare semblance that I loved it first . v 1 260
Tell me for which of my bad parts didst thou first fall in love with me? v 2 60
But for which of my good parts did you first suffer love for me? . v 2 65

First. We'll have dancing afterward.—First, of my word *Much Ado* v 4 123
The first and second cause will not serve my turn *L. L. Lost* i 2 183
I shall know, sir, when I have done it.—Why, villain, thou must know first iii 1 160
What, what? first praise me and again say no? iv 1 14
Am I the first that have been perjured so? iv 3 51
Consider what you first did swear unto iv 3 291
Love, first learned in a lady's eyes, Lives not alone immured in the brain iv 3 327
But be first advised, In conflict that you get the sun of them iv 3 368
First, from the park let us conduct them thither iv 3 374
Since love's argument was first on foot, Let not the cloud of sorrow justle it v 2 757
First, good Peter Quince, say what the play treats on *M. N. Dream* i 2 8
So, with two seeming bodies, but one heart; Two of the first iii 2 213
Make choice of which your highness will see first v 1 43
The trusty Thisby, coming first by night v 1 141
First, rehearse your song by rote, To each word a warbling note v 1 404
Shoot another arrow that self way Which you did shoot the first *M. of V.* i 1 149
Bring your latter hazard back again And thankfully rest debtor for the first i 1 152
First, forward to the temple: after dinner Your hazard shall be made ii 1 44
Where is the horse that doth untread again His tedious measures with the unbated fire That he did pace them first? ii 6 12
The first, of gold, who this inscription bears ii 7 4
First, never to unfold to any one Which casket 'twas I chose ii 9 10
When I did first impart my love to you, I freely told you iii 2 256
First go with me to church and call me wife iii 2 305
I will anon: first, let us go to dinner iii 5 91
Every offence is not a hate at first iv 1 68
You taught me first to beg; and now methinks You teach me how a beggar should be answer'd iv 1 439
You shall not entreat him to a second, that have so mightily persuaded him from a first *As Y. Like It* i 2 219
You touch'd my vein at first ii 7 94
Till he be first sufficed, . . . I will not touch a bit ii 7 131
At first the infant, Mewling and puking in the nurse's arms ii 7 143
You must borrow me Gargantua's mouth first iii 2 239
The common executioner . . . Falls not the axe upon the humbled neck But first begs pardon iii 5 6
I would kiss before I spoke.—Nay, you were better speak first iv 1 73
The first, the Retort Courteous; the second, the Quip Modest v 4 96
Pisa renowned for grave citizens Gave me my being and my father first, A merchant of great traffic *T. of Shrew* i 1 11
Both our inventions meet and jump in one.—Tell me thine first i 1 196
But I will charm him first to keep his tongue i 1 214
I should knock you first, And then I know after who comes by the worst i 2 13
Whom would to God I had well knock'd at first i 2 34
The first's for me; let her go by i 2 256
And will not promise her to any man Until the elder sister first be wed i 2 263
I knew you at the first You were a moveable ii 1 197
Sunday is the wedding-day.—I'll see thee hang'd on Sunday first ii 1 301
I am your neighbour, and was suitor first ii 1 336
First, as you know, my house within the city Is richly furnished ii 1 348
First were we sad, fearing you would not come; Now sadder iii 2 100
'Tis like you'll prove a jolly surly groom, That take it on you at the first so roundly iii 2 216
I pray thee, news.—First, know, my horse is tired iv 1 56
What, master, read you? first resolve me that iv 2 7
First, tell me, have you ever been at Pisa? iv 2 93
Let's follow, to see the end of this ado.—First kiss me, Kate, and we will v 1 148
And he whose wife is most obedient To come at first when he doth send for her, Shall win the wager v 2 68
Come on, I say; and first begin with her v 2 133
There was never virgin got till virginity was first lost *All's Well* i 1 140
As when thy father and myself in friendship First tried our soldiership i 2 26
You are loved, sir; They that least lend it you shall lack you first i 2 68
He was first smoked by the old lord Lafeu iii 6 111
First, give me trust, the count he is my husband iii 7 8
First demand of him how many horse the duke is strong iv 3 148
Put it up again.—Nay, I'll read it first, by your favour iv 3 244
Not altogether so great as the first in goodness iv 3 320
His majesty, out of a self-gracious remembrance, did first propose iv 5 78
O my good lord, you were the first that found me!—Was I, in sooth? and I was the first that lost thee v 2 45
At first I stuck my choice upon her, ere my heart Durst make too bold a herald of my tongue v 3 44
Here we'll stay To see our widower's second marriage-day.—Which better than the first, O dear heaven, bless! v 3 71
You, that have turn'd off a first so noble wife, May justly diet me v 3 220
O, when mine eyes did see Olivia first, Methought she purged the air of pestilence! *T. Night* i 1 19
In his bosom! In what chapter of his bosom?—To answer by the method, in the first of his heart i 5 244
Best first go see your lodging.—I am not weary iii 3 20
Though I struck him first, yet it's no matter for that iv 1 38
I would I were the first that ever dissembled in such a gown iv 2 6
The captain that did bring me first on shore Hath my maid's garments v 1 281
It was she First told me thou wast mad v 1 357
If you first sinn'd with us and that with us You did continue fault *W. T.* i 2 84
My last good deed was to entreat his stay: What was my first? i 2 98
Your highness Will take again your queen as yours at first i 2 336
Let him that makes but trifles of his eyes First hand me ii 3 63
On mine own accord I'll off; But first I'll do my errand ii 3 64
I ne'er heard yet That any of these bolder vices wanted Less impudence to gainsay what they did Than to perform it first iii 2 58
But, first, how the poor souls roared, and the sea mocked them iii 3 100
Let's first see moe ballads; we'll buy the other things anon iv 4 277
They throng who should buy first, as if my trinkets had been hallowed iv 4 612
The stars, I see, will kiss the valleys first v 1 206
And there was the first gentleman-like tears that ever we shed v 2 156
But yet speak; first, you, my liege. Comes it not something near? v 3 22
O, thus she stood, Even with such life of majesty, warm life, As now it coldly stands, when first I woo'd her! v 3 36
Perform'd in this wide gap of time since first We were dissever'd v 3 154
For our advantage; therefore hear us first *K. John* ii 1 206
Our colours do return in those same hands That did display them when we first march'd forth ii 1 320

First. I was never so bethump'd with words Since I first call'd my brother's father dad *K. John* ii 1 467
Speak England first, that hath been forward first To speak unto this city ii 1 482
I am well assured That I did so when I was first assured ii 1 535
O, let thy vow First made to heaven, first be to heaven perform'd! iii 1 266
Thy later vows against thy first Is in thyself rebellion to thyself iii 1 288
Your breath first kindled the dead coal of wars v 2 83
This England never did, nor never shall, Lie at the proud foot of a conqueror, But when it first did help to wound itself v 7 114
First, heaven be the record to my speech! *Richard II.* i 1 30
To the cure Of those physicians that first wounded thee ii 1 99
The ripest fruit first falls, and so doth he ii 1 153
I am the last of noble Edward's sons, Of whom thy father, Prince of Wales, was first ii 1 172
Hold out my horse, and I will first be there ii 1 300
Had you first died, and he been thus trod down ii 3 126
If on the first, how heinous e'er it be, To win thy after-love I pardon thee v 3 34
Do not say, 'stand up;' Say 'pardon' first, and afterwards 'stand up' v 3 112
Flatter themselves That they are not the first of fortune's slaves v 5 24
Will't please you to fall to?—Taste of it first, as thou art wont to do v 5 99
Where I first bow'd my knee Unto this king of smiles *1 Hen. IV.* i 3 245
Lend me thy lantern, quoth he? marry, I'll see thee hanged first ii 1 45
What is your will with me?—First, pardon me, my lord ii 4 556
I would the state of time had first been whole Ere he by sickness had been visited iv 1 25
My lord, We were the first and dearest of your friends v 1 33
But what mean I To speak so true at first? *2 Hen. IV.* Ind. 28
When we mean to build, We first survey the plot, then draw the model i 3 42
But, for all our loves, First let them try themselves ii 3 56
'When Arthur first in court'—Empty the jordan ii 4 36
I'll see her damned first; to Pluto's damned lake ii 4 169
By whose fell working I was first advanced iv 5 207
Doth any name particular belong Unto the lodging where I first did swoon? iv 5 234
First my fear; then my courtesy; last my speech Epil. 1
If that you will France win, Then with Scotland first begin *Hen. V.* i 2 168
As gardeners do with ordure hide those roots That shall first spring ii 4 40
You must first go yourself to hazard, ere you have them iii 7 95
Suffolk first died: and York, all haggled over, Comes to him iv 6 11
The king hath granted every article: His daughter first v 2 361
Henry the Fifth he first train'd to the wars *1 Hen. VI.* i 4 79
Of all exploits since first I follow'd arms ii 1 43
Didst thou at first, to flatter us withal, Make us partakers of a little gain? ii 1 51
Then how or which way should they first break in? ii 1 71
Since Henry Monmouth first began to reign ii 5 23
First, lean thine aged back against mine arm ii 5 43
Ascribes the glory of his conquest got First to my God iii 4 12
When first this order was ordain'd, my lords, Knights of the garter were of noble birth iv 1 33
First let me know, and then I'll answer you iv 1 88
I was provoked by him; And he first took exceptions at this badge iv 1 105
Let this dissension first be tried by fight iv 1 116
Accept it, Somerset.—Nay, let it rest where it began at first iv 1 121
The life thou gavest me first was lost and done iv 6 7
You shall first receive The sum of money which I promised v 1 51
First, let me tell you whom you have condemn'd v 4 36
A' comes, methinks, and the queen with him. I'll be the first, sure *2 Hen. VI.* i 3 8
Why I am unmeet: First, for I cannot flatter thee in pride i 3 169
First of the king: what shall of him become? i 4 32
Edward the Third, my lords, had seven sons: The first, Edward the Black Prince ii 2 11
In this private plot be we the first That shall salute our rightful sovereign ii 2 60
Holden at Bury the first of this next month ii 4 71
First note that he is near you in descent iii 1 21
And, had I first been put to speak my mind, I think I should have told your grace's tale iii 1 43
And wolves are gnarling who shall gnaw thee first iii 1 192
For that is good deceit Which mates him first that first intends deceit iii 1 265
First let my words stab him, as he hath me iv 1 66
Let's go fight with them: but first, go and set London bridge on fire iv 6 16
First let me ask of these, If they can brook I bow a knee to man v 1 109
I am resolved for death or dignity.—The first I warrant thee v 1 195
Plantagenet shall speak first: hear him, lords *3 Hen. VI.* i 1 121
First shall war unpeople this my realm i 1 126
At a strife? What is your quarrel? how began it first? i 2 5
First will I see the coronation; And then to Brittany ii 6 96
First, to do greetings to thy royal person iii 3 52
But, with the first of all your chief affairs, Let me entreat iv 6 58
So first the harmless sheep doth yield his fleece And next his throat v 6 8
Hadst thou been kill'd when first thou didst presume, Thou hadst not lived to kill a son of mine v 6 35
But first I'll turn yon fellow in his grave; And then return lamenting to my love *Richard III.* i 2 261
I do the wrong, and first begin to brawl i 3 324
The first that there did greet my stranger soul, Was my great father-in-law i 4 48
First, madam, I entreat true peace of you ii 1 62
First, he commends him to your noble lordship.—And then? iii 2 8
To speak, and to avoid the first, And then, in speaking, not to incur the last iii 7 151
First he was contract to Lady Lucy iii 7 179
Go'st not to the duke?—First, mighty sovereign, let me know your mind iv 4 446
The first was I that help'd thee to the crown v 3 167
Conscience is but a word that cowards use, Devised at first to keep the strong in awe v 3 310
The first and happiest hearers of the town *Hen. VIII.* Prol. 24
To climb steep hills Requires slow pace at first i 1 132
Speak freely.—First, it was usual with him i 2 132
He would have all as merry As, first, good company, good wine, good welcome, Can make good people i 4 6
Henry of Buckingham, Who first raised head against usurping Richard ii 1 108
To leave a thousand-fold more bitter than 'Tis sweet at first to acquire ii 3 9
My conscience first received a tenderness, Scruple, and prick ii 4 170
First, methought I stood not in the smile of heaven ii 4 186
First I began in private With you, my Lord of Lincoln ii 4 206
Remember How under my oppression I did reek, When I first moved you ii 4 208

First. The question did at first so stagger me . *Hen. VIII.* ii 4 212
And the first he view'd, He did it with a serious mind . . iii 2 79
The Duke of Suffolk is the first, and claims To be high-steward . iv 1 17
O, my lord, The times and titles now are alter'd strangely With me since first you knew me . . . . iv 2 113
What is your pleasure with me?—Noble lady, First, mine own service . iv 2 115
Misdemean'd yourself, and not a little, Toward the king first, then his laws . . . . v 3 15
I told ye all, When we first put this dangerous stone a-rolling, 'Twould fall upon ourselves . . . . v 3 104
A' should not bear it so, a' should eat swords first . *Troi. and Cres.* ii 3 228
I wish'd myself a man, Or that we women had men's privilege Of speaking first . . . . iii 2 137
The first was Menelaus' kiss; this, mine . . . . . iv 5 32
There's many a Greek and Trojan dead, Since first I saw yourself and Diomed . . . . iv 5 215
First, all you peers of Greece, go to my tent . . . iv 5 271
Against him first: he's a very dog to the commonalty . . *Coriolanus* i 1 28
I receive the general food at first, Which you do live upon . . i 1 135
Thou rascal, that art worst in blood to run, Lead'st first to win some vantage . . . . i 1 164
The rabble should have first unroof'd the city, Ere so prevail'd with me i 1 222
Can not Better be held nor more attain'd than by A place below the first i 1 270
I sprang not more in joy at first hearing he was a man-child than now in first seeing he had proved himself a man . . . i 3 17
Better to starve, Than crave the hire which first we do deserve . . ii 3 121
So then the Volsces stand but as at first . . . . iii 1 4
As thou hast said My praises made thee first a soldier . . iii 2 108
Know thou first, I loved the maid I married . . . . iv 5 119
More dances my rapt heart Than when I first my wedded mistress saw Bestride my threshold . . . . . . iv 5 123
Let me commend thee first to those that shall Say yea to thy desires . iv 5 150
He bears himself more proudlier, Even to my person, than I thought he would When first I did embrace him . . . . iv 7 10
First he was A noble servant to them; but he could not Carry his honours even . . . . iv 7 35
First, the gods bless you for your tidings; next, Accept my thankfulness v 4 61
Ten years are spent since first he undertook This cause . *T. Andron.* i 1 31
To the bay From whence at first she weigh'd her anchorage . . i 1 73
First thrash the corn, then after burn the straw . . . ii 3 123
Sensibly fed Of that self-blood that first gave life to you . . iv 2 123
First hang the child, that he may see it sprawl . . . v 1 51
The all-seeing sun Ne'er saw her match since first the world begun *Rom. and Jul.* i 2 98
That presses them and learns them first to bear . . . . i 4 93
Love, who first did prompt me to inquire; He lent me counsel . . ii 2 80
I think you are happy in this second match, For it excels your first; or if it did not, Your first is dead . . . . . iii 5 225
I am a man That from my first have been inclined to thrift *T. of Athens* i 1 118
Ceremony was but devised at first To set a gloss on faint deeds . i 2 15
I see no sense for't, But his occasions might have woo'd me first . iii 3 15
I'ld rather than the worth of thrice the sum, Had sent to me first . iii 3 23
What, dost thou go? Soft! take thy physic first—thou too—and thou iii 6 110
More money, bounteous Timon.—More whore, more mischief first . iv 3 168
First mend my company, take away thyself . . . . iv 3 283
Let us first see peace in Athens . . . . . . iv 3 461
Nor are they living Who were the motives that you first went out . v 4 27
Since Cassius first did whet me against Cæsar, I have not slept *J. Cæsar* ii 1 61
Two months hence up higher toward the north He first presents his fire ii 1 110
O'er-read, At your best leisure, this his humble suit.—O Cæsar, read mine first . . . . iii 1 6
Casca, you are the first that rears your hand . . . iii 1 30
Let each man render me his bloody hands: First, Marcus Brutus . . iii 1 185
I will myself into the pulpit first, And show the reason of our Cæsar's death . . . . iii 1 236
This day I breathed first: time is come round, And where I did begin, there shall I end . . . . v 3 23
Give me your hand first. Fare you well, my lord . . . v 5 49
He's here in double trust; First, as I am his kinsman . *Macbeth* i 7 13
He chid the sisters When first they put the name of king upon me . iii 1 58
Swelter'd venom sleeping got, Boil thou first i' the charmed pot . iv 1 9
He will not be commanded: here's another, More potent than the first iv 1 76
And thy hair, Thou other gold-bound brow, is like the first . . iv 1 114
Lay on, Macduff, And damn'd be him that first cries 'Hold, enough!' v 8 34
Henceforth be earls, the first that ever Scotland In such an honour named v 8 63
Look you, sir, Inquire me first what Danskers are in Paris *Hamlet* ii 1 7
Upon our first, he sent out to suppress His nephew's levies . . ii 2 61
Still harping on my daughter: yet he knew me not at first . . ii 2 190
Whose end, both at the first and now, was and is, to hold, as 'twere, the mirror up to nature . . . . iii 2 23
In second husband let me be accurst! None wed the second but who kill'd the first . . . . iii 2 190
Like a man to double business bound, I stand in pause where I shall first begin, And both neglect . . . . . iii 3 42
First, her father slain: Next, your son gone . . . iv 5 79
When I shall, first asking your pardon thereunto, recount the occasion iv 7 46
Was he a gentleman?—A' was the first that ever bore arms . . v 1 37
If Hamlet give the first or second hit, Or quit in answer of the third exchange . . . . v 2 279
Give him the cup.—I'll play this bout first; set it by awhile . . v 2 295
Goneril, Our eldest-born, speak first . . . . . *Lear* i 1 55
My lord of Burgundy, We first address towards you . . . i 1 193
If I speak like myself in this, let him be whipped that first finds it so . i 4 180
Natures of such deep trust we shall much need; You we first seize on . ii 1 118
He that first lights on him Holla the other . . . . iii 1 54
In, boy; go first. You houseless poverty,—Nay, get thee in . . iii 4 26
First let me talk with this philosopher. What is the cause of thunder? iii 4 159
Will you lie down and rest upon the cushions?—I'll see their trial first iii 6 37
Arraign her first; 'tis Goneril . . . . . . iii 6 48
Wherefore to Dover? Let him first answer that . . . iii 7 53
O, let me kiss that hand!—Let me wipe it first; it smells of mortality . iv 6 136
That eyeless head of thine was first framed flesh To raise my fortunes . iv 6 231
Take them away: good guard, Until their greater pleasures first be known v 3 2
We are not the first Who, with best meaning, have incurr'd the worst . v 3 3
Ere they shall make us weep: we'll see 'em starve first . . v 3 25
Not by old gradation, where each second Stood heir to the first *Othello* i 1 38
We must not think the Turk is so unskilful To leave that latest which concerns him first . . . . i 3 28
First, I must tell thee this—Desdemona is directly in love with him ii 1 220
She first loved the Moor, but for bragging and telling her fantastical lies ii 1 225

First. When devils will the blackest sins put on, They do suggest at first with heavenly shows . . . . *Othello* ii 3 358
Yet fruits that blossom first will first be ripe . . . . ii 3 383
What handkerchief! Why, that the Moor first gave to Desdemona . iii 3 308
Dangerous conceits are, in their natures, poisons, Which at the first are scarce found to distaste . . . . iii 3 327
First, to be hanged, and then to confess . . . . iv 1 39
Ay, 'twas he that told me first: An honest man he is . . . v 2 147
With that recognizance and pledge of love Which I first gave her . v 2 215
Fulvia thy wife first came into the field . . . *Ant. and Cleo.* i 2 92
Yet at the first I saw the treasons planted . . . . i 3 25
Small to greater matters must give way.—Not if the small come first . ii 2 12
When she first met Mark Antony, she pursed up his heart . . ii 2 191
First, madam, he is well.—Why, there's more gold . . . ii 5 31
Most meet That first we come to words . . . . . ii 6 3
This is fought indeed! Had we done so at first, we had droven them home . . . . iv 7 5
If she first meet the curled Antony, He'll make demand of her, and spend that kiss Which is my heaven to have . . . v 2 304
I thank him, makes no stranger of me; we are familiar at first *Cymbeline* i 4 112
Here comes a flattering rascal; upon him Will I first work . . i 5 28
Which first, perchance, she'll prove on cats and dogs, Then afterward up higher . . . . i 5 38
Ravening first the lamb Longs after for the garbage . . . i 6 49
First, a very excellent good-conceited thing; after, a wonderful sweet air ii 3 18
This yellow Iachimo, in an hour,—was't not?—Or less,—at first? . ii 5 15
With shame—The first that ever touch'd him . . . . iii 1 25
The first of Britain which did put His brows within a golden crown . iii 1 60
But first, how get hence: Why should excuse be born or e'er begot? . iii 2 66
My report was once First with the best of note . . . iii 3 58
He that strikes The venison first shall be the lord o' the feast . iii 3 75
Ne'er long'd my mother so To see me first, as I have now . . iii 4 3
To bed then.—I'll wake mine eye-balls blind first . . . iii 4 104
And am almost A man already.—First, make yourself but like one . iii 4 170
With that suit upon my back, will I ravish her: first kill him . . iii 5 142
The ground that gave them first has them again . . . iv 2 289
First pay me for the nursing of thy sons . . . . v 5 322
How parted with your brothers? how first met them? . . . v 5 386
Take that life, beseech you, Which I so often owe; but your ring first . v 5 415
And what was first but fear what might be done, Grows elder now and cares it be not done . . . . *Pericles* i 2 14
That man and wife Draw lots who first shall die to lengthen life . i 4 46
Who is the first that doth prefer himself? . . . . ii 2 17
Even at the first Thy loss is more than can thy portage quit . . iii 1 34
He that will give most shall have her first . . . . iv 2 64
To fetch his daughter home, who first is gone . . . . iv 4 20
First, I would have you note, this is an honourable man . . iv 6 53
Tell me one thing first.—Come now, your one thing . . . iv 6 166
But I am For other service first: toward Ephesus Turn our blown sails v 1 255
I will, my lord. Beseech you, first go with me to my house . . v 3 65

First affection. This forenamed maid hath yet in her the continuance of her first affection . . . . . . *Meas. for Meas.* iii 1 249
First and last. Ay, grief, I fear me, both at first and last . 1 *Hen. VI.* v 5 102
Sit down: at first And last the hearty welcome . . . *Macbeth* iii 4 1
Would hazard the winning both of first and last . . . *Cymbeline* i 4 102
First approach. Mark his first approach before my lady . . *T. Night* ii 5 218
At the first approach you must kneel, then kiss his foot . *T. Andron.* iv 3 110
First assault. Without rescue in the first assault or ransom afterward *All's Well* i 3 120
First battle. You, worthy uncle, Shall . . . Lead our first battle *Macb.* v 6 4
First beginners. A sin in war, Damn'd in the first beginners! *Cymbeline* v 3 37
First-begotten. The first-begotten and the lawful heir . 1 *Hen. VI.* ii 5 65
First being. All love the womb that their first being bred . *Pericles* i 1 107
First-born. Like an envious sneaping frost That bites the first-born infants of the spring . . . . *L. L. Lost* i 1 101
The courtesy of nations allows you my better, in that you are the first-born; but the same tradition takes not away my blood *As Y. Like It* i 1 50
I'll go sleep, if I can; if I cannot, I'll rail against all the first-born of Egypt . . . . ii 5 63
Let one spirit of the first-born Cain Reign in all bosoms! . 2 *Hen. IV.* i 1 157
I am his first-born son, that was the last That wore the imperial diadem of Rome . . . . *T. Andron.* i 1 5
Thrice noble Titus, spare my first-born son . . . . i 1 120
He dies upon my scimitar's sharp point That touches this my first-born son . . . . iv 2 92
First boy. We'll play with them the first boy for a thousand ducats *Mer. of Venice* iii 2 216
First bringer. Yet the first bringer of unwelcome news Hath but a losing office . . . . 2 *Hen. IV.* i 1 100
First budger. Let the first budger die the other's slave! . *Coriolanus* i 8 5
First career. Or, if misfortune miss the first career . *Richard II.* i 2 49
First choice. Let's have the first choice. Follow me, girls *W. Tale* iv 4 319
First cock. And look thou meet me ere the first cock crow *M. N. Dream* ii 1 267
There is ne'er a king christen could be better bit than I have been since the first cock . . . . 1 *Hen. IV.* ii 1 20
He begins at curfew, and walks till the first cock . . . *Lear* iii 4 121
First complaint. Said to be something imperfect in favouring the first complaint . . . . *Coriolanus* ii 1 54
First-conceived. Can chase away the first-conceived sound . 2 *Hen. VI.* iii 2 44
First conception. The passions of the mind, That have their first conception by mis-dread, Have after-nourishment and life by care *Pericles* i 2 12
First conditions. Once more offer'd The first conditions . *Coriolanus* v 3 14
First corse. And who still hath cried, From the first corse till he that died to-day, 'This must be so' . . . . . *Hamlet* i 2 105
First create. O loving hate! O any thing, of nothing first create! *R. and J.* i 1 183
First dash. She takes upon her bravely at first dash . 1 *Hen. VI.* i 2 71
First day. Is not, sir, my doublet as fresh as the first day I wore it? I mean, in a sort . . . . *Tempest* ii 1 103
First decree. And turn pre-ordinance and first decree Into the law of children . . . . *J. Cæsar* iii 1 38
First departing. They stay The first departing of the king *Richard II.* i 2 290
First duke. We here create thee the first duke of Suffolk . 2 *Hen. VI.* i 1 64
William de la Pole, first duke of Suffolk . . . . . i 2 30
First employer. Troilus the first employer of pandars . *Much Ado* v 2 31
First encounter. Let me be thus bold with you To give you over at this first encounter . . . . *T. of Shrew* i 2 105
Upon the first encounter, drave them.—Well, what worst? *Ant. and Cleo.* i 2 98
First face. I have felt so many quirks of joy and grief, That the first face of neither, on the start, Can woman me unto't . . *All's Well* iii 2 52
First false speaking. My first false speaking Was this upon myself *Macb.* iv 3 130

First father. From son to son, some four or five descents Since the first father wore it . *All's Well* iii 7 25
First fight. And had the maidenhood Of thy first fight . 1 *Hen. VI.* iv 6 18
First fruit. My second joy And first-fruits of my body . . *W. Tale* iii 2 98
She was the first fruit of my bachelorship . . 1 *Hen. VI.* v 4 13
First gift. To part so slightly with your wife's first gift . *Mer. of Venice* v 1 167
I gave her such a one; 'twas my first gift . *Othello* iii 3 436
First giver. Heat them and they retort that heat again To the first giver *Troi. and Cres.* iii 3 102
First glance. But I was won, my lord, With the first glance . . iii 2 126
First griefs. When thy first griefs were but a mere conceit *T. of Athens* v 4 14
First head. I assure ye, it was a buck of the first head . *L. L. Lost* iv 2 10
All the treasons for these eighteen years Complotted and contrived in this land Fetch from false Mowbray their first head . *Richard II.* i 1 97
First hour. As my mother was, the first hour I was born . *Mer. Wives* ii 2 39
There is no hope that ever I will stay, If the first hour I shrink and run away . . . . 1 *Hen. VI.* iv 5 31
First house. A gentleman of the very first house, of the first and second cause . . . . *Rom. and Jul.* ii 4 25
First humane principle. The first humane principle I would teach them should be, to forswear thin potations . . 2 *Hen. IV.* iv 3 133
First in question. Old Escalus, Though first in question, is thy secondary . . . . *Meas. for Meas.* i 1 47
First interrogatory. The first inter'gatory That my Nerissa shall be sworn on is . . . . *Mer. of Venice* v 1 300
First knave. Thou art the first knave that e'er madest a duke *M. for M.* v 1 361
First lord. Many so arrive at second masters, Upon their first lord's neck *T. of Athens* iv 3 513
But die thy thoughts when thy first lord is dead . . *Hamlet* iii 2 225
First male child. Since the birth of Cain, the first male child, To him that did but yesterday suspire . . . . . . *K. John* iii 4 79
First man. Was the first man that leap'd . . . *Tempest* i 2 214
I was the first man That e'er received gift from him . *T. of Athens* iii 3 16
First meeting. Not a relation for a breakfast nor Befitting this first meeting . . . . *Tempest* v 1 165
And at first meeting loved; Continued so, until we thought he died *Cymbeline* v 5 379
First merriment. Our first merriment hath made thee jealous *T. of S.* iv 5 76
First motion. Between the acting of a dreadful thing And the first motion, all the interim is Like a phantasma, or a hideous dream *J. Cæsar* ii 1 64
First motive. Thy father's wealth Was the first motive that I woo'd thee *Mer. Wives* iii 4 14
First mouthed, to be last swallowed . . . . *Hamlet* iv 2 20
First murder. As if it were Cain's jaw-bone, that did the first murder! . v 1 85
First of all. But first of all, How we may steal from hence . *Cymbeline* iii 2 63
First of April. The first of April died Your noble mother . *K. John* iv 2 120
First of difference. That, from your first of difference and decay, Have follow'd your sad steps . . . . . . *Lear* v 3 288
First of manhood. And many unrough youths that even now Protest their first of manhood . . . . . . *Macbeth* v 2 11
First of May. Exceeds her as much in beauty as the first of May doth the last of December . . . . . . *Much Ado* i 1 194
First opening. At the first opening of the gorgeous east . . *L. L. Lost* iv 3 223
First order. But he, poor soul, by your first order died . *Richard III.* ii 1 87
First or last, your fine Egyptian cookery Shall have the fame *A. and C.* ii 6 63
First pace. So every step, Exampled by the first pace that is sick Of his superior, grows to an envious fever . . *Troi. and Cres.* i 3 132
First place. Make not a city feast of it, to let the meat cool ere we can agree upon the first place . . . . *T. of Athens* iii 6 77
First proportion. Whose power was in the first proportion . 1 *Hen. IV.* iv 4 15
First queen. Walk'd your first queen's ghost, it should take joy To see her in your arms . . . . *W. Tale* v 1 80
That Shall be when your first queen's again in breath . . v 1 83
First rank. Like a gallant horse fall'n in first rank . *Troi. and Cres.* iii 3 161
First remembrance. This was her first remembrance from the Moor *Oth.* iii 3 291
First row. The first row of the pious chanson will show you more *Hamlet* ii 2 438
First sacrifice. Ere the first sacrifice, within this hour *Troi. and Cres.* iv 2 66
First service. The first service thou dost me, fetch that suit hither: let it be thy first service . . . . . *Cymbeline* iii 5 130
First show. If these four Worthies in their first show thrive, These four will change habits, and present the other five . . *L. L. Lost* v 2 541
There is five in the first show.—You are deceived; 'tis not so v 2 543
First sight. At the first sight They have changed eyes . . *Tempest* i 2 440
Who ever loved that loved not at first sight? . . . *As Y. Like It* iii 5 82
She will sing any man at first sight . . . *Troi. and Cres.* v 2 9
First son. My first son, Whither wilt thou go? . . . *Coriolanus* iv 1 33
First stone. From my cold heart let heaven engender hail, And poison it in the source; and the first stone Drop in my neck! *Ant. and Cleo.* iii 13 160
First stroke. He that strikes the first stroke, I'll run him up to the hilts *Hen. V.* ii 1 68
First suit. The first suit is hot and hasty, like a Scotch jig . *Much Ado* ii 1 78
First swath. Hadst thou, like us from our first swath, proceeded The sweet degrees that this brief world affords . . *T. of Athens* iv 3 252
First sword. Since the first sword was drawn about this question *Troi. and Cres.* ii 2 18
First thing. Rob me the exchequer the first thing thou doest 1 *Hen. IV.* iii 3 205
The first thing we do, let's kill all the lawyers . . . 2 *Hen. VI.* iv 2 83
Ay, that's the first thing that we have to do . . . 3 *Hen. VI.* iv 3 62
First thrust. He that makes the first thrust, I'll kill him . *Hen. V.* ii 1 104
First time. It is the first time that ever I heard breaking of ribs was sport for ladies . . . . *As Y. Like It* i 2 146
The first time that I ever saw him Methought he was a brother . v 4 28
'Tis not the first time I have constrained one to call me knave *T. Night* ii 3 71
You have shot over.—'Tis not the first time you were overshot *Hen. VI.* iii 7 134
'Tis the first time that ever I was forced to scold . . *Coriolanus* v 6 105
You all do know this mantle: I remember The first time ever Cæsar put it on; 'Twas on a summer's evening . . . . *J. Cæsar* iii 2 175
The first time that we smell the air, We wawl and cry . . *Lear* iv 6 183
First to last. When from the first to last betwixt us two Tears our recountments had most kindly bathed . . *As Y. Like It* iv 3 140
Behold, From first to last, the onset and retire Of both your armies *K. John* ii 1 326
I ask'd his blessing, and from first to last Told him my pilgrimage *Lear* v 3 195
Know of your love?—He did, from first to last: why dost thou ask? *Othello* iii 3 96
That can From first to last resolve you . . . . . *Pericles* v 3 61
First truth. This is the first truth that e'er thine own tongue was guilty of . . . . *All's Well* iv 1 35
First view. On the first view to say, to swear, I love thee *M. N. Dream* iii 1 144
First view. My appointments have in them a need Greater than shows itself at the first view . . . . . . *All's Well* ii 5 73
We are reconciled; and the first view shall kill All repetition . . v 3 21
First way. If you bring not Marcius, we'll proceed In our first way *Cor.* iii 1 334
First white hair. Whom I have weekly sworn to marry since I perceived the first white hair on my chin . . . . 2 *Hen. IV.* i 2 270
First wife. This ring was mine; I gave it his first wife . . *All's Well* v 3 280
First year. The pissing-conduit run nothing but claret wine this first year of our reign . . . . 2 *Hen. VI.* iv 6 4
Firstling. Our play Leaps o'er the vaunt and firstlings of those broils, Beginning in the middle . . . . . *Troi. and Cres.* Prol. 27
The very firstlings of my heart shall be The firstlings of my hand *Macb.* iv 1 147
Fish. What strange fish Hath made his meal on thee? . . *Tempest* ii 1 112
What have we here? a man or a fish? dead or alive? . . . ii 2 25
A fish: he smells like a fish; a very ancient and fish-like smell . . ii 2 26
A strange fish! Were I in England now, as once I was, and had but this fish painted . . . . ii 2 28
This is no fish, but an islander, that hath lately suffered by a thunderbolt ii 2 37
I'll pluck thee berries; I'll fish for thee and get thee wood enough . ii 2 165
No more dams I ll make for fish; Nor fetch in firing At requiring . ii 2 184
Thou deboshed fish, thou, was there ever man a coward that hath drunk so much? . . . . iii 2 30
Wilt thou tell a monstrous lie, being but half a fish and half a monster? iii 2 32
One of them Is a plain fish, and, no doubt, marketable . . . v 1 266
They are both as whole as a fish . . . . *T. G. of Ver.* ii 5 20
The luce is the fresh fish; the salt fish is an old coat . . *Mer. Wives* i 1 22
The beast, the fishes and the winged fowls Are their males' subjects and at their controls . . . . . *Com. of Errors* ii 1 18
With intellectual sense and souls, Of more pre-eminence than fish and fowls . . . . ii 1 23
Either at flesh or fish, A table full of welcome makes scarce one dainty dish . . . . iii 1 22
When fowls have no feathers and fish have no fin . . . . iii 1 79
For a fish without a fin, there's a fowl without a feather . . . iii 1 82
Bait the hook well; this fish will bite . . . *Much Ado* ii 3 114
The pleasant'st angling is to see the fish Cut with her golden oars the silver stream . . . . iii 1 26
Fish not, with this melancholy bait, For this fool gudgeon *Mer. of Venice* i 1 101
What's that good for?—To bait fish withal . . . . . iii 1 55
I love not many words.—No more than a fish loves water . *All's Well* iii 6 92
I will henceforth eat no fish of fortune's buttering . . . . v 2 9
Here's another ballad of a fish, that appeared upon the coast *W. Tale* iv 4 279
It was thought she was a woman and was turned into a cold fish . . iv 4 284
Caught the water though not the fish . . . . v 2 91
A dragon and a finless fish . . . . . 1 *Hen. IV.* iii 1 151
Why, she's neither fish nor flesh; a man knows not where to have her . iii 3 144
It had froze them up, As fish are in a pond . . . 2 *Hen. IV.* i 1 200
Ten thousand men that fishes gnaw'd upon . . *Richard III.* i 4 25
As ravenous fishes, do a vessel follow That is new-trimm'd . *Hen. VIII.* i 2 79
Whiles others fish with craft for great opinion, I with great truth catch mere simplicity . . . . *Troi. and Cres.* iv 4 105
As is the osprey to the fish, who takes it By sovereignty of nature *Cor.* iv 7 34
More dangerous Than baits to fish, or honey-stalks to sheep *T. Andron.* iv 4 91
I am a pretty piece of flesh.—'Tis well thou art not fish *Rom. and Jul.* i 1 36
The fish lives in the sea, and 'tis much pride For fair without the fair within to hide . . . . i 3 89
An alligator stuff'd, and other skins Of ill-shaped fishes . . . . v 1 44
We cannot live on grass, on berries, water, As beasts and birds and fishes.—Nor on the beasts themselves, the birds, and fishes; You must eat men . . . . *T. of Athens* iv 3 426
A man may fish with the worm that hath eat of a king, and eat of the fish that hath fed of that worm . . . . . . *Hamlet* iv 3 28
To fear judgement; to fight when I cannot choose; and to eat no fish *Lear* i 4 18
He fishes, drinks, and wastes The lamps of night in revel *Ant. and Cleo.* i 4 4
My music playing far off, I will betray Tawny-finn'd fishes . . . ii 5 12
The imperious seas breed monsters, for the dish Poor tributary rivers as sweet fish . . . . *Cymbeline* iv 2 36
Let it to the sea, And tell the fishes he's the queen's son, Cloten . . iv 2 153
They say they're [the porpus] half fish, half flesh . . . *Pericles* ii 1 27
I marvel how the fishes live in the sea.—Why, as men do a-land . . ii 1 29
Canst thou catch any fishes, then?—I never practised it . . . ii 1 70
Here's nothing to be got now-a-days, unless thou canst fish for't . . ii 1 74
We'll have flesh for holidays, fish for fasting-days . . . . ii 1 86
Here's a fish hangs in the net, like a poor man's right in the law . . ii 1 122
Fished. I mean, in a sort.—That sort was well fished for . . *Tempest* ii 1 104
And his pond fish'd by his next neighbour . . . *W. Tale* i 2 195
Fisher. Would have reft the fishers of their prey . . *Com. of Errors* i 1 116
The fisher with his pencil, and the painter with his nets *Rom. and Jul.* i 2 41
From the finny subject of the sea These fishers tell the infirmities of men *Pericles* ii 1 53
Fishermen. They would melt me out of my fat drop by drop and liquor fishermen's boots with me . . . . . . *Mer. Wives* iv 5 100
They three were taken up By fishermen of Corinth, as we thought *Com. of Errors* i 1 112
By and by rude fishermen of Corinth By force took Dromio . . v 1 351
The fishermen, that walk upon the beach, Appear like mice . . *Lear* iv 6 17
Peace be at your labour, honest fishermen . . . . *Pericles* ii 1 56
Fishified. O flesh, flesh, how art thou fishified! . . . *Rom. and Jul.* ii 4 40
Fish-like. A very ancient and fish-like smell . . . . *Tempest* ii 2 27
Fish-meal. And making many fish-meals, that they fall into a kind of male green-sickness . . . . 2 *Hen. IV.* iv 3 99
Fishmonger. Do you know me, my lord?—Excellent well; you are a fishmonger . . . . *Hamlet* ii 2 174
He knew me not at first; he said I was a fishmonger: he is far gone . ii 2 190
Fishpond. A musk-cat, that Has fallen into the unclean fishpond of her displeasure . . . . *All's Well* v 2 22
Fish Street. Up Fish Street! down Saint Magnus' Corner! 2 *Hen. VI.* iv 8 1
Fisnomy. A' has an English name; but his fisnomy is more hotter in France than there . . . . *All's Well* iv 5 42
Fist. Not a word of his But buffets better than a fist . . *K. John* ii 1 465
An I but fist him once . . . . 2 *Hen. IV.* ii 1 23
Give me thy fist, thy fore-foot to me give: Thy spirits are most tall *Hen. V.* ii 1 71
Of parents good, of fist most valiant . . . . iv 1 46
Whom with my bare fists I would execute . . . . . 1 *Hen. VI.* i 4 36
Nor hold the sceptre in his childish fist . . . . . 2 *Hen. VI.* v 1 245
Thy hand is but a finger to my fist, Thy leg a stick compared with this iv 10 51
And wring the awful sceptre from his fist . . . . 3 *Hen. VI.* ii 1 154
He would pun thee into shivers with his fist . . . *Troi. and Cres.* ii 1 43
If I go to him, with my armed fist I'll pash him o'er the face . . ii 3 212

Fisting each other's throat . . . *Coriolanus* iv 5 131
To the choleric fisting of every rogue Thy ear is liable . . *Pericles* iv 6 177
Fistula. What is it, my good lord, the king languishes of?—A fistula, my lord.—I heard not of it before . . *All's Well* i 1 39
Fit. His more braver daughter could control thee, If now 'twere fit to do't . . . . *Tempest* i 2 440
He's in his fit now and does not talk after the wisest . . . ii 2 76
If he have never drunk wine afore, it will go near to remove his fit ii 2 79
In these fits I leave them . . . . iii 3 91
'Tis an office of great worth And you an officer fit for the place *T. G. of V.* i 2 45
Fit me with such weeds As may beseem some well-reputed page . ii 7 42
That fits as well as 'Tell me, good my lord, What compass will you wear your farthingale?' . . . . ii 7 50
And here an engine fit for my proceeding . . . . . iii 1 138
One Julia, that his changing thoughts forget, Would better fit his chamber . . . . iv 4 125
As fit, by all men's judgements, As if the garment had been made for me . . . . iv 4 167
Full of good And fit for great employment . . . . . v 4 157
Trust me, I thought on her: she'll fit it . . . *Mer. Wives* ii 1 166
In state as wholesome as in state 'tis fit, Worthy the owner . v 5 63
More fit to do another such offence Than die for this *Meas. for Meas.* ii 3 14
Fit thy consent to my sharp appetite . . . . . . ii 4 161
And fit his mind to death, for his soul's rest . . . . ii 4 187
The maid will I frame and make fit for his attempt . . . iii 1 266
Every true man's apparel fits your thief . . . . . iv 2 46
I have found you out a stand most fit . . . . . iv 6 10
Consenting to the safeguard of your honour, I thought your marriage fit v 1 425
Belike his wife, acquainted with his fits, On purpose shut the doors *Com. of Errors* iv 3 91
Thy jealous fits Have scared thy husband from the use of wits . v 1 85
Look, what will serve is fit: 'tis once, thou lovest, And I will fit thee with the remedy . . . . *Much Ado* i 1 320
It better fits my blood to be disdained of all . . . . i 3 29
We'll fit the kid-fox with a pennyworth . . . . . ii 3 44
Think you of a worse title, and I will fit her to it . . . iii 2 114
It would better fit your honour to change your mind . . . iii 2 119
Fit in his place and time.—In reason nothing . . *L. L. Lost* i 1 98
O heresy in fair, fit for these days! . . . . . . iv 1 22
One o' these maids' girdles for your waist should be fit . . . iv 1 50
By my troth, most pleasant: how both did fit it! . . . . iv 1 131
Vulgar wit! When it comes so smoothly off, so obscenely, as it were, so fit . . . . iv 1 145
None so fit as to present the Nine Worthies . . . . v 1 130
Look you arm yourself To fit your fancies to your father's will *M. N. D.* i 1 118
Every man's name, which is thought fit, through all Athens, to play i 2 5
Fit for treasons, stratagems and spoils . . *Mer. of Venice* v 1 85
I love to cope him in these sullen fits . . . *As Y. Like It* ii 1 67
As it is a spare life, look you, it fits my humour well . . . iii 2 20
And take a lodging fit to entertain Such friends . *T. of Shrew* i 1 44
Schoolmasters will I keep within my house, Fit to instruct her youth . i 1 95
Was it fit for a servant to use his master so? . . . . . i 2 31
For learning and behaviour Fit for her turn, well read in poetry . i 2 170
Get a man,—whate'er he be, It skills not much, we'll fit him to our turn iii 2 134
This doth fit the time, And gentlewomen wear such caps as these . iv 3 69
These fix'd evils sit so fit in him . . . . . *All's Well* i 1 113
Nay, I'll fit you, And not be all day neither . . . . ii 1 93
Oft expectation fails and most oft there Where most it promises, and oft it hits Where hope is coldest and despair most fits . . . . ii 1 147
That's a bountiful answer that fits all questions.—It is like a barber's chair that fits all buttocks . . . . ii 2 16
Will your answer serve fit to all questions?—As fit as ten groats is for the hand of an attorney . . . . ii 2 20
From below your duke to beneath your constable, it will fit any question ii 2 33
It must be an answer of most monstrous size that must fit all demands ii 2 35
It were fit you knew him; lest, reposing too far in his virtue . iii 6 14
A wise man's art: For folly that he wisely shows is fit . *T. Night* iii 1 74
Do not then walk too open.—It doth not fit me . . . . iii 3 38
Ungracious wretch, Fit for the mountains and the barbarous caves! . iv 1 52
What fit is this, good lady? . . . . . . *W. Tale* iii 2 175
Well you fit our ages With flowers of winter . . . . . iv 4 78
No milliner can so fit his customers with gloves . . . . iv 4 192
Get you hence, for I must go Where it fits not you to know . . iv 4 304
For some other reasons, my grave sir, Which 'tis not fit you know . iv 4 423
I will bring these two moles, these blind ones, aboard him; if he think it fit to shore them again . . . . iv 4 869
This is worshipful society And fits the mounting spirit like myself *K. John* i 1 206
I had a thing to say, But I will fit it with some better time . . iii 3 26
And he will look as hollow as a ghost, As dim and meagre as an ague's fit iii 4 85
Even in the instant of repair and health, The fit is strongest . . iii 4 114
Fit for bloody villany, Apt, liable to be employ'd in danger . . iv 2 225
This ague fit of fear is over-blown . . . . *Richard II.* iii 2 190
To the latter end of a fray and the beginning of a feast Fits a dull fighter and a keen guest. . . . . 1 *Hen. IV.* iv 2 86
Impatient of his fit, breaks like a fire Out of his keeper's arms 2 *Hen. IV.* i 1 142
I would thou wert a man's tailor, that thou mightst mend him and make him fit to go . . . . iii 2 176
These fits Are with his highness very ordinary . . . . . iv 4 114
It fits us then to be as provident As fear may teach us . . *Hen. V.* ii 4 11
Is it fit this soldier keep his oath? . . . . iv 7 138
My wooing is fit for thy understanding . . . . v 2 125
A goodly prize, fit for the devil's grace . . . . . 1 *Hen. VI.* v 3 33
Happy for so sweet a child, Fit to be made companion with a king . v 3 149
Approves her fit for none but for a king . . . . . . v 5 69
Whose church-like humours fits not for a crown . . . 2 *Hen. VI.* i 1 247
That were a state fit for his holiness . . . . i 3 67
That time best fits the work we have in hand . . . . . i 4 23
This staff of honour raught, there let it stand Where it best fits to be . ii 3 44
See the lists and all things fit: Here let them end it . . . ii 3 54
Thou art not king, Not fit to govern and rule multitudes . . . v 1 94
I am a subject fit to jest withal, But far unfit to be a sovereign 3 *Hen. VI.* iii 2 91
Most fit For your best health and recreation . . . *Richard III.* iii 1 66
All the good our English Have got by the late voyage is but merely A fit or two o' the face . . . . *Hen. VIII.* i 3 7
And fit it with such furniture as suits The greatness of his person . i 1 99
Thou art a cure fit for a king . . . . ii 2 76
Therefore, madam, It's fit this royal session do proceed . . . ii 4 66
I feel The last fit of my greatness . . . . iii 1 78
O negligence! Fit for a fool to fall by . . . . . . iii 2 214
It fits we thus proceed, or else no witness Would come against you . v 1 107
Fit. Well said, my lord! well, you say so in fits . . *Troi. and Cres.* iii 1 62
Better would it fit Achilles much To throw down Hector than Polyxena iii 3 207
You have a vice of mercy in you, Which better fits a lion than a man . v 3 38
And fit it is, Because I am the store-house . . . *Coriolanus* i 1 136
Tell Valeria, We are fit to bid her welcome . . . . . . i 3 47
He cannot but with measure fit the honours Which we devise him . ii 2 127
Go fit you to the custom . . . . ii 2 146
Hast not the soft way which, thou dost confess, Were fit for thee to use iii 2 83
'Tis fit You make strong party, or defend yourself By calmness or by absence . . . . iii 2 93
A better head her glorious body fits Than his . . . *T. Andron.* i 1 187
One fit to bandy with thy lawless sons, To ruffle in the commonwealth i 1 312
Arm thy heart, and fit thy thoughts, To mount aloft . . . . ii 1 12
I am as able and as fit as thou To serve, and to deserve my mistress' grace ii 1 33
Till I find the stream To cool this heat, a charm to calm these fits . ii 1 134
This valley fits the purpose passing well . . . . . . ii 3 84
Nay, barbarous Tamora, For no name fits thy nature but thy own! . ii 3 119
Why dost thou laugh? it fits not with this hour . . . . iii 1 267
Unless some fit or frenzy do possess her . . . . . . iv 1 17
Come, go with me into mine armoury; Lucius, I'll fit thee . . iv 1 114
That is as fit as can be to serve for your oration . . . . iv 3 95
Shall we be thus afflicted in his wreaks, His fits, his frenzy? . . iv 4 12
This closing with him fits his lunacy . . . . v 2 70
Whate'er I forge to feed his brain-sick fits, Do you uphold and maintain v 2 71
Put off these frowns, An ill-beseeming semblance for a feast.—It fits, when such a villain is a guest . . . . . . *Rom. and Jul.* i 5 77
Help me sort such needful ornaments As you think fit to furnish me . iv 2 35
With instruments upon them, fit to open These dead men's tombs . v 3 200
He does neither affect company, nor is he fit for't, indeed *T. of Athens* i 2 31
Thou art a fool, and fit for thy master . . . . . . ii 1 52
Fit I meet them . . . . v 1 57
When the fit was on him, I did mark How he did shake . . *J. Cæsar* i 2 120
Leave him out.—Indeed he is not fit . . . . ii 1 153
Let's carve him as a dish fit for the gods, Not hew him as a carcass fit for hounds . . . . ii 1 173
There is no hour so fit As Cæsar's death's hour . . . . . iii 1 153
Is it fit, The three-fold world divided, he should stand One of the three to share it? . . . . iv 1 13
Then comes my fit again: I had else been perfect . . . *Macbeth* iii 4 21
The fit is momentary; upon a thought He will again be well . . iii 4 55
If such a one be fit to govern, speak: I am as I have spoken.—Fit to govern! No, not to live . . . . iv 3 101
It fits your wisdom so far to believe it . . . . . *Hamlet* i 3 25
Let's follow; 'tis not fit thus to obey him . . . . . . i 4 88
Your visitation shall receive such thanks As fits a king's remembrance ii 2 26
If you hold it fit, after the play Let his queen mother all alone entreat him To show his grief . . . . iii 1 189
Thoughts black, hands apt, drugs fit, and time agreeing . . . iii 2 266
Am I then revenged, To take him in the purging of his soul, When he is fit and season'd for his passage? . . . . iii 3 86
These profound heaves: You must translate: 'tis fit we understand them . . . . iv 1 2
In his lawless fit, Behind the arras hearing something stir, Whips out his rapier, cries, 'A rat, a rat!' . . . . iv 1 8
But so much was our love, We would not understand what was most fit iv 1 20
Botch the words up fit to their own thoughts . . . . . iv 5 10
Weigh what convenience both of time and means May fit us to our shape . . . . iv 7 151
This is mere madness: And thus awhile the fit will work on him . v 1 308
I will forestal their repair hither, and say you are not fit . . v 2 229
You have begot me, bred me, loved me: I Return those duties back as are right fit, Obey you, love you . . . . *Lear* i 1 99
So much as I have perused, I find it not fit for your o'er-looking . i 2 40
But I have heard him oft maintain it to be fit . . . . . i 2 77
All with me's meet that I can fashion fit . . . . . . i 2 200
That which ordinary men are fit for, I am qualified in . . . i 4 37
Which I least thought it fit To answer from our home . . . ii 1 125
To take the indisposed and sickly fit For the sound man . . . ii 4 112
Must make content with his fortunes fit, For the rain it raineth every day . . . . iii 2 76
The revenges we are bound to take upon your traitorous father are not fit for your beholding . . . . iii 7 9
I thought it fit To send the old and miserable king To some retention v 3 45
If she be black, and thereto have a wit, She'll find a white that shall her blackness fit . . . . *Othello* ii 1 134
He is a soldier fit to stand by Cæsar And give direction . . . ii 3 127
If you think fit, or that it may be done, Give me advantage of some brief discourse With Desdemona alone . . . . iii 1 54
It be fit that Cassio have his place, For, sure, he fills it up with great ability . . . . iii 3 246
We must think men are not gods, Nor of them look for such observances As fit the bridal . . . . iii 4 150
If I do find him fit, I'll move your suit And seek to effect it . . iii 4 166
This is his second fit; he had one yesterday . . . . . . iv 1 52
I find thee Most fit for business: go make thee ready . *Ant. and Cleo.* iii 3 40
Thou hast forspoke my being in these wars, And say'st it is not fit . iii 7 4
The foul'st best fits My latter part of life . . . . . . iv 6 38
As the fits and stirs of's mind Could best express . . . *Cymbeline* i 3 12
Fit That all the plagues of hell should at one time Encounter such revolt . . . . i 6 110
If he shall think it fit, A saucy stranger in his court to mart . . i 6 150
And you his mistress, only For the most worthiest fit! . . . . i 6 162
It is not fit your lordship should undertake every companion that you give offence to.—No, I know that: but it is fit I should commit offence to my inferiors.—Ay, it is fit for your lordship only . . ii 1 28
Is it fit I went to look upon him? is there no derogation in't? . . ii 1 46
A riding-suit, no costlier than would fit A franklin's housewife . . iii 2 78
Fore-thinking this, I have already fit—'Tis in my cloak-bag—doublet, hat, hose . . . . iii 4 171
To some shade, And fit you to your manhood . . . . . iii 4 195
It fits us therefore ripely Our chariots and our horsemen be in readiness iii 5 22
How fit his garments serve me! Why should his mistress, who was made by him that made the tailor, not be fit too? . . . . . . iv 1 2
'Tis said a woman's fitness comes by fits . . . . . . iv 1 6
Thy name well fits thy faith, thy faith thy name . . . . iv 2 381
With faces fit for masks, or rather fairer Than those for preservation cased . . . . v 3 21
And will fit you With dignities becoming your estates . . . v 5 21
The fit and apt construction of thy name, Being Leo-natus . . . v 5 444
It is fit, What being more known grows worse, to smother it . *Pericles* i 1 105

Fit. Which pleasure fits an husband, not a father . . . *Pericles* i 1 129
It fits thee not to ask the reason why, Because we bid it . . . i 1 157
Whereas reproof, obedient and in order, Fits kings, as they are men . i 2 43
And I, as fits my nature, do obey you . . . . . . ii 1 4
If it be a day fits you, search out of the calendar, and nobody look after it . . . . ii 1 58
It's fit it should be so; for princes are A model . . . ii 2 10
Were more than you expect, or more than's fit . . . ii 3 5
Sir, yonder is your place.—Some other is more fit . . . ii 3 23
Fit a word. O, how fit a word Is that vile name to perish on my sword! *M. N. Dream* ii 2 106
Fit counsellor and servant for a prince . . . . *Pericles* i 2 63
Fit disposition. I crave fit disposition for my wife . . *Othello* i 3 237
Fit fellow. I find him a fit fellow . . . . . *Hen. VIII.* ii 2 117
Fit man. The most senseless and fit man for the constable . *Much Ado* iii 3 23
If I can by any means light on a fit man . . . *T. of Shrew* i 1 112
Fit occasion. You may have very fit occasion for't . . *T. Night* iii 4 190
Fit of madness. What's a fever but a fit of madness? . *Com. of Errors* v 1 76
This ill day A most outrageous fit of madness took him . . . v 1 139
Fits o' the season. And best knows The fits o' the season . *Macbeth* iv 2 17
Fit o' the time. But that The violent fit o' the time craves it as physic For the whole state . . . . . . *Coriolanus* iii 2 33
Fit rewards. In time will find their fit rewards . . *Hen. VIII.* iii 2 245
Fit time. These letters at fit time deliver me . . *Meas. for Meas.* iv 5 1
To prison, till fit time Of law and course of direct session Call thee *Othello* i 2 85
Fit welcome. I look'd not for you yet, nor am provided For your fit welcome . . . . *Lear* ii 4 236
Fitchew. A fitchew, a toad, a lizard, an owl . . . *Troi. and Cres.* v 1 67
The fitchew, nor the soiled horse, goes to't With a more riotous appetite. Down from the waist they are Centaurs . . . . *Lear* iv 6 124
'Tis such another fitchew! marry, a perfumed one . . . *Othello* iv 1 150
Fitful. After life's fitful fever he sleeps well . . . *Macbeth* iii 2 23
Fitly. Even so most fitly As you malign our senators . *Coriolanus* i 1 116
Cats, that can judge as fitly of his worth As I can of those mysteries . iv 2 34
My steward!—Here, my lord.—So fitly? . . . *T. of Athens* iii 4 111
If aught within that little seeming substance . . may fitly like your grace, She's there, and she is yours . . . . . *Lear* i 1 203
I will fitly bring you to hear my lord speak . . . . . i 2 184
I can compare our rich misers to nothing so fitly as to a whale *Pericles* ii 1 33
Fitment. 'Twas a fitment for The purpose I then follow'd . *Cymbeline* v 5 409
When she should do for clients her fitment . . . *Pericles* iv 6 6
Fitness. Dispossessing all my other parts Of necessary fitness *M. for M.* ii 4 23
Have you, I say, an answer of such fitness for all questions? *All's Well* ii 2 31
'Tis a needful fitness That we adjourn this court till further day *Hen. VIII.* ii 4 231
The still and mental parts, That do contrive how many hands shall strike, When fitness calls them on . . . *Troi. and Cres.* i 3 202
Of no more soul nor fitness for the world Than camels in the war *Coriol.* ii 1 266
They have made themselves, and their fitness now Does unmake you . . . . *Macbeth* i 7 53
If his fitness speaks, mine is ready . . . . . *Hamlet* v 2 209
Were't my fitness To let these hands obey my blood, They are apt enough to dislocate and tear Thy flesh and bones . . . *Lear* iv 2 63
'Tis said a woman's fitness comes by fits . . . *Cymbeline* iv 1 6
Fitted. He may be so fitted That his soul sicken not . *Meas. for Meas.* ii 4 40
I have been drinking all night; I am not fitted for't . . . iv 3 47
I hope to see you one day fitted with a husband . . *Much Ado* ii 1 61
Well fitted in arts, glorious in arms: Nothing becomes him ill *L. L. Lost* ii 1 45
No time shall be omitted That will betime, and may by us be fitted . iv 3 382
And, I hope, here is a play fitted . . . . *M. N. Dream* i 2 67
For in all the play There is not one word apt, one player fitted . . v 1 65
Sure, that part Was aptly fitted and naturally perform'd *T. of Shrew* Ind. 1 87
She better would have fitted me . . . . . *3 Hen. VI.* iv 1 54
Unfrequented plots there are Fitted by kind for rape and villany *T. An.* ii 1 116
Well are you fitted, had you but a Moor . . . . . v 2 85
A document in madness, thoughts and remembrance fitted *Hamlet* iv 5 179
And in time, When she had fitted you with her craft . . *Cymbeline* v 5 55
Fitter. Dispose of her To some more fitter place . . *Meas. for Meas.* ii 2 17
He is my brother too: but fitter time for that . . . . . v 1 498
There is no fitter matter . . . . . . *All's Well* iv 5 81
Thou art fitter to be worn in my cap than to wait at my heels *2 Hen. IV.* i 2 17
There are other men fitter to go out than I . . . . . i 2 126
In some better place, Fitter for sickness and for crazy age *1 Hen. VI.* iii 2 89
Fitter is my study and my books Than wanton dalliance . . . v 1 22
The fitter for the King of heaven, that hath him *Richard III.* i 2 105
He was fitter for that place than earth . . . . . . i 2 108
The question of Cordelia and her father Requires a fitter place . *Lear* v 3 59
She is a goodly creature.—The fitter, then, the gods should have her *Per.* iv 1 10
Fittest. This course I fittest choose . . . *Com. of Errors* iv 3 96
Devise the fittest time and safest way To hide us from pursuit *As Y. L. It* i 3 137
I have heard it said, the fittest time to corrupt a man's wife is when she's fallen out with her husband . . . . *Coriolanus* iv 3 33
He wakes; speak to him.—Madam, do you; 'tis fittest . . . *Lear* iv 7 43
'Bout midnight, more: The herbs that have on them cold dew o' the night Are strewings fitt'st for graves . . . . *Cymbeline* iv 2 285
Fitteth. I am ill at reckoning; it fitteth the spirit of a tapster *L. L. Lost* i 2 42
It fitteth not a prelate so to plead . . . . *1 Hen. VI.* iii 1 57
Best fitteth my degree or your condition . . . . *Richard III.* iii 7 143
Fitting. A silly answer and fitting well a sheep . . . *T. G. of Ver.* i 1 81
And any thing that is fitting to be known, discover . . *W. Tale* iv 4 741
News fitting to the night, Black, fearful, comfortless and horrible *K. John* v 6 19
Embrace we then this opportunity As fitting best . . *1 Hen. VI.* ii 1 14
Are all things fitting for that royal time? . . . *Richard III.* iii 4 4
Left nothing fitting for the purpose Untouch'd, or slightly handled . iii 7 18
Acquaint him with it, As needful in our loves, fitting our duty *Hamlet* i 1 173
And fitting for a princess Descended of so many royal kings *Ant. and Cleo.* v 2 329
Ask of Cymbeline what boon thou wilt, Fitting my bounty . *Cymbeline* v 5 98
Fitzwater, thou art damn'd to hell for this . . . *Richard II.* iv 1 43
Fitzwater, I do remember well The very time Aumerle and you did talk iv 1 60
Thy pains, Fitzwater, shall not be forgot: Right noble is thy merit . v 6 17
Five. Full fathom five thy father lies; Of his bones are coral made *Temp.* i 2 396
They say there's but five upon this isle . . . . . iii 2 6
We find Each putter-out of five for one will bring us Good warrant of . iii 3 48
By this, I think, the dial points at five . . . *Com. of Errors* v 1 118
The whole world again Cannot pick out five such . . *L. L. Lost* v 2 548
Strike more dead Than common sleep of all these five the sense *M. N. D.* iv 1 87
Rayed with the yellows, past cure of the fives . . *T. of Shrew* iii 2 54
There's four or five, to great Saint Jaques bound . . *All's Well* iii 5 98
Some four or five attend him; All, if you will . . . *T. Night* i 4 36
The eldest is eleven; The second and the third, nine, and some five *W. T.* ii 1 145

Five. The prince once set a dish of apple-johns before him, and told him there were five more Sir Johns . . . . . . *2 Hen. IV.* ii 4 6
Thou art as valorous as Hector of Troy, worth five of Agamemnon . ii 4 237
With four or five most vile and ragged foils . . . *Hen. V.* iv Prol. 50
I think there be six Richmonds in the field; Five have I slain to-day *Richard III.* v 4 12
The five best senses Acknowledged thee their patron *T. of Athens* i 2 129
From this present hour of five till the bell have told eleven . *Othello* ii 2 11
Devils do the gods great harm in their women; for in every ten that they make, the devils mar five . . . . *Ant. and Cleo.* v 2 279
Were you a gamester at five or at seven?—Earlier too, sir . *Pericles* iv 6 81
Five and thirty. I swam, ere I could recover the shore, five and thirty leagues off and on . . . . . . *Tempest* iii 2 16
How giddily a' [fashion] turns about all the hot bloods between fourteen and five-and-thirty . . . . . . *Much Ado* iii 3 141
Five and twenty. How old are you, friend?—Five and twenty, sir.—A ripe age . . . . *As Y. Like It* v 1 21
Our present musters grow upon the file To five and twenty thousand *2 Hen. IV.* i 3 11
What, is the king but five and twenty thousand? . . . . i 3 68
None else of name; and of all other men But five and twenty *Hen. V.* iv 8 111
Will but amount to five and twenty thousand . . . *3 Hen. VI.* ii 1 181
Five and twenty valiant sons, Half of the number that King Priam had *T. Andron.* i 1 79
Come pentecost as quickly as it will, Some five and twenty years *R. and J.* i 5 39
Besides my former sum, Which makes it five and twenty *T. of Athens* ii 1 3
Bring but five and twenty: to no more Will I give place or notice *Lear* ii 4 251
What, must I come to you With five and twenty, Regan? said you so? . ii 4 257
Thy fifty yet doth double five-and-twenty, And thou art twice her love ii 4 262
What need you five and twenty, ten, or five? . . . . ii 4 264
Five days. This advertisement is five days old . . . *1 Hen. IV.* iii 2 172
These five days have I hid me in these woods . . *2 Hen. VI.* iv 10 3
Look on me well: I have eat no meat these five days . . iv 10 41
Five days we do allot thee, for provision To shield thee from diseases *Lear* i 1 176
Five descents. From son to son, some four or five descents *All's Well* iii 7 24
Five ducats. To pay five ducats, five, I would not farm it *Hamlet* iv 4 20
Five-fathom. Of healths five-fathom deep . . . *Rom. and Jul.* i 4 85
Five-finger-tied. With another knot, five-finger-tied *Troi. and Cres.* v 2 157
Five flower-de-luces. Deck'd with five flower-de-luces on each side *1 Hen. VI.* i 2 99
Five-fold. Thy tongue, thy face, thy limbs, actions and spirit, Do give thee five-fold blazon . . . . . . *T. Night* i 5 312
Five Frenchmen. There hath at least five Frenchmen died to-night *1 Hen. VI.* ii 2 9
Five hours. Within these five hours lived Lord Hastings *Richard III.* iii 6 8
She hath not been entranced Above five hours . . . *Pericles* iii 2 95
Five hundred. Your wife is as honest a 'omans as I will desires among five thousand, and five hundred too . . . *Mer. Wives* iii 3 237
Five hundred ducats, villain, for a rope?—I'll serve you, sir, five hundred at the rate . . . . . . *Com. of Errors* iv 4 13
I have five hundred crowns, The thrifty hire I saved . *As Y. Like It* ii 3 38
A' pops me out At least from fair five hundred pound a year . *K. John* i 1 69
A half-faced groat five hundred pound a year! . . . . . i 1 94
Your face hath got five hundred pound a year, Yet sell your face for five pence and 'tis dear . . . . i 1 152
Good Sir John, let me have five hundred of my thousand . *2 Hen. IV.* v 5 89
Five hundred poor I have in yearly pay . . . . *Hen. V.* iv 1 315
Of the which, Five hundred were but yesterday dubb'd knights . iv 8 91
Beside five hundred prisoners of esteem . . . *1 Hen. VI.* iii 4 8
With five thousand men?—Ay, with five hundred, father, for a need *3 Hen. VI.* i 2 68
I'll have five hundred voices of that sound.—I twice five hundred *Coriol.* ii 3 219
This monument five hundred years hath stood . . *T. Andron.* i 1 350
Five justices' hands at it, and witnesses more . . . *W. Tale* iv 4 288
Five leagues. Ere the ships could meet by twice five leagues *Com. of Er.* i 1 101
Five marks. Of which he made five marks, ready money *Meas. for Meas.* iv 3 7
Five men. Come thou and thy five men, and if I do not leave you all as dead as a door-nail . . . . . . *2 Hen. VI.* iv 10 42
Five men to twenty! though the odds be great, I doubt not, uncle, of our victory . . . . *3 Hen. VI.* i 2 72
Five moons. They say five moons were seen to-night . *K. John* iv 2 182
Five o'clock. Soon at five o'clock, Please you, I'll meet with you *C. of Er.* i 2 26
He had of me a chain: at five o'clock I shall receive the money for the same . . . . iv 1 10
'Tis almost five o'clock, cousin; 'tis time you were ready . *Much Ado* iii 4 52
Five of the clock. Let it be so hasted that supper be ready at the farthest by five of the clock . . . . *Mer. of Venice* ii 2 122
Five or six thousand; but very weak and unserviceable . *All's Well* iv 3 151
One Mistress Tale-porter, and five or six honest wives *W. Tale* iv 4 273
Some five or six and thirty of his knights, Hot questrists after him *Lear* iii 7 16
Five pence. Where, for one shot of five pence, thou shalt have five thousand welcomes . . . . . . *T. G. of Ver.* ii 5 10
Your face hath got five hundred pound a year, Yet sell your face for five pence and 'tis dear . . . . *K. John* i 1 152
Five pound. Three pound of sugar, five pound of currants *W. Tale* iv 3 40
Five removes. Here's a petition from a Florentine, Who hath for four or five removes come short To tender it herself . . *All's Well* v 3 131
Five-score. The moon was a month old when Adam was no more, And raught not to five weeks when he came to five-score . *L. L. Lost* iv 2 41
A wither'd hermit, five-score winters worn, Might shake off fifty, looking in her eye . . . . iv 3 242
Five sentences. The gentleman had drunk himself out of his five sentences.—It is his five senses: fie, what the ignorance is! *M. Wives* i 1 179
Five shillings to one on't . . . . . . *Much Ado* iii 3 84
Five summers have I spent in furthest Greece . . *Com. of Errors* i 1 133
Till twice five summers have enrich'd our fields . . *Richard II.* i 3 141
Five talents is his debt, His means most short . . *T. of Athens* i 1 95
When he was poor, Imprison'd, and in scarcity of friends, I clear'd him with five talents . . . . ii 2 235
Bid him suppose some good necessity Touches his friend, which craves to be remember'd With those five talents . . . . . ii 2 238
Five thousand. Where, for one shot of five pence, thou shalt have five thousand welcomes . . . . . . *T. G. of Ver.* ii 5 10
Your wife is as honest a 'omans as I will desires among five thousand, and five hundred too . . . . . . *Mer. Wives* iii 3 237
Was worth five thousand of you all . . . *Meas. for Meas.* i 2 61
He hath been five thousand years a boy . . . *L. L. Lost* v 2 11
Why, now thou hast unwish'd five thousand men . . *Hen. V.* iv 3 76
We'll meet her in the field.—What, with five thousand men? . *3 Hen. VI.* i 2 67
Thou and Oxford, with five thousand men, Shall cross the seas . . iii 3 234

Five thousand. And late, five thousand: to Varro and to Isidore He owes nine thousand . . . . . *T. of Athens* ii 1 1
Five thousand crowns, my lord.—Five thousand drops pays that . . iii 4 96
Five times, Marcius, I have fought with thee . . *Coriolanus* i 10 7
Five times he hath return'd Bleeding to Rome . . . *T. Andron.* i 1 33
Take our good meaning, for our judgement sits Five times in that ere once in our five wits . . . . . *Rom. and Jul.* i 4 47
With five times so much conversation, I should get ground of your fair mistress, make her go back . . . . *Cymbeline* i 4 113
It is a thing I made, which hath the king Five times redeem'd from death i 5 63
Five to one. There's five to one; besides, they all are fresh . *Hen. V.* iv 3 4
Five tribunes to defend their vulgar wisdoms . . *Coriolanus* i 1 219
Five vowels. The third of the five vowels, if you repeat them *L. L. Lost* v 1 56
Five weeks. You would lift the moon out of her sphere, if she would continue in it five weeks without changing . . . *Tempest* ii 1 184
What was a month old at Cain's birth, that's not five weeks old as yet? *L. L. Lost* iv 2 36
The moon was a month old when Adam was no more, And raught not to five weeks when he came to five-score . . . . . iv 2 41
Five wits. In our last conflict four of his five wits went halting off *M. Ado* i 1 66
Alas, sir, how fell you besides your five wits? . . *T. Night* iv 2 92
Take our good meaning, for our judgement sits Five times in that ere once in our five wits . . . . . *Rom. and Jul.* i 4 47
Thou hast more of the wild-goose in one of thy wits than, I am sure, I have in my whole five . . . . . . ii 4 78
Bless thy five wits! . . . . . . *Lear* iii 4 59; iii 6 60
Five women. Had I not Four or five women once that tended me? *Tempest* i 2 47
Five years since there was some speech of marriage . *Meas. for Meas.* v 1 217
Since which time of five years I never spake with her . . v 1 222
How long hast thou to serve, Francis?—Forsooth, five years . 1 *Hen. IV.* ii 4 46
Fix. One that fixes No bourn 'twixt his and mine . . *W. Tale* i 2 133
Fix thy foot.—Let the first budger die the other's slave! . *Coriolanus* i 8 4
I earnestly did fix mine eye Upon the wasted building . *T. Andron.* v 1 22
Think on that, And fix most firm thy resolution . . *Othello* v 1 5
Fixed. The hour is fixed; the match is made . . *Mer. Wives* ii 2 303
You orphan heirs of fixed destiny, Attend your office . . v 5 43
Fixing our eyes on whom our care was fix'd . . *Com. of Errors* i 1 85
That give a name to every fixed star . . . . *L. L. Lost* i 1 89
An ass's nole I fixed on his head . . . . *M. N. Dream* iii 2 17
These fix'd evils sit so fit in him . . . . . *All's Well* i 1 113
My intents are fix'd and will not leave me . . . . i 1 244
There thy fixed foot shall grow . . . . . *T. Night* i 4 17
Took it deeply, Fasten'd and fix'd the shame on 't in himself . *W. Tale* ii 3 15
The statue is but newly fix'd, the colour's Not dry . . . v 3 47
By this time from their fixed beds of lime Had been dishabited *K. John* ii 1 219
Five moons were seen to-night; Four fixed, and the fifth did whirl about iv 2 183
And meteors fright the fixed stars of heaven . . *Richard II.* ii 4 9
To which is fixed, as an aim or butt, Obedience . . *Hen. V.* i 2 186
And her foot, look you, is fixed upon a spherical stone . . iii 6 37
The fix'd sentinels almost receive The secret whispers of each other's watch . . . . iv Prol. 6
The horsemen sit like fixed candlesticks, With torch-staves in their hand iv 2 45
Why are thine eyes fix'd to the sullen earth? . 2 *Hen. VI.* i 2 5
Deliver'd strongly through my fixed teeth . . . iii 2 313
Mine hair be fix'd on end, as one distract . . . . iii 2 318
An eternal plant, Whereof the root was fix'd in virtue's ground 3 *Hen. VI.* iii 3 125
If yet your gentle souls fly in the air And be not fix'd in doom perpetual, Hover about me with your airy wings! . *Richard III.* iv 4 12
If we did think His contemplation were above the earth, And fix'd on spiritual object . . . . . *Hen. VIII.* iii 2 132
Shall star-like rise, as great in fame as she was, And so stand fix'd . v 5 48
Whose patience Is, as a virtue, fix'd . . . *Troi. and Cres.* i 2 5
Never did young man fancy With so eternal and so fix'd a soul . v 2 166
You have found, Scaling his present bearing with his past, That he's your fixed enemy . . . . . *Coriolanus* ii 3 258
'Tis a worthy lord.—Nay, that's most fix'd . . *T. of Athens* i 1 9
Whose eyes are on this sovereign lady fix'd . . . . i 1 68
And fix'd his head upon our battlements . . . *Macbeth* i 2 23
That the Everlasting had not fix'd His canon 'gainst self-slaughter! *Ham.* i 2 131
And fix'd his eyes upon you?—Most constantly . . . i 2 234
It is a massy wheel, Fix'd on the summit of the highest mount . iii 3 18
Like an engine, wrench'd my frame of nature From the fix'd place *Lear* i 4 291
You know the fiery quality of the duke; How unremoveable and fix'd he is . . . . ii 4 94
Where the greater malady is fix'd, The lesser is scarce felt . iii 4 8
But, alas, to make me A fixed figure for the time of scorn To point his slow unmoving finger at! . . . . . *Othello* iv 2 54
Fixing our eyes on whom our care was fix'd . *Com. of Errors* i 1 85
To please the eye indeed By fixing it upon a fairer eye . *L. L. Lost* i 1 81
Takes prisoner the wild motion of mine eye, Fixing it only here . *Cymb.* i 6 104
Fixture. The firm fixture of thy foot would give an excellent motion to thy gait in a semi-circled farthingale . . . *Mer. Wives* iii 3 67
Fixure. The fixure of her eye has motion in't . . . *W. Tale* v 3 67
Divert and crack, rend and deracinate The unity and married calm of states Quite from their fixure! . . . *Troi. and Cres.* i 3 101
Flag. These flags of France, that are advanced here . . *K. John* ii 1 207
Stand for your own; unwind your bloody flag . . *Hen. V.* i 2 101
This token serveth for a flag of truce . . . 1 *Hen. VI.* iii 1 138
A breath, a bubble, A sign of dignity, a garish flag . *Richard III.* iv 4 89
Set up the bloody flag against all patience . . *Coriolanus* ii 1 84
And death's pale flag is not advanced there . . *Rom. and Jul.* v 3 96
I must show out a flag and sign of love, Which is indeed but sign *Othello* i 1 157
Like to a vagabond flag upon the stream, Goes to and back *Ant. and Cleo.* i 4 45
'Twas a shame no less Than was his loss, to course your flying flags . iii 13 11
By the semblance Of their white flags display'd, they bring us peace *Per.* i 4 72
Flagging. Who, with their drowsy, slow and flagging wings, Clip dead men's graves . . . . 2 *Hen. VI.* iv 1 5
Flagon. A' poured a flagon of Rhenish on my head once . *Hamlet* v 1 197
Flail. Like an idle thresher with a flail, Fell gently down . 3 *Hen. VI.* ii 1 131
Flake. Had you not been their father, these white flakes Had challenged pity of them . . . . *Lear* iv 7 30
Flaky. And flaky darkness breaks within the east . *Richard III.* v 3 86
Flame. On the topmast, The yards and bowsprit, would I flame *Tempest* i 2 200
If he be chaste, the flame will back descend And turn him to no pain *Mer. Wives* v 5 89
Whose flames aspire As thoughts do blow them, higher and higher . v 5 101
'Let me not live,' quoth he, 'After my flame lacks oil' . *All's Well* i 2 59
In so true a flame of liking Wish chastely and love dearly . . i 3 217
The honour, sir, that flames in your fair eyes, Before I speak, too threateningly replies . . . . ii 3 86

Flame. If I did love you in my master's flame, With such a suffering, such a deadly life, In your denial I would find no sense . *T. Night* i 5 283
Quenching the flame of bold rebellion Even with the rebels' blood 2 *Hen. IV.* Ind. 26
Array'd in flames like to the prince of fiends . . *Hen. V.* iii 3 16
His face is all bubukles, and whelks, and knobs, and flames o' fire . iii 6 109
Through their paly flames Each battle sees the other's umber'd face iv Prol. 8
Burns under feigned ashes of forged love And will at last break out into a flame . . . . 1 *Hen. VI.* iii 1 191
O, let the vile world end, And the premised flames of the last day Knit earth and heaven together! . . . . 2 *Hen. VI.* v 2 41
And burns me up with flames that tears would quench . 3 *Hen. VI.* ii 1 84
Put in her tender heart the aspiring flame Of golden sovereignty *Richard III.* iv 4 328
To feed for aye her lamp and flames of love . . *Troi. and Cres.* iii 2 167
By the flame of yonder glorious heaven . . . . v 6 23
But a small thing would make it flame again . . *Coriolanus* iv 3 21
Can you think to blow out the intended fire your city is ready to flame in? . . . . v 2 49
Our gentle flame Provokes itself . . . . *T. of Athens* i 1 23
As Æneas, our great ancestor, Did from the flames of Troy upon his shoulder The old Anchises bear . . . . *J. Cæsar* i 2 113
Held up his left hand, which did flame and burn Like twenty torches . i 3 16
Grease that's sweaten From the murderer's gibbet throw Into the flame *Macbeth* iv 1 67
I to sulphurous and tormenting flames Must render up myself *Hamlet* i 5 3
Run barefoot up and down, threatening the flames With bisson rheum . ii 2 528
Upon the heat and flame of thy distemper Sprinkle cool patience . . iii 4 123
There lives within the very flame of love A kind of wick or snuff that will abate it . . . . iv 7 115
You nimble lightnings, dart your blinding flames Into her scornful eyes! *Lear* ii 4 167
Through fire and through flame, and through ford and whirlipool . . iii 4 53
The flame o' the taper Bows toward her, and would under-peep her lids, To see the enclosed lights . . . . . *Cymbeline* ii 2 19
Murder's as near to lust as flame to smoke . . . *Pericles* i 1 138
Flame-coloured. It does indifferent well in a flame-coloured stock *T. N.* i 3 144
A fair hot wench in flame-coloured taffeta . . 1 *Hen. IV.* i 2 11
Flamed. In every cabin I flamed amazement . . . *Tempest* i 2 198
Flamen. Seld-shown flamens Do press among the popular throngs *Coriolanus* ii 1 229
Hoar the flamen, That scolds against the quality of flesh *T. of Athens* iv 3 155
Flaming. Beauty that the tyrant oft reclaims Shall to my flaming wrath be oil and flax . . . . 2 *Hen. VI.* v 2 55
He having colour enough, and the other higher, is too flaming a praise for a good complexion . . . . . *Troi. and Cres.* i 2 113
Senseless Ilium, Seeming to feel this blow, with flaming top Stoops to his base . . . . *Hamlet* ii 2 497
To flaming youth let virtue be as wax, And melt in her own fire . iii 4 84
If I quench thee, thou flaming minister, I can again thy former light restore, Should I repent me . . . . *Othello* v 2 8
Flaminius, honest Flaminius; you are very respectively welcome, sir *T. of Athens* iii 1 6
What hast thou there under thy cloak, pretty Flaminius? . . . iii 1 15
Flaminius, I have noted thee always wise . . . . iii 1 33
Draw nearer, honest Flaminius. Thy lord's a bountiful gentleman . iii 1 41
Flanders. To Lynn, my lord, And ship from thence to Flanders 3 *Hen. VI.* iv 5 21
You made bold To carry into Flanders the great seal . *Hen. VIII.* iii 2 319
Flannel. I am not able to answer the Welsh flannel . . *Mer. Wives* v 5 172
Flap. Thou green sarcenet flap for a sore eye . . *Troi. and Cres.* v 1 36
Flap-dragon. Thou art easier swallowed than a flap-dragon . *L. L. Lost* v 1 45
Drinks off candles' ends for flap-dragons, and rides the wild-mare 2 *Hen. IV.* ii 4 267
Flap-dragoned. To see how the sea flap-dragoned it . . *W. Tale* iii 3 100
Flap-eared. A whoreson beetle-headed, flap-ear'd knave! . *T. of Shrew* iv 1 160
Flap-jack. We'll have flesh for holidays, fish for fasting-days, and more-o'er puddings and flap-jacks . . . . . . *Pericles* ii 1 87
Flaring. With ribands pendent, flaring 'bout her head . *Mer. Wives* iv 6 42
Flash. Secure of thunder's crack or lightning flash . *T. Andron.* ii 1 3
Timon will be left a naked gull, Which flashes now a phœnix *T. of Athens* ii 1 32
I did present myself Even in the aim and very flash of it *J. Cæsar* i 3 52
The flash and outbreak of a fiery mind . . . . *Hamlet* ii 1 33
Flashes of merriment, that were wont to set the table on a roar . v 1 210
Every hour He flashes into one gross crime or other . . *Lear* i 3 4
O, still Thy deafening, dreadful thunders; gently quench Thy nimble, sulphurous flashes! . . . . *Pericles* iii 1 6
Flashing. Pistol's cock is up, And flashing fire will follow . *Hen. V.* ii 1 56
Flask. The carved-bone face on a flask . . . *L. L. Lost* v 2 619
Like powder in a skilless soldier's flask, Is set a-fire . *Rom. and Jul.* iii 3 132
Flat. All the infections that the sun sucks up From bogs, fens, flats, on Prosper fall! . . . . *Tempest* ii 2 2
I'll fall flat; Perchance he will not mind me . . . . ii 2 16
Nibbling sheep, And flat meads thatch'd with stover . . iv 1 63
You are too flat And mar the concord with too harsh a descant *T. G. of V.* i 2 93
That in the captain's but a choleric word, Which in the soldier is flat blasphemy.—Art avised o' that? . . . *Meas. for Meas.* ii 2 131
The flat transgression of a school-boy . . . . *Much Ado* ii 1 229
This is flat perjury, to call a prince's brother villain . . iv 2 44
Flat burglary as ever was committed . . . . . iv 2 52
The boy hath sold him a bargain, a goose, that's flat . *L. L. Lost* iii 1 102
Flat treason 'gainst the kingly state of youth . . . iv 3 293
I should not see the sandy hour-glass run, But I should think of shallows and of flats . . . . *Mer. of Venice* i 1 26
The Goodwins, I think they call the place; a very dangerous flat and fatal . . . . iii 1 5
This is flat knavery, to take upon you another man's name *T. of Shrew* v 1 37
Rebellion, flat rebellion! . . . . . . *K. John* iii 1 298
Half my power this night, Passing these flats, are taken by the tide . v 6 40
Those prisoners you shall keep.—Nay, I will; that's flat . 1 *Hen. IV.* i 3 218
I'll not march through Coventry with them, that's flat . . iv 2 43
But pardon, gentles all, The flat unraised spirits . . *Hen. V.* Prol. 9
He, like a puling cuckold, would drink up The lees and dregs of a flat tamed piece . . . . *Troi. and Cres.* iv 1 62
To unbuild the city and to lay all flat.—What is the city but the people? *Coriolanus* iii 1 198
That is the way to lay the city flat . . . . . iii 1 204
Down with the nose, Down with it flat . . . *T. of Athens* iv 3 158
O God! God! How weary, stale, flat and unprofitable, Seem to me all the uses of this world! . . . . *Hamlet* i 2 133

Flat. The ocean, overpeering of his list, Eats not the flats with more impetuous haste . . . . *Hamlet* iv 5 100
You must not think That we are made of stuff so flat and dull . . iv 7 31
Till of this flat a mountain you have made, To o'ertop old Pelion . v 1 275
All-shaking thunder, Smite flat the thick rotundity o' the world! *Lear* iii 2 7
To fortify her judgement, which else an easy battery might lay flat *Cymb.* i 4 23
Up to yond hill; Your legs are young; I'll tread these flats . . iii 3 11
Flat-long. What a blow was there given!—An it had not fallen flat-long *Tempest* ii 1 181
Flatly. He tells me flatly, there is no mercy for me in heaven *M. of Ven.* iii 5 34
He tells you flatly what his mind is . . . . *T. of Shrew* i 2 77
He flatly says he'll not lay down his arms . . *K. John* v 2 126
And tell me flatly I am no proud Jack, like Falstaff . 1 *Hen. IV.* ii 4 12
Flatness. That he did but see The flatness of my misery! . *W. Tale* iii 2 123
Flatter. Call her divine.—I will not flatter her.—O, flatter me; for love delights in praises . . . . . . *T. G. of Ver.* ii 4 147
Flatter and praise, commend, extol their graces . . . iii 1 102
Think not I flatter, for I swear I do not . . . . iv 3 12
Yet the painter flatter'd her a little, Unless I flatter with myself too much . . . . iv 4 193
To flatter up these powers of mine with rest . . *L. L. Lost* v 2 824
But wherefore should I go? I am not bid for love; they flatter me *Mer. of Venice* ii 5 13
'Tis not her glass, but you, that flatters her . . *As Y. Like It* iii 5 54
Desire him not to flatter with his lord . . . *T. Night* v 1 322
Further I will not flatter you, my lord . . . . *K. John* ii 1 516
We thank you both: yet one but flatters us . . . *Richard II.* i 1 25
I mock my name, great king, to flatter thee.—Should dying men flatter with those that live?—No, no, men living flatter those that die . ii 1 87
I hardly yet have learn'd To insinuate, flatter, bow, and bend my limbs iv 1 165
Thoughts tending to content flatter themselves That they are not the first of fortune's slaves . . . . v 5 23
I cannot flatter; I do defy The tongues of soothers . . 1 *Hen. IV.* iv 1 6
I dare not swear thou lovest me; yet my blood begins to flatter me that thou dost . . . . *Hen. V.* v 2 239
At first, to flatter us withal, Make us partakers of a little gain 1 *Hen. VI.* ii 1 51
Fair Margaret knows That Suffolk doth not flatter, face, or feign . . v 3 142
So should I give consent to flatter sin . . . . . v 5 25
How evil it beseems thee, To flatter Henry and forsake thy brother! 3 *Hen. VI.* iv 7 85
'Tis sin to flatter; 'good' was little better . . . . v 6 3
Since you teach me how to flatter you, Imagine I have said farewell *Richard III.* i 2 224
Because I cannot flatter and speak fair, Smile in men's faces . . i 3 47
Flatter my sorrows with report of it . . . . . iv 4 245
I am a villain: yet I lie, I am not. Fool, of thyself speak well: fool, do not flatter . . . . v 3 192
He that will give good words to thee will flatter Beneath abhorring *Coriolanus* i 1 171
Now, to seem to affect the malice and displeasure of the people is as bad as that which he dislikes, to flatter them for their love . . ii 2 26
Masters of the people, Your multiplying spawn how can he flatter? ii 2 82
I will, sir, flatter my sworn brother, the people, to earn a dearer estimation of them . . . . ii 3 102
For the mutable, rank-scented many, let them Regard me as I do not flatter . . . . iii 1 67
He would not flatter Neptune for his trident, Or Jove for's power to thunder . . . . iii 1 256
I know thou hadst rather Follow thine enemy in a fiery gulf Than flatter him in a bower . . . . iii 2 92
Andronicus, I do not flatter thee, But honour thee . . *T. Andron.* i 1 212
I scorn thy meat; 'twould choke me, for I should ne'er flatter thee *T. of Athens* i 2 39
Bid them flatter thee; O, thou shalt find— A fool of thee . . iv 3 231
Thou flatter'st misery.—I flatter not; but say thou art a caitiff iv 3 235
Do not think I flatter; For what advancement may I hope from thee? *Hamlet* iii 2 61
He cannot flatter, he, An honest mind and plain, he must speak truth! *Lear* ii 2 104
Lepidus flatters both, Of both is flatter'd; but he neither loves *A. and C.* ii 1 14
To flatter Cæsar, would you mingle eyes With one that ties his points? iii 13 156
They do abuse the king that flatter him . . . . *Pericles* i 2 38
When Signior Sooth here does proclaim a peace, He flatters you . i 2 45
Flattered. And yet the painter flatter'd her a little . . *T. G. of Ver.* iv 4 192
I have trod a measure; I have flattered a lady . *As Y. Like It* v 4 46
I have fondly flatter'd her withal . . . . *T. of Shrew* iv 2 31
Now shall he try his friends that flatter'd him . *Richard II.* ii 2 85
Where be the bending peers that flatter'd thee? . *Richard III.* iv 4 95
There have been many great men that have flattered the people, who ne'er loved them . . . . *Coriolanus* ii 2 9
He that loves to be flattered is worthy o' the flatterer . *T. of Athens* i 1 232
Why shouldst thou hate men? They never flatter'd thee . . iv 3 270
When I tell him he hates flatterers, He says he does, being then most flattered. Let me work . . . . . . *J. Cæsar* ii 1 208
Why should the poor be flatter'd? . . . . *Hamlet* iii 2 64
Yet better thus, and known to be contemn'd, Than still contemn'd and flatter'd . . . . *Lear* iv 1 2
Ha! Goneril, with a white beard! They flattered me like a dog . iv 6 98
'Tis thus; Who tells me true, though in his tale lie death, I hear him as he flatter'd . . . . *Ant. and Cleo.* i 2 103
Lepidus flatters both, Of both is flatter'd; but he neither loves . ii 1 15
The thing the which is flatter'd, but a spark, To which that blast gives heat and stronger glowing . . . . . . *Pericles* i 2 40
Flatterer. Even here I will put off my hope and keep it No longer for my flatterer . . . . *Tempest* iii 3 8
And fear to find Mine eye too great a flatterer for my mind . *T. Night* i 5 328
A thousand flatterers sit within thy crown . . . *Richard II.* ii 1 100
The king is not himself, but basely led By flatterers . . . ii 1 242
He is a flatterer, A parasite, a keeper back of death . . . ii 2 69
When I was a king, my flatterers Were then but subjects; being now a subject, I have a king here to my flatterer . . . . . iv 1 306
Let him that is no coward nor no flatterer, But dare maintain the party of the truth, Pluck a red rose . . . . 1 *Hen. VI.* ii 4 31
If thine eye be not a flatterer, Come thou on my side . *Richard III.* i 4 271
When drums and trumpets shall I' the field prove flatterers, let courts and cities be Made all of false-faced soothing! . . . *Coriolanus* i 9 43
Call'd them Time-pleasers, flatterers, foes to nobleness . . iii 1 45
From the glass-faced flatterer To Apemantus . . . *T. of Athens* i 1 58
He that loves to be flattered is worthy o' the flatterer . . . i 1 233
Would all those flatterers were thine enemies! . . . . i 2 83

Flatterer. This is the world's soul; and just of the same piece Is every flatterer's spirit . . . . *T. of Athens* iii 2 72
Who dares In purity of manhood stand upright, And say 'This man's a flatterer'? . . . . iv 3 15
Thy flatterers yet wear silk, drink wine, lie soft . . . iv 3 206
Be thou a flatterer now, and seek to thrive By that which has undone thee iv 3 210
If thou hadst not been born the worst of men, Thou hadst been a knave and flatterer . . . . iv 3 276
What things in the world canst thou nearest compare to thy flatterers? —Women nearest; but men, men are the things themselves . . iv 3 319
Unicorns may be betray'd with trees, And bears with glasses, elephants with holes, Lions with toils and men with flatterers . *J. Cæsar* ii 1 206
When I tell him he hates flatterers, He says he does, being then most flattered . . . . ii 1 207
One of two bad ways you must conceit me, Either a coward or a flatterer iii 1 193
A friendly eye could never see such faults.—A flatterer's would not . iv 3 91
O you flatterers!—Flatterers! Now, Brutus, thank yourself . . v 1 44
I know, sir, I am no flatterer . . . . . . *Lear* ii 2 117
Sit down: thou art no flatterer: I thank thee for it . . *Pericles* i 2 60
Flatterest. Thou, now a-dying, say'st thou flatterest me *Richard II.* ii 1 90
Thou flatter'st misery.—I flatter not; but say thou art a caitiff *T. of A.* iv 3 234
Flattering. You are a flattering boy: now I see you'll be a courtier *Mer. Wives* iii 2 7
Though I cannot be said to be a flattering honest man . *Much Ado* i 3 32
That flattering tongue of yours won me . . . *As Y. Like It* iv 1 188
Even as a flattering dream or worthless fancy . *T. of Shrew* Ind. 1 44
I beheld myself Drawn in the flattering table of her eye . *K. John* ii 1 503
It is stopp'd with other flattering sounds, As praises *Richard II.* ii 1 17
O flattering glass, Like to my followers in prosperity, Thou dost beguile me! . . . . iv 1 279
Flattering himself in project of a power . . . 2 *Hen. IV.* i 3 29
Thou dost give me flattering busses . . . . ii 4 291
For all this flattering gloss, He will be found a dangerous protector 2 *Hen. VI.* i 1 163
I'll cut the causes off, Flattering me with impossibilities 3 *Hen. VI.* iii 2 143
The flattering index of a direful pageant . . . *Richard III.* iv 4 85
I will insult on him; Flattering myself, as if it were the Moor *T. An.* iii 2 72
If I may trust the flattering truth of sleep . . *Rom. and Jul.* v 1 1
Unsafe the while, that we Must lave our honours in these flattering streams, And make our faces vizards . . . . *Macbeth* iii 2 33
For love of grace, Lay not that flattering unction to your soul *Hamlet* iii 4 145
When he, conjunct, and flattering his displeasure, Tripp'd me behind *Lear* ii 2 125
Here comes a flattering rascal; upon him Will I first work *Cymbeline* i 5 27
Be it lying, note it, The woman's; flattering, hers; deceiving, hers . ii 5 23
Flattering-sweet. All this is but a dream, Too flattering-sweet to be substantial . . . . *Rom. and Jul.* ii 2 141
Flattery. Think'st thou I am so shallow, so conceitless, To be seduced by thy flattery? . . . . *T. G. of Ver.* iv 2 97
When the sweet breath of flattery conquers strife . *Com. of Errors* iii 2 28
Ay, marry, there; some flattery for this evil . . *L. L. Lost* iv 3 286
Even till I shrink with cold, I smile and say 'This is no flattery' *As Y. Like It* ii 1 10
He does me double wrong That wounds me with the flatteries of his tongue . . . . *Richard II.* iii 2 216
If speaking truth In this fine age were not thought flattery 1 *Hen. IV.* iv 1 2
I will cap that proverb with 'There is flattery in friendship' *Hen. V.* iii 7 125
What drink'st thou oft, instead of homage sweet, But poison'd flattery? iv 1 268
Having neither the voice nor the heart of flattery about me . . v 2 315
Without all colour Of base insinuating flattery I pluck this 1 *Hen. VI.* ii 4 35
By flattery hath he won the commons' hearts . . 2 *Hen. VI.* iii 1 28
Would I had never trod this English earth, Or felt the flatteries that grow upon it! . . . . *Hen. VIII.* iii 1 144
I come not To hear such flattery now, and in my presence . . v 3 124
And the words I utter Let none think flattery, for they'll find 'em truth v 5 17
Or never trust to what my tongue can do I' the way of flattery *Coriol.* iii 2 137
He water'd his new plants with dews of flattery, Seducing so my friends v 6 23
Now, farewell, flattery: die, Andronicus . . . *T. Andron.* iii 1 254
Spend our flatteries, to drink those men Upon whose age we void it up again, With poisonous spite and envy . . . . *T. of Athens* i 2 142
That men's ears should be To counsel deaf, but not to flattery! . i 2 257
Who, stuck and spangled with your flatteries, Washes it off . . iii 6 101
A discovery of the infinite flatteries that follow youth and opulency . v 1 37
I kiss thy hand, but not in flattery . . . . *J. Cæsar* iii 1 52
Think'st thou that duty shall have dread to speak, When power to flattery bows? To plainness honour's bound . . . *Lear* i 1 150
Old fools are babes again; and must be used With checks as flatteries . i 3 20
She is persuaded I will marry her, out of her own love and flattery, not out of my promise . . . . *Othello* iv 1 133
Mine eyes Were not in fault, for she was beautiful; Mine ears, that heard her flattery . . . . *Cymbeline* v 5 64
They do abuse the king that flatter him: For flattery is the bellows blows up sin . . . . *Pericles* i 2 39
No visor does become black villany So well as soft and tender flattery . iv 4 45
Flaunt. In these my borrow'd flaunts . . . . . *W. Tale* iv 4 23
Flavius. Call at Flavius' house, And tell him where I stay *M. for M.* iv 5 6
Bid them bring the trumpets to the gate; But send me Flavius first . iv 5 10
Flavius,— My lord?—The little casket bring me hither *T. of Athens* i 2 163
More news too: Marullus and Flavius, for pulling scarfs off Cæsar's images, are put to silence . . . . *J. Cæsar* i 2 289
Labeo and Flavius, set our battles on: 'Tis three o'clock . . v 3 108
Flaw. Falling in the flaws of her own youth . . . *Meas. for Meas.* ii 3 11
My love to thee is sound, sans crack or flaw . . *L. L. Lost* v 2 415
As sudden As flaws congealed in the spring of day . . 2 *Hen. IV.* iv 4 35
Do calm the fury of this mad-bred flaw . . . . 2 *Hen. VI.* iii 1 354
Like a great sea-mark, standing every flaw . . . *Coriolanus* v 3 74
O, these flaws and starts, Impostors to true fear . . *Macbeth* iii 4 63
O, that that earth, which kept the world in awe, Should patch a wall to expel the winter's flaw! . . . . *Hamlet* v 1 239
I have full cause of weeping; but this heart Shall break into a hundred thousand flaws, Or ere I'll weep . . . . . *Lear* ii 4 288
Observe how Antony becomes his flaw . . . *Ant. and Cleo.* iii 12 34
Courage enough: I do not fear the flaw; It hath done to me the worst *Pericles* iii 1 39
Flawed. France hath flaw'd the league . . . . *Hen. VIII.* i 1 95
Which hath flaw'd the heart Of all their loyalties . . . . i 2 21
But his flaw'd heart, Alack, too weak the conflict to support! . *Lear* v 3 196
Flax. What, a hodge-pudding? a bag of flax? . . . *Mer. Wives* v 5 159
Excellent; it hangs like flax on a distaff? . . . . *T. Night* i 3 108
And beauty that the tyrant oft reclaims Shall to my flaming wrath be oil and flax . . . . 2 *Hen. VI.* v 2 55

Flax. I'll fetch some flax and whites of eggs To apply to his bleeding face *Lear* iii 7 106
Flaxen. His beard was as white as snow, All flaxen was his poll *Hamlet* iv 5 196
Flax-wench. Deserves a name As rank as any flax-wench . *W. Tale* i 2 277
Flay. With her nails She'll flay thy wolvish visage . . *Lear* i 4 330
Flayed. The gentleman is half flayed already . . *W. Tale* iv 4 655
He has a son, who shall be flayed alive; then 'nointed over with honey iv 4 812
Remember 'stoned,' and 'flayed alive' . . . . . . iv 4 835
Though my case be a pitiful one, I hope I shall not be flayed out of it . iv 4 845
Who's yonder, That does appear as he were flay'd? . . *Coriolanus* i 6 22
Flaying. What flaying? boiling? In leads or oils? . . *W. Tale* iii 2 177
Vagabond exile, flaying, pent to linger But with a grain a day *Coriolanus* iii 3 89
Flea. He shall die a flea's death . . . *Mer. Wives* iv 2 158
If a' have no more man's blood in's belly than will sup a flea *L. L. Lost* v 2 698
Thou flea, thou nit, thou winter-cricket thou! . . *T. of Shrew* iv 3 110
If he were opened, and you find so much blood in his liver as will clog the foot of a flea, I'll eat the rest of the anatomy . . *T. Night* iii 2 67
This be the most villanous house in all London road for fleas 1 *Hen. IV.* ii 1 16
Your chamber-lie breeds fleas like a loach . . . . . ii 1 23
A' saw a flea stick upon Bardolph's nose, and a' said it was a black soul burning in hell-fire . . . . *Hen. V.* ii 3 42
That's a valiant flea that dare eat his breakfast on the lip of a lion . iii 7 156
Fleance. Goes Fleance with you?—Ay, my good lord . . *Macbeth* iii 1 36
Fleance his son, that keeps him company, Whose absence is no less material to me Than is his father's . . . . . . iii 1 135
O, full of scorpions is my mind, dear wife! Thou know'st that Banquo, and his Fleance, lives . . . . iii 2 37
O, treachery! Fly, good Fleance, fly, fly, fly! Thou mayst revenge . iii 3 17
Thou art the best o' the cut-throats: yet he's good That did the like for Fleance . . . . iii 4 18
Most royal sir, Fleance is 'scaped.—Then comes my fit again . . iii 4 20
Banquo walk'd too late; Whom, you may say, if't please you, Fleance kill'd, For Fleance fled . . . . iii 6 6
They should find What 'twere to kill a father; so should Fleance . . iii 6 20
Flecked darkness like a drunkard reels From forth day's path *Rom. and Jul.* ii 3 3
Fled. Why then, She's fled unto that peasant . . *T. G. of Ver.* v 2 35
Whither they are fled: Dispatch, sweet gentlemen, and follow me . v 2 47
We'll follow him that's fled; The thicket is beset . . . . v 3 10
Do not say they be fled; Germans are honest men . *Mer. Wives* iv 5 73
Then they fled Into this abbey, whither we pursued them *Com. of Errors* v 1 154
And then you fled into this abbey here . . . . . v 1 263
Your brother the bastard is fled from Messina . . *Much Ado* v 1 193
Pluck up, my heart, and be sad. Did he not say, my brother was fled? v 1 209
He is composed and framed of treachery: And fled he is upon this villany v 1 258
Here stand a pair of honourable men; A third is fled, that had a hand in it v 1 277
Don John is the author of all, who is fled and gone . . . v 2 101
Speak again: Thou runaway, thou coward, art thou fled? *M. N. Dream* iii 2 405
And, as she fled, her mantle she did fall . . . . . v 1 143
Now am I dead, Now am I fled; My soul is in the sky . . . v 1 307
O my daughter! Fled with a Christian! O my Christian ducats! *Mer. of Venice* ii 8 16
Acqaint my mother with my hate to her, And wherefore I am fled *All's W.* ii 3 305
His wife some two months since fled from his house . . . iv 3 57
Lest that the treachery of the two fled hence Be left her to perform *W. T.* ii 1 195
Fled from his father, from his hopes, and with A shepherd's daughter v 1 184
The life, the right and truth of all this realm Is fled to heaven *K. John* iv 3 145
All their powerful friends are fled to him . . . *Richard II.* ii 2 55
Resign'd his stewardship, And all the household servants fled with him ii 2 60
Go all which way it will! The nobles they are fled, the commons they are cold . . . . ii 2 88
Our countrymen are gone and fled, As well assured Richard their king is dead . . . . ii 4 16
Thy friends are fled to wait upon thy foes . . . . . . ii 4 23
Hearing thou wert dead, Are gone to Bolingbroke, dispersed and fled . iii 2 74
But now the blood of twenty thousand men Did triumph in my face, and they are fled . . . . iii 2 77
And all his men Upon the foot of fear, fled with the rest 1 *Hen. IV.* v 5 20
Arrows fled not swifter toward their aim Than did our soldiers 2 *Hen. IV.* i 1 123
The rogue fled from me like quicksilver . . . . . . ii 4 248
Cowardly fled, not having struck one stroke . 1 *Hen. VI.* i 1 134
I would ne'er have fled, But that they left me 'midst my enemies . . i 2 23
The day begins to break, and night is fled . . . . . ii 2 1
Rouen hangs her head for grief That such a valiant company are fled . iii 2 125
For fly he could not, if he would have fled; And fly would Talbot never iv 4 43
He is not Talbot's blood, That basely fled when noble Talbot stood . iv 5 17
You fled for vantage, every one will swear; But, if I bow, they'll say it was for fear . . . . iv 5 28
That which we have fled During the life, let us not wrong it dead . . iv 7 49
For with his soul fled all my worldly solace . . 2 *Hen. VI.* iii 2 151
What, is he fled? Go some, and follow him . . . . . iv 8 68
He is fled, my lord, and all his powers do yield . . . . iv 9 10
The unconquered soul of Cade is fled . . . . . . iv 10 70
'Tis not enough our foes are this time fled, Being opposites of such repairing nature . . . . v 3 21
I know our safety is to follow them; For, as I hear, the king is fled . v 3 24
So fled his enemies my warlike father . . . . 3 *Hen. VI.* ii 1 19
And we in them no hope to win the day; So that we fled . . . ii 1 137
'Twas odds, belike, when valiant Warwick fled . . . . . ii 1 148
You said so much before, and yet you fled . . . . . ii 2 106
Fly, father, fly! for all your friends are fled . . . . . ii 5 125
But think you, lords, that Clifford fled with them?—No, 'tis impossible ii 6 37
Edward is escaped from your brother, And fled, as he hears since, to Burgundy . . . . iv 6 79
The queen is valued thirty thousand strong, And Somerset, with Oxford, fled to her . . . . v 3 15
Dorset's fled To Richmond, in those parts beyond the sea *Richard III.* iv 2 46
Bad news, my lord: Ely is fled to Richmond . . . . . iv 3 46
Proclaim a pardon to the soldiers fled That in submission will return to us v 5 16
Either to harbour fled, Or made a toast for Neptune . *Troi. and Cres.* i 3 44
When the splitting wind Makes flexible the knees of knotted oaks, And flies fled under shade . . . . i 3 51
Yet oft, When blows have made me stay, I fled from words . *Coriolanus* ii 2 76
Be you remember'd, Marcus, she's gone, she's fled . . *T. Andron.* iv 3 5
And gladly shunn'd who gladly fled from me . . *Rom. and Jul.* i 1 136
Tybalt hit the life Of stout Mercutio, and then Tybalt fled . . iii 1 174
This was my lord's best hope; now all are fled, Save only the gods *T. of A.* iii 3 36
Where is Antony?—Fled to his house amazed . . *J. Cæsar* iii 1 96
O judgement! thou art fled to brutish beasts, And men have lost their reason . . . . iii 2 109
This morning are they fled away and gone . . . . . v 1 84
Fled. Malcolm and Donaldbain, the king's two sons, Are stol'n away and fled . . . . *Macbeth* ii 4 26
There's but one down; the son is fled.—We have lost Best half of our affair iii 3 20
The worm that's fled Hath nature that in time will venom breed . iii 4 29
Whom, you may say, if't please you, Fleance kill'd, For Fleance fled . iii 6 7
Macduff is fled to England.—Fled to England! . . . . . iv 1 142
Our exiled friends abroad That fled the snares of watchful tyranny . v 8 67
Where is the villain, Edmund?—Fled this way, sir . . . *Lear* ii 1 44
Full suddenly he fled.—Let him fly far . . . . . . ii 1 58
Dogs leap the hatch, and all are fled . . . . . . iii 6 76
Fled from her wish and yet said 'Now I may' . . . *Othello* ii 1 152
Cassio, I believe, received From him that fled some strange indignity . ii 3 245
Toward Peloponnesus are they fled . . . . *Ant. and Cleo.* iii 10 31
I have fled myself; and have instructed cowards To run . . . iii 11 7
What though you fled From that great face of war, whose several ranges Frighted each other? why should he follow? . . . . . . iii 13 4
No; but he fled forward still, toward your face . . *Cymbeline* i 2 16
'Tis certain she is fled. Go in and cheer the king . . . . iii 5 66
When I have slain thee with my proper hand, I'll follow those that even now fled hence . . . . iv 2 98
Cried to those that fled, 'Our Britain's harts die flying, not our men' . v 3 23
Why fled you from the court? and whither? . . . . . v 5 387
Prince Pericles is fled.—As thou Wilt live, fly after . . *Pericles* i 1 162
I hither fled, Under the covering of a careful night . . . . i 2 80
Fledged. Shylock, for his own part, knew the bird was fledged *Mer. of Ven.* iii 1 32
Whose chin is not yet fledged . . . . . . 2 *Hen. IV.* i 2 23
Flee. I shoot thee at the swain.—Thump then and I flee . *L. L. Lost* iii 1 66
Fleece. Sunny locks Hang on her temples like a golden fleece *Mer. of Ven.* i 1 170
We are the Jasons, we have won the fleece.—I would you had won the fleece that he hath lost . . . . iii 2 244
And wish, for her sake more than for mine own, My fortunes were more able to relieve her; But I am shepherd to another man And do not shear the fleeces that I graze . . . . . *As Y. Like It* ii 4 79
Down with them; fleece them . . . . . . 1 *Hen. IV.* ii 2 90
Worthy Saint Michael and the Golden Fleece . . . 1 *Hen. VI.* iv 7 69
So many years ere I shall shear the fleece . . . 3 *Hen. VI.* ii 5 37
So first the harmless sheep doth yield his fleece And next his throat . v 6 8
My fleece of woolly hair that now uncurls Even as an adder *T. Andron.* ii 3 34
Fleeced. Or foul felonious thief that fleeced poor passengers 2 *Hen. VI.* iii 1 129
Fleer. Tush, tush, man; never fleer and jest at me . . *Much Ado* v 1 58
What dares the slave Come hither, cover'd with an antic face, To fleer and scorn at our solemnity? . . . . . . *Rom. and Jul.* i 5 59
And mark the fleers, the gibes, and notable scorns, That dwell in every region of his face . . . . *Othello* iv 1 83
Fleered. One rubb'd his elbow thus, and fleer'd, and swore . *L. L. Lost* v 2 109
Fleering. A man That is no fleering tell-tale . . . *J. Cæsar* i 3 117
Fleet. Of the king's ship The mariners say how thou hast disposed And all the rest o' the fleet . . . . *Tempest* i 2 226
And for the rest o' the fleet Which I dispersed, they all have met again i 2 232
And sail so expeditious that shall catch Your royal fleet far off . . v 1 316
I am sure he is in the fleet: I would he had boarded me . *Much Ado* ii 1 148
How all the other passions fleet to air! . . . *Mer. of Venice* iii 2 108
Even from the gallows did his fell soul fleet . . . . . iv 1 135
Fleet the time carelessly, as they did in the golden world *As Y. Like It* i 1 124
If Echo were as fleet, I would esteem him worth a dozen such *T. of S.* Ind. 1 26
With the most noble bottom of our fleet . . . . . *T. Night* v 1 60
Shall fleet, In dreadful trial of our kingdom's king . . . *K. John* ii 1 285
Carry Sir John Falstaff to the Fleet: Take all his company along 2 *Hen. IV.* v 5 97
His brave fleet With silken streamers the young Phœbus fanning *Hen. V.* iii Prol. 5
For so appears this fleet majestical, Holding due course to Harfleur iii Prol. 16
So cares and joys abound, as seasons fleet . . . 2 *Hen. VI.* ii 4 4
Shalt waft them over with our royal fleet . . . 3 *Hen. VI.* iii 3 253
They all confirm A Turkish fleet, and bearing up to Cyprus . . *Othello* i 3 8
Have there injointed them with an after fleet . . . . . i 3 35
What shall we hear of this?—A segregation of the Turkish fleet . . ii 1 10
If that the Turkish fleet Be not enshelter'd and embay'd, they are drown'd ii 1 17
A noble ship of Venice Hath seen a grievous wreck and sufferance On most part of their fleet . . . . ii 1 24
Tidings now arrived, importing the mere perdition of the Turkish fleet ii 2 4
In Cæsar's fleet Are those that often have 'gainst Pompey fought *A. and C.* ii 7 37
Our sever'd navy too Have knit again, and fleet, threatening most sea-like iii 13 171
This foul Egyptian hath betrayed me: My fleet hath yielded to the foe iv 12 11
To darkness fleet souls that fly backwards . . . . *Cymbeline* v 3 25
Fleeter than arrows, bullets, wind, thought, swifter things . *L. L. Lost* v 2 261
Swift As breathed stags, ay, fleeter than the roe . . *T. of Shrew* Ind. 2 50
Fleeting. Clarence is come; false, fleeting, perjured Clarence *Richard III.* i 4 55
That thou, residing here, go'st yet with me, And I, hence fleeting, here remain with thee . . . . *Ant. and Cleo.* i 3 104
Now the fleeting moon No planet is of mine . . . . . v 2 240
Fleming. I will rather trust a Fleming with my butter . *Mer. Wives* ii 2 316
Flemish. What an unweighed behaviour hath this Flemish drunkard picked? . . . . ii 1 23
Flesh. Whose throats had hanging at 'em Wallets of flesh . . *Tempest* iii 3 46
Methinks his flesh is punished, he shall have no desires . *Mer. Wives* iv 4 24
But if he start, It is the flesh of a corrupted heart . . . . . v 5 91
I shall follow it as the flesh and fortune shall better determine *M. for M.* ii 1 267
I do digest the poison of thy flesh . . . . . *Com. of Errors* ii 2 145
Either at flesh or fish, A table full of welcome makes scarce one dainty dish iii 1 22
The mountain of mad flesh that claims marriage of me . . . iv 4 159
And salt too little which may season give To her foul-tainted flesh! *M. Ado* iv 1 145
As pretty a piece of flesh as any is in Messina . . . . . iv 2 85
Such is the simplicity of man to hearken after the flesh . . *L. L. Lost* i 1 220
My sweet ounce of man's flesh! my incony Jew! . . . . . iii 1 136
This is the liver-vein, which makes flesh a deity, A green goose a goddess iv 3 74
Let the forfeit Be nominated for an equal pound Of your fair flesh *M. of V.* i 3 151
A pound of man's flesh taken from a man Is not so estimable, profitable neither, As flesh of muttons, beefs, or goats . . . . . . i 3 166
More difference between thy flesh and hers than between jet and ivory iii 1 42
I am sure, if he forfeit, thou wilt not take his flesh: what's that good for? iii 1 54
He would rather have Antonio's flesh Than twenty times the value . iii 2 288
I shall hardly spare a pound of flesh To-morrow to my bloody creditor iii 3 33
Now exact'st the penalty, Which is a pound of this poor merchant's flesh iv 1 23
You'll ask me, why I rather choose to have A weight of carrion flesh than to receive Three thousand ducats . . . . iv 1 41
The pound of flesh, which I demand of him, Is dearly bought . . iv 1 99
The Jew shall have my flesh, blood, bones and all, Ere thou shalt lose for me one drop of blood . . . . iv 1 112
This bond is forfeit; And lawfully by this the Jew may claim A pound of flesh . . . . iv 1 232
Are there balance here to weigh The flesh? . . . . . . iv 1 256

Flesh. A pound of that same merchant's flesh is thine: The court awards it *Mer. of Venice* iv 1 299
And you must cut this flesh from off his breast . . . . iv 1 302
The words expressly are 'a pound of flesh:' Take then thy bond, take thou thy pound of flesh . . . . . . iv 1 307
Therefore prepare thee to cut off the flesh. Shed thou no blood, nor cut thou less nor more But just a pound of flesh . . . . iv 1 324
A thing stuck on with oaths upon your finger And so riveted with faith unto your flesh . . . . v 1 169
Thou worms-meat, in respect of a good piece of flesh indeed! *As Y. L. It* iii 2 68
And here upon his arm The lioness had torn some flesh away . . iv 3 148
And better 'twere that both of us did fast, Since, of ourselves, ourselves are choleric, Than feed it with such over-roasted flesh *T. of S.* iv 1 178
Why thou wilt maary.— . . . I am driven on by the flesh . *All's Well* i 3 31
And this night he fleshes his will in the spoil of her honour . . iv 3 19
If she had partaken of my flesh, and cost me the dearest groans of a mother, I could not have owed her a more rooted love . . . . iv 5 11
As witty a piece of Eve's flesh as any in Illyria . . *T. Night* i 5 30
Every dram of woman's flesh is false, If she be . . *W. Tale* ii 1 138
She was a woman and was turned into a cold fish for she would not exchange flesh with one that loved her . . . . iv 4 285
And now he feasts, mousing the flesh of men . . *K. John* ii 1 354
Within this wall of flesh There is a soul counts thee her creditor . . iii 3 20
Brave our fields, And flesh his spirit in a warlike soil . . . v 1 71
One of our souls had wander'd in the air, Banish'd this frail sepulchre of our flesh, As now our flesh is banish'd from this land *Richard II.* i 3 196
As if this flesh which walls about our life Were brass impregnable . iii 2 167
Thy seat is up on high; Whilst my gross flesh sinks downward, here to die . . . . v 5 113
'Sblood, I'll not bear mine own flesh so far afoot again . . *1 Hen. IV.* ii 2 37
This horse-back-breaker, this huge hill of flesh . . . . ii 4 269
Why, she's neither fish nor flesh; a man knows not where to have her . iii 3 144
Thou seest I have more flesh than another man, and therefore more frailty . . . . iii 3 188
They wound my thoughts worse than thy sword my flesh . . . v 4 80
What, old acquaintance! could not all this flesh Keep in a little life? . v 4 102
You were advised his flesh was capable Of wounds and scars . *2 Hen. IV.* i 1 172
By this light flesh and corrupt blood, thou art welcome . . . ii 4 320
For suffering flesh to be eaten in thy house, contrary to the law . . ii 4 372
His grace says that which his flesh rebels against . . . . ii 4 379
The wild dog Shall flesh his tooth on every innocent . . . iv 5 133
When flesh is cheap and females dear . . . . . . v 3 20
Name not religion, for thou lovest the flesh . . . *1 Hen. VI.* i 1 41
Fester'd members rot but by degree, Till bones and flesh and sinews fall away . . . . iii 1 193
Did flesh his puny sword in Frenchmen's blood . . . . iv 7 36
God knows thou art a collop of my flesh . . . . . v 4 18
Men's flesh preserved so whole do seldom win . *2 Hen. VI.* iii 1 301
And like an empty eagle Tire on the flesh of me and of my son! *3 Hen. VI.* i 1 269
And at each word's deliverance Stab poniards in our flesh . . . ii 1 98
Cold fearful drops stand on my trembling flesh . . *Richard III.* v 3 181
We all are men, In our own natures frail, and capable Of our flesh *Hen. VIII.* v 3 12
Good traders in the flesh, set this in your painted cloths *Troi. and Cres.* v 10 46
His doubled spirit Re-quicken'd what in flesh was fatigate . *Coriolanus* ii 2 121
Best of my flesh, Forgive my tyranny . . . . v 3 42
Hew his limbs, and on a pile Ad manes fratrum sacrifice his flesh *T. An.* i 1 98
When my heart, all mad with misery, Beats in this hollow prison of my flesh . . . . iii 2 10
Eating the flesh that she herself hath bred . . . . . v 3 62
I am a pretty piece of flesh.—'Tis well thou art not fish . *Rom. and Jul.* i 1 35
Patience perforce with wilful choler meeting Makes my flesh tremble in their different greeting . . . . i 5 92
O flesh, flesh, how art thou fishified! . . . . . . ii 4 40
O nature, what hadst thou to do in hell, When thou didst bower the spirit of a fiend In mortal paradise of such sweet flesh? . . . iii 2 82
Farewell: buy food, and get thyself in flesh . . . . . v 1 84
And shake the yoke of inauspicious stars From this world-wearied flesh v 3 112
Hoar the flamen, That scolds against the quality of flesh *T. of Athens* iv 3 156
Let the famish'd flesh slide from the bone, Ere thou relieve the beggar iv 3 535
I'll fight till from my bones my flesh be hack'd . . . *Macbeth* v 3 32
O, that this too too solid flesh would melt! . . . . *Hamlet* i 2 129
The heart-ache and the thousand natural shocks That flesh is heir to . iii 1 63
Father and mother is man and wife; man and wife is one flesh . . iv 3 54
From her fair and unpolluted flesh May violets spring! . . . v 1 262
With you, goodman boy, an you please: come, I'll flesh ye . . *Lear* ii 2 49
We'll no more meet, no more see one another: But yet thou art my flesh, my blood, my daughter; Or rather a disease that's in my flesh ii 4 224
Is it the fashion, that discarded fathers Should have thus little mercy on their flesh? Judicious punishment! 'twas this flesh begot Those pelican daughters . . . . iii 4 75
In his anointed flesh stick boarish fangs . . . . . iii 7 58
That eyeless head of thine was first framed flesh To raise my fortunes . iv 6 231
You shall be yet far fairer than you are.—He means in flesh *A. and C.* i 2 17
On the Alps It is reported thou didst eat strange flesh . . . i 4 67
The record of what injuries you did us, Though written in our flesh, we shall remember As things but done by chance . . . . . v 2 119
If you buy ladies' flesh at a million a dram, you cannot preserve it from tainting . . . . *Cymbeline* i 4 147
Why should we be tender To let an arrogant piece of flesh threat us? . iv 2 127
How now, my flesh, my child! What, makest thou me a dullard in this act? . . . . v 5 264
I am no viper, yet I feed On mother's flesh which did me breed *Pericles* i 1 65
And she an eater of her mother's flesh . . . . . . i 1 130
They say they're [the porpus] half fish, half flesh . . . . ii 1 27
We'll have flesh for holidays, fish for fasting-days . . . . ii 1 85
Look, who kneels here! Flesh of thy flesh . . . . . v 3 46

Flesh and blood, You, brother mine . . . . . . *Tempest* v 1 74
Thy pulse Beats as of flesh and blood . . . . . . v 1 114
I pray thee, peace. I will be flesh and blood . . . *Much Ado* v 1 34
But I would see his own person in flesh and blood . . *L. L. Lost* i 1 186
O, let us embrace! As true we are as flesh and blood can be . . iv 3 215
If thou be Launcelot, thou art mine own flesh and blood *Mer. of Venice* ii 2 98
My own flesh and blood to rebel!—Out upon it, old carrion! rebels it at these years?—I say, my daughter is my flesh and blood . . . iii 1 37
I will therefore tarry in despite of the flesh and the blood *T. of Shrew* Ind. 2 130
A wicked creature, as you and all flesh and blood are . . *All's Well* i 3 38
He that comforts my wife is the cherisher of my flesh and blood; he that cherishes my flesh and blood loves my flesh and blood; he that loves my flesh and blood is my friend . . . . i 3 50
Flesh and blood. Put your grace in your pocket, sir, for this once, and let your flesh and blood obey it . . . . . . *T. Night* v 1 36
She being none of your flesh and blood, your flesh and blood has not offended the king; and so your flesh and blood is not to be punished by him . . . . *W. Tale* iv 4 710
Cover your heads and mock not flesh and blood With solemn reverence *Richard II.* iii 2 171
Methinks the realms of England, France and Ireland Bear that proportion to my flesh and blood As did the fatal brand Althæa burn'd *2 Hen. VI.* i 1 233
Then let no man but I Do execution on my flesh and blood *T. Andron.* iv 2 84
Men are flesh and blood, and apprehensive . . . *J. Cæsar* iii 1 67
This eternal blazon must not be To ears of flesh and blood . *Hamlet* i 5 22
Our flesh and blood is grown so vile, my lord, That it doth hate what gets it . . . . *Lear* iii 4 150
For flesh and blood, sir, white and red, you shall see a rose . *Pericles* iv 6 37
But are you flesh and blood? Have you a working pulse? . . . v 1 154

Flesh and bones. They are apt enough to dislocate and tear Thy flesh and bones . . . . *Lear* iv 2 66

Flesh and fell. The good-years shall devour them, flesh and fell . . v 3 24

Fleshed. Put up your iron: you are well fleshed . . . *T. Night* iv 1 43
Full bravely hast thou flesh'd Thy maiden sword . . *1 Hen. IV.* v 4 133
The head Which princes, flesh'd with conquest, aim to hit . *2 Hen. IV.* i 1 149
The kindred of him hath been flesh'd upon us . . . *Hen. V.* ii 4 50
The flesh'd soldier, rough and hard of heart . . . . iii 3 11
Although they were flesh'd villains, bloody dogs . . *Richard III.* iv 3 6

Flesh-fly. Than to suffer The flesh-fly blow my mouth . . *Tempest* iii 1 63

Fleshly. In the body of this fleshly land . . . . *K. John* iv 2 245

Fleshment. In the fleshment of this dread exploit, Drew on me . *Lear* ii 2 130

Fleshmonger. And was the duke a fleshmonger? . . *Meas. for Meas.* v 1 337

Flew. I, for my part, knew the tailor that made the wings she flew withal *Mer. of Venice* iii 1 30
Here, there, and every where, enraged he flew . . . *1 Hen. VI.* i 1 124
What a point, my lord, your falcon made, And what a pitch she flew above the rest! . . . . *2 Hen. VI.* ii 1 6
Hats, cloaks,—Doublets, I think,—flew up . . . *Hen. VIII.* iv 1 74
Make distinct the very breach whereout Hector's great spirit flew *Troi. and Cres.* iv 5 246
Who, thereat enraged, Flew on him, and amongst them fell'd him dead *Lear* iv 2 76

Flewed. My hounds are bred out of the Spartan kind, So flew'd, so sanded . . . . *M. N. Dream* iv 1 125

Flexible. Women are soft, mild, pitiful and flexible . . *3 Hen. VI.* i 4 141
When the splitting wind Makes flexible the knees of knotted oaks *Troi. and Cres.* i 3 50

Flexure. Will it give place to flexure and low bending? . . *Hen. V.* iv 1 272
His legs are legs for necessity, not for flexure . . . *Troi. and. Cres.* ii 3 115

Flibbertigibbet. This is the foul fiend Flibbertigibbet . . *Lear* iii 4 120
Flibbertigibbet, of mopping and mowing, who since possesses chambermaids and waiting-women . . . . iv 1 64

Flickering. Like the wreath of radiant fire On flickering Phœbus' front ii 2 114

Flier. For the followers fortune widens them, Not for the fliers *Coriolanus* i 4 45
Following the fliers at the very heels, With them he enters . . . i 4 49
He stopp'd the fliers; And by his rare example made the coward Turn terror into sport . . . . ii 2 107
You, it seems, come from the fliers.—I did . . . *Cymbeline* v 3 2

Flies. Why, this it is to be a peevish girl, That flies her fortune when it follows her . . . . *T. G. of Ver.* v 2 50
Love like a shadow flies when substance love pursues; Pursuing that that flies, and flying what pursues . . . . *Mer. Wives* ii 2 215
Apollo flies, and Daphne holds the chase . . . *M. N. Dream* ii 1 231
Bootless speed, When cowardice pursues and valour flies . . . ii 1 234
Then my taxing like a wild-goose flies, Unclaim'd of any man *As Y. L. It* ii 7 86
When I consider What great creation and what dole of honour Flies where you bid it? . . . . *All's Well* ii 3 177
Slaves of chance and flies Of every wind that blows . . *W. Tale* iv 4 551
Where he is to behold him with flies blown to death . . . . iv 4 820
As the thing that's heavy in itself Upon enforcement flies with greatest speed, So did our men, heavy in Hotspur's loss . *2 Hen. IV.* i 1 120
Thus with imagined wing our swift scene flies . . . *Hen. V.* iii Prol. 1
Like flies at Bartholomew-tide, blind, though they have their eyes . v 2 336
Between two hawks, which flies the higher pitch . . *1 Hen. VI.* ii 4 11
Fly, to revenge my death, if I be slain.—He that flies so will ne'er return iv 5 19
Yet have I gold flies from another coast . . . . *2 Hen. VI.* i 2 93
We'll all assist you; he that flies shall die . . . *3 Hen. VI.* i 1 30
Gracious God! My soul flies through these wounds to seek out Thee . i 4 178
The common people swarm like summer flies; And whither fly the gnats? . . . . ii 6 8
They never then had sprung like summer flies . . . . . ii 6 17
So flies the reckless shepherd from the wolf . . . . . v 6 7
So when he opens his purse to give us our reward, thy conscience flies out.—Let it go . . . . *Richard III.* i 4 133
True hope is swift, and flies with swallow's wings . . . . v 2 23
When the splitting wind Makes flexible the knees of knotted oaks, And flies fled under shade . . . . *Troi. and Cres.* i 3 51
A sword employ'd is perilous, And reason flies the object of all harm . ii 2 41
Flies the grasps of love With wings more momentary-swift than thought iv 2 13
With no less confidence Than boys pursuing summer butterflies, Or butchers killing flies . . . . *Coriolanus* iv 6 95
Who is this? my niece, that flies away so fast! . . . *T. Andron.* ii 4 11
Now to the Goths, as swift as swallow flies . . . . . iv 2 172
That we should be thus afflicted with these strange flies *Rom. and Jul.* ii 4 34
Flies may do this, but I from this must fly . . . . . iii 3 41
And like the current flies Each bound it chafes . . *T. of Athens* i 1 24
Flies an eagle flight, bold and forth on, Leaving no tract behind . . i 1 49
One cloud of winter showers, These flies are couch'd . . . . ii 2 181
Time's flies, Cap and knee slaves, vapours, and minute-jacks! . . iii 6 106
How will you live?—As birds do, mother.—What, with worms and flies? *Macbeth* iv 2 32
The great man down, you mark his favourite flies . . . *Hamlet* iii 2 214
As flies to wanton boys, are we to the gods, They kill us for their sport *Lear* iv 1 38
Though he in a fertile climate dwell, Plague him with flies . *Othello* i 1 71
As summer flies are in the shambles, That quicken even with blowing . iv 2 66
Our separation so abides, and flies, That thou, residing here, go'st yet with me, And I, hence fleeting, here remain with thee *Ant. and Cleo.* i 3 102
The breese upon her, like a cow in June, Hoists sails and flies . . iii 10 15
And, like a doting mallard, Leaving the fight in height, flies after her . iii 10 21
Lie graveless, till the flies and gnats of Nile Have buried them for prey! iii 13 166
Our valour is to chase what flies . . . . *Cymbeline* iii 3 42

Flies. I'll hide my master from the flies, as deep As these poor pickaxes can dig . . . . *Cymbeline* iv 2 388
No more, thou thunder-master, show Thy spite on mortal flies . v 4 31
You are like one that superstitiously Doth swear to the gods that winter kills the flies . . . . *Pericles* iv 3 50
Though they did change me to the meanest bird That flies i' the purer air . . . . iv 6 109
Flieth. The Duke of Alençon flieth to his side . 1 *Hen. VI.* i 1 95
Flight. With all the cunning manner of our flight Determined of *T. G. of Ver.* ii 4 180
I'll give her father notice Of their disguising and pretended flight . ii 6 37
And when the flight is made to one so dear, Of such divine perfection . ii 7 12
'Twas Ariadne passioning For Theseus' perjury and unjust flight . . iv 4 173
These likelihoods confirm her flight . . . . . . v 2 43
Thou art death's fool; For him thou labour'st by thy flight to shun And yet runn'st toward him still . . . *Meas. for Meas.* iii 1 12
He set up his bills here in Messina and challenged Cupid at the flight *Much Ado* i 1 40
Your brother John is ta'en in flight, And brought with armed men back v 4 127
A time that lovers' flights doth still conceal . *M. N. Dream* i 1 212
I will go tell him of fair Hermia's flight . . . . i 1 246
Come, my lord, and in our flight Tell me how it came this night . iv 1 104
Tongue, lose thy light; Moon, take thy flight . . . . v 1 310
When I had lost one shaft, I shot his fellow of the self-same flight The self-same way . . . . . . *Mer. of Venice* i 1 141
You knew, none so well, none so well as you, of my daughter's flight iii 1 28
Devise the fittest time and safest way To hide us from pursuit that will be made After my flight . . . . . *As Y. Like It* i 3 139
Away, and for our flight.—Bravely, coragio! . . *All's Well* ii 5 97
That pitiful rumour may report my flight, To consolate thine ear . . iii 2 130
Camillo's flight, Added to their familiarity . . *W. Tale* ii 1 174
I bless the time When my good falcon made her flight across Thy father's ground.—Now Jove afford you cause! . . . . . . iv 4 15
He's irremoveable, Resolved for flight . . . . . . iv 4 519
This follows, if you will not change your purpose But undergo this flight iv 4 554
I know not what impediment this complaint may be to the flight of my master . . . . iv 4 730
We will untread the steps of damned flight . . . *K. John* v 4 52
Away, my friends! New flight; And happy newness, that intends old right . . . . v 4 60
As confident as is the falcon's flight Against a bird . . . *Richard II.* i 3 61
Quite from the flight of all thy ancestors . . . 1 *Hen. IV.* iii 2 31
In his flight, Stumbling in fear, was took . . . 2 *Hen. IV.* i 1 130
Whither away! to save myself by flight . . . 1 *Hen. VI.* iii 2 105
They that of late were daring with their scoffs Are glad and fain by flight to save themselves . . . . iii 2 114
There are squadrons pitch'd, To wall thee from the liberty of flight . iv 2 24
I'll direct thee how thou shalt escape By sudden flight . . . iv 5 11
Flight cannot stain the honour you have won . . . . iv 5 26
Yes, your renowned name: shall flight abuse it? . . . . iv 5 41
Talk no more of flight, it is no boot . . . . . iv 6 52
Like the night-owl's lazy flight . . . . . 3 *Hen. VI.* ii 1 130
Even with those wings Which sometime they have used with fearful flight . . . . ii 2 30
Bootless is flight, they follow us with wings; And weak we are . . ii 3 12
No way to fly, nor strength to hold out flight . . . . ii 6 24
Our soldiers put to flight, And, as thou seest, ourselves in heavy plight iii 3 36
My lord, I like not of this flight of Edward's . . . . iv 6 89
I do not speak of flight, of fear, of death . . . *Troi. and Cres.* v 10 12
Backs red, and faces pale With flight and agued fear! . . *Coriolanus* i 4 38
By uproar sever'd, like a flight of fowl Scatter'd by winds *T. Andron.* v 3 68
Flies an eagle flight, bold and forth on, Leaving no tract behind *T. of A.* i 1 49
And pursy insolence shall break his wind With fear and horrid flight . v 4 13
Banquo, thy soul's flight, If it find heaven, must find it out to-night *Macbeth* iii 1 141
Ere the bat hath flown His cloister'd flight . . . . iii 2 41
His flight was madness: when our actions do not, Our fears do make us traitors . . . . iv 2 3
As little is the wisdom, where the flight So runs against all reason . iv 2 13
Good night, sweet prince; And flights of angels sing thee to thy rest! *Ham.* v 2 371
Thou'ldst shun a bear; But if thy flight lay toward the raging sea, Thou'ldst meet the bear i' the mouth . . . . . *Lear* iii 4 10
O, he has given example for our flight, Most grossly, by his own! *Ant. and Cleo.* iii 10 28
This paper is the history of my knowledge Touching her flight *Cymbeline* iii 5 100
Whose life, But that her flight prevented it, she had Ta'en off by poison v 5 46
By flight I'll shun the danger which I fear . . . *Pericles* i 1 142
Flighty. Time, thou anticipatest my dread exploits: The flighty purpose never is o'ertook Unless the deed go with it . . . *Macbeth* iv 1 145
Flinch. If I break time, or flinch in property Of what I spoke, unpitied let me die . . . . *All's Well* ii 1 190
If he flinch, chide me for it . . . . . *Troi. and Cres.* iii 2 114
Fling. And here I'll fling the pillow, there the bolster . *T. of Shrew* iv 1 204
The mouth of passage shall we fling wide ope . . . *K. John* ii 1 449
Else would I have a fling at Winchester . . . 1 *Hen. VI.* iii 1 64
Who loves the king and will embrace his pardon, Fling up his cap 2 *Hen. VI.* iv 8 15
I had rather chop this hand off at a blow, And with the other fling it at thy face, Than bear so low a sail. . . . . . 3 *Hen. VI.* v 1 51
I charge thee, fling away ambition: By that sin fell the angels *Hen. VIII.* iii 2 440
Flint. Fire enough for a flint, pearl enough for a swine . . *L. L. Lost* iv 2 90
From brassy bosoms and rough hearts of flint . . *Mer. of Venice* iv 1 31
Love make his heart of flint that you shall love! . . . *T. Night* i 5 305
Julius Cæsar's ill-erected tower, To whose flint bosom my condemned lord Is doom'd a prisoner . . . . . . *Richard II.* v 1 3
Notwithstanding, being incensed, he's flint . . . 2 *Hen. IV.* iv 4 33
The ruthless flint doth cut my tender feet . . . 2 *Hen. VI.* ii 4 34
Mine eyes should sparkle like the beaten flint . . . . iii 2 317
O, I could hew up rocks and fight with flint, I am so angry . . v 1 24
I would to God my heart were flint . . . . *Richard III.* i 3 140
It lies as coldly in him as fire in a flint . . . *Troi. and Cres.* iii 3 257
Whilst, with no softer cushion than the flint, I kneel before thee *Coriol.* v 3 53
But be your heart to them As unrelenting flint to drops of rain *T. An.* ii 3 141
My heart is not compact of flint nor steel . . . . . v 3 88
O, so light a foot Will ne'er wear out the everlasting flint *Rom. and Jul.* ii 6 17
The fire i' the flint Shows not till it be struck . . . *T. of Athens* i 1 22
Searching the window for a flint, I found This paper, thus seal'd *J. Cæsar* ii 1 36
You are yoked with a lamb That carries anger as the flint bears fire . iv 3 111
For charitable prayers, Shards, flints and pebbles should be thrown on her: Yet here she is allow'd her virgin crants . . . *Hamlet* v 1 254
Flint. Throw my heart Against the flint and hardness of my fault *Ant. and Cleo.* iv 9 16
Weariness Can snore upon the flint, when resty sloth Finds the down pillow hard . . . . *Cymbeline* iii 6 34
Make raging battery upon shores of flint . . . . *Pericles* iv 4 43
Flint castle. Go to Flint castle: there I'll pine away . *Richard II.* iii 2 209
Flinty. Which gratitude Through flinty Tartar's bosom would peep forth, and answer, thanks . . . . *All's Well* iv 4 7
Till their soul-fearing clamours have brawl'd down The flinty ribs of this contemptuous city . . . . *K. John* ii 1 384
May tear a passage through the flinty ribs Of this hard world *Richard II.* v 5 20
Let us resolve to scale their flinty bulwarks . . . 1 *Hen. VI.* ii 1 27
Uneath may she endure the flinty streets, To tread them . 2 *Hen. VI.* ii 4 8
Thy flinty heart, more hard than they, Might in thy palace perish Margaret . . . . iii 2 99
Thou stern, obdurate, flinty, rough, remorseless . . . 3 *Hen. VI.* i 4 142
Were thy heart as hard as steel, As thou hast shown it flinty by thy deeds, I come to pierce it . . . . ii 1 202
Come nearer. Then I love thee, Because thou art a woman, and disclaim'st Flinty mankind . . . . . . *T. of Athens* iv 3 491
The flinty and steel couch of war My thrice-driven bed of down . *Othello* i 3 231
Flirt-gill. Scurvy knave! I am none of his flirt-gills *Rom. and Jul.* ii 4 162
Float. Did never float upon the swelling tide . . . *K. John* ii 1 74
But float upon a wild and violent sea Each way and move . *Macbeth* iv 2 21
Floated. Where is that son That floated with thee on the fatal raft? *Com. of Errors* v 1 348
Floating straight, obedient to the stream, Was carried towards Corinth . i 1 87
When the sea was calm all boats alike Show'd mastership in floating *Cor.* iv 1 7
Flock. And crows are fatted with the murrion flock . *M. N. Dream* ii 1 97
I am a tainted wether of the flock, Meetest for death . *Mer. of Venice* iv 1 114
They say many young gentlemen flock to him every day *As Y. Like It* i 1 123
His flocks and bounds of feed Are now on sale . . . . ii 4 83
What is he that shall buy his flock and pasture? . . . . ii 4 88
If it stand with honesty, Buy thou the cottage, pasture and the flock . ii 4 92
Come, to our flock . . . . iii 5 81
How will she love, when the rich golden shaft Hath kill'd the flock of all affections else That live in her! . . . . . . *T. Night* i 1 36
Come on, And bid us welcome to your sheep-shearing, As your good flock shall prosper . . . . *W. Tale* iv 4 70
I should leave grazing, were I of your flock, And only live by gazing . iv 4 109
Beat Cut's saddle, put a few flocks in the point . . 1 *Hen. IV.* ii 1 7
And drive all thy subjects afore thee like a flock of wild-geese . ii 4 152
And more and less do flock to follow him . . . 2 *Hen. IV.* i 1 209
When that your flock, assembled by the bell, Encircled you . . iv 2 5
They flock together in consent, like so many wild-geese . . . v 1 78
Till they have snared the shepherd of the flock . . 2 *Hen. VI.* ii 2 73
Let him die, in that he is a fox, By nature proved an enemy to the flock iii 1 258
Muster'd my soldiers, gather'd flocks of friends . . . 3 *Hen. VI.* ii 1 112
So many hours must I tend my flock . . . . . . ii 5 31
And many giddy people flock to him . . . . iv 8 5
Every hour more competitors Flock to their aid . . *Richard III.* iv 4 507
They could do no less, Out of the great respect they bear to beauty, But leave their flocks . . . . *Hen. VIII.* i 4 70
'Mongst this flock of drunkards . . . . *Othello* ii 3 61
Flood. Thou'lt lose the flood, and, in losing the flood, lose thy voyage *T. G. of Ver.* ii 3 47
And the delighted spirit To bathe in fiery floods . *Meas. for Meas.* iii 1 122
O, train me not, sweet mermaid with thy note, To drown me in thy sister's flood of tears . . . . *Com. of Errors* iii 2 46
'Tis in grain; Noah's flood could not do it . . . . . iii 2 108
What need the bridge much broader than the flood? . . . *Much Ado* i 1 318
Over park, over pale, Thorough flood, thorough fire . *M. N. Dream* ii 1 5
The moon, the governess of floods, Pale in her anger, washes all the air ii 1 103
Marking the embarked traders on the flood . . . . . ii 1 127
Damned spirits all, That in crossways and floods have burial . . iii 2 383
Like signiors and rich burghers on the flood . . *Mer. of Venice* i 1 10
You may as well go stand upon the beach And bid the main flood bate iv 1 72
Therefore the poet Did feign that Orpheus drew trees, stones and floods v 1 80
There is, sure, another flood toward, and these couples are coming to the ark. Here comes a pair of very strange beasts . *As Y. Like It* v 4 35
Like envious floods o'er-run her lovely face . . . *T. of Shrew* Ind. 2 67
Great floods have flown From simple sources . . . . *All's Well* ii 1 142
This accident and flood of fortune So far exceed all instance . *T. Night* iv 3 11
So, by a roaring tempest on the flood, A whole armado of convicted sail Is scatter'd . . . . *K. John* iii 4 1
I was amazed Under the tide: but now I breathe again Aloft the flood iv 2 139
Like a bated and retired flood, Leaving our rankness and irregular course v 4 53
Were in the Washes all unwarily Devoured by the unexpected flood . v 7 64
Three times did they drink, Upon agreement, of swift Severn's flood 1 *Hen. IV.* i 3 103
Such a flood of greatness fell on you. . . . . v 1 48
So looks the strand whereon the imperious flood Hath left a witness'd usurpation . . . . 2 *Hen. IV.* i 1 62
Let not Nature's hand Keep the wild flood confined! let order die! . i 1 154
Ebb back to the sea, Where it shall mingle with the state of floods . v 2 132
Never came reformation in a flood, With such a heady currance *Hen. V.* i 1 33
The land Salique is in Germany, Between the floods of Sala and of Elbe i 2 45
Let floods o'erswell, and fiends for food howl on! . . . . ii 1 97
Behold, the English beach Pales in the flood with men . . . . v Prol. 10
Return thee therefore with a flood of tears, And wash away thy country's stained spots . . . . 1 *Hen. VI.* iii 3 56
My heart is drown'd with grief, Whose flood begins to flow within mine eyes, My body round engirt with misery . . 2 *Hen. VI.* iii 1 199
Sometime the flood prevails, and then the wind . . . 3 *Hen. VI.* ii 5 9
The holding-anchor lost, And half our sailors swallow'd in the flood . v 4 5
But still the envious flood Kept in my soul . . . . *Richard III.* i 4 37
Who pass'd, methought, the melancholy flood, With that grim ferryman i 4 45
By sudden floods and fall of waters . . . . iv 4 512
As doth a rock against the chiding flood . . . . *Hen. VIII.* iii 2 197
Between our Ilium and where she resides, Let it be call'd the wild and wandering flood . . . . *Troi. and Cres.* i 1 105
His youth in flood, I'll prove this truth with my three drops of blood . i 3 300
Like a bold flood o'er-bear . . . . *Coriolanus* iv 5 137
As meadows, yet not dry, With miry slime left on them by a flood *T. An.* iii 1 126
All the water in the ocean Can never turn the swan's black legs to white, Although she lave them hourly in the flood . . . . . iv 2 103
Floods of tears will drown my oratory, And break my utterance . . v 3 90
The bark thy body is, Sailing in this salt flood . . . *Rom. and Jul.* iii 5 135
You see this confluence, this great flood of visitors . . *T. of Athens* i 1 42
Made his everlasting mansion Upon the beached verge of the salt flood v 1 219

Flood. Darest thou, Cassius, now Leap in with me into this angry flood? *J. Cæsar* i 2 103
When went there by an age, since the great flood, But it was famed with more than with one man? i 2 152
Sweet friends, let me not stir you up To such a sudden flood of mutiny iii 2 215
There is a tide in the affairs of men, Which, taken at the flood, leads on to fortune iv 3 219
What if it tempt you toward the flood, my lord? *Hamlet* i 4 69
Of moving accidents by flood and field, Of hair-breadth scapes *Othello* i 3 135
What from the cape can you discern at sea?—Nothing at all: it is a high-wrought flood ii 1 2
I never did like molestation view On the enchafed flood ii 1 17
With his eyes in flood with laughter: It is a recreation to be by *Cymb.* i 6 74
Half the flood Hath their keel cut: but fortune's mood Varies *Per.* iii Gower 45
Flood-gate. For tears do stop the flood-gates of her eyes *1 Hen. IV.* ii 4 435
My particular grief Is of so flood-gate and o'erbearing nature *Othello* i 3 56
Floor. Do fear The smallest monstrous mouse that creeps on floor *M. N. Dream* v 1 223
The floor of heaven Is thick inlaid with patines of bright gold *M. of Ven.* v 1 58
Good troth, I have stol'n nought, nor would not, though I had found Gold strew'd i' the floor *Cymbeline* iii 6 50
Reposing on a cushion.—Where?—O' the floor; His arms thus leagued iv 2 212
Flora. No shepherdess, but Flora Peering in April's front *W. Tale* iv 4 3
Florence. Vincentio's son brought up in Florence *T. of Shrew* i 1 14
I have bills for money by exchange From Florence and must here deliver them iv 2 90
And Florence is denied before he comes *All's Well* i 2 12
Madam, he's gone to serve the duke of Florence iii 2 54
Towards Florence is he?—Ay, madam.—And to be a soldier? iii 2 71
He hath perverted a young gentlewoman here in Florence iv 3 18
Well, is this captain in the duke of Florence's camp? iv 3 219
That is an advertisement to a proper maid in Florence iv 3 240
In Florence was it from a casement thrown me, Wrapp'd in a paper v 3 93
You shall as easy Prove that I husbanded her bed in Florence v 3 126
He stole from Florence, taking no leave, and I follow him to his country v 3 143
He's now in Florence.—Write from us to him; post-post-haste *Othello* i 3 45
Florentine. Bestowed much honour on a young Florentine *Much Ado* i 1 11
I will some other be, some Florentine, Some Neapolitan *T. of Shrew* i 1 209
The Florentines and Senoys are by the ears *All's Well* i 2 1
With caution that the Florentine will move us For speedy aid i 2 6
I, with a troop of Florentines, will suddenly surprise him iii 6 23
I'll Discover that which shall undo the Florentine iv 1 80
If your life be saved, will you undertake to betray the Florentine? iv 3 326
Here's a petition from a Florentine, Who hath for four or five removes come short To tender it herself v 3 130
I am, my lord, a wretched Florentine, Derived from the ancient Capilet v 3 158
A great arithmetician, One Michael Cassio, a Florentine *Othello* i 1 20
I never knew A Florentine more kind and honest iii 1 43
Florentius. Be she as foul as was Florentius' love *T of Shrew* i 2 69
Florizel. A son o' the king's, which Florizel I now name to you *W. Tale* iv 1 22
Say to me, when sawest thou the Prince Florizel, my son? iv 2 29
I have served Prince Florizel and in my time wore three-pile iv 3 13
One that gives out himself Prince Florizel, Son of Polixenes v 1 85
Flote. Are upon the Mediterranean flote, Bound sadly home *Tempest* i 2 234
Flour. That all From me do back receive the flour of all, And leave me but the bran *Coriolanus* i 1 149
Flourish. Your title to him Doth flourish the deceit *Meas. for Meas.* iv 1 75
Good Lord Boyet, my beauty, though but mean, Needs not the painted flourish of your praise *L. L. Lost* ii 1 14
Lend me the flourish of all gentle tongues iv 3 238
Then music is Even as the flourish when true subjects bow To a new-crowned monarch *Mer. of Venice* iii 2 49
Otherwise a seducer flourishes, and a poor maid is undone *All's Well* v 3 146
Or flourish to the height of my degree *1 Hen. VI.* ii 4 111
Till Lionel's issue fails, his should not reign: It fails not yet, but flourishes in thee *2 Hen. VI.* ii 2 57
Wither one rose, and let the other flourish *3 Hen. VI.* ii 5 101
Poor painted queen, vain flourish of my fortune! *Richard III.* i 3 241
I call'd thee then vain flourish of my fortune iv 4 82
A flourish, trumpets! strike alarum, drums! iv 4 148
Good angels guard thy battle! live, and flourish! v 3 138
Edward's unhappy sons do bid thee flourish v 3 158
And ever flourish, When I shall dwell with worms! *Hen. VIII.* iv 2 125
He shall flourish, And, like a mountain cedar, reach his branches v 5 53
Why do the emperor's trumpets flourish thus? *T. Andron.* iv 2 49
Old Montague is come, And flourishes his blade in spite of me *R. and J.* i 1 85
You shall see him a palm in Athens again, and flourish with the highest. Therefore 'tis not amiss we tender our loves *T. of Athens* v 1 13
Since brevity is the soul of wit, And tediousness the limbs and outward flourishes, I will be brief *Hamlet* ii 2 91
As love between them like the palm might flourish v 2 40
To this effect, sir; after what flourish your nature will v 2 187
Britain be fortunate and flourish in peace and plenty *Cymbeline* v 4 145; v 5 442
He hopes by you his fortunes yet may flourish *Pericles* ii 2 47
Flourished. If I could find example Of thousands that had struck anointed kings And flourish'd after, I'ld not do't *W. Tale* i 2 359
Like the lily, That once was mistress of the field and flourish'd *Hen. VIII.* iii 1 152
Give that changing piece To him that flourish'd for her *T. Andron.* i 1 310
And all of us fell down, Whilst bloody treason flourish'd over us *J. Cæsar* iii 2 196
Flourisheth. 'Tis age that nourisheth.—But youth in ladies' eyes that flourisheth *T. of Shrew* ii 1 342
Flourishing. Unfrequented woods, I better brook than flourishing peopled towns *T. G. of Ver.* v 4 3
One flourishing branch of his most royal root . . . Is hack'd down *Rich. II.* i 2 18
Renowned Titus, flourishing in arms *T. Andron.* i 1 38
Flout 'em and scout 'em And scout 'em and flout 'em *Tempest* iii 2 130
What, wilt thou flout me thus unto my face, Being forbid? *Com. of Errors* i 2 91
Dost thou jeer and flout me in the teeth? Think'st thou I jest? ii 2 22
Ere you flout old ends any further, examine your conscience *Much Ado* i 1 290
That she should be so immodest to write to one that she knew would flout her ii 3 148
I should flout him, if he writ to me; yea, though I love him, I should ii 3 150
Fashion-monging boys, That lie and cog and flout, deprave and slander v 1 95
A college of wit-crackers cannot flout me out of my humour v 4 102
Never flout at me for what I have said v 4 108
O poverty in wit, kingly-poor flout! *L. L. Lost* v 2 269
Dart thy skill at me; Bruise me with scorn, confound me with a flout v 2 397
A man replete with mocks, Full of comparisons and wounding flouts v 2 854
But you must flout my insufficiency *M. N. Dream* ii 2 128
Why will you suffer her to flout me thus? iii 2 327
Flout. Though Nature hath given us wit to flout at Fortune, hath not Fortune sent in this fool to cut off the argument? *As Y. Like It* i 2 48
Ne'er a fantastical knave of them all shall flout me out of my calling iii 3 109
Her silence flouts me, and I'll be revenged *T. of Shrew* ii 1 29
By heaven, these scroyles of Angiers flout you, kings *K. John* ii 1 373
Let him perceive how ill we brook his treason And what offence it is to flout his friends *1 Hen. VI.* iv 1 75
I could have given my uncle's grace a flout *Richard III.* ii 4 24
You bring me to do, and then you flout me too *Troi. and Cres.* iv 2 27
Where the Norweyan banners flout the sky *Macbeth* i 2 49
Flouted. Shall I be flouted thus by dunghill grooms? *1 Hen. VI.* i 3 14
Why, madam, have I offer'd love for this, To be so flouted? *Richard III.* ii 1 78
He flouted us downright.—No, 'tis his kind of speech *Coriolanus* ii 3 168
Sorrow flouted at is double death *T. Andron.* iii 1 246
Flouting. And wherefore; for they say every why hath a wherefore.—Why, first,—for flouting me *Com. of Errors* ii 2 46
Speak you this with a sad brow? or do you play the flouting Jack? *M. Ado* i 1 186
We shall be flouting; we cannot hold *As Y. Like It* v 1 13
Flow. I am standing water.—I'll teach you how to flow *Tempest* ii 1 222
One so strong That could control the moon, make flows and ebbs v 1 270
Scarce confesses That his blood flows *Meas. for Meas.* i 3 52
Being that I flow in grief, The smallest twine may lead me *Much Ado* iv 1 251
The night of dew that on my cheeks down flows *L. L. Lost* iv 3 29
The sea will ebb and flow, heaven show his face iv 3 216
Doth it [pride] not flow as hugely as the sea? *As Y. Like It* ii 7 72
Let us from point to point this story know, To make the even truth in pleasure flow *All's Well* v 3 326
I'll use that tongue I have: if wit flow from't As boldness from my bosom, let't not be doubted I shall do good *W. Tale* ii 2 52
The fortune of us that are the moon's men doth ebb and flow like the sea, being governed, as the sea is, by the moon *1 Hen. IV.* i 2 36
In as high a flow as the ridge of the gallows i 2 43
And flow henceforth in formal majesty *2 Hen. IV.* v 2 133
With grief, Whose flood begins to flow within mine eyes *2 Hen. VI.* iii 1 199
You are the fount that makes small brooks to flow *3 Hen. VI.* iv 8 54
Such noble scenes as draw the eye to flow We now present *Hen. VIII.* Prol. 4
This top-proud fellow, Whom from the flow of gall I name not i 1 152
What expense by the hour Seems to flow from him! iii 2 109
Yea, watch His pettish lunes, his ebbs, his flows *Troi. and Cres.* ii 3 139
Go off: You flow to great distraction v 2 41
Make our eyes flow with joy, hearts dance with comforts *Coriolanus* v 3 99
Thy eyes, which I may call the sea, Do ebb and flow with tears *R. and J.* iii 5 134
Let the health go round.—Let it flow this way *T. of Athens* i 2 55
Flow this way! A brave fellow! he keeps his tides well i 2 56
That he will neither know how to maintain it, Nor cease his flow of riot ii 2 3
I have Prompted you in the ebb of your estate And your great flow of debts ii 2 151
I have retired me to a wasteful cock, And set mine eyes at flow ii 2 172
Their blood is caked, 'tis cold, it seldom flows ii 2 225
Scorn'dst our brain's flow v 4 76
And we'll wear out, In a wall'd prison, packs and sects of great ones, That ebb and flow by the moon *Lear* v 3 19
They take the flow o' the Nile By certain scales i' the pyramid *A. and C.* ii 7 20
Who is so full of grace, that it flows over On all that need v 2 24
Even then The princely blood flows in his cheek, he sweats *Cymbeline* iii 3 93
Flow, flow, You heavenly blessings, on her! iii 5 166
He did not flow From honourable sources *Pericles* iv 3 27
Flowed. Your verse Flow'd with her beauty once *W. Tale* v 1 102
The river hath thrice flow'd, no ebb between *2 Hen. IV.* iv 4 125
The tide of blood in me Hath proudly flow'd in vanity till now v 2 130
And no more words till they have flow'd their fill *3 Hen. VI.* ii 5 72
Now is he for the numbers that Petrarch flowed in *Rom. and Jul.* ii 4 41
Flower. With thy saffron wings upon my flowers Diffusest honey-drops, refreshing showers *Tempest* iv 1 78
Disdain to root the summer-swelling flower *T. G. of Ver.* ii 4 162
Look you scour With juice of balm and every precious flower *Mer. Wives* v 5 66
In emerald tufts, flowers purple, blue, and white v 5 74
Fairies use flowers for their charactery v 5 77
Do as the carrion does, not as the flower *Meas. for Meas.* ii 2 167
Smelling out the odoriferous flowers of fancy *L. L. Lost* iv 2 129
Masks and merry hours Forerun fair Love, strewing her way with flowers iv 3 380
This is the flower that smiles on every one, To show his teeth v 2 331
I am that flower,— That mint.—That columbine v 2 661
Crowns him with flowers and makes him all her joy *M. N. Dream* ii 1 27
A little western flower, Before milk-white, now purple with love's wound ii 1 166
Fetch me that flower; the herb I shew'd thee once ii 1 169
Hast thou the flower there? Welcome, wanderer ii 1 247
Lull'd in these flowers with dances and delight ii 1 254
On whose eyes I might approve This flower's force in stirring love ii 2 69
The flowers of odious savours sweet,— Odours, odours iii 1 84
Sing while thou on pressed flowers dost sleep iii 1 162
When she weeps, weeps every little flower, Lamenting some enforced chastity iii 1 204
Flower of this purple dye, Hit with Cupid's archery iii 2 102
Like two artificial gods, Have with our needles created both one flower iii 2 204
Had rounded With coronet of fresh and fragrant flowers iv 1 57
Dian's bud o'er Cupid's flower Hath such force and blessed power iv 1 78
How that a life was but a flower In spring-time *As Y. Like It* v 3 29
A silver basin Full of rose-water and bestrew'd with flowers *T. of Shrew* Ind. 1 56
Passing courteous, But slow in speech, yet sweet as spring-time flowers ii 1 248
If thou be'st yet a fresh uncropped flower, Choose thou thy husband *All's Well* v 3 327
Away before me to sweet beds of flowers *T. Night* i 1 40
As there is no true cuckold but calamity, so beauty's a flower i 5 57
For women are as roses, whose fair flower Being once display'd, doth fall that very hour ii 4 39
Not a flower, not a flower sweet, On my black coffin let there be strown ii 4 60
You're welcome, sir. Give me those flowers there *W. Tale* iv 4 73
Well you fit our ages With flowers of winter iv 4 79
The fairest flowers o' the season Are our carnations and streak'd gillyvors iv 4 81
Here's flowers for you; Hot lavender, mints, savory, marjoram iv 4 103
These are flowers Of middle summer, and I think they are given To men of middle age iv 4 106
I would I had some flowers o' the spring that might Become your time of day iv 4 113
O Proserpina, For the flowers now, that frighted thou let'st fall From Dis's waggon! daffodils, That come before the swallow dares iv 4 117

Flower. Come, take your flowers . . . . . . *W. Tale* iv 4 132
Suppose the singing birds musicians, The grass whereon thou tread'st the presence strew'd, The flowers fair ladies . *Richard II.* i 3 290
Be like crooked age, To crop at once a too long wither'd flower . ii 1 134
When they from thy bosom pluck a flower, Guard it, I pray thee, with a lurking adder . . . . iii 2 19
Ten thousand bloody crowns of mothers' sons Shall ill become the flower of England's face . . . . iii 3 97
Noisome weeds, which without profit suck The soil's fertility from wholesome flowers . . . . iii 4 39
The whole land Is full of weeds, her fairest flowers choked up . iii 4 44
Out of this nettle, danger, we pluck this flower, safety . 1 *Hen. IV.* ii 3 11
Like the bee, culling from every flower The virtuous sweets 2 *Hen. IV.* iv 5 75
I saw him fumble with the sheets and play with flowers and smile *Hen. V.* ii 3 15
I am bound to you, That you on my behalf would pluck a flower 1 *Hen. VI.* ii 4 129
The paleness of this flower Bewray'd the faintness of my master's heart iv 1 106
Thou hast slain The flower of Europe for his chivalry . 3 *Hen. VI.* ii 1 71
Because sweet flowers are slow and weeds make haste . *Richard III.* ii 4 15
My tender babes! My unblown flowers, new-appearing sweets . iv 4 10
To his music plants and flowers Ever sprung . *Hen. VIII.* iii 1 6
Strew me over With maiden flowers, that all the world may know I was a chaste wife to my grave . . . . . . iv 2 169
Where every flower Did, as a prophet, weep what it foresaw . *T. and C.* i 2 9
Is not that a brave man? he's one of the flowers of Troy, I can tell you i 2 203
Come knights from east to west, And cull their flower, Ajax shall cope the best . . . . ii 3 275
Flower of warriors, How is't with Titus Lartius? . . . *Coriolanus* i 6 32
Make triumphant fires; strew flowers before them . . . v 5 3
As fresh as morning dew distill'd on flowers . . *T. Andron.* ii 3 201
I hang the head As flowers with frost or grass beat down with storms . iv 4 71
He's a man of wax.—Verona's summer hath not such a flower.—Nay, he's a flower; in faith, a very flower . . *Rom. and Jul.* i 3 77
This bud of love, by summer's ripening breath, May prove a beauteous flower . . . . ii 2 122
I must up-fill this osier cage of ours With baleful weeds and precious-juiced flowers . . . . ii 3 8
Within the infant rind of this small flower Poison hath residence . . ii 3 23
Nay, I am the very pink of courtesy.—Pink for flower . . . ii 4 62
He is not the flower of courtesy, but, I'll warrant him, as gentle as a lamb . . . . ii 5 44
Like an untimely frost Upon the sweetest flower of all the field . iv 5 29
There she lies, Flower as she was, deflowered by him . . . iv 5 37
Our bridal flowers serve for a buried corse . . . . iv 5 89
Give me those flowers. Do as I bid thee, go . . . . v 3 9
Sweet flower, with flowers thy bridal bed I strew,—O woe! . . v 3 12
He came with flowers to strew his lady's grave . . . . v 3 281
Do you now strew flowers in his way That comes in triumph? *J. Cæsar* i 1 55
Look like the innocent flower, But be the serpent under't . *Macbeth* i 5 66
Good men's lives Expire before the flowers in their caps . . iv 3 172
To dew the sovereign flower and drown the weeds . . . v 2 30
Larded with sweet flowers; Which bewept to the grave did go *Hamlet* iv 5 37
Where souls do couch on flowers, we'll hand in hand . *Ant. and Cleo.* iv 14 51
Whiles yet the dew's on ground, gather those flowers . *Cymbeline* i 5 1
His steeds to water at those springs On chaliced flowers that lies . ii 3 25
With fairest flowers Whilst summer lasts and I live here, Fidele, I'll sweeten thy sad grave . . . . iv 2 218
Thou shalt not lack The flower that's like thy face, pale primrose . iv 2 221
Furr'd moss besides, when flowers are none, To winter-ground thy corse iv 2 228
We have done our obsequies: come, lay him down.—Here's a few flowers iv 2 283
You were as flowers, now wither'd: even so These herblets shall . . iv 2 286
These flowers are like the pleasures of the world; This bloody man, the care on't . . . . iv 2 296
Poor shadows of Elysium, hence, and rest Upon your never-withering banks of flowers . . . . v 4 98
Though they feed On sweetest flowers, yet they poison breed *Pericles* i 1 133
See how she gins to blow Into life's flower again! . . . iii 2 96
I will rob Tellus of her weed, To strew thy green with flowers . . iv 1 15
Come, give me your flowers, ere the sea mar it . . . . iv 1 27
Flower-de-luce. Lilies of all kinds, The flower-de-luce being one *W. Tale* iv 4 127
What sayest thou, my fair flower-de-luce? . . . *Hen. V.* v 2 224
Cropp'd are the flower-de-luces in your arms . 1 *Hen. VI.* i 1 80
Here is my keen-edged sword, Deck'd with five flower-de-luces on each side . . . . i 2 99
A sceptre shall it have, have I a soul, On which I'll toss the flower-de-luce of France . . . . 2 *Hen. VI.* v 1 11
Flowered. Like stinging bees in hottest summer's day Led by their master to the flowered fields . . . *T. Andron.* v 1 15
I am the very pink of courtesy.—Pink for flower.—Right.—Why, then is my pump well flowered . . . . *Rom. and Jul.* ii 4 64
Floweret. Within the pretty flowerets' eyes Like tears . *M. N. Dream* iv 1 60
Nor bruise her flowerets with the armed hoofs . 1 *Hen. IV.* i 1 8
Flowering. Your fresh-fair virgins and your flowering infants *Hen. V.* iii 3 14
Detain'd me all my flowering youth Within a loathsome dungeon 1 *Hen. VI.* ii 5 56
Or as the snake roll'd in a flowering bank . . . 2 *Hen. VI.* iii 1 228
O serpent heart, hid with a flowering face! . *Rom. and Jul.* iii 2 73
Flower-soft. With the touches of those flower-soft hands *Ant. and Cleo.* ii 2 215
Flowery. Think you I can a resolution fetch From flowery tenderness? *Meas. for Meas.* iii 1 83
What angel wakes me from my flowery bed? . *M. N. Dream* iii 1 132
Come, sit thee down upon this flowery bed . . . . iv 1 1
The flowery way that leads to the broad gate and the great fire *All's Well* iv 5 56
Flowing. Be in their flowing cups freshly remember'd . . *Hen. V.* iv 3 55
Were our tears wanting to this funeral, These tidings would call forth their flowing tides . . . . . . 1 *Hen. VI.* i 1 83
Honour to you no less flowing Than Marchioness of Pembroke *Hen. VIII.* ii 3 62
Flowing and swelling o'er with arts and exercise . *Troi. and Cres.* iv 4 80
Have I to-night fluster'd with flowing cups . . *Othello* ii 3 60
Flown. Great floods have flown From simple sources . *All's Well* ii 1 142
Having flown over many knavish professions, he settled only in rogue *W. Tale* iv 3 105
But health, alack, with youthful wings is flown . 2 *Hen. IV.* iv 5 229
Ere the bat hath flown His cloister'd flight . . *Macbeth* iii 2 40
Bring up the brown bills. O, well flown, bird! i' the clout . *Lear* iv 6 92
Or, wing'd with fervour of her love, she's flown . . *Cymbeline* iii 5 61
Fluellen. Captain Fluellen, you must come presently to the mines *Hen. V.* iii 2 58
I say gud-day, Captain Fluellen.—God-den to your worship, good Captain James . . . . iii 2 88
How now, Captain Fluellen! come you from the bridge? . . . iii 6 1
What men have you lost, Fluellen? . . . . . . iii 6 102
Fluellen. Know'st thou Fluellen?—Yes.—Tell him, I'll knock his leek about his pate . . . . *Hen. V.* iv 1 52
Captain Fluellen!—So! in the name of Jesu Christ, speak lower . . iv 1 64
What think you, Captain Fluellen? is it fit this soldier keep his oath? iv 7 137
Here, Fluellen; wear thou this favour for me and stick it in thy cap . iv 7 160
Follow Fluellen closely at the heels . . . . . . iv 7 179
For I do know Fluellen valiant And, touch'd with choler, hot as gunpowder . . . . iv 7 187
Fluent. It is a theme as fluent as the sea . . . . iii 7 36
Flung. He trod the water, Whose enmity he flung aside . *Tempest* ii 1 116
Accused him strongly; which he fain Would have flung from him *Hen. VIII.* ii 1 25
Matrons flung gloves, Ladies and maids their scarfs and handkerchers, Upon him as he pass'd . . . . . *Coriolanus* ii 1 279
He's flung in rage from this ingrateful seat Of monstrous friends *T. of A.* iv 2 45
Broke their stalls, flung out, Contending 'gainst obedience . *Macbeth* ii 4 16
Flush. Now the time is flush . . . . *T. of Athens* v 4 8
With all his crimes broad blown, as flush as May . . *Hamlet* iii 3 81
The borders maritime Lack blood to think on't, and flush youth revolt: No vessel can peep forth . . . . *Ant. and Cleo.* i 4 52
Flushing. Ere yet the salt of most unrighteous tears Had left the flushing in her galled eyes, She married . . . . *Hamlet* i 2 155
Flustered. The very elements of this warlike isle Have I to-night fluster'd with flowing cups . . . . . *Othello* ii 3 60
Flute. Francis Flute, the bellows-mender.—Here . *M. N. Dream* i 2 44
Flute, you must take Thisby on you.—What is Thisby? a wandering knight? . . . . i 2 46
Heigh-ho! Peter Quince! Flute, the bellows-mender! Snout, the tinker! . . . . iv 1 207
The oars were silver, Which to the tune of flutes kept stroke *A. and C.* ii 2 200
These drums! these trumpets, flutes! what! . . . . . iv 7 138
Fluttered. I Flutter'd your Volscians in Corioli: Alone I did it *Coriolanus* v 6 116
Flux. Thus misery doth part The flux of company . *As Y. Like It* ii 1 52
Civet is of a baser birth than tar, the very uncleanly flux of a cat . iii 2 70
Fly. Be't to fly, To swim, to dive into the fire, to ride . *Tempest* i 2 190
The very instant that I saw you, did My heart fly to your service . . iii 1 65
Her peacocks fly amain: Approach, rich Ceres, her to entertain . . iv 1 74
Do chase the ebbing Neptune and do fly him When he comes back . v 1 35
On the bat's back I do fly After summer merrily . . . . v 1 91
Much less shall she that hath Love's wings to fly . *T. G. of Ver.* ii 7 11
I fly not death, to fly his deadly doom: Tarry I here, I but attend on death: But, fly I hence, I fly away from life . . . . iii 1 185
Upon their sight, We two in great amazedness will fly . *Mer. Wives* iv 4 55
I am undone! Fly, run, hue and cry, villain! I am undone! . . iv 5 93
Nay, do not fly; I think we have watch'd you now . . . . v 5 107
As from a bear a man would run for life, So fly I from her that would be my wife . . . . *Com. of Errors* iii 2 160
'Fly pride,' says the peacock: mistress, that you know . . . iv 3 81
Hark, hark! I hear him, mistress: fly, be gone! . . . . v 1 184
Muster your wits; stand in your own defence; Or hide your heads like cowards, and fly hence . . . . . . *L. L. Lost* v 2 86
Lysander and myself will fly this place . . *M. N. Dream* i 1 203
Ere he do leave this grove, Thou shalt fly him and he shall seek thy love ii 1 246
No marvel though Demetrius Do, as a monster, fly my presence thus . ii 2 97
O strange! we are haunted. Pray, masters! fly, masters! Help! . iii 1 108
Away his fellows fly; And, at our stamp, here o'er and o'er one falls . iii 2 24
I follow'd fast, but faster he did fly . . . . iii 2 416
Do them reverence, As they fly by them with their woven wings *M. of V.* i 1 14
O, ten times faster Venus' pigeons fly To seal love's bonds new-made! . ii 6 5
In the morning early will we both Fly toward Belmont . . . iv 1 457
Devise with me how we may fly, Whither to go and what to bear with us . . . . *As Y. Like It* i 3 102
I fly thee, for I would not injure thee . . . . . . iii 5 9
Her frown might kill me.—By this hand, it will not kill a fly . . iv 1 111
Stop that, 'twill fly with the smoke out at the chimney . . . iv 1 165
Softly and swiftly, sir; for the priest is ready.—I fly . . *T. of Shrew* v 1 3
What is infirm from your sound parts shall fly . . *All's Well* ii 1 170
Now, Dian, from thy altar do I fly . . . . . . ii 3 80
And all the honours that can fly from us Shall on them settle . . iii 1 20
This is not well, rash and unbridled boy, To fly the favours of so good a king . . . . iii 2 31
O you leaden messengers, That ride upon the violent speed of fire, Fly with false aim . . . . iii 2 113
I wonder, sir, sith wives are monsters to you, And that you fly them as you swear them lordship, Yet you desire to marry . . . . v 3 156
Fly away, fly away, breath; I am slain by a fair cruel maid . *T. Night* ii 4 54
Methinks his words do from such passion fly, That he believes himself . iii 4 407
And aid them, for their better safety, to fly away by night *W. Tale* iii 2 21
If that shepherd be not in hand-fast, let him fly . . . . iv 4 796
Be Mercury, set feathers to thy heels, And fly like thought . *K. John* iv 2 175
Fly, noble English, you are bought and sold . . . . . v 4 10
Who was he that said King John did fly an hour or two before? . . v 5 17
Since the more fair and crystal is the sky, The uglier seem the clouds that in it fly . . . . *Richard II.* i 1 42
Confess thy treasons ere thou fly the realm . . . . . i 3 198
Where one on his side fights, thousands will fly . . . . ii 2 147
All souls that will be safe fly from my side . . . . . iii 2 80
A rendezvous, a home to fly unto . . . . . 1 *Hen. IV.* iv 1 57
We were enforced, for safety sake, to fly Out of your sight . . v 1 65
That arrows fled not swifter toward their aim Than did our soldiers, aiming at their safety, Fly from the field . . . . 2 *Hen. IV.* i 1 125
O, fly to Scotland, Till that the nobles and the armed commons Have of their puissance made a little taste . . . . ii 3 50
O, with what wings shall his affections fly Towards fronting peril! . iv 4 65
His soul Shall stand sore charged for the wasteful vengeance That shall fly with them . . . . *Hen. V.* i 2 284
And so our scene must to the battle fly . . . . . . iv Prol. 48
They have no wings to fly from God . . . . iv 1 177
The knavish crows Fly o'er them, all impatient for their hour . . iv 2 52
Not a piece of feather in our host—Good argument, I hope, we will not fly . . . . iv 3 113
Tarry, sweet soul, for mine, then fly abreast . . . . iv 6 17
And so I shall catch the fly, your cousin, in the latter end . . v 2 340
Another would fly swift, but wanteth wings . . . 1 *Hen. VI.* i 1 75
O, whither shall we fly from this reproach?—We will not fly, but to our enemies' throats . . . . i 1 97
Him I forgive my death that killeth me When he sees me go back one foot or fly . . . . i 2 21
I fear no woman.—And while I live, I'll ne'er fly from a man . . i 2 103
My grisly countenance made others fly . . . . i 4 47

Fly. Sheep run not half so treacherous from the wolf . . . As you fly from your oft-subdued slaves . . . . *1 Hen. VI.* i 5 32
What! will you fly, and leave Lord Talbot? . . . . iii 2 107
For fly he could not, if he would have fled; And fly would Talbot never, though he might . . . . iv 4 43
Is my name Talbot? and am I your son? And shall I fly? . . . . iv 5 13
Fly, to revenge my death, if I be slain.—He that flies so will ne'er return iv 5 18
Then let me stay; and, father, do you fly . . . . iv 5 21
Upon my blessing, I command thee go.—To fight I will, but not to fly the foe . . . . iv 5 37
If death be so apparent, then both fly.—And leave my followers here? . iv 5 44
Together live and die; And soul with soul from France to heaven fly . iv 5 55
Wilt thou yet leave the battle, boy, and fly, Now thou art seal'd the son of chivalry? . . . . iv 6 28
Fly, to revenge my death when I am dead . . . . iv 6 30
All these and more we hazard by thy stay; All these are saved if thou wilt fly away . . . . iv 6 41
Before young Talbot from old Talbot fly, The coward horse that bears me fall and die! . . . . iv 6 46
Surely, by all the glory you have won, An if I fly, I am not Talbot's son iv 6 51
The regent conquers, and the Frenchmen fly. Now help, ye charming spells . . . . v 3 1
O fairest beauty, do not fear nor fly! . . . . v 3 46
Were it not good your grace could fly to heaven? . . . *2 Hen. VI.* ii 1 17
Humphrey has done a miracle to-day.—True; made the lame to leap and fly away . . . . ii 1 162
But you have done more miracles than I; You made in a day, my lord, whole towns to fly . . . . ii 1 164
And, fly thou how thou canst, they'll tangle thee . . . . . . ii 4 55
Where's our general?—Here I am, thou particular fellow.—Fly, fly, fly! iv 2 120
That those which fly before the battle ends May, even in their wives' and children's sight, Be hang'd up for example . . . . . . iv 2 188
Cade hath gotten London bridge: The citizens fly and forsake their houses . . . . iv 4 50
Ignorance is the curse of God, Knowledge the wing wherewith we fly to heaven . . . . iv 7 79
Alas, he hath no home, no place to fly to . . . . iv 8 40
Let no soldier fly. He that is truly dedicate to war Hath no self-love . v 2 36
What are you made of? you'll nor fight nor fly . . . . . . v 2 74
And to secure us By what we can, which can no more but fly . . . v 2 77
I would speak blasphemy ere bid you fly: But fly you must . . . . v 2 85
But when the duke is slain, they'll quickly fly . . . . *3 Hen. VI.* i 1 69
Sound drums and trumpets, and the king will fly . . . . . . i 1 118
Ah, whither shall I fly to 'scape their hands? . . . . i 3 1
Fly, like ships before the wind Or lambs pursued by hunger-starved wolves . . . . i 4 4
The fatal followers do pursue; And I am faint and cannot fly their fury i 4 23
So cowards fight when they can fly no further . . . . i 4 40
Whose frown hath made thee faint and fly ere this . . . . . . i 4 48
Cry 'Charge upon our foes!' But never once again turn back and fly . ii 1 185
In the towns, as they do march along, Proclaims him king, and many fly to him . . . . ii 2 71
Then 'twas my turn to fly, and now 'tis thine.—You said so much before, and yet you fled . . . . ii 2 105
What counsel give you? whither shall we fly? . . . . ii 3 11
I'll kill my horse, because I will not fly . . . . ii 3 24
Give them leave to fly that will not stay . . . . ii 3 50
Fly, father, fly! for all your friends are fled . . . . ii 5 125
And whither fly the gnats but to the sun? . . . . ii 6 9
No way to fly, nor strength to hold out flight . . . . ii 6 24
What are they that fly there?—Richard and Hastings . . . . . iv 3 27
Come, therefore, let us fly while we may fly . . . . iv 4 34
Ah, couldst thou fly!—Why, then I would not fly . . . . . . v 2 32
Sweet rest his soul! Fly, lords, and save yourselves . . . . . . v 2 48
To let you understand, If case some one of you would fly from us . . v 4 34
To fly the boar before the boar pursues, Were to incense the boar to follow us And make pursuit . . . . *Richard III.* iii 2 28
But I disdain'd it, and did scorn to fly . . . . iii 4 85
If yet your gentle souls fly in the air And be not fix'd in doom perpetual iv 4 11
Wilt thou, O God, fly from such gentle lambs, And throw them in the entrails of the wolf? . . . . iv 4 22
Fly to the duke: Post thou to Salisbury . . . . iv 4 443
Thou wilt revolt, and fly to him, I fear . . . . iv 4 478
I doubt not but his friends will fly to us . . . . v 2 19
Then fly. What, from myself? Great reason why: Lest I revenge . . v 3 185
Where my chaff And corn shall fly asunder . . . . . *Hen. VIII.* v 1 111
Now, good angels Fly o'er thy royal head, and shade thy person! . . . v 1 160
Fly like chidden Mercury from Jove, Or like a star disorb'd *Tr. and Cr.* ii 2 45
It will not in circumvention deliver a fly from a spider . . . . . ii 3 17
From Cupid's shoulder pluck his painted wings, And fly with me to Cressid! . . . . iii 2 16
And with his arms outstretch'd, as he would fly, Grasps in the comer . iii 3 167
And thou shalt hunt a lion, that will fly With his face backward . . iv 1 19
Fly not; for shouldst thou take the river Styx, I would swim after . . v 4 20
Thou dost miscall retire: I do not fly . . . . v 4 22
They fly or die, like scaled sculls Before the belching whale . . . . v 5 22
Wilt thou not, beast, abide? Why, then fly on, I'll hunt thee for thy hide . . . . v 6 31
If I fly, Marcius, Holloa me like a hare . . . . . . *Coriolanus* i 8 6
My valour's poison'd With only suffering stain by him; for him Shall fly out of itself . . . . i 10 19
Do they still fly to the Roman?—I do not know what witchcraft's in him iv 7 1
Sir, if you'ld save your life, fly to your house . . . . v 4 38
What dost thou strike at, Marcus, with thy knife?—At that that I have kill'd, my lord; a fly . . . . *T. Andron.* iii 2 53
I have but kill'd a fly.—But how, if that fly had a father and mother? . iii 2 59
Poor harmless fly, That, with his pretty buzzing melody, Came here to make us merry! and thou hast kill'd him . . . . iii 2 63
Pardon me, sir; it was a black ill-favour'd fly . . . . iii 2 66
We are not brought so low, But that between us we can kill a fly . . iii 2 77
Which made me down to throw my books, and fly,—Causeless, perhaps iv 1 25
Sweet scrolls to fly about the streets of Rome! . . . . iv 4 16
Is the sun dimm'd, that gnats do fly in it? . . . . iv 4 82
I have done a thousand dreadful things As willingly as one would kill a fly . . . . v 1 142
Ope the door, That so my sad decrees may fly away . . . . . . v 2 11
But no more deep will I endart mine eye Than your consent gives strength to make it fly . . . . *Rom. and Jul.* i 3 99
As he fell, did Romeo turn and fly. This is the truth . . . . . iii 1 179
Flies may do this, but I from this must fly: They are free men . . iii 3 41

Fly. Tempt not a desperate man; Fly hence, and leave me *Rom. and Jul.* v 3 60
I will fly, like a dog, the heels o' the ass . . . . . *T. of Athens* i 1 282
His promises fly so beyond his state That what he speaks is all in debt i 2 203
Fly, damned baseness, To him that worships thee! . . . . . . iii 1 50
If thou hatest curses, Stay not; fly, whilst thou art blest and free . iv 3 542
These growing feathers pluck'd from Cæsar's wing Will make him fly an ordinary pitch, Who else would soar . . . . . . *J. Cæsar* i 1 78
His coward lips did from their colour fly . . . . i 2 122
Be not affrighted; Fly not; stand still: ambition's debt is paid . . iii 1 83
Crows and kites Fly o'er our heads and downward look on us . . . v 1 86
O, look, Titinius, look, the villains fly! . . . . v 3 1
Fly further off, my lord, fly further off . . . . v 3 9
Fly, therefore, noble Cassius, fly far off.—This hill is far enough . . v 3 11
Fly, fly, my lord; there is no tarrying here . . . . v 5 30
Fly, fly, fly!—Fly, my lord, fly.—Hence! I will follow . . . . . v 5 43
Fly, good Fleance, fly, fly, fly! Thou mayst revenge . . *Macbeth* iii 3 17
Some holy angel Fly to the court of England and unfold His message! iii 6 46
What had he done, to make him fly the land? . . . . iv 2 1
Wisdom! to leave his wife, to leave his babes, His mansion and his titles in a place From whence himself does fly? . . . . . . iv 2 8
Whither should I fly? I have done no harm . . . . iv 2 73
Bring me no more reports; let them fly all . . . . v 3 1
Then fly, false thanes, And mingle with the English epicures . . . v 3 7
Give me my staff. Seyton, send out. Doctor, the thanes fly from me v 3 49
They have tied me to a stake; I cannot fly, But, bear-like, I must fight the course . . . . v 7 1
We'll e'en to't like French falconers, fly at any thing we see. *Hamlet* ii 2 450
Rather bear those ills we have Than fly to others that we know not of . iii 1 82
My words fly up, my thoughts remain below . . . . iii 3 97
Unpeg the basket on the house's top, Let the birds fly . . . . . iii 4 194
Repair thou to me with as much speed as thou wouldst fly death . . iv 6 24
Fly this place; Intelligence is given where you are hid . . . *Lear* ii 1 22
Light, ho, here! Fly, brother. Torches, torches! . . . . . . ii 1 34
Let him fly far: Not in this land shall he remain uncaught . . . . ii 1 58
Winter's not gone yet, if the wild-geese fly that way . . . . . ii 4 47
The wren goes to't, and the small gilded fly Does lecher in my sight . iv 6 114
She that being anger'd, her revenge being nigh, Bade her wrong stay and her displeasure fly . . . . *Othello* ii 1 154
With as little a web as this will I ensnare as great a fly as Cassio . . ii 1 170
Thy freer thoughts May not fly forth of Egypt . . *Ant. and Cleo.* i 5 12
And never Fly off our loves again!—Happily, amen! . . . . . ii 2 155
This was but as a fly by an eagle . . . . ii 2 186
Spur through Media, Mesopotamia, and the shelters whither The routed fly . . . . iii 1 9
The Antoniad, the Egyptian admiral, With all their sixty, fly . . . iii 10 3
Fly, And make your peace with Cæsar.—Fly! not we . . . . . iii 11 5
Bid them all fly; For when I am revenged upon my charm, I have done all. Bid them all fly; begone . . . . iv 12 15
Thy death and fortunes bid thy followers fly . . . . iv 14 111
Or, like the Parthian, I shall flying fight; Rather, directly fly *Cymbeline* i 6 21
His spirits fly out Into my story: say 'Thus mine enemy fell' . . . iii 3 90
I think Foundations fly the wretched . . . . iii 6 7
The smile mocking the sigh, that it would fly From so divine a temple iv 2 54
What are you That fly me thus? some villain mountaineers? . . . iv 2 71
Thus smiling, as some fly had tickled slumber, Not as death's dart . iv 2 210
Their blood thinks scorn, Till it fly out and show them princes born . iv 4 54
It is a day turn'd strangely: or betimes Let's re-inforce, or fly . . v 2 18
To darkness fleet souls that fly backwards . . . . v 3 25
Forthwith they fly Chickens, the way which they stoop'd eagles . . v 3 41
If he'll do as he is made to do, I know he'll quickly fly my friendship too v 3 62
Help, Jupiter; or we appeal, And from thy justice fly . . . . . v 4 92
Prince Pericles is fled.—As thou Wilt live, fly after . . . *Pericles* i 1 163
Believe me, la, I never kill'd a mouse, nor hurt a fly . . . . . iv 1 78
The petty wrens of Tarsus will fly hence, And open this to Pericles . iv 3 22
When I did fly from Tyre, I left behind an ancient substitute . . . v 3 50

Fly-bitten. These fly-bitten tapestries . . . . . . *2 Hen. IV.* ii 1 159
Fly-blowing. I shall not fear fly-blowing . . . . . . *Tempest* v 1 284
Fly-blown. Stinking and fly-blown lies here at our feet . *1 Hen. VI.* iv 7 76

Flying. My thoughts do harbour with my Silvia nightly, And slaves they are to me that send them flying . . . . . *T. G. of Ver.* iii 1 141
Think upon my grief, a lady's grief, And on the justice of my flying hence iv 3 29
Love like a shadow flies when substance love pursues; Pursuing that that flies, and flying what pursues . . . . . *Mer. Wives* ii 2 216
Flying between the cold moon and the earth, Cupid all arm'd *M. N. D.* ii 1 156
And thou art flying to a fresher clime . . . . . . *Richard II.* i 3 285
Rides at high speed and with his pistol kills a sparrow flying *1 Hen. IV.* ii 4 380
Believe me, lords, for flying at the brook, I saw not better sport these seven years' day . . . . *2 Hen. VI.* ii 1 1
With thy lips to stop my mouth; So shouldst thou either turn my flying soul . . . . iii 2 397
Like a brace of greyhounds Having the fearful flying hare in sight *3 Hen. VI.* ii 5 130
Flying for succour to his servant Banister . . . . *Hen. VIII.* ii 1 109
As doth a battle, when they charge on heaps The enemy flying *T. and C.* iii 2 30
There is nor flying hence nor tarrying here . . . . . *Macbeth* v 5 48
Mere fetches; The images of revolt and flying off . . . . . *Lear* ii 4 91
'Twas a shame no less Than was his loss, to course your flying flags, And leave his navy gazing . . . . *Ant. and Cleo.* iii 13 11
Or, like the Parthian, I shall flying fight; Rather, directly fly *Cymbeline* i 6 20
And but the backs of Britons seen, all flying Through a strait lane . v 3 6
Our Britain's harts die flying, not our men . . . . v 3 24

Foal. Neighing in likeness of a filly foal . . . . . *M. N. Dream* ii 1 46
Give my horse to Timon, Ask nothing, give it him, it foals me, straight, And able horses . . . . *T of Athens* i 1 9

Foam. Ajax hath lost a friend And foams at mouth . . *Troi. and Cres.* v 5 36
Where the light foam of the sea may beat Thy grave-stone daily *T. of A.* iv 3 379
'Tis thou [gold] that rigg'st the bark and plough'st the foam . . . v 1 53
I have seen The ambitious ocean swell and rage and foam . . *J. Cæsar* i 3 7
The lethargy must have his quiet course: If not, he foams at mouth *Oth.* iv 1 55
My navy; at whose burthen The anger'd ocean foams . *Ant. and Cleo.* ii 6 21

Foamed. He fell down in the market-place, and foamed at mouth *J. C.* i 2 255
Came to me With his sword drawn; foam'd at the mouth . *Cymbeline* v 5 276

Foaming. All but mariners Plunged in the foaming brine . . *Tempest* i 2 211
Be Mowbray's sins so heavy in his bosom, That they may break his foaming courser's back! . . . . *Richard II.* i 2 51
Among foaming bottles and ale-washed wits . . . . . *Hen. V.* iii 6 82
And once again bestride our foaming steeds . . . . *3 Hen. VI.* ii 1 183
For do but stand upon the foaming shore, The chidden billow seems to pelt the clouds . . . . *Othello* ii 1 11

Foamy. From the rude sea's enraged and foamy mouth Did I redeem *T. N.* v 1 81

Fob. You must not think to fob off our disgrace with a tale *Coriolanus* i 1 97
Fobbed as it is with the rusty curb of old father antic the law 1 *Hen. IV.* i 2 68
Fodder. The sheep for fodder follow the shepherd . . *T. G. of Ver.* i 1 92
Foe. O time most accurst, 'Mongst all foes that a friend should be the worst! . . . . v 4 72
'Twere pity two such friends should be long foes . . . . . v 4 118
I see what thou wert, if Fortune thy foe were not, Nature thy friend *Mer. Wives* iii 3 70
A huge infectious troop Of pale distemperatures and foes to life *C. of Er.* v 1 82
That oft in field, with targe and shield, did make my foe to sweat *L. L. Lost* v 2 556
Why . . . Lay breath so bitter on your bitter foe . *M. N. Dream* iii 2 44
Strangers and foes do sunder, and not kiss . . . *All's Well* ii 5 91
Sent him forth From courtly friends, with camping foes to live . iii 4 14
The better for my foes and the worse for my friends . *T. Night* v 1 13
Now my foes tell me plainly I am an ass: so that by my foes, sir, I profit in the knowledge of myself, and by my friends I am abused . v 1 20
Why then, the worse for my friends and the better for my foes . v 1 26
With purpled hands, Dyed in the dying slaughter of their foes *K. John* ii 1 323
And dost thou now fall over to my foes? . . . . iii 1 127
I alone, alone do me oppose Against the pope and count his friends my foes . . . . iii 1 171
Yet, I know, Our party may well meet a prouder foe . . . v 1 79
My noble Lord of Lancaster, The honourable father to my foe *Richard II.* i 1 136
Nor friends nor foes, to me welcome you are . . . . . ii 3 170
Thy friends are fled to wait upon thy foes . . . . . ii 4 23
Feed not thy sovereign's foe, my gentle earth . . . . . iii 2 12
To fear the foe, since fear oppresseth strength, Gives in your weakness strength unto your foe . . . . iii 2 181
I'll give thee scope to beat, Since foes have scope to beat both thee and me iii 3 141
May my hands rot off And never brandish more revengeful steel Over the glittering helmet of my foe! . . . . iv 1 51
Let's go: I am the king's friend, and will rid his foe . . . . v 4 11
But wherefore do I tell these news to thee? Why, Harry, do I tell thee of my foes, Which art my near'st and dearest enemy? 1 *Hen. IV.* iii 2 122
His foes are so enrooted with his friends . . . . 2 *Hen. IV.* iv 1 207
It is most meet we arm us 'gainst the foe . . . *Hen. V.* ii 4 15
Fortune is Bardolph's foe, and frowns on him . . . . . . iii 6 41
Were enow To purge this field of such a hilding foe . . . . iv 2 29
And ne'er throughout the year to church thou go'st Except it be to pray against thy foes . . . . 1 *Hen. VI.* i 1 43
When I have chased all thy foes from hence, Then will I think upon a recompense.—Meantime look gracious . . . . i 2 115
A foe to citizens, One that still motions war and never peace . . i 3 62
And know us by these colours for thy foes . . . . . . ii 4 105
We and our wives and children all will fight And have our bodies slaughter'd by thy foes . . . . iii 1 101
And so thrive Richard as thy foes may fall! . . . . . . iii 1 174
For friendly counsel cuts off many foes . . . . iii 1 185
Now shine it like a comet of revenge, A prophet to the fall of all our foes! iii 2 32
In his litter sick Came to the field and vanquished his foes . . iii 2 96
And see the cities and the towns defaced By wasting ruin of the cruel foe iii 3 46
Was not the Duke of Orleans thy foe? And was he not in England prisoner? . . . . iii 3 69
Join our powers, And seek how we may prejudice the foe . . . iii 3 91
Esteem none friends but such as are his friends, And none your foes but such as shall pretend Malicious practices against his state . iv 1 6
Doth my uncle Burgundy revolt?—He doth, my lord, and is become your foe . . . . iv 1 65
In heart desiring still You may behold confusion of your foes . . iv 1 77
I command thee go.—To fight I will, but not to fly the foe . . iv 5 37
Imagine him a Frenchman and thy foe . . . . iv 7 26
In his infancy Crowned in Paris in despite of foes . 2 *Hen. VI.* i 1 94
Fear not thou, until thy foot be snared, Nor never seek prevention of thy foes . . . . ii 4 57
Had I twenty times so many foes, And each of them had twenty times their power . . . . ii 4 60
And to preserve my sovereign from his foe, Say but the word, and I will be his priest . . . . iii 1 271
Foe as he was to me, Might liquid tears . . . recall his life, I would be blind with weeping . . . . iii 2 59
But both of you were vow'd Duke Humphrey's foes . . . . iii 2 182
'Tis not enough our foes are this time fled, Being opposites of such repairing nature . . . . v 3 21
Accursed be he that seeks to make them foes! . . . 3 *Hen. VI.* i 1 205
All my followers to the eager foe Turn back and fly . . . . i 4 3
Even my foes will shed fast-falling tears, And say 'Alas!' . . . i 4 162
Environed he was with many foes, And stood against them . . . ii 1 50
Or shall we on the helmets of our foes Tell our devotion? . . . ii 1 163
And once again cry 'Charge upon our foes!' But never once again turn back ii 1 184
Our foes are nigh, And this soft courage makes your followers faint . ii 2 56
Why stand we like soft-hearted women here, Wailing our losses, whiles the foe doth rage? . . . . ii 3 26
If with thy will it stands That to my foes this body must be prey . ii 3 39
The foe is merciless, and will not pity . . . . ii 6 25
Now the battle's ended, If friend or foe, let him be gently used . ii 6 45
Thou shalt not dread The scatter'd foe that hopes to rise again . ii 6 93
Henry your foe is taken, And brought your prisoner to your palace gate iii 2 118
The more we stay, the stronger grows our foe . . . . . iii 3 40
I came from Edward as ambassador, But I return his sworn and mortal foe iii 3 257
I rather wish you foes than hollow friends . . . . . . iv 1 139
Either betray'd by falsehood of his guard Or by his foe surprised . iv 4 9
The Bishop of York, Fell Warwick's brother and by that our foe . iv 4 12
So other foes may set upon our backs. Stand we in good array . v 1 61
I here proclaim myself thy mortal foe . . . . v 1 94
Ah, who is nigh? come to me, friend or foe, And tell me who is victor? v 2 5
I must yield my body to the earth And, by my fall, the conquest to my foe v 2 10
Henry, your sovereign, Is prisoner to the foe . . . . . . v 4 77
If any here, By false intelligence, or wrong surmise, Hold me a foe *Richard III.* ii 1 55
Two deep enemies, Foes to my rest and my sweet sleep's disturbers . iv 2 74
If you do fight against your country's foes, Your country's fat shall pay your pains the hire . . . . v 3 257
Arm, arm, my lord; the foe vaunts in the field.—Come, bustle, bustle v 3 288
Advance our standards, set upon our foes . . . . . . v 3 348
Heat not a furnace for your foe so hot That it do singe yourself *Hen. VIII.* i 1 140
I hold my most malicious foe, and think not At all a friend to truth . ii 4 83
Her foes shake like a field of beaten corn, And hang their heads with sorrow . . . . v 5 32
Feast with us before you go And find the welcome of a noble foe *T. and C.* i 3 309
Whose present courage may beat down our foes . . . . . . ii 2 201
Foe. I'll leave the foe And make my wars on you . . . *Coriolanus* i 4 39
If he should still malignantly remain Fast foe to the plebeii . . ii 3 192
Call'd them Time-pleasers, flatterers, foes to nobleness . . . . iii 1 45
A traitorous innovator, A foe to the public weal . . . . . iii 1 176
Making not reservation of yourselves, Still your own foes . . . iii 3 131
So, fellest foes, Whose passions and whose plots have broke their sleep iv 4 18
With his sons, a terror to our foes, Hath yoked a nation strong *T. An.* i 1 29
To quit the bloody wrongs upon her foes . . . . i 1 141
My foes I do repute you every one; So, trouble me no more . . . i 1 366
To ease the gnawing vulture of thy mind, By working wreakful vengeance on thy foes . . . . v 2 32
Bring in the empress and her sons, The emperor himself and all thy foes v 2 117
Revenge now goes To lay a complot to betray thy foes . . . . v 2 147
Thy foes are bound. Sirs, stop their mouths, let them not speak to me v 2 167
From forth the fatal loins of these two foes A pair of star-cross'd lovers take their life . . . . *Rom. and Jul.* Prol. 5
Thou shalt not stir a foot to seek a foe . . . . i 1 87
This is a Montague, our foe, A villain that is hither come in spite . i 5 63
Is she a Capulet? O dear account! my life is my foe's debt . . . i 5 120
But to his foe supposed he must complain . . . . . . ii Prol. 7
Being held a foe, he may not have access To breathe such vows as lovers use to swear . . . . ii Prol. 9
I bear no hatred, blessed man, for, lo, My intercession likewise steads my foe . . . . ii 3 54
I would I could not think it: that thought is bounty's foe *T. of Athens* ii 2 241
Seeing his reputation touch'd to death, He did oppose his foe . . iii 5 20
Sleep upon 't, And let the foes quietly cut their throats? . . . iii 5 44
If there were no foes, that were enough To overcome him . . . iii 5 70
I have kept back their foes, While they have told their money . . iii 5 106
In, and prepare: Ours is the fall, I fear; our foes the snare . . v 2 17
Shaking the bloody fingers of thy foes, Most noble! . . *J. Cæsar* iii 1 198
I am the son of Marcus Cato, ho! A foe to tyrants, and my country's friend . . . . v 4 5
So they Doubly redoubled strokes upon the foe . . . *Macbeth* i 2 38
Those That would make good of bad, and friends of foes . . . ii 4 41
We have met with foes That strike beside us . . . . . . v 7 28
Would I had met my dearest foe in heaven Or ever I had seen that day! *Hamlet* i 2 182
Is 't writ in your revenge, That, swoopstake, you will draw both friend and foe? . . . . iv 5 142
When we our betters see bearing our woes, We scarcely think our miseries our foes . . . . *Lear* iii 6 110
All friends shall taste The wages of their virtue, and all foes The cup of their deservings . . . . v 3 303
Of being taken by the insolent foe And sold to slavery . . . *Othello* i 3 137
All is lost; This foul Egyptian hath betrayed me: My fleet hath yielded to the foe . . . . *Ant. and Cleo.* iv 12 11
Such a foe, good heavens! . . . . *Cymbeline* iii 6 27
Our foe was princely; And though you took his life, as being our foe, Yet bury him as a prince . . . . iv 2 249
Who dares not stand his foe, I'll be his friend . . . . . . v 3 60
Came crying 'mongst his foes, A thing of pity! . . . . . . v 4 46
They bring us peace, And come to us as favourers, not as foes *Pericles* i 4 73
Foeman. The foeman may with as great aim level at the edge of a penknife . . . . 2 *Hen. IV.* iii 2 285
Is this our foeman's face? Ah, no, no, no, it is mine only son! 3 *Hen. VI.* ii 5 82
Foemen. Unto his dastard foemen is betray'd . . . 1 *Hen. VI.* i 1 144
What valiant foemen, like to autumn's corn, Have we mow'd down! 3 *Hen. VI.* v 7 3
That hath more scars of sorrow in his heart Than foemen's marks upon his batter'd shield . . . . *T. Andron.* iv 1 127
Fog. Have suck'd up from the sea Contagious fogs . *M. N. Dream* ii 1 90
The starry welkin cover thou anon With drooping fog as black as Acheron iii 2 357
In which thou art more puzzled than the Egyptians in their fog *T. Night* iv 2 48
Southward.—Why that way?—To lose itself in a fog . *Coriolanus* ii 3 34
We'll breathe the welkin dim, And stain the sun with fog *T. Andron.* iii 1 213
Fair is foul, and foul is fair: Hover through the fog and filthy air *Macb.* i 1 12
Blasts and fogs upon thee! . . . . *Lear* i 4 321
Infect her beauty, You fen-suck'd fogs, drawn by the powerful sun! . ii 4 169
Nor here, nor here, Nor what ensues, but have a fog in them, That I cannot look through . . . . *Cymbeline* iii 2 81
Foggy. Like foggy south puffing with wind and rain *As Y. Like It* iii 5 50
Is not their climate foggy, raw and dull? . . . . *Hen. V.* iii 5 16
My little spirit, see, Sits in a foggy cloud, and stays for me . *Macbeth* iii 5 35
Foh. 'Steal!' foh! a fico for the phrase! . . . . *Mer. Wives* i 3 33
Come, sir; come, sir; come, sir; foh, sir! . . *Meas. for Meas.* v 1 356
Pray you, sir, deliver me this paper.—Foh! prithee, stand away *All's W.* v 2 17
I'll tell you what,— Foh, foh! come, tell a pin . *Troi. and Cres.* v 2 22
Foh, foh! adieu; you palter.—In faith, I do not: come hither once again v 2 48
Fie upon't! foh! About, my brain! . . . . *Hamlet* ii 2 617
Fie, foh, and fum, I smell the blood of a British man . . . *Lear* iii 4 188
Foh! one may smell in such a will most rank, Foul disproportion *Othello* iii 3 232
As honest As you that thus abuse me.—As I! foh! fie upon thee! . v 1 123
Foi. Fe, fe, fe, fe! ma foi, il fait fort chaud . . . . *Mer. Wives* i 4 53
Les doigts? ma foi, j'oublie les doigts . . . . . *Hen. V.* iii 4 9
Ma foi, je ne veux point que vous abaissiez votre grandeur . . . v 2 274
Foil. Some defect in her Did quarrel with the noblest grace she owed And put it to the foil . . . . *Tempest* iii 1 46
Blunt as the fencer's foils, which hit, but hurt not . . . *Much Ado* v 2 13
I would be loath to foil him . . . . *As Y. Like It* i 1 136
The wrestler That did but lately foil the sinewy Charles . . . ii 2 14
The sullen passage of thy weary steps Esteem as foil wherein thou art to set The precious jewel of thy home return . . *Richard II.* i 3 266
Attract more eyes Than that which hath no foil to set it off . 1 *Hen. IV.* i 2 239
With four or five most vile and ragged foils . . . *Hen. V.* iv Prol. 50
One sudden foil shall never breed distrust . . . 1 *Hen. VI.* iii 3 11
Then take my soul, my body, soul and all, Before that England give the French the foil . . . . v 3 23
And make him, naked, foil a man at arms . . . 3 *Hen. VI.* v 4 42
A base foul stone, made precious by the foil Of England's chair *Rich. III.* v 3 250
The adventurous knight shall use his foil and target . . *Hamlet* ii 2 334
He, being remiss, Most generous and free from all contriving, Will not peruse the foils . . . . iv 7 137
Let the foils be brought, the gentleman willing . . . . . v 2 182
Give us the foils. Come on.—Come, one for me.—I'll be your foil, Laertes . . . . v 2 265
Give them the foils, young Osric. Cousin Hamlet, You know the wager? v 2 270
These foils have all a length?—Ay, my good lord . . . . . v 2 276
Foiled. Wherein if I be foiled, there is but one shamed that was never gracious . . . . *As Y. Like It* i 2 199

Foiled. If he were foil'd, Why then, we did our main opinion crush In taint of our best man . . . *Troi. and Cres.* i 3 372
For that I have not wash'd My nose that bled, or foil'd some debile wretch, . . . You shout me forth . . . *Coriolanus* i 9 48
Foin. To see thee fight, to see thee foin, to see thee traverse *Mer. Wives* ii 3 24
He will foin like any devil . . . *2 Hen. IV.* ii 1 17
Come; no matter vor your foins . . . *Lear* iv 6 251
Foining. I'll whip you from your foining fence . . . *Much Ado* v 1 84
When wilt thou leave fighting o' days and foining o' nights? . *2 Hen. IV.* ii 4 252
Fois. Je reciterai une autre fois ma leçon ensemble . . . *Hen. V.* iii 4 61
C'est assez pour une fois: allons-nous à dîner . . . iii 4 65
Foison. Nature should bring forth, Of it own kind, all foison . *Tempest* ii 1 163
Earth's increase, foison plenty, Barns and garners never empty . iv 1 110
That from the seedness the bare fallow brings To teeming foison *M. for M.* i 4 43
Scotland hath foisons to fill up your will, Of your mere own *Macbeth* iv 3 88
They know, By the height, the lowness, or the mean, if dearth Or foison follow: the higher Nilus swells, The more it promises *Ant. and Cleo.* ii 7 23
Foix. Grandpré, Roussi, and Fauconberg, Foix, Lestrale. . *Hen. V.* iii 5 45
Lusty earls, Grandpré and Roussi, Fauconberg and Foix . . . iv 8 104
Fold. Thus will I fold them one upon another: Now kiss, embrace, contend, do what you will . . . *T. G. of Ver.* i 2 128
The fold stands empty in the drowned field . . . *M. N. Dream* ii 1 96
We will descend and fold him in our arms . . . *Richard II.* i 3 54
Dost thou thirst, base Trojan, To have me fold up Parca's fatal web? *Hen. V.* v 1 21
Were't not madness, then, To make the fox surveyor of the fold? *2 Hen. VI.* iii 1 253
But more in Troilus thousand fold I see . . . *Troi. and Cres.* i 2 310
The weak wanton Cupid Shall from your neck unloose his amorous fold iii 3 223
And wonder greatly that man's face can fold In pleasing smiles such murderous tyranny . . . *T. Andron.* ii 3 266
Hast thou a knife? come, let me see it. Here, Marcus, fold it in the oration . . . iv 3 116
Like a shepherd, Approach the fold and cull the infected forth *T. of A.* v 4 43
Fold it, write upon't, read it, afterwards seal it . . . *Macbeth* v 1 7
To dismantle So many folds of favour . . . *Lear* i 1 221
Mine eyes are weak: Fold down the leaf where I have left . *Cymbeline* ii 2 4
Folded. The folded meaning of your words' deceit . . *Com. of Errors* iii 2 36
Regent of love-rhymes, lord of folded arms . . . *L. L. Lost* iii 1 183
They shoot but calm words folded up in smoke . . . *K. John* ii 1 229
Thy cloudy wrath Hath in eternal darkness folded up . *Richard III.* i 3 269
And cannot passionate our tenfold grief With folded arms *T. Andron.* iii 2 7
Folded the writ up in form of the other, Subscribed it . . *Hamlet* v 2 51
Fold-in. The fires i' the lowest hell fold-in the people! . . *Coriolanus* iii 3 68
The man is noble and his fame folds-in This orb o' the earth . . . v 6 126
Folio. Write, pen; for I am for whole volumes in folio . . *L. L. Lost* i 2 192
Folk. We must give folks leave to prate . . . *Mer. Wives* i 4 128
Old folks, you know, have discretion, as they say, and know the world ii 2 134
Walk aside the true folk, and let the traitors stay . . *L. L. Lost* iv 3 213
These pretty country folks would lie, In spring time . *As Y. Like It* v 3 25
Here's no knavery! See, to beguile the old folks, how the young folks lay their heads together! . . . *T. of Shrew* i 2 139
How likes Gremio these quick-witted folks? . . . v 2 38
In winter's tedious nights sit by the fire With good old folks *Richard II.* v 1 41
And the old folk, time's doting chronicles, Say it did so. . *2 Hen. IV.* iv 4 126
O monstrous coward! what, to come behind folks? . . *2 Hen. VI.* iv 7 89
But old folks, many feign as they were dead . . *Rom. and Jul.* ii 5 16
The more pity that great folk should have countenance in this world to drown or hang themselves . . . *Hamlet* v 1 30
Fools are not mad folks.—Do you call me fool? . . *Cymbeline* ii 3 105
Will poor folks lie, That have afflictions on them? . . . iii 6 9
Follies. But you are so without these follies, that these follies are within you and shine through you . . . *T. G. of Ver.* ii 1 39
As you have one eye upon my follies, as you hear them unfolded, turn another into the register of your own. . . . *Mer. Wives* ii 2 193
And follies doth emmew As falcon doth the fowl . *Meas. for Meas.* iii 1 91
After he hath laughed at such shallow follies in others . . *Much Ado* ii 3 11
Lovers cannot see The pretty follies that themselves commit *Mer. of Ven.* ii 6 37
You, that are thus so tender o'er his follies, Will never do him good *W. T.* ii 3 128
And so your follies fight against yourself . . . *Richard II.* iii 2 182
Was this the face that faced so many follies, And was at last out-faced? iv 1 285
I think thou art enamoured On his follies . . . *1 Hen. IV.* v 2 71
A sounder man than Surrey can be, And all that love his follies *Hen. VIII.* iii 2 275
O my follies! then Edgar was abused. Kind gods, forgive me that! *Lear* iii 7 91
Follow.—No; I will resist such entertainment . . . *Tempest* i 2 464
Come, follow. Speak not for him . . . i 2 501
I'll bear him no more sticks, but follow thee, Thou wondrous man . ii 2 167
The sound is going away; let's follow it, and after do our work.—Lead, monster; we'll follow . . . iii 2 157
I would I could see this taborer; he lays it on.—Wilt come? I'll follow iii 2 161
I do beseech you That are of suppler joints, follow them swiftly . iii 3 107
For a little Follow, and do me service . . . iv 1 267
The sheep for fodder follow the shepherd; the shepherd for food follows not the sheep: thou for wages followest thy master; thy master for wages follows not thee . . . *T. G. of Ver.* i 1 92
Here follow her vices.—Close at the heels of her virtues . . iii 1 324
It follows not that she will love Sir Thurio . . . iii 2 50
Whither they are fled: Dispatch, sweet gentlemen, and follow me . v 2 48
This it is to be a peevish girl, That flies her fortune when it follows her v 2 50
And I will follow, more for Silvia's love Than hate of Eglamour . v 2 53
And I will follow, more to cross that love Than hate for Silvia . v 2 55
He hath outrun us, But Moyses and Valerius follow him . . v 3 8
We'll follow him that's fled; The thicket is beset; he cannot 'scape . v 3 10
Let him follow. Let me see thee froth and lime: I am at a word; follow *Mer. Wives* i 3 14
Follow him. A tapster is a good trade . . . i 3 17
Follow my heels, Rugby . . . i 4 132
I follow, mine host, I follow . . . ii 1 202
I had rather, forsooth, go before you like a man than follow him like a dwarf . . . iii 2 6
Follow your friend's counsel . . . iii 3 145
Nay, follow him, gentlemen: see the issue of his search . . iii 3 185
You must pray, and not follow the imaginations of your own heart iv 2 163
Will you follow, gentlemen? I beseech you, follow . . iv 2 206
Follow. Strange things in hand, Master Brook! Follow . . v 1 31
Be pold, I pray you; follow me into the pit . . . v 4 2
And follows close the rigour of the statute . . *Meas. for Meas.* i 4 67
I shall follow it as the flesh and fortune shall better determine . i 1 267
Hooking both right and wrong to the appetite, To follow as it draws! . ii 4 177
This being granted in course,—and now follows all. . . iii 1 259
We must follow the leaders.—In every good thing . . *Much Ado* ii 1 157

Follow. The ladies follow her and but one visor remains . *Much Ado* ii 1 163
All disquiet, horror and perturbation follows her . . . ii 1 268
If you will follow me, I will show you enough . . . iii 2 123
Mass, and my elbow itched; I thought there would a scab follow . iii 3 107
Come, follow me, boy; come, sir boy, come, follow me . . v 1 83
How follows that?—Fit in his place and time . . *L. L. Lost* i 1 98
For the following, sir?—As it shall follow in my correction . . i 1 215
Now will I begin your moral, and do you follow with my l'envoy . . iii 1 94
Moth, follow.—Like the sequel, I . . . iii 1 134
With duty and desire we follow you . . . *M. N. Dream* i 1 127
The more I hate, the more he follows me . . . i 1 198
Follow me no more.—You draw me, you hard-hearted adamant . . ii 1 194
Leave you your power to draw, And I shall have no power to follow you ii 1 198
Only give me leave, Unworthy as I am, to follow you . . . ii 1 207
If thou follow me, do not believe But I shall do thee mischief in the wood . . . ii 1 236
I'll follow thee and make a heaven of hell, To die upon the hand I love so well . . . ii 1 243
I'll follow you, I'll lead you about a round, Through bog, through bush iii 1 109
Have you not set Lysander, as in scorn, To follow me and praise my eyes? . . . iii 2 223
Take on as you would follow, But yet come not . . . iii 2 258
To Athens will I bear my folly back And follow you no further . iii 2 316
Now follow, if thou darest, to try whose right, Of thine or mine, is most in Helena.—Follow! nay, I'll go with thee, cheek by jole . iii 2 336
I will be with thee straight.—Follow me, then, To plainer ground . iii 2 403
Follow my voice: we'll try no manhood here . . . iii 2 412
Do not you think The duke was here, and bid us follow him? . iv 1 200
And he did bid us follow to the temple.—Why, then, we are awake: let's follow . . . iv 1 202
I urge this childhood proof, Because what follows is pure innocence *Mer. of Venice* i 1 145
It is a good divine that follows his own instructions: I can easier teach twenty what were good to be done, than be one of the twenty to follow mine own teaching . . . i 2 16
All the boys in Venice follow him, Crying, his stones, his daughter . ii 8 23
Follow not; I'll have no speaking: I will have my bond . . iii 3 16
I'll follow him no more with bootless prayers. He seeks my life . . iii 3 20
That I follow thus A losing suit against him . . . iv 1 61
Of a strange nature is the suit you follow . . . iv 1 177
Which if thou follow, this strict court of Venice Must needs give sentence . . . iv 1 204
I will follow thee, To the last gasp, with truth and loyalty *As Y. Like It* ii 3 69
You foolish shepherd, wherefore do you follow her? . . . iii 5 49
Then it follows thus; Thou shalt be master . . *T. of Shrew* i 1 206
Come, sir; we will better it in Pisa.—I follow you . . . iv 4 72
Husband, let's follow, to see the end of this ado . . . v 1 147
That we, the poorer born, Whose baser stars do shut us up in wishes, Might with effects of them follow our friends . . *All's Well* i 1 198
I follow him not By any token of presumptuous suit . . . i 3 203
Now, fair one, does your business follow us? . . . ii 1 102
But follows it, my lord, to bring me down Must answer for your raising? ii 3 119
I follow him to his country for justice . . . v 3 144
She uses me with a more exalted respect than any one else that follows her. What should I think on't . . . *T. Night* ii 5 32
What follows? the numbers altered! 'No man must know' . . ii 5 111
A should follow, but O does.—And O shall end, I hope . . ii 5 143
Every one of these letters are in my name. Soft! here follows prose . ii 5 154
Follow me.—To the gates of Tartar, thou most excellent devil of wit! . ii 5 225
If you desire the spleen, and will laugh yourselves into stitches, follow me . . . iii 2 73
I'll follow this good man, and go with you . . . iv 3 32
To do this deed, Promotion follows . . . *W. Tale* i 2 357
Why, what need we Commune with you of this, but rather follow Our forceful instigation? . . . ii 1 162
Come, follow us; We are to speak in public . . . ii 1 196
Go thou away: I'll follow instantly . . . iii 3 14
That for thy mother's fault art thus exposed To loss and what may follow! . . . iii 3 51
And what to her adheres, which follows after, Is the argument of Time iv 1 28
What follows this? . . . I have put you out: But to your protestation iv 4 376
Mark thou my words: Follow us to the court . . . iv 4 443
This follows, if you will not change your purpose . . . iv 4 553
I will but look upon the hedge and follow you . . . iv 4 857
Make proselytes Of who she but bid follow.—How! not women? . v 1 109
Therefore follow me And mark what way I make . . . v 1 232
Which lames report to follow it and undoes description to do it . v 2 62
Come, follow us: we'll be thy good masters . . . v 2 188
What follows if we disallow of this? . . . *K. John* i 1 16
Wilt thou forsake thy fortune, Bequeath thy land to him and follow me? . . . i 1 149
I'll follow you unto the death.—Nay, I would have you go before me thither . . . i 1 154
Till then, fair boy, Will I not think of home, but follow arms . ii 1 31
I fear some outrage, and I'll follow her . . . iii 4 106
Bear away that child And follow me with speed . . . iv 3 157
To grace the gentry of a land remote, And follow unacquainted colours here . . . v 2 32
She and my aunt Percy Shall follow in your conduct speedily *1 Hen. IV.* iii 1 197
I'll follow, as they say, for reward . . . v 4 166
And more and less do flock to follow him. . . *2 Hen. IV.* i 1 209
But how I should be your patient to follow your prescriptions . . i 2 147
You follow the young prince up and down, like his ill angel . . i 2 185
How ill it follows, after you have laboured so hard, you should talk so idly! . . . ii 2 31
I am your shadow, my lord; I'll follow you . . . ii 2 174
'The time shall come,' thus did he follow it, 'The time will come' . iii 1 75
And to see how many of my old acquaintance are dead!—We shall all follow . . . iii 2 39
The heat is past; follow no further now: Call in the powers . . iv 3 27
You shall bear to comfort him, And we with sober speed will follow you iv 3 86
Come, Sir John.—I'll follow you, good Master Robert Shallow . v 1 67
O, let their bodies follow, my dear liege . . . *Hen. V.* i 2 130
It follows then the cat must stay at home . . . i 2 174
Pistol's cock is up, And flashing fire will follow . . . ii 1 56
Or else what follows?—Bloody constraint . . . ii 4 96
Follow, follow: Grapple your minds to sternage of this navy . iii Prol. 17
Who is he . . . that will not follow These cull'd and choice-drawn cavaliers? . . . iii Prol. 23
Follow your spirit, and upon this charge Cry 'God for Harry, England!' iii 1 33

Follow. And follows so the ever-running year, With profitable labour, to his grave . . . *Hen. V.* iv 1 293

And he that will not follow Bourbon now, Let him go hence . . iv 5 12

My brother Gloucester, Follow Fluellen closely at the heels . . iv 7 179

Follow, and see there be no harm between them . . . iv 7 190

The liberty that follows our places stops the mouth of all find-faults . v 2 297

Placed behind With purpose to relieve and follow them . 1 *Hen. VI.* i 1 133

Ascend, brave Talbot; we will follow thee . . . . ii 1 28

After that things are set in order here, We'll follow them . . ii 2 33

If Talbot do but thunder, rain will follow . . . . ii 2 59

Cowardly knight! ill fortune follow thee! . . . . iii 2 109

We will entice the Duke of Burgundy To leave the Talbot and to follow us . . . iii 3 20

Then follow thou thy desperate sire of Crete, Thou Icarus . . iv 6 54

Pride went before, ambition follows him . . 2 *Hen. VI.* i 1 180

I'll follow presently. Follow I must; I cannot go before . . i 2 60

I will follow Eleanor, And listen after Humphrey, how he proceeds . i 3 151

Follow the knave; and take this drab away . . . . ii 1 156

Come, fellow, follow us for thy reward . . . . ii 3 108

That erst did follow thy proud chariot-wheels . . . . ii 4 13

When he please to make commotion, 'Tis to be fear'd they all will follow him . . . iii 1 30

We'll follow Cade, we'll follow Cade! . . . . . iv 8 35

A Clifford! we'll follow the king and Clifford . . . . iv 8 55

What, is he fled? Go some, and follow him . . . . iv 8 68

Follow me, soldiers: we'll devise a mean To reconcile you all . . iv 8 71

I know our safety is to follow them . . . . . v 3 23

Whom should he follow but his natural king? . . . 3 *Hen. VI.* i 1 82

Nay, go not from me; I will follow thee . . . . . i 1 213

The northern lords that have forsworn thy colours Will follow mine . i 1 252

When I return with victory from the field I'll see your grace: till then I'll follow her . . . i 1 262

Our ranks are broke, and ruin follows us: What counsel give you? . ii 3 10

Bootless is flight, they follow us with wings . . . . ii 3 12

This noble queen And prince shall follow with a fresh supply . . iii 3 237

You that love me and Warwick, follow me . . . . iv 1 123

Myself in person will straight follow you . . . . iv 1 133

You that will follow me to this attempt, Applaud the name of Henry . iv 2 26

Honour now or never! But follow me, and Edward shall be ours . iv 3 25

When I have fought with Pembroke and his fellows, I'll follow you . iv 3 55

But when the fox hath once got in his nose, He'll soon find means to make the body follow . . . iv 7 26

For Edward will defend the town and thee, And all those friends that deign to follow me . . . iv 7 39

When the lion fawns upon the lamb, The lamb will never cease to follow him . . . iv 8 50

It follows in his thought that I am he . . . . *Richard III.* i 1 59

Go you before, and I will follow you . . . . . i 1 144

Or, like obedient subjects, follow him To his new kingdom of perpetual rest . . . ii 2 45

To fly the boar before the boar pursues, Were to incense the boar to follow us . . . iii 2 29

The rest, that love me, rise and follow me . . . . iii 4 81

Without her, follows to this land and me, To thee, herself, and many a Christian soul, Death, desolation, ruin and decay . . . iv 4 407

Those whom we fight against Had rather have us win than him they follow . . . v 3 244

They thus directed, we will follow In the main battle . . . v 3 298

He's gone to the king; I'll follow and outstare him . *Hen. VIII.* i 1 129

Now this follows,—Which, as I take it, is a kind of puppy To the old dam i 1 174

Which ever, As ravenous fishes, do a vessel follow That is new-trimm'd i 2 79

That good fellow, If I command him, follows my appointment . ii 2 133

You bear a gentle mind, and heavenly blessings Follow such creatures . ii 3 58

It faints me, To think what follows . . . . . ii 3 104

Then follows, that I weigh'd the danger which my realms stood in By this . . . ii 4 196

How eagerly ye follow my disgraces, As if it fed ye! . . . iii 2 240

Follow your envious courses, men of malice . . . . iii 2 243

Well, sir, what follows?—Sir, I have brought my lord the archbishop . v 1 79

I grieve at what I speak, And am right sorry to repeat what follows . v 1 96

And what follows then? Commotions, uproars, with a general taint . v 3 27

Untune that string, And, hark, what discord follows! . *Troi. and Cres.* i 3 110

This chaos, when degree is suffocate, Follows the choking . . . i 3 126

There is no lady . . . More ready to cry out 'Who knows what follows?' . . . ii 2 13

Do not you follow the young Lord Paris?—Ay, sir, when he goes before me . . . iii 1 2

The bitter disposition of the time Will have it so. On, lord; we'll follow you . . . iv 1 49

Follow his torch; he goes to Calchas' tent: I'll keep you company . v 1 92

He that takes that doth take my heart withal.—I had your heart before, this follows it . . . v 2 83

Follow me, sirs, and my proceedings eye . . . . . v 7 7

We must follow you; Right worthy you priority . . . *Coriolanus* i 1 250

Nay, let them follow: The Volsces have much corn . . . i 1 252

Worshipful mutiners, Your valour puts well forth: pray, follow . . i 1 255

So many so minded, Wave thus, to express his disposition, And follow Marcius . . . i 6 75

Follows it that I am known well enough too? . . . . ii 1 69

Whither do you follow your eyes so fast? . . . . . ii 1 109

Won, With fame, a name to Caius Marcius; these In honour follows Coriolanus . . . ii 1 182

Therefore follow me, and I'll direct you how you shall go . . . ii 3 51

Purpose so barr'd, it follows, Nothing is done to purpose . . . iii 1 148

Obey, I charge thee, And follow to thine answer . . . . iii 1 177

He must come, Or what is worst will follow . . . . iii 1 336

Rather Follow thine enemy in a fiery gulf Than flatter him in a bower . iii 2 91

Follow him, As he hath follow'd you, with all despite . . . iii 3 138

I'll follow thee a month, devise with thee Where thou shalt rest . . iv 1 38

Follow your function, go, and batten on cold bits . . . iv 5 35

They follow him, Against us brats, with no less confidence Than boys pursuing summer butterflies . . . iv 6 92

The most noble corse that ever herald Did follow to his urn . . v 6 146

Follow, my lord, and I'll soon bring her back . . *T. Andron.* i 1 289

I have horse will follow where the game Makes way, and run like swallows . . . ii 2 23

Thou shalt not bail them: see thou follow me . . . . ii 3 299

My aunt Lavinia Follows me every where, I know not why . . . iv 1 2

We'll follow where thou lead'st, Like stinging bees in hottest summer's day . . . v 1 13

Follow. I beseech you, follow straight.—We follow thee *Rom. and Jul.* i 3 104

What's he that follows there, that would not dance? . . . i 5 134

And follow thee my lord throughout the world . . . . ii 2 148

Follow me this jest now till thou hast worn out thy pump . . ii 4 65

Follow me close, for I will speak to them . . . . . iii 1 40

Every one prepare To follow this fair corse unto her grave . . iv 5 93

Some better than his value, on the moment Follow his strides *T. of A.* i 1 80

I do not always follow lover, elder brother and woman; sometime the philosopher . . . ii 2 130

The swallow follows not summer more willing than we your lordship . iii 6 31

I'll follow and inquire him out: I'll ever serve his mind . . iv 2 48

Follow thy drum; With man's blood paint the ground, gules, gules . iv 3 58

With a discovery of the infinite flatteries that follow youth and opulency v 1 37

What tributaries follow him to Rome? . . . . *J. Cæsar* i 1 38

Accoutred as I was, I plunged in And bade him follow . . . i 2 106

If the redress will follow, thou receivest Thy full petition . . ii 1 57

For he will never follow any thing That other men begin . . ii 1 151

Set on your foot, And with a heart new-fired I follow you . . ii 1 332

The throng that follows Cæsar at the heels . . . . ii 4 34

But will follow The fortunes and affairs of noble Brutus Thorough the hazards of this untrod state . . . iii 1 134

Prepare the body then, and follow us . . . . . iii 1 253

Then follow me, and give me audience, friends . . . . iii 2 2

Those that will follow Cassius, go with him . . . . iii 2 6

We'll hear him, we'll follow him, we'll die with him . . . iii 2 212

Bid him set on his powers betimes before, And we will follow . . iv 3 309

Fly, my lord, fly.—Hence! I will follow . . . . . v 5 43

Take him to follow thee, That did the latest service to my master . v 5 66

The love that follows us sometime is our trouble . . *Macbeth* i 6 11

Now follows, that you know . . . . . . *Hamlet* i 2 17

It must follow, as the night the day, Thou canst not then be false to any man . . . i 3 79

It will not speak; then I will follow it.—Do not, my lord . . i 4 63

It waves me forth again: I'll follow it . . . . . i 4 68

It waves me still. Go on; I'll follow thee.—You shall not go, my lord i 4 79

I say, away! Go on; I'll follow thee.—He waxes desperate with imagination . . . i 4 86

Let's follow; 'tis not fit thus to obey him.—Have after . . . i 4 88

Nay, that follows not.—What follows, then, my lord? . . . ii 2 432

Follow him, friends: we'll hear a play to-morrow . . . . ii 2 560

Follow that lord; and look you mock him not . . . . ii 2 570

Crook the pregnant hinges of the knee Where thrift may follow fawning iii 2 67

Look you now, what follows: Here is your husband . . . iii 4 63

Follow him at foot; tempt him with speed aboard; delay it not . iv 3 56

Follow her close; give her good watch . . . . . iv 5 75

One woe doth tread upon another's heel, So fast they follow . . iv 7 165

Let's follow, Gertrude: How much I had to do to calm his rage! Now fear I this will give it start again; Therefore let's follow . iv 7 192

But to follow him thither with modesty enough, and likelihood to lead it v 1 229

Who is this they follow? And with such maimed rites? This doth betoken The corse they follow did with desperate hand Fordo it own life . . . v 1 241

I am constant to my purposes; they follow the king's pleasure . . v 2 209

Drink off this potion. Is thy union here? Follow my mother . . v 2 338

Heaven make thee free of it! I follow thee. I am dead, Horatio . v 2 343

Treachery, and all ruinous disorders, follow us disquietly to our graves *Lear* i 2 123

So that it follows, I am rough and lecherous . . . . i 2 141

I read this other day, what should follow these eclipses . . . i 2 153

Follow me; thou shalt serve me: if I like thee no worse after dinner . i 4 43

If thou follow him, thou must needs wear my coxcomb . . . i 4 116

If my cap would buy a halter: So the fool follows after . . . i 4 344

Commanded me to follow, and attend The leisure of their answer . ii 4 36

Follow me not; Stay here . . . . ii 4 59

All that follow their noses are led by their eyes but blind men . . ii 4 70

I would have none but knaves follow it, since a fool gives it . . ii 4 78

That sir which serves and seeks for gain, And follows but for form, Will pack when it begins to rain . . . ii 4 80

Whose easy-borrow'd pride Dwells in the fickle grace of her he follows ii 4 189

What need you five and twenty, ten, or five, To follow in a house where twice so many Have a command to tend you? . . . ii 4 265

Come forth.—Away! the foul fiend follows me! . . . . iii 4 46

Follow me, that will to some provision Give thee quick conduct . . iii 6 103

Let's follow the old earl, and get the Bedlam To lead him where he would iii 7 103

Would I could meet him, madam! I should show What party I do follow iv 5 40

Take thou this note; go follow them to prison . . . . v 3 27

I would not follow him then.—O, sir, content you; I follow him to serve my turn upon him . . . *Othello* i 1 40

In following him, I follow but myself . . . . . i 1 58

Put money in thy purse; follow thou the wars; defeat thy favour . i 3 345

I do follow here in the chase, not like a hound that hunts, but one that fills up the cry . . . ii 3 369

To follow still the changes of the moon With fresh suspicions . . iii 3 178

And let worse follow worse, till the worst of all follow him laughing to his grave! . . . *Ant. and Cleo.* i 2 68

A man who is the abstract of all faults That all men follow . . . i 4 10

At thy heel Did famine follow . . . . . . i 4 59

The oars were silver, Which to the tune of flutes kept stroke, and made The water which they beat to follow faster . . . ii 2 201

Your commission's ready; Follow me, and receive't . . . ii 3 42

Mark Antony Will e'en but kiss Octavia, and we'll follow . . . ii 4 3

And what may follow, To try a larger fortune . . . . ii 6 33

They know, By the height, the lowness, or the mean, if dearth Or foison follow . . . ii 7 23

For this, I'll never follow thy pall'd fortunes more . . . ii 7 88

Whilst yet with Parthian blood thy sword is warm, The fugitive Parthians follow . . . iii 1 7

I'll yet follow The wounded chance of Antony . . . . iii 10 35

What though you fled From that great face of war, whose several ranges Frighted each other? why should he follow? . . . iii 13 6

He that can endure To follow with allegiance a fall'n lord Does conquer him that did his master conquer . . . iii 13 44

Be thou sorry To follow Cæsar in his triumph, since Thou hast been whipp'd for following him . . . iii 13 136

Follow the noise so far as we have quarter; Let's see how it will give off iv 3 22

You that will fight, Follow me close; I'll bring you to't . . iv 4 34

Follow his chariot, like the greatest spot Of all thy sex . . . iv 12 35

Signior Iachimo will not from it. Pray, let us follow 'em . *Cymbeline* i 4 185

Let's follow him, and pervert the present wrath He hath against himself ii 4 151

What your own love will out of this advise you, follow . . . iii 2 46

Follow. My revenge is now at Milford : would I had wings to follow it ! *Cymbeline* iii 5 161
When I have slain thee with my proper hand, I'll follow those that even now fled hence . . . . iv 2 98
The sceptre, learning, physic, must All follow this, and come to dust . iv 2 269
I'll follow, sir. But first, an't please the gods, I'll hide my master . iv 2 387
And leaving so his service, follow you, So please you entertain me . iv 2 393
Let thy effects So follow, to be most unlike our courtiers . . . v 4 136
Your neck, sir, is pen, book and counters ; so the acquittance follows . v 4 174
Happy what follows ! Thou hast as chiding a nativity As fire, air, water, earth, and heaven can make . . . . *Pericles* iii 1 31
Get this done as I command you.—Performance shall follow . . . iv 2 67
Followed. I have follow'd it, Or it hath drawn me rather . *Tempest* i 2 393
Calf-like they my lowing follow'd through Tooth'd briers . . . iv 1 179
Bestowed much on her ; followed her with a doting observance *M. Wives* ii 2 202
What secret hath held you here, that you followed not to Leonato's? *Much Ado* i 1 207
Begin, sir ; you are my elder.—Well followed . . . . *L. L. Lost* v 2 610
It should have followed in the end of our show . . . . v 2 898
He follow'd you ; for love I follow'd him . . . . *M. N. Dream* iii 2 311
I follow'd fast, but faster he did fly . . . . iii 2 416
And I in fury hither follow'd them . . . . iv 1 167
Good sentences and well pronounced.—They would be better, if well followed . . . . *Mer. of Venice* i 2 12
She would have followed her exile, or have died to stay behind her *As Y. Like It* i 1 114
You are there followed by a faithful shepherd . . . . . . v 2 87
Follow'd well, would demonstrate them now But goers backward *All's W.* i 2 47
Though the devil lead the measure, such are to be followed . . . ii 1 58
O, had I but followed the arts ! . . . . *T. Night* i 3 99
How with a sportful malice it was follow'd . . . . . . v 1 373
Therefore mark my counsel, Which must be even as swiftly follow'd as I mean to utter it . . . . *W. Tale* i 2 409
And the words that follow'd Should be 'Remember mine' . . . v 1 66
But I followed me close, came in foot and hand . . . . 1 *Hen. IV.* ii 4 240
A hue and cry Hath follow'd certain men unto this house . . . ii 4 557
As pages follow'd him Even at the heels in golden multitudes . . iv 3 72
O, such a day, So fought, so follow'd and so fairly won ! 2 *Hen. IV.* i 1 21
He's follow'd both with body and with mind . . . . . . i 1 203
You see this chase is hotly follow'd . . . . . . *Hen. V.* ii 4 68
Of all exploits since first I follow'd arms . . . . 1 *Hen. VI.* ii 1 43
And follow'd with a rabble that rejoice To see my tears . . 2 *Hen. VI.* ii 4 32
We follow'd then our lord, our lawful king . . . *Richard III.* i 3 147
When he that is my husband now Came to me, as I follow'd Henry's corse iv 1 67
That dead saint which then I weeping follow'd . . . . . iv 1 70
Where be the thronging troops that follow'd thee? . . . . . iv 4 96
Follow'd with the general throng and sweat Of thousand friends *Hen. VIII.* Prol. 28
Every man, After the hideous storm that follow'd, was A thing inspired i 1 90
New customs, Though they be never so ridiculous, Nay, let 'em be unmanly, yet are follow'd . . . . i 3 4
But, what follow'd ?—At length her grace rose . . . . . iv 1 81
My wretched women, that so long Have follow'd both my fortunes faithfully . . . . iv 2 141
We'll beat them to their wives, As they us to our trenches followed *Cor.* i 4 42
Follow him, As he hath follow'd you, with all despite . . . . iii 3 139
I have ever follow'd thee with hate . . . . iv 5 104
Why follow'd not, when she said 'Tybalt's dead,' Thy father, or thy mother, nay, or both? . . . . *Rom. and Jul.* iii 2 118
How this lord is follow'd !—The senators of Athens : happy man ! *T. of A.* i 1 39
Never learn'd The icy precepts of respect, but follow'd The sugar'd game iv 3 258
Brutus stabb'd ; And as he pluck'd his cursed steel away, Mark how the blood of Cæsar follow'd it . . . . *J. Cæsar* iii 2 182
A little month, or ere those shoes were old With which she follow'd my poor father's body . . . . *Hamlet* i 2 148
To see my mother's wedding.—Indeed, my lord, it follow'd hard upon . i 2 179
Are they so followed ?—No, indeed, are they not . . . . . ii 2 349
Lov'd as my father, as my master follow'd . . . . *Lear* i 1 143
But kept a reservation to be follow'd With such a number . . . ii 4 255
Where is my lord of Gloucester ?—Follow'd the old man forth . . ii 4 298
The bloody proclamation to escape, That follow'd me so near . . v 3 184
The banish'd Kent ; who in disguise Follow'd his enemy king . . v 3 220
That, from your first of difference and decay, Have follow'd your sad steps v 3 289
We cannot all be masters, nor all masters Cannot be truly follow'd *Othello* i 1 44
What was he that you followed with your sword ? What had he done to you ? . . . . ii 3 285
I follow'd that I blush to look upon . . . . . *Ant. and Cleo.* iii 11 12
My lord, Forgive my fearful sails ! I little thought You would have follow'd . . . . iii 11 56
The soldier That has this morning left thee, would have still Follow'd thy heels . . . . iv 5 6
O Antony ! I have follow'd thee to this . . . . v 1 36
O, behold, How pomp is follow'd ! mine will now be yours . . . v 2 151
Follow'd him, till he had melted from The smallness of a gnat to air *Cymbeline* i 3 20
I was confederate with the Romans : so Follow'd my banishment . . iii 3 69
'Twas a fitment for The purpose I then follow'd . . . . . v 5 410
Follower. Say, my spirit, How fares the king and 's followers ? *Tempest* v 1 7
You have an exchequer of words, and, I think, no other treasure to give your followers . . . . *T. G. of Ver.* ii 4 45
I must turn away some of my followers . . . . . *Mer. Wives* i 3 5
You were wont to be a follower, but now you are a leader . . . iii 2 2
Time himself is bald and therefore to the world's end will have bald followers.—I knew 'twould be a bald conclusion *Com. of Errors* ii 2 109
Dreams and sighs, Wishes and tears, poor fancy's followers *M. N. Dream* i 1 155
If it be preferment To leave a rich Jew's service, to become The follower of so poor a gentleman . . . . *Mer. of Venice* ii 2 157
Thither will I invite the duke and all 's contented followers *As Y. Like It* v 2 17
If 'twere so, She could not sway her house, command her followers *T. N.* iv 3 17
A gentleman, and follower of my lady's . . . . v 1 284
Your followers I will whisper to the business . . . . *W. Tale* i 2 437
What became of his bark and his followers ?—Wrecked the same instant v 2 74
Discharge my followers : let them hence away . . *Richard II.* iii 2 217
Grievous crimes Committed by your person and your followers . . iv 1 224
O flattering glass, Like to my followers in prosperity, Thou dost beguile me ! . . . . iv 1 280
He is a man Who with a double surety binds his followers . 2 *Hen. IV.* i 1 191
How accompanied ? . . . —With Poins, and his other continual followers iv 4 53
The prince will in the perfectness of time Cast off his followers . . iv 4 75
He hath intent his wonted followers Shall all be very well provided for v 5 104
Follower. Crowns and coronets, Promised to Harry and his followers *Hen. V.* ii Prol. 11
Tell him, for conclusion, he hath betrayed his followers . . . iii 6 143
To mope with his fat-brained followers so far out of his knowledge ! . iii 7 144
The constable desires thee thou wilt mind Thy followers of repentance iv 8 85
For a flag of truce Betwixt ourselves and all our followers 1 *Hen. VI.* iii 1 139
Then both fly.—And leave my followers here to fight and die ? . . iv 5 45
A wonder and a pointing-stock To every idle rascal follower . 2 *Hen. VI.* ii 4 47
My followers' base and ignominious treasons makes me betake me to my heels . . . . iv 8 66
I'll keep London with my soldiers.—And I to Norfolk with my followers 3 *Hen. VI.* i 1 208
All my followers to the eager foe Turn back and fly . . . . i 4 3
Hark ! the fatal followers do pursue ; And I am faint and cannot fly . i 4 22
This soft courage makes your followers faint . . . . . . ii 2 57
But why commands the king That his chief followers lodge in towns about him ? . . . . iv 3 13
Brave followers, yonder stands the thorny wood . . . . . v 4 67
Some followers of mine own, At the lower end of the hall, hurl'd up their caps, And some ten voices cried . . . . *Richard III.* iii 7 34
Where are thy tenants and thy followers ? . . . . iv 4 481
For both our honour and our shame in this Are dogg'd with two strange followers . . . . *Troi. and Cres.* i 3 365
'Tis for the followers fortune widens them, Not for the fliers . *Coriolanus* i 4 44
Till, at the last, I seem'd his follower, not partner . . . . v 6 39
My loving followers, Plead my successive title with your swords *T. An.* i 1 3
Romans, friends, followers, favourers of my right . . . . . i 1 9
Dismiss your followers and, as suitors should, Plead your deserts in peace . . . . i 1 44
That, for your honour and your state, Will use you nobly and your followers . . . . i 1 260
Marry, go before to field, he'll be your follower ; Your worship in that sense may call him 'man' . . . . . . *Rom. and Jul.* iii 1 61
What, fifty of my followers at a clap ! Within a fortnight ! . . *Lear* i 4 316
Perchance She have restrain'd the riots of your followers . . . ii 4 145
What, fifty followers ? Is it not well ? What should you need of more? ii 4 240
For his particular, I'll receive him gladly, But not one follower . . ii 4 296
Beware my follower. Peace, Smulkin ; peace, thou fiend ! . . . iii 4 146
What does he mean ?—To make his followers weep . *Ant. and Cleo.* iv 2 24
Thy death and fortunes bid thy followers fly . . . . . . iv 14 111
Woe, woe are we, sir, you may not live to wear All your true followers out . . . . iv 14 134
Thou canst not, in the course of gratitude, but be a diligent follower of mine : wilt thou serve me ? . . . . *Cymbeline* iii 5 121
Followest. A loyal sir To him thou follow'st . . . . *Tempest* v 1 70
Thou for wages followest thy master . . . . . *T. G. of Ver.* i 1 94
Following. Had made provision for her following me . *Com. of Errors* i 1 48
In what manner ?—In manner and form following, sir . *L. L. Lost* i 1 207
Sitting with her upon the form, and taken following her into the park ; which, put together, is in manner and form following . . . . i 1 209
For the following, sir ?—As it shall follow in my correction . . . i 1 214
And then we, Following the signs, woo'd but the sign of she . . . v 2 469
With pretty and with swimming gait Following . . *M. N. Dream* ii 1 131
There is no following her in this fierce vein . . . . . . iii 2 82
I in fury hither follow'd them, Fair Helena in fancy following me . . iv 1 168
From the presence of the sun, Following darkness like a dream . . v 1 393
I will buy with you, sell with you, talk with you, walk with you, and so following, but I will not eat with you . . . *Mer. of Venice* i 3 37
Not following My leash unwillingly . . . . *W. Tale* iv 4 476
Following the mirror of all Christian kings . . . . *Hen. V.* ii Prol. 6
And his advantage following your decease . . . . 2 *Hen. VI.* iii 1 25
Thou art a traitor to the crown In following this usurping Henry 3 *Hen. VI.* i 1 81
Each following day Became the next day's master . . . *Hen. VIII.* i 1 16
Following the fliers at the very heels, With them he enters . *Coriolanus* i 4 49
With a rearward following Tybalt's death, 'Romeo is banished' *R. and J.* iii 2 121
If, on the tenth day following, Thy banish'd trunk be found . . *Lear* i 1 179
Knowing nought, like dogs, but following . . . . ii 2 86
To have her gentleman abused, assaulted, For following her affairs . . ii 2 157
Let go thy hold when a great wheel runs down a hill, lest it break thy neck with following it . . . . ii 4 74
In following him, I follow but myself . . . . *Othello* i 1 58
See suitors following and not look behind . . . . ii 1 158
And Cassio following him with determined sword, To execute upon him ii 3 227
If thou the next night following enjoy not Desdemona . . . . iv 2 220
Be thou sorry To follow Cæsar in his triumph, since Thou hast been whipp'd for following him . . . . *Ant. and Cleo.* iii 13 137
And ourselves Will in that kingdom spend our following days *Pericles* v 3 81
Folly. Servant-monster ! the folly of this island ! . . . . *Tempest* iii 2 5
A folly bought with wit, Or else a wit by folly vanquished *T. G. of Ver.* i 1 34
Even so by love the young and tender wit Is turn'd to folly . . . i 1 48
Lord, Lord ! to see what folly reigns in us ! . . . . i 2 15
My penance is to call Lucetta back And ask remission for my folly past i 2 65
What should I see then?—Your own present folly and her passing deformity . . . . ii 1 81
What seem I that I am not ?—Wise.—What instance of the contrary ?—Your folly.—And how quote you my folly ? . . . . ii 4 17
My jerkin is a doublet.—Well, then, I'll double your folly . . . ii 4 21
Wilt thou aspire to guide the heavenly car And with thy daring folly burn the world ? . . . . iii 1 155
The folly of my soul dares not present itself . . . . *Mer Wives* ii 2 253
He gives her folly motion and advantage . . . . iii 2 35
Why, this is your own folly. Did not I tell you ? . . . . . . v 5 206
Either this is envy in you, folly, or mistaking . . . *Meas. for Meas.* iii 2 149
It is no addition to her wit, nor no great argument of her folly *Much Ado* ii 3 243
I'll drop the paper : Sweet leaves, shade folly . . . . *L. L. Lost* iv 3 44
Folly, in wisdom hatch'd, Hath wisdom's warrant and the help of school v 2 70
Folly in fools bears not so strong a note As foolery in the wise . . v 2 75
In this spleen ridiculous appears, To check their folly, passion's solemn tears . . . . v 2 118
His folly, Helena, is no fault of mine.—None, but your beauty *M. N. D.* i 1 200
So you will let me quiet go, To Athens will I bear my folly back . . iii 2 315
If thou remember'st not the slightest folly That ever love did make thee run into, Thou hast not loved . . . . . *As Y. Like It* ii 4 34
But as all is mortal in nature, so is all nature in love mortal in folly . ii 4 57
They that are most galled with my folly, They most must laugh . . ii 7 50
The wise man's folly is anatomized Even by the squandering glances of the fool . . . . ii 7 56
Therein suits His folly to the mettle of my speech . . . . . ii 7 82
Most friendship is feigning, most loving mere folly . . . . . ii 7 181
But all's brave that youth mounts and folly guides . . . . iii 4 49

Folly. He uses his folly like a stalking-horse and under the presentation of that he shoots his wit . . . . . . *As Y. Like It* v 4 111
Full oft we see Cold wisdom waiting on superfluous folly . *All's Well* i 1 116
You lack not folly to commit them, and have ability enough . . . i 3 11
Your son, As mad in folly, lack'd the sense to know Her estimation home . . . . v 3 3
Infirmity, that decays the wise, doth ever make the better fool.—God send you, sir, a speedy infirmity, for the better increasing your folly! . . . . *T. Night* i 5 85
The Lady Olivia's fool?—No, indeed, sir; the Lady Olivia has no folly iii 1 38
For folly that he wisely shows is fit; But wise men, folly-fall'n, quite taint their wit . . . . iii 1 74
Vent thy folly somewhere else: Thou know'st not me.—Vent my folly! iv 1 10
Vent my folly! I am afraid this great lubber, the world, will prove a cockney . . . . iv 1 14
How sometimes nature will betray its folly, Its tenderness! . *W. Tale* i 2 151
I may be negligent, foolish and fearful; In every one of these no man is free, But that his negligence, his folly, fear, Among the infinite doings of the world, Sometime puts forth . . . . . i 2 252
If ever I were wilful-negligent, It was my folly . . . . . i 2 256
By oath remove or counsel shake The fabric of his folly . . . . i 2 429
Our feasts In every mess have folly and the feeders Digest it with a custom . . . . iv 4 11
Then I lost—All mine own folly—the society, Amity too, of your brave father . . . . v 1 135
Your fault was not your folly: Needs must you . . *K. John* i 1 262
Must I do so? and must I ravel out My weaved-up folly? *Richard II.* iv 1 229
In every thing the purpose must weigh with the folly . . *2 Hen. IV.* ii 2 196
Covering discretion with a coat of folly . . . . . *Hen. V.* ii 4 38
England shall repent his folly, see his weakness, and admire our sufferance . . . . iii 6 132
Too much folly is it, well I wot, To hazard all our lives in one small boat! . . . . *1 Hen. VI.* iv 6 32
His valour is crushed into folly, his folly sauced with discretion *T. and C.* i 2 24
The common curse of mankind, folly and ignorance, be thine! . . ii 3 31
The amity that wisdom knits not, folly may easily untie . . . ii 3 110
What folly I commit, I dedicate to you . . . . . . iii 2 110
Pardon me this brag; His insolence draws folly from my lips . . iv 5 258
Sweet honey Greek, tempt me no more to folly . . . . . v 2 18
Confess yourselves wondrous malicious, Or be accused of folly *Coriolanus* i 1 92
Nor did you think it folly To keep your great pretences veil'd . . i 2 19
We call a nettle but a nettle and The faults of fools but folly . . ii 1 208
He said 'twas folly, For one poor grain or two, to leave unburnt . v 1 26
What folly 'tis to hazard life for ill! . . . . *T. of Athens* iii 5 37
What, quite unmann'd in folly? . . . . . . *Macbeth* iii 4 73
I am in this earthly world; where to do harm Is often laudable, to do good sometime Accounted dangerous folly . . . . . . iv 2 77
A speech of fire, that fain would blaze, But that this folly douts it *Ham.* iv 7 192
To plainness honour's bound, When majesty stoops to folly . . *Lear* i 1 151
Beat at this gate, that let thy folly in, And thy dear judgement out! . i 4 293
'Tis his own blame; hath put himself from rest, And must needs taste his folly . . . . ii 4 294
Even her folly help'd her to an heir . . . . . . *Othello* ii 1 138
Hath all those requisites in him that folly and green minds look after . ii 1 251
She turn'd to folly . . . . v 2 132
Though age from folly could not give me freedom, It does from childishness . . . . *Ant. and Cleo.* i 3 57
Be deaf to my unpitied folly, And all the gods go with you! . . i 3 98
The loyalty well held to fools does make Our faith mere folly . iii 13 43
Languish A drop of blood a day; and, being aged, Die of this folly! *Cymbeline* i 1 158
Dost thou think in time She will not quench and let instructions enter Where folly now possesses? . . . . i 5 48
That it was folly in me, thou mayst say, And prove it in thy feeling . v 5 67

Folly-fallen. But wise men, folly-fall'n, quite taint their wit . *T. Night* iii 1 75

Fond. But wherefore waste I time to counsel thee That art a votary to fond desire? . . . . *T. G. of Ver.* i 1 52
If this fond Love were not a blinded god . . . . . iv 4 201
As fond fathers, Having bound up the threatening twigs of birch, Only to stick it in their children's sight . . . *Meas. for Meas.* i 3 23
Not with fond shekels of the tested gold . . . . . ii 2 149
Ever till now, When men were fond, I smiled and wonder'd how . . ii 2 187
By heaven, fond wretch, thou know'st not what thou speak'st . . v 1 105
How many fond fools serve mad jealousy! . . *Com. of Errors* ii 1 116
That he may prove More fond on her than she upon her love *M. N. Dream* ii 1 266
O, I am out of breath in this fond chase! . . . . . ii 2 88
Shall we their fond pageant see? Lord, what fools these mortals be! . iii 2 114
You see how simple and how fond I am . . . . . . iii 2 317
Not learning more than the fond eye doth teach . *Mer. of Venice* ii 9 27
I do wonder, Thou naughty gaoler, that thou art so fond To come abroad with him at his request . . . . iii 3 9
Why would you be so fond to overcome The bonny priser? *As Y. Like It* ii 3 7
A world Of pretty, fond, adoptious christendoms . . . *All's Well* i 1 188
Fond done, done fond . . . . i 3 76
This is a fond and desperate creature, Whom sometime I have laugh'd with . . . . v 3 178
And I, poor monster, fond as much on him . . . . *T. Night* ii 2 35
Are you so fond of your young prince as we Do seem to be of ours? *W. T.* i 2 164
Fond boy, If I may ever know thou dost but sigh . . . . iv 4 437
You are as fond of grief as of your child . . . . *K. John* iii 4 92
Then, have I reason to be fond of grief? . . . . . . iii 4 98
We make woe wanton with this fond delay . . . *Richard II.* v 1 101
Thou fond mad woman, Wilt thou conceal this dark conspiracy? . . v 2 95
Away, fond woman! were he twenty times my son, I would appeach him . . . . v 2 101
O thou fond many, with what loud applause Didst thou beat heaven with blessing! . . . . *2 Hen. IV.* i 3 91
I laugh to see your ladyship so fond . . . . . *1 Hen. VI.* ii 3 45
Fond man, remember that thou hast a wife . . . . . v 3 80
If it be fond, call it a woman's fear . . . . *2 Hen. VI.* iii 1 36
Ah, what's more dangerous than this fond affiance! . . . . iii 1 74
I wonder he is so fond To trust the mockery of unquiet slumbers *Richard III.* iii 2 26
I, too fond, might have prevented this . . . . . . iii 4 83
Who, but for dreaming on this fond exploit, For want of means, poor rats, had hang'd themselves . . . . v 3 330
'Tis fond to wail inevitable strokes, As 'tis to laugh at em *Coriolanus* iv 1 26
When she, poor hen, fond of no second brood, Has cluck'd thee to the wars . . . . v 3 162
What begg'st thou, then? fond woman, let me go . . *T. Andron.* ii 3 172
Fond. I am too fond, And therefore thou mayst think my 'haviour light *Rom. and Jul.* ii 2 98
Thou fond mad man, hear me but speak a word . . . . . iii 3 52
Fond nature bids us all lament, Yet nature's tears are reason's merriment . . . . iv 5 82
Grant I may never prove so fond, To trust man on his oath or bond . . *T. of Athens* i 2 65
Why do fond men expose themselves to battle, And not endure all threats? . . . . iii 5 42
Be not fond, To think that Cæsar bears such rebel blood . *J. Cæsar* iii 1 39
I'll wipe away all trivial fond records . . . . *Hamlet* i 5 99
Carries them through and through the most fond and winnowed opinions v 2 200
I begin to find an idle and fond bondage in the oppression of aged tyranny. . . . . *Lear* i 2 52
Old fond eyes, Beweep this cause again, I'll pluck ye out . . . i 4 323
I am a very foolish fond old man, Fourscore and upward . . . iv 7 60
It is my shame to be so fond; but it is not in my virtue to amend it *Oth.* i 3 320
These are old fond paradoxes to make fools laugh i' the alehouse . . ii 1 139
All my fond love thus do I blow to heaven . . . . . iii 3 445
If you are so fond over her iniquity, give her patent to offend . . iv 1 208
He lies to the heart: She was too fond of her most filthy bargain . . v 2 157
For which their father, Then old and fond of issue, took such sorrow that he quit being . . . . *Cymbeline* i 1 37

Fonder than ignorance, Less valiant than the virgin in the night *Troi. and Cres.* i 1 10

Fondly. How fondly dost thou reason! . . . *Com. of Errors* iv 2 57
I have fondly flatter'd her withal . . . . . *T. of Shrew* iv 2 31
If you fondly pass our proffer'd offer . . . . . *K. John* ii 1 258
As a long-parted mother with her child Plays fondly with her tears and smiles in meeting . . . . *Richard II.* iii 2 9
Sorrow and grief of heart Makes him speak fondly, like a frantic man . iii 3 185
How fondly dost thou spur a forward horse! . . . . . v 1 72
Fondly brought here and foolishly sent hence . . . . *2 Hen. IV.* iv 2 119
What my great-grandfather and grandsire got My careless father fondly gave away . . . . *3 Hen. VI.* ii 2 38
Which fondly you would here impose on me . . . *Richard III.* iii 7 147

Fondness. In obsequious fondness Crowd to his presence *Meas. for Meas.* ii 4 28
My fear hath catch'd your fondness . . . . . *All's Well* i 3 176
Been, out of fondness, superstitious to him . . . *Hen. VIII.* iii 1 131

Font. Had I been judge, thou shouldst have had ten more [godfathers], To bring thee to the gallows, not the font . . . *Mer. of Venice* iv 1 400
I have no name, no title, No, not that name was given me at the font *Richard II.* iv 1 256

Fontibell. They told me that your name was Fontibell . *All's Well* iv 2 1

Food. Some food we had and some fresh water . . . *Tempest* i 2 160
Thy food shall be The fresh-brook muscles, wither'd roots and husks . i 2 462
The shepherd for food follows not the sheep . . . *T. G. of Ver.* i 1 93
O, know'st thou not his looks are my soul's food? . . . . ii 7 15
Pity the dearth that I have pined in, By longing for that food so long a time ii 7 17
Young ravens must have food . . . . *Mer. Wives* i 3 38
It would give eternal food to his jealousy . . . . . . ii 1 104
My food, my fortune and my sweet hope's aim . *Com. of Errors* iii 2 63
In food, in sport and life-preserving rest To be disturb'd, would mad or man or beast . . . . v 1 83
Is it possible disdain should die while she hath such meet food? *M. Ado* i 1 122
This may prove food to my displeasure . . . . . . i 3 68
And one day in a week to touch no food . . . . *L. L. Lost* i 1 39
But if thou strive, poor soul, what art thou then? Food for his rage . iv 1 95
Starve our sight From lovers' food till morrow deep midnight *M. N. D.* i 1 223
But, like in sickness, did I loathe this food . . . . . iv 1 178
Fed with the same food, hurt with the same weapons . *Mer. of Venice* iii 1 63
Therefore, thou gaudy gold, Hard food for Midas, I will none of thee . iii 2 102
What, wouldst thou have me go and beg my food? . *As Y. Like It* ii 3 31
One of you question yond man If he for gold will give us any food . ii 4 65
Seeking the food he eats And pleased with what he gets . . . . ii 5 42
I can go no further: O, I die for food! . . . . . . ii 6 2
If this uncouth forest yield any thing savage, I will either be food for it or bring it for food to thee . . . . ii 6 7
As I do live by food, I met a fool . . . . ii 7 14
I almost die for food; and let me have it . . . . . . ii 7 104
But forbear your food a little while, Whiles, like a doe, I go to find my fawn And give it food . . . . ii 7 127
Pacing through the forest, Chewing the food of sweet and bitter fancy . iv 3 102
Did he leave him there, Food to the suck'd and hungry lioness? . . iv 3 127
Get me some repast; I care not what, so it be wholesome food *T. of S.* iv 3 16
If music be the food of love, play on; Give me excess of it . *T. Night* i 1 1
My life, my joy, my food, my all the world! My widow-comfort! *K. John* iii 4 104
With eager feeding food doth choke the feeder . . . *Richard II.* ii 1 37
Where no man never comes but that sad dog That brings me food . . v 5 71
Good enough to toss; food for powder, food for powder . *1 Hen. IV.* iv 2 71
No, Percy, thou art dust, And food for— For worms . . . . v 4 86
She either gives a stomach and no food; Such are the poor . *2 Hen. IV.* iv 4 105
Let floods o'erswell, and fiends for food howl on! . . . *Hen. V.* ii 1 97
The very blood to suck!—And that's but unwholesome food, they say . ii 3 59
Like lions wanting food, Do rush upon us as their hungry prey *1 Hen. VI.* i 2 27
But still sweet love is food for fortune's tooth . . *Troi. and Cres.* iv 5 293
I receive the general food at first, Which you do live upon . *Coriolanus* i 1 135
There let him stand, and rave, and cry for food . . *T. Andron.* v 3 180
Shut up in prison, kept without my food . . . . *Rom. and Jul.* i 2 56
Farewell: buy food, and get thyself in flesh . . . . . v 1 84
And, in despite, I'll cram thee with more food . . . . . v 3 48
Honest water, which ne'er left man i' the mire: This and my food are equals; there's no odds . . . . *T. of Athens* i 2 61
Duty and zeal to your unmatched mind, Care of your food and living . iv 3 524
A tithed death—If thy revenges hunger for that food Which nature loathes . . . . v 4 32
Shark'd up a list of lawless resolutes, For food and diet . . *Hamlet* i 1 99
Nor earth to me give food, nor heaven light! . . . . . iii 2 226
On my knees I beg That you'll vouchsafe me raiment, bed, and food *Lear* ii 4 158
Is it not as this mouth should tear this hand For lifting food to't? . iii 4 16
But mice and rats, and such small deer, Have been Tom's food for seven long year . . . . iii 4 145
And bring you where both fire and food is ready . . . . . iii 4 158
Croak not, black angel; I have no food for thee . . . . . iii 6 34
O dear son Edgar, The food of thy abused father's wrath! . . . iv 1 24
Food that to him now is as luscious as locusts . . . . *Othello* i 3 354
They [men] are all but stomachs, and we all but food . . . . iii 4 104
Music, moody food Of us that trade in love . . . *Ant. and Cleo.* ii 5 1
Throw between them all the food thou hast, They'll grind the one the other . . . . iii 5 15

Food. My hunger's gone; but even before, I was At point to sink for food *Cymbeline* iii 6 17
Who wanteth food, and will not say he wants it, Or can conceal his hunger till he famish? *Pericles* i 4 11
Thy food is such As hath been belch'd on by infected lungs iv 6 178
Fool. Not a holiday fool there but would give a piece of silver *Tempest* ii 2 30
I am a fool To weep at what I am glad of iii 1 73
Travellers ne'er did lie, Though fools at home condemn 'em iii 3 27
You fools! I and my fellows Are ministers of Fate iii 3 60
What a wardrobe here is for thee!—Let it alone, thou fool; it is but trash iv 1 224
The dropsy drown this fool! what do you mean To dote thus? iv 1 230
What a thrice-double ass Was I, to take this drunkard for a god And worship this dull fool! v 1 297
You call me fool.—So, by your circumstance, I fear you'll prove *T. G. of V.* i 1 36
He that is so yoked by a fool, Methinks, should not be chronicled for wise i 1 40
What a fool is she, that knows I am a maid, And would not force the letter to my view! i 2 53
Thou mistakest me.—Why, fool, I meant not thee ii 5 51
'Tis not to have you gone; For why, the fools are mad, if left alone iii 1 99
I am but a fool, look you; and yet I have the wit to think my master is a kind of a knave iii 1 261
Thou canst not read.—Come, fool, come; try me in thy paper iii 1 299
Alas, poor fool! why do I pity him? iv 4 98
You are well derived.—True; from a gentleman to a fool v 2 24
I care not for her, I: I hold him but a fool that will endanger His body for a girl that loves him not v 4 133
Though Page be a secure fool, and stands so firmly *Mer. Wives* ii 1 241
Good mother, do not marry me to yond fool iii 4 87
Will you cast away your child on a fool, and a physician? iii 4 100
The virtuous creature, that hath the jealous fool to her husband! iv 2 137
Come, you are a tedious fool: to the purpose *Meas. for Meas.* ii 1 119
Wrench awe from fools and tie the wiser souls To thy false seeming! ii 4 14
If I do lose thee, I do lose a thing That none but fools would keep iii 1 8
Thou [life] art death's fool iii 1 11
O heaven, the vanity of wretched fools! v 1 164
And was the duke a fleshmonger, a fool, and a coward? v 1 337
You, sirrah, that knew me for a fool, a coward, One all of luxury v 1 505
Unfeeling fools can with such wrongs dispense *Com. of Errors* ii 1 103
How many fond fools serve mad jealousy! ii 1 116
Because that I familiarly sometimes Do use you for my fool ii 2 27
No longer will I be a fool, To put the finger in the eye and weep ii 2 205
And the while His man with scissors nicks him like a fool v 1 175
Peace, fool! thy master and his man are here v 1 178
And my uncle's fool, reading the challenge, subscribed for Cupid *M. Ado* i 1 41
What is he for a fool that betroths himself to unquietness? i 3 49
A very dull fool; only his gift is in devising impossible slanders ii 1 143
There's a partridge wing saved, for the fool will eat no supper that night ii 1 156
The prince's fool! Ha? It may be I go under that title because I am merry ii 1 211
Lest I should prove the mother of fools ii 1 295
I thank it, poor fool, it keeps on the windy side of care ii 1 326
I do much wonder that one man, seeing how much another man is a fool when he dedicates his behaviours to love ii 3 9
Till he have made an oyster of me, he shall never make me such a fool ii 3 28
He is no fool for fancy, as you would have it appear he is iii 2 38
I may as well say the fool's the fool iii 3 130
My cousin's a fool, and thou art another iii 4 11
What means the fool, trow?—Nothing I iii 4 59
I am not such a fool to think what I list, nor I list not to think what I can iii 4 82
Call me a fool; Trust not my reading nor my observations iv 1 166
I speak not like a dotard nor a fool, As under privilege of age to brag v 1 59
What your wisdoms could not discover, these shallow fools have brought to light v 1 240
A hard rhyme; for 'school,' 'fool,' a babbling rhyme; very ominous endings v 2 39
What time o' day?—The hour that fools should ask *L. L. Lost* ii 1 123
Is the fool sick?—Sick at the heart ii 1 184
It would ill become me to be vain, indiscreet, or a fool iv 2 31
Set thee down, sorrow! for so they say the fool said, and so say I, and I the fool iv 3 5
The clown bore it, the fool sent it, and the lady hath it: sweet clown, sweeter fool, sweetest lady! iv 3 16
Now, in thy likeness, one more fool appear! iv 3 46
What fool is not so wise To lose an oath to win a paradise? iv 3 72
Here sit I in the sky, And wretched fools' secrets heedfully o'er-eye iv 3 80
I confess.—What?—That you three fools lack'd me fool to make up the mess iv 3 207
Fools you were these women to forswear, Or keeping what is sworn, you will prove fools iv 3 355
We are wise girls to mock our lovers so.—They are worse fools v 2 59
That he should be my fool and I his fate v 2 68
None are so surely caught, when they are catch'd, As wit turn'd fool v 2 70
Folly, in wisdom hatch'd, Hath wisdom's warrant and the help of school And wit's own grace to grace a learned fool v 2 72
Folly in fools bears not so strong a note As foolery in the wise v 2 75
Let us complain to them what fools were here v 2 302
I dare not call them fools; but this I think, When they are thirsty, fools would fain have drink v 2 371
For in my eye,— I am a fool, and full of poverty v 2 380
I am yours, and all that I possess!—All the fool mine? v 2 384
The pedant, the braggart, the hedge-priest, the fool and the boy v 2 546
Begot of that loose grace Which shallow laughing hearers give to fools v 2 870
Lord, what fools these mortals be! *M. N. Dream* iii 2 115
Seeking sweet favours for this hateful fool, I did upbraid her iv 1 54
Man is but a patch'd fool, if he will offer to say what methought I had iv 1 215
Let me play the fool: With mirth and laughter let old wrinkles come *Mer. of Venice* i 1 79
Almost damn those ears Which, hearing them, would call their brothers fools i 1 99
To gaze on Christian fools with varnish'd faces ii 5 33
What says that fool of Hagar's offspring, ha? ii 5 44
There be fools alive, I wis, Silver'd o'er; and so was this ii 9 68
Still more fool I shall appear By the time I linger here ii 9 73
Thus hath the candle singed the moth. O, these deliberate fools! ii 9 80
This is the fool that lent out money gratis iii 3 2
Be made a soft and dull-eyed fool, To shake the head, relent, and sigh iii 3 14
How every fool can play upon the word! iii 5 48

Fool. The fool hath planted in his memory An army of good words *Mer. of Venice* iii 5 71
I do know A many fools, that stand in better place iii 5 73
Hath not Fortune sent in this fool to cut off the argument? *As Y. Like It* i 2 49
For always the dulness of the fool is the whetstone of the wits i 2 58
The more pity, that fools may not speak wisely what wise men do foolishly i 2 92
Since the little wit that fools have was silenced, the little foolery that wise men have makes a great show i 2 95
Thou art a fool: she robs thee of thy name i 3 82
I cannot live out of her company.—You are a fool i 3 89
What if we assay'd to steal The clownish fool out of your father's court? i 3 132
Shall we go and kill us venison? And yet it irks me the poor dappled fools ii 1 22
Thus the hairy fool, Much marked of the melancholy Jacques, Stood ii 1 40
The more fool I; when I was at home, I was in a better place ii 4 17
Holla, you clown!—Peace, fool: he's not thy kinsman ii 4 67
Here shall he see Gross fools as he, An if he will come to me ii 5 58
'Tis a Greek invocation, to call fools into a circle ii 5 61
A fool, a fool! I met a fool i' the forest, A motley fool! ii 7 12
I met a fool; Who laid him down and bask'd him in the sun ii 7 14
Rail'd on Lady Fortune in good terms, In good set terms and yet a motley fool ii 7 17
Call me not fool till heaven hath sent me fortune ii 7 19
I did hear The motley fool thus moral on the time ii 7 29
My lungs began to crow like chanticleer, That fools should be so deep-contemplative ii 7 31
O noble fool! A worthy fool! Motley's the only wear ii 7 33
What fool is this?—O worthy fool! One that hath been a courtier ii 7 35
O that I were a fool! I am ambitious for a motley coat ii 7 42
As large a charter as the wind, To blow on whom I please; for so fools have ii 7 49
He that a fool doth very wisely hit Doth very foolishly, although he smart, Not to seem senseless of the bob ii 7 53
The wise man's folly is anatomized Even by the squandering glances of the fool ii 7 57
Out, fool!—For a taste: If a hart do lack a hind, Let him seek out Rosalind iii 2 105
Peace, you dull fool! I found them on a tree iii 2 121
I was seeking for a fool when I found you.—He is drowned in the brook: look but in, and you shall see him.—There I shall see mine own figure.—Which I take to be either a fool or a cipher iii 2 303
A material fool! iii 3 32
'Tis such fools as you That makes the world full of ill-favour'd children iii 5 52
I had rather have a fool to make me merry than experience to make me sad iv 1 28
Let her never nurse her child herself, for she will breed it like a fool! iv 1 179
You are a fool And turn'd into the extremity of love iv 3 22
The fool doth think he is wise, but the wise man knows himself to be a fool v 1 34
A pair of very strange beasts, which in all tongues are called fools v 4 38
Is not this a rare fellow, my lord? he's as good at any thing and yet a fool v 4 110
I take him for the better dog.—Thou art a fool *T. of Shrew* Ind. 1 26
And paint your face and use you like a fool i 1 65
Though her father be very rich, any man is so very a fool to be married to hell i 1 129
My remedy is then, to pluck it out.—Ay, if the fool could find it ii 1 213
Go, fool, and whom thou keep'st command ii 1 259
Your father were a fool To give thee all ii 1 402
He was a frantic fool, Hiding his bitter jests in blunt behaviour iii 2 12
But what a fool am I to chat with you! iii 2 123
Tut, she's a lamb, a dove, a fool to him! iii 2 159
I see a woman may be made a fool, If she had not spirit to resist iii 2 222
Away, you three-inch fool! iv 1 27
The more fool you, for laying on my duty v 2 12
I know him a notorious liar, Think him a great way fool *All's Well* i 1 112
I will be a fool in question, hoping to be the wiser by your answer ii 2 41
I play the noble housewife with the time, To entertain't so merrily with a fool ii 2 63
Thou art a witty fool; I have found thee.—Did you find me in yourself, sir? ii 4 32
Much fool may you find in you, even to the world's pleasure ii 4 36
But shall we have this dialogue between the fool and the soldier? iv 3 112
He was whipped for getting the shrieve's fool with child iv 3 213
Dian, the count's a fool, and full of gold iv 3 238
For count of this, the count's a fool, I know it iv 3 258
He will lie, sir, with such volubility, that you would think truth were a fool iv 3 285
Whether dost thou profess thyself, a knave or a fool?—A fool, sir, at a woman's service, and a knave at a man's iv 5 24
I will subscribe for thee, thou art both knave and fool iv 5 35
Though you are a fool and a knave, you shall eat v 2 57
But a year in all these ducats: he's a very fool and a prodigal *T. Night* i 3 25
Besides that he's a fool, he's a great quarreller i 3 31
Do you think you have fools in hand?—Sir, I have not you by the hand i 3 69
God give them wisdom that have it; and those that are fools, let them use their talents i 5 15
Those wits, that think they have thee, do very oft prove fools i 5 37
What says Quinapalus? 'Better a witty fool than a foolish wit' i 5 39
Take the fool away.—Do you not hear, fellows? Take away the lady i 5 42
You're a dry fool; I'll no more of you: besides, you grow dishonest i 5 45
Give the dry fool drink, then is the fool not dry i 5 48
The lady bade take away the fool; therefore, I say again, take her away i 5 58
Give me leave to prove you a fool?—Can you do it?—Dexteriously i 5 64
Why mournest thou?—Good fool, for my brother's death i 5 73
His soul is in heaven, fool.—The more fool, madonna, to mourn for your brother's soul being in heaven i 5 75
Take away the fool, gentlemen.—What think you of this fool? i 5 78
Infirmity, that decays the wise, doth ever make the better fool i 5 83
He will not pass his word for twopence that you are no fool i 5 87
I saw him put down the other day with an ordinary fool i 5 91
I take these wise men, that crow so at these set kind of fools, no better than the fools' zanies i 5 96
There is no slander in an allowed fool, though he do nothing but rail i 5 101
Now Mercury endue thee with leasing, for thou speakest well of fools! i 5 106
Thou hast spoke for us, madonna, as if thy eldest son should be a fool i 5 121
What's a drunken man like, fool?—Like a drowned man, a fool and a madman i 5 138
One draught above heat makes him a fool; the second mads him i 5 140

Fool. He is but mad yet, madonna; and the fool shall look to the madman *T. Night* i 5 146
Here comes the fool, i' faith.—How now, my hearts! ii 3 15
By my troth, the fool has an excellent breast ii 3 19
I had rather than forty shillings I had such a leg, and so sweet a breath to sing, as the fool has ii 3 22
Begin, fool: it begins 'Hold thy peace.'—I shall never begin if I hold my peace ii 3 72
Then to break promise with him and make a fool of him ii 3 138
I will plant you two, and let the fool make a third ii 3 189
A fool that the lady Olivia's father took much delight in ii 4 11
We will fool him black and blue: shall we not? ii 5 12
I knew 'twas I; for many do call me fool ii 5 90
I do not now fool myself, to let imagination jade me ii 5 178
Art not thou the Lady Olivia's fool?—No, indeed, sir iii 1 36
She will keep no fool, sir, till she be married iii 1 38
Fools are as like husbands as pilchards are to herrings; the husband's the bigger iii 1 39
I am indeed not her fool, but her corrupter of words iii 1 41
But the fool should be as oft with your master as with my mistress iii 1 45
Wise enough to play the fool; And to do that well craves a kind of wit iii 1 67
I would you were as I would have you be!—Would it be better, madam, than I am? I wish it might, for now I am your fool iii 1 156
He has heard that word of some great man and now applies it to a fool iv 1 13
Wise men that give fools money get themselves a good report iv 1 23
'Tell me how thy lady does.'—Fool!—'My lady is unkind, perdy.'—Fool!—'Alas, why is she so?'—Fool, I say! iv 2 80
Good fool, as ever thou wilt deserve well at my hand, help me to a candle iv 2 86
Fool, there was never man so notoriously abused iv 2 94
I am as well in my wits, fool, as thou art.—But as well? then you are mad indeed, if you be no better in your wits than a fool iv 2 95
Fool, fool, fool, I say!—Alas, sir, be patient iv 2 110
Good fool, help me to some light and some paper iv 2 113
Good fool, some ink, paper and light; and convey what I will set down iv 2 117
Fool, I'll requite it in the highest degree iv 2 128
You can fool no more money out of me at this throw v 1 44
Look then to be well edified when the fool delivers the madman v 1 299
Alas, poor fool, how have they baffled thee! v 1 377
By the Lord, fool, I am not mad v 1 382
A fool That seest a game play'd home, the rich stake drawn, And takest it all for jest *W. Tale* i 2 247
If industriously I play'd the fool, it was my negligence i 2 257
Do not weep, good fools; There is no cause ii 1 118
Either thou art most ignorant by age, Or thou wert born a fool ii 1 174
A fool, inconstant And damnable ingrateful iii 2 187
Sir, forgive a foolish woman: The love I bore your queen—lo, fool again! iii 2 229
Who of force must know The royal fool thou copest with iv 4 435
What a fool Honesty is! and Trust, his sworn brother, a very simple gentleman! iv 4 606
Women and fools, break off your conference *K. John* ii 1 150
A ramping fool, to brag and stamp and swear Upon my party! iii 1 122
A lunatic lean-witted fool, Presuming on an ague's privilege *Richard II.* ii 1 115
Wife, thou art a fool. Boy, let me see the writing v 2 68
What a wasp-stung and impatient fool Art thou! *1 Hen. IV.* i 3 236
My lord fool, out of this nettle, danger, we pluck this flower, safety ii 3 10
Thou clay-brained guts, thou knotty-pated fool ii 4 252
Carded his state, Mingled his royalty with capering fools iii 2 63
A fool go with thy soul, whither it goes! v 3 22
But thought's the slave of life, and life time's fool v 4 81
Let it alone; I'll make other shift: you'll be a fool still *2 Hen. IV.* ii 1 170
If they become me not, he was a fool that taught them me ii 1 205
Now the Lord lighten thee! thou art a great fool ii 1 209
Come, you virtuous ass, you bashful fool, must you be blushing? ii 2 81
Thus we play the fools with the time, and the spirits of the wise sit in the clouds and mock us ii 2 154
Thou art welcome.—How, you fat fool! I scorn you ii 4 322
Fools and cowards; which some of us should be too, but for inflammation iv 3 102
How ill white hairs become a fool and jester! v 5 52
'Tis a gull, a fool, a rogue, that now and then goes to the wars *Hen. V.* iii 6 70
If the enemy is an ass and a fool and a prating coxcomb, is it meet, think you, that we should also, look you, be an ass and a fool and a prating coxcomb? iv 1 78
Be friends, you English fools, be friends: we have French quarrels enow iv 1 239
Subject to the breath Of every fool iv 1 252
Belike your lordship takes us then for fools *1 Hen. VI.* iii 2 62
I'll be the first, sure.—Come back, fool *2 Hen. VI.* i 3 9
So many weeks ere the poor fools will ean *3 Hen. VI.* ii 5 36
What a peevish fool was that of Crete, That taught his son the office of a fowl! And yet, for all his wings, the fool was drown'd v 6 18
Fool, fool! thou whet'st a knife to kill thyself *Richard III.* i 3 244
When he wakes! why, fool, he shall never wake till the judgement-day i 4 105
I will converse with iron-witted fools And unrespective boys iv 2 28
Relenting fool, and shallow, changing woman! iv 4 431
I am a villain: yet I lie, I am not. Fool, of thyself speak well: fool, do not flatter v 3 192
To rank our chosen truth with such a show As fool and fight is *Hen. VIII.* Prol. 19
This masque Was cried incomparable; and the ensuing night Made it a fool i 1 28
Leave those remnants Of fool and feather i 3 25
He was a fool; For he would needs be virtuous ii 2 132
O negligence! Fit for a fool to fall by iii 2 214
She's a fool to stay behind her father; let her to the Greeks *T. and C.* i 1 83
Peace, you ungracious clamours! peace, rude sounds! Fools on both sides! i 1 93
Asses, fools, dolts! chaff and bran, chaff and bran! porridge after meat! i 2 262
The wise and fool, the artist and unread, The hard and soft, seem all affined i 3 24
Thou art proclaimed a fool, I think ii 1 26
I know that, fool.—Ay, but that fool knows not himself ii 1 71
Peace, fool!—I would have peace and quietness, but the fool will not ii 1 89
Will you set your wit to a fool's?—No, I warrant you; for a fool's will shame it ii 1 94
I will keep where there is wit stirring and leave the faction of fools ii 1 131
Patroclus is a fool.—You rascal!—Peace fool! I have not done.—He is a privileged man. Proceed ii 3 60
Agamemnon is a fool; Achilles is a fool; Thersites is a fool, and, as aforesaid, Patroclus is a fool ii 3 63
Agamemnon is a fool to offer to command Achilles; Achilles is a fool to be commanded of Agamemnon; Thersites is a fool to serve such a fool, and Patroclus is a fool positive ii 3 67
Why am I a fool?—Make that demand of the prover. It suffices me thou art ii 3 71

Fool. Achilles hath inveigled his fool from him *Troi. and Cres.* ii 3 99
It was a strong composure a fool could disunite ii 3 109
See, we fools! Why have I blabb'd? who shall be true to us? iii 2 131
But an unkind self, that itself will leave, To be another's fool iii 2 157
The fool slides o'er the ice that you should break iii 3 215
I'll send the fool to Ajax and desire him To invite the Trojan lords iii 3 235
From whence, fragment?—Why, thou full dish of fool, from Troy v 1 10
I'll be your fool no more.—Thy better must v 2 32
Away, you fool; it [blood] more becomes a man Than gilt his trophy *Cor.* i 3 42
A brace of unmeriting, proud, violent, testy magistrates, alias fools ii 1 48
We call a nettle but a nettle and The faults of fools but folly ii 1 208
Rather than fool it so, Let the high office and the honour go ii 3 128
If you are learn'd, Be not as common fools iii 1 100
Are you mankind?—Ay, fool; is that a shame? Note but this fool iv 2 17
Present My throat to thee and to thy ancient malice; Which not to cut would show thee but a fool iv 5 103
Who resist Are mock'd for valiant ignorance, And perish constant fools iv 6 105
And patient fools, Whose children he hath slain, their base throats tear With giving him glory v 6 52
Are you such fools To square for this? *T. Andron.* ii 1 99
What fool hath added water to the sea? iii 1 68
Let fools do good, and fair men call for grace iii 1 205
Drown the lamenting fool in sea-salt tears iii 2 20
Part, fools! Put up your swords; you know not what you do *R. and J.* i 1 71
Pretty fool, To see it tetchy and fall out with the dug! i 3 31
'Wilt thou not, Jule?' quoth he; And, pretty fool, it stinted and said 'Ay' i 3 48
Her vestal livery is but sick and green And none but fools do wear it ii 2 9
O, I am fortune's fool! iii 1 141
I would the fool were married to her grave! iii 5 141
Peace, you mumbling fool! Utter your gravity o'er a gossip's bowl iii 5 174
To have a wretched puling fool, A whining mammet, in her fortune's tender, To answer 'I'll not wed' iii 5 185
To see meat fill knaves and wine heat fools *T. of Athens* i 1 271
Fare thee well, fare thee well.—Thou art a fool to bid me farewell twice i 1 273
We make ourselves fools, to disport ourselves i 2 141
Thus honest fools lay out their wealth on court'sies i 2 241
Here comes the fool with Apemantus: let's ha' some sport with 'em ii 2 47
How dost, fool?—Dost dialogue with thy shadow? ii 2 51
There's the fool hangs on your back already ii 2 56
Where's the fool now?—He last asked the question ii 2 59
Speak to 'em fool.—How do you, gentlemen?—Gramercies, good fool ii 2 67
No usurer but has a fool to his servant: my mistress is one, and I am her fool ii 2 103
What is a whoremaster, fool?—A fool in good clothes, and something like thee ii 2 113
Thou art not altogether a fool.—Nor thou altogether a wise man ii 2 122
Come with me, fool, come.—I do not always follow lover ii 2 129
Ha! now I see thou art a fool, and fit for thy master iii 1 52
It may prove an argument of laughter To the rest, and 'mongst lords I be thought a fool iii 3 21
You fools of fortune, trencher-friends, time's flies, Cap and knee slaves! iii 6 106
Slaves and fools, Pluck the grave wrinkled senate from the bench! iv 1 4
The learned pate Ducks to the golden fool: all is oblique iv 3 18
Spare not the babe, Whose dimpled smiles from fools exhaust their mercy iv 3 119
A madman so long, now a fool iv 3 221
O, thou shalt find— A fool of thee iv 3 232
Why dost thou seek me out?—To vex thee.—Always a villain's office or a fool's iv 3 237
Thou art the cap of all the fools alive iv 3 363
Why old men fool and children calculate *J. Cæsar* i 3 65
Be not fond, To think that Cæsar bears such rebel blood That will be thaw'd from the true quality With that which melteth fools iii 1 42
Wisely I say, I am a bachelor.—That's as much as to say, they are fools that marry iii 3 20
He was but a fool that brought My answer back iv 3 84
What should the wars do with these jigging fools? iv 3 137
Mine eyes are made the fools o' the other senses *Macbeth* ii 1 44
No boasting like a fool; This deed I'll do before this purpose cool iv 1 153
I am so much a fool, should I stay longer, It would be my disgrace and your discomfort iv 2 28
Then the liars and swearers are fools, for there are liars and swearers enow to beat the honest men iv 2 56
And all our yesterdays have lighted fools The way to dusty death v 5 22
Why should I play the Roman fool, and die On mine own sword? v 8 1
Tender yourself more dearly; Or . . . you'll tender me a fool *Hamlet* i 3 109
And we fools of nature So horridly to shake our disposition i 4 54
These tedious old fools! ii 2 223
Let the doors be shut upon him, that he may play the fool no where but in's own house iii 1 136
Or, if thou wilt needs marry, marry a fool iii 1 143
Villanous, and shows a most pitiful ambition in the fool that uses it iii 2 49
They fool me to the top of my bent iii 2 401
Thou wretched, rash, intruding fool, farewell! I took thee for thy better iii 4 31
Cannot you tell that? every fool can tell that v 1 159
As if we were villains by necessity; fools by heavenly compulsion *Lear* i 2 132
Did my father strike my gentleman for chiding of his fool? i 3 1
Old fools are babes again; and must be used With checks as flatteries i 3 19
Where's my knave? my fool? Go you, and call my fool hither i 4 46
What says the fellow there? Call the clotpoll back. Where's my fool, ho? i 4 52
But where's my fool? I have not seen him this two days i 4 77
Since my young lady's going into France, sir, the fool hath much pined away i 4 80
Go you, call hither my fool. O, you sir, you, come you hither i 4 84
Sirrah, you were best take my coxcomb.—Why, fool? i 4 110
This is nothing, fool.—Then 'tis like the breath of an unfee'd lawyer i 4 141
He will not believe a fool.—A bitter fool! i 4 149
Dost thou know the difference, my boy, between a bitter fool and a sweet fool? i 4 152
The sweet and bitter fool Will presently appear i 4 158
Dost thou call me fool, boy?—All thy other titles thou hast given away i 4 162
This is not altogether fool, my lord.—No, faith, lords and great men will not let me i 4 165
And ladies too, they will not let me have all fool to myself i 4 169
Fools had ne'er less wit in a year; For wise men are grown foppish i 4 181
That such a king should play bo-peep, And go the fools among i 4 194
Keep a schoolmaster that can teach thy fool to lie: I would fain learn to lie i 4 196
I had rather be any kind o' thing than a fool: and yet I would not be thee i 4 203
I am better than thou art now; I am a fool, thou art nothing i 4 213
Not only, sir, this your all-licensed fool, But other of your insolent retinue i 4 220
More knave than fool i 4 337

Fool. Nuncle Lear, tarry and take the fool with thee . . . *Lear* i 4 339
If my cap would buy a halter: So the fool follows after . . . i 4 344
Yes, indeed: thou wouldst make a good fool . . . i 5 41
If thou wert my fool, nuncle, I'ld have thee beaten for being old before thy time . . . i 5 45
Smile you my speeches, as I were a fool? . . . ii 2 88
None of these rogues and cowards But Ajax is their fool . . . ii 2 132
I would have none but knaves follow it, since a fool gives it . . . ii 4 78
But I will tarry; the fool will stay, And let the wise man fly: The knave turns fool that runs away; The fool no knave, perdy . . . ii 4 83
Where learned you this, fool?—Not i' the stocks, fool . . . ii 4 87
Fool me not so much To bear it tamely; touch me with noble anger . ii 4 278
O fool, I shall go mad!—Let us withdraw; 'twill be a storm . ii 4 289
Who is with him?—None but the fool; who labours to out-jest His heart-struck injuries . . . iii 1 16
Here's a night pities neither wise man nor fool . . . iii 2 13
Here's grace and a cod-piece; that's a wise man and a fool . . . iii 2 41
Poor fool and knave, I have one part in my heart That's sorry yet for thee . . . iii 2 72
This cold night will turn us all to fools and madmen . . . iii 4 80
Bad is the trade that must play fool to sorrow, Angering itself and others iv 1 40
To thee a woman's services are due: My fool usurps my body . iv 2 28
That not know'st Fools do those villains pity who are punish'd Ere they have done their mischief . . . iv 2 54
Whiles thou, a moral fool, sit'st still, and criest 'Alack, why does he so?' . . . iv 2 58
O vain fool!—Thou changed and self-cover'd thing, for shame . iv 2 61
When we are born, we cry that we are come To this great stage of fools iv 6 187
I am even The natural fool of fortune. Use me well . . . iv 6 195
And my poor fool is hang'd! . . . v 3 305
Thus do I ever make my fool my purse . . . *Othello* i 3 389
These are old fond paradoxes to make fools laugh i' the alehouse . ii 1 140
To do what?—To suckle fools and chronicle small beer . . . ii 1 161
My sick fool Roderigo, Whom love hath turn'd almost the wrong side out ii 3 53
To be now a sensible man, by and by a fool, and presently a beast! O strange! . . . ii 3 310
This honest fool Plies Desdemona to repair his fortunes . . . ii 3 359
O wretched fool, That livest to make thine honesty a vice! . . . iii 3 375
I should be wise, for honesty's a fool And loses that it works for . iii 3 382
Fools as gross As ignorance made drunk . . . iii 3 404
Work on, My medicine, work! Thus credulous fools are caught . iv 1 46
I was a fine fool to take it. I must take out the work? . . . iv 1 155
You are a fool; go to . . . iv 2 148
What should such a fool Do with so good a woman? . . . v 2 233
For a special purpose Which wrought to his desire.—O fool! fool! fool! v 2 323
The triple pillar of the world transform'd Into a strumpet's fool *A. and C.* i 1 13
I'll seem the fool I am not; Antony Will be himself . . . i 1 42
Out, fool! I forgive thee for a witch . . . i 2 40
The nature of bad news infects the letter.—When it concerns the fool or coward . . . i 2 100
Cross him in nothing.—Thou teachest like a fool; the way to lose him i 3 10
Cries, 'Fool Lepidus!' And threats the throat of that his officer . iii 5 18
The loyalty well held to fools does make Our faith mere folly . iii 13 42
Yet come a little,—Wishers were ever fools,—O, come, come, come! . iv 15 37
That's the way To fool their preparation . . . v 2 225
Poor venomous fool, Be angry, and dispatch . . . v 2 308
Till you had measured how long a fool you were upon the ground *Cymb.* i 2 25
She shines not upon fools, lest the reflection should hurt her . i 2 34
Would he had been one of my rank!—To have smelt like a fool . ii 1 18
You are a fool granted; therefore your issues, being foolish, do not derogate . . . ii 1 50
Fools are not mad folks.—Do you call me fool?—As I am mad, I do . ii 3 106
I am sprited with a fool, Frighted, and anger'd worse . . . ii 3 144
Thus may poor fools Believe false teachers . . . iii 4 86
For when fools Shall— Who is here? What, are you packing, sirrah? iii 5 79
Thou art some fool; I am loath to beat thee . . . iv 2 85
Those that I reverence those I fear, the wise: At fools I laugh . iv 2 96
This Cloten was a fool, an empty purse; There was no money in't . iv 2 113
Yet I not doing this, the fool had borne My head as I do his . . iv 2 116
Ay me, most credulous fool, Egregious murderer, thief! . . . v 5 210
Opinion's but a fool, that makes us scan The outward habit by the inward man . . . *Pericles* ii 2 56
To wisdom he's a fool that will not yield . . . ii 4 54
Or tie my treasure up in silken bags, To please the fool and death . iii 2 42
This is the rarest dream that e'er dull sleep Did mock sad fools withal v 1 164
Fool-begged. If thou live to see like right bereft, This fool-begg'd patience in thee will be left . . . *Com. of Errors* ii 1 41
Fool-born. Reply not to me with a fool-born jest . . . 2 *Hen. IV.* v 5 59
Fool gudgeon. Fish not, with this melancholy bait, For this fool gudgeon, this opinion . . . *Mer. of Venice* i 1 102
Fool multitude. The fool multitude, that choose by show . . . ii 9 26
Fool's bolt. According to the fool's bolt, sir, and such dulcet diseases *As Y. Like It* v 4 67
The better at proverbs, by how much 'A fool's bolt is soon shot' *Hen. V.* iii 7 132
Fool's eyes. When thou wakest, with thine own fool's eyes peep *M. N. D.* iv 1 89
Your eyes drop millstones, when fools' eyes drop tears . *Richard III.* i 3 354
Fool's head. You shall have An fool's-head of your own . . *Mer. Wives* i 4 134
Did I deserve no more than a fool's head? . . . *Mer. of Venice* ii 9 59
With one fool's head I came to woo, But I go away with two . . ii 9 75
Fool's heart. Lend me a fool's heart and a woman's eyes *T. of Athens* v 1 160
Fool's paradise. If ye should lead her into a fool's paradise *R. and J.* ii 4 175
Fool's play. O, 'tis fair play.—Fool's play, by heaven . *Troi. and Cres.* v 3 43
Fool's speed. This fool's speed Be cross'd with slowness! *Cymbeline* iii 5 167
Fooled. Being fool'd, by foolery thrive! . . . *All's Well* iv 3 374
You are fool'd, discarded and shook off . . . 1 *Hen. IV.* i 3 178
She is fool'd With a most false effect . . . *Cymbeline* i 5 42
Foolery. Now he shall see his own foolery . . . *Mer. Wives* iv 2 38
Well, sir, there rest in your foolery . . . *Com. of Errors* iv 3 34
Unless he have a fancy to this foolery, as it appears he hath *Much Ado* iii 2 37
What a scene of foolery have I seen, Of sighs, of groans! *L. L. Lost* iv 3 163
Folly in fools bears not so strong a note As foolery in the wise . v 2 76
The little foolery that wise men have makes a great show *As Y. Like It* i 2 96
They are but burs, cousin, thrown upon thee in holiday foolery . i 3 14
Being fool'd, by foolery thrive! . . . *All's Well* iv 3 374
And that may you be bold to say in your foolery . . . *T. Night* i 5 13
Foolery, sir, does walk about the orb like the sun, it shines every where iii 1 43
Mad indeed, stark mad! for all Thy by-gone fooleries were but spices of it . . . *W. Tale* iii 2 185
Here has been too much homely foolery already . . . iv 4 341
Manhood is call'd foolery, when it stands Against a falling fabric *Coriol.* iii 1 246
Foolery. As much foolery as I have, so much wit thou lackest *T. of A.* ii 2 124
It was mere foolery; I did not mark it . . . *J. Cæsar* i 2 236
There was more foolery yet, if I could remember it . . . i 2 291
It is but foolery; but it is such a kind of gain-giving, as would perhaps trouble a woman . . . *Hamlet* v 2 225
But this is foolery . . . *Cymbeline* iii 2 75
Foolhardiness. Mark me, and do the like.—Fool-hardiness; not I *Coriol.* i 4 46
Foolhardy. I find my tongue is too foolhardy . . . *All's Well* iv 1 32
Open the door, secure, foolhardy king . . . *Richard II.* v 3 43
Fooling. Who in this kind of merry fooling am nothing to you *Tempest* ii 1 177
But, after all this fooling, I would not have it so . *Meas. for Meas.* i 2 71
Let's have no more fooling about it . . . *Mer. of Venice* ii 2 88
Wit, an't be thy will, put me into good fooling! . . . *T. Night* i 5 36
Now you see, sir, how your fooling grows old, and people dislike it . i 5 119
In sooth, thou wast in very gracious fooling last night . . . ii 3 23
Excellent! why, this is the best fooling, when all is done . . . ii 3 31
Beshrew me, the knight's in admirable fooling . . . ii 3 86
While I stand fooling here . . . *Richard II.* v 5 60
I do not like this fooling.—Nor I, by Pluto . . *Troi. and Cres.* v 2 101
Foolish. Thou think'st there is no more such shapes as he, Having seen but him and Caliban: foolish wench! . . . *Tempest* i 2 479
Fie, fie, how wayward is this foolish love! . . . *T. G. of Ver.* i 2 57
My foolish rival, that her father likes Only for his possessions are so huge ii 4 174
For 'tis no trusting to yond foolish lout . . . iv 4 71
Shall we send that foolish carrion, Mistress Quickly, to him? *Mer. Wives* iii 3 205
To build upon a foolish woman's promise . . . iii 5 42
Thou art as foolish Christian creatures as I would desires . . iv 1 73
So play the foolish throngs with one that swoons . . *Meas. for Meas.* ii 4 24
Thou foolish friar, and thou pernicious woman . . . v 1 241
When the sun shines let foolish gnats make sport . . *Com. of Errors* ii 2 30
Arrest me, foolish fellow, if thou darest . . . iv 1 75
Foolish, blunt, unkind, Stigmatical in making, worse in mind . . iv 2 21
A foolish extravagant spirit, full of forms, figures, shapes, objects *L. L. L.* iv 2 68
Fair gentle sweet, Your wit makes wise things foolish . . . v 2 374
To your huge store Wise things seem foolish and rich things but poor . v 2 378
A foolish mild man; an honest man, look you, and soon dashed . . v 2 584
And make and mar The foolish Fates . . . *M. N. Dream* i 2 40
Indeed, who would set his wit to so foolish a bird? . . . iii 1 137
Who is't that hinders you?—A foolish heart, that I leave here behind iii 2 319
He, of all the men that ever my foolish eyes looked upon, was the best deserving a fair lady . . . *Mer. of Venice* i 2 130
These foolish drops do something drown my manly spirit . . . ii 3 13
Bring again these foolish runaways . . . *As Y. Like It* ii 2 21
You foolish shepherd, wherefore do you follow her? . . . iii 5 49
The foolish coroners of that age found it was 'Hero of Sestos' . iv 1 105
I count it but time lost to hear such a foolish song . . . v 3 41
No duty? Where is the foolish knave I sent before?—Here, sir; as foolish as I was before . . . *T. of Shrew* iv 1 130
What a foolish duty call you this?—I would your duty were as foolish too v 2 125
One Count Rousillon, a foolish idle boy . . . *All's Well* iv 3 242
He looks like a poor, decayed, ingenious, foolish, rascally knave . v 2 25
I heard my lady talk of it yesterday; and of a foolish knight *T. Night* i 3 16
Better a witty fool than a foolish wit . . . i 5 39
Besides, you waste the treasure of your time with a foolish knight . ii 5 86
Go to, thou art a foolish fellow: Let me be clear of thee . . . iv 1 3
I prithee, foolish Greek, depart from me: There's money for thee . iv 1 19
What foolish boldness brought thee to their mercies? . . . v 1 73
A foolish thing was but a toy, For the rain it raineth every day . v 1 400
I may be negligent, foolish and fearful . . . *W. Tale* i 2 250
Cleft the heart That could conceive a gross and foolish sire . . iii 2 198
Sir, forgive a foolish woman: The love I bore your queen—lo, fool again! iii 2 228
Lame, foolish, crooked, swart, prodigious, Patch'd with foul moles *K. John* iii 1 46
How now, foolish rheum! Turning dispiteous torture out of door! . iv 1 33
Foolish boy, the king is left behind . . . *Richard II.* ii 3 97
Peace, foolish woman.—I will not peace . . . v 2 80
Ransom straight His brother-in-law, the foolish Mortimer . 1 *Hen. IV.* i 3 80
A villanous trick of thine eye and a foolish hanging of thy nether lip . ii 4 446
Make blind itself with foolish tenderness . . . iii 2 91
But for these foolish officers, I beseech you I may have redress against them . . . 2 *Hen. IV.* ii 1 117
What foolish master taught you these manners? . . . ii 1 202
Dries me there all the foolish and dull and crudy vapours . . iv 3 106
The foolish over-careful fathers Have broke their sleep with thoughts . iv 5 68
O foolish youth! Thou seek'st the greatness that will overwhelm thee . iv 5 97
They, by observing of him, do bear themselves like foolish justices . v 1 75
Foolish curs, that run winking into the mouth of a Russian bear! *Hen. V.* iii 7 153
Never trust his word after! come, 'tis a foolish saying . . . iv 1 214
What is the trust or strength of foolish man? . . . 1 *Hen. VI.* iii 2 112
Henry my lord is cold in great affairs, Too full of foolish pity 2 *Hen. VI.* iii 1 225
Tut, that's a foolish observation . . . 3 *Hen. VI.* ii 6 108
So foolish sorrow bids your stones farewell . . . *Richard III.* iv 1 104
The boy is foolish, and I fear not him . . . iv 2 56
O foolish Cressid! I might have still held off . . . *Troi. and Cres.* iv 2 17
This foolish, dreaming, superstitious girl Makes all these bodements . v 3 79
Rascally tisick so troubles me, and the foolish fortune of this girl . v 3 102
That same scurvy doting foolish young knave's sleeve of Troy . . v 4 4
Like Romans, neither foolish in our stands, Nor cowardly in retire *Coriol.* i 6 2
No, foolish tribune, no; no son of mine . . . *T. Andron.* i 1 343
We have a trifling foolish banquet towards . . . *Rom. and Jul.* i 5 124
Back, foolish tears, back to your native spring . . . iii 2 102
How foolish do your fears seem now, Calpurnia! . . . *J. Cæsar* ii 2 105
A foolish thought, to say a sorry sight . . . *Macbeth* ii 2 22
'Tis true 'tis pity; And pity 'tis 'tis true: a foolish figure . . *Hamlet* ii 2 98
Who was in life a foolish prating knave . . . iii 4 215
A knavish speech sleeps in a foolish ear . . . iv 2 26
On whose foolish honesty My practices ride easy . . . *Lear* i 2 197
No more; the text is foolish.—Wisdom and goodness to the vile seem vile iv 2 37
I am a very foolish fond old man, Fourscore and upward . . . iv 7 60
Pray you now, forget and forgive: I am old and foolish . . . iv 7 84
She never yet was foolish that was fair . . . *Othello* ii 1 137
What miserable praise hast thou for her that's foul and foolish?—There's none so foul and foolish thereunto, But does foul pranks which fair and wise ones do . . . ii 1 141
A thing for me? it is a common thing— Ha!—To have a foolish wife . iii 3 304
Prick'd to't by foolish honesty and love . . . iii 3 412
And to see how he prizes the foolish woman your wife! . . . iv 1 186
How foolish are our minds! If I do die before thee, prithee, shroud me In one of those same sheets . . . iv 3 23
Is't long or round?—Round even to faultiness.—For the most part, too, they are foolish that are so . . . *Ant. and Cleo.* iii 3 34

Foolish. Thou foolish thing! They were again together . . *Cymbeline* i 1 150
A foolish suitor to a wedded lady, That hath her husband banish'd . i 6 2
You are a fool granted; therefore your issues, being foolish, do not derogate ii 1 51
If I could get this foolish Imogen, I shall have gold enough . . ii 3 9
You're a young foolish sapling, and must be bowed . . *Pericles* iv 2 93
Why, are you foolish? Can it be undone? . . . . iv 3 1
Foolish-compounded. The brain of this foolish-compounded clay, man *2 Hen. IV.* i 2 8
Foolishly. Thus foolishly lost at a game of tick-tack . *Meas. for Meas.* i 2 196
That fools may not speak wisely what wise men do foolishly *As Y. Like It* i 2 93
He that a fool doth very wisely hit Doth very foolishly, although he smart, Not to seem senseless of the bob . . . . . ii 7 54
Fondly brought here and foolishly sent hence . . . . *2 Hen. IV.* iv 2 119
I will indeed no longer endure it, nor am I yet persuaded to put up in peace what already I have foolishly suffered . . . *Othello* iv 2 181
Foolishness. Have done your foolishness And tell me . *Com. of Errors* i 2 72
Foot it featly here and there; And, sweet sprites, the burthen bear *Tempest* i 2 380
What? I say, My foot my tutor? Put thy sword up . . . i 2 469
I will kiss thy foot: I prithee, be my god . . . . . ii 2 153
I'll kiss thy foot; I'll swear myself thy subject . . . . ii 2 157
Tread softly, that the blind mole may not Hear a foot fall . . . iv 1 195
Ye that on the sands with printless foot Do chase the ebbing Neptune v 1 34
Sometimes the beam of her view gilded my foot . . *Mer. Wives* i 3 69
Take heed, have open eye, for thieves do foot by night . . ii 1 126
The firm fixture of thy foot would give an excellent motion to thy gait in a semi-circled farthingale . . . . iii 3 67
While other jests are something rank on foot . . . . . iv 6 22
His death, Which I did think with slower foot came on . *Meas. for Meas.* v 1 400
No longer from head to foot than from hip to hip . *Com. of Errors* iii 2 115
With a good leg and a good foot, uncle, and money enough . *Much Ado* ii 1 15
Bring you the length of Prester John's foot . . . . . ii 1 276
One foot in sea and one on shore, To one thing constant never . ii 3 66
From the crown of his head to the sole of his foot, he is all mirth . iii 2 10
Her shoe, which is baser, guided by her foot, which is basest *L. L. Lost* i 2 174
I profane my lips on thy foot, my eyes on thy picture . . iv 1 86
When shall you hear that I Will praise a hand, a foot, a face, an eye? . iv 3 184
Look, here's thy love: my foot and her face see . . . . iv 3 277
No, to the death, we will not move a foot . . . . . v 2 146
Do not you know my lady's foot by the squier? . . . . v 2 474
I do adore thy sweet grace's slipper.—Loves her by the foot . . v 2 674
Since love's argument was first on foot, Let not the cloud of sorrow justle it . . . . v 2 757
Who even but now did spurn me with his foot, To call me goddess *M. N. Dream* iii 2 225
And foot me as you spurn a stranger cur Over your threshold *Mer. of Venice* i 3 119
Never dare misfortune cross her foot, Unless she do it under this excuse ii 4 36
I would my daughter were dead at my foot, and the jewels in her ear! . iii 1 92
Would she were hearsed at my foot, and the ducats in her coffin! . . iii 1 94
All the embossed sores and headed evils, That thou with license of free foot hast caught . . . . *As Y. Like It* ii 7 68
Every hour would detect the lazy foot of Time as well as a clock.—And why not the swift foot of Time? . . . . iii 2 322
Though he go as softly as foot can fall . . . . . . iii 2 346
A mighty power; which were on foot, In his own conduct . . . v 4 162
And in his waning age Set foot under thy table . . *T. of Shrew* ii 1 404
Am I but three inches? why, thy horn is a foot; and so long am I . iv 1 30
Out, you rogue! you pluck my foot awry . . . . . . iv 1 150
What say you to a neat's foot?—'Tis passing good . . . . iv 3 17
There will we mount, and thither walk on foot . . . . iv 3 188
Place your hands below your husband's foot . . . . . v 2 177
France is a dog-hole, and it no more merits The tread of a man's foot *All's Well* ii 3 292
Will speed her foot again, Led hither by pure love . . . . iii 4 37
The inaudible and noiseless foot of Time Steals ere we can effect them . v 3 41
There thy fixed foot shall grow Till thou have audience . . *T. Night* i 4 17
Wilt thou set thy foot o' my neck?—Or o' mine either? . . . ii 5 206
And you find so much blood in his liver as will clog the foot of a flea iii 2 66
On the like occasion whereon my services are now on foot . *W. Tale* i 1 3
Jumps twelve foot and a half by the squier . . . . . iv 4 347
Proceed: No foot shall stir.—Music, awake her . . . . v 3 98
I would give it every foot to have this face . . . *K. John* i 1 146
That white-faced shore, Whose foot spurns back the ocean's roaring tides . . . . ii 1 24
And wheresoe'er this foot of mine doth tread, He lies before me . . iii 3 62
The path which shall directly lead Thy foot to England's throne . . iii 4 130
Methinks I see this hurly all on foot . . . . . . iii 4 169
When I strike my foot Upon the bosom of the ground, rush forth . . iv 1 2
That blood which owed the breadth of all this isle, Three foot of it doth hold . . . . iv 2 100
Nay, but make haste; the better foot before . . . . . iv 2 170
Nor attend the foot That leaves the print of blood where'er it walks . iv 3 25
If thou but frown on me, or stir thy foot, . . . I'll strike thee dead . iv 3 96
That, like a lion foster'd up at hand, It may lie gently at the foot of peace . . . . v 2 76
England never did, nor never shall, Lie at the proud foot of a conqueror v 7 113
Where ever Englishman durst set his foot . . . . . *Richard II.* i 1 66
Interchangeably hurl down my gage Upon this overweening traitor's foot . . . . i 1 147
Myself I throw, dread sovereign, at thy foot . . . . . i 1 165
Nimble mischance, that art so light of foot . . . . . iii 4 92
Now in as low an ebb as the foot of the ladder . . . *1 Hen. IV.* i 2 42
If I travel but four foot by the squier further afoot, I shall break my wind . . . . ii 2 13
I'll starve ere I'll rob a foot further . . . . . . ii 2 23
I'll sew nether stocks and mend them and foot them too . . . ii 4 130
I followed me close, came in foot and hand . . . . . ii 4 241
But afoot he will not budge a foot.—Yes, Jack, upon instinct . . ii 4 388
I'll procure this fat rogue a charge of foot . . . . . ii 4 597
When I from France set foot at Ravenspurgh . . . . . iii 2 95
I have procured thee, Jack, a charge of foot . . . . . iii 3 209
All his men Upon the foot of fear, fled with the rest . . . v 5 20
A cause on foot Lives so in hope as in an early spring We see the appearing buds . . . . *2 Hen. IV.* i 3 37
Fifteen hundred foot, five hundred horse, Are march'd up . . . ii 1 186
And laid his love and life under my foot . . . . . . iii 1 63
Stoop tamely to the foot of majesty . . . . iv 2 42
With mine own picture on the top on't, Colevile kissing my foot . iv 3 54
Let every man now task his thought, That this fair action may on foot be brought . . . . *Hen. V.* i 2 310

Foot. Comment appelez-vous le pied et la robe?—De foot, madame; et de coun . . . . *Hen. V.* iii 4 54
And her foot, look you, is fixed upon a spherical stone, which rolls . iii 6 37
Swear by her foot, that she may tread out the oath . . . . iii 7 103
Him I forgive my death that killeth me When he sees me go back one foot or fly . . . . *1 Hen. VI.* i 2 21
Nay, stand thou back; I will not budge a foot . . . . . i 3 38
Stoop then and set your knee against my foot . . . . . iii 1 169
Unite Your troops of horsemen with his bands of foot . . . . iv 1 165
Talk no more of flight, it is no boot; If son to Talbot, die at Talbot's foot . . . . iv 6 53
But fear not thou, until thy foot be snared . . . . *2 Hen. VI.* ii 4 56
To mow down thorns that would annoy our foot, Is worthy praise . iii 1 67
My foot shall fight with all the strength thou hast . . . . iv 10 53
And tread it under foot with all contempt . . . . . . v 1 209
This happy day Is not itself, nor have we won one foot, If Salisbury be lost . . . . v 3 6
What valour were it, when a cur doth grin, For one to thrust his hand between his teeth, When he might spurn him with his foot away? *3 Hen. VI.* i 4 58
Who 'scapes the lurking serpent's mortal sting? Not he that sets his foot upon her back . . . . ii 2 16
Wishing his foot were equal with his eye . . . . . . iii 2 137
A pretty foot, A cherry lip, a bonny eye . . . . *Richard III.* i 1 93
I'll strike thee to my foot, And spurn upon thee . . . . . i 2 41
My foreward shall be drawn out all in length, Consisting equally of horse and foot . . . . v 3 294
Thomas Earl of Surrey Shall have the leading of this foot and horse . v 3 297
His horse is slain, and all on foot he fights, Seeking for Richmond . v 4 4
As much as one sound cudgel of four foot . . . could distribute *Hen. VIII.* v 4 19
And 'tis this fever that keeps Troy on foot . . . *Troi. and Cres.* i 3 135
I would thou didst itch from head to foot and I had the scratching of thee . . . . ii 1 30
They clap the lubber Ajax on the shoulder, As if his foot were on brave Hector's breast . . . . iii 3 140
There's language in her eye, her cheek, her lip, Nay, her foot speaks . iv 5 56
Fix thy foot.—Let the first budger die the other's slave! . *Coriolanus* i 8 4
From face to foot He was a thing of blood . . . . . . ii 2 112
The service of the foot Being once gangrened, is not then respected For what before it was . . . . iii 1 306
I'ld with thee every foot . . . . iv 1 57
And to be on foot at an hour's warning . . . . . . iv 3 49
We have a power on foot . . . . iv 5 125
I cannot help it now, Unless, by using means, I lame the foot Of our design . . . . iv 7 7
Come on, my lords, the better foot before . . . . *T. Andron.* ii 3 192
At the first approach you must kneel, then kiss his foot . . . iv 3 111
Thou shalt not stir a foot to seek a foe . . . . *Rom. and Jul.* i 1 87
A hall, a hall! give room! and foot it, girls. More light, you knaves . i 5 28
By her fine foot, straight leg and quivering thigh . . . . . ii 1 19
It is nor hand, nor foot, Nor arm, nor face, nor any other part . . ii 2 40
And all my fortunes at thy foot I'll lay And follow thee my lord . . ii 2 147
And for a hand, and a foot, and a body, though they be not to be talked on, yet they are past compare . . . . ii 5 42
O, so light a foot Will ne'er wear out the everlasting flint . . ii 6 16
So shall no foot upon the churchyard tread . . . But thou shalt hear it v 3 5
What cursed foot wanders this way to-night? . . . . . . v 3 19
Let him slip down, Not one accompanying his declining foot *T. of Athens* i 1 88
Show Lord Timon that mean eyes have seen The foot above the head . i 1 94
It requires swift foot . . . . v 1 231
Set but thy foot Against our rampired gates, and they shall ope . . v 4 46
I will set this foot of mine as far As who goes farthest . . *J. Cæsar* i 3 119
Then you scratch'd your head, And too impatiently stamp'd with your foot . . . . ii 1 244
Set on your foot, And with a heart new-fired I follow you . . . ii 1 331
As low as to thy foot doth Cassius fall, To beg enfranchisement for Publius iii 1 56
Nor our strong sorrow Upon the foot of motion . . . *Macbeth* ii 3 131
I wish your horses swift and sure of foot . . . . . . iii 1 38
Arm'd, my lord.—From top to toe?—My lord, from head to foot *Hamlet* i 2 228
Head to foot Now is he total gules . . . . ii 2 478
Follow him at foot; tempt him with speed aboard; Delay it not . . iv 3 56
Keep thy foot out of brothels, thy hand out of plackets . . *Lear* iii 4 99
Fellows, hold the chair. Upon these eyes of thine I'll set my foot . iii 7 68
You are now within a foot Of the extreme verge . . . . . iv 6 25
How near's the other army?—Near and on speedy foot . . . iv 6 217
From the extremest upward of thy head To the descent and dust below thy foot . . . . v 3 137
He, swift of foot, Outran my purpose . . . . . . *Othello* ii 3 232
At whose foot, To mend the petty present, I will piece Her opulent throne with kingdoms . . . . *Ant. and Cleo.* i 5 44
Our foot Upon the hills adjoining to the city Shall stay with us . iv 10 4
I have nothing Of woman in me: now from head to foot I am marble-constant . . . . v 2 239
Boldness be my friend! Arm me, audacity, from head to foot! . *Cymb.* i 6 19
Two winking Cupids Of silver, each on one foot standing . . . ii 4 90
Thus mine enemy fell, And thus I set my foot on's neck . . . iii 3 92
To the court I'll knock her back, foot her home again . . . iii 5 148
His foot Mercurial; his Martial thigh; The brawns of Hercules . iv 2 310
The holy eagle Stoop'd, as to foot us . . . . v 4 116
Foot of ground. Charge! and give no foot of ground! . . *3 Hen. VI.* i 4 15
Foot of honour. A foot of honour better than I was; But many a many foot of land the worse . . . . *K. John* i 1 182
Foot on foot. A note infallible Of breaking honesty—horsing foot on foot *W. Tale* i 2 288
Foot to foot. We Have used to conquer, standing on the earth, And fighting foot to foot . . . . *Ant. and Cleo.* iii 7 67
Football. That like a football you do spurn me thus . *Com. of Errors* ii 1 83
Nor tripped neither, you base foot-ball player . . . . *Lear* i 4 95
Footboy. And not like a Christian footboy . . . *T. of Shrew* iii 2 72
Like peasant foot-boys do they keep the walls . . *1 Hen. VI.* iii 2 69
Who holds his state at door, 'mongst pursuivants, Pages, and footboys *Hen. VIII.* v 2 25
Wait like a lousy footboy At chamber-door . . . . . . v 3 139
Foot-cloth. Bare-headed plodded by my foot-cloth mule . *2 Hen. VI.* iv 1 54
Thou dost ride in a foot-cloth, dost thou not? . . . . . iv 7 51
Three times to-day my foot-cloth horse did stumble, And startled *Rich. III.* iii 4 86
Footed. He is footed in this land already . . . . *Hen. V.* ii 4 143
There's part of a power already footed . . . . . . *Lear* iii 3 14
Withold footed thrice the old; He met the night-mare, and her nine-fold iii 4 125
What confederacy have you with the traitors Late footed in the kingdom? iii 7 45

Footfall. Then like hedgehogs which Lie tumbling in my barefoot way and mount Their pricks at my footfall . . . . *Tempest* ii 2 12
Footing. These fresh nymphs encounter every one In country footing . iv 1 138
But, hark, I hear the footing of a man . . . . *Mer. of Venice* v 1 24
There your charity would have lacked footing . . *W. Tale* iii 3 114
Shall we, upon the footing of our land, Send fair-play orders? *K. John* v 1 66
Who strongly hath set footing in this land . . . *Richard II.* ii 2 48
As full of peril and adventurous spirit As to o'er-walk a current roaring loud On the unsteadfast footing of a spear. . . . 1 *Hen. IV.* i 3 193
When Talbot hath set footing once in France . . . 1 *Hen. VI.* iii 3 64
Seek not a scorpion's nest, Nor set no footing on this unkind shore 2 *Hen. VI.* iii 2 87
As we paced along Upon the giddy footing of the hatches *Richard III.* i 4 17
That little thought, when she set footing here, She should have bought her dignities so dear . . . . *Hen. VIII.* iii 1 183
'Twixt his stretch'd footing and the scaffoldage . . *Troi. and Cres.* i 3 156
Can it be That so degenerate a strain as this Should once set footing in your generous bosoms? . . . . ii 2 155
Blind fear, that seeing reason leads, finds safer footing than blind reason stumbling without fear . . . . iii 2 77
Whose footing here anticipates our thoughts A se'nnights speed *Othello* ii 1 76
Foot-land rakers. I am joined with no foot-land rakers, no long-staff sixpenny strikers . . . . 1 *Hen. IV.* ii 1 81
Foot-licker. And I, thy Caliban, For aye thy foot-licker . *Tempest* iv 1 219
Footman. By a horseman, or a footman?—A footman, sweet sir, a footman.—Indeed, he should be a footman by the garments he has left with thee . . . . *W. Tale* iv 3 67
And by the waggon-wheel Trot, like a servile footman, all day long *T. An.* v 2 55
Distract your army, which doth most consist Of war-mark'd footmen *Ant. and Cleo.* iii 7 45
Footpath. Jog on, jog on, the foot-path way . . . . *W. Tale* iv 3 132
Both stile and gate, horse-way and foot-path . . . . *Lear* iv 1 58
Footstep. Yet, to avoid deceit, I mean to learn; For it shall strew the footsteps of my rising . . . . *K. John* i 1 216
Footstool. And made our footstool of security . . . 3 *Hen. VI.* v 7 14
Fop. Go to the creating a whole tribe of fops . . . . *Lear* i 2 14
Fopped. I think it is scurvy, and begin to find myself fopped in it *Othello* iv 2 197
Foppery. Drove the grossness of the foppery into a received belief *M. W.* v 5 132
To say the truth, I had as lief have the foppery of freedom as the morality of imprisonment . . . . . *Meas. for Meas.* i 2 138
Let not the sound of shallow foppery enter My sober house *Mer. of Venice* ii 5 35
This is the excellent foppery of the world . . . . *Lear* i 2 128
Foppish. Wise men are grown foppish, They know not how their wits to wear . . . . i 4 182
For. I'll warrant him for drowning . . . . . . *Tempest* i 1 49
To have no screen between this part he play'd And him he play'd it for i 2 108
This Is the third man that e'er I saw, the first That e'er I sigh'd for . i 2 446
Speak not you for him; he's a traitor . . . . . . i 2 460
I will give him some relief, if it be but for that . . . . ii 2 70
I will not take too much for him; he shall pay for him that hath him . ii 2 80
I Have given you here a thrid of mine own life, Or that for which I live iv 1 4
The sheep for fodder follow the shepherd . . . *T. G. of Ver.* i 1 92
I was taken up for laying them down: Yet here they shall not lie, for catching cold . . . . i 2 136
And yet I was last chidden for being too slow . . . . . ii 1 12
I pray thee, out with 't, and place it for her chief virtue . . . iii 1 340
Tell my lady I claim the promise for her heavenly picture . . iv 4 92
To hide our love Till time had made them for us . *Meas. for Meas.* i 2 157
You may not so extenuate his offence For I have had such faults . . ii 1 28
I know him for a man divine and holy; Not scurvy . . . . v 1 144
Those, for their parents were exceeding poor, I bought . *Com. of Errors* i 1 57
My wife . . . Made daily motions for our home return . . . . i 1 60
Forced me to seek delays for them and me. And this it was, for other means was none . . . . i 1 75
Denied my house for his, me for his wife . . . . . . ii 2 161
O, for my beads! I cross me for a sinner . . . . . . ii 2 190
She that doth call me husband, even my soul Doth for a wife abhor . iii 2 164
'Tis for me to be patient; I am in adversity . . . . . iv 4 20
I dare, and do defy thee for a villain . . . . v 1 32
What is he for a fool that betroths himself to unquietness? . *Much Ado* i 3 49
This is not so well as I looked for, but the best that ever I heard.—Ay, the best for the worst . . . . *L. L. Lost* i 1 282
Write, pen; for I am for whole volumes in folio . . . . . i 2 191
I marvel thy master hath not eaten thee for a word . . . . v 1 43
Even such a husband Hast thou of me as she is for a wife *Mer. of Venice* iii 5 89
Why should this a desert be? For it is unpeopled? . . *As Y. Like It* iii 2 134
The rather for I have some sport in hand . . . *T. of Shrew* Ind. 1 91
Though bride and bridegroom wants For to supply the places at the table iii 2 249
The conceit is deeper than you think for . . . . . . iv 3 163
Entreat you That presently you take your way for home . *All's Well* ii 5 69
Lay a more noble thought upon mine honour Than for to think that I would sink it here . . . . v 3 181
But more than that, he loved her: for indeed he was mad for her . v 3 260
You may as well Forbid the sea for to obey the moon . . *W. Tale* i 2 427
And, for the babe Is counted lost for ever, Perdita, I prithee, call't . iii 3 32
And for these great affairs do ask some charge . . . *Richard II.* ii 1 159
How shall we do for money for these wars? . . . . . . ii 2 104
He might have more diseases than he knew for . . . 2 *Hen. IV.* i 2 6
Do, an thou darest for thy heart . . . . ii 4 242
If you look for a good speech now, you undo me: for what I have to say is of mine own making . . . . Epil. 4
These cheeks are pale for watching for your good . . . 2 *Hen. VI.* iv 7 90
My heart for anger burns; I cannot brook it . . . 3 *Hen. VI.* i 1 60
And, for the time shall not seem tedious, I'll tell thee . . . iii 1 9
And, for I should not deal in her soft laws, She did corrupt frail nature iii 2 154
And, for my name of George begins with G, It follows in his thought that I am he. . . . . *Richard III.* i 1 58
Oh for my husband, for my dear lord Edward! . . . . . ii 2 71
To be thus opposite with heaven, For it requires the royal debt it lent you ii 2 95
Of all one pain, save for a night of groans Endured of her . . . iv 4 303
A horse! a horse! my kingdom for a horse! . . . . . . v 4 13
I can watch you for telling how I took the blow . . *Troi. and Cres.* i 2 293
Did curse Against the Volsces, for they had so vilely Yielded *Coriolanus* iii 1 10
Here lacks but your mother for to say amen.—And that would she for twenty thousand more . . . . *T. Andron.* iv 2 44
And move the gods To send down Justice for to wreak our wrongs . iv 3 51
That fair for which love groan'd for and would die . *Rom. and Jul.* ii Prol. 3
My lord, his throat is cut; that I did for him . . . . *Macbeth* iii 4 16
I am for the air; this night I'll spend Unto a dismal and a fatal end . iii 5 20
How wilt thou do for a father?—Nay, how will you do for a husband? iv 2 38
For. If thy speech be sooth, I care not if thou dost for me as much *Macbeth* v 5 41
So much for him. Now for ourself and for this time of meeting *Hamlet* i 2 25
Were you not sent for? Is it your own inclining? . . . . . . ii 2 283
Say on: he's for a jig or a tale of bawdry, or he sleeps . . . ii 2 522
Good my lord, How does your honour for this many a day? . . . iii 1 91
Which for to prevent, I have in quick determination Thus set it down iii 1 175
How now! a rat? Dead, for a ducat, dead! . . . . . . iii 4 23
A pick-axe, and a spade, a spade, For and a shrouding sheet: O, a pit of clay for to be made For such a guest is meet . . . . . v 1 103
A pestilence on him for a mad rogue! . . . . v 1 196
If for I want that glib and oily art, To speak and purpose not . *Lear* i 1 227
If thou be as poor for a subject as he is for a king, thou art poor enough i 4 22
Fellow, I know thee.—What dost thou know me for? . . . . ii 2 14
Heaven defend your good souls, that you think I will your serious and great business scant For she is with me . . . . . *Othello* i 3 269
Haply, for I am black And have not those soft parts of conversation . iii 3 263
They are not ever jealous for the cause, But jealous for they are jealous iii 4 160
Out, fool! I forgive thee for a witch . . . . . *Ant. and Cleo.* i 2 40
Doubt not, sir; I knew it for my bond . . . . i 4 84
The bright day is done, And we are for the dark . . . . . v 2 194
He's for his master, And enemy to my son . . . . *Cymbeline* i 5 28
Thou wouldst have told this tale for virtue, not For such an end . . i 6 143
O, for a horse with wings! . . . . iii 2 50
Then why should we be tender To let an arrogant piece of flesh threat us, . . For we do fear the law? . . . . iv 2 129
And with dead cheeks advise thee to desist For going on death's net *Per.* i 1 40
O'erboard thrown me For to seek my mother . . . . . . iv 2 71
For all. The priest was good enough, for all the old gentleman's saying *As Y. Like It* v 1 3
And yet, for all his wings, the fool was drown'd . . . 3 *Hen. VI.* v 6 20
My father is not dead, for all your saying . . . . *Macbeth* iv 2 37
There are verier knaves desire to live, for all he be a Roman *Cymbeline* v 4 209
For all that, cousin, let him be a handsome fellow . . . *Much Ado* ii 1 57
For all that, an if she did not hate him deadly, she would love him dearly . . . . v 1 177
Then I'll repent, And wish, for all that, that I had not kill'd them *Mer. of Venice* iii 4 73
For all this. Mistress, look out at window, for all this . . . . . ii 5 41
For all this same, I'll hide me hereabout . . . . *Rom. and Jul.* v 3 43
But, for all this, thou shalt have as many dolours for thy daughters *Lear* ii 4 54
For any thing I know . . . . 2 *Hen. IV.* Epil. 31
For aught that I could ever read, Could ever hear . . *M. N. Dream* i 1 132
Nor is he dead, for aught that I can tell . . . . . . iii 2 76
Yet, for aught I see, they are as sick that surfeit with too much *M. of V.* i 2 5
Being perhaps, for aught I see, two and thirty, a pip out *T. of Shrew* i 2 32
It might be yours or hers, for aught I know . . . . *All's Well* v 3 281
Hubert told me he did live.—So, on my soul, he did, for aught he knew *K. John* v 1 43
Hold those justs and triumphs?—For aught I know . . *Richard II.* v 2 53
For aught I see, this city must be famish'd . . . . 1 *Hen. VI.* i 4 68
And may, for aught thou know'st, affected be . . . *T. Andron.* ii 1 28
Honest, my lord!—Honest! ay, honest.—My lord, for aught I know *Oth.* iii 3 104
Who, for aught I know, May be, nor can I think the contrary, As great *Pericles* ii 5 78
For because. Not for because Your brows are blacker . . *W. Tale* ii 1 7
But for because he hath not woo'd me yet . . . . *K. John* ii 1 588
And for because the world is populous . . . . *Richard II.* v 5 3
For it. I'll die for't but some woman had the ring . *Mer. of Venice* v 1 208
To the health of our general!—I am for it . . . . . *Othello* ii 3 89
For long. Which have for long run by the hideous law . *Meas. for Meas.* i 4 63
For my hand, Both our inventions meet and jump in one *T. of Shrew* i 1 194
For my head. I dare not for my head fill my belly . *Meas. for Meas.* iv 3 160
For my life, to break with him about Beatrice . . . . *Much Ado* iii 2 76
Dead, for my life!—Even so; my tale is told . . . *L. L. Lost* v 2 728
Now, for my life, the knave doth court my love . . *T. of Shrew* iii 1 49
No, no, forsooth; I dare not for my life . . . . iv 3 1
I should not for my life but weep with him . . . . 3 *Hen. VI.* i 4 170
Now, for my life, she's wandering to the Tower . . *Richard III.* iv 1 3
For nothing. Where I shall have my music for nothing . . *Tempest* iii 2 154
That chain will I bestow—Be it for nothing but to spite my wife *C. of Er.* iii 1 118
For once. I'll be so bold to break the seal for once . . *T. G. of Ver.* iii 1 139
Farewell at once, for once, for all, and ever . . . *Richard II.* ii 2 148
Why not Ned and I For once allow'd the skilful pilot's charge? 3 *Hen. VI.* v 4 20
My lord, you shall o'er-rule my mind for once . . . *Richard III.* iii 1 57
For that It is not night when I do see your face . . *M. N. Dream* ii 1 220
I hate him for he is a Christian, But more for that in low simplicity He lends out money gratis . . . . *Mer. of Venice* i 3 44
Do not extort thy reasons from this clause, For that I woo *T. Night* iii 1 166
The rather, For that I saw the tyrant's power a-foot . . *Macbeth* iv 3 185
For the best. I hope all's for the best . . . . . 3 *Hen. VI.* iii 3 170
For the heavens, rouse up a brave mind . . . . *Mer. of Venice* ii 2 12
For the nonce. I have cases of buckram for the nonce . . 1 *Hen. IV.* i 2 201
This is a riddling merchant for the nonce . . . . 1 *Hen. VI.* ii 3 57
I'll have prepared him A chalice for the nonce . . . . *Hamlet* iv 7 161
For the world. No, my dear'st love, I would not for the world *Tempest* v 1 173
He'll be forsworn.—Not for the world, fair madam . . *L. L. Lost* ii 1 99
And say thee nay, So thou wilt woo; but else, not for the world *R. and J.* ii 2 97
For why, the fools are mad, if left alone . . . . *T. G. of Ver.* iii 1 99
Trembled and shook; for why, he stamp'd and swore . *T. of Shrew* iii 2 169
For why the senseless brands will sympathize . . . *Richard II.* v 1 46
Overflow'd and drown'd; For why my bowels cannot hide her woes *T. Andron.* iii 1 231
For you. They are for you.—Ay, ay: you writ them, sir, at my request; But I will none of them; they are for you *T. G. of Ver.* ii 1 131
I am for you, though it cost me ten nights' watchings . . *Much Ado* ii 1 386
The most peaceable way for you, if you do take a thief, is to let him show himself . . . . iii 3 61
Sit, sit, and a song.—We are for you: sit i' the middle *As Y. Like It* v 3 10
Nay, if you be an undertaker, I am for you . . . . *T. Night* iii 4 350
Come, sir, now I am for you again . . . . . . *W. Tale* ii 1 22
Quarrel, sir! no, sir.—If you do, sir, I am for you . . *Rom. and Jul.* i 1 61
Sir, I am for you.—Keep up your bright swords . . . . *Othello* i 2 58
But one cup: I'll drink for you . . . . ii 3 39
For your lives. Stir not, for your lives . . . . . 2 *Hen. VI.* iii 4 18
Forage. And he from forage will incline to play . . . *L. L. Lost* iv 1 93
Forage, and run To meet displeasure farther from the doors . *K. John* v 1 59
Stood smiling to behold his lion's whelp Forage in blood . . *Hen. V.* i 2 110
Forager. When that the general is not like the hive To whom the foragers shall all repair, What honey is expected? . . . *Troi. and Cres.* i 3 82

Forbade. He swears she's a witch; forbade her my house . *Mer. Wives* iv 2 88
Forbad my tongue to speak of Mortimer . . . . . 1 *Hen. IV.* i 3 220
Coriolanus He would not answer to: forbad all names . *Coriolanus* v 1 12
Forbear. Better forbear till Proteus make return . . *T. G. of Ver.* ii 7 14
Villain, forbear.—Why, sir, I'll strike nothing . . . . . iii 1 202
Love, lend me patience to forbear awhile . . . . . v 4 27
Forbear, forbear, I say! it is my lord the duke . . . . v 4 122
Villany, take your rapier.—Forbear; here's company . *Mer. Wives* ii 3 17
Focative is caret.—And that's a good root.—'Oman, forbear . . iv 1 57
This nor hurts him nor profits you a jot; Forbear it therefore *M. for M.* iv 3 129
Till he come home again, I would forbear . . *Com. of Errors* ii 1 31
To hear? or forbear laughing?—To hear meekly, sir, and to laugh moderately; or to forbear both . . . . . *L. L. Lost* i 1 198
I say, sing.—Forbear till this company be past . . . . i 2 131
Peace, peace! forbear: Your oath once broke, you force not to forswear v 2 439
In choosing wrong, I lose your company: therefore forbear awhile . *Mer. of Venice* iii 2 3
Forbear, and eat no more.—Why, I have eat none yet . *As Y. Like It* ii 7 88
But forbear, I say: He dies that touches any of this fruit . . ii 7 97
Forbear your food a little while, Whiles, like a doe, I go to find my fawn ii 7 127
Fiddler, forbear; you grow too forward, sir . . . *T. of Shrew* iii 1 1
I can hardly forbear hurling things at him . . . . *T. Night* iii 2 87
Let no man mock me, For I will kiss her.—Good my lord, forbear *W. Tale* v 3 80
Either forbear, Quit presently the chapel, or resolve you For more amazement . . . . v 3 85
Bagot, forbear; thou shalt not take it up . . . . *Richard II.* iv 1 30
Canst thou not forbear me half an hour? . . . . 2 *Hen. IV.* iv 5 110
My lord, it were your duty to forbear . . . . 1 *Hen VI.* iii 1 52
If you love me, as you say you do, Let me persuade you to forbear awhile iii 1 105
Forbear! for that which we have fled During the life, let us not wrong it dead . . . . iv 7 49
Ah, Nell, forbear! thou aimest all awry . . . . . 2 *Hen. VI.* ii 4 58
Lay not thy hands on me; forbear, I say; Their touch affrights me . iii 2 46
So bad a death argues a monstrous life.—Forbear to judge . . iii 3 31
Unless you be possess'd with devilish spirits, You cannot but forbear to murder me . . . . iv 7 81
Let this my sword report what speech forbears . . . . iv 10 57
Forbear awhile; we'll hear a little more . . . . 3 *Hen. VI.* iii 1 27
My lords, forbear this talk; here comes the king . . . . iv 1 6
My love, forbear to fawn upon their frowns . . . . . iv 1 75
And withal Forbear your conference with the noble duke *Richard III.* i 1 104
Forbear to sleep the nights, and fast the days . . . . iv 4 118
This is too much; Forbear, for shame, my lords . . . *Hen. VIII.* v 3 86
Villains, forbear! we are the empress' sons . . . *T. Andron.* v 2 163
Gentlemen, for shame, forbear this outrage! . . . *Rom. and Jul.* iii 1 90
Meantime forbear, And let mischance be slave to patience . . v 3 220
For love of God, forbear him . . . . *Hamlet* v 1 296
O, vassal! miscreant!—Dear sir, forbear . . . . . . *Lear* i 1 164
At my entreaty forbear his presence till some little time hath qualified the heat of his displeasure . . . . i 2 175
I'll forbear; And am fall'n out with my more headier will . . . ii 4 110
With the little godliness I have, I did full hard forbear him . *Othello* i 2 10
Rub him about the temples.—No, forbear . . . . . . iv 1 53
Forbear me. There's a great spirit gone! . . . *Ant. and Cleo.* i 2 125
Tempt him not so too far; I wish, forbear . . . . . i 3 11
Forbear; And give true evidence to his love, which stands An honourable trial . . . . i 3 73
Hear me speak a word.—Forbear me till anon . . . . . . ii 7 44
I could well forbear't. It's monstrous labour, when I wash my brain ii 7 104
We must forbear: here comes the gentleman . . . . *Cymbeline* i 1 68
Beseech your majesty, Forbear sharp speeches . . . . . iii 5 39
Ghost unlaid forbear thee!—Nothing ill come near thee! . . . iv 2 278
Peace, peace! see further; he eyes us not; forbear . . . . v 5 124
For honour's cause, forbear your suffrages: If that you love Prince Pericles, forbear . . . . *Pericles* ii 4 41
A twelvemonth longer, let me entreat you to Forbear the absence of your king . . . . ii 4 46
Forbearance. I shall crave your forbearance a little . *Meas. for Meas.* iv 1 22
True noblesse would Learn him forbearance from so foul a wrong *Rich. II.* iv 1 120
Tut, tut, here is a mannerly forbearance . . . . 1 *Hen. VI.* ii 4 19
Have a continent forbearance till the speed of his rage goes slower *Lear* i 2 182
One of your great knowing Should learn, being taught, forbearance *Cymb.* ii 3 103
Me of my lawful pleasure she restrain'd And pray'd me oft forbearance ii 5 10
Forbid. And oftentimes have purposed to forbid Sir Valentine her company and my court . . . . *T. G. of Ver.* iii 1 26
An old cozening quean! Have I not forbid her my house? *Mer. Wives* iv 2 181
That do coin heaven's image In stamps that are forbid . *Meas. for Meas.* ii 4 46
What, wilt thou flout me thus unto my face, Being forbid? *Com. of Errors* i 2 92
God forbid it should be so.—If my passion change not shortly, God forbid it should be otherwise . . . . *Much Ado* i 1 219
Where honeysuckles, ripen'd by the sun, Forbid the sun to enter . . iii 1 9
As to show a child his new coat and forbid him to wear it . . . iii 2 7
I will swear to study so, To know the thing I am forbid to know *L. L. L.* i 1 60
To study where I well may dine, When I to feast expressly am forbid . i 1 62
Though the mourning brow of progeny Forbid the smiling courtesy of love . . . . v 2 755
When thou wakest, let love forbid Sleep his seat on thy eyelid *M. N. D.* ii 2 80
As well forbid the mountain pines To wag their high tops *Mer. of Venice* iv 1 75
And I expressly am forbid to touch it, For it engenders choler *T. of S.* iv 1 174
Let it be forbid, sir; so should I be a great deal of his act . *All's Well* iv 3 54
Fortune forbid my outside have not charm'd her! . . . *T. Night* ii 2 19
Deceived In that which seems so.—Be it forbid, my lord! . *W. Tale* i 2 241
You may as well Forbid the sea for to obey the moon . . . . i 2 427
The higher powers forbid! . . . . iii 2 203
How can the law forbid my tongue to curse? . . . . *K. John* iii 1 190
From whose obedience I forbid my soul . . . . iv 3 64
Now, afore God—God forbid I say true! . . . . . *Richard II.* ii 1 200
Now God in heaven forbid!—Ah, madam, 'tis too true . . . ii 2 51
The king of heaven forbid our lord the king Should so with civil and uncivil arms Be rush'd upon! . . . . iii 3 101
And thou shalt know The treason that my haste forbids me show . . v 3 50
He forbids it, Being free from vainness and self-glorious pride *Hen. V.* v Prol. 19
I may not open; The Cardinal of Winchester forbids . . 1 *Hen. VI.* i 3 19
And therefore do they cry, though you forbid . . 2 *Hen. VI.* iii 2 264
And when thou fail'st—as God forbid the hour!—Must Edward fall 3 *Hen. VI.* ii 1 190
If she be obdurate To mild entreaties, God in heaven forbid We should infringe the holy privilege Of blessed sanctuary! . . *Richard III.* iii 1 40
Entreats.—That at her hands which the king's King forbids . . iv 4 346
The leisure and enforcement of the time Forbids to dwell upon . . v 3 239

Forbid. Will the king Digest this letter of the cardinal's? The Lord forbid! . . . . *Hen. VIII.* iii 2 54
Now heavens forbid such scarcity of youth! . . . *Troi. and Cres.* i 3 302
And Jove forbid there should be done amongst us Such things! . . . ii 2 127
Jupiter forbid, And say in thunder 'Achilles go to him' . . . ii 3 208
The obligation of our blood forbids A gory emulation 'twixt us twain . iv 5 122
Give me leave To take that course by your consent and voice, Which you do here forbid me . . . . v 3 75
Shall I be married then to-morrow morning? No, no: this shall forbid it: lie thou there . . . . *Rom. and Jul.* iv 3 23
Join with me to forbid him her resort; Myself have spoke in vain *T. of A.* i 1 127
He shall live a man forbid . . . . *Macbeth* i 3 21
You should be women, And yet your beards forbid me to interpret That you are so . . . . i 3 46
I am forbid To tell the secrets of my prison-house . . . . *Hamlet* i 5 13
Too much of water hast thou, poor Ophelia, And therefore I forbid my tears . . . . iv 7 187
This courtesy, forbid thee, shall the duke Instantly know . . *Lear* iii 3 22
Stay till I have read the letter.—I was forbid it . . . . . v 1 47
The heavens forbid But that our loves and comforts should increase! *Oth.* ii 1 195
And to ourselves do that Which heaven hath forbid the Ottomites . . ii 3 171
Are you hurt, lieutenant?—Ay, past all surgery.—Marry, heaven forbid! ii 3 261
My leg is cut in two.—Marry, heaven forbid! . . . . . v 1 72
You shall paint when you are old.—Wrinkles forbid! . *Ant. and Cleo.* i 2 19
Heaven forbid That kings should let their ears hear their faults hid! *Per.* i 2 61
Pray see me buried.—Die quoth-a? Now gods forbid! . . . . ii 1 82
God forbid! *Mer. of Venice* ii 2; *T. of Shrew* iv 2; v 1; *Richard II.* iv 1; 1 *Hen. IV.* v 2; v 4; 2 *Hen. IV.* v 1; *Hen. V.* i 2; 2 *Hen. VI.* iii 2; iv 4; 3 *Hen. VI.* i 2; iii 2; iv 1; v 4; *Richard III.* iii 7; *Hen. VIII.* ii 2; *T. Andron.* iv 3; *Rom. and Jul.* i 3
The gods forbid! *M. N. Dream* iii 2; *All's Well* iii 5; *Troi. and Cres.* v 10; *Coriolanus* iii 1; *Ant. and Cleo.* iv 2; v 2
Forbidden. A needful course, Before we enter his forbidden gates *L. L. L.* ii 1 26
Why have those banish'd and forbidden legs Dared once to touch a dust of England's ground? . . . . *Richard II.* ii 3 90
Forbidden late to carry any weapon, Have fill'd their pockets full of pebble stones . . . . 1 *Hen. VI.* iii 1 79
If we be forbidden stones, we'll fall to it with our teeth . . . . iii 1 89
The prince expressly hath Forbidden bandying in Verona streets *R. and J.* iii 1 92
Forbiddenly. That you have touch'd his queen Forbiddenly . *W. Tale* i 2 417
Forborne the getting of a lawful race . . . . . . *Ant. and Cleo.* iii 13 107
Force. What a fool is she, that knows I am a maid, And would not force the letter to my view! . . . . *T. G. of Ver.* i 2 54
Which, unreversed, stands in effectual force . . . . . . iii 1 223
Much is the force of heaven-bred poesy . . . . iii 2 72
I'll woo you like a soldier, at arms' end, And love you 'gainst the nature of love,—force ye . . . . v 4 58
I'll force thee yield to my desire.—Ruffian, let go . . . . . v 4 59
Has he affections in him, That thus can make him bite the law by the nose, When he would force it? . . . . . *Meas. for Meas.* iii 1 110
By and by rude fishermen of Corinth By force took Dromio *Com. of Er.* v 1 352
Never could maintain his part but in the force of his will . *Much Ado* i 1 239
And take her hearing prisoner with the force And strong encounter of my amorous tale . . . . i 1 326
Our late edict shall strongly stand in force . . . . *L. L. Lost* i 1 11
We must of force dispense with this decree . . . . . . i 1 148
Peace! forbear: Your oath once broke, you force not to forswear . . v 2 440
On whose eyes I might approve This flower's force in stirring love *M. N. Dream* ii 2 69
And thy fair virtue's force perforce doth move me . . . . . iii 1 143
That, when he waked, of force she must be eyed . . . . . iii 2 40
Dian's bud o'er Cupid's flower Hath such force and blessed power . iv 1 79
Even in the force and road of casualty . . . *Mer. of Venice* ii 9 30
Of force Must yield to such inevitable shame As to offend . . . iv 1 56
Fie upon your law! There is no force in the decrees of Venice . . iv 1 102
His sceptre shows the force of temporal power . . . . . iv 1 190
Dear sir, of force I must attempt you further . . . . . . iv 1 421
Your gentleness shall force More than your force move us *As Y. Like It* ii 7 102
I am sure, there is no force in eyes That can do hurt . . . . iii 5 26
All the secrets of our camp I'll show, Their force, their purposes *All's W.* iv 1 94
When oil and fire, too strong for reason's force, O'erbears it and burns on v 3 7
Fate, show thy force: ourselves we do not owe . . . *T. Night* i 5 329
To force that on you, in a shameful cunning, Which you knew none of yours . . . . iii 1 127
Force me to keep you as a prisoner, Not like a guest . . *W. Tale* i 2 52
Force her hence.—Let him that makes but trifles of his eyes First hand me . . . . ii 3 61
Had force and knowledge More than was ever man's . . . . . iv 4 385
Who of force must know The royal fool thou copest with . . . iv 4 434
Shall then my father's will be of no force To dispossess that child which is not his?—Of no more force to dispossess me, sir, Than was his will to get me . . . . *K. John* i 1 130
Against whose fury and unmatched force The aweless lion could not wage the fight . . . . i 1 265
Then turn your forces from this paltry siege . . . . . . ii 1 54
His marches are expedient to this town, His forces strong . . . ii 1 61
Use our commission in his utmost force . . . . iii 3 11
For do we must what force will have us do . . . *Richard II.* iii 3 207
Will this content you, Kate?—It must of force . . . 1 *Hen. IV.* ii 3 120
Some twelve days hence Our general forces at Bridgenorth shall meet . iii 2 178
I am sorry I should force you to believe That which I would to God I had not seen . . . . 2 *Hen. IV.* i 1 105
Who is it like should lead his forces hither? . . . . i 3 81
What is the news, my lord?—Come all his forces back? . . . . ii 1 185
And put the world's whole strength Into one giant arm, it shall not force This lineal honour from me . . . . iv 5 45
On your imaginary forces work . . . . *Hen. V.* Prol. 18
O noble English, that could entertain With half their forces the full pride of France! . . . . i 2 112
That my great-grandfather Never went with his forces into France . i 2 147
Pouring, like the tide into a breach, With ample and brim fulness of his force . . . . i 2 150
Linger your patience on; and we'll digest The abuse of distance; force a play . . . . ii Prol. 32
Will cut their passage through the force of France . . . . . ii 2 16
Est-il impossible d'échapper la force de ton bras? . . . . . iv 4 17
Where is my strength, my valour, and my force? . . . 1 *Hen. VI.* i 5 1
A witch, by fear, not force, like Hannibal, Drives back our troops . i 5 21
If it chance the one of us do fail, The other yet may rise against their force . . . . ii 1 32

Force. And those occasions, uncle, were of force . . 1 *Hen. VI.* iii 1 157
But gather we our forces out of hand And set upon our boasting enemy iii 2 102
My forces and my power of men are yours . . . iii 3 83
All our general force Might with a sally of the very town Be buckled with . . . iv 4 3
Who with me Set from our o'ermatch'd forces forth for aid . . . iv 4 11
The fraud of England, not the force of France, Hath now entrapp'd the noble-minded Talbot . . . iv 4 36
That pure blood of mine Which thou didst force from Talbot, my brave boy . . . iv 6 24
Whether it be through force of your report . . . v 5 79
Maine is lost; That Maine which by main force Warwick did win 2 *Hen. VI.* i 1 210
Give me leave To show some reason, of no little force . . . i 3 166
Which now they hold by force and not by right . . . ii 2 30
Or like an overcharged gun, recoil, And turn the force of them upon thyself . . . iii 2 332
Stafford and his brother are hard by, with the king's forces . . . iv 2 122
Or dare to bring thy force so near the court . . . v 1 22
Then what intends these forces thou dost bring? . . . v 1 60
To do a murderous deed, to rob a man, To force a spotless virgin's chastity . . . v 1 186
For hither we have broken in by force . . . 3 *Hen. VI.* i 1 29
Well hath Clifford play'd the orator, Inferring arguments of mighty force ii 2 44
And force the tyrant from his seat by war . . . iii 3 206
There shall I rest secure from force and fraud . . . iv 4 33
Away betimes, before his forces join, And take the great-grown traitor unawares . . . iv 8 62
At Southam I did leave him with his forces . . . v 1 9
Nay, rather, wilt thou draw thy forces hence? . . . v 1 25
George of Clarence sweeps along, Of force enough to bid his brother battle . . . v 1 77
Sweetly in force unto her fair life's end . . . *Richard III.* iv 4 351
Thus doth he force the swords of wicked men To turn their own points on their masters' bosoms . . . v 1 23
O Thou, whose captain I account myself, Look on my forces with a gracious eye! . . . v 3 109
The force of his own merit makes his way . . . *Hen. VIII.* i 1 64
Free pardon to each man that has denied The force of this commission . i 2 101
Now unite in your complaints, And force them with a constancy . iii 2 2
The rude son should strike his father dead: Force should be right *Troi. and Cres.* i 3 116
Force him with praises: pour in, pour in; his ambition is dry . ii 3 232
Shall more obey than to the edge of steel Or force of Greekish sinews . iii 1 166
I'll play the hunter for thy life With all my force, pursuit and policy . iv 1 18
Time, force, and death, Do to this body what extremes you can . iv 2 107
With such a careless force and forceless care . . . v 5 40
Where I thought to crush him in an equal force, True sword to sword, I'll potch at him . . . *Coriolanus* i 10 14
As for my country I have shed my blood, Not fearing outward force . iii 1 77
Why force you this?—Because that now it lies you on to speak . iii 2 51
Mine ears against your suits are stronger than Your gates against my force . . . v 2 95
And strike her home by force, if not by words . . . *T. Andron.* ii 1 118
Being the time the potion's force should cease . *Rom. and Jul.* v 3 249
What heart, head, sword, force, means, but is Lord Timon's? *T. of Athens* ii 2 176
Yet our old love made a particular force, And made us speak like friends v 2 8
Good reasons must, of force, give place to better . *J. Cæsar* iv 3 203
What soldiers, whey-face?—The English force, so please you . *Macbeth* v 3 18
In a dream of passion, Could force his soul so to his own conceit *Hamlet* ii 2 579
The power of beauty will sooner transform honesty from what it is to a bawd than the force of honesty can translate beauty into his likeness iii 1 113
And what's in prayer but this two-fold force? . . . iii 3 48
Return, and force Their scanted courtesy . . . *Lear* iii 2 66
Here is the guess of their true strength and forces By diligent discovery v 1 52
Made friends of them, jointing their force 'gainst Cæsar . *Ant. and Cleo.* i 2 96
Labienus—This is stiff news—hath, with his Parthian force, Extended Asia from Euphrates . . . i 2 104
Our force by land Hath nobly held; our sever'd navy too Have knit again . . . iii 13 169
To-night I'll force The wine peep through their scars . . . iii 13 190
His best force Is forth to man his galleys . . . iv 11 2
Yea, very force entangles Itself with strength: seal then, and all is done iv 14 48
I will try the forces Of these thy compounds on such creatures *Cymbeline* i 5 18
Whose every touch would force the feeler's soul To the oath of loyalty . i 6 101
This secret Will force him think I have pick'd the lock and ta'en The treasure . . . ii 2 41
Is Lucius general of the forces?—Ay.—Remaining now in Gallia? . iii 7 11
But now my heavy conscience sinks my knee, As then your force did . v 5 414
With hostile forces he'll o'erspread the land . . . *Pericles* i 2 24
The common body, By you relieved, would force me to my duty . iii 3 22
Force perforce Keep Stephen Langton . . . from that holy see *K. John* iii 1 142
As the state stood then, Was force perforce compell'd to banish him 2 *Hen. IV.* iv 1 116
With venom of suggestion—As, force perforce, the age will pour it in . iv 4 46
And, force perforce, I'll make him yield the crown . . . 2 *Hen. VI.* i 1 258
Forced. That would have forced your honour and your love *T. G. of Ver.* v 4 22
She doth evitate and shun A thousand irreligious cursed hours, Which forced marriage would have brought upon her . *Mer. Wives* v 5 243
He hath forced me to tell him he is indeed Justice . *Meas. for Meas.* iii 2 268
Forced me to seek delays for them and me . *Com. of Errors* i 1 75
That I am forced to lay my reverence by . . . *Much Ado* v 1 64
I must, forsooth, be forced To give my hand opposed against my heart *T. of Shrew* iii 2 8
For ever Unvenerable be thy hands, if thou Takest up the princess by that forced baseness Which he has put upon't! . *W. Tale* ii 3 78
With these forced thoughts, I prithee, darken not The mirth o' the feast iv 4 41
'Tis not a visitation framed, but forced By need and accident . v 1 91
His little kingdom of a forced grave . . . *K. John* iv 2 98
Like the forced gait of a shuffling nag . . . 1 *Hen. IV.* iii 1 135
But he hath forced us to compel this offer . . . 2 *Hen. IV.* iv 1 147
And on it have bestow'd more contrite tears Than from it issued forced drops of blood . . . *Hen. V.* iv 1 314
The pretty and sweet manner of it forced Those waters from me . iv 6 28
For what is wedlock forced but a hell, An age of discord? . 1 *Hen. VI.* v 5 62
Enforced thee! art thou king, and wilt be forced? . . 3 *Hen. VI.* i 1 230
Now sways it this way, like a mighty sea Forced by the tide to combat with the wind; Now sways it that way, like the selfsame sea Forced to retire by fury of the wind . . . ii 5 6
A banish'd man, And forced to live in Scotland a forlorn . . iii 3 26

Forced. Which forced such way, That many mazed considerings did throng *Hen. VIII.* ii 4 184
Thou hast forced me, Out of thy honest truth, to play the woman . iii 2 429
Wit larded with malice and malice forced with wit . *Troi. and Cres.* v 1 64
That I was forced to wheel Three or four miles about . *Coriolanus* i 6 19
'Tis the first time that ever I was forced to scold . . . v 6 106
Forced in the ruthless, vast, and gloomy woods . . *T. Andron.* iv 1 53
Cursed be that heart that forced us to this shift! . . . iv 1 72
Her spotless chastity, Inhuman traitors, you constrain'd and forced . v 2 178
Would I were gently put out of office Before I were forced out! *T. of A.* i 2 208
The people . . . Do stand but in a forced affection . . . *J. Cæsar* iv 3 205
Were they not forced with those that should be ours, We might have met them dareful, beard to beard . . . *Macbeth* v 5 5
Nor windy suspiration of forced breath . . . *Hamlet* i 2 79
Of deaths put on by cunning and forced cause . . . v 2 394
With others whom the rigour of our state Forced to cry out . *Lear* v 1 23
Did you by indirect and forced courses Subdue and poison this young maid's affections? . . . *Othello* i 3 111
So shall I clothe me in a forced content . . . iii 4 120
Of thy intents desires instruction, That she preparedly may frame herself To the way she's forced to . . . *Ant. and Cleo.* v 1 56
In their thick breaths, Rank of gross diet, shall we be enclouded, And forced to drink their vapour . . . v 2 213
Forceful. But rather follow Our forceful instigation . *W. Tale* ii 1 163
Forceless. With such a careless force and forceless care . *Troi. and Cres.* v 5 40
Forcible. Thou hast frighted the word out of his right sense, so forcible is thy wit . . . *Much Ado* v 2 56
Let that suffice, most forcible Feeble . . . 2 *Hen. IV.* iii 2 179
But I have reasons strong and forcible . . . 3 *Hen. VI.* i 2 3
Forcibly. Enforce these rights so forcibly withheld . . . *K. John* i 1 18
Forcibly prevents Our lock'd embrasures . . . *Troi. and Cres.* iv 4 38
Forcing. These proclamations, So forcing faults upon Hermione, I little like . . . *W. Tale* iii 1 16
If your pure maidens fall into the hand Of hot and forcing violation *Hen. V.* iii 3 21
Most like a gentleman.—But with much forcing of his disposition *Hamlet* iii 1 12
Ford. Which of you know Ford of this town? . . . *Mer. Wives* i 3 39
Briefly, I do mean to make love to Ford's wife . . . i 3 48
Go bear thou this letter to Mistress Page; and thou this to Mistress Ford . . . i 3 81
And I to Ford shall eke unfold How Falstaff, varlet vile, His dove will prove . . . i 3 105
What? thou liest! Sir Alice Ford! These knights will hack . . ii 1 51
Letter for letter, but that the name of Page and Ford differs! . ii 1 72
He wooes both high and low, both rich and poor, Both young and old, one with another, Ford . . . ii 1 118
He loves the gallimaufry: Ford, perpend.—Love my wife! . . ii 1 119
There is one Mistress Ford, sir:—I pray, come a little nearer this ways ii 2 45
Well, Mistress Ford; what of her?—Why, sir, she's a good creature . ii 2 55
Master Ford, her husband, will be from home . . . ii 2 91
Has Ford's wife and Page's wife acquainted each other how they love me? . . . ii 2 113
Mistress Ford and Mistress Page, have I encompassed you? . . ii 2 158
There is a gentlewoman in this town; her husband's name is Ford . ii 2 199
As to lay an amiable siege to the honesty of this Ford's wife . ii 2 244
As I am a gentleman, you shall, if you will, enjoy Ford's wife . ii 2 265
Want no Mistress Ford, Master Brook; you shall want none . . ii 2 270
I am blest in your acquaintance. Do you know Ford, sir? . . ii 2 280
I would you knew Ford, sir, that you might avoid him if you saw him . ii 2 288
I must excuse myself, Master Ford.—And so must I, sir . . iii 2 54
Sir John is come in at your back-door, Mistress Ford . . iii 3 25
Mistress Ford, I cannot cog, I cannot prate, Mistress Ford . . iii 3 50
Mistress Ford, Mistress Ford! here's Mistress Page at the door . iii 3 92
O Mistress Ford, what have you done? You're shamed! . . iii 3 101
O well-a-day, Mistress Ford! having an honest man to your husband, to give him such cause of suspicion! . . . iii 3 106
Help to cover your master, boy. Call your men, Mistress Ford . iii 3 152
Good Master Ford, be contented: you wrong yourself too much . iii 3 177
You use me well, Master Ford, do you? . . . iii 3 215
You do yourself mighty wrong, Master Ford.—Ay, ay; I must bear it. iii 3 222
Fie, fie, Master Ford! are you not ashamed? . . . iii 3 229
Mistress Ford! I have had ford enough; I was thrown into the ford; I have my belly full of ford . . . iii 5 36
You come to know what hath passed between me and Ford's wife? . iii 5 63
Comes in one Mistress Page; gives intelligence of Ford's approach; and, in her invention and Ford's wife's distraction, they conveyed me into a buck-basket . . . iii 5 86
A couple of Ford's knaves, his hinds, were called forth by their mistress iii 5 99
You shall cuckold Ford.—Hum! ha! is this a vision? . . iii 5 140
Awake, Master Ford! there's a hole made in your best coat, Master Ford . . . iii 5 143
Is he at Master Ford's already, think'st thou?—Sure he is by this . iv 1 1
Mistress Ford desires you to come suddenly . . . iv 1 5
Mistress Ford, your sorrow hath eaten up my sufferance . . iv 2 1
Not only, Mistress Ford, in the simple office of love . . iv 2 4
What, ho, gossip Ford! what, ho!—Step into the chamber, Sir John . iv 2 9
Three of Master Ford's brothers watch the door with pistols . iv 2 52
Why, this passes, Master Ford; you are not to go loose any longer . iv 2 127
Indeed, Master Ford, this is not well, indeed.—So say I too, sir . iv 2 132
Mistress Ford, the honest woman, the modest wife . . . iv 2 135
Master Ford, you must pray, and not follow the imaginations of your own heart . . . iv 2 162
As jealous as Ford, that searched a hollow walnut for his wife's leman iv 2 170
Go, Mistress Ford, Send quickly to Sir John, to know his mind . iv 4 82
Mistress Ford, good heart, is beaten black and blue . . iv 5 114
That same knave Ford, her husband, hath the finest mad devil of jealousy . . . v 1 19
I'll tell you strange things of this knave Ford . . . v 1 30
He hath enjoyed nothing of Ford's but his buck-basket, his cudgel . v 5 116
You yet shall hold your word; For he to-night shall lie with Mistress Ford . . . v 5 259
Through fire and through flame, and through ford and whirlipool . *Lear* iii 4 53
Fordid. To lay the blame upon her own despair, That she fordid herself v 3 255
Fordo. This is the very ecstasy of love, Whose violent property fordoes itself . . . *Hamlet* ii 1 103
The corse they follow did with desperate hand Fordo it own life . v 1 244
This is the night That either makes me or fordoes me quite . *Othello* v 1 129
Fordone. All with weary task fordone . . . *M. N. Dream* v 1 381
Your eldest daughters have fordone themselves . . . *Lear* v 3 291
Fore-advised. Thus to have said, As you were fore-advised . *Coriolanus* ii 3 199

Forecast. Alas, that Warwick had no more forecast! . . . 3 *Hen. VI.* v 1 42

Fore-end. Where I have lived at honest freedom, paid More pious debts to heaven than in all The fore-end of my time . . . *Cymbeline* iii 3 73

Forefather. Conceit is still derived From some forefather grief *Rich. II.* ii 2 35

Our forefathers had no other books but the score and the tally 2 *Hen. VI.* iv 7 37

If I digg'd up thy forefathers' graves And hung their rotten coffins up in chains, It could not slake mine ire, nor ease my heart. 3 *Hen. VI.* i 3 27

And madly play with my forefathers' joints . . . *Rom. and Jul.* iv 3 51

Forefinger. As Tib's rush for Tom's forefinger . . . *All's Well* ii 2 24

No bigger than an agate-stone On the fore-finger of an alderman *R. and J.* i 4 56

Forefoot. Give me thy fist, thy fore-foot to me give . . . *Hen. V.* ii 1 71

Forego. Do not, for one repulse, forego the purpose . . . *Tempest* iii 3 12

Or the light loss of England for a friend: Forego the easier . *K. John* iii 1 207

My native English now I must forego . . . . . *Richard II.* i 3 160

My manors, rents, revenues I forego . . . . . iv 1 212

Let us not forego That for a trifle that was bought with blood! 1 *Hen. VI.* iv 1 149

Must I needs forgo So good, so noble and so true a master? *Hen. VIII.* iii 2 422

I am unarm'd; forego this vantage, Greek . . . *Troi. and Cres.* v 8 9

Quite forego The way which promises assurance . . *Ant. and Cleo.* iii 7 46

Foregoer. Honours thrive, When rather from our acts we them derive Than our foregoers . . . . *All's Well* ii 3 144

Foregone. By our remembrances of days foregone . . . . i 3 140

Lost all my mirth, forgone all custom of exercises . . . *Hamlet* ii 2 308

But this denoted a foregone conclusion . . . . . *Othello* iii 3 428

Forehand. And so extenuate the 'forehand sin . . . *Much Ado* iv 1 51

Carried you a forehand shaft a fourteen and fourteen and a half 2 *Hen. IV.* iii 2 52

Had the fore-hand and vantage of a king . . . . *Hen. V.* iv 1 297

Whom opinion crowns The sinew and the forehand of our host *Tr. and Cr.* i 3 143

Forehead. Apes With foreheads villanous low . . . *Tempest* iv 1 250

But her forehead's low, and mine's as high . . . *T. G. of Ver.* iv 4 198

And so buffets himself on the forehead . . . *Mer. Wives* iv 2 26

Where France?—In her forehead . . . . *Com. of Errors* iii 2 126

I will have a recheat winded in my forehead . . . *Much Ado* i 1 243

Pluck off the bull's horns and set them in my forehead . . . . i 1 266

Ill, to example ill, Would from my forehead wipe a perjured note *L. L. L.* iv 3 125

Nor did not with unbashful forehead woo The means of weakness *As Y. Like It* ii 3 50

So is the forehead of a married man more honourable than the bare brow of a bachelor . . . . iii 3 60

He shall be whipped through the army with this rhyme in's forehead *All's Well* iv 3 263

The expressure of his eye, forehead, and complexion . *T. Night* ii 3 171

Copy of the father, eye, nose, lip, The trick of's frown, his forehead *W. Tale* ii 3 100

In his forehead sits A bare-ribb'd death . . . . *K. John* v 2 176

To look with forehead bold and big enough . . . . 2 *Hen. IV.* i 3 8

Hidest thou that forehead with a golden crown? . . *Richard III.* iv 4 140

Would not lose So rich advantage of a promised glory As smiles upon the forehead of this action . . . . . *Troi. and Cres.* ii 2 205

By my troth, sweet lord, thou hast a fine forehead . . . . iii 1 117

Look'd not lovelier Than Hector's forehead when it spit forth blood *Cor.* i 3 45

One that converses more with the buttock of the night than with the forehead of the morning . . . . ii 1 57

By Rosaline's bright eyes, By her high forehead and her scarlet lip *Rom. and Jul.* ii 1 18

We ourselves compell'd Even to the teeth and forehead of our faults, To give in evidence . . . . *Hamlet* iii 3 63

Takes off the rose From the fair forehead of an innocent love . . iii 4 43

I have a pain upon my forehead here.—'Faith, that's with watching *Oth.* iii 3 284

And her forehead As low as she would wish it . . *Ant. and Cleo.* iii 3 36

Forehorse. I shall stay here the forehorse to a smock . . *All's Well* ii 1 30

Foreign. The watery kingdom, whose ambitious head Spits in the face of heaven, is no bar To stop the foreign spirits . . *Mer. of Venice* ii 7 46

And choice breeds A native slip to us from foreign seeds . *All's Well* i 3 152

Still secure And confident from foreign purposes . . *K. John* ii 1 28

Never such a power For any foreign preparation Was levied . . . iv 2 111

My state is braved, Even at my gates, with ranks of foreign powers . iv 2 244

Swearing allegiance and the love of soul To stranger blood, to foreign royalty . . . . v 1 11

Must I not serve a long apprenticehood To foreign passages? *Richard II.* i 3 272

And sigh'd my English breath in foreign clouds . . . . iii 1 20

Be it thy course to busy giddy minds With foreign quarrels 2 *Hen. IV.* iv 5 215

That he should, for a foreign purse, so sell His sovereign's life *Hen. V.* ii 2 10

May it be possible, that foreign hire Could out of thee extract one spark of evil That might annoy my finger? . . . . . . ii 2 100

One drop of blood drawn from thy country's bosom Should grieve thee more than streams of foreign gore . . . . 1 *Hen. VI.* iii 3 55

Beside, what infamy will there arise, When foreign princes shall be certified! . . . . iv 1 144

This tongue hath parley'd unto foreign kings For your behoof 2 *Hen. VI.* iv 7 82

Such alliance Would more have strengthen'd this our commonwealth 'Gainst foreign storms . . . . . . 3 *Hen. VI.* iv 1 38

And lose no hour, Till we meet Warwick with his foreign power . . iv 1 149

That with a fearful soul Leads discontented steps in foreign soil *Rich. III.* iv 4 312

If not to fight with foreign enemies, Yet to beat down these rebels here iv 4 531

Abusing better men than they can be, Out of a foreign wisdom *Hen. VIII.* i 3 29

And hither make, as great ambassadors From foreign princes . . i 4 56

Fearing he would rise, he was so virtuous, Kept him a foreign man still ii 2 129

Then, that in all you writ to Rome, or else To foreign princes, 'Ego et Rex meus' Was still inscribed . . . . iii 2 314

As a foreign recreant, be led With manacles thorough our streets . *Cor.* v 3 114

Sometime she driveth o'er a soldier's neck, And then dreams he of cutting foreign throats . . . . . . *Rom. and Jul.* i 4 83

Malice domestic, foreign levy, nothing, Can touch him further *Macbeth* iii 2 25

And foreign mart for implements of war . . . . . *Hamlet* i 1 74

Turn'd her To foreign casualties . . . . . . *Lear* iv 3 46

They slack their duties, And pour our treasures into foreign laps *Othello* iv 3 89

I love the king your father, and yourself, With more than foreign heart *Pericles* iv 1 34

Foreigner. O, let me have no subject enemies, When adverse foreigners affright my towns! . . . . *K. John* iv 2 172

Foreknowing that the truth will fall out so . . . . . iv 2 154

Which, happily, foreknowing may avoid . . . . *Hamlet* i 1 134

Foreknowledge. I told him you were asleep; he seems to have a foreknowledge of that . . . . *T. Night* i 5 151

Foremost. Goes foremost in report through Italy . . . *Much Ado* iii 1 97

In which you, father, shall have foremost hand . . 2 *Hen. IV.* v 2 140

Being one o' the lowest, basest, poorest, Of this most wise rebellion, thou go'st foremost . . . . *Coriolanus* i 1 162

Foremost. My wife comes foremost . . . . *Coriolanus* v 3 22

The foremost man of all this world . . . . . . *J. Cæsar* iv 3 22

Forenamed. This forenamed maid hath yet in her the continuance of her first affection . . . . *Meas. for Meas.* iii 1 248

Forenoon. You wear out a good wholesome forenoon . . *Coriolanus* ii 1 78

Let me be married to three kings in a forenoon . . *Ant. and Cleo.* i 2 26

Fore-past. My fore-past proofs, howe'er the matter fall, Shall tax my fears of little vanity . . . . *All's Well* v 3 121

Fore-rank. Comprised Within the fore-rank of our articles . *Hen. V.* v 2 97

Fore-recited. Bid him recount The fore-recited practices . *Hen. VIII.* i 2 127

Forerun. Revels, dances, masks and merry hours Forerun fair Love *L. L. Lost* iv 3 380

These signs forerun the death or fall of kings . . . *Richard II.* ii 4 15

Woe is forerun with woe . . . . iii 4 28

But heaviness foreruns the good event . . . . 2 *Hen. IV.* iv 2 82

O, this same thought did but forerun my need . . *Rom. and Jul.* v 1 53

Forerunner. There is a forerunner come . . . *Mer. of Venice* i 2 136

Arthur, that great forerunner of thy blood . . . . *K. John* ii 1 2

There comes with them a forerunner . . . . . *T. of Athens* i 2 124

Forerunning more requital . . . . . . *Meas. for Meas.* v 1 8

Foresaid. Cracking the stones of the foresaid prunes . . . . ii 1 110

On my privilege I have with the parents of the foresaid child *L. L. Lost* iv 2 163

This, in our foresaid holy father's name . . . *K. John* iii 1 145

Ermengare, Daughter to Charles the foresaid duke of Lorraine *Hen. V.* i 2 83

To alter the king's course, And break the foresaid peace . *Hen. VIII.* i 1 190

Those foresaid lands So by his father lost . . . . *Hamlet* i 1 103

Foresaw. Every flower Did, as a prophet, weep what it foresaw In Hector's wrath . . . . *Troi. and Cres.* i 2 10

Foresay. Let ordinance Come as the gods forsay it . . . *Cymbeline* iv 2 146

Foresee. My master through his art forsees the danger . . *Tempest* ii 1 297

You foresee not what impediments Drag back our expedition 1 *Hen. IV.* iv 3 18

I foresee with grief The utter loss of all the realm of France . 1 *Hen. VI.* v 4 111

Cassandra doth forsee . . . . *Troi. and Cres.* v 3 64

Take the bridge quite away Of him that, his particular to foresee, Smells from the general weal . . . . *T. of Athens* iv 3 159

Good sir, give me good fortune.—I make not, but foresee.—Pray, then, foresee me one . . . . *Ant. and Cleo.* i 2 14

Foreseeing those fell mischiefs Our reasons laid before him *Hen. VIII.* v 1 49

Foreshow. Your looks foreshow You have a gentle heart . *Pericles* iv 1 86

Foreshowed. Which foreshow'd our princely eagle, The imperial Cæsar, should again unite . . . . *Cymbeline* v 5 473

Foreskirt. Honour's train Is longer than his foreskirt . *Hen. VIII.* ii 3 98

Forespent. You shall find his vanities forespent Were but the outside of the Roman Brutus . . . . *Hen. V.* ii 4 36

His goodness forespent on us, We must extend our notice . *Cymbeline* ii 3 64

Fore-spurrer. This fore-spurrer comes before his lord . *Mer. of Venice* ii 9 95

Forest. The forest is not three leagues off . . . . *T. G. of Ver.* v 1 11

As he in penance wander'd through the forest . . . . . v 2 38

Herne the hunter, Sometime a keeper here in Windsor forest *Mer. Wives* iv 4 29

I am here a Windsor stag; and the fattest, I think, i' the forest . . v 5 15

Do not these fair yokes Become the forest better than the town? . . v 5 112

To trace the forests wild . . . . *M. N. Dream* ii 1 25

In dale, forest or mead, By paved fountain or by rushy brook . . ii 1 83

Through the forest have I gone, But Athenian found I none . . . ii 2 66

In the forest of Arden, and a many merry men with him *As Y. Like It* i 1 120

Whither shall we go?—To seek my uncle in the forest of Arden . . i 3 109

Well, this is the forest of Arden . . . . ii 4 15

If this uncouth forest yield any thing savage, I will either be food for it or bring it for food to thee . . . . ii 6 6

A fool, a fool! I met a fool i' the forest, A motley fool! . . . . ii 7 12

Every eye which in this forest looks Shall see thy virtue witness'd . iii 2 7

Whether wisely or no, let the forest judge . . . . . . iii 2 130

Doth he know that I am in this forest and in man's apparel? . . . iii 2 242

There's no clock in the forest.—Then there is no true lover in the forest iii 2 319

Here in the skirts of the forest, like fringe upon a petticoat . . . iii 2 354

There is a man haunts the forest, that abuses our young plants . . iii 2 378

And by the way you shall tell me where in the forest you live . . iii 2 453

Who hath promised to meet me in this place of the forest and to couple us iii 3 45

He attends here in the forest on the duke your father . . . iii 4 36

Where in the purlieus of this forest stands A sheep-cote? . . . iv 3 77

Pacing through the forest, Chewing the food of sweet and bitter fancy . iv 3 101

There is a youth here in the forest lays claim to you . . . . v 1 7

Wast born i' the forest here?—Ay, sir, I thank God . . . . v 1 24

A great magician, Obscured in the circle of this forest . . . . v 4 34

This is the motley-minded gentleman that I have so often met in the forest v 4 42

Every day Men of great worth resorted to this forest . . . . v 4 161

First, in this forest let us do those ends That here were well begun . v 4 176

What is this forest call'd?—'Tis Gaultree Forest . . . 2 *Hen. IV.* iv 1 1

West of this forest, scarcely off a mile, In goodly form comes on the enemy . . . . iv 1 19

And made the forest tremble when they roar'd . . . 3 *Hen. VI.* v 7 12

To see the general hunting in this forest . . . . *T. Andron.* ii 3 59

The commonwealth of Athens is become a forest of beasts *T. of Athens* iv 3 352

O world, thou wast the forest to this hart . . . . *J. Cæsar* iii 1 207

Who can impress the forest, bid the tree Unfix his earth-bound root? *Macbeth* iv 1 95

Till Birnam forest come to Dunsinane . . . . v 3 60

A forest of feathers . . . . *Hamlet* iii 2 286

With shadowy forests and with champains rich'd . . . . *Lear* i 1 65

Forest bear. Whose hand is that the forest bear doth lick? . 3 *Hen. VI.* ii 2 13

Forest-born. This boy is forest-born . . . . . *As Y. Like It* v 4 30

Forest side. Attended him In secret ambush on the forest side 3 *Hen. VI.* iv 6 83

Forest walks. The forest walks are wide and spacious . *T. Andron.* ii 1 114

Forest woods. Dispark'd my parks and fell'd my forest woods *Richard II.* iii 1 23

Forestall. Might not you Forestall our sport? . . . . *L. L. Lost* v 2 473

Forestall prescience and esteem no act But that of hand *Troi. and Cres.* i 3 199

I shall forestall thee . . . . iv 5 230

I will forestal their repair hither, and say you are not fit . *Hamlet* v 2 228

May This night forestall him of the coming day! . . . *Cymbeline* iii 5 69

Forestalled. I had forestall'd this dear and deep rebuke . 2 *Hen. IV.* iv 5 141

Never shall you see that I will beg A ragged and forestall'd remission . v 2 38

To be forestalled ere we come to fall, Or pardon'd being down *Hamlet* iii 3 49

Forester. Then, forester, my friend, where is the bush That we must stand and play the murderer in? . . . . . . *L. L. Lost* iv 1 7

And, like a forester, the groves may tread . . . *M. N. Dream* iii 2 390

Go, one of you, find out the forester . . . . iv 1 108

Dispatch, I say, and find the forester . . . . iv 1 113

Do you hear, forester?—Very well: what would you? . *As Y. Like It* iii 2 315

Have you no song, forester, for this purpose? . . . . . . iv 2 6

Diana's foresters, gentlemen of the shade, minions of the moon 1 *Hen. IV.* i 2 29

Foretell. 'Tis good speed; foretells The great Apollo suddenly will have The truth of this appear . . . . . . *W. Tale* ii 3 199
His pure brain . . . Doth by the idle comments that it makes Foretell the ending of mortality . . . . . . *K. John* v 7 5
I am a prophet new inspired And thus expiring do foretell of him *Rich. II.* ii 1 32
Hollow whistling in the leaves Foretells a tempest . . . 1 *Hen. IV.* v 1 6
This man's brow, like to a title-leaf, Foretells the nature of a tragic volume: So looks the strand . . . . . . 2 *Hen. IV.* i 1 61
But what art thou, whose heavy looks foretell Some dreadful story? 3 *Hen. VI.* ii 1 43
When he performs, astronomers foretell it . . . *Troi. and Cres.* v 1 100
Foretelling. So went on, Foretelling this same time's condition 2 *Hen. IV.* iii 1 78
Forethink. Every man Prophetically doth forethink thy fall 1 *Hen. IV.* iii 2 38
Fore-thinking this, I have already fit . . . . *Cymbeline* iii 4 171
Forethought. Alter not the doom Forethought by heaven! . *K. John* iii 1 312
Foretold. These our actors, As I foretold you, were all spirits *Tempest* iv 1 149
For many men that stumble at the threshold Are well foretold that danger lurks within . . . . 3 *Hen. VI.* iv 7 12
About the hour of eight, which he himself Foretold should be his last *Hen. VIII.* iv 2 27
I foretold you then what would ensue . . . . *Troi. and Cres.* iv 5 217
Fore-vouched. Or your fore-vouch'd affection Fall'n into taint . *Lear* i 1 223
Foreward. My foreward shall be drawn out all in length *Richard III.* v 3 293
Forewarn him that he use no scurrilous words in 's tunes . . *W. Tale* iv 4 215
Forewarned. I will arm me, being thus forewarn'd . . 3 *Hen. VI.* iv 1 113
We were forewarned of your coming . . . . iv 7 17
Forfeit. Your brother's life Falls into forfeit . . . *Meas. for Meas.* i 4 66
Your brother is a forfeit of the law . . . . ii 2 71
Alas, alas! Why, all the souls that were were forfeit once . . ii 2 73
Double and treble admonition, and still forfeit in the same kind! . iii 2 206
No greater forfeit to the law than Angelo who hath sentenced him . iv 2 167
Stand like the forfeits in a barber's shop, As much in mock as mark . v 1 323
Thy slanders I forgive; and therewithal Remit thy other forfeits . v 1 526
Our states are forfeit: seek not to undo us . . . . *L. L. Lost* v 2 425
How can this be true, That you stand forfeit? . . . . . . v 2 427
Let the forfeit Be nominated for an equal pound Of your fair flesh *Mer. of Venice* i 3 149
Why, fear not, man; I will not forfeit it . . . . i 3 158
I am sure, if he forfeit, thou wilt not take his flesh . . . . iii 1 53
I will have the heart of him, if he forfeit . . . . . . iii 1 132
My estate is very low, my bond to the Jew is forfeit . . . . iii 2 319
By our holy Sabbath have I sworn To have the due and forfeit of my bond . . . . iv 1 37
I crave the law, The penalty and forfeit of my bond . . . iv 1 207
I will be bound to pay it ten times o'er, On forfeit of my hands, my head . . . . iv 1 212
This bond is forfeit . . . . iv 1 230
Thy wealth being forfeit to the state, Thou hast not left the value of a cord . . . . iv 1 365
I dare be bound again, My soul upon the forfeit . . . . . v 1 252
With the divine forfeit of his soul . . . . . *All's Well* iii 6 34
His brains are forfeit to the next tile that falls . . . . . iv 3 216
And he that throws not up his cap for joy Shall for the fault make forfeit of his head . . . . . . 3 *Hen. VI.* ii 1 197
Speak at once what is it thou demand'st.—The forfeit, sovereign, of my servant's life . . . . *Richard III.* ii 1 99
To forfeit all your goods, lands, tenements . . . *Hen. VIII.* iii 2 342
Despising many forfeits and subduements . . . *Troi. and Cres.* iv 5 187
If ever you disturb our streets again, Your lives shall pay the forfeit of the peace . . . . *Rom. and Jul.* i 1 104
And expire the term Of a despised life closed in my breast By some vile forfeit of untimely death . . . . i 4 111
Friend or brother, He forfeits his own blood that spills another *T. of A.* iii 5 88
Did forfeit, with his life, all those his lands Which he stood seized of *Hamlet* i 1 88
That he could not But think her bond of chastity quite crack'd, I having ta'en the forfeit . . . . *Cymbeline* v 5 208
Forfeited. Undone, and forfeited to cares for ever! . . *All's Well* iii 3 284
His vows are forfeited to me . . . . v 3 142
Shall we buy treason? and indent with fears, When they have lost and forfeited themselves? . . . . 1 *Hen. IV.* i 3 88
There without ransom to lie forfeited . . . . iv 3 96
'Tis all engaged, some forfeited and gone . . . *T. of Athens* ii 2 155
Forfeiter. Though forfeiters you cast in prison, yet You clasp young Cupid's tables . . . . *Cymbeline* iii 2 38
Forfeiting. We save a valiant gentleman By forfeiting a traitor 1 *Hen. VI.* iv 3 27
Beside forfeiting Our own brains, and the opinion that we bring *Hen. VIII.* Prol. 19
Forfeiture. If he should break his day, what should I gain By the exaction of the forfeiture? . . . . . . *Mer. of Venice* i 3 165
But none can drive him from the envious plea Of forfeiture, of justice . iii 2 285
I oft deliver'd from his forfeitures Many that have at times made moan to me . . . . iii 3 22
I am sure the duke Will never grant this forfeiture to hold . . . iii 3 25
Thou wilt not only loose the forfeiture, But, touch'd with human gentleness and love, Forgive a moiety of the principal . . . iv 1 24
To cut the forfeiture from that bankrupt there . . . . iv 1 122
Why doth the Jew pause? take thy forfeiture.—Give me my principal iv 1 335
Thou shalt have nothing but the forfeiture, To be so taken at thy peril, Jew . . . . iv 1 343
'Twas due on forfeiture, my lord, six weeks And past . *T. of Athens* ii 2 30
Forfend. There's no disjunction to be made, but by—As heavens forfend!—your ruin . . . . *W. Tale* iv 4 541
O, forfend it, God, That in a Christian climate souls refined Should show so heinous, black, obscene a deed! . . . *Richard II.* iv 1 129
Now heaven forfend! the holy maid with child! . . . 1 *Hen. VI.* v 4 65
Gloucester is dead.—Marry, God forfend! . . . 2 *Hen. VI.* iii 2 30
And when thou fail'st—as God forbid the hour!—Must Edward fall, which peril heaven forfend! . . . . . . 3 *Hen. VI.* ii 1 191
The gods of Rome forfend I should be author to dishonour you! *T. An.* i 1 434
I would not kill thy unprepared spirit; No; heaven forfend! I would not kill thy soul . . . . *Othello* v 2 32
My mistress here lies murder'd in her bed,— O heavens forfend! . . v 2 186
Forfended. Have you never found my brother's way To the forfended place? . . . . *Lear* v 1 11
Forgave. In such a night Did pretty Jessica, like a little shrew, Slander her love, and he forgave it her . . . . . . *Mer. of Venice* v 1 22
Cried 'Alas, good soul!' and forgave him with all their hearts *J. Cæsar* i 2 275
Forge. Come, to the forge with it then; shape it: I would not have things cool . . . . *Mer. Wives* iv 2 239

Forge. Here he comes, to beguile two hours in a sleep, and then to return and swear the lies he forges . . . . *All's Well* iv 1 26
To me the difference forges dread . . . . *W. Tale* iv 4 17
In the quick forge and working-house of thought . . . *Hen. V.* v Prol. 23
By the forge that stithied Mars his helm, I'll kill thee . *Troi. and Cres.* iv 5 255
What his breast forges, that his tongue must vent . . *Coriolanus* iii 1 258
Whate'er I forge to feed his brain-sick fits, Do you uphold *T. Andron.* v 2 71
That I should forge Quarrels unjust against the good and loyal *Macbeth* iv 3 82
I should make very forges of my cheeks, That would to cinders burn up modesty, Did I but speak thy deeds . . . . . . *Othello* iv 2 74
Forged. The best wishes that can be forged in your thoughts be servants to you! . . . . *All's Well* i 1 85
I will turn thy falsehood to thy heart, Where it was forged *Richard II.* iv 1 40
We stand opposed by such means As you yourself have forged 1 *Hen. IV.* v 1 68
Seal this lawless bloody book Of forged rebellion with a seal divine 2 *Hen. IV.* iv 1 92
Think not, although in writing I preferr'd The manner of thy vile outrageous crimes, That therefore I have forged . . 1 *Hen. VI.* iii 1 12
Burns under feigned ashes of forged love . . . . iii 1 190
With forged quaint conceit To set a gloss upon his bold intent . . iv 1 102
'Twas dangerous for him To ruminate on this so far, until It forged him some design . . . . *Hen. VIII.* i 2 181
Titleless, Till he had forged himself a name o' the fire Of burning Rome *Coriolanus* v 1 14
Denmark Is by a forged process of my death Rankly abused . *Hamlet* i 5 37
Never did the Cyclops' hammers fall On Mars's armour forged for proof eterne With less remorse . . . . ii 2 512
Damn'd Pisanio Hath with his forged letters,—damn'd Pisanio—From this most bravest vessel of the world Struck the main-top! *Cymbeline* iv 2 318
Forgery. These are the forgeries of jealousy . . . *M. N. Dream* ii 1 81
And now, to soothe your forgery and his, Sends me a paper to persuade me patience . . . . 3 *Hen. VI.* iii 3 175
And there put on him What forgeries you please . . . *Hamlet* ii 1 20
I, in forgery of shapes and tricks, Come short of what he did . . iv 7 90
Forget. Dost thou forget From what a torment I did free thee? *Tempest* i 2 250
The latter end of his commonwealth forgets the beginning . . ii 1 157
I forget: But these sweet thoughts do even refresh my labours . . iii 1 13
I prattle Something too wildly and my father's precepts I therein do forget . . . . iii 1 59
I will forget that Julia is alive . . . . *T. G. of Ver.* ii 6 27
What might we do to make the girl forget The love of Valentine? . . iii 2 29
One Julia, that his changing thoughts forget . . . . . . iv 4 124
I here forget all former griefs, Cancel all grudge . . . . . v 4 142
It is qui, quæ, quod: if you forget your 'quies,' your 'quæs,' and your 'quods,' you must be preeches . . . . . *Mer. Wives* iv 1 79
Our dance of custom round about the oak Of Herne the hunter, let us not forget . . . . v 5 80
But, whilst I live, forget to drink after thee . . . *Meas. for Meas.* i 2 40
Though it be not written down, yet forget not that I am an ass *M. Ado* iv 2 80
Do not forget to specify, when time and place shall serve, that I am an ass . . . . v 1 263
While it doth study to have what it would It doth forget to do the thing it should . . . . *L. L. Lost* i 1 145
I would forget her; but a fever she Reigns in my blood and will remember'd be . . . . iv 3 95
Forget the shames that you have stain'd me with . *Mer. of Venice* i 3 140
Unless you could teach me to forget a banished father . *As Y. Like It* i 2 5
I will forget the condition of my estate, to rejoice in yours . . i 2 16
Meantime, forget this new-fall'n dignity And fall into our rustic revelry . . . . v 4 182
When he wakes, Would not the beggar then forget himself? *T. of Shrew* Ind. 1 41
I could not forget you, for I never saw you before in all my life . v 1 51
Be this sweet Helen's knell, and now forget her . . . *All's Well* v 3 67
Let me be punish'd, that have minded you Of what you should forget *W. Tale* iii 2 227
Do as the heavens have done, forget your evil; With them forgive yourself . . . . v 1 5
Whilst I remember Her and her virtues, I cannot forget My blemishes in them . . . . v 1 7
For new-made honour doth forget men's names . . . . *K. John* i 1 187
We like not this; thou dost forget thyself . . . . . . iii 1 134
'Tis like I should forget myself: O, if I could, what grief should I forget! . . . . iii 4 49
If I were mad, I should forget my son . . . . iii 4 57
I would not have you, lord, forget yourself . . . . . iv 3 83
Forget, forgive; conclude and be agreed . . . . . *Richard II.* i 1 156
How dare thy joints forget To pay their awful duty to our presence? . iii 3 75
Or that I could forget what I have been, Or not remember what I must be now! . . . . iii 3 138
Fear, and not love, begets his penitence: Forget to pity him . . v 3 57
Thou'lt forget me when I am gone.—By my troth, thou'lt set me a-weeping, an thou sayest so . . . . 2 *Hen. IV.* ii 4 300
How might a prince of my great hopes forget So great indignities? . v 2 68
Your highness pleased to forget my place . . . . . . v 2 77
And shall forget the office of our hand Sooner . . . . *Hen. V.* ii 2 33
Old men forget; yet all shall be forgot . . . . iv 3 49
Before we go, let's not forget The noble Duke of Bedford 1 *Hen. VI.* iii 2 131
I charge you, as you love our favour, Quite to forget this quarrel . iv 1 136
Forget this grief.—Ah, Gloucester, teach me to forget myself! 2 *Hen. VI.* ii 4 26
That winter lion, who in rage forgets Aged contusions and all brush of time . . . . v 3 2
You forget That we are those which chased you from the field 3 *Hen. VI.* i 1 89
Did I forget that by the house of York My father came untimely to his death? . . . . iii 3 186
Turn'd my hate to love; And I forgive and quite forget old faults iii 3 200
At last by notes of household harmony They quite forget their loss of liberty . . . . iv 6 15
But we now forget Our title to the crown and only claim Our dukedom iv 7 45
Let me put in your minds, if you forget, What you have been *Richard III.* i 3 131
Shall I forget myself to be myself?—Ay, if yourself's remembrance wrong yourself . . . . iv 4 420
Did my commission Bid ye so far forget yourselves? . . *Hen. VIII.* v 3 142
Great thunder-darter of Olympus, forget that thou art Jove! *Tr. and Cr.* ii 3 11
But they Upon their ancient malice will forget With the least cause these his new honours . . . . *Coriolanus* ii 1 244
Think upon me! hang 'em! I would they would forget me . . . ii 3 63
Forget not With what contempt he wore the humble weed . . . ii 3 228
And, being angry, does forget that ever He heard the name of death . iii 1 259
And when I do forget The least of these unspeakable deserts, Romans, forget your fealty to me . . . . *T. Andron.* i 1 255

Forget. As if we should forget we had no hands, If Marcus did not name the word of hands! *T. Andron.* iii 2 32
Forget to think of her.—O, teach me how I should forget to think *Rom. and Jul.* i 1 231
He that is strucken blind cannot forget The precious treasure of his eyesight lost i 1 238
Farewell: thou canst not teach me to forget i 1 243
I never shall forget it,—Of all the days of the year, upon that day i 3 24
An I should live a thousand years, I never should forget it i 3 47
I shall forget, to have thee still stand there, Remembering how I love thy company.—And I'll still stay, to have thee still forget ii 2 173
I would forget it fain; But, O, it presses to my memory iii 2 109
To forget their faults, I drink to you *T. of Athens* i 2 112
O, forget What we are sorry for ourselves in thee v 1 141
Forget not, in your speed, Antonius, To touch Calpurnia *J. Cæsar* i 2 6
With himself at war, Forgets the shows of love to other men i 2 47
Bay not me; I'll not endure it: you forget yourself, To hedge me in iv 3 29
Urge me no more, I shall forget myself iv 3 35
I do forget. Do not muse at me, my most worthy friends *Macbeth* iii 4 84
I am glad to see you well: Horatio,—or I do forget myself.—The same *Hamlet* i 2 161
Necessary 'tis that we forget To pay ourselves what to ourselves is debt iii 2 202
Do not forget: this visitation Is but to whet thy almost blunted purpose iii 4 110
And labour'd much How to forget that learning v 2 35
I will forget my nature *Lear* i 5 35
Bear with me: Pray you now, forget and forgive: I am old and foolish iv 7 84
But men are men; the best sometimes forget *Othello* ii 3 241
I being absent and my place supplied, My general will forget my love iii 3 18
A fine woman! a fair woman! a sweet woman!—Nay, you must forget that iv 1 190
Why do you send so thick?—Who's born that day When I forget to send to Antony, Shall die a beggar *Ant. and Cleo.* i 5 64
To forget them quite Were to remember that the present need Speaks to atone you ii 2 100
I am much sorry, sir, You put me to forget a lady's manners *Cymbeline* ii 3 110
Well, then, here's the point: You must forget to be a woman iii 4 157
You must Forget that rarest treasure of your cheek, Exposing it iii 4 163
Forget Your laboursome and dainty trims iii 4 166
Shall we rest us here, And by relating tales of others' griefs, See if 'twill teach us to forget our own? *Pericles* i 4 3
Forgetful. This forgetful man 1 *Hen. IV.* i 3 161
The queen is comfortless, and we forgetful In our long absence *Hen. VIII.* ii 3 105
That rash humour which my mother gave me Makes me forgetful *J. Cæsar* iv 3 121
Bear with me, good boy, I am much forgetful iv 3 255
Forgetfulness. Some foul mischance Torment me for my love's forgetfulness! *T. G. of Ver.* ii 2 12
And steep my senses in forgetfulness 2 *Hen. IV.* iii 1 8
In the swallowing gulf Of blind forgetfulness and dark oblivion *Richard III.* iii 7 129
That we have been familiar, Ingrate forgetfulness shall poison *Coriolanus* v 2 92
They confess Toward thee forgetfulness too general, gross *T. of Athens* v 1 147
Forgetive. Makes it apprehensive, quick, forgetive 2 *Hen. IV.* iv 3 107
Forgettest. I must Once in a month recount what thou hast been, Which thou forget'st *Tempest* i 2 263
Happy thou art not; For what thou hast not, still thou strivest to get, And what thou hast, forget'st *Meas. for Meas.* iii 1 23
Forgetting. The powers, delaying, not forgetting *Tempest* iii 3 73
Forgetting, like a good man, your late censure *Hen. VIII.* iii 1 64
And I'll still stay, to have thee still forget, Forgetting any other home *Rom. and Jul.* ii 2 176
Mindless of thy worth, Forgetting thy great deeds *T. of Athens* iv 3 94
Making so bold, My fears forgetting manners *Hamlet* v 2 17
Forgive. O, forgive me my sins!—He that dies pays all debts *Tempest* iii 2 139
I do forgive thee, Unnatural though thou art v 1 78
I do forgive Thy rankest fault; all of them v 1 131
Forgive me that I do not dream on thee *T. G. of Ver.* ii 4 172
Forgive me, Valentine: if hearty sorrow Be a sufficient ransom for offence, I tender't here v 4 74
Forgive them what they have committed here And let them be recall'd v 4 154
I was then frugal of my mirth: Heaven forgive me! *Mer. Wives* ii 1 28
Well, heaven forgive you and all of us, I pray! ii 2 58
Heaven forgive my sins at the day of judgement! iii 3 226
Alas, what noise?—Heaven forgive our sins! v 5 35
Well, heaven forgive him! and forgive us all! *Meas. for Meas.* ii 1 37
Thy slanders I forgive; and therewithal Remit thy other forfeits v 1 525
I protest I love thee.—Why, then, God forgive me! *Much Ado* iv 1 283
I forgive thy duty: adieu *L. L. Lost* iv 2 147
If he would despise me, I would forgive him *Mer. of Venice* i 2 68
Cursed be my tribe, If I forgive him! i 3 53
Forgive a moiety of the principal; Glancing an eye of pity on his losses iv 1 26
Portia, forgive me this enforced wrong v 1 240
His taken labours bid him me forgive *All's Well* iii 4 12
Come to what is important in't: I forgive you the praise *T. Night* i 5 204
O good Antonio, forgive me your trouble ii 1 35
Sir, royal sir, forgive a foolish woman *W. Tale* iii 2 228
Do as the heavens have done, forget your evil; With them forgive yourself v 1 6
God shall forgive you Cœur-de-lion's death The rather that you give his offspring life *K. John* ii 1 12
Then God forgive the sin of all those souls! ii 1 283
Thrust but these men away, and I'll forgive you iv 1 83
Forgive the comment that my passion made Upon thy feature iv 2 263
Forget, forgive; conclude and be agreed *Richard II.* i 1 156
Thou hast done much harm upon me, Hal; God forgive thee for it! 1 *Hen. IV.* i 2 103
O, the devil take such cozeners! God forgive me! i 3 255
God forgive them that so much have sway'd Your majesty's good thoughts away from me! iii 2 130
Hostess, I forgive thee: go, make ready breakfast iii 3 192
How I came by the crown, O God forgive! 2 *Hen. IV.* iv 5 219
And I repent my fault more than my death; Which I beseech your highness to forgive *Hen. V.* ii 2 153
Yet, forgive me, God, That I do brag thus! iii 6 159
Him I forgive my death that killeth me When he sees me go back 1 *Hen. VI.* i 2 20
Forgive me, country, and sweet countrymen iii 3 81
Forgive me, God, For judgement only doth belong to thee 2 *Hen. VI.* iii 2 139
He dies, and makes no sign. O God, forgive him! iii 3 29
I forgive and quite forget old faults 3 *Hen. VI.* iii 3 200
O, God forgive my sins, and pardon thee! v 6 60

Forgive. If thy revengeful heart cannot forgive *Richard III.* i 2 174
If I chance to talk a little wild, forgive me; I had it from my father *Hen. VIII.* i 4 26
I heartily forgive 'em: Yet let 'em look they glory not in mischief ii 1 65
Forgive me frankly.—Sir Thomas Lovell, I as free forgive you As I would be forgiven: I forgive all ii 1 81
Speak how I fell. I have done; and God forgive me!—O, this is full of pity! ii 1 136
Pray, forgive me, If I have used myself unmannerly iii 1 175
Heaven forgive me! Ever God bless your highness! iii 2 135
My heart weeps to see him So little of his great self.—I forgive him iii 2 336
The veins unfill'd, our blood is cold, and then We pout upon the morning, are unapt To give or to forgive *Coriolanus* v 1 53
Forgive my tyranny; but do not say For that 'Forgive our Romans' v 3 43
God forgive me, Marry, and amen, how sound is she asleep! *Rom. and Jul.* iv 5 7
Forgive me, cousin! Ah, dear Juliet, Why art thou yet so fair? v 3 101
Forgive my general and exceptless rashness, You perpetual-sober gods! *T. of Athens* iv 3 502
If he 'scape, Heaven forgive him too! *Macbeth* iv 3 235
More needs she the divine than the physician. God, God forgive us all! v 1 83
But, O, what form of prayer Can serve my turn? 'Forgive me my foul murder'? That cannot be *Hamlet* iii 3 52
Forgive me this my virtue; For in the fatness of these pursy times Virtue itself of vice must pardon beg iii 4 152
Kind gods, forgive me that, and prosper him! *Lear* iii 7 92
Bear with me: Pray you now, forget and forgive: I am old and foolish iv 7 84
If thou'rt noble, I do forgive thee.—Let's exchange charity v 3 166
Forgive us our sins!—Gentlemen, let's look to our business *Othello* ii 3 116
O grace! O heaven forgive me! Are you a man? have you a soul or sense! iii 3 373
O, heaven forgive us!—I cry you mercy, then iv 2 88
Out, fool! I forgive thee for a witch *Ant. and Cleo.* i 2 40
Forgive me; Since my becomings kill me, when they do not Eye well to you i 3 95
My lord, Forgive my fearful sails! I little thought You would have follow'd iii 11 55
O Antony, Nobler than my revolt is infamous, Forgive me iv 9 20
The power that I have on you is to spare you; The malice towards you to forgive you *Cymbeline* v 5 419
Heavens forgive it! *Pericles* iv 3 39
Forgiven. I have forgiven and forgotten all *All's Well* v 3 9
If the sins of your youth are forgiven you, you're well to live *W. Tale* iii 3 125
All the gentlewomen here have forgiven me 2 *Hen. IV.* Epil. 23
I as free forgive you As I would be forgiven *Hen. VIII.* ii 1 83
Yet rich conceit Taught thee to make vast Neptune weep for aye On thy low grave, on faults forgiven *T. of Athens* v 4 79
Forgiveness. But, O, how oddly will it sound that I Must ask my child forgiveness! *Tempest* v 1 198
Your hangman is a more penitent trade than your bawd; he doth oftener ask forgiveness *Meas. for Meas.* iv 2 54
Asks thee the son forgiveness, As 'twere i' the father's person *W. Tale* iv 4 560
Cries 'O, thy mother, thy mother!' then asks Bohemia forgiveness v 2 57
More sins for this forgiveness prosper may *Richard II.* v 3 84
Forgiveness, horse! why do I rail on thee? v 5 90
Exchange forgiveness with me, noble Hamlet *Hamlet* v 2 340
Ask her forgiveness? Do you but mark how this becomes the house *Lear* ii 4 154
When thou dost ask me blessing, I'll kneel down, And ask of thee forgiveness v 3 11
Forgot. Hast thou forgot The foul witch Sycorax? *Tempest* i 2 257
I had forgot that foul conspiracy iv 1 139
For long agone I have forgot to court *T. G. of Ver.* iii 1 85
A little time will melt her frozen thoughts And worthless Valentine shall be forgot iii 2 10
She dreams on him that has forgot her love iv 4 86
Out upon't! what have I forgot? *Mer. Wives* i 4 180
Now, William, some declensions of your pronouns.—Forsooth, I have forgot iv 1 78
When once our grace we have forgot, Nothing goes right *Meas. for Meas.* iv 4 36
And may it be that you have quite forgot A husband's office? *C. of Er.* iii 2 1
Why, this was quite forgot.—So study evermore is overshot *L. L. Lost* i 1 142
The hobby-horse is forgot iii 1 30; *Hamlet* iii 2 145
But have you forgot your love?—Almost I had *L. L. Lost* iii 1 34
To speak troth, I have forgot our way *M. N. Dream* ii 2 36
Is it all forgot? All school-days' friendship, childhood innocence? iii 2 201
Alack, alack, I fear my Thisby's promise is forgot! v 1 174
Three thousand ducats.—And for three months.—I had forgot *Mer. of Ven.* i 3 68
Thou bitter sky, That dost not bite so nigh As benefits forgot *As Y. L. It* ii 7 186
I have forgot your name; but, sure, that part Was aptly fitted *T. of S.* Ind. 1 86
Have you so soon forgot the entertainment? iii 1 2
Come hither, you rogue. What, have you forgot me? v 1 50
What was he like? I have forgot him *All's Well* i 1 93
Hast thou forgot thyself? is it so long? *T. Night* v 1 144
O Perdita, what have we twain forgot! Pray you, a word *W. Tale* iv 4 674
Pardon, madam: The one I have almost forgot v 1 104
I had forgot to tell your lordship, To-day, as I came by, I called there *Richard II.* ii 2 93
For that is not forgot Which ne'er I did remember ii 3 37
I had forgot myself: am I not king? iii 2 83
Thy pains, Fitzwater, shall not be forgot; Right noble is thy merit v 6 17
If manhood, good manhood, be not forgot upon the face of the earth 1 *Hen. IV.* ii 4 142
A plague upon it! I have forgot the map.—No, here it is iii 1 6
If that the king Have any way your good deserts forgot iv 3 46
Forgot your oath to us at Doncaster v 1 58
My nephew's trespass may be well forgot; It hath the excuse of youth v 2 16
It angered him to the heart: but he hath forgot that 2 *Hen. IV.* ii 4 10
We meet like men that had forgot to speak v 2 22
Old men forget; yet all shall be forgot, But he'll remember *Hen. V.* iv 3 49
I have forgot his name.—Sir John Falstaff.—That is he iv 7 53
Hath he forgot he is his sovereign? 1 *Hen. VI.* iv 1 52
Methought this staff, mine office-badge in court, Was broke in twain; by whom I have forgot 2 *Hen. VI.* i 2 26
But if she have forgot Honour and virtue ii 1 194
Show what cruelty ye can, That this my death may never be forgot! iv 1 133
Why, Warwick, hath thy knee forgot to bow? v 1 161
Hath she forgot already that brave prince, Edward, her lord? *Richard III.* i 2 240
'Tis time to speak; my pains are quite forgot i 3 117
'Zounds, he dies: I had forgot the reward i 4 128
Almost forgot my prayers to content him *Hen. VIII.* iii 1 132
When time is old and hath forgot itself *Troi. and Cres.* iii 2 192

Forgot. Please it our general to pass strangely by him, As if he were forgot . . . . *Troi. and Cres.* iii 3 40
Neither gave to me Good word nor look : what, are my deeds forgot? . iii 3 144
Which are devour'd As fast as they are made, forgot as soon As done . iii 3 149
I have forgot my father ; I know no touch of consanguinity . . . iv 2 102
By Jupiter! forgot. I am weary ; yea, my memory is tired . *Coriolanus* i 9 90
Your name, I think, is Adrian.—It is so, sir : truly, I have forgot you . iv 3 3
Like a dull actor now, I have forgot my part, and I am out . . . v 3 41
Even when their sorrows almost were forgot . . *T. Andron.* v 1 137
I have forgot why I did call thee back . . . . *Rom. and Jul.* ii 2 171
With Rosaline, my ghostly father? no ; I have forgot that name . . ii 3 46
I cannot think but your age has forgot me ; It could not else be *T. of A.* iii 5 93
Hug their diseased perfumes, and have forgot That ever Timon was . iv 3 207
Have you forgot me, sir?—Why dost ask that? I have forgot all men ; Then, if thou grant'st thou'rt a man, I have forgot thee . . . iv 3 480
I must tell you, then : You have forgot the will I told you of *J. Cæsar* iii 2 243
I have almost forgot the taste of fears . . . . *Macbeth* v 5 9
Have you forgot me?—No, by the rood, not so . . . *Hamlet* iii 4 14
I must to England ; you know that?—Alack, I had forgot . . iii 4 201
As the world were now but to begin, Antiquity forgot, custom not known iv 5 104
I am very sorry, good Horatio, That to Laertes I forgot myself . . v 2 76
Thy half o' the kingdom hast thou not forgot, Wherein I thee endow'd *Lear* ii 4 183
Great thing of us forgot! . . . . v 3 236
Have you forgot all sense of place and duty? . . . *Othello* ii 3 167
How comes it, Michael, you are thus forgot?—I pray you, pardon me . ii 3 188
But, for the handkerchief,— By heaven, I would most gladly have forgot it iv 1 19
I had forgot thee : O, come in, Emilia : Soft ; by and by . . v 2 103
Speak no more.—That truth should be silent I had almost forgot *A. and C.* ii 2 110
My lord, I fear, Has forgot Britain.—And himself . . *Cymbeline* i 6 113
I had almost forgot To entreat your grace but in a small request . . i 6 180
The exile of her minion is too new ; She hath not yet forgot him . . ii 3 47
Her andirons—I had forgot them—were two winking Cupids Of silver . ii 4 89
I forgot to ask him one thing ; I'll remember't anon . . . iii 5 133
Great griefs, I see, medicine the less ; for Cloten Is quite forgot . iv 2 244
Go travel for a while, Till that his rage and anger be forgot . *Pericles* i 2 107
What I have been I have forgot to know ; But what I am, want teaches me . . . . iii 1 75
The unfriendly elements Forgot thee utterly . . . . . iii 1 59
Forgotten. My former love Is by a newer object quite forgotten *T. G. of V.* ii 4 195
How many actions most ridiculous Hast thou been drawn to by thy fantasy?—Into a thousand that I have forgotten . *As Y. Like It* ii 4 32
I have forgiven and forgotten all . . . . . *All's Well* v 3 9
On a forgotten matter we can hardly make distinction of our hands *T. N.* ii 3 174
Thou hast forgotten to demand that truly which thou wouldst truly know . . . . *1 Hen. IV.* i 2 5
An I have not forgotten what the inside of a church is made of . . iii 3 8
Only compound me with forgotten dust . . *2 Hen. IV.* iv 5 116
May this be wash'd in Lethe, and forgotten? . . . . v 2 72
But all Was either pitied in him or forgotten . . *Hen. VIII.* ii 1 29
When I am forgotten, as I shall be, And sleep in dull cold marble . iii 2 432
My dull brain was wrought With things forgotten . . *Macbeth* i 3 150
If he had been forgotten, It had been as a gap in our great feast . iii 1 11
O heavens! die two months ago, and not forgotten yet? . *Hamlet* iii 2 139
O, my oblivion is a very Antony, And I am all forgotten *Ant. and Cleo.* i 3 91
Fork. Thou dost fear the soft and tender fork Of a poor worm *M. for M.* iii 1 16
Adder's fork and blind-worm's sting, Lizard's leg and howlet's wing *Macb.* iv 1 16
Let it fall rather, though the fork invade The region of my heart *Lear* i 1 146
Yond simpering dame, Whose face between her forks presages snow . iv 6 121
Forked. With forked heads Have their round haunches gored *As Y. L. It* ii 1 24
Inch-thick, knee-deep, o'er head and ears a fork'd one! . . *W. Tale* i 2 186
When a' was naked, he was, for all the world, like a forked radish *2 Hen. IV.* iii 2 334
Were there a serpent seen, with forked tongue . . *2 Hen. VI.* iii 2 259
Which of these hairs is Paris my husband? 'The forked one,' quoth he *Troi. and Cres.* i 2 178
Unaccommodated man is no more but such a poor, bare, forked animal as thou art . . . . *Lear* iii 4 113
Even then this forked plague is fated to us When we do quicken *Othello* iii 3 276
A forked mountain, or blue promontory With trees upon't *A. and C.* iv 14 5
Forlorn. Poor forlorn Proteus, passionate Proteus . . *T. G. of Ver.* i 2 124
Thou gentle nymph, cherish thy forlorn swain! . . . . v 4 12
Go with speed To some forlorn and naked hermitage . *L. L. Lost* v 2 805
As well as one so great and so forlorn May hold together *W. Tale* ii 2 22
So forlorn, that his dimensions to any thick sight were invincible *2 Hen. IV.* iii 2 335
Now for the honour of the forlorn French! . . . . *1 Hen. VI.* i 2 19
I, his forlorn duchess, Was made a wonder and a pointing-stock *2 Hen. VI.* ii 4 45
Art thou, like the adder, waxen deaf? Be poisonous too and kill thy forlorn queen . . . . iii 2 77
Shall I stab the forlorn swain?—First let my words stab him . iv 1 65
And thou, poor soul, Art then forsaken, as thou went'st forlorn! *3 Hen. VI.* iii 1 54
A banish'd man, And forced to live in Scotland a forlorn . . iii 3 26
The trees, though summer, yet forlorn and lean . *T. Andron.* ii 3 94
Some say that ravens foster forlorn children . . . ii 3 153
Long have I been forlorn, and all for thee : Welcome, dread Fury . v 2 81
Like a forlorn and desperate castaway, Do shameful execution on herself v 3 75
Wast thou fain, poor father, To hovel thee with swine, and rogues forlorn? . . . . *Lear* iv 7 39
The forlorn soldier, that so nobly fought . . . . *Cymbeline* v 5 405
Form. Believe me, sir, It carries a brave form . . . *Tempest* i 2 411
Nor can imagination form a shape, Besides yourself, to like of . iii 1 56
With an hour's heat Dissolves to water and doth lose his form *T. G. of V.* iii 2 8
O thou senseless form, Thou shalt be worshipp'd! . . . iv 4 203
If the gentle spirit of moving words Can no way change you to a milder form . . . . v 4 56
A fault done first in the form of a beast . . . *Mer. Wives* v 5 10
O place, O form, How often dost thou with thy case, thy habit, Wrench awe from fools and tie the wiser souls To thy false seeming! *M. for M.* ii 4 12
Glasses . . . ; Which are as easy broke as they make forms . . ii 4 126
By cold gradation and well-balanced form, We shall proceed . . iv 3 104
So may Angelo, In all his dressings, characts, titles, forms, Be an arch-villain . . . . v 1 56
Thou hast thine own form.—No, I am an ape . . *Com. of Errors* ii 2 200
Be brief ; only to the plain form of marriage . . . *Much Ado* iv 1 2
And such a grief for such, In every lineament, branch, shape, and form v 1 14
In manner and form following . . . . . . *L. L. Lost* i 1 207
I was seen with her in the manor-house, sitting with her upon the form i 1 209
It is the manner of a man to speak to a woman : for the form,—in some form . . . . i 1 213
Form. Proud with his form, in his eye pride express'd . . *L. L. Lost* ii 1 237
Full of forms, figures, shapes, objects, ideas, apprehensions . . . iv 2 68
This is the ape of form, monsieur the nice . . . . . v 2 325
Their form confounded makes most form in mirth . . . . v 2 520
Extremely forms All causes to the purpose of his speed . . . v 2 750
Like the eye, Full of strange shapes, of habits and of forms . . . v 2 773
One To whom you are but as a form in wax By him imprinted *M. N. Dream* i 1 49
Things base and vile, holding no quantity, Love can transpose to form i 1 233
And as imagination bodies forth The forms of things unknown . . v 1 15
And if my form lie there, Then I am yours . . *Mer. of Venice* ii 7 61
The which he vents In mangled forms . . . . *As Y. Like It* ii 7 42
Such disguise as haply shall become The form of my intent *T. Night* i 2 55
Easy is it for the proper-false In women's waxen hearts to set their forms! ii 2 31
Nothing of that wonderful promise, to read him by his form . . iii 4 291
If spirits can assume both form and suit You come to fright us . v 1 242
Camest in smiling, And in such forms which here were presupposed . v 1 358
Whom I from meaner form Have bench'd and rear'd to worship *W. Tale* i 2 313
Praise her but for this her without-door form . . . . ii 1 69
From henceforth bear his name whose form thou bear'st *K. John* i 1 160
Not alone in habit and device, Exterior form, outward accoutrement . i 1 211
All form is formless, order orderless . . . . . . iii 1 253
Stuffs out his vacant garments with his form . . . . iii 4 97
I will not keep this form upon my head, When there is such disorder in my wit . . . . iii 4 101
The antique and well-noted face Of plain old form is much disfigured . iv 2 22
And you have slander'd nature in my form . . . . iv 2 256
Could thought, without this object, Form such another? . . . iv 3 45
Even as a form of wax Resolveth from his figure 'gainst the fire . v 4 24
But I do love the favour and the form Of this most fair occasion . v 4 50
You are born To set a form upon that indigest . . . . v 7 26
I am a scribbled form, drawn with a pen Upon a parchment . . . v 7 32
Like perspectives, which rightly gazed upon Show nothing but confusion, eyed awry Distinguish form . . . . *Richard II.* ii 2 20
Throw away respect, Tradition, form and ceremonious duty . . iii 2 173
Why should we in the compass of a pale Keep law and form? . . iii 4 41
He apprehends a world of figures here, But not the form . *1 Hen IV.* i 3 210
It never yet did hurt To lay down likelihoods and forms of hope *2 Hen. IV.* i 3 35
By the necessary form of this King Richard might create a perfect guess iii 1 87
In goodly form comes on the enemy . . . . . . iv 1 20
To dress the ugly form Of base and bloody insurrection . . iv 1 39
Acquitted by a true substantial form . . . . . iv 1 173
The time misorder'd doth, in common sense, Crowd us and crush us to this monstrous form . . . . iv 2 34
The blood weeps from my heart when I do shape In forms imaginary . iv 4 59
For now a time is come to mock at form : Harry the Fifth is crown'd . iv 5 119
With forms being fetch'd From glistering semblances of piety *Hen. V.* ii 2 116
Now and then goes to the wars, to grace himself at his return into London under the form of a soldier . . . . . . iii 6 72
The ceremonies of the wars, and the cares of it, and the forms of it . iv 1 74
Art thou aught else but place, degree and form, Creating awe and fear? iv 1 263
Shall name your highness in this form and with this addition . v 2 366
Did he not, contrary to form of law, Devise strange deaths? *2 Hen. VI.* iii 1 58
That afterwards We may digest our complots in some form *Richard III.* iii 1 200
What, think you . . . we would, against the form of law, Proceed thus rashly? . . . . iii 5 42
The right idea of your father, Both in your form and nobleness of mind iii 7 14
I'll draw the form and model of our battle . . . . . v 3 24
The mind growing once corrupt, They turn to vicious forms . *Hen. VIII.* i 2 117
Though perils did Abound, as thick as thought could make 'em, and Appear in forms more horrid . . . . iii 2 196
Season, form, Office and custom, in all line of order *Troi. and Cres.* i 3 87
We may not think the justness of each act Such and no other than event doth form it . . . . ii 2 120
And put on A form of strangeness as we pass along . . . iii 3 51
But eye to eye opposed Salutes each other with each other's form . iii 3 108
To what form but that he is, should wit larded with malice and malice forced with wit turn him too? . . . . v 1 63
And this whole night Hath nothing been but shapes and forms of slaughter v 3 12
Take to you, as your predecessors have, Your honour with your form *Coriolanus* ii 2 148
Where he shall answer, by a lawful form, In peace, to his utmost peril iii 1 325
Serious vanity! Mis-shapen chaos of well-seeming forms! *Rom. and Jul.* i 1 185
Fain would I dwell on form, fain, fain deny What I have spoke . ii 2 88
Stand so much on the new form, that they cannot sit at ease on the old bench . . . . ii 4 36
Hold thy desperate hand : Art thou a man? thy form cries out thou art iii 3 109
Thy noble shape is but a form of wax, Digressing from the valour of a man iii 3 126
Which so took effect As I intended, for it wrought on her The form of death v 3 246
'Tis a good form.—And rich : here is a water, look ye *T. of Athens* i 1 17
To bring manslaughter into form and set quarrelling Upon the head of valour . . . . iii 5 27
So is he now in execution Of any bold or noble enterprise, However he puts on this tardy form . . . . . . *J. Cæsar* i 2 303
Fierce fiery warriors fought upon the clouds, In ranks and squadrons and right form of war . . . . ii 2 20
Pluck down benches.—Pluck down forms, windows, any thing . . iii 2 264
This sober form of yours hides wrongs . . . . iv 2 40
I see thee yet, in form as palpable As this which now I draw *Macbeth* ii 1 40
That fair and warlike form In which the majesty of buried Denmark Did sometimes march . . . . *Hamlet* i 1 47
With all forms, moods, shapes of grief, That can denote me truly . . i 2 82
Both in time, Form of the thing, each word made true and good . . i 2 210
Some habit that too much o'er-leavens The form of plausive manners . i 4 30
And there assume some other horrible form . . . . . i 4 72
I'll wipe away all trivial fond records, All saws of books, all forms . i 5 100
How infinite in faculty! in form and moving how express and admirable! ii 2 317
A broken voice, and his whole function suiting With forms to his conceit ii 2 583
The glass of fashion and the mould of form, The observed of all observers iii 1 161
That unmatch'd form and feature of blown youth Blasted with ecstasy iii 1 167
What he spake, though it lack'd form a little, Was not like madness . iii 1 171
The very age and body of the time his form and pressure . . . iii 2 27
But, O, what form of prayer Can serve my turn? . . . . iii 3 51
A combination and a form indeed, Where every god did seem to set his seal iii 4 60
His form and cause conjoin'd, preaching to stones, Would make them capable . . . . iii 4 126
Folded the writ up in form of the other, Subscribed it . . . v 2 51
That sir which serves and seeks for gain, And follows but for form Will pack when it begins to rain . . . . . . *Lear* ii 4 80
We may not pass upon his life Without the form of justice . . . iii 7 25

Form. Others there are Who, trimm'd in forms and visages of duty, Keep yet their hearts attending on themselves . . . . . *Othello* i 1 50
Putting on the mere form of civil and humane seeming . . . ii 1 243
Her will, recoiling to her better judgement, May fall to match you with her country forms . . . . iii 3 237
What place? what time? what form? what likelihood? . . . iv 2 138
Or that mine eyes, mine ears, or any sense, Delighted them in any other form . . . . iv 2 155
Nature wants stuff To vie strange forms with fancy . *Ant. and Cleo.* v 2 98
Plate of rare device, and jewels Of rich and exquisite form . *Cymbeline* i 6 190
And now, This ornament Makes me look dismal will I clip to form *Per.* v 3 74
Formal. To make of him a formal man again . . *Com. of Errors* v 1 105
With eyes severe and beard of formal cut, Full of wise saws *As Y. Like It* ii 7 155
Are you so formal, sir? . . . . . . *T. of Shrew* iii 1 61
Formal in apparel, In gait and countenance surely like a father . iv 2 64
Why, this is evident to any formal capacity . . . *T. Night* ii 5 128
And flow henceforth in formal majesty . . . . 2 *Hen. IV.* v 2 133
Like the formal vice, Iniquity, I moralize two meanings in one word *Richard III.* iii 1 82
With untired spirits and formal constancy . . . *J. Cæsar* ii 1 227
No noble rite nor formal ostentation . . . . *Hamlet* iv 5 215
If not well, Thou shouldst come like a Fury crown'd with snakes, Not like a formal man . . . . . . *Ant. and Cleo.* ii 5 41
Formally. Instruct me How I may formally in person bear me *M. for M.* i 3 47
And formally, according to our law, Depose him . . . *Richard II.* i 3 29
Form'd by the eye and therefore, like the eye, Full of strange shapes *L. L. L.* v 2 772
I did think, by the excellent constitution of thy leg, it was formed under the star of a galliard . . . . . . *T. Night* i 3 142
A wondrous miracle, The shadow of myself form'd in her eye *K. John* ii 1 498
Nor doth he of himself know them for aught Till he behold them form'd in the applause Where they're extended . . *Troi. and Cres.* iii 3 119
Former. The remembrance of my former love Is by a newer object quite forgotten . . . . *T. G. of Ver.* ii 4 194
I here forget all former griefs, Cancel all grudge . . . v 4 142
Let me entreat you speak the former language . *Meas. for Meas.* ii 4 140
The former Hero! Hero that is dead! . . . . *Much Ado* v 4 65
True delight In the sight Of thy former lady's eye . . *M. N. Dream* iii 2 457
You to your former honour I bequeath . . . *As Y. Like It* v 4 192
In peril to incur your former malady . . . *T. of Shrew* Ind. 2 124
But do forswear her, As one unworthy all the former favours . iv 2 30
This simulation is not as the former . . . . *T. Night* ii 5 152
What were more holy Than to rejoice the former queen is well? *W. Tale* v 1 30
She shall not be so young As was your former . . . . v 1 79
Had I not the dash of my former life in me . . . . v 2 122
We do lock Our former scruple in our strong-barr'd gates . *K. John* ii 1 370
Speak again; not all thy former tale, But this one word . . iii 1 25
Learn, good soul, To think our former state a happy dream *Richard II.* v 1 18
His former strength may be restored With good advice . 2 *Hen. IV.* iii 1 42
That action, hence borne out, May waste the memory of the former days iv 5 216
So shall the world perceive, That I have turn'd away my former self . v 5 62
You should rouse yourself, As did the former lions of your blood *Hen. V.* i 2 124
I pray thee, bear my former answer back . . . . iv 3 90
Which to reduce into our former favour You are assembled . . v 2 63
And bless us with her former qualities . . . . v 2 67
Darest thou maintain the former words thou spakest? . 1 *Hen. VI.* iii 4 31
The over-daring Talbot Hath sullied all his gloss of former honour . iv 4 6
Bethink thee once again, And in thy thought o'er-run my former time! 3 *Hen. VI.* i 4 45
I was, I must confess, Great Albion's queen in former golden days . iii 3 7
Let former grudges pass, And henceforth I am thy true servitor . iii 3 195
I will revenge his wrong to Lady Bona And replant Henry in his former state . . . . iii 3 198
I will never more remember Our former hatred . . *Richard III.* ii 1 24
Each following day Became the next day's master, till the last Made former wonders its . . . . . . *Hen. VIII.* i 1 18
That former fabulous story, Being now seen possible enough, got credit i 1 36
The former agents, if they did complain, What could the belly answer? *Coriolanus* i 1 127
It is your former promise.—Sir, it is . . . . i 1 242
He hath in this action outdone his former deeds doubly . . ii 1 150
Out of that I'll work Myself a former fortune . . . . v 3 202
He owes nine thousand; besides my former sum . *T. of Athens* ii 1 2
Offering the fortunes of his former days, The former man may make him v 1 127
Coming from Sardis, on our former ensign Two mighty eagles fell *J. Cæsar* v 1 80
Pronounce his present death, And with his former title greet Macbeth *Macbeth* i 2 65
This sore night Hath trifled former knowings . . . . . ii 4 4
Whilst our poor malice Remains in danger of her former tooth . iii 2 15
My former speeches have but hit your thoughts, Which can interpret further . . . . iii 6 1
Thy hair, Thou other gold-bound brow, is like the first. A third is like the former . . . . iv 1 115
So by my former lecture and advice, Shall you my son . . *Hamlet* ii 1 67
You are so sick of late, So far from cheer and from your former state . iii 2 174
If you come slack of former services, You shall do well . *Lear* i 3 9
What's the news with you?—Madam, my former suit . *Othello* iii 4 110
Or say they strike us, Or scant our former having in despite . iv 3 92
If I quench thee, thou flaming minister, I can again thy former light restore . . . . v 2 9
You have seen and proved a fairer former fortune Than that which is to approach . . . . *Ant. and Cleo.* i 2 33
Thou must not take my former sharpness ill: I will employ thee back again iii 3 38
Wisdom and fortune combating together, If that the former dare but what it can, No chance may shake it . . . . . iii 13 80
My good stars, that were my former guides, Have empty left their orbs iii 13 145
Please your thoughts In feeding them with those my former fortunes . iv 15 53
Some dying; some their friends O'er-borne i' the former wave *Cymbeline* v 3 48
Virtue and cunning . . . ; immortality attends the former . *Pericles* iii 2 30
Formerly. Thou hast incurr'd The danger formerly by me rehearsed *M. of V.* iv 1 362
'Tis [virginity] a withered pear; it was formerly better . *All's Well* i 1 176
Is less frequent to his princely exercises than formerly . . *W. Tale* iv 2 37
That never They shall abound as formerly . . *Hen. VIII.* i 1 83
Hear from me still, and never of me aught But what is like me formerly *Cor.* iv 1 53
Accuses him of letters he had formerly wrote to Pompey *Ant. and Cleo.* iii 5 11
Formless. All form is formless, order orderless . *K. John* iii 1 253
What's past and what's to come is strew'd with husks And formless ruin of oblivion . . . . *Troi. and Cres.* iv 5 167
Fornication. Given to fornications, and to taverns . *Mer. Wives* v 5 166
Might have been accused in fornication, adultery . *Meas. for Meas.* ii 1 82
Condemn'd upon the act of fornication . . . . v 1 70
Fornication. She that accuses him of fornication, In self-same manner doth accuse my husband . . . . . *Meas. for Meas.* v 1 195
Bless me, what a fry of fornication is at door! . . *Hen. VIII.* v 4 36
Fornicatress. See you the fornicatress be removed . . *Meas. for Meas.* ii 2 23
Forres. How far is't call'd to Forres? . . . . *Macbeth* i 3 39
Forrest. Dighton and Forrest, whom I did suborn To do this ruthless piece of butchery . . . . *Richard III.* iv 3 4
'Thus,' quoth Forrest, 'girdling one another Within their innocent alabaster arms' . . . . iv 3 10
'A book of prayers on their pillow lay; Which once,' quoth Forrest, 'almost changed my mind' . . . . iv 3 15
Forsake. Make tigers tame and huge leviathans Forsake unsounded deeps to dance on sands . . . . . . *T. G. of Ver* iii 2 81
He that came behind you, sir, like an evil angel, and bid you forsake your liberty . . . . *Com. of Errors* iv 3 20
Thou hast power to choose, and they none to forsake . *All's Well* ii 3 62
I see that men make ropes in such a scarre That we'll forsake ourselves iv 2 39
I must Forsake the court: to do't, or no, is certain To me a break-neck *W. T.* i 2 362
Wilt thou forsake thy fortune, Bequeath thy land to him and follow me? *K. John* i 1 148
Of old I know them; rather with their teeth The walls they'll tear down than forsake the siege . . . . . 1 *Hen. VI.* i 2 40
Even with the earth Shall lay your stately and air-braving towers, If you forsake the offer of their love . . . . . . iv 2 14
See, they forsake me! Now the time is come . . . . v 3 24
Home to your cottages, forsake this groom . . . 2 *Hen. VI.* iv 2 132
The citizens fly and forsake their houses . . . . . iv 4 50
And here pronounce free pardon to them all That will forsake thee . iv 8 10
How evil it beseems thee, To flatter Henry and forsake thy brother! 3 *Hen VI.* iv 7 85
My parks, my walks, my manors that I had, Even now forsake me . v 2 25
Poor Clarence did forsake his father, Warwick *Richard III.* i 3 135
Who told me how the poor soul did forsake The mighty Warwick? . ii 1 109
Sweet partner, I must not yet forsake you: let's be merry . *Hen. VIII.* i 4 104
And, till my soul forsake, Shall cry for blessings on him . . ii 1 89
I must now forsake ye: the last hour Of my long weary life is come upon me ii 1 132
Were your godheads to borrow of men, men would forsake the gods *T. of A.* iii 6 84
She was in love, and he she loved proved mad And did forsake her *Othello* iv 3 28
You must forsake this room, and go with us . . . . v 2 330
Forsake thy seat, I do beseech thee, captain, And hear me *Ant. and Cleo.* ii 7 43
Forsaken. To make him a garland, as being forsaken . . *Much Ado* ii 1 226
Forsaken your pernicious faction And join'd with Charles 1 *Hen. VI.* iv 1 59
And thou, poor soul, Art then forsaken, as thou went'st forlorn! 3 *Hen. VI.* iii 1 54
Is Rosaline, whom thou didst love so dear, So soon forsaken? *R. and J.* ii 3 67
Most rich, being poor; Most choice, forsaken; and most loved, despised! *Lear* i 1 254
Forsaketh. Or one that, at a triumph having vow'd To try his strength, forsaketh yet the lists . . . . . . 1 *Hen. VI.* v 5 32
Forslow no longer, make we hence amain . . . 3 *Hen. VI.* ii 3 56
Forsook. Belike she thinks that Proteus hath forsook her *T. G. of Ver.* iv 4 151
In their sport Forsook his scene and enter'd in a brake *M. N. Dream* iii 2 15
How fares your majesty?—Poison'd,—ill fare—dead, forsook . *K. John* v 7 35
He hath forsook the court, Broken his staff of office . *Richard II.* ii 3 26
No one in this presence But his red colour hath forsook his cheeks *Rich. III.* ii 1 85
Our dastard nobles, who Have all forsook me . . *Coriolanus* iv 5 82
His comfortable temper has forsook him . . . *T. of Athens* iii 4 72
Hath she forsook so many noble matches, Her father and her country? *Oth.* iv 2 125
Forsooth. I thank you, forsooth . . . . *Mer. Wives* i 1 277; 280
I had rather, forsooth, go before you like a man . . . . iii 2 5
Whither bear you this?—To the laundress, forsooth . . . iii 3 163
And, forsooth, to search his house for his wife's love . . iii 5 78
Forsooth, I have forgot . . . . iv 1 78
Whence come you?—From the two parties, forsooth . . . iv 5 107
This pernicious slave, Forsooth, took on him as a conjurer *Com. of Errors* v 1 242
Very crotchets that he speaks; Note, notes, forsooth, and nothing *M. Ado* ii 3 59
And I, forsooth, in love! I, that have been love's whip! . *L. L. Lost* iii 1 175
But that, forsooth, the bouncing Amazon, Your buskin'd mistress and your warrior love, To Theseus must be wedded. . *M. N. Dream* ii 1 70
And tender me, forsooth, affection? . . . . . . iii 2 230
With her personage, her tall personage, Her height, forsooth, she hath prevail'd with him . . . . iii 2 293
All, forsooth, deifying the name of Rosalind . *As Y. Like It* iii 2 380
I must, forsooth, be forced To give my hand . . . *T. of Shrew* iii 2 8
No, no, forsooth; I dare not for my life . . . . . iv 3 1
I am going, forsooth: the business is for Helen to come hither *All's Well* i 3 100
He will, forsooth, have all my prisoners . . . . 1 *Hen. IV.* i 3 140
How long hast thou to serve, Francis?—Forsooth, five years . . ii 4 46
And now, forsooth, takes on him to reform Some certain edicts . iv 3 78
As well they may upbraid me with my crown, Because, forsooth, the king of Scots is crown'd . . . . . . 1 *Hen. VI.* iv 1 157
She hath been liberal and free.—And yet, forsooth, she is a virgin pure v 4 83
That my master was? no, forsooth: my master said that he was 2 *Hen. VI.* i 3 33
Because the king, forsooth, will have it so . . . . . i 3 118
Forsooth, a blind man at Saint Alban's shrine . . . hath received his sight ii 1 63
What's thy name?—Peter, forsooth.—Peter! what more?—Thump . ii 3 82
And you, forsooth, had the good duke to keep . . . . iii 2 183
Who are they that complain unto the king, That I, forsooth, am stern and love them not? . . . . *Richard III.* i 3 44
Nay, forsooth, my friends . . . live not here . . . *Hen. VIII.* i 1 87
And wot you what I found There,—on my conscience, put unwittingly? Forsooth, an inventory . . . . iii 2 124
Then, forsooth, the faint defects of age Must be the scene of mirth *T. and C.* i 3 172
But thou wilt frame Thyself, forsooth, hereafter theirs . *Coriolanus* iii 2 85
Wouldst thou speak with us?—Yea, forsooth . . . *T. Andron.* iv 4 40
Yes, forsooth, I will hold my tongue . . . . . *Lear* i 4 214
And what was he? Forsooth, a great arithmetician . . . *Othello* i 1 19
Yes, forsooth: I wish you joy o' the worm . . *Ant. and Cleo.* v 2 281
Ay, forsooth *Mer. Wives* i 4; ii 1; ii 2; v 2; *Rom. and Jul.* iv 2
Forspent. A gentleman, almost forspent with speed . . 2 *Hen. IV.* i 1 37
Forspent with toil, as runners with a race, I lay me down a little while to breathe . . . . 3 *Hen. VI.* ii 3 1
Forspoke. Thou hast forspoke my being in these wars, And say'st it is not fit.—Well, is it? . . . . *Ant. and Cleo.* iii 7 3
Forswear not thyself, sweet youth, for I am not welcome *T. G. of Ver.* ii 5 3
Love bade me swear and Love bids me forswear . . . . ii 6 6
You'll forswear this again.—I'll be hanged first . *Meas. for Meas.* iii 2 177
Yes, marry, did I: but I was fain to forswear it . . . iv 3 183
Who heard me to deny it or forswear it? . . . *Com. of Errors* v 1 25
Then fools you were these women to forswear . . . *L. L. Lost* iv 3 355
Your oath once broke, you force not to forswear . . . . . v 2 440

Forswear. As waggish boys in game themselves forswear . *M. N. Dream* i 1 240
Loathe him; then entertain him, then forswear him . *As Y. Like It* iii 2 437
To forswear the full stream of the world and to live in a nook merely monastic . . . iii 2 440
To swear and to forswear; according as marriage binds and blood breaks v 4 58
If you be so contented, Forswear Bianca and her love for ever *T. of Shrew* iv 2 26
I firmly vow Never to woo her more, but do forswear her . . . iv 2 29
Deny him, forswear him, or else we are all undone . . . v 1 114
If it be so, you have wound a goodly clew; If it be not, forswear't *All's W.* i 3 189
An I thought that, I'ld forswear it . . . . *T. Night* i 3 93
For meddle you must, that's certain, or forswear to wear iron about you iii 4 276
Let villany itself forswear't . . . . *W. Tale* i 2 361
Forswear themselves as often as they speak . . . . . v 1 200
All pomp and majesty I do forswear . . . . . *Richard II.* iv 1 211
If he fight longer than he sees reason, I'll forswear arms . *1 Hen. IV.* i 2 208
I'll forswear keeping house, afore I'll be in these tirrits and frights *2 Hen. IV.* ii 4 219
To forswear thin potations and to addict themselves to sack . . iv 3 134
If you be not swinged, I'll forswear half-kirtles . . . . v 4 23
Thou usest to forswear thyself: 'Twas sin before, but now 'tis charity *3 Hen. VI.* v 5 75
Accuse some innocent and forswear myself . . . *T. Andron.* v 1 130
Did my heart love till now? forswear it, sight! . . *Rom. and Jul.* i 5 54
Give us some gold, good Timon: hast thou more?—Enough to make a whore forswear her trade . . . . *T. of A.* iv 3 133
Comfort forswear me! . . . . *Othello* iv 2 159
Forswearing. For false forswearing and for murder too . *Richard III.* i 4 207
Which he mended thus, By now forswearing that he is forsworn *1 Hen. IV.* v 2 39
Forswore. I never prospered since I forswore myself at primero *M. Wives* iv 5 103
Which he forswore most monstrously to have . . . *Com. of Errors* v 1 11
I never did deny it.—Yes, that you did, sir, and forswore it too . v 1 24
You first forswore it on the mart: And thereupon I drew my sword on you . . . . v 1 261
He swore a thing to me on Monday night, which he forswore on Tuesday morning; there's a double tongue . . . *Much Ado* v 1 169
A woman I forswore; but I will prove, Thou being a goddess, I forswore not thee: My vow was earthly . . . . *L. L. Lost* iv 3 64
Why, love forswore me in my mother's womb . *3 Hen. VI.* iii 2 153
Yea, and forswore himself,—Which Jesu pardon! . . *Richard III.* i 3 136
Forsworn. Her and her blind boy's scandal'd company I have forsworn *Tempest* iv 1 91
To leave my Julia, shall I be forsworn; To love fair Silvia, shall I be forsworn; To wrong my friend, I shall be much forsworn *T. G. of V.* ii 6 1
Hath she forsworn me?—No, Valentine.—No Valentine, if Silvia have forsworn me . . . . iii 1 212
She hath despised me most, Forsworn my company . . . . iii 2 4
She bids me think how I have been forsworn . . . . iv 2 10
Take, O, take those lips away, That so sweetly were forsworn *M. for M.* iv 1 2
That Angelo's forsworn; is it not strange? . . . . . v 1 38
And true he swore, though yet forsworn he were . *Com. of Errors* iv 2 10
They are both forsworn: In this the madman justly chargeth them . v 1 212
If you swear, my lord, you shall not be forsworn . . *Much Ado* i 1 155
Necessity will make us all forsworn . . . . . *L. L. Lost* i 1 150
I am forsworn on 'mere necessity' . . . . i 1 155
I shall be forsworn, which is a great argument of falsehood, if I love . i 2 175
Our Lady help my lord! he'll be forsworn . . . . . ii 1 98
If love make me forsworn, how shall I swear to love? . . . iv 2 109
Though to myself forsworn, to thee I'll faithful prove . . . iv 2 111
I am forsworn!—Why, he comes in like a perjure, wearing papers . iv 3 47
Do not call it sin in me, That I am forsworn for thee . . . iv 3 116
We cannot cross the cause why we were born; Therefore of all hands must we be forsworn . . . . iv 3 219
Are we not all in love?—Nothing so sure; and thereby all forsworn . iv 3 283
In that each of you have forsworn his book, Can you still dream and pore? . . . . iv 3 297
Not looking on a woman's face, You have in that forsworn the use of eyes iv 3 310
O, we have made a vow to study, lords, And in that vow we have forsworn our books . . . . iv 3 319
It is religion to be thus forsworn . . . . iv 3 363
Light wenches may prove plagues to men forsworn . . . iv 3 385
We are again forsworn, in will and error . . . . . v 2 471
Yet swear not, lest ye be forsworn again . . . . . v 2 842
I have forsworn his bed and company . . . . *M. N. Dream* ii 1 62
I could teach you How to choose right, but I am then forsworn *M. of V.* iii 2 11
You'll make me wish a sin, That I had been forsworn . . . iii 2 14
The mustard was good, and yet was not the knight forsworn *As Y. Like It* i 2 71
If you swear by that that is not, you are not forsworn . . . i 2 82
Would all the world but he had quite forsworn! . . *T. of Shrew* iv 2 35
Nay, I have ta'en you napping, gentle love, And have forsworn you . iv 2 47
You jest: but have you both forsworn me?—Mistress, we have . . iv 2 48
Tell me, thou fellow, is not France forsworn? . . . *K. John* iii 1 62
You are forsworn, forsworn; You came in arms to spill mine enemies' blood . . . . iii 1 101
The truth thou art unsure To swear, swears only not to be forsworn . iii 1 284
But thou dost swear only to be forsworn; And most forsworn, to keep what thou dost swear . . . . iii 1 286
He is forsworn, if e'er those eyes of yours Behold another day break . v 4 31
I task the earth to the like, forsworn Aumerle . . . *Richard II.* iv 1 52
I have forsworn his company hourly any time this two and twenty years, and yet I am bewitched . . . . *1 Hen. IV.* ii 2 16
Which he mended thus, By now forswearing that he is forsworn . . v 2 39
How now, sir! you villain!—Do you think I'll be forsworn? *Hen. V.* iv 8 13
The northern lords that have forsworn thy colours Will follow mine *3 Hen. VI.* i 1 251
God forbid your grace should be forsworn.—I shall be . . . . i 2 18
Foh, foh! come, tell a pin: you are forsworn . . . *Troi. and Cres.* v 2 22
Those doves' eyes, Which can make gods forsworn . . . *Coriolanus* v 3 28
The thing I have forsworn to grant may never Be held by you denials . v 3 80
She hath forsworn to love, and in that vow Do I live dead *Rom. and Jul.* i 1 229
All perjured, All forsworn, all naught, all dissemblers . . . iii 2 87
Nor what is mine shall never do thee good: Trust to't, bethink you; I'll not be forsworn . . . . iii 5 197
Is it more sin to wish me thus forsworn, Or to dispraise my lord with that same tongue Which she hath praised him with above compare So many thousand times? . . . . iii 5 236
I am yet Unknown to woman, never was forsworn . . . *Macbeth* iv 3 126
Fort. Fe, fe! ma foi, il fait fort chaud . . . *Mer. Wives* i 4 53
Surprised our forts And sent the ragged soldiers wounded home *2 Hen. VI.* iv 1 89
Oft breaking down the pales and forts of reason . . . *Hamlet* i 4 28
Forted. A forted residence 'gainst the tooth of time . . *Meas. for Meas.* v 1 12
Forth. Know thus far forth . . . . *Tempest* i 2 177
O, if a virgin, And your affection not gone forth, I'll make you The queen of Naples . . . . i 2 448
And, sowing the kernels of it in the sea, bring forth more islands . . ii 1 93
But nature should bring forth, Of it own kind, all foison, all abundance ii 1 162
And sends me forth—For else his project dies . . . . ii 1 298
She will become thy bed, I warrant. And bring thee forth brave brood iii 2 113
I have bedimm'd The noontide sun, call'd forth the mutinous winds . v 1 42
Graves at my command Have waked their sleepers, oped, and let 'em forth v 1 49
I am Prospero and that very duke Which was thrust forth of Milan . v 1 160
I will requite you with as good a thing; At least bring forth a wonder . v 1 170
For it is you that have chalk'd forth the way Which brought us hither . v 1 203
Put forth their sons to seek preferment out . . . *T. G. of Ver.* i 3 7
I shall inquire you forth . . . . ii 4 186
At that time the jealous rascally knave her husband will be forth *M. W.* ii 2 276
A couple of Ford's knaves, his hinds, were called forth by their mistress iii 5 100
Behold what honest clothes you send forth to bleaching! . . . iv 2 126
Let them from forth a sawpit rush at once With some diffused song . iv 4 53
Hath answer'd my affection, So far forth as herself might be her chooser iv 6 11
For if our virtues Did not go forth of us, 'twere all alike As if we had them not . . . . *Meas. for Meas.* i 1 35
The heavens give safety to your purposes!—Lead forth and bring you back in happiness! . . . . i 1 75
They put forth to steal . . . . i 2 14
There spake my brother; there my father's grave Did utter forth a voice iii 1 87
Our soul Cannot but yield you forth to public thanks . . . v 1 7
Whom it concerns to hear this matter forth . . . . . . v 1 255
Like a drop of water That in the ocean seeks another drop, Who, falling there to find his fellow forth, Unseen, inquisitive, confounds himself *Com. of Errors* i 2 37
The heedful slave Is wander'd forth, in care to seek me out . . . ii 2 3
If any ask you for your master, Say he dines forth . . . . ii 2 212
If any bark put forth, come to the mart, Where I will walk . . . iii 2 155
Is there any ship puts forth to-night? may we be gone? . . . iv 3 35
Say, wherefore didst thou lock me forth to-day? . . . . iv 4 98
I did not, gentle husband, lock thee forth . . . . . iv 4 100
Then let your servants bring my husband forth . . . . v 1 93
The abbess shuts the gates on us And will not suffer us to fetch him out, Nor send him forth . . . . v 1 158
You'll be made bring Deformed forth, I warrant you . . *Much Ado* iii 3 186
You must call forth the watch that are their accusers.—Yea, marry, that's the eftest way. Let the watch come forth . . . . iv 2 36
Call her forth, brother; here's the friar ready . . . . . v 4 39
Now step I forth to whip hypocrisy . . . . . *L. L. Lost* iv 3 151
Call them forth quickly; we will do so.—Holla! approach . . . v 2 899
Turn melancholy forth to funerals . . . . . *M. N. Dream* i 1 15
If thou lovest me then, Steal forth thy father's house to-morrow night . i 1 164
Call forth your actors by the scroll. Masters, spread yourselves . . i 2 16
Anon his Thisbe must be answered, And forth my mimic comes . . iii 2 19
And as imagination bodies forth The forms of things unknown . . v 1 14
The graves all gaping wide, Every one lets forth his sprite . . . v 1 388
Had I such venture forth, The better part of my affections would Be with my hopes abroad . . . . *Mer. of Venice* i 1 15
I shot his fellow of the self-same flight The self-same way with more advised watch, To find the other forth . . . . i 1 143
Therefore go forth; Try what my credit can in Venice do . . . i 1 179
What is your will?—I am bid forth to supper, Jessica . . . . ii 5 11
By Jacob's staff, I swear, I have no mind of feasting forth to-night . ii 5 37
The Dardanian wives, With bleared visages, come forth to view The issue iii 2 59
'Mong other things I shall digest it.—Well, I'll set you forth . . iii 5 95
I must away this night toward Padua, And it is meet I presently set forth iv 1 404
And bring your music forth into the air . . . . . . v 1 53
I set forth as soon as you And even but now return'd . . . v 1 271
Now unmuzzle your wisdom.—Stand you both forth now *As Y. Like It* i 2 75
On my life, his malice 'gainst the lady Will suddenly break forth . i 2 295
Alas, what danger will it be to us, Maids as we are, to travel forth so far! i 3 111
The wretched animal heaved forth such groans . . . . ii 1 36
It may well be called Jove's tree, when it drops forth such fruit . . iii 2 250
He went but forth to wash him in the Hellespont . . . . iv 1 103
He hath ta'en his bow and arrows and is gone forth to sleep . . iv 3 5
Women's gentle brain Could not drop forth such giant-rude invention . iv 3 34
Since this bar in law makes us friends, it shall be so far forth friendly maintained . . . . *T. of Shrew* i 1 140
Draw forth thy weapon, we are beset with thieves . . . . iii 2 238
It was the friar of orders grey, As he forth walked on his way . . iv 1 149
Come, tailor, let us see these ornaments; Lay forth the gown . . iv 3 62
Call forth an officer. Carry this mad knave to the goal . . . v 1 94
Swinge me them soundly forth unto their husbands . . . . v 2 104
Exempted be from me the arrogance To choose from forth the royal blood of France . . . . *All's Well* ii 1 199
Fair maid, send forth thine eye: this youthful parcel Of noble bachelors stand at my bestowing . . . . ii 3 58
Whose great decision hath much blood let forth And more thirsts after iii 1 3
Then go thou forth; And fortune play upon thy prosperous helm! . . iii 3 6
Sent him forth From courtly friends, with camping foes to live . . iii 4 13
Come, bring forth this counterfeit module, has deceived me . . . iv 3 113
Bring him forth: has sat i' the stocks all night . . . . iv 3 116
Which gratitude Through flinty Tartar's bosom would peep forth . . iv 4 7
So stand thou forth; The time is fair again . . . . . v 3 35
The heavens have thought well on thee, Lafeu, To bring forth this discovery . . . . v 3 151
My desire, More sharp than filed steel, did spur me forth . *T. Night* iii 3 5
The rather by these arguments of fear, Set forth in your pursuit . . iii 3 13
Hast thou forgot thyself? is it so long? Call forth the holy father . v 1 145
No sneaping winds at home, to make us say 'This is put forth too truly' . . . . *W. Tale* i 2 14
His folly, fear, Among the infinite doings of the world, Sometime puts forth i 2 254
Put apart these your attendants, I Shall bring Emilia forth . . ii 2 15
The good queen, For she is good, hath brought you forth a daughter . ii 3 65
Therefore bring forth, And in Apollo's name, his oracle . . . iii 2 118
Whereof I reckon The casting forth to crows thy baby-daughter To be or none or little . . . . iii 2 192
But let Time's news Be known when 'tis brought forth . . . iv 1 27
Methinks I see Leontes opening his free arms and weeping His welcomes forth . . . . iv 4 560
The which shall point you forth at every sitting What you must say . iv 4 572
With thought of such affections, Step forth mine advocate . . . v 1 221
We'll set forth In best appointment all our regiments . . *K. John* ii 1 295
Our colours do return in those same hands That did display them when we first march'd forth . . . . ii 1 320

Forth. Fortune shall cull forth Out of one side her happy minion *K. John* ii 1 391
Here's a large mouth, indeed, That spits forth death and mountains! . ii 1 458
Arise forth from the couch of lasting night, Thou hate and terror to prosperity . . . . iii 4 27
None so small advantage shall step forth To check his reign . . . iii 4 151
Rush forth, And bind the boy which you shall find with me . . . iv 1 3
Young lad, come forth; I have to say with you . . . . . iv 1 8
Here's a prophet, that I brought with me From forth the streets of Pomfret . . . . iv 2 148
From forth this morsel of dead royalty, The life, the right and truth of all this realm Is fled to heaven . . . . iv 3 143
I pray you, bear me hence From forth the noise and rumour of the field v 4 45
Not so deep a maim As to be cast forth in the common air *Richard II.* i 3 157
Go, say I sent thee forth to purchase honour . . . . . i 3 282
Where doth the world thrust forth a vanity—So it be new? . . ii 1 24
From forth thy reach he would have laid thy shame . . . ii 1 106
Now hath my soul brought forth her prodigy . . . . ii 2 64
From forth the ranks of many thousand French . . . . ii 3 102
Bring forth these men. Bushy and Green, I will not vex your souls . iii 1 1
Beshrew thee, cousin, which didst lead me forth Of that sweet way I was in to despair! . . . . iii 2 204
His eye, As bright as is the eagle's, lightens forth Controlling majesty iii 3 69
Call forth Bagot. Now, Bagot, freely speak thy mind . . . iv 1 1
The lion dying thrusteth forth his paw, And wounds the earth . . v 1 29
My wife to France: from whence, set forth in pomp . . . v 1 78
I see some sparks of better hope, which elder years May happily bring forth v 3 22
How shall we part with them in setting forth?—Why, we will set forth before or after them . . . . *1 Hen. IV.* i 2 188
When the unhappy king . . . did set forth Upon his Irish expedition . i 3 149
O esperance! Bid Butler lead him forth into the park . . . . ii 3 75
Thither shall you go too; To-day will I set forth, to-morrow you . . ii 3 119
Diseased nature oftentimes breaks forth In strange eruptions . . iii 1 27
My good Lord of Worcester will set forth To meet your father . . iii 1 84
Doth he keep his bed?—He did, my lord, four days ere I set forth . iv 1 22
The king himself in person is set forth, Or hitherwards intended speedily iv 1 91
The Prince of Wales stepp'd forth before the king . . . . v 2 46
His lordship is walk'd forth into the orchard . . . *2 Hen. IV.* i 1 4
His forward spirit Would lift him where most trade of danger ranged: Yet did you say 'Go forth'. . . . . i 1 175
What hath this bold enterprise brought forth? . . . . . i 1 178
Come, we will all put forth, body and goods . . . . . i 1 186
Lend me a thousand pound to furnish me forth . . . . . i 2 251
The powers that you already have sent forth Shall bring this prize in . iii 1 100
Send discoverers forth To know the numbers of our enemies . . . iv 1 3
Answer them directly How far forth you do like their articles . . iv 2 53
But Peace puts forth her olive every where . . . . . iv 4 87
On this unworthy scaffold to bring forth So great an object . *Hen. V.* Prol. 10
I am coming on, To venge me as I may and to put forth My rightful hand i 2 292
But, till the king come forth, and not till then . . . . ii Prol. 41
Fetch forth the lazar kite of Cressid's kind . . . . . ii 1 80
Then forth, dear countrymen: let us deliver Our puissance into the hand of God . . . . ii 2 189
'Tis meet we all go forth To view the sick and feeble parts of France . ii 4 21
Now forth, lord constable and princes all, And quickly bring us word of England's fall . . . . iii 5 67
For forth he goes and visits all his host, Bids them good morrow . iv Prol. 32
Go forth and fetch their conquering Cæsar in . . . . . v Prol. 28
Like prisoners wildly overgrown with hair, Put forth disorder'd twigs . v 2 44
The even mead, that erst brought sweetly forth The freckled cowslip . v 2 48
These tidings would call forth their flowing tides . . *1 Hen. VI.* i 1 83
For none but Samsons and Goliases It sendeth forth to skirmish . . i 2 34
Raise this tedious siege And drive the English forth the bounds of France i 2 54
My keen-edged sword . . . Out of a great deal of old iron I chose forth i 2 101
Bring forth the body of old Salisbury, And here advance it . . . ii 2 4
Engenders thunder in his breast And makes him roar these accusations forth . . . . iii 1 40
Dare ye come forth and meet us in the field? . . . . . iii 2 61
English John Talbot, captains, calls you forth . . . . . iv 2 3
Who with me Set from our o'ermatch'd forces forth for aid . . iv 4 11
Then call our captains and our colours forth . . . . . v 3 128
Bring forth that sorceress condemn'd to burn . . . . . v 4 1
Put forth thy hand, reach at the glorious gold . . . *2 Hen. VI.* i 2 11
Cursed the gentle gusts And he that loosed them forth their brazen caves iii 2 89
Therefore bring forth the soldiers of our prize . . . . . iv 1 8
In our voiding lobby hast thou stood And duly waited for my coming forth . . . . iv 1 62
O that I were a god, to shoot forth thunder! . . . . . iv 1 104
Clifford, I say, come forth and fight with me . . . . . v 2 5
Let us pursue him ere the writs go forth . . . . . . v 3 26
Let's set our men in order, And issue forth and bid them battle *3 Hen. VI.* i 2 71
My ashes, as the phœnix, may bring forth A bird that will revenge . i 4 35
And watch'd him how he singled Clifford forth . . . . ii 1 12
Even then that sunshine brew'd a shower for him, That wash'd his father's fortunes forth of France . . . . ii 2 157
From London by the king was I press'd forth . . . . . ii 5 64
He lopp'd the branch In hewing Rutland when his leaves put forth . ii 6 48
Bring forth that fatal screech-owl to our house . . . . ii 6 56
Bring forth the gallant, let us hear him speak . . . . . v 5 12
Thy mother felt more than a mother's pain, And yet brought forth less than a mother's hope . . . . v 6 50
In these windows that let forth thy life . . . . *Richard III.* i 2 12
And let the soul forth that adoreth thee . . . . . . i 2 177
But still the envious flood Kept in my soul, and would not let it forth i 4 38
Are you call'd forth from out a world of men To slay the innocent? . i 4 186
I am not barren to bring forth complaints . . . . . . ii 2 67
May send forth plenteous tears to drown the world . . . . ii 2 70
To draw forth your noble ancestry From the corruption of abusing times iii 7 198
From forth the kennel of thy womb hath crept A hell-hound . . iv 4 47
That call'd your grace To breakfast once forth of my company . . iv 4 176
Bid him bring his power: I will lead forth my soldiers to the plain . v 3 291
Base lackey peasants, Whom their o'ercloyed country vomits forth . v 3 318
To-day he puts forth The tender leaves of hopes . . *Hen. VIII.* iii 2 352
No sun shall ever usher forth mine honours . . . . . iii 2 410
I was a chaste wife to my grave: embalm me, Then lay me forth . . iv 2 171
My accusers, Be what they will, may stand forth face to face . . v 3 47
From the Athenian bay Put forth toward Phrygia . *Troi. and Cres.* Prol. 7
I think he went not forth to-day . . . . i 2 239
The worthiness of praise distains his worth, If that the praised himself bring the praise forth . . . . i 3 242
Doth boil, As 'twere from forth us all, a man distill'd Out of our virtues i 3 350

Forth. When thou art forth in the incursions, thou strikest as slow as another . . . . *Troi. and Cres.* ii 1 32
How Hecuba cries out! How poor Andromache shrills her dolours forth! v 3 84
We'll forth and fight, Do deeds worth praise and tell you them at night v 3 92
Sigh'd forth proverbs, That hunger broke stone walls . *Coriolanus* i 1 209
And throw forth greater themes For insurrection's arguing . . . i 1 224
Worshipful mutiners, Your valour puts well forth . . . . . i 1 255
Some parcels of their power are forth already, And only hitherward . i 2 32
Forth he goes, Like to a harvest-man that's task'd to mow . . . i 3 38
Not lovelier Than Hector's forehead when it spit forth blood . . i 3 45
Pardon me; indeed, I will not forth.—In truth, la, go with me . . i 3 99
Thus it is: the Volsces have an army forth . . . . . . i 3 108
Hark! our drums Are bringing forth our youth . . . . . i 4 16
They fear us not, but issue forth their city . . . . . . i 4 23
We render you the tenth, to be ta'en forth, Before the common distribution i 9 34
You shout me forth In acclamations hyperbolical . . . . . i 9 50
Whoever gave that counsel, to give forth The corn o' the storehouse gratis iii 1 113
If the time thrust forth A cause for thy repeal . . . . . iv 1 40
When I am forth, Bid me farewell, and smile . . . . . iv 1 49
We should by this, to all our lamentation, If he had gone forth consul, found it . . . . iv 6 35
Thrusts forth his horns again into the world . . . . . . iv 6 44
Back, I say, go; lest I let forth your half-pint of blood . . . . v 2 60
That brought you forth this boy, to keep your name Living to time . v 3 126
Till from forth this place I lead espoused my bride along with me *T. An.* i 1 327
Your Moor and you Are singled forth to try experiments . . . ii 3 69
Remember, boys, I pour'd forth tears in vain . . . . . ii 3 163
Is torn from forth that pretty hollow cage . . . . . . iii 1 84
That my tongue may utter forth The venomous malice of my swelling heart! . . . . v 3 12
I am the turned forth, be it known to you . . . . . . v 3 109
Throw her forth to beasts and birds of prey: Her life was beast-like . v 3 198
From forth the fatal loins of these two foes A pair of star-cross'd lovers take their life . . . . *Rom. and Jul.* Prol. 5
An hour before the worshipp'd sun Peer'd forth the golden window of the east . . . . i 1 126
Nurse, where's my daughter? call her forth to me . . . . . i 3 1
And flecked darkness like a drunkard reels From forth day's path . ii 3 4
Romeo, come forth; come forth, thou fearful man . . . . iii 3 1
And call thee back With twenty hundred thousand times more joy Than thou went'st forth in lamentation . . . . iii 3 154
I'll play the housewife for this once. What, ho! They are all forth . iv 2 44
For shame, bring Juliet forth; her lord is come . . . . . iv 5 22
Seal'd up the doors, and would not let us forth . . . . . v 2 11
Bring forth the parties of suspicion . . . . v 3 222
I entreated her come forth, And bear this work of heaven with patience v 3 260
When comes your book forth? . . . . *T. of Athens* i 1 26
What a mental power This eye shoots forth! . . . . . . i 1 32
Flies an eagle flight, bold and forth on, Leaving no tract behind . . i 1 49
I will choose Mine heir from forth the beggars of the world . . . i 1 138
So soon as dinner's done, we'll forth again . . . . . . ii 2 14
Is my lord ready to come forth?—No, indeed, he is not . . . . iii 4 35
Yield him, . . . From forth thy plenteous bosom, one poor root! . . iv 3 186
Within this mile break forth a hundred springs . . . . . iv 3 421
Approach the fold and cull the infected forth, But kill not all together v 4 43
Will you sup with me to-night, Casca?—No, I am promised forth *J. Cæsar* i 2 293
It is the bright day that brings forth the adder . . . . . ii 1 14
But it is doubtful yet, Whether Cæsar will come forth to-day, or no . ii 1 194
Think you to walk forth? You shall not stir out of your house to-day ii 2 8
Cæsar shall forth: the things that threaten'd me Ne'er look'd but on my back . . . . ii 2 10
Cæsar shall go forth; for these predictions Are to the world in general ii 2 28
The heavens themselves blaze forth the death of princes . . . ii 2 31
What say the augurers?—They would not have you to stir forth to-day ii 2 38
Plucking the entrails of an offering forth, They could not find a heart . ii 2 39
Cæsar shall go forth.—Alas, my lord, Your wisdom is consumed in confidence . . . . ii 2 48
Do not go forth to-day: call it my fear That keeps you in the house . ii 2 50
Bring me word, boy, if thy lord look well, For he went sickly forth . ii 4 14
Then walk we forth, even to the market-place . . . . . iii 1 108
What, shall we forth?—Ay, every man away: Brutus shall lead . . iii 1 119
Had I as many eyes as thou hast wounds, Weeping as fast as they stream forth thy blood, It would become me . . . . iii 1 201
I have no will to wander forth of doors, Yet something leads me forth . iii 3 3
He must be taught and train'd and bid go forth; A barren-spirited fellow iv 1 35
If that thou be'st a Roman, take it forth . . . . . . iv 3 103
Make forth; the generals would have some words . . . . v 1 25
Why didst thou send me forth, brave Cassius? Did I not meet thy friends? v 3 80
Implored your highness' pardon, and set forth A deep repentance *Macbeth* i 4 6
Bring forth men-children only . . . . i 7 72
And Sent forth great largess to your offices . . . . . . ii 1 14
By magot-pies and choughs and rooks brought forth The secret'st man of blood . . . . iii 4 125
Siward, with ten thousand warlike men, Already at a point, was setting forth . . . . iv 3 135
Well; more anon.—Comes the king forth, I pray you? . . . . iv 3 140
I have seen her rise from her bed, . . . take forth paper, fold it, write upon't v 1 6
Producing forth the cruel ministers Of this dead butcher . . . v 8 68
The funeral baked meats Did coldly furnish forth the marriage tables *Hamlet* i 2 181
It waves me forth again: I'll follow it . . . . i 4 68
Forth at your eyes your spirits wildly peep . . . . . . iii 4 119
Breaking forth In rank and not-to-be-endured riots . . . . *Lear* i 4 222
Fetch forth the stocks! As I have life and honour, There shall he sit till noon . . . . ii 2 140
Half breathless, panting forth From Goneril his mistress salutations . ii 4 31
Give me my servant forth. Go tell the duke and 's wife I'ld speak with them . . . . ii 4 116
Bid them come forth and hear me, Or at their chamber-door I'll beat the drum . . . . ii 4 118
Where is my lord of Gloucester?—Follow'd the old man forth . . ii 4 298
Something he left imperfect in the state, which since his coming forth is thought of . . . . iv 3 4
Once or twice she heaved the name of 'father' Pantingly forth . . iv 3 28
A century send forth; Search every acre in the high-grown field . . iv 4 6
But are my brother's powers set forth?—Ay, madam . . . . iv 5 1
Our troops set forth to-morrow: stay with us; The ways are dangerous iv 5 16
I pray you, sir, go forth, And give us truth who 'tis that is arrived *Othello* ii 1 57
'Tis but a man gone. Forth, my sword: he dies . . . . . v 1 10
Forth of my heart those charms, thine eyes, are blotted . . . . v 1 35

Forth. Uncle, I must come forth.—If thou attempt it, it will cost thee dear . . . . *Othello* v 2 254
Where is that viper? bring the villain forth . . . . . v 2 285
O, then we bring forth weeds, When our quick minds lie still *A. and C.* i 2 113
Your old smock brings forth a new petticoat . . . . i 2 175
No vessel can peep forth, but 'tis as soon Taken as seen . . i 4 53
Being unseminar'd, thy freer thoughts May not fly forth of Egypt . i 5 12
That she did make defect perfection, And, breathless, power breathe forth ii 2 237
'But yet'! 'But yet' is as a gaoler to bring forth Some monstrous malefactor . . . . ii 5 52
Welcome hither: Your letters did withhold our breaking forth . . iii 6 79
With news the time's with labour, and throes forth, Each minute, some iii 7 81
Of late, when I cried 'Ho!' Like boys unto a muss, kings would start forth . . . . iii 13 91
Call forth my household servants: let's to-night Be bounteous . iv 2 9
He goes forth gallantly. That he and Cæsar might Determine this great war! . . . . iv 4 36
Go forth, Agrippa, and begin the fight: Our will is Antony be took alive iv 6 1
Order for sea is given; They have put forth the haven . . iv 10 7
His best force Is forth to man his galleys . . . . iv 11 3
This grave charm,—Whose eye beck'd forth my wars . . . iv 12 26
Let the world see His nobleness well acted, which your death Will never let come forth . . . . v 2 46
Antony Shall be brought drunken forth . . . . . v 2 219
Were you but riding forth to air yourself, Such parting were too petty *Cymbeline* i 1 110
Attend you here the door of our stern daughter? Will she not forth? ii 3 43
The boy Fidele's sickness Did make my way long forth . . iv 2 149
Step you forth; Give answer to this boy, and do it freely . . v 5 130
Call forth your soothsayer . . . . . . v 5 426
The lofty cedar, royal Cymbeline, Personates thee: and thy lopp'd branches point Thy two sons forth . . . . v 5 455
He must not live to trumpet forth my infamy . . *Pericles* i 1 145
Put forth to seas, Where when men been, there's seldom ease . ii Gower 27
The grisled north Disgorges such a tempest forth . . iii Gower 48
Your honour has through Ephesus pour'd forth Your charity . iii 2 43
Well, call forth, call forth.—For flesh and blood, sir, white and red . iv 6 36
Yet I was mortally brought forth, and am No other than I appear . v 1 105
At sea in childbed died she, but brought forth A maid-child call'd Marina v 3 5
And (or) so forth *L. L. Lost* iv 2; *T. Night* i 5; iii 4; *2 Hen. IV.* v 3; *Hamlet* ii 1
Come forth *Tempest* i 2; ii 2; *Mer. Wives* iii 3; iv 2; *M. for M.* iv 1; *K. John* iv 1; *Lear* iii 4
From this day (time) forth *J. Cæsar* iv 3; *Hamlet* i 3; iv 4; *Oth.* v 2; *Cymbeline* iii 5
Stand forth *M. N. Dream* i 1; iii 1; *Mer. of Ven.* iv 1; *Richard II.* iv 1; *2 Hen. VI.* ii 3; *Hen. VIII.* i 2
Forthcoming. I charge you see that he be forthcoming *T. of Shrew* v 1 96
We'll see your trinkets here all forthcoming . . . *2 Hen. VI.* i 4 56
By this means Your lady is forthcoming yet at London . . ii 1 179
Forthlight. Master Forthlight the tilter . . . *Meas. for Meas.* iv 3 17
Forthright. My old bones ache: here's a maze trod indeed Through forth-rights and meanders! . . . . *Tempest* iii 3 3
If you give way, Or hedge aside from the direct forthright *Troi. and Cres.* iii 3 158
Forthwith. Bear me forthwith unto his creditor . *Com. of Errors* iv 4 123
Then meet me forthwith at the notary's . *Mer. of Venice* i 3 173
Hence forthwith, To feast and sport us at thy father's house *T. of Shrew* iv 3 184
Go and entreat my wife To come to me forthwith . . . v 2 87
You must part forthwith . . . . *Richard II.* v 1 70
Forthwith a power of English shall we levy . . *1 Hen. IV.* i 1 22
Bonfires in France forthwith I am to make . . *1 Hen. VI.* i 1 153
Thy hour is not yet come: I must go victual Orleans forthwith . i 5 14
And now forthwith shall articles be drawn Touching the jointure *3 Hen. VI.* iii 3 135
I'll join mine eldest daughter and my joy To him forthwith . . iii 3 243
See that forthwith Duke Edward be convey'd Unto my brother . iv 3 52
I'll hence forthwith unto the sanctuary . . . iv 4 31
It is more than needful Forthwith that Edward be pronounced a traitor iv 6 54
Forthwith we'll send him hence to Brittany, Till storms be past . iv 6 97
Forthwith from Ludlow the young prince be fetch'd . *Richard III.* ii 2 121
The queen shall be acquainted Forthwith for what you come *Hen. VIII.* ii 2 109
That forthwith You be convey'd to the Tower a prisoner . . v 3 88
And I will give a taste of it forthwith . *Troi. and Cres.* i 3 389
Forthwith, Ere the first sacrifice, within this hour, We must give up . iv 2 65
Lavinia shall forthwith Be closed in our household's monument *T. And.* v 3 193
I your commission will forthwith dispatch . *Hamlet* iii 3 3
Get you to bed on the instant; I will be returned forthwith . *Othello* iv 3 8
Forthwith they fly Chickens, the way which they stoop'd eagles *Cymb.* v 3 41
Fortification. This fortification, gentlemen, shall we see't? *Othello* iii 2 5
Fortified. He's fortified against any denial . . . *T. Night* i 5 153
What he hath won, that hath he fortified . . . *K. John* iii 4 10
We are well fortified And strong enough to issue out and fight *1 Hen. VI.* iv 2 19
Once again assail your ears, That are so fortified against our story *Hamlet* i 1 32
Fortify. Or else We fortify in paper and in figures . *2 Hen. IV.* i 3 56
Go you and enter Harfleur; there remain, And fortify it strongly *Hen. V.* iii 3 53
I count each one And view the Frenchmen how they fortify . *1 Hen. VI.* i 4 61
Therefore fortify your hold, my lord.—Ay, with my sword . *3 Hen. VI.* i 2 52
Great Dunsinane he strongly fortifies . . . *Macbeth* v 2 12
To fortify her judgement, which else an easy battery might lay flat *Cymb.* i 4 21
Fortinbras. By Fortinbras of Norway . . . Dared to the combat *Hamlet* i 1 82
Our valiant Hamlet . . . Did slay this Fortinbras . . . i 1 86
Which had return'd To the inheritance of Fortinbras, Had he been vanquisher . . . . i 1 92
Young Fortinbras, Of unimproved mettle hot and full . . i 1 95
Young Fortinbras, Holding a weak supposal of our worth . . i 2 17
We have here writ To Norway, uncle of young Fortinbras . . i 2 28
Sends out arrests On Fortinbras; which he, in brief, obeys . . ii 2 68
Fortinbras Craves the conveyance of a promised march Over his kingdom iv 4 2
Who commands them, sir?—The nephew to old Norway, Fortinbras . iv 4 14
I came to't that day that our last king Hamlet overcame Fortinbras . v 1 157
Young Fortinbras, with conquest come from Poland . . v 2 361
I do prophesy the election lights On Fortinbras: he has my dying voice v 2 367
Fortitude. Infused with a fortitude from heaven . *Tempest* i 2 154
Despairing of his own arm's fortitude, To join with witches! *1 Hen. VI.* ii 1 17
I am able now, methinks, Out of a fortitude of soul I feel *Hen. VIII.* iii 2 388
Devotion, patience, courage, fortitude, I have no relish of them *Macbeth* iv 3 94
The fortitude of the place is best known to you . . *Othello* i 3 222
Fortnight. Upon All-hallowmas last, a fortnight afore Michaelmas *M. W.* i 1 212
A fortnight hold we this solemnity, In nightly revels . *M. N. Dream* v 1 376
Fee me an officer; bespeak him a fortnight before . *Mer. of Venice* iii 1 131
Fortnight. For what offence have I this fortnight been A banish'd woman? . . . . . . *1 Hen. IV.* ii 3 41
Your majesty hath been this fortnight ill . . . *2 Hen. IV.* iii 1 104
Ere a fortnight make me elder, I'll send some packing *Richard III.* iii 2 62
They have had inkling this fortnight what we intend to do . *Coriolanus* i 1 59
A fortnight and odd days . . . . *Rom. and Jul.* i 3 15
What, fifty of my followers at a clap! Within a fortnight! . *Lear* i 4 317
Fortress. This fortress built by Nature for herself . *Richard II.* ii 1 43
Let them practise and converse with spirits: God is our fortress *1 Hen. VI.* ii 1 26
This arm, that hath reclaim'd To your obedience fifty fortresses . iii 4 6
Let not the piece of virtue, which is set Betwixt us as the cement of our love, To keep it builded, be the ram to batter The fortress of it *Ant. and Cleo.* iii 2 31
Fortuna de la guerra . . . . . *L. L. Lost* v 2 533
Si fortuna me tormenta, spero contenta . *2 Hen. IV.* v 5 102
Fortunate. Doth not the gentleman Deserve as full as fortunate a bed As ever Beatrice shall couch upon? . . *Much Ado* iii 1 45
So fortunate, But miserable most, to love unloved . *M. N. Dream* iii 2 233
And the issue there create Ever shall be fortunate . . . v 1 413
To hold a rival place with one of them, I have a mind presages me such thrift, That I should questionless be fortunate . *Mer. of Venice* i 1 176
Bless you, my fortunate lady!—I hope, sir, I have your good will *All's Well* ii 4 14
Fortunate mistress,—let my prophecy Come home to ye! *W. Tale* iv 4 662
Nothing so strong and fortunate as I . . *1 Hen. IV.* v 1 38
Thou shalt be fortunate, If thou receive me for thy warlike mate *1 Hen. VI.* i 2 91
Then on, my lords; and France be fortunate! . . . v 2 21
For thou art fortunate in all thy deeds . *3 Hen. VI.* iv 6 25
Well-minded Clarence, be thou fortunate! . . . iv 8 27
I am most fortunate, thus accidentally to encounter you . *Coriolanus* iv 3 39
'Tis not the difference of a year or two Makes me less gracious or thee more fortunate . . . . *T. Andron.* ii 1 32
It was a vision fair and fortunate . . . *J. Cæsar* ii 2 84
As he was fortunate, I rejoice at it; as he was valiant, I honour him . iii 2 27
The wheel'd seat Of fortunate Cæsar, drawn before him, branded His baseness that ensued . . . *Ant. and Cleo.* iv 14 76
Britain be fortunate and flourish in peace and plenty *Cymbeline* v 4 144; v 5 442
Fortunately. You are fortunately met . *M. N. Dream* iv 1 182
Who hath most fortunately been inform'd Of my obscured course *Lear* ii 2 174
Is your general wived?—Most fortunately . . *Othello* ii 1 61
Fortunate-Unhappy. THE FORTUNATE-UNHAPPY . . . *T. Night* ii 5 173
Fortune. Bountiful Fortune, Now my dear lady . *Tempest* i 2 178
If now I court not but omit, my fortunes Will ever after droop . i 2 183
Thou let'st thy fortune sleep—die, rather . . . ii 1 216
How does your content Tender your own good fortune? . . ii 1 270
For all is but fortune . . . . . v 1 257
Some to the wars, to try their fortune there . *T. G. of Ver.* i 3 8
Wishing me with him, partner of his fortune . . i 3 59
I read your fortune in your eye. Was this the idol that you worship so? ii 4 143
Myself do want my servants' fortune . . . iii 1 147
Longer might have stay'd, If crooked fortune had not thwarted me . iv 1 22
Have you any thing to take to?—Nothing but my fortune . iv 1 43
A most unholy match, Which heaven and fortune still rewards with plagues . . . . iv 3 31
Witness good bringing up, fortune and truth . . . iv 4 74
This it is to be a peevish girl, That flies her fortune when it follows her v 2 50
He shall not knit a knot in his fortunes with the finger of my substance: if he take her, let him take her simply . *Mer. Wives* iii 2 76
I see what thou wert, if Fortune thy foe were not, Nature thy friend iii 3 69
Now heaven send thee good fortune! A kind heart he hath . iii 4 105
To know if it were my master's fortune to have her or no.—'Tis, 'tis his fortune.—What, sir?—To have her, or no . . iv 5 49
I shall follow it as the flesh and fortune shall better determine *M. for M.* ii 1 268
Fortune hath conveyed to my understanding . . . iii 1 189
With him, the portion and sinew of her fortune, her marriage-dowry . iii 1 230
If any thing fall to you upon this, more than thanks and good fortune . iv 2 191
I came to her from Claudio, and desired her To try her gracious fortune v 1 76
Fortune had left to both of us alike What to delight in *Com. of Errors* i 1 106
My fortune and my sweet hope's aim, My sole earth's heaven . iii 2 63
What then became of them I cannot tell; I to this fortune that you see me in . . . . v 1 355
And hear at large discoursed all our fortunes . . . v 1 395
Take of me my daughter, and with her my fortunes . *Much Ado* ii 1 314
To be a well-favour'd man is the gift of fortune; but to write and read comes by nature . . . . . iii 3 15
I have only been Silent so long and given way unto This course of fortune . . . . iv 1 159
Nor age so eat up my invention, Nor fortune made such havoc of my means . . . . iv 1 197
Belonging to whom?—To my fortunes and me . . *L. L. Lost* ii 1 224
My fortunes every way as fairly rank'd, If not with vantage *M. N. Dream* i 1 101
I thank my fortune for it, My ventures are not in one bottom trusted *Mer. of Venice* i 1 41
Nor is my whole estate Upon the fortune of this present year . i 1 44
All my fortunes are at sea; Neither have I money nor commodity . i 1 177
If your miseries were in the same abundance as your good fortunes are i 2 5
I pray you, lead me to the caskets To try my fortune . . ii 1 24
The greater throw May turn by fortune from the weaker hand . ii 1 34
And so may I, blind fortune leading me, Miss that which one unworthier may attain, And die with grieving . . . . ii 1 36
Good fortune then! To make me blest or cursed'st among men . ii 1 45
O rare fortune! here comes the man: to him, father . . ii 2 118
If any man in Italy have a fairer table which doth offer to swear upon a book, I shall have good fortune . . . . ii 2 168
Well, if Fortune be a woman, she's a good wench for this gear . ii 2 175
If my fortune be not crost, I have a father, you a daughter, lost . ii 5 56
I do in birth deserve her, and in fortunes, In graces . . ii 7 32
If I do fail in fortune of my choice, Immediately to leave you . ii 9 15
Fortune now To my heart's hope! . . . . ii 9 19
Who shall go about To cozen fortune and be honourable? . . ii 9 38
Give me a key for this, And instantly unlock my fortunes here . ii 9 52
Prove it so, Let fortune go to hell for it, not I . . iii 2 21
But let me to my fortune and the caskets . . . iii 2 39
Here's the scroll, The continent and summary of my fortune . iii 2 131
Since this fortune falls to you, Be content and seek no new . iii 2 134
If you be well pleased with this And hold your fortune for your bliss . iii 2 137
Your fortune stood upon the casket there, And so did mine too . iii 2 203
I got a promise of this fair one here To have her love, provided that your fortune Achieved her mistress . . . . iii 2 209
Herein Fortune shows herself more kind Than is her custom . iv 1 267

Fortune. Give me the poor allottery my father left me by testament; with that I will go buy my fortunes *As Y. Like It* i 1 78
Let us sit and mock the good housewife Fortune from her wheel i 2 35
Now thou goest from Fortune's office to Nature's: Fortune reigns in gifts of the world, not in the lineaments of Nature i 2 43
When Nature hath made a fair creature, may she not by Fortune fall into the fire? Though Nature hath given us wit to flout at Fortune, hath not Fortune sent in this fool to cut off the argument? i 2 47
Indeed, there is Fortune too hard for Nature, when Fortune makes Nature's natural the cutter-off of Nature's wit i 2 51
Peradventure this is not Fortune's work neither, but Nature's i 2 54
How shall I answer you?—As wit and fortune will i 2 110
One out of suits with fortune i 2 258
My pride fell with my fortunes; I'll ask him what he would i 2 264
Happy is your grace, That can translate the stubbornness of fortune Into so quiet and so sweet a style ii 1 19
At seventeen years many their fortunes seek; But at fourscore it is too late ii 3 73
Fortune cannot recompense me better Than to die well ii 3 75
And wish, for her sake more than for mine own, My fortunes were more able to relieve her ii 4 77
Rail'd on Lady Fortune in good terms, In good set terms ii 7 16
Call me not fool till heaven hath sent me fortune ii 7 19
I will not trouble you As yet, to question you about your fortunes ii 7 172
The residue of your fortune, Go to my cave and tell me ii 7 196
Give me your hand, And let me all your fortunes understand ii 7 200
He comes armed in his fortune iv 1 61
I know into what straits of fortune she is driven v 2 71
Share the good of our returned fortune v 4 180
To deck his fortune with his virtuous deeds *T. of Shrew* i 1 16
Scatters young men through the world To seek their fortunes i 2 51
By good fortune I have lighted well On this young man i 2 168
My father dead, my fortune lives for me; And I do hope good days and long i 2 192
Means but well, Whatever fortune stays him from his word iii 2 23
Not the worst of all your fortunes That you are like to Sir Vincentio iv 2 104
The fouler fortune mine, and there an end v 2 98
The mightiest space in fortune nature brings To join like likes *All's Well* i 1 237
Have fought with equal fortune and continue A braving war i 2 2
Fortune, she said, was no goddess, that had put such difference betwixt their two estates i 3 115
Love make your fortunes twenty times above Her that so wishes! ii 3 88
And in your bed Find fairer fortune, if you ever wed! ii 3 98
Do thine own fortunes that obedient right Which both thy duty owes ii 3 167
Good fortune and the favour of the king Smile upon this contract ii 3 184
I hope, sir, I have your good will to have mine own good fortunes ii 4 16
My homely stars have fail'd To equal my great fortune ii 5 81
We, Great in our hope, lay our best love and credence Upon thy promising fortune iii 3 3
Go thou forth; And fortune play upon thy prosperous helm! iii 3 7
You have show'd me that which well approves You're great in fortune iii 7 14
I am now, sir, muddied in fortune's mood v 2 5
Fortune's displeasure is but sluttish, if it smell so strongly v 2 7
I will henceforth eat no fish of fortune's buttering v 2 9
A paper from fortune's close-stool to give to a nobleman! v 2 18
Here is a purr of fortune's, sir, or of fortune's cat,—but not a musk-cat v 2 20
I am a man whom fortune hath cruelly scratched v 2 28
I bade her, if her fortunes ever stood Necessitied to help, that by this token I would relieve her v 3 84
But when I had subscribed To mine own fortune and inform'd her fully v 3 97
Thou shalt live as freely as thy lord, To call his fortunes thine *T. Night* i 4 40
What is your parentage?—Above my fortunes, yet my state is well i 5 297; 309
Fortune forbid my outside have not charm'd her! She made good view of me ii 2 19
The parts that fortune hath bestow'd upon her, Tell her, I hold as giddily as fortune ii 4 86
'Tis but fortune; all is fortune ii 5 27
My fortunes having cast me on your niece give me this prerogative ii 5 77
You might see more detraction at your heels than fortunes before you ii 5 150
The fellow of servants, and not worthy to touch Fortune's fingers ii 5 171
Why, then, build me thy fortunes upon the basis of valour iii 2 35
He is sad and civil, And suits well for a servant with my fortunes iii 4 6
Yet doth this accident and flood of fortune So far exceed all instance iv 3 11
Take thy fortunes up; Be that thou know'st thou art v 1 151
Till each circumstance Of place, time, fortune, do cohere and jump v 1 259
All the occurrence of my fortune since Hath been between this lady and this lord v 1 264
For myself, I'll put My fortunes to your service *W. Tale* i 2 440
As by strange fortune It came to us ii 3 179
To my kingly guest Unclasp'd my practice, quit his fortunes here iii 2 168
Which may, if fortune please, both breed thee, pretty, And still rest thine iii 3 48
O lady Fortune, Stand you auspicious! iv 4 51
Let myself and fortune Tug for the time to come iv 4 507
I think you know my fortunes Do all lie there iv 4 601
Fortune speed us! Thus we set on, Camillo, to the sea-side iv 4 681
If I had a mind to be honest, I see Fortune would not suffer me iv 4 862
Though Fortune, visible an enemy, Should chase us with my father, power no jot Hath she to change our loves v 1 216
Already appearing in the blossoms of their fortune v 2 136
Wilt thou forsake thy fortune, Bequeath thy land to him and follow me? *K. John* i 1 148
Good fortune come to thee! For thou wast got i' the way of honesty i 1 180
Have sold their fortunes at their native homes, Bearing their birthrights proudly on their backs, To make a hazard of new fortunes here ii 1 71
Fortune shall cull forth Out of one side her happy minion ii 1 391
At thy birth, dear boy, Nature and Fortune join'd to make thee great iii 1 52
But Fortune, O, She is corrupted, changed and won from thee iii 1 54
France is a bawd to Fortune and King John, That strumpet Fortune! iii 1 60
Thou Fortune's champion that dost never fight But when her humorous ladyship is by To teach thee safety! iii 1 118
Bidding me depend Upon thy stars, thy fortune and thy strength iii 1 126
I may not wish the fortune thine iii 1 333
Lady, with me, with me thy fortune lies iii 1 337
There where my fortune lives, there my life dies iii 1 338
No, no; when Fortune means to men most good, She looks upon them with a threatening eye iii 4 119
Nor met with fortune other than at feasts, Full of warm blood, of mirth v 2 58
As thy cause is right, So be thy fortune in this royal fight! *Richard II.* i 3 56
However God or fortune cast my lot i 3 85

Fortune. Wooing poor craftsmen with the craft of smiles And patient underbearing of his fortune *Richard II.* i 4 29
Methinks, Some unborn sorrow, ripe in fortune's womb, Is coming towards me ii 2 10
And, as my fortune ripens with thy love, It shall be still thy true love's recompense ii 3 48
Which, till my infant fortune comes to years, Stands for my bounty ii 3 66
Thy friends are fled to wait upon thy foes, And crossly to thy good all fortune goes ii 4 24
Myself, a prince by fortune of my birth iii 1 16
To-day, to-day, unhappy day, too late, O'erthrows thy joys, friends, fortune iii 2 72
Think the world is full of rubs, And that my fortune runs against the bias iii 4 5
Their fortunes both are weigh'd: In your lord's scale is nothing but himself iii 4 84
They are not the first of fortune's slaves, Nor shall not be the last v 5 24
Who is sweet Fortune's minion and her pride *1 Hen. IV.* i 1 83
The fortune of us that are the moon's men doth ebb and flow like the sea i 2 35
When his infant fortune came to age i 3 253
To bear our fortunes in our own strong arms i 3 298
We should on, To see how fortune is disposed to us iv 1 38
The very list, the very utmost bound Of all our fortunes iv 1 52
Wherein the fortune of ten thousand men Must bide the touch iv 4 9
In short space It rain'd down fortune showering on your head v 1 47
To save the blood on either side, Try fortune with him in a single fight v 1 100
I embrace this fortune patiently, Since not to be avoided it falls on me v 5 12
When he saw The fortune of the day quite turn'd from him v 5 18
And, in the fortune of my lord your son, Prince Harry slain outright *2 Hen. IV.* i 1 15
Came not till now to dignify the times, Since Cæsar's fortunes i 1 23
Must I marry your sister?—God send the wench no worse fortune! ii 2 152
Si fortune me tormente, sperato me contento ii 4 195
He is retired, to ripe his growing fortunes iv 1 13
Who knows on whom fortune would then have smiled? iv 1 133
We ready are to try our fortunes To the last man iv 2 43
Will Fortune never come with both hands full? iv 4 103
I would not take a knighthood for my fortune v 3 133
I am fortune's steward—get on thy boots: we'll ride all night v 3 137
Giddy Fortune's furious fickle wheel, That goddess blind *Hen. V.* iii 6 29
Fortune is painted blind, with a muffler afore her eyes, to signify to you that Fortune is blind iii 6 33
She [Fortune] is painted also with a wheel, to signify to you, which is the moral of it, that she is turning, and inconstant iii 6 35
Fortune is an excellent moral iii 6 40
Fortune is Bardolph's foe, and frowns on him iii 6 41
O méchante fortune! Do not run away iv 5 5
Doth Fortune play the huswife with me now? v 1 85
Fortune made his sword; By which the world's best garden he achieved Epil. 6
Now am I like that proud insulting ship Which Cæsar and his fortune bare at once *1 Hen. VI.* i 2 139
Cowardly knight! ill fortune follow thee! iii 2 109
Fortune in favour makes him lag behind iii 3 34
No more my fortune can, But curse the cause I cannot aid the man iv 3 43
But dies, betray'd to fortune by your strife iv 4 39
To Dover; where inshipp'd Commit them to the fortune of the sea v 1 50
I am a soldier and unapt to weep Or to exclaim on fortune's fickleness v 3 134
I will not be slack To play my part in Fortune's pageant *2 Hen. VI.* i 2 67
His fortunes I will weep and 'twixt each groan Say 'Who's a traitor?' iii 1 221
'Tis meet that lucky ruler be employ'd; Witness the fortune he hath had iii 1 292
Thy fortune, York, hadst thou been regent there, Might happily have proved far worse than his iii 1 305
My Lord of York, try what your fortune is iii 1 309
We then should see the bottom Of all our fortunes v 2 79
This breach now in our fortunes made May readily be stopp'd v 2 82
We will live To see their day and them our fortune give v 2 89
How ill-beseeming is it in thy sex To triumph, like an Amazonian trull, Upon their woes whom fortune captivates! *3 Hen. VI.* i 4 115
His manly face, which promiseth Successful fortune ii 2 41
Leave us to our fortune.—Why, that's my fortune too; therefore I'll stay ii 2 75
Or bide the mortal fortune of the field ii 2 83
Even then that sunshine brew'd a shower for him, That wash'd his father's fortunes forth of France ii 2 157
Never stand still, Till either death hath closed these eyes of mine Or fortune given me measure of revenge ii 3 32
Good fortune bids us pause, And smooth the frowns of war with peaceful looks ii 6 31
I must take like seat unto my fortune, And to my humble seat conform myself iii 3 10
Yield not thy neck To fortune's yoke iii 3 17
And meaner than myself have had like fortune iv 1 71
Though fortune's malice overthrow my state, My mind exceeds the compass of her wheel iv 3 46
I may conquer fortune's spite By living low, where fortune cannot hurt me iv 6 20
May seem as wise as virtuous, By spying and avoiding fortune's malice iv 6 28
On thy fortune I repose myself.—Why, then, though loath, yet must I be content iv 6 47
Thus far fortune maketh us amends iv 7 2
If you'll not here proclaim yourself our king, I'll leave you to your fortune iv 7 55
If fortune serve me, I'll requite this kindness iv 7 78
Thus far our fortune keeps an upward course v 3 1
But stoop with patience to my fortune.—So part we sadly v 5 6
Poor painted queen, vain flourish of my fortune! *Richard III.* i 3 241
Oh, who shall hinder me to wail and weep, To chide my fortune? ii 2 35
Your state of fortune and your due of birth iii 7 120
The right and fortune of his happy stars iii 7 172
Since you will buckle fortune on my back, To bear her burthen iii 7 228
Go thou to Richmond, and good fortune guide thee! iv 1 92
I call'd thee then vain flourish of my fortune iv 4 82
Heaven and fortune bar me happy hours! Day, yield me not thy light! iv 4 400
Fortune and victory sit on thy helm! v 3 79
And put thy fortune to the arbitrement Of bloody strokes v 3 89
Yet thus far we are one in fortunes: both Fell by our servants *Hen. VIII.* ii 1 121
When they once perceive The least rub in your fortunes, fall away Like water ii 1 129

Fortune. That blind priest, like the eldest son of fortune, Turns what he list *Hen. VIII.* ii 2 21
Of her That, when the greatest stroke of fortune falls, Will bless the king ii 2 36
That quarrel, fortune ii 3 14
Fie, fie, fie upon This compell'd fortune! ii 3 87
You have, by fortune and his highness' favours, Gone slightly o'er low steps ii 4 111
Alas, poor wenches, where are now your fortunes! iii 1 148
I know A way, if it take right, in spite of fortune Will bring me off again iii 2 219
That so long Have follow'd both my fortunes faithfully iv 2 141
The fineness of which metal is not found In fortune's love *Troi. and Cres.* i 3 23
So Doth valour's show and valour's worth divide In storms of fortune i 3 47
And with an accent tuned in selfsame key Retorts to chiding fortune i 3 54
And do a deed that fortune never did ii 2 90
Exposed myself, From certain and possess'd conveniences, To doubtful fortunes iii 3 8
Greatness, once fall'n out with fortune, Must fall out with men too iii 3 75
'Tis not so with me: Fortune and I are friends iii 3 88
How some men creep in skittish fortune's hall! iii 3 134
But still sweet love is food for fortune's tooth iv 5 293
Rascally tisick so troubles me, and the foolish fortune of this girl v 3 102
Thou anon shalt hear of me again; Till when, go seek thy fortune v 6 19
'Tis for the followers fortune widens them, Not for the fliers *Coriolanus* i 4 44
Now the fair goddess, Fortune, Fall deep in love with thee! i 5 21
He would pawn his fortunes To hopeless restitution iii 1 15
This man has marr'd his fortune iii 1 254
Would put you to your fortune and The hazard of much blood iii 2 60
I would dissemble with my nature where My fortunes and my friends at stake required I should do so in honour iii 2 63
Fortune's blows, When most struck home, being gentle wounded, craves A noble cunning iv 1 7
To prove more fortunes Thou'rt tired iv 5 99
Pride, Which out of daily fortune ever taints The happy man iv 7 38
For myself, son, I purpose not to wait on fortune till These wars determine v 3 119
Out of that I'll work Myself a former fortune v 3 202
Why, noble lords, Will you be put in mind of his blind fortune? v 6 118
And to my fortunes and the people's favour Commit my cause *T. Andron.* i 1 54
With honour and with fortune is return'd i 1 67
Whose fortunes Rome's best citizens applaud i 1 164
Your fortunes are alike in all, That in your country's service drew your swords i 1 174
Whose wisdom hath her fortune conquered i 1 336
Now climbeth Tamora Olympus' top, Safe out of fortune's shot ii 1 2
Had you not by wondrous fortune come ii 3 112
I am content.—And ours with thine, befall what fortune will v 3 3
Can you read?—Ay, mine own fortune in my misery *Rom. and Jul.* i 2 60
And all my fortunes at thy foot I'll lay And follow thee my lord ii 2 147
Hie you to the cell.—Hie to high fortune! Honest nurse, farewell ii 5 80
O, I am fortune's fool! iii 1 141
Like a misbehaved and sullen wench, Thou pout'st upon thy fortune iii 3 144
O fortune, fortune! all men call thee fickle iii 5 60
Be fickle, fortune; For then, I hope, thou wilt not keep him long iii 5 62
To have a wretched puling fool, A whining mammet, in her fortune's tender, To answer 'I'll not wed' iii 5 186
Unhappy fortune! by my brotherhood, The letter was not nice v 2 17
His large fortune Upon his good and gracious nature hanging *T. of A.* i 1 55
I have upon a high and pleasant hill Feign'd Fortune to be throned i 1 64
Whom Fortune with her ivory hand wafts to her i 1 70
'Tis conceived to scope. This throne, this Fortune, and this hill i 1 73
When Fortune in her shift and change of mood Spurns down her late beloved i 1 84
Paintings I can show That shall demonstrate these quick blows of Fortune's i 1 91
To build his fortune I will strain a little, For 'tis a bond in men i 1 143
Never may That state or fortune fall into my keeping, Which is not owed to you! i 1 150
Long may he live in fortunes! i 1 293
More welcome are ye to my fortunes Than my fortunes to me i 2 19
What a precious comfort 'tis, to have so many, like brothers, commanding one another's fortunes! i 2 109
The best of happiness, Honour and fortunes, keep with you! i 2 235
Men and men's fortunes could I frankly use As I can bid thee speak ii 2 188
You Mistake my fortunes; I am wealthy in my friends ii 2 193
Ne'er speak, or think, That Timon's fortunes 'mong his friends can sink ii 2 240
It pleases time and fortune to lie heavy Upon a friend of mine iii 5 10
You fools of fortune, trencher-friends, time's flies, Cap and knee slaves! iii 6 106
Not One friend to take his fortune by the arm, And go along with him! iv 2 7
So his familiars to his buried fortunes Slink all away iv 2 10
Say, As 'twere a knell unto our master's fortunes, 'We have seen better days' iv 2 26
Rich, only to be wretched, thy great fortunes Are made thy chief afflictions iv 2 43
Twinn'd brothers of one womb, . . . touch them with several fortunes iv 3 5
For nature, To whom all sores lay siege, can bear great fortune But by contempt of nature iv 3 7
Every grise of fortune Is smooth'd by that below iv 3 16
I know thee well; But in thy fortunes am unlearn'd and strange iv 3 56
When neighbour states, But for thy sword and fortune, trod upon them iv 3 95
A poor unmanly melancholy sprung From change of fortune iv 3 204
Whom Fortune's tender arm With favour never clasp'd iv 3 250
Offering the fortunes of his former days, The former man may make him v 1 127
But will follow The fortunes and affairs of noble Brutus *J. Cæsar* iii 1 135
Joy for his fortune; honour for his valour; and death for his ambition iii 2 29
Fortune is merry, And in this mood will give us any thing iii 2 271
There is a tide in the affairs of men, Which, taken at the flood, leads on to fortune iv 3 219
And, Romans, yet ere night We shall try fortune in a second fight v 3 110
Fortune, on his damned quarrel smiling, Show'd like a rebel's whore *Macbeth* i 2 14
Disdaining fortune, with his brandish'd steel, . . . carved out his passage i 2 17
Our separated fortune Shall keep us both the safer ii 3 144
It was he in the times past which held you So under fortune iii 1 78
So weary with disasters, tugg'd with fortune iii 1 112
The malevolence of fortune nothing Takes from his high respect iii 6 28
Let me find him, fortune! And more I beg not v 7 22
Being nature's livery, or fortune's star *Hamlet* i 4 32

Fortune. On fortune's cap we are not the very button.—Nor the soles of her shoe? *Hamlet* ii 2 233
In the secret parts of fortune? O, most true; she is a strumpet ii 2 239
What have you, my good friends, deserved at the hands of fortune? ii 2 246
Out, out, thou strumpet, Fortune! All you gods, In general synod, take away her power! ii 2 515
'Gainst Fortune's state would treason have pronounced ii 2 534
To suffer The slings and arrows of outrageous fortune iii 1 58
A man that fortune's buffets and rewards Hast ta'en with equal thanks iii 2 72
They are not a pipe for fortune's finger To sound what stop she please iii 2 75
'Tis not strange That even our loves should with our fortunes change iii 2 211
For 'tis a question left us yet to prove, Whether love lead fortune, or else fortune love iii 2 213
Hitherto doth love on fortune tend iii 2 216
If the rest of my fortunes turn Turk with me iii 2 287
Take thy fortune; Thou find'st to be too busy is some danger iii 4 32
To all that fortune, death and danger dare, Even for an egg-shell iv 4 52
The queen carouses to thy fortune, Hamlet v 2 300
For me, with sorrow I embrace my fortune v 2 399
Mend your speech a little, Lest it may mar your fortunes *Lear* i 1 97
Since that respects of fortune are his love, I shall not be his wife i 1 251
Let your study Be to content your lord, who hath received you At fortune's alms i 1 281
Keeps our fortunes from us till our oldness cannot relish them i 2 50
When we are sick in fortune,—often the surfeit of our own behaviour i 2 129
Briefness and fortune, work! ii 1 20
A good man's fortune may grow out at heels ii 2 164
Fortune, good night: smile once more; turn thy wheel! ii 2 180
Fortune, that arrant whore, Ne'er turns the key to the poor ii 4 52
Must make content with his fortunes fit, For the rain it raineth every day iii 2 76
How malicious is my fortune, that I must repent to be just! iii 5 10
To be worst, The lowest and most dejected thing of fortune, Stands still in esperance, lives not in fear iv 1 3
If thou wilt weep my fortunes, take my eyes iv 6 180
I am even The natural fool of fortune. Use me well iv 6 195
A most poor man, made tame to fortune's blows iv 6 225
That eyeless head of thine was first framed flesh To raise my fortunes iv 6 232
Hence; Lest that the infection of his fortune take Like hold on thee iv 6 237
Fortune love you! v 1 46
Myself could else out-frown false fortune's frown v 3 6
If thou dost As this instructs thee, thou dost make thy way To noble fortunes v 3 30
You have shown to-day your valiant strain, And fortune led you well v 3 41
Despite thy victor sword and fire-new fortune, Thy valour v 3 132
But what art thou That hast this fortune on me? v 3 165
If fortune brag of two she loved and hated, One of them we behold v 3 280
What a full fortune does the thick-lips owe! *Othello* i 1 66
Tying her duty, beauty, wit and fortunes In an extravagant and wheeling stranger Of here and every where i 1 136
My demerits May speak unbonneted to as proud a fortune As this i 2 23
The battles, sieges, fortunes, That I have pass'd i 3 130
What cannot be preserved when fortune takes Patience her injury a mockery makes i 3 206
You must therefore be content to slubber the gloss of your new fortunes i 3 228
My downright violence and storm of fortunes May trumpet to the world i 3 250
To his honours and his valiant parts Did I my soul and fortunes consecrate i 3 255
Who stands so eminent in the degree of this fortune as Cassio does? ii 1 241
My fortunes against any lay worth naming ii 3 329
I am desperate of my fortunes if they check me here ii 3 337
This honest fool Plies Desdemona to repair his fortunes ii 3 360
I'ld whistle her off and let her down the wind, To prey at fortune iii 3 263
A man that all his time Hath founded his good fortunes on your love iii 4 94
And shut myself up in some other course, To fortune's alms iii 4 122
Would you would bear your fortune like a man! iv 1 62
Would it not make one weep?—It is my wretched fortune iv 2 128
He knows not yet of his honourable fortune iv 2 241
She had a song of 'willow'; An old thing 'twas, but it express'd her fortune iv 3 29
That handkerchief thou speak'st of I found by fortune v 2 226
And seize upon the fortunes of the Moor, For they succeed on you v 2 366
Good sir, give me good fortune.—I make not, but foresee *Ant. and Cleo.* i 2 13
Nay, hear him.—Good now, some excellent fortune! i 2 25
You have seen and proved a fairer former fortune Than that which is to approach i 2 33
We'll know all our fortunes.—Mine, and most of our fortunes, to-night, shall be—drunk to bed i 2 44
Prithee, tell her but a worky-day fortune.—Your fortunes are alike i 2 55
Am I not an inch of fortune better than she? i 2 59
If you were but an inch of fortune better than I, where would you choose it? i 2 61
Our worser thoughts heavens mend! Alexas,—come, his fortune, his fortune! i 2 65
Therefore, dear Isis, keep decorum, and fortune him accordingly! i 2 77
Say to me, Whose fortunes shall rise higher, Cæsar's or mine? ii 3 16
Cæsar and he are greater friends than ever.—Make thee a fortune from me ii 5 49
Say 'tis not so, a province I will give thee, And make thy fortunes proud ii 5 69
And what may follow, To try a larger fortune ii 6 34
I know not What counts harsh fortune casts upon my face ii 6 55
Pompey doth this day laugh away his fortune.—If he do, sure, he cannot weep't back again ii 6 110
I have ever held my cap off to thy fortunes ii 7 63
For this, I'll never follow thy pall'd fortunes more ii 7 88
Now Pleased fortune does of Marcus Crassus' death Make me revenger iii 1 2
Good fortune, worthy soldier; and farewell iii 2 22
Our fortune lies Upon this jump iii 8 5
Our fortune on the sea is out of breath, And sinks most lamentably iii 10 25
With half the bulk o' the world play'd as I pleased, Making and marring fortunes iii 11 65
Fortune knows We scorn her most when most she offers blows iii 11 73
Lord of his fortunes he salutes thee, and Requires to live in Egypt iii 12 11
Fortune pursue thee!—Bring him through the bands iii 12 25
Women are not In their best fortunes strong iii 12 30
I see men's judgements are A parcel of their fortunes iii 13 32
It much would please him, That of his fortunes you should make a staff iii 13 68
Wisdom and fortune combating together, If that the former dare but what it can, No chance may shake it iii 13 79
He thinks, being twenty times of better fortune, He is twenty men to one iv 2 3

Fortune. If fortune be not ours to-day, it is Because we brave her . . . *Ant. and Cleo.* iv 4 4
O, my fortunes have Corrupted honest men! . . . . . iv 5 16
His fretted fortunes give him hope, and fear, Of what he has, and has not iv 12 8
Fortune and Antony part here; even here Do we shake hands . iv 12 19
My mistress loved thee, and her fortunes mingled With thine entirely iv 14 24
Thy death and fortunes bid thy followers fly . . . iv 14 111
Let me rail so high, That the false housewife Fortune break her wheel iv 15 44
But please your thoughts In feeding them with those my former fortunes iv 15 53
Not being Fortune, he's but Fortune's knave, A minister of her will . v 2 3
Pray you, tell him I am his fortune's vassal . . . v 2 29
His fortunes all lie speechless and his name Is at last gasp . *Cymbeline* i 5 52
Cassibelan, who was once at point—O giglot fortune!—to master Cæsar's sword . . . . iii 1 31
Thy mind to her is now as low as were Thy fortunes . . . iii 2 11
You shall find me, wretched man, a thing The most disdain'd of fortune iii 4 20
If you could wear a mind Dark as your fortune is . . . iii 4 147
Patiently and constantly thou hast stuck to the bare fortune of that beggar . . . . iii 5 119
Not beneath him in fortunes, beyond him in the advantage of the time iv 1 11
Fortune, put them into my hand! . . . . . iv 1 25
Inform us of thy fortunes, for it seems They crave to be demanded . iv 2 361
Fortune brings in some boats that are not steer'd . . . iv 3 46
Wherein Our pleasure his full fortune doth confine . . . v 4 110
Till fortune, tired with doing bad, Threw him ashore . *Pericles* ii Gower 37
Let it suffice the greatness of your powers To have bereft a prince of all his fortunes . . . . ii 1 9
Were my fortunes equal to my desires, I could wish to make one there . ii 1 117
Thanks, fortune, yet, that, after all my crosses, Thou givest me somewhat ii 1 127
If that ever my low fortune's better, I'll pay your bounties . . ii 1 148
He hopes by you his fortunes yet may flourish . . . . ii 2 47
'Tis more by fortune, lady, than by merit.—Call it by what you will . ii 3 12
Half the flood Hath their keel cut: but fortune's mood Varies again iii Gower 46
'Tis a good constraint of fortune it [the sea] belches upon us . . iii 2 55
Your shafts of fortune, though they hurt you mortally, Yet glance full wanderingly on us . . . . iii 3 6
You have fortunes coming upon you . . . . . . iv 2 126
She did distain my child, and stood between Her and her fortunes . iv 3 32
And bear his courses to be ordered By Lady Fortune . . . iv 4 48
A maid, though most ungentle fortune Have placed me in this sty . iv 6 103
Though wayward fortune did malign my state . . . . v 1 90
My fortunes—parentage—good parentage—To equal mine!—was it not thus? . . . . v 1 98
Her fortunes brought the maid aboard us . . . . . v 3 11
Although assail'd with fortune fierce and keen, Virtue preserved v 3 Gower 88
Fortuned. You will wonder what hath fortuned . . *T. G. of Ver.* v 4 169
Fortune-tell. I'll conjure you, I'll fortune-tell you . . *Mer. Wives* iv 2 196
Fortune-teller. A threadbare juggler and a fortune-teller *Com. of Errors* v 1 239
Fortune-telling. We do not know what's brought to pass under the profession of fortune-telling . . . . *Mer. Wives* iv 2 184
Forty. I had rather than forty shillings I had my Book of Songs and Sonnets here . . . . i 1 205
And, I think, forty more; all great doers in our trade . *Meas. for Meas.* iv 3 20
A ring he hath of mine worth forty ducats . . . *Com. of Errors* iv 3 84
This course I fittest choose; For forty ducats is too much to lose . iv 3 97
I'll put a girdle round about the earth In forty minutes *M. N. Dream* ii 1 176
'The humour of forty fancies' pricked in't for a feather *T. of Shrew* iii 2 70
I had rather than forty shillings I had such a leg . . . *T. Night* ii 3 20
I had rather than forty pound I were at home . . . . . v 1 180
Forty thousand fathom above water . . . . . . *W. Tale* iv 4 281
The language I have learn'd these forty years, My native English, now I must forego . . . . *Richard II.* i 3 159
I have lost a seal-ring of my grandfather's worth forty mark 1 *Hen. IV.* iii 3 95
Three or four bonds of forty pound a-piece, and a seal-ring . . iii 3 117
To thirty thousand.—Forty let it be . . . . . . iv 1 130
You shall have forty, sir.—Go to; stand aside . . . 2 *Hen. IV.* iii 2 248
Moy shall not serve; I will have forty moys . . . *Hen. V.* iv 4 14
I myself fight not once in forty year . . . . 1 *Hen. VI.* i 3 91
How tastes it? is it better? forty pence, no . . . *Hen. VIII.* ii 3 89
Within these forty hours Surrey durst better Have burnt that tongue than said so . . . . iii 2 253
When I might see from far some forty truncheoners draw to her succour v 4 54
On fair ground I could beat forty of them . . . *Coriolanus* iii 1 243
I have been thy soldier forty years . . . . *T. Andron.* i 1 193
And in this borrow'd likeness of shrunk death Thou shalt continue two and forty hours . . . . *Rom. and Jul.* iv 1 105
I see that thou art poor: Hold, there is forty ducats . . . v 1 59
Forty thousand brothers Could not, with all their quantity of love, Make up my sum . . . . *Hamlet* v 1 292
My letters say a hundred and seven galleys.—And mine, a hundred and forty.—And mine, two hundred . . . . . *Othello* i 3 4
O, that the slave had forty thousand lives! One is too poor . . iii 3 442
I saw her once Hop forty paces through the public street *Ant. and Cleo.* ii 2 234
Forty days longer we do respite you . . . . . *Pericles* i 1 116
Forty-eight. I have years on my back forty eight . . . *Lear* i 4 42
Forward. His forward voice now is to speak well of his friend *Tempest* ii 2 94
Now, forward with your tale. Prithee, stand farther off . . . i 2 91
The most forward bud Is eaten by the canker ere it blow *T. G. of Ver.* i 1 45
You'll still be too forward.—And yet I was last chidden for being too slow ii 1 11
But let our plot go forward . . . . . . *Mer. Wives* iv 4 13
I beseech you Look forward on the journey you shall go *Meas. for Meas.* iv 3 61
Nay, forward, old man; do not break off so . . *Com. of Errors* i 1 97
A very forward March-chick! How came you to this? . *Much Ado* i 3 58
I will owe thee an answer for that: and now forward with thy tale . iii 3 109
And now forward; for we have put thee in countenance . *L. L. Lost* v 2 623
But I will forward with my device . . . . . . v 2 669
If he come not, then the play is marred: it goes not forward, doth it? *M. N. Dream* iv 2 6
If our sport had gone forward, we had all been made men . . iv 2 17
Forward to the temple: after dinner Your hazard shall be made *M. of Ven.* ii 1 44
We will make it our suit to the duke that the wrestling might not go forward . . . . *As Y. Like It* i 2 193
A man's good wit seconded with the forward child Understanding . iii 3 14
Go forward; this contents: The rest will comfort . . *T. of Shrew* i 1 168
Am bold to show myself a forward guest Within your house . . ii 1 51
Baccare! you are marvellous forward . . . . . . ii 1 73
You grow too forward, sir . . . . iii 1 1
How fiery and forward our pedant is! . . . . . . iii 1 48
Gentlemen, forward to the bridal dinner . . . . . . iii 2 221
They shall go forward, Kate, at thy command . . . . . iii 2 224

Forward. Forward, I pray, since we have come so far *T. of Shrew* iv 5 12
Forward, forward! thus the bowl should run, And not unluckily against the bias . . . . iv 5 24
I set him there; Whoever charges on his forward breast, I am the caitiff that do hold him to't . . . . . . *All's Well* iii 2 116
Let's take the instant by the forward top; For we are old . . v 3 39
She is as forward of her breeding as She is i' the rear our birth *W. Tale* iv 4 591
Speak England first, that hath been forward first To speak . *K. John* ii 1 482
Or rather then set forward; for 'twill be Two long days' journey . iv 3 19
And dares him to set forward to the fight . . . *Richard II.* i 3 109
Sound, trumpets; and set forward, combatants . . . . i 3 117
How fondly dost thou spur a forward horse! . . . . . iv 1 72
When a jest is so forward, and afoot too! . . . . 1 *Hen. IV.* ii 2 50
And are they not some of them set forward already? . . . ii 3 30
We are prepared. I will set forward to-night . . . . . ii 3 38
On Wednesday next, Harry, you shall set forward . . . . iii 2 173
What need I be so forward with him that calls not on me? . . v 1 130
And bending forward struck his armed heels Against the panting sides of his poor jade . . . . 2 *Hen. IV.* i 1 44
His forward spirit Would lift him where most trade of danger ranged . i 1 173
Your grace of York, in God's name, then, set forward . . . iv 1 227
Go forward and be choked with thy ambition! . . . 1 *Hen. VI.* ii 4 112
Makes them thus forward in his banishment . . 2 *Hen. VI.* iii 2 253
But angry, wrathful, and inclined to blood, If you go forward . . iv 2 135
Then are we in order when we are most out of order. Come, march forward iv 2 200
And long live thou and these thy forward sons! . . 3 *Hen. VI.* i 1 203
You promised knighthood to our forward son: Unsheathe your sword . ii 2 58
But love to go Whither the queen intends. Forward; away! . . ii 5 139
If that go forward, Henry's hope is done . . . . . . iii 3 58
We'll forward towards Warwick and his mates . . . . iv 7 82
Nor forward of revenge, though they much err'd . . . . iv 8 46
I have often heard my mother say I came into the world with my legs forward . . . . v 6 71
Short summers lightly have a forward spring . . . *Richard III.* iii 1 94
A parlous boy; Bold, quick, ingenious, forward, capable . . . iii 1 155
And hopes to find you forward Upon his party for the gain thereof . iii 2 46
The tender love I bear your grace, my lord, Makes me most forward . iii 4 66
But on thy side I may not be too forward . . . . . v 3 94
Let him on. Go forward.—On my soul, I'll speak but truth *Hen. VIII.* i 2 177
But the sharp thorny points Of my alleged reasons drive this forward . ii 4 225
Let his grace go forward, And dare us with his cap like larks . . iii 2 281
As, let 'em have their rights, they are ever forward . . . . iv 1 9
Northumberland Arrested him at York, and brought him forward . . iv 2 13
But when goes this forward?—To-morrow; to-day; presently *Coriolanus* iv 5 228
Friends, that have been thus forward in my right, I thank you all *T. Andron.* i 1 56
Can I go forward when my heart is here? . . . *Rom. and Jul.* ii 1 1
A violet in the youth of primy nature, Forward, not permanent *Hamlet* i 3 8
Nor do we find him forward to be sounded . . . . . iii 1 7
The villain would not stand me.—No; but he fled forward still *Cymbeline* i 2 16
Our expectation that it would be thus Hath made us forward . . iii 5 29
Set we forward; let A Roman and a British ensign wave . . . v 5 479
Forwarding. In forwarding this dear expedience . . . 1 *Hen. IV.* i 1 33
Forwardness. His own peril on his forwardness . . *As Y. Like It* i 2 159
Bedford, if thou be slack, I'll fight it out.—Gloucester, why doubt'st thou of my forwardness? . . . . 1 *Hen. VI.* i 1 100
Stanley, I will requite thy forwardness . . . . 3 *Hen. VI.* iv 5 23
This cheers my heart, to see your forwardness . . . . . v 4 65
This forwardness Makes our hopes fair . . . . *Cymbeline* iv 2 342
Forwearied in this action of swift speed, Brave harbourage . *K. John* ii 1 233
Fosset-seller. You wear out a good wholesome forenoon in hearing a cause between an orange-wife and a fosset-seller . . *Coriolanus* ii 1 79
Foster. Some say that ravens foster forlorn children . *T. Andron.* ii 3 153
If you love me, sir.—Even as my life my blood that fosters it *Pericles* ii 5 89
She is dead. Nurses are not the fates, To foster it, nor ever to preserve iv 3 15
Fostered. If I be not by her fair influence Foster'd . . *T. G. of Ver.* iii 1 184
Like a lion foster'd up at hand . . . . . . *K. John* v 2 75
For that our kingdom's earth should not be soil'd With that dear blood which it hath fostered . . . . *Richard II.* i 3 126
One bred of alms and foster'd with cold dishes . . . *Cymbeline* iii 3 119
Fostering. My soul's earth's god, and body's fostering patron *L. L. Lost* i 1 223
Foster-nurse. Which I did store to be my foster-nurse *As Y. Like It* ii 3 40
Our foster-nurse of nature is repose . . . . . . *Lear* iv 4 12
Fought. He hath fought with a warrener.—How say you? . *Mer. Wives* i 4 28
Sir, there is a fray to be fought . . . . ii 1 208
Had we fought, I doubt we should have been too young for them *M. Ado* v 1 118
I have had four quarrels, and like to have fought one . *As Y. Like It* v 4 49
Have fought with equal fortune and continue A braving war *All's Well* i 2 2
But O, the noble combat that 'twixt joy and sorrow was fought! *W. Tale* v 2 80
Richard, that robb'd the lion of his heart And fought the holy wars *K. John* ii 1 4
A noble combat hast thou fought Between compulsion and a brave respect! . . . . v 2 43
Fought For Jesu Christ in glorious Christian field . . *Richard II.* iv 1 92
His captain Christ, Under whose colours he had fought so long . . iv 1 100
Thirty, at least, he fought with . . . . . 1 *Hen. IV.* ii 2 211
What, fought you with them all?—All! I know not what you call all . ii 4 203
If I fought not with fifty of them, I am a bunch of radish . . ii 4 205
Now, sirs: by'r lady, you fought fair; so did you, Peto . . ii 4 329
O Douglas, hadst thou fought at Holmedon thus, I never had triumph'd v 3 14
We rose both at an instant and fought a long hour by Shrewsbury clock v 4 151
O, such a day, So fought, so follow'd and so fairly won! . 2 *Hen. IV.* i 1 21
Your son did thus and thus; Your brother thus: so fought the noble Douglas . . . . i 1 77
God, and not we, hath safely fought to-day . . . . . iv 2 121
Have in these parts from morn till even fought . . . *Hen. V.* iii 1 20
And if he be not fought withal, my lord, Let us not live in France . iii 5 2
Whiles any speaks That fought with us upon Saint Crispin's day . iv 3 67
The field of Agincourt, Fought on the day of Crispin Crispianus . iv 7 94
The Plack Prince of Wales, as I have read in the chronicles, fought a most prave pattle here in France . . . . iv 7 98
But with this acknowledgement, That God fought for us . . . iv 8 125
The battles of the Lord of hosts he fought . . . 1 *Hen. VI.* i 1 31
Whilst a field should be dispatch'd and fought, You are disputing of your generals . . . . i 1 72
And fought so long, till that his thighs with darts Were almost like a sharp-quill'd porpentine . . . . 2 *Hen. VI.* iii 1 362
Well hast thou fought to-day; By the mass, so did we all . . v 3 15
After the bloody fray at Wakefield fought . . . 3 *Hen. VI.* ii 1 107
We at Saint Alban's met, Our battles join'd, and both sides fiercely fought ii 1 121
When I have fought with Pembroke and his fellows, I'll follow you . iv 3 54

Fought. And towards London they do bend their course, If by the way they be not fought withal . . . . . . *Richard III.* iv 5 15
I knew thy grandsire, And once fought with him . *Troi. and Cres.* iv 5 197
Yea, Troilus? O, well fought, my youngest brother! . . . v 6 12
I would wish me only he.—You have fought together . . *Coriolanus* i 1 236
Well fought; we are come off Like Romans . . . . . i 6 1
We have at disadvantage fought and did Retire to win our purpose . i 6 49
I do beseech you, By all the battles wherein we have fought. . . i 6 56
Alone I fought in your Corioli walls, And made what work I pleased . i 8 8
Five times, Marcius, I have fought with thee . . . . . i 10 8
They fought together, but Aufidius got off.—And 'twas time for him too ii 1 140
He fought Beyond the mark of others . . . . ii 2 92
Your voices: for your voices I have fought; Watch'd for your voices . ii 3 133
I'll chop off my hands too; For they have fought for Rome *T. Andron.* iii 1 73
As true a dog as ever fought at head . . . . v 1 102
And basely cozen'd Of that true hand that fought Rome's quarrel out . v 3 102
When I have fought with the men, I will be cruel with the maids *Rom. and Jul.* i 1 26
Came more and more and fought on part and part, Till the prince came i 1 121
Some twenty of them fought in this black strife . . . . . iii 1 183
I dreamt my master and another fought, And that my master slew him v 3 138
Fierce fiery warriors fought upon the clouds . . . . *J. Cæsar* ii 2 19
Who like a good and hardy soldier fought 'Gainst my captivity *Macbeth* i 2 4
In the unshrinking station where he fought . . . . . . v 8 42
Yet so far hath discretion fought with nature . . . . *Hamlet* i 2 5
My point and period will be throughly wrought, Or well or ill, as this day's battle's fought . . . . *Lear* iv 7 98
I, Your partner in the cause 'gainst which he fought . *Ant. and Cleo.* ii 2 59
At Pharsalia, Where Cæsar fought with Pompey . . . . . iii 7 33
In Cæsar's fleet Are those that often have 'gainst Pompey fought . . iii 7 38
This is fought indeed! Had we done so at first, we had droven them home iv 7 4
And have fought Not as you served the cause, but as 't had been Each man's like mine . . . . iv 8 5
He hath fought to-day As if a god, in hate of mankind, had Destroy'd in such a shape . . . . iv 8 24
Rather play'd than fought And had no help of anger . . . *Cymbeline* i 1 162
For all was lost, But that the heavens fought . . . . . . v 3 4
The poor soldier that so richly fought, Whose rags shamed gilded arms v 5 3
The forlorn soldier, that so nobly fought . . . . v 5 405
I saw you lately, When you caught hurt in parting two that fought *Per.* iv 1 88
Foughtest. Did famine follow; whom thou fought'st against *A. and C.* i 4 59
Foul. The reasonable shore That now lies foul and muddy . *Tempest* v 1 82
I have spirit to do any thing that appears not foul in the truth of my spirit.—Virtue is bold . . . . . *Meas. for Meas.* iii 1 213
But fare thee well, most foul, most fair! farewell! . . *Much Ado* iv 1 104
A giving hand, though foul, shall have fair praise . . *L. L. Lost* iv 1 23
Come, come, you talk greasily; your lips grow foul . . . . iv 1 139
Her amber hair for foul hath amber quoted . . . . . . iv 3 87
'Fair' in 'all hail' is foul, as I conceive . . . . . . v 2 340
When blood is nipp'd and ways be foul, Then nightly sings the staring owl v 2 926
I am not a slut, though I thank the gods I am foul . *As Y. Like It* iii 3 39
Foul is most foul, being foul to be a scoffer . . . . . . iii 5 62
Grim death, how foul and loathsome is thine image! . *T. of Shrew* Ind. 1 35
O, that a mighty man of such descent, Of such possessions and so high esteem, Should be infused with so foul a spirit! . . . Ind. 2 17
Be she as foul as was Florentius' love, As old as Sibyl . . . i 2 69
What is she but a foul contending rebel? . . . . v 2 159
For then we wound our modesty and make foul the clearness of our deservings, when of ourselves we publish them . . . *All's Well* i 3 6
So foul a sky clears not without a storm . . . . *K. John* iv 2 108
And foul imaginary eyes of blood Presented thee more hideous . . iv 2 265
Ah, foul shrewd news! beshrew thy very heart! I did not think to be so sad . . . . v 5 14
How God and good men hate so foul a liar . . . *Richard II.* i 1 114
That he is a traitor, foul and dangerous . . . . i 3 39
Then true noblesse would Learn him forbearance from so foul a wrong iv 1 120
Breaking through the foul and ugly mists Of vapours . . 1 *Hen. IV.* i 2 226
For nothing can seem foul to those that win . . . . . . v 1 8
Shall we fall foul for toys? . . . . 2 *Hen. IV.* ii 4 183
Then you perceive the body of our kingdom How foul it is . . . iii 1 39
If you grow foul with me, Pistol, I will scour you with my rapier *Hen. V.* ii 1 59
Who, like a foul and ugly witch, doth limp So tediously away . . iv Prol 21
In their pale dull mouths the gimmal bit Lies foul with chew'd grass . iv 2 50
Consume to ashes, Thou foul accursed minister of hell! . . 1 *Hen. VI.* v 4 93
A bloody murderer, Or foul felonious thief . . . . 2 *Hen. VI.* iii 1 129
From their misty jaws Breathe foul contagious darkness in the air . iv 1 7
This breast [is free] from harbouring foul deceitful thoughts . . . iv 7 109
Foul indigested lump, As crooked in thy manners as thy shape! . . v 1 157
A foul mis-shapen stigmatic, Mark'd by the destinies to be avoided 3 *Hen. VI.* ii 2 136
Foul wrinkled witch, what makest thou in my sight? . *Richard III.* i 3 164
That bottled spider, that foul bunch-back'd toad! . . . . . iv 4 81
No, no, they would not do so foul a deed . . . *T. Andron.* iii 1 118
O, why should nature build so foul a den? . . . . iv 1 59
Accursed the offspring of so foul a fiend! . . . . iv 2 79
And bakes the elf-locks in foul sluttish hairs . . . *Rom. and Jul.* i 4 90
How fairly this lord strives to appear foul! . . . *T. of Athens* iii 3 32
'Tis inferr'd to us, His days are foul and his drink dangerous . . iii 5 74
Thus much of this [gold] will make black white, foul fair, Wrong right iv 3 28
Fair is foul, and foul is fair: Hover through the fog and filthy air *Macbeth* i 1 11
So foul and fair a day I have not seen . . . . i 3 38
Though all things foul would wear the brows of grace, Yet grace must still look so . . . . iv 3 23
Revenge his foul and most unnatural murder . . . . . *Hamlet* i 5 25
Murder most foul, as in the best it is; But this most foul, strange and unnatural . . . . i 5 27
A foul and pestilent congregation of vapours . . . . . . ii 2 314
My imaginations are as foul As Vulcan's stithy . . . . . iii 2 88
Join'd Your high engender'd battles 'gainst a head So old and white as this. O! O! 'tis foul! . . . . *Lear* iii 2 24
If you do find me foul in her report, The trust, the office I do hold of you, Not only take away . . . . *Othello* i 3 117
They were parted With foul and violent tempest . . . . . ii 1 34
What miserable praise hast thou for her that's foul and foolish?—There's none so foul and foolish thereunto, But does foul pranks . . ii 1 141
I will chop her into messes: cuckold me!—O, 'tis foul in her . . iv 1 213
If she be not honest, chaste, and true, There's no man happy; the purest of their wives Is foul as slander . . . . iv 2 19
To preserve this vessel for my lord From any other foul unlawful touch iv 2 84
The sweetest innocent That e'er did lift up eye.—O, she was foul! . v 2 200

Foul. Hath nature given them eyes . . . ? and can we not Partition make with spectacles so precious 'Twixt fair and foul? *Cymbeline* i 6 38
Foul act. And future ages groan for this foul act . . *Richard II.* iv 1 138
Foul adulteress. And then they call'd me foul adulteress *T. Andron.* ii 3 109
Foul ambition. Virtue is choked with foul ambition 2 *Hen. VI.* iii 1 143
Foul blot. Nature, drawing of an antique, Made a foul blot *Much Ado* iii 1 64
Foul body. I will through and through Cleanse the foul body of the infected world . . . . *As Y. Like It* ii 7 60
Foul bogs. They that ride so and ride not warily, fall into foul bogs *Hen. V.* iii 7 61
Foul bombard. Looks like a foul bombard that would shed his liquor *Tempest* ii 2 21
Foul breath. Foul wind is but foul breath, and foul breath is noisome *Much Ado* v 2 53
Foul cause. How innocent I was From any private malice in his end, His noble jury and foul cause can witness . . . *Hen. VIII.* iii 2 269
Foul charms. Thou hast practised on her with foul charms . *Othello* i 2 73
Foul clothes. His hinds were called forth by their mistress to carry me in the name of foul clothes to Datchet-lane . . *Mer. Wives* iii 5 101
Well: on went he for a search, and away went I for foul clothes . . iii 5 108
Foul collier. Hang him, foul collier! . . . . . . *T. Night* iii 4 130
Foul conspiracy. I had forgot that foul conspiracy . . *Tempest* iv 1 139
Foul contempt. Ingrateful Rome requites with foul contempt *T. Andron.* v 1 12
Foul corruption. The foul corruption of a sweet child's death *K. John* iv 2 81
Foul crimes. And for the day confined to fast in fires, Till the foul crimes done in my days of nature Are burnt and purged away *Hamlet* i 5 12
Foul death. On whom foul death hath made this slaughter . *Pericles* iv 4 37
Foul deed. For which foul deed The powers, delaying, not forgetting, have Incensed the seas and shores . . . . . . *Tempest* iii 3 72
They that stabb'd Cæsar shed no blood at all, Did not offend, nor were not worthy blame, If this foul deed were by to equal it . 3 *Hen. VI.* v 5 55
This foul deed shall smell above the earth With carrion men *J. Cæsar* iii 1 274
Foul deeds will rise, Though all the earth o'erwhelm them, to men's eyes *Hamlet* i 2 257
Foul defacer. That foul defacer of God's handiwork *Richard III.* iv 4 51
Foul deformity. Blush, blush, thou lump of foul deformity . . i 2 57
Foul derision. To bait me with this foul derison . . *M. N. Dream* iii 2 197
Foul desire. If foul desire had not conducted you . *T. Andron.* ii 3 79
Foul despair. How shall poor Henry live, Unless thou rescue him from foul despair? . . . . 3 *Hen. VI.* iii 3 215
Foul devil, for God's sake, hence, and trouble us not . *Richard III.* i 2 50
Foul disease. But, like the owner of a foul disease, To keep it from divulging, let it feed Even on the pith of life . . . *Hamlet* iv 1 21
Kill thy physician, and the fee bestow Upon thy foul disease . *Lear* i 1 167
Foul disgrace. To thy foul disgrace And utter ruin . . 3 *Hen. VI.* i 1 253
Foul disproportion. Foh! one may smell in such a will most rank, Foul disproportion, thoughts unnatural . . . . . . *Othello* iii 3 233
Foul effect. Is it not fair writ?—Too fairly, Hubert, for so foul effect *K. John* iv 1 38
Foul Egyptian. This foul Egyptian hath betrayed me . *Ant. and Cleo.* iv 12 10
Foul ends. But With colours fairer painted their foul ends . *Tempest* i 2 143
Foul escape. Rome will despise her for this foul escape . *T. Andron.* iv 2 113
Foul expulsion. A wooer More hateful than the foul expulsion is Of thy dear husband . . . . *Cymbeline* ii 1 65
Foul-faced. Black scandal or foul-faced reproach *Richard III.* iii 7 231
Foul fault. And then another fault in the semblance of a fowl; think on't, Jove; a foul fault! . . . . *Mer. Wives* v 5 12
You will mistake each other.—A! that's a foul fault . *Hen. V.* iii 2 148
Foul fiend of France, and hag of all despite! . . 1 *Hen. VI.* iii 2 52
Methoughts, a legion of foul fiends Environ'd me about . *Richard III.* i 4 58
Away! the foul fiend follows me! . . . . *Lear* iii 4 46
Whom the foul fiend hath led through fire and through flame . . iii 4 52
Do poor Tom some charity, whom the foul fiend vexes . . . iii 4 62
Take heed o' the foul fiend: obey thy parents . . . . . iii 4 82
Defy the foul fiend. Still through the hawthorn blows the cold wind . iii 4 101
This is the foul fiend Flibbertigibbet: he begins at curfew . . iii 4 120
When the foul fiend rages, eats cow-dung for sallets . . . . iii 4 137
Pray, innocent, and beware the foul fiend . . . . . . iii 6 9
The foul fiend bites my back . . . . iii 6 18
The foul fiend haunts poor Tom in the voice of a nightingale . . iii 6 31
Bless thee, good man's son, from the foul fiend! . . . . . iv 1 61
Foul gap. Mean mischief and break a foul gap into the matter *W. Tale* iv 4 198
Foul hand. With foul hand Defile the locks of your shrill-shrieking daughters . . . . *Hen. V.* iii 3 34
Foul head. Balm his foul head in warm distilled waters *T. of Shrew* Ind. 1 48
Foul hill. Imprimis, we came down a foul hill . . . . . . iv 1 69
Foul incest. Not so bad As with foul incest to abuse your soul *Pericles* i 1 126
Foul inconstancy. The agent of thy foul inconstancy . 2 *Hen. VI.* i 2 115
Foul injustice. Miscarried By underhand corrupted foul injustice *Rich. III.* v 1 6
Foul intrusion. That may with foul intrusion enter in And dwell upon your grave . . . . *Com. of Errors* iii 1 103
Foul issue. So horrible, so bloody, must Lead on to some foul issue *W. T.* ii 3 153
Foul knave. It is a deadly sorrow to behold a foul knave uncuckolded *Ant. and Cleo.* i 2 76
Foul lake. The foul lake O'erstunk their feet . . . . *Tempest* iv 1 183
Foul linen. And throw foul linen upon him . . . . *Mer. Wives* iii 3 139
They have marvellous foul linen . . . . 2 *Hen. IV.* v 1 38
Foul means. By fair or foul means we must enter in . 3 *Hen. VI.* iv 7 14
Foul mischance Torment me for my love's forgetfulness! *T. G. of Ver.* ii 2 11
Foul misleading. To plague thee for thy foul misleading me 3 *Hen. VI.* v 1 97
Foul misplaced. I'll have this crown of mine cut from my shoulders Ere I will see the crown so foul misplaced . . . . . *Richard III.* iii 2 44
Foul moles. Patch'd with foul moles and eye-offending marks *K. John* iii 1 47
Foul mouth. In foul mouth And in the witness of his proper ear *Meas. for Meas.* v 1 309
In the vault, To whose foul mouth no healthsome air breathes in *R. and J.* iv 3 34
Foul-mouthed. Wilt thou ever be a foul-mouthed and calumnious knave? *All's Well* i 3 60
He speaks most vilely of you, like a foul-mouthed man as he is 1 *Hen. IV.* iii 3 122
Foul mouthedest. It is the foul-mouth'd'st rogue in England 2 *Hen. IV.* ii 4 77
Foul murder. Seek, and know how this foul murder comes *Rom. and Jul.* v 3 198
'Forgive me my foul murder'? That cannot be . . . *Hamlet* iii 3 52
O, my good lord, yonder's foul murders done! . . . . *Othello* v 2 106
Foul offender. Call these foul offenders to their answers . 2 *Hen. VI.* ii 1 203
My dreadful name, Revenge, which makes the foul offender quake *T. An.* v 2 40
Foul ones. Those articles, my lord, are in the king's hand: But, thus much, they are foul ones . . . . *Hen. VIII.* iii 2 300
Foul opinion. The foul opinion You had of her pure honour gains or loses Your sword or mine . . . . *Cymbeline* ii 4 58
Foul oyster. As your pearl in your foul oyster . . *As Y. Like It* v 4 64
Foul play. What foul play had we, that we came from thence? *Tempest* i 2 60

Foul play. By foul play, as thou say'st, were we heaved thence, But blessedly holp hither *Tempest* i 2 62
We neglected time, Play'd foul play with our oaths *L. L. Lost* v 2 766
It is apparent foul play; and 'tis shame *K. John* iv 2 93
A fearful head they are, If promises be kept on every hand, As ever offer'd foul play in a state *1 Hen. IV.* iii 2 169
My father's spirit in arms! all is not well; I doubt some foul play *Hamlet* i 2 256
Consider You are my guests: do me no foul play, friends *Lear* iii 7 31
And for an honest attribute cry out 'She died by foul play' *Pericles* iv 3 19
Foul practice. The foul practice Hath turn'd itself on me *Hamlet* v 2 328
Foul pranks. There's none so foul and foolish thereunto, But does foul pranks which fair and wise ones do *Othello* ii 1 143
Foul proceeding. For testimony of her foul proceedings *T. Andron.* v 3 8
Whoe'er he be that in this foul proceeding Hath thus beguiled your daughter of herself And you of her *Othello* i 3 65
Foul profanation. Great men may jest with saints; 'tis wit in them, But in the less foul profanation *Meas. for Meas.* ii 2 128
Foul rebellion. Shall falter under foul rebellion's arms *Richard II.* iii 2 26
Foul redemption. Lawful mercy Is nothing kin to foul redemption *Meas. for Meas.* ii 4 113
Foul revolt. O foul revolt of French inconstancy! *K. John* iii 1 322
Foul rout. Give me to know How this foul rout began *Othello* ii 3 210
Foul scorn. And take foul scorn to fawn on him *1 Hen. VI.* iv 4 35
Foul shame. Lest to thy harm thou move our patience.—Foul shame upon you! you have all moved mine *Richard III.* i 3 249
Foul shirts. Rammed me in with foul shirts and smocks *Mer. Wives* iii 5 91
Foul show. See how belief may suffer by foul show! *Pericles* iv 4 23
Foul sin. Most mischievous foul sin, in chiding sin *As Y. Like It* ii 7 64
Ere foul sin gathering head Shall break into corruption *Richard II.* v 1 58; *2 Hen. IV.* iii 1 76
Let your mother in: I know she is come to pray for your foul sin *Rich. II.* v 3 82
Foul slut. To cast away honesty upon a foul slut were to put good meat into an unclean dish *As Y. Like It* iii 3 36
Foul speeches. His backward voice is to utter foul speeches *Tempest* ii 2 96
Foul-spoken coward, that thunder'st with thy tongue, And with thy weapon nothing darest perform! *T. Andron.* ii 1 58
Foul stigmatic, that's more than thou canst tell *2 Hen. VI.* v 1 215
Foul stone. A base foul stone, made precious by the foil Of England's chair, where he is falsely set *Richard III.* v 3 250
Foul subornation is predominant And equity exiled *2 Hen. VI.* iii 1 145
Foul swine. This foul swine Lies now even in the centre of this isle *Richard III.* v 2 10
Foul-tainted. And salt too little which may season give To her foul-tainted flesh! *Much Ado* iv 1 145
Foul taunts. And after many scorns, many foul taunts, They took his head *3 Hen. VI.* ii 1 64
Foul terrors. All the foul terrors in dark-seated hell *2 Hen. VI.* iii 2 328
Foul thief. O thou foul thief, where hast thou stow'd my daughter? *Oth.* i 2 62
Foul thing. 'Tis a foul thing when a cur cannot keep himself in all companies! *T. G. of Ver.* iv 4 11
When good manners shall lie all in one or two men's hands and they unwashed too, 'tis a foul thing *Rom. and Jul.* i 5 6
Where's that palace whereinto foul things Sometimes intrude not? *Oth.* iii 3 137
Foul thoughts. An index and obscure prologue to the history of lust and foul thoughts ii 1 264
Will break to powder, And finish all foul thoughts *Ant. and Cleo.* iv 9 18
Foul throat. In thy foul throat thou liest *Richard III.* i 2 93
Foul toads. A cistern for foul toads To knot and gender in! *Othello* iv 2 61
Foul traitor. With a foul traitor's name stuff I thy throat *Richard II.* i 1 44
Is a foul traitor to proud Hereford's king iv 1 135
Foul treason. Treason! foul treason! Villain! traitor! slave! v 2 72
Foul way. Fie on all tired jades, on all mad masters, and all foul ways! *T. of Shrew* iv 1 2
I am a foul way out *T. Night* ii 3 201
The commonwealth their boots? will she hold out water in foul way? *1 Hen. IV.* ii 1 93
Foul weather. It is foul weather in us all, good sir, When you are cloudy.—Foul weather?—Very foul *Tempest* ii 1 141
You and you are sure together, As the winter to foul weather *As Y. L. It* v 4 142
We'll make foul weather with despised tears *Richard II.* iii 3 161
Home without boots, and in foul weather too! *1 Hen. IV.* iii 1 68
Who's there, besides foul weather?—One minded like the weather *Lear* iii 1 1
Foul whisperings are abroad *Macbeth* v 1 79
Foul wind. Foul words is but foul wind, and foul wind is but foul breath, and foul breath is noisome *Much Ado* v 2 52
Foul witch. The foul witch Sycorax *Tempest* i 2 258
Foul womb. Through the foul womb of night The hum of either army stilly sounds *Hen. V.* iv Prol. 4
Foul word. Only foul words; and thereupon I will kiss thee *Much Ado* v 2 50
Foul words is but foul wind, and foul wind is but foul breath v 2 52
Fair payment for foul words is more than due *L. L. Lost* iv 1 19
I am toiling in a pitch,—pitch that defiles: defile! a foul word iv 3 4
Foul wrong. Answering one foul wrong, Lives not to act another *M. for M.* ii 2 103
With tears drawn from her eyes by your foul wrongs *Richard II.* iii 1 15
Now, by the world— 'Tis full of thy foul wrongs *Richard III.* iv 4 374
Fouled. His stockings foul'd, Ungarter'd, and down-gyved *Hamlet* ii 1 79
Fouler. Your virtue hath a license in't, Which seems a little fouler than it is *Meas. for Meas.* ii 4 146
The fouler fortune mine, and there an end *T. of Shrew* v 2 98
A fouler fact Did never traitor in the land commit *2 Hen. VI.* i 3 176
Fouler than heart can think thee, thou canst make No excuse *Rich. III.* i 2 83
Never hung poison on a fouler toad. Out of my sight! i 2 148
Think that thy babes were fairer than they were, And he that slew them fouler than he is iv 4 121
O, 'tis foul in her.—With mine officer!—That's fouler *Othello* iv 1 215
It's monstrous labour, when I wash my brain, And it grows fouler *Ant. and Cleo.* ii 7 106
Foulest. But write her fair words still in foulest letters *2 Hen. IV.* iv 4 104
O, 'twas the foulest deed to slay that babe! *Richard III.* i 3 183
Turn me away; and let the foul'st contempt Shut door upon me *Hen. VIII.* ii 4 42
Let us, like merchants, show our foulest wares, And think, perchance, they'll sell; if not, The lustre of the better *Troi. and Cres.* i 3 359
I will go seek Some ditch wherein to die; the foul'st best fits My latter part of life *Ant. and Cleo.* iv 6 38
Foully. Dost thou desire her foully for those things That make her good? *Meas. for Meas.* ii 2 174
I am afeard the life of Helen, lady, Was foully snatch'd *All's Well* v 3 154
We in the world's wide mouth Live scandalized and foully spoken of *1 Hen. IV.* i 3 154
I fear Thou play'dst most foully for't *Macbeth* iii 1 3

Foulness. Who loved her so, that, speaking of her foulness, Wash'd it with tears *Much Ado* iv 1 155
Praised be the gods for thy foulness! sluttishness may come *As Y. L. It* iii 3 40
He's fallen in love with your foulness iii 5 66
The honour of it Does pay the act of it; as, i' the contrary, The foulness is the punishment *Hen. VIII.* iii 2 183
It is no vicious blot, murder, or foulness, No unchaste action *Lear* i 1 230
Found. Her brother found a wife Where he himself was lost *Tempest* v 1 210
The best news is, that we have safely found Our king and company v 1 221
Hence, and bestow your luggage where you found it.—Or stole it v 1 299
Good wind, blow not a word away Till I have found each letter *T. G. of V.* i 2 119
All this I speak in print, for in print I found it ii 1 175
If he had found the young man, he would have been horn-mad *Mer. Wives* i 4 51
'Tis true, Master Shallow.—It would be found so ii 3 53
I found thee of more value Than stamps in gold or sums in sealed bags iii 4 15
He's not to be found *Meas. for Meas.* i 2 180
And He that might the vantage best have took Found out the remedy ii 2 75
We have found upon him, sir, a strange picklock iii 2 18
My brother justice have I found so severe, that he hath forced me to tell him he is indeed Justice iii 2 267
And well could wish You had not found me here so musical iv 1 11
I respect you.—Good friar, I know you do, and have found it iv 1 54
I have found you out a stand most fit iv 6 10
Let this friar be found v 1 133
What ruins are in me that can be found, By him not ruin'd? *Com. of Er.* ii 1 96
I found it [Ireland] out by the bogs iii 2 120
Where Scotland?—I found it by the barrenness iii 2 123
I see, sir, you have found the goldsmith now iv 3 46
If he found her accordant, he meant to take the present time *Much Ado* i 2 14
I found him here as melancholy as a lodge in a warren ii 1 221
The world was very guilty of such a ballad some three ages since: but I think now 'tis not to be found *L. L. Lost* i 2 118
You found his mote; the king your mote did see iv 3 161
For when would you, my lord, or you, or you, Have found the ground of study's excellence? iv 3 300
For when would you, my liege, or you, or you, In leaden contemplation have found out Such fiery numbers? iv 3 321
To wail friends lost Is not by much so wholesome-profitable As to rejoice at friends but newly found v 2 761
Through the forest have I gone, But Athenian found I none *M. N. Dream* ii 2 67
Thou art not by mine eye, Lysander, found; Mine ear, I thank it, brought me to thy sound iii 2 181
Tell me how it came this night That I sleeping here was found iv 1 106
And I have found Demetrius like a jewel, Mine own, and not mine own iv 1 196
How I caught it, found it, or came by it, What stuff 'tis made of, whereof it is born, I am to learn *Mer. of Venice* i 1 3
Since you have found Antonio, We two will leave you i 1 69
And by adventuring both I oft found both i 1 144
Hast thou found my daughter?—I often came where I did hear of her iii 1 84
As I have ever found thee honest-true, So let me find thee still iii 4 46
If that thou be'st found So near our public court as twenty miles, Thou diest for it *As Y. Like It* i 3 45
In the morning early They found the bed untreasured of their mistress ii 2 7
Searching of thy wound, I have by hard adventure found mine own ii 4 45
I found them on a tree.—Truly, the tree yields bad fruit iii 2 121
Look here what I found on a palm-tree iii 2 186
I found him under a tree, like a dropped acorn iii 2 248
I was seeking for a fool when I found you iii 2 304
The foolish coroners of that age found it was 'Hero of Sestos' iv 1 106
We met, and found the quarrel was upon the seventh cause v 4 51
Till I found it to be true, I never thought it possible or likely *T. of. Shrew* i 1 153
While idly I stood looking on, I found the effect of love in idleness i 1 156
Virginity by being once lost may be ten times found *All's Well* i 1 143
I wish might be found in the calendar of my past endeavours i 3 4
In what he did profess, well found ii 1 105
I have now found thee; when I lose thee again, I care not ii 3 216
Thou art a witty fool; I have found thee.—Did you find me in yourself? ii 4 32
Prepared I was not For such a business; therefore am I found So much unsettled ii 5 67
I have found Myself in my incertain grounds to fail As often as I guess'd iii 1 14
I spoke with her but once And found her wondrous cold iii 6 121
Which I will over-pay and pay again When I have found it iii 7 17
For it will come to pass That every braggart shall be found an ass iv 3 372
You were the first that found me!—Was I, in sooth? and I was the first that lost thee v 2 46
Where did you find it, then?—I found it not v 3 275
When I was like this maid, I found you wondrous kind v 3 311
The most . . . fatal opposite that you could possibly have found *T. N.* iii 4 294
I found this credit, That he did range the town to seek me out iv 3 6
You'll be found, Be you beneath the sky *W. Tale* i 2 179
The king shall live without an heir, if that which is lost be not found iii 2 137
Show those things you found about her, those secret things iv 4 713
King Leontes shall not have an heir Till his lost child be found v 1 40
I was by at the opening of the fardel, heard the old shepherd deliver the manner how he found it v 2 5
Methought I heard the shepherd say, he found the child v 2 8
Nothing but bonfires: the oracle is fulfilled; the king's daughter is found v 2 25
Has the king found his heir?—Most true v 2 32
Our king, being ready to leap out of himself for joy of his found daughter v 2 55
All the instruments which aided to expose the child were even then lost when it was found v 2 79
Turn, good lady; Our Perdita is found v 3 121
Where hast thou been preserved? where lived? how found Thy father's court? v 3 124
And there My mate, that's never to be found again, Lament till I am lost v 3 134
Thou hast found mine; But how, is to be question'd v 3 138
Whom I found With many hundreds treading on his heels *K. John* iv 2 148
Or, when he doom'd this beauty to a grave, Found it too precious-princely for a grave iv 3 40
They found him dead and cast into the streets, An empty casket v 1 39
On pain to be found false and recreant *Richard II.* i 3 106; 111
A weary way From Ravenspurgh to Cotswold will be found ii 3 9
He should have found his uncle Gaunt a father ii 3 127
So Judas did to Christ: but he, in twelve, Found truth in all but one iv 1 171
I would to God, my lords, he might be found: Inquire at London v 3 4
You have found me; for accordingly You tread upon my patience *1 Hen. IV.* i 3 3
We think ourselves unsatisfied, Till he hath found a time to pay us home i 3 288
There is nothing but roguery to be found in villanous man ii 4 138
Rebellion lay in his way, and he found it v 1 28

Found. But Priam found the fire ere he his tongue . 2 *Hen. IV.* i 1 74
For he hath found to end one doubt by death Revives two greater . iv 1 199
As the year Had found some months asleep and leap'd them over . iv 4 124
I found the prince in the next room, Washing with kindly tears his gentle cheeks . iv 5 83
When I here came in, And found no course of breath within your majesty . iv 5 151
France hath in thee found out A nest of hollow bosoms . *Hen. V.* ii Prol. 20
Be assured, you'll find a difference, As we his subjects have in wonder found . ii 4 135
'Tis sure they found some place But weakly guarded . 1 *Hen. VI.* ii 1 73
I should revive the soldiers' hearts, Because I ever found them as myself iii 2 98
Can this be so, That in alliance, amity and oaths, There should be found such false dissembling guile? . iv 1 63
Had York and Somerset brought rescue in, We should have found a bloody day . iv 7 34
He will be found a dangerous protector . 2 *Hen. VI.* i 1 164
A staff is quickly found to beat a dog . iii 1 171
You would not feast him like a friend; And 'tis well seen he found an enemy . iii 2 185
If, after three days' space, thou here be'st found . iii 2 295
If thou be found by me, thou art but dead . iii 2 387
Our scouts have found the adventure very easy . 3 *Hen. VI.* iv 2 18
It [conscience] made me once restore a purse of gold that I found *Richard III.* i 4 144
And, by just computation of the time, Found that the issue was not his begot . iii 5 90
This is the day that, in King Edward's time, I wish'd might fall on me, when I was found False to his children . v 1 14
This found I on my tent this morning . v 3 303
I'll make My royal choice.—Ye have found him, cardinal . *Hen. VIII.* i 4 86
Is he found guilty?—Yes, truly is he, and condemn'd upon't . ii 1 7
So his peers, upon this evidence, Have found him guilty of high treason ii 1 27
Fall away Like water from ye, never found again But where they mean to sink ye . ii 1 130
But that slander, sir, Is found a truth now . ii 1 154
Have great care I be not found a talker.—Sir, you cannot . ii 2 79
His spell in that is out: the king hath found Matter against him . iii 2 20
And wot you what I found There,—on my conscience, put unwittingly? iii 2 122
I pray you, tell me, If what I now pronounce you have found true . iii 2 163
The duke by law Found his deserts . iii 2 267
Found thee a way, out of his wreck, to rise in . iii 2 437
And found the blessedness of being little . iv 2 66
Pray you, speak no more to me: I will leave all as I found it *Tr. and Cr.* i 1 91
The fineness of which metal is not found In fortune's love . i 3 22
The nature of the sickness found, Ulysses, What is the remedy? . i 3 140
And when I have the bloody Hector found, Empale him with your weapons . v 7 4
How then?—Then his good report should have been my son; I therein would have found issue . *Coriolanus* i 3 23
But you have found, Scaling his present bearing with his past, That he's your fixed enemy . ii 3 256
We should, by this, to all our lamentation, If he had gone forth consul, found it so . iv 6 35
What faults he made before the last, I think Might have found easy fines v 6 65
Though you left me like a churl, I found a friend . *T. Andron.* i 1 487
A speedier course than lingering languishment Must we pursue, and I have found the path . ii 1 111
We know not where you left him all alive; But, out, alas! here have we found him dead . ii 3 258
If it be proved! you see it is apparent. Who found this letter? . ii 3 293
O, thus I found her, straying in the park, Seeking to hide herself . iii 1 88
Here's no sound jest! the old man hath found their guilt . iv 2 26
I wrote the letter that thy father found And hid the gold . v 1 106
'Tis in vain To seek him here that means not to be found *Rom. and Jul.* ii 1 42
Young Romeo will be older when you have found him than he was when you sought him . ii 4 127
So ho!—What hast thou found?—No hare, sir . ii 4 137
Let Romeo hence in haste, Else, when he's found, that hour is his last iii 1 200
I dreamt my lady came and found me dead . v 1 6
Here's Romeo's man; we found him in the churchyard . v 3 182
It cannot hold; no reason Can found his state in safety . *T. of Athens* ii 1 13
You would throw them off, And say, you found them in mine honesty . ii 2 144
I am proud, say, that my occasions have found time to use 'em . ii 2 200
They have all been touch'd and found base metal . iii 3 6
Searching the window for a flint, I found This paper . *J. Cæsar* ii 1 36
Certain he was not ambitious.—If it be found so, some will dear abide it iii 2 119
Here's a parchment with the seal of Cæsar; I found it in his closet . iii 2 134
When you do find him, or alive or dead, He will be found like Brutus . v 4 25
Yet in all my life I found no man but he was true to me . v 5 35
For Brutus only overcame himself, And no man else hath honour by his death.—So Brutus should be found . v 5 58
So were their daggers, which unwiped we found Upon their pillows *Macb.* ii 3 108
If you will take a homely man's advice, Be not found here . iv 2 69
My children too?—Wife, children, servants, all That could be found . iv 3 212
I have found The very cause of Hamlet's lunacy . *Hamlet* ii 2 48
He hath found The head and source of all your son's distemper . ii 2 54
He truly found It was against your highness . ii 2 64
Why, 'tis found so.—It must be 'se offendendo;' it cannot be else . v 1 8
Where I found, Horatio,—O royal knavery!—an exact command . v 2 18
As much as child e'er loved, or father found . *Lear* i 1 60
If, on the tenth day following, Thy banish'd trunk be found in our dominions, The moment is thy death . i 1 180
I found it thrown in at the casement of my closet . i 2 64
Found you no displeasure in him by word or countenance? . i 2 171
The one in motley here, The other found out there . i 4 161
I had thought, by making this well known unto you, To have found a safe redress . i 4 225
Not in this land shall he remain uncaught; And found—dispatch . ii 1 60
I dissuaded him from his intent, And found him pight to do it . ii 1 67
Your son and daughter found this trespass worth The shame . ii 4 44
When we have found the king,—in which your pain That way, I'll this,—he that first lights on him Holla the other . iii 1 53
There I found 'em, there I smelt 'em out . iv 6 104
But have you never found my brother's way To the forfended place? . v 1 10
You were best go in.—Not I; I must be found . *Othello* i 2 30
Being not at your lodging to be found, The senate hath sent about three several quests To search you out.—'Tis well I am found by you . i 2 45
And found good means To draw from her a prayer of earnest heart . i 3 151
I never found man that knew how to love himself . i 3 315

Found. You shall be well desired in Cyprus; I have found great love amongst them . *Othello* ii 1 207
A pestilent complete knave; and the woman hath found him already . ii 1 253
I found them close together, At blow and thrust . ii 3 237
I am glad I have found this napkin . iii 3 290
Dangerous conceits are, in their natures, poisons, Which at the first are scarce found to distaste . iii 3 327
I found not Cassio's kisses on her lips . iii 3 341
I found it in my chamber. I like the work well . iii 4 188
I will be found most cunning in my patience . iv 1 91
I should have found in some place of my soul A drop of patience . iv 2 52
I saw the handkerchief.—He found it then; I never gave it him . v 2 66
And told no more Than what he found himself was apt and true . v 2 177
That handkerchief thou speak'st of I found by fortune . v 2 226
She give it Cassio! no, alas! I found it, And I did give't my husband . v 2 230
Here is a letter Found in the pocket of the slain Roderigo . v 2 309
Here's another discontented paper, Found in his pocket too . v 2 315
How came you, Cassio, by that handkerchief That was my wife's?—I found it in my chamber . v 2 320
Being done unknown, I should have found it afterwards well done *Ant. and Cleo.* ii 7 85
When Antony found Julius Cæsar dead, He cried almost to roaring; and he wept When at Philippi he found Brutus slain . iii 2 56
I found you as a morsel cold upon Dead Cæsar's trencher . iii 13 116
For when she saw—Which never shall be found—you did suspect She had disposed with Cæsar . iv 14 122
I found her trimming up the diadem On her dead mistress . v 2 345
But found their courage Worthy his frowning at . *Cymbeline* ii 4 22
Found no opposition But what he look'd for should oppose . ii 5 17
I have stol'n nought, nor would not, though I had found Gold strew'd i' the floor . iii 6 49
How found you him?—Stark, as you see . iv 2 209
Have I not found it Murderous to the senses? . iv 2 327
There wants no diligence in seeking him, And will, no doubt, be found iv 3 21
Having found the back-door open Of the unguarded hearts . v 3 45
So 'tis reported: But none of 'em can be found . v 3 88
Woe is my heart That the poor soldier that so richly fought... cannot be found . v 5 5
When I waked, I found This label on my bosom . v 5 429
I sought a husband, in which labour I found that kindness in a father *Pericles* i 1 67
He has found the meaning: But I will gloze with him . i 1 109
He hath found the meaning, for which we mean To have his head . i 1 143
Which by my knowledge found, the sinful father Seem'd not to strike, but smooth . i 2 77
Thou that wast born at sea, buried at Tarsus, And found at sea again!. v 1 199
I oped the coffin, Found there rich jewels . v 3 24
Now do I long to hear how you were found; How possibly preserved . v 3 56
Go with me to my house, Where shall be shown you all was found with her v 3 66

Foundation. God save the foundation! . *Much Ado* v 1 327
Whose foundation Is piled upon his faith . *W. Tale* i 2 429
If I mistake In those foundations which I build upon . ii 1 101
There is no sure foundation set on blood . *K. John* iv 2 104
At my birth The frame and huge foundation of the earth Shaked 1 *Hen. IV.* iii 1 16
Consent upon a sure foundation, Question surveyors . 2 *Hen. IV.* i 3 52
To bring the roof to the foundation, And bury all . *Coriolanus* iii 1 205
Though palaces and pyramids do slope Their heads to their foundations *Macbeth* iv 1 58
I think Foundations fly the wretched . *Cymbeline* iii 6 7

Founded. Whole as the marble, founded as the rock . *Macbeth* iii 4 22
A man that all his time Hath founded his good fortunes on your love *Oth.* iii 4 94

Founder. Pharamond The founder of this law and female bar . *Hen. V.* i 2 42
After defunction of King Pharamond, Idly supposed the founder of this law . i 2 59
In this point All his tricks founder . *Hen. VIII.* iii 2 40

Foundered. Phœbus' steeds are founder'd . *Tempest* iv 1 30
I have foundered nine score and odd posts . 2 *Hen. IV.* iv 3 39

Foundest. By whose direction found'st thou out this place? *Rom. and Jul.* ii 2 79

Fount. Meet me at the consecrated fount . *Meas. for Meas.* iv 3 102
You are the fount that makes small brooks to flow . 3 *Hen. VI.* iv 8 54
As clear as founts in July when We see each grain of gravel . *Hen. VIII.* i 1 154

Fountain. In grove or green, By fountain clear . *M. N. Dream* ii 1 29
By paved fountain or by rushy brook, Or in the beached margent of the sea . ii 1 84
The skies, the fountains, every region near Seem'd all one mutual cry . iv 1 121
I will weep for nothing, like Diana in the fountain . *As Y. Like It* iv 1 155
A woman moved is like a fountain troubled, Muddy, ill-seeming, thick, bereft of beauty . *T. of Shrew* v 2 142
Thou sheer, immaculate and silver fountain! . *Richard II.* v 3 61
What too curious dreg espies my sweet lady in the fountain of our love?—More dregs than water . *Troi. and Cres.* iii 2 71
My mind is troubled, like a fountain stirr'd . iii 3 311
Would the fountain of your mind were clear again, that I might water an ass at it! . iii 3 313
A crimson river of warm blood, Like to a bubbling fountain *T. Andron.* ii 4 23
And thou, and I, sit round about some fountain, Looking all downwards iii 1 123
And in the fountain shall we gaze so long Till the fresh taste be taken from that clearness, And made a brine-pit with our bitter tears . iii 1 127
With purple fountains issuing from your veins . *Rom. and Jul.* i 1 92
She dreamt to-night she saw my statua, Which, like a fountain with an hundred spouts, Did run pure blood . *J. Cæsar* ii 2 77
The spring, the head, the fountain of your blood Is stopp'd . *Macbeth* ii 3 103
The fountain from the which my current runs, Or else dries up *Othello* iv 2 59

Four. One that I saved from drowning, when three or four of his blind brothers and sisters went to it . *T. G. of Ver.* iv 4 4
He thrusts me himself into the company of three or four gentlemanlike dogs . iv 4 19
Vat be all you, one, two, tree, four, come for? . *Mer. Wives* ii 3 22
My daughter and my little son And three or four more of their growth iv 4 48
In our last conflict four of his five wits went halting off . *Much Ado* i 1 66
Of what complexion?—Of all the four, or the three, or the two, or one of the four.—Tell me precisely . *L. L. Lost* i 2 83
Until the goose came out of door, And stay'd the odds by adding four iii 1 93; 99
Now the number is even.—True, true; we are four . iv 3 211
We four indeed confronted were with four In Russian habit . v 2 367
Yet but three? Come one more; Two of both kinds makes up four *M. N. Dream* iii 2 438
If I could bid the fifth welcome with so good a heart as I can bid the other four farewell, I should be glad . *Mer. of Venice* i 2 141
Some three or four of you Go give him courteous conduct to this place. iv 1 147

Four. And three or four loving lords have put themselves into voluntary exile with him . . . . *As Y. Like It* i 1 106
I'll leave her houses three or four as good *T. of Shrew* ii 1 368
They say five moons were seen to-night; Four fixed, and the fifth did whirl about The other four in wondrous motion . *K. John* iv 2 183
Hath from the number of his banish'd years Pluck'd four away *Rich. II.* i 3 211
Heigh-ho! an it be not four by the day, I'll be hanged . 1 *Hen. IV.* ii 1 1
Sirs, you four shall front them in the narrow lane . . . ii 2 62
There be four of us here have ta'en a thousand pound this day morning ii 4 175
A hundred upon poor four of us.—What, a hundred, man? . ii 4 180
I am eight times thrust through the doublet, four through the hose . ii 4 185
How was it?—We four set upon some dozen— Sixteen at least, my lord ii 4 193
These four came all a-front, and mainly thrust at me . . ii 4 222
Seven? why, there were but four even now.—In buckram?—Ay, four, in buckram . . . . ii 4 225
We two saw you four set on four and bound them . . ii 4 279
You had not four such swinge-bucklers in all the inns o' court 2 *Hen. IV.* iii 2 24
You must have but four here, sir: and so, I pray you, go in with me to dinner . . . . iii 2 201
Which men shall I have?—Four of which you please . . iii 2 259
Come, Sir John, which four will you have?—Do you choose for me . iii 2 263
Divide your happy England into four; Whereof take you one quarter *Hen. V.* i 2 214
Four of their lords I'll change for one of ours . . . 1 *Hen. VI.* i 1 151
Come, let us four to dinner . . . . ii 4 133
You four, from hence to prison back again . . 2 *Hen. VI.* ii 3 5
You shall have four, if you'll be ruled by him . 3 *Hen. VI.* iii 2 30
What is't o'clock?—Upon the stroke of four . . *Richard III.* iii 2 5
How far into the morning is it, lords?—Upon the stroke of four . v 3 235
Please you to march; And four shall quickly draw out my command *Coriolanus* i 6 84
I'll lay fourteen of my teeth,—And yet, to my teen be it spoken, I have but four,—She is not fourteen . . . *Rom. and Jul.* i 3 13
Which four successive kings In Denmark's crown have worn *Hamlet* v 2 284
By the four opposing coigns Which the world together joins *Pericles* iii Gower 17
Four and twenty times the pilot's glass Hath told the thievish minutes how they pass . . . . *All's Well* ii 1 168
Four and twenty nosegays for the shearers . . . *W. Tale* iv 3 44
And money lent you, four and twenty pound . 1 *Hen. IV.* iii 3 85
Four barons. They that bear The cloth of honour over her, are four barons Of the Cinque-ports . . . . *Hen. VIII.* iv 1 48
Four bonds. Three or four bonds of forty pound a-piece 1 *Hen. IV.* iii 3 117
Four captains Bear Hamlet, like a soldier, to the stage *Hamlet* v 2 406
Four complexions. Is that one of the four complexions? *L. L. Lost* i 2 87
Four corners. From the four corners of the earth they come *Mer. of Ven.* ii 7 39
Four days. I crave but four days' respite . *Meas. for Meas.* iv 2 170
Hath this been proclaimed?—Four days ago . *L. L. Lost* i 1 122
Four days will quickly steep themselves in night *M. N. Dream* i 1 7
Doth he keep his bed?—He did, my lord, four days ere I set forth 1 *Hen. IV.* iv 1 22
Or I will peat his pate four days . . . *Hen. V.* v 1 43
'Tis not four days gone Since I heard thence *Coriolanus* i 2 6
I had rather fast from all four days Than drink so much in one *A. and C.* ii 7 108
Four dozen. If I were sawed into quantities, I should make four dozen of such bearded hermits' staves . . 2 *Hen. IV.* v 1 70
Four elements. Does not our life consist of the four elements? *T. Night* ii 3 10
Four feasts. I perceive, Four feasts are toward *Ant. and Cleo.* ii 6 75
Four foot. If I travel but four foot by the squier further afoot, I shall break my wind . . . . . 1 *Hen. IV.* ii 2 12
As much as one sound cudgel of four foot—You see the poor remainder—could distribute, I made no spare . . *Hen. VIII.* v 4 19
Four hairs. Not past three or four hairs on his chin *Troi. and Cres.* i 2 121
Four happy days bring in Another moon . *M. N. Dream* i 1 2
Four Harry ten shillings in French crowns . 2 *Hen. IV.* iii 2 236
Four hours. Ay, and have been so any time these four hours *W. Tale* v 2 148
Sometimes he walks four hours together Here in the lobby *Hamlet* ii 2 160
Four hundred. Of knights, esquires, and gallant gentlemen, Eight thousand and four hundred . . . *Hen. V.* iv 8 90
Four hundred twenty-six. Within the year of our redemption Four hundred twenty-six . . . . i 2 61
Four-inched. To ride on a bay trotting-horse over four-inched bridges *Lear* iii 4 57
Four lagging winters and four wanton springs *Richard II.* i 3 214
Four languages. And speaks three or four languages *T. Night* i 3 27
Four legs. I have not 'scaped drowning to be afeard now of your four legs . . . . *Tempest* ii 2 62
As proper a man as ever went on four legs cannot make him give ground ii 2 63
This is some monster of the isle with four legs . . ii 2 68
Four legs and two voices: a most delicate monster! . ii 2 93
Four loggerheads. Three or four loggerheads amongst three or four score hogsheads . . . . 1 *Hen. IV.* ii 4 4
Four miles. I was forced to wheel Three or four miles about *Coriolanus* i 6 20
Four milk-white horses, trapp'd in silver . *T. of Athens* i 2 189
Four negatives. If your four negatives make your two affirmatives *T. N.* v 1 23
Four nights will quickly dream away the time . *M. N. Dream* i 1 9
Four o'clock. You, sirrah, provide your block and your axe to-morrow four o'clock . . . . . *Meas. for Meas.* iv 2 56
'Tis now but four o'clock: we have two hours To furnish us *Mer. of Venice* ii 4 8
To-morrow morning, by four o'clock, early at Gadshill! . 1 *Hen. IV.* i 2 139
Is it four o'clock?—It is.—Then go we in . . *Hen. V.* i 1 93
Towards three or four o'clock Look for the news *Richard III.* ii 5 101
Four of the clock. Let Claudio be executed by four of the clock *M. for M.* iv 2 124
If thou canst awake by four o' the clock, I prithee, call me *Cymbeline* ii 2 6
Four or five. Had I not Four or five women once that tended me? *Temp.* i 2 47
There's four or five, to great Saint Jaques bound . *All's Well* iii 5 98
From son to son, some four or five descents . . . iii 7 24
Who hath for four or five removes come short To tender it herself . v 3 131
Some four or five attend him; All, if you will. . . *T. Night* i 4 36
With four or five most vile and ragged foils . *Hen. V.* iv Prol. 50
Four pasterns. I will not change my horse with any that treads but on four pasterns . . . . iii 7 12
Four pound of prunes, and as many of raisins o' the sun . *W. Tale* iv 3 51
Four quarrels. I have had four quarrels, and like to have fought one *As Y. Like It* v 4 48
Four red roses. Their lips were four red roses on a stalk *Richard III.* iv 3 12
Four rogues in buckram let drive at me— What, four? thou saidst but two even now.—Four, Hal; I told thee four.—Ay, ay, he said four 1 *Hen. IV.* ii 4 216
Four strangers. The four strangers seek for you, madam, to take their leave . . . . *Mer. of Venice* i 2 135
Four suits of peach-coloured satin . . . *Meas. for Meas.* iv 3 11
Four tall fellows. With my long sword I would have made you four tall fellows skip like rats . . . . . *Mer. Wives* ii 1 237
Four terms. The wearing out of six fashions, which is four terms, or two actions . . . . 2 *Hen. IV.* v 1 90
Four thousand. Three or four thousand chequins were as pretty a proportion to live quietly . . . . *Pericles* iv 2 28
Four threes. Pray, let's see these four threes of herdsmen . *W. Tale* iv 4 344
Four throned ones. What four throned ones could have weigh'd Such a compounded one? . . . . . . *Hen. VIII.* i 1 11
Four times. I was three or four times in the thought they were not fairies . . . . *Mer. Wives* v 5 129
Paid money that I borrowed, three or four times . 1 *Hen. IV.* iii 3 21
So a' cried out 'God, God, God!' three or four times . *Hen. V.* ii 3 20
I have looked upon the world for four times seven years *Othello* i 3 313
Four to one she'll none of me . . . . . *T. Night* i 3 112
Four Volsces. Which of you But is four Volsces? . . *Coriolanus* i 6 78
Four wenches. Three or four wenches, where I stood, cried 'Alas!' *J. C.* i 2 274
Four winds. For the four winds blow in from every coast Renowned suitors . . . . *Mer. of Venice* i 1 168
Four woodcocks. Dumain transform'd! four woodcocks in a dish! *L. L. Lost* iv 3 82
Four worthies. If these four Worthies in their first show thrive, These four will change habits, and present the other five . . . . v 2 541
Four yard. Is digt himself four yard under the countermines *Hen. V.* iii 2 66
Four years. On Ash-Wednesday was four year, in the afternoon *M. of V.* ii 5 27
In regard of me He shortens four years of my son's exile *Richard II.* i 3 217
Fourscore. I have lived fourscore years and upward . *Mer. Wives* iii 1 56
A man of fourscore pound a year . . . *Meas. for Meas.* ii 1 127
Are you of fourscore pounds a year?—Yes, an't please you, sir . . ii 1 204
Your daughter spent . . . in one night fourscore ducats *Mer. of Venice* iii 1 114
Fourscore ducats at a sitting! fourscore ducats! . . . iii 1 116
From seventeen years till now almost fourscore Here lived I *As Y. L. It* ii 3 71
At seventeen years many their fortunes seek; But at fourscore it is too late ii 3 74
On Wednesday the fourscore of April, forty thousand fathom above water . . . . *W. Tale* iv 4 280
Three or four loggerheads amongst three or four score hogsheads 1 *Hen. IV.* ii 4 5
In all shapes that man goes up and down in from fourscore to thirteen, this spirit walks in . . . . . . *T. of Athens* ii 2 120
I have been your tenant, and your father's tenant, these fourscore years *Lear* iv 1 14
A very foolish fond old man, Fourscore and upward, not an hour more nor less . . . . iv 7 61
Fourscore three. You have undone a man of fourscore three . *W. Tale* iv 4 464
Fourteen. All the hot bloods between fourteen and five-and-thirty *M. Ado* iii 3 141
If she say I am not fourteen pence on the score for sheer ale *T. of Shrew* Ind. 2 24
But if thou be'st not an ass, I am a youth of fourteen . *All's Well* ii 3 107
These wise men that give fools money get themselves a good report—after fourteen years' purchase . . . . . *T. Night* iv 1 24
Fourteen they shall not see, To bring false generations . *W. Tale* ii 1 147
He came into the world Full fourteen weeks before the course of time *K. John* i 1 113
Those blessed feet Which fourteen hundred years ago were nail'd For our advantage on the bitter cross . . . . 1 *Hen. IV.* i 1 26
How many hast thou killed to-day? 'Give my roan horse a drench,' says he; and answers 'Some fourteen,' an hour after . . ii 4 121
Nor shall we need his help these fourteen days . . . iii 1 88
He cannot draw his power this fourteen days . . . iv 1 126
Carried you a forehand shaft a fourteen and fourteen and a half 2 *Hen. IV.* iii 2 53
We cannot lodge and board a dozen or fourteen gentlewomen *Hen. V.* ii 1 35
Within fourteen days At Bristol I expect my soldiers . 2 *Hen. VI.* iii 1 327
My child is yet a stranger in the world; She hath not seen the change of fourteen years . . . . *Rom. and Jul.* i 2 9
I'll lay fourteen of my teeth,—And yet, to my teen be it spoken, I have but four,—She is not fourteen . . . . i 3 12
Of all days in the year, Come Lammas-eve at night shall she be fourteen i 3 17; 21
Sir, March is wasted fourteen days.—'Tis good . *J. Cæsar* ii 1 59
For that I am some twelve or fourteen moonshines Lag of a brother *Lear* i 2 5
Who at fourteen years He sought to murder . . . *Pericles* v 3 8
What this fourteen years no razor touch'd . . . . v 3 75
Fourth. The fourth turn'd on the toe, and down he fell . *L. L. Lost* v 2 114
He hath a third at Mexico, a fourth for England . *Mer. of Venice* i 3 21
The fourth, the Reproof Valiant . . . . *As Y. Like It* v 4 98
Third, or fourth, or fifth borough, I'll answer him by law *T. of Shrew* Ind. 1 13
And long live Henry, fourth of that name! . . *Richard II.* iv 1 112
He From John of Gaunt doth bring his pedigree, Being but fourth of that heroic line . . . . 1 *Hen. VI.* ii 5 78
Henry doth claim the crown from John of Gaunt, The fourth son 2 *Hen. VI.* ii 2 55
The fourth would return for conscience sake . . *Coriolanus* ii 3 36
Why do you show me this? A fourth! Start, eyes! . . *Macbeth* iv 1 116
There was a fourth man, in a silly habit, That gave the affront *Cymbeline* v 3 86
What is the fourth?—A burning torch . . . *Pericles* ii 2 31
Foutre. A foutre for the world and worldlings base! . 2 *Hen. IV.* v 3 103
A foutre for thine office! . . . . v 3 121
Fowl. And then another fault in the semblance of a fowl; think on't, Jove; a foul fault! . . . . *Mer. Wives* v 5 11
Even for our kitchens We kill the fowl of season . *Meas. for Meas.* ii 2 85
And follies doth emmew As falcon doth the fowl . . iii 1 92
The winged fowls Are their males' subjects and at their controls *C. of Er.* ii 1 18
With intellectual sense and souls, Of more pre-eminence than fish and fowls . . . . ii 1 23
When fowls have no feathers and fish have no fin . . . iii 1 79
For a fish without a fin, there's a fowl without a feather . . iii 1 82
Alas, poor hurt fowl! now will he creep into sedges . *Much Ado* ii 1 209
O, ay: stalk on, stalk on; the fowl sits . . . . . ii 3 95
What is the opinion of Pythagoras concerning wild fowl? . *T. Night* iv 2 55
Such as fear the report of a caliver worse than a struck fowl 1 *Hen. IV.* iv 2 21
Had not your man put up the fowl so suddenly, We had had more sport 2 *Hen. VI.* ii 1 45
Why, what a peevish fool was that of Crete, That taught his son the office of a fowl! . . . . 3 *Hen. VI.* v 6 19
Like a flight of fowl Scatter'd by winds and high tempestuous gusts *T. An.* v 3 68
You know, strange fowl light upon neighbouring ponds . *Cymbeline* i 4 97
Fowler. As wild geese that the creeping fowler eye . *M. N. Dream* iii 2 20
Fox. Thou hast entertain'd A fox to be the shepherd of thy lambs *T. G. of V.* iv 4 97
Search, seek, find out: I'll warrant we'll unkennel the fox *Mer. Wives* iii 3 174
Furred with fox and lamb-skins too . . . *Meas. for Meas.* iii 2 9
O, poor souls, Come you to seek the lamb here of the fox? . . v 1 300
The fox, the ape, and the humble-bee, Were still at odds . *L. L. Lost* iii 1 96
A very fox for his valour.—True; and a goose for his discretion *M. N. D.* v 1 234
His valour cannot carry his discretion; and the fox carries the goose . v 1 237

Fox. His discretion, I am sure, cannot carry his valour; for the goose carries not the fox . . . . . . *M. N. Dream* v 1 240
Tut, a toy! An old Italian fox is not so kind, my boy . *T. of Shrew* ii 1 405
O, will you eat no grapes, my royal fox? Yes, but you will my noble grapes, an if My royal fox could reach them . . *All's Well* ii 1 73
We'll make you some sport with the fox ere we case him . . iii 6 111
Sir Toby will be sworn that I am no fox . . . *T. Night* i 5 86
Sowter will cry upon't for all this, though it be as rank as a fox . ii 5 136
No more truth in thee than in a drawn fox . . 1 *Hen. IV.* iii 3 129
For treason is but trusted like the fox . . . . . v 2 9
To wake a wolf is as bad as to smell a fox . . 2 *Hen. IV.* i 2 176
O Signieur Dew, thou diest on point of fox . . *Hen. V.* iv 4 9
The fox barks not when he would steal the lamb . 2 *Hen. VI.* iii 1 55
Were't not madness, then, To make the fox surveyor of the fold? . . iii 1 253
Let him die, in that he is a fox, By nature proved an enemy to the flock iii 1 257
But when the fox hath once got in his nose, He'll soon find means to make the body follow . . . . 3 *Hen. VI.* iv 7 25
This holy fox, Or wolf, or both,—for he is equal ravenous As he is subtle, and as prone to mischief As able to perform't . . *Hen. VIII.* i 1 158
As fox to lamb, as wolf to heifer's calf . . *Troi. and Cres.* iii 2 200
He that trusts to you, Where he should find you lions, finds you hares; Where foxes, geese . . . . . *Coriolanus* i 1 176
If thou wert the lion, the fox would beguile thee: if thou wert the lamb, the fox would eat thee . . . . . . *T. of Athens* iv 3 331
If thou wert the fox, the lion would suspect thee . . . iv 3 332
Hide fox, and all after . . . . . . *Hamlet* iv 2 33
A fox, when one has caught her, And such a daughter . . *Lear* i 4 340
Fox in stealth, wolf in greediness, dog in madness, lion in prey . iii 4 96
Thou, sapient sir, sit here. Now, you she foxes! . . . iii 6 24
Ingrateful fox! 'tis he.—Bind fast his corky arms . . . iii 7 28
He that parts us shall bring a brand from heaven, And fire us hence like foxes . . . . v 3 23
Subtle as the fox for prey, Like warlike as the wolf for what we eat *Cymb.* iii 3 40
Foxship. Hadst thou foxship To banish him that struck more blows for Rome Than thou hast spoken words? . . *Coriolanus* iv 2 18
Fracted. His heart is fracted and corroborate . . . *Hen. V.* ii 1 130
My reliances on his fracted dates Have smit my credit . *T. of Athens* ii 1 22
Fraction. Their fraction is more our wish than their faction *Troi. and Cres.* ii 3 107
The fractions of her faith, orts of her love . . . . v 2 158
After distasteful looks and these hard fractions . . *T. of Athens* ii 2 220
Fragile. With other incident throes That nature's fragile vessel doth sustain . . . . v 1 204
Fragment. The body of your discourse is sometime guarded with fragments *Much Ado* i 1 288
From whence, fragment?—Why, thou full dish of fool, from Troy *T. and C.* v 1 9
The fragments, scraps, the bits and greasy relics Of her o'er-eaten faith v 2 159
Go, get you home, you fragments! . . . . *Coriolanus* i 1 226
It is some poor fragment, some slender ort of his remainder *T. of Athens* iv 3 400
I found you as a morsel cold upon Dead Cæsar's trencher; nay, you were a fragment Of Cneius Pompey's . . *Ant. and Cleo.* iii 13 117
And now our cowards, Like fragments in hard voyages, became The life o' the need . . . . *Cymbeline* v 3 44
Fragrant. Make our beds of roses, And a thousand fragrant poses *M. Wives* iii 1 20
With coronet of fresh and fragrant flowers . . *M. N. Dream* iv 1 57
The fields are fragrant and the woods are green . *T. Andron.* ii 2 2
One hour's storm will drown the fragrant meads . . . ii 4 54
Frail. Pricking goss and thorns, Which enter'd their frail shins *Tempest* iv 1 181
We are all frail . . . . *Meas. for Meas.* ii 4 121
Nay, women are frail too.—Ay, as the glasses where they view themselves ii 4 124
Nay, call us ten times frail; For we are soft as our complexions are . ii 4 128
Babbling, drunkenness, Or any taint of vice whose strong corruption Inhabits our frail blood . . . . . . *T. Night* iii 4 391
His pure brain, Which some suppose the soul's frail dwelling-house *K. John* v 7 3
This frail sepulchre of our flesh . . . . . *Richard II.* i 3 196
My ransom is this frail and worthless trunk . . *Hen. V.* iii 6 163
She did corrupt frail nature with some bribe, To shrink mine arm up 3 *Hen. VI.* iii 2 155
Look your faith be firm, Or else his head's assurance is but frail *Rich. III.* iv 4 498
And nature does require Her times of preservation, which perforce I, her frail son, amongst my brethren mortal, Must give my tendance to *Hen. VIII.* iii 2 148
We all are men, In our own natures frail, and capable Of our flesh . v 3 11
A frail vow betwixt an erring barbarian and a supersubtle Venetian *Oth.* i 3 362
In wisdom never was so frail To change the cod's head for the salmon's tail ii 1 155
Heart, once be stronger than thy continent, Crack thy frail case! *A. and C.* iv 14 41
The one is but frail and the other casual . . . *Cymbeline* i 4 100
Your Italy contains none so accomplished a courtier to convince the honour of my mistress, if, in the holding or loss of that, you term her frail . . . . i 4 106
I thank thee, who hath taught My frail mortality to know itself *Pericles* i 1 42
Frailest. That eyes, that are the frail'st and softest things *As Y. Like It* iii 5 12
Frailty. A secure fool, and stands so firmly on his wife's frailty *M. Wives* ii 1 242
Bid her think what a man is: let her consider his frailty . . ii 5 52
But that frailty hath examples for his falling, I should wonder *M. for M.* iii 1 190
Framed to himself, by the instruction of his frailty, many deceiving promises . . . . iii 2 260
Alas, our frailty is the cause, not we! For such as we are made of, such we be . . . . *T. Night* ii 2 32
Chants a doleful hymn to his own death, And from the organ-pipe of frailty sings His soul and body to their lasting rest . . *K. John* v 7 23
I have more flesh than another man, and therefore more frailty 1 *Hen. IV.* iii 3 189
Out of which frailty And want of wisdom, you, that best should teach us, Have misdemean'd yourself . . . . . *Hen. VIII.* v 3 12
And sometimes we are devils to ourselves, When we will tempt the frailty of our powers . . . . . . *Troi. and Cres.* iv 4 98
When we have our naked frailties hid . . . . *Macbeth* ii 3 132
Let me not think on't—Frailty, thy name is woman! . *Hamlet* i 2 146
Is't frailty that thus errs? It is so too: and have not we affections, Desires for sport, and frailty, as men have? . . . *Othello* iv 3 100
Frailties which before Have often shamed our sex . . *Ant. and Cleo.* v 2 123
Frame. And frame some feeling line . . . . *T. G. of Ver.* iii 2 76
We are made to be no stronger Than faults may shake our frames *M. for M.* ii 4 133
The maid will I frame and make fit for his attempt . . . iii 1 266
Her madness hath the oddest frame of sense . . . . . v 1 61
It is needful that you frame the season for your own harvest . *Much Ado* i 3 26
Chid I for that at frugal nature's frame? . . . . . iv 1 130
Whose spirits toil in frame of villanies . . . . . iv 1 191
A woman, that is like a German clock, Still a-repairing, ever out of frame, And never going aright . . . . *L. L. Lost* iii 1 193
Like to Lysander sometime frame thy tongue . . *M. N. Dream* iii 2 360

Frame. O wherefore, Nature, didst thou lions frame? . *M. N. Dream* v 1 296
Frame your mind to mirth and merriment . . . *T. of Shrew* Ind. 2 137
'Tis no time to jest, And therefore frame your manners to the time . i 1 232
Like a common and an outward man, That the great figure of a council frames By self-unable motion . . . . . *All's Well* iii 1 12
But, fair soul, In your fine frame hath love no quality? . . . iv 2 4
O, she that hath a heart of that fine frame To pay this debt of love but to a brother, How will she love! . . . . . *T. Night* i 1 33
The very mould and frame of hand, nail, finger . . *W. Tale* ii 3 103
Now were I happy, if His going I could frame to serve my turn . . iv 4 520
The frame and huge foundation of the earth Shaked like a coward 1 *Hen. IV.* iii 1 16
His apparel is built upon his back and the whole frame stands upon pins: prick him no more . . . . . . 2 *Hen. IV.* iii 2 155
We may meet; And either end in peace, which God so frame! . . iv 1 180
Were the whole frame here, It is of such a spacious lofty pitch, Your roof were not sufficient to contain't . . . . 1 *Hen. VI.* ii 3 54
Faith, I have been a truant in the law, And never yet could frame my will to it; And therefore frame the law unto my will . . . ii 4 8
By wicked means to frame our sovereign's fall . . 2 *Hen. VI.* iii 1 52
Fear frames disorder, and disorder wounds Where it should guard . v 2 32
And frame my face to all occasions . . . . 3 *Hen. VI.* iii 2 185
You know no more than others; but you frame Things that are known alike; which are not wholesome . . . . . *Hen. VIII.* i 2 44
But thou wilt frame Thyself, forsooth, hereafter theirs . *Coriolanus* iii 2 84
I think 'twill serve, if he Can thereto frame his spirit . . . iii 2 97
Thou art my warrior; I help to frame thee . . . . . v 3 63
Though I cannot make true wars, I'll frame convenient peace . . v 3 191
One do I personate of Lord Timon's frame . . . *T. of Athens* i 1 69
Men At duty, more than I could frame employment . . . iv 3 262
But let the frame of things disjoint, both the worlds suffer . *Macbeth* iii 2 16
Or thinking by our late dear brother's death Our state to be disjoint and out of frame . . . . *Hamlet* i 2 20
This goodly frame, the earth, seems to me a sterile promontory . . ii 2 310
Put your discourse into some frame and start not so wildly from my affair iii 2 321
The gallows-maker; for that frame outlives a thousand tenants . . v 1 49
Frame the business after your own wisdom . . . . . *Lear* i 2 107
That, like an engine, wrench'd my frame of nature From the fix'd place i 4 290
Some bloody passion shakes your very frame . . . *Othello* v 2 44
Those flower-soft hands, That yarely frame the office . *Ant. and Cleo.* ii 2 216
That she preparedly may frame herself To the way she's forced to . v 1 55
Frame yourself To orderly soliciting . . . . . *Cymbeline* ii 3 51
'Tis wonder That an invisible instinct should frame them To royalty unlearn'd . . . . iv 2 177
The beauty of this sinful dame Made many princes thither frame *Per.* i Gower 32
Hear you, mistress; either frame Your will to mine,—and you, sir, hear you . . . . ii 5 81
Framed. Yet had he framed to himself, by the instruction of his frailty, many deceiving promises of life . . . *Meas. for Meas.* iii 2 259
Nature never framed a woman's heart Of prouder stuff . *Much Ado* iii 1 49
Framed by thy villany!—My villany?—Thine, Claudio; thine, I say . v 1 71
He is composed and framed of treachery . . . . . v 1 257
And here he hath framed a letter . . . . . *L. L. Lost* iv 2 142
Nature hath framed strange fellows in her time . *Mer. of Venice* i 1 51
'Tis not a visitation framed, but forced By need and accident *W. Tale* v 1 91
I framed to the harp Many an English ditty lovely well . 1 *Hen. IV.* iii 1 123
For thou art framed of the firm truth of valour . . *Hen. V.* iv 3 14
His head by nature framed to wear a crown . . 3 *Hen. VI.* iv 6 72
Framed in the prodigality of nature, Young, valiant, wise *Richard III.* i 2 244
The most replenished sweet work of nature, That from the prime creation e'er she framed . . . . iv 3 19
The honour'd mould Wherein this trunk was framed . . *Coriolanus* v 3 23
Here's a young lad framed of another leer . . . *T. Andron.* iv 2 119
No big-boned men framed of the Cyclops' size; But metal, Marcus . iv 3 46
'Twas time and griefs That framed him thus . . . *T. of Athens* v 1 126
That eyeless head of thine was first framed flesh To raise my fortunes *Lear* iv 6 231
He hath a person and a smooth dispose To be suspected, framed to make women false . . . . *Othello* i 3 404
She's framed as fruitful As the free elements . . . . . ii 3 347
When nature framed this piece, she meant thee a good turn . *Pericles* iv 2 150
Framing. In framing an artist, art hath thus decreed, To make some good, but others to exceed . . . . ii 3 15
Frampold. She leads a very frampold life with him, good heart *M. Wives* ii 2 94
France. Let the court of France show me such another . . . . iii 3 57
By gar, 'tis no the fashion of France; it is not jealous in France . . iii 3 183
Where France?—In her forehead; armed and reverted *Com. of Errors* iii 2 125
Where England?— . . . I guess it stood in her chin, by the salt rheum that ran between France and it . . . . iii 2 132
The daughter of the King of France, On serious business . *L. L. Lost* ii 1 30
And go well satisfied to France again . . . . . . ii 1 153
On Saturday we will return to France . . . . . . iv 1 6
To a lady of France that he call'd Rosaline . . . . . iv 1 107
That was a man when King Pepin of France was a little boy . . . iv 1 122
Lay these glozes by: Shall we resolve to woo these girls of France? . iv 3 371
And lay my arms before the legs of this sweet lass of France . . v 2 558
He bought his doublet in Italy, his round hose in France *Mer. of Venice* i 2 81
It is the stubbornest young fellow of France . . . *As Y. Like It* i 1 149
Exempted be from me the arrogance To choose from forth the royal blood of France . . . . *All's Well* ii 1 199
France is a dog-hole, and it no more merits The tread of a man's foot . ii 3 291
To other regions France is a stable; we that dwell in't jades . . ii 3 301
We marvel much our cousin France Would in so just a business shut his bosom . . . . iii 1 7
Till I have no wife, I have nothing in France . . . . . iii 2 77
Nothing in France, until he have no wife! . . . . . . iii 2 81
You came, I think, from France?—I did so . . . . . . iii 5 49
He stole from France, As 'tis reported, for the king had married him . iii 5 55
Will he travel higher, or return again into France? . . . . . iv 3 51
His lordship will next morning for France . . . . . . iv 3 91
What greeting will you to my Lord Lafeu? I am for France . . . iv 3 353
I am for France too: we shall speak of you there . . . . iv 3 364
A' has an English name; but his fisnomy is more hotter in France than there . . . . iv 5 42
I have seen you in the court of France.—I have been sometimes there . v 1 10
Now, say, Chatillon, what would France with us?—Thus, after greeting, speaks the King of France . . . . *K. John* i 1 1
Philip of France, in right and true behalf Of thy deceased brother . i 1 7
Here have we war for war and blood for blood, Controlment for controlment: so answer France . . . . i 1 20
Be thou as lightning in the eyes of France . . . . . . i 1 24

France. Constance would not cease Till she had kindled France and all the world *K. John* i 1 33
We must speed For France, for France, for it is more than need i 1 179
The right thou hast in France, Together with that pale, that white-faced shore ii 1 22
Peace be to France, if France in peace permit Our just and lineal entrance to our own; If not, bleed France, and peace ascend to heaven ii 1 84
Peace be to England, if that war return From France to England ii 1 90
From whom hast thou this great commission, France? ii 1 110
Who is it thou dost call usurper, France? ii 1 120
I do defy thee, France. Arthur of Bretagne, yield thee to my hand ii 1 155
I'll give thee more Than e'er the coward hand of France can win ii 1 158
Who is it that hath warn'd us to the walls?—'Tis France, for England ii 1 202
These flags of France, that are advanced here Before the eye and prospect of your town, Have hither march'd to your endamagement ii 1 207
Who by the hand of France this day hath made Much work for tears in many an English mother ii 1 302
No plume in any English crest That is removed by a staff of France ii 1 318
France, hast thou yet more blood to cast away? ii 1 334
England, thou hast not saved one drop of blood, In this hot trial, more than we of France; Rather, lost more ii 1 342
Let France and England mount Their battering cannon charged to the mouths ii 1 381
France, shall we knit our powers And lay this Angiers even with the ground? ii 1 398
Austria and France shoot in each other's mouth: I'll stir them to it ii 1 414
Not a word of his But buffets better than a fist of France ii 1 465
I see a yielding in the looks of France; Mark, how they whisper ii 1 474
Philip of France, if thou be pleased withal, Command thy son and daughter to join hands ii 1 531
France, whose armour conscience buckled on ii 1 564
This all-changing word, Clapp'd on the outward eye of fickle France ii 1 583
O boy, then where art thou? France friend with England, what becomes of me? iii 1 35
Fortune . . . with her golden hand hath pluck'd on France To tread down fair respect of sovereignty iii 1 57
France is a bawd to Fortune and King John, That strumpet Fortune! iii 1 60
Is not France forsworn? Envenom him with words, or get thee gone iii 1 62
This blessed day Ever in France shall be kept festival iii 1 76
Philip of France, on peril of a curse, Let go the hand of that arch-heretic iii 1 191
Raise the power of France upon his head, Unless he do submit himself to Rome iii 1 193
Look'st thou pale, France? do not let go thy hand.—Look to that devil; lest that France repent iii 1 195
France, thou mayst hold a serpent by the tongue iii 1 258
France, thou shalt rue this hour within this hour iii 1 323
That bald sexton Time, Is it as he will? well then, France shall rue iii 1 325
France, I am burn'd up with inflaming wrath iii 1 340
That nothing can allay, nothing but blood, The blood, and dearest-valued blood, of France iii 1 343
Bloody England into England gone, O'erbearing interruption, spite of France iii 4 9
I remember, when I was in France, Young gentlemen would be as sad as night, Only for wantonness iv 1 14
Pour down thy weather: how goes all in France?—From France to England iv 2 109
Where is my mother's care, That such an army could be drawn in France? iv 2 118
What! mother dead! How wildly then walks my estate in France! iv 2 128
Under whose conduct came those powers of France? iv 2 129
Who brought that letter from the cardinal?—The Count Melun, a noble lord of France iv 3 15
Hail, noble prince of France! The next is this, King John hath reconciled Himself to Rome v 2 68
Since last I went to France to fetch his queen *Richard II.* i 1 131
Hie thee to France And cloister thee in some religious house v 1 22
Good sometime queen, prepare thee hence for France v 1 37
With all swift speed you must away to France v 1 54
I towards the north, Where shivering cold and sickness pines the clime; My wife to France v 1 78
Weep thou for me in France, I for thee here v 1 87
When I from France set foot at Ravenspurgh *1 Hen. IV.* iii 2 95
We bear our civil swords and native fire As far as France *2 Hen. IV.* v 5 113
And make you merry with fair Katharine of France Epil. 30
Can this cockpit hold The vasty fields of France? *Hen. V.* Prol. 12
In regard of causes now in hand, Which I have open'd to his grace at large, As touching France i 1 79
Titles to some certain dukedoms And generally to the crown and seat of France i 1 88
Some things of weight That task our thoughts, concerning us and France i 2 6
Religiously unfold Why the law Salique that they have in France Or should, or should not, bar us in our claim i 2 11
There is no bar To make against your highness' claim to France But this i 2 36
Which Salique land the French unjustly glose To be the realm of France i 2 41
Doth it well appear the Salique law Was not devised for the realm of France i 2 55
King Pepin . . . Did . . . Make claim and title to the crown of France i 2 68
Lewis the Tenth . . . Could not keep quiet in his conscience, Wearing the crown of France i 2 80
The line of Charles the Great Was re-united to the crown of France i 2 85
So do the kings of France unto this day i 2 90
Edward the Black Prince, Who on the French ground play'd a tragedy, Making defeat on the full power of France i 2 107
O noble English, that could entertain With half their forces the full pride of France And let another half stand laughing by! i 2 112
Whose hearts have left their bodies here in England And lie pavilion'd in the fields of France i 2 129
My great-grandfather Never went with his forces into France But that the Scot on his unfurnish'd kingdom Came pouring i 2 147
When all her chivalry hath been in France And she a mourning widow i 2 157
Impounded as a stray The King of Scots; whom she did send to France i 2 161
If that you will France win, Then with Scotland first begin i 2 167
Therefore to France, my liege. Divide your happy England into four; Whereof take you one quarter into France i 2 213
France being ours, we'll bend it to our awe, Or break it all to pieces i 2 224
There we'll sit, Ruling in large and ample empery O'er France i 2 227

France. Your highness, lately sending into France, Did claim some certain dukedoms *Hen. V.* i 2 246
There's nought in France That can be with a nimble galliard won i 2 251
We will, in France, by God's grace, play a set Shall strike his father's crown into the hazard i 2 262
That all the courts of France will be disturb'd With chaces i 2 265
And show my sail of greatness When I do rouse me in my throne of France i 2 275
That I will dazzle all the eyes of France, Yea, strike the Dauphin blind i 2 279
We have now no thought in us but France, Save those to God i 2 302
France hath in thee found out A nest of hollow bosoms ii Prol. 20
Have, for the gilt of France,—O guilt indeed!—Confirm'd conspiracy with fearful France ii Prol. 26
This grace of kings must die, If hell and treason hold their promises, Ere he take ship for France ii Prol. 30
And thence to France shall we convey you safe, And bring you back ii Prol. 37
And we'll be all three sworn brothers to France ii 1 14
Come, shall I make you two friends? We must to France together ii 1 95
The powers we bear with us Will cut their passage through the force of France ii 2 16
Lightly conspired, And sworn unto the practices of France ii 2 90
For me, the gold of France did not seduce ii 2 155
Lords, for France; the enterprise whereof Shall be to you, as us, like glorious ii 2 182
The signs of war advance; No king of England, if not king of France ii 2 193
Yoke-fellows in arms, Let us to France; like horse-leeches, my boys ii 3 57
'Tis meet we all go forth To view the sick and feeble parts of France ii 4 22
The crown And all wide-stretched honours that pertain By custom and the ordinance of times Unto the crown of France ii 4 84
Caves and womby vaultages of France Shall chide your trespass ii 4 124
That you shall read In your own losses, if he stay in France ii 4 139
Follow These cull'd and choice-drawn cavaliers to France iii Prol. 24
Je ne voudrais prononcer ces mots devant les seigneurs de France pour tout le monde iii 4 59
And if he be not fought withal, my lord, Let us not live in France iii 5 3
They will give Their bodies to the lust of English youth To new-store France with bastard warriors iii 5 31
Charles Delabreth, high constable of France iii 5 40; iv 8 97
This your air of France Hath blown that vice in me iii 6 160
We will come on, Though France himself and such another neighbour Stand in our way iii 6 166
He is simply the most active gentleman of France iii 7 106
A good soft pillow for that good white head Were better than a churlish turf of France iv 1 15
Why do you stay so long, my lords of France? iv 2 38
Who hath sent thee now?—The Constable of France iv 3 89
And those that leave their valiant bones in France, Dying like men, though buried in your dunghills, They shall be famed iv 3 98
The smell whereof shall breed a plague in France iv 3 103
I was not angry since I came to France Until this instant iv 7 58
As I have read in the chronicles, fought a most prave pattle here in France iv 7 99
As any is in the universal world, or in France, or in England! iv 8 11
Jacques of Chatillon, admiral of France iv 8 98
Great Master of France, the brave Sir Guichard Dolphin iv 8 100
To Calais; and to England then; Where ne'er from France arrived more happy men iv 8 131
The emperor's coming in behalf of France, To order peace between them v Prol. 38
And omit All the occurrences, whatever chanced, Till Harry's back-return again to France v Prol. 41
Your eyes advance, After your thoughts, straight back again to France v Prol. 45
News have I, that my Nell is dead i' the spital Of malady of France v 1 87
Unto our brother France, and to our sister, Health and fair time of day! v 2 2
My duty to you both, on equal love, Great Kings of France and England! v 2 24
Why that the naked, poor and mangled Peace . . . Should not in this best garden of the world, Our fertile France, put up her lovely visage? Alas, she hath from France too long been chased v 2 37
It is not possible you should love the enemy of France, Kate: but, in loving me, you should love the friend of France v 2 181
I love France so well that I will not part with a village of it v 2 183
When France is mine and I am yours, then yours is France and you are mine v 2 185
Je quand sur le possession de France, et quand vous avez le possession de moi, . . . donc votre est France et vous êtes mienne v 2 192
Your majestee ave fausse French enough to deceive de most sage demoiselle dat is en France v 2 235
England is thine, Ireland is thine, France is thine, and Henry Plantagenet is thine v 2 259
Les dames et demoiselles pour être baisées, devant leur noces, il n'est pas la coutume de France v 2 281
Dat it is not be de fashion pour les ladies of France v 2 285
It is not a fashion for the maids in France to kiss before they are married v 2 290
The King of France . . . shall name your highness in this form and with this addition, in French, Notre très-cher fils Henri, Roi d'Angleterre, Héritier de France v 2 365
The contending kingdoms Of France and England, whose very shores look pale With envy of each other's happiness v 2 378
That never war advance His bleeding sword 'twixt England and fair France v 2 383
Henry the Sixth, in infant bands crown'd King Of France and England Epil. 10
Whose state so many had the managing, That they lost France Epil. 12
Sad tidings bring I to you out of France, Of loss, of slaughter *1 Hen. VI.* i 1 58
Regent I am of France. Give me my steeled coat. I'll fight for France i 1 85
France is revolted from the English quite, Except some petty towns i 1 90
An army have I muster'd in my thoughts, Wherewith already France is overrun i 1 102
Talbot . . . Whom all France with their chief assembled strength Durst not presume to look once in the face i 1 139
Bonfires in France forthwith I am to make, To keep our great Saint George's feast withal i 1 153
Raise this tedious siege And drive the English forth the bounds of France i 2 54
Wretched shall France be only in my name i 4 97
France, triumph in thy glorious prophetess! Recover'd is the town of Orleans i 6 8
All France will be replete with mirth and joy, When they shall hear i 6 15

France. Transported shall be at high festivals Before the kings and queens of France . . . . 1 *Hen. VI.* i 6 27
No longer on Saint Denis will we cry, But Joan la Pucelle shall be France's saint . . . . i 6 29
Coward of France! how much he wrongs his fame! . . . . . ii 1 16
And what a terror he had been to France . . . . . . ii 2 17
So much applauded through the realm of France . . . . . ii 2 36
Is this the scourge of France? Is this the Talbot, so much fear'd abroad? . . . . ii 3 15
Now will it best avail your majesty To cross the seas and to be crown'd in France: The presence of a king engenders love . . . iii 1 180
We may march in England or in France, Not seeing what is likely to ensue . . . . iii 1 187
Qui est là?—Paysans, pauvres gens de France . . . . . . iii 2 14
France, thou shalt rue this treason with thy tears . . . . . iii 2 36
That hardly we escaped the pride of France . . . . . . iii 2 40
Foul fiend of France, and hag of all despite! . . . . . . iii 2 52
Signior, hang! base muleters of France! . . . . iii 2 68
Prick'd on by public wrongs sustain'd in France . . . . . iii 2 78
If we could do that, France were no place for Henry's warriors . . iii 3 22
For ever should they be expulsed from France And not have title of an earldom . . . . iii 3 25
Who craves a parley with the Burgundy?—The princely Charles of France . . . . iii 3 38
Brave Burgundy, undoubted hope of France! . . . . . . iii 3 41
Look on fertile France, And see the cities and the towns defaced . . iii 3 44
See, see the pining malady of France; Behold the wounds . . . iii 3 49
Besides, all French and France exclaims on thee, Doubting thy birth . iii 3 60
When Talbot hath set footing once in France . . . . . . iii 3 64
Is this the Lord Talbot, uncle Gloucester, That hath so long been resident in France? . . . . iii 4 14
And join'd with Charles, the rightful King of France. O monstrous treachery! . . . . iv 1 60
Crossing the sea from England into France . . . . . . iv 1 89
Remember where we are; In France, amongst a fickle wavering nation iv 1 138
King Henry's peers and chief nobility Destroy'd themselves, and lost the realm of France! . . . . iv 1 147
York, we institute your grace To be our regent in these parts of France iv 1 163
If he miscarry, farewell wars in France . . . . iv 3 16
Thou princely leader of our English strength, Never so needful on the earth of France, Spur to the rescue . . . . iv 3 18
To Bourdeaux, York! Else, farewell Talbot, France, and England's honour . . . . iv 3 23
We mourn, France smiles; we lose, they daily get . . . . . iv 3 32
The fraud of England, not the force of France, Hath now entrapp'd the noble-minded Talbot . . . . iv 4 36
Together live and die; And soul with soul from France to heaven fly . iv 5 55
The regent hath with Talbot broke his word And left us to the rage of France his sword . . . . iv 6 3
And like me to the peasant boys of France, To be shame's scorn! . . iv 6 48
Great marshal to Henry the Sixth Of all his wars within the realm of France . . . . iv 7 71
O, that I could but call these dead to life! It were enough to fright the realm of France . . . . iv 7 82
From their ashes shall be rear'd A phœnix that shall make all France afeard . . . . iv 7 93
A godly peace concluded of Between the realms of England and of France . . . . v 1 6
A man of great authority in France, Proffers his only daughter to your grace . . . . v 1 18
We mean Shall be transported presently to France . . . . . v 1 40
Then march to Paris, royal Charles of France, And keep not back your powers in dalliance . . . . v 2 4
Then on, my lords; and France be fortunate! . . . . . . v 2 21
Ye familiar spirits, that are cull'd Out of the powerful regions under earth, Help me this once, that France may get the field . . . v 3 12
Now the time is come That France must vail her lofty-plumed crest . v 3 25
Now, France, thy glory droopeth to the dust . . . . . . v 3 29
Damsel of France, I think I have you fast . . . . . . v 3 30
Reignier of France, I give thee kingly thanks . . . . . . v 3 163
I foresee with grief The utter loss of all the realm of France . . v 4 112
It is thus agreed That peaceful truce shall be proclaim'd in France . v 4 117
Of such great authority in France As his alliance will confirm our peace v 5 41
Take, therefore, shipping; post, my lord, to France; Agree to any covenants . . . . v 5 87
I had in charge at my depart for France, As procurator . . 2 *Hen. VI.* i 1 2
In presence of the Kings of France and Sicil, The Dukes of Orleans, Calaber, Bretagne . . . . i 1 6
Did he so often lodge in open field, In winter's cold and summer's parching heat, To conquer France? . . . . i 1 82
And victorious Warwick Received deep scars in France and Normandy i 1 87
Debating to and fro How France and Frenchmen might be kept in awe i 1 92
Defacing monuments of conquer'd France . . . . i 1 102
For France, 'tis ours; and we will keep it still.—Ay, uncle, we will keep it, if we can; But now it is impossible . . . . . i 1 106
France should have torn and rent my very heart, Before I would have yielded . . . . i 1 126
She should have stay'd in France and starved in France . . . . i 1 135
And say, when I am gone, I prophesied France will be lost ere long . i 1 146
Thy late exploits done in the heart of France, When thou wert regent . i 1 196
I meant Maine, Which I will win from France, or else be slain . . i 1 213
England, France and Ireland Bear that proportion to my flesh and blood As did the fatal brand Althæa burn'd . . . . . . i 1 232
Cold news for me, for I had hope of France, Even as I have of fertile England's soil . . . . i 1 237; iii 1 87
And stolest away the ladies' hearts of France . . . . . . i 3 55
If York have ill demean'd himself in France, Then let him be denay'd the regentship . . . . i 3 106
Thy sale of offices and towns in France, If they were known, as the suspect is great, Would make thee quickly hop without thy head . i 3 138
York is meetest man To be your regent in the realm of France . . i 3 164
Till France be won into the Dauphin's hands . . . . . . i 3 173
Deposed the rightful king, Sent his poor queen to France . . . ii 2 25
Did he not, in his protectorship, Levy great sums of money through the realm For soldiers' pay in France? . . . . iii 1 62
What news from France?—That all your interest in those territories Is utterly bereft you; all is lost . . . . iii 1 83
'Tis thought, my lord, that you took bribes of France . . . . iii 1 104
Stay'd the soldiers' pay; By means whereof his highness hath lost France iii 1 106
Nor ever had one penny bribe from France . . . . . . iii 1 109
France. 'Tis meet that lucky ruler be employ'd; Witness the fortune he hath had in France . . . . 2 *Hen. VI.* iii 1 292
He never would have stay'd in France so long.—No, not to lose it all . iii 1 295
To France, sweet Suffolk: let me hear from thee . . . . . iii 2 405
By thee Anjou and Maine were sold to France . . . . . . iv 1 86
I go of message from the queen to France; I charge thee waft me safely iv 1 113
Here's the Lord Say, which sold the towns in France . . . . iv 7 23
For giving up of Normandy unto Mounsieur Basimecu, the dauphin of France . . . . iv 7 31
Lest they consult about the giving up of some more towns in France . iv 7 142
Henry the Fifth, that made all France to quake . . . . . iv 8 17
Will he conduct you through the heart of France, And make the meanest of you earls and dukes? . . . . iv 8 38
To France, to France, and get what you have lost . . . . . iv 8 51
A sceptre shall it have, have I a soul, On which I'll toss the flower-de-luce of France . . . . v 1 11
Talk not of France, sith thou hast lost it all . . . 3 *Hen. VI.* i 1 110
Their colours, often borne in France, And now in England to our heart's great sorrow, Shall be my winding-sheet . . . . . . i 1 127
Many a battle have I won in France, When as the enemy hath been ten to one . . . . i 2 74
She-wolf of France, but worse than wolves of France! . . . . i 4 111
His father revell'd in the heart of France, And tamed the king . . ii 2 150
Even then that sunshine brew'd a shower for him, That wash'd his father's fortunes forth of France . . . . ii 2 157
From whence shall Warwick cut the sea to France, And ask the Lady Bona ii 6 89
And, having France thy friend, thou shalt not dread The scatter'd foe ii 6 92
My queen and son are gone to France for aid . . . . . . iii 1 28
No, mighty King of France: now Margaret Must strike her sail . . iii 3 4
Tell thy grief; It shall be eased, if France can yield relief . . . iii 3 20
Welcome, brave Warwick! What brings thee to France? . . . iii 3 46
Henry the Fifth, Who by his prowess conquered all France . . . iii 3 86
Methinks these peers of France should smile at that . . . . iii 3 91
You have a father able to maintain you; And better 'twere you troubled him than France . . . . iii 3 155
Is this the alliance that he seeks with France? . . . . . . iii 3 177
That Lewis of France is sending over masquers To revel it with him and his new bride . . . . iii 3 224
I long till Edward fall by war's mischance, For mocking marriage with a dame of France . . . . iii 3 255
Alas, you know, 'tis far from hence to France . . . . . . iv 1 4
How like you our choice . . . ?—As well as Lewis of France . . . iv 1 11
Yet, to have join'd with France in such alliance Would more have strengthen'd this our commonwealth 'Gainst foreign storms . . iv 1 36
Of itself England is safe, if true within itself?—But the safer when 'tis back'd with France . . . . iv 1 41
'Tis better using France than trusting France . . . . . . iv 1 42
Now, messenger, what letters or what news From France? . . . iv 1 85
Let me entreat, for I command no more, That Margaret your queen and my son Edward Be sent for, to return from France with speed . iv 6 61
The queen from France hath brought a puissant power: Even now we heard the news . . . . v 2 31
The friends of France our shrouds and tacklings . . . . . . v 4 18
Reignier, her father, to the king of France Hath pawn'd the Sicils . v 7 38
Away with her, and waft her hence to France . . . . . . v 7 41
I'll win our ancient right in France again, Or die a soldier *Richard III.* iii 1 92
Noble York My princely father then had wars in France . . . iii 5 88
I did; with his contract with Lady Lucy, And his contract by deputy in France . . . . iii 7 6
His own bastardy, As being got, your father then in France . . . iii 7 10
Afterward by substitute betroth'd To Bona, sister to the King of France iii 7 182
A dire induction am I witness to, And will to France . . . . iv 4 6
These English woes will make me smile in France . . . . . iv 4 115
Lash hence these overweening rags of France, These famish'd beggars . v 3 328
Well met. How have ye done Since last we saw in France? *Hen. VIII.* i 1 2
France hath flaw'd the league, and hath attach'd Our merchants' goods i 1 95
Only to show his pomp as well in France As here at home . . . i 1 163
His fears were, that the interview betwixt England and France might, through their amity, Breed him some prejudice . . . . . i 1 181
And the pretence for this Is named, your wars in France . . . . i 2 60
Not long before your highness sped to France, The duke being at the Rose i 2 151
Is't possible the spells of France should juggle Men into such strange mysteries? . . . . i 3 1
Leave those remnants Of fool and feather that they got in France . i 3 25
What wouldst thou have, Laertes?—My dread lord, Your leave and favour to return to France . . . . *Hamlet* i 2 51
That duty done, My thoughts and wishes bend again toward France . i 2 55
They in France of the best rank and station Are of a most select and generous chief in that . . . . i 3 73
Her brother is in secret come from France . . . . . . iv 5 88
Since he went into France, I have been in continual practice . . v 2 221
Attend the lords of France and Burgundy, Gloucester . . . . *Lear* i 1 35
France and Burgundy, Great rivals in our youngest daughter's love . i 1 46
To whose young love The vines of France and milk of Burgundy Strive to be interess'd . . . . i 1 86
Call France; who stirs? Call Burgundy . . . . i 1 128
Here's France and Burgundy, my noble lord . . . . i 1 191
Is queen of us, of ours, and our fair France . . . . . . i 1 260
Thou hast her, France: let her be thine; for we Have no such daughter i 1 265
There is further compliment of leave-taking between France and him . i 1 307
Kent banish'd thus! and France in choler parted! And the king gone to-night! . . . . i 2 23
Since my young lady's going into France, sir, the fool hath much pined away . . . . i 4 80
The hot-blooded France, that dowerless took Our youngest born . . ii 4 215
Which are to France the spies and speculations Intelligent of our state iii 1 24
But, true it is, from France there comes a power Into this scatter'd kingdom . . . . iii 1 30
Which approves him an intelligent party to the advantages of France . iii 5 13
Show him this letter: the army of France is landed . . . . . iii 7 2
Come, sir, what letters had you late from France? . . . . . iii 7 42
France spreads his banners in our noiseless land . . . . . iv 2 56
Why the King of France is so suddenly gone back know you the reason? iv 3 1
Who hath he left behind him general?—The Marshal of France, Monsieur La Far . . . . iv 3 9
Therefore great France My mourning and important tears hath pitied . iv 4 25
Am I in France?—In your own kingdom, sir.—Do not abuse me . . iv 7 76
For this business, It toucheth us, as France invades our land . . v 1 25
I have seen him in France: we had very many there could behold the sun with as firm eyes as he . . . . *Cymbeline* i 4 11

France. Less attemptable than any the rarest of our ladies in France *Cymb.* i 4 66
Being so far provoked as I was in France, I would abate her nothing . i 4 72
Have mingled sums To buy a present for the emperor; Which I, the factor for the rest, have done In France . . . . i 6 189
Frances. I will enfranchise thee.—O, marry me to one Frances *L. L. Lost* iii 1 122
Franchise. And Your franchises, whereon you stood, confined Into an auger's bore . . . . *Coriolanus* iv 6 86
Whose repair and franchise Shall, by the power we hold, be our good deed, Though Rome be therefore angry . . . . *Cymbeline* iii 1 57
Franchised. Still keep My bosom franchised and allegiance clear *Macbeth* ii 1 28
Franchisement. Il est content de vous donner la liberté, le franchisement *Hen. V.* iv 4 56
Franciæ. Noster Henricus, Rex Angliæ, et Hæres Franciæ . . . v 2 370
Francis. Good partner, go, get you to Francis Seacole . *Much Ado* iii 5 62
Friar Francis, be brief; only to the plain form of marriage . . iv 1 1
Francis Flute, the bellows-mender.—Here, Peter Quince *M. N. Dream* i 2 44
At the Saint Francis here beside the port . . . *All's Well* iii 5 39
Sir Robert Waterton and Francis Quoint . . . *Richard II.* ii 1 284
Call them all by their christen names, as Tom, Dick, and Francis 1 *Hen. IV.* ii 4 9
And do thou never leave calling 'Francis' . . . . . ii 4 35
I'll show thee a precedent.—Francis!—Thou art perfect.—Francis!—Anon ii 4 38
Francis!—Anon, anon.—Anon, Francis? No, Francis; but to-morrow, Francis; or Francis, o' Thursday . . . . . ii 4 71
Some sack, Francis.—Anon, anon, sir . . . 2 *Hen. IV.* ii 4 305
Who knocks so loud at door? Look to the door there, Francis . ii 4 382
Black George Barnes, and Francis Pickbone . . . . iii 2 23
Francis Feeble!—Here, sir.—What trade art thou, Feeble? . iii 2 158
Holy Saint Francis, what a change is here! . . *Rom. and Jul.* ii 3 65
Saint Francis be my speed! how oft to-night Have my old feet stumbled! v 3 121
Franciscan. Holy Franciscan friar! brother, ho! . . . . . v 2 1
Francisco. Is he dead, my Ethiopian? is he dead, my Francisco? *M. W.* ii 3 28
'Tis now struck twelve; get thee to bed, Francisco . . *Hamlet* i 1 7
François. Le François que vous parlez, il est meilleur que l'Anglois lequel je parle . . . . *Hen. V.* v 2 199
Frank. How now, sweet Frank! why art thou melancholy? *Mer. Wives* ii 1 155
Frank nature, rather curious than in haste, Hath well composed thee *All's Well* i 2 20
Thy frank election make; Thou hast power to choose . . ii 3 61
Where sups he? doth the old boar feed in the old frank? . 2 *Hen. IV.* ii 2 160
Therefore with frank and with uncurbed plainness Tell us *Hen. V.* i 2 244
All cause unborn, could never be the motive Of our so frank donation *Coriolanus* iii 1 130
For what purpose, love?—But to be frank, and give it thee again *R. and J.* ii 2 131
Your old kind father, whose frank heart gave all . . . *Lear* iii 4 20
Bearing with frank appearance Their purposes toward Cyprus *Othello* i 3 38
'Tis a good hand, A frank one.—You may, indeed, say so . . iii 4 44
Franked. He is frank'd up to fatting for his pains . . *Richard III.* i 3 314
My son George Stanley is frank'd up in hold . . . . iv 5 3
Franker. Now I shall have reason To show the love and duty that I bear you With franker spirit . . . . *Othello* iii 3 195
Frankfort. There, there! a diamond gone, cost me two thousand ducats in Frankfort! . . . . *Mer. of Venice* iii 1 89
Franklin. Let boors and franklins say it, I'll swear it . . *W. Tale* v 2 173
A franklin in the wild of Kent hath brought three hundred marks 1 *Hen. IV.* ii 1 60
A riding-suit, no costlier than would fit A franklin's housewife *Cymbeline* iii 2 79
Frankly. O, were it but my life, I'ld throw it down for your deliverance As frankly as a pin . . . . . *Meas. for Meas.* iii 1 106
I do beseech your grace, for charity, If ever any malice in your heart Were hid against me, now to forgive me frankly . *Hen. VIII.* ii 1 81
Speak frankly as the wind . . . . . *Troi. and Cres.* i 3 253
My half-supp'd sword, that frankly would have fed, Pleased with this dainty bait, thus goes to bed . . . . v 8 19
And highly moved to wrath To be controll'd in that he frankly gave *T. Andron.* i 1 420
Men and men's fortunes could I frankly use As I can bid thee speak *T. of A.* ii 2 188
Very frankly he confess'd his treasons . . . . *Macbeth* i 4 5
Seeing, unseen, We may of their encounter frankly judge *Hamlet* iii 1 34
I embrace it freely; And will this brother's wager frankly play . v 2 264
One unperfectness shows me another, to make me frankly despise myself.—Come, you are too severe . . . . . *Othello* ii 3 299
Frankness. Pardon the frankness of my mirth . . . *Hen. V.* v 2 318
Frantic. Go bind this man, for he is frantic too . *Com. of Errors* iv 4 116
Anne intelligis, domine? to make frantic, lunatic . . . *L. L. Lost* v 1 29
The lover, all as frantic, Sees Helen's beauty in a brow of Egypt *M. N. D.* v 1 10
If that I do not dream or be not frantic,—As I do trust I am not *As Y. L. It* i 3 51
A frantic fool, Hiding his bitter jests in blunt behaviour *T. of Shrew* iii 2 12
Sorrow and grief of heart Makes him speak fondly, like a frantic man *Richard II.* iii 3 185
Thou frantic woman, what dost thou make here? . . . . . v 3 89
Let frantic Talbot triumph for a while . . . 1 *Hen. VI.* iii 3 5
False-boding woman, end thy frantic curse . . *Richard III.* i 3 247
O, preposterous And frantic outrage, end thy damned spleen! . . ii 4 64
Sly frantic wretch, that holp'st to make me great . *T. Andron.* iv 4 59
Die, frantic wretch, for this accursed deed! . . . . . v 3 64
Franticly. Fie, fie, how franticly I square my talk! . . . . iii 2 31
Frateretto calls me; and tells me Nero is an angler . . . *Lear* iii 6 7
Fratrum. And on a pile Ad manes fratrum sacrifice his flesh *T. Andron.* i 1 98
Fraud. His heart as far from fraud as heaven from earth *T. G. of Ver.* ii 7 78
The fraud of men was ever so, Since summer first was leavy *Much Ado* ii 3 74
The fraud of England, not the force of France, Hath now entrapp'd the noble-minded Talbot . . . . 1 *Hen. VI.* iv 4 36
There shall I rest secure from force and fraud . . 3 *Hen. VI.* iv 4 33
Fraudful. Take heed, my lord; the welfare of us all Hangs on the cutting short that fraudful man . . . . . . 2 *Hen. VI.* iii 1 81
Fraught. There miscarried A vessel of our country richly fraught *M. of V.* ii 8 30
Antonio That took the Phœnix and her fraught from Candy . *T. Night* v 1 64
I am so fraught with curious business that I leave out ceremony *W. Tale* iv 4 525
Ships, Fraught with the ministers and instruments Of cruel war *Troi. and Cres.* Prol. 4
As the bark, that hath discharged her fraught, Returns . *T. Andron.* i 1 71
Make use of that good wisdom, Whereof I know you are fraught . *Lear* i 4 241
Swell, bosom, with thy fraught, For 'tis of aspics' tongues! . *Othello* iii 3 449
Hence, from my sight! If after this command thou fraught the court With thy unworthiness, thou diest . . . . . *Cymbeline* i 1 126
Fraughtage. Our fraughtage, sir, I have convey'd aboard *Com. of Errors* iv 1 87
The deep-drawing barks do there disgorge Their warlike fraughtage *Troi. and Cres.* Prol. 13
Fraughting. I would Have sunk the sea within the earth or ere It should the good ship so have swallow'd and The fraughting souls within her . . . . *Tempest* i 2 13

Fray. There is a fray to be fought between Sir Hugh the Welsh priest and Caius the French doctor . . . . . *Mer. Wives* ii 1 208
You are almost come to part almost a fray . . . *Much Ado* v 1 114
Welcome, pure wit! thou partest a fair fray . . . *L. L. Lost* v 2 484
When truth kills truth, O devilish-holy fray! . . *M. N. Dream* iii 2 129
Your hands than mine are quicker for a fray, My legs are longer though iii 2 342
Heavens shield Lysander, if they mean a fray! . . . . iii 2 447
Live thou, I live: with much much more dismay I view the fight than thou that makest the fray . . . . . . *Mer. of Venice* iii 2 62
Speak of frays Like a fine bragging youth, and tell quaint lies . . iii 4 68
Come you to part the fray? 'Con tutto il cuore, ben trovato' *T. of Shrew* i 2 23
To the latter end of a fray and the beginning of a feast Fits a dull fighter and a keen guest . . . . 1 *Hen. IV.* iv 2 85
Death hath not struck so fat a deer to-day, Though many dearer, in this bloody fray . . . . v 4 108
After the bloody fray at Wakefield fought . . . 3 *Hen. VI.* ii 1 107
Right glad I am he was not at this fray . . . *Rom. and Jul.* i 1 124
O me! What fray was here? Yet tell me not, for I have heard it all . i 1 179
Where are the vile beginners of this fray? . . . . . iii 1 146
Who began this bloody fray?—Tybalt, here slain, whom Romeo's hand did slay . . . . iii 1 156
Prithee, listen well; I heard a bustling rumour, like a fray . *J. Cæsar* ii 4 18
Frayed. She does so blush, and fetches her wind so short, as if she were frayed with a sprite . . . . *Troi. and Cres.* iii 2 34
Freckle. In those freckles live their savours . . *M. N. Dream* ii 1 13
Freckled. A freckled whelp hag-born . . . . . *Tempest* i 2 283
The freckled cowslip, burnet and green clover . . *Hen. V.* v 2 49
Frederick. Frederick the great soldier who miscarried at sea *M. for M.* iii 1 217
Her brother Frederick was wrecked at sea . . . . . iii 1 224
One that old Frederick, your father, loves . . *As Y. Like It* i 2 87
And would not change that calling, To be adopted heir to Frederick . i 2 246
Duke Frederick, hearing how that every day Men of great worth resorted to this forest, Address'd a mighty power . . . . . . v 4 160
Free. Dost thou forget From what a torment I did free thee? . *Tempest* i 2 251
Spirit, fine spirit! I'll free thee Within two days for this . . i 2 420
Delicate Ariel, I'll set thee free for this . . . . . i 2 442
Thou shalt be as free As mountain winds . . . . . . i 2 498
One stroke Shall free thee from the tribute which thou payest . . ii 1 293
Thought is free . . . . iii 2 132; *T. Night* i 3 73
Quickly, spirit; Thou shalt ere long be free . . . . . v 1 87
Bravely, my diligence. Thou shalt be free . . . . . v 1 241
Set Caliban and his companions free; Untie the spell . . . v 1 252
To the elements Be free, and fare thou well! . . . . . v 1 318
Prayer, Which pierces so that it assaults Mercy itself and frees all faults . . . . Epil. 18
As you from crimes would pardon'd be, Let your indulgence set me free Epil. 20
That my love may appear plain and free . . . *T. G. of Ver.* v 4 82
I have done myself wrong, have I not?—Yes, that thou hast, whether thou art tainted or free . . . . . *Meas. for Meas.* i 2 44
That will free your life, But fetter you till death . . . . iii 1 66
That we were all, as some would seem to be, From our faults, as faults from seeming, free! . . . . iii 2 41
Is as free from touch or soil with her As she from one ungot . . v 1 141
And now, dear maid, be you as free to us . . . . . v 1 393
Where would you had remain'd until this time, Free from these slanders and this open shame! . . . . . . *Com. of Errors* iv 4 70
Will you with free and unconstrained soul Give me this maid? *Much Ado* iv 1 25
A most acute juvenal; volable and free of grace! . . *L. L. Lost* iii 1 67
You are not free, For the Lord's tokens on you do I see.—No, they are free that gave these tokens to us . . . . v 2 422
Shall I say to you, Let them be free, marry them to your heirs? *M. of V.* iv 1 94
Are not these woods More free from peril than the envious court? *As Y. Like It* ii 1 4
If he be free, Why then my taxing like a wild-goose flies, Unclaim'd of any man . . . . ii 7 85
By helping Baptista's eldest daughter to a husband we set his youngest free for a husband . . . . *T. of Shrew* i 1 143
Are not the streets as free For me as for you? . . . . . i 2 233
The younger then is free and not before . . . . . . i 2 264
Achieve the elder, set the younger free For our access . . . i 2 268
I will be free Even to the uttermost, as I please, in words . . iv 3 79
Health shall live free and sickness freely die . . . *All's Well* ii 1 171
Whom I know Is free for me to ask, thee to bestow . . . ii 1 203
He is too good and fair for death and me; Whom I myself embrace, to set him free . . . . iii 4 17
In voices well divulged, free, learn'd and valiant . . *T. Night* i 5 279
My remembrance is very free and clear from any image of offence . iii 4 249
Come on.—I will be free from thee. What wouldst thou now? . iv 1 44
Negligent, foolish and fearful; In every one of these no man is free *W. T.* i 2 251
Such allow'd infirmities that honesty Is never free of . . . . i 2 264
A gracious innocent soul, More free than he is jealous . . . ii 3 30
No life, I prize it not a straw, but for mine honour, Which I would free iii 2 112
Though full of our displeasure, yet we free thee From the dead blow of it! . . . . iv 4 444
Lions more confident, mountains and rocks More free from motion *K. John* ii 1 453
And free from other misbegotten hate . . . . *Richard II.* i 1 33
So as thou livest in peace, die free from strife . . . . . v 6 27
Deliver him Up to his pleasure, ransomless and free . 1 *Hen. IV.* v 5 28
I have three pound to free Mouldy and Bullcalf . 2 *Hen. IV.* iii 2 261
Spare in diet, Free from gross passion or of mirth or anger . *Hen. V.* ii 2 132
Let man go free And let not hemp his wind-pipe suffocate . . iii 6 44
He forbids it, Being free from vainness and self-glorious pride . v Prol. 20
Will'd me to leave my base vocation And free my country . 1 *Hen. VI.* i 2 81
They set him free without his ransom paid, In spite of Burgundy . iii 3 72
If this servile usage once offend, Go and be free again as Suffolk's friend v 3 59
My hand would free her, but my heart says no . . . . v 3 61
Princes should be free.—And so shall you, If happy England's royal king be free.—Why, what concerns his freedom unto me? . . v 3 114
Free from oppression or the stroke of war . . . . . v 3 155
It's sign she hath been liberal and free . . . . . v 4 82
The purest spring is not so free from mud As I am clear from treason 2 *Hen. VI.* iii 1 101
With that dread King that took our state upon him To free us from his father's wrathful curse . . . . iii 2 155
Free from a stubborn opposite intent . . . . . . iii 2 251
These hands are free from guiltless blood-shedding . . . . iv 7 108
Be as free as heart can wish or tongue can tell . . . . iv 7 132
From that torment I will free myself, Or hew my way out 3 *Hen. VI.* iii 2 180
He shall here find his friends with horse and men To set him free . iv 5 13
But, Warwick, after God, thou set'st me free . . . . . iv 6 16

Free. Untainted, unexamined, free, at liberty. Here's a good world! *Richard III.* iii 6 9
If you do free your children from the sword, Your children's children quit it in your age . . . v 3 261
I as free forgive you As I would be forgiven . . . . *Hen. VIII.* ii 1 82
And free us from his slavery.—We had need pray . . . ii 2 44
If he know That I am free of your report, he knows I am not of your wrong . . . ii 4 99
I do excuse you; yea, upon mine honour, I free you from't . . ii 4 157
Would all other women Could speak this with as free a soul as I do! . iii 1 32
To deliver, Like free and honest men, our just opinions . . . . iii 1 60
Courtiers as free, as debonair, unarm'd, As bending angels *Troi. and Cres.* i 3 235
Let me be privileged by my place and message, To be a speaker free . iv 4 133
His heart and hand both open and both free . . . . iv 5 100
Thou art too gentle and too free a man . . . . iv 5 139
Were he the butcher of my son, he should Be free as is the wind *Coriol.* i 9 89
For they have pardons, being ask'd, as free As words to little purpose . iii 2 88
I would say 'Thou liest' unto thee with a voice as free As I do pray the gods . . . . iii 3 73
He hath spices of them all, not all, For I dare so far free him . . iv 7 47
Never known before But to be rough, unswayable and free . . . v 6 26
Let us go: Ransomless here we set our prisoners free . *T. Andron.* i 1 274
And this shall free thee from this present shame . *Rom. and Jul.* iv 1 118
I'll pay the debt, and free him.—Your lordship ever binds him *T. of A.* i 1 103
That thought is bounty's foe; Being free itself, it thinks all others so . ii 2 242
Have I been ever free, and must my house Be my retentive enemy, my gaol? . . . . iii 4 81
If thou hatest curses, Stay not; fly, whilst thou art blest and free . iv 3 542
Before black-corner'd night, Find what thou want'st by free and offer'd light . . . . v 1 48
I was born free as Cæsar; so were you: We both have fed as well as he *J. Cæsar* i 2 97
O conspiracy, Shamest thou to show thy dangerous brow by night, When evils are most free? . . . . ii 1 79
Nor with such free and friendly conference As he hath used of old . iv 2 17
So, I am free; yet would not so have been, Durst I have done my will . v 3 47
Where is thy master?—Free from the bondage you are in . . . v 5 54
Being unprepared, Our will became the servant to defect; Which else should free have wrought . . . . *Macbeth* ii 1 19
Free from our feasts and banquets bloody knives, Do faithful homage and receive free honours . . . . iii 6 35
The time is free . . . . v 8 55
You yourself Have of your audience been most free and bounteous *Ham.* i 3 93
Make mad the guilty and appal the free, Confound the ignorant . . ii 2 590
Niggard of question; but, of our demands, Most free in his reply . . iii 1 14
O limed soul, that, struggling to be free, Art more engaged! . . . iii 3 68
Being remiss, Most generous and free from all contriving . . . iv 7 136
Let my disclaiming from a purposed evil Free me so far in your most generous thoughts . . . . v 2 253
Heaven make thee free of it! I follow thee . . . . v 2 343
No port is free; no place, That guard, and most unusual vigilance, Does not attend my taking . . . . *Lear* ii 3 3
O, are you free? Some other time for that . . . . . . ii 4 134
When the mind's free, The body's delicate . . . . . . iii 4 11
Bear free and patient thoughts . . . . iv 6 80
For if such actions may have passage free, Bond-slaves and pagans shall our statesmen be . . . . *Othello* i 2 98
But to be free and bounteous to her mind . . . . i 3 266
The Moor is of a free and open nature . . . . i 3 405
She is of so free, so kind, so apt, so blessed a disposition . . . ii 3 325
This advice is free I give and honest, Probal to thinking . . . ii 3 343
Out of the way, that your converse and business May be more free . iii 1 41
I am not bound to that all slaves are free to. Utter my thoughts? . iii 3 135
Loves company, Is free of speech, sings, plays and dances well . . iii 3 185
I would not have your free and noble nature, Out of self-bounty, be abused . . . . iii 3 199
Hold her free, I do beseech your honour . . . . iii 3 255
I slept the next night well, was free and merry . . . . . iii 3 340
If thou say so, villain, Thou kill'st thy mistress: but well and free, If thou so yield him, there is gold . . . . . *Ant. and Cleo.* ii 5 27
If Antony Be free and healthful,—so tart a favour! . . . . . ii 5 38
Thou say'st free.—Free, madam! no; I made no such report: He's bound unto Octavia . . . . ii 5 56
When I did make thee free, sworest thou not then To do this? . . iv 14 81
You must know, Till the injurious Romans did extort This tribute from us, we were free . . . . *Cymbeline* iii 1 49
He wrings at some distress.—Would I could free't! . . . . . iii 6 80
Give me The penitent instrument to pick that bolt, Then, free for ever! v 4 11
I am called to be made free.—I'll be hang'd then . . . . . v 4 202
Know this of me, Antiochus from incest lived not free . . *Pericles* i 4 2
O, that the gods Would set me free from this unhallow'd place! . . iv 6 107
Free access and favour . . . . *T. of Shrew* ii 1 98
Free air. And through him Drink the free air . . . . *T. of Athens* i 1 83
Free an offer. Making God so free an offer . . . . *Hen. V.* iv 1 193
Free arms. Opening his free arms and weeping His welcomes *W. Tale* iv 4 559
Free awe. And thy free awe Pays homage to us . . . *Hamlet* iv 3 63
Free breath. For mine own part, I breathe free breath . *L. L. Lost* v 2 732
What earthy name to interrogatories Can task the free breath of a sacred king? Thou canst not, cardinal, devise a name . . *K. John* iii 1 148
Free comfort. He bears the sentence well that nothing bears But the free comfort which from thence he hears . . . . *Othello* i 3 213
Free condition. I would not my unhoused free condition Put into circumscription and confine For the sea's worth . . . . . i 2 26
Free consent. I yield thee my free consent . . . . *3 Hen. VI.* iv 6 36
Free contempt. He did solicit you in free contempt . . *Coriolanus* ii 3 208
Free dependant. I am your free dependant . . . *Meas. for Meas.* iv 3 95
Free descent. I lay my claim To my inheritance of free descent *Rich. II.* ii 3 136
Free desire. Courageously and with a free desire . . . . . i 3 115
Free determination. Than to make up a free determination 'Twixt right and wrong . . . . *Troi. and Cres.* ii 2 170
Free disposition. Guiltless and of free disposition . . . *T. Night* i 5 99
Free drift. My free drift Halts not particularly . . . *T. of Athens* i 1 45
Free duty. With his free duty recommends you thus . . . *Othello* i 3 41
Free election. And leave us to our free election . . . *Pericles* ii 4 33
Free elements. She's framed as fruitful As the free elements *Othello* ii 3 348
Free entertainment. Provided I have your commendation for my more free entertainment . . . . *Cymbeline* i 4 167
Free face. This entertainment May a free face put on . . . *W. Tale* i 2 112
Free foot. And all the embossed sores and headed evils, That thou with license of free foot hast caught . . . . . . *As Y. Like It* ii 7 68
Free-footed. We will fetters put upon this fear, Which now goes too free-footed . . . . *Hamlet* iii 3 26
Free heart. In grateful virtue I am bound To your free heart *T. of Athens* i 2 6
Let us speak Our free hearts each to other . . . . *Macbeth* i 3 155
Free-hearted. And how does that honourable, complete, free-hearted gentleman of Athens? . . . . *T. of Athens* iii 1 9
Free honours. Do faithful homage and receive free honours . *Macbeth* iii 6 36
Free hours. To think that man . . . will his free hours languish for Assured bondage . . . . *Cymbeline* i 6 72
Free leave. Never to marry but by my free leave . . . . *W. Tale* v 1 70
Free lords, cold snow melts with the sun's hot beams . *2 Hen. VI.* iii 1 223
Free love. Out of his free love, hath presented to you . *T. of Athens* i 2 188
Free lungs. Your lord, I mean—laughs from's free lungs . *Cymbeline* i 6 68
Free maids. The free maids that weave their thread with bones *T. Night* ii 4 46
Free march. Strike a free march to Troy! . . . . *Troi. and Cres.* v 10 30
Free men. Flies may do this, but I from this must fly: They are free men, but I am banished . . . . *Rom. and Jul.* iii 3 42
Had you rather Cæsar were living and die all slaves, than that Cæsar were dead, to live all free men? . . . . *J. Cæsar* iii 2 25
Free pardon. Ignomy in ransom and free pardon Are of two houses *Meas. for Meas.* ii 4 111
And here pronounce free pardon to them all That will forsake thee *2 Hen. VI.* iv 8 9
Send our letters, with Free pardon to each man . . . *Hen. VIII.* i 2 100
Free person. So have we thought it good From our free person she should be confined . . . . *W. Tale* ii 1 194
Free power. Take with you free power to ratify, Augment, or alter *Hen. V.* v 2 86
Free purses. O'ercharging your free purses with large fines . *1 Hen. VI.* i 3 64
Free scope. The fated sky Gives us free scope . . . . *All's Well* i 1 233
Free souls. We that have free souls, it touches us not . . *Hamlet* iii 2 252
Free speech. Give me leave To have free speech with you *Meas. for Meas.* i 1 78
Your highness curbs me From giving reins and spurs to my free speech *Richard II.* i 1 55
Free speech and fearless I to thee allow . . . . i 1 123
And stood within the blank of his displeasure For my free speech *Othello* iii 4 129
Free things. Leaving free things and happy shows behind . . *Lear* iii 6 112
Free-town. To old Free-town, our common judgement-place *Rom. and Jul.* i 1 109
Free undertaking. Your free undertaking cannot miss A thriving issue *W. Tale* ii 2 44
Free visitation. Is it a free visitation? Come, deal justly . *Hamlet* ii 2 284
Free voices. All the clerks, I mean the learned ones, in Christian kingdoms Have their free voices. . . . . . *Hen. VIII.* ii 2 94
Free will. Good my lord, To come thus was I not constrain'd, but did On my free will . . . . *Ant. and Cleo.* iii 6 57
Freed. If I would yield him my virginity, Thou mightst be freed *M. for M.* iii 1 99
By law and process of great nature thence Freed and enfranchised *W. T.* ii 2 61
No man's pie is freed From his ambitious finger . . . . *Hen. VIII.* i 1 52
Freedom, hey-day! hey-day, freedom! freedom, hey-day, freedom! *Tempest* ii 2 190
With a heart as willing As bondage e'er of freedom: here's my hand . iii 1 89
Shortly shall all my labours end, and thou Shalt have the air at freedom iv 1 266
I shall miss thee; But yet thou shalt have freedom . . . . . v 1 96
To say the truth, I had as lief have the foppery of freedom as the morality of imprisonment . . . . *Meas. for Meas.* i 2 138
Gnawing with my teeth my bonds in sunder, I gain'd my freedom *C. of Er.* v 1 250
Doth impeach the freedom of the state, If they deny him justice *M. of V.* iii 2 280
Let the danger light Upon your charter and your city's freedom . . iv 1 39
Shall I play my freedom at tray-trip, and become thy bond-slave? *T. N.* ii 5 208
Verily, I speak it in the freedom of my knowledge . . . *W. Tale* i 1 12
And in the end, Having my freedom, boast of nothing else But that I was a journeyman to grief . . . . *Richard II.* i 3 273
Why, what concerns his freedom unto me? . . . . *1 Hen. VI.* v 3 116
I thought ye would never have given out these arms till you had recovered your ancient freedom . . . . *2 Hen. VI.* iv 8 28
Cozen'd Of comfort, kingdom, kindred, freedom, life . *Richard III.* iv 4 223
May his highness live in freedom, And this man out of prison? *Hen. VIII.* i 2 200
Where, I know, You cannot with such freedom purge yourself . . v 1 102
I request you To give my poor host freedom.—O, well begg'd! *Coriolanus* i 9 87
Silenced their pleaders and Dispropertied their freedoms . . . ii 1 264
And, Romans, fight for freedom in your choice . . . *T. Andron.* i 1 17
Or a keeper with my freedom; Or my friends, if I should need 'em *T. of Athens* i 2 69
I kiss thy hand, but not in flattery, Cæsar; Desiring thee that Publius Cimber may Have an immediate freedom of repeal . . *J. Cæsar* iii 1 54
Liberty! Freedom! Tyranny is dead! Run hence, proclaim, cry it about the streets . . . . iii 1 78
Cry out 'Liberty, freedom, and enfranchisement!'. . . . . . iii 1 81
Waving our red weapons o'er our heads, Let's all cry 'Peace, freedom and liberty!' . . . . iii 1 110
Freedom lives hence, and banishment is here . . . . . . *Lear* i 1 184
Though age from folly could not give me freedom, It does from childishness . . . . *Ant. and Cleo.* i 3 57
Brutus, With the arm'd rest, courtiers of beauteous freedom . . . ii 6 17
This rock and these demesnes have been my world; Where I have lived at honest freedom . . . . *Cymbeline* iii 3 71
To satisfy, If of my freedom 'tis the main part, take No stricter render of me than my all . . . . v 4 16
Freelier. I should freelier rejoice in that absence wherein he won honour than in the embracements of his bed . . . . . *Coriolanus* i 3 3
Freely. And some donation freely to estate On the blest lovers *Tempest* iv 1 85
That I am freely dissolved, and dissolutely . . . . *Mer. Wives* i 1 259
But when they weep and kneel, All their petitions are as freely theirs As they themselves would owe them . . . . *Meas. for Meas.* i 4 82
Speak freely, Syracusian, what thou wilt . . . . *Com. of Errors* v 1 285
Will you with free and unconstrained soul Give me this maid, your daughter?—As freely, son, as God did give her me . . . *Much Ado* iv 1 27
I will weep a while longer.—I will not desire that.—You have no reason; I do it freely . . . . iv 1 260
I am half yourself, And I must freely have the half of any thing *M. of V.* iii 2 252
I freely told you, all the wealth I had Ran in my veins, I was a gentleman . . . . iii 2 257
We freely cope your courteous pains withal . . . . iv 1 412
Freely give unto you this young scholar . . . . *T. of Shrew* ii 1 79
Freely have they leave To stand on either part . . . . *All's Well* i 2 14
Health shall live free and sickness freely die . . . . . . ii 1 171
We'll see what may be done, so you confess freely . . . . . iv 3 276
Thou shalt live as freely as thy lord, To call his fortunes thine *T. Night* i 4 39
Most freely I confess, myself and Toby Set this device . . . . v 1 367
You pay a great deal too dear for what's given freely . . . *W. Tale* i 1 19
Whose love had spoke, Even since it could speak, from an infant, freely iii 2 71
Ourselves will hear The accuser and the accused freely speak *Richard II.* i 1 17

Freely. Provided that my banishment repeal'd And lands restored again be freely granted . . . . *Richard II.* iii 3 41
Call forth Bagot. Now, Bagot, freely speak thy mind . . . . iv 1 2
Before I freely speak my mind herein . . . . iv 1 327
That freely render'd me these news for true . . . . *2 Hen. IV.* i 1 27
If you knew what pains I have bestow'd to breed this present peace, You would drink freely . . . . iv 2 75
Our history shall with full mouth Speak freely of our acts . *Hen. V.* i 2 231
Give us leave Freely to render what we have in charge . . . . i 2 238
This prisoner freely give I thee . . . . *2 Hen. VI.* iv 1 12
Why, then, thy husband's lands I freely give thee . . *3 Hen. VI.* iii 2 55
Speak freely what you think.—Then this is mine opinion . . . iv 1 28
Speak freely.—First, it was usual with him . . . *Hen. VIII.* i 2 131
That noble lady, Or gentleman, that is not freely merry, Is not my friend i 4 36
In committing freely Your scruple to the voice of Christendom . . ii 2 87
Scholars allow'd freely to argue for her . . . . ii 2 113
Opposing freely The beauty of her person to the people . . . iv 1 67
My accusers, Be what they will, may stand forth face to face, And freely urge against me . . . . v 3 48
It is spoke freely out of many mouths—How probable I do not know *Coriolanus* iv 6 64
Hear me speak.—Freely, good father . . . . *T. of Athens* i 1 110
You mistake my love: I gave it freely ever . . . . . . i 2 10
And come freely To gratulate thy plenteous bosom. . . . . i 2 130
To such as may the passive drugs of it Freely command. . . . iv 3 255
Hath it slept since? And wakes it now, to look so green and pale At what it did so freely? . . . . *Macbeth* i 7 38
Nor have we herein barr'd Your better wisdoms, which have freely gone With this affair along . . . . *Hamlet* i 2 15
Here give up ourselves, in the full bent To lay our service freely at your feet . . . . ii 2 31
The lady shall say her mind freely, or the blank verse shall halt for't . ii 2 338
I embrace it freely . . . . v 2 263
My boat sails freely, both with wind and stream . . . . *Othello* ii 3 65
Confess yourself freely to her . . . . ii 3 324
I think it freely . . . . ii 3 335
You shall have time To speak your bosom freely . . . . . iii 1 58
Therefore confess thee freely of thy sin . . . . v 2 53
The three-nook'd world Shall bear the olive freely . *Ant. and Cleo.* iv 6 7
Fear nothing: Make your full reference freely to my lord . . . v 2 23
Our cage We make a quire, as doth the prison'd bird, And sing our bondage freely . . . . *Cymbeline* iii 3 44
My page; I'll be thy master: walk with me; speak freely . . . v 5 119
Step you forth; Give answer to this boy, and do it freely . . . v 5 131
Since you have given me leave to speak, Freely will I speak *Pericles* i 2 102
Princes in this should live like gods above, Who freely give to every one ii 3 60
Freeman. Come now, keep thine oath; Now be a freeman . *J. Cæsar* v 3 41
Freeness. Nobly doom'd! We'll learn our freeness of a son-in-law *Cymbeline* v 5 421
Freer. Fare you well: we shall have the freer wooing at Master Page's *Mer. Wives* iii 2 86
Never did captive with a freer heart Cast off his chains of bondage *Rich. II.* i 3 88
That their punishment Might have the freer course. . . . *Lear* iv 2 95
'Tis well for thee, That, being unseminar'd, thy freer thoughts May not fly forth of Egypt . . . . *Ant. and Cleo.* i 5 11
Thou shalt be then freer than a gaoler; no bolts for the dead *Cymbeline* v 4 204
Freestone-coloured. A leathern hand, A freestone-colour'd hand *As Y. L. It* iv 3 25
Freeze, freeze, thou bitter sky, That dost not bite so nigh As benefits forgot . . . . ii 7 184
Greybeard, thy love doth freeze.—But thine doth fry . *T. of Shrew* ii 1 340
My very lips might freeze to my teeth . . . . iv 1 7
Cool the hearts Of all his people and freeze up their zeal . *K. John* iii 4 150
This makes bold mouths: Tongues spit their duties out, and cold hearts freeze Allegiance in them . . . . *Hen. VIII.* i 2 61
Nay, you must not freeze; Two women placed together makes cold weather . . . . i 4 21
Orpheus with his lute made trees, And the mountain tops that freeze, Bow themselves . . . . iii 1 4
I have a faint cold fear thrills through my veins, That almost freezes up the heat of life . . . . *Rom. and Jul.* iv 3 16
I could a tale unfold whose lightest word Would harrow up thy soul, freeze thy young blood . . . . *Hamlet* i 5 16
Fie upon her! she's able to freeze the god Priapus . . . *Pericles* iv 6 3
Freezeth. Tut, tut, thou art all ice, thy kindness freezeth *Richard III.* iv 2 22
Freezing. How, In this our pinching cave, shall we discourse The freezing hours away? . . . . *Cymbeline* iii 3 39
French. Peace, I say, Gallia and Gaul, French and Welsh! *Mer. Wives* iii 1 99
How meanest thou? brawling in French? . . . . *L. L. Lost* iii 1 10
He hath neither Latin, French, nor Italian . . *Mer. of Venice* i 2 75
In the narrow seas that part The French and English . . . . ii 8 29
Like one of our French withered pears, it looks ill, it eats drily *All's Well* i 1 175
Those girls of Italy, take heed of them: They say, our French lack language to deny, If they demand . . . . ii 1 20
They are bastards to the English; the French ne'er got 'em . . . ii 3 101
If there be here German, or Dane, low Dutch, Italian, or French, let him speak to me . . . . iv 1 79
All preparation for a bloody siege And merciless proceeding by these French Confronts your city's eyes . . . . . *K. John* ii 1 214
Behold, the French amazed vouchsafe a parle . . . . . . ii 1 226
Victory, with little loss, doth play Upon the dancing banners of the French ii 1 308
If but a dozen French Were there in arms, they would be as a call To train ten thousand English to their side . . . . iii 4 173
Who are arrived?—The French, my lord; men's mouths are full of it . iv 2 161
Told of a many thousand warlike French That were embattailed . . iv 2 199
Go meet the French And from his holiness use all your power . . v 1 5
Upon your oath of service to the pope, Go I to make the French lay down their arms . . . . v 1 24
Death, whose office is this day To feast upon whole thousands of the French . . . . v 2 178
The French fight coldly, and retire themselves . . . . . . v 3 13
Up once again; put spirit in the French: If they miscarry, we miscarry too . . . . v 4 2
If the French be lords of this loud day, He means to recompense the pains you take By cutting off your heads . . . . . . v 4 14
But when he frown'd, it was against the French . . *Richard II.* ii 1 178
Rescued the Black Prince, that young Mars of men, From forth the ranks of many thousand French . . . . ii 3 102
Speak it in French, king; say, 'pardonne moi' . . . . . v 3 119
The chopping French we do not understand . . . . . . v 3 124
One power against the French, And one against Glendower . *2 Hen. IV.* i 3 71
French. He leaves his back unarm'd, the French and Welsh Baying him at the heels . . . . *2 Hen. IV.* i 3 79
But who is substituted 'gainst the French, I have no certain notice . i 3 84
'No woman shall succeed in Salique land:' Which Salique land the French unjustly glose To be the realm of France . . *Hen. V.* i 2 40
Charles the Great, having subdued the Saxons, There left behind and settled certain French . . . . i 2 47
Nor did the French possess the Salique land Until four hundred one and twenty years After defunction of King Pharamond . . . . . i 2 56
Charles the Great Subdued the Saxons, and did seat the French Beyond the river Sala . . . . i 2 62
We must not only arm to invade the French, But lay down our proportions to defend Against the Scot . . . . i 2 136
The French, advised by good intelligence Of this most dreadful preparation, Shake in their fear . . . . ii Prol. 12
Suppose the ambassador from the French comes back . . . iii Prol. 28
Enter Harfleur; there remain, And fortify it strongly 'gainst the French iii 3 53
The French is gone off, look you; and there is gallant and most prave passages . . . . iii 6 96
Nothing taken but paid for, none of the French upbraided or abused . iii 6 117
And those few I have Almost no better than so many French . . iii 6 156
The confident and over-lusty French Do the low-rated English play at dice . . . . iv Prol. 18
The French may lay twenty French crowns to one, they will beat us . iv 1 242
Bestow yourself with speed: The French are bravely in their battles set iv 3 69
Ask me this slave in French What is his name. . . . . . iv 4 24
I'll fer him, and firk him, and ferret him: discuss the same in French unto him.—I do not know the French for fer, and ferret, and firk . iv 4 30
The French might have a good prey of us, if he knew of it . . . iv 4 80
But all's not done; yet keep the French the field . . . . . iv 6 2
The French have reinforced their scatter'd men . . . . . iv 6 36
Here comes the herald of the French, my liege . . . . . iv 7 69
Here is the number of the slaughter'd French . . . . . . iv 8 79
This note doth tell me of ten thousand French That in the field lie slain iv 8 85
The lamentation of the French Invites the King of England's stay at home . . . . v Prol. 36
And, princes French, and peers, health to you all! . . . . . v 2 8
Your eyes, which hitherto have borne in them Against the French, that met them in their bent, The fatal balls of murdering basilisks . . v 2 16
I cannot tell vat is dat.—No, Kate? I will tell thee in French . . v 2 188
It is as easy for me, Kate, to conquer the kingdom as to speak so much more French . . . . v 2 196
I shall never move thee in French, unless it be to laugh at me . . v 2 197
Compound a boy, half French, half English . . . . . . v 2 221
Your majestee ave fausse French enough to deceive de most sage demoiselle dat is en France . . . . v 2 233
Now, fie upon my false French! By mine honour, in true English, I love thee . . . . v 2 236
Shall name your highness in this form and with this addition, in French v 2 367
That English may as French, French Englishmen, Receive each other . v 2 395
Or shall we think the subtle-witted French Conjurers and sorcerers? *1 Hen. VI.* i 1 25
Unto the French the dreadful judgement-day So dreadful will not be as was his sight . . . . i 1 29
Wounds will I lend the French instead of eyes . . . . . i 1 87
A dismal fight Betwixt the stout Lord Talbot and the French . . i 1 106
By three and twenty thousand of the French Was round encompassed . i 1 113
The French exclaim'd, the devil was in arms . . . . . . i 1 125
We will rush on them. Now for the honour of the forlorn French! . i 2 19
Here, said they, is the terror of the French, The scarecrow that affrights our children so . . . . i 4 42
When I am dead and gone, Remember to avenge me on the French . i 4 94
My lord, my lord, the French have gather'd head . . . . . i 4 100
Pray God she prove not masculine ere long, If underneath the standard of the French She carry armour as she hath begun . . . . ii 1 23
All French and France exclaims on thee, Doubting thy birth. . . iii 3 60
In all I was six thousand strong And that the French were almost ten to one . . . . iv 1 21
Ten thousand French have ta'en the sacrament To rive their dangerous artillery Upon no Christian soul but English Talbot . . . . iv 2 28
Upon my death the French can little boast; In yours they will . . iv 5 24
Made him from my side to start Into the clustering battle of the French iv 7 13
Had death been French, then death had died to-day . . . . iv 7 28
Rushing in the bowels of the French, He left me proudly, as unworthy fight . . . . iv 7 42
The stout Parisians do revolt And turn again unto the warlike French . v 2 3
Then take my soul, my body, soul and all, Before that England give the French the foil . . . . v 3 23
Perhaps I shall be rescued by the French . . . . v 3 104
The states of Christendom . . . Have earnestly implored a general peace Betwixt our nation and the aspiring French . . . . . . v 4 99
Anjou and Maine are given to the French; Paris is lost . . *2 Hen. VI.* i 1 214
Anjou and Maine both given unto the French! Cold news for me . . i 1 236
Let Somerset be regent o'er the French . . . . i 3 209
He can speak French; and therefore he is a traitor . . . . iv 2 176
Were't not a shame, that whilst you live at jar, The fearful French, whom you late vanquished, Should make a start o'er seas and vanquish you? . . . . iv 8 44
Henry the Fifth, Who made the Dauphin and the French to stoop *3 Hen. VI.* i 1 108
To-day the French, All clinquant, all in gold, like heathen gods, Shone down the English. . . . . *Hen. VIII.* i 1 18
Men fear'd the French would prove perfidious, To the king's danger . i 2 156
I've seen myself, and served against, The French, And they can well on horseback . . . . *Hamlet* iv 7 84
French ambassador. The French ambassador upon that instant Craved audience . . . . *Hen. V.* i 1 91
By the Bishop of Bayonne, then French ambassador . . *Hen. VIII.* ii 4 172
French bet. That's the French bet against the Danish . . *Hamlet* v 2 170
French brawl. Will you win your love with a French brawl? *L. L. Lost* iii 1 9
French causes. And now to our French causes . . . . *Hen. V.* ii 2 60
French city. Who cannot see many a fair French city for one fair French maid that stands in my way . . . . v 2 345
French council. There is more eloquence in a sugar touch of them than in the tongues of the French council . . . . v 2 304
French count. They say the French count has done most honourable service . . . . *All's Well* iii 5 3
French courtier. And ransom him to any French courtier for a new-devised courtesy . . . . *L. L. Lost* i 2 65
French crown. Ay, and more.—A French crown more . *Meas. for Meas.* i 2 52

French crown. Remuneration! why, it is a fairer name than French crown . . . . *L. L. Lost* iii 1 142
Some of your French crowns have no hair at all . . *M. N. Dream* i 2 99
As your French crown for your taffeta punk . . . *All's Well* ii 2 23
And here's four Harry ten shillings in French crowns for you 2 *Hen. IV.* iii 2 237
The French may lay twenty French crowns to one, they will beat us *Hen. V.* iv 1 243
It is no English treason to cut French crowns . . . . . iv 1 245
For his father's sake, Henry the Fifth, in whose time boys went to span-counter for French crowns . . . . 2 *Hen. VI.* iv 2 166
French-crown-colour. Your French-crown-colour beard, your perfect yellow . . . . *M. N. Dream* i 2 97
French curs. A little herd of England's timorous deer, Mazed with a yelping kennel of French curs! . . . . . 1 *Hen. VI.* iv 2 47
French Dauphin. 'Tis the French Dauphin sueth to thee thus . i 2 112
French doctor. The very yea and the no is, the French doctor *Mer. Wives* i 4 99
There is a fray to be fought between Sir Hugh the Welsh priest and Caius the French doctor . . . . ii 1 209
French earl. Well, Diana, take heed of this French earl . *All's Well* iii 5 12
French falconers. We'll e'en to't like French falconers . . *Hamlet* ii 2 450
French fathers. And deface The patterns that by God and by French fathers Had twenty years been made . . . . *Hen. V.* ii 4 61
French gallants. To give each naked curtle-axe a stain, That our French gallants shall to-day draw out . . . . . . iv 2 22
French going out. Why the devil, Upon this French going out, took he upon him, Without the privity o' the king, to appoint Who should attend on him? . . . . *Hen. VIII.* i 1 73
French ground. Edward the Black Prince, Who on the French ground play'd a tragedy . . . . *Hen. V.* i 2 106
French heart. If you will love me soundly with your French heart, I will be glad to hear you confess it brokenly . . . . . v 2 105
French hose. Your French hose off, and in your strait strossers . . iii 7 56
Here's an English tailor come hither, for stealing out of a French hose *Macbeth* ii 3 16
French inconstancy. O foul revolt of French inconstancy! . *K. John* iii 1 322
French journey. Demand What was the speech among the Londoners Concerning the French journey . . . . . *Hen. VIII.* i 2 155
French king. Here comes in embassy The French king's daughter *L. L. Lost* i 1 136
Here are the articles of contracted peace Between our sovereign and the French king Charles . . . . 2 *Hen. VI.* i 1 41
Warwick Is thither gone, to crave the French king's sister 3 *Hen. VI.* iii 1 30
Every true heart weeps for't: all that dare Look into these affairs see this main end, The French king's sister . . . *Hen. VIII.* ii 2 42
It shall be to the Duchess of Alençon, The French king's sister . . iii 2 86
French knight. But, mistress, do you know the French knight that cowers i' the hams? . . . . *Pericles* iv 2 113
French lord. How say you by the French lord, Monsieur Le Bon? *Mer. of Venice* i 2 58
French maid. Who cannot see many a fair French city for one fair French maid that stands in my way . . . . . . *Hen. V.* v 2 345
French nobility. Stood smiling to behold his lion's whelp Forage in blood of French nobility . . . . i 2 110
French nods. Duck with French nods and apish courtesy *Richard III.* i 3 49
French part. But now promise, Kate, you will endeavour for your French part of such a boy . . . . *Hen. V.* v 2 228
French peers. The English are embattled, you French peers . . iv 2 14
French physician. Doctor Caius, the renowned French physician *M. W.* iii 1 61
French quarrels. You English fools, be friends: we have French quarrels enow, if you could tell how to reckon . . *Hen. V.* iv 1 240
French rapiers. Six French rapiers and poniards, with their assigns *Ham.* v 2 156
French salutation. Bon jour! there's a French salutation to your French slop . . . . *Rom. and Jul.* ii 4 47
French soldiers. They will pluck The gay new coats o'er the French soldiers' heads . . . . *Hen. V.* iv 3 118
French song. A French song and a fiddle has no fellow . *Hen. VIII.* i 3 41
French swords. Six Barbary horses against six French swords *Hamlet* v 2 168
French thrift. Falstaff will learn the humour of the age, French thrift, you rogues . . . . *Mer. Wives* i 3 93
French tongue. Give 'em welcome; you can speak the French tongue *Hen. VIII.* i 4 57
French velvet. I had as lief be a list of an English kersey as be piled, as thou art piled, for a French velvet . . . *Meas. for Meas.* i 2 35
French word. Submission, Dauphin! 'tis a mere French word 1 *Hen. VI.* iv 7 54
Frenchman. The Frenchman hath good skill in his rapier *Mer. Wives* ii 1 230
To be a Dutchman to-day, a Frenchman to-morrow . *Much Ado* iii 2 33
I think the Frenchman became his surety . . . . *Mer. of Venice* i 2 88
I reason'd with a Frenchman yesterday . . . . ii 8 27
Whether I live or die, be you the sons Of worthy Frenchmen *All's Well* ii 1 12
Which is the Frenchman?—He; That with the plume . . . iii 5 80
Since Frenchmen are so braid, Marry that will, I live and die a maid . iv 2 73
Demand of him, whether one Captain Dumain be i' the camp, a Frenchman iv 3 200
Who's that? a Frenchman?—Faith, sir, a' has an English name . iv 5 40
Wade to the market-place in Frenchmen's blood . . . *K. John* ii 1 42
Their armours, that march'd hence so silver-bright, Hither return all gilt with Frenchmen's blood . . . . ii 1 316
Which I could with a ready guess declare, Before the Frenchman speak a word of it . . . . *Hen. V.* i 1 97
I thought upon one pair of English legs Did march three Frenchmen . iii 6 159
I count each one And view the Frenchmen how they fortify 1 *Hen. VI.* i 4 61
Frenchmen, I'll be a Salisbury to you . . . . i 4 106
Convey me Salisbury into his tent, And then we'll try what these dastard Frenchmen dare . . . . i 4 111
This happy night the Frenchmen are secure, Having all day caroused . ii 1 11
For every drop of blood was drawn from him There hath at least five Frenchmen died to-night . . . . ii 2 9
If I to-day die not with Frenchmen's rage, To-morrow I shall die with mickle age . . . . iv 6 34
Done like a Frenchman: turn, and turn again! . . . . . iii 3 85
Brave death by speaking, whether he will or no; Imagine him a Frenchman and thy foe . . . . iv 7 26
Did flesh his puny sword in Frenchmen's blood . . . . . iv 7 36
Is Talbot slain, the Frenchmen's only scourge? . . . . . iv 7 77
The Frenchmen fly. Now help, ye charming spells and periapts . v 3 1
Such strict and severe covenants As little shall the Frenchmen gain thereby . . . . v 4 115
His alliance will confirm our peace And keep the Frenchmen in allegiance v 5 43
How France and Frenchmen might be kept in awe . . 2 *Hen. VI.* i 1 92
Nay, answer, if you can: the Frenchmen are our enemies . . . iv 2 179
Better ten thousand base-born Cades miscarry Than you should stoop unto a Frenchman's mercy . . . . iv 8 50
Frenchman. And set a double varnish on the fame The Frenchman gave you . . . . *Hamlet* iv 7 134
There is a Frenchman his companion, one An eminent monsieur *Cymb.* i 6 64
It is a recreation to be by And hear him mock the Frenchman . i 6 76
Frenchwoman. Was't I! yea, I it was, proud Frenchwoman . 2 *Hen. VI.* i 3 143
And every drop cries vengeance for his death, 'Gainst thee, fell Clifford, and thee, false Frenchwoman . . . . . . 3 *Hen. VI.* i 4 149
Frenzy. Her husband hath the finest mad devil of jealousy in him, Master Brook, that ever governed frenzy . . . *Mer. Wives* v 1 21
Yielding to him humours well his frenzy . . . . *Com. of Errors* iv 4 84
The poet's eye, in a fine frenzy rolling . . . . *M. N. Dream* v 1 12
And melancholy is the nurse of frenzy . . . . *T. of Shrew* Ind. 2 135
A most extracting frenzy of mine own From my remembrance clearly banish'd his . . . . *T. Night* v 1 288
The Lady Constance in a frenzy died Three days before . . *K. John* iv 2 122
Behold, distraction, frenzy and amazement, Like witless antics, one another meet . . . . *Troi. and Cres.* v 3 85
I'll haunt thee like a wicked conscience still, That mouldeth goblins swift as frenzy's thoughts . . . . v 10 29
Nor can I guess, Unless some fit or frenzy do possess her *T. Andron.* iv 1 17
Shall we be thus afflicted in his wreaks, His fits, his frenzy? . . iv 4 12
Not frenzy, not Absolute madness could so far have raved To bring him here alone . . . . *Cymbeline* iv 2 134
Where, in a frenzy, in my master's garments, . . . away he posts . . v 5 282
Frequent. And is less frequent to his princely exercises . *W. Tale* iv 2 36
Inquire at London, 'mongst the taverns there, For there, they say, he daily doth frequent . . . . *Richard II.* v 3 6
This thy creature By night frequents my house . . *T. of Athens* i 1 117
And prostitute me to the basest groom That doth frequent your house *Pericles* iv 6 202
Fresh. Our garments are now as fresh as when we put them on first *Tempest* ii 1 68
We were talking that our garments seem now as fresh as when we were at Tunis . . . . ii 1 97
Is not, sir, my doublet as fresh as the first day I wore it? . . . ii 1 102
They Will not, nor cannot, use such vigilance As when they are fresh . iii 3 17
What is in Silvia's face, but I may spy More fresh in Julia's? *T. G. of Ver.* v 4 115
'Tis painted about with the story of the Prodigal, fresh and new *M. W.* iv 5 9
With coronet of fresh and fragrant flowers . . . *M. N. Dream* iv 1 57
Young budding virgin, fair and fresh and sweet . . *T. of Shrew* iv 5 37
If thou be'st yet a fresh uncropped flower, Choose thou thy husband *All's Well* v 3 327
O spirit of love! how quick and fresh art thou . . . *T. Night* i 1 9
Which she would keep fresh And lasting in her sad remembrance . . i 1 31
But a month ago I went from hence, And then 'twas fresh in murmur . i 2 32
Of great estate, of fresh and stainless youth . . . . . i 5 278
Cast thy humble slough and appear fresh . . . . . . ii 5 162
If it prove, Tempests are kind and salt waves fresh in love . . iii 4 419
One that indeed physics the subject, makes old hearts fresh *W. Tale* i 1 44
How green you are and fresh in this old world! . . *K. John* iii 4 145
Such crimson tempest should bedrench The fresh green lap of fair King Richard's land . . . . *Richard II.* iii 3 47
And wash him fresh again with true-love tears . . . . . v 1 10
Neat, and trimly dress'd, Fresh as a bridegroom! . . . 1 *Hen. IV.* i 3 34
Thus did I keep my person fresh and new . . . . . iii 2 55
There's five to one; besides, they all are fresh . . . *Hen. V.* iv 3 4
Thy friendship makes us fresh . . . . 1 *Hen. VI.* iii 3 86
Who finds the heifer dead and bleeding fresh And sees fast by a butcher with an axe, But will suspect 'twas he that made the slaughter? 2 *Hen. VI.* iii 2 188
'Tis so lately alter'd, that the old name Is fresh about me *Hen. VIII.* iv 1 99
The fresh and yet unbruised Greeks do pitch Their brave pavilions *Troi. and Cres.* Prol. 14
Here art thou in appointment fresh and fair . . . . . . iv 5 1
As fresh as morning dew distill'd on flowers . . . *T. Andron.* ii 3 201
Valiant Mars! Thou ever young, fresh, loved and delicate wooer! *T. of Athens* iv 3 385
Look fresh and merrily; Let not our looks put on our purposes *J. Cæsar* ii 1 224
I am fresh of spirit and resolved To meet all perils very constantly . v 1 91
Indeed, she's a most fresh and delicate creature . . . *Othello* ii 3 20
Her name, that was as fresh As Dian's visage, is now begrimed and black . . . . iii 3 386
The locking-up the spirits a time, To be more fresh, reviving *Cymbeline* i 5 42
Whose remembrance Is yet fresh in their grief. . . . . . . ii 4 15
How fresh she looks! They were too rough That threw her in the sea *Pericles* iii 2 79
Fresh admirer. And ever since a fresh admirer Of what I saw there *Hen. VIII.* i 1 3
Fresh alacrity. With a bridegroom's fresh alacrity . *Troi. and Cres.* iv 4 147
Fresh appetite. To give satiety a fresh appetite . . . *Othello* ii 1 231
Fresh array. Who gave me fresh array and entertainment *As Y. Like It* iv 3 144
Fresh blood. With sighs of love, that costs the fresh blood dear *M. N. D.* iii 2 97
Why hast thou lost the fresh blood in thy cheeks? . . . 1 *Hen. IV.* ii 3 47
Fresh-brook. Thy food shall be The fresh-brook muscles. . . *Tempest* i 2 463
Fresh cheek. If ever,—as that ever may be near,—You meet in some fresh cheek the power of fancy . . . . . . *As Y. Like It* iii 5 29
Fresh complexion. Whose fresh complexion and whose heart together Affliction alters . . . . *W. Tale* iv 4 585
Fresh cups. 'Tis strange he hides him in fresh cups, soft beds *Cymbeline* v 3 71
Fresh days. Joy and fresh days of love Accompany your hearts! *M. N. D.* v 1 29
Fresh embassies and suits, Nor from the state nor private friends, hereafter Will I lend ear to . . . . *Coriolanus* v 3 17
Fresh expectation troubled not the land With any long'd-for change *K. John* iv 2 7
Fresh-fair. Your fresh-fair virgins and your flowering infants *Hen. V.* iii 3 14
Fresh female buds. Even such delight Among fresh female buds shall you this night Inherit . . . . *Rom. and Jul.* i 2 29
Fresh fish. The luce is the fresh fish . . . . . *Mer. Wives* i 1 22
And you, O fate! A very fresh-fish here . . . . . *Hen. VIII.* ii 3 86
Fresh garments. In the heaviness of his sleep We put fresh garments on him . . . . *Lear* iv 7 22
Rise; thou art my child. Give me fresh garments . . . . *Pericles* v 1 216
Fresh horses. Go: fresh horses! And gracious be the issue! *W. Tale* iii 1 21
Fresh kings are come to Troy . . . . . . *Troi. and Cres.* ii 3 272
Fresh lap. The seasons alter: hoary-headed frosts Fall in the fresh lap of the crimson rose . . . . *M. N. Dream* ii 1 108
Fresh legerity. Newly move, With casted slough and fresh legerity *Hen. V.* iv 1 23
Fresh lily. How bravely thou becomest thy bed, fresh lily! *Cymbeline* ii 2 15
Fresh men. Some six or seven fresh men set upon us . 1 *Hen. IV.* ii 4 200

Fresh morning. 'Tis fresh morning with me When you are by at night *Tempest* iii 1 33
Those fresh morning drops upon the rose . . . . *L. L. Lost* iv 3 27
With tears augmenting the fresh morning's dew . . *Rom. and Jul.* i 1 138
Fresh-new. This poor infant, this fresh-new sea-farer . . *Pericles* iii 1 41
Fresh nymphs. Your rye-straw hats put on And these fresh nymphs encounter every one In country footing . . . . . *Tempest* iv 1 137
Fresh ones. Let's have fresh ones, whate'er we pay for them *Pericles* iv 2 10
Fresh piece. And thou, fresh piece Of excellent witchcraft . *W. Tale* iv 4 433
Fresh princess. Kisses the hands Of your fresh princess . . . iv 4 562
Fresh rays. As thy eye-beams, when their fresh rays have smote The night of dew that on my cheeks down flows . . . *L. L. Lost* iv 3 28
Fresh springs. And show'd thee all the qualities o' the isle, The fresh springs, brine-pits . . . . *Tempest* i 2 338
Fresh streams. As many fresh streams meet in one salt sea . *Hen. V.* i 2 209
The fresh streams ran by her, and murmur'd her moans . . *Othello* iv 3 45
Fresh suits. Shall we go send them dinners and fresh suits? . *Hen. V.* iv 2 57
Fresh supply. And, as occasion serves, this noble queen And prince shall follow with a fresh supply . . . . . . 3 *Hen. VI.* iii 3 237
'Tis their fresh supplies.—It is a day turn'd strangely . . *Cymbeline* v 2 16
Fresh suspicions. Think'st thou I'ld make a life of jealousy, To follow still the changes of the moon With fresh suspicions? . . *Othello* iii 3 179
Fresh tapster. A withered serving-man [makes] a fresh tapster *M. Wives* i 3 19
Fresh taste. Till the fresh taste be taken from that clearness *T. And.* iii 1 128
Fresh tears. When I did name her brothers, then fresh tears Stood on her cheeks . . . . iii 1 111
Fresh tree. Under a fresh tree's shade . . . . . 3 *Hen. VI.* ii 5 49
Fresh water. Some food we had and some fresh water . . *Tempest* i 2 160
Fresh whore. Ever your fresh whore and your powdered bawd *M. for M.* iii 2 61
Fresher. On their sustaining garments not a blemish, But fresher than before . . . . *Tempest* i 2 219
Tell me truly too, Hast thou beheld a fresher gentlewoman? *T. of Shrew* iv 5 29
I have ere now, sir, been better known to you, when I have held familiarity with fresher clothes . . . . . . *All's Well* v 2 4
And thou art flying to a fresher clime . . . . . *Richard II.* i 3 285
My poor soldiers tell me, yet ere night They'll be in fresher robes *Hen. V.* iv 3 117
There's fresher air, my lord, In the next chamber . . . *Hen. VIII.* i 4 101
That slander, sir, Is found a truth now; for it grows again Fresher than e'er it was . . . . ii 1 155
I would have been much more a fresher man, Had I expected thee *Troi. and Cres.* v 6 20
Freshes. I'll not show him Where the quick freshes are . . *Tempest* iii 2 75
Freshest. Turn then my freshest reputation to A savour that may strike the dullest nostril! . . . . *W. Tale* i 2 420
So shall I do To the freshest things now reigning . . . . . iv 1 13
Let him choose Out of my files, his projects to accomplish, My best and freshest men . . . . *Coriolanus* v 6 35
Freshly beheld Our royal, good and gallant ship . . . *Tempest* v 1 236
Now puts the drowsy and neglected act Freshly on me . *Meas. for Meas.* i 2 175
Looks he as freshly as he did? . . . . *As Y. Like It* iii 2 243
Freshly looks and over-bears attaint With cheerful semblance *Hen. V.* iv Prol. 39
Be in their flowing cups freshly remember'd . . . . . . iv 3 55
Yet freshly pitied in our memories . . . . . . *Hen. VIII.* v 3 31
Being dead many years, shall after revive, be jointed to the old stock and freshly grow . . . . *Cymbeline* v 4 143; v 5 440
Freshness. Our garments, being, as they were, drenched in the sea, hold notwithstanding their freshness . . . . *Tempest* ii 1 63
Whose youth and freshness Wrinkles Apollo's . . . *Troi. and Cres.* ii 2 78
Fret. Good sister, let us dine and never fret: A man is master of his liberty: Time is their master . . . . . *Com. of Errors* ii 1 6
Do not fret yourself too much in the action . . . *M. N. Dream* iv 1 14
I did but tell her she mistook her frets . . . . *T. of Shrew* ii 1 150
'Frets, call you these?' quoth she; 'I'll fume with them' . . . ii 1 153
Nay, look not big, nor stamp, nor stare, nor fret . . . . . iii 2 230
He frets like a gummed velvet . . . . 1 *Hen. IV.* ii 2 2
Their wounded steeds Fret fetlock deep in gore . . . . *Hen. V.* iv 7 82
Charles, it shall be thine, Let Henry fret and all the world repine 1 *Hen. VI.* v 2 20
So York must sit and fret and bite his tongue . . . . 2 *Hen. VI.* i 1 230
Stamp, rave, and fret, that I may sing and dance . . . 3 *Hen. VI.* i 4 91
He is vex'd at something.—I would 'twere something that would fret the string, The master-cord on's heart! . . . . *Hen. VIII.* iii 2 106
Yon gray lines That fret the clouds are messengers of day . *J. Cæsar* ii 1 104
Fret till your proud heart break; Go show your slaves how choleric you are . . . . iv 3 42
Be lion-mettled, proud; and take no care Who chafes, who frets *Macb.* iv 1 91
A poor player That struts and frets his hour upon the stage . . . v 5 25
Though you can fret me, yet you cannot play upon me . . *Hamlet* iii 2 388
With cadent tears fret channels in her cheeks . . . . *Lear* i 4 307
He frets That Lepidus of the triumvirate Should be deposed *A. and C.* iii 6 27
Fretful. You are so fretful, you cannot live long . . 1 *Hen. IV.* iii 3 13
Away! though parting be a fretful corrosive, It is applied to a deathful wound . . . . 2 *Hen. VI.* iii 2 404
To stand an end, Like quills upon the fretful porpentine . *Hamlet* i 5 20
Where's the king?—Contending with the fretful element . . *Lear* iii 1 4
Fretted. With stinking clothes that fretted in their own grease *M. Wives* iii 5 115
Till they have fretted us a pair of graves Within the earth *Richard II.* iii 3 167
This majestical roof fretted with golden fire . . . . *Hamlet* ii 2 313
And, by starts, His fretted fortunes give him hope, and fear *A. and C.* iv 12 8
The roof o' the chamber With golden cherubins is fretted . *Cymbeline* ii 4 88
Fretten. You may as well forbid the mountain pines To wag their high tops and to make no noise, When they are fretten with the gusts of heaven . . . . *Mer. of Venice* iv 1 77
Fretting. Command these fretting waters from your eyes *Meas. for Meas.* iv 3 151
'Twas a commodity lay fretting by you: 'Twill bring you gain *T. of Shr.* ii 1 330
And he may well in fretting spend his gall . . . . 1 *Hen. VI.* i 2 16
As doth a sail, fill'd with a fretting gust, Command an argosy 3 *Hen. VI.* ii 6 35
Friar. By the bare scalp of Robin Hood's fat friar . . *T. G. of Ver.* iv 1 36
Instruct me How I may formally in person bear me Like a true friar *Meas. for Meas* i 3 48
What's your will, good friar?— . . . I come to visit the afflicted spirits ii 3 2
'Bless you, good father friar.—And you, good brother father . . . iii 2 13
What news, friar, of the duke?—I know none . . . . . . iii 2 90
Something too crabbed that way, friar . . . . iii 2 105
It is impossible to extirp it [lechery] quite, friar . . . . . iii 2 110
Thou art deceived in me, friar. But no more of this . . . . iii 2 179
Farewell, good friar: I prithee, pray for me . . . . . . iii 2 191
This friar hath been with him, and advised him . . . . . iii 2 224
Do you persuade yourself that I respect you?—Good friar, I know you do iv 1 54
I am come to advise you, comfort you and pray with you.—Friar, not I iv 3 56
Friar. I would Friar Peter— O, peace! the friar is come *Meas. for Meas.* iv 6 9
'Tis a meddling friar; I do not like the man . . . . . . v 1 127
Words against me! this is a good friar, belike! . . . . . . v 1 131
Let this friar be found.—But yesternight, my lord, she and that friar, I saw them at the prison: a saucy friar . . . . v 1 133
Thou foolish friar, and thou pernicious woman, Compact with her that's gone . . . . v 1 241
There is another friar that set them on; Let him be sent for . . . v 1 248
We shall find this friar a notable fellow.—As any in Vienna . . . v 1 268
Why, thou unreverend and unhallow'd friar . . . . v 1 307
Sneak not away, sir; for the friar and you Must have a word anon . v 1 363
Go take her hence, and marry her instantly. Do you the office, friar . v 1 383
Come hither, Isabel. Your friar is now your prince . . . . v 1 387
There was a friar told me of this man . . . . v 1 484
Friar, advise him; I leave him to your hand . . . . . . v 1 490
Come, Friar Francis, be brief; only to the plain form of marriage *M. Ado* iv 1 1
To be married to her: friar, you come to marry her . . . . . iv 1 7
Stand thee by, friar. Father, by your leave . . . . . . iv 1 24
Signior Leonato, let the friar advise you . . . . iv 1 246
Friar, I must entreat your pains, I think.—To do what, signior? . . v 4 18
Honourable marriage: In which, good friar, I shall desire your help . v 4 31
Call her forth, brother; here's the friar ready . . . . . . v 4 39
You shall not, till you take her hand Before this friar and swear to marry her . . . . v 4 57
Before this holy friar, I am your husband, if you like of me . . . v 4 58
It was the friar of orders grey, As he forth walked on his way *T. of Shr.* iv 1 148
As the nun's lip to the friar's mouth . . . . . *All's Well* ii 2 28
He hath confessed himself to Morgan, whom he supposes to be a friar . iv 3 125
And all the priests and friars in my realm Shall in procession sing her endless praise . . . . 1 *Hen. VI.* i 6 19
A Chartreux friar, His confessor; who fed him every minute With words of sovereignty . . . . *Hen. VIII.* i 2 148
'Banished'? O friar, the damned use that word in hell *Rom. and Jul.* iii 3 47
O holy friar, O, tell me, holy friar, Where is my lady's lord, where's Romeo? . . . . iii 3 81
Tell me, friar, tell me, In what vile part of this anatomy Doth my name lodge? . . . . iii 3 105
I'll to the friar, to know his remedy . . . . iii 5 241
Tell me not, friar, that thou hear'st of this, Unless thou tell me how I may prevent it . . . . iv 1 50
I'll send a friar with speed To Mantua, with my letters to thy lord . iv 1 123
This reverend holy friar, All our whole city is much bound to him . iv 2 31
What if it be a poison, which the friar Subtly hath minister'd . . iv 3 24
Dost thou not bring me letters from the friar? How doth my lady? . v 1 13
Hast thou no letters to me from the friar?—No, my good lord . . v 1 31
Holy Franciscan friar! brother, ho! . . . . v 2 1
This same should be the voice of Friar John . . . . . . v 2 2
O comfortable friar! where is my lord? . . . . v 3 148
Here is a friar, that trembles, sighs, and weeps . . . . . v 3 184
A great suspicion: stay the friar too . . . . v 3 187
Here is a friar, and slaughter'd Romeo's man . . . . . . v 3 199
Friar John Was stay'd by accident, and yesternight Return'd my letter back . . . . v 3 250
This letter doth make good the friar's words . . . . . . v 3 286
Friday. The duke, I say to thee again, would eat mutton on Fridays. He's not past it yet . . . . *Meas. for Meas.* iii 2 192
I will grant it.—Then love me, Rosalind.—Yes, faith, will I, Fridays and Saturdays and all . . . . *As Y. Like It* iv 1 116
An she were not kin to me, she would be as fair on Friday as Helen is on Sunday . . . . *Troi. and Cres.* i 1 78
Friend. The wreck of all my friends . . . are but light to me *Tempest* i 2 488
Thy case, dear friend, Shall be my precedent . . . . . . ii 1 290
My master through his art forsees the danger That you, his friend, are in . . . . ii 1 298
You cannot tell who's your friend: open your chaps again . . . ii 2 89
His forward voice now is to speak well of his friend . . . . ii 2 95
I am Trinculo—be not afeard—thy good friend Trinculo . . . ii 2 106
Nor have I seen More that I may call men than you, good friend . iii 1 51
What harmony is this? My good friends, hark! . . . . . iii 3 18
First, noble friend, Let me embrace thine age . . . . . . v 1 120
Welcome, my friends all! . . . . v 1 125
And what news else Betideth here in absence of thy friend *T. G. of Ver.* i 1 59
He leaves his friends to dignify them more; I leave myself, my friends and all, for love . . . . i 1 65
'Tis a word or two Of commendations sent from Valentine, Deliver'd by a friend . . . . i 3 54
What maintenance he from his friends receives, Like exhibition thou shalt have . . . . i 3 68
I have writ your letter Unto the secret nameless friend of yours . ii 1 111
She hath given you a letter.—That's the letter I writ to her friend . ii 1 166
What say you to a letter from your friends Of much good news? . . ii 4 51
Your friends are well and have them much commended . . . . ii 4 123
To wrong my friend, I shall be much forsworn . . . . . . ii 6 3
I to myself am dearer than a friend, For love is still most precious in itself ii 6 23
Valentine I'll hold an enemy, Aiming at Silvia as a sweeter friend ii 6 30
My friend This night intends to steal away your daughter . . . iii 1 10
I rather chose To cross my friend in his intended drift . . . iii 1 18
Love of you, not hate unto my friend, Hath made me publisher of this pretence . . . . iii 1 46
There is a messenger That stays to bear my letters to my friends . iii 1 53
I have sought To match my friend Sir Thurio to my daughter . . iii 1 62
She I mean is promised by her friends Unto a youthful gentleman . iii 1 106
Friend Valentine, a word.—My ears are stopt . . . . . . iii 1 204
That thou art banished—O, that's the news!—From hence, from Silvia and from me thy friend . . . . iii 1 218
It must with circumstance be spoken By one whom she esteemeth as his friend . . . . iii 2 37
'Tis an ill office for a gentleman, Especially against his very friend . iii 2 41
The office is indifferent, Being entreated to it by your friend . . iii 2 45
And, for your friend's sake, will be glad of you . . . . . iii 2 63
Temper her by your persuasion To hate young Valentine and love my friend iii 2 65
My friends,— That's not so, sir: we are your enemies . . . . iv 1 7
When I protest true loyalty to her, She twits me with my falsehood to my friend . . . . iv 2 8
Say that she be; yet Valentine thy friend Survives . . . . iv 2 109
Who calls?—Your servant and your friend . . . . iv 3 4
'Friend,' quoth I, 'you mean to whip the dog?' . . . . . . iv 4 27
Thou counterfeit to thy true friend! . . . . v 4 53
In love Who respects friend? . . . . v 4 54
Let go that rude uncivil touch, Thou friend of an ill fashion! . . . v 4 61

Friend. Thou common friend, that's without faith or love, For such is a friend now . . . . *T. G. of Ver.* v 4 62
Now I dare not say I have one friend alive ; thou wouldst disprove me v 4 66
O time most accurst, 'Mongst all foes that a friend should be the worst ! v 4 72
'Twere pity two such friends should be long foes . . . . . . v 4 118
It is petter that friends is the sword, and end it . . . *Mer. Wives* i 1 42
Here is Got's plessing, and your friend, and Justice Shallow . . . . i 1 77
A justice of peace sometime may be beholding to his friend for a man . i 1 284
Alas, he speaks but for his friend.—It is no matter-a ver dat . . i 4 120
And one that is your friend, I can tell you that by the way . . . i 4 149
I have grated upon my good friends for three reprieves . . . . ii 2 6
I am damned in hell for swearing to gentlemen my friends . . . ii 2 10
Master Slender's serving-man, and friend Simple by your name . . iii 1 2
I desire you that we may be friends . . . . iii 1 121
I see what thou wert, if Fortune thy foe were not, Nature thy friend . iii 3 70
If you have a friend here, convey, convey him out . . . . . iii 3 124
There is a gentleman my dear friend ; and I fear not mine own shame so much as his peril . . . . iii 3 129
Follow your friend's counsel. I'll in . . . . iii 3 146
I will not be your friend nor enemy . . . . iii 4 93
The doctor is well money'd, and his friends Potent at court . . . iv 4 88
There is a friend of mine come to town . . . . iv 5 78
One word, good friend. Lucio, a word with you . . *Meas. for Meas.* i 2 146
Only for propagation of a dower Remaining in the coffer of her friends i 2 155
Implore her, in my voice, that she make friends To the strict deputy . i 2 185
I'll to her.—I thank you, good friend . . . . i 2 197
He hath got his friend with child . . . . i 4 29
Where were you born, friend?—Here in Vienna, sir . . . . . ii 1 202
A journey, And death unloads thee. Friend hast thou none . . . iii 1 28
I cry bail. Here's a gentleman and a friend of mine . . . . iii 2 44
Seldom when The steeled gaoler is the friend of men . . . . . iv 2 90
His friends still wrought reprieves for him . . . . iv 2 140
What are you?—Your friends, sir ; the hangman . . . . . . iv 3 28
There's other of our friends Will greet us here anon . . . . . iv 5 12
Our old and faithful friend, we are glad to see you . . . . . . v 1 2
Thanks, good friend Escalus, for thy much goodness . . . . . v 1 534
Try all the friends thou hast in Ephesus ; Beg thou, or borrow *Com. of Er.* i 1 153
Salute me As if I were their well-acquainted friend . . . . . iv 3 2
You have done wrong to this my honest friend . . . . . . v 1 19
Hath he not lost much wealth by wreck of sea? Buried some dear friend? v 1 50
If any friend will pay the sum for him, He shall not die . . . . v 1 131
Haply I see a friend will save my life And pay the sum that may deliver me . . . . v 1 283
There is a fat friend at your master's house, That kitchen'd me for you v 1 414
I will hold friends with you, lady.—Do, good friend . . . *Much Ado* i 1 91
My dear friend Leonato hath invited you all . . . . i 1 149
Your loving friend, Benedick.—Nay, mock not, mock not . . . . i 1 286
O, I cry you mercy, friend ; go you with me, and I will use your skill . i 2 27
Lady, will you walk about with your friend? . . . . ii 1 90
In love of your brother's honour, who hath made this match, and his friend's reputation . . . . ii 2 38
Yes, in truth it is, sir.—What is it, my good friends? . . . . . iii 5 9
Give not this rotten orange to your friend . . . . iv 1 33
I stand dishonour'd, that have gone about To link my dear friend to a common stale . . . . iv 1 66
Nor my bad life reft me so much of friends . . . . iv 1 198
Strength of limb and policy of mind, Ability in means and choice of friends iv 1 201
Is there any way to show such friendship?—A very even way, but no such friend . . . . iv 1 266
We'll be friends first.—You dare easier be friends with me than fight with mine enemy . . . . iv 1 299
That I had any friend would be a man for my sake ! . . . . . iv 1 320
What is your name, friend?—Borachio . . . . iv 2 11
I will never love that which my friend hates . . . . v 2 72
Come, come, we are friends : let's have a dance ere we are married . v 4 119
Forester, my friend, where is the bush? . . . . . . *L. L. Lost* iv 1 7
O, thy letter, thy letter ! he's a good friend of mine : Stand aside . . iv 1 54
A noble gentleman, and my familiar, I do assure ye, very good friend . v 1 101
You'll ne'er be friends with him . . . . v 2 13
Why take we hands, then?—Only to part friends . . . . . . v 2 220
Nor never come in vizard to my friend, Nor woo in rhyme . . . . v 2 404
Well said, old mocker : I must needs be friends with thee . . . . v 2 552
To wail friends lost Is not by much so wholesome-profitable As to rejoice at friends but newly found . . . . v 2 759
At the twelvemonth's end I'll change my black gown for a faithful friend v 2 844
Or else it stood upon the choice of friends . . . . *M. N. Dream* i 1 139
From Athens turn away our eyes, To seek new friends . . . . . i 1 219
But, gentle friend, for love and courtesy Lie further off . . . . . ii 2 56
Good night, sweet friend : Thy love ne'er alter till thy sweet life end ! ii 2 60
The more the pity that some honest neighbours will not make them friends iii 1 149
And will you rent our ancient love asunder, To join with men in scorning your poor friend? . . . . iii 2 216
Good morrow, friends. Saint Valentine is past . . . . . . iv 1 144
Joy, gentle friends ! joy and fresh days of love Accompany your hearts ! v 1 29
The death of a dear friend would go near to make a man look sad . . v 1 294
And, farewell, friends ; Thus Thisby ends : Adieu, adieu, adieu . . v 1 352
This palpable-gross play hath well beguiled The heavy gait of night. Sweet friends, to bed . . . . v 1 375
Give me your hands, if we be friends . . . . v 1 444
I would have stay'd till I had made you merry, If worthier friends had not prevented me . . . . *Mer. of Venice* i 1 61
To supply the ripe wants of my friend, I'll break a custom . . . . i 3 64
If thou wilt lend this money, lend it not As to thy friends . . . . i 3 134
When did friendship take A breed for barren metal of his friend? . . i 3 135
Why, look you, how you storm ! I would be friends with you . . . i 3 139
Your worship's friend and Launcelot, sir . . . . ii 2 58
Put on Your boldest suit of mirth, for we have friends That purpose merriment . . . . ii 2 211
Sweet friends, your patience for my long abode . . . . . . ii 6 21
'Tis nine o'clock : our friends all stay for you . . . . . . ii 6 63
Thwarted my bargains, cooled my friends, heated mine enemies . . . iii 1 59
So sweet a bar Should sunder such sweet friends . . . . . . iii 2 120
I might in virtues, beauties, livings, friends, Exceed account . . . iii 2 158
What, and my old Venetian friend Salerio? . . . . iii 2 222
I bid my very friends and countrymen, Sweet Portia, welcome . . . iii 2 226
Ere I ope his letter, I pray you, tell me how my good friend doth . iii 2 236
Some dear friend dead ; else nothing in the world Could turn so much the constitution Of any constant man . . . . iii 2 248
I have engaged myself to a dear friend, Engaged my friend to his mere enemy, To feed my means . . . . iii 2 264

Friend. Here is a letter, lady ; The paper as the body of my friend *Mer. of Venice* iii 2 267
Is it your dear friend that is thus in trouble?—The dearest friend to me iii 2 293
Treble that, Before a friend of this description Shall lose a hair . . iii 2 303
Call me wife, And then away to Venice to your friend . . . . . iii 2 306
When it is paid, bring your true friend along . . . . iii 2 310
Bid your friends welcome, show a merry cheer . . . . iii 2 314
But let me hear the letter of your friend . . . . iii 2 316
Repent but you that you shall lose your friend, And he repents not that he pays your debt . . . . iv 1 278
I and my friend Have by your wisdom been this day acquitted . . iv 1 408
Who comes so fast in silence of the night?—A friend.—A friend ! what friend? your name, I pray you, friend? . . . . v 1 26
Give welcome to my friend. This is the man, this is Antonio . . . v 1 133
Even he that did uphold the very life Of my dear friend . . . . v 1 215
In the hearing of these many friends, I swear to thee . . . . . v 1 241
I shall do my friends no wrong, for I have none to lament me *As Y. L. It* i 2 202
If we did derive it from our friends, What's that to me? . . . . i 3 64
Being there alone, Left and abandon'd of his velvet friends . . . ii 1 50
Good even to you, friend.—And to you, gentle sir, and to you all . . ii 4 69
What a life is this, That your poor friends must woo your company? . ii 7 10
Thy sting is not so sharp As friend remember'd not . . . . . ii 7 189
He that wants money, means and content is without three good friends iii 2 27
Violated vows 'Twixt the souls of friend and friend . . . . . iii 2 142
How now ! back, friends ! Shepherd, go off a little . . . . . iii 2 167
It is a hard matter for friends to meet . . . . iii 2 195
I knew what you would prove : my friends told me as much . . . iv 1 187
Good even to you, sir.—Good even, gentle friend . . . . . . v 1 18
How old are you, friend?—Five and twenty, sir . . . . . . v 1 20
Therefore, put you in your best array ; bid your friends . . . . v 2 79
I have been politic with my friend, smooth with mine enemy . . . v 4 47
And take a lodging fit to entertain Such friends . . . . *T. of Shrew* i 1 45
Since this bar in law makes us friends, it shall be so far forth friendly maintained . . . . i 1 140
Keep house and ply his book, welcome his friends . . . . . . i 1 201
For a while I take my leave, To see my friends in Padua, but of all My best beloved and approved friend, Hortensio . . . . i 2 2
My old friend Grumio ! and my good friend Petruchio ! How do you? . i 2 21
Tell me now, sweet friend, what happy gale Blows you to Padua? . . i 2 48
But thou 'rt too much my friend, And I'll not wish thee to her . . i 2 63
'Twixt such friends as we Few words suffice . . . . i 2 65
Now shall my friend Petruchio do me grace . . . . i 2 131
Do as adversaries do in law, Strive mightily, but eat and drink as friends i 2 279
How now, my friend ! why dost thou look so pale? . . . . . . ii 1 143
He'll woo a thousand, 'point the day of marriage, Make feasts, invite friends . . . . iii 2 16
Gentlemen and friends, I thank you for your pains . . . . . . iii 2 186
Neighbours and friends, though bride and bridegroom wants For to supply the places at the table . . . . iii 2 248
Keep thy friend Under thy own life's key . . . . . . *All's Well* i 1 75
A mother and a mistress and a friend, A phœnix, captain and an enemy i 1 181
Follow our friends, And show what we alone must think . . . . i 1 198
Remember thy friends : get thee a good husband, and use him as he uses thee . . . . i 1 229
Wherein our dearest friend Prejudicates the business . . . . . i 2 7
I am out o' friends, madam ; and I hope to have friends for my wife's sake.—Such friends are thine enemies . . . . i 3 42
You're shallow, madam, in great friends . . . . i 3 45
He that loves my flesh and blood is my friend : ergo, he that kisses my wife is my friend . . . . i 3 53
My friends were poor, but honest ; so's my love . . . . . . i 3 201
Sir, I am a poor friend of yours, that loves you . . . . . . ii 2 45
The solemn feast Shall more attend upon the coming space, Expecting absent friends . . . . ii 3 189
Here he comes : I pray you, make us friends ; I will pursue the amity ii 5 14
Sent him forth From courtly friends, with camping foes to live . . iii 4 14
This is your devoted friend, sir, the manifold linguist . . . . iv 3 264
That shall you, and take your leave of all your friends . . . . iv 3 347
Ever a friend whose thoughts more truly labour To recompense your love iv 4 17
There's a quart d'écu for you : let the justices make you and fortune friends . . . . v 2 36
Oft our displeasures, to ourselves unjust, Destroy our friends and after weep their dust . . . . v 3 64
You have them ill to friend Till your deeds gain them . . . . v 3 182
What country, friends, is this?—This is Illyria, lady . . . *T. Night* i 2 1
Give me some music. Now, good morrow, friends . . . . . . ii 4 1
Not a friend, not a friend greet My poor corpse . . . . . . ii 4 62
Save thee, friend, and thy music : dost thou live by thy tabor? . . iii 1 1
Thy friend, as thou usest him, and thy sworn enemy . . . . . iii 4 186
His dishonesty appears in leaving his friend here in necessity . . iii 4 422
I prithee, gentle friend, Let thy fair wisdom, not thy passion, sway . iv 1 55
Belong you to the Lady Olivia, friends?—Ay, sir ; we are some of her trappings . . . . v 1 9
The better for my foes and the worse for my friends.—Just the contrary ; the better for thy friends . . . . v 1 14
By my foes, sir, I profit in the knowledge of myself, and by my friends I am abused . . . . v 1 22
Why then, the worse for my friends and the better for my foes . . v 1 25
Excellent.—By my troth, sir, no ; though it please you to be one of my friends . . . . v 1 29
I have spoke to the purpose twice: The one for ever earn'd a royal husband ; The other for some while a friend . . . . *W. Tale* i 2 108
Mine honest friend, Will you take eggs for money? . . . . . . i 2 160
Now my sworn friend and then mine enemy . . . . i 2 167
Fear o'ershades me : Good expedition be my friend ! . . . . . i 2 458
Both disobedience and ingratitude To you and toward your friend . . iii 2 70
I chose Camillo for the minister to poison My friend . . . . . iii 2 162
Pray you, bid These unknown friends to's welcome . . . . . iv 4 65
It is A way to make us better friends, more known . . . . . iv 4 66
Now, my fair'st friend, I would I had some flowers o' the spring that might Become your time of day . . . . iv 4 112
These I lack, To make you garlands of, and my sweet friend, To strew him o'er . . . . iv 4 128
Take hands, a bargain ! And, friends unknown, you shall bear witness to't iv 4 395
You have ever been my father's honour'd friend . . . . . . iv 4 504
Come, lady, come. Farewell, my friend . . . . iv 4 673
Go, Cleomenes ; Yourself, assisted with your honour'd friends . . . v 1 113
Give you all greetings that a king, at friend, Can send his brother . v 1 140
Your honour not o'erthrown by your desires, I am friend to them and you v 1 231
If it be ne'er so false, a true gentleman may swear it in the behalf of his friend v 2 176

Friend. In sooth, good friend, your father might have kept This calf *K. John* i 1 123
Be friends awhile and both conjointly bend Your sharpest deeds of malice ii 1 379
False blood to false blood join'd! gone to be friends! . . . iii 1 2
O boy, then where art thou? France friend with England, what becomes of me? . . . iii 1 35
I alone, alone do me oppose Against the pope and count his friends my foes iii 1 171
A heavy curse from Rome, Or the light loss of England for a friend . iii 1 206
And then we shall be blest To do your pleasure and continue friends . iii 1 252
My good friend, thy voluntary oath Lives in this bosom, dearly cherished iii 3 23
I am much bounden to your majesty.—Good friend, thou hast no cause iii 3 30
I'll tell thee what, my friend, He is a very serpent in my way . iii 3 60
Is not Angiers lost? Arthur ta'en prisoner? divers dear friends slain? . iii 4 7
To that drop ten thousand wiry friends Do glue themselves in sociable grief iii 4 64
I have heard you say That we shall see and know our friends in heaven iii 4 77
Alas, I then have chid away my friend! He hath a stern look . iv 1 87
He show'd his warrant to a friend of mine . . . iv 2 70
Amazement hurries up and down The little number of your doubtful friends . . . v 1 36
And is't not pity, O my grieved friends? . . . v 2 24
I did not think the king so stored with friends . . . v 4 1
Away, my friends! New flight; And happy newness, that intends old right . . . v 4 60
Who's there? speak, ho! speak quickly, or I shoot.—A friend. What art thou? . . . v 6 2
I will upon all hazards well believe Thou art my friend . . . v 6 8
Which since we cannot do to make you friends, Be ready . *Richard II.* i 1 197
Let us take a ceremonious leave And loving farewell of our several friends i 3 51
To what purpose dost thou hoard thy words, That thou return'st no greeting to thy friends? . . . i 3 254
'Tis doubt, When time shall call him home from banishment, Whether our kinsman come to see his friends . . . i 4 22
With 'Thanks, my countrymen, my loving friends' . . . i 4 34
But when he frown'd, it was against the French And not against his friends . . . ii 1 179
Beaumond and Willoughby, With all their powerful friends, are fled to him ii 2 55
Now shall he try his friends that flatter'd him . . . ii 2 85
Be sure I count myself in nothing else so happy As in a soul remembering my good friends . . . ii 3 47
Nor friends nor foes, to me welcome you are . . . ii 3 170
Thy friends are fled to wait upon thy foes . . . ii 4 23
To-day, to-day, unhappy day, too late, O'erthrows thy joys, friends, fortune . . . iii 2 72
I live with bread like you, feel want, Taste grief, need friends . iii 2 176
Who lately landed With some few private friends upon this coast . iii 3 4
And we are barren and bereft of friends . . . iii 3 84
Let's fight with gentle words Till time lend friends and friends their helpful swords . . . iii 3 132
Letters came last night To a dear friend . . . iii 4 70
Aumerle that was; But that is lost for being Richard's friend . v 2 42
Have I no friend will rid me of this living fear? . . . v 4 2
Come, let's go: I am the king's friend, and will rid his foe . v 4 11
Rode he on Barbary? Tell me, gentle friend, How went he under him? v 5 81
Therefore, friends, As far as to the sepulchre of Christ . *1 Hen. IV.* i 1 18
Here is a dear, a true industrious friend . . . i 1 62
For I shall never hold that man my friend Whose tongue shall ask me for one penny cost . . . i 3 90
The friends you have named uncertain; the time itself unsorted . ii 3 12
Our plot is a good plot as ever was laid; our friends true and constant ii 3 19
A good plot, good friends, and full of expectation; an excellent plot, very good friends . . . ii 3 20
Call you that backing of your friends? A plague upon such backing! . ii 4 166
Within that space you may have drawn together Your tenants, friends iii 1 90
I'll give thrice as much land To any well-deserving friend . iii 1 138
Ta'en him once, Enlarged him and made a friend of him . iii 2 115
I am good friends with my father and may do any thing . iii 3 203
His friends by deputation could not So soon be drawn . iv 1 32
I must go write again To other friends; and so farewell . iv 4 41
My lord, We were the first and dearest of your friends . v 1 33
They and you, yea, every man Shall be my friend again and I'll be his . v 1 108
Fellows, soldiers, friends, Better consider what you have to do . v 2 76
Make up, Lest your retirement do amaze your friends . v 4 6
To the highest of the field, To see what friends are living, who are dead v 4 165
As a sullen bell, Remember'd tolling a departing friend . *2 Hen. IV.* i 1 103
Make friends with speed: Never so few, and never yet more need . i 1 214
And, my most noble friends, I pray you all, Speak plainly your opinions i 3 2
As to one it pleases me, for fault of a better, to call my friend . ii 2 45
I'll be friends with thee, Jack: thou art going to the wars . ii 4 71
In which doing, I have done the part of a careful friend . ii 4 349
Since Richard and Northumberland, great friends, Did feast together . iii 1 58
A good-limbed fellow; young, strong, and of good friends . iii 2 114
I will take such order that thy friends shall ring for thee . iii 2 198
Stand my friend; and here's four Harry ten shillings in French crowns for you . . . iii 2 236
And, for mine own part, have a desire to stay with my friends . iii 2 241
Good master corporal captain, for my old dame's sake, stand my friend iii 2 245
My friends and brethren in these great affairs, I must acquaint you . iv 1 6
His foes are so enrooted with his friends That, plucking to unfix an enemy, He doth unfasten so and shake a friend . . . iv 1 209
And thou shalt prove a shelter to thy friends . . . iv 4 42
Let there be no noise made, my gentle friends . . . iv 5 1
Now, where is he that will not stay so long Till his friend sickness hath determined me? . . . iv 5 82
All my friends, which thou must make thy friends, Have but their stings and teeth newly ta'en out . . . iv 5 205
A friend i' the court is better than a penny in purse . . . v 1 34
But a knave should have some countenance at his friend's request . v 1 49
The knave is mine honest friend, sir; therefore, I beseech your worship, let him be countenanced . . . v 1 55
O, good my lord, you have lost a friend indeed . . . v 2 27
I am thy Pistol and thy friend, And helter-skelter have I rode to thee . v 3 97
Blessed are they that have been my friends . . . v 3 145
What, are Ancient Pistol and you friends yet? . . . *Hen. V.* ii 1 4
I will bestow a breakfast to make you friends . . . ii 1 13
Come, shall I make you two friends? We must to France together . ii 1 94
An thou wilt be friends, be friends: an thou wilt not, why, then, be enemies . . . ii 1 107
You see this chase is hotly follow'd, friends.—Turn head, and stop pursuit . . . ii 4 68
Once more unto the breach, dear friends, once more . . . iii 1 1
There stands your friend for the devil . . . iii 7 128

Friend. Bids them good morrow with a modest smile And calls them brothers, friends . . . *Hen. V.* iv Prol. 34
Qui va là?—A friend.—Discuss unto me; art thou officer? . . . iv 1 36
Art thou his friend?—And his kinsman too . . . iv 1 58
Who goes there?—A friend.—Under what captain serve you? . . iv 1 94
Be friends, you English fools, be friends . . . iv 1 239
I will go with thee: The day, my friends and all things stay for me . iv 1 326
Disorder, that hath spoil'd us, friend us now! . . . iv 5 17
Did, in his ales and his angers, look you, kill his best friend . . iv 7 41
Our king is not like him in that: he never killed any of his friends . iv 7 43
If any man challenge this, he is a friend to Alençon . . . iv 7 164
He is my dear friend, an please you . . . iv 7 174
Apprehend him: he's a friend of the Duke Alençon's . . . iv 8 19
Give him the crowns: And, captain, you must needs be friends with him iv 8 65
I will tell you, asse my friend . . . v 1 5
But, in loving me, you should love the friend of France . . . v 2 182
His crown shall be the ransom of my friend . . . *1 Hen. VI.* i 1 150
Thou art no friend to God or to the king . . . i 3 25
The regions of Artois, Wallon and Picardy are friends to us . . ii 1 10
Wherefore is Charles impatient with his friend? . . . ii 1 54
I'll find friends to wear my bleeding roses . . . ii 4 72
For these my friends in spite of thee shall wear . . . ii 4 106
Richard Plantagenet, my friend, is he come? . . . ii 5 34
My friends and loving countrymen, This token serveth for a flag of truce iii 1 137
The presence of a king engenders love Amongst his subjects and his loyal friends, As it disanimates his enemies . . . iii 1 182
I'll by a sign give notice to our friends . . . iii 2 8
See, noble Charles, the beacon of our friend . . . iii 2 29
They set him free . . . In spite of Burgundy and all his friends . iii 3 73
Esteem none friends but such as are his friends . . . iv 1 5
And what offence it is to flout his friends . . . iv 1 75
It grieves his highness: good my lords, be friends . . . iv 1 133
They shall find dear deer of us, my friends . . . iv 2 54
Away! vexation almost stops my breath, That sunder'd friends greet in the hour of death . . . iv 3 42
If this servile usage once offend, Go and be free again as Suffolk's friend v 3 59
Thou art no father nor no friend of mine . . . v 4 9
An enemy unto you all, And no great friend, I fear me, to the king *2 Hen. VI.* i 1 150
Pirates may make cheap pennyworths of their pillage And purchase friends . . . i 1 223
For it is known we were but hollow friends . . . iii 2 66
'Tis like you would not feast him like a friend . . . iii 2 184
O, go not yet! Even thus two friends condemn'd Embrace and kiss . iii 2 353
If he revenge it not, yet will his friends . . . iv 1 146
And you that be the king's friends, follow me . . . iv 2 191
Nor knows he how to live but by the spoil, Unless by robbing of your friends . . . iv 8 42
Tell me, my friend, art thou the man that slew him? . . . v 1 71
Call Buckingham, and all the friends thou hast, I am resolved for death v 1 193
Vow'd revenge On him, his sons, his favourites and his friends *3 Hen. VI.* i 1 56
Of thee and these thy sons, Thy kinsmen and thy friends, I'll have more lives . . . i 1 96
Muster'd my soldiers, gather'd flocks of friends . . . ii 1 112
Fell gently down, as if they struck their friends . . . ii 1 132
With all the friends that thou, brave Earl of March, . . . canst procure ii 1 179
Would thy best friends did know How it doth grieve me that thy head is here! . . . ii 2 54
Fly, father, fly! for all your friends are fled . . . ii 5 125
My love and fear glued many friends to thee . . . ii 6 5
Now the battle's ended, If friend or foe, let him be gently used . ii 6 45
When Clifford cannot spare his friends an oath. I know by that he's dead . . . ii 6 78
And, having France thy friend, thou shalt not dread The scatter'd foe . ii 6 92
Our Earl of Warwick, Edward's greatest friend . . . iii 3 45
Edward, King of Albion, My lord and sovereign, and thy vowed friend iii 3 50
Before thy coming Lewis was Henry's friend.—And still is friend to him iii 3 143
I forgive and quite forget old faults, And joy that thou becomest King Henry's friend.—So much his friend, ay, his unfeigned friend . iii 3 201
What danger or what sorrow can befall thee, So long as Edward is thy constant friend? . . . iv 1 77
But say, is Warwick friends with Margaret?—Ay, gracious sovereign . iv 1 115
I rather wish you foes than hollow friends . . . iv 1 139
Speak suddenly, my lords, are we all friends?—Fear not that, my lord iv 2 4
Else might I think that Clarence, Edward's brother, Were but a feigned friend . . . iv 2 11
For Warwick and his friends, God and Saint George! . . . iv 2 29
'Tis the Lord Hastings, the king's chiefest friend . . . iv 3 11
Guess thou the rest; King Edward's friends must down . . . iv 4 28
He shall here find his friends with horse and men To set him free . iv 5 12
Now that God and friends Have shaken Edward from the regal seat . iv 6 1
We must enter in, For hither will our friends repair to us . . iv 7 15
Why stand you in a doubt? Open the gates: we are King Henry's friends iv 7 28
For Edward will defend the town and thee, And all those friends that deign to follow me . . . iv 7 39
Our trusty friend, unless I be deceived . . . iv 7 41
The bruit thereof will bring you many friends . . . iv 7 64
I have true-hearted friends, Not mutinous in peace, yet bold in war . iv 8 9
Oxford, wondrous well beloved, In Oxfordshire shalt muster up thy friends iv 8 18
Who should that be? belike, unlook'd-for friends . . . v 1 14
Sail how thou canst, have wind and tide thy friend . . . v 1 53
Ah, who is nigh? come to me, friend or foe, And tell me who is victor? v 2 5
We are advertised by our loving friends That they do hold their course v 3 18
And Montague our topmast; what of him? Our slaughter'd friends the tackles . . . v 4 15
The friends of France our shrouds and tacklings . . . v 4 18
I never sued to friend nor enemy . . . *Richard III.* i 2 168
You envy my advancement and my friends' . . . i 3 75
A weeder-out of his proud adversaries, A liberal rewarder of his friends i 3 124
Thy friends suspect for traitors while thou livest, And take deep traitors for thy dearest friends! . . . i 3 223
Wherein, my friends, have I offended you?—Offended us you have not . i 4 182
My friend, I spy some pity in thy looks . . . i 4 270
Now in peace my soul shall part to heaven, Since I have set my friends at peace on earth . . . ii 1 6
When I have most need to employ a friend, And most assured that he is a friend, Deep, hollow, treacherous, and full of guile, Be he unto me! ii 1 36
Stood the state so? No, no, good friends, God wot . . . ii 3 18
God keep you from them, and from such false friends!—God keep me from false friends! but they were none . . . iii 1 15

Friend. And bid my friend, for joy of this good news, Give Mistress Shore one gentle kiss the more — *Richard III.* iii 1 184
Your friends at Pomfret, they do need the priest — iii 2 115
Be patient, they are friends, Ratcliff and Lovel — iii 5 21
Which now the loving haste of these our friends, Somewhat against our meaning, have prevented — iii 5 54
'Thanks, gentle citizens and friends,' quoth I — iii 7 38
Earnest in the service of my God, Neglect the visitation of my friends — iii 7 107
Consorted with the citizens, Your very-worshipful and loving friends — iii 7 138
Then, on the other side, I check'd my friends — iii 7 150
Let us to our holy task again. Farewell, good cousin; farewell, gentle friends — iii 7 247
Darest thou resolve to kill a friend of mine? — iv 2 70
Lo, at their births good stars were opposite.—No, to their lives bad friends were contrary — iv 4 216
To the shore Throng many doubtful hollow-hearted friends — iv 4 435
Some light-foot friend post to the Duke of Norfolk — iv 4 440
My good lord, my friends are in the north.—Cold friends to Richard — iv 4 485
Please it your majesty to give me leave, I'll muster up my friends — iv 4 489
Now in Devonshire, as I by friends am well advertised — iv 4 501
Hath any well-advised friend proclaim'd Reward to him that brings the traitor? — iv 4 517
Fellows in arms, and my most loving friends — v 2 1
In God's name, cheerly on, courageous friends — v 2 14
His friends will fly to us.—He hath no friends but who are friends for fear — v 2 19
Sweet discourse, Which so long sunder'd friends should dwell upon — v 3 100
Your friends are up, and buckle on their armour — v 3 211
What thinkest thou, will our friends prove all true?—No doubt, my lord — v 3 213
God and your arms be praised, victorious friends — v 5 1
Will leave us never an understanding friend — *Hen. VIII.* Prol. 22
Follow'd with the general throng and sweat Of thousand friends — Prol. 29
Be to yourself As you would to your friend — i 1 136
His will is most malignant; and it stretches Beyond you, to your friends — i 2 142
That noble lady, Or gentleman, that is not freely merry, Is not my friend — i 4 37
His noble friends and fellows, whom to leave Is only bitter to him — ii 1 73
For those you make friends And give your hearts to, when they once perceive The least rub in your fortunes, fall away Like water from ye — ii 1 127
Which of your friends Have I not strove to love? — ii 4 29
What friend of mine That had to him derived your anger, did I Continue in my liking? — ii 4 31
Spare me, till I may Be by my friends in Spain advised — ii 4 55
I hold my most malicious foe, and think not At all a friend to truth — ii 4 84
Your hopes and friends are infinite — iii 1 82
Can you think, lords, That any Englishman dare give me counsel? Or be a known friend? — iii 1 85
My friends, They that must weigh out my afflictions, They that my trust must grow to, live not here — iii 1 87
Let me speak myself, Since virtue finds no friends — iii 1 126
Where no pity, No friends, no hope; no kindred weep for me — iii 1 150
Think us Those we profess, peace-makers, friends, and servants — iii 1 167
Should, notwithstanding that your bond of duty, As 'twere in love's particular, be more To me, your friend, than any — iii 2 190
Indeed, to gain the popedom, And fee my friends in Rome — iii 2 213
When it comes, Cranmer will find a friend will not shrink from him — iv 1 107
A man in much esteem with the king, and truly A worthy friend — iv 1 110
Good, my lord, . . . Stand these poor people's friend — iv 2 157
Give your friend Some touch of your late business — v 1 12
Thy truth and thy integrity is rooted In us, thy friend — v 1 115
I thank you; You are always my good friend — v 3 59
Make me no more ado, but all embrace him: Be friends, for shame! — v 3 160
Do my Lord of Canterbury A shrewd turn, and he is your friend for ever — v 3 178
Are all these Your faithful friends o' the suburbs? — v 4 76
Well, the gods are above; time must friend or end — *Troi. and Cres.* i 2 84
As honour, loss of time, travail, expense, Wounds, friends, and what else dear — ii 2 5
Friend, you! pray you, a word: do not you follow the young Lord Paris? — iii 1 1
Friend, know me better; I am the Lord Pandarus — iii 1 11
You are in the state of grace.—Grace! not so, friend — iii 1 16
Friend, we understand not one another: I am too courtly — iii 1 29
My dear lord and most esteemed friend, your brother — iii 1 69
'Tis not so with me: Fortune and I are friends — iii 3 88
With such a costly loss of wealth and friends — iv 1 60
But I'll be true.—And I'll grow friend with danger — iv 4 72
To-morrow do I meet thee, fell as death; To-night all friends — iv 5 270
Ajax hath lost a friend And foams at mouth, and he is arm'd and at it — v 5 35
My good friends, mine honest neighbours, Will you undo yourselves? — *Coriolanus* i 1 63
I tell you, friends, most charitable care Have the patricians of you — i 1 67
Note me this, good friend; Your most grave belly was deliberate — i 1 131
'True is it, my incorporate friends,' quoth he, 'That I receive the general food' — i 1 134
'You, my good friends,'—this says the belly, mark me — i 1 145
Where, I know, Our greatest friends attend us — i 1 249
March from hence, To help our fielded friends! — i 4 12
Prosperity be thy page.—Thy friend no less Than those she placeth highest! — i 5 24
By interims and conveying gusts we have heard The charges of our friends — i 6 6
By the vows We have made to endure friends — i 6 58
Nature teaches beasts to know their friends — ii 1 7
You have been a scourge to her enemies, you have been a rod to her friends — ii 3 98
We hope to find you our friend; and therefore give you our voices heartily — ii 3 111
The gods give him joy, and make him good friend to the people! — ii 3 142
I'll have five hundred voices of that sound.—I twice five hundred and their friends to piece 'em — ii 3 220
Get you hence instantly, and tell those friends, They have chose a consul — ii 3 221
My nobler friends, I crave their pardons — iii 1 64
Be that you seem, truly your country's friend — iii 1 218
Stand fast: We have as many friends as enemies — iii 1 232
I prithee, noble friend, home to thy house; Leave us to cure this cause — iii 1 234
Honour and policy, like unsever'd friends, I' the war do grow together — iii 2 42
I would dissemble with my nature where My fortunes and my friends at stake required I should do so in honour — iii 2 63
Hear me, my masters, and my common friends — iii 3 108
My sweet wife, my dearest mother, and My friends of noble touch — iv 1 49
Friends now fast sworn, Whose double bosoms seem to wear one heart — iv 4 12
By some chance, Some trick not worth an egg, shall grow dear friends — iv 4 21
What would you have, friend? whence are you? Here's no place for you — iv 5 7

Friend. A thousand welcomes! And more a friend than e'er an enemy — *Coriolanus* iv 5 152
Come, we are fellows and friends: he was ever too hard for him — iv 5 194
He has as many friends as enemies; which friends, sir, as it were, durst not, look you, sir, show themselves, as we term it, his friends whilst he's in directitude — iv 5 219
Here do we make his friends Blush that the world goes well — iv 6 4
Is not much miss'd, but with his friends — iv 6 13
His best friends, if they Should say 'Be good to Rome,' they charged him even As those should do that had deserved his hate — iv 6 111
I offer'd to awaken his regard For's private friends — v 1 24
As a discontented friend, grief-shot With his unkindness — v 1 44
Good my friends, If you have heard your general talk of Rome, And of his friends there, it is lots to blanks, My name hath touch'd your ears — v 2 8
For I have ever verified my friends, Of whom he's chief — v 2 17
Never admitted A private whisper, no, not with such friends That thought them sure of you — v 3 7
Fresh embassies and suits, Nor from the state nor private friends, hereafter Will I lend ear to — v 3 18
Friend, Art thou certain this is true? is it most certain? — v 4 46
He water'd his new plants with dews of flattery, Seducing so my friends — v 6 24
Romans, friends, followers, favourers of my right — *T. Andron.* i 1 9
Princes, that strive by factions and by friends Ambitiously for rule — i 1 18
I will here dismiss my loving friends — i 1 53
Friends, that have been thus forward in my right, I thank you all — i 1 56
The people of Rome, Whose friend in justice thou hast ever been — i 1 180
My faction if thou strengthen with thy friends, I will most thankful be — i 1 214
There lie thy bones, sweet Mutius, with thy friends — i 1 387
A father and a friend to thee and Rome — i 1 423
Lose not so noble a friend on vain suppose — i 1 440
And let it be mine honour, good my lord, That I have reconciled your friends and you — i 1 467
We must all be friends: The tribune and his nephews kneel for grace — i 1 479
Though you left me like a churl, I found a friend — i 1 487
You are my guest, Lavinia, and your friends — i 1 490
Are you so desperate grown, to threat your friends? — ii 1 40
For shame, be friends, and join for that you jar — ii 1 103
Do this, and purchase us thy lasting friends — ii 3 275
Give signs, sweet girl, for here are none but friends — iv 1 61
And secretly to greet the empress' friends — iv 2 174
Approved warriors, and my faithful friends — v 1 1
Set deadly enmity between two friends — v 1 131
Oft have I digg'd up dead men from their graves, And set them upright at their dear friends' doors — v 1 136
I am not Tamora; She is thy enemy, and I thy friend — v 2 29
And see the ambush of our friends be strong — v 3 9
Speak, Rome's dear friend, as erst our ancestor — v 3 80
Who drown'd their enmity in my true tears, And oped their arms to embrace me as a friend — v 3 108
O, pardon me; For when no friends are by, men praise themselves — v 3 118
Friends should associate friends in grief and woe — v 3 169
Some loving friends convey the emperor hence — v 3 191
Have you importuned him by any means?—Both by myself and many other friends — *Rom. and Jul.* i 1 152
My very friend hath got his mortal hurt In my behalf — iii 1 115
He cries aloud, 'Hold, friends! friends, part!' — iii 1 170
Who now the price of his dear blood doth owe?—Not Romeo, prince, he was Mercutio's friend — iii 1 189
O Tybalt, Tybalt, the best friend I had! O courteous Tybalt! — iii 2 61
A divine, a ghostly confessor, A sin-absolver, and my friend profess'd — iii 3 50
The law that threaten'd death becomes thy friend And turns it to exile — iii 3 139
Till we can find a time To blaze your marriage, reconcile your friends — iii 3 151
Do you like this haste? We'll keep no great ado,—a friend or two — iii 4 23
We'll have some half a dozen friends, And there an end — iii 4 27
Art thou gone so? love, lord, ay, husband, friend! — iii 5 43
So shall you feel the loss, but not the friend Which you weep for.—Feeling so the loss, I cannot choose but ever weep the friend — iii 5 76
Lay hand on heart, advise: An you be mine, I'll give you to my friend — iii 5 193
The world is not thy friend nor the world's law — v 1 72
Who's there?—Here's one, a friend, and one that knows you well — v 3 123
I am not of that feather to shake off My friend when he must need me. I do know him A gentleman that well deserves a help — *T. of Athens* i 1 101
What have you there, my friend?—A piece of painting — i 1 154
No, I will do nothing at thy bidding: make thy requests to thy friend — i 1 279
Or a keeper with my freedom; Or my friends, if I should need 'em — i 2 70
You had rather be at a breakfast of enemies than a dinner of friends — i 2 79
There's no meat like 'em: I could wish my best friend at such a feast — i 2 82
O, no doubt, my good friends, but the gods themselves have provided that I shall have much help from you: how had you been my friends else? — i 2 91
What need we have any friends, if we should ne'er have need of 'em? — i 2 99
What better or properer can we call our own than the riches of our friends? — i 2 107
Who dies, that bears not one spurn to their graves Of their friends' gift? — i 2 147
O my friends, I have one word to say to you — i 2 173
Happier is he that has no friend to feed Than such that do e'en enemies exceed — i 2 209
I weigh my friend's affection with mine own; I'll tell you true — i 2 222
Methinks, I could deal kingdoms to my friends, And ne'er be weary — i 2 226
Ready for his friends — i 2 236
Mine honest friend, I prithee, but repair to me next morning — ii 2 24
Nay, good my lord,— Contain thyself, good friend — ii 2 26
Canst thou the conscience lack, To think I shall lack friends? — ii 2 185
In some sort, these wants of mine are crown'd, That I account them blessings; for by these Shall I try friends — ii 2 192
You Mistake my fortunes; I am wealthy in my friends — ii 2 193
When he was poor, Imprison'd and in scarcity of friends, I clear'd him — ii 2 234
Bid him suppose some good necessity Touches his friend — ii 2 237
Ne'er speak, or think, That Timon's fortunes 'mong his friends can sink — ii 2 240
Let molten coin be thy damnation, Thou disease of a friend, and not himself! — iii 1 56
He is my very good friend, and an honourable gentleman — iii 2 2
Commend me to thy honourable virtuous lord, my very exquisite friend — iii 2 32
Who can call him His friend that dips in the same dish? — iii 2 73
Nor came any of his bounties over me, To mark me for his friend — iii 2 86
His friends, like physicians, Thrive, give him over — iii 3 11
Now all are fled, Save only the gods: now his friends are dead — iii 3 37
What do ye ask of me, my friend?—We wait for certain money here, sir — iii 4 45
Go, bid all my friends again, Lucius, Lucullus, and Sempronius: All, sirrah, all — iii 4 111

Friend. It pleases time and fortune to lie heavy Upon a friend of mine *T. of Athens* iii 5 11
Friend or brother, He forfeits his own blood that spills another iii 5 88
I hope it is not so low with him as he made it seem in the trial of his several friends iii 6 7
My noble lord,— Ah, my good friend, what cheer? iii 6 44
My worthy friends, will you draw near?—I'll tell you more anon iii 6 66
For these my present friends, as they are to me nothing, so in nothing bless them, and to nothing are they welcome iii 6 93
Not One friend to take his fortune by the arm, And go along with him! iv 2 7
But only painted, like his varnish'd friends iv 2 36
He's flung in rage from this ingrateful seat Of monstrous friends iv 2 46
Get thee gone.—I am thy friend, and pity thee iv 3 97
The mere want of gold, and the falling-from of his friends, drove him into this melancholy iv 3 402
What viler thing upon the earth than friends Who can bring noblest minds to basest ends! iv 3 470
This breaking of his has been but a try for his friends v 1 11
Your friends fall'n off, Whose thankless natures—O abhorred spirits! v 1 62
But therefore Came not my friend nor I v 1 82
My honest-natured friends, I must needs say you have a little fault v 1 89
Lord Timon! Timon! Look out, and speak to friends v 1 131
Tell my friends, Tell Athens, in the sequence of degree From high to low v 1 210
I met a courier, one mine ancient friend v 2 6
Yet our old love made a particular force, And made us speak like friends v 2 9
You bear too stubborn and too strange a hand Over your friend *J. Cæsar* i 2 36
But let not therefore my good friends be grieved i 2 43
Till then, my noble friend, chew upon this i 2 171
I do know him by his gait; He is a friend i 3 133
And, gentle friends, Let's kill him boldly, but not wrathfully ii 1 171
Friends, disperse yourselves; but all remember What you have said ii 1 222
So near will I be, That your best friends shall wish I had been further ii 2 125
Good friends, go in, and taste some wine with me; And we, like friends, will straightway go together ii 2 126
Stand fast together, lest some friend of Cæsar's Should chance iii 1 87
So are we Cæsar's friends, that have abridged His time of fearing death iii 1 104
Soft! who comes here? A friend of Antony's iii 1 122
I know that we shall have him well to friend.—I wish we may iii 1 143
The enemies of Cæsar shall say this; Then, in a friend, it is cold modesty iii 1 213
Will you be prick'd in number of our friends; Or shall we on? iii 1 216
Friends am I with you all and love you all, Upon this hope iii 1 220
And in the pulpit, as becomes a friend, Speak in the order of his funeral iii 1 229
Then follow me, and give me audience, friends iii 2 2
If there be any in this assembly, any dear friend of Cæsar's iii 2 19
If then that friend demand why Brutus rose against Cæsar, this is my answer iii 2 21
Friends, Romans, countrymen, lend me your ears; I come to bury Cæsar iii 2 78
He was my friend, faithful and just to me: But Brutus says he was ambitious iii 2 90
We will hear Cæsar's will.—Have patience, gentle friends, I must not read it iii 2 145
Good friends, sweet friends, let me not stir you up iii 2 214
I come not, friends, to steal away your hearts: I am no orator, as Brutus is iii 2 220
You know me all, a plain blunt man, That love my friend iii 2 223
Why, friends, you go to do you know not what iii 2 240
I am going to Cæsar's funeral.—As a friend or an enemy?—As a friend. iii 3 23
Let our alliance be combined, Our best friends made, our means stretch'd iv 1 44
Thou hast described A hot friend cooling iv 2 19
When Marcus Brutus grows so covetous, To lock such rascal counters from his friends iv 3 80
A friend should bear his friend's infirmities, But Brutus makes mine greater iv 3 86
Love, and be friends, as two such men should be iv 3 131
You must note beside, That we have tried the utmost of our friends iv 3 214
That I may rest assured Whether yond troops are friend or enemy v 3 18
Coward that I am, to live so long, To see my best friend ta'en before my face! v 3 35
Why didst thou send me forth, brave Cassius? Did I not meet thy friends? v 3 81
Friends, I owe more tears To this dead man than you shall see me pay. v 3 101
I am the son of Marcus Cato, ho! A foe to tyrants, and my country's friend v 4 5
And I am Brutus, Marcus Brutus, I; Brutus, my country's friend v 4 8
This is not Brutus, friend; but, I assure you, A prize no less in worth v 4 26
I had rather have Such men my friends than enemies v 4 29
Come, poor remains of friends, rest on this rock v 5 1
That's not an office for a friend, my lord v 5 29
Hail, brave friend! Say to the king the knowledge of the broil *Macbeth* i 2 5
Very gladly.—Till then, enough. Come, friends i 3 156
Who's there?—A friend.—What, sir, not yet at rest? The king's a-bed ii 1 11
Was it so late, friend, ere you went to bed, That you do lie so late? ii 3 24
Those that would make good of bad, and friends of foes ii 4 41
Certain friends that are both his and mine, Whose loves I may not drop iii 1 121
We will require her welcome.—Pronounce it for me, sir, to all our friends iii 4 7
Sit, worthy friends: my lord is often thus, And hath been from his youth iii 4 53
Your noble friends do lack you.—I do forget. Do not muse at me, my most worthy friends iii 4 84
I drink to the general joy o' the whole table, And to our dear friend Banquo iii 4 90
What I can redress, As I shall find the time to friend, I will iv 3 10
Honour, love, obedience, troops of friends, I must not look to have v 3 25
I would the friends we miss were safe arrived v 8 35
As calling home our exiled friends abroad v 8 66
Who's there?—Friends to this ground.—And liegemen to the Dane *Hamlet* i 1 15
Cast thy nighted colour off, And let thine eye look like a friend on Denmark i 2 69
Your poor servant ever.—Sir, my good friend; I'll change that name i 2 163
Those friends thou hast, and their adoption tried, Grapple them to thy soul i 3 62
Neither a borrower nor a lender be; For loan oft loses both itself and friend i 3 76
Good friends, As you are friends, scholars and soldiers, Give me one poor request i 5 140
I know his father and his friends, And in part him ii 1 14
He closes with you in this consequence; 'Good sir,' or so, or 'friend' ii 1 46

Friend. Welcome, my good friends! Say, Voltimand, what from our brother Norway? *Hamlet* ii 2 58
Friend, look to't.—How say you by that? ii 2 187
My most dear lord!—My excellent good friends! ii 2 228
What have you, my good friends, deserved at the hands of fortune? ii 2 245
And sure, dear friends, my thanks are too dear a halfpenny ii 2 281
O, my old friend! thy face is valanced since I saw thee last ii 2 442
Follow him, friends: we'll hear a play to-morrow ii 2 560
Dost thou hear me, old friend; can you play the Murder of Gonzago? ii 2 562
My good friends, I'll leave you till night: you are welcome to Elsinore ii 2 572
The poor advanced makes friends of enemies iii 2 215
Hitherto doth love on fortune tend; For who not needs shall never lack a friend iii 2 217
Who in want a hollow friend doth try, Directly seasons him his enemy. iii 2 218
You do, surely, bar the door upon your own liberty, if you deny your griefs to your friend iii 2 353
By and by is easily said. Leave me, friends iii 2 405
Friends both, go join you with some further aid iv 1 33
We'll call up our wisest friends; And let them know iv 1 38
Swoopstake, you will draw both friend and foe, Winner and loser. iv 5 142
To his good friends thus wide I'll ope my arms iv 5 145
Make choice of whom your wisest friends you will, And they shall hear iv 5 204
You must put me in your heart for friend iv 7 2
O, yet defend me, friends; I am but hurt v 2 335
Remember him hereafter as my honourable friend *Lear* i 1 28
Banishment of friends, dissipation of cohorts, nuptial breaches i 2 161
How now, my noble friend! since I came hither, Which I can call but now, I have heard strange news ii 1 88
Our good old friend, Lay comforts to your bosom ii 1 127
Good dawning to thee, friend: art of this house? ii 2 1
I am sorry for thee, friend; 'tis the duke's pleasure ii 2 159
I'll tell thee, friend, I am almost mad myself iii 4 170
I loved him, friend; No father his son dearer iii 4 173
Come hither, friend: where is the king my master?—Here, sir iii 6 93
Good friend, I prithee, take him in thy arms iii 6 95
Lay him in't, And drive towards Dover, friend iii 6 98
Towards Dover; where they boast To have well-armed friends iii 7 20
Good my friends, consider You are my guests: do me no foul play, friends iii 7 30
Good friend, be gone: Thy comforts can do me no good at all; Thee they may hurt iv 1 16
My son Came then into my mind; and yet my mind Was then scarce friends with him iv 1 37
Come hither, friend: Tell me what more thou know'st iv 2 97
Here, friend, 's another purse; in it a jewel Well worth a poor man's taking iv 6 28
Alive or dead? Ho, you sir! friend! Hear you, sir! speak! iv 6 46
Take that of me, my friend, who have the power To seal the accuser's lips iv 6 173
The letters that he speaks of May be my friends iv 6 262
Come, father, I'll bestow you with a friend iv 6 293
At this time We sweat and bleed: the friend hath lost his friend v 3 55
'Tis noble Kent, your friend.—A plague upon you, murderers, traitors all! v 3 268
You lords and noble friends, know our intent v 3 296
All friends shall taste The wages of their virtue v 3 302
Friends of my soul v 3 319
What lights come yond?—Those are the raised father and his friends *Othello* i 2 29
The goodness of the night upon you, friends! i 2 35
And bade me, if I had a friend that loved her, I should but teach him how to tell my story i 3 164
I have professed me thy friend and I confess me knit to thy deserving i 3 342
Our friends at least.—I pray you, sir, go forth ii 1 57
This likewise is a friend.—See for the news ii 1 96
News, friends: our wars are done, the Turks are drown'd ii 1 204
O, they are our friends; but one cup: I'll drink for you ii 3 38
Friends all but now, even now, In quarter, and in terms like bride and groom ii 3 179
Dost thou hear, my honest friend?—No, I hear not your honest friend iii 1 22
I shall seem to notify unto her.—Do, good my friend iii 1 32
Thou dost conspire against thy friend, Iago, If thou but think'st him wrong'd and makest his ear A stranger to thy thoughts iii 3 142
Cassio's my worthy friend—My lord, I see you're moved iii 3 223
From hence I'll love no friend, sith love breeds such offence iii 3 380
My friend is dead; 'tis done at your request iii 3 474
O Cassio, whence came this? This is some token from a newer friend iii 4 181
To be naked with her friend in bed An hour or more, not meaning any harm? iv 1 3
Forsook so many noble matches, Her father and her country and her friends iv 2 126
O good Iago, What shall I do to win my lord again? Good friend, go to him iv 2 150
Iago, honest and just, That hast such noble sense of thy friend's wrong! v 1 32
Know we this face or no? Alas, my friend and my dear countryman! v 1 89
He that lies slain here, Cassio, Was my dear friend v 1 102
I say thy husband: dost understand the word? My friend, thy husband v 2 154
That war had end, and the time's state Made friends of them *A. and C.* i 2 96
The letters too Of many our contriving friends in Rome Petition us at home i 2 189
Noble friends, That which combined us was most great ii 2 17
If thou say Antony lives, is well, Or friends with Cæsar, or not captive to him, I'll set thee in a shower of gold ii 5 44
Madam, he's well.—Well said.—And friends with Cæsar ii 5 47
Cæsar and he are greater friends than ever ii 5 48
Prithee, friend, Pour out the pack of matter to mine ear ii 5 53
He's friends with Cæsar; In state of health thou say'st; and thou say'st free ii 5 55
I do not know Wherefore my father should revengers want, Having a son and friends ii 6 12
You have my father's house,—But, what? we are friends ii 7 135
My heart parted betwixt two friends That do afflict each other! iii 6 77
Friends, come hither: I am so lated in the world, that I Have lost my way iii 11 2
Friends, be gone; I have myself resolved upon a course Which has no need of you iii 11 8
Friends, be gone: you shall Have letters from me to some friends that will Sweep your way for you iii 11 15
So she From Egypt drive her all-disgraced friend iii 12 22

Friend. Hear it apart.—None but friends: say boldly.—So, haply, are they friends to Antony *Ant. and Cleo.* iii 13 47
If Cæsar please, our master Will leap to be his friend iii 13 51
Mine honest friends, I turn you not away iv 2 29
My hearty friends, You take me in too dolorous a sense iv 2 38
Enter the city, clip your wives, your friends, Tell them your feats iv 8 8
I'll give thee, friend, An armour all of gold; it was a king's iv 8 26
And carouse together Like friends long lost iv 12 13
I have done my work ill friends: O, make an end Of what I have begun iv 14 105
Bear me, good friends, where Cleopatra bides iv 14 131
Carry me now, good friends, And have my thanks for all iv 14 139
Assist, good friends.—O, quick, or I am gone iv 15 31
We have no friend But resolution, and the briefest end iv 15 90
Look you sad, friends? The gods rebuke me, but it is tidings To wash the eyes of kings v 1 26
My mate in empire, Friend and companion in the front of war v 1 44
Hear me, good friends,—But I will tell you at some meeter season v 1 48
His voice was propertied As all the tuned spheres, and that to friends v 2 84
Immoment toys, things of such dignity As we greet modern friends withal v 2 167
Our care and pity is so much upon you, That we remain your friend v 2 189
Who to my father was a friend, to me Known but by letter *Cymbeline* i 1 98
I never do him wrong, But he does buy my injuries, to be friends i 1 105
Your son's my father's friend; he takes his part i 1 165
Whom I commend to you as a noble friend of mine i 4 33
Though I profess myself her adorer, not her friend i 4 74
Had I admittance and opportunity to friend i 4 116
Who cannot be new built, nor has no friends, So much as but to prop him i 5 59
Boldness be my friend! Arm me, audacity, from head to foot! i 6 18
Myself and other noble friends Are partners in the business i 6 183
There's an Italian come; and, 'tis thought, one of Leonatus' friends ii 1 41
I hope you know that we Must not continue friends.—Good sir, we must ii 4 49
Be sprightly, for you fall 'mongst friends.—'Mongst friends, If brothers iii 6 75
My friends, The boy hath taught us manly duties iv 2 396
For friends kill friends, and the disorder's such As war were hoodwink'd v 2 15
Some slain before; some dying; some their friends O'er-borne v 3 47
Who dares not stand his foe, I'll be his friend v 3 60
Wilt have him live? Is he thy kin? thy friend?—He is a Roman v 5 111
This we desire, As friends to Antioch, we may feast in Tyre *Pericles* i 3 40
He asks of you, that never used to beg.—No, friend, cannot you beg? ii 1 67
Hark you, my friend; you said you could not beg.—I did but crave ii 1 89
Are all your beggars whipped, then?—O, not all, my friend, not all ii 1 95
An armour, friends! I pray you, let me see it ii 1 126
What mean you, sir?—To beg of you, kind friends, this coat of worth ii 1 142
Ay, but hark you, my friend; 'twas we that made up this garment ii 1 154
Only, my friend, I yet am unprovided Of a pair of bases ii 1 166
This world to me is like a lasting storm, Whirring me from my friends iv 1 21
Thou look'st Like one I loved indeed. What were thy friends? v 1 126
What were thy friends? How lost thou them? Thy name? v 1 140
My companion friends, If this but answer to my just belief, I'll well remember you v 1 238
Friended. For the fault's love is the offender friended *Meas. for Meas.* iv 2 116
Not friended by his wish, to your high person His will is most malignant; and it stretches Beyond you *Hen. VIII.* i 2 140
And be friended With aptness of the season *Cymbeline* ii 3 52
Friending. What so poor a man as Hamlet is May do, to express his love and friending to you, God willing, shall not lack *Hamlet* i 5 186
Friendless. Alas, I am a woman, friendless, hopeless! *Hen. VIII.* iii 1 80
Friendliness. Of such childish friendliness *Coriolanus* ii 3 183
Friendly. Not depending on his friendly wish *T. G. of Ver.* i 3 62
Then you do not love me?—No, truly, but in friendly recompense *M. Ado* v 4 83
It is not friendly, 'tis not maidenly *M. N. Dream* iii 2 217
The fiend gives the more friendly counsel: I will run, fiend *Mer. of Venice* ii 2 32
For I must tell you friendly in your ear, Sell when you can *As Y. Like It* iii 5 59
Give them friendly welcome every one: Let them want nothing *T. of Shrew* Ind. 1 103
Since this bar in law makes us friends, it shall be so far forth friendly maintained i 1 141
And in my house you shall be friendly lodged iv 2 107
And let me buy your friendly help thus far *All's Well* iii 7 15
I will seem friendly, as thou hast advised me *W. Tale* i 2 350
Thence, A prosperous south-wind friendly, we have cross'd v 1 161
Why answer not the double majesties This friendly treaty? *K. John* ii 1 481
Let's drink together friendly and embrace *2 Hen. IV.* iv 2 63
In the way of argument, look you, and friendly communication *Hen. V.* iii 2 104
For friendly counsel cuts off many foes *1 Hen. VI.* iii 1 185
Therefore are we certainly resolved To draw conditions of a friendly peace v 1 38
Give me assurance with some friendly vow *3 Hen. VI.* iv 1 141
I desire To reconcile me to his friendly peace *Richard III.* ii 1 59
For I must think of that which company Would not be friendly to *Hen. VIII.* v 1 76
Translate his malice towards you into love, Standing your friendly lord *Coriolanus* ii 3 198
O, come, go in, And take our friendly senators by the hands iv 5 138
Tradesmen singing in their shops and going About their functions friendly iv 6 9
I ask your voices and your suffrages: Will you bestow them friendly? *T. Andron.* i 1 219
Did you not use his daughter very friendly? iv 2 40
O churl! drunk all, and left no friendly drop To help me after! *R. and J.* v 3 163
Nothing but himself which looks like man Is friendly with him *T. of A.* v 1 122
So thou wilt send thy gentle heart before, To say thou'lt enter friendly v 4 49
Nor with such free and friendly conference As he hath used of old *J. C.* iv 2 17
A friendly eye could never see such faults.—A flatterer's would not iv 3 90
The gods to-day stand friendly! v 1 94
Now, my friendly knave, I thank thee: there's earnest of thy service *Lear* i 4 103
Now let thy friendly hand Put strength enough to't iv 6 234
I will have my lord and you again As friendly as you were *Othello* iii 3 7
Your mother came to Sicily and did find Her welcome friendly *A. and C.* ii 6 47
Your hand, my lord.—Receive it friendly *Cymbeline* iii 5 13
Let A Roman and a British ensign wave Friendly together v 5 481
My authority shall not see thee, or else look friendly upon thee *Pericles* iv 6 97
Friendship. That which I would discover The law of friendship bids me to conceal *T. G. of Ver.* iii 1 5
I desire you in friendship *Mer. Wives* iii 1 89
Friendship. Friendship is constant in all other things Save in the office and affairs of love: Therefore all hearts in love use their own tongues *Much Ado* ii 1 182
Is there any way to show such friendship?—A very even way, but no such friend iv 1 265
And hold fair friendship with his majesty *L. L. Lost* ii 1 141
O, is it all forgot? All school-days' friendship? *M. N. Dream* iii 2 202
When did friendship take A breed for barren metal of his friend? *M. of V.* i 3 134
To buy his favour, I extend this friendship: If he will take it, so i 3 169
I do in friendship counsel you To leave this place *As Y. Like It* i 2 273
Most friendship is feigning, most loving mere folly ii 7 181
When thy father and myself in friendship First tried our soldiership *All's Well* i 2 25
To mingle friendship far is mingling bloods *W. Tale* i 2 109
With a countenance as clear As friendship wears at feasts i 2 344
And my profit therein the heaping friendships iv 2 22
Hal, if thou see me down in the battle and bestride me, so; 'tis a point of friendship.—Nothing but a colossus can do thee that friendship *1 Hen. IV.* v 1 122
Liquor likewise will I give to thee, And friendship shall combine *Hen. V.* ii 1 114
Die and be damn'd! and figo for thy friendship! iii 6 60
I will cap that proverb with 'There is flattery in friendship' iii 7 125
Trouble us no more; But join in friendship *1 Hen. VI.* iii 1 145
Thy friendship makes us fresh.—And doth beget new courage in our breasts iii 3 86
They are so link'd in friendship *3 Hen. VI.* iv 1 116
He little thought of this divided friendship *Richard III.* i 4 244
You have no cause to hold my friendship doubtful iv 4 493
Nor no more assurance Of equal friendship *Hen. VIII.* ii 4 18
Desert in service, Love, friendship, charity, are subjects all To envious and calumniating time *Troi. and Cres.* iii 3 173
Because thou canst not ease thy smart By friendship nor by speaking iv 4 21
I will be gone, sir, and not trouble you.—So shalt thou show me friendship. Take thou that *Rom. and Jul.* v 3 41
Where there is true friendship, there needs none *T. of Athens* i 2 18
Friendship's full of dregs i 2 239
This is no time to lend money, especially upon bare friendship iii 1 45
Has friendship such a faint and milky heart, It turns in less than two nights? iii 1 57
That their society, as their friendship, may Be merely poison! iv 1 31
Who would be so mock'd with glory? or to live But in a dream of friendship? iv 2 34
What friendship may I do thee?—None, but to Maintain my opinion iv 3 70
Promise me friendship, but perform none iv 3 72
Better than to close In terms of friendship with thine enemies *J. Cæsar* iii 1 203
But, in the beaten way of friendship, what make you at Elsinore? *Ham.* ii 2 277
Love cools, friendship falls off, brothers divide *Lear* i 2 116
Hard by here is a hovel; Some friendship will it lend you 'gainst the tempest iii 2 62
If I do vow a friendship, I'll perform it To the last article *Othello* iii 3 21
For't cannot be We shall remain in friendship, our conditions So differing in their acts *Ant. and Cleo.* ii 2 115
You shall find, the band that seems to tie their friendship together will be the very strangler of their amity ii 6 129
I know he'll quickly fly my friendship too *Cymbeline* v 3 62
Frieze. No jutty, frieze, Buttress, nor coign of vantage *Macbeth* i 6 6
Fright. O, 'twas a din to fright a monster's ear! *Tempest* ii 1 314
Fright me with urchin-shows, pitch me i' the mire ii 2 5
Here's a fellow frights English out of his wits *Mer Wives* ii 1 143
First, an intolerable fright, to be detected with a jealous rotten bell-wether iii 5 110
The devil will shake her chain and fright us with it *Com. of Errors* iv 3 77
And why?—To fright them hence with that dread penalty *L. L. Lost* i 1 128
No devil will fright thee then so much as she iv 3 275
An you should do it too terribly, you would fright the duchess *M. N. D.* i 2 77
If that you should fright the ladies out of their wits i 2 82
Are not you he That frights the maidens of the villagery? ii 1 35
This is to make an ass of me; to fright me, if they could iii 1 124
And what's worse, To fright the animals and to kill them *As Y. Like It* ii 1 62
This will so fright them both that they will kill one another *T. Night* iii 4 214
If spirits can assume both form and suit You come to fright us v 1 243
Come on, and do your best To fright me with your sprites *W. Tale* ii 1 28
On her frights and griefs, Which never tender lady hath borne greater, She is something before her time deliver'd ii 2 23
Spare your threats: The bug which you would fright me with I seek iii 2 93
Startles and frights consideration, Makes sound opinion sick *K. John* iv 2 25
What, shall they seek the lion in his den, And fright him there? v 1 58
Might from our quiet confines fright fair peace *Richard II.* i 3 137
And fright our native peace with self-born arms ii 3 80
And meteors fright the fixed stars of heaven ii 4 9
Where hateful death put on his ugliest mask To fright our party *2 Hen. IV.* i 1 67
I'll forswear keeping house, afore I'll be in these tirrits and frights ii 4 221
That, when I come to woo ladies, I fright them *Hen. V.* v 2 246
It were enough to fright the realm of France *1 Hen. VI.* iv 7 82
Out of my sight! Upon thy eye-balls murderous tyranny Sits in grim majesty, to fright the world *2 Hen. VI.* iii 2 50
Nay, do not fright us with an angry look v 1 126
Mounting barbed steeds To fright the souls of fearful adversaries *Rich. III.* i 1 11
Whose ugly and unnatural aspect May fright the hopeful mother i 2 24
Frights, changes, horrors, Divert and crack, rend and deracinate *T. and C.* i 3 98
Or rudely visit them in parts remote, To fright them, ere destroy *Coriol.* iv 5 149
And would not, but in fury, fright my youth *T. Andron.* i 1 24
Ay, let the county take you in your bed; He'll fright you up *R. and J.* iv 5 11
I never stood on ceremonies, Yet now they fright me *J. Cæsar* ii 2 14
To fright you thus, methinks, I am too savage *Macbeth* iv 2 70
Silence that dreadful bell: it frights the isle From her propriety *Othello* ii 3 175
Lest by his clamour—as it so fell out—The town might fall in fright ii 3 232
Therefore these stops of thine fright me the more iii 3 120
Frighted. Thou hast frighted the word out of his right sense *Much Ado* v 2 55
Hath that awaken'd you?—Ay, but not frighted me *T. of Shrew* v 2 43
For the flowers now, that frighted thou let'st fall From Dis's waggon! *W. Tale* iv 4 117
Find we a time for frighted peace to pant *1 Hen. IV.* i 1 2
And the herds Were strangely clamorous to the frighted fields iii 1 40
O gentle sleep, Nature's soft nurse, how have I frighted thee? *2 Hen. IV.* iii 1 6
But those, we fear, We have frighted with our trumpets *Hen. VIII.* Epil. 4
Where ladies shall be frighted, And, gladly quaked, hear more *Coriol.* i 9 5
And being thus frighted swears a prayer or two And sleeps again *R. and J.* i 4 87
Shall I be frighted when a madman stares? *J. Cæsar* iv 3 40
What, frighted with false fire! *Hamlet* iii 2 277

Frighted. What though you fled From that great face of war, whose several ranges Frighted each other? *Ant. and Cleo.* iii 13 6
To be furious, Is to be frighted out of fear iii 13 196
I am sprited with a fool, Frighted, and anger'd worse *Cymbeline* ii 3 145
Frighted from my country, did wed At Pentapolis the fair Thaisa *Pericles* v 3 3
Frightful. Their music frightful as the serpent's hiss! 2 *Hen. VI.* iii 2 326
Thy school-days frightful, desperate, wild, and furious *Richard III.* iv 4 169
Frighting. Thou shalt be punish'd for thus frighting me *K. John* iii 1 11
Frighting her pale-faced villages with war *Richard II.* ii 3 94
A plague break thy neck for frighting me! *Troi. and Cres.* v 4 34
Fringe. Like fringe upon a petticoat *As Y. Like It* iii 2 354
Her eyelids . . . Begin to part their fringes of bright gold *Pericles* iii 2 101
Fringed. The fringed curtains of thine eye advance *Tempest* i 2 408
Frippery. O, ho, monster! we know what belongs to a frippery iv 1 226
Frisk. We were as twinn'd lambs that did frisk i' the sun *W. Tale* i 2 67
Fritter. Have I lived to stand at the taunt of one that makes fritters of English? *Mer. Wives* v 5 151
Frivolous. To leave frivolous circumstances *T. of Shrew* v 1 28
For so slight and frivolous a cause 1 *Hen. VI.* iv 1 112
Your oath, my lord, is vain and frivolous 3 *Hen. VI.* i 2 27
Frize. Shall I have a coxcomb of frize? *Mer. Wives* v 5 146
My invention Comes from my pate as birdlime does from frize *Othello* ii 1 127
Fro. I was employ'd in passing to and fro 1 *Hen. VI.* ii 1 69
Early and late, debating to and fro 2 *Hen. VI.* i 1 91
Was ever feather so lightly blown to and fro as this multitude? iv 8 58
Frock. That to the use of actions fair and good He likewise gives a frock or livery *Hamlet* iii 4 164
Frog. Eye of newt and toe of frog, Wool of bat and tongue of dog *Macb.* iv 1 14
That eats the swimming frog, the toad, the tadpole, the wall-newt *Lear* iii 4 134
Frogmore. Go you through the town to Frogmore *Mer. Wives* ii 3 78
Go about the fields with me through Frogmore ii 3 90
There comes my master, Master Shallow, and another gentleman, from Frogmore iii 1 33
Froissart, a countryman of ours, records 1 *Hen. VI.* i 2 29
Frolic. Following darkness like a dream, Now are frolic *M. N. Dream* v 1 394
If thou account'st it shame, lay it on me; And therefore frolic *T. of S.* iv 3 184
From. Which is from my remembrance *Tempest* i 2 65
The setting of thine eye and cheek proclaim A matter from thee ii 1 230
It is my promise, And they expect it from me iv 1 42
Why, couldst thou perceive so much from her? *T. G. of Ver.* i 1 142
I had other things to have spoken with her too from him *Mer. Wives* iv 5 42
He would give't thee, from this rank offence, So to offend him still *Meas. for Meas.* iii 1 100
To cram a maw or clothe a back From such a filthy vice iii 2 24
If aught possess thee from me, it is dross, Usurping ivy *Com. of Errors* ii 2 179
Not to be so odd and from all fashions *Much Ado* iii 1 72
Happiest of all is that her gentle spirit Commits itself to yours to be directed, As from her lord *Mer. of Venice* iii 2 167
I wish you all the joy that you can wish; For I am sure you can wish none from me iii 2 193
Uncapable of pity, void and empty From any dram of mercy iv 1 6
And so, from hour to hour, we ripe and ripe *As Y. Like It* ii 7 26
Upon agreement from us to his liking, Will undertake to woo *T. of Shrew* i 2 183
Why, then the maid is mine from all the world ii 1 386
I am from humble, he from honour'd name *All's Well* i 3 162
Humbly entreating from your royal thoughts A modest one ii 1 130
I have, sir, as I was commanded from you, Spoke with the king ii 5 59
But this is from my commission *T. Night* i 5 201
For a pension of thousands to be paid from the Sophy ii 5 197
You must not now deny it is your hand: Write from it, if you can v 1 340
Who in that sale sells pardon from himself *K. John* iii 1 167
I am best pleased to be from such a deed iv 1 86
Which robs my tongue from breathing native breath *Richard II.* i 3 173
Our scene is alter'd from a serious thing v 3 79
Quite from the flight of all thy ancestors 1 *Hen. IV.* iii 2 31
Holds from all soldiers chief majority iii 2 109
Stand from him, fellow: wherefore hang'st upon him? 2 *Hen. IV.* ii 1 74
And heir from heir shall hold this quarrel up iv 2 48
Stand from him, give him air; he'll straight be well iv 4 116
I must speak with him from the pridge *Hen. V.* iii 6 91
So great an honour As one man more, methinks, would share from me iv 3 32
Quite from the answer of his degree iv 7 142
Giving full trophy, signal and ostent Quite from himself to God v Prol. 22
From thee to die were torture more than death 2 *Hen. VI.* iii 2 401
We will not from the helm to sit and weep 3 *Hen. VI.* v 4 21
That thou dost love my daughter from thy soul: So from thy soul's love didst thou love her brothers; And from my heart's love I do thank thee *Richard III.* iv 4 258
This top-proud fellow, Whom from the flow of gall I name not *Hen. VIII.* i 1 152
Ay, utterly Grow from the king's acquaintance iii 1 161
Heaven, from thy endless goodness, send prosperous life! v 5 1
And will be led At your request a little from himself *Troi. and Cres.* ii 3 191
O, doubt not that; I speak from certainties *Coriolanus* i 2 31
Mark you His absolute 'shall'?—'Twas from the canon iii 1 90
His particular to foresee, Smells from the general weal *T. of Athens* iv 3 160
But thus condition'd: thou shalt build from men iv 3 533
Clean from the purpose of the things themselves *J. Cæsar* i 3 35
Why birds and beasts from quality and kind, Why old men fool i 3 64
Quite from the main opinion he held once Of fantasy, of dreams ii 1 196
He bade me, from him, call thee thane of Cawdor *Macbeth* i 3 105
For't must be done to-night, And something from the palace iii 1 132
To feed were best at home; From thence the sauce to meat is ceremony iii 4 36
For from broad words . . . I hear Macduff lives in disgrace iii 6 21
But what, in faith, make you from Wittenberg? *Hamlet* i 2 168
For any thing so overdone is from the purpose of playing iii 2 22
The orbs From whom we do exist, and cease to be *Lear* i 1 114
I have this present evening from my sister Been well inform'd of them ii 1 103
Of differences, which I least thought it fit To answer from our home ii 1 126
Do not believe That, from the sense of all civility, I thus would play *Oth.* i 1 132
Make thee a fortune from me *Ant. and Cleo.* ii 5 49
Be pleased to tell us—For this is from the present ii 6 30
Promise . . . what she requires; add more, From thine invention, offers iii 12 29
Words him, I doubt not, a great deal from the matter *Cymbeline* i 4 17
Will this hold, think you?—Signior Iachimo will not from it i 4 184
From every one The best she hath, and she, of all compounded iii 5 72
To royalty unlearn'd, honour untaught, Civility not seen from other iv 2 179
Whose containing Is so from sense in hardness v 5 431
Like an arrow shot From a well-experienced archer hits the mark *Pericles* i 1 164
From above. My profession's sacred from above 1 *Hen. VI.* i 2 114
From among. Perhaps she cull'd it from among the rest *T. Andron.* iv 1 44

From behind. They threw me off from behind one of them *Mer. Wives* iv 5 69
Come, come from behind; I know thee well 1 *Hen. VI.* i 2 66
From below your duke to beneath your constable *All's Well* ii 2 32
Pluck stout men's pillows from below their heads *T. of Athens* iv 3 32
From forth. Let them from forth a sawpit rush at once *Mer. Wives* iv 4 53
To choose from forth the royal blood of France *All's Well* ii 1 199
A prophet, that I brought with me From forth the streets *K. John* iv 2 148
From forth this morsel of dead royalty, The life . . . Is fled iv 3 143
Bear me hence From forth the noise and rumour of the field v 4 45
From forth thy reach he would have laid thy shame *Richard II.* ii 1 106
Rescued the Black Prince, that young Mars of men, From forth the ranks of many thousand French ii 3 102
From forth the kennel of thy womb hath crept A hell-hound *Rich. III.* iv 4 47
As 'twere from forth us all, a man distill'd Out of our virtues *T. and C.* i 3 350
Till from forth this place I lead espoused my bride *T. Andron.* i 1 327
From forth the fatal loins of these two foes *Rom. and Jul.* Prol. 5
I will choose Mine heir from forth the beggars of the world *T. of Athens* i 1 138
From forth thy plenteous bosom, one poor root! iv 3 186
From home. He breaks the pale And feeds from home *Com. of Errors* ii 1 101
Now powers from home and discontents at home Meet in one line *K. John* iv 3 151
From off. Take this transformed scalp From off the head *M. N. Dream* iv 1 70
Till thou canst rail the seal from off my bond *Mer. of Venice* iv 1 139
And you must cut this flesh from off his breast iv 1 302
Dare not shake the snow from off their cassocks *All's Well* iv 3 191
Would I might never stir from off this place *K. John* i 1 145
From off our towers we might behold, From first to last ii 1 325
To wash your blood From off my hands *Richard II.* iii 1 6
The cloak of night being pluck'd from off their backs iii 2 45
I give this heavy weight from off my head And this unwieldy sceptre from my hand, The pride of kingly sway from out my heart iv 1 204
May make a peaceful and a sweet retire From off these fields *Hen. V.* iv 3 87
From off this brier pluck a white rose with me 1 *Hen. VI.* ii 4 30
From off the gates of York fetch down the head 3 *Hen. VI.* ii 6 52
In peril of precipitation From off the rock Tarpeian *Coriolanus* iii 3 103
Bid me leap, rather than marry Paris, From off the battlements *R. and J.* iv 1 78
He was carried From off our coast, twice beaten *Cymbeline* iii 1 26
From out. How little is the cost I have bestow'd In purchasing the semblance of my soul From out the state of hellish misery! *M. of V.* iii 4 21
To whip this dwarfish war, these pigmy arms, From out the circle of his territories *K. John* v 2 136
From out the fiery portal of the east *Richard II.* iii 3 64
Are you call'd forth from out a world of men To slay the innocent? *Richard III.* i 4 186
From under. When from under this terrestrial ball He fires the proud tops of the eastern pines *Richard II.* iii 2 41
Raising up wicked spirits from under ground 2 *Hen. VI.* ii 1 174
Front. 'Accost' is front her, board her, woo her, assail her *T. Night* i 3 59
No shepherdess, but Flora Peering in April's front *W. Tale* iv 4 3
Why stand these royal fronts amazed thus? *K. John* ii 1 356
Sirs, you four shall front them in the narrow lane 1 *Hen. IV.* ii 2 62
At my nativity The front of heaven was full of fiery shapes iii 1 14
What well-appointed leader fronts us here? 2 *Hen. IV.* iv 1 25
Two mighty monarchies, Whose high upreared and abutting fronts The perilous narrow ocean parts asunder *Hen. V.* Prol. 21
But death doth front thee with apparent spoil 1 *Hen. VI.* iv 2 26
Boldly stand and front him to his face 2 *Hen. VI.* v 1 86
All abreast, Charged our main battle's front 3 *Hen. VI.* i 1 8
Grim-visaged war hath smooth'd his wrinkled front *Richard III.* i 1 9
And front but in that file Where others tell steps with me *Hen. VIII.* i 2 42
Yonder walls, that partly front your town *Troi. and Cres.* iv 5 219
Our powers, with smiling fronts encountering *Coriolanus* i 6 8
Think to front his revenges with the easy groans of old woman? v 2 44
Front to front Bring thou this fiend of Scotland and myself *Macbeth* iv 3 232
Had he his hurts before?—Ay, on the front v 8 47
Hyperion's curls; the front of Jove himself; An eye like Mars *Hamlet* iii 4 56
Like the wreath of radiant fire On flickering Phœbus' front *Lear* ii 2 114
The very head and front of my offending Hath this extent, no more *Oth.* i 3 80
To take the safest occasion by the front To bring you in again iii 1 52
Those his goodly eyes . . . now bend, now turn, The office and devotion of their view Upon a tawny front *Ant. and Cleo.* i 1 6
Both what by sea and land I can be able To front this present time i 4 79
My mate in empire, Friend and companion in the front of war v 1 44
Fronted. Those wars Which fronted mine own peace ii 2 61
Frontier. And majesty might never yet endure The moody frontier of a servant brow 1 *Hen. IV.* i 3 19
Of palisadoes, frontiers, parapets, Of basilisks, of cannon, culverin ii 3 55
Goes it against the main of Poland, sir, Or for some frontier? *Hamlet* iv 4 16
Fronting. With what wings shall his affections fly Towards fronting peril! 2 *Hen. IV.* iv 4 66
Like a gate of steel Fronting the sun *Troi. and Cres.* iii 3 122
Frontlet. How now, daughter! what makes that frontlet on? Methinks you are too much of late i' the frown *Lear* i 4 208
Frost. To do me business in the veins o' the earth When it is baked with frost *Tempest* i 2 256
You have such a February face, So full of frost, of storm *Much Ado* v 4 42
Biron is like an envious sneaping frost That bites the first-born infants of the spring *L. L. Lost* i 1 100
If frosts and fasts, hard lodging and thin weeds Nip not the gaudy blossoms of your love v 2 811
Hoary-headed frosts Fall in the fresh lap of the crimson rose *M. N. D.* ii 1 107
Your suit is cold. Cold, indeed; and labour lost: Then, farewell, heat, and welcome, frost! *Mer. of Venice* ii 7 75
Is she so hot a shrew as she's reported?—She was, good Curtis, before this frost *T. of Shrew* iv 1 23
It blots thy beauty as frosts do bite the meads v 2 139
Which to prove fruit, Hope gives not so much warrant as despair That frosts will bite them 2 *Hen. IV.* i 3 41
The third day comes a frost, a killing frost *Hen. VIII.* iii 2 355
Chaste as the icicle That's curdied by the frost from purest snow *Cor.* v 3 66
These tidings nip me, and I hang the head As flowers with frost *T. An.* iv 4 71
Death lies on her like an untimely frost Upon the sweetest flower of all the field *Rom. and Jul.* iv 5 28
Since frost itself as actively doth burn And reason pandars will *Hamlet* iii 4 87
Frosty. My age is as a lusty winter, Frosty, but kindly *As Y. Like It* ii 3 53
Who can hold a fire in his hand By thinking on the frosty Caucasus? *Richard II.* i 3 295
Ay, by my faith, that bears a frosty sound 1 *Hen. IV.* iv 1 128
Shall our quick blood, spirited with wine, Seem frosty? *Hen. V.* iii 5 22
Let us not hang like roping icicles Upon our houses' thatch, whiles a more frosty people Sweat drops of gallant youth in our rich fields! iii 5 24

Frosty. O, where is loyalty? If it be banish'd from the frosty head 2 *Hen. VI.* v 1 167
For all the frosty nights that I have watch'd . . . *T. Andron.* iii 1 5
My frosty signs and chaps of age, Grave witnesses of true experience . v 3 77
Frosty-spirited. What a frosty-spirited rogue is this! . . 1 *Hen. IV.* ii 3 21
Froth and scum, thou liest! . . . . *Mer. Wives* i 1 167
Let me see thee froth and lime . . . . i 3 15
Look into Master Froth here, sir; a man of fourscore pound a year *Meas. for Meas.* ii 1 127
How could Master Froth do the constable's wife any harm? . . . ii 1 165
Master Froth, I would not have you acquainted with tapsters . . ii 1 214
Swallowed with yest and froth, as you'ld thrust a cork into a hogshead *W. Tale* iii 3 95
Go, suck the subtle blood o' the grape, Till the high fever seethe your blood to froth, And so 'scape hanging . . . *T. of Athens* iv 3 433
Who once a day with his embossed froth The turbulent surge shall cover v 1 220
Froward. She is peevish, sullen, froward, Proud . . *T. G. of Ver.* iii 1 68
That wench is stark mad or wonderful froward . . *T. of Shrew* i 1 69
She is intolerable curst And shrewd and froward, so beyond all measure i 2 90
For she's not froward, but modest as the dove . . . . ii 1 295
If she be froward, Then hast thou taught Hortensio to be untoward . iv 5 78
See where she comes and brings your froward wives . . . . v 2 119
When she is froward, peevish, sullen, sour, And not obedient. . . v 2 157
Come, come, your froward and unable worms! . . . . . . v 2 169
'Tis a good hearing when children are toward.—But a harsh hearing when women are froward . . . . v 2 183
Thou art a most pernicious usurer, Froward by nature . 1 *Hen. VI.* iii 1 18
Ah, froward Clarence! how evil it beseems thee! . . 3 *Hen. VI.* iv 7 84
Frown. The sole drift of my purpose doth extend Not a frown further *Tempest* v 1 30
Were I so minded, I here could pluck his highness' frown upon you . v 1 127
How angerly I taught my brow to frown! . . . . . *T. G. of Ver.* i 2 62
Sir Thurio frowns on you.—Ay, boy, it's for love.—Not of you . . ii 4 3
If she do frown, 'tis not in hate of you, But rather to beget more love in you . . . . iii 1 96
Look strange and frown: Some other mistress hath thy sweet aspects *Com. of Errors* ii 2 112
I frown upon him, yet he loves me still.—O that your frowns would teach my smiles such skill! . . . . . . *M. N. Dream* i 1 194
He doth nothing but frown, as who should say 'If you will not have me, choose' . . . . *Mer. of Venice* i 2 50
I do frown on thee with all my heart; And if mine eyes can wound, now let them kill thee . . . . *As Y. Like It* iii 5 15
Her frown might kill me.—By this hand, it will not kill a fly . . iv 1 110
Say that she frown; I'll say she looks as clear As morning roses *T. of S.* ii 1 173
Thou canst not frown, thou canst not look askance, Nor bite the lip . ii 1 249
Gentles, methinks you frown . . . . iii 2 95
Look not pale, Bianca; thy father will not frown . . . . . v 1 144
To bandy word for word and frown for frown . . . . . . v 2 172
I frown the while; and perchance wind up my watch . . *T. Night* ii 5 65
Bade me . . . To put on yellow stockings and to frown . . . . v 1 346
Copy of the father, eye, nose, lip, The trick of 's frown, his forehead *W. T.* ii 3 100
The heavens with that we have in hand are angry And frown upon 's . iii 3 6
The day frowns more and more . . . . iii 3 54
The grappling vigour and rough frown of war . . . . *K. John* iii 1 104
These eyes that never did nor never shall So much as frown on you . iv 1 58
Perchance it frowns More upon humour than advised respect . . iv 2 213
If thou but frown on me, or stir thy foot . . . . iv 3 96
And heaven itself doth frown upon the land . . . . . . iv 3 159
To dog his heels and curtsy at his frowns . . . 1 *Hen. IV.* iii 2 127
Approach The ragged'st hour that time and spite dare bring To frown upon the enraged Northumberland! . . . . . . 2 *Hen. IV.* i 1 152
The sun looks pale, Killing their fruit with frowns . . *Hen. V.* iii 5 18
Fortune is Bardolph's foe, and frowns on him . . . . . . iii 6 41
But, if you frown upon this proffer'd peace, You tempt the fury 1 *Hen. VI.* iv 2 9
These brows of mine, Whose smile and frown, like to Achilles' spear, Is able with the change to kill and cure. . . . . . 2 *Hen. VI.* v 1 100
Frowns, words and threats Shall be the war that Henry means to use 3 *Hen. VI.* i 1 72
Whose frown hath made thee faint and fly ere this . . . . . i 4 48
Smile, gentle heaven! or strike, ungentle death! For this world frowns ii 3 7
Good fortune bids us pause, And smooth the frowns of war with peaceful looks . . . . ii 6 32
Our fair queen and mistress Smiles at her news, while Warwick frowns at his . . . . iii 3 168
My love, forbear to fawn upon their frowns . . . . iv 1 75
Shield thee from Warwick's frown; And pray that I may repossess the crown . . . . iv 5 28
Do not frown upon my faults, For I will henceforth be no more unconstant . . . . v 1 101
Let my woes frown on the upper hand . . . . . *Richard III.* iv 4 37
The sun will not be seen to-day; The sky doth frown and lour . . v 3 283
For the selfsame heaven That frowns on me looks sadly upon him . v 3 287
I am fearful: wherefore frowns he thus? . . . . . *Hen. VIII.* v 1 87
In the wind and tempest of her frown . . . . . *Troi. and Cres.* i 3 26
Frown on, you heavens, effect your rage with speed! . . . . v 10 6
You will rather show our general louts How you can frown than spend a fawn upon 'em . . . . *Coriolanus* iii 2 67
Prepare thy brow to frown: know'st thou me yet? . . . . . iv 5 69
Cheer the heart That dies in tempest of thy angry frown . *T. Andron.* i 1 458
And virtue stoops and trembles at her frown . . . . . . ii 1 11
I will frown as I pass by, and let them take it as they list *Rom. and Jul.* i 1 46
Put off these frowns, An ill-beseeming semblance for a feast . . . i 5 75
If thou think'st I am too quickly won, I'll frown and be perverse . . ii 2 96
Methinks you are too much of late i' the frown . . . . . *Lear* i 4 209
Myself could else out-frown false fortune's frown . . . . . v 3 6
Even his stubbornness, his checks, his frowns,—Prithee, unpin me,—have grace and favour in them . . . . *Othello* iv 3 20
Our graver business Frowns at this levity . . . . *Ant. and Cleo.* ii 7 128
You do not meet a man but frowns . . . . . . *Cymbeline* i 1 1
Fear no more the frown o' the great; Thou art past the tyrant's stroke iv 2 264
And may save, But to look back in frown . . . . v 3 28
If there be such a dart in princes' frowns, How durst thy tongue move anger to our face? . . . . *Pericles* i 2 53
Feast here awhile, Until our stars that frown lend us a smile . . i 4 108
Frowned. But when he frown'd, it was against the French *Richard II.* ii 1 178
All without desert have frown'd on me . . . . *Richard III.* ii 1 67
Smile heaven upon this fair conjunction, That long have frown'd upon their enmity! . . . . v 5 21
Against a graver bench Than ever frown'd in Greece . *Coriolanus* iii 1 107
Frowned. So frown'd he once, when, in an angry parle, He smote the sledded Polacks on the ice . . . . *Hamlet* i 1 62
Frowning. A better bad habit of frowning . . . *Mer. of Venice* i 2 64
Wear yet upon their chins The beards of Hercules and frowning Mars . iii 2 85
As fast as she answers thee with frowning looks, I'll sauce her *As Y. L. It* iii 5 68
Hang'd in the frowning wrinkle of her brow! . . . . . *K. John* ii 1 505
Face to face, And frowning brow to brow. . . . . *Richard II.* i 1 16
Knit his brows, As frowning at the favours of the world . 2 *Hen. VI.* i 2 4
Have given their verdict up Unto the frowning judge . *Richard III.* i 4 190
The penance lies on you, if these fair ladies Pass away frowning *Hen. VIII.* i 4 33
He parted frowning from me, as if ruin Leap'd from his eyes . . . iii 2 205
The grey-eyed morn smiles on the frowning night . . *Rom. and Jul.* ii 3 1
Thou wast a pretty fellow when thou hadst no need to care for her frowning . . . . *Lear* i 4 211
When Julius Cæsar Smiled at their lack of skill, but found their courage Worthy his frowning at . . . . *Cymbeline* ii 4 23
He goes hence frowning: but it honours us That we have given him cause . . . . iii 5 18
Frowningly. Look'd he frowningly?—A countenance more in sorrow than in anger . . . . *Hamlet* i 2 231
Froze. And all the conduits of my blood froze up . *Com. of Errors* v 1 313
This word, rebellion, it had froze them up, As fish are in a pond 2 *Hen. IV.* i 1 199
With . . . cold-moving nods They froze me into silence . *T. of Athens* ii 2 222
Frozen. A little time will melt her frozen thoughts . . *T. G. of Ver.* iii 2 9
Twenty adieus, my frozen Muscovits . . . . . . *L. L. Lost* v 2 265
And milk comes frozen home in pail . . . . v 2 925
My master and mistress are almost frozen to death . . *T. of Shrew* iv 1 40
Even to the frozen ridges of the Alps . . . . . *Richard II.* i 1 64
Six frozen winters spent, Return with welcome home from banishment i 3 211
Darest with thy frozen admonition Make pale our cheek . . . . ii 1 117
Throw in the frozen bosoms of our part Hot coals of vengeance! 2 *Hen. VI.* v 2 35
When we both lay in the field Frozen almost to death . *Richard III.* ii 1 115
That kiss is comfortless As frozen water to a starved snake *T. Andron.* iii 1 252
The wind, who wooes Even now the frozen bosom of the north *R. and J.* i 4 101
Fructify. Such barren plants are set before us, that we thankful should be, Which we of taste and feeling are, for those parts that do fructify in us more than he . . . . *L. L. Lost* iv 2 30
Frugal. I was then frugal of my mirth . . . . *Mer. Wives* ii 1 28
Chid I for that at frugal nature's frame? . . . . . *Much Ado* iv 1 130
Fruit. The weakest kind of fruit Drops earliest . . *Mer. of Venice* iv 1 115
Forbear, I say: He dies that touches any of this fruit . *As Y. Like It* ii 7 98
Truly, the tree yields bad fruit . . . . iii 2 123
Graff it with a medlar: then it will be the earliest fruit i' the country . iii 2 126
It may well be called Jove's tree, when it drops forth such fruit . . iii 2 250
If you will then see the fruits of the sport, mark . . . *T. Night* ii 5 217
Shall have no sun to ripe The bloom that promiseth a mighty fruit *K. John* ii 1 473
The ripest fruit first falls, and so doth he; His time is spent *Richard II.* ii 1 153
They might have lived to bear and he to taste Their fruits of duty . iii 4 63
If then the tree may be known by the fruit, as the fruit by the tree 1 *Hen. IV.* ii 4 471
Which to prove fruit, Hope gives not so much warrant as despair 2 *Hen. IV.* i 3 39
But I pray God the fruit of her womb miscarry! . . . . . . v 4 15
And wholesome berries thrive and ripen best Neighbour'd by fruit of baser quality . . . . *Hen. V.* i 1 62
On whom, as in despite, the sun looks pale, Killing their fruit with frowns iii 5 18
She was the first fruit of my bachelorship . . . . 1 *Hen. VI.* v 4 13
Murder not then the fruit within my womb . . . . v 4 63
And noble stock Was graft with crab-tree slip; whose fruit thou art 2 *Hen. VI.* iii 2 214
'Tis the fruits of love I mean.—The fruits of love I mean 3 *Hen. VI.* iii 2 58
The leaves and fruit maintain'd with beauty's sun . . . . . iii 3 126
Lest with my sighs or tears I blast or drown King Edward's fruit. . iv 4 24
An indigested and deformed lump, Not like the fruit of such a goodly tree . . . . v 6 52
And, that I love the tree from whence thou sprang'st, Witness the loving kiss I give the fruit . . . . v 7 32
This is the fruit of rashness! . . . . *Richard III.* ii 1 134
The royal tree hath left us royal fruit . . . . iii 7 167
The fruit she goes with I pray for heartily . . . . *Hen. VIII.* v 1 20
Like fair fruit in an unwholesome dish, Are like to rot untasted *T. and C.* ii 3 129
As Hercules Did shake down mellow fruit . . . . *Coriolanus* iv 6 100
And here's the base fruit of his burning lust . . *T. Andron.* v 1 43
Hang him on this tree, And by his side his fruit of bastardy . . . v 1 48
Now will he sit under a medlar tree, And wish his mistress were that kind of fruit As maids call medlars . . . . . *Rom. and Jul.* ii 1 35
My news shall be the fruit to that great feast . . . . . *Hamlet* ii 2 52
Which done, she took the fruits of my advice . . . . . . ii 2 145
Like fruit unripe, sticks on the tree; But fall, unshaken, when they mellow be . . . . iii 2 200
The purchase made, the fruits are to ensue . . . . . *Othello* ii 3 9
Fruits that blossom first will first be ripe . . . . ii 3 383
Alas, good Cassio!—This is the fruit of whoring . . . . . v 1 116
Then was I as a tree Whose boughs did bend with fruit . . *Cymbeline* iii 3 61
Hang there like fruit, my soul, Till the tree die! . . . . . v 5 263
To taste the fruit of yon celestial tree, Or die in the adventure *Pericles* i 1 21
Before thee stands this fair Hesperides, With golden fruit, but dangerous i 1 28
Fruit-dish. A fruit-dish, a dish of some three-pence . *Meas. for Meas.* ii 1 95
Fruiterer. One Sampson Stockfish, a fruiterer . . . 2 *Hen. IV.* iii 2 36
Fruitful. One fruitful meal would set me to't . . . *Meas. for Meas.* iv 3 161
Weed this wormwood from your fruitful brain . . . . *L. L. Lost* v 2 857
I am arrived for fruitful Lombardy . . . . *T. of Shrew* i 1 3
Besides two thousand ducats by the year Of fruitful land . . . ii 1 372
Thy promises are like Adonis' gardens That one day bloom'd and fruitful were the next . . . . 1 *Hen. VI.* i 6 7
And suffer you to breathe in fruitful peace . . . . v 4 127
Usurping boar, That spoil'd your summer fields and fruitful vines *Richard III.* v 2 8
A hand as fruitful as the land that feeds us . . . . *Hen. VIII.* i 3 56
A recompense more fruitful Than their offence can weigh down *T. of A.* v 1 153
Nor the fruitful river in the eye, Nor the dejected 'haviour . *Hamlet* i 2 80
Suspend thy purpose, if thou didst intend To make this creature fruitful! *Lear* i 4 299
She's framed as fruitful As the free elements . . . . *Othello* ii 3 347
Nay, if an oily palm be not a fruitful prognostication . *Ant. and Cleo.* i 2 53
Ram thou thy fruitful tidings in mine ears, That long time have been barren . . . . ii 5 24
In Britain where was he That could stand up his parallel; Or fruitful object be In eye of Imogen? . . . . *Cymbeline* v 4 55

Fruitfully. You understand me?—Most fruitfully . . . *All's Well* ii 2 73
If your will want not, time and place will be fruitfully offered . *Lear* iv 6 270
Fruitfulness. This argues fruitfulness and liberal heart . . *Othello* iii 4 38
Fruition. So am I driven by breath of her renown Either to suffer shipwreck or arrive Where I may have fruition of her love . 1 *Hen. VI.* v 5 9
Fruitless. Chanting faint hymns to the cold fruitless moon *M. N. Dream* i 1 73
All this derision Shall seem a dream and fruitless vision . . iii 2 371
How many fruitless pranks This ruffian hath botch'd up . *T. Night* iv 1 59
Upon my head they placed a fruitless crown . . . *Macbeth* iii 1 61
Fruit-tree. Her fruit-trees all unpruned, her hedges ruin'd *Richard II.* iii 4 45
We at time of year Do wound the bark, the skin of our fruit-trees . iii 4 58
That tips with silver all these fruit-tree tops . . . *Rom. and Jul.* ii 2 108
Frush. I like thy armour well; I'll frush it and unlock the rivets all, But I'll be master of it . . . . . . *Troi. and Cres.* v 6 29
Frustrate. The sea mocks Our frustrate search on land . . *Tempest* iii 3 10
To frustrate prophecies and to raze out Rotten opinion . 2 *Hen. IV.* v 2 127
All the crew are gone, To frustrate both his oath and what beside 3 *Hen. VI.* ii 1 175
'Twas yet some comfort, When misery could beguile the tyrant's rage, And frustrate his proud will . . . . *Lear* iv 6 64
Being so frustrate, tell him he mocks The pauses that he makes *A. and C.* v 1 2
Frutify. My father, being, I hope, an old man, shall frutify unto you *Mer. of Venice* ii 2 142
Fry. Greybeard, thy love doth freeze.—But thine doth fry *T. of Shrew* ii 1 340
Is a whale to virginity and devours up all the fry it finds . *All's Well* iv 3 250
What a fry of fornication is at door! . . . . *Hen. VIII.* v 4 36
Fry, lechery, fry! . . . . *Troi. and Cres.* v 2 57
Thou shag-hair'd villain!—What, you egg! Young fry of treachery! *Macbeth* iv 2 84
A' plays and tumbles, driving the poor fry before him . . *Pericles* ii 1 34
Fubbed off, and fubbed off, and fubbed off, from this day to that 2 *Hen. IV.* ii 1 37
Fuel. Fetch us in fuel; and be quick, thou'rt best . . . *Tempest* i 2 366
The fuel is gone that maintained that fire . . . *Hen. V.* ii 3 45
Nay, then, this spark will prove a raging fire, If wind and fuel be brought to feed it with . . . . . . 2 *Hen. VI.* iii 1 303
I need not add more fuel to your fire, For well I wot ye blaze 3 *Hen. VI.* v 4 70
Fuerza. Piu por dulzura que por fuerza . . . *Pericles* ii 2 27
Fugitive. And thou be thrust out like a fugitive . . . 1 *Hen. VI.* iii 3 67
Whilst yet with Parthian blood thy sword is warm, The fugitive Parthians follow; spur through Media . . . *Ant. and Cleo.* iii 1 7
Let the world rank me in register A master-leaver and a fugitive . . iv 9 22
Fulfil. For servants must their master's minds fulfil . *Com. of Errors* iv 1 113
Charity itself fulfils the law . . . . . *L. L. Lost* iv 3 364
This is desperate, sir.—So call it: but it does fulfil my vow . *W. Tale* iv 4 497
And wilt thou, then, Spurn at his edict and fulfil a man's? *Richard III.* i 4 203
If you bear me hard, Now, whilst your purpled hands do reek and smoke, Fulfil your pleasure . . . . . . *J. Cæsar* iii 1 159
To fulfil his prince' desire, Sends word of all that haps in Tyre *Per.* ii Gower 21
Fulfilled. The gods Will have fulfill'd their secret purposes . *W. Tale* v 1 36
The oracle is fulfilled; the king's daughter is found . . . v 2 25
One eye declined for the loss of her husband, another elevated that the oracle was fulfilled . . . . v 2 82
But see his exequies fulfill'd in Rouen . . . 1 *Hen. VI.* iii 2 133
If not, i' the name of God, Your pleasure be fulfill'd! . . *Hen VIII.* ii 4 57
But their pleasures Must be fulfill'd, and I attend with patience . v 2 19
The ears are senseless that should give us hearing, To tell him his commandment is fulfill'd . . . . *Hamlet* v 2 381
Fulfilling. With massy staples And corresponsive and fulfilling bolts *Troi. and Cres.* Prol. 18
Full. I am full of pleasure: Let us be jocund . . . . *Tempest* iii 2 125
The isle is full of noises . . . . iii 2 144
All sanctimonious ceremonies may With full and holy rite be minister'd iv 1 17
So full of valour that they smote the air . . . . . iv 1 172
For love, thou know'st, is full of jealousy. . . *T. G. of Ver.* ii 4 177
The gentleman Is full of virtue, bounty, worth . . . . iii 1 65
Even from a heart As full of sorrows as the sea of sands. . . . iv 3 33
I know they are stuff'd with protestations And full of new-found oaths iv 4 135
They are reformed, civil, full of good And fit for great employment . v 4 156
'Pless my soul, how full of chollors I am, and trempling of mind! *M. W.* iii 1 11
I was thrown into the ford; I have my belly full of ford . . . iii 5 37
Pray heaven it be not full of knight again . . . . . iv 2 115
You are wise and full of gibes and vlouting-stocks . . . . iv 5 82
In our remove be thou at full ourself . . . *Meas. for Meas.* i 1 44
Thou art full of error; I am sound . . . . . . i 2 54
Your brother and his lover have embraced: As those that feed grow full i 4 41
Do me the favour to dilate at full What hath befall'n of them *C. of Er.* i 1 123
They say this town is full of cozenage . . . . . . i 2 97
A table full of welcome makes scarce one dainty dish . . . iii 1 23
For then were you a child.—You have it full, Benedick . . *Much Ado* i 1 110
The wedding, mannerly-modest, as a measure, full of state and ancientry ii 1 80
More moving-delicate and full of life, Into the eye and prospect of his soul . . . . iv 1 230
Thou art full of piety, as shall be proved upon thee by good witness . iv 2 81
With nothing But what was true and very full of proof . . . v 1 105
What's the matter, That you have such a February face, So full of frost? v 4 42
A foolish extravagant spirit, full of forms, figures, shapes . *L. L. Lost* iv 2 68
O that your face were not so full of O's!—A pox of that jest! . . v 2 45
You took the moon at full, but now she's changed . . . . v 2 214
Trim gallants, full of courtship and of state . . . . . v 2 363
I am a fool, and full of poverty . . . . v 2 380
These summer-flies Have blown me full of maggot ostentation . . v 2 409
Love is full of unbefitting strains, All wanton as a child. . . . v 2 770
Like the eye, Full of strange shapes, of habits and of forms . . . v 2 773
We have received your letters full of love . . . . . v 2 787
Your grace is perjured much, Full of dear guiltiness . . . . v 2 801
A man replete with mocks, Full of comparisons and wounding flouts . v 2 854
Full of vexation come I, with complaint Againt my child *M. N. Dream* i 1 22
I'll streak her eyes, And make her full of hateful fantasies . . ii 1 258
Here come the lovers, full of joy and mirth . . . . . v 1 28
Being so full of unmannerly sadness . . . . *Mer. of Venice* i 2 54
There's a post come from my master, with his horn full of good news . v 1 47
Since nought so stockish, hard and full of rage, But music for the time doth change his nature . . . . v 1 81
And yet I am sure you are not satisfied Of these events at full . . v 1 297
Full of ambition, an envious emulator of every man's good parts *As Y. L. It* i 1 149
Full of noble device, of all sorts enchantingly beloved . . . . i 1 173
Here comes Monsieur Le Beau.—With his mouth full of news . . i 2 98
O, how full of briers is this working-day world! . . . . . i 3 12
Here comes the duke.—With his eyes full of anger . . . . i 3 42
Anon a careless herd, Full of the pasture, jumps along by him . . ii 1 53
Full. I love to cope him in these sullen fits, For then he's full of matter *As Y. Like It* ii 1 68
Then a soldier, Full of strange oaths and bearded like the pard . . ii 7 150
With eyes severe and beard of formal cut, Full of wise saws . . ii 7 156
You are full of pretty answers . . . . iii 2 287
Fantastical, apish, shallow, inconstant, full of tears, full of smiles . iii 2 432
His kissing is as full of sanctity as the touch of holy bread . . iii 4 14
'Tis such fools as you That makes the world full of ill-favour'd children iii 5 53
Let one attend him with a silver basin Full of rose-water *T. of Shrew* Ind. 1 56
Content thee, for I have it full . . . . i 1 203
Unto a mad-brain rudesby full of spleen . . . . . . iii 2 10
Full of windgalls, sped with spavins, rayed with the yellows . . iii 2 53
Come, your are so full of cony-catching! . . . . iv 1 45
I am so full of businesses, I cannot answer thee acutely . . *All's Well* i 1 220
For your passions Have to the full appeach'd . . . . . i 3 197
What at full I know, thou know'st no part . . . . . . ii 1 135
A very tainted fellow, and full of wickedness . . . . . iii 2 89
Dian, the count's a fool, and full of gold . . . . . . iv 3 238
So full of shapes is fancy That it alone is high fantastical . *T. Night* i 1 14
A dry jest, sir.—Are you full of them?—Ay, sir . . . . . i 3 82
I hold the olive in my hand; my words are as full of peace as matter . i 5 226
Fare ye well at once: my bosom is full of kindness . . . . ii 1 40
This is a practice As full of labour as a wise man's art . . . iii 1 73
It is no matter how witty, so it be eloquent and full of invention . . iii 2 47
Thy intercepter, full of despite, bloody as the hunter, attends thee . iii 4 242
Your heart is full of something that does take Your mind from feasting *W. Tale* iv 4 357
Though full of our displeasure, yet we free thee From the dead blow of it iv 4 444
Thou must know the king is full of grief . . . . . . iv 4 792
With a powerless hand, But with a heart full of unstained love *K. John* ii 1 16
The cannons have their bowels full of wrath . . . . . ii 1 210
Oppress'd with wrongs and therefore full of fears . . . . iii 1 13
Full of unpleasing blots and sightless stains, Lame, foolish, crooked . iii 1 45
Is all too wanton and too full of gawds To give me audience . . iii 3 36
Do not seek to stuff My head with more ill news, for it is full . . iv 2 134
Full of idle dreams, Not knowing what they fear, but full of fear . . iv 2 145
Who are arrived?—The French, my lord; men's mouths are full of it . iv 2 161
Full of warm blood, of mirth, of gossiping . . . . . . v 2 59
High-stomach'd are they both, and full of ire . . . . *Richard II.* i 1 18
One vial full of Edward's sacred blood . . . Is crack'd . . . i 2 17
O, full of careful business are his looks! . . . . . . ii 2 75
We'll play at bowls.—'Twill make me think the world is full of rubs iii 4 4
Our sea-walled garden, the whole land, Is full of weeds . . . iii 4 44
Like a deep well That owes two buckets, filling one another, The emptier ever dancing in the air, The other down, unseen and full of water . iv 1 187
Mine eyes are full of tears, I cannot see . . . . . . iv 1 244
Your brows are full of discontent, Your hearts of sorrow . . . iv 1 331
His prayers are full of false hypocrisy; Ours of true zeal . . . v 3 107
As full of valour as of royal blood: Both have I spill'd . . . v 5 114
My soul is full of woe, That blood should sprinkle me to make me grow v 6 45
If you will go, I will stuff your purses full of crowns . . 1 *Hen. IV.* i 2 147
As full of peril and adventurous spirit As to o'er-walk a current roaring loud . . . . i 3 191
A good plot, good friends, and full of expectation . . . . . ii 3 20
The parties sure, And our induction full of prosperous hope . . . iii 1 2
At my birth The front of heaven was full of fiery shapes . . . iii 1 38
Being with his presence glutted, gorged and full . . . . . iii 2 84
Thy looks are full of speed.—So hath the business that I come to speak of iii 2 162
Our hands are full of business: let's away . . . . . . iii 2 179
As full of spirit as the month of May, And gorgeous as the sun . . iv 1 101
The better part of ours [horses] are full of rest . . . . . iv 3 27
Suspicion all our lives shall be stuck full of eyes . . . . . v 2 8
Contention, like a horse Full of high feeding, madly hath broke loose 2 *Hen. IV.* i 1 10
This is the news at full . . . . i 1 135
Thou, beastly feeder, art so full of him, That thou provokest thyself to cast him up . . . . i 3 95
Our battle is more full of names than yours, Our men more perfect . iv 1 154
Full of nimble fiery and delectable shapes . . . . . . iv 3 107
Will Fortune never come with both hands full? . . . . . iv 4 103
I am here, brother, full of heaviness . . . . iv 5 8
The king is full of grace and fair regard . . . . . . *Hen. V.* i 1 22
Congreeing in a full and natural close, Like music . . . . . i 2 182
To-morrow shall you know our mind at full . . . . . . ii 4 140
He is as full of valour as of kindness; Princely in both . . . iv 3 15
He was full of jests, and gipes, and knaveries, and mocks . . . iv 7 51
What says she, fair one? that the tongues of men are full of deceits? . v 2 121
Lords, view these letters full of bad mischance . . . 1 *Hen. VI.* i 1 89
God's mother deigned to appear to me And in a vision full of majesty . i 2 79
Have fill'd their pockets full of pebble stones . . . . . iii 1 80
'Twas full of darnel; do you like the taste? . . . . . iii 2 44
Of noble birth, Valiant and virtuous, full of haughty courage . . iv 1 35
We'll see these things effected to the full . . . . 2 *Hen. VI.* i 2 84
My lord, I long to hear it at full.—Sweet York, begin . . . . ii 2 6
My lord, break we off; we know your mind at full . . . . . ii 2 77
Mine eyes are full of tears, my heart of grief . . . . . . ii 3 17
Gloucester is a man Unsounded yet and full of deep deceit . . . iii 1 57
Henry my lord is cold in great affairs, Too full of foolish pity . . iii 1 225
But see, his face is black and full of blood . . . . . . iii 2 168
And boding screech-owls make the concert full! . . . . . iii 2 327
Sweet is the country, because full of riches . . . . . . iv 7 67
Long sitting to determine poor men's causes Hath made me full of sickness . . . . iv 7 94
They are soldiers, Witty, courteous, liberal, full of spirit . 3 *Hen. VI.* i 2 43
With my talk and tears, Both full of truth . . . . . . iii 3 159
Mine, such as fill my heart with unhoped joys.—Mine, full of sorrow . iii 3 173
These news I must confess are full of grief . . . . . . iv 4 13
His looks are full of peaceful majesty . . . . iv 6 71
O, I have pass'd a miserable night, So full of ugly sights! *Richard III.* i 4 3
So full of dismal terror was the time! . . . . i 4 7
It [conscience] fills one full of obstacles . . . . . . i 4 143
Deep, hollow, treacherous, and full of guile, Be he unto me! . . . ii 1 38
I pray thee, peace: my soul is full of sorrow . . . . . . ii 1 96
In his full and ripen'd years . . . . ii 3 14
O, full of danger is the Duke of Gloucester! . . . . . . ii 3 27
Truly, the souls of men are full of dread . . . . ii 3 38
Ye cannot reason almost with a man That looks not heavily and full of fear . . . . ii 3 40
Full of wise care is this your counsel, madam . . . . . . iv 1 48
Why should calamity be full of words? . . . . iv 4 126

Full. Now, by the world— 'Tis full of thy foul wrongs . *Richard III.* iv 4 374
My anointed body By thee was punched full of deadly holes . . . v 3 125
A serious brow, Sad, high, and working, full of state and woe *Hen. VIII.* Prol. 3
Where this heaven of beauty Shall shine at full upon them . . i 4 60
I have done; and God forgive me!—O, this is full of pity! . . . ii 1 137
If the duke be guiltless, 'Tis full of woe . . . . . ii 1 140
I left him private, Full of sad thoughts and troubles . . . ii 2 16
Good my lord, You are full of heavenly stuff . . . . . iii 2 137
The citizens, I am sure, have shown at full their royal minds . iv 1 8
Full of repentance, Continual meditations, tears, and sorrows . iv 2 27
Having his ear full of his airy fame, Grows dainty of his worth *Troi. and Cres.* i 3 144
How if he had boils? full, all over, generally? . . . . ii 1 2
As full of envy at his greatness as Cerberus is at Proserpina's beauty . ii 1 36
Nor the remainder viands We do not throw in unrespective sieve, Because we now are full . . . . . . ii 2 72
Dear lord, you are full of fair words . . . . iii 1 50
Nell, he is full of harmony.—Truly, lady, no . . . . iii 1 56
Their rhymes, Full of protest, of oath and big compare, Want similes . iii 2 182
The grief is fine, full, perfect, that I taste . . . . . iv 4 3
Hear why I speak it, love: The Grecian youths are full of quality . iv 4 78
Go to my tent; There in the full convive we . . . . iv 5 272
Wheezing lungs, bladders full of imposthume . . . . . v 1 24
O, then conclude Minds sway'd by eyes are full of turpitude . . v 2 112
You would be another Penelope; yet, they say, all the yarn she spun in Ulysses' absence did but fill Ithaca full of moths . *Coriolanus* i 3 94
Thou art too full Of the wars' surfeits, to go rove . . . . iv 1 45
Let me have war, say I; it exceeds peace as far as day does night; it's spritely, waking, audible, and full of vent . . . . iv 5 238
This Volumnia Is worth of cousuls, senators, patricians, A city full; of tribunes, such as you, A sea and land full. . . . . . v 4 57
The palace full of tongues, of eyes, and ears . . *T. Andron.* ii 1 127
A charitable wish and full of love . . . . iv 2 43
My report is just and full of truth . . . . v 3 115
What saucy merchant was this, that was so full of his ropery? *R. and J.* ii 4 153
Thy head is as full of quarrels as an egg is full of meat . . . iii 1 24
My state, Which, well thou know'st, is cross and full of sin . . iv 3 5
I am sure, you have your hands full all, In this so sudden business . iv 3 11
My heart itself plays 'My heart is full of woe:' O, play me some merry dump . . . . iv 5 107
Art thou so bare and full of wretchedness, And fear'st to die? . . v 1 68
The letter was not nice but full of charge Of dear import . . . v 2 18
Her beauty makes This vault a feasting presence full of light . . v 3 86
Friendship's full of dregs . . . . . . *T. of Athens* i 2 239
How full of valour did he bear himself In the last conflict! . . . iii 5 65
Full of decay and failing . . . . iv 3 466
Does the rumour hold for true, that he's so full of gold? . . . v 1 4
Thou hast painfully discover'd: are his files As full as thy report? . v 2 2
Who ever knew the heavens menace so?—Those that have known the earth so full of faults . . . . . . *J. Cæsar* i 3 45
Our reasons are so full of good regard That were you, Antony, the son of Cæsar, You should be satisfied . . . . iii 1 224
My noble master will appear Such as he is, full of regard and honour . iv 2 12
Whilst we, lying still, Are full of rest, defence, and nimbleness . . iv 3 202
Now is that noble vessel full of grief, That it runs over even at his eyes v 5 13
Welcome hither: I have begun to plant thee, and will labour To make thee full of growing . . . . *Macbeth* i 4 29
Yet do I fear thy nature: It is too full o' the milk of human kindness . i 5 18
O, full of scorpions is my mind, dear wife! . . . . . iii 2 36
The table's full.—Here is a place reserved, sir.—Where?—Here . . iii 4 46
Give me some wine; fill full. I drink to the general joy o' the whole table . . . . iii 4 88
And sundry blessings hang about his throne, That speak him full of grace . . . . iv 3 159
I have supp'd full with horrors . . . . v 5 13
It is a tale Told by an idiot, full of sound and fury, Signifying nothing v 5 27
Young Fortinbras, Of unimproved mettle hot and full . . *Hamlet* i 1 96
He took my father grossly, full of bread; With all his crimes broad blown . . . . iii 3 80
His liberty is full of threats to all; To you yourself, to us, to every one iv 1 14
O, come away! My soul is full of discord and dismay . . . . iv 1 45
Which imports at full, By letters congruing to that effect, The present death of Hamlet . . . . iv 3 65
So full of artless jealousy is guilt, It spills itself in fearing to be spilt . iv 5 19
An absolute gentleman, full of most excellent differences . . . v 2 111
You see how full of changes his age is . . . . . *Lear* i 1 291
Thy master, whom thou lovest, Shall find thee full of labours . . i 4 7
When were you wont to be so full of songs? . . . . . . i 4 185
Away to horse: Inform her full of my particular fear . . . . i 4 360
You see me here, you gods, a poor old man, As full of grief as age . ii 4 276
He's full of alteration And self-reproving . . . . . . v 1 3
In madness, Being full of supper and distempering draughts . *Othello* i 1 99
I cannot believe that in her; she's full of most blessed condition . . ii 1 254
She's a most exquisite lady.—And, I'll warrant her, full of game . . ii 3 19
He'll be as full of quarrel and offence As my young mistress' dog . . ii 3 52
It shall be full of poise and difficult weight And fearful to be granted . iii 3 82
I know thou'rt full of love and honesty, And weigh'st thy words . . iii 3 118
I had rather have lost my purse Full of crusadoes . . . . iii 4 26
They eat us hungerly, and when they are full, They belch us . . iii 4 105
Speak, for my heart is full . . . . v 2 175
And my auguring hope Says it will come to the full . *Ant. and Cleo.* ii 1 11
Love, I am full of lead. Some wine, within there, and our viands! . iii 11 72
'Tis a brave army, And full of purpose . . . . . . iv 3 12
Who is so full of grace, that it flows over On all that need . . . v 2 24
It gave me present hunger To feed again, though full . . *Cymbeline* ii 4 138
So children temporal fathers do appease; Gods are more full of mercy . v 4 13
Their tables were stored full, to glad the sight . . . *Pericles* i 4 28
Search the market narrowly; Mytilene is full of gallants . . . iv 2 4
Full a glory. But I will rise there with so full a glory That I will dazzle all the eyes of France . . . . *Hen. V.* i 2 278
Full a month. Not full a month Between their births . . *W. Tale* v 1 117
Full a voice. I did never know so full a voice issue from so empty a heart . . . . *Hen. V.* iv 4 72
Full accomplished. The vision Which I made known to Lucius . . . at this instant Is full accomplish'd . . . . . . *Cymbeline* v 5 470
Full accord. With full accord to all our just demands . . *Hen. V.* v 2 71
Full-acorned. Like a full-acorn'd boar, a German one . *Cymbeline* ii 5 16
Full affections. Have I with all my full affections Still met the king? loved him next heaven? . . . . *Hen. VIII.* iii 1 129
Full arming. Point from point, to the full arming of the verity *All's Well* iv 3 72
Full as dearly. Do you love your children?—Ay, full as dearly as I love myself . . . . *3 Hen. VI.* iii 2 37
Full as fantastical. Like a Scotch jig, and full as fantastical *Much Ado* ii 1 79
Full as fortunate. Doth not the gentleman Deserve as full as fortunate a bed As ever Beatrice shall couch upon? . . . . . . iii 1 45
Full as long. The precedent was full as long a-doing . *Richard III.* iii 6 7
Full as lovely. If I had such a tire, this face of mine Were full as lovely as is this of hers . . . . *T. G. of Ver.* iv 4 191
Full as many. And spur thee on with full as many lies As may be holloa'd in thy treacherous ear . . . . . *Richard II.* iv 1 53
With full as many signs of deadly hate As lean-faced Envy *2 Hen. VI.* iii 2 314
Full as much. Whose life's as tender to me as my soul! And full as much, for more there cannot be . . . . . *T. G. of Ver.* v 4 38
Full as oft. And full as oft came Edward to my side . . *3 Hen. VI.* i 4 11
Full as proud. In full as proud a place As broad Achilles *Troi. and Cres.* i 3 189
Full as strong. Her faction will be full as strong as ours . *3 Hen. VI.* v 3 17
Full assurance. Plight me the full assurance of your faith . *T. Night* iv 3 26
Full bags. Balm'd and entreasured With full bags of spices! . *Pericles* iii 2 66
Full bent. Her affections have their full bent . . . . *Much Ado* ii 3 232
In the full bent To lay our service freely at your feet . . *Hamlet* ii 2 30
Thaliard came full bent with sin And had intent to murder him *Per.* ii Gower 23
Full bravely hast thou flesh'd Thy maiden sword . . *1 Hen. IV.* v 4 133
Full Cæsar. That he should dream, Knowing all measures, the full Cæsar will Answer his emptiness! . . . . *Ant. and Cleo.* iii 13 35
Full cause. We shall give you The full cause of our coming *Hen. VIII.* iii 1 29
I have full cause of weeping; but this heart Shall break into a hundred thousand flaws, Or ere I'll weep. . . . . . . *Lear* ii 4 287
Full-charged. I stood i' the level Of a full-charged confederacy *Hen. VIII.* i 2 3
Full circle. The wheel is come full circle; I am here . *Lear* v 3 174
Full clear. What he with his oath And all probation will make up full clear, Whensoever he's convented . . . *Meas. for Meas.* v 1 157
Full commission. Hath the Prince John a full commission? *2 Hen. IV.* iv 1 162
The Moor himself at sea, And is in full commission here for Cyprus *Oth.* ii 1 29
Full complete. To see the minutes how they run, How many make the hour full complete . . . . *3 Hen. VI.* ii 5 26
Full consent. Your breath of full consent bellied his sails *Troi. and Cres.* ii 2 74
But I attest the gods, your full consent Gave wings to my propension . ii 2 132
Full content. So will I In England work your grace's full content *2 Hen. VI.* i 3 70
Full course. Mangling by starts the full course of their glory *Hen. V.* Epil. 4
Full dearly. Many a soul Shall pay full dearly for this encounter *1 Hen. IV.* v 1 84
Full desire. Till we Have seal'd thy full desire . . *T. of Athens* v 4 54
Full disgrace. I am out, Even to a full disgrace . . . *Coriolanus* v 3 42
Full dish. Thou full dish of fool . . . . . *Troi. and Cres.* v 1 10
Full expired. Till term of eighteen months Be full expired . *2 Hen. VI.* i 1 68
Full eye. I might have look'd upon my queen's full eyes . *W. Tale* v 1 53
A full eye will wax hollow . . . . *Hen. V.* v 2 170
Full fain. I wad full fain hear some question 'tween you tway . iii 2 127
Full fairly. Our soldiers stand full fairly for the day . *1 Hen. IV.* v 3 29
Full fast. Night's swift dragons cut the clouds full fast . *M. N. Dream* iii 2 379
Full fathom five thy father lies; Of his bones are coral made *Tempest* i 2 396
Full-flowing. I am not well; else I should answer From a full-flowing stomach . . . . *Lear* v 3 74
Full fortune. What a full fortune does the thick-lips owe! . *Othello* i 1 66
Wherein Our pleasure his full fortune doth confine . . *Cymbeline* v 4 110
Full-fortuned. The full-fortuned Cæsar . . . . *Ant. and Cleo.* iv 15 24
Full fourteen weeks before the course of time . . . *K. John* i 1 113
Full-fraught. Wailful sonnets, whose composed rhymes Should be full-fraught with serviceable vows . . . . . *T. G. of Ver.* iii 2 70
Thy fall hath left a kind of blot, To mark the full-fraught man *Hen V.* ii 2 139
Full function. The office did Distinctly his full function . *Hen. VIII.* i 1 45
Full gently. Who look'd full gently on his warlike queen . *3 Hen. VI.* ii 1 123
Full ghastly. Staring full ghastly like a strangled man . *2 Hen. VI.* iii 2 170
Full-gorged. Till she stoop she must not be full-gorged . *T. of Shrew* iv 1 194
Full grown. A wench full grown, Even ripe for marriage-rite *Per.* iv Gower 16
Full half an hour. How long hath he been there?—Full half an hour *Rom. and Jul.* v 3 130
Full hand. A city on whom plenty held full hand . . . *Pericles* i 4 22
Full hard. I did full hard forbear him . . . . . *Othello* i 2 10
Full heart. My full heart Remains in use with you . . *Ant. and Cleo.* i 3 43
Full-hearted. The enemy full-hearted, Lolling the tongue with slaughtering, having work More plentiful than tools to do't . . *Cymbeline* v 3 7
Full height. And bend up every spirit To his full height . . *Hen. V.* iii 1 17
Full hogshead. Can a weak empty vessel bear such a huge full hogshead? . . . . *2 Hen. IV.* ii 4 68
Full-hot. Anger is like A full-hot horse, who being allow'd his way, Self-mettle tires him . . . . *Hen. VIII.* i 1 133
Full intent. To-morrow shall you bear our full intent Back . *Hen. V.* ii 4 114
Coming with a full intent To dash our late decree . . . *3 Hen. VI.* ii 1 117
And now be it known to you my full intent . . . *T Andron.* iv 2 151
Full joyous. Who will of thy arrival be full joyous . . *T. of Shrew* iv 5 70
Full liberty. There is full liberty of feasting from this present hour of five till the bell hath told eleven . . . . . . *Othello* ii 2 10
Full license. And taunt my faults With such full license *Ant. and Cleo.* i 2 112
Full life. Survey With thy chaste eye, from thy pale sphere above, Thy huntress' name that my full life doth sway . . *As Y. Like It* iii 2 4
Full like. Thou want'st a rough pash and the shoots that I have, To be full like me . . . . *W. Tale* i 2 129
Full line. With full line of his authority . . . *Meas. for Meas.* i 4 56
Full little, God knows, looking Either for such men or such business *Hen. VIII.* i 1 75
Full low. And lie full low, graved in the hollow ground . *Richard II.* iii 2 140
Full-manned. Our overplus of shipping will we burn; And, with the rest full-mann'd, from the head of Actium Beat the approaching Cæsar . . . . *Ant. and Cleo.* iii 7 52
Full many a lady I have eyed with best regard . . . *Tempest* iii 1 39
The plain-song cuckoo gray, Whose note full many a man doth mark *M. N. Dream* iii 1 135
Full measure. Carouse full measure . . . . . *T. of Shrew* iii 2 227
Full meridian. And, from that full meridian of my glory, I haste now to my setting . . . . *Hen. VIII.* iii 2 224
Full merrily Hath this brave manage, this career, been run *L. L. Lost* v 2 481
Full merrily the humble-bee doth sing, Till he hath lost his honey *Trio. and Cres.* v 10 42
Full mess. The bounteous housewife, nature, on each bush Lays her full mess before you . . . . *T. of Athens* iv 3 424
Full moon. And I in the clear sky of fame o'ershine you as much as the full moon doth the cinders of the element . . . *2 Hen. IV.* iv 3 57
As I stood here below, methought his eyes Were two full moons . *Lear* iv 6 70

Full mouth. Our history shall with full mouth Speak freely of our acts *Hen. V.* i 2 230
Full numbers. A victory is twice itself when the achiever brings home full numbers *Much Ado* i 1 9
Full of face. So buxom, blithe, and full of face *Pericles* i Gower 23
Full of heart. Strong joints, true swords; and, Jove's accord, Nothing so full of heart *Troi. and Cres.* i 3 239
Full of tide. The swan's down-feather, That stands upon the swell at full of tide, And neither way inclines *Ant. and Cleo.* iii 2 49
Full of view. To behold his visage, Even to my full of view *T. and C.* iii 3 241
You should tread a course Pretty and full of view *Cymbeline* iii 4 150
Full oft we see Cold wisdom waiting on superfluous folly *All's Well* i 1 115
For I have heard my grandsire say full oft *T. Andron.* iv 1 18
Thy father hath full oft For his ungrateful country done the like iv 1 110
Full oft 'tis seen, Our means secure us *Lear* iv 1 21
Full often hath she gossip'd by my side *M. N. Dream* ii 1 125
O wall, full often hast thou heard my moans! v 1 190
Full often, like a shag-hair'd crafty kern, Hath he conversed 2 *Hen. VI.* iii 1 367
Full often struck a doe, And borne her cleanly by the keeper's nose *T. An.* ii 1 93
Full petition. If the redress will follow, thou receivest Thy full petition at the hand of Brutus *J. Cæsar* ii 1 58
Full points. Come we to full points here; and are etceteras nothing? 2 *Hen. IV.* ii 4 198
Full poor. Prospero, master of a full poor cell *Tempest* i 2 20
Full power. Making defeat on the full power of France *Hen. V.* i 2 107
Thus comes the English with full power upon us ii 4 1
Full pride. O noble English, that could entertain With half their forces the full pride of France! i 2 112
Full proportions. The lists and full proportions are all made Out of his subject *Hamlet* i 2 32
Full prospect. Nothing that can be can come between me and the full prospect of my hopes *T. Night* iii 4 90
Full puissance. And come against us in full puissance 2 *Hen. IV.* i 3 77
Full purpose. To veil full purpose *Meas. for Meas.* iv 6 4
Full quit. To be full quit of those my banishers *Coriolanus* iv 5 89
Full reference. Many things, having full reference To one consent, may work contrariously *Hen. V.* i 2 205
Make your full reference freely to my lord *Ant. and Cleo.* v 2 23
Full relation. For the intent and purpose of the law Hath full relation to the penalty *Mer. of Venice* iv 1 248
Full-replete. So full-replete with choice of all delights 1 *Hen. VI.* v 5 17
Full resolved. I now am full resolved to take a wife *T. G. of Ver.* iii 1 76
For that I am prepared and full resolved. Foul-spoken coward! *T. An.* ii 1 57
Full ripe. But that we thought not good to bruise an injury till it were full ripe *Hen. V.* iii 6 130
Full sacrifice. Words, vows, gifts, tears, and love's full sacrifice, He offers in another's enterprise *Troi. and Cres.* i 2 308
Full salt. When I have deck'd the sea with drops full salt *Tempest* i 2 155
Full satisfaction. We shall make full satisfaction *Com. of Errors* v 1 399
Full scarce. Having full scarce six thousand in his troop 1 *Hen. VI.* i 1 112
Full sea. On such a full sea are we now afloat *J. Cæsar* iv 3 222
Full seeming. You sign your place and calling, in full seeming, With meekness and humility *Hen. VIII.* ii 4 108
Full senate. Whom our full senate Call all in all sufficient *Othello* iv 1 275
Full show. You must not make the full show of this *Much Ado* i 3 20
Full sick. I meant to rectify my conscience,—which I then did feel full sick, and yet not well *Hen. VIII.* ii 4 204
Full so black. No face is fair that is not full so black *L. L. Lost* iv 3 253
Full so valiant. He is full so valiant *Macbeth* i 4 54
Full soldier. The man commands Like a full soldier *Othello* ii 1 36
Full soon the canker death eats up that plant *Rom. and Jul.* ii 3 30
Full sorry. I am full sorry That he approves the common liar *A. and C.* i 1 59
Full soul. For several virtues Have I liked several women; never any With so full soul *Tempest* iii 1 44
Full state. And with the same full state paced back again *Hen. VIII.* iv 1 93
Full stomach. When I do it, I shall do it on a full stomach *L. L. Lost* i 2 154
Full stop. Come, the full stop *Mer. of Venice* iii 1 17
Full stream. To forswear the full stream of the world *As Y. Like It* iii 2 440
Full suddenly. Gasted by the noise I made, Full suddenly he fled *Lear* ii 1 58
Full sum. But the full sum of me Is sum of something *Mer. of Venice* iii 2 159
Full supremacy. O'er my spirit Thy full supremacy thou knew'st *A. and C.* iii 11 59
Full surely. And, when he thinks, good easy man, full surely His greatness is a-ripening, nips his root, And then he falls *Hen. VIII.* iii 2 356
Full surfeits, and the dryness of his bones, Call on him for't *Ant. and Cleo.* i 4 27
Full third part. Our spoils we have brought home Do more than counterpoise a full third part The charges of the action *Coriolanus* v 6 78
Full thirty thousand marks of English coin *K. John* ii 1 530
Full thirty times hath Phœbus' cart gone round *Hamlet* iii 2 165
Full three months. 'Tis full three months since I did see him last *Rich. II.* v 3 2
Full three score. Of fighting men they have full three score thousand *Hen. V.* iv 3 3
Full three thousand ducats *Mer. of Venice* i 3 57
Full tilth. Even so her plenteous womb Expresseth his full tilth and husbandry *Meas. for Meas.* i 4 44
Full time. You shall have your full time of imprisonment iv 2 12
This is a poor epitome of yours, Which by the interpretation of full time May show like all yourself *Coriolanus* v 3 69
Full trophy. Giving full trophy, signal and ostent Quite from himself to God *Hen. V.* v Prol. 21
Full true. Which men full true shall find *All's Well* i 3 65
Full two years. 'Twas full two years ere I could get a tooth *Richard III.* ii 4 29
Full view. Which when the people Had the full view of, such a noise arose As the shrouds make at sea *Hen. VIII.* iv 1 71
Full voice. Being pass'd for consul with full voice *Coriolanus* iii 3 59
Full wanderingly. Your shafts of fortune, though they hurt you mortally, Yet glance full wanderingly on us *Pericles* iii 3 7
Full weak. The legions now in Gallia are Full weak to undertake our wars *Cymbeline* iii 7 5
Full weight. Herein I see thou lovest me not with the full weight that I love thee *As Y. Like It* i 2 9
Full well. It becomes thy oath full well, Thou to me thy secrets tell *W. T.* iv 4 306
I know this face full well 1 *Hen. IV.* v 3 19
Full well he knows He cannot so precisely weed this land 2 *Hen. IV.* iv 1 204
To make commotion, as full well he can 2 *Hen. VI.* iii 1 358
Full well hath Clifford play'd the orator 3 *Hen. VI.* ii 2 43
Full well, Andronicus, Agree these deeds with that proud brag *T. Andron.* i 1 305
With the little skill I have, Full well shalt thou perceive how much I dare ii 1 44
Full well I wot the ground of all this grudge ii 1 48
Danger knows full well That Cæsar is more dangerous than he *J. Cæsar* ii 2 44
A plain blunt man, That love my friend; and that they know full well iii 2 223
Full-winged. Often, to our comfort, shall we find The sharded beetle in a safer hold Than is the full-wing'd eagle *Cymbeline* iii 3 21
Full year. Thou didst promise To bate me a full year *Tempest* i 2 250
Fullam. Gourd and fullam holds, And high and low beguiles the rich and poor *Mer. Wives* i 3 94
Fuller. The spinsters, carders, fullers, weavers *Hen. VIII.* i 2 33
The enemy, marching along by them, By them shall make a fuller number up, Come on refresh'd *J. Cæsar* iv 3 208
A fuller blast ne'er shook our battlements *Othello* ii 1 6
Fullest. One that but performs The bidding of the fullest man *A. and C.* iii 13 87
Fully. That to the observer doth thy history Fully unfold *Meas. for Meas.* i 1 30
I do present you with a man of mine, ... To instruct her fully in those sciences, Whereof I know she is not ignorant *T. of Shrew* ii 1 57
Nathaniel's coat, sir, was not fully made iv 1 135
Inform'd her fully I could not answer in that course of honour *All's Well* v 3 97
Here had the conquest fully been seal'd up, If Sir John Fastolfe had not play'd the coward 1 *Hen. VI.* i 1 130
Although not there At once and fully satisfied *Hen. VIII.* ii 4 148
Having fully dined before *Coriolanus* i 9 11
And leaves nothing undone that may fully discover him their opposite ii 2 23
I wish I had a cause to seek him there, To oppose his hatred fully iii 1 20
Wherefore ere this time Had you not fully laid my state before me? *T. of Athens* ii 2 134
It will stuff his suspicion more fully *Lear* iii 5 22
Fie, wrangling queen! ... whose every passion fully strives To make itself, in thee, fair and admired! *Ant. and Cleo.* i 1 50
Our hour Is fully out.—Come on, then iv 9 33
Fulness. And she a fair divided excellence, Whose fulness of perfection lies in him *K. John* ii 1 440
Like the tide into a breach, With ample and brim fulness of his force *Hen. V.* i 2 150
Such is the fulness of my heart's content 2 *Hen. VI.* i 1 35
My plenteous joys, Wanton in fulness, seek to hide themselves In drops of sorrow *Macbeth* i 4 34
To lapse in fulness Is sorer than to lie for need *Cymbeline* iii 6 12
Fulsome. The fulsome ewes, Who then conceiving did in eaning time Fall parti-colour'd lambs *Mer. of Venice* i 3 87
It is as fat and fulsome to mine ear As howling after music *T. Night* v 1 112
And stop this gap of breath with fulsome dust *K. John* iii 4 32
I, that was wash'd to death with fulsome wine, Poor Clarence! *Rich. III.* v 3 132
Lie with her! that's fulsome.—Handkerchief—confessions! *Othello* iv 1 37
Fulvia. Nay, hear them, Antony: Fulvia perchance is angry *Ant. and Cleo.* i 1 20
Where's Fulvia's process? Cæsar's I would say? both? i 1 28
Else so thy cheek pays shame When shrill-tongued Fulvia scolds i 1 32
Excellent falsehood! Why did he marry Fulvia, and not love her? i 1 41
Fulvia thy wife first came into the field.—Against my brother Lucius?—Ay i 2 92
Name Cleopatra as she is call'd in Rome; Rail thou in Fulvia's phrase i 2 111
Fulvia thy wife is dead.—Where died she?—In Sicyon i 2 122
Fulvia is dead.—Sir?—Fulvia is dead.—Fulvia!—Dead i 2 162
If there were no more women but Fulvia, then had you indeed a cut i 2 173
The death of Fulvia, with more urgent touches, Do strongly speak to us i 2 187
Though you in swearing shake the throned gods, Who have been false to Fulvia i 3 29
And that which most with you should safe my going, Is Fulvia's death i 3 56
Can Fulvia die?—She's dead, my queen i 3 58
Now I see, I see, In Fulvia's death, how mine received shall be i 3 65
So Fulvia told me. I prithee, turn aside and weep for her i 3 75
Truth is, that Fulvia, To have me out of Egypt, made wars here ii 2 94
Fum. Fie, foh, and fum, I smell the blood of a British man *Lear* iii 4 188
Fumble. I saw him fumble with the sheets and play with flowers *Hen. V.* ii 3 14
He fumbles up into a loose adieu *Troi. and Cres.* iv 4 48
What dost thou wrap and fumble in thine arms? *T. Andron.* iv 2 58
Fumblest. Thou fumblest, Eros; and my queen's a squire More tight at this than thou *Ant. and Cleo.* iv 4 14
Fume. Their rising senses Begin to chase the ignorant fumes that mantle Their clearer reason *Tempest* v 1 67
'Frets, call you these?' quoth she; 'I'll fume with them' *T. of Shrew* ii 1 153
Her fume needs no spurs, She'll gallop far enough 2 *Hen. VI.* i 3 153
Love is a smoke raised with the fume of sighs *Rom. and Jul.* i 1 196
That memory, the warder of the brain, Shall be a fume *Macbeth* i 7 66
A bolt of nothing, shot at nothing, Which the brain makes of fumes *Cymbeline* iv 2 301
Fuming. Keep his brain fuming *Ant. and Cleo.* ii 1 24
Fumiter. Crown'd with rank fumiter and furrow-weeds *Lear* iv 4 3
Fumitory. Her fallow leas The darnel, hemlock and rank fumitory Doth root upon *Hen. V.* v 2 45
Function. 'Twas a commandment to command the captain and all the rest from their functions *Meas. for Meas.* i 2 14
Mine were the very cipher of a function, To fine the faults ii 2 39
You have paid the heavens your function iii 2 264
Gives to every power a double power, Above their functions *L. L. Lost* iv 3 332
Dark night, that from the eye his function takes *M. N. Dream* iii 2 177
What is he of basest function That says his bravery is not on my cost, Thinking that I mean him? *As Y. L. It* ii 7 79
I am not tall enough to become the function well *T. Night* iv 2 8
And all the ceremony of this compact Seal'd in my function v 1 164
Move still, still so, And own no other function *W. Tale* iv 4 143
Therefore doth heaven divide The state of man in divers functions *Hen. V.* i 2 184
To lay apart their particular functions and wonder at him iii 7 41
Each hath his place and function to attend: I am left out 1 *Hen. VI.* i 1 173
Thou art reverent Touching thy spiritual function, not thy life iii 1 50
The office did Distinctly his full function *Hen. VIII.* i 1 45
Your hand and heart, Your brain, and every function of your power iii 2 187
Doth invert the attest of eyes and ears, As if those organs had deceptious functions, Created only to calumniate *Troi. and Cres.* v 2 123
Follow your function, go, and batten on cold bits *Coriolanus* iv 5 35
Tradesmen singing in their shops and going About their functions friendly iv 6 9
Function Is smother'd in surmise, and nothing is But what is not *Macbeth* i 3 140
And his whole function suiting With forms to his conceit *Hamlet* ii 2 582
My operant powers their functions leave to do iii 2 184
Even as her appetite shall play the god With his weak function *Othello* ii 3 354
Some of your function, mistress; Leave procreants alone and shut the door iv 2 27
All offices of nature should again Do their due functions *Cymbeline* v 5 258
Fundamental. You heard The fundamental reasons of this war *All's Well* iii 1 2
That love the fundamental part of state More than you doubt the change on't, that prefer A noble life before a long *Coriolanus* iii 1 151
Funeral. This is a very scurvy tune to sing at a man's funeral *Tempest* ii 2 47
Turn melancholy forth to funerals *M. N. Dream* i 1 14
My noble prince, With other princes that may best be spared, Shall wait upon your father's funeral *K. John* v 7 98

Funeral. Were our tears wanting to this funeral, These tidings would call forth their flowing tides . . . . 1 *Hen. VI.* i 1 82
Mourn not, except thou sorrow for my good; Only give order for my funeral . . . . ii 5 112
My sighing breast shall be thy funeral bell . . . . . 3 *Hen. VI.* ii 5 117
But safer triumph is this funeral pomp, That hath aspired to Solon's happiness And triumphs over chance in honour's bed . *T. Andron.* i 1 176
Wise Laertes' son Did graciously plead for his funerals . . . . i 1 381
I have given her physic, And you must needs bestow her funeral . iv 2 163
No funeral rite, nor man in mourning weeds, No mournful bell shall ring v 3 196
All things that we ordained festival, Turn from their office to black funeral; Our instruments to melancholy bells . . *Rom. and Jul.* iv 5 85
As becomes a friend, Speak in the order of his funeral . . *J. Cæsar* iii 1 230
You know not what you do: do not consent That Antony speak in his funeral . . . . iii 1 233
You shall not in your funeral speech blame us, But speak all good . iii 1 245
Else shall you not have any hand at all About his funeral . . . iii 1 249
Come I to speak in Cæsar's funeral . . . . iii 2 89
I am going to Cæsar's funeral.—As a friend or an enemy?—As a friend . iii 3 22
His funerals shall not be in our camp, Lest it discomfort us . . . v 3 105
With mirth in funeral and with dirge in marriage . . . *Hamlet* i 2 12
I came to see your father's funeral.—I pray thee, do not mock me . i 2 176
The funeral baked meats Did coldly furnish forth the marriage tables . i 2 180
His obscure funeral—No trophy, sword, nor hatchment o'er his bones . iv 5 213
Our army shall In solemn show attend this funeral . *Ant. and Cleo.* v 2 367
Or dead, give's cause to mourn his funeral . . . . *Pericles* ii 4 32
Fur. You fur your gloves with reason . . . . *Troi. and Cres.* ii 2 38
The lion and the belly-pinched wolf Keep their fur dry . . . *Lear* iii 1 14
Furbish. And furbish new the name of John a Gaunt, Even in the lusty haviour of his son . . . . *Richard II.* i 3 76
Furbished. With furbish'd arms and new supplies of men Began a fresh assault . . . . *Macbeth* i 2 32
Furies. Approach, ye Furies fell! O Fates, come, come! *M. N. Dream* v 1 289
Talked of Satan and of Limbo and of Furies . . . . *All's Well* v 3 261
Then, Pistol, lay thy head in Furies' lap . . . . . 2 *Hen. IV.* v 3 110
In his rages, and his furies, and his wraths, and his cholers . *Hen V.* iv 7 37
Seize on him, Furies, take him to your torments! . . *Richard III.* i 4 57
Furious. Give ground, if you see him furious . . . *T. Night* iii 4 334
In the intestine shock And furious close of civil butchery . 1 *Hen. IV.* i 1 13
And that furious Scot, The bloody Douglas . . . . 2 *Hen. IV.* i 1 126
Colevile of the dale, a most furious knight and valorous enemy . iv 3 42
O braggart vile and damned furious wight! . . . . *Hen. V.* ii 1 64
By cruel fate, And giddy Fortune's furious fickle wheel . . . . iii 6 29
More furious raging broils Than yet can be imagined or supposed 1 *Hen VI.* iv 1 185
Peace, good queen, And whet not on these furious peers . 2 *Hen. VI.* ii 1 34
Thy school-days frightful, desperate, wild, and furious . *Richard III.* iv 4 169
Know ye not, in Rome How furious and impatient they be? *T. Andron.* ii 1 76
Here comes the furious Tybalt back again.—Alive, in triumph! *R. and J.* iii 1 126
Who can be wise, amazed, temperate and furious, Loyal and neutral, in a moment? No man . . . . *Macbeth* ii 3 114
To be furious, Is to be frighted out of fear . . . *Ant. and Cleo.* iii 13 195
You are most hot and furious when you win . . . *Cymbeline* ii 3 7
Fear no more the heat o' the sun, Nor the furious winter's rages . iv 2 259
Furlong. Now would I give a thousand furlongs of sea for an acre of barren ground, long heath, brown furze, any thing . . *Tempest* i 1 68
You may ride's With one soft kiss a thousand furlongs ere With spur we heat an acre . . . . *W. Tale* i 2 95
Furnace. Then the lover, Sighing like furnace . . *As Y. L. It* ii 7 148
Heat not a furnace for your foe so hot That it do singe yourself *Hen. VIII.* i 1 140
He furnaces The thick sighs from him . . . . . *Cymbeline* i 6 66
Furnace-burning. I cannot weep; for all my body's moisture Scarce serves to quench my furnace-burning heart . . . 3 *Hen. VI.* ii 1 80
Furnish. Kiss the book: I will furnish it anon with new contents *Tempest* ii 2 146
Take a note of what I stand in need of, To furnish me . *T. G. of Ver.* ii 7 85
Have thy counsel Which is the best to furnish me to-morrow *Much Ado* iii 1 103
That shall be rack'd, even to the uttermost, To furnish thee to Belmont, to fair Portia . . . . *Mer. of Venice* i 1 182
Tubal, a wealthy Hebrew of my tribe, Will furnish me . . . . i 3 59
We have two hours To furnish us . . . . ii 4 9
What heaven more will, That thee may furnish . . . *All's Well* i 1 78
His present gift Shall furnish me to those Italian fields . . . ii 3 307
Your opposite hath in him what youth, strength, skill and wrath can furnish man withal . . . . *T. Night* iii 4 255
The revenue whereof shall furnish us For our affairs in hand *Richard II.* i 4 46
Will your lordship lend me a thousand pound to furnish me forth? 2 *Hen. IV.* i 2 251
Furnish him with all appertinents Belonging to his honour . *Hen. V.* ii 2 87
His training such, That he may furnish and instruct great teachers *Hen. VIII.* i 2 113
To furnish Rome, and to prepare the ways You have for dignities . . iii 2 328
Good Diomed, Furnish you fairly for this interchange . *Troi. and Cres.* iii 3 33
Sort such needful ornaments As you think fit to furnish me *R. and J.* iv 2 35
Having great and instant occasion to use fifty talents, hath sent to your lordship to furnish him . . . . *T. of Athens* iii 1 20
There is not so much left, to furnish out A moderate table . . . iii 4 116
The funeral baked meats Did coldly furnish forth the marriage tables *Ham.* i 2 181
I will withdraw, To furnish me with some swift means of death *Othello* iii 3 478
Furnished. He furnish'd me From mine own library with volumes *Temp.* i 2 166
Claudio must die to-morrow: let him be furnished with divines *M. for M.* iii 2 221
I am not furnish'd with the present money . . . *Com. of Errors* iv 1 34
What gold and jewels she is furnish'd with . . . *Mer. of Venice* ii 4 32
We turned o'er many books together: he is furnished with my opinion iv 1 157
He was furnished like a hunter . . . . *As Y. Like It* iii 2 258
I am not furnished like a beggar, therefore to beg will not become me Epil. 10
My house within the city Is richly furnished with plate and gold *T. of S.* ii 1 349
We are not furnish'd like Bohemia's son . . . . . . *W. Tale* iv 4 599
All furnish'd, all in arms; All plumed like estridges . 1 *Hen. IV.* iv 1 97
Semblably furnish'd like the king himself . . . . v 3 21
He is furnish'd with no certainties . . . . 2 *Hen. IV.* i 1 31
He then that is not furnish'd in this sort Doth but usurp the sacred name of knight . . . . 1 *Hen. VI.* iv 1 39
The horses your lordship sent for, with all the care I had, I saw well chosen, ridden, and furnished . . . . *Hen. VIII.* ii 2 3
There ye shall meet about this weighty business. My Wolsey, see it furnish'd . . . . ii 2 141
'Tis furnish'd well with men, And men are flesh and blood . *J. Cæsar* iii 1 66
I shall be furnish'd to inform you rightly . . . *Ant. and Cleo.* i 4 77
When he was less furnished than now he is with that which makes him both without and within . . . . *Cymbeline* i 4 8
If she be furnish'd with a mind so rare, She is alone the Arabian bird . i 6 16
Furnished. He well may be a stranger, for he comes To an honour'd triumph strangely furnished . . . . *Pericles* ii 2 53
Furnishings. Something deeper, Whereof perchance these are but furnishings . . . . *Lear* iii 1 29
Furniture. Neither art thou the worse For this poor furniture *T. of Shrew* iv 3 182
I'ld give bay Curtal and his furniture, My mouth no more were broken than these boys' . . . . *All's Well* ii 3 65
And there receive Money and order for their furniture . 1 *Hen. IV.* iii 3 226
Somerset will keep me here, Without discharge, money, or furniture 2 *Hen. VI.* i 3 172
Fit it with such furniture as suits The greatness of his person *Hen. VIII.* ii 1 99
Furnival. Lord Furnival of Sheffield, The thrice-victorious Lord of Falconbridge . . . . 1 *Hen. VI.* iv 7 66
Furor. 'Ira furor brevis est;' but yond man is ever angry *T. of Athens* i 2 28
Furred. Allowed by order of law a furred gown to keep him warm; and furred with fox and lamb-skins too . . . *Meas. for Meas.* iii 2 8
Now of late, not able to travel with her furred pack, she washes bucks here at home . . . . 2 *Hen. VI.* iv 2 51
Through tatter'd clothes small vices do appear; Robes and furr'd gowns hide all . . . . *Lear* iv 6 169
Yea, and furr'd moss besides, when flowers are none . *Cymbeline* iv 2 228
Furrow. You sunburnt sicklemen, of August weary, Come hither from the furrow and be merry . . . . *Tempest* iv 1 135
Thou canst help time to furrow me with age, But stop no wrinkle *Rich. II.* i 3 229
Furrowed. Draw the huge bottoms through the furrow'd sea *Hen. V.* iii Prol. 12
Furrow-weed. Crown'd with rank fumiter and furrow-weeds . . *Lear* iv 4 3
Further. Hear a little further And then I'll bring thee to the present business . . . . *Tempest* i 2 135
Run into no further danger: interrupt the monster one word further . iii 2 76
I can go no further, sir; My old bones ache . . . . iii 3 1
The sole drift of my purpose doth extend Not a frown further . . . v 1 30
What they made there, I know not. Well, I will look further into't *Mer. Wives* ii 1 245
Let's obey his humour a little further: come, gentlemen . . . iv 2 210
If they can find in their hearts the poor unvirtuous fat knight shall be any further afflicted, we two will still be the ministers . . . iv 2 233
Well, I will muse no further . . . . v 5 253
I will go further than I meant, to pluck all fears out of you *M. for M.* iv 2 206
A stubborn soul, That apprehends no further than this world . . v 1 486
Ere you flout old ends any further, examine your conscience *Much Ado* i 1 290
We will hear further of it by your daughter: let it cool the while . . ii 3 211
To Athens will I bear my folly back And follow you no further *M. N. D.* iii 2 316
Torn with briers, I can no further crawl, no further go . . . . iii 2 444
What if I stray'd no further, but chose here? . . *Mer. of Venice* ii 7 35
I must attempt you further: Take some remembrance of us, as a tribute iv 1 421
I will no further offend you than becomes me for my good *As Y. Like It* i 1 83
No further in sport neither than with safety of a pure blush thou mayst in honour come off again . . . . i 2 31
I pray you, bear with me; I cannot go no further . . . . . ii 4 10
I can go no further: O, I die for food! Here lie I down . . . . ii 6 1
I durst go no further than the Lie Circumstantial . . . . . v 4 89
I will speak with you further anon . . . . *All's Well* i 3 133
I hope I need not to advise you further . . . . iii 5 27
To requite you further, I will bestow some precepts of this virgin . . iii 5 102
And extend to you what further becomes his greatness . . . . iii 6 74
And by midnight look to hear further from me . . . . . . iii 6 82
If you misdoubt me that I am not she, I know not how I shall assure you further . . . . iii 7 2
Prithee, get thee further.—Pray you, sir, deliver me this paper . . v 2 15
Inquire further after me; I had talk of you last night . . . . v 2 56
Away with him! We'll sift this matter further . . . . . . v 3 124
I neither can nor will deny But that I know them: do they charge me further? . . . . v 3 167
Trip no further, pretty sweeting; Journeys end in lovers meeting *T. N.* ii 3 43
Since you make your pleasure of your pains, I will no further chide you iii 3 3
What wouldst thou now? If thou darest tempt me further, draw thy sword . . . . iv 1 45
Bring her along with you, it may awake my bounty further . . . v 1 47
These things further thought on, To think me as well a sister as a wife v 1 324
No further enemy to you Than the constraint of hospitable zeal *K. John* ii 1 243
Further I will not flatter you, my lord . . . . ii 1 516
Which for our goods we do no further ask . . . . iv 2 64
And be no further harmful than in show . . . . v 2 77
Further I say and further will maintain Upon his bad life *Richard II.* i 1 98
Mistake not, uncle, further than you should.—Take not, good cousin, further than you should . . . . iii 3 14
And shall it in more shame be further spoken, That you are fool'd? 1 *Hen. IV.* i 3 177
No further go in this Than I by letters shall direct your course . . i 3 292
If I travel but four foot by the squier further afoot, I shall break my wind . . . . ii 2 13
I'll starve ere I'll rob a foot further . . . . ii 2 23
How! so far?—Not an inch further . . . . ii 3 117
As if thou never walk'st further than Finsbury . . . . . . iii 1 257
And further, I have learn'd, The king himself in person is set forth . iv 1 90
Did he win The hearts of all that he did angle for, Proceeded further . iv 3 85
Nor claim no further than your new-fall'n right, The seat of Gaunt . v 1 44
To approve my youth further, I will not . . . . . 2 *Hen. IV.* i 2 214
The heat is past; follow no further now: Call in the powers . . . iv 3 27
For us, we will consider of this further . . . . . . *Hen. V.* ii 4 113
Question, my lords, no further of the case, How or which way 1 *Hen. VI.* ii 1 72
And dimm'd mine eyes, that I can read no further . . . 2 *Hen. VI.* i 1 55
Item, It is further agreed between them . . . . i 1 57
So cowards fight when they can fly no further . . . . 3 *Hen. VI.* i 4 40
Then further, all dissembling set aside, Tell me for truth . . . iii 3 119
And, as I further have to understand, Is new committed . . . iv 4 10
To consider further that What his high hatred would effect wants not A minister in his power . . . . *Hen. VIII.* i 1 106
You shall to the Tower, till you know How he determines further . . i 1 214
I have no further gone in this than by A single voice . . . . i 2 69
But benefit no further Than vainly longing . . . . i 2 80
I shall anon advise you Further in the proceeding . . . . . i 2 108
There's mischief in this man: canst thou say further? . . . . i 2 187
How far I have proceeded; Or how far further shall . . . . . ii 4 91
Confine yourself To Asher House, my Lord of Winchester's, Till you hear further from his highness . . . . iii 2 232
Further, sir, Stands in the gap and trade of moe preferments . . v 1 35
I should have ta'en some pains to bring together Yourself and your accusers; and to have heard you, Without indurance, further . v 1 121
For my part, I'll not meddle nor make no further . *Troi. and Cres.* i 1 14

Further. There is expectance here from both the sides, What further you will do *Troi. and Cres.* iv 5 147
Before we proceed any further, hear me speak *Coriolanus* i 1 1
Plagues Plaster you o'er, that you may be abhorr'd Further than seen! i 4 33
I will make much of your voices, and so trouble you no further ii 3 117
Now you have left your voices, I have no further with you ii 3 181
Pass no further.—Ha! what is that?—It will be dangerous to go on: no further iii 1 24
A mind That shall remain a poison where it is, Not poison any further iii 1 88
Lest his infection, being of catching nature, Spread further iii 1 311
I muse my mother Does not approve me further iii 2 8
Or never trust to what my tongue can do I' the way of flattery further iii 2 137
Shall I be charged no further than this present? Must all determine here? iii 3 42
Consider further, That when he speaks not like a citizen, You find him like a soldier iii 3 52
Know, I pray you,— I'll know no further iii 3 87
Bid them all home; he's gone, and we'll no further iv 2 1
I would have thee gone: And yet no further than a wanton's bird *Rom. and Jul.* ii 2 178
Dost return to pry In what I further shall intend to do v 3 34
Can vengeance be pursued further than death? v 3 55
Well; what further?—One only daughter have I *T. of Athens* i 1 120
Wait attendance Till you hear further from me i 1 162
Sermon me no further: No villanous bounty yet hath pass'd my heart ii 2 181
Trouble him no further; thus you still shall find him v 1 216
Nor construe any further my neglect *J. Cæsar* i 2 45
I would not, so with love I might entreat you, Be any further moved i 2 167
I urged you further; then you scratch'd your head ii 1 243
So near will I be, That your best friends shall wish I had been further ii 2 125
From hence to Inverness, And bind us further to you *Macbeth* i 4 43
When I burned in desire to question them further, they made themselves air i 5 4
We will speak further.—Only look up clear i 5 72
We will proceed no further in this business: He hath honour'd me of late i 7 31
This place is too cold for hell. I'll devil-porter it no further ii 3 20
And question this most bloody piece of work, To know it further ii 3 135
You made it known to us.—I did so, and went further iii 1 85
Malice domestic, foreign levy, nothing, Can touch him further iii 2 26
My former speeches have but hit your thoughts, Which can interpret further iii 6 2
I dare not speak much further: But cruel are the times iv 2 17
Giving to you no further personal power To business with the king *Ham.* i 2 36
Which is no further Than the main voice of Denmark goes withal i 3 27
Where wilt thou lead me? speak; I'll go no further i 5 1
With an entreaty, herein further shown, That it might please you ii 2 76
How may we try it further? ii 2 159
Let's further think of this; Weigh what convenience both of time and means May fit us to our shape iv 7 149
Without debatement further, more or less v 2 45
We shall further think on't.—We must do something, and i' the heat *Lear* i 1 311
I will look further into't. But where's my fool? i 4 76
Acquaint my daughter no further with any thing you know i 5 2
I will talk further with you.—No, do not iii 1 43
Poor Tom's a-cold. I cannot daub it further iv 1 54
Then shall you go no further. It is the cowish terror of his spirit iv 2 11
No further conscionable than in putting on the mere form of civil and humane seeming *Othello* ii 1 242
I would I might entreat your honour To scan this thing no further iii 3 245
I do beseech you, sir, trouble yourself no further iv 3 1
Enforce no further The griefs between ye *Ant. and Cleo* ii 2 99
I am not married, Cæsar: let me hear Agrippa further speak ii 2 126
Let me have thy hand: Further this act of grace ii 2 149
Trouble yourselves no further: pray you, hasten Your generals after ii 4 1
Would you praise Cæsar, say 'Cæsar:' go no further iii 2 13
No further, sir.—You take from me a great part of myself iii 2 23
'Tis easy to't; and there I will attend What further comes iii 10 33
Cæsar entreats, Not to consider in what case thou stand'st, Further than he is Cæsar iii 13 55
Peace! Hark further iv 9 11
You do extend These thoughts of horror further than you shall Find cause v 2 63
Give me directly to understand you have prevailed, I am no further your enemy *Cymbeline* i 4 172
Had I not brought The knowledge of your mistress home, I grant We were to question further ii 4 52
Away! no further with your din Express impatience v 4 111
Further to boast were neither true nor modest, Unless I add, we are honest v 5 18
Peace, peace! see further; he eyes us not; forbear v 5 124
But we saw him dead.—Be silent; let's see further v 5 127
What became of him I further know not v 5 286
You shall not need, my fellow peers of Tyre, Further to question me *Per.* i 3 12
If further yet you will be satisfied, Why . . . He would depart i 3 16
And further he desires to know of you, Of whence you are ii 3 79
But I'll see further: Perhaps they will but please themselves upon her iv 1 100
Further act. Persuaded him from any further act *2 Hen. VI.* v 3 10
Further aid. Friends both, go join you with some further aid *Hamlet* iv 1 33
Further benefit. Give it you In earnest of a further benefit *1 Hen. VI.* v 3 16
Further charge. My lord hath sent you this note; and by me this further charge, that you swerve not *Meas. for Meas.* iv 2 106
Further compliment. There is further compliment of leave-taking *Lear* i 1 306
Further conference. Stand aside, While I use further conference with Warwick *3 Hen. VI.* iii 3 111
Further danger. Run into no further danger *Tempest* iii 2 76
Keep you where you are, though there were no further danger known but the modesty which is so lost *All's Well* iii 5 29
Further day. We adjourn this court till further day *Hen. VIII.* ii 4 232
Further deed. Without any further deed to have them at all into their estimation and report *Coriolanus* ii 2 31
Further delay. Without any further delay than this very evening *Lear* i 2 100
Further edge. Give him a further edge, And drive his purpose on *Hamlet* iii 1 26
Further evil. Is't not to be damn'd, To let this canker of our nature come In further evil? v 2 70
Further fear. To thy further fear, Nay, to thy mere confusion *Cymbeline* iv 2 91
Further gait. To suppress His further gait herein *Hamlet* i 2 31
Further good. It is an earnest of a further good That I mean *Cymbeline* i 5 65
Further grief. And for a further grief,—God give you joy! *Pericles* ii 5 87
Further halting. Come nearer; No further halting: satisfy me *Cymbeline* iii 5 92
Further harm. No further harm Than so much loss of time *Coriolanus* iii 1 284
But for a satisfaction of my thought; No further harm *Othello* iii 3 98
Further leisure. Ere further leisure yield them further means *Richard II.* i 4 40
Further life. For further life in this world I ne'er hope *Hen. VIII.* ii 1 69
Further matter. My thoughts aim at a further matter *3 Hen. VI.* iv 1 125
Further means. Ere further leisure yield them further means *Richard II.* i 4 40
Further misery. Let us, that have our tongues, Plot some device of further misery *T. Andron.* iii 1 134
Further necessity. There's no further necessity of qualities can make her be refused *Pericles* iv 2 52
Further off. For my sake, my dear, Lie further off yet *M. N. Dream* ii 2 44
But, gentle friend, for love and courtesy Lie further off ii 2 57
My lord, fly further off; Mark Antony is in your tents, my lord *J. Cæsar* v 3 9
Be you well assured He shall in strangeness stand no further off Than in a politic distance *Othello* iii 3 12
Further out. His eye-balls further out than when he lived *2 Hen. VI.* iii 2 169
Further pleasure. Presently Attend his further pleasure *All's Well* ii 4 54
Come you this afternoon, To know our further pleasure *Rom. and Jul.* i 1 108
Further reason. I will hear further reason for this *Othello* iv 2 251
Further recompense. Do not look for further recompense Than thine own gladness that thou art employ'd *As Y. Like It* iii 5 97
Further revenge. May we . . . pursue him with any further revenge? *Mer. Wives* iv 2 221
Further satisfying. If you seek For further satisfying *Cymbeline* iii 4 134
Further scope. His coming hither hath no further scope Than for his lineal royalties *Richard II.* iii 3 112
Further search. Let's make further search For my poor son *Tempest* iii 3 323
Further service. No further service, doctor, Until I send for thee *Cymb.* i 5 44
Further settling. Trouble him no more Till further settling *Lear* iv 7 82
Further space. And they are ready To-morrow, or at further space v 3 53
Further time. And here commit you to my lord cardinal To keep, until your further time of trial *2 Hen. VI.* iii 1 138
Further trade. Have you any further trade with us? *Hamlet* iii 2 346
Further travel. Since he went from Egypt 'tis A space for further travel *Ant. and Cleo.* ii 1 31
Further trial. Till further trial in those charges *Hen. VIII.* v 1 103
He hath resisted law, And therefore law shall scorn him further trial *Coriolanus* iii 1 268
Further use. Which should, indeed, give us a further use *All's Well* ii 3 41
Which once attain'd, Your highness knows, comes to no further use But to be known and hated *2 Hen. IV.* iv 4 72
Further view. Mine eyes did sicken at the sight, and could not Endure a further view *Ant. and Cleo.* iii 10 18
Further warrant. Wonder not till further warrant *Much Ado* iii 2 115
Further woe. What further woe conspires against mine age? *Rom. and Jul.* v 3 212
Furtherance. By your furtherance I am clothed in steel *Pericles* ii 1 160
Omit no happy hour That may give furtherance to our expedition *Hen. V.* i 2 301
Cannot my body nor blood-sacrifice Entreat you to your wonted furtherance? Then take my soul *1 Hen. VI.* v 3 21
Furtherer. Thy brother was a furtherer in the act *Tempest* v 1 73
Furthermore, I pray you, show my youth old Shylock's house *Mer. of Ven.* iv 2 10
And furthermore, we'll have the Lord Say's head *2 Hen. VI.* iv 2 169
Furthermore tell him, we desire to know of him, Of whence he is *Pericles* ii 3 73
Furthest. Five summers have I spent in furthest Greece *Com. of Errors* i 1 133
I will fetch you a toothpicker now from the furthest inch of Asia *M. Ado* ii 1 275
To the furthest verge That ever was survey'd by English eye *Richard II.* i 1 93
Soon as the all-cheering sun Should in the furthest east begin to draw The shady curtains from Aurora's bed *Rom. and Jul.* i 1 141
Fury. This music crept by me upon the waters, Allaying both their fury and my passion With its sweet air *Tempest* i 2 392
Silver! there it goes, Silver!—Fury, Fury! there, Tyrant, there! hark! iv 1 258
Yet with my nobler reason 'gainst my fury Do I take part v 1 26
The fury of ungovern'd youth *T. G. of Ver.* iv 1 45
He would never have boarded me in this fury *Mer. Wives* ii 1 92
A fiend, a fury, pitiless and rough; A wolf, nay, worse *Com. of Errors* iv 2 35
Sent him home, Whilst to take order for the wrongs I went That here and there his fury had committed v 1 147
Her cousin, an she were not possessed with a fury, exceeds her *Much Ado* i 1 193
I keep her as a vessel of thy law's fury *L. L. Lost* i 1 278
What zeal, what fury hath inspired thee now? iv 3 229
I in fury hither follow'd them, Fair Helena in fancy following me *M. N. Dream* iv 1 167
I do oppose My patience to his fury, and am arm'd To suffer *Mer. of Ven.* iv 1 11
Where two raging fires meet together They do consume the thing that feeds their fury *T. of Shrew* ii 1 134
A most hideous opinion of his rage, skill, fury and impetuosity *T. Night* iii 4 213
The fury spent, anon Did this break from her *W. Tale* iii 3 26
Till the fury of his highness settle, Come not before him iv 4 482
Against whose fury and unmatched force The aweless lion could not wage the fight *K. John* i 1 265
Not Death himself In mortal fury half so peremptory ii 1 454
Let belief and life encounter so As doth the fury of two desperate men iii 1 32
By all the blood that ever fury breathed v 2 127
Chasing the royal blood With fury from his native residence *Richard II.* ii 1 119
An oath of mickle might; and fury shall abate *Hen. V.* ii 1 70
Tell him my fury shall abate, and I The crowns will take iv 4 50
The duke Hath banish'd moody discontented fury *1 Hen. VI.* iii 1 123
You tempt the fury of my three attendants, Lean famine, quartering steel, and climbing fire iv 2 10
Mad ire and wrathful fury makes me weep iv 3 28
Dizzy-eyed fury and great rage of heart Suddenly made him from my side to start iv 7 11
Proud prelate, in thy face I see thy fury *2 Hen. VI.* i 1 143
Do calm the fury of this mad-bred flaw iii 1 354
Like Ajax Telamonius, On sheep or oxen could I spend my fury v 1 27
The sight of any of the house of York Is as a fury to torment my soul *3 Hen. VI.* i 3 31
I am faint and cannot fly their fury: And were I strong, I would not shun their fury i 4 23
I dare your quenchless fury to more rage i 4 28
Like the selfsame sea Forced to retire by fury of the wind ii 5 8
This, in respect, a child: And men ne'er spend their fury on a child v 5 57
How now, Thersites! what, lost in the labyrinth of thy fury! *Tr. and Cr.* ii 3 2
The prayers of priests nor times of sacrifice, Embarquements all of fury *Coriolanus* i 10 22
Whose fury not dissembled speaks his griefs *T. Andron.* i 1 438
And would not, but in fury, fright my youth iv 1 24
As she in fury shall Cut off the proud'st conspirator that lives iv 4 25
Welcome, dread Fury, to my woful house v 2 82
O, why should wrath be mute, and fury dumb? v 3 184

Fury. Mercutio slain! Away to heaven, respective lenity, And fire-eyed fury be my conduct now! *Rom. and Jul.* iii 1 129
Thy wild acts denote The unreasonable fury of a beast iii 3 111
Put not another sin upon my head, By urging me to fury v 3 63
With a noble fury and fair spirit *T. of Athens* iii 5 18
In that beastly fury He has been known to commit outrages iii 5 71
It is a cause worthy my spleen and fury, That I may strike at Athens iii 5 113
Know you the quality of Lord Timon's fury? iii 6 118
Make large confusion; and, thy fury spent, Confounded be thyself! iv 3 127
And make thine own self the conquest of thy fury iv 3 341
Domestic fury and fierce civil strife Shall cumber all the parts of Italy; Blood and destruction shall be so in use *J. Cæsar* iii 1 263
O, yet I do repent me of my fury, That I did kill them *Macbeth* ii 3 112
Some say he's mad; others that lesser hate him Do call it valiant fury v 2 14
It is a tale Told by an idiot, full of sound and fury, Signifying nothing v 5 27
Which the impetuous blasts, with eyeless rage, Catch in their fury *Lear* iii 1 9
In the fury of his heart, when the foul fiend rages, eats cow-dung for sallets iii 4 136
In her prophetic fury sew'd the work *Othello* iii 4 72
I understand a fury in your words, But not the words iv 2 32
Thou shouldst come like a Fury crown'd with snakes *Ant. and Cleo.* ii 5 40
Plant those that have revolted in the van, That Antony may seem to spend his fury Upon himself iv 6 10
But better 'twere Thou fell'st into my fury, for one death Might have prevented many iv 12 41
Look For fury not to be resisted. Thus defied, I thank thee *Cymbeline* iii 1 68
I never saw Such noble fury in so poor a thing v 5 8
Furze. Long heath, brown furze, any thing *Tempest* i 1 70
Through Tooth'd briers, sharp furzes, pricking goss and thorns iv 1 180

Fust. Sure, he . . . gave us not That capability and god-like reason To fust in us unused *Hamlet* iv 4 39
Fustian. The serving-men in their new fustian *T. of Shrew* iv 1 49
A fustian riddle! *T. Night* ii 5 119
I cannot endure such a fustian rascal *2 Hen. IV.* ii 4 203
Swagger? swear? and discourse fustian with one's own shadow? *Othello* ii 3 282
Fustilarian. You fustilarian! I'll tickle your catastrophe *2 Hen. IV.* ii 1 66
Fusty. At this fusty stuff The large Achilles . . . From his deep chest laughs out a loud applause *Troi. and Cres.* i 3 161
A' were as good crack a fusty nut with no kernel ii 1 111
The dull tribunes, That, with the fusty plebeians, hate thine honours *Coriolanus* i 9 7
Future. And all the fair effects of future hopes *T. G. of Ver.* i 1 50
Like a prophet, Looks in a glass, that shows what future evils, Either new, or by remissness new-conceived *Meas. for Meas.* ii 2 95
What in time proceeds May token to the future our past deeds *All's Well* iv 2 63
For present comfort and for future good *W. Tale* v 1 32
And future ages groan for this foul act *Richard II.* iv 1 138
And give me signs of future accidents *1 Hen. VI.* v 3 4
My heart's on future mischief set *2 Hen. VI.* v 2 84
Make use now, and provide For thine own future safety *Hen. VIII.* iii 2 421
Three talents on the present; in future, all *T. of Athens* i 1 141
The future comes apace: What shall defend the interim? ii 2 157
I feel now The future in the instant *Macbeth* i 5 59
That future strife May be prevented now *Lear* i 1 45
Learn'd indeed were that astronomer That knew the stars as I his characters; He'ld lay the future open *Cymbeline* iii 2 29
Futurity. Nor present sorrows, Nor purposed merit in futurity, Can ransom me into his love again *Othello* iii 4 117

G

G. About a prophecy, which says that G Of Edward's heirs the murderer shall be *Richard III.* i 1 39
For my name of George begins with G, It follows in his thought that I am he i 1 58
Gabble. Wouldst gabble like A thing most brutish *Tempest* i 2 356
Choughs' language, gabble enough, and good enough *All's Well* iv 1 22
Have you no wit, manners, nor honesty, but to gabble like tinkers? *T. N.* ii 3 95
Gaberdine. My best way is to creep under his gaberdine *Tempest* ii 2 40
I hid me under the dead moon-calf's gaberdine for fear of the storm ii 2 115
And spit upon my Jewish gaberdine *Mer. of Venice* i 3 113
Gabriel. And Gabriel's pumps were all unpink'd i' the heel *T. of Shrew* iv 1 136
Gad. And with a gad of steel will write these words *T. Andron.* iv 1 103
And the king gone to-night! subscribed his power! Confined to exhibition! All this done Upon the gad! *Lear* i 2 26
Gadding. How now, my headstrong! where have you been gadding? *Rom. and Jul.* iv 2 16
Gadshill. Now shall we know if Gadshill have set a match *1 Hen. IV.* i 2 118
By four o'clock, early at Gadshill! there are pilgrims going to Canterbury i 2 139
Gadshill lies to-night in Rochester i 2 143
Falstaff, Bardolph, Peto and Gadshill shall rob those men i 2 182
When thou rannest up Gadshill in the night to catch my horse iii 3 43
Your day's service at Shrewsbury hath a little gilded over your night's exploit on Gad's-hill *2 Hen. IV.* i 2 170
And you knew me, as you did when you ran away by Gad's-hill ii 4 333
Gage. Pale trembling coward, there I throw my gage *Richard II.* i 1 69
Interchangeably hurl down my gage Upon this overweening traitor's foot i 1 146
Throw down, my son, the Duke of Norfolk's gage i 1 161
Rage must be withstood: Give me his gage i 1 174
Take but my shame, And I resign my gage i 1 176
Cousin, throw up your gage; do you begin i 1 186
There is my gage, the manual seal of death, That marks thee out for hell iv 1 25
There is my gage, Aumerle, in gage to thine iv 1 34
There I throw my gage, To prove it on thee to the extremest point iv 1 46
Some honest Christian trust me with a gage, That Norfolk lies iv 1 83
Lords appellants, Your differences shall all rest under gage Till we assign you to your days of trial iv 1 105
Shall it for shame be spoken . . . That men of your nobility and power Did gage them both in an unjust behalf? *1 Hen. IV.* i 3 173
Give me any gage of thine, and I will wear it in my bonnet *Hen. V.* iv 1 223
'Tis the gage of one that I should fight withal, if he be alive iv 7 127
Gaged. Wherein my time something too prodigal Hath left me gaged *Mer. of Venice* i 1 130
Against the which, a moiety competent Was gaged by our king *Hamlet* i 1 91
Gagged. Unless you laugh and minister occasion to him, he is gagged *T. Night* i 5 94
Why laugh you at such a barren rascal? an you smile not, he's gagged v 1 384
Gaging. Both taxing me and gaging me to keep An oath *Troi. and Cres.* v 1 46
Gagne. J'ai gagné deux mots d'Anglois vitement *Hen. V.* iii 4 14
Gain. If haply won, perhaps a hapless gain *T. G. of Ver.* i 1 32
He gains by death that hath such means to die *Com. of Errors* iii 2 51
I will loose his bonds And gain a husband by his liberty v 1 340
If study's gain be thus and this be so, Study knows that which yet it doth not know *L. L. Lost* i 1 67
What should I gain By the exaction of the forfeiture? *Mer. of Venice* i 3 165
Who chooseth me shall gain what many men desire ii 7 37
Laughed at my losses, mocked at my gains, scorned my nation iii 1 58
But I, his brother, gain nothing under him but growth *As Y. Like It* i 1 14
'Twill bring you gain, or perish on the seas *T. of Shrew* ii 1 331
The gain I seek is, quiet in the match ii 1 332
If both gain, all The gift doth stretch itself as 'tis received *All's Well* ii 1 3
How mightily some other times we drown our gain in tears! *All's Well* iv 3 79
For my thoughts, you have them ill to friend Till your deeds gain them v 3 183
The loss, the gain, the ordering on't, is all Properly ours *W. Tale* ii 1 169
That for thine own gain shouldst defend mine honour *K. John* ii 1 242
Gain, be my lord, for I will worship thee ii 1 598
But what shall I gain by young Arthur's fall? iii 4 141

Gain. Your care is gain of care, by new care won *Richard II.* iv 1 197
And to thy worth will add right worthy gains v 6 12
The gain proposed Choked the respect of likely peril fear'd *2 Hen. IV.* i 1 183
We offer'd to the king, And might by no suit gain our audience iv 1 76
Wherein, to gain the language, 'Tis neeedful that the most immodest word Be look'd upon and learn'd iv 4 69
And I had many living to upbraid My gain of it by their assistances iv 5 194
Didst thou at first, to flatter us withal, Make us partakers of a little gain, That now our loss might be ten times so much? *1 Hen. VI.* ii 1 52
By me they nothing gain an if I stay iv 6 36
Unchain your spirits now with spelling charms And try if they can gain your liberty v 3 32
With such strict and severe covenants As little shall the Frenchmen gain v 4 115
My mind presageth happy gain and conquest *3 Hen. VI.* v 1 71
And of our labours thou shalt reap the gain v 7 20
When they are gone, then must I count my gains *Richard III.* i 1 162
Up and down my sons were toss'd, For me to joy and weep their gain and loss ii 4 59
Hopes to find you forward Upon his party for the gain thereof iii 2 47
Not as protector, steward, substitute, Or lowly factor for another's gain iii 7 134
Murder her brothers, and then marry her! Uncertain way of gain! iv 2 64
Advantaging their loan with interest Of ten times double gain of happiness iv 4 324
But if I thrive, the gain of my attempt The least of you shall share v 3 267
Bid him strive To gain the love o' the commonalty *Hen. VIII.* i 2 170
To gain the popedom, And fee my friends in Rome iii 2 212
Lords, one remain; So I grow stronger, you more honour gain v 3 182
Our sufferance is a gain to them *Coriolanus* i 1 22
You must think, if we give you any thing, we hope to gain by you ii 3 78
And might not gain so great a happiness As have thy love *T. Andron.* ii 4 20
Graves only be men's works and death their gain! *T. of Athens* v 1 225
Better be with the dead, Whom we, to gain our peace, have sent to peace, Than on the torture of the mind to lie In restless ecstasy *Macbeth* iii 2 20
Now spurs the lated traveller apace To gain the timely inn iii 3 7
O, well done! I commend your pains; And every one shall share i' the gains iv 1 40
To gain a little patch of ground That hath in it no profit but the name *Hamlet* iv 4 18
I will win for him an I can; if not, I will gain nothing but my shame v 2 184
That sir which serves and seeks for gain, And follows but for form, Will pack when it begins to rain *Lear* ii 4 79
Neglecting an attempt of ease and gain *Othello* i 3 29
Whether he kill Cassio, Or Cassio him, or each do kill the other, Every way makes my gain v 1 14
Ambition, The soldier's virtue, rather makes choice of loss, Than gain which darkens him *Ant. and Cleo.* iii 1 24
Gains or loses Your sword or mine, or masterless leaves both *Cymbeline* ii 4 59
Such gain the cap of him that makes 'em fine, Yet keeps his book uncross'd iii 3 25
To gain his colour I'ld let a parish of such Clotens blood iv 2 167
View Her countless glory, which desert must gain *Pericles* i 1 31
I'll show you those in troubles reign, Losing a mite, a mountain gain ii Gower 8
He is a happy king, since he gains from his subjects the name of good ii 1 109
Never did my actions yet commence A deed might gain her love ii 5 54
You must seem to do that fearfully which you commit willingly, despise profit where you have most gain iv 2 129
If that thy master would gain by me, Proclaim that I can sing, weave iv 6 193
Gained. Gnawing with my teeth my bonds in sunder, I gain'd my freedom *Com. of Errors* v 1 250
Thy grace being gain'd cures all disgrace in me *L. L. Lost* iv 3 67
Yes, I have gained my experience *As Y. Like It* iv 1 26
Must be as boisterously maintain'd as gain'd *K. John* iii 4 136
The time was blessedly lost wherein such preparation was gained *Hen. V.* iv 1 192
And this her easy-held imprisonment Hath gain'd thy daughter princely liberty *1 Hen. VI.* v 3 140
I mine own gain'd knowledge should profane *Othello* i 3 390
Thanks to you, That call'd me timelier than my purpose hither; For I have gain'd by't *Ant. and Cleo.* ii 6 53

Gained. He served with glory and admired success, So gain'd the sur- addition Leonatus . . . . *Cymbeline* i 1 33
Who hath gain'd Of education all the grace . . . *Pericles* iv Gower 8
Gainer. Wilt thou, after the expense of so much money, be now a gainer? Good body, I thank thee . . . . . *Mer. Wives* ii 2 147
Gain-giving. It is such a kind of gain-giving, as would perhaps trouble a woman . . . . *Hamlet* v 2 226
Gainsaid. You are too great to be by me gainsaid . . . 2 *Hen. IV.* i 1 91
Gainsay. I ne'er heard yet That any of these bolder vices wanted Less impudence to gainsay what they did Than to perform it first *W. Tale* iii 2 57
And whosoe'er gainsays King Edward's right, By this I challenge him 3 *Hen. VI.* iv 7 74
What I should say My tears gainsay . . . . . v 4 74
If it be known to him That I gainsay my deed, how may he wound, And worthily, my falsehood! . . . . . . *Hen. VIII.* ii 4 96
But the just gods gainsay That any drop thou borrow'dst from thy mother, My sacred aunt, should by my mortal sword Be drain'd! *Troi. and Cres.* iv 5 132
Gainsaying. In that I'll no gainsaying . . . *W. Tale* i 2 19
Gait. Great Juno comes; I know her by her gait . . *Tempest* iv 1 102
Does he not hold up his head, as it were, and strut in his gait? *Mer. Wives* i 4 31
The firm fixture of thy foot would give an excellent motion to thy gait in a semi-circled farthingale . . . . . . iii 3 68
When shall you hear that I Will praise a hand, a foot, a face, an eye, A gait? . . . . *L. L. Lost* iv 3 185
His eye ambitious, his gait majestical, and his general behaviour vain . v 1 12
With pretty and with swimming gait . . . *M. N. Dream* ii 1 130
This palpable-gross play hath well beguiled The heavy gait of night . v 1 375
With this field-dew consecrate, Every fairy take his gait . . v 1 423
I know the boy will well usurp the grace, Voice, gait and action of a gentlewoman: I long to hear him . . . . *T. of Shrew* Ind. 1 132
Did ever Dian so become a grove As Kate this chamber with her princely gait? . . . . ii 1 261
Formal in apparel, In gait and countenance surely like a father . . iv 2 65
There do muster true gait . . . . *All's Well* ii 1 56
Therefore, good youth, address thy gait unto her . . . *T. Night* i 4 15
By the colour of his beard, the shape of his leg, the manner of his gait ii 3 171
To go, sir, to enter.—I will answer you with gait and entrance . . iii 1 93
Hath not my gait in it the measure of the court? . . . *W. Tale* iv 4 756
'Tis like the forced gait of a shuffling nag . . . 1 *Hen. IV.* iii 1 135
He had no legs that practised not his gait . . . . 2 *Hen. IV.* ii 3 23
In speech, in gait, In diet, in affections of delight, In military rules . ii 3 28
Should with his lion gait walk the whole world . . . *Hen. V.* ii 2 122
In face, in gait, in speech, he doth resemble . . . 2 *Hen. VI.* iii 1 373
Straight Springs out into fast gait; then stops again . *Hen. VIII.* iii 2 116
Her eyes, her hair, her cheek, her gait, her voice . *Troi. and Cres.* i 1 54
'Tis he, I ken the manner of his gait; He rises on the toe . . iv 5 14
Pass by and curse thy fill, but pass and stay not here thy gait *T. of A.* v 4 73
I do know him by his gait . . . . *J. Cæsar* i 3 132
To suppress His further gait herein . . . . *Hamlet* i 2 31
Neither having the accent of Christians nor the gait of Christian, pagan, nor man, have so strutted and bellowed . . . . . . iii 2 35
Good gentleman, go your gait, and let poor volk pass . . . *Lear* iv 6 242
Methought thy very gait did prophesy A royal nobleness . . . v 3 175
I know his gait, 'tis he . . . . *Othello* v 1 23
Dull of tongue, and dwarfish! What majesty is in her gait? Re- member, If e'er thou look'dst on majesty . . *Ant. and Cleo.* iii 3 20
Galathe. Now here he fights on Galathe his horse . . *Troi. and Cres.* v 5 20
Gale. And promise you calm seas, auspicious gales . . . *Tempest* v 1 314
What happy gale Blows you to Padua here from old Verona? *T. of Shrew* i 2 48
A little gale will soon disperse that cloud . . . 3 *Hen. VI.* v 3 10
Turn their halcyon beaks With every gale and vary of their masters *Lear* ii 2 85
Galen. What says my Æsculapius? my Galen? my heart of elder? *M. W.* ii 3 29
He has no more knowledge in Hibocrates and Galen . . . . iii 1 67
Both of Galen and Paracelsus . . . . *All's Well* ii 3 12
I have read the cause of his effects in Galen . . . 2 *Hen. IV.* i 2 133
The most sovereign prescription in Galen is but empiricutic *Coriolanus* ii 1 128
Gall. 'Twould be my tyranny to strike and gall them For what I bid them do . . . . *Meas. for Meas.* i 3 36
I pity those I do not know, Which a dismiss'd offence would after gall . ii 2 102
What king so strong Can tie the gall up in the slanderous tongue? . iii 2 199
Thou grievest my gall.—Gall! bitter . . . . . *L. L. Lost* v 2 237
Let there be gall enough in thy ink, though thou write with a goose- pen, no matter: about it . . . . *T. Night* iii 2 52
Stand by, or I shall gall you, Faulconbridge.—Thou wert better gall the devil, Salisbury . . . . *K. John* iv 3 94
Hear you, cousin; a word.—All studies here I solemnly defy, Save how to gall and pinch this Bolingbroke . . . . . 1 *Hen. IV.* i 3 229
I am loath to gall a new-healed wound . . . . . 2 *Hen. IV.* i 2 166
You do measure the heat of our livers with the bitterness of your galls i 2 199
But the gout galls the one, and the pox pinches the other . . . i 2 258
Your father's enemies Have steep'd their galls in honey . . *Hen. V.* ii 2 30
And he may well in fretting spend his gall . . . 1 *Hen. VI.* i 2 16
Gall, worse than gall, the daintiest that they taste! . . 2 *Hen. VI.* iii 2 322
This top-proud fellow, Whom from the flow of gall I name not *Hen. VIII.* i 1 152
Whose gall coins slanders like a mint . . . . *Troi. and Cres.* i 3 193
But when they would seem soldiers, they have galls, Good arms, strong joints, true swords . . . . i 3 237
You have the honey still, but these the gall; So to be valiant is no praise ii 2 144
O deadly gall, and theme of all our scorns! . . . . . . iv 5 30
Out, gall!—Finch-egg! . . . . v 1 40
A choking gall and a preserving sweet . . . . *Rom. and Jul.* i 1 200
This intrusion shall Now seeming sweet convert to bitter gall . . i 5 94
Come to my woman's breasts, And take my milk for gall! . . *Macbeth* i 5 49
Gall of goat, and slips of yew Sliver'd in the moon's eclipse . . iv 1 27
The canker galls the infants of the spring . . . . *Hamlet* i 3 39
I am pigeon-liver'd and lack gall To make oppression bitter . . ii 2 605
That, if I gall him slightly, It may be death . . . . . iv 7 148
The toe of the peasant comes so near the heel of the courtier, he galls his kibe . . . . v 1 153
A pestilent gall to me! . . . . *Lear* i 4 127
Drew from my heart all love, And added to the gall . . . . i 4 292
I do know, the state, However this may gall him with some check, Cannot with safety cast him . . . . *Othello* i 1 149
These sentences, to sugar, or to gall, Being strong on both sides, are equivocal . . . . i 3 216
Let it not gall your patience, good Iago, That I extend my manners . ii 1 98
We have galls, and though we have some grace, Yet have we some revenge . . . . iv 3 93
I'll drink the words you send, Though ink be made of gall *Cymbeline* i 1 101

Gallant. This gallant which thou seest Was in the wreck . *Tempest* i 2 413
We, in all her trim, freshly beheld Our royal, good and gallant ship . v 1 237
O wicked, wicked world! One that is well-nigh worn to pieces with age to show himself a young gallant! . . . . . *Mer. Wives* ii 1 22
Nay, keep your way, little gallant . . . . iii 2 1
Gallants, I am not as I have been . . . . . *Much Ado* iii 2 15
All the gallants of the town are come to fetch you to church . . iii 4 96
A sweet gallant, surely! . . . . iv 1 319
Katharine her name.—A gallant lady . . . . *L. L. Lost* ii 1 196
This most gallant, illustrate, and learned gentleman . . . . v 1 128
Joshua, yourself; myself and this gallant gentleman, Judas . . v 1 133
The gallants shall be task'd; For, ladies, we will every one be mask'd . v 2 126
Ladies, withdraw: the gallants are at hand . . . . . . v 2 308
This gallant pins the wenches on his sleeve . . . . . . v 2 321
Trim gallants, full of courtship and of state . . . . . . v 2 363
A lover, that kills himself most gallant for love . . *M. N. Dream* i 2 25
Never did I hear Such gallant chiding . . . . iv 1 120
Where is this young gallant that is so desirous to lie with his mother earth?—Ready, sir . . . . *As Y. Like It* i 2 212
Thou art a gallant youth: I would thou hadst told me of another father i 2 242
A gallant curtle-axe upon my thigh, A boar-spear in my hand . . i 3 119
Fetch that gallant hither; If he be absent, bring his brother . . ii 2 17
Come, where be these gallants? who's at home? . . *T. of Shrew* iii 2 89
Why, so this gallant will command the sun . . . . . . iv 3 198
'Tis a most gallant fellow. I would he loved his wife . *All's Well* iii 5 81
Has sat i' the stocks all night, poor gallant knave . . . . iv 3 117
The gallant militarist,—that was his own phrase . . . . . iv 3 161
It is a gallant child; one that indeed physics the subject *W. Tale* i 1 42
This gallant head of war . . . . *K. John* v 2 113
Know the gallant monarch is in arms . . . . v 2 148
And what said the gallant? . . . . *Richard II.* v 3 15
The gallant Hotspur there, Young Harry Percy . . . 1 *Hen. IV.* i 1 52
Is not this an honourable spoil? A gallant prize? . . . . . i 1 75
Gallants, lads, boys, hearts of gold, all the titles of good fellowship . ii 4 306
This gallant Hotspur, this all-praised knight . . . . . iii 2 140
A head Of gallant warriors, noble gentlemen . . . . . iv 4 26
A gallant knight he was, his name was Blunt . . . . . v 3 20
A tall gentleman, by heaven, and a most gallant leader . 2 *Hen. IV.* ii 2 68
Whiles a more frosty people Sweat drops of gallant youth . *Hen. V.* iii 5 25
But I did see him do as gallant service . . . . . . iii 6 17
By the white hand of my lady, he's a gallant prince . . . iii 7 102
To horse, you gallant princes! straight to horse! . . . . iv 2 15
Scarce blood enough in all their sickly veins To give each naked curtle- axe a stain, That our French gallants shall to-day draw out . . iv 2 22
O, 'tis a gallant king!—Ay, he was porn at Monmouth . . . iv 7 11
Knights, esquires, and gallant gentlemen, Eight thousand and four hundred . . . . iv 8 89
Good morrow, gallants! want ye corn for bread? . . 1 *Hen. VI.* iii 2 41
Like a gallant in the brow of youth, Repairs him with occasion 2 *Hen. VI.* v 3 4
And, gallant Warwick, do but answer this . . . 3 *Hen. VI.* v 1 40
Bring forth the gallant, let us hear him speak . . . . . v 5 12
The reformation of our travell'd gallants . . . . *Hen. VIII.* i 3 19
She is a gallant creature, and complete In mind and feature . . iii 2 49
Hector's a gallant man.—As may be in the world, lady *Troi. and Cres.* i 2 40
Is't not a gallant man too, is't not? Why, this is brave now . . i 2 231
This challenge that the gallant Hector sends . . . . . i 3 321
Like a gallant horse fall'n in first rank, Lie there for pavement . iii 3 161
I have, thou gallant Trojan, seen thee oft Labouring for destiny . iv 5 183
God give you joy, sir, of your gallant bride! . . . *T. Andron.* i 1 400
The fields are near, and you are gallant grooms . . . . . iv 2 164
That gallant spirit hath aspired the clouds . . *Rom. and Jul.* iii 1 122
The gallant, young and noble gentleman, The County Paris . . iii 5 114
But hollow men, like horses hot at hand, Make gallant show . *J. Cæsar* iv 2 24
The enemy comes on in gallant show . . . . v 1 13
This gallant Had witchcraft in't; he grew unto his seat . . *Hamlet* iv 7 85
Without are a brace of Cyprus gallants . . . . *Othello* ii 3 31
What, man! 'tis a night of revels: the gallants desire it . . . ii 3 46
Goodly and gallant shall be false and perjured From thy great fail *Cymb.* iii 4 65
Sure, he's a gallant gentleman.—He's but a country gentleman *Pericles* ii 3 32
Search the market narrowly; Mytilene is full of gallants . . . iv 2 4
Welcome, fair one! Is't not a goodly presence?—She's a gallant lady . v 1 66
Gallantest. Dost overshine the gallant'st dames of Rome . *T. Andron.* i 1 317
Gallantly. His cuisses on his thighs, gallantly arm'd . 1 *Hen. IV.* iv 1 105
The Duke of Exeter has very gallantly maintained the pridge *Hen. V.* iii 6 95
He goes forth gallantly . . . . . . *Ant. and Cleo.* iv 4 36
Gallantry. And all the gallantry of Troy . . . *Troi. and Cres.* iii 1 149
Gallant-springing brave Plantagenet, That princely novice *Richard III.* i 4 227
Galled. My state being gall'd with my expense *Mer. Wives* iii 4 5
They that are most galled with my folly, They most must laugh *As Y. L. It* ii 7 50
A' has a little gall'd me, I confess . . . . . *T. of Shrew* v 2 60
Who mayst see Plainly as heaven sees earth and earth sees heaven, How I am gall'd . . . . *W. Tale* i 2 316
Wherein have you been galled by the king? . . . . 2 *Hen. IV.* iv 1 89
Let the brow o'erwhelm it As fearfully as doth a galled rock O'erhang and jutty his confounded base . . . . . . *Hen. V.* iii 1 12
That foul defacer of God's handiwork, That excellent grand tyrant of the earth, That reigns in galled eyes of weeping souls . *Richard III.* iv 4 53
So looks the chafed lion Upon the daring huntsman that has gall'd him; Then makes him nothing . . . . *Hen. VIII.* iii 2 207
My fear is this, Some galled goose of Winchester would hiss *Tr. and Cr.* v 10 55
Or else it would have gall'd his surly nature . . . *Coriolanus* ii 3 203
The Bull, being gall'd, gave Aries such a knock . . *T. Andron.* iv 3 71
Ere yet the salt of most unrighteous tears Had left the flushing in her galled eyes, She married . . . . *Hamlet* i 2 155
Let the galled jade wince, our withers are unwrung . . . . iii 2 253
Gallery. Your gallery Have we pass'd through, not without much content In many singularities . . . . *W. Tale* v 3 10
Long time thy shadow hath been thrall to me, For in my gallery thy picture hangs . . . . 1 *Hen. VI.* ii 3 37
Avoid the gallery. Ha! I have said. Be gone . . . *Hen. VIII.* v 1 86
We will withdraw Into the gallery . . . . *Pericles* ii 2 59
Galley. Two galliases, And twelve tight galleys . . . *T. of Shrew* ii 1 381
Once, in a sea-fight, 'gainst the count his galleys I did some service *T. N.* iii 3 26
The galleys Have sent a dozen sequent messengers . . . *Othello* i 2 40
My letters say a hundred and seven galleys . . . . . . i 3 3
What, ho!—A messenger from the galleys.—Now, what's the business? i 3 13
Aboard my galley I invite you all . . . . . *Ant. and Cleo.* ii 6 82
His best force Is forth to man his galleys. To the vales . . . iv 11 3
Gallia. Peace, I say, Gallia and Gaul, French and Welsh! *Mer. Wives* iii 1 99
And you withal shall make all Gallia shake . . . . . *Hen. V.* i 2 216

Gallia. And patches will I get unto these cudgell'd scars, And swear I got them in the Gallia wars . . . . *Hen. V.* v 1 94
And from the pride of Gallia rescued thee . . . *1 Hen. VI.* iv 6 15
Whose life was England's glory, Gallia's wonder . . . . iv 7 48
Those powers that the queen Hath raised in Gallia have arrived *3 Hen. VI.* v 3 8
From Gallia I cross'd the seas on purpose and on promise To see your grace.—I thank you for your pains . . . . . *Cymbeline* i 6 201
You shall hear The legions now in Gallia sooner landed In our not-fearing Britain than have tidings Of any penny tribute paid . . ii 4 18
The powers that he already hath in Gallia Will soon be drawn to head . iii 5 24
The legions now in Gallia are Full weak to undertake our wars . . iii 7 4
Is Lucius general of the forces?—Ay.—Remaining now in Gallia? . . iii 7 12
The legions garrison'd in Gallia, After your will, have cross'd the sea . iv 2 333
The Roman legions, all from Gallia drawn, Are landed on your coast . iv 3 24
Gallian. I am possess'd With more than half the Gallian territories *1 Hen. VI.* v 4 139
There is a Frenchman his companion, one An eminent monsieur, that, it seems, much loves A Gallian girl at home . . . *Cymbeline* i 6 66
Galliard. What is thy excellence in a galliard? . *T. Night* i 3 127
Why dost thou not go to church in a galliard and come home in a coranto? . . . . i 3 137
I did think, by the excellent constitution of thy leg, it was formed under the star of a galliard . . . . i 3 142
There's nought in France That can be with a nimble galliard won *Hen. V.* i 2 252
Galliases. Besides two galliases, And twelve tight galleys *T. of Shrew* ii 1 380
Gallimaufry. He loves the gallimaufry . . . *Mer. Wives* ii 1 119
A dance which the wenches say is a gallimaufry of gambols . *W. Tale* iv 4 335
Galling the gleaned land with hot assays . . . *Hen. V.* i 2 151
I have seen you gleeking and galling at this gentleman . . . v 1 78
Galling His kingly hands, haling ropes . . . . *Pericles* iv 1 54
Gallon. Item, Sauce, 4d. Item, Sack, two gallons, 5s. 8d. . *1 Hen. IV.* ii 4 587
Gallop. What pace is this that thy tongue keeps?—Not a false gallop *Much Ado* iii 4 94
Whither away so fast? A true man or a thief that gallops so? *L. L. Lost* iv 3 187
This is the very false gallop of verses . . . *As Y. Like It* iii 2 119
Who Time ambles withal, who Time trots withal, who Time gallops withal . . . . iii 2 329
Who doth he [Time] gallop withal?—With a thief to the gallows . . iii 2 344
For yet a many of your horsemen peer And gallop o'er the field *Hen. V.* iv 7 89
She'll gallop far enough to her destruction . . . *2 Hen. VI.* i 3 154
Gallops the zodiac in his glistering coach . . . *T. Andron.* ii 1 7
She gallops night by night Through lovers' brains . *Rom. and Jul.* i 4 70
Sometime she gallops o'er a courtier's nose, And then dreams he of smelling out a suit . . . . i 4 77
Gallop apace, you fiery-footed steeds, Towards Phœbus' lodging . . iii 2 1
Galloping. I did hear The galloping of horse: who was't came by? *Macb.* iv 1 140
Gallow. The wrathful skies Gallow the very wanderers of the dark *Lear* iii 2 44
Galloway. Know we not Galloway nags? . . . . *2 Hen. IV.* ii 4 205
Gallowglasses. A mighty power Of gallowglasses and stout kerns Is marching hitherward . . . . *2 Hen. VI.* iv 9 26
From the western isles Of kerns and gallowglasses is supplied *Macbeth* i 2 13
Gallows. He hath no drowning mark upon him; his complexion is perfect gallows . . . . *Tempest* i 1 32
I prophesied, if a gallows were on land, This fellow could not drown . v 1 217
What with the gallows and what with poverty, I am custom-shrunk *Meas. for Meas.* i 2 84
Ay, and a shrewd unhappy gallows too . . . . *L. L. Lost* v 2 12
Even from the gallows did his fell soul fleet . . . *Mer. of Venice* iv 1 135
Thou shouldst have had ten more, To bring thee to the gallows, not the font . . . . iv 1 400
Who doth he [Time] gallop withal?—With a thief to the gallows *As Y. Like It* iii 2 345
Gallows and knock are too powerful on the highway . . *W. Tale* iv 3 28
In as high a flow as the ridge of the gallows . . . . *1 Hen. IV.* i 2 43
Shall there be gallows standing in England when thou art king? . . i 2 66
If I hang, I'll make a fat pair of gallows . . . . . . ii 1 74
An you do not make him hanged among you, the gallows shall have wrong . . . . *2 Hen. IV.* ii 2 105
These tardy tricks of yours will, on my life, One time or other break some gallows' back . . . . iv 3 32
A damned death! Let gallows gape for dog; let man go free *Hen. V.* iii 6 44
And you three shall be strangled on the gallows . . . *2 Hen. VI.* ii 3 8
Rebellious hinds, the filth and scum of Kent, Mark'd for the gallows . iv 2 131
I belong to the larder.—Belong to the gallows, and be hanged! *Hen. VIII.* v 4 6
The gallows does well; but how does it well? it does well to those that do ill: now thou dost ill to say the gallows is built stronger than the church: argal, the gallows may do well to thee . . . . *Hamlet* v 1 52
Unless a man would marry a gallows and beget young gibbets *Cymbeline* v 4 207
Gallowses. O, there were desolation of gaolers and gallowses! . . v 4 214
Gallows-maker. What is he that builds stronger than either the mason, the shipwright, or the carpenter?—The gallows-maker . *Hamlet* v 1 49
Gallus, go you along. Where's Dolabella? . . . *Ant. and Cleo.* v 1 69
Gam. Sir Richard Ketly, Davy Gam esquire: None else of name *Hen. V.* iv 8 109
Gambol. Hop in his walks and gambol in his eyes . . *M. N. Dream* iii 1 168
Golden locks Which make such wanton gambols with the wind *Mer. of Venice* iii 2 93
A dance which the wenches say is a gallimaufry of gambols . *W. Tale* iv 4 335
Other gambol faculties a' has, that show a weak mind . . *2 Hen. IV.* ii 4 273
I the matter will re-word; which madness Would gambol from *Hamlet* iii 4 144
Where be your gibes now? your gambols? your songs . . . . v 1 209
Gambold. Is not a comonty a Christmas gambold? . . *T. of Shrew* Ind. 2 140
Game. Foolishly lost at a game of tick-tack . . . *Meas. for Meas.* i 2 196
The gentles are at their game . . . . . . *L. L. Lost* iv 2 172
So shall we stay, mocking intended game, And they, well mock'd, depart . . . . v 2 155
It is not so, I swear; We have had pastimes here and pleasant game . v 2 360
As waggish boys in game themselves forswear, So the boy Love is perjured . . . . *M. N. Dream* i 1 240
Ay, that way goes the game . . . . iii 2 289
Or else a fool That seest a game play'd home, the rich stake drawn, And takest it all for jest . . . . *W. Tale* i 2 248
So thrive it in your game! . . . . *K. John* iv 2 95
Have I not here the best cards for the game, To win this easy match? . v 2 105
Before the game is afoot, thou still let'st slip . . . *1 Hen. IV.* i 3 278
The game's afoot . . . . *Hen. V.* iii 1 32
Such rewards As victors wear at the Olympian games . . *3 Hen. VI.* ii 3 53
He knows the game: how true he keeps the wind! . . . . . iii 2 14
Under the colour of his usual game . . . . iv 5 11
This way lies the game.—Nay, this way, man . . . . . . iv 5 14
Nor sweeten talk, Nor play at subtle games; fair virtues all *Tr. and Cr.* iv 4 89
Game. Set them down For sluttish spoils of opportunity And daughters of the game . . . . *Troi. and Cres.* iv 5 63
The bull has the game: ware horns, ho! . . . . v 7 12
I have horse will follow where the game Makes way . *T. Andron.* ii 2 23
The game was ne'er so fair, and I am done . . *Rom. and Jul.* i 4 39
If our betters play at that game, we must not dare To imitate them *T. of A.* i 2 12
Never learn'd The icy precepts of respect, but follow'd The sugar'd game . . . . iv 3 259
The games are done and Cæsar is returning . . . . *J. Cæsar* i 2 178
I'll warrant her, full of game . . . . *Othello* ii 3 19
If thou dost play with him at any game, Thou art sure to lose *A. and. C.* ii 3 25
Hark, the game is roused! . . . . *Cymbeline* iii 3 98
The game is up . . . . iii 3 107
Gamesome. Pleasant, gamesome, passing courteous . *T. of Shrew* ii 1 247
I am not gamesome: I do lack some part Of that quick spirit that is in Antony. Let me not hinder . . . . . . *J. Cæsar* i 2 28
None a stranger there So merry and so gamesome . . . *Cymbeline* i 6 60
Gamester. Keep a gamester from the dice, and a good student from his book, and it is wonderful . . . . *Mer. Wives* iii 1 37
You are a gentleman and a gamester, sir . . . . . *L. L. Lost* i 2 44
Now will I stir this gamester: I hope I shall see an end of him *As Y. L. It* i 1 170
Young gamester, your father were a fool To give thee all *T. of Shrew* ii 1 402
And was a common gamester to the camp . . . . *All's Well* v 3 188
The gentler gamester is the soonest winner . . . . *Hen. V.* iii 6 119
You are a merry gamester, My Lord Sands.—Yes, if I make my play *Hen. VIII.* i 4 45
Were you a gamester at five or at seven?—Earlier too, sir, if now I be one . . . . *Pericles* iv 6 81
Gaming. As gaming, my lord.—Ay, or drinking, fencing, swearing *Ham.* ii 1 24
There was a' gaming; there o'ertook in's rouse; There falling out at tennis . . . . ii 1 58
At gaming, swearing, or about some act That has no relish of salvation in't . . . . iii 3 91
Gammon. I have a gammon of bacon and two razes of ginger . *1 Hen. IV.* ii 1 26
Gamut. I must begin with rudiments of art; To teach you gamut in a briefer sort . . . . *T. of Shrew* iii 1 67
Why, I am past my gamut long ago.—Yet read the gamut of Hortensio iii 1 71
'Gamut' I am, the ground of all accord, 'A re,' to plead Hortensio's passion . . . . iii 1 73
Call you this gamut? tut, I like it not . . . . iii 1 79
'Gan. That furious Scot . . . 'Gan vail his stomach . . *2 Hen. IV.* i 1 129
When, by and by, the din of war gan pierce His ready sense *Coriolanus* ii 2 119
Turn'd coward But by example—O, a sin in war Damn'd in the first beginners!—gan to look The way that they did . . *Cymbeline* v 3 37
Mine Italian brain 'Gan in your duller Britain operate Most vilely . v 5 197
Gangrened. The service of the foot Being once gangrened, is not then respected For what before it was . . . . .*Coriolanus* iii 1 307
Ganymede. Therefore look you call me Ganymede . . *As Y. L. It* i 3 127
Here comes young Master Ganymede, my new mistress's brother . . iii 2 91
Why, how now, Ganymede! sweet Ganymede! . . . . . iv 3 158
There is more in it. Cousin Ganymede!—Look, he recovers . . iv 3 160
And so am I for Phebe.—And I for Ganymede.—And I for Rosalind . v 2 92
Gaol. Bid him bring his pen and inkhorn to the gaol . . *Much Ado* iii 5 64
Set down our excommunication and meet me at the gaol . . . iii 5 69
Carry this mad knave to the gaol . . . . . . *T. of Shrew* v 1 95
Carry me to the gaol!—Stay, officer: he shall not go to prison . v 1 97
I'll slit the villain's nose, that would have sent me to the gaol . . v 1 135
Break open the gaols and let out the prisoners . . *2 Hen. VI.* iv 3 18
And must my house Be my retentive enemy, my gaol? . *T. of Athens* iii 4 82
Then am I the prisoner, and his bed my gaol . . . . . *Lear* iv 6 272
Gaoler. Seldom when The steeled gaoler is the friend of men *M. for M.* iv 2 90
Thou art doom'd to die. Gaoler, take him to thy custody *Com. of Errors* i 1 156
Will you murder me? Thou gaoler, thou, I am thy prisoner . . . iv 4 112
Come, gaoler, bring me where the goldsmith is . . . . . iv 4 145
Gaoler, look to him: tell not me of mercy . . . *Mer. of Venice* iii 3 1
I do wonder, Thou naughty gaoler, that thou art so fond To come abroad with him at his request . . . . iii 3 9
Not your gaoler, then, But your kind hostess . . . *W. Tale* i 2 59
And dull unfeeling barren ignorance Is made my gaoler . . *Richard II.* i 3 169
And his injury The gaoler to his pity . . . . . *Coriolanus* v 1 65
'But yet' is a gaoler to bring forth Some monstrous malefactor *A. and C.* ii 5 52
You're my prisoner, but Your gaoler shall deliver you the keys That lock up your restraint . . . . *Cymbeline* i 1 73
Thou shalt be then freer than a gaoler; no bolts for the dead . . v 4 204
O, there were desolation of gaolers and gallowses! . . . . v 4 213
Gap. I slide O'er sixteen years and leave the growth untried Of that wide gap . . . . *W. Tale* iv 1 7
Some stretch-mouthed rascal would, as it were, mean mischief and break a foul gap into the matter . . . . iv 4 198
In this wide gap of time since first We were dissever'd . . . . v 3 154
And stop this gap of breath with fulsome dust . . . *K. John* iii 4 32
Stands in the gap and trade of moe preferments . . . *Hen. VIII.* v 1 36
When two authorities are up, Neither supreme, how soon confusion May enter 'twixt the gap of both . . . . . . *Coriolanus* iii 1 111
If he had been forgotten, It had been as a gap in our great feast *Macb.* iii 1 12
It would make a great gap in your own honour . . . . *Lear* i 2 91
That I might sleep out this great gap of time . . . *Ant. and Cleo.* i 5 5
The air; which, but for vacancy, Had gone to gaze on Cleopatra too And made a gap in nature . . . . ii 2 223
For the gap That we shall make in time, from our hence-going And our return, to excuse . . . . *Cymbeline* iii 2 64
Who stand i' the gaps to teach you The stages of our story . *Pericles* iv 4 8
Gape. He'll be hang'd yet, Though every drop of water swear against it And gape at widest to glut him . . . . *Tempest* i 1 63
It was mine art . . . that made gape The pine and let thee out . . i 2 292
They gape and point At your industrious scenes and acts of death *K. John* ii 1 375
Which gape and rub the elbow at the news Of hurlyburly innovation *1 Hen. IV.* v 1 77
The grave doth gape For thee thrice wider than for other men *2 Hen. IV.* v 5 57
The grave doth gape, and doting death is near; Therefore exhale *Hen. V.* ii 1 65
Let gallows gape for dog; let man go free . . . . . . iii 6 44
May that ground gape and swallow me alive, Where I shall kneel to him that slew my father! . . . . *3 Hen. VI.* i 1 161
Either heaven with lightning strike the murderer dead, Or earth, gape open wide and eat him quick! . . . . *Richard III.* i 2 65
Earth gapes, hell burns, fiends roar, saints pray . . . . . iv 4 75
Now old desire doth in his death-bed lie, And young affection gapes to be his heir . . . . *Rom. and Jul.* ii Prol. 2
I'll speak to it, though hell itself should gape And bid me hold my peace . . . . *Hamlet* i 2 245

Gape. Would you, the supervisor, grossly gape on—Behold her topp'd? *Oth.* iii 3 395
Gaping. The time of night That the graves all gaping wide *M. N. Dream* v 1 387
Every word in it a gaping wound, Issuing life-blood *Mer. of Venice* iii 2 268
Some men there are love not a gaping pig . . . . iv 1 47
As there is no firm reason to be render'd, Why he cannot abide a gaping pig iv 1 54
Let grievous, ghastly, gaping wounds Untwine the Sisters Three! *2 Hen. IV.* ii 4 212
Behold the ordnance on their carriages, With fatal mouths gaping *Hen. V.* iii Prol. 27
Ye rude slaves, leave your gaping . . . *Hen. VIII.* v 4 3
Who art thou that lately didst descend Into this gaping hollow? *T. An.* ii 3 249
Never leave gaping till they've swallowed the whole parish . *Pericles* ii 1 37
Garb. He could not speak English in the native garb *Hen. V.* v 1 80
But commanding peace Even with the same austerity and garb As he controll'd the war . . . *Coriolanus* iv 7 44
Let me comply with you in this garb . . . *Hamlet* ii 2 390
Constrains the garb Quite from his nature . . *Lear* ii 2 103
Abuse him to the Moor in the rank garb . . . *Othello* ii 1 315
Garbage. So lust, though to a radiant angel link'd, Will sate itself in a celestial bed, And prey on garbage . . *Hamlet* i 5 57
Ravening first the lamb Longs after for the garbage . . *Cymbeline* i 6 50
Garboil. At thy sovereign leisure read The garboils she awaked *A. and C.* i 3 61
So much uncurable, her garboils . . . . . ii 2 67
Garçon. By gar, I am cozened: I ha' married un garçon, a boy *Mer. Wives* v 5 218
Garde. Dieu vous garde, monsieur.—Et vous aussi; votre serviteur *T. N.* iii 1 78
Garden. He hath a garden circummured with brick . *Meas. for Meas.* iv 1 28
A little door Which from the vineyard to the garden leads . . iv 1 33
And, moreover, God saw him when he was hid in the garden . *Much Ado* v 1 182
From the west corner of thy curious-knotted garden . *L. L. Lost* i 1 250
Fruitful Lombardy, The pleasant garden of great Italy . *T. of Shrew* i 1 4
I knew a wench married in an afternoon as she went to the garden for parsley to stuff a rabbit . . . . iv 4 100
Let the garden door be shut, and leave me to my hearing . *T. Night* iii 1 103
If you would seek us, We are yours i' the garden . *W. Tale* i 2 178
Of that kind Our rustic garden's barren . . . iv 4 84
Then make your garden rich in gillyvors, And do not call them bastards iv 4 98
What sport shall we devise here in this garden? *Richard II.* iii 4 1
Our sea-walled garden, the whole land, Is full of weeds . . iii 4 43
O, what pity is it That he had not so trimm'd and dress'd his land As we this garden! . . . . . iii 4 57
Thou, old Adam's likeness, set to dress this garden . . iii 4 73
The Welshmen did good service in a garden where leeks did grow *Hen. V.* iv 7 103
In this best garden of the world, Our fertile France . . v 2 36
Fortune made his sword; By which the world's best garden he achieved Epil. 7
Thy promises are like Adonis' gardens, That one day bloom'd and fruitful were the next . . . *1 Hen. VI.* i 6 6
We were too loud; The garden here is more convenient . . ii 4 4
Suffer them now, and they'll o'ergrow the garden . *2 Hen. VI.* iii 1 32
I climbed into this garden, to see if I can eat grass, or pick a sallet . iv 10 8
Is't not enough to break into my garden, And, like a thief, to come to rob my grounds? . . . . iv 10 35
Wither, garden; and be henceforth a burying-place to all that do dwell in this house . . . . iv 10 67
I saw good strawberries in your garden . . *Richard III.* iii 4 34
'Tis an unweeded garden, That grows to seed . . *Hamlet* i 2 135
He poisons him i' the garden for's estate . . . iii 2 272
To use his eyes for garden water-pots . . . *Lear* iv 6 200
Our bodies are our gardens, to the which our wills are gardeners . *Othello* i 3 323
Where's Antony?—He's walking in the garden—thus . *Ant. and Cleo.* iii 5 17
I'll fetch a turn about the garden, pitying The pangs of barr'd affections *Cymbeline* i 1 81
Gardener. But stay, here come the gardeners: Let's step into the shadow of these trees . . *Richard II.* iii 4 24
Gardener, for telling me these news of woe, Pray God the plants thou graft'st may never grow . . . iii 4 100
Gardeners do with ordure hide those roots That shall first spring *Hen. V.* ii 4 39
And Adam was a gardener.—And what of that? *2 Hen. VI.* iv 2 142
There is no ancient gentlemen but gardeners, ditchers, and grave-makers *Hamlet* v 1 34
Our bodies are our gardens, to the which our wills are gardeners *Othello* i 3 324
Garden-house. This is the body That took away the match from Isabel, And did supply thee at thy garden-house . *Meas. for Meas.* v 1 212
But Tuesday night last gone in's garden-house He knew me as a wife . v 1 229
Gardez ma vie, et je vous donnerai deux cents écus . *Hen. V.* iv 4 44
Gardiner. Call Gardiner to me, my new secretary . *Hen. VIII.* ii 2 116
Stokesly and Gardiner; the one of Winchester, Newly preferr'd from the king's secretary, The other, London . . . iv 1 101
Gardon, O sweet Gardon! better than remuneration . *L. L. Lost* iii 1 171
Gargantua. You must borrow me Gargantua's mouth first *As Y. Like It* iii 2 238
Gargrave. Sir Thomas Gargrave, and Sir William Glansdale *1 Hen. VI.* i 4 63
Sir Thomas Gargrave, hast thou any life? Speak unto Talbot . i 4 88
Garish. A garish flag, To be the aim of every dangerous shot *Richard III.* iv 4 89
And pay no worship to the garish sun . *Rom. and Jul.* iii 2 25
Garland. She excels each mortal thing Upon the dull earth dwelling: To her let us garlands bring . . *T. G. of Ver.* iv 2 53
What fashion will you wear the garland of? about your neck? *Much Ado* ii 1 196
I offered him my company to a willow-tree, either to make him a garland, as being forsaken, or to bind him up a rod . . ii 1 226
It had not been amiss the rod had been made, and the garland too; for the garland he might have worn himself, and the rod he might have bestowed on you . . . . . ii 1 235
O, these I lack, To make you garlands of! . . *W. Tale* iv 4 128
And all the budding honours on thy crest I'll crop, to make a garland for my head . . . . *1 Hen. IV.* v 4 73
So thou the garland wear'st successively . *2 Hen. IV.* iv 5 202
If the deed were ill, Be you contented, wearing now the garland . v 2 84
Tell him, in hope he'll prove a widower shortly, I'll wear the willow garland for his sake . . . *3 Hen. VI.* iii 3 228; iv 1 100
Till Richard wear the garland of the realm.—How! wear the garland! dost thou mean the crown? . . *Richard III.* iii 2 40
Bound with triumphant garlands will I come And lead thy daughter to a conqueror's bed . . . . iv 4 333
They promised me eternal happiness; And brought me garlands, Griffith, which I feel I am not worthy yet to wear *Hen. VIII.* iv 2 91
Call him noble that was now your hate, Him vile that was your garland *Coriolanus* i 1 188
Therefore, be it known . . . that Caius Marcius Wears this war's garland i 9 60
He comes the third time home with the oaken garland . . ii 1 138
And in the brunt of seventeen battles since He lurch'd all swords of the garland . . . . . ii 2 105
Garland. Take this garland on thy brow; Thy Brutus bid me give it thee *J. Cæsar* v 3 85
There with fantastic garlands did she come Of crow-flowers, nettles *Ham.* iv 7 169
As peace should still her wheaten garland wear . . v 2 41
Sing all a green willow must be my garland . *Othello* iv 3 51
O, that I knew this husband, which, you say, must charge his horns with garlands! . . . . *Ant. and Cleo.* i 2 5
Thy grand captain Antony Shall set thee on triumphant chariots and Put garlands on thy head . . . . iii 1 11
O, wither'd is the garland of the war, The soldier's pole is fall'n . iv 15 64
Garlic. Though she smelt brown bread and garlic . *Meas. for Meas.* iii 2 195
Eat no onions nor garlic, for we are to utter sweet breath *M. N. Dream* iv 2 43
Mopsa must be your mistress: marry, garlic, To mend her kissing with! *W. Tale* iv 4 162
I had rather live With cheese and garlic in a windmill *1 Hen. IV.* iii 1 162
Garlic-eater. You that stood so much Upon the voice of occupation and The breath of garlic-eaters! . . . *Coriolanus* iv 6 98
Garment. Lend thy hand, And pluck my magic garment from me *Tempest* i 2 24
Rich garments, linens, stuffs and necessaries, Which since have steaded much . . . . . . i 2 164
On their sustaining garments not a blemish, But fresher than before . i 2 218
Hence! hang not on my garments . . . . i 2 474
Our garments, being, as they were, drenched in the sea . ii 1 61
Methinks our garments are now as fresh as when we put them on first . ii 1 68
Our garments seem now as fresh as when we were at Tunis . ii 1 96
Look how well my garments sit upon me; Much feater than before ii 1 272
I thank thee for that jest; here's a garment for't . iv 1 241
An excellent pass of pate; there's another garment for't . iv 1 244
Which served me as fit, by all men's judgements, As if the garment had been made for me . . . . *T. G. of Ver.* iv 4 168
Did not I tell you how you should know my daughter by her garments? *Mer. Wives* v 5 208
There is something in the wind, that we cannot get in.—You would say so, master, if your garments were thin . . *Com. of Errors* iii 1 70
A devil in an everlasting garment hath him . . iv 2 33
And saw me court Margaret in Hero's garments . *Much Ado* v 1 245
Thou shalt know the man By the Athenian garments he hath on *M. N. D.* ii 1 264
Did not you tell me I should know the man By the Athenian garments? iii 2 349
And, look, what notes and garments he doth give thee . *Mer. of Venice* iii 4 51
Winter garments must be lined, So must slender Rosalind *As Y. Like It* iii 2 111
Then should I know you by description; Such garments and such years iv 3 86
Our purses shall be proud, our garments poor . *T. of Shrew* iv 3 173
Whose judgements are Mere fathers of their garments . *All's Well* i 2 62
I would the cutting of my garments would serve the turn . iv 1 50
The captain that did bring me first on shore Hath my maid's garments *T. Night* v 1 282
He should be a footman by the garments he has left with thee *W. Tale* iv 3 70
Think there's a necessity in't,—and change garments with this gentleman iv 4 649
His garments are rich, but he wears them not handsomely . iv 4 776
With countenance of such distraction that they were to be known by garment, not by favour . . . . . v 2 53
Stuffs out his vacant garments with his form . . *K. John* iii 4 97
Cases of buckram . . . , to immask our noted outward garments *1 Hen. IV.* i 2 202
Beslubber our garments with it and swear it was the blood of true men ii 4 342
I will wear a garment all of blood And stain my favours . iii 2 135
To face the garment of rebellion With some fine colour . . v 1 74
God save your majesty!—This new and gorgeous garment, majesty, Sits not so easy on me as you think . . . *2 Hen. IV.* v 2 44
It yearns me not if men my garments wear . . *Hen. V.* iv 3 26
As a common man; witness the night, your garments, your lowliness . iv 8 55
Thy garments are not spotted with our blood . *Richard III.* i 3 283
Frozen almost to death, how he did lap me Even in his own garments . ii 1 116
This tempest, Dashing the garment of this peace . *Hen. VIII.* i 1 93
May I change these garments?—You may, sir . *Coriolanus* ii 3 154
Hence, rotten thing! or I shall shake thy bones Out of thy garments . iii 1 180
New honours come upon him, Like our strange garments, cleave not to their mould But with the aid of use . . *Macbeth* i 3 145
Her garments, heavy with their drink, Pull'd the poor wretch from her melodious lay To muddy death . . . *Hamlet* iv 7 182
Only I do not like the fashion of your garments . . *Lear* iii 6 84
In nothing am I changed But in my garments . . . iv 6 10
In the heaviness of his sleep We put fresh garments on him . iv 7 22
All the skill I have Remembers not these garments . . iv 7 67
His meanest garment, That ever hath but clipp'd his body, is dearer In my respect than all the hairs above thee, Were they all made such men *Cymbeline* ii 3 138
You have abused me: 'His meanest garment!'—Ay, I said so, sir . ii 3 155
Poor I am stale, a garment out of fashion; And, for I am richer than to hang by the walls, I must be ripp'd . . . iii 4 53
Hast any of thy late master's garments in thy possession? . . iii 5 125
I would these garments were come . . . . iii 5 136
She held the very garment of Posthumus in more respect than my noble and natural person . . . . . iii 5 138
Be those the garments?—Ay, my noble lord . . . iii 5 151
How fit his garments serve me! . . . . . iv 1 3
Thy mistress enforced; thy garments cut to pieces before thy face . iv 1 19
The garments of Posthumus! I know the shape of's leg: this is his hand . . . . iv 2 308
Be not, as is our fangled world, a garment Nobler than that it covers . v 4 134
In my master's garments, Which he enforced from me, away he posts . v 5 282
'Twas we that made up this garment through the rough seams of the waters . . . . . *Pericles* ii 1 155
Come, young one, I like the manner of your garments well . . iv 2 145
Give me fresh garments . . . . . v 1 216
Garner. Foison plenty, Barns and garners never empty . *Tempest* iv 1 111
Nay, let them follow: The Volsces have much corn; take these rats thither To gnaw their garners . . . *Coriolanus* i 1 254
Garnered. But there, where I have garner'd up my heart, Where either I must live, or bear no life . . . *Othello* iv 2 57
Garnish. I should be obscured.—So are you, sweet, Even in the lovely garnish of a boy . . . . *Mer. of Venice* ii 6 45
With taper-light To seek the beauteous eye of heaven to garnish *K. John* iv 2 15
Garnished With such bedecking ornaments of praise . *L. L. Lost* ii 1 78
I do know A many fools, that stand in better place, Garnish'd like him, that for a tricksy word Defy the matter . *Mer. of Venice* iii 5 74
Garnish'd and deck'd in modest complement . *Hen. V.* ii 2 134
Garret. He did speak them to me in the garret one night *2 Hen. VI.* i 3 194
Garrison. Only reserved, you claim no interest In any of our towns of garrison . . . . . *1 Hen. VI.* v 4 168
Mine own proper store . . . Have I dispursed to the garrisons *2 Hen. VI.* iii 1 117

Garrisoned. Why, then the Polack never will defend it.—Yes, it is already garrison'd . . . *Hamlet* iv 4 24
To them the legions garrison'd in Gallia . . . have cross'd the sea *Cymb.* iv 2 333
Garter. He, being in love, could not see to garter his hose *T. G. of Ver.* ii 1 83
The three party is, lastly and finally, mine host of the Garter *Mer. Wives* i 1 143
Mine host of the Garter!—What says my bully-rook? . . . i 3 1
Till he hath pawned his horses to mine host of the Garter . . ii 1 100
Does he lie at the Garter?—Ay, marry, does he . . . ii 1 187
Look where my ranting host of the Garter comes . . . ii 1 197
Good mine host o' the Garter, a word with you . . . ii 1 211
I'll be judgement by mine host of the Garter . . . iii 1 98
Peace, I say! hear mine host of the Garter. Am I politic? am I subtle? iii 1 103
This same scall, scurvy, cogging companion, the host of the Garter . iii 1 124
Like to the Garter's compass, in a ring . . . v 5 70
If he that writ it had played Pyramus and hanged himself in Thisbe's garter, it would have been a fine tragedy . . *M. N. Dream* v 1 366
Let their heads be sleekly combed, their blue coats brushed and their garters of an indifferent knit . . *T. of Shrew* iv 1 94
Why dost thou garter up thy arms o' this fashion? . *All's Well* ii 3 265
Go, hang thyself in thine own heir-apparent garters! . . 1 *Hen. IV.* ii 2 47
The Gordian knot of it he will unloose, Familiar as his garter *Hen. V.* i 1 47
I vow'd, base knight, when I did meet thee next, To tear the garter from thy craven's leg, Which I have done . 1 *Hen. VI.* iv 1 15
When first this order was ordain'd, my lords, Knights of the garter were of noble birth, Valiant and virtuous, full of haughty courage . iv 1 34
Now, by my George, my garter, and my crown,— Profaned, dishonour'd, and the third usurp'd . . . *Richard III.* iv 4 366
The garter, blemish'd, pawn'd his knightly virtue . . iv 4 370
Ha, ha! he wears cruel garters. Horses are tied by the heads, dogs and bears by the neck, monkeys by the loins, and men by the legs *Lear* ii 4 7
Lend me a garter. So. O, for a chair, To bear him easily hence! *Othello* v 1 82
Gartered with a red and blue list . . . *T. of Shrew* iii 2 69
Gash. A perilous gash, a very limb lopp'd off . . 1 *Hen. IV.* iv 1 43
Kisses the gashes That bloodily did yawn upon his face . *Hen. V.* iv 6 13
Instead of oil and balm, Thou lay'st in every gash that love hath given me The knife that made it . . . *Troi. and Cres.* i 1 62
Every gash was an enemy's grave . . . *Coriolanus* ii 1 171
But I am faint, my gashes cry for help . . *Macbeth* i 2 42
Safe in a ditch he bides, With twenty trenched gashes on his head . iii 4 27
Each new day a gash Is added to her wounds . . . iv 3 40
Whiles I see lives, the gashes Do better upon them . . v 8 2
With joyful tears Wash the congealment from your wounds, and kiss The honour'd gashes whole . . . *Ant. and Cleo.* iv 8 11
Strike me, honour'd sir; Give me a gash, put me to present pain *Pericles* v 1 193
Gashed. His gash'd stabs look'd like a breach in nature . *Macbeth* ii 3 119
Gaskin. I am resolved on two points.—That if one break, the other will hold; or, if both break, your gaskins fall . *T. Night* i 5 27
Gasp. I will follow thee, To the last gasp . *As Y. Like It* ii 3 70
I cannot look greenly nor gasp out my eloquence . *Hen. V.* v 2 149
Distrustful recreants! Fight till the last gasp . 1 *Hen. VI.* i 2 127
And in his bosom spend my latter gasp . . . ii 5 38
Suddenly a grievous sickness took him, That makes him gasp and stare and catch the air . . . 2 *Hen. VI.* iii 2 371
Where your brave father breathed his latest gasp . 3 *Hen. VI.* ii 1 108
And to the latest gasp cried out for Warwick . . . v 2 41
His fortunes all lie speechless and his name Is at last gasp . *Cymbeline* i 5 53
Gasping to begin some speech, her eyes Became two spouts . *W. Tale* iii 3 25
And I, a gasping new-deliver'd mother . . *Richard II.* ii 2 65
A bleeding land, Gasping for life . . . 2 *Hen. IV.* i 1 208
Gasted by the noise I made, Full suddenly he fled . . *Lear* ii 1 57
Gastness. Do you perceive the gastness of her eye? . . *Othello* v 1 106
Gat. Whom nature gat For men to see, and seeing wonder at . *Pericles* ii 2 6
Gate. One midnight Fated to the purpose did Antonio open The gates of Milan . . . *Tempest* i 2 130
To that vineyard is a planched gate . . . *Meas. for Meas.* iv 1 30
Who do prepare to meet him at the gates, There to give up their power iv 3 136
Why meet him at the gates, and redeliver our authorities there? . iv 4 6
Bid them bring the trumpets to the gate; But send me Flavius first . iv 5 9
The generous and gravest citizens Have hent the gates . . iv 6 14
Come, sir, to dinner. Dromio, keep the gate . *Com. of Errors* ii 2 208
Shall I be porter at the gate?—Ay; and let none enter, lest I break your pate . . . ii 2 219
What a coil is there, Dromio? who are those at the gate? . . iii 1 48
Go fetch me something: I'll break ope the gate . . . iii 1 73
The abbess shuts the gates on us And will not suffer us to fetch him out v 1 156
Well, then, go you into hell?—No, but to the gate . *Much Ado* ii 1 45
For thee I'll lock up all the gates of love . . . iv 1 106
Why had I not with charitable hand Took up a beggar's issue at my gates? . . . iv 1 134
Climb o'er the house to unlock the little gate . *L. L. Lost* i 1 109
Strong-jointed Samson! I do excel thee in my rapier as much as thou didst me in carrying gates . . . i 2 79
Before we enter his forbidden gates, To know his pleasure . . ii 1 26
You may not come, fair princess, in my gates . . . ii 1 172
Through Athens' gates have we devised to steal . *M. N. Dream* i 1 213
And shivering shocks Shall break the locks Of prison gates . . i 2 36
Till the eastern gate, all fiery-red, Opening on Neptune with fair blessed beams, Turns into yellow gold . . . iii 2 391
Whiles we shut the gates upon one wooer, another knocks *Mer. of Venice* i 2 147
Madam, there is alighted at your gate A young Venetian . . ii 9 86
That eyes, that are the frail'st and softest things, Who shut their coward gates on atomies, Should be call'd tyrants! . *As Y. Like It* iii 5 13
Knock me at this gate And rap me well . . . *T. of Shrew* i 2 11
I bade the rascal knock upon your gate And could not get him for my heart to do it . . . i 2 37
Knock at the gate! O heavens! Spake you not these words plain, 'Sirrah, knock me here, rap me here, knock me well, and knock me soundly'? And come you now with, 'knocking at the gate'? . i 2 39
What's he that knocks as he would beat down the gate? . . v 1 18
I am for the house with the narrow gate . . *All's Well* iv 5 53
For the flowery way that leads to the broad gate and the great fire . iv 5 57
There is at the gate a young gentleman much desires to speak with you *T. Night* i 5 107
What is he at the gate, cousin?—A gentleman . . . i 5 125
There's one at the gate.—Ay, marry, what is he? . . i 5 134
I heard you were saucy at my gates . . . i 5 210
Make me a willow-cabin at your gate, And call upon my soul within the house . . . i 5 287
Follow me.—To the gates of Tartar, thou most excellent devil of wit! . ii 5 226
'Gainst knaves and thieves men shut their gate . . . v 1 404

Gate. Other men have gates and those gates open'd, As mine, against their will . . . *W. Tale* i 2 197
Welcome before the gates of Angiers, duke . . . *K. John* ii 1 17
Confronts your city's eyes, your winking gates . . . ii 1 215
With much expedient march Have brought a countercheck before your gates . . . ii 1 224
Till that time Have we ramm'd up our gates against the world . ii 1 272
Open wide your gates, And let young Arthur, Duke of Bretagne, in . ii 1 300
Open your gates and give the victors way . . . ii 1 324
We do lock Our former scruple in our strong-barr'd gates . . ii 1 370
This union shall do more than battery can To our fast-closed gates . ii 1 447
Citizens of Angiers, ope your gates, Let in that amity which you have made ii 1 536
Who keeps the gate here, ho? . . . 2 *Hen. IV.* i 1 1
Please it your honour, knock but at the gate, And he himself will answer i 1 5
By his gates of breath There lies a downy feather which stirs not . iv 5 31
Porters crowding in Their heavy burdens at his narrow gate . *Hen. V.* i 2 201
The gates of mercy shall be all shut up . . . iii 3 10
Great king, We yield our town and lives to thy soft mercy. Enter our gates iii 3 49
Open your gates. Come, uncle Exeter, Go you and enter Harfleur . iii 3 51
Where be these warders, that they wait not here? Open the gates 1 *Hen. VI.* i 3 4
Break up the gates, I'll be your warrantize . . . i 3 13
Where is best place to make our battery next?—I think, at the north gate i 4 66
These are the city gates, the gates of Rouen . . . iii 2 1
Go to the gates of Bourdeaux, trumpeter; Summon their general . iv 2 1
Open your city gates; Be humble to us; call my sovereign yours . iv 2 5
Will cry for vengeance at the gates of heaven . . . v 4 53
Hath my sword therefore broke through London gates? . 2 *Hen. VI.* iv 8 24
Heaven, set ope thy everlasting gates, To entertain my vows! . . iv 9 13
Sufficeth that I have maintains my state And sends the poor well pleased from my gate . . . iv 10 25
With colours spread March'd through the city to the palace gates 3 *Hen. VI.* i 1 92
Open Thy gate of mercy, gracious God! My soul flies through these wounds to seek out Thee . . . i 4 177
Off with his head, and set it on York gates . . . i 4 179
See how the morning opes her golden gates! . . . ii 1 21
They took his head, and on the gates of York They set the same . ii 1 65
Yet that thy brazen gates of heaven may ope, And give sweet passage to my sinful soul! . . . ii 3 40
From off the gates of York fetch down the head, Your fathers' head . ii 6 52
Your foe is taken, And brought your prisoner to your palace gate . iii 2 119
What then remains, we being thus arrived From Ravenspurgh haven before the gates of York, But that we enter, as into our dukedom? iv 7 8
The gates made fast! Brother, I like not this . . . iv 7 10
We were forewarned of your coming, And shut the gates for safety . iv 7 18
Why, master mayor, why stand you in a doubt? Open the gates . iv 7 28
We are King Henry's friends.—Ay, say you so? the gates shall then be open'd . . . iv 7 29
These gates must not be shut But in the night or in the time of war . iv 7 35
Now, Warwick, wilt thou ope the city gates, Speak gentle words? . v 1 21
The gates are open, let us enter too . . . v 1 60
If we talk of reason, Let's shut our gates and sleep . *Troi. and Cres.* ii 2 47
Like a gate of steel Fronting the sun, receives and renders back His figure and his heat . . . iii 3 121
I'll call mine uncle down; He shall unbolt the gates.—Trouble him not iv 2 3
Instance, O instance! strong as Pluto's gates . . . v 2 153
I'll bring you to the gates.—Accept distracted thanks . . v 2 188
Our gates, Which yet seem shut, we have but pinn'd with rushes . *Cor.* i 4 17
So, now the gates are ope: now prove good seconds . . i 4 43
Following the fliers at the very heels, With them he enters; who, upon the sudden, Clapp'd to their gates . . . i 4 51
Hence, and shut your gates upon's. Our guider, come . . i 7 6
Know, Rome, that all alone Marcius did fight Within Corioli gates . ii 1 180
Alone he enter'd The mortal gate of the city, which he painted With shunless destiny; aidless came off . . . ii 2 115
Even when the navel of the state was touch'd, They would not thread the gates . . . iii 1 124
Never more To enter our Rome gates . . . iii 3 104
Go, see him out at gates, and follow him, As he hath follow'd you, with all despite . . . iii 3 138
Let's see him out at gates come. The gods preserve our noble tribunes! iii 3 142
Bring me but out at gate. Come, my sweet wife . . iv 1 47
Whether to knock against the gates of Rome, Or rudely visit them in parts remote, To fright them, ere destroy . . . iv 5 147
He'll go, he says, and sowl the porter of Rome gates by the ears . iv 5 214
You have pushed out your gates the very defender of them . . v 2 42
I have been blown out of your gates with sighs . . . v 2 81
Mine ears against your suits are stronger than Your gates against my force v 2 95
Ne'er through an arch so hurried the blown tide, As the recomforted through the gates . . . v 4 51
With bloody passage led your wars even to The gates of Rome . . v 6 77
Open the gates, and let me in.—Tribunes, and me . . *T. Andron.* i 1 62
And make proud Saturnine and his empress Beg at the gates . . iii 1 299
It did me good, before the palace gate To brave the tribune . . iv 2 35
Myself unkindly banished, The gates shut on me, and turn'd weeping out v 3 105
Send thy man away.—Peter, stay at the gate . . *Rom. and Jul.* ii 5 20
No porter at his gate, But rather one that smiles and still invites All that pass by. It cannot hold . . . *T. of Athens* ii 1 10
And enter in our ears like great triumphers In their applauding gates . v 1 200
Set but thy foot Against our rampired gates, and they shall ope . v 4 47
Go to the gate; somebody knocks . . . *J. Cæsar* ii 1 60
Brutus and Cassius Are rid like madmen through the gates of Rome . iii 2 274
They are, my lord, without the palace gate.—Bring them before us *Macb.* iii 1 47
So all men do, from hence to the palace gate Make it their walk . iii 3 13
To bed, to bed! there's knocking at the gate: come, come, come, come v 1 74
It courses through The natural gates and alleys of the body . *Hamlet* i 5 67
Beat at this gate, that let thy folly in, And thy dear judgement out! *Lear* i 4 293
If wolves had at thy gate howl'd that stern time, Thou shouldst have said 'Good porter, turn the key' . . . iii 7 63
Go thrust him out at gates, and let him smell His way to Dover . iii 7 93
You, mistress, That have the office opposite to Saint Peter, And keep the gate of hell! . . . *Othello* iv 2 92
The lark at heaven's gate sings, And Phœbus 'gins arise . *Cymbeline* ii 3 22
This gate Instructs you how to adore the heavens . . . iii 3 2
The gates of monarchs Are arch'd so high that giants may jet through iii 3 4
And on the gates of Lud's-town set your heads . . . iv 2 99
For he's no man on whom perfections wait That, knowing sin within, will touch the gate . . . *Pericles* i 1 80
Gather. Now does my project gather to a head . . . *Tempest* v 1 1
O, let me say no more! Gather the sequel by that went before *C. of Er.* i 1 96
The reason that I gather he is mad . . . iv 3 87

Gather. Bring him yet to me, And I of him will gather patience *Much Ado* v 1 19
Having come to Padua To gather in some debts *T. of Shrew* iv 4 25
And, hoodwink'd as thou art, will lead thee on To gather from thee *All's W.* iv 1 91
By this we gather You have tripp'd since *W. Tale* i 2 75
Thus may we gather honey from the weed *Hen. V.* iv 1 11
Now there rests no other shift but this; To gather our soldiers 1 *Hen. VI.* ii 1 76
Thou art my heir; the rest I wish thee gather ii 5 96
Market men That come to gather money for their corn iii 2 5
Gather we our forces out of hand And set upon our boasting enemy iii 2 102
Then gather strength and march unto him straight iv 1 73
For your expenses and sufficient charge, Among the people gather up a tenth v 5 93
Get you to Smithfield and gather head 2 *Hen. VI.* iv 5 10
I seek not to wax great by others' waning, Or gather wealth, I care not, with what envy iv 10 23
That thereby he may gather The ground of your ill-will *Richard III.* i 3 68
So by your companies To draw him on to pleasures, and to gather, So much as from occasion you may glean *Hamlet* ii 2 15
Now gather, and surmise ii 2 108
Gather by him, as he is behaved, If't be the affliction of his love or no iii 1 35
You may gather more *Lear* iv 5 32
Half way down Hangs one that gathers samphire, dreadful trade! iv 6 15
Whiles yet the dew's on ground, gather those flowers *Cymbeline* i 5 1
And by them gather Their several virtues and effects i 5 22
Gathered. In such a night Medea gather'd the enchanted herbs That did renew old Æson *Mer. of Venice* v 1 13
My lord, the French have gather'd head 1 *Hen. VI.* i 4 100
I find thou art no less than fame hath bruited And more than may be gather'd by thy shape ii 3 69
My lord, there's an army gathered together in Smithfield 2 *Hen. VI.* iv 6 13
Muster'd my soldiers, gather'd flocks of friends 3 *Hen. VI.* ii 1 112
They had gather'd a wise council to them Of every realm *Hen. VIII.* ii 4 51
Fresh tears Stood on her cheeks, as doth the honey-dew Upon a gather'd lily almost wither'd *T. Andron.* iii 1 113
Rome never had more cause. The Goths have gather'd head iv 4 63
Thy Cæsar knighted me; my youth I spent Much under him; of him I gather'd honour *Cymbeline* iii 1 71
Gathering. The time shall not be many hours of age More than it is ere foul sin gathering head Shall break into corruption *Richard II.* v 1 58; 2 *Hen. IV.* iii 1 76
Gaudeo. Videsne quis venit?—Video, et gaudeo *L. L. Lost* v 1 34
Gaudy. If frosts and fasts . . . Nip not the gaudy blossoms of your love v 2 812
Thou gaudy gold, Hard food for Midas, I will none of thee *Mer. of Venice* iii 2 101
The gaudy, blabbing and remorseful day Is crept into the bosom of the sea 2 *Hen. VI.* iv 1 1
Costly thy habit as thy purse can buy, But not express'd in fancy; rich, not gaudy; For the apparel oft proclaims the man *Hamlet* i 3 71
Come, Let's have one other gaudy night *Ant. and Cleo.* iii 13 183
Gauge. You shall not gauge me By what we do to-night *Mer. of Venice* ii 2 208
Gaul. Peace, I say, Gallia and Gaul, French and Welsh! *Mer. Wives* iii 1 99
Gaultier. Thy name is Gaultier, being rightly sounded.—Gaultier or Walter, which it is, I care not 2 *Hen. VI.* iv 1 37
Gaultree. What is this forest call'd?—'Tis Gaultree Forest 2 *Hen. IV.* iv 1 2
Gaunt. Old John of Gaunt, time-honour'd Lancaster *Richard II.* i 1 1
Ah, Gaunt, his blood was thine! that bed, that womb, That metal, that self-mould, that fashion'd thee Made him a man i 2 22
Call it not patience, Gaunt; it is despair i 2 29
Farewell, old Gaunt. Thou goest to Coventry, there to behold Our cousin Hereford and fell Mowbray fight i 2 44
Farewell, old Gaunt: thy sometimes brother's wife With her companion grief must end her life i 2 54
And furbish new the name of John a Gaunt, Even in the lusty haviour of his son i 3 76
Old John of Gaunt is grievous sick, my lord, Suddenly taken i 4 54
What comfort, man? how is't with aged Gaunt?—O, how that name befits my composition! Old Gaunt indeed, and gaunt in being old ii 1 72
And who abstains from meat that is not gaunt? ii 1 76
Watching breeds leanness, leanness is all gaunt ii 1 78
Gaunt am I for the grave, gaunt as a grave ii 1 82
My liege, old Gaunt commends him to your majesty ii 1 147
We do seize to us The plate, coin, revenues and moveables, Whereof our uncle Gaunt did stand possess'd ii 1 162
Not Gaunt's rebukes, nor England's private wrongs ii 1 166
Is not Gaunt dead, and doth not Hereford live? Was not Gaunt just, and is not Harry true? ii 1 191
As when brave Gaunt, thy father, and myself Rescued the Black Prince ii 3 100
You are my father, for methinks in you I see old Gaunt alive ii 3 118
He should have found his uncle Gaunt a father, To rouse his wrongs ii 3 127
By the buried hand of warlike Gaunt iii 3 109
I am not John of Gaunt, your grandfather; but yet no coward 1 *Hen. IV.* ii 2 70
Nor claim no further than your new-fall'n right, The seat of Gaunt v 1 45
John a Gaunt loved him well, and betted much money on his head 2 *Hen. IV.* iii 2 49
Talks as familiarly of John a Gaunt as if he had been sworn brother to him iii 2 345
I saw it, and told John a Gaunt he beat his own name iii 2 349
Whereas he From John of Gaunt doth bring his pedigree 1 *Hen. VI.* ii 5 77
Next to whom Was John of Gaunt, the Duke of Lancaster 2 *Hen. VI.* ii 2 14
Duke of Lancaster, The eldest son and heir of John of Gaunt ii 2 22
Henry doth claim the crown from John of Gaunt, The fourth son ii 2 54
Such hope have all the line of John of Gaunt! 3 *Hen. VI.* i 1 19
Then Warwick disannuls great John of Gaunt, Which did subdue the greatest part of Spain iii 3 81
And, after John of Gaunt, Henry the Fourth iii 3 83
Gauntlet. Their thimbles into armed gauntlets change *K. John* v 2 156
A scaly gauntlet now with joints of steel Must glove this hand 2 *Hen. IV.* i 1 146
By Mars his gauntlet, thanks! *Troi. and Cres.* iv 5 177
There's my gauntlet; I'll prove it on a giant *Lear* iv 6 91
Gave. Confined together In the same fashion as you gave in charge *Temp.* v 1 8
Our ship—Which, but three glasses since, we gave out split—Is tight v 1 223
I, a lost mutton, gave your letter to her, a laced mutton, and she, a laced mutton, gave me, a lost mutton, nothing for my labour *T. G. of V.* i 1 101
From whom?—That the contents will show.—Say, say, who gave it thee? i 2 37
Did you perceive her earnest?—She gave me none, except an angry word ii 1 164
Yourself, sweet lady; for you gave the fire ii 4 37
When I was sick, you gave me bitter pills, And I must minister the like ii 4 149
Even that power which gave me first my oath Provokes me to this ii 6 4
I gave him gentle looks, thereby to find That which thyself hast now disclosed to me iii 1 31
This ring I gave him when he parted from me, To bind him to remember iv 4 102
I have heard him say a thousand times His Julia gave it him iv 4 140
Gave. Let me see: Why, this is the ring I gave to Julia *T. G. of Ver.* v 4 93
How camest thou by this ring? At my depart I gave this unto Julia v 4 97
Behold her that gave aim to all thy oaths v 4 101
Who even now gave me good eyes too, examined my parts *Mer. Wives* i 3 66
And gave such orderly and well-behaved reproof to all uncomeliness ii 1 59
A league from Epidamnum had we sail'd, Before the always wind-obeying deep Gave any tragic instance of our harm *Com. of Errors* i 1 65
Gave healthful welcome to their shipwreck'd guests i 1 115
Where have you left the money that I gave you? i 2 54
Where is the gold I gave in charge to thee?—To me, sir? why, you gave no gold to me i 2 70
Where is the thousand marks I gave thee, villain? ii 1 65
The gold I gave to Dromio is laid up Safe at the Centaur ii 2 1; 16
Thank me, sir! for what?—Marry, sir, for this something that you gave me for nothing ii 2 53
If the skin were parchment and the blows you gave were ink iii 1 13
You know I gave it you half an hour since.—You gave me none iv 1 65
Where's the money?—Why, sir, I gave the money for the rope iv 4 12
He lent it me awhile; and I gave him use for it, a double heart *Much Ado* ii 1 288
And prodigally gave them all to you *L. L. Lost* ii 1 12
Thou fellow, a word: Who gave thee this letter? iv 1 103
They are free that gave these tokens to us v 2 424
And to confirm it plain, You gave me this: but take it, sir, again v 2 453
The armipotent Mars, of lances the almighty, Gave Hector a gift v 2 651
She in mild terms begg'd my patience, I then did ask of her her changeling child; Which straight she gave me *M. N. Dream* iv 1 65
You do me wrong; In faith, I gave it to the judge's clerk *Mer. of Venice* v 1 143
Gave it a judge's clerk! no, God's my judge, The clerk will ne'er wear hair on's face that had it v 1 157
By this hand, I gave it to a youth, A kind of boy, a little scrubbed boy v 1 161
I gave my love a ring and made him swear Never to part with it v 1 170
My Lord Bassanio gave his ring away Unto the judge that begg'd it v 1 179
If you did know to whom I gave the ring, If you did know for whom I gave the ring And would conceive for what I gave the ring And how unwillingly I left the ring v 1 193
If you had known the virtue of the ring, Or half her worthiness that gave the ring, Or your own honour to contain the ring v 1 200
By heaven, it is the same I gave the doctor!—I had it of him v 1 257
Besides this nothing that he so plentifully gives me, the something that nature gave me his countenance seems to take from me *As Y. Like It* i 1 18
He led me to the gentle duke, Who gave me fresh array iv 3 144
Pisa renowned for grave citizens Gave me my being *T. of Shrew* i 1 11
Grumio gave order how it should be done.—I gave him no order; I gave him the stuff iv 3 118
With that she sighed as she stood, And gave this sentence then *All's Well* i 3 80
On's bed of death Many receipts he gave me; chiefly one ii 1 108
That gave him out incurable,— Why, there 'tis; so say I too ii 3 16
When I gave it Helen, I bade her, if her fortunes ever stood Necessitied to help, that by this token I would relieve her v 3 83
'Twas mine, 'twas Helen's, Whoever gave it you v 3 105
She call'd the saints to surety That she would never put it from her finger, Unless she gave it to yourself in bed v 3 110
Yet for all that He gave it to a commoner o' the camp, If I be one v 3 194
This ring was his of late.—And this was it I gave him, being abed v 3 228
Where did you buy it? or who gave it you?—It was not given me v 3 272
How could you give it him?—I never gave it him v 3 277
This ring was mine; I gave it his first wife v 3 280
This is the air; that is the glorious sun; This pearl she gave me *T. Night* iv 3 2
His life I gave him and did thereto add My love, without retention v 1 83
We have cross'd, To execute the charge my father gave me *W. Tale* v 1 162
The oracle Gave hope thou wast in being v 3 127
My father gave me honour, yours gave land *K. John* i 1 164
The latest breath that gave the sound of words Was deep-sworn faith iii 1 230
Shall that victorious hand be feebled here, That in your chambers gave you chastisement? v 2 147
Whereto thy tongue a party-verdict gave *Richard II.* i 3 234
But you gave leave to my unwilling tongue i 3 245
But if I could, by Him that gave me life, I would attach you all ii 3 155
And there at Venice gave His body to that pleasant country's earth iv 1 97
No joyful tongue gave him his welcome home v 2 29
A pouncet-box, which ever and anon He gave his nose 1 *Hen. IV.* i 3 39
While I question my puny drawer to what end he gave me the sugar ii 4 33
And he of Wales, that gave Amamon the bastinado ii 4 370
And gave the tongue a helpful ornament iii 1 125
And gave his countenance, against his name iii 2 65
A poor unminded outlaw sneaking home, My father gave him welcome iv 3 59
Laid gifts before him, proffer'd him their oaths, Gave him their heirs iv 3 72
He gave you all the duties of a man; Trimm'd up your praises v 2 56
I'll take it upon my death, I gave him this wound in the thigh v 4 155
With that, he gave his able horse the head 2 *Hen. IV.* i 1 43
For the box of the ear that the prince gave you, he gave it like a rude prince i 2 218
And the boy that I gave Falstaff: a' had him from me Christian ii 2 75
Yea, for my sake, even to the eyes of Richard Gave him defiance iii 1 65
Thirty thousand.—The just proportion that we gave them out iv 1 23
Give that which gave thee life unto the worms iv 5 117
My gracious liege, You won it, wore it, kept it, gave it me iv 5 222
I gave bold way to my authority And did commit you v 2 82
Gave thee no instance why thou shouldst do treason *Hen. V.* ii 2 119
And all my mother came into mine eyes And gave me up to tears iv 6 32
This was my glove; here is the fellow of it; and he that I gave it to in change promised to wear it iv 8 30
Porter, remember what I gave in charge 1 *Hen. VI.* ii 3 1
I gave thee life and rescued thee from death.—O, twice my father! iv 6 5
I gave a noble to the priest The morn that I was wedded to her mother v 4 23
I would the milk Thy mother gave thee when thou suck'dst her breast, Had been a little ratsbane for thy sake! v 4 28
The happiest gift that ever marquess gave 2 *Hen. VI.* i 1 15
Till Suffolk gave two dukedoms for his daughter i 3 90
I never gave them condign punishment iii 1 130
Is all things well, According as I gave directions? iii 2 12
The ruthless queen gave him to dry his cheeks A napkin steeped in the harmless blood Of sweet young Rutland 3 *Hen. VI.* ii 1 61
Say unto his child, 'What my great-grandfather and grandsire got My careless father fondly gave away' ii 2 38
The noble gentleman gave up the ghost ii 3 22
O boy, thy father gave thee life too soon, And hath bereft thee of thy life too late!—Woe above woe! ii 5 92
Here burns my candle out; ay, here it dies, Which, whiles it lasted, gave King Henry light ii 6 2

Gave. 'Tis but his policy to counterfeit, Because he would avoid such bitter taunts Which in the time of death he gave our father 3 *Hen. VI.* ii 6 67
Matter of marriage was the charge he gave me, But dreadful war shall answer . . . iii 3 258
And Warwick, doing what you gave in charge, Is now dishonoured . iv 1 32
'Twas I that gave the kingdom to thy brother . . . . . . v 1 34
I will not ruinate my father's house, Who gave his blood to lime the stones together . . . . v 1 84
Gave himself, All thin and naked, to the numb cold night *Richard III.* ii 1 116
If to have done the thing you gave in charge Beget your happiness, be happy then . . . . iv 3 25
Whose hand soever lanced their tender hearts, Thy head, all indirectly, gave direction . . . . iv 4 225
Order gave each thing view . . . . *Hen. VIII.* i 1 44
Nay, gave notice He was from thence discharged . . . ii 4 33
And that gave to me Many a groaning throe . . . . . ii 4 198
The packet, Cromwell, Gave't you the king? . . . . . . iii 2 77
With his own hand gave me; Bade me enjoy it, with the place and honours . . . . iii 2 247
Now, who'll take it?—The king, that gave it . . . . . iii 2 251
But I think your grace, Out of the pain you suffer'd, gave no ear to't . iv 2 8
Honourably received him; To whom he gave these words . . iv 2 20
He gave his honours to the world again, His blessed part to heaven . iv 2 29
Of his own body he was ill, and gave The clergy ill example . . iv 2 43
My mind gave me, In seeking tales and informations Against this man v 3 109
How much are we bound to heaven In daily thanks, that gave us such a prince . . . . v 3 115
I gave ye Power as he was a counsellor to try him, Not as a groom v 3 142
That unbodied figure of the thought That gave't surmised shape *Troi. and Cres.* i 3 17
Praise him that got thee, she that gave thee suck . . . . ii 3 252
Neither gave to me Good word nor look . . . . . . iii 3 143
As if that whatsoever god who leads him Were slily crept into his human powers And gave him graceful posture . . . *Coriolanus* ii 1 237
Whoever gave that counsel, to give forth The corn o' the storehouse gratis . . . . iii 1 113
We are the greater poll, and in true fear They gave us our demands . iii 1 135
And yet my mind gave me his clothes made a false report of him . . iv 5 157
Like beasts And cowardly nobles, gave way unto your clusters . . iv 6 122
Gave him way In all his own desires; nay, let him choose . . . v 6 32
Highly moved to wrath To be controll'd in that he frankly gave *T. An.* i 1 420
Our mother, unadvised, Gave you a dancing-rapier by your side . . ii 1 39
O, let me teach thee! for my father's sake, That gave thee life . . ii 3 159
'Tis Ovid's Metamorphoses; My mother gave it me . . . . iv 1 43
Sensibly fed Of that self-blood that first gave life to you . . iv 2 123
The Bull, being gall'd, gave Aries such a knock . . . . iv 3 71
And for my tidings gave me twenty kisses . . . . . . v 1 120
I gave thee mine before thou didst request it: And yet I would it were to give again.—Wouldst thou withdraw it? . . . *Rom. and Jul.* ii 2 128
You gave us the counterfeit fairly last night . . . . . ii 4 47
And gave him what becomed love I might . . . . . . iv 2 26
Then gave I her, so tutor'd by my art, A sleeping potion . . . v 2 243
You mistake my love: I gave it freely ever . . . *T. of Athens* i 2 10
You gave Good words the other day of a bay courser I rode on: it is yours . . . . i 2 216
He gave me a jewel th' other day, and now he has beat it out of my hat iii 6 122
'Tis said he gave unto his steward a mighty sum . . . . v 1 8
Whose star-like nobleness gave life and influence To their whole being! v 1 66
With an angry wafture of your hand, Gave sign for me to leave you *J. C.* ii 1 247
So often shall the knot of us be call'd The men that gave their country liberty . . . . iii 1 118
And that they know full well That gave me public leave to speak of him iii 2 224
That rash humour which my mother gave me Makes me forgetful . . iv 3 120
O Cassius, Brutus gave the word too early . . . . . . v 3 5
Those that gave the thane of Cawdor to me Promised no less to them *Macbeth* i 3 119
I believe drink gave thee the lie last night . . . . . ii 3 41
I prescripts gave her, That she should lock herself from his resort *Ham.* ii 2 142
I never gave you aught.—My honour'd lord, you know right well you did iii 1 96
I will bestow him, and will answer well The death I gave him . . iii 4 177
He that made us with such large discourse, Looking before and after, gave us not That capability and god-like reason To fust in us unused iv 4 37
A pirate of very warlike appointment gave us chase . . . . iv 6 16
He made confession of you, And gave you such a masterly report . . iv 7 97
And set a double varnish on the fame The Frenchman gave you . . iv 7 134
Subscribed it, gave't the impression, placed it safely . . . v 2 52
He never gave commandment for their death . . . . . . v 2 385
If I gave them all my living, I'ld keep my coxcombs myself . *Lear* i 4 120
'Tis like the breath of an unfee'd lawyer; you gave me nothing for't . i 4 143
What was the offence you gave him?—I never gave him any . . . ii 2 121
Commanded me to follow, and attend The leisure of their answer; gave me cold looks . . . . ii 4 37
I gave you all— And in good time you gave it . . . . . ii 4 253
I never gave you kingdom, call'd you children, You owe me no subscription . . . . iii 2 17
Your old kind father, whose frank heart gave all,—O, that way madness lies . . . . iii 4 20
Gave her dear rights To his dog-hearted daughters . . . . iv 3 46
She gave strange œillades and most speaking looks . . . . iv 5 25
My story being done, She gave me for my pains a world of sighs . *Othello* i 3 159
What handkerchief! Why, that the Moor first gave to Desdemona . iii 3 308
And then Cried 'Cursed fate that gave thee to the Moor!' . . . iii 3 426
I gave her such a one; 'twas my first gift.—I know not that . . . iii 3 436
You may, indeed, say so; For 'twas that hand that gave away my heart iii 4 45
The hearts of old gave hands; But our new heraldry is hands, not hearts . . . . iii 4 46
Lend me thy handkerchief.—Here, my lord.—That which I gave you . iii 4 53
She, dying, gave it me; And bid me, when my fate would have me wive, To give it her . . . . iii 4 63
I never gave him cause.—But jealous souls will not be answer'd so . iii 4 158
What did you mean by that same handkerchief you gave me even now? iv 1 155
To see how he prizes the foolish woman your wife! she gave it him . iv 1 186
That handkerchief which I so loved and gave thee Thou gavest to Cassio v 2 48
I never gave him token.—By heaven, I saw my handkerchief in's hand v 2 61
He found it then; I never gave it him . . . . v 2 67
That recognizance and pledge of love Which I first gave her . . . v 2 215
It was a handkerchief, an antique token My father gave my mother . v 2 217
Dear general, I never gave you cause.—I do believe it . . . . v 2 299
Hardly gave audience, or Vouchsafed to think he had partners *A. and C.* i 4 7
Unto her He gave the stablishment of Egypt . . . . . . iii 6 9

Gave. Great Media, Parthia, and Armenia, He gave to Alexander *Ant. and Cleo.* iii 6 15
Oft before gave audience, As 'tis reported, so . . . . . . iii 6 18
The hearts That spaniel'd me at heels, to whom I gave Their wishes, do discandy . . . . iv 12 21
But he added to your having; gave you some ground . . *Cymbeline* i 2 19
Here the leaf's turn'd down Where Philomel gave up . . . ii 2 46
She gave it me, and said She prized it once . . . . . ii 4 103
It gave me present hunger To feed again, though full . . . ii 4 137
My tailor made them not.—Hence, then, and thank The man that gave them thee . . . . iv 2 85
The ground that gave them first has them again . . . . iv 2 289
All curses madded Hecuba gave the Greeks, And mine to boot . . iv 2 313
The drug he gave me, which he said was precious And cordial to me . iv 2 326
Ditch'd, and wall'd with turf; Which gave advantage to an ancient soldier . . . . v 3 15
There was a fourth man, in a silly habit, That gave the affront with them . . . . v 3 87
The gods throw stones of sulphur on me, if That box I gave you was not thought by me A precious thing . . . . v 5 241
Given his mistress that confection Which I gave him for cordial . . v 5 247
Nature this dowry gave, to glad her presence . . . *Pericles* i 1 9
Were all too little to content and please, Although they gave their creatures in abundance . . . . i 4 36
The king my father gave you such a ring . . . . . . v 3 39
Gavest. Dost thou hear? gavest thou my letter to Julia? *T. G. of Ver.* i 1 99
That woman there! She whom thou gavest to me to be my wife *Com. of Errors* v 1 198
For the sugar thou gavest me, 'twas a pennyworth, wast't not? 1 *Hen. IV.* ii 4 65
Thou, like a kind fellow, gavest thyself away gratis . 2 *Hen. IV.* iv 3 75
The life thou gavest me first was lost and done, Till with thy warlike sword, despite of fate, To my determined time thou gavest new date 1 *Hen. VI.* iv 6 9
And then, to dry them, gavest the duke a clout . *Richard III.* i 3 177
From all That might have mercy on the fault thou gavest him *Hen. VIII.* iii 2 262
Take the villain back again, That late thou gavest me . *Rom. and Jul.* iii 1 131
Thou gavest thine ears like tapsters that bid welcome To knaves *T. of A.* iv 3 215
When thou clovest thy crown i' the middle, and gavest away both parts, thou borest thy ass on thy back o'er the dirt . . . *Lear* i 4 176
Thou hadst little wit in thy bald crown, when thou gavest thy golden one away . . . . i 4 178
When thou gavest them the rod, and put'st down thine own breeches . i 4 189
That handkerchief which I so loved and gave thee Thou gavest to Cassio *Othello* v 2 49
O, get thee from my sight; Thou gavest me poison . . . *Cymbeline* v 5 237
Gawd. With bracelets of thy hair, rings, gawds, conceits *M. N. Dream* i 1 33
As the remembrance of an idle gawd Which in my childhood I did dote upon . . . . iv 1 172
For these other gawds, Unbind my hands, I'll pull them off myself *T. of Shrew* ii 1 3
And the proud day, Attended with the pleasures of the world, Is all too wanton and too full of gawds To give me audience . *K. John* iii 3 36
All with one consent praise new-born gawds . . . *Troi. and Cres.* iii 3 176
Gawsey. Sir Nicholas Gawsey hath for succour sent, And so hath Clifton . . . —Make up to Clifton: I'll to Sir Nicholas Gawsey 1 *Hen. IV.* v 4 45
Gay. Do their gay vestments his affections bait? . *Com. of Errors* ii 1 94
My gay apparel for an almsman's gown . . . *Richard II.* iii 3 149
'Tis nothing but some bond, that he is enter'd into For gay apparel . v 2 66
They will pluck The gay new coats o'er the French soldiers' heads *Hen. V.* iv 3 118
And deck my body in gay ornaments, And witch sweet ladies 3 *Hen. VI.* iii 2 149
Never lack'd gold and yet went never gay . . . . *Othello* ii 1 151
I dare him therefore To lay his gay comparisons apart . *Ant. and Cleo.* iii 13 26
Gayness. Our gayness and our gilt are all besmirch'd . . *Hen. V.* iv 3 110
Gaze. She that you gaze on so as she sits at supper? . . *T. G. of Ver.* ii 1 46
Peruse the traders, gaze upon the buildings . . *Com. of Errors* i 2 13
Gaze where you should, and that will clear your sight . . . iii 2 57
All eyes saw his eyes enchanted with gazes . . . *L. L. Lost* ii 1 247
A lover's eyes will gaze an eagle blind . . . . . . iv 3 334
Nor thrust your head into the public street To gaze on Christian fools *Mer. of Venice* ii 5 33
Their savage eyes turn'd to a modest gaze By the sweet power of music v 1 78
Well said, master; mum! and gaze your fill . . . *T. of Shrew* i 1 73
Wherefore gaze this goodly company, As if they saw some wondrous monument? . . . . iii 2 96
Not a month 'Fore your queen died, she was more worth such gazes Than what you look on now . . . . *W. Tale* v 1 226
No longer shall you gaze on't, lest your fancy May think anon it moves v 3 60
Seen, but with such eyes As, sick and blunted with community, Afford no extraordinary gaze . . . . 1 *Hen. IV.* iii 2 78
Gaze on, and grovel on thy face, Until thy head be circled with the same 2 *Hen. VI.* i 2 9
Look how they gaze! See how the giddy multitude do point! . . ii 4 20
Had you such leisure in the time of death To gaze upon the secrets of the deep?—Methought I had . . . . . . *Richard III.* i 4 35
Gives all gaze and bent of amorous view On the fair Cressid *T. and C.* iv 5 282
When youth with comeliness plucked all gaze his way . *Coriolanus* i 3 8
And in the fountain shall we gaze so long Till the fresh taste be taken from that clearness . . . . *T. Andron.* iii 1 127
From our troops I stray'd To gaze upon a ruinous monastery . . . v 1 21
As is a winged messenger of heaven Unto the white-upturned wondering eyes Of mortals that fall back to gaze on him . *Rom. and Jul.* ii 2 30
Here all eyes gaze on us.—Men's eyes were made to look, and let them gaze . . . . iii 1 56
You look pale and gaze And put on fear . . . . . *J. Cæsar* i 3 59
Yield thee, coward, And live to be the show and gaze o' the time *Macbeth* v 8 24
'Tis a pageant, To keep us in false gaze . . . . . *Othello* i 3 19
The air; which, but for vacancy, Had gone to gaze on Cleopatra too *Ant. and Cleo.* ii 2 222
And with our sprightly port make the ghosts gaze . . . . iv 14 52
None would look on her, But cast their gazes on Marina's face *Pericles* iv 3 33
Gazed. Never gazed the moon Upon the water as he'll stand and read As 'twere my daughter's eyes . . . . *W. Tale* iv 4 172
Like perspectives, which rightly gazed upon Show nothing but confusion, eyed awry Distinguish form . . . . *Richard II.* ii 2 18
Like dumb statuas or breathing stones, Gazed each on other *Richard III.* iii 7 26
I am a maid, My lord, that ne'er before invited eyes, But have been gazed on like a comet . . . . *Pericles* v 1 87

Gazer. Come, basilisk, And kill the innocent gazer with thy sight 2 *Hen. VI.* iii 2 53
I'll slay more gazers than the basilisk . . . . 3 *Hen. VI.* iii 2 187
A courser, whose delightful steps Shall make the gazer joy . *Pericles* ii 1 165
Gazing. Dost thou know her by my gazing on her? . . *T. G. of Ver.* ii 1 51
At length the sun, gazing upon the earth, Dispersed those vapours *C. of Er.* i 1 89
It is a fault that springeth from your eye.—For gazing on your beams . iii 2 56
A sin prevailing much in youthful men, Who give their eyes the liberty of gazing . . . . v 1 53
Gazing in mine eyes, feeling my pulse . . . . . . v 1 243
It is engender'd in the eyes, With gazing fed . . *Mer. of Venice* iii 2 68
Still gazing in a doubt Whether those peals of praise be his or no . . iii 2 145
I should leave grazing, were I of your flock, And only live by gazing *W. T.* iv 4 110
Presenteth them unto the gazing moon So many horrid ghosts *Hen. V.* iv Prol. 27
Why are thine eyes fix'd to the sullen earth, Gazing on that which seems to dim thy sight? What seest thou there? . . 2 *Hen. VI.* i 2 6
Ill can thy noble mind abrook The abject people gazing on thy face . ii 4 11
Nay, if thou be that princely eagle's bird, Show thy descent by gazing 'gainst the sun . . . . 3 *Hen. VI.* ii 1 92
'Twas a shame no less Than was his loss, to course your flying flags, And leave his navy gazing . . . . *Ant. and Cleo.* iii 13 12
Thou dost look Like Patience gazing on kings' graves . *Pericles* v 1 139
Gear. Disguised like Muscovites, in shapeless gear . *L. L. Lost* v 2 303
I'll grow a talker for this gear . . . . *Mer. of Venice* i 1 110
If Fortune be a woman, she's a good wench for this gear . . ii 2 176
To this gear the sooner the better . . . . 2 *Hen. VI.* i 4 17
I will remedy this gear ere long, Or sell my title for a glorious grave . iii 1 91
Come, shall we to this gear? . . . . *Richard III.* i 4 158
Will this gear ne'er be mended? . . . . *Troi. and Cres.* i 1 6
And Cupid grant all tongue-tied maidens here Bed, chamber, Pandar to provide this gear! . . . . iii 2 220
Come, to this gear. You are a good archer, Marcus . *T. Andron.* iv 3 52
Here's goodly gear!—A sail, a sail!—Two, two; a shirt and a smock *Rom. and Jul.* ii 4 107
Let me have A dram of poison, such soon-speeding gear . . . v 1 60
Geck. The most notorious geck and gull That e'er invention play'd on *T. N.* v 1 351
To become the geck and scorn O' th' other's villany . *Cymbeline* v 4 67
Geese. I have stood on the pillory for geese he hath killed *T. G. of Ver.* iv 4 35
Tell Mistress Anne the jest, how my father stole two geese out of a pen *Mer. Wives* iii 4 41
Since I plucked geese, played truant and whipped top . . v 1 27
The spring is near when green geese are a-breeding . *L. L. Lost* i 1 97
Where he should find you lions, finds you hares; Where foxes, geese *Cor.* i 1 176
You souls of geese, That bear the shapes of men, how have you run! . i 4 34
There is ten thousand— Geese, villain?—Soldiers, sir . *Macbeth* v 3 13
Geffrey. In right and true behalf Of thy deceased brother Geffrey's son, Arthur Plantagenet . . . . . *K. John* i 1 8
Look here upon thy brother Geffrey's face; These eyes, these brows, were moulded out of his . . . . ii 1 99
This little abstract doth contain that large Which died in Geffrey . . ii 1 102
That Geffrey was thy elder brother born, And this his son . . ii 1 104
England was Geffrey's right And this is Geffrey's . . . ii 1 105
Liker in feature to his father Geffrey Than thou and John in manners . ii 1 126
I was Geffrey's wife; Young Arthur is my son, and he is lost . . iii 4 46
Is it my fault that I was Geffrey's son? No, indeed, is't not. . iv 1 22
Geld. Does your worship mean to geld and splay all the youth? *M. for M.* ii 1 242
I'll geld 'em all; fourteen they shall not see . . *W. Tale* ii 1 147
'Twas nothing to geld a codpiece of a purse . . . . . iv 4 623
Gelded. We much rather had depart withal And have the money by our father lent Than Aquitaine so gelded as it is . . *L. L. Lost* ii 1 149
Bereft and gelded of his patrimony . . . . *Richard II.* ii 1 237
Lord Say hath gelded the commonwealth . . . 2 *Hen. VI.* iv 2 174
Let me be gelded like a spaniel. Come your ways . . *Pericles* iv 6 133
Gelding. I will rather trust a Fleming with my butter, . . . or a thief to walk my ambling gelding . . . . *Mer. Wives* ii 2 319
Lend me thy lantern, to see my gelding in the stable . 1 *Hen. IV.* ii 1 39
Bid the ostler bring my gelding out of the stable . . . ii 1 105
Gelding the opposed continent as much As on the other side it takes from you . . . . iii 1 110
Gelida. Precor gelida quando pecus omne sub umbra Ruminat *L. L. Lost* iv 2 95
Gelidus timor occupat artus, it is thee I fear . 2 *Hen. VI.* iv 1 117
Gelt. Would he were gelt that had it . . . *Mer. of Venice* v 1 144
Gem. Never so rich a gem Was set in worse than gold . . . ii 7 54
Of six preceding ancestors, that gem, Conferr'd by testament to the sequent issue, Hath it been owed and worn . . *All's Well* v 3 196
'Tis that miracle and queen of gems That nature pranks her in *T. Night* ii 4 88
Reflecting gems, Which woo'd the slimy bottom of the deep *Richard III.* i 4 31
From this lady may proceed a gem To lighten all this isle . *Hen. VIII.* ii 3 78
I know him well: he is the brooch indeed And gem of all the nation *Ham.* iv 7 95
Forborne the getting of a lawful race, And by a gem of women *A. and C.* iii 13 108
Geminy. Like a geminy of baboons . . . . *Mer. Wives* ii 2 8
Gender. Hast thou no understandings for thy cases and the numbers of the genders? . . . . iv 1 73
The great love the general gender bear him . . . *Hamlet* iv 7 18
Supply it with one gender of herbs, or distract it with many . *Othello* i 3 326
Keep it as a cistern for foul toads To knot and gender in! . . . iv 2 62
General. We parley to you: Are you content to be our general? *T. G. of Ver.* iv 1 61
Even so The general, subject to a well-wish'd king, Quit their own part, and in obsequious fondness Crowd to his presence *Meas. for Meas.* ii 4 27
Sole imperator and great general Of trotting 'paritors . *L. L. Lost* iii 1 187
The general of our horse thou art; and we, Great in our hope *All's Well* iii 3 1
The general is content to spare thee yet . . . . . iv 1 89
You are a merciful general. Our general bids you answer to what I shall ask . . . . iv 3 144
I perceive, sir, by the general's looks, we shall be fain to hang you . iv 3 268
I'll whisper with the general, and know his pleasure . . . iv 3 329
Whose private with me of the Dauphin's love Is much more general than these lines import . . . . . . *K. John* iv 3 17
So are the horses of the enemy In general, journey-bated . 1 *Hen. IV.* iv 3 26
Health and fair greeting from our general, The prince . 2 *Hen. IV.* iv 1 27
My brother general, the commonwealth, To brother born an household cruelty, I make my quarrel in particular . . . . . . iv 1 94
Here come I from our princely general To know your griefs . . iv 1 141
To determine Of what conditions we shall stand upon.—That is intended in the general's name . . . . iv 1 166
This will I show the general. Please you, lords, In sight of both our battles . . . . iv 1 178
Here comes our general.—The heat is past; follow no further now . iv 3 26
As heir general, being descended Of Blithild, which was daughter to King Clothair . . . . *Hen. V.* i 2 66
General. What a beard of the general's cut and a horrid suit of the camp will do . . . . *Hen. V.* iii 6 81
Were now the general of our gracious empress, As in good time he may, from Ireland coming . . . . v Prol. 30
And whilst a field should be dispatch'd and fought, You are disputing of your generals . . . . 1 *Hen. VI.* i 1 73
Trumpeter; Summon their general unto the wall . . . . iv 2 2
Success unto our valiant general, And happiness to his accomplices! . v 2 8
Where's our general?—Hear I am, thou particular fellow 2 *Hen. VI.* iv 2 118
And I myself, Rather than bloody war shall cut them short, Will parley with Jack Cade their general . . . . iv 4 13
A woman's general; what should we fear? . . 3 *Hen. VI.* i 2 69
Their woes are parcell'd, mine are general . . *Richard III.* ii 2 81
Retail'd to all posterity, Even to the general all-ending day . . iii 1 78
When that the general is not like the hive To whom the foragers shall all repair, What honey is expected? . . . *Troi. and Cres.* i 3 81
The general's disdain'd By him one step below, he by the next . . i 3 129
Abilities, gifts, natures, shapes, Severals and generals of grace exact . i 3 180
With one voice Call Agamemnon head and general . . . . i 3 222
For the success, Although particular, shall give a scantling Of good or bad unto the general . . . . i 3 342
I was advertised their great general slept, Whilst emulation in the army crept . . . . ii 2 211
You feed too much on this dislike.—Our noble general, do not do so . ii 3 237
Please it our great general To call together all his state of war . ii 3 270
Please it our general to pass strangely by him, As if he were forgot . iii 3 39
What, comes the general to speak with me? You know my mind . . iii 3 55
Would you, my lord, aught with the general?—No.—Nothing, my lord iii 3 58
What think you of this man that takes me for the general? . . iii 3 263
Our general doth salute you with a kiss.—Yet is the kindness but particular; 'Twere better she were kiss'd in general . . . . iv 5 19
Thanks and good night to the Greeks' general.—Good night, my lord . v 1 80
Were I the general, thou shouldst have my office Ere that correction . v 6 4
For what miscarries Shall be the general's fault, though he perform To the utmost of a man . . . . *Coriolanus* i 1 271
Has our general met the enemy?—They lie in view; but have not spoke i 4 3
Down with them! And hark, what noise the general makes! To him! . i 5 10
I thank you, general; But cannot make my heart consent to take A bribe to pay my sword . . . . i 9 36
I, that now Refused most princely gifts, am bound to beg Of my lord general . . . . i 9 81
The senate has letters from the general, wherein he gives my son the whole name of the war . . . . ii 1 148
O, welcome home: And welcome, general: and ye're welcome all . ii 1 199
The present consul, and last general In our well-found successes . . ii 2 47
My sometime general, I have seen thee stern . . . . . iv 1 23
Why, here's he that was wont to thwack our general . . . . iv 5 189
I do not say 'thwack our general;' but he was always good enough for him iv 5 192
Our general himself makes a mistress of him . . . . . iv 5 207
Our general is cut i' the middle and but one half of what he was yesterday iv 5 210
You hear what he hath said Which was sometime his general . . v 1 2
You must return: our general Will no more hear from thence . . v 2 5
I tell thee, fellow, Thy general is my lover . . . . . v 2 14
Always factionary on the party of your general . . . . . v 2 31
You are a Roman, are you?—I am, as thy general is . . . . v 2 39
Our general has sworn you out of reprieve and pardon . . . . v 2 53
I mean, thy general.—My general cares not for you . . . . v 2 58
I neither care for the world nor your general . . . . . v 2 109
He that hath a will to die by himself fears it not from another: let your general do his worst . . . . v 2 112
The worthy fellow is our general: he's the rock, the oak . . . v 2 116
Most welcome!—How is it with our general? . . . . . v 6 10
Lucius general of the Goths? These tidings nip me . *T. Andron.* iv 4 69
Then will I be general of your woes, And lead you even to death *R. and J.* v 3 219
Forgive my general and exceptless rashness . . . *T. of Athens* iv 3 502
They confess Toward thee forgetfulness too general, gross . . . v 1 147
I know no personal cause to spurn at him, But for the general *J. Cæsar* ii 1 12
These predictions Are to the world in general as to Cæsar . . . ii 2 29
The greater part, the horse in general, Are come with Cassius . . iv 2 29
Let me go in to see the generals; There is some grudge between 'em . iv 3 124
What's the matter?—For shame, you generals! what do you mean? . iv 3 130
Prepare you, generals: The enemy comes on in gallant show . . v 1 12
Make forth; the generals would have some words.—Stir not until the signal . . . . v 1 25
What says my general?—Messala, This is my birth-day . . . . v 1 70
Here comes the general. Brutus is ta'en . . . . v 4 17
He only, in a general honest thought And common good to all, made one of them . . . . v 5 71
Founded as the rock, As broad and general as the casing air *Macbeth* iii 4 23
The play, I remember, pleased not the million; 'twas caviare to the general: but it was . . . an excellent play . . . *Hamlet* ii 2 457
Who hath he left behind him general?—The Marshal of France *Lear* iv 3 8
General, Take thou my soldiers, prisoners, patrimony . . . v 3 74
The duke does greet you, general, And he requires your haste-post-haste appearance, Even on the instant . . . . *Othello* i 2 36
General, be advised; He comes to bad intent . . . . . i 2 55
But, good lieutenant, is your general wived? . . . . . ii 1 60
How now! who has put in?—'Tis one Iago, ancient to the general . ii 1 66
It is Othello's pleasure, our noble and valiant general . . . . ii 2 2
Heaven bless the isle of Cyprus and our noble general Othello! . ii 2 12
Our general cast us thus early for the love of his Desdemona . . ii 3 14
To the health of our general!—I am for it, lieutenant . . . ii 3 88
For mine own part,—no offence to the general, nor any man of quality, —I hope to be saved . . . . ii 3 110
It were well The general were put in mind of it. Perhaps he sees it not ii 3 137
Have you forgot all sense of place and duty? Hold! the general speaks to you . . . . ii 3 168
Thus it is, general. Montano and myself being in speech . . ii 3 224
What, man! there are ways to recover the general again . . . ii 3 273
Our general's wife is now the general . . . . . . ii 3 320
Something that's brief; and bid 'Good morrow, general' . . . iii 1 2
The general so likes your music, that he desires you, for love's sake, to make no more noise with it . . . . iii 1 12
But, as they say, to hear music the general does not greatly care . iii 1 18
If the gentlewoman that attends the general's wife be stirring, tell her iii 1 27
The general and his wife are talking of it; And she speaks for you stoutly iii 1 46
I being absent and my place supplied, My general will forget my love . iii 3 18
Ha! ha! false to me?—Why, how now, general! no more of that . . iii 3 334
Leave you! wherefore?—I do attend here on the general . . . iii 4 193
How is it, general? have you not hurt your head?—Dost thou mock me? iv 1 60

General. Save you, worthy general!—With all my heart . *Othello* iv 1 229
Bear him carefully from hence; I'll fetch the general's surgeon . . v 1 100
What is the matter? How now, general!—O, are you come, Iago? . v 2 168
Dear general, I never gave you cause.—I do believe it, and I ask you pardon . . . . v 2 299
This dotage of our general's O'erflows the measure . . *Ant. and Cleo.* i 1 1
Trouble yourselves no further: pray you, hasten Your generals after . ii 4 2
Had our general Been what he knew himself, it had gone well . . iii 10 26
The morn is fair. Good morrow, general . . . . . iv 4 24
Is Lucius general of the forces? . . . . . . *Cymbeline* iii 7 11
Tell their general we attend him here, To know for what he comes *Pericles* i 4 79
Thou art a grave and noble counsellor, Most wise in general . . . v 1 185
General a vice. It [lechery] is too general a vice, and severity must cure it . . . . *Meas. for Meas.* iii 2 106
General applause. This general applause and loving shout Argues your wisdoms and your love . . . *Richard III.* iii 7 39
General assault. A savageness in unreclaimed blood, Of general assault *Hamlet* ii 1 35
General behaviour. His general behaviour vain, ridiculous . *L. L. Lost* v 1 13
General camp. I had been happy if the general camp, Pioners and all, had tasted her sweet body . . . . . . *Othello* iii 3 345
General care. Nor doth the general care Take hold on me, for my particular grief Is of so flood-gate and o'erbearing nature . . i 3 54
General cause. What concern they? The general cause? or is it a fee-grief Due to some single breast? . . . . . *Macbeth* iv 3 196
General censure. Their virtues else—be they as pure as grace, As infinite as man may undergo—Shall in the general censure take corruption . . . . *Hamlet* i 4 35
General ceremony. What have kings, that privates have not too, Save ceremony, save general ceremony? . . . . *Hen. V.* iv 1 256
General challenger. He is the general challenger: I come but in, as others do . . . . *As Y. Like It* i 2 180
General coffers. He hath brought many captives home to Rome, Whose ransoms did the general coffers fill . . . . *J. Cæsar* iii 2 94
General course. My lord of York commends the plot and the general course of the action . . . . . . *1 Hen. IV.* ii 3 23
General current. As not a soldier of this season's stamp Should go so general current through the world . . . . . iv 1 5
General dependants. There's a great abatement of kindness appears as well in the general dependants as in the duke himself . *Lear* i 4 65
General doom. Then, dreadful trumpet, sound the general doom! For who is living, if those two are gone? . . . *Rom. and Jul.* iii 2 67
General ear. And cleave the general ear with horrid speech . *Hamlet* ii 2 589
General enemy. We must straight employ you Against the general enemy Ottoman . . . . *Othello* i 3 49
General excrement. The earth's a thief, That feeds and breeds by a composture stolen From general excrement . . *T. of Athens* iv 3 445
General filths. To general filths Convert o' the instant! . . iv 1 6
General food. 'True is it, my incorporate friends,' quoth he, 'That I receive the general food' . . . . . . *Coriolanus* i 1 135
General force. Some twelve days hence Our general forces at Bridgenorth shall meet . . . . . . *1 Hen. IV.* iii 2 178
Too rashly plotted: all our general force Might with a sally of the very town Be buckled with . . . . . . *1 Hen. VI.* iv 4 3
General gender. Why to a public count I might not go, Is the great love the general gender bear him . . . . *Hamlet* iv 7 18
General good. No less importing than our general good *Richard III.* iii 7 68
If it be aught toward the general good, Set honour in one eye and death i' the other, And I will look on both indifferently . *J. Cæsar* i 2 85
General graces. Whose general graces speak That which none else can utter . . . . *Ant. and Cleo.* ii 2 132
General grievances. This schedule, For this contains our general grievances . . . . *2 Hen. IV.* iv 1 169
General groan. Never alone Did the king sigh, but with a general groan *Hamlet* iii 3 23
General honour. Revenges to your heart, And general honour *Meas. for Meas.* iv 3 141
General hunting. Who hath abandoned her holy groves To see the general hunting in this forest . . . . *T. Andron.* ii 3 59
General ignorance. Where gentry, title, wisdom, Cannot conclude but by the yea and no Of general ignorance . . *Coriolanus* iii 1 146
General joy. But that time offer'd sorrow; This, general joy *Hen. VIII.* iv 1 7
Fill full. I drink to the general joy o' the whole table . *Macbeth* iii 4 89
General leprosy. Itches, blains, Sow all the Athenian bosoms; and their crop Be general leprosy! . . . . . *T. of Athens* iv 1 30
General louts. Show our general louts How you can frown *Coriolanus* iii 2 66
General mock. Would ever have, to incur a general mock, Run from her guardage to the sooty bosom Of such a thing as thou *Othello* i 2 69
General name. However it is spread in general name, Relates in purpose only to Achilles . . . . . . *Troi. and Cres.* i 3 322
The blot and enemy to our general name! . . *T. Andron.* ii 3 183
General offence. Methinks, thou art a general offence, and every man should beat thee . . . . *All's Well* ii 3 270
General part. Though in general part we were opposed, Yet our old love made a particular force . . . . *T. of Athens* v 2 7
General peace. Have earnestly implored a general peace . *1 Hen. VI.* v 4 98
General petition. They [your lips] should sooner persuade Harry of England than a general petition of monarchs . . . *Hen. V.* v 2 305
General praise. And her epitaphs In glittering golden characters express A general praise to her . . . . . . *Pericles* iv 3 45
General prophecy. And, not consulting, broke Into a general prophecy *Hen. VIII.* i 1 92
General riot. Thou wouldst have plunged thyself In general riot; melted down thy youth . . . . . . *T. of Athens* iv 3 256
General services. Alike conversant in general services, and more remarkable in single oppositions . . . . . *Cymbeline* iv 1 13
General sex. To square the general sex By Cressid's rule *Troi. and Cres.* v 2 132
General shout. Another general shout! I do believe that these applauses are For some new honours that are heap'd on Cæsar *J. Cæsar* i 2 132
General sovereignty. Such as his reading And manifest experience had collected For general sovereignty . . . . *All's Well* i 3 230
General state. The other half comes to the general state *Mer. of Venice* iv 1 371
Is it so concluded?—By Priam and the general state of Troy *Tr. and Cr.* iv 2 69
The general state, I fear, Can scarce entreat you to be odd with him . iv 5 264
General suit. Only their ends You have respected; stopp'd your ears against The general suit of Rome . . . . . *Coriolanus* v 3 6
General sway. To gripe the general sway into your hand . *1 Hen. IV.* v 1 57
General synod. Out, thou strumpet, Fortune! All you gods, In general synod, take away her power! . . . . . *Hamlet* ii 2 516
General taint. With a general taint Of the whole state . *Hen. VIII.* v 3 28
General throng. Follow'd with the general throng and sweat Of thousand friends . . . . *Hen. VIII.* Prol. 28
General tongue. Rome, the nurse of judgement, Invited by your noble self, hath sent One general tongue unto us . . . . ii 2 96
Speak to me home, mince not the general tongue . . *Ant. and Cleo.* i 2 109
General trumpet. Now let the general trumpet blow his blast! *2 Hen. VI.* v 2 43
General use. Ten thousand dollars to our general use . *Macbeth* i 2 62
General voice. For all the country in a general voice Cried hate upon him . . . . *2 Hen. IV.* iv 1 136
General warranty. But with such general warranty of heaven As I might love . . . . *Othello* v 2 60
General way. I have been bold—For that I knew it the most general way—To them to use your signet . . . *T. of Athens* ii 2 209
General weal. Take the bridge quite away Of him that, his particular to foresee, Smells from the general weal . . . . iv 3 160
General welcome. Ladies, a general welcome from his grace Salutes ye all . . . . *Hen. VIII.* i 4 1
General woe. Our present business Is general woe . . . . *Lear* v 3 319
General wonder. All the grace, Which makes her both the heart and place Of general wonder . . . . . *Pericles* iv Gower 11
General world. As prodigal of all dear grace As Nature was in making graces dear When she did starve the general world beside And prodigally gave them all to you . . . . . *L. L. Lost* ii 1 11
Wouldst thou disgorge into the general world . . . *As Y. Like It* ii 7 69
General wreck. Hence grew the general wreck and massacre *1 Hen. VI.* i 1 135
General wrong. They are pitiful; And pity to the general wrong of Rome—As fire drives out fire, so pity pity—Hath done this deed on Cæsar . . . . *J. Cæsar* iii 1 170
Generally allowed for your many war-like . . . preparations . *Mer. Wives* ii 2 236
You were best to call them generally, man by man . . *M. N. Dream* i 2 2
I thank God I am not a woman, to be touched with so many giddy offences as he hath generally taxed their whole sex withal *As Y. L. It* iii 2 367
To whom we all rest generally beholding . . . *T. of Shrew* i 2 274
He that so generally is at all times good must of necessity hold his virtue to you . . . . *All's Well* i 1 8
As to be—generally thankful . . . . ii 3 44
Wherein the king stands generally condemn'd . . . *Richard II.* ii 2 132
They are generally fools and cowards . . . *2 Hen. IV.* iv 3 102
Of his true titles to some certain dukedoms And generally to the crown and seat of France . . . . *Hen. V.* i 1 88
This is noted, And generally, whoever the king favours . *Hen. VIII.* ii 1 47
How if he had boils? full, all over, generally? . *Troi. and Cres.* ii 1 3
And, generally, in all shapes that man goes up and down in *T. of Athens* ii 2 119
Generation. More gentle-kind than of Our human generation *Tempest* iii 3 33
Ere twice the sun hath made his journal greeting To the under generation, you shall find Your safety manifested . . *Meas. for Meas.* iv 3 93
When the work of generation was Between these woolly breeders *M. of V.* i 3 83
Fourteen they shall not see, To bring false generations . *W. Tale* ii 1 148
Being but the second generation Removed . . . . *K. John* ii 1 181
And these two beget A generation of still-breeding thoughts *Richard II.* v 5 8
So success of mischief shall be born And heir from heir shall hold this quarrel up Whiles England shall have generation . *2 Hen. IV.* iv 2 49
Is this the generation of love? hot blood, hot thoughts, and hot deeds? Why, they are vipers: is love a generation of vipers? *Troi. and Cres.* iii 1 144
Thy mother's of my generation: what's she, if I be a dog? *T. of Athens* i 1 204
He that makes his generation messes To gorge his appetite . *Lear* i 1 119
The gods revenge it upon me and mine, To the end of generation! *Per.* iii 3 25
She's able to freeze the god Priapus, and undo a whole generation . iv 6 4
Generative. He is a motion generative; that's infallible *Meas. for Meas.* iii 2 119
Generosity. To break the heart of generosity . . *Coriolanus* i 1 215
Generous. The generous and gravest citizens Have hent the gates *Meas. for Meas.* iv 6 13
The posterior of the day, most generous sir, is liable, congruent and measurable for the afternoon . . . . . *L. L. Lost* v 1 96
This is not generous, not gentle, not humble . . . . . v 2 632
Generous, guiltless and of free disposition . . . *T. Night* i 5 98
Can it be That so degenerate a strain as this Should once set footing in your generous bosoms? . . . . . *Troi. and Cres.* ii 2 155
They in France of the best rank and station Are of a most select and generous chief in that . . . . . . *Hamlet* i 3 74
He, being remiss, Most generous and free from all contriving . iv 7 136
Let my disclaiming from a purposed evil Free me so far in your most generous thoughts . . . . v 2 253
My dimensions are as well compact, My mind as generous . *Lear* i 2 8
The generous islanders By you invited do attend your presence *Othello* iii 3 280
Genitive. What is your genitive case plural, William?—Genitive case!—Ay.—Genitive,—horum, harum, horum . . *Mer. Wives* iv 1 59
Genitivo. Nominativo, hig, hag, hog; pray you, mark: genitivo, hujus iv 1 45
Genius. The strong'st suggestion Our worser genius can, shall never melt Mine honour into lust . . . . . . *Tempest* iv 1 27
One of these men is Genius to the other; And so of these *Com. of Errors* v 1 332
His very genius hath taken the infection of the device . *T. Night* iii 4 142
So forlorn, that his dimensions to any thick sight were invincible: a' was the very genius of famine . . . . *2 Hen. IV.* iii 2 337
Hark! you are call'd: some say the Genius so Cries 'come' to him that instantly must die . . . . . . *Troi. and Cres.* iv 4 52
The Genius and the mortal instruments Are then in council . *J. Cæsar* ii 1 66
And, under him, My Genius is rebuked . . . . *Macbeth* iii 1 56
Gennet. You'll have coursers for cousins and gennets for germans *Othello* i 1 113
Genoa. What news from Genoa? hast thou found my daughter? *M. of V.* iii 1 84
Antonio, as I heard in Genoa,— What, what, what? ill luck, ill luck? iii 1 103
In Genoa?—Your daughter spent in Genoa, as I heard, in one night four-score ducats . . . . iii 1 112
Baptista may remember me, Near twenty years ago, in Genoa *T. of Shr.* iv 4 4
Genoux. Sur mes genoux je vous donne mille remercîmens . *Hen. V.* iv 4 57
Gens. Qui est là?—Paysans, pauvres gens de France . *1 Hen. VI.* iii 2 14
What say you of Kent?—Nothing but this; 'tis 'bonna terra, mala gens' *2 Hen. VI.* iv 7 61
Gentile. Now, by my hood, a Gentile and no Jew . *Mer. of Venice* ii 6 51
Gentilhomme. Je pense que vous êtes gentilhomme de bonne qualité *Hen. V.* iv 4 2
Je suis gentilhomme de bonne maison . . . . . . iv 4 43
Gentility. A dangerous law against gentility! . . *L. L. Lost* i 1 129
As much as in him lies, mines my gentility with my education *As Y. L. It* i 1 22
Gentle. Make not too rash a trial of him, for He's gentle . *Tempest* i 2 468
O, she is Ten times more gentle than her father's crabbed . . iii 1 8
In truth, sir, and she is pretty, and honest, and gentle . *Mer. Wives* i 4 149
I'll make him dance. Will you go, gentles? . . . . . iii 2 92
Gentle and fair, your brother kindly greets you . *Meas. for Meas.* i 4 24
Pretty and witty, wild and yet, too, gentle . . *Com. of Errors* iii 1 110

Gentle. Such a gentle sovereign grace, Of such enchanting presence and discourse — *Com. of Errors* iii 2 165
Good wits will be jangling; but, gentles, agree — *L. L. Lost* ii 1 225
Away! the gentles are at their game, and we will to our recreation — iv 2 172
This is not generous, not gentle, not humble — v 2 632
Gentles, perchance you wonder at this show — *M. N. Dream* v 1 128
Gentles, do not reprehend: If you pardon, we will mend — v 1 436
He's gentle, never schooled and yet learned — *As Y. Like It* i 1 172
Why do people love you? And wherefore are you gentle, strong and valiant? — ii 3 6
I find you passing gentle. 'Twas told me you were rough — *T. of Shrew* ii 1 244
How does my father? Gentles, methinks you frown — iii 2 95
When you are gentle, you shall have one too, And not till then — iv 3 71
Which no less adorns Our gentry than our parents' noble names, In whose success we are gentle — *W. Tale* i 2 394
Be merry, gentle; Strangle such thoughts as these — iv 4 46
We must be gentle, now we are gentlemen — v 2 164
As gentle and as jocund as to jest Go I to fight — *Richard II.* i 3 95
But pardon, gentles all, The flat unraised spirits — *Hen. V.* Prol. 8
And the scene Is now transported, gentles, to Southampton — ii Prol. 35
Mine was not bridled.—O then belike she was old and gentle — iii 7 55
Mean and gentle all Behold, as may unworthiness define — iv Prol. 45
Be he ne'er so vile, This day shall gentle his condition — iv 3 63
As mild and gentle as the cradle-babe — *2 Hen. VI.* iii 2 392
O, he was gentle, mild, and virtuous!—The fitter for the King of heaven, that hath him — *Richard III.* i 2 104
We know your tenderness of heart And gentle, kind, effeminate remorse iii 7 211
I will be mild and gentle in my speech.—And brief, good mother — iv 4 160
And display'd the effects Of disposition gentle — *Hen. VIII.* ii 4 87
I know you have a gentle, noble temper, A soul as even as a calm — iii 1 165
Those that tame wild horses Pace 'em not in their hands to make 'em gentle — v 3 22
No less noble, much more gentle, and altogether more tractable — *Troi. and Cres.* ii 3 160
Thou art too gentle and too free a man — iv 5 139
Most gentle and most valiant Hector, welcome — iv 5 227
As gentle tell me, of what honour was This Cressida in Troy? — iv 5 287
'Tis a condition they account gentle — *Coriolanus* ii 3 104
O gentle, aged men! Unbind my sons — *T. Andron.* iii 1 23
Alas, that love, so gentle in his view, Should be so tyrannous and rough in proof! — *Rom. and Jul.* i 1 175
Good morrow to thee, gentle Apemantus!—Till I be gentle, stay thou for thy good morrow — *T. of Athens* i 1 179
O, pardon me, thou bleeding piece of earth, That I am meek and gentle with these butchers! — *J. Cæsar* iii 1 255
His life was gentle, and the elements So mix'd in him — v 5 73
This gentle and unforced accord of Hamlet Sits smiling to my heart *Ham.* i 2 123
Her voice was ever soft, Gentle, and low, an excellent thing in woman — *Lear* v 3 273
You shall see How hardly I was drawn into this war; How calm and gentle I proceeded still In all my writings — *Ant. and Cleo.* v 1 75
It shall content me best: be gentle to her — v 2 68
If you apply yourself to our intents, Which towards you are most gentle, you shall find A benefit in this change — v 2 127
As sweet as balm, as soft as air, as gentle,—O Antony! — v 2 314
He said he was gentle, but unfortunate; Dishonestly afflicted *Cymbeline* iv 2 39
They are as gentle As zephyrs blowing below the violet — iv 2 171
Divinest patroness, and midwife gentle To those that cry by night *Per.* iii 1 11
Now, mild may be thy life! — Quiet and gentle thy conditions! — iii 1 29
Gentle a condition. And then, of so gentle a condition!—Ay, too gentle.—Nay, that's certain — *Othello* iv 1 204
Gentle Aaron! Did ever raven sing so like a lark? — *T. Andron.* iii 1 157
O gentle Aaron, we are all undone! Now help, or woe betide thee evermore! — iv 2 55
Gentle adieus. Detain no jot, I charge thee: write to him—I will subscribe—gentle adieus and greetings — *Ant. and Cleo.* iv 5 14
Gentle air. For what doth cherish weeds but gentle air? *3 Hen. VI.* ii 6 21
Gentle answer. We all expect a gentle answer, Jew *Mer. of Venice* iv 1 34
Gentle Apemantus. Good morrow to thee, gentle Apemantus!—Till I be gentle, stay thou for thy good morrow — *T. of Athens* i 1 178
Gentle as a lamb. He is not the flower of courtesy, but, I'll warrant him, as gentle as a lamb — *Rom. and Jul.* ii 5 45
Gentle Audrey. We shall find a time, Audrey; patience, gentle Audrey.—Faith, the priest was good enough — *As Y. Like It* v 1 2
Gentle babe. My gentle babe Marina — *Pericles* iii 3 12
Gentle bath. I could wish You were conducted to a gentle bath *Coriol.* i 6 63
Gentle beast. Grant pasture for me.—Not so, gentle beast — *L. L. Lost* ii 1 222
A very gentle beast, and of a good conscience — *M. N. Dream* v 1 230
Gentle blood. Like a hedge-born swain That doth presume to boast of gentle blood — *1 Hen. VI.* iv 1 44
To worry lambs and lap their gentle blood — *Richard III.* iv 4 50
Gentle bosom. Wherein we step after a stranger march Upon her gentle bosom — *K. John* v 2 28
Gored the gentle bosom of peace with pillage and robbery — *Hen. V.* iv 1 174
Gentle brain. Women's gentle brain Could not drop forth such giant-rude invention — *As Y. Like It* iv 3 33
Gentle breath of yours my sails Must fill — *Tempest* Epil. 11
All this uttered With gentle breath, calm look — *Rom. and Jul.* iii 1 161
Gentle brother, get you in again; Comfort my sister — *Com. of Errors* iii 2 25
O my gentle brothers, Have we thus met? — *Cymbeline* v 5 374
Gentle brow. Make a riot on the gentle brow Of true sincerity *K. John* iii 1 247
Gentle Brutus. And be not jealous on me, gentle Brutus — *J. Cæsar* i 2 71
Kneel not, gentle Portia.—I should not need, if you were gentle Brutus ii 1 279
Gentle business. It was a gentle business, and becoming The action of good women — *Hen. VIII.* ii 3 54
Gentle Casca. Tell us the manner of it, gentle Casca — *J. Cæsar* i 2 234
Gentle Catesby. Go, gentle Catesby, And, as it were far off, sound thou Lord Hastings — *Richard III.* iii 1 169
Gentle cheeks. I found the prince in the next room, Washing with kindly tears his gentle cheeks — *2 Hen. IV.* iv 5 84
Gentle citizens. 'Thanks, gentle citizens and friends,' quoth I — *Richard III.* iii 7 38
Gentle Clarence, welcome unto Warwick; And welcome, Somerset — *3 Hen. VI.* iv 2 6
Gentle Claudio. I hope it is some pardon or reprieve For the most gentle Claudio — *Meas. for Meas.* iv 2 75
Gentle concord. How comes this gentle concord in the world? *M. N. D.* iv 1 148
Gentle condition. You are my eldest brother; and, in the gentle condition of blood, you should so know me — *As Y. Like It* i 1 48
Gentle conference. With gentle conference, soft and affable *T. of Shrew* ii 1 253
Gentle Constance. Patience, good lady! comfort, gentle Constance! — *K. John* iii 4 22
Gentle convertite. But since you are a gentle convertite, My tongue shall hush again this storm of war — v 1 19
Gentle counsel. What, dost thou scorn me for my gentle counsel? — *Richard III.* i 3 297
Gentle cousin, Let us go thank him and encourage him — *As Y. Like It* i 2 251
I kiss your hand.—Farewell, gentle cousin.—Coz, farewell — *K. John* iii 3 17
O my gentle cousin, Hear'st thou the news abroad, who are arrived? — iv 2 159
Then let me hear Of you, my gentle cousin — *1 Hen. IV.* i 1 31
Health to my lord and gentle cousin, Mowbray — *2 Hen. IV.* iv 2 78
Gentle coz. Content thee, gentle coz, let him alone — *Rom. and Jul.* i 5 67
Gentle creditors. Which, if like an ill venture it come unluckily home, I break, and you, my gentle creditors, lose — *2 Hen. IV.* Epil. 13
Gentle daughter. On Thurio, whom your gentle daughter hates — *T. G. of Ver.* iii 1 14
Fear me not.—Nor, gentle daughter, fear you not at all *Meas. for Meas.* iv 1 71
If e'er the Jew her father come to heaven, It will be for his gentle daughter's sake — *Mer. of Venice* ii 4 35
Loving wife, and gentle daughter, Give even way unto my rough affairs — *2 Hen. IV.* ii 3 1
Gentle day. The gentle day, Before the wheels of Phœbus, round about Dapples the drowsy east with spots of grey — *Much Ado* v 3 25
And here will rest me. Come, thou gentle day! — *M. N. Dream* iii 2 418
Gentle Desdemona. But that I love the gentle Desdemona — *Othello* i 2 25
Gentle duke. In brief, he led me to the gentle duke — *As Y. Like It* iv 3 143
Gentle earl. Be patient, gentle Earl of Westmoreland.—Patience is for poltroons, such as he — *3 Hen. VI.* i 1 61
Gentle earth. Feed not thy sovereign's foe, my gentle earth *Richard II.* iii 2 12
Gentle empress, 'Tis thought you have a goodly gift in horning *T. Andron.* ii 3 66
Gentle entertainment. The queen desires you to use some gentle entertainment to Laertes before you fall to play — *Hamlet* v 2 216
Gentle Eros. Nay, weep not, gentle Eros; there is left us Ourselves to end ourselves — *Ant. and Cleo.* iv 14 21
Gentle exercise. To gentle exercise and proof of arms — *1 Hen. IV.* v 2 55
Gentle eye. And snarleth in the gentle eyes of peace — *K. John* iv 3 150
O thou eternal Mover of the heavens, Look with a gentle eye upon this wretch! O, beat away the busy meddling fiend! — *2 Hen. VI.* iii 3 20
Gentle eye-drops. Would, by beholding him, have wash'd his knife With gentle eye-drops — *2 Hen. IV.* iv 5 88
Gentle fine. The gentle fine is this: My lips, two blushing pilgrims, ready stand To smooth that rough touch with a tender kiss *R. and J.* i 5 96
Gentle flame. Our gentle flame Provokes itself — *T. of Athens* i 1 23
Gentle friend, for love and courtesy Lie further off — *M. N. Dream* ii 2 56
Joy, gentle friends! joy and fresh days of love Accompany your hearts! v 1 29
Good even to you, sir.—Good even, gentle friend — *As Y. Like It* v 1 18
Gentle friend, Let thy fair wisdom, not thy passion, sway — *T. Night* iv 1 55
Rode he on Barbary? Tell me, gentle friend, How went he under him? — *Richard II.* v 5 81
Let there be no noise made, my gentle friends — *2 Hen. IV.* iv 5 1
Farewell, good cousin; farewell, gentle friends — *Richard III.* iii 7 247
Gentle friends, Let's kill him boldly, but not wrathfully — *J. Cæsar* ii 1 171
We will hear Cæsar's will.—Have patience, gentle friends — iii 2 145
Gentle gentlemen. Fare you well, gentle gentlemen — *2 Hen. IV.* iii 2 321
Gentle girl, assist me; And even in kind love I do conjure thee *T. G. of V.* ii 7 1
Come, let's fall to; and, gentle girl, eat this: Here is no drink! *T. An.* iii 2 34
Gentle gods. You gentle gods, give me but this [wife] I have, And sear up my embracements from a next! — *Cymbeline* i 1 115
Gentle Gratiano. And pardon me, my gentle Gratiano — *Mer. of Venice* v 1 260
Gentle grave. Rather a ditch in Egypt Be gentle grave unto me! — *Ant. and Cleo.* v 2 58
Gentle greeting. This is the most despiteful gentle greeting, The noblest hateful love — *Troi. and Cres.* iv 1 32
Gentle Guildenstern. Thanks, Rosencrantz and gentle Guildenstern.—Thanks, Guildenstern and gentle Rosencrantz — *Hamlet* ii 2 33
Gentle gusts. What did I then, but cursed the gentle gusts? *2 Hen. VI.* iii 2 88
Gentle hands. Your gentle hands lend us, and take our hearts *All's W.* Epil. 340
Gentle Harry Percy. And 'gentle Harry Percy,' and 'kind cousin;' O, the devil take such cozeners! — *1 Hen. IV.* i 3 254
Gentle head. Rest your gentle head upon her lap, And she will sing — iii 1 215
Gentle hearers. For, gentle hearers, know, To rank our chosen truth with such a show — *Hen. VIII.* Prol. 17
Gentle hearing. Speak to his gentle hearing kind commends *Richard II.* iii 3 126
Gentle heart. You, ladies, you, whose gentle hearts do fear The smallest monstrous mouse — *M. N. Dream* v 1 222
Much good do it unto thy gentle heart! — *T. of Shrew* iv 3 51
He hath a stern look, but a gentle heart — *K. John* iv 1 88
And their gentle hearts To fierce and bloody inclination — v 2 157
Teach a soldier terms Such as will enter at a lady's ear And plead his love-suit to her gentle heart — *Hen. V.* v 2 101
Nor with sour looks afflict his gentle heart — *T. Andron.* i 1 441
Send thy gentle heart before, To say thou'lt enter friendly *T. of Athens* v 4 48
And your looks foreshow You have a gentle heart — *Pericles* iv 1 87
Gentle-hearted. And here's to right our gentle-hearted king *3 Hen. VI.* i 4 176
Gentle heaven. Smile, gentle heaven! or strike, ungentle death! — ii 3 6
O, pity, pity, gentle heaven, pity! — ii 5 96
But, gentle heavens, Cut short all intermission — *Macbeth* iv 3 231
Gentle Helena. Stay, gentle Helena; hear my excuse — *M. N. Dream* iii 2 245
Gentle help. By whose gentle help I was preserved — *T. Night* v 1 262
Gentle herald. Come thou no more for ransom, gentle herald *Hen. V.* iv 3 122
Gentle Hermia. There, gentle Hermia, may I marry thee *M. N. Dream* i 1 161
Gentle hind. The tiger now hath seized the gentle hind — *Richard III.* ii 4 50
Gentle Hubert. O my gentle Hubert, We owe thee much! — *K. John* iii 3 19
Gentle husband. I did not, gentle husband, lock thee forth *Com. of Er.* iv 4 100
Gentle Isabella, Turn you the key, and know his business *Meas. for Meas.* i 4 7
Gentle Jessica. Tell gentle Jessica I will not fail her — *Mer. of Venice* ii 4 20
Gentle Jew. Hie thee, gentle Jew. The Hebrew will turn Christian — i 3 179
Gentle Joan. Deny me not, I prithee, gentle Joan — *1 Hen. VI.* v 4 20
Gentle joy. And kiss thy fair large ears, my gentle joy — *M. N. Dream* iv 1 4
Gentle Julia. Have patience, gentle Julia.—I must, where is no remedy — *T. G. of Ver.* ii 2 1
Gentle Kate. This evening must I leave you, gentle Kate — *1 Hen. IV.* ii 3 109
Thou wilt not utter what thou dost not know; And so far will I trust thee, gentle Kate.—How! so far? — ii 3 115
Gentle keeper, stay by me; My soul is heavy — *Richard III.* i 4 73
Gentle-kind. Their manners are more gentle-kind than of Our human generation you shall find Many — *Tempest* iii 3 32
Came of a gentle kind and noble stock — *Pericles* v 1 68
Gentle king. And we, in pity of the gentle king, Had slipp'd our claim until another age — *3 Hen. VI.* ii 2 161

Gentle king. Not willing any longer conference, Since thou deniest the gentle king to speak . . . 3 *Hen. VI.* ii 2 172
Gentle kinsman, go, And thrust thyself into their companies *K. John* iv 2 166
Gentle kiss. Giving a gentle kiss to every sedge . . *T. G. of Ver.* ii 7 29
Give Mistress Shore one gentle kiss to the more . . . *Richard III.* iii 1 185
Gentle knave, good night; I will not do thee so much wrong to wake thee . . . . *J. Cæsar* iv 3 269
Gentle knight. My gentle knight, give me your thoughts . *Hen. V.* ii 2 14
Go, gentle knight, Stand by our Ajax . . *Troi. and Cres.* iv 5 88
Gentle lady. Sir Proteus, gentle lady, and your servant *T. G. of Ver.* iv 2 91
Good morrow, gentle lady.—Good morrow, kind sir . . . iv 3 46
He and his competitors in oath Were all address'd to meet you, gentle lady, Before I came . . . . . *L. L. Lost* ii 1 83
The princess comes to hunt here in the park, And in her train there is a gentle lady . . . . iii 1 166
If you were men, as men you are in show, You would not use a gentle lady so; To vow, and swear . . . *M. N. Dream* iii 2 152
My gentle lady, I wish you all the joy that you can wish *Mer. of Venice* iii 2 191
Gentle lady, When I did first impart my love to you, I freely told you, all the wealth I had Ran in my veins . . . . . . iii 2 255
But, gentle Lady Anne, To leave this keen encounter of our wits *Rich. III.* i 2 114
The advancement of your children, gentle lady.—Up to some scaffold? iv 4 241
O gentle lady, 'Tis not for you to hear what I can speak *Macbeth* ii 3 88
O gentle lady, do not put me to't; For I am nothing, if not critical *Othello* ii 1 119
He quit being, and his gentle lady, Big of this gentleman our theme, deceased As he was born . . . . *Cymbeline* i 1 38
Gentle lamb. In peace was never gentle lamb more mild *Richard II.* ii 1 174
Wilt thou, O God, fly from such gentle lambs? *Richard III.* iv 2 22
Gentle Lavinia, let me kiss thy lips . . . *T. Andron.* iii 1 120
Gentle liege. Sweet York, be patient. Hear me, gentle liege *Richard II.* v 3 91
Gentle limbs. You have made the days and nights as one, To wear your gentle limbs in my affairs . . . . . *All's Well* v 1 4
Gentle Longaville, where lies thy pain? . . . . *L. L. Lost* iv 3 172
Gentle looks. I gave him gentle looks, thereby to find That which thyself hast now disclosed to me . . . . *T. G. of Ver.* iii 1 31
To whom do lions cast their gentle looks? Not to the beast that would usurp their den . . . . 3 *Hen. VI.* ii 2 11
Gentle lord. What England says, say briefly, gentle lord *K. John* ii 1 52
Good day to you, gentle lord archbishop . . . 2 *Hen. IV.* iv 2 2
O, calm thee, gentle lord; although I know There is enough *T. Andron.* iv 1 83
Gentle lords, let's part; You see we have burnt our cheeks *Ant. and Cleo.* ii 7 128
Gentle love. I have ta'en you napping, gentle love . *T. of Shrew* iv 2 46
Look, if my gentle love be not raised up! . . . *Othello* ii 3 250
Gentle lover. I'll apply To your eye, Gentle lover, remedy *M. N. Dream* iii 2 452
Gentle Lucetta, fit me with such weeds As may beseem *T. G. of Ver.* ii 7 42
Gentle madam; I unworthy am To woo so fair a dame . . 1 *Hen. VI.* v 3 123
Nay, gentle madam, to him, comfort him.—Do, most dear queen *A. and C.* iii 11 25
Gentle madam, no.—You lie, up to the hearing of the gods . . v 2 94
Gentle maid. Please it this matron and this gentle maid To eat with us to-night . . . . *All's Well* iii 5 100
Gentle maiden. Wherefore, gentle maiden, Do you neglect them? *W. Tale* iv 4 85
Gentle Marcius. My gentle Marcius, worthy Caius . . . *Coriolanus* ii 1 189
Gentle Marcus. Go, gentle Marcus, to thy nephew Lucius *T. Andron.* v 2 122
Gentle Margaret. Stay, gentle Margaret, and hear me speak 3 *Hen. VI.* i 1 257
Gentle mariner, Alter thy course for Tyre . . . *Pericles* iii 1 75
Gentle Master Slender, come; we stay for you . . *Mer. Wives* i 1 313
Gentle Master Fenton, Yet seek my father's love . . . . iii 4 18
Gentle master, I received no gold . . . . *Com. of Errors* iv 4 101
O my gentle master! O my sweet master! . . . *As Y. Like It* ii 3 2
Your virtues, gentle master, Are sanctified and holy traitors to you . ii 3 12
Gentle means. Those that do teach young babes Do it with gentle means and easy tasks . . . . *Othello* iv 2 112
Gentle Mercutio, put thy rapier up . . . . *Rom. and Jul.* iii 1 87
Gentle mind. You bear a gentle mind, and heavenly blessings Follow such creatures . . . . *Hen. VIII.* ii 3 57
Gentle mistress. Which of you two did dine with me to-day?—I, gentle mistress . . . . *Com. of Errors* v 1 370
Good morrow, gentle mistress: where away? . . *T. of Shrew* iv 5 27
Come hither, gentle mistress: Do you perceive in all this noble company Where most you owe obedience? . . . . . *Othello* i 3 178
Gentle mortal, sing again: Mine ear is much enamour'd *M. N. Dream* iii 1 140
Gentle murmur. The current that with gentle murmur glides, Thou know'st, being stopp'd, impatiently doth rage . *T. G. of Ver.* ii 7 25
Gentle my liege,— You do but lose your labour . . *Meas. for Meas.* v 1 433
Gentle my lord, turn back.—I will bethink me . . 1 *Hen. IV.* ii 2 143
Gentle my lord, Let me entreat you speak the former language . ii 4 139
Gentle my lord, You scarce can right me throughly then *W. Tale* ii 1 98
Gentle my lord, sleek o'er your rugged looks; Be bright and jovial *Macb.* iii 2 27
Gentle nation. They speak us fair, give us gold: methinks they are such a gentle nation . . . . *Com. of Errors* iv 4 158
Gentle neighbours. Hush, my gentle neighbours! Lend me your hands *Pericles* iii 2 107
Gentle Nell. Be patient, gentle Nell; forget this grief . . 2 *Hen. VI.* ii 4 26
Gentle Nell: I pray thee, sort thy heart to patience . . . ii 4 67
Gentle niece. Hath ta'en displeasure 'gainst his gentle niece *As Y. L. It* i 2 290
Speak, gentle niece, what stern ungentle hands Have lopp'd and hew'd and made thy body bare? . . . . *T. Andron.* ii 4 16
Gentle night. Come, gentle night, come, loving, black-brow'd night, Give me my Romeo . . . . *Rom. and Jul.* iii 2 20
Gentle Norfolk. Thanks, gentle Norfolk: stay by me, my lords 3 *Hen. VI.* i 1 31
Stir with the lark to-morrow, gentle Norfolk . . . *Richard III.* v 3 56
Gentle Northumberland, If thy offences were upon record, Would it not shame thee? . . . . *Richard II.* iv 1 229
Gentle nurse, I pray thee, leave me to myself to-night . *Rom. and Jul.* iv 3 1
Gentle nymph, cherish thy forlorn swain! . . . *T. G. of Ver.* v 4 12
Gentle Octavia, Let your best love draw to that point, which seeks Best to preserve it . . . . *Ant. and Cleo.* iii 4 20
Gentle offer. We must embrace This gentle offer . . . *K. John* iv 3 13
Gentle one. Good gentle one, give me modest assurance if you be the lady of the house . . . . *T. Night* i 5 191
I am one of those gentle ones that will use the devil himself with courtesy iv 2 37
Gentle order. Impose Some gentle order . . . . *K. John* iii 1 251
Gentle Pandarus. O gentle Pandarus, From Cupid's shoulder pluck his painted wings! . . . . *Troi. and Cres.* iii 2 14
Gentle pardon. I cry you gentle pardon; These bloody accidents must excuse my manners . . . . *Othello* v 1 93
Gentle Paris. Woo her, gentle Paris, get her heart, My will to her consent is but a part . . . . *Rom. and Jul.* i 2 16
Gentle parle. Our trumpet call'd you to this gentle parle . *K. John* ii 1 205
Gentle part. In the duke's behalf I'll give my voice, Which, I presume, he'll take in gentle part . . . . . . *Richard III.* iii 4 21
Gentle pass. Charming the narrow seas To give you gentle pass *Hen. V.* ii Prol. 39
Gentle Patience. Let's sit down quiet, For fear we wake her: softly, gentle Patience . . . . *Hen. VIII.* iv 2 82
Gentle peace. My speech entreats That I may know the let, why gentle Peace Should not expel these inconveniences . . . *Hen. V.* v 2 65
Still in thy right hand carry gentle peace, To silence envious tongues *Hen. VIII.* iii 2 445
Gentle people. But, gentle people, give me aim awhile, For nature puts me to a heavy task . . . . . . *T. Andron.* v 3 149
Gentle Percy. I thank thee, gentle Percy . . . *Richard II.* ii 3 45
We thank thee, gentle Percy, for thy pains . . . . . v 6 11
Gentle person. There's many a gentle person made a Jack *Richard III.* i 3 73
Gentle Phebe. My gentle Phebe bid me give you this *As Y. Like It* iv 3 7
Gentle physic. 'Tis like a pardon after execution: That gentle physic, given in time, had cured me . . . . . *Hen. VIII.* iv 2 122
Gentle Portia. Kneel not, gentle Portia.—I should not need, if you were gentle Brutus . . . . *J. Cæsar* ii 1 278
Gentle princes. To gratulate the gentle princes there . *Richard III.* iv 1 10
These gentle princes—For such and so they are—these twenty years Have I train'd up. . . . . *Cymbeline* v 5 336
Gentle princess. The rather, gentle princess, because I love thee cruelly *Hen. V.* v 2 215
Say, gentle princess, would you not suppose Your bondage happy, to be made a queen? . . . . 1 *Hen. VI.* v 3 110
Gentle Proteus. What think'st thou of the gentle Proteus? *T. G. of Ver.* i 2 14
O gentle Proteus, Love's a mighty lord . . . . . ii 4 136
Gentle provost. This is a gentle provost: seldom when The steeled gaoler is the friend of men . . . . *Meas. for Meas.* iv 2 89
Gentle Publius. Therefore bind them, gentle Publius . *T. Andron.* v 2 158
Gentle Puck. My gentle Puck, come hither. Thou rememberest Since once I sat upon a promontory . . . . *M. N. Dream* ii 1 148
And, gentle Puck, take this transformed scalp From off the head of this Athenian swain . . . . iv 1 69
Gentle pulpiter. O most gentle pulpiter! what tedious homily of love have you wearied your parishioners withal! *As Y. Like It* iii 2 163
Gentle queen. I would not change this hue, Except to steal your thoughts, my gentle queen . . . . . *Mer. of Venice* ii 1 12
Cease, gentle queen, these execrations . . . 2 *Hen. VI.* iii 2 305
Be patient, gentle queen, and I will stay . . . 3 *Hen. VI.* i 1 214
Let's away to London And see our gentle queen how well she fares . v 5 89
O Tamora, be called a gentle queen, And with thine own hands kill me! *T. Andron.* ii 3 168
But, my gentle queen, Where is our daughter? . . . *Cymbeline* ii 5 29
Gentle rain. The quality of mercy is not strain'd, It droppeth as the gentle rain from heaven . . . . *Mer. of Venice* iv 1 185
Gentle riddance. A gentle riddance . . . . ii 7 78
Gentle Romans. Thanks, gentle Romans: may I govern so, To heal Rome's harms, and wipe away her woe! . . . . *T. Andron.* v 3 147
You gentle Romans,— Peace, ho! let us hear him . . *J. Cæsar* iii 2 77
Gentle Romeo. Nay, gentle Romeo, we must have you dance *R. and J.* i 4 13
O gentle Romeo, If thou dost love, pronounce it faithfully . . ii 2 93
Gentle scroll. A gentle scroll. Fair lady, by your leave; I come by note, to give and to receive . . . . . *Mer. of Venice* iii 2 140
Gentle senses. The air Nimbly and sweetly recommends itself Unto our gentle senses . . . . *Macbeth* i 6 3
Gentle servant. I thank you, gentle servant: 'tis very clerkly done *T. G. of Ver.* ii 1 114
Gentle Severn. When on the gentle Severn's sedgy bank . 1 *Hen. IV.* i 3 98
Gentle shapes. Oh, that deceit should steal such gentle shapes! *Rich. III.* ii 2 27
Gentle signior; We lack'd your counsel and your help to-night . *Othello* i 3 50
Gentle Silvius. I am sorry for thee, gentle Silvius.—Wherever sorrow is, relief would be . . . . *As Y. Like It* iii 5 85
Gentle sir. Good even to you, friend.—And to you, gentle sir . ii 4 70
This do and do it kindly, gentle sirs . . . *T. of Shrew* Ind. 1 66
Gentle sir, methinks you walk like a stranger . . . . . ii 1 86
Gentle sir.—Happily met; the happier for thy son . . . . iv 5 58
Thanks, gentle sir. Come, let us four to dinner . . 1 *Hen. VI.* ii 4 132
Hail, gentle sir.—Sir, speed you: what's your will? . . *Lear* iv 6 212
Gentle sister, who hath martyr'd thee? . . . . *T. Andron.* iii 1 81
Gentle sleep. Draws the sweet infant breath of gentle sleep . *Richard II.* i 3 133
O sleep, O gentle sleep, Nature's soft nurse . . . 2 *Hen. IV.* iii 1 5
Gentle-sleeping. And there awake God's gentle-sleeping peace *Rich. III.* i 3 288
Gentle Somerset. Thanks, gentle Somerset; sweet Oxford, thanks 3 *Hen. VI.* v 4 58
Gentle son Edward, thou wilt stay with me? . . . . . i 1 259
O gentle son, Upon the heat and flame of thy distemper Sprinkle cool patience. Whereon do you look? . . . . *Hamlet* iii 4 122
Gentle sorrow. But dust was thrown upon his sacred head; Which with such gentle sorrow he shook off . . . . . . *Richard II.* v 2 31
Gentle souls. If yet your gentle souls fly in the air And be not fix'd in doom perpetual, Hover about me! . . . . . *Richard III.* iv 4 11
Gentle spectators. Imagine me, Gentle spectators, that I now may be In fair Bohemia . . . . *W. Tale* iv 1 20
Gentle speech. Entreat your captain To soft and gentle speech.—I shall entreat him To answer like himself . . . . *Ant. and Cleo.* ii 2 3
Gentle spirit. If the gentle spirit of moving words Can no way change you to a milder form . . . . *T. G. of Ver.* v 4 55
Happiest of all is that her gentle spirit Commits itself to yours to be directed, As from her lord . . . . . . *Mer. of Venice* iii 2 165
Gentle stream. I'll be as patient as a gentle stream . *T. G. of Ver.* ii 7 34
Gentle Suffolk. Let me plead for gentle Suffolk!—Ungentle queen, to call him gentle Suffolk! . . . . 2 *Hen. VI.* iii 2 289
Gentle suit. You may not, my lord, despise her gentle suit . 1 *Hen. VI.* ii 2 47
Gentle sweet. This jest is dry to me. Fair gentle sweet, Your wit makes wise things foolish . . . . *L. L. Lost* v 2 373
Why, gentle sweet, you shall see no such thing . . *M. N. Dream* v 1 87
Gentle Thetis. Let the ruffian Boreas once enrage The gentle Thetis *T. and C.* i 3 39
Gentle thoughts. Madam, I come to whet your gentle thoughts On his behalf . . . . *T. Night* iii 1 116
Gentle three. Let me bail these gentle three . . *Meas. for Meas.* v 1 362
Gentle tongue. Lend me the flourish of all gentle tongues *L. L. Lost* iv 3 238
What, will you tear Impatient answers from my gentle tongue? *M. N. D.* iii 2 287
Gentle travail. God safely quit her of her burthen, and With gentle travail! . . . . *Hen. VIII.* v 1 71
Gentle tribune. Thanks, gentle tribune, noble brother Marcus *T. Andron.* i 1 171
Gentle truce. Health to you, valiant sir, During all question of the gentle truce . . . . *Troi. and Cres.* iv 1 11

Gentle Tyrrel. Didst thou see them dead?—I did, my lord.—And buried, gentle Tyrrel? . . . . *Richard III.* iv 3 28

Gentle uncle. Thanks, gentle uncle. Come, lords, away *Richard II.* iii 1 42

How fares our cousin, noble Lord of York?—I thank you, gentle uncle *Richard III.* iii 1 102

Gentle Varrius. There's other of our friends Will greet us here anon, my gentle Varrius . . . . . . *Meas. for Meas.* iv 5 13

Gentle vessel. Dangerous rocks, Which touching but my gentle vessel's side, Would scatter all her spices on the stream *Mer. of Venice* i 1 32

Gentle villain. O gentle villain, do not turn away! *Richard III.* i 3 163

Gentle visitation. What would you with the princess?—Nothing but peace and gentle visitation . . . . . . *L. L. Lost* v 2 179; 181

Gentle visitors. Here's ado, To lock up honesty and honour from The access of gentle visitors . . . . *W. Tale* ii 2 11

Gentle Warwick. Where is the Duke of Norfolk, gentle Warwick? *3 Hen. VI.* ii 1 142

Gentle Warwick, Let me embrace thee in my weary arms . . . ii 3 44

Gentle wax. Leave, gentle wax: and, manners, blame us not . *Lear* iv 6 264

Gentle weal. Ere humane statute purged the gentle weal . *Macbeth* iii 4 76

Gentle wife. O, shall I say, I thank you, gentle wife?—Not so *L. L. Lost* v 2 836

Gentle wishes. Let your fair eyes and gentle wishes go with me to my trial . . . . *As Y. Like It* i 2 198

Gentle words. Let's fight with gentle words Till time lend friends *Richard II.* iii 3 131

Seeing gentle words will not prevail, Assail them with the army *2 Hen. VI.* iv 2 184

Speak gentle words and humbly bend thy knee . . . *3 Hen. VI.* v 1 22

Now, this no more dishonours you at all Than to take in a town with gentle words . . . . *Coriolanus* iii 2 59

Gentle wounded. Fortune's blows, When most struck home, being gentle wounded, craves A noble cunning . . . . . iv 1 8

Gentle youth. She is beholding to thee, gentle youth . *T. G. of Ver.* iv 4 178

Good gentle youth, tempt not a desperate man . *Rom. and Jul.* v 3 59

Gentlefolks. The queen's kindred are made gentlefolks . *Richard III.* i 1 95

Gentleman. I know the gentleman To be of worth . *T. G. of Ver.* ii 4 55

Complete in feature and in mind With all good grace to grace a gentleman ii 4 74

This gentleman is come to me, With commendation . . . ii 4 78

This is the gentleman I told your ladyship Had come along with me . ii 4 87

Have done, have done; here comes the gentleman . . . ii 4 99

The gentleman Is full of virtue, bounty, worth and qualities . . . iii 1 64

She I mean is promised by her friends Unto a youthful gentleman of worth iii 1 107

As thou art a gentleman of blood, Advise me . . . . iii 1 121

'Tis an ill office for a gentleman, Especially against his very friend . iii 2 40

We'll have you merry: I'll bring you where you shall hear music and see the gentleman that you asked for . . . . . iv 2 31

Thou art a gentleman—Think not I flatter, for I swear I do not . . iv 3 11

You are well derived.—True; from a gentleman to a fool . . . v 2 24

Where is the gentleman that was with her? . . . . . v 3 6

Thou art a gentleman and well derived . . . . . . v 4 146

A gentleman born, master parson; who writes himself 'Armigero' *M. W.* i 1 8

The gentleman had drunk himself out of his five sentences . . i 1 178

Yet I live like a poor gentleman born . . . . . . i 1 286

Truly, an honest gentleman: but Anne loves him not . . . i 4 177

How now, bully-rook! thou'rt a gentleman. Cavaleiro-justice, I say! . ii 1 200

Sir, I am a gentleman that have spent much: my name is Brook . ii 2 166

A gentleman of excellent breeding, admirable discourse, of great admittance . . . . ii 2 234

And last, as I am a gentleman, you shall, if you will, enjoy Ford's wife ii 2 264

Master Shallow, and another gentleman, from Frogmore . . iii 1 32

Yonder is a most reverend gentleman . . . . . iii 1 52

The gentleman is of no having: he kept company with the wild prince iii 2 73

A gentleman that he says is here now in the house . . . iii 3 115

What shall I do? There is a gentleman my dear friend . . . iii 3 129

As I am a gentleman, I'll give thee A hundred pound in gold . iv 6 4

Alas, this gentleman, Whom I would save, had a most noble father! *Meas. for Meas.* ii 1 6

Well, sir; what did this gentleman to her?—I beseech you, sir, look in this gentleman's face . . . . ii 1 151

I spy comfort; I cry bail. Here's a gentleman and a friend of mine . iii 2 44

A gentleman of all temperance . . . . iii 2 251

I have laboured for the poor gentleman to the extremest shore of my modesty . . . . iii 2 265

This gentleman told somewhat of my tale,— Right . . . v 1 84

Not scurvy, nor a temporary meddler, As he's reported by this gentleman . . . . v 1 146

Three odd ducats more Than I stand debted to this gentleman *C. of Er.* iv 1 31

Both wind and tide stays for this gentleman . . . . iv 1 46

In the street I met him And in his company that gentleman . . v 1 226

I see, lady, the gentleman is not in your books . . *Much Ado* i 1 78

So some gentleman or other shall 'scape a predestinate scratched face . i 1 135

How tartly that gentleman looks! I never can see him but I am heart-burned . . . . ii 1 3

When I know the gentleman, I'll tell him what you say . . . ii 1 150

The gentleman that danced with her told her she is much wronged by you . . . . ii 1 244

Doth not the gentleman Deserve as full as fortunate a bed As ever Beatrice shall couch upon? . . . . iii 1 44

If fair-faced, She would swear the gentleman should be her sister . iii 1 62

So rare a gentleman as Signior Benedick.—He is the only man of Italy iii 1 91

A' goes up and down like a gentleman: I remember his name . . iii 3 135

I am a gentleman, sir, and my name is Conrade.—Write down, master gentleman Conrade . . . . iv 2 15

I'll whip you from your foining fence; Nay, as I am a gentleman, I will v 1 85

'Nay,' said I, 'the gentleman is wise:' 'Certain,' said she, 'a wise gentleman' . . . . v 1 166

Come, cousin, I am sure you love the gentleman . . . . v 4 84

And, as I am a gentleman, betook myself to walk . . *L. L. Lost* i 1 236

You are a gentleman and a gamester, sir . . . . . i 2 44

The king is a noble gentleman, and my familiar, I do assure ye . v 1 100

This most gallant, illustrate, and learned gentleman . . . v 1 129

Joshua, yourself; myself and this gallant gentleman, Judas . . v 1 134

Thrice-worthy gentleman!—Shall I tell you a thing? . . . v 1 151

As she is mine, I may dispose of her: Which shall be either to this gentleman Or to her death . . . . . . *M. N. Dream* i 1 43

Be kind and courteous to this gentleman; Hop in his walks . . iii 1 167

Your name, honest gentleman?—Peaseblossom . . . . iii 1 187

Giant-like ox-beef hath devoured many a gentleman of your house . iii 1 198

Master young gentleman, I pray you, which is the way to master Jew's? *Mer. of Venice* ii 2 40

The young gentleman, according to Fates and Destinies and such odd sayings, the Sisters Three and such branches of learning, is indeed deceased . . . . ii 2 64

Gentleman. If it be preferment To leave a rich Jew's service, to become The follower of so poor a gentleman . . . *Mer. of Venice* ii 2 157

A kinder gentleman treads not the earth . . . . . . ii 8 35

I freely told you, all the wealth I had Ran in my veins, I was a gentleman . . . . iii 2 258

If you knew to whom you show this honour, How true a gentleman . iii 4 6

The gentleman That lately stole his daughter . . . . . iv 1 384

Gratify this gentleman, For, in my mind, you are much bound to him . iv 1 406

Worthy gentleman, I and my friend Have by your wisdom been this day acquitted . . . . iv 1 408

Call you that keeping for a gentleman of my birth? *As Y. Like It* i 1 10

Allow me such exercises as may become a gentleman . . . i 1 76

Young gentleman, your spirits are too bold for your years . . i 2 183

Gentleman, Wear this for me, one out of suits with fortune . . i 2 257

Fare you well, fair gentleman.—Can I not say, I thank you? . . i 2 260

The priest was good enough, for all the old gentleman's saying . v 1 4

I know you are a gentleman of good conceit . . . . . v 2 58

Well met, honest gentleman.—By my troth, well met . . . v 3 7

This is the motley-minded gentleman that I have so often met . v 4 41

Belike, some noble gentleman that means, Travelling some journey, to repose him here . . . . *T. of Shrew* Ind. 1 75

An affable and courteous gentleman . . . . i 2 98

I have met a gentleman Hath promised me to help me to another . . i 2 172

Here is a gentleman whom by chance I met . . . . . i 2 182

This gentleman is happily arrived, My mind presumes, for his own good and ours . . . . i 2 213

A noble gentleman, To whom my father is not all unknown . . i 2 240

What! this gentleman will out-talk us all . . . . . i 2 248

Gratify this gentleman, To whom we all rest generally beholding . i 2 273

Was ever gentleman thus grieved as I? . . . . . . ii 1 37

Give me leave. I am a gentleman of Verona, sir . . . . ii 1 47

Nay, come again, Good Kate; I am a gentleman . . . . ii 1 220

If you strike me, you are no gentleman; And if no gentleman, why then no arms . . . . ii 1 223

Not like a Christian footboy or a gentleman's lackey . . . iii 2 73

Such a one as leaves a gentleman, And makes a god of such a cullion . iv 2 19

Sir, this is the gentleman I told you of . . . . . . iv 4 20

So qualified as may beseem The spouse of any noble gentleman . iv 5 67

Why, how now, gentleman! why, this is flat knavery . . . v 1 36

You seem a sober ancient gentleman by your habit . . . v 1 75

Who was with him?—A servant only, and a gentleman *All's Well* iii 2 86

I have told my neighbour how you have been solicited by a gentleman his companion . . . . iii 5 16

A gentleman that serves the count Reports but coarsely of her . iii 5 59

Is't not a handsome gentleman?—I like him well . . . . iii 5 83

My master hath been an honourable gentleman: tricks he hath had in him, which gentlemen have . . . . v 3 239

He did love her, sir, as a gentleman loves a woman . . . v 3 245

There is at the gate a young gentleman much desires to speak with you *T. Night* i 5 108

What is he at the gate, cousin?—A gentleman.—A gentleman! what gentleman?—'Tis a gentleman here—a plague o' these pickle-herring! . . . . i 5 126

What is your parentage?—Above my fortunes, yet my state is well: I am a gentleman . . . . i 5 298; 310

Save you, gentleman.—And you, sir.—Dieu vous garde, monsieur . iii 1 76

The young gentleman of the Count Orsino's is returned . . . iii 4 62

The behaviour of the young gentleman gives him out to be of good capacity . . . . iii 4 203

And drive the gentleman . . . into a most hideous opinion of his rage . iii 4 211

Gentleman, God save thee.—And you, sir . . . . . iii 4 238

Stay you by this gentleman till my return . . . . . iii 4 282

The gentleman will, for his honour's sake, have one bout with you . iii 4 336

He has promised me, as he is a gentleman and a soldier, he will not hurt you . . . . iii 4 338

If this young gentleman Have done offence, I take the fault on me . iii 4 343

As I am a gentleman, I will live to be thankful to thee for't . . iv 2 88

Who has done this, Sir Andrew?—The count's gentleman . . . v 1 183

My gentleman, Cesario?—'Od's lifelings, here he is! . . . v 1 186

How now, gentleman! how is't with you?—That's all one . . v 1 199

At Malvolio's suit, A gentleman, and follower of my lady's . . v 1 284

They say, poor gentleman, he's much distract . . . . . v 1 287

A gentleman of the greatest promise that ever came into my note *W. Tale* i 1 39

How like, methought, I then was to this kernel, This squash, this gentleman . . . . i 2 160

You are certainly a gentleman, thereto Clerk-like experienced . . i 2 391

How the poor gentleman roared and the bear mocked him . . iii 3 102

Nor the bear half dined on the gentleman: he's at it now . . iii 3 108

I'll go see if the bear be gone from the gentleman and how much he hath eaten . . . . iii 3 133

What a fool Honesty is! and Trust, his sworn brother, a very simple gentleman! . . . . iv 4 607

Think there's a necessity in't,—and change garments with this gentleman . . . . iv 4 650

Nay, prithee, dispatch: the gentleman is half flayed already . . iv 4 654

When I shall see this gentleman, thy speeches Will bring me to consider that which may Unfurnish me of reason . . . . . . v 1 121

Good gentleman! the wrongs I have done thee stir Afresh within me . v 1 148

You have a holy father, A graceful gentleman . . . . . v 1 171

Here comes a gentleman that haply knows more . . . . v 2 22

You denied to fight with me this other day, because I was no gentleman born . . . . v 2 141

See you these clothes? say you see them not and think me still no gentleman born . . . . v 2 142

Give me the lie, do, and try whether I am not now a gentleman born . v 2 145

But I was a gentleman born before my father . . . . . v 2 150

You may say it, but not swear it.—Not swear it, now I am a gentleman? v 2 172

If it be ne'er so false, a true gentleman may swear it in the behalf of his friend . . . . v 2 175

Your faithful subject I, a gentleman Born in Northamptonshire *K. John* i 1 50

Large lengths of seas and shores Between my father and my mother lay, . . . When this same lusty gentleman was got . . . i 1 108

That smooth-faced gentleman, tickling Commodity . . . ii 1 573

Spoke like a sprightful noble gentleman . . . . . . iv 2 177

Hurl down my gage . . . , To prove myself a loyal gentleman Even in the best blood chamber'd in his bosom . . . . . *Richard II.* i 1 148

A loyal, just and upright gentleman . . . . i 3 87

In peace was never gentle lamb more mild Than was that young and princely gentleman . . . . ii 1 175

A happy gentleman in blood and lineaments, By you unhappied . iii 1 9

Gentleman. Leaving me no sign, Save men's opinions and my living blood, To show the world I am a gentleman *Richard II.* iii 1 27
And, as I am a gentleman, I credit him iii 3 120
He is a worthy gentleman, Exceedingly well read *1 Hen. IV.* iii 1 165
I was as virtuously given as a gentleman need to be iii 3 17
I do not think a braver gentleman . . . is now alive v 1 89
This earth that bears thee dead Bears not alive so stout a gentleman v 4 93
A gentleman well bred and of good name *2 Hen. IV.* i 1 26
After him came spurring hard A gentleman, almost forspent with speed i 1 37
Why should that gentleman that rode by Travers Give then such instances of loss?—Who, he? He was some hilding fellow i 1 55
To bear a gentleman in hand, and then stand upon security! i 2 42
You said so before.—As I am a gentleman. Come, no more words of it ii 1 150
I am a gentleman; thou art a drawer ii 4 311
A tall gentleman, by heaven, and a most gallant leader iii 2 67
Was reputed then In England the most valiant gentleman iv 1 132
Honest gentleman, I know not your breeding v 3 111
Is altogether directed by an Irishman, a very valiant gentleman *Hen. V.* iii 2 71
A marvellous falorous gentleman, that is certain iii 2 82
He is simply the most active gentleman of France iii 7 105
A valiant and most expert gentleman iii 7 139
I am a gentleman of a company.—Trail'st thou the puissant pike? iv 1 39
What are you?—As good a gentleman as the emperor iv 1 42
A good old commander and a most kind gentleman iv 1 98
Art thou a gentleman? what is thy name? discuss iv 4 5
O, Signieur Dew should be a gentleman: Perpend my words iv 4 7
He prays you to save his life: he is a gentleman of a good house iv 4 48
It may be his enemy is a gentleman of great sort iv 7 141
Though he be as good a gentleman as the devil is, as Lucifer iv 7 144
I have seen you gleeking and galling at this gentleman twice or thrice v 1 78
Let him that is a true-born gentleman And stands upon the honour of his birth . . . pluck a white rose *1 Hen. VI.* ii 4 27
Poor gentleman! his wrong doth equal mine ii 5 22
So should we save a valiant gentleman By forfeiting a traitor iv 3 26
While he, renowned noble gentleman, Yields up his life unto a world of odds iv 4 24
I never saw but Humphrey Duke of Gloucester Did bear him like a noble gentleman *2 Hen. VI.* i 1 184
I am a gentleman: Rate me at what thou wilt, thou shalt be paid iv 1 29
We will not leave one lord, one gentleman iv 2 194
The noble gentleman gave up the ghost *3 Hen. VI.* ii 3 22
In quarrel of the house of York The worthy gentleman did lose his life iii 2 7
A sweeter and a lovelier gentleman, Framed in the prodigality of nature, Young, valiant, wise *Richard III.* i 2 243
Since every Jack became a gentleman, There's many a gentle person made a Jack i 3 72
My servant's life; Who slew to-day a riotous gentleman ii 1 100
Finds the testy gentleman so hot, As he will lose his head ere give consent iii 4 39
I know a discontented gentleman, Whose humble means match not his haughty mind iv 2 36
Inquire me out some mean-born gentleman, Whom I will marry straight to Clarence' daughter iv 2 54
Let be call'd before us That gentleman of Buckingham's *Hen. VIII.* i 2 5
The gentleman is learned, and a most rare speaker i 2 111
You shall hear—This was his gentleman in trust i 2 125
That noble lady, Or gentleman, that is not freely merry, Is not my friend i 4 36
A bold brave gentleman. That should be The Duke of Suffolk? iv 1 40
There is staying A gentleman, sent from the king, to see you iv 2 106
You're a gentleman Of mine own way v 1 27
The gentleman, That was sent to me from the council, pray'd me To make great haste v 2 1
You depend upon a noble gentleman; I must needs praise him *T. and C.* iii 1 6
I knew thou wouldst be his death. O, poor gentleman! iv 2 91
Bold gentleman, Prosperity be thy page!—Thy friend no less! *Coriolanus* i 5 23
What are you?—A gentleman.—A marvellous poor one.—True, so I am.—Pray you, poor gentleman, take up some other station iv 5 29
This noble gentleman, Lord Titus here, Is in opinion and in honour wrong'd *T. Andron.* i 1 415
What say you? can you love the gentleman? *Rom. and Jul.* i 3 79
He bears him like a portly gentleman; And, to say truth, Verona brags of him i 5 68
Come hither, nurse. What is yond gentleman?—The son and heir of old Tiberio i 5 130
Trust me, gentleman, I'll prove more true Than those that have more cunning ii 2 100
A gentleman of the very first house, of the first and second cause ii 4 25
A gentleman, nurse, that loves to hear himself talk ii 4 155
Like an honest gentleman, and a courteous, and a kind, and a handsome ii 5 56
Your love says, like an honest gentleman, Where is your mother? ii 5 62
This gentleman, the prince's near ally, My very friend, hath got his mortal hurt iii 1 114
Honest gentleman! That ever I should live to see thee dead! iii 2 62
The gallant, young and noble gentleman iii 5 114
Doth she not count her blest, Unworthy as she is, that we have wrought So worthy a gentleman to be her bridegroom? iii 5 146
A gentleman of noble parentage, Of fair demesnes, youthful iii 5 181
O, he's a lovely gentleman! Romeo's a dishclout to him iii 5 220
I do know him A gentleman that well deserves a help *T. of Athens* i 1 102
This gentleman of mine hath served me long i 1 142
Well fare you, gentleman: give me your hand; We must needs dine together i 1 163
That honourable gentleman, Lord Lucullus, entreats your company to-morrow i 2 193
And how does that honourable, complete, free-hearted gentleman? iii 1 10
A noble gentleman 'tis, if he would not keep so good a house iii 1 23
Thy lord's a bountiful gentleman: but thou art wise iii 1 42
He is my very good friend, and an honourable gentleman iii 2 2
Say, that I cannot pleasure such an honourable gentleman iii 2 63
O valiant cousin! worthy gentleman! *Macbeth* i 2 24
The thane of Cawdor lives, A prosperous gentleman i 3 73
He was a gentleman on whom I built An absolute trust i 4 13
'Good sir,' or so, or 'friend,' or 'gentleman,' According to the phrase or the addition Of man and country *Hamlet* ii 1 46
I know the gentleman; I saw him yesterday, or t'other day, Or then, or then ii 1 55
Did he receive you well?—Most like a gentleman iii 1 11
Why, now you speak Like a good child and a true gentleman iv 5 148
Two months since, Here was a gentleman of Normandy iv 7 83

Gentleman. Was he a gentleman?—A' was the first that ever bore arms *Hamlet* v 1 36
An absolute gentleman, full of most excellent differences v 2 111
You shall find in him the continent of what part a gentleman would see v 2 116
Why do we wrap the gentleman in our more rawer breath? v 2 129
What imports the nomination of this gentleman? v 2 134
Let the foils be brought, the gentleman willing, and the king hold his purpose v 2 182
I've done you wrong; But pardon't, as you are a gentleman v 2 238
Do you know this noble gentleman, Edmund?—No, my lord *Lear* i 1 25
Did my father strike my gentleman for chiding of his fool? i 3 1
My sister may receive it much more worse, To have her gentleman abused ii 2 156
I am a gentleman of blood and breeding iii 1 40
The prince of darkness is a gentleman: Modo he's call'd, and Mahu iii 4 148
Prithee, nuncle, tell me whether a madman be a gentleman or a yeoman? iii 6 11
He's a yeoman that has a gentleman to his son; for he's a mad yeoman that sees his son a gentleman before him iii 6 13
Burning shame Detains him from Cordelia.—Alack, poor gentleman! iv 3 49
Good gentleman, go your gait, and let poor volk pass iv 6 242
I shall never love thee after. Why, thou silly gentleman! *Othello* i 3 308
Sir, this gentleman Steps in to Cassio, and entreats his pause ii 3 228
Alas, what does this gentleman conceive? How do you, madam? iv 2 95
Alas, good gentleman! alas, good Cassio! v 1 115
Hath referr'd herself Unto a poor but worthy gentleman: she's wedded *Cymbeline* i 1 7
And had, besides this gentleman in question, Two other sons i 1 34
His gentle lady, Big of this gentleman our theme, deceased As he was born i 1 39
We must forbear: here comes the gentleman i 1 68
I beseech you all, be better known to this gentleman i 4 31
This gentleman at that time vouching . . . his to be more fair i 4 62
That lady is not now living, or this gentleman's opinion by this worn out i 4 68
A noble gentleman of Rome, Comes from my lord with letters i 6 10
Thou wrong'st a gentleman, who is as far From thy report as thou from honour i 6 145
When a gentleman is disposed to swear, it is not for any standers-by to curtail his oaths ii 1 11
Who's there that knocks?—A gentleman.—No more? ii 3 82
My boon is, that this gentleman may render Of whom he had this ring v 5 135
This gentleman, my Cadwal, Arviragus, Your younger princely son v 5 359
Where with it I may appear a gentleman *Pericles* ii 1 147
Sure, he's a gallant gentleman.—He's but a country gentleman ii 3 32
A gentleman of Tyre; my name, Pericles; My education been in arts and arms ii 3 81
He thanks your grace; names himself Pericles, A gentleman of Tyre ii 3 87
A stranger and distressed gentleman, That never aim'd so high to love your daughter, But bent all offices to honour her ii 5 46

Gentleman-like. He thrusts me himself into the company of three or four gentlemanlike dogs *T. G. of Ver.* iv 4 19
A most lovely gentleman-like man *M. N. Dream* i 2 90
Obscuring and hiding from me all gentleman-like qualities *As Y. Like It* i 1 72
And there was the first gentleman-like tears that ever we shed *W. Tale* v 2 156
I will tell her, sir, that you do protest; which, as I take it, is a gentlemanlike offer *Rom. and Jul.* ii 4 190

Gentlemen, who are of such sensible and nimble lungs *Tempest* ii 1 173
You are gentlemen of brave mettle; you would lift the moon out of her sphere ii 1 182
Of all the fair resort of gentlemen That every day with parle encounter me, In thy opinion which is worthiest love? *T. G. of Ver.* i 2 4
'Tis a passing shame That I, unworthy body as I am, Should censure thus on lovely gentlemen i 2 19
Other gentlemen of good esteem Are journeying to salute the emperor i 3 40
A fine volley of words, gentlemen, and quickly shot off ii 4 33
No more, gentlemen, no more: here comes my father ii 4 47
Let us into the city presently To sort some gentlemen well skill'd in music iii 2 92
About it, gentlemen!—We'll wait upon your grace till after supper iii 2 95
Know, then, that some of us are gentlemen iv 1 44
Now, gentlemen, Let's tune, and to it lustily awhile iv 2 24
I thank you for your music, gentlemen. Who is that that spake? iv 2 86
Dispatch, sweet gentlemen, and follow me v 2 48
You hear all these matters denied, gentlemen; you hear it *Mer. Wives* i 1 193
Wife, bid these gentlemen welcome i 1 201
Come, gentlemen, I hope we shall drink down all unkindness i 1 203
I am damned in hell for swearing to gentlemen my friends ii 2 10
There has been knights, and lords, and gentlemen, with their coaches ii 2 65
I shall procure-a you de good guest, de earl, de knight, de lords, de gentlemen ii 3 96
Trust me, a mad host. Follow, gentlemen, follow iii 1 115
Gentlemen, I have dreamed to-night; I'll tell you my dream iii 3 171
Up, gentlemen; you shall see sport anon: follow me, gentlemen iii 3 179
Nay, follow him, gentlemen; see the issue of his search iii 3 185
Let's go in, gentlemen; but, trust me, we'll mock him iii 3 244
Good gentlemen, let him not strike the old woman iv 2 190
Will you follow, gentlemen? I beseech you, follow; see but the issue iv 2 206
Let's obey his humour a little further: come, gentlemen iv 2 211
Let me speak with the gentlemen: they speak English? iv 3 7
Bore many gentlemen, myself being one, In hand and hope of action *Meas. for Meas.* i 4 51
When gentlemen are tired, gives them a sob and 'rests them *Com. of Er.* iv 3 24
How many gentlemen have you lost in this action? *Much Ado* i 1 5
Gentlemen both, we will not wake your patience v 1 102
Gentlemen and soldiers, pardon me; I will not combat in my shirt *L. L. Lost* v 2 710
Though you mock me, gentlemen, Let her not hurt me *M. N. Dream* iii 2 299
Go, gentlemen, Will you prepare you for this masque to-night? *Mer. of Ven.* ii 4 22
On, gentlemen; away! Our masquing mates by this time for us stay ii 6 58
Gentlemen, my master Antonio is at his house iii 1 77
Many young gentlemen flock to him every day *As Y. Like It* i 1 123
Truly, young gentlemen, though there was no great matter in the ditty v 3 35
Gentlemen, importune me no farther *T. of Shrew* i 1 48
Gentlemen, that I may soon make good What I have said, Bianca, get you in i 1 74
Gentlemen, content ye; I am resolved i 1 90
Gentlemen, God save you i 2 219
If you be gentlemen, Do me this right; hear me with patience i 2 238
God save you, gentlemen!—And you, good sir! ii 1 41

Gentlemen. Lead these gentlemen To my daughters; and tell them both, These are their tutors *T. of Shrew* ii 1 109
Be patient, gentlemen; I choose her for myself ii 1 304
Father, and wife, and gentlemen, adieu; I will to Venice ii 1 323
Faith, gentlemen, now I play a merchant's part ii 1 328
Content you, gentlemen: I will compound this strife ii 1 343
Well, gentlemen, I am thus resolved ii 1 394
Why, gentlemen, you do me double wrong iii 1 16
Gentlemen and friends, I thank you for your pains iii 2 186
Gentlemen, forward to the bridal dinner iii 2 221
Yet, for our gentlemen that mean to see The Tuscan service, freely have they leave To stand on either part *All's Well* i 2 13
Gentlemen, Heaven hath through me restored the king to health ii 3 69
Think upon patience. Pray you, gentlemen iii 2 50
Brought you this letter, gentlemen?—Ay, madam iii 2 65
You're welcome, gentlemen iii 2 94
Tricks he hath had in him, which gentlemen have v 3 240
My father and the gentlemen are in sad talk *W. Tale* iv 4 316
But thy sons and daughters will be all gentlemen born v 2 138
You were best say these robes are not gentlemen born v 2 143
We must be gentle, now we are gentlemen v 2 165
Young gentlemen would be as sad as night, Only for wantonness *K. John* iv 1 15
Wrath-kindled gentlemen, be ruled by me *Richard II.* i 1 152
Come, gentlemen, let's all go visit him: Pray God we may make haste, and come too late! i 4 63
Well met, gentlemen: I hope the king is not yet shipp'd for Ireland ii 2 41
Gentlemen, will you go muster men? ii 2 108
And all your southern gentlemen in arms Upon his party iii 2 202
Diana's foresters, gentlemen of the shade, minions of the moon *1 Hen. IV.* i 2 29
We'll call up the gentlemen: they will along with company ii 1 50
There are two gentlemen Have in this robbery lost three hundred marks ii 4 568
Drawn together Your tenants, friends and neighbouring gentlemen iii 1 90
Ancients, corporals, lieutenants, gentlemen of companies iv 2 26
And a head Of gallant warriors, noble gentlemen iv 4 26
Arm, gentlemen; to arms! for I have thrown A brave defiance v 2 42
O gentlemen, the time of life is short! v 2 82
Good morrow, honest gentlemen *2 Hen. IV.* iii 2 61
Fie! this is hot weather, gentlemen iii 2 101
Fare you well, gentlemen both: I thank you: I must a dozen mile to-night iii 2 309
Fare you well, gentle gentlemen iii 2 321
O that the living Harry had the temper Of him, the worst of these three gentlemen! v 2 16
If the gentlemen will not, then the gentlemen do not agree with the gentlewomen Epil. 23
How now, gentlemen! What see you in those papers? *Hen. V.* ii 2 71
Gentlemen both, you will mistake each other iii 2 146
And gentlemen in England now a-bed Shall think themselves accursed they were not here iv 3 64
Of knights, esquires, and gallant gentlemen, Eight thousand and four hundred iv 8 89
Lords, knights, squires, And gentlemen of blood and quality iv 8 95
Great lords and gentlemen, what means this silence? *1 Hen. VI.* ii 4 1
Stay, lords and gentlemen, and pluck no more ii 4 39
They keep the walls And dare not take up arms like gentlemen iii 2 70
Myself and divers gentlemen beside Were there surprised and taken prisoners iv 1 25
Give them leave to speak. Say, gentlemen, what makes you thus exclaim? iv 1 83
After the slaughter of so many peers, So many captains, gentlemen v 4 104
What, think you much to pay two thousand crowns, And bear the name and port of gentlemen? *2 Hen. VI.* iv 1 19
It was never merry world in England since gentlemen came up iv 2 10
All scholars, lawyers, courtiers, gentlemen, They call false caterpillars iv 4 36
Stir up in Suffolk, Norfolk and in Kent, The knights and gentlemen *3 Hen. VI.* iv 8 13
Lords, knights, and gentlemen, what I should say My tears gainsay v 4 73
O, gentlemen, see, see! dead Henry's wounds Open their congeal'd mouths and bleed afresh! *Richard III.* i 2 55
All without desert have frown'd on me; Dukes, earls, lords, gentlemen ii 1 68
Valiant gentlemen, Let us survey the vantage of the field v 3 14
Come, gentlemen, Let us consult upon to-morrow's business v 3 44
Once more, good night, kind lords and gentlemen v 3 107
Cry mercy, lords and watchful gentlemen, That you have ta'en a tardy sluggard here v 3 224
For what is he they follow? truly, gentlemen, A bloody tyrant v 3 245
Go, gentlemen, every man unto his charge v 3 307
Fight, gentlemen of England! fight, bold yeomen! Draw, archers! v 3 338
Gentlemen, The penance lies on you, if these fair ladies Pass away frowning.—For my little cure, Let me alone *Hen. VIII.* i 4 31
Ladies, you are not merry: gentlemen, Whose fault is this? i 4 42
By all your good leaves, gentlemen; here I'll make My royal choice i 4 85
A health, gentlemen! Let it go round i 4 96
Our issues, Who, if he live, will scarce be gentlemen iii 2 292
Come, gentlemen, ye shall go my way, which Is to the court iv 1 114
But for our gentlemen, The common file—a plague! tribunes for them! *Coriolanus* i 6 42
Direct my sail! On, lusty gentlemen.—Strike, drum *Rom. and Jul.* i 4 113
Welcome, gentlemen! ladies that have their toes Unplagued with corns will have a bout with you i 5 18
Welcome, gentlemen! I have seen the day That I have worn a visor and could tell A whispering tale in a fair lady's ear i 5 23
Gentlemen, prepare not to be gone; We have a trifling foolish banquet i 5 123
I thank you all; I thank you, honest gentlemen; good night i 5 126
God ye good morrow, gentlemen.—God ye good den ii 4 115
Gentlemen, can any of you tell me where I may find the young Romeo? ii 4 124
I will speak to them. Gentlemen, good den: a word with one of you iii 1 41
Gentlemen, for shame, forbear this outrage! iii 1 90
Please you, gentlemen, The time is unagreeable to this business *T. of A.* ii 2 40
I was sending to use Lord Timon myself, these gentlemen can witness iii 2 56
If I might beseech you, gentlemen, to repair some other hour iii 4 68
With all my heart, gentlemen both; and how fare you? iii 6 27
Gentlemen, our dinner will not recompense this long stay iii 6 34
Good gentlemen, look fresh and merrily *J. Cæsar* ii 1 224
I know not, gentlemen, what you intend iii 1 151
Gentlemen all,—alas, what shall I say? My credit now stands on such slippery ground iii 1 190
I thank you, gentlemen *Macbeth* i 3 129
Kind gentlemen, your pains Are register'd where every day I turn The leaf to read them i 3 150

Gentlemen. Gentlemen, rise; his highness is not well *Macbeth* iii 4 52
Where are these gentlemen? Come, bring me where they are iv 1 155
Till I may deliver, Upon the witness of these gentlemen, This marvel *Ham.* i 2 194
Two nights together had these gentlemen . . . Been thus encounter'd? i 2 196
Unhand me, gentlemen. By heaven, I'll make a ghost of him that lets me! i 4 84
Come hither, gentlemen, And lay your hands again upon my sword i 5 157
So, gentlemen, With all my love I do commend me to you i 5 183
Good gentlemen, he hath much talk'd of you ii 2 19
Go, some of you, And bring these gentlemen where Hamlet is ii 2 37
Gentlemen, you are welcome to Elsinore ii 2 387
Well be with you, gentlemen! ii 2 398
Good gentlemen, give him a further edge, And drive his purpose on iii 1 26
There is no ancient gentlemen but gardeners, ditchers, and grave-makers v 1 33
Hamlet, Hamlet!—Gentlemen,— Good my lord, be quiet v 1 288
Gentlemen, let's look to our business. Do not think, gentlemen, I am drunk: this is my ancient *Othello* ii 3 116
Nay, good lieutenant,—alas, gentlemen;—Help, ho! ii 3 158
Montano,—gentlemen,—Have you forgot all sense of place and duty? ii 3 166
This fortification, gentlemen, shall we see't?—We'll wait upon your lordship iii 2 5
Light, gentlemen: I'll bind it with my shirt v 1 73
Gentlemen all, I do suspect this trash To be a party in this injury v 1 85
Stay you, good gentlemen. Look you pale, mistress? v 1 105
I pray you, look upon her: Do you see, gentlemen? nay, guiltiness will speak v 1 109
Kind gentlemen, let's go see poor Cassio dress'd v 1 124
Good gentlemen, let me have leave to speak: 'Tis proper I obey him, but not now v 2 195
Filth, thou liest.—By heaven, I do not, I do not, gentlemen v 2 232
They were parted By gentlemen at hand *Cymbeline* i 1 164
Let him be so entertained amongst you as suits, with gentlemen of your knowing, to a stranger of his quality i 4 29
Let us leave here, gentlemen.—Sir, with all my heart i 4 109
Gentlemen, enough of this: it came in too suddenly i 4 130
Gentlemen of Italy, most willing spirits, That promise noble service iv 2 338
A supply Of Roman gentlemen, by the senate sent iv 3 26
In Cambria are we born, and gentlemen: Further to boast were neither true nor modest, Unless I add, we are honest v 5 17
O, gentlemen, help! Mine and your mistress! v 5 229
These two young gentlemen, that call me father And think they are my sons, are none of mine v 5 328
We are gentlemen That neither in our hearts nor outward eyes Envy the great nor do the low despise *Pericles* ii 3 24
Come, gentlemen, we sit too long on trifles, And waste the time ii 3 92
Thanks, gentlemen, to all; all have done well, But you the best ii 3 108
Gentlemen, Why do you stir so early? iii 2 11
I pray you, give her air. Gentlemen, This queen will live iii 2 92
Yes, indeed shall you, and taste gentlemen of all fashions iv 2 83
We'll have no more gentlemen driven away. Come your ways, I say iv 6 138
Call up some gentlemen.—Ho, gentlemen! my lord calls v 1 6
Gentlemen, there's some of worth would come aboard; I pray ye, greet them fairly v 1 9

Gentleness. So, of his gentleness, Knowing I loved my books, he furnish'd me From mine own library with volumes *Tempest* i 2 165
The truth you speak doth lack some gentleness And time to speak it in ii 1 137
Your gentleness Was guilty of it *L. L. Lost* v 2 745
I must confess I thought you lord of more true gentleness *M. N. Dream* ii 2 132
Touch'd with human gentleness and love *Mer. of Venice* iv 1 25
What would you have? Your gentleness shall force More than your force move us to gentleness *As Y. Like It* ii 7 103
Let gentleness my strong enforcement be ii 7 118
Sit you down in gentleness And take upon command what help we have ii 7 124
The gentleness of all the gods go with thee! *T. Night* ii 1 45
No way but gentleness: gently, gently: the fiend is rough iii 4 123
Thy rare qualities, sweet gentleness, Thy meekness saint-like *Hen. VIII.* ii 4 137
Manhood, learning, gentleness, virtue, youth, liberality, and such like, the spice and salt that season a man *Troi. and Cres.* i 2 276
In humane gentleness, Welcome! iv 1 20
And will with deeds requite thy gentleness *T. Andron.* i 1 237
I have not from your eyes that gentleness And show of love as I was wont to have *J. Cæsar* i 2 33
This milky gentleness and course of yours Though I condemn not *Lear* i 4 364

Gentler. No mates for you, Unless you were of gentler, milder mould *T. of Shrew* i 1 60
We marry A gentler scion to the wildest stock *W. Tale* iv 4 93
For when lenity and cruelty play for a kingdom, the gentler gamester is the soonest winner *Hen. V.* iii 6 119
By a slave, no gentler than my dog, His fairest daughter is contaminated iv 5 15
A braver soldier never couched lance, A gentler heart did never sway in court *1 Hen. VI.* iii 2 135
I am descended of a gentler blood: Thou art no father nor no friend of mine v 4 8
Inquire your way, Which you are out of, with a gentler spirit *Coriolanus* iii 1 55
A gentler judgement vanish'd from his lips, Not body's death, but body's banishment *Rom. and Jul.* iii 3 10
He put it by thrice, every time gentler than other *J. Cæsar* i 2 230
How goes it now? he looks gentler than he did *Othello* iv 3 11

Gentlest. Then give you up to the mask'd Neptune and The gentlest winds of heaven *Pericles* iii 3 37

Gentlewoman. Doth this Sir Proteus that we talk on Often resort unto this gentlewoman? *T. G. of Ver.* iv 2 74
When didst thou see me heave up my leg and make water against a gentlewoman's farthingale? iv 4 41
Gentlewoman, good day! I pray you, be my mean iv 4 113
Poor gentlewoman! my master wrongs her much iv 4 146
A virtuous gentlewoman, mild and beautiful! iv 4 185
I know the young gentlewoman; she has good gifts *Mer. Wives* i 1 63
Desire this honest gentlewoman, your maid, to speak a good word i 4 87
There is a gentlewoman in this town; her husband's name is Ford ii 2 198
He will maintain you like a gentlewoman iii 4 45
A gentlewoman of mine, Who, falling in the flaws of her own youth, Hath blister'd her report *Meas. for Meas.* ii 3 10
But mark how heavily this befell to the poor gentlewoman iii 1 227
Here's a gentlewoman denies all that you have said v 1 282
Did you converse, sir, with this gentlewoman? *Com. of Errors* ii 2 162
And this fair gentlewoman, her sister here, Did call me brother v 1 373
I have to-night wooed Margaret, the Lady Hero's gentlewoman *M. Ado* iii 3 154
The princess' gentlewoman Confesses that she secretly o'erheard *As Y. Like It* ii 2 10

Gentlewoman. 'Twas where you woo'd the gentlewoman so well *T. of Shrew* Ind. 1 85
The boy will well usurp the grace, Voice, gait and action of a gentlewoman . . . . Ind. 1 132
Young and beauteous, Brought up as best becomes a gentlewoman . i 2 87
Tell me truly too, Hast thou beheld a fresher gentlewoman? . . iv 5 29
The sister to my wife, this gentlewoman, Thy son by this hath married iv 5 62
This young gentlewoman had a father,—O, that 'had'! . *All's Well* i 1 19
Was this gentlewoman the daughter of Gerard de Narbon? . . i 1 42
I will now hear; what say you of this gentlewoman? . . . . i 3 2
Tell my gentlewoman I would speak with her . . . . . . i 3 72
I know, madam, you love your gentlewoman entirely . . . i 3 103
He hath perverted a young gentlewoman here in Florence . iv 3 17
The most virtuous gentlewoman that ever nature had praise for creating . . . . iv 5 9
Let him approach: call in my gentlewoman . . . . *T. Night* i 5 172
Dear gentlewoman, How fares our gracious lady? . . *W. Tale* ii 2 20
A proper gentlewoman, sir, and a kinswoman of my master's. 2 *Hen. IV.* ii 2 169
How vilely did you speak of me even now before this honest, virtuous, civil gentlewoman! . . . . ii 4 328
See now, whether pure fear and entire cowardice doth not make thee wrong this virtuous gentlewoman? . . . . . . ii 4 354
And at night, when you come into your closet, you'll question this gentlewoman about me . . . . . *Hen. V.* v 2 211
The late queen's gentlewoman, a knight's daughter . *Hen. VIII.* iii 2 94
God ye good den, fair gentlewoman.—Is it good den? . *Rom. and Jul.* ii 4 116
What a man are you!—One, gentlewoman, that God hath made . . ii 4 121
A very gross kind of behaviour, as they say: for the gentlewoman is young . . . . ii 4 177
Truly it were an ill thing to be offered to any gentlewoman . . ii 4 180
If this had not been a gentlewoman, she should have been buried out o' Christian burial . . . . *Hamlet* v 1 27
Your name, fair gentlewoman?—This admiration, sir, is much o' the savour Of other your new pranks . . . . . *Lear* i 4 257
If the gentlewoman that attends the general's wife be stirring *Othello* iii 1 26
A gentleman.—No more?—Yes, and a gentlewoman's son . *Cymbeline* ii 3 83

Gentlewomen. That must your daughter and her gentlewomen carry *Much Ado* ii 3 223
Gentlewomen all, Withdraw into a chamber by yourselves . . . v 4 10
And gentlewomen wear such caps as these . . . *T. of Shrew* iv 3 70
All the gentlewomen here have forgiven me: if the gentlemen will not, then the gentlemen do not agree with the gentlewomen 2 *Hen. IV.* Epil. 22
Gentlewomen that live honestly by the prick of their needles . *Hen. V.* ii 1 35
The jealous o'erworn widow and herself, Since that our brother dubb'd them gentlewomen, Are mighty gossips . . . *Richard III.* i 1 82
Her gentlewomen, like the Nereides, So many mermaids, *Ant. and Cleo.* ii 2 211

Gently. I will be correspondent to command And do my spiriting gently *Tempest* i 2 298
I will roar you as gently as any sucking dove . . *M. N. Dream* i 2 85
So doth the woodbine the sweet honeysuckle Gently entwist . . iv 1 48
When the sweet wind did gently kiss the trees . . *Mer. of Venice* v 1 2
Speak you so gently? Pardon me, I pray you: I thought that all things had been savage here . . . . . *As Y. Like It* ii 7 106
Carry him gently to my fairest chamber . . . . *T. of Shrew* Ind. 1 46
Take him up gently and to bed with him . . . . . . Ind 1 72
We must deal gently with him . . . . *T. Night* iii 4 106
Gently, gently: the fiend is rough, and will not be roughly used . iii 4 123
Being something gently considered, I'll bring you where he is *W. Tale* iv 4 825
It may lie gently at the foot of peace, And be no further harmful *K. John* v 2 76
By that sword I swear, Which gently laid my knighthood on my shoulder . . . . *Richard II.* i 1 79
Who gently would dissolve the bands of life, Which false hope lingers . ii 2 71
I told him gently of our grievances, Of his oath-breaking . 1 *Hen. IV.* v 2 37
You may stroke him as gently as a puppy greyhound . 2 *Hen. IV.* ii 4 106
Your humble patience pray, Gently to hear, kindly to judge *Hen. V.* Prol. 34
I kiss these fingers for eternal peace, And lay them gently on thy tender side. Who art thou? say . . . . . 1 *Hen. VI.* v 3 49
The king, Who look'd full gently on his warlike queen . 3 *Hen. VI.* ii 1 123
Or like an idle thresher with a flail, Fell gently down . . . ii 1 132
Now the battle's ended, If friend or foe, let him be gently used . ii 6 45
Must gently be preserved, cherish'd, and kept . . *Richard III.* ii 2 119
So may he rest; his faults lie gently on him! . . . *Hen. VIII.* iv 2 31
And bring our emperor gently in thy hand . . . *T. Andron.* v 3 138
Would I were gently put out of office Before I were forced out! *T. of A.* i 2 207
Hark! he is arrived. March gently on to meet him . *J. Cæsar* iv 2 31
This way, my lord; the castle's gently render'd . . *Macbeth* v 7 24
Do not saw the air too much with your hand, thus, but use all gently *Hamlet* iii 2 6
What's amiss, May it be gently heard . . . *Ant. and Cleo.* ii 2 20
If thou and nature can so gently part, The stroke of death is as a lover's pinch, Which hurts, and is desired . . . . . . v 2 297
O, still Thy deafening, dreadful thunders; gently quench Thy nimble, sulphurous flashes! . . . . *Pericles* iii 1 5

Gentry. Thou shouldst not alter the article of thy gentry *Mer. Wives* ii 1 53
It well may serve A nursery to our gentry . . . *All's Well* i 2 16
Which no less adorns Our gentry than our parents' noble names *W. Tale* i 2 393
To grace the gentry of a land remote . . . . *K. John* v 2 31
Attainted, Corrupted, and exempt from ancient gentry . 1 *Hen. VI.* ii 4 93
He makes up the file Of all the gentry . . . . *Hen. VIII.* i 1 76
He would miss it rather Than carry it but by the suit of the gentry *Coriolanus* ii 1 254
Where gentry, title, wisdom, Cannot conclude but by the yea and no Of general ignorance . . . . iii 1 144
I have a file Of all the gentry: there is Siward's son *Macbeth* v 2 9
If it will please you To show us so much gentry and good will *Hamlet* ii 2 22
To speak feelingly of him, he is the card or calendar of gentry . v 2 114
This is the tenour of the emperor's writ: . . . that we do incite The gentry to this business . . . . . *Cymbeline* iii 7 7
I am brought hither Among the Italian gentry . . . . v 1 18
If that thy gentry, Britain, go before This lout as he exceeds our lords, the odds Is that we scarce are men and you are gods . v 2 8

George. Whither go you, George? Hark you . . *Mer. Wives* ii 1 153
You'll come to dinner, George . . . . ii 1 162
Good George, be not angry: I knew of your purpose . . . v 5 213
Hugh Oatcake, sir, or George Seacole; for they can write and read *M. Ado* iii 3 11
Saint George's half-cheek in a brooch . . . . *L. L. Lost* v 2 620
Now, by Saint George, I am too young for you . . *T. of Shrew* ii 1 238
And if his name be George, I'll call him Peter . . *K. John* i 1 186
Saint George, that swinged the dragon, and e'er since Sits on his horse back at mine hostess' door . . . . ii 1 288
Mine innocency and Saint George to thrive! . . . *Richard II.* i 3 84
Little John Doit of Staffordshire, and black George Barnes 2 *Hen. IV.* iii 2 22
We lay all night in the windmill in Saint George's field . . . iii 2 207
Upon this charge Cry 'God for Harry, England, and Saint George!' *Hen. V.* iii 1 34
Shall not thou and I, between Saint Denis and Saint George, compound a boy? . . . . v 2 220
To my task will I; Bonfires in France forthwith I am to make, To keep our great Saint George's feast . . . . . 1 *Hen. VI.* i 1 154
God and Saint George, Talbot and England's right, Prosper our colours! iv 2 55
Saint George and victory! fight, soldiers, fight . . . . iv 6 1
Knight of the noble order of Saint George, Worthy Saint Michael . . iv 7 68
Look on my George; I am a gentleman . . . . 2 *Hen. VI.* iv 1 29
Meet me to-morrow in Saint George's field, You shall have pay . v 1 46
Where are your mess of sons to back you now? The wanton Edward, and the lusty George? . . . . 3 *Hen. VI.* i 4 74
Lord George your brother, Norfolk and myself, In haste, post-haste, are come . . . . ii 1 138
And when came George from Burgundy to England? . . . . ii 1 143
Then strike up drums: God and Saint George for us! . . . . ii 1 204
Unsheathe your sword, good father; cry 'Saint George!' . . . ii 2 80
Let me be Duke of Clarence, George of Gloucester . . . . ii 6 106
For Warwick and his friends, God and Saint George! . . . . iv 2 29
And lo, where George of Clarence sweeps along . . . . . v 1 76
Lords, to the field; Saint George and victory! . . . . . v 1 113
Lascivious Edward, and thou perjured George, And thou mis-shapen Dick . . . . v 5 34
Upon what cause?—Because my name is George . . *Richard III.* i 1 46
For my name of George begins with G, It follows in his thought that I am he . . . . i 1 58
He cannot live, I hope; and must not die Till George be pack'd with post-horse up to heaven . . . . i 1 146
Now, by my George, my garter, and my crown,— Profaned, dishonour'd iv 4 366
The George, profaned, hath lost his holy honour . . . . iv 4 369
But, hear you, leave behind Your son, George Stanley . . . iv 4 497
My son George Stanley is frank'd up in hold: If I revolt, off goes young George's head . . . . iv 5 3
Bid him bring his power Before sunrising, lest his son George fall Into the blind cave of eternal night . . . . v 3 61
But on thy side I may not be too forward, Lest, being seen, thy brother, tender George, Be executed . . . . v 3 95
God and Saint George! Richmond and victory! . . . . . v 3 270
He doth deny to come.—Off with his son George's head! . . . v 3 344
After the battle let George Stanley die . . . . . . v 3 346
Our ancient word of courage, fair Saint George, Inspire us! . . . v 3 349
But, tell me, is young George Stanley living? . . . . . v 5 9

Gerard. He was famous, sir, in his profession, and it was his great right to be so: Gerard de Narbon . . . . . *All's Well* i 1 30
Was this gentlewoman the daughter of Gerard de Narbon? . . . i 1 42
Gerard de Narbon was my father; In what he did profess, well found . ii 1 104

German. The Germans desire to have three of your horses *Mer. Wives* iv 3 1
Like three German devils, three Doctor Faustuses . . . . iv 5 70
Do not say they be fled; Germans are honest men . . . . iv 5 73
A German from the waist downward, all slops . . *Much Ado* iii 2 35
Like a German clock, Still a-repairing, ever out of frame . *L. L. Lost* iii 1 192
How like you the young German, the Duke of Saxony's nephew? *M. of V.* i 2 90
If there be here German, or Dane, low Dutch, Italian, or French, let him speak to me . . . . *All's Well* iv 1 78
The story of the Prodigal, or the German hunting in water-work 2 *Hen. IV.* ii 1 157
Holding in disdain the German women For some dishonest manners *Hen. V.* i 2 48
Edward from Belgia, With hasty Germans and blunt Hollanders 3 *Hen. VI.* iv 8 2
Wert thou a leopard, thou wert german to the lion . *T. of Athens* iv 3 344
The phrase would be more german to the matter, if we could carry cannon by our sides . . . . *Hamlet* v 2 165
You'll have coursers for cousins and gennets for germans . . *Othello* i 1 114
Your Dane, your German, and your swag-bellied Hollander—Drink, ho!—are nothing to your English . . . . ii 3 80
Like a full-acorn'd boar, a German one . . . . *Cymbeline* ii 5 16

Germane. Those that are germane to him, though removed fifty times, shall all come under the hangman . . . . . *W. Tale* iv 4 802

Germany. He bought his doublet in Italy, his round hose in France, his bonnet in Germany . . . . *Mer. of Venice* i 2 81
Once dispatch'd him in an embassy To Germany . . *K. John* i 1 100
Their own authors faithfully affirm That the land Salique is in Germany *Hen. V.* i 2 44
Which Salique, as I said, 'twixt Elbe and Sala, Is at this day in Germany call'd Meisen . . . . i 2 53
Our neighbours, The upper Germany, can dearly witness . *Hen. VIII.* v 3 30
Edgar, his banished son, is with the Earl of Kent in Germany . *Lear* iv 7 91

Germen. Though the treasure Of nature's germens tumble all together *Macbeth* iv 1 59
All germens spill at once, That make ingrateful man! . . . *Lear* iii 2 8

Gertrude. He tells me, my dear Gertrude, he hath found The head and source of all your son's distemper . . . . . *Hamlet* ii 2 54
Sweet Gertrude, leave us too; For we have closely sent for Hamlet hither iii 1 28
What have I seen to-night!—What, Gertrude? How does Hamlet?—Mad as the sea and wind . . . . iv 1 6
He weeps for what is done.—O Gertrude, come away! . . . . iv 1 28
Come, Gertrude, we'll call up our wisest friends; And let them know iv 1 38
O Gertrude, Gertrude, When sorrows come, they come not single spies iv 5 77
O my dear Gertrude, this, Like to a murdering-piece, in many places Gives me superfluous death . . . . iv 5 94
Let him go, Gertrude; do not fear our person . . . . iv 5 122
Let's follow, Gertrude: How much I had to do to calm his rage! . iv 7 192
Good Gertrude, set some watch over your son . . . . . v 1 319
Gertrude, do not drink.—I will, my lord; I pray you, pardon me . v 2 301

Gest. A month behind the gest Prefix'd for's parting . . *W. Tale* i 2 41
We have beat him to his camp: run one before, And let the queen know of our gests . . . . *Ant. and Cleo.* iv 8 2

Gesture. I cannot too much muse Such shapes, such gesture . *Tempest* iii 3 37
If you do love Rosalind so near the heart as your gesture cries it out, when your brother marries Aliena, shall you marry her *As Y. Like It* v 2 69
There was speech in their dumbness, language in their very gesture *W. T.* v 2 15
Their gesture sad Investing lank-lean cheeks and war-worn coats *Hen. V.* iv Prol. 25
How big imagination Moves in this lip! to the dumbness of the gesture One might interpret . . . . *T. of Athens* i 1 33
As her winks, and nods, and gestures yield them . . . *Hamlet* iv 5 11
I say, but mark his gesture . . . . *Othello* iv 1 88

Gesture. His unbookish jealousy must construe Poor Cassio's smiles, gestures, and light behaviour, Quite in the wrong *Othello* iv 1 103
His gesture imports it iv 1 142
Get. If I can recover him and keep him tame and get to Naples with him *Tempest* ii 2 71
I'll fish for thee and get thee wood enough ii 2 165
I'll get the Young scamels from the rock. Wilt thou go with me? ii 2 175
'Ban, 'Ban, Cacaliban Has a new master: get a new man ii 2 189
Thou shalt never get such a secret from me but by a parable.—'Tis well that I get it so *T. G. of Ver.* ii 5 40
By seven o'clock I'll get you such a ladder iii 1 126
Let me see thy cloak: I'll get me one of such another length iii 1 133
If that be all the difference in his love, I'll get me such a colour'd periwig iv 4 196
What he gets more of her than sharp words, let it lie on my head *M. W.* ii 1 190
I warrant you, they could never get an eye-wink of her ii 2 72
They could never get her so much as sip on a cup with the proudest of them all ii 2 76
I see I cannot get thy father's love iii 4 1
Go get us properties And tricking for our fairies iv 4 78
I'll do what I can to get you a pair of horns v 1 7
Happy thou art not; For what thou hast not, still thou strivest to get, And what thou hast, forget'st *Meas. for Meas.* iii 1 22
I commend you to your own content.—He that commends me to mine own content Commends me to the thing I cannot get *Com. of Errors* i 2 34
An you use these blows long, I must get a sconce for my head ii 2 37
Either get thee from the door or sit down at the hatch iii 1 33
Sir knave! go get you from the door iii 1 64
There is something in the wind, that we cannot get in iii 1 69
Get you home And fetch the chain iii 1 114
Hold you still: I'll fetch my sister, to get her good will iii 2 70
I will not stay to-night . . . ; Therefore away, to get our stuff aboard iv 4 162
Some get within him, take his sword away v 1 34
Once did I get him bound and sent him home v 1 145
Alas! he gets nothing by that *Much Ado* i 1 65
Prove that ever I lose more blood with love than I will get again with drinking i 1 253
Such a man would win any woman in the world, if a' could get her good-will ii 1 18
Thou wilt never get thee a husband, if thou be so shrewd of thy tongue ii 1 20
Get you to heaven, Beatrice, get you to heaven; here's no place for you maids ii 1 47
And cry heigh-ho for a husband!—Lady Beatrice, I will get you one ii 1 334
If I do not love her, I am a Jew. I will go get her picture ii 3 273
Call at all the ale-houses, and bid those that are drunk get them to bed iii 3 45
Get you some of this distilled Carduus Benedictus iii 4 73
Only get the learned writer to set down our excommunication iii 5 68
Prince, thou art sad; get thee a wife v 4 124
Then will she get the upshoot by cleaving the pin *L. L. Lost* iv 1 138
If you my favour mean to get, A twelvemonth shall you spend v 2 830
If I had wit enough to get out of this wood, I have enough *M. N. Dream* iii 1 153
Tell me then that he is well.—An if I could, what should I get therefore? iii 2 78
Get you your weapons in your hand, and kill me a red-hipped humble-bee iv 1 10
I will get Peter Quince to write a ballad of this dream iv 1 220
Get your apparel together, good strings to your beards iv 2 35
I cannot get a service, no; I have ne'er a tongue in my head *M. of Ven.* ii 2 165
If a Christian did not play the knave and get thee, I am much deceived ii 3 12
Who chooseth me shall get as much as he deserves ii 7 7
I may be married too.—With all my heart, so thou canst get a wife iii 2 197
I shall grow jealous of you shortly, Launcelot, if you thus get my wife into corners.—Nay, you need not fear us iii 5 32
I'll see if I can get my husband's ring iv 2 13
Get you with him, you old dog.—Is 'old dog' my reward? *As Y. Like It* i 1 85
Dispatch you with your safest haste And get you from our court i 3 44
Let's away, And get our jewels and our wealth together i 3 136
Seeking the food he eats And pleased with what he gets ii 5 43
I earn that I eat, get that I wear, owe no man hate iii 2 78
Get you to church, and have a good priest that can tell you what marriage is iii 3 86
What's that, I pray?—Marry, sir, to get a husband for her sister *T. of S.* i 1 123
Happy man be his dole! He that runs fastest gets the ring i 1 145
He took some care To get her cunning schoolmasters to instruct her i 1 192
I bade the rascal knock upon your gate And could not get him for my heart to do it i 2 38
Then tell me, if I get your daughter's love, What dowry shall I have? ii 1 120
Supposed Lucentio Must get a father, call'd 'supposed Vincentio' ii 1 410
Fathers commonly Do get their children; but in this case of wooing, A child shall get a sire ii 1 412
Son unto Vincentio of Pisa, 'Sigeia tellus,' disguised thus to get your love iii 1 33
I am to get a man,—whate'er he be, It skills not much iii 2 133
Get me some repast: I care not what, so it be wholesome food iv 3 15
You shall have the mustard, Or else you get no beef of Grumio iv 3 28
Your commendations, madam, get from her tears *All's Well* i 1 53
Get thee a good husband, and use him as he uses thee i 1 229
When thou canst get the ring upon my finger which never shall come off iii 2 59
Prithee, get thee further v 2 15
Get you to your lord; I cannot love him *T. Night* i 5 298
One more, Cesario, Get thee to yond same sovereign cruelty ii 4 83
Get ye all three into the box-tree ii 5 18
'Odours,' 'pregnant' and 'vouchsafed:' I'll get 'em all three all ready iii 1 102
Get him to say his prayers, good Sir Toby, get him to pray iii 4 131
Therefore, get you on and give him his desire iii 4 270
These wise men that give fools money get themselves a good report iv 1 23
Get him to bed, and let his hurt be look'd to v 1 214
Go, get aboard; Look to thy bark: I'll not be long *W. Tale* iii 3 7
I think it not uneasy to get the cause of my son's resort thither iv 2 56
Of that kind Our rustic garden's barren; and I care not To get slips of them iv 4 85
That you may—For I do fear eyes over—to shipboard Get undescried iv 4 669
Why, being younger born, Doth he lay claim to thine inheritance?—I know not why, except to get the land *K. John* i 1 73
Well, sir, by this you cannot get my land i 1 97
How if my brother, Who, as you say, took pains to get this son, Had of your father claim'd this son for his? i 1 121
My mother's son did get your father's heir i 1 128
Of no more force to dispossess me, sir, Than was his will to get me i 1 133
Sir Robert could do well: marry, to confess, Could he get me? i 1 237
By this light, were I to get again, Madam, I would not wish a better father i 1 259
If I get down, and do not break my limbs, I'll find a thousand shifts to get away iv 3 6
Sirrah, get thee to Plashy, to my sister Gloucester *Richard II.* ii 2 90
They well deserve to have, That know the strong'st and surest way to get iii 3 201
Get. Mount thee upon his horse; Spur post, and get before him to the king *Richard II.* v 2 112
Get thee before to Coventry; fill me a bottle of sack *1 Hen. IV.* iv 2 1
He walk'd o'er perils, on an edge, More likely to fall in than to get o'er *2 Hen. IV.* i 1 171
Get posts and letters, and make friends with speed i 1 214
I will sooner have a beard grow in the palm of my hand than he shall get one on his cheek i 2 25
An I could get me but a wife in the stews, I were manned, horsed, and wived i 2 59
I can get no remedy against this consumption of the purse i 2 264
Is't such a matter to get a pottle-pot's maidenhead? ii 2 83
Get you down stairs.—Here's a goodly tumult! ii 4 218
And then, when they marry, they get wenches iv 3 101
I thee defy again. O hound of Crete, think'st thou my spouse to get? *Hen. V.* ii 1 77
Get you therefore hence, Poor miserable wretches, to your death ii 2 177
Gets him to rest, cramm'd with distressful bread iv 1 287
And patches will I get unto these cudgell'd scars, And swear I got them in the Gallia wars v 1 93
If ever thou beest mine, Kate, as I have a saving faith within me tells me thou shalt, I get thee with scambling v 2 217
Swift-winged with desire to get a grave *1 Hen. VI.* ii 5 15
I would see his heart out, ere the priest Should ever get that privilege of me iii 1 121
Let's get us from the walls; For Talbot means no goodness by his looks iii 2 71
Either to get the town again or die iii 2 79
We mourn, France smiles; we lose, they daily get; All 'long of this vile traitor iv 3 32
Ye familiar spirits, . . . Help me this once, that France may get the field v 3 12
Go, get you to my house; I will reward you for this venturous deed *2 Hen. VI.* iii 2 8
This get I by his death: ay me, unhappy! To be a queen, and crown'd with infamy! iii 2 70
Come, and get thee a sword, though made of a lath iv 2 1
But get you to Smithfield and gather head iv 5 10
To France, to France, and get what you have lost iv 8 51
Thou wilt betray me, and get a thousand crowns of the king iv 10 29
We shall to London get, where you are loved v 2 81
Then get your husband's lands, to do them good *3 Hen. VI.* iii 2 40
What love, think'st thou, I sue so much to get? iii 2 61
And yet I know not how to get the crown, For many lives stand between me and home iii 2 172
Can I do this, and cannot get a crown? iii 2 194
He could gnaw a crust at two hours old: 'Twas full two years ere I could get a tooth *Richard III.* ii 4 29
My husband lost his life to get the crown iii 4 57
Get a prayer-book in your hand, And stand betwixt two churchmen iii 7 47
If your back Cannot vouchsafe this burthen, 'tis too weak Ever to get a boy.—How you do talk! *Hen. VIII.* ii 3 44
Go, get thee from me, Cromwell; I am a poor fall'n man iii 2 412
How got they in, and be hang'd?—Alas, I know not; how gets the tide in? v 4 18
Never, before This happy child, did I get any thing v 5 66
Come in, come in: I'll go get a fire *Troi. and Cres.* iii 2 62
If my lord get a boy of you, you'll give him me iii 2 112
Unless the fiddler Apollo get his sinews to make catlings on iii 3 305
I'll potch at him some way Or wrath or craft may get him *Coriolanus* i 10 16
Would return for conscience sake, to help to get thee a wife ii 3 37
Go, get you to your house; be gone, away! iii 1 230
I cannot get him out o' the house: prithee, call my master to him iv 5 22
As for thee, boy, go get thee from my sight *T. Andron.* iii 1 284
Or get some little knife between thy teeth, And just against thy heart make thou a hole iii 2 16
I will go get a leaf of brass, And with a gad of steel will write these words iv 1 102
First hang the child, that he may see it sprawl; . . . Get me a ladder v 1 53
Gentle Paris, get her heart, My will to her consent is but a part *R. and J.* i 2 16
Get thee to thy love, as was decreed, Ascend her chamber iii 3 146
Get thee to church o' Thursday, Or never after look me in the face iii 5 162
Farewell: buy food, and get thyself in flesh v 1 84
I could not send it,—here it is again,—Nor get a messenger to bring it thee v 2 15
Get me an iron crow, and bring it straight Unto my cell v 2 21
Every man has his fault, and honesty is his: I ha' told him on't, but I could ne'er get him from't *T. of Athens* iii 1 30
If he covetously reserve it, how shall's get it? iv 3 408
Why dost thou lead these men about the streets?—Truly, sir, to wear out their shoes, to get myself into more work *J. Cæsar* i 1 34
Get me a taper in my study, Lucius: When it is lighted, come and call me ii 1 7
I'll get me to a place more void ii 4 37
Thy heart is big, get thee apart and weep. Passion, I see, is catching iii 1 282
Pindarus, get higher on that hill; My sight was ever thick v 3 20
Go get him surgeons. Who comes here?—The worthy thane of Ross *Macb.* i 2 44
Thou shalt get kings, though thou be none i 3 67
Go get some water, And wash this filthy witness from your hand ii 2 46
How will you live?—As birds do, mother.—What, with worms and flies?—With what I get iv 2 33
Of all men else I have avoided thee: But get thee back v 8 5
Get from him why he puts on this confusion *Hamlet* iii 1 2
Get thee to a nunnery: why wouldst thou be a breeder of sinners? iii 1 122
Get thee to a nunnery, go: farewell. Or, if thou wilt needs marry, marry a fool iii 1 142
They are coming to the play; I must be idle: Get you a place iii 2 96
You shall see anon how the murderer gets the love of Gonzago's wife iii 2 275
Get me a fellowship in a cry of players, sir iii 2 288
Where the dead body is bestow'd, my lord, We cannot get from him iv 3 13
Go, get thee to Yaughan: fetch me a stoup of liquor v 1 67
Get you to my lady's chamber, and tell her, let her paint an inch thick v 1 212
Let me not stay a jot for dinner; go get it ready *Lear* i 4 8
Our flesh and blood is grown so vile, my lord, That it doth hate what gets it iii 4 151
Get horses for your mistress iii 7 20
Let's follow the old earl, and get the Bedlam To lead him where he would iii 7 103
Get thee glass eyes; And, like a scurvy politician, seem To see the things thou dost not iv 6 174
Nay, if you get it, you shall get it with running iv 6 206
Get more tapers; Raise all my kindred *Othello* i 1 167

Get. I can discover him, if you please To get good guard and go along *Oth.* i 1 180
Get weapons, ho! And raise some special officers of night . . . i 1 182
I had rather to adopt a child than get it . . . . . . i 3 191
Let me see now: To get his place and to plume up my will In double knavery—How, how?—Let's see . . . . i 3 399
Get me some poison, Iago; this night: I'll not expostulate with her . iv 1 216
Some cogging, cozening slave, to get some office . . . . iv 2 132
I am not valiant neither, But every puny whipster gets my sword . v 2 244
I shall break The cause of our expedience to the queen, And get her leave to part . . . . *Ant. and Cleo.* i 2 186
Get me ink and paper: He shall have every day a several greeting . i 5 76
Cæsar gets money where He loses hearts . . . . ii 1 13
Get thee back to Cæsar. Tell him thy entertainment . . . iii 13 139
Yet ha' we A brain that nourishes our nerves, and can Get goal for goal of youth . . . . iv 8 22
Those things I bid you do, get them dispatch'd . . . *Cymbeline* i 3 39
If I could get this foolish Imogen, I should have gold enough . . ii 3 9
O, get thee from my sight; Thou gavest me poison . . . . . v 5 236
If I can get him within my pistol's length, I'll make him sure enough *Pericles* i 1 168
Gets more with begging than we can do with working . . . . ii 1 68
What a man cannot get, he may lawfully deal for—his wife's soul . . ii 1 120
Her reason to herself is only known, Which yet from her by no means can I get . . . . ii 5 6
Get fire and meat for these poor men . . . . iii 2 3
Lend me your hands; to the next chamber bear her. Get linen . . iii 2 109
Marina gets All praises, which are paid as debts, And not as given iv Gower 33
Is it a shame to get when we are old? . . . . iv 2 32
Get this done as I command you.—Performance shall follow . . . iv 2 66
We must either get her ravished, or be rid of her . . . . . iv 6 5
Get access. May we not get access to her, my lord? . . . . ii 5 7
Get clear. How to get clear of all the debts I owe . . *Mer. of Venice* i 1 134
Get ground. If they get ground and vantage of the king, Then join you with them . . . . 2 *Hen. IV.* ii 3 53
With five times so much conversation, I should get ground of your fair mistress . . . . *Cymbeline* i 4 114
Get on thy boots: we'll ride all night . . . . . . 2 *Hen. IV.* v 3 137
Get on your cloak, and haste you to Lord Timon . . *T. of Athens* ii 1 15
Get on your nightgown, lest occasion call us . . . *Macbeth* ii 2 70
Gets possession. For slander lives upon succession, For ever housed where it gets possession . . . . *Com. of Errors* iii 1 106
Get the better. And I will strive with things impossible; Yea, get the better of them . . . . *J. Cæsar* ii 1 326
Get the start. It doth amaze me A man of such a feeble temper should So get the start of the majestic world . . . . i 2 130
Get the sun. But be first advised, In conflict that you get the sun of them . . . . *L. L. Lost* iv 3 369
Get thee away.—Many a man would take you at your word *Com. of Errors* i 2 16
Get thee away, and take Thy beagles with thee . . . *T. of Athens* iv 3 174
Get thee gone. Go get thee gone; fetch me an iron crow *Com. of Errors* iii 1 84
Get thee gone; Buy thou a rope and bring it home to me . . . iv 1 19
Hence, get thee gone, and follow me no more . . . *M. N. Dream* ii 1 194
Waste no time in words, But get thee gone . . . *Mer. of Venice* iii 4 55
Send the deed after me, And I will sign it.—Get thee gone, but to it . iv 1 397
Dally not with the gods, but get thee gone . . . *T. of Shrew* iv 4 68
Envenom him with words, or get thee gone And leave those woes alone *K. John* iii 1 63
Get thee gone; for I do see Danger and disobedience in thine eye 1 *Hen. IV.* i 3 15
What! canst thou not forbear me half an hour? Then get thee gone and dig my grave thyself . . . . 2 *Hen. IV.* iv 5 111
So, get thee gone, that I may know my grief . . . 2 *Hen. VI.* iii 2 346
Thou hast spoke too much already: get thee gone . . 3 *Hen. VI.* i 1 258
Get thee gone; I see thou art not for my company . . *T. Andron.* iii 2 57
Get thee gone, And hire those horses; I'll be with thee straight *Rom. and Jul.* v 1 32
I prithee, beat thy drum, and get thee gone . . . *T. of Athens* iv 3 96
Run to the senate-house; Stay not to answer me, but get thee gone *Jul. Cæsar* ii 4 2
Get thee gone: to-morrow We'll hear, ourselves, again . . *Macbeth* iii 4 31
Get thee gone; good night. Mine eyes do itch; Doth that bode weeping? . . . . *Othello* iv 3 58
Get thee gone: Say to Ventidius I would speak with him *Ant. and Cleo.* ii 3 30
Get thee hence, and find my dog again, Or ne'er return again *T. G. of V.* iv 4 64
O Dorset, speak not to me, get thee hence! . . . *Richard III.* iv 1 39
I dare no longer stay.—Go, get thee hence, for I will not away *R. and J.* v 3 160
Go, get thee hence: Hadst thou Narcissus in thy face, to me Thou wouldst appear most ugly . . . . *Ant. and Cleo.* ii 5 95
Get thee in.—What, will you not suffer me? . . . *T. of Shrew* ii 1 30
Prithee, get thee in: would thou hadst ne'er been born! *Troi. and Cres.* iv 2 89
In, boy; go first. You houseless poverty,—Nay, get thee in . . *Lear* iii 4 27
Get thee to bed, and rest; for thou hast need . . *Rom. and Jul.* iv 3 13
Get thee to bed. Is this a dagger which I see? . . . *Macbeth* ii 1 32
'Tis now struck twelve; get thee to bed, Francisco . . . *Hamlet* i 1 7
Get up. I think I am as like to ride the mare, if I have any vantage of ground to get up . . . . 2 *Hen. IV.* ii 1 85
You i' the camlet, get up o' the rail . . . . . . *Hen. VIII.* v 4 93
Get you away. Pray, get you out.—Away!—Away! get you away *Cor.* iv 5 16
Get you away; I'll send for you anon . . . . . *Othello* iv 1 269
Get you gone. Go get you gone, and let the papers lie . *T. G. of Ver.* i 2 100
Take no repulse, whatever she doth say; For 'get you gone,' she doth not mean 'away!' . . . . iii 1 101
Get you gone, and let me hear no more of you . . *Meas. for Meas.* ii 1 216
Why, get you gone: who is't that hinders you?—A foolish heart *M. N. Dream* iii 2 318
What does this knave here? Get you gone, sirrah . . . *All's Well* i 3 8
Get you gone, And do as I have bid you . . . . . *Hen. VIII.* v 1 155
Now, pray, sir, get you gone: You have done a brave deed *Coriolanus* iv 2 37
So, trouble me no more, but get you gone . . . *T. Andron.* i 1 367
Well, get you gone: o' Thursday be it, then . . . *Rom. and Jul.* iii 4 30
Get you gone, be strong and prosperous In this resolve . . . iv 1 122
Get you gone: Put on a most importunate aspect . . *T. of Athens* ii 1 27
Get you gone; And hasten your return . . . . . . *Lear* i 4 362
Get you hence. *T. of Shrew* iv 1; *Hen. V.* i 2; 2 *Hen. VI.* iii 2; *Coriolanus* ii 3
If without more words you will get you hence . . . *T. of Shrew* i 2 232
Get you hence, for I must go Where it fits not you to know . *W. Tale* iv 4 303
Get you hence, sirrah; saucy fellow, hence! . . . *J. Cæsar* iv 3 134
Get you in again; Comfort my sister, cheer her, call her wife *Com. of Er.* iii 2 25
Well, sir, get you in: I will not long be troubled with you *As Y. Like It* i 1 80
Get you in. That I may soon make good What I have said, Bianca, get you in . . . . *T. of Shrew* i 1 75
I am offended with you: Upon the love you bear me, get you in *Troi. and Cres.* v 3 78
Get you to bed; faith, you'll be sick to-morrow . . *Rom. and Jul.* iv 4 7
Get you to bed again; it is not day . . . . . . *J. Cæsar* ii 1 39
Get you to bed on the instant; I will be returned forthwith . *Othello* iv 3 7
And then with what haste you can get you to bed . . . *Pericles* ii 5 93
Get your living. It were pity you should get your living by reckoning, sir . . . . *L. L. Lost* v 2 497
To offer to get your living by the copulation of cattle . *As Y. Like It* iii 2 84
Getter. Peace is a very apoplexy, . . . a getter of more bastard children than war's a destroyer of men . . . . . . *Coriolanus* iv 5 240
Gettest. If Percy be alive, thou get'st not my sword . . 1 *Hen. IV.* v 3 52
If thou gettest any leave of me, hang me; if thou takest leave, thou wert better be hanged . . . . 2 *Hen. IV.* i 2 100
Getting. It is for getting Madam Julietta with child . *Meas. for Meas.* i 2 73
Ere he would have hanged a man for the getting a hundred bastards, he would have paid for the nursing a thousand . . . . iii 2 125
I was once before him for getting a wench with child . . . . iv 3 179
I would rather have one of your father's getting . . . *Much Ado* ii 1 336
I shall answer that better to the commonwealth than you can the getting up of the negro's belly . . . . . . *Mer. of Venice* iii 5 41
'Tis none of his own getting . . . . *As Y. Like It* iii 3 56
That's the loss of men, though it be the getting of children . *All's Well* iii 2 44
He was whipped for getting the shrieve's fool with child . . . iv 3 212
For there is nothing in the between but getting wenches with child *W. Tale* iii 3 62
Though he were unsatisfied in getting, Which was a sin . *Hen. VIII.* iv 2 55
Have I my pillow left unpress'd in Rome, Forborne the getting of a lawful race, And by a gem of women? . . . . *Ant. and Cleo.* iii 13 107
Ghastly. Wherefore this ghastly looking?—What's the matter? *Tempest* ii 1 309
Let grievous, ghastly, gaping wounds Untwine the Sisters Three! 2 *Hen. IV.* ii 4 212
Staring full ghastly like a strangled man . . . . 2 *Hen. VI.* iii 2 170
So full of ugly sights, of ghastly dreams . . . . *Richard III.* i 4 3
Ghastly looks Are at my service, like enforced smiles . . . . iii 5 8
A hundred ghastly women, Transformed with their fear . . *J. Cæsar* i 3 23
Ghost. Her brother's ghost his paved bed would break . *Meas. for Meas.* v 1 440
Ægeon art thou not? or else his ghost? . . . . *Com. of Errors* v 1 337
Ghosts, wandering here and there, Troop home to churchyards *M. N. Dream* iii 2 381
Were I the ghost that walk'd, I'ld bid you mark Her eye . . *W. Tale* v 1 63
But she shall be such As, walk'd your first queen's ghost, it should take joy To see her in your arms . . . . v 1 80
He will look as hollow as a ghost . . . . . . *K. John* iii 4 84
Some haunted by the ghosts they have deposed; Some poison'd by their wives . . . . *Richard II.* iii 2 158
Never, O never, do his ghost the wrong To hold your honour more precise and nice With others than with him! . . . . 2 *Hen. IV.* ii 3 39
Presenteth them unto the gazing moon So many horrid ghosts *Hen. V.* iv Prol. 28
Henry the Fifth, thy ghost I invocate: Prosper this realm! . 1 *Hen. VI.* i 1 52
If Henry were recall'd to life again, These news would cause him once more yield the ghost . . . . i 1 67
The famish'd English, like pale ghosts, Faintly besiege us . . . i 2 7
I think this upstart is old Talbot's ghost . . . . iv 7 87
I trust the ghost of Talbot is not there: Now he is gone, my lord, you need not fear . . . . v 2 16
And spirits walk and ghosts break up their graves . . 2 *Hen. VI.* i 4 22
Oft have I seen a timely-parted ghost, Of ashy semblance . . . iii 2 161
I'll cope with thee And do some service to Duke Humphrey's ghost . iii 2 231
Sometime he talks as if Duke Humphrey's ghost Were by his side . iii 2 373
The noble gentleman gave up the ghost . . . . . 3 *Hen. VI.* ii 3 22
Be it lawful that I invocate thy ghost! . . . . . *Richard III.* i 2 8
And often did I strive To yield the ghost: but still the envious flood Kept in my soul . . . . i 4 37
Why, what should you fear?—Marry, my uncle Clarence' angry ghost . iii 1 144
Blind sight, dead life, poor mortal living ghost . . . . . iv 4 26
O, look! methinks I see my cousin's ghost . . . *Rom. and Jul.* iv 3 55
Why all these fires, why all these gliding ghosts . . . *J. Cæsar* i 3 63
Dying men did groan, And ghosts did shriek and squeal about the streets . . . . ii 2 24
Their shadows seem A canopy most fatal, under which Our army lies, ready to give up the ghost . . . . v 1 89
The ghost of Cæsar hath appear'd to me Two several times by night . v 5 17
Towards his design Moves like a ghost . . . . . *Macbeth* ii 1 56
If thou be'st slain and with no stroke of mine, My wife and children's ghosts will haunt me still . . . . v 7 16
Still am I call'd. Unhand me, gentlemen. By heaven, I'll make a ghost of him that lets me! . . . . *Hamlet* i 4 85
Alas, poor ghost!—Pity me not, but lend thy serious hearing . . i 5 4
Remember thee! Ay, thou poor ghost, while memory holds a seat In this distracted globe. Remember thee! . . . . i 5 96
There needs no ghost, my lord, come from the grave To tell us this . i 5 125
Touching this vision here, It is an honest ghost, that let me tell you . i 5 138
It is a damned ghost that we have seen, And my imaginations are as foul As Vulcan's stithy . . . . iii 2 87
I'll take the ghost's word for a thousand pound . . . . . iii 2 297
Vex not his ghost: O, let him pass! . . . . *Lear* v 3 313
Where souls do couch on flowers, we'll hand in hand, And with our sprightly port make the ghosts gaze . . . . . *Ant. and Cleo.* iv 14 52
Ghost unlaid forbear thee!—Nothing ill come near thee! . *Cymbeline* iv 2 278
Help; Or we poor ghosts will cry To the shining synod of the rest . v 4 88
Hush! How dare you ghosts Accuse the thunderer? . . . . v 4 94
Ghosted. Since Julius Cæsar, Who at Philippi the good Brutus ghosted *Ant. and Cleo.* ii 6 13
Ghostly. Here comes your ghostly father: do we jest now? *M. for M.* iv 3 51
Friar Lodowick.—A ghostly father, belike . . . . . . v 1 126
The ghostly father now hath done his shrift . . . 3 *Hen. VI.* iii 2 107
Hence will I to my ghostly father's cell, His help to crave *Rom. and Jul.* ii 2 189
Wast thou with Rosaline?—With Rosaline, my ghostly father? no . ii 3 45
Good even to my ghostly confessor . . . . ii 6 21
Being a divine, a ghostly confessor, A sin-absolver . . . . . iii 3 49
Giant. It is excellent To have a giant's strength; but it is tyrannous To use it like a giant . . . . *Meas. for Meas.* ii 2 108
The poor beetle, that we tread upon, In corporal sufferance finds a pang as great As when a giant dies . . . . iii 1 81
He is then a giant to an ape; but then is an ape a doctor to such a man *Much Ado* v 1 205
Some mollification for your giant, sweet lady . . . . *T. Night* i 5 218

Giant. Old sir Robert's son? Colbrand the giant, that same mighty man? *K. John* i 1 225
Those baby eyes That never saw the giant world enraged . . . v 2 57
Sirrah, you giant, what says the doctor to my water? . . *2 Hen. IV.* i 2 1
Put the world's whole strength Into one giant arm, it shall not force This lineal honour from me. . . . . iv 5 45
A giant traitor! . . . . *Hen. VIII.* i 2 199
The baby figure of the giant mass Of things to come at large *Tr. and Cr.* i 3 345
A stirring dwarf we do allowance give Before a sleeping giant . ii 3 147
Like a giant's robe Upon a dwarfish thief. . . . . *Macbeth* v 2 21
There's my gauntlet; I'll prove it on a giant . . . . *Lear* iv 6 91
The gates of monarchs Are arch'd so high that giants may jet through *Cymbeline* iii 3 5
Giant-dwarf. This senior-junior, giant-dwarf, Dan Cupid . *L. L. Lost* iii 1 182
Giantess. I had rather be a giantess, and lie under Mount Pelion *M. W.* ii 1 81
Giant-like. That same cowardly, giant-like ox-beef hath devoured many a gentleman of your house . . . . . *M. N. Dream* iii 1 197
What is the cause, Laertes, That thy rebellion looks so giant-like? *Ham.* iv 5 121
Giant-rude. Women's gentle brain Could not drop forth such giant-rude invention . . . . *As Y. Like It* iv 3 34
Gib. Who, that's but a queen, fair, sober, wise, Would from a paddock, from a bat, a gib, Such dear concernings hide? . . *Hamlet* iii 4 190
Gibber. The sheeted dead Did squeak and gibber in the Roman streets . i 1 116
Gibbet. At a word, hang no more about me, I am no gibbet for you *Mer. Wives* ii 2 17
Unloaded all the gibbets and pressed the dead bodies . *1 Hen. IV.* iv 2 40
Come off and on swifter than he that gibbets on the brewer's bucket *2 Hen. IV.* iii 2 282
Grease that's sweaten From the murderer's gibbet throw Into the flame *Macbeth* iv 1 66
Rather make My country's high pyramides my gibbet! . *Ant. and Cleo.* v 2 61
Unless a man would marry a gallows and beget young gibbets, I never saw one so prone . . . . *Cymbeline* v 4 207
Gibbet-maker. What says Jupiter?—O, the gibbet-maker! he says that he hath taken them down . . . . . . *T. Andron.* iv 3 80
Gib cat. I am as melancholy as a gib cat or a lugged bear . *1 Hen. IV.* i 2 83
Gibe. A lousy knave, to have his gibes and his mockeries! *Mer. Wives* iii 3 259
You are wise and full of gibes and vlouting-stocks . . . . iv 5 82
Where be your gibes now? your gambols? your songs? . . *Hamlet* v 1 209
And mark the fleers, the gibes, and notable scorns, That dwell in every region of his face . . . . *Othello* iv 1 83
With taunts Did gibe my missive out of audience . . *Ant. and Cleo.* ii 2 74
Ready in gibes, quick-answer'd, saucy . . . . . *Cymbeline* iii 4 161
Giber. You are well understood to be a perfecter giber for the table than a necessary bencher in the Capitol . . . . . *Coriolanus* ii 1 91
Gibing. Why, that's the way to choke a gibing spirit . . *L. L. Lost* v 2 868
To laugh at gibing boys . . . . *1 Hen. IV.* iii 2 66
Gibingly. Which most gibingly, ungravely, he did fashion After the inveterate hate he bears you . . . . . . *Coriolanus* ii 3 233
Giddily. How giddily a' [fashion] turns about all the hot bloods between fourteen and five-and-thirty . . . . . . *Much Ado* iii 3 140
Prizes not quantity of dirty lands; The parts that fortune hath bestow'd upon her, Tell her, I hold as giddily as fortune . . *T. Night* ii 4 87
Giddiness. Neither call the giddiness of it in question . *As Y. Like It* v 2 6
Giddy. Art not thou thyself giddy with the fashion too? . *Much Ado* iii 3 150
For man is a giddy thing, and this is my conclusion . . . . v 4 109
Giddy in spirit, still gazing in a doubt . . . *Mer. of Venice* iii 2 145
I am not a woman, to be touched with so many giddy offences *As Y. Like It* iii 2 367
More giddy in my desires than a monkey . . . . . . iv 1 153
Am starved for meat, giddy for lack of sleep . . *T. of Shrew* iv 3 9
He that is giddy thinks the world turns round . . . . . v 2 20
Our [men's] fancies are more giddy and unfirm, More longing, wavering *T. Night* ii 4 34
Arm . . . thy nobler parts Against these giddy loose suggestions *K. John* iii 1 292
Thou hast made me giddy With these ill tidings . . . . . iv 2 131
Go, ye giddy goose . . . . *1 Hen. IV.* iii 1 232
An habitation giddy and unsure Hath he that buildeth on the vulgar heart. O thou fond many! . . . . *2 Hen. IV.* i 3 89
Upon the high and giddy mast Seal up the ship-boy's eyes . . iii 1 18
And now my sight fails, and my brain is giddy . . . . iv 4 110
Be it thy course to busy giddy minds With foreign quarrels . . iv 5 214
The Scot, Who hath been still a giddy neighbour to us . . *Hen. V.* i 2 145
A vain, giddy, shallow, humorous youth . . . . ii 4 28
And giddy Fortune's furious fickle wheel. . . . . iii 6 29
That many have their giddy brains knock'd out . . *1 Hen. VI.* iii 1 83
See how the giddy multitude do point, And nod their heads! *2 Hen. VI.* ii 4 21
And many giddy people flock to him . . . . . *3 Hen. VI.* iv 8 5
As we paced along Upon the giddy footing of the hatches *Richard III.* i 4 17
I am giddy; expectation whirls me round . . . *Troi. and Cres.* iii 2 19
And giddy censure Will then cry out . . . . . *Coriolanus* i 1 272
With the shadow of his wings He can at pleasure stint their melody: Even so mayst thou the giddy men of Rome . . . *T. Andron.* iv 4 87
To scatter and disperse the giddy Goths . . . . v 2 78
Turn giddy, and be holp by backward turning. . . *Rom. and Jul.* i 2 48
Giddy-paced. Of these most brisk and giddy-paced times . *T. Night* ii 4 6
Gift. Here, afore Heaven, I ratify this my rich gift . . *Tempest* iv 1 8
As my gift and thine own acquisition Worthily purchased, take my daughter . . . . iv 1 13
Win her with gifts, if she respect not words . . . *T. G. of Ver.* iii 1 89
Too true, too holy, To be corrupted with my worthless gifts . . . iv 2 6
A dog as big as ten of yours, and therefore the gift the greater . . iv 4 62
I thank your grace; the gift hath made me happy . . . . v 4 148
I know the young gentlewoman; she has good gifts . . *Mer. Wives* i 1 64
Seven hundred pounds and possibilities is goot gifts . . . . . i 1 66
Coach after coach, letter after letter, gift after gift . . . . ii 2 67
I'll have my brains ta'en out and buttered, and give them to a dog for a new-year's gift . . . . iii 5 9
With such gifts that heaven shall share with you . . *Meas. for Meas.* ii 2 147
He would not, but by gift of my chaste body To his concupiscible intemperate lust, Release my brother . . . . v 1 97
I see a man here needs not live by shifts, When in the streets he meets such golden gifts . . . . *Com. of Errors* iii 2 188
A very dull fool; only his gift is in devising impossible slanders *M. Ado* ii 1 143
To be a well-favoured man is the gift of fortune . . . . . iii 3 15
He comes too short of you.—Gifts that God gives . . . . . iii 5 47
And what have I to give you back, whose worth May counterpoise this rich and precious gift? . . . . iv 1 29
This is a gift that I have, simple, simple; a foolish extravagant spirit *L. L. Lost* iv 2 67

Gift. The gift is good in those in whom it is acute, and I am thankful for it *L. L. Lost* iv 2 73
The armipotent Mars, of lances the almighty, Gave Hector a gift . v 2 651
I was never curst; I have no gift at all in shrewishness *M. N. Dream* iii 2 301
Besides commends and courteous breath, Gifts of rich value *Mer. of Ven.* ii 9 91
That he do record a gift, Here in the court, of all he dies possess'd . iv 1 388
Clerk, draw a deed of gift . . . . iv 1 394
That 'scuse serves many men to save their gifts . . . . . . iv 1 444
You were to blame, I must be plain with you, To part so slightly with your wife's first gift . . . . v 1 167
I give to you and Jessica, From the rich Jew, a special deed of gift . v 1 292
Let us sit and mock the good housewife Fortune from her wheel, that her gifts may henceforth be bestowed equally . . *As Y. Like It* i 2 35
The bountiful blind woman doth most mistake in her gifts to women . i 2 39
Fortune reigns in gifts of the world, not in the lineaments of Nature . i 2 44
If ladies be but young and fair, They have the gift to know it . . ii 7 38
Heaven would that she these gifts should have . . . . . iii 2 161
I will not take her on gift of any man . . . . iii 3 69
A woman's gift To rain a shower of commanded tears . . *T. of Shrew* Ind. 1 124
Your gifts are so good, here's none will hold you . . . . . i 1 107
Neighbour, this is a gift very grateful, I am sure of it . . . ii 1 76
Her dispositions she inherits, which makes fair gifts fairer . *All's Well* i 1 47
The gift doth stretch itself as 'tis received, And is enough for both . ii 1 4
Wherein the honour Of my dear father's gift stands chief in power . ii 1 115
A second time receive The confirmation of my promised gift . . . ii 3 56
Here, take her hand, Proud scornful boy, unworthy this good gift . ii 3 158
His present gift Shall furnish me to those Italian fields . . . ii 3 306
And hath all the good gifts of nature . . . . . . *T. Night* i 3 29
He hath the gift of a coward to allay the gust he hath in quarrelling . i 3 32
'Tis thought among the prudent he would quickly have the gift of a grave . . . . i 3 34
Wherefore have these gifts a curtain before 'em? . . . . . i 3 134
Their encounters, though not personal, have been royally attorneyed with interchange of gifts, letters, loving embassies . . *W. Tale* i 1 31
The gifts she looks from me are pack'd and lock'd Up in my heart . iv 4 369
Of Nature's gifts thou mayst with lilies boast . . . . *K. John* iii 1 53
Laid gifts before him, proffer'd him their oaths . . *1 Hen. IV.* iv 3 71
I, that have not well the gift of tongue . . . . v 2 78
All the other gifts appertinent to man . . . . . *2 Hen. IV.* i 2 194
By gift of heaven, By law of nature and of nations . . . *Hen. V.* ii 4 79
He perforce must do thee right, because he hath not the gift to woo in other places . . . . v 2 162
As liking of the lady's virtuous gifts, Her beauty . . *1 Hen. VI.* v 1 43
Her virtues graced with external gifts Do breed love's settled passions . v 5 3
The happiest gift that ever marquess gave . . . . *2 Hen. VI.* i 1 15
Prayers and tears have moved me, gifts could never . . . . iv 7 73
Large gifts have I bestow'd on learned clerks . . . . . . iv 7 76
Is not a dukedom, sir, a goodly gift?—Ay, by my faith . . *3 Hen. VI.* v 1 31
I'll do thee service for so good a gift . . . . v 1 33
'Twas I that gave the kingdom to thy brother.—Why then 'tis mine, if but by Warwick's gift.—Thou art no Atlas for so great a weight: And, weakling, Warwick takes his gift again . . . . v 1 35
A greater gift than that I'll give my cousin.—A greater gift! *Rich. III.* iii 1 115
O, then, I see, you will part but with light gifts . . . . . iii 1 118
I claim your gift, my due by promise . . . . iv 2 91
His own merit makes his way; A gift that heaven gives for him *Hen. VIII.* i 1 65
And which gifts, Saving your mincing, the capacity Of your soft cheveril conscience would receive, If you might please to stretch it ii 3 30
Words, vows, gifts, tears, and love's full sacrifice, He offers *Tr. and Cr.* i 2 308
All our abilities, gifts, natures, shapes, Severals and generals of grace . i 3 179
The secrets of nature Have not more gift in taciturnity . . . iv 2 75
Well composed with gifts of nature, Flowing and swelling o'er with arts iv 4 79
I, that now Refused most princely gifts, am bound to beg . *Coriolanus* i 9 80
How proud I am of thee and of thy gifts Rome shall record . *T. Andron.* i 1 254
Gentle empress, 'Tis thought you have a goodly gift in horning . . ii 3 67
And with his gifts present Your lordships . . . . iv 2 14
But me more good, to see so great a lord Basely insinuate and send us gifts . . . . iv 2 38
No gift to him, But breeds the giver a return exceeding . *T. of Athens* i 1 289
Who dies, that bears not one spurn to their graves Of their friends' gift? . . . . i 2 147
I am so far already in your gifts,— So are we all . . . . . i 2 178
He commands us to provide, and give great gifts, And all out of an empty coffer . . . . i 2 198
A gift, I warrant. Why, this hits right . . . . iii 1 5
In my conscience, I was the first man That e'er received gift from him. iii 3 17
He wears jewels now of Timon's gift, For which I wait for money . . iii 4 19
For your own gifts, make yourselves praised: but reserve still to give . iii 6 80
As rich men deal gifts, Expecting in return twenty for one . . . iv 3 516
He and myself Have travail'd in the great shower of your gifts . . v 1 73
According to the gift which bounteous nature Hath in him closed *Macb.* iii 1 98
With this strange virtue, He hath a heavenly gift of prophecy . . iv 3 157
With witchcraft of his wit, with traitorous gifts . . . . *Hamlet* i 5 43
O wicked wit and gifts, that have the power So to seduce! . . . i 5 44
To decline Upon a wretch whose natural gifts were poor To those of mine! . . . . i 5 51
To the noble mind Rich gifts wax poor when givers prove unkind . . iii 1 101
I gave her such a one; 'twas my first gift.—I know not that . *Othello* iii 3 436
If she lost it Or made a gift of it, my father's eye Should hold her loathed . . . . iii 4 61
Gold and jewels that I bobb'd from him, As gifts to Desdemona . . v 1 17
I will boot thee with what gift beside Thy modesty can beg *Ant. and Cleo.* ii 5 71
The one may be sold, or given, if there were wealth enough for the purchase, or merit for the gift: the other is not a thing for sale, and only the gift of the gods . . . . *Cymbeline* i 4 91
Her pretty action did outsell her gift, And yet enrich'd it too . . ii 4 102
Whom best I love I cross; to make my gift, The more delay'd, delighted v 4 101
My shipwreck now's no ill, Since I have here my father's gift in's will *Pericles* ii 1 140
Since men take women's gifts for impudence . . . . ii 3 69
O you gods! Why do you make us love your goodly gifts, And snatch them straight away? . . . . iii 1 23
Yet my good will is great, though the gift small . . . . . . iii 4 18
Gig. To see great Hercules whipping a gig . . . . *L. L. Lost* iv 3 167
Thou disputest like an infant: go, whip thy gig . . . . . . v 1 70
I will whip about your infamy circum circa,—a gig of a cuckold's horn v 1 73
Giglot. Away with those giglots too, and with the other! *Meas. for Meas.* v 1 352
Young Talbot was not born To be the pillage of a giglot wench *1 Hen. VI.* iv 7 41
The famed Cassibelan, who was once at point—O giglot fortune!—to master Cæsar's sword . . . . *Cymbeline* iii 1 31

Gilbert. Sir Gilbert Talbot, Sir William Stanley . . *Richard III.* iv 5 10
One Gilbert Peck, his chancellor . . . . *Hen. VIII.* i 1 219; ii 1 20
Gild. The sun begins to gild the western sky . . *T. G. of Ver.* v 1 1
I will make fast the doors, and gild myself With some more ducats *Mer. of Venice* ii 6 49
Shall gild her bridal bed and make her rich In titles, honours *K. John* ii 1 491
To gild refined gold, to paint the lily, To throw a perfume on the violet iv 2 11
And those his golden beams to you here lent Shall point on me and gild my banishment . . . . *Richard II.* i 3 147
For my part, if a lie may do thee grace, I'll gild it with the happiest terms I have . . . . 1 *Hen. IV.* v 4 162
England shall double gild his treble guilt . . . 2 *Hen. IV.* iv 5 129
The sun doth gild our armour: up, my lords! . . . *Hen. V.* iv 2 1
No sun shall ever usher forth mine honours, Or gild again the noble troops that waited Upon my smiles . . . . *Hen. VIII.* iii 2 411
Whilst some with cunning gild their copper crowns, With truth and plainness I do wear mine bare . . . . *Troi. and Cres.* iv 4 107
Theme of all our scorns! For which we lose our heads to gild his horns iv 5 31
If he do bleed, I'll gild the faces of the grooms withal . *Macbeth* ii 2 56
Gilded. Where should they Find this grand liquor that hath gilded 'em? *Tempest* v 1 280
Sometimes the beam of her view gilded my foot, sometimes my portly belly . . . . *Mer. Wives* i 3 69
Gilded tombs do worms infold . . . . . *Mer of Venice* ii 7 69
About his neck A green and gilded snake had wreathed itself *As Y. L. It* iv 3 109
That away, Men are but gilded loam or painted clay . *Richard II.* i 1 179
Your day's service at Shrewsbury hath a little gilded over your night's exploit in Gad's-hill . . . . 2 *Hen. IV.* i 2 169
I saw him run after a gilded butterfly . . . *Coriolanus* i 3 66
How would he hang his slender gilded wings, And buzz! *T. Andron.* iii 2 61
The gilded newt and eyeless venom'd worm . . *T. of Athens* iv 3 182
In the corrupted currents of this world Offence's gilded hand may shove by justice . . . but 'tis not so above . . . . *Hamlet* iii 3 58
The wren goes to't, and the small gilded fly Does lecher . *Lear* iv 6 114
And pray, and sing, and tell old tales, and laugh At gilded butterflies . v 3 13
I arrest thee On capital treason; and, in thine attaint, This gilded serpent . . . . v 3 84
Thou didst drink The stale of horses, and the gilded puddle *Ant. and Cleo.* i 4 62
Coming from him, that great medicine hath With his tinct gilded thee. i 5 37
Gilded pale looks, Part shame, part spirit renew'd . . *Cymbeline* v 3 34
Whose rags shamed gilded arms, whose naked breast Stepp'd before targes of proof . . . . v 5 4
Gilliams. Is Gilliams with the packet gone?—He is, my lord . 1 *Hen. IV.* ii 3 68
Gillian. Maud, Bridget, Marian, Cicely, Gillian, Ginn! . *Com. of Errors* iii 1 31
Gillyvor. Streak'd gillyvors, Which some call nature's bastards *W. Tale* iv 4 82
Make your garden rich in gillyvors, And do not call them bastards . iv 4 98
Gilt. A gilt nutmeg.—A lemon.—Stuck with cloves . . . *L. L. Lost* v 2 652
The double gilt of this opportunity you let time wash off . *T. Night* iii 2 26
Their armours, that march'd hence so silver-bright, Hither return all gilt with Frenchmen's blood . . . . . . *K. John* ii 1 316
If you do not all show like gilt two-pences to me . . 2 *Hen. IV.* iv 3 55
Have, for the gilt of France,—O guilt indeed!—Confirm'd conspiracy with fearful France . . . . *Hen. V.* ii Prol. 26
Our gayness and our gilt are all besmirch'd With rainy marching . iv 3 110
Iron of Naples hid with English gilt . . . . 3 *Hen. VI.* ii 2 139
Their dwarfish pages were As cherubins, all gilt . . *Hen. VIII.* i 1 23
If I could have remembered a gilt counterfeit, thou wouldst not have slipped out of my contemplation . . . . *Troi. and Cres.* ii 3 27
Give to dust that is a little gilt More laud than gilt o'er-dusted . iii 3 178
Away, you fool! it [blood] more becomes a man Than gilt his trophy *Coriolanus* i 3 43
And, having gilt the ocean with his beams, Gallops the zodiac *T. Andron.* ii 1 6
When thou wast in thy gilt and thy perfume, they mocked thee *T. of A.* iv 3 302
Gimmal. In their pale dull mouths the gimmal bit Lies foul with chew'd grass . . . . *Hen. V.* iv 2 49
Gimmor. By some odd gimmors or device Their arms are set like clocks, still to strike on . . . . 1 *Hen. VI.* i 2 41
Gin. Now is the woodcock near the gin . . . . *T. Night* ii 5 92
By gins, by snares, by subtlety, Sleeping or waking, 'tis no matter how 2 *Hen. VI.* iii 1 262
Ay, ay, so strives the woodcock with the gin . . 3 *Hen. VI.* i 4 61
Thou'ldst never fear the net nor lime, The pitfall nor the gin. *Macbeth* iv 2 35
'Gin. Their great guilt, Like poison given to work a great time after, Now 'gins to bite the spirits . . . . . . *Tempest* iii 3 106
As whence the sun 'gins his reflection Shipwrecking storms and direful thunders break . . . . *Macbeth* i 2 25
I gin to be aweary of the sun, And wish the estate o' the world were now undone . . . . v 5 49
The glow-worm shows the matin to be near, And 'gins to pale his uneffectual fire: Adieu, adieu! . . . . . . *Hamlet* i 5 90
The lark at heaven's gate sings, And Phœbus 'gins arise . *Cymbeline* ii 3 23
See how she gins to blow Into life's flower again! . . *Pericles* iii 2 95
Ging. There's a knot, a ging, a pack, a conspiracy against me *Mer. Wives* iv 2 123
Ginger. He's in for a commodity of brown paper and old ginger *Meas. for Meas.* iv 3 6
Ginger was not much in request, for the old women were all dead . iv 3 8
As lying a gossip in that as ever knapped ginger . *Mer. of Venice* iii 1 10
Yes, by Saint Anne, and ginger shall be hot i' the mouth too . *T. Night* ii 3 126
A race or two of ginger, but that I may beg . . . *W. Tale* iv 3 50
A gammon of bacon and two razes of ginger . . . 1 *Hen. IV.* ii 1 27
He's of the colour of the nutmeg.—And of the heat of the ginger *Hen. V.* iii 7 21
Gingerbread. Thou shouldst have it to buy gingerbread . *L. L. Lost* v 1 75
Gingerly. What is't that you took up so gingerly? . . *T. G. of Ver.* i 2 70
Ginn. Maud, Bridget, Marian, Cicely, Gillian, Ginn! . *Com. of Errors* iii 1 31
Gipe. He was full of jests, and gipes, and knaveries, and mocks *Hen. V.* iv 7 52
Gipsy. Both in a tune, like two gipsies on a horse . *As Y. Like It* v 3 16
Cleopatra a gipsy; Helen and Hero hildings . . *Rom. and Jul.* ii 4 44
And is become the bellows and the fan To cool a gipsy's lust *Ant. and Cleo.* i 1 10
Like a right gipsy, hath, at fast and loose, Beguiled me . . . iv 12 28
Gird. I thank thee for that gird, good Tranio . . *T. of Shrew* v 2 58
Men of all sorts take a pride to gird at me . . . 2 *Hen. IV.* i 2 7
Sweet king! the bishop hath a kindly gird . . 1 *Hen. VI.* iii 1 131
In reguerdon of that duty done, I gird thee with the valiant sword of York . . . . iii 1 171
Create thee the first duke of Suffolk, And gird thee with the sword 2 *Hen. VI.* i 1 65
Being moved, he will not spare to gird the gods . . *Coriolanus* i 1 260
Girded. Behold the ordnance on their carriages, With fatal mouths gaping on girded Harfleur . . . . *Hen. V.* iii Prol. 27
Girding with grievous siege castles and towns . . . . . i 2 152
Girdle. He changes more and more: I think he be angry indeed.—If he be, he knows how to turn his girdle . . . . . *Much Ado* v 1 143
An your waist, mistress, were as slender as my wit, One o' these maids' girdles for your waist should be fit . . . . *L. L. Lost* iv 1 50
I'll put a girdle round about the earth In forty minutes *M. N. Dream* ii 1 175
Those sleeping stones, That as a waist doth girdle you about . *K. John* ii 1 217
Dost thou think I'll fear thee as I fear thy father? nay, an I do, I pray God my girdle break . . . . 1 *Hen. IV.* iii 3 171
Wear nothing but high shoes, and bunches of keys at their girdles 2 *Hen. IV.* i 2 45
To see The beachy girdle of the ocean Too wide for Neptune's hips . iii 1 50
On your imaginary forces work. Suppose within the girdle of these walls Are now confined two mighty monarchies . *Hen. V.* Prol. 19
All our bills.—Knock me down with 'em: cleave me to the girdle *T. of Athens* iii 4 91
Six French rapiers and poniards, with their assigns, as girdle, hangers *Hamlet* v 2 157
But to the girdle do the gods inherit, Beneath is all the fiends' . *Lear* iv 6 128
You shall find us in our salt-water girdle . . . . *Cymbeline* iii 1 81
Girdled with maiden walls that war hath never entered . *Hen. V.* v 2 349
Spur to the rescue of the noble Talbot, Who now is girdled with a waist of iron And hemm'd about with grim destruction . 1 *Hen. VI.* iv 3 20
Girdlest. O thou wall, That girdlest in those wolves, dive in the earth, And fence not Athens! . . . . . . *T. of Athens* iv 1 2
Girdling one another Within their innocent alabaster arms *Richard III.* iv 3 10
Girl. What foul play had we, that we came from thence? Or blessed was't we did?—Both, both, my girl . . . . *Tempest* i 2 61
Gentle girl, assist me; And even in kind love I do conjure thee *T. G. of V.* ii 7 1
Why, then, your ladyship must cut your hair.—No, girl . . . ii 7 45
She persevers so. What might we do to make the girl forget? . iii 2 29
This it is to be a peevish girl, That flies her fortune when it follows her v 2 49
I hold him but a fool that will endanger His body for a girl that loves him not . . . . v 4 134
Anne is a good girl, and I wish— Out, alas! . . . *Mer. Wives* i 4 35
What need you tell me that? I think so, when I took a boy for a girl . v 5 203
I was taken with Jaquenetta, and Jaquenetta is a true girl . *L. L. Lost* i 1 315
I do love that country girl that I took in the park with the rational hind . . . . i 2 123
God save your life!—Have with thee, my girl . . . . iv 2 151
Lay these glozes by: Shall we resolve to woo these girls of France . iv 3 371
We are wise girls to mock our lovers so . . . . . v 2 58
Jessica, my girl, Look to my house. I am right loath to go *Mer. of Ven.* ii 5 15
Justice! find the girl; She hath the stones upon her, and the ducats . ii 8 21
Which, to term in gross, Is an unlesson'd girl, unschool'd . . iii 2 161
Shall we be sunder'd? shall we part, sweet girl? . . *As Y. Like It* i 3 100
There's a girl goes before the priest; and certainly a woman's thought runs before her actions . . . . iv 1 140
For I will love thee ne'er the less, my girl . . . *T. of Shrew* i 1 77
I pine, I perish, Tranio, If I achieve not this young modest girl . i 1 161
Stand aside. Poor girl! she weeps. Go ply thy needle . . ii 1 24
Go, girl; I cannot blame thee now to weep . . . . iii 2 27
'Tis a groom indeed, A grumbling groom, and that the girl shall find . iii 2 155
Those girls of Italy, take heed of them . . . . *All's Well* ii 1 19
In those unfledged days was my wife a girl . . . *W. Tale* i 2 78
Fancies too weak for boys, too green and idle For girls of nine . iii 2 183
Let's have the first choice. Follow me, girls . . . . iv 4 320
No measure keeps in grief: Therefore, no dancing, girl; some other sport . . . . *Richard II.* iii 4 9
Between two girls, which hath the merriest eye . . 1 *Hen. VI.* ii 4 15
Kneel down and take my blessing, good my girl. Wilt thou not stoop? v 4 25
Why, here's a girl! I think she knows not well, There were so many, whom she may accuse . . . . v 4 80
'Tis a girl, Promises boys hereafter . . . . . *Hen. VIII.* v 1 165
Said I for this, the girl was like to him? I will have more, or else unsay't . . . . v 1 174
And all the Greekish girls shall tripping sing, 'Great Hector's sister did Achilles win' . . . . *Troi. and Cres.* iii 3 211
This foolish, dreaming, superstitious girl Makes all these bodements . v 3 79
Here's a letter come from yond poor girl.—Let me read . . . v 3 99
A whoreson rascally tisick so troubles me, and the foolish fortune of this girl . . . . v 3 103
Wound it with sighing, girl, kill it with groans . . *T. Andron.* iii 2 15
Come, let's fall to; and, gentle girl, eat this: Here is no drink! . iii 2 34
Some book there is that she desires to see. Which is it, girl, of these? iv 1 32
Wert thou thus surprised, sweet girl, Ravish'd and wrong'd? . . iv 1 51
Give signs, sweet girl, for here are none but friends . . . iv 1 61
Because the girl should not survive her shame . . . . v 3 41
What, lamb! what, lady-bird! God forbid! Where's this girl? *R. and J.* i 3 4
Go, girl, seek happy nights to happy days . . . . . i 3 106
A hall, a hall! give room! and foot it, girls . . . . . i 5 28
Well, girl, thou weep'st not so much for his death, As that the villain lives . . . . iii 5 79
But now I'll tell thee joyful tidings, girl . . . . . iii 5 105
How now! a conduit, girl? what, still in tears? Evermore showering? iii 5 130
My heart is wondrous light, Since this same wayward girl is so reclaim'd . . . . iv 2 47
Alas, it cried 'Give me some drink, Titinius,' As a sick girl . *J. Cæsar* i 2 128
If trembling I inhabit then, protest me The baby of a girl . *Macbeth* iii 4 106
You speak like a green girl, Unsifted in such perilous circumstance *Hamlet* i 3 101
Where didst thou see her? O unhappy girl! With the Moor, say'st thou? . . . . *Othello* i 1 164
Cold, cold, my girl! Even like thy chastity . . . . . v 2 275
What, girl! though grey Do something mingle with our younger brown, yet ha' we A brain that nourishes our nerves *Ant. and Cleo.* iv 8 19
Young boys and girls Are level now with men . . . . . iv 15 65
My noble girls! Ah, women, women, look, Our lamp is spent, it's out! iv 15 84
He words me, girls, he words me, that I should not Be noble to myself v 2 191
That, it seems, much loves A Gallian girl at home . . *Cymbeline* i 6 66
Golden lads and girls all must, As chimney-sweepers, come to dust . iv 2 262
Briefly die their joys That place them on the truth of girls and boys . v 5 107
Thou art a man, and I Have suffer'd like a girl . . . *Pericles* v 1 138
I am wild in my beholding. O heavens bless my girl! . . . v 1 225
Girt. Like to his island girt in with the ocean . . . 3 *Hen. VI.* iv 8 20
Girth. One girth six times pieced and a woman's crupper of velure *T. of Shrew* iii 2 61
Gis. By Gis and by Saint Charity, Alack, and fie for shame! . *Hamlet* iv 5 59
Give. Now would I give a thousand furlongs of sea for an acre of barren ground, long heath, brown furze, any thing . . . *Tempest* i 1 68
Thou art inclined to sleep; 'tis a good dulness, And give it way . . i 2 186

Give. Since thou dost give me pains, Let me remember thee what thou hast promised . . . . *Tempest* i 2 242
Madest much of me, wouldst give me Water with berries in't . . i 2 333
And that you will some good instruction give How I may bear me here i 2 424
He receives comfort like cold porridge.—The visitor will not give him o'er so . . . . ii 1 11
He will carry this island home in his pocket and give it his son for an apple . . . . ii 1 91
Not a holiday fool there but would give a piece of silver . . ii 2 30
They will not give a doit to relieve a lame beggar . . . . ii 2 33
I will give him some relief, if it be but for that . . . ii 2 70
Open your mouth; here is that which will give language to you . ii 2 86
If you'll sit down, I'll bear your logs the while: pray, give me that iii 1 24
That dare not offer What I desire to give, and much less take What I shall die to want . . . . iii 1 78
Give him blows And take his bottle from him . . . . . iii 2 72
As you like this, give me the lie another time.—I did not give the lie . iii 2 85
Sounds and sweet airs, that give delight and hurt not . . . iii 2 145
Give us kind keepers, heavens! What were these? . . . . iii 3 20
Go bring the rabble, O'er whom I give thee power, here to this place . iv 1 38
Look thou be true; do not give dalliance Too much the rein . . iv 1 51
Good my lord, give me thy favour still . . . . . . iv 1 204
Give us particulars of thy preservation; How thou hast met us here . v 1 135
Over the boots? nay, give me not the boots . . *T. G. of Ver.* i 1 27
Give her no token but stones; for she's as hard as steel . . . i 1 148
Give me a note: your ladyship can set . . . . i 2 81
Give ye good even! here's a million of manners . . . . ii 1 104
He should give her interest, and she gives it him . . . . ii 1 108
You have an exchequer of words, and, I think, no other treasure to give your followers . . . . ii 4 45
I'll give her father notice Of their disguising and pretended flight . ii 6 36
Never give her o'er; For scorn at first makes after-love the more . iii 1 94
Longer than swiftest expedition Will give thee time to leave . . . iii 1 165
I have a sonnet that will serve the turn To give the onset . . . iii 2 94
Now must we to her window, And give some evening music to her ear . iv 2 17
I give consent to go along with you, Recking as little what betideth me iv 3 39
Well, give her that ring and therewithal This letter . . . . iv 4 90
Bring my picture there. Go give your master this . . . . iv 4 123
I give thee this For thy sweet mistress' sake, because thou lovest her . iv 4 181
But one fair look; A smaller boon than this I cannot beg And less than this, I am sure, you cannot give . . . . v 4 25
All that was mine in Silvia I give thee . . . . v 4 83
And Julia herself did give it me; And Julia herself hath brought it . v 4 98
Seven hundred pounds of moneys, and gold and silver, is her grandsire upon his death's bed—Got deliver to a joyful resurrections!—give, when she is able to overtake seventeen years old . . *Mer. Wives* i 1 54
Give her this letter; for it is a 'oman that altogether's acquaintance with Mistress Anne Page . . . . i 2 7
She discourses, she carves, she gives the leer of invitation . . . i 3 49
You jack'nape, give-a this letter to Sir Hugh; by gar, it is a shallenge . i 4 113
Give me some counsel!—What's the matter, woman? . . . . ii 1 42
Appoint him a meeting; give him a show of comfort in his suit . . ii 1 98
It would give eternal food to his jealousy . . . . . . ii 1 104
I'll give you a pottle of burnt sack to give me recourse to him . . ii 1 222
She gives you to notify that her husband will be absence from his house . . . . ii 2 85
I will tell you, sir, if you will give me the hearing . . . . ii 2 182
Not only bought many presents to give her . . . . . . ii 2 206
Spend all I have; only give me so much of your time in exchange of it ii 2 242
Give me my gown; or else keep it in your arms . . . . iii 1 34
Shall I lose my doctor? no; he gives me the potions and the motions . iii 1 105
He gives me the proverbs and the no-verbs. Give me thy hand, terrestrial; so. Give me thy hand, celestial; so . . . . iii 1 107
He gives her folly motion and advantage . . . . iii 2 35
The clock gives me my cue, and my assurance bids me search . . iii 2 46
Give your men the charge; we must be brief . . . . . . iii 3 7
The firm fixture of thy foot would give an excellent motion to thy gait iii 3 67
Having an honest man to your husband, to give him such cause of suspicion! . . . . iii 3 107
And give him another hope, to betray him to another punishment . . iii 3 207
I am not such a sickly creature, I give heaven praise . . . . iii 4 61
Give my sweet Nan this ring: there's for thy pains . . . . iii 4 104
I'll have my brains ta'en out and buttered, and give them to a dog . iii 5 8
Comes in one Mistress Page; gives intelligence of Ford's approach . iii 5 85
I'll give thee A hundred pound in gold more than your loss . . . iv 6 4
And, in the lawful name of marrying, To give our hearts united ceremony iv 6 51
When I give the watch-'ords, do as I pid you: come, come; trib, trib . v 4 3
Seese is not good to give putter; your belly is all putter . . . v 5 148
Heaven give thee joy! What cannot be eschew'd must be embraced . v 5 250
Master Fenton, Heaven give you many, many merry days! . . . . v 5 254
Your own science Exceeds, in that, the lists of all advice My strength can give you . . . . *Meas. for Meas.* i 1 7
The heavens give safety to your purposes! . . . . i 1 74
Why I desire thee To give me secret harbour, hath a purpose . . . i 3 4
Sith 'twas my fault to give the people scope . . . . . . i 3 35
To give fear to use and liberty, Which have for long run by the hideous law i 4 62
When maidens sue, Men give like gods . . . . i 4 81
No longer staying but to give the mother Notice of my affair . . . i 4 86
I could not give you three-pence again.—No, indeed . . . . ii 1 107
Heaven give thee moving graces! . . . . ii 2 36
Give't not o'er so: to him again, entreat him; Kneel down before him ii 2 43
So you must be the first that gives this sentence, And he, that suffers . ii 2 106
I had rather give my body than my soul.—I talk not of your soul . ii 4 56
He shall die for it.—He shall not, Isabel, if you give me love . . ii 4 144
I have begun, And now I give my sensual race the rein . . . . ii 4 160
Why give you me this shame? Think you I can a resolution fetch From flowery tenderness? . . . . iii 1 81
He would give't thee, from this rank offence, So to offend him still . iii 1 100
What think you of it?—The image of it gives me content already . . iii 1 270
If for this night he entreat you to his bed, give him promise of satisfaction iii 1 275
Must upon a warranted need give him a better proclamation . . . iii 2 152
But, hark, what noise? Heaven give your spirits comfort! By and by iv 2 73
Give him leave to escape hence, he would not . . . . . . iv 2 156
I will give him a present shrift and advise him for a better place . . iv 2 223
This nor hurts him nor profits you a jot; Forbear it therefore; give your cause to heaven . . . . iv 3 129
One of our covent, and his confessor, Gives me this instance . . . iv 3 134
Here is Lord Angelo shall give you justice: Reveal yourself to him . v 1 27
Give us some seats. Come, cousin Angelo; In this I'll be impartial . v 1 165
Good my lord, give me the scope of justice; My patience here is touch'd v 1 234

Give. O, give me pardon, That I, your vassal, have employ'd and pain'd Your unknown sovereignty! . . . . . *Meas. for Meas.* v 1 390
Now your jest is earnest: Upon what bargain do you give it me? *C. of Er.* ii 2 25
I'll make you amends next, to give you nothing for something . . ii 2 54
Nay, come, I pray you, sir, give me the chain . . . . . . iv 1 45
The chain!—Why, give it to my wife and fetch your money . . . iv 1 54
I do obey thee till I give thee bail . . . . iv 1 80
Hie thee straight: Give her this key, and tell her, in the desk . . iv 1 103
Some invite me; Some other give me thanks for kindnesses . . . iv 3 5
He, sir, that takes pity on decayed men and gives them suits of durance iv 3 26
One that thinks a man always going to bed and says 'God give you good rest!' . . . . iv 3 33
Give me the ring of mine you had at dinner . . . . . . iv 3 69
But she, more covetous, would have a chain. Master, be wise: an if you give it her, The devil will shake her chain and fright us with it iv 3 76
I'll give thee, ere I leave thee, so much money, To warrant thee . . iv 4 2
Youthful men, Who give their eyes the liberty of gazing . . . v 1 53
Whom I beseech To give me ample satisfaction . . . . . . v 1 252
That she brought me up, I likewise give her most humble thanks *M. Ado* i 1 241
I can give you intelligence of an intended marriage . . . . . i 3 46
It is the base, though bitter, disposition of Beatrice that puts the world into her person, and so gives me out . . . . ii 1 216
Name the day of marriage, and God give thee joy! . . . . . ii 1 312
If you three will but minister such assistance as I shall give you direction ii 1 385
Prays, curses; 'O sweet Benedick! God give me patience!' . . . ii 3 154
They say too that she will rather die than give any sign of affection . ii 3 236
Never gives to truth and virtue that Which simpleness and merit purchaseth . . . . iii 1 69
Well, give them their charge, neighbour Dogberry . . . . . iii 3 7
Why, give God thanks, and make no boast of it . . . . . iii 3 19
God give me joy to wear it! for my heart is exceeding heavy . . . iii 4 24
He comes too short of you.—Gifts that God gives . . . . . iii 5 47
My lord, they stay for you to give your daughter to her husband . . iii 5 59
Give me this maid, your daughter?—As freely, son, as God did give her me.—And what have I to give you back? . . . . iv 1 26
Give not this rotten orange to your friend . . . . iv 1 33
And salt too little which may season give To her foul-tainted flesh! . iv 1 144
Give not me counsel; Nor let no comforter delight mine ear . . . v 1 5
Counsel turns to passion, which before Would give perceptial medicine to rage . . . . v 1 24
Give me no counsel: My griefs cry louder than advertisement . . . v 1 31
Beshrew my hand, If it should give your age such cause of fear . . v 1 56
Give him another staff: this last was broke cross . . . . . v 1 138
Give her the right you should have given her cousin, And so dies my revenge . . . . v 1 300
I humbly give you leave to depart . . . . v 1 334
I give thee the bucklers.—Give us the swords; we have bucklers of our own v 2 17
Death, in guerdon of her wrongs, Gives her fame which never dies . v 3 6
This same is she, and I do give you her.—Why, then she's mine . . v 4 54
Godfathers of heaven's lights That give a name to every fixed star *L. L. Lost* i 1 89
And every godfather can give a name . . . . i 1 93
Give me the paper; let me read the same; And to the strict'st decrees I'll write my name . . . . i 1 116
Be it as the style shall give us cause to climb in the merriness . . i 1 201
'Fair' I give you back again; and 'welcome' I have not yet . . . ii 1 91
I'll give you Aquitaine and all that is his, An you give him for my sake but one loving kiss . . . . ii 1 247
Take this key, give enlargement to the swain . . . . . . iii 1 5
Most rude melancholy, valour gives thee place . . . . . . iii 1 69
I give thee thy liberty, set thee from durance . . . . . . iii 1 129
What's the price of this inkle?—One penny.—No, I'll give you a remuneration . . . . iii 1 140
To whom shouldst thou give it?—From my lord to my lady . . . iv 1 104
Here comes one with a paper: God give him grace to groan! . . . iv 3 20
So sweet a kiss the golden sun gives not To those fresh morning drops . iv 3 25
As doth thy face through tears of mine give light . . . . . iv 3 32
Beauty doth varnish age, as if new-born, And gives the crutch the cradle's infancy . . . . iv 3 245
O, who can give an oath? where is a book? . . . . . . iv 3 250
And gives to every power a double power, Above their functions . . iv 3 331
Hold, take thou this, my sweet, and give me thine . . . . . v 2 132
Will you give horns, chaste lady? do not so . . . . . . v 2 252
Then wish me better; I will give you leave . . . . . . v 2 342
To the manner of the days, In courtesy gives undeserving praise . . v 2 366
I am yours, and all that I possess!—All the fool mine?—I cannot give you less . . . . v 2 384
God give thee joy of him! . . . . v 2 448
My faith and this the princess I did give . . . . v 2 454
For the ass to the Jude; give it him:—Jud-as, away! . . . . v 2 631
Rein thy tongue.—I must rather give it the rein . . . . . v 2 663
Then if I have much love, I'll give you some . . . . . . v 2 840
That loose grace Which shallow laughing hearers give to fools . . v 2 870
Whose unwished yoke My soul consents not to give sovereignty *M. N. D.* i 1 82
Were the world mine, Demetrius being bated, The rest I'ld give to be to you translated . . . . i 1 191
I give him curses, yet he gives me love . . . . i 1 196
Have you the lion's part written? pray you, if it be, give it me . . i 2 69
And you come To give their bed joy and prosperity . . . . . ii 1 73
Give me that boy, and I will go with thee . . . . ii 1 143
Here is my bed: sleep give thee all his rest! . . . . . . ii 2 64
Who would give a bird the lie, though he cry 'cuckoo' never so? . . iii 1 138
Go with me; I'll give thee fairies to attend on thee . . . . iii 1 160
Wilt thou give him me?—I had rather give his carcass to my hounds . iii 2 63
These vows are Hermia's: will you give her o'er? . . . . . iii 2 130
I had no judgement when to her I swore.—Nor none, in my mind, now you give her o'er . . . . iii 2 135
Give me your neaf, Mounsieur Mustardseed . . . . iv 1 20
Is not this the day That Hermia should give answer of her choice? . iv 1 141
And gives to airy nothing A local habitation and a name . . . . v 1 16
The kinder we, to give them thanks for nothing . . . . . . v 1 89
Through the house give glimmering light, By the dead and drowsy fire v 1 398
Give him direction for this merry bond . . . . *Mer. of Venice* i 3 174
The fiend gives the more friendly counsel . . . . ii 2 31
Let's have no more fooling about it, but give me your blessing . . ii 2 89
Give him a present! give him a halter: I am famished in his service . ii 2 112
Give me your present to one Master Bassanio, who, indeed, gives rare new liveries . . . . ii 2 115
Give him a livery More guarded than his fellows . . . . . ii 2 163
Give him this letter; do it secretly; And so farewell . . . . ii 3 7
'Who chooseth me must give and hazard all he hath.' Must give: for what? ii 7 16

Give. I'll then nor give nor hazard aught for lead . . *Mer. of Venice* ii 7 21
You shall look fairer, ere I give or hazard . . . . ii 9 22
Give me a key for this, And instantly unlock my fortunes here . ii 9 51
Fair lady, by your leave; I come by note, to give and to receive . iii 2 141
This house, these servants and this same myself Are yours, my lord: I give them with this ring . . . . iii 2 173
And, look, what notes and garments he doth give thee . . . iii 4 51
What if my house be troubled with a rat And I be pleased to give ten thousand ducats To have it baned? . . . . iv 1 45
So can I give no reason, nor I will not, More than a lodged hate iv 1 59
Some three or four of you Go give him courteous conduct to this place iv 1 148
It is twice blest; It blesseth him that gives and him that takes . iv 1 187
This strict court of Venice Must needs give sentence 'gainst the merchant iv 1 205
I do beseech the court To give the judgement . . . . . iv 1 244
Your wife would give you little thanks for that, If she were by . iv 1 288
The court awards it, and the law doth give it . . . . . iv 1 300
This bond doth give thee here no jot of blood . . . . . iv 1 306
Give me my principal, and let me go.—I have it ready for thee; here it is iv 1 336
Why, then the devil give him good of it! I'll stay no longer question iv 1 345
I pray you, give me leave to go from hence; I am not well . . iv 1 395
Give me your gloves, I'll wear them for your sake . . . . iv 1 426
Alas, it is a trifle! I will not shame myself to give you this . . iv 1 431
The dearest ring in Venice will I give you, And find it out by proclamation iv 1 435
She made me vow That I should neither sell nor give nor lose it . iv 1 443
Run and overtake him; Give him the ring . . . . . . iv 1 453
Inquire the Jew's house out, give him this deed And let him sign it . iv 2 1
We shall have old swearing That they did give the rings away to men . iv 2 16
Let me give light, but let me not be light . . . . . . v 1 129
I thank you, madam. Give welcome to my friend . . . . v 1 133
About a hoop of gold, a paltry ring That she did give me . . . v 1 148
You swore to me, when I did give it you, That you would wear it till your hour of death . . . . v 1 152
You give your wife too unkind a cause of grief . . . . v 1 175
I think you would have begg'd The ring of me to give the worthy doctor v 1 222
Give him this And bid him keep it better than the other . . v 1 254
Ay, and I'll give them him without a fee. There do I give to you and Jessica, From the rich Jew, a special deed of gift . . . v 1 290
Besides this nothing that he so plentifully gives me, the something that nature gave me his countenance seems to take from me *As Y. L. It* i 1 18
My father charged you in his will to give me good education . . i 1 70
Give me the poor allottery my father left me by testament . . i 1 76
I will physic yo r rankness, and yet give no thousand crowns neither . i 1 91
If he come to-m rrow, I'll give him his payment . . . . i 1 166
That could give more, but that her hand lacks means . . . . i 2 259
Wilt thou change fathers? I will give thee mine . . . . . i 3 93
Here is the gold; All this I give you . . . . ii 3 46
One of you question yond man If he for gold will give us any food . ii 4 65
But I give heaven thanks and make no boast of them . . . . ii 5 37
I'll give you a verse to this note that I made yesterday . . . ii 5 48
Whiles, like a doe, I go to find my fawn And give it food . . . ii 7 129
Give us some music; and, good cousin, sing . . . . . ii 7 173
Give me audience, good madam.—Proceed . . . . . . iii 2 251
If I could meet that fancy-monger, I would give him some good counsel iii 2 382
One of the points in the which women still give the lie to their consciences iii 2 409
Well, the gods give us joy! . . . . iii 3 47
Is there none here to give the woman?—I will not take her on gift of any man.—Truly, she must be given, or the marriage is not lawful. —Proceed, proceed: I'll give her . . . . iii 3 68
My gentle Phebe bid me give you this: I know not the contents . iv 3 7
Nature, stronger than his just occasion, Made him give battle . . iv 3 131
And to give this napkin Dyed in his blood unto the shepherd youth . iv 3 155
That would I, had I kingdoms to give with her . . . . . v 4 8
But if you do refuse to marry me, You'll give yourself to this most faithful shepherd? . . . . v 4 14
Keep you your word, O duke, to give your daughter . . . . v 4 19
He durst not give me the Lie Direct . . . . v 4 90
To you I give myself, for I am yours. To you I give myself . . . v 4 122
Give them friendly welcome every one: Let them want nothing *T. of S.* Ind. 1 103
Anon I'll give thee more instructions . . . . Ind. 1 130
If you give me any conserves, give me conserves of beef . . . Ind. 2 7
Give him gold enough and marry him to a puppet or an aglet-baby . i 2 78
Let me be thus bold with you To give you over at this first encounter . i 2 105
And do you tell me of a woman's tongue, That gives not half so great a blow to bear As will a chestnut in a farmer's fire? . . . . . i 2 209
Sir, give him head: I know he'll prove a jade . . . . . i 2 249
Freely give unto you this young scholar, that hath been long studying ii 1 79
If she do bid me pack, I'll give her thanks, As though she bid me stay ii 1 178
Your father were a fool To give thee all, and in his waning age Set foot under thy table . . . . ii 1 403
God give him joy!—Ay, and he'll tame her . . . . . . iv 2 52
And give assurance to Baptista Minola . . . . iv 2 69
Take thou the bill, give me thy mete-yard . . . . . . iv 3 153
Stand good father to me now, Give me Bianca for my patrimony . . iv 4 22
Let's away.—Nay, I will give thee a kiss: now pray thee, love, stay . v 1 153
The fated sky Gives us free scope, only doth backward pull . *All's Well* i 1 233
I quickly were dissolved from my hive, To give some labourers room . i 2 67
O, then, give pity To her, whose state is such that cannot choose But lend and give where she is sure to lose! . . . . i 3 219
To give great Charlemain a pen in's hand And write to her a love-line . ii 1 80
I cannot give thee less, to be call'd grateful . . . . . . ii 1 132
Such thanks I give As one near death to those that wish him live . . ii 1 133
To my endeavours give consent; Of heaven, not me, make an experiment ii 1 156
Give me with thy kingly hand What husband in thy power I will command ii 1 196
Give me some help here, ho! . . . . ii 1 212
Give Helen this, And urge her to a present answer back . . . ii 2 66
Great transcendence: which should, indeed, give us a further use . ii 3 41
I'ld give bay Curtal and his furniture, My mouth no more were broken ii 3 65
I give Me and my service, ever whilst I live, Into your guiding power . ii 3 109
Give me thy hand.—My lord, you give me most egregious indignity . ii 3 226
The commission of your birth and virtue gives you heraldry . . ii 3 279
I do know him well, and common speech Gives him a worthy pass . ii 5 58
If you give him not John Drum's entertainment . . . . . iii 6 40
Give me trust, the count he is my husband . . . . . . iii 7 8
I must give myself some hurts, and say I got them in exploit: yet slight ones will not carry it; . . . and great ones I dare not give . . iv 1 40
Stand no more off, But give thyself unto my sick desires . . . iv 2 35
Give me that ring.—I'll lend it thee, my dear; but have no power To give it from me . . . . iv 2 39
Will you give me a copy of the sonnet you writ to Diana? . . . iv 3 354
And I would give his wife my bauble, sir, to do her service . . iv 5 32

Give. There's my purse: I give thee not this to suggest thee from thy master . . . . *All's Well* iv 5 46
Please you To give this poor petition to the king . . . . v 1 19
Stand away: a paper from fortune's close-stool to give to a nobleman! v 2 18
Give a favour from you To sparkle in the spirits of my daughter . . v 3 74
Send for your ring, I will return it home, And give me mine again . v 3 224
How could you give it him?—I never gave it him . . . . . v 3 277
If music be the food of love, play on; Give me excess of it . *T. Night* i 1 2
Well, God give them wisdom that have it . . . . i 5 14
For give the dry fool drink, then is the fool not dry . . . . i 5 48
Let him be the devil, an he will, I care not: give me faith, say I . . i 5 137
Give me my veil: come, throw it o'er my face . . . . . . i 5 175
Give me modest assurance if you be the lady of the house . . . i 5 192
Give us the place alone: we will hear this divinity . . . . . i 5 235
Thy face, thy limbs, actions and spirit, Do give thee five-fold blazon . i 5 312
If that the youth will come this way to-morrow, I'll give him reasons for't i 5 325
If you prized my lady's favour at any thing more than contempt, you would not give means for this uncivil rule . . . . ii 3 132
Give me some music. Now, good morrow, friends . . . . . ii 4 1
It gives a very echo to the seat Where Love is throned . . . ii 4 21
Give me now leave to leave thee.—Now, the melancholy god protect thee ii 4 74
There is no woman's sides Can bide the beating of so strong a passion As love doth give my heart . . . . ii 4 98
Give her this jewel; say, My love can give no place, bide no denay . ii 4 127
My fortunes having cast me on your niece give me this prerogative . ii 5 78
I will not give my part of this sport for a pension of thousands . ii 5 196
I'll not stay a jot longer.—Thy reason, dear venom, give thy reason . iii 2 2
But read.—Give me. 'Youth, whatsoever thou art, thou art but a scurvy fellow' . . . . iii 4 162
If this letter move him not, his legs cannot: I'll give't him . . . iii 4 189
A terrible oath, with a swaggering accent sharply twanged off, gives manhood more approbation . . . . iii 4 198
The behaviour of the young gentleman gives him out to be of good capacity iii 4 203
Give them way till he take leave, and presently after him . . . iii 4 216
What shall you ask of me that I'll deny, That honour saved may upon asking give?—Nothing but this; your true love . . . . . iii 4 232
How with mine honour may I give him that Which I have given to you? iii 4 234
Hob, nob, is his word; give't or take't . . . . iii 4 263
Therefore, get you on and give him his desire . . . . . . iii 4 271
He gives me the stuck in with such a mortal motion, that it is inevitable iii 4 303
Let him let the matter slip, and I'll give him my horse, grey Capilet . iii 4 314
There's money for thee: if you tarry longer, I shall give worse payment iv 1 21
These wise men that give fools money get themselves a good report . iv 1 23
This is, to give a dog, and in recompense desire my dog again . . v 1 7
O, you give me ill counsel.—Put your grace in your pocket . . . v 1 34
Noble sir, Be pleased that I shake off these names you give me . . v 1 76
We will give you sleepy drinks . . . . *W. Tale* i 1 15
I'll give him my commission To let him there a month behind the gest Prefix'd . . . . i 2 40
I am angling now, Though you perceive me not how I give line . . i 2 181
Mightst bespice a cup, To give mine enemy a lasting wink . . . i 2 317
Give scandal to the blood o' the prince my son, Who I do think is mine i 2 330
I'll give no blemish to her honour, none . . . . i 2 341
Come on, then, And give't me in mine ear . . . . ii 1 32
Give me the boy: I am glad you did not nurse him . . . . . ii 1 56
A bed-swerver, even as bad as those That vulgars give bold'st titles . ii 1 94
Yet shall the oracle Give rest to the minds of others . . . . ii 1 191
Traitors! Will you not push her out? Give her the bastard . . . ii 3 75
Take up the bastard; Take't up, I say; give't to thy crone . . . ii 3 76
Give us better credit: We have always truly served you . . . . ii 3 147
I turn my glass and give my scene such growing As you had slept between iv 1 16
Then my account I well may give, And in the stocks avouch it . . iv 3 21
These your unusual weeds to each part of you Do give a life . . . iv 4 2
You're welcome, sir. Give me those flowers there . . . . . iv 4 73
When you sing, I'ld have you buy and sell so, so give alms, Pray so . iv 4 138
Your youth, And the true blood which peepeth fairly through't, Do plainly give you out an unstain'd shepherd . . . . iv 4 149
Golden quoifs and stomachers, For my lads to give their dears . . iv 4 227
He has paid you more, which will shame you to give him again . . iv 4 243
I give my daughter to him, and will make Her portion equal his . . iv 4 396
Sent by the king your father To greet him and to give him comforts . iv 4 568
We'll make an instrument of this, omit Nothing may give us aid . . iv 4 638
It becomes none but tradesmen, and they often give us soldiers the lie iv 4 746
He seems to be of great authority: close with him, give him gold . iv 4 831
Well, give me the moiety. Are you a party in this business? . . iv 4 842
I will give you as much as this old man does when the business is performed . . . . iv 4 851
Give me the office To choose you a queen . . . . v 1 77
Give you all greetings that a king, at friend, Can send his brother . v 1 140
Give me the lie, do, and try whether I am not now a gentleman born . v 2 144
Give me your good report to the prince my master . . . . . v 2 162
On my knee I give heaven thanks I was not like to thee! . . *K. John* i 1 83
Would I might never stir from off this place, I would give it every foot to have this face . . . . i 1 146
Our country manners give our betters way . . . . i 1 156
Give me your hand: My father gave me honour, yours gave land . . i 1 163
Embrace him, love him, give him welcome hither . . . . . ii 1 11
God shall forgive you Cœur-de-lion's death The rather that you give his offspring life . . . . ii 1 13
Till your strong hand shall help to give him strength . . . . ii 1 33
I'll give thee more Than e'er the coward hand of France can win . . ii 1 157
Give grandam kingdom, and it grandam will Give it a plum, a cherry, and a fig . . . . ii 1 161
Shall we give the signal to our rage And stalk in blood to our possession? ii 1 265
Open your gates and give the victors way . . . . ii 1 324
Her happy minion, To whom in favour she shall give the day . . . ii 1 393
The mouth of passage shall we fling wide ope, And give you entrance . ii 1 450
He gives the bastinado with his tongue: Our ears are cudgell'd . . ii 1 463
Then do I give Volquessen, Touraine, Maine, Poictiers and Anjou . ii 1 527
This league that we have made Will give her sadness very little cure . ii 1 546
I believe you think them false That give you cause to prove my saying true iii 1 28
Law cannot give my child his kingdom here . . . . iii 1 187
Too wanton and too full of gawds To give me audience . . . . iii 3 37
Had you such a loss as I, I could give better comfort than you do . iii 4 100
Give me the iron, I say, and bind him here . . . . iv 1 75
Let him come back, that his compassion may Give life to yours . . iv 1 90
Although my will to give is living, The suit which you demand is gone and dead . . . . iv 2 83
Now I breathe again Aloft the flood, and can give audience To any tongue iv 2 139
Shall give a holiness, a purity, To the yet unbegotten sin of times . iv 3 53

Give. The holy legate comes apace, To give us warrant from the hand of heaven *K. John* v 2 66
My arm shall give thee help to bear thee hence v 4 58
I have a kind soul that would give you thanks And knows not how to do it v 7 108
Rage must be withstood: Give me his gage *Richard II.* i 1 174
Thou hast many years to live.—But not a minute, king, that thou canst give i 3 226
The apprehension of the good Gives but the greater feeling to the worse i 3 301
I am denied to sue my livery here, And yet my letters-patents give me leave ii 3 130
And for the right of that We all have strongly sworn to give him aid ii 3 150
To fear the foe, since fear oppresseth strength, Gives in your weakness strength unto your foe iii 2 181
I'll give thee scope to beat, Since foes have scope to beat both thee and me iii 3 140
I'll give my jewels for a set of beads, My gorgeous palace for a hermitage iii 3 147
Will his majesty Give Richard leave to live till Richard die? iii 3 174
What you will have, I'll give, and willing too iii 3 206
Give some supportance to the bending twigs iii 4 32
So much dishonour my fair stars, On equal terms to give him chastisement? iv 1 22
What subject can give sentence on his king? iv 1 121
Give me the crown. Here, cousin, seize the crown iv 1 181
Part of your cares you give me with your crown iv 1 194
The cares I give I have, though given away iv 1 198
I give this heavy weight from off my head And this unwieldy sceptre from my hand iv 1 204
Give me the glass, and therein will I read iv 1 276
Give me leave to go.—Whither?—Whither you will iv 1 313
Though he divide the realm and give thee half, It is too little v 1 60
One kiss shall stop our mouths, and dumbly part; Thus give I mine, and thus take I thy heart.—Give me mine own again v 1 96
Give me my boots, I say; saddle my horse v 2 77
Give me leave that I may turn the key, That no man enter v 3 36
For ever will I walk upon my knees, And never see day that the happy sees, Till thou give joy v 3 95
Blessing on his heart that gives it me! For 'tis a sign of love v 5 64
Take hence the rest, and give them burial here v 5 119
I'll give thee thy due, thou hast paid all there *1 Hen. IV.* i 2 59
He was never yet a breaker of proverbs: he will give the devil his due i 2 132
Good cousin, give me audience for a while.—I cry you mercy i 3 211
Give it him, To keep his anger still in motion i 3 225
That is the next way to give poor jades the bots ii 1 10
If they meet not with Saint Nicholas' clerks, I'll give thee this neck ii 1 68
Give me my horse, you rogues; give me my horse, and be hanged! ii 2 32
I give thee this pennyworth of sugar, clapped even now into my hand ii 4 24
I will give thee for it a thousand pound: ask me when thou wilt ii 4 68
'Give my roan horse a drench,' says he ii 4 119
Give me a cup of sack, boy ii 4 128
I would give a thousand pound I could run as fast as thou canst ii 4 162
Give me them that will face me. Give me a cup of sack ii 4 167
Down fell their hose.—Began to give me ground: but I followed me close ii 4 240
Give you a reason on compulsion! if reasons were as plentiful as blackberries, I would give no man a reason upon compulsion, I ii 4 263
Give him as much as will make him a royal man, and send him back again ii 4 320
What doth gravity out of his bed at midnight? Shall I give him his answer? ii 4 326
Give me a cup of sack to make my eyes look red ii 4 422
I'll give thrice so much land To any well-deserving friend iii 1 137
Yet doth he give us bold advertisement, That with our small conjunction we should on, To see how fortune is disposed iv 1 36
Will you give me money, captain?—Lay out, lay out iv 2 4
You give him then advantage.—Not a whit iv 3 2
My father and my uncle and myself Did give him that same royalty he wears iv 3 55
Give me life: which if I can save, so v 3 63
Upon mine honour, for a silken point I'll give my barony *2 Hen. IV.* i 1 54
Why should that gentleman . . . Give then such instances of loss? i 1 56
If ye will needs say I am an old man, you should give me rest i 2 243
Hope gives not so much warrant as despair i 3 40
Loving wife, and gentle daughter, Give even way unto my rough affairs ii 3 2
You muddy rascal, is that all the comfort you give me? ii 4 44
Die men like dogs! give crowns like pins! Have we not Hiren here? ii 4 188
Give me my rapier, boy.—I pray thee, Jack, I pray thee, do not draw ii 4 215
Thou dost give me flattering busses ii 4 291
And thy father is to give me thanks for it ii 4 350
Give me my sword and cloak ii 4 395
Canst thou, O partial sleep, give thy repose To the wet sea-boy? iii 1 26
Give me the spirit, Master Shallow iii 2 278
Give me this man: he presents no mark to the enemy iii 2 284
O, give me the spare men, and spare me the great ones iii 2 288
Give me always a little, lean, old, chapt, bald shot iii 2 294
Bardolph, give the soldiers coats iii 2 311
To tell you from his grace That he will give you audience iv 1 143
All too confident To give admittance to a thought of fear iv 1 153
It illumineth the face, which as a beacon gives warning to all the rest iv 3 117
If God doth give successful end To this debate iv 4 1
But, being moody, give him line and scope iv 4 39
She either gives a stomach and no food; Such are the poor, in health; or else a feast And takes away the stomach iv 4 105
Stand from him, give him air; he'll straight be well iv 4 116
Give that which gave thee life unto the worms iv 5 117
England shall give him office, honour, might iv 5 130
With the least affection of a welcome Give entertainment to the might of it iv 5 174
A merry heart! Good Master Silence, I'll give you a health for that anon v 3 25
Give me pardon, sir: if, sir, you come with news from the court v 3 114
I will leer upon him as a' comes by; and do but mark the countenance that he will give me v 5 8
We will, according to your strengths and qualities, Give you advancement v 5 74
Unless you should give me your doublet and stuff me out with straw v 5 87
To give a greater sum Than ever at one time the clergy yet Did *Hen. V.* i 1 79
The hour, I think, is come To give him hearing i 1 93
Whose wrongs give edge unto the swords That make such waste i 2 27
And therefore, living hence, did give ourself To barbarous license i 2 270
Omit no happy hour That may give furtherance to our expedition i 2 301
Charming the narrow seas To give you gentle pass ii Prol. 39
Give me thy fist, thy fore-foot to me give: Thy spirits are most tall ii 1 71
A noble shalt thou have, and present pay; And liquor likewise will I give ii 1 113

Give. And you, my gentle knight, give me your thoughts *Hen. V.* ii 2 14
You show great mercy, if you give him life ii 2 50
The taste whereof, God of his mercy give You patience to endure! ii 2 179
My love, give me thy lips. Look to my chattels and my movables ii 3 49
We'll give them present audience. Go, and bring them ii 4 67
Hear the shrill whistle which doth order give To sounds confused iii Prol. 9
I would give all my fame for a pot of ale and safety iii 2 13
To our best mercy give yourselves iii 3 3
Let us quit all And give our vineyards to a barbarous people iii 5 4
And they will give Their bodies to the lust of English youth iii 5 29
Say to England that we send To know what willing ransom he will give iii 5 63
We give express charge, that in our marches through the country, there be nothing compelled from the villages iii 6 114
I will take up that with 'Give the devil his due' iii 7 126
And then give them great meals of beef and iron and steel iii 7 161
With busy hammers closing rivets up, Give dreadful note of preparation iv Prol. 14
A largess universal like the sun His liberal eye doth give to every one iv Prol. 44
Give me any gage of thine, and I will wear it in my bonnet iv 1 223
Here's my glove: give me another of thine.—There.—This will I also wear iv 1 226
O, be sick, great greatness, And bid thy ceremony give thee cure! iv 1 269
Scarce blood enough in all their sickly veins To give each naked curtle-axe a stain iv 2 21
Give their fasting horses provender, And after fight with them iv 2 58
O Signieur Dew, thou diest on point of fox, Except, O signieur, thou do give to me Egregious ransom iv 4 10
Owy, cuppele gorge, permafoy, Peasant, unless thou give me crowns iv 4 40
And for his ransom he will give you two hundred crowns iv 4 49
He gives you, upon his knees, a thousand thanks iv 4 63
Then every soldier kill his prisoners; Give the word through iv 6 38
I will give treason his payment into plows, I warrant you iv 8 14
This is the glove of Alençon, that your majesty is give me iv 8 40
Give me thy glove, soldier: look, here is the fellow of it iv 8 41
Fill this glove with crowns, And give it to this fellow iv 8 62
Give him the crowns: And, captain, you must needs be friends with him iv 8 64
Whose want gives growth to the imperfections Which you have cited v 2 69
Give me your answer; i' faith, do: and so clap hands v 2 132
And thereupon give me your daughter.—Take her, fair son v 2 375
Regent I am of France. Give me my steeled coat. I'll fight for France *1 Hen. VI.* i 1 85
Thou art a witch, And straightway give thy soul to him thou servest i 5 7
Renounce your soil, give sheep in lions' stead i 5 29
Fain would mine eyes be witness with mine ears, To give their censure ii 3 10
O, tell me when my lips do touch his cheeks, That I may kindly give one fainting kiss ii 5 40
Vouchsafe To give me hearing what I shall reply iii 1 28
I will yield to thee; Love for thy love and hand for hand I give iii 1 135
All the whole inheritance I give That doth belong unto the house of York iii 1 164
Talk with him And give him chastisement for this abuse iv 1 69
They are return'd, my lord, and give it out That he is march'd to Bourdeaux iv 3 3
Give me their bodies, that I may bear them hence And give them burial iv 7 85
And means to give you battle presently.—Somewhat too sudden, sirs v 2 13
I'll lop a member off and give it you In earnest of a further benefit v 3 15
Then take my soul, my body, soul and all, Before that England give the French the foil v 3 23
I prithee, give me leave to curse awhile v 3 43
Sweet madam, give me hearing in a cause v 3 106
Consent, and for thy honour give consent, Thy daughter shall be wedded v 3 136
Upon thy princely warrant, I descend To give thee answer v 3 144
Give thee her hand, for sign of plighted faith v 3 162
I give thee kingly thanks, Because this is in traffic of a king v 3 163
That, in regard King Henry gives consent, Of mere compassion v 4 124
Give consent That Margaret may be England's royal queen.—So should I give consent to flatter sin v 5 23
Reignier sooner will receive than give v 5 47
Seal up your lips, and give no words but mum *2 Hen. VI.* i 2 89
Dame Eleanor gives gold to bring the witch: Gold cannot come amiss i 2 91
The king is old enough himself To give his censure i 3 120
Give me my fan: what, minion! can ye not? I cry you mercy, madam; was it you? i 3 141
God be praised, that to believing souls Gives light in darkness! ii 1 67
I banish her my bed and company And give her as a prey to law and shame ii 1 198
Give me leave to go; Sorrow would solace and mine age would ease ii 3 20
Here, Robin, an if I die, I give thee my apron ii 3 75
In the morn, When every one will give the time of day iii 1 14
What counsel give you in this weighty cause? iii 1 289
'Twas men I lack'd and you will give them me: I take it kindly iii 1 345
What instance gives Lord Warwick for his vow? iii 2 159
And after all this fearful homage done, Give thee thy hire iii 2 225
If thou be'st death, I'll give thee England's treasure iii 3 2
Show me where he is: I'll give a thousand pound to look upon him iii 3 13
Give me some drink, and bid the apothecary Bring the strong poison iii 3 17
Master, this prisoner freely give I thee iv 1 12
A thousand crowns, or else lay down your head.—And so much shall you give, or off goes yours iv 1 17
A petty sum!—I'll give it, sir; and therefore spare my life iv 1 23
Give him a box o' the ear and that will make 'em red again iv 7 91
Give me but the ten meals I have lost, and I'ld defy them all iv 10 66
I cannot give due action to my words, Except a sword or sceptre balance it v 1 8
We give thee for reward a thousand marks v 1 79
His sons, he says, shall give their words for him v 1 137
Now is it manhood, wisdom and defence, To give the enemy way v 2 76
And we will live To see their day and them our fortune give v 2 89
Sons, peace!—Peace, thou! and give King Henry leave to speak *3 Hen. VI.* i 1 120
Richard cried 'Charge! and give no foot of ground!' i 4 15
I give thee this to dry thy cheeks withal i 4 83
Were thy heart as hard as steel, As thou hast shown it flinty by thy deeds, I come to pierce it, or to give thee mine ii 1 203
For God's sake, lords, give signal to the fight ii 2 100
Give no limits to my tongue: I am a king, and privileged to speak ii 2 119
What counsel give you? whither shall we fly?—Bootless is flight ii 3 11
Yet that thy brazen gates of heaven may ope, And give sweet passage to my sinful soul! ii 3 41
Gives not the hawthorn-bush a sweeter shade To shepherds? ii 5 42

Give. Give me thy gold, if thou hast any gold; For I have bought it with an hundred blows *3 Hen. VI.* ii 5 80
But she's come to beg, Warwick, to give iii 1 42
I think he means to beg a child of her.— . . . He'll rather give her two iii 2 28
What service wilt thou do me, if I give them? iii 2 44
Thy husband's lands I freely give thee.—I take my leave iii 2 55
And give my tongue-tied sorrows leave to speak iii 3 22
Let me give humble thanks for all at once iii 3 221
She is fair and virtuous, Therefore delay not, give thy hand to Warwick iii 3 246
Yes, I accept her, for she well deserves it; And here, to pledge my vow, I give my hand iii 3 250
Your grace hath not done well, To give the heir and daughter of Lord Scales Unto the brother of your loving bride iv 1 52
Give me assurance with some friendly vow iv 1 141
Ay, but give me worship and quietness; I like it better iv 3 16
Warwick and Clarence, give me both your hands iv 6 38
Is not a dukedom, sir, a goodly gift?—Ay, by my faith, for a poor earl to give v 1 32
Add water to the sea And give more strength to that which hath too much v 4 9
Give signal to the fight, and to it, lords! v 4 72
In God's name, lords, Be valiant and give signal to the fight v 4 82
And, that I love the tree from whence thou sprang'st, Witness the loving kiss I give the fruit v 7 32
But I shall live, my lord, to give them thanks That were the cause of my imprisonment.—No doubt, no doubt *Richard III.* i 1 127
Vouchsafe to wear this ring.—To take is not to give i 2 203
God give your grace good rest! i 4 75
When he opens his purse to give us our reward, thy conscience flies out i 4 133
Give me a cup of wine.—You shall have wine enough, my lord, anon i 4 166
Have I a tongue to doom my brother's death, And shall the same give pardon to a slave? ii 1 103
Give me no help in lamentation; I am not barren to bring forth complaints ii 2 66
Will you go To give your censures in this weighty business? ii 2 144
Uncle, give me this dagger.—My dagger, little cousin? with all my heart iii 1 110
A beggar, brother?—Of my kind uncle, that I know will give; And being but a toy, which is no grief to give iii 1 113
A greater gift than that I'll give my cousin iii 1 115
To mitigate the scorn he gives his uncle, He prettily and aptly taunts himself iii 1 133
And so break off your talk, And give us notice of his inclination iii 1 178
For joy of this good news, Give Mistress Shore one gentle kiss the more iii 1 185
But, that I'll give my voice on Richard's side, . . . God knows I will not iii 2 53
We give thee up our guiltless blood to drink iii 3 14
In the duke's behalf I'll give my voice, Which, I presume, he'll take in gentle part iii 4 20
Finds the testy gentleman so hot, As he will lose his head ere give consent iii 4 40
For reverence to some alive, I give a sparing limit to my tongue iii 7 194
God give your graces both A happy and a joyful time of day! iv 1 5
Give me some breath, some little pause, my lord, Before I positively speak iv 2 24
If ancient sorrow be most reverend, Give mine the benefit of seniory iv 4 36
Men shall deal unadvisedly sometimes, Which after hours give leisure to repent iv 4 293
If I did take the kingdom from your sons, To make amends, I'll give it to your daughter iv 4 295
We must have knocks; ha! must we not?—We must both give and take v 3 6
The weary sun . . . Gives signal of a goodly day to-morrow v 3 21
Give me some ink and paper in my tent v 3 23
And so, God give you quiet rest to-night! v 3 43
Give me a watch. Saddle white Surrey for the field to-morrow v 3 63
So, I am satisfied. Give me a bowl of wine v 3 72
God give us leisure for these rites of love! v 3 101
Give me another horse: bind up my wounds. Have mercy, Jesu! v 3 177
Why, then 'tis time to arm and give direction v 3 236
Tell the clock there. Give me a calendar. Who saw the snn to-day? v 3 276
Such as give Their money out of hope they may believe *Hen. VIII.* Prol. 7
Out of his self-drawing web, he gives us note, The force of his own merit makes his way i 1 63
A gift that heaven gives for him, which buys A place next to the king i 1 65
Pray, give me favour, sir. This cunning cardinal The articles o' the combination drew As himself pleased i 1 168
To as much end As give a crutch to the dead i 1 172
I would your highness Would give it quick consideration i 2 66
'Tis time to give 'em physic, their deseases Are grown so catching i 3 36
They are set here for examples.—True, they are so; But few now give so great ones. i 3 63
Go, give 'em welcome; you can speak the French tongue i 4 57
To the water side I must conduct your grace; Then give my charge up ii 1 96
Those you make friends And give your hearts to, when they once perceive The least rub in your fortunes, fall away ii 1 128
Yet I can give you inkling Of an ensuing evil, if it fall, Greater than this ii 1 140
I would your grace would give us but an hour Of private conference ii 2 80
'Tis sweet at first to acquire,—after this process, To give her the avaunt! ii 3 10
Shut door upon me, and so give me up To the sharp'st kind of justice ii 4 43
Then mark the inducement. Thus it came; give heed to't ii 4 169
We shall give you The full cause of our coming iii 1 28
Can you think, lords, That any Englishman dare give me counsel? iii 1 84
I am joyful To meet the least occasion that may give me Remembrance iii 2 7
I, her frail son, amongst my brethren mortal, Must give my tendance to iii 2 149
Give him a little earth for charity! iv 2 23
And, to add greater honours to his age Than man could give him, he died fearing God iv 2 68
Beseeching him to give her virtuous breeding iv 2 134
Give your friend Some touch of your late business v 1 12
Give me thy hand, stand up: Prithee, let's walk v 1 115
Give her an hundred marks. I'll to the queen.—An hundred marks! v 1 170
I take my cause Out of the gripes of cruel men, and give it To a most noble judge v 3 100
Take my blessing: God protect thee! Into whose hand I give thy life v 5 12
You shall see him nod at me.—Will he give you the nod? *Troi. and Cres.* i 2 212
Paris is dirt to him; and, I warrant, Helen, to change, would give an eye to boot i 2 260
Give me ribs of steel! I shall split all In pleasure of my spleen i 3 177
For the success, Although particular, shall give a scantling Of good or bad unto the general i 3 341
Give pardon to my speech i 3 357

Give. Among ourselves Give him allowance for the better man *Troi. and Cres.* i 3 377
Now I begin to relish thy advice; And I will give a taste of it forthwith i 3 389
A stirring dwarf we do allowance give Before a sleeping giant ii 3 146
Let Mars divide eternity in twain, And give him half ii 3 257
You spy! what do you spy? Come, give me an instrument iii 1 104
What he shall receive of us in duty Gives us more palm in beauty than we have iii 1 170
O, be thou my Charon, And give me swift transportance! iii 2 12
You have bereft me of all words, lady.—Words pay no debts, give her deeds iii 2 58
If my lord get a boy of you, you'll give him me iii 2 113
I'll give my word for her too iii 2 117
I do beseech you, as in way of taste, To give me now a little benefit iii 3 14
And they will almost Give us a prince of blood, a son of Priam iii 3 26
Give to dust that is a little gilt More laud than gilt o'er-dusted iii 3 178
An operation more divine Than breath or pen can give expressure to iii 3 204
Those wounds heal ill that men do give themselves iii 3 229
Give him note of our approach, With the whole quality wherefore iv 1 43
Sleep kill those pretty eyes, And give as soft attachment to thy senses iv 2 5
The like allayment could I give my grief iv 4 8
I will corrupt the Grecian sentinels, To give thee nightly visitation iv 4 75
I'll give her to thy hand; And by the way possess thee what she is iv 4 113
Give with thy trumpet a loud note to Troy, Thou dreadful Ajax iv 5 3
In kissing, do you render or receive?—Both take and give iv 5 37
I'll make my match to live, The kiss you take is better than you give iv 5 38
I'll give you boot, I'll give you three for one.—You're an odd man; give even, or give none iv 5 40
Why then for Venus' sake, give me a kiss. iv 5 49
So glib of tongue, That give accosting welcome ere it comes iv 5 59
For what he has he gives, what thinks he shows: Yet gives he not till judgement guide his bounty iv 5 101
That I may give the local wound a name iv 5 244
But gives all gaze and bent of amorous view On the fair Cressid iv 5 282
Give me some token for the surety of it.—I'll fetch you one v 2 60
He loved me—O false wench!—Give't me again v 2 70
Takes my glove, And gives memorial dainty kisses to it, As I kiss thee v 2 80
I'll give you something else.—I will have this: whose was it? v 2 86
Do not give advantage To stubborn critics, apt, without a theme v 2 130
Patroclus will give me any thing for the intelligence v 2 192
We would give much, to use violent thefts, And rob in the behalf of charity v 3 21
Give some groans, Though not for me, yet for your aching bones v 10 50
And could be content to give him good report for't *Coriolanus* i 1 33
He that will give good words to thee will flatter Beneath abhorring i 1 171
Give me excuse, good madam; I will obey you in every thing hereafter i 3 114
I'll nor sell nor give him: lend you him I will For half a hundred years i 4 6
Our powers, with smiling fronts encountering, May give you thankful sacrifice i 6 9
More cruel to your good report than grateful To us that give you truly i 9 55
My noble steed, known to the camp, I give him, With all his trim belonging i 9 61
I request you To give my poor host freedom.—O, well begg'd! i 9 87
Give your dispositions the reins, and be angry at your pleasures ii 1 33
If the drink you give me touch my palate adversely, I make a crooked face ii 1 61
A letter for me! it gives me an estate of seven years' health ii 1 125
Wherein he gives my son the whole name of the war ii 1 149
That he will give them make I as little question As he is proud to do't ii 1 246
But yet my caution was more pertinent Than the rebuke you give it ii 2 68
He covets less Than misery itself would give ii 2 131
I cannot Put on the gown, stand naked and entreat them, For my wounds' sake, to give their suffrage ii 2 142
He will require them, As if he did contemn what he requested Should be in them to give ii 2 162
Are you all resolved to give your voices? But that's no matter ii 3 40
You must think, if we give you any thing, we hope to gain by you ii 3 77
But this is something odd.—An 'twere to give again,—but 'tis no matter ii 3 89
I will counterfeit the bewitchment of some popular man and give it bountiful to the desirers ii 3 109
We hope to find you our friend; and therefore give you our voices heartily ii 3 112
The gods give you joy, sir, heartily! ii 3 118
Whoever gave that counsel, to give forth The corn o' the storehouse gratis iii 1 113
Why, shall the people give One that speaks thus their voice? iii 1 118
I'll give my reasons, More worthier than their voices iii 1 119
Must I with base tongue give my noble heart A lie that it must bear? iii 2 100
Make them be strong and ready for this hint, When we shall hap to give't iii 3 24
I would not buy Their mercy at the price of one fair word; Nor check my courage for what they can give iii 3 92
Give him deserved vexation iii 3 140
I'll enter: if he slay me, He does fair justice; if he give me way, I'll do his country service iv 4 25
Has the porter his eyes in his head, that he gives entrance to such companions? iv 5 13
The veins unfill'd, our blood is cold, and then We pout upon the morning, are unapt To give or to forgive v 1 53
And each in either side Give the all-hail to thee v 3 139
Yet give us our dispatch: I am hush'd until our city be a-fire v 3 180
We have all Great cause to give great thanks v 4 63
Your judgements, my grave lords, Must give this cur the lie v 6 107
Give us the proudest prisoner of the Goths *T. Andron.* i 1 96
I give him you, the noblest that survives, The eldest son of this distressed queen i 1 102
Give me a staff of honour for mine age, But not a sceptre i 1 198
I give thee thanks in part of thy deserts, And will with deeds requite thy gentleness i 1 236
Go, give that changing piece To him that flourish'd for her with his sword i 1 309
Let us give him burial, as becomes: Give Mutius burial with our brethren i 1 347
God give you joy, sir, of your gallant bride! i 1 400
Only thus much I give your grace to know i 1 413
With horn and hound we'll give your grace bonjour i 1 494
Give the king this fatal-plotted scroll. Now question me no more ii 3 47
Give me thy poniard; you shall know, my boys, Your mother's hand shall right your mother's wrong ii 3 120
That he thereby may give a likely guess ii 3 207
Give me a sword, I'll chop off my hands too iii 1 72

Give. But that which gives my soul the greatest spurn, Is dear Lavinia *T. Andron.* iii 1 101
Like a lark, That gives sweet tidings of the sun's uprise . . . iii 1 159
I'll deceive them both : Lend me thy hand, and I will give thee mine . iii 1 188
Good Aaron, give his majesty my hand : Tell him it was a hand that warded him From thousand dangers . . . . iii 1 194
Give me thy knife, I will insult on him . . . . . . iii 2 71
Give signs, sweet girl, for here are none but friends . . . iv 1 61
She is brought a-bed.—Well, God give her good rest! . . . iv 2 63
Nurse, give it me ; my sword shall soon dispatch it . . . iv 2 86
Go pack with him, and give the mother gold . . . . . iv 2 155
Good boy, in Virgo's lap ; give it Pallas . . . . . . iv 3 64
He should not choose But give them to his master for a present.—Why, there it goes : God give his lordship joy! . . . . . . iv 3 75
Make no more ado, But give your pigeons to the emperor . . iv 3 103
Give me pen and ink. Sirrah, can you with a grace deliver a supplication? . . . . iv 3 106
How can I grace my talk, Wanting a hand to give it action? . . v 2 18
Now give some surance that thou art Revenge . . . . . v 2 46
That gives our Troy, our Rome, the civil wound . . . . v 3 87
Gentle people, give me aim awhile, For nature puts me to a heavy task v 3 149
Have done with woes : Give sentence on this execrable wretch . v 3 177
Convey the emperor hence, And give him burial in his father's grave . v 3 192
Give me my long sword, ho!—A crutch, a crutch! . *Rom and Jul.* i 1 82
Could we but learn from whence his sorrows grow, We would as willingly give cure as know . . . . i 1 161
But no more deep will I endart mine eye Than your consent gives strength to make it fly . . . . i 3 99
Give me a torch : I am not for this ambling . . . . . i 4 11
Give me a case to put my visage in : A visor for a visor! . . . i 4 29
A hall, a hall! give room! and foot it, girls . . . . . i 5 28
O trespass sweetly urged! Give me my sin again . . . . . i 5 112
I gave thee mine before thou didst request it : And yet I would it were to give again.—Wouldst thou withdraw it? for what purpose, love? —But to be frank, and give it thee again . . . . ii 2 128
My bounty is as boundless as the sea, My love as deep ; the more I give to thee, The more I have . . . . ii 2 134
For nought so vile that on the earth doth live But to the earth some special good doth give . . . . ii 3 18
What counterfeit did I give you?—The slip, sir . . . . . ii 4 50
The exchange of joy That one short minute gives me in her sight . ii 6 5
You shall find me apt enough to that, sir, an you will give me occasion iii 1 45
I beg for justice, which thou, prince, must give . . . . iii 1 185
Come, gentle night, come, loving, black-brow'd night, Give me my Romeo . . . . iii 2 21
Give me some aqua vitæ : These griefs, these woes, these sorrows make me old . . . . iii 2 88
Give this ring to my true knight, And bid him come to take his last farewell . . . . iii 2 142
I'll give thee armour to keep off that word . . . . . iii 3 54
Here, sir, a ring she bid me give you, sir : Hie you, make haste . iii 3 163
Shall give him such an unaccustomed dram . . . . . . iii 5 91
Ay, sir ; but she will none, she gives you thanks . . . . iii 5 140
Doth she not give us thanks? Is she not proud? doth she not count her blest? . . . . iii 5 143
An you be mine, I'll give you to my friend ; An you be not, hang, beg, starve . . . . iii 5 193
Her father counts it dangerous That she doth give her sorrow so much sway . . . . iv 1 10
If, in thy wisdom, thou canst give no help, Do thou but call my resolution wise, And with this knife I'll help it . . . . . iv 1 52
Out of thy long-experienced time, Give me some present counsel . iv 1 61
And, if thou darest, I'll give thee remedy . . . . . . iv 1 76
Hold, then ; go home, be merry, give consent To marry Paris . . iv 1 89
Give me, give me! O, tell not me of fear! . . . . . . iv 1 121
Love give me strength! and strength shall help afford . . . iv 1 125
Have I thought long to see this morning's face, And doth it give me such a sight as this? . . . . iv 5 42
I will then give it you soundly.—What will you give us?—No money . iv 5 113
Then will I give you the serving-creature . . . . . . iv 5 117
What says Romeo? Or, if his mind be writ, give me his letter . . v 2 3
Give me thy torch, boy : hence, and stand aloof . . . . . v 3 1
Give me those flowers. Do as I bid thee, go . . . . . v 3 9
The boy gives warning something doth approach . . . . . v 3 18
Give me that mattock and the wrenching iron . . . . . v 3 22
Give me the light : upon thy life, I charge thee, Whate'er thou hear'st or seest, stand all aloof . . . . v 3 25
This letter he early bid me give his father . . . . . . v 3 275
Give me the letter ; I will look on it . . . . v 3 278
No more Can I demand.—But I can give thee more . . . . v 3 298
Give him thy daughter : What you bestow, in him I'll counterpoise *T. of Athens* i 1 144
My lord, 'tis rated As those which sell would give . . . . i 1 169
Pray, entertain them ; give them guide to us . . . . . i 1 252
Thou art a fool to bid me farewell twice.—Why, Apemantus?—Shouldst have kept one to thyself, for I mean to give thee none . . . i 1 276
There's none Can truly say he gives, if he receives . . . . i 2 11
I come to observe : I give thee warning on't.—I take no heed of thee . i 2 33
He commands us to provide, and give great gifts, And all out of an empty coffer . . . . i 2 198
'Tis not enough to give ; Methinks, I could deal kingdoms to my friends i 2 225
I am sworn not to give regard to you . . . . i 2 251
If I want gold, steal but a beggar's dog, And give it Timon . . ii 1 6
If I would sell my horse, and buy twenty more Better than he, why, give my horse to Timon, Ask nothing, give it him, it foals me, straight, And able horses . . . . ii 1 8
Give me breath. I do beseech you, good my lords, keep on . . ii 2 34
The world is but a word : Were it all yours to give it in a breath, How quickly were it gone! . . . . ii 2 162
Five talents. That had, give't these fellows To whom 'tis instant due ii 2 238
A towardly prompt spirit—give thee thy due . . . . . . iii 1 37
His friends, like physicians, Thrive, give him over . . . . iii 3 12
But reserve still to give, lest your deities be despised . . . iii 6 81
Make the meat be beloved more than the man that gives it . . iii 6 86
One day he gives us diamonds, next day stones . . . . . iii 6 131
Place thieves And give them title, knee and approbation With senators iv 3 36
How came the noble Timon to this change?—As the moon does, by wanting light to give . . . . iv 3 67
Give them diseases, leaving with thee their lust . . . . iv 3 84
Give us some gold, good Timon : hast thou more? . . . . iv 3 132

Give. What wouldst thou do with the world, Apemantus, if it lay in thy power?—Give it the beasts, to be rid of the men *T. of Athens* iv 3 323
Steal no less for this I give you ; and gold confound you howsoe'er! . iv 3 452
Whose eyes do never give But thorough lust and laughter . . . iv 3 491
Give to dogs What thou deny'st to men ; let prisons swallow 'em . . iv 3 536
I'll give you gold, Rid me these villains from your companies . . v 1 103
Confound them by some course, and come to me, I'll give you gold enough . . . . v 1 107
To give thy rages balm, To wipe out our ingratitude with loves . . v 4 16
Which give some soil perhaps to my behaviours . . . *J. Cæsar* i 2 42
Alas, it cried 'Give me some drink, Titinius,' As a sick girl . . i 2 127
Which gives men stomach to digest his words With better appetite . i 2 305
The exhalations whizzing in the air Give so much light that I may read ii 1 45
Let me work ; For I can give his humour the true bent . . . ii 1 210
The senate have concluded To give this day a crown to mighty Cæsar . ii 2 94
I am ashamed I did yield to them. Give me my robe, for I will go . ii 2 107
Here will I stand till Cæsar pass along, And as a suitor will I give him this . . . . ii 3 12
Upon this hope, that you shall give me reasons Why and wherein . iii 1 221
Let us be satisfied.—Then follow me, and give me audience . . . iii 2 2
Give him a statue with his ancestors . . . . iii 2 55
To every Roman citizen he gives, To every several man, seventy five drachmas . . . . iii 2 246
Fortune is merry, And in this mood will give us any thing . . . iii 2 272
Stand, ho!—Give the word, ho! and stand . . . . . . iv 2 2
Enlarge your griefs, And I will give you audience . . . . iv 2 47
I, that denied thee gold, will give my heart . . . . . . iv 3 104
Give me a bowl of wine. In this I bury all unkindness . . . iv 3 158
Give me the gown. Where is thy instrument?—Here in the tent . . iv 3 239
I was sure your lordship did not give it me . . . . . . iv 3 254
Mark Antony, shall we give sign of battle?—No, Cæsar . . . . v 1 23
In your bad strokes, Brutus, you give good words . . . . . v 1 30
By which I did blame Cato for the death Which he did give himself . v 1 103
Ride, and give these bills Unto the legions on the other side . . v 2 1
Sudden push gives them the overthrow. Ride, ride . . . . v 2 5
They Put on my brows this wreath of victory, And bid me give it thee . v 3 83
Take this garland on thy brow ; Thy Brutus bid me give it thee . . v 3 86
Give him all kindness : I had rather have Such men my friends than enemies . . . . v 4 28
'Give me,' quoth I : 'Aroint thee, witch!' the rump-fed ronyon cries *Macbeth* i 3 5
I'll give thee a wind.—Thou'rt kind.—And I another . . . . i 3 11
We are sent To give thee from our royal master thanks . . . i 3 101
Give me your favour : my dull brain was wrought With things forgotten . . . . i 3 149
Give him tending ; He brings great news . . . . i 5 38
Nights and days to come Give solely sovereign sway and masterdom . i 5 71
Words to the heat of deeds too cold breath gives . . . . . ii 1 61
The fatal bellman, Which gives the stern'st good-night . . . . ii 2 4
Look on't again I dare not.—Infirm of purpose! Give me the daggers ii 2 53
Hark! I hear horses.—Give us a light there, ho! . . . . . iii 3 9
You do not give the cheer : the feast is sold That is not often vouch'd, while 'tis a-making, 'Tis given with welcome . . . . . . iii 4 33
Give me some wine : fill full. I drink to the general joy o' the whole table . . . . iii 4 88
We may again Give to our tables meat, sleep to our nights . . . iii 6 34
I'll charm the air to give a sound, While you perform your antic round iv 1 129
Seize upon Fife ; give to the edge o' the sword His wife, his babes . iv 1 151
Give sorrow words : the grief that does not speak Whispers the o'erfraught heart and bids it break . . . . iv 3 209
Well, march we on, To give obedience where 'tis truly owed . . . v 2 26
I'll fight till from my bones my flesh be hack'd. Give me my armour . v 3 33
Come, put mine armour on ; give me my staff. Seyton, send out . . v 3 48
Make all our trumpets speak ; give them all breath . . . . v 6 9
Thou bloodier villain Than terms can give thee out! . . . . v 8 8
Give you good night.—O, farewell . . . . *Hamlet* i 1 16
I do beseech you, give him leave to go.—Take thy fair hour, Laertes . i 2 61
'Tis sweet and commendable in your nature, Hamlet, To give these mourning duties to your father . . . . i 2 88
Whatsoever else shall hap to-night, Give it an understanding, but no tongue . . . . i 2 250
As the winds give benefit And convoy is assistant, do not sleep . . i 3 2
As he in his particular act and place May give his saying deed . . i 3 27
Give thy thoughts no tongue, Nor any unproportion'd thought his act . i 3 59
Give every man thy ear, but few thy voice ; Take each man's censure . i 3 68
What is between you? give me up the truth . . . . . . i 3 98
I would not . Have you so slander any moment leisure, As to give words or talk with the Lord Hamlet . . . . i 3 134
As you are friends, scholars and soldiers, Give me one poor request . i 5 142
This is wondrous strange!—And therefore as a stranger give it welcome i 5 165
Give him this money and these notes . . . . ii 1 1
Give first admittance to the ambassadors . . . . ii 2 51
Makes vow before his uncle never more To give the assay of arms . . ii 2 71
Gives him three thousand crowns in annual fee . . . . . . ii 2 73
That it might please you to give quiet pass Through your dominions . ii 2 77
Give twenty, forty, fifty, an hundred ducats a-piece for his picture in little ii 2 382
Come, give us a taste of your quality ; come, a passionate speech . ii 2 451
Gives me the lie i' the throat, As deep as to the lungs? who does me this? ii 2 601
Give him a further edge, And drive his purpose on to these delights . iii 1 26
How smart a lash that speech doth give my conscience! . . . . iii 1 50
In that sleep of death what dreams may come When we have shuffled off this mortal coil, Must give us pause . . . . iii 1 68
This was sometime a paradox, but now the time gives it proof . . iii 1 115
Imagination to give them shape, or time to act them in . . . . iii 1 128
If thou dost marry, I'll give thee this plague for thy dowry . . . iii 1 139
You must acquire and beget a temperance that may give it smoothness iii 2 9
Give me that man That is not passion's slave . . . . . . iii 2 76
Give him heedful note ; For I mine eyes will rivet to his face . . iii 2 89
Nor earth to me give food, nor heaven light! . . . . . . iii 2 226
Give it breath with your mouth, and it will discourse most eloquent music . . . . iii 2 373
How in my words soever she be shent, To give them seals never, my soul, consent! . . . . iii 2 417
And we ourselves compell'd, Even to the teeth and forehead of our faults, To give in evidence . . . . iii 3 64
To give the world assurance of a man . . . . iii 4 62
Proclaim no shame When the compulsive ardour gives the charge . iii 4 86
He likewise gives a frock or livery, That aptly is put on . . . iii 4 164
As my great power thereof may give thee sense . . . . . iv 3 61
Follow her close ; give her good watch, I pray you . . . . . iv 5 75

Give. Like to a murdering-piece, in many places Gives me superfluous death *Hamlet* iv 5 96
O thou vile king, Give me my father! iv 5 116
That both the worlds I give to negligence, Let come what comes iv 5 134
I would give you some violets, but they withered all when my father died iv 5 184
We will our kingdom give, Our crown, our life, and all that we call ours iv 5 207
We shall jointly labour with your soul To give it due content iv 5 212
Give these fellows some means to the king iv 6 13
And long purples That liberal shepherds give a grosser name iv 7 171
How much I had to do to calm his rage! Now fear I this will give it start again iv 7 194
Give me your pardon, sir: I've done you wrong; But pardon't v 2 237
Give us the foils. Come on.—Come, one for me v 2 265
Give them the foils, young Osric. Cousin Hamlet, You know the wager? v 2 270
If Hamlet give the first or second hit, Or quit in answer of the third exchange, Let all the battlements their ordnance fire v 2 279
Give me the cups; And let the kettle to the trumpet speak v 2 285
Stay; give me drink. Hamlet, this pearl is thine; Here's to thy health v 2 293
Give him the cup.—I'll play this bout first; set it by awhile v 2 294
As thou'rt a man, Give me the cup: let go; by heaven, I'll have't v 2 354
To the ambassadors of England gives This warlike volley v 2 362
The ears are senseless that should give us hearing v 2 380
Give me the map there. Know that we have divided In three our kingdom *Lear* i 1 38
Here I give Her father's heart from her! i 1 127
Give but that portion which yourself proposed, And here I take Cordelia i 1 245
Give me the letter, sir.—I shall offend, either to detain or give it i 2 41
Give me an egg, nuncle, and I'll give thee two crowns i 4 170
But let his disposition have that scope That dotage gives it i 4 315
I can tell why a snail has a house.—Why?—Why, to put his head in; not to give it away to his daughters i 5 32
Seeking to give Losses their remedies ii 2 176
The country gives me proof and precedent Of Bedlam beggars ii 3 13
When a wise man gives thee better counsel, give me mine again: I would have none but knaves follow it, since a fool gives it ii 4 76
Give me my servant forth. Go tell the duke and's wife I'ld speak with them ii 4 116
Thy tender-hefted nature shall not give Thee o'er to harshness ii 4 174
But, for true need,—You heavens, give me that patience, patience I need! ii 4 274
Who gives any thing to poor Tom? whom the foul fiend hath led iii 4 51
What, have his daughters brought him to this pass? Couldst thou save nothing? Didst thou give them all? iii 4 66
He gives the web and the pin, squints the eye, and makes the hare-lip iii 4 122
Follow me, that will to some provision Give thee quick conduct iii 6 104
He that will think to live till he be old, Give me some help! iii 7 70
Give me thy sword. A peasant stand up thus! iii 7 80
I bleed apace: Untimely comes this hurt: give me your arm iii 7 98
Give me thy arm: Poor Tom shall lead thee iv 1 81
I must change arms at home, and give the distaff Into my husband's hands iv 2 17
If you do find him, pray you, give him this iv 5 33
Give me your hand: you are now within a foot Of the extreme verge iv 6 25
Give me your arm: Up: so. How is't? Feel you your legs? You stand iv 6 64
Give the word.—Sweet marjoram.—Pass iv 6 93
Give me an ounce of civet, good apothecary, to sweeten my imagination iv 6 132
And give the letters which thou find'st about me To Edmund iv 6 254
This sword of mine shall give them instant way v 3 149
Well thought on: take my sword, Give it the captain v 3 251
Give me a taper! call up all my people! *Othello* i 1 142
Or put upon you what restraint and grievance The law, with all his might to enforce it on, Will give him cable i 2 17
There is no composition in these news That gives them credit i 3 2
I here do give thee that with all my heart Which, but thou hast already, with all my heart I would keep from thee i 3 193
O, let the heavens Give him defence against the elements ii 1 45
Go forth, And give us truth who 'tis that is arrived ii 1 58
Give renew'd fire to our extincted spirits! ii 1 81
A sail!—They give their greeting to the citadel: This likewise is a friend ii 1 95
'Tis my breeding That gives me this bold show of courtesy ii 1 100
Would she give you so much of her lips As of her tongue she oft bestows on me, You'ld have enough ii 1 101
It gives me wonder great as my content To see you here before me ii 1 185
To give satiety a fresh appetite, loveliness in favour, sympathy in years ii 1 231
He gives your Hollander a vomit, ere the next pottle can be filled ii 3 86
He is a soldier fit to stand by Cæsar And give direction ii 3 128
Give me answer to it.—Worthy Othello, I am hurt to danger ii 3 196
Give me to know How this foul rout began ii 3 209
When this advice is free I give and honest, Probal to thinking ii 3 343
Give me advantage of some brief discourse With Desdemona alone iii 1 55
These letters give, Iago, to the pilot; And by him do my duties to the senate iii 2 1
Before Emilia here I give thee warrant of thy place iii 3 20
Thy solicitor shall rather die Than give thy cause away iii 3 28
Give thy worst of thoughts The worst of words iii 3 132
I'll have the work ta'en out, And give't Iago: what he will do with it Heaven knows, not I iii 3 297
What will you give me now For that same handkerchief? iii 3 305
Look, here it is.—A good wench; give it me.—What will you do with't? iii 3 313
If it be not for some purpose of import, Give't me again iii 3 317
Be sure of it; give me the ocular proof iii 3 360
If imputation and strong circumstances, Which lead directly to the door of truth, Will give you satisfaction iii 3 408
That handkerchief Did an Egyptian to my mother give iii 4 56
She, dying, gave it me; And bid me, when my fate would have me wive, To give it her iii 4 63
To lose't or give't away were such perdition As nothing else could match iii 4 67
But if I give my wife a handkerchief,— What then?—Why, then, 'tis hers iv 1 10
She is protectress of her honour too: May she give that? iv 1 15
How do you now, lieutenant?—The worser that you give me the addition Whose want even kills me iv 1 105
She gives it out that you shall marry her: Do you intend it? iv 1 118
Give it your hobby-horse: wheresoever you had it, I'll take out no work iv 1 160
If you are so fond over her iniquity, give her patent to offend iv 1 209
Good Emilia, Give me my nightly wearing, and adieu iv 3 16
O, I am spoil'd, undone by villains! Give me some help v 1 55
When I have pluck'd the rose, I cannot give it vital growth again v 2 14
That handkerchief thou speak'st of I found by fortune and did give my husband v 2 226
She give it Cassio! no, alas! I found it, And I did give't my husband v 2 230

Give. Good sir, give me good fortune.—I make not, but foresee *A. and C.* i 2 13
Your fortunes are alike.—But how, but how? give me particulars i 2 57
And let her die too, and give him a worse! and let worse follow worse! i 2 67
Why, sir, give the gods a thankful sacrifice i 2 167
In each thing give him way, cross him in nothing i 3 9
I am sick and sullen.—I am sorry to give breathing to my purpose i 3 14
Though age from folly could not give me freedom, It does from childishness i 3 57
Which are, or cease, As you shall give the advice i 3 68
And give true evidence to his love, which stands An honourable trial i 3 74
Let us grant, it is not Amiss to tumble on the bed of Ptolemy; To give a kingdom for a mirth i 4 18
Men's reports Give him much wrong'd i 4 40
Ha, ha! Give me to drink mandragora.—Why, madam? i 5 4
I will give thee bloody teeth, If thou with Cæsar paragon again My man i 5 70
Give me some music; music, moody food Of us that trade in love ii 5 1
Give me mine angle; we'll to the river ii 5 10
The gold I give thee will I melt and pour Down thy ill-uttering throat ii 5 34
Will this description satisfy him?—With the health that Pompey gives him ii 7 57
Though thou think me poor, I am the man Will give thee all the world ii 7 71
Look, here I have you; thus I let you go, And give you to the gods iii 2 64
Let all the number of the stars give light To thy fair way! iii 2 65
And gives his potent regiment to a trull, That noises it against us iii 6 95
Give me a kiss; Even this repays me iii 11 70
He partly begs To be desired to give iii 13 67
Give him no breath, but now Make boot of his distraction iv 1 8
What mean you, sir, To give them this discomfort? Look, they weep iv 2 34
So, so; come, give me that: this way; well said. Fare thee well, dame iv 4 28
Antony Hath after thee sent all thy treasure . . . —I give it you.—Mock not iv 6 24
I'll give thee, friend, An armour all of gold; it was a king's iv 8 26
By starts, His fretted fortunes give him hope, and fear iv 12 8
Vanish, or I shall give thee thy deserving, And blemish Cæsar's triumph iv 12 32
Draw thy sword, and give me Sufficing strokes for death iv 14 116
I am dying, Egypt, dying: Give me some wine, and let me speak a little iv 15 42
But you, gods, will give us Some faults to make us men v 1 32
Give her what comforts The quality of her passion shall require v 1 62
If he please To give me conquer'd Egypt for my son, He gives me so much of mine own v 2 19
We intend so to dispose you as Yourself shall give us counsel v 2 187
Give it nothing, I pray you, for it is not worth the feeding.—Will it eat me? v 2 279
Give me my robe, put on my crown; I have Immortal longings in me v 2 283
I hear him mock The luck of Cæsar, which the gods give men To excuse their after wrath v 2 289
I am fire and air; my other elements I give to baser life v 2 293
O lady, weep no more, lest I give cause To be suspected of more tenderness Than doth become a man *Cymbeline* i 1 93
Give me but this [wife] I have, And sear up my embracements from a next! i 1 115
Ere I could Give him that parting kiss i 3 34
And give me directly to understand you have prevailed i 4 171
I was going, sir, To give him welcome i 6 55
Give me your pardon. I have spoke this, to know i 6 162
I give him satisfaction? Would he had been one of my rank! ii 1 16
It is not fit your lordship should undertake every companion that you give offence to ii 1 29
I am advised to give her music o' mornings; they say it will penetrate ii 3 13
The thanks I give Is telling you that I am poor of thanks ii 3 93
By her own command Shall give thee opportunity iii 2 19
I shall give thee opportunity at Milford-Haven iii 4 28
But we'll even All that good time will give us iii 4 185
I'll love him as my brother: And such a welcome as I'ld give to him After long absence, such is yours iii 6 73
But what occasion Hath Cadwal now to give it motion? iv 2 188
O! Give colour to my pale cheek with thy blood iv 2 330
Britain, I have kill'd thy mistress; peace! I'll give no wound to thee v 1 21
We are Romans and will give you that Like beasts which you shun beastly v 3 26
You good gods, give me The penitent instrument to pick that bolt! v 4 9
Ask of Cymbeline what boon thou wilt, Fitting my bounty and thy state, I'll give it v 5 98
I'll tell you, sir, in private, if you please To give me hearing v 5 116
Step you forth; Give answer to this boy, and do it freely v 5 131
O, give me cord, or knife, or poison, Some upright justicer! v 5 213
To the judgement of your eye I give, my cause who best can justify *Pericles* i Gower 42
Her thoughts the king Of every virtue gives renown to men! i 1 14
O you powers That give heaven countless eyes to view men's acts i 1 73
Then give my tongue like leave to love my head i 1 108
Peace, peace, and give experience tongue i 2 37
A spark, To which that blast gives heat and stronger glowing i 2 41
Why . . . He would depart, I'll give some light unto you i 3 18
Those which see them fall Have scarce strength left to give them burial i 4 49
And give them life whom hunger starved half dead i 4 96
The good in conversation, To whom I give my benison ii Gower 10
Till fortune, tired with doing bad, Threw him ashore, to give him glad ii Gower 38
My veins are chill, And have no more of life than may suffice To give my tongue that heat to ask your help ii 1 79
Why, do 'e take it, and the gods give thee good on't! ii 1 153
To whom this wreath of victory I give, And crown you king ii 3 10
And gives them what he will, not what they crave ii 3 47
Princes in this should live like gods above, Who freely give to every one that comes To honour them ii 3 60
That all those eyes adored them ere their fall Scorn now their hand should give them burial ii 4 12
Be resolved he lives to govern us, Or dead, give's cause to mourn his funeral ii 4 32
And for a further grief,—God give you joy!—What, are you both pleased? ii 5 87
We here below Recall not what we give, and therein may Use honour with you iii 1 25
Nor have I time To give thee hallow'd to thy grave iii 1 60
Give this to the 'pothecary, And tell me how it works iii 2 9
Which doth give me A more content in course of true delight iii 2 38

Give. Here I give to understand, If e'er this coffin drive a-land *Pericles* iii 2 68
Who finds her, give her burying; She was the daughter of a king . . iii 2 72
I pray you, give her air. Gentlemen, This queen will live . . . iii 2 91
Beseeching you To give her princely training . . . . . . iii 3 16
Give you up to the mask'd Neptune and The gentlest winds of heaven . iii 3 36
Come, give me your flowers, ere the sea mar it . . . . . . iv 1 27
Cry 'He that will give most shall have her first' . . . . . iv 2 64
Were I chief lord of all this spacious world, I'ld give it to undo the deed . . . . iv 3 6
No less than it gives a good report to a number to be chaste . . iv 6 43
Her gain She gives the cursed bawd . . . . v Gower 11
And makes them hungry, The more she gives them speech . . . v 1 114
Strike me, honour'd sir; Give me a gash, put me to present pain . . v 1 193
Give me fresh garments . . . . v 1 216
Give me my robes. I am wild in my beholding . . . . . . v 1 224
It is not good to cross him; give him way . . . . . . v 1 232
And give them repetition to the life . . . . v 1 247
And give you gold for such provision As our intents will need . . v 1 258
This, my last boon, give me, For such kindness must relieve me . . v 2 3
Give you good morrow *Mer. Wives* ii 2; ii 3; iii 5; *L. L. Lost* iv 2; *Richard III.* ii 3
Give away. I give away myself for you and dote upon the exchange *Much Ado* ii 1 319
This ring: Which when you part from, lose, or give away, Let it presage the ruin of your love . . . . *Mer. of Venice* iii 2 174
I thank you all, That have beheld me give away myself . *T. of Shrew* iii 2 195
If you shall marry, You give away this hand, and that is mine; You give away heaven's vows, and those are mine; You give away myself, which is known mine . . . . *All's Well* v 3 170
With mine own hands I give away my crown . . . *Richard II.* iv 1 208
I thank your grace for this high courtesy, Which I shall give away immediately . . . . *1 Hen. IV.* v 5 33
Our King Henry gives away his own, To match with her . *2 Hen. VI.* i 1 130
What is't to them? 'Tis thine they give away, and not their own . i 1 221
And give away The benefit of our levies . . . . . . *Coriolanus* v 6 66
I fear me thou wilt give away thyself in paper shortly . *T. of Athens* i 2 247
That lord that counsell'd thee To give away thy land . . . *Lear* i 4 155
Give back, or else embrace thy death . . . . . *T. G. of Ver.* v 4 126
She could not sway her house, command her followers, Take and give back affairs and their dispatch . . . . *T. Night* iv 3 18
Give ear to his motions, Master Slender . . . . . *Mer. Wives* i 1 221
Break the neck of the wax, and every one give ear . . *L. L. Lost* iv 1 59
Pretty mistresses, give ear: Immediately they will again be here . v 2 286
Therefore perpend, my princess, and give ear . . . . *T. Night* v 1 308
Give ear, sir, to my sister . . . . *Lear* ii 4 236
Give fire: she is my prize, or ocean whelm them all! . . *Mer. Wives* ii 2 143
Fear we broadsides? no, let the fiend give fire . . . *2 Hen. IV.* ii 4 196
Give ground. As proper a man as ever went on four legs cannot make him give ground . . . . *Tempest* ii 2 64
Give ground, if you see him furious . . . . *T. Night* iii 4 334
Give guess. I cannot, by the progress of the stars, Give guess how near to day . . . . *J. Cæsar* ii 1 3
Give lost. The crown and comfort of my life, your favour, I do give lost *W. Tale* iii 2 96
Give notice to such men of sort and suit as are to meet him *M. for M.* iv 4 19
That we find the slothful watch but weak, I'll by a sign give notice *1 Hen. VI.* iii 2 8
Give notice, that no manner of person At any time have recourse unto the princes . . . . *Richard III.* iii 5 108
Give off. Did not the prophet Say that before Ascension-day at noon My crown I should give off? . . . . *K. John* v 1 27
Let's see how it will give off . . . . *Ant. and Cleo.* iv 3 23
Give order to my servants that they take No note at all of our being absent hence . . . . *Mer. of Venice* v 1 119
Mourn not . . . ; Only give order for my funeral . . . *1 Hen. VI.* i 5 112
Give order that these bodies High on a stage be placed to the view *Ham.* v 2 388
Give out. You'll be glad to give out a commission for more heads *Meas. for Meas.* ii 1 253
Therefore give out you are of Epidamnum . . . . *Com. of Errors* i 2 1
I will give out divers schedules of my beauty . . . . *T. Night* i 5 263
One that gives out himself Prince Florizel, Son of Polixenes *W. Tale* v 1 85
Give out That Anne my wife is sick and like to die . . *Richard III.* iv 2 57
Side factions and give out Conjectural marriages . . . *Coriolanus* i 1 197
These pencill'd figures are Even such as they give out . *T. of Athens* i 1 160
An older and a better soldier none That Christendom gives out *Macbeth* iv 3 192
She that, so young, could give out such a seeming . . . *Othello* iii 3 209
Give over. Shall we give o'er and drown? . . . . . . *Tempest* i 1 41
Talk not to me; my mind is heavy: I will give over all . *Mer. Wives* iv 6 2
Embrace your own safety and give over this attempt . *As Y. Like It* i 2 189
And shall I now give o'er the yielded set? . . . . . *K. John* v 2 107
I must give over this life, and I will give it over . . . *1 Hen. IV.* i 2 107
The which, if you give o'er To stormy passion, must perforce decay *2 Hen. IV.* i 1 164
Who, half through, Gives o'er and leaves his part-created cost . i 3 60
The work ish give over, the trompet sound the retreat . *Hen. V.* iii 2 94
What devise you on? Shall we give over Orleans, or no? . *1 Hen. VI.* i 2 125
I'll believe him as an enemy, and give over my trade . *T. of Athens* iv 3 460
Give o'er the play.—Give me some light: away! . . . *Hamlet* iii 2 279
I will give over my suit . . . . *Othello* iv 2 201
If none will do, let her remain; but I'll never give o'er . *Cymbeline* ii 3 17
Three or four thousand chequins were as pretty a proportion to live quietly, and so give over . . . . *Pericles* iv 2 29
You scorn: believe me, 'twere best I did give o'er . . . . . v 1 168
Give place. Farewell.—Let all the rest give place . . . *T. Night* ii 4 82
Fellow, give place; here is no longer stay . . . . *Richard II.* v 5 95
Will it give place to flexure and low bending? . . . . *Hen. V.* iv 1 272
Give place: by heaven, thou shalt rule no more O'er him . *2 Hen. VI.* v 1 104
Give place.—What, urge you your petitions in the street? . *J. Cæsar* iii 1 10
Of your philosophy you make no use, If you give place to accidental evils . . . . iv 3 146
Bring but five and twenty: to no more Will I give place or notice *Lear* ii 4 252
It hath pleased the devil drunkenness to give place to the devil wrath *Othello* ii 3 298
Give thanks you have lived so long . . . . *Tempest* i 1 26
Will you give thanks, sweet Kate; or else shall I? . . *T. of Shrew* iv 1 162
I stood i' the level Of a full-charged confederacy, and give thanks To you that choked it . . . . *Hen. VIII.* i 2 3
Feasts are too proud to give thanks to the gods . . *T. of Athens* i 2 62
Give up. Do you your office, or give up your place . . *Meas. for Meas.* ii 2 13
Or, to redeem him, Give up your body to such sweet uncleanness . . ii 4 54
Give up. Who do prepare to meet him at the gates, There to give up their power . . . . *Meas. for Meas.* iv 3 137
For which I do discharge you of your office: Give up your keys . . v 1 467
We will give up our right in Aquitaine . . . . . *L. L. Lost* ii 1 140
Give up thy staff: Henry will to himself Protector be . *2 Hen. VI.* ii 3 23
Give up your staff, sir, and the king his realm . . . . . . ii 3 31
I dare not make myself so guilty, To give up willingly that noble title Your master wed me to . . . . *Hen. VIII.* iii 1 140
We must give up to Diomedes' hand The Lady Cressida . *Troi. and Cres.* iv 2 67
Their shadows seem A canopy most fatal, under which Our army lies, ready to give up the ghost . . . . *J. Cæsar* v 1 89
But we both obey, And here give up ourselves . . . . *Hamlet* ii 2 30
Iago doth give up The execution of his wit, hands, heart *Othello* iii 3 465
Give up yourself merely to chance and hazard, From firm security *Ant. and Cleo.* iii 7 48
Give way. To the brightest beams Distracted clouds give way *All's Well* v 3 35
As every present time doth boast itself Above a better gone, so must thy grave Give way to what's seen now . . . . . *W. Tale* v 1 98
Why, then, give way, dull clouds, to my quick curses! . *Richard III.* i 3 196
What he deserves of you and me I know; What we can do to him, though now the time Gives way to us, I much fear . *Hen. VIII.* iii 2 16
Be of good cheer; They shall no more prevail than we give way to . v 1 143
If you give way, Or hedge aside from the direct forthright, Like to an enter'd tide, they all rush by . . . . . *Troi. and Cres.* iii 3 157
Give way there, and go on! . . . . *Coriolanus* ii 1 210
Tribunes, give way; he shall to the market-place . . . . . iii 1 31
It must omit Real necessities, and give way the while To unstable slightness . . . . iii 1 147
Yonder comes a poet and a painter: the plague of company light upon thee! I will fear to catch it and give way . . . *T. of Athens* iv 3 358
Look about you: security gives way to conspiracy . . . *J. Cæsar* ii 3 8
Merciful powers, Restrain in me the cursed thoughts that nature Gives way to in repose! . . . . *Macbeth* ii 1 9
For mine own good, All causes shall give way . . . . . . iii 4 136
That nature thus gives way to loyalty, something fears me to think of *Lear* iii 5 4
I know not, Menas, How lesser enmities may give way to greater *A. and C.* ii 1 43
Small to greater matters must give way.—Not if the small come first . ii 2 11
Fie! you must give way . . . . *Cymbeline* ii 1 158
If the peevish baggage would but give way to customers . *Pericles* iv 6 20
Given. What a blow was there given!—An it had not fallen flat-long *Temp.* ii 1 180
Like poison given to work a great time after, Now 'gins to bite the spirits iii 3 105
I Have given you here a thrid of mine own life, Or that for which I live iv 1 3
To the dread rattling thunder Have I given fire . . . . . v 1 45
My dukedom since you have given me again, I will requite you . . v 1 168
He would have given it you; but I, being in the way, Did in your name receive it: pardon the fault, I pray . . . . *T. G. of Ver.* i 2 39
She hath given you a letter.—That's the letter I writ to her friend . ii 1 165
His worst fault is, that he is given to prayer . . . . *Mer. Wives* i 4 13
She is given too much to allicholy and musing. . . . . . i 4 164
I had myself twenty angels given me this morning . . . . . ii 2 73
Have given largely to many to know what she would have given . . ii 2 207
On that token, The maid hath given consent to go with him . . . iv 6 45
And have given ourselves without scruple to hell . . . . . v 5 156
And given to fornications, and to taverns and sack and wine . . . v 5 166
And given his deputation all the organs Of our own power *Meas. for Meas.* i 1 21
Who, if she had been a woman cardinally given, might have been accused ii 1 81
If the devil have given thee proofs for sin, Thou wilt prove his . . iii 2 31
He must before the deputy, sir; he has given him warning . . . iii 2 36
What pleasure was he given to?—Rather rejoicing to see another merry iii 2 248
Good morning to you, fair and gracious daughter.—The better, given me by so holy a man . . . . iv 3 117
And given me justice, justice, justice, justice! . . . . . v 1 25
What he [Time] hath scanted men in hair he hath given them in wit *Com. of Errors* ii 2 82
Give her the right you should have given her cousin . . *Much Ado* v 1 300
Be so good as read me this letter: it was given me by Costard *L. L. Lost* iv 2 93
Your lion, that holds his poll-axe sitting on a close-stool, will be given to Ajax . . . . v 2 581
You have put me out of countenance.—False'; we have given thee faces v 2 625
Thou hast given her rhymes And interchanged love-tokens *M. N. Dream* i 1 28
I should use thee worse, For thou, I fear, hast given me cause to curse iii 2 46
An the duke had not given him sixpence a day for playing Pyramus, I'll be hanged . . . . iv 2 22
I would not have given it for a wilderness of monkeys . *Mer. of Venice* iii 1 127
Good sir, this ring was given me by my wife . . . . . . iv 1 441
Sweet lady, you have given me life and living . . . . . . v 1 286
I am given, sir, secretly to understand . . . . . *As Y. Like It* i 1 129
Though Nature hath given us wit to flout at Fortune . . . . . i 2 48
I should have given him tears unto entreaties . . . . . . i 2 250
When a man thanks me heartily, methinks I have given him a penny . ii 5 28
Lovers are given to poetry. . . . . iii 3 20
Truly, she must be given, or the marriage is not lawful . . . . iii 3 70
Would I had given him the best horse in Padua to begin his wooing! *T. of Shrew* i 1 147
Thanks be given, she's very well and wants nothing . *All's Well* ii 4 4
I have writ my letters, casketed my treasure, Given order for our horses . . . . ii 5 27
If I had given you this at over-night, She might have been o'erta'en . iii 4 23
You have not given him his mother's letter? . . . . . . iv 3 1
He hath given her his monumental ring, and thinks himself made . iv 3 20
Where did you buy it? or who gave it you?—It was not given me . . v 3 273
Love sought is good, but given unsought is better . . . *T. Night* iii 1 168
The quality of the time and quarrel Might well have given us bloody argument . . . . iii 3 32
How with mine honour may I give him that Which I have given to you? iii 4 235
He has broke my head across and has given Sir Toby a bloody coxcomb v 1 179
Has here writ a letter to you; I should have given't you to-day morning v 1 293
You have put me into darkness and given your drunken cousin rule over me v 1 312
Tell me, . . . Why you have given me such clear lights of favour . v 1 344
You pay a great deal too dear for what's given freely . . *W. Tale* i 1 19
Say that she were gone, Given to the fire, a moiety of my rest Might come to me again . . . . ii 3 8
These are flowers Of middle summer, and I think they are given To men of middle age . . . . iv 4 107
The gifts she looks from me are pack'd and lock'd Up in my heart; which I have given already, But not deliver'd . . . . . iv 4 370
They do not give us the lie.—Your worship had like to have given us one iv 4 750
The adverse winds, Whose leisure I have stay'd, have given him time To land his legions . . . . *K. John* ii 1 58

Given. O that these hands could so redeem my son, As they have given these hairs their liberty! . . . . *K. John* iii 4 72
I find myself a traitor with the rest; For I have given here my soul's consent To undeck the pompous body of a king *Richard II.* iv 1 249
I have no name, no title, No, not that name was given me at the font . iv 1 256
If the rascal have not given me medicines to make me love him 1 *Hen. IV.* ii 2 19
And given my treasures and my rights of thee To thick-eyed musing . ii 3 48
If that man should be lewdly given, he deceiveth me . . . . ii 4 469
I was as virtuously given as a gentleman need to be . . . . iii 3 16
If thou wert any way given to virtue, I would swear by thy face . . iii 3 38
Filthy dowlas: I have given them away to bakers' wives . . . iii 3 79
Lord, Lord, how this world is given to lying! . . . . . . v 4 149
Lands which men devout By testament have given to the church *Hen. V.* i 1 10
The Duke of Gloucester, to whom the order of the siege is given . iii 2 70
But Exeter hath given the doom of death For pax of little price . iii 6 46
The glove which I have given him for a favour May haply purchase him a box o' th' ear . . . . iv 7 180
And thou hast given me most bitter terms . . . . . . iv 8 44
To celebrate the joy that God hath given us . . . 1 *Hen. VI.* i 6 14
The most unnatural wounds, Which thou thyself hast given her woful breast . . . . iii 3 51
I have awhile given truce unto my wars . . . . iii 4 3
The French were almost ten to one, Before we met or that a stroke was given . . . . iv 1 22
For thou hast given me in this beauteous face A world of earthly blessings to my soul . . . . 2 *Hen. VI.* i 1 21
Hath given the duchy of Anjou and Maine Unto the poor King Reignier i 1 110
Anjou and Maine are given to the French; Paris is lost . . . . i 1 214
So am I given in charge, may't please your grace . . . . ii 4 80
The duke is virtuous, mild and too well given To dream on evil . iii 1 72
Come to me again And given me notice of their villanies . . . iii 1 370
His brother's death Hath given them heart and courage to proceed . iv 4 35
I prithee, pardon me, That I have given no answer all this while . v 1 33
Thus war hath given thee peace, for thou art still . . . . . v 2 29
Given unto the house of York such head As thou shalt reign but by their sufferance . . . . 3 *Hen. VI.* i 1 233
Till either death hath closed these eyes of mine Or fortune given me measure of revenge . . . . ii 3 32
O Phœbus, hadst thou never given consent That Phaëthon should check thy fiery steeds! . . . . ii 6 11
Back'd with God and with the seas Which He hath given for fence impregnable . . . . iv 1 44
His majesty hath straitly given in charge That no man shall have private conference, Of what degree soever . . *Richard III.* i 1 85
Many fair promotions Are daily given . . . . i 3 81
What lawful quest have given their verdict up Unto the frowning judge? i 4 189
I could have given my uncle's grace a flout . . . . . . ii 4 24
And given in earnest what I begg'd in jest . . . . . . v 1 22
I cannot tell What heaven hath given him . . . . *Hen. VIII.* i 1 67
The devil is a niggard, Or has given all before . . . . . i 1 71
You have half our power: The other moiety, ere you ask, is given . i 2 12
Your grace has given a precedent of wisdom Above all princes . . ii 2 86
What cause Hath my behaviour given to your displeasure? . . . ii 4 20
There's order given for her coronation . . . . iii 2 46
That gentle physic, given in time, had cured me . . . . . iv 2 122
If heaven had pleased to have given me longer life And able means . iv 2 152
Who hath so far Given ear to our complaint, of his great grace . . v 1 48
I look'd You would have given me your petition . . . . . v 1 118
Instead of oil and balm, Thou lay'st in every gash that love hath given me The knife that made it . . . . . . *Troi. and Cres.* i 1 62
Something not worth in me such rich beholding As they have often given iii 3 92
She hath not given so many good words breath As for her Greeks and Trojans suffer'd death . . . . iv 1 73
Have issued, And given to Lartius and to Marcius battle . *Coriolanus* i 6 11
When corn was given them gratis, you repined . . . . . iii 1 43
Lack not virtue, no, nor power, but that Which they have given to beggars iii 1 74
Have you thus Given Hydra here to choose an officer? . . . . iii 1 93
Given hostile strokes, and that not in the presence Of dreaded justice . iii 3 97
An he had been cannibally given, he might have broiled and eaten him too iv 5 200
And, in a violent popular ignorance, given your enemy your shield . v 2 43
This morning for ten thousand of your throats I'ld not have given a doit v 4 60
And given up, For certain drops of salt, your city Rome . . . v 6 92
Here Goths have given me leave to sheathe my sword . *T. Andron.* i 1 85
Pray to the devils; the gods have given us over . . . . . iv 2 48
Ye see I have given her physic, And you must needs bestow her funeral iv 2 162
And when thou hast given it the emperor, Knock at my door . . iv 3 118
I doubt whether their legs be worth the sums That are given for 'em. Friendship's full of dregs . . . . *T. of Athens* i 2 239
Unwisely, not ignobly, have I given . . . . ii 2 183
More whore, more mischief first; I have given you earnest . . . iv 3 168
Why shouldst thou hate men? They never flatter'd thee: what hast thou given? . . . . iv 3 270
He's not dangerous; He is a noble Roman and well given . *J. Cæsar* i 2 197
He is given To sports, to wildness and much company . . . . ii 1 188
He loves me well, and I have given him reasons . . . . . ii 1 219
Hath given me some worthy cause to wish Things done, undone . . iv 2 8
Why hath it given me earnest of success, Commencing in a truth? *Macbeth* i 3 132
I have given suck, and know How tender 'tis to love the babe that milks me . . . . i 7 54
What hath quench'd them hath given me fire . . . . ii 2 2
And mine eternal jewel Given to the common enemy of man . . . iii 1 69
The feast is sold That is not often vouch'd, while 'tis a-making, 'Tis given with welcome . . . . iii 4 35
But at his touch—Such sanctity hath heaven given his hand—They presently amend . . . . iv 3 144
'Tis his main hope: For where there is advantage to be given, Both more and less have given him the revolt . . . . v 4 11
'Tis told me, he hath very oft of late Given private time to you *Hamlet* i 3 92
And hath given countenance to his speech, my lord . . . . . i 3 113
With a larger tether may he walk Than may be given you . . . i 3 126
What, have you given him any hard words of late? . . . . . ii 1 107
I have a daughter—have while she is mine—Who, in her duty and obedience, mark, Hath given me this . . . . ii 2 108
And more above, hath his solicitings . . . All given to mine ear . . ii 2 128
Or given my heart a winking, mute and dumb . . . . . . ii 2 137
God has given you one face, and you make yourselves another . . iii 1 149
They were given me by Claudio; he received them Of him that brought them . . . . iv 7 40
I have been with your father, and given him notice . . . *Lear* ii 1 3
O sir, fly this place; Intelligence is given where you are hid . . ii 1 23

Given. Hast thou given all to thy two daughters? And art thou come to this? . . . . *Lear* iii 4 49
Your daughter, if you have not given her leave, I say again, hath made a gross revolt . . . . *Othello* i 1 134
'Fore God, they have given me a rouse already . . . . . ii 3 66
He hath devoted and given up himself to the contemplation, mark, and denotement of her parts and graces . . . . ii 3 322
Given to captivity me and my utmost hopes . . . . iv 2 51
And yet he hath given me satisfying reasons . . . . v 1 9
Sextus Pompeius Hath given the dare to Cæsar . *Ant. and Cleo.* i 2 191
You may go: Would she had never given you leave to come! . . . i 3 21
I could have given less matter A better ear . . . . . . ii 1 31
When the best hint was given him, he not took't, Or did it from his teeth iii 4 9
He hath given his empire Up to a whore . . . . iii 6 66
O, he has given example for our flight, Most grossly, by his own! . . iii 10 28
Order for sea is given; They have put forth the haven . . . . iv 10 6
A very honest woman, but something given to lie . . . . . v 2 252
The one may be sold, or given, if there were wealth enough for the purchase, or merit for the gift . . . . *Cymbeline* i 4 90
Which the gods have given you?—Which, by their graces, I will keep . i 4 94
I have given him that Which, if he take, shall quite unpeople her . i 5 78
What, are men mad? Hath nature given them eyes? . . . . . i 6 32
When you have given good morning to your mistress, Attend the queen and us . . . . ii 3 66
Let it be granted you have seen all this—and praise Be given to your remembrance . . . . ii 4 93
He goes hence frowning: but it honours us That we have given him cause iii 5 19
Her chambers are all lock'd; and there's no answer That will be given iii 5 44
To-day how many would have given their honours To have saved their carcases! . . . . v 3 66
'If Pisanio Have,' said she, 'given his mistress that confection Which I gave him for cordial, she is served As I would serve a rat' . . . v 5 246
Since you have given me leave to speak, Freely will I speak. *Pericles* i 2 101
The rough seas, that spare not any man, Took it in rage, though calm'd have given't again . . . . ii 1 138
Yours, sir, We have given order to be next our own . . . . . ii 3 111
Marina gets All praises, which are paid as debts, And not as given iv Gower 35

Given away. My rights and royalties Pluck'd from my arms perforce and given away To upstart unthrifts . . . . . . *Richard II.* ii 3 121
The cares I give I have, though given away . . . . iv 1 198
Idle old man, That still would manage those authorities That he hath given away! . . . . *Lear* i 3 18
Dost thou call me fool, boy?—All thy other titles thou hast given away i 4 163

Given out. I thought ye would never have given out these arms till you had recovered your ancient freedom . . . . . 2 *Hen. VI.* iv 8 26
'Tis given out that, sleeping in my orchard, A serpent stung me *Hamlet* i 5 35
I will prove that two on's are as good As I have given out him *Cymbeline* v 5 312

Given over. But thou art altogether given over . . 1 *Hen. IV.* iii 3 40
I have given over, I will speak no more: Do what you will . 2 *Hen. IV.* ii 3 5
Have the pioners given o'er? . . . . *Hen. V.* iii 2 92

Given to understand. There the duke was given to understand *M. of Ven.* ii 8 7
At Shrewsbury, As I am truly given to understand . . 1 *Hen. IV.* iv 4 11

Given way. I have only been Silent so long and given way unto This course of fortune . . . . *Much Ado* iv 1 158
All the power of his wits have given way to his impatience . . *Lear* iii 6 4

Giver. We thank the giver.—Who is that, servant?—Yourself *T. G. of Ver.* ii 4 35
Heat them and they retort that heat again To the first giver *T. and C.* iii 3 102
No gift to him, But breeds the giver a return exceeding . *T. of Athens* i 1 290
To the noble mind Rich gifts wax poor when givers prove unkind *Hamlet* iii 1 101

Givest. Under whose conduct came those powers of France That thou for truth givest out are landed here? . . . . *K. John* iv 2 130
That not only givest Me cause to wail but teachest me the way How to lament the cause . . . . *Richard II.* iv 1 300
And givest such sarcenet surety for thy oaths . . . 1 *Hen. IV.* iii 1 256
Thou that givest whores indulgences to sin . . . . 1 *Hen. VI.* i 3 35
Thou givest so long, Timon, I fear me thou wilt give away thyself *T. of A.* i 2 246
I'll take the gold thou givest me, Not all thy counsel . . . . iv 3 129
And weigh'st thy words before thou givest them breath . *Othello* iii 3 119
After all my crosses, Thou givest me somewhat to repair myself *Pericles* ii 1 128

Giveth. Which giveth many wounds when one will kill . 1 *Hen. VI.* ii 5 110

Giving a gentle kiss to every sedge He overtaketh . . *T. G. of Ver.* ii 7 29
He's as far from jealousy as I am from giving him cause *Mer. Wives* ii 1 108
A giving hand, though foul, shall have fair praise . . *L. L. Lost* iv 1 23
I neither lend nor borrow By taking nor by giving of excess *Mer. of Venice* i 3 63
She would not hold out enemy for ever, For giving it to me . . . iv 1 448
Giving thy sum of more To that which had too much . *As Y. Like It* ii 1 48
Giving her them again, said with weeping tears 'Wear these for my sake' . . . . ii 4 53
By giving love your sorrow and my grief Were both extermined . . iii 5 88
That breathes upon a bank of violets, Stealing and giving odour! *T. Night* i 1 7
Till I have set a glory to this hand, By giving it the worship of revenge *K. John* iv 3 72
Curbs me From giving reins and spurs to my free speech . *Richard II.* i 1 55
Giving him breath, The traitor lives, the true man's put to death . . v 3 72
Thou variest no more from picking of purses than giving direction doth from labouring . . . . 1 *Hen. IV.* ii 1 56
And hath his quick wit wasted in giving reckonings . . . . iii 2 193
Giving full trophy, signal and ostent Quite from himself to God *Hen. V.* v Prol. 21
Giving my verdict on the white rose side . . . . . 1 *Hen. VI.* ii 4 48
What canst thou answer to my majesty for giving up of Normandy? 2 *Hen. VI.* iv 7 30
Lest they consult about the giving up of some more towns in France . iv 7 141
By giving the house of Lancaster leave to breathe, It will outrun you 3 *Hen. VI.* i 2 13
Or as thy father and his father did, Giving no ground unto the house of York . . . . ii 6 16
'Tis but reason that I be released From giving aid which late I promised iii 3 148
I am not in the giving vein to-day . . . . . . *Richard III.* iv 2 119
For your stubborn answer About the giving back the great seal to us, The king shall know it . . . . *Hen. VIII.* iii 2 347
Giving itself the lie, would pluck reproof and rebuke from every ear *Cor.* ii 2 37
Every one of us has a single honour, in giving him our own voices with our own tongues . . . . ii 3 49
Their base throats tear With giving him glory . . . . . . v 6 54
By giving liberty unto thine eyes; Examine other beauties *Rom. and Jul.* i 1 233
Could you not take some occasion without giving? . . . . . iii 1 47
And humbly prays you That with your other noble parts you'll suit In giving him his right . . . . *T. of Athens* ii 2 24
Giving our holy virgins to the stain Of contumelious, beastly, mad-brain'd war . . . . v 1 176

Giving. Giving myself a voluntary wound Here, in the thigh *J. Cæsar* ii 1 300
Equivocates him in a sleep, and, giving him the lie, leaves him *Macbeth* ii 3 39
Giving to you no further personal power To business with the king *Hamlet* i 2 36
These blazes, daughter, Giving more light than heat, extinct in both i 3 118
Giving out. His givings-out were of an infinite distance From his true-meant design *Meas. for Meas.* i 4 54
Or such ambiguous giving out, to note That you know aught of me *Ham.* i 5 178
This is the monkey's own giving out *Othello* iv 1 131
Thunder shall not so awake the beds of eels as my giving out her beauty stir up the lewdly-inclined *Pericles* iv 2 155
Giving over. The sore terms we stand upon with the gods will be strong with us for giving over iv 2 39
Glad. I am a fool To weep at what I am glad of *Tempest* iii 1 74
So glad of this as they I cannot be, Who are surprised withal iii 1 92
And, for your friend's sake, will be glad of you *T. G. of Ver.* iii 2 63
Were you banish'd for so small a fault?—I was, and held me glad of such a doom iv 1 32
I am of the church, and will be glad to do my benevolence *Mer. Wives* i 1 32
I am glad to see your worships well i 1 80
I am glad to see you, good Master Slender i 1 89
I am glad I am so acquit of this tinder-box i 3 27
I am glad he went not in himself i 4 50
I am glad he is so quiet i 4 94
Speak, good Master Brook: I shall be glad to be your servant ii 2 185
I shall be glad if he have deceived me iii 1 12
If you know yourself clear, why, I am glad of it iii 3 124
Truly, I am so glad you have nobody here iv 2 18
I am glad the fat knight is not here.—Why, does he talk of him? iv 2 29
I am glad the knight is not here; now he shall see his own foolery iv 2 36
I thank your worship: I shall make my master glad with these tidings iv 5 57
I am glad, though you have ta'en a special stand to strike at me, that your arrow hath glanced v 5 247
You'll be glad to give out a commission for more heads *Meas. for Meas.* ii 1 253
As they are chosen, they are glad to choose me for them ii 1 283
Hath made him that gracious denial which he is most glad to receive iii 1 167
I would be glad to receive some instruction from my fellow partner iv 2 18
Our old and faithful friend, we are glad to see you v 1 2
I am glad to see you in this merry vein *Com. of Errors* ii 2 20
He hath an uncle here in Messina will be very much glad of it *Much Ado* i 1 19
And though I be but a poor man, I am glad to hear it iii 5 30
I am glad that all things sort so well v 4 7
Pray you, do my commendations; I would be glad to see it *L. L. Lost* ii 1 182
And so far am I glad it so did sort As this their jangling I esteem a sport *M. N. Dream* iii 2 352
I am glad this parcel of wooers are so reasonable *Mer. of Venice* i 2 118
I should be glad of his approach i 2 142
Father, I am glad you are come ii 2 115
I am glad 'tis night, you do not look on me ii 6 34
I am glad on't: I desire no more delight Than to be under sail ii 6 67
He cannot choose but break.—I am very glad of it: I'll plague him; I'll torture him: I am glad of it iii 1 121
I know he will be glad of our success iii 2 243
I am heartily glad I came hither to you *As Y. Like It* i 1 165
Owe no man hate, envy no man's happiness, glad of other men's good iii 2 79
I am glad of your departure: adieu iii 2 311
I am in all affected as yourself; Glad that you thus continue your resolve To suck the sweets of sweet philosophy *T. of Shrew* i 1 27
I am glad he's come, howsoe'er he comes.—Why, sir, he comes not iii 2 76
I'll make him glad to seem Vincentio iv 2 68
That you are well restored, my lord, I'm glad: Let the rest go *All's W.* ii 3 154
I am heartily sorry that he'll be glad of this iv 3 75
Wouldst thou not be glad to have the niggardly rascally sheep-biter come by some notable shame? *T. Night* ii 5 5
Give me the boy: I am glad you did not nurse him *W. Tale* ii 1 56
I am glad at heart To be so rid o' the business iii 3 14
Are not you grieved that Arthur is his prisoner?—As heartily as he is glad he hath him *K. John* iii 4 124
I am not glad that such a sore of time Should seek a plaster v 2 12
Glad am I that your highness is so arm'd To bear the tidings *Richard II.* iii 2 104
His father loves him not And would be glad he met with some mischance *1 Hen. IV.* i 3 232
By the Lord, lads, I am glad you have the money ii 4 304
Marry, And I am glad of it with all my heart iii 1 128
I am glad to see your lordship abroad *2 Hen. IV.* i 2 107
I am glad to see you, by my troth, Master Shallow iii 2 204
I do not doubt you.—I am glad of it v 2 77
I am glad to see your worship.—I thank thee with all my heart v 1 63
We are glad the Dauphin is so pleasant with us *Hen. V.* i 2 259
As we are now glad to behold your eyes v 2 14
I will be glad to hear you confess it brokenly with your English tongue v 2 106
I am glad thou canst speak no better English v 2 126
What, all unready so?—Unready! ay, and glad we 'scaped so well *1 Hen. VI.* ii 1 40
They that of late were daring with their scoffs Are glad and fain by flight to save themselves iii 2 114
Were glad to be employ'd To show how quaint an orator you are *2 Hen. VI.* iii 2 273
Henry's late presaging prophecy Did glad my heart with hope *3 Hen. VI.* iv 6 93
Well met, my lord; I am glad to see your honour *Richard III.* iii 2 110
That's clapp'd upon the court-gate.— . . . I'm glad 'tis there *Hen. VIII.* i 3 21
I am glad they are going, For, sure, there's no converting of 'em i 3 42
I am glad Your grace is grown so pleasant i 4 89
Subject to your countenance, glad or sorry As I saw it inclined ii 4 26
I should be glad to hear such news as this Once every hour iii 2 24
I deem you an ill husband, and am glad To have you therein my companion iii 2 142
I am glad your grace has made that right use of it iii 2 386
I am glad I came this way so happily v 2 8
Most reverend Nestor, I am glad to clasp thee *Troi. and Cres.* iv 5 204
The Volsces are in arms.—I am glad on't *Coriolanus* i 1 229
Sweet madam.—I am glad to see your ladyship i 3 53
A curse begin at very root on's heart, That is not glad to see thee! ii 1 203
Most glad of your company.—You take my part from me, sir; I have the most cause to be glad of yours iv 3 54
That would be glad to have This true which they so seem to fear iv 6 151
I am glad thou hast set thy mercy and thy honour At difference in thee v 3 200
Thus lovingly reserved The cordial of mine age to glad my heart! *T. Andron.* i 1 166
Right glad I am he was not at this fray *Rom. and Jul.* i 1 124
I am glad on t; this is well: stand up: This is as't should be iv 2 28
Good day, sir.—I am glad you're well *T. of Athens* i 1 1
Glad. I am glad that my weak words Have struck but thus much show of fire from Brutus *J. Cæsar* i 2 176
When he perceived the common herd was glad he refused the crown i 2 266
Am I not stay'd for, Cinna?—I am glad on't i 3 137
For mine own part, I shall be glad to learn of noble men iv 3 54
I understand you not, my lord.—I am glad of it *Hamlet* iv 2 25
And such a tongue As I am glad I have not, though not to have it Hath lost me in your liking *Lear* i 1 235
I am glad to see your highness.—Regan, I think you are; I know what reason I have to think so: if thou shouldst not be glad, I would divorce me from thy mother's tomb ii 4 130
For your sake, jewel, I am glad at soul I have no other child *Othello* i 3 196
I am glad on't; 'tis a worthy governor ii 1 30
Away at once with love or jealousy!—I am glad of it iii 3 193
I am glad I have found this napkin: This was her first remembrance iii 3 290
I am glad on't.—Indeed!—My lord?—I am glad to see you mad iv 1 249
Excuse my manners, That so neglected you.—I am glad to see you v 1 95
I am glad thy father's dead: Thy match was mortal to him v 2 204
We have cause to be glad that matters are so well digested *Ant. and Cleo.* ii 2 178
Not a courtier . . . hath a heart that is not Glad at the thing they scowl at.—And why so? *Cymbeline* i 1 15
They were parted By gentlemen at hand.—I am very glad on't i 1 164
I was glad I did atone my countryman and you i 4 42
I am glad I was up so late; for that's the reason I was up so early ii 3 37
I am most glad You think of other place iii 4 143
I am glad to be constrain'd to utter that Which torments me to conceal v 5 141
To glad your ear, and please your eyes *Pericles* i Gower 4
To glad her presence, The senate-house of planets all did sit, To knit in her their best perfections i 1 9
Their tables were stored full, to glad the sight, And not so much to feed on as delight i 4 28
Would now be glad of bread, and beg for it i 4 41
Till fortune, tired with doing bad, Threw him ashore, to give him glad ii Gower 38
Your presence glads our days: honour we love ii 3 21
Say if you had, Who takes offence at that would make me glad? ii 5 72
Are you so peremptory? I am glad on't with all my heart ii 5 74
I am glad to see your honour in good health iv 6 24
I am glad to see you well *2 Hen. IV.* iii 2; *Hamlet* i 2; ii 2
I am right glad *Temp.* iii 3; *Hen. VIII.* v 1; *T. of A.* iii 1; *Cymb.* v 5
I am very glad to see you *As Y. Like It* iii 3; *Hamlet* i 2; *Othello* iv 1
Glad father. Now all the blessings Of a glad father compass thee about! *Tempest* v 1 180
Glad tidings. Health and glad tidings to your majesty! *2 Hen. VI.* iv 9 7
Gladded. That my kingdom, Well worthy the best heir o' the world, should not Be gladded in't by me *Hen. VIII.* ii 4 196
Gladding. To the gladding of Your highness with an heir v 1 71
Gladly. You will demand of me why I do this?—Gladly *Meas. for Meas.* i 3 18
Try your penitence, if it be sound, Or hollowly put on.—I'll gladly learn ii 3 23
Which though myself would gladly have embraced *Com. of Errors* i 1 70
I would gladly have him see his company anatomized *All's Well* iv 3 37
I would most gladly know the issue of it *W. Tale* v 2 9
His weary joints would gladly rise, I know *Richard II.* v 3 105
But gladly would be better satisfied *2 Hen. IV.* i 3 6
He is not the man that he would gladly make show to the world he is *Hen. V.* iii 6 87
Where ladies shall be frighted, And, gladly quaked, hear more *Coriolanus* i 9 6
And gladly shunn'd who gladly fled from me *Rom. and Jul.* i 1 136
Let us speak Our free hearts each to other.—Very gladly *Macbeth* i 3 155
For his particular, I'll receive him gladly *Lear* ii 4 295
I would most gladly have forgot it *Othello* iv 1 19
And would gladly Look him i' the face *Ant. and Cleo.* v 2 31
Gladness. Do not look for further recompense Than thine own gladness that thou art employ'd *As Y. Like It* iii 5 98
Sorrow, that is couch'd in seeming gladness, Is like that mirth fate turns to sudden sadness *Troi. and Cres.* i 1 39
Dispatch we The business we have talk'd of.—With most gladness *A. and C.* ii 2 169
Glamis. All hail, Macbeth! hail to thee, thane of Glamis! *Macbeth* i 3 48
By Sinel's death I know I am thane of Glamis; But how of Cawdor? i 3 71
Glamis, and thane of Cawdor! The greatest is behind i 3 116
Glamis thou art, and Cawdor; and shalt be What thou art promised i 5 16
Thou'ldst have, great Glamis, That which cries 'Thus thou must do' i 5 23
Great Glamis! worthy Cawdor! Greater than both, by the all-hail hereafter! i 5 55
Glamis hath murder'd sleep, and therefore Cawdor Shall sleep no more ii 2 42
Thou hast it now: king, Cawdor, Glamis, all, As the weird women promised iii 1 1
Glance. Were't not affection chains thy tender days To the sweet glances of thy honour'd love *T. G. of Ver.* i 1 4
To call him villain? and then to glance from him To the duke? *M. for M.* v 1 311
As the eye doth roll To every varied object in his glance *L. L. Lost* v 2 775
How canst thou thus for shame, Titania, Glance at my credit with Hippolyta, Knowing I know thy love to Theseus? *M. N. Dream* ii 1 75
The poet's eye, in a fine frenzy rolling, Doth glance from heaven to earth v 1 13
If not, The wise man's folly is anatomized Even by the squandering glances of the fool *As Y. Like It* ii 7 57
The jest did glance away from me *T. of Shrew* v 2 61
Dart not scornful glances from those eyes, To wound thy lord v 2 137
Lift our heads to heaven, And never more abase our sight so low As to vouchsafe one glance unto the ground *2 Hen. VI.* i 2 16
And if we did but glance a far-off look, Immediately he was upon his knee iii 1 10
I was won, my lord, With the first glance *Troi. and Cres.* iii 2 126
They yet glance by and scarcely bruise *Lear* v 3 148
Your shafts of fortune, though they hurt you mortally, Yet glance full wanderingly on us *Pericles* iii 3 7
Glanced. Your arrow hath glanced.—Well, what remedy? *Mer. Wives* v 5 249
In company I often glanced it *Com. of Errors* v 1 66
Wherein obscurely Cæsar's ambition shall be glanced at *J. Cæsar* i 2 324
Glancing an eye of pity on his losses *Mer. of Venice* iv 1 27
Glanders. Possessed with the glanders *T. of Shrew* iii 2 51
Glansdale. Sir Thomas Gargrave, and Sir William Glansdale, Let me have your express opinions *1 Hen. VI.* i 4 63
Glare. Thy blood is cold; Thou hast no speculation in those eyes Which thou dost glare with! *Macbeth* iii 4 96
Wherein do you look?—On him, on him! Look you, how pale he glares! *Hamlet* iii 4 125
Look, where he stands and glares! Wantest thou eyes at trial, madam? *Lear* iii 6 25
Glared. I met a lion, Who glared upon me, and went surly by *J. Cæsar* i 3 21

Glass. Past the mid season.—At least two glasses . . . *Tempest* i 2 240
No woman's face remember, Save, from my glass, mine own . . iii 1 50
Our ship—Which, but three glasses since, we gave out split—Is tight . v 1 223
Her eyes are grey as glass, and so are mine . . *T. G. of Ver.* iv 4 197
And, like a prophet, Looks in a glass . . . . *Meas. for Meas.* ii 2 95
Women are frail too.—Ay, as the glasses where they view themselves . ii 4 125
Methinks you are my glass, and not my brother . *Com. of Errors* v 1 417
Here, good my glass, take this for telling true: Fair payment for foul words is more than due . . . . *L. L. Lost* iv 1 18
Then thou wilt keep My tears for glasses, and still make me weep . iv 3 40
When Phœbe doth behold Her silver visage in the watery glass *M. N. Dream* i 1 210
What wicked and dissembling glass of mine Made me compare with Hermia's sphery eyne? . . . ii 2 98
Set a deep glass of rhenish wine on the contrary casket *Mer. of Venice* i 2 104
'Tis not her glass, but you, that flatters her . . . *As Y. Like It* iii 5 54
It is a figure in rhetoric that drink, being poured out of a cup into a glass, by filling the one doth empty the other . . . v 1 46
You will not pay for the glasses you have burst?—No, not a denier *T. of Shrew* Ind. 1 7
Then show it me.—Had I a glass, I would.—What, you mean my face? ii 1 234
Or four and twenty times the pilot's glass Hath told the thievish minutes how they pass . . . *All's Well* ii 1 168
I my brother know Yet living in my glass . . . *T. Night* iii 4 415
If this be so, as yet the glass seems true . . . v 1 272
She would not live The running of one glass . . *W. Tale* i 2 306
I turn my glass and give my scene such growing As you had slept between . . . iv 1 16
I should blush To see you so attired, sworn, I think, To show myself a glass . . . iv 4 14
Not a ribbon, glass, pomander, brooch, table-book, ballad, knife . iv 4 609
Even in the glasses of thine eyes I see thy grieved heart . *Richard II.* i 3 208
Read o'er this paper while the glass doth come . . . iv 1 269
Give me the glass, and therein will I read. No deeper wrinkles yet? . iv 1 276
O flattering glass, Like to my followers in prosperity, Thou dost beguile me! . . . iv 1 279
Glasses, glasses, is the only drinking . . . . 2 *Hen. IV.* ii 1 155
He was indeed the glass Wherein the noble youth did dress themselves ii 3 21
He was the mark and glass, copy and book, That fashion'd others . ii 3 31
That never looks in his glass for love of any thing he sees there *Hen. V.* v 2 154
Ere the glass, that now begins to run, Finish the process of his sandy hour, These eyes . . . Shall see thee wither'd . 1 *Hen. VI.* iv 2 35
Like the sun 'gainst glass, Or like an overcharged gun, recoil 2 *Hen. VI.* iii 2 330
A brood of traitors have we here!—Look in a glass, and call thy image so . . . v 1 142
Shine out, fair sun, till I have bought a glass, That I may see my shadow as I pass . . . *Richard III.* i 2 263
And I for comfort have but one false glass, Which grieves me . . ii 2 53
My kingdom stands on brittle glass . . . iv 2 62
And like a glass Did break i' the rinsing . . . *Hen. VIII.* i 1 166
But more in Troilus thousand fold I see Than in the glass of Pandar's praise may be; Yet hold I off . . . *Troi. and Cres.* i 2 311
Pride is his own glass, his own trumpet, his own chronicle . . ii 3 165
Pride hath no other glass To show itself but pride . . iii 3 47
And schoolboys' tears take up The glasses of my sight! . *Coriolanus* iii 2 117
I, your glass, Will modestly discover to yourself That of yourself which you yet know not of . . . *J. Cæsar* i 2 68
That unicorns may be betray'd with trees, And bears with glasses . ii 1 205
Yet the eighth appears, who bears a glass Which shows me many more *Macbeth* iv 1 119
The glass of fashion and the mould of form, The observed of all *Hamlet* iii 1 161
You go not till I set you up a glass Where you may see the inmost part of you . . . iii 4 19
There was never yet fair woman but she made mouths in a glass . *Lear* iii 2 36
Get thee glass eyes; And, like a scurvy politician, seem To see the things thou dost not . . . iv 6 174
To the more mature A glass that feated them . . *Cymbeline* i 1 49
It is not vain-glory for a man and his glass to confer in his own chamber iv 1 9
Fair glass of light, I loved you, and could still . . *Pericles* i 1 76
Whose men and dames so jetted and adorn'd, Like one another's glass . i 4 27
To me he seems like diamond to glass . . . ii 3 36
Crack the glass of her virginity, and make the rest malleable . . iv 6 151
Glassed. Who, tendering their own worth from where they were glass'd, Did point you to buy them, along as you pass'd . *L. L. Lost* ii 1 244
Glass-faced. From the glass-faced flatterer To Apemantus *T. of Athens* i 1 58
Glass-gazing, superserviceable, finical rogue . . . *Lear* ii 2 19
Glassy. Most ignorant of what he's most assured, His glassy essence, like an angry ape, Plays such fantastic tricks . *Meas. for Meas.* ii 2 120
As plays the sun upon the glassy streams . 1 *Hen. VI.* v 3 62
That shows his hoar leaves in the glassy stream . . . *Hamlet* iv 7 168
Glazed. Sorrow's eye, glazed with blinding tears, Divides one thing entire to many objects . . . *Richard II.* ii 2 16
Gleam. By thy gracious, golden, glittering gleams, I trust to take of truest Thisby sight . . . *M. N. Dream* v 1 279
Glean. I shall think it a most plenteous crop To glean the broken ears after the man That the main harvest reaps . . *As Y. Like It* iii 5 102
Which is a wonder how his grace should glean it . . *Hen. V.* i 1 53
What harm can your bisson conspectuities glean out of this character? *Coriolanus* ii 1 71
And to gather, So much as from occasion you may glean *Hamlet* ii 2 16
Gleaned. How much low peasantry would then be glean'd From the true seed of honour! . . . *Mer. of Venice* ii 9 46
Not for Bohemia, nor the pomp that may Be thereat glean'd . *W. Tale* iv 4 500
Galling the gleaned land with hot assays . . . *Hen. V.* i 2 151
When he needs what you have gleaned, it is but squeezing you *Hamlet* iv 2 21
Gleaning. Yes, that goodness Of gleaning all the land's wealth into one, Into your own hands, cardinal, by extortion . *Hen. VIII.* iii 2 284
Gleeful. Wherefore look'st thou sad, When every thing doth make a gleeful boast? . . . *T. Andron.* ii 3 11
Gleek. Nay, I can gleek upon occasion . . *M. N. Dream* iii 1 150
Now where's the Bastard's braves, and Charles his gleeks? 1 *Hen. VI.* iii 2 123
What will you give us?—No money, on my faith, but the gleek *R. and J.* iv 5 115
Gleeking. I have seen you gleeking and galling at this gentleman *Hen. V.* v 1 78
Glendower. Come, lords, away, To fight with Glendower *Richard II.* iii 1 43
To fight Against the irregular and wild Glendower . . 1 *Hen. IV.* i 1 40
Betray'd The lives of those that he did lead to fight Against that great magician, damn'd Glendower . . . i 3 83
Hand to hand, He did confound the best part of an hour In changing hardiment with great Glendower . . . i 3 101
Thou dost belie him; He never did encounter with Glendower . . i 3 114
Glendower. He durst as well have met the devil alone As Owen Glendower for an enemy . . . 1 *Hen. IV.* i 3 117
When time is ripe, which will be suddenly, I'll steal to Glendower . i 3 295
Lord Edmund Mortimer, my lord of York, and Owen Glendower . . ii 3 27
What a plague call you him?—O, Glendower.—Owen, Owen, the same . ii 4 374
Could the world pick thee out three such enemies again as that fiend Douglas, that spirit Percy, and that devil Glendower? . . ii 4 405
Lord Mortimer, and cousin Glendower, Will you sit down? . . iii 1 3
He wisheth you in heaven.—And you in hell, as oft as he hears Owen Glendower spoke of . . . iii 1 12
All westward, Wales beyond the Severn shore, And all the fertile land within that bound, To Owen Glendower . . . iii 1 78
My father Glendower is not ready yet, Nor shall we need his help . iii 1 87
O that Glendower were come! . . . iv 1 124
My father and Glendower being both away, The powers of us may serve iv 1 131
With Owen Glendower's absence thence, Who with them was a rated sinew too . . . iv 4 16
Myself and you, son Harry, will towards Wales, To fight with Glendower v 5 40
One power against the French, And one against Glendower . 2 *Hen. IV.* i 3 72
I have received A certain instance that Glendower is dead . . iii 1 103
This Edmund, . . . but for Owen Glendower, had been king. 2 *Hen. VI.* ii 2 41
Glib. I had rather glib myself than they Should not produce fair issue *W. Tale* ii 1 149
O, these encounterers, so glib of tongue! . . *Troi. and Cres.* iv 5 58
As well of glib and slippery creatures as Of grave . *T. of Athens* i 1 53
I want that glib and oily art, To speak and purpose not. . *Lear* i 1 227
Glide. The current that with gentle murmur glides . . *T. G. of Ver.* ii 7 25
Every one lets forth his sprite, In the church-way paths to glide *M. N. D.* v 1 389
It unlink'd itself, And with indented glides did slip away *As Y. Like It* iv 3 113
O, she is lame! love's heralds should be thoughts, Which ten times faster glide than the sun's beams . . *Rom. and Jul.* ii 5 5
If one of mean affairs May plod it in a week, why may not I Glide thither in a day? . . . *Cymbeline* iii 2 54
Glided. Were there a serpent seen, with forked tongue, That slily glided towards your majesty . . . 2 *Hen. VI.* iii 2 260
Glideth. More water glideth by the mill Than wots the miller of *T. An.* ii 1 85
Gliding. Why all these fires, why all these gliding ghosts *J. Cæsar* i 3 63
Glimmer. My wasting lamps some fading glimmer left . *Com. of Errors* v 1 315
So evident That it will glimmer through a blind man's eye . 1 *Hen. VI.* ii 4 24
The west yet glimmers with some streaks of day . . *Macbeth* iii 3 5
Glimmering. Didst thou not lead him through the glimmering night From Perigenia? . . . *M. N. Dream* ii 1 77
As bright, as clear, As yonder Venus in her glimmering sphere . . iii 2 61
Through the house give glimmering light, By the dead and drowsy fire v 1 398
Glimpse. Whether it be the fault and glimpse of newness *Meas. for Meas.* i 2 162
There is no man hath a virtue that he hath not a glimpse of *Tr. and Cr.* i 2 25
In complete steel Revisit'st thus the glimpses of the moon *Hamlet* i 4 53
Glister. All that glisters is not gold; Often have you heard that told *Mer. of Venice* ii 7 65
How he glisters Thorough my rust! . . . *W. Tale* iii 2 171
Away, and glister like the god of war . . . *K. John* v 1 54
Glistering. And make stale The glistering of this present . *W. Tale* iv 1 14
Like glistering Phaethon, Wanting the manage of unruly jades *Rich. II.* iii 3 178
With forms being fetch'd From glistering semblances of piety *Hen. V.* ii 2 117
To be perk'd up in a glistering grief, And wear a golden sorrow *Hen. VIII.* ii 3 21
Gallops the zodiac in his glistering coach. . *T. Andron.* ii 1 7
Glittering. By thy gracious, golden, glittering gleams *M. N. Dream* v 1 279
Plays the alchemist, Turning with splendour of his precious eye The meagre cloddy earth to glittering gold . . . *K. John* iii 1 80
His glittering arms he will commend to rust . . *Richard II.* iii 3 116
Never brandish more revengeful steel Over the glittering helmet of my foe! . . . iv 1 51
My reformation, glittering o'er my fault, Shall show more goodly and attract more eyes . . . 1 *Hen. IV.* i 2 237
Glittering in golden coats, like images . . . iv 1 100
What is here? Gold? yellow, glittering, precious gold? *T. of Athens* iv 3 26
Her epitaphs In glittering golden characters . . *Pericles* iv 3 44
Globe. The solemn temples, the great globe itself, Yea, all which it inherit, shall dissolve . . . *Tempest* iv 1 153
She is spherical, like a globe; I could find out countries in her *C. of Er.* iii 2 116
We the globe can compass soon, Swifter than the wandering moon *M. N. Dream* iv 1 102
When the searching eye of heaven is hid, Behind the globe *Richard II.* iii 2 38
Thou globe of sinful continents, what a life dost thou lead! . 2 *Hen. IV.* ii 4 309
Wheresoe'er thou art in this world's globe, I'll have an Iris that shall find thee out. . . . 2 *Hen. VI.* iii 2 406
And make a sop of all this solid globe . . *Troi. and Cres.* i 3 113
Be thy waggoner, And whirl along with thee about the globe *T. Andron.* v 2 49
While memory holds a seat In this distracted globe . . *Hamlet* i 5 97
The warm sun! Approach, thou beacon to this under globe! . *Lear* ii 2 170
The affrighted globe Should yawn at alteration . . *Othello* v 2 100
Glooming. A glooming peace this morning with it brings *Rom. and Jul.* v 3 305
Gloomy. Darkness and the gloomy shade of death Environ you! 1 *Hen. VI.* v 4 89
In the ruthless, vast, and gloomy woods . . . *T. Andron.* iv 1 53
Glorified. I will not return Till my attempt so much be glorified As to my ample hope was promised . . . *K. John* v 2 111
Glorify. O, two such silver currents, when they join, Do glorify the banks that bound them in . . . ii 1 442
Death's dishonourable victory We with our stately presence glorify 1 *Hen. VI.* i 1 21
Tell us here the circumstance, That we for thee may glorify the Lord 2 *Hen. VI.* ii 1 75
Glorious. In that glorious supposition think He gains by death *C. of Er.* iii 2 50
So the life that died with shame Lives in death with glorious fame *Much Ado* v 3 8
Study is like the heaven's glorious sun . . . *L. L. Lost* i 1 84
Of sovereign parts he is esteem'd; Well fitted in arts, glorious in arms . ii 1 45
This is the air; that is the glorious sun . . *T. Night* iv 3 1
And kiss him with a glorious victory . . . *K. John* ii 1 394
To solemnize this day the glorious sun Stays in his course . . iii 1 77
By the glorious worth of my descent, This arm shall do it . *Richard II.* i 1 107
God for his Richard hath in heavenly pay A glorious angel . . iii 2 61
Banish'd Norfolk fought For Jesu Christ in glorious Christian field . iv 1 93
In the closing of some glorious day . . . 1 *Hen. IV.* iii 2 133
I shall make this northern youth exchange His glorious deeds for my indignities. Percy is but my factor, good my lord, To engross up glorious deeds on my behalf . . . iii 2 146
The enterprise whereof Shall be to you, as us, like glorious . *Hen. V.* ii 2 183
In this glorious and well-foughten field We kept together in our chivalry iv 6 18
A far more glorious star thy soul will make Than Julius Cæsar 1 *Hen. VI.* i 1 55

Glorious. France, triumph in thy glorious prophetess! Recover'd is the town of Orleans — 1 *Hen. VI.* i 6 8
Never glorious sun reflex his beams Upon the country where you make abode! — v 4 87
Her father is no better than an earl, Although in glorious titles he excel — v 5 38
Put forth thy hand, reach at the glorious gold — 2 *Hen. VI.* i 2 11
I will remedy this gear ere long, Or sell my title for a glorious grave — iii 1 92
Like to the glorious sun's transparent beams — iii 1 353
Now, by my faith, lords, 'twas a glorious day — v 3 29
And cried 'A crown, or else a glorious tomb!' — 3 *Hen. VI.* i 4 16
See how the morning opes her golden gates, And takes her farewell of the glorious sun! — ii 1 22
Do I see three suns?—Three glorious suns, each one a perfect sun — ii 1 26
Until my mis-shaped trunk that bears this head Be round impaled with a glorious crown — iii 2 171
I spy a black, suspicious, threatening cloud, That will encounter with our glorious sun — v 3 5
Now is the winter of our discontent Made glorious summer by this sun of York — *Richard III.* i 1 2
Therefore is the glorious planet Sol In noble eminence enthroned — *Troi. and Cres.* i 3 89
Whose glorious deeds, but in these fields of late, Made emulous missions 'mongst the gods themselves — iii 3 188
Let all untruths stand by thy stained name, And they'll seem glorious — v 2 180
No, by the flame of yonder glorious heaven, He shall not carry him — v 6 23
The glorious gods sit in hourly synod about thy particular prosperity! — *Coriolanus* v 2 74
A better head her glorious body fits — *T. Andron.* i 1 187
Thou art As glorious to this night, being o'er my head, As is a winged messenger of heaven — *Rom. and Jul.* ii 2 27
Would in action glorious I had lost Those legs that brought me! *Othello* ii 3 186
All quality, Pride, pomp and circumstance of glorious war! — iii 3 354
But most miserable Is the desire that's glorious — *Cymbeline* i 6 7
The purchase is to make men glorious; Et bonum quo antiquius, eo melius — *Pericles* i Gower 9
I loved you, and could still, Were not this glorious casket stored with ill — i 1 77
Not an hour, In the day's glorious walk, or peaceful night — i 2 4
Against the face of death, I sought the purchase of a glorious beauty — i 2 72
To remember what he does, Build his statue to make him glorious ii Gower 14
Gloriously. When his love he doth espy, Let her shine as gloriously As the Venus of the sky — *M. N. Dream* iii 2 106
Glory. The uncertain glory of an April day — *T. G. of Ver.* i 3 85
She determines Herself the glory of a creditor — *Meas. for Meas.* i 1 40
That young start-up hath all the glory of my overthrow — *Much Ado* i 3 69
Cupid is no longer an archer: his glory shall be ours — ii 1 401
Maiden pride, adieu! No glory lives behind the back of such — iii 1 110
His disgrace is to be called boy; but his glory is to subdue men *L. L. Lost* i 2 186
So it is sometimes, Glory grows guilty of detested crimes — iv 1 31
Do but behold the tears that swell in me, And they thy glory through my grief will show — iv 3 38
That have I told my love, In glory of my kinsman — *M. N. Dream* v 1 47
So doth the greater glory dim the less — *Mer. of Venice* v 1 93
Ha, majesty! how high thy glory towers, When the rich blood of kings is set on fire! — *K. John* ii 1 350
What have you lost by losing of this day?—All days of glory, joy — iii 4 117
Till I have set a glory to this hand, By giving it the worship of revenge iv 3 71
Thus have I yielded up into your hand The circle of my glory — v 1 2
Happily may your sweet self put on The lineal state and glory of the land! — v 7 102
I see thy glory like a shooting star Fall to the base earth — *Richard II.* ii 4 19
Arm, arm, my name! a puny subject strikes At thy great glory — iii 2 87
To dim his glory and to stain the track Of his bright passage — iii 3 66
And threat the glory of my precious crown — iii 3 90
You may my glories and my state depose, But not my griefs; still am I king of those — iv 1 192
Made glory base and sovereignty a slave, Proud majesty a subject — iv 1 251
A brittle glory shineth in this face: As brittle as the glory is the face — iv 1 287
I will call him to so strict account, That he shall render every glory up, Yea, even the slightest worship — 1 *Hen. IV.* iii 2 150
Think not, Percy, To share with me in glory any more — v 4 64
I will rise there with so full a glory That I will dazzle all the eyes *Hen. V.* i 2 278
Divest yourself, and lay apart The borrow'd glories that by gift of heaven, By law of nature and of nations, 'long To him and to his heirs — ii 4 79
Let him cry 'Praise and glory on his head!' — iv Prol. 31
What! shall we curse the planets of mishap That plotted thus our glory's overthrow? — 1 *Hen. VI.* i 1 24
In complete glory she reveal'd herself — i 2 83
Glory is like a circle in the water, Which never ceaseth to enlarge itself i 2 133
She hath beheld the man Whose glory fills the world with loud report — ii 2 43
Before whose glory I was great in arms — ii 5 24
Yet heavens have glory for this victory! — iii 2 117
Ascribes the glory of his conquest got First to my God and next unto your grace — iii 4 11
This is the latest glory of thy praise That I, thy enemy, due thee withal iv 2 33
Surely, by all the glory you have won, An if I fly, I am not Talbot's son iv 6 50
Whose life was England's glory, Gallia's wonder — iv 7 48
To the Dauphin's tent, To know who hath obtained the glory of the day iv 7 52
I shall be well content with any choice Tends to God's glory — v 1 27
Now, France, thy glory droopeth to the dust — v 3 29
Will you pale your head in Henry's glory, And rob his temples? 3 *Hen. VI.* i 4 103
Blame me not: 'Tis love I bear thy glories makes me speak — ii 1 158
Had he match'd according to his state, He might have kept that glory — ii 2 153
Lo, now my glory smear'd in dust and blood! — v 2 23
Long mayst thou live To bear his image and renew his glories! — v 4 54
Outlive thy glory, like my wretched self! — *Richard III.* i 3 203
Princes have but their titles for their glories, An outward honour for an inward toil — i 4 78
Your due of birth, The lineal glory of your royal house — iii 7 121
And in the vapour of my glory smother'd — iii 7 164
Go, go, poor soul, I envy not thy glory — iv 1 64
Farewell, thou woful welcomer of glory! — iv 1 90
The high imperial type of this earth's glory — iv 4 244
The crown, usurp'd, disgraced his kingly glory — iv 4 371
When Those suns of glory, those two lights of men, Met — *Hen. VIII.* i 1 6
Then you lost The view of earthly glory — i 1 14
I heartily forgive 'em: Yet let 'em look they glory not in mischief — ii 1 66
From that full meridian of my glory, I haste now to my setting — iii 2 224
In a sea of glory, But far beyond my depth — iii 2 360
Vain pomp and glory of this world, I hate ye: I feel my heart new open'd — iii 2 365
Glory. All my glories In that one woman I have lost for ever *Hen. VIII.* iii 2 408
Wolsey, that once trod the ways of glory — iii 2 435
The greatest monarch now alive may glory In such an honour — v 3 164
What glory our Achilles shares from Hector, Were he not proud, we all should share with him — *Troi. and Cres.* i 3 367
Were it not glory that we more affected Than the performance of our heaving spleens — ii 2 195
Would not lose So rich advantage of a promised glory — ii 2 204
Let Æneas live, If to my sword his fate be not the glory, A thousand complete courses of the sun! — iv 1 26
The glory of our Troy doth this day lie On his fair worth — iv 4 149
And, in the last, When he had carried Rome and that we look'd For no less spoil than glory — *Coriolanus* v 6 44
And patient fools, Whose children he hath slain, their base throats tear With giving him glory — v 6 54
Let it be your glory To see her tears — *T. Andron.* ii 3 139
That book in many's eyes doth share the glory, That in gold clasps locks in the golden story — *Rom. and Jul.* i 3 91
When we for recompense have praised the vile, It stains the glory in that happy verse Which aptly sings the good — *T. of Athens* i 1 16
Like madness is the glory of this life, As this pomp shows to a little oil and root — i 2 139
O, the fierce wretchedness that glory brings us! — iv 2 30
Who would be so mock'd with glory? or to live But in a dream of friendship? — iv 2 33
Dost thou lie so low? Are all thy conquests, glories, triumphs, spoils, Shrunk to this little measure? — *J. Cæsar* iii 1 149
His glory not extenuated, wherein he was worthy — iii 2 42
Do grace to Cæsar's corpse, and grace his speech Tending to Cæsar's glories — iii 2 63
I shall have glory by this losing day — v 5 36
Let's away, To part the glories of this happy day — v 5 81
Was never call'd to bear my part, Or show the glory of our art *Macbeth* iii 5 9
Would not let him partake in the glory of the action *Ant. and Cleo.* iii 5 9
False-play'd my glory Unto an enemy's triumph — iv 14 19
Their story is No less in pity than his glory which Brought them to be lamented — v 2 365
He served with glory and admired success — *Cymbeline* i 1 32
Embolden'd with the glory of her praise, Think death no hazard *Pericles* i 1 4
Her face, like heaven, enticeth thee to view Her countless glory — i 1 31
And make a conquest of unhappy me, Whereas no glory's got to overcome — i 4 70
As jewels lose their glory if neglected, So princes their renowns — ii 2 12
Yon king's to me like to my father's picture, Which tells me in that glory once he was — ii 3 38
Even in the height and pride of all his glory — ii 4 6
Gloss. Our garments, being, as they were, drenched in the sea, hold notwithstanding their freshness and glosses — *Tempest* ii 1 63
That would be as great a soil in the new gloss of your marriage as to show a child his new coat and forbid him to wear it — *Much Ado* iii 2 6
The only soil of his fair virtue's gloss, If virtue's gloss will stain with any soil, Is a sharp wit — *L. L. Lost* ii 1 47
'Tis [virginity] a commodity will lose the gloss with lying *All's Well* i 1 167
With forged quaint conceit To set a gloss upon his bold intent 1 *Hen. VI.* iv 1 103
Sullied all his gloss of former honour By this . . . wild adventure — iv 4 6
For all this flattering gloss, He will be found a dangerous protector — 2 *Hen. VI.* i 1 163
That's the plain truth: your painted gloss discovers, To men that understand you, words and weakness — *Hen. VIII.* v 3 71
Yet all his virtues, Not virtuously on his own part beheld, Do in our eyes begin to lose their gloss — *Troi. and Cres.* ii 3 128
Ceremony was but devised at first To set a gloss on faint deeds *T. of A.* i 2 16
Worn now in their newest gloss, Not cast aside so soon — *Macbeth* i 7 34
Be content to slubber the gloss of your new fortunes — *Othello* i 3 227
Gloster. Unreverent Gloster!—Thou art reverent Touching thy spiritual function, not thy life — 1 *Hen. VI.* iii 1 49
Gloucester. In the county of Gloucester, justice of peace — *Mer. Wives* i 1 5
That he did plot the Duke of Gloucester's death — *Richard II.* i 1 100
For Gloucester's death, I slew him not; but to my own disgrace Neglected my sworn duty in that case — i 1 132
But Thomas, my dear lord, my life, my Gloucester — i 2 16
The best way is to venge my Gloucester's death — i 2 36
My brother Gloucester, plain well-meaning soul, Whom fair befal in heaven 'mongst happy souls! — ii 1 128
Not Gloucester's death, nor Hereford's banishment, Not Gaunt's rebukes ii 1 165
To my sister Gloucester; Bid her send me presently a thousand pound ii 2 90
What dost thou know of noble Gloucester's death? — iv 1 3
In that dead time when Gloucester's death was plotted — iv 1 10
Vauntingly thou spakest it, That thou wert cause of noble Gloucester's death — iv 1 37
Humphrey, my son of Gloucester, Where is the prince your brother? — 2 *Hen. IV.* iv 4 12
Warwick! Gloucester! Clarence!—Doth the king call? — iv 5 48
The Duke of Gloucester would speak with you — *Hen. V.* iii 2 59
The Duke of Gloucester, to whom the order of the siege is given — iii 2 69
Gloucester, 'tis true that we are in great danger — iv 1 1
My brother Gloucester's voice? Ay; I know thy errand, I will go with thee — iv 1 323
My dear Lord Gloucester, and my good Lord Exeter — iv 3 9
Warwick and Talbot, Salisbury and Gloucester — iv 3 54
My Lord of Warwick, and my brother Gloucester, Follow Fluellen closely — iv 7 178
Gloucester, whate'er we like, thou art protector And lookest to command the prince and realm — 1 *Hen. VI.* i 1 37
Bedford, if thou be slack, I'll fight it out.—Gloucester, why doubt'st thou of my forwardness? — i 1 100
Open the gates; 'tis Gloucester that calls — i 3 4
It is the noble Duke of Gloucester.—Whoe'er he be, you may not be let in — i 3 6
Open the gates; here's Gloucester that would enter — i 3 17
Gloucester, thou wilt answer this before the pope.—Winchester goose! i 3 52
Here's Gloucester, a foe to citizens, One that still motions war — i 3 62
Gloucester, we will meet; to thy cost, be sure — i 3 82
Abominable Gloucester, guard thy head; For I intend to have it ere long — i 3 87
In the next parliament Call'd for the truce of Winchester and Gloucester ii 4 118
With written pamphlets studiously devised, Humphrey of Gloucester — iii 1 3
Gloucester, I do defy thee. Lords, vouchsafe To give me hearing — iii 1 27
Uncles of Gloucester and of Winchester, The special watchmen of our English weal, I would prevail — iii 1 65

Gloucester. The Duke of Gloucester's men, Forbidden late to carry any weapon . . . . . . 1 *Hen. VI.* iii 1 78
Pray, uncle Gloucester, mitigate this strife . . . iii 1 88
Duke of Gloucester, I will yield to thee; Love for thy love and hand for hand . . . . iii 1 134
Kind Duke of Gloucester, How joyful am I made by this contract! iii 1 142
When Gloucester says the word, King Henry goes . . . . . . iii 1 184
Is this the Lord Talbot, uncle Gloucester? . . . . . . iii 4 13
Humphrey of Gloucester, thou shalt well perceive That, neither in birth or for authority, The bishop will be overborne by thee . v 1 58
Thanks, uncle Winchester, Gloucester, York, Buckingham . 2 *Hen. VI.* i 1 69
My Lord of Gloucester, now ye grow too hot . . . . . i 1 137
Calling him 'Humphrey, the good Duke of Gloucester' . . . . i 1 159
If Gloucester be displaced, he'll be protector . . . . . i 1 177
I never saw but Humphrey Duke of Gloucester Did bear him like a noble gentleman . . . . i 1 183
He that breaks a stick of Gloucester's grove Shall lose his head . . i 2 33
I cannot go before, While Gloucester bears this base and humble mind i 2 62
Suffolk, England knows thine insolence.—And thy ambition, Gloucester ii 1 32
Believe me, cousin Gloucester, Had not your man put up the fowl so suddenly, We had had more sport . . . . ii 1 44
Why, how now, uncle Gloucester!—Talking of hawking; nothing else . ii 1 49
Gloucester, see here the tainture of thy nest, And look thyself be faultless ii 1 188
That hath dishonour'd Gloucester's honest name . . . . . . ii 1 199
Thomas of Woodstock, Duke of Gloucester . . . . . . ii 2 16
Stand forth, Dame Eleanor Cobham, Gloucester's wife . . . . ii 3 1
Stay, Humphrey Duke of Gloucester: ere thou go, Give up thy staff . ii 3 22
And Humphrey Duke of Gloucester scarce himself, That bears so shrewd a maim . . . . ii 3 40
Ah, Gloucester, hide thee from their hateful looks! . . . . . ii 4 23
Gentle Nell; forget this grief.—Ah, Gloucester, teach me to forget myself! . . . . ii 4 27
I muse my Lord of Gloucester is not come . . . . . . iii 1 1
Gloucester is a man Unsounded yet and full of deep deceit . . . iii 1 56
Gloucester is as innocent From meaning treason to our royal person As is the suckling lamb . . . . iii 1 69
Pardon, my liege, that I have stay'd so long.—Nay, Gloucester, know that thou art come too soon . . . . iii 1 95
Gloucester, 'tis my special hope That you will clear yourself from all suspect . . . . iii 1 139
Even so myself bewails good Gloucester's case With sad unhelpful tears iii 1 217
I will weep and 'twixt each groan Say 'Who's a traitor? Gloucester he is none' . . . . iii 1 222
Gloucester's show Beguiles him as the mournful crocodile . . . iii 1 225
This Gloucester should be quickly rid the world, To rid us from the fear we have of him . . . . iii 1 233
Proceed no straiter 'gainst our uncle Gloucester Than from true evidence iii 2 20
Dead in his bed, my lord; Gloucester is dead . . . . . iii 2 29
In life but double death, now Gloucester's dead . . . . . iii 2 55
Ah, woe is me for Gloucester, wretched man! . . . . . . iii 2 72
Is all thy comfort shut in Gloucester's tomb? . . . . . . iii 2 78
Richard, I will create thee Duke of Gloucester, And George, of Clarence . . .—Let me be Duke of Clarence, George of Gloucester; For Gloucester's dukedom is too ominous . . . . . 3 *Hen. VI.* ii 6 103
Now, brother of Gloucester, Lord Hastings, and the rest, Stand you thus close, to steal the bishop's deer? . . . . iv 5 16
He was convey'd by Richard Duke of Gloucester And the Lord Hastings iv 6 81
'Good Gloucester' and 'good devil' were alike, And both preposterous v 6 4
Clarence and Gloucester, love my lovely queen . . . . . v 7 26
His minority Is put unto the trust of Richard Gloucester *Richard III.* i 3 12
He desires to make atonement Betwixt the Duke of Gloucester and your brothers . . . . i 3 37
Brother of Gloucester, you mistake the matter . . . . . . i 3 62
Come, come, we know your meaning, brother Gloucester . . . . i 3 74
My Lord of Gloucester, I have too long borne Your blunt upbraidings . i 3 103
My Lord of Gloucester, in those busy days . . . We follow'd then our lord i 3 145
And, in my company, my brother Gloucester . . . . . . i 4 11
Upon the giddy footing of the hatches, Methought that Gloucester stumbled . . . . i 4 18
So I am, to let him live.—Back to the Duke of Gloucester, tell him so . i 4 118
Where is thy conscience now?—In the Duke of Gloucester's purse . . i 4 131
I will send you to my brother Gloucester, Who shall reward you . . i 4 235
You are deceived, your brother Gloucester hates you . . . . i 4 238
Bid Gloucester think of this, and he will weep . . . . . i 4 245
There wanteth now our brother Gloucester here, To make the perfect period of this peace . . . . ii 1 43
You cannot guess who caused your father's death.—Grandam, we can; for my good uncle Gloucester Told me . . . . ii 2 20
O, full of danger is the Duke of Goucester! . . . . . . ii 3 27
'Ay,' quoth my uncle Goucester, 'Small herbs have grace' . . . ii 4 12
Who hath committed them?—The mighty dukes Gloucester and Buckingham . . . . ii 4 45
Uncle Gloucester, if our brother come, Where shall we sojourn? . . iii 1 61
This day had plotted, in the council-house To murder me and my good Lord of Gloucester . . . . iii 5 39
My niece Plantagenet Led in the hand of her kind aunt of Gloucester . iv 1 2
Attend the lords of France and Burgundy, Gloucester . . . . *Lear* i 1 35
Go you before to Gloucester with these letters . . . . . . i 5 1
Occasions, noble Gloucester, of some poise . . . . . . ii 1 122
Why, Gloucester, Gloucester, I'ld speak with the Duke of Cornwall . ii 4 97
Where is my lord of Gloucester?—Follow'd the old man forth . . ii 4 297
True or false, it hath made thee earl of Gloucester . . . . . iii 5 19
Seek out the villain Gloucester.—Hang him instantly . . . . iii 7 3
Farewell, dear sister: farewell, my lord of Gloucester . . . . iii 7 13
My lord of Gloucester hath convey'd him hence . . . . . . iii 7 15
Go seek the traitor Gloucester, Pinion him like a thief, bring him before us . . . . iii 7 22
Of Gloucester's treachery, And of the loyal service of his son . . iv 2 6
My most dear Gloucester! O, the difference of man and man! . . . iv 2 25
Cornwall's dead; Slain by his servant, going to put out The other eye of Gloucester.—Gloucester's eyes! . . . . iv 2 72
O poor Gloucester! Lost he his other eye?—Both, both, my lord . . iv 2 80
One way I like this well; But being widow, and my Gloucester with her iv 2 85
Gloucester, I live To thank thee for the love thou show'dst the king . iv 2 95
It was great ignorance, Gloucester's eyes being out, To let him live . iv 5 9
Gloucester's bastard son Was kinder to his father than my daughters . iv 6 116
I know thee well enough; thy name is Gloucester . . . . . iv 6 181
Who is conductor of his people?—As 'tis said, the bastard son of Gloucester . . . . iv 7 89
Thou art arm'd, Gloucester: let the trumpet sound . . . . . v 3 90

Gloucester. If any man . . . will maintain upon Edmund, supposed Earl of Gloucester, that he is a manifold traitor . . . . *Lear* v 3 112
What's he that speaks for Edmund Earl of Gloucester?—Himself . v 3 125
This is practice, Gloucester: By the law of arms thou wast not bound to answer . . . . v 3 151

Gloucestershire. My cousin loves you.—Ay, that I do; as well as I love any woman in Gloucestershire . . . . *Mer. Wives* iii 4 44
I'll make the best in Gloucestershire know on 't . . . . . v 5 191
Noble lord, I am a stranger here in Gloucestershire . *Richard II.* ii 3 3
The rebels have consumed with fire Our town of Cicester in Gloucestershire . . . . v 6 3
What do you call the place?—A plague upon it, it is in Gloucestershire 1 *Hen. IV.* i 3 243
Our meeting Is Bridgenorth: and, Harry, you shall march Through Gloucestershire . . . . iii 2 176
I beseech you, give me leave to go Through Gloucestershire 2 *Hen. IV.* iv 3 88
I'll through Gloucestershire; and there will I visit Master Robert Shallow . . . . iv 3 138

Glove. Sir, your glove.—Not mine; my gloves are on . *T. G. of Ver.* ii 1 1
Did you pick Master Slender's purse?—Ay, by these gloves, did he *M. Wives* i 1 156
Cost me two shilling and two pence a-piece of Yead Miller, by these gloves . . . . i 1 161
Froth and scum, thou liest!—By these gloves, then, 'twas he . . i 1 168
These gloves the count sent me; they are an excellent perfume *M. Ado* iii 4 62
What was sent to you from fair Dumain?—Madam, this glove *L. L. Lost* v 2 48
I here protest, By this white glove,—how white the hand, God knows! v 2 411
Give me your gloves, I'll wear them for your sake . . *Mer. of Venice* iv 1 426
I verily did think That her old gloves were on, but 'twas her hands: She has a huswife's hand . . . . . . *As Y. Like It* iv 3 26
This woman's an easy glove, my lord; she goes off and on . *All's Well* v 3 278
A sentence is but a cheveril glove to a good wit . . . *T. Night* iii 1 13
No milliner can so fit his customers with gloves . . . *W. Tale* iv 4 193
Gloves as sweet as damask roses . . . . iv 4 222
It will also be the bondage of certain ribbons and gloves . . . iv 4 236
Come, you promised me a tawdry-lace and a pair of sweet gloves . iv 4 253
Not a ribbon, glass, pomander, brooch, table-book, ballad, knife, tape, glove . . . . iv 4 610
And from the common'st creature pluck a glove . . . *Richard II.* v 3 17
A scaly gauntlet now with joints of steel Must glove this hand 2 *Hen. IV.* i 1 147
As familiar with men's pockets as their gloves or their handkerchers *Hen. V.* iii 2 51
Here's my glove: give me another of thine . . . . . iv 1 226
If ever thou come to me and say, after to-morrow, 'This is my glove,' by this hand, I will take thee a box on the ear . . . . . iv 1 231
Soldier, why wearest thou that glove in thy cap? . . . . . iv 7 125
Who, if alive and ever dare to challenge this glove, I have sworn to take him a box o' th' ear: or if I can see my glove in his cap, which he swore, as he was a soldier, he would wear if alive, I will strike it out soundly . . . . iv 7 132
When Alençon and myself were down together, I plucked this glove from his helm . . . . iv 7 162
I would fain see the man, that has but two legs, that shall find himself aggriefed at this glove . . . . iv 7 170
The glove which I have given him for a favour May haply purchase him a box o' th' ear . . . . iv 7 180
Know you this glove?—Know the glove! I know the glove is a glove . iv 8 6
Look your grace, has struck the glove which your majesty is take out of the helmet of Alençon . . . . iv 8 27
This was my glove; here is the fellow of it . . . . . iv 8 29
I met this man with my glove in his cap, and I have been as good as my word . . . . iv 8 33
This is the glove of Alençon, that your majesty is give me . . iv 8 39
Give me thy glove, soldier: look, here is the fellow of it . . . iv 8 41
Here, uncle Exeter, fill this glove with crowns, And give it to this fellow . . . . iv 8 61
You fur your gloves with reason . . . . *Troi. and Cres.* ii 2 38
I will throw my glove to Death himself, That there's no maculation in thy heart . . . . iv 4 65
Wear this sleeve.—And you this glove. When shall I see you? . . iv 4 73
Your quondam wife swears still by Venus' glove . . . . . iv 5 179
Takes my glove, And gives memorial dainty kisses to it, As I kiss thee v 2 79
Matrons flung gloves, Ladies and maids their scarfs . . *Coriolanus* ii 1 279
See, how she leans her cheek upon her hand! Oh, that I were a glove upon that hand, That I might touch that cheek! . *Rom. and Jul.* ii 2 24
Throw thy glove, Or any token of thine honour else . . *T. of Athens* v 4 49
Then there's my glove . . . . v 4 54
That curled my hair; wore gloves in my cap . . . . *Lear* iii 4 88
This is not a boon; 'Tis as I should entreat you wear your gloves *Othello* iii 3 77
To fetch her fan, her gloves, her mask, nor nothing? . . . . iv 2 9
He did keep The deck, with glove, or hat, or handkerchief, Still waving *Cymbeline* i 3 11

Glover. A great round beard, like a glover's paring-knife . *Mer. Wives* i 4 21

Glow. Now the wasted brands do glow . . . . *M. N. Dream* v 1 382
Between the pale complexion of true love And the red glow of scorn *As Y. Like It* iii 4 57
You will but make it blush And glow with shame . . . *K. John* iv 1 114
The angry spot doth glow on Cæsar's brow . . . . *J. Cæsar* i 2 183
Heaven's face doth glow . . . . *Hamlet* iii 4 48
With divers-colour'd fans, whose wind did seem To glow the delicate cheeks which they did cool . . . . . *Ant. and Cleo.* ii 2 209
There is something glows upon my cheek, And whispers in mine ear *Per.* v 1 96

Glowed. Those his goodly eyes, That o'er the files and musters of the war Have glow'd like plated Mars . . . . *Ant. and Cleo.* i 1 4

Glowing. Cooled, glowing hot, in that surge, like a horse-shoe *Mer. Wives* iii 5 122
This lies glowing, I can tell you, and is almost mature . *Coriolanus* iv 3 26
A spark, To which that blast gives heat and stronger glowing *Pericles* i 2 41

Glow-worm. Twenty glow-worms shall our lanterns be . *Mer. Wives* v 5 82
Light them at the fiery glow-worm's eyes . . . *M. N. Dream* iii 1 173
The glow-worm shows the matin to be near, And 'gins to pale *Hamlet* i 5 89
Now his son's like a glow-worm in the night, The which hath fire in darkness, none in light . . . . *Pericles* ii 3 43

Gloze. Now to plain-dealing; lay these glozes by . . . *L. L. Lost* iv 3 370
More Than they whom youth and ease have taught to glose *Richard II.* ii 1 10
Salique land the French unjustly glose To be the realm of France *Hen. V.* i 2 40
Thus it shall become High-witted Tamora to gloze with all *T. Andron.* iv 4 35
He has found the meaning: But I will gloze with him . . *Pericles* i 1 110

Glozed. You have both said well, And on the cause and question now in hand Have glozed, but superficially . . . *Troi. and Cres.* ii 2 165

Glue. Ten thousand wiry friends Do glue themselves in sociable grief *K. John* iii 4 65

Glue. Thy tears would wash this cold congealed blood That glues my lips and will not let me speak . . . 3 *Hen. VI.* v 2 38
Glued. My love and fear glued many friends to thee . . . ii 6 5
Go to; have your lath glued within your sheath Till you know better how to handle it . . . *T. Andron.* ii 1 41
Glut. He'll be hang'd yet, Though every drop of water swear against it And gape at widest to glut him . . . *Tempest* i 1 63
Glutted. Being with his presence glutted, gorged and full 1 *Hen. IV.* iii 2 84
Glutton. Ragged as Lazarus in the painted cloth, where the glutton's dogs licked his sores . . . iv 2 28
Let him be damned, like the glutton! pray God his tongue be hotter! 2 *Hen. IV.* i 2 39
So, thou common dog, didst thou disgorge Thy glutton bosom . i 3 98
Gluttonous. Then they could smile and fawn upon his debts And take down the interest into their gluttonous maws . . *T. of Athens* iii 4 52
Gluttony. I make them! gluttony and diseases make them; I make them not.—If the cook help to make the gluttony, you help to make the diseases . . . 2 *Hen. IV.* ii 4 46
Gnarled. Split'st the unwedgeable and gnarled oak . *Meas. for Meas.* ii 2 116
Gnarling sorrow hath less power to bite The man that mocks at it and sets it light . . . *Richard II.* i 3 292
And wolves are gnarling who Shall gnaw thee first . . 2 *Hen. VI.* iii 1 192
Gnat. When the sun shines let foolish gnats make sport . *Com. of Errors* ii 2 30
O me, with what strict patience have I sat, To see a king transformed to a gnat! . . . *L. L. Lost* iv 3 166
The painter plays the spider and hath woven A golden mesh to entrap the hearts of men Faster than gnats in cobwebs . *Mer. of Venice* iii 2 123
A grain, a dust, a gnat, a wandering hair, Any annoyance . *K. John* iv 1 93
And whither fly the gnats but to the sun? . . . 3 *Hen. VI.* ii 6 9
Is the sun dimm'd, that gnats do fly in it? . . . *T. Andron.* iv 4 82
Her waggoner a small grey-coated gnat . . . *Rom. and Jul.* i 4 64
Till the flies and gnats of Nile Have buried them for prey! *A. and C.* iii 13 166
Follow'd him, till he had melted from The smallness of a gnat to air *Cymbeline* i 3 21
Like to gnats, Which make a sound, but kill'd are wonder'd at *Pericles* ii 3 62
Gnaw. Civil dissension is a viperous worm That gnaws the bowels of the commonwealth . . . 1 *Hen. VI.* iii 1 73
And wolves are gnarling who shall gnaw thee first . . 2 *Hen. VI.* iii 1 192
Grew so fast That he could gnaw a crust at two hours old *Richard III.* ii 4 28
Take these rats thither To gnaw their garners . . . *Coriolanus* i 1 254
The canker gnaw thy heart! . . . *T. of Athens* iv 3 49
The thought whereof Doth, like a poisonous mineral, gnaw my inwards *Othello* ii 1 306
Heaven pardon him!—A halter pardon him! and hell gnaw his bones! iv 2 136
Why gnaw you so your nether lip? Some bloody passion shakes your very frame . . . v 2 43
Gnawed. I was his bondman, sir, But he, I thank him, gnaw'd in two my cords . . . *Com. of Errors* v 1 289
Ten thousand men that fishes gnaw'd upon . . *Richard III.* i 4 25
Gnawing with my teeth my bonds in sunder, I gain'd my freedom *Com. of Errors* v 1 249
Rend off thy silver hair, thy other hand Gnawing with thy teeth *T. An.* iii 1 262
I am Revenge; sent from the infernal kingdom, To ease the gnawing vulture of thy mind . . . v 2 31
Gnawn. My coffers ransacked, my reputation gnawn at . *Mer. Wives* ii 2 307
Go make thyself like a nymph o' the sea . . . *Tempest* i 2 301
So, king, go safely on to seek thy son . . . ii 1 327
We'll not run, Monsieur Monster.—Nor go neither . . . iii 2 22
Why, what did I? I did nothing. I'll go farther off . . . iii 2 81
Before you can say 'come' and 'go,' And breathe twice and cry 'so, so' iv 1 44
Go bring it hither, For stale to catch these thieves.—I go, I go . iv 1 187
Wit shall not go unrewarded while I am king of this country . iv 1 242
With such discourse as, I not doubt, shall make it Go quick away . v 1 304
I must go send some better messenger . . *T. G. of Ver.* i 1 159
Dinner is ready, and your father stays.—Well, let us go . . i 2 132
To-morrow be in readiness to go: Excuse it not, for I am peremptory . i 3 70
No more of stay! to-morrow thou must go . . . i 3 75
Your father calls for you: He is in haste; therefore, I pray you, go . i 3 89
Wilt thou go?—Well, I will go . . . ii 3 64
If thou wilt, go with me to the alehouse; if not, thou art an Hebrew . ii 5 56
Thou hast not so much charity in thee as to go to the ale with a Christian ii 5 61
Thou wouldst as soon go kindle fire with snow . . . ii 7 19
Then let me go and hinder not my course . . . ii 7 33
If you think so, then stay at home and go not.—Nay, that I will not . ii 7 62
Go with me to my chamber, To take a note of what I stand in need of . ii 7 83
But, hark thee; I will go to her alone . . . iii 1 127
O, could their master come and go as lightly! . . . iii 1 142
Soho, soho!—What seest thou?—Him we go to find . . . iii 1 191
And must I go to him?—Thou must run to him . . . iii 1 386
Come, go with us, we'll bring thee to our crews . . . iv 1 74
You know that love Will creep in service where it cannot go . . iv 2 20
My love is buried. . . . Go to thy lady's grave and call hers thence . iv 2 117
To bear me company and go with me . . . iv 3 34
When will you go?—This evening coming . . . iv 3 42
Go get thee hence, and find my dog again . . . iv 4 64
Go presently and take this ring with thee, Deliver it to Madam Silvia . iv 4 76
Go thou with her to the west end of the wood; There is our captain . v 3 9
Let go that rude uncivil touch, Thou friend of an ill fashion! . . v 4 60
Go to the casement, and see if you can see my master . *Mer. Wives* i 4 1
I'll go watch.—Go; and we'll have a posset for't soon at night . i 4 7
Run in here, good young man; go into this closet . . . i 4 39
John! what, John, I say! Go, John, go inquire for my master . . i 4 41
Pray you, go and vetch me in my closet un boitier vert, a box . . i 4 46
Prevent, or go thou, Like Sir Actæon he, with Ringwood at thy heels . ii 1 121
How now, Meg!—Whither go you, George? Hark you . . . ii 1 153
If you should fight, you go against the hair of your professions . ii 3 41
Go you through the town to Frogmore . . . ii 3 78
Whither go you?—Truly, sir, to see your wife . . . iii 2 9
For it is as positive as the earth is firm that Falstaff is there: I will go iii 2 50
I have good cheer at home; and I pray you all go with me . . iii 2 53
I will show you a monster. Master doctor, you shall go; so shall you iii 2 83
Will you go, gentles?—Have with you to see this monster . . iii 2 92
I'll go hide me.—Do so. Go tell thy master I am alone . . iii 3 35
What, John! Robert! John! Go take up these clothes here quickly . iii 3 155
They can tell you how things go better than I can . . . iii 4 69
Go fetch me a quart of sack; put a toast in't . . . iii 5 3
Go brew me a pottle of sack finely.—With eggs, sir?—Simple of itself . iii 5 29
If I have horns to make one mad, let the proverb go with me: I'll be horn-mad . . . iii 5 154
Which way should he go? how should I bestow him? . . . iv 2 47
Go. Let's go dress him like the witch of Brentford . . *Mer. Wives* iv 2 100
Master Slender sent to her, seeing her go thorough the streets . iv 5 32
You shall hear how things go; and, I warrant, to your content . iv 5 126
When Slender sees his time To take her by the hand and bid her go, She shall go . . . iv 6 37
On that token, The maid hath given consent to go with him . . iv 6 45
Let's go learn the truth of it . . . *Meas. for Meas.* i 2 82
Away, sir! you must go.—One word, good friend . . . i 2 145
Go to your bosom; Knock there, and ask your heart what it doth know ii 2 136
I am going with instruction to him. Grace go with you, Benedicite! . ii 3 39
Ay, but to die, and go we know not where; To lie in cold obstruction . iii 1 118
You must die; go to your knees and make ready . . . iii 1 171
Advise this wronged maid to stead up your appointment, go in your place iii 1 261
He were as good go a mile on his errand . . . iii 2 38
Pattern in himself to know, Grace to stand, and virtue go . . iii 2 278
I will go further than I meant, to pluck all fears out of you . iv 2 206
I beseech you Look forward on the journey you shall go . . iv 3 61
Pace your wisdom In that good path that I would wish it go . . iv 3 138
Heaven shield your grace from woe, As I, thus wrong'd, hence unbelieved go! . . . v 1 119
I will go darkly to work with her . . . v 1 279
Many a man would take you at your word, And go indeed *Com. of Errors* i 2 18
Walk with me about the town, And then go to my inn and dine with me i 2 23
Time is their master, and when they see time They'll go or come . ii 1 9
I'll say as they say and persever so And in this mist at all adventures go ii 2 218
While I go to the goldsmith's house, go thou And buy a rope's end . iv 1 15
Vouchsafe to take the pains To go with us . . . v 1 394
Go to a gossips' feast, and go with me . . . v 1 405
And now let's go hand in hand, not one before another . . v 1 425
In what key shall a man take you, to go in the song? . *Much Ado* i 1 188
The fine is, for the which I may go the finer, I will live a bachelor . i 1 247
Go you with me, and I will use your skill . . . i 2 27
Shall we go prove what's to be done? . . . i 3 75
Well, then, go you into hell?—No, but to the gate . . . ii 1 44
And people sin upon purpose, because they would go thither . . ii 1 267
I will go on the slightest errand now to the Antipodes that you can devise ii 1 272
I warrant thee, Claudio, the time shall not go dully by us . . ii 1 379
I will presently go learn their day of marriage . . . ii 2 57
Then sigh not so, but let them go, And be you blithe and bonny . ii 3 68
If I do not love her, I am a Jew. I will go get her picture . . ii 3 273
Then go we near her, that her ear lose nothing . . . iii 1 32
Take no note of him, but let him go . . . iii 3 30
Let us go sit here upon the church-bench till two . . . iii 3 95
We charge you let us obey you to go with us . . . iii 3 189
Master constable, you go not the way to examine . . . iv 2 35
And yet, ere I go, let me go with that I came . . . v 2 47
Will you come presently?—Will you go hear this news? . . . v 2 103
And moreover I will go with thee to thy uncle's . . . v 2 106
For the which, with songs of woe, Round about her tomb they go . v 3 15
And go we, lords, to put in practice that . . . *L. L. Lost* i 1 308
Proud of employment, willingly I go . . . ii 1 35
And go well satisfied to France again . . . ii 1 153
Trip and go, my sweet; deliver this paper into the royal hand of the king . . . iv 2 145
Disfigure not his slop.—This same shall go . . . iv 3 59
Go with speed To some forlorn and naked hermitage . . . v 2 804
I must go seek some dewdrops here . . . *M. N. Dream* ii 1 14
Go with us; If not, shun me, and I will spare your haunts . . ii 1 141
Leave me? do not go.—Stay, on thy peril: I alone will go . . ii 2 87
Out of this wood do not desire to go: Thou shalt remain here . . iii 1 155
I do love thee: therefore, go with me; I'll give thee fairies . . iii 1 159
I will purge thy mortal grossness so That thou shalt like an airy spirit go iii 1 164
About the wood go swifter than the wind . . . iii 2 94
I go, I go; look how I go, Swifter than arrow from the Tartar's bow . iii 2 100
Why should he stay, whom love doth press to go? . . . iii 2 184
So you will let me quiet go, To Athens will I bear my folly back . iii 2 314
Let me go: You see how simple and how fond I am . . . iii 2 316
All this coil is 'long of you: Nay, go not back.—I will not trust you iii 2 340
Torn with briers, I can no further crawl, no further go . . . iii 2 444
Thus have I, Wall, my part discharged so; And, being done, thus Wall away doth go . . . v 1 207
I will go and purse the ducats straight, See to my house *Mer. of Venice* i 3 175
I must go with you to Belmont.—Why, then you must . . . ii 2 187
Lest through thy wild behaviour I be misconstrued in the place I go to ii 2 197
But wherefore should I go? I am not bid for love; they flatter me . ii 5 12
But yet I'll go in hate, to feed upon The prodigal Christian . . ii 5 14
I am right loath to go: There is some ill a-brewing towards my rest . ii 5 16
I beseech you, sir, go: my young master doth expect your reproach . ii 5 19
The wind is come about; Bassanio presently will go aboard . . ii 6 65
Madam, I go with all convenient speed . . . iii 4 56
Go to thy fellows; bid them cover the table, serve in the meat . iii 5 63
Go one, and call the Jew into the court . . . iv 1 14
I take this offer, then; pay the bond thrice And let the Christian go . iv 1 319
Give me my principal, and let me go.—I have it ready for thee . iv 1 336
I pray you, give me leave to go from hence; I am not well . . iv 1 395
But go we in, I pray thee, Jessica . . . v 1 36
And suffer'd him to go displeased away . . . v 1 213
Let your fair eyes and gentle wishes go with me to my trial *As Y. Like It* i 2 198
Gentle cousin, Let us go thank him and encourage him . . . i 2 252
Devise with me how we may fly, Whither to go and what to bear . . i 3 103
Now go we in content To liberty and not to banishment . . . i 3 139
Whither, Adam, wouldst thou have me go?—No matter whither . . ii 3 29
What, wouldst thou have me go and beg my food? . . . ii 3 31
Whiles, like a doe, I go to find my fawn And give it food . . ii 7 128
The residue of your fortune, Go to my cave and tell me . . . ii 7 197
Though he go as softly as foot can fall, he thinks himself too soon there iii 2 346
Dispatch us here under this tree, or shall we go with you to your chapel? iii 3 66
Go thou with me, and let me counsel thee . . . iii 3 96
I see no more in you Than without candle may go dark to bed . . iii 5 39
And from hence I go, To make these doubts all even . . . v 4 24
Why, and I trust I may go too, may I not? . . . *T. of Shrew* i 1 102
You may go to the devil's dam: your gifts are so good . . . i 1 106
I pray you, sir, let him go while the humour lasts . . . i 2 107
She is sweeter than perfume itself To whom they go to . . . i 2 154
Well, go with me and be not so discomfited . . . ii 1 164
Will you go with us, Or shall I send my daughter Kate to you? . . ii 1 167
Go to my chamber; put on clothes of mine.—Not I, believe me . . iii 2 115
If you knew my business, You would entreat me rather go than stay . iii 2 194
Then go with me to make the matter good . . . iv 2 114
I'll instruct you: Go with me to clothe you as becomes you . . . iv 2 120

Go. I will not go to-day; and ere I do, It shall be what o'clock I say it is *T. of Shrew* iv 3 196
Nothing but cross'd!—Say as he says, or we shall never go . iv 5 11
You shall not choose but drink before you go . v 1 12
Go to your mistress; Say, I command her come to me . v 2 95
For where an unclean mind carries virtuous qualities there commendations go with pity *All's Well* i 1 49
If I may have your ladyship's good will to go to the world . i 3 19
I am driven on by the flesh; and he must needs go that the devil drives i 3 31
Love you my son?—Do not you love him, madam?—Go not about . i 3 194
The property by what it is should go, Not by the title . ii 3 137
That you are well restored, my lord, I'm glad: Let the rest go . ii 3 155
Go with me to my chamber, and advise me . ii 3 311
Let death and honesty Go with your impositions, I am yours . iv 4 29
Will you go hunt, my lord? *T. Night* i 1 16
Marry, now I let go your hand, I am barren . i 3 84
Will you stay no longer? nor will you not that I go with you? . ii 1 2
The gentleness of all the gods go with thee! . ii 1 45
Shall I bid him go?—What an if you do?—Shall I bid him go, and spare not? . ii 3 118
Go shake your ears . ii 3 134
What you mean by bidding me taste my legs.—I mean, to go, sir, to enter . iii 1 92
Go call him hither. I am as mad as he . iii 4 15
I am one that had rather go with sir priest than sir knight . iii 4 298
Let him alone: I'll go another way to work with him . iv 1 35
Let go thy hand.—Come, sir, I will not let you go . iv 1 40
Thou shalt not choose but go: Do not deny . iv 1 61
Let him say so then, and let him go; But let him swear so, and he shall not stay, We'll thwack him hence *W. Tale* i 2 35
Verily, You shall not go: a lady's 'Verily''s As potent as a lord's. Will you go yet? . i 2 50
If word nor oath Prevail not, go and see . iii 2 205
Make your best haste, and go not Too far i' the land . iii 3 10
Go thou away: I'll follow instantly . iii 3 13
Let my sheep go: come, good boy, the next way home.—Go you the next way . iii 3 131
But shall I go mourn for that, my dear? . iv 3 15
Get you hence, for I must go Where it fits not you to know . iv 4 303
Me too, let me go thither.—Or thou goest to the grange or mill . iv 4 308
You have let him go And nothing marted with him . iv 4 362
Have you thought on A place whereto you'll go? . iv 4 548
Walk before toward the sea-side; go on the right hand . iv 4 856
Upon which errand I now go toward him . v 1 232
Come to thy grandam, child.—Do, child, go to it grandam, child *K. John* ii 1 160
Go we, as well as haste will suffer us, To this unlook'd for, unprepared pomp . ii 1 559
On peril of a curse, Let go the hand of that arch-heretic . iii 1 192
Upon my knee I beg, go not to arms Against mine uncle . iii 1 308
Which is the side that I must go withal? I am with both . iii 1 327
I had a thing to say, but let it go . iii 3 33
My blessing go with thee!—For England, cousin, go . iii 3 71
Go, stand within; let me alone with him . iv 1 85
Go closely in with me: Much danger do I undergo for thee . iv 1 133
The colour of the king doth come and go Between his purpose and his conscience . iv 2 76
I'll go with thee, And find the inheritance of this poor child . iv 2 96
As good to die and go, as die and stay . iv 3 8
Go I to make the French lay down their arms . v 1 24
Leave the field And send him word by me which way you go . v 3 7
Whither dost thou go?—What's that to thee? . v 6 3
As much good stay with thee as go with me! *Richard II.* i 2 57
Depart not so; Though this be all, do not so quickly go . i 2 64
As gentle and as jocund as to jest Go I to fight . i 3 96
Since thou hast far to go, bear not along The clogging burthen of a guilty soul . i 3 199
Six years we banish him, and he shall go.—Cousin, farewell . i 3 248
Well, he is gone; and with him go these thoughts . i 4 37
But if you faint, as fearing to do so, Stay and be secret, and myself will go . ii 1 298
The wind sits fair for news to go to Ireland, But none returns . ii 2 123
But we must win your grace to go with us To Bristol castle . ii 3 163
It may be I will go with you: but yet I'll pause . ii 3 168
Let them go To ear the land that hath some hope to grow . iii 2 211
Noble lords, Go to the rude ribs of that ancient castle . iii 3 32
Must he lose The name of king? o' God's name, let it go . iii 3 146
Go thou, and like an executioner, Cut off the heads of too fast growing sprays . iii 4 33
Then give me leave to go.—Whither?—Whither you will . iv 1 313
Then whither he goes, thither let me go . v 1 85
Come, let's go: I am the king's friend, and will rid his foe . v 4 10
Go thou, and fill another room in hell . v 5 108
Bootless 'tis to tell you we will go: Therefore we meet not now *1 Hen. IV.* i 1 29
We that take purses go by the moon . i 2 15
If you will go, I will stuff your purses full of crowns . i 2 146
If I tarry at home and go not, I'll hang you for going . i 2 150
I will lay him down such reasons for this adventure that he shall go . i 2 169
No further go in this Than I by letters shall direct your course . i 3 292
Now could thou and I rob the thieves and go merrily to London . ii 2 99
But if you go,— So far afoot, I shall be weary, love . ii 3 86
I must not have you henceforth question me Whither I go . ii 3 107
Whither I go, thither shall you go too . ii 3 118
You are as slow As hot Lord Percy is on fire to go . iii 1 269
As not a soldier of this season's stamp Should go so general current through the world . iv 1 5
A fool go with thy soul, whither it goes! . v 3 22
And yet, in some respects, I grant, I cannot go: I cannot tell *2 Hen. IV.* i 2 190
O yet, for God's sake, go not to these wars! . ii 3 9
I must go and meet with danger there, Or it will seek me in another place . ii 3 48
Hollow pamper'd jades of Asia, Which cannot go but thirty mile a-day . ii 4 179
If I be not sent away post, I will see you again ere I go . ii 4 408
I would thou wert a man's tailor, that thou mightst mend him and make him fit to go . iii 2 176
I had as lief be hanged, sir, as go . iii 2 238
Let it go which way it will, he that dies this year is quit for the next . iii 2 254
And away again would a' go, and again would a' come . iii 2 305
That the great body of our state may go In equal rank . v 2 136
An the child I now go with do miscarry, thou wert better thou hadst struck thy mother, thou paper-faced villain . v 4 10

Go. Come, I charge you both go with me; for the man is dead *2 Hen. IV.* v 4 18
Fear no colours: go with me to dinner . v 5 94
Then go we in, to know his embassy . *Hen. V.* i 1 95
Go, my dread lord, to your great-grandsire's tomb . i 2 103
For humours do abound: Knocks go and come; God's vassals drop and die . iii 2 8
Ay, or go to death; and ay'll pay't as valorously as I may . iii 2 124
I know thy errand, I will go with thee . iv 1 324
Good luck go with thee!—Farewell, kind lord . iv 3 11
But yet, before we go, let's not forget The noble duke *1 Hen. VI.* iii 2 131
I go, my lord, in heart desiring still You may behold confusion of your foes . iv 1 76
Go cheerfully together and digest Your angry choler on your enemies iv 1 167
I command thee go.—To fight I will, but not to fly the foe . iv 5 36
Stay, go, do what you will, the like do I . iv 5 50
And so, I pray you, go, in God's name, and leave us *2 Hen. VI.* i 4 12
Thither go these news, as fast as horse can carry them . i 4 78
Give me leave to go; Sorrow would solace and mine age would ease . ii 3 20
Art thou gone too? all comfort go with thee! For none abides with me ii 4 87
Go; speak not to me; even now be gone. O, go not yet! . iii 2 353
I go.—And take my heart with thee . iii 2 408
I go of message from the queen to France; I charge thee waft me safely iv 1 113
Therefore come you with us and let him go . iv 1 141
The nobility think scorn to go in leather aprons . iv 2 13
For thereby is England mained, and fain to go with a staff . iv 2 172
Spare none but such as go in clouted shoon; For they are thrifty honest men . iv 2 195
Now go some and pull down the Savoy; others to the inns of court . iv 7 1
Honester men than thou go in their hose and doublets . iv 7 56
What, is he fled? Go some, and follow him . iv 8 68
Nay, go not from me; I will follow thee.—Be patient . *3 Hen. VI.* i 1 213
My heart, sweet boy, shall be thy sepulchre, For from my heart thine image ne'er shall go . ii 5 116
Not that I fear to stay, but love to go Whither the queen intends . ii 5 138
Go where you will, the king shall be commanded . iii 1 92
Go you before, and I will follow you *Richard III.* i 1 144
Thy conscience flies out.—Let it go; there's few or none will entertain it i 4 134
He holds me dear: Go you to him from me.—Ay, so we will . i 4 240
Go we to determine Who they shall be that straight shall post to Ludlow ii 2 141
My dear cousin, I, like a child, will go by thy direction . ii 2 153
What, will you go unto the Tower, my lord? . iii 1 140
And with a heavy heart, Thinking on them, go I unto the Tower . iii 1 150
Where is your boar-spear, man? Fear you the boar, and go so unprovided? iii 2 75
Come; I in all haste was sent.—And I in all unwillingness will go . iv 1 58
Go thou to Richmond, and good fortune guide thee! . iv 1 92
Go thou to Richard, and good angels guard thee! . iv 1 93
Go thou to sanctuary, and good thoughts possess thee! . iv 1 94
To her I go, a jolly thriving wooer . iv 3 43
Why, what wouldst thou do there before I go? . iv 4 454
Go with me, like good angels, to my end . *Hen. VIII.* ii 1 75
Give us but an hour Of private conference.—We are busy; go . ii 2 81
Great-bellied women, That had not half a week to go . iv 1 77
Whilst I sit meditating On that celestial harmony I go to . iv 2 80
That my teaching And the strong course of my authority Might go one way v 3 36
Must I go like a traitor thither? . v 3 96
Come, go we then together . *Troi. and Cres.* i 1 119
Feast with us before you go And find the welcome of a noble foe . i 3 308
If he fail, Yet go we under our opinion still That we have better men i 3 383
If you'll avouch 'twas wisdom Paris went—As you must needs, for you all cried 'Go, go' . ii 2 85
Troy burns, or else let Helen go . ii 2 112
We'll consecrate the steps that Ajax makes When they go from Achilles ii 3 194
This lord go to him! Jupiter forbid, And say in thunder 'Achilles go to him' . ii 3 208
If I go to him, with my armed fist I'll pash him o'er the face . ii 3 212
Ajax shall cope the best.—Go we to council. Let Achilles sleep . ii 3 276
You cannot shun Yourself.—Let me go and try . iii 2 154
If to-morrow be a fair day, by eleven o'clock it will go one way or other iii 3 297
How now, how now! how go maidenheads? . iv 2 23
Who's that at door? good uncle, go and see . iv 2 36
O you immortal gods! I will not go.—Thou must.—I will not . iv 2 100
Honour or go or stay; My major vow lies here, this I'll obey . v 1 48
Good night and welcome, both at once, to those That go or tarry . v 1 85
You shall not go: one cannot speak a word, But it straight starts you v 2 100
By all the everlasting gods, I'll go! . v 3 5
Ay, but thou shalt not go.—I must not break my faith . v 3 70
With comfort go: Hope of revenge shall hide our inward woe . v 10 30
Where go you With bats and clubs? . *Coriolanus* i 1 56
And when he caught it, he let it go again; and after it again . i 3 67
I will wish her speedy strength, and visit her with my prayers; but I cannot go thither . i 3 88
Go you to the city; Learn how 'tis held . i 10 27
For the love of Juno, let's go . ii 1 111
Rather than fool it so, Let the high office and the honour go . ii 3 129
He'll go, he says, and sowl the porter of Rome gates by the ears . iv 5 213
No, I'll not go: you hear what he hath said . v 1 1
No, I'll not meddle.—Pray you, go to him.—What should I do? . v 1 39
I have sat too long.—Nay, go not from us thus . v 3 131
What begg'st thou, then? fond woman, let me go *T. Andron.* ii 3 172
My hand shall go.—By heaven, it shall not go! . iii 1 177
Go with me: I'll to thy closet; and go read with thee Sad stories . iii 2 81
Then go successantly, and plead to him . iv 4 113
Thou villain Capulet,—Hold me not, let me go . *Rom. and Jul.* i 1 86
Come, go with me. Go, sirrah, trudge about . i 2 34
We mean well in going to this mask; But 'tis no wit to go . i 4 49
Go, then; for 'tis in vain To seek him here that means not to be found ii 1 41
I have more care to stay than will to go: Come, death, and welcome! . iii 5 23
Or bid me go into a new-made grave And hide me with a dead man . iv 1 84
Get you gone.—I go, sir.—'I go, sir!'—Take the bonds along with you *T. of Athens* ii 1 33
Takes no account How things go from him, nor resumes no care . ii 2 4
I am sick of that grief too, as I understand how all things go . iii 6 20
What, dost thou go? Soft! take thy physic first . iii 6 109
Thou'lt go, strong thief, When gouty keepers of thee cannot stand . iv 3 45
Go you down that way towards the Capitol; This way will I . *J. Cæsar* i 1 68
Give me my robe, for I will go . ii 2 107
They would go and kiss dead Cæsar's wounds . iii 2 137
Why, friends, you go to do you know not what . iii 2 240
Some to Decius' house, and some to Casca's; some to Ligarius': away, go! iii 3 43
Think not, thou noble Roman, That ever Brutus will go bound to Rome v 1 112

Go. I go, and it is done; the bell invites me. Hear it not, Duncan *Macb.* ii 1 62
I'll go no more: I am afraid to think what I have done . ii 2 50
Some of all professions that go the primrose way to the everlasting bonfire ii 3 21
God's benison go with you; and with those That would make good of bad! ii 4 40
Go not my horse the better, I must become a borrower of the night iii 1 26
Do you find Your patience so predominant in your nature That you can let this go? Are you so gospell'd? . iii 1 88
We are men, my liege.—Ay, in the catalogue ye go for men . iii 1 92
Stand not upon the order of your going, But go at once . iii 4 120
Round about the cauldron go; In the poison'd entrails throw . iv 1 4
The flighty purpose never is o'ertook Unless the deed go with it . iv 1 146
Go we to the king; our power is ready; Our lack is nothing but our leave iv 3 236
I do beseech you, give him leave to go.—Take thy fair hour, Laertes *Ham.* i 2 61
It waves you to a more removed ground: But do not go with it . i 4 62
And for mine own poor part, Look you, I'll go pray . i 5 132
You may go so far.—My lord, that would dishonour him . ii 1 26
Come, go with me: I will go seek the king . ii 1 101
Come, go we to the king: This must be known . ii 1 117
Go to your rest; at night we'll feast together: Most welcome home! . ii 2 84
What is't but to be nothing else but mad? But let that go . ii 2 95
To a nunnery, go, and quickly too. Farewell . iii 1 145
It shall be so: Madness in great ones must not unwatch'd go . iii 1 196
My thoughts remain below: Words without thoughts never to heaven go iii 3 98
You go not till I set you up a glass Where you may see the inmost part of you . iii 4 19
We go to gain a little patch of ground That hath in it no profit but the name . iv 4 18
That, for a fantasy and trick of fame, Go to their graves like beds . iv 4 62
Which bewept to the grave did go With true-love showers . iv 5 38
Go to thy death-bed: He never will come again . iv 5 193
The other motive, Why to a public count I might not go . iv 7 17
If the man go to this water, and drown himself, it is, will he, nill he, he goes v 1 18
As thou'rt a man, Give me the cup: let go; by heaven, I'll have't . v 2 354
Go to the creating a whole tribe of fops, Got 'tween asleep and wake *Lear* i 2 14
That such a king should play bo-peep, And go the fools among . i 4 194
Let go thy hold when a great wheel runs down a hill . ii 4 73
Good my lord, take his offer; go into the house . iii 4 161
Importune him once more to go, my lord; His wits begin to unsettle . iii 4 166
Go thou farther off; Bid me farewell, and let me hear thee going . iv 6 30
Let go his arm.—Chill not let go, zir, without vurther 'casion . iv 6 238
All my reports go with the modest truth; Nor more nor clipp'd, but so iv 7 5
I'll bring you comfort.—Grace go with you, sir! . v 2 4
I have a journey, sir, shortly to go; My master calls me, I must not say no v 3 321
Letting go safely by The divine Desdemona . *Othello* ii 1 72
Good Iago, Go to the bay and disembark my coffers . ii 1 210
Go where thou art billeted: Away, I say; thou shalt know more hereafter ii 3 386
Nor answer have I none, But what should go by water . iv 2 104
What shall I do to win my lord again? Good friend, go to him . iv 2 150
That song to-night Will not go from my mind . iv 3 31
Where should Othello go? Now, how dost thou look now? . v 2 271
Soft you; a word or two before you go . v 2 338
Sometimes, when he is not Antony, He comes too short of that great property Which still should go with Antony . *Ant. and Cleo.* i 1 59
Go, you wild bedfellow, you cannot soothsay . i 2 51
O, let him marry a woman that cannot go! . i 2 66
You may go: Would she had never given you leave to come! . i 3 20
Seek no colour for your going, But bid farewell, and go . i 3 33
By the fire That quickens Nilus' slime, I go from hence Thy soldier . i 3 69
And all the gods go with you! upon your sword Sit laurel victory! . i 3 99
Let him for ever go:—let him not—Charmian, Though he be painted one way like a Gorgon, The other way's a Mars . ii 5 115
Look, here I have you; thus I let you go, And give you to the gods . iii 2 63
I'll bring thee word Straight, how 'tis like to go . iv 12 3
Bruised pieces, go; You have been nobly borne. From me awhile . iv 14 42
Her beauty and her brain go not together . *Cymbeline* i 2 32
O, that I had her here, to tear her limb-meal! I will go there and do't ii 4 148
One that rode to's execution, man, Could never go so slow . iii 2 73
It shall be so. Boys, we'll go dress our hunt . iii 6 90
I am very sick.—Go you to hunting; I'll abide with him . iv 2 6
Look you, sir, you know not which way you shall go . v 4 182
He must hence depart to Tyre: His queen with child makes her desire —Which who shall cross?—along to go . *Pericles* iii Gower 41
Let her go: There's no hope she will return . iv 1 98
For your bride goes to that with shame which is her way to go with warrant . iv 2 139
Will you not go the way of women-kind? . iv 6 159
There is something glows upon my cheek, And whispers in mine ear 'Go not till he speak' . v 1 97
Go a bat-fowling. We would so, and then go a bat-fowling *Tempest* ii 1 185
Go a-ducking. Let the Egyptians And the Phœnicians go a-ducking *Ant. and Cleo.* iii 7 65
Go about the fields with me through Frogmore . *Mer. Wives* ii 3 89
A marvellous witty fellow, I assure you; but I will go about with him *Much Ado* iv 2 28
Man is but an ass, if he go about to expound this dream *M. N. Dream* iv 1 212
Who shall go about To cozen fortune and be honourable? *Mer. of Venice* ii 9 37
That I kindle the boy thither; which now I'll go about *As Y. Like It* i 1 180
A fellow, sir, that I have known to go about with troll-my-dames *W. Tale* iv 3 91
That have more in them than you'ld think, sister.—Ay, good brother, or go about to think . iv 4 219
Is no honest man, neither to his father nor to me, to go about to make me the king's brother-in-law . iv 4 720
You may as well go about to turn the sun to ice with fanning *Hen. V.* iv 1 212
And here take my leave, To go about my preparation . *1 Hen. VI.* i 1 166
I am not able to stand alone: You go about to torture me in vain *2 Hen VI.* ii 1 146
Let your reason with your choler question What 'tis you go about *Hen. VIII.* i 1 131
He must, and will. Prithee now, say you will, and go about it *Coriol.* iii 2 98
Go about it. Put him to choler straight . iii 3 24
Posters of the sea and land, Thus do go about, about . *Macbeth* i 3 34
His horses go about.—Almost a mile . iii 3 11
Why do you go about to recover the wind of me? . *Hamlet* iii 2 361
O dear father, It is thy business that I go about . *Lear* iv 4 24
Go after him; for he perhaps shall need Some messenger . *K. John* iv 2 178
Ask me not what I know.—Go after her: she's desperate . *Lear* v 3 161
Do but go after, And mark how he continues . *Othello* iv 1 291
Go all. Why, so! go all which way it will! . *Richard II.* ii 2 87
But why should honour outlive honesty? Let it go all . *Othello* v 2 246
Go alone. Stay, then; I'll go alone. Fear comes upon me *Rom. and Jul.* v 3 135
Go along with me: I'll tell you all, Master Brook . *Mer. Wives* v 1 25
Go along: I must employ you in some business . *M. N. Dream* i 1 123
He'll go along o'er the wide world with me . *As Y. Like It* i 3 134
I'll go along with you.—You have no cause . *Richard III.* ii 4 67
Soft! I will go along; An if you leave me so, you do me wrong *Rom. and Jul.* i 1 201
Go a progress. To show you how a king may go a progress through the guts of a beggar . *Hamlet* iv 3 33
Go away. With one fool's head I came to woo, But I go away with two *Mer. of Venice* ii 9 76
Since I have your good leave to go away, I will make haste . iii 2 326
My lord will go away to-night; A very serious business calls on him *All's Well* ii 4 40
I prithee, lady, go away with me . *K. John* iii 4 20
Look not upon me, for thine eyes are wounding: Yet do not go away *2 Hen. VI.* iii 2 52
He should have leave to go away betimes, Lest in our need he might infect another . *3 Hen. VI.* v 4 45
They approach sadly, and go away merry . *T. of Athens* ii 2 106
It beckons you to go away with it, As if it some impartment did desire To you alone . *Hamlet* i 4 58
Go back. Come, Hector, come, go back . *Troi. and Cres.* v 3 62
What, goest thou back? thou shalt Go back, I warrant thee *Ant. and Cleo.* v 2 156
Go bare. Our head shall go bare till merit crown it . *Troi. and Cres.* iii 2 99
Go before. They say, if money go before, all ways do lie open *Mer. Wives* ii 2 175
I had rather, forsooth, go before you like a man . iii 2 5
Go before into the Park: we two must go together . v 3 4
God defend but God should go before such villains! . *Much Ado* iv 2 22
I will go before and show him their examination . iv 2 68
I multiply With one 'We thank you' many thousands moe That go before it.—Stay your thanks . *W. Tale* i 2 9
I'll follow you unto the death.—Nay, I would have you go before me thither . *K. John* i 1 155
My father is sore sick: Our news shall go before us . *2 Hen. IV.* iv 3 84
Follow I must; I cannot go before . *2 Hen. VI.* i 2 61
Peter, take my fan, and go before, and apace . *Rom. and Jul.* ii 4 232
Go before to field, he'll be your follower; Your worship in that sense may call him 'man' . iii 1 61
Go before, nurse: commend me to thy lady . iii 3 155
If that thy gentry, Britain, go before This lout as he exceeds our lords, the odds Is that we scarce are men and you are gods *Cymbeline* v 2 8
Go between. Look you, he may come and go between you both *M. Wives* ii 2 130
I did go between them, as I said; but more than that, he loved her *All's Well* v 3 258
But, as you requested, Yourself shall go between's . *Ant. and Cleo.* iii 4 25
Go buy. I'll go buy them vizards . *Mer. Wives* iv 6 69
A robe of white.—That silk will I go buy . iv 4 73
Then fare thee well: I must go buy spices for our sheep-shearing *W. Tale* iv 3 124
Go by. Mine were the very cipher of a function, To fine the faults whose fine stands in record, And let go by the actor . *Meas. for Meas.* ii 2 41
Go by, Jeronimy: go to thy cold bed, and warm thee . *T. of Shrew* Ind. 1 9
Let her go by.—Yea, leave that labour to great Hercules . i 2 256
Which lets go by some sixteen years and makes her As she lived now *W. Tale* v 3 31
And Crispin Crispian shall ne'er go by, From this day to the ending of the world, But we in it shall be remembered . *Hen. V.* iv 3 57
Follow me, and I'll direct you how you shall go by him . *Coriolanus* ii 3 51
Lips, let sour words go by and language end . *T. of Athens* v 1 223
Lapsed in time and passion, let's go by The important acting *Hamlet* iii 4 107
Who lets go by no vantages that may Prefer you . *Cymbeline* ii 3 50
Go current. And yet go current from suspicion . *Richard III.* ii 1 94
Go down upon him, you have power enough . *Hen. V.* iii 5 53
Go even. Rather shunned to go even with what I heard . *Cymbeline* i 4 47
Go far. I'll husband them so well, They shall go far with little *Hamlet* iv 5 139
Go first. Yourself shall go first.—Not I, sir; pray you, keep on.—Truly, I will not go first . *Mer. Wives* i 1 320
In, boy; go first. You houseless poverty,—Nay, get thee in *Lear* iii 4 26
Go forth. For if our virtues Did not go forth of us, 'twere all alike As if we had them not . *Meas. for Meas.* i 1 35
Therefore go forth; Try what my credit can in Venice do *Mer. of Venice* i 1 179
Go forth and fetch their conquering Cæsar in . *Hen. V.* v Prol. 28
Let us pursue him ere the writs go forth . *2 Hen. VI.* v 3 26
Go forward. But let our plot go forward . *Mer. Wives* iv 4 13
Can I go forward when my heart is here? . *Rom. and Jul.* ii 1 1
Go free. Let man go free And let not hemp his wind-pipe suffocate *Hen. V.* iii 6 44
Go great with tigers, dragons, wolves, and bears . *T. of Athens* iv 3 189
Go hang. For she had a tongue with a tang, Would cry to a sailor, Go hang! . *Tempest* ii 2 53
Then to sea, boys, and let her go hang! . ii 2 56
Go hang yourself, you naughty mocking uncle! . *Troi. and Cres.* iv 2 26
Go hang, sir, hang! Tell me of that? away! . *Ant. and Cleo.* ii 7 59
Go hard. It shall go hard but I'll prove it . *T. G. of Ver.* i 1 86
It shall go hard but I will better the instruction . *Mer. of Venice* iii 1 75
It will go hard with poor Antonio . iii 2 292
It shall go hard if Cambio go without her . *T. of Shrew* iv 4 109
They use to write it on the top of letters; 'twill go hard with you *2 Hen. VI.* iv 2 108
Go hence a little and I shall conduct you . *As Y. Like It* iii 4 58
And yet we should, for perpetuity, Go hence in debt . *W. Tale* i 2 6
Let him go hence, and with his cap in hand, Like a base pandar *Hen. V.* iv 5 13
Go hence, to have more talk of these sad things . *Rom. and Jul.* v 3 307
Prithee, go hence; Or I shall show the cinders of my spirits *A. and C.* v 2 172
Go home. Some of you go home with me to dinner . *Mer. Wives* iii 2 80
Go home, John Rugby; I come anon . iii 2 87
Let us every one go home, And laugh this sport o'er by a country fire . v 5 255
Well, sit you out: go home, Biron: adieu . *L. L. Lost* i 1 110
And he that will not fight for such a hope, Go home to bed *3 Hen. VI.* v 4 56
Go home, And show no sign of fear . *Coriolanus* iv 6 152
Go ill. Jack shall have Jill; Nought shall go ill . *M. N. Dream* iii 2 462
Doubting things go ill often hurts more Than to be sure they do *Cymbeline* i 6 95
Go in. I may not go in without your worship . *Mer. Wives* i 1 288
How does good Mistress Anne?—Go in with us and see . ii 1 171
He's too big to go in there. What shall I do? . iii 3 142
Let's go in, gentlemen; but, trust me, we'll mock him . iii 3 244
She must needs go in; Her father will be angry . iii 4 96
Go in to him, and fetch him out.—He is coming, sir . *Meas. for Meas.* iv 3 36
Go in with me, and I will tell you my drift . *Much Ado* ii 1 402
Come, go in; I'll show thee some attires . iii 1 101
Well, Jessica, go in: Perhaps I will return immediately . *Mer. of Venice* ii 5 51
Go in, sirrah; bid them prepare for dinner . iii 5 51

Go in. Sweet soul, let's in, and there expect their coming. And yet no matter: why should we go in? *Mer. of Venice* v 1 50
Let us go in; And charge us there upon inter'gatories v 1 297
Go in with me; and counsel every man The aptest way *2 Hen. IV.* i 1 212
Go in with me to dinner.—Come, I will go drink with you iii 2 202
Go in and cheer the town: we'll forth and fight *Troi. and Cres.* v 3 92
Let him that will a screech-owl aye be call'd, Go in to Troy v 10 17
O, come, go in, And take our friendly senators by the hands *Coriolanus* iv 5 137
Portia, go in awhile; And by and by thy bosom shall partake *J. Cæsar* ii 1 304
I must go in. Ay me, how weak a thing The heart of woman is! ii 4 39
Let us go in together; And still your fingers on your lips, I pray *Hamlet* i 5 187
Enter here.—Prithee, go in thyself; seek thine own ease *Lear* iii 4 23
This tempest will not give me leave to ponder On things would hurt me more. But I'll go in iii 4 25
Poor Tom's a-cold.—Go in with me iii 4 153
Desire him to go in; trouble him no more Till further settling iv 7 81
Those are the raised father and his friends: You were best go in *Othello* i 2 30
Your napkin is too little: Let it alone. Come, I'll go in with you iii 3 288
Go in, and weep not; all things shall be well iv 2 171
Go in and rest.—We'll not be long away.—Pray, be not sick *Cymbeline* iv 2 43
Go in couples. I'll go in couples with her; Than when I feel and see her no farther trust her *W. Tale* ii 1 135
Go in peace. The treason and you go in peace away together *L. L. Lost* iv 3 192
Go in peace, Humphrey, no less beloved Than when thou wert protector *2 Hen. VI.* ii 3 26
Go in person. I bespoke the officer To go in person with me to my house *Com. of Errors* v 1 234
Go in quest. If lusty love should go in quest of beauty, Where should he find it fairer than in Blanch? *K. John* ii 1 426
Go in search. If zealous love should go in search of virtue, Where should he find it purer than in Blanch? ii 1 428
Go like lightning. And to't they go like lightning *Rom. and Jul.* iii 1 177
Go loose. You are not to go loose any longer *Mer. Wives* iv 2 128
Go mad. The young prince will go mad: a plague upon Antenor! *T. and C.* iv 2 78
This heart Shall break into a hundred thousand flaws, Or ere I'll weep. O fool, I shall go mad! *Lear* ii 4 289
Go naked. Let it go naked, men may see't the better *T. of Athens* v 1 70
Go near. If he have never drunk wine afore, it will go near to remove his fit *Tempest* ii 2 78
You are little better than false knaves; and it will go near to be thought so shortly *Much Ado* iv 2 24
The death of a dear friend would go near to make a man look sad *M. N. D.* v 1 294
You shall go near To call them both a pair of crafty knaves *2 Hen. VI.* i 2 102
Go no farther. Let me go no farther to mine answer *Much Ado* v 1 236
Go no further. I can go no further, sir; My old bones ache *Tempest* iii 3 1
I pray you, bear with me; I cannot go no further *As Y. Like It* ii 4 9
I can go no further: O, I die for food! Here lie I down ii 6 1
I durst go no further than the Lie Circumstantial v 4 89
Where wilt thou lead me? speak; I'll go no further *Hamlet* i 5 1
Go no further. It is the cowish terror of his spirit *Lear* iv 2 11
Would you praise Cæsar, say 'Cæsar:' go no further *Ant. and Cleo.* iii 2 13
Go off. Shepherd, go off a little. Go with him, sirrah *As Y. Like It* iii 2 167
Go off; I discard you: let me enjoy my private: go off *T. Night* iii 4 99
No more, Pistol; I would not have you go off here *2 Hen. IV.* ii 4 147
Having charge from you to stand, Will not go off until they hear you speak iv 2 100
Good my lord, go off: You flow to great distraction *Troi. and Cres.* v 2 40
I would the friends we miss were safe arrived.—Some must go off *Macb.* v 8 36
Go on before; I shall inquire you forth *T. G. of Ver.* ii 4 186
Go on, good Eglamour, Out at the postern by the abbey-wall v 1 8
If you go on thus, you will kill yourself *Much Ado* v 1 1
Go on, and I will follow thee, To the last gasp *As Y. Like It* ii 3 69
Go on, and fetch our horses back again. Evermore cross'd *T. of Shrew* iv 5 9
Be magnanimous in the enterprise and go on *All's Well* iii 6 71
This action I now go on Is for my better grace *W. Tale* ii 1 121
Go on, go on: Thou canst not speak too much iii 2 215
Go on before; I'll talk with this good fellow *Richard III.* iii 2 97
Give way there, and go on! *Coriolanus* ii 1 210
Let them go on; This mutiny were better put in hazard ii 3 263
It will be dangerous to go on: no further.—What makes this change? iii 1 26
Go on,—here's gold,—go on; Be as a planetary plague *T. of Athens* iv 3 107
With your will, go on; We'll along ourselves, and meet them *J. Cæsar* iv 3 224
Go on, And see whether Brutus be alive or dead v 4 29
It waves me still. Go on; I'll follow thee.—You shall not go, my lord *Hamlet* i 4 79
Sith I am enter'd in this cause so far, Prick'd to't by foolish honesty and love, I will go on *Othello* iii 3 413
She can turn, and turn, and yet go on, And turn again; and she can weep iv 1 264
Go on wheels. Would it were all, That it might go on wheels! *A. and C.* ii 7 99
Go out. May I not go out ere he come? *Mer. Wives* iv 2 51
I'll go out then.—If you go out in your own semblance, you die, Sir John. Unless you go out disguised iv 2 66
Think'st thou the fiery fever will go out With titles blown from adulation? Will it give place to flexure? *Hen. V.* iv 1 270
To go out of my dialect, which you discommend so much *Lear* ii 2 115
Away, I say; go out, and cry a mutiny *Othello* ii 3 157
Go over. Stepp'd in so far that, should I wade no more, Returning were as tedious as go o'er *Macbeth* iii 4 138
Go over shoes. A man may go over shoes in the grime of it *Com. of Errors* iii 2 106
Go right. Never going aright, being a watch, But being watch'd that it may still go right *L. L. Lost* iii 1 195
And when I wander here and there, I then do most go right *W. Tale* iv 3 18
Go round. A health, gentlemen! Let it go round *Hen. VIII.* i 4 97
Let the health go round.—Let it flow this way, my good lord *T. of Athens* i 2 54
Cup us, till the world go round, Cup us, till the world go round! *A. and C.* ii 7 124
Does the world go round?—How come these staggers on me? *Cymbeline* v 5 232
Go see. Shall we go see the reliques of this town? *T. Night* iii 3 19
First go see your lodging.—I am not weary, and 'tis long to night iii 3 20
Will you go see the order of the course?—Not I *J. Cæsar* i 2 25
Go sleep. I am very heavy.—Go sleep, and hear us *Tempest* ii 1 190
Go slip-shod. Be merry; thy wit shall ne'er go slip-shod *Lear* i 5 12
Go sore. If you went in pain, master, this 'knave' would go sore *C. of Er.* iii 1 65
Go tell thy master I am alone *Mer. Wives* iii 3 37
I will go tell him of fair Hermia's flight *M. N. Dream* i 1 246
Decius, go tell them Cæsar will not come *J. Cæsar* ii 2 68
Go through. I do it for some piece of money, and go through with all *Meas. for Meas.* ii 1 285
The rough brake That virtue must go through *Hen. VIII.* i 2 76
Never till now Did I go through a tempest dropping fire *J. Cæsar* i 3 10

Go thy way *M. N. Dream* ii 1; iii 2; *T. Night* i 5; *Troi. and Cres.* i 2
Go thy ways; I'll make more of thy old body than I have done *M. W.* ii 2 144
Go thy ways, I begin to be aweary of thee *All's Well* iv 5 59
Believe none of us. Go thy ways to a nunnery *Hamlet* iii 1 132
Go thy ways *T. of Shrew* iv 5; v 2; *All's Well* iv 5; 1 *Hen. IV.* ii 4; *Hen. VIII.* ii 4; *T. Andron.* i 1; *R. and J.* ii 5; *Per.* iii 1; iv 6
Go to, carry this.—And this.—Ay, and this *Tempest* iv 1 253
Go to; away!—Hence, and bestow your luggage where you found it v 1 297
Go to, sir: tell me, do you know Madam Silvia? *T. G. of Ver.* ii 1 14
She is given too much to allicholy and musing: but for you—well, go to *Mer. Wives* i 4 165
You are not young, no more am I; go to then, there's sympathy ii 1 7
Mistress Ford and Mistress Page, have I encompassed you? go to; via! ii 2 159
Go to, then: we'll use this unwholesome humidity iii 3 42
One that knows the law, go to; and a rich fellow enough, go to *M. Ado* iv 2 86
Go to, thou art a witty fool; I have found thee *All's Well* iv 4 32
Though you are a fool and a knave, you shall eat; go to, follow v 2 58
Go to, go to, thou art a foolish fellow *T. Night* iv 1 3
Go to, go to! How she holds up the neb, the bill to him! *W. Tale* i 2 182
A parlous boy: go to, you are too shrewd *Richard III.* ii 4 35
Ye are too bold: Go to; I'll make ye know your times of business *Hen. VIII.* ii 2 72
Go to, go to; You take a precipice for no leap of danger v 1 138
I say, he shall: go to; Am I the master here, or you? go to *R. and J.* i 5 79
Go to, go to; you have known what you should not *Macbeth* v 1 51
Go to (*used as a terminal through the plays*).
Go to bed when she list, rise when she list, all is as she will *Mer. Wives* ii 2 124
To be up after midnight and to go to bed then, is early: so that to go to bed after midnight is to go to bed betimes *T. Night* ii 3 7
I'll go burn some sack; 'tis too late to go to bed now ii 3 207
Wilt thou go to bed, Malvolio?—To bed! ay, sweet-heart iii 4 32
We'll go to supper i' the morning. So, so, so.—And I'll go to bed at noon *Lear* iii 6 92
Go to buffets. O, I could divide myself and go to buffets! 1 *Hen. IV.* ii 3 35
Go to church. When mean you to go to church?—To-morrow *Much Ado* ii 1 371
Should I go to church And see the holy edifice of stone? *Mer. of Venice* i 1 29
He hath some meaning in his mad attire: We will persuade him, be it possible, To put on better ere he go to church *T. of Shrew* iii 2 128
Why dost thou not go to church in a galliard and come home in a coranto? My very walk should be a jig *T. Night* i 3 136
Come, is the bride ready to go to church?—Ready to go, but never to return *Rom. and Jul.* iv 5 33
Go to dinner. I will anon: first, let us go to dinner *Mer. of Venice* iii 5 91
Go to grass. And in Cheapside shall my palfry go to grass *2 Hen. VI.* iv 2 75
Go to hazard. Who will go to hazard with me? *Hen. V.* iii 7 93
Go to hell. If I would but go to hell for an eternal moment or so, I could be knighted *Mer. Wives* ii 1 49
Prove it so, Let fortune go to hell for it, not I. *Mer. of Venice* iii 2 21
I would I might go to hell among the rogues *J. Cæsar* i 2 270
Go to horse. It shall be seven ere I go to horse *T. of Shrew* iv 3 193
Go to it. You are too blunt: go to it orderly ii 1 45
So Guildenstern and Rosencrantz go to't *Hamlet* v 2 56
Did you go to't so young? Were you a gamester at five? *Pericles* iv 6 80
Go to kennel, Pompey; go *Meas. for Meas.* iii 2 89
Go to prison. He shall not go to prison.—Talk not, Signior Gremio: I say he shall go to prison *T. of Shrew* v 1 98
Go to shrift. Have you got leave to go to shrift to-day? *Rom. and Jul.* ii 5 68
Go to supper. We'll go to supper i' the morning. So, so, so *Lear* iii 6 90
Go to the door. Here's no place for you: pray, go to the door *Coriolanus* iv 5 9
Now go to the door, and stay there till we call *Macbeth* iii 1 73
Go to the wars. Thou shalt go to the wars in a gown *2 Hen. IV.* iii 2 196
What would you have me do? go to the wars, would you? *Pericles* iv 6 180
Go to war. Bring action hither, this cannot go to war *Troi. and Cres.* ii 3 145
But not such a wife.—Would we had all such wives, that the men might go to wars with the women! *Ant. and Cleo.* ii 2 66
Go to ward. Ere they will have me go to ward, They'll pawn their swords *2 Hen. VI.* v 1 112
Go together. We two must go together *Mer. Wives* v 3 5
Your hand, Leonato; we will go together *Much Ado* i 1 161
Go together, You precious winners all *W. Tale* v 3 130
One word, sweet queen: Of Cæsar seek your honour, with your safety. O!—They do not go together *Ant. and Cleo.* iv 15 47
Go under. It may be I go under that title because I am merry *Much Ado* ii 1 212
All these engines of lust are not the things they go under *All's Well* iii 5 22
Go up; I'll bring linen for him straight *Mer. Wives* iv 2 102
Let him go up into the public chair; We'll hear him *J. Cæsar* iii 2 68
You shall nose him as you go up the stairs into the lobby *Hamlet* iv 3 39
I must go up and down like a cock that nobody can match *Cymbeline* ii 1 23
Go visit. Come, you must go visit the good lady that lies in *Coriolanus* i 3 85
Go walk. You may go walk, and give me leave a while *T. of Shrew* iii 1 59
Go warm. If only to go warm were gorgeous, Why, nature needs not what thou gorgeous wear'st *Lear* ii 4 271
Go well. All shall yet go well.—What can go well, when we have run so ill? *K. John* iii 4 4
If things go well, Opinion that so sticks on Marcius shall Of his demerits rob Cominius *Coriolanus* i 1 274
Does't not go well? Cassio hath beaten thee, And thou, by that small hurt, hath cashier'd Cassio *Othello* ii 3 380
Go without. I hope I shall make shift to go without him *Mer. of Venice* i 2 97
Pardon me, madam, I may not go without you to the kings.—Thou mayst, thou shalt; I will not go with thee *K. John* iii 1 66
He has done nobly, and cannot go without any honest man's voice *Coriolanus* ii 3 139
Seek thou rather to be hanged in compassing thy will than to be drowned and go without her *Othello* i 3 368
Go woolward. I have no shirt; I go woolward for penance *L. L. Lost* v 2 717
Go wrong. Or else it must go wrong with you and me *K. John* i 1 41
We go wrong.—No, yonder 'tis; There, where we see the lights *T. and C.* v 1 74
Go your gait. Good gentleman, go your gait *Lear* iv 6 242
Go your way to her, for I see love hath made thee a tame snake *As Y. Like It* iv 3 69
Go your ways, and ask of Doctor Caius' house which is the way *M. Wives* i 2 1
Go your ways, and play, go iv 1 81
Go your ways, go your ways; I knew what you would prove *As Y. L. It* iv 1 186
Goad. Most dangerous Is that temptation that doth goad us on To sin in loving virtue *Meas. for Meas.* ii 2 182
Which being spotted Is goads, thorns, nettles, tails of wasps *W. Tale* i 2 329
Goaded with most sharp occasions *All's Well* v 1 14
This shall seem, as partly 'tis, their own, Which we have goaded onward *Coriolanus* ii 3 271

Goal. But to the goal *W. Tale* i 2 96

Yet ha' we A brain that nourishes our nerves, and can Get goal for goal of youth *Ant. and Cleo.* iv 8 22

Then honour be but a goal to my will, This day I'll rise *Pericles* ii 1 171

Goat. Am I ridden with a Welsh goat too? shall I have a coxcomb of frize? *Mer. Wives* v 5 146

Flesh taken from a man Is not so estimable, profitable neither, As flesh of muttons, beefs, or goats *Mer. of Venice* i 3 168

I will fetch up your goats, Audrey *As Y. Like It* iii 3 2

I am here with thee and thy goats iii 3 7

The goats ran from the mountains, and the herds Were strangely clamorous to the frighted fields *1 Hen. IV.* iii 1 39

Gorgeous as the sun at midsummer; Wanton as youthful goats iv 1 103

Thou damned and luxurious mountain goat, Offer'st me brass? *Hen. V.* iv 4 20

Not for Cadwallader and all his goats v 1 29

Hence, old goat!—We'll surety him.—Aged sir, hands off *Coriolanus* iii 1 177

And feed on curds and whey, and suck the goat *T. Andron.* iv 2 178

Liver of blaspheming Jew, Gall of goat, and slips of yew *Macbeth* iv 1 27

Exchange me for a goat, When I shall turn the business of my soul To such exsufflicate and blown surmises *Othello* iii 3 180

It is impossible you should see this, Were they as prime as goats iii 3 403

Goats and monkeys! iv 1 274

Scarce ever look'd on blood, But that of coward hares, hot goats *Cymb.* iv 4 37

Goatish. An admirable evasion of whoremaster man, to lay his goatish disposition to the charge of a star! *Lear* i 2 138

Gobbet. And, like ambitious Sylla, overgorged With gobbets of thy mother's bleeding heart *2 Hen. VI.* iv 1 85

Into as many gobbets will I cut it As wild Medea young Absyrtus did v 2 58

Gobbo, Launcelot Gobbo, good Launcelot, or good Gobbo, or good Launcelot Gobbo *Mer. of Venice* ii 2 4

Go-between. Her assistant or go-between *Mer. Wives* ii 2 273

Goblet. I do think him as concave as a covered goblet *As Y. Like It* iii 4 26

My figured goblets for a dish of wood *Richard II.* iii 3 150

Thou didst swear to me upon a parcel-gilt goblet *2 Hen. IV.* ii 1 94

Goblin. Go charge my goblins that they grind their joints *Tempest* iv 1 259

O spite of spites! We talk with goblins, owls and sprites *Com. of Errors* ii 2 192

I am fear'd in field and town: Goblin, lead them up and down *M. N. D.* iii 2 399

A sad tale's best for winter: I have one Of sprites and goblins *W. Tale* ii 1 26

I'll haunt thee like a wicked conscience still, That mouldeth goblins swift as frenzy's thoughts *Troi. and Cres.* v 10 29

Be thou a spirit of health or goblin damn'd *Hamlet* i 4 40

With, ho! such bugs and goblins in my life v 2 22

God. His art is of such power, It would control my dam's god, Setebos *Tempest* i 2 373

It sounds no more: and, sure, it waits upon Some god o' the island i 2 389

That's a brave god and bears celestial liquor ii 2 122

Look down, you gods, And on this couple drop a blessed crown! v 1 201

What a thrice-double ass Was I, to take this drunkard for a god! v 1 296

If this fond Love were not a blinded god *T. G. of Ver.* iv 4 201

If I be drunk, I'll be drunk with those that have the fear of God *M. Wives* i 1 189

Now, the hot-blooded gods assist me! v 5 2

Omnipotent Love! how near the god drew to the complexion of a goose! v 5 8

When gods have hot backs, what shall poor men do? v 5 12

When maidens sue, Men give like gods *Meas. for Meas.* i 4 81

We may pity, though not pardon thee.—O, had the gods done so, I had not now Worthily term'd them merciless to us! *Com. of Errors* i 1 99

Pray God our cheer May answer my good will iii 1 19

Are you a god? would you create me new? Transform me then iii 2 39

One that thinks a man always going to bed and says 'God give you good rest!' iv 3 33

O husband, God doth know you dined at home iv 4 68

God and the rope-maker bear me witness! iv 4 93

God, for thy mercy! they are loose again iv 4 148

God help the noble Claudio! if he have caught the Benedick *Much Ado* i 1 88

I thank God and my cold blood, I am of your humour i 1 131

God keep your ladyship still in that mind! i 1 134

So I commit you— To the tuition of God i 1 283

It is said, 'God sends a curst cow short horns;' but to a cow too curst he sends none.—So, by being too curst, God will send you no horns ii 1 25

Not till God make men of some other metal than earth ii 1 62

God match me with a good dancer!—Amen.—And God keep him out of my sight when the dance is done! ii 1 111

I would to God some scholar would conjure her ii 1 264

O God, sir, here's a dish I love not: I cannot endure my Lady Tongue ii 1 283

Name the day of marriage, and God give thee joy! ii 1 312

Her hair shall be of what colour it please God ii 3 37

I pray God his bad voice bode no mischief ii 3 83

May be she doth but counterfeit.—Faith, like enough.—O God, counterfeit! ii 3 109

Prays, curses; 'O sweet Benedick! God give me patience!' ii 3 154

Before God! and, in my mind, very wise ii 3 192

If he do fear God, a' must necessarily keep peace ii 3 201

The man doth fear God, howsoever it seems not in him ii 3 205

God hath blessed you with a good name: to be a well-favoured man is the gift of fortune iii 3 13

Give God thanks, and make no boast of it iii 3 20

Call the rest of the watch together and thank God you are rid of a knave iii 3 31

God give me joy to wear it! for my heart is exceeding heavy iii 4 24

God send every one their heart's desire! iii 4 60

O, God help me! God help me! how long have you professed apprehension? iii 4 67

I thank God I am as honest as any man living that is an old man iii 5 15

God help us! it is a world to see iii 5 38

Well, God's a good man; an two men ride of a horse, one must ride behind iii 5 39

God is to be worshipp'd; all men are not alike; alas, good neighbour! iii 5 42

Indeed, neighbour, he comes too short of you.—Gifts that God gives iii 5 47

Give me this maid, your daughter?—As freely, son, as God did give her me iv 1 27

O, God defend me! how am I beset! What kind of catechising call you this? iv 1 78

O God, that I were a man! I would eat his heart in the market-place iv 1 308

Masters, do you serve God?—Yea, sir, we hope iv 2 18

Write down, that they hope they serve God: and write God first; for God defend but God should go before such villains! iv 2 21

'Fore God, they are both in a tale iv 2 32

They have writ the style of gods And made a push at chance and sufferance v 1 37

God. Shall I speak a word in your ear?—God bless me from a challenge! *Much Ado* v 1 145

And, moreover, God saw him when he was hid in the garden v 1 181

You break jests as braggarts do their blades, which, God be thanked, hurt not v 1 190

God save the foundation! v 1 327

God keep your worship! I wish your worship well; God restore you to health! v 1 332

If a merry meeting may be wished, God prohibit it! v 1 335

Serve God, love me and mend. There will I leave you v 2 95

How low soever the matter, I hope in God for high words.—A high hope for a low heaven: God grant us patience! *L. L. Lost* i 1 195

God defend the right! i 1 216

My soul's earth's god, and body's fostering patron i 1 223

I thank God I have as little patience as another man; and therefore I can be quiet i 2 170

God bless my ladies! are they all in love? ii 1 77

Now, God save thy life!—And yours from long living! ii 1 191

God comfort thy capacity! iv 2 44

God give you good morrow, master Parson iv 2 84

You have done this in the fear of God, very religiously iv 2 153

Here comes one with a paper: God give him grace to groan! iv 3 20

God amend us, God amend! we are much out o' the way iv 3 76

God bless the king!—What present hast thou there? iv 3 189

When Love speaks, the voice of all the gods Make heaven drowsy iv 3 344

Pecks up wit as pigeons pease, And utters it again when God doth please v 2 316

So hold your vow: Nor God, nor I, delights in perjured men v 2 346

So God help me, la!—My love to thee is sound, sans crack or flaw v 2 414

Or else die my lover.—God give thee joy of him! v 2 448

Doth this man serve God?—Why ask you? v 2 526

He's a god or a painter; for he makes faces v 2 648

Be advised, fair maid: To you your father should be as a god *M. N. Dream* i 1 47

To bring in—God shield us!—a lion among ladies, is a most dreadful thing iii 1 31

Like two artificial gods, Have with our needles created both one flower iii 2 203

Why, then you left me—O, the gods forbid!—In earnest, shall I say? iii 2 276

A paramour is, God bless us, a thing of naught iv 2 14

Is the better; he for a man, God warrant us; she for a woman, God bless us v 1 326

God defend me from these two! *Mer. of Venice* i 2 57

God made him, and therefore let him pass for a man i 2 60

I pray God grant them a fair departure i 2 121

An honest exceeding poor man and, God be thanked, well to live ii 2 55

Tell me, is my boy, God rest his soul, alive or dead? ii 2 75

I will run as far as God has any ground ii 2 118

God bless your worship!—Gramercy! wouldst thou aught with me? ii 2 127

You have the grace of God, sir, and he hath enough ii 2 160

Some god direct my judgement! ii 7 13

Hath an argosy cast away, coming from Tripolis.—I thank God, I thank God iii 1 107

Pray God, Bassanio come To see me pay his debt, and then I care not! iii 3 35

If two gods should play some heavenly match And on the wager lay two earthly women, And Portia one iii 5 84

It is enthroned in the hearts of kings, It is an attribute to God himself; And earthly power doth then show likest God's When mercy seasons justice iv 1 195

But God sort all! You are welcome home, my lord v 1 132

God's my judge, The clerk will ne'er wear hair on's face that had it v 1 157

I am helping you to mar that which God made *As Y. Like It* i 1 36

God be with my old master! he would not have spoke such a word i 1 87

I'll never wrestle for prize more: and so God keep your worship! i 1 168

God help thee, shallow man! God make incision in thee! thou art raw iii 2 74

He hath but a little beard.—Why, God will send more, if the man will be thankful iii 2 220

I thank God I am not a woman, to be touched with so many giddy offences iii 2 366

Truly, I would the gods had made thee poetical iii 3 16

Do you wish then that the gods had made me poetical? iii 3 23

I am not fair; and therefore I pray the gods make me honest iii 3 34

I am not a slut, though I thank the gods I am foul iii 3 38

Well, the gods give us joy! iii 3 47

Almost chide God for making you that countenance you are iv 1 36

By my troth, and in good earnest, and so God mend me iv 1 193

Art thou god to shepherd turn'd, That a maiden's heart hath burn'd? iv 3 40

God ye good even, William.—And good even to you, sir v 1 16

Wast born i' the forest here?—Ay, sir, I thank God.—'Thank God;' a good answer v 1 26

God rest you merry, sir v 1 65

Honour, high honour and renown, To Hymen, god of every town! v 4 152

Would to God I had well knock'd at first *T. of Shrew* i 2 34

I know not what to say: but give me your hands; God send you joy! ii 1 321

Such a one as leaves a gentleman, And makes a god of such a cullion iv 2 20

God give him joy!—Ay, and he'll tame her iv 2 52

As far as Rome; And so to Tripoli, if God lend me life iv 2 76

Let us see't. O mercy, God! what masquing stuff is here? iv 3 87

She's like to be Lucentio's wife.—I pray the gods she may with all my heart!—Dally not with the gods, but get thee gone iv 4 67

Then, God be bless'd, it is the blessed sun iv 5 18

I have seen them in the church together: God send 'em good shipping! v 1 43

What am I, sir! nay, what are you, sir? O immortal gods! O fine villain! v 1 68

Pray God, sir, your wife send you not a worse.—I hope, better v 2 84

And, being a winner, God give you good night! v 2 187

Now shall he—I know not what he shall. God send him well! *All's Well* i 1 190

I think I shall never have the blessing of God till I have issue o' my body i 3 27

Would God would serve the world so all the year! i 3 87

Love no god, that would not extend his might, only where qualities were level i 3 117

You might be my daughter-in-law: God shield you mean it not! i 3 174

If God have lent a man any manners, he may easily put it off at court ii 2 8

Is not this Helen?—'Fore God, I think so ii 3 51

To imperial Love, that god most high, Do my sighs stream ii 3 81

Whom I serve above is my master.—Who? God?—Ay, sir ii 3 262

She's not in heaven, whither God send her quickly! ii 4 12

God delay our rebellion! as we are ourselves, what things are we! iv 3 23

Of that I have made a bold charter; but I thank my God it holds yet iv 5 98

Dost thou put upon me at once both the office of God and the devil? v 2 52

Well, God give them wisdom that have it *T. Night* i 5 14

God. God bless thee, lady!—Take the fool away *T. Night* i 5 41

God send you, sir, a speedy infirmity, for the better increasing your folly! i 5 84

Is't not well done?—Excellently done, if God did all i 5 254

The gentleness of all the gods go with thee! ii 1 45

For the love o' God, peace! ii 3 92

Now, the melancholy god protect thee ii 4 75

God comfort thee! Why dost thou smile so and kiss thy hand so oft? iii 4 35

God have mercy upon one of our souls! iii 4 183

Pray God defend me! iii 4 331

Pray God, he keep his oath! iii 4 341

But O how vile an idol proves this god! iii 4 399

For the love of God, a surgeon! Send one presently v 1 175

For the love of God, your help! v 1 180

The gods themselves, Wotting no more than I, are ignorant *W. Tale* iii 2 76

I'll serve you As I would do the gods iii 2 208

A thousand knees Ten thousand years together . . . could not move the gods To look that way thou wert iii 2 214

This your sheep-shearing Is as a meeting of the petty gods iv 4 4

The gods themselves, Humbling their deities to love, have taken The shapes of beasts upon them iv 4 25

And the fire-robed god, Golden Apollo, a poor humble swain, As I seem now iv 4 29

He sings 'em over as they were gods or goddesses iv 4 209

Sure the gods do this year connive at us, and we may do any thing extempore iv 4 691

The gods Will have fulfill'd their secret purposes v 1 35

The blessed gods Purge all infection from our air whilst you Do climate here! v 1 168

You gods, look down And from your sacred vials pour your graces Upon my daughter's head! v 3 121

God shall forgive you Cœur-de-lion's death The rather that you give his offspring life *K. John* ii 1 12

In the name of God How comes it then that thou art call'd a king? ii 1 106

God hath made her sin and her the plague On this removed issue ii 1 185

Then God forgive the sin of all those souls! ii 1 283

At the other hill Command the rest to stand. God and our right! ii 1 299

How God and good men hate so foul a liar *Richard II.* i 1 114

O, God defend my soul from such deep sin! i 1 187

God's is the quarrel; for God's substitute, His deputy anointed in His sight, Hath caused his death i 2 37

Where, then, alas, may I complain myself?—To God, the widow's champion i 2 43

To defend my loyalty and truth To God, my king and my succeeding issue i 3 20

By the grace of God and this mine arm i 3 22

To prove him, in defending of myself, A traitor to my God, my king, and me i 3 24

God in thy good cause make thee prosperous! i 3 78

However God or fortune cast my lot i 3 85

Stands here for God, his sovereign and himself i 3 105

A traitor to his God, his king and him i 3 108

To God, his sovereign and to him disloyal i 3 114

Swear by the duty that you owe to God—Our part therein we banish i 3 180

You never shall, so help you truth and God! Embrace each other's love i 3 183

But what thou art, God, thou, and I do know i 3 204

Now put it, God, in the physician's mind To help him to his grave immediately! i 4 59

Pray God we may make haste, and come too late! i 4 64

Now, afore God—God forbid I say true! ii 1 200

God save your majesty! and well met, gentlemen ii 2 41

I would to God, So my untruth had not provoked him to it ii 2 100

God for his Richard hath in heavenly pay A glorious angel iii 2 60

If he serve God, We'll serve Him too and be his fellow so iii 2 98

That we cannot mend; They break their faith to God as well as us iii 2 101

Show us the hand of God That hath dismiss'd us from our stewardship iii 3 77

O God, O God! that e'er this tongue of mine, That laid the sentence of dread banishment On yon proud man, should take it off again! iii 3 133

Would God that any in this noble presence Were enough noble to be upright judge Of noble Richard! iv 1 117

O, forfend it, God, That in a Christian climate souls refined Should show so heinous, black, obscene a deed! iv 1 129

A subject speaks, Stirr'd up by God, thus boldly for his king iv 1 133

God pardon all oaths that are broke to me! God keep all vows unbroke that swear to thee! iv 1 214

God save King Harry, unking'd Richard says, And send him many years! iv 1 220

Did scowl on gentle Richard; no man cried 'God save him!' v 2 28

Had not God, for some strong purpose, steel'd The hearts of men v 2 34

You will be there, I know.—If God prevent not, I purpose so v 2 55

I would to God, my lords, he might be found v 3 4

God save your grace! I do beseech your majesty, To have some conference v 3 26

I pardon him, as God shall pardon me v 3 131

With all my heart I pardon him.—A god on earth thou art v 3 136

Come, my old son: I pray God make thee new v 3 146

God save thy grace,—majesty I should say *1 Hen. IV.* i 2 18

I would to God thou and I knew where a commodity of good names were to be bought i 2 92

Thou hast done much harm upon me, Hal; God forgive thee for it! i 2 103

God give thee the spirit of persuasion and him the ears of profiting i 2 170

When the unhappy king,—Whose wrongs in us God pardon!—did set forth i 3 149

As both of you—God pardon it!—have done i 3 174

Pray God you have not murdered some of them ii 4 209

If sack and sugar be a fault, God help the wicked! ii 4 517

Now God help thee!—To the Welsh lady's bed.—What's that? iii 1 246

'As true as I live,' and 'as God shall mend me,' and 'as sure as day' iii 1 254

I know not whether God will have it so, For some displeasing service I have done iii 2 4

God forgive them that so much have sway'd Your majesty's good thoughts away from me! iii 2 130

This, in the name of God, I promise here iii 2 153

Why, a thing to thank God on.—I am no thing to thank God on iii 3 134

Nay, an I do, I pray God my girdle break iii 3 171

God be thanked for these rebels, they offend none but the virtuous iii 3 213

Pray God my news be worth a welcome iv 1 87

Would to God You were of our determination! iv 3 32

When he heard him swear and vow to God iv 3 60

And God befriend us, as our cause is just! v 1 120

Thou owest God a death.—'Tis not due yet; I would be loath to pay him v 1 127

God. God keep lead out of me! I need no more weight than mine own bowels *1 Hen. IV.* v 3 35

Before God, Hal, if Percy be alive, thou get'st not my sword v 3 51

Would to God Thy name in arms were now as great as mine! v 4 69

He that rewards me, God reward him! v 4 167

I bring you certain news from Shrewsbury.—Good, an God will! *2 Hen. IV.* i 1 13

I am sorry I should force you to believe That which I would to God I had not seen i 1 106

His face is a face-royal: God may finish it when he will i 2 26

Like the glutton! pray God his tongue be hotter! i 2 40

God give your lordship good time of day i 2 106

Well, God mend him! I pray you, let me speak with you i 2 124

God send the prince a better companion!—God send the companion a better prince! i 2 223

I would to God my name were not so terrible to the enemy as it is i 2 244

Well, be honest, be honest; and God bless your expedition! i 2 249

Before God, I am exceeding weary ii 2 1

From a God to a bull? a heavy descension! it was Jove's case ii 2 192

O thou dull god [sleep], why liest thou with the vile In loathsome beds? iii 1 15

O God! that one might read the book of fate! iii 1 45

'Fore God, a likely fellow! iii 2 186

I care not; a man can die but once: we owe God a death iii 2 251

God keep you, Master Silence: I will not use many words with you iii 2 308

In sight of both our battles we may meet; And either end in peace, which God so frame! iv 1 180

Who hath not heard it spoken How deep you were within the books of God? iv 2 17

To us the imagined voice of God himself iv 2 19

Under the counterfeited zeal of God iv 2 27

Pursue the scatter'd stray: God, and not we, hath safely fought to-day iv 2 121

If God doth give successful end To this debate that bleedeth at our doors iv 4 1

Lo, here it sits, Which God shall guard iv 5 44

Let God for ever keep it from my head! iv 5 175

God put it in thy mind to take it hence, That thou mightst win the more thy father's love iv 5 179

How I came by the crown, O God forgive! iv 5 219

Laud be to God! even there my life must end iv 5 236

And, God consigning to my good intents, No prince nor peer shall have just cause to say, God shorten Harry's happy life one day! v 2 143

'Fore God, you have here a goodly dwelling and a rich v 3 6

Do nothing but eat, and make good cheer, And praise God for the merry year v 3 19

I would to God that I might die, that I might have thee hanged v 4 1

I pray God the fruit of her womb miscarry! v 4 15

O God, that right should thus overcome might! v 4 27

God bless thy lungs, good knight v 5 9

God save thy grace, King Hal! my royal Hal! v 5 43

For God doth know, so shall the world perceive v 5 61

God and his angels guard your sacred throne! *Hen. V.* i 2 7

For God doth know how many now in health Shall drop their blood i 2 18

We charge you, in the name of God, take heed i 2 23

This lies all within the will of God, To whom I do appeal i 2 289

We have now no thought in us but France, Save those to God i 2 303

God before, We'll chide this Dauphin at his father's door i 2 307

'Fore God, his grace is bold, to trust these traitors ii 2 1

Arrest them to the answer of the law; And God acquit them! ii 2 144

Our purposes God justly hath discover'd; And I repent my fault ii 2 151

But God be thanked for prevention ii 2 158

I in sufferance heartily will rejoice, Beseeching God and you to pardon me ii 2 160

God quit you in his mercy! Hear your sentence ii 2 166

The taste whereof, God of his mercy give You patience to endure! ii 2 179

Since God so graciously hath brought to light This dangerous treason ii 2 185

Let us deliver Our puissance into the hand of God ii 2 190

So a' cried out 'God, God, God!' three or four times. Now I, to comfort him, bid him a' should not think of God ii 3 20

The patterns that by God and by French fathers Had twenty years been made ii 4 61

Cry 'God for Harry, England, and Saint George!' iii 1 34

'Tis shame for us all: so God sa' me, 'tis shame to stand still iii 2 118

He is not—God be praised and blessed!—any hurt in the world iii 6 10

The Duke of Exeter doth love thee well.—Ay, I praise God iii 6 24

Yet, forgive me, God, That I do brag thus! iii 6 159

Yet, God before, tell him we will come on iii 6 165

Though they can outstrip men, they have no wings to fly from God iv 1 178

Making God so free an offer, He let him outlive that day iv 1 193

What kind of god art thou, that suffer'st more Of mortal griefs than do thy worshippers? iv 1 258

If they do this,—As, if God please, they shall,—my ranson then Will soon be levied iv 3 120

Now, soldiers, march along: And how thou pleasest, God, dispose the day! iv 3 132

The day is yours.—Praised be God, and not our strength, for it! iv 7 90

God pless it and preserve it, as long as it pleases his grace, and his majesty too! iv 7 113

I need not to be ashamed of your majesty, praised be God, so long as your majesty is an honest man.—God keep me so! iv 7 119

I would fain see it once, an please God of his grace that I might see iv 7 172

Here is—praised be God for it!—a most contagious treason iv 8 22

I pray you to serve God, and keep you out of prawls, and prabbles iv 8 68

O God, thy arm was here; And not to us, but to thy arm alone, Ascribe we all! iv 8 111

Take it, God, For it is none but thine! iv 8 116

And be it death proclaimed through our host To boast of this or take that praise from God Which is his only iv 8 120

With this acknowledgement, That God fought for us iv 8 125

Giving full trophy, signal and ostent Quite from himself to God v Prol. 22

God pless you, Aunchient Pistol! you scurvy, lousy knave, God pless you! v 1 18

Before God, Kate, I cannot look greenly nor gasp out my eloquence v 2 148

God save your majesty! my royal cousin v 2 307

God, the best maker of all marriages, Combine your hearts in one! v 2 387

Receive each other. God speak this Amen! v 2 396

Thy wife is proud; she holdeth thee in awe, More than God or religious churchmen may *1 Hen. VI.* i 1 40

Thou art no friend to God or to the king i 3 25

Here's Beaufort, that regards nor God nor king i 3 60

Good God, these nobles should such stomachs bear! i 3 90

To celebrate the joy that God hath given us i 6 14

God. Pray God she prove not masculine ere long . . . *1 Hen. VI.* ii 1 22
God is our fortress, in whose conquering name Let us resolve to scale their flinty bulwarks . . . ii 1 26
So help me God, as I dissemble not!—So help me God, as I intend it not! . . . iii 1 140
Ascribes the glory of his conquest got First to my God . . . iii 4 12
God save King Henry, of that name the sixth! . . . iv 1 2
This shall ye do, so help you righteous God! . . . iv 1 8
God and Saint George, Talbot and England's right! . . . iv 2 55
God comfort him in this necessity! If he miscarry, farewell wars . iv 3 15
O God, that Somerset, who in proud heart Doth stop my cornets, were in Talbot's place! . . . iv 3 24
Then God take mercy on brave Talbot's soul! . . . iv 3 34
God preserve the good Duke Humphrey! . . . *2 Hen. VI.* i 1 162
So God help Warwick, as he loves the land, And common profit of his country! . . . i 1 205
By the grace of God, and Hume's advice . . . i 2 72
But God in mercy so deal with my soul, As I in duty love my king! . i 3 160
Pray God the Duke of York excuse himself! . . . i 3 181
God is my witness, I am falsely accused by the villain . . . i 3 191
By the eternal God, whose name and power Thou tremblest at, answer i 4 28
To see how God in all his creatures works! Yea, man and birds are fain of climbing high . . . ii 1 7
God be praised, that to believing souls Gives light in darkness! . ii 1 66
Thou see'st not well.—Yes, master, clear as day, I thank God and Saint Alban . . . ii 1 108
O God, seest Thou this, and bearest so long? . . . ii 1 154
O God, what mischiefs work the wicked ones! . . . ii 1 186
In sight of God and us, your guilt is great . . . ii 3 2
God shall be my hope, My stay, my guide and lantern to my feet . . ii 3 24
God and King Henry govern England's realm . . . ii 3 30
O Lord bless me! I pray God! for I am never able to deal with my master . . . ii 3 77
Fellow, thank God, and the good wine in thy master's way . . . ii 3 99
God in justice hath reveal'd to us The truth and innocence of this poor fellow . . . ii 3 105
So help me God, as I have watch'd the night! . . . iii 1 110
I say no more than truth, so help me God! . . . iii 1 120
Pray God he may acquit him of suspicion! . . . iii 2 25
O heavenly God!—How fares my gracious lord? . . . iii 2 37
Forgive me, God, For judgement only doth belong to thee . . . iii 2 139
Stare and catch the air, Blaspheming God and cursing men on earth iii 2 372
He dies, and makes no sign. O God, forgive him! . . . iii 3 29
O that I were a god, to shoot forth thunder! . . . iv 1 104
God save your majesty!—I thank you, good people . . . iv 2 77
I thank God, I have been so well brought up that I can write my name iv 2 112
God, our hope, will succour us.—My hope is gone . . . iv 4 55
Seeing ignorance is the curse of God, Knowledge the wing wherewith we fly to heaven . . . iv 7 78
If when you make your prayers, God should be so obdurate as yourselves, How would it fare with your departed souls? . . . iv 7 122
Fling up his cap, and say 'God save his majesty!' . . . iv 8 15
You are strong and manly; God on our side, doubt not of victory . iv 8 54
I pray God I may never eat grass more . . . iv 10 43
I beseech God on my knees thou mayst be turned to hobnails . . iv 10 62
The head of Cade! Great God, how just art Thou! . . . v 1 68
Open Thy gate of mercy, gracious God! My soul flies through these wounds to seek out Thee . . . *3 Hen. VI.* i 4 177
And when thou fail'st—as God forbid the hour!—Must Edward fall . ii 1 190
Then strike up drums: God and Saint George for us! . . . ii 1 204
Withhold revenge, dear God! 'tis not my fault . . . ii 2 7
Here on my knee I vow to God above, I'll never pause again, never stand still . . . ii 3 29
On this molehill will I sit me down. To whom God will, there be the victory! . . . ii 5 15
O God! methinks it were a happy life, To be no better than a homely swain . . . ii 5 21
O God! it is my father's face, Whom in this conflict I unwares have kill'd . . . ii 5 61
Pardon me, God, I knew not what I did! And pardon, father! . . ii 5 69
O, pity, God, this miserable age! . . . ii 5 88
Your king's name be obey'd: And what God will, that let your king perform . . . iii 1 100
Let us be back'd with God and with the seas . . . iv 1 43
So God help Montague as he proves true! . . . iv 1 143
For Warwick and his friends, God and Saint George! . . . iv 2 29
Now that God and friends Have shaken Edward from the regal seat . iv 6 1
But, Warwick, after God, thou set'st me free, And chiefly therefore I thank God and thee . . . iv 6 16
And only claim Our dukedom till God please to send the rest . . iv 7 47
By the grace of God, king of England and France, and lord of Ireland . iv 7 72
O, God forgive my sins, and pardon thee! . . . v 6 60
Which done, God take King Edward to his mercy, And leave the world for me to bustle in! . . . *Richard III.* i 1 151
O God, which this blood madest, revenge his death! . . . i 2 62
Villain, thou know'st no law of God nor man . . . i 2 70
God grant me too Thou mayst be damned for that wicked deed! . . i 2 102
Having God, her conscience, and these bars against me, And I nothing i 2 235
God make your majesty joyful as you have been! . . . i 3 19
God grant him health! Did you confer with him? . . . i 3 35
Whom God preserve better than you would wish! . . . i 3 59
God grant we never may have need of you!—Meantime, God grants that we have need of you . . . i 3 76
Small joy have I in being England's queen.—And lessen'd be that small, God, I beseech thee! . . . i 3 111
Yea, and forswore himself,—which Jesu pardon!—Which God revenge! i 3 137
I would to God my heart were flint, like Edward's . . . i 3 140
And God, not we, hath plagued thy bloody deed.—So just is God, to right the innocent . . . i 3 181
God, I pray him, That none of you may live your natural age! . . i 3 212
O God, that seest it, do not suffer it! . . . i 3 271
Ascend the sky, And there awake God's gentle-sleeping peace . . i 3 288
Live each of you the subjects to his hate, And he to yours, and all of you to God's! . . . i 3 303
God pardon them that are the cause of it! . . . i 3 315
With a piece of scripture, Tell them that God bids us do good for evil . i 3 335
God give your grace good rest! . . . i 4 75
And, like a traitor to the name of God, Didst break that vow . . i 4 210
If God will be revenged for this deed, O, know you yet, he doth it publicly . . . i 4 221

God. Make peace with God, for you must die, my lord.—Hast thou that holy feeling in thy soul, To counsel me to make my peace with God, And art thou yet to thy own soul so blind, That thou wilt war with God by murdering me? . . . *Richard III.* i 4 256
God punish me With hate in those where I expect most love! . . ii 1 34
This do I beg of God, When I am cold in zeal to you or yours . . ii 1 39
I thank my God for my humility . . . ii 1 72
I would to God all strifes were well compounded . . . ii 1 74
God grant that some, less noble and less loyal, . . Deserve not worse! ii 1 91
O God, I fear thy justice will take hold On me, and you, and mine, and yours for this! . . . ii 1 131
God will revenge it; whom I will importune With daily prayers . . ii 2 14
God is much displeased That you take with unthankfulness his doing . ii 2 89
God bless thee; and put meekness in thy mind! . . . ii 2 107
For emulation now . . . Will touch us all too near, if God prevent not ii 3 26
But, if God sort it so, 'Tis more than we deserve . . . ii 3 36
But leave it all to God. Whither away?—Marry, we were sent for . ii 3 45
God keep you from them, and from such false friends!—God keep me from false friends! but they were none . . . iii 1 15
God bless your grace with health and happy days! . . . iii 1 18
God keep your lordship in that gracious mind! . . . iii 2 56
Pray God, I say, I prove a needless coward! . . . iii 2 90
God hold it, to your honour's good content! . . . iii 2 107
God keep the prince from all the pack of you! . . . iii 3 5
O, remember, God, To hear her prayers for them, as now for us! . iii 3 18
Be satisfied, dear God, with our true blood . . . iii 3 21
O momentary grace of mortal men, Which we more hunt for than the grace of God! . . . iii 4 99
God and our innocency defend and guard us! . . . iii 5 20
I bid them that did love their country's good Cry 'God save Richard!' iii 7 22
So God help me, they spake not a word . . . iii 7 24
And some ten voices cried 'God save King Richard!' . . . iii 7 36
Earnest in the service of my God, Neglect the visitation of my friends . iii 7 106
Even that, I hope, which pleaseth God above, And all good men . iii 7 109
But, God be thanked, there's no need of me . . . iii 7 165
God bless your grace! we see it, and will say it . . . iii 7 237
God give your graces both A happy and a joyful time of day! . . iv 1 5
I would to God that the inclusive verge Of golden metal that must round my brow Were red-hot steel! . . . iv 1 59
And die, ere man can say, God save the queen! . . . iv 1 63
Wilt thou, O God, fly from such gentle lambs, And throw them in the entrails of the wolf? . . . iv 4 22
O upright, just, and true-disposing God, How do I thank thee! . . iv 4 55
Triumph not in my woes! God witness with me, I have wept for thine iv 4 60
Cancel his bond of life, dear God, I pray . . . iv 4 77
Wherein dost thou joy? Who sues to thee and cries 'God save the queen'? . . . iv 4 94
Art thou my son?—Ay, I thank God, my father, and yourself . . iv 4 155
That God, the law, my honour and her love, Can make seem pleasing . iv 4 341
Why then, by God— God's wrong is most of all . . . iv 4 377
Kings it [hope] makes gods, and meaner creatures kings . . . v 2 24
And so, God give you quiet rest to-night! . . . v 3 43
God give us leisure for these rites of love! . . . v 3 101
God and good angels fight on Richmond's side; And Richard falls . v 3 175
Yet remember this, God and our good cause fight upon our side . . v 3 240
Then, in the name of God and all these rights, Advance your standards v 3 263
God and Saint George! Richmond and victory! . . . v 3 270
God and your arms be praised, victorious friends; The day is ours . v 5 1
And let their heirs, God, if thy will be so, Enrich the time to come! . v 5 32
That she may long live here, God say amen! . . . v 5 41
The French, All clinquant, all in gold, like heathen gods . *Hen. VIII.* i 1 19
Ask God for temperance; that's the appliance only Which your disease requires . . . i 1 124
God mend all!—There's something more would out of thee; what say'st? i 2 201
The king will know him one day.—Pray God he do! . . . ii 2 23
Who's there, ha?—Pray God he be not angry . . . ii 2 64
If not, i' the name of God, Your pleasure be fulfill'd! . . . ii 4 56
Be patient yet.—I will, when you are humble; nay, before, Or God will punish me . . . ii 4 75
But with thanks to God for such A royal lady . . . ii 4 152
Ye speak like honest men; pray God, ye prove so! . . . iii 1 69
Now, God incense him, And let him cry Ha! louder! . . . iii 2 61
Ever God bless your highness! . . . iii 2 136
The worst Is your displeasure with the king.—God bless him! . . iii 2 392
Let all the ends thou aim'st at be thy country's, Thy God's, and truth's iii 2 448
Had I but served my God with half the zeal I served my king . . iii 2 455
To add greater honours to his age Than man could give him, he died fearing God . . . iv 2 68
God safely quit her of her burthen, and With gentle travail! . . . v 1 70
God and your majesty Protect mine innocence! . . . v 1 140
God turn their hearts! I never sought their malice . . . v 2 15
And that I would not for a cow, God save her! . . . v 4 27
God protect thee! Into whose hand I give thy life . . . v 5 11
God shall be truly known . . . v 5 37
O gods, how do you plague me! I cannot come to Cressid but by Pandar; And he's as tetchy . . . *Troi. and Cres.* i 1 97
Well, the gods are above; time must friend or end . . . i 2 83
Which is that god in office, guiding men? . . . i 3 231
'Tis mad idolatry To make the service greater than the god . . . ii 2 57
But I attest the gods, your full consent Gave wings to my propension . ii 2 132
Forget that thou art Jove, the king of gods . . . iii 3 12
The gods grant,—O my lord!—What should they grant? . . . iii 2 67
To be wise and love Exceeds man's might; that dwells with gods above iii 2 164
Whose glorious deeds, but in these fields of late, Made emulous missions 'mongst the gods themselves . . . iii 3 189
And almost, like the gods, Does thoughts unveil in their dumb cradles iii 3 199
O the gods! what's the matter!—Prithee, get thee in . . . iv 2 88
O you immortal gods! I will not go.—Thou must . . . iv 2 100
O you gods divine! Make Cressid's name the very crown of falsehood, If ever she leave Troilus! . . . iv 2 105
That the bless'd gods, as angry with my fancy, . . . take thee from me iv 4 27
Have the gods envy?—Ay, ay, ay, ay; 'tis too plain a case . . iv 4 30
The just gods gainsay That any drop thou borrow'dst from thy mother, My sacred aunt, should by my mortal sword Be drain'd! . . . iv 5 132
It would discredit the blest gods, proud man, To answer such a question iv 5 247
O, all you gods! O pretty, pretty pledge! . . . v 2 77
By all the everlasting gods, I'll go! . . . v 3 5
The gods have heard me swear.—The gods are deaf to hot and peevish vows . . . v 3 15
For the love of all the gods, Let's leave the hermit pity with our mothers v 3 44

God. Farewell: the gods with safety stand about thee! . *Troi. and Cres.* v 3 94
If in his death the gods have us befriended, Great Troy is ours . . v 9 9
Hector is slain.—Hector! the gods forbid!—He's dead . . . v 10 3
Sit, gods, upon your thrones, and smile at Troy! . . . . v 10 7
But dare all imminence that gods and men Address their dangers in . v 10 13
For the gods know I speak this in hunger for bread . . *Coriolanus* i 1 24
For the dearth, The gods, not the patricians, make it, and Your knees to them, not arms, must help . . . . i 1 75
You cry against the noble senate, who, Under the gods, keep you in awe i 1 191
That the gods sent not Corn for the rich men only . . . . i 1 211
Being moved, he will not spare to gird the gods.—Be-mock the modest moon . . . . i 1 260
The gods assist you!—And keep your honours safe! . . . . i 2 36
Ye Roman gods! Lead their successes as we wish our own . . i 6 6
Who's yonder, That does appear as he were flay'd? O gods! . . i 6 22
Let the first budger die the other's slave, And the gods doom him after! i 8 6
We thank the gods Our Rome hath such a soldier . . . . i 9 8
The gods begin to mock me. I, that now Refused most princely gifts, am bound to beg . . . . i 9 79
O, he is wounded; I thank the gods for't.—So do I too, if it be not too much . . . . ii 1 133
The gods grant them true!—True! pow, wow . . . . . ii 1 156
God save your good worships! Marcius is coming home . . . ii 1 159
You have, I know, petition'd all the gods For my prosperity! . . ii 1 187
Now, the gods crown thee! . . . . ii 1 196
As if that whatsoever god who leads him Were slily crept into his human powers . . . . ii 1 235
O me, the gods! You must not speak of that . . . . . ii 3 60
The gods give you joy, sir, heartily! . . . . ii 3 118
The gods give him joy, and make him good friend to the people! . ii 3 142
We pray the gods he may deserve your loves . . . . . ii 3 165
You speak o' the people, As if you were a god to punish, not A man of their infirmity . . . . iii 1 81
The good gods forbid That our renowned Rome . . . Should now eat up her own! . . . . iii 1 290
For them! I cannot do it to the gods; Must I then do't to them . iii 2 38
The honour'd gods Keep Rome in safety! . . . . . . iii 3 33
With a voice as free As I do pray the gods . . . . . iii 3 74
The gods preserve our noble tribunes! . . . . . . iii 3 143
O the gods!—I'll follow thee a month . . . . . . iv 1 37
By the good gods, I'ld with thee every foot . . . . . iv 1 56
The hoarded plague o' the gods Requite your love! . . . . iv 2 11
I would the gods had nothing else to do But to confirm my curses! . iv 2 45
You bless me, gods! . . . . iv 5 141
The gods preserve you both!—God-den, our neighbours . . . iv 6 20
Now the gods keep you!—Farewell, farewell . . . . . iv 6 25
The gods have well prevented it, and Rome Sits safe . . . iv 6 36
He is their god: he leads them like a thing Made by some other deity than nature . . . . iv 6 90
Show no sign of fear.—The gods be good to us! . . . . iv 6 154
The glorious gods sit in hourly synod about thy particular prosperity! v 2 74
The good gods assuage thy wrath, and turn the dregs of it upon this varlet . . . . v 2 83
Those doves' eyes, Which can make gods forsworn . . . . v 3 28
You gods! I prate, And the most noble mother of the world Leave unsaluted . . . . v 3 48
Thine enmity's most capital: thou barr'st us Our prayers to the gods . v 3 105
Thou hast affected the fine strains of honour, To imitate the graces of the gods . . . . v 3 150
The gods will plague thee, That thou restrain'st from me the duty which To a mother's part belongs . . . . v 3 166
The gods look down, and this unnatural scene They laugh at . . . v 3 184
He wants nothing of a god but eternity and a heaven to throne in . v 4 25
The gods be good unto us!—No, in such a case the gods will not be good unto us . . . . v 4 33
First, the gods bless you for your tidings; next, Accept my thankfulness v 4 61
Call all your tribes together, praise the gods, And make triumphant fires v 5 2
Hear'st thou, Mars?—Name not the god, thou boy of tears! . . v 6 101
Wilt thou draw near the nature of the gods? Draw near them then in being merciful: Sweet mercy is nobility's true badge *T. Andron.* i 1 117
The self-same gods that arm'd the Queen of Troy With opportunity . i 1 136
And here I swear by all the Roman gods . . . . . . i 1 322
God give you joy, sir, of your gallant bride! . . . . . i 1 400
The gods of Rome forfend I should be author to dishonour you! . i 1 434
By the gods that warlike Goths adore, This petty brabble will undo us all . . . . ii 1 61
O, why should nature build so foul a den, Unless the gods delight in tragedies? . . . . iv 1 60
And here display, at last, What God will have discover'd for revenge iv 1 74
And pray the Roman gods confound you both? . . . . . iv 2 6
Let us go; and pray to all the gods For our beloved mother in her pains iv 2 46
Pray to the devils; the gods have given us over . . . . iv 2 48
She is brought a-bed.—Well, God give her good rest! . . . iv 2 63
And, sith there's no justice in earth nor hell, We will solicit heaven and move the gods . . . . iv 3 50
There's not a god left unsolicited . . . . iv 3 60
Why, there it goes: God give his lordship joy! . . . . iv 3 76
My lords, you know, as know the mightful gods . . . . iv 4 5
God and Saint Stephen give you good den . . . . . iv 4 42
Thou believest no god: That granted, how canst thou believe an oath? v 1 71
I know An idiot holds his bauble for a god And keeps the oath which by that god he swears . . . . v 1 79
Vow By that same god, what god soe'er it be, That thou adorest . v 1 82
Susan and she—God rest all Christian souls!—Were of an age *R. and J.* i 3 18
Well, Susan is with God; She was too good for me . . . . i 3 19
My husband—God be with his soul! A' was a merry man . . . i 3 39
Peace, I have done. God mark thee to his grace! . . . . i 3 59
God shall mend my soul! You'll make a mutiny among my guests! . i 5 81
Swear by thy gracious self, Which is the god of my idolatry . . ii 2 114
The sweeter rest was mine.—God pardon sin! wast thou with Rosaline? ii 3 44
God ye good morrow, gentlemen.—God ye good den, fair gentlewoman . ii 4 115
One, gentlewoman, that God hath made for himself to mar . . ii 4 121
Now, afore God, I am so vexed, that every part about me quivers . ii 4 170
O God, she comes! O honey nurse, what news? . . . . ii 5 18
Go thy ways, wench; serve God. What, have you dined at home? . ii 5 46
Claps me his sword upon the table and says, 'God send me no need of thee!' . . . . iii 1 7
O God! did Romeo's hand shed Tybalt's blood?—It did, it did . . iii 2 71
O God, I have an ill-divining soul! . . . . iii 5 54
God pardon him! I do, with all my heart . . . . . . iii 5 83

God. We scarce thought us blest That God had lent us but this only child . . . . *Rom. and Jul.* iii 5 166
O God!—O nurse, how shall this be prevented? . . . . . iii 5 206
God shield I should disturb devotion! . . . . iv 1 41
God join'd my heart and Romeo's, thou our hands . . . . iv 1 55
Now, afore God! this reverend holy friar, All our whole city is much bound to him . . . . iv 2 31
I call the gods to witness, I will choose Mine heir from forth the beggars of the world, And dispossess her all . . . *T. of Athens* i 1 137
The gods preserve ye!—Well fare you, gentleman . . . . i 1 162
Traffic confound thee, if the gods will not!—If traffic do it, the gods do it.—Traffic's thy god; and thy god confound thee! . . . . i 1 244
It hath pleased the gods to remember my father's age, And call him to long peace . . . . i 2 2
O you gods, what a number of men eat Timon, and he sees 'em not! . i 2 39
Feasts are too proud to give thanks to the gods . . . . i 2 62
Immortal gods, I crave no pelf; I pray for no man but myself . . i 2 63
The gods themselves have provided that I shall have much help from you i 2 92
O you gods, think I, what need we have any friends, if we should ne'er have need of 'em? . . . . i 2 98
So the gods bless me, When all our offices have been oppress'd . . ii 2 166
You gods, reward them! Prithee, man, look cheerly . . . . ii 2 222
O you gods, I feel my master's passion! . . . . . . iii 1 58
Now, before the gods, I am ashamed on't . . . . . . iii 2 19
Now, before the gods, I am not able to do,—the more beast, I say . iii 2 54
This was my lord's best hope; now all are fled, Save only the gods . iii 3 37
I'm weary of this charge, the gods can witness . . . . iii 4 25
Methinks he should the sooner pay his debts, And make a clear way to the gods.—Good gods!—We cannot take this for answer, sir . . iii 4 77
Tear me, take me, and the gods fall upon you! . . . . . iii 4 100
Now the gods keep you old enough; that you may live Only in bone! . iii 5 104
Soldiers should brook as little wrongs as gods . . . . . iii 5 117
Sit, sit. The gods require our thanks . . . . . . iii 6 77
Were your godheads to borrow of men, men would forsake the gods . iii 6 85
The rest of your fees, O gods—the senators of Athens . . . —what is amiss in them, you gods, make suitable for destruction . . . iii 6 89
Piety, and fear, Religion to the gods, peace, justice, truth . . iv 1 16
The gods confound—hear me, you good gods all—The Athenians! . iv 1 37
Let me be recorded by the righteous gods, I am as poor as you . . iv 2 4
For bounty, that makes gods, does still mar men . . . . iv 2 41
No, gods, I am no idle votarist: roots, you clear heavens! . . iv 3 26
Ha, you gods! why this? what this, you gods? . . . . . iv 3 30
If thou wilt not promise, the gods plague thee, for thou art a man! . iv 3 73
The gods confound them all in thy conquest; And thee after! . . iv 3 103
I know, you'll swear, terribly swear Into strong shudders and to heavenly agues The immortal gods . . . . iv 3 138
A beastly ambition, which the gods grant thee t' attain to! . . iv 3 329
Thou visible god [gold], That solder'st close impossibilities! . . iv 3 387
O you gods! Is yond despised and ruinous man my lord? . . . iv 3 464
The gods are witness, Ne'er did poor steward wear a truer grief . iv 3 486
Forgive my general and exceptless rashness, You perpetual-sober gods! iv 3 503
Here, take: the gods out of my misery Have sent thee treasure . iv 3 531
What a god's gold, That he is worshipp'd in a baser temple Than where swine feed! 'Tis thou that rigg'st the bark . . . . . . v 1 50
I leave you To the protection of the prosperous gods, As thieves to keepers . . . . v 1 186
Pray to the gods to intermit the plague . . . . *J. Cæsar* i 1 59
Let the gods so speed me as I love The name of honour more than I fear death . . . . i 2 88
And this man Is now become a god, and Cassius is A wretched creature i 2 116
I did mark How he did shake: 'tis true, this god did shake . . i 2 121
Ye gods, it doth amaze me A man of such a feeble temper should So get the start of the majestic world . . . . i 2 128
Now, in the names of all the gods at once, Upon what meat doth this our Cæsar feed, That he is grown so great? . . . . . . i 2 148
Either there is a civil strife in heaven, Or else the world, too saucy with the gods, Incenses them to send destruction . . . . . i 3 12
It is the part of men to fear and tremble, When the most mighty gods by tokens send Such dreadful heralds . . . . i 3 55
Therein, ye gods, you make the weak most strong; Therein, ye gods, you tyrants do defeat . . . . i 3 91
Let's carve him as a dish fit for the gods, Not hew him as a carcass . ii 1 173
O ye gods, Render me worthy of this noble wife! . . . . . ii 1 302
By all the gods that Romans bow before, I here discard my sickness! . ii 1 320
What can be avoided Whose end is purposed by the mighty gods? . . ii 2 27
The gods do this in shame of cowardice . . . . . . ii 2 41
The mighty gods defend thee! Thy lover, 'ARTEMIDORUS' . . . ii 3 9
For Brutus, as you know, was Cæsar's angel: Judge, O you gods, how dearly Cæsar loved him! . . . . iii 2 186
Judge me, you gods! wrong I mine enemies? . . . . . . iv 2 38
You are Brutus that speak this, Or, by the gods, this speech were else your last . . . . iv 3 14
O ye gods, ye gods! must I endure all this?—All this! ay, more . . iv 3 41
Be ready, gods, with all your thunderbolts; Dash him to pieces! . . iv 3 81
And died so?—Even so.—O ye immortal gods! . . . . . iv 3 157
Art thou some god, some angel, or some devil, That makest my blood cold? . . . . iv 3 279
The gods to-day stand friendly, that we may, Lovers in peace, lead on our days to age! . . . . v 1 94
By your leave, gods:—this is a Roman's part . . . . . v 3 89
The gods defend him from so great a shame! . . . . . v 4 23
One cried 'God bless us!' and 'Amen' the other . . . . *Macbeth* ii 2 27
I could not say 'Amen,' When they did say 'God bless us!' . . . ii 2 30
Fears and scruples shake us: In the great hand of God I stand . . ii 3 136
Now, God help thee, poor monkey! But how wilt thou do for a father? iv 2 59
To offer up a weak poor innocent lamb To appease an angry god . . iv 3 17
But God above Deal between thee and me! . . . . . . iv 3 120
Good God, betimes remove The means that makes us strangers! . . iv 3 162
Well, well, well,—Pray God it be, sir . . . . v 1 64
More needs she the divine than the physician. God, God forgive us all! v 1 83
They say he parted well, and paid his score: And so, God be with him! v 8 53
What think you on't?—Before my God, I might not this believe *Hamlet* i 1 56
O God! God! How weary, stale, flat and unprofitable, Seem to me all the uses of this world! . . . . i 2 132
O God! a beast, that wants discourse of reason, Would have mourn'd longer . . . . i 2 150
I have been so affrighted!—With what, i' the name of God? . . . ii 1 76
I hold my duty, as I hold my soul, Both to my God and to my gracious king . . . . ii 2 45
If the sun breed maggots in a dead dog, being a god kissing carrion . ii 2 182

God. O God, I could be bounded in a nutshell and count myself a king *Hamlet* ii 2 260
In action how like an angel! in apprehension how like a god! ii 2 319
Pray God, your voice, like a piece of uncurrent gold, be not cracked ii 2 447
'Fore God, my lord, well spoken, with good accent and good discretion ii 4 488
Out, out, thou strumpet, Fortune! All you gods, In general synod, take away her power! ii 2 515
But if the gods themselves did see her then When she saw Pyrrhus ii 2 535
Would have made milch the burning eyes of heaven, And passion in the gods ii 2 541
God has given you one face, and you make yourselves another iii 1 149
God bless you, sir! iii 2 390; iv 6 6
A combination and a form indeed, Where every god did seem to set his seal iii 4 61
Lord, we know what we are, but know not what we may be. God be at your table! iv 5 43
God ha' mercy on his soul! And of all Christian souls, I pray God iv 5 199
Do you see this, O God? iv 5 201
One that would circumvent God, might it not? v 1 88
O, he is mad, Laertes.—For love of God, forbear him v 1 296
Now, by Apollo, king, Thou swear'st thy gods in vain *Lear* i 1 163
The gods to their dear shelter take thee! i 1 185
Gods, gods! 'tis strange that from their cold'st neglect My love should kindle to inflamed respect i 1 257
I grow; I prosper: Now, gods, stand up for bastards! i 2 22
Now, gods that we adore, whereof comes this? i 4 312
The revenging gods 'Gainst parricides did all their thunders bend ii 1 47
O the blest gods! so will you wish on me, When the rash mood is on ii 4 171
You see me here, you gods, a poor old man, As full of grief as age ii 4 275
Let the great gods, That keep this dreadful pother o'er our heads, Find out their enemies now iii 2 49
The gods reward your kindness! iii 6 5
By the kind gods, 'tis most ignobly done To pluck me by the beard iii 7 35
Give me some help! O cruel! O you gods! iii 7 70
Then Edgar was abused. Kind gods, forgive me that, and prosper him! iii 7 92
O gods! Who is't can say 'I am at the worst'? I am worse than e'er I was iv 1 27
As flies to wanton boys, are we to the gods, They kill us for their sport iv 1 38
Fairies and gods Prosper it with thee! iv 6 29
O you mighty gods! This world I do renounce iv 6 34
Think that the clearest gods, who make them honours Of men's impossibilities, have preserved thee iv 6 73
But to the girdle do the gods inherit, Beneath is all the fiends' iv 6 128
You ever-gentle gods, take my breath from me iv 6 221
O you kind gods, Cure this great breach in his abused nature! iv 7 14
Upon such sacrifices, my Cordelia, The gods themselves throw incense v 3 21
False to thy gods, thy brother, and thy father v 3 134
The gods are just, and of our pleasant vices Make instruments to plague us v 3 170
Lay the blame upon her own despair, That she fordid herself.—The gods defend her! v 3 256
You are one of those that will not serve God, if the devil bid you *Othello* i 1 109
God's above all; and there be souls must be saved, and there be souls must not be saved ii 3 105
She may make, unmake, do what she list, Even as her appetite shall play the god With his weak function ii 3 353
We must think men are not gods, Nor of them look for such observances As fit the bridal iii 4 148
Why, sir, give the gods a thankful sacrifice *Ant. and Cleo.* i 2 167
I have no power upon you; hers you are.—The gods best know i 3 24
Why should I think you can be mine and true, Though you in swearing shake the throned gods? i 3 28
All the gods go with you! upon your sword Sit laurel victory! i 3 99
If the great gods be just, they shall assist The deeds of justest men ii 1 1
We yet not know. Be't as our gods will have't! ii 1 50
Before the gods my knee shall bow my prayers To them for you ii 3 3
The gods confound thee! dost thou hold there still?—Should I lie, madam? ii 5 92
The senators alone of this great world, Chief factors for the gods ii 6 10
So, the gods keep you, And make the hearts of Romans serve your ends! iii 2 36
Look, here I have you; thus I let you go, And give you to the gods iii 2 64
The good gods will mock me presently, When I shall pray iii 4 15
And the high gods, To do you justice, make them ministers Of us iii 6 87
Gods and goddesses, All the whole synod of them! iii 10 4
Thy beck might from the bidding of the gods Command me iii 11 60
He is a god, and knows What is most right iii 13 60
Now, gods and devils! Authority melts from me iii 13 89
The wise gods seel our eyes; In our own filth drop our clear judgements iii 13 112
To let a fellow that will take rewards And say 'God quit you!' be familiar! iii 13 124
That I might do you service So good as you have done.—The gods forbid! iv 2 19
Tend me to-night two hours, I ask no more, And the gods yield you for't! iv 2 33
The gods make this a happy day to Antony! iv 5 1
He hath fought to-day As if a god, in hate of mankind, had Destroy'd in such a shape iv 8 25
I have lived in such dishonour, that the gods Detest my baseness iv 14 56
Put colour in thy cheek.—The gods withhold me! iv 14 69
It were for me To throw my sceptre at the injurious gods iv 15 76
The gods rebuke me, but it is tidings To wash the eyes of kings v 1 27
But you, gods, will give us Some faults to make us men v 1 32
Cæsar cannot live To be ungentle.—So the gods preserve thee! v 1 60
You lie, up to the hearing of the gods v 2 95
Sir, the gods Will have it thus; my master and my lord I must obey v 2 115
The gods! it smites me Beneath the fall I have v 2 171
Shall we be enclouded, And forced to drink their vapour.—The gods forbid! v 2 213
O the good gods!—Nay, that's certain.—I'll never see't v 2 221
I know that a woman is a dish for the gods, if the devil dress her not v 2 276
These same whoreson devils do the gods great harm in their women; for in every ten that they make, the devils mar five v 2 277
I hear him mock The luck of Cæsar, which the gods give men To excuse their after wrath v 2 289
Dissolve, thick cloud, and rain; that I may say, The gods themselves do weep! v 2 303
How, how! another [wife]? You gentle gods, give me but this I have! *Cymbeline* i 1 115
O the gods! When shall we see again? i 1 123
The gods protect you! And bless the good remainders of the court! i 1 128

God. The gift of the gods.—Which the gods have given you?—Which, by their graces, I will keep *Cymbeline* i 4 93
I will have it no lay.—By the gods, it is one i 4 160
It is an office of the gods to venge it, Not mine to speak on't i 6 92
He sits 'mongst men like a descended god i 6 169
But the gods made you, Unlike all others, chaffless i 6 177
To your protection I commend me, gods ii 2 8
You good gods, Let what is here contain'd relish of love iii 2 29
You clasp young Cupid's tables. Good news, gods! iii 2 39
Thou art all the comfort The gods will diet me with iii 4 183
May the gods Direct you to the best! iii 4 195
All gold and silver rather turn to dirt! As 'tis no better reckon'd, but of those Who worship dirty gods iii 6 56
Pardon me, gods! I'ld change my sex to be companion with them iii 6 87
These are kind creatures. Gods, what lies I have heard! iv 2 32
Displace our heads where—thank the gods!—they grow iv 2 122
Let ordinance Come as the gods foresay it iv 2 146
O gods and goddesses! These flowers are like the pleasures of the world iv 2 295
If there be Yet left in heaven as small a drop of pity As a wren's eye, fear'd gods, a part of it! iv 2 305
Last night the very gods show'd me a vision iv 2 346
If I do lie and do No harm by it, though the gods hear, I hope They'll pardon it iv 2 378
But first, an't please the gods, I'll hide my master from the flies iv 2 387
Gods! if you Should have ta'en vengeance on my faults, I never Had lived to put on this v 1 7
Gods, put the strength o' the Leonati in me! v 1 31
The odds Is that we scarce are men, and you are gods v 2 10
You good gods, give me The penitent instrument to pick that bolt! v 4 9
So children temporal fathers do appease; Gods are more full of mercy v 4 13
Then, Jupiter, thou king of gods, Why hast thou thus adjourn'd The graces for his merits due? v 4 77
His royal bird Prunes the immortal wing and cloys his beak, As when his god is pleased v 4 119
Stand by my side, you whom the gods have made Preservers of my throne v 5 1
Since the gods Will have it thus, that nothing but our lives May be call'd ransom, let it come v 5 78
If this be so, the gods do mean to strike me To death with mortal joy v 5 234
The gods throw stones of sulphur on me v 5 240
O gods! I left out one thing which the queen confess'd v 5 243
I slew him there.—Marry, the gods forfend! v 5 287
Laud we the gods; And let our crooked smokes climb to their nostrils v 5 476
You gods that made me man, and sway in love *Pericles* i 1 19
Would draw heaven down, and all the gods, to hearken i 1 83
Kings are earth's gods; in vice their law's their will i 1 103
The gods of Greece protect you! And we'll pray for you i 4 97
Pray see me buried.—Die quoth-a? Now gods forbid! ii 1 82
In like necessity—The which the gods protect thee from! ii 1 135
Why, do'e take it, and the gods give thee good on't! ii 1 152
Honour we love; For who hates honour hates the gods above ii 3 22
Princes in this should live like gods above, Who freely give to every one ii 3 59
Now, by the gods, he could not please me better ii 3 72
Now, by the gods, I pity his misfortune ii 3 90
The most high gods not minding longer To withhold the vengeance ii 4 3
Thou hast bewitch'd my daughter, and thou art A villain.—By the gods, I have not ii 5 51
Now, by the gods, I do applaud his courage ii 5 58
I'll thus your hopes destroy; And for a further grief,—God give you joy! ii 5 87
Thou god of this great vast, rebuke these surges! iii 1 1
O you gods! Why do you make us love your goodly gifts, And snatch them straight away? We here below Recall not what we give iii 1 22
Now, the good gods Throw their best eyes upon't! iii 1 36
Immortality attends the former, Making a man a god iii 2 31
O you most potent gods! what's here? a corse!—Most strange! iii 2 63
Besides this treasure for a fee, The gods require his charity! iii 2 75
Take from my heart all thankfulness! The gods Make up the rest! iii 3 4
The gods revenge it upon me and mine, To the end of generation! iii 3 24
Whether there Deliver'd, by the holy gods, I cannot rightly say iii 4 7
She is a goodly creature.—The fitter, then, the gods should have her iv 1 10
Pray; but be not tedious, For the gods are quick of ear iv 1 70
The sore terms we stand upon with the gods will be strong with us for giving over iv 2 38
The gods have done their part in you.—I accuse them not iv 2 74
The gods defend me!—If it please the gods to defend you by men, then men must comfort you iv 2 95
Of all the faults beneath the heavens, the gods Do like this worst iv 3 20
You are like one that superstitiously Doth swear to the gods iv 3 50
How a dozen of virginities?—Now, the gods to bless your honour! iv 6 23
O, that the gods Would set me free from this unhallow'd place! iv 6 106
Persever in that clear way thou goest, And the gods strengthen thee!—The good gods preserve you! iv 6 114
She makes our profession as it were to stink afore the face of the gods iv 6 145
Hark, hark, you gods!—She conjures: away with her! iv 6 155
O, that the gods Would safely deliver me from this place! iv 6 190
The gods preserve you!—And you, sir, to outlive the age I am v 1 14
Sir king, all hail! the gods preserve you! Hail, royal sir! v 1 39
The most just gods For every graff would send a caterpillar v 1 59
Come, let us leave her; And the gods make her prosperous! v 1 80
And thou by some incensed god sent hither To make the world to laugh at me v 1 144
Down on thy knees, thank the holy gods as loud As thunder threatens us v 1 200
No more, you gods! your present kindness Makes my past miseries sports v 3 40
And who to thank, Besides the gods, for this great miracle v 3 58
This man, Through whom the gods have shown their power v 3 60
The gods can have no mortal officer More like a god than you v 3 63
God be with you! *L. L. Lost* iii 1; *As Y. Like It* iii 2; iv 1; v 3; *T. N.* iv 2; *Hen. V.* iv 1; iv 3; v 1; 1 *Hen. VI.* iii 2; *T. and C.* iii 3; *T. An.* iv 3; *Macb.* iii 1; *Hamlet* ii 1; ii 2; iv 4; iv 5; *Oth.* i 3; iii 3
God bless the mark! *Mer. of Ven.* ii 2 25; *Othello* i 1 33
God help the while! 1 *Hen. IV.* ii 4 145; *Richard III.* ii 3 8
God save the mark! 1 *Hen. IV.* i 3 56; *Rom. and Jul.* iii 2 53
I praise God for you *Much Ado* v 1; *L. L. Lost* v 1; *All's Well* v 2

God Achilles. Yet god Achilles still cries 'Excellent!' *Troi. and Cres.* i 3 169

God Almighty. He wills you, in the name of God Almighty, That you divest yourself *Hen. V.* ii 4 77
God Almighty! There is some soul of goodness in things evil iv 1 3
What, art thou lame?—Ay, God Almighty help me! 2 *Hen. VI.* ii 1 95

God-a-mercy, Grumio! then he shall have no odds *T. of Shrew* iv 3 154
Good den, sir Richard!—God-a-mercy, fellow! *K. John* i 1 185

God-a-mercy. God-a-mercy! so should I be sure to be heart-burned 1 *Hen. IV.* iii 3 58
God-a-mercy, old heart! thou speak'st cheerfully . . *Hen. V.* iv 1 34
God-a-mercy, that thou wilt believe me . . *Troi. and Cres.* v 4 33
How does my good Lord Hamlet?—Well, God-a-mercy . . *Hamlet* ii 2 172
God Bel. Like god Bel's priests in the old church-window . *Much Ado* iii 3 143
God damn me. And thereof comes that the wenches say 'God damn me' *Com. of Errors* iv 3 54
God-daughter. And your fairest daughter and mine, my god-daughter Ellen . . . . 2 *Hen. IV.* iii 2 8
God defend the lute should be like the case! . . . . *Much Ado* ii 1 97
For God defend but God should go before such villains! . . . iv 2 21
By my oath—Which God defend a knight should violate! *Richard II.* i 3 18
And God defend but still I should stand so . . . 1 *Hen. IV.* iv 3 38
Which God defend that I should wring from him! . . *Richard III.* iii 7 173
God-den to your worship, good Captain James . . . *Hen. V.* iii 2 89
God-den, our neighbours.—God-den to you all. . . *Coriolanus* iv 6 20
God-den, good fellow.—God gi' god-den. I pray, sir, can you read? *Rom. and Jul.* i 2 57
speak no treason.—O, God ye god-den.—May not one speak? . . iii 5 173
God dig-you-den all! Pray you, which is the head lady? . *L. L. Lost* iv 1 42
God forbid. It is not so, nor 'twas not so, but, indeed, God forbid it should be so . . . . *Much Ado* i 1 219
In plain terms, gone to heaven.—Marry, God forbid! . *Mer. of Venice* ii 2 69
Of Mantua, sir? marry, God forbid! And come to Padua? *T. of Shrew* iv 2 78
Art thou ashamed of me?—No, sir, God forbid . . . . v 1 151
Now afore God—God forbid I say true! . . . . *Richard II.* ii 1 200
In God's name, I'll ascend the regal throne.—Marry, God forbid! . . iv 1 114
There is no seeming mercy in the king.—Did you beg any? God forbid! 1 *Hen. IV.* v 2 36
God forbid any malice should prevail! . . . . . 2 *Hen. VI.* iii 2 23
God forbid so many simple souls Should perish by the sword! . . iv 4 10
God forbid your grace should be forsworn.—I shall be . 3 *Hen. VI.* i 2 18
I fear her not, unless she chance to fall.—God forbid that! . . . iii 2 25
God forbid that I should wish them sever'd Whom God hath join'd together . . . . iv 1 21
If any such be here—as God forbid!—Let him depart . . . . v 4 48
Marry, God forbid his grace should say us nay! . . *Richard III.* iii 7 81
My favour To him that does best: God forbid else . *Hen. VIII.* ii 2 115
God forbid I should be so bold to press to heaven in my young days *T. Andron.* iv 3 90
What, lamb! what, lady-bird! God forbid! Where's this girl? *R. and J.* i 3 4
God forgive me. I protest I love thee.—Why, then, God forgive me! *M. Ado* iv 1 283
O, the devil take such cozeners! God forgive me! . . 1 *Hen. IV.* i 3 255
Speak how I fell. I have done; and God forgive me! . *Hen. VIII.* ii 1 136
God forgive me, Marry, and amen, how sound is she asleep! *Rom. and Jul.* iv 5 7
God for his mercy! what a tide of woes Comes rushing on this woeful land at once! . . . . *Richard II.* ii 2 98
God for his mercy, what treachery is here! . . . . . v 2 75
God he knows. Which, God he knows, I saw not . *Com. of Errors* v 1 229
But, God he knows, thy share thereof [of beauty] is small . 3 *Hen. VI.* i 4 129
On what occasion, God he knows, not I . . . *Richard III.* iii 1 26
For God he knows, and you may partly see, How far I am from the desire iii 7 235
God help, poor souls, how idly do they talk! . *Com. of Errors* iv 4 132
And his wits are not so blunt as, God help, I would desire they were *M. Ado* iii 5 12
God Hercules. 'Tis the god Hercules, whom Antony loved, Now leaves him . . . . *Ant. and Cleo.* iv 3 16
God 'ild you for your last company . . . . *As Y. Like It* iii 3 76
I like him very well.—God 'ild you, sir; I desire you of the like . v 4 56
Herein I teach you How you shall bid God 'ild us for your pains *Macbeth* i 6 13
How do you, pretty lady?—Well, God 'ild you! . . . *Hamlet* iv 5 41
God in heaven forbid!—Ah, madam, 'tis too true . . *Richard II.* ii 2 51
God in heaven forbid We should infringe the holy privilege Of blessed sanctuary! . . . . *Richard III.* iii 1 40
Now God in heaven bless thee! Hark you, sir . . *Rom. and Jul.* ii 4 206
God in heaven bless her! You are to blame, my lord, to rate her so . iii 5 169
God knows I loved my niece; And she is dead . . . . *Much Ado* v 1 87
Will they return?—They will, they will, God knows . . *L. L. Lost* v 2 290
By this white glove,—how white the hand, God knows! . . . v 2 411
Which we, God knows, have turn'd another way, To our own vantage *K. John* ii 1 549
I greatly care not: God knows I had as lief be none as one *Richard II.* v 2 49
One that hath abundance of charge too, God knows what . 1 *Hen. IV.* v 1 64
God knows, whether those that bawl out the ruins of thy linen shall inherit his kingdom . . . . 2 *Hen. IV.* ii 2 26
God knows, I had no such intent, But that necessity so bow'd the state iii 1 72
God knows, my son, By what by-paths and indirect crook'd ways I met this crown . . . . iv 5 184
God knows, and you know . . . . *Hen. V.* iv 7 36
God knows thou art a collop of my flesh . . . . 1 *Hen. VI.* v 4 18
This was my dream: what it doth bode, God knows . 2 *Hen. VI.* i 2 31
Camest thou here by chance, Or of devotion, to this holy shrine?—God knows, of pure devotion . . . . ii 1 89
But how he died God knows, not Henry . . . . . . iii 2 131
God knows how long it is I have to live . . . . . . v 3 17
My sons, God knows what hath bechanced them . . 3 *Hen. VI.* i 4 6
To bar my master's heirs in true descent, God knows I will not *Rich. III.* iii 2 55
I have stay'd for thee, God knows, in anguish, pain and agony . . iv 4 163
Full little, God knows, looking Either for such men or such business *Hen. VIII.* iii 1 75
Farewell! God knows when we shall meet again . . *Rom. and Jul.* iv 3 14
God Neptune. The city strived God Neptune's annual feast to keep *Pericles* v Gower 17
God of battles. O God of battles! steel my soldiers' hearts . *Hen. V.* iv 1 306
God of day. Doth with his lofty and shrill-sounding throat Awake the god of day . . . . *Hamlet* i 1 152
God of gold. Plutus, the god of gold, Is but his steward *T. of Athens* i 1 287
God of heaven. He is a traitor, foul and dangerous, To God of heaven, King Richard and to me . . . . *Richard II.* i 3 40
There were two honours lost, yours and your son's. For yours, the God of heaven brighten it! . . . . 2 *Hen. IV.* ii 3 17
Rather let my head Stoop to the block than these knees bow to any Save to the God of heaven . . . . . . 2 *Hen. VI.* iv 1 126
Great God of heaven, say Amen to all! . . . . *Richard III.* v 5 8
The God of heaven Both now and ever bless her! . . *Hen. VIII.* v 1 164
God of Jupiter. Cæsar? Why, he's the Jupiter of men.—What's Antony? The god of Jupiter . . . . *Ant. and Cleo.* iii 2 10
God of love. O god of love! I know he doth deserve As much as may be yielded to a man . . . . *Much Ado* iii 1 47
The god of love, That sits above, And knows me, and knows me . . v 2 26

God of power. Had I been any god of power, I would Have sunk the sea within the earth . . . . *Tempest* i 2 10
God of rhyme. Assist me, some extemporal god of rhyme . *L. L. Lost* i 2 189
God of sleep. And on your eyelids crown the god of sleep 1 *Hen. IV.* iii 1 217
God of soldiers. The god of soldiers, With the consent of supreme Jove, inform Thy thoughts with nobleness! . . . . . *Coriolanus* v 3 70
God of war. Away, and glister like the god of war . . . *K. John* v 1 54
To look upon the hideous god of war In disadvantage . . 2 *Hen. IV.* ii 3 35
Nor great Alcides, nor the god of war, Shall seize this prey *T. Andron.* iv 2 95
This to Mercury; This to Apollo; this to the god of war . . . iv 4 15
God omnipotent Is mustering in his clouds on our behalf *Richard II.* iii 3 85
God Priapus. She's able to freeze the god Priapus . . *Pericles* iv 6 4
God save the king! Will no man say amen? . . . *Richard II.* iv 1 172
God save the king! God save the king! . . . . 2 *Hen. VI.* iv 8 19; iv 9 22
God save the king!—Whence camest thou, worthy thane? . *Macbeth* i 2 47
God save thee. Whilst all tongues cried 'God save thee!' *Richard II.* v 2 11
God save thee, my sweet boy! . . . . 2 *Hen. IV.* v 5 47
God save ye. Whither away so fast?—O, God save ye! Even to the hall *Hen. VIII.* ii 1 1
God save you. My lord and brother, God save you! . . *Much Ado* iii 2 82
God save you, brother.—And you, fair sister . . . *As Y. Like It* v 2 20
God save you, sir!—And you, sir! you are welcome . *T. of Shrew* iv 2 72
God save you, pilgrim! whither are you bound? . . . *All's Well* iii 5 35
God save you, sir! where have you been broiling? . . *Hen. VIII.* iv 1 56
What courage, sir? God save you!—Courage enough . . *Pericles* iii 1 38
God speed fair Helena! whither away?—Call you me fair? *M. N. Dream* i 1 180
A brace of draymen bid God speed him well . . . *Richard II.* i 4 32
God speed the Parliament! who shall be the speaker? . 1 *Hen. VI.* iii 2 60
Neighbours, God speed!—Give you good morrow, sir *Richard III.* ii 3 6
God willing. And what so poor a man as Hamlet is May do, to express his love and friending to you, God willing, shall not lack *Hamlet* i 5 187
God wot. Stood the state so? No, no, good friends, God wot *Richard III.* ii 3 18
Why, 'As by lot, God wot,' and then, you know . . . *Hamlet* ii 2 435
God's angel. My oath should be 'By this fire, that's God's angel' 1 *Hen. IV.* iii 3 40
God's arm strike with us! 'tis a fearful odds . . . . *Hen. V.* iv 3 5
God's benison go with you! . . . . *Macbeth* ii 4 40
God's blessing. Whose daughter?—Her mother's, I have heard.—God's blessing on your beard! . . . . *L. L. Lost* ii 1 203
I'll stay at home And pray God's blessing into thy attempt . *All's Well* i 3 260
God's blessing of your good heart! and so she is . . . 2 *Hen. IV.* ii 4 329
God's blest mother! I swear he is true-hearted . . *Hen. VIII.* v 1 153
God's body! the turkeys in my pannier are quite starved . 1 *Hen. IV.* ii 1 29
God's bodykins. I will use them according to their desert.—God's bodykins, man, much better . . . . *Hamlet* ii 2 554
God's book. Sins Such as by God's book are adjudged to death 2 *Hen. VI.* ii 3 4
God's bread! it makes me mad . . . . . . *Rom. and Jul.* iii 5 177
God's creatures. You lisp, and nick-name God's creatures . *Hamlet* iii 1 151
God's curse light upon you all! . . . . . . 2 *Hen. VI.* iv 8 33
God's delight. If sanctimony be the gods' delight, If there be rule in unity itself, This is not she . . . . *Troi. and Cres.* v 2 140
God's dew. It is you Have blown this coal betwixt my lord and me; Which God's dew quench! . . . . *Hen. VIII.* ii 4 80
God's enemy. One that hath ever been God's enemy: Then, if you fight against God's enemy, God will in justice ward you as his soldiers *Richard III.* v 3 252
God's dreadful law. How canst thou urge God's dreadful law to us, When thou hast broke it in so dear degree? . . . . i 4 214
God's fair ordinance. By God's fair ordinance conjoin together! . . v 5 31
God's glory. I shall be well content with any choice Tends to God's glory and my country's weal . . . . 1 *Hen. VI.* v 1 27
God's good grace. By God's good grace his son shall reign *Richard III.* ii 3 10
God's good pleasure. Peace to his soul, if God's good pleasure be! 2 *Hen. VI.* iii 3 26
God's good will. Would I were dead! if God's good will were so; For what is in this world but grief and woe? . . . . 3 *Hen. VI.* ii 5 19
God's goodness hath been great to thee . . . . . 2 *Hen. VI.* ii 1 84
God's grace. To prove, by God's grace and my body's valour *Richard II.* i 3 37
We will, in France, by God's grace, play a set . . . . *Hen. V.* i 2 262
God's ground. As arrant a villain and a Jacksauce, as ever his black shoe trod upon God's ground . . . . iv 7 149
God's hand. We are in God's hand, brother, not in theirs . . . iii 6 178
God's handiwork. That foul defacer of God's handiwork *Richard III.* iv 4 51
God's help. By God's help, And yours . . . . . . *Hen. V.* i 2 222
God's holy mother. I cannot blame her: by God's holy mother, She hath had too much wrong . . . . *Richard III.* i 3 306
God's just ordinance. Either thou wilt die, by God's just ordinance . iv 4 183
God's lady. O God's lady dear! Are you so hot? . . *Rom. and Jul.* ii 5 63
God's lid. By God's lid, it does one's heart good . *Troi. and Cres.* i 2 228
God's light, I was never called so in mine own house before 1 *Hen. IV.* iii 3 71
God's light, with two points on your shoulder? much! . 2 *Hen. IV.* ii 4 142
God's light, these villains will make the word as odious as the word 'occupy' . . . . ii 4 159
God's love. For God's love, let me hear . . . . . . *Hamlet* i 2 195
God's majesty. The figure of God's majesty, His captain *Richard II.* iv 1 125
God's making. He speaks not like a man of God's making *L. L. Lost* v 2 528
Is he of God's making? What manner of man? . . *As Y. Like It* iii 2 216
God's me, my horse! What say'st thou, Kate? . . . 1 *Hen. IV.* ii 3 97
God's mercy, maiden! does it curd thy blood To say I am thy mother? What's the matter? . . . . *All's Well* i 3 155
God's mother deigned to appear to me . . . . . 1 *Hen. VI.* i 2 78
Now, by God's mother, priest, I'll shave your crown for this 2 *Hen. VI.* ii 1 51
Thou art a widow, and thou hast some children; And, by God's mother, I, being but a bachelor, Have other some . . . 3 *Hen. VI.* iii 2 103
God's my life, where's the sexton? . . . . . *Much Ado* iv 2 72
Starveling! God's my life, stolen hence, and left me asleep! *M. N. D.* iv 1 209
God's name. But keep your way, i' God's name; I have done *Much Ado* i 1 144
Borrows money in God's name, the which he hath used so long and never paid that now men grow hard-hearted and will lend nothing for God's sake . . . . v 1 319
But if you have a stomach, to't i' God's name . . *T. of Shrew* i 2 195
Come on, i God's name; once more toward our father's. . . iv 5 1
In God's name and the king's, say who thou art . . *Richard II.* i 3 11
But what, o' God's name, doth become of this? . . . . ii 1 251
Must he lose The name of king? o' God's name, let it go . . iii 3 146
In God's name, I'll ascend the regal throne.—Marry, God forbid! . iv 1 113
Then come, o' God's name; I fear no woman . . 1 *Hen. VI.* i 2 102
And so, I pray you, go, in God's name, and leave us . 2 *Hen. VI.* i 4 12
O' God's name, see the lists and all things fit: Here let them end it . ii 3 54
He has a familiar under his tongue; he speaks not o' God's name . iv 7 115

God's name. We charge you, in God's name, and the king's, To go with us . . . . 3 *Hen. VI.* iii 1 97
In God's name, lead ; your king's name be obey'd : And what God will, that let your king perform . . . . iii 1 99
Then, in God's name, lords, Be valiant and give signal to the fight . v 4 81
In God's name what are you, and how came you hither? *Richard III.* i 4 85
In God's name, cheerly on, courageous friends, To reap the harvest v 2 14
God's officers. Wilt thou kill God's officers and the kings? . 2 *Hen. IV.* ii 1 56
God's own soldier. Whom zeal and charity brought to the field As God's own soldier . . . . . *K. John* ii 1 566
God's patience. Here will be an old abusing of God's patience and the king's English . . . . . *Mer. Wives* i 4 5
God's peace! I would not lose so great an honour . . *Hen. V.* iv 3 31
Assembled here in arms this day against God's peace and the king's 1 *Hen. VI.* i 3 75
And without trial fell ; God's peace be with him! . . *Hen. VIII.* ii 1 111
God's sake. For God's sake, hold your hands! . . . *Com. of Errors* i 2 93
Hold, sir, for God's sake! now your jest is earnest . . . ii 2 24
Men grow hard-hearted and will lend nothing for God's sake *Much Ado* v 1 321
For God's sake, a pot of small ale . . . . *T. of Shrew* Ind. 2 1
O yet, for God's sake, go not to these wars! . . . 2 *Hen. IV.* ii 3 9
Foul devil, for God's sake, hence, and trouble us not . *Richard III.* i 2 50
For God's sake, entertain good comfort, And cheer his grace . . i 3 4
God's secret judgement: I did dream to-night The duke was dumb 2 *Hen. VI.* iii 2 31
God's sending. I shall lessen God's sending that way; for it is said, 'God sends a curst cow short horns' . . . . *Much Ado* ii 1 24
God's soldier. Why then, God's soldier be he! . . . *Macbeth* v 8 47
God's sonties. By God's sonties, 'twill be a hard way to hit *Mer. of Venice* ii 2 47
God's spies. And take upon's the mystery of things, As if we were God's spies . . . . *Lear* v 3 17
God's substitute, His deputy anointed in His sight . . . *Richard II.* i 2 37
God's vassals. Knocks go and come ; God's vassals drop and die *Hen. V.* iii 2 8
God's will! I pray thee, wish not one man more . . . . . iv 3 23
God's will! my liege, would you and I alone, Without more help, could fight this royal battle! . . . . iv 3 74
God's will and his pleasure, captain, I beseech you now, come . iv 8 2
Thou shalt die.—You say very true, scauld knave, when God's will is . v 1 34
Now, by God's will, thou wrong'st him, Somerset . . . 1 *Hen. VI.* ii 4 82
Cold news, Lord Somerset : but God's will be done!—Cold news for me 2 *Hen. VI.* iii 1 86
O, God's will! much better She ne'er had known pomp . . *Hen. VIII.* ii 3 12
God's will, What simpleness is this! . . . . *Rom. and Jul.* iii 3 76
God's will, lieutenant, hold! You will be shamed for ever . *Othello* ii 3 162
God's wrathful agent. Whiles we, God's wrathful agent, do correct Their proud contempt . . . . . . *K. John* ii 1 87
God's wrong. Why then, by God— God's wrong is most of all *Richard III.* iv 4 377
Godded. Loved me above the measure of a father; Nay, godded me, indeed . . . . *Coriolanus* v 3 11
Goddess. Most sure, the goddess On whom these airs attend! *Tempest* i 2 421
Is she the goddess that hath sever'd us, And brought us thus together? v 1 187
Like a thrifty goddess, she determines Herself the glory of a creditor, Both thanks and use . . . . . . *Meas. for Meas.* i 1 39
Pardon, goddess of the night, Those that slew thy virgin knight *M. Ado* v 3 12
A woman I forswore; but I will prove, Thou being a goddess, I forswore not thee : My vow was earthly . . . . . *L. L. Lost* iv 3 65
This is the liver-vein, which makes flesh a deity, A green goose a goddess iv 3 75
I were the fairest goddess on the ground . . . . . . v 2 36
O Helen, goddess, nymph, perfect, divine! . . . *M. N. Dream* iii 2 137
To call me goddess, nymph, divine and rare, Precious, celestial? . . iii 2 226
Our natural wits too dull to reason of such goddesses . *As Y. Like It* i 2 56
A guide, a goddess, and a sovereign, A counsellor . . . *All's Well* i 1 183
Fortune, she said, was no goddess, that had put such difference betwixt their two estates ; Love no god . . . . i 3 116
Titled goddess ; And worth it, with addition! . . . . . iv 2 2
Good goddess Nature, which hast made it So like to him that got it *W. T.* ii 3 104
Why, he sings 'em over as they were gods or goddesses . . . iv 4 210
Most dearly welcome! And your fair princess,—goddess! . . . v 1 131
And giddy Fortune's furious fickle wheel, That goddess blind *Hen. V.* iii 6 30
Patience herself, what goddess e'er she be, Doth lesser blench at sufferance than I do . . . . *Troi. and Cres.* i 1 27
Had I a sister were a grace, or a daughter a goddess, he should take his choice . . . . i 2 257
Now the fair goddess, Fortune, Fall deep in love with thee! *Coriolanus* i 5 21
To wanton with this queen, This goddess, this Semiramis *T. Andron.* ii 1 22
Thou, nature, art my goddess . . . . *Lear* i 2 1
Hear, nature, hear ; dear goddess, hear! . . . . . . i 4 297
Dear goddess, hear that prayer of the people! . . *Ant. and Cleo.* i 2 73
She In the habiliments of the goddess Isis That day appear'd . . iii 6 17
Gods and goddesses, All the whole synod of them! . . . . iii 10 4
O thou goddess, Thou divine Nature, how thyself thou blazon'st In these two princely boys! . . . . *Cymbeline* iv 2 169
But, soft! no bedfellow!—O gods and goddesses! . . . . . iv 2 295
Celestial Dian, goddess argentine, I will obey thee . . . *Pericles* v 1 251
A maid-child call'd Marina ; who, O goddess, Wears yet thy silver livery v 3 6
Goddess-like. And me, poor lowly maid, Most goddess-like prank'd up *W. Tale* iv 4 10
Undergoes, More goddess-like than wife-like, such assaults *Cymbeline* iii 2 8
She dances As goddess-like to her admired lays . . *Pericles* v Gower 4
Godfather. These earthly godfathers of heaven's lights . *L. L. Lost* i 1 88
And every godfather can give a name . . . . i 1 93
In christening shalt thou have two godfathers . . *Mer. of Venice* iv 1 398
Alack, my lord, that fault is none of yours ; He should, for that, commit your godfathers . . . . *Richard III.* i 1 48
A fair young maid that yet wants baptism, You must be godfather *Hen. VIII.* v 3 163
Here will be father, godfather, and all together . . . . . v 4 39
Godhead. That was the way to make his godhead wax . *L. L. Lost* v 2 10
Why, thy godhead laid apart, Warr'st thou with a woman's heart? *As Y. Like It* iv 3 44
Were your godheads to borrow of men, men would forsake the gods *T. of Athens* iii 6 84
Be content ; Your low-laid son our godhead will uplift . *Cymbeline* v 4 103
God-like. Ay, that is study's god-like recompense . . . *L. L. Lost* i 1 58
You have a noble and a true conceit Of god-like amity . *Mer. of Venice* iii 4 3
With due observance of thy godlike seat . . . *Troi. and Cres.* i 3 31
Gave us not That capability and god-like reason To fust in us unused *Hamlet* iv 4 38
In the rest you said Thou hast been godlike perfect . . *Pericles* v 1 208
Godliness. I warrant you, he will not hear of godliness . . *T. Night* iii 4 135
Godliness. With the little godliness I have, I did full hard forbear him *Othello* i 2 9
Godly. I'll ne'er be drunk whilst I live again, but in honest, civil, godly company . . . . *Mer. Wives* i 1 187
They humbly sue unto your excellence To have a godly peace 1 *Hen. VI.* v 1 5
Fie, for godly shame! . . . . *Troi. and Cres.* ii 2 32
A kind of godly jealousy—Which, I beseech you, call a virtuous sin—Makes me afeard . . . . iv 4 82
Godson. What, did my father's godson seek your life? . . *Lear* ii 1 93
Goer-back. I would they were in Afric both together ; Myself by with a needle, that I might prick The goer-back . . . . *Cymbeline* i 1 169
Goer backward. Would demonstrate them now But goers backward *All's Well* i 2 48
Goer-between. Let all pitiful goers-between be called to the world's end after my name . . . . *Troi. and Cres.* iii 2 208
Goes. Hey, Mountain, hey!—Silver! there it goes, Silver! . *Tempest* iv 1 257
For being ignorant to whom it goes I writ at random . *T. G. of Ver.* ii 1 116
Knew it was Crab, and goes me to the fellow that whips the dogs . iv 4 26
The report goes she has all the rule of her husband's purse *Mer. Wives* i 3 58
The wealth I have waits on my consent, and my consent goes not that way iii 2 79
Her husband goes this morning a-birding . . . . . . iii 5 46
He hath an abstract for the remembrance of such places, and goes to them by his note . . . . iv 2 64
There is an old tale goes . . . . iv 4 28
We shall write to you . . . How it goes with us . . *Meas. for Meas.* i 1 58
Like an o'ergrown lion in a cave, That goes not out to prey . . . i 3 23
The baby beats the nurse, and quite athwart Goes all decorum . . . i 3 31
He that goes in the calf's skin that was killed for the Prodigal *C. of Er.* iv 3 18
Thus goes every one to the world but I, and I am sunburnt *Much Ado* ii 1 330
For shape, for bearing, argument and valour, Goes foremost in report . iii 1 97
Loving goes by haps : Some Cupid kills with arrows, some with traps . iii 1 105
Clap's into 'Light o' love ;' that goes without a burden . . . iii 4 44
Your wit ambles well ; it goes easily . . . . v 1 159
What a pretty thing man is when he goes in his doublet and hose and leaves off his wit! . . . . v 1 203
Now mercy goes to kill, And shooting well is then accounted ill *L. L. Lost* iv 1 24
My lady goes to kill horns . . . . iv 1 113
As she goes, what upward lies The street should see as she walk'd over-head . . . . iv 3 280
You must understand he goes but to see a noise that he heard *M. N. D.* iii 1 93
Puppet? why so? ay, that way goes the game . . . . . . iii 2 289
It goes not forward, doth it?—It is not possible . . . . . iv 2 6
Hanging and wiving goes by destiny . . . . *Mer. of Venice* ii 9 83
Now he goes, With no less presence, but with much more love . . iii 2 53
Thus it goes :—If it do come to pass That any man turn ass *As Y. L. It* ii 5 51
As there is no more plenty in it, it goes much against my stomach . iii 2 21
Who goes there, ha?—Peace, Grumio! it is the rival of my love *T. of S.* i 2 141
Yet oftentimes he goes but mean-apparell'd . . . . . . iii 2 75
Tell me, how goes the world?—A cold world . . . . . . iv 1 36
Who comes here? One that goes with him : I love him for his sake *A. W.* i 1 110
Then my dial goes not true : I took this lark for a bunting . . . ii 5 6
You are not fallen From the report that goes upon your goodness . . v 1 13
Goes as fairly as to say a careful man and a great scholar . *T. Night* iv 2 10
Where goes Cesario?—After him I love . . . . v 1 137
Who is't that goes with me? Beseech your highness, My women may be with me . . . . *W. Tale* ii 1 116
Which is enough, I'll warrant, As this world goes, to pass for honest . ii 3 72
Howe'er the business goes, you have made fault I' the boldness of your speech . . . . iii 2 218
A merry heart goes all the day, Your sad tires in a mile-a . . . iv 3 134
Goes to the tune of 'Two maids wooing a man' . . . . . iv 4 295
Lest men should say 'Look, where three-farthings goes!' . . *K. John* i 1 143
You are the hare of whom the proverb goes, Whose valour plucks dead lions by the beard . . . . ii 1 137
How goes all in France?—From France to England . . . . iv 2 109
How goes the day with us? O, tell me, Hubert.—Badly, I fear . . v 3 1
Off goes his bonnet to an oyster-wench . . . . . *Richard II.* i 4 31
And crossly to thy good all fortune goes . . . . ii 4 24
Then whither he goes, thither let me go . . . . v 1 85
A fool go with thy soul, whither it goes! . . . . 1 *Hen. IV.* v 3 22
Other offenders we will pause upon. How goes the field? . . . v 5 16
What's he that goes there?—Falstaff, an 't please your lordship 2 *Hen. IV.* i 2 66
For all the soil of the achievement goes With me into the earth . . iv 5 190
The devilish cannon touches, And down goes all before them *Hen. V.* iii Prol. 34
Now and then goes to the wars, to grace himself at his return into London iii 6 71
For forth he goes and visits all his host, Bids them good morrow . iv Prol. 32
Who goes there?—A friend.—Under what captain serve you? . . iv 1 93
What means he now? Go ask him whither he goes . . 1 *Hen. VI.* ii 3 28
When Gloucester says the word, King Henry goes . . . . . iii 1 184
There goes the Talbot, with his colours spread . . . . . iii 3 31
And thus he goes, As did the youthful Paris once to Greece . . . v 5 103
A thousand crowns, or else lay down your head.—And so much shall you give, or off goes yours . . . . 2 *Hen. VI.* iv 1 17
Who goes there?—Stay, or thou diest! . . . . . 3 *Hen. VI.* iv 3 26
How now, sirrah! how goes the world with thee? . . . *Richard III.* iii 2 98
If I revolt, off goes young George's head . . . . iv 5 4
This candle burns not clear : 'tis I must snuff it ; Then out it goes *Hen. VIII.* iii 2 97
What's become of Katharine, The princess dowager? how goes her business? . . . . iv 1 23
Tell me how he died . . . —Well, the voice goes, madam . . . iv 2 11
The fruit she goes with I pray for heartily, that it may find Good time v 1 20
He was harness'd light, And to the field goes he . . *Troi. and Cres.* i 2 9
What was his cause of anger?—The noise goes, this . . . . i 2 12
How he looks, and how he goes! O admirable youth! . . . . i 2 254
And this neglection of degree it is That by a pace goes backward . . i 3 128
For honour travels in a strait so narrow, Where one but goes abreast . iii 3 155
And in what fashion . . . he goes Upon this present action . *Coriolanus* i 1 282
Forth he goes, Like to a harvest-man that's task'd to mow . . . i 3 38
Bring me word thither How the world goes, that to the pace of it I may spur on my journey . . . . i 10 32
But when goes this forward?—To-morrow ; to-day ; presently . . iv 5 228
Why, there it goes : God give his lordship joy! . . . *T. Andron.* iv 3 76
That shows thee a weak slave ; for the weakest goes to the wall *R. and J.* i 1 18
Love goes toward love, as schoolboys from their books . . . . ii 2 157
He that cannot lick his fingers goes not with me . . . . . iv 2 8
How goes the world?—It wears, sir, as it grows . . . *T. of Athens* i 1 2
How goes the world, that I am thus encounter'd With clamorous demands? . . . . ii 2 37
What shall defend the interim? and at length How goes our reckoning? ii 2 159

Goes. If it be a just and true report that goes of his having *T. of Athens* v 1 18
And I will set this foot of mine as far As who goes farthest . *J. Cæsar* i 3 120
Thou seest the world, Volumnius, how it goes: Our enemies have beat us to the pit . . . . v 5 22
Duncan comes here to-night.—And when goes hence?—To-morrow, as he purposes . . . . *Macbeth* i 5 60
How goes the night, boy?—The moon is down; I have not heard the clock . . . . ii 1 1
Goes the king hence to-day?—He does: he did appoint so . . ii 3 58
How goes the world, sir, now?—Why, see you not? . . . . ii 4 21
Goes Fleance with you?—Ay, my good lord: our time does call upon's iii 1 36
This tune goes manly . . . . iv 3 235
Who is't that can inform me?—That can I; At least, the whisper goes so *Hamlet* i 1 80
And with solemn march Goes slow and stately by them . . . i 2 202
Which is no further Than the main voice of Denmark goes withal . i 3 28
He took me by the wrist and held me hard; Then goes he to the length of all his arm . . . . ii 1 88
To be honest, as this world goes, is to be one man picked out of ten thousand . . . . ii 2 179
Indeed it goes so heavily with my disposition . . . . . ii 2 309
We will fetters put upon this fear, Which now goes too free-footed . iii 3 26
And so he goes to heaven; And so am I revenged . . . . iii 3 74
And that his soul may be as damn'd and black As hell, whereto it goes iii 3 95
Look, where he goes, even now, out at the portal! . . . . iii 4 136
Goes it against the main of Poland, sir, Or for some frontier? . iv 4 15
If the man go to this water, and drown himself, it is, will he, nill he, he goes . . . . v 1 19
But goes thy heart with this?—Ay, good my lord . . . *Lear* i 1 107
Have a continent forbearance till the speed of his rage goes slower . i 2 183
Yet you see how this world goes.—I see it feelingly . . . iv 6 151
A man may see how this world goes with no eyes . . . iv 6 154
'Tis the curse of service, Preferment goes by letter and affection *Othello* i 1 36
'Faith, the cry goes that you shall marry her.—Prithee, say true . iv 1 127
Like to a vagabond flag upon the stream, Goes to and back . *A. and C.* i 4 46
Being barber'd ten times o'er, goes to the feast . . . ii 2 229
He goes hence frowning: but it honours us That we have given him cause *Cymbeline* iii 5 18
Lucius hath wrote already to the emperor How it goes here . . iii 5 22
Your bride goes to that with shame which is her way to go with warrant *Pericles* iv 2 138
Goes about. And see how he goes about to abuse me! *Meas. for Meas.* iii 2 215
Goes abroad. I hope your lordship goes abroad by advice . 2 *Hen. IV.* i 2 109
Goes against. Their villany goes against my weak stomach . *Hen. V.* iii 2 56
Goes along. Old Helicanus goes along behind . . . *Pericles* iv 4 16
Goes away. He goes away in a cloud: call him, call him *T. of Athens* iii 4 42
Goes before. He goes before me and still dares me on . *M. N. Dream* iii 2 413
There's a girl goes before the priest . . . . *As Y. Like It* iv 1 140
Do not you follow the young Lord Paris?—Ay, sir, when he goes before me.—You depend upon him, I mean? . . *Troi. and Cres.* iii 1 3
Goes down. How goes the night, boy?—The moon is down; I have not heard the clock.—And she goes down at twelve *Macbeth* ii 1 3
Goes even. Were you a woman, as the rest goes even, I should my tears let fall upon your cheek . . . . . *T. Night* v 1 246
Goes false. The story then goes false, you threw it him . *All's Well* v 3 229
Goes forth. He goes forth gallantly . . . *Ant. and Cleo.* iv 4 36
Goes hard. When a man's servant shall play the cur with him, look you, it goes hard . . . . *T. G. of Ver.* iv 4 2
My life, sir! how, I pray? for that goes hard . . *T. of Shrew* iv 2 80
The world goes hard When Clifford cannot spare his friends an oath 3 *Hen. VI.* ii 6 77
Goes it. How goes it now, sir? this news which is called true is so like an old tale . . . . *W. Tale* v 2 29
Be not a niggard of your speech: how goes't? . . . *Macbeth* iv 3 180
How goes it now? he looks gentler than he did . . *Othello* iv 3 11
How goes it with my brave Mark Antony? . . . *Ant. and Cleo.* i 5 38
How goes it here?—All dead . . . . v 2 332
Goes loose. How dangerous is it that this man goes loose! . *Hamlet* iv 3 2
Goes off and on. This woman's an easy glove, my lord; she goes off and on at pleasure . . . . *All's Well* v 3 279
Goes on. It goes on, I see, As my soul prompts it . . *Tempest* i 2 419
With the same 'haviour that your passion bears Goes on my master's grief . . . . *T. Night* iii 4 227
Goes on crutches. Time goes on crutches till love have all his rites *Much Ado* ii 1 372
Goes out. Welcome ever smiles, And farewell goes out sighing *T. and C.* iii 3 169
Goes right. Alack, when once our grace we have forgot, Nothing goes right . . . . *Meas. for Meas.* iv 4 37
Goes to bed. The marigold, that goes to bed wi' the sun *W. Tale* iv 4 105
Pleased with this dainty bait, thus goes to bed . *Troi. and Cres.* v 8 20
Goes to it. The wren goes to't, and the small gilded fly Does lecher in my sight . . . . *Lear* iv 6 114
The fitchew, nor the soiled horse, goes to't With a more riotous appetite iv 6 124
Goes to rest. Alarbus goes to rest; and we survive . . *T. Andron.* i 1 133
Goes up and down like a gentleman: I remember his name . *Much Ado* iii 3 134
Ajax goes up and down the field, asking for himself . *Troi. and Cres.* iii 3 244
In all shapes that man goes up and down in from fourscore to thirteen, this spirit walks in . . . . *T. of Athens* ii 2 119
When think you that the sword goes up again? . . . *J. Cæsar* v 1 52
But the great one that goes up the hill, let him draw thee after . *Lear* ii 4 75
Goes upright. And time Goes upright with his carriage . . *Tempest* v 1 3
Goes well. The third he caper'd, and cried, 'All goes well' . *L. L. Lost* v 2 113
Yet all goes well, yet all our joints are whole . . 1 *Hen. IV.* iv 1 83
All hitherto goes well; The common people by numbers swarm to us 3 *Hen. VI.* iv 2 1
Here do we make his friends Blush that the world goes well *Coriolanus* iv 6 5
Goes worse. And all goes worse than I have power to tell *Richard II.* iii 2 120
Goest about to apply a moral medicine to a mortifying mischief *Much Ado* i 3 12
Whither goest thou?—Marry, sir, to bid my old master the Jew to sup to-night with my new master . . . . . *Mer. of Venice* ii 4 16
Come, go with me; peruse this as thou goest . . . . ii 4 39
Nay, now thou goest from Fortune's office to Nature's . *As Y. Like It* i 2 43
Me too, let me go thither.—Or thou goest to the grange or mill *W. Tale* iv 4 309
What thy soul holds dear, imagine it To lie that way thou go'st *Rich. II.* i 3 287
Thou lovest the flesh, And ne'er throughout the year to church thou go'st Except it be to pray against thy foes . . 1 *Hen. VI.* i 1 42
Why stand'st thou still, and go'st not to the duke? . *Richard III.* iv 4 445
Why the great toe?—For that, being one o' the lowest, basest, poorest, Of this most wise rebellion, thou go'st foremost . . *Coriolanus* i 1 162
Lend less than thou owest, Ride more than thou goest . . *Lear* i 4 134

Goest. Fellow, where goest?—Is it a beggar-man?—Madman and beggar too . . . . *Lear* iv 1 31
What, goest thou back? thou shalt Go back, I warrant thee *Ant. and Cleo.* v 2 155
Persever in that clear way thou goest, And the gods strengthen thee! *Pericles* iv 6 113
Gogs-wouns. 'Ay, by gogs-wouns,' quoth he . . . *T. of Shrew* iii 2 162
Going. The sound is going away; let's follow it . . *Tempest* iii 2 157
You chid at Sir Proteus for going ungartered . . . *T. G. of Ver.* ii 1 79
Am going with Sir Proteus to the Imperial's court . . . . ii 3 4
Letters to my friends, And I am going to deliver them . . . . iii 1 54
Thou hast stayed so long that going will scarce serve the turn . . iii 1 388
My daughter takes his going grievously . . . . iii 2 14
Trust me, I was going to your house.—And, trust me, I was coming to you . . . . *Mer. Wives* ii 1 34
And now she's going to my wife, and Falstaff's boy with her . . iii 2 36
Throw foul linen upon him, as if it were going to bucking . . iii 3 140
The duke himself will be to-morrow at court, and they are going to meet him . . . . iv 3 3
I am that way going to temptation, Where prayers cross *Meas. for Meas.* ii 2 158
As I hear, must die to-morrow, And I am going with instruction to him ii 3 38
I am now going to resolve him . . . . iii 1 194
Art going to prison, Pompey?—Yes, faith, sir.—Why, 'tis not amiss . iii 2 63
I am going to visit the prisoner. Fare you well . . . . iii 2 272
One that thinks a man always going to bed . . *Com. of Errors* iv 3 32
A woman, that is like a German clock, Still a-repairing, ever out of frame, And never going aright . . . . . *L. L. Lost* iii 1 194
I remember the style.—Else your memory is bad, going o'er it erewhile iv 1 99
Do this expediently and turn him going . . . *As Y. Like It* iii 1 18
Till you met your wife's wit going to your neighbour's bed . . iv 1 170
Trow you whither I am going? . . . . *T. of Shrew* i 2 165
And I in going, madam, weep o'er my father's death anew . *All's Well* i 1 3
I am going, forsooth: the business is for Helen to come hither . . i 3 100
I was in that credit with them at that time that I knew of their going to bed . . . . v 3 263
I will waylay thee going home . . . . *T. Night* iii 4 176
But I, Though you would seek to unsphere the stars with oaths, Should yet say 'Sir, no going' . . . . *W. Tale* i 2 49
I have a kinsman not past three quarters of a mile hence, unto whom I was going . . . . iv 3 86
Is there not milking-time, when you are going to bed, or kiln-hole? . iv 4 247
Now were I happy, if His going I could frame to serve my turn . . iv 4 520
The kings and the princes, our kindred, are going to see the queen's picture . . . . v 2 187
And others more, going to seek the grave Of Arthur . . *K. John* iv 2 164
There are pilgrims going to Canterbury with rich offerings . 1 *Hen. IV.* i 2 140
If I tarry at home and go not, I'll hang you for going . . . i 2 150
'Tis going to the king's exchequer.—You lie, ye rogue; 'tis going to the king's tavern . . . . ii 2 58
Is now going with some charge to the Lord John of Lancaster 2 *Hen. IV.* i 2 72
I hear you are going with Lord John of Lancaster . . . . i 2 228
I am undone by his going; I warrant you, he's an infinitive thing upon my score . . . . ii 1 25
My honour is at pawn; And, but my going, nothing can redeem it . ii 3 8
Thou art going to the wars; and whether I shall ever see thee again or no, there is nobody cares . . . . ii 4 71
Stout resolved mates! Are you now going to dispatch this deed? *Richard III.* i 3 341
'Tis better with me now Than when I met thee last where now we meet: Then was I going prisoner to the Tower . . . . . iii 2 102
Why the devil, Upon this French going out, took he upon him, Without the privity o' the king, to appoint Who should attend on him? *Hen. VIII.* i 1 73
I am glad they are going, For, sure, there's no converting of 'em . i 3 42
Whither were you a-going?—To the cardinal's: Your lordship is a guest too . . . . i 3 50
'Tis not well. She's going away.—Call her again . . . . ii 4 124
Lady Anne . . . This day was view'd in open as his queen, Going to chapel iii 2 405
Mark her eyes!—She is going, wench: pray, pray . . . . iv 2 99
It passed.—So let it now; for it has been a great while going by *T. and C.* i 2 184
Nor, by my will, assubjugate his merit, As amply titled as Achilles is, By going to Achilles . . . . ii 3 204
Nor doth the eye itself, That most pure spirit of sense, behold itself, Not going from itself . . . . iii 3 107
Mother, I am going to the market-place; Chide me no more *Coriolanus* iii 2 131
Look, I am going: Commend me to my wife . . . . . . iii 2 134
Our tradesmen singing in their shops and going About their functions iv 6 8
The nobles in great earnestness are going All to the senate-house . iv 6 57
Coming and going with thy honey breath . . . . *T. Andron.* ii 4 25
I am going with my pigeons to the tribunal plebs . . . . iv 3 91
We mean well in going to this mask; But 'tis no wit to go *Rom. and Jul.* i 4 48
What's he that now is going out of door? . . . . . . i 5 132
Going to find a bare-foot brother out, One of our order . . . v 2 5
And threaten'd me with death, going in the vault, If I departed not . v 3 276
Whither art going?—To knock out an honest Athenian's brains *T. of A.* i 1 191
Thou art going to Lord Timon's feast? . . . . i 1 269
I shall unfold to thee, as we are going To whom it must be done *J. Cæsar* ii 1 330
And you shall speak In the same pulpit whereto I am going . . iii 1 250
What is your name?—Whither are you going?—Where do you dwell? . iii 3 6
What is my name? Whither am I going? Where do I dwell? . . iii 3 15
Proceed; directly.—Directly, I am going to Cæsar's funeral . . iii 3 22
Pluck but his name out of his heart, and turn him going . . . iii 3 39
Thou marshall'st me the way that I was going . . . *Macbeth* ii 1 42
Stand not upon the order of your going, But go at once . . . iii 4 119
For your intent In going back to school in Wittenberg, It is most retrograde to our desire . . . . *Hamlet* i 2 113
He's going to his mother's closet: Behind the arras I'll convey myself iii 3 27
Since my young lady's going into France, sir, the fool hath much pined away . . . . *Lear* i 4 79
Then comes the time, who lives to see't, That going shall be used with feet . . . . iii 2 94
Advise the duke, where you are going, to a most festinate preparation iii 7 10
Slain by his servant, going to put out The other eye of Gloucester . iv 2 71
Bid me farewell, and let me hear thee going . . . . . iv 6 31
Men must endure Their going hence, even as their coming hither . v 2 10
Be it as you shall privately determine, Either for her stay or going *Othello* i 3 277
I was coming to your house.—And I was going to your lodging . . iii 4 172
If you will watch his going thence, which I will fashion . . iv 2 242
Whose quality, going on, The sides o' the world may danger *A. and C.* i 2 198
Pray you, seek no colour for your going, But bid farewell, and go . i 3 32
When you sued staying, Then was the time for words: no going then . i 3 34

Going. And that which most with you should safe my going, Is Fulvia's death *Ant. and Cleo.* i 3 55
Provide your going ; Choose your own company iii 4 36
The soul and body rive not more in parting Than greatness going off iv 13 6
Now my spirit is going ; I can no more iv 15 58
I was going, sir, To give him welcome *Cymbeline* i 6 54
To whom being going, almost spent with hunger, I am fall'n in this offence iii 6 63
To the mountains ; there secure us. To the king's party there's no going iv 4 9
Farewell ; you're angry.—Still going? v 3 64
There are none want eyes to direct them the way I am going v 4 193
With dead cheeks advise thee to desist For going on death's net *Pericles* i 1 40
There's no going but by their consent iv 6 208

Gold. Set it down With gold on lasting pillars *Tempest* v 1 208
The water nectar and the rocks pure gold *T. G. of Ver.* ii 4 171
Seven hundred pounds of moneys, and gold and silver *Mer. Wives* i 1 52
She is a region in Guiana, all gold and bounty i 3 76
His dove will prove, his gold will hold, And his soft couch defile i 3 107
All musk, and so rushling, I warrant you, in silk and gold ii 2 69
Wooing thee, I found thee of more value Than stamps in gold iii 4 16
I'll give thee A hundred pound in gold more than your loss iv 6 5
Not with fond shekels of the tested gold *Meas. for Meas.* ii 2 149
Where is the gold I gave in charge to thee?—To me, sir? why, you gave no gold to me.—Come on, sir knave *Com. of Errors* i 2 70
When I desired him to come home to dinner, He ask'd me for a thousand marks in gold : 'Tis dinner-time,' quoth I ; 'My gold!' quoth he ii 1 61
The gold bides still, That others touch, and often touching will Wear gold ii 1 110
The gold I gave to Dromio is laid up Safe at the Centaur ii 2 1
You know no Centaur? you received no gold? ii 2 9
You sent me hence, Home to the Centaur, with the gold you gave me ii 2 16
Villain, thou didst deny the gold's receipt And told'st me of a mistress ii 2 17
I beat him And charged him with a thousand marks in gold iii 1 8
To the utmost carat, The fineness of the gold and chargeful fashion iv 1 29
Master, here's the gold you sent me for iv 3 12
What gold is this? what Adam dost thou mean? iv 3 15
Wherefore didst thou lock me forth to-day? And why dost thou deny the bag of gold?—I did not, gentle husband, lock thee forth.—And, gentle master, I received no gold iv 4 99
You saw they speak us fair, give us gold iv 4 157
Cloth o' gold, and cuts, and laced with silver, set with pearls *Much Ado* iii 4 19
Fear not, man : we'll tip thy horns with gold v 4 44
One, her hairs were gold, crystal the other's eyes *L. L. Lost* iv 3 142
The cowslips tall her pensioners be : In their gold coats spots you see ; Those be rubies, fairy favours *M. N. Dream* ii 1 11
Turns into yellow gold his salt green streams iii 2 393
The lottery, that he hath devised in these three chests of gold, silver and lead *Mer. of Venice* i 2 33
Or is your gold and silver ewes and rams?—I cannot tell i 3 96
What gold and jewels she is furnish'd with ii 4 32
The first, of gold, who this inscription bears ii 7 4
Let's see once more this saying graved in gold ii 7 36
Shall I think in silver she's immured, Being ten times undervalued to tried gold? ii 7 53
Never so rich a gem Was set in worse than gold ii 7 55
They have in England A coin that bears the figure of an angel Stamped in gold ii 7 57
All that glisters is not gold ; Often have you heard that told ii 7 65
Fortune now To my heart's hope! Gold ; silver ; and base lead ii 9 20
Thou stickest a dagger in me : I shall never see my gold again iii 1 116
Thou gaudy gold, Hard food for Midas, I will none of thee iii 2 101
You shall have gold To pay the petty debt twenty times over iii 2 308
Look how the floor of heaven Is thick inlaid with patines of bright gold v 1 59
What's the matter?—About a hoop of gold, a paltry ring v 1 147
Beauty provoketh thieves sooner than gold *As Y. Like It* i 3 112
Here is the gold ; All this I give you. Let me be your servant ii 3 45
Question yond man If he for gold will give us any food ii 4 65
If that love or gold Can in this desert place buy entertainment, Bring us where we may rest ourselves and feed ii 4 71
I will your very faithful feeder be And buy it with your gold ii 4 100
Their harness studded all with gold and pearl *T. of Shrew* Ind. 2 44
Why, give him gold enough and marry him to a puppet or an aglet-baby i 2 78
Were my state far worser than it is, I would not wed her for a mine of gold.—Hortensio, peace! thou know'st not gold's effect i 2 92
My house within the city Is richly furnished with plate and gold ii 1 349
Cushions boss'd with pearl, Valance of Venice gold in needlework ii 1 356
Why, sir, what 'cerns it you if I wear pearl and gold? v 1 78
Take this purse of gold, And let me buy your friendly help *All's Well* iii 7 14
Not possible, with well-weighing sums of gold, to corrupt him to a revolt iv 3 204
Dian, the count's a fool, and full of gold iv 3 238
When he swears oaths, bid him drop gold, and take it iv 3 252
I need not to ask you if gold will corrupt him to revolt iv 3 309
For saying so, there's gold *T. Night* i 2 18
Thou shalt not be the worse for me : there's gold v 1 31
Gold! all gold!—This is fairy gold, boy, and 'twill prove so *W. Tale* iii 3 126
Close with him, give him gold ; and though authority be a stubborn bear, yet he is oft led by the nose with gold iv 4 831
An't please you, sir, to undertake the business for us, here is that gold I have iv 4 837
I am courted now with a double occasion, gold and a means to do the prince my master good iv 4 865
Plays the alchemist, Turning with splendour of his precious eye The meagre cloddy earth to glittering gold *K. John* iii 1 80
By the merit of vile gold, dross, dust, Purchase corrupted pardon of a man iii 1 165
Bell, book, and candle shall not drive me back, When gold and silver becks me to come on iii 3 13
To gild refined gold, to paint the lily, To throw a perfume on the violet iv 2 11
When they shall know what men are rich, They shall subscribe them for large sums of gold *Richard II.* i 4 50
And he shall spend mine honour with his shame, As thriftless sons their scraping fathers' gold v 3 69
A purse of gold most resolutely snatched on Monday night and most dissolutely spent on Tuesday morning *1 Hen. IV.* i 2 38
A franklin in the wild of Kent hath brought three hundred marks with him in gold ii 1 61
Gallants, lads, boys, hearts of gold ii 4 307
Never call a true piece of gold a counterfeit : thou art essentially mad ii 4 540

Gold. I will inset you neither in gold nor silver, but in vile apparel *2 Hen. IV.* i 2 20
Why, that's well said ; a good heart's worth gold ii 4 35
And learning a mere hoard of gold kept by a devil iv 3 125
A hoop of gold to bind thy brothers in iv 4 43
How quickly nature falls into revolt When gold becomes her object! iv 5 67
They have engross'd and piled up The canker'd heaps of strange-achieved gold iv 5 72
Therefore, thou best of gold art worst of gold iv 5 161
The singing masons building roofs of gold *Hen. V.* i 2 198
That almost mightst have coin'd me into gold ii 2 98
For me, the gold of France did not seduce ; Although I did admit it as a motive ii 2 155
A heart of gold, A lad of life, an imp of fame ; Of parents good iv 1 44
The crown imperial, The intertissued robe of gold and pearl iv 1 279
I am not covetous for gold, Nor care I who doth feed upon my cost iv 3 24
Instead of gold, we'll offer up our arms ; Since arms avail not now *1 Hen. VI.* i 1 46
And doth deserve a coronet of gold iii 3 89
I never read but England's kings have had Large sums of gold and dowries with their wives *2 Hen. VI.* i 1 129
Put forth thy hand, reach at the glorious gold. What, is't too short? i 2 11
Hume must make merry with the duchess' gold i 2 87
Dame Eleanor gives gold to bring the witch : Gold cannot come amiss, were she a devil. Yet have I gold flies from another coast i 2 91
Sort how it will, I shall have gold for all i 2 107
Are my chests fill'd up with extorted gold? Is my apparel sumptuous? iv 7 105
This hand was made to handle nought but gold v 1 7
That gold must round engirt these brows of mine v 1 99
Give me thy gold, if thou hast any gold ; For I have bought it with an hundred blows *3 Hen. VI.* ii 5 80
Wedges of gold, great anchors, heaps of pearl *Richard III.* i 4 26
It [conscience] made me once restore a purse of gold that I found i 4 144
Now do I play the touch, To try if thou be current gold indeed iv 2 9
Know'st thou not any whom corrupting gold Would tempt? iv 2 34
Gold were as good as twenty orators, And will, no doubt, tempt him to any thing.—What is his name? iv 2 38
The French, All clinquant, all in gold, like heathen gods *Hen. VIII.* i 1 19
When the way was made, And paved with gold i 1 188
My surveyor is false ; the o'er-great cardinal Hath show'd him gold i 1 223
Tell him from me I'll hide my silver beard in a gold beaver *Tr. and Cr.* i 3 296
Is that a wonder? The providence that's in a watchful state Knows almost every grain of Plutus' gold iii 3 197
I would not have been so fidiused for all the chests in Corioli, and the gold that's in them *Coriolanus* ii 1 145
I tell you, he does sit in gold, his eye Red as 'twould burn Rome v 1 63
I will be bright, and shine in pearl and gold *T. Andron.* ii 1 19
I would not for a million of gold The cause were known to them ii 1 49
He that had wit would think that I had none, To bury so much gold under a tree . . . Let him that thinks of me so abjectly Know that this gold must coin a stratagem ii 3 2
And so repose, sweet gold, for their unrest ii 3 8
My gracious lord, here is the bag of gold ii 3 280
Go pack with him, and give the mother gold iv 2 155
I wrote the letter that thy father found And hid the gold v 1 107
Nor ope her lap to saint-seducing gold *Rom. and Jul.* i 1 220
That book in many's eyes doth share the glory, That in gold clasps locks in the golden story i 3 92
It is 'music with her silver sound,' because musicians have no gold for sounding iv 5 143
There is thy gold, worse poison to men's souls, Doing more murders in this loathsome world, Than these poor compounds that thou mayst not sell v 1 80
I will raise her statue in pure gold v 3 299
He pours it out ; Plutus, the god of gold, Is but his steward *T. of Athens* i 1 287
If I want gold, steal but a beggar's dog, And give it Timon, why, the dog coins gold ii 1 5
Poor rogues, and usurers' men! bawds between gold and want! ii 2 61
Whilst I have gold, I'll be his steward still iv 2 50
What is here? Gold? yellow, glittering, precious gold? iv 3 26
I have but little gold of late, brave Timon, The want whereof doth daily make revolt In my penurious band iv 3 90
Here is some gold for thee.—Keep it, I cannot eat it iv 3 100
Put up thy gold : go on,—here's gold,—go on ; Be as a planetary plague iv 3 107
There's gold to pay thy soldiers : Make large confusion iv 3 126
Hast thou gold yet? I'll take the gold thou givest me, Not all thy counsel iv 3 129
Give us some gold, good Timon : hast thou more? iv 3 132
More gold : what then? Believe't, that we'll do any thing for gold iv 3 150
There's more gold : Do you damn others, and let this damn you! iv 3 164
Tell them there I have gold ; look, so I have iv 3 289
Here is no use for gold.—The best and truest ; For here it sleeps, and does no hired harm iv 3 290
I'll say thou'st gold : Thou wilt be throng'd to shortly iv 3 394
Where should he have this gold? It is some poor fragment, some slender ort of his remainder iv 3 399
The mere want of gold, and the falling-from of his friends, drove him into this melancholy iv 3 401
Rascal thieves, Here's gold. Go, suck the subtle blood o' the grape iv 3 432
Love not yourselves : away, Rob one another. There's more gold iv 3 448
Steal no less for this I give you ; and gold confound you howsoe'er! iv 3 452
Does the rumour hold for true, that he's so full of gold? v 1 4
Timandra had gold of him : he likewise enriched poor straggling soldiers v 1 6
Wilt thou whip thine own faults in other men? Do so, I have gold for thee v 1 41
What a god's gold, That he is worshipp'd in a baser temple Than where swine feed! 'Tis thou that rigg'st the bark v 1 50
Ye're honest men : ye've heard that I have gold ; I am sure you have : speak truth v 1 79
I'll give you gold, Rid me these villains from your companies v 1 103
Confound them by some course, and come to me, I'll give you gold enough v 1 107
Hence, pack! there's gold ; you came for gold, ye slaves v 1 115
You are an alchemist ; make gold of that. Out, rascal dogs! v 1 117
He shall but bear them as the ass bears gold, To groan and sweat *J. C.* iv 1 21
To sell and mart your offices for gold To undeservers iv 3 11
I did send to you For certain sums of gold, which you denied me iv 3 70
I did send To you for gold to pay my legions, Which you denied me iv 3 76
A heart Dearer than Plutus' mine, richer than gold iv 3 102
I, that denied thee gold, will give my heart iv 3 104

Gold. Pray God, your voice, like a piece of uncurrent gold, be not cracked *Hamlet* ii 2 448
When usurers tell their gold i' the field . . . . . *Lear* iii 2 89
Plate sin with gold, And the strong lance of justice hurtless breaks . iv 6 169
Never lack'd gold and yet went never gay, Fled from her wish *Othello* ii 1 151
Prithee, keep up thy quillets. There's a poor piece of gold for thee . iii 1 26
He calls me to a restitution large Of gold and jewels that I bobb'd from him . v 1 16
The poop was beaten gold; Purple the sails . . . *Ant. and Cleo.* ii 2 197
There is gold, and here My bluest veins to kiss . . . ii 5 28
First, madam, he is well.—Why, there's more gold. . . . ii 5 31
The gold I give thee will I melt and pour Down thy ill-uttering throat. ii 5 34
I'll set thee in a shower of gold, and hail Rich pearls upon thee . . ii 5 45
There's gold for thee. Thou must not take my former sharpness ill . iii 3 37
On a tribunal silver'd, Cleopatra and himself in chairs of gold . iii 6 4
I have a ship Laden with gold; take that, divide it; fly. . . . iii 11 5
How wouldst thou have paid My better service, when my turpitude Thou dost so crown with gold! . . . . . iv 6 34
I'll give thee, friend, An armour all of gold; it was a king's . . iv 8 27
I will wage against your gold, gold to it . . . . *Cymbeline* i 4 144
She your jewel, this your jewel, and my gold are yours . . i 4 166
I will fetch my gold and have our two wagers recorded . . . i 4 180
Diseased ventures That play with all infirmities for gold . . i 6 124
What If I do line one of their hands? 'Tis gold Which buys admittance ii 3 72
'Tis gold Which makes the true man kill'd and saves the thief . . ii 3 75
What Can it [gold] not do and undo? . . . . . ii 3 78
There is gold for you; Sell me your good report . . . . ii 3 87
If I had lost it, I should have lost the worth of it in gold . . ii 4 42
I have stol'n nought, nor would not, though I had found Gold strew'd i' the floor . . . . . iii 6 50
All gold and silver rather turn to dirt! As 'tis no better reckon'd, but of those Who worship dirty gods . . . iii 6 54
Wager'd with him Pieces of gold 'gainst this which then he wore . . v 5 183
Here's poison, and here's gold; We hate the prince of Tyre *Pericles* i 1 155
An hand environed with clouds, Holding out gold that's by the touch-stone tried . . . . . ii 2 37
If the sea's stomach be o'ercharged with gold, 'Tis a good constraint of fortune it belches upon us . . . . iii 2 54
Her eyelids . . . Begin to part their fringes of bright gold . . iii 2 101
Will you use him kindly? He will line your apron with gold . . iv 6 64
Here's gold for thee: Persever in that clear way thou goest . . iv 6 112
Let us beseech you That for our gold we may provision have. . v 1 56
And give you gold for such provision As our intents will need . . v 1 258
Gold-bound. Thy hair, Thou other gold-bound brow, is like the first. A third is like the former . . . *Macbeth* iv 1 114
Golden. I would with such perfection govern, sir, To excel the golden age . . . . . *Tempest* ii 1 168
Whose golden touch could soften steel and stones . . *T. G. of Ver.* iii 2 79
Sail like my pinnace to these golden shores . . *Mer. Wives* i 3 89
Spread o'er the silver waves thy golden hairs . . *Com. of Errors* iii 2 48
I see a man here needs not live by shifts, When in the streets he meets such golden gifts . . . . iii 2 188
To see the fish Cut with her golden oars the silver stream . *Much Ado* iii 1 27
But, for the elegancy, facility, and golden cadence of poesy, caret *L. L. Lost* iv 2 126
So sweet a kiss the golden sun gives not To those fresh morning drops. iv 3 26
Let me not die your debtor, My red dominical, my golden letter . v 2 44
By Cupid's strongest bow, By his best arrow with the golden head *M. N. Dream* i 1 170
By thy gracious, golden, glittering gleams . . . . v 1 279
A golden mind stoops not to shows of dross . . . *Mer. of Venice* ii 7 20
But here an angel in a golden bed Lies all within . . . ii 7 58
What says the golden chest? ha! let me see . . . . ii 9 23
Those crisped snaky golden locks Which make such wanton gambols with the wind . . . . . iii 2 92
A golden mesh to entrap the hearts of men . . . . iii 2 122
And fleet the time carelessly, as they did in the golden world *As Y. L. It* i 1 125
With silken coats and caps and golden rings, With ruffs. *T. of Shrew* iv 3 55
How will she love, when the rich golden shaft Hath kill'd the flock of all affections else That live in her! . . . . *T. Night* i 1 35
His counsel now might do me golden service . . . . iv 3 8
When that is known and golden time convents, A solemn combination shall be made Of our dear souls . . . . . v 1 391
And the fire-robed god, Golden Apollo, a poor humble swain . *W. Tale* iv 4 30
Golden quoifs and stomachers, For my lads to give their dears . iv 4 226
And with her [Fortune's] golden hand hath pluck'd on France *K. John* iii 1 57
What hath it done, That it in golden letters should be set? . . iii 1 85
And embrace His golden uncontroll'd enfranchisement . . *Richard II.* i 3 90
His golden beams to you here lent Shall point on me and gild my banishment . . . . . i 3 146
To lift shrewd steel against our golden crown . . . . iii 2 59
Now is this golden crown like a deep well . . . . iv 1 184
Tell me, sweet lord, what is't that takes from thee Thy stomach, pleasure and thy golden sleep? . . . . *1 Hen. IV.* ii 3 44
Thy golden sceptre for a leaden dagger . . . . . ii 4 419
The hour before the heavenly-harness'd team Begins his golden progress iii 1 222
Glittering in golden coats, like images . . . . . iv 1 100
Pages follow'd him Even at the heels in golden multitudes . . iv 3 73
O polish'd perturbation! golden care! That keep'st the ports of slumber open wide To many a watchful night! . . . *2 Hen. IV.* iv 5 23
A sleep That from this golden rigol hath divorced So many English kings iv 5 36
Tidings do I bring and lucky joys And golden times and happy news . v 3 100
A foutre for the world and worldlings base! I speak of Africa and golden joys . . . . . . v 3 104
And from his coffers Received the golden earnest of our death *Hen. V.* ii 2 169
Standing, Up in the air, crown'd with the golden sun . . ii 4 58
Let us banquet royally, After this golden day of victory . *1 Hen. VI.* i 6 31
To put a golden sceptre in thy hand And set a precious crown upon thy head . . . . . . v 3 118
Set this diamond safe In golden palaces, as it becomes . . . v 3 170
That's the golden mark I seek to hit . . . *2 Hen. VI.* i 1 243
The golden circuit on my head, Like to the glorious sun's transparent beams . . . . . . iii 1 352
See how the morning opes her golden gates, And takes her farewell of the glorious sun! . . . . . *3 Hen. VI.* ii 1 21
His viands sparkling in a golden cup, His body couched in a curious bed ii 5 52
To cross me from the golden time I look for . . . . iii 2 127
And more unlikely Than to accomplish twenty golden crowns! . . iii 2 152
I was, I must confess, Great Albion's queen in former golden days . iii 3 7
That cropp'd the golden prime of this sweet prince. . *Richard III.* i 2 248

Golden. As if the golden fee for which I plead Were for myself *Rich. III.* iii 5 96
To bear the golden yoke of sovereignty . . . . . iii 7 146
I would to God that the inclusive verge Of golden metal that must round my brow Were red-hot steel! . . . . . . iv 1 60
Never yet one hour in his bed Have I enjoy'd the golden dew of sleep . iv 1 84
Hidest thou that forehead with a golden crown? . . . . iv 4 140
Put in her tender heart the aspiring flame Of golden sovereignty . . iv 4 329
The weary sun hath made a golden set . . . . . v 3 19
To be perk'd up in a glistering grief, And wear a golden sorrow *Hen. VIII.* ii 3 22
Too flaming a praise for a good complexion. I had as lief Helen's golden tongue had commended Troilus for a copper nose . *Troi. and Cres.* i 2 114
As when the golden sun salutes the morn . . . *T. Andron.* ii 1 5
Each wreathed in the other's arms, Our pastimes done, possess a golden slumber . . . . . . ii 3 26
For I can smooth and fill his aged ear With golden promises . . . iv 4 97
An hour before the worshipp'd sun Peer'd forth the golden window of the east, A troubled mind drave me to walk abroad *Rom. and Jul.* i 1 126
That book in many's eyes doth share the glory, That in gold clasps locks in the golden story . . . . . . i 3 92
Where unbruised youth with unstuff'd brain Doth couch his limbs, there golden sleep doth reign . . . . . . ii 3 38
Thou cutt'st my head off with a golden axe, And smilest upon the stroke iii 3 22
The learned pate Ducks to the golden fool: all is oblique *T. of Athens* iv 3 18
And chastise with the valour of my tongue All that impedes thee from the golden round . . . . . *Macbeth* i 5 29
I have bought Golden opinions from all sorts of people . . . i 7 33
Here lay Duncan, His silver skin laced with his golden blood . . ii 3 118
Hanging a golden stamp about their necks, Put on with holy prayers . iv 3 153
This majestical roof fretted with golden fire . . . *Hamlet* ii 2 313
As patient as the female dove, When that her golden couplets are disclosed v 1 310
His purse is empty already; all's golden words are spent . . v 2 136
Thou hadst little wit in thy bald crown, when thou gavest thy golden one away . . . . *Lear* i 4 179
And golden Phœbus never be beheld Of eyes again so royal! *A. and C.* v 2 320
And winking Mary-buds begin To ope their golden eyes . *Cymbeline* ii 3 27
The roof o' the chamber With golden cherubins is fretted . . ii 4 88
Who was the first of Britain which did put His brows within a golden crown . . . . iii 1 61
Golden lads and girls all must, As chimney-sweepers, come to dust . iv 2 262
So am I, That have this golden chance and know not why . . v 4 132
Before thee stands this fair Hesperides, With golden fruit . *Pericles* i 1 28
Should at these early hours Shake off the golden slumber of repose . iii 2 23
Her epitaphs In glittering golden characters express A general praise to her iv 3 44
Golden fleece. Her sunny locks Hang on her temples like a golden fleece *Mer. of Venice* i 1 170
Worthy Saint Michael and the Golden Fleece . . . *1 Hen. VI.* iv 7 69
Goldenly. My brother Jaques he keeps at school, and report speaks goldenly of his profit . . . *As Y. Like It* i 1 6
Goldsmith. While I go to the goldsmith's house, go thou And buy a rope's end . . . . . *Com. of Errors* iv 1 15
But, soft! I see the goldsmith. Get thee gone; Buy thou a rope . iv 1 19
But neither chain nor goldsmith came to me . . . . iv 1 24
I see, sir, you have found the goldsmith now . . . . iv 3 46
Thou hast suborn'd the goldsmith to arrest me . . . . iv 4 85
Whose suit is he arrested at?—One Angelo, a goldsmith . . iv 4 135
Bring me where the goldsmith is: I long to know the truth hereof at large iv 4 145
That goldsmith there, were he not pack'd with her, Could witness it . v 1 219
There did this perjured goldsmith swear me down . . . v 1 227
You say he dined at home; the goldsmith here Denies that saying . v 1 273
Have you not been acquainted with goldsmiths' wives? *As Y. Like It* iii 2 288
Golgotha. This land be call'd The field of Golgotha . *Richard II.* iv 1 144
Except they meant to bathe in reeking wounds, Or memorize another Golgotha, I cannot tell . . . . . *Macbeth* i 2 40
Goliases. None but Samsons and Goliases It sendeth forth to skirmish. One to ten! . . . . . . *1 Hen. VI.* i 2 33
Goliath. For in the shape of man, Master Brook, I fear not Goliath with a weaver's beam . . . . . *Mer. Wives* v 1 23
Gondola. In a gondola were seen together Lorenzo and his amorous Jessica . . . . . *Mer. of Venice* ii 8 8
I will scarce think you have swam in a gondola . . *As Y. Like It* iv 1 38
Gondolier. With a knave of common hire, a gondolier . . *Othello* i 1 126
Gone. But 'tis gone. No, it begins again . . . . *Tempest* i 2 394
I not doubt He came alive to land.—No, no, he's gone . . . ii 1 122
Take his bottle from him: when that's gone He shall drink nought but brine . . . . . . iii 2 73
Let us not burthen our remembrance with A heaviness that's gone . v 1 200
Wilt thou be gone? Sweet Valentine, adieu! . . *T. G. of Ver.* i 1 11
Will ye be gone!—That you may ruminate . . . . i 2 49
Go get you gone, and let the papers lie . . . . . i 2 100
What, gone without a word? Ay, so true love should do: it cannot speak ii 2 16
My foolish rival . . . Is gone with her along, and I must after . . ii 4 176
But, Valentine being gone, I'll quickly cross By some sly trick blunt Thurio's dull proceeding . . . . . ii 6 40
No matter who's displeased when you are gone . . . . ii 7 66
For which the youthful lover now is gone And this way comes he . iii 1 41
If she do chide, 'tis not to have you gone . . . . iii 1 98
Take no repulse, whatever she doth say; For 'get you gone,' she doth not mean 'away!' . . . . . . iii 1 101
Is your countryman According to our proclamation gone?—Gone, my good lord . . . . . . iii 2 12
Where is Launce?—Gone to seek his dog . . . . . iv 2 78
I will follow, more to cross that love Than hate for Silvia that is gone for love . . . . v 2 56
You may be gone; it is not good you tarry here . . *Mer. Wives* i 4 117
I would have sworn his disposition would have gone to the truth of his words . . . . ii 1 61
Be gone, and come when you are called . . . . . iii 3 19
There's an old woman, a fat woman, gone up into his chamber . . iv 5 13
There was, mine host, an old fat woman even now with me; but she's gone iv 5 26
They are gone but to meet the duke, villain: do not say they be fled . iv 5 72
They had gone down too, but that a wise burgher put in for them *Meas. for Meas.* i 2 102
This is the point. The duke is very strangely gone from hence . i 4 50
All hope is gone, Unless you have the grace by your fair prayer . . i 4 68
Get you gone, and let me hear no more of you . . . . ii 1 217
What's your will, father?—That now you are come, you will be gone . iii 1 180
I know you'ld fain be gone! An officer! To prison with her! . . v 1 120
Tuesday night last gone in's garden-house He knew me as a wife . . v 1 229
Thou foolish friar, and thou pernicious woman, Compact with her that's gone . . . . v 1 242

Gone. Is the duke gone? Then is your cause gone too . *Meas. for Meas.* v 1 301
If it prove so, I will be gone the sooner . *Com. of Errors* i 2 103
And from the mart he's somewhere gone to dinner . ii 1 5
Go get thee gone; fetch me an iron crow . iii 1 84
'Tis time, I think, to trudge, pack and be gone . iii 2 158
No evil lost is wail'd when it is gone . iv 2 24
'Tis time that I were gone: It was two ere I left him . iv 2 53
Is there any ship puts forth to-night? may we be gone? . iv 3 36
I conjure thee to leave me and be gone . iv 3 68
And I'll be gone, sir, and not trouble you . iv 3 71
Hark, hark! I hear him, mistress: fly, be gone!—Come, stand by me . v 1 184
Thirty-three years have I but gone in travail Of you, my sons . v 1 400
For trouble being gone, comfort should remain . *Much Ado* i 1 100
I am gone, though I am here: there is no love in you . iv 1 295
Thy slander hath gone through and through her heart . v 1 68
Don John is the author of all, who is fled and gone . v 2 101
Send you many lovers!—Amen, so you be none.—Nay, then will I be gone . *L. L. Lost* ii 1 128
What then, do you see? Ay, our way to be gone.—You are too hard for me ii 1 258
Will these turtles be gone?—Hence, sirs; away! . iv 3 212
Is this your perfectness? be gone, you rogue! . v 2 173
Bid them so be gone.—She says, you have it, and you may be gone . v 2 182
God save you! Where's the princess?—Gone to her tent . v 2 311
The party is gone, fellow Hector, she is gone; she is two months on her way v 2 678
I'll be gone: Our queen and all her elves come here anon *M. N. Dream* ii 1 16
Here comes Oberon.—And here my mistress. Would that he were gone! ii 1 59
Hence, get thee gone, and follow me no more . ii 1 194
Through the forest have I gone, But Athenian found I none . ii 2 66
So awake when I am gone; For I must now to Oberon . ii 2 82
What, out of hearing? gone? no sound, no word? Alack, where are you? speak . ii 2 152
If e'er I loved her, all that love is gone . iii 2 170
Why, get you gone: who is't that hinders you?—A foolish heart . iii 2 318
Get you gone, you dwarf; You minimus, of hindering knot-grass made iii 2 328
Damned spirits all, That in crossways and floods have burial, Already to their wormy beds are gone . iii 2 384
And still dares me on: When I come where he calls, then he is gone . iii 2 414
Fairies, be gone, and be all ways away . iv 1 46
Our intent Was to be gone from Athens . iv 1 157
If our sport had gone forward, we had all been made men . iv 2 17
How chance Moonshine is gone before Thisbe comes back? . v 1 318
This cherry nose, These yellow cowslip cheeks, Are gone, are gone . v 1 340
Deceased, or, as you would say in plain terms, gone to heaven *Mer. of Venice* ii 2 68
I desire no more delight Than to be under sail and gone to-night . ii 6 68
Without more speech, my lord, You must be gone from hence immediately ii 9 8
If I do fail in fortune of my choice, Immediately to leave you and be gone ii 9 16
I will ever be your head: So be gone: you are sped . ii 9 72
A diamond gone, cost me two thousand ducats in Frankfort! . iii 1 88
Loss upon loss! the thief gone with so much, and so much to find the thief iii 1 97
O love, dispatch all business, and be gone! . iii 2 325
Waste no time in words, But get thee gone . iii 4 55
Well, you are gone both ways.—I shall be saved by my husband . iii 5 20
Send the deed after me, And I will sign it.—Get thee gone, but do it . iv 1 397
But you see my finger Hath not the ring upon it; it is gone . v 1 188
She robs thee of thy name; And thou wilt show more bright and seem more virtuous When she is gone . *As Y. Like It* i 3 84
Wherever they are gone, That youth is surely in their company . ii 2 15
He is but even now gone hence: Here was he merry, hearing of a song ii 7 3
Would have gone near To fall in love with him . iii 5 126
Sirrah, be gone, or talk not, I advise you . *T. of Shrew* i 1 44
O excellent motion! Fellows, let's be gone.—The motion's good indeed i 2 280
I must be gone.—Faith, mistress, then I have no cause to stay . iii 1 85
You may be jogging whiles your boots are green; For me, I'll not be gone till I please myself . iii 2 214
Go, get thee gone, thou false deluding slave . iv 3 31
Go take it hence; be gone, and say no more . iv 3 167
Dally not with the gods, but get thee gone . iv 4 68
He's gone, and my idolatrous fancy Must sanctify his reliques *All's Well* i 1 108
What does this knave here? Get you gone, sirrah . i 3 9
Get you gone, sir; I'll talk with you more anon . i 3 68
You'll be gone, sir knave, and do as I command you . i 3 94
Be gone to-morrow; and be sure of this, What I can help thee to thou shalt not miss . i 3 261
Is she gone to the king?—She is.—Will she away to-night? . ii 5 22
Madam, my lord is gone, for ever gone.—Do not say so . iii 2 48
Madam, he's gone to serve the Duke of Florence . iii 2 54
I will be gone; My being here it is that holds thee hence . iii 2 125
I will be gone, That pitiful rumour may report my flight . iii 2 129
I am Saint Jaques' pilgrim, thither gone . iii 4 4
When haply he shall hear that she is gone, He will return . iii 4 35
We have lost our labour; they are gone a contrary way . iii 5 8
My lord that's gone made himself much sport out of him . iv 5 67
I do beseech you, whither is he gone? . v 1 27
Crying, 'That's good that's gone.' Our rash faults Make trivial price of serious things we have . v 3 60
If you be not mad, be gone; if you have reason, be brief *T. Night* i 5 212
Farewell, dear heart, since I must needs be gone . ii 3 110
I prithee, be gone.—I am gone, sir, And anon, sir, I'll be with you again iv 2 129
Gone already! Inch-thick, knee-deep, o'er head and ears a fork'd one! *W. Tale* i 2 185
'Tis far gone, When I shall gust it last . i 2 218
Say that she were gone, Given to the fire, a moiety of my rest Might come to me again . ii 3 7
Away with her!—I pray you, do not push me; I'll be gone . ii 3 125
Your favour I do give lost; for I do feel it gone, But know not how it went iii 2 96
The prince your son, with mere conceit and fear Of the queen's speed, is gone.—How! gone!—Is dead . iii 2 146
What's gone and what's past help Should be past grief . iii 2 223
This is the chase: I am gone for ever . iii 3 58
I'll go see if the bear be gone from the gentleman and how much he hath eaten . iii 3 133
Is it not too far gone? 'Tis time to part them . iv 4 354
Will't please you, sir, be gone? I told you what would come of this . iv 4 457
He is gone aboard a new ship to purge melancholy and air himself . iv 4 789
He must know 'tis none of your daughter nor my sister; we are gone else iv 4 851
There is none worthy, Respecting her that's gone . v 1 35
As every present time doth boast itself Above a better gone . v 1 97
Thither with all greediness of affection are they gone . v 2 112
Legitimation, name, and all is gone . *K. John* i 1 248

Gone. Gone to be married! gone to swear a peace! False blood to false blood join'd! gone to be friends! . *K. John* iii 1 1
Fellow, be gone: I cannot brook thy sight . iii 1 36
Get thee gone And leave those woes alone which I alone Am bound to under-bear . iii 1 63
And bloody England into England gone, O'erbearing interruption . iii 4 8
If that young Arthur be not gone already, Even at that news he dies . iii 4 163
Although my will to give is living, The suit which you demand is gone and dead . iv 2 84
Avaunt, thou hateful villain, get thee gone!—I am no villain . iv 3 77
Your nobles will not hear you, but are gone To offer service to your enemy . v 1 33
Art thou gone so? I do but stay behind To do the office for thee of revenge . v 7 70
What is six winters? they are quickly gone . *Richard II.* i 3 260
Well, he is gone; and with him go these thoughts . i 4 37
York is too far gone with grief, Or else he never would compare between ii 1 184
He is gone to save far off, Whilst others come to make him lose at home ii 2 80
My lord, your son was gone before I came.—He was? Why, so! . ii 2 86
Our countrymen are gone and fled, As well assured Richard their king is dead . ii 4 16
For all the Welshmen, hearing thou wert dead, Are gone to Bolingbroke iii 2 74
And Salisbury Is gone to meet the king, who lately landed . iii 3 3
I'll beg one boon, And then be gone and trouble you no more . iv 1 303
So, now I have mine own again, be gone, That I may strive to kill it with a groan . v 1 99
Get thee gone; for I do see Danger and disobedience in thine eye *1 Hen. IV.* i 3 15
Who struck this heat up after I was gone? . i 3 139
Is Gilliams with the packet gone?—He is, my lord, an hour ago . ii 3 68
Shall we be gone?—The moon shines fair; you may away by night . iii 1 141
So, be gone; We will not now be troubled with reply . v 1 112
Where's Bardolph?—He's gone into Smithfield to buy your worship a horse . *2 Hen. IV.* i 2 56
We are time's subjects, and time bids be gone . i 3 110
Didst thou not, when she was gone down stairs, desire me to be no more so familiarity with such poor people? . ii 1 107
Be gone, good ancient: this will grow to a brawl anon . ii 4 186
I pray thee, Jack, be quiet; the rascal's gone . ii 4 225
Thou'lt forget me when I am gone.—By my troth, thou'lt set me a-weeping, an thou sayest so . ii 4 300
'Tis not ten years gone Since . iii 1 57
She has nobody to do any thing about her when I am gone; and she is old . iii 2 247
The dangers of the days but newly gone . iv 1 80
The army is discharged all and gone.—Let them go . iv 3 137
Where is the prince your brother?—I think he's gone to hunt . iv 4 14
Let me see him: He is not here.—This door is open; he is gone this way iv 5 56
Then get thee gone and dig my grave thyself . iv 5 111
My father is gone wild into his grave, For in his tomb lie my affections v 2 123
Well, the fuel is gone that maintained that fire . *Hen. V.* ii 3 45
Shall we shog? the king will be gone from Southampton . ii 3 47
When I am dead and gone, Remember to avenge me on the French *1 Hen. VI.* i 4 93
Unbidden guests Are often welcomest when they are gone . ii 2 56
Let us now persuade you.—Not to be gone from hence . iii 2 94
Thou shalt escape By sudden flight: come, dally not, be gone . iv 5 11
Where is my other life? mine own is gone; O, where's young Talbot? . iv 7 1
The ghost of Talbot is not there: Now he is gone, my lord, you need not fear . v 2 17
Be gone, I say; for, till you do return, I rest perplexed . v 5 94
And say, when I am gone, I prophesied France will be lost ere long *2 Hen. VI.* i 1 145
The state of Normandy Stands on a tickle point, now they are gone . i 1 216
Still revelling like lords till all be gone . i 1 224
The wind was very high; And, ten to one, old Joan had not gone out . ii 1 4
When I am dead and gone, May honourable peace attend thy throne! . ii 3 37
What, gone, my lord, and bid me not farewell! . ii 4 85
Art thou gone too? all comfort go with thee! For none abides with me ii 4 87
So, get thee gone, that I may know my grief . iii 2 346
Go; speak not to me; even now be gone. O, go not yet! . iii 2 352
God, our hope, will succour us.—My hope is gone, now Suffolk is deceased iv 4 56
Now thou art gone, we have no staff, no stay . *3 Hen. VI.* ii 1 69
And now to London all the crew are gone . ii 1 174
My queen and son are gone to France for aid . iii 1 28
The great commanding Warwick Is thither gone . iii 1 30
Clarence and Somerset both gone to Warwick! . iv 1 127
I'll leave you to your fortune and be gone To keep them back . iv 7 55
Where's Richard gone?—To London, all in post . v 5 83
King Henry and the prince his son are gone: Clarence, thy turn is next v 6 89
Clarence still breathes; Edward still lives and reigns: When they are gone, then must I count my gains . *Richard III.* i 1 162
His soul thou canst not have; therefore, be gone . i 2 48
The heavens have blessed you with a goodly son, To be your comforter when he is gone . i 3 10
Why wither not the leaves the sap being gone? . ii 2 42
What stay had I but Edward? and he's gone.—What stay had we but Clarence? and he's gone?—What stays had I but they? and they are gone . ii 2 74
Is Catesby gone?—He is; and, see, he brings the mayor along . iii 5 12
O, let me think on Hastings, and be gone To Brecknock, while my fearful head is on! . iv 2 125
Thus both are gone with conscience and remorse . iv 3 20
Thou wouldst be gone to join with Richmond: I will not trust you, sir iv 4 491
He's gone to the king; I'll follow and outstare him . *Hen. VIII.* i 1 128
For me, I have no further gone in this than by A single voice . i 2 69
You have, by fortune and his highness' favours, Gone slightly o'er low steps . ii 4 112
O Cromwell, The king has gone beyond me . iii 2 408
Are ye all gone, And leave me here in wretchedness behind ye? . iv 2 83
Avoid the gallery. Ha! I have said. Be gone . v 1 86
Get you gone, And do as I have bid you . v 1 155
Was Hector armed and gone ere ye came to Ilium? . *Troi. and Cres.* i 2 49
Helen was not up, was she?—Hector was gone, but Helen was not up . i 2 51
Ne'er look, ne'er look; the eagles are gone: crows and daws, crows and daws! . i 2 265
What, are you gone again? you must be watched ere you be made tame iii 2 45
I would be gone: Where is my wit? I know not what I speak . iii 2 157
Why sigh you so profoundly? where's my lord? gone! Tell me . iv 2 84
What's the matter?—Thou must be gone, wench, thou must be gone . iv 2 95

Gone. Thou must to thy father, and be gone from Troilus *Troi. and Cres.* iv 2 97
Be gone, I say : the gods have heard me swear v 3 15
Hector is gone : Who shall tell Priam so, or Hecuba? v 10 14
Hence to your homes, be gone!—Nay, let them follow *Coriolanus* i 1 252
'Tis not four days gone Since I heard thence i 2 6
Be gone, away! All will be naught else.—Get you gone iii 1 230
The people's enemy is gone, is gone!—Our enemy is banish'd! he is gone! iii 3 136
Bid them all home ; he's gone, and we'll no further iv 2 1
Will you be gone?—You shall stay too iv 2 14
Now, pray, sir, get you gone : You have done a brave deed iv 2 37
My rage is gone ; And I am struck with sorrow v 6 148
Die he must, To appease their groaning shadows that are gone *T. Andron.* i 1 126
So, trouble me no more, but get you gone i 1 367
This way to death my wretched sons are gone iii 1 98
Get thee gone ; I see thou art not for my company iii 2 57
For love of her that's gone, Perhaps she cull'd it from among the rest iv 1 43
Terras Astræa reliquit : Be you remember'd, Marcus, she's gone, she's fled iv 3 5
Go, get you gone ; and pray be careful all iv 3 21
We'll measure them a measure, and be gone *Rom. and Jul.* i 4 10
And could tell A whispering tale in a fair lady's ear, Such as would please : 'tis gone, 'tis gone i 5 26
Gentlemen, prepare not to be gone ; We have a trifling foolish banquet towards i 5 123
Anon, anon! Come, let's away ; the strangers all are gone i 5 146
I would have thee gone : And yet no further than a wanton's bird ii 2 177
I am sped. Is he gone, and hath nothing? iii 1 95
The prince will doom thee death, If thou art taken : hence, be gone, away! iii 1 140
We are undone! Alack the day! he's gone, he's kill'd, he's dead! iii 2 39
Who is living, if those two are gone?—Tybalt is gone, and Romeo banished iii 2 68
Wilt thou be gone? it is not yet near day : It was the nightingale iii 5 1
I must be gone and live, or stay and die iii 5 11
Therefore stay yet ; thou need'st not to be gone iii 5 16
It is not day.—It is, it is : hie hence, be gone, away! iii 5 26
O, now be gone ; more light and light it grows iii 5 35
Art thou gone so? love, lord, ay, husband, friend! iii 5 43
Tell my lady I am gone, Having displeased my father, to Laurence' cell iii 5 231
What, is my daughter gone to Friar Laurence?—Ay, forsooth iv 2 11
Faith, we may put up our pipes, and be gone iv 5 97
I will be gone, sir, and not trouble you.—So shalt thou show me friendship v 3 40
Fly hence, and leave me : think upon these gone v 3 60
O, be gone! By heaven, I love thee better than myself v 3 63
My master knows not but I am gone hence v 3 132
He is gone happy, and has left me rich *T. of Athens* i 2 4
Answer not ; I am gone.—E'en so thou outrunnest grace ii 2 92
Let all my land be sold.—'Tis all engaged, some forfeited and gone ii 2 155
The world is but a word : Were it all yours to give it in a breath, How quickly were it gone! ii 2 163
When the means are gone that buy this praise, The breath is gone whereof this praise is made ii 2 178
All gone! and not One friend to take his fortune by the arm! iv 2 6
Till now you have gone on and fill'd the time With all licentious measure v 4 3
As proper men as ever trod upon neat's leather have gone upon my handiwork *J. Cæsar* i 1 29
Be gone! Run to your houses, fall upon your knees i 1 57
He's gone To seek you at your house i 3 149
Stay not to answer me, but get thee gone : Why dost thou stay? ii 4 2
Is Cæsar yet gone to the Capitol?—Madam, not yet ii 4 24
The ides of March are come.—Ay, Cæsar ; but not gone iii 1 2
Portia, art thou gone?—No more, I pray you iv 3 166
This morning are they fled away and gone v 1 84
Our day is gone ; Clouds, dews, and dangers come ; our deeds are done! v 3 63
Her husband's to Aleppo gone, master o' the Tiger *Macbeth* i 3 7
He is already named, and gone to Scone To be invested ii 4 31
Is Banquo gone from court?—Ay, madam, but returns again to-night iii 2 1
Get thee gone : to-morrow We'll hear, ourselves, again iii 4 31
Hence, horrible shadow! Unreal mockery, hence! Why, so : being gone, I am a man again iii 4 107
Get you gone, And at the pit of Acheron Meet me i' the morning iii 5 14
Thither Macduff Is gone to pray the holy king iii 6 30
Where are they? Gone? Let this pernicious hour Stand aye accursed! iv 1 133
I charge thee, speak!—'Tis gone, and will not answer *Hamlet* i 1 52
'Tis here!—'Tis here!—'Tis gone! We do it wrong i 1 142
Nor have we herein barr'd Your better wisdoms, which have freely gone With this affair along i 2 15
He said I was a fishmonger : he is far gone, far gone ii 2 190
Where is he gone?—To draw apart the body he hath kill'd iv 1 23
He is dead and gone, lady, He is dead and gone iv 5 29
First, her father slain : Next, your son gone iv 5 80
Nature her custom holds, Let shame say what it will : when these are gone, The woman will be out iv 7 189
Therefore be gone Without our grace, our love, our benison *Lear* i 1 267
And the king gone to-night! subscribed his power! Confined to exhibition! i 2 24
Winter's not gone yet, if the wild-geese fly that way ii 4 46
If he ask for me, I am ill, and gone to bed iii 3 18
Trouble him not, his wits are gone iii 6 94
Some other of the lords dependants Are gone with him towards Dover iii 7 19
Do as I bid thee, or rather do thy pleasure ; Above the rest, be gone iv 1 50
Is gone, In pity of his misery, to dispatch His nighted life iv 5 11
Now, fellow, fare thee well.—Gone, sir : farewell iv 6 41
She's gone for ever! I know when one is dead, and when one lives v 3 259
I might have saved her ; now she's gone for ever! Cordelia, Cordelia! stay a little v 3 270
Gone she is ; And what's to come of my despised time Is nought but bitterness *Othello* i 1 161
To mourn a mischief that is past and gone Is the next way to draw new mischief on i 3 204
For I am declined Into the vale of years,—yet that's not much—She's gone iii 3 267
Othello's occupation's gone!—Is't possible, my lord? iii 3 357
All my fond love thus do I blow to heaven. 'Tis gone iii 3 446
Is't lost? is't gone? speak, is it out o' the way? iii 4 80
When he is gone, I would on great occasion speak with you iv 1 58
'Tis but a man gone. Forth, my sword : he dies v 1 10
She's, like a liar, gone to burning hell : 'Twas I that kill'd her v 2 129

Gone. He's gone, but his wife's kill'd.—'Tis a notorious villain *Othello* v 2 238
There's a great spirit gone! Thus did I desire it *Ant. and Cleo.* i 2 126
She's good, being gone ; The hand could pluck her back that shoved her on i 2 130
I must be gone i 2 140
The air ; which, but for vacancy, Had gone to gaze on Cleopatra too ii 2 222
He is gone ; The other three are sealing iii 2 2
That Herod's head I'll have : but how, when Antony is gone? iii 3 5
This should be answer'd.—'Tis done already, and the messenger gone iii 6 31
Who's gone this morning?—Who! One ever near thee iv 5 6
His chests and treasure He has not with him.—Is he gone? iv 5 11
'Tis well thou'rt gone, If it be well to live iv 12 39
Assist, good friends.—O, quick, or I am gone iv 15 31
Our strength is all gone into heaviness, That makes the weight iv 15 33
The odds is gone, And there is nothing left remarkable iv 15 66
You must be gone ; And I shall here abide the hourly shot *Cymbeline* i 1 88
The gods protect you! And bless the good remainders of the court! I am gone i 1 130
I hope it be not gone to tell my lord That I kiss aught but he ii 3 152
Why hast thou gone so far, To be unbent when thou hast ta'en thy stand? iii 4 110
Where is she gone? Haply, despair hath seized her, Or, wing'd with fervour of her love, she's flown iii 5 60
Gone she is To death or to dishonour ; and my end Can make good use of either iii 5 62
Now I think on thee, My hunger's gone iii 6 16
Why, he but sleeps : If he be gone, he'll make his grave a bed iv 2 216
Thou thy worldly task hast done, Home art gone, and ta'en thy wages iv 2 261
'Ods pittikins! can it be six mile yet?—I have gone all night iv 2 294
But his Jovial face—Murder in heaven?—How!—'Tis gone iv 2 312
Imogen, The great part of my comfort, gone iv 3 5
Her son gone, So needful for this present : it strikes me, past The hope of comfort iv 3 7
I nothing know where she remains, why gone, Nor when she purposes return iv 3 14
But, O scorn! Gone! they went hence so soon as they were born v 4 126
The day Was yours by accident ; had it gone with us, We should not, when the blood was cool, have threaten'd Our prisoners with the sword v 5 76
But her son Is gone, we know not how nor where v 5 273
Swore, If I discover'd not which way she was gone, It was my instant death v 5 277
The breath is gone, and the sore eyes see clear *Pericles* i 1 99
Doth speak sufficiently he's gone to travel.—How! the king gone! i 3 14
But since he's gone, the king's seas must please i 3 28
I must needs be gone ; My twelve months are expired iii 3 1
I have gone through for this piece, you see iv 2 47
Nor none can know, Leonine being gone iv 3 30
To fetch his daughter home, who first is gone iv 4 20
Did you ever hear the like?—No, nor never shall do in such a place as this, she being once gone iv 5 3
My heart Leaps to be gone into my mother's bosom v 3 45

Gone a-birding. Her husband is this morning gone a-birding *Mer. Wives* iii 5 131

Gone about. I stand dishonour'd, that have gone about To link my dear friend to a common stale *Much Ado* iv 1 65
Ay, marry, I'll be gone about it straight.—And so will I *Mer. of Venice* ii 4 25
May I be bold to acquaint his grace you are gone about it? *All's Well* iii 6 85
Be my horses ready?—Thy asses are gone about 'em *Lear* i 5 37

Gone along. With him is Gratiano gone along *Mer. of Venice* ii 8 2

Gone back. Why the King of France is so suddenly gone back know you the reason? *Lear* iv 3 2

Gone barefoot. Condition, I had gone barefoot to India *Troi. and Cres.* i 2 80

Gone before. All his successors gone before him hath done't *Mer. Wives* i 1 14
Sith every action that hath gone before, Whereof we have record, trial did draw Bias and thwart *Troi. and Cres.* i 3 13
Let's after him, Whose care is gone before to bid us welcome *Macbeth* i 4 57
You see this fellow that is gone before ; He is a soldier fit to stand by Cæsar And give direction *Othello* ii 3 126

Gone between and between, but small thanks for my labour *T. and C.* i 1 71

Gone by. The particular accidents gone by Since I came *Tempest* v 1 305
Which of the peers Have uncontemn'd gone by him? *Hen. VIII.* iii 2 10
With martial stalk hath he gone by our watch *Hamlet* i 1 66
When saw you my father last?—Why, the night gone by *Lear* i 2 168
Had superfluous kings for messengers Not many moons gone by *Ant. and Cleo.* iii 12 6

Gone forth. O, if a virgin, And your affection not gone forth, I'll make you The queen of Naples *Tempest* i 2 448
He hath ta'en his bow and arrows and is gone forth to sleep *As Y. L. It* iv 3 5
We should by this, to all our lamentation, If he had gone forth consul, found it so *Coriolanus* iv 6 35

Gone off. The French is gone off, look you *Hen. V.* iii 6 96
The cardinal's and Sir Thomas Lovell's heads Should have gone off *Hen. VIII.* i 2 186

Gone round. So long that nineteen zodiacs have gone round *M. for M.* i 2 172
Full thirty times hath Phœbus' cart gone round Neptune's salt wash *Ham.* iii 2 165

Gone well. Had our general Been what he knew himself, it had gone well *Ant. and Cleo.* iii 10 27

Goneril, Our eldest-born, speak first *Lear* i 1 54
No less in space, validity, and pleasure, Than that conferr'd on Goneril i 1 84
I cannot be so partial, Goneril, To the great love I bear you i 4 334
Half breathless, panting forth From Goneril his mistress salutations ii 4 32
In such a night as this! O Regan, Goneril! Your old kind father iii 4 19
Pur! the cat is gray.—Arraign her first ; 'tis Goneril iii 6 48
Come hither, mistress. Is your name Goneril?—She cannot deny it iii 6 52
O Goneril! You are not worth the dust which the rude wind Blows in your face. I fear your disposition iv 2 29
Ha! Goneril, with a white beard! They flattered me like a dog iv 6 97
Your—wife, so I would say—Affectionate servant, GONERIL iv 6 277
To take the widow Exasperates, makes mad her sister Goneril v 1 60

Gonzago. Old friend ; can you play the Murder of Gonzago? *Hamlet* ii 2 563
Gonzago is the duke's name ; his wife, Baptista iii 2 249
You shall see anon how the murderer gets the love of Gonzago's wife iii 2 275

Gonzalo. Some fresh water that A noble Neapolitan, Gonzalo, . . . did give us *Tempest* i 2 161
God save his majesty!—Long live Gonzalo! ii 1 169
Lords that can prate As amply and unnecessarily As this Gonzalo ii 1 265
And when I rear my hand, do you the like, To fall it on Gonzalo ii 1 296
Him that you term'd, sir, 'The good old lord, Gonzalo' v 1 15
Holy Gonzalo, honourable man, Mine eyes, even sociable to the show of thine v 1 62
O good Gonzalo, My true preserver, and a loyal sir To him thou follow'st! v 1 68

Good. In all her trim, freshly beheld Our royal, good and gallant ship *Tempest* v 1 237
Of many good I think him best *T. G. of Ver.* i 2 21
'Twere good, I think, your lordship sent him thither i 3 29
'Twere good you knocked him ii 4 7
If he make this good, He is as worthy for an empress' love ii 4 75
My duty pricks me on to utter that Which else no worldly good should draw from me iii 1 9
Time is the nurse and breeder of all good iii 1 243
She will often praise her liquor.—If her liquor be good, she shall iii 1 352
As you unwind her love from him, Lest it should ravel and be good to none, You must provide to bottom it on me iii 2 52
Recking as little what betideth me As much I wish all good befortune you iv 3 41
They are reformed, civil, full of good, And fit for great employment v 4 156
Much good do it your good heart! *Mer. Wives* i 1 83
His meaning is good.—Ay, I think my cousin meant well i 1 264
I ken the wight: he is of substance good i 3 41
The humour rises; it is good: humour me the angels i 3 63
But notwithstanding, man, I'll do you your master what good I can i 4 98
You may be gone; it is not good you tarry here i 4 117
Shall I do any good, thinkest thou? shall I not lose my suit? i 4 152
'Twas a good sensible fellow: well ii 1 151
'Tis not good that children should know any wickedness ii 2 133
Said I well?—By gar, 'tis good; vell said.—Let us wag, then ii 3 100
Ay, dat is very good; excellent.—Peace, I say! iii 1 101
Dat is good; by gar, with all my heart! iii 3 257
What I have suffered to bring this woman to evil for your good iii 5 98
He is a good sprag memory iv 1 84
Seese is not good to give putter; your belly is all putter v 5 148
So to enforce or qualify the laws As to your soul seems good *M. for M.* i 1 67
A word with you.—A hundred, if they'll do you any good i 2 147
You do blaspheme the good in mocking me i 4 38
And make us lose the good we oft might win By fearing to attempt i 4 78
It is an open room and good for winter ii 1 136
Dost thou desire her foully for those things That make her good? ii 2 175
As good To pardon him that hath from nature stolen A man already made ii 4 42
You are ignorant, Or seem so craftily; and that's not good ii 4 75
Let me be ignorant, and in nothing good ii 4 76
What's the comfort.—Why, As all comforts are; most good, most good indeed iii 1 56
The hand that hath made you fair hath made you good iii 1 185
To the love I have in doing good a remedy presents itself iii 1 204
He were as good go a mile on his errand iii 2 38
Why, 'tis good; it is the right of it; it must be so iii 2 60
Good my lord, be good to me; your honour is accounted a merciful man iii 2 202
'Tis good; though music oft hath such a charm To make bad good, and good provoke to harm iv 1 14
I pray you, be acquainted with this maid; She comes to do you good iv 1 52
Who can do good on him? Well, go, prepare yourself iv 2 71
You must be so good, sir, to rise and be put to death iv 3 29
I will keep her ignorant of her good iv 3 113
Might reproach your life And choke your good to come v 1 427
I have a motion much imports your good v 1 541
As good to wink, sweet love, as look on night *Com. of Errors* iii 2 58
Is't good to soothe him in these contraries? iv 4 82
To do him all the grace and good I could v 1 164
What I told you then, I hope I shall have leisure to make good v 1 375
My liege, your highness now may do me good *Much Ado* i 1 292
Thou shalt see how apt it is to learn Any hard lesson that may do thee good i 1 295
I can tell you strange news that you yet dreamt not of.—Are they good? —As the event stamps them i 2 6
It is very true.—It were good that Benedick knew of it ii 3 160
Tell Benedick of it, and hear what a' will say.—Were it good, think you? ii 3 179
He is a very proper man.—He hath indeed a good outward happiness ii 3 190
It were not good She knew his love, lest she make sport at it iii 1 57
Disloyal?—The word is too good to paint out her wickedness iii 2 112
Nay, that were a punishment too good for them iii 3 4
I'll wear this.—By my troth, 's not so good iii 4 9
That is some good: But not for that dream I on this strange course iv 1 213
I will make it good how you dare, with what you dare, and when you dare v 1 147
He hath wit to make an ill shape good, And shape to win grace *L. L. Lost* ii 1 59
Much too little of that good I saw Is my report to his great worthiness ii 1 62
Let it blood.—Would that do it good?—My physic says 'ay' ii 1 187
Sir, your pennyworth is good, an your goose be fat iii 1 103
The gift is good in those in whom it is acute, and I am thankful for it iv 2 73
Good master Parson, be so good as read me this letter iv 2 92
Your mistresses dare never come in rain, For fear their colours should be wash'd away.—'Twere good, yours did iv 3 272
Are good at such eruptions and sudden breaking out of mirth v 1 120
I will roar, that I will do any man's heart good to hear me *M. N. Dream* i 2 73
We'll rest us, Hermia, if you think it good, And tarry ii 2 37
If to do were as easy as to know what were good to do *Mer. of Venice* i 2 14
I can easier teach twenty what were good to be done, than be one of the twenty to follow mine own teaching i 2 17
Was this inserted to make interest good? i 3 95
'Tis good we do so ii 4 28
I never did repent for doing good, Nor shall not now iii 4 10
There is but one hope in it that can do you any good iii 5 8
'Twere good you do so much for charity iv 1 261
Why, then the devil give him good of it! I'll stay no longer question iv 1 345
Nothing is good, I see, without respect v 1 99
I will no further offend you than becomes me for my good *As Y. Like It* i 1 84
I'll stand to it, the pancakes were naught and the mustard was good i 2 70
Books in the running brooks, Sermons in stones and good in every thing ii 1 17
What, for a counter, would I do but good? ii 7 63
Glad of other men's good, content with my harm iii 2 79
He asked me of what parentage I was; I told him, of as good as he iii 4 40
'Tis good to be sad and say nothing.—Why then, 'tis good to be a post iv 1 8
Are you not good?—I hope so.—Why then, can one desire too much of a good thing? iv 1 121
'So so' is good, very good, very excellent good; and yet it is not; it is but so so v 1 29
It shall be to your good v 2 11
In some little measure draw a belief from you, to do yourself good v 2 64
Shall share the good of our returned fortune v 4 180
Silver made it good At the hedge-corner, in the coldest fault *T. of S.* Ind. 1 19
I would not lose the dog for twenty pound.—Why, Belman is as good as he Ind. 1 22
They thought it good you hear a play And frame your mind to mirth Ind. 2 136
That I may soon make good What I have said i 1 74
Good. Go to the devil's dam: your gifts are so good, here's none will hold you *T. of Shrew* i 1 107
If thou ask me why, sufficeth, my reasons are both good and weighty i 1 253
She would think scolding would do little good upon him i 2 110
If you speak me fair, I'll tell you news indifferent good for either i 2 181
This gentleman is happily arrived, My mind presumes, for his own good and ours i 2 214
Let's be gone.—The motion's good indeed and be it so i 2 281
I'll leave her houses three or four as good, Within rich Pisa walls ii 1 368
'Tis in my head to do my master good ii 1 408
'Twere good, methinks, to steal our marriage iii 2 142
Then go with me to make the matter good iv 2 114
What say you to a neat's foot?—'Tis passing good iv 3 18
Much good do it unto thy gentle heart! iv 3 51
Here comes your boy; 'Twere good he were school'd iv 4 9
A good swift simile, but something currish v 2 54
He that so generally is at all times good must of necessity hold his virtue to you; whose worthiness would stir it up *All's Well* i 1 9
I have those hopes of her good that her education promises i 1 46
Among nine bad if one be good, There's yet one good in ten i 3 82
You are too young, too happy, and too good, To make yourself a son out of my blood ii 3 102
Good alone Is good without a name ii 3 135
Check thy contempt: Obey our will, which travails in thy good ii 3 165
Good, very good; it is so then: good, very good; let it be concealed awhile ii 3 282
But we must do good against evil ii 5 53
There's nothing here that is too good for him But only she iii 2 82
He is too good and fair for death and me iii 4 16
The web of our life is of a mingled yarn, good and ill together iv 3 84
Turns a sour offence, Crying, 'That's good that's gone' v 3 60
Art thou good at these kickshawses, knight? *T. Night* i 3 122
He that is well hanged in this world needs to fear no colours.—Make that good i 5 7
A good lenten answer i 5 9
To be turned away, is not that as good as a hanging to you? i 5 19
Excellent good, i' faith.—Good, good ii 3 46
Love sought is good, but given unsought is better iii 1 168
The triplex, sir, is a good tripping measure v 1 41
'Good' should be pertinent; But, so it is, it is not *W. Tale* i 2 221
That Canst with thine eyes at once see good and evil i 2 303
So have we thought it good From our free person she should be confined ii 1 193
No court in Europe is too good for thee ii 2 3
Let't not be doubted I shall do good ii 2 54
And would by combat make her good, so were I A man ii 3 60
The good queen, For she is good, hath brought you forth a daughter ii 3 65
You, that are thus so tender o'er his follies, Will never do him good ii 3 129
I, that please some, try all, both joy and terror Of good and bad iv 1 2
Let's before as he bids us: he was provided to do us good iv 4 861
From the all that are took something good, To make a perfect woman v 1 14
For present comfort and for future good v 1 32
Here come those I have done good to against my will v 2 134
Creep time ne'er so slow, Yet it shall come for me to do thee good *K. John* iii 3 32
No, no; when Fortune means to men most good, She looks upon them with a threatening eye iii 4 119
You have bid us ask his liberty; Which for our goods we do no further ask iv 2 64
As good to die and go, as die and stay iv 3 8
Here to make good the boisterous late appeal *Richard II.* i 1 4
What I speak My body shall make good upon this earth i 1 37
A miscreant, Too good to be so and too bad to live i 1 40
By that and all the rites of knighthood else, Will I make good against thee i 1 76
And further will maintain Upon his bad life to make all this good i 1 99
As much good stay with thee as go with me! i 2 57
The apprehension of the good Gives but the greater feeling to the worse i 3 300
By bad courses may be understood That their events can never fall out good ii 1 214
Out with it boldly, man; Quick is mine ear to hear of good towards him ii 1 234
No good at all that I can do for him; Unless you call it good to pity him ii 1 235
And crossly to thy good all fortune goes ii 4 24
The news is very fair and good, my lord iii 3 5
I could weep, madam, would it do you good.—And I could sing, would weeping do me good iii 4 21
Good king, great king, and yet not greatly good iv 1 263
Thy overflow of good converts to bad, And thy abundant goodness shall excuse This deadly blot in thy digressing son v 3 64
O would the deed were good! For now the devil, that told me I did well, Says that this deed is chronicled in hell v 5 115
Wherein is he good, but to taste sack and drink it? *1 Hen. IV.* ii 4 501
One that no persuasion can do good upon iii 1 200
Swear me, Kate, like a lady as thou art, A good mouth-filling oath iii 1 259
The sack that thou hast drunk me would have bought me lights as good cheap at the dearest chandler's in Europe iii 3 51
Were it good To set the exact wealth of all our states All at one cast iv 1 45
Good, an God will!—As good as heart can wish *2 Hen. IV.* i 1 13
He said, sir, the water itself was a good healthy water i 2 4
My master is deaf.—I am sure he is, to the hearing of any thing good i 2 81
Good my lord, be good to me. I beseech you, stand to me ii 1 69
I'll drink no more than will do me good, for no man's pleasure, I ii 4 128
What humour's the prince of?—A good shallow young fellow ii 4 257
It would have done a man's heart good to see iii 2 54
Very singular good! in faith, well said, Sir John, very well said iii 2 120
No man is too good to serve's prince iii 2 253
So: very well: go to: very good, exceeding good iii 2 293
Our cause the best; Then reason will our hearts should be as good iv 1 157
Our corn shall seem as light as chaff And good from bad find no partition iv 1 196
Let it do something, my good lord, that may do me good iv 3 66
With excellent endeavour of drinking good and good store of fertile sherris iv 3 131
What wind blew you hither, Pistol?—Not the ill wind which blows no man to good v 3 91
And withal devise something to do thyself good v 3 140
It is not so good to come to the mines; for, look you *Hen. V.* iii 2 62
We thought not good to bruise an injury till it were full ripe iii 6 129
The prescript praise and perfection of a good and particular mistress iii 7 50
'Tis good for men to love their present pains Upon example iv 1 18
A lad of life, an imp of fame; Of parents good, of fist most valiant iv 1 46
If the cause be not good, the king himself hath a heavy reckoning iv 1 140
There is more good toward you peradventure than is in your knowledge iv 8 4

Good. Wherefore should you be so pashful? your shoes is not so good *Hen. V.* iv 8 76
God fought for us.—Yes, my conscience, he did us great good iv 8 126
Will you be so good, scauld knave, as eat it? v 1 31
Bite, I pray you; it is good for your green wound v 1 44
Thou dost see I eat.—Much good do you, scauld knave, heartily v 1 55
Throw none away; the skin is good for your broken coxcomb v 1 57
Ay, leeks is good: hold you, there is a groat to heal your pate v 1 61
Let a Welsh correction teach you a good English condition v 1 83
Haply a woman's voice may do some good, When articles too nicely urged be stood on v 2 93
Improvident soldiers! had your watch been good, This sudden mischief never could have fall'n 1 *Hen. VI.* ii 1 58
Mourn not, except thou sorrow for my good ii 5 111
Or make my ill the advantage of my good ii 5 129
I am as good— As good! Thou bastard of my grandfather! iii 1 41
Employ thee then, sweet virgin, for our good iii 3 16
Your purpose is both good and reasonable v 1 36
O, burn her, burn her! hanging is too good v 4 33
Join we together, for the public good, In what we can 2 *Hen. VI.* i 1 199
And will they undertake to do me good?—This they have promised i 2 77
Were it not good your grace could fly to heaven? ii 1 17
And if thy claim be good, The Nevils are thy subjects to command ii 2 7
I have watch'd the night, Ay, night by night, in studying good for England iii 1 111
And with dimm'd eyes Look after him and cannot do him good iii 1 219
And yet herein I judge mine own wit good iii 1 232
He shall be encountered with a man as good as himself iv 2 125
If we mean to thrive and do good, break open the gaols iv 3 17
These cheeks are pale for watching for your good iv 7 90
Doubt not so to deal As all things shall redound unto your good iv 9 47
I think this word 'sallet' was born to do me good iv 10 12
I'll warrant they'll make it good v 1 122
Why faint you, lords? My title's good, and better far than his 3 *Hen. VI.* i 1 130
What good is this to England and himself! i 1 177
Thou art as opposite to every good As the Antipodes are unto us i 4 134
What hap? what hope of good?—Our hap is loss, our hope but sad despair ii 3 8
To do them good, I would sustain some harm.—Then get your husband's lands, to do them good iii 2 39
I am too mean to be your queen, And yet too good to be your concubine iii 2 98
As good to chide the waves as speak them fair v 4 24
My good lord:—my lord, I should say rather; 'Tis sin to flatter; 'good' was little better v 6 3
You know no rules of charity, Which renders good for bad *Richard III.* i 2 69
I was too hot to do somebody good, That is too cold in thinking of it now i 3 311
With a piece of scripture, Tell them that God bids us do good for evil i 3 335
Me seemeth good, that, with some little train, Forthwith from Ludlow the young prince be fetch'd ii 2 120
Why, my young cousin, it is good to grow ii 4 9
I bid them that did love their country's good Cry 'God save Richard!' iii 7 21
Matters of great moment, No less importing than our general good iii 7 68
My lord, he fears you mean no good to him.—Sorry I am my noble cousin should Suspect me, that I mean no good to him iii 7 87
Your sleepy thoughts, Which here we waken to our country's good iii 7 124
Gold were as good as twenty orators, And will, no doubt, tempt him iv 2 38
But think how I may do thee good, And be inheritor of thy desire iv 3 33
I intend more good to you and yours Than ever you or yours were by me wrong'd!—What good is cover'd with the face of heaven, To be discover'd, that can do me good? iv 4 237
Shall I be tempted of the devil thus?—Ay, if the devil tempt thee to do good iv 4 419
Hoyday, a riddle! neither good nor bad! Why dost thou run so many mile about? iv 4 460
Bless thee from thy mother, Who prays continually for Richmond's good v 3 84
I love myself. Wherefore? for any good That I myself have done unto myself? v 3 187
All the good our English Have got by the late voyage is but merely A fit or two o' the face *Hen. VIII.* i 3 5
This is a mere distraction; You turn the good we offer into envy iii 1 113
Madam, you wander from the good we aim at iii 1 138
Evermore they pointed To the good of your most sacred person iii 2 173
For your highness' good I ever labour'd More than mine own iii 2 191
As you are truly noble, As you respect the common good iii 2 290
So farewell to the little good you bear me iii 2 350
Must I needs forgo So good, so noble and so true a master? iii 2 423
May it please your highness To hear me speak his good now? iv 2 47
One of which fell with him, Unwilling to outlive the good that did it iv 2 60
The good I stand on is my truth and honesty v 1 122
Not only good and wise, but most religious v 3 116
You were ever good at sudden commendations v 3 122
They fell on; I made good my place v 4 57
All the virtues that attend the good Shall still be doubled on her v 5 28
Good grows with her: In her days every man shall eat in safety v 5 33
All the expected good we're like to hear Epil. 8
Now good or bad, 'tis but the chance of war *Troi. and Cres.* Prol. 31
O, a brave man!—Is a' not? it does a man's heart good i 2 221
By God's lid, it does one's heart good i 2 229
He's not hurt: why, this will do Helen's heart good now, ha! i 2 234
And posts, like the commandment of a king, Sans check to good and bad i 3 94
Shall make it good, or do his best to do it i 3 274
For the success, Although particular, shall give a scantling Of good or bad unto the general i 3 342
A' were as good crack a fusty nut with no kernel ii 1 111
Here is good broken music.—You have broke it, cousin iii 1 52
It may do good: pride hath no other glass To show itself but pride iii 3 47
Beshrew your heart! you'll ne'er be good, Nor suffer others iv 2 30
He was a soldier good; But, by great Mars, the captain of us all, Never like thee iv 5 197
Great Hector was a man as good as he v 9 6
We are accounted poor citizens, the patricians good *Coriolanus* i 1 16
Take Convenient numbers to make good the city i 5 13
Make good this ostentation, and you shall Divide in all with us i 6 86
With whom we may articulate, For their own good and ours i 9 78
The augurer tells me we shall have news to-night.—Good or bad? ii 1 3
You wear out a good wholesome forenoon in hearing a cause ii 1 77
He waved indifferently 'twixt doing them neither good nor harm ii 2 20
'Shall'! O good but most unwise patricians! iii 1 91
Not having the power to do the good it would, For the ill which doth control't iii 1 160
Good. I do love My country's good with a respect more tender, More holy and profound *Coriolanus* iii 3 112
More noble blows than ever thou wise words: And for Rome's good iv 2 22
Strange things from Rome; all tending to the good of their adversaries iv 3 45
If they Should say 'Be good to Rome,' they charged him even As those should do that had deserved his hate iv 6 112
Show no sign of fear.—The gods be good to us! iv 6 154
The gods be good unto us!—No, in such a case the gods will not be good unto us v 4 33
Surnamed Pius For many good and great deserts to Rome *T. Andron.* i 1 24
A Roman now adopted happily, And must advise the emperor for his good i 1 464
Many good morrows to your majesty; Madam, to you as many and as good ii 2 12
I may help thee out; Or, wanting strength to do thee so much good ii 3 238
Let fools do good, and fair men call for grace iii 1 205
It did me good, before the palace gate To brave the tribune . . . —But me more good, to see so great a lord Basely insinuate iv 2 35
You were as good to shoot against the wind. To it, boy! iv 3 57
Too like the sire for ever being good v 1 50
I fear the emperor means no good to us v 3 10
For peace, for love, for league, and good to Rome v 3 23
Well, Susan is with God; She was too good for me *Rom. and Jul.* i 3 20
For nought so vile that on the earth doth live But to the earth some special good doth give, Nor aught so good but strain'd from that fair use Revolts from true birth ii 3 18
That it would do you good to hear it ii 4 227
Now, good sweet nurse,—O Lord, why look'st thou sad? ii 5 21
If good, thou shamest the music of sweet news By playing it to me with so sour a face ii 5 23
Is thy news good, or bad? answer to that; Say either ii 5 35
Let me be satisfied, is't good or bad? ii 5 37
Nor what is mine shall never do thee good: Trust to't, bethink you iii 5 196
Is dead; or 'twere as good he were, As living here and you no use of him iii 5 226
Well, he may chance to do some good on her iv 2 13
This letter doth make good the friar's words v 3 286
When we for recompense have praised the vile, It stains the glory in that happy verse Which aptly sings the good *T. of Athens* i 1 17
Here is a touch; is't good?—I will say of it, It tutors nature i 1 36
Invite them without knives; Good for their meat, and safer for their lives i 2 46
What a beggar his heart is, Being of no power to make his wishes good i 2 202
If thou wert not sullen, I would be good to thee.—No, I'll nothing i 2 243
I'd such a courage to do him good iii 3 24
As you are great, be pitifully good iii 5 52
Strange, unusual blood, When man's worst sin is, he does too much good! iv 2 39
Good as the best v 1 24
Good honest men! Thou draw'st a counterfeit Best in all Athens v 1 83
If it be aught toward the general good, Set honour in one eye and death i' the other, And I will look on both indifferently *J. Cæsar* i 2 85
Who's there?—A Roman.—Casca, by your voice.—Your ear is good i 3 42
If it will please Cæsar To be so good to Cæsar as to hear me ii 4 29
Speak all good you can devise of Cæsar, And say you do't by our permission iii 1 246
As I slew my best lover for the good of Rome, I have the same dagger for myself iii 2 50
The evil that men do lives after them; The good is oft interred with their bones; So let it be with Cæsar iii 2 81
'Tis good you know not that you are his heirs iii 2 150
I do not think it good.—Your reason? iv 3 198
If I do live, I will be good to thee iv 3 266
In a general honest thought And common good to all v 5 72
This is the sergeant Who like a good and hardy soldier fought *Macbeth* i 2 4
This supernatural soliciting Cannot be ill, cannot be good i 3 131
If good, why do I yield to that suggestion Whose horrid image doth unfix my hair And make my seated heart knock at my ribs? i 3 134
This have I thought good to deliver thee, my dearest partner i 5 11
Alas, the day! What good could they pretend? ii 4 24
Those That would make good of bad, and friends of foes ii 4 41
Why, by the verities on thee made good, May they not be my oracles as well And set me up in hope? iii 1 8
This I made good to you In our last conference iii 1 79
Thou art the best o' the cut-throats: yet he's good That did the like iii 4 17
For mine own good, All causes shall give way iii 4 135
Cool it with a baboon's blood, Then the charm is firm and good iv 1 38
I am in this earthly world; where to do harm Is often laudable, to do good sometime Accounted dangerous folly iv 2 76
A good and virtuous nature may recoil In an imperial charge iv 3 19
I should forge Quarrels unjust against the good and loyal iv 3 83
It is not nor it cannot come to good: But break, my heart *Hamlet* i 2 158
Both in time, Form of the thing, each word made true and good i 2 210
There is nothing either good or bad, but thinking makes it so ii 2 256
'The mobled queen?'—That's good; 'mobled queen' is good ii 2 527
You are as good as a chorus, my lord iii 2 255
In the fatness of these pursy times Virtue itself of vice must pardon beg, Yea, curb and woo for leave to do him good iii 4 155
That to the use of actions fair and good He likewise gives a frock or livery iii 4 163
'Twere good you let him know iii 4 188
Good.—So is it, if thou knew'st our purposes iv 3 48
What is a man, If his chief good and market of his time Be but to sleep and feed? a beast, no more iv 4 34
'Twere good she were spoken with iv 5 14
Here lies the water; good: here stands the man; good v 1 17
No medicine in the world can do thee good v 2 325
Our potency made good, take thy reward *Lear* i 1 175
If the matter were good, my lord, I durst swear it were his i 2 68
These late eclipses in the sun and moon portend no good to us i 2 113
Who is too good to pity thee iii 7 90
I'll never care what wickedness I do, If this man come to good iii 7 100
Thy comforts can do me no good at all; Thee they may hurt iv 1 17
This speech of yours hath moved me, And shall perchance do good v 3 200
Some good I mean to do, Despite of mine own nature v 3 243
With my good biting falchion I would have made them skip v 3 276
Very good; well kissed! an excellent courtesy! 'tis so, indeed *Othello* ii 1 176
Since it is as it is, mend it for your own good ii 3 305
How am I then a villain To counsel Cassio to this parallel course, Directly to his good? Divinity of hell! ii 3 356
By how much she strives to do him good, She shall undo her credit ii 3 364

Good. It were not for your quiet nor your good, Nor for my manhood, honesty, or wisdom, To let you know my thoughts . *Othello* iii 3 152
I'll see you soon.—'Tis very good ; I must be circumstanced . . iii 4 201
He had my handkerchief.—Ay, what of that ?—That's not so good now iv 1 23
Good, good : the justice of it pleases : very good . iv 1 222
Trouble yourself no further.—O, pardon me ; 'twill do me good to walk iv 3 2
Are you of good or evil ?—As you shall prove us, praise us . . . v 1 65
Shall she come in ? were't good ?—I think she stirs again . . v 2 94
O thou Othello, that wert once so good, Fall'n in the practice of a damned slave, What shall be said to thee ? . . . . . . v 2 291
She's good, being gone ; The hand could pluck her back that shoved her on . . . . *Ant. and Cleo.* i 2 130
We, ignorant of ourselves, Beg often our own harms, which the wise powers Deny us for our good . . . . ii 1 7
What power is in Agrippa, If I would say, 'Agrippa, be it so,' To make this good ?—The power of Cæsar . . . . ii 2 145
Pour out the pack of matter to mine ear, The good and bad together . ii 5 55
Though it be honest, it is never good To bring bad news . . ii 5 85
I could do more to do Antonius good, But 'twould offend him . iii 1 25
She is low-voiced.—That's not so good : he cannot like her long . iii 3 17
That I might do you service So good as you have done . . iv 2 19
Very good. Give it nothing, I pray you, for it is not worth the feeding v 2 270
The fire of rage is in him, and 'twere good You lean'd unto his sentence *Cymbeline* i 1 77
As fair and as good—a kind of hand-in-hand comparison—had been something too fair and too good for any lady in Britain . . . i 4 75
It is an earnest of a further good That I mean to thee . . . i 5 65
Here are letters for you.—Their tenour good, I trust . . . ii 4 36
Thersites' body is as good as Ajax', When neither are alive . . iv 2 252
A very valiant Briton and a good, That here by mountaineers lies slain iv 3 369
I may wander From east to occident, cry out for service, Try many, all good, serve truly, never Find such another master . . . . iv 2 373
Made good the passage ; cried to those that fled . . . . v 3 23
Since, Jupiter, our son is good, Take off his miseries . . . v 4 85
Let thy effects So follow, to be most unlike our courtiers, As good as promise . . . . v 4 137
I would we were all of one mind, and one mind good . . . v 4 213
Since she is living, let the time run on To good or bad . . v 5 129
He was too good to be Where ill men were . . . . v 5 158
How of descent As good as we ? . . . . v 5 309
But I will prove that two on's are as good As I have given out him . v 5 311
Your danger's ours.—And our good his.—Have at it then . . v 5 315
Like an hypocrite, The which is good in nothing but in sight *Pericles* i 1 123
The care I had and have of subjects' good On thee I lay . . . i 2 118
The good in conversation, To whom I give my benison, Is still at Tarsus . . . . ii Gower 9
For though he strive To killen bad, keep good alive . . . ii Gower 20
He is a happy king, since he gains from his subjects the name of good by his government . . . . ii 1 110
Why, do'e take it, and the gods give thee good on't ! . . . . ii 1 153
In framing an artist, art hath thus decreed, To make some good, but others to exceed ; And you are her labour'd scholar . . . . ii 3 16
Come, come, I know 'tis good for you. Walk half an hour . . iv 1 45
And they with continual action are even as good as rotten . . iv 2 9
If you were born to honour, show it now ; If put upon you, make the judgement good That thought you worthy of it . . . . . iv 6 100
If thou dost Hear from me, it shall be for thy good . . . iv 6 123
It is not good to cross him ; give him way . . . . . . v 1 232
Good a commander. I will rather sue to be despised than to deceive so good a commander . . . . *Othello* ii 3 279
Good a continuer. I would my horse had the speed of your tongue, and so good a continuer . . . . *Much Ado* i 1 143
Good a deed. As good a deed as to drink when a man's a-hungry *T. Night* ii 3 135
An 'twere not as good a deed as drink, to turn true man . 1 *Hen. IV.* ii 2 23
Good a gentleman. As good a gentleman as the emperor . *Hen. V.* iv 1 42
Though he be as good a gentleman as the devil is . . . . iv 7 144
Good a gift. I'll do thee service for so good a gift . . 3 *Hen. VI.* v 1 33
Good a grace. Nor the judge's robe, Become them with one half so good a grace As mercy does . . . . *Meas. for Meas.* ii 2 62
Good a heart. If I could bid the fifth welcome with so good a heart as I can bid the other four farewell . . . . . *Mer. of Venice* i 2 141
Good a house. A noble gentleman 'tis, if he would not keep so good a house . . . . *T. of Athens* iii 1 24
Good a king. This is not well, rash and unbridled boy, To fly the favours of so good a king . . . . *All's Well* iii 2 31
Good a lady. I could wish he would modestly examine himself, to see how much he is unworthy so good a lady . . . . . *Much Ado* ii 3 217
So good a lady that no tongue could ever Pronounce dishonour of her *Hen. VIII.* ii 3 3
Good a man. As good a man as he, sir, whoe'er I am . .2 *Hen. IV.* iv 3 12
Being as good a man as yourself, both in the disciplines of war *Hen. V.* iii 2 140
I do not know you so good a man as myself . . . . . iii 2 143
Why, what is he? as good a man as York. . . . 1 *Hen. VI.* iii 4 36
I serve as good a man as you.—No better.—Well, sir . *Rom. and Jul.* i 1 62
Good a mean. Many a man would take you at your word, And go indeed, having so good a mean . . . . *Com. of Errors* i 2 18
Good a mind. Continue still in this so good a mind . 2 *Hen. VI.* iv 9 17
Good a proficient. I am so good a proficient in one quarter of an hour, that I can drink with any tinker . . . . . 1 *Hen. IV.* ii 4 19
Good a quarrel. No more than well becomes So good a quarrel and so bad a peer . . . . 2 *Hen. VI.* ii 1 28
Good a thing. I will requite you with as good a thing . *Tempest* v 1 169
Good a trick. As good a trick as ever hangman served thief *T. of Athens* ii 2 99
Good a wife. He has much worthy blame laid upon him for shaking off so good a wife . . . . *All's Well* iv 3 8
Good a will. Cæsar, now be still : I kill'd not thee with half so good a will . . . . *J. Cæsar* v 5 51
Good a woman. What should such a fool Do with so good a woman? *Oth.* v 2 234
Good accent. Well spoken, with good accent and good discretion *Hamlet* ii 2 489
Good acceptance. How did this offer seem received, my lord ?—With good acceptance . . . . *Hen. V.* i 1 83
Good actor. And was accounted a good actor . . . . *Hamlet* iii 2 106
Good acts. I have been The book of his good acts . . *Coriolanus* v 2 15
Good addition. I mean to stride your steed, and at all times To undercrest your good addition To the fairness of my power . . . i 9 72
Good advantage. Nor lose the good advantage of his grace By seeming cold or careless of his will . . . . . . 2 *Hen. IV.* iv 4 28
You have now the good advantage of the night . . . *Lear* ii 1 24
Good advice. To give the onset to thy good advice . . *T. G. of Ver.* iii 2 94
Thy son is banish'd upon good advice . . . . . *Richard II.* i 3 233
Good advice. May be restored With good advice and little medicine 2 *Hen. IV.* iii 1 43
We will prosecute by good advice Mortal revenge . . *T. Andron.* iv 1 92
We should have else desired your good advice . . . *Macbeth* iii 1 21
Good aid. By the good aid that I of you shall borrow . *All's Well* iii 7 11
Good air. Beggars all, Sir John : marry, good air . . 2 *Hen. IV.* v 3 9
Good ale. She brews good ale.—And thereof comes the proverb: 'Blessing of your heart, you brew good ale' . . . . *T. G. of Ver.* iii 1 304
Good amendment. I see a good amendment of life in thee . 1 *Hen. IV.* i 2 114
Good amends. Now Lord be thanked for my good amends ! *T. of Shrew* Ind. 2 99
Good ancestors. This youth, howe'er distress'd, appears he hath had Good ancestors . . . . *Cymbeline* iv 2 48
Good angel. Now, good angels Preserve the king . . . *Tempest* ii 1 306
Let's write good angel on the devil's horn . . *Meas. for Meas.* ii 4 16
O, my sweet beef, I must still be good angel to thee . 1 *Hen. IV.* iii 3 199
There is a good angel about him ; but the devil outbids him too 2 *Hen. IV.* ii 4 362
Go thou to Richard, and good angels guard thee ! . . *Richard III.* iv 1 93
Good angels guard thy battle ! live, and flourish ! . . . v 3 138
Good angels guard thee from the boar's annoy ! . . . . v 3 156
God and good angels fight on Richmond's side ; And Richard falls . v 3 175
Go with me, like good angels, to my end . . . *Hen. VIII.* ii 1 75
Good angels keep it from us ! What may it be ? You do not doubt my faith ? . . . . ii 1 142
Now, good angels Fly o'er thy royal head, and shade thy person ! . . v 1 159
Good answer. I thank God.—'Thank God ;' a good answer *As Y. Like It* v 1 27
Good Antonio. Let good Antonio look he keep his day . *Mer. of Venice* ii 8 25
The good Antonio, the honest Antonio . . . . . . iii 1 14
Good apparel. Find her the infernal Ate in good apparel . *Much Ado* ii 1 263
Good appliance. I heard of an Egyptian That had nine hours lien dead, Who was by good appliance recovered . . . . *Pericles* iii 2 86
Good archer. Come, to this gear. You are a good archer *T. Andron.* iv 3 52
Good argument. There's not a piece of feather in our host—Good argument, I hope, we will not fly . . . . *Hen. V.* iv 3 113
I had good argument for kissing once . . . *Troi. and Cres.* iv 5 26
Good armour. I have known when he would have walked ten mile a-foot to see a good armour . . . . *Much Ado* ii 3 17
Good arms. 'Bove the contentious waves he kept, and oar'd Himself with his good arms . . . . *Tempest* ii 1 119
They have galls, Good arms, strong joints . . . *Troi. and Cres.* i 3 238
Good array. Stand we in good array . . . . . 3 *Hen. VI.* v 1 62
Good as my word. So I have promised, and I'll be as good as my word *M. W.* iii 4 112
For that I promised you, I'll be as good as my word . . *T. Night* iii 4 357
I will be as good as my word : this that you heard was but a colour 2 *Hen. IV.* v 5 90
And I have been as good as my word . . . . . *Hen. V.* iv 8 33
Good as thy word. Darest thou be as good as thy word now? 1 *Hen. IV.* iii 3 164
Good at any thing. He's as good at any thing and yet a fool *As Y. Like It* v 4 110
Good beards. As many as have good beards or good faces . . . Epil 22
Good beauties. I do wish That your good beauties be the happy cause Of Hamlet's wildness . . . . *Hamlet* iii 1 39
Good belly. The senators of Rome are this good belly . *Coriolanus* i 1 152
Good bilbo. Like a good bilbo, in the circumference of a peck *Mer. Wives* iii 5 112
Good blade. A very good blade ! a very tall man ! . . *Rom. and Jul.* ii 4 31
Good block. When we are born, we cry that we are come To this great stage of fools : this' a good block . . . . *Lear* iv 6 187
Good blossom. O, that this good blossom could be kept ! . 2 *Hen. IV.* ii 2 101
Good blunt fellow. A good blunt fellow . . . . . *K. John* i 1 71
Good boatswain, have care. Where's the master ? . . *Tempest* i 1 10
Good body, I thank thee. Let them say 'tis grossly done *Mer. Wives* ii 2 148
Good bow. Jesu, Jesu, dead ! a' drew a good bow ; and dead ! 2 *Hen. IV.* iii 2 48
Good bowler. He is a marvellous good neighbour, faith, and a very good bowler . . . . *L. L. Lost* v 2 587
Good boy. Thou 'rt a good boy : this secrecy of thine shall be a tailor to thee . . . . *Mer. Wives* iii 3 33
A Corinthian, a lad of mettle, a good boy . . . . 1 *Hen. IV.* ii 4 13
Good breath. Now is my day's work done ; I'll take good breath *T. and C.* v 8 3
Good breeding. He that hath learned no wit by nature nor art may complain of good breeding . . . . . . *As Y. Like It* iii 2 31
Good bricklayer. An honest man, and a good bricklayer . 2 *Hen. VI.* iv 2 43
Good bringing up. Which . . . Witness good bringing up *T. G. of Ver.* iv 4 74
And liberal To mine own children in good bringing up . . *T. of Shrew* i 1 99
Good brother. Could my good brother suffer you to do it? . . *Lear* iv 2 44
If it be sin to say so, sir, I yoke me In my good brother's fault *Cymbeline* iv 2 20
Good Brutus. Who at Philippi the good Brutus ghosted *Ant. and Cleo.* ii 6 13
Good bushes. Yet to good wine they do use good bushes *As Y. Like It* Epil. 6
Good cabbage. Goot worts.—Good worts ! good cabbage . *Mer. Wives* i 1 124
Good capacity. Of good capacity and breeding . . . *T. Night* iii 4 204
Good capon. In fair round belly with good capon lined . *As Y. L. It* ii 7 154
Good captain. Gower is a good captain . . . . . *Hen. V.* iv 7 156
Good care. Well ; keep good quarter and good care to-night . *K. John* v 5 20
Good carriage. Samson, master : he was a man of good carriage *L. L. Lost* i 2 74
Making them women of good carriage . . . . *Rom. and Jul.* i 4 94
Good case. She hath been in good case, and the truth is, poverty hath distracted her . . . . 2 *Hen. IV.* ii 1 115
Good cause. Hoping you'll find good cause to whip them all *Meas. for Meas.* ii 1 142
Have I not cause to weep ?—As good cause as one would desire *As Y. L. It* iii 4 5
God in thy good cause make thee prosperous ! . . . *Richard II.* i 3 78
Remember this, God and our good cause fight upon our side *Richard III.* v 3 240
Good caution. For thy good caution, thanks . . . . *Macbeth* iv 1 73
Good cheer. I have good cheer at home . . . . *Mer. Wives* iii 2 52
Well, I will meet you, so I may have good cheer . . . *Much Ado* v 1 153
Therefore be of good cheer, for truly I think you are damned *M. of Ven.* iii 5 5
Good cheer, Antonio ! What, man, courage yet ! . . . . iv 1 111
Be of good cheer, youth : you a man ! you lack a man's heart *As Y. Like It* iv 3 164
My banquet is to close our stomachs up, After our great good cheer *T. of S.* v 2 10
We shall Do nothing but eat, and make good cheer . . . 2 *Hen. IV.* v 3 18
'How now, Sir John !' quoth I : 'what, man ! be o' good cheer' *Hen. V.* ii 3 19
O unpleasing news !—Be of good cheer : mother, how fares your grace? *Richard III.* iv 1 38
Be of good cheer ; They shall no more prevail than we give way to *Hen. VIII.* v 1 142
Good cheer ; There is no harm intended to your person . . *J. Cæsar* iii 1 89
How do you, women ? What, what ! good cheer ! . . *Ant. and Cleo.* iv 15 83
Be of good cheer ; You're fall'n into a princely hand, fear nothing . v 2 21
Good child. Why, now you speak Like a good child . . . *Hamlet* iv 5 148
Good Christians. And void of all profanation in the world that good Christians ought to have . . . . *Meas. for Meas.* ii 1 56
Good city. Unless, by not so doing, our good city Cleave in the midst, and perish . . . . *Coriolanus* iii 2 27
Good clothes. What is a whoremaster, fool ?—A fool in good clothes, and something like thee . . . . *T. of Athens* ii 2 114

Good clothes. She has a good face, speaks well, and has excellent good clothes *Pericles* iv 2 52
Good colour. His hair is of a good colour *As Y. Like It* iii 4 11
Good comfort. I thank you for that good comfort *Mer. Wives* iii 4 54
My clerk hath some good comforts too for you *Mer. of Venice* v 1 289
I thank ye; and be blest for your good comfort! *As Y. Like It* ii 7 135
Comfort, good comfort! We must to the king *W. Tale* iv 4 848
So much to my good comfort, as it is Now piercing to my soul v 3 33
Be of good comfort *K. John* v 3 9; v 7 25
Entertain good comfort, And cheer his grace *Richard III.* i 3 4
Yet this good comfort bring I to your grace iv 4 522
And heartily entreats you take good comfort *Hen. VIII.* iv 2 119
Good command. A word of exceeding good command 2 *Hen. IV.* iii 2 84
Good company; with them shall Proteus go *T. G. of Ver.* i 3 43
Peace here; grace and good company! *Meas. for Meas.* iii 1 44
You have no employment for me?—None, but to desire your good company *Much Ado* ii 1 281
Arm'd With his good will and thy good company *T. of Shrew.* i 1 6
He would have all as merry As, first, good company, good wine, good welcome, Can make good people *Hen. VIII.* i 4 6
Good compass. Lived well and in good compass 1 *Hen. IV.* iii 3 22
Good complexion. Too flaming a praise for a good complexion *T. and C.* i 2 113
Good conceit. The good conceit I hold of thee—For thou hast shown some sign of good desert—Makes me the better to confer with thee *T. G. of Ver.* iii 2 17
I know you are a gentleman of good conceit *As Y. Like It* v 2 59
Good-conceited. A very excellent good-conceited thing *Cymbeline* ii 3 18
Good conclusion. Beauteous as ink; a good conclusion *L. L. Lost* v 2 41
Good condition. The town is ta'en!—'Twill be deliver'd back on good condition *Coriolanus* i 10 2
What good condition can a treaty find I' the part that is at mercy? i 10 6
Good conscience. And the witness of a good conscience *M. Wives* iv 2 221
And done in the testimony of a good conscience *L. L. Lost* iv 2 2
A very gentle beast, and of a good conscience *M. N. Dream* v 1 230
Now, my masters, for a true face and good conscience 1 *Hen. IV.* ii 4 551
A good conscience will make any possible satisfaction 2 *Hen. IV.* Epil. 21
Good constraint. 'Tis a good constraint of fortune *Pericles* iii 2 55
Good construction. And my pretext to strike at him admits A good construction *Coriolanus* v 6 21
Good content. God hold it, to your honour's good content! *Richard III* iii 2 107
Good convenience. Lay upon him all the honour, That good convenience claims *All's Well* iii 2 75
Good correction. Under your good correction *Meas. for Meas.* ii 2 10
Good counsel. Lose my time, War with good counsel *T. G. of Ver.* i 1 68
I thank your worship for your good counsel *Meas. for Meas.* ii 1 266
Let her wear it out with good counsel *Much Ado* ii 3 208
Such a hare is madness the youth, to skip o'er the meshes of good counsel the cripple *Mer. of Venice* i 2 22
I would give him some good counsel, for he seems to have the quotidian of love upon him *As Y. Like It* iii 2 383
Two faults, madonna, that drink and good counsel will amend *T. Night* i 5 48
Cast your good counsels Upon his passion *W. Tale* iv 4 506
Good counsel, marry: learn it, learn it, marquess *Richard III.* i 3 261
Black and portentous must this humour prove, Unless good counsel may the cause remove *Rom. and Jul.* i 1 148
I could have stay'd here all the night To hear good counsel iii 3 160
And so I thank you for your good counsel. Come, my coach! Good night, ladies; good night, sweet ladies; good night, good night *Ham.* iv 5 72
This man hath had good counsel:—a hundred knights! *Lear* i 4 345
Good counsellors lack no clients *Meas. for Meas.* i 2 109
Can he that speaks with the tongue of an enemy be a good counsellor? 2 *Hen. VI.* iv 2 182
Good countryman. For I am Welsh, you know, good countryman *Hen. V.* iv 7 110
Good courage. Away, then, with good courage! *K. John* v 1 78
Good cover. Are they good?—As the event stamps them: but they have a good cover *Much Ado* i 2 8
Good creature. What of her?—Why, sir, she's a good creature *M. Wives* ii 2 56
I warrant, good creature, wheresoe'er she is, Her heart weighs sadly *All's W.* iii 5 69
And yet my conscience says She's a good creature *Hen. VIII.* v 1 25
Good credit. Lord Cerimon hath letters of good credit, sir, My father's dead *Pericles* v 3 77
Good dancer. God match me with a good dancer!—Amen *Much Ado* ii 1 111
Good dawning to thee, friend; art of this house? *Lear* ii 2 1
Good day and happiness, dear Rosalind! *As Y. Like It* iv 1 30
And I do hope good days and long to see *T. of Shrew* i 2 193
Fair lovely maid, once more good day to thee iv 5 33
By this good day, I know not the phrase 2 *Hen. IV.* iii 2 81
So happy be the issue, brother England, Of this good day *Hen. V.* v 2 13
Good day at once.—Welcome, good brother *T. of Athens* iii 4 7
Good day *T. G. of Ver.* iv 4; *M. Ado* v 1; *W. Tale* i 2; 2 *Hen. IV.* iv 2; 3 *Hen. VI.* v 6; *Rich. III.* i 1; *Hen. VIII.* ii 2; *Troi. and Cres.* iii 3; *Coriolanus* i 3; *T. of Athens* i 1
Good day's work. Now have I done a good day's work *Richard III.* ii 1 1
Good deceit. For that is good deceit Which mates him first that first intends deceit 2 *Hen. VI.* iii 1 264
Good deed. So shines a good deed in a naughty world *Mer. of Venice* v 1 91
Yet, good deed, Leontes, I love thee not a jar o' the clock behind *W. Tale* i 2 42
One good deed dying tongueless Slaughters a thousand waiting upon that i 2 92
My last good deed was to entreat his stay: What was my first? i 2 97
If there be any of him left, I'll bury it.—That's a good deed iii 3 137
'Tis a lucky day, boy, and we'll do good deeds on't iii 3 143
An 'twere not as good deed as drink, to break the pate on thee 1 *Hen. IV.* ii 1 32
But his few bad words are matched with as few good deeds *Hen. V.* iii 2 42
'Tis well said again; And 'tis a kind of good deed to say well *Hen. VIII.* iii 2 153
Those scraps are good deeds past *Troi. and Cres.* iii 3 148
If one good deed in all my life I did, I do repent it *T. Andron* v 3 189
O monument And wonder of good deeds evilly bestow'd! *T. of Athens* iv 3 467
Whose repair and ranchise Shall, by the power we hold, be our good deed *Cymbeline* iii 1 58
I would not thy good deeds should from my lips Pluck a hard sentence v 5 288
Good demand. Tush, tush!—A good demand *Coriolanus* iii 2 45
Good den. God save you!—Good den, brother *Much Ado* iii 2 83
Good den, good den.—Good day to both of you v 1 46
Good den, sir Richard!—God-a-mercy, fellow! *K. John* i 1 185
Cod and Saint Stephen give you good den *T. Andron.* iv 4 43
God ye good den, fair gentlewoman.—Is it good den? *Rom. and Jul.* ii 4 116
Gentlemen, good den: a word with one of you iii 1 41
Good deputy. What is the news from this good deputy? *Meas. for Meas.* iv 1 27
Good descending. Didst thou not say, when I did push thee back, that thou camest From good descending? *Pericles* v 1 129

Good desert. Thou hast shown some sign of good desert *T. G. of Ver.* iii 2 18
If that the king Have any way your good deserts forgot 1 *Hen. IV.* iv 3 46
For these good deserts, We here create you Earl of Shrewsbury 1 *Hen. VI.* iii 4 25
My lord protector will, I doubt it not, See you well guerdon'd for these good deserts 2 *Hen. VI.* i 4 49
Good devil. 'Good Gloucester' and 'good devil' were alike, And both preposterous 3 *Hen. VI.* v 6 4
Good diet. Past cure of the thing you wot of, unless they kept very good diet *Meas. for Meas.* ii 1 116
Good digestion. A good digestion to you all *Hen. VIII.* i 4 62
Now, good digestion wait on appetite, And health on both! *Macbeth* iii 4 38
Good dinner. I would I were as sure of a good dinner *T. of Shrew* i 2 218
Good direction. A good direction, warlike sovereign *Richard III.* v 3 302
Good discourse. Of good discourse, an excellent musician *Much Ado* ii 3 35
Good discourser. The tract of every thing Would by a good discourser lose some life *Hen. VIII.* i 1 41
Good discretion. All this was order'd by the good discretion Of the right reverend Cardinal i 1 50
Well spoken, with good accent and good discretion *Hamlet* ii 2 489
Good dish. They are not China dishes, but very good dishes *M. for M.* ii 1 97
Telling us she had a good dish of prawns 2 *Hen. IV.* ii 1 104
Good disposition. Then westward-ho! Grace and good disposition Attend your ladyship! *T. Night* iii 1 146
Good divine. It is a good divine that follows his own instructions *M. of V.* i 2 15
Good divinity. To say 'ay' and 'no' to every thing that I said!—'Ay' and 'no' too was no good divinity *Lear* iv 6 101
Good doers. Talkers are no good doers *Richard III.* i 3 352
Good dog. 'Tis a good dog.—A cur, sir.—Sir, he's a good dog, and a fair dog *Mer. Wives* i 1 96
Good double beer. Here's a pot of good double beer, neighbour 2 *Hen. VI.* ii 3 64
Good dowry. Will you, upon good dowry, marry her? *Mer. Wives* i 1 246
Good dreams. I am most joyful, madam, such good dreams Possess your fancy *Hen. VIII.* iv 2 93
Good drum. He's a good drum, my lord, but a naughty orator *All's W.* v 3 253
Good dry oats. I could munch your good dry oats *M. N. Dream* iv 1 36
Good duke. You, forsooth, had the good duke to keep 2 *Hen. VI.* iii 2 183
Good dulness. Thou art inclined to sleep; 'tis a good dulness *Tempest* i 2 185
Good ear. I have a reasonable good ear in music. Let's have the tongs and the bones *M. N. Dream* iv 1 31
Good earnest. But love no man in good earnest *As Y. Like It* i 2 30
Turning these jests out of service, let us talk in good earnest i 3 26
In good earnest, and so God mend me iv 1 192
Are you moved, my lord?—No, in good earnest *W. Tale* i 2 150
Good easy man. When he thinks, good easy man, full surely His greatness is a-ripening, nips his root *Hen. VIII.* iii 2 356
Good education. My father charged you in his will to give me good education *As Y. Like It* i 1 71
Good effects. And your large speeches may your deeds approve, That good effects may spring from words of love *Lear* i 1 188
Good end. They say he made a good end *Hamlet* iv 5 186
Good English. I will never mistrust my wife again, till thou art able to woo her in good English *Mer. Wives* v 5 142
I love her; and that is good English *Hen. V.* v 2 311
Good enough. And tells you currish thanks is good enough for such a present *T. G. of Ver.* iv 4 53
O that I had a title good enough to keep his name company! *Mer. of Ven.* iii 1 15
The priest was good enough, for all the old gentleman's saying *As Y. L. It* v 1 3
Choughs' language, gabble enough, and good enough *All's Well* iv 1 22
These clothes are good enough to drink in *T. Night* i 3 11
I have no exquisite reason for't, but I have reason good enough ii 3 158
I did never see such pitiful rascals.—Tut, tut; good enough to toss 1 *Hen. IV.* iv 2 71
He's a man good enough: he's one o' the soundest judgements in Troy *Troi. and Cres.* i 2 207
Why do you say 'thwack our general'?—I do not say 'thwack our general;' but he was always good enough for him *Coriolanus* iv 5 193
Thou then look'dst like a villain; now methinks Thy favour's good enough *Cymbeline* iii 4 51
Good epilogues. Good plays prove the better by the help of good epilogues *As Y. Like It* Epil. 7
Good epithet. Suffer love! a good epithet! *Much Ado* v 2 67
Good escape. Had he 'scaped, methinks we should have heard The happy tidings of his good escape 3 *Hen. VI.* ii 1 7
Good esquires. Six thousand and two hundred good esquires *Hen. V.* i 1 14
Good esteem. With other gentlemen of good esteem *T. G. of Ver.* i 3 40
She is of good esteem, Her dowry wealthy *T. of Shrew* iv 5 64
Than from true evidence of good esteem 2 *Hen. VI.* iii 2 21
Good even. O, give ye good even! here's a million of manners *T. G. of V.* ii 1 104
Madam, good even to your ladyship iv 2 85
I follow. Good even and twenty, good Master Page! *Mer. Wives* ii 1 202
God ye good even, William.—And good even to you, sir *As Y. Like It* v 1 16
Good even *Meas. for Meas.* iii 2; iv 3; *As Y. Like It* ii 4; iii 3; v 1; *Rom. and Jul.* ii 6; *J. Cæsar* i 3; *Hamlet* i 2
Good event. Against ill chances men are ever merry; But heaviness foreruns the good event 2 *Hen. IV.* iv 2 82
Good ewes. A score of good ewes may be worth ten pounds iii 2 56
Good exclamation. I hear as good exclamation on your worship as of any man in the city *Much Ado* iii 5 28
Good excuse. Not being well married, it will be a good excuse for me hereafter to leave my wife *As Y. Like It* iii 3 94
Good exercise. The rich advantage of good exercise *K. John* iv 2 60
Good expedition. Fear o'ershades me: Good expedition be my friend and comfort! *W. Tale* i 2 458
Good eye. Who even now gave me good eyes too *Mer. Wives* i 3 67
I have a good eye, uncle; I can see a church by daylight *Much Ado* ii 1 85
Good face. As many as have good beards or good faces *As Y. Like It* Epil. 22
Yet they lie deadly that tell you you have good faces *Coriolanus* ii 1 67
She has a good face, speaks well, and has excellent good clothes *Pericles* iv 2 51
Good-faced. No, good-faced sir; no, sweet sir *W. Tale* iv 3 123
Good faith, it is such another Nan *Mer. Wives* i 4 159
Trow you what he call'd me?—Qualm, perhaps.—Yes, in good faith *L. L. Lost* v 2 280
And do you, Gratiano, mean good faith?—Yes, faith, my lord *M. of Ven.* iii 2 212
Apt, in good faith; very apt. Well, go thy way *T. Night* i 5 28
Sick of a calm; yea, good faith.—So is all her sect 2 *Hen. IV.* ii 4 40
Fight closer, or, good faith, you'll catch a blow 3 *Hen. VI.* iii 2 23
What are you sewing here? A fine spot, in good faith *Coriolanus* i 3 56
I beseech you, remember— Nay, good my lord; for mine ease, in good faith *Hamlet* v 2 110
Good faith, how foolish are our minds! *Othello* iv 3 23

Good falcon. I bless the time When my good falcon made her flight across Thy father's ground . . . *W. Tale* iv 4 15
Good fate. Stand fast, good Fate, to his hanging . . . *Tempest* i 1 33
Good father. And pity her for her good father's sake *As Y. Like It* i 2 293
I pray you, stand good father to me now . . . *T. of Shrew* iv 4 21
I am content, in a good father's care, To have him match'd . . . iv 4 31
I thank my good father, I am able to maintain it . . . v 1 78
It much repairs me To talk of your good father *All's Well* i 2 31
Good favour. By your good favour,—for surely, sir, a good favour you have . . . *Meas. for Meas.* iv 2 33
You are a little, By your good favour, too sharp *Hen. VIII.* v 3 74
Good feature. Thou hast, Sebastian, done good feature shame *T. Night* iii 4 400
Good fellow. That shrewd and knavish sprite Call'd Robin Goodfellow *M. N. Dream* ii 1 34
There be good fellows in the world, an a man could light on them *T. of S.* i 1 132
Well said; thou'rt a good fellow.—Faith, I'll bear no base mind 2 *Hen. IV.* iii 2 256
If he be not fellow with the best king, thou shalt find the best king of good fellows . . . *Hen. V.* v 2 262
Go on before; I'll talk with this good fellow. How now, sirrah *Rich. III.* iii 2 97
That good fellow, If I command him, follows my appointment *Hen. VIII.* ii 2 133
Good fellows all, The latest of my wealth I'll share amongst you *T. of A.* iv 2 22
These good fellows will bring thee where I am *Hamlet* iv 6 27
He's a good fellow, I can tell you that; He'll strike, and quickly too *Lear* v 3 284
Good fellowship. There's neither honesty, manhood, nor good fellowship in thee . . . 1 *Hen. IV.* i 2 156
Lads, boys, hearts of gold, all the titles of good fellowship come to you! ii 4 307
Tell me true, Even in the soul of sound good-fellowship *Troi. and Cres.* iv 1 52
Good fire. The master I speak of ever keeps a good fire . *All's Well* iv 5 51
Good flock. Come on, And bid us welcome to your sheep-shearing, As your good flock shall prosper . . . *W. Tale* iv 4 70
Good fool, as ever thou wilt deserve well at my hand . . *T. Night* iv 2 86
Good fool, help me to some light and some paper . . . iv 2 113
Yes, indeed: thou wouldst make a good fool . . . *Lear* i 5 41
Good fooling. Wit, an't be thy will, put me into good fooling! *T. Night* i 5 35
Good foot. With a good leg and a good foot, uncle, and money enough in his purse . . . *Much Ado* ii 1 15
Good for. What's that good for? . . . *Mer. of Venice* iii 1 54
Good for nothing but taking up; and that thou'rt scarce worth *All's Well* ii 3 218
Good form. 'Tis a good form . . . *T. of Athens* i 1 17
Good fortune. And how does your content Tender your own good fortune? . . . *Tempest* ii 1 270
Now heaven send thee good fortune! . . . *Mer. Wives* iii 4 105
If any thing fall to you upon this, more than thanks and good fortune *Meas. for Meas.* iv 2 191
You would be, sweet madam, if your miseries were in the same abundance as your good fortunes are . . . *Mer. of Venice* i 2 4
Good fortune then! To make me blest or cursed'st among men . . ii 1 45
If any man in Italy have a fairer table which doth offer to swear upon a book, I shall have good fortune . . . ii 2 168
By good fortune I have lighted well On this young man . *T. of Shrew* i 2 168
Good fortune and the favour of the king Smile upon this contract *All's W.* ii 3 184
I hope, sir, I have your good will to have mine own good fortunes . ii 4 16
Good fortune come to thee! For thou wast got i' the way of honesty *K. John* i 1 180
Now breathe we, lords: good fortune bids us pause . . 3 *Hen. VI.* ii 6 31
Go thou to Richmond, and good fortune guide thee! *Richard III.* iv 1 92
A man that all his time Hath founded his good fortunes on your love *Othello* iii 4 94
Give me good fortune.—I make not, but foresee . . *Ant. and Cleo.* i 2 13
Good fortune, worthy soldier; and farewell . . . iii 2 22
Good friar. Words against me! this is a good friar, belike! *Meas. for Meas.* v 1 131
Good-Friday. Sir Robert might have eat his part in me Upon Good-Friday and ne'er broke his fast . . . *K. John* i 1 235
Jack! how agrees the devil and thee about thy soul, that thou soldest him on Good-Friday last for a cup of Madeira and a cold capon's leg? 1 *Hen. IV.* i 2 128
Good friend. Be not afeard—thy good friend Trinculo . *Tempest* ii 2 106
Nor have I seen More that I may call men than you, good friend, And my dear father . . . iii 1 51
What harmony is this? My good friends, hark! . . . iii 3 18
I have grated upon my good friends for three reprieves . *Mer. Wives* ii 2 6
O, thy letter, thy letter! he's a good friend of mine: Stand aside *L. L. L.* iv 1 54
The king is a noble gentleman, and my familiar, I do assure ye, very good friend . . . v 1 101
Ere I ope his letter, I pray you, tell me how my good friend doth *Mer. of Venice* iii 2 236
And that he that wants money, means and content is without three good friends . . . *As Y. Like It* iii 2 27
And be sure I count myself in nothing else so happy As in a soul remembering my good friends . . . *Richard II.* ii 3 47
A good plot, good friends, and full of expectation . . 1 *Hen. IV.* ii 3 19
I am good friends with my father and may do any thing . . iii 3 203
A good-limbed fellow; young, strong, and of good friends 2 *Hen. IV.* iii 2 114
I thank you; You are always my good friend . . *Hen. VIII.* v 3 59
The gods give him joy, and make him good friend to the people! *Coriol.* ii 3 142
He is my very good friend, and an honourable gentleman *T. of Athens* iii 2 2
Your poor servant ever.—Sir, my good friend; I'll change that name with you . . . *Hamlet* i 2 163
My most dear lord!—My excellent good friends! . . . ii 2 228
To his good friends thus wide I'll ope my arms . . . iv 5 145
Good gentleman. O my brother, Good gentleman! . . *W. Tale* v 1 148
Alas, good gentleman! alas, good Cassio! . . . *Othello* v 1 115
Good gift. She has good gifts.—Seven hundred pounds and possibilities is goot gifts . . . *Mer. Wives* i 1 64
Here, take her hand, Proud scornful boy, unworthy this good gift *All's Well* ii 3 158
And hath all the good gifts of nature . . . *T. Night* i 3 29
Good girl. Anne is a good girl, and I wish . . . *Mer. Wives* i 4 35
'Good Gloucester' and 'good devil' were alike . . 3 *Hen. VI.* v 6 4
Good gods. The good gods assuage thy wrath . . *Coriolanus* v 2 83
The gods confound—hear me, you good gods all—The Athenians! *T. of A.* iv 1 37
The good gods will mock me presently, When I shall pray *Ant. and Cleo.* iii 4 15
You good gods, Let what is here contain'd relish of love . *Cymbeline* iii 2 29
Now, the good gods Throw their best eyes upon't! . . *Pericles* ii 1 36
Good government. Let men say we be men of good government 1 *Hen. IV.* i 2 31
He deserves so to be called for his peaceable reign and good government *Pericles* ii 1 108
Good grace. With all good grace to grace a gentleman . *T. G. of Ver.* ii 4 74
Truly, the moon shines with a good grace . . . *M. N. Dream* v 1 273
Swears with a good grace, and wears his boots very smooth 2 *Hen. IV.* ii 4 270
Good grace. The Lord preserve thy good grace! by my troth, welcome 2 *Hen. IV.* ii 4 315
No, no; by God's good grace his son shall reign . . *Richard III.* ii 3 10
What cause . . . , That thus you should proceed to put me off, And take your good grace from me? . . . *Hen. VIII.* ii 4 22
With what else needful your good grace shall think To be sent after me *Othello* i 3 287
Good grandam. There's a good grandam, boy, that would blot thee *K. John* ii 1 133
Good ground. I leap down: Good ground, be pitiful and hurt me not! . iv 3 2
Then on good ground we fear, If we do fear this body hath a tail *Cymb.* iv 2 143
Good guard, Until their greater pleasures first be known . . *Lear* v 3 1
I think I can discover him, if you please To get good guard . *Othello* i 1 180
Never anger Made good guard for itself . . . *Ant. and Cleo.* iv 1 10
Good guest. I shall procure-a you de good guest, de earl *Mer. Wives* ii 3 95
Good hand. But release me from my bands With the help of your good hands . . . *Tempest* Epil. 10
Give me your good hand, give me your worship's good hand 2 *Hen. IV.* iii 2 91
Ill art thou repaid For that good hand thou sent'st the emperor *T. An.* iii 1 236
This is the incarnate devil That robb'd Andronicus of his good hand . v 1 41
'Tis a good hand, A frank one.—You may, indeed, say so *Othello* iii 4 43
Quick, quick, good hands.—Hold, worthy lady, hold . *Ant. and Cleo.* v 2 39
Good hap. Wish me partaker in thy happiness When thou dost meet good hap . . . *T. G. of Ver.* i 1 15
What's her name in the cap?—Rosaline, by good hap . *L. L. Lost* ii 1 210
Until the heavens, envying earth's good hap, Add an immortal title *Richard II.* i 1 23
And he shall signify from time to time Every good hap to you that chances here . . . *Rom. and Jul.* iii 3 171
By good hap, yonder's my lord; I have sweat to see his honour *T. of A.* iii 2 27
Good hare-finder. Cupid is a good hare-finder . . . *Much Ado* i 1 186
Good haste. Thou hast made good haste: Come, we will walk *M. for M.* iv 5 11
Good hay, sweet hay, hath no fellow . . . *M. N. Dream* iv 1 37
Good head-piece. He that has a house to put's head in has a good head-piece . . . *Lear* iii 2 26
Good health. Your father's in good health . . *T. G. of Ver.* ii 4 50
How does his highness?—Madam, in good health . . *Hen. VIII.* iv 2 124
I am glad to see your honour in good health . . . *Pericles* iv 6 24
Good hearing. 'Tis a good hearing when children are toward . *T. of Shrew* v 2 182
Good heart. Cheerly, good hearts! Out of our way, I say . *Tempest* i 1 29
Much good do it your good heart! . . . *Mer. Wives* i 1 83
Good heart, what grace hast thou, thus to reprove These worms? *L. L. L.* iv 3 153
Well then, take a good heart and counterfeit to be a man *As Y. Like It* iv 3 174
That's well said; a good heart's worth gold . . . 2 *Hen. IV.* ii 4 34
God's blessing of your good heart! and so she is . . . ii 4 329
But a good heart, Kate, is the sun and the moon . . *Hen. V.* v 2 170
I rather weep.—Good heart, at what?—At thy good heart's oppression.—Why, such is love's transgression . . . *Rom. and Jul.* i 1 190
Good heart, and, i' faith, I will tell her as much . . . ii 4 184
And I eat root. Much good dich thy good heart, Apemantus! *T. of Athens* i 2 73
Bid her have good heart: She soon shall know of us . *Ant. and Cleo.* v 1 56
Good heavens. Such a foe, good heavens! . . . *Cymbeline* iii 6 27
Good heed. Take good heed You charge not in your spleen a noble person *Hen. VIII.* i 2 173
Good honour. And do bring in here before your good honour two notorious benefactors . . . *Meas. for Meas.* ii 1 50
Good hope. His designs crave haste, his haste good hope *Richard II.* ii 2 44
Madam, good hope; his grace speaks cheerfully . . *Richard III.* i 3 34
I have good hope Thou didst not know on't . . . *Lear* i 4 191
Good horns. Many a man has good horns, and knows no end of them. Well, that is the dowry of his wife . . . *As Y. Like It* iii 3 54
Good horse. In such great letters as they write 'Here is good horse to hire' . . . *Much Ado* i 1 268
So, the good horse is mine.—I'll buy him of you . . *Coriolanus* i 4 5
Good host. Take the shadow of this tree For your good host . *Lear* v 2 2
Good hour of night, Sir Thomas! . . . *Hen. VIII.* v 1 5
Good house. He is a gentleman of a good house . . *Hen. V.* iv 4 48
Good householders. I press me none but good householders . 1 *Hen. IV.* iv 2 16
Good housekeeper. To be said an honest man and a good housekeeper goes as fairly as to say a careful man and a great scholar . *T. Night* iv 2 10
Good housewife. Let us sit and mock the good housewife Fortune from her wheel . . . *As Y. Like It* i 2 34
Good humour. Be avised, sir, and pass good humours . . *Mer. Wives* i 1 169
The good humour is to steal at a minute's rest . . . i 3 30
Aggravate your choler.—These be good humours, indeed! . 2 *Hen. IV.* ii 4 177
These be good humours! your honour wins bad humours . *Hen. V.* iii 2 27
Good husband. You will turn good husband now, Pompey *Meas. for Meas.* iii 2 73
I will do any modest office, my lord, to help my cousin to a good husband *Much Ado* ii 1 391
While I play the good husband at home, my son and my servant spend all at the university . . . *T. of Shrew* v 1 71
Get thee a good husband, and use him as he uses thee . *All's Well* i 1 229
Will deserve . . . A right good husband, let him be a noble *Hen. VIII.* iv 2 146
Good husbandry. Which is both healthful and good husbandry *Hen. V.* iv 1 7
He bears all things fairly, And shows good husbandry . *Coriolanus* iv 7 22
Good inspirations. Your father was ever virtuous; and holy men at their death have good inspirations . . . *Mer. of Venice* i 2 31
Good instruction. And that you will some good instruction give How I may bear me here . . . *Tempest* i 2 424
Good intelligence. Advised by good intelligence . . *Hen. V.* ii Prol. 12
Good intent. My good intent May carry through itself . . *Lear* i 4 2
Good interpretation. A crown's worth of good interpretation 2 *Hen. IV.* ii 2 99
Good-jer. We must give folks leave to prate: what, the good-jer! *M. Wives* i 4 129
Good jest. My uncle can tell you good jests of him . . . iii 4 39
It would be . . . laughter for a month and a good jest for ever 1 *Hen. IV.* ii 2 101
Good joy. It is now our time, That have stood by and seen our wishes prosper, To cry, good joy: good joy, my lord and lady! *Mer. of Ven.* iii 2 190
Good judgement. You have good judgement in horsemanship *Hen. V.* iii 7 58
Being in his right wits and his good judgements . . . iv 7 50
There's nothing in her yet: The fellow has good judgement *A. and C.* iii 3 28
Good Kent. Ah, that good Kent! He said it would be thus . *Lear* iv 4 168
O thou good Kent, how shall I live and work, To match thy goodness? iv 7 1
Good king, great king, and yet not greatly good . . *Richard II.* iv 1 263
The king is a good king: but it must be as it may . . *Hen. V.* ii 1 131
Eat him quick, As thou dost swallow up this good king's blood! *Rich III.* i 2 66
Good king, to be so mightily abused! . . . *T. Andron.* ii 3 87
'Tis call'd the evil: A most miraculous work in this good king *Macbeth* iv 3 147
The good King Simonides, do you call him? . . . *Pericles* ii 1 105
I am the daughter to King Pericles, If good King Pericles be . . v 1 181
Good knave. A good knave, i' faith, and well fed . . . *All's Well* ii 4 39

Good knave. The knave counterfeits well; a good knave . *T. Night* iv 2 22
Good knight. A good backsword man. How doth the good knight? *2 Hen. IV.* iii 2 70
Good lads. I shall command all the good lads in Eastcheap . *1 Hen. IV.* ii 4 15
Good lads, how do ye both?—As the indifferent children of the earth *Ham.* ii 2 229
Good lady. 'Twas a good lady: we may pick a thousand salads ere we light on such another herb . *All's Well* iv 5 14
I was about to tell you, since I heard of the good lady's death . iv 5 73
Who of herself is a good lady and would not have knaves thrive long under her . v 2 33
You must go visit the good lady that lies in . *Coriolanus* i 3 85
Her mother is the lady of the house, And a good lady . *Rom. and Jul.* i 5 116
Good leave. He gives them good leave to wander . *As Y. Like It* i 1 109
Since I have your good leave to go away, I will make haste *Mer. of Ven.* iii 2 326
Wilt thou give us leave awhile?—Good leave, good Philip *K. John* i 1 231
You have good leave to leave us. *1 Hen. IV.* i 3 20
Leave our cousin Katherine here with us: . . . —She hath good leave *Hen. V.* v 2 98
Good leave have you; for you will have leave . *3 Hen. VI.* iii 2 34
By all your good leaves, gentlemen; here I'll make My royal choice *Hen. VIII.* i 4 85
Good leg. With a good leg and a good foot, uncle, and money enough *Much Ado* ii 1 15
A good leg will fall; a straight back will stoop . *Hen. V.* v 2 167
Good leisure. Deceiving promises of life; which I by my good leisure have discredited to him . *Meas. for Meas.* iii 2 261
Good l'envoy. A good l'envoy, ending in the goose . *L. L. Lost* iii 1 100
Good lesson. I shall the effect of this good lesson keep . *Hamlet* i 3 45
Good letters. Whose learning and good letters peace hath tutor'd *2 Hen. IV.* iv 1 44
Good life. So, with good life And observation strange, my meaner ministers Their several kinds have done . *Tempest* iii 3 86
Defend your reputation, or bid farewell to your good life for ever *M. W.* iii 3 127
In respect of itself, it is a good life; but in respect that it is a shepherd's life, it is naught . *As Y. Like It* iii 2 14
Would you have a love-song, or a song of good life?—A love-song, a love-song.—Ay, ay; I care not for good life . *T. Night* ii 3 37
Good light. By this good light, this is a very shallow monster! *Tempest* ii 2 147
A nest of traitors!—I am none, by this good light . *W. Tale* ii 3 82
Good-limbed. A good-limbed fellow; young, strong. *2 Hen. IV.* iii 2 113
Good livery. A noble scar is a good livery of honour . *All's Well* iv 5 106
Good looks. Who builds his hopes in air of your good looks, Lives like a drunken sailor on a mast *Richard III.* iii 4 100
Good Lord, how you take it! . *Tempest* ii 1 80
O that I had my wish!—And I had mine!—And I mine too, good Lord! *L. L. Lost* iv 3 93
Good Lord, how bright and goodly shines the moon! . *T. of Shrew* iv 5 2
He is my good lord: whom I serve above is my master . *All's Well* iii 3 261
I must wait upon my good lord here; I thank you . *2 Hen. IV.* ii 1 196
Let it do something, my good lord, that may do me good . iv 3 65
Stand my good lord, pray, in your good report . iv 3 89
Ay, my good lord:—my lord, I should say rather; 'Tis sin to flatter; 'good' was little better . *3 Hen. VI.* v 6 2
So fare you well, my little good lord cardinal . *Hen. VIII.* iii 2 349
Thy very bountiful good lord and master . *T. of Athens* iii 1 11
But when to my good lord I prove untrue, I'll choke myself *Cymbeline* i 5 86
Good lordship. Commend me bountifully to his good lordship; and I hope his honour will conceive the fairest of me . *T. of Athens* iii 2 59
Good love. What good love may I perform for you?. *K. John* iv 1 49
Good lover. I post from love: good lover, let me go . *L. L. Lost* iv 3 188
Winchester Is held no great good lover of the archbishop's . *Hen. VIII.* iv 1 104
Good luck. As good luck would have it *Mer. Wives* iii 5 84
This is the third time; I hope good luck lies in odd numbers . v 1 2
Strew good luck, ouphes, on every sacred room . v 5 61
Pray thou for us; And good luck grant thee thy Demetrius! *M. N. Dream* i 1 221
You do their work, and they shall have good luck . ii 1 41
Good luck, an't be thy will! what have we here? . *W. Tale* iii 3 69
Be opposite all planets of good luck To my proceedings! *Richard III* iv 4 402
Good lustre. A good lustre of conceit in a tuft of earth . *L. L. Lost* iv 2 89
Good man. Look where he comes; and my good man too . *Mer. Wives* ii 1 107
There is such a league between my good man and he! . iii 2 25
Are you good men and true?—Yea, or else it were pity . *Much Ado* iii 3 1
Well, God's a good man; an two men ride of a horse, one must ride behind . iii 5 39
I'll lay my head to any good man's hat . *L. L. Lost* i 5 310
Thou canst not hit it, hit it, hit it, Thou canst not hit it, my good man iv 1 128
Antonio is a good man . . . : my meaning in saying he is a good man is to have you understand me that he is sufficient . *Mer. of Venice* i 3 12
If ever sat at any good man's feast *As Y. Like It* ii 7 115
Have with holy bell been knoll'd to church And sat at good men's feasts ii 7 122
And thank heaven, fasting, for a good man's love . iii 5 58
I'll follow this good man, and go with you *T. Night* iv 3 32
Whoop, do me no harm, good man *W. Tale* iv 4 199
Since these good men are pleased, let them come in . iv 4 349
How God and good men hate so foul a liar . *Richard II.* i 1 114
There live not three good men unhanged in England . *1 Hen. IV.* ii 4 144
This story shall the good man teach his son . *Hen. V.* iv 3 56
I'll tell you there is good men porn at Monmouth . iv 7 55
The Lord protect him, for he's a good man! Jesu bless him! *2 Hen. VI.* i 3 6
Was it not she and that good man of worship?. . *Richard III.* i 1 66
'Tis death to me to be at enmity; I hate it, and desire all good men's love ii 1 61
Even that, I hope, which pleaseth God above, And all good men . iii 7 110
With that excellence That angels love good men with . *Hen. VIII.* ii 2 35
This good man, This just and learned priest, Cardinal Campeius . ii 2 96
Now I think on't, They should be good men; their affairs as righteous iii 1 22
Forgetting, like a good man, your late censure. . iii 1 64
Look, the good man weeps! He's honest, on mine honour . v 1 152
Good man, sit down. Now let me see the proudest He, that dares most, but wag his finger at thee . v 3 130
This man, This good man,—few of you deserve that title . v 3 138
Good man, the wounds that he does bear for Rome! . *Coriolanus* iv 2 28
O heavens, can you hear a good man groan, And not relent? *T. Andron.* iv 1 123
Are you so gospell'd To pray for this good man? . *Macbeth* iii 1 89
And like good men Bestride our down-fall'n birthdom . iv 3 3
Good men's lives Expire before the flowers in their caps, Dying or ere they sicken . iv 3 171
A good man's fortune may grow out at heels . *Lear* ii 2 164
Be aidant and remediate In the good man's distress! . iv 4 18
Some good man bear him carefully from hence *Othello* v 1 99
So I bequeath a happy peace to you And all good men . *Pericles* i 1 51
Good manhood. If manhood, good manhood, be not forgot upon the face of the earth, then am I a shotten herring . *1 Hen. IV.* ii 4 142
Good manners. Or else a rude despiser of good manners. *As Y. Like It* ii 7 92
If thou never wast at court, thou never sawest good manners . iii 2 42
If thou never sawest good manners, then thy manners must be wicked . iii 2 43
Good manners at the court are as ridiculous in the country as the behaviour of the country is most mockable at the court . iii 2 47
We quarrel in print, by the book; as you have books for good manners v 4 95
Well, I am school'd: good manners be your speed!. *1 Hen. IV.* iii 1 190
I had thought They had parted so much honesty among 'em, At least, good manners, as not thus to suffer A man of his place . *Hen. VIII.* v 2 29
When good manners shall lie all in one or two men's hands and they unwashed too, 'tis a foul thing . *Rom. and Jul.* i 5 4
Good mark-man. A right good mark-man! . i 1 212
Good master. From my lord Biron, a good master of mine . *L. L. Lost* iv 1 106
Come, follow us: we'll be thy good masters . *W. Tale* v 2 188
O my good master!—Prithee, away.—'Tis noble Kent, your friend *Lear* v 3 267
My very noble and approved good masters . *Othello* i 3 77
Good matter. A good matter, surely: comes there any more of it? *T. of S.* i 1 255
Good mean. Tell me some good mean How, with my honour, I may undertake A journey . *T. G. of Ver.* ii 7 5
I had never so good means, as desire, to make myself acquainted with you *Mer. Wives* ii 2 188
And found good means To draw from her a prayer of earnest heart *Othello* i 3 151
Good meaning. Take our good meaning, for our judgement sits Five times in that ere once in our five wits . *Rom. and Jul.* i 4 46
I am no honest man if there be any good meaning towards you . *Lear* i 2 189
Good meat, sir, is common; that every churl affords . *Com. of Errors* iii 1 24
And to cast away honesty upon a foul slut were to put good meat into an unclean dish *As Y. Like It* iii 3 36
And an old hare hoar Is very good meat in lent . *Rom. and Jul.* ii 4 143
Good meeting. You have displaced the mirth, broke the good meeting, With most admired disorder *Macbeth* iii 4 109
Good melancholy. 'Let me not live,'—This his good melancholy oft began *All's Well* i 2 56
Good member. You are a good member of the commonwealth *L. L. Lost* iv 2 78
He says, you are no good member of the commonwealth *Mer. of Venice* iii 5 37
Good memory. A good memory, And witness of the malice and displeasure Which thou shouldst bear me *Coriolanus* iv 5 77
Good metals. Good sparks and lustrous, a word, good metals *All's Well* ii 1 41
Good mettle. That rascal hath good mettle in him . *1 Hen. IV.* ii 4 383
Good mind. Which had been done, But that the good mind of Camillo tardied My swift command . *W. Tale* iii 2 163
Nor measure our good minds By this rude place we live in . *Cymbeline* iii 6 65
Good mischief. Do that good mischief which may make this island Thine own for ever. *Tempest* iv 1 217
Good mistress. A quiet night; and my good mistress will Remember in my prayers . *Hen. VIII.* v 1 77
Good moon-calf. Moon-calf, speak once in thy life, if thou beest a good moon-calf . *Tempest* iii 2 25
Good moral. A good moral, my lord: it is not enough to speak, but to speak true . *M. N. Dream* v 1 120
Good morning to you, fair and gracious daughter . *Meas. for Meas.* iv 3 116
When you have given good morning to your mistress, Attend the queen *Cymbeline* ii 3 66
Good morrow. Madam and mistress, a thousand good-morrows *T. G. of V.* ii 1 102
A thousand times good morrow.—As many, worthy lady, to yourself . iv 3 6
God give you good morrow, master Parson . *L. L. Lost* iv 2 84
But what a fool am I to chat with you, When I should bid good morrow to my bride! . *T. of Shrew* iii 2 124
It is good morrow, is it not?—Indeed, my lord, I think it be two o'clock *1 Hen. IV.* ii 4 573
Many good morrows to your majesty!—Is it good morrow, lords?—'Tis one o'clock, and past.—Why, then, good morrow . *2 Hen. IV.* iii 1 32
Bids them good morrow with a modest smile And calls them brothers *Hen. V.* iv Prol. 33
Do my good morrow to them, and anon Desire them all to my pavilion iv 1 26
Many good morrows to my noble lord!—Good morrow, Catesby *Rich. III.* iii 2 35
There's some conceit or other likes him well, When he doth bid good-morrow with such a spirit . iii 4 52
Good morrow.—Ay, and good next day too . *Troi. and Cres.* iii 3 68
I would not buy Their mercy . . . ; Nor check my courage for what they can give, To have't with saying 'Good morrow' . *Coriolanus* iii 3 93
Many good morrows to your majesty; Madam, to you as many *T. Andron.* ii 2 11
Good morrow, cousin.—Is the day so young?—But new struck nine *Rom. and Jul.* i 1 166
It argues a distemper'd head So soon to bid good morrow to thy bed . ii 3 34
God ye good morrow, gentlemen.—God ye good den . ii 4 115
Vouchsafe good morrow from a feeble tongue . *J. Cæsar* ii 1 313
Or of a courtier; which could say 'Good morrow, sweet lord!' *Hamlet* v 1 91
Play here; I will content your pains; Something that's brief; and bid 'Good morrow, general . *Othello* iii 1 2
And keep their impious turbans on, without Good morrow to the sun *Cymbeline* iii 3 7
Give you good morrow *Mer. Wives* ii 2; iii 3; iii 5; *Richard III.* ii 3; *Lear* ii 2
Good mother. There's a good mother, boy, that blots thy father *K. John* ii 1 132
I will be mild and gentle in my speech.—And brief, good mother *Rich. III.* iv 4 161
Good murder. And when thou find'st a man that's like thyself, Good Murder, stab him . *T. Andron.* v 2 100
Good musician. What, will my daughter prove a good musician? *T. of S.* ii 1 145
Good my complexion! dost thou think, though I am caparisoned like a man, I have a doublet and hose in my disposition? *As Y. Like It* iii 2 204
Good my glass, take this for telling true . *L. L. Lost* iv 1 18
Good my lord, give me thy favour still . *Tempest* iv 1 204
Good my lord, be good to me *Meas. for Meas.* iii 2 202; *2 Hen. IV.* ii 1 69
Let's be merry, Good my lord cardinal . *Hen. VIII.* i 4 105
I beg of you to know me, good my lord, To accept my grief *T. of Athens* iv 3 494
I beseech you, remember— Nay, good my lord; for mine ease, in good faith . *Hamlet* v 2 109
Good my mother, peace! I would that I were low laid in my grave *K. John* iii 1 163
Good name. Indeed, he hath an excellent good name . *Much Ado* iii 1 98
God hath blessed you with a good name . iii 3 14
I would to God thou and I knew where a commodity of good names were to be bought . *1 Hen. IV.* i 2 93
Even those some Envy your great deservings and good name . iv 3 35
A gentleman well bred and of good name . *2 Hen. IV.* i 1 26
I am in good name and fame with the very best . ii 4 81
He will keep that good name still.—I know him to be valiant *Hen. V.* iii 7 111
And thy good name Live with authority . *T. of Athens* v 1 165

Good name in man and woman, dear my lord, Is the immediate jewel of their souls: Who steals my purse steals trash; . . But he that filches from me my good name Robs me of that which not enriches him And makes me poor indeed . . . *Othello* iii 3 155
Sell me your good report.—How! my good name? or to report of you What I shall think is good? . . . . . . *Cymbeline* ii 3 89
Good nature. Which good natures Could not abide to be with *Tempest* i 2 359
Perhaps he sees it not; or his good nature Prizes the virtue that appears in Cassio, And looks not on his evils . . . . . *Othello* ii 3 138
Good necessity. Bid him suppose some good necessity Touches his friend *T. of Athens* ii 2 236
Good neighbour. An old, an old instance, Beatrice, that lived in the time of good neighbours . . . . . . *Much Ado* v 2 79
A marvellous good neighbour, faith, and a very good bowler *L. L. Lost* v 2 586
Good news. What say you to a letter from your friends Of much good news? . . . . *T. G. of Ver.* ii 4 52
My ears are stopt and cannot hear good news . . . . . iii 1 205
I thank thee, good Tubal: good news, good news! ha, ha! *Mer. of Venice* iii 1 111
There's a post come from my master, with his horn full of good news . v 1 47
Fever burns me up, And will not let me welcome this good news *K. John* v 3 15
And wherefore should these good news make me sick? 2 *Hen. IV.* iv 4 102
Heard he the good news yet? Tell it him.—He alter'd much upon the hearing it . . . . iv 5 11
Shall dunghill curs confront the Helicons? And shall good news be baffled? . . . . v 3 109
What! I do bring good news . . . . v 3 134
For joy of this good news, Give Mistress Shore one gentle kiss the more *Richard III.* iii 1 184
And thereupon he sends you this good news . . . . . iii 2 48
Good news or bad, that thou comest in so bluntly? . . . . iv 3 45
Good news, good news; the ladies have prevail'd . *Coriolanus* v 4 43
This is good news: I will go meet the ladies . . . . . v 4 54
Thou still hast been the father of good news . . . *Hamlet* ii 2 42
I know, by that same eye, there's some good news . *Ant. and Cleo.* i 3 19
You clasp young Cupid's tables. Good news, gods! . *Cymbeline* iii 2 39
Thou bring'st good news; I am called to be made free . . . v 4 201
Good next day. Good morrow.—Ay, and good next day too *T. and C.* iii 3 69
Good night. Be more abstemious, Or else, good night your vow! *Temp.* iv 1 54
Good night to your redress! . . . . . . *Meas. for Meas.* v 1 301
Bids me a thousand times good night . . . . *Much Ado* iii 3 157
Now, unto thy bones good night! Yearly will I do this rite . . v 3 22
Come our lovely lady nigh; So, good night, with lullaby *M. N. Dream* ii 2 19
Good night, sweet friend: Thy love ne'er alter till thy sweet life end! . ii 2 60
So, good night unto you all. Give me your hands . . . . v 1 443
Is this your speeding? nay, then, good night our part! . *T. of Shrew* ii 1 303
And, being a winner, God give you good night! . . . . . v 2 187
On both yourself and me Cry lost, and so good night! . . *W. Tale* i 2 411
After such bloody toil, we bid good night . . . . *K. John* v 5 6
And ere thou bid good night, to quit their griefs, Tell thou the lamentable tale of me . . . . *Richard II.* v 1 43
If he fall in, good night! or sink or swim . . . 1 *Hen. IV.* i 3 194
And sware they were his fancies or his good-nights . 2 *Hen. IV.* iii 2 343
My tongue is weary; when my legs are too, I will bid you good night Epil. 35
And Anne my wife hath bid the world good night . *Richard III.* iv 3 39
Pembroke keeps his regiment: Good Captain Blunt, bear my good-night to him . . . . v 3 30
Sweet sir, you honour me.—And so, good night . *Troi. and Cres.* v 1 94
And so, good night.—Nay, but you part in anger . . . . v 2 44
Good night, good night! as sweet repose and rest Come to thy heart as that within my breast! . . . . *Rom. and Jul.* ii 2 123
Three words, dear Romeo, and good night indeed . . . . ii 2 142
A thousand times good night!—A thousand times the worse, to want thy light . . . . ii 2 155
Good night, good night! parting is such sweet sorrow, That I shall say good night till it be morrow . . . . ii 2 185
Good night: Get thee to bed, and rest; for thou hast need . . iv 3 12
Good night: Early to-morrow will we rise, and hence . *J. Cæsar* iv 3 229
The fatal bellman, Which gives the stern'st good-night . *Macbeth* ii 2 4
At once, good night: Stand not upon the order of your going . iii 4 118
Good night; and better health Attend his majesty!—A kind good night to all! . . . . iii 4 120
So, good night: My mind she has mated, and amazed my sight . v 1 85
Give you good night.—O, farewell . . . . . *Hamlet* i 1 16
Once more, good night: And when you are desirous to be bless'd, I'll blessing beg of you . . . . iii 4 170
So, again, good night. I must be cruel, only to be kind . . iii 4 177
Mother, good night. Indeed this counsellor Is now most still . iii 4 213
Good night, ladies; good night, sweet ladies; good night, good night . iv 5 72
Good night, sweet prince; And flights of angels sing thee to thy rest! . v 2 370
Fortune, good night: smile once more; turn thy wheel! . . *Lear* ii 2 180
I am come To bid my king and master aye good night . . . v 3 235
Let it be so. Good night to every one . . . . *Othello* i 3 289
What needs more words? Good night. Good Antony, your hand *A. and C.* ii 7 132
Ay, are you thereabouts? Why, then, good night indeed . . . iii 10 30
Brother, good night: to-morrow is the day.—It will determine one way iv 3 1
Good nose. A good nose is requisite also, to smell out work for the other senses . . . . *W. Tale* iv 4 686
Good note. A good note; that keeps you from the blow of the law *T. N.* iii 4 168
Take good note What Cæsar doth, what suitors press to him *J. Cæsar* ii 4 14
Take but good note, and you shall see in him The triple pillar of the world transform'd Into a strumpet's fool . . . *Ant. and Cleo.* i 1 11
Good now, hold thy tongue . . . . . . *Com. of Errors* iv 4 22
Now, good now, Say so but seldom . . . . . *W. Tale* v 1 19
Ay, good now, love, love, nothing but love . . *Troi. and Cres.* iii 1 122
Good now, sit down, and tell me, he that knows . . *Hamlet* i 1 70
Good now, some excellent fortune! Let me be married *Ant. and Cleo.* i 2 25
Good now, play one scene Of excellent dissembling . . . i 3 78
Good nurse. I pray thee, speak; good, good nurse, speak *Rom. and Jul.* ii 5 28
As my good nurse Lychorida hath oft Deliver'd weeping *Pericles* v 1 161
Good observance. But take a taste of my finding him, and relish it with good observance . . . . *As Y. Like It* iii 2 247
Good occasion. Am right glad to catch this good occasion *Hen. VIII.* v 1 109
Had I so good occasion to lie long As you . . *Troi. and Cres.* iv 1 3
Good office. I would I could do a good office between you *Mer. Wives* i 1 102
We are come to you to do a good office, master parson . . . iii 1 49
Good old Abraham. Sweet peace conduct his sweet soul to the bosom Of good old Abraham! . . . . *Richard II.* iv 1 104
Good old chronicle. Let me embrace thee, good old chronicle *T. and C.* iv 5 202
Good old commander. A good old commander and a most kind gentleman . . . . *Hen. V.* iv 1 97

Good old folks. In winter's tedious nights sit by the fire With good old folks . . . . *Richard II.* v 1 41
Good old friend. Our good old friend, Lay comforts to your bosom *Lear* ii 1 127
Good old lord. Him that you term'd, sir, 'The good old lord' *Tempest* v 1 15
Good old man. A good old man, sir; he will be talking . *Much Ado* iii 5 36
Nay, do not quarrel with us, good old man . . . . . . v 1 50
Yet, to satisfy this good old man, I would bend under any heavy weight v 1 286
O good old man, how well in thee appears The constant service of the antique world, When service sweat for duty! . . *As Y. Like It* ii 3 56
Good old man, Thou art right welcome as thy master is . . . . ii 7 197
The good old man would fain that all were well . 3 *Hen. VI.* iv 7 31
Amen; and make me die a good old man! That is the butt-end of a mother's blessing . . . . *Richard III.* ii 2 109
Take up this good old man, and cheer the heart . . *T. Andron.* i 1 457
And, in this brainish apprehension, kills The unseen good old man *Ham.* iv 1 12
Good old Mantuan! I may speak of thee as the traveller doth of Venice *L. L. Lost* iv 2 96
Good old York. What shall good old York there see But empty lodgings? *Richard II.* i 2 67
What stir Keeps good old York there with his men of war? . . . ii 3 52
Good one. Well read in poetry And other books, good ones . *T. of Shrew* i 2 171
Four and twenty nosegays for the shearers, three-man-song-men all, and very good ones . . . . *W. Tale* iv 3 45
He was a scholar, and a ripe and good one; Exceeding wise *Hen. VIII.* iv 2 51
Masters of the people, Your multiplying spawn how can he flatter—That's thousand to one good one? . . . . . *Coriolanus* ii 2 83
He is a good one, and his worthiness Does challenge much respect *Othello* ii 1 212
And was the best of all Amongst the rarest of good ones . *Cymbeline* v 5 160
Good opinion. I speak not this that you should bear a good opinion of my knowledge . . . . *As Y. Like It* v 2 60
The king's majesty Commends his good opinion of you . *Hen. VIII.* ii 3 61
Let us have him, for his silver hairs Will purchase us a good opinion *J. Cæsar* ii 1 145
Seldom but that pity begets you a good opinion . . *Pericles* iv 2 131
Good opportunities. I have good opportunities for the ork *Mer. Wives* ii 1 15
Good orators, when they are out, they will spit . . *As Y. Like It* iv 1 75
Good pancakes. A certain knight that swore by his honour they were good pancakes . . . . i 2 67
Good pantler. A' would have made a good pantler . . 2 *Hen. IV.* ii 4 258
Good parent. And my trust, Like a good parent, did beget of him A falsehood in its contrary . . . . *Tempest* i 2 94
Good parentage—To equal mine!—was it not thus? . . *Pericles* v 1 98
Good part. Setting the attraction of my good parts aside I have no other charms . . . . *Mer. Wives* ii 2 110
But though my cates be mean, take them in good part *Com. of Errors* iii 1 28
So politic a state of evil that they will not admit any good part to intermingle with them . . . . *Much Ado* v 2 64
But for which of my good parts did you first suffer love for me? . v 2 65
And he makes it a great appropriation to his own good parts, that he can shoe him himself . . . . *Mer. of Venice* i 2 46
An envious emulator of every man's good parts . *As Y. Like It* i 1 150
'Twere no good part To take on me to keep and kill thy heart *Rich. II.* v 1 97
One that knows what belongs to reason; and canst use the time well, if the time use thee well: good parts in thee . . *T. of Athens* iii 1 40
Good pastime. Hush, master! here's some good pastime toward *T. of S.* i 1 68
Good pasture. That good pasture makes fat sheep . . *As Y. Like It* iii 2 28
Good path. Pace your wisdom In that good path . *Meas. for Meas.* iv 3 138
Good people. If these be good people in a commonweal that do nothing but use their abuses in common houses, I know no law . . . ii 1 41
He would have all as merry As, first, good company, good wine, good welcome, Can make good people . . . . . . *Hen. VIII.* i 4 7
All good people, Pray for me! I must now forsake ye . . . ii 1 131
Good person. To the prejudice of her present state, Or touch of her good person . . . . ii 4 155
Good persuasion. A good persuasion: therefore, hear me *M. N. Dream* i 1 156
Good phrases are surely, and ever were, very commendable 2 *Hen. IV.* iii 2 76
Good picture. Who was he That, otherwise than noble nature did, Hath alter'd that good picture? . . . . *Cymbeline* iv 2 365
Good piece. A very good piece of work, I assure you . *M. N. Dream* i 2 14
Thou worms-meat, in respect of a good piece of flesh indeed! *As Y. L. It* iii 2 68
'Tis a good piece.—So 'tis: this comes off well and excellent *T. of Athens* i 1 28
Good pity. Who, by the art of known and feeling sorrows, Am pregnant to good pity . . . . *Lear* iv 6 227
Good play. A good play needs no epilogue . . . *As Y. Like It* Epil. 4
Good plays prove the better by the help of good epilogues . . Epil. 6
Nor cannot insinuate with you in the behalf of a good play . . Epil. 9
Primo, secundo, tertio, is a good play . . . . . *T. Night* v 1 39
Good pleasure. What is your good pleasure with me? . 2 *Hen. IV.* iii 2 65
I would desire the duke to use his good pleasure . . *Hen. V.* iii 6 57
Peace to his soul, if God's good pleasure be! . . 2 *Hen. VI.* iii 3 26
Dwell I but in the suburbs Of your good pleasure? . . *J. Cæsar* ii 1 286
Good plots, they are laid; and our revolted wives share damnation together *Mer. Wives* iii 2 39
A good plot, good friends, and full of expectation . . 1 *Hen. IV.* ii 3 19
Good prayers. To your good prayers will scarcely say amen *Richard III.* i 3 21
Good precedence. I do not like 'But yet,' it does allay The good precedence; fie upon 'But yet'! . . . . . *Ant. and Cleo.* ii 5 51
Good preparation. We have not made good preparation *Mer. of Venice* ii 4 4
Good presence. Here is like to be a good presence of Worthies *L. L. Lost* v 2 536
Good prey. The French might have a good prey of us . . *Hen. V.* iv 4 81
Good priest. Get you to church, and have a good priest . *As Y. Like It* iii 3 86
Good prince. He, good prince, having all lost . . . *Pericles* ii Gower 33
Good proceeding. Proceeded well, to stop all good proceeding! *L. L. Lost* i 1 95
And make this haste as your own good proceeding . . *All's Well* ii 4 50
Good protector. Under the covering of a careful night, Who seem'd my good protector . . . . *Pericles* i 2 82
Good purpose. Look upon his honour; 'tis for a good purpose *M. for M.* ii 1 155
May I never To this good purpose, that so fairly shows, Dream of impediment! . . . . *Ant. and Cleo.* ii 2 147
You shall bereave yourself Of my good purposes . . . . . v 2 131
Good quality. The owner of no one good quality . . . *All's Well* iii 6 12
Good quarrel. A good quarrel to draw emulous factions *Troi. and Cres.* ii 3 79
I dare draw as soon as another man, if I see occasion in a good quarrel, and the law on my side . . . . *Rom. and Jul.* ii 4 168
Good quarter. Well; keep good quarter and good care to-night *K. John* v 5 20
Good queen. At the good queen's entreaty.—At the queen's be't: 'good' should be pertinent . . . . *W. Tale* i 2 220
I come From your good queen.—Good queen!—Good queen, my lord, Good queen; I say good queen . . . . ii 3 58
The good queen, For she is good, hath brought you forth a daughter . ii 3 64

Good queen. Have, out of malice To the good queen, possess'd him with a scruple . . . . *Hen. VIII.* ii 1 158
Good rapier. Wear thy good rapier bare, and put it home . *Othello* v 1 2
Good rapine. And when it is thy hap To find another that is like to thee, Good Rapine, stab him . . . *T. Andron.* v 2 103
Good reason. Reason my son Should choose himself a wife, but as good reason The father . . . should hold some counsel . . *W. Tale* iv 4 418
And good reason, for thereby is England mained . 2 *Hen. VI.* iv 2 171
Good reasons must, of force, give place to better . . *J. Cæsar* iv 3 203
Good rebuke. A good rebuke, Which might have well becomed the best of men . . . . *Ant. and Cleo.* iii 7 26
Good receipt. That his good receipt Shall for my legacy be sanctified By the luckiest stars in heaven . . . . *All's Well* i 3 250
Good regard. Our reasons are so full of good regard . *J. Cæsar* iii 1 224
Good remainders. The gods protect you! And bless the good remainders of the court! . . . . *Cymbeline* i 1 129
Good remembrance. His good remembrance, sir, Lies richer in your thoughts than on his tomb . . . . *All's Well* i 2 48
Good repast. If I prove a good repast to the spectators, the dish pays the shot . . . . *Cymbeline* v 4 157
Good report. For the good report I hear of you . *T. of Shrew* iv 4 28
These wise men that give fools money get themselves a good report *T. Night* iv 1 24
And to give me your good report to the prince my master *W. Tale* v 2 162
Stand my good lord, pray, in your good report . . 2 *Hen. IV.* iv 3 89
And could be content to give him good report for't, but that he pays himself with being proud . . . . . . *Coriolanus* i 1 33
But had he died in the business, madam; how then?—Then his good report should have been my son. . . . . . i 3 22
Too modest are you; More cruel to your good report than grateful To us i 9 54
She makes a very good report o' the worm . . *Ant. and Cleo.* v 2 255
Sell me your good report.—How! my good name? or to report of you What I shall think is good? . . . . . *Cymbeline* ii 3 88
It gives a good report to a number to be chaste . . . *Pericles* iv 6 43
Good repose the while!—Thanks, sir: the like to you! . *Macbeth* ii 1 29
Good repute. A man of good repute, carriage, bearing . *L. L. Lost* i 1 271
Sweet my child, let them be men of good repute and carriage . i 2 72
Good respect. I am almost ashamed To say what good respect I have of thee . . . . *K. John* iii 3 28
There's a letter for you.—Delivered with good respect . 2 *Hen. IV.* ii 2 109
Thou art a fellow of a good respect . . . . *J. Cæsar* v 5 45
Good rest. And so, good rest.—As wretches have o'ernight *T. G. of Ver.* iv 2 133
One that thinks a man always going to bed and says 'God give you good rest!'—Well, sir, there rest . . *Com. of Errors* iv 3 33
He took good rest to-night; 'Tis hoped his sickness is discharged *W. Tale* ii 3 10
God give your grace good rest! Sorrow breaks seasons . *Richard III.* i 4 75
She is brought a-bed.—Well, God give her good rest! . *T. Andron.* iv 2 63
Good returns. I'll pawn my victories, all My honours to you, upon his good returns. . . . . *T. of Athens* iii 5 82
Good riddance. A good riddance . . . . . *Troi. and Cres.* ii 1 132
Good room. The revellers are entering, brother: make good room *M. Ado* ii 1 88
Good root. Focative is caret.—And that's a good root . *Mer. Wives* iv 1 56
Good round sum. 'Tis a good round sum . . . *Mer. of Venice* i 3 104
Good sadness. In good sadness, sir, I am sorry . . . *Mer. Wives* iii 5 125
Is my husband coming?—Ay, in good sadness, is he . . . iv 2 93
Now, in good sadness, son Petruchio, I think thou hast the veriest shrew of all.—Well, I say no . . . . . *T. of Shrew* v 2 63
We'll search.—In good sadness, I do not know . . *All's Well* iv 3 230
Good sake. You're welcome, sir; and he, for your good sake *T. of Shrew* ii 1 61
Good scab. I' faith, Wart; thou'rt a good scab . . 2 *Hen. IV.* iii 2 295
Good scholar. I dare say my cousin William is become a good scholar . iii 2 11
Good 'scuse. And laid good 'scuse upon your ecstasy . *Othello* iv 1 80
Good seconds. Now the gates are ope: now prove good seconds *Coriol.* i 4 43
Good seeming. All good seeming, By thy revolt, O husband, shall be thought Put on for villany . . . . . *Cymbeline* iii 4 56
Good selves. O that you could turn your eyes toward the napes of your necks, and make but an interior survey of your good selves! *Coriol.* ii 1 44
Good sense—less. Very brief, and to exceeding good sense—less *T. Night* iii 4 174
Good sentences and well pronounced.—They would be better, if well followed . . . . *Mer. of Venice* i 2 11
Good servant. Every good servant does not all commands . *Cymbeline* v 1 6
Good service. He hath done good service, lady, in these wars *Much Ado* i 1 48
But he hath since done good service at Shrewsbury . 2 *Hen. IV.* i 2 71
The Welshmen did good service in a garden where leeks did grow *Hen. V.* iv 7 103
'Twere not amiss He were created knight for his good service 2 *Hen. VI.* v 1 77
One that wouldst be a bawd, in way of good service . *Lear* ii 2 21
In me 'tis villany; In thee't had been good service . *Ant. and Cleo.* ii 7 81
But, like a master Married to your good service, stay till death . iv 2 31
If it be so to do good service, never Let me be counted serviceable *Cymb.* iii 2 14
Good shape. Is not birth, beauty, good shape, . . . the spice and salt that season a man? . . . . . . *Troi. and Cres.* i 2 275
Good sharp fellow. A good sharp fellow: I will send for him *Much Ado* i 2 19
Good sherris-sack. A good sherris-sack hath a two-fold operation in it 2 *Hen. IV.* iv 3 103
Good ship. I would Have sunk the sea within the earth or ere It should the good ship so have swallow'd . . . . . *Tempest* i 2 12
Good shipping. God send 'em good shipping! . . *T. of Shrew* v 1 43
Good show. Stand here, make a good show . . . *T. Night* iii 4 317
Good sign. If he were dead, you'ld weep for him: if you would not, it were a good sign that I should quickly have a new father *Macbeth* iv 2 62
She's a good sign, but I have seen small reflection of her wit. *Cymbeline* i 2 32
Good silling. 'Tis a good silling, I warrant you . . . *Hen. V.* iv 8 76
Good sir. Thou attend'st not.—O, good sir, I do . . *Tempest* i 2 88
A word, good sir; I fear you have done yourself some wrong. . . i 2 442
It is foul weather in us all, good sir, When you are cloudy . . ii 1 141
He closes with you in this consequence; 'Good sir,' or so, or 'friend' *Hamlet* ii 1 46
Good skill. The Frenchman hath good skill in his rapier *Mer. Wives* ii 1 230
Good soft pillow. A good soft pillow for that good white head *Hen. V.* iv 1 14
Good soldier. I am damned in hell for swearing to gentlemen my friends, you were good soldiers . . . . . *Mer. Wives* ii 2 10
Money is a good soldier, sir, and will on . . . . . . ii 2 176
And a good soldier too, lady.—And a good soldier to a lady . *Much Ado* i 1 53
Good soldier-breeder. Thou must therefore needs prove a good soldier-breeder . . . . *Hen. V.* v 2 219
Good sometime queen, prepare thee hence for France . *Richard II.* v 1 37
Good son. I have forgot that name, and that name's woe.—That's my good son . . . . *Rom. and Jul.* ii 3 47
Good song. A good song.—And an ill singer, my lord . . *Much Ado* ii 3 77
Good sooth. Well drawn, monster, in good sooth! . . . *Tempest* ii 2 150
Good sooth. In good sooth, the vice is of a great kindred; it is well allied *Meas. for Meas.* iii 2 108
Good troth, you do me wrong, good sooth, you do . . *M. N. Dream* ii 2 129
In good sooth! Heart! you swear like a comfit-maker's wife. 'Not you, in good sooth,' and 'as true as I live,' and 'as God shall mend me,' and 'as sure as day' . . . . . . 1 *Hen. IV.* iii 1 252
Good sooth, I care not for you . . . . . . *Pericles* i 1 86
Good sort. What prisoners of good sort are taken? . . *Hen. V.* iv 8 80
Good soul. But she, good soul, had as lief see a toad . *Rom. and Jul.* ii 4 215
And heaven defend your good souls, that you think I will your serious and great business scant For she is with me . . . *Othello* i 3 267
That their good souls may be appeased with slaughter . . *Cymbeline* v 5 72
Good sparks and lustrous, a word, good metals . . *All's Well* ii 1 41
Good speech. If you look for a good speech now, you undo me 2 *Hen. IV.* Epil 4
Good speed. I will come after you with what good speed Our means will make us means . . . . *All's Well* v 1 34
Twenty three days They have been absent: 'tis good speed . *W. Tale* ii 3 199
O'er-read these letters, And well consider of them: make good speed 2 *Hen. IV.* iii 1 3
Good spirits. For what advancement may I hope from thee That no revenue hast but thy good spirits, To feed and clothe thee? *Hamlet* iii 2 63
Good sport. Fair princess, you have lost much good sport *As Y. Like It* i 2 106
Hark, what good sport is out of town to-day!—Better at home, if 'would I might' were 'may' . . . . *Troi. and Cres.* i 1 116
Yet was his mother fair; there was good sport at his making . *Lear* i 1 23
Good stars. Lo, at their births good stars were opposite. *Richard III.* iv 4 215
When my good stars, that were my former guides, Have empty left their orbs, and shot their fires Into the abysm of hell *Ant. and Cleo.* iii 13 145
Good store. Of all the horses, Whereof we have ta'en good and good store, of all The treasure . . . . . . *Coriolanus* i 9 32
Good strawberries. I saw good strawberries in your garden *Richard III.* iii 4 34
Good strings to your beards, new ribbons to your pumps . *M. N. Dream* iv 2 36
Good student. Keep a gamester from the dice, and a good student from his book, and it is wonderful . . . . *Mer. Wives* iii 1 38
Nor lean enough to be thought a good student . . *T. Night* iv 2 9
Good subject. If he appeal the duke on ancient malice; Or worthily, as a good subject should . . . . . . *Richard II.* i 1 10
Good success. If your title to the crown be weak, As may appear by Edward's good success. . . . . 3 *Hen. VI.* iii 3 146
Such a nature, Tickled with good success, disdains the shadow Which he treads on at noon . . . . . . *Coriolanus* i 1 264
Mistrust of good success hath done this deed . . . *J. Cæsar* v 3 66
Not sure, though hoping, of this good success, I ask'd his blessing *Lear* v 3 194
Good supporters are you . . . . . . *Meas. for Meas.* v 1 18
Good sweet. And now, good sweet, say thy opinion . *Mer. of Venice* iii 5 76
Good swimmer. Leander the good swimmer . . . . *Much Ado* v 2 30
Good sword. I would my son Were in Arabia, and thy tribe before him, His good sword in his hand . . . . . *Coriolanus* iv 2 25
With this good sword, That ran through Cæsar's bowels . *J. Cæsar* v 3 41
Good tailor. A good workman, a very good tailor . . *All's Well* ii 5 21
Good tall fellow. Which many a good tall fellow had destroy'd 1 *Hen. IV.* i 3 62
Good temper. What man of good temper would endure this tempest of exclamation? . . . . 2 *Hen. IV.* ii 1 87
Good temperality. You are in an excellent good temperality . . ii 4 25
Good terms. And rail'd on Lady Fortune in good terms, In good set terms . . . . *As Y. Like It* ii 7 16
If you would walk off, I would prick your guts a little, in good terms *Hen. V.* ii 1 62
Parted you in good terms? . . . . *Lear* i 2 171
Good testimony. Within this hour bring me word 'tis done, And by good testimony . . . . *W. Tale* ii 3 136
Good thing. If the ill spirit have so fair a house, Good things will strive to dwell with't . . . . *Tempest* i 2 459
Good things should be praised . . . . . *T. G. of Ver.* iii 1 353
Like a good thing, being often read, Grown fear'd and tedious *M. for M.* ii 4 8
We must follow the leaders.—In every good thing . . *Much Ado* ii 1 158
Can one desire too much of a good thing? . . . *As Y. Like It* iv 1 124
It was alway yet the trick of our English nation, if they have a good thing, to make it too common . . . . . 2 *Hen. IV.* i 2 241
Yes, faith; and let it be an excellent good thing . . . ii 2 37
Since sudden sorrow Serves to say thus, 'some good thing comes to-morrow' . . . . iv 2 84
Good things of day begin to droop and drowse. . . . *Macbeth* iii 2 52
Speak to me: If there be any good thing to be done . . *Hamlet* i 1 130
Good thou, save me a piece of marchpane . . *Rom. and Jul.* i 5 8
Good thoughts. Your own good thoughts excuse me . . *L. L. Lost* ii 1 176
From that supernal judge, that stirs good thoughts . . *K. John* ii 1 112
Restore yourselves Into the good thoughts of the world again 1 *Hen. IV.* i 3 182
And God forgive them that so much have sway'd Your majesty's good thoughts away from me! . . . . iii 2 131
Go thou to sanctuary, and good thoughts possess thee! . *Richard III.* iv 1 94
With all kind love, good thoughts, and reverence . . *J. Cæsar* iii 1 176
Let Rome be thus Inform'd.—Who, queasy with his insolence Already, will their good thoughts call from him . . *Ant. and Cleo.* iii 6 21
Good tidings. What good tidings comes with you? . . 2 *Hen. IV.* i 1 33
Good tidings, my Lord Hastings; for the which I do arrest thee, traitor, of high treason . . . . iv 2 106
So tart a favour To trumpet such good tidings! . *Ant. and Cleo.* ii 5 39
Good time. Bring forth more islands.—Ay.—Why, in good time *Tempest* ii 1 95
And, in good time! now will we break with him . *T. G. of Ver.* i 3 44
Pray you, use your patience: in good time . . *Mer. Wives* iii 1 84
No loss shall touch her by my company.—In good time *Meas. for Meas.* iii 1 183
In very good time: speak not you to him till we call upon you . v 1 286
The meat wants that I have.—In good time, sir; what's that? *C. of Errors* ii 2 58
Learn to jest in good time: there's a time for all things. . . ii 2 65
The fault will be in the music, cousin, if you be not wooed in good time *Much Ado* ii 1 73
She is spread of late Into a goodly bulk: good time encounter her! *W. T.* ii 1 20
Were now the general of our gracious empress, As in good time he may, from Ireland coming, Bringing rebellion . . . *Hen. V.* v Prol. 31
And, in good time, here comes the noble duke. . . *Richard III.* ii 1 45
And, in good time, here comes the sweating lord . . . iii 1 24
The fruit she goes with I pray for heartily, that it may find Good time, and live . . . . *Hen. VIII.* v 1 22
We stood to't in good time . . . . . . *Coriolanus* iv 6 10
I must to the learned.—In good time . . . *Rom. and Jul.* i 2 45
What a wicked beast was I to disfurnish myself against such a good time, when I might ha' shown myself honourable! . . . *T. Athens* iii 2 50
I gave you all— And in good time you gave it . . . *Lear* ii 4 253
This counter-caster, He, in good time, must his lieutenant be *Othello* i 1 32
But we'll even All that good time will give us . . . *Cymbeline* iii 4 185

Good time. I wish my brother make good time with him, You say he is so fell . . . . *Cymbeline* iv 2 108
Good time of day unto my gracious lord! *Richard III.* i 1 122; i 3 18
God give your lordship good time of day . . . 2 *Hen. IV.* i 2 107
The good time of day to you, sir.—I also wish it to you *T. of Athens* iii 6 1
Good tongue. Keep a good tongue in your head . . *Tempest* iii 2 40
To taint that honour every good tongue blesses . *Hen. VIII.* iii 1 55
Your good tongue, More than the instant army we can make, Might stop our countryman . . . . . . *Coriolanus* v 1 36
Good trade. A tapster is a good trade . . . *Mer. Wives* i 3 18
Good traders in the flesh, set this in your painted cloths . *Troi. and Cres.* v 10 46
Good trading. It is like we shall have good trading that way 1 *Hen. IV.* ii 4 401
Good traveller. A good traveller is something at the latter end of a dinner . . . . *All's Well* ii 5 30
Good troth, you do me wrong, good sooth, you do *M. N. Dream* ii 2 129
Nay, good troth.—Yes, troth, and troth; you would not be a queen? *Hen. VIII.* ii 3 33
That this is from some mistress, some remembrance: No, in good troth *Othello* iii 4 187
Good troth, I have stol'n nought, nor would not . . . *Cymbeline* iii 6 48
Good truth. If the good truth were known . . *W. Tale* ii 1 199
In good truth, the poet makes a most excellent description of it *Hen. V.* iii 6 38
Reconciled my thoughts To thy good truth and honour . . *Macbeth* iv 3 117
Good turn. For your kindness I owe you a good turn . *Meas. for Meas.* iv 2 62
She's apt to learn and thankful for good turns . *T. of Shrew* ii 1 166
Oft good turns Are shuffled off with such uncurrent pay . *T. Night* iii 3 15
Is she not then beholding to the man That brought her for this high good turn so far? Yes, and will nobly him remunerate . *T. Andron.* i 1 397
I'll look you out a good turn, Servilius . . . *T. of Athens* iii 2 67
But they knew what they did; I am to do a good turn for them *Hamlet* iv 6 22
He's bound unto Octavia.—For what good turn? *Ant. and Cleo.* ii 5 58
When nature framed this piece, she meant thee a good turn . *Pericles* iv 2 151
Good usage. At whose hands He hath good usage . . 3 *Hen. VI.* iv 5 6
Good use. What I saw, to my good use I remembered . *W. Tale* iv 4 616
I make as good use of it as many a man doth of a Death's-head 1 *Hen. IV.* iii 3 33
This Davy serves you for good uses; he is your serving-man . 2 *Hen. IV.* v 3 11
Gone she is To death or to dishonour; and my end Can make good use of either . . . . *Cymbeline* iii 5 64
Good valour. I will reward thee Once for thy spritely comfort, and tenfold For thy good valour . . . . . *Ant. and Cleo.* iv 7 16
Good varlet. A good varlet, a very good varlet, Sir John . 2 *Hen. IV.* v 3 13
Good velvet. Thou art good velvet . . . *Meas. for Meas.* i 2 33
Good view. She made good view of me . . . *T. Night* ii 2 20
Good voice. Your good voice, sir; what say you? . . *Coriolanus* ii 3 84
Good voyage. That always makes a good voyage of nothing . *T. Night* ii 4 81
Good wager. For a good wager, first begins to crow . . *Tempest* ii 1 28
Good warrant. Which now we find Each putter-out of five for one will bring us Good warrant of . . . . iii 3 49
Good watch. Follow her close; give her good watch . . *Hamlet* iv 5 75
Good wax, thy leave. Blest be You bees that make these locks! *Cymb.* iii 2 35
Good way. Call him in. 'Twill be a good way . . *As Y. Like It* i 1 99
Good wearing. Sparkles this stone as it was wont? or is't not Too dull for your good wearing? . . . . *Cymbeline* ii 4 41
Good welcome. Pray God our cheer May answer my good will and your good welcome here . . . . . *Com. of Errors* iii 1 20
Good wench. If Fortune be a woman, she's a good wench for this gear *Mer. of Venice* ii 2 175
She's a good wench.—She's a beagle, true-bred . . *T. Night* ii 3 194
Look, here it is.—A good wench; give it me . . . *Othello* iii 3 313
Good white head. A good soft pillow for that good white head *Hen. V.* iv 1 14
Good whore. A very tall man! a very good whore! . . *Rom. and Jul.* ii 4 32
Good wife. Good morrow, good wife.—Not so . . *Mer. Wives* ii 2 35
Good will. I should do it With much more ease; for my good will is to it, And yours it is against . . . . . . *Tempest* iii 1 30
Thou art not ignorant what dear good will I bear . *T. G. of Ver.* iv 3 14
This ring I gave him . . . , To bind him to remember my good will . iv 4 103
Can you carry your good will to the maid? . . . *Mer. Wives* i 1 238
I hope I have your good will, father Page.—You have . . iii 2 61
I must advance the colours of my love And not retire: let me have your good will . . . . iii 4 86
I'll to the doctor: he hath my good will, And none but he . . iv 4 84
I tell you for good will, look you: you are wise . . . iv 5 81
Our cheer May answer my good will and your good welcome *Com. of Errors* iii 1 20
Hold you still: I'll fetch my sister, to get her good will . . iii 2 70
Heart and good-will you might; But surely, master, not a rag of money iv 4 88
Such a man would win any woman in the world, if a' could get her good-will . . . . *Much Ado* ii 1 18
I told him true, that your grace had got the good will of this young lady ii 1 223
I have broke with her father, and his good will obtained . . ii 1 311
But, for my will, my will is your good will May stand with ours . . v 4 28
And here, with all good will, with all my heart, In Hermia's love I yield you up my part . . . . *M. N. Dream* iii 2 164
If we offend, it is with our good will. That you should think, we come not to offend, But with good will . . . . v 1 108
And by my father's love and leave am arm'd With his good will *T. of S.* i 1 6
Sorry am I that our good will effects Bianca's grief . . . . i 1 86
Have you married my daughter without asking my good will? . . v 1 137
If I may have your ladyship's good will to go to the world . *All's Well* i 3 19
I do beg your good will in this case.—In what case? . . . i 3 23
I hope, sir, I have your good will to have mine own good fortunes . ii 4 15
To do that office of thine own good will Which tired majesty did make thee offer, The resignation of thy state . . . . *Richard II.* iv 1 177
I will do my good will, sir: you can have no more . 2 *Hen. IV.* iii 2 167
I will none of your money.—It is with a good will . . *Hen. V.* iv 8 73
Doth this churlish superscription Pretend some alteration in good will? What's here? . . . . 1 *Hen. VI.* iv 1 54
Would I were dead! if God's good will were so . . 3 *Hen. VI.* ii 5 19
I thank you both for your good wills; Ye speak like honest men *Hen. VIII.* iii 1 68
He that has but effected his good will Hath overta'en mine act *Coriolanus* i 9 18
It shall be to him then as our good wills, A sure destruction . . ii 1 258
Yet your good will Must have that thanks from Rome . . . v 1 45
If it will please you To show us so much gentry and good will . *Hamlet* ii 2 22
The let-alone lies not in your good will . . . . . *Lear* v 3 79
As well as I can, madam.—And when good will is show'd, though't come too short, The actor may plead pardon . . . . . *Ant. and Cleo.* ii 5 8
My recompense is thanks, that's all; Yet my good will is great *Pericles* iii 4 18
Good wind. Be calm, good wind, blow not a word away . *T. G. of Ver.* i 2 118
Good window. So, my good window of lattice, fare thee well *All's Well* ii 3 224
Good wine. If it be true that good wine needs no bush . *As Y. Like It* Epil. 3
Yet to good wine they do use good bushes . . . . Epil. 5
Good wine. Thank God, and the good wine in thy master's way 2 *Hen. VI.* ii 3 99
He would have all as merry As, first, good company, good wine, good welcome, Can make good people . . . . . . *Hen. VIII.* i 4 6
Good wine is a good familiar creature, if it be well used . . *Othello* ii 3 313
Good wing. The composition that your valour and fear makes in you is a virtue of a good wing . . . . *All's Well* i 1 218
Good wisdom. I would you would make use of that good wisdom, Whereof I know you are fraught . . . . . . *Lear* i 4 240
Good wish. O, a good wish upon you! you will try . . *As Y. Like It* i 3 24
To the unknown beloved, this, and my good wishes . *T. Night* ii 5 102
Joy and good wishes To our most fair and princely cousin! . *Hen. V.* v 2 3
Farewell, my lord: good wishes, praise and prayers . . 1 *Hen. VI.* v 3 173
Good wit. That I had my good wit out of the 'Hundred Merry Tales' *M. Ado* ii 1 135
'Nay,' said I, 'a good wit': 'Just,' said she, 'it hurts nobody' . . v 1 164
Yet was Solomon so seduced, and he had a very good wit . *L. L. Lost* i 2 181
Good wits will be jangling: but, gentles, agree . . . . ii 1 225
A man's good wit seconded with the forward child Understanding *As. Y. Like It* iii 3 13
We that have good wits have much to answer for . . . . v 1 12
A sentence is but a cheveril glove to a good wit . . . *T. Night* iii 1 13
A good wit will make use of any thing . . . . 2 *Hen. IV.* i 2 277
They say Poins has a good wit.—He a good wit? hang him! . . ii 4 260
This rudeness is a sauce to his good wit . . . . . *J. Cæsar* i 2 304
Good witness. Thou art full of piety, as shall be proved upon thee by good witness . . . . *Much Ado* iv 2 82
I have good witness of this . . . . 2 *Hen. VI.* i 3 204
Good woman. One good woman in ten, madam . . . *All's Well* i 3 86
An we might have a good woman born but one every blazing star . . i 3 90
It was a gentle business, and becoming The action of good women *Hen. VIII.* ii 3 55
Only in The merciful construction of good women . . . . . Epil. 10
Good wombs have borne bad sons . . . . . . *Tempest* i 2 120
Good word. Where your good word cannot advantage him, Your slander never can endamage him . . . . *T. G. of Ver.* iii 2 42
Speak a good word to Mistress Anne Page for my master . *Mer. Wives* i 4 88
I have heard of the lady, and good words went with her name *M. for M.* iii 1 219
Amen, so I had mine: is not that a good word? . . . *L. L. Lost* iv 3 94
The king was weeping-ripe for a good word . . . . . . v 2 274
The fool hath planted in his memory An army of good words *Mer. of Venice* iii 5 72
Whate'er you think, good words, I think, were best . . *K. John* iv 3 28
Of much less value is my company Than your good words *Richard II.* ii 3 20
The guilt of conscience take thou for thy labour, But neither my good word nor princely favour . . . . v 6 42
An excellent good word before it was ill sorted . . 2 *Hen. IV.* ii 4 161
Good words, Thersites.—What's the quarrel? . . . *Troi. and Cres.* ii 1 97
Neither gave to me Good word nor look . . . . . . iii 3 144
She hath not given so many good words breath . . . . . iv 1 73
We have ever your good word.—He that will give good words to thee will flatter Beneath abhorring . . . . *Coriolanus* i 1 170
You gave Good words the other day of a bay courser I rode on *T. of Athens* i 2 217
Good words are better than bad strokes, Octavius.—In your bad strokes, Brutus, you give good words . . . . *J. Cæsar* v 1 29
Good work. You have made Good work, you and your cry! *Coriolanus* iv 6 148
You have made good work! A pair of tribunes that have rack'd for Rome v 1 15
Good workman. A good workman, a very good tailor . . *All's Well* ii 5 21
The king's council are no good workmen . . . 2 *Hen. VI.* iv 2 16
Good world. Here's a good world! Knew you of this fair work? *K. John* iv 3 116
Here's a good world the while! Why who's so gross, That seeth not this palpable device? . . . . *Richard III.* iii 6 10
Good worship. How dost thou?—The better that it pleases your good worship to ask . . . . *Mer. Wives* i 4 144
I hope, sir, your good worship will be my bail . *Meas. for Meas.* iii 2 75
Thou wilt amend thy life?—Ay, an it like your good worship *W. Tale* v 2 167
Good worts. Good worts.—Good worts! good cabbage . *Mer. Wives* i 1 123
Good wrestling. I would have told you of good wrestling *As Y. Like It* i 2 116
Good-year. What the good-year, my lord! why are you thus out of measure sad? . . . . *Much Ado* i 3 1
What the good-year! one must bear, and that must be you . 2 *Hen. IV.* ii 4 64
What the good-year! do you think I would deny her? . . . ii 4 191
The good-years shall devour them, flesh and fell, Ere they shall make us weep: we'll see 'em starve first . . . . *Lear* v 3 24
Good yoke. How a good yoke of bullocks at Stamford fair? 2 *Hen. IV.* iii 2 42
Good young man. Run in here, good young man; go into this closet *M. W.* i 4 39
Good young princes. How many good young princes would do so, their fathers being so sick as yours at this time is? . . . 2 *Hen. IV.* ii 2 33
Good youth, he went but forth to wash him in the Hellespont *As Y. Like It* iv 1 103
Goodlier. I have no ambition To see a goodlier man . . . *Tempest* i 2 483
If he were honester He were much goodlier . . . . *All's Well* iii 5 83
Goodliest. She is the goodliest woman That ever lay by man *Hen. VIII.* iv 1 69
Hath sent by me The goodliest weapons of his armoury . *T. Andron.* iv 2 11
Patience and sorrow strove Who should express her goodliest . *Lear* iv 3 19
Goodly. Thou mightst call him A goodly person . . . *Tempest* i 2 416
Vines with clustering bunches growing, Plants with goodly burthen bowing . . . . iv 1 113
How many goodly creatures are there here! How beauteous mankind is! . . . . v 1 182
If these be true spies which I wear in my head, here's a goodly sight . v 1 260
By my modesty, a goodly broker! . . . . . . *T. G. of Ver.* i 2 41
And partly, seeing you are beautified With goodly shape . . . iv 1 56
'Tis a goodly credit for you . . . . *Mer. Wives* iv 2 199
She became A joyful mother of two goodly sons . . *Com. of Errors* i 1 51
We are like to prove a goodly commodity, being taken up *Much Ado* iii 3 190
A maid, and stuffed! there's goodly catching of cold . . . iii 4 65
A goodly count, Count Comfect; a sweet gallant, surely! . . . iv 1 318
A goodly apple rotten at the heart . . . . . *Mer. of Venice* i 3 102
Goodly Lord, what a wit-snapper are you! . . . . iii 5 55
By my fay, a goodly nap . . . . *T. of Shrew* Ind. 2 83
For though you lay here in this goodly chamber, Yet would you say ye were beaten out of door . . . . Ind. 2 86
Where did you study all this goodly speech? . . . . . . ii 1 264
Wherefore gaze this goodly company, As if they saw some wondrous monument? . . . . iii 2 96
Good Lord, how bright and goodly shines the moon! . . . . iv 5 2
She says you have some goodly jest in hand: She will not come . . v 2 91
Within ten year it will make itself ten, which is a goodly increase *All's W.* i 1 160
If it be so, you have wound a goodly clew; If it be not, forswear't . i 3 188
I know a man that had this trick of melancholy sold a goodly manor for a song . . . . iii 2 9
Whether there be a scar under't or no, the velvet knows; but 'tis a goodly patch of velvet . . . . iv 5 102

Goodly. She is spread of late Into a goodly bulk *W. Tale* ii 1 20
Say 'she is a goodly lady,' and The justice of your hearts will thereto add 'Tis pity she's not honest' . ii 1 66
When you have said 'she's goodly,' come between Ere you can say 'she's honest' ii 1 75
A daughter, and a goodly babe, Lusty and like to live . ii 2 26
What might I have been, Might I a son and daughter now have look'd on, Such goodly things as you! . v 1 178
Shall show more goodly and attract more eyes . 1 *Hen. IV.* i 2 238
A goodly portly man, i' faith, and a corpulent . ii 4 464
Thou, that threw'st dust upon his goodly head 2 *Hen. IV.* i 3 103
Here's goodly stuff toward! . ii 4 214
Here's a goodly tumult! I'll forswear keeping house . ii 4 219
In goodly form comes on the enemy . iv 1 20
'Fore God, you have here a goodly dwelling and a rich v 3 6
A goodly prize, fit for the devil's grace! . 1 *Hen. VI.* v 3 33
Thou, being a king, blest with a goodly son, Didst yield consent to disinherit him . 3 *Hen. VI.* ii 2 23
Were it not pity that this goodly boy Should lose his birthright? ii 2 34
Is not a dukedom, sir, a goodly gift?—Ay, by my faith . v 1 31
Is not Oxford here another anchor? And Somerset another goodly mast? . v 4 17
An indigested and deformed lump, Not like the fruit of such a goodly tree . v 6 52
The heavens have bless'd you with a goodly son, To be your comforter *Richard III.* i 3 9
What! we have many goodly days to see . iv 4 320
Gives signal of a goodly day to-morrow . v 3 21
Troy must not be, nor goodly Ilion stand . *Troi. and Cres.* ii 2 109
'O heart,' as the goodly saying is, '—O heart, heavy heart' . iv 4 15
The goodly transformation of Jupiter there, his brother, the bull . v 1 59
Stand, thou Greek; thou art a goodly mark: No? wilt thou not? . v 6 27
Most putrefied core, so fair without, Thy goodly armour thus hath cost thy life . v 8 2
A goodly medicine for my aching bones! O world! world! world! v 10 35
Here's goodly work! . *Coriolanus* iii 1 261
A goodly city is this Antium. City, 'Tis I that made thy widows . iv 4 1
A goodly house: the feast smells well; but I Appear not like a guest . iv 5 5
Ye're goodly things, you voices! . iv 6 147
A goodly lady, trust me; of the hue That I would choose . *T. Andron.* i 1 261
'Tis thought you have a goodly gift in horning . ii 3 67
Dismounted from your snow-white goodly steed . ii 3 76
A goodly humour, is it not, my lords? . iv 4 19
This goodly summer with your winter mix'd . v 2 172
Here's goodly gear!—A sail, a sail! . *Rom. and Jul.* ii 4 107
Excellent! Your lordship's a goodly villain *T. of Athens* iii 3 27
But if he sack fair Athens, And take our goodly aged men by the beards v 1 175
Here from gracious England have I offer Of goodly thousands *Macbeth* iv 3 44
I saw him once; he was a goodly king *Hamlet* i 2 186
Denmark's a prison.—Then is the world one.—A goodly one . ii 2 251
This goodly frame, the earth, seems to me a sterile promontory . ii 2 310
Help, masters!—Here's a goodly watch indeed! *Othello* ii 3 160
Was this fair paper, this most goodly book, Made to write 'whore' upon? . iv 2 71
Those his goodly eyes, That o'er the files and musters of the war Have glow'd like plated Mars *Ant. and Cleo.* i 1 2
Certainly, I have heard the Ptolemies' pyramises are very goodly things ii 7 40
A goodly day not to keep house, with such Whose roof's as low as ours! *Cymbeline* iii 3 1
Goodly and gallant shall be false and perjured From thy great fail iii 4 65
Like goodly buildings left without a roof Soon fall to ruin *Pericles* ii 4 36
O you gods! Why do you make us love your goodly gifts, And snatch them straight away? . iii 1 23
She is a goodly creature.—The fitter, then, the gods should have her . iv 1 9
Seeing this goodly vessel ride before us, I made to it . v 1 18
This was a goodly person, Till the disaster that, one mortal night, Drove him to this v 1 36
Here is The lady that I sent for. Welcome, fair one! Is't not a goodly presence? . v 1 66

Goodman. Come hither, goodman baldpate: do you know me? *M. for M.* v 1 328
Goodman Verges, sir, speaks a little off the matter . *Much Ado* iii 5 10
Dictynna, goodman Dull.—What is Dictynna?—A title to Phœbe *L. L. L.* iv 2 37
Via, goodman Dull! thou hast spoken no word all this while v 1 156
I am your goodman.—My husband and my lord . *T. of Shrew* Ind. 2 107
Pare thy nails, dad; Adieu, good man devil . *T. Night* iv 2 141
Since the old days of goodman Adam . 1 *Hen. IV.* ii 4 106
By'r lady, I think a' be, but goodman Puff of Barson . 2 *Hen. IV.* v 3 93
Goodman death, goodman bones! . v 4 32
Against John Goodman, my lord cardinal's man, for keeping my house 2 *Hen. VI.* i 3 19
He shall be endured: What, goodman boy! I say, he shall *Rom. and Jul.* i 5 79
Nay, but hear you, goodman delver,— Give me leave . *Hamlet* v 1 14
With you, goodman boy, and you please: come, I'll flesh ye; come on *Lear* ii 2 48

Goodness. Abhorred slave, Which any print of goodness wilt not take, Being capable of all ill! *Tempest* i 2 352
Goodness that is cheap in beauty makes beauty brief in goodness *Meas. for Meas.* iii 1 185
Virtue is bold, and goodness never fearful . iii 1 215
Bliss and goodness on you! . iii 2 2?8
There is so great a fever on goodness, that the dissolution of it must cure it . iii 2 236
We have made inquiry of you; and we hear Such goodness of your justice . v 1 6
Thanks, good friend Escalus, for thy much goodness . v 1 534
She derives her honesty and achieves her goodness . *All's Well* i 1 52
And thy goodness Share with thy birthright! . i 1 72
Not altogether so great as the first in goodness, but greater a great deal in evil . iv 3 320
You are not fallen From the report that goes upon your goodness . v 1 13
Our natural goodness Imparts this . *W. Tale* ii 1 164
Your goodness is so evident That your free undertaking cannot miss . ii 2 43
The need I have of thee thine own goodness hath made . iv 2 13
And your father's blest . . . with you Worthy his goodness . v 1 176
Thy overflow of good converts to bad, And thy abundant goodness shall excuse This deadly blot in thy digressing son . *Richard II.* v 3 65
God Almighty! There is some soul of goodness in things evil, Would men observingly distil it out . *Hen. V.* iv 1 4
Let's get us from the walls; For Talbot means no goodness by his looks 1 *Hen. VI.* iii 2 72
Goodness. Poor soul, God's goodness hath been great to thee 2 *Hen. VI.* ii 1 84
Therefore, for goodness' sake, and as you are known . *Hen. VIII.* Prol. 23
Goodness and he fill up one monument! . ii 1 94
Must now confess, if they have any goodness, The trial just and noble . ii 2 91
For goodness' sake, consider what you do; How you may hurt yourself iii 1 159
And, to confirm his goodness, Tied it by letters-patents . iii 2 249
Whilst your great goodness, out of holy pity, Absolved him with an axe iii 2 263
All goodness Is poison to thy stomach . iii 2 282
That goodness Of gleaning all the land's wealth into one, Into your own hands . iii 2 283
The goodness of your intercepted packets You writ to the pope . iii 2 286
Your goodness, Since you provoke me, shall be most notorious . iii 2 287
In which I have commended to his goodness The model of our chaste loves . iv 2 131
Heaven, from thy endless goodness, send prosperous life, long, and ever happy, to the high and mighty princess of England, Elizabeth! . v 5 1
Few now living can behold that goodness—A pattern to all princes living . v 5 22
Her brain-sick raptures Cannot distaste the goodness of a quarrel *Troi. and Cres.* ii 2 123
Breathed, as it were, To an untirable and continuate goodness *T. of Athens* i 1 11
Hollow welcomes, Recanting goodness, sorry ere 'tis shown . i 2 17
Poor honest lord, brought low by his own heart, Undone by goodness! iv 2 38
Tyranny! lay thou thy basis sure, For goodness dare not check thee *Macbeth* iv 3 33
And the chance of goodness Be like our warranted quarrel! . iv 3 136
Nothing is at a like goodness still; For goodness, growing to a plurisy, Dies in his own too much . *Hamlet* iv 7 118
Wisdom and goodness to the vile seem vile . *Lear* iv 2 38
How shall I live and work, To match thy goodness? My life will be too short . iv 7 2
You know the goodness I intend upon you: Tell me—but truly . v 1 7
The goodness of the night upon you, friends! What is the news? *Othello* i 2 35
She holds it a vice in her goodness not to do more than she is requested ii 3 327
Out of her own goodness make the net That shall enmesh them all . ii 3 367
I must not think there are Evils enow to darken all his goodness *Ant. and Cleo.* i 4 11
Good madam, hear me.—Well, go to, I will; But there's no goodness in thy face . ii 5 37
The worm is not to be trusted but in the keeping of wise people; for, indeed, there is no goodness in the worm . v 2 268
Exceeds in goodness the hugeness of your unworthy thinking *Cymbeline* i 4 156
The credit that thy lady hath of thee Deserves thy trust, and thy most perfect goodness Her assured credit . i 6 158
His goodness forespent on us, We must extend our notice . ii 3 64
Your very goodness and your company O'erpays all I can do . ii 4 9
I believe you; Your honour and your goodness teach me to't *Pericles* iii 3 26
A curse upon him, die he like a thief, That robs thee of thy goodness! . iv 6 122
All goodness that consists in bounty Expect even here . v 1 70

Goodrig. Lord Talbot of Goodrig and Urchinfield . 1 *Hen. VI.* iv 7 64

Goodwife Keech, the butcher's wife . 2 *Hen. IV.* ii 1 101

Goods. I leave at thy dispose My goods, my lands . *T. G. of Ver.* ii 7 87
He dies, His goods confiscate to the duke's dispose *Com. of Errors* i 1 21
And the great care of goods at random left Drew me from kind embracements of my spouse . i 1 43
Lest that your goods too soon be confiscate . i 2 2
What stuff of mine hast thou embark'd?—Your goods that lay at host . v 1 410
If thou dost shed One drop of Christian blood, thy lands and goods Are, by the laws of Venice, confiscate *Mer. of Venice* iv 1 310
The party 'gainst the which he doth contrive Shall seize one half his goods . iv 1 353
To quit the fine for one half of his goods, I am content . iv 1 381
It is said, 'many a man knows no end of his goods' *As Y. Like It* iii 3 53
Crowns in my purse I have and goods at home . *T. of Shrew* i 2 57
Left solely heir to all his lands and goods, Which I have better'd . ii 1 118
She is my goods, my chattels; she is my house, My household stuff . iii 2 232
We seize into our hands His plate, his goods, his money *Richard II.* ii 1 210
My father's goods are all distrain'd and sold . ii 3 131
Come, we will all put forth, body and goods . 2 *Hen. IV.* i 1 186
While as the silly owner of the goods Weeps over them . 2 *Hen. VI.* i 1 225
Lands, goods, horse, armour, any thing I have, Is his to use . v 1 52
Pronounced a traitor, And all his lands and goods be confiscate 3 *Hen. VI.* iv 6 55
Go; And thither bear your treasure and your goods *Richard III.* iv 4 69
France hath flaw'd the league, and hath attach'd Our merchants' goods at Bourdeaux . *Hen. VIII.* i 1 96
To forfeit all your goods, lands, tenements, Chattels . iii 2 342

Goodwin. The Goodwins, I think they call the place; a very dangerous flat and fatal. *Mer. of Venice* iii 1 4
The great supply That was expected by the Dauphin here, Are wreck'd three nights ago on Goodwin Sands *K. John* v 3 11
And your supply, which you have wish'd so long, Are cast away and sunk on Goodwin Sands . v 5 13

Goose. Though thou canst swim like a duck, thou art made like a goose *Tempest* ii 2 135
O omnipotent Love! how near the god drew to the complexion of a goose! . *Mer. Wives* v 5 9
Until the goose came out of door, Staying the odds by adding four *L. L. Lost* iii 1 98
The boy hath sold him a bargain, a goose, that's flat. Sir, your pennyworth is good, an your goose be fat . iii 1 102
Let me see; a fat l'envoy; ay, that's a fat goose . iii 1 105
Thus came your argument in; Then the boy's fat l'envoy, the goose that you bought . iii 1 110
I smell some l'envoy, some goose, in this . iii 1 123
This is the liver-vein, which makes flesh a deity, A green goose a goddess . iv 3 75
A very fox for his valour.—True; and a goose for his discretion *M. N. D.* v 1 235
His valour cannot carry his discretion; and the fox carries the goose.—His discretion, I am sure, cannot carry his valour; for the goose carries not the fox . v 1 238
The nightingale, if she should sing by day, When every goose is cackling, would be thought No better a musician than the wren *M. of V.* v 1 105
As a puisny tilter, that spurs his horse but on one side, breaks his staff like a noble goose *As Y. Like It* iii 4 48
Go, ye giddy goose . 1 *Hen. IV.* iii 1 232
Winchester goose, I cry, a rope! a rope! Now beat them hence 1 *Hen. VI.* i 3 53
My fear is this, Some galled goose of Winchester would hiss *T. and C.* v 10 55
Was I with you there for the goose?—Thou wast never with me for any thing when thou wast not there for the goose . *Rom. and Jul.* ii 4 78
I will bite thee by the ear for that jest.—Nay, good goose, bite not . ii 4 82

Goose. A most sharp sauce.—And is it not well served in to a sweet goose? . . . . *Rom. and Jul.* ii 4 86
I stretch it out for that word 'broad;' which added to the goose, proves thee far and wide a broad goose . . . ii 4 90
Come in, tailor; here you may roast your goose . *Macbeth* ii 3 17
Goose, if I had you upon Sarum plain, I'ld drive ye cackling home to Camelot.—What, art thou mad, old fellow? . . . *Lear* ii 2 89
Gooseberry. Are not worth a gooseberry . . . 2 *Hen. IV.* i 2 196
Goose look. Cream-faced loon! Where got'st thou that goose look? *Macb.* v 3 12
Goose-pen. Let there be gall enough in thy ink, though thou write with a goose-pen, no matter . . . *T. Night* iii 2 53
Goose-quill. Many wearing rapiers are afraid of goose-quills . *Hamlet* ii 2 359
Goot. There is also another device in my prain, which peradventure prings goot discretions . . . . *Mer. Wives* i 1 44
It were a goot motion if we leave our pribbles and prabbles . . i 1 55
Pauca verba, Sir John; goot worts.—Good worts! good cabbage . . i 1 123
Fery goot: I will make a prief of it in my note-book . . i 1 146
Gorbellied. Hang ye, gorbellied knaves, are ye undone? . 1 *Hen. IV.* ii 2 93
Gorboduc. Very wittily said to a niece of King Gorboduc . *T. Night* iv 2 16
Gordian. The Gordian knot of it he will unloose . . . *Hen. V.* i 1 46
As slippery as the Gordian knot was hard! . . *Cymbeline* ii 2 34
Gore. Lay them in gore, Since you have shore With shears his thread of silk. Tongue, not a word . . . . . *M. N. Dream* v 1 346
But silence, like a Lucrece knife, With bloodless stroke my heart doth gore . . . . *T. Night* ii 5 117
York, all haggled over, Comes to him, where in gore he lay insteep'd *Hen. V.* iv 6 12
Their wounded steeds Fret fetlock deep in gore . . . iv 7 82
One drop of blood drawn from thy country's bosom Should grieve thee more than streams of foreign gore . 1 *Hen. VI.* iii 3 55
If by this crime he owes the law his life, Why, let the war receive't in valiant gore; For law is strict . . . *T. of Athens* iii 5 84
Their daggers Unmannerly breech'd with gore . . . *Macbeth* ii 3 122
Roasted in wrath and fire, And thus o'er-sized with coagulate gore *Ham.* ii 2 484
Gore-blood. All bedaub'd in blood, All in gore-blood *Rom. and Jul.* iii 2 56
Gored. With forked heads Have their round haunches gored *As Y. Like It* ii 1 25
O, let no noble eye profane a tear For me, if I be gored with Mowbray's spear . . . . *Richard II.* i 3 60
Gored the gentle bosom of peace with pillage and robbery . *Hen. V.* iv 1 174
Paris is gored with Menelaus' horn . . *Troi. and Cres.* i 1 115
I see my reputation is at stake; My fame is shrewdly gored . . iii 3 229
You twain Rule in this realm, and the gored state sustain . *Lear* v 3 320
Gorge. He cracks his gorge, his sides, With violent hefts . *W. Tale* ii 1 44
'Couple a gorge!' That is the word . . . . *Hen. V.* ii 1 75
Ce soldat ici est disposé tout à cette heure de couper votre gorge . iv 4 38
She, whom the spital-house and ulcerous sores Would cast the gorge at, this embalms and spices . . . . *T. of Athens* iv 3 40
How abhorred in my imagination it is! my gorge rises at it *Hamlet* v 1 207
He that makes his generation messes To gorge his appetite . . *Lear* i 1 120
Begin to heave the gorge, disrelish and abhor . . . *Othello* ii 1 236
Gorged. Being with his presence glutted, gorged and full 1 *Hen. IV.* iii 2 84
Thou womb of death, Gorged with the dearest morsel of the earth *Rom. and Jul.* v 3 46
Gorgeous. The cloud-capp'd towers, the gorgeous palaces . *Tempest* iv 1 152
At the first opening of the gorgeous east . . . *L. L. Lost* iv 3 223
My jewels for a set of beads, My gorgeous palace for a hermitage *Rich. II.* iii 3 148
And gorgeous as the sun at midsummer . . . 1 *Hen. IV.* iv 1 102
This new and gorgeous garment, majesty, Sits not so easy on me 2 *Hen. IV.* v 2 44
So seems this gorgeous beauty to mine eyes . . . 1 *Hen. VI.* v 3 64
O, that deceit should dwell In such a gorgeous palace! . *Rom. and Jul.* iii 2 85
If only to go warm were gorgeous, Why, nature needs not what thou gorgeous wear'st, Which scarcely keeps thee warm . . *Lear* ii 4 271
Gorget. And, with a palsy-fumbling on his gorget, Shake in and out the rivet . . . . *Troi. and Cres.* i 3 174
Gorging and feeding from our soldiers' hands . . *J. Cæsar* v 1 82
Gorgon. Destroy your sight With a new Gorgon . . . *Macbeth* ii 3 77
Though he be painted one way like a Gorgon, The other way's a Mars *Ant. and Cleo.* ii 5 116
Gormandise. Thou shalt not gormandise, As thou hast done with me:—What, Jessica!—And sleep and snore . . . *Mer. of Venice* ii 5 3
Gormandizing. Leave gormandizing; know the grave doth gape For thee thrice wider than for other men . . . 2 *Hen. IV.* v 5 57
Gory. The obligation of our blood forbids A gory emulation . *T. and C.* iv 5 123
What mean these masterless and gory swords? . *Rom. and Jul.* v 3 142
Thou canst not say I did it: never shake Thy gory locks at me *Macbeth* iii 4 51
Gosling. I'll never Be such a gosling to obey instinct . *Coriolanus* v 3 35
Whip thee, gosling: I think I shall have something to do with you *Per.* iv 2 91
Gospel. A madman's epistles are no gospels . . . *T. Night* v 1 295
Gospelled. Are you so gospell'd To pray for this good man? . *Macbeth* iii 1 88
Goss. Through Tooth'd briers, sharp furzes, pricking goss . *Tempest* iv 1 180
Gossamer. A lover may bestride the gossamer That idles in the wanton summer air, And yet not fall . . . *Rom. and Jul.* ii 6 18
Hadst thou been aught but gossamer, feathers, air . . *Lear* iv 6 49
Gossip. Yet 'tis not a maid, for she hath had gossips . *T. G. of Ver.* iii 1 269
What, ho, gossip Ford! what, ho!—Step into the chamber *Mer. Wives* iv 2 9
Go to a gossips' feast, and go with me . . . *Com. of Errors* v 1 405
With all my heart, I'll gossip at this feast . . . . v 1 407
Sometime lurk I in a gossip's bowl . . . . *M. N. Dream* ii 1 47
If my gossip Report be an honest woman of her word . *Mer. of Venice* iii 1 7
As lying a gossip in that as ever knapped ginger . . . . iii 1 9
With a world Of pretty, fond, adoptious christendoms, That blinking Cupid gossips . . . . *All's Well* i 1 189
And make the babbling gossip of the air Cry out . . *T. Night* i 5 292
Needful conference About some gossips for your highness . *W. Tale* ii 3 41
Did not goodwife Keech, the butcher's wife, come in then and call me gossip Quickly? coming in to borrow a mess of vinegar? 2 *Hen. IV.* ii 1 102
Are mighty gossips in this monarchy . . . *Richard III.* i 1 83
My noble gossips, ye have been too prodigal: I thank ye heartily *Hen. VIII.* v 5 13
A long-tongued babbling gossip . . . . . *T. Andron.* iv 2 150
Speak to my gossip Venus one fair word . . *Rom. and Jul.* ii 1 11
Hold your tongue, Good prudence; smatter with your gossips, go . iii 5 172
Peace, you mumbling fool! Utter your gravity o'er a gossip's bowl . iii 5 175
Gossiped. Full often hath she gossip'd by my side . *M. N. Dream* ii 1 125
Gossiping. Will you walk in to see their gossiping? . *Com of Errors* v 1 419
Full of warm blood, of mirth, of gossiping . . *K. John* v 2 59
Gossip-like. I will leave you now to your gossip-like humour . *Much Ado* v 1 188
Got. Thou poisonous slave, got by the devil himself! . *Tempest* i 2 319
Who hath got, as I take it, an ague . . . . . ii 2 68
I say, by sorcery he got this isle; From me he got it . . . iii 2 60

Got. Since they did plot The means that dusky Dis my daughter got *Tempest* iv 1 89
Let me not, Since I have my dukedom got . . . . . Epil. 6
And show thee all the treasure we have got . . *T. G. of Ver.* iv 1 75
Our youth got me to play the woman's part . . . . iv 4 165
There is no fear of Got in a riot: the council, look you, shall desire to hear the fear of Got, and not to hear a riot . . . *Mer. Wives* i 1 37
Got deliver to a joyful resurrections! . . . . . . i 1 53
Got pless your house here!—Who's there? . . . . . i 1 74
Here is Got's plessing, and your friend . . . . . i 1 76
So Got udge me, that is a virtuous mind . . . . . i 1 191
Got's lords and his ladies! you must speak possitable . . . i 1 243
Got's will, and his passion of my heart! . . . . . iii 1 62
Serve Got, and leave your desires, and fairies will not pinse you . v 5 136
Who hath got the right Anne?—My heart misgives me . . . v 5 224
He hath got his friend with child . . . . *Meas. for Meas.* i 4 29
She is with child; And he that got it, sentenced . . . ii 3 13
The one ne'er got me credit, the other mickle blame . *Com. of Errors* iii 1 45
What, have you got the picture of old Adam new-apparelled? . . iv 3 13
The prince hath got your Hero.—I wish him joy of her . *Much Ado* ii 1 199
I told him true, that your grace had got the good will of this young lady ii 1 223
Your father got excellent husbands, if a maid could come by them . ii 1 337
And some such strange bull leap'd your father's cow, And got a calf . v 4 50
What a beard hast thou got! thou hast got more hair on thy chin than Dobbin my fill-horse has on his tail . . . *Mer. of Venice* ii 2 99
So thou canst get a wife.—I thank your lordship, you have got me one. iii 2 198
I got a promise of this fair one here To have her love . . . iii 2 208
You may partly hope that your father got you not . . . . iii 5 12
Let not that doctor e'er come near my house: Since he hath got the jewel that I loved . . . . v 1 224
This order hath Baptista ta'en, That none shall have access unto Bianca Till Katharine the curst have got a husband . . *T. of Shrew* i 2 128
No doubt but he hath got a quiet catch . . . . . ii 1 333
And there was never virgin got till virginity was first lost . *All's Well* i 1 140
Sure, they are bastards to the English; the French ne'er got 'em . . ii 3 101
I must give myself some hurts, and say I got them in exploit . . iv 1 41
And now you should be as your mother was When your sweet self was got . . . . iv 2 10
A scar nobly got, or a noble scar, is a good livery of honour . . iv 5 105
Confess 'twas hers, and by what rough enforcement You got it from her v 3 108
She got the ring; And I had that which any inferior might . . v 3 217
And at that time he got his wife with child . . . . . v 3 302
Good goddess Nature, which hast made it So like to him that got it *W. T.* ii 3 105
Hurried Here to this place, i' the open air, before I have got strength . iii 2 107
They were warmer that got this than the poor thing is here . . . iii 3 76
Large lengths of seas and shores Between my father and my mother lay, . . . When this same lusty gentleman was got . . *K. John* i 1 108
Your face hath got five hundred pound a year . . . . . i 1 152
Blessed be the hour, by night or day, When I was got, sir Robert was away! . . . . i 1 166
Good fortune come to thee! For thou wast got i' the way of honesty . i 1 181
Who lives and dares but say thou didst not well When I was got, I'll send his soul to hell . . . . i 1 272
Got with swearing 'Lay by' and spent with crying 'Bring in' 1 *Hen. IV.* i 2 40
Your money!—Villains!—Got with much ease. Now merrily to horse . ii 2 111
What never-dying honour hath he got Against renowned Douglas! . . iii 2 106
I have got, in exchange of a hundred and fifty soldiers, three hundred and odd pounds . . . . iv 2 14
Belike then my appetite was not princely got . . . . 2 *Hen. IV.* ii 2 12
Hath got the voice in hell for excellence . . . . *Hen V.* ii 2 113
That's all the riches I got in his service . . . . . . ii 3 46
And patches will I get unto these cudgell'd scars, And swear I got them in the Gallia wars . . . . v 1 94
Beshrew my father's ambition! he was thinking of civil wars when he got me . . . . v 2 243
Ascribes the glory of his conquest got First to my God . 1 *Hen. VI.* iii 4 11
And did my brother Bedford toil his wits, To keep by policy what Henry got? . . . . 2 *Hen. VI.* i 1 84
Are the cities, that I got with wounds, Deliver'd up again with peaceful words? . . . . i 1 121
Had Henry got an empire by his marriage, And all the wealthy kingdoms . . . . i 1 153
Thus got the house of Lancaster the crown . . . . . . ii 2 29
Wear it as a herald's coat, To emblaze the honour that thy master got . iv 10 76
We have not got that which we have . . . . v 3 20
Henry the Fourth by conquest got the crown.—'Twas by rebellion 3 *Hen. VI.* i 1 132
The army of the queen hath got the field . . . . . . i 4 1
Say unto his child, 'What my great-grandfather and grandsire got My careless father fondly gave away' . . . . ii 2 37
Whoever got thee, there thy mother stands . . . . . ii 2 133
The air hath got into my deadly wounds . . . . . . ii 6 27
I'll tell you how these lands are to be got . . . . . iii 2 42
But when the fox hath once got in his nose, He'll soon find means to make the body follow . . . . iv 7 25
That's not my fear; my meed hath got me fame . . . . iv 8 38
Humbly complaining to her deity Got my lord chamberlain his liberty *Richard III.* i 1 77
His own bastardy, As being got, your father then in France . . iii 7 10
By her, in his unlawful bed, he got This Edward . . . . iii 7 190
All the good our English Have got by the late voyage . . *Hen. VIII.* i 3 6
Leave those remnants Of fool and feather that they got in France . i 3 25
The sly whoresons Have got a speeding trick to lay down ladies . . i 3 40
And got your leave To make this present summons . . . . ii 4 218
Innumerable substance—By what means got, I leave to your own conscience . . . . iii 2 327
How got they in, and be hang'd?—Alas, I know not; how gets the tide in? . . . . v 4 17
Men prize the thing ungain'd more than it is: That she was never yet that ever knew Love got so sweet as when desire did sue *Troi. and Cres.* i 2 317
Praise him that got thee, she that gave thee suck . . . . i 3 252
Is't possible? no sooner got but lost? . . . . . . iv 2 76
Diomed has got that same scurvy doting foolish young knave's sleeve . v 4 3
You cowards! you were got in fear, Though you were born in Rome *Coriolanus* i 3 36
I had rather have my wounds to heal again Than hear say how I got them . . . . ii 2 74
Look, sir, my wounds! I got them in my country's service . . ii 3 58
And that the spoil got on the Antiates Was ne'er distributed . . iii 3 4

Got. The plebeians have got your fellow-tribune And hale him up and down . . . . *Coriolanus* v 4 39
Now, by the burning tapers of the sky, That shone so brightly when this boy was got, He dies . . . . . *T. Andron.* iv 2 90
My very friend hath got his mortal hurt In my behalf . *Rom. and Jul.* iii 1 115
Thy face is much abused with tears.—The tears have got small victory iv 1 30
No kin else, On whom I may confer what I have got *T. of Athens* i 1 122
Ye've got a humour there Does not become a man . . . . . i 2 26
Thou mightst have sooner got another service . . . . . iv 3 511
Nought's had, all's spent, Where our desire is got without content *Macb.* iii 2 5
Toad, that under cold stone Days and nights has thirty one Swelter'd venom sleeping got . . . . iv 1 8
Only got the tune of the time and outward habit of encounter *Hamlet* v 2 198
A whole tribe of fops, Got 'tween asleep and wake . . *Lear* i 2 15
Strong and fasten'd villain! Would he deny his letter? I never got him . . . . ii 1 80
Got praises of the king For him attempting who was self-subdued ii 2 128
Gloucester's bastard son Was kinder to his father than my daughters Got 'tween the lawful sheets . . . . . . iv 6 118
The dark and vicious place where thee he got Cost him his eyes v 3 172
O heaven! How got she out? O treason of the blood! . . *Othello* i 1 170
Reputation is an idle and most false imposition; oft got without merit, and lost without deserving . . . . . . ii 3 269
My queen and Eros Have by their brave instruction got upon me A nobleness in record . . . . . *Ant. and Cleo.* iv 14 98
I am his fortune's vassal, and I send him The greatness he has got . v 2 30
What got he by that? You have broke his pate with your bowl *Cymb.* ii 1 7
Though now our voices Have got the mannish crack, sing him to the ground . . . . iv 2 236
She never loved you, only Affected greatness got by you, not you . . v 5 38
By villany I got this ring: 'twas Leonatus' jewel . . . v 5 143
This her bracelet,—O cunning, how I got it! . . . . v 5 205
Thou hast lost by this a kingdom.—No, my lord; I have got two worlds by't . . . . v 5 374
And make a conquest of unhappy me, Whereas no glory's got *Pericles* i 4 70
For here's nothing to be got now-a-days, unless thou canst fish for't . ii 1 73

Got clear. On the instant they got clear of our ship *Hamlet* iv 6 19

Got credit. That former fabulous story, Being now seen possible enough, got credit . . . . *Hen. VIII.* i 1 37

Got leave. Have you got leave to go to shrift to-day? . *Rom. and Jul.* ii 5 68

Got off. They fought together, but Aufidius got off . . *Coriolanus* ii 1 141

Got possession. Upon a true contract I got possession of Julietta's bed *Meas. for Meas.* i 2 150

Goth. As the most capricious poet, honest Ovid, was among the Goths.—O knowledge ill-inhabited! . . . . . *As Y. Like It* iii 3 9
Accited home From weary wars against the barbarous Goths *T. Andron.* i 1 28
Here Goths have given me leave to sheathe my sword . . . i 1 85
Give us the proudest prisoner of the Goths, That we may hew his limbs i 1 96
These are their brethren, whom you Goths beheld Alive and dead i 1 122
Tamora, the Queen of Goths—When Goths were Goths and Tamora was queen . . . . i 1 139
He comforts you Can make you greater than the Queen of Goths . . i 1 269
Speak, Queen of Goths, dost thou applaud my choice? . . . i 1 321
I swear, If Saturnine advance the Queen of Goths, She will a handmaid be to his desires . . . . i 1 330
By the gods that warlike Goths adore, This petty brabble will undo us all . . . . ii 1 61
And then they call'd me foul adulteress, Lascivious Goth . . . ii 3 110
Thou must not stay: Hie to the Goths, and raise an army there . iii 1 286
Now will I to the Goths, and raise a power, To be revenged on Rome iii 1 300
We will prosecute by good advice Mortal revenge upon these traitorous Goths . . . . iv 1 93
Now to the Goths, as swift as swallow flies . . . . . iv 2 172
Kinsmen, his sorrows are past remedy. Join with the Goths . . iv 3 32
Arm, arm, my lord;—Rome never had more cause. The Goths have gather'd head . . . . iv 4 63
Is warlike Lucius general of the Goths? These tidings nip me . . iv 4 69
With all the art I have, To pluck proud Lucius from the warlike Goths iv 4 110
But who comes here, led by a lusty Goth? . . . . . v 1 19
Thus he rates the babe,—'For I must bear thee to a trusty Goth' . v 1 34
O worthy Goth, this is the incarnate devil That robb'd Andronicus . v 1 40
Lord Lucius, and you princes of the Goths, The Roman emperor greets you v 1 156
I'll find some cunning practice out of hand, To scatter and disperse the giddy Goths . . . . v 2 78
Send for Lucius, thy thrice-valiant son, Who leads towards Rome a band of warlike Goths . . . . v 2 113
Go, gentle Marcus, to thy nephew Lucius; Thou shalt inquire him out among the Goths . . . . v 2 123
Bring with him Some of the chiefest princes of the Goths . . v 2 125
Welcome, my gracious lord; welcome, dread queen; Welcome, ye warlike Goths . . . . v 3 27

Gotten. He was gotten in drink: is not the humour conceited? *M. Wives* i 3 25
With much ado at length have gotten leave *Richard II.* v 5 74
Jake Cade hath gotten London bridge: The citizens fly . *2 Hen. VI.* iv 4 49
How haps it, . . . You told not how Henry the Sixth hath lost All that which Henry the Fifth had gotten? . *3 Hen. VI.* iii 3 90
Doubt not of the day, And, that once gotten, doubt not of large pay iv 7 88

Gottest. As thou got'st Milan, I'll come by Naples . . *Tempest* ii 1 291
By what means got'st thou to be released? Discourse, I prithee *1 Hen. VI.* i 4 25
Thou cream-faced loon! Where got'st thou that goose look? *Macbeth* v 3 12

Gourd and fullam holds, And high and low beguiles the rich and poor *Mer. Wives* i 3 94

Gout. Do curse the gout, serpigo, and the rheum . *Meas. for Meas.* iii 1 31
A priest that lacks Latin and a rich man that hath not the gout *As Y. L. It* iii 2 338
But the gout galls the one, and the pox pinches the other . *2 Hen. IV.* i 2 258
A pox of this gout! or, a gout of this pox! for the one or the other plays the rogue with my great toe . . . . . . i 2 273
I see thee still, And on thy blade and dudgeon gouts of blood *Macbeth* ii 1 46
Yet am I better Than one that's sick o' the gout . . *Cymbeline* v 4 5

Gouty. He is a gouty Briareus, many hands and no use . *Troi. and Cres.* i 2 30
Thou'lt go, strong thief, When gouty keepers of thee cannot stand *T. of Athens* iv 3 46

Govern. I would with such perfection govern, sir, To excel the golden age *Tempest* ii 1 167
But truer stars did govern Proteus' birth . . *T. G. of Ver.* ii 7 74
And with full line of his authority, Governs Lord Angelo *Meas. for Meas.* i 4 57
Why, let it be as humours and conceits shall govern . *Mer. of Venice* iii 5 69
Who governs here?—A noble duke, in nature as in name . *T. Night* i 2 24
Let not the world see fear and sad distrust Govern the motion of a kingly eye: Be stirring as the time . . . . *K. John* v 1 47

Govern. I have no tongue, sir.—And for mine, sir, I will govern it *2 Hen. IV.* ii 2 180
He being of age to govern of himself . . . *2 Hen. VI.* i 1 166
God and King Henry govern England's realm . . . . . ii 3 30
Come, wife, let's in, and learn to govern better . . . . iv 9 48
Not fit to govern and rule multitudes . . . . . . v 1 94
For how can tyrants safely govern home, Unless abroad they purchase great alliance? . . . . *3 Hen. VI.* iii 3 69
Alas! how should you govern any kingdom, That know not how to use ambassadors? . . . . iv 3 35
Himself, No doubt, shall then and till then govern well *Richard III.* ii 3 15
The duke Shall govern England . . . . . . *Hen. VIII.* i 2 171
Though Venus govern your desires, Saturn is dominator over mine *T. Andron.* ii 3 30
But yet let reason govern thy lament . . . . . . iii 1 219
Sly frantic wretch, that holp'st to make me great, In hope thyself should govern Rome and me . . . . iv 4 60
May I govern so, To heal Rome's harms, and wipe away her woe! . . v 3 147
To stay the providence of some high powers That govern us below *J. C.* v 1 108
If such a one be fit to govern, speak: I am as I have spoken.—Fit to govern! No, not to live . . . . . . *Macbeth* iv 3 101
Govern these ventages with your fingers and thumb *Hamlet* iii 2 372
It is the stars, The stars above us, govern our conditions . *Lear* iv 3 35
Go after her: she's desperate; govern her . . . . . v 3 161
From this hour The heart of brothers govern in our loves! *Ant. and Cleo.* ii 2 150
Thy spirit Is all afraid to govern thee near him; But, he away, 'tis noble ii 3 29
Be resolved he lives to govern us, Or dead, give's cause to mourn *Pericles* ii 4 31
Advanced in time to great and high estate, Is left to govern . . . iv 4 15
If he govern the country, you are bound to him indeed . . . iv 6 59

Governance. What, shall King Henry be a pupil still Under the surly Gloucester's governance? . . . . . . *2 Hen. VI.* i 3 50

Governed. Her husband hath the finest mad devil of jealousy in him, Master Brook, that ever governed frenzy *Mer. Wives* v 1 20
A due sincerity govern'd his deeds, Till he did look on me *Meas. for Meas.* v 1 451
In our last conflict four of his five wits went halting off, and now is the whole man governed with one . . . . . *Much Ado* i 1 67
Nay, but his jesting spirit; which is now crept into a lute-string and now governed by stops . . . . ii 2 61
Thy currish spirit Govern'd a wolf . . . *Mer. of Venice* iv 1 134
The fortune of us that are the moon's men doth ebb and flow like the sea, being governed, as the sea is, by the moon . . *1 Hen. IV.* i 2 36
You are altogether governed by humours . . . . . iii 1 237
A hare-brain'd Hotspur, govern'd by a spleen . . . . v 2 19
Our state may go In equal rank with the best govern'd nation *2 Hen. IV.* v 2 137
I, being govern'd by the watery moon, May send forth plenteous tears *Richard III.* ii 2 69
Woe to that land that's govern'd by a child! . . . . . ii 3 11
Tell my lord the emperor How I have govern'd our determined jest *T. Andron.* v 2 139
The noblest mind he carries That ever govern'd man . *T. of Athens* i 1 292
Woe the while! our fathers' minds are dead, And we are govern'd with our mothers' spirits . . . . *J. Cæsar* i 3 83
His corporal motion govern'd by my spirit . . . . . iv 1 33
Be govern'd by your knowledge, and proceed I' the sway of your own will *Lear* iv 7 19
What thou endurest, Betwixt a father by thy step-dame govern'd! *Cymb.* ii 1 63

Governess. The moon, the governess of floods . . *M. N. Dream* ii 1 103

Government. The government I cast upon my brother And to my state grew stranger . . . . *Tempest* i 2 75
Of government the properties to unfold, Would seem in me to affect speech and discourse . . . . . . *Meas. for Meas.* i 1 3
I will open my lips in vain, or discover his government . . iii 1 199
And, indeed, his fact, till now in the government of Lord Angelo, came not to an undoubtful proof . . . . iv 2 141
A sound, but not in government . . . . *M. N. Dream* v 1 124
All must be even in our government . . . . *Richard II.* iii 4 36
Let men say we be men of good government . . *1 Hen. IV.* i 2 31
Defect of manners, want of government, Pride, haughtiness . . iii 1 184
Who leads his power? Under whose government come they along? . iv 1 19
Till these rebels, now afoot, Come underneath the yoke of government *2 Hen. IV.* iv 4 10
For Government, though high and low and lower, Put into parts, doth keep in one consent . . . . *Hen. V.* i 2 181
Under the sweet shade of your government . . . . . ii 2 28
Had all your quarters been as safely kept As that whereof I had the government, We had not been thus shamefully surprised *1 Hen. VI.* ii 1 64
Is this the government of Britain's isle? . . *2 Hen. VI.* i 3 47
'Tis government that makes them seem divine . . *3 Hen. VI.* i 4 132
I here resign my government to thee, For thou art fortunate in all thy deeds . . . . iv 6 24
Now join your hands, and with your hands your hearts, That no dissension hinder government . . . . iv 6 40
In bearing weight of government, While he enjoys the honour and his ease iv 6 51
In him there is a hope of government . . . . *Richard III.* ii 3 12
We heartily solicit Your gracious self to take on you the charge And kingly government of this your land . . . . . . iii 7 132
Wife-like government, Obeying in commanding . . . *Hen. VIII.* ii 4 138
Each part, deprived of supple government, Shall, stiff and stark and cold, appear like death . . . . . . *Rom. and Jul.* iv 1 102
Fear not my government . . . . *Othello* iii 3 256
As I think, they do command him home, Deputing Cassio in his government iv 1 248
Quite besides The government of patience! . . . *Cymbeline* ii 4 150
This Tarsus, o'er which I have the government . . . *Pericles* i 4 21
He deserves so to be called for his peaceable reign and good government ii 1 108
He is a happy king, since he gains from his subjects the name of good by his government . . . . ii 1 110

Governor. Whether that the body public be A horse whereon the governor doth ride . . . . *Meas. for Meas.* i 2 164
This new governor Awakes me all the enrolled penalties . . . i 2 169
To be directed, As from her lord, her governor, her king *Mer. of Venice* iii 2 167
And dart not scornful glances from those eyes, To wound thy lord, thy king, thy governor . . . . *T. of Shrew* v 2 138
We create, in absence of ourself, Our uncle York lord governor *Rich. II.* ii 1 220
How yet resolves the governor of the town? . . . *Hen. V.* iii 3 1
To Eltham will I, where the young king is, Being ordain'd his special governor . . . . *1 Hen. VI.* i 1 171
Run and bring me word; And thou shalt find me at the governor's . i 4 20
Now, governor of Paris, take your oath . . . . . . iv 1 3
I am glad on't; 'tis a worthy governor . . . . *Othello* ii 1 30
My hopes do shape him for the governor . . . . . . ii 1 55

Governor. To you, lord governor, Remains the censure of this hellish villain *Othello* v 2 367
He's the governor of this country, and a man whom I am bound to *Per.* iv 6 57
You are of honourable parts, and are the governor of this place iv 6 87
What is your place?—I am the governor of this place you lie before v 1 21
Gower. Master Gower, shall I entreat you with me to dinner? *2 Hen. IV.* ii 1 194
Gower is a good captain, and is good knowledge and literatured *Hen. V.* iv 7 156
Knowest thou Gower?—He is my dear friend, an please you iv 7 173
Stand away, Captain Gower; I will give treason his payment into plows iv 8 14
To sing a song that old was sung, From ashes ancient Gower is come *Pericles* i Gower 2
What shall be next, Pardon old Gower,—this longs the text ii Gower 40
Gown. Put off that gown, Trinculo; by this hand, I'll have that gown *Tempest* iv 1 227
I was trimm'd in Madam Julia's gown, Which served me as fit *T. G. of V.* iv 4 166
Pray you, give me my gown; or else keep it in your arms *Mer. Wives* iii 1 34
There is no woman's gown big enough for him iv 2 72
My maid's aunt, the fat woman of Brentford, has a gown above iv 2 78
We'll come dress you straight: put on the gown the while iv 2 85
Kneel down before him, hang upon his gown: You are too cold *Meas. for Meas.* ii 2 44
Allowed by order of law a furred gown to keep him warm iii 2 8
Your gown's a most rare fashion, i' faith *Much Ado* iii 4 15
I saw the Duchess of Milan's gown that they praise so.—O, that exceeds, they say.—By my troth, 's but a night-gown in respect of yours iii 4 16
One that hath two gowns and every thing handsome about him iv 2 88
I'll change my black gown for a faithful friend *L. L. Lost* v 2 844
Thy gown? why, ay: come, tailor, let us see't. O mercy! *T. of Shrew* iv 3 86
I see she's like to have neither cap nor gown iv 3 93
I never saw a better-fashion'd gown, More quaint, more pleasing iv 3 101
Thou hast marr'd her gown.—Your worship is deceived; the gown is made Just as my master had direction iv 3 115
If ever I said loose-bodied gown, sew me in the skirts of it iv 3 136
The gown is not for me.—You are i' the right, sir: 'tis for my mistress iv 3 156
Take up my mistress' gown for thy master's use! iv 3 161
Tailor, I'll pay thee for thy gown to-morrow iv 3 168
Wear the surplice of humility over the black gown of a big heart *All's W.* i 3 99
In my branched velvet gown *T. Night* ii 5 54
I prithee, put on this gown and this beard iv 2 1
I would I were the first that ever dissembled in such a gown iv 2 7
Thou mightst have done this without thy beard and gown iv 2 70
My gay apparel for an almsman's gown *Richard II.* iii 3 149
My skin hangs about me like an old lady's loose gown *1 Hen. IV.* iii 3 4
You shall have it, though I pawn my gown *2 Hen. IV.* ii 1 172
Come, thou shalt go to the wars in a gown iii 2 197
She vaunted . . . , The very train of her worst wearing gown Was better worth than all my father's land *2 Hen. VI.* i 3 88
What colour is my gown of?—Black, forsooth: coal-black as jet ii 1 111
I think, jet did he never see.—But cloaks and gowns, before this day, a many ii 1 115
In black mourning gowns, Numbering our Ave-Maries *3 Hen. VI.* ii 1 161
I cannot Put on the gown, stand naked and entreat them *Coriolanus* ii 2 141
Here he comes, and in the gown of humility: mark his behaviour ii 3 44
If it may stand with the tune of your voices that I may be consul, I have here the customary gown ii 3 93
Here's the book I sought for so; I put it in the pocket of my gown *J. C.* iv 3 253
Through tatter'd clothes small vices do appear; Robes and furr'd gowns hide all. Plate sin with gold *Lear* iv 6 169
'Zounds, sir, you're robb'd; for shame, put on your gown *Othello* i 1 86
I would not do such a thing for a joint-ring, nor for measures of lawn, nor for gowns, petticoats, nor caps iv 3 74
I have a gown here; come, put it on; keep thee warm *Pericles* ii 1 83
Thou shalt have my best gown to make thee a pair ii 1 169
Grace. Some defect in her Did quarrel with the noblest grace she owed And put it to the foil *Tempest* iii 1 45
Heavens rain grace On that which breeds between 'em! iii 1 75
His daughter and I will be king and queen,—save our graces! iii 2 115
A grace it had, devouring iii 3 84
With her sovereign grace, Here on this grass-plot iv 1 72
By this hand, I'll have that gown.—Thy grace shall have it iv 1 229
I will pay thy graces Home both in word and deed v 1 70
Of whose soft grace For the like loss I have her sovereign aid v 1 142
Now, blasphemy, That swear'st grace o'erboard, not an oath on shore? v 1 219
I'll be wise hereafter And seek for grace v 1 295
Truth hath better deeds than words to grace it *T. G. of Ver.* ii 2 18
Complete in feature and in mind With all good grace to grace a gentleman ii 4 74
Cannot your Grace win her to fancy him?—No, trust me iii 1 67
What would your Grace have me to do in this? iii 1 80
Flatter and praise, commend, extol their graces iii 1 102
Do curse the grace that with such grace hath bless'd them iii 1 146
Longer than I prove loyal to your grace Let me not live to look upon your grace iii 2 20
We'll wait upon your grace till after supper, And afterward determine iii 2 96
The heaven such grace did lend her, That she might admired be iv 2 42
Your grace is welcome to a man disgraced v 4 123
I dare be bold With our discourse to make your grace to smile v 4 163
I think the boy hath grace in him; he blushes.—I warrant you, my lord, more grace than boy v 4 165
I will not be absence at the grace *Mer. Wives* i 1 274
They have not so little grace, I hope ii 2 117
If any in Vienna be of worth To undergo such ample grace and honour, It is Lord Angelo *Meas. for Meas.* i 1 24
Always obedient to your grace's will, I come to know your pleasure i 1 26
I think thou never wast where grace was said.—No? a dozen times at least i 2 20
Grace is grace, despite of all controversy: as, for example, thou thyself art a wicked villain, despite of all grace i 2 25
It rested in your grace To unloose this tied-up justice when you pleased i 3 31
All hope is gone, Unless you have the grace by your fair prayer To soften Angelo i 4 69
Heaven give thee moving graces! ii 2 36
Nor the judge's robe, Become them with one half so good a grace As mercy does ii 2 62
Grace go with you, Benedicite! ii 3 39
Peace here; grace and good company! iii 1 44
Grace, being the soul of your complexion, shall keep the body of it ever fair iii 1 187
Pattern in himself to know, Grace to stand, and virtue go iii 2 278
You shall have your bosom on this wretch, Grace of the duke iv 3 140
When once our grace we have forgot, Nothing goes right iv 4 36
Happy return be to your royal grace!—Many and hearty thankings v 1 3
Grace. Heaven shield your grace from woe, As I, thus wrong'd, hence unbelieved go! *Meas. for Meas.* v 1 118
For certain words he spake against your grace In your retirement v 1 129
A man that never yet Did, as he vouches, misreport your grace v 1 148
I perceive your grace, like power divine, Hath look'd upon my passes v 1 374
Immediate sentence then and sequent death Is all the grace I beg v 1 379
His company must do his minions grace, Whilst I at home starve for a merry look *Com. of Errors* ii 1 87
Less in your knowledge and your grace you show not Than our earth's wonder iii 2 31
Possess'd with such a gentle sovereign grace, Of such enchanting presence and discourse iii 2 165
And never rise until my tears and prayers Have won his grace to come v 1 116
To do him all the grace and good I could v 1 164
Never came trouble to my house in the likeness of your grace *Much Ado* i 1 100
I would your grace would constrain me to tell i 1 208
He is in love. With who? now that is your grace's part i 1 215
He hath ta'en you newly into his grace i 3 24
I had rather be a canker in a hedge than a rose in his grace i 3 29
Graces will appear, and there's an end ii 1 128
I told him true, that your grace had got the good will of this young lady ii 1 223
Will your grace command me any service to the world's end? ii 1 271
His grace hath made the match, and all grace say Amen to it ii 1 314
Hath your grace ne'er a brother like you? ii 1 336
Your grace is too costly to wear every day. But, I beseech your grace, pardon me ii 1 341
I cry you mercy, uncle. By your grace's pardon ii 1 353
Till all graces be in one woman, one woman shall not come in my grace ii 3 30
How still the evening is, As hush'd on purpose to grace harmony! ii 3 41
If half thy outward graces had been placed About thy thoughts! iv 1 102
All the grace that she hath left Is that she will not add to her damnation A sin of perjury iv 1 173
And then grace us in the disgrace of death *L. L. Lost* i 1 3
I only swore to study with your grace And stay here in your court i 1 51
A maid of grace and complete majesty i 1 137
Every man with his affects is born, Not by might master'd but by special grace i 1 153
I myself reprehend his own person, for I am his grace's tharborough i 1 185
By thy sweet grace's officer, Anthony Dull i 1 270
Be now as prodigal of all dear grace As Nature was in making graces dear ii 1 9
He hath wit to make an ill shape good, And shape to win grace ii 1 60
I hear your grace hath sworn out house-keeping ii 1 104
Sweet health and fair desires consort your grace! ii 1 178
A most acute juvenal; volable and free of grace! iii 1 67
If, before repast, it shall please you to gratify the table with a grace iv 2 161
God give him grace to groan! iv 3 20
Thy grace being gain'd cures all disgrace in me iv 3 67
What grace hast thou, thus to reprove These worms for loving? iv 3 153
I must tell thee, it will please his grace, by the world v 1 107
That is the way to make an offence gracious, though few have the grace to do it v 1 147
The help of school And wit's own grace to grace a learned fool v 2 72
O, I am stabb'd with laughter! Where's her grace? v 2 80
Not a man of them shall have the grace, Despite of suit, to see a lady's face v 2 128
Nor to their penn'd speech render we no grace v 2 147
And we that sell by gross, the Lord doth know, Have not the grace to grace it with such show v 2 320
I do adore thy sweet grace's slipper.—Loves her by the foot v 2 672
Even that falsehood, in itself a sin, Thus purifies itself and turns to grace v 2 786
Your grace is perjured much, Full of dear guiltiness v 2 800
That loose grace Which shallow laughing hearers give to fools v 2 869
O, then, what graces in my love do dwell, That he hath turn'd a heaven unto a hell! *M. N. Dream* i 1 206
The more my prayer, the lesser is my grace ii 2 89
What though I be not so in grace as you, So hung upon with love? iii 2 232
If you have any pity, grace, or manners iii 2 241
And, hearing our intent, Came here in grace of our solemnity iv 1 139
Think what thou wilt, I am thy lover's grace v 1 197
Truly, the moon shines with a good grace v 1 273
Hand in hand, with fairy grace, Will we sing, and bless this place v 1 406
While grace is saying, hood mine eyes Thus with my hat *Mer. of Venice* ii 2 202
I do in birth deserve her, and in fortunes, In graces and in qualities ii 7 33
And wear my dagger with the braver grace iii 4 65
I think the best grace of wit will shortly turn into silence iii 5 49
Your grace hath ta'en great pains to qualify His rigorous course iv 1 7
I have possess'd your grace of what I purpose iv 1 35
Your grace shall understand that at the receipt of your letter I am very sick iv 1 150
I humbly do desire your grace of pardon: I must away this night iv 1 402
If he do not mightily grace himself on thee, he will practise against thee by poison, entrap thee *As Y. Like It* i 1 155
They are as innocent as grace itself i 3 56
Happy is your grace, That can translate the stubbornness of fortune Into so quiet and so sweet a style ii 1 18
The roynish clown, at whom so oft Your grace was wont to laugh ii 2 9
Much commend The parts and graces of the wrestler ii 2 13
To some kind of men Their graces serve them but as enemies ii 3 11
Within this roof The enemy of all your graces lives ii 3 18
Nature charged That one body should be fill'd With all graces wide-enlarged iii 2 151
Have the grace to consider that tears do not become a man iii 4 2
So holy and so perfect is my love, And I in such a poverty of grace iii 5 100
Neither do I labour for a greater esteem than may in some little measure draw a belief from you, to do yourself good and not to grace me v 2 64
I know the boy will well usurp the grace, Voice, gait and action of a gentlewoman *T. of Shrew* Ind. 1 131
Now shall my friend Petruchio do me grace i 2 131
Bless you with such grace As 'longeth to a lover's blessed case! iv 2 44
These great tears grace his remembrance more Than those I shed *All's W.* i 1 91
Tell true.—I will tell truth; by grace itself I swear i 3 226
I'ld venture The well-lost life of mine on his grace's cure i 3 254
'Tis our hope, sir, After well-enter'd soldiers, to return And find your grace in health ii 1 7
Hopest thou my cure?—The great'st grace lending grace ii 1 163
Holy seems the quarrel Upon your grace's part iii 1 5
I hope your own grace will keep you where you are iii 5 28

Grace. I will grace the attempt for a worthy exploit . *All's Well* iii 6 71
May I be bold to acquaint his grace you are gone about it? . . iii 6 84
She was the sweet-marjoram of the salad, or rather, the herb of grace . iv 5 18
It lies in you, my lord, to bring me in some grace, for you did bring me out . . . . v 2 50
God and the devil? One brings thee in grace and the other brings thee out . . . . v 2 53
Vanquish'd thereto by the fair grace and speech Of the poor suppliant . v 3 133
Her infinite cunning, with her modern grace, Subdued me to her rate . v 3 216
Lady, you are the cruell'st she alive, If you will lead these graces to the grave And leave the world no copy . . . *T. Night* i 5 260
He does it with a better grace, but I do it more natural . . . . ii 3 89
Grace and good disposition Attend your ladyship! . . . . iii 1 146
Put your grace in your pocket, sir, for this once, and let your flesh and blood obey it.—Well, I will be so much a sinner . . . . v 1 35
Grace to boot! Of this make no conclusion . . . *W. Tale* i 2 80
It has an elder sister, Or I mistake you: O, would her name were Grace! i 2 99
'Tis grace indeed. Why, lo you now, I have spoke to the purpose twice i 2 105
This action I now go on Is for my better grace . . . . ii 1 122
How I was in your grace, How merited to be so . . . . iii 2 48
Now grown in grace Equal with wondering . . . . . iv 1 24
Grace and remembrance be to you both! . . . . . . iv 4 76
A ram-tender, to offer to have his daughter come into grace! . . iv 4 806
Every wink of an eye some new grace will be born . . . . v 2 120
It is a surplus of your grace, which never My life may last to answer . v 3 7
For she was as tender As infancy and grace . . . . . v 3 27
You gods, look down And from your sacred vials pour your graces Upon my daughter's head! . . . . v 3 122
Out of your grace, devise, ordain, impose Some gentle order . *K. John* iii 1 250
Your grace shall stay behind So strongly guarded . . . . iii 3 1
That the time's enemies may not have this To grace occasions . . iv 2 62
To grace the gentry of a land remote, And follow unacquainted colours here v 2 31
I did confess it, and exactly begg'd Your grace's pardon . *Richard II.* i 1 141
Stand in arms, To prove, by God's grace and my body's valour . . i 3 37
And so by chance Did grace our hollow parting with a tear . . i 4 9
I shall not need transport my words by you; Here comes his grace in person . . . . ii 3 82
Grace me no grace, nor uncle me no uncle . . . . . ii 3 87
That word 'grace' In an ungracious mouth is but profane . . . ii 3 88
It stands your grace upon to do him right . . . . . ii 3 138
But we must win your grace to go with us To Bristol castle . . . ii 3 163
How brooks your grace the air, After your late tossing on the breaking seas? . . . . iii 2 2
Comfort, my liege: why looks your grace so pale? . . . . iii 2 75
Base court, where kings grow base, To come at traitors' calls and do them grace . . . . iii 3 181
What, was I born to this, that my sad look Should grace the triumph of great Bolingbroke? . . . . iii 4 99
Here in this place I'll set a bank of rue, sour herb of grace . . iii 4 105
God save your grace! I do beseech your majesty, To have some conference with your grace alone . . . . v 3 27
Ill mayst thou thrive, if thou grant any grace! . . . . . v 3 99
Grace my mournings here; In weeping after this untimely bier . . v 6 51
God save thy grace,—majesty I should say, for grace thou wilt have none,— What, none? . . . . *1 Hen. IV.* i 2 19
Which for sport sake are content to do the profession some grace . . ii 1 79
An the fire of grace be not quite out of thee, now shalt thou be moved . ii 4 421
Thou art violently carried away from grace: there is a devil haunts thee ii 4 492
I would your grace would take me with you: whom means your grace? ii 4 506
And that's the dearest grace it renders you . . . . . iii 1 182
The Archbishop's grace of York, Douglas, Mortimer . . . . iii 2 119
So I told him, my lord; and I said I heard your grace say so . . iii 3 121
I would you would accept of grace and love.—And may be so we shall . iv 3 112
Is now alive To grace this latter age with noble deeds . . . v 1 92
Will they take the offer of our grace, . . . every man Shall be my friend v 1 106
And chid his truant youth with such a grace . . . . . v 2 63
Cheerly, my lord: how fares your grace? . . . . . . v 4 44
If a lie may do thee grace, I'll gild it with the happiest terms I have . v 4 161
Did not we send grace, Pardon and terms of love to all of you? . . v 5 2
And did grace the shame Of those that turn'd their backs . *2 Hen. IV.* i 1 129
He may keep his own grace, but he's almost out of mine . . . i 2 32
This is the right fencing grace, my lord; tap for tap, and so part fair . ii 1 206
God save your grace!—And yours, most noble Bardolph! . . . ii 2 78
He heard of your grace's coming to town: there's a letter for you . . ii 2 108
Jumps upon joined-stools, and swears with a good grace . . . ii 4 270
O, the Lord preserve thy good grace! by my troth, welcome to London ii 4 315
What says your grace?—His grace says that which his flesh rebels against ii 4 378
Unto your grace do I in chief address The substance of my speech . iv 1 31
Wherefore do you so ill translate yourself Out of the speech of peace that bears such grace? . . . . iv 1 48
In God's name, then, set forward.—Before, and greet his grace . . iv 1 228
Between the grace, the sanctities of heaven And our dull workings . iv 2 21
Employ the countenance and grace of heaven, As a false favourite doth his prince's name, In deeds dishonourable . . . . . . iv 2 24
And will maintain my word: And thereupon I drink unto your grace . iv 2 68
Blunt not his love, Nor lose the good advantage of his grace . . . iv 4 28
By which his grace must mete the lives of others . . . . . iv 4 77
What would your majesty? How fares your grace? . . . . iv 5 50
Though no man be assured what grace to find, You stand in coldest expectation . . . . v 2 30
I will make the king do you grace: I will leer upon him as a' comes by v 5 6
God save thy grace, King Hal! my royal Hal! . . . . . v 5 43
Make less thy body hence, and more thy grace . . . . . v 5 56
The king is full of grace and fair regard . . . . . *Hen. V.* i 1 22
Which I have open'd to his grace at large, As touching France . . i 1 78
A Christian king; Unto whose grace our passion is as subject As are our wretches fetter'd in our prisons . . . . i 2 242
We will, in France, by God's grace, play a set . . . . . i 2 262
And by their hands this grace of kings must die . . . . ii Prol. 28
'Fore God, his grace is bold, to trust these traitors . . . . ii 2 1
Labour shall refresh itself with hope, To do your grace incessant services . . . . ii 2 38
Question your grace the late ambassadors . . . . . . ii 4 31
Whiles yet the cool and temperate wind of grace O'erblows the filthy and contagious clouds Of heady murder, spoil and villany . . . iii 3 30
Je ne doute point d'apprendre, par la grace de Dieu . . . . iii 4 44
Saying our grace is only in our heels, And that we are most lofty runaways . . . . iii 5 34
A rogue, that now and then goes to the wars, to grace himself at his return into London under the form of a soldier . . . . . iii 6 71

Grace. God pless it and preserve it, as long as it pleases his grace! *Hen. V.* iv 7 114
It is necessary, look your grace, that he keeps his vow and his oath . iv 7 146
Your grace doo's me as great honours as can be desired . . . . iv 7 167
I would fain see it once, an please God of his grace that I might see . iv 7 172
Oui, vraiment, sauf votre grace, ainsi dit-il . . . . . . v 2 214
To win the Dauphin's grace, Thrust Talbot with a spear . *1 Hen. VI.* i 1 137
Though thy speech doth fail, One eye thou hast, to look to heaven for grace . . . . i 4 83
I muse we met not with the Dauphin's grace, His new-come champion . ii 2 19
We grace the yeomen by conversing with him . . . . . . ii 4 81
We know your grace to be a man Just and upright . . . . . iii 1 94
An if your grace mark every circumstance, You have great reason . iii 1 153
Your grace may starve perhaps before that time . . . . . iii 2 48
Ascribes the glory of his conquest got First to my God and next unto your grace . . . . iii 4 12
York should have sent him aid.—And York as fast upon your grace exclaims . . . . iv 4 30
How doth your grace affect their motion?—Well, my good lord . . v 1 7
Proffers his only daughter to your grace In marriage . . . . v 1 19
A goodly prize, fit for the devil's grace! . . . . v 3 33
What answer makes your grace unto my suit? . . . . . . v 3 150
Those two counties I will undertake Your grace shall well and quietly enjoy . . . . v 3 159
Her virtues that surmount, And natural graces that extinguish art . v 3 192
Chosen from above, By inspiration of celestial grace . . . . v 4 40
Because you want the grace that others have, You judge it straight a thing impossible To compass wonders . . . . v 4 46
Her grace in speech, Her words y-clad with wisdom's majesty *2 Hen. VI.* i 1 32
We here discharge your grace from being regent I' the parts of France . i 1 66
What say'st thou? majesty! I am but grace . . . . . . i 2 71
By the grace of God, and Hume's advice, Your grace's title shall be multiplied . . . . i 2 72
So will I In England work your grace's full content . . . . i 3 70
Whether your grace be worthy, yea or no, Dispute not that . . . i 3 110
If he be old enough, what needs your grace To be protector of his excellence? . . . . i 3 121
Your grace shall give me leave, my Lord of York, To be the post . . i 4 80
Were it not good your grace could fly to heaven! . . . . . ii 1 17
As more at large your grace shall understand . . . . . . ii 1 177
I summon your grace to his majesty's parliament . . . . . ii 4 70
I think I should have told your grace's tale . . . . . . iii 1 44
'Twill make them cool in zeal unto your grace . . . . . . iii 1 177
We intend to try his grace to-day, If he be guilty, as 'tis published . iii 2 16
What answer makes your grace to the rebels' supplication? . . . iv 4 7
So might your grace's person be in danger . . . . . . iv 4 45
Seditious to his grace and to the state . . . . v 1 37
I present your grace a traitor's head, The head of Cade . . . . v 1 66
Thy hand is made to grasp a palmer's staff, And not to grace an awful princely sceptre . . . . v 1 98
Obey, audacious traitor; kneel for grace.—Wouldst have me kneel? . v 1 108
And in my conscience do repute his grace The rightful heir . . . v 1 177
But is your grace dead, my Lord of Somerset? . . . *3 Hen. VI.* i 1 18
Thou factious Duke of York, descend my throne, And kneel for grace . i 1 75
When I return with victory from the field I'll see your grace . . . i 1 262
About what?—About that which concerns your grace and us . . . i 2 8
God forbid your grace should be forsworn.—I shall be, if I claim by open war . . . . i 2 18
What would your grace have done unto him now? . . . . . i 4 65
Now, perjured Henry! wilt thou kneel for grace? . . . . . ii 2 81
Ask mercy and obtain no grace . . . . ii 6 69
Why, then I will do what your grace commands . . . . . iii 2 49
'Twill grieve your grace my sons should call you father . . . . iii 2 100
And yet methinks your grace hath not done well . . . . . iv 1 51
Your grace hath still been famed for virtuous . . . . . . iv 6 26
Yet in this one thing let me blame your grace, For choosing me . . iv 6 30
These graces challenge grace . . . . iv 8 48
What will your grace have done with Margaret? . . . . . v 7 37
What means this armed guard That waits upon your grace? *Richard III.* i 1 43
Entertain good comfort, And cheer his grace with quick and merry words . . . . i 3 5
Good time of day unto your royal grace! . . . . i 3 18
Good hope; his grace speaks cheerfully.—God grant him health! . . i 3 34
By holy Paul, they love his grace but lightly . . . . . . i 3 45
To whom in all this presence speaks your grace?—To thee, that hast nor honesty nor grace . . . . i 3 54
Madam, his majesty doth call for you; And for your grace; and you . i 3 321
Why looks your grace so heavily to-day?—O, I have pass'd a miserable night! . . . . i 4 1
I do beseech your majesty To take our brother Clarence to your grace . ii 1 76
And not a man of you Had so much grace to put it in my mind . . ii 1 120
Madam, my mother, I do cry you mercy; I did not see your grace . ii 2 105
That is the butt-end of a mother's blessing: I marvel why her grace did leave it out . . . . ii 2 111
No, no; by God's good grace his son shall reign . . . . . ii 3 10
Then the king Had virtuous uncles to protect his grace . . . . ii 3 21
Small herbs have grace, great weeds do grow apace . . . . . ii 4 13
I could have given my uncle's grace a flout, To touch his growth . . ii 4 24
For my part, I'll resign unto your grace The seal I keep . . . ii 4 70
Your grace attended to their sugar'd words . . . . . . iii 1 13
God bless your grace with health and happy days! . . . . . iii 1 18
The tender prince Would fain have come with me to meet your grace . iii 1 29
Lord cardinal, will your grace Persuade the queen? . . . . . iii 1 32
It is too heavy for your grace to wear.—I weigh it lightly . . . iii 1 120
Your grace knows how to bear with him.—You mean, to bear me . . iii 1 127
I'll claim that promise at your grace's hands . . . . . . iii 1 197
Your grace, we think, should soonest know his mind . . . . . iii 4 9
His grace looks cheerfully and smooth to-day . . . . . . iii 4 50
The tender love I bear your grace, my lord, Makes me most forward . iii 4 65
And I myself secure in grace and favour . . . . iii 4 93
O momentary grace of mortal men, Which we more hunt for than the grace of God! . . . . iii 4 98
And both are ready in their offices, At any time, to grace my stratagems iii 5 11
Your grace's word shall serve, As well as I had seen and heard him speak . . . . iii 5 62
He doth entreat your grace To visit him to-morrow or next day . . iii 7 59
The mayor and citizens . . . Are come to have some conference with his grace . . . . iii 7 69
God forbid his grace should say us nay!—I fear he will . . . . iii 7 81
His grace not being warn'd thereof before . . . . iii 7 86
I come in perfect love to him; And so once more return and tell his grace iii 7 91

Grace. What is your grace's pleasure?—Even that, I hope, which pleaseth God above . . . . *Richard III.* iii 7 108
Would it might please your grace, At our entreaties, to amend that fault! iii 7 114
My lord, this argues conscience in your grace . . . . . iii 7 174
God bless your grace! we see it, and will say it . . . . iii 7 237
To-morrow, then, we will attend your grace . . . . . iii 7 244
God give your graces both A happy and a joyful time of day! . iv 1 5
Mother, how fares your grace?—O Dorset, speak not to me, get thee hence! . . . . iv 1 38
Speak suddenly; be brief.—Your grace may do your pleasure . iv 2 21
I will resolve your grace immediately . . . . . . iv 2 26
I am thus bold to put your grace in mind Of what you promised me . iv 2 113
Humphrey Hour, that call'd your grace To breakfast once . . iv 4 175
Unavoided is the doom of destiny.—True, when avoided grace makes destiny . . . . iv 4 218
My babes were destined to a fairer death, If grace had bless'd thee with a fairer life . . . . iv 4 220
Let me know your mind, What from your grace I shall deliver to him . iv 4 447
I'll muster up my friends, and meet your grace . . . . iv 4 489
This long-usurped royalty . . . Have I pluck'd off, to grace thy brows v 5 6
Propp'd by ancestry, whose grace Chalks successors their way *Hen. VIII.* i 1 59
Like it your grace, The state takes notice of the private difference Betwixt you . . . . i 1 100
Let there be letters writ to every shire, Of the king's grace and pardon i 2 104
Hath into monstrous habits put the graces That once were his . . i 2 122
Ladies, a general welcome from his grace Salutes ye all . . . i 4 1
Place you that side; I'll take the charge of this: His grace is entering i 4 21
Your grace is noble: Let me have such a bowl may hold my thanks . i 4 38
I told your grace they would talk anon . . . . . . i 4 49
Because they speak no English, thus they pray'd To tell your grace . i 4 66
They have done my poor house grace; for which I pay 'em A thousand thanks . . . . i 4 73
Such a one, they all confess, There is indeed; which they would have your grace Find out . . . . i 4 83
I am glad Your grace is grown so pleasant . . . . . . i 4 90
Your grace, I fear, with dancing is a little heated.—I fear, too much i 4 99
Commend me to his grace . . . . ii 1 86
To the water side I must conduct your grace . . . . . ii 1 95
Good day to both your graces . . . . ii 2 14
I would your grace would give us but an hour Of private conference . ii 2 80
Your grace has given a precedent of wisdom Above all princes . . ii 2 86
Your grace must needs deserve all strangers' loves . . . . ii 2 102
To be commanded For ever by your grace, whose hand has raised me . ii 2 120
A thousand pound a year, annual support, Out of his grace he adds . ii 3 65
That thus you should proceed to put me off, And take your good grace from me . . . . ii 4 22
His grace Hath spoken well and justly . . . . . . ii 4 64
Pray their graces To come near. What can be their business with me? iii 1 18
Your graces find me here part of a housewife, I would be all . . iii 1 24
Out of his noble nature, Zeal and obedience he still bore your grace . iii 1 63
Good your graces, Let me have time and counsel for my cause . . iii 1 78
I would your grace Would leave your griefs, and take my counsel . . iii 1 91
If your grace Could but be brought to know our ends are honest . . iii 1 153
And bear the inventory Of your best graces in your mind . . . iii 2 138
Your royal graces, Shower'd on me daily, have been more than could My studied purposes requite . . . . iii 2 166
For your great graces Heap'd upon me, poor undeserver, I Can nothing render but allegiant thanks . . . . iii 2 174
Let his grace go forward, And dare us with his cap like larks . . iii 2 281
How does your grace?—Why, well; Never so truly happy, my good Cromwell . . . . iii 2 376
The king has cured me, I humbly thank his grace . . . . iii 2 381
I am glad your grace has made that right use of it . . . . iii 2 386
Her grace sat down To rest awhile, some half an hour or so . . iv 1 65
At length her grace rose, and with modest paces Came to the altar . iv 1 82
How does your grace?—O Griffith, sick to death! . . . . iv 2 1
I think your grace, Out of the pain you suffer'd, gave no ear to't . iv 2 7
Do you note How much her grace is alter'd on the sudden? . . iv 2 96
First, mine own service to your grace; the next, The king's request that I would visit you . . . . iv 2 115
That his noble grace would have some pity Upon my wretched women iv 2 139
Who hath so far Given ear to our complaint, of his great grace . . v 1 48
Your grace must wait till you be call'd for . . . . . v 2 7
I'll show your grace the strangest sight . . . . . . v 2 19
Let him come in.—Your grace may enter now . . . . . v 3 7
Thus far, My most dread sovereign, may it like your grace To let my tongue excuse all . . . . v 3 148
And to your royal grace, and the good queen, My noble partners, and myself, thus pray . . . . v 5 5
All princely graces, That mould up such a mighty piece as this is . v 5 26
Had I a sister were a grace, or a daughter a goddess, he should take his choice. O admirable man! . . . . *Troi. and Cres.* i 2 257
All our abilities, gifts, natures, shapes, Severals and generals of grace exact . . . . i 3 180
You are in the state of grace.—Grace! not so, friend; honour and lordship are my titles . . . . iii 1 15
In each grace of these There lurks a still and dumb-discoursive devil . iv 4 91
Your soldiers use him as the grace 'fore meat, Their talk at table *Coriol.* iv 7 3
To grace him only That thought he could do more, a very little I have yielded to . . . . v 3 15
If I cannot persuade thee Rather to show a noble grace to both parts . v 3 121
Thou hast affected the fine strains of honour, To imitate the graces of the gods . . . . v 3 150
Dost thou think I'll grace thee with that robbery, thy stol'n name Coriolanus in Corioli? . . . . v 6 89
And in this match I hold me highly honour'd of your grace *T. Andron.* i 1 245
Only thus much I give your grace to know . . . . . . i 1 413
And make them know what 'tis to let a queen Kneel in the streets and beg for grace in vain . . . . i 1 455
We must all be friends: The tribune and his nephews kneel for grace . i 1 480
With horn and hound we'll give your grace bonjour . . . . i 1 494
I am as able and as fit as thou To serve, and to deserve my mistress' grace . . . . ii 1 34
I promised your grace a hunter's peal.—And you have rung it lustily . ii 2 13
No grace? no womanhood? Ah, beastly creature! . . . . ii 3 182
Let fools do good, and fair men call for grace . . . . . iii 1 205
Can you deliver an oration to the emperor with a grace?—Nay, truly, sir, I could never say grace in all my life . . . . . iv 3 99
Can you with a grace deliver a supplication? . . . . . iv 3 107
How can I grace my talk, Wanting a hand to give it action? . . v 2 17

Grace. Villains, for shame you could not beg for grace . *T. Andron.* v 2 180
God mark thee to his grace! Thou wast the prettiest babe *Rom. and Jul.* i 3 59
O, mickle is the powerful grace that lies In herbs, plants, stones . ii 3 15
Two such opposed kings encamp them still In man as well as herbs, grace and rude will . . . . ii 3 28
She whom I love now Doth grace for grace and love for love allow . ii 3 86
How this grace Speaks his own standing! . . . *T. of Athens* i 1 30
Whose present grace to present slaves and servants Translates his rivals i 1 71
You have done our pleasures much grace, fair ladies . . . i 2 151
E'en so thou outrunnest grace . . . . ii 2 93
I should prove so base, To sue, and be denied such common grace . iii 5 95
What tributaries follow him to Rome, To grace in captive bonds his chariot-wheels? . . . . *J. Cæsar* i 1 39
We will grace his heels With the most boldest and best hearts of Rome iii 1 120
Stay here with Antony: Do grace to Cæsar's corpse, and grace his speech iii 2 62
You greet with present grace and great prediction . . . *Macbeth* i 3 55
We love him highly, And shall continue our graces towards him . . i 6 30
All is but toys: renown and grace is dead; The wine of life is drawn . ii 3 99
Please't your highness To grace us with your royal company.—The table's full . . . . iii 4 45
He shall spurn fate, scorn death, and bear His hopes 'bove wisdom, grace and fear . . . . iii 5 31
With such grace That the malevolence of fortune nothing Takes from his high respect . . . . iii 6 27
Come in, without there!—What's your grace's will? . . . iv 1 135
Though all things foul would wear the brows of grace, Yet grace must still look so . . . . iv 3 23
All these are portable, With other graces weigh'd . . . . iv 3 90
The king-becoming graces, As justice, verity, temperance . . . iv 3 91
Sundry blessings hang about his throne, That speak him full of grace . iv 3 159
This, and what needful else That calls upon us, by the grace of Grace, We will perform . . . . v 8 72
If there be any good thing to be done, That may to thee do ease and grace to me, Speak to me . . . . *Hamlet* i 1 131
Time be thine, And thy best graces spend it at thy will! . . . i 2 63
In grace whereof, No jocund health that Denmark drinks to-day, But the great cannon to the clouds shall tell . . . . . . i 2 124
A double blessing is a double grace: Occasion smiles upon a second leave i 3 53
Be they as pure as grace, As infinite as man may undergo . . . i 4 33
Angels and ministers of grace defend us! Be thou a spirit of health . i 4 39
This not to do, So grace and mercy at your most need help you, Swear i 5 180
Thyself do grace to them, and bring them in . . . . . ii 2 53
Your grace hath screen'd and stood between Much heat and him . . iii 4 3
Such an act That blurs the grace and blush of modesty . . . . iii 4 41
See, what a grace was seated on this brow; Hyperion's curls . . iii 4 55
For love of grace, Lay not that flattering unction to your soul . . iii 4 144
Conscience and grace, to the profoundest pit! I dare damnation . . iv 5 132
Like the spring that turneth wood to stone, Convert his gyves to graces iv 7 21
Your grace hath laid the odds o' the weaker side.—I do not fear it . v 2 272
No less than life, with grace, health, beauty, honour . . . *Lear* i 1 59
If aught within that little seeming substance, Or all of it, with our displeasure pieced, And nothing more, may fitly like your grace, She's there . . . . i 1 203
No unchaste action, or dishonour'd step, That hath deprived me of your grace . . . . i 1 232
Therefore be gone Without our grace, our love, our benison . . . i 1 268
Stood I within his grace, I would prefer him to a better place . . i 1 276
I serve you, madam: Your graces are right welcome . . . . ii 1 131
Show too bold malice Against the grace and person of my master . ii 2 138
Let me beseech your grace not to do so . . . . ii 2 147
Hail to your grace!—I am glad to see your highness . . . . ii 4 129
Whose easy-borrow'd pride Dwells in the fickle grace of her he follows ii 4 189
What means your grace?—Who stock'd my servant? . . . . ii 4 190
Marry, here's grace and a cod-piece; that's a wise man and a fool . iii 2 40
Close pent-up guilts, Rive your concealing continents, and cry These dreadful summoners grace . . . . iii 2 59
How fares your grace?—What's he?—Who's there? What is't you seek? iii 4 130
What, hath your grace no better company? . . . . . . iii 4 147
What mean your graces? Good my friends, consider You are my guests iii 7 30
If e'er your grace had speech with man so poor, Hear me one word . v 1 38
If ever I return to you again, I'll bring you comfort.—Grace go with you! v 2 4
I hold you but a subject of this war, Not as a brother.—That's as we list to grace him . . . . v 3 61
In his own grace he doth exalt himself, More than in your addition . v 3 67
Good your grace, pardon me . . . . *Othello* i 3 52
Little shall I grace my cause In speaking for myself . . . . i 3 88
With what else needful your good grace shall think To be sent after me i 3 287
The grace of heaven, Before, behind thee and on every hand, Enwheel thee! . . . . ii 1 85
He hath devoted and given up himself to the contemplation, mark, and denotement of her parts and graces . . . . ii 3 323
If I have any grace or power to move you, His present reconciliation take . . . . iii 3 46
O grace! O heaven forgive me! Are you a man? have you a soul or sense? . . . . iii 3 373
Even his stubbornness, his checks, his frowns, . . . have grace and favour in them . . . . iv 3 21
We have galls, and though we have some grace, Yet have we some revenge . . . . iv 3 93
If you bethink yourself of any crime Unreconciled as yet to heaven and grace . . . . v 2 27
Whose general graces speak That which none else can utter *A. and C.* ii 2 132
Let me have thy hand: Further this act of grace . . . . . ii 2 149
And of thee craves The circle of the Ptolemies for her heirs, Now hazarded to thy grace . . . . iii 12 19
Give me grace to lay My duty on your hand . . . . . . iii 13 81
Grace grow where those drops fall! . . . . iv 2 38
Do not please sharp fate To grace it with you sorrows . . . iv 14 136
Who is so full of grace, that it flows over On all that need . . v 2 24
That will pray in aid for kindness, Where he for grace is kneel'd to . v 2 28
As she would catch another Antony In her strong toil of grace . . v 2 351
A touch more rare Subdues all pangs, all fears.—Past grace? obedience? —Past hope, and in despair; that way, past grace . *Cymbeline* i 1 136
Which the gods have given you?—Which, by their graces, I will keep . i 4 95
But 'tis your graces That from my mutest conscience to my tongue Charms this report out . . . . i 6 115
I had almost forgot To entreat your grace but in a small request . i 6 181
I cross'd the seas on purpose and on promise To see your grace . . i 6 203
Madam, all joy befal your grace!—And you! . . . . . iii 5 9
Nature hath meal and bran, contempt and grace . . . . . iv 2 27

Grace. Why hast thou thus adjourn'd The graces for his merits due! *Cymbeline* v 4 79
He shall be happy that can find him, if Our grace can make him so . v 5 7
Thou hast look'd thyself into my grace, And art mine own . . v 5 94
Or, by our greatness and the grace of it, Which is our honour . v 5 132
Blithe, and full of face, As heaven had lent her all his grace *Pericles* i Gower 24
Graces her subjects, and her thoughts the king Of every virtue . i 1 13
Your grace is welcome to our town and us.—Which welcome we'll accept i 4 106
Here take your place: Marshal the rest, as they deserve their grace . ii 3 19
I am at your grace's pleasure . . . . . . ii 3 112
It is your grace's pleasure to commend; Not my desert . . . ii 5 29
Your grace, that fed my country with your corn . . . . iii 3 18
We'll bring your grace e'en to the edge o' the shore, Then give you up . iii 3 35
Look to your little mistress, on whose grace You may depend hereafter iii 3 40
All the grace, Which makes her both the heart and place Of general wonder . . . . iv Gower 9
And what this fourteen years no razor touch'd, To grace thy marriage-day, I'll beautify . . . . v 3 76
An't like your grace *Temp.* iv 1; *Meas. for Meas.* v 1; *2 Hen. VI.* ii 1
Beseech your grace *L. L. Lost* iv 3; *M. N. Dream* i 1; *As Y. L. It* i 2; i 3; *W. Tale* i 2; *Rich. II.* ii 3; v 2; *1 Hen. IV.* v 5; *2 Hen. IV.* iv 3; *Rich. III.* i 1; *Hen. VIII.* ii 1; *Lear* iii 4; *Cymbeline* i 5
Please it your grace *T. G. of Ver.* iii 1; *Much Ado* i 1; *2 Hen. IV.* iii 1; *2 Hen. VI.* iv 9; *Othello* i 3
Please your grace *Com. of Errors* v 1; *L. L. Lost* ii 1; *M. N. Dr.* v 1; *Mer. of Venice* iv 1; *2 Hen. IV.* ii 1; iv 1; iv 5; *2 Hen. VI.* i 1; i 3; ii 1; ii 4; *Hen. VIII.* i 1; i 4; iii 1; v 3; *Othello* i 3
Thank your grace *T. G. of Ver.* v 4; *1 Hen. IV.* v 5; *Hen. VIII.* i 1; *Lear* ii 1; *Othello* i 3; *Pericles* ii 3

Grace of God. By the grace of God and this mine arm . *Richard II.* i 3 22
You have the grace of God, sir, and he hath enough *Mer. of Venice* ii 2 160
By the grace of God, and Hume's advice . . . . . *2 Hen. VI.* i 2 72
By the grace of God, king of England and France . . *3 Hen. VI.* iv 7 71
O momentary grace of mortal men, Which we more hunt for than the grace of God! . . . . *Richard III.* iii 4 99

Graced. Tunis was never graced before with such a paragon to their queen . . . . *Tempest* ii 1 74
. . . . *T. G. of Ver.* i 3 58
How well beloved, And daily graced by the emperor . *T. G. of Ver.* i 3 58
And graced Your kindness better . . . . *W. Tale* v 1 22
Whom they doted on And bless'd and graced indeed . *2 Hen. IV.* iv 1 139
Her virtues graced with external gifts Do breed love's settled passions in my heart . . . . *1 Hen. VI.* v 5 3
And graced thy poor sire with his bridal-day . . *3 Hen. VI.* ii 2 155
And we are graced with wreaths of victory . . . . v 3 2
What comfortable hour canst thou name, That ever graced me in thy company?—Faith, none, but Humphrey Hour . *Richard III.* iv 4 174
The imperial metal, circling now thy brow, Had graced the tender temples of my child . . . . iv 4 383
Fame, at the which he aims, In whom already he's well graced *Coriolanus* i 1 268
Thy wit wants edge, And manners, to intrude where I am graced *T. An.* ii 1 27
Here had we now our country's honour roof'd, Were the graced person of our Banquo present . . . . . *Macbeth* iii 4 41
More like a tavern or a brothel Than a graced palace . . . *Lear* i 4 267
He would have . . . graced The thankings of a king *Cymbeline* v 5 406

Graceful. A fine, quaint, graceful and excellent fashion . *Much Ado* iii 4 22
You have a holy father, A graceful gentleman . . *W. Tale* v 1 171
As if that whatsoever god who leads him Were slily crept into his human powers And gave him graceful posture . . *Coriolanus* ii 1 237
Could not with graceful eyes attend those wars . *Ant. and Cleo.* ii 2 60
Which the knight himself With such a graceful courtesy deliver'd *Pericles* ii 2 41
This so darks In Philoten all graceful marks . . . iv Gower 36

Graceless. Will not so graceless be to be ingrate . *T. of Shrew* i 2 270
What is she but a foul contending rebel And graceless traitor? . v 2 160
The graceless action of a heavy hand . . . *K. John* iv 3 58
Graceless! wilt thou deny thy parentage? . . . *1 Hen. VI.* v 4 14
O graceless men! they know not what they do . *2 Hen. VI.* iv 4 38

Gracing. Or add a royal number to the dead, Gracing the scroll that tells of this war's loss . . . . . . *K. John* ii 1 348

Gracious. 'More wealth than faults.'—Why, that word makes the faults gracious . . . . *T. G. of Ver.* iii 1 378
And never shall it more be gracious . . . . *Much Ado* iv 1 109
That is the way to make an offence gracious . . *L. L. Lost* iv 1 147
To make it the more gracious, I shall sing it at her death *M. N. Dream* iv 1 224
By thy gracious, golden, glittering gleams . . . . . v 1 279
If I be foiled, there is but one shamed that was never gracious *As Y. L. It* i 2 200
A gracious innocent soul, More free than he is jealous . *W. Tale* ii 3 29
Go: fresh horses! And gracious be the issue! . . . . iii 1 22
Kings are no less unhappy, their issue not being gracious . . iv 2 30
For he is gracious, if he be observed . . . . *2 Hen. IV.* iv 4 30
Heaven and our Lady gracious hath it pleased To shine on my contemptible estate . . . . *1 Hen. VI.* i 2 74
Meantime look gracious on thy prostrate thrall . . . . i 2 117
Heaven, be thou gracious to none alive, If Salisbury wants mercy! . i 4 85
But is he gracious in the people's eye?—The more that Henry was unfortunate . . . . *3 Hen. VI.* iii 3 117
If this rule were true, he should be gracious . . *Richard III.* ii 4 20
You have a daughter call'd Elizabeth, Virtuous and fair, royal and gracious . . . . iv 4 204
He's loving and most gracious . . . . . *Hen. VIII.* iii 1 94
Which hath our several honours all engaged To make it gracious *Troi. and Cres.* ii 2 125
If ever Bassianus . . . Were gracious in the eyes of royal Rome *T. An.* i 1 11
Rome, be as just and gracious unto me As I am confident and kind to thee . . . . i 1 60
Great defender of this Capitol, Stand gracious to the rites that we intend! i 1 78
If ever Tamora Were gracious in those princely eyes of thine . . i 1 429
'Tis not the difference of a year or two Makes me less gracious . . ii 1 32
So hallow'd and so gracious is the time . . . . *Hamlet* i 1 164
Gracious, so please you, We will bestow ourselves . . . . iii 1 44
Thy state is the more gracious; for 'tis a vice to know him . . v 2 86
A father, and a gracious aged man . . . . . *Lear* iv 2 41
The Ottomites, reverend and gracious, Steering with due course *Othello* i 3 33

Gracious acceptance. I leave him to your gracious acceptance *M. of V.* iv 1 165

Gracious brother. Our gracious brother, I will go with them *Hen. V.* v 2 92

Gracious conqueror, Victorious Titus, rue the tears I shed . *T. Andron.* i 1 104

Gracious couple. Stood begetting wonder as You, gracious couple, do *W. Tale* v 1 134

Gracious creature. There was not such a gracious creature born *K. John* iii 4 81

Gracious dam. Cleft the heart That could conceive a gross and foolish sire Blemish'd his gracious dam . . . . . . *W. Tale* iii 2 199

Gracious daughter. Good morning to you, fair and gracious daughter *Meas. for Meas.* iv 3 116

Gracious denial. That gracious denial which he is most glad to receive iii 1 166

Gracious drops. O, now you weep; and, I perceive, you feel The dint of pity: these are gracious drops . . . . *J. Cæsar* iii 2 198

Gracious duke. O gracious duke, Harp not on that. *Meas. for Meas.* v 1 63
Most gracious duke, with thy command Let him be brought forth *C. of Er.* v 1 159
Justice, most gracious duke, O, grant me justice! . . . . v 1 190
My gracious duke, This man hath bewitch'd the bosom of my child *M. N. Dream* i 1 26
My gracious duke, Be it so she will not here before your grace Consent to marry . . . . i 1 38
Who crown'd the gracious duke in high despite . *3 Hen. VI.* ii 1 59
Most gracious duke, To my unfolding lend your prosperous ear . *Othello* i 3 244

Gracious Duncan. For them the gracious Duncan have I murder'd *Macb.* iii 1 66
The gracious Duncan Was pitied of Macbeth . . . . iii 6 3

Gracious emperor. O gracious emperor! O gentle Aaron! *T. Andron.* iii 1 157

Gracious empress. The general of our gracious empress. *Hen. V.* v Prol. 30

Gracious England. And here from gracious England have I offer Of goodly thousands. . . . . *Macbeth* iv 3 43
Gracious England hath Lent us good Siward and ten thousand men . iv 3 189

Gracious eye. O Thou, whose captain I account myself, Look on my forces with a gracious eye! . . . . . *Richard III.* v 3 109

Gracious father. My gracious father, by your kingly leave . *3 Hen. VI.* ii 2 63
How monstrous It was for Malcolm and for Donalbain To kill their gracious father . . . . *Macbeth* iii 6 10

Gracious favours. When I call to mind your gracious favours *T. G. of V.* iii 1 6
His bedfellow, Whom he hath dull'd and cloy'd with gracious favours *Hen. V.* ii 2 9

Gracious figure. What would your gracious figure? *Hamlet* iii 4 104

Gracious fooling. Thou wast in very gracious fooling last night *T. Night* ii 3 22

Gracious fortune. Desired her To try her gracious fortune *Meas. for Meas.* v 1 76

Gracious God. Open Thy gate of mercy, gracious God! . *3 Hen. VI.* i 4 177

Gracious governor. Lucius, all hail, Rome's gracious governor! *T. An.* v 3 146

Gracious hand. Commend the paper to his gracious hand . *All's Well* v 1 31
Deliver up my title in the queen To your most gracious hands *2 Hen. VI.* i 1 13
If thy poor devoted suppliant may But beg one favour at thy gracious hand, Thou dost confirm his happiness for ever . *Richard III.* i 2 208

Gracious head. Currents that spring from one most gracious head *Richard II.* iii 3 108

Gracious Henry. Comfort, my sovereign! gracious Henry, comfort! *2 Hen. VI.* iii 2 38

Gracious king. As deputy unto that gracious king . . *1 Hen. VI.* v 3 161
A gracious king that pardons all offences Malice ne'er meant . *Hen. VIII.* ii 2 68
I assure my good liege, I hold my duty, as I hold my soul, Both to my God and to my gracious king . . . . . *Hamlet* ii 2 45

Gracious lady. Dear gentlewoman, How fares our gracious lady? *W. Tale* ii 2 21
'Tis nothing but conceit, my gracious lady . . *Richard II.* ii 2 33
Is all unknown to me, my gracious lady . . *Richard III.* ii 4 48
My gracious lady, go; And thither bear your treasure . . ii 4 68
All comfort, joy, in this most gracious lady . . . *Hen. VIII.* v 5 7
O gracious lady, Since I received command to do this business I have not slept one wink.—Do't, and to bed then . *Cymbeline* iii 4 101

Gracious Lavinia, Rome's rich ornament . . . *T. Andron.* i 1 52

Gracious leave. Bow them to your gracious leave and pardon *Hamlet* i 2 56

Gracious liege, . . . Your brother did employ my father much *K. John* i 1 95
My gracious liege, You won it, wore it, kept it, gave it me *2 Hen. IV.* iv 5 221
My gracious liege, this too much lenity . . . must be laid aside *3 Hen. VI.* ii 2 9
My Lord of Norfolk,— Here, most gracious liege . *Richard III.* v 3 4

Gracious lord. My gracious lord, that which I would discover The law of friendship bids me to conceal . . . *T. G. of Ver.* iii 1 4
Most gracious lord, I hope you will not mock me with a husband *M. for M.* v 1 421
I came from Corinth, my most gracious lord . . *Com. of Errors* v 1 365
I thank you, gracious lords, For all your fair endeavours . *L. L. Lost* v 2 739
Pardon, my gracious lord; for I submit My fancy to your eyes *All's Well* ii 3 174
My gracious lord, I may be negligent . . . *W. Tale* i 2 249
My gracious lord, Shall I be your playfellow? . . . . ii 1 2
My gracious lord, To chide at your extremes it not becomes me . . iv 4 5
My gracious lord, I tender you my service . . *Richard II.* ii 3 41
Nor near nor farther off, my gracious lord, Than this weak arm . iii 2 64
My gracious lord,— Fair cousin, you debase your princely knee . . iii 3 189
My gracious lord, I come but for mine own . . . . iii 3 196
This match'd with other did, my gracious lord . . . *1 Hen. IV.* i 1 49
One of them is well known, my gracious lord . . . . ii 4 559
I shall hereafter, my thrice gracious lord, Be more myself . . iii 2 92
My gracious lord, you look beyond him quite . . *2 Hen. IV.* iv 4 67
My gracious lord! my father! This sleep is sound indeed . . iv 5 34
Where is my gracious Lord of Canterbury? . . . *Hen. V.* i 2 1
Gracious lord, Stand for your own; unwind your bloody flag . . i 2 100
My gracious lords, . . . I must inform you of a dismal fight . *1 Hen. VI.* i 1 103
Great King of England and my gracious lord . . *2 Hen. VI.* i 1 24
Pardon me, gracious lord; Some sudden qualm hath struck me at the heart . . . . i 1 53
Ah, gracious lord, these days are dangerous . . . . iii 1 142
O heavenly God!—How fares my gracious lord? . . . . iii 2 37
My gracious lord, entreat him, speak him fair . . . . iv 1 120
My gracious lord, retire to Killingworth . . . . . iv 4 39
My gracious lord, here in the parliament Let us assail the family of York *3 Hen. VI.* i 1 64
Farewell, my gracious lord; I'll to my castle . . . . . i 1 206
Right gracious lord, I cannot brook delay . . . . . iii 2 18
How many children hast thou, widow? . . . —Three, my most gracious lord iii 2 29
No, gracious lord, except I cannot do it . . . . . iii 2 47
'Tis better said than done, my gracious lord . . . . iii 2 90
My gracious lord, Henry your foe is taken, And brought your prisoner iii 2 118
Good time of day unto my gracious lord! . . . *Richard III.* i 1 122
What doth she say . . . ?—Nothing that I respect, my gracious lord . i 3 296
He did, my gracious lord, begin that place . . . . . ii 1 70
I'll tell you what, my cousin Buckingham,— What, my gracious lord? iii 1 90
'Tis a vile thing to die, my gracious lord, When men are unprepared . iii 2 64
And I will love thee, and prefer thee too.—'Tis done, my gracious lord iv 2 83
Abate the edge of traitors, gracious Lord! . . . . . v 5 35
Arise, My good and gracious Lord of Canterbury . . . *Hen. VIII.* v 1 92
My gracious lord, here is the bag of gold . . . *T. Andron.* ii 3 280
My gracious lord, no tribune hears you speak . . . . iii 1 32
My gracious lord, my lovely Saturnine, Lord of my life . . . iv 4 27
Welcome, my gracious lord; welcome, dread queen . . . . v 3 26
O, seek not to entrap me, gracious lord . . . . *Pericles* ii 5 45

Gracious madam, in our king's behalf, I am commanded. *3 Hen. VI.* iii 3 59
Yet, gracious madam, bear it as you may . . . . . . iv 4 14

Gracious madam. I do beseech You, gracious madam, to unthink your speaking . . . . *Hen. VIII.* ii 4 104
Gracious majesty. Come thou near.—Most gracious majesty,— Didst thou behold Octavia? . . . . *Ant. and Cleo.* iii 3 7
Gracious mark. Your high self, The gracious mark o' the land *W. Tale* iv 4 8
Gracious meeting. Of this good day and of this gracious meeting *Hen. V.* v 2 13
Gracious message. Give to a gracious message An host of tongues; but let ill tidings tell Themselves . . . . . *Ant. and Cleo.* ii 5 86
Gracious mind. God keep your lordship in that gracious mind! *Richard III.* iii 2 56
Gracious mistress. To satisfy your highness the entreaties Of our most gracious mistress . . . . *W. Tale* i 2 233
Gracious moon. My love, her mistress, is a gracious moon . *L. L. Lost* iv 3 230
Gracious mother! Why doth your highness look so pale? *T. Andron.* ii 3 89
Good morrow to your majesty and to my gracious mother . *Cymbeline* ii 3 40
Gracious my lord, You know your father's temper . *W. Tale* iv 4 477
Gracious my lord, I should report that which I say I saw . *Macbeth* v 5 30
Alack, bare-headed! Gracious my lord, hard by here is a hovel *Lear* iii 2 61
Gracious nature. So his gracious nature Would think upon you for your voices . . . . *Coriolanus* ii 3 195
His large fortune Upon his good and gracious nature hanging *T. of Athens* i 1 56
Gracious offers. I come with gracious offers from the king 1 *Hen. IV.* iv 3 30
Gracious Olivia,— What do you say, Cesario? . . . *T. Night* v 1 108
Gracious order. I am a brother Of gracious order . . *Meas. for Meas.* iii 2 232
Gracious pardon. By your most gracious pardon, I sing but after you *Ant. and Cleo.* i 5 72
Gracious parts. Remembers me of all his gracious parts . . *K. John* iii 4 96
Gracious patience. By your gracious patience, I will a round unvarnish'd tale deliver . . . . *Othello* i 3 89
Gracious person. Do no stain to your own gracious person *Meas. for Meas.* iii 1 208
In dimension and the shape of nature A gracious person . *T. Night* i 5 281
Gracious pleasure. What is your gracious pleasure? . . *Macbeth* v 3 30
I have not sounded him, nor he deliver'd His gracious pleasure *Richard III.* iii 4 18
Gracious prince. My gracious prince, and honourable peers 1 *Hen. VI.* iii 4 1
Happy were England, Would this gracious prince Take on himself the sovereignty thereof . . . . . . *Richard III.* iii 7 78
Most gracious prince, Lend favourable ears to our request . . iii 7 100
Gracious promise. From him pluck'd Either his gracious promise, which you might, As cause had call'd you up, have held him to *Coriolanus* ii 3 201
Gracious queen. Good expedition be my friend, and comfort The gracious queen! . . . . *W. Tale* i 2 459
Gracious regent. From the most gracious regent of this land *Richard II.* ii 3 77
Gracious season. You are my father too, and did relieve me, To see this gracious season . . . . *Cymbeline* v 5 401
Gracious self. I love the king And through him what is nearest to him, which is Your gracious self . . . . . *W. Tale* iv 4 534
We heartily solicit Your gracious self to take on you the charge *Richard III.* iii 7 131
Swear by thy gracious self, Which is the god of my idolatry *Rom. and Jul.* ii 2 113
Gracious silence. My gracious silence, hail! . . . *Coriolanus* ii 1 192
Gracious sir. How fares my gracious sir? . . . . *Tempest* v 1 253
Most gracious sir, In humblest manner I require your highness *Hen. VIII.* ii 4 143
Gracious sir, Here are your sons again . . . . *Cymbeline* v 5 347
Gracious sovereign. My gracious sovereign, Howe'er it pleases you to take it so, The ring was never hers . . . . . *All's Well* v 3 87
Gracious sovereign, Whether I have been to blame or no, I know not v 3 128
Many years of happy days befal My gracious sovereign! . *Richard II.* i 1 21
Then hear me, gracious sovereign, and you peers . . *Hen. V.* i 2 33
They of those marches, gracious sovereign, Shall be a wall sufficient . i 2 140
My gracious sovereign, as I rode from Calais . . 1 *Hen. VI.* iv 1 9
Grant me the combat, gracious sovereign . . . . . . iv 1 78
All health unto my gracious sovereign! . . . 2 *Hen. VI.* i 1 82
Come hither, gracious sovereign, view this body . . . . iii 2 149
Is Warwick friends with Margaret?—Ay, gracious sovereign 3 *Hen. VI.* iv 1 116
Cousin of Buckingham!—My gracious sovereign? . . *Richard III.* iv 2 2
Prove me, my gracious sovereign . . . . iv 2 69
My gracious sovereign, on the western coast Rideth a puissant navy . iv 4 433
Gracious triumpher in the eyes of Rome! . . . . *T. Andron.* i 1 170
Gracious uncle. My gracious uncle— Tut, tut! Grace me no grace, nor uncle me no uncle . . . . *Richard II.* ii 3 85
My gracious uncle, let me know my fault . . . . . ii 3 106
Gracious utterance. With all the gracious utterance thou hast Speak to his gentle hearing . . . . iii 3 125
Gracious voice. In law, what plea so tainted and corrupt But, being season'd with a gracious voice, Obscures the show of evil? *M. of V.* iii 2 76
Gracious words. Delivers in such apt and gracious words . *L. L. Lost* ii 1 73
Those gracious words revive my drooping thoughts . 3 *Hen. VI.* iii 3 21
Graciously. Let me be ignorant, and in nothing good, But graciously to know I am no better . . . . . . *Meas. for Meas.* ii 4 77
Since God so graciously hath brought to light This dangerous treason *Hen. V.* ii 2 185
And wise Laertes' son Did graciously plead for his funerals . *T. Andron.* i 1 381
Then, at my suit, look graciously on him . . . . . i 1 439
What he will do graciously, I will thankfully receive . *Pericles* iv 6 65
Gradation. By cold gradation and well-balanced form *Meas. for Meas.* iv 3 104
Preferment goes by letter and affection, And not by old gradation *Othello* i 1 37
Graff. The tree yields bad fruit.—I'll graff it with you, and then I shall graff it with a medlar . . . . *As Y. Like It* iii 2 124
The most just gods For every graff would send a caterpillar . *Pericles* v 1 60
Graffing. We will eat a last year's pippin of my own graffing 2 *Hen. IV.* v 3 3
Graft. And noble stock Was graft with crab-tree slip . 2 *Hen. VI.* iii 2 214
Her royal stock graft with ignoble plants . . . *Richard III.* iii 7 127
Grafted. His plausive words He scatter'd not in ears, but grafted them, To grow there and to bear . . . . . . *All's Well* i 2 54
A servant grafted in my serious trust And therein negligent . *W. Tale.* i 2 246
Such . . . rude society As thou art match'd withal and grafted to 1 *Hen. IV.* iii 2 15
By the faith of men, We have some old crab-trees here at home that will not Be grafted to your relish . . . . . *Coriolanus* ii 1 206
In whom I know All the particulars of vice so grafted . . *Macbeth* iv 3 51
Grafter. Our scions, put in wild and savage stock, Spirt up so suddenly into the clouds, And overlook their grafters . . . *Hen. V.* iii 5 9
Graftest. Pray God the plants thou graft'st may never grow *Richard II.* iii 4 101
Grain. Thou art not thyself; For thou exist'st on many a thousand grains That issue out of dust . . . . . *Meas. for Meas.* iii 1 20
That 's a fault that water will mend.—No, sir, 'tis in grain *Com. of Errors* iii 2 108
His reasons are as two grains of wheat hid in two bushels of chaff *Mer. of Venice* i 1 115
'Tis in grain, sir; 'twill endure wind and weather . . *T. Night* i 5 255
There's not a grain of it the face to sweeten Of the whole dungy earth *W. T.* ii 1 156
A grain, a dust, a gnat, a wandering hair, Any annoyance . *K. John* iv 1 93
Now he weighs time Even to the utmost grain . . . *Hen. V.* ii 4 138
As clear as founts in July when We see each grain of gravel . *Hen. VIII* i 1 155
Grain. As knots, by the conflux of meeting sap, Infect the sound pine and divert his grain Tortive and errant from his course of growth *T. and C.* i 3 8
Is that a wonder? The providence that 's in a watchful state Knows almost every grain of Plutus' gold . . . . iii 3 197
Suffer us to famish, and their store-houses crammed with grain *Coriolanus* i 1 83
They say there's grain enough! . . . . i 1 200
Made you against the grain To voice him consul . . . . ii 3 241
Pent to linger But with a grain a day, I would not buy Their mercy . iii 3 90
He said twas folly, For one poor grain or two, to leave unburnt . v 1 27
For one poor grain or two! I am one of those; his mother, wife, his child, And this brave fellow too, we are the grains: You are the musty chaff . . . . v 1 28
If you can look into the seeds of time, And say which grain will grow and which will not . . . . *Macbeth* i 3 59
If he say so, may his pernicious soul Rot half a grain a day! . *Othello* v 2 156
As it ebbs, the seedsman Upon the slime and ooze scatters his grain, And shortly comes to harvest . . . . . *Ant. and Cleo.* ii 7 25
Grained. Though now this grained face of mine be hid In sap-consuming winter's drizzled snow . . . . . . *Com. of Errors* v 1 311
Where against My grained ash an hundred times hath broke *Coriolanus* iv 5 114
There I see such black and grained spots As will not leave their tinct *Ham.* iii 4 90
Gramercy! wouldst thou aught with me? . . . . *Mer. of Venice* ii 2 128
Gramercies, Tranio, well dost thou advise . . . *T. of Shrew* i 1 41
Gramercies, lad, go forward; this contents . . . . . i 1 168
Gramercy, fellow: there, drink that for me . . *Richard III.* iii 2 108
We'll give your grace bonjour.—Be it so, Titus, and gramercy too *T. An.* i 1 495
Gramercy, lovely Lucius: what's the news? . . . . . iv 2 7
Gramercies, good fool: how does your mistress? . *T. of Athens* ii 2 69
Would we could see you at Corinth!—Good! gramercy . . . ii 2 74
Grammar. O, 'tis a verse in Horace; I know it well: I read it in the grammar long ago . . . . *T. Andron.* iv 2 23
Grammar school. Corrupted the youth of the realm in erecting a grammar school . . . . 2 *Hen. VI.* iv 7 37
Grand. Refusing her grand hests, she did confine thee . . *Tempest* i 2 274
Where should they Find this grand liquor that hath gilded 'em? . . v 1 280
But it is tell-a me dat you make grand preparation . . *Mer. Wives* iv 5 88
Whither are you bound?—To Saint Jaques le Grand . . *All's Well* iii 5 37
Her pretence is a pilgrimage to Saint Jaques le Grand . . . iv 3 58
The grand conspirator, Abbot of Westminster, With clog of conscience *Richard II.* v 6 19
Follow me!—Suivez-vous le grand capitaine . . . *Hen. V.* iv 4 70
That excellent grand tyrant of the earth . . . *Richard III.* iv 4 52
Produce the grand sum of his sins, the articles Collected *Hen. VIII.* iii 2 293
Making so bold . . . to unseal Their grand commission . . *Hamlet* v 2 18
Thy grand captain Antony Shall set thee on triumphant chariots *Ant. and Cleo.* iii 1 9
I was of late as petty to his ends As is the morn-dew on the myrtle-leaf To his grand sea . . . . iii 12 10
Grandam. To weep, like a young wench that had buried her grandam; to fast, like one that takes diet . . . . . . *T. G. of Ver.* ii 1 24
My grandam, having no eyes, look you, wept herself blind . . ii 3 13
She might ha' been a grandam ere she died: And so may you *L. L. Lost* v 2 17
Like one well studied in a sad ostent To please his grandam *M. of Venice* ii 2 206
What is the opinion of Pythagoras concerning wild fowl?—That the soul of our grandam might haply inhabit a bird . . . . *T. Night* iv 2 56
And fear to kill a woodcock, lest thou dispossess the soul of thy grandam iv 2 65
I am thy grandam, Richard; call me so . . . . *K. John* i 1 168
There's a good grandam, boy, that would blot thee . . . . ii 1 133
Come to thy grandam, child.—Do, child, go to it grandam, child; Give grandam kingdom, and it grandam will Give it a plum, a cherry, and a fig: There's a good grandam . . . . ii 1 159
His grandam's wrongs, and not his mother's shames, Draws those heaven-moving pearls from his poor eyes . . . . ii 1 168
A wicked will; A woman's will; a canker'd grandam's will! . . . ii 1 194
Grandam, I will not wish thy wishes thrive . . . . . . iii 1 334
Thy grandam loves thee; and thy uncle will As dear be to thee as thy father was . . . . iii 3 3
Grandam, I will pray, If ever I remember to be holy, For your fair safety . . . . iii 3 14
Ourgrandam earth, having this distemperature, In passion shook 1 *Hen. IV.* iii 1 34
A handsome stripling too: I wis your grandam had a worser match *Richard III.* i 3 102
Tell me, good grandam, is our father dead?—No, boy . . . ii 2 1
It were lost sorrow to wail one that's lost.—Then, grandam, you conclude that he is dead . . . . ii 2 12
You cannot guess who caused your father's death.—Grandam, we can . ii 2 20
Think you my uncle did dissemble, grandam?—Ay, boy . . . ii 2 31
Grandam, one night, as we did sit at supper, My uncle Rivers talk'd how I did grow . . . . ii 4 10
Grandam, this would have been a biting jest . . . . . ii 4 30
Who told thee this?—Grandam, his nurse.—His nurse! why, she was dead ere thou wert born . . . . ii 4 32
What should you fear?—Marry, my uncle Clarence' angry ghost: My grandam told me he was murder'd there . . . . iii 1 145
A grandam's name is little less in love Than is the doting title of a mother iv 4 299
My lady Was fairer than his grandam and as chaste . *Troi. and Cres.* i 3 209
A woman's story at a winter's fire, Authorized by her grandam *Macbeth* iii 4 66
Grandchild. And in her hand The grandchild to her blood *Coriolanus* v 3 24
Grande affaire. Je m'en vais a la cour—la grande affaire . *Mer. Wives* i 4 54
Grandeur. Je ne veux point que vous abaissiez votre grandeur en baisant la main d'une de votre seigneurie indigne serviteur . . *Hen. V.* v 2 275
Grandfather. Who begot thee?—Marry, the son of my grandfather *T. G. of Ver.* iii 1 295
He is Cupid's grandfather and learns news of him . . *L. L. Lost* ii 1 254
For, sure, Æacides Was Ajax, call'd so from his grandfather *T. of Shrew* iii 1 53
Indeed, I am not John of Gaunt, your grandfather . . 1 *Hen. IV.* ii 2 71
I have lost a seal-ring of my grandfather's worth forty mark . . iii 3 94
Three or four bonds of forty pound a-piece, and a seal-ring of my grandfather's . . . . iii 3 118
Your grandfather of famous memory . . . . . *Hen. V.* iv 7 95
His grandfather was Lionel Duke of Clarence . . . 1 *Hen. VI.* ii 4 83
Henry the Fourth, grandfather to this king, Deposed his nephew Richard ii 5 63
But he shall know I am as good— As good! Thou bastard of my grandfather! . . . . iii 1 42
Thy grandfather, Roger Mortimer, Earl of March . . . 3 *Hen. VI.* i 1 106
My father and my grandfather were kings . . . . . . iii 1 77
Thy famous grandfather Doth live again in thee . . . . . v 4 52
Some mad message from his mad grandfather . . . . *T. Andron.* iv 2 3
Nor thy tailor, rascal, Who is thy grandfather: he made those clothes, Which, as it seems, make thee . . . . *Cymbeline* iv 2 82

Grandjuror. You are grandjurors, are ye? we'll jure ye . . 1 *Hen. IV.* ii 2 96
Grand-jurymen. And they have been grand-jurymen since before Noah was a sailor . . . *T. Night* iii 2 17
Grandmother. I should sin To think but nobly of my grandmother: Good wombs have borne bad sons . . *Tempest* i 2 119
Who begot thee?—Marry, the son of my grandfather.—O illiterate loiterer! it was the son of thy grandmother . . *T. G. of Ver.* iii 1 297
With a child of our grandmother Eve, a female . . *L. L. Lost* i 1 266
Fair Queen Isabel, his grandmother, Was lineal of the Lady Ermengare *Hen. V.* i 2 81
Grandpré, Roussi, and Fauconberg, Foix, Lestrale . . . iii 5 44; iv 8 104
Who hath measured the ground?—The Lord Grandpré . . . iii 7 138
Grandsire. Seven hundred pounds of moneys, and gold and silver, is her grandsire upon his death's-bed—Got deliver to a joyful resurrections!—give, when she is able to overtake seventeen years old . . . *Mer. Wives* i 1 53
Did her grandsire leave her seven hundred pound? . . . i 1 59
Sit like his grandsire cut in alabaster . . . *Mer. of Venice* i 1 84
Do, good old grandsire; and withal make known Which way thou travellest . . . *T. of Shrew* iv 5 50
For that my grandsire was an Englishman, Awakes my conscience *K. John* v 4 42
O, had thy grandsire with a prophet's eye Seen how his son's son should destroy his sons . . . *Richard II.* ii 1 104
By the honourable tomb he swears, That stands upon your royal grandsire's bones . . . iii 3 106
Guarded with grandsires, babies and old women . . *Hen. V.* iii Prol. 20
Think'st thou that I will leave my kingly throne, Wherein my grandsire and my father sat? . . . 3 *Hen. VI.* i 1 125
Say unto his child, 'What my great-grandfather and grandsire got My careless father fondly gave away' . . . ii 2 37
Nestor, one that was a man When Hector's grandsire suck'd *Troi. and Cres.* i 3 292
Whose wit was mouldy ere your grandsires had nails on their toes . ii 1 115
I knew thy grandsire, And once fought with him: he was a soldier good iv 5 196
Good grandsire, leave these bitter deep laments . . *T. Andron.* iii 2 46
The tender boy, in passion moved, Doth weep to see his grandsire's heaviness . . . iii 2 49
Help, grandsire, help! my aunt Lavinia Follows me every where . . iv 1 1
I have heard my grandsire say full oft, Extremity of griefs would make men mad . . . iv 1 18
What book is that she tosseth so?—Grandsire, 'tis Ovid's Metamorphoses iv 1 42
Thou'lt do thy message, wilt thou not?—Ay, with my dagger in their bosoms, grandsire.—No, boy, not so . . . iv 1 118
My grandsire, well advised, hath sent by me The goodliest weapons of his armoury . . . iv 2 10
Thy grandsire loved thee well: Many a time he danced thee on his knee v 3 161
O grandsire, grandsire! even with all my heart Would I were dead! . v 3 172
I am proverb'd with a grandsire phrase . . . *Rom. and Jul.* i 4 37
Is not this a lamentable thing, grandsire, that we should be thus afflicted? ii 4 33
The hellish Pyrrhus Old grandsire Priam seeks . . . *Hamlet* ii 2 486
The devil will make a grandsire of you . . . *Othello* i 1 91
Sleep, thou hast been a grandsire, and begot A father to me . *Cymbeline* v 4 123
Grange. At the moated grange resides this dejected Mariana *M. for M.* iii 1 277
Or thou goest to the grange or mill.—If to either, thou dost ill *W. Tale* iv 4 309
What tell'st thou me of robbing? this is Venice; My house is not a grange . . . *Othello* i 1 106
Grant. Being once perfected how to grant suits, How to deny them *Temp.* i 2 79
Will you grant with me That Ferdinand is drown'd? . . . ii 1 243
I grant, sweet love, that I did love a lady; But she is dead *T. G. of Ver.* iv 2 105
Grant one boon that I shall ask of you.—I grant it . . . v 4 150
Heaven grant us its peace, but not the King of Hungary's! *Meas. for Meas.* i 2 4
There went but a pair of shears between us.—I grant . . . i 2 30
What obscured light the heavens did grant . . *Com. of Errors* i 1 67
O, grant me justice! Even for the service that long since I did thee . v 1 190
The fairest grant is the necessity. Look, what will serve is fit *Much Ado* i 1 319
God grant us patience!—To hear? or forbear laughing? . *L. L. Lost* i 1 197
You sheep, and I pasture: shall that finish the jest?—So you grant pasture for me . . . ii 1 222
Now, at the latest minute of the hour, Grant us your loves . . v 2 798
Pray thou for us; And good luck grant thee thy Demetrius! *M. N. Dream* i 1 221
I grant you, friends, if that you should fright the ladies . . i 2 81
A more swelling port Than my faint means would grant continuance *M. of V.* i 1 125
I pray God grant them a fair departure . . . i 2 121
Since I am a dog, beware my fangs: The duke shall grant me justice . iii 3 8
The duke Will never grant this forfeiture to hold . . . iii 3 25
Grant me two things, I pray you, Not to deny me, and to pardon me . iv 1 423
Ask me what you will, I will grant it . . . *As Y. Like It* iv 1 114
But seeing you should love her? and loving woo? and, wooing, she should grant? . . . v 2 4
Sir, will you hear my suit?—And grant it . . . *All's Well* ii 3 83
My wish receive, Which great Love grant! . . . ii 3 91
Unless her prayers, whom heaven delights to hear And loves to grant . iii 4 28
I follow him to his country for justice: grant it me, O king! . . v 3 145
Grant me another request.—Any thing . . . *T. Night* v 1 3
You can say none of this: well, grant it then And tell me . . v 1 342
And well become the agent; 't may, I grant . . . *W. Tale* i 2 114
'Tis a sickness denying thee any thing; a death to grant this . . iv 2 3
At your request My father will grant precious things as trifles . . v 1 222
O, if thou grant my need, Which only lives but by the death of faith *K. John* iii 1 211
I will both hear and grant you your requests . . . iv 2 46
Turn thy face in peace; We grant thou canst outscold us . . v 2 160
May it please you, lords, to grant the commons' suit . *Richard II.* iv 1 154
Ill mayst thou thrive, if thou grant any grace! . . . v 3 99
Yes, Jack, upon instinct.—I grant ye, upon instinct . 1 *Hen. IV.* ii 4 390
I grant you I was down and out of breath . . . v 4 149
And yet, in some respects, I grant, I cannot go . . 2 *Hen. IV.* i 2 190
Grant that our hopes, yet likely of fair birth, Should be still-born . i 3 63
We catch of you; grant that, my poor virtue, grant that . . ii 4 50
May well be charm'd asleep With grant of our most just and right desires . . . iv 2 40
O God forgive; And grant it may with thee in true peace live! . . iv 5 220
I grant your worship that he is a knave, sir . . . v 1 47
An if your father's highness Do not, in grant of all demands at large, Sweeten the bitter mock . . . *Hen. V.* ii 4 121
Grant him there; there seen, Heave him away upon your winged thoughts . . . v Prol. 7
Having any occasion to write for matter of grant . . . v 2 366
Grant me the combat, gracious sovereign.—And me, my lord, grant me the combat too.—This is my servant . . 1 *Hen. VI.* iv 1 78
My body shall Pay recompense, if you will grant my suit . . . v 3 19
Grant. Your highness shall do well to grant her suit . 3 *Hen. VI.* iii 2 8
I see the lady hath a thing to grant, Before the king will grant her humble suit . . . iii 2 12
Be pitiful, dread lord, and grant it then . . . iii 2 32
My humble thanks, my prayers; That love which virtue begs and virtue grants . . . iii 2 63
My mind will never grant what I perceive Your highness aims at . . iii 2 67
Grant That virtuous Lady Bona, thy fair sister, To England's king . iii 3 55
Heavens grant that Warwick's words bewitch him not! . . . iii 3 112
Let us hear your firm resolve.—Your grant, or your denial, shall be mine iii 3 130
It was my will and grant; And for this once my will shall stand for law iv 1 49
Didst thou not kill this king?—I grant ye.—Dost grant me, hedgehog? then, God grant me too Thou mayst be damned! . *Richard III.* i 2 102
For divers unknown reasons, I beseech you, Grant me this boon . . i 2 219
His grace speaks cheerfully.—God grant him health! . . . i 3 35
God grant we never may have need of you!—Meantime, God grants that we have need of you . . . i 3 76
God grant that some, less noble and less loyal, . . . Deserve not worse! ii 1 91
You straight are on your knees for pardon, pardon; And I, unjustly too, must grant it you . . . ii 1 125
O, make them joyful, grant their lawful suit! . . . iii 7 203
How often have I wished me thus!—Wished, my lord! The gods grant,—O my lord!—What should they grant? . *Troi. and Cres.* iii 2 67
And Cupid grant all tongue-tied maidens here Bed, chamber, Pandar! . iii 2 219
The gods grant them true!—True! pow, wow . . *Coriolanus* ii 1 156
Grant that, and tell me, In peace what each of them by the other lose . iii 2 43
By the entreaty and grant of the whole table . . . iv 5 212
The thing I have forsworn to grant may never Be held by you denials . v 3 80
O, no more, no more! You have said you will not grant us any thing . v 3 87
Saints do not move, though grant for prayers' sake *Rom. and Jul.* i 5 107
Grant I may never prove so fond, To trust man on his oath or bond *T. of Athens* i 2 65
To kill, I grant, is sin's extremest gust . . . iii 5 54
And grant, as Timon grows, his hate may grow To the whole race of mankind! . . . iv 1 39
A beastly ambition, which the gods grant thee t' attain to! . . . iv 3 330
Grant I may ever love, and rather woo Those that would mischief me! iv 3 474
Crown him?—that;—And then, I grant, we put a sting in him *J. Cæsar* ii 1 16
I grant I am a woman; but withal A woman that Lord Brutus took to wife: I grant I am a woman; but withal A woman well-reputed, Cato's daughter . . . ii 1 292
Brutus hath a suit That Cæsar will not grant . . . ii 4 43
Grant that, and then is death a benefit . . . iii 1 103
If you would grant the time.—At your kind'st leisure . *Macbeth* ii 1 24
I grant him bloody, Luxurious, avaricious, false, deceitful . . iv 3 57
Mad let us grant him, then: and now remains That we find out the cause *Hamlet* ii 2 100
All ports I'll bar; the villain shall not 'scape; The duke must grant me that . . . *Lear* ii 1 83
Marry, before your ladyship, I grant, She puts her tongue a little in her heart, And chides with thinking . . . *Othello* ii 1 106
I do beseech thee, grant me this, To leave me but a little to myself . iii 3 84
It hath not appeared.—I grant indeed it hath not appeared . . iv 2 214
Let us grant, it is not Amiss to tumble on the bed of Ptolemy *Ant. and Cleo.* i 4 16
Out of her impatience . . . , I grieving grant Did you too much disquiet ii 2 69
That Without the which a soldier, and his sword, Grants scarce distinction . . . iii 1 29
I grant him part; but then, in his Armenia, And other of his conquer'd kingdoms, I Demand the like . . . iii 6 35
Bids thee study on what fair demands Thou mean'st to have him grant thee . . . v 2 11
I think He'll grant the tribute, send the arrearages . . *Cymbeline* ii 4 13
Had I not brought The knowledge of your mistress home, I grant We were to question further . . . ii 4 51
Not seen of late? Grant, heavens, that which I fear Prove false! . . iii 5 52
Thy words, I grant, are bigger, for I wear not My dagger in my mouth . iv 2 78
The liver, heart and brain of Britain, By whom I grant she lives . . v 5 15
If you require a little space for prayer, I grant it . . *Pericles* iv 1 69
Granted. This being granted in course,—and now follows all *M. for M.* iii 1 259
But is there no quick recreation granted? . . . *L. L. Lost* i 1 162
Acordo linta. Come on; thou art granted space . . *All's Well* iv 1 98
If that my cousin king be King of England, It must be granted I am Duke of Lancaster . . . *Richard II.* ii 3 124
At his feet to lay my arms and power, Provided that my banishment repeal'd And lands restored again be freely granted . . . iii 3 41
Which on thy royal party granted once, His glittering arms he will commend to rust . . . iii 3 115
Which, for divers reasons . . . , Will easily be granted . 1 *Hen. IV.* i 3 264
But thy speaking of my tongue, and I thine, most truly-falsely, must needs be granted to be much at one . . . *Hen. V.* v 2 204
The king hath granted every article: His daughter first . . . v 2 360
Chid and rated at, And the offender granted scope of speech 2 *Hen. VI.* iii 1 176
The soldiers should have toss'd me on their pikes Before I would have granted to that act . . . 3 *Hen. VI.* i 1 245
I can tell you both Her suit is granted for her husband's lands . . iii 2 117
The benefit thereof is always granted To those whose dealings have deserved the place . . . *Richard III.* iii 1 48
His suit was granted Ere it was ask'd . . . *Hen. VIII.* i 1 186
Which, if granted, As he made semblance of his duty, would Have put his knife into him . . . i 2 197
Let this be granted, and Achilles' horse Makes many Thetis' sons *Troi. and Cres.* i 3 211
And a petition granted them, a strange one . . . *Coriolanus* i 1 214
What is granted them?—Five tribunes to defend their vulgar wisdoms . i 1 218
When we granted that, Here was 'I thank you for your voices: thank you' . . . ii 3 178
Were you in my stead, would you have heard A mother less? or granted less? . . . v 3 193
Thou believest no god: That granted, how canst thou believe an oath? *T. Andron.* v 1 72
This granted,—as it is a most pregnant and unforced position *Othello* ii 1 239
It shall be full of poise and difficult weight And fearful to be granted . iii 3 83
I begg'd His pardon for return.—Which soon he granted *Ant. and Cleo.* iii 6 60
Requires to live in Egypt: which not granted, He lessens his requests iii 12 12
You are a fool granted . . . *Cymbeline* ii 1 50
Let it be granted you have seen all this—and praise Be given to your remembrance . . . ii 4 92
For him And his succession granted Rome a tribute . . . iii 1 8
With slaughter Of you their captives, which ourself have granted . . v 5 73

Grantest. I have forgot all men; Then, if thou grant'st thou'rt a man, I have forgot thee . . . . . . *T. of Athens* iv 3 481
Granting. I am so far from granting thy request That I despise thee for thy wrongful suit . . . . *T. G. of Ver.* iv 2 101
You granting of my suit, If that be sin, I'll make it my morn prayer To have it added to the faults of mine . . . *Meas. for Meas.* ii 4 70
Grape. 'Twas in the Bunch of Grapes, where indeed you have a delight to sit, have you not? . . . . ii 1 133
Feed him with apricocks and dewberries, With purple grapes *M. N. D.* iii 1 170
When he had a desire to eat a grape, would open his lips when he put it into his mouth; meaning thereby that grapes were made to eat *As Y. Like It* v 1 37
O, will you eat no grapes, my royal fox? Yes, but you will my noble grapes, an if My royal fox could reach them . . . *All's Well* ii 1 73
There's one grape yet; I am sure thy father drunk wine . . ii 3 105
The tartness of his face sours ripe grapes . . . *Coriolanus* v 4 18
Go, suck the subtle blood o' the grape, Till the high fever seethe your blood to froth, And so 'scape hanging . . . *T. of Athens* iv 3 432
The wine she drinks is made of grapes . . . . *Othello* ii 1 257
With thy grapes our hairs be crown'd . . . *Ant. and Cleo.* ii 7 123
Now no more The juice of Egypt's grape shall moist this lip . . v 2 285
Grapple. I was as willing to grapple as he was to board . *L. L. Lost* ii 1 218
With which such scathful grapple did he make With the most noble bottom of our fleet . . . . *T. Night* v 1 59
And grapple with him ere he come so nigh . . . *K. John* v 1 61
And grapple thee unto a pagan shore . . . . v 2 36
Send danger from the east unto the west, So honour cross it from the north to south, And let them grapple . . . . 1 *Hen. IV.* i 3 197
Grapple your minds to sternage of this navy . . . *Hen. V.* iii Prol. 18
Bear the arms of York, To grapple with the house of Lancaster 2 *Hen. VI.* i 1 257
Grapples you to the heart and love of us . . . . *Macbeth* iii 1 106
Those friends thou hast, and their adoption tried, Grapple them to thy soul with hoops of steel . . . . *Hamlet* i 3 63
We put on a compelled valour, and in the grapple I boarded them . iv 6 18
Grappling. The grappling vigour and rough frown of war . *K. John* iii 1 104
Grasp. Thy hand is made to grasp a palmer's staff . . 2 *Hen. VI.* v 1 97
With his arms outstretch'd, as he would fly, Grasps in the comer *Troi. and Cres.* iii 3 168
But flies the grasps of love With wings more momentary-swift than thought . . . . iv 2 13
I would not . . . For the whole space that's in the tyrant's grasp *Macb.* iv 3 36
Grasped. His hands abroad display'd, as one that grasp'd And tugg'd for life . . . . 2 *Hen. VI.* iii 2 172
And bloody steel grasp'd in their ireful hands . . . . 3 *Hen. VI.* ii 5 132
And sell the mighty space of our large honours For so much trash as may be grasped thus? I had rather be a dog . . . *J. Cæsar* iv 3 26
And with those hands, that grasp'd the heaviest club, Subdue my worthiest self. The witch shall die . . . . *Ant. and Cleo.* iv 12 46
Grass. How lush and lusty the grass looks! how green! . . *Tempest* ii 1 52
She rides me and I long for grass. 'Tis so, I am an ass . *Com. of Errors* ii 2 202
To tread a measure with her on this grass . . . *L. L. Lost* v 2 185
Decking with liquid pearl the bladed grass . . . *M. N. Dream* i 1 211
Plucking the grass, to know where sits the wind . . *Mer. of Venice* i 1 18
I am no great Nebuchadnezzar, sir; I have not much skill in grass *All's Well* iv 5 22
The grass whereon thou tread'st the presence strew'd . . *Richard II.* i 3 289
And bedew Her pastures' grass with faithful English blood . . . iii 3 100
Grew like the summer grass, fastest by night, Unseen . . *Hen. V.* i 1 65
Mowing like grass Your fresh-fair virgins and your flowering infants . iii 3 13
In their pale dull mouths the gimmal bit Lies foul with chew'd grass . iv 2 50
On a mountain top, Where biting cold would never let grass grow 2 *Hen. VI.* iii 2 337
And in Cheapside shall my palfry go to grass . . . . . . iv 2 75
I climbed into this garden, to see if I can eat grass, or pick a sallet . iv 10 9
If I do not leave you all as dead as a door-nail, I pray God I may never eat grass more . . . . iv 10 44
As flowers with frost or grass beat down with storms . *T. Andron.* iv 4 71
We cannot live on grass, on berries, water, As beasts . *T. of Athens* iv 3 425
Ay, sir but, 'While the grass grows,—the proverb is something musty *Hamlet* iii 2 358
Grass-green. At his head a grass-green turf, At his heels a stone . . iv 5 31
Grasshopper. The cover of the wings of grasshoppers . *Rom. and Jul.* i 4 60
Grass-plot. Here on this grass-plot, in this very place . *Tempest* iv 1 73
Grassy. While here we march Upon the grassy carpet of this plain *Richard II.* iii 3 50
Grate. Looked through the grate, like a geminy of baboons *Mer. Wives* ii 2 8
I had rather hear a brazen canstick turn'd, Or a dry wheel grate 1 *Hen. IV.* iii 1 132
What peer hath been suborn'd to grate on you? . . . 2 *Hen. IV.* iv 1 90
Wont through a secret grate of iron bars In yonder tower . 1 *Hen. VI.* i 4 10
Here, through this grate, I count each one And view the Frenchmen . i 4 60
News, my good lord, from Rome.—Grates me: the sum *Ant. and Cleo.* i 1 18
Grated. I have grated upon my good friends for three reprieves *Mer. Wives* ii 2 6
And mighty states characterless are grated To dusty nothing *T. and C.* iii 2 195
Grateful. Neighbour, this is a gift very grateful . . . *T. of Shrew* ii 1 76
I cannot give thee less, to be call'd grateful . . . *All's Well* ii 1 132
Too modest are you; More cruel to your good report than grateful To us that give you truly . . . . *Coriolanus* i 9 54
In grateful virtue I am bound To your free heart . . *T. of Athens* i 2 5
Gratiano. Here comes Bassanio, your most noble kinsman, Gratiano and Lorenzo . . . . *Mer. of Venice* i 1 58
I hold the world but as the world, Gratiano; A stage . . . . i 1 77
I must be one of these same dumb wise men, For Gratiano never lets me speak . . . . i 1 107
Gratiano speaks an infinite deal of nothing, more than any man . . i 1 114
Desire Gratiano to come anon to my lodging . . . . . . ii 2 124
But hear thee, Gratiano; Thou art too wild, too rude and bold of voice ii 2 189
Meet me and Gratiano At Gratiano's lodging some hour hence . . ii 4 26
Fie, fie, Gratiano! where are all the rest? 'Tis nine o'clock . . ii 6 62
I saw Bassanio under sail: With him is Gratiano gone along . . . ii 8 2
And do you, Gratiano, mean good faith?—Yes, faith, my lord . . iii 2 212
Go, Gratiano, run and overtake him; Give him the ring . . . . iv 1 452
Now, in faith, Gratiano, You give your wife too unkind a cause of grief v 1 174
And pardon me, my gentle Gratiano . . . . v 1 260
Signior Gratiano? I cry you gentle pardon . . . . . *Othello* v 1 93
Gratiano, keep the house, And seize upon the fortunes of the Moor . v 2 365
Gratify. Please you to gratify the table with a grace . *L. L. Lost* iv 2 161
Gratify this gentleman, For, in my mind, you are much bound to him *Mer. of Venice* iv 1 406
Gratify this gentleman, To whom we all rest generally beholding *T. of S.* i 2 273
To gratify his noble service that Hath thus stood for his country *Coriol.* ii 2 44

Gratify. To gratify the good Andronicus, And gratulate his safe return *T. Andron.* i 1 220
To gratify your honourable youth, The hope of Rome . . . . . iv 2 12
She did gratify his amorous works With that recognizance and pledge of love Which I first gave her . . . . *Othello* v 2 213
In these sear'd hopes, I barely gratify your love . . . *Cymbeline* ii 4 7
The which when any shall not gratify, Or pay you with unthankfulness in thought, Be it our wives, our children . . . . *Pericles* i 4 101
Gratii. Guiltian, Cosmo, Lodowick, and Gratii . . . . *All's Well* iv 3 186
Gratillity. I did impeticos thy gratillity . . . . . *T. Night* ii 3 27
Grating. And grating shock of wrathful iron arms . . . *Richard II.* i 3 136
Grating so harshly all his days of quiet . . . . . *Hamlet* iii 1 3
Gratis. Thinkest thou I'll endanger my soul gratis? . . *Mer. Wives* ii 2 16
He lends out money gratis and brings down The rate of usance *M. of V.* i 3 45
This is the fool that lent out money gratis . . . . iii 3 2
A halter gratis; nothing else, for God's sake . . . . . . iv 1 379
Thou, like a kind fellow, gavest thyself away gratis . 2 *Hen. IV.* iv 3 76
When corn was given them gratis, you repined . . . *Coriolanus* iii 1 43
Whoever gave that counsel, to give forth The corn o' the storehouse gratis iii 1 114
This kind of service Did not deserve corn gratis . . . . . iii 1 125
The lover shall not sigh gratis . . . . *Hamlet* ii 2 335
Gratitude. Which gratitude Through flinty Tartar's bosom would peep forth, And answer, thanks . . . . *All's Well* iv 4 6
Whose gratitude Towards her deserved children is enroll'd *Coriolanus* iii 1 291
Bond of childhood, Effects of courtesy, dues of gratitude . . *Lear* ii 4 182
Thou canst not, in the course of gratitude, but be a diligent follower of mine: wilt thou serve me? . . . . *Cymbeline* iii 5 121
Gratulate. There's more behind that is more gratulate . *Meas. for Meas.* v 1 535
To gratulate the gentle princes there . . . . . *Richard III.* iv 1 10
To gratify the good Andronicus, And gratulate his safe return *T. Andron.* i 1 221
Come freely To gratulate thy plenteous bosom . . . *T. of Athens* i 2 131
Graves at my command Have waked their sleepers . . . . *Tempest* v 1 48
Every third thought shall be my grave . . . . v 1 311
Heap on your head A pack of sorrows which would press you down, Being unprevented, to your timeless grave . . . *T. G. of Ver.* iii 1 21
For in his grave Assure thyself my love is buried.—Sweet lady, let me rake it from the earth.—Go to thy lady's grave and call hers thence iv 2 114
Thy true love died, Upon whose grave thou vow'dst pure chastity . iv 3 21
More grave and wrinkled than the aims and ends Of burning youth *Meas. for Meas.* i 3 5
There my father's grave Did utter forth a voice . . . . . iii 1 86
The wicked'st caitiff on the ground May seem as shy, as grave, as just, as absolute . . . . v 1 54
Enter in And dwell upon your grave when you are dead . *Com. of Errors* iii 1 104
With his bad legs, falls into the cinque pace faster and faster, till he sink into his grave . . . . *Much Ado* ii 1 83
Graves, yawn and yield your dead, Till death be uttered, Heavily, heavily v 3 19
Now it is the time of night That the graves all gaping wide *M. N. Dream* v 1 387
It were too gross To rib her cerecloth in the obscure grave *Mer. of Venice* ii 7 51
That you would wear it till your hour of death And that it should lie with you in your grave . . . . v 1 154
Here lie I down, and measure out my grave . . . *As Y. Like It* ii 6 3
And thou return unexperienced to thy grave . . . . *T. of Shrew* iv 1 86
The mere word's a slave Debosh'd on every tomb, on every grave *All's W.* ii 3 145
When you have spoken it, 'tis dead, and I am the grave of it . . . iv 3 16
Our rash faults Make trivial price of serious things we have, Not knowing them until we know their grave . . . . v 3 62
'Tis thought among the prudent he would quickly have the gift of a grave . . . . *T. Night* i 3 35
If you will lead these graces to the grave And leave the world no copy i 5 260
Lay me, O, where Sad true lover never find my grave, To weep there! . ii 4 66
Since when, my watch hath told me, toward my grave I have travell'd but two hours . . . . v 1 165
So disgraced a part, whose issue Will hiss me to my grave . *W. Tale* i 2 189
If it be so, We need no grave to bury honesty . . . . . ii 1 155
And my near'st of kin Cry fie upon my grave! . . . . . . iii 2 55
One grave shall be for both: upon them shall The causes of their death appear . . . . iii 2 237
You have undone a man of fourscore three, That thought to fill his grave in quiet . . . . iv 4 465
As monstrous to our human reason As my Antigonus to break his grave v 1 42
As every present time doth boast itself Above a better gone, so must thy grave Give way to what's seen now . . . . v 1 97
O grave and good Paulina, the great comfort That I have had of thee! . v 3 1
Come, I'll fill your grave up: stir, nay, come away . . . . . v 3 101
For I saw her, As I thought, dead, and have in vain said many A prayer upon her grave . . . . v 3 141
By this brave duke came early to his grave . . . . *K. John* ii 1 5
I would that I were low laid in my grave: I am not worth this coil . ii 1 164
He shall not offend your majesty.—Death.—My lord?—A grave . . iii 3 66
Look, who comes here! a grave unto a soul . . . . . . iii 4 17
Find the inheritance of this poor child, His little kingdom of a forced grave . . . . iv 2 98
And others more, going to seek the grave Of Arthur . . . . . iv 2 164
Or, when he doom'd this beauty to a grave, Found it too precious-princely for a grave . . . . iv 3 40
Despite of death that lives upon my grave . . . . *Richard II.* i 1 168
Such grief That words seemed buried in my sorrow's grave . . . i 4 15
Now put it, God, in the physician's mind To help him to his grave immediately! . . . . i 4 60
Gaunt am I for the grave, gaunt as a grave . . . . . . ii 1 82
Convey me to my bed, then to my grave . . . . ii 1 137
Let them die that age and sullens have; For both hast thou, and both become the grave . . . . ii 1 140
Of comfort no man speak: Let's talk of graves, of worms and epitaphs iii 2 145
My large kingdom for a little grave, A little little grave, an obscure grave iii 3 153
Shedding tears? As thus, to drop them still upon one place, Till they have fretted us a pair of graves . . . . iii 3 167
There lies Two kinsmen digg'd their graves with weeping eyes . . iii 3 169
With clog of conscience and sour melancholy Hath yielded up his body to the grave . . . . v 6 21
Thy ignominy sleep with thee in the grave! . . . . . 1 *Hen. IV.* v 4 100
They that, when Richard lived, would have him die, Are now become enamour'd on his grave . . . . 2 *Hen. IV.* i 3 102
To-day might I, hanging on Hotspur's neck, Have talk'd of Monmouth's grave . . . . ii 3 45
Turning your books to graves, your ink to blood, Your pens to lances . iv 1 50
What! canst thou not forbear me half an hour? Then get thee gone and dig my grave thyself . . . . iv 5 111
My father is gone wild into his grave, For in his tomb lie my affections v 2 123

Graves. The grave doth gape For thee thrice wider than for other men *2 Hen. IV.* v 5 57

Else our grave, Like Turkish mute, shall have a tongueless mouth *Hen. V.* i 2 231

The grave doth gape, and doting death is near; Therefore exhale . ii 1 65

Show men dutiful? Why, so didst thou: seem they grave and learned? ii 2 128

The organs, though defunct and dead before, Break up their drowsy grave . iv 1 22

And follows so the ever-running year, With profitable labour, to his grave . iv 1 294

A many of our bodies shall no doubt Find native graves . iv 3 96

And here will Talbot mount, or make his grave . *1 Hen. VI.* ii 1 34

Until it wither with me to my grave Or flourish to the height of my degree . ii 4 110

Swift-winged with desire to get a grave, As witting I no other comfort have . ii 5 15

What joy shall noble Talbot have To bid his young son welcome to his grave? . iv 3 40

I have what I would have, Now my old arms are young John Talbot's grave . iv 7 32

Ban-dogs howl And spirits walk and ghosts break up their graves *2 Hen. VI.* i 4 22

I will remedy this gear ere long, Or sell my title for a glorious grave . iii 1 92

View this body.—That is to see how deep my grave is made . iii 2 150

Who, with their drowsy, slow and flagging wings, Clip dead men's graves . iv 1 6

If mine arm be heaved in the air, Thy grave is digg'd already in the earth iv 10 55

Hence will I drag thee headlong by the heels Unto a dunghill which shall be thy grave . iv 10 87

Wilt thou go dig a grave to find out war? . v 1 169

In duty bend thy knee to me That bows unto the grave with mickle age v 1 174

If I digg'd up thy forefathers' graves And hung their rotten coffins up in chains, It could not slake mine ire, nor ease my heart *3 Hen. VI.* i 3 27

Let our bloody colours wave! And either victory, or else a grave . ii 2 174

Would bring white hairs unto a quiet grave . ii 5 40

Your brother Richard mark'd him for the grave . ii 6 40

For who lived king, but I could dig his grave? . v 2 21

And wet his grave with my repentant tears . *Richard III.* i 2 216

I'll turn yon fellow in his grave; And then return lamenting to my love i 2 261

In him your comfort lives: Drown desperate sorrow in dead Edward's grave . ii 2 99

Go thou to sanctuary, and good thoughts possess thee! I to my grave, where peace and rest lie with me! . iv 1 95

Woe's scene, world's shame, grave's due by life usurp'd . iv 4 27

O, that thou wouldst as well afford a grave As thou canst yield a melancholy seat! Then would I hide my bones . iv 4 31

Thy womb let loose, to chase us to our graves . iv 4 54

Untimely smother'd in their dusky graves . iv 4 70

Too deep and dead; Too deep and dead, poor infants, in their grave . iv 4 363

Nor build their evils on the graves of great men . *Hen. VIII.* ii 1 67

No black envy Shall mark my grave . ii 1 86

Should Do no more offices of life to't than The grave does to the dead . ii 4 191

No kindred weep for me; Almost no grave allow'd me . iii 1 151

Strew me over With maiden flowers, that all the world may know I was a chaste wife to my grave . iv 2 170

Till Cranmer, Cromwell, her two hands, and she, Sleep in their graves . v 1 32

You shall not be The grave of your deserving . *Coriolanus* i 9 20

Your beards deserve not so honourable a grave as to stuff a botcher's cushion . ii 1 98

Every gash was an enemy's grave . ii 1 172

Why, You grave but reckless senators . iii 1 92

Think Upon the wounds his body bears, which show Like graves . iii 3 51

Wears my stripes impress'd upon him; that Must bear my beating to his grave . v 6 109

And shall she carry this unto her grave? . *T. Andron.* ii 3 127

Into the swallowing womb Of this deep pit, poor Bassianus' grave . ii 3 240

Bassianus 'tis we mean—Do thou so much as dig the grave for him . ii 3 270

Oft have I digg'd up dead men from their graves, And set them upright v 1 135

That fought Rome's quarrel out, And sent her enemies unto the grave . v 3 103

Commit him to the grave; Do him that kindness, and take leave of him v 3 170

Convey the emperor hence, And give him burial in his father's grave . v 3 192

Ancient citizens Cast by their grave beseeming ornaments *Rom. and Jul.* i 1 100

If he be married, My grave is like to be my wedding bed . i 5 137

The earth that's nature's mother is her tomb; What is her burying grave that is her womb . ii 3 10

And bad'st me bury love.—Not in a grave, To lay one in, another out to have . ii 3 83

Fall upon the ground, as I do now, Taking the measure of an unmade grave . iii 3 70

Wilt thou wash him from his grave with tears? . iii 5 71

I would the fool were married to her grave! . iii 5 141

Or bid me go into a new-made grave And hide me with a dead man . iv 1 84

Every one prepare To follow this fair corse unto her grave . iv 5 93

Come, cordial and not poison, go with me To Juliet's grave . v 1 86

So shall no foot upon the churchyard tread, Being loose, unfirm, with digging up of graves, But thou shalt hear it . v 3 6

The obsequies that I for thee will keep Nightly shall be to strew thy grave v 3 17

I'll bury thee in a triumphant grave; A grave? O, no! a lantern, slaughter'd youth . v 3 83

How oft to-night Have my old feet stumbled at graves! . v 3 122

What manners is in this, To press before thy father to a grave? . v 3 215

I writ to Romeo, That he should hither come as this dire night, To help to take her from her borrow'd grave . v 3 248

He came with flowers to strew his lady's grave . v 3 281

As well of glib and slippery creatures as Of grave . *T. of Athens* i 1 54

Who dies, that bears not one spurn to their graves Of their friends' gift? i 2 146

Slaves and fools, Pluck the grave wrinkled senate from the bench . iv 1 5

As we do turn our backs From our companion thrown into his grave . iv 2 9

Do you damn others, and let this damn you, And ditches grave you all! iv 3 166

Then, Timon, presently prepare thy grave; Lie where the light foam of the sea may beat Thy grave-stone daily . iv 3 378

Graves only be men's works and death their gain! Sun, hide thy beams! . v 1 225

There does not live a man. Dead, sure; and this his grave . v 3 5

Yet rich conceit Taught thee to make vast Neptune weep for aye On thy low grave . v 4 79

And peep about To find ourselves dishonourable graves . *J. Cæsar* i 2 138

This dreadful night, That thunders, lightens, opens graves, and roars . i 3 74

Graves have yawn'd, and yielded up their dead . ii 2 18

As from your graves rise up, and walk like sprites! . *Macbeth* ii 3 84

Your good advice, Which still hath been both grave and prosperous . iii 1 22

Graves. Whose heavy hand hath bow'd you to the grave And beggar'd yours . *Macbeth* iii 1 90

Duncan is in his grave: After life's fitful fever he sleeps well . iii 2 22

If charnel-houses and our graves must send Those that we bury back, our monuments Shall be the maws of kites . iii 4 71

It cannot Be call'd our mother, but our grave; where nothing, But who knows nothing, is once seen to smile . iv 3 166

I tell you yet again, Banquo's buried; he cannot come out on's grave . v 1 71

The graves stood tenantless and the sheeted dead Did squeak and gibber in the Roman streets . *Hamlet* i 1 115

There needs no ghost, my lord, come from the grave To tell us this . i 5 125

Will you walk out of the air, my lord?—Into my grave . ii 2 210

This counsellor Is now most still, most secret and most grave . iii 4 214

For a fantasy and trick of fame, Go to their graves like beds . iv 4 62

Which bewept to the grave did go With true-love showers . iv 5 38

And in his grave rain'd many a tear . iv 5 166

Make her grave straight: the crowner hath sat on her, and finds it Christian burial . v 1 4

I will speak to this fellow. Whose grave's this, sirrah?—Mine, sir . v 1 127

I thought thy bride-bed to have deck'd, sweet maid, And not have strew'd thy grave . v 1 269

Dost thou come here to whine? To outface me with leaping in her grave? . v 1 301

This grave shall have a living monument . v 1 320

So be my grave my peace, as here I give Her father's heart from her! *Lear* i 1 127

Treachery, and all ruinous disorders, follow us disquietly to our graves i 2 124

Thou wert better in thy grave than to answer with thy uncovered body this extremity of the skies . iii 4 105

You do me wrong to take me out o' the grave . iv 7 45

Most potent, grave, and reverend signiors . *Othello* i 3 76

Ha! no more moving? Still as the grave . v 2 94

Let her die too, and give him a worse! and let worse follow worse, till the worst of all follow him laughing to his grave! . *Ant. and Cleo.* i 2 69

Rather a ditch in Egypt Be gentle grave unto me! . v 2 58

No grave upon the earth shall clip in it A pair so famous . v 2 362

They took thee for their mother, And every day do honour to her grave *Cymbeline* iii 3 105

Maids, matrons, nay, the secrets of the grave This viperous slander enters iii 4 40

Why, he but sleeps: If he be gone, he'll make his grave a bed . iv 2 216

With fairest flowers Whilst summer lasts and I live here, Fidele, I'll sweeten thy sad grave . iv 2 220

Let us bury him, And not protract with admiration what Is now due debt. To the grave! . iv 2 233

Quiet consummation have; And renowned be thy grave! . iv 2 281

Herbs that have on them cold dew o' the night Are strewings fitt'st for graves . iv 2 285

I ha' strew'd his grave, And on it said a century of prayers . iv 2 390

Let us Find out the prettiest daisied plot we can, And make him with our pikes and partisans A grave . iv 2 400

Having thrown him from your watery grave, Here to have death *Pericles* ii 1 10

Time's the king of men, He's both their parent, and he is their grave . ii 3 46

If in the world he live, we'll seek him out; If in his grave he rest, we'll find him there . ii 4 30

Nor have I time To give thee hallow'd to thy grave . iii 1 60

The purple violets, and marigolds, Shall as a carpet hang upon thy grave . iv 1 17

Thou dost look Like Patience gazing on kings' graves . v 1 139

Thou art a grave and noble counsellor, Most wise in general . v 1 184

Grave admonishments. Thy grave admonishments prevail with me *1 Hen. VI.* ii 5 98

Grave aspect. She will attend it better in thy youth Than in a nuncio's of more grave aspect . *T. Night* i 4 28

Grave belly. Your most grave belly was deliberate . *Coriolanus* i 1 132

Grave Brabantio. Most grave Brabantio, In simple and pure soul I come to you . *Othello* i 1 106

Grave citizens. Pisa renowned for grave citizens . *T. of Shrew* i 1 10

In Pisa have I often been, Pisa renowned for grave citizens . iv 2 95

Grave charm. O this false soul of Egypt! this grave charm *A. and C.* iv 12 25

Grave counsel. For then this land was famously enrich'd With politic grave counsel . *Richard III.* ii 3 20

Grave ears. Justly to your grave ears I'll present How I did thrive in this fair lady's love, And she in mine . *Othello* i 3 124

Grave elders. Please you, Most reverend and grave elders . *Coriolanus* ii 2 46

Grave fathers. Hear me, grave fathers! noble tribunes, stay! *T. An.* iii 1 1

Grave lords. Your judgements, my grave lords, Must give this cur the lie . *Coriolanus* v 6 106

Grave man. Cousin of Buckingham, and you sage, grave men *Rich. III.* iii 7 227

I must be content to bear with those that say you are reverend grave men, yet they lie deadly . *Coriolanus* ii 1 66

Ask for me to-morrow, and you shall find me a grave man *Rom. and Jul.* iii 1 102

Grave masters. Bound servants, steal! Large-handed robbers your grave masters are . *T. of Athens* iv 1 11

Grave ornaments. For clothing me in these grave ornaments *1 Hen. VI.* v 1 54

Grave sir, hail! I come To answer thy best pleasure . *Tempest* i 2 189

For some other reasons, my grave sir, Which 'tis not fit you know *W. Tale* iv 4 422

Grave tribunes, once more I entreat of you . *T. Andron.* iii 1 31

Grave wearers. Celestial habits, Methinks I so should term them, and the reverence Of the grave wearers . *W. Tale* iii 1 6

Grave weeds. And, were they but attired in grave weeds, Rome could afford no tribune like to these . *T. Andron.* iii 1 43

Grave witnesses. My frosty signs and chaps of age, Grave witnesses of true experience . v 3 78

Graved. Let's see once more this saying graved in gold . *Mer. of Venice* ii 7 36

And lie full low, graved in the hollow ground . *Richard II.* iii 2 140

Gravel Unfit to live or die: O gravel heart! . *Meas. for Meas.* iv 3 68

As c[illegible] as founts in July when We see each grain of gravel *Hen. VIII.* i 1 155

Loads [illegible]' gravel i' the back, lethargies, cold palsies . *Troi. and Cres.* v 1 22

Graveless. My brave Egyptians all, By the discandying of this pelleted storm, Lie graveless . *Ant. and Cleo.* iii 13 166

Gravelled. When you were gravelled for lack of matter . *As Y. Like It* iv 1 74

Gravely. If thou dost it half so gravely, so majestically . *1 Hen. IV.* ii 4 478

Grave-maker. There is no ancient gentlemen but gardeners, ditchers, and grave-makers . *Hamlet* v 1 34

Say 'a grave-maker:' the houses that he makes last till doomsday . v 1 66

How long hast thou been a grave-maker? . v 1 154

Grave-making. Has this fellow no feeling of his business, that he sings at grave-making? . v 1 74

Graven. Hidest thou that forehead with a golden crown, Where should be graven, if that right were right, The slaughter of the prince? *Richard III.* iv 4 141

Graveness. His sables and his weeds, Importing health and graveness *Hamlet* iv 7 82
Graver. We two will walk, my lord, And leave you to your graver steps *W. Tale* i 2 173
Let some graver eye Pierce into that . . . . *Hen. VIII.* i 1 67
Against a graver bench Than ever frown'd in Greece . *Coriolanus* iii 1 106
Our graver business Frowns at this levity . . *Ant. and Cleo.* ii 7 127
To the more mature A glass that feated them, and to the graver A child that guided dotards . . . . *Cymbeline* i 1 49
This is but a custom in your tongue; you bear a graver purpose, I hope i 4 151
Gravest. The generous and gravest citizens Have hent the gates *Meas. for Meas.* iv 6 13
Grave-stone. Lie where the light foam of the sea may beat Thy grave-stone daily . . . . *T. of Athens* iv 3 380
Thither come, And let my grave-stone be your oracle . . v 1 222
And on his grave-stone this insculpture, which With wax I brought away . . . . v 4 67
Gravity. Is at most odds with his own gravity and patience *Mer. Wives* iii 1 54
I have lived fourscore years and upward; I never heard a man of his place, gravity and learning, so wide of his own respect . iii 1 57
My gravity, Wherein—let no man hear me—I take pride *Meas. for Meas.* ii 4 9
How ill agrees it with your gravity To counterfeit thus grossly! *Com. of Errors* ii 2 170
The blood of youth burns not with such excess As gravity's revolt to wantonness . . . . *L. L. Lost* v 2 74
Have misbecomed our oaths and gravities . . . . v 2 778
To be dress'd in an opinion Of wisdom, gravity . *Mer. of Venice* i 1 92
'Tis not for gravity to play at cherry-pit with Satan . *T. Night* iii 4 129
What doth gravity out of his bed at midnight? . . . *1 Hen. IV.* ii 4 325
There is not a white hair on your face but should have his effect of gravity . . . . *2 Hen. IV.* i 2 183
With my weak wit, And to such men of gravity and learning *Hen. VIII.* iii 1 73
Peace, you mumbling fool! Utter your gravity o'er a gossip's bowl *Rom. and Jul.* iii 5 175
Our youths and wildness shall no whit appear, But all be buried in his gravity.—O, name him not . . . . . *J. Cæsar* ii 1 149
The gravity and stillness of your youth The world hath noted *Othello* ii 3 191
Gravy. His effect of gravity.—His effect of gravy, gravy . *2 Hen. IV.* i 2 184
Gray. *See* Grey
Graymalkin. I come, Graymalkin!—Paddock calls . . . *Macbeth* i 1 8
Gray's Inn. One Sampson Stockfish, a fruiterer, behind Gray's Inn *2 Hen. IV.* iii 2 36
Graze. About the sixth hour; when beasts most graze *L. L. Lost* i 1 238
I am shepherd to another man And do not shear the fleeces that I graze *As Y. Like It* ii 4 79
The greatest of my pride is to see my ewes graze and my lambs suck . iii 2 81
Graze where you will, you shall not house with me. *Rom. and Jul.* iii 5 190
Like to the empty ass, to shake his ears, And graze in commons *J. Cæsar* iv 1 27
Whose solid virtue The shot of accident, nor dart of chance, Could neither graze nor pierce . . . . . . *Othello* iv 1 279
You have locks upon you; So graze as you find pasture . *Cymbeline* v 4 2
Grazed. When Jacob grazed his uncle Laban's sheep . *Mer. of Venice* i 3 72
Grazing. I should leave grazing, were I of your flock, And only live by gazing . . . . *W. Tale* iv 4 109
Like to the bullet's grazing, Break out into a second course of mischief *Hen. V.* iv 3 105
Grease. Till the wicked fire of lust have melted him in his own grease *Mer. Wives* ii 1 69
Stinking clothes that fretted in their own grease . . . iii 5 116
I was more than half stewed in grease, like a Dutch dish . . iii 5 121
She's the kitchen wench and all grease . . *Com. of Errors* iii 2 97
Is not the grease of a mutton as wholesome as the sweat of a man? *As Y. Like It* iii 2 57
Greases his pure mind, That from it all consideration slips *T. of Athens* iv 3 195
Grease that's sweaten From the murderer's gibbet throw Into the flame *Macbeth* iv 1 65
Greasily. Come, come, you talk greasily; your lips grow foul *L. L. Lost* iv 1 139
Greasy. Let's consult together against this greasy knight *Mer. Wives* ii 1 112
Foul shirts and smocks, socks, foul stockings, greasy napkins . iii 5 92
While greasy Joan doth keel the pot. . . . *L. L. Lost* v 2 930
Sweep on, you fat and greasy citizens; 'Tis just the fashion *As Y. Like It* ii 1 55
We are still handling our ewes, and their fells, you know, are greasy . iii 2 55
Thou knotty-pated fool, thou whoreson, obscene, greasy tallow-catch *1 Hen. IV.* ii 4 252
The bits and greasy relics Of her o'er-eaten faith . *Troi. and Cres.* v 2 159
That made the air unwholesome, when you cast Your stinking greasy caps . . . . *Coriolanus* iv 6 131
Mechanic slaves With greasy aprons, rules, and hammers *Ant. and Cleo.* v 2 210
Great. A falsehood in its contrary as great As my trust was . *Tempest* i 2 95
You the like loss!—As great to me as late . . . . v 1 145
And, of so great a favour growing proud . . *T. G. of Ver.* ii 4 161
Let there be some more test made of my metal, Before so noble and so great a figure Be stamp'd upon it . . . . *Meas. for Meas.* i 1 50
The poor beetle, that we tread upon, In corporal sufferance finds a pang as great As when a giant dies . . . . . . iii 1 80
There is so great a fever on goodness, that the dissolution of it must cure it . . . . iii 2 235
How darest thou trust So great a charge from thine own custody? *Com. of Errors* i 2 61
As great a soil in the new gloss of your marriage . . *Much Ado* iii 2 5
If my face were but as fair as yours, My favour were as great *L. L. Lost* v 2 33
Pompey surnamed the Big,— The Great.—It is, 'Great,' sir . . v 2 554
I hope I was perfect: I made a little fault in 'Great' . . v 2 562
Greater than great, great, great, great Pompey! Pompey the Huge! . v 2 691
When I thought What harm a wind too great at sea might do *Mer. of Ven.* i 1 24
'Tis a word too great for any mouth of this age's size . *As Y. Like It* iii 2 239
Their love is not so great, Hortensio, but we may blow our nails together, and fast it fairly out . . . . . . *T. of Shrew* i 1 108
That gives not half so great a blow to hear As will a chestnut in a farmer's fire . . . . i 2 209
If you accept them, then their worth is great . . . . ii 1 102
Though little fire grows great with little wind. . . . ii 1 135
Too little payment for so great a debt . . . . . v 2 154
My mind hath been as big as one of yours, My heart as great . v 2 171
Whose skill was almost as great as his honesty . . *All's Well* i 1 21
Believing thee a vessel of too great a burthen . . . ii 3 216
He is very great in knowledge and accordingly valiant . . ii 5 9
Let that go: My haste is very great: farewell; hie home . . ii 5 81
Great in our hope, lay our best love and credence Upon thy promising fortune . . . . iii 3 2

Great. He might at some great and trusty business in a main danger fail you . . . . *All's Well* iii 6 16
You have show'd me that which well approves You're great in fortune. iii 7 14
Not altogether so great as the first in goodness, but greater a great deal in evil . . . . iv 3 320
If my heart were great, 'Twould burst at this . . . . iv 3 366
I can serve as great a prince as you are . . . . . . iv 5 39
Some are born great, some achieve greatness, and some have greatness thrust upon 'em *T. Night* ii 5; iii 4; v 1
I do I know not what, and fear to find Mine eye too great a flatterer for my mind . . . . *T. Night* i 5 328
Say that some lady, as perhaps there is, Hath for your love as great a pang of heart . . . . ii 4 93
The matter, I hope, is not great, sir, begging but a beggar . iii 1 61
Be that thou know'st thou art, and then thou art As great as that thou fear'st . . . . v 1 153
As she's rare, Must it [his jealousy] be great . . *W. Tale* i 2 453
As well as one so great and so forlorn May hold together . ii 2 22
Kneel thou down Philip, but rise more great, Arise sir Richard *K. John* i 1 161
At thy birth, dear boy, Nature and Fortune join'd to make thee great . iii 1 52
My grief's so great That no supporter but the huge firm earth Can hold it up . . . . iii 1 71
Thou wretch, thou coward! Thou little valiant, great in villany! . iii 1 116
As little prince, having so great a title To be more prince, as may be . iv 1 10
Why look you sad? Be great in act, as you have been in thought . v 1 45
Inferior eyes, That borrow their behaviours from the great, Grow great v 1 51
What doth our cousin lay to Mowbray's charge? It must be great that can inherit us So much as of a thought of ill in him . *Richard II.* i 1 85
For our coffers, with too great a court And liberal largess, are grown somewhat light . . . . i 4 43
My heart is great; but it must break with silence, Ere't be disburden'd ii 1 228
Base men by his endowments are made great . . . . ii 3 139
Through our security, Grows strong and great in substance and in power iii 2 35
Strives Bolingbroke to be as great as we? Greater he shall not be . iii 2 97
O that I were as great As is my grief, or lesser than my name! . iii 3 136
Had he done so to great and growing men, They might have lived to bear . . . . iii 4 61
Being so great, I have no need to beg.—Yet ask.—And shall I have?—You shall . . . . iv 1 309
And your whole plot too light for the counterpoise of so great an opposition . . . . *1 Hen. IV.* ii 3 14
When men restrain their breath On some great sudden hest . . ii 3 65
The powers of us may serve so great a day . . . . iv 1 132
Grew by our feeding to so great a bulk . . . . . v 1 62
Would to God Thy name in arms were now as great as mine! . v 4 70
If I do grow great, I'll grow less; for I'll purge, and leave sack . v 4 168
You are too great to be by me gainsaid: Your spirit is too true *2 Hen. IV.* i 1 91
Your means are very slender, and your waste is great . . i 2 160
In the perfumed chambers of the great, Under the canopies of costly state . . . . iii 1 12
Great and puffed up with this retinue, doth any deed of courage . iv 3 121
I will be the man yet that shall make you great . . . v 5 85
Spirits that have dared On this unworthy scaffold to bring forth So great an object . . . . *Hen. V.* Prol. 11
Not ready To raise so great a siege . . . . . iii 3 47
This becomes the great . . . . iii 5 55
The perdition of th' athversary hath been very great, reasonable great . iii 6 104
I would not lose so great an honour . . . . . . iv 3 31
I pray you, is not pig great? the pig, or the great, or the mighty, or the huge . . . . iv 7 16
Was ever known so great and little loss On one part and on the other? . . . . iv 8 115
Great is the rumour of this dreadful knight, And his achievements *1 Hen. VI.* ii 3 7
And think me honoured To feast so great a warrior in my house . ii 3 82
Before whose glory I was great in arms . . . . . ii 5 24
I have heard you preach That malice was a great and grievous sin. . iii 1 128
Let me stay; and, father, do you fly: Your loss is great . . v 5 22
From the great and new-made Duke of Suffolk . . . *2 Hen. VI.* i 2 95
If they were known, as the suspect is great, Would make thee quickly hop . . . . i 3 139
Great is his comfort in this earthly vale . . . . . ii 1 70
Poor soul, God's goodness hath been great to thee . . . ii 1 84
Would ye not think his cunning to be great, that could restore this cripple? . . . . ii 1 133
In sight of God and us, your guilt is great . . . . ii 3 2
By devilish policy art thou grown great . . . . . iv 1 83
I seek not to wax great by others' waning, Or gather wealth, I care not iv 10 22
Why thou . . . Should raise so great a power without his leave . v 1 21
Scarce can I speak, my choler is so great. . . . . v 1 23
Though the odds be great, I doubt not, uncle, of our victory. *3 Hen. VI.* i 2 72
Thou art no Atlas for so great a weight . . . . . v 1 36
A thousand hearts are great within my bosom. . . *Richard III.* v 3 347
Think you see them great, And follow'd with the general throng *Hen. VIII.* Prol. 27
To whom as great a charge as little honour He meant to lay upon . i 1 77
And one as great as you are? Why, what a shame was this! . v 3 140
Her ashes new create another heir, As great in admiration as herself . v 5 43
Shall star-like rise, as great in fame as she was, And so stand fix'd . v 5 47
Let it please both, Thou great, and wise, to hear Ulysses speak *Troi. and Cres.* i 3 69
Weigh you the worth and honour of a king So great as our dread father in a scale Of common ounces? . . . . ii 2 27
Then marvel not, thou great and complete man . . . iii 3 181
In the extremity of great and little, Valour and pride excel themselves. iv 5 78
It is decreed Hector the great must die . . . . . v 7 8
The dearth is great; The people mutinous . . . *Coriolanus* i 2 10
Thou hast made my heart Too great for what contains it . . v 6 104
And might not gain so great a happiness As have thy love *T. Andron.* ii 4 20
To see so great a lord Basely insinuate . . . . . iv 2 37
Sly frantic wretch, that holp'st to make me great, In hope thyself should govern Rome and me . . . . iv 4 59
My master is the great rich Capulet . . . . *Rom. and Jul.* i 2 84
Pardon, good Mercutio, my business was great . . . ii 4 54
Having great and instant occasion to use fifty talents *T. of Athens* iii 1 18
O my lords, As you are great, be pitifully good . . . iii 5 52
Go great with tigers, dragons, wolves, and bears; Teem with new monsters! . . . . iv 3 189
Upon what meat doth this our Cæsar feed, That he is grown so great? *J. Cæsar* i 2 150

Great. Think not, thou noble Roman, That ever Brutus will go bound to Rome; He bears too great a mind . . . . . *J. Cæsar* v 1 113
The gods defend him from so great a shame! . . . . v 4 23
Thou wouldst be great; Art not without ambition . . . *Macbeth* i 5 19
By these I see, So great a day as this is cheaply bought . . . v 8 37
Where love is great, the littlest doubts are fear; Where little fears grow great, great love grows there . . . . . *Hamlet* iii 2 181
Rightly to be great Is not to stir without great argument . . . iv 4 53
Sith that both charge and danger Speak 'gainst so great a number *Lear* ii 4 243
To quarrel with your great opposeless wills . . . . iv 6 38
With as little a web as this will I ensnare as great a fly as Cassio *Othello* ii 1 170
It gives me wonder great as my content To see you here before me . ii 1 185
Though peradventure I stand accountant for as great a sin . . . ii 1 302
And your name is great In mouths of wisest censure . . . . ii 3 192
That which combined us was most great . . . *Ant. and Cleo.* ii 2 18
What is his strength by land?—Great and increasing . . . . ii 2 165
A lower place, note well, May make too great an act . . . . iii 1 13
When one so great begins to rage, he's hunted Even to falling . . iv 1 7
Our size of sorrow, Proportion'd to our cause, must be as great As that which makes it . . . . iv 15 5
Antony is dead.—The breaking of so great a thing should make A greater crack . . . . v 1 14
It is great To do that thing that ends all other deeds . . . . v 2 4
Your loss is as yourself, great; and you bear it As answering to the weight . . . . v 2 101
Thou art then As great as is thy master . . . . . *Cymbeline* i 5 51
Jewels Of rich and exquisite form; their values great . . . . i 6 190
Fear no more the frown o' the great; Thou art past the tyrant's stroke . . . . iv 2 264
Great the slaughter is Here made by the Roman; great the answer be Britons must take . . . . v 3 78
Since he's so great can make his will his act . . . . *Pericles* i 2 18
All poverty was scorn'd, and pride so great, The name of help grew odious . . . . i 4 30
It pleaseth you, my royal father, to express My commendations great . ii 2 9
Neither in our hearts nor outward eyes Envy the great nor do the low despise . . . . ii 3 26
For though This king were great, his greatness was no guard To bar heaven's shaft, but sin had his reward . . . . . . ii 4 14
May be, nor can I think the contrary, As great in blood as I myself . ii 5 80
My recompense is thanks, that's all; Yet my good will is great . . iii 4 18
Late Advanced in time to great and high estate . . . . . iv 4 14
Great abatement. There's a great abatement of kindness . . *Lear* i 4 64
Great ability. He fills it up with great ability . . . *Othello* iii 3 247
Great accompt. And let us, ciphers to this great accompt, On your imaginary forces work . . . . *Hen. V.* Prol. 17
Great Achilles Doth long to see unarm'd the valiant Hector *Troi. and Cres.* iv 5 152
Great Achilles Is arming, weeping, cursing, vowing vengeance . . v 5 30
Great action. He sold the blood and labour Of our great action *Coriolanus* v 6 48
Great addition. Where great additions swell's, and virtue none, It is a dropsied honour . . . . *All's Well* ii 3 134
And bear hence A great addition earned in thy death . *Troi. and Cres.* iv 5 141
Great admittance. Of great admittance, authentic in your place and person . . . . *Mer. Wives* ii 2 235
Great ado. We'll keep no great ado,—a friend or two . *Rom. and Jul.* iii 4 23
Great affairs. And for these great affairs do ask some charge *Richard II.* ii 1 159
My friends and brethren in these great affairs . . . . 2 *Hen. IV.* iv 1 6
My lord is cold in great affairs, Too full of foolish pity . 2 *Hen. VI.* iii 1 224
I was a pack-horse in his great affairs . . . . *Richard III.* i 3 122
Great affections wrestling in thy bosom . . . . . *K. John* v 2 41
Great affinity. Of great fame in Cyprus And great affinity . *Othello* iii 1 49
Great affliction. In most great affliction of spirit . . *Hamlet* iii 2 323
And, in your sights, Shake patiently my great affliction off . . *Lear* iv 6 36
Great Agamemnon. With due observance of thy godlike seat, Great Agamemnon . . . . *Troi. and Cres.* i 3 32
Sometime, great Agamemnon, Thy topless deputation he puts on . . i 3 151
Great Agamemnon comes to meet us here . . . . . . iv 5 159
Great aim. The foeman may with as great aim level at the edge of a penknife . . . . 2 *Hen. IV.* iii 2 285
Great Ajax. But our great Ajax bravely beat down him *Troi. and Cres.* iii 3 213
Jove bless great Ajax!—Hum! . . . . iii 3 281
Great Albion's queen in former golden days . . . 3 *Hen. VI.* iii 3 7
Great Alcides. It lies as sightly on the back of him As great Alcides' shows upon an ass . . . . *K. John* ii 1 144
But where's the great Alcides of the field? . . . 1 *Hen. VI.* iv 7 60
Nor great Alcides, nor the god of war, Shall seize this . *T. Andron.* iv 2 95
Great Alexander. The crown will find an heir: great Alexander Left his to the worthiest . . . . *W. Tale* v 1 47
Great alliance. How can tyrants safely govern home, Unless abroad they purchase great alliance? . . . . . 3 *Hen. VI.* iii 3 70
Great allies. You to your land and love and great allies *As Y. Like It* v 4 195
Great amazedness. We two in great amazedness will fly *Mer. Wives* iv 4 55
Great amiss. Each toy seems prologue to some great amiss . *Hamlet* iv 5 18
Great ancestor. [Censorinus] . . . Was his great ancestor . *Coriolanus* ii 3 253
As Æneas, our great ancestor, Did from the flames of Troy upon his shoulder The old Anchises bear . . . . *J. Cæsar* i 2 112
Great anchors. Wedges of gold, great anchors, heaps of pearl *Richard III.* i 4 26
Great Andronicus. Brave slip, sprung from the great Andronicus *T. Andron.* v 1 9
Great Antiochus. That would be son to great Antiochus . *Pericles* i 1 26
The great Antiochus, 'Gainst whom I am too little to contend . . i 2 16
Great Apollo suddenly will have The truth of this appear . *W. Tale* ii 3 200
Great Apollo Turn all to the best! . . . . iii 1 14
This seal'd-up oracle, by the hand deliver'd Of great Apollo's priest . iii 2 129
Now blessed be the great Apollo!—Praised! . . . . . iii 2 138
Great appropriation. He makes it a great appropriation to his own good parts . . . . *Mer. of Venice* i 2 46
Great argosies. No less Than three great argosies . . *T. of Shrew* ii 1 380
Great argument. It is no addition to her wit, nor no great argument of her folly . . . . *Much Ado* ii 3 243
I shall be forsworn, which is a great argument of falsehood, if I love *L. L. Lost* i 2 175
This was a great argument of love in her toward you . . *T. Night* iii 2 12
Rightly to be great Is not to stir without great argument . *Hamlet* iv 4 54
Great arithmetician. A great arithmetician . . . . . *Othello* i 1 19
Great article. I take him to be a soul of great article . . *Hamlet* v 2 122
Great aspect. Under the allowance of your great aspect . . *Lear* ii 2 112
Great assay. Their malady convinces The great assay of art . *Macbeth* iv 3 143
Great assembly. By whom this great assembly is contrived . *Hen. V.* v 2 6
Great attempt. In this haughty great attempt They laboured 1 *Hen. VI.* ii 5 79
Great attraction. The sun's a thief, and with his great attraction Robs the vast sea . . . . *T. of Athens* iv 3 439
Great attributes. If I should swear by God's great attributes, I loved you dearly, would you believe my oaths? . . . *All's Well* iv 2 25
Great Aufidius. Able to bear against the great Aufidius A shield as hard as his . . . . *Coriolanus* i 6 79
Great Augustus. Your king Hath heard of great Augustus . *Cymbeline* ii 4 11
Great authority. By his great authority . . . . . *W. Tale* ii 1 53
He seems to be of great authority: close with him . . . . iv 4 830
A man of great authority in France . . . . . 1 *Hen. VI.* v 1 18
Of such great authority in France As his alliance will confirm our peace . . . . v 5 41
Great axe. Where the offence is let the great axe fall . . *Hamlet* iv 5 218
Great baby. That great baby you see there is not yet out of his swaddling-clouts . . . . ii 2 400
Great behest. Let us with care perform his great behest . *Cymbeline* v 4 122
Great-bellied, and longing, as I said, for prunes . *Meas. for Meas.* ii 1 102
Great-bellied women, That had not half a week to go . *Hen. VIII.* iv 1 76
Great belly. I am the fellow with the great belly, and he my dog 2 *Hen. IV.* i 2 165
The fat knight with the great-belly doublet . . . . *Hen. V.* iv 7 51
O, they eat lords; so they come by great bellies . . *T. of Athens* i 1 210
Great benefactors, sprinkle our society with thankfulness . . . iii 6 79
Great bidding. Denies his person At our great bidding? . *Macbeth* iii 4 129
Great Birnam wood. Until Great Birnam wood to high Dunsinane hill Shall come against him . . . . iv 1 93
Great birth. For then I should not love thee, no, nor thou Become thy great birth . . . . *K. John* iii 1 50
Great body. That the great body of our state may go In equal rank with the best govern'd nation . . . . . . 2 *Hen. IV.* v 2 136
Great Bolingbroke. But in the balance of great Bolingbroke, Besides himself, are all the English peers . . . . *Richard II.* iii 4 87
That my sad look Should grace the triumph of great Bolingbroke . . iii 4 99
Great Bolingbroke, Mounted upon a hot and fiery steed . . . v 2 7
He doth bestride a bleeding land, Gasping for life under great Bolingbroke 2 *Hen. IV.* i 1 208
Great bond. Cancel and tear to pieces that great bond Which keeps me pale! . . . . *Macbeth* iii 2 49
Great bounty. I thank thee, king, For thy great bounty *Richard II.* iv 1 300
Great breach. However, yet there is no great breach . *Hen. VIII.* iv 1 106
O you kind gods, Cure this great breach in his abused nature! . *Lear* iv 7 15
Great buildings. Who can speak broader than he that has no house to put his head in? such may rail against great buildings *T. of Athens* iii 4 65
Great bulk. Though the great bulk Achilles be thy guard, I'll cut thy throat . . . . *Troi. and Cres.* iv 4 130
Great burthen. I cannot weep; . . . Nor can my tongue unload my heart's great burthen . . . . 3 *Hen. VI.* ii 1 81
Great business. You shall put This night's great business into my dispatch . . . . *Macbeth* i 5 69
Great business must be wrought ere noon . . . . . iii 5 22
You think I will your serious and great business scant . . *Othello* i 3 268
Great buyer. This fellow might be in's time a great buyer of land *Hamlet* v 1 112
Great Cæsar. Speak to great Cæsar as he comes along . *J. Cæsar* ii 4 38
Mine's a suit That touches Cæsar nearer: read it, great Cæsar . . iii 1 7
Is there no voice . . . To sound more sweetly in great Cæsar's ear? . iii 1 50
Great Cæsar,— Doth not Brutus bootless kneel? . . . . iii 1 75
Great Cæsar fell. O, what a fall was there, my countrymen! . . iii 2 193
All the conspirators save only he Did that they did in envy of great Cæsar v 5 70
Royal wench! She made great Cæsar lay his sword to bed *Ant. and Cleo.* ii 2 232
Say to great Cæsar this: in deputation I kiss his conquering hand . iii 13 74
That I might hear thee call great Cæsar ass Unpolicied! . . . v 2 310
Great cannon. The great cannon to the clouds shall tell . *Hamlet* i 2 126
Great captain. She that I spake of, our great captain's captain *Othello* ii 1 74
Great cardinals. The two great cardinals Wait . . . *Hen. VIII.* iii 1 16
Great care. The great care of goods at random left . *Com. of Errors* i 1 43
It seems he hath great care to please his wife . . . . . ii 1 56
My life itself . . . Thanks you for this great care . . *Hen. VIII.* i 2 2
My good lord, have great care I be not found a talker . . . ii 2 78
Great carriage. He was a man of good carriage, great carriage *L. L. Lost* i 2 74
Great catch. Hector shall have a great catch . . *Troi. and Cres.* i 1 110
Great cause. A great cause of the night is lack of the sun *As Y. Like It* iii 2 29
We therefore have great cause of thankfulness . . . *Hen. V.* ii 2 32
We have no great cause to desire the approach of day . . . iv 1 89
We have all Great cause to give great thanks . . . *Coriolanus* v 4 63
Though, between them [women] and a great cause, they should be esteemed nothing . . . . *Ant. and Cleo.* i 2 143
Great chairs. Now breathless wrong Shall sit and pant in your great chairs of ease . . . . *T. of Athens* v 4 11
Great Cham. Fetch you a hair off the great Cham's beard . *Much Ado* ii 1 277
Great chamber. Or I would I might never come in mine own great chamber again . . . . *Mer. Wives* i 1 157
You are looked for and called for . . . in the great chamber *Rom. and Jul.* i 5 14
Leave a casement of the great chamber window, where we play, open *M. N. Dream* iii 1 58
Great charge. 'Tis a great charge to come under one body's hand *Mer. Wives* i 4 104
Are you avised o' that? you shall find it a great charge . . . i 4 107
They will along with company, for they have great charge . 1 *Hen IV.* ii 1 51
And many such-like 'As'es of great charge . . . . *Hamlet* v 2 43
Great Charlemain. To give great Charlemain a pen in's hand *All's Well* ii 1 80
Great charms. Now the fair goddess, Fortune, Fall deep in love with thee; and her great charms Misguide thy opposers' swords! *Coriolanus* i 5 22
Great chief. Farewell, great chief. Shall I strike now? *Ant. and Cleo.* iv 14 93
Great child. The great child of honour, Cardinal Wolsey *Hen. VIII.* iv 2 6
Great clatter. By this great clatter, one of greatest note Seems bruited. Let me find him, fortune! . . . . *Macbeth* v 7 21
Great clerks have purposed To greet me with premeditated welcomes *M. N. Dream* v 1 93
Great Cœur-de-lion. In this late-betrayed town Great Cœur-de-lion's heart was buried . . . . 1 *Hen. VI.* iii 2 83
Great coil. For the wedding being there to-morrow, there is a great coil to-night . . . . *Much Ado* iii 3 100
Great combatant. That the appalled air May pierce the head of the great combatant . . . . *Troi. and Cres.* iv 5 5
Great comfort. I have great comfort from this fellow . *Tempest* i 1 30
To thy great comfort in this mystery of ill opinions . *Mer. Wives* ii 1 72
Good Paulina, the great comfort That I have had of thee! . *W. Tale* v 3 1
Great command. Still subsisting Under your great command *Coriolanus* v 6 74
But that great command o'ersways the order . . . . *Hamlet* v 1 251
Great commander. And such fellows are perfect in the great commanders' names . . . . *Hen. V.* iii 6 73

Great commander. The vulture of sedition Feeds in the bosom of such great commanders . . . . 1 *Hen. VI.* iv 3 48
Agamemnon, Thou great commander, nerve and bone of Greece *Troi. and Cres.* i 3 55
Great commanding Warwick Is thither gone . . . . 3 *Hen. VI.* iii 1 29
Great commission. From whom hast thou this great commission? *K. John* ii 1 110
Great competitor. It is not Cæsar's natural vice to hate Our great competitor . . . . *Ant. and Cleo.* i 4 3
Great compt. That thou didst love her, strikes some scores away From the great compt . . . . *All's Well* v 3 57
Great confusion. Then shall the realm of Albion Come to great confusion: Then comes the time . . . . . . *Lear* iii 2 92
Great constancy. And grows to something of great constancy *M. N. D.* v 1 26
Great Constantine. Helen, the mother of great Constantine 1 *Hen. VI.* i 2 142
Great contention. The great contention of the sea and skies Parted our fellowship . . . . *Othello* ii 1 92
Great count. Or to the worth Of the great count himself *All's Well* iii 5 63
Great court. But our great court Made me to blame in memory *Cymb.* iii 5 50
Great courtier. This cannot be but a great courtier . *W. Tale* iv 4 775
Great creating. There is an art which in their piedness shares With great creating nature . . . . iv 4 88
Great creation. What great creation and what dole of honour Flies where you bid it . . . . *All's Well* ii 3 176
Great credit. That she loves him, 'tis apt and of great credit *Othello* ii 1 296
Great danger. 'Tis true that we are in great danger . *Hen. V.* iv 1 1
We'll deliver you Of your great danger . . . . *Coriolanus* v 6 15
The great danger Which this man's life did owe you . . v 6 138
When they are in great danger, I recover them . . *J. Cæsar* i 2 28
Great deal. But 'tis no matter; better a little chiding than a great deal of heart-break . . . . *Mer. Wives* v 3 11
And for a week escape a great deal of discoveries . . *All's Well* iii 6 99
Let it be forbid, sir; so should I be a great deal of his act . iv 3 55
Not altogether so great as the first in goodness, but greater a great deal in evil . . . . iv 3 321
You pay a great deal too dear for what's given freely . *W. Tale* i 1 18
A great deal of your wit, too, lies in your sinews . *Troi. and Cres.* ii 1 108
A little proudly, and great deal misprizing The knight opposed . iv 5 74
'Tis no great matter; for a very little thief of occasion will rob you of a great deal of patience . . . . . *Coriolanus* ii 1 32
How unluckily it happened, that I should purchase the day before for a little part, and undo a great deal of honour! . *T. of Athens* iii 2 53
Words him, I doubt not, a great deal from the matter . *Cymbeline* i 4 17
You are a great deal abused in too bold a persuasion . . i 4 124
Great debts. But my chief care Is to come fairly off from the great debts . . . . *Mer. of Venice* i 1 128
Great decay. What comfort to this great decay may come Shall be applied . . . . *Lear* v 3 297
Great decision. Whose great decision hath much blood let forth And more thirsts after . . . . . . *All's Well* iii 1 3
Great deeds. Forgetting thy great deeds . . *T. of Athens* iv 3 94
Great defence. And every one did bear Thy praises in his kingdom's great defence . . . . *Macbeth* i 3 99
Great defender. Thou great defender of this Capitol . *T. Andron.* i 1 77
Great deputy, the welkin's vicegerent and sole dominator . *L. L. Lost* i 1 221
In us, that are our own great deputy . . . . *K. John* ii 1 365
Great deserts. Andronicus, surnamed Pius For many good and great deserts to Rome . . . . *T. Andron.* i 1 24
Great deservings. And even those some Envy your great deservings and good name . . . . . . 1 *Hen. IV.* iv 3 35
Great designs. I have been long a sleeper; but, I hope, My absence doth neglect no great designs . . . . *Richard III.* iii 4 25
And be not peevish-fond in great designs . . . . iv 4 417
And from this hour The heart of brothers govern in our loves And sway our great designs! . . . . . *Ant. and Cleo.* ii 2 151
Great desire. I have a great desire to a bottle of hay . *M. N. Dream* iv 1 37
Since for the great desire I had To see fair Padua . . *T. of Shrew* i 1 1
Great devotion. I have no great devotion to the deed . *Othello* v 1 8
Great difference betwixt our Bohemia and your Sicilia . *W. Tale* i 1 4
Great dignity. The great dignity that his valour hath here acquired for him . . . . *All's Well* iv 3 79
Call home To high promotions and great dignity *Richard III.* iv 4 314
Great disaster. Sent it us Upon her great disaster . *All's Well* v 3 112
Great discreetly. We will afterwards ork upon the cause with as great discreetly as we can . . . . *Mer. Wives* i 1 148
Great discretion. He avoids them with great discretion . *Much Ado* ii 3 198
Great disguiser. O, death's a great disguiser . *Meas. for Meas.* iv 2 186
Great disparagement. And passed sentence may not be recall'd But to our honour's great disparagement . . . *Com. of Errors* i 1 149
Great dispositions. I have a great dispositions to cry . *Mer. Wives* iii 1 22
Great distraction. You flow to great distraction . . *Troi. and Cres.* v 2 41
Great divine. Thus by Apollo's great divine seal'd up . *W. Tale* iii 1 19
Great doers. All great doers in our trade. . *Meas. for Meas.* iv 3 20
Great doom. Up, up, and see The great doom's image! . . *Macbeth* ii 3 83
Great Douglas. This infant warrior in his enterprizes Discomfited great Douglas . . . . 1 *Hen. IV.* iii 2 114
Great Duke. This day, great duke, she shut the doors upon me *C. of Er.* v 1 204
Great Duke of Lancaster, I come to thee From plume-pluck'd Richard *Richard II.* iv 1 107
Be merciful, great duke, to men of mould . . *Hen. V.* iii 2 23
Abate thy manly rage, Abate thy rage, great duke! . . . iii 2 25
Why doth the great Duke Humphrey knit his brows? . 2 *Hen. VI.* i 2 3
To hear what shall become Of the great Duke of Buckingham *Hen. VIII.* ii 1 3
The great duke Came to the bar . . . . ii 1 11
Great Dunsinane he strongly fortifies . . . . *Macbeth* v 2 12
Great Earl of Washford, Waterford and Valence . 1 *Hen. VI.* iv 7 63
Great earnestness. The nobles in great earnestness are going All to the senate-house . . . . *Coriolanus* iv 6 57
Great eater. I am a great eater of beef . . . *T. Night* i 3 90
Great Edward. Wert thou not brother to great Edward's son *Richard II.* ii 1 121
Great Egypt. Say, the firm Roman to great Egypt sends This treasure of an oyster . . . . *Ant. and Cleo.* i 5 43
Great emperor. Saturninus Rome's great emperor . . *T. Andron.* i 1 232
Great employment. And fit for great employment . . *T. G. of Ver.* v 4 157
Thy great employment Will not bear question . . . *Lear* v 3 32
Great empress. Sweeter to me than life!—No more, great empress *T. An.* ii 3 52
Great enemy. Say their great enemy is gone . . . *Coriolanus* iv 2 6
The only son of your great enemy . . . . *Rom. and Jul.* i 5 139
Great England. To entertain great England's lawful king 2 *Hen. VI.* v 1 4
Great enterprise. A larger dare to our great enterprise . 1 *Hen. IV.* iv 1 78
Great errand. There is no lady living So meet for this great errand *W. T.* ii 2 46

Great estate. Of great estate, of fresh and stainless youth . *T. Night* i 5 278
By whose death he's stepp'd Into a great estate . . *T. of Athens* ii 2 233
Great exceptions. Your cousin, my lady, takes great exceptions to your ill hours . . . . *T. Night* i 3 6
Great exchange. Oft have you—often have you thanks therefore—Desired my Cressid in right great exchange . . *Troi. and Cres.* iii 3 21
Great expedition. Of great expedition and knowledge in th' aunchient wars . . . . *Hen. V.* iii 2 82
Great exploit. Imagination of some great exploit Drives him beyond the bounds of patience . . . . . . 1 *Hen. IV.* i 3 199
Great extremity. The queen's in labour, They say, in great extremity; and fear'd She'll with the labour end . . . *Hen. VIII.* v 1 19
Great face. You fled From that great face of war . *Ant. and Cleo.* iii 13 5
Great fail. Goodly and gallant shall be false and perjured From thy great fail . . . . *Cymbeline* iii 4 66
Great fairy. To this great fairy I'll commend thy acts . *Ant. and Cleo.* iv 8 12
Great fame. He you hurt is of great fame in Cyprus . *Othello* iii 1 48
Great father-in-law. The first that there did greet my stranger soul, Was my great father-in-law . . . . . *Richard III.* i 4 49
Great favour. He'll smile and take't for a great favour . *T. Night* iii 2 89
We thank you all for this great favour done . . 2 *Hen. VI.* ii 1 71
Great fear. So great fear of my name 'mongst them was spread 1 *Hen. VI.* i 4 50
And all great fears, which now import their dangers, Would then be nothing: truths would be tales . . . *Ant. and Cleo.* ii 2 135
Great feast. They have been at a great feast of languages . *L. L. Lost* v 1 40
If he had been forgotten, It had been as a gap in our great feast *Macbeth* iii 1 12
My news shall be the fruit to that great feast . . *Hamlet* ii 2 52
Great fellow. You great fellow, Stand close up . *Hen. VIII.* v 4 91
Let Neptune hear me bid a loud farewell To these great fellows *Ant. and Cleo.* ii 7 140
Great fights. In the scuffles of great fights hath burst The buckles . i 1 7
Great fighter. You have yourself been a great fighter . *Mer. Wives* ii 3 44
Great figure. That the great figure of a council frames . *All's Well* iii 1 12
Great fire. I am a woodland fellow, sir, that always loved a great fire . iv 5 50
The flowery way that leads to the broad gate and the great fire . iv 5 57
Great floods have flown From simple sources . . . . ii 1 142
You see this confluence, this great flood of visitors . . *T. of Athens* i 1 42
When went there by an age, since the great flood, But it was famed with more than with one man? . . . . . *J. Cæsar* i 2 152
Great flow. I have Prompted you in the ebb of your estate And your great flow of debts . . . . *T. of Athens* ii 2 151
Great folk. The more pity that great folk should have countenance in this world to drown or hang themselves . . . . *Hamlet* v 1 30
Great fool. The Lord lighten thee! thou art a great fool . 2 *Hen. IV.* ii 1 209
Great forerunner. That great forerunner of thy blood . . *K. John* ii 1 2
Great fortune. Wherein toward me my homely stars have fail'd To equal my great fortune . . . . *All's Well* ii 5 81
Thy great fortunes Are made thy chief afflictions . *T. of Athens* iv 2 43
Not nature, To whom all sores lay siege, can bear great fortune . iv 3 7
Great friend. You're shallow, madam, in great friends . . *All's Well* i 3 45
Richard and Northumberland, great friends, Did feast together 2 *Hen. IV.* iii 1 58
And no great friend, I fear me, to the king . . . 2 *Hen. VI.* i 1 150
Great gap. It would make a great gap in your own honour . *Lear* i 2 91
That I might sleep out this great gap of time . . *Ant. and Cleo.* i 5 5
Great general Of trotting 'paritors . . . . . *L. L. Lost* iii 1 187
I was advertised their great general slept . . *Troi. and Cres.* ii 2 211
Please it our great general To call together all his state of war . ii 3 270
Great gifts. He commands us to provide, and give great gifts, And all out of an empty coffer . . . . . . *T. of Athens* i 2 198
Great Glamis. Thou'ldst have, great Glamis, That which cries 'Thus thou must do, if thou have it' . . . . . *Macbeth* i 5 23
Great Glamis! worthy Cawdor! Greater than both, by the all-hail hereafter! . . . . i 5 55
Great Glendower. He did confound the best part of an hour In changing hardiment with great Glendower . . . . 1 *Hen. IV.* i 3 101
Great globe. The solemn temples, the great globe itself . . *Tempest* iv 1 153
Great glory. Arm, arm, my name! a puny subject strikes At thy great glory . . . . *Richard II.* iii 2 87
Great God, how just art Thou! . . . . 2 *Hen. VI.* v 1 68
Great God of heaven, say Amen to all! . . . *Richard III.* v 5 8
Let the great gods, That keep this dreadful pother o'er our heads, Find out their enemies now . . . . *Lear* iii 2 49
If the great gods be just, they shall assist The deeds of justest men *Ant. and Cleo.* ii 1 1
Great good. Yes, my conscience, he did us great good . *Hen. V.* iv 8 126
Great good cheer. My banquet is to close our stomachs up, After our great good cheer . . . . *T. of Shrew* v 2 10
Great good lover. He of Winchester Is held no great good lover of the archbishop's . . . . *Hen. VIII.* iv 1 104
Great grace. For your great graces Heap'd upon me, poor undeserver . iii 2 174
Of his great grace And princely care foreseeing those fell mischiefs . v 1 48
Great-grandfather. Derived from Edward, his great-grandfather *Hen. V.* i 1 89
My great-grandfather Never went with his forces into France . . i 2 146
Say unto his child, 'What my great-grandfather and grandsire got My careless father fondly gave away' . . . . 3 *Hen. VI.* ii 2 37
Great-grandsire. A little time before That our great-grandsire, Edward, sick'd and died . . . . . . 2 *Hen. IV.* iv 4 128
Go, my dread lord, to your great-grandsire's tomb . *Hen. V.* i 2 103
Great greatness. O, be sick, great greatness, And bid thy ceremony give thee cure! . . . . iv 1 268
Great grief. To our great grief we pronounce . . . *W. Tale* iii 2 1
To me and to the state of my great grief Let kings assemble . *K. John* iii 1 70
Great griefs, I see, medicine the less . . . . *Cymbeline* iv 2 243
Great grievance. Your subjects Are in great grievance . . *Hen. VIII.* i 2 20
Great gross one. 'No,' said I, 'a great wit:' 'Right,' says she, 'a great gross one' . . . . *Much Ado* v 1 163
Great-grown. Take the great-grown traitor unawares . 3 *Hen. VI.* iv 8 63
Great guilt. Their great guilt, Like poison given to work a great time after, Now 'gins to bite the spirits . . . . . *Tempest* iii 3 104
Great hand. In the great hand of God I stand . . . *Macbeth* ii 3 136
Great happiness. The victory fell on us.—Great happiness! . . i 2 58
Great harm. These same whoreson devils do the gods great harm in their women . . . . *Ant. and Cleo.* v 2 277
Great haste. Well, farewell; I am in great haste now . *Mer. Wives* i 4 174
I am now in great haste, as it may appear unto you . *Much Ado* iii 5 54
And yet the gentleman . . . pray'd me To make great haste *Hen. VIII.* v 2 3
Great heap. How prove you that, in the great heap of your knowledge?—Ay, marry, now unmuzzle . . . . . . *As Y. Like It* i 2 72
Great heart. And with a great heart heave away this storm . *K. John* v 2 55
Fare thee well, great heart! Ill-weaved ambition! . . 1 *Hen. IV.* v 4 87

Great Hector's sword had lack'd a master *Troi. and Cres.* i 3 76
You shall do more Than all the island kings,—disarm great Hector iii 1 167
Great Hector's sister did Achilles win iii 3 212
I am sick withal, To see great Hector in his weeds of peace iii 3 239
From heart of very heart, great Hector, welcome iv 5 171
Good night, great Hector.—Give me your hand v 1 90
Yet bragless let it be; Great Hector was a man as good as he v 9 6
Great Hercules. To see great Hercules whipping a gig *L. L. Lost* iv 3 167
Great Hercules is presented by this imp, Whose club kill'd Cerberus v 2 592
Leave that labour to great Hercules *T. of Shrew* i 2 257
Great Herod. There did persuade Great Herod to incline himself to Cæsar *Ant. and Cleo.* iv 6 14
Great honours. Doo's me as great honours as can be desired *Hen. V.* iv 7 167
Great hope. O, out of that 'no hope' What great hope have you! *Temp.* ii 1 240
Bid herself assay him: I have great hope in that *Meas. for Meas.* i 2 187
How might a prince of my great hopes forget So great indignities? *2 Hen. IV.* v 2 68
For, being green, there is great hope of help *2 Hen. VI.* iii 1 287
Great Hostilius. Who, after great Hostilius, here was king *Coriolanus* ii 3 248
Great hurt. Who hath done To thee particularly and to all the Volsces Great hurt iv 5 73
Great Hyperion. Burns With entertaining great Hyperion *Troi. and Cres.* ii 3 207
Great ignorance. It was great ignorance, Gloucester's eyes being out, To let him live *Lear* iv 5 9
Great Ilion. Did in great Ilion thus translate him to me *Troi. and Cres.* iv 5 112
Great image. Thou mightst behold the great image of authority *Lear* iv 6 162
Great imagination. And so, with great imagination Proper to madmen, led his powers to death *2 Hen. IV.* i 3 31
Great impeachment. Which would be great impeachment to his age, In having known no travel *T. G. of Ver.* i 3 15
Great import. Of great import indeed, too, but let that pass *L. L. Lost* v 1 105
Great importance. Maria writ The letter at Sir Toby's great importance *T. Night* v 1 371
Great indignation. At which my nose is in great indignation *Tempest* iv 1 200
Great indignities. Give me ample satisfaction For these deep shames and great indignities *Com. of Errors* v 1 253
How might a prince of my great hopes forget So great indignities? *2 Hen. IV.* v 2 69
Great infamy. Sir John, you live in great infamy i 2 157
Great infection. He hath a great infection, sir, as one would say, to serve *Mer. of Venice* ii 2 133
Great injunctions. By great injunctions I am bound *Meas. for Meas.* iv 3 100
Great Italy. Lombardy, The pleasant garden of great Italy *T. of Shrew* i 1 4
Great John of Gaunt. Then Warwick disannuls great John of Gaunt *3 Hen. VI.* iii 3 81
Great journey. O, many Have broke their backs with laying manors on 'em For this great journey *Hen. VIII.* i 1 85
Great Jove. Made great Jove to humble him to her hand *T. of Shrew* i 1 174
Nought else But the protractive trials of great Jove *Troi. and Cres.* i 3 20
Great Jove, Othello guard, And swell his sail! *Othello* ii 1 77
Great judgement. Which hath Honour'd with confirmation your great judgement In the election *Cymbeline* i 6 174
Great Julius. Did not great Julius bleed for justice' sake? *J. Cæsar* iv 3 19
Great Juno. High'st queen of state, Great Juno, comes *Tempest* iv 1 102
Wedding is great Juno's crown: O blessed bond! *As Y. Like It* v 4 147
Had I great Juno's power, . . . Mercury should fetch thee up *A. and C.* iv 15 34
Dainty trims, wherein You made great Juno angry *Cymbeline* iii 4 168
Great Jupiter be praised! Lucius is taken v 3 84
Great Jupiter, upon his eagle back'd, Appear'd to me v 5 427
In the temple of great Jupiter Our peace we'll ratify v 5 482
Great justice. His life is parallel'd Even with the stroke and line of his great justice *Meas. for Meas.* iv 2 83
Great kindred. In good sooth, the vice is of a great kindred iii 2 108
Great king, I am no strumpet, by my life *All's Well* v 3 293
A great king's daughter The mother to a hopeful prince *W. Tale* iii 2 40
Hear us, great kings: vouchsafe awhile to stay *K. John* ii 1 416
Calmly run on in obedience Even to our ocean, to our great King John v 4 57
I mock my name, great king, to flatter thee *Richard II.* ii 1 87
Good king, great king, and yet not greatly good iv 1 263
A woman, and thy aunt, great king; 'tis I. Speak with me, pity me v 3 76
Great king, within this coffin I present Thy buried fear v 6 30
Comest thou again for ransom?—No, great king *Hen. V.* iv 7 73
O, give us leave, great king, To view the field in safety! iv 7 84
My duty to you both, on equal love, Great Kings of France and England! v 2 24
O Kate, nice customs curtsy to great kings v 2 294
Great King of England and my gracious lord *2 Hen. VI.* i 1 24
The great King of kings Hath in the tables of his law commanded That thou shalt do no murder *Richard III.* i 4 200
Whence camest thou, worthy thane?—From Fife, great king *Macbeth* i 2 48
That this great king may kindly say, Our duties did his welcome pay iv 1 131
For you, great king, I would not from your love make such a stray *Lear* i 1 211
Our great king himself doth woo me oft For my confections *Cymbeline* i 5 14
Hail, great king! To sour your happiness, I must report The queen is dead v 5 25
Thou hadst, great king, a subject who Was call'd Belarius v 5 316
Great king, Few love to hear the sins they love to act *Pericles* i 1 91
Great kinsman. And, in this rage, with some great kinsman's bone, As with a club, dash out my desperate brains *Rom. and Jul.* iv 3 53
Great knowing. One of your great knowing Should learn, being taught, forbearance *Cymbeline* ii 3 102
Great land. To enjoy thy banish'd lord and this great land! ii 1 70
Great largess. Sent forth great largess to your offices *Macbeth* ii 1 14
Great leading. Being men of such great leading as you are *1 Hen. IV.* iv 3 17
Great leaves. When great leaves fall, the winter is at hand *Richard III.* ii 3 33
Great letters. In such great letters as they write, 'Here is good horse to hire' *Much Ado* i 1 267
Great liberty. He hath good usage and great liberty *3 Hen. VI.* iv 5 6
Great like. Say that he thrive, as 'tis great like he will *2 Hen. VI.* iii 1 379
Great limb. This swain, because of his great limb or joint, shall pass Pompey the Great *L. L. Lost* v 1 135
Great lord. By me entreats, great lord, thou wouldst vouchsafe To visit her poor castle *1 Hen. VI.* ii 2 40
Great lords and gentlemen, what means this silence? ii 4 1
Then judge, great lords, if I have done amiss iv 1 27
These great lords and Margaret our queen Do seek subversion of thy harmless life? Thou never didst them wrong *2 Hen. VI.* iii 1 207
Great lords, from Ireland am I come amain iii 1 282
The great Lord of Northumberland . . . Cheer'd up the drooping army *3 Hen. VI.* i 1 4
Great Lord of Warwick, if we should recount Our baleful news ii 1 96

Great lord. Great lords, wise men ne'er sit and wail their loss *3 Hen. VI.* v 4 1
Thou art, great lord, my father's sister's son *Troi. and Cres.* iv 5 120
Great lords, be, as your titles witness, Imperious *T. Andron.* v 1 5
In some work, some dedication To the great lord *T. of Athens* i 1 20
Great loss. You may thank yourself for this great loss *Tempest* ii 1 123
Great love. If there be no great love in the beginning, yet heaven may decrease it upon better acquaintance *Mer. Wives* i 1 254
My wish receive, Which great Love grant! *All's Well* ii 3 91
They think my little stomach to the war And your great love to me restrains you thus *Troi. and Cres.* iii 3 221
His great love, sharp as his spur, hath holp him To his home before us *Macbeth* i 6 23
Where little fears grow great, great love grows there *Hamlet* iii 2 182
The other motive . . . Is the great love the general gender bear him iv 7 18
I cannot be so partial, Goneril, To the great love I bear you *Lear* i 4 335
You shall be well desired in Cyprus; I have found great love amongst them *Othello* ii 1 207
Great lubber. This great lubber, the world *T. Night* iv 1 14
Great lubberly boy. And she's a great lubberly boy *Mer. Wives* v 5 195
Great magician. Whom he reports to be a great magician *As Y. Like It* v 4 33
That great magician, damn'd Glendower *1 Hen. IV.* i 3 83
Great maker. Peace is a great maker of cuckolds *Coriolanus* iv 5 244
Great man. Could great men thunder As Jove himself does, Jove would ne'er be quiet *Meas. for Meas.* ii 2 110
Great men may jest with saints; 'tis wit in them ii 2 127
What great men have been in love? *L. L. Lost* i 2 68
He has heard that word of some great man *T. Night* iv 1 13
A great man, I'll warrant; I know by the picking on's teeth *W. Tale* iv 4 779
Small curs are not regarded when they grin; But great men tremble when the lion roars *2 Hen. VI.* iii 1 19
Great men oft die by vile bezonians iv 1 134
Great men have reaching hands: oft have I struck Those that I never saw iv 7 86
Nor build their evils on the graves of great men *Hen. VIII.* ii 1 67
Can thy spirit wonder A great man should decline? iii 2 375
There have been many great men that have flattered the people *Coriol.* ii 2 8
Great men should drink with harness on their throats *T. of Athens* i 2 53
Great men shall press For tinctures, stains, relics and cognizance *J. C.* ii 2 88
Even so great men great losses should endure iv 3 193
There's hope a great man's memory may outlive his life half a year *Ham.* iii 2 140
The great man down, you mark his favourite flies iii 2 214
Lords and great men will not let me *Lear* i 4 166
This it is to have a name in great men's fellowship *Ant. and Cleo.* ii 7 13
Great men, That had a court no bigger than this cave *Cymbeline* iii 6 82
Great Mark Antony is now a widower *Ant. and Cleo.* ii 2 121
Great Mars, I put myself into thy file *All's Well* iii 3 9
And drave great Mars to faction *Troi. and Cres.* iii 3 190
He was a soldier good; But, by great Mars, the captain of us all, Never like thee iv 5 198
Great marshal to Henry the Sixth *1 Hen. VI.* iv 7 70
Great marvel. Sing, boy; my spirit grows heavy in love.—And that's great marvel *L. L. Lost* i 2 128
Great master. All hail, great master! grave sir, hail! *Tempest* i 2 189
Great Master of France, the brave Sir Guichard Dolphin *Hen. V.* iv 8 100
Bending his sword To his great master *Lear* iv 2 75
Great matter. There's some great matter she'ld employ me in *T. G. of Ver.* iv 3 3
There was no great matter in the ditty *As Y. Like It* v 3 36
A million of beating may come to a great matter *W. Tale* iv 3 63
I thought she had some great matter there in hand v 2 113
Instinct is a great matter; I was now a coward on instinct *1 Hen. IV.* ii 4 301
Go with me; I have great matters to impart to thee *2 Hen. VI.* iii 2 299
Well, well, sir, well.—Why, 'tis no great matter *Coriolanus* ii 1 31
He was mad: he shall recover his wits there; or, if he do not, it's no great matter there *Hamlet* v 1 167
Great meals. Give them great meals of beef and iron and steel *Hen. V.* iii 7 161
Great measure. Did he break out into tears?—In great measure *M. Ado* i 1 25
Great Media, Parthia, and Armenia, He gave to Alexander *Ant. and Cleo.* iii 6 14
Great medicine. That great medicine hath With his tinct gilded thee i 5 36
Great mercy. You show great mercy, if you give him life *Hen. V.* ii 2 50
Great metropolis. The great metropolis and see of Rome *K. John* v 2 72
Great minds, of partial indulgence To their benumbed wills *Troi. and Cres.* ii 2 178
Great miracle. And who to thank, Besides the gods, for this great miracle *Pericles* v 3 58
Great moment. Matters of great moment *Richard III.* iii 7 67
Great morning. It is great morning *Troi. and Cres.* iv 3 1; *Cymbeline* iv 2 61
Great Myrmidon. That will physic the great Myrmidon *Troi. and Cres.* i 3 378
Great name. Had his great name profaned with their scorns *1 Hen. IV.* iii 2 64
Whose . . . great name in arms Holds from all soldiers chief majority iii 2 108
I am content that he shall take the odds Of his great name and estimation v 1 98
Great natural. This drivelling love is like a great natural *Rom. and Jul.* ii 4 96
Great nature. By law and process of great nature thence Freed *W. Tale* ii 2 60
And my young boy Hath an aspect of intercession, which Great nature cries 'Deny not' *Coriolanus* v 3 33
Balm of hurt minds, great nature's second course *Macbeth* ii 2 39
Great nature, like his ancestry, Moulded the stuff so fair *Cymbeline* v 4 48
Great navy. Our great navy's rigg'd.—For Italy *Ant. and Cleo.* iii 5 20
Great Nebuchadnezzar. I am no great Nebuchadnezzar, sir; I have not much skill in grass *All's Well* iv 5 21
Great need. Him and his worth and our great need of him You have right well conceited *J. Cæsar* i 3 161
Great nephew. The emperor, the queen's great nephew *Hen. VIII.* ii 2 26
Great Neptune. Will all great Neptune's ocean wash this blood Clean from my hand? *Macbeth* ii 2 60
Great Northumberland. Our supplies live largely in the hope Of great Northumberland *2 Hen. IV.* i 3 13
That great Northumberland, then false to him, Would of that seed grow to a greater falseness iii 1 89
Great number. Belike you slew great number of his people *T. Night* iii 3 29
Great oaths. How deep?—Thirty fathom.—Three great oaths would scarce make that be believed *All's Well* iv 1 64
Great observer. He reads much; He is a great observer *J. Cæsar* i 2 202
Great occasion. My master is awaked by great occasion To call upon his own *T. of Athens* ii 2 21
When he is gone, I would on great occasion speak with you *Othello* iv 1 59
Great of birth. He doth object I am too great of birth *Mer. Wives* iii 4 4
Great of heart. This did I fear, but thought he had no weapon; For he was great of heart *Othello* v 2 361
Great offence. The nature of his great offence is dead *All's Well* v 3 23

Great offence. An if there be No great offence belongs to't, give your friend Some touch of your late business . . . . *Hen. VIII.* v 1 12
Great offender. His royal self in judgement comes to hear The cause betwixt her and this great offender . . . . v 3 121
Great office. Hath been So clear in his great office . . . *Macbeth* i 7 18
My great office will sometimes Divide me from your bosom *Ant. and Cleo.* ii 3 1
Great one. No ceremony that to great ones 'longs . . *Meas. for Meas.* ii 2 59
Slight ones will not carry it; . . . and great ones I dare not give *All's W.* iv 1 43
What great ones do the less will prattle of . . . . . *T. Night* i 2 33
Be certain what you do, sir, lest your justice Prove violence; in the which three great ones suffer . . . . *W. Tale* ii 1 128
O, give me the spare men, and spare me the great ones . 2 *Hen. IV.* iii 2 289
This night he makes a supper, and a great one, To many lords *Hen. VIII.* i 3 52
They are set here for examples.—True, they are so; But few now give so great ones . . . . i 3 63
Madness in great ones must not unwatch'd go . . . . *Hamlet* iii 1 196
But the great one that goes up the hill, let him draw thee after . *Lear* ii 4 75
Packs and sects of great ones, That ebb and flow by the moon . . v 3 18
Three great ones of the city, In personal suit . . . . *Othello* i 1 8
'Tis the plague of great ones; Prerogatived are they less than the base. iii 3 273
Men's natures wrangle with inferior things, Though great ones are their object . . . . iii 4 145
I marvel how the fishes live in the sea.—Why, as men do a-land; the great ones eat up the little ones . . . . . *Pericles* ii 1 31
Great oneyers, such as can hold in, such as will strike . . 1 *Hen. IV.* ii 1 84
Great opinion. It lends a lustre and more great opinion . . . . . iv 1 77
Alas, it is my vice, my fault: Whiles others fish with craft for great opinion, I with great truth catch mere simplicity *Troi. and Cres.* iv 4 105
Writings all tending to the great opinion That Rome holds of his name *J. Cæsar* i 2 322
Great opposer. His great opposer, Coriolanus, being now in no request of his country . . . . *Coriolanus* iv 3 36
Great oppression. Too great oppression for a tender thing *Rom. and Jul.* i 4 24
Great ordnance. Have I not heard great ordnance in the field? *T. of Shrew* i 2 204
Great P's. And thus makes she her great P's . . . . . *T. Night* ii 5 97
Great pails. They threw on him Great pails of puddled mire *Com. of Er.* v 1 173
Great pains. Alas, it hath been great pains to you . . *Meas. for Meas.* ii 1 279
Your grace hath ta'en great pains to qualify His rigorous course *M. of V.* iv 1 7
I have taken great pains to con it . . . . . . *T. Night* i 5 185
I took great pains to study it, and 'tis poetical. . . . . . . i 5 206
Great palace. Had our great palace the capacity To camp this host, we all would sup together . . . . *Ant. and Cleo.* iv 8 32
Great part. To say nothing, to do nothing, to know nothing, and to have nothing, is to be a great part of your title . . . . . *All's Well* ii 4 26
His own impatience Takes from Aufidius a great part of blame *Coriol.* v 6 147
You take from me a great part of myself; Use me well in't *A. and C.* iii 2 24
Imogen, The great part of my comfort, gone . . . . *Cymbeline* iv 3 5
Great patience. When she has done most, Yet will I add an honour, a great patience . . . . *Hen. VIII.* iii 1 137
Great patricians shall attend and shrug . . . . . *Coriolanus* i 9 4
Great patron. As my great patron thought on in my prayers . *Lear* i 1 144
Great peard. I like not when a 'oman has a great peard; I spy a great peard under his muffler . . . . *Mer. Wives* iv 2 204
Great perplexity. And all our house in a great perplexity *T. G. of Ver.* ii 3 9
Great person. Supposing that they saw the king's ship wreck'd And his great person perish . . . . *Tempest* i 2 237
Great persuasion. I yield upon great persuasion . . . *Much Ado* v 4 95
Great perturbation. A great perturbation in nature, to receive at once the benefit of sleep, and do the effects of watching! . . *Macbeth* v 1 10
Great pin. And swallow my sword like a great pin . . 2 *Hen. VI.* iv 10 32
Great pirate. These roguing thieves serve the great pirate Valdes; And they have seized Marina . . . . *Pericles* iv 1 97
Great pitch. Enterprises of great pitch and moment . . *Hamlet* iii 1 86
Great pity. Though it be a great pity, yet it is necessary . *W. Tale* iv 4 804
And that it was great pity, so it was . . . . . 1 *Hen. IV.* i 3 59
'Tis great pity that the noble Moor Should hazard such a place as his own second With one of an ingraft infirmity . . . . *Othello* ii 3 143
Great place. Whose credit with the judge, or own great place, Could fetch your brother . . . . *Meas. for Meas.* ii 4 92
Know you where you are?—Respect to your great place! . . . . v 1 294
Great Plantagenet. But how is it that great Plantagenet Is crown'd so soon? . . . . 3 *Hen. VI.* i 4 99
Great Pompey. Great thanks, great Pompey . . . . *L. L. Lost* v 2 560
Greater than great, great, great, great Pompey! Pompey the Huge! . v 2 691
To see great Pompey pass the streets of Rome . . . *J. Cæsar* i 1 47
Great Pompey Would stand and make his eyes grow in my brow *A. and C.* i 5 31
Great pool. Our Britain seems as of it, but not in't; In a great pool a swan's nest . . . . *Cymbeline* iii 4 142
Great potentates. This gentleman is come to me, With commendation from great potentates . . . . *T. G. of Ver.* ii 4 79
Great power, great transcendence . . . . . . *All's Well* ii 3 40
With a great power of English and of Scots, Are by the sheriff of York-shire overthrown . . . . 2 *Hen. IV.* iv 4 98
A holy prophetess new risen up Is come with a great power . 1 *Hen. VI.* i 4 103
Away, away, to meet the queen's great power! . . . 3 *Hen. VI.* v 2 50
Defying Those whose great power must try him . . . *Coriolanus* iii 3 80
And, England, if my love thou hold'st at aught—As my great power thereof may give thee sense . . . . *Hamlet* iv 3 61
Great powers, If you will take this audit, take this life . . *Cymbeline* v 4 26
Great praise. And too little for a great praise . . . . *Much Ado* i 1 175
Great predecessor. In the right Of your great predecessor . . *Hen. V.* i 2 248
Great prediction Of noble having and of royal hope . . . *Macbeth* i 3 55
Great preparation. Indeed he hath made great preparation . *Much Ado* i 1 280
Great prerogative. The great prerogative and rite of love, Which, as your due, time claims, he does acknowledge . . . . *All's Well* ii 4 42
Great presage. In his visage no great presage of cruelty . *T. Night* ii 2 69
Great preservation. Were't not that, by great preservation, We live to tell it you . . . . *Richard III.* iii 5 36
Great pretences. Nor did you think it folly To keep your great pretences veil'd . . . . *Coriolanus* i 2 20
Great Priam. A cousin-german to great Priam's seed . *Troi. and Cres.* iv 5 121
Great Priamus. I am yours, You valiant offspring of great Priamus . ii 2 207
Great price. It is a great price For a small vice . . . . *Othello* iv 3 68
Great princes. High dukes, great princes, barons, lords . . *Hen. V.* iii 5 46
Let him be sent, great princes, And he shall buy my daughter *T. and C.* iii 3 27
Great profaneness. Apollo, pardon My great profaneness 'gainst thine oracle! . . . . *W. Tale* iii 2 155
Great progenitors. Our great progenitors had conquered . 1 *Hen. VI.* v 4 110
Great property. He comes too short of that great property Which still should go with Antony . . . . *Ant. and Cleo.* i 1 58
Great provoker. Drink, sir, is a great provoker of three things *Macbeth* ii 3 27
Great purpose. I am thwarted quite From my great purpose *Troi. and Cres.* v 1 43
Great quantity. He likewise enriched poor straggling soldiers with great quantity . . . . *T. of Athens* v 1 7
Great quarrel. For all my blood in Rome's great quarrel shed *T. Andron.* iii 1 4
Great quarreller. For besides that he's a fool, he's a great quarreller *T. N.* i 3 31
Great queen. I had rather be a country servant-maid Than a great queen, with this condition . . . . *Richard III.* i 3 108
Great quell. Who shall bear the guilt Of our great quell . . *Macbeth* i 7 72
Great rage of heart Suddenly made him from my side to start 1 *Hen. VI.* iv 7 11
The great rage, You see, is kill'd in him . . . . . . *Lear* iv 7 78
Great ragged horns. Walk round about an oak, with great ragg'd horns *Mer. Wives* iv 4 31
Great reason; for 'past cure is still past care' . . . . *L. L. Lost* v 2 28
A traveller! By my faith, you have great reason to be sad *As Y. Like It* iv 1 21
You have great reason to do Richard right . . . . 1 *Hen. VI.* iii 1 154
Then fly. What, from myself? Great reason why: Lest I revenge *Richard III.* v 3 185
Great reason that my noble lord be rated For sauciness . . *T. Andron.* ii 3 81
Great revenge. Let's make us medicines of our great revenge *Macbeth* iv 3 214
Had all his hairs been lives, my great revenge Had stomach for them all.—Alas! he is betray'd . . . . *Othello* v 2 74
Great revenue. A dowager Of great revenue . . . . *M. N. Dream* i 1 158
The common curse of mankind, folly and ignorance, be thine in great revenue! heaven bless thee from a tutor! . . . *Troi. and Cres.* ii 3 31
Great rewards. I cheer'd them up with justice of our cause, With promise of high pay and great rewards . . . . . 3 *Hen. VI.* ii 1 134
Great right. To do a great right, do a little wrong . . *Mer. of Venice* iv 1 216
He was famous, sir, in his profession, and it was his great right *All's Well* i 1 30
Great rivals in our youngest daughter's love . . . . . *Lear* i 1 47
Great Rome. And sack great Rome with Romans . . *Coriolanus* iii 1 316
I have received letters from great Rome . . . . *T. Andron.* v 1 2
From you great Rome shall suck Reviving blood . . . *J. Cæsar* ii 2 87
Wouldst thou be window'd in great Rome and see Thy master thus? *Ant. and Cleo.* iv 14 72
Great round beard. Does he not wear a great round beard? . *Mer. Wives* i 4 20
Great Saint George. To keep our great Saint George's feast withal 1 *Hen. VI.* i 1 154
Great scene. Fat Falstaff Hath a great scene . . . . *Mer. Wives* iv 6 17
Great scholar. A careful man and a great scholar . . . *T. Night* iv 2 11
Great seas have dried When miracles have by the greatest been denied. Oft expectation fails . . . . *All's Well* ii 1 143
Lest this great sea of joy's rushing upon me O'erbear the shores of my mortality, And drown me . . . . *Pericles* v 1 194
Great seal. Who commands you To render up the great seal *Hen. VIII.* iii 2 229
You made bold To carry into Flanders the great seal . . . . iii 2 319
For your stubborn answer About the giving back the great seal to us, The king shall know it . . . . iii 2 347
Great sea-mark. Stick i' the wars Like a great sea-mark . *Coriolanus* v 3 74
Great seats. For your great seats now quit you of great shames *Hen. V.* iii 5 47
Great self. To dissever so Our great self and our credit . *All's Well* ii 1 126
My heart weeps to see him So little of his great self . *Hen. VIII.* iii 2 336
Great sender. Like a remorseful pardon slowly carried, To the great sender turns a sour offence . . . . *All's Well* v 3 59
Great shadow. That are the substance Of that great shadow 2 *Hen VI.* i 1 14
Great shames. For your great seats now quit you of great shames *Hen. V.* iii 5 47
Great show. Since the little wit that fools have was silenced, the little foolery that wise men have makes a great show . *As Y. Like It* i 2 96
Great shower. He and myself Have travail'd in the great shower of your gifts . . . . *T. of Athens* v 1 73
Great showing. Of very soft society and great showing . . *Hamlet* v 2 113
Great Sicilius. He deserved the praise o' the world, As great Sicilius' heir . . . . *Cymbeline* v 4 51
Great sickness. Which argues a great sickness in his judgement that makes it . . . . *T. of Athens* v 1 31
Great sign. A great sign, sir, that he will look sad . . *L. L. Lost* i 2 3
Great sin. It is great sin to swear unto a sin, But greater sin to keep a sinful oath . . . . 2 *Hen. VI.* v 1 182
Great sir. This great sir will yet stay longer . . . . *W. Tale* i 2 212
Please you, great sir, Bohemia greets you from himself by me . . v 1 180
Great sir, they shall be brought you to my house . . . *Pericles* v 3 26
Great size. You are potently opposed; and with a malice Of as great size. Ween you of better luck? . . . . *Hen. VIII.* v 1 135
Great-sized. A great-sized monster of ingratitudes . . *Troi. and Cres.* iii 3 147
Thou great-sized coward, No space of earth shall sunder our two hates v 10 26
Great snare. Comest thou smiling from The world's great snare un-caught! . . . . *Ant. and Cleo.* iv 8 18
Great soldier. The sister of Frederick the great soldier *Meas. for Meas.* iii 1 217
Let the trumpets blow, That this great soldier may his welcome know *Troi. and Cres.* iv 5 276
Great solemnity. We'll hold a feast in great solemnity . *M. N. Dream* iv 1 190
See High order in this great solemnity . . . . *Ant. and Cleo.* v 2 369
Great son. Thou know'st, great son, The end of war's uncertain *Coriolanus* v 3 140
Great sorrow. With such a deep demeanour in great sorrow 2 *Hen. IV.* iv 5 85
Their colours, often borne in France, And now in England to our heart's great sorrow, Shall be my winding-sheet . . . . . 3 *Hen. VI.* i 1 128
Great sort. It may be his enemy is a gentleman of great sort *Hen. V.* iv 7 142
Great sphere. O sun, Burn the great sphere thou movest in! *Ant. and Cleo.* iv 15 10
Great spirit. What sign is it when a man of great spirit grows melan-choly?—A great sign, sir, that he will look sad . . *L. L. Lost* i 2 2
Make distinct the very breach whereout Hector's great spirit flew *Troi. and Cres.* iv 5 246
There's a great spirit gone! . . . . *Ant. and Cleo.* i 2 126
Great sport. Who set the body and the limbs Of this great sport together, as you guess? . . . . *Hen. VIII.* i 1 47
Great stage. When we are born, we cry that we are come To this great stage of fools . . . . *Lear* iv 6 187
Great stars. That their great stars Throned and set high . . . . iii 1 22
Great state. With what great state he heard their embassy . *Hen. V.* ii 4 32
Great stock. Sweet stem from York's great stock . . 1 *Hen. VI.* ii 5 41
And you Recoil from your great stock . . . . . *Cymbeline* i 6 128
Great store. Prepared great store of wedding cheer . . *T. of Shrew* iii 2 188
We shall have Great store of room, no doubt, left for the ladies *Hen. VIII.* v 4 77
Great subsidies. I have not been desirous of their wealth, Nor much oppress'd them with great subsidies . . . . . . 3 *Hen. VI.* iv 8 45
Great sums. Did he not . . . Levy great sums of money? 2 *Hen. VI.* iii 1 61
Great supper. I came yonder from a great supper . . . *Much Ado* i 3 44
Let us to the great supper: their cheer is the greater that I am subdued i 3 73
Great supply. The great supply That was expected by the Dauphin here, Are wreck'd . . . . *K. John* v 3 9

Great supremacy. So under Him that great supremacy, Where we do reign, we will alone uphold . . . . *K. John* iii 1 156
Great suspicion. A great suspicion: stay the friar too . *Rom. and Jul.* v 3 187
Great swarths. An affectioned ass, that cons state without book and utters it by great swarths . . . . *T. Night* ii 3 162
Great sway. Should not our father Bear the great sway of his affairs with reasons? . . . . *Troi. and Cres.* ii 2 35
Great swing. For the great swing and rudeness of his poise . . i 3 207
Great teachers. His training such, That he may furnish and instruct great teachers . . . . *Hen. VIII.* i 2 113
Great tears. And these great tears grace his remembrance more Than those I shed for him . . . . *All's Well* i 1 91
Great testimony. There is too great testimony in your complexion that it was a passion of earnest . . . . . . *As Y. Like It* iv 3 171
Great thanks, great Pompey . . . . . . *L. L. Lost* v 2 560
I return great thanks, And in submission will attend on her . *1 Hen. VI.* ii 2 51
We have all Great cause to give great thanks . . . . *Coriolanus* v 4 63
Great thaw. That I was duller than a great thaw . . *Much Ado* ii 1 251
Great Theseus. A play Intended for great Theseus' nuptial-day *M. N. D.* iii 2 12
Great Thetis. Now, great Thetis' son! . . . . . *Troi. and Cres.* iii 3 94
Great thief. You have been a great thief by sea . . *Ant. and Cleo.* ii 6 96
Great thing. When great things labouring perish in their birth *L. L. Lost* v 2 521
And now, Octavius, Listen great things . . . . . . *J. Cæsar* iv 1 41
Great thing of us forgot! . . . . *Lear* v 3 236
Great thunder-darter. O thou great thunder-darter of Olympus, forget that thou art Jove! . . . . *Troi. and Cres.* ii 3 11
Great time. Like poison given to work a great time after . *Tempest* iii 3 105
Great Timon, noble, worthy, royal Timon! . . . *T. of Athens* ii 2 177
Great toe. A pox of this gout! or, a gout of this pox! for the one or the other plays the rogue with my great toe . . . *2 Hen. IV.* i 2 274
You, the great toe of this assembly?—I the great toe! why the great toe?—For that, being one o' the lowest . . . . *Coriolanus* i 1 159
Great tool. Some strange Indian with the great tool come to court *Hen. VIII.* v 4 35
Great towers. That these great towers, trophies and schools should fall For private faults in them . . . . . . *T. of Athens* v 4 25
Great towns. The loss of those great towns Will make him burst his lead and rise from death . . . . *1 Hen. VI.* i 1 63
Great traffic. A merchant of great traffic . . . . *T. of Shrew* i 1 12
Great transcendence. Great power, great transcendence *All's Well* ii 3 40
Great traveller. Brave Master Shooty the great traveller *Meas. for Meas.* iv 3 18
Great triumphers. And enter in our ears like great triumphers In their applauding gates . . . . *T. of Athens* v 1 199
Great Troy is ours, and our sharp wars are ended . . *Troi. and Cres.* v 9 10
Great tyranny! lay thou thy basis sure . . . . . *Macbeth* iv 3 32
Great-uncle. Your great-uncle Edward the Black Prince *Hen. V.* i 2 105; iv 7 96
Great value. This breast of mine hath buried Thoughts of great value *J. Cæsar* i 2 50
Great vast. Thou god of this great vast, rebuke these surges! *Pericles* iii 1 1
Great vow. By all your vows of love and that great vow Which did incorporate and make us one . . . . *J. Cæsar* ii 1 272
Great voyage. He will repent the breadth of his great voyage *Pericles* iv 1 37
Great wager. He has laid a great wager on your head . *Hamlet* v 2 106
Great war. He goes forth gallantly. That he and Cæsar might Determine this great war in single fight! . . . . *Ant. and Cleo.* iv 4 37
Great wart. The great wart on my left arm . . *Com. of Errors* iii 2 148
Great Warwick. Now methinks I hear great Warwick speak *3 Hen. VI.* ii 1 186
Great way. Think him a great way fool, solely a coward . *All's Well* i 1 112
The sun arises, Which is a great way growing on the south . *J. Cæsar* ii 1 107
Great weeds do grow apace . . . . *Richard III.* ii 4 13
Great weight. No way excuse his soils, when we do bear So great weight in his lightness . . . . *Ant. and Cleo.* i 4 25
Great welcome. Small cheer and great welcome makes a merry feast.—Ay to a niggardly host . . . . . *Com. of Errors* iii 1 26
Great wheel. Let go thy hold when a great wheel runs down a hill *Lear* ii 4 73
Great while. A great while ago the world begun . . *T. Night* v 1 414
As thou hast not done a great while . . . . . *2 Hen. IV.* ii 2 24
So let it now; for it has been a great while going by . *Troi. and Cres.* i 2 183
Why, sir, his hide is so tanned with his trade, that he will keep out water a great while . . . . *Hamlet* v 1 187
Great wit. A great wit: 'Right,' says she, 'a great gross one' *Much Ado* v 1 163
Great with child. Sir, she came in great with child . *Meas. for Meas.* ii 1 91
Great with woe. I am great with woe, and shall deliver weeping *Pericles* v 1 107
Great work. Much more, in this great work, Which is almost to pluck a kingdom down . . . . *2 Hen. IV.* i 3 48
Great world. My little body is aweary of this great world *Mer. of Venice* i 2 2
This great world Shall so wear out to nought . . . *Lear* iv 6 137
And little of this great world can I speak, More than pertains to feats of broil and battle . . . . *Othello* i 3 86
The senators alone of this great world, Chief factors for the gods *A. and C.* ii 6 9
Great worth. 'Tis an office of great worth . . . *T. G. of Ver.* i 2 44
Every day Men of great worth resorted to this forest . *As Y. Like It* v 4 161
Disgrace to your great worths and shame to me . *Troi. and Cres.* ii 2 151
Great worthiness. And much too little of that good I saw Is my report to his great worthiness . . . . . . *L. L. Lost* ii 1 63
Great wrong. If thou consider rightly of the matter, Cæsar has had great wrong . . . . *J. Cæsar* iii 2 115
Great York. That, Talbot dead, great York might bear the name *1 Hen. VI.* iv 4 9
And who is England's king but great York's heir? . . *Richard III.* iv 4 473
Greater. Master of a full poor cell, And thy no greater father *Tempest* i 2 21
I'll knit it up in silken strings. . . . To be fantastic may become a youth Of greater time than I shall show to be . . *T. G. of Ver.* ii 7 48
For the greater hides the less . . . . iii 1 372
A dog as big as ten of yours, and therefore the gift the greater . iv 4 63
I will do a greater thing than that, upon your request . *Mer. Wives* i 1 248
The greater file of the subject held the duke to be wise *Meas. for Meas.* iii 2 144
Is no greater forfeit to the law than Angelo who hath sentenced him . iv 2 167
You make my bonds still greater.—O, your desert speaks loud v 1 8
Their cheer is the greater that I am subdued . . . *Much Ado* i 3 74
But on this travail look for greater birth . . . . . . iv 1 215
Beg a greater matter; Thou now request'st but moonshine in the water *L. L. Lost* v 2 207
Greater than great, great, great, great Pompey! Pompey the Huge! . v 2 691
What, can you do me greater harm than hate? . . . *M. N. Dream* iii 2 271
The greater throw May turn by fortune from the weaker hand *M. of V.* ii 1 33
So doth the greater glory dim the less . . . . v 1 93
Why, how now, Adam! no greater heart in thee? . . *As Y. Like It* ii 6 4
Ay, and greater wonders than that.—O, I know where you are . . v 2 31
Neither do I labour for a greater esteem . . . . v 2 62

Greater. And make assurance here in Padua Of greater sums than I have promised . . . . *T. of Shrew* iii 2 137
Thou mayst slide from my shoulder to my heel with no greater a run but my head and my neck . . . . iv 1 16
A need Greater than shows itself at the first view . . . *All's Well* ii 5 73
But greater a great deal in evil: he excels his brother for a coward . iv 3 320
Yet, for a greater confirmation, For in an act of this importance 'twere Most piteous to be wild . . . . *W. Tale* ii 1 180
On her frights and griefs, Which never tender lady hath borne greater . ii 2 24
Nothing she does or seems But smacks of something greater than herself . . . . iv 4 158
A greater power than we denies all this . . . . *K. John* iii 1 368
O, no! the apprehension of the good Gives but the greater feeling to the worse . . . . *Richard II.* i 3 301
Strives Bolingbroke to be as great as we? Greater he shall not be . iii 2 98
I am greater than a king: For when I was a king, my flatterers Were then but subjects . . . . iv 1 305
Would to God Thy name in arms were now as great as mine!—I'll make it greater ere I part from thee . . . . . . *1 Hen. IV.* v 4 71
I would my means were greater, and my waist slenderer . *2 Hen. IV.* i 2 162
Would of that seed grow to a greater falseness . . . . . . iii 1 90
To end one doubt by death Revives two greater in the heirs of life . iv 1 200
To give a greater sum Than ever at one time the clergy yet Did *Hen. V.* i 1 79
We are in great danger; The greater therefore should our courage be . iv 1 2
And if to live, The fewer men, the greater share of honour . . iv 3 22
And to survey his dead and earthy image, What were it but to make my sorrow greater? . . . . *3 Hen. VI.* iii 2 148
It is great sin to swear unto a sin, But greater sin to keep a sinful oath v 1 183
I am resolved to bear a greater storm Than any thou canst conjure up . v 1 198
Commanded always by the greater gust . . . . *2 Hen. VI.* iii 1 88
The harder match'd, the greater victory . . . . v 1 70
A greater gift than that I'll give my cousin.—A greater gift! *Rich. III.* iii 1 115
'Tis full of woe: yet I can give you inkling Of an ensuing evil, if it fall, Greater than this . . . . *Hen. VIII.* ii 1 142
I am able now, methinks, Out of a fortitude of soul I feel, To endure more miseries and greater far Than my weak-hearted enemies dare offer . . . . iii 2 389
Never greater, Nor, I'll assure you, better taken, sir . . . iv 1 11
And, to add greater honours to his age Than man could give him, he died fearing God . . . . iv 2 67
'Tis mad idolatry To make the service greater than the god *Troi. and Cres.* ii 2 57
In self-assumption greater Than in the note of judgement . . . ii 3 133
Light boats sail swift, though greater hulks draw deep . . . ii 3 277
And throw forth greater themes For insurrection's arguing . *Coriolanus* i 1 224
He seeks their hate with greater devotion than they can render it him ii 2 21
But that's no matter, the greater part carries it . . . . ii 3 41
This mutiny were better put in hazard, Than stay, past doubt, for greater . . . . ii 3 265
We are the greater poll, and in true fear They gave us our demands . iii 1 134
On whom depending, their obedience fails To the greater bench . . iii 1 166
But a greater soldier than he, you wot one.—Who, my master? . iv 5 170
I take him to be the greater soldier . . . . iv 5 176
He comforts you Can make you greater than the Queen of Goths *T. An.* i 1 269
A greater power than we can contradict Hath thwarted our intents *Rom. and Jul.* v 3 153
The greater scorns the lesser . . . . . . *T. of Athens* iv 3 6
Such men as he be never at heart's ease Whiles they behold a greater than themselves, And therefore are they very dangerous *J. Cæsar* i 2 209
The greater part, the horse in general, Are come with Cassius . iv 2 29
A friend should bear his friend's infirmities, But Brutus makes mine greater than they are . . . . iv 3 87
Lesser than Macbeth, and greater.—Not so happy, yet much happier *Macbeth* i 3 65
For an earnest of a greater honour . . . . i 3 104
Great Glamis! worthy Cawdor! Greater than both, by the all-hail hereafter! . . . . i 5 56
Where the greater malady is fix'd, The lesser is scarce felt . . *Lear* iii 4 8
Good guard, Until their greater pleasures first be known . . . v 3 2
For nothing canst thou to damnation add Greater than that . *Othello* iii 3 373
Which I have greater reason to believe now than ever . . . . iv 2 217
They are greater storms and tempests than almanacs can report *A. and C.* i 2 154
I know not, Menas, How lesser enmities may give way to greater . ii 1 43
But small to greater matters must give way.—Not if the small come first . . . . ii 2 11
Cæsar and he are greater friends than ever . . . . . . ii 5 48
It raises the greater war between him and his discretion . . . ii 7 10
The greater cantle of the world is lost With very ignorance . . iii 10 6
The breaking of so great a thing should make A greater crack . . v 1 15
Thou art then As great as is thy master, greater . . . *Cymbeline* i 5 51
Yet 'tis greater skill In a true hate, to pray they have their will . ii 5 33
We will fear no poison, which attends In place of greater state . . iii 3 78
Virtue and cunning were endowments greater Than nobleness and riches *Pericles* iii 2 27
Greatest. She as far surpasseth Sycorax As great'st does least *Temp.* iii 2 111
Your bum is the greatest thing about you . . . *Meas. for Meas.* ii 1 228
The sweet youth's in love.—The greatest note of it is his melancholy *Much Ado* iii 2 54
Which is the greatest lady, the highest?—The thickest and the tallest *L. L. Lost* iv 1 46
This is the greatest error of all the rest . . . . *M. N. Dream* v 1 250
The magnificoes Of greatest port have all persuaded with him *M. of V.* iii 2 283
The greatest of my pride is to see my ewes graze . . *As Y. Like It* iii 2 80
And he of both That can assure my daughter greatest dower Shall have my Bianca's love . . . . *T. of Shrew* ii 1 345
My father's skill, which was the greatest Of his profession . *All's Well* i 3 249
He that of greatest works is finisher Oft does them by the weakest minister . . . . ii 1 139
Great seas have dried When miracles have by the greatest been denied . ii 1 144
Hopest thou my cure?—The great'st grace lending grace . . . ii 1 163
Reprieve him from the wrath Of greatest justice . . . . . iii 4 29
My greatest grief, Though little he do feel it, set down sharply . . iii 4 32
It is reported that he has taken their greatest commander . . . iii 5 6
Which were the greatest obloquy i' the world In me to lose . . iv 2 44
The last was the greatest, but that I have not ended yet . . . iv 3 105
One of the greatest in the Christian world Shall be my surety . . iv 4 2
But to himself The greatest wrong of all . . . . v 3 15
A gentleman of the greatest promise that ever came into my note *W. T.* i 1 39
Worse than the great'st infection That e'er was heard or read! . . i 2 423
Both are alike; and both alike we like. One must prove greatest *K. John* ii 1 332
Herein all breathless lies The mightiest of thy greatest enemies *Rich. II.* v 6 32

Greatest. As the thing that's heavy in itself Upon enforcement flies with greatest speed, So did our men . . . . . 2 *Hen. IV.* i 1 120
Thou art now one of the greatest men in this realm . . . v 3 92
It is the greatest admiration in the universal world . . *Hen. V.* iv 1 66
The saying is true, 'The empty vessel makes the greatest sound' . . iv 4 74
Or else reproach be Talbot's greatest fame! . . 1 *Hen. VI.* iii 2 76
The greatest miracle that e'er ye wrought . . . . . v 4 66
Thy plainness and thy housekeeping Hath won the greatest favour 2 *Hen. VI.* i 1 192
And so says York, for he hath greatest cause . . . . i 1 207
The greatest man in England but the king . . . . . ii 2 82
Thy greatest help is quiet, gentle Nell . . . . . ii 4 67
Our Earl of Warwick, Edward's greatest friend . . 3 *Hen. VI.* iii 3 45
Great John of Gaunt, Which did subdue the greatest part of Spain . iii 3 82
Bid him levy straight The greatest strength and power he can make *Richard III.* iv 4 449
When the greatest stroke of fortune falls, Will bless the king *Hen. VIII.* ii 2 36
I sent your message; who return'd her thanks In the great'st humbleness . . . . v 1 65
The greatest monarch now alive may glory In such an honour . . v 3 164
Our greatest friends attend us . . . . . *Coriolanus* i 1 249
Both your voices blended, the great'st taste Most palates theirs . . iii 1 103
But that which gives my soul the greatest spurn . . *T. Andron.* iii 1 101
I am the greatest, able to do least, Yet most suspected . *Rom. and Jul.* v 3 223
The greatest of your having lacks a half To pay your present debts *T. of Athens* ii 2 153
I count it one of my greatest afflictions, say, that I cannot pleasure such an honourable gentleman . . . . . . iii 2 62
Your greatest want is, you want much of meat . . . . . iv 3 419
Glamis, and thane of Cawdor! The greatest is behind . . *Macbeth* i 3 117
By this great clatter, one of greatest note Seems bruited . . . v 7 21
The greatest discords be That e'er our hearts shall make! . *Othello* ii 1 200
They are so still, Or thou, the greatest soldier of the world, Art turn'd the greatest liar . . . . *Ant. and Cleo.* i 3 39
Whip him. Were't twenty of the greatest tributaries . . . iii 13 96
Follow his chariot, like the greatest spot Of all thy sex . . . iv 12 35
Wherein I lived, the greatest prince o' the world, The noblest . . iv 15 54
Be it known, that we, the greatest, are misthought For things that others do . . . . v 2 176
A lady So fair . . . Would make the great'st king double . *Cymbeline* i 6 121

Greatly. I greatly fear my money is not safe . . *Com. of Errors* i 2 105
And their daughters profit very greatly under you . . . *L. L. Lost* iv 2 78
We cannot greatly condemn our success . . . . *All's Well* iii 6 58
Good king, great king, and yet not greatly good . . *Richard II.* iv 1 263
I know not, nor I greatly care not: God knows I had as lief be none as one . . . . v 2 48
Small time, but in that small most greatly lived . . . *Hen. V.* Epil. 5
It skills not greatly who impugns our doom . . . 2 *Hen. VI.* iii 1 281
They cannot greatly sting to hurt, Yet look to have them buzz 3 *Hen. VI.* ii 6 94
And wonder greatly that man's face can fold In pleasing smiles such murderous tyranny . . . . *T. Andron.* ii 3 266
But greatly to find quarrel in a straw When honour's at the stake *Hamlet* iv 4 55
But, as they say, to hear music the general does not greatly care *Othello* iii 1 18
I do not greatly care to be deceived, That have no use for trusting *Ant. and Cleo.* v 2 14

Greatness. If thy greatness will Revenge it on him . . . *Tempest* iii 2 61
I do beseech thy greatness, give him blows And take his bottle from him . . . . iii 2 72
No might nor greatness in mortality Can censure 'scape *Meas. for Meas.* iii 2 196
O place and greatness! millions of false eyes Are stuck upon thee . iv 1 60
Some certain special honours it pleaseth his greatness to impart *L. L. Lost* v 1 113
Most esteemed greatness, will you hear? . . . . . . v 2 894
His own learning, the greatness whereof I cannot enough commend *Mer. of Venice* iv 1 158
Upon mine honour, And in the greatness of my word . *As Y. Like It* i 3 91
And extend to you what further becomes his greatness . . *All's Well* iii 6 74
In my stars I am above thee; but be not afraid of greatness . *T. Night* ii 5 157
Some are born great, some achieve greatness and some have greatness thrust upon 'em . . . . ii 5 158; iii 4 47; v 1 389
'Be not afraid of greatness:' 'twas well writ . . . . . iii 4 42
Your greatness Hath not been used to fear . . . *W. Tale* iv 4 17
He comes not Like to his father's greatness . . . . . v 1 89
Thou art perjured too, And soothest up greatness . . *K. John* iii 1 121
Foul play; and 'tis shame That greatness should so grossly offer it . iv 2 94
Lest I, by marking of your rage, forget Your worth, your greatness . iv 3 86
As holding of the pope Your sovereign greatness and authority . . v 1 4
Our house, my sovereign liege, little deserves The scourge of greatness to be used on it; And that same greatness too which our own hands Have holp to make so portly . . . . . 1 *Hen. IV.* i 3 11
Amend this fault: Though sometimes it show greatness, courage, blood iii 1 181
Tell me else, Could such inordinate and low desires . . . Accompany the greatness of thy blood? . . . . iii 2 16
Many tales devised, Which oft the ear of greatness needs must hear . iii 2 24
He presently, as greatness knows itself, Steps me a little higher than his vow . . . . iv 3 74
And such a flood of greatness fell on you . . . . . . v 1 48
It discolours the complexion of my greatness to acknowledge it 2 *Hen. IV.* ii 2 6
These humble considerations make me out of love with my greatness . ii 2 15
Necessity so bow'd the state That I and greatness were compell'd to kiss iii 1 74
Alack, what mischiefs might he set abroach In shadow of such greatness! iv 2 15
And noble offices thou mayst effect Of mediation, after I am dead, Between his greatness and thy other brethren . . . . . iv 4 26
O foolish youth! Thou seek'st the greatness that will overwhelm thee iv 5 98
Not less happy, having such a son, That would deliver up his greatness so v 2 111
I will keep my state, Be like a king and show my sail of greatness *Hen. V.* i 2 274
O England! model to thy inward greatness, Like little body with a mighty heart . . . . ii Prol. 16
Making God so free an offer, He let him outlive that day to see His greatness . . . . iv 1 195
We must bear all. O hard condition, Twin-born with greatness . . iv 1 251
O, be sick, great greatness, And bid thy ceremony give thee cure! . iv 1 268
Though Humphrey's pride And greatness of his place be grief to us 2 *Hen. VI.* i 1 173
As for words, whose greatness answers words, Let this my sword report iv 10 56
As I had rather hide me from my greatness, Being a bark to brook no mighty sea, Than in my greatness covet to be hid . *Richard III.* iii 7 161
Fit it with such furniture as suits The greatness of his person *Hen. VIII.* ii 1 100
I feel The last fit of my greatness . . . . iii 1 78
I have touch'd the highest point of all my greatness . . . . iii 2 223
Farewell! a long farewell, to all my greatness! This is the state of man iii 2 351
When he thinks, good easy man, full surely His greatness is a-ripening . . . . *Hen. VIII.* iii 2 357
You are to blame, Knowing she will not lose her wonted greatness, To use so rude behaviour . . . . iv 2 102
Shall read the perfect ways of honour, And by those claim their greatness v 5 39
His honour and the greatness of his name Shall be, and make new nations v 5 52
Where's then the saucy boat Whose weak untimber'd sides but even now Co-rivall'd greatness? . . . . . *Troi. and Cres.* i 3 44
Such to-be-pitied and o'er-wrested seeming He acts thy greatness in . i 3 158
As full of envy at his greatness as Cerberus is at Proserpina's beauty . ii 1 37
If any thing more than your sport and pleasure Did move your greatness . . . . ii 3 118
Possess'd he is with greatness, And speaks not to himself but with a pride . . . . ii 3 180
Greatness, once fall'n out with fortune, Must fall out with men too . iii 3 75
Who deserves greatness Deserves your hate . . . *Coriolanus* i 1 180
Do you hear how we are shent for keeping your greatness back? . v 2 105
The abuse of greatness is, when it disjoins Remorse from power *J. Cæsar* ii 1 18
This have I thought good to deliver thee, my dearest partner of greatness, that thou mightst not lose the dues of rejoicing, by being ignorant of what greatness is promised thee . . *Macbeth* i 5 12
So many As will to greatness dedicate themselves, Finding it so inclined iv 3 75
His greatness weigh'd, his will is not his own; For he himself is subject to his birth . . . . *Hamlet* i 3 17
But mine honesty Shall not make poor my greatness . *Ant. and Cleo.* ii 2 93
Cleopatra does confess thy greatness; Submits her to thy might . . iii 12 16
The soul and body rive not more in parting Than greatness going off . iv 13 6
Lest, in her greatness, by some mortal stroke She do defeat us . . v 1 64
Tell him I am his fortune's vassal, and I send him The greatness he has got . . . . v 2 30
And I shall see Some squeaking Cleopatra boy my greatness . . . v 2 220
O noble strain! O worthiness of nature! breed of greatness! *Cymbeline* iv 2 25
Poor wretches that depend On greatness' favour dream as I have done . v 4 128
She confess'd she never loved you, only Affected greatness got by you . v 5 38
By our greatness and the grace of it, Which is our honour . . . v 5 132
Let it suffice the greatness of your powers To have bereft a prince of all his fortunes . . . . *Pericles* ii 1 8
His greatness was no guard To bar heaven's shaft, but sin had his reward ii 4 14

Grecian. In such a night Troilus methinks mounted the Troyan walls And sigh'd his soul toward the Grecian tents . . *Mer. of Venice* v 1 5
Troilus had his brains dashed out with a Grecian club . *As Y. Like It* iv 1 98
Was this fair face the cause, quoth she, Why the Grecians sacked Troy? Fond done, done fond . . . . . . *All's Well* i 3 75
Look, how many Grecian tents do stand Hollow upon this plain *Troi. and Cres.* i 3 79
To rouse a Grecian that is true in love: If any come, Hector shall honour him . . . . i 3 279
The Grecian dames are sunburnt and not worth The splinter of a lance i 3 282
If there be not in our Grecian host One noble man . . . . i 3 293
Who marvels then, when Helenus beholds A Grecian and his sword, if he do set The very wings of reason to his heels? . . . . ii 2 43
For an old aunt whom the Greeks held captive, He brought a Grecian queen . . . . ii 2 78
Why keep we her? the Grecians keep our aunt: Is she worth keeping? ii 2 80
To see these Grecian lords!—why, even already They clap the lubber Ajax iii 3 138
Six-or-seven-times-honoured captain-general of The Grecian army. . iii 3 279
For every false drop in her bawdy veins A Grecian's life hath sunk . iv 1 70
There is at hand Paris your brother, and Deiphobus, The Grecian Diomed iv 2 64
Walk into her house; I'll bring her to the Grecian presently . . iv 3 6
I must then to the Grecians?—No remedy.—A woful Cressid! . . iv 4 57
I will corrupt the Grecian sentinels, To give thee nightly visitation . iv 4 74
The Grecian youths are full of quality . . . . . . iv 4 78
Fair virtues all, To which the Grecians are most prompt and pregnant. iv 4 90
Come you hither; And bring Æneas and the Grecian with you . . iv 4 102
Grecian, thou dost not use me courteously . . . . . . iv 4 123
This hand is Grecian all, And this is Trojan . . . . . iv 5 125
I would desire My famous cousin to our Grecian tents . . . iv 5 151
The fall of every Phrygian stone will cost A drop of Grecian blood . iv 5 224
You wisest Grecians, pardon me this brag . . . . . iv 5 257
We have had pelting wars, since you refused The Grecians' cause . . iv 5 268
When many times the captive Grecian falls, Even in the fan and wind of your fair sword, You bid them rise, and live. . . . . v 3 40
Whereupon the Grecians begin to proclaim barbarism . . . . v 4 17
Hark! a retire upon our Grecian part.—The Trojan trumpets sound the like. . . . . v 8 15
Look'd not lovelier Than Hector's forehead when it spit forth blood At Grecian sword, contemning . . . . . *Coriolanus* i 3 46

'Gree. How dost thou and thy master agree? I have brought him a present. How 'gree you now? . . . . . *Mer. of Venice* ii 2 108

Greece. Thou art a Castalian-King-Urinal. Hector of Greece, my boy! *Mer. Wives* ii 3 35
Five summers have I spent in furthest Greece . . . *Com. of Errors* i 1 133
As Stephen Sly and old John Naps of Greece . . *T. of Shrew* Ind. 2 95
And thus he goes, As did the youthful Paris once to Greece 1 *Hen. VI.* v 5 104
Helen of Greece was fairer far than thou . . . . 3 *Hen. VI.* ii 2 146
From isles of Greece The princes orgulous, their high blood chafed, Have to the port of Athens sent their ships . *Troi. and Cres.* Prol. 1
I had rather be such a man as Troilus than Agamemnon and all Greece i 2 267
Agamemnon, Thou great commander, nerve and bone of Greece . i 3 55
Such As Agamemnon and the hand of Greece Should hold up high in brass i 3 63
If there be one among the fair'st of Greece That holds his honour higher than his ease . . . . i 3 265
The plague of Greece upon thee, thou mongrel beef-witted lord! . . ii 1 13
I would make thee the loathsomest scab in Greece . . . . ii 1 31
Troilus had rather Troy were borne to Greece Than Cressid borne from Troy . . . . iv 1 46
I tell thee, lord of Greece, She is as far high-soaring o'er thy praises . iv 4 125
Hail, all you state of Greece! what shall be done To him that victory commands? . . . . iv 5 65
First, all you peers of Greece, go to my tent; There in the full convive we . . . . iv 5 271
Against a graver bench Than ever frown'd in Greece . *Coriolanus* iii 1 107
Whoever gave that counsel, to give forth The corn o' the storehouse gratis, as 'twas used Sometime in Greece . . . . . iii 1 115
The gods of Greece protect you! And we'll pray for you! . *Pericles* i 4 97
Here's them in our country of Greece gets more with begging than we can do with working . . . . ii 1 68

'Greed. All the means Plotted and 'greed on for my happiness *T. G. of Ver.* ii 4 183
Are there no other tokens Between you 'greed? . . *Meas. for Meas.* iv 1 42
Consented That you shall be my wife; your dowry 'greed on *T. of Shrew* ii 1 272

'Greed. We have 'greed so well together, That upon Sunday is the wedding-day *T. of Shrew* ii 1 299
This 'greed upon, To part with unhack'd edges *Ant. and Cleo.* ii 6 37
Greedily. And greedily devour the treacherous bait *Much Ado* iii 1 28
Greediness. Thither with all greediness of affection are they gone *W. Tale* v 2 111
The insatiate greediness of his desires *Richard III.* iii 7 7
If thou wert the wolf, thy greediness would afflict thee, and oft thou shouldst hazard thy life for thy dinner *T. of Athens* iv 3 337
Wolf in greediness, dog in madness, lion in prey *Lear* iii 4 96
Greedy. She did so course o'er my exteriors with such a greedy intention *Mer. Wives* i 3 73
So keen and greedy to confound a man *Mer. of Venice* iii 2 278
So many greedy looks of young and old *Richard II.* v 2 13
Stopping my greedy ear with their bold deeds *2 Hen. IV.* i 1 78
She'ld come again, and with a greedy ear Devour up my discourse *Othello* i 3 149
Alack, no remedy!—to the greedy touch Of common-kissing Titan *Cymbeline* iii 4 165
Greek. 'Tis a Greek invocation, to call fools into a circle *As Y. Like It* ii 5 61
Cunning in Greek, Latin, and other languages *T. of Shrew* ii 1 81
I here bestow a simple instrument, And this small packet of Greek and Latin books ii 1 101
I prithee, foolish Greek, depart from me *T. Night* iv 1 19
Compare with Cæsars, and with Cannibals, And Trojan Greeks *2 Hen. IV.* ii 4 181
And stood against them, as the hope of Troy Against the Greeks *3 Hen. VI.* ii 1 52
On Dardan plains The fresh and yet unbruised Greeks do pitch Their brave pavilions *Troi. and Cres.* Prol. 14
On one and other side, Trojan and Greek, Sets all on hazard Prol. 21
The Greeks are strong and skilful to their strength, Fierce to their skill i 1 7
She's a fool to stay behind her father; let her to the Greeks; and so I'll tell her i 1 84
There is among the Greeks A lord of Trojan blood, nephew to Hector i 2 12
Then she's a merry Greek indeed i 2 118
There is among the Greeks Achilles, a better man than Troilus i 2 268
Call you yourself Æneas?—Ay, Greek, that is my name i 3 246
And every Greek of mettle, let him know, What Troy means fairly shall be spoke aloud i 3 258
Hector, in view of Trojans and of Greeks, Shall make it good i 3 273
A lady, wiser, fairer, truer, Than ever Greek did compass in his arms i 3 276
Thus once again says Nestor from the Greeks: 'Deliver Helen' ii 2 2
Though no man lesser fears the Greeks than I ii 2 8
It was thought meet Paris should do some vengeance on the Greeks ii 2 73
For an old aunt whom the Greeks held captive, He brought a Grecian queen ii 2 77
A roisting challenge sent amongst The dull and factious nobles of the Greeks ii 2 209
Then marvel not . . . That all the Greeks begin to worship Ajax iii 3 182
A valiant Greek, Æneas,—take his hand iv 1 7
His purpose meets you: 'twas to bring this Greek To Calchas' house iv 1 36
Since she could speak, She hath not given so many good words breath As for her Greeks and Trojans suffer'd death iv 1 74
The hour prefix'd Of her delivery to this valiant Greek iv 3 2
A woful Cressid 'mongst the merry Greeks! When shall we see again? iv 4 58
Fair Greek, If e'er thou stand at mercy of my sword, Name Cressid iv 4 115
Most dearly welcome to the Greeks, sweet lady iv 5 18
Half Hector comes to seek This blended knight, half Trojan and half Greek iv 5 86
Were thy commixtion Greek and Trojan so That thou couldst say 'This hand is Grecian all, And this is Trojan; the sinews of this leg All Greek, and this all Troy' iv 5 124
And I have seen thee pause and take thy breath, When that a ring of Greeks have hemm'd thee in iv 5 193
Ah, sir, there's many a Greek and Trojan dead, Since first I saw yourself iv 5 214
Fall Greeks; fail fame; honour or go or stay; My major vow lies here v 1 47
Thanks and good night to the Greeks' general v 1 80
Sweet honey Greek, tempt me no more to folly v 2 18
Do not hold me to mine oath; Bid me do any thing but that, sweet Greek v 2 27
By Jove, I will be patient.—Guardian!—why, Greek! v 2 47
Ay, Greek; and that shall be divulged well In characters as red as Mars v 2 163
Hark, Greek: as much as I do Cressid love, So much by weight hate I her Diomed v 2 167
I do stand engaged to many Greeks, Even in the faith of valour v 3 68
What art thou, Greek? art thou for Hector's match? v 4 28
The strawy Greeks, ripe for his edge, Fall down before him v 5 24
Come, both you cogging Greeks; have at you both! v 6 11
Stand, stand, thou Greek; thou art a goodly mark: No? wilt thou not? v 6 27
I am unarm'd; forego this vantage, Greek.—Strike, fellows, strike v 8 9
The Greeks upon advice did bury Ajax That slew himself *T. Andron.* i 1 379
That baleful burning night When subtle Greeks surprised King Priam's Troy v 3 84
Did Cicero say any thing?—Ay, he spoke Greek *J. Cæsar* i 2 282
For mine own part, it was Greek to me i 2 287
Anon he finds him Striking too short at Greeks *Hamlet* ii 2 491
All curses madded Hecuba gave the Greeks, And mine to boot *Cymbeline* iv 2 313
Greekish. Knit all the Greekish ears To his experienced tongue *T. and C.* i 3 67
With surety stronger than Achilles' arm 'Fore all the Greekish heads i 3 221
Shall more obey than to the edge of steel Or force of Greekish sinews iii 1 166
And all the Greekish girls shall tripping sing, 'Great Hector's sister did Achilles win' iii 3 211
By Jove multipotent, Thou shouldst not bear from me a Greekish member Wherein my sword had not impressure made Of our rank feud iv 5 130
I have, thou gallant Trojan, seen thee oft Labouring for destiny make cruel way Through ranks of Greekish youth iv 5 185
There's many a Greek and Trojan dead, Since first I saw yourself and Diomed In Ilion, on your Greekish embassy iv 5 216
I'll heat his blood with Greekish wine to-night v 1 1
That Greekish whoremasterly villain, with the sleeve v 4 7
Green. How lush and lusty the grass looks! how green! *Tempest* ii 1 53
The ground indeed is tawny.—With an eye of green in't ii 1 55
Why hath thy queen Summon'd me hither, to this short-grass'd green? iv 1 83
You demi-puppets that By moonshine do the green sour ringlets make v 1 37
We'll dress Like urchins, ouphes and fairies, green and white *M. Wives* iv 4 49
That quaint in green she shall be loose enrobed, With ribands pendent iv 6 41
Master doctor, my daughter is in green v 3 2
Fairies, black, grey, green, and white, You moonshine revellers v 5 41
Green let it be, More fertile-fresh than all the field to see v 5 71
I knew of your purpose; turned my daughter into green v 5 215
By gar, I am cozened.—Why, did you take her in green? v 5 221
Of what complexion.—Of the sea-water green, sir *L. L. Lost* i 2 86
Green. Green indeed is the colour of lovers *L. L. Lost* i 2 90
When wheat is green, when hawthorn buds appear *M. N. Dream* i 1 185
And I serve the fairy queen, To dew her orbs upon the green ii 1 9
And now they never meet in grove or green, By fountain clear ii 1 28
The quaint mazes in the wanton green For lack of tread are undistinguishable ii 1 99
His eyes were green as leeks v 1 342
About his neck A green and gilded snake had wreathed itself *As Y. L. It* iv 3 109
You may be jogging whiles your boots are green *T. of Shrew* iii 2 213
So bedazzled with the sun That every thing I look on seemeth green iv 5 47
She pined in thought, And with a green and yellow melancholy She sat like patience on a monument *T. Night* ii 4 116
Fancies to weak for boys, too green and idle For girls of nine *W. Tale* iii 2 182
We tread In warlike march these greens before your town *K. John* ii 1 242
How green you are and fresh in this old world! iii 4 145
Bagot here and Green Observed his courtship *Richard II.* i 4 23
So, Green, thou art the midwife to my woe ii 2 62
Bushy and Green, I will not vex your souls—Since presently your souls must part your bodies iii 1 2
Where is Bagot? What is become of Bushy? where is Green? iii 2 123
Is Bushy, Green, and the Earl of Wiltshire dead?—Ay, all of them iii 2 141; iii 4 53
Three misbegotten knaves in Kendal green came at my back *1 Hen. IV.* ii 4 246
Why, how couldst thou know these men in Kendal Green? ii 4 257
Reverend Feeble. Who is next?—Peter Bullcalf o' the green *2 Hen. IV.* iii 2 183
I remember at Mile-end Green, when I lay at Clement's Inn iii 2 298
Thou art not firm enough, since griefs are green iv 5 204
For, being green, there is great hope of help *2 Hen. VI.* iii 1 287
So much the more dangerous, By how much the estate is green *Rich. III.* ii 2 127
Since it is but green, it should be put To no apparent likelihood of breach ii 2 135
Were your days As green as Ajax' and your brain so temper'd *T. and C.* ii 3 265
The fields are fragrant and the woods are green *T. Andron.* ii 2 2
Her vestal livery is but sick and green *Rom. and Jul.* ii 2 8
An eagle, madam, Hath not so green, so quick, so fair an eye As Paris iii 5 222
Where bloody Tybalt, yet but green in earth, Lies festering in his shroud iv 3 42
Wakes it now, to look so green and pale At what it did so freely? *Macb.* i 7 37
The multitudinous seas incarnadine, Making the green one red ii 2 63
Though yet of Hamlet our dear brother's death The memory be green *Ham.* i 2 2
My salad days, When I was green in judgement *Ant. and Cleo.* i 5 74
His present is A wither'd branch, that's only green at top *Pericles* ii 2 43
I will rob Tellus of her weed, To strew thy green with flowers iv 1 15
Green-a box. Un boitier vert, a box, a green-a box *Mer. Wives* i 4 47
Green boy. That yon green boy shall have no sun to ripe The bloom that promiseth a mighty fruit *K. John* ii 1 472
Green clover. The freckled cowslip, burnet and green clover *Hen. V.* v 2 49
Green corn. And the green corn Hath rotted ere his youth attain'd a beard *M. N. Dream* ii 1 94
Green cornfield. That o'er the green corn-field did pass In the spring time *As Y. Like It* v 3 19
Green earthen pots, bladders and musty seeds *Rom. and Jul.* v 1 46
Green-eyed. And shuddering fear, and green-eyed jealousy *Mer. of Venice* iii 2 110
It is the green-eyed monster which doth mock The meat it feeds on *Oth.* iii 3 166
Green fields. And a' babbled of green fields *Hen. V.* ii 3 18
Green figs. Feed him with apricocks and dewberries, With purple grapes, green figs *M. N. Dream* iii 1 170
Green girl. You speak like a green girl *Hamlet* i 3 101
Green goose. The spring is near when green geese are a-breeding *L. L. Lost* i 1 97
This is the liver-vein, which makes flesh a deity, A green goose a goddess iv 3 75
Green hair. An't had been a green hair, I should have laughed too.—They laughed not so much at the hair *Troi. and Cres.* i 2 166
Green holly. Heigh-ho! sing, heigh-ho! unto the green holly *As Y. L. It* ii 7 180
Green land. Leave your crisp channels and on this green land Answer your summons *Tempest* iv 1 130
Green lap. Such crimson tempest should bedrench The fresh green lap of fair King Richard's land *Richard II.* iii 3 47
Who are the violets now That strew the green lap of the new come spring? v 2 47
Green leaf. The green leaves quiver with the cooling wind *T. Andron.* ii 3 14
An oak but with one green leaf on it would have answered her *Much Ado* ii 1 247
Green mantle. Drinks the green mantle of the standing pool *Lear* iii 4 138
Green minds. Is handsome, young, and hath all those requisites in him that folly and green minds look after *Othello* ii 1 251
Green Neptune. Jupiter Became a bull, and bellow'd; the green Neptune A ram, and bleated *W. Tale* iv 4 28
And o'er green Neptune's back With ships made cities *Ant. and Cleo.* iv 14 58
Green plot. This green plot shall be our stage *M. N. Dream* iii 1 3
Green sarcenet flap. Thou green sarcenet flap for a sore eye, thou tassel of a prodigal's purse *Troi. and Cres.* v 1 36
Green-sickness. And making many fish-meals, that they fall into a kind of male green-sickness *2 Hen. IV.* iv 3 100
Out, you green-sickness carrion! out, you baggage! *Rom. and Jul.* iii 5 157
Troubled With the green sickness *Ant. and Cleo.* iii 2 6
Now, the pox upon her green-sickness for me! *Pericles* iv 6 14
Green sleeves. They do no more adhere and keep place together than the Hundreth Psalm to the tune of 'Green Sleeves' *Mer. Wives* ii 1 64
Let it thunder to the tune of Green Sleeves v 5 22
Green-sward. This is the prettiest low-born lass that ever Ran on the green-sward *W. Tale* iv 4 157
Green timber. And, like green timber, warp, warp *As Y. Like It* iii 3 90
Green velvet. Saw myself unbreech'd, In my green velvet coat *W. Tale* i 2 156
Green virginity. To general filths Convert o' the instant, green virginity, Do't in your parents' eyes! *T. of Athens* iv 1 7
Green willow. Sing all a green willow must be my garland *Othello* iv 3 51
Green wit. She had a green wit *L. L. Lost* i 2 94
Green wound. I told thee they were ill for a green wound *2 Hen. IV.* ii 1 106
It is good for your green wound and your ploody coxcomb *Hen. V.* v 1 44
Greener. Between the promise of his greener days And these he masters now ii 4 136
Greenly. I cannot look greenly nor gasp out my eloquence v 2 149
We have done but greenly, In hugger-mugger to inter him *Hamlet* iv 5 83
Greenwich. Being at Greenwich, After your highness had reproved the duke About Sir William Blomer *Hen. VIII.* i 2 188
Greenwood. Under the greenwood tree Who loves to lie with me, And turn his merry note *As Y. Like It* ii 5 1
Greet. Gentle and fair, your brother kindly greets you *Meas. for Meas.* i 4 24
There's other of our friends Will greet us here anon iv 5 13
We meet, With visages display'd, to talk and greet *L. L. Lost* v 2 144
When we greet, With eyes best seeing, heaven's fiery eye v 2 374

Greet. Great clerks have purposed To greet me with premeditated welcomes *M. N. Dream* v 1 94
Bellario greets your grace *Mer. of Venice* iv 1 120
Jumps along by him And never stays to greet him *As Y. Like It* ii 1 54
My mother greets me kindly: is she well?—She is not well *All's Well* ii 4 1
Not a friend greet My poor corpse, where my bones shall be thrown *T. Night* ii 4 62
Sent by the king your father To greet him and to give him comforts *W. Tale* iv 4 568
To greet a man not worth her pains, much less The adventure of her person v 1 155
Bohemia greets you from himself by me; Desires you to attach his son v 1 181
The appellant in all duty greets your highness *Richard II.* i 3 52
So, weeping, smiling, greet I thee, my earth iii 2 10
He greets me well, sir. I knew him a good backsword man *2 Hen. IV.* iii 2 69
Set forward.—Before, and greet his grace iv 1 228
From our brother England?—From him; and thus he greets your majesty *Hen. V.* ii 4 76
Speed him hence: Let him greet England with our sharp defiance iii 5 37
The sun shall greet them, And draw their honours reeking up to heaven iv 3 100
Away! vexation almost stops my breath, That sunder'd friends greet in the hour of death *1 Hen. VI.* iv 3 42
I do greet your excellence With letters of commission from the king v 4 94
If thou meanest well, I greet thee well *2 Hen. VI.* v 1 14
To greet mine own land with my wishful sight *3 Hen. VI.* iii 1 14
The first that there did greet my stranger soul, Was my great father-in-law, renowned Warwick *Richard III.* i 4 48
My lord, the mayor of London comes to greet you iii 1 17
She's wandering to the Tower, On pure heart's love to greet the tender princes iv 1 4
Go you and greet him in his tent: 'Tis said he holds you well *T. and C.* ii 3 189
They're come from field: let us to Priam's hall, To greet the warriors iii 1 162
Greet him not, Or else disdainfully, which shall shake him more iii 3 52
A merrier day did never yet greet Rome *Coriolanus* v 4 45
There greet in silence, as the dead are wont *T. Andron.* i 1 90
With all the humbleness I may, I greet your honours iv 2 5
And secretly to greet the empress' friends iv 2 174
You princes of the Goths, The Roman emperor greets you all by me v 1 157
Greet him from me; Bid him suppose some good necessity Touches his friend, which craves to be remember'd *T. of Athens* ii 2 235
The Athenians, By two of their most reverend senate, greet thee v 1 132
The senators of Athens greet thee, Timon.—I thank them v 1 139
To do you salutation from his master.—He greets me well *J. Cæsar* iv 2 6
Pronounce his present death, And with his former title greet Macbeth *Macbeth* i 2 65
My noble partner You greet with present grace and great prediction i 3 55
This diamond he greets your wife withal, By the name of most kind hostess ii 1 15
Go, captain, from me greet the Danish king *Hamlet* iv 4 1
Your haste Is now urged on you.—We will greet the time *Lear* v 1 54
The duke does greet you, general, And he requires your haste *Othello* i 2 36
I greet thy love, Not with vain thanks, but with acceptance bounteous iii 3 469
Senators of Venice greet you.—I kiss the instrument of their pleasures iv 1 230
I cannot hope Cæsar and Antony shall well greet together *Ant. and Cleo.* ii 1 39
Immoment toys, things of such dignity As we greet modern friends withal v 2 167
Leonatus is in safety And greets your highness dearly *Cymbeline* i 6 13
If you please To greet your lord with writing, do't to-night i 6 206
Why so sadly Greet you our victory? you look like Romans v 5 24
Yet I find It greets me as an enterprise of kindness *Pericles* iv 3 38
There's some of worth would come aboard; I pray ye, greet them fairly v 1 10
And pretty din The regent made in Mytilene To greet the king v 2 274
Greeted. I do not know from what part of the world I should be greeted, if not from lord Hamlet *Hamlet* iv 6 5
Greeting. Ere twice the sun hath made his journal greeting To the under generation *Meas. for Meas.* iv 3 92
Salutation and greeting to you all! *As Y. Like It* v 4 39
Welcome, you;—how now, you;—what, you;—fellow, you;—and thus much for greeting *T. of Shrew* iv 1 115
Thou shalt have my leave and love, Means and attendants and my loving greetings To those of mine in court *All's Well* ii 3 258
Captain, what greeting will you to my Lord Lafeu? I am for France iv 3 152
And from him Give you all greetings *W. Tale* v 1 140
Thus, after greeting, speaks the King of France *K. John* i 1 2
I turn to thee, And mark my greeting well *Richard II.* i 1 36
To what purpose dost thou hoard thy words, That thou return'st no greeting to thy friends? i 3 254
Take special care my greetings be deliver'd iii 1 39
Sir John Falstaff, knight, to the son of the king, nearest his father, Harry Prince of Wales, greeting *2 Hen. IV.* ii 2 131
Health and fair greeting from our general iv 1 27
We hear Your greeting is from him, not from the king *Hen. V.* i 2 236
To whom expressly I bring greeting too ii 4 112
I accept thy greeting. Art thou a messenger, or come of pleasure? *2 Hen. VI.* v 1 15
First, to do greetings to thy royal person *3 Hen. VI.* iii 3 52
This is the most despiteful gentle greeting *Troi. and Cres.* iv 1 32
Let me confirm my princely brother's greeting iv 5 174
I have received not only greetings, But with them change of honours *Coriolanus* ii 1 213
Patience perforce with wilful choler meeting Makes my flesh tremble in their different greeting *Rom. and Jul.* i 5 92
The reason that I have to love thee Doth much excuse the appertaining rage To such a greeting iii 1 67
I will omit no opportunity That may convey my greetings, love, to thee iii 5 50
I pray you, do my greeting.—Trouble him no further *T. of Athens* v 1 215
Bear my greeting to the senators And tell them that I will not come *J. Cæsar* ii 2 61
You stop our way With such prophetic greeting *Macbeth* i 3 78
We here dispatch You, good Cornelius, and you, Voltimand, For bearers of this greeting to old Norway *Hamlet* i 2 35
Most fair return of greetings and desires ii 2 60
They give their greeting to the citadel *Othello* ii 1 94
He shall have every day a several greeting *Ant. and Cleo.* i 5 77
Supplying every stage With an augmented greeting iii 6 55
Write to him—I will subscribe—gentle adieus and greetings iv 5 14
Cæsar sends greeting to the Queen of Egypt v 2 9
Gregory. Where meet we?—At Saint Gregory's well *T. G. of Ver.* iv 2 84
Where is Nathaniel, Gregory, Philip?—Here, here, sir; here, sir *T. of S.* iv 1 125
There were none fine but Adam, Ralph, and Gregory iv 1 139
Gregory. Turk Gregory never did such deeds in arms as I have done this day *1 Hen. IV.* v 3 46
You sent a large commission To Gregory de Cassado *Hen. VIII.* iii 2 321
Gregory, o' my word, we'll not carry coals *Rom. and Jul.* i 1 1
Gregory, remember thy swashing blow i 1 69
Gremio. If you, Hortensio, Or Signior Gremio, you, know any such, Prefer them hither *T. of Shrew* i 1 96
Tush, Gremio, though it pass your patience and mine to endure i 1 130
He that runs fastest gets the ring. How say you, Signior Gremio? i 1 146
Gremio, 'tis now no time to vent our love: Listen to me i 2 179
That she's the choice love of Signior Gremio.—That she's the chosen of Signior Hortensio i 2 236
You will have Gremio to keep you fair.—Is it for him you do envy me so? ii 1 17
Good morrow, neighbour Gremio. God save you, gentlemen! ii 1 40
You are too blunt: go to it orderly.—You wrong me, Signior Gremio ii 1 46
Baccare! you are marvellous forward.—O, pardon me, Signior Gremio. ii 1 74
Pray, accept his service.—A thousand thanks, Signior Gremio ii 1 85
Say, Signior Gremio, what can you assure her? ii 1 347
I'll leave her houses three or four as good, Within rich Pisa walls, as any one Old Signior Gremio has ii 1 370
What, have I pinch'd you, Signior Gremio? ii 1 373
Gremio, 'tis known my father hath no less Than three great argosies ii 1 379
Why, then the maid is mine from all the world, By your firm promise: Gremio is out-vied ii 1 387
Be bride to you, if you make this assurance; If not, to Signior Gremio ii 1 399
We'll over-reach the greybeard, Gremio, The narrow-prying father, Minola iii 2 147
Signior Gremio, came you from the church? iii 2 151
Old Gremio is hearkening still; And happily we might be interrupted. iv 4 53
He shall not go to prison.—Talk not, Signior Gremio: I say he shall go to prison v 1 99
How likes Gremio these quick-witted folks? v 2 38
Grew. And to my state grew stranger *Tempest* i 2 76
Talk with Margaret, How her acquaintance grew with this lewd fellow *Much Ado* v 1 341
That the rude sea grew civil at her song *M. N. Dream* ii 1 152
So we grew together, Like to a double cherry, seeming parted iii 2 208
Having no other reason But that his beard grew thin *T. of Shrew* iii 2 177
Grew a twenty years removed thing While one would wink *T. Night* v 1 92
And all men's ears grew to his tunes *W. Tale* iv 4 186
Grew so in love with the wenches' song, that he would not stir iv 4 618
Grew a companion to the common streets *1 Hen. IV.* iii 2 68
Grew by our feeding to so great a bulk That even our love durst not come near your sight For fear of swallowing v 1 62
Which daily grew to quarrel and to bloodshed *2 Hen. IV.* iv 5 195
Which, no doubt, Grew like the summer grass, fastest by night *Hen. V.* i 1 65
Hence grew the general wreck and massacre *1 Hen. VI.* i 1 135
In argument upon a case, Some words there grew 'twixt Somerset and me ii 5 46
Grew so fast That he could gnaw a crust at two hours old *Richard III.* ii 4 27
When mine oratory grew to an end iii 7 20
My woman's heart Grossly grew captive to his honey words iv 1 80
How they clung In their embracement, as they grew together *Hen. VIII.* i 1 10
He fell sick suddenly, and grew so ill He could not sit his mule iv 2 15
This gallant Had witchcraft in't; he grew unto his seat *Hamlet* iv 7 86
Whereupon she grew round-wombed *Lear* i 1 14
Speak yet, how grew your quarrel? ii 2 66
His grief grew puissant, and the strings of life Began to crack v 3 216
As if he pluck'd up kisses by the roots That grew upon my lips *Othello* iii 3 424
I have heard that Julius Cæsar Grew fat with feasting there *A. and C.* ii 6 66
An autumn 'twas That grew the more by reaping v 2 88
Failing of her end by his strange absence, Grew shameless-desperate *Cymbeline* v 5 58
Which fear so grew in me, I hither fled *Pericles* i 2 80
And pride so great, The name of help grew odious to repeat i 4 31
Grewest. I would thou grew'st unto the shores o' the haven *Cymbeline* i 3 1
O sweetest, fairest lily! My brother wears thee not the one half so well As when thou grew'st thyself iv 2 203
Grey. Her eyes are grey as glass, and so are mine *T. G. of Ver.* iv 4 197
Fairies, black, grey, green, and white, You moonshine revellers *M. Wives* v 5 41
With grey hairs and bruise of many days, Do challenge thee *Much Ado* v 1 65
Round about Dapples the drowsy east with spots of grey v 3 27
The sparrow and the lark, The plain-song cuckoo gray *M. N. Dream* iii 1 134
For if but once thou show me thy grey light, I'll find Demetrius iii 2 419
It was the friar of orders grey, As he forth walked on his way *T. of S.* iv 1 148
Item, two grey eyes, with lids to them; item, one neck *T. Night* i 5 266
I'll give him my horse, grey Capilet iii 4 315
So sure as this beard's grey *W. Tale* ii 3 162
That grey iniquity, that father ruffian, that vanity in years *1 Hen. IV.* ii 4 499
It stuck upon him as the sun In the grey vault of heaven *2 Hen. IV.* ii 3 19
Sir Thomas Grey, knight, of Northumberland *Hen. V.* ii Prol. 25
Scroop and Grey, in their dear care And tender preservation of our person, Would have him punish'd ii 2 58
And, sir knight, Grey of Northumberland, this same is yours ii 2 68
I arrest thee of high treason, by the name of Thomas Grey, knight ii 2 150
These grey locks, the pursuivants of death, Nestor-like aged *1 Hen. VI.* ii 5 5
At Saint Alban's field This lady's husband, Sir Richard Grey, was slain, His lands then seized on *3 Hen. VI.* iii 2 2
What! has your king married the Lady Grey? iii 3 174
What think you Of this new marriage with the Lady Grey? iv 1 2
Tell me some reason why the Lady Grey Should not become my wife iv 1 25
My Lady Grey his wife, Clarence, 'tis she That tempers him *Richard III.* i 1 64
You and your husband Grey Were factious for the house of Lancaster i 3 127
And withal whet me To be revenged on Rivers, Vaughan, Grey i 3 333
Of you, Lord Rivers, and, Lord Grey, of you; That all without desert have frown'd on me ii 1 66
Lord Rivers and Lord Grey are sent to Pomfret ii 4 42
O monstrous, monstrous! and so falls it out With Rivers, Vaughan, Grey iii 2 67
Come, Grey, come, Vaughan, let us all embrace: And take our leave iii 3 24
Rivers, Vaughan, Grey, Untimely smother'd in their dusky graves iv 4 69
Where is kind Hastings, Rivers, Vaughan, Grey? iv 4 147
Hastings, and Edward's children, Rivers, Grey, Holy King Henry v 1 3
Think upon Grey, and let thy soul despair! v 3 141
The hunt is up, the morn is bright and grey *T. Andron.* ii 2 1
Thisbe a grey eye or so, but not to the purpose *Rom. and Jul.* ii 4 45
Yon grey is not the morning's eye, 'Tis but the pale reflex of Cynthia's brow iii 5 19
Yon gray lines That fret the clouds are messengers of day *J. Cæsar* ii 1 103

Grey. The satirical rogue says here that old men have grey beards *Hamlet* ii 2 199
Whose life I have spared at suit of his gray beard . . . . . *Lear* ii 2 68
Spare my gray beard, you wagtail? . . . . ii 2 72
Pur! the cat is gray.—Arraign her first; 'tis Goneril . . . . iii 6 47
Though grey Do something mingle with our younger brown, yet ha' we A brain that nourishes our nerves . . . . . *Ant. and Cleo.* iv 8 19
Greybeard, thy love doth freeze.—But thine doth fry . *T. of Shrew* ii 1 340
We'll over-reach the greybeard, Gremio, The narrow-prying father . iii 2 147
What will you do, good grey-beard? break a lance? . 1 *Hen. VI.* iii 2 50
This word 'love,' which greybeards call divine . . 3 *Hen. VI.* v 6 81
Have I in conquest stretch'd mine arm so far, To be afeard to tell gray-beards the truth? . . . . *J. Cæsar* ii 2 67
Grey-coated. Her waggoner a small grey-coated gnat . *Rom. and Jul.* i 4 64
Grey-eyed. The grey-eyed morn smiles on the frowning night . . ii 3 1
Greyhound. How does your fallow greyhound, sir? . . *Mer. Wives* i 1 91
Thy wit is as quick as the greyhound's mouth; it catches *Much Ado* v 2 11
It runs against Hector.—Ay, and Hector's a greyhound . *L. L. Lost* v 2 665
Thy greyhounds are as swift As breathed stags . *T. of Shrew* Ind. 2 49
Lucentio slipp'd me like his greyhound, Which runs himself and catches for his master . . . . v 2 52
You say true: Why, what a candy deal of courtesy This fawning grey-hound then did proffer me! . . . . 1 *Hen. IV.* i 3 252
You may stroke him as gently as a puppy greyhound . 2 *Hen. IV.* ii 4 107
You stand like greyhounds in the slips, Straining upon the start *Hen. V.* iii 1 31
Like a brace of greyhounds Having the fearful flying hare in sight 3 *Hen. VI.* ii 5 129
Like a fawning greyhound in the leash, To let him slip at will *Coriolanus* i 6 38
And has sent your honour two brace of greyhounds . *T. of Athens* i 2 195
As hounds and greyhounds, mongrels, spaniels, curs, Shoughs *Macbeth* iii 1 93
Mastiff, greyhound, mongrel grim, Hound or spaniel, brach or lym *Lear* iii 6 71
Grief. He's something stain'd With grief that's beauty's canker *Tempest* i 2 415
When every grief is entertain'd that's offer'd, Comes to the entertainer—A dollar.—Dolour comes to him . . . . ii 1 16
She at least is banish'd from your eye, Who hath cause to wet the grief on't . . . . ii 1 127
Let grief and sorrow still embrace his heart That doth not wish you joy! v 1 214
A little time, my lord, will kill that grief . . . *T. G. of Ver.* iii 2 15
I have heard thee say No grief did ever come so near thy heart . iv 3 19
But think upon my grief, a lady's grief, And on the justice of my flying hence . . . . iv 3 28
I here forget all former griefs, Cancel all grudge . . . . v 4 142
The vile conclusion I now begin with grief and shame to utter *Meas. for Meas.* v 1 96
To speak my griefs unspeakable . . . . . *Com. of Errors* i 1 33
Grief hath changed me since you saw me last . . . . . v 1 297
Go to a gossips' feast, and go with me; After so long grief, such festivity! . . . . v 1 406
How sweetly you do minister to love, That know love's grief by his complexion! . . . . *Much Ado* i 1 315
Every one can master a grief but he that has it . . . . iii 2 28
Being that I flow in grief, The smallest twine may lead me . . . iv 1 251
And upon the grief of this suddenly died . . . . . . iv 2 65
'Tis not wisdom thus to second grief Against yourself . . . v 1 2
As thus for thus and such a grief for such, In every lineament, branch v 1 13
Patch grief with proverbs, make misfortune drunk With candle-wasters v 1 17
Men Can counsel and speak comfort to that grief Which they themselves not feel; but, tasting it, Their counsel turns to passion . . . v 1 21
Give me no counsel: My griefs cry louder than advertisement . . v 1 32
Do but behold the tears that swell in me, And they thy glory through my grief will show . . . . *L. L. Lost* iv 3 38
How shall she know my griefs? I'll drop the paper . . . . iv 3 43
Thy love is far from charity, That in love's grief desirest society . iv 3 128
Where lies thy grief, O, tell me? . . . . iv 3 171
I understand you not: my griefs are double . . . . . v 2 762
Honest plain words best pierce the ear of grief . . . . v 2 763
These griefs and losses have so bated me . . . . *Mer. of Venice* iii 3 32
You give your wife too unkind a cause of grief . . . . . v 1 175
Do not seek . . . To bear your griefs yourself and leave me out *As Y. L. It* i 3 105
If you do sorrow at my grief in love, By giving love your sorrow and my grief Were both extermined . . . . iii 5 87
Sorry am I that our good will effects Bianca's grief. . . *T. of Shrew* i 1 87
This I know, She is not for your turn, the more my grief . . ii 1 63
Moderate lamentation is the right of the dead, excessive grief the enemy to the living.—If the living be enemy to the grief, the excess makes it soon mortal . . . . *All's Well* i 1 65
I have felt so many quirks of joy and grief . . . . . iii 2 51
If thou engrossest all the griefs are thine, Thou robb'st me of a moiety iii 2 68
My greatest grief, Though little he do feel it, set down sharply . iii 4 32
Grief would have tears, and sorrow bids me speak . . . iii 4 42
The tenderness of her nature became a prey to her grief. . . . iv 3 61
She sat like patience on a monument, Smiling at grief . *T. Night* ii 4 118
With the same 'haviour that your passion bears Goes on my master's grief . . . . iii 4 227
But I have That honourable grief lodged here which burns Worse than tears drown . . . . *W. Tale* ii 1 111
On her frights and griefs, Which never tender lady hath borne greater. ii 2 23
This sessions, to our great grief we pronounce, Even pushes 'gainst our heart . . . . iii 2 1
For life, I prize it As I weigh grief, which I would spare . . . iii 2 44
What's gone and what's past help Should be past grief . . . iii 2 224
If thou beest capable of things serious, thou must know the king is full of grief . . . . iv 4 792
To take off so much grief from you as he Will piece up in himself . v 3 55
I will instruct my sorrows to be proud: For grief is proud . *K. John* iii 1 69
To me and to the state of my great grief Let kings assemble . . iii 1 70
My grief's so great That no supporter but the huge firm earth Can hold it up . . . . iii 1 71
O, this will make my mother die with grief! . . . . . iii 3 5
'Tis like I should forget myself: O, if I could, what grief should I forget! . . . . iii 4 50
Being not mad but sensible of grief, My reasonable part produces reason iii 4 53
Ten thousand wiry friends Do glue themselves in sociable grief . iii 4 65
You hold too heinous a respect of grief.—He talks to me that never had a son . . . . iii 4 90
You are as fond of grief as of your child.—Grief fills the room up of my absent child, Lies in his bed . . . . iii 4 92
Saying, 'What lack you?' and 'Where lies your grief?' . . . iv 1 48
The fire is dead with grief, Being create for comfort . . . iv 1 106
Good words, I think, were best.—Our griefs, and not our manners, reason now . . . . iv 3 29

Grief. There is little reason in your grief; Therefore 'twere reason you had manners. . . . . *K. John* iv 3 30
Pay the time but needful woe, Since it hath been beforehand with our griefs . . . . v 7 111
Grief boundeth where it falls, Not with the empty hollowness *Richard II.* i 2 58
Thy grief is but thy absence for a time.—Joy absent, grief is present . i 3 258
What is six winters? they are quickly gone.—To men in joy; but grief makes one hour ten . . . . i 3 261
Boast of nothing else But that I was a journeyman to grief . . . i 3 274
Such grief That words seem'd buried in my sorrow's grave . . . i 4 14
Within me grief hath kept a tedious fast; And who abstains from meat that is not gaunt? . . . . ii 1 75
York is too far gone with grief, Or else he never would compare between ii 1 184
I know no cause Why I should welcome such a guest as grief . . ii 2 7
Each substance of a grief hath twenty shadows, Which shows like grief itself . . . . ii 2 14
Find shapes of grief, more than himself, to wail . . . . . ii 2 22
Conceit is still derived From some forefather grief . . . . ii 2 35
For nothing hath begot my something grief; Or something hath the nothing that I grieve . . . . ii 2 36
We are on the earth, Where nothing lives but crosses, cares and grief . ii 2 79
I live with bread like you, feel want, Taste grief, need friends . iii 2 176
O that I were as great As is my grief, or lesser than my name! . . iii 3 137
Sorrow and grief of heart Makes him speak fondly, like a frantic man . iii 3 184
My legs can keep no measure in delight, When my poor heart no measure keeps in grief. . . . . iii 4 8
If of grief, being altogether had, It adds more sorrow to my want of joy iii 4 15
Full of tears am I, Drinking my griefs, whilst you mount up on high . iv 1 189
Still my griefs are mine: You may my glories and my state depose, But not my griefs; still am I king of those . . . . iv 1 191
'Tis very true, my grief lies all within; And these external manners of laments Are merely shadows to the unseen grief . . . . . iv 1 295
Most beauteous inn, Why should hard-favour'd grief be lodged in thee? v 1 14
Join not with grief, fair woman, do not so, To make my end too sudden v 1 16
To quit their griefs, Tell thou the lamentable tale of me. . . . v 1 43
In wooing sorrow let's be brief, Since, wedding it, there is such length in grief . . . . v 1 94
Combating with tears and smiles, The badges of his grief and patience. v 2 33
Out of my grief and my impatience, Answer'd neglectingly . 1 *Hen. IV.* i 3 51
A plague of sighing and grief! it blows a man up like a bladder . . ii 4 365
The king hath sent to know The nature of your griefs . . . iv 3 42
He bids you name your griefs; and with all speed You shall have your desires . . . . iv 3 48
Can honour set to a leg? no: or an arm? no: or take away the grief of a wound? no . . . . v 1 134
The big year, swoln with some other grief, Is thought with child 2 *Hen. IV.* Ind. 13
Even so my limbs, Weaken'd with grief, being now enraged with grief, Are thrice themselves . . . . i 1 144
To speak truth, This present grief had wiped it from my mind . . i 1 211
It hath it original from much grief, from study . . . . i 2 131
And find our griefs heavier than our offences . . . . . iv 1 69
Have the summary of all our griefs, When time shall serve, to show . iv 1 73
When we are wrong'd and would unfold our griefs, We are denied access iv 1 77
That you should have an inch of any ground To build a grief on . . iv 1 110
Here come I from our princely general To know your griefs . . iv 1 142
I sent your grace The parcels and particulars of our grief . . iv 2 36
These griefs shall be with speed redress'd; Upon my soul, they shall . iv 2 59
My grief Stretches itself beyond the hour of death . . . . iv 4 56
I had forestall'd this dear and deep rebuke Ere you with grief had spoke iv 5 142
Thou art not firm enough, since griefs are green . . . . iv 5 204
What kind of god art thou, that suffer'st more Of mortal griefs than do thy worshippers? What are thy rents? . . . . . . *Hen. V.* iv 1 259
This day Shall change all griefs and quarrels into love . . . v 2 20
Weak shoulders, overborne with burthening grief . . . 1 *Hen. VI.* ii 5 10
Rouen hangs her head for grief That such a valiant company are fled . iii 2 124
I foresee with grief The utter loss of all the realm of France . . v 4 111
Conduct me where, from company, I may revolve and ruminate my grief.—Ay, grief, I fear me, both at first and last . . . . . v 5 101
His grief, Your grief, the common grief of all the land . 2 *Hen. VI.* i 1 76
Wherefore weeps Warwick . . .?—For grief that they are past recovery i 1 116
Though Humphrey's pride And greatness of his place be grief to us . i 1 173
Sorrow and grief have vanquish'd all my powers . . . . ii 1 183
Mine eyes are full of tears, my heart of grief . . . . . ii 3 17
Forget this grief.—Ah, Gloucester, teach me to forget myself! . . ii 4 26
My heart is drown'd with grief, Whose flood begins to flow within mine eyes . . . . iii 1 198
So, get thee gone, that I may know my grief . . . . . iii 2 346
Oft have I heard that grief softens the mind And makes it fearful . iv 4 1
I remember it to my grief . . . . 3 *Hen. VI.* i 1 93
And I, with grief and sorrow, to the court . . . . . . i 1 210
And when with grief he wept, The ruthless queen gave him to dry his cheeks A napkin steeped in the harmless blood Of sweet young Rutland . . . . ii 1 60
To weep is to make less the depth of grief: Tears then for babes . ii 1 85
Would I were dead! if God's good will were so; For what is in this world but grief and woe? . . . . ii 5 20
Be blind with tears, and break o'ercharged with grief . . . . ii 5 78
Woe above woe! grief more than common grief! . . . . . ii 5 94
She, poor wretch, for grief can speak no more . . . . . iii 1 47
Be plain, Queen Margaret, and tell thy grief . . . . . iii 3 19
These news I must confess are full of grief; Yet, gracious madam, bear it . . . . iv 4 13
My mildness hath allay'd their swelling griefs. . . . . . iv 8 42
And, after many lengthen'd hours of grief, Die neither mother, wife, nor England's queen! . . . . *Richard III.* i 3 208
What cause have I, Thine being but a moiety of my grief, To overgo thy plaints! . . . . ii 2 60
My dread lord; so must I call you now.—Ay, brother, to our grief . iii 1 98
And being but a toy, which is no grief to give . . . . . iii 1 114
I with grief and extreme age shall perish And never look upon thy face again . . . . iv 4 185
But that still use of grief makes wild grief tame . . . . iv 4 229
The subjects' grief Comes through commissions . . *Hen. VIII.* i 2 56
Than to be perk'd up in a glistering grief, And wear a golden sorrow . ii 3 21
In sweet music is such art, Killing care and grief of heart . . iii 1 13
I would your grace Would leave your griefs, and take my counsel . iii 1 92
What grief hath set the jaundice on your cheeks? . . *Troi. and Cres.* i 3 2
Why tell you me of moderation? The grief is fine, full, perfect, that I taste . . . . iv 4 3

Grief. If I could temporise with my affection, . . . The like allayment could I give my grief *Troi. and Cres.* iv 4 8
My love admits no qualifying dross; No more my grief iv 4 10
Whose fury not dissembled speaks his griefs *T. Andron.* i 1 438
Be ruled by me, be won at last; Dissemble all your griefs and discontents i 1 443
Though grieved with killing grief ii 3 260
My grief was at the height before thou camest, And now, like Nilus, it disdaineth bounds iii 1 70
Cease your tears; for, at your grief, See how my wretched sister sobs iii 1 136
Thy griefs their sports, thy resolution mock'd iii 1 239
Now no more will I control thy griefs: Rend off thy silver hair iii 1 260
But now nor Lucius nor Lavinia lives But in oblivion and hateful griefs iii 1 296
Want our hands, And cannot passionate our tenfold grief With folded arms iii 2 6
Grief has so wrought on him, He takes false shadows for true substances iii 2 79
I have heard my grandsire say full oft, Extremity of griefs would make men mad iv 1 19
Witness these trenches made by grief and care v 2 23
Nor can I utter all our bitter grief, But floods of tears will drown my oratory v 3 89
Friends should associate friends in grief and woe v 3 169
Griefs of mine own lie heavy in my breast *Rom. and Jul.* i 1 192
This love that thou hast shown Doth add more grief to too much of mine own i 1 195
One desperate grief cures with another's languish i 2 49
And kill the envious moon, Who is already sick and pale with grief ii 2 5
By and by, I come:—To cease thy suit, and leave me to my grief ii 2 153
These griefs, these woes, these sorrows make me old iii 2 89
If sour woe delights in fellowship And needly will be rank'd with other griefs iii 2 117
But that a joy past joy calls out on me, It were a grief, so brief to part iii 3 174
Some grief shows much of love; But much of grief shows still some want of wit iii 5 73
Is there no pity sitting in the clouds, That sees into the bottom of my grief? iii 5 199
I already know thy grief; It strains me past the compass of my wits iv 1 46
When griping grief the heart doth wound, And doleful dumps the mind oppress iv 5 128
With which grief, It is supposed, the fair creature died v 3 50
My wife is dead to-night; Grief of my son's exile hath stopp'd her breath v 3 211
You, to remove that siege of grief from her, Betroth'd and would have married her perforce To County Paris v 3 237
I am sick of that grief too, as I understand how all things go *T. of Athens* iii 6 19
I will present My honest grief unto him iv 3 477
Ne'er did poor steward wear a truer grief For his undone lord iv 3 487
I beg of you to know me, good my lord, To accept my grief iv 3 495
'Twas time and griefs That framed him thus v 1 125
To ease them of their griefs, Their fears of hostile strokes, their aches, losses v 1 201
Noble and young, When thy first griefs were but a mere conceit v 4 14
These walls of ours Were not erected by their hands from whom You have received your griefs v 4 24
Thou abhorr'dst in us our human griefs, Scorn'dst our brain's flow v 4 75
But, O grief, Where hast thou led me? *J. Cæsar* i 3 111
Be factious for redress of all these griefs i 3 118
Dear my lord, Make me acquainted with your cause of grief ii 1 256
What private griefs they have, alas, I know not, That made them do it iii 2 217
Speak your griefs softly: I do know you well iv 2 42
In my tent, Cassius, enlarge your griefs, And I will give you audience iv 2 46
When grief, and blood ill-temper'd, vexeth him iv 3 115
I am sick of many griefs.—Of your philosophy you make no use iv 3 144
Upon what sickness?—Impatient of my absence, And grief iv 3 153
Now is that noble vessel full of grief, That it runs over even at his eyes v 5 13
We shall make our griefs and clamour roar Upon his death *Macbeth* i 7 78
What's the newest grief?—That of an hour's age doth hiss the speaker iv 3 174
The grief that does not speak Whispers the o'er-fraught heart iv 3 209
Let's make us medicines of our great revenge, To cure this deadly grief iv 3 215
Let grief Convert to anger; blunt not the heart, enrage it iv 3 228
It us befitted To bear our hearts in grief *Hamlet* i 2 3
With all forms, moods, shapes of grief, That can denote me truly i 2 82
'Tis unmanly grief; It shows a will most incorrect to heaven i 2 94
Might move More grief to hide than hate to utter love ii 1 119
The origin and commencement of his grief Sprung from neglected love iii 1 185
Let his queen mother all alone entreat him To show his grief iii 1 191
The violence of either grief or joy Their own enactures with themselves destroy; Where joy most revels, grief doth most lament; Grief joys, joy grieves, on slender accident iii 2 206
Bar the door upon your own liberty, if you deny your griefs to your friend iii 2 352
O, this is the poison of deep grief iv 5 76
I am guiltless of your father's death, And am most sensibly in grief for it iv 5 150
I must commune with your grief, Or you deny me right iv 5 202
What is he whose grief Bears such an emphasis? v 1 277
The bravery of his grief did put me Into a towering passion v 2 79
A poor old man, As full of grief as age; wretched in both! *Lear* ii 4 276
Truth to tell thee, The grief hath crazed my wits iii 4 175
Then the mind much sufferance doth o'erskip, When grief hath mates iii 6 114
Did your letters pierce the queen to any demonstration of grief? iv 3 12
Away she started To deal with grief alone iv 3 34
Better I were distract: So should my thoughts be sever'd from my griefs iv 6 289
'Twixt two extremes of passion, joy and grief, Burst smilingly v 3 198
His grief grew puissant, and the strings of life Began to crack v 3 216
My particular grief Is of so flood-gate and o'er-bearing nature That it engluts and swallows other sorrows *Othello* i 3 55
When remedies are past, the griefs are ended By seeing the worst i 3 202
He robs himself that spends a bootless grief i 3 209
He bears both the sentence and the sorrow That, to pay grief, must of poor patience borrow i 3 215
So humbled That he hath left part of his grief with me, To suffer with him iii 3 53
O'erwhelmed with your grief—A passion most unsuiting such a man iv 1 77
O villany!—I thought so then:—I'll kill myself for grief:—O villany, villany! v 2 192
Pure grief Shore his old thread in twain v 2 205
This grief is crowned with consolation *Ant. and Cleo.* i 2 174
To enforce no further The griefs between ye: to forget them quite ii 2 100
Being dried with grief, will break to powder, And finish all foul thoughts iv 9 17
I do feel, By the rebound of yours, a grief that smites My very heart at root v 2 104
O, that husband! My supreme crown of grief! *Cymbeline* i 6 4
Or look upon our Romans, whose remembrance Is yet fresh in their grief ii 4 15
Let that grieve him: Some griefs are med'cinable iii 2 33
I speak not out of weak surmises, but from proof as strong as my grief iii 4 25
My heart: Fear not; 'tis empty of all things but grief: Thy master is not there, who was indeed The riches of it iii 4 71
Grief and patience, rooted in him both, Mingle their spurs together iv 2 57
Grief. Let the stinking elder, grief, untwine His perishing root! *Cymb.* iv 2 59
And lamenting toys Is jollity for apes and grief for boys iv 2 194
Great griefs, I see, medicine the less iv 2 243
To my grief, I am The heir of his reward v 5 12
Peaceful night, The tomb where grief should sleep *Pericles* i 2 5
Bear with patience Such griefs as you yourself do lay upon yourself i 2 66
By relating tales of others' griefs, See if 'twill teach us to forget our own i 4 2
Even such our griefs are; Here they're but felt, and seen with mischief's eyes i 4 7
Know that our griefs are risen to the top, And now at length they overflow ii 4 23
Your griefs! for what? wrong not your prince you love ii 4 25
And for a further grief,—God give you joy!—What, are you both pleased? ii 5 87
Not spoken To any one, nor taken sustenance But to prorogue his grief v 1 26
The main grief springs from the loss Of a beloved daughter and a wife v 1 29
She speaks, My lord, that, may be, hath endured a grief Might equal yours v 1 88
Thou thought'st thy griefs might equal mine, If both were open'd v 1 132
Grief-shot With his unkindness *Coriolanus* v 1 44
Grievance. Commend thy grievance to my holy prayers *T. G. of Ver.* i 1 17
The night's dead silence Will well become such sweet-complaining grievance iii 2 86
I pity much your grievances iv 3 37
I told him gently of our grievances, Of his oath-breaking *1 Hen. IV.* v 2 37
For this contains our general grievances *2 Hen. IV.* iv 1 169
Is weary Of dainty and such picking grievances iv 1 198
I promised you redress of these same grievances iv 2 113
Your subjects Are in great grievance *Hen. VIII.* i 2 20
Step aside; I'll know his grievance, or be much denied *Rom. and Jul.* i 1 163
Withdraw unto some private place, And reason coldly of your grievances iii 1 55
Put upon you what restraint and grievance The law, with all his might to enforce it on, Will give him cable *Othello* i 2 15
Grieve. He grieves my very heart-strings *T. G. of Ver.* iv 2 61
It grieves me for the death of Claudio; But there's no remedy *M. for M.* ii 1 294
You might pardon him, And neither heaven nor man grieve at the mercy ii 2 50
Thou, that hast no unkind mate to grieve thee *Com. of Errors* ii 1 38
Would it not grieve a woman to be overmastered with a piece of valiant dust? to make an account of her life to a clod? *Much Ado* ii 1 63
Yet do not suddenly, for it may grieve him *Mer. of Venice* ii 8 34
Grieve not that I am fallen to this for you iv 1 266
Sir, grieve not you; you are welcome notwithstanding v 1 239
This is it, Adam, that grieves me *As Y. Like It* i 1 23
The melancholy Jaques grieves at that ii 1 26
At which time would I, being but a moonish youth, grieve, be effeminate iii 2 430
How it grieves me to see thee wear thy heart in a scarf! v 2 22
It grieves me Much more for what I cannot do for you Than what befalls myself. You stand amazed *T. Night* iii 4 369
Be't known, From him that has most cause to grieve it should be, She's an adulteress *W. Tale* ii 1 77
How will this grieve you, When you shall come to clearer knowledge! ii 1 96
He shall not need to grieve At knowing of thy choice iv 4 426
O, it grieves my soul, That I must draw this metal from my side To be a widow-maker! *K. John* v 2 15
At some thing it grieves, More than with parting from my lord *Rich. II.* ii 2 12
Or something hath the nothing that I grieve ii 2 37
But I shall grieve you to report the rest ii 2 95
The king himself; who, Douglas, grieves at heart So many of his shadows thou hast met And not the very king *1 Hen. IV.* v 4 29
Do not you grieve at this; I shall be sent for in private to him *2 Hen. IV.* v 5 82
I grieve to hear what torments you endured *1 Hen. VI.* i 4 57
Nor grieve that Rouen is so recovered: Care is no cure iii 3 2
One drop of blood drawn from thy country's bosom Should grieve thee more than streams of foreign gore iii 3 55
It grieves his highness: my good lords, be friends iv 1 133
But wherefore grieve I at an hour's poor loss? *2 Hen. VI.* iii 2 381
It grieves my soul to leave thee unassail'd v 2 18
I prithee, grieve, to make me merry, York *3 Hen. VI.* i 4 86
Would thy best friends did know How it doth grieve me that thy head is here! ii 2 55
'Twill grieve your grace my sons should call you father iii 2 100
Murder whiles I smile, And cry 'Content' to that which grieves my heart iii 2 183
One false glass, Which grieves me when I see my shame in him *Rich. III.* ii 2 54
Such news, my lord, as grieves me to unfold ii 4 39
It grieves many: The gentleman is learn'd *Hen. VIII.* i 2 110
The cause He may a little grieve at ii 1 39
Would it not grieve an able man to leave So sweet a bedfellow? ii 2 142
Who grieves much for your weakness iv 2 117
I grieve at what I speak, And am right sorry to repeat what follows v 1 95
But it must grieve young Pyrrhus now at home *Troi. and Cres.* iii 3 209
You part in anger.—Doth that grieve thee? O wither'd truth! v 2 45
I wear it on my helm, And grieve his spirit that dares not challenge it v 2 94
Pray now, no more: my mother, Who has a charter to extol her blood, When she does praise me grieves me *Coriolanus* i 9 15
Have you with heed perused What I have written to you?—We have.—And grieve to hear't v 6 63
I have done a thousand dreadful things . . . And nothing grieves me heartily indeed But that I cannot do ten thousand more *T. Andron.* v 1 143
And yet no man like he doth grieve my heart *Rom. and Jul.* iii 5 84
It grieves me to see so many dip their meat in one man's blood *T. of Athens* i 2 41
If then thy spirit look upon us now, Shall it not grieve thee? *J. Cæsar* iii 1 196
To kill their gracious father? damned fact! How it did grieve Macbeth! *Macbeth* iii 6 11
Show his eyes, and grieve his heart; Come like shadows, so depart! iv 1 110
Now this overdone, or come tardy off, though it make the unskilful laugh, cannot but make the judicious grieve *Hamlet* iii 2 30
Grief joys, joy grieves, on slender accident iii 2 209
We dearly grieve For that which thou hast done iv 3 43
You shall not grieve Lending me this acquaintance *Lear* iv 3 55
It grieves my husband, As if the case were his *Othello* iii 3 3
Let that grieve him: Some griefs are med'cinable *Cymbeline* iii 2 32
I grieve myself To think, when thou shalt be disedged by her iii 4 95
But We grieve at chances here iv 3 35
And—which more may grieve thee, As it doth me v 5 144
Come to the matter.—All too soon I shall, Unless thou wouldst grieve quickly v 5 170
I thought it princely charity to grieve them *Pericles* i 2 100
It shall no longer grieve without reproof ii 4 19
Grieved. Myself, my brother and this grieved count Did see her *M. Ado* iv 1 90
Grieved I, I had but one? Chid I for that at frugal nature's frame? iv 1 129
I have too grieved a heart To take a tedious leave *Mer. of Venice* ii 7 76
Be not thou more grieved than I am.—I have more cause *As Y. Like It* i 3 94
Was ever gentleman thus grieved as I? *T. of Shrew* ii 1 37

Grieved. Thy son by this hath married. Wonder not, Nor be not grieved *T. of Shrew* iv 5 64
Are not you grieved that Arthur is his prisoner? *K. John* iii 4 123
And is't not pity, O my grieved friends? v 2 24
A trespass that doth vex my grieved soul *Richard II.* i 1 138
Even in the glasses of thine eyes I see thy grieved heart i 3 209
Make me, that nothing have, with nothing grieved iv 1 216
Was ever king so grieved for subjects' woe? *3 Hen. VI.* ii 5 111
The grieved commons Hardly conceive of me *Hen. VIII.* i 2 104
Which so grieved him That he ran mad and died ii 2 130
Though grieved with killing grief *T. Andron.* iii 3 260
I have heard, and grieved, How cursed Athens *T. of Athens* iv 3 92
Let not therefore my good friends be grieved *J. Cæsar* i 2 43
Whereat grieved, That so his sickness, age and impotence Was falsely borne in hand, sends out arrests *Hamlet* ii 2 65
Hearing that you prepared for war, acquainted My grieved ear *A. and C.* iii 6 59
It grieved my heart to hear what pitiful cries they made to us *Pericles* ii 1 21
Grievest. Thou grievest my gall.—Gall! bitter *L. L. Lost* v 2 237
Grieving. I cannot be a man with wishing, therefore I will die a woman with grieving *Much Ado* iv 1 326
Miss that which one unworthier may attain, And die with grieving *Mer. of Venice* ii 1 38
The effects of his fond jealousies so grieving *W. Tale* iv 1 18
Honest Iago, that look'st dead with grieving, Speak *Othello* ii 3 177
I grieving grant Did you too much disquiet *Ant. and Cleo.* ii 2 69
Grievingly I think *Hen. VIII.* i 1 87
Grievous. If lost, why then a grievous labour won *T. G. of Ver.* i 1 33
Which else would stand under grievous imposition *Meas. for Meas.* i 2 194
A grievous fault! Say, woman, didst thou so?—No, my good lord *Com. of Errors* v 1 206
By your wisdom been this day acquitted Of grievous penalties *M. of V.* iv 1 410
Old John of Gaunt is grievous sick, my lord, Suddenly taken *Richard II.* i 4 54
The commons hath he pill'd with grievous taxes, And quite lost their hearts ii 1 246
These grievous crimes Committed by your person and your followers iv 1 223
The complaints I hear of thee are grievous *1 Hen. IV.* ii 4 487
He is grievous sick.—'Zounds! how has he the leisure to be sick? iv 1 16
Let grievous, ghastly, gaping wounds Untwine the Sisters Three! *2 Hen. IV.* ii 4 212
Girding with grievous siege castles and towns *Hen. V.* i 2 152
I have heard you preach That malice was a great and grievous sin *1 Hen. VI.* iii 1 128
And torture him with grievous lingering death *2 Hen. VI.* iii 2 247
Suddenly a grievous sickness took him, That makes him gasp and stare iii 2 370
'Tis very grievous to be thought upon *Richard III.* i 1 141
If heaven have any grievous plague in store Exceeding those i 3 217
The secret mischiefs that I set abroach I lay unto the grievous charge of others i 3 326
By Christ's dear blood shed for our grievous sins i 4 195
Like Pilate, would I wash my hands Of this most grievous guilty murder i 4 280
A grievous burthen was thy birth to me iv 4 167
I have, and most unwillingly, of late Heard many grievous, I do say, my lord, Grievous complaints of you *Hen. VIII.* v 1 99
If it were so, it was a grievous fault *J. Cæsar* iii 2 84
A noble ship of Venice Hath seen a grievous wreck *Othello* ii 1 23
Grievously. My daughter takes his going grievously *T. G. of Ver.* iii 2 14
And has been grievously peaten as an old 'oman *Mer. Wives* iv 4 22
He beat me grievously, in the shape of a woman v 1 21
I do suspect thee very grievously *K. John* iv 3 134
It was a grievous fault, And grievously hath Cæsar answer'd it *J. Cæsar* iii 2 85
What are you here that cry so grievously? *Othello* v 1 53
Griffin. The dove pursues the griffin *M. N. Dream* ii 1 232
A clip-wing'd griffin and a moulten raven, A couching lion *1 Hen. IV.* iii 1 152
Griffith. How does your grace?—O Griffith, sick to death! *Hen. VIII.* iv 2 1
Didst thou not tell me, Griffith, as thou led'st me, That the great child of honour, Cardinal Wolsey, Was dead? iv 2 5
Prithee, good Griffith, tell me how he died: If well, he stepp'd before me iv 2 9
Yet thus far, Griffith, give me leave to speak him, And yet with charity iv 2 32
Hear me speak his good now?—Yes, good Griffith; I were malicious else iv 2 47
But such an honest chronicler as Griffith iv 2 72
Good Griffith, Cause the musicians play me that sad note I named my knell iv 2 77
They promised me eternal happiness; And brought me garlands, Griffith iv 2 91
Mine eyes grow dim. Farewell, My lord. Griffith, farewell iv 2 165
Grim. Dull melancholy, Kinsman to grim and comfortless despair *Com. of Errors* v 1 80
Then was Venus like her mother, for her father is but grim *L. L. Lost* ii 1 255
So should a murderer look, so dead, so grim *M. N. Dream* iii 2 57
Grim death, how foul and loathsome is thine image! *T. of Shrew* Ind. 1 35
If thou, that bid'st me be content, wert grim, . . . I would not care, I then would be content *K. John* iii 1 43
I am sworn brother, sweet, To grim Necessity *Richard II.* v 1 21
A second Hector, for his grim aspect *1 Hen. VI.* ii 3 20
And hemm'd about with grim destruction iv 3 21
Upon thy eye-balls murderous tyranny Sits in grim majesty *2 Hen. VI.* iii 2 50
That grim ferryman which poets write of *Richard III.* i 4 46
Thy grim looks and The thunder-like percussion of thy sounds *Coriolanus* i 4 58
Thou hast a grim appearance, and thy face Bears a command in't iv 5 66
Would to the bleeding and the grim alarm Excite the mortified man *Macb.* v 2 4
Mastiff, greyhound, mongrel grim, Hound or spaniel *Lear* iii 6 71
Young and rose-lipp'd cherubin,—Ay, there, look grim as hell! *Othello* iv 2 64
I know this act shows horrible and grim v 2 203
So for her many a wight did die, As yon grim looks do testify *Per.* 1 Gower 40
Grime. A man may go over shoes in the grime of it *Com. of Errors* iii 2 106
My face I'll grime with filth; Blanket my loins *Lear* ii 3 9
Grim-look'd night! O night with hue so black! *M. N. Dream* v 1 171
Grimly. The skies look grimly And threaten present blusters *W. Tale* iii 3 3
They cannot tell; look grimly, And dare not speak *Ant. and Cleo.* iv 12 5
Grim-visaged war hath smooth'd his wrinkled front *Richard III.* i 1 9
Grin. Come, grin on me, and I will think thou smilest *K. John* iii 4 34
Small curs are not regarded when they grin *2 Hen. VI.* iii 1 18
See, how the pangs of death do make him grin! iii 3 24
Against the senseless winds shalt grin in vain iv 1 77
What valour were it, when a cur doth grin, For one to thrust his hand between his teeth? *3 Hen. VI.* i 4 56
And to grin like lions Upon the pikes o' the hunters *Cymbeline* v 3 38
Grind. Go charge my goblins that they grind their joints With dry convulsions *Tempest* iv 1 259
Grind. They to dust should grind it And throw't against the wind *Cor.* iii 2 103
Hark, villains! I will grind your bones to dust *T. Andron.* v 2 187
When that they are dead, Let me go grind their bones to powder small. v 2 199
A pair of chaps, no more; And throw between them all the food thou hast, They'll grind the one the other *Ant. and Cleo.* iii 5 16
Grinding. He that will have a cake out of the wheat must needs tarry the grinding.—Have I not tarried?—Ay, the grinding; but you must tarry the bolting *Troi. and Cres.* i 1 16
No leisure bated, No, not to stay the grinding of the axe *Hamlet* v 2 24
Grindstone. Let the porter let in Susan Grindstone *Rom. and Jul.* i 5 10
Grinning. Scoffing his state and grinning at his pomp *Richard II.* iii 2 163
I like not such grinning honour as Sir Walter hath *1 Hen. IV.* v 3 62
Not one now, to mock your own grinning? quite chap-fallen? *Hamlet* v 1 212
Gripe. And he that speaks doth gripe the hearer's wrist *K. John* iv 2 190
Seek you to seize and gripe into your hands The royalties? *Richard II.* ii 1 189
No hand of blood and bone Can gripe the sacred handle of our sceptre iii 3 80
You took occasion to be quickly woo'd To gripe the general sway *1 Hen. IV.* v 1 57
Raught me his hand, And, with a feeble gripe, says, 'Dear my lord' *Hen. V.* iv 6 22
But weep with him, To see how inly sorrow gripes his soul *3 Hen. VI.* i 4 171
I take my cause Out of the gripes of cruel men *Hen. VIII.* v 3 100
And put a barren sceptre in my gripe *Macbeth* iii 1 62
And then, sir, would he gripe and wring my hand *Othello* iii 3 421
Join gripes with hands Made hard with hourly falsehood *Cymbeline* i 6 106
We have yet many among us can gripe as hard as Cassibelan iii 1 40
But, feeling woe, Gripe not at earthly joys as erst they did *Pericles* i 1 49
Griped. We live not to be grip'd by meaner persons *Hen. VIII.* ii 2 136
Griping. When griping grief the heart doth wound *Rom. and Jul.* iv 5 128
Grise. I pity you.—That's a degree to love.—No, not a grize *T. Night* iii 1 135
Every grise of fortune Is smooth'd by that below *T. of Athens* iv 3 16
Lay a sentence, Which, as a grise or step, may help these lovers *Othello* i 3 200
Grisled. The grisled north Disgorges such a tempest forth *Pericles* iii Gower 47
Grisly. This grisly beast, which Lion hight by name *M. N. Dream* v 1 140
My grisly countenance made others fly *1 Hen. VI.* i 4 47
Grissel. For patience she will prove a second Grissel *T. of Shrew* ii 1 297
Grizzle. O thou dissembling cub! what wilt thou be When time hath sow'd a grizzle on thy case? *T. Night* v 1 168
Grizzled. His beard was grizzled,—no?—It was, as I have seen it in his life, A sable silver'd *Hamlet* i 2 240
To the boy Cæsar send this grizzled head, And he will fill thy wishes to the brim With principalities *Ant. and Cleo.* iii 13 17
Groan. Thou didst vent thy groans As fast as mill-wheels strike *Tempest* i 2 280
Thy groans Did make wolves howl i 2 287
To be in love, where scorn is bought with groans *T. G. of Ver.* i 1 29
With penitential groans, With nightly tears and daily heart-sore sighs ii 4 131
Deep groans, nor silver-shedding tears, Could penetrate her uncompassionate sire iii 1 230
Bid sorrow wag, cry 'hem!' when he should groan *Much Ado* v 1 16
Midnight, assist our moan; Help us to sigh and groan v 3 17
I would you heard it groan.—Is the fool sick? *L. L. Lost* ii 1 183
The anointed sovereign of sighs and groans, Liege of all loiterers iii 1 184
Well, I will love, write, sigh, pray, sue and groan iii 1 206
God give him grace to groan! iv 3 20
O, what a scene of foolery have I seen, Of sighs, of groans! iv 3 164
When shall you see me write a thing in rhyme? Or groan for love? iv 3 182
Sickly ears, Deaf'd with the clamours of their own dear groans v 2 874
With mirth and laughter let old wrinkles come, And let my liver rather heat with wine Than my heart cool with mortifying groans *M. of V.* i 1 82
The wretched animal heaved forth such groans *As Y. Like It* ii 1 36
You ne'er oppress'd me with a mother's groan *All's Well* i 3 153
Made a groan of her last breath, and now she sings in heaven iv 3 62
If she had partaken of my flesh, and cost me the dearest groans of a mother, I could not have owed her a more rooted love iv 5 12
With groans that thunder love, with sighs of fire *T. Night* i 5 275
And what hear there for welcome but my groans? *Richard II.* i 2 70
And future ages groan for this foul act iv 1 138
Go, count thy way with sighs; I mine with groans v 1 89
Twice for one step I'll groan, the way being short v 1 91
Be gone, That I may strive to kill it with a groan v 1 100
The sound that tells what hour it is Are clamorous groans v 5 56
So sighs and tears and groans Show minutes, times, and hours v 5 57
Till fields and blows and groans applaud our sport! *1 Hen. IV.* i 3 302
The orphans' cries, The dead men's blood, the pining maidens' groans *Hen. V.* ii 4 107
Hear, hear how dying Salisbury doth groan! It irks his heart he cannot be revenged *1 Hen. VI.* i 4 104
And follow'd with a rabble that rejoice To see my tears and hear my deep-fet groans *2 Hen. VI.* ii 4 33
His fortunes I will weep and 'twixt each groan Say, 'Who's a traitor?' iii 1 221
Might liquid tears or heart-offending groans Or blood-consuming sighs recall his life, I would be blind with weeping, sick with groans iii 2 60
Would curses kill, as doth the mandrake's groan, I would invent iii 2 310
A deadly groan, like life and death's departing *3 Hen. VI.* ii 6 43
Deliver'd with a groan, 'O, farewell, Warwick!' v 2 46
Of all one pain, save for a night of groans Endured of her *Richard III.* iv 4 303
And with that blood will make 'em one day groan for't *Hen. VIII.* ii 1 106
Oh! oh! groans out for ha! ha! ha! *Troi. and Cres.* iii 1 136
If you cannot weep, yet give some groans v 10 50
City, 'Tis I that made thy widows: many an heir Of these fair edifices 'fore my wars Have I heard groan and drop *Coriolanus* iv 4 4
Think to front his revenges with the easy groans of old women? v 2 45
Wound it with sighing, girl, kill it with groans *T. Andron.* iii 2 15
O heavens, can you hear a good man groan, And not relent? iv 1 123
Tell me in sadness, who is that you love.—What, shall I groan and tell thee?—Groan! why, no *Rom. and Jul.* i 1 206
Thy old groans ring yet in my ancient ears ii 3 74
Unless the breath of heart-sick groans, Mist-like, infold me from the search iii 3 72
Religion groans at it *T. of Athens* iii 2 83
And that same eye whose bend doth awe the world Did lose his lustre: I did hear him groan *J. Cæsar* i 2 124
Horses did neigh, and dying men did groan, And ghosts did shriek ii 2 23
Bear them as the ass bears gold, To groan and sweat under the business iv 1 22
Groans and shrieks that rend the air Are made, not mark'd *Macbeth* iv 3 168
I have not art to reckon my groans: but that I love thee best *Hamlet* ii 2 121
Never alone Did the king sigh, but with a general groan iii 3 23
Such groans of roaring wind and rain I never Remember to have heard *Lear* iii 2 47
Two or three groan: it is a heavy night: These may be counterfeits *Oth.* v 1 42

Groan. Cannot remove nor choke the strong conception That I do groan withal . . . . *Othello* v 2 56
In the midst a tearing groan did break The name of Antony *A. and C.* iv 14 31
Could not find death where I did hear him groan . . . *Cymbeline* v 3 69
He had rather Groan so in perpetuity than be cured . . . v 4 6
He made a groan at it, and swore he would see her to-morrow *Pericles* iv 2 117
Groaned. Under my burthen groan'd . . . . . *Tempest* i 2 156
Hadst thou groan'd for him As I have done, thou wouldst be more pitiful. But now I know thy mind . . . . *Richard II.* v 2 102
That fair for which love groan'd for and would die . *Rom. and Jul.* ii Prol. 3
Groaning. What shall be done, sir, with the groaning Juliet? *M. for M.* ii 2 15
Visit the speechless sick and still converse With groaning wretches *L. L. Lost* v 2 862
Sighing every minute and groaning every hour . . . *As Y. Like It* iii 2 321
That gave to me Many a groaning throe . . . . *Hen. VIII.* ii 4 199
Die he must, To appease their groaning shadows that are gone *T. Andron.* i 1 126
Is not this better now than groaning for love? . . . *Rom. and Jul.* ii 4 92
Groaning underneath this age's yoke. . . . . . *J. Cæsar* i 2 61
This foul deed shall smell above the earth With carrion men, groaning for burial . . . . iii 1 275
It would cost you a groaning to take off my edge . . . *Hamlet* iii 2 259
Groat. Seven groats in mill-sixpences . . . . *Mer. Wives* i 1 158
As fit as ten groats is for the hand of an attorney . . *All's Well* ii 2 22
A half-faced groat five hundred pound a year! . . . . *K. John* i 1 94
The cheapest of us is ten groats too dear . . . . *Richard II.* v 5 68
What money is in my purse?—Seven groats and two pence 2 *Hen. IV.* i 2 263
Ay, leeks is good: hold you, there is a groat to heal your pate.—Me a groat! . . . . *Hen. V.* v 1 62
I take thy groat in earnest of revenge . . . . . v 1 67
Or any groat I hoarded to my use, Be brought against me . 2 *Hen. VI.* iii 1 113
Woollen vassals, things created To buy and sell with groats *Coriolanus* iii 2 10
Groin. Are you not hurt i' the groin? . . . . 2 *Hen. IV.* ii 4 227
Groom. A bridegroom say you? 'tis a groom indeed, A grumbling groom, and that the girl shall find . . . . . *T. of Shrew* iii 2 154
'Tis like you'll prove a jolly surly groom . . . . . iii 2 215
You logger-headed and unpolish'd grooms! What, no attendance? . iv 1 128
I was a poor groom of thy stable, king, When thou wert king *Richard II.* v 5 72
Shall I be flouted thus by dunghill grooms? . . 1 *Hen. VI.* i 3 14
Vanquish'd as I am, I yield to thee, Or to the meanest groom 2 *Hen. VI.* ii 1 185
The honourable blood of Lancaster Must not be shed by such a jaded groom . . . . iv 1 52
Sooner dance upon a bloody pole Than stand uncover'd to the vulgar groom . . . . iv 1 128
Lay your weapons down; Home to your cottages, forsake this groom . iv 2 132
I'll ha' more. An ordinary groom is for such payment . . *Hen. VIII.* v 1 172
A fellow-counsellor, 'Mong boys, grooms, and lackeys . . . v 2 18
I gave ye Power as he was a counsellor to try him, Not as a groom . v 3 144
The fields are near, and you are gallant grooms . . *T. Andron.* iv 2 164
The surfeited grooms Do mock their charge with snores . . *Macbeth* ii 2 5
Go carry them; and smear The sleepy grooms with blood.—I'll go no more . . . . ii 2 50
If he do bleed, I'll gild the faces of the grooms withal . . . ii 2 56
Persuade me rather to be slave and sumpter To this detested groom *Lear* ii 4 220
In terms like bride and groom Devesting them for bed . . *Othello* ii 3 180
Thou wert too base To be his groom . . . . . *Cymbeline* ii 3 132
Were you a woman, youth, I should woo hard but be your groom . . iii 6 70
And prostitute me to the basest groom That doth frequent your house *Pericles* iv 6 201
Groped. In the dark Groped I to find out them . . . *Hamlet* v 2 14
Groping for trouts in a peculiar river . . . *Meas. for Meas.* i 2 91
Gros. Ce sont mots de son mauvais, corruptible, gros, et impudique *Hen. V.* iii 4 56
Gross. This unwholesome humidity, this gross watery pumpion *M. Wives* iii 3 43
I never saw him so gross in his jealousy till now . . . . iii 3 201
It wants matter to prevent so gross o'erreaching as this . . . . v 5 144
But it chances The stealth of our most mutual entertainment With character too gross is writ on Juliet . . . *Meas. for Meas.* i 2 159
Shall we serve heaven With less respect than we do minister To our gross selves? Good, good my lord, bethink you . . . . ii 2 87
To be received plain, I'll speak more gross . . . . . ii 4 82
'A great wit:' 'Right,' says she, 'a great gross one' . . *Much Ado* v 1 164
The grosser manner of these world's delights He throws upon the gross world's baser slaves . . . . . . *L. L. Lost* i 1 30
You know how much the gross sum of deuce-ace amounts to . . i 2 49
Love's tongue proves dainty Bacchus gross in taste . . . . iv 3 339
Well-liking wits they have; gross, gross; fat, fat . . . . v 2 268
We that sell by gross, the Lord doth know, Have not the grace to grace it with such show . . . . v 2 319
By the near guess of my memory, I cannot instantly raise up the gross Of full three thousand ducats . . . . *Mer. of Venice* i 3 56
It were too gross To rib her cerecloth in the obscure grave . . ii 7 50
Which, to term in gross, Is an unlesson'd girl, unschool'd, unpractised iii 2 160
Here shall he see Gross fools as he . . . . *As Y. Like It* ii 5 58
Chosen out of the gross band of the unfaithful . . . . iv 1 199
Now to all sense 'tis gross You love my son . . . *All's Well* i 3 178
I will wash off gross acquaintance, I will be point-devise . *T. Night* ii 5 177
And I hate thee, Pronounce thee a gross lout, a mindless slave *W. Tale* i 2 301
Which was as gross as ever touch'd conjecture, That lack'd sight only ii 1 176
A gross hag! And, lozel, thou art worthy to be hang'd . . . ii 3 108
That could conceive a gross and foolish sire Blemish'd his gracious dam iii 2 198
Though they come to him by the gross . . . . . . iv 4 208
Even in condition of the worst degree, In gross rebellion *Richard II.* ii 3 109
Mount, my soul! thy seat is up on high; Whilst my gross flesh sinks downward . . . . v 5 113
These lies are like their father that begets them; gross as a mountain, open, palpable . . . . 1 *Hen. IV.* ii 4 250
A gross fat man.—As fat as butter . . . . ii 4 560
What is the gross sum that I owe thee? . . . . 2 *Hen. IV.* ii 1 91
So, like gross terms, The prince will in the perfectness of time Cast off his followers . . . . iv 4 73
Though the truth of it stands off as gross As black and white *Hen. V.* ii 2 103
Free from gross passion or of mirth or anger . . . . . ii 2 132
In gross brain little wots What watch the king keeps to maintain the peace . . . . iv 1 299
O gross and miserable ignorance! . . . . . 2 *Hen. VI.* iv 2 178
I will acquaint his majesty With those gross taunts . *Richard III.* i 3 106
Why, who's so gross, That seeth not this palpable device? . . iii 6 10
It were a very gross kind of behaviour, as they say . *Rom. and Jul.* ii 4 176
You cannot make gross sins look clear . . . . *T. of Athens* iii 5 38
See him dissemble, Know his gross patchery, love him, feed him . . v 1 99
Gross. They confess Toward thee forgetfulness too general, gross *T. of A.* v 1 147
In the gross and scope of my opinion, This bodes some strange eruption to our state . . . . *Hamlet* i 1 68
Things rank and gross in nature Possess it merely . . . . . i 2 136
Examples gross as earth exhort me . . . . iv 4 46
Every hour He flashes into one gross crime or other . . . *Lear* i 3 4
And choughs that wing the midway air Show scarce so gross as beetles iv 6 14
Your daughter, if you have not given her leave, I say again, hath made a gross revolt . . . . *Othello* i 1 135
Judge me the world, if 'tis not gross in sense . . . . . i 2 72
As salt as wolves in pride, and fools as gross As ignorance made drunk iii 3 404
Dost thou in conscience think,—tell me, Emilia,—That there be women do abuse their husbands In such gross kind? . . . . . iv 3 63
Most heathenish and most gross! . . . . v 2 313
In their thick breaths, Rank of gross diet, shall we be enclouded *A. and C.* v 2 212
Grosser. The grosser manner of these world's delights . . *L. L. Lost* i 1 29
Be copy now to men of grosser blood . . . . . *Hen. V.* iii 1 24
That [we do] worst, as oft, Hitting a grosser quality, is cried up For our best act . . . . *Hen. VIII.* i 2 84
Long purples That liberal shepherds give a grosser name . *Hamlet* iv 7 171
I am to pray you not to strain my speech To grosser issues . *Othello* iii 3 219
Grossly. To counterfeit thus grossly with your slave! . *Com. of Errors* ii 2 171
Let them say 'tis grossly done; so it be fairly done, no matter *M. Wives* ii 2 149
Thy best of rest is sleep, And that thou oft provokest; yet grossly fear'st Thy death, which is no more . . . . *Meas. for Meas.* iii 1 18
I am sorry, one so learned and so wise As you, Lord Angelo, have still appear'd, Should slip so grossly . . . . v 1 477
Whilst this muddy vesture of decay Doth grossly close it in *M. of Venice* v 1 65
Are we cuckolds ere we have deserved it?—Speak not so grossly . . v 1 266
Thine eyes See it so grossly shown in thy behaviours . . *All's Well* i 3 184
A spirit I am indeed; But am in that dimension grossly clad *T. Night* v 1 244
Led so grossly by this meddling priest . . . . . *K. John* iii 1 163
Though you and all the rest so grossly led . . . . . . iii 1 168
Foul play; and 'tis shame That greatness should so grossly offer it . iv 2 94
He slanders thee most grossly.—So he doth you . . 1 *Hen. IV.* iii 3 150
Working so grossly in a natural cause . . . . . *Hen. V.* ii 2 107
My woman's heart Grossly grew captive to his honey words *Richard III.* iv 1 80
He took my father grossly, full of bread . . . . . *Hamlet* iii 3 80
With what poor judgement he hath now cast her off appears too grossly *Lear* i 1 295
Would you, the supervisor, grossly gape on? . . . . *Othello* iii 3 395
O, he has given example for our flight, Most grossly, by his own! *Ant. and Cleo.* iii 10 29
Grossness. Hiding the grossness with fair ornament . *Mer. of Venice* iii 2 80
Drove the grossness of the foppery into a received belief *Mer. Wives* v 5 131
I will purge thy mortal grossness so That thou shalt like an airy spirit go. Peaseblossom! Cobweb! Moth! . . . . . *M. N. Dream* iii 1 163
Can ever believe such impossible passages of grossness . . *T. Night* iii 2 77
Weigh it but with the grossness of this age . . . *Richard III.* ii 1 46
Whose grossness little characters sum up . . *Troi. and Cres.* i 3 325
Ground. Now would I give a thousand furlongs of sea for an acre of barren ground, long heath, brown furze, any thing . . *Tempest* i 1 69
The ground indeed is tawny.—With an eye of green in't . . . ii 1 54
Lead off this ground; and let's make further search For my poor son . ii 1 323
As proper a man as ever went on four legs cannot make him give ground ii 2 64
Beat the ground For kissing of their feet . . . . . . iv 1 173
If the ground be overcharged, you were best stick her . *T. G. of Ver.* i 1 107
Her chamber is aloft, far from the ground . . . . . . iii 1 114
Like a fair house built on another man's ground . . *Mer. Wives* ii 2 225
All our houses of resort in the suburbs be pulled down?—To the ground . . . . *Meas. for Meas.* i 2 106
Having waste ground enough, Shall we desire to raze the sanctuary? . ii 2 170
The wicked'st caitiff on the ground May seem as shy . . . . v 1 53
Then is he the ground Of my defeatures . . . . *Com. of Errors* ii 1 97
Look where Beatrice, like a lapwing, runs Close by the ground *M. Ado* iii 1 25
Now for the ground which; which, I mean, I walked upon . *L. L. Lost* i 1 241
I do affect the very ground, which is base, where her shoe, which is baser, guided by her foot, which is basest, doth tread . . . . i 2 172
Strucken blind Kisses the base ground with obedient breast . . iv 3 225
When would you, my lord, or you, or you, Have found the ground of study's excellence Without the beauty of a woman's face? . . . iv 3 300
They are the ground, the books, the academes From whence doth spring the true Promethean fire . . . . iv 3 303
I were the fairest goddess on the ground . . . . . . v 2 36
With that, they all did tumble on the ground . . . . . v 2 115
Here the maiden, sleeping sound, On the dank and dirty ground *M. N. D.* ii 2 75
But who is here? Lysander! on the ground! Dead? or asleep? . . ii 2 100
I will be with thee straight.—Follow me, then, To plainer ground . iii 2 404
On the ground Sleep sound: I'll apply To your eye, Gentle lover, remedy iii 2 448
Take hands with me, And rock the ground whereon these sleepers be . iv 1 91
That I sleeping here was found With these mortals on the ground . iv 1 107
O lovely wall, That stand'st between her father's ground and mine! . v 1 176
I will not rest till I have run some ground . . . *Mer. of Venice* ii 2 111
I will run as far as God has any ground . . . . . . ii 2 118
The weakest kind of fruit Drops earliest to the ground . . . iv 1 116
Though it be pity to see such a sight, it well becomes the ground *As Y. Like It* iii 2 256
Lay couching, head on ground, with catlike watch . . . . iv 3 116
Say thou wilt walk; we will bestrew the ground . . *T. of Shrew* Ind. 2 42
'Gamut' I am, the ground of all accord . . . . iii 1 73
I have found Myself in my incertain grounds to fail . . *All's Well* iii 1 15
Barefoot plod I the cold ground upon, With sainted vow . . . iii 4 6
But I shall lose the grounds I work upon . . . . . . iii 7 3
It is his grounds of faith that all that look on him love him . *T. Night* ii 3 164
Surely as your feet hit the ground they step on . . . . . iii 4 306
Give ground, if you see him furious . . . . iii 4 334
Though I confess, on base and ground enough . . . . . v 1 78
When we know the grounds and authors of it . . . . . . v 1 361
My ground to do't Is the obedience to a master . . . *W. Tale* i 2 353
Lack I credit?—I had rather you did lack than I, my lord, Upon this ground . . . . ii 1 159
And you shall help to put him i' the ground . . . . . iii 3 141
I bless the time When my good falcon made her flight across Thy father's ground.—Now Jove afford you cause! . . . . iv 4 16
Whose sons lie scattered on the bleeding ground . . . *K. John* ii 1 304
France, shall we knit our powers And lay this Angiers even with the ground? . . . . ii 1 399
And when that we have dash'd them to the ground, Why then defy each other . . . . ii 1 405
Who of itself is peised well, Made to run even upon even ground . . . ii 1 576
When I strike my foot Upon the bosom of the ground, rush forth . iv 1 3

Ground. Good ground, be pitiful and hurt me not! . . . *K. John* iv 3 2

When English measure backward their own ground In faint retire . . . v 5 3

On some known ground of treachery in him . . . *Richard II.* i 1 11

Or any other ground inhabitable, Where ever Englishman durst set his foot . . . i 1 65

Then, England's ground, farewell; sweet soil, adieu! . . . i 3 306

Why have those banish'd and forbidden legs Dared once to touch a dust of England's ground? . . . ii 3 91

Look not to the ground, Ye favourites of a king: are we not high? . . . iii 2 87

And lie full low, graved in the hollow ground . . . iii 2 140

For what can we bequeath Save our deposed bodies to the ground? . . . iii 2 150

Let us sit upon the ground And tell sad stories of the death of kings . . . iii 2 155

The blood of English shall manure the ground, And future ages groan . . . iv 1 137

Never will I rise up from the ground Till Bolingbroke have pardon'd thee . . . v 2 116

Our knees shall kneel till to the ground they grow . . . v 3 106

So proudly as if he disdain'd the ground . . . v 5 83

Like bright metal on a sullen ground . . . *1 Hen. IV.* i 2 236

Dive into the bottom of the deep, Where fathom-line could never touch the ground . . . i 3 204

Eight yards of uneven ground is threescore and ten miles afoot with me . . . ii 2 27

Lay thine ear close to the ground and list if thou canst hear the tread of travellers . . . ii 2 34

Began to give me ground: but I followed me close . . . ii 4 240

No man so potent breathes upon the ground But I will beard him . . . iv 1 11

Gallantly arm'd, Rise from the ground like feather'd Mercury . . . iv 1 106

I saw him dead, Breathless and bleeding on the ground . . . v 4 137

I think I am as like to ride the mare, if I have any vantage of ground to get up . . . *2 Hen. IV.* ii 1 85

By this heavenly ground I tread on . . . ii 1 152

If they get ground and vantage of the king, Then join you with them . . . ii 3 53

Which should not find a ground to root upon, Unless on you . . . iii 1 91

The hopes we have in him touch ground And dash themselves to pieces . . . iv 1 17

And, by the ground they hide, I judge their number Upon or near the rate of thirty thousand . . . iv 1 21

That you should have an inch of any ground To build a grief on . . . iv 1 109

His passions, like a whale on ground, Confound themselves with working . . . iv 4 40

The Black Prince, Who on the French ground play'd a tragedy . . . *Hen. V.* i 2 106

If we be hinder'd, We shall your tawny ground with your red blood Discolour . . . iii 6 170

Who hath measured the ground? . . . iii 7 137

A Jacksauce, as ever his black shoe trod upon God's ground . . . iv 7 149

Sharp stakes pluck'd out of hedges They pitched in the ground *1 Hen. VI.* i 1 118

And with my nails digg'd stones out of the ground . . . i 4 45

I'll maintain my words On any plot of ground in Christendom . . . ii 4 89

Like to a wither'd vine That droops his sapless branches to the ground . . . ii 5 12

Now, Rouen, I'll shake thy bulwarks to the ground . . . iii 2 17

Lift our heads to heaven, And never more abase our sight so low As to vouchsafe one glance unto the ground . . . *2 Hen. VI.* i 2 16

Raising up wicked spirits from under ground . . . ii 1 174

This dishonour in thine age Will bring thy head with sorrow to the ground! . . . ii 3 19

If . . . thou here be'st found On any ground that I am ruler of . . . iii 2 296

Now, by the ground that I am banish'd from, Well could I curse away a winter's night . . . iii 2 334

Thy lips that kiss'd the queen shall sweep the ground . . . iv 1 75

Come to rob my grounds, Climbing my walls in spite of me the owner iv 10 36

May that ground gape and swallow me alive, Where I shall kneel to him that slew my father! . . . *3 Hen. VI.* i 1 161

Richard cried 'Charge! and give no foot of ground!' . . . i 4 15

That this my body Might in the ground be closed up in rest! . . . ii 1 76

Giving no ground unto the house of York . . . ii 6 16

Trod my title down, And with dishonour laid me on the ground . . . iii 3 9

An eternal plant, Whereof the root was fix'd in virtue's ground . . . iii 3 125

What, will the aspiring blood of Lancaster Sink in the ground? . . . v 6 62

That thereby he may gather The ground of your ill-will . . . *Richard III.* i 3 69

On that ground I'll build a holy descant . . . iii 7 49

I would these dewy tears were from the ground . . . iv 3 284

Starts; Stops on a sudden, looks upon the ground . . . *Hen. VIII.* iii 2 114

A most unspotted lily shall she pass To the ground . . . v 5 63

If they love they know not why, they hate upon no better a ground *Coriol.* ii 2 13

On fair ground I could beat forty of them . . . iii 1 242

While I remain above the ground, you shall Hear from me still . . . iv 1 51

Like to a bowl upon a subtle ground, I have tumbled past the throw . . . v 2 20

He moves like an engine, and the ground shrinks before his treading . . . v 4 20

Full well I wot the ground of all this grudge . . . *T. Andron.* ii 1 48

An should the empress know This discord's ground, the music would not please . . . ii 1 70

But hope to pluck a dainty doe to ground . . . ii 2 26

The green leaves quiver with the cooling wind And make a chequer'd shadow on the ground . . . ii 3 15

Throw your mistemper'd weapons to the ground . . . *Rom. and Jul.* i 1 94

I have a soul of lead So stakes me to the ground I cannot move . . . i 4 16

Fall upon the ground, as I do now, Taking the measure of an unmade grave . . . iii 3 69

Where's Romeo?—There on the ground, with his own tears made drunk iii 3 83

An unaccustom'd spirit Lifts me above the ground with cheerful thoughts v 1 5

Lay thee all along, Holding thine ear close to the hollow ground . . . v 3 4

The ground is bloody; search about the churchyard . . . v 3 172

We see the ground whereon these woes do lie; But the true ground of all these piteous woes We cannot without circumstance descry . . . v 3 179

With man's blood paint the ground, gules, gules . . . *T. of Athens* iv 3 59

My credit now stands on such slippery ground . . . *J. Cæsar* iii 1 191

Bid our commanders lead their charges off A little from this ground . . . iv 2 49

The people 'twixt Philippi and this ground Do stand but in a forced affection . . . iv 3 204

Is not that he that lies upon the ground?—He lies not like the living . . . v 3 57

I'll catch it ere it come to ground . . . *Macbeth* iii 5 25

I will not yield, To kiss the ground before young Malcolm's feet . . . v 8 28

Who's there?—Friends to this ground . . . *Hamlet* i 1 15

With what courteous action It waves you to a more removed ground . . . i 4 61

Hic et ubique? then we'll shift our ground . . . i 5 156

I'll have grounds More relative than this . . . ii 2 632

Full thirty times hath Phœbus' cart gone round Neptune's salt wash and Tellus' orbed ground . . . iii 2 166

To gain a little patch of ground That hath in it no profit but the name iv 4 18

I cannot choose but weep, to think they should lay him i' the cold ground iv 5 70

How the knave jowls it to the ground, as if it were Cain's jaw-bone! . . . v 1 84

Faith, e'en with losing his wits.—Upon what ground?—Why, here in Denmark . . . v 1 175

She should in ground unsanctified have lodged Till the last trumpet . . . v 1 252

Ground. Till our ground, Singeing his pate against the burning zone, Make Ossa like a wart! . . . *Hamlet* v 1 304

'Tis on such ground, and to such wholesome end, As clears her . . . *Lear* ii 4 146

Methinks the ground is even.—Horrible steep. . . . iv 6 3

At Rhodes, at Cyprus, and on other grounds Christian and heathen *Oth.* i 1 29

But that I did proceed upon just grounds To this extremity . . . v 2 138

Broad-fronted Cæsar, When thou wast here above the ground, I was A morsel for a monarch . . . *Ant. and Cleo.* i 5 30

You have land enough of your own: but he added to your having; gave you some ground . . . *Cymbeline* i 2 20

Till you had measured how long a fool you were upon the ground . . . i 2 26

With five times so much conversation, I should get ground of your fair mistress . . . i 4 114

Whiles yet the dew's on ground, gather those flowers . . . i 5 1

He on the ground, my speech of insultment ended on his dead body . . . iii 5 144

For two nights together Have made the ground my bed . . . iii 6 3

Then on good ground we fear, If we do fear this body hath a tail . . . iv 2 143

Though now our voices Have got the mannish crack, sing him to the ground . . . iv 2 236

The ground that gave them first has them again . . . iv 2 289

Stand, stand! We have the advantage of the ground . . . v 2 11

What fairies haunt this ground? . . . v 4 133

A nobler sir ne'er lived 'Twixt sky and ground . . . v 5 146

Let's quit this ground, And smoke the temple with our sacrifices . . . v 5 397

I have ground the axe myself; Do you but strike the blow . . . *Pericles* i 2 58

What need we fear? The ground's the lowest, and we are half way there i 4 78

Let us salute him, Or know what ground's made happy by his breath . . . ii 4 28

An if she were a thornier piece of ground than she is, she shall be ploughed . . . iv 6 154

Upon what ground is his distemperature?—'Twould be too tedious to repeat . . . v 1 27

Grounded upon no other argument But that the people praise her for her virtues And pity her . . . *As Y. Like It* i 2 291

I think, proceeds From wayward sickness, and no grounded malice . . . *Richard III.* i 3 29

How grounded he his title to the crown, Upon our fail? . . . *Hen. VIII.* i 2 144

Groundling. To split the ears of the groundlings . . . *Hamlet* iii 2 12

Grove. Ye elves of hills, brooks, standing lakes and groves . . . *Tempest* v 1 33

And now they never meet in grove or green . . . *M. N. Dream* ii 1 28

Thou shalt not from this grove Till I torment thee for this injury . . . ii 1 146

Ere he do leave this grove, Thou shalt fly him and he shall seek thy love ii 1 245

Take thou some of it, and seek through this grove . . . ii 1 259

How now, mad spirit! What night-rule now about this haunted grove? iii 2 5

And, like a forester, the groves may tread . . . iii 2 390

For, besides the groves, The skies, the fountains, every region near Seem'd all one mutual cry . . . iv 1 120

Did ever Dian so become a grove As Kate this chamber? . . . *T. of Shrew* ii 1 260

Amongst a grove, the very straightest plant . . . *1 Hen. IV.* i 1 82

He that breaks a stick of Gloucester's grove Shall lose his head *2 Hen. VI.* i 2 33

An if thou darest, This evening, on the east side of the grove . . . ii 1 43

Are ye advised? the east side of the grove?—Cardinal, I am with you . . . ii 1 48

Their sweetest shade a grove of cypress trees! . . . iii 2 323

I am attended at the cypress grove: I pray you—'Tis south the city mills . . . *Coriolanus* i 10 30

Or is it Dian, habited like her, Who hath abandoned her holy groves? . . . *T. Andron.* ii 3 58

Underneath the grove of sycamore That westward rooteth *Rom. and Jul.* i 1 128

Within this three mile may you see it coming; I say, a moving grove . . . *Macbeth* v 5 38

Like to groves, being topp'd, they higher rise . . . *Pericles* i 4 9

Grovel. Gaze on, and grovel on thy face . . . *2 Hen. VI.* i 2 9

Mother Jourdain, be you prostrate and grovel on the earth . . . i 4 14

Grovelling. Many a widow's husband grovelling lies . . . *K. John* ii 1 305

Grow. I prithee, let me bring thee where crabs grow . . . *Tempest* ii 2 171

No sweet aspersion shall the heavens let fall To make this contract grow iv 1 19

As with age his body uglier grows, So his mind cankers . . . iv 1 191

The more she spurns my love, The more it grows . . . *T. G. of Ver.* iv 2 15

If matters grow to your likings . . . *Mer. Wives* i 1 79

I hope, upon familiarity will grow more contempt . . . i 1 258

As those that feed grow full . . . *Meas. for Meas.* i 4 41

I trust it will grow to a most prosperous perfection . . . iii 1 271

Twice treble shame on Angelo, To weed my vice and let his grow! . . . iii 2 284

There's no time for a man to recover his hair that grows bald by nature . . . *Com. of Errors* ii 2 74

Shall love, in building, grow so ruinous? . . . iii 2 4

Knowing how the debt grows, I will pay it . . . iv 1 124

Say, how grows it due?—Due for a chain your husband had of him . . . iv 4 137

Grow this to what adverse issue it can, I will put it in practice *M. Ado* ii 2 52

That now men grow hard-hearted and will lend nothing for God's sake v 1 321

Your light grows dark by losing of your eyes . . . *L. L. Lost* i 1 79

He weeds the corn and still lets grow the weeding . . . i 1 96

But like of each thing that in season grows . . . i 1 107

Boy, what sign is it when a man of great spirit grows melancholy? . . . i 2 2

Sing, boy; my spirit grows heavy in love . . . i 2 127

Such short-lived wits do wither as they grow . . . ii 1 54

Out of question so it is sometimes, Glory grows guilty of detested crimes iv 1 31

Come, come, you talk greasily; your lips grow foul . . . iv 1 139

Nay then, two treys, and if you grow so nice, Metheglin, wort, and malmsey . . . v 2 232

Then die a calf, before your horns do grow . . . v 2 253

A light for Monsieur Judas! it grows dark, he may stumble . . . v 2 633

Grows, lives, and dies in single blessedness.—So will I grow, so live, so die, my lord, Ere I will yield my virgin patent up . . . *M. N. Dream* i 1 79

Read the names of the actors, and so grow to a point . . . i 2 10

We have laugh'd to see the sails conceive And grow big-bellied . . . ii 1 129

Where the wild thyme blows, Where oxlips and the nodding violet grows ii 1 250

So sorrow's heaviness doth heavier grow For debt that bankrupt sleep doth sorrow owe . . . iii 2 84

How ripe in show Thy lips, those kissing cherries, tempting grow! . . . iii 2 140

And grows to something of great constancy . . . v 1 26

When shall we laugh? say, when? You grow exceeding strange *M. of V.* i 1 67

Farewell: I'll grow a talker for this gear . . . i 1 110

I fear he will prove the weeping philosopher when he grows old . . . i 2 53

The Hebrew will turn Christian: he grows kind . . . i 3 180

My father did something smack, something grow to, he had a kind of taste ii 2 18

It should seem, then, that Dobbin's tail grows backward . . . ii 2 103

My ships have all miscarried, my creditors grow cruel, my estate is very low . . . iii 2 318

If we grow all to be pork-eaters, we shall not shortly have a rasher iii 5 26

I shall grow jealous of you shortly . . . iii 5 31

Grow. And discourse grow commendable in none only but parrots *Mer. of Venice* iii 5 50
The spirit of my father grows strong in me . . . *As Y. Like It* i 1 74
Is it even so? begin you to grow upon me? . . . . . i 1 90
Thus men may grow wiser every day . . . . . i 2 145
It grows something stale with me . . . . . ii 4 63
If he, compact of jars, grow musical, We shall have shortly discord in the spheres . . . . ii 7 5
Weed your better judgements Of all opinion that grows rank in them . ii 7 46
For I tell you, sirs, If you should smile he grows impatient *T. of Shrew* Ind. 1 99
Abate the over-merry spleen Which otherwise would grow into extremes Ind. 1 138
No profit grows where is no pleasure ta'en . . . . i 1 39
Farther than at home Where small experience grows . . . . i 2 52
Whence grows this insolence? . . . . ii 1 23
Though little fire grows great with little wind, Yet extreme gusts will blow out fire and all . . . . ii 1 135
Fiddler, forbear; you grow too forward, sir . . . . . iii 1 1
Methinks I hear him now; his plausive words He scatter'd not in ears, but grafted them, To grow there and to bear . . *All's Well* i 2 55
I grow to you, and our parting is a tortured body . . . ii 1 36
It is in us to plant thine honour where We please to have it grow . ii 3 164
You do so grow in my requital As nothing can unroot you . . v 1 5
Tell them, there thy fixed foot shall grow . . . *T. Night* i 4 17
I'll no more of you: besides, you grow dishonest . . . . i 5 46
Now you see, sir, how your fooling grows old, and people dislike it . i 5 119
Alas, that they are so; To die, even when they to perfection grow! . ii 4 42
I am almost sick for one [a beard]; though I would not have it grow on my chin . . . . iii 1 54
The man grows mad: away with him! Come, come, sir . . . iii 4 405
Or will not else thy craft so quickly grow, That thine own trip shall be thine overthrow? . . . . v 1 169
How should this grow?—I know not . . . *W. Tale* i 2 431
The one He chides to hell and bids the other grow Faster than thought or time . . . . iv 4 564
Though indirect, Yet indirection thereby grows direct . . *K. John* iii 1 276
This day grows wondrous hot; Some airy devil hovers in the sky . . iii 2 1
Grow great by your example and put on The dauntless spirit of resolution . . . . v 1 52
Mine honour is my life; both grow in one . . . *Richard II.* i 1 182
Through our security, Grows strong and great in substance and in power iii 2 35
Let them go To ear the land that hath some hope to grow . . iii 2 212
Base court, where kings grow base, To come at traitors' calls . . iii 3 180
Pray God the plants thou graft'st may never grow . . . iii 4 101
For ever may my knees grow to the earth . . . . . v 3 30
Our knees shall kneel till to the ground they grow . . . . v 3 106
My soul is full of woe, That blood should sprinkle me to make me grow v 6 46
One of them is fat and grows old: God help the while! . . 1 *Hen. IV.* ii 4 145
The camomile, the more it is trodden on the faster it grows . . ii 4 442
Another king! they grow like Hydra's heads . . . . v 4 25
If I do grow great, I'll grow less; for I'll purge, and leave sack . v 4 167
I will sooner have a beard grow in the palm of my hand than he shall get one on his cheek . . . . . . 2 *Hen. IV.* i 2 24
I lay aside that which grows to me! . . . . . . i 2 100
Our present musters grow upon the file To five and twenty thousand . i 3 10
That it may grow and sprout as high as heaven, For recordation . ii 3 60
Be gone, good ancient: this will grow to a brawl anon . . . ii 4 186
A merry song, come: it grows late; we'll to bed . . . ii 4 299
Perceive the body of our kingdom How foul it is; what rank diseases grow . . . . iii 1 39
Would of that seed grow to a greater falseness . . . . iii 1 90
For your part, Bullcalf, grow till you come unto it: I will none of you iii 2 270
Our peace will, like a broken limb united, Grow stronger for the breaking iv 1 223
The strawberry grows underneath the nettle . . . *Hen. V.* i 1 60
If you grow foul with me, Pistol, I will scour you with my rapier . ii 1 59
We carry not a heart with us from hence That grows not in a fair consent ii 2 22
The Welshmen did good service in a garden where leeks did grow . iv 7 103
Fallows, meads, and hedges, Defective in their natures, grow to wildness v 2 55
Grow like savages,—as soldiers will That nothing do but meditate on blood . . . . v 2 59
A black beard will turn white; a curled pate will grow bald . . v 2 169
And, now the matter grows to compromise, Stand'st thou aloof? 1 *Hen. VI.* v 4 149
Now ye grow too hot: It was the pleasure of my lord the king 2 *Hen. VI.* i 1 137
The winds grow high; so do your stomachs, lords . . . ii 1 55
And stop the rage betime, Before the wound do grow uncurable . . iii 1 286
Naked on a mountain top, Where biting cold would never let grass grow iii 2 337
The more we stay, the stronger grows our foe . . 3 *Hen. VI.* iii 3 40
When we grow stronger, then we'll make our claim . . . iv 7 59
Why grow the branches now the root is wither'd? . . *Richard III.* ii 2 41
Why, my young cousin, it is good to grow . . . . . ii 4 9
My uncle Rivers talk'd how I did grow More than my brother . . ii 4 11
Small herbs have grace, great weeds do grow apace . . . ii 4 13
I would not grow so fast, Because sweet flowers are slow and weeds make haste . . . . ii 4 14
High-reaching Buckingham grows circumspect . . . . iv 2 31
But that slander, sir, Is found a truth now: for it grows again Fresher than e'er it was . . . . *Hen. VIII.* ii 1 154
Take thy lute, wench: my soul grows sad with troubles . . . iii 1 1
They that my trust must grow to, live not here . . . . iii 1 89
Would I had never trod this English earth, Or felt the flatteries that grow upon it! . . . . iii 1 144
You may hurt yourself, ay, utterly Grow from the king's acquaintance . iii 1 161
But to stubborn spirits They swell, and grow as terrible as storms . iii 1 164
Tell him, in death I bless'd him, For so I will. Mine eyes grow dim. Farewell . . . . iv 2 164
So I grow stronger, you more honour gain . . . . . v 3 182
What a multitude are here! They grow still too; from all parts they are coming . . . . v 4 72
Good grows with her: In her days every man shall eat in safety . . v 5 33
And like a vine grow to him . . . . v 5 50
Checks and disasters Grow in the veins of actions highest rear'd *T. and C.* i 3 6
Grows to an envious fever Of pale and bloodless emulation . . . i 3 133
Having his ear full of his airy fame, Grows dainty of his worth . . i 3 145
Why should a man be proud? How doth pride grow? . . . . ii 3 162
But I'll be true.—And I'll grow friend with danger . . . . iv 4 72
Let grow thy sinews till their knots be strong . . . . v 3 33
And policy grows into an ill opinion . . . . v 4 18
When steel grows soft as the parasite's silk . . . *Coriolanus* i 9 45
Your helps are many, or else your actions would grow wondrous single ii 1 40
It is a purposed thing, and grows by plot . . . . . iii 1 38
Honour and policy, like unsever'd friends, I' the war do grow together. iii 2 43
Grow. By some chance, Some trick not worth an egg, shall grow dear friends . . . . *Coriolanus* iv 4 21
Here grow no damned grudges; here are no storms . . *T. Andron.* i 1 154
Full well shalt thou perceive how much I dare.—Ay, boy, grow ye so brave? . . . . ii 1 45
Who marks the waxing tide grow wave by wave . . . . iii 1 95
Could we but learn from whence his sorrows grow, We would as willingly give cure as know . . . . . *Rom. and Jul.* i 1 160
No less! nay, bigger; women grow by men . . . . . i 3 95
Hie you, make haste, for it grows very late . . . . . iii 3 164
O, now be gone; more light and light it grows . . . . iii 5 35
How goes the world?—It wears, sir, as it grows . . *T. of Athens* i 1 3
And nature, as it grows again toward earth, Is fashion'd for the journey ii 2 227
Grant, as Timon grows, his hate may grow To the whole race of mankind! iv 1 39
I have a tree, which grows here in my close, That mine own use invites me to cut down . . . . v 1 208
A serpent's egg Which, hatch'd, would, as his kind, grow mischievous *J. Cæsar* ii 1 33
O, I grow faint. Run, Lucius, and commend me to my lord; Say I am merry . . . . ii 4 43
When Marcus Brutus grows so covetous, To lock such rascal counters . iv 3 79
If you can look into the seeds of time, And say which grain will grow *Macb.* i 3 59
And hold thee to my heart.—There if I grow, The harvest is your own . i 4 32
He grows worse and worse; Question enrages him . . . . iii 4 117
There grows In my most ill-composed affection such A stanchless avarice . . . . iv 3 76
This avarice Sticks deeper, grows with more pernicious root . . . iv 3 85
'Tis an unweeded garden That grows to seed . . . *Hamlet* i 2 136
For nature, crescent, does not grow alone In thews and bulk . . . i 3 11
As this temple waxes, The inward service of the mind and soul Grows wide . . . . i 3 14
And you, my sinews, grow not instant old, But bear me stiffly up . i 5 94
Do they grow rusty?—Nay, their endeavour keeps in the wonted pace . ii 2 352
If they should grow themselves to common players—as it is most like . ii 2 364
Where little fears grow great, great love grows there . . . iii 2 182
My spirits grow dull, and fain I would beguile The tedious day with sleep iii 2 236
Ay, sir, but, 'While the grass grows,'—the proverb is something musty iii 2 358
Hazard so near us as doth hourly grow Out of his lunacies . . . iii 3 6
Drown'd! O, where?—There is a willow grows aslant a brook . . iv 7 167
Their defeat Does by their own insinuation grow . . . . v 2 59
I grow; I prosper: Now, gods, stand up for bastards! . . . *Lear* i 2 21
His knights grow riotous, and himself upbraids us On every trifle . i 3 6
What grows of it, no matter; advise your fellows so . . . . i 3 23
But now grow fearful, By what yourself too late have spoke and done . i 4 225
A good man's fortune may grow out at heels . . . . . ii 2 164
The king grows mad; I'll tell thee, friend, I am almost mad myself . iii 4 170
And all the idle weeds that grow In our sustaining corn . . . . iv 4 5
Why, then, your other senses grow imperfect By your eyes' anguish . iv 6 5
My sickness grows upon me . . . . v 3 105
Men whose heads Do grow beneath their shoulders . . . . *Othello* i 3 145
Our loves and comforts should increase, Even as our days do grow . ii 1 197
This crack of your love shall grow stronger than it was before . . ii 3 331
Though other things grow fair against the sun, Yet fruits that blossom first will first be ripe . . . . ii 3 382
It is now high supper-time, and the night grows to waste . . . iv 2 249
I have rubb'd this young quat almost to the sense, And he grows angry v 1 12
Then murder's out of tune, and sweet revenge grows harsh . . . v 2 116
Great Pompey Would stand and make his eyes grow in my brow *A. and C.* i 5 32
I earnestly beseech, Touch you the sourest points with sweetest terms, Nor curstness grow to the matter . . . . ii 2 25
It's monstrous labour, when I wash my brain, And it grows fouler . ii 7 106
But his whole action grows Not in the power on't . . . . iii 7 69
But when we in our viciousness grow hard—O misery on't! . . . iii 13 111
Grace grow where those drops fall! . . . . iv 2 38
Should we be taking leave As long a term as yet we have to live, The loathness to depart would grow . . . . . *Cymbeline* i 1 108
Not born where't grows, But worn a bait for ladies . . . . iii 4 58
Grow, patience! And let the stinking elder, grief, untwine His perishing root with the increasing vine! . . . . iv 2 58
He'ld take us in, Displace our heads where—thank the gods!—they grow iv 2 122
Valour That wildly grows in them, but yields a crop As if it had been sow'd . . . . iv 2 180
Which, being dead many years, shall after revive, be jointed to the old stock, and freshly grow . . . . v 4 143; v 5 440
It is fit, What being more known grows worse, to smother it . *Pericles* i 1 106
And what was first but fear what might be done, Grows elder now . i 2 15
Who am no more but as the tops of trees, Which fence the roots they grow by . . . . i 2 30
And tyrants' fears Decrease not, but grow faster than the years . . i 2 85
So with his steerage shall your thoughts grow on . . . . iv 4 19
Here comes that which grows to the stalk; never plucked yet . . iv 6 45
Groweth. Our fine musician groweth amorous . . . *T. of Shrew* iii 1 63
Growing. Hence his ambition growing—Dost thou hear? . . *Tempest* i 2 105
Vines with clustering bunches growing, Plants with goodly burthen bowing . . . . iv 1 112
And, of so great a favour growing proud . . . *T. G. of Ver.* ii 4 161
Lest, growing ruinous, the building fall . . . . . . v 4 9
The sum that I do owe to you Is growing to me by Antipholus *C. of Er.* iv 1 8
Things growing are not ripe until their season . . *M. N. Dream* ii 2 117
And give my scene such growing As you had slept between . *W. Tale* iv 1 16
That wear upon your virgin branches yet Your maidenheads growing . iv 4 116
Had he done so to great and growing men, They might have lived to bear and he to taste Their fruits of duty . . . *Richard II.* iii 4 61
Whereupon He is retired, to ripe his growing fortunes . 2 *Hen. IV.* iv 1 13
The winter coming on and sickness growing Upon our soldiers *Hen. V.* iii 3 55
Were growing time once ripen'd to my will . . . 1 *Hen. VI.* ii 4 99
Or bathed thy growing with our heated bloods . . 3 *Hen. VI.* ii 2 169
Like to the morning's war, When dying clouds contend with growing light ii 5 2
He was the wretched'st thing when he was young, So long a-growing *Richard III.* ii 4 19
The mind growing once corrupt, They turn to vicious forms . *Hen. VIII.* i 2 116
Still growing in a majesty and pomp . . . . ii 3 7
Which ever has and ever shall be growing, Till death, that winter, kill it iii 2 178
This growing image of thy fiend-like face . . . *T. Andron.* v 1 45
These growing feathers pluck'd from Cæsar's wing Will make him fly an ordinary pitch, Who else would soar . . . . . *J. Cæsar* i 1 77
The sun arises, Which is a great way growing on the south . . ii 1 107
Welcome hither: I have begun to plant thee, and will labour To make thee full of growing . . . . *Macbeth* i 4 29
For goodness, growing to a plurisy, Dies in his own too much *Hamlet* iv 7 118

Growing. Comes in my father And like the tyrannous breathing of the north Shakes all our buds from growing . . *Cymbeline* i 3 37
Thy head, which now is growing upon thy shoulders, shall within this hour be off . . . . iv 1 17
Grown. Who with age and envy Was grown into a hoop *Tempest* i 2 259
Is like a good thing, being often read, Grown fear'd and tedious *M. for M.* ii 4 9
Why are you grown so rude? what change is this? *M. N. Dream* iii 2 262
Are you grown so high in his esteem, Because I am so dwarfish? . iii 2 294
I'll knock your knave's pate.—My master is grown quarrelsome *T. of Shrew* i 2 13
And words are grown so false, I am loath to prove reason with them *T. N.* iii 1 28
'Tis safer to Avoid what's grown than question how 'tis born *W. Tale* i 2 433
Now grown in grace Equal with wondering . . . . iv 1 24
Beyond the imagination of his neighbours, is grown into an unspeakable estate . . . . iv 2 46
Is not your father grown incapable Of reasonable affairs? . . . iv 4 408
Our coffers, with too great a court . . . , are grown somewhat light *Rich. II.* i 4 44
The king's grown bankrupt, like a broken man . . . . ii 1 257
O monstrous! eleven buckram men grown out of two! . . 1 *Hen. IV.* ii 4 244
The English army is grown weak and faint . . . . 1 *Hen. VI.* i 1 158
This brawl to-day, Grown to this faction in the Temple-garden . . ii 4 125
This late dissension grown betwixt the peers Burns under feigned ashes iii 1 189
Full of haughty courage, Such as were grown to credit by the wars . iv 1 36
Is your priesthood grown peremptory? Tantæne animis cœlestibus iræ? 2 *Hen. VI.* ii 1 23
By devilish policy art thou grown great . . . . . iv 1 83
To Bedlam with him! is the man grown mad? . . . . . v 1 131
I cannot tell: the world is grown so bad, That wrens make prey where eagles dare not perch . . . . . . *Richard III.* i 3 70
I hope he is much grown since last I saw him . . . . ii 4 5
'Tis time to give 'em physic, their diseases Are grown so catching *Hen. VIII.* i 3 37
I am glad Your grace is grown so pleasant . . . . . i 4 90
Though he be grown so desperate to be honest . . . . iii 1 86
Ajax is grown self-will'd, and bears his head In such a rein *Troi. and Cres.* i 3 188
Who in this dull and long-continued truce Is rusty grown . . i 3 263
My thoughts were like unbridled children, grown Too headstrong for their mother . . . . iii 2 130
A woman impudent and mannish grown Is not more loathed than an effeminate man In time of action . . . . . . iii 3 217
He's grown a very land-fish, languageless, a monster . . . iii 3 264
He is grown Too proud to be so valiant . . . . *Coriolanus* i 1 262
'Tis he: O, he is grown most kind of late . . . . . iv 6 11
This Marcius is grown from man to dragon: he has wings . . v 4 13
Are you so desperate grown, to threat your friends? . *T. Andron.* ii 1 40
Quench the fire, the room is grown too hot . . *Rom. and Jul.* i 5 30
My true love is grown to such excess I cannot sum up sum of half my wealth . . . . ii 6 33
Till strange love, grown bold, Think true love acted simple modesty . iii 2 15
Upon what meat doth this our Cæsar feed, That he is grown so great? *J. C.* i 2 150
What a blunt fellow is this grown to be! . . . . . . i 2 299
Prodigious grown And fearful, as these strange eruptions are . . i 3 77
He is superstitious grown of late, Quite from the main opinion he held once . . . . ii 1 195
There the grown serpent lies; the worm that's fled Hath nature that in time will venom breed, No teeth for the present . . *Macbeth* iii 4 29
As if increase of appetite had grown By what it fed on . . *Hamlet* i 2 144
What's the news?—None, my lord, but that the world's grown honest ii 2 242
Diseases desperate grown By desperate appliance are relieved, Or not at all . . . . iv 3 9
The age is grown so picked that the toe of the peasant comes so near the heel of the courtier, he galls his kibe . . . . . v 1 151
Fools had ne'er less wit in a year; For wise men are grown foppish *Lear* i 4 182
Our flesh and blood is grown so vile, my lord, That it doth hate what gets it . . . . iii 4 150
The hated, grown to strength, Are newly grown to love . *Ant. and Cleo.* i 3 48
Quietness, grown sick of rest, would purge By any desperate change . i 3 53
I have told him, Lepidus was grown too cruel . . . . . iii 6 32
Are grown The mortal bugs o' the field . . . . *Cymbeline* v 3 50
One daughter, and a wench full grown, Even ripe for marriage-rite *Pericles* iv Gower 16
Growth. My little son And three or four more of their growth *Mer. Wives* iv 4 48
But I, his brother, gain nothing under him but growth . *As Y. Like It* i 1 15
Three proper young men, of excellent growth and presence . . i 2 130
Let me stay the growth of his beard . . . . . . iii 2 221
I slide O'er sixteen years and leave the growth untried . *W. Tale* iv 1 6
All tallow: if I did say of wax, my growth would approve the truth 2 *Hen. IV.* i 2 180
Whose want gives growth to the imperfections Which you have cited *Hen. V.* v 2 69
My son of York Hath almost overta'en him in his growth *Richard III.* ii 4 7
I could have given my uncle's grace a flout, To touch his growth nearer than he touch'd mine . . . . ii 4 25
My lord, You said that idle weeds are fast in growth . . . iii 1 103
It stands me much upon, To stop all hopes whose growth may damage me iv 2 60
Divert his grain Tortive and errant from his course of growth *T. and C.* i 3 9
When I have pluck'd the rose, I cannot give it vital growth again *Othello* v 2 14
Grub. There is differency between a grub and a butterfly; yet your butterfly was a grub . . . . *Coriolanus* v 4 11
Her chariot is an empty hazel-nut Made by the joiner squirrel or old grub, Time out o' mind the fairies' coachmakers . *Rom. and Jul.* i 4 68
What torch is yond, that vainly lends his light To grubs and eyeless skulls? v 3 126
Grubbed. But for the stock, Sir Thomas, I wish it grubb'd up now *Hen. VIII.* v 1 23
Grudge. Served Without or grudge or grumblings . . . *Tempest* i 2 249
I here forget all former griefs, Cancel all grudge . . *T. G. of Ver.* v 4 143
I will feed fat the ancient grudge I bear him . . *Mer. of Venice* i 3 48
So perish they That grudge one thought against your majesty! 1 *Hen. VI.* iii 1 176
Your private grudge, my Lord of York, will out . . . . iv 1 109
Let former grudges pass, And henceforth I am thy true servitor 3 *Hen. VI.* iii 3 195
If ever any grudge were lodged between us . . . *Richard III.* ii 1 65
Here grow no damned grudges; here are no storms, No noise *T. Andron.* i 1 154
Full well I wot the ground of all this grudge . . . . ii 1 48
From ancient grudge break to new mutiny . . . *Rom. and Jul.* Prol. 3
There is some grudge between 'em, 'tis not meet They be alone *J. Cæsar* iv 3 125
'Tis not in thee To grudge my pleasures . . . . . *Lear* ii 4 177
Grudged. They have grudged us contribution . . . *J. Cæsar* iv 3 206
Grudging. He eats his meat without grudging . . . *Much Ado* iii 4 90
How will their grudging stomachs be provoked! . . . 1 *Hen. VI.* iv 1 141
By heaven, my heart is purged from grudging hate . . *Richard III.* ii 1 9
Gruel. Make the gruel thick and slab . . . . . *Macbeth* iv 1 32
Grumble. What, do you grumble? I'll be with you straight *T. of Shrew* iv 1 170
What art thou that dost grumble there i' the straw? Come forth *Lear* iii 4 44
Grumblest. Thou grumblest and railest every hour . . *Troi. and Cres.* ii 1 35
Grumbling. Served Without or grudge or grumblings . . *Tempest* i 2 249
A groom indeed, A grumbling groom, and that the girl shall find *T. of Shrew* iii 2 155
Somerset, Buckingham, And grumbling York . . . . 2 *Hen. VI.* i 3 73
With his grumbling voice Was wont to cheer his dad in mutinies 3 *Hen. VI.* i 4 76
Grumio; knock, I say.—Knock, sir! whom should I knock? . *T. of Shrew* i 2 5
What's the matter? My old friend Grumio! and my good friend Petruchio! . . . . i 2 21
Rise, Grumio, rise: we will compound this quarrel.—Nay, 'tis no matter i 2 27
Whom would to God I had well knock'd at first, Then had not Grumio come by the worst . . . . i 2 35
Patience; I am Grumio's pledge: Why, this's a heavy chance 'twixt him and you, Your ancient, trusty, pleasant servant Grumio . . i 2 45
Who goes there, ha?—Peace, Grumio! it is the rival of my love . i 2 142
What an ass it is!—Peace, sirrah!—Grumio, mum! . . . . i 2 163
Grumio, my horse.—Ay, sir, they be ready: the oats have eaten the horses iii 2 206
Grumio, Draw forth thy weapon, we are beset with thieves . . iii 2 237
Is my master and his wife coming, Grumio?—O, ay . . . iv 1 19
I prithee, good Grumio, tell me, how goes the world?—A cold world . iv 1 35
There's fire ready; and therefore, good Grumio, the news . . iv 1 42
And thereby hangs a tale.—Let's ha't, good Grumio.—Lend thine ear . iv 1 61
Welcome home, Grumio!—How now, Grumio!—What, Grumio!—Fellow Grumio . . . . iv 1 109
A fat tripe finely broil'd?—I like it well: good Grumio, fetch it me . iv 3 21
You shall have the mustard, Or else you get no beef of Grumio . . iv 3 28
Grumio gave order how it should be done.—I gave him no order; I gave him the stuff . . . . iv 3 118
God-a-mercy, Grumio! then he shall have no odds . . . . iv 3 154
Sirrah Grumio, go to your mistress; Say, I command her come to me . v 2 95
Grund. Ay'll de gud service, or ay'll lig i' the grund for it . *Hen. V.* iii 2 124
Grunt. Neigh, and bark, and grunt, and roar, and burn . *M. N. Dream* iii 1 113
Who would fardels bear, To grunt and sweat under a weary life? *Hamlet* iii 1 77
Guard. We two, my lord, Will guard your person . . . *Tempest* ii 1 197
'Tis best we stand upon our guard, Or that we quit this place . . ii 1 321
Whose wraths to guard you from . . . is nothing but heart-sorrow . iii 3 79
Stands at a guard with envy; scarce confesses That his blood flows *Meas. for Meas.* i 3 51
The damned'st body to invest and cover In prenzie guards! . . . iii 1 97
He broke from those that had the guard of him . *Com. of Errors* v 1 149
Come, stand by me; fear nothing. Guard with halberds! . . . v 1 185
The body of your discourse is sometime guarded with fragments, and the guards are but slightly basted on neither . . . . *Much Ado* i 1 289
One that will do the deed Though Argus were her eunuch and her guard *L. L. Lost* iii 1 201
Rhymes are guards on wanton Cupid's hose: Disfigure not his slop . iv 3 58
See to my house, left in the fearful guard Of an unthrifty knave *M. of Ven.* i 3 176
She is arm'd for him and keeps her guard In honestest defence *All's Well* iii 5 76
He's out of his guard already . . . . *T. Night* i 5 93
Your ladyship were best to have some guard about you, if he come . iii 4 12
If you hold your life at any price, betake you to your guard . . iii 4 253
Heaven guard my mother's honour and my land! . . . . *K. John* i 1 70
To guard a title that was rich before, To gild refined gold, to paint the lily iv 2 10
And when they from thy bosom pluck a flower, Guard it, I pray thee, with a lurking adder . . . . *Richard II.* iii 2 20
If angels fight, Weak men must fall, for heaven still guards the right . iii 2 62
Hence, thou sickly quoif! Thou art a guard too wanton for the head 2 *Hen. IV.* i 1 148
Some guard these traitors to the block of death, Treason's true bed . iv 2 122
Blunt, lead him hence; and see you guard him sure . . . iv 3 81
This imperial crown . . . Lo, here it sits, Which God shall guard . iv 5 44
And He that wears the crown immortally Long guard it yours! . . iv 5 145
To trip the course of law and blunt the sword That guards the peace . v 2 88
The heavens thee guard and keep, most royal imp of fame! . . v 5 45
God and his angels guard your sacred throne! . . . . . *Hen. V.* i 2 7
My army but a weak and sickly guard; Yet, God before, tell him we will come . . . . iii 6 164
For there is none to guard it but boys . . . . . . iv 4 82
Fight till the last gasp; I will be your guard . . . . 1 *Hen. VI.* i 2 127
Abominable Gloucester, guard thy head; For I intend to have it ere long i 3 87
A guard of chosen shot I had That walked about me every minute while i 4 53
By some apparent sign Let us have knowledge at the court of guard . ii 1 4
I marvel how he sped.—Tut, holy Joan was his defensive guard . . ii 1 49
He is your prisoner.—Sirs, take away the duke, and guard him sure 2 *Hen. VI.* iii 1 188
Were't not all one, an empty eagle were set To guard the chicken from a hungry kite? . . . . iii 1 249
They will guard you, whether you will or no, From such fell serpents . iii 2 265
Fear frames disorder, and disorder wounds Where it should guard . v 2 33
And but attended by a simple guard, We may surprise and take him 3 *Hen. VI.* iv 2 16
At unawares may beat down Edward's guard And seize himself . . iv 2 23
Wherefore else guard we his royal tent, But to defend his person? . iv 3 21
This is his tent; and see where stand his guard. Courage, my masters! iv 3 23
Betray'd by falsehood of his guard Or by his foe surprised . . . iv 4 8
And, often but attended with weak guard, Comes hunting this way . iv 5 7
What means this armed guard That waits upon your grace? *Richard III.* i 1 42
God and our innocency defend and guard us! . . . . . . iii 5 20
Go thou to Richard, and good angels guard thee! . . . . . iv 1 93
Bid my guard watch; leave me. Ratcliff, about the mid of night come v 3 76
Good angels guard thy battle! live, and flourish! . . . . . v 3 138
And wake in joy; Good angels guard thee from the boar's annoy! . v 3 156
You are strangely troublesome. Let some o' the guard be ready there *Hen. VIII.* v 3 95
If we have lost so many tenths of ours, To guard a thing not ours nor worth to us . . . . *Troi. and Cres.* ii 2 22
Though the great bulk Achilles be thy guard, I'll cut thy throat . iv 4 130
Henceforth guard thee well; For I'll not kill thee there, nor there, nor there . . . . iv 5 253
I bid good night. Ajax commands the guard to tend on you . . v 1 79
There is between my will and all offences A guard of patience . . v 2 54
Ajax, your guard, stays to conduct you home . . . . . . v 2 184
Hie you to your bands: Let us alone to guard Corioli . *Coriolanus* i 2 27
Where I find him, were it At home, upon my brother's guard, even there, Against the hospitable canon, would I Wash my fierce hand in's heart i 10 25
Give him deserved vexation. Let a guard Attend us through the city . iii 3 140
You guard like men; 'tis well: but, by your leave, I am an officer of state v 2 2
Traitors, avaunt! Where is the emperor's guard? Treason! *T. Andron.* i 1 283
Doors, that were ne'er acquainted with their wards Many a bounteous year, must be employ'd Now to guard sure their master *T. of Athens* iii 3 40

Guard. Let no man Come to our tent till we have done our conference.
Let Lucius and Titinius guard our door *J. Cæsar* iv 2 52
Have you had quiet guard?—Not a mouse stirring *Hamlet* i 1 10
Save me, and hover o'er me with your wings, You heavenly guards! iii 4 104
Where are my Switzers? Let them guard the door iv 5 97
The scrimers of their nation, He swore, had neither motion, guard, nor eye iv 7 102
My father hath set guard to take my brother *Lear* ii 1 18
No place, That guard, and most unusual vigilance, Does not attend my taking ii 3 4
Good guard, Until their greater pleasures first be known v 3 1
I thought it fit To send the old and miserable king To some retention and appointed guard v 3 47
With no worse nor better guard But with a knave of common hire *Othello* i 1 125
I think I can discover him, if you please To get good guard i 1 180
Cast water on the burning bear, And quench the guards of the ever-fixed pole ii 1 15
Great Jove, Othello guard, And swell his sail with thine own powerful breath! ii 1 77
The lieutenant to-night watches on the court of guard ii 1 220
Good Michael, look you to the guard to-night ii 3 1
To manage private and domestic quarrel, In night, and on the court and guard of safety! 'Tis monstrous ii 3 216
Come, guard the door without; let him not pass, But kill him rather v 2 241
Never anger Made good guard for itself *Ant. and Cleo.* iv 1 10
The messenger Came on my guard; and at thy tent is now iv 6 23
Let us bear him To the court of guard; he is of note iv 9 32
How! not dead? not dead? The guard, ho! O, dispatch me! iv 14 104
Call my guard, I prithee.—What, ho, the emperor's guard! iv 14 128
Look out o' the other side your monument; His guard have brought him thither iv 15 9
Guard her till Cæsar come.—Royal queen!—O Cleopatra! thou art taken v 2 36
For the queen, I'll take her to my guard v 2 67
And put your children To that destruction which I'll guard them from v 2 132
From fairies and the tempters of the night Guard me, beseech ye *Cymbeline* ii 2 10
Found no opposition But what he look'd for should oppose and she Should from encounter guard ii 5 19
His greatness was no guard To bar heaven's shaft *Pericles* ii 4 14

Guardage.—Run from her guardage to the sooty bosom Of such a thing as thou, to fear, not to delight *Othello* i 2 70

Guardant. When my angry guardant stood alone, Tendering my ruin and assail'd of none 1 *Hen. VI.* iv 7 9
Perceive that a Jack guardant cannot office me from my son *Coriolanus* v 2 67

Guarded. The body of your discourse is sometime guarded with fragments *Much Ado* i 1 288
Give him a livery More guarded than his fellows' *Mer. of Venice* ii 2 164
Your grace shall stay behind So strongly guarded *K. John* iii 3 2
Led on by bloody youth, guarded with rags 2 *Hen. IV.* iv 1 34
Guarded with grandsires, babies, and old women *Hen. V.* iii Prol. 20
'Tis sure they found some place But weakly guarded 1 *Hen. VI.* ii 1 74
My lord protector, see them guarded And safely brought to Dover v 1 48
A fellow In a long motley coat guarded with yellow *Hen. VIII.* Prol. 16
Let the ports be guarded: keep your duties, As I have set them down *Cor.* i 7 1
But where is he?—Without, my lord; guarded, to know your pleasure *Ham.* iv 3 14
That a king's children should be so convey'd, So slackly guarded *Cymbeline* i 1 64
We have the advantage of the ground; The lane is guarded v 2 12

Guardian. I am sorry for her, as I have just cause, being her uncle and her guardian *Much Ado* ii 3 174
That judge hath made me guardian to this boy *K. John* ii 1 115
Now, my sweet guardian! Hark, a word with you *Troi. and Cres.* v 2 7
I will be patient.—Guardian!—why, Greek!—Foh, foh! adieu; you palter v 2 47
The sacred storehouse of his predecessors, And guardian of their bones *Macbeth* ii 4 35
I gave you all— And in good time you gave it.—Made you my guardians *Lear* ii 4 254

Gud. It sall be vary gud, gud feith, gud captains bath: and I sall quit you with gud leve *Hen. V.* iii 2 109
Ay'll de gud service, or ay'll lig i' the grund for it iii 2 123

Gud-day. I say gud-day, Captain Fluellen.—God-den to your worship iii 2 88

Gudgeon. But fish not, with this melancholy bait, For this fool gudgeon, this opinion *Mer. of Venice* i 1 102

Guerdon. Death, in guerdon of her wrongs, Gives her fame *Much Ado* v 3 5
There's thy guerdon; go.—Gardon, O sweet gardon! better than remuneration *L. L. Lost* iii 1 170

Guerdoned. See you well guerdon'd for these good deserts 2 *Hen. VI.* i 4 49
And am I guerdon'd at the last with shame? Shame on himself! 3 *Hen. VI.* iii 3 191

Guerra. We will put it, as they say, to fortuna de la guerra *L. L. Lost* v 2 534

Guess. Well, I guess the sequel; And yet I will not name it *T. G. of Ver.* ii 1 122
And redeliver our authorities there?—I guess not *Meas. for Meas.* iv 4 8
I guess it stood in her chin, by the salt rheum that ran *Com. of Errors* iii 2 130
We may guess by this what you are *Much Ado* i 1 111
And are apparell'd thus, Like Muscovites or Russians, as I guess *L. L. Lost* v 2 121
By the near guess of my memory *Mer. of Venice* i 3 55
I partly guess; for I have loved ere now.—No, Corin, being old, thou canst not guess *As Y. Like It* ii 4 24
As I guess By the stern brow and waspish action Which she did use as she was writing of it, It bears an angry tenour iv 3 8
More Than words can witness, or your thoughts can guess *T. of Shrew* ii 1 338
It is not so with Him that all things knows As 'tis with us that square our guess by shows *All's Well* ii 1 153
For I can guess that by thy honest aid Thou kept'st a wife herself v 3 329
What incidency thou dost guess of harm Is creeping toward me *W. Tale* i 2 403
He will allow no speech, which I do guess You do not purpose to him iv 4 479
It is my Lord of Berkeley, as I guess *Richard II.* ii 3 68
My good lord, I guess their tenour 1 *Hen. IV.* iv 4 7
King Richard might create a perfect guess 2 *Hen. IV.* iii 1 88
Which I could with a ready guess declare *Hen. V.* i 1 96
Better far, I guess, That we do make our entrance several ways 1 *Hen. VI.* ii 1 29
I am ignorant and cannot guess ii 5 60
Tell me their words as near as thou canst guess them 3 *Hen. VI.* iv 1 90
Guess thou the rest iv 4 28
By thy guess, how nigh is Clarence now? v 1 8
As I guess, To make a bloody supper in the Tower v 5 84
Shallow innocents, You cannot guess who caused your father's death *Richard III.* ii 2 19
But canst thou guess that he doth aim at it? iii 2 45
And, as I guess, Upon the like devotion as yourselves iv 1 8
I know not, mighty sovereign, but by guess.—Well, sir, as you guess? iv 4 466
Unless for that, my liege, I cannot guess.—Unless for that he comes to be your liege, You cannot guess wherefore the Welshman comes iv 4 475

Guess. Who did guide, I mean, who set the body and the limbs Of this great sport together, as you guess? *Hen. VIII.* i 1 47
What has happen'd?—You may guess quickly what ii 1 7
Now, by thy looks I guess thy message v 1 162
We might guess they relieved us humanely *Coriolanus* i 1 18
As I guess, Marcius, Their bands i' the vaward are the Antiates i 6 52
Guess, but by my entertainment with him v 2 68
That he thereby may give a likely guess *T. Andron.* ii 3 207
Canst thou not guess wherefore she plies thee thus?—My lord, I know not, I, nor can I guess iv 1 15
I cannot, by the progress of the stars, Give guess how near to-day *J. C.* ii 1 3
Hum! I guess at it *Macbeth* iv 3 203
Here is the guess of their true strength and forces *Lear* v 1 52
How many, as you guess?—Of thirty sail *Othello* i 3 36
Though I perchance am vicious in my guess iii 3 145
Throw your vile guesses in the devil's teeth, From whence you have them iii 4 184
Guess at her years, I prithee *Ant. and Cleo.* iii 3 29
Though you can guess what temperance should be, You know not what it is iii 13 121
To this hour no guess in knowledge Which way they went *Cymbeline* i 1 60

Guessed. Him he knew well, and guess'd that it was she *T. G. of Ver.* v 2 39
Dare not Say what I think of it, since I have found Myself in my incertain grounds to fail As often as I guess'd *All's Well* iii 1 16
Well guess'd, believe me; for that was my meaning 3 *Hen. VI.* iv 5 22

Guessingly. I have a letter guessingly set down *Lear* iii 7 47

Guest. Now, my young guest, methinks you're allycholly *T. G. of Ver.* iv 2 26
And, moreover, bully,—but first, master guest *Mer. Wives* ii 3 77
I shall procure-a you de good guest, de earl, de knight, de lords ii 3 96
I have turned away my other guests: they must come off iv 3 13
Gave healthful welcome to their shipwreck'd guests *Com. of Errors* i 1 115
A merry feast.—Ay to a niggardly host and more sparing guest iii 1 27
I would not yield to be your house's guest *L. L. Lost* v 2 354
At supper shalt thou see Lorenzo, who is thy new master's guest *M. of V.* ii 3 6
Am bold to show myself a forward guest Within your house *T. of Shrew* ii 1 51
Provide the feast, father, and bid the guests; I will be sure my Katharine shall be fine ii 1 318
Will you go yet? Force me to keep you as a prisoner, Not like a guest *W. Tale* i 2 53
My prisoner? or my guest? by your dread 'Verily,' One of them you shall be.—Your guest, then, madam i 2 55
To my kingly guest Unclasp'd my practice, quit his fortunes here iii 2 167
Your guests are coming: Lift up your countenance iv 4 48
See, your guests approach: Address yourself to entertain them sprightly iv 4 52
You must be tittle-tattling before all our guests iv 4 249
A father Is at the nuptial of his son a guest That best becomes the table iv 4 406
I know no cause Why I should welcome such a guest as grief *Richard II.* ii 2 7
Most beauteous inn, Why should hard-favour'd grief be lodged in thee, When triumph is become an alehouse guest? v 1 15
Standest thou still, and hearest such a calling? Look to the guests 1 *Hen. IV.* ii 4 91
Love thy husband, look to thy servants, cherish thy guests iii 3 194
To the latter end of a fray and the beginning of a feast Fits a dull fighter and a keen guest iv 2 86
Therefore take heed what guests you receive 2 *Hen. IV.* ii 4 101
To-night in Harfleur will we be your guest; To-morrow for the march *Hen. V.* iii 3 57
Unbidden guests Are often welcomest when they are gone 1 *Hen. VI.* ii 2 55
Your lordship is a guest too.—O, tis true *Hen. VIII.* i 3 51
You're welcome, my fair guests: that noble lady, Or gentleman, that is not freely merry, Is not my friend i 4 35
Ye shall go my way, which Is to the court, and there ye shall be my guests iv 1 115
For time is like a fashionable host That slightly shakes his parting guest by the hand *Troi. and Cres.* iii 3 166
The feast smells well; but I Appear not like a guest *Coriolanus* iv 5 6
Prithee, tell my master what a strange guest he has here iv 5 38
You are my guest, Lavinia, and your friends *T. Andron.* i 1 490
Whereto I have invited many a guest, Such as I love *Rom. and Jul.* i 2 21
The guests are come, supper served up, you called, my young lady asked for i 3 100
An ill-beseeming semblance for a feast.—It fits, when such a villain is a guest: I'll not endure him i 5 77
You'll make a mutiny among my guests! You will set cock-a-hoop! i 5 82
So many guests invite as here are writ iv 2 1
Henceforth be no feast, Whereat a villain's not a welcome guest *T. of A.* iii 6 113
This guest of summer, The temple-haunting martlet *Macbeth* i 6 3
Fair and noble hostess, We are your guest to-night i 6 25
Here's our chief guest.—If he had been forgotten, It had been as a gap in our great feast iii 1 11
Be bright and jovial among your guests to-night iii 2 28
O, a pit of clay for to be made For such a guest is meet *Hamlet* v 1 105
Good my friends, consider You are my guests: do me no foul play *Lear* iii 7 31
Seem'd not to know What guests were in her eyes iv 3 23
She replied, It should be better he became her guest *Ant. and Cleo.* ii 2 226
Make yourself my guest Whilst you abide here.—Humbly, sir, I thank you ii 2 249
Why should this change of thoughts, The sad companion, dull-eyed melancholy, Be my so used a guest? *Pericles* i 2 3
You are princes and my guests.—But you, my knight and guest ii 3 8

Guest-cavaleire. Hast thou no suit against my knight, my guest-cavaleire?—None, I protest *Mer. Wives* ii 1 221

Guest-justice. Pardon, guest-justice i 3 59

Guest-wise. My heart to her but as guest-wise sojourn'd *M. N. Dream* iii 2 171

Guiana. She is a region in Guiana, all gold and bounty *Mer. Wives* i 3 76

Guichard. Great Master of France, the brave Sir Guichard Dolphin *Hen. V.* iv 8 100

Guide. Some heavenly power guide us Out of this fearful country! *Temp.* v 1 105
Why, Phaethon, . . . Wilt thou aspire to guide the heavenly car? *T. G. of Ver.* iii 1 154
But, lest the devil that guides him should aid him, I will search impossible places *Mer. Wives* iii 5 150
Heaven guide him to thy husband's cudgel, and the devil guide his cudgel afterwards! iv 2 90
And twenty glow-worms shall our lanterns be, To guide our measure v 5 83
In love the heavens themselves do guide the state v 5 245
By the affection that now guides me most, I'll prove a tyrant *Meas. for Meas.* ii 4 168
I warrant you, if my instructions may be your guide iv 2 181
But all's brave that youth mounts and folly guides *As Y. Like It* iii 4 49
A guide, a goddess, and a sovereign, A counsellor, a traitress *All's Well* i 1 183

Guide. Discomfort guides my tongue And bids me speak of nothing but despair . . . . *Richard II.* iii 2 65
Do what you will; your wisdom be your guide . . . *2 Hen. IV.* ii 3 6
God shall be my hope, My stay, my guide and lantern to my feet *2 Hen. VI.* ii 3 25
Good fortune guide thee! . . . . *Richard III.* iv 1 92
Who did guide, I mean, who set the body and the limbs Of this great sport together, as you guess? . . . . *Hen. VIII.* i 1 45
Or those that with the fineness of their souls By reason guide *T. and C.* i 3 210
Fair desires, in all fair measure, fairly guide them! . . . iii 1 48
Yet gives he not till judgement guide his bounty . . . . . iv 5 102
Here comes himself to guide you.—Welcome, brave Hector . . . v 1 76
If souls guide vows, if vows be sanctimonies . . . . . . v 2 139
Guide, if thou canst, This after me, when I have writ my name Without the help of any hand at all . . . . . *T. Andron.* iv 1 69
Heaven guide thy pen to print thy sorrows plain! . . . . iv 1 75
Come, bitter conduct, come, unsavoury guide! . . *Rom. and Jul.* v 3 116
Pray, entertain them; give them guide to us . . . *T. of Athens* i 1 252
And, when my face is cover'd, as 'tis now, Guide thou the sword *J. Cæsar* v 3 45
He hath a wisdom that doth guide his valour To act in safety *Macbeth* iii 1 53
Became his guide, Led him, begg'd for him, saved him from despair *Lear* v 3 190
My blood begins my safer guides to rule . . . . . *Othello* ii 3 205
My good stars, that were my former guides, Have empty left their orbs, and shot their fires Into the abysm of hell . . *Ant. and Cleo.* iii 13 145
And that you'ld guide me to your sovereign's court . . *Pericles* ii 1 146
Her relapse is mortal. Come, come; And Æsculapius guide us! . . iii 2 111
Guided. Where her shoe, which is baser, guided by her foot, which is basest, doth tread . . . . *L. L. Lost* i 2 173
We have been guided by thee hitherto And of thy cunning had no diffidence: One sudden foil shall never breed distrust *1 Hen. VI.* iii 3 9
Say, you chose him More after our commandment than as guided By your own true affections . . . . *Coriolanus* ii 3 238
To the more mature A glass that feated them, and to the graver A child that guided dotards . . . . *Cymbeline* i 1 50
Rather shunned to go even with what I heard than in my every action to be guided by others' experiences . . . . . . i 4 48
Guider. Our guider, come; to the Roman camp conduct us . *Coriolanus* i 7 7
Guiderius. The heir of Cymbeline and Britain, who The king his father call'd Guiderius . . . . *Cymbeline* iii 3 88
This gentleman, whom I call Polydore, Most worthy prince, as yours, is true Guiderius . . . . v 5 358
Guiderius had Upon his neck a mole, a sanguine star . . . . v 5 363
Guiding. I give Me and my service, ever whilst I live, Into your guiding power . . . . *All's Well* ii 3 111
Jove send her A better guiding spirit! . . . . . *W. Tale* ii 3 127
Which is that god in office, guiding men? . . . *Troi. and Cres.* i 3 231
Guidon. I stay but for my guidon: to the field! . . . *Hen. V.* iv 2 60
Guienne, Champagne, Rheims, Orleans, Paris, Guysors, Poictiers, are all quite lost . . . . *1 Hen. VI.* i 1 60
Guildenstern. Welcome, dear Rosencrantz and Guildenstern! *Hamlet* ii 2 1
Thanks, Rosencrantz and gentle Guildenstern.—Thanks, Guildenstern ii 2 33
How dost thou, Guildenstern? Ah, Rosencrantz! Good lads, how do ye both? . . . . ii 2 229
Hark you, Guildenstern; and you too: at each ear a hearer . . . ii 2 399
Ho, Guildenstern! Friends both, go join you with some further aid! . iv 1 32
Ho, Guildenstern! bring in my lord . . . . iv 3 16
Rosencrantz and Guildenstern hold their course for England. . . iv 6 28
So Guildenstern and Rosencrantz go to't . . . . . . v 2 56
His commandment is fulfill'd, That Rosencrantz and Guildenstern are dead . . . . v 2 382
Guilder. I am bound To Persia and want guilders for my voyage *C. of Er.* iv 1 4
Guildford. The Guildfords are in arms; And every hour more competitors Flock to their aid . . . . *Richard III.* iv 4 505
With Sir Henry Guildford This night to be comptrollers . *Hen. VIII.* i 3 66
You are young, Sir Harry Guildford . . . . i 4 9
Guildhall. The mayor towards Guildhall hies him in all post *Richard III.* iii 5 73
Towards three or four o'clock Look for the news that the Guildhall affords . . . . iii 5 102
Guile. Can this be so, That in alliance, amity and oaths, There should be found such false dissembling guile? . . . . *1 Hen. VI.* iv 1 63
A friend, Deep, hollow, treacherous, and full of guile . *Richard III.* ii 1 38
And with a virtuous vizard hide foul guile . . . . . . ii 2 28
Poor Clarence, by thy guile betray'd to death! . . . . . v 3 133
Guiled. Thus ornament is but the guiled shore To a most dangerous sea *Mer. of Venice* iii 2 97
Guileful. A third thinks, without expense at all, By guileful fair words peace may be obtain'd . . . . *1 Hen. VI.* i 1 77
I train'd thy brethren to that guileful hole . . . *T. Andron.* v 1 104
Guilt. Thy conscience Is so possess'd with guilt . . . *Tempest* i 2 471
Their great guilt, Like poison given to work a great time after . . iii 3 104
My shame and guilt confounds me . . . . . *T. G. of Ver.* v 4 73
A murderous guilt shows not itself more soon Than love that would seem hid: love's night is noon . . . . *T. Night* iii 1 159
Since we so openly Proceed in justice, which shall have due course, Even to the guilt or the purgation . . . . . . *W. Tale* iii 2 7
Thieves are not judged but they are by to hear, Although apparent guilt be seen in them . . . . *Richard II.* iv 1 124
My guilt be on my head, and there an end . . . . . . v 1 69
The guilt of conscience take thou for thy labour . . . . . v 6 41
England shall double gild his treble guilt . . . . *2 Hen. IV.* iv 5 129
Have, for the gilt of France,—O guilt indeed!—Confirm'd conspiracy *Hen. V.* ii Prol. 26
Peradventure have on them the guilt of premeditated and contrived murder . . . . iv 1 170
In sight of God and us, your guilt is great . . . . *2 Hen. VI.* ii 3 2
For by his death we do perceive his guilt . . . . . . ii 3 104
I shall not want false witness to condemn me, Nor store of treasons to augment my guilt . . . . iii 1 169
His guilt should be but idly posted over, Because his purpose is not executed . . . . iii 1 255
But that the guilt of murder bucklers thee And I should rob the deathsman of his fee . . . . iii 2 216
Which laid their guilt upon my guiltless shoulders . . *Richard III.* i 2 98
His apparent open guilt omitted, I mean, his conversation with Shore's wife . . . . iii 5 30
Let them not speak a word; the guilt is plain . . . *T. Andron.* ii 3 301
Here's no sound jest! the old man hath found their guilt . . . iv 2 26
Shall she live to betray this guilt of ours, A long-tongued babbling gossip? . . . . iv 2 149
Who shall bear the guilt Of our great quell . . . . . *Macbeth* i 7 71
Guilt. I'll gild the faces of the grooms withal; For it must seem their guilt . . . . *Macbeth* ii 2 57
If his occulted guilt Do not itself unkennel in one speech . *Hamlet* iii 2 85
My stronger guilt defeats my strong intent . . . . . . iii 3 40
So full of artless jealousy is guilt, It spills itself in fearing to be spilt . iv 5 19
Close pent-up guilts, Rive your concealing continents, and cry *Lear* iii 2 57
The heaviness and guilt within my bosom Takes off my manhood *Cymb.* v 2 1
Guiltian, Cosmo, Lodowick, and Gratii . . . . . *All's Well* iv 3 185
Guiltier. May in the sworn twelve have a thief or two Guiltier than him they try . . . . *Meas. for Meas.* ii 1 21
I should be guiltier than my guiltiness, To think I can be undiscernible v 1 372
Guiltily. Bloody and guilty, guiltily awake! . . . . *Richard III.* v 3 146
Guiltiness. The guiltiness of my mind, the sudden surprise of my powers *Mer. Wives* v 5 130
If it confess A natural guiltiness such as is his . . *Meas. for Meas.* ii 2 139
I should be guiltier than my guiltiness, To think I can be undiscernible v 1 372
Her blush is guiltiness, not modesty . . . . . . *Much Ado* iv 1 43
Your grace is perjured much, Full of dear guiltiness . . *L. L. Lost* v 2 801
Think on Buckingham, And die in terror of thy guiltiness! *Richard III.* v 3 170
They vanish tongue-tied in their guiltiness . . . . *J. Cæsar* i 1 67
Guiltiness will speak, Though tongues were out of use . . *Othello* v 1 109
Why I should fear I know not, Since guiltiness I know not . . . v 2 39
Guiltless. As fast lock'd up in sleep as guiltless labour . *Meas. for Meas.* iv 2 69
If this sweet lady lie not guiltless here Under some biting error *M. Ado* iv 1 171
I am but as a guiltless messenger . . . . . . *As Y. Like It* iv 3 12
To be generous, guiltless and of free disposition . . . *T. Night* i 5 99
Whose guiltless drops Are every one a woe, a sore complaint *Hen. V.* i 2 25
And all to make away my guiltless life . . . . . *2 Hen. VI.* iii 1 167
Thrust from the crown By shameful murder of a guiltless king . . iv 1 95
These hands are free from guiltless blood-shedding . . . . iv 7 108
Which laid their guilt upon my guiltless shoulders . . *Richard III.* i 2 98
O, spare my guiltless wife and my poor children! . . . . . i 4 72
I will not reason what is meant hereby, Because I will be guiltless . i 4 95
We give thee up our guiltless blood to drink . . . . . . iii 3 14
My guiltless blood must cry against 'em . . . . . *Hen. VIII.* ii 1 68
If the duke be guiltless, 'Tis full of woe . . . . ii 1 139
I am guiltless of your father's death, And am most sensibly in grief *Hamlet* iv 5 149
I am guiltless, as I am ignorant Of what hath moved you . . *Lear* i 4 295
Congregated sands,—Traitors ensteep'd to clog the guiltless keel *Othello* ii 1 70
And many worthy and chaste dames even thus, All guiltless, meet reproach . . . . iv 1 48
A guiltless death I die.—O, who hath done this deed?—Nobody; I myself . . . . v 2 122
Guilty. With whispering and most guilty diligence . *Meas. for Meas.* iv 1 39
Lest myself be guilty to self-wrong, I'll stop mine ears . *Com. of Errors* iii 2 168
Whilst upon me the guilty doors were shut And I denied to enter . . iv 4 66
The world was very guilty of such a ballad some three ages since *L. L. L.* i 2 116
So it is sometimes, Glory grows guilty of detested crimes . . . iv 1 31
I heard your guilty rhymes, observed your fashion . . . . iv 3 139
Guilty, my lord, guilty! I confess, I confess . . . . . iv 3 205
If over-boldly we have borne ourselves In the converse of breath: your gentleness Was guilty of it . . . . v 2 746
I am not guilty of Lysander's blood; Nor is he dead . *M. N. Dream* iii 2 75
Till I come again, No bed shall e'er be guilty of my stay *Mer. of Venice* iii 2 328
I confess me much guilty, to deny so fair and excellent ladies *As Y. Like It* i 2 196
This is the first truth that e'er thine own tongue was guilty of *All's Well* iv 1 36
Wherefore hast thou accused him all this while?—Because he's guilty, and he is not guilty . . . . v 3 290
We should have answer'd heaven Boldly 'not guilty' . . . *W. Tale* i 2 74
He who shall speak for her is afar off guilty But that he speaks . . ii 1 104
Nor guilty of, If any be, the trespass of the queen . . . . . ii 2 62
He is not guilty of her coming hither.—You're liars all . . . . ii 3 144
The testimony on my part no other But what comes from myself, it shall scarce boot me To say 'not guilty' . . . . iii 2 27
But as the unthought-on accident is guilty To what we wildly do . . iv 4 549
If I in act, consent, or sin of thought, Be guilty . . . . *K. John* iv 3 136
If guilty dread have left thee so much strength As to take up mine honour's pawn, then stoop . . . . *Richard II.* i 1 73
Since thou hast far to go, bear not along The clogging burthen of a guilty soul . . . . i 3 200
His hands were guilty of no kindred blood . . . . ii 1 182
And darts his light through every guilty hole . . . . . . iii 2 43
As I intend to thrive in this new world, Aumerle is guilty . . . iv 1 79
I'll make a voyage to the Holy Land, To wash this blood off from my guilty hand: March sadly after . . . . v 6 50
Either envy, therefore, or misprision Is guilty of this fault . *1 Hen. IV.* i 3 28
I'll be no longer guilty of this sin . . . . ii 4 267
Yield, and this avoid, Or, guilty in defence, be thus destroy'd *Hen. V.* iii 3 43
No more is the king guilty of their damnation than he was before guilty of those impieties for the which they are now visited . . . . iv 1 183
His trespass yet lives guilty in thy blood . . . . *1 Hen. VI.* ii 4 94
And shall my youth be guilty of such blame? . . . . . . iv 5 47
Who can accuse me? wherein am I guilty? . . . . *2 Hen. VI.* iii 1 103
Say we intend to try his grace to-day, If he be guilty . . . . iii 2 17
Then you, belike, suspect these noblemen As guilty of Duke Humphrey's timeless death . . . . iii 2 187
A proper man, of mine honour; unless I find him guilty, he shall not die iv 2 103
For of that sin My mild entreaty shall not make you guilty *3 Hen. VI.* iii 1 91
For Somerset, off with his guilty head. Go, bear them hence . . v 5 3
Suspicion always haunts the guilty mind; The thief doth fear each bush v 6 11
How fain, like Pilate, would I wash my hands Of this most grievous guilty murder done! . . . . *Richard III.* i 4 280
Mark'd you not How that the guilty kindred of the queen Look'd pale? ii 1 135
Not for all this land Would I be guilty of so deep a sin . . . iii 1 43
Within the guilty closure of thy walls Richard the second here was hack'd to death . . . . iii 3 11
The most arch act of piteous massacre That ever yet this land was guilty of . . . . iv 3 3
With guilty fear, Let fall thy lance: despair, and die! . . . . v 3 142
Bloody and guilty, guiltily awake, And in a bloody battle end thy days! v 3 146
All several sins, all used in each degree, Throng to the bar, crying all, Guilty! guilty! I shall despair . . . . v 3 199
Is he found guilty?—Yes, truly is he, and condemn'd upon't *Hen. VIII.* ii 1 7
He pleaded still not guilty and alleged Many sharp reasons to defeat the law . . . . ii 1 13
So his peers, upon this evidence, Have found him guilty of high treason ii 1 27
I dare not make myself so guilty, To give up willingly that noble title . iii 1 139
If you can blush and cry 'guilty,' cardinal, You'll show a little honesty iii 2 305
And find out murderers in their guilty caves . . . . *T. Andron* v 2 52

Guilty. Lavinia 'tween her stumps doth hold The basin that receives your guilty blood . . . . *T. Andron.* v 2 184
I would forget it fain; But, O, it presses to my memory, Like damned guilty deeds to sinners' minds . . . . . *Rom. and Jul.* iii 2 111
What an unkind hour Is guilty of this lamentable chance! . . . v 3 146
When every drop of blood That every Roman bears, and nobly bears, Is guilty of a several bastardy. . . . . . *J. Cæsar* ii 1 138
And then it started like a guilty thing Upon a fearful summons *Hamlet* i 1 148
In their birth—wherein they are not guilty, Since nature cannot choose his origin . . . . i 4 25
Having ever seen in the prenominate crimes The youth you breathe of guilty . . . . ii 1 44
Make mad the guilty and appal the free, Confound the ignorant . . ii 2 590
I have heard That guilty creatures sitting at a play Have by the very cunning of the scene Been struck so to the soul that presently They have proclaim'd their malefactions . . . . . ii 2 618
He that is not guilty of his own death shortens not his own life . . v 1 21
We make guilty of our disasters the sun, the moon, and the stars . *Lear* i 2 130
Guilty-like. I cannot think it, That he would steal away so guilty-like, Seeing you coming . . . . . . *Othello* iii 3 39
Guinea-hen. I would drown myself for the love of a guinea-hen . . i 3 317
Guinover. That was a woman when Queen Guinover of Britain was a little wench . . . . *L. L. Lost* iv 1 125
Guise. Is this the guise, Is this the fashion in the court of England? Is this the government of Britain's isle? . . . . . *2 Hen. VI.* i 3 45
How rarely does it meet with this time's guise, When man was wished to love his enemies . . . . . . *T. of Athens* iv 3 472
This is her very guise; and, upon my life, fast asleep . . *Macbeth* v 1 22
To shame the guise o' the world, I will begin The fashion, less without and more within . . . . . . *Cymbeline* v 1 32
Gules. With man's blood paint the ground, gules, gules . *T. of Athens* iv 3 59
Head to foot Now is he total gules . . . . . . *Hamlet* ii 2 479
Gulf. As easy mayst thou fall A drop of water in the breaking gulf And take unmingled thence that drop again . . . *Com. of Errors* ii 2 128
His approaches makes as fierce As waters to the sucking of a gulf *Hen. V.* ii 4 10
Certainly thou art so near the gulf, Thou needs must be englutted . iv 3 82
Thyself the sea Whose envious gulf did swallow up his life *3 Hen. VI.* v 6 25
In the swallowing gulf Of blind forgetfulness and dark oblivion *Rich. III.* iii 7 128
That only like a gulf it did remain I' the midst o' the body *Coriolanus* i 1 101
Thou had'st rather Follow thine enemy in a fiery gulf Than flatter him in a bower . . . . iii 2 91
Maw and gulf Of the ravin'd salt-sea shark . . . . *Macbeth* iv 1 23
Like a gulf, doth draw What's near it with it . . . . *Hamlet* iii 3 16
Roast me in sulphur! Wash me in steep-down gulfs of liquid fire! *Othello* v 2 280
Gull. I should think this a gull, but that the white-bearded fellow speaks it: knavery cannot, sure, hide himself in such reverence *Much Ado* ii 3 123
If I do not gull him into a nayword . . . . . *T. Night* ii 3 145
Yond gull Malvolio is turned heathen, a very renegado . . . iii 2 73
An ass-head and a coxcomb and a knave, a thin-faced knave, a gull! . v 1 213
And made the most notorious geck and gull That e'er invention play'd on v 1 351
As that ungentle gull, the cuckoo's bird, Useth the sparrow . *1 Hen. IV.* v 1 60
'Tis a gull, a fool, a rogue, that now and then goes to the wars *Hen. V.* iii 6 70
I do beweep to many simple gulls . . . . . *Richard III.* i 3 328
When every feather sticks in his own wing, Lord Timon will be left a naked gull, Which flashes now a phœnix . . . *T. of Athens* ii 1 31
O gull! O dolt! As ignorant as dirt! thou hast done a deed *Othello* v 2 163
Gull-catcher. Here comes my noble gull-catcher . . *T. Night* ii 5 205
Gulled. That same demon that hath gull'd thee thus . . *Hen. V.* ii 2 121
Gum. The gum down-roping from their pale-dead eyes . . . iv 2 48
Our poesy is as a gum, which oozes . . . . . *T. of Athens* i 1 21
Pluck'd my nipple from his boneless gums, And dash'd the brains out *Macbeth* i 7 57
Their eyes purging thick amber and plum-tree gum . . *Hamlet* ii 2 201
Drop tears as fast as the Arabian trees Their medicinal gum . *Othello* v 2 351
Gummed. He frets like a gummed velvet . . . . *1 Hen. IV.* ii 2 2
Gun. Sword, pike, knife, gun, or need of any engine, Would I not have *Tempest* ii 1 161
Is that lead slow which is fired from a gun? . . . *L. L. Lost* iii 1 63
Rising and cawing at the gun's report, Sever themselves *M. N. Dream* iii 2 22
And talk so like a waiting-gentlewoman Of guns and drums . *1 Hen. IV.* i 3 56
But for these vile guns, He would himself have been a soldier . . i 3 63
Like an overcharged gun, recoil . . . . . . *2 Hen. VI.* iii 2 331
And then down falls again.—As if that name, Shot from the deadly level of a gun, Did murder her . . . . . *Rom. and Jul.* iii 3 103
Gunner. The master, the swabber, the boatswain and I, The gunner and his mate, Loved Mall, Meg and Marian . . . *Tempest* ii 2 49
The nimble gunner With linstock now the devilish cannon touches *Hen. V.* iii Prol. 32
Gunpowder. 'Zounds, I am afraid of this gunpowder Percy, though he be dead . . . . *1 Hen. IV.* v 4 123
As strong As aconitum or rash gunpowder . . . *2 Hen. IV.* iv 4 48
Touch'd with choler, hot as gunpowder . . . . *Hen. V.* iv 7 188
Gun-stone. This mock of his Hath turn'd his balls to gun-stones . . i 2 282
Gurnet. If I be not ashamed of my soldiers, I am a soused gurnet *1 Hen. IV.* iv 2 13
Gurney. James Gurney, wilt thou give us leave awhile? . . *K. John* i 1 230
Gust. You may as well forbid the mountain pines To wag their high tops and to make no noise, When they are fretten with the gusts of heaven . . . . *Mer. of Venice* iv 1 77
Though little fire grows great with little wind, Yet extreme gusts will blow out fire and all . . . . . . *T. of Shrew* ii 1 136
He hath the gift of a coward to allay the gust he hath in quarrelling *T. Night* i 3 33
'Tis far gone, When I shall gust it last . . . . *W. Tale* i 2 219
Like as rigour of tempestuous gusts Provokes the mightiest hulk against the tide . . . . *1 Hen. IV.* v 5 5
Cursed the gentle gusts And he that loosed them forth . *2 Hen. VI.* iii 2 88
As doth a sail, fill'd with a fretting gust, Command an argosy to stem the waves . . . . *3 Hen. VI.* ii 6 35
Commanded always by the greater gust; Such is the lightness of you common men . . . . iii 1 88
By interims and conveying gusts we have heard The charges *Coriolanus* i 6 5
By uproar sever'd, like a flight of fowl Scatter'd by winds and high tempestuous gusts . . . . *T. Andron* v 3 69
To kill, I grant, is sin's extremest gust . . . *T of Athens* iii 5 54
Gusty. Once, upon a raw and gusty day . . . . . *J. Cæsar* i 2 100
Gut. Let vultures gripe thy guts! for gourd and fullam holds *Mer. Wives* i 3 94
Revenged I will be, as sure as his guts are made of puddings . . ii 1 32
Is it not strange that sheeps' guts should hale souls out of men's bodies? *Much Ado* ii 3 61
Thou clay-brained guts, thou knotty-pated fool . . *1 Hen. IV.* ii 4 251
You carried your guts away as nimbly, with as quick dexterity . . ii 4 285
That huge bombard of sack, that stuffed cloak-bag of guts . . ii 4 498
I pray God my girdle break.—O, if it should, how would thy guts fall about thy knees! . . . . iii 3 172
It is all filled up with guts and midriff . . . . . iii 3 175
If you would walk off, I would prick your guts a little . . *Hen. V.* ii 1 61
Who wears his wit in his belly and his guts in his head . *Troi. and Cres.* ii 1 80
I'll lug the guts into the neighbour room . . . . *Hamlet* iii 4 212
To show you how a king may go a progress through the guts of a beggar iv 3 33
Guts-griping, ruptures, catarrhs, loads o' gravel i' the back *Troi. and Cres.* v 1 21
Gutter'd rocks and congregated sands,—Traitors ensteep'd . *Othello* ii 1 69
Guy. I am not Samson, nor Sir Guy, nor Colbrand, To mow 'em down *Hen. VIII.* v 4 22
Guynes. 'Twixt Guynes and Arde: I was then present, saw them salute i 1 7
Guysors. Orleans, Paris, Guysors, Poictiers, are all quite lost *1 Hen. VI.* i 1 61
Gyve. If you will take it on you to assist him, it shall redeem you from your gyves . . . . *Meas. for Meas.* iv 2 12
The villains march wide betwixt the legs, as if they had gyves on *1 Hen. IV.* iv 2 44
Like a poor prisoner in his twisted gyves . . . *Rom. and Jul.* ii 2 180
Dipping all his faults in their affection, Would, like the spring that turneth wood to stone, Convert his gyves to graces . *Hamlet* iv 7 21
I will gyve thee in thine own courtship . . . . *Othello* ii 1 171
Must I repent? I cannot do it better than in gyves . . *Cymbeline* v 4 14

H

H. For a hawk, a horse, or a husband?—For the letter that begins them all, H . . . . *Much Ado* iii 4 56
I had a wound here that was like a T, But now 'tis made an H *Ant. and Cleo.* iv 7 8
Ha, ha, ha! So, you're paid . . . . . . *Tempest* ii 1 36
Ha! let me see: ay, give it me, it's mine. . . . *T. G. of Ver.* ii 1 3
Am I a woodman, ha? . . . . *Mer. Wives* v 5 31
Why, then, some be of laughing, as, ah, ha, he! . . . *Much Ado* iv 1 23
Sola, sola! wo ha, ho! sola, sola! . . . . *Mer. of Venice* v 1 39
The shrug, the hum or ha, these petty brands That calumny doth use *W. Tale* ii 1 71
These shrugs, these hums and ha's, When you have said 'she's goodly,' come between Ere you can say 'she's honest' . . . . . ii 1 74
Doth turn oh! oh! to ha! ha! he! So dying love lives still: Oh! oh! a while, but ha! ha! ha! Oh! oh! groans out for ha! ha! ha? *Troi. and Cres.* iii 1 133
Ah, ha, boy! say'st thou so? art thou there, truepenny? . *Hamlet* i 5 150
Ha, ha! Give me to drink mandragora . . . . *Ant. and Cleo.* i 5 3
Haberdasher. There was a haberdasher's wife of small wit *Hen. VIII.* v 4 49
Habiliment. My riches are these poor habiliments . *T. G. of Ver.* iv 1 13
Even in these honest mean habiliments: Our purses shall be proud, our garments poor . . . . *T. of Shrew* iv 3 172
Why he cometh hither Thus plated in habiliments of war . *Richard II.* i 3 28
Thus, in this strange and sad habiliment, I will encounter with Andronicus, And say I am Revenge . . . . *T. Andron.* v 2 1
She In the habiliments of the goddess Isis That day appear'd *A. and C.* iii 6 17
Habit. In what habit will you go along?—Not like a woman *T. G. of Ver.* ii 7 39
How use doth breed a habit in a man! . . . . . . v 4 1
O Proteus, let this habit make thee blush! . . . . . v 4 104
Habit. And in that habit, When Slender sees his time To take her by the hand and bid her go, She shall go . . . . *Mer. Wives* iv 6 36
Supply me with the habit and instruct me How I may formally in person bear me Like a true friar . . . . . *Meas. for Meas.* i 3 46
O place, O form, How often dost thou with thy case, thy habit, Wrench awe from fools! . . . . ii 4 13
My mind promises with my habit no loss shall touch her by my company iii 1 181
Not changing heart with habit, I am still Attorney'd at your service . v 1 389
Here she comes in the habit of a light wench . . *Com. of Errors* iv 3 52
Every lovely organ of her life Shall come apparell'd in more precious habit, More moving-delicate . . . . . . *Much Ado* iv 1 229
We four indeed confronted were with four In Russian habit . *L. L. Lost* v 2 368
Never more to dance, Nor never more in Russian habit wait . . . v 2 401
These four will change habits, and present the other five . . . v 2 542
Like the eye, Full of strange shapes, of habits and of forms . . . v 2 773
A better bad habit of frowning . . . . . . *Mer. of Venice* i 2 63
Put on a sober habit, Talk with respect and swear but now and then . ii 2 199
In such a habit, That they shall think we are accomplished With that we lack . . . . iii 4 60
I will speak to him like a saucy lackey and under that habit play the knave with him . . . . *As Y. Like It* iii 2 314
Fie, doff this habit, shame to your estate, An eye-sore! . *T. of Shrew* iii 2 102
As the sun breaks through the darkest clouds, So honour peereth in the meanest habit . . . . iv 3 176
You seem a sober ancient gentleman by your habit . . . . v 1 76
With a kind of injunction drives me to these habits of her liking *T. Night* ii 5 184
A sad face, a reverend carriage, a slow tongue, in the habit of some sir of note . . . . iii 4 81
One face, one voice, one habit, and two persons, A natural perspective! v 1 223

Habit. When in other habits you are seen, Orsino's mistress and his fancy's queen . . . . *T. Night* v 1 396
The celestial habits, Methinks I so should term them . . *W. Tale* iii 1 4
Not alone in habit and device, Exterior form, outward accoutrement *K. John* i 1 210
They will know us by our horses, by our habits . . . 1 *Hen. IV.* i 2 196
You know me by my habit.—Well then I know thee . . *Hen. V.* iii 6 121
Hath into monstrous habits put the graces That once were his *Hen. VIII.* i 2 122
If you have any justice, any pity; If ye be any thing but churchmen's habits . . . . iii 1 117
Strike me the counterfeit matron; It is her habit only that is honest, Herself's a bawd . . . . *T. of Athens* iv 3 113
Why this spade? this place? This slave-like habit? and these looks of care? . . . . iv 3 205
If thou didst put this sour-cold habit on To castigate thy pride, 'twere well . . . . iv 3 239
Costly thy habit as thy purse can buy, But not express'd in fancy *Hamlet* i 3 70
Some habit that too much o'er-leavens The form of plausive manners . i 4 29
Look, how it steals away! My father, in his habit as he lived! . . iii 4 135
That monster, custom, who all sense doth eat, Of habits devil, is angel yet in this . . . . iii 4 162
Only got the tune of the time and outward habit of encounter . . v 2 198
In this habit Met I my father with his bleeding rings . . *Lear* v 3 188
These thin habits and poor likelihoods Of modern seeming . . *Othello* i 3 108
Let me make men know More valour in me than my habits show *Cymb.* v 1 30
There was a fourth man, in a silly habit, That gave the affront with them . . . . v 3 86
Opinion's but a fool, that makes us scan The outward habit by the inward man . . . . *Pericles* ii 2 57

Habitation. A breath thou art, Servile to all the skyey influences, That dost this habitation, where thou keep'st, Hourly afflict *M. for M.* iii 1 10
Gives to airy nothing A local habitation and a name *M. N. Dream* v 1 17
To smell pork; to eat of the habitation which your prophet the Nazarite conjured the devil into . . . . . *Mer. of Venice* i 3 34
An habitation giddy and unsure Hath he that buildeth on the vulgar heart . . . . 2 *Hen. IV.* i 3 89

Habited. She shall be habited as it becomes The partner of your bed *W. Tale* iv 4 557
Rome's royal empress . . . ? Or is it Dian, habited like her? *T. Andron.* ii 3 57

Hack. These knights will hack . . . . *Mer. Wives* ii 1 52
Let them keep their limbs whole and hack our English . . . . iii 1 79
He teaches him to hick and to hack, which they'll do fast enough of themselves . . . . iv 1 68
What a slave art thou, to hack thy sword as thou hast done, and then say it was in fight! . . . . . . 1 *Hen. IV.* ii 4 288
Hew them to pieces, hack their bones asunder . . 1 *Hen. VI.* iv 7 47
Look you what hacks are on his helmet! . . . . *Troi. and Cres.* i 2 222
There's laying on, take't off who will, as they say: there be hacks! . i 2 225
Our course will seem too bloody, Caius Cassius, To cut the head off and then hack the limbs . . . . *J. Cæsar* ii 1 163

Hacked. Is hack'd down, and his summer leaves all faded . *Richard II.* i 2 20
My sword hacked like a hand-saw—ecce signum! . . 1 *Hen IV.* ii 4 187
Tell me now in earnest, how came Falstaff's sword so hacked?—Why, he hacked it with his dagger . . . . ii 4 335
Richard the second here was hack'd to death . . *Richard III.* iii 3 12
And, though we leave it with a root, thus hack'd, The air will drink the sap . . . . *Hen. VIII.* i 2 97
How his sword is bloodied, and his helm more hacked than Hector's! *Troi. and Cres.* i 2 253
Mangled Myrmidons, That noseless, handless, hack'd and chipp'd, come to him . . . . v 5 34
When your vile daggers Hack'd one another in the sides of Cæsar *J. C.* v 1 40
I'll fight till from my bones my flesh be hack'd. Give me my armour *Macbeth* v 3 32
Bear our hack'd targets like the men that owe them . *Ant. and Cleo.* iv 8 31

Hacket. Ask Marian Hacket, the fat ale-wife of Wincot . *T. of Shrew* Ind. 2 23
Sometimes you would call out for Cicely Hacket.—Ay, the woman's maid of the house . . . . Ind. 2 91

Hackney. The hobby-horse is but a colt, and your love perhaps a hackney *L. L. Lost.* iii 1 33

Had. A brave vessel, Who had, no doubt, some noble creature in her *Temp.* i 2 7
Had I not Four or five women once that tended me?—Thou hadst . i 2 46
I had peopled else This isle with Calibans . . . . . i 2 350
He is drunk now: where had he wine? . . . . . . v 1 278
Or else I often had been miserable . . . . *T. G. of Ver.* iv 1 35
I think verily he had been hanged for't; sure as I live, he had suffered for't . . . . iv 4 16
My desires had instance and argument to commend themselves *M. Wives* ii 2 256
Where had you this pretty weathercock? . . . . . . iii 2 18
I had other things to have spoken with her too from him . . iv 5 41
O,—sixpence, that I had o' Wednesday last To pay the saddler for my mistress' crupper? The saddler had it, sir; I kept it not *Com. of Errors* i 2 55
Told me what privy marks I had about me . . . . . iii 2 146
If my breast had not been made of faith . . . , She had transform'd me iii 2 151
Consent to pay thee that I never had! . . . . . . iv 1 74
He did bespeak a chain for me, but had it not . . . . . iv 4 139
We had like to have had our two noses snapped off. . . *Much Ado* v 1 115
It is the same I gave the doctor!—I had it of him . . *Mer. of Venice* v 1 258
I thought that all things had been savage here . . *As Y. Like It* ii 7 107
This young gentlewoman had a father,—O, that 'had'! . . *All's Well* i 1 19
The main consents are had . . . . v 3 69
I had thought, sir, to have held my peace until You had drawn oaths from him not to stay . . . . *W. Tale* i 2 28
They will bring all; whose spiritual counsel had, Shall stop or spur me ii 1 186
Do not give us the lie.—Your worship had like to have given us one . iv 4 750
I had thought, my lord, to have learn'd his health of you *Richard II.* ii 3 24
If of grief, being altogether had, It adds more sorrow to my want of joy iii 4 15
'Faith, for their poverty, I know not where they had that 1 *Hen. IV.* iv 2 77
The boy that I gave Falstaff: a' had him from me Christian 2 *Hen. IV.* ii 2 76
A new link to the bucket must needs be had . . . . . v 1 24
These wounds I had on Crispin's day. Old men forget . *Hen. V.* iv 3 48
I thought King Henry had resembled thee In courage . 2 *Hen. VI.* i 3 56
Which he had thought to have murder'd wrongfully . . . . ii 3 107
I had thought I had had men of some understanding And wisdom *Hen. VIII.* v 3 135
Who rather had, Though they themselves did suffer by't *Coriolanus* iv 6 5
Those five talents. That had, give't these fellows . . *T. of Athens* ii 2 238
Nought's had, all's spent, Where our desire is got without content *Macb.* iii 2 4
Nine or ten times I had thought to have yerk'd him here . *Othello* i 2 5

Had. Give it your hobby-horse: wheresoever you had it, I'll take out no work on't . . . . *Othello* iv 1 161
Then had you indeed a cut, and the case to be lamented *Ant. and Cleo.* i 2 173
It is my birth-day: I had thought to have held it poor . . iii 13 186

Had as lief. I had as lief you would tell me of a mess of porridge *M. W.* iii 1 63
I had as lief bear so much lead . . . . iv 2 117
To say the truth, I had as lief have the foppery of freedom as the morality of imprisonment . . . . . *Meas. for Meas.* i 2 137
I had as lief have heard the night-raven . . . . . *Much Ado* ii 3 83
I had as lief thou didst break his neck as his finger. . *As Y. Like It* i 1 152
But, good faith, I had as lief have been myself alone . . . iii 2 269
I had as lief be wooed of a snail.—Of a snail? . . . . . iv 1 52
I had as lief take her dowry with this condition . . *T. of Shrew* i 1 135
Policy I hate: I had as lief be a Brownist as a politician *T. Night* iii 2 33
I greatly care not: God knows I had as lief be none as one *Richard II.* v 2 49
I had as lief they would put ratsbane in my mouth . . 2 *Hen. IV.* i 2 47
In very truth, sir, I had as lief be hanged, sir, as go . . . iii 2 238
She, good soul, had as lief see a toad, a very toad, as see him *R. and J.* ii 4 215
I had as lief not be as live to be In awe of such a thing as I myself *J. C.* i 2 95
I had as lief the town-crier spoke my lines . . . *Hamlet* iii 2 4
I had as lief have a reed that will do me no service as a partisan I could not heave . . . . *Ant. and Cleo.* ii 7 13

Had as lieve hear the devil as a drum . . . . 1 *Hen. IV.* iv 2 19
I would not be a Roman, . . . I had as lieve be a condemned man *Coriol.* iv 5 186

Had better. He had better starve Than but once think this place becomes thee not . . . . *Hen. VIII.* v 3 132

Had rather. I had rather wink than look on them . . *T. G. of Ver.* v 2 14
I had rather than forty shillings I had my Book of Songs *Mer. Wives* i 1 205
Walk in.—I had rather walk here, I thank you . . . . . i 1 293
I had rather be a giantess, and lie under Mount Pelion . . . ii 1 81
I had rather hear them scold than fight . . . . . . ii 1 239
I had rather than a thousand pound he were out of the house . . iii 3 130
For shame! never stand 'you had rather' and 'you had rather' . . iii 3 133
I had rather be set quick i' the earth And bowl'd to death with turnips! iii 4 90
But I had rather it would please you I might be whipt . *Meas. for Meas.* v 1 511
I had rather hear my dog bark at a crow than a man swear he loves me *Much Ado* i 1 132
I had rather be a canker in a hedge than a rose in his grace . . i 3 28
I had rather lie in the woollen . . . . ii 1 33
Which I had rather seal with my death than repeat over to my shame . v 1 247
I had rather pray a month with mutton and porridge . . *L. L. Lost* i 1 304
I had rather give his carcass to my hounds . . . *M. N. Dream* iii 2 64
I had rather have a handful or two of dried peas . . . . iv 1 41
I had rather be married to a death's-head . . . *Mer. of Venice* i 2 55
I had rather he should shrive me than wive me . . . . . i 2 144
Whether till the next night she had rather stay, Or go to bed now . v 1 302
I had rather bear with you than bear you . . . *As Y. Like It* ii 4 11
I had rather hear you chide than this man woo . . . . . iii 5 65
I had rather than forty shillings I had such a leg . . *T. Night* ii 3 20
But I had rather You would have bid me argue like a father . *Richard II.* i 3 237
I had rather be a kitten and cry mew . . . . . 1 *Hen. IV.* iii 1 129
I had rather have my horse to my mistress . . . . *Hen. V.* iii 7 61
To tell you plain, I had rather lie in prison . . . 3 *Hen. VI.* iii 2 70
I had rather chop this hand off at a blow . . . . . . v 1 50
I had rather be a country servant-maid Than a great queen *Richard III.* i 3 107
I had rather had eleven die nobly for their country than one voluptuously surfeit out of action . . . . *Coriolanus* i 3 26
You had rather be at a breakfast of enemies than a dinner of friends *T. of Athens* i 2 78
Brutus had rather be a villager Than to repute himself a son of Rome Under these hard conditions . . . . *J. Cæsar* i 2 172
By heaven, I had rather coin my heart, And drop my blood for drachmas iv 3 72
I had rather to adopt a child than get it . . . . . *Othello* i 3 191
I had rather heat my liver with drinking . . . *Ant. and Cleo.* i 2 23
I had rather seal my lips, than, to my peril, Speak that which is not . v 2 146
I had rather not be so noble as I am . . . . . *Cymbeline* ii 1 20
I hate you; which I had rather You felt than make't my boast . iii 3 115
I had rather Have skipp'd from sixteen years of age to sixty . . iv 2 198

Hadst. Unless thou tell'st me where thou hadst this ring, Thou diest within this hour . . . . *All's Well* v 3 284
I sent thee sixpence for thy leman: hadst it? . . . . . *T. Night* ii 3 26
Thou wert better thou hadst struck thy mother . . . 2 *Hen. IV.* v 4 11

Hæc. Thus declined, Singulariter, nominativo, hic, hæc, hoc *Mer. Wives* iv 1 43

Hæres. Præclarissimus filius noster Henricus, Rex Angliæ, et Hæres Franciæ . . . . *Hen. V.* v 2 370

Hag. This blue-eyed hag was hither brought with child . . *Tempest* i 2 269
Nominativo, hig, hag, hog; pray you, mark; genitivo, hujus *Mer. Wives* iv 1 44
Come down, you witch, you hag, you; come down, I say! . . . iv 2 187
Out of my door, you witch, you hag, you baggage, you polecat! . . iv 2 194
A gross hag! . . . . *W. Tale* ii 3 108
Foul fiend of France, and hag of all despite! . . . 1 *Hen. VI.* iii 2 52
Fell banning hag, enchantress, hold thy tongue! . . . . . v 3 42
And wedded be thou to the hags of hell . . . . 2 *Hen. VI.* iv 1 79
Have done thy charm, thou hateful wither d hag! . . . *Richard III.* i 3 215
This is the hag, when maids lie on their backs, That presses them and learns them first to bear . . . . *Rom. and Jul.* i 4 92
How now, you secret, black, and midnight hags! What is't you do? *Macbeth* iv 1 48
Filthy hags! Why do you show me this? A fourth! Start, eyes! . iv 1 115
You unnatural hags, I will have such revenges on you both . *Lear* ii 4 281

Hagar. What says that fool of Hagar's offspring, ha? *Mer. of Venice* ii 5 44

Hag-born. A freckled whelp hag-born . . . . . . *Tempest* i 2 283

Haggard. Her spirits are as coy and wild As haggerds of the rock *M. Ado* iii 1 36
Another way I have to man my haggard, To make her come *T. of Shrew* iv 1 196
I have loved this proud disdainful haggard . . . . . iv 2 39
Like the haggard, check at every feather That comes before his eye *T. N.* iii 1 71
If I do prove her haggard, Though that her jesses were my dear heart-strings, I'ld whistle her off. . . . . *Othello* iii 3 260

Haggish. On us both did haggish age steal on . . . *All's Well* i 2 29

Haggled. Suffolk first died: and York, all haggled over, Comes to him *Hen. V.* iv 6 11

Hag-seed, hence! Fetch us in fuel; and be quick . . . *Tempest* i 2 365

Hai. Ah, the immortal passado! the punto reverso! the hai! *R. and J.* ii 4 27

Hail. All hail, great master! grave sir, hail! I come To answer *Tempest* i 2 189
Hail, many-colour'd messenger, that ne'er Dost disobey the wife of Jupiter . . . . iv 1 76
Hail kissing-comfits and snow eringoes . . . . . *Mer. Wives* v 5 22
Hail, virgin, if you be, as those cheek-roses Proclaim you are! *M. for M.* i 4 16
Hail to you, provost! so I think you are. . . . . . . ii 3 1
All hail, the richest beauties on the earth! . . . . *L. L. Lost* v 2 158

Hail. All hail, sweet madam, and fair time of day !—'Fair' in 'all hail' is foul, as I conceive *L. L. Lost* v 2 339
He hail'd down oaths that he was only mine ; And when this hail some heat from Hermia felt, So he dissolved, and showers of oaths did melt *M. N. Dream* i 1 244
Hail, mortal !—Hail !—Hail !—Hail ! iii 1 178
Thou mayst see a sunshine and a hail In me at once *All's Well* v 3 33
Hail, most royal sir !—What is the news i' the court ?—None rare *W. Tale* i 2 366
Hail, you anointed deputies of heaven ! *K. John* iii 1 136
Did they not sometime cry, 'all hail !' to me? So Judas did to Christ *Richard II.* iv 1 169
Hail, royal prince !—Thanks, noble peer ; The cheapest of us is ten groats too dear v 5 67
All hail, my lords ! Which of this princely train Call ye the warlike Talbot, for his acts So much applauded ? *1 Hen. VI.* ii 2 34
To say the truth, so Judas kiss'd his master, And cried 'all hail !' when as he meant all harm *3 Hen. VI.* v 7 34
Hail, all you state of Greece ! what shall be done ? *Troi. and Cres.* iv 5 65
But, O, thy wife !—My gracious silence, hail ! *Coriolanus* ii 1 192
Hail, lords ! I am return'd your soldier v 6 71
Hail, Rome, victorious in thy mourning weeds ! *T. Andron.* i 1 70
Lucius, all hail, Rome's royal emperor ! v 3 141
Hail to thee, worthy Timon, and to all That of his bounties taste ! *T. of A.* i 2 128
Hail, worthy Timon !—Our late noble master ! v 1 58
Cæsar, all hail ! good morrow, worthy Cæsar : I come to fetch you to the senate-house *J. Cæsar* ii 2 58
Crying 'Long live ! hail, Cæsar !' v 1 32
Hail, brave friend ! Say to the king the knowledge of the broil *Macbeth* i 2 5
All hail, Macbeth ! hail to thee, thane of Glamis !—All hail, Macbeth ! hail to thee, thane of Cawdor !—All hail, Macbeth, that shalt be king hereafter ! i 3 48
Hail !—Hail !—Hail !—Lesser than Macbeth, and greater i 3 62
As thick as hail Came post with post i 3 97
And referred me to the coming on of time, with 'Hail, king that shalt be !' i 5 10
Hail, king ! for so thou art : behold, where stands The usurper's cursed head v 8 54
Whose voices I desire aloud with mine : Hail, King of Scotland ! v 8 59
Hail to your lordship !—I am glad to see you well *Hamlet* i 2 160
Hail to thee, noble master !—Ha ! Makest thou this shame thy pastime ? *Lear* ii 4 4
Good morrow to you both.—Hail to your grace !—I am glad to see your highness ii 4 129
Hail to thee, lady ! and the grace of heaven, Before, behind thee and on every hand, Enwheel thee round ! *Othello* ii 1 85
I'll set thee in a shower of gold, and hail Rich pearls upon thee *A. and C.* ii 5 45
Hail, Cæsar, and my lord ! hail, most dear Cæsar ! iii 6 39
If I be so, From my cold heart let heaven engender hail iii 13 159
Hail, thou fair heaven ! We house i' the rock, yet use thee not so hardly As prouder livers do *Cymbeline* iii 3 7
Hail, great king ! To sour your happiness, I must report The queen is dead v 5 25
Sir king, all hail ! the gods preserve you ! Hail, royal sir ! *Pericles* v 1 39
See, she will speak to him.—Hail, sir ! my lord, lend ear.—Hum, ha ! v 1 83
Hail, Dian ! to perform thy just command, I here confess myself the king of Tyre v 3 1
Hail, madam, and my queen !—I know you not v 3 49

Hailed. For ere Demetrius look'd on Hermia's eyne, He hail'd down oaths that he was only mine *M. N. Dream* i 1 243
Then prophet-like They hail'd him father to a line of kings *Macbeth* iii 1 60

Hailstone. Vanish like hailstones, go ; Trudge *Mer. Wives* i 3 90
You are no surer, no, Than is the coal of fire upon the ice, Or hailstone in the sun *Coriolanus* i 1 178

Hair. Not so much perdition as an hair Betid to any creature *Tempest* i 2 30
With hair up-staring,—then like reeds, not hair i 2 213
Not a hair perish'd : On their sustaining garments not a blemish i 2 217
Now, jerkin, you are like to lose your hair and prove a bald jerkin iv 1 237
Why, then, your ladyship must cut your hair *T. G. of Ver.* ii 7 44
There's not a hair on 's head but 'tis a Valentine iii 1 192
She hath more hair than wit, and more faults than hairs iii 1 361
The hair that covers the wit is more than the wit iii 1 371
Her hair is auburn, mine is perfect yellow iv 4 194
She has brown hair, and speaks small like a woman *Mer. Wives* i 1 49
If you should fight, you go against the hair of your professions ii 3 41
There's no time for a man to recover his hair that grows bald by nature.—May he not do it by fine and recovery ?—Yes, to pay a fine for a periwig and recover the lost hair of another man *Com. of Errors* ii 2 74
Why is Time such a niggard of hair, being, as it is, so plentiful an excrement ? ii 2 78
What he hath scanted men in hair he hath given them in wit ii 2 82
But there's many a man hath more hair than wit.—Not a man of those but he hath the wit to lose his hair ii 2 84
Namely, no time to recover hair lost by nature ii 2 104
Spread o'er the silver waves thy golden hairs, And as a bed I'll take them iii 2 48
Some devils ask but the parings of one's nail, A rush, a hair iv 3 73
They threw on him Great pails of puddled mire to quench the hair v 1 173
Fetch you a hair off the great Cham's beard, do you any embassage *Much Ado* ii 1 277
Her hair shall be of what colour it please God ii 3 36
Upon her knees she falls, weeps, sobs, beats her heart, tears her hair ii 3 153
If the hair were a thought browner iii 4 14
With grey hairs and bruise of many days, Do challenge thee to trial of a man v 1 65
Her amber hair for foul hath amber quoted *L. L. Lost* iv 3 87
Ay me ! says one ; O Jove ! the other cries ; One, her hairs were gold iv 3 142
That painting and usurping hair Should ravish doters with a false aspect iv 3 259
As sweet and musical As bright Apollo's lute, strung with his hair iv 3 343
As is the razor's edge invisible, Cutting a smaller hair than may be seen v 2 258
With bracelets of thy hair, rings, gawds, conceits *M. N. Dream* i 1 33
Some of your French crowns have no hair at all i 2 100
Be it ounce, or cat, or bear, Pard, or boar with bristled hair ii 2 31
If my hair do but tickle me, I must scratch iv 1 28
Would you desire lime and hair to speak better ? v 1 166
Often kiss'd thy stones, Thy stones with lime and hair knit up in thee v 1 193
Superfluity comes sooner by white hairs *Mer. of Venice* i 2 9
Thou hast got more hair on thy chin than Dobbin my fill-horse has on his tail ii 2 100
I am sure he had more hair of his tail than I have of my face ii 2 104
Here in her hairs The painter plays the spider iii 2 120

Hair. Treble that, Before a friend of this description Shall lose a hair *Mer. of Venice* iii 2 304
If the scale do turn But in the estimation of a hair iv 1 331
The clerk will ne'er wear hair on's face that had it v 1 158
His very hair is of the dissembling colour *As Y. Like It* iii 4 7
I' faith, his hair is of a good colour.—An excellent colour iii 4 11
'Tis not your inky brows, your black silk hair, Your bugle eyeballs iii 5 46
He said mine eyes were black and my hair black iii 5 130
A wretched ragged man, o'ergrown with hair, Lay sleeping on his back iv 3 107
Let them curtsy with their left legs and not presume to touch a hair of my master's horse-tail till they kiss their hands *T. of Shrew* iv 1 96
By my old beard, And every hair that's on 't *All's Well* v 3 77
Then hadst thou had an excellent head of hair.—Why, would that have mended my hair ?—Past question *T. Night* i 3 101
Now Jove, in his next commodity of hair, send thee a beard ! iii 1 51
Black brows, they say, Become some women best, so that there be not Too much hair there *W. Tale* ii 1 10
Have made themselves all men of hair, they call themselves Saltiers iv 4 333
I am not mad : this hair I tear is mine ; My name is Constance *K. John* iii 4 45
O, what love I note In the fair multitude of those her hairs ! iii 4 62
Bind up your hairs.—Yes, that I will ; and wherefore will I do it ? iii 4 68
O that these hands could so redeem my son, As they have given these hairs their liberty ! iii 4 72
A dust, a gnat, a wandering hair, Any annoyance in that precious sense iv 1 93
And all the shrouds wherewith my life should sail Are turned to one thread, one little hair v 7 54
If I do not beat thee out of thy kingdom with a dagger of lath, . . . I'll never wear hair on my face more *1 Hen. IV.* ii 4 153
That he is old, the more the pity, his white hairs do witness it ii 4 514
In the way of bargain, mark ye me, I'll cavil on the ninth part of a hair iii 1 140
The tithe of a hair was never lost in my house before iii 3 66
Bardolph was shaved and lost many a hair iii 3 69
The quality and hair of our attempt Brooks no division iv 1 61
God may finish it when he will, 'tis not a hair amiss yet *2 Hen. IV.* i 2 27
There is not a white hair on your face but should have his effect of gravity i 2 182
Weekly sworn to marry since I perceived the first white hair on my chin i 2 271
The weight of a hair will turn the scales between their avoirdupois ii 4 276
How ill white hairs become a fool and jester ! v 5 52
Whose chin is but enrich'd With one appearing hair *Hen. V.* iii Prol. 23
He bounds from the earth, as if his entrails were hairs iii 7 14
I tell thee, constable, my mistress wears his own hair iii 7 65
Like prisoners wildly overgrown with hair v 2 43
His hair uprear'd, his nostrils stretch'd with struggling *2 Hen. VI.* iii 2 171
Look, on the sheets his hair, you see, is sticking iii 2 174
Mine hair be fix'd on end, as one distract iii 2 318
Comb down his hair ; look, look ! it stands upright, Like lime-twigs iii 3 15
Shame to thy silver hair, Thou mad misleader of thy brain-sick son ! v 1 162
Would bring white hairs unto a quiet grave *3 Hen. VI.* ii 5 40
This hand, fast wound about thy coal-black hair v 1 54
My hair doth stand on end to hear her curses *Richard III.* i 3 304
A shadow like an angel, with bright hair Dabbled in blood i 4 53
All thy best parts bound together Weigh'd not a hair of his *Hen. VIII.* iii 2 259
An her hair were not somewhat darker than Helen's—well, go to—there were no more comparison between the women *Troi. and Cres.* i 1 41
Pour'st in the open ulcer of my heart Her eyes, her hair, her cheek i 1 54
He is melancholy without cause, and merry against the hair i 2 28
He has not past three or four hairs on his chin i 2 122
And she takes upon her to spy a white hair on his chin i 2 154
At what was all this laughing ?—Marry, at the white hair that Helen spied on Troilus' chin.—An't had been a green hair, I should have laughed too i 2 164
They laughed not so much at the hair as at his pretty answer i 2 168
Here's but two and fifty hairs on your chin, and one of them is white i 2 172
That white hair is my father, and all the rest are his sons. 'Jupiter !' quoth she, 'which of these hairs is Paris my husband ?' i 2 176
You'll remember your brother's excuse ?—To a hair iii 1 157
If I be false, or swerve a hair from truth iii 2 191
Tear my bright hair and scratch my praised cheeks iv 2 113
See him pluck Aufidius down by the hair, As children from a bear *Coriolanus* i 3 33
And not a hair upon a soldier's head Which will not prove a whip iv 6 133
My fleece of woolly hair that now uncurls Even as an adder when she doth unroll To do some fatal execution *T. Andron.* ii 3 34
Rend off thy silver hair, thy other hand Gnawing with thy teeth iii 1 261
Go, drag the villain hither by the hair ; Nor age nor honour shall shape privilege iv 4 56
And bakes the elf-locks in foul sluttish hairs, Which once entangled much misfortune bodes *Rom. and Jul.* i 4 90
Thou desirest me to stop in my tale against the hair ii 4 100
Thou wilt quarrel with a man that hath a hair more, or a hair less, in his beard iii 1 19
Then mightst thou speak, then mightst thou tear thy hair, And fall upon the ground iii 3 68
For his silver hairs Will purchase us a good opinion *J. Cæsar* ii 1 144
Beg a hair of him for memory, And, dying, mention it within their wills iii 2 139
Art thou some god, some angel, or some devil, That makest my blood cold and my hair to stare ? iv 3 280
That suggestion Whose horrid image doth unfix my hair *Macbeth* i 3 135
Thy hair, Thou other gold-bound brow, is like the first iv 1 113
My fell of hair Would at a dismal treatise rouse and stir As life were in't v 5 11
Had I as many sons as I have hairs, I would not wish them to a fairer death v 8 48
And each particular hair to stand an end *Hamlet* i 5 19
Your bedded hair, like life in excrements, Start up, and stand an end iii 4 121
My face I'll grime with filth ; Blanket my loins ; elf all my hair in knots *Lear* ii 3 10
Tears his white hair, Which the impetuous blasts, with eyeless rage, Catch in their fury, and make nothing of iii 1 7
A serving-man, proud in heart and mind ; that curled my hair iii 4 88
These hairs, which thou dost ravish from my chin, Will quicken, and accuse thee iii 7 38
And told me I had white hairs in my beard ere the black ones were there iv 6 99
Had all his hairs been lives, my great revenge Had stomach for them all *Othello* v 2 74
Much is breeding, Which, like the courser's hair, hath yet but life, And not a serpent's poison *Ant. and Cleo.* i 2 200
Her years, Her inclination, let him not leave out The colour of her hair ii 5 114
In thy fats our cares be drown'd, With thy grapes our hairs be crown'd ii 7 123
Her hair, what colour ?—Brown, madam : and her forehead As low as she would wish it iii 3 35
My very hairs do mutiny ; for the white Reprove the brown for rashness iii 11 13

Hair. His meanest garment, That ever hath but clipp'd his body, is dearer In my respect than all the hairs above thee . . . *Cymbeline* ii 3 140
Unscissar'd shall this hair of mine remain, Though I show ill in't *Pericles* iii 3 29
Take you the marks of her, the colour of her hair, complexion, height . iv 2 62
I have cried her almost to the number of her hairs . . . . iv 2 101
He swears Never to wash his face, nor cut his hairs: He puts on sackcloth iv 4 28
Hair-breadth scapes i' the imminent deadly breach . . . *Othello* i 3 136
Hairless. White-beards have arm'd their thin and hairless scalps *Richard II.* iii 2 112
Hair's breadth. I profess requital to a hair's breadth . *Mer. Wives* iv 2 3
Hairy. Thou didst conclude hairy men plain dealers without wit *Com. of Errors* ii 2 87
Methinks I am marvellous hairy about the face . . *M. N. Dream* iv 1 27
She his hairy temples then had rounded With coronet of fresh and fragrant flowers . . . . iv 1 56
The hairy fool, Much marked of the melancholy Jaques . *As Y. Like It* ii 1 40
We are but plain fellows, sir.—A lie; you are rough and hairy *W. Tale* iv 4 744
Hal. Now, Hal, what time of day is it, lad? . . . . *1 Hen. IV.* i 2 1
Indeed, you come near me now, Hal . . . . . . i 2 14
But, Hal, I prithee, trouble me no more with vanity . . . . i 2 91
Thou hast done much harm upon me, Hal; God forgive thee for it! . i 2 103
Before I knew thee, Hal, I knew nothing . . . . . . i 2 104
Why, Hal, 'tis my vocation, Hal; 'tis no sin . . . . . i 2 116
I prithee, good Prince Hal, help me to my horse, good king's son . ii 2 43
Where hast been, Hal?—With three or four loggerheads . . . ii 4 3
I tell thee what, Hal, if I tell thee a lie, spit in my face . . . ii 4 214
What, four? thou saidst but two even now.—Four, Hal; I told thee four ii 4 220
Dost thou hear me, Hal?—Ay, and mark thee too, Jack . . . ii 4 233
For it was so dark, Hal, that thou couldst not see thy hand . . ii 4 247
No more of that, Hal, an thou lovest me! . . . . . ii 4 312
When I was about thy years, Hal, I was not an eagle's talon in the waist ii 4 363
But tell me, Hal, art not thou horrible afeard? . . . . ii 4 402
Dost thou hear, Hal? never call a true piece of gold a counterfeit . ii 4 539
Do I owe you a thousand pound?—A thousand pound, Hal! a million iii 3 155
Darest thou be as good as thy word now?—Why, Hal, thou knowest, as thou art but man, I dare . . . . iii 3 165
Now, Hal, to the news at court: for the robbery, lad, how is that answered? . . . . iii 3 197
What, Hal! how now, mad wag! what a devil dost thou in Warwickshire? iv 2 55
Tell me, Jack, whose fellows are these that come after?—Mine, Hal, mine iv 2 69
Hal, if thou see me down in the battle and bestride me, so . . v 1 121
I would 'twere bed-time, Hal, and all well . . . . . v 1 125
What, is it in the case?—Ay, Hal; 'tis hot, 'tis hot . . . v 3 55
Well said, Hal! to it, Hal! Nay, you shall find no boy's play here . v 4 75
I know how to handle you.—No abuse, Hal, o' mine honour; no abuse *2 Hen. IV.* ii 4 340
God save thy grace, King Hal! my royal Hal! . . . . . v 5 43
Halberd. Guard with halberds! . . . . . *Com. of Errors* v 1 185
He would waken him.—Unless our halberds did shut up his passage *3 Hen. VI.* iv 3 20
Advance thy halberd higher than my breast, Or, by Saint Paul, I'll strike thee to my foot . . . . . *Richard III.* i 2 40
Halcyon. Expect Saint Martin's summer, halcyon days . *1 Hen. VI.* i 2 131
Turn their halcyon beaks With every gale and vary of their masters *Lear* ii 2 84
Hale. Is it not strange that sheeps' guts should hale souls out of men's bodies? . . . . *Much Ado* ii 3 62
I think oxen and wainropes cannot hale them together . *T. Night* iii 2 64
I'll hale the Dauphin headlong from his throne . . *1 Hen. VI.* i 1 149
Although ye hale me to a violent death . . . . . . v 4 64
Hale him away, and let him talk no more . . *2 Hen. VI.* iv 1 131
The name of Henry the Fifth hales them to an hundred mischiefs . iv 8 59
That the appalled air May pierce the head of the great combatant And hale him hither . . . . . . *Troi. and Cres.* iv 5 6
The plebeians have got your fellow-tribune And hale him up and down *Coriolanus* v 4 40
To hale thy vengeful waggon swift away . . . . *T. Andron.* v 2 51
And hither hale that misbelieving Moor . . . . . v 3 143
So hangs, and lolls, and weeps upon me; so hales, and pulls me *Othello* iv 1 144
Haled. Thus strangers may be haled and abused . . *T. of Shrew* v 1 111
Haled out to murder . . . . *W. Tale* iii 2 102
Haled thither By most mechanical and dirty hand . . *2 Hen. IV.* v 5 37
Even like a man new haled from the rack, So fare my limbs *1 Hen. VI.* ii 5 3
Half. And now farewell Till half an hour hence . . . *Tempest* iii 1 91
Being but half a fish and half a monster . . . . . . iii 2 32
Take all, or half, for easing me of the carriage . . *Mer. Wives* ii 2 179
How long have you been in this place of constable?—Seven year and a half, sir.— . . . You say, seven years together?—And a half, sir *Meas. for Meas.* ii 1 274
Nor the judge's robe Become them with one half so good a grace As mercy ii 2 62
Even now, even here, not half an hour since . *Com. of Errors* ii 2 14
You know I gave it you half an hour since . . . . . iv 1 65
You know I gave it you half an hour since
And half Count John's melancholy in Signior Benedick's face *Much Ado* ii 1 13
O Hero, what a Hero hadst thou been, If half thy outward graces had been placed About thy thoughts and counsels of thy heart! . . iv 1 102
And speak off half a dozen dangerous words . . . . . v 1 97
And make a dark night too of half the day . . . *L. L. Lost* i 1 45
Being but the one half of an entire sum Disbursed by my father . ii 1 131
Restore But that one half which is unsatisfied, We will give up our right ii 1 139
Nor shines the silver moon one half so bright . . . . . iv 3 30
He clepeth a calf, cauf; half, hauf; neighbour vocatur nebour . . v 1 25
The letter is too long by half a mile . . . . . . v 2 54
Under the cool shade of a sycamore I thought to close mine eyes some half an hour . . . . v 2 90
Well run, dice! There's half-a-dozen sweets . . . . . v 2 234
You have a double tongue within your mask, And would afford my speechless vizard half . . . . v 2 246
No, I'll not be your half . . . . v 2 249
Here is my bed: sleep give thee all his rest!—With half that wish the wisher's eyes be press'd! . . . . . . *M. N. Dream* ii 2 65
You must name his name, and half his face must be seen . . iii 1 37
He hath disgraced me, and hindered me half a million; laughed at my losses . . . . *Mer. of Venice* iii 1 57
One half of me is yours, the other half yours . . . . iii 2 16
No metal can . . . bear half the keenness Of thy sharp envy . . iv 1 125
The party 'gainst the which he doth contrive Shall seize one half his goods iv 1 353
Half thy wealth, it is Antonio's; The other half comes to the general state iv 1 370
So please my lord the duke and all the court To quit the fine for one half of his goods, I am content; so he will let me have The other half in use . . . . iv 1 381
Half. If you had known the virtue of the ring, Or half her worthiness that gave the ring . . . . . . *Mer. of Venice* v 1 200
She may perhaps call him half a score knaves . . . *T. of Shrew* i 2 111
A woman's tongue, That gives not half so great a blow to hear As will a chestnut in a farmer's fire . . . . i 2 209
After my death the one half of my lands . . . . . . ii 1 122
Son, I'll be your half, Bianca comes.—I'll have no halves . . v 2 78
Half of the which dare not shake the snow from off their cassocks *All's W.* iv 3 190
His left cheek is a cheek of two pile and a half . . . . iv 5 103
I would not have him miscarry for the half of my dowry . *T. Night* iii 4 70
I'll make division of my present with you: Hold, there's half my coffer iii 4 381
This youth that you see here I snatch'd one half out of the jaws of death iii 4 394
Denied me mine own purse, Which I had recommended to his use Not half an hour before . . . . v 1 95
Thou hast the one half of my heart . . . . . *W. Tale* i 2 348
I think there is not half a kiss to choose Who loves another best . iv 4 175
Not the worst of the three but jumps twelve foot and a half by the squier iv 4 348
But without this match, The sea enraged is not half so deaf . *K. John* ii 1 451
Not Death himself In mortal fury half so peremptory As we . . ii 1 454
Half my power this night, Passing these flats, are taken by the tide v 6 39
Who half an hour since came from the Dauphin . . . . v 7 83
Though he divide the realm and give thee half, It is too little *Richard II.* v 1 60
Old Sir John, with half-a-dozen more, are at the door . *1 Hen. IV.* ii 4 93
If thou dost it half so gravely, so majestically . . . . ii 4 478
There's but a shirt and a half in all my company; and the half shirt is two napkins tacked together . . . . iv 2 46
With hard labour tame and dull, That not a horse is half the half of himself . . . . iv 3 24
Drew Priam's curtain in the dead of night, And would have told him half his Troy was burnt . . . . *2 Hen. IV.* i 1 73
Had my sweet Harry had but half their numbers, To-day might I, hanging on Hotspur's neck, Have talk'd of Monmouth's grave . ii 3 43
And carried you a forehand shaft a fourteen and fourteen and a half iii 2 53
Have you provided me here half a dozen sufficient men? . . . iii 2 102
Yet not so sound and half so deeply sweet . . . . . iv 5 26
To stab at half an hour of my life . . . . iv 5 109
If it pass against us, We lose the better half of our possession *Hen. V.* i 1 8
And let another half stand laughing by, All out of work . . . i 2 213
Of England's coat one half is cut away . . . *1 Hen. VI.* i 1 81
Sheep run not half so treacherous from the wolf . . . . i 5 30
I am possess'd With more than half the Gallian territories . . iv 4 139
Not all these lords do vex me half so much As that proud dame *2 Hen. VI.* i 3 78
Well guerdon'd for these good deserts.—Not half so bad as thine . i 4 50
Hadst thou but loved him half so well as I . . . *3 Hen. VI.* i 1 220
The holding-anchor lost, And half our sailors swallow'd in the flood . v 4 5
Now thy proud neck bears half my burthen'd yoke . *Richard III.* iv 4 111
His regiment lies half a mile at least South . . . . . v 3 37
Half your suit Never name to us; you have half our power: The other moiety, ere you ask, is given . . . . . *Hen. VIII.* i 2 10
Had the cardinal But half my lay thoughts in him . . . . i 4 11
I have half a dozen healths To drink to these fair ladies . . . i 4 105
Tell him You met him half in heaven . . . . . . ii 1 88
I will not wish ye half my miseries; I have more charity . . iii 1 108
Had I but served my God with half the zeal I served my king . iii 2 455
While her grace sat down To rest awhile, some half an hour or so . iv 1 66
Great-bellied women, That had not half a week to go . . . iv 1 77
Would you were half so honest! Men's prayers then would seek you, not their fears . . . . v 3 82
Shall pride carry it?—An 'twould, you'ld carry half . *Troi. and Cres.* ii 3 229
Let Mars divide eternity in twain, And give him half . . . ii 3 257
I foretold you then what would ensue: My prophecy is but half his journey yet . . . . iv 5 218
Were half to half the world by the ears and he Upon my party, I'ld revolt *Coriolanus* i 1 237
Half all Cominius' honours are to Marcius, Though Marcius earn'd them not i 1 277
O' my troth, I looked upon him o' Wednesday half an hour together . i 3 64
Lend you him I will For half a hundred years . . . . . i 4 7
How far off lie these armies?—Within this mile and half . . . i 4 8
Else had I, sir, Half an hour since brought my report . . . i 6 21
Take The one half of my commission . . . . . . iv 5 144
Our general is cut i' the middle and but one half of what he was yesterday iv 5 211
Would half my wealth Would buy this for a lie! . . . . iv 6 160
Of five and twenty valiant sons, Half of the number that King Priam had, Behold the poor remains, alive and dead! . . *T. Andron.* i 1 80
O cruel, irreligious piety!—Was ever Scythia half so barbarous? . . i 1 131
Renowned Titus, more than half my soul,— Dear father . . . i 1 373
And that you'll say, ere half an hour pass . . . . . iii 1 192
Peace, tawny slave, half me and half thy dam! . . . . . iv 2 27
Not half so big as a round little worm . . . *Rom. and Jul.* i 4 65
The clock struck nine when I did send the nurse; In half an hour she promised to return . . . . ii 5 2
My true love is grown to such excess I cannot sum up sum of half my wealth . . . . ii 6 34
We'll have some half a dozen friends, And there an end . . . iii 4 27
How long hath he been there?—Full half an hour . . . . v 3 130
Our entertainment, Which was not half so beautiful . *T. of Athens* i 2 153
The greatest of your having lacks a half To pay your present debts . ii 2 153
If his occasion were not virtuous, I should not urge it half so faithfully iii 2 46
The best half should have return'd to him, So much I love his heart . iii 2 91
Who, then, dares to be half so kind again? . . . . . iv 2 40
And half their faces buried in their cloaks . . . *J. Cæsar* ii 1 74
Unfold to me, yourself, your half, Why you are heavy . . . ii 1 274
Nor no instrument Of half that worth as those your swords . . iii 1 155
Cæsar, now be still: I kill'd not thee with half so good a will . v 5 51
To half a soul and to a notion crazed . . . . . *Macbeth* iii 1 83
We have lost Best half of our affair . . . . iii 3 21
Then there's hope a great man's memory may outlive his life half a year . . . . *Hamlet* iii 2 141
Get me a fellowship in a cry of players, sir?—Half a share.—A whole one, I . . . . iii 2 290
Thou hast cleft my heart in twain.—O, throw away the worser part of it, And live the purer with the other half . . . . . . iii 4 158
In thee there is not half an hour of life . . . . . . v 2 326
When I shall wed, That lord whose hand must take my plight shall carry Half my love with him, half my care and duty . . *Lear* i 1 104
If our father would sleep till I waked him, you should enjoy half his revenue . . . . i 2 56
She hath abated me of half my train; Look'd black upon me . . ii 4 161
Thy half o' the kingdom hast thou not forgot, Wherein I thee endow'd . ii 4 183
You will return and sojourn with my sister, Dismissing half your train ii 4 207

Half. Fathom and half, fathom and half! Poor Tom! . . . *Lear* iii 4 37
If thou shouldst dally half an hour, his life, With thine, and all that offer to defend him, Stand in assured loss . . . . iii 6 100
Your heart is burst, you have lost half your soul . . . *Othello* i 1 87
If she confess that she was half the wooer, Destruction on my head, if my bad blame Light on the man! . . . . i 3 176
The jewels you have had from me . . . would half have corrupted a votarist . . . . iv 2 189
Kill me to-morrow: let me live to-night!—Nay, if you strive,— But half an hour!—Being done, there is no pause . . . . . v 2 82
May his pernicious soul Rot half a grain a day! . . . . v 2 156
Thou hast not half that power to do me harm As I have to be hurt . v 2 162
Welcome from Egypt, sir.—Half the heart of Cæsar! . *Ant. and Cleo.* ii 2 175
So half my Egypt were submerged and made A cistern for scaled snakes! ii 5 94
With half the bulk o' the world play'd as I pleased, Making and marring fortunes . . . . iii 11 64
At such a point, When half to half the world opposed . . . iii 13 9
He that will believe all that they [women] say, shall never be saved by half that they do . . . . v 2 257
Half all men's hearts are his . . . . . *Cymbeline* i 6 168
Changing still One vice, but of a minute old, for one Not half so old . ii 5 32
My brother wears thee not the one half so well As when thou grew'st thyself . . . . iv 2 202
How far is his court distant from this shore?—Marry, sir, half a day's journey . . . . *Pericles* ii 1 112
Half the flood Hath their keel cut . . . . . iii Gower 45
Come, I know 'tis good for you. Walk half an hour, Leonine, at the least . . . . iv 1 46
Half-achieved. I will not leave the half-achieved Harfleur Till in her ashes she lie buried . . . . . . *Hen. V.* iii 3 8
Half afeard. Where is the fellow?—Half afeard to come *Ant. and Cleo.* iii 3 1
I am half afeard Thou wilt say anon he is some kin to thee *Mer. of Venice* ii 9 96
Half afraid. I am half afraid he will have need of washing *Mer. Wives* iii 3 193
Half asleep. How do you, my good lady?—'Faith, half asleep *Othello* iv 2 97
Half attached. May worthy Troilus be half attach'd With that which here his passion doth express? . . . . . *Troi. and Cres.* v 2 161
Half blasted. You were half blasted ere I knew you *Ant. and Cleo.* iii 13 105
Half-blooded fellow, yes . . . . *Lear* v 3 80
Half-blown. Of Nature's gifts thou mayst with lilies boast And with the half-blown rose . . . . *K. John* iii 1 54
Half breathless. Stew'd in his haste, half breathless . . *Lear* ii 4 31
Half-can. Wild Half-can that stabbed Pots . . *Meas. for Meas.* iv 3 19
Half-cap. With certain half-caps and cold-moving nods They froze me into silence . . . . *T. of Athens* ii 2 221
Half-checked. With a half-checked bit . . . *T. of Shrew* iii 2 57
Half-cheek. Saint George's half-cheek in a brooch . *L. L. Lost* v 2 620
Half-conquered. Now it is half-conquer'd, must I back? . *K. John* v 2 95
Half dead. And twit with cowardice a man half dead? . *1 Hen. VI.* iii 2 55
Fisting each other's throat, And waked half dead with nothing *Coriolanus* iv 5 132
And give them life whom hunger starved half dead . . *Pericles* i 4 96
Half dined. Nor the bear half dined on the gentleman . *W. Tale* iii 3 108
Half drunk. By mine honour, half drunk . . . *T. Night* i 5 124
Half eclipsed. My joy of liberty is half eclipsed *3 Hen. VI.* iv 6 63
Half English. Compound a boy, half French, half English . *Hen. V.* v 2 221
Half-face. He hath a half-face, like my father. With half that face would he have all my land . . . . . . *K. John* i 1 92
Half-faced. A half-faced groat five hundred pound a year! . . i 1 94
But out upon this half-faced fellowship! . . . *1 Hen. IV.* i 3 208
This same half-faced fellow, Shadow; give me this man . *2 Hen. IV.* iii 2 283
Whose hopeful colours Advance our half-faced sun . *2 Hen. VI.* iv 1 98
Half fish. I saw the porpus how he bounced and tumbled; they say they're half fish, half flesh . . . . . . *Pericles* ii 1 27
Half flayed. Dispatch: the gentleman is half flayed already . *W. Tale* iv 4 655
Half French. Compound a boy, half French, half English . *Hen. V.* v 2 221
Half Hector stays at home; Half heart, half hand, half Hector comes to seek This blended knight, half Trojan and half Greek *Troi. and Cres.* iv 5 84
Half hour. Within this half hour will he be asleep . . *Tempest* iii 2 122
He has been yonder i' the sun practising behaviour to his own shadow this half hour . . . . *T. Night* ii 5 21
A blind man . . . , Within this half-hour, hath received his sight *2 Hen. VI.* ii 1 64
Never,—O fault!—reveal'd myself unto him, Until some half-hour past *Lear* v 3 193
About some half-hour hence, I pray you, speak with me . *Cymbeline* i 1 176
Half-kirtle. If you be not swinged, I'll forswear half-kirtles *2 Hen. IV.* v 4 24
Half lunatic. You have show'd a tender fatherly regard, To wish me wed to one half lunatic . . . . *T. of Shrew* ii 1 289
Half made. This Ajax is half made of Hector's blood: In love whereof, half Hector stays at home . . . . . *Troi. and Cres.* iv 5 83
Half made up. Sent before my time Into this breathing world, scarce half made up . . . . *Richard III.* i 1 21
Half malcontent. How like you our choice, That you stand pensive, as half malcontent? . . . . *3 Hen. VI.* iv 1 10
Half-moon. In a semicircle, Or a half-moon . . . *W. Tale* ii 1 11
'Anon, anon, sir! Score a pint of bastard in the Half-moon,' or so *1 Hen. IV.* ii 4 30
And cuts me from the best of all my land A huge half-moon . . iii 1 100
Half myself. I would have daffed all other respects and made her half myself . . . . *Much Ado* ii 3 177
Half once. Adieu; Twice to your visor, and half once to you . *L. L. Lost* v 2 227
Half out. Your eyes, half out, weep out at Pandar's fall *Troi. and Cres.* v 10 49
Half part. He is the half part of a blessed man, Left to be finished by such as she . . . . *K. John* ii 1 437
Half-part, mates, half-part . . . . *Pericles* iv 1 95
Halfpence. She tore the letter into a thousand halfpence . *Much Ado* ii 3 147
They were all like one another as half-pence are . . *As Y. Like It* iii 2 372
Bardolph stole a lute-case, bore it twelve leagues, and sold it for three half-pence . . . . *Hen. V.* iii 2 47
Halfpenny. He cannot creep into a halfpenny purse . *Mer. Wives* iii 5 149
What is a remuneration?—Marry, sir, halfpenny farthing . *L. L. Lost* iii 1 149
Thou halfpenny purse of wit, thou pigeon-egg of discretion . . v 1 77
My hat to a halfpenny . . . . v 2 563
There shall be in England seven halfpenny loaves sold for a penny *2 Hen. VI.* iv 2 71
Sure, dear friends, my thanks are too dear a halfpenny . . *Hamlet* ii 2 282
Half-pennyworth. But one half-pennyworth of bread to this intolerable deal of sack! . . . . *1 Hen. IV.* ii 4 591
Half-pint. I say, go; lest I let forth your half-pint of blood . *Coriolanus* v 2 60
Half ripe. You'll be rotten ere you be half ripe . *As Y. Like It* iii 2 127
Half sense. Speak things in doubt, That carry but half sense. *Hamlet* iv 5 7
Half sleep. I shall reply amazedly, Half sleep, half waking *M. N. Dream* iv 1 152
Half stints. The combatants being kin Half stints their strife before their strokes begin . . . . *Troi. and Cres.* iv 5 93
Half-supped. My half-supp'd sword, that frankly would have fed, Pleased with this dainty bait, thus goes to bed . . . . . v 8 19
Half-sword. If I were not at half-sword with a dozen of them. *1 Hen. IV.* ii 4 182
Half tales. Truths would be tales, Where now half tales be truths *A. and C.* ii 2 137
Half through, Gives o'er and leaves his part-created cost . *2 Hen. IV.* i 3 59
I am half through; The one part suffer'd, the other will I do . *Coriolanus* ii 3 130
Half Trojan. This blended knight, half Trojan and half Greek *T. and C.* iv 5 86
Half Troy. Come in: I would not for half Troy have you seen here . iv 2 42
Half waking. I shall reply amazedly, Half sleep, half waking *M. N. D.* iv 1 152
Half way. I wis it is not half way to her heart . . *T. of Shrew* i 1 62
Half way down Hangs one that gathers samphire . . . *Lear* iv 6 14
What need we fear? The ground 's the lowest, and we are half way there *Pericles* i 4 78
Half Windsor. With half Windsor at his heels . . *Mer. Wives* iii 3 121
Half won is match well made: match, and well make it . . *All's Well* iv 3 254
Half-worker. Is there no way for men to be but women Must be half-workers? . . . . *Cymbeline* ii 5 2
Half-world. Now o'er the one half-world Nature seems dead . *Macbeth* ii 1 49
Half-yard. Thou yard, three-quarters, half-yard, quarter, nail! *T. of Shrew* iv 3 109
Half yourself. I am half yourself, And I must freely have the half of anything That this same paper brings you . . . *Mer. of Venice* iii 2 251
Halidom. By my halidom, I was fast asleep . . *T. G. of Ver.* iv 2 136
Haling. Galling His kingly hands, haling ropes . . *Pericles* iv 1 55
Hall. And Tom bears logs into the hall . . . *L. L. Lost* v 2 924
That light we see is burning in my hall . . . *Mer. of Venice* v 1 89
The prettiest Kate in Christendom, Kate of Kate Hall . *T. of Shrew* ii 1 189
'Tis merry in hall when beards wag all . . . *2 Hen. IV.* v 3 37
Some followers of mine own, At the lower end of the hall *Richard III.* iii 7 35
Whither away so fast?—O, God save ye! Even to the hall . *Hen. VIII.* ii 1 2
Let us to Priam's hall, To greet the warriors . *Troi. and Cres.* iii 1 161
How some men creep in skittish fortune's hall, Whiles others play the idiots! . . . . iii 3 134
As many as be here of pandar's hall, Your eyes, half out, weep out . v 10 48
A hall, a hall! give room! and foot it, girls. More light *Rom. and Jul.* i 5 28
Let's briefly put on manly readiness And meet i' the hall together *Macb.* ii 3 140
Sir, I will walk here in the hall . . . . . *Hamlet* v 2 180
Who brings back to him, that you attend him in the hall . . v 2 205
Halloing. What halloing and what stir is this to-day? *T. G. of Ver.* v 4 13
For my voice, I have lost it with halloing and singing of anthems *2 Hen. IV.* i 2 213
Halloo your name to the reverberate hills . . . *T. Night* i 5 291
Pillicock sat on Pillicock-hill: Halloo, halloo, loo, loo! . . *Lear* iii 4 79
Hallooed. He hallooed but even now. Whoa, ho, hoa! . *W. Tale* iii 3 78
Hallow. Sword, I will hallow thee for this thy deed . *2 Hen. VI.* iv 10 72
Hallowed. I'll have the cudgel hallowed and hung o'er the altar *Mer. Wives* iv 2 216
Not a mouse Shall disturb this hallow'd house . . *M. N. Dream* v 1 395
As if my trinkets had been hallowed and brought a benediction *W. Tale* iv 4 613
Whom we raise, We will make fast within a hallow'd verge *2 Hen. VI.* i 4 25
Nor my prayers Are not words duly hallow'd . . . *Hen. VIII.* ii 3 68
Nor witch hath power to charm, So hallow'd and so gracious is the time *Hamlet* i 1 164
The worms were hallow'd that did breed the silk . . *Othello* iii 4 73
Nor have I time To give thee hallow'd to thy grave . . *Pericles* iii 1 60
Hallowmas. To speak puling, like a beggar at Hallowmas *T. G. of Ver.* ii 1 27
Whose father died at Hallowmas: was't not at Hallowmas? *Meas. for Meas.* ii 1 128
She came adorned hither like sweet May, Sent back like Hallowmas *Rich. II.* v 1 80
Halt. She will outstrip all praise And make it halt behind her *Tempest* iv 1 11
O, let me see thee walk: thou dost not halt . . *T. of Shrew* ii 1 258
And yet I come not well.—And yet you halt not . . . . iii 2 91
'Tis no matter if I do halt; I have the wars for my colour . *2 Hen. IV.* i 2 275
That dogs bark at me as I halt by them . . . *Richard III.* i 1 23
On me, that halt and am unshapen thus? . . . . . . i 2 251
My free drift Halts not particularly . . . . *T. of Athens* i 1 46
Cripple our senators, that their limbs may halt As lamely as their manners! iv 1 24
The lady shall say her mind freely, or the blank verse shall halt for't *Ham.* ii 2 339
Our wars are done. The desperate tempest hath so bang'd the Turks, That their designment halts . . . . *Othello* ii 1 22
Come thee on.—I'll halt after . . . . . *Ant. and Cleo.* iv 7 16
Halter. Give him a present! give him a halter . . *Mer. of Venice* ii 2 113
A halter gratis; nothing else, for God's sake . . . . . iv 1 379
Choler, my lord, if rightly taken.—No, if rightly taken, halter *1 Hen. IV.* ii 4 357
I hope I shall as soon be strangled with a halter as another . . ii 4 548
Humbly thus, with halters on their necks, Expect your highness' doom *2 Hen. VI.* iv 9 11
A halter, soldiers! hang him on this tree . . . *T. Andron.* v 1 47
Such a daughter Should sure to the slaughter, If my cap would buy a halter . . . . *Lear* i 4 343
Hath laid knives under his pillow, and halters in his pew . . . iii 4 55
Heaven pardon him!—A halter pardon him! and hell gnaw his bones! *Oth.* iv 2 136
Haltered. Like A halter'd neck which does the hangman thank For being yare about him . . . . *Ant. and Cleo.* iii 13 130
Halting. In our last conflict four of his five wits went halting off *M. Ado* i 1 66
Here's a paper written in his hand, A halting sonnet . . . . v 4 87
Here comes Sir Toby halting; you shall hear more . . . *T. Night* v 1 196
Not trusting to this halting legate here . . . . *K. John* v 2 174
To serve bravely is to come halting off, you know . . *2 Hen. IV.* ii 4 54
No further halting: satisfy me home What is become of her . *Cymbeline* iii 5 92
Halves. I'll have no halves; I'll bear it all myself . . *T. of Shrew* v 2 79
Ham. Such a case as yours constrains a man to bow in the hams *Rom. and Jul.* ii 4 57
They have a plentiful lack of wit, together with most weak hams *Hamlet* ii 2 203
The French knight that cowers i' the hams . . . *Pericles* iv 2 114
Hames Castle. Away with Oxford to Hames Castle straight *3 Hen. VI.* v. 5 2
Hamlet. Our valiant Hamlet—For so this side of our known world esteem'd him—Did slay this Fortinbras . . . . . *Hamlet* i 1 84
By the same covenant, And carriage of the article design'd, His fell to Hamlet . . . . i 1 95
Let us impart what we have seen to-night Unto young Hamlet . . i 1 170
Though yet of Hamlet our dear brother's death The memory be green . i 2 1
But now, my cousin Hamlet, and my son,— A little more than kin . i 2 64
Good Hamlet, cast thy nighted colour off, And let thine eye look like a friend . . . . i 2 68
'Tis sweet and commendable in your nature, Hamlet, To give these mourning duties to your father . . . . i 2 87
Let not thy mother lose her prayers, Hamlet: I pray thee, stay with us i 2 118
This gentle and unforced accord of Hamlet Sits smiling to my heart . i 2 123
For Hamlet and the trifling of his favour, Hold it a fashion and a toy . i 3 5
So please you, something touching the Lord Hamlet . . . . i 3 89
For Lord Hamlet, Believe so much in him, that he is young . . . i 3 123

Hamlet. I would not, in plain terms, from this time forth, Have you so slander any moment leisure, As to give words or talk with the Lord Hamlet . . . *Hamlet* i 3 134
I'll call thee Hamlet, King, father, royal Dane: O, answer me! . . i 4 44
Hamlet, hear: 'Tis given out that, sleeping in my orchard, A serpent stung me . . . . i 5 34
O Hamlet, what a falling-off was there! . . . . . . i 5 47
Adieu, adieu! Hamlet, remember me . . . . . . i 5 91
My lord, my lord,— Lord Hamlet,— Heaven secure him!—So be it! i 5 113
What so poor a man as Hamlet is May do, to express his love and friending i 5 185
Lord Hamlet, with his doublet all unbraced; No hat upon his head . ii 1 78
Something have you heard Of Hamlet's transformation . . . ii 2 5
Go, some of you, And bring these gentlemen where Hamlet is . . ii 2 37
I have found The very cause of Hamlet's lunacy . . . . ii 2 49
Thus: 'In her excellent white bosom, these, etc.'—Came this from Hamlet? . . . . ii 2 114
Thine evermore, most dear lady, whilst this machine is to him, HAMLET ii 2 124
Lord Hamlet is a prince, out of thy star . . . . . ii 2 141
How does my good Lord Hamlet?—Well, God-a-mercy . . . ii 2 171
You go to seek the Lord Hamlet; there he is.—God save you, sir! . ii 2 224
We have closely sent for Hamlet hither, That he, as 'twere by accident, may here Affront Ophelia . . . . iii 1 29
I do wish That your good beauties be the happy cause Of Hamlet's wildness . . . . iii 1 40
You need not tell us what Lord Hamlet said; We heard it all . . iii 1 187
How fares our cousin Hamlet?—Excellent, i' faith . . . . iii 2 97
I have nothing with this answer, Hamlet; these words are not mine . iii 2 101
My dear Hamlet, sit by me.—No, good mother, here's metal more attractive . . . . iii 2 114
Mother, what's the matter?—Hamlet, thou hast thy father much offended iii 4 9
Why, how now, Hamlet!—What's the matter now?—Have you forgot me? iii 4 13
O Hamlet, speak no more: Thou turn'st mine eyes into my very soul iii 4 88
No more, sweet Hamlet!—A murderer and a villain . . . . iii 4 96
Speak to her, Hamlet.—How is it with you, lady? . . . . iii 4 115
O Hamlet, thou hast cleft my heart in twain . . . . . iii 4 156
How does Hamlet?—Mad as the sea and wind, when both contend . iv 1 6
Hamlet in madness hath Polonius slain . . . . . . iv 1 34
Hamlet! Lord Hamlet!—But soft, what noise? who calls on Hamlet? O, here they come . . . . iv 2 2
Now, Hamlet, where's Polonius?—At supper.—At supper! where?—Not where he eats . . . . iv 3 17
Hamlet, this deed, for thine especial safety,—Which we do tender . iv 3 42
Every thing is bent For England.—For England!—Ay, Hamlet.—Good iv 3 48
Farewell, dear mother.—Thy loving father, Hamlet.—My mother . iv 3 52
Which imports at full, By letters congruing to that effect, The present death of Hamlet . . . . iv 3 67
I do not know from what part of the world I should be greeted, if not from lord Hamlet . . . . iv 6 5
Farewell. He that thou knowest thine, HAMLET . . . . . iv 6 31
How now! what news?—Letters, my lord, from Hamlet: This to your majesty . . . . iv 7 36
From Hamlet! who brought them?—Sailors, my lord, they say . . iv 7 38
Know you the hand?—'Tis Hamlet's character . . . . . iv 7 52
You have been talk'd of since your travel much, And that in Hamlet's hearing . . . . iv 7 73
This report of his Did Hamlet so envenom with his envy . . . iv 7 104
But, to the quick o' the ulcer:—Hamlet comes back . . . iv 7 125
Keep close within your chamber. Hamlet return'd shall know you are come home . . . . iv 7 131
I came to't that day that our last king Hamlet overcame Fortinbras . v 1 156
The very day that young Hamlet was born; he that is mad, and sent into England . . . . v 1 161
I hoped thou shouldst have been my Hamlet's wife . . . . v 1 267
This is I, Hamlet the Dane.—The devil take thy soul! . . . v 1 281
Pluck them asunder.—Hamlet, Hamlet!—Gentlemen,— Good my lord, be quiet . . . . v 1 287
Come, Hamlet, come, and take this hand from me . . . . v 2 236
Was't Hamlet wrong'd Laertes? Never Hamlet: If Hamlet from himself be ta'en away, And when he's not himself does wrong Laertes, Then Hamlet does it not, Hamlet denies it . . . . . v 2 244
Hamlet is of the faction that is wrong'd; His madness is poor Hamlet's enemy . . . . v 2 249
Cousin Hamlet, You know the wager?—Very well, my lord . . v 2 270
If Hamlet give the first or second hit, Or quit in answer of the third exchange, Let all the battlements their ordnance fire . . . v 2 279
The king shall drink to Hamlet's better breath . . . . . v 2 282
Now the king drinks to Hamlet . . . . v 2 289
Stay; give me drink. Hamlet, this pearl is thine; Here's to thy health v 2 293
He's fat, and scant of breath. Here, Hamlet, take my napkin, rub thy brows . . . . v 2 299
The queen carouses to thy fortune, Hamlet.—Good madam! . . . v 2 300
O my dear Hamlet,—The drink, the drink! I am poison'd . . . v 2 320
Ho! let the door be lock'd: Treachery! Seek it out.—It is here, Hamlet v 2 324
Hamlet, thou art slain; No medicine in the world can do thee good . v 2 324
Exchange forgiveness with me, noble Hamlet . . . . . v 2 340
Let four captains Bear Hamlet, like a soldier, to the stage . . v 2 407
Hammer. I saw a smith stand with his hammer, thus . . *K. John* iv 2 193
I cannot do it; yet I'll hammer it out . . . *Richard II.* v 5 5
Charge you and discharge you with the motion of a pewterer's hammer *2 Hen. IV.* iii 2 281
With busy hammers closing rivets up . . . *Hen. V.* iv Prol. 13
I give thee my apron: and, Will, thou shalt have my hammer *2 Hen. VI.* ii 3 76
Never did the Cyclops' hammers fall On Mars's armour forged for proof eterne With less remorse . . . . . . *Hamlet* ii 2 511
Mechanic slaves With greasy aprons, rules, and hammers *Ant. and Cleo.* v 2 210
Hammered. Who but to-day hammer'd of this design . . *W. Tale* ii 2 49
Are you more stubborn-hard than hammer'd iron? . . *K. John* iv 1 67
Hammering. Whereon this month I have been hammering *T. G. of Ver.* i 3 18
And wilt thou still be hammering treachery? . . . *2 Hen. VI.* i 2 47
Blood and revenge are hammering in my head . . . *T. Andron.* ii 3 39
Hamper. She'll hamper thee, and dandle thee like a baby *2 Hen. VI.* i 3 148
Hampton. To kill us here in Hampton . . . . *Hen. V.* ii 2 91
Suppose that you have seen The well-appointed king at Hampton pier iii Prol. 4
Hamstring. Whose conceit Lies in his hamstring . . *Troi. and Cres.* i 3 154
Hand. We will not hand a rope more . . . . . *Tempest* i 1 25
Lend thy hand, And pluck my magic garment from me . . . i 2 23
Come unto these yellow sands, And then take hands . . . i 2 377
Draw together; And when I rear my hand, do you the like . . ii 1 295
By this bottle! which I made of the bark of a tree with mine own hands ii 2 128
Here's my hand.—And mine, with my heart in't . . . . . iii 1 90
Hand. By this hand, I will supplant some of your teeth . . *Tempest* iii 2 56
By this hand, I'll turn my mercy out o' doors . . . . . iii 2 78
Give me thy hand: I am sorry I beat thee . . . . . iii 2 119
That for which I live; who once again I tender to thy hand . . iv 1 5
Give me thy hand. I do begin to have bloody thoughts . . . iv 1 219
Put off that gown, Trinculo; by this hand, I'll have that gown . iv 1 227
Give me your hands: Let grief and sorrow still embrace his heart That doth not wish you joy! . . . . v 1 213
But release me from my bands With the help of your good hands . . Epil. 10
O hateful hands, to tear such loving words! Injurious wasps! *T. G. of V.* i 2 105
Here is her hand, the agent of her heart . . . . . i 3 46
Seal the bargain with a holy kiss.—Here is my hand for my true constancy . . . . ii 2 8
Our maid howling, our cat wringing her hands . . . . ii 3 9
Wringing her hands, whose whiteness so became them As if but now they waxed pale for woe . . . . iii 1 227
Neither bended knees, pure hands held up, Sad sighs, deep groans . iii 1 229
She can milk; look you, a sweet virtue in a maid with clean hands . iii 1 278
Who should be trusted, when one's own right hand Is perjured to the bosom? . . . . v 4 67
Come, come, a hand from either: Let me be blest to make this happy close . . . . v 4 116
He is as tall a man of his hands as any is between this and his head *M. W.* i 4 27
'Tis a great charge to come under one body's hand . . . . i 4 105
Troth, sir, all is in his hands above: but notwithstanding . . . i 4 154
This is the very same; the very hand, the very words . . . ii 1 85
Will you go with us? we have sport in hand . . . . . ii 1 205
My hand, bully; thou shalt have egress and regress;—said I well? . ii 1 225
Leaving the fear of God on the left hand and hiding mine honour in my necessity . . . . ii 2 24
Have you received no promise of satisfaction at her hands? . . . ii 2 218
Now, could I come to her with any detection in my hand . . . ii 2 255
I will first make bold with your money; next, give me your hand . ii 2 263
Give me thy hand, terrestrial; so. Give me thy hand, celestial; so . iii 1 108
Never stand 'you had rather' and 'you had rather:' your husband's here at hand . . . . iii 3 135
But fate, ordaining he should be a cuckold, held his hand . . iii 5 107
With rounds of waxen tapers on their heads, And rattles in their hands iv 4 51
When Slender sees his time To take her by the hand and bid her go . iv 6 37
And when the doctor spies his vantage ripe, To pinch her by the hand iv 6 44
I will be revenged, and I will deliver his wife into your hand. Follow. Strange things in hand, Master Brook! . . . . . . v 1 32
Take her by the hand, away with her to the deanery . . . . v 3 3
Bore many gentlemen, myself being one, In hand and hope of action *Meas. for Meas.* i 4 52
By this hand, sir, his wife is a more respected person than any of us all ii 1 172
The hand that hath made you fair hath made you good . . . iii 1 184
For putting the hand in the pocket and extracting it clutched . . iii 2 48
Take, then, this your companion by the hand, Who hath a story ready iv 1 55
Give me your hand, And let the subject see, to make them know That outward courtesies would fain proclaim Favours that keep within . v 1 13
You must walk by us on our other hand; And good supporters are you v 1 17
This is the hand which, with a vow'd contract, Was fast belock'd in thine v 1 209
Do yet but kneel by me; Hold up your hands, say nothing; I'll speak all v 1 443
Advise him; I leave him to your hand . . . . . . v 1 491
For your lovely sake, Give me your hand and say you will be mine . v 1 497
What mean you, sir? for God's sake, hold your hands! . *Com. of Errors* i 2 93
Is your tardy master now at hand?—Nay, he's at two hands with me . ii 1 44
Beshrew his hand, I scarce could understand it . . . . ii 1 49
That never touch well welcome to thy hand, That never meat sweet-savour'd in thy taste . . . . ii 2 118
And from my false hand cut the wedding-ring . . . . . ii 2 139
That you beat me at the mart, I have your hand to show . . . iii 1 12
If by strong hand you offer to break in Now in the stirring passage of the day . . . . iii 1 98
Where Scotland?—I found it by the barrenness; hard in the palm of the hand . . . . iii 2 124
Hold thy tongue.—Nay, rather persuade him to hold his hands . . iv 4 24
And have nothing at his hands for my service but blows . . . iv 4 33
Give me your hand and let me feel your pulse.—There is my hand, and let it feel your ear . . . . iv 4 56
It shall privilege him from your hands Till I have brought him to his wits v 1 95
With time's deformed hand Have written strange defeatures in my face v 1 298
Lead on?—Your hand, Leonato; we will go together . . *Much Ado* i 1 161
That liked, but had a rougher task in hand . . . . . i 1 301
It is your brother's right hand.—Who? the most exquisite Claudio . i 3 51
Here's his dry hand up and down . . . . ii 1 124
I will requite thee, Taming my wild heart to thy loving hand . . iii 1 112
If we know him to be a thief, shall we not lay hands on him? . . iii 3 58
O Fate! take not away thy heavy hand . . . . . . iv 1 116
Why had I not with charitable hand Took up a beggar's issue? . . iv 1 133
If they speak but truth of her, These hands shall tear her . . iv 1 193
Bear her in hand until they come to take hands . . . . iv 1 306
By this hand, I love thee.—Use it for my love some other way than swearing by it . . . . iv 1 327
I will kiss your hand, and so I leave you . . . . . iv 1 336
Nay, never lay thy hand upon thy sword; I fear thee not . . . v 1 54
Beshrew my hand, If it should give your age such cause of fear: In faith, my hand meant nothing to my sword . . . . . . v 1 55
Here stand a pair of honourable men; A third is fled, that had a hand in it v 1 277
Deserve well at my hands by helping me to the speech of Beatrice . v 2 2
Take her hand Before this friar and swear to marry her . . . v 4 56
Give me your hand: before this holy friar, I am your husband, if you like of me . . . . v 4 58
Here's a paper written in his hand, A halting sonnet . . . . v 4 86
Here's another Writ in my cousin's hand, stolen from her pocket . . v 4 89
A miracle! here's our own hands against our hearts . . . . v 4 91
Subscribe your names, That his own hand may strike his honour down That violates the smallest branch herein . . . . *L. L. Lost* i 1 20
Meantime receive such welcome at my hand . . . . . ii 1 169
Your hands in your pocket like a man after the old painting . . iii 1 20
To her white hand see thou do commend This seal'd-up counsel . iii 1 169
A giving hand, though foul, shall have fair praise . . . . iv 1 23
Wide o' the bow hand! i' faith, your hand is out . . . . iv 1 135
An if my hand be out, then belike your hand is in . . . . iv 1 137
To see him walk before a lady and to bear her fan! To see him kiss his hand! . . . . iv 1 148
To the snow-white hand of the most beauteous Lady Rosaline . . iv 2 136
Deliver this paper into the royal hand of the king: it may concern much iv 2 146
But, alack, my hand is sworn Ne'er to pluck thee from thy thorn . iv 3 111

Hand. When shall you hear that I Will praise a hand, a foot, a face, an eye? *L. L. Lost* iv 3 184
Therefore of all hands must we be forsworn iv 3 219
Then homeward every man attach the hand Of his fair mistress iv 3 375
Ay, or I would these hands might never part v 2 57
We will not dance.—Why take we hands, then?—Only to part friends v 2 220
Ladies, withdraw: the gallants are at hand.—Whip to our tents v 2 308
This is he That kiss'd his hand away in courtesy v 2 324
I here protest, By this white glove,—how white the hand, God knows! v 2 411
If this thou do deny, let our hands part, Neither intitled in the other's heart v 2 821
Commit yourself Into the hands of one that loves you not *M. N. Dream* ii 1 216
And make a heaven of hell, To die upon the hand I love so well ii 1 244
When at your hands did I deserve this scorn? ii 2 124
Captain of our fairy band, Helena is here at hand iii 2 111
That pure congealed white, high Taurus' snow, Fann'd with the eastern wind, turns to a crow When thou hold'st up thy hand iii 2 143
As if our hands, our sides, voices and minds, Had been incorporate iii 2 207
Your hands than mine are quicker for a fray, My legs are longer though iii 2 342
Get you your weapons in your hand, and kill me a red-hipped humble-bee iv 1 11
Take hands with me, And rock the ground whereon these sleepers be iv 1 90
The ear of man hath not seen, man's hand is not able to taste iv 1 218
What revels are in hand? Is there no play? v 1 36
The actors are at hand v 1 116
Come, come to me, With hands as pale as milk v 1 345
And the blots of Nature's hand Shall not in their issue stand v 1 416
Give me your hands, if we be friends v 1 444
The greater throw May turn by fortune from the weaker hand *M. of Ven.* ii 1 34
Turn up on your right hand at the next turning, but, at the next turning of all, on your left; marry, at the very next turning, turn of no hand ii 2 42
I know the hand: in faith, 'tis a fair hand; And whiter than the paper it writ on Is the fair hand that writ ii 4 12
Weigh thy value with an even hand ii 7 25
His eye being big with tears, Turning his face, he put his hand behind him, And with affection wondrous sensible He wrung Bassanio's hand ii 8 47
A day in April never came so sweet, To show how costly summer was at hand ii 9 94
Hath not a Jew hands, organs, dimensions, senses, affections, passions? iii 1 62
Your hand, Salerio: what's the news from Venice? iii 2 241
I commit into your hands The husbandry and manage of my house iii 4 24
See thou render this Into my cousin's hand, Doctor Bellario iii 4 50
I have work in hand That you yet know not of iii 4 57
I will be bound to pay it ten times o'er, On forfeit of my hands, my head iv 1 212
I'll take this ring from you: Do not draw back your hand; I'll take no more iv 1 428
In such a night Stood Dido with a willow in her hand v 1 10
Signify, I pray you, Within the house, your mistress is at hand v 1 52
Your husband is at hand; I hear his trumpet: We are no tell-tales, madam v 1 122
Now, by this hand, I gave it to a youth, A kind of boy v 1 161
I were best to cut my left hand off And swear I lost the ring defending it v 1 177
Wilt thou lay hands on me, villain?—I am no villain *As Y. Like It* i 1 58
Wert thou not my brother, I would not take this hand from thy throat till this other had pulled out thy tongue for saying so i 1 63
That could give more, but that her hand lacks means i 2 259
A gallant curtle-axe upon my thigh, A boar-spear in my hand i 3 120
I remember the kissing of her batlet and the cow's dugs that her pretty chopt hands had milked ii 4 50
Give me your hand, And let me all your fortunes understand ii 7 199
All things that thou dost call thine Worth seizure do we seize into our hands iii 1 10
You told me you salute not at the court, but you kiss your hands iii 2 50
Why, do not your courtier's hands sweat? iii 2 56
Besides, our hands are hard.—Your lips will feel them the sooner iii 2 60
The courtier's hands are perfumed with civet iii 2 65
By the white hand of Rosalind, I am that he, that unfortunate he iii 2 414
I am very glad to see you: even a toy in hand here, sir iii 3 77
To have seen much and to have nothing, is to have rich eyes and poor hands iv 1 25
I saw her hand: she has a leathern hand, A freestone-colour'd hand iv 3 25
I verily did think That her old gloves were on, but 'twas her hands: She has a huswife's hand iv 3 26
She never did invent this letter; This is a man's invention and his hand iv 3 29
The murmuring stream Left on your right hand brings you to the place iv 3 81
'If you said so, then I said so;' and they shook hands and swore brothers v 4 107
Join her hand with his Whose heart within his bosom is v 4 120
Here's eight that must take hands To join in Hymen's bands v 4 134
Will't please your lordship cool your hands? *T. of Shrew* Ind. 1 58
You are come to me in happy time; The rather for I have some sport in hand Ind. 1 91
Will't please your mightiness to wash your hands? Ind. 2 78
That made great Jove to humble him to her hand i 1 174
Till the father rid his hands of her, Master, your love must live a maid i 1 186
For my hand, Both our inventions meet and jump in one i 1 194
All books of love, see that at any hand i 2 147
What have you to do?—Not her that chides, sir, at any hand, I pray i 2 227
But for these other gawds, Unbind my hands, I'll pull them off myself ii 1 4
I prithee, sister Kate, untie my hands ii 1 21
That covenants may be kept on either hand ii 1 128
And bow'd her hand to teach her fingering ii 1 151
I know not what to say: but give me your hands; God send you joy! ii 1 320
Basins and ewers to lave her dainty hands ii 1 350
I must, forsooth, be forced To give my hand opposed against my heart iii 2 9
Whose hand, she being now at hand, thou shalt soon feel iv 1 32
And not presume to touch a hair of my master's horse-tail till they kiss their hands iv 1 97
How near is our master?—E'en at hand, alighted by this iv 1 120
I tell you, sir, she bears me fair in hand iv 2 3
Here is my hand, and here I firmly vow Never to woo her more iv 2 28
Lay hands on the villain: I believe a' means to cozen somebody v 1 39
She says you have some goodly jest in hand v 2 91
And craves no other tribute at thy hands But love, fair looks v 2 152
And place your hands below your husband's foot v 2 177
If he please, My hand is ready; may it do him ease v 2 179
At this time His tongue obey'd his hand *All's Well* i 2 41
To give great Charlemain a pen in's hand And write to her a love-line ii 1 80
Give me with thy kingly hand What husband in thy power I will command ii 1 196
Here is my hand; the premises observed, Thy will by my performance shall be served ii 1 204

Hand. He that cannot make a leg, put off's cap, kiss his hand and say nothing, has neither leg, hands, lip, nor cap *All's Well* ii 2 11
As fit as ten groats is for the hand of an attorney ii 2 22
This healthful hand, whose banish'd sense Thou hast repeal'd ii 3 54
Be not afraid that I your hand should take; I'll never do you wrong ii 3 95
Here, take her hand, Proud scornful boy, unworthy this good gift ii 3 157
Take her by the hand, And tell her she is thine ii 3 180
I take her hand.—Good fortune and the favour of the king Smile upon this contract ii 3 183
I have spoken better of you than you have or will to deserve at my hand ii 5 52
And, after some dispatch in hand at court, Thither we bend again iii 2 56
But the boldness of his hand, haply, which his heart was not consenting to iii 2 79
And that with his own hand he slew the duke's brother iii 5 6
Let him fetch off his drum in any hand iii 6 45
By the hand of a soldier, I will undertake it iii 6 76
Hold your hands; though I know his brains are forfeit to the next tile that falls iv 3 215
Commend the paper to his gracious hand v 1 31
If you shall marry, You give away this hand, and that is mine v 3 170
Your gentle hands lend us, and take our hearts Epil. 340
Do you think you have fools in hand?—Sir, I have not you by the hand *T. N.* i 3 69
Bring your hand to the buttery-bar and let it drink i 3 74
I am not such an ass but I can keep my hand dry i 3 79
Now I let go your hand, I am barren i 3 84
I hold the olive in my hand; my words are as full of peace as matter i 5 226
Whose red and white Nature's own sweet and cunning hand laid on i 5 258
My lady has a white hand, and the Myrmidons are no bottle-ale houses ii 3 28
On a forgotten matter we can hardly make distinction of our hands ii 3 175
I extend my hand to him thus, quenching my familiar smile with an austere regard ii 5 72
This is my lady's hand: these be her very C's, her U's and her T's ii 5 95
It is, in contempt of question, her hand ii 5 98
If this fall into thy hand, revolve. In my stars I am above thee ii 5 155
Thy Fates open their hands; let thy blood and spirit embrace them ii 5 159
Give me your hand, sir.—My duty, madam, and most humble service iii 1 105
This was looked for at your hand, and this was balked iii 2 26
Go, write it in a martial hand; be curst and brief iii 2 45
It did come to his hands, and commands shall be executed iii 4 29
I think we do know the sweet Roman hand iii 4 31
God comfort thee! Why dost thou smile so and kiss thy hand so oft? iii 4 36
Thou hast an open hand. These wise men that give fools money get themselves a good report iv 1 22
Let go thy hand.—Come, sir, I will not let you go iv 1 40
As ever thou wilt deserve well at my hand, help me to a candle iv 2 87
Confirm'd by mutual joinder of your hands v 1 160
Give me thy hand; And let me see thee in thy woman's weeds v 1 279
Here is my hand: you shall from this time be Your master's mistress v 1 333
Peruse that letter. You must not now deny it is your hand: Write from it, if you can, in hand or phrase v 1 339
I confess, much like the character: But out of question 'tis Maria's hand v 1 355
Though absent, shook hands, as over a vast, and embraced *W. Tale* i 1 33
Ere I could make thee open thy white hand And clap thyself my love i 2 103
Give me thy hand: Be pilot to me and thy places shall Still neighbour mine i 2 447
Let him that makes but trifles of his eyes First hand me ii 3 63
For ever Unvenerable be thy hands, if thou Takest up the princess by that forced baseness! ii 3 77
His smiles, The very mould and frame of hand, nail, finger ii 3 103
What needs these hands? You, that are thus so tender o'er his follies, Will never do him good ii 3 127
The bastard brains with these my proper hands Shall I dash out ii 3 139
This seal'd-up oracle, by the hand deliver'd Of great Apollo's priest iii 2 128
The heavens with that we have in hand are angry And frown upon's iii 3 5
Lend me thy hand, I'll help thee: come, lend me thy hand iv 3 72
Your hand, my Perdita: so turtles pair, That never mean to part iv 4 154
Five justices' hands at it, and witnesses more than my pack will hold iv 4 288
I take thy hand, this hand, As soft as dove's down and as white as it iv 4 373
How prettily the young swain seems to wash The hand was fair before! iv 4 378
Take hands, a bargain! And, friends unknown, you shall bear witness to't iv 4 394
Come, your hand; And, daughter, yours.—Soft, swain, awhile, beseech you iv 4 401
Kisses the hands Of your fresh princess iv 4 561
An open ear, a quick eye, and a nimble hand, is necessary for a cut-purse iv 4 686
Show the inside of your purse to the outside of his hand, and no more ado iv 4 834
Go on the right hand: I will but look upon the hedge and follow you iv 4 856
There was casting up of eyes, holding up of hands v 2 51
I thought she had some great matter there in hand v 2 114
The king's son took me by the hand, and called me brother v 2 152
I'll swear to the prince thou art a tall fellow of thy hands and that thou wilt not be drunk; but I know thou art no tall fellow of thy hands v 2 178
I'll swear it, and I would thou wouldst be a tall fellow of thy hands v 2 181
Dear queen, that ended when I but began, Give me that hand of yours to kiss v 3 46
I'll make the statue move indeed, descend And take you by the hand v 3 89
Nay, present your hand: When she was young you woo'd her; now in age Is she become the suitor? v 3 107
And put the same into young Arthur's hand, Thy nephew *K. John* i 1 14
A soldier, by the honour-giving hand Of Cœur-de-lion knighted i 1 53
Give me your hand: My father gave me honour, yours gave land i 1 163
The aweless lion could not wage the fight, Nor keep his princely heart from Richard's hand i 1 267
I give you welcome with a powerless hand, But with a heart full of unstained love ii 1 15
Till your strong hand shall help to give him strength ii 1 33
They are at hand, To parley or to fight; therefore prepare ii 1 77
Lo, in this right hand, whose protection Is most divinely vow'd upon the right Of him it holds, stands young Plantagenet ii 1 236
The dancing banners of the French, Who are at hand, triumphantly display'd ii 1 309
Our colours do return in those same hands That did display them when we first march'd forth ii 1 319
Come Our lusty English, all with purpled hands ii 1 322
And by this hand I swear, That sways the earth this climate overlooks ii 1 343
She in beauty, education, blood, Holds hand with any princess ii 1 494
Command thy son and daughter to join hands ii 1 532
Young princes, close your hands.—And your lips too ii 1 533
Not that I have the power to clutch my hand, When his fair angels would salute my palm; But for my hand, as unattempted yet, Like a poor beggar, raileth on the rich ii 1 589

Hand. What means that hand upon that breast of thine? . *K. John* iii 1 21
And with her [Fortune's] golden hand hath pluck'd on France . iii 1 57
We will alone uphold, Without the assistance of a mortal hand . iii 1 158
And meritorious shall that hand be call'd, Canonized and worshipp'd . iii 1 176
Let go the hand of that arch-heretic; And raise the power of France . iii 1 192
Look'st thou pale, France? do not let go thy hand . . . . . iii 1 195
Lest that France repent, And by disjoining hands, hell lose a soul . iii 1 197
This royal hand and mine are newly knit . . . . . . iii 1 226
No longer than we well could wash our hands To clap this royal bargain up iii 1 234
These hands, so lately purged of blood, So newly join'd in love . iii 1 239
France, thou mayst hold . . . A fasting tiger safer by the tooth Than keep in peace that hand which thou dost hold . . . . . iii 1 261
I may disjoin my hand, but not my faith.—So makest thou faith an enemy to faith . . . . iii 1 262
I am with both: each army hath a hand . . . . . . iii 1 328
So, I kiss your hand.—Farewell, gentle cousin . . . . . iii 3 16
Give me thy hand. I had a thing to say . . . . . . iii 3 25
O that these hands could so redeem my son, As they have given these hairs their liberty! . . . . iii 4 71
A sceptre snatch'd with an unruly hand Must be as boisterously maintain'd iii 4 135
And with my hand at midnight held your head . . . . iv 1 45
We cannot hold mortality's strong hand . . . . . . iv 2 82
With his shears and measure in his hand, Standing on slippers . iv 2 196
Why urgest thou so oft young Arthur's death? Thy hand hath murder'd him . . . . iv 2 205
Didst let thy heart consent, And consequently thy rude hand to act . iv 2 240
This hand of mine Is yet a maiden and an innocent hand . . iv 2 251
The graceless action of a heavy hand, If that it be the work of any hand iv 3 58
It is the shameful work of Hubert's hand . . . . . . iv 3 62
Nor conversant with ease and idleness, Till I have set a glory to this hand iv 3 71
A thousand businesses are brief in hand, And heaven itself doth frown iv 3 158
Thus have I yielded up into your hand The circle of my glory . v 1 1
Take again From this my hand, as holding of the pope Your sovereign greatness and authority . . . . v 1 3
The jewel of life By some damn'd hand was robb'd and ta'en away . v 1 41
We cannot deal but with the very hand Of stern injustice . . v 2 22
Thou shalt thrust thy hand as deep Into the purse of rich prosperity . v 2 60
Like a lion foster'd up at hand . . . . v 2 75
That hand which had the strength, even at your door, To cudgel you . . . Shall that victorious hand be feebled here, That in your chambers gave you chastisement? . . . . v 2 137
Even at hand a drum is ready braced That shall reverberate all as loud v 2 169
At hand, Not trusting to this halting legate here, . . . Is warlike John v 2 173
Since correction lieth in those hands Which made the fault . *Richard II.* i 2 4
His summer leaves all faded, By envy's hand and murder's bloody axe . i 2 21
Let me kiss my sovereign's hand, And bow my knee . . . i 3 46
A dearer merit . . . Have I deserved at your highness' hands . . i 3 158
Or, being open, put into his hands That knows no touch to tune the harmony . . . . i 3 164
Lay on our royal sword your banish'd hands . . . . . i 3 179
Who can hold a fire in his hand By thinking on the frosty Caucasus? . i 3 294
The revenue whereof shall furnish us For our affairs in hand . . i 4 47
His noble hand Did win what he did spend and spent not that Which his triumphant father's hand had won . . . . ii 1 179
His hands were guilty of no kindred blood . . . . . . ii 1 182
Seek you to seize and gripe into your hands The royalties? . . ii 1 189
We seize into our hands His plate, his goods, his money and his lands . ii 1 209
If I know how or which way to order these affairs Thus thrust disorderly into my hands, Never believe me . . . . ii 2 110
My heart this covenant makes, my hand thus seals it . . . ii 3 50
To wash your blood From off my hands, here in the view of men I will unfold some causes of your deaths . . . . iii 1 6
Barkloughly castle call they this at hand? . . . . . . iii 2 1
Dear earth, I do salute thee with my hand, Though rebels wound thee with their horses' hoofs . . . . iii 2 6
Greet I thee, my earth, And do thee favours with my royal hands . iii 2 11
Their peace is made With heads, and not with hands . . . iii 2 138
Henry Bolingbroke On both his knees doth kiss King Richard's hand . iii 3 36
No hand of blood and bone Can gripe the sacred handle of our sceptre . iii 3 79
That lift your vassal hands against my head . . . . . iii 3 89
Thy thrice noble cousin Harry Bolingbroke doth humbly kiss thy hand iii 3 104
By the buried hand of warlike Gaunt . . . . iii 3 109
Give me your hands: nay, dry your eyes; Tears show their love . . iii 3 202
An if I do not, may my hands rot off! . . . . iv 1 49
And his high sceptre yields To the possession of thy royal hand . iv 1 110
Little are we beholding to your love, And little look'd for at your helping hands . . . . iv 1 161
Here, cousin; On this side my hand, and on that side yours . . iv 1 183
I give this heavy weight from off my head And this unwieldy sceptre from my hand . . . . iv 1 205
With mine own hands I give away my crown . . . . . iv 1 208
Though some of you with Pilate wash your hands Showing an outward pity . . . . iv 1 239
Must we part?—Ay, hand from hand, my love, and heart from heart . v 1 82
Where rude misgovern'd hands from windows' tops Threw dust and rubbish . . . . v 2 5
But heaven hath a hand in these events . . . . . . v 2 37
And interchangeably set down their hands, To kill the king at Oxford . v 2 98
Stay thy revengeful hand; thou hast no cause to fear . . . v 3 42
My heart is not confederate with my hand.—It was, villain, ere thy hand did set it down . . . . v 3 53
I do not sue to stand; Pardon is all the suit I have in hand . . v 3 130
That jade hath eat bread from my royal hand; This hand hath made him proud with clapping him . . . . v 5 85
Villain, thy own hand yields thy death's instrument . . . . v 5 107
That hand shall burn in never-quenching fire That staggers thus my person . . . . v 5 109
Thy fierce hand Hath with the king's blood stain'd the king's own land v 5 110
Thou hast wrought A deed of slander with thy fatal hand . . . v 6 35
I'll make a voyage to the Holy Land, To wash this blood off from my guilty hand . . . . v 6 50
Was by the rude hands of that Welshman taken . . . *1 Hen. IV.* i 1 41
That same greatness too which our own hands Have holp to make so portly . . . . i 3 12
What, ho! chamberlain!—At hand, quoth pick-purse.—That's even as fair as—at hand, quoth the chamberlain . . . . . . ii 1 53
Give me thy hand: thou shalt have a share in our purchase . . ii 1 100
Some heavy business hath my lord in hand, And I must know it . . ii 3 66
Come out of that fat room, and lend me thy hand to laugh a little . ii 4 2
Clapped even now into my hand by an under-skinker . . . . ii 4 26

Hand. Washes his hands, and says to his wife 'Fie upon this quiet life!' *1 Hen. IV.* ii 4 116
But I followed me close, came in foot and hand . . . . . ii 4 241
It was so dark, Hal, that thou couldst not see thy hand . . . ii 4 248
Be near at hand, For we shall presently have need of you . . iii 2 2
A fearful head they are, If promises be kept on every hand . . iii 2 168
Our hands are full of business: let's away; Advantage feeds him fat . iii 2 179
Rob me the exchequer the first thing thou doest, and do it with unwashed hands too . . . . iii 3 206
I am out of fear Of death or death's hand for this one-half year . iv 1 136
Kiss your hand, When yet you were in place and in account Nothing so strong . . . . v 1 36
Quickly woo'd To gripe the general sway into your hand . . . v 1 57
I might have let alone The insulting hand of Douglas over you . . v 4 54
And both the Blunts Kill'd by the hand of Douglas . . *2 Hen. IV.* i 1 17
A scaly gauntlet now with joints of steel Must glove this hand . . i 1 147
Let heaven kiss earth! now let not Nature's hand Keep the wild flood confined! . . . . i 1 153
I will sooner have a beard grow in the palm of my hand than he shall get one on his cheek . . . . i 2 24
To bear a gentleman in hand, and then stand upon security! . . i 2 42
Have you not a moist eye? a dry hand? a yellow cheek? . . . i 2 204
God send the companion a better prince! I cannot rid my hands of him i 2 226
We should not step too far Till we had his assistance by the hand . i 3 21
The king, my lord, and Harry Prince of Wales Are near at hand . ii 1 147
That I am a second brother and that I am a proper fellow of my hands ii 2 72
Were these inward wars once out of hand . . . . . . iii 1 107
Come on, sir; give me your hand, sir, give me your hand, sir . . iii 2 2
Give me your good hand, give me your worship's good hand . . . iii 2 91
Put me a caliver into Wart's hand . . . . iii 2 290
To lay a heavy and unequal hand Upon our honours . . . . iv 1 102
The prince is here at hand: pleaseth your lordship To meet his grace . iv 1 225
He hath a tear for pity and a hand Open as day for melting charity . iv 4 31
Prince John your son doth kiss your grace's hand . . . . iv 4 83
Will Fortune never come with both hands full? . . . . . iv 4 103
Unless some dull and favourable hand Will whisper music to my weary spirit . . . . iv 5 2
It seem'd in me But as an honour snatch'd with boisterous hand . iv 5 192
I do commit into your hand The unstained sword that you have used to bear . . . . v 2 113
There is my hand. You shall be as a father to my youth . . . v 2 117
In which you, father, shall have foremost hand . . . . . v 2 140
Haled thither By most mechanical and dirty hand . . . . . v 5 38
In regard of causes now in hand, Which I have open'd . . *Hen. V.* i 1 77
While that the armed hand doth fight abroad, The advised head defends itself at home . . . . i 2 178
And to put forth My rightful hand in a well-hallow'd cause . . . i 2 293
And by their hands this grace of kings must die . . . . ii Prol. 28
Now, by this hand, I swear, I scorn the term . . . . . ii 1 32
And shall forget the office of our hand, Sooner than quittance of desert ii 2 33
So a' bade me lay more clothes on his feet: I put my hand into the bed and felt them, and they were as cold as any stone . . . . ii 3 24
And all our princes captived by the hand Of that black name . . ii 4 55
In liberty of bloody hand shall range With conscience wide as hell . iii 3 12
If your pure maidens fall into the hand Of hot and forcing violation . iii 3 20
Look to see The blind and bloody soldier with foul hand Defile the locks of your shrill-shrieking daughters . . . . iii 3 34
La main? elle est appelée de hand.—De hand. Et les doigts? . . iii 4 7
I have merited some love at his hands . . . . iii 6 25
We are in God's hand, brother, not in theirs . . . . . iii 6 178
By the white hand of my lady . . . . iii 7 101
By this hand, I will take thee a box on the ear . . . . . iv 1 231
Who twice a-day their wither'd hands hold up Toward heaven, to pardon blood . . . . iv 1 316
There is not work enough for all our hands . . . . . . iv 2 19
The horsemen sit like fixed candlesticks, With torch-staves in their hand . . . . iv 2 46
He hath fallen into the hands of one, as he thinks, the most brave . iv 4 65
And with his cap in hand, Like a base pandar, hold the chamber-door . iv 5 13
He smiled me in the face, raught me his hand . . . . . iv 6 21
Well, bawd I'll turn, And something lean to cutpurse of quick hand . v 1 91
Whose tenours . . . You have enscheduled briefly in your hands . . v 2 73
Give me your answer; i' faith, do: and so clap hands and a bargain . v 2 133
Take me by the hand, and say 'Harry of England, I am thine' . . v 2 255
Upon that I kiss your hand, and I call you my queen . . . . v 2 271
He ne'er lift up his hand but conquered . . . . *1 Hen. VI.* i 1 16
Be not dismay'd, for succour is at hand . . . . i 2 50
Stay, stay thy hands! thou art an Amazon . . . . . . i 2 104
My heart and hands thou hast at once subdued . . . . . i 2 109
Accursed fatal hand That hath contrived this woful tragedy! . . . i 4 76
Heaven, be thou gracious to none alive, If Salisbury wants mercy at thy hands! . . . . i 4 86
Thou shalt not die whiles—He beckons with his hand and smiles on me i 4 92
Now, by this maiden blossom in my hand, I scorn thee . . . . ii 4 75
Hold your slaughtering hands and keep the peace . . . . . iii 1 87
Why look you still so stern and tragical?—Here, Winchester, I offer thee my hand . . . . iii 1 126
I will yield to thee; Love for thy love and hand for hand I give . iii 1 135
Gather we our forces out of hand And set upon our boasting enemy . iii 2 102
A letter was deliver'd to my hands, Writ to your grace . . . . iv 1 11
'Tis much when sceptres are in children's hands . . . . . iv 1 192
On either hand thee there are squadrons pitch'd, To wall thee . . iv 2 23
Both be suddenly surprised By bloody hands, in sleeping on your beds! v 3 41
Do not fear nor fly! For I will touch thee but with reverent hands . v 3 47
My hand would free her, but my heart says no . . . . . v 3 61
Put a golden sceptre in thy hand And set a precious crown upon thy head . . . . v 3 118
Give thee her hand, for sign of plighted faith . . . . . . v 3 162
And here at hand the Dauphin and his train Approacheth . . . v 4 100
Deliver up my title in the queen To your most gracious hands *2 Hen. VI.* i 1 13
Clapping their hands, and crying with loud voice . . . . . i 1 160
The silly owner of the goods Weeps over them and wrings his hapless hands . . . . i 1 226
Put forth thy hand, reach at the glorious gold. What, is't too short? . i 2 11
But, to the matter that we have in hand . . . . i 3 162
Till France be won into the Dauphin's hands . . . . . . i 3 173
That time best fits the work we have in hand . . . . . . i 4 23
Lay hands upon these traitors and their trash . . . . . . i 4 44
This staff of honour raught, there let it stand Where it best fits to be, in Henry's hand . . . . ii 3 44

Hand. And charity chased hence by rancour's hand . . *2 Hen. VI.* iii 1 144
Here is my hand, the deed is worthy doing.—And so say I . . . iii 1 278
Take thou this task in hand.—I am content . . . . . . iii 1 318
Yet be well assured You put sharp weapons in a madman's hands . . iii 1 347
The king and all the peers are here at hand . . . . . iii 2 10
Lay not thy hands on me; forbear, I say; Their touch affrights me . iii 2 46
Some violent hands were laid on Humphrey's life . . . . . iii 2 138
And with my fingers feel his hand unfeeling . . . . . iii 2 145
I do believe that violent hands were laid Upon the life . . . iii 2 156
His hands abroad display'd, as one that grasp'd And tugg'd for life . iii 2 172
Give me thy hand, That I may dew it with my mournful tears . . iii 2 339
O, could this kiss be printed in thy hand! . . . . . . iii 2 343
If thou think'st on heaven's bliss, Hold up thy hand, make signal . iii 3 28
Hast thou not kiss'd thy hand and held my stirrup? . . . . iv 1 53
This hand of mine hath writ in thy behalf And therefore shall it charm thy riotous tongue . . . . iv 1 63
Brutus' bastard hand Stabb'd Julius Cæsar . . . . . . iv 1 136
There's no better sign of a brave mind than a hard hand . . . iv 2 22
He should stand in fear of fire, being burnt i' the hand for stealing of sheep . . . . iv 2 67
When have I aught exacted at your hands, But to maintain the king? . iv 7 74
Great men have reaching hands: oft have I struck Those that I never saw . . . . iv 7 86
These hands are free from guiltless blood-shedding . . . . . iv 7 108
Thy hand is but a finger to my fist, Thy leg a stick compared with this iv 10 51
This hand was made to handle nought but gold . . . . . v 1 7
Thy hand is made to grasp a palmer's staff, And not to grace an awful princely sceptre . . . . v 1 97
Here is a hand to hold a sceptre up . . . . v 1 102
I wonder how the king escaped our hands . . . . . *3 Hen. VI.* i 1 1
Ah, whither shall I fly to 'scape their hands? . . . . . i 3 1
What valour were it, when a cur doth grin, For one to thrust his hand between his teeth? . . . . i 4 57
That raught at mountains with outstretched arms, Yet parted but the shadow with his hand . . . . i 4 69
A crown for York! and, lords, bow low to him: Hold you his hands, whilst I do set it on . . . . i 4 95
You should not be king Till our King Henry had shook hands with death . . . . i 4 102
Such comfort come to thee As now I reap at thy too cruel hand! . . i 4 166
By many hands your father was subdued . . . . ii 1 56
This strong right hand of mine Can pluck the diadem from faint Henry's head . . . . ii 1 152
Whose hand is that the forest bear doth lick? Not his that spoils her young before her face . . . . ii 2 13
Many fly to him: Darraign your battle, for they are at hand . . . ii 2 72
Your legs did better service than your hands . . . . . . ii 2 104
I throw my hands, mine eyes, my heart to thee . . . . . ii 3 36
Brother, give me thy hand; and, gentle Warwick, Let me embrace thee ii 3 44
This is the hand that stabb'd thy father York; And this the hand that slew thy brother Rutland; And here's the heart that triumphs in their death And cheers these hands . . . . ii 4 6
And I, who at his hands received my life, Have by my hands of life bereaved him . . . . ii 5 68
And bloody steel grasp'd in their ireful hands . . . . . . ii 5 132
The foe is merciless, and will not pity; For at their hands I have deserved no pity . . . . ii 6 26
If this right hand would buy two hours' life, That I in all despite might rail at him, This hand should chop it off . . . . ii 6 80
Why linger we? let us lay hands upon him.—Forbear awhile . . . iii 1 26
My eye's too quick, my heart o'erweens too much, Unless my hand and strength could equal them . . . . iii 2 145
Humbly to kiss your hand and with my tongue To tell the passion . iii 3 61
Yet shall you have all kindness at my hand That your estate requires . iii 3 149
She is fair and virtuous, Therefore delay not, give thy hand to Warwick iii 3 246
I accept her, for she well deserves it; And here, to pledge my vow, I give my hand . . . . iii 3 250
They shall obey, and love thee too, Unless they seek for hatred at my hands . . . . iv 1 80
I hold it cowardice To rest mistrustful where a noble heart Hath pawn'd an open hand in sign of love . . . . iv 2 9
At whose hands He hath good usage and great liberty . . . . iv 5 5
Give me both your hands: Now join your hands, and with your hands your hearts . . . . iv 6 38
His head by nature framed to wear a crown, His hand to wield a sceptre iv 6 73
We will proclaim you out of hand; The bruit thereof will bring you many friends . . . . iv 7 63
In sign of truth, I kiss your highness' hand . . . . . . iv 8 26
Then Clarence is at hand; I hear his drum.—It is not his, my lord . v 1 11
They are at hand, and you shall quickly know . . . . . . v 1 15
Humbly bend thy knee, Call Edward king and at his hands beg mercy . v 1 23
Strike now, or else the iron cools.—I had rather chop this hand off at a blow . . . . v 1 50
This hand, fast wound about thy coal-black hair . . . . . v 1 54
To deserve well at my brother's hands, I here proclaim myself thy mortal foe . . . . v 1 93
Sweet brother, take my hand, And with thy lips keep in my soul awhile! . . . . v 2 34
Edward is at hand, Ready to fight; therefore be resolute . . . . v 4 60
I do love thee so, That I will shortly send thy soul to heaven, If heaven will take the present at our hands . . . . *Richard III.* i 1 120
Stabb'd by the selfsame hand that made these wounds! . . . . i 2 11
Cursed be the hand that made these fatal holes! . . . . . i 2 14
He is dead; and slain by Edward's hand.—In thy foul throat thou liest i 2 92
That hand, which, for thy love, did kill thy love, Shall, for thy love, kill a far truer love . . . . i 2 190
If thy poor devoted suppliant may But beg one favour at thy gracious hand . . . . i 2 208
She may help you to many fair preferments, And then deny her aiding hand therein . . . . i 3 96
I'll kiss thy hand, In sign of league and amity with thee . . . i 3 280
Be assured We come to use our hands and not our tongues . . . i 3 353
I am, in this, commanded to deliver The noble Duke of Clarence to your hands . . . . i 4 93
Depart and lay no hands on me: The deed you undertake is damnable . i 4 196
He holds vengeance in his hands, To hurl upon their heads that break his law . . . . i 4 204
How fain, like Pilate, would I wash my hands Of this most grievous guilty murder done! . . . . i 4 279
Rivers and Hastings, take each other's hand: Dissemble not your hatred ii 1 7

Hand. And with my hand I seal my true heart's love . *Richard III.* ii 1 10
Wife, love Lord Hastings, let him kiss your hand . . . . . ii 1 21
'Tis call'd ungrateful, With dull unwillingness to repay a debt Which with a bounteous hand was kindly lent . . . . ii 2 93
When great leaves fall, the winter is at hand . . . . . . ii 3 33
I'll claim that promise at your grace's hands.—And look to have it yielded with all willingness . . . . iii 1 197
They do need the priest; Your honour hath no shriving work in hand . iii 2 116
I never look'd for better at his hands . . . . iii 5 50
Which in a set hand fairly is engross'd . . . . iii 6 2
Get a prayer-book in your hand, And stand betwixt two churchmen . iii 7 47
See, a book of prayer in his hand, True ornaments to know a holy man iii 7 98
Who meets us here? my niece Plantagenet Led in the hand of her kind aunt . . . . iv 1 2
When scarce the blood was well wash'd from his hands Which issued from my other angel husband . . . . iv 1 68
Give me thy hand. Thus high, by thy advice And thy assistance, is King Richard seated . . . . iv 2 3
If ancient sorrow be most reverend, Give mine the benefit of seniory, And let my woes frown on the upper hand . . . . . . iv 4 37
But at hand, at hand, Ensues his piteous and unpitied end . . . iv 4 73
Whose hand soever lanced their tender hearts, Thy head, all indirectly, gave direction . . . . iv 4 224
Say that the king, which may command, entreats.—That at her hands which the king's King forbids . . . . iv 4 346
Put in their hands thy bruising irons of wrath . . . . . . v 3 110
With one hand on his dagger, Another spread on's breast . *Hen. VIII.* i 2 204
A hand as fruitful as the land that feeds us; His dews fall every where i 3 56
The fairest hand I ever touch'd! O beauty, Till now I never knew thee! . . . . i 4 75
To your highness' hand I tender my commission . . . . . ii 2 103
Give me your hand: much joy and favour to you . . . . . ii 2 118
But to be commanded For ever by your grace, whose hand has raised me ii 2 120
Put my sick cause into his hands that hates me? . . . . . iii 1 118
Gave't you the king?—To his own hand, in's bedchamber . . . iii 2 77
As my hand has open'd bounty to you, My heart dropp'd love . . iii 2 184
Your hand and heart, Your brain, and every function of your power . iii 2 186
Who commands you To render up the great seal presently Into our hands . . . . iii 2 230
That seal, You ask with such a violence, the king, Mine and your master, with his own hand gave me . . . . iii 2 247
That goodness Of gleaning all the land's wealth into one, Into your own hands . . . . iii 2 285
Those articles, my lord, are in the king's hand . . . . . iii 2 299
Still in thy right hand carry gentle peace, To silence envious tongues . iii 2 445
May I be bold to ask what that contains, That paper in your hand? . iv 1 14
Till Cranmer, Cromwell, her two hands, and she, Sleep in their graves . v 1 31
The archbishop Is the king's hand and tongue . . . . . . v 1 38
I have news to tell you: come, come, give me your hand . . . v 1 94
Give me thy hand, stand up: Prithee, let's walk . . . . . v 1 115
Those that tame wild horses Pace 'em not in their hands to make 'em gentle . . . . v 3 22
Ye have made a fine hand, fellows: There's a trim rabble let in . . v 4 74
Take my blessing: God protect thee! Into whose hand I give thy life v 5 12
Her hand, In whose comparison all whites are ink . *Troi. and Cres.* i 1 55
If she be fair, 'tis the better for her; an she be not, she has the mends in her own hands . . . . i 1 68
He is a gouty Briareus, many hands and no use . . . . . i 2 30
She came and puts me her white hand to his cloven chin . . . i 2 131
She has a marvellous white hand, I must needs confess . . . . i 2 151
Forestall prescience and esteem no act But that of hand . . . i 3 200
The still and mental parts, That do contrive how many hands shall strike . . . . i 3 201
So that the ram that batters down the wall . . . They place before his hand that made the engine . . . . i 3 208
Let me touch your hand; To our pavilion shall I lead you, sir . . i 3 304
You all clapp'd your hands, And cried 'Inestimable!' . . . . ii 2 87
And on the cause and question now in hand Have glozed, but superficially . . . . ii 2 164
What exploit's in hand? where sups he to-night? . . . . . iii 1 89
I'll be the witness. Here I hold your hand, here my cousin's . . iii 2 205
Like a fashionable host That slightly shakes his parting guest by the hand . . . . iii 3 166
Take his hand,—Witness the process of your speech . . . . iv 1 7
By Venus' hand I swear, No man alive can love in such a sort . . iv 1 22
There is at hand Paris your brother, and Deiphobus The Grecian Diomed iv 2 62
Within this hour, We must give up to Diomedes' hand The Lady Cressida . . . . iv 2 67
They are at hand and ready to effect it . . . . iv 2 70
And to his hand when I deliver her, Think it an altar . . . . iv 3 7
At the port, lord, I'll give her to thy hand . . . . . . iv 4 113
Give me your hand, and, as we walk, To our own selves bend we our needful talk . . . . iv 4 140
Half heart, half hand, half Hector comes to seek This blended knight . iv 5 85
His heart and hand both open and both free; For what he has he gives iv 5 100
This hand is Grecian all, And this is Trojan . . . . . . iv 5 125
Give me thy hand, my cousin; I will go eat with thee . . . . iv 5 157
To-morrow do I meet thee, fell as death; To-night all friends.—Thy hand upon that match . . . . iv 5 270
What work's, my countrymen, in hand? where go you With bats? *Coriol.* i 1 56
His bloody brow With his mail'd hand then wiping, forth he goes . i 3 38
There, Against the hospitable canon, would I Wash my fierce hand in's heart . . . . i 10 27
Your hand, and yours: Ere in our own house I do shade my head, The good patricians must be visited . . . . ii 1 210
Aged sir, hands off.—Hence, rotten thing! . . . . iii 1 178
Lay hands upon him, And bear him to the rock . . . . . iii 1 222; 227
He shall be thrown down the Tarpeian rock With rigorous hands . . iii 1 267
The noble tribunes are the people's mouths, And we their hands . . iii 1 272
I prithee now, my son, Go to them, with this bonnet in thy hand . . iii 2 73
Within thine eyes sat twenty thousand deaths, In thy hands clutch'd as many millions . . . . iii 3 71
I would my son Were in Arabia, and thy tribe before him, His good sword in his hand.—What then? . . . . iv 2 25
O, come, go in, And take our friendly senators by the hands . . . iv 5 138
Your hand: most welcome!—Here's a strange alteration! . . . iv 5 153
By my hand, I had thought to have strucken him with a cudgel . . iv 5 155
Sanctifies himself with's hand and turns up the white o' the eye to his discourse . . . . iv 5 208
You have made fair hands, You and your crafts! . . . . . . iv 6 117

Hand. Dismiss'd me Thus, with his speechless hand — *Coriolanus* v 1 67
And in her hand The grandchild to her blood — v 3 23
This boy, that cannot tell what he would have, But kneels and holds up hands for fellowship — v 3 175
O, bless me here with thy victorious hand! — *T. Andron.* i 1 163
That proud brag of thine, That said'st I begg'd the empire at thy hands — i 1 307
With his own hand did slay his youngest son, In zeal to you — i 1 418
A solemn hunting is in hand; There will the lovely Roman ladies troop — ii 1 112
Vengeance is in my heart, death in my hand, Blood and revenge are hammering in my head — ii 3 38
Make pillage of her chastity And wash their hands in Bassianus' blood — ii 3 45
You shall know, my boys, Your mother's hand shall right your mother's wrong — ii 3 121
Be call'd a gentle queen, And with thine own hands kill me in this place! — ii 3 169
O brother, help me with thy fainting hand—If fear hath made thee faint — ii 3 233
Reach me thy hand, that I may help thee out — ii 3 237
Thy hand once more; I will not loose again, Till thou art here aloft, or I below — ii 3 243
Go home, call for sweet water, wash thy hands.—She hath no tongue to call, nor hands to wash; And so let's leave her — ii 4 6
I should go hang myself.—If thou hadst hands to help thee knit the cord — ii 4 10
What stern ungentle hands Have lopp'd and hew'd and made thy body bare Of her two branches? — ii 4 16
O, had the monster seen those lily hands Tremble, like aspen-leaves, upon a lute, And make the silken strings delight to kiss them! — ii 4 44
Lavinia, what accursed hand Hath made thee handless in thy father's sight? — iii 1 66
I'll chop off my hands too; For they have fought for Rome, and all in vain — iii 1 72
'Tis well, Lavinia, that thou hast no hands; For hands, to do Rome service, are but vain — iii 1 79
Thou hast no hands, to wipe away thy tears; Nor tongue, to tell me who hath martyr'd thee — iii 1 106
Shall we cut away our hands, like thine? Or shall we bite our tongues? — iii 1 130
Let Marcus, Lucius, or thyself, old Titus, Or any one of you, chop off your hand, And send it to the king — iii 1 153
With all my heart, I'll send the emperor My hand — iii 1 161
That noble hand of thine, That hath thrown down so many enemies, Shall not be sent: my hand will serve the turn — iii 1 163
Which of your hands hath not defended Rome? — iii 1 168
My hand hath been but idle; let it serve To ransom my two nephews — iii 1 172
Nay, come, agree whose hand shall go along, For fear they die — iii 1 175
My hand shall go.—By heaven, it shall not go! — iii 1 177
Agree between you; I will spare my hand.—Then I'll go fetch an axe — iii 1 184
Lend me thy hand, and I will give thee mine — iii 1 188
Give his majesty my hand: Tell him it was a hand that warded him From thousand dangers — iii 1 194
And for thy hand Look by and by to have thy sons with thee — iii 1 201
Here I lift this one hand up to heaven, And bow this feeble ruin to the earth — iii 1 207
Ill art thou repaid For that good hand thou sent'st the emperor — iii 1 236
Here are the heads of thy two noble sons; And here's thy hand, in scorn to thee sent back — iii 1 238
See, thy two sons' heads, Thy warlike hand, thy mangled daughter here — iii 1 256
Rend off thy silver hair, thy other hand Gnawing with thy teeth — iii 1 261
Come, brother, take a head; And in this hand the other will I bear — iii 1 281
These arms! Bear thou my hand, sweet wench, between thy teeth — iii 1 283
Thy niece and I, poor creatures, want our hands, And cannot passionate our tenfold grief With folded arms — iii 2 5
This poor right hand of mine Is left to tyrannize upon my breast — iii 2 7
Teach her not thus to lay Such violent hands upon her tender life — iii 2 22
What violent hands can she lay on her life? Ah, wherefore dost thou urge the name of hands? — iii 2 25
O, handle not the theme, to talk of hands, Lest we remember still that we have none. Fie, fie, how franticly I square my talk, As if we should forget we had no hands, If Marcus did not name the word of hands! — iii 2 29
Guide, if thou canst, This after me, when I have writ my name Without the help of any hand at all — iv 1 71
Nor the god of war Shall seize this prey out of his father's hands — iv 2 96
Give your pigeons to the emperor: By me thou shalt have justice at his hands — iv 3 104
I'll be at hand, sir; see you do it bravely.—I warrant you, sir — iv 3 113
This is the incarnate devil That robb'd Andronicus of his good hand — v 1 41
They cut thy sister's tongue and ravish'd her And cut her hands — v 1 93
I play'd the cheater for thy father's hand — v 1 111
When, for his hand, he had his two sons' heads — v 1 115
How can I grace my talk, Wanting a hand to give it action? — v 2 18
Mighty Tamora: Is not thy coming for my other hand? — v 2 27
I'll find some cunning practice out of hand — v 2 77
Bind them, gentle Publius. Caius and Valentine, lay hands on them — v 2 159
My hand cut off and made a merry jest — v 2 175
Both her sweet hands, her tongue, and that more dear Than hands or tongue, her spotless chastity, Inhuman traitors, you constrain'd and forced — v 2 176
This one hand yet is left to cut your throats — v 2 182
The trumpets show the emperor is at hand — v 3 16
Was it well done of rash Virginius To slay his daughter with his own right hand? — v 3 37
And basely cozen'd Of that true hand that fought Rome's quarrel out — v 3 102
And bring our emperor gently in thy hand, Lucius our emperor — v 3 138
Where civil blood makes civil hands unclean — *Rom. and Jul.* Prol. 4
From those bloody hands Throw your mistemper'd weapons to the ground — i 1 93
To wield old partisans, in hands as old, Canker'd with peace — i 1 101
When good manners shall lie all in one or two men's hands and they unwashed too, 'tis a foul thing — i 5 5
What lady is that, which doth enrich the hand Of yonder knight? — i 5 43
I'll watch her place of stand, And, touching hers, make blessed my rude hand — i 5 53
If I profane with my unworthiest hand This holy shrine, the gentle fine is this — i 5 95
Good pilgrim, you do wrong your hand too much — i 5 99
For saints have hands that pilgrims' hands do touch, And palm to palm is holy palmers' kiss — i 5 101
O, then, dear saint, let lips do what hands do; They pray, grant thou — i 5 105
See, how she leans her cheek upon her hand! O, that I were a glove upon that hand, That I might touch that cheek! — ii 2 23

Hand. It is nor hand, nor foot, Nor arm, nor face, nor any other part — *Rom. and Jul.* ii 2 40
No further than a wanton's bird; Who lets it hop a little from her hand — ii 2 179
The bawdy hand of the dial is now upon the prick of noon — ii 4 119
And for a hand, and a foot, and a body, though they be not to be talked on, yet they are past compare — ii 5 41
Do thou but close our hands with holy words, Then love-devouring death do what he dare — ii 6 6
Who began this bloody fray?—Tybalt, here slain, whom Romeo's hand did slay — iii 1 157
With one hand beats Cold death aside, and with the other sends It back — iii 1 165
Why dost thou wring thy hands?—Ah, well-a-day! he's dead, he's dead! — iii 2 36
O God! did Romeo's hand shed Tybalt's blood?—It did, it did — iii 2 71
What sorrow craves acquaintance at my hand, That I yet know not? — iii 3 5
They [flies] may seize On the white wonder of dear Juliet's hand — iii 3 36
Did murder her; as that name's cursed hand Murder'd her kinsman — iii 3 104
Hold thy desperate hand: Art thou a man? thy form cries out thou art — iii 3 108
Give me thy hand; 'tis late: farewell; good night — iii 3 172
That is, because the traitor murderer lives.—Ay, madam, from the reach of these my hands — iii 5 86
Tell him so yourself, And see how he will take it at your hands — iii 5 126
Lay hand on heart, advise — iii 5 192
God join'd my heart and Romeo's, thou our hands — iv 1 55
Ere this hand, by thee to Romeo seal'd, Shall be the label to another deed — iv 1 56
I am sure, you have your hands full all, In this so sudden business — iv 3 11
My dreams presage some joyful news at hand — v 1 2
O, give me thy hand, One writ with me in sour misfortune's book! — v 3 81
O, what more favour can I do to thee, Than with that hand that cut thy youth in twain To sunder his that was thine enemy? — v 3 99
What's here? a cup, closed in my true love's hand? Poison, I see — v 3 161
Whom Fortune with her ivory hand wafts to her — *T. of Athens* i 1 70
All his dependants Which labour'd after him to the mountain's top Even on their knees and hands — i 1 87
My hand to thee; mine honour on my promise — i 1 148
Well fare you, gentleman: give me your hand; We must needs dine together — i 1 163
Commend me to your master—and the cap Plays in the right hand — ii 1 19
'Gainst the authority of manners, pray'd you To hold your hand more close — ii 2 148
Let each take some; Nay, put out all your hands. Not one word more — iv 2 28
I'll beat thee, but I should infect my hands — iv 3 369
Time, with his fairer hand, Offering the fortunes of his former days, The former man may make him — v 1 126
These walls of ours Were not erected by their hands from whom You have received your griefs — v 4 23
You bear too stubborn and too strange a hand Over your friend — *J. Cæsar* i 2 35
Come on my right hand, for this ear is deaf, And tell me truly — i 2 213
Being offered him, he put it by with the back of his hand, thus — i 2 222
The rabblement hooted and clapped their chopped hands — i 2 246
I will this night, In several hands, in at his windows throw — i 2 320
A common slave—you know him well by sight—Held up his left hand, which did flame and burn Like twenty torches join'd, and yet his hand, Not sensible of fire, remain'd unscorch'd — i 3 16
Every bondman in his own hand bears The power to cancel his captivity — i 3 101
Hold, my hand: Be factious for redress of all these griefs — i 3 117
Like the work we have in hand, Most bloody, fiery, and most terrible — i 3 129
I make thee promise: If the redress will follow, thou receivest Thy full petition at the hand of Brutus! — ii 1 58
Give me your hands all over, one by one.—And let us swear our resolution — ii 1 112
It shall be said, his judgement ruled our hands — ii 1 147
With an angry wafture of your hand, Gave sign for me to leave you — ii 1 246
I am not sick, if Brutus have in hand Any exploit worthy the name of honour.—Such an exploit have I in hand — ii 1 316
Many lusty Romans Came smiling, and did bathe their hands in it — ii 2 79
Press near and second him.—Casca, you are the first that rears your hand — iii 1 30
I kiss thy hand, but not in flattery — iii 1 52
Great Cæsar,— Doth not Brutus bootless kneel?—Speak, hands, for me! — iii 1 76
Stoop, And let us bathe our hands in Cæsar's blood Up to the elbows — iii 1 106
If you bear me hard, Now, whilst your purpled hands do reek and smoke, Fulfil your pleasure — iii 1 158
Though now we must appear bloody and cruel, As, by our hands and this our present act, You see we do, yet see you but our hands — iii 1 166
Let each man render me his bloody hand: First, Marcus Brutus — iii 1 184
Next, Caius Cassius, do I take your hand; Now, Decius Brutus, yours — iii 1 186
Therefore I took your hands, but was, indeed, Sway'd from the point — iii 1 218
Else shall you not have any hand at all About his funeral — iii 1 248
Woe to the hand that shed this costly blood! — iii 1 258
Lend me your hand — iii 1 297
Though he had no hand in his death, shall receive the benefit of his dying — iii 2 46
What now, Lucilius! is Cassius near?—He is at hand — iv 2 4
If he be at hand, I shall be satisfied — iv 2 9
But hollow men, like horses hot at hand, Make gallant show — iv 2 23
Than to wring From the hard hands of peasants their vile trash — iv 3 74
Do you confess so much? Give me your hand.—And my heart too — iv 3 117
Their battles are at hand; They mean to warn us at Philippi here — v 1 4
Octavius, lead your battle softly on, Upon the left hand of the even field.—Upon the right hand I; keep thou the left — v 1 17
Thou canst not die by traitors' hands, Unless thou bring'st them with thee — v 1 56
Give me thy hand, Messala: Be thou my witness — v 1 73
And there they perch'd, Gorging and feeding from our soldiers' hands — v 1 82
Wilt thou, Strato?—Give me your hand first. Fare you well, my lord — v 5 49
Which ne'er shook hands, nor bade farewell to him, Till he unseam'd him from the nave to the chaps — *Macbeth* i 2 21
Let not light see my black and deep desires: The eye wink at the hand — i 4 52
Bear welcome in your eye, Your hand, your tongue — i 5 66
Give me your hand; Conduct me to mine host — i 6 28
Is this a dagger which I see before me, The handle toward my hand? — ii 1 34
One cried 'God bless us!' and 'Amen' the other; As they had seen me with these hangman's hands — ii 2 28
Go get some water, And wash this filthy witness from your hand — ii 2 47
What hands are here? ha! they pluck out mine eyes — ii 2 59
Will all great Neptune's ocean wash this blood Clean from my hand? No, this my hand will rather The multitudinous seas incarnadine — ii 2 61
My hands are of your colour; but I shame To wear a heart so white — ii 2 64

Hand. Their hands and faces were all badged with blood . *Macbeth* ii 3 107
Thence to be wrench'd with an unlineal hand, No son of mine succeeding iii 1 63
How you were borne in hand, how cross'd, the instruments, Who wrought iii 1 81
Whose heavy hand hath bow'd you to the grave And beggar'd yours . iii 1 90
With thy bloody and invisible hand Cancel and tear to pieces that great bond! . . . . iii 2 48
Strange things I have in head, that will to hand . . . . iii 4 139
That a swift blessing May soon return to this our suffering country Under a hand accursed! . . . . iii 6 49
The very firstlings of my heart shall be The firstlings of my hand . iv 1 148
I think withal There would be hands uplifted in my right . iv 3 42
But at his touch—Such sanctity hath heaven given his hand—They presently amend . . . . iv 3 144
What is it she does now? Look how she rubs her hands . v 1 31
It is an accustomed action with her, to seem thus washing her hands v 1 33
What, will these hands ne'er be clean? . . . . v 1 48
All the perfumes of Arabia will not sweeten this little hand . v 1 58
Wash your hands, put on your nightgown; look not so pale . v 1 68
There's knocking at the gate: come, come, come, come, give me your hand . . . . v 1 75
Now does he feel His secret murders sticking on his hands . v 2 17
I hope the days are near at hand That chambers will be safe . v 4 1
Who, as 'tis thought, by self and violent hands Took off her life . v 8 70
By strong hand And terms compulsatory. . . *Hamlet* i 1 102
The head is not more native to the heart, The hand more instrumental to the mouth . . . . i 2 48
I knew your father; These hands are not more like . . i 2 212
You shall not go, my lord.—Hold off your hands.—Be ruled . i 4 80
By a brother's hand Of life, of crown, of queen, at once dispatch'd . i 5 74
Without more circumstance at all, I hold it fit that we shake hands and part . . . . i 5 128
Come hither, gentlemen, And lay your hands again upon my sword . i 5 158
With his other hand thus o'er his brow, He falls to such perusal of my face As he would draw it . . . . . . ii 1 89
Grieved, That so his sickness, age and impotence Was falsely borne in hand . . . . ii 2 67
Gentlemen, you are welcome to Elsinore. Your hands, come then . ii 2 388
Do not saw the air too much with your hand, thus, but use all gently . iii 2 5
Since love our hearts and Hymen did our hands Unite commutual . iii 2 169
Thoughts black, hands apt, drugs fit, and time agreeing . . iii 2 266
What if this cursed hand Were thicker than itself with brother's blood? iii 3 43
In the corrupted currents of this world Offence's gilded hand may shove by justice . . . . iii 3 58
Leave wringing of your hands: peace! sit you down, And let me wring your heart . . . . iii 4 34
Eyes without feeling, feeling without sight, Ears without hands or eyes iii 4 79
Caps, hands, and tongues, applaud it to the clouds . . . iv 5 107
If by direct or by collateral hand They find us touch'd . . iv 5 206
Know you the hand?—'Tis Hamlet's character . . iv 7 52
Delays as many As there are tongues, are hands, are accidents . iv 7 122
The hand of little employment hath the daintier sense . . v 1 77
The corse they follow did with desperate hand Fordo it own life . v 1 243
Hold off thy hand.—Pluck them asunder.—Hamlet, Hamlet! . v 1 286
Come, Hamlet, come, and take this hand from me . . . v 2 236
You mock me, sir.—No, by this hand . . . . v 2 269
The treacherous instrument is in thy hand, Unbated and envenom'd . v 2 327
When I shall wed, That lord whose hand must take my plight shall carry Half my love with him . . . . *Lear* i 1 103
And here I take Cordelia by the hand, Duchess of Burgundy . . i 1 246
Had he a hand to write this? a heart and brain to breed it in? . i 2 60
It is his hand, my lord; but I hope his heart is not in the contents . i 2 72
O Regan, wilt thou take her by the hand?—Why not by the hand, sir? ii 4 197
Give me your hand: have you no more to say? . . . iii 1 51
Hide thee, thou bloody hand . . . . . . iii 2 53
Is it not as this mouth should tear this hand For lifting food to't? . iii 4 15
False of heart, light of ear, bloody of hand . . . iii 4 95
Keep thy foot out of brothels, thy hand out of plackets . . iii 4 100
If the matter of this paper be certain, you have mighty business in hand iii 5 17
With robbers' hands my hospitable favours You should not ruffle thus iii 7 40
To whose hands have you sent the lunatic king? . . . iii 7 46
Hold your hand, my lord: I have served you ever since I was a child . iii 7 72
I must change arms at home, and give the distaff Into my husband's hands . . . . iv 2 18
Were't my fitness To let these hands obey my blood, They are apt enough to dislocate and tear Thy flesh and bones . . . iv 2 64
More convenient is he for my hand Than for your lady's . . iv 5 31
Give me your hand: you are now within a foot Of the extreme verge . iv 6 25
Let go my hand. Here, friend, 's another purse; in it a jewel . iv 6 27
O, let me kiss that hand!—Let me wipe it first; it smells of mortality. iv 6 135
Thou rascal beadle, hold thy bloody hand! . . . . iv 6 164
O, here he is: lay hand upon him. Sir, Your most dear daughter . iv 6 192
Now let thy friendly hand Put strength enough to't . . . iv 6 234
I will not swear these are my hands: let's see; I feel this pin prick . iv 7 55
O, look upon me, sir, And hold your hands in benediction o'er me . iv 7 58
Away, old man; give me thy hand; away! King Lear hath lost . . v 2 5
Hold your hands, Both you of my inclining, and the rest . *Othello* i 2 81
Men do their broken weapons rather use Than their bare hands . i 3 175
The grace of heaven, Before, behind thee and on every hand, Enwheel thee round! . . . . ii 1 86
Didst thou not see her paddle with the palm of his hand? . . ii 1 260
When these mutualities so marshal the way, hard at hand comes the master ii 1 268
This is my right hand, and this is my left: I am not drunk now . ii 3 118
Hold your hand.—Let me go, sir, Or I'll knock you o'er the mazzard . ii 3 154
I'll know thy thoughts.—You cannot, if my heart were in your hand . iii 3 163
Wring my hand, Cry 'O sweet creature!' and then kiss me hard . iii 3 421
Have you not sometimes seen a handkerchief Spotted with strawberries in your wife's hand? . . . . iii 3 435
Witness that here Iago doth give up The execution of his wit, hands, heart, To wrong'd Othello's service! . . . . iii 3 466
Give me your hand: this hand is moist, my lady.—It yet hath felt no age nor known no sorrow . . . . iii 4 36
This hand of yours requires A sequester from liberty, fasting and prayer iii 4 39
'Tis a good hand, A frank one.—You may, indeed, say so; For 'twas that hand that gave away my heart.—A liberal hand . . . iii 4 43
The hearts of old gave hands; But our new heraldry is hands, not hearts iii 4 46
And, by this hand, she falls me thus about my neck . . iv 1 139
Did you see the handkerchief?—Was that mine?—Yours, by this hand iv 1 185
My heart is turned to stone; I strike it, and it hurts my hand . iv 1 194
Put in every honest hand a whip To lash the rascals naked through the world . . . . iv 2 142

Hand. Her hand on her bosom, her head on her knee, Sing willow, willow, willow . . . . *Othello* iv 3 43
Be near at hand; I may miscarry in't.—Here, at thy hand: be bold . v 1 6
By heaven, I saw my handkerchief in's hand . . . v 2 62
There lies your niece, Whose breath, indeed, these hands have newly stopp'd . . . . v 2 202
I saw it in his hand: It was a handkerchief, an antique token . v 2 215
Of one whose hand, Like the base Indian, threw a pearl away . v 2 346
Is't you, sir, that know things?—In nature's infinite book of secrecy A little I can read.—Show him your hand . . *Ant. and Cleo.* i 2 10
Lo, now, if it lay in their hands to make me a cuckold! . . i 2 80
The hand could pluck her back that shoved her on . . i 2 131
It only stands Our lives upon to use our strongest hands . . ii 1 51
Let me have thy hand: Further this act of grace . . . ii 2 148
There is my hand. A sister I bequeath you . . . ii 2 151
The silken tackle Swell with the touches of those flower-soft hands . ii 2 215
A hand that kings Have lipp'd, and trembled kissing . . ii 5 29
These hands do lack nobility, that they strike A meaner than myself . ii 5 82
Lie they upon thy hand, And be undone by 'em! . . . ii 5 105
Let me have your hand: I did not think, sir, to have met you here . ii 6 49
Let me shake thy hand; I never hated thee . . . ii 6 75
All men's faces are true, whatsome'er their hands are . . ii 6 103
Let's all take hands, Till that the conquering wine hath steep'd our sense In soft and delicate Lethe . . . . . . ii 7 112
All take hands. Make battery in our ears with the loud music . ii 7 114
What needs more words? Good night. Good Antony, your hand . ii 7 133
I'll try you on the shore.—And shall, sir: give's your hand . . ii 7 134
Say to great Cæsar this: in deputation I kiss his conquering hand . iii 13 75
Give me grace to lay My duty on your hand . . . . iii 13 82
So saucy with the hand of she here,—what's her name, Since she was Cleopatra? . . . . iii 13 98
To let a fellow that will take rewards And say 'God quit you!' be familiar with My playfellow, your hand! . . . . . . iii 13 125
Henceforth The white hand of a lady fever thee, Shake thou to look on't iii 13 138
Give me thy hand, Thou hast been rightly honest . . . iv 2 10
Give me thy hand; To this great fairy I'll commend thy acts . iv 8 11
Behold this man; Commend unto his lips thy favouring hand . iv 8 23
Fortune and Antony part here; even here Do we shake hands . iv 12 20
And with those hands, that grasp'd the heaviest club, Subdue my worthiest self . . . . iv 12 46
What thou wouldst do Is done unto thy hand . . . iv 14 29
My resolution and my hands I'll trust; None about Cæsar . . iv 15 49
That self hand, Which writ his honour in the acts it did . . v 1 21
Be of good cheer; You're fall'n into a princely hand, fear nothing . v 2 22
O Cleopatra! thou art taken, queen.—Quick, quick, good hands . v 2 39
Who in the wars o' the time Died with their swords in hand . *Cymbeline* i 1 36
They were parted By gentlemen at hand.—I am very glad on't . i 1 164
Your hand; a covenant: we will have these things set down by lawful counsel . . . . i 4 177
This hand, whose touch, Whose every touch, would force the feeler's soul To the oath of loyalty . . . . i 6 100
Join gripes with hands Made hard with hourly falsehood . . . i 6 106
What If I do line one of their hands? 'Tis gold Which buys admittance ii 3 72
Good morrow, fairest: sister, your sweet hand.—Good morrow, sir . ii 3 91
We have yet many among us can gripe as hard as Cassibelan: I do not say I am one; but I have a hand . . . . . . iii 1 42
Thou told'st me, when we came from horse, the place Was near at hand iii 4 2
My husband's hand! That drug-damn'd Italy hath out-craftied him . iii 4 14
Let thine own hands take away her life: I shall give thee opportunity . iii 4 28
Hence, vile instrument! Thou shalt not damn my hand . . iii 4 76
I must die; And if I do not by thy hand, thou art No servant of thy master's . . . . iii 4 77
Against self-slaughter There is a prohibition so divine That cravens my weak hand . . . . iii 4 80
Your hand, my lord.—Receive it friendly; but from this time forth I wear it as your enemy . . . . iii 5 12
It is Posthumus' hand; I know't . . . . . . iii 5 108
Give me thy hand; here's my purse . . . . . iii 5 124
Fortune, put them into my hand! . . . . . . iv 1 26
When I have slain thee with my proper hand, I'll follow those . iv 2 97
Swore With his own single hand he'ld take us in . . . iv 2 121
This is his hand; His foot Mercurial; his Martial thigh . . iv 2 309
Lay hands on him; a dog! . . . . v 3 91
Your daughter, whom she bore in hand to love With such integrity . v 5 43
There's other work in hand: I see a thing Bitter to me as death . v 5 103
Lapp'd In a most curious mantle, wrought by the hand Of his queen mother . . . . v 5 361
Whom heavens, in justice, both on her and hers, Have laid most heavy hand . . . . v 5 465
Never was a war did cease, Ere bloody hands were wash'd, with such a peace . . . . v 5 485
A city on whom plenty held full hand . . . . *Pericles* i 4 22
An hand environed with clouds, Holding out gold . . . ii 2 36
That all those eyes adored them ere their fall Scorn now their hand should give them burial . . . . ii 4 12
Then you love us, we you, and we'll clasp hands . . . ii 4 57
If my tongue Did e'er solicit, or my hand subscribe To any syllable that made love to you . . . . ii 5 69
Man and wife: Nay, come, your hands and lips must seal it too . ii 5 85
Hush, my gentle neighbours! Lend me your hands; to the next chamber bear her . . . . iii 2 108
Cried 'Good seamen!' to the sailors, galling His kingly hands, haling ropes . . . . iv 1 55
You are light into my hands, where you are like to live.—The more my fault To scape his hands where I was like to die . . . iv 2 77
Give me your hand *Mer. Wives* iv 2; *Meas. for Meas.* i 1; *M. of Ven.* iv 1; *As Y. L. It* iv 1; v 1; *All's Well* v 2; *W. T.* v 2; *2 Hen. IV.* v 1; *Coriolanus* iv 1; *Lear* iii 4; iv 6; *Ant. and Cleo.* ii 6; iv 8

Hand and seal. Here is the hand and seal of the duke . *Meas. for Meas.* iv 2 207
Here is your hand and seal for what I did.—O, when the last account 'twixt heaven and earth Is to be made, then shall this hand and seal Witness against us to damnation! . . . . *K. John* iv 2 215
Proceeded Under your hands and seals . . . . *Hen. VIII.* ii 4 222

Hand in hand. Lock hand in hand; yourselves in order set . *Mer. Wives* v 5 81
Now let's go hand in hand, not one before another . . *Com. of Errors* v 1 425
Hand in hand, in sad conference . . . . *Much Ado* i 3 62
Hand in hand, with fairy grace, Will we sing . . *M. N. Dream* v 1 406
Let us to't pell-mell; If not to heaven, then hand in hand to hell *Rich. III.* v 3 313
Good old chronicle, That hast so long walk'd hand in hand with time *Troi. and Cres.* iv 5 203

Hand in hand. Will, hand in hand, all headlong cast us down *T. Andron.* v 3 132
And if you say we shall, Lo, hand in hand, Lucius and I will fall . v 3 136
The weird sisters, hand in hand, Posters of the sea and land . *Macbeth* i 3 32
It went hand in hand even with the vow I made to her in marriage *Hamlet* i 5 49
Where souls do couch on flowers, we'll hand in hand . *Ant. and Cleo.* iv 14 51
As fair and as good—a kind of hand-in-hand comparison . *Cymbeline* i 4 75
Hand of death. The sudden hand of death close up mine eye! *L. L. Lost* v 2 825
See them deliver'd over To execution and the hand of death *Richard II.* iii 1 30
But that the earthy and cold hand of death Lies on my tongue *1 Hen. IV.* v 4 84
The hand of death hath raught him . *Ant. and Cleo.* iv 9 30
Hand of fortune. What have you, my good friends, deserved at the hands of fortune? . *Hamlet* ii 2 246
Hand of France. Out of my dear love I'll give thee more Than e'er the coward hand of France can win . *K. John* ii 1 158
Who by the hand of France this day hath made Much work for tears in many an English mother . ii 1 302
Hand of God. Show us the hand of God That hath dismiss'd us from our stewardship . *Richard II.* iii 3 77
Let us deliver Our puissance into the hand of God . *Hen. V.* ii 2 190
Fears and scruples shake us: In the great hand of God I stand *Macbeth* ii 3 136
Hand of Greece. Such As Agamemnon and the hand of Greece Should hold up high in brass . *Troi. and Cres.* i 3 63
Hand of heaven. Sway'd and fashion'd by the hand of heaven *M. of Ven.* i 3 94
To be the— Very hand of heaven.—Ay, so I say . *All's Well* ii 3 37
Look, where the holy legate comes apace, To give us warrant from the hand of heaven . *K. John* v 2 66
Hand of justice. Having such a son, That would deliver up his greatness so Into the hands of justice . *2 Hen. IV.* v 2 112
Hand of man. Excels whatever yet you look'd upon Or hand of man hath done . *W. Tale* v 3 17
Hand of Mars. Who should withhold me? Not fate, obedience, nor the hand of Mars . *Troi. and Cres.* v 3 52
Hand of nature. A fellow by the hand of nature mark'd, Quoted and sign'd to do a deed of shame . *K. John* iv 2 221
Hand of peace. Whose beard the silver hand of peace hath touch'd *2 Hen. IV.* iv 1 43
Hand of sin. Poison and treason are the hands of sin *Pericles* i 1 139
Hand of time. The hand of time Shall draw this brief into as huge a volume . *K. John* ii 1 102
Hand of war. This fortress built by Nature for herself Against infection and the hand of war . *Richard II.* ii 1 44
Mothers shall but smile when they behold Their infants quarter'd with the hands of war . *J. Cæsar* iii 1 268
Hand to hand. In single opposition, hand to hand, He did confound the best part of an hour . *1 Hen. IV.* i 3 99
Hand to hand he would have vanquish'd thee . *3 Hen. VI.* ii 1 73
This man, whom hand to hand I slew in fight . ii 5 56
Handed. When I was young And handed love as you do, I was wont To load my she with knacks . *W. Tale* iv 4 359
What false Italian, As poisonous-tongued as handed, hath prevail'd On thy too ready hearing? . *Cymbeline* iii 2 5
Hand-fast. If that shepherd be not in hand-fast, let him fly . *W. Tale* iv 4 795
The agent for his master And the remembrancer of her to hold The hand-fast to her lord . *Cymbeline* i 5 78
Handful. That handful of wit! . *L. L. Lost* iv 1 149
I had rather have a handful or two of dried peas . *M. N. Dream* iv 1 41
Handicraft. He hath simply the best wit of any handicraft man in Athens iv 2 10
Handicrafts-men. Virtue is not regarded in handicrafts-men . *2 Hen. VI.* iv 2 12
Handiwork. We know his handiwork . *K. John* i 1 238
That foul defacer of God's handiwork . *Richard III.* iv 4 51
As proper men as ever trod upon neat's leather have gone upon my handiwork . *J. Cæsar* i 1 30
Handkercher. And how, and why, and where This handkercher was stain'd . *As Y. Like It* iv 3 98
Did your brother tell you how I counterfeited to swoon when he showed me your handkerchief? . v 2 30
Good Tom Drum, lend me a handkercher. *All's Well* v 3 322
When your head did but ache, I knit my handkercher about your brows *K. John* iv 1 42
They would have me as familiar with men's pockets as their gloves or their handkerchers . *Hen. V.* iii 2 52
Matrons flung gloves, Ladies and maids their scarfs and handkerchers *Coriolanus* ii 1 280
Handkerchief. Who has not only his innocence, which seems much, to justify him, but a handkerchief and rings of his . *W. Tale* v 2 71
Therefore present to her,—as sometime Margaret Did to thy father, steep'd in Rutland's blood,—A handkerchief . *Richard III.* iv 4 276
What will you give me now For that same handkerchief?—What handkerchief?—What handkerchief! Why, that the Moor first gave to Desdemona . *Othello* iii 3 306
Have you not sometimes seen a handkerchief Spotted with strawberries in your wife's hand . iii 3 434
Such a handkerchief—I am sure it was your wife's—did I to-day See Cassio wipe his beard with . iii 3 437
Where should I lose that handkerchief, Emilia?—I know not, madam . iii 4 23
I have a salt and sorry rheum offends me; Lend me thy handkerchief . iii 4 52
That handkerchief Did an Egyptian to my mother give . iii 4 55
Fetch me the handkerchief: my mind misgives . iii 4 89
The handkerchief!—I pray, talk me of Cassio.—The handkerchief! . iii 4 92
There's some wonder in this handkerchief: I am most unhappy in the loss of it . iii 4 101
But if I give my wife a handkerchief,— What then?—Why, then, 'tis hers . iv 1 10
But for the handkerchief,— By heaven, I would most gladly have forgot it . iv 1 18
He had my handkerchief.—Ay, what of that?—That's not so good now iv 1 22
Handkerchief—confessions—handkerchief!—To confess, and be hanged iv 1 37
Pish! Noses, ears, and lips.—Is't possible?—Confess—handkerchief!. iv 1 43
What did you mean by that same handkerchief you gave me even now? iv 1 154
By heaven, that should be my handkerchief! . iv 1 164
And did you see the handkerchief?—Was that mine? . iv 1 183
That handkerchief which I so loved and gave thee Thou gavest to Cassio v 2 48
I never gave him token.—By heaven, I saw my handkerchief in's hand v 2 62
I saw the handkerchief.—He found it then; I never gave it him . v 2 66
It was a handkerchief, an antique token My father gave my mother . v 2 216
That handkerchief thou speak'st of I found by fortune and did give my husband . v 2 225
How came you, Cassio, by that handkerchief That was my wife's? . v 2 319
Then waved his handkerchief?—And kiss'd it, madam.—Senseless linen! happier therein than I! . *Cymbeline* i 3 6
Handkerchief. He did keep The deck, with glove, or hat, or handkerchief, Still waving . *Cymbeline* i 3 11
Handle. When Mistress Bridget lost the handle of her fan, I took't upon mine honour thou hadst it not . *Mer. Wives* ii 2 12
Give me leave to question; you shall see how I'll handle her *M. for M.* v 1 273
Points more than all the lawyers in Bohemia can learnedly handle *W. T.* iv 4 207
No hand of blood and bone Can gripe the sacred handle of our sceptre *Richard II.* iii 3 80
I know how to handle you . *2 Hen. IV.* ii 4 339
A' did in some sort, indeed, handle women; but then he was rheumatic *Hen. V.* ii 3 39
You thought, because he could not speak English in the native garb, he could not therefore handle an English cudgel . v 1 81
And not to wear, handle, or use any sword, weapon, or dagger *1 Hen. VI.* i 3 78
This hand was made to handle nought but gold . *2 Hen. VI.* v 1 7
Go to; have your lath glued within your sheath Till you know better how to handle it . *T. Andron.* ii 1 42
O, handle not the theme, to talk of hands . iii 2 29
Is this a dagger which I see before me, The handle toward my hand? *Macbeth* ii 1 34
That fellow handles his bow like a crow-keeper . *Lear* iv 6 87
Handled. I think, if you handled her privately, she would sooner confess *Meas. for Meas.* v 1 276
How wert thou handled being prisoner? . *1 Hen. VI.* i 4 24
A stouter champion never handled sword. . iii 4 19
Left nothing fitting for the purpose Untouch'd, or slightly handled, in discourse . *Richard III.* iii 7 19
Handless. Noseless, handless, hack'd and chipp'd . *Troi. and Cres.* v 5 34
Speak, Lavinia, what accursed hand Hath made thee handless? *T. An.* iii 1 67
Handlest in thy discourse, O, that her hand . *Troi. and Cres.* i 1 55
Handling. We are still handling our ewes, and their fells, you know, are greasy . *As Y. Like It* iii 2 54
A rotten case abides no handling . *2 Hen. IV.* iv 1 161
Then they will endure handling, which before would not abide looking on . *Hen. V.* v 2 337
Humble as the ripest mulberry That will not hold the handling *Coriol.* iii 2 80
Handmaid. But from her handmaid do return this answer . *T. Night* i 1 25
Stay, let thy humble handmaid speak to thee . *1 Hen. VI.* iii 3 42
Speak my thanks and my obedience, As from a blushing handmaid *Hen. VIII.* ii 3 72
She will a handmaid be to his desires, A loving nurse . *T. Andron.* i 1 331
Fear and niceness—The handmaids of all women . *Cymbeline* iii 4 159
Handsaw. My sword hacked like a hand-saw—ecce signum! . *1 Hen. IV.* ii 4 187
When the wind is southerly I know a hawk from a handsaw *Hamlet* ii 2 397
Handsome. O, what a world of vile ill-favour'd faults Looks handsome in three hundred pounds a-year! *Mer. Wives* iii 4 33
But yet for all that, cousin, let him be a handsome fellow *Much Ado* ii 1 58
One that hath two gowns and every thing handsome about him . iv 2 89
If a man will be beaten with brains, a' shall wear nothing handsome . v 4 105
Is't not a handsome gentleman?—I like him well . *All's Well* iii 5 83
Prove that ever I dress myself handsome till thy return . *2 Hen. IV.* ii 4 303
A bachelor, a handsome stripling too *Richard III.* i 3 101
They were young and handsome, and of the best breed in the north *Hen. VIII.* ii 2 4
An honest gentleman, and a courteous, and a kind, and a handsome *Rom. and Jul.* ii 5 57
And by very much more handsome than fine . *Hamlet* ii 2 466
The knave is handsome, young, and hath all those requisites in him that folly and green minds look after. *Othello* ii 1 250
A proper man.—A very handsome man.—He speaks well . iv 3 36
It is a heart-breaking to see a handsome man loose-wived *Ant. and Cleo.* i 2 75
Now, afore me, a handsome fellow! Come, thou shalt go home *Pericles* ii 1 84
Handsomely. As you look To have my pardon, trim it handsomely *Temp.* v 1 293
His garments are rich, but he wears them not handsomely *W. Tale* iv 4 777
An if we miss to meet him handsomely . *T. Andron.* ii 3 268
Handsomeness. I will beat thee into handsomeness . *Troi. and Cres.* ii 1 16
Handwriting. If the skin were parchment and the blows you gave were ink, Your own handwriting would tell you what I think *Com. of Er.* iii 1 14
Handy-dandy, which is the justice, which is the thief? . *Lear* iv 6 157
Hang, cur! hang, you whoreson, insolent noisemaker! . *Tempest* i 1 46
Hence! hang not on my garments . i 2 474
For she had a tongue with a tang, Would cry to a sailor, Go hang! . ii 2 53
Then to sea, boys, and let her go hang! . ii 2 56
And even with such-like valour men hang and drown Their proper selves iii 3 59
I will plague them all, Even to roaring. Come, hang them on this line iv 1 193
Merrily, merrily shall I live now Under the blossom that hangs on the bough . v 1 94
'Out with the dog!' says one: 'What cur is that?' says another: 'Whip him out,' says the third: 'Hang him up,' says the duke *T. G. of Ver.* iv 4 24
Hang the trifle, woman! take the honour *Mer. Wives* ii 1 46
Do you think there is truth in them?—Hang 'em, slaves! . ii 1 179
Hang no more about me, I am no gibbet for you . ii 2 17
Hang him, poor cuckoldy knave! I know him not . ii 2 281
Hang him, mechanical salt-butter rogue! I will stare him out of his wits ii 2 290
I will awe him with my cudgel: it shall hang like a meteor o'er the cuckold's horns . ii 2 292
As idle as she may hang together, for want of company . iii 2 13
Hang him, dishonest rascal! . iii 3 196
Accusativo, hung, hang, hog.—'Hang-hog' is Latin for bacon . iv 1 49
Hang him, dishonest varlet! we cannot misuse him enough . iv 2 104
Hang her, witch!—By yea and no, I think the 'oman is a witch indeed iv 2 201
I would not have you acquainted with tapsters: they will draw you, Master Froth, and you will hang them . *Meas. for Meas.* ii 1 216
If you head and hang all that offend that way but for ten year together ii 1 251
Entreat him; Kneel down before him, hang upon his gown: You are too cold . ii 2 44
If you will hang me for it, you may; but I had rather it would please you I might be whipt . v 1 510
'My mistress, sir,' quoth I; 'Hang up thy mistress! I know not thy mistress; out on thy mistress!' . *Com. of Errors* ii 1 67
He will hang upon him like a disease *Much Ado* i 1 86
I will have a recheat winded in my forehead, or hang my bugle in an invisible baldrick . i 1 243
And hang me up at the door of a brothel-house for the sign of blind Cupid . i 1 255
If I do, hang me in a bottle like a cat and shoot at me . i 1 259
It were an alms to hang him . ii 3 165
Hang him, truant! there's no true drop of blood in him . iii 2 18
I have the toothache.—Draw it.—Hang it!—You must hang it first, and draw it afterwards . iii 2 23

Hang. I would not hang a dog by my will, much more a man *Much Ado* iii 3 66
I'll lock up all the gates of love, And on my eyelids shall conjecture hang iv 1 107
And on your family's old monument Hang mournful epitaphs iv 1 209
Hang her an epitaph upon her tomb And sing it to her bones v 1 293
Hang thou there upon the tomb, Praising her when I am dumb v 3 9
But, if thou marry, Hang me by the neck, if horns that year miscarry *L. L. Lost* iv 1 114
I will not love: if I do, hang me; i' faith, I will not iv 3 9
The corner-cap of society, The shape of Love's Tyburn that hangs up simplicity iv 3 54
Will they not, think you, hang themselves to-night? v 2 270
What mean you, sir?—To make Judas hang himself v 2 608
When icicles hang by the wall And Dick the shepherd blows his nail v 2 922
They would shriek; and that were enough to hang us all.—That would hang us, every mother's son *M. N. Dream* i 2 79
If that you should fright the ladies out of their wits, they would have no more discretion but to hang us i 2 83
I must go seek some dewdrops here And hang a pearl in every cowslip's ear ii 1 15
Hang off, thou cat, thou burr! vile thing, let loose! iii 2 260
Let not him that plays the lion pare his nails, for they shall hang out for the lion's claws iv 2 42
Her sunny locks Hang on her temples like a golden fleece *Mer. of Venice* i 1 170
Beg that thou mayst have leave to hang thyself iv 1 364
What passion hangs these weights upon my tongue? *As Y. Like It* i 2 269
Hang there, my verse, in witness of my love iii 2 1
Tongues I'll hang on every tree, That shall civil sayings show iii 2 135
Hangs odes upon hawthorns and elegies on brambles iii 2 379
Are you he that hangs the verses on the trees? iii 2 411
Carry him gently to my fairest chamber, And hang it round with all my wanton pictures *T. of Shrew* Ind. 1 47
Will he woo her? ay, or I'll hang her i 2 198
Be mad and merry, or go hang yourselves iii 2 228
He that hangs himself is a virgin: virginity murders itself *All's Well* i 1 150
I know that knave; hang him! one Parolles: a filthy officer iii 5 17
Marry, hang you!—And your courtesy, for a ring-carrier! iii 5 94
I perceive, sir, by the general's looks, we shall be fain to hang you iv 3 269
Let them hang themselves in their own straps *T. Night* i 3 13
Excellent; it [your hair] hangs like flax on a distaff i 3 108
My lady will hang thee for thy absence.—Let her hang me i 5 4
Marry, hang thee, brock! ii 5 114
Where you will hang like an icicle on a Dutchman's beard iii 2 29
'Tis not for gravity to play at cherry-pit with Satan: hang him, foul collier! iii 4 130
Go, hang yourselves all! you are idle shallow things iii 4 136
Should all despair That have revolted wives, the tenth of mankind Would hang themselves *W. Tale* i 2 200
Stay her tongue.—Hang all the husbands That cannot do that feat, you'll leave yourself Hardly one subject ii 3 110
Hang him, he'll be made an example iv 4 847
She hangs about his neck: If she pertain to life let her speak too v 3 112
Now, by the sky that hangs above our heads, I like it well *K. John* ii 1 397
And hang a calf's-skin on those recreant limbs iii 1 129; 131; 133; 199
Hang no more in doubt.—Hang nothing but a calf's-skin, most sweet lout iii 1 219
My reasonable part produces reason How I may be deliver'd of these woes, And teaches me to kill or hang myself iii 4 56
A rush will be a beam To hang thee on iv 3 130
Suppose Devouring pestilence hangs in our air And thou art flying to a fresher clime *Richard II.* i 3 284
What seal is that, that hangs without thy bosom? Yea, look'st thou pale? v 2 56
If any plague hang over us, 'tis he v 3 3
Do not thou, when thou art king, hang a thief *1 Hen. IV.* i 2 70
If I tarry at home and go not, I'll hang you for going i 2 150
If I hang, I'll make a fat pair of gallows; for if I hang, old Sir John hangs with me, and thou knowest he is no starveling ii 1 74
Go, hang thyself in thine own heir-apparent garters! ii 2 46
Hang ye, gorbellied knaves, are ye undone? No, ye fat chuffs ii 2 93
Hang him! let him tell the king: we are prepared ii 3 36
Hang me up by the heels for a rabbit-sucker ii 4 479
Those musicians that shall play to you Hang in the air a thousand leagues from hence iii 1 227
My skin hangs about me like an old lady's loose gown iii 3 3
If thou gettest any leave of me, hang me; if thou takest leave, thou wert better be hanged *2 Hen. IV.* i 2 101
Hang yourself, you muddy conger, hang yourself! ii 4 58
Hang him, swaggering rascal! let him not come hither ii 4 76
Hang him, rogue! he lives upon mouldy stewed prunes and dried cakes ii 4 158
They say Poins has a good wit.—He a good wit? hang him, baboon! ii 4 261
And hangs resolved correction in the arm That was uprear'd to execution iv 1 213
Let us not hang like roping icicles Upon our houses' thatch *Hen. V.* iii 5 23
Will hang upon my tongue like a new-married wife about her husband's neck v 2 189
In my gallery thy picture hangs *1 Hen. VI.* ii 3 37
Signior, no.—Signior, hang! base muleters of France iii 2 68
Rouen hangs her head for grief That such a valiant company are fled iii 2 124
Till mischief and despair Drive you to break your necks or hang yourselves v 4 91
Hang up your ensigns, let your drums be still v 4 174
Alas, my lord, hang me, if ever I spake the words *2 Hen. VI.* i 3 200
Thus droops this lofty pine and hangs his sprays ii 3 45
Nor stir at nothing till the axe of death Hang over thee ii 4 50
It [my shame] will hang upon my richest robes And show itself ii 4 108
The welfare of us all Hangs on the cutting short that fraudful man iii 1 81
Hang him with his pen and ink-horn about his neck iv 2 116
Sword, I will hallow thee for this thy deed, And hang thee o'er my tomb iv 10 73
Thou canst make No excuse current, but to hang thyself *Richard III.* i 2 84
Mark how well the sequel hangs together: Eleven hours I spent to write it iii 6 4
Like the lily, That once was mistress of the field and flourish'd, I'll hang my head and perish *Hen. VIII.* iii 1 153
O, how wretched Is that poor man that hangs on princes' favours! iii 2 367
Her foes shake like a field of beaten corn, And hang their heads with sorrow v 5 33
Not for the worth that hangs upon our quarrel *Troi. and Cres.* ii 3 217
He hangs the lip at something iii 1 152
To have done is to hang Quite out of fashion, like a rusty mail iii 3 151
Go hang yourself, you naughty mocking uncle! iv 2 26
Hang ye! Trust ye? With every minute you do change a mind *Coriolanus* i 1 185
They say, The city is well stored.—Hang 'em! They say! i 1 194

Hang. Hang 'em! They said they were an-hungry; sigh'd forth proverbs *Coriolanus* i 1 208
They threw their caps As they would hang them on the horns o' the moon i 1 217
That it was no better than picture-like to hang by the wall i 3 12
Think upon me! hang 'em! I would they would forget me ii 3 62
Let them hang.—Ay, and burn too iii 2 23
Chaste as the icicle That's curdied by the frost from purest snow And hangs on Dian's temple v 3 67
If you fail in our request, the blame May hang upon your hardness v 3 91
An 'twere my case, I should go hang myself *T. Andron.* ii 4 9
How would he hang his slender gilded wings, And buzz lamenting doings! iii 2 61
Go, take him away, and hang him presently iv 4 45
These tidings nip me, and I hang the head As flowers with frost or grass beat down with storms iv 4 70
Hang him on this tree, And by his side his fruit of bastardy v 1 47
First hang the child, that he may see it sprawl v 1 51
It seems she hangs upon the cheek of night Like a rich jewel in an Ethiope's ear *Rom. and Jul.* i 5 47
Hang up philosophy! Unless philosophy can make a Juliet iii 3 57
Hang thee, young baggage! disobedient wretch! iii 5 161
Hang, beg, starve, die in the streets, For, by my soul, I'll ne'er acknowledge thee iii 5 194
What a pestilent knave is this same!—Hang him, Jack! iv 5 149
Contempt and beggary hangs upon thy back v 1 71
I will kiss thy lips; Haply some poison yet doth hang on them v 3 165
Hang thyself!—No, I will do nothing at thy bidding *T. of Athens* i 1 277
Hang him, he'll abuse us.—A plague upon him, dog! ii 2 49
There's the fool hangs on your back already.—No, thou stand'st single ii 2 56
Hang thee, monster!—Pardon him, sweet Timandra iv 3 87
When Jove Will o'er some high-viced city hang his poison In the sick air iv 3 109
Were all the wealth I have shut up in thee, I'ld give thee leave to hang it iv 3 280
Hang them or stab them, drown them in a draught, Confound them by some course v 1 105
Whoso please To stop affliction, let him take his haste, Come hither, ere my tree hath felt the axe, And hang himself v 1 215
Night hangs upon mine eyes; my bones would rest *J. Cæsar* v 5 41
Sleep shall neither night nor day Hang upon his pent-house lid *Macbeth* i 3 20
Upon the corner of the moon There hangs a vaporous drop profound iii 5 24
Must they all be hanged that swear and lie?—Every one.—Who must hang them?—Why, the honest men iv 2 54
There are liars and swearers enow to beat the honest men and hang up them iv 2 58
And sundry blessings hang about his throne, That speak him full of grace iv 3 158
Now does he feel his title Hang loose about him, like a giant's robe Upon a dwarfish thief v 2 21
Hang those that talk of fear. Give me mine armour v 3 36
Hang out our banners on the outward walls; The cry is still 'They come' v 5 1
If thou speak'st false, Upon the next tree shalt thou hang alive v 5 39
How is it that the clouds still hang on you?—Not so, my lord *Hamlet* i 2 66
She would hang on him, As if increase of appetite had grown By what it fed on i 2 143
There, on the pendent boughs her coronet weeds Clambering to hang, an envious sliver broke iv 7 174
And the more pity that great folk should have countenance in this world to drown or hang themselves v 1 31
Now, all the plagues that in the pendulous air Hang fated o'er men's faults light on thy daughters! *Lear* iii 4 70
Seek out the villain Gloucester.—Hang him instantly.—Pluck out his eyes iii 7 4
Half way down Hangs one that gathers samphire, dreadful trade! iv 6 15
The usurer hangs the cozener iv 6 167
O my dear father! Restoration hang Thy medicine on my lips! iv 7 26
He hath commission from thy wife and me To hang Cordelia in the prison v 3 253
I am glad at soul I have no other child; For thy escape would teach me tyranny, To hang clogs on them *Othello* i 3 198
O, thereby hangs a tail.—Whereby hangs a tale, sir? iii 1 8
So prove it, That the probation bear no hinge nor loop To hang a doubt on iii 3 366
So hangs, and lolls, and weeps upon me; so hales, and pulls me iv 1 143
Hang her! I do but say what she is: so delicate with her needle iv 1 198
I have much to do, But to go hang my head all at one side, And sing it iv 3 32
When your diver Did hang a salt-fish on his hook *Ant. and Cleo.* ii 5 17
Go hang, sir, hang! ii 7 59
My enfranched bondman, whom He may at pleasure whip, or hang, or torture iii 13 150
That life, a very rebel to my will, May hang no longer on me iv 9 15
Rather make My country's high pyramides my gibbet, And hang me up in chains! v 2 62
We, Your scutcheons and your signs of conquest, shall Hang in what place you please v 2 136
'Tis gold Which makes the true man kill'd and saves the thief; Nay, sometime hangs both thief and true man *Cymbeline* ii 3 77
Poor I am stale, a garment out of fashion; And, for I am richer than to hang by the walls, I must be ripp'd iii 4 54
Hang there like fruit, my soul, Till the tree die! v 5 263
Here's a fish hangs in the net, like a poor man's right in the law *Pericles* ii 1 123
The purple violets, and marigolds, Shall as a carpet hang upon thy grave iv 1 17
Marry, hang her up for ever! iv 6 146
Marry, hang you! She's born to undo us iv 6 158
It nips me unto listening, and thick slumber Hangs upon mine eyes v 1 236
Thereby hangs a tale *Mer. Wives* i 4; *As Y. Like It* ii 7; *T. of Shrew* iv 1; *Othello* iii 1

Hanged. If he be not born to be hanged, our case is miserable *Tempest* i 1 35
He'll be hang'd yet, Though every drop of water swear against it i 1 61
I reckon this always, that a man is never undone till he be hanged *T. G. of Ver.* ii 5 5
If I had not had more wit than he, to take a fault upon me that he did, I think verily he had been hanged for't iv 4 16
My cousin meant well.—Ay, or else I would I might be hanged, la! *M. W.* i 1 266
I'll make the best in Gloucestershire know on't; would I were hanged, la, else! v 5 191
Ere he would have hanged a man for the getting a hundred bastards, he would have paid for the nursing a thousand *Meas. for Meas.* iii 2 124
You'll forswear this again.—I'll be hanged first: thou art deceived in me iii 2 178
What mystery there should be in hanging, if I should be hanged, I cannot imagine iv 2 42

Hanged. Master Barnardine! you must rise and be hanged *M. for M.* iv 3 24
He that drinks all night, and is hanged betimes in the morning, may sleep the sounder all the next day . . . . iv 3 49
Show your sheep-biting face, and be hanged an hour! . . . . v 1 360
Please you I might be whipt.—Whipt first, sir, and hanged after . v 1 513
He shall marry her: the nuptial finish'd, Let him be whipt and hang'd v 1 519
And he had been a dog that should have howled thus, they would have hanged him . . . . *Much Ado* ii 3 82
You are my elder.—Well followed: Judas was hanged on an elder *L. L. L.* v 2 610
Then shall Hector be whipped for Jaquenetta that is quick by him and hanged for Pompey that is dead by him . . . . . . v 2 687
An the duke had not given him sixpence a day for playing Pyramus, I'll be hanged; he would have deserved it . . . *M. N. Dream* iv 2 23
If he that writ it had played Pyramus and hanged himself in Thisbe's garter, it would have been a fine tragedy . . . . . . v 1 366
Thy currish spirit Govern'd a wolf, who, hang'd for human slaughter, Even from the gallows did his fell soul fleet . . *Mer. of Venice* iv 1 134
Therefore thou must be hang'd at the state's charge . . . . iv 1 367
How thy name should be hanged and carved upon these trees *As Y. L. It* iii 2 182
Sunday is the wedding-day.—I'll see thee hang'd on Sunday first *T. of S.* ii 1 301
He that is well hanged in this world needs to fear no colours . *T. Night* i 5 5
You will be hanged for being so long absent; or, to be turned away . i 5 17
Thou art worthy to be hang'd, That wilt not stay her tongue *W. Tale* ii 3 109
Hang'd in the frowning wrinkle of her brow! . . . . *K. John* ii 1 505
This is pity now, That, hang'd and drawn and quarter'd, there should be In such a love so vile a lout as he . . . . ii 1 508
On that day at noon, whereon he says I shall yield up my crown, let him be hang'd . . . . iv 2 157
If you will not, tarry at home and be hanged . . . . 1 *Hen. IV.* i 2 148
Heigh-ho! an it be not four by the day, I'll be hanged . . . . ii 1 2
Come, and be hanged! hast no faith in thee? . . . . . ii 1 34
Lend me thy lantern, quoth he? marry, I'll see thee hanged first . . ii 1 44
Poins! Poins, and be hanged! Poins!—Peace, ye fat-kidneyed rascal! . ii 2 4
If the rascal have not given me medicines to make me love him, I'll be hanged . . . . ii 2 20
Give me my horse, you rogues; give me my horse, and be hanged! . ii 2 32
There's enough to make us all.—To be hanged . . . . . ii 2 61
Stand fast.—Now cannot I strike him, if I should be hanged . . . ii 2 77
If thou takest leave, thou wert better be hanged . . . 2 *Hen. IV.* i 2 102
And you do not make him hanged among you, the gallows shall have wrong . . . . ii 2 104
I had as lief be hanged, sir, as go . . . . iii 2 238
I would to God that I might die, that I might have thee hanged . . v 4 2
For he hath stolen a pax, and hanged must a' be . . . *Hen. V.* iii 6 42
If ever I live to see it, I will challenge it.—Thou darest as well be hanged iv 1 235
They are both hanged; and so would this be, if he durst steal any thing iv 4 77
Sirrah, or you must fight, or else be hang'd . . . . 2 *Hen. VI.* i 3 222
Even in their wives' and children's sight, Be hang'd up for example . iv 2 190
Because they could not read, thou hast hanged them . . . . iv 7 49
Will you needs be hanged with your pardons about your necks? . . iv 8 22
Wilt thou go along?—Better do so than tarry and be hang'd 3 *Hen. VI.* iv 5 26
Who, but for dreaming on this fond exploit, For want of means, poor rats, had hang'd themselves . . . . . . *Richard III.* v 3 331
I belong to the larder.—Belong to the gallows, and be hanged! *Hen. VIII.* v 4 6
How got they in, and be hang'd?—Alas, I know not; how gets the tide in? . . . . v 4 17
I will see you hanged, like clotpoles, ere I come any more *Troi. and Cres.* ii 1 128
Would I were hanged, but I thought there was more in him *Coriolanus* iv 5 166
The man must not be hanged till the next week . . *T. Andron.* iv 3 82
You must be hanged.—Hanged! by'r lady, then I have brought up a neck to a fair end . . . . iv 4 47
My man.—But I'll be hang'd, sir, if he wear your livery *Rom. and Jul.* iii 1 60
Ho, ho, confess'd it! hang'd it, have you not? . . . *T. of Athens* i 2 22
There will little learning die then, that day thou art hanged . . . ii 2 87
Some that were hang'd, No matter:—wear them, betray with them . iv 3 145
Speak, and be hang'd: For each true word, a blister! . . . . v 1 134
I can as well be hanged as tell the manner of it . . . *J. Cæsar* i 2 235
Here's a farmer, that hanged himself on the expectation of plenty *Macb.* ii 3 5
Every one that does so is a traitor, and must be hanged.—And must they all be hanged that swear and lie?—Every one . . . . iv 2 50
And my poor fool is hanged! No, no, no life! . . . . *Lear* v 3 305
Seek thou rather to be hanged in compassing thy joy than to be drowned and go without her . . . . *Othello* i 3 367
To confess, and be hanged for his labour;—first, to be hanged . iv 1 38
I will be hang'd, if some eternal villain . . . Have not devised this slander; I'll be hang'd else . . . . iv 2 130
Let Neptune hear we bid a loud farewell To these great fellows: sound and be hang'd, sound out! . . . . *Ant. and Cleo.* ii 7 140
For this pains Cæsar hath hang'd him . . . . iv 6 16
It was hang'd With tapestry of silk and silver . . . . *Cymbeline* ii 4 63
I am called to be made free.—I'll be hang'd then . . . . . v 4 203
If I do it not, I am sure to be hanged at home: 'tis dangerous *Pericles* i 3 3
Well, I perceive I shall not be hang'd now, although I would . . i 3 27

Hanger. Six French rapiers and poniards, with their assigns, as girdle, hangers, and so . . . . *Hamlet* v 2 157
The carriages, sir, are the hangers.—The phrase would be more german to the matter, if we could carry cannon by our sides: I would it might be hangers till then . . . . v 2 164

Hangest. Stand from him, fellow: wherefore hang'st upon him? 2 *Hen. IV.* ii 1 74

Hangeth. Ripe as the pomewater, who now hangeth like a jewel in the ear of caelo . . . . *L. L. Lost* iv 2 4
Reproach and dissolution hangeth over him . . . *Richard II.* ii 1 258

Hang-hog is Latin for bacon, I warrant you . . . *Mer. Wives* iv 1 50

Hanging. Stand fast, good Fate, to his hanging . . . *Tempest* i 1 33
Dew-lapp'd like bulls, whose throats had hanging at 'em Wallets of flesh iii 3 45
Vouchsafe me yet your picture for my love, The picture that is hanging in your chamber . . . . *T. G. of Ver.* iv 2 122
There are pretty orders beginning, I can tell you: it is but heading and hanging . . . . *Meas. for Meas.* ii 1 250
A good favour you have, but that you have a hanging look . . iv 2 35
What mystery there should be in hanging, if I should be hanged, I cannot imagine . . . . iv 2 42
This may prove worse than hanging . . . . v 1 365
Marrying a punk, my lord, is pressing to death, whipping, and hanging v 1 529
They say he wears a key in his ear and a lock hanging by it . *Much Ado* v 1 318
My conscience, hanging about the neck of my heart . . *Mer. of Venice* ii 2 14
The ancient saying is no heresy, Hanging and wiving goes by destiny . ii 9 83
My hangings all of Tyrian tapestry . . . . . . *T. of Shrew* ii 1 351
To be turned away, is not that as good as a hanging to you? . *T. Night* i 5 19
Hanging. Many a good hanging prevents a bad marriage . . *T. Night* i 5 20
He that wears her like her medal, hanging About his neck . *W. Tale* i 2 307
Beating and hanging are terrors to me: for the life to come, I sleep out the thought of it . . . . iv 3 30
I am sorry that by hanging thee I can But shorten thy life one week . iv 4 432
If they have overheard me now, why, hanging . . . . . . iv 4 640
Every shop, church, session, hanging, yields a careful man work . . iv 4 701
I mean, thou shalt have the hanging of the thieves . . . 1 *Hen. IV.* i 2 75
I doubt not but to die a fair death for all this, if I 'scape hanging . ii 2 15
A villanous trick of thine eye and a foolish hanging of thy nether lip . ii 4 446
Had my sweet Harry had but half their numbers, To-day might I, hanging on Hotspur's neck, Have talk'd of Monmouth's grave 2 *Hen. IV.* ii 3 44
Who take the ruffian billows by the top, Curling their monstrous heads and hanging them With deafening clamour in the slippery clouds . iii 1 23
Like over-ripen'd corn, Hanging the head at Ceres' plenteous load 2 *Hen. VI.* i 2 2
Like rich hangings in a homely house, So was his will in his old feeble body . . . . v 3 12
Whose heavy looks foretell Some dreadful story hanging on thy tongue 3 *Hen. VI.* ii 1 44
A thrifty shoeing-horn in a chain, hanging at his brother's leg *T. and C.* v 1 62
The state of hanging, or of some death more long in spectatorship, and crueller in suffering . . . . *Coriolanus* v 2 70
He must not die So sweet a death as hanging . . . *T. Andron.* v 1 146
Small consequence yet hanging in the stars Shall bitterly begin his fearful date With this night's revels . . . . *Rom. and Jul.* i 4 107
His large fortune Upon his good and gracious nature hanging *T. of Athens* i 1 56
Go, suck the subtle blood o' the grape, Till the high fever seethe your blood to froth, And so 'scape hanging . . . . iv 3 434
He cures, Hanging a golden stamp about their necks . . *Macbeth* iv 3 153
I kill'd the slave that was a-hanging thee.—'Tis true, my lords . *Lear* v 3 274
On such creatures as We count not worth the hanging . *Cymbeline* i 5 20
A storm or robbery, call it what you will, Shook down my mellow hangings . . . . iii 3 63
Hanging is the word, sir: if you be ready for that, you are well cooked v 4 155
I am sure hanging's the way of winking . . . . v 4 197

Hangman. Stolen from me by the hangman boys . . *T. G. of Ver.* iv 4 60
I will be content to be a lawful hangman . . . *Meas. for Meas.* iv 2 18
Your hangman is a more penitent trade than your bawd . . . . iv 2 53
Who makes that noise there? What are you?—Your friends, sir; the hangman . . . . iv 3 28
The little hangman [Cupid] dare not shoot at him . . . *Much Ado* iii 2 11
No metal can, No, not the hangman's axe, bear half the keenness Of thy sharp envy . . . . *Mer. of Venice* iv 1 125
But now Some hangman must put on my shroud . . . *W. Tale* iv 4 468
Those that are germane to him, though removed fifty times, shall all come under the hangman . . . . iv 4 803
Thou shalt have the hanging of the thieves and so become a rare hangman . . . . 1 *Hen. IV.* i 2 76
Obtaining of suits, whereof the hangman hath no lean wardrobe . . i 2 82
The agents, or base second means, The cords, the ladder, or the hangman i 3 166
I'll give thee this neck.—No, I'll none of it: I pray thee, keep that for the hangman . . . . ii 1 70
What talkest thou to me of the hangman? . . . . ii 1 73
Leaden spoons, Irons of a doit, doublets that hangmen would Bury with those that wore them . . . . *Coriolanus* i 5 7
Worth all your predecessors since Deucalion, though peradventure some of the best of 'em were hereditary hangmen . . . . . . ii 1 103
As good a trick as ever hangman served thief . . . *T. of Athens* ii 2 100
One cried 'God bless us!' and 'Amen' the other; As they had seen me with these hangman's hands . . . . *Macbeth* ii 2 28
By heaven, I rather would have been his hangman . . . . *Othello* i 1 34
To proclaim it civilly, were like A halter'd neck which does the hangman thank For being yare about him . . . . *Ant. and Cleo.* iii 13 130
But a man that were to sleep your sleep, and a hangman to help him to bed, I think he would change places with his officer . *Cymbeline* v 4 179
I must have your maidenhead taken off, or the common hangman shall execute it. Come your ways . . . . *Pericles* iv 6 137
Serve by indenture to the common hangman: Any of these ways are yet better than this . . . . iv 6 187

Hannibal. O thou wicked Hannibal! . . . . *Meas. for Meas.* ii 1 183
Prove this, thou wicked Hannibal, or I'll have mine action of battery on thee . . . . ii 1 187
This Hector far surmounted Hannibal . . . . . *L. L. Lost* v 2 677
A witch, by fear, not force, like Hannibal, Drives back our troops 1 *Hen. VI.* i 5 21

Hap. Make yourself ready in your cabin for the mischance of the hour, if it so hap . . . . *Tempest* i 1 28
Wish me partaker in thy happiness When thou dost meet good hap *T. G. of Ver.* i 1 15
Happy but for me, And by me, had not our hap been bad *Com. of Errors* i 1 39
Knowing whom it was their hap to save . . . . i 1 114
If it proves so, then loving goes by haps . . . . . . *Much Ado* iii 1 105
What's her name in the cap?—Rosaline, by good hap . *L. L. Lost* ii 1 210
Whose hap shall be to have her Will not so graceless be to be ingrate *T. of Shrew* i 2 269
Wherefore should I doubt? Hap what hap may, I'll roundly go about her . . . . iv 4 108
What else may hap to time I will commit . . . . *T. Night* i 2 60
Until the heavens, envying earth's good hap, Add an immortal title *Richard II.* i 1 23
More blessed hap did ne'er befall our state . . . 1 *Hen. VI.* i 6 10
Or how haps it I seek not to advance Or raise myself? . . . . iii 1 31
Try your hap against the Irishmen?—I will, my lord . 2 *Hen. VI.* iii 1 314
What hap? what hope of good?—Our hap is loss . . 3 *Hen. VI.* ii 3 8
How haps it, in this smooth discourse, You told not? . . . . iii 3 88
More direful hap betide that hated wretch! . . . *Richard III.* i 2 17
By Him that raised me to this careful height From that contented hap which I enjoy'd . . . . i 3 84
For 'tis ill hap, If they [men] hold when their ladies bid 'em clap *Hen. VIII.* Epil. 13
Strong and ready for this hint, When we shall hap to give 't them *Coriol.* iii 3 24
When it is thy hap To find another that is like to thee . . *T. Andron* v 2 101
By whom our heavy haps had their beginning . . . . . . v 3 202
Hence will I to my ghostly father's cell, His help to crave, and my dear hap to tell . . . . *Rom. and Jul.* ii 2 190
He shall signify from time to time Every good hap to you that chances here . . . . iii 3 171
See, by good hap, yonder's my lord . . . . . . *T. of Athens* iii 2 27

Hap. Whatsoever else shall hap to-night, Give it an understanding *Hamlet* i 2 249
Till I know 'tis done, Howe'er my haps, my joys were ne'er begun . iv 3 70
What will hap more to-night, safe 'scape the king! . . . . *Lear* iii 6 121
Be it art or hap, He hath spoken true: the very dice obey him *A. and C.* ii 3 32
To fulfil his prince' desire, Sends word of all that haps in Tyre *Per.* ii Gower 22
Hapless. If haply won, perhaps a hapless gain . . . *T. G. of Ver.* i 1 32
Come, Valentine.—O my dear Silvia! Hapless Valentine! . . . iii 1 260
Hapless Ægeon, whom the fates have mark'd! . . . *Com. of Errors* i 1 141
His days may finish ere that hapless time . . . 1 *Hen. VI.* iii 1 201
Wrings his hapless hands And shakes his head . . 2 *Hen. VI.* ii 1 226
See, ruthless queen, a hapless father's tears . . . . 3 *Hen. VI.* i 4 156
And I, the hapless male to one sweet bird . . . . . . v 6 15
Haply. When thou haply seest Some rare note-worthy object *T. G. of Ver.* i 1 12
If haply won, perhaps a hapless gain . . . . i 1 32
Seem you that you are not?—Haply I do.—So do counterfeits . . ii 4 11
This love of theirs myself have often seen, Haply when they have judged me fast asleep . . . . iii 1 25
Haply, in private.—And in assemblies too . . . . *Com. of Errors* v 1 60
Haply I see a friend will save my life . . . . v 1 283
Haply my presence May well abate the over-merry spleen *T. of Shrew* Ind. 1 136
Here let us breathe and haply institute A course of learning . . . i 1 8
I have thrust myself into this maze, Haply to wive and thrive as best I may. . . . . i 2 56
My heart as great, my reason haply more, To bandy word for word . v 2 171
Had from the conversation of my thoughts Haply been absent *All's Well* i 3 241
'Tis but the boldness of his hand, haply . . . . iii 2 80
When haply he shall hear that she is gone, He will return . . . iii 4 35
Haply thou mayst inform Something to save thy life . . . . iv 1 91
Be my aid For such disguise as haply shall become . . *T. Night* i 2 54
Haply your eye shall light upon some toy You have desire to purchase iii 3 44
The soul of our grandam might haply inhabit a bird . . . . iv 2 57
Here comes a gentleman that haply knows more . . . *W. Tale* v 2 22
With no certainties More than he haply may retail from me 2 *Hen. IV.* i 1 32
The glove which I have given him for a favour May haply purchase him a box o' th' ear . . . . *Hen. V.* iv 7 181
Haply a woman's voice may do some good, When articles too nicely urged be stood on . . . . v 2 93
The commons haply rise, to save his life . . . . . 2 *Hen. VI.* iii 1 240
But if we haply scape, As well we may . . . . v 2 79
And I, that haply take them from him now, May yet ere night yield both my life and them. . . . . 3 *Hen. VI.* ii 5 58
Which haply by much company might be urged . . *Richard III.* ii 2 137
The citizens, who haply may Misconstrue us in him . . . . iii 5 60
You might haply think Tongue-tied ambition, not replying, yielded . iii 7 144
Send to her . . . A pair of bleeding hearts; thereon engrave Edward and York; then haply she will weep . . . . iv 4 273
I have been The book of his good acts, whence men have read His fame unparallel'd, haply amplified . . . . . . *Coriolanus* v 2 16
I will kiss thy lips; Haply some poison yet doth hang on them *R. and J.* v 3 165
Haply the seas and countries different With variable objects shall expel This something-settled matter in his heart . . . *Hamlet* iii 1 179
And haply one as kind For husband shalt thou— O, confound the rest iii 2 186
Haply, when I shall wed, That lord whose hand must take my plight shall carry Half my love with him, half my care and duty . *Lear* i 1 102
He is rash and very sudden in choler, and haply may strike at you *Oth.* ii 1 280
Haply, for I am black And have not those soft parts of conversation . iii 3 263
If haply you my father do suspect An instrument of this your calling back . . . . iv 2 44
None but friends: say boldly.—So, haply, are they friends to Antony *Ant. and Cleo.* iii 13 48
Haply you shall not see me more; or if, A mangled shadow . . . iv 2 26
Haply this life is best, If quiet life be best . . . . *Cymbeline* iii 3 29
Yea, haply, near The residence of Posthumus; so nigh at least . . iii 4 150
Haply, despair hath seized her . . . . iii 5 60
May haply be a little angry for my so rough usage . . . . . iv 1 21
For mine own part, unfold a dangerous speech, Though, haply, well for you . . . . v 5 314
Happed. Tell my lord and lady what hath happ'd . . *Othello* v 1 127
Happen. If this should ever happen, thou wouldst be horn-mad *Much Ado* i 1 271
In the loss that may happen, it concerns you something to know it *All's W.* i 3 125
But also to effect Whatever I shall happen to devise . *Richard II.* iv 1 330
Yet am I arm'd against the worst can happen . . . 3 *Hen. VI.* iv 1 128
I would be all, against the worst may happen . . *Hen. VIII.* iii 1 25
What can happen To me above this wretchedness? . . . . . iii 1 122
Lest more mischance, On plots and errors, happen . . . *Hamlet* v 2 406
Happened. Of every These happen'd accidents . . . . *Tempest* v 1 250
And, if you will, tell what hath happened . . . *T. of Shrew* iv 4 64
It hath happened all as I would have had it . . . . *All's Well* iii 2 1
That hereafter ages may behold What ruin happen'd in revenge of him 1 *Hen. VI.* ii 2 11
Were you there?—Yes, indeed, was I.—Pray, speak what has happen'd *Hen. VIII.* ii 1 6
How unluckily it happened, that I should purchase the day before for a little part, and undo a great deal of honour! . . *T. of Athens* iii 2 52
Happier. You are the happier woman . . . . . . *M. Wives* ii 1 110
Happier than this, She is not bred so dull but she can learn *M. of Ven.* iii 2 163
Happy the parents of so fair a child; Happier the man, whom favourable stars Allot thee for his lovely bed-fellow! . . . *T. of Shrew* iv 5 40
Happily met; the happier for thy son . . . . iv 5 59
What his happier affairs may be, are to me unknown . . *W. Tale* iv 2 34
Against the envy of less happier lands . . . . *Richard II.* ii 1 49
Which makes me A little happier than my wretched father *Hen. VIII.* ii 1 120
This is a happier and more comely time . . . . *Coriolanus* iv 6 27
Happier is he that has no friend to feed Than such that do e'en enemies exceed . . . . *T. of Athens* i 2 209
Lesser than Macbeth, and greater.—Not so happy, yet much happier *Macbeth* i 3 66
That I am wretched Makes thee the happier . . . . . *Lear* iv 1 69
And kiss'd it, madam.—Senseless linen! happier therein than I! . *Cymb.* i 3 7
Some falls are means the happier to arise. . . . . iv 2 403
And happier much by his affliction made. . . . . v 4 108
Happiest of all is that her gentle spirit Commits itself to yours to be directed, As from her lord . . . . . . *Mer. of Venice* iii 2 165
If a lie may do thee grace, I'll gild it with the happiest terms I have 1 *Hen. IV.* v 4 162
The happiest youth, viewing his progress through, What perils past, what crosses to ensue, Would shut the book, and sit him down and die . . . . 2 *Hen. IV.* iii 1 54
The happiest gift that ever marquess gave, The fairest queen 2 *Hen. VI.* i 1 15
As you are known The first and happiest hearers of the town *Hen. VIII.* Prol. 24
Happily. He writes How happily he lives, how well beloved *T. G. of Ver.* i 3 57
You shall hear more ere morning.—Happily You something know *Meas. for Meas.* iv 2 98
Parts that become thee happily enough . . . . *Mer. of Venice* ii 2 191
I come to wive it wealthily in Padua; If wealthily, then happily *T. of S.* i 2 76
This gentleman is happily arrived, My mind presumes, for his own good i 2 213
You are happily met . . . . iv 4 19
And happily we might be interrupted . . . . iv 4 54
Happily met; the happier for thy son . . . . iv 5 59
Happily I have arrived at the last Unto the wished haven of my bliss v 1 130
I wish it happily effected . . . . *All's Well* iv 5 84
This afternoon will post To consummate this business happily *K. John* v 7 95
And happily may your sweet self put on The lineal state and glory! . v 7 101
Which elder years May happily bring forth . . . *Richard II.* v 3 22
Our powers at once, As I will fashion it, shall happily meet . 1 *Hen. IV.* i 3 297
Thy fortune, York, hadst thou been regent there, Might happily have proved far worse than his . . . . 2 *Hen. VI.* iii 1 306
He stepp'd before me, happily For my example . . . . *Hen. VIII.* iv 2 10
This is about that which the bishop spake: I am happily come hither . v 1 85
I am glad I came this way so happily . . . . v 2 9
I am incorporate in Rome, A Roman now adopted happily . *T. Andron* i 1 463
Cast your nets; Happily you may catch her in the sea . . . . iv 3 8
The County Paris, at Saint Peter's Church, Shall happily make thee there a joyful bride . . . . *Rom. and Jul.* iii 5 116
Happily met, my lady and my wife!—That may be, sir, when I may be a wife . . . . iv 1 18
The king hath happily received, Macbeth, The news of thy success *Macb.* i 3 89
Which, happily, foreknowing may avoid . . . . . . *Hamlet* i 1 134
Happily he's the second time come to them [his swaddling-clouts] . ii 2 402
Her will, recoiling to her better judgement, May fall to match you with her country forms And happily repent . . . . *Othello* iii 3 238
And never Fly off our loves again!—Happily, amen! . *Ant. and Cleo.* ii 2 155
These our ships, you happily may think Are like the Trojan horse *Pericles* i 4 92
Happiness. Wish me partaker in thy happiness When thou dost meet good hap . . . . *T. G. of Ver.* i 1 14
All happiness bechance to thee in Milan!—As much to you at home! . i 1 61
O, that our fathers would applaud our loves, To seal our happiness! . i 3 49
And all the means Plotted and 'greed on for my happiness . . . ii 4 183
One feast, one house, one mutual happiness . . . . . . v 4 173
Lead forth and bring you back in happiness! . . *Meas. for Meas.* i 1 75
When you depart from me, sorrow abides and happiness takes his leave . . . . *Much Ado* i 1 102
I love none.—A dear happiness to women . . . . i 1 129
He hath indeed a good outward happiness . . . . ii 3 191
Society, saith the text, is the happiness of life . . . *L. L. Lost* iv 2 168
It is no mean happiness, therefore, to be seated in the mean . *M. of Ven.* i 2 7
Envy no man's happiness, glad of other men's good . *As Y. Like It* iii 2 79
Good day and happiness, dear Rosalind! . . . . iv 1 30
How bitter a thing it is to look into happiness through another man's eyes! . . . . v 2 48
That treats of happiness By virtue specially to be achieved . *T. of Shrew* i 1 19
Wisdom, courage, all That happiness and prime can happy call *All's Well* ii 1 185
Who had even tuned his bounty to sing happiness to him . . . iv 3 12
What have you lost by losing of this day?—All days of glory, joy and happiness . . . . *K. John* iii 4 117
Each day still better other's happiness! . . . . . *Richard II.* i 1 22
More health and happiness betide my liege Than can my care-tuned tongue deliver him! . . . . iii 2 91
What is the news?—First, to thy sacred state wish I all happiness . v 6 6
Like fearful war, To diet rank minds sick of happiness . 2 *Hen IV.* iv 1 64
Health to my sovereign, and new happiness Added to that that I am to deliver! . . . . iv 4 81
Health, peace, and happiness to my royal father! . . . . . iv 5 227
Thou bring'st me happiness and peace, son John . . . . . iv 5 228
That shall convert those tears By number into hours of happiness . v 2 61
The contending kingdoms Of France and England, whose very shores look pale With envy of each other's happiness . . . . *Hen. V.* v 2 379
Success unto our valiant general, And happiness to his accomplices! 1 *Hen. VI.* v 2 9
Long live Queen Margaret, England's happiness!—We thank you all 2 *Hen. VI.* i 1 37
All happiness unto my lord the king! . . . . . iii 1 93; v 1 124
And if thy poor devoted suppliant may But beg one favour at thy gracious hand, Thou dost confirm his happiness for ever *Richard III.* i 2 209
I fear our happiness is at the highest . . . . i 3 41
If to have done the thing you gave in charge Beget your happiness, be happy then . . . . iv 3 26
Compare dead happiness with living woe . . . . iv 4 119
Advantaging their loan with interest Of ten times double gain of happiness . . . . iv 4 324
Thy beauteous princely daughter! In her consists my happiness and thine . . . . iv 4 406
His overthrow heap'd happiness upon him . . . . *Hen. VIII.* iv 2 64
They promised me eternal happiness; And brought me garlands, Griffith iv 2 90
She shall be, to the happiness of England, An aged princess . . . v 5 57
That hath aspired to Solon's happiness . . . . . *T. Andron.* i 1 177
And might not gain so great a happiness As have thy love . . . ii 4 20
Let rich music's tongue Unfold the imagined happiness that both Receive in either by this dear encounter . . . *Rom. and Jul.* ii 6 28
Happiness courts thee in her best array . . . . iii 3 142
Bowing his head against the steepy mount To climb his happiness *T. of A.* i 1 76
Fare you well.—All happiness to your honour! . . . . . . i 1 109
Might we but have that happiness, my lord, that you would once use our hearts . . . . i 2 86
The best of happiness, Honour and fortunes, keep with you! . . . i 2 234
To conclude, The victory fell on us.—Great happiness! . . *Macbeth* i 2 58
A happiness that often madness hits on . . . . . . *Hamlet* ii 2 213
She is indeed perfection.—Well, happiness to their sheets! . *Othello* ii 3 29
There is no other way; 'tis she must do't: And, lo, the happiness! . iii 4 108
I'ld have thee live; For, in my sense, 'tis happiness to die . . v 2 290
Like enough, high-battled Cæsar will Unstate his happiness! *A. and C.* iii 13 30
So he wishes you all happiness, that remains loyal to his vow *Cymbeline* iii 2 46
Fare you well.— . . . Happiness! . . . . iii 5 17
To sour your happiness, I must report The queen is dead . . . v 5 26
Be my helps . . . To compass such a boundless happiness! . . *Pericles* i 1 24
Of all say'd yet, I wish thee happiness! . . . . i 1 60
This wreath of victory I give, And crown you king of this day's happiness ii 3 11
Happy. My youthful travel therein made me happy . *T. G. of Ver.* iv 1 34
Unhappy were you, madam, ere I came; But by my coming I have made you happy . . . . v 4 30

Happy. I thank your grace; the gift hath made me happy *T. G. of Ver.* v 4 148

Happy thou art not; For what thou hast not, still thou strivest to get, And what thou hast, forget'st *Meas. for Meas.* iii 1 21

Make it your comfort, So happy is your brother v 1 404

In Syracusa was I born, and wed Unto a woman, happy but for me, And by me, had not our hap been bad *Com. of Errors* i 1 38

Here must end the story of my life; And happy were I in my timely death i 1 139

Be happy, lady; for you are like an honourable father *Much Ado* i 1 112

I were but little happy, if I could say how much ii 1 318

Happy are they that hear their detractions and can put them to mending ii 3 237

Happy be Theseus, our renowned duke!—Thanks, good Egeus *M. N. D.* i 1 20

But earthlier happy is the rose distill'd i 1 76

How happy some o'er other some can be! i 1 226

Happy is Hermia, wheresoe'er she lies; For she hath blessed and attractive eyes ii 2 90

Happy in this, she is not yet so old But she may learn *Mer. of Venice* iii 2 162

If you do keep your promises in love But justly, . . . Your mistress shall be happy *As Y. Like It* i 2 257

Happy is your grace, That can translate the stubbornness of fortune Into so quiet and so sweet a style ii 1 18

By how much I shall think my brother happy in having what he wishes for v 2 51

Well mayst thou woo, and happy be thy speed! *T. of Shrew* ii 1 139

Happy the parents of so fair a child! iv 5 39

And, to be short, what not, that's sweet and happy v 2 110

All That happiness and prime can happy call *All's Well* ii 1 185

You are too young, too happy, and too good ii 3 102

I thank my stars I am happy *T. Night* ii 5 185

If nothing lets to make us happy both But this v 1 256

Now were I happy, if His going I could frame to serve my turn *W. Tale* iv 4 519

Happy be you! All that you speak shows fair iv 4 635

Happy be he whose cloak and cincture can Hold out this tempest *K. John* iv 3 155

When we were happy we had other names v 4 8

Ah, would the scandal vanish with my life, How happy then were my ensuing death! *Richard II.* ii 1 68

I count myself in nothing else so happy As in a soul remembering my good friends ii 3 46

For ever will I walk upon my knees, And never see day that the happy sees v 3 94

Be happy, he will trouble you no more *2 Hen. IV.* iv 5 128

Happy am I, that have a man so bold, That dares do justice on my proper son; And not less happy, having such a son v 2 108

Thou art less happy being fear'd Than they in fearing *Hen. V.* iv 1 265

He esteems himself happy that he hath fallen into the hands of one, as he thinks, the most brave iv 4 64

So happy be the issue, brother England, Of this good day v 2 12

Would you not suppose Your bondage happy, to be made a queen? *1 Hen. VI.* v 3 111

Happy for so sweet a child, Fit to be made companion with a king v 3 148

Or count them happy that enjoy the sun *2 Hen. VI.* ii 4 39

If my death might make this island happy iii 1 148

And thought thee happy when I shook my head iv 1 55

And happy always was it for that son Whose father for his hoarding went to hell *3 Hen. VI.* ii 2 47

And make me happy in your unity *Richard III.* ii 1 31

Happy were England, would this gracious prince Take on himself the sovereignty thereof iii 7 78

And make, no doubt, us happy by his reign iii 7 170

God give your graces both A happy and a joyful time of day! iv 1 6

Am I happy in thy news?—If to have done the thing you gave in charge Beget your happiness, be happy then iv 3 24

Life, honour, name and all That made me happy at one stroke has taken For ever from the world *Hen. VIII.* ii 1 117

I care not, so much I am happy Above a number ii 1 33

May you be happy in your wish! iii 2 43

Never so truly happy, my good Cromwell. I know myself now iii 2 377

Those men are happy; and so are all are near her iv 1 50

And, sure, those men are happy that shall have 'em iv 2 147

Send prosperous life, long, and ever happy! v 5 2

All comfort, joy, in this most gracious lady, Heaven ever laid up to make parents happy, May hourly fall upon ye! v 5 8

Be happy that my arms are out of use *Troi. and Cres.* v 6 16

How happy art thou, then, From these devourers to be banished! *T. An.* iii 1 56

I would thou wert so happy by thy stay, To hear true shrift *Rom. and Jul.* i 1 164

For this alliance may so happy prove, To turn your households' rancour to pure love ii 3 91

There art thou happy iii 3 137; 138; 140

I think you are happy in this second match, For it excels your first iii 5 224

He is gone happy, and has left me rich *T. of Athens* iii 2 4

Go, live rich and happy; But thus condition'd: thou shalt build from men iv 3 532

Lesser than Macbeth, and greater.—Not so happy, yet much happier *Macb.* i 3 66

Happy, in that we are not over-happy *Hamlet* ii 2 232

A proclaim'd prize! Most happy! That eyeless head of thine was first framed flesh To raise my fortunes *Lear* iv 6 230

About it; and write happy when thou hast done v 3 35

A maid so tender, fair and happy, So opposite to marriage *Othello* i 2 66

If it were now to die, 'Twere now to be most happy ii 1 192

I had been happy, if the general camp, Pioneers and all, had tasted her sweet body, So I had nothing known iii 3 345

If she be not honest, chaste, and true, There's no man happy iv 2 18

But I will hope Of better deeds to-morrow. Rest you happy! *A. and C.* i 1 62

Thus I let you go, And give you to the gods.—Adieu; be happy! i 2 64

Had I been thief-stol'n, As my two brothers, happy! *Cymbeline* i 6 6

Tell me how Wales was made so happy as To inherit such a haven iii 2 62

Tell him Wherein you're happy,—which you'll make him know, If that his head have ear in music iii 4 177

He shall be happy that can find him, if Our grace can make him so v 5 6

My good master, I will yet do you service.—Happy be you! v 5 404

Let us salute him, Or know what ground's made happy by his breath *Pericles* ii 4 28

Thou art the rudeliest welcome to this world That ever was prince's child. Happy what follows! iii 1 31

She is all happy as the fairest of all iv 1 49

Perform my bidding, or thou livest in woe; Do it, and happy v 1 249

Happy being. The tenour of them doth but signify My health and happy being at your court *T. G. of Ver.* iii 1 57

Happy birth. O error, soon conceived, Thou never comest unto a happy birth, But kill'st the mother that engender'd thee! *J. Cæsar* v 3 70

Happy breed. This happy breed of men, this little world *Richard II.* ii 1 45

Happy cause. Ophelia, I do wish That your good beauties be the happy cause Of Hamlet's wildness *Hamlet* iii 1 39

Happy child. Thou hast made me now a man! never, before This happy child, did I get any thing *Hen. VIII.* v 5 66

Happy close. Let me be blest to make this happy close *T. G. of Ver.* v 4 117

Happy dagger. O happy dagger! This is thy sheath *Rom. and Jul.* v 3 169

Happy day. Our nuptial hour Draws on apace; four happy days bring in Another moon *M. N. Dream* i 1 2

Many years of happy days befal My gracious sovereign! *Richard II.* i 1 20

One day too late, I fear me, noble lord, Hath clouded all thy happy days on earth: O, call back yesterday! iii 2 68

This happy day Is not itself, nor have we won one foot, If Salisbury be lost *2 Hen. VI.* v 3 5

Long die thy happy days before thy death! *Richard III.* i 3 207

I would not spend another such a night, Though 'twere to buy a world of happy days i 4 6

God bless your grace with health and happy days! iii 1 18

To-morrow, then, I judge a happy day iii 4 6

Go, girl, seek happy nights to happy days *Rom. and Jul.* i 3 106

And let's away, To part the glories of this happy day *J. Cæsar* v 5 81

The gods make this a happy day to Antony! *Ant. and Cleo.* iv 5 1

Happy dream. Think our former state a happy dream *Richard II.* v 1 18

Happy earth. For thou hast made the happy earth thy hell *Richard III.* i 2 51

Happy end. But on, my liege; for very little pains Will bring this labour to an happy end *K. John* iii 2 10

Happy England. Divide your happy England into four *Hen. V.* i 2 214

And so shall you, If happy England's royal king be free *1 Hen. VI.* v 3 115

Happy evening. Lady, a happy evening! *T. G. of Ver.* v 1 7

Happy fair. Demetrius loves your fair: O happy fair! *M. N. Dream* i 1 182

Happy farewell. Once more a happy farewell *3 Hen. VI.* iv 8 31

Happy father. Thou happy father *Lear* iv 6 72

Happy few. We few, we happy few, we band of brothers *Hen. V.* iv 3 60

Happy gain. My mind presageth happy gain *3 Hen. VI.* v 1 71

Happy gale. What happy gale Blows you to Padua? *T. of Shrew* i 2 48

Happy gentleman. A happy gentleman in blood and lineaments, By you unhappied and disfigured clean *Richard II.* iii 1 9

Happy havens. All places that the eye of heaven visits Are to a wise man ports and happy havens i 3 276

Happy helm. And you yourself shall steer the happy helm *2 Hen. VI.* i 3 103

Happy holding. You were straited For a reply, at least if you make a care Of happy holding her *W. Tale* iv 4 367

Happy hollow. By the happy hollow of a tree Escaped *Lear* ii 3 2

Happy horse. O happy horse, to bear the weight of Antony! *A. and C.* i 5 21

Happy hour. You have stayed me in a happy hour *Much Ado* i 1 285

O most courageous day! O most happy hour! *M. N. Dream* iv 2 28

Fair thoughts and happy hours attend on you! *Mer. of Venice* iii 4 41

Omit no happy hour That may give furtherance to our expedition *Hen. V.* i 2 300

Mine uncles, You are come to Sandal in a happy hour *3 Hen. VI.* i 2 63

Heaven and fortune bar me happy hours! *Richard III.* iv 4 400

Lord Timon's happy hours are done and past *T. of Athens* iii 2 6

Happy issue. No doubt we'll bring it to a happy issue *Richard III.* iii 7 54

Happy king. A king of beasts, indeed; if aught but beasts, I had been still a happy king of men *Richard II.* v 1 36

He is a happy king, since he gains from his subjects the name of good *Per.* ii 1 109

Happy life. No prince nor peer shall have just cause to say, God shorten Harry's happy life one day! *2 Hen. IV.* v 2 145

Methinks it were a happy life, To be no better than a homely swain *3 Hen. VI.* ii 5 21

Happy low, lie down! Uneasy lies the head that wears a crown *2 Hen. IV.* iii 1 30

Happy man be his dole! *Mer. Wives* iii 4; *T. of Shrew* i 1; *W. Tale* i 2; *1 Hen. IV.* ii 2

To England then; Where ne'er from France arrived more happy men *Hen. V.* iv 8 131

Pride, Which out of daily fortune ever taints The happy man *Coriolanus* iv 7 39

O happy man! they have befriended thee *T. Andron.* iii 1 52

How this lord is follow'd!—The senators of Athens: happy man! *T. of A.* i 1 40

Happy masks that kiss fair ladies' brows *Rom. and Jul.* i 1 236

Happy messenger. I will be thankful To any happy messenger from thence *T. G. of Ver.* ii 4 53

Happy minion. Then, in a moment, Fortune shall cull forth Out of one side her happy minion *K. John* ii 1 392

Happy mother. And rob me of a happy mother's name *Richard II.* v 2 93

Shall I go win my daughter to thy will?—And be a happy mother by the deed *Richard III.* iv 4 427

Younger than she are happy mothers made *Rom. and Jul.* i 2 12

Happy newness, that intends old right *K. John* v 4 61

Happy news. I should rejoice now at this happy news *2 Hen. IV.* iv 4 109

Tidings do I bring and lucky joys And golden times and happy news of price v 3 100

Happy night. This happy night the Frenchmen are secure *1 Hen. VI.* ii 1 11

Go, girl, seek happy nights to happy days *Rom. and Jul.* i 3 106

Happy number. Every of this happy number That have endured shrewd days and nights with us *As Y. Like It* v 4 178

Happy peace. And I have made a happy peace with him *K. John* v 1 63

So I bequeath a happy peace to you And all good men *Pericles* i 1 50

Happy prologues to the swelling act Of the imperial theme *Macbeth* i 3 128

Happy race. Live, and beget a happy race of kings! *Richard III.* v 3 157

Happy return be to your royal grace! *Meas. for Meas.* v 1 3

Happy rivals. We may yet again have access to our fair mistress and be happy rivals *T. of Shrew* i 1 119

Happy season. You wish me health in very happy season *2 Hen. IV.* v 2 79

Happy shows. Who alone suffers suffers most i' the mind, Leaving free things and happy shows behind *Lear* iii 6 112

Happy smilets. Those happy smilets, That play'd on her ripe lip, seem'd not to know What guests were in her eyes iv 3 21

Happy souls. Plain well-meaning soul, Whom fair befal in heaven 'mongst happy souls! *Richard II.* ii 1 129

Happy speed. Has had most favourable and happy speed *Othello* ii 1 67

Happy star reign now! Here comes Bohemia *W. Tale* i 2 363

The right and fortune of his happy stars *Richard III.* iii 7 172

Was't not a happy star Led us to Rome? *T. Andron.* iv 2 32

Happy storm. When with a happy storm they were surprised ii 3 23

Happy stratagem. Saint Denis bless this happy stratagem! *1 Hen. VI.* iii 2 18

Happy thing. 'Tis a happy thing To be the father unto many sons *3 Hen. VI.* iii 2 104

Happy throne. Boundless intemperance In nature is a tyranny; it hath been The untimely emptying of the happy throne *Macbeth* iv 3 68

Happy tidings. Methinks we should have heard The happy tidings of his good escape *3 Hen. VI.* ii 1 7

Happy time. You are come to me in happy time *T. of Shrew* Ind. 1 90

In happy time; This man may help me to his majesty's ear *All's Well* v 1 6

A happy time of day!—Happy, indeed, as we have spent the day *Rich. III.* ii 1 47

Happy time. Madam, in happy time, what day is that? *Rom. and Jul.* iii 5 112

And you are come in very happy time, To bear my greeting . *J. Cæsar* ii 2 60

The king and queen and all are coming down.—In happy time *Hamlet* v 2 214

In happy time, Iago.—You have not been a-bed, then?—Why, no *Othello* iii 1 32

Happy torment. O happy torment! . . . . *Mer. of Venice* iii 2 37

Happy vantage. O happy vantage of a kneeling knee! . *Richard II.* v 3 132

Happy verse. When we for recompense have praised the vile, It stains the glory in that happy verse Which aptly sings the good *T. of Athens* i 1 16

Happy victory. Disgraced me in my happy victories 1 *Hen. IV.* iv 3 97

Sleep thou a quiet sleep; Dream of success and happy victory! *Rich. III.* v 3 165

O my mother, mother! O! You have won a happy victory to Rome *Cor.* v 3 186

Happy wedding torch. This is the happy wedding torch That joineth Rouen unto her countrymen . . . 1 *Hen. VI.* iii 2 26

Happy wedlock hours. Where she kneels and prays For happy wedlock hours . . . . *Mer. of Venice* v 1 32

Happy wife. For happy wife, a most distressed widow *Richard III.* iv 4 98

Happy word. They did not bless us with one happy word . *L. L. Lost* v 2 370

Happy wreck. I shall have share in this most happy wreck . *T. Night* v 1 273

Happy years. They shall yet belie thy happy years, That say thou art a man . . . . i 4 30

Take from my mouth the wish of happy years . . . . *Richard II.* i 3 94

Harbinger. Apparel vice like virtue's harbinger . . *Com. of Errors* iii 2 12

And yonder shines Aurora's harbinger . . . *M. N. Dream* iii 2 380

I'll be myself the harbinger and make joyful The hearing of my wife with your approach . . . . . . *Macbeth* i 4 45

Give them all breath, Those clamorous harbingers of blood and death . v 6 10

Fierce events, As harbingers preceding still the fates . . *Hamlet* i 1 122

Harbour. Safely in harbour Is the king's ship . . . *Tempest* i 2 226

Dare you presume to harbour wanton lines? . . *T. G. of Ver.* i 2 42

My thoughts do harbour with my Silvia nightly . . . iii 1 140

They are sent by me, That they should harbour where their lord would be iii 1 149

Why I desire thee To give me secret harbour, hath a purpose. *M. for M.* i 3 4

Loath to leave unsought Or that or any place that harbours men *Com. of Errors* i 1 137

If the wind blow any way from shore, I will not harbour in this town to-night . . . . iii 2 154

Lodged in my heart, Though so denied fair harbour in my house *L. L. Lost* ii 1 175

Three of your argosies Are richly come to harbour suddenly *Mer. of Venice* v 1 277

Though she harbours you as her kinsman . . . *T. Night* ii 3 103

Where shame doth harbour, even in Mowbray's face . *Richard II.* i 1 195

In his simple show he harbours treason . . . . 2 *Hen. VI.* iii 1 54

Let pale-faced fear keep with the mean-born man, And find no harbour in a royal heart . . . . iii 1 336

If it be banish'd from the frosty head, Where shall it find a harbour? . v 1 168

O monstrous fault, to harbour such a thought! . . 3 *Hen. VI.* iii 2 164

Now, for this night, let's harbour here in York . . . iv 7 79

Either to harbour fled, Or made a toast for Neptune *Troi. and Cres.* i 3 44

All thy powers Shall make their harbour in our town . *T. of Athens* v 4 53

In this plainness Harbour more craft and more corrupter ends *Lear* ii 2 108

There's one gone to the harbour?—Ay, madam . . *Othello* ii 1 121

Do thou meet me presently at the harbour. Come hither . . ii 1 215

My treasure's in the harbour, take it . . *Ant. and Cleo.* iii 11 11

To show what coast thy sluggish crare Might easiliest harbour in *Cymb.* iv 2 206

Harbourage. Crave harbourage within your city walls . *K. John* ii 1 234

We do not look for reverence, but for love, And harbourage for ourself, our ships, and men . . . . *Pericles* i 4 100

Harboured. Though all these English and their discipline Were harbour'd in their rude circumference . . . . . *K. John* ii 1 262

Harbouring. These hands are free from guiltless blood-shedding, This breast from harbouring foul deceitful thoughts. 2 *Hen. VI.* iv 7 109

Hard. Alas, now, pray you, Work not so hard . . . . *Tempest* iii 1 16

It shall go hard but I'll prove it by another . . *T. G. of Ver.* i 1 86

Being so hard to me that brought your mind, I fear she'll prove as hard to you in telling your mind . . . . i 1 146

Give her no token but stones; for she's as hard as steel . . . i 1 149

When a man's servant shall play the cur with him, look you, it goes hard iv 4 2

I have been drinking hard all night . . . . *Meas. for Meas.* iv 3 56

Unkindness blunts it more than marble hard . *Com. of Errors* ii 1 93

Master, knock the door hard.—Let him knock till it ache . . iii 1 58

Where Scotland?—I found it by the barrenness; hard in the palm of the hand . . . . iii 2 123

These are barren tasks, too hard to keep, Not to see ladies . *L. L. Lost* i 1 47

Or, having sworn too hard a keeping oath, Study to break it . . . i 1 65

Cupid's butt-shaft is too hard for Hercules' club . . . . i 2 182

What then, do you see?—Ay, our way to be gone.—You are too hard for me . . . . ii 1 257

Was that the king, that spurred his horse so hard? . . . . iv 1 1

She's too hard for you at pricks, sir: challenge her to bowl . . iv 1 140

Is it not hard, Nerissa, that I cannot choose one nor refuse none? *Mer. of Venice* i 2 27

It shall go hard but I will better the instruction . . . . iii 1 75

If law, authority and power deny not, It will go hard with poor Antonio iii 2 292

You may as well do any thing most hard, As seek to soften that . . iv 1 78

Since nought so stockish, hard and full of rage, But music for the time doth change his nature . . . . v 1 81

Indeed, there is Fortune too hard for Nature . . *As Y. Like It* i 2 51

Besides, our hands are hard.—Your lips will feel them the sooner . . iii 2 60

He [Time] trots hard with a young maid between the contract of her marriage and the day it is solemnized . . . . iii 2 331

Time's pace is so hard that it seems the length of seven year . . . iii 2 334

The common executioner, Whose heart the accustom'd sight of death makes hard . . . . iii 5 4

Shepherd, ply her hard . . . . iii 5 77

Careless of your life?—My life, sir! how, I pray? for that goes hard *T. of Shrew* iv 2 80

I'll roundly go about her: It shall go hard if Cambio go without her . iv 4 109

This is hard and undeserved measure, my lord . . . *All's Well* ii 3 273

'Tis hard: A young man married is a man that's marr'd. . . . ii 3 314

That were hard to compass; Because she will admit no kind of suit *T. N.* i 2 44

It is too hard a knot for me to untie! . . . . ii 2 42

You'll kiss me hard and speak to me as if I were a baby still. *W. Tale* ii 1 5

Upon my knee, Made hard with kneeling, I do pray to thee . *K. John* iii 1 310

With hard bright steel and hearts harder than steel . *Richard II.* iii 2 111

As hard to come as for a camel To thread the postern of a small needle's eye . . . . v 5 16

Yea, but I doubt they will be too hard for us . . 1 *Hen. IV.* i 2 204

Who bears hard His brother's death . . . . i 3 270

Snorting like a horse.—Hark, how hard he fetches breath . . ii 4 579

After him came spurring hard A gentleman, almost forspent with speed 2 *Hen. IV.* i 1 36

Hard. How ill it follows, after you have laboured so hard, you should talk so idly! . . . . 2 *Hen. IV.* ii 2 32

Hold hard the breath and bend up every spirit To his full height *Hen. V.* iii 1 16

The splitting rocks . . . . would not dash me with their ragged sides, Because thy flinty heart, more hard than they, Might in thy palace perish, Margaret . . . . 2 *Hen. VI.* iii 2 99

What is thy name?—Emmanuel.—They use to write it on the top of letters: 'twill go hard with you . . . . iv 2 108

Were thy heart as hard as steel, As thou hast shown it flinty by thy deeds, I come to pierce it, or to give thee mine . . 3 *Hen. VI.* ii 1 201

The world goes hard When Clifford cannot spare his friends an oath . ii 6 77

He plies her hard; and much rain wears the marble . . . iii 2 50

What, at your book so hard? . . . . v 6 1

'Tis hard to draw them thence, So sweet is zealous contemplation *Richard III.* iii 7 93

Spur your proud horses hard, and ride in blood . . . . v 3 340

You suffer Too hard an exclamation . . . . . *Hen. VIII.* i 2 52

Then stops again, Strikes his breast hard . . . . . . iii 2 117

I will play no more to-night; My mind's not on't; you are too hard for me . . . . v 1 57

And spirit of sense Hard as the palm of ploughman . *Troi. and Cres.* i 1 59

The artist and unread, The hard and soft, seem all affined and kin . i 3 25

Why was my Cressid then so hard to win?—Hard to seem won . iii 2 124

Which of you But is four Volsces? none of you but is Able to bear against the great Aufidius A shield as hard as his . *Coriolanus* i 6 80

He was ever too hard for him; I have heard him say so himself . iv 5 195

He was too hard for him directly, to say the troth on't . . iv 5 197

A stone is soft as wax,—tribunes more hard than stones *T. Andron.* iii 1 45

'Tis not hard, I think, For men so old as we to keep the peace *Rom. and Jul.* i 2 2

The orchard walls are high and hard to climb, And the place death . ii 2 63

I come, I come! Who knocks so hard? whence come you? what's your will? . . . . iii 3 78

Thy nature did commence in sufferance, time Hath made thee hard in't. Why shouldst thou hate men? . . . . . *T. of Athens* iv 3 269

Fawn on men and hug them hard And after scandal them . *J. Cæsar* i 2 75

Cæsar doth bear me hard; but he loves Brutus . . . . i 2 317

Caius Ligarius doth bear Cæsar hard. . . . . . . ii 1 215

How hard it is for women to keep counsel! . . . . . ii 4 9

If you bear me hard, Now, whilst your purpled hands do reek and smoke, Fulfil your pleasure . . . . iii 1 157

Such welcome and unwelcome things at once 'Tis hard to reconcile *Macbeth* iv 3 139

What said he?—He took me by the wrist and held me hard . *Hamlet* ii 1 87

And 't shall go hard But I will delve one yard below their mines . . iii 4 207

I have watched and travell'd hard; Some time I shall sleep out . *Lear* ii 2 162

How, in one house, Should many people, under two commands, Hold amity? 'Tis hard; almost impossible . . . . ii 4 245

Bind him, I say.—Hard, hard. O filthy traitor! . . . . . iii 7 32

With the little godliness I have, I did full hard forbear him . *Othello* i 2 10

If sanctimony and a frail vow betwixt an erring barbarian and a super-subtle Venetian be not too hard for my wits . . . . . . i 3 364

Let me but bind it hard, within this hour It will be well . . . iii 3 286

Kiss me hard, As if he pluck'd up kisses by the roots . . . iii 3 422

But when we in our viciousness grow hard—O misery on't!—the wise gods seel our eyes . . . . *Ant. and Cleo.* iii 13 111

Shall from this practice but make hard your heart . . . *Cymbeline* i 5 24

Join gripes with hands Made hard with hourly falsehood . . . . i 6 107

As slippery as the Gordian knot was hard! . . . . . . ii 2 34

The stone's too hard to come by.—Not a whit, Your lady being so easy ii 4 46

We have yet many among us can gripe as hard as Cassibelan . . . iii 1 41

The art o' the court, As hard to leave as keep . . . . . iii 3 47

How hard it is to hide the sparks of nature! . . . . . . iii 3 79

Weariness Can snore upon the flint, when resty sloth Finds the down pillow hard . . . . iii 6 35

Were you a woman, youth, I should woo hard but be your groom . . iii 6 70

For death-like dragons here affright thee hard . . . . *Pericles* i 1 29

Hard adventure. Searching of thy wound, I have by hard adventure found mine own . . . . *As Y. Like It* ii 4 45

Hard at door. Your master is hard at door . . . *Mer. Wives* iv 2 111

Hard at hand comes the master and main exercise . . *Othello* ii 1 268

Hard at study. My father Is hard at study . . . . *Tempest* iii 1 20

Hard beset. Daughter Silvia, you are hard beset . . *T. G. of Ver.* ii 4 49

Hard bondage. Alas, poor lady! 'Tis a hard bondage to become the wife Of a detesting lord . . . . *All's Well* iii 5 67

Hard by. Be ready here hard by in the brew-house . . *Mer. Wives* iii 3 10

How near is he, Mistress Page?—Hard by; at street end . . . iv 2 40

They are all couched in a pit hard by Herne's oak . . . . v 3 14

He attendeth here hard by, To know your answer . . *Mer. of Venice* iv 1 145

If you will know my house, 'Tis at the tuft of olives here hard by *As Y. Like It* iii 5 76

She'll none of me: the count himself here hard by woos her . *T. Night* i 3 114

Where are our disguises?—Here, hard by: stand close . 1 *Hen. IV.* ii 2 79

What is this castle call'd that stands hard by? . . . *Hen. V.* iv 7 91

Sir Humphrey Stafford and his brother are hard by. . 2 *Hen. VI.* iv 2 121

She is hard by with twenty thousand men; And therefore fortify 3 *Hen. VI.* i 2 51

Hard by here is a hovel; Some friendship will it lend you . . *Lear* iii 2 61

Hard commands. My duty cannot suffer To obey in all your daughters' hard commands . . . . iii 4 154

Hard condition. O hard condition, Twin-born with greatness! *Hen. V.* iv 1 250

A hard condition for a maid to consign to . . . . . . v 2 326

Under these hard conditions as this time Is like to lay upon us *J. Cæsar* i 2 174

Hard conscience. My conscience is but a kind of hard conscience *Mer. of Venice* ii 2 30

Hard consent. At last Upon his will I seal'd my hard consent *Hamlet* i 2 60

Hard construction. Under your hard construction must I sit *T. Night* iii 1 126

Hard cure. This rest might yet have balm'd thy broken sinews, Which, if convenience will not allow, Stand in hard cure . . . *Lear* iii 6 107

Hard dealings. What these Christians are, Whose own hard dealings teaches them suspect The thoughts of others! . . *Mer. of Venice* i 3 163

Hard distress. In pity of my hard distress . . . . 1 *Hen. VI.* ii 5 87

Hard fate. He dies.—Hard fate! he might have died in war *T. Athens* iii 5 75

Hard-favoured. Is she not hard-favoured, sir? . . . *T. G. of Ver.* ii 1 53

I might have some hope thou didst feign.—Would you not have me honest?—No, truly, unless thou wert hard-favoured *As Y. Like It* iii 3 29

Why should hard-favour'd grief be lodged in thee? . . *Richard. II.* v 1 14

Disguise fair nature with hard-favour'd rage . . . *Hen. V.* iii 1 8

O thou, whose wounds become hard-favour'd death, Speak! 1 *Hen. VI.* iv 7 23

Where is that devil's butcher, Hard-favour'd Richard? . . 3 *Hen. VI.* v 5 78

Hard food. Thou gaudy gold, Hard food for Midas . . *Mer. of Venice* iii 2 102

Hard fractions. After distasteful looks and these hard fractions, With certain half-caps . . . *T. of Athens* ii 2 220
Hard hand. There's no better sign of a brave mind than a hard hand *2 Hen. VI.* iv 2 22
To wring From the hard hands of peasants their vile trash . *J. Cæsar* iv 3 74
Hard-handed men that work in Athens here . *M. N. Dream* v 1 72
Hard heart. One whose hard heart is button'd up with steel . *C. of Er.* iv 2 34
I would I could find in my heart that I had not a hard heart . *Much Ado* i 1 128
And sung this ballad against the hard hearts of maids . *W. Tale* iv 4 282
O, be to me, though thy hard heart say no, Nothing so kind, but something pitiful! . . . *T. Andron.* ii 3 155
O you hard hearts, you cruel men of Rome . . . *J. Cæsar* i 1 41
Is there any cause in nature that makes these hard hearts? . . *Lear* iii 6 82
Hard-hearted. Men grow hard-hearted and will lend nothing *Much Ado* v 1 321
Follow me no more.—You draw me, you hard-hearted adamant *M. N. D.* ii 1 195
I will not be so hard-hearted; I will give out divers schedules of my beauty: it shall be inventoried . . . *T. Night* i 5 262
Believe not this hard-hearted man! Love loving not itself none other can.—Thou frantic woman . . . *Richard II.* v 3 87
Ah, my sour husband, my hard-hearted lord! . . . v 3 121
Hard-hearted Clifford, take me from the world . . . *3 Hen. VI.* i 4 167
That same pale hard-hearted wench, that Rosaline, Torments him so *Rom. and Jul.* ii 4 4
Hard house—More harder than the stones whereof 'tis raised . . *Lear* iii 2 63
Hard journey. When Duncan is asleep—Whereto the rather shall his day's hard journey Soundly invite him . . . *Macbeth* i 7 62
Hard knots. Blunt wedges rive hard knots . . *Troi. and Cres.* i 3 316
Hard labour. Their courage with hard labour tame and dull . *1 Hen. IV.* iv 3 23
Hard language. Be not too rough in terms; For he is fierce and cannot brook hard language . . . *2 Hen. VI.* iv 9 45
Hard lesson. See how apt it is to learn Any hard lesson . . *Much Ado* i 1 295
Hard life. The certainty of this hard life . . . *Cymbeline* iv 4 27
Hard lodging. If frosts and fasts, hard lodging and thin weeds Nip not the gaudy blossoms of your love . . . *L. L. Lost* v 2 811
Hard luck. Or else 'twere hard luck . . . *W. Tale* v 2 158
Hard matter. It is a hard matter for friends to meet . *As Y. Like It* iii 2 194
Hard of hearing. Well have you heard, but something hard of hearing *T. of Shrew* ii 1 184
Hard of heart. The flesh'd soldier, rough and hard of heart . *Hen. V.* iii 3 11
Hard opinion. As thou lovest me, do him not that wrong To bear a hard opinion of his truth . . . *T. G. of Ver.* ii 7 81
For any thing I know, Falstaff shall die of a sweat, unless already a' be killed with your hard opinions . . . *2 Hen. IV.* Epil. 32
Hard point. He's at some hard point . . . *Cymbeline* iii 4 16
Hard rein. The hard rein which both of them have borne . . *Lear* iii 1 27
Hard rhyme. I can find out no rhyme to 'lady' but 'baby,' an innocent rhyme; for 'scorn,' 'horn,' a hard rhyme . . . *Much Ado* v 2 38
Hard rock. And here you sty me In this hard rock . . *Tempest* i 2 343
Hard-ruled. I' the bosom of Our hard-ruled king . *Hen. VIII.* iii 2 101
Hard sentence. I would not thy good deeds should from my lips Pluck a hard sentence . . . *Cymbeline* v 5 289
Hard temper. Hearts of most hard temper Melt . . *Hen. VIII.* ii 3 11
Hard things. There is two hard things; that is, to bring the moonlight into a chamber . . . *M. N. Dream* iii 1 49
Hard thoughts. Punish me not with your hard thoughts *As Y. Like It* i 2 196
Take to you no hard thoughts . . . *Ant. and Cleo.* v 2 117
Hard upon. I think it was to see my mother's wedding.—Indeed, my lord, it follow'd hard upon . . . *Hamlet* i 2 179
Hard use. My strange and self-abuse Is the initiate fear that wants hard use . . . *Macbeth* iii 4 143
Hard voyages. Our cowards, Like fragments in hard voyages, became The life o' the need . . . *Cymbeline* v 3 44
Hard way. By God's sonties, 'twill be a hard way to hit *Mer. of Venice* ii 2 47
Your fair discourse hath been as sugar, Making the hard way sweet *Rich. II.* ii 3 7
Hard words. Have you given him any hard words of late? . *Hamlet* ii 1 107
Hard world. Through the flinty ribs Of this hard world . *Richard II.* v 5 21
Harden'd be the hearts Of all that hear me! . . . *W. Tale* iii 2 53
Hardening. To the infection of my brains And hardening of my brows . i 2 146
Harder. As well do any thing most hard, As seek to soften that—than which what's harder?—His Jewish heart . . . *Mer. of Venice* iv 1 79
How sometimes nature will betray its folly, Its tenderness, and make itself a pastime To harder bosoms! . . . *W. Tale* i 2 153
With hard bright steel and hearts harder than steel . *Richard II.* iii 2 111
The harder match'd, the greater victory . . . *3 Hen. VI.* v 1 70
Thinking it harder for our mistress to devise imposition enough than for us to undergo any difficulty imposed . . . *Troi. and Cres.* iii 2 85
This hard house—More harder than the stones whereof 'tis raised *Lear* iii 2 64
Now, now, now, now: Pull off my boots: harder, harder . . . iv 6 177
Or ise try whether your costard or my ballow be the harder . iv 6 247
You must Forget that rarest treasure of your cheek, Exposing it—but, O, the harder heart! . . . *Cymbeline* iii 4 164
Hardest. And the hardest voice of her behaviour, to be Englished rightly, is, 'I am Sir John Falstaff's' . . . *Mer. Wives* i 3 51
Hardest-timbered. And many strokes, though with a little axe, Hew down and fell the hardest-timber'd oak . . . *3 Hen. VI.* ii 1 55
Hardiest. When the hardiest warriors did retire, Richard cried 'Charge!' i 4 14
Hardiment.—He did confound the best part of an hour In changing hardiment with great Glendower . . . *1 Hen. IV.* i 3 101
For thus popp'd Paris in his hardiment, And parted thus you and your argument . . . *Trio and Cres.* iv 5 28
Like hardiment Posthumus hath To Cymbeline perform'd . *Cymbeline* v 4 75
Hardiness. And our nation lose The name of hardiness . . *Hen. V.* i 2 220
Plenty and peace breeds cowards: hardness ever Of hardiness is mother *Cymbeline* iii 6 22
Hardly. Truly, sir, I think you'll hardly win her . . *T. G. of Ver.* i 1 141
When I look on you, I can hardly think you my master . . . ii 1 33
'Tis very clerkly done.—Now trust me, madam, it came hardly off . ii 1 115
I can hardly believe that, since you know not what you speak *M. for M.* iii 2 162
I shall hardly spare a pound of flesh To-morrow . *Mer. of Venice* iii 3 33
I was never so berhymed since Pythagoras' time, that I was an Irish rat, which I can hardly remember . . . *As Y. Like It* iii 2 188
Ay, it stands so that I may hardly tarry so long . . *T. of Shrew* Ind. 2 127
Such a storm That mortal ears might hardly endure the din . . . i 1 178
Or to drown my clothes, and say I was stripped.—Hardly serve *All's Well* iv 1 59
On a forgotten matter we can hardly make distinction of our hands *T. N.* ii 3 174
I can hardly forbear hurling things at him . . . iii 2 87
I could hardly entreat him back: he attends your ladyship's pleasure iii 4 63
Stay her tongue.—Hang all the husbands That cannot do that feat, you'll leave yourself Hardly one subject . . . *W. Tale* ii 3 112
Hardly Will he endure your sight as yet, I fear . . . iv 4 480
Hardly. Myself, well mounted, hardly have escaped . . *K. John* v 6 42
We have stay'd ten days, And hardly kept our countrymen together *Rich. II.* ii 4 2
I hardly yet have learn'd To insinuate, flatter, bow, and bend my limbs iv 1 164
I could be sad, and sad indeed too.—Very hardly upon such a subject *2 Hen. IV.* ii 2 47
She is pistol-proof, sir; you shall hardly offend her . . . ii 4 125
Which I beseech you to let me have home with me.—That can hardly be v 5 81
Will hang upon my tongue like a new-married wife about her husband's neck, hardly to be shook off . . . *Hen. V.* v 2 191
And hardly keeps his men from mutiny . . . *1 Hen. VI.* i 1 160
That hardly we escaped the pride of France . . . iii 2 40
Have done, for more I hardly can endure . . . *2 Hen. VI.* i 4 41
These oracles are hardly attain'd, And hardly understood . . i 4 74
Why hast thou broken faith with me, Knowing how hardly I can brook abuse? . . . v 1 92
His passion moves me so That hardly can I check my eyes from tears *3 Hen. VI.* i 4 151
If I unwittingly . . . Have aught committed that is hardly borne *Rich. III.* ii 1 57
The grieved commons Hardly conceive of me . . . *Hen. VIII.* i 2 105
We shall hardly in our ages see Their banners wave again *Coriolanus* iii 1 7
I was hardly moved to come to thee . . . v 2 78
And what remains will hardly stop the mouth Of present dues *T. Athens* ii 2 156
And he that's once denied will hardly speed . . . iii 2 69
Profit again should hardly draw me here . . . *Macbeth* v 3 62
The very conveyances of his lands will hardly lie in this box . *Hamlet* v 1 120
And hardly shall I carry out my side, Her husband being alive . *Lear* v 1 61
Hardly gave audience, or Vouchsafed to think he had partners *A. and C.* i 4 7
You shall see How hardly I was drawn into this war . . . v 1 74
Hail, thou fair heaven! We house i' the rock, yet use thee not so hardly As prouder livers do . . . *Cymbeline* iii 3 8
Here's a fish hangs in the net, like a poor man's right in the law; 'twill hardly come out . . . *Pericles* ii 1 124
Hardness. If you fail in our request, the blame May hang upon your hardness . . . *Coriolanus* v 3 91
I do agnize A natural and prompt alacrity I find in hardness . . *Othello* i 3 234
O, hardness to dissemble!—How do you, Desdemona? . . . iii 4 34
Throw my heart Against the flint and hardness of my fault *A. and C.* iv 9 16
Plenty and peace breeds cowards: hardness ever Of hardiness is mother *Cymbeline* iii 6 21
Is so from sense in hardness, that I can Make no collection of it . . v 5 431
Hardy. That you be never so hardy to come again in his affairs *T. Night* ii 2 10
Threefold renown'd For hardy and undoubted champions . *3 Hen. VI.* v 7 6
How now, my hardy, stout resolved mates! . . . *Richard III.* i 3 340
Buckingham, back'd with the hardy Welshmen, Is in the field . iv 3 47
Who like a good and hardy soldier fought 'Gainst my captivity *Macbeth* i 2 4
Makes each petty artery in this body As hardy as the Nemean lion's nerve . . . *Hamlet* i 4 83
Hare. Such a hare is madness the youth, to skip o'er the meshes of good counsel the cripple . . . *Mer. of Venice* i 2 21
Her love is not the hare that I do hunt . . . *As Y. Like It* iv 3 18
A very dishonest paltry boy, and more a coward than a hare . *T. Night* iii 4 421
You are the hare of whom the proverb goes, Whose valour plucks dead lions by the beard . . . *K. John* ii 1 137
What sayest thou to a hare, or the melancholy of Moor-ditch? *1 Hen. IV.* i 2 87
O, the blood more stirs To rouse a lion than to start a hare! . . i 3 198
Hang me up by the heels for a rabbit-sucker or a poulter's hare . ii 4 481
Like a brace of greyhounds Having the fearful flying hare in sight *3 Hen. VI.* ii 5 130
They that have the voice of lions and the act of hares . *Troi. and Cres.* iii 2 96
He that trusts to you, Where he should find you lions, finds you hares *Coriolanus* i 1 175
If I fly, Marcius, Holloa me like a hare . . . i 8 7
No hare, sir; unless a hare, sir, in a lenten pie . . *Rom. and Jul.* ii 4 138
An old hare hoar, And an old hare hoar, Is very good meat in lent: But a hare that is hoar Is too much for a score, When it hoars ere it be spent . . . ii 4 141
Dismay'd not this Our captains, Macbeth and Banquo?—Yes; As sparrows eagles, or the hare the lion . . . *Macbeth* i 2 35
Score their backs, And snatch 'em up, as we take hares, behind *A. and C.* iv 7 13
Scarce ever look'd on blood, But that of coward hares, hot goats *Cymb.* iv 4 37
Harebell. Thou shalt not lack The flower that's like thy face, pale primrose, nor The azured harebell, like thy veins . . . iv 2 222
Hare-brained. A hare-brain'd Hotspur, govern'd by a spleen . *1 Hen. IV.* v 2 19
They are hare-brain'd slaves, And hunger will enforce them to be more eager: Of old I know them . . . *1 Hen. VI.* i 2 37
Hare-finder. Cupid is a good hare-finder . . . *Much Ado* i 1 186
Hare-heart. Manhood and honour Should have hare-hearts *Troi. and Cres.* ii 2 48
Hare-lip. Never mole, hare-lip, nor scar, Nor mark prodigious *M. N. D.* v 1 418
He gives the web and the pin, squints the eye, and makes the hare-lip *Lear* iii 4 123
Harfleur. This fleet majestical, Holding due course to Harfleur *Hen. V.* iii Prol. 17
With fatal mouths gaping on girded Harfleur . . . iii Prol. 27
I will not leave the half-achieved Harfleur Till in her ashes she lie buried iii 3 8
Therefore, you men of Harfleur, Take pity of your town and of your people . . . iii 3 27
Go you and enter Harfleur; there remain, And fortify it strongly . . iii 3 52
To-night in Harfleur will we be your guest; To-morrow for the march . iii 3 57
Sweeps through our land With pennons painted in the blood of Harfleur iii 5 49
Tell him we could have rebuked him at Harfleur, but that we thought not good to bruise an injury till it were full ripe . . . iii 6 129
Ha'rford-west. At Ha'rford-west, in Wales . . . *Richard III.* iv 5 7
Hark in thine ear . . . *Tempest* i 2 318; *Pericles* i 2 76
Hark what thou else shalt do me . . . *Tempest* i 2 495
What harmony is this? My good friends, hark! . . . iii 3 18
Fury, Fury! there, Tyrant, there! hark! hark! . . . iv 1 258
Hark you hither! . . . *Mer. Wives* iii 4 21; *2 Hen. IV.* ii 4 165
Hark how I'll bribe you . . . *Meas. for Meas.* ii 2 145
But hark, a voice! stay thou but here awhile . . . *M. N. Dream* iii 1 88
But, hark, I hear the footing of a man . . . *Mer. of Venice* v 1 24
Hark you, the king is coming, and I must speak with him . *Hen. V.* iii 6 90
Ah, hark! the fatal followers do pursue . . . *3 Hen. VI.* ii 4 22
Why, hark ye, hark ye! and are you such fools To square for this? *T. An.* ii 1 99
Peace! Hark further . . . *Ant. and Cleo.* iv 9 11
Hark, hark! the lark at heaven's gate sings . . . *Cymbeline* ii 3 22
Hark, hark, you gods?—She conjures: away with her! . . *Pericles* iv 6 155
Harlot. Dissembling harlot, thou art false in all . . *Com. of Errors* iv 4 104
While she with harlots feasted in my house . . . v 1 205
For the harlot king Is quite beyond mine arm . . . *W. Tale* ii 3 4
That monstrous witch, Consorted with that harlot strumpet Shore *Richard III.* iii 4 73
Away, my disposition, and possess me Some harlot's spirit! *Coriolanus* iii 2 112

Harlot. Helen and Hero hildings and harlots . *Rom. and Jul.* ii 4 45
To trust man on his oath or bond ; Or a harlot, for her weeping *T. of Athens* i 2 67
Then was a blessed time.—As thine is now, held with a brace of harlots iv 3 79
If it be no more, Portia is Brutus' harlot, not his wife . *J. Cæsar* ii 1 287
The harlot's cheek, beautied with plastering art, Is not more ugly *Ham.* iii 1 51
Brands the harlot Even here, between the chaste unsmirched brow Of my true mother . . . . iv 5 118
Harlot-brow. And tear the stain'd skin off my harlot-brow *Com. of Errors* ii 2 138
Harlotry. He doth it as like one of these harlotry players as ever I see! 1 *Hen. IV.* ii 4 437
A peevish self-will'd harlotry . . . . iii 1 199 ; *Rom. and Jul.* iv 2 14
He sups to-night with a harlotry, and thither will I go to him *Othello* iv 2 239
Harm. Tell your piteous heart There's no harm done O, woe the day!—No harm. I have done nothing but in care of thee . . *Tempest* i 2 15
Doth your honour see any harm in his face? . . . *Meas. for Meas.* ii 1 159
How could Master Froth do the constable's wife any harm? . . . ii 1 165
A little more lenity to lechery would do no harm in him . . . iii 2 104
But indeed I can do you little harm ; you'll forswear this again . . iii 2 176
Music oft hath such a charm To make bad good, and good provoke to harm iv 1 15
A league from Epidamnum had we sail'd, Before the always wind-obeying deep Gave any tragic instance of our harm . . *Com. of Errors* i 1 65
They will surely do us no harm : you saw they speak us fair . . iv 4 156
Is there any harm in 'the heavier for a husband'? None, I think *M. Ado* iii 4 35
To turn all beauty into thoughts of harm . . . . iv 1 108
Bend not all the harm upon yourself; Make those that do offend you suffer too . . . . v 1 39
When I was wont to think no harm all night . . *L. L. Lost* i 1 44
Most power to do most harm, least knowing ill . . . . ii 1 58
Mislead night-wanderers, laughing at their harm . . *M. N. Dream* ii 1 39
Never harm, Nor spell, nor charm, Come our lovely lady nigh . . ii 2 17
And let the prologue seem to say, we will do no harm with our swords iii 1 19
Kill her dead? Although I hate her, I'll not harm her so . . . iii 2 270
What, can you do me greater harm than hate? . . . . . . iii 2 271
Be not afraid ; she shall not harm thee, Helena.—No, sir, she shall not iii 2 321
When I thought What harm a wind too great at sea might do *M. of Ven.* i 1 24
Glad of other men's good, content with my harm . . *As Y. Like It* iii 2 80
Frame your mind to mirth and merriment, Which bars a thousand harms and lengthens life . . . . . *T. of Shrew* Ind. 2 138
She is an irksome brawling scold : If that be all, masters, I hear no harm i 2 189
Ask me if I am a courtier: it shall do you no harm to learn . *All's Well* ii 2 39
In his sleep he does little harm, save to his bed-clothes about him . iv 3 287
I am a great eater of beef and I believe that does harm to my wit *T. Night* i 3 91
What incidency thou dost guess of harm Is creeping toward me *W. Tale* i 2 403
Slights him with 'Whoop, do me no harm, good man' . . . . iv 4 201
Fear not, man ; here's no harm intended to thee . . . . . iv 4 642
What other harm have I, good lady, done, But spoke the harm that is by others done?—Which harm within itself so heinous is As it makes harmful all that speak of it . . . . . . *K. John* iii 1 38
And so I would be here, but that I doubt My uncle practises more harm to me . . . . iv 1 20
Consume away in rust, But for containing fire to harm mine eye . . iv 1 66
By my troth, the instrument is cold And would not harm me . . iv 1 105
Nay, speak thy mind ; and let him ne'er speak more That speaks thy words again to do thee harm! . . . . . . *Richard II.* ii 1 231
Alack, alack, for woe, That any harm should stain so fair a show! . iii 3 71
Thou hast done much harm upon me, Hal; God forgive thee for it! 1 *Hen. IV.* i 2 103
To say I know more harm in him than in myself, were to say more than I know . . . . ii 4 512
My face does you no harm.—No, I'll be sworn . . . . . iii 3 32
Is marching hitherwards ; with him Prince John.—No harm : what more? iv 1 90
He never did harm, that I heard of.—Nor will do none to-morrow *Hen. V.* iii 7 109
Follow, and see there be no harm between them . . . . . iv 7 190
Blame him not ; I dare presume, sweet prince, he thought no harm 1 *Hen. VI.* iv 1 179
My spirit can no longer bear these harms . . . . iv 7 30
He lies inhearsed in the arms Of the most bloody nurser of his harms! iv 7 46
Buckingham, doth York intend no harm to us, That thus he marcheth with thee arm in arm? . . . . 2 *Hen. VI.* v 1 56
I never did thee harm : why wilt thou slay me?—Thy father hath 3 *Hen. VI.* i 3 38
To do them good, I would sustain some harm . . . . iii 2 39
So doth my heart misgive me, in these conflicts What may befall him, to his harm and ours . . . . iv 6 95
Great lords, wise men ne'er sit and wail their loss, But cheerly seek how to redress their harms . . . . v 4 2
So Judas kiss'd his master, And cried 'all hail!' when as he meant all harm v 7 34
No other harm but loss of such a lord.—The loss of such a lord includes all harm . . . . *Richard III.* i 3 8
Cannot a plain man live and think no harm? . . . . . . i 3 51
Lest to thy harm thou move our patience . . . . i 3 248
None can cure their harms by wailing them . . . . . . ii 2 103
As well the fear of harm, as harm apparent, In my opinion, ought to be prevented . . . . ii 2 130
I envy not thy glory ; To feed my humour, wish thyself no harm . . iv 1 65
From this league Peep'd harms that menaced him . . *Hen. VIII.* i 1 183
You know an enemy intends you harm . . . . *Troi. and Cres.* ii 2 39
And reason flies the object of all harm . . . . ii 2 41
'Tis this naming of him does him harm . . . . ii 3 239
We'll put you, Like one that means his proper harm, in manacles *Coriolanus* i 9 57
What harm can your bisson conspectuities glean out of this character? ii 1 70
He waved indifferently 'twixt doing them neither good nor harm . . ii 2 20
Which shall turn you to no further harm Than so much loss of time . iii 1 284
This tiger-footed rage, when it shall find The harm of unscann'd swiftness iii 1 313
She loves thee, boy, too well to do thee harm . . . *T. Andron.* iv 1 6
May I govern so, To heal Rome's harms, and wipe away her woe! . v 3 148
I never did thee harm.—Yes, thou spokest well of me.—Call'st thou that harm?—Men daily find it . . . . . . *T. of Athens* iv 3 172
Here is no use for gold.—The best and truest ; For here it sleeps, and does no hired harm . . . . iv 3 291
Know'st thou any harm's intended towards him?—None that I know will be, much that I fear may chance . . . . *J. Cæsar* ii 4 31
There is no harm intended to your person, Nor to no Roman else . . iii 1 90
'Twere best he speak no harm of Brutus here . . . . . . iii 2 73
Oftentimes, to win us to our harm, The instruments of darkness tell us truths, Win us with honest trifles . . . . . . *Macbeth* i 3 123
I, the mistress of your charms, The close contriver of all harms . . iii 5 7
For none of woman born Shall harm Macbeth . . . . . . iv 1 81
I have done no harm. But I remember now I am in this earthly world ; where to do harm Is often laudable . . . . iv 2 75
Harm. Why then, alas, Do I put up that womanly defence, To say I have done no harm? . . . . *Macbeth* iv 2 79
Esteem him as a lamb, being compared With my confineless harms . iv 3 55
Whose nature is so far from doing harms, That he suspects none . *Lear* i 2 196
Let me still take away the harms I fear, Not fear still to be taken . i 4 352
If he be taken, he shall never more Be fear'd of doing harm . . . ii 1 113
And for one blast of thy minikin mouth, Thy sheep shall take no harm iii 6 46
Let this kiss Repair those violent harms . . . . iv 7 28
But for a satisfaction of my thought; No further harm . . . *Othello* iii 3 98
Or to be naked with her friend in bed An hour or more, not meaning any harm?—Naked in bed, Iago, and not mean harm! . . . . . iv 1 4
But then I saw no harm, and then I heard Each syllable . . . . iv 2 4
Thou hast not half that power to do me harm As I have to be hurt . v 2 162
Ten thousand harms, more than the ills I know, My idleness doth hatch *Ant. and Cleo.* i 2 133
We, ignorant of ourselves, Beg often our own harms . . . . . ii 1 6
These same whoreson devils do the gods great harm in their women . v 2 278
Harm not yourself with your vexation : I am senseless of your wrath *Cymbeline* i 1 134
Ha! No harm, I trust, is done?—There might have been . . . i 1 161
I do suspect you, madam ; But you shall do no harm . . . . i 5 32
Good masters, harm me not : Before I enter'd here, I call'd . . . iii 6 46
No exorciser harm thee!—Nor no witchcraft charm thee! . . . . iv 2 276
If I do lie and do No harm by it, though the gods hear, I hope They'll pardon it . . . . iv 2 378
He hath done no Briton harm, Though he have served a Roman . . v 5 90
That I suffer'd Was all the harm I did . . . . v 5 336
Harm-doing. By my life, She never knew harm-doing . *Hen. VIII.* ii 3 5
Harmed. Though yet he never harm'd me, here I quit him . *All's Well* v 3 300
She hath been then more fear'd than harm'd . . . . *Hen. V.* i 2 155
I saw't not, thought it not, it harm'd not me . . . . *Othello* iii 3 339
Harmful. Which harm within itself so heinous is As it makes harmful all that speak of it . . . . *K. John* iii 1 41
Using conceit alone, Without eyes, ears, and harmful sound of words . iii 3 51
Lie gently at the foot of peace, And be no further harmful than in show v 2 77
Necessary you were waked, Lest, being suffer'd in that harmful slumber, The mortal worm might make the sleep eternal . . 2 *Hen. VI.* iii 2 262
This too much lenity And harmful pity must be laid aside . 3 *Hen. VI.* ii 2 10
More mild, but yet more harmful, kind in hatred . . *Richard III.* iv 4 172
More attask'd for want of wisdom Than praised for harmful mildness *Lear* i 4 367
But not without that harmful stroke, which since Hath pluck'd him after iv 2 77
Harmless. Your fairy, which you say is a harmless fairy, has done little better than played the Jack with us . . . . . . *Tempest* iv 1 197
That's more to me than my wetting : yet this is your harmless fairy . iv 1 212
Why he cannot abide a gaping pig ; Why he, a harmless necessary cat *Mer. of Venice* iv 1 55
Great pity, so it was, This villanous salt-petre should be digg'd Out of the bowels of the harmless earth . . . . . 1 *Hen. IV.* i 3 61
As all you know, Harmless Richard was murder'd traitorously 2 *Hen. VI.* ii 2 27
As is the sucking lamb or harmless dove . . . . iii 1 71
Do seek subversion of thy harmless life . . . . iii 1 208
The dam runs lowing up and down, Looking the way her harmless young one went . . . . iii 1 215
A napkin steeped in the harmless blood Of sweet young Rutland 3 *Hen. VI.* ii 1 62
Whiles lions war and battle for their dens, Poor harmless lambs abide their enmity . . . . ii 5 75
So first the harmless sheep doth yield his fleece And next his throat . v 6 8
I took him for the plainest harmless creature That breathed *Richard III.* iii 5 25
Poor harmless fly, That, with his pretty buzzing melody, Came here to make us merry! . . . . *T. Andron.* iii 2 63
And she, like harmless lightning, throws her eye On him . *Cymbeline* v 5 394
Harmonious. A most majestic vision, and Harmonious charmingly *Temp.* iv 1 119
Uttering such dulcet and harmonious breath . . . *M. N. Dream* ii 1 151
Harmony. The harmony of their tongues hath into bondage Brought my too diligent ear . . . . *Tempest* iii 1 41
What harmony is this? My good friends, hark!—Marvellous sweet music! . . . . iii 3 18
How still the evening is, As hush'd on purpose to grace harmony! *M. Ado* ii 3 41
His own vain tongue Doth ravish like enchanting harmony . *L. L. Lost* i 1 168
The voice of all the gods Make heaven drowsy with the harmony . . iv 3 345
Soft stillness and the night Become the touches of sweet harmony *Mer. of Venice* v 1 57
Such harmony is in immortal souls . . . . v 1 63
This is The patroness of heavenly harmony . . . . *T. of Shrew* iii 1 5
Give me leave to read philosophy, And while I pause, serve in your harmony . . . . iii 1 14
Into his hands That knows no touch to tune the harmony *Richard II.* i 3 165
They say the tongues of dying men Enforce attention like deep harmony ii 1 6
When such strings jar, what hope of harmony? . . . 2 *Hen. VI.* ii 1 57
After many moody thoughts At last by notes of household harmony They quite forget their loss of liberty . . . . 3 *Hen. VI.* iv 6 14
Whilst I sit meditating On that celestial harmony I go to *Hen. VIII.* iv 2 80
He is full of harmony . . . . *Troi. and Cres.* iii 1 56
Had he heard the heavenly harmony Which that sweet tongue hath made . . . . *T. Andron.* ii 4 48
But these cannot I command to any utterance of harmony . *Hamlet* iii 2 378
The fingers of the powers above do tune The harmony of this peace *Cymb.* v 5 467
My ears were never better fed With such delightful pleasing harmony *Pericles* ii 5 28
With her sweet harmony And other chosen attractions . . . . . v 1 45
Harness. Their harness studded all with gold and pearl . *T. of Shrew* Ind. 2 44
He doth fill fields with harness in the realm . . 1 *Hen. IV.* iii 2 101
Doff thy harness, youth ; I am to-day i' the vein of chivalry *T. and C.* v 3 31
Great men should drink with harness on their throats . . *T. of Athens* i 2 53
Come, wrack! At least we'll die with harness on our back . *Macbeth* v 5 52
Leap thou, attire and all, Through proof of harness to my heart! *A. and C.* iv 8 15
Harnessed. This harness'd masque and unadvised revel . . *K. John* v 2 132
Before the sun rose he was harness'd light . . . *Troi. and Cres.* i 2 8
Harp. His word is more than the miraculous harp! . . . *Tempest* ii 1 87
Harp not on that, nor do not banish reason For inequality *Meas. for Meas.* v 1 64
To be sung By an Athenian eunuch to the harp . . *M. N. Dream* v 1 45
My tongue's use is to me no more Than an unstringed viol or a harp *Richard II.* i 3 162
I framed to the harp Many an English ditty lovely well . 1 *Hen. IV.* iii 1 123
Harp not on that string, madam ; that is past.—Harp on it still shall I till heart-strings break . . . . *Richard III.* iv 4 364
Say, you ne'er had done't—Harp on that still—but by our putting on *Coriolanus* ii 3 260
Harped. Thou hast harp'd my fear aright . . . . . . *Macbeth* iv 1 74

Harper. Nor woo in rhyme, like a blind harper's song . *L. L. Lost* v 2 405
Harpier cries 'Tis time, 'tis time . . . . . . *Macbeth* iv 1 3
Harping. Still harping on my daughter . . . . *Hamlet* ii 2 189
Harping on what I am, Not what he knew I was . *Ant. and Cleo.* iii 13 142
Harpy. Bravely the figure of this harpy hast thou Perform'd . *Tempest* iii 3 83
Rather than hold three words' conference with this harpy . *Much Ado* ii 1 279
Thou art like the harpy, Which, to betray, dost, with thine angel's face, Seize with thine eagle's talons . . . . . *Pericles* iv 3 46
Harried. A proper man.—Indeed, he is so : I repent me much That so I harried him . . . . *Ant. and Cleo.* iii 3 43
Harrow. Let the Volsces Plough Rome, and harrow Italy . *Coriolanus* v 3 34
Most like : it harrows me with fear and wonder . . . *Hamlet* i 1 44
I could a tale unfold whose lightest word Would harrow up thy soul . i 5 16
Harry Bolingbroke doth humbly kiss thy hand . . *Richard II.* iii 3 104
Harry England (Hen. V.) Bar Harry England, that sweeps through our land With pennons painted in the blood of Harfleur . . *Hen. V.* iii 5 48
Harry Hereford. When, Harry, when? Obedience bids I should not bid again . . . . *Richard II.* i 1 162
Is Harry Hereford arm'd?—Yea, at all points . . . . . i 3 1
Harry of Hereford, Lancaster and Derby, Receive thy lance . . i 3 100; 104
He loves you, on my life, and holds you dear As Harry Duke of Hereford ii 1 144
Is not Gaunt dead, and doth not Hereford live? Was not Gaunt just, and is not Harry true? . . . . ii 1 192
Received intelligence That Harry Duke of Hereford, Rainold Lord Cobham . . . . ii 1 279
Harry Monmouth (afterwards Hen. V.) Whilst I, by looking on the praise of him, See riot and dishonour stain the brow Of my young Harry . . . . 1 *Hen. IV.* i 1 86
Then would I have his Harry, and he mine . . . . . i 1 90
Harry, I do not only marvel where thou spendest thy time . . ii 4 439
There is a thing, Harry, which thou hast often heard of and it is known to many in our land by the name of pitch . . . . . . ii 4 453
For, Harry, now I do not speak to thee in drink but in tears . . ii 4 457
If that man should be lewdly given, he deceiveth me ; for, Harry, I see virtue in his looks . . . . ii 4 470
Now, Harry, whence come you?—My noble lord, from Eastcheap . ii 4 484
Banish not him thy Harry's company : banish plump Jack, and banish all the world . . . . ii 4 525
God pardon thee! yet let me wonder, Harry, At thy affections . . iii 2 29
Gorged and full. And in that very line, Harry, standest thou . . iii 2 85
Why, Harry, do I tell thee of my foes, Which art my near'st and dearest enemy? . . . . iii 2 122
This gallant Hotspur, this all-praised knight, And your unthought-of Harry . . . . iii 2 141
On Wednesday next, Harry, you shall set forward ; On Thursday we ourselves will march . . . . iii 2 173
Our meeting Is Bridgenorth : and, Harry, you shall march Through Gloucestershire . . . . iii 2 175
I saw young Harry, with his beaver on, His cuisses on his thighs . iv 1 104
Harry to Harry shall, hot horse to horse, Meet and ne'er part till one drop down a corse . . . . iv 1 122
That no man might draw short breath to-day But I and Harry Monmouth! v 2 50
I prithee, Harry, withdraw thyself ; thou bleed'st too much . . . v 4 2
If I mistake not, thou art Harry Monmouth.—Thou speak'st as if I would deny my name . . . . v 4 59
O, Harry, thou hast robb'd me of my youth! . . . . . v 4 77
Myself and you, son Harry, will towards Wales . . . . v 5 39
My office is To noise abroad that Harry Monmouth fell . 2 *Hen. IV.* Ind. 29
And, in the fortune of my lord your son, Prince Harry slain outright . i 1 16
Harry Monmouth's brawn, the hulk Sir John, Is prisoner . . . i 1 19
Harry Monmouth ; whose swift wrath beat down The never-daunted Percy . . . . i 1 109
Well, the king hath severed you and Prince Harry . . . . i 2 228
Against the Welsh, himself and Harry Monmouth . . . . i 3 83
The king, my lord, and Harry Prince of Wales Are near at hand . . ii 1 146
To the son of the king, nearest his father, Harry Prince of Wales . . ii 2 130
Hereof [from sherris] comes it that Prince Harry is valiant . . iv 3 127
Come hither to me, Harry. Depart the chamber, leave us here alone . iv 5 90
I never thought to hear you speak again.—Thy wish was father, Harry, to that thought . . . . iv 5 93
Harry the Fifth is crown'd : up, vanity! Down, royal state! . . iv 5 120
For the fifth Harry from curb'd license plucks The muzzle of restraint iv 5 131
Come hither, Harry, sit thou by my bed ; And hear, I think, the very latest counsel That ever I shall breathe . . . . . . iv 5 182
My Harry, Be it thy course to busy giddy minds With foreign quarrels iv 5 213
No prince nor peer shall have just cause to say, God shorten Harry's happy life one day! . . . . v 2 145
Sir John, thy tender lambkin now is king ; Harry the Fifth's the man v 3 123
Then should the warlike Harry, like himself, Assume the port of Mars *Hen. V.* Prol. 5
Crowns imperial, crowns and coronets, Promised to Harry and his followers . . . . ii Prol. 11
Think we King Harry strong ; And, princes, look you strongly arm to meet him . . . . ii 4 48
Tells Harry that the king doth offer him Katharine his daughter . iii Prol. 29
And upon this charge Cry 'God for Harry, England, and Saint George!' iii 1 34
Thus says my king : Say thou to Harry of England . . . . iii 6 125
Alas, poor Harry of England! he longs not for the dawning as we do . iii 7 140
Behold, as may unworthiness define, A little touch of Harry in the night . . . . iv Prol. 47
The Lord in heaven bless thee, noble Harry!—God-a-mercy, old heart! iv 1 33
What is thy name?—Harry le Roy.—Le Roy! a Cornish name . . iv 1 49
Familiar in his mouth as household words, Harry the king, Bedford and Exeter . . . . iv 3 53
Once more I come to know of thee, King Harry, If for thy ransom thou wilt now compound . . . . iv 3 79
Much more, and much more cause, Did they this Harry . . v Prol. 35
Omit All the occurrences, whatever chanced, Till Harry's back-return v Prol. 41
Take me by the hand, and say 'Harry of England, I am thine' . . v 2 255
And they should sooner persuade Harry of England than a general petition of monarchs . . . . v 2 305
Harry Percy. It is my son, young Harry Percy, Sent from my brother Worcester, whencesoever. Harry, how fares your uncle? *Richard II.* ii 3 21
Welcome, Harry : what, will not this castle yield?—The castle royally is mann'd . . . . iii 3 20
The gallant Hotspur there, Young Harry Percy . . . 1 *Hen. IV.* i 1 53
Those prisoners in your highness' name demanded, Which Harry Percy here at Holmedon took . . . . i 3 24
Whate'er Lord Harry Percy then had said To such a person . . . i 3 71
And 'gentle Harry Percy,' and 'kind cousin' . . . . . . i 3 254

Harry Percy. For what offence have I this fortnight been A banish'd woman from my Harry's bed? Tell me, sweet lord . . 1 *Hen. IV.* ii 3 42
In faith, I'll know your business, Harry, that I will . . . ii 3 83
I'll break thy little finger, Harry, An if thou wilt not tell me all things true . . . . ii 3 90
I know you wise, but yet no farther wise Than Harry Percy's wife . ii 3 111
'O my sweet Harry,' says she, 'how many hast thou killed to-day?' . ii 4 118
The king with mighty and quick-raised power Meets with Lord Harry . iv 4 13
But there is Mordake, Vernon, Lord Harry Percy . . . . iv 4 24
Good cousin, let not Harry know, In any case, the offer of the king . v 2 24
My name is Harry Percy.—Why, then I see A very valiant rebel . . v 4 61
Nor can one England brook a double reign, Of Harry Percy and the Prince of Wales.—Nor shall it, Harry . . . . v 4 67
Said he young Harry Percy's spur was cold? Of Hotspur Coldspur? 2 *Hen. IV.* i 1 49
When my heart's dear Harry Threw many a northward look to see his father . . . . ii 3 12
Had my sweet Harry had but half their numbers, To-day might I, hanging on Hotspur's neck, Have talk'd of Monmouth's grave . . ii 3 43
Harry ten shillings. Here's four Harry ten shillings in French crowns for you . . . . iii 2 236
Harry the Fourth. The Lord of Stafford dear to-day hath bought Thy likeness, for instead of thee, King Harry, This sword hath ended him . . . . 1 *Hen. IV.* v 3 8
Why is Rumour here? I run before King Harry's victory . 2 *Hen. IV.* Ind. 23
Bear me to that chamber ; there I'll lie ; In that Jerusalem shall Harry die iv 5 241
Here come the heavy issue of dead Harry : O that the living Harry had the temper Of him, the worst of these three gentlemen! . . . . v 2 14
Not Amurath an Amurath succeeds, But Harry Harry . . . . v 2 49
Yet weep that Harry's dead ; and so will I ; But Harry lives, that shall convert those tears By number into hours of happiness . . . . v 2 59
Under which king, Bezonian? speak, or die.—Under King Harry.—Harry the Fourth? or Fifth?—Harry the Fourth . . . . v 3 120
Harry the Sixth. Servant in arms to Harry King of England 1 *Hen. VI.* iv 2 4
No, Harry, Harry, 'tis no land of thine ; Thy place is fill'd 3 *Hen. VI.* iii 1 15
When holy Harry died, and my sweet son . . . . *Richard III.* iv 4 25
I had a Harry, till a Richard kill'd him . . . . . . iv 4 41
O Harry's wife, triumph not in my woes! . . . . . . iv 4 59
Harry the Sixth bids thee despair and die! . . . . . . v 3 127
Harry, that prophesied thou shouldst be king, Doth comfort thee in thy sleep . . . . v 3 129
Harsh. And mar the concord with too harsh a descant . . *T. G. of Ver.* i 2 94
They [my news] are harsh, untuneable and bad . . . . . iii 1 208
For it can never be They will digest this harsh indignity . *L. L. Lost* v 2 288
The words of Mercury are harsh after the songs of Apollo . . . v 2 940
On thy soul, harsh Jew, Thou makest thy knife keen . *Mer. of Venice* iv 1 123
Tedious it were to tell, and harsh to hear . . . *T. of Shrew* iii 2 107
'Tis a good hearing when children are toward.—But a harsh hearing when women are froward . . . . v 2 183
Is it not a language I speak?—A most harsh one . . . *All's Well* ii 3 198
How dares thy harsh rude tongue sound this unpleasing news? *Rich. II.* iii 4 74
Harsh rage, Defect of manners, want of government, Pride 1 *Hen. IV.* iii 1 183
Into the harsh and boisterous tongue of war . . 2 *Hen. IV.* iv 1 49
I would invent as bitter-searching terms, As curst, as harsh 2 *Hen. VI.* iii 2 312
Why, trow'st thou, Warwick, That Clarence is so harsh? . 3 *Hen. VI.* v 1 86
Plain and not honest is too harsh a style . . . *Richard III.* iv 4 360
Bid the music leave, They are harsh and heavy to me . . *Hen. VIII.* iv 2 95
To whose soft seizure The cygnet's down is harsh . . *Troi. and Cres.* i 1 58
A name unmusical to the Volscians' ears, And harsh in sound to thine *Coriolanus* iv 5 65
Out of tune, Straining harsh discords and unpleasing sharps *R. and J.* iii 5 28
Like sweet bells jangled, out of tune and harsh . . . *Hamlet* iii 1 166
And in this harsh world draw thy breath in pain, To tell my story . v 2 359
Then murder's out of tune, And sweet revenge grows harsh . *Othello* v 2 116
Let's not confound the time with conference harsh . *Ant. and Cleo.* i 1 45
Well, I know not What counts harsh fortune casts upon my face . . ii 6 55
No more ado With that harsh, noble, simple nothing . . *Cymbeline* iii 4 135
No longer exercise Upon a valiant race thy harsh And potent injuries . v 4 83
Play'd upon before your time, Hell only danceth at so harsh a chime *Per.* i 1 85
Saying this Loud music is too harsh for ladies' heads . . . ii 3 97
Harshly. 'Twill sound harshly in her ears . . . . *Com. of Errors* iv 4 7
Feast your ears with the music awhile, if they will fare so harshly o' the trumpet's sound . . . . *T. of Athens* iii 6 37
Grating so harshly all his days of quiet . . . . . *Hamlet* iii 1 3
Harshness. He's composed of harshness . . . . . *Tempest* iii 1 9
Turn'd her obedience, which is due to me, To stubborn harshness *M. N. Dream* i 1 38
Thy tender-hefted nature shall not give Thee o'er to harshness . *Lear* ii 4 175
Harsh-resounding trumpets' dreadful bray . . . . *Richard II.* i 3 135
Harsh-sounding. He sung, in rude harsh-sounding rhymes . *K. John* iv 2 150
Hart. If a hart do lack a hind, Let him seek out Rosalind *As Y. Like It* iii 2 107
Will you go hunt, my lord?—What, Curio?—The hart . . *T. Night* i 1 17
That instant was I turn'd into a hart . . . . i 1 21
The hart Achilles Keeps thicket . . . . . . *Troi. and Cres.* ii 3 269
Please your majesty To hunt the panther and the hart with me *T. An.* i 1 493
Here wast thou bay'd, brave hart ; Here didst thou fall . . *J. Cæsar* iii 1 204
O world, thou wast the forest to this hart ; And this, indeed, O world, the heart of thee . . . . iii 1 207
Why, let the stricken deer go weep, The hart ungalled play . *Hamlet* iii 2 283
The swiftest harts have posted you by land . . . . *Cymbeline* ii 4 27
Our Britain's harts die flying, not our men . . . . . . v 3 24
Harum. Genitive case!—Ay.—Genitive,—horum, harum, horum *M. W.* iv 1 63
Harvest. Spring come to you at the farthest In the very end of harvest! *Tempest* iv 1 115
It is needful that you frame the season for your own harvest . *Much Ado* i 3 27
Scarce show a harvest of their heavy toil . . . . . *L. L. Lost* iv 3 326
I shall think it a most plenteous crop To glean the broken ears after the man That the main harvest reaps . . . . *As Y. Like It* iii 5 103
And yet, when wit and youth is come to harvest, Your wife is like to reap a proper man . . . . *T. Night* iii 1 143
I trust ere long to choke thee with thine own And make thee curse the harvest of that corn . . . . 1 *Hen. VI.* iii 2 47
And reap the harvest which that rascal sow'd . . . 2 *Hen. VI.* iii 1 381
And of our labours thou shalt reap the gain.—I'll blast his harvest 3 *Hen. VI.* v 7 21
He is kind.—Right, As snow in harvest . . . . *Richard III.* i 4 249
Though we have spent our harvest of this king, We are to reap the harvest of his son . . . . ii 2 115
To reap the harvest of perpetual peace By this one bloody trial . . v 2 15
There if I grow, The harvest is your own . . . . . *Macbeth* i 4 33

Harvest. The seedsman Upon the slime and ooze scatters his grain, And shortly comes to harvest . . . . *Ant. and Cleo.* ii 7 26
In's spring became a harvest, lived in court . . *Cymbeline* i 1 46
Thou hast the harvest out of thine own report *Pericles* iv 2 152
Harvest-home. There's my harvest-home . . . *Mer. Wives* ii 2 287
His chin new reap'd Show'd like a stubble-land at harvest-home 1 *Hen. IV.* i 3 35
Harvest-man. Like to a harvest-man that's task'd to mow Or all or lose his hire . . . . . *Coriolanus* i 3 39
Has. Nobody but has his fault; but let that pass *Mer. Wives* i 4 15
Indeed, he has no pace, but runs where he will . *All's Well* iv 5 70
Away with him! he has a familiar under his tongue . 2 *Hen. VI.* iv 7 114
Hast. Good, yet remember whom thou hast aboard . . *Tempest* i 1 20
Happy thou art not; For what thou hast not, still thou strivest to get, And what thou hast, forget'st . *Meas. for Meas.* iii 1 22
If thou hast her not i' the end, call me cut . . . *T. Night* ii 3 202
Now hast thou thy desire . . . . . *K. John* i 1 176
I had rather kill two enemies.—Why, there thou hast it *Richard III.* iv 2 73
Haste. Your father calls for you: He is in haste . *T. G. of Ver.* i 3 89
I'll presently attend you.—Will you make haste?—I will . . ii 4 190
An if thou seest my boy, Bid him make haste and meet me . iii 1 258
Well, farewell; I am in great haste now . . . *Mer. Wives* i 4 174
Take this basket on your shoulders: that done, trudge with it in all haste iii 3 14
I am in haste; go along with me: I'll tell you all . . v 1 25
Our haste from hence is of so quick condition . . *Meas. for Meas.* i 1 54
We may bring you something on the way.—My haste may not admit it . i 1 63
It lies much in your holding up. Haste you speedily to Angelo . iii 1 273
Break off thy song, and haste thee quick away: Here comes a man of comfort . . . . . . iv 1 7
I shall attend your leisure: but make haste . . . iv 1 57
What noise? That spirit's possess'd with haste That wounds the unsisting postern with these strokes . . . . iv 2 91
I thank thee, Varrius; thou hast made good haste . . iv 5 11
Haste still pays haste, and leisure answers leisure; Like doth quit like v 1 415
To the very block Where Claudio stoop'd to death, and with like haste v 1 420
Neither my husband nor the slave return'd, That in such haste I sent to seek his master! . . . . *Com. of Errors* ii 1 2
Here! go; the desk, the purse! sweet, now, make haste . . iv 2 29
I sent you money to redeem you, By Dromio here, who came in haste for it iv 4 87
I am now in great haste, as it may appear unto you . . *Much Ado* iii 5 54
We have some haste, Leonato.—Some haste, my lord! well, fare you well v 1 48
There will I leave you too, for here comes one in haste . . v 2 96
Haste, signify so much; while we attend . . . *L. L. Lost* ii 1 33
His tongue, all impatient to speak and not see, Did stumble with haste ii 1 239
Wings and no eyes figure unheedy haste . . . *M. N. Dream* i 1 237
This must be done with haste, For night's swift dragons cut the clouds iii 2 378
But, notwithstanding, haste; make no delay . . . iii 2 394
Return in haste, for I do feast to-night My best-esteem'd acquaintance: hie thee, go . . . . . *Mer. of Venice* ii 2 180
Since I have your good leave to go away, I will make haste . . iii 2 327
And therefore haste away, For we must measure twenty miles to-day . iii 4 83
The Jew shall have all justice; soft! no haste . . . iv 1 321
Away! make haste: thou know'st where I will tarry . . iv 2 18
Dispatch you with your safest haste . . . *As Y. Like It* i 3 43
See this dispatch'd with all the haste thou canst . *T. of Shrew* Ind. 1 129
My business asketh haste, And every day I cannot come to woo . . ii 1 115
Who woo'd in haste and means to wed at leisure . . . iii 2 11
But so it is, my haste doth call me hence . . . iii 2 189
When you are gentle, you shall have one too, And not till then.—That will not be in haste . . . . . . iv 3 72
Frank nature, rather curious than in haste, Hath well composed thee *All's Well* i 2 20
Come your ways.—This haste hath wings indeed . . . ii 1 96
I am there before my legs.—Haste you again . . . ii 2 74
And make this haste as your own good proceeding . . . ii 4 50
Let that go: My haste is very great: farewell; hie home . . ii 5 82
Stay not, but in haste to horse.—I shall not break your bidding . ii 5 92
It requires haste of your lordship.—I mean, the business is not ended . iv 3 109
He hence removed last night and with more haste Than is his use . v 1 23
To her in haste; give her this jewel; say, My love can give no place *T. N.* ii 4 126
Blame not this haste of mine. If you mean well, Now go with me . iv 3 22
Make your best haste . . . . . . *W. Tale* iii 3 10
But who comes in such haste in riding-robes? . . *K. John* i 1 217
We shall repent each drop of blood That hot rash haste so indirectly shed ii 1 49
Go we, as well as haste will suffer us, To this unlook'd for, unprepared pomp . . . . ii 1 559
Haste before: And, ere our coming, see thou shake the bags Of hoarding abbots . . . . iii 3 6
Nay, but make haste; the better foot before . . . . iv 2 170
Slippers, which his nimble haste Had falsely thrust upon contrary feet iv 2 197
O, haste thee to the peers, Throw this report on their incensed rage! . iv 2 260
Answer not, but to my closet bring The angry lords with all expedient haste . . . . iv 2 268
Lords, I am hot with haste in seeking you: Arthur doth live . iv 3 74
In haste whereof, most heartily I pray Your highness to assign our trial day.—Wrath-kindled gentlemen, be ruled by me *Richard II.* i 1 150
And hath sent post haste To entreat your majesty to visit him . i 4 55
Pray God we may make haste, and come too late! . . . i 4 64
His designs crave haste, his haste good hope . . . ii 2 44
Bloody with spurring, fiery-red with haste . . . ii 3 58
This haste was hot in question . . . . 1 *Hen. IV.* i 1 34
I'll haste the writer and withal Break with your wives . . iii 1 143
But, sirrah, make haste: Percy is already in the field . . iv 2 81
Bear this sealed brief With winged haste to the lord marshal . iv 4 2
If you knew How much they do import, you would make haste . iv 4 5
Therefore, lord constable, haste on Montjoy . . *Hen. V.* iii 5 61
I will the banner from a trumpet take, And use it for my haste . iv 2 62
I'll to the Tower with all the haste I can, To view the artillery 1 *Hen VI.* i 1 167
And therefore haste I to the parliament . . . . ii 5 127
Whither away, Sir John Fastolfe, in such haste?—Whither away! to save myself . . . . iii 2 104
As I rode from Calais, To haste unto your coronation . . iv 1 10
Then let's make haste away, and look unto the main . 2 *Hen. VI.* i 1 208
How now! what news? why comest thou in such haste? . . iv 4 26
In haste, post-haste, are come to join with you . . 3 *Hen. VI.* ii 1 139
Yet am I arm'd against the worst can happen; And haste is needful . iv 1 129
The time and case requireth haste . . . . . iv 5 18
It is his policy To haste thus fast, to find us unprovided . . v 4 63
Had I not reason, think ye, to make haste, And seek their ruin? . v 6 72
Because sweet flowers are slow and weeds make haste . *Richard III.* ii 4 15
Make all the speedy haste you may . . . . . iii 1 60
Haste. Which now the loving haste of these our friends, Somewhat against our meaning, have prevented . . . *Richard III.* iii 5 54
I in all haste was sent.—And I in all unwillingness will go . . iv 1 57
And brief, good mother; for I am in haste.—Art thou so hasty? . iv 4 161
Sent thither, and in haste too, Lest he should help his father *Hen. VIII.* ii 1 43
From that full meridian of my glory, I haste now to my setting . iii 2 225
My haste made me unmannerly . . . . . . v 2 105
What's the matter? It seems you are in haste . . . v 1 11
Yet the gentleman, That was sent to me from the council, pray'd me To make great haste . . . . v 2 3
Are you bound thither?—In all swift haste . . *Troi. and Cres.* i 1 119
Let's have your company, or, if you please, Haste there before us . iv 1 40
Tell you the lady what she is to do, And haste her to the purpose . iv 3 5
Injurious time now with a robber's haste Crams his rich thievery up . iv 4 44
Haste we, Diomed, To reinforcement, or we perish all . . v 5 15
I, with those that have the spirit, will haste To help Cominius *Coriolanus* i 5 14
Let's hence, And with our fair entreaties haste them on . . v 1 74
O, let us hence; I stand on sudden haste.—Wisely and slow; they stumble that run fast . . . . *Rom. and Jul.* ii 3 93
What haste? can you not stay awhile? Do you not see that I am out of breath? . . . . ii 5 29
Will you pluck your sword out of his pilcher by the ears? make haste . iii 1 84
Let Romeo hence in haste, Else, when he's found, that hour is his last iii 1 199
Hie you, make haste, for it grows very late . . . iii 3 164
Will you be ready? do you like this haste? We'll keep no great ado . iii 4 22
I wonder at this haste; that I must wed Ere he, that should be husband, comes to woo . . . . iii 5 119
And I am nothing slow to slack his haste . . . . iv 1 3
Hastes our marriage, To stop the inundation of her tears . . iv 1 11
Now do you know the reason of this haste.—I would I knew not why it should be slow'd . . . . iv 1 15
Hie, make haste, Make haste; the bridegroom he is come already . iv 4 25
Get on your cloak, and haste you to Lord Timon; Importune him *T. of Athens* ii 1 15
Whoso please To stop affliction, let him take his haste, Come hither . v 1 213
Those that with haste will make a mighty fire Begin it with weak straws *J. Cæsar* i 3 107
Stand close awhile, for here comes one in haste . . . i 3 131
Where haste you so?—To find out you . . . . i 3 133
Leave me with haste. Lucius, who's that knocks? . . . ii 1 309
What a haste looks through his eyes . . . . *Macbeth* i 2 46
Come, let's make haste; she'll soon be back again . . . iii 5 36
And modest wisdom plucks me From over-credulous haste . . iv 3 120
Bid them make haste.—I think I hear them . . . *Hamlet* i 1 13
This sweaty haste Doth make the night joint-labourer with the day . i 1 77
Farewell, and let your haste commend your duty . . . i 2 39
The morning cock crew loud, And at the sound it shrunk in haste away . i 2 219
Stay'd it long?—While one with moderate haste might tell a hundred . i 2 238
Haste me to know't . . . . i 5 29
Bid the players make haste. Will you two help to hasten them? . iii 2 54
Arm you, I pray you, to this speedy voyage . . . —We will haste us . iii 3 26
Speak fair, and bring the body Into the chapel. I pray you, haste in this . . . . iv 1 37
Away! for every thing is seal'd and done That else leans on the affair: pray you, make haste . . . . iv 3 59
The ocean . . . Eats not the flats with more impetuous haste . . iv 5 100
Let us haste to hear it, And call the noblest to the audience . . v 2 397
He's coming hither; now, i' the night, i' the haste . . . *Lear* ii 1 26
Resolve me, with all modest haste, which way Thou mightst deserve . ii 4 25
Came there a reeking post, Stew'd in his haste, half breathless . ii 4 31
Your haste Is now urged on you.—We will greet the time . . v 1 53
Take my sword, Give it the captain.—Haste thee, for thy life . . v 3 251
Which ever as she could with haste dispatch, She'ld come again *Othello* i 3 148
The affair cries haste, And speed must answer it . . . i 3 278
What's your pleasure, sir?—I must with haste from hence *Ant. and Cleo.* i 2 136
Haste we for it: Yet, ere we put ourselves in arms, dispatch we The business we have talk'd of . . . . ii 2 167
With what haste The weight we must convey with's will permit . . iii 1 35
Make your soonest haste; So your desires are yours . . . iii 4 27
I have spoke already, and it is provided; Go put it to the haste . v 2 196
Whiles yet the dew's on ground, gather those flowers; Make haste *Cymbeline* i 5 2
I have such a heart that both mine ears Must not in haste abuse . i 6 131
Let your breath cool yourself, telling your haste . . *Pericles* i 1 161
Speak out thy sorrows which thou bring'st in haste . . . i 4 58
And then with what haste you can get you to bed . . . ii 5 93
The mutiny he there hastes t' oppress . . . . iii Gower 29
The gods are quick of ear, and I am sworn To do my work with haste . iv 1 71
Hasted. Let it be so hasted that supper be ready at the farthest by five of the clock . . . . . . *Mer. of Venice* ii 2 121
Hasten. You shall be employ'd To hasten on his expedition *T. G. of Ver.* i 3 77
Do not plunge thyself too far in anger, lest thou hasten thy trial *All's W.* ii 3 223
Bid her hasten all the house to bed . . . *Rom. and Jul.* iii 3 156
Bid the players make haste. Will you two help to hasten them? *Hamlet* iii 2 55
Get you gone; And hasten your return . . . . *Lear* i 4 363
To my brother; Hasten his musters and conduct his powers . . iv 2 16
Pray you, hasten Your generals after . . . *Ant. and Cleo.* ii 4 1
Hastening. Whiles he was hastening, in the chase, it seems, Of this fair couple . . . . *W. Tale* v 1 189
Haste-post-haste. He requires your haste-post-haste appearance *Othello* i 2 37
Hastily. Here comes the prince and Claudio hastily . . *Much Ado* v 1 45
Hearing how hastily you are to depart, I am come to advise you *Meas. for Meas.* iv 3 54
Lead us from hence . . .: hastily lead away . . . *W. Tale* v 3 155
How now, good lady! What brings you here to court so hastily? *K. John* i 1 221
Hasting. Are both landed, Hasting to the court . . *W. Tale* ii 3 197
Hastings. The question then, Lord Hastings, standeth thus . 2 *Hen. IV.* i 3 15
Good day to you, gentle lord archbishop; And so to you, Lord Hastings iv 2 3
You are too shallow, Hastings, much too shallow . . . iv 2 50
Good tidings, my Lord Hastings; for the which I do arrest thee, traitor iv 2 106
Bishop Scroop, Hastings and all Are brought to the correction of your law . . . . iv 4 84
For this one speech Lord Hastings well deserves To have the heir of the Lord Hungerford . . . . 3 *Hen. VI.* iv 1 47
But, ere I go, Hastings and Montague, Resolve my doubt . . iv 1 134
So God help Montague as he proves true!—And Hastings as he favours Edward's cause! . . . . iv 1 144
What nobleman is that That with the king here resteth in his tent?—'Tis the Lord Hastings . . . . iv 3 11
What are they that fly there?—Richard and Hastings: let them go . iv 3 28

Hastings. My Lord Hastings and Sir William Stanley, Leave off to wonder why I drew you hither . . . . 3 *Hen. VI.* iv 5 1
Hastings, and the rest, Stand you thus close, to steal the bishop's deer? iv 5 16
How made he escape?—He was convey'd by Richard Duke of Gloucester And the Lord Hastings . . . . iv 6 82
Lord Hastings, and the rest, Yet thus far fortune maketh us amends . iv 7 1
Her brother there, That made him send Lord Hastings to the Tower *Richard III.* i 1 68
Heard ye not what an humble suppliant Lord Hastings was to her? . i 1 75
But who comes here? the new-deliver'd Hastings? . . . . i 1 121
You may deny that you were not the cause Of my Lord Hastings' late imprisonment.—She may . . . . i 3 91
Rivers and Dorset, you were standers by, And so wast thou, Lord Hastings, when my son Was stabb'd with bloody daggers . . i 3 211
I do beweep to many simple gulls; Namely, to Hastings, Derby . . i 3 329
Rivers and Hastings, take each other's hand; Dissemble not your hatred ii 1 7
So prosper I, as I swear perfect love!—And I, as I love Hastings! . ii 1 17
Wife, love Lord Hastings, let him kiss your hand . . . . ii 1 21
Here, Hastings; I will never more remember Our former hatred . . ii 1 23
Dorset, embrace him; Hastings, love lord marquess . . . . ii 1 25
Come, Hastings, help me to my closet. Oh, poor Clarence! . . . ii 1 133
Fie, what a slug is Hastings, that he comes not To tell us! . . . iii 1 22
Lord Hastings, go with him, And from her jealous arms pluck him perforce . . . . iii 1 35
Come on, Lord Hastings, will you go with me?—I go, my lord . . iii 1 58
Is it not an easy matter To make William Lord Hastings of our mind? iii 1 162
What will he?—He will do all in all as Hastings doth . . . . iii 1 168
Sound thou Lord Hastings, How he doth stand affected to our purpose iii 1 170
What shall we do, if we perceive Lord Hastings will not yield? . . iii 1 192
Then cursed she Hastings, then cursed she Buckingham . . . . iii 3 17
Lord Hastings, you and he are near in love.—I thank his grace, I know he loves me well . . . . iii 4 14
Had not you come upon your cue, my lord, William Lord Hastings had pronounced your part . . . . iii 4 28
Than my Lord Hastings no man might be bolder . . . . . iii 4 30
A word with you.—Catesby hath sounded Hastings in our business . iii 4 38
Margaret, now thy heavy curse Is lighted on poor Hastings' wretched head! . . . . iii 4 95
Here is the head of that ignoble traitor, The dangerous and unsuspected Hastings.—So dear I loved the man . . . . iii 5 23
This is the indictment of the good Lord Hastings . . . . . iii 6 1
Within these five hours lived Lord Hastings, Untainted, unexamined iii 6 8
Let me think on Hastings, and be gone To Brecknock, while my fearful head is on! . . . . iv 2 125
The adulterate Hastings, Rivers, Vaughan, Grey, Untimely smother'd in their dusky graves . . . . iv 4 69
Where is kind Hastings, Rivers, Vaughan, Grey? . . . . . iv 4 147
Hastings, and Edward's children, Rivers, Grey, Holy King Henry . v 1 3
Think on Lord Hastings: despair, and die! . . . . . . v 3 148
Hasty. Hot and hasty, like a Scotch jig, and full as fantastical *M. Ado* ii 1 78
Are you so hasty now? well, all is one.—Nay, do not quarrel with us . v 1 49
Take no unkindness of his hasty words . . . . *T. of Shrew* iv 3 169
If thou but frown on me, or stir thy foot, Or teach thy hasty spleen to do me shame, I'll strike thee dead . . . . *K. John* iv 3 97
Full of ire, In rage deaf as the sea, hasty as fire . . *Richard II.* i 1 19
Being upon hasty employment in the king's affairs . . 2 *Hen. IV.* ii 1 139
Is he so hasty that he doth suppose My sleep my death? . . . iv 5 61
Yet hasty marriage seldom proveth well . . . . 3 *Hen. VI.* iv 1 18
Edward from Belgia, With hasty Germans and blunt Hollanders . . iv 8 2
I am in haste.—Art thou so hasty? I have stay'd for thee, God knows, in anguish, pain, and agony . . . . . . *Richard III.* iv 4 162
Be not so hasty to confound my meaning . . . . iv 4 261
And something spoke in choler, ill, and hasty . . . *Hen. VIII.* ii 1 34
Hasty and tinder-like upon too trivial motion . . . *Coriolanus* ii 1 55
Their people Will be as rash in the repeal, as hasty To expel him thence iv 7 32
As violently as hasty powder fired . . . . . *Rom. and Jul.* v 1 64
Much enforced, shows a hasty spark, And straight is cold again *J. Cæsar* iv 3 112
The need we have to use you did provoke Our hasty sending . *Hamlet* ii 2 4
To cut off my train, To bandy hasty words, to scant my sizes . *Lear* ii 4 178
I'll stay Till hasty Polydore return, and bring him . . . *Cymbeline* iv 2 165
Hasty-footed. The hours that we have spent, When we have chid the hasty-footed time For parting us . . . . . *M. N. Dream* iii 2 200
Hasty-witted. An hasty-witted body Would say . . . *T. of Shrew* v 2 40
Hat. Make holiday; your rye-straw hats put on . . . . *Tempest* iv 1 136
Fetch me the hat and rapier in my cell: I will discase me . . . v 1 84
This hat is Nan, our maid: I am the dog . . . . *T. G. of Ver.* ii 3 23
By this hat, then, he in the red face had it . . . *Mer. Wives* i 1 173
He might put on a hat, a muffler, and a kerchief, and so escape . iv 2 73
And there's her thrummed hat and her muffler too . . . . iv 2 81
He wears his faith but as the fashion of his hat . . . *Much Ado* i 1 76
A' brushes his hat o' mornings; what should that bode? . . . . iii 2 41
The fashion of a doublet, or a hat, or a cloak, is nothing to a man . iii 3 125
I'll lay my head to any good man's hat . . . . . *L. L. Lost* i 1 310
With your hat penthouse-like o'er the shop of your eyes . . . . iii 1 17
My hat to a halfpenny . . . . v 2 563
Some sleeves, some hats, some yielders all things catch . *M. N. Dream* iii 2 30
Hood mine eyes Thus with my hat, and sigh, and say 'amen' *Mer. of Venice* ii 2 203
Is his head worth a hat, or his chin worth a beard? . *As Y. Like It* iii 2 217
Take my colour'd hat and cloak . . . . . . *T. of Shrew* i 1 212
In a new hat and an old jerkin, a pair of old breeches . . . . iii 2 43
An old hat and 'the humour of forty fancies' pricked in't for a feather iii 2 69
There was no link to colour Peter's hat . . . . iv 1 137
A velvet hose! a scarlet cloak! and a copatain hat! . . . . . v 1 70
Delicate fine hats and most courteous feathers . . . . *All's Well* iv 5 111
Take your sweetheart's hat And pluck it o'er your brows . . *W. Tale* iv 4 664
Nay, you shall have no hat. Come, lady, come . . . . . . iv 4 672
And, putting off his hat, said, 'I will now take my leave' . 2 *Hen. IV.* ii 4 7
I'll canvass thee in thy broad cardinal's hat . . . . 1 *Hen. VI.* i 3 36
Under my feet I stamp thy cardinal's hat: In spite of pope . . . i 3 49
They, for their truth, might better wear their heads Than some that have accused them wear their hats . . . . . . *Richard III.* iii 2 95
You have caused Your holy hat to be stamp'd on the king's coin *Hen. VIII.* iii 2 325
Hats, cloaks,—Doublets, I think,—flew up . . . . iv 1 73
The wisdom of their choice is rather to have my hat than my heart *Cor.* ii 3 105
And with his hat, thus waving it in scorn, 'I would be consul,' says he ii 3 175
He gave me a jewel th' other day, and now he has beat it out of my hat: did you see my jewel? . . . . *T. of Athens* iii 6 123
Their hats are pluck'd about their ears . . . . . *J. Cæsar* ii 1 73
Hat. What, man! ne'er pull your hat upon your brows; Give sorrow words . . . . *Macbeth* iv 3 208
No hat upon his head; his stockings foul'd, Ungarter'd . . *Hamlet* ii 1 79
By his cockle hat and staff, And his sandal shoon . . . . . iv 5 25
With glove, or hat, or handkerchief, Still waving . . . *Cymbeline* i 3 11
I have already fit—'Tis in my cloak-bag—doublet, hat, hose, all . . iii 4 172
Hatch. Either get thee from the door or sit down at the hatch *C. of Er.* iii 1 33
A little from the right, In at the window, or else o'er the hatch *K. John* i 1 171
That hand which had the strength, even at your door, To cudgel you and make you take the hatch . . . . v 2 138
Such things become the hatch and brood of time . . 2 *Hen. IV.* iii 1 86
'Tis true; the raven doth not hatch a lark . . . . *T. Andron.* ii 3 149
I do doubt the hatch and the disclose Will be some danger . *Hamlet* iii 1 174
With throwing thus my head, Dogs leap the hatch, and all are fled *Lear* iii 6 76
Ten thousand harms, more than the ills I know, My idleness doth hatch *Ant. and Cleo.* i 2 134
Hatched. And so in progress to be hatch'd and born . *Meas. for Meas.* ii 2 97
Folly, in wisdom hatch'd, Hath wisdom's warrant . . . *L. L. Lost* v 2 70
'Tis hatch'd and shall be so . . . . *T. of Shrew* i 1 211
A cockatrice hast thou hatch'd to the world . . . . *Richard III.* iv 1 55
Such [speeches] again As venerable Nestor, hatch'd in silver *T. and C.* i 3 65
Think him as a serpent's egg Which, hatch'd, would, as his kind, grow mischievous, And kill him in the shell . . . . *J. Cæsar* ii 1 33
And confused events New hatch'd to the woeful time . . . *Macbeth* ii 3 64
Repented The evils she hatch'd were not effected . . . *Cymbeline* v 5 60
If in our youths we could pick up some pretty estate, 'twere not amiss to keep our door hatched . . . . *Pericles* iv 2 37
Hatches. The mariners all under hatches stow'd . . . . *Tempest* i 2 230
There shalt thou find the mariners asleep Under the hatches . . . v 1 99
And—how we know not—all clapp'd under hatches . . . . . v 1 231
If he come under my hatches, I'll never to sea again . *Mer. Wives* ii 1 96
I stood upon the hatches in the storm . . . . . 2 *Hen. VI.* iii 2 103
Who from my cabin tempted me to walk Upon the hatches *Richard III.* i 4 13
As we paced along Upon the giddy footing of the hatches . . . . i 4 17
Sir, we have a chest beneath the hatches, caulked and bitumed *Pericles* iii 1 72
Hatchet. Ye shall have a hempen caudle then and the help of hatchet 2 *Hen. VI.* iv 7 96
Hatching. Which in the hatching, It seem'd, appear'd to Rome *Coriolanus* i 2 21
Hatchment. No trophy, sword, nor hatchment o'er his bones *Hamlet* iv 5 214
Hate. One word more Shall make me chide thee, if not hate thee *Tempest* i 2 476
They all do hate him As rootedly as I . . . . iii 2 102
But barren hate, Sour-eyed disdain, and discord shall bestrew The union of your bed with weeds so loathly That you shall hate it both iv 1 19
To plead for love deserves more fee than hate . . . *T. G. of Ver.* i 2 48
You have determined to bestow her on Thurio, whom your gentle daughter hates . . . . iii 1 14
For love of you, not hate unto my friend, Hath made me publisher of this . . . . iii 1 46
If she do frown, 'tis not in hate of you, But rather to beget more love . iii 1 96
Three things that women highly hold in hate . . . . . . iii 2 33
But she'll think that it is spoke in hate.—Ay, if his enemy deliver it . iii 2 34
You may temper her by your persuasion To hate young Valentine . . iii 2 65
I will follow, more for Silvia's love Than hate of Eglamour that goes with her.—And I will follow, more to cross that love Than hate for Silvia . . . . v 2 54
Our radiant queen hates sluts and sluttery . . . . *Mer. Wives* v 5 50
I something do excuse the thing I hate, For his advantage that I dearly love.—We are all frail . . . . *Meas. for Meas.* ii 4 119
Refuse me, hate me, torture me to death! . . . . . *Much Ado* iv 1 186
If she did not hate him deadly, she would love him dearly . . . v 1 178
I will never love that which my friend hates . . . . . . v 2 72
So much I hate a breaking cause to be Of heavenly oaths *L. L. Lost* v 2 355
The more I hate, the more he follows me . . . . *M. N. Dream* i 1 198
Can you not hate me, as I know you do, But you must join in souls to mock me too? . . . . iii 2 149
Superpraise my parts, When I am sure you hate me with your hearts . iii 2 154
Could not this make thee know, The hate I bear thee made me leave thee so? . . . . iii 2 190
Precious, celestial? Wherefore speaks he this To her he hates? . . iii 2 228
Although I hate her, I'll not harm her so.—What, can you do me greater harm than hate?—Hate me! wherefore? . . . . . . iii 2 270
Be certain, nothing truer; 'tis no jest That I do hate thee . . . iii 2 281
To sleep by hate, and fear no enmity? . . . . iv 1 150
I hate him for he is a Christian . . . . . . *Mer. of Venice* i 3 43
He hates our sacred nation, and he rails . . . . i 3 49
I'll go in hate, to feed upon The prodigal Christian . . . . . ii 5 14
You know yourself, Hate counsels not in such a quality . . . . iii 2 6
I oft deliver'd from his forfeitures Many that have at times made moan to me; Therefore he hates me . . . . iii 3 24
I give no reason, nor I will not, More than a lodged hate . . . iv 1 60
Do all men kill the things they do not love?—Hates any man the thing he would not kill? . . . . iv 1 67
Every offence is not a hate at first.—What, wouldst thou have a serpent sting thee twice? . . . . iv 1 68
My soul, yet I know not why, hates nothing more than he *As Y. Like It* i 1 172
I should hate him, for my father hated his father dearly; yet I hate not Orlando.—No, faith, hate him not, for my sake . . . . . . i 3 34
Owe no man hate, envy no man's happiness, glad of other men's good . iii 2 78
For my part, I love him not nor hate him not; and yet I have more cause to hate him than to love him . . . . iii 5 127
For the love you bear to women—as I perceive by your simpering, none of you hates them . . . . Epil. 17
Let not your hate encounter with my love For loving where you do *All's Well* i 3 214
Both my revenge and hate Loosing upon thee, in the name of justice . ii 3 171
I'll send her to my house, Acquaint my mother with my hate to her . ii 3 304
O strange men! That can such sweet use make of what they hate . iv 4 22
Thou didst hate her deadly, And she is dead . . . . . . v 3 117
A false conclusion: I hate it as an unfilled can . . . . *T. Night* ii 3 6
An't be any way, it must be with valour; for policy I hate . . . iii 2 33
I hate ingratitude more in a man Than lying, vainness, babbling . . iii 4 388
He's a rogue, and a passy measures panyn: I hate a drunken rogue . v 1 207
I hate thee, Pronounce thee a gross lout, a mindless slave . *W. Tale* i 2 300
Nothing do I see in you, Though churlish thoughts themselves should be your judge, That I can find should merit any hate . . *K. John* ii 1 520
Thou hate and terror to prosperity . . . . iii 4 28
Free from other misbegotten hate . . . . *Richard II.* i 1 33
How God and good men hate so foul a liar . . . . i 1 114
Swords and lances arbitrate The swelling difference of your settled hate i 1 201
For our eyes do hate the dire aspect Of civic wounds . . . . . i 3 127

Hate. Nor reconcile This louring tempest of your home-bred hate *Rich. II.* i 3 187
And what they will inform, Merely in hate, 'gainst any of us all, That will the king severely prosecute . . . . ii 1 243
Our nearness to the king in love Is near the hate of those love not the king . . . . ii 2 128
Their love Lies in their purses, and whoso empties them By so much fills their hearts with deadly hate . . . ii 2 131
Sweet love, I see, changing his property, Turns to the sourest and most deadly hate . . . . iii 2 136
I'll hate him everlastingly That bids me be of comfort any more . . iii 2 207
The love of wicked men converts to fear; That fear to hate, and hate turns one or both To worthy danger and deserved death . . v 1 67
Though I did wish him dead, I hate the murderer, love him murdered . v 6 40
When a jest is so forward, and afoot too! I hate it . . 1 *Hen. IV.* ii 2 50
Bacon-fed knaves! they hate us youth: down with them; fleece them ii 2 89
For all the country in a general voice Cried hate upon him 2 *Hen. IV.* iv 1 137
If I be measured rightly, Your majesty hath no just cause to hate me . v 2 66
As cognizance of my blood-drinking hate . . . 1 *Hen. VI.* ii 4 108
He that can do all in all With her that hateth thee and hates us all 2 *Hen. VI.* ii 4 52
Beaufort's red sparkling eyes blab his heart's malice, And Suffolk's cloudy brow his stormy hate . . . iii 1 155
With full as many signs of deadly hate As lean-faced Envy . . iii 2 314
Lord Say, the traitors hate thee; Therefore away with us to Killingworth . . . . iv 4 43
But that I hate thee deadly, I should lament thy miserable state 3 *Hen. VI.* i 4 84
These words have turn'd my hate to love; And I forgive and quite forget old faults . . . . iii 3 199
And ten times more beloved Than if thou never hadst deserved our hate v 1 104
And hate the idle pleasures of these days . . . *Richard III.* i 1 31
In deadly hate the one against the other . . . . i 1 35
To take her in her heart's extremest hate, With curses in her mouth . i 2 232
Be you, good lord, assured I hate not you for her proud arrogance . i 3 24
Live each of you the subjects to his hate, And he to yours, and all of you to God's! . . . . i 3 302
Oh, if you love my brother, hate not me; I am his brother, and I love him well . . . . i 4 232
Your brother Gloucester hates you.—O, no, he loves me . . . i 4 238
He that set you on To do this deed will hate you for the deed . . i 4 262
By heaven, my heart is purged from grudging hate . . . ii 1 9
Whenever Buckingham doth turn his hate On you or yours . . ii 1 32
God punish me With hate in those where I expect most love! . . ii 1 35
We have done deeds of charity; Made peace of enmity, fair love of hate ii 1 50
'Tis death to me to be at enmity; I hate it . . . . ii 1 61
They who brought me in my master's hate, I live to look upon their tragedy . . . . iii 2 58
Never a man in Christendom That can less hide his love or hate than he iii 4 54
He hates me for my father Warwick . . . . iv 1 86
She cannot choose but hate thee, Having bought love with such a bloody spoil . . . . iv 4 289
Alas, I rather hate myself For hateful deeds committed by myself! . v 3 189
All the commons Hate him perniciously . . . . *Hen. VIII.* ii 1 50
Put my sick cause into his hands that hates me? . . . iii 1 118
Vain pomp and glory of this world, I hate ye . . . iii 2 365
Love thyself last: cherish those hearts that hate thee . . . iii 2 443
This is of purpose laid by some that hate me—God turn their hearts! . v 2 14
I do hate a proud man, as I hate the engendering of toads *Troi. and Cres.* ii 3 169
As much as I do Cressid love, So much by weight hate I her Diomed . v 2 168
No space of earth shall sunder our two hates . . . v 10 27
Who deserves greatness Deserves your hate . . . *Coriolanus* i 1 181
Call him noble that was now your hate, Him vile that was your garland i 1 187
There is the man of my soul's hate, Aufidius, Piercing our Romans i 5 11
I do hate thee Worse than a promise-breaker.—We hate alike: Not Afric owns a serpent I abhor More than thy fame and envy . . i 8 1
The dull tribunes, That, with the fusty plebeians, hate thine honours . i 9 7
The prayers of priests nor times of sacrifice, Embarquements all of fury, shall lift up Their rotten privilege and custom 'gainst My hate i 10 24
If they love they know not why, they hate upon no better a ground ii 2 12
For Coriolanus neither to care whether they love or hate him manifests the true knowledge he has in their disposition . . . ii 2 14
He seeks their hate with greater devotion than they can render it him ii 2 21
Enforce his pride, And his old hate unto you . . . iii 3 228
Gibingly, ungravely, he did fashion After the inveterate hate he bears you ii 3 234
You common cry of curs! whose breath I hate As reek o' the rotten fens iii 3 120
My birth-place hate I, and my love's upon This enemy town . . iv 4 23
I have ever follow'd thee with hate . . . . iv 5 104
It [peace] makes men hate one another.—Reason; because they then less need one another . . . . iv 5 245
They charged him even As those should do that had deserved his hate iv 6 113
I am, as thy general is.—Then you should hate Rome, as he does . v 2 40
I have received letters from great Rome, Which signify what hate they bear their emperor . . . *T. Andron.* v 1 3
Talk of peace! I hate the word, As I hate hell . . *Rom. and Jul.* i 1 77
Canker'd with peace, to part your canker'd hate . . . i 1 102
Here's much to do with hate, but more with love . . . i 1 181
O brawling love! O loving hate! O any thing, of nothing first create! i 1 182
My only love sprung from my only hate! Too early seen unknown! . i 5 140
My life were better ended by their hate, Than death prorogued, wanting of thy love . . . . ii 2 77
The hate I bear thee can afford No better term than this,—thou art a villain . . . . iii 1 63
I have an interest in your hate's proceeding . . . iii 1 193
Wilt thou slay thyself? And slay thy lady too that lives in thee, By doing damned hate upon thyself? . . . iii 3 118
I will not marry yet; and, when I do, I swear, It shall be Romeo, whom you know I hate . . . . iii 5 123
Proud can I never be of what I hate; But thankful even for hate, that is meant love . . . . iii 5 148
See, what a scourge is laid upon your hate, That heaven finds means to kill your joys with love . . . v 3 292
That I were a lord!—What wouldst do then, Apemantus?—E'en as Apemantus does now; hate a lord with my heart *T. of Athens* i 1 236
I hate not to be banish'd; It is a cause worthy my spleen and fury . iii 5 112
Grant, as Timon grows, his hate may grow To the whole race of mankind! iv 1 39
I am Misanthropos, and hate mankind . . . . iv 3 53
Yield him, who all thy human sons doth hate, From forth thy plenteous bosom, one poor root! . . . . iv 3 185
I love thee better now than e'er I did.—I hate thee worse . . iv 3 234
Why shouldst thou hate men? They never flatter'd thee . . iv 3 269

Hate. Eat it.—On what I hate I feed not.—Dost hate a medlar? *T. of A.* iv 3 306
Thou shalt build from men; Hate all, curse all, show charity to none iv 3 534
Here lie I, Timon; who, alive, all living men did hate . . v 4 72
But when I tell him he hates flatterers, He says he does, being then most flattered . . . . *J. Cæsar* ii 1 207
When thou didst hate him worst, thou lovedst him better Than ever thou lovedst Cassius . . . . iv 3 106
Who neither beg nor fear Your favours nor your hate . . *Macbeth* i 3 61
Some say he's mad; others that lesser hate him Do call it valiant fury v 2 13
Might move More grief to hide than hate to utter love . *Hamlet* ii 1 119
Unfriended, new-adopted to our hate, Dower'd with our curse . *Lear* i 1 206
I would not from your love make such a stray, To match you where I hate i 1 213
Our flesh and blood is grown so vile, my lord, That it doth hate what gets it . . . . iii 4 151
Thou call'st on him that hates thee . . . . iii 7 88
O world! But that thy strange mutations make us hate thee, Life would not yield to age . . . . iv 1 11
Let sorrow split my heart, if ever I Did hate thee or thy father! . v 3 178
O, let him pass! he hates him much That would upon the rack of this tough world Stretch him out longer . . . . v 3 313
Thou told'st me thou didst hold him in thy hate . . *Othello* i 1 7
Though I do hate him as I do hell-pains . . . . i 1 155
I hate the Moor: my cause is hearted; thine hath no less reason . i 3 373
Yield up, O love, thy crown and hearted throne To tyrannous hate! . iii 3 449
An honest man he is, and hates the slime That sticks on filthy deeds . v 2 148
An honourable murderer, if you will; For nought I did in hate . v 2 295
In time we hate that which we often fear . . *Ant. and Cleo.* i 3 12
It is not Cæsar's natural vice to hate Our great competitor . . i 4 2
I cannot hate thee worser than I do, If thou again say 'Yes' . ii 5 90
He hath fought to-day As if a god, in hate of mankind, had Destroy'd in such a shape . . . . iv 8 25
I care not for you, And am so near the lack of charity—To accuse myself—I hate you . . . . *Cymbeline* ii 3 115
Yet 'tis greater skill In a true hate, to pray they have their will . ii 5 34
I love and hate her: for she's fair and royal . . . iii 5 70
I will conclude to hate her, nay, indeed, To be revenged upon her . iii 5 78
Here's poison, and here's gold; We hate the prince of Tyre *Pericles* i 1 156
Honour we love; For who hates honour hates the gods above . . ii 3 22
Hated. As the heresies that men do leave Are hated most of those they did deceive, So thou, my surfeit and my heresy, Of all be hated, but the most of me! . . . . *M. N. Dream* ii 2 140
And from thy hated presence part I so: See me no more . . iii 2 80
Thy love! out, tawny Tartar, out! Out, loathed medicine! hated potion! iii 2 264
I should hate him, for my father hated his father dearly *As Y. Like It* i 3 34
The time was that I hated thee, And yet it is not that I bear thee love iii 5 92
And my approach be shunn'd, Nay, hated too! . . *W. Tale* i 2 423
What is the business?—O sir, I shall be hated to report it! . . ii 2 144
If to be fat be to be hated, then Pharaoh's lean kine are to be loved 1 *Hen. IV.* ii 4 519
Comes to no further use But to be known and hated . 2 *Hen. IV.* iv 4 73
Ah, Clifford, murder not this innocent child, Lest thou be hated both of God and man! . . . . 3 *Hen. VI.* i 3 9
That hated wretch, That makes us wretched . . *Richard III.* i 2 17
Whom I most hated living, thou hast made me, With thy religious truth and modesty, Now in his ashes honour . . *Hen. VIII.* iv 2 73
Your old enemy, Who is of Rome worse hated than of you *Coriolanus* i 2 13
That of all things upon the earth he hated Your person most . iii 1 14
Made him fear'd, So hated, and so banish'd . . . iv 7 48
Despised, distressed, hated, martyr'd, kill'd! . . *Rom. and Jul.* iv 5 59
Henceforth hated be Of Timon man and all humanity! . *T. of Athens* iii 6 114
An thou hadst hated meddlers sooner, thou shouldst have loved thyself better . . . . iv 3 309
How fain would I have hated all mankind! . . . iv 3 506
Hated by one he loves; braved by his brother . . *J. Cæsar* iv 3 96
And on the sixth [day] to turn thy hated back Upon our kingdom *Lear* i 1 178
If fortune brag of two she loved and hated, One of them we behold v 3 280
The hated, grown to strength, Are newly grown to love *Ant. and Cleo.* i 3 48
Let me shake thy hand; I never hated thee . . . ii 6 76
And hated For being preferr'd so well . . . *Cymbeline* ii 3 135
Thus, unknown, Pitied nor hated, to the face of peril Myself I'll dedicate v 1 28
Hateful. O hateful hands, to tear such loving words! . *T. G. of Ver.* i 2 105
Is as hateful to me as the reek of a lime-kiln . . *Mer. Wives* iii 3 85
Death is a fearful thing—And shamed life a hateful *Meas. for Meas.* iii 1 117
Thou art suborn'd against his honour In hateful practice . . v 1 107
You'll not be perjured, 'tis a hateful thing . . *L. L. Lost* iv 3 157
And make her full of hateful fantasies . . . *M. N. Dream* ii 1 258
Seeking sweet favours for this hateful fool . . . iv 1 50
I will undo This hateful imperfection of her eyes . . . iv 1 68
Canonized and worshipp'd as a saint, That takes away by any secret course Thy hateful life . . . . *K. John* iii 1 179
Idle merriment, A passion hateful to my purposes . . . iii 3 47
Avaunt, thou hateful villain, get thee gone!—I am no villain . . iv 3 77
For little office The hateful commons will perform for us *Richard II.* ii 2 138
He calls us rebels, traitors; and will scourge With haughty arms this hateful name in us . . . . 1 *Hen. IV.* v 2 41
Where hateful death put on his ugliest mask To fright our party 2 *Hen. IV.* i 1 66
The 'solus' in thy teeth, and in thy throat, And in thy hateful lungs! *Hen. V.* ii 1 52
And nothing teems But hateful docks, rough thistles, kecksies, burs . v 2 52
Hide thee from their hateful looks, And, in thy closet pent up 2 *Hen. VI.* ii 4 23
He's disposed as the hateful raven . . . . iii 1 76
Yet Æolus would not be a murderer, But left that hateful office unto thee . . . . iii 2 93
Revenged may she be on that hateful duke! . . 3 *Hen. VI.* i 1 266
Have done thy charm, thou hateful wither'd hag! . *Richard III.* i 3 215
Urge his hateful luxury, And bestial appetite in change of lust . iii 5 80
Alas, I rather hate myself For hateful deeds committed by myself! . v 3 190
The noblest hateful love that e'er I heard of . *Troi. and Cres.* iv 1 33
A hateful truth . . . . . . iv 4 33
As hateful as Cocytus' misty mouth . . . *T. Andron.* ii 3 236
Bite our tongues, and in dumb shows Pass the remainder of our hateful days . . . . iii 1 132
But now nor Lucius nor Lavinia lives But in oblivion and hateful griefs iii 1 296
Go grind their bones to powder small And with this hateful liquor temper it . . . . v 2 200
My name, dear saint, is hateful to myself . *Rom. and Jul.* ii 2 55
Tell me, that I may sack The hateful mansion . . . iii 3 108
Accursed, unhappy, wretched, hateful day! . . . iv 5 43
O day! O day! O hateful day! Never was seen so black a day as this iv 5 52
Is man so hateful to thee, That art thyself a man? . *T. of Athens* iv 3 51

Hateful. O hateful error, melancholy's child . . . . *J. Cæsar* v 3 67
The devil himself could not pronounce a title More hateful to mine ear *Macbeth* v 7 9
May all the building in my fancy pluck Upon my hateful life *Lear* iv 2 87
When men revolted shall upon record Bear hateful memory *Ant. and Cleo.* iv 9 9
A wooer More hateful than the foul expulsion is Of thy dear husband *Cymbeline* ii 1 65
Hater. I shall prove A lover of thy drum, hater of love . *All's Well* iii 3 11
He was my master; and I wore my life To spend upon his haters *Ant. and Cleo.* v 1 9
Hatest. If thou hatest curses, Stay not; fly . . *T. of Athens* iv 3 541
Hateth. The more I love, the more he hateth me . *M. N. Dream* i 1 199
He that can do all in all With her that hateth thee and hates us all *2 Hen. VI.* ii 4 52
Who hateth him and honours not his father, . . . that made all France to quake, Shake he his weapon at us . . . . iv 8 16
Hatfield. Edward the Third, my lords, had seven sons: . . . The second, William of Hatfield . . . . . . ii 2 12
But William of Hatfield died without an heir . . . . ii 2 33
Hath. Methinks he hath no drowning mark upon him *Tempest* i 1 31
He shall pay for him that hath him, and that soundly . . . ii 2 81
The harmony of their tongues hath into bondage Brought my too diligent ear . . . . iii 1 41
Heaven send thee good fortune! A kind heart he hath . *Mer. Wives* iii 4 106
Howsoever he hath had intelligence . . . . . iv 2 94
He hath neither Latin, French, nor Italian . . *Mer. of Venice* i 2 74
But since he hath Served well for Rome . . *Coriolanus* iii 3 82
I am sped. Is he gone, and hath nothing? . *Rom. and Jul.* iii 1 95
Tybalt, that an hour Hath been my kinsman! . . . . iii 1 118
He that hath her—I mean, that married her, alack, good man! And therefore banish'd . . . . *Cymbeline* i 1 17
Hating. Murder, as hating what himself hath done, Doth lay it open to urge on revenge . . . . . *K. John* iv 3 37
The Nevils all . . . , As hating thee, are rising up in arms *2 Hen. VI.* iv 1 93
Hatred. Tempt not too much the hatred of my spirit . *M. N. Dream* ii 1 211
That hatred is so far from jealousy, To sleep by hate . . iv 1 149
With immodest hatred The child-bed privilege denied . *W. Tale* iii 2 103
That the contending kingdoms Of France and England, whose very shores look pale With envy of each other's happiness, May cease their hatred . . . . *Hen. V.* v 2 380
Unless they seek for hatred at my hands . . . . *3 Hen. VI.* iv 1 80
I'll in, to urge his hatred more to Clarence, With lies *Richard III.* i 1 147
Tears in her eyes, The bleeding witness of her hatred by . i 2 234
Your interior hatred, Which in your outward actions shows itself i 3 65
And turn you all your hatred now on me? . . . . i 3 190
Take each other's hand; Dissemble not your hatred, swear your love . ii 1 8
I will never more remember Our former hatred, so thrive I and mine! . ii 1 24
More mild, but yet more harmful, kind in hatred . . . iv 4 172
What his high hatred would effect wants not A minister in his power *Hen. VIII.* i 1 107
Suggest the people in what hatred He still hath held them *Coriolanus* ii 1 261
I wish I had a cause to seek him there, To oppose his hatred fully . iii 1 20
I bear no hatred, blessed man . . . . *Rom. and Jul.* ii 3 53
Haud credo. 'Twas not a haud credo; 'twas a pricket . *L. L. Lost* iv 2 12
My haud credo for a deer.—I said the deer was not a haud credo . iv 2 20
Haught. No lord of thine, thou haught insulting man . *Richard II.* iv 1 254
With Clifford and the haught Northumberland . *3 Hen. VI.* ii 1 169
The queen's sons and brothers haught and proud . *Richard III.* ii 3 28
Haughtiness. Pride, haughtiness, opinion and disdain *1 Hen. IV.* iii 1 185
Haughty. And will scourge With haughty arms this hateful name in us v 2 41
That haughty prelate, Whom Henry, our late sovereign, ne'er could brook . . . . *1 Hen. VI.* i 3 23
This cardinal's more haughty than the devil . . . . i 3 85
In this haughty great attempt They laboured to plant the rightful heir ii 5 79
These haughty words of hers Have batter'd me like roaring cannon-shot iii 3 78
Valiant and virtuous, full of haughty courage . . . . iv 1 35
Let us watch the haughty cardinal: His insolence is more intolerable Than all the princes in the land beside . *2 Hen. VI.* i 1 174
The haughty cardinal, More like a soldier than a man o' the church i 1 185
Beside the haughty protector, have we Beaufort The imperious churchman i 3 71
Whose haughty spirit, winged with desire, Will cost my crown *3 Hen. VI.* i 1 267
Whose humble means match not his haughty mind *Richard III.* iv 2 37
The haughty prelate Bishop of Exeter . . . . iv 4 502
I'll trust, by leisure, him that mocks me once; Thee never, nor thy traitorous haughty sons . . . . . *T. Andron.* i 1 302
This is that banish'd haughty Montague . . *Rom. and Jul.* v 3 49
Haunch. Divide me like a bribe buck, each a haunch *Mer. Wives* v 5 28
With forked heads Have their round haunches gored *As Y. Like It* ii 1 25
A summer bird, Which ever in the haunch of winter sings *2 Hen. IV.* iv 4 92
Haunt. You wrong me, sir, thus still to haunt my house *Mer. Wives* iii 4 73
And held in idle price to haunt assemblies *Meas. for Meas.* i 3 9
One that claims me, one that haunts me, one that will have me *C. of Er.* iii 2 82
Shun me, and I will spare your haunts . . *M. N. Dream* ii 1 142
I charge thee, hence, and do not haunt me thus . . . ii 2 85
This our life exempt from public haunt Finds tongues in trees *As Y. L. It* ii 1 15
There is a man haunts the forest, that abuses our young plants . iii 2 377
He haunts wakes, fairs and bear-baitings . . . *W. Tale* iv 3 109
There is a devil haunts thee in the likeness of an old fat man *1 Hen. IV.* ii 4 492
I do haunt thee in the battle thus Because some tell me that thou art a king . . . . v 3 4
And never noted in him any study, Any retirement, any sequestration From open haunts and popularity . . . *Hen. V.* i 1 59
Suspicion always haunts the guilty mind . . . *3 Hen. VI.* v 6 11
Your beauty, which did haunt me in my sleep . . *Richard III.* i 2 122
When thou wed'st, let sorrow haunt thy bed! . . . . iv 1 74
A whole week by days, Did haunt you in the field . *Troi. and Cres.* iv 1 10
I'll haunt thee like a wicked conscience still . . . v 10 28
We talk here in the public haunt of men . . *Rom. and Jul.* iii 1 53
Where they most breed and haunt, I have observed, The air is delicate *Macbeth* i 6 9
If thou be'st slain and with no stroke of mine, My wife and children's ghosts will haunt me still . . . . . . v 7 16
Whose providence Should have kept short, restrain'd and out of haunt, This mad young man . . . . . *Hamlet* iv 1 18
The foul fiend haunts poor Tom in the voice of a nightingale . *Lear* iii 6 31
I have charged thee not to haunt about my doors . . *Othello* i 1 96
She was here even now; she haunts me in every place . . iv 1 136
Let the devil and his dam haunt you! . . . . iv 1 153
Make the ghosts gaze: Dido and her Æneas shall want troops, And all the haunt be ours . . . . . *Ant. and Cleo.* iv 14 54

Haunt. What fairies haunt this ground? . . . *Cymbeline* v 4 133
Haunted. Our court, you know, is haunted With a refined traveller *L. L. Lost* i 1 163
O monstrous! O strange! we are haunted . . *M. N. Dream* iii 1 108
How now, mad spirit! What night-rule now about this haunted grove? iii 2 5
Haunted by the ghosts they have deposed . . *Richard II.* iii 2 158
Bred out of that bloody strain That haunted us in our familiar paths *Hen. V.* ii 4 52
With female fairies will his tomb be haunted . . *Cymbeline* iv 2 217
Haunting. The least of which haunting a nobleman Loseth men's hearts *1 Hen. IV.* iii 1 186
What do you mean by this haunting of me? . . . *Othello* iv 1 152
Hautboy. The case of a treble hautboy was a mansion for him *2 Hen. IV.* iii 2 351
Have. Good boatswain, have care. Where's the master? . *Tempest* i 1 10
Shall we give o'er and drown? Have you a mind to sink? . . i 1 42
Wipe thou thine eyes; have comfort . . . . . i 2 25
Be merry; you have cause, So have we all, of joy . . . ii 1 1
So to Naples, Where I have hope to see the nuptial . . . v 1 308
Now therefore would I have thee to my tutor . . *T. G. of Ver.* iii 1 84
Have you the tongues?—My youthful travel therein made me happy . iv 1 33
I'll ne'er believe that; I have to show to the contrary . *Mer. Wives* ii 1 38
I had other things to have spoken with her . . . . iv 5 41
O, pardon me, my lord; it oft falls out, To have what we would have, we speak not what we mean . . . *Meas. for Meas.* ii 4 118
Your mistress sent to have me home to dinner? . *Com. of Errors* ii 2 10
She would have made Hercules have turned spit . . *Much Ado* ii 1 261
Light them at the fiery glow-worm's eyes, To have my love to bed *M. N. D.* iii 1 174
Inquire, and so will I, Where money is, and I no question make To have it of my trust . . . . . . *Mer. of Venice* i 1 185
Have by some surgeon, Shylock, on your charge, To stop his wounds . iv 1 257
If you had pleased to have defended it With any terms of zeal . . v 1 204
A lean cheek, which you have not, a blue eye and sunken, which you have not, an unquestionable spirit, which you have not, a beard neglected, which you have not . . . . *As Y. Like It* iii 2 392
Art thou learned?—No, sir.—Then learn this of me: to have is to have v 1 44
Or wilt thou sleep? we'll have thee to a couch . . *T. of Shrew* Ind. 2 39
I have no more; And she can have no more than all I have . . ii 1 383
This has put me in heart. Have to my widow! . . . . v 5 78
Well, go thy ways, old lad; for thou shalt ha't . . . v 2 181
Till I have no wife, I have nothing in France . . *All's Well* iii 2 77; 102
When you find him out, you have him ever after . . . . iii 6 101
You beg a single penny more: come, you shall ha't . . . v 2 40
I think I have the back-trick simply as strong as any man . *T. Night* i 3 131
You might have saved me my pains, to have taken it away yourself . ii 2 6
There shall you have me . . . . iii 3 42
But once before I spoke to the purpose: when? Nay, let me have't *W. T.* i 2 101
I have one Of sprites and goblins.—Let's have that, good sir . . ii 1 25
Have is have, however men do catch . . . . *K. John* i 1 173
A man knows not where to have her . . . . . *1 Hen. IV.* iii 3 145
Thou or any man knows where to have me . . . . . iii 3 147
A' would have made a good pantler, a' would ha' chipped bread well *2 Hen. IV.* ii 4 258
Have at the very eye of that proverb with 'A pox of the devil' *Hen. V.* iii 7 129
Desire him to have borne His bruised helmet . . . Before him v Prol. 17
Weening to redeem And have install'd me in the diadem . *1 Hen. VI.* ii 5 89
If I were covetous, ambitious or perverse, As he will have me . . iii 1 30
Let him have all the rigour of the law . . . *2 Hen. VI.* i 3 199
In despite of the devils and hell, have through the very middest of you! iv 8 63
We have not got that which we have . . . . . . v 3 20
Come then, away; let's ha' no more ado . . *3 Hen. VI.* iv 5 27
Have not to do with him, beware of him . . . *Richard III.* i 3 292
I will have more, or scold it out of him . . . *Hen. VIII.* v 1 173
Cannot make boast to have that which he hath . . *Troi. and Cres.* iii 3 98
Without any further deed to have them at all into their estimation *Cor.* ii 2 31
I have no further with you . . . . ii 3 181
Let me have war, say I; it exceeds peace as far as day does night . iv 5 236
A verse in Horace; right, you have it . . . *T. Andron.* iv 2 24
They have made worms' meat of me: I have it, And soundly too *R. and J.* iii 1 112
What wouldst thou have to Athens?—Thee thither . . *T. of Athens* iv 3 287
Have an eye to Cinna; trust not Trebonius . . . *J. Cæsar* ii 3 2
I would have had thee there, and here again . . . . ii 4 4
Come, let me clutch thee. I have thee not, and yet I see thee still *Macb.* ii 1 35
You have me, have you not? . . . . *Hamlet* ii 1 68
I have nothing with this answer, Hamlet; these words are not mine . iii 2 101
Will you ha' the truth on't? . . . . v 1 26
I thought thy bride-bed to have deck'd, sweet maid, And not have strew'd thy grave . . . . v 1 268
Have more than thou showest, Speak less than thou knowest *Lear* i 4 131
We will have more of this to-morrow . . . . *Othello* i 3 379
Let her have your knees. Hail to thee, lady! . . . . ii 1 84
Her honour is an essence that's not seen; They have it very oft that have it not . . . . iv 1 17
Where have you this? 'tis false . . . . *Ant. and Cleo.* ii 1 18
I have seen thee fight, When I have envied thy behaviour . . ii 6 76
I ha' praised ye, When you have well deserved ten times As much as I have said you did . . . . ii 6 78
Must I be unfolded With one that I have bred? The gods! it smites me Beneath the fall I have . . . . v 2 171
Here's my ring.—I will have it no lay . . . *Cymbeline* i 4 159
Have after. To what issue will this come? . . . *Hamlet* i 4 89
Have at him. Let him lend me the money, and have at him! *2 Hen. IV.* ii 2 217
I'll venture one have-at-him . . . . . *Hen. VIII.* ii 2 85
Have at it. 'Tis my occupation; have at it with you . *W. Tale* iv 4 302
Have at it then, by leave . . . . . *Cymbeline* v 5 315
Have at you with a proverb—Shall I set in my staff?—Have at you with another . . . . *Com. of Errors* iii 1 51
Have at you, then, affection's men at arms . . *L. L. Lost* iv 3 290
Since you have begun, Have at you for a bitter jest or two! *T. of Shrew* v 2 45
Have at thee with a downright blow! . . . *2 Hen. VI.* ii 3 92
Ye blew the fire that burns ye: now have at ye! . *Hen. VIII.* v 3 113
Come, both you cogging Greeks; have at you both! . *Troi. and Cres.* v 6 11
Then have at you with my wit! I will dry-beat you . *Rom. and Jul.* iv 5 125
Wilt thou provoke me? then have at thee, boy! . . . . v 3 70
Have at you now!—Part them; they are incensed . . *Hamlet* v 2 313
Have done. To have done is to hang Quite out of fashion *Troi. and Cres.* iii 3 151
Have to it. And then have to't afresh . . . *T. of Shrew* i 1 143
Have to thee. That's my office.—Spoke like an officer: ha' to thee, lad! v 2 37
Have with you. You'll come to dinner . . . *Mer. Wives* ii 1 161
Will you go, An-heires?—Have with you . . . . . ii 1 229
Shall we wag?—Have with you. I had rather hear them scold than fight ii 1 239
Will you go, gentles?—Have with you to see this monster . . . iii 2 93

Have with you. God save your life!—Have with thee, my girl *L. L. Lost* iv 2 151
Will you go, coz?—Have with you. Fare you well . . *As Y. Like It* i 2 268
Farewell until I meet thee next.—Have with thee . . 1 *Hen. VI.* ii 4 114
Come, come, have with you. Wot you what, my lord? . *Richard III.* iii 2 92
Have with you, prince. My courteous lord, adieu . *Troi. and Cres.* v 2 185
Haven. And happily I have arrived at the last Unto the wished haven of my bliss . . . . *T. of Shrew* v 1 131
All places that the eye of heaven visits Are to a wise man ports and happy havens . . . . *Richard II.* i 3 276
Arrived From Ravenspurgh haven before the gates of York 3 *Hen. VI.* iv 7 8
Order for sea is given; They have put forth the haven . *Ant. and Cleo.* iv 10 7
He would not suffer me To bring him to the haven . . *Cymbeline* i 1 171
I would thou grew'st unto the shores o' the haven, And question'dst every sail . . . . i 3 1
Tell me how Wales was made so happy as To inherit such a haven . iii 2 63
O'erlook What shipping and what lading's in our haven . . *Pericles* i 2 49
Haver. It is held That valour is the chiefest virtue, and Most dignifies the haver . . . . *Coriolanus* ii 2 89
Having both the key Of officer and office . . . . . *Tempest* i 2 83
Thou think'st there is no more such shapes as he, Having seen but him i 2 479
The gentleman is of no having . . . . . . *Mer. Wives* iii 2 73
You need not fear, lady, the having any of these lords . *Mer. of Venice* i 2 109
Having that, do choke their service up Even with the having *As Y. L. It* ii 3 61
Simply your having in beard is a younger brother's revenue . . iii 2 396
I'll lend you something: my having is not much . . *T. Night* iii 4 379
I would not have you to think that my desire of having is the sin of covetousness . . . . v 1 50
The place of your dwelling, your names, your ages, of what having *W. T.* iv 4 740
Our content Is our best having . . . . . . *Hen. VIII.* ii 3 23
Pared my present havings, to bestow My bounties upon you . . . iii 2 159
That man, how dearly ever parted, How much in having, or without or in, Cannot make boast to have that which he hath, Nor feels not what he owes, but by reflection . . . . *Troi. and Cres.* iii 3 97
Back,—that's the utmost of your having: back . . *Coriolanus* v 2 62
What sadness lengthens Romeo's hours?—Not having that, which, having, makes them short . . . . *Rom. and Jul.* i 1 170
The greatest of your having lacks a half To pay your present debts.—Let all my land be sold . . . . *T. of Athens* ii 2 153
If it be a just and true report that goes of his having . . . . v 1 18
You greet with present grace and great prediction Of noble having *Macbeth* i 3 56
Him you would sound, Having ever seen in the prenominate crimes The youth you breathe of guilty . . . . *Hamlet* ii 1 43
Or say they strike us, Or scant our former having in despite . *Othello* iv 3 92
You have land enough of your own: but he added to your having *Cymb.* i 2 19
For his sake I wish the having of it . . . . . . *Pericles* ii 1 145
'Haviour. I will keep the haviour of reputation . . *Mer. Wives* i 3 86
With the same 'haviour that your passion bears Goes on my master's grief . . . . *T. Night* iii 4 226
And furbish new the name of John a Gaunt, Even in the lusty haviour of his son . . . . *Richard II.* i 3 77
And therefore thou mayst think my 'haviour light . . *Rom. and Jul.* ii 2 99
Nor the dejected 'haviour of the visage . . . . . *Hamlet* i 2 81
Brought up with him, And sith so neighbour'd to his youth and haviour ii 2 12
Put thyself Into a haviour of less fear . . . . *Cymbeline* iii 4 9
Havoc. Nor fortune made such havoc of my means . *Much Ado* iv 1 197
Away with him! Who hath made this havoc with them? . *T. Night* v 1 209
And wide havoc made For bloody power to rush upon your peace *K. John* ii 1 220
Cry, 'havoc!' kings; back to the stained field, You equal potents! . ii 1 357
Moody beggars, starving for a time Of pellmell havoc and confusion 1 *Hen. IV.* v 1 82
To tear and havoc more than she can eat . . . . *Hen. V.* i 2 173
Do not cry havoc, where you should but hunt With modest warrant *Coriol.* iii 1 275
Cry 'Havoc,' and let slip the dogs of war . . . *J. Cæsar* iii 1 273
This quarry cries on havoc . . . . *Hamlet* v 2 375
Hawk. I have a fine hawk for the bush . . . *Mer. Wives* iii 3 247
Heigh-ho!—For a hawk, a horse, or a husband? . . *Much Ado* ii 4 55
Thou hast hawks will soar Above the morning lark . *T. of Shrew* Ind. 2 45
Twenty crowns! I'll venture so much of my hawk or hound, But twenty times so much upon my wife . . . . v 2 72
When I bestride him, I soar, I am a hawk: he trots the air . *Hen. V.* iii 7 16
Between two hawks, which flies the higher pitch . . 1 *Hen. VI.* ii 4 11
The king and queen do mean to hawk . . . . 2 *Hen. VI.* i 2 58
No marvel, an it like your majesty, My lord protector's hawks do tower so well . . . . ii 1 10
When the wind is southerly I know a hawk from a handsaw . *Hamlet* ii 2 397
Hawked. A falcon, towering in her pride of place, Was by a mousing owl hawk'd at and kill'd . . . . *Macbeth* ii 4 13
Hawking. Without hawking or spitting or saying we are hoarse *As Y. L. It* v 3 12
Dost thou love hawking? thou hast hawks will soar . *T. of Shrew* Ind. 2 45
His arched brows, his hawking eye, his curls . . . *All's Well* i 1 105
Talking of hawking; nothing else, my lord . . . 2 *Hen. VI.* ii 1 50
Hawthorn. Hangs odes upon hawthorns and elegies on brambles *As Y. L. It* iii 2 380
Through the sharp hawthorn blows the cold wind . . . *Lear* iii 4 47
Still through the hawthorn blows the cold wind . . . . iii 4 102
Hawthorn-brake. This green plot shall be our stage, this hawthorn-brake our tiring-house . . . . *M. N. Dream* iii 1 4
Hawthorn-bud. Like a many of these lisping hawthorn-buds *Mer. Wives* iii 3 77
When wheat is green, when hawthorn buds appear . *M. N. Dream* i 1 185
Hawthorn-bush. Gives not the hawthorn-bush a sweeter shade To shepherds looking on their silly sheep, Than doth a rich embroider'd canopy To kings? . . . . 3 *Hen. VI.* ii 5 42
Hay. I will play On the tabor . . . , and let them dance the hay *L. L. Lost* v 1 161
Methinks I have a great desire to a bottle of hay: good hay, sweet hay, hath no fellow . . . . *M. N. Dream* iv 1 37
While we lie tumbling in the hay . . . . . . *W. Tale* iv 3 12
The sun shines hot; and, if we use delay, Cold biting winter mars our hoped-for hay . . . . 3 *Hen. VI.* iv 8 61
I will drain him dry as hay . . . . *Macbeth* i 3 18
'Twas her brother that, in pure kindness to his horse, buttered his hay *Lear* ii 4 128
Hay-stack. Set fire on barns and hay-stacks in the night, And bid the owners quench them with their tears . . . . *T. Andron.* v 1 133
Hazard. One cannot climb it Without apparent hazard of his life *T. G. of V.* iii 1 116
Madam, this service I have done for you, . . . To hazard life . . v 4 21
In the boldness of my cunning, I will lay myself in hazard *Meas. for Meas.* iv 2 166
Or bring your latter hazard back again . . . *Mer. of Venice* i 1 151
After dinner Your hazard shall be made . . . . . . ii 1 45
Who chooseth me must give and hazard all he hath . . . . ii 7 9
Men that hazard all Do it in hope of fair advantages . . . . ii 7 18
I'll then nor give nor hazard aught for lead . . . . . ii 7 21
To these injunctions every one doth swear That comes to hazard for my worthless self . . . . *Mer. of Venice* ii 9 18
You shall look fairer, ere I give or hazard . . . . . . ii 9 22
I pray you, tarry: pause a day or two Before you hazard . . . iii 2 2
Thou this to hazard needs must intimate Skill infinite . *All's Well* ii 1 186
We'll strive to bear it for your worthy sake To the extreme edge of hazard iii 3 6
To the hazard Of all incertainties himself commended . . *W. Tale* iii 2 169
Which fault lies on the hazards of all husbands That marry wives *K. John* i 1 119
To make a hazard of new fortunes here . . . . ii 1 71
I will upon all hazards well believe Thou art my friend . . . . v 6 7
I will ease my heart, Albeit I make a hazard of my head . 1 *Hen. IV.* i 3 128
To set so rich a main On the nice hazard of one doubtful hour . iv 1 48
In hearty prayers That your attempts may overlive the hazard 2 *Hen. IV.* iv 1 15
Play a set Shall strike his father's crown into the hazard . *Hen. V.* i 2 263
Who will go to hazard with me for twenty prisoners?—You must first go yourself to hazard, ere you have them . . . . iii 7 93
O, too much folly is it, well I wot, To hazard all our lives in one small boat! . . . . 1 *Hen. VI.* iv 6 33
All these and more we hazard by thy stay . . . . . iv 6 40
I have set my life upon a cast, And I will stand the hazard of the die *Richard III.* v 4 10
On one and other side, Trojan and Greek, Sets all on hazard *T. and C.* Prol. 22
Let them go on; This mutiny were better put in hazard, Than stay, past doubt, for greater . . . . *Coriolanus* ii 3 264
Which else would put you to your fortune and The hazard of much blood iii 2 61
You wot well My hazards still have been your solace . . . iv 1 28
He hath left undone That which shall break his neck or hazard mine . iv 7 25
What folly 'tis to hazard life for ill! . . . . *T. of Athens* iii 5 37
If thou wert the wolf, thy greediness would afflict thee, and oft thou shouldst hazard thy life for thy dinner . . . . iv 3 338
We stand much hazard, if they bring not Timon . . . . . v 2 5
And by the hazard of the spotted die Let die the spotted . . . v 4 34
Will follow The fortunes and affairs of noble Brutus Thorough the hazards of this untrod state . . . . *J. Cæsar* iii 1 136
Swell billow and swim bark! The storm is up, and all is on the hazard v 1 68
The terms of our estate may not endure Hazard so near us as doth hourly grow Out of his lunacies . . . . *Hamlet* iii 3 6
'Tis great pity that the noble Moor Should hazard such a place as his own second With one of an ingraft infirmity . . . . *Othello* ii 3 144
Give up yourself merely to chance and hazard, From firm security *Ant. and Cleo.* iii 7 48
A that way accomplished courtier would hazard the winning *Cymbeline* i 4 101
The hazard therefore due fall on me by The hands of Romans! . . iv 4 46
Think death no hazard in this enterprise . . . . *Pericles* i 1 5
Hazarded. Whom whilst I labour'd of a love to see, I hazarded the loss of whom I loved . . . . *Com. of Errors* i 1 132
Of thee craves The circle of the Ptolemies for her heirs, Now hazarded to thy grace . . . . *Ant. and Cleo.* iii 12 19
Hazel-eyes. Thou wilt quarrel with a man for cracking nuts, having no other reason but because thou hast hazel eyes . . *Rom. and Jul.* iii 1 22
Hazel-nut. As brown in hue As hazel nuts and sweeter . *T. of Shrew* ii 1 257
Her chariot is an empty hazel-nut . . . . *Rom. and Jul.* i 4 67
Hazel-twig. Like the hazel-twig Is straight and slender . *T. of Shrew* ii 1 255
He whom next thyself Of all the world I loved . . . *Tempest* i 2 68
He will be talking.—Which, of he or Adrian? . . . . . ii 1 26
He that is so yoked by a fool . . . . *T. G. of Ver.* i 1 40
By this hat, then, he in the red face had it . . . *Mer. Wives* i 1 173
Prevent, or go thou, Like Sir Actæon he, with Ringwood at thy heels . ii 1 122
Sir John Falstaff!—He, he; I can never hit on's name. There is such a league between my good man and he! . . . . ii 2 24
He hath my good will, And none but he, to marry with Nan Page . iv 4 84
An idiot; And he my husband best of all affects . . . . . iv 4 87
He that might the vantage best have took . . . *Meas. for Meas.* ii 2 74
How would you be, If He, which is the top of judgement, should But judge you as you are? . . . . ii 2 76
The chain, Which, God he knows, I saw not . . . *Com. of Errors* v 1 229
What's he?—I am sure you know him well enough . . . *Much Ado* ii 1 137
The king he is hunting the deer; I am coursing myself . *L. L. Lost* iv 3 1
The third he caper'd, and cried, 'All goes well' . . . . . v 2 113
Are not you he That frights the maidens of the villagery? *M. N. Dream* ii 1 34
There is no firm reason to be rendered, Why he cannot abide a gaping pig; Why he, a harmless necessary cat; Why he, a woollen bag-pipe *Mer. of Venice* iv 1 54
My soul, yet I know not why, hates nothing more than he *As Y. Like It* i 1 172
He that doth the ravens feed . . . . ii 3 43
What did he when thou sawest him? What said he? How looked he? Wherein went he? What makes he here? Did he ask for me? . . iii 2 232
Are you he that hangs the verses on the trees? . . . . . iii 2 411
I am that he, that unfortunate he . . . . iii 2 414
Leander, he would have lived many a fair year . . . . . iv 1 100
I'll have no father, if you be not he: I'll have no husband, if you be not he . . . . v 4 128
I'll bring mine action on the proudest he That stops my way *T. of Shrew* iii 2 236
The count he wooes your daughter . . . . . *All's Well* iii 7 17
My brother he is in Elysium. Perchance he is not drown'd *T. Night* i 2 4
What is he at the gate, cousin?—A gentleman . . . . . i 5 124
Where heaven He knows how we shall answer him . . . *K. John* v 7 60
And not by Phœbus, he, 'that wandering knight so fair' . 1 *Hen. IV.* i 2 16
Cursed the gentle gusts And he that loosed them forth . 2 *Hen. VI.* iii 2 89
He that loves him best The proudest he that holds up Lancaster 3 *Hen. VI.* i 1 45
Here I stand to answer thee, Or any he the proudest of thy sort . . ii 2 97
Which, God he knows, Seldom or never jumpeth with the heart *Rich. III.* iii 1 10
And his own letter, The honourable board of council out, Must fetch him in he papers . . . . *Hen. VIII.* i 1 80
Now let me see the proudest He, that dares most, but wag his finger at thee . . . . v 3 131
If I spared any That had a head to hit, either young or old, He or she . v 4 25
I would have peace and quietness, but the fool will not: he there: that he: look you there . . . . *Troi. and Cres.* i 1 91
Shall he be worshipp'd Of that we hold an idol more than he? . . ii 3 199
Both merits poised, each weighs nor less nor more; But he as he . . iv 1 66
Were I any thing but what I am, I would wish me only he . *Coriolanus* i 1 236
But He, that hath the steerage of my course, Direct my sail! *Rom. and Jul.* i 4 112
Villain and he be many miles asunder . . . . iii 5 82
And yet no man like he doth grieve my heart . . . . . iii 5 84
The bridegroom he is come already: Make haste . . . . . iv 4 26
Mortal drugs I have; but Mantua's law Is death to any he that utters them . . . . v 1 67
'Tis better thee without than he within . . . . *Macbeth* iii 4 14
Who still hath cried, From the first corse till he that died to-day *Hamlet* i 2 105

He. He cannot flatter, he, An honest mind and plain, he must speak truth! . . . *Lear* ii 2 104
I do not think So fair an outward and such stuff within Endows a man but he.—You speak him far . . . *Cymbeline* i 1 24
I hope it be not gone to tell my lord That I kiss aught but he . ii 3 153
Head. His bold head 'Bove the contentious waves he kept . *Tempest* ii 1 117
My strong imagination sees a crown Dropping upon thy head . ii 1 209
If it should thunder as it did before, I know not where to hide my head ii 2 23
Thy eyes are almost set in thy head.—Where should they be set else? . iii 2 10
Keep a good tongue in your head . iii 2 41
I'll yield him thee asleep, Where thou mayst knock a nail into his head iii 2 69
While thou livest, keep a good tongue in thy head . iii 2 121
There were such men Whose heads stood in their breasts . iii 3 47
Whose wraths to guard you from—Which here, in this most desolate isle, else falls Upon your heads . iii 3 81
Now does my project gather to a head: My charms crack not . v 1 1
If these be true spies which I wear in my head, here's a goodly sight v 1 260
His head unmellow'd, but his judgement ripe . *T. G. of Ver.* ii 4 70
Heap on your head A pack of sorrows which would press you down . iii 1 19
There's not a hair on's head but 'tis a Valentine . iii 1 192
Slender, I broke your head: what matter have you against me?—Marry, sir, I have matter in my head against you . *Mer. Wives* i 1 125
He is as tall a man of his hands as any is between this and his head i 4 27
Does he not hold up his head, as it were, and strut in his gait? i 4 30
If I have not Anne Page, I shall turn your head out of my door . i 4 132
Faith, thou hast some crotchets in thy head . ii 1 160
And what he gets more of her than sharp words, let it lie on my head . ii 1 191
A man may be too confident: I would have nothing lie on my head . ii 1 195
In the circumference of a peck, hilt to point, heel to head . iii 5 114
Come on, sirrah; hold up your head; answer your master, be not afraid . iv 1 20
Go, go, sweet Sir John: Mistress Page and I will look some linen for your head . iv 2 83
With rounds of waxen tapers on their heads, And rattles in their hands iv 4 50
With ribands pendent, flaring 'bout her head . iv 6 42
Away, I say; time wears: hold up your head, and mince . v 1 9
Within these three days his head to be chopped off . *Meas. for Meas.* i 2 69
Thy head stands so tickle on thy shoulders . i 2 176
If you head and hang all that offend that way but for ten year together, you'll be glad to give out a commission for more heads . ii 1 251
Had he twenty heads to tender down On twenty bloody blocks, he'ld yield them up . ii 4 180
None, but such remedy as, to save a head, To cleave a heart in twain . iii 1 62
Whose settled visage and deliberate word Nips youth i' the head . iii 1 91
Can you cut off a man's head?—If the man be a bachelor, sir, I can; but if he be a married man, he's his wife's head, and I can never cut off a woman's head . iv 2 2
For my better satisfaction, let me have Claudio's head sent me by five . iv 2 126
The hour limited, and an express command, under penalty, to deliver his head . iv 2 177
Let this Barnardine be this morning executed, and his head borne to Angelo . iv 2 183
Shave the head, and tie the beard; and say it was the desire of the penitent . iv 2 187
Call your executioner, and off with Barnardine's head . iv 2 223
A man of Claudio's years; his beard and head Just of his colour . iv 3 76
Quick, dispatch, and send the head to Angelo . iv 3 96
Here is the head; I'll carry it myself.—Convenient is it. Make a swift return . iv 3 106
He hath released him, Isabel, from the world: His head is off . iv 3 120
To the head of Angelo Accuse him home and home . iv 3 147
I dare not for my head fill my belly; one fruitful meal would set me to't . iv 3 160
Condemn'd upon the act of fornication To lose his head . v 1 71
His purpose surfeiting, he sends a warrant For my poor brother's head v 1 103
That I saved, Who should have died when Claudio lost his head . v 1 493
That brought you home The head of Ragozine for Claudio's . v 1 539
Between you I shall have a holy head . *Com. of Errors* ii 1 80
Sconce call you it? so you would leave battering, I had rather have it a head . ii 2 36
I must get a sconce for my head and insconce it too . ii 2 38
It seems his sleeps were hinder'd by thy railing, And thereof comes it that his head is light . v 1 72
She would not have his head on her shoulders for all Messina *Much Ado* i 1 115
There will the devil meet me, like an old cuckold, with horns on his head ii 1 47
I know you by the waggling of your head . ii 1 120
You shake the head at so long a breathing . ii 1 377
From the crown of his head to the sole of his foot, he is all mirth . iii 2 9
Know, Claudio, to thy head, Thou hast so wrong'd mine innocent child v 1 62
I thank him; he hath bid me to a calf's head and a capon . v 1 156
When shall we set the savage bull's horns on the sensible Benedick's head? . v 1 184
I'll lay my head to any good man's hat . *L. L. Lost* i 1 310
Which is the head lady?—Thou shalt know her, fellow, by the rest that have no heads . iv 1 45
It was a buck of the first head . iv 2 10
Bows not his vassal head and strucken blind Kisses the base ground iv 3 224
When the suspicious head of theft is stopp'd . iv 3 336
Thou art not so long by the head as honorificabilitudinitatibus . v 1 44
What is a, b, spelt backward, with the horn on his head?—Ba, pueritia v 1 51
I do beseech thee, remember thy courtesy; I beseech thee, apparel thy head . v 1 104
Stand in your own defence; Or hide your heads like cowards . v 2 86
I Pompey am,— With libbard's head on knee.—Well said, old mocker v 2 551
A cittern-head.—The head of a bodkin . v 2 615
Hide thy head, Achilles: here comes Hector in arms . v 2 635
I'll avouch it to his head . *M. N. Dream* i 1 106
By Cupid's strongest bow, By his best arrow with the golden head . i 1 170
Find you out a bed; For I upon this bank will rest my head . ii 2 40
When I did him at this advantage take, An ass's nole I fixed on his head iii 2 17
Speak! In some bush? Where dost thou hide thy head? . iii 2 406
Stick musk-roses in thy sleek smooth head, And kiss thy fair large ears iv 1 3
Scratch my head, Peaseblossom. Where's Mounsieur Cobweb? . iv 1 7
Take this transformed scalp From off the head of this Athenian swain iv 1 70
Silence awhile. Robin, take off this head. Titania, music call . iv 1 85
Their heads are hung With ears that sweep away the morning dew . iv 1 125
I beg the law, the law, upon his head . iv 1 160
He should have worn the horns on his head . v 1 245
I cannot get a service, no; I have ne'er a tongue in my head *Mer. of Ven.* ii 2 166
Nor thrust your head into the public street To gaze on Christian fools . ii 5 32

Head. The watery kingdom, whose ambitious head Spits in the face of heaven . *Mer. of Venice* ii 7 44
Did I deserve no more than a fool's head? Is that my prize? . ii 9 59
Take what wife you will to bed, I will ever be your head . ii 9 71
With one fool's head I came to woo, But I go away with two . ii 9 75
A bankrupt, a prodigal, who dare scarce show his head on the Rialto . iii 1 48
Tell me where is fancy bred, Or in the heart or in the head? . iii 2 64
Upon supposed fairness, often known To be the dowry of a second head iii 2 95
I'll not be made a soft and dull-eyed fool, To shake the head, relent . iii 3 15
I never knew so young a body with so old a head . iv 1 164
My deeds upon my head! . iv 1 206
Bound to pay it ten times o'er, On forfeit of my hands, my head, my heart . iv 1 212
Which, like the toad, ugly and venomous, Wears yet a precious jewel in his head . *As Y. Like It* ii 1 14
It irks me the poor dappled fools, Being native burghers of this desert city, Should in their own confines with forked heads Have their round haunches gored . ii 1 24
Is his head worth a hat, or his chin worth a beard? . iii 2 217
I'll write it straight; The matter's in my head and in my heart . iii 5 137
Though he comes slowly, he carries his house on his head . iv 1 55
We must have your doublet and hose plucked over your head . iv 1 207
It would do well to set the deer's horns upon his head . iv 2 5
A lioness, with udders all drawn dry, Lay couching, head on ground iv 3 116
Cover thy head; nay, prithee, be covered. How old are you? . v 1 19
Balm his foul head in warm distilled waters . *T. of Shrew* Ind. 1 48
Kind embracements, tempting kisses, And with declining head into his bosom . Ind. 1 119
An old trot with ne'er a tooth in her head . i 2 80
To beguile the old folks, how the young folks lay their heads together! i 2 139
Give him head: I know he'll prove a jade . i 2 249
She struck me on the head, And through the instrument my pate made way . ii 1 154
'Tis in my head to do my master good . ii 1 408
Thou mayst slide from my shoulder to my heel with no greater a run but my head and my neck . iv 1 16
Let their heads be sleekly combed, their blue coats brushed . iv 1 93
Head, and butt! an hasty-witted body Would say your head and butt were head and horn . v 2 40
Thy husband is thy lord, thy life, thy keeper, Thy head, thy sovereign v 2 147
What heaven more will, That thee may furnish and my prayers pluck down, Fall on thy head! . *All's Well* i 1 79
Howsome'er their hearts are severed in religion, their heads are both one i 3 58
Now I see The mystery of your loneliness, and find Your salt tears' head i 3 178
I'll like a maid the better, whilst I have a tooth in my head . ii 3 49
To pluck his indignation on thy head . iii 2 32
Come, headsman, off with his head.—O Lord, sir, let me live! . iv 3 343
Most courteous feathers, which bow the head and nod at every man iv 5 112
I know your favour well, Though now you have no sea-cap on your head *T. Night* iii 4 364
He has broke my head across and has given Sir Toby a bloody coxcomb too . v 1 178
You broke my head for nothing . v 1 188
With toss-pots still had drunken heads . v 1 412
To me comes a creature, Sometimes her head on one side, some another *W. Tale* iii 3 20
Pins and poking-sticks of steel, What maids lack from head to heel iv 4 229
And how she longed to eat adders' heads and toads carbonadoed . iv 4 268
Any silk, any thread, Any toys for your head, Of the new'st and finest? . iv 4 326
'Nointed over with honey, set on the head of a wasp's nest . iv 4 813
Would preferment drop on my head . v 2 123
From your sacred vials pour your graces Upon my daughter's head! . v 3 123
That still I lay upon my mother's head . *K. John* i 1 76
Now, by the sky that hangs above our heads, I like it well . ii 1 397
Makes it take head from all indifferency, From all direction . ii 1 579
What dost thou mean by shaking of thy head? Why dost thou look so sadly? . iii 1 19
We, under heaven, are supreme head . iii 1 155
And raise the power of France upon his head . iii 1 193
I will denounce a curse upon his head.—Thou shalt not need . iii 1 319
Austria's head lie there, While Philip breathes . iii 2 3
I will not keep this form upon my head, When there is such disorder in my wit . iii 4 101
When your head did but ache, I knit my handkercher about your brows iv 1 41
And with my hand at midnight held your head . iv 1 45
Hath blown his spirit out, And strew'd repentant ashes on his head . iv 1 111
Do not seek to stuff My head with more ill news, for it is full . iv 2 134
If you be afeard to hear the worst, Then let the worst unheard fall on your head . iv 2 136
Hadst thou but shook thy head or made a pause When I spake darkly . iv 2 231
As to my ample hope was promised Before I drew this gallant head of war . v 2 113
He means to recompense the pains you take By cutting off your heads v 4 16
All the treasons for these eighteen years Complotted and contrived in this land Fetch from false Mowbray their first head . *Richard II.* i 1 97
Will rain hot vengeance on offenders' heads . i 2 8
Doth with a twofold vigour lift me up To reach at victory above my head . i 3 72
A thousand flatterers sit within thy crown, Whose compass is no bigger than thy head . ii 1 101
This tongue that runs so roundly in thy head Should run thy head from thy unreverent shoulders . ii 1 122
You pluck a thousand dangers on your head . ii 1 205
I would to God, So my untruth had not provoked him to it, The king had cut off my head with my brother's . ii 2 102
If we prevail, their heads shall pay for it . iii 2 126
Their peace is made With heads, and not with hands . iii 2 138
Ay, all of them at Bristol lost their heads . iii 2 142
Cover your heads and mock not flesh and blood With solemn reverence iii 2 171
Richard not far from hence hath hid his head . iii 3 6
Alack the heavy day When such a sacred king should hide his head . iii 3 8
To shorten you, For taking so the head, your whole head's length . iii 3 13
Lest you mistake the heavens are o'er our heads . iii 3 17
That lift your vassal hands against my head . iii 3 89
Currents that spring from one most gracious head . iii 3 108
Where subjects' feet May hourly trample on their sovereign's head; For on my heart they tread now whilst I live; And buried once, why not upon my head? . iii 3 157
And like an executioner, Cut off the heads of too fast growing sprays . iii 4 34

Head. Is not my arm of length, That reacheth from the restful English court As far as Calais, to mine uncle's head? *Richard II.* iv 1 13
I will undo myself: I give this heavy weight from off my head . iv 1 204
Ere foul sin gathering head Shall break into corruption v 1 58; *2 Hen. IV.* iii 1 76
My guilt be on my head, and there an end *Richard II.* v 1 69
From windows' tops Threw dust and rubbish on King Richard's head . v 2 6
But dust was thrown upon his sacred head . . . . . v 2 30
I have to London sent The heads of Oxford, Salisbury, Blunt, and Kent v 6 8
Thou hast wrought A deed of slander with thy fatal hand Upon my head and all this famous land . . . . . . v 6 36
Go wander thorough shades of night, And never show thy head by day nor light . . . . v 6 44
If you and I do not rob them, cut this head off from my shoulders *1 Hen. IV.* i 2 185
Severn's flood; Who then, affrighted with their bloody looks, Ran fearfully among the trembling reeds, And hid his crisp head . i 3 106
For I will ease my heart, Albeit I make a hazard of my head . . i 3 128
You, that set the crown Upon the head of this forgetful man . . i 3 161
'Tis no little reason bids us speed, To save our heads by raising of a head i 3 284
A plague on thee! hast thou never an eye in thy head? canst not hear? ii 1 32
Three times hath Henry Bolingbroke made head Against my power . iii 1 64
On the wanton rushes lay you down And rest your gentle head upon her lap . . . . iii 1 215
Come, quick, quick, that I may lay my head in thy lap . . . iii 1 231
Wouldst thou have thy head broken?—No.—Then be still . . iii 1 242
Turns head against the lion's armed jaws . . . . . iii 2 102
I will redeem all this on Percy's head . . . . . iii 2 132
Would they were multitudes, and on my head My shames redoubled! . iii 2 143
A mighty and a fearful head they are, If promises be kept . . iii 2 167
If we without his help can make a head To push against a kingdom . iv 1 80
With hearts in their bellies no bigger than pins' heads . . iv 2 24
Cut me off the heads Of all the favourites . . . . . iv 3 85
And in conclusion drove us to seek out This head of safety . . iv 3 103
A head Of gallant warriors, noble gentlemen . . . . iv 4 25
Hath drawn The special head of all the land together . . . iv 4 28
In short space It rain'd down fortune showering on your head . v 1 47
For safety sake, to fly Out of your sight and raise this present head v 1 66
By my hopes, This present enterprise set off his head . . . v 1 88
All his offences live upon my head And on his father's . . . v 2 20
O, would the quarrel lay upon our heads! . . . . . v 2 48
Thou crossest me? what honour dost thou seek Upon my head? . . v 3 3
Hold up thy head, vile Scot, or thou art like Never to hold it up again! v 4 39
All the budding honours on thy crest I'll crop, to make a garland for my head . . . . v 4 73
Let them that should reward valour bear the sin upon their own heads v 4 154
The blunt monster with uncounted heads, The still-discordant wavering multitude . . . . . *2 Hen. IV.* Ind. 18
The king before the Douglas' rage Stoop'd his anointed head as low as death . . . . Ind. 32
With that, he gave his able horse the head . . . . . i 1 43
Thou shakest thy head and hold'st it fear or sin To speak a truth . i 1 95
Hence, thou sickly quoif! Thou art a guard too wanton for the head . i 1 148
And summ'd the account of chance, before you said 'Let us make head' i 1 168
I was born about three of the clock in the afternoon, with a white head i 2 211
Not a dangerous action can peep out his head but I am thrust upon it . i 2 239
Whether our present five and twenty thousand May hold up head . . i 3 17
His divisions, as the times do brawl, Are in three heads . . . i 3 71
Thou, that threw'st dust upon his goodly head . . . . i 3 103
Cut me off the villain's head: throw the quean in the channel . ii 1 51
When the prince broke thy head for liking his father to a singing-man . ii 1 97
Doth begin to melt And drop upon our bare unarmed heads . . ii 4 394
Who take the ruffian billows by the top, Curling their monstrous heads iii 1 23
Then happy low, lie down! Uneasy lies the head that wears a crown . iii 1 31
I see him break Skogan's head at the court-gate . . . . iii 2 33
And betted much money on his head . . . . . . iii 2 51
Like a forked radish, with a head fantastically carved upon it with a knife . . . . iii 2 334
The cinders of the element, which show like pins' heads to her . iv 3 59
Let all the tears that should bedew my hearse Be drops of balm to sanctify thy head . . . . iv 5 115
Accusing it, I put it on my head, To try with it, as with an enemy . iv 5 166
Let God for ever keep it from my head And make me as the poorest vassal is! . . . . iv 5 175
And I myself know well How troublesome it sat upon my head . . iv 5 187
Shall good news be baffled? Then, Pistol, lay thy head in Furies' lap . v 3 110
The sin upon my head, dread sovereign! . . . . *Hen. V.* i 2 97
While that the armed hand doth fight abroad, The advised head defends itself at home . . . . i 2 179
Doing the execution and the act For which we have in head assembled them . . . . ii 2 18
Turn head, and stop pursuit . . . . ii 4 69
Let them know Of what a monarchy you are the head . . . ii 4 73
And on your head Turning the widows' tears, the orphans' cries . ii 4 105
Let it pry through the portage of the head Like the brass cannon . iii 1 10
Never broke any man's head but his own, and that was against a post . iii 2 43
So Chrish save me, I will cut off your head . . . . iii 2 145
Your fathers taken by the silver beards, And their most reverend heads dash'd to the walls . . . . iii 3 37
For if their heads had any intellectual armour, they could never wear such heavy head-pieces . . . . iii 7 147
Have their heads crushed like rotten apples . . . . iii 7 154
Praise and glory on his head! . . . . . . iv Prol. 31
A good soft pillow for that good white head Were better than a churlish turf of France . . . . iv 1 14
When all those legs and arms and heads, chopped off in a battle, shall join together at the latter day . . . . . . iv 1 142
'Tis certain, every man that dies ill, the ill upon his own head . iv 1 198
And their poor jades Lob down their heads, dropping the hides and hips iv 2 47
They will pluck The gay new coats o'er the French soldiers' heads . iv 3 118
Guard thy head; For I intend to have it ere long . *1 Hen. VI.* i 3 87
My lord, my lord, the French have gather'd head . . . i 4 100
The shame hereof will make me hide my head . . . . i 5 39
Declare the cause My father, Earl of Cambridge, lost his head . ii 5 54
Rouen hangs her head for grief That such a valiant company are fled . iii 2 124
Lord bishop, set the crown upon his head.—God save King Henry! . iv 1 1
Turn on the bloody hounds with heads of steel . . . . iv 2 51
Now the time is come That France must vail her lofty-plumed crest And let her head fall into England's lap . . . . . v 3 26
Put a golden sceptre in thy hand And set a precious crown upon thy head . . . . v 3 119

Head. Wrings his hapless hands And shakes his head . . *2 Hen. VI.* i 1 227
Nor wear the diadem upon his head, Whose church-like humours fits not for a crown . . . . i 1 246
Why droops my lord, like over-ripen'd corn, Hanging the head at Ceres' plenteous load? . . . . i 2 2
Gaze on, and grovel on thy face, Until thy head be circled with the same i 2 10
Lift our heads to heaven, And never more abase our sight so low . i 2 14
And on the pieces of the broken wand Were placed the heads of Edmund Duke of Somerset, And William de la Pole . . . . i 2 29
He that breaks a stick of Gloucester's grove Shall lose his head . i 2 34
Dame Margaret kneel'd to me And on my head did set the diadem . i 2 40
Carry him to Rome, And set the triple crown upon his head . . i 3 66
If they were known, as the suspect is great, Would make thee quickly hop without thy head . . . . i 3 140
Base dunghill villain and mechanical, I'll have thy head for this . i 3 197
The protector's wife, The ringleader and head of all this rout . ii 1 170
Heaping confusion on their own heads thereby . . . . ii 1 187
This dishonour in thine age Will bring thy head with sorrow to the ground! . . . . ii 3 19
See how the giddy multitude do point, And nod their heads! . . ii 4 22
My sovereign lady, with the rest, Causeless have laid disgraces on my head . . . . iii 1 162
All of you have laid your heads together—Myself had notice . . iii 1 165
The golden circuit on my head, Like to the glorious sun's transparent beams . . . . iii 1 352
A thousand crowns, or else lay down your head . . . . iv 1 16
And thought thee happy when I shook my head . . . . iv 1 55
Convey him hence and on our long-boat's side Strike off his head . iv 1 69
Rather let my head Stoop to the block than these knees bow to any Save to the God of heaven and to my king . . . . . iv 1 124
Let his head and lifeless body lie, Until the queen his mistress bury it iv 1 142
We'll have the Lord Say's head for selling the dukedom of Maine . iv 2 170
Can he that speaks with the tongue of an enemy be a good counsellor, or no?—No, no; and therefore we'll have his head . . . iv 2 183
Here may his head lie on my throbbing breast: But where's the body? iv 4 5
Lord Say, Jack Cade hath sworn to have thy head . . . iv 4 19
Get you to Smithfield and gather head . . . . . iv 5 10
I'll see if his head will stand steadier on a pole, or no . . iv 7 100
Go, take him away, I say, and strike off his head presently . iv 7 116
And strike off his head, and bring them both upon two poles hither . iv 7 118
The proudest peer in the realm shall not wear a head on his shoulders, unless he pay me tribute . . . . iv 7 128
Let them break your backs with burthens, take your houses over your heads . . . . iv 8 31
I see them lay their heads together to surprise me . . . iv 8 61
And he that brings his head unto the king Shall have a thousand crowns . . . . iv 8 69
And get a thousand crowns of the king by carrying my head to him . iv 10 30
And there cut off thy most ungracious head . . . . iv 10 88
Comes York to claim his right, And pluck the crown from feeble Henry's head . . . . v 1 2
Lo, I present your grace a traitor's head, The head of Cade . . v 1 66
The head of Cade! Great God, how just art Thou! O, let me view his visage . . . . v 1 68
For thousand Yorks he shall not hide his head, But boldly stand . v 1 85
That head of thine doth not become a crown . . . . . v 1 96
O, where is faith? O, where is loyalty? If it be banish'd from the frosty head . . . . v 1 167
Thus do I hope to shake King Henry's head . . . *3 Hen. VI.* i 1 20
Father, tear the crown from the usurper's head.—Sweet father, do so; set it on your head . . . . i 1 114
And given unto the house of York such head As thou shalt reign but by their sufferance . . . . i 1 233
And will you pale your head in Henry's glory, And rob his temples? i 4 103
Off with the crown; and, with the crown, his head . . . i 4 107
My soul to heaven, my blood upon your heads! . . . . i 4 168
Off with his head, and set it on York gates; So York may overlook the town of York . . . . i 4 179
They took his head, and on the gates of York They set the same . ii 1 65
Here we heard you were, Making another head to fight again . . ii 1 141
This strong right hand of mine Can pluck the diadem from faint Henry's head . . . . ii 1 153
And he that throws not up his cap for joy Shall for the fault make forfeit of his head . . . . ii 1 197
Yonder's the head of that arch-enemy That sought to be encompass'd with your crown . . . . ii 2 2
How it doth grieve me that thy head is here! . . . . ii 2 55
Wilt thou kneel for grace, And set thy diadem upon my head? . . ii 2 82
If thou deny, their blood upon thy head . . . . . ii 2 129
From off the gates of York fetch down the head, Your father's head . ii 6 52
Off with the traitor's head, And rear it in the place your father's stands ii 6 85
My crown is in my heart, not on my head; Not deck'd with diamonds . iii 1 62
Until my mis-shaped trunk that bears this head Be round impaled with a glorious crown . . . . iii 2 170
He comes towards London, To set the crown once more on Henry's head iv 4 27
Although my head still wear the crown, I here resign my government to thee . . . . iv 6 23
His head by nature framed to wear a crown, His hand to wield a sceptre iv 6 72
Do but answer this: What is the body when the head is off? . . v 1 41
This hand . . . Shall, whiles thy head is warm and new cut off, Write in the dust this sentence . . . . v 1 55
For Somerset, off with his guilty head . . . . . . v 5 3
He's sudden, if a thing comes in his head . . . . . v 5 86
Teeth hadst thou in thy head when thou wast born . . . v 6 53
I'll blast his harvest, if your head were laid . . . . v 7 21
Take heed; for he holds vengeance in his hands, To hurl upon their heads that break his law . . . . . *Richard III.* i 4 205
Why do you look on us, and shake your head? . . . . ii 2 5
Chop off his head, man; somewhat we will do . . . . iii 1 193
The princes both make high account of you; For they account his head upon the bridge . . . . iii 2 72
They, for their truth, might better wear their heads Than some that have accused them wear their hats . . . . . . iii 2 94
Now Margaret's curse is fall'n upon our heads . . . . iii 3 15
Finds the testy gentleman so hot, As he will lose his head ere give consent . . . . iii 4 40
Off with his head! Now, by Saint Paul I swear, I will not dine until I see the same . . . . iii 4 78
Margaret, now thy heavy curse Is lighted on poor Hastings' wretched head! . . . . iii 4 95

Head. The duke would be at dinner: Make a short shrift; he longs to see your head *Richard III.* iii 4 97
Come, lead me to the block; bear him my head iii 4 108
Here is the head of that ignoble traitor, The dangerous . . . Hastings iii 5 22
O, let me think on Hastings, and be gone To Brecknock, while my fearful head is on! iv 2 126
Thy head, all indirectly, gave direction iv 4 225
Up to some scaffold, there to lose their heads iv 4 242
Look your faith be firm, Or else his head's assurance is but frail iv 4 498
If I revolt, off goes young George's head iv 5 4
That high All-Seer that I dallied with Hath turn'd my feigned prayer on my head And given in earnest v 1 21
And every one did threat To-morrow's vengeance on the head of Richard v 3 206
Fairest-boding dreams That ever enter'd in a drowsy head v 3 228
Draw, archers, draw your arrows to the head! v 3 339
He doth deny to come.—Off with his son George's head! v 3 344
The cardinal's and Sir Thomas Lovell's heads Should have gone off *Hen. VIII.* i 2 185
Henry of Buckingham, Who first raised head against usurping Richard ii 1 108
It calls, I fear, too many curses on their heads That were the authors ii 1 138
Even the billows of the sea Hung their heads, and then lay by iii 1 11
Like the lily, . . . I'll hang my head and perish iii 1 153
The heads of all thy brother cardinals, With thee and all thy best parts bound together, Weigh'd not a hair of his iii 2 257
If I blush, It is to see a nobleman want manners.—I had rather want those than my head iii 2 309
Now, good angels Fly o'er thy royal head, and shade thy person! v 1 160
I'll scratch your heads: you must be seeing christenings? v 4 9
But if I spared any That had a head to hit, either young or old, He or she, cuckold or cuckold-maker, Let me ne'er hope to see a chine again v 4 24
That fire-drake did I hit three times on the head v 4 46
Railed upon me till her pinked porringer fell off her head v 4 51
And on your heads Clap round fines for neglect v 4 83
You great fellow, Stand close up, or I'll make your head ache v 4 92
Her foes shake like a field of beaten corn, And hang their heads with sorrow v 5 33
If you love an addle egg as well as you love an idle head, you would eat chickens i' the shell *Troi. and Cres.* i 2 147
And bears his head In such a rein, in full as proud a place i 3 188
'Fore all the Greekish heads, which with one voice Call Agamemnon head i 3 221
Who wears his wit in his belly and his guts in his head ii 1 80
By my head, 'tis pride ii 3 95
You shall not bob us out of our melody: if you do, our melancholy upon your head! iii 1 76
Our head shall go bare till merit crown it iii 2 99
There were wit in this head, an 'twould out iii 3 256
Did not I tell you? Would he were knock'd i' the head! iv 2 35
This brave shall oft make thee to hide thy head iv 4 139
That the appalled air May pierce the head of the great combatant iv 5 5
For which we lose our heads to gild his horns iv 5 31
You fillip me o' the head iv 5 45
Stand fast, and wear a castle on thy head! v 2 187
Troilus, thou coward Troilus, show thy head!—Troilus, I say! v 6 1
The kingly-crowned head, the vigilant eye, The counsellor heart *Coriol.* i 1 119
He'll beat Aufidius' head below his knee And tread upon his neck i 3 49
Ere in our own house I do shade my head ii 1 211
I had rather have one scratch my head i' the sun When the alarum were struck ii 2 79
At sixteen years, When Tarquin made a head for Rome ii 2 92
Our heads are some brown, some black, some auburn, some bald ii 3 20
Tullus Aufidius then had made new head?—He had iii 1 1
To show bare heads In congregations, to yawn, be still and wonder iii 2 10
Waving thy head, Which often, thus, correcting thy stout heart iii 2 77
The beast With many heads butts me away iv 1 2
Has the porter his eyes in his head, that he gives entrance to such companions? iv 5 13
Not a hair upon a soldier's head Which will not prove a whip iv 6 133
You lords and heads o' the state, perfidiously He has betray'd your business v 6 91
Put it on, And help to set a head on headless Rome.—A better head her glorious body fits Than his that shakes for age and feebleness *T. An.* i 1 186
Blood and revenge are hammering in my head ii 3 39
Look by and by to have thy sons with thee. Their heads, I mean iii 1 203
For that good hand thou sent'st the emperor, Here are the heads of thy two noble sons iii 1 237
See, thy two sons' heads, Thy warlike hand, thy mangled daughter here iii 1 255
These two heads do seem to speak to me, And threat me iii 1 272
Come, brother, take a head; And in this hand the other will I bear iii 1 280
Arm, my lord;—Rome never had more cause. The Goths have gather'd head iv 4 63
And I hang the head As flowers with frost or grass beat down with storms iv 4 70
As true a dog as ever fought at head v 1 102
When, for his hand, he had his two sons' heads v 1 115
And when thy car is loaden with their heads, I will dismount v 2 53
I'll make a paste, And of the paste a coffin I will rear, And make two pasties of your shameful heads v 2 190
And in that paste let their vile heads be baked v 2 201
I will be cruel with the maids, and cut off their heads.—The heads of the maids? *Rom. and Jul.* i 1 28
He swung about his head and cut the winds i 1 118
What if her eyes were there, they in her head? The brightness of her cheek would shame those stars ii 2 18
Thou art As glorious to this night, being o'er my head, As is a winged messenger of heaven ii 2 27
It argues a distemper'd head So soon to bid good morrow to thy bed ii 3 33
Lord, how my head aches! what a head have I! It beats as it would fall in twenty pieces ii 5 49
Thy head is as full of quarrels as an egg is full of meat, and yet thy head hath been beaten as addle as an egg for quarrelling iii 1 24
By my head, here come the Capulets.—By my heel, I care not iii 1 38
Mercutio's soul Is but a little way above our heads, Staying for thine iii 1 132
Thou cutt'st my head off with a golden axe, And smilest upon the stroke iii 3 22
The lark, whose notes do beat The vaulty heaven so high above our heads iii 5 22
I have a head, sir, that will find out logs, And never trouble Peter iv 4 17
Put not another sin upon my head, By urging me to fury v 3 62
Till we can clear these ambiguities, And know their spring, their head v 3 218

Head. The sun, for sorrow, will not show his head *Rom. and Jul.* v 3 306
Bowing his head against the steepy mount To climb his happiness *T. of A.* i 1 75
Show Lord Timon that mean eyes have seen The foot above the head i 1 94
When, for some trifling present, you have bid me Return so much, I have shook my head and wept ii 2 146
What heart, head, sword, force, means, but is Lord Timon's? Great Timon! ii 2 176
They do shake their heads, and I am here No richer in return ii 2 211
Who can speak broader than he that has no house to put his head in? iii 4 64
And set quarrelling Upon the head of valour iii 5 28
Let's shake our heads, and say, As 'twere a knell unto our master's fortunes iv 2 25
This [gold] Will . . . Pluck stout men's pillows from below their heads iv 3 32
Those that understood him smiled at one another and shook their heads *J. Cæsar* i 2 286
Our course will seem too bloody, Caius Cassius, To cut the head off and then hack the limbs ii 1 163
For Mark Antony, think not of him; For he can do no more than Cæsar's arm When Cæsar's head is off ii 1 183
Then you scratch'd your head, And too impatiently stamp'd with your foot ii 1 243
Waving our red weapons o'er our heads, Let's all cry 'Peace, freedom!' iii 1 109
Brutus and Cassius Are levying powers: we must straight make head iv 1 42
And chastisement doth therefore hide his head iv 3 16
And in their steads do ravens, crows and kites, Fly o'er our heads v 1 86
Yet, countrymen, O, yet hold up your heads! v 4 1
Till he unseam'd him from the nave to the chaps, And fix'd his head upon our battlements *Macbeth* i 2 23
The spring, the head, the fountain of your blood Is stopp'd ii 3 103
Upon my head they placed a fruitless crown iii 1 61
Safe in a ditch he bides, With twenty trenched gashes on his head iii 4 27
Strange things I have in head, that will to hand iii 4 139
Though castles topple on their warders' heads; Though palaces and pyramids do slope Their heads to their foundations iv 1 56
Rebellion's head, rise never till the wood Of Birnam rise iv 1 97
When I shall tread upon the tyrant's head, Or wear it on my sword iv 3 45
Hail, king! for so thou art: behold, where stands The usurper's cursed head v 8 55
The chief head Of this post-haste and romage in the land *Hamlet* i 1 106
The head is not more native to the heart i 2 47
Once methought It lifted up it head and did address Itself to motion i 2 216
Unto the voice and yielding of that body Whereof he is the head i 3 24
But sent to my account With all my imperfections on my head i 5 79
No hat upon his head; his stockings foul'd, Ungarter'd ii 1 79
And thrice his head thus waving up and down, He raised a sigh so piteous ii 1 93
His head over his shoulder turn'd, He seem'd to find his way without his eyes ii 1 97
He hath found The head and source of all your son's distemper ii 2 55
His sword, Which was declining on the milky head Of reverend Priam ii 2 500
A clout upon that head Where late the diadem stood ii 2 529
Shall I lie in your lap?—No, my lord.—I mean, my head upon your lap? iii 2 121
At his head a grass-green turf, At his heels a stone iv 5 31
Young Laertes, in a riotous head, O'erbears your officers iv 5 101
Bring you in fine together And wager on your heads iv 7 135
A' poured a flagon of Rhenish on my head once v 1 197
O, treble woe Fall ten times treble on that cursed head! v 1 270
To o'ertop old Pelion, or the skyish head Of blue Olympus v 1 276
No leisure bated, No, not to stay the grinding of the axe, My head should be struck off v 2 25
Put your bonnet to his right use; 'tis for the head v 2 96
Bade me signify to you that he has laid a great wager on your head v 2 106
This lapwing runs away with the shell on his head v 2 194
And, in this upshot, purposes mistook Fall'n on the inventors' heads v 2 396
For, you know, nuncle, The hedge-sparrow fed the cuckoo so long, That it had it head bit off by it young *Lear* i 4 236
I can tell why a snail has a house.—Why?—Why, to put his head in i 5 32
Horses are tied by the heads, dogs and bears by the neck ii 4 8
Vaunt-couriers to oak-cleaving thunderbolts, Singe my white head! iii 2 6
That have with two pernicious daughters join'd Your high engender'd battles 'gainst a head So old and white as this iii 2 23
He that has a house to put's head in has a good head-piece iii 2 25
The cod-piece that will house Before the head has any, The head and he shall louse iii 2 28
Let the great gods, That keep this dreadful pother o'er our heads, Find out their enemies now iii 2 50
Your houseless heads and unfed sides, Your loop'd and window'd raggedness iii 4 30
Tom will throw his head at them. Avaunt, you curs! iii 6 67
For, with throwing thus my head, Dogs leap the hatch, and all are fled iii 6 75
The sea, with such a storm as his bare head In hell-black night endured, would have buoy'd up, And quench'd the stelled fires iii 7 59
A cliff, whose high and bending head Looks fearfully in the confined deep iv 1 76
Decline your head: this kiss, if it durst speak, Would stretch thy spirits up into the air iv 2 22
Milk-liver'd man! That bear'st a cheek for blows, a head for wrongs iv 2 51
Half way down Hangs one that gathers samphire, dreadful trade! Methinks he seems no bigger than his head iv 6 16
That minces virtue, and does shake the head To hear of pleasure's name iv 6 122
No eyes in your head, nor no money in your purse? iv 6 149
That eyeless head of thine was first framed flesh To raise my fortunes iv 6 231
From the extremest upward of thy head To the descent and dust below thy foot v 3 136
Back do I toss these treasons to thy head v 3 146
The very head and front of my offending Hath this extent *Othello* i 3 80
Rough quarries, rocks and hills whose heads touch heaven i 3 141
The Anthropophagi and men whose heads Do grow beneath their shoulders i 3 144
Destruction on my head, if my bad blame Light on the man! i 3 177
All indign and base adversities Make head against my estimation! i 3 275
She that in wisdom never was so frail To change the cod's head for the salmon's tail ii 1 156
Abandon all remorse; On horror's head horrors accumulate iii 3 370
Have you not hurt your head?—Dost thou mock me?—I mock you! no iv 1 60
If any wretch have put this in your head, Let heaven requite it! iv 2 15
Had they rain'd All kinds of sores and shames on my bare head iv 2 49
I have much to do, But to go hang my head all at one side, And sing it iv 3 32
Her hand on her bosom, her head on her knee, Sing willow, willow, willow iv 3 43
Let Antony look over Cæsar's head And speak as loud as Mars *A. and C.* ii 2 5
Or I'll spurn thine eyes Like balls before me; I'll unhair thy head ii 5 64
Shall set thee on triumphant chariots and Put garlands on thy head iii 1 11
That Herod's head I'll have: but how, when Antony is gone? iii 3 4
From the head of Actium Beat the approaching Cæsar iii 7 52
Her head's declined, and death will seize her iii 11 47

Head. To the boy Cæsar send this grizzled head, And he will fill thy wishes to the brim With principalities.—That head, my lord? *Ant. and Cleo.* iii 13 17
Let our best heads Know, that to-morrow the last of many battles We mean to fight . . . iv 1 10
Had we done so at first, we had droven them home With clouts about their heads . . . iv 7 6
Which you'll make him know, If that his head have ear in music *Cymb.* iii 4 178
The powers that he already hath in Gallia Will soon be drawn to head iii 5 25
What mortality is! Posthumus, thy head, which now is growing upon thy shoulders, shall within this hour be off . . . iv 1 17
And on the gates of Lud's-town set your heads . . . iv 2 99
Yet I not doing this, the fool had borne My head as I do his . . iv 2 117
What hast thou done?—I am perfect what: cut off one Cloten's head . iv 2 118
Swore With his own single hand he'ld take us in, Displace our heads . iv 2 122
Are outlaws, and in time May make some stronger head . . iv 2 139
We do fear this body hath a tail More perilous than the head . . iv 2 145
I have ta'en His head from him: I'll throw't into the creek . . iv 2 151
Gentle As zephyrs blowing below the violet, Not wagging his sweet head iv 2 173
We must lay his head to the east; My father hath a reason for't . iv 2 255
Alas, Where is thy head? where's that? Ay me! where's that? . . iv 2 321
Pisanio might have kill'd thee at the heart, And left this head on . iv 2 323
Your death has eyes in's head then; I have not seen him so pictured v 4 184
'Twas at a feast,—O, would Our viands had been poison'd, or at least Those which I heaved to head! . . . v 5 157
I cut off's head; And am right glad he is not standing here . . v 5 295
The benediction of these covering heavens Fall on their heads like dew! v 5 351
All love the womb that their first being bred, Then give my tongue like leave to love my head . . . *Pericles* i 1 108
Heaven, that I had thy head! he has found the meaning . . . i 1 109
He hath found the meaning, for which we mean To have his head . . i 1 144
Till Pericles be dead, My heart can lend no succour to my head . . i 1 171
Whose towers bore heads so high they kiss'd the clouds . . . i 4 24
I will not have excuse, with saying this Loud music is too harsh for ladies' heads . . . ii 3 97
This kingdom is without a head,—Like goodly buildings left without a roof ii 4 35
The men of Tyrus on the head Of Helicanus would set on The crown iii Gower 26
Let me rest.—A pillow for his head: So, leave him all . . . v 1 237
Head and ears. O'er head and ears a fork'd one! . . *W. Tale* i 2 186
Head and shoulders. Though we would have thrust virtue out of our hearts by the head and shoulders . . . *Mer. Wives* v 5 156
Head lady. Which is the head lady?—Thou shalt know her, fellow, by the rest that have no heads . . . *L. L. Lost* iv 1 43
Head of hair. Then hadst thou had an excellent head of hair *T. Night* i 3 100
Head to foot. No longer from head to foot than from hip to hip *C. of Er.* iii 2 115
My fingers itch.—I would thou didst itch from head to foot and I had the scratching of thee . . . *Troi. and Cres.* ii 1 29
Arm'd, my lord.—From top to toe?—My lord, from head to foot *Hamlet* i 2 228
Head to foot Now is he total gules; horridly trick'd With blood . . ii 2 478
Now from head to foot I am marble-constant . . *Ant. and Cleo.* v 2 239
Boldness be my friend! Arm me, audacity, from head to foot! *Cymbeline* i 6 19
Headed. All the embossed sores and headed evils . . *As Y. Like It* ii 7 67
Headier. I'll forbear; And am fall'n out with my more headier will *Lear* ii 4 111
Heading. There are pretty orders beginning, I can tell you: it is but heading and hanging . . . *Meas. for Meas.* ii 1 250
Headland. Again, sir, shall we sow the headland with wheat? *2 Hen. IV.* v 1 16
Headless. Sometime a hound, A hog, a headless bear . *M. N. Dream* iii 1 112
And smooth my way upon their headless necks . . . *2 Hen. VI.* i 2 65
And help to set a head on headless Rome . . . *T. Andron.* i 1 186
A headless man! The garments of Posthumus! . . *Cymbeline* iv 2 308
That headless man I thought had been my lord . . . v 5 299
Headlong. And throw the rider headlong in the lists . *Richard II.* i 2 52
Another way To pluck him headlong from the usurped throne . . v 1 65
I'll hale the Dauphin headlong from his throne . . . *1 Hen. VI.* i 1 149
Hence will I drag thee headlong by the heels . . *2 Hen. VI.* iv 10 86
Will, hand in hand, all headlong cast us down . . *T. Andron.* v 3 132
I'll look no more; Lest my brain turn, and the deficient sight Topple down headlong . . . *Lear* iv 6 24
Head-lugged. Whose reverence even the head-lugg'd bear would lick . iv 2 42
Headpiece. By some severals Of head-piece extraordinary . *W. Tale* i 2 227
For if their heads had any intellectual armour, they could never wear such heavy head-pieces . . . *Hen. V.* iii 7 149
He that has a house to put's head in has a good head-piece . . *Lear* iii 2 26
Headshake. With arms encumber'd thus, or this head-shake . *Hamlet* i 5 174
Headsman. Come, headsman, off with his head . . . *All's Well* iv 3 342
Head-stall. A head-stall of sheep's leather . . *T. of Shrew* iii 2 58
Headstrong. The needful bits and curbs to headstrong weeds *M. for M.* i 3 20
Headstrong liberty is lash'd with woe . . . *Com. of Errors* ii 1 15
And thus I'll curb her mad and headstrong humour . *T. of Shrew* iv 1 212
Tell these headstrong women What duty they do owe their lords . . v 2 130
Such a headstrong potent fault it is, That it but mocks reproof *T. Night* iii 4 224
When his headstrong riot hath no curb . . . . *2 Hen. IV.* iv 4 62
Peace, headstrong Warwick! . . . . . *2 Hen. VI.* i 3 178
I have seduced a headstrong Kentishman, John Cade of Ashford . . iii 1 356
My thoughts were like unbridled children, grown Too headstrong for their mother. See, we fools! . . . *Troi. and Cres.* iii 2 131
How now, my headstrong! where have you been gadding? *Rom. and Jul.* iv 2 16
Heady. And all the currents of a heady fight . . . *1 Hen. IV.* ii 3 58
Never came reformation in a flood, With such a heady currance *Hen. V.* i 1 34
Whiles yet the cool and temperate wind of grace O'erblows the filthy and contagious clouds Of heady murder . . . . iii 3 32
Heady-rash, provoked with raging ire . . . *Com. of Errors* v 1 216
Heal. My state being gall'd with my expense, I seek to heal it only by his wealth . . . . *Mer. Wives* iii 4 6
It is a rupture that you may easily heal . . . *Meas. for Meas.* ii 1 245
Faster than his tongue Did make offence his eye did heal it up *As Y. L. It* iii 5 117
We will heal up all . . . . *K. John* ii 1 550
And heal the inveterate canker of one wound By making many . . v 2 14
Ay, leeks is good: hold you, there is a groat to heal your pate *Hen. V.* v 1 62
God b' wi' you, and keep you, and heal your pate . . . v 1 71
My pity hath been balm to heal their wounds . . . *3 Hen. VI.* iv 8 41
Those wounds heal ill that men do give themselves . *Troi. and Cres.* iii 3 229
Your honours' pardon: I had rather have my wounds to heal again Than hear say how I got them . . . . *Coriolanus* ii 2 73
May I govern so, To heal Rome's harms, and wipe away her woe! *T. An.* v 3 148
But must not break my back to heal his finger . . *T. of Athens* ii 1 24
What wound did ever heal but by degrees? . . . *Othello* ii 3 377
Healed. My bosom as a bed Shall lodge thee till thy wound be throughly heal'd . . . . *T. G. of Ver.* i 2 115
Subject to the same diseases, healed by the same means. *Mer. of Venice* iii 1 65
Healing. 'Tis spoken, To the succeeding royalty he leaves The healing benediction . . . . *Macbeth* iv 3 156
When we debate Our trivial difference loud, we do commit Murder in healing wounds . . . . *Ant. and Cleo.* ii 2 22
Health. Your father's in good health: What say you to a letter? *T. G. of Ver.* ii 4 50
And how do yours?—I left them all in health.—How does your lady? . ii 4 124
The tenour of them doth but signify My health and happy being . . iii 1 57
I will, out of thine own confession, learn to begin thy health *M. for M.* i 2 39
I wish your worship well; God restore you to health! . . *M. Ado* v 1 334
Sweet health and fair desires consort your grace! . . *L. L. Lost* ii 1 178
A beard, fair health, and honesty; With three-fold love I wish you . v 2 834
But, like in sickness, did I loathe this food; But, as in health, come to my natural taste, Now I do wish it . . . *M. N. Dream* iv 1 179
We have been praying for our husbands' healths . *Mer. of Venice* v 1 114
As being overjoy'd To see her noble lord restored to health *T. of Shrew* Ind. 1 121
We may contrive this afternoon, And quaff carouses to our mistress' health . . . . i 2 277
'A health!' quoth he, as if He had been aboard, carousing to his mates iii 2 172
Dine with my father, drink a health to me; For I must hence . . iii 2 198
Therefore a health to all that shot and miss'd . . . . v 2 51
'Tis our hope, sir, . . . to return And find your grace in health *All's Well* ii 1 7
Health, at your bidding, serve your majesty! . . . . ii 1 18
Health shall live free and sickness freely die . . . . ii 1 171
Heaven hath through me restored the king to health . . . ii 3 70
She is not well; but yet she has her health . . . . ii 4 2
He's drunk nightly . . . —With drinking healths to my niece *T. Night* i 3 40
He has his health and ampler strength indeed Than most have of his age *W. Tale* iv 4 414
Even in the instant of repair and health, The fit is strongest *K. John* iii 4 113
For the health and physic of our right, We cannot deal but with the very hand Of stern injustice and confused wrong . . . v 2 21
I am in health, I breathe, and see thee ill . . . *Richard II.* ii 1 92
How fares your uncle?—I had thought, my lord, to have learn'd his health of you . . . . ii 3 24
More health and happiness betide my liege, Than can my care-tuned tongue deliver him! . . . . iii 2 91
His health was never better worth than now . . . *1 Hen. IV.* iv 1 27
The lives of all your loving complices Lean on your health . *2 Hen. IV.* i 1 164
I most humbly beseech your lordship to have a reverent care of your health . . . . i 2 114
In bodily health, sir.—Marry, the immortal part needs a physician . ii 2 111
Health and fair greeting from our general, The prince, Lord John . iv 1 27
Health to my lord and gentle cousin, Mowbray.—You wish me health in very happy season; For I am, on the sudden, something ill . . iv 2 78
Health to my sovereign, and new happiness Added to that that I am to deliver! . . . . iv 4 81
She either gives a stomach and no food; Such are the poor, in health . iv 4 106
Health, peace, and happiness to my royal father! . . . iv 5 227
Health, alack, with youthful wings is flown From this bare wither'd trunk . . . . iv 5 229
Good Master Silence, I'll give you a health for that anon . . v 3 25
Health and long life to you, Master Silence.—Fill the cup . . v 3 54
God doth know how many now in health Shall drop their blood *Hen. V.* i 2 18
Who when they were in health, I tell thee, herald, I thought upon one pair of English legs Did march three Frenchmen . . . iii 6 157
Canst thou, when thou command'st the beggar's knee, Command the health of it? . . . . iv 1 274
To our sister, Health and fair time of day! . . . . v 2 3
And, princes French, and peers, health to you all! . . . v 2 8
All health unto my gracious sovereign! . . . *2 Hen. VI.* iii 1 82
Health and glad tidings to your majesty! . . . . iv 9 7
Health and all happiness to my lord the king!—I thank thee, Clifford . v 1 124
No doubt his majesty Will soon recover his accustom'd health *Rich. III.* i 3 2
Madam, good hope; his grace speaks cheerfully.—God grant him health! i 3 35
How fares the prince?—Well, madam, and in health . . . ii 4 40
God bless your grace with health and happy days! . . . iii 1 18
And shall be thought most fit For your best health and recreation . iii 1 67
This, to confirm my welcome; And to you all, good health . *Hen. VIII.* i 4 38
A health, gentlemen! Let it go round . . . . . i 4 96
I have half a dozen healths To drink to these fair ladies . . . i 4 105
To his highness; Whose health and royalty I pray for . . . ii 3 73
How does his highness?—Madam, in good health.—So may he ever do! iv 2 124
For your health and your digestion sake, An after-dinner's breath *T. and C.* ii 3 120
Health to you, valiant sir, During all question of the gentle truce . iv 1 10
Our bloods are now in calm; and, so long, health! . . . iv 1 15
A letter for me! it gives me an estate of seven years' health *Coriolanus* ii 1 126
He and his shall know that justice lives In Saturninus' health *T. An.* iv 4 24
Feather of lead, bright smoke, cold fire, sick health! . *Rom. and Jul.* i 1 186
Of breaches, ambuscadoes, Spanish blades, Of healths five-fathom deep i 4 85
Let the health go round.—Let it flow this way . . *T. of Athens* i 2 54
Those healths will make thee and thy state look ill . . . i 2 57
Even to the state's best health, I have Deserved this hearing . . ii 2 206
His health is well, sir.—I am right glad that his health is well . iii 1 12
His comfortable temper has forsook him; he's much out of health . iii 4 72
If it be so far beyond his health, Methinks he should the sooner pay his debts, And make a clear way to the gods . . . . iii 4 75
Honour, health, and compassion to the senate! . . . . iii 5 5
My long sickness Of health and living now begins to mend . . v 1 190
Wherefore rise you now? It is not for your health thus to commit Your weak condition to the raw cold morning . . . *J. Cæsar* ii 1 235
I am not well in health, and that is all.—Brutus is wise, and, were he not in health, He would embrace the means to come by it . . ii 1 257
I shall forget myself; Have mind upon your health, tempt me no farther . . . . iv 3 36
Who wear our health but sickly in his life, Which in his death were perfect . . . . *Macbeth* iii 1 107
Now, good digestion wait on appetite, And health on both! . . . iii 4 39
Come, love and health to all; Then I'll sit down. Give me some wine. iii 4 87
Good night; and better health Attend his majesty! . . . iii 4 120
Find her disease, And purge it to a sound and pristine health . . v 3 52
No jocund health that Denmark drinks to-day, But the great cannon to the clouds shall tell . . . . . . *Hamlet* i 2 125
On his choice depends The safety and health of this whole state . . i 3 21
Be thou a spirit of health or goblin damn'd . . . . i 4 40
His sables and his weeds, Importing health and graveness . . iv 7 82
Larded with many several sorts of reasons Importing Denmark's health v 2 21
Stay; give me drink. Hamlet, this pearl is thine; Here's to thy health v 2 294
No less than life, with grace, health, beauty, honour . . . *Lear* i 1 59
Infirmity doth still neglect all office Whereto our health is bound . ii 4 108

Health. He's mad that trusts in the tameness of a wolf, a horse's health, a boy's love . . . . *Lear* iii 6 20
That would fain have a measure to the health of black Othello *Othello* ii 3 32
To the health of our general!—I am for it, lieutenant; and I'll do you justice . . . . ii 3 88
Bring in the banquet quickly; wine enough Cleopatra's health to drink *Ant. and Cleo.* i 2 12
In state of health thou say'st; and thou say'st free . ii 5 56
I have a health for you.—I shall take it . . . . ii 6 142
A health to Lepidus!—I am not so well as I should be, but I'll ne'er out ii 7 33
Will this description satisfy him?—With the health that Pompey gives him . . . . ii 7 57
This health to Lepidus!—Bear him ashore. I'll pledge it for him ii 7 90
Continues well my lord? His health, beseech you?—Well, madam *Cymb.* i 6 56
Let what is here contain'd relish of love, Of my lord's health . iii 2 31
Brother, farewell.—I wish ye sport.—You health. So please you, sir . iv 2 31
We drink this health to you.—We thank your grace . *Pericles* ii 3 52
I am glad to see your honour in good health.—You may so . iv 6 25
Healthful. Gave healthful welcome to their shipwreck'd guests *C. of Er.* i 1 115
This healthful hand, whose banish'd sense Thou hast repeal'd *All's Well* ii 3 54
Early stirrers, Which is both healthful and good husbandry *Hen. V.* iv 1 7
Well met. How have ye done Since last we saw in France?—I thank your grace, Healthful . . . . . . *Hen. VIII.* i 1 3
Such an exploit have I in hand, Ligarius, Had you a healthful ear to hear of it . . . . *J. Cæsar* ii 1 319
Ecstasy! My pulse, as yours, doth temperately keep time, And makes as healthful music . . . . . . *Hamlet* iii 4 141
Let our finger ache, and it indues Our other healthful members even to that sense Of pain . . . . . . *Othello* iii 4 147
If Antony Be free and healthful,—so tart a favour! *Ant. and Cleo.* ii 5 38
Health-giving. To the most wholesome physic of thy health-giving air *L. L. L.* i 1 236
Healthsome. Shall I not, then, be stifled in the vault, To whose foul mouth no healthsome air breathes in? . *Rom. and Jul.* iv 3 34
Healthy. I am sound.—Nay, not as one would say, healthy *Meas. for Meas.* i 2 55
He said, sir, the water itself was a good healthy water . 2 *Hen. IV.* i 2 4
Heap on your head A pack of sorrows . . . *T. G. of Ver.* iii 1 19
How prove you that, in the great heap of your knowledge? *As Y. Like It* i 2 72
For this they have engross'd and piled up The canker'd heaps of strange-achieved gold . . . . . . 2 *Hen. IV.* iv 5 72
Let us on heaps go offer up our lives . . . *Hen. V.* iv 5 18
All her husbandry doth lie on heaps, Corrupting in it our fertility . v 2 39
Hence, heap of wrath, foul indigested lump! . . 2 *Hen. VI.* v 1 157
Great anchors, heaps of pearl, Inestimable stones . *Richard III.* i 4 26
Amongst this princely heap, if any here . . . . Hold me a foe . . ii 1 53
Alas, why would you heap these cares on me? . . . . iii 7 204
As doth a battle, when they charge on heaps The enemy flying *T. and C.* iii 2 29
Bury all, which yet distinctly ranges, In heaps and piles of ruin *Cor.* iii 1 207
All on a heap, like to a slaughter'd lamb . . *T. Andron.* ii 3 223
Your potent and infectious fevers heap On Athens! . *T. of Athens* iv 1 22
When I have laid proud Athens on a heap . . . . iv 3 101
Even such heaps and sums of love and wealth As shall to thee blot out what wrongs were theirs . . . . v 1 155
There were drawn Upon a heap a hundred ghastly women *J. Cæsar* i 3 23
Because thine eye Presumes to reach, all thy whole heap must die *Pericles* i 1 33
Heaped. With measure heap'd in joy, to the measures fall *As Y. Like It* v 4 185
And heap'd sedition on his crown at home . . 3 *Hen. VI.* ii 2 158
For your great graces Heap'd upon me, poor undeserver *Hen. VIII.* iii 2 175
His overthrow heap'd happiness upon him . . . . iv 2 64
If the measure of thy joy Be heap'd like mine . *Rom. and Jul.* ii 6 25
These applauses are For some new honours that are heap'd on Cæsar *J. C.* i 2 134
For those of old, And the late dignities heap'd up to them, We rest your hermits . . . . *Macbeth* i 6 19
Heapest. O disloyal thing, That shouldst repair my youth, thou heap'st A year's age on me . . . . *Cymbeline* i 1 132
Heaping. And my profit therein the heaping friendships . *W. Tale* iv 2 22
Heaping confusion on their own heads thereby . . 2 *Hen VI.* ii 1 187
Heapt. And mountainous error be too highly heapt For truth to o'er-peer *Coriolanus* ii 3 127
Hear. Where is the master, boatswain?—Do you not hear him? *Tempest* i 1 14
Dost thou hear?—Your tale, sir, would cure deafness . . i 2 106
Hear a little further And then I'll bring thee to the present business i 2 135
Sit still, and hear the last of our sea-sorrow. Here in this island we arrived . . . . i 2 170
Hark, hark! I hear The strain of strutting chanticleer . . i 2 384
Sea-nymphs hourly ring his knell: Ding-dong.—Hark! now I hear them i 2 404
This is . . . no sound That the earth owes. I hear it now above me i 2 407
What wert thou, if the King of Naples heard thee?—A single thing, as I am now, that wonders To hear thee speak of Naples . . . i 2 433
He does hear me; And that he does I weep . . . . i 2 433
Laugh me asleep, for I am very heavy?—Go sleep, and hear us . ii 1 190
His spirits hear me And yet I needs must curse . . . ii 2 3
And another storm brewing; I hear it sing i' the wind . . ii 2 20
Hear my soul speak: The very instant that I saw you, did My heart fly to your service . . . . iii 1 63
Do not approach Till thou dost hear me call . . . iv 1 50
Pray you, tread softly, that the blind mole may not Hear a foot fall . iv 1 195
That rejoice To hear the solemn curfew . . . . v 1 40
I long To hear the story of your life, which must Take the ear strangely v 1 312
Let me hear from thee by letters Of thy success in love . *T. G. of Ver.* i 1 57
There shall he practise tilts and tournaments, Hear sweet discourse . i 3 31
If this be he you oft have wish'd to hear from.—Mistress, it is . ii 4 103
When you have done, we look to hear from you . . . ii 4 120
Be gone! I will not hear thy vain excuse . . . . iii 1 168
My ears are stopt and cannot hear good news, So much of bad already hath possess'd them . . . . iii 1 205
Peace! we'll hear him.—Ay, by my beard, will we, for he's a proper man iv 1 9
I'll bring you where you shall hear music and see the gentleman . iv 2 31
But shall I hear him speak?—Ay, that you shall.—That will be music . iv 2 33
Is he among these?—Ay: but, peace! let's hear 'em . . iv 2 38
I likewise hear that Valentine is dead.—And so suppose am I . iv 2 113
I would to Valentine, To Mantua, where I hear he makes abode . iv 3 23
How like a dream is this I see and hear! Love, lend me patience v 4 26
'Tis your penance but to hear The story of your loves discovered . v 4 170
The council shall hear it; it is a riot.—It is not meet the council hear a riot; there is no fear of Got in a riot: the council, look you, shall desire to hear the fear of Got, and not to hear a riot *Mer. Wives* i 1 35
We three, to hear it and end it beween them . . . . i 1 144
He hears with ears.—The tevil and his tam! what phrase is this, 'He hears with ear'? . . . . i 1 150
You hear all these matters denied, gentlemen; you hear it . . i 1 193
Hear. I beseech you, be not so phlegmatic. Hear the truth of it *Mer. Wives* i 4 80
I hear the parson is no jester . . . . . . ii 1 217
I had rather hear them scold than fight . . . . ii 1 239
Come a little nearer this ways.—I warrant thee, nobody hears . ii 2 51
I hear you are a scholar,—I will be brief with you . . . ii 2 186
As you have one eye upon my follies, as you hear them unfolded, turn another into the register of your own. . . . . . ii 2 193
Peace, I say! hear mine host of the Garter . . . . iii 1 102
A man may hear this shower sing in the wind . . . . iii 2 37
I marvel I hear not of Master Brook; he sent me word to stay within . iii 5 58
And did he search for you, and could not find you?—You shall hear . iii 5 84
What duke should that be comes so secretly? I hear not of him . iv 3 6
You shall hear how things go; and, I warrant, to your content . iv 5 126
I will hear you, Master Fenton; and I will at the least keep your counsel iv 6 6
You do amaze her: hear the truth of it . . . . v 5 233
As I hear, the provost hath A warrant for his execution *Meas. for Meas.* i 4 73
Do you hear how he misplaces? . . . . ii 1 90
Get you gone, and let me hear no more of you . . . . ii 1 217
What, do I love her, That I desire to hear her speak again? . . ii 2 178
Your partner, as I hear, must die to-morrow . . . . ii 3 37
My gravity, Wherein—let no man hear me—I take pride . . ii 4 10
Bring me to hear them speak, where I may be concealed . . iii 1 52
Let me hear you speak farther . . . . iii 1 212
As near the dawning, provost, as it is, You shall hear more ere morning iv 2 98
Let's hear.—Whatsoever you may hear to the contrary, let Claudio be executed . . . . iv 2 122
He wants advice.—He will hear none . . . . . iv 2 155
He is coming, sir, he is coming; I hear his straw rustle . . iv 3 37
We hear Such goodness of your justice . . . . . v 1 5
Her shall you hear disproved to her eyes, Till she herself confess it . v 1 161
Whom it concerns to hear this matter forth . . . . v 1 255
We will hear you speak: Look you speak justly . . . v 1 297
A wretched soul, bruised with adversity, We bid be quiet when we hear it cry; But were we burden'd . . . . *Com. of Errors* ii 1 35
How dearly would it touch thee to the quick, Shouldst thou but hear I were licentious! . . . . ii 2 133
Or sleep I now and think I hear all this? . . . . ii 2 185
Sir, dispatch.—You hear how he importunes me . . . iv 1 53
I do arrest you, sir: you hear the suit.—I do obey thee . . iv 1 79
A chain, a chain! Do you not hear it ring?—What, the chain? . iv 2 51
The hours come back! that did I never hear . . . . iv 2 55
Who heard me to deny it or forswear it?—These ears of mine, thou know'st, did hear thee. . . . . v 1 26
Hark, hark! I hear him, mistress: fly, be gone!—Come, stand by me . v 1 184
My wasting lamps some fading glimmer left, My dull deaf ears a little use to hear . . . . v 1 316
If this be not a dream I see and hear . . . . . v 1 376
Go with us into the abbey here And hear at large discoursed all our fortunes . . . . v 1 395
I had rather hear my dog bark at a crow than a man swear he loves me *Much Ado* i 1 132
You should hear reason.—And when I have heard it, what blessing brings it? . . . . i 3 6
Thus answer I in name of Benedick, But hear these ill news with the ears of Claudio . . . . ii 1 180
And now had he rather hear the tabor and the pipe . . . ii 3 15
Come, shall we hear this music?—Yea, my good lord . . . ii 3 39
We'll hear that song again.—O, good my lord, tax not so bad a voice . ii 3 45
I pray you, tell Benedick of it, and hear what a' will say . . ii 3 178
I hear how I am censured: they say I will bear myself proudly . ii 3 233
Happy are they that hear their detractions and can put them to mending ii 3 238
Beatrice, like a lapwing, runs Close by the ground, to hear our conference . . . . iii 1 25
Yet tell her of it: hear what she will say . . . . iii 1 81
Yea, or to paint himself? for the which, I hear what they say of him . iii 2 59
I have studied eight or nine wise words to speak to you, which these hobby-horses must not hear . . . . iii 2 75
In private?—If it please you: yet Count Claudio may hear . . iii 2 88
If you hear a child cry in the night, you must call to the nurse . iii 3 69
How if the nurse be asleep and will not hear us? . . . . iii 3 72
The ewe that will not hear her lamb when it baes will never answer a calf when he bleats . . . . iii 3 75
Well, masters, we hear our charge: let us go sit here upon the church-bench . . . . iii 3 94
Didst thou not hear somebody?—No; 'twas the vane on the house . iii 3 137
I hear as good exclamation on your worship as of any man in the city; and though I be but a poor man, I am glad to hear it . . iii 5 28
I am sorry you must hear . . . . iv 1 89
Myself, my brother and this grieved count Did see her, hear her . iv 1 91
If they wrong her honour, The proudest of them shall well hear of it . iv 1 194
So will it fare with Claudio: When he shall hear she died upon his words iv 1 225
As you hear of me, so think of me. Go, comfort your cousin . . iv 1 338
I will not hear you.—No? Come, brother; away! I will be heard . v 1 107
You have killed a sweet lady, and her death shall fall heavy on you. Let me hear from you . . . . v 1 151
Either I must shortly hear from him, or I will subscribe him a coward. v 2 58
Will you go hear this news, signior?—I will live in thy heart . . v 2 103
I love to hear him lie And I will use him for my minstrelsy *L. L. Lost* i 1 176
God grant us patience!—To hear? or forbear laughing?—To hear meekly, sir, and to laugh moderately; or to forbear both . . i 1 198
Will you hear this letter with attention?—As we would hear an oracle . i 1 217
Did you hear the proclamation?—I do confess much of the hearing it . i 1 286
I am less proud to hear you tell my worth Than you much willing to be counted wise In spending your wit . . . . ii 1 17
I hear your grace hath sworn out house-keeping . . . . ii 1 104
Do you hear, my mad wenches?—No.—What then, do you see? . . ii 1 256
Thus dost thou hear the Nemean lion roar 'Gainst thee, thou lamb . iv 1 90
What vane? what weathercock? did you ever hear better? . . iv 1 97
Will you hear an extemporal epitaph on the death of the deer? . iv 2 50
Let me hear a staff, a stanze, a verse; lege, domine . . . iv 2 107
What will Biron say when that he shall hear Faith so infringed? . iv 3 145
When shall you hear that I Will praise a hand, a foot, a face, an eye? iv 3 183
It did move him to passion, and therefore let's hear it . . iv 3 202
A lover's ear will hear the lowest sound, When the suspicious head of theft is stopp'd . . . . iv 3 335
You hear his learning . . . . v 1 54
Tell her, we measure them by weary steps.—She hears herself . . v 2 195
Bleat softly then; the butcher hears you cry . . . . v 2 255
But will you hear? the king is my love sworn . . . . v 2 282

Hear. A jest's prosperity lies in the ear Of him that hears it, never in the tongue Of him that makes it . . . . . . *L. L. Lost* v 2 872
If sickly ears, Deaf'd with the clamours of their own dear groans, Will hear your idle scorns, continue then . . . . . . v 2 875
Will you hear the dialogue that the two learned men have compiled? . v 2 895
For aught that I could ever read, Could ever hear . . *M. N. Dream* i 1 133
I will roar, that I will do any man's heart good to hear me . . i 2 73
Certain stars shot madly from their spheres, To hear the sea-maid's music . . . . ii 1 154
Alack, where are you? speak, an if you hear; Speak, of all loves! . ii 2 153
And I will sing, that they shall hear I am not afraid . . . iii 1 127
Stay, gentle Helena; hear my excuse: My love, my life, my soul, fair Helena! . . . . iii 2 245
What, wilt thou hear some music, my sweet love? . . . . iv 1 29
Fairy king, attend, and mark: I do hear the morning lark . . iv 1 99
My love shall hear the music of my hounds . . . . . iv 1 111
Never did I hear Such gallant chiding . . . . . . iv 1 119
Judge when you hear . . . . iv 1 132
You are fortunately met: Of this discourse we more will hear anon . iv 1 183
I will tell you every thing, right as it fell out.—Let us hear . . iv 2 33
And I do not doubt but to hear them say, it is a sweet comedy . iv 2 45
We will hear it.—No, my noble lord; It is not for you . . . v 1 76
I will hear that play; For never anything can be amiss, When simpleness and duty tender it . . . . v 1 81
Now will I to the chink, To spy an I can hear my Thisby's face . v 1 195
No remedy, my lord, when walls are so wilful to hear without warning v 1 211
Will it please you to see the epilogue, or to hear a Bergomask dance? . v 1 360
He hears merry tales and smiles not . . . . *Mer. of Venice* i 2 52
Do you hear?—I am debating of my present store . . . . i 3 53
Hear you me, Jessica: Lock up my doors; and when you hear the drum . . . , Clamber not you up to the casements . . . . . ii 5 28
You were best to tell Antonio what you hear; Yet do not suddenly . ii 8 33
Do you hear whether Antonio have had any loss at sea or no? . . iii 1 44
Hast thou found my daughter?—I often came where I did hear of her . iii 1 85
But let me hear the letter of your friend . . . . . . iii 2 316
This comes too near the praising of myself; Therefore no more of it: hear other things . . . . iii 4 23
You hear the learn'd Bellario, what he writes . . . . . iv 1 167
Your wife would give you little thanks for that, If she were by, to hear you make the offer . . . . iv 1 289
Hark, I hear the footing of a man.—Who comes so fast? . . . v 1 24
Such harmony is in immortal souls; But whilst this muddy vesture of decay Doth grossly close it in, we cannot hear it . . . . v 1 65
I am never merry when I hear sweet music . . . . . . v 1 69
If they but hear perchance a trumpet sound, Or any air of music . v 1 75
Your husband is at hand; I hear his trumpet . . . . . v 1 122
As I hear, he was much bound for you . . . . . . v 1 137
Go apart, Adam, and thou shalt hear how he will shake me up *As Y. Like It* i 1 29
I cannot hear of any that did see her . . . . . . ii 2 4
When I did hear The motley fool thus moral on the time . . . ii 7 28
Didst thou hear these verses?—O, yes, I heard them all, and more too . iii 2 172
Didst thou hear without wondering how thy name should be hanged and carved upon these trees? . . . . iii 2 181
Do you hear, forester?—Very well: what would you? . . . iii 2 315
Chide a year together: I had rather hear you chide than this man woo iii 5 65
Yet words do well When he that speaks them pleases those that hear . iii 5 112
Will you hear the letter?—So please you, for I never heard it yet . iv 3 36
Warr'st thou with a woman's heart? Did you ever hear such railing? . iv 3 46
Who do you speak to, 'Why blame you me to love you?'—To her that is not here, nor doth not hear . . . . v 2 117
I count it but time lost to hear such a foolish song . . . . v 3 41
There is a lord will hear you play to-night . . . *T. of Shrew* Ind. 1 93
I long to hear him call the drunkard husband . . . . Ind. 1 133
I do not sleep: I see, I hear, I speak; I smell sweet savours . Ind. 2 72
They thought it good you hear a play And frame your mind to mirth Ind. 2 136
Hark, Tranio! thou may'st hear Minerva speak . . . . . i 1 84
She is an irksome brawling scold: If that be all, masters, I hear no harm . . . . i 2 189
A woman's tongue, That gives not half so great a blow to hear As will a chestnut in a farmer's fire . . . . i 2 209
Did you yet ever see Baptista's daughter?—No, sir; but hear I do that he hath two . . . . i 2 253
Good morrow, Kate; for that's your name, I hear.—Well have you heard ii 1 183
My instrument's in tune.—Let's hear. O fie! the treble jars . . iii 1 39
'Hic steterat Priami,' take heed he hear us not, 'regia,' presume not . iii 1 44
And yet we hear not of our son-in-law. What will be said? . . iii 2 3
Is it not news, to hear of Petruchio's coming?—Is he come?—Why, no, sir . . . . iii 2 33
Tedious it were to tell, and harsh to hear . . . . . . iii 2 107
Hark, hark! I hear the minstrels play . . . . . . iii 2 185
This is to feel a tale, not to hear a tale.—And therefore 'tis called a sensible tale . . . . iv 1 65
Cock's passion, silence! I hear my master . . . . . . iv 1 121
And, for the good report I hear of you . . . . . . iv 4 28
Curious I cannot be with you, Signior Baptista, of whom I hear so well iv 4 37
He would always say—Methinks I hear him now; his plausive words He scatter'd not in ears, but grafted them. . . . *All's Well* i 2 53
I will now hear; what say you of this gentlewoman? . . . . i 3 1
I must not hear thee; fare thee well, kind maid . . . . ii 1 148
Sir, will you hear my suit?—And grant it.—Thanks, sir . . . ii 3 82
Do you hear, monsieur? a word with you . . . . . . ii 3 191
Where I will never come Whilst I can shake my sword or hear the drum ii 5 96
You shall hear I am run away: know it before the report come . . iii 2 24
Why should he be killed?—So say I, madam, if he run away, as I hear he does . . . . iii 2 43
For my part, I only hear your son was run away . . . . iii 2 46
Unless her prayers, whom heaven delights to hear And loves to grant, reprieve him . . . . iii 4 27
When haply he shall hear that she is gone, He will return . . . iii 4 35
Know you such a one?—But by the ear, that hears most nobly of him . iii 5 53
Let him fetch off his drum, which you hear him so confidently undertake to do . . . . iii 6 21
I would I had any drum of the enemy's . . . You shall hear one anon . iv 1 68
Keep him muffled Till we do hear from them . . . . . iv 1 101
Knock at my chamber-window: I'll order take my mother shall not hear iv 2 55
What hear you of these wars?—I hear there is an overture of peace . iv 3 44
I mean, the business is not ended, as fearing to hear of it hereafter . iv 3 111
If your lordship be in't, as I believe you are, you must have the patience to hear it . . . . iv 3 133
Look not so upon me; we shall hear of your lordship anon . . . iv 3 222

Hear. Take the fool away.—Do you not hear, fellows? Take away the lady . . . . *T. Night* i 5 43
We'll once more hear Orsino's embassy . . . . i 5 176
And allowed your approach rather to wonder at you than to hear you . i 5 211
We will hear this divinity. Now, sir, what is your text? . . . i 5 235
Where are you roaming? O, stay and hear; your true love's coming . ii 3 41
To hear by the nose, it is dulcet in contagion . . . . . ii 3 58
I had rather hear you to solicit that Than music from the spheres . iii 1 120
Let me hear you speak.—I pity you . . . . iii 1 133
I warrant you, he will not hear of godliness . . . . . iii 4 134
Go with me to my house, And hear thou there how many fruitless pranks iv 1 59
Here comes Sir Toby halting; you shall hear more . . . . . v 1 196
I would not be a stander-by to hear My sovereign mistress clouded so *W. Tale* i 2 279
I will tell it softly; Yond crickets shall not hear it . . . . ii 1 31
La you now, you hear: When she will take the rein I let her run . ii 3 50
To prate and talk for life and honour 'fore Who please to come and hear iii 2 43
Harden'd be the hearts Of all that hear me, and my near'st of kin Cry fie upon my grave! . . . . iii 2 54
Therefore proceed. But yet hear this; mistake me not . . . iii 2 110
If you did but hear the pedlar at the door, you would never dance again iv 4 181
We can both sing it: if thou 'lt bear a part, thou shalt hear . . iv 4 299
But to your protestation; let me hear What you profess . . . iv 4 379
Can he speak? hear? Know man from man? dispute his own estate? . iv 4 410
Hark, Perdita. I'll hear you by and by.—He's irremoveable . . iv 4 518
I understand the business, I hear it: to have an open ear, a quick eye . iv 4 684
Has the old man e'er a son, sir, do you hear, an't like you, sir? . iv 4 811
Then I'ld shriek, that even your ears Should rift to hear me . . v 1 66
That which you hear you'll swear you see, there is such unity in the proofs . . . . v 2 34
What you can make her do, I am content to look on: what to speak, I am content to hear . . . . v 3 93
Start not; her actions shall be holy as You hear my spell is lawful . v 3 105
For thou shalt hear that I . . . have preserved Myself to see the issue v 3 125
Silence, good mother; hear the embassy . . . . . *K. John* i 1 6
So much my conscience whispers in your ear, Which none but heaven and you and I shall hear . . . . i 1 43
Hear the crier.—What the devil art thou? . . . . . . ii 1 134
Let us hear them speak Whose title they admit, Arthur's or John's . ii 1 199
Our trumpet call'd you to this gentle parle— For our advantage; therefore hear us first . . . . ii 1 206
Peace! no more.—O, tremble, for you hear the lion roar . . . ii 1 294
Hear us, great kings: vouchsafe awhile to stay . . . . . ii 1 416
Rouse from sleep that fell anatomy Which cannot hear a lady's feeble voice . . . . iii 4 41
When he shall hear of your approach, If that young Arthur be not gone already, Even at that news he dies . . . . iii 4 162
Perceive how willingly I will both hear and grant you your requests . iv 2 46
Where is my mother's care, That such an army could be drawn in France, And she not hear of it? . . . . iv 2 119
And, as I hear, my lord, The Lady Constance in a frenzy died . . iv 2 121
But if you be afeard to hear the worst, Then let the worst unheard fall on your head . . . . iv 2 135
And he that speaks doth gripe the hearer's wrist, Whilst he that hears makes fearful action . . . . iv 2 191
Your nobles will not hear you, but are gone To offer service to your enemy . . . . v 1 33
Now hear our English king; For thus his royalty doth speak in me . v 2 128
Which then our leisure would not let us hear . . . . *Richard II.* i 1 5
Ourselves will hear The accuser and the accused freely speak . . i 1 16
And what hear there for welcome but my groans? Therefore commend me . . . . i 2 70
Though Richard my life's counsel would not hear, My death's sad tale may yet undeaf his ear . . . . ii 1 15
Quick is mine ear to hear of good towards him . . . . . ii 1 234
We hear this fearful tempest sing, Yet seek no shelter . . . . ii 1 263
We hear no tidings from the king; Therefore we will disperse ourselves ii 4 3
Thieves are not judged but they are by to hear . . . . . iv 1 123
I never long'd to hear a word till now . . . . v 3 115
Music do I hear? Ha, ha! keep time . . . . v 5 41
But for the concord of my state and time Had not an ear to hear my true time broke . . . . v 5 48
The latest news we hear Is that the rebels have consumed with fire Our town of Cicester . . . . v 6 1
But whether they be ta'en or slain we hear not . . . . . v 6 4
Then let me hear Of you, my gentle cousin Westmoreland . . 1 *Hen. IV.* i 1 30
That what thou speakest may move and what he hears may be believed i 2 172
Whose daughter, as we hear, the Earl of March Hath lately married . i 3 84
Henceforth Let me not hear you speak of Mortimer . . . . i 3 119
You shall hear in such a kind from me As will displease you . . . i 3 121
Send us your prisoners, or you will hear of it . . . . . i 3 124
Nettled and stung with pismires, when I hear Of this vile politician . i 3 240
Hast thou never an eye in thy head? canst not hear? . . . . ii 1 32
Lay thine ear close to the ground and list if thou canst hear the tread of travellers . . . . ii 2 35
Stand close; I hear them coming.—Come, my masters, let us share . ii 2 103
Away, you rogue! dost thou not hear them call? . . . . . ii 4 88
Come, let's hear, Jack; what trick hast thou now? . . . . ii 4 293
I blushed to hear his monstrous devices . . . . . . ii 4 344
The complaints I hear of thee are grievous.—'Sblood, my lord, they are false . . . . ii 4 486
He wisheth you in heaven.—And you in hell, as oft as he hears Owen Glendower spoke of . . . . iii 1 11
I had rather hear a brazen canstick turn'd, Or a dry wheel grate . . iii 1 131
I'll sit and hear her sing: By that time will our book, I think, be drawn iii 1 223
Lie still, ye thief, and hear the lady sing in Welsh.—I had rather hear Lady, my brach, howl in Irish . . . . iii 1 238
Of many tales devised, Which oft the ear of greatness needs must hear . iii 2 24
I am on fire To hear this rich reprisal is so nigh And yet not ours . iv 1 118
That's the worst tidings that I hear of yet . . . . . iv 1 127
Such a commodity of warm slaves, as had as lieve hear the devil as a drum . . . . iv 2 19
Tut, I came not to hear this.—Then to the point . . . . iv 3 89
I have a truant been to chivalry; And so I hear he doth account me too v 1 95
Doth he feel it [honour]? no. Doth he hear it? no. Tis insensible, then . . . . v 1 139
Never did I hear Of any prince so wild a libertine . . . . v 2 71
Who, as we hear, Are busily in arms . . . . v 5 38
I hear for certain, and do speak the truth . . . . 2 *Hen. IV.* i 1 188
I hear his majesty is returned with some discomfort . . . . i 2 117

Hear. I hear, moreover, his highness is fallen into this same whoreson apoplexy *2 Hen. IV.* i 2 122
You hear not what I say to you.—Very well, my lord, very well i 2 136
I hear you are going with Lord John of Lancaster i 2 228
I am well spoke on; I can hear it with mine own ears ii 2 70
Find out Sneak's noise; Mistress Tearsheet would fain hear some music ii 4 13
You would bless you to hear what he said ii 4 103
To hear and absolutely to determine Of what conditions iv 1 164
To hear with reverence Your exposition on the holy text iv 2 6
The leaders, having charge from you to stand, Will not go off until they hear you speak iv 2 100
Toward the court, my lords: I hear the king my father is sore sick iv 3 83
I never thought to hear you speak again iv 5 92
Sit thou by my bed; And hear, I think, the very latest counsel iv 5 183
Hear your own dignity so much profaned v 2 93
When thou dost hear I am as I have been, Approach me v 5 64
As we hear you do reform yourselves, We will . . . Give you advancement v 5 72
I cannot now speak: I will hear you soon v 5 100
Your humble patience pray, Gently to hear, kindly to judge *Hen. V.* Prol. 34
We are blessed in the change.—Hear him but reason in divinity i 1 38
Hear him debate of commonwealth affairs, You would say it hath been all in all his study i 1 41
List his discourse of war, and you shall hear A fearful battle render'd you in music i 1 43
Save that there was not time enough to hear i 1 84
I'll wait upon you, and I long to hear it i 1 98
We would be resolved, Before we hear him, of some things of weight i 2 5
Speak, my lord; For we will hear, note and believe in heart i 2 30
For hear her but exampled by herself i 2 156
We hear Your greeting is from him, not from the king i 2 235
Desires you let the dukedoms that you claim Hear no more of you i 2 257
God quit you in his mercy! Hear your sentence ii 2 166
Hear the shrill whistle which doth order give To sounds confused iii Prol. 9
Therefore, go speak: the duke will hear thy voice iii 6 48
The enemy is loud; you hear him all night iv 1 76
So fare thee well: Thou never shalt hear herald any more iv 3 127
Your majesty hear now, saving your majesty's manhood iv 8 35
I will be glad to hear you confess it brokenly with your English tongue v 2 106
Is it you whose voice I hear? Open the gates *1 Hen. VI.* i 3 16
I grieve to hear what torments you endured i 4 57
Hear, hear how dying Salisbury doth groan! i 4 104
All France will be replete with mirth and joy, When they shall hear how we have play'd the men i 6 16
This is my servant: hear him, noble prince.—And this is mine iv 1 80
I were best to leave him, for he will not hear v 3 82
Let me hear no more!—What, what, my lord! are you so choleric? *2 Hen. VI.* i 2 50
Will her ladyship behold and hear our exorcisms? i 4 4
I know not how it stands; Sorry I am to hear what I have heard ii 1 193
My lord, I long to hear it at full.—Sweet York, begin ii 2 6
A rabble that rejoice To see my tears and hear my deep-fet groans ii 4 33
What have we done? Didst ever hear a man so penitent? iii 2 4
Have calm'd their spleenful mutiny, Until they hear the order of his death iii 2 129
As bitter-searching terms, As curst, as harsh and horrible to hear iii 2 312
To France, sweet Suffolk: let me hear from thee iii 2 405
Our safety is to follow them; For, as I hear, the king is fled v 3 24
Hear him, lords; And be you silent and attentive too *3 Hen. VI.* i 1 121
I cannot stay to hear these articles.—Nor I i 1 180
Art thou king, and wilt be forced? I shame to hear thee speak i 1 231
Nay, stay; let's hear the orisons he makes i 4 110
Say how he died, for I will hear it all ii 1 49
Nor now my scandal, Richard, dost thou hear ii 1 151
Ay, now methinks I hear great Warwick speak ii 1 186
Tell me, didst thou never hear That things ill-got had ever bad success? ii 2 45
He nor sees nor hears us what we say.—O, would he did! ii 6 63
Forbear awhile; we'll hear a little more iii 1 27
And, as I hear, the great commanding Warwick Is thither gone iii 1 29
Nero will be tainted with remorse, To hear and see her plaints iii 1 41
Shall I not hear my task?—An easy task; 'tis but to love a king iii 2 52
Let us hear your firm resolve.—Your grant, or your denial, shall be mine iii 3 129
I hear, yet say not much, but think the more iv 1 83
Edward is escaped from your brother, And fled, as he hears since iv 6 79
Men well inclined to hear what thou command'st iv 8 16
Then Clarence is at hand; I hear his drum.—It is not his, my lord v 1 11
The drum your honour hears marcheth from Warwick.—Who should that be? v 1 13
Where slept our scouts, or how are they seduced, That we could hear no news? v 1 20
But at last I well might hear, deliver'd with a groan, 'O, farewell!' v 2 46
Have arrived our coast And, as we hear, march on to fight with us v 3 9
I will not hear them speak.—For my part, I'll not trouble thee with words v 5 4
Let us hear him speak. What! can so young a thorn begin to prick? v 5 12
Ere ye come there, be sure to hear some news v 5 48
Didst thou not hear me swear I would not do it? v 5 74
Thou camest— I'll hear no more: die, prophet, in thy speech v 6 57
I invocate thy ghost, To hear the lamentations of poor Anne! *Richard III.* i 2 9
And thou unfit for any place but hell.—Yes, one place else, if you will hear me name it i 2 110
York and Edward wept, To hear the piteous moan that Rutland made i 2 158
My hair doth stand on end to hear her curses i 3 304
Be sudden in the execution, Withal obdurate, do not hear him plead i 3 347
What was your dream? I long to hear you tell it i 4 8
No marvel, my lord, though it affrighted you; I promise you, I am afraid to hear you tell it i 4 65
Look'd pale when they did hear of Clarence' death ii 1 136
Hear you the news abroad?—Ay, that the king is dead ii 3 3
Last night, I hear, they lay at Northampton ii 4 1
I hope he is much grown since last I saw him.—But I hear, no ii 4 6
How, my pretty York? I pray thee, let me hear it ii 4 26
Shall we hear from you, Catesby, ere we sleep?—You shall, my lord iii 1 188
O, remember, God, To hear her prayers for them, as now for us! iii 3 19
But since you come too late of our intents, Yet witness what you hear we did intend iii 5 70
Dorset is fled to Richmond.—I hear that news, my lord iv 2 89
Hover about me with your airy wings And hear your mother's lamentation! iv 4 14
Let not the heavens hear these tell-tale women Rail on the Lord's anointed iv 4 149

Hear. Then patiently hear my impatience *Richard III.* iv 4 156
O, let me speak!—Do then; but I'll not hear iv 4 159
Prepare her ears to hear a wooer's tale iv 4 327
I hear their drum.—Fight, gentlemen of England! fight, bold yeomen! v 3 337
What traitor hears me, and says not amen? v 5 22
Only they That come to hear a merry bawdy play *Hen. VIII.* Prol. 14
I am sorry To hear this of him; and could wish he were Something mistaken i 1 194
In person I'll hear him his confessions justify i 2 6
Sit by us; you shall hear—This was his gentleman in trust i 2 124
Whereof We cannot feel too little, hear too much i 2 128
A choice hour To hear from him a matter of some moment i 2 163
What news, Sir Thomas Lovell?—Faith, my lord, I hear of none i 3 17
Even to the hall, to hear what shall become Of the great Duke ii 1 2
When he was brought again to the bar, to hear His knell rung out ii 1 31
You that thus far have come to pity me, Hear what I say ii 1 57
Did you not of late days hear A buzzing of a separation? ii 1 147
I should be glad to hear such news as this Once every hour iii 2 24
We shall see him For it an archbishop.—So I hear iii 2 74
Speedily I wish To hear from Rome iii 2 90
May be, he hears the king Does whet his anger to him iii 2 91
Hear the king's pleasure, cardinal iii 2 228
Can ye endure to hear this arrogance? And from this fellow? iii 2 278
Let 'em alone, and draw the curtain close: We shall hear more anon v 2 35
His royal self in judgement comes to hear The cause v 3 120
But know, I come not To hear such flattery now, and in my presence v 3 124
Others, to hear the city Abused extremely, and to cry 'That's witty!' Epil. 5
All the expected good we're like to hear Epil. 8
Hark! do you not hear the people cry 'Troilus'? *Troi. and Cres.* i 2 244
Agamemnon, . . . hear what Ulysses speaks i 3 58
Yet let it please both, Thou great, and wise, to hear Ulysses speak i 3 69
When rank Thersites opes his mastic jaws, We shall hear music i 3 74
And doth think it rich To hear the wooden dialogue and sound i 3 155
'Tis for Agamemnon's ears.—He hears nought privately that comes from Troy i 3 249
Thou bitch-wolf's son, canst thou not hear? Feel, then ii 1 12
Young men, whom Aristotle thought Unfit to hear moral philosophy ii 2 167
Nay, this shall not hedge us out: we'll hear you sing, certainly iii 1 66
Come, come, I'll hear no more of this; I'll sing you a song now iii 1 114
I long to hear how they sped to-day iii 1 155
Be true.—O heavens! 'be true' again!—Hear why I speak it, love iv 4 77
Do you hear, my lord? do you hear?—What now? v 3 97
But thou anon shalt hear of me again; Till when, go seek thy fortune v 6 18
Well, I'll hear it, sir: yet you must not think to fob off our disgrace with a tale *Coriolanus* i 1 96
The other instruments Did see and hear, devise, instruct, walk, feel i 1 105
Patience awhile, you'll hear the belly's answer i 1 130
Let's hence, and hear How the dispatch is made, and in what fashion i 1 280
Methinks I hear hither your husband's drum i 3 32
He had rather see the swords, and hear a drum, than look upon his schoolmaster i 3 60
Then shall we hear their 'larum, and they ours i 4 9
Where ladies shall be frighted, And, gladly quaked, hear more i 9 6
I have some wounds upon me, and they smart To hear themselves remember'd i 9 29
I have seen the dumb men throng to see him and The blind to hear him speak ii 1 279
Please you To hear Cominius speak?—Most willingly ii 2 66
Never shame to hear What you have nobly done ii 2 71
I had rather have one scratch my head i' the sun When the alarum were struck than idly sit To hear my nothings monster'd ii 2 81
He had rather venture all his limbs for honour Than one on's ears to hear it ii 2 85
We'll hear no more. Pursue him to his house, and pluck him thence iii 1 308
They are prepared With accusations, as I hear, more strong iii 2 140
Devise with thee Where thou shalt rest, that thou mayst hear of us iv 1 39
Hear from me still, and never of me aught But what is like me formerly.—That's worthily As any ear can hear iv 1 52
If that I could for weeping, you should hear,—Nay, and you shall hear some iv 2 13
You have done a brave deed. Ere you go, hear this iv 2 38
I am joyful to hear of their readiness iv 3 51
We hear not of him, neither need we fear him; His remedies are tame iv 6 1
Where is he, hear you?—Nay, I hear nothing: his mother and his wife Hear nothing from him iv 6 17
Faith, we hear fearful news iv 6 139
You hear what he hath said Which was sometime his general v 1 1
Nay, if he coy'd To hear Cominius speak, I'll keep at home v 1 7
He'll never hear him.—Not?—I tell you, he does sit in gold, his eye Red as 'twould burn Rome v 1 62
Who, as I hear, mean to solicit him For mercy to his country v 1 72
You must return: our general Will no more hear from thence v 2 6
I will not hear thee speak. This man, Aufidius, Was my beloved v 2 98
Do you hear how we are shent for keeping your greatness back? v 2 104
If you fail in our request, the blame May hang upon your hardness: therefore hear us v 3 91
Mark; for we'll Hear nought from Rome in private v 3 93
Have you with heed perused What I have written to you?—We have.—And grieve to hear't v 6 63
This admits no excuse.—He approaches: you shall hear him v 6 70
And all the bitterest terms That ever ear did hear *T. Andron.* ii 3 111
You lament in vain: The tribunes hear you not; no man is by iii 1 28
No tribune hears you speak.—Why, 'tis no matter, man: if they did hear, They would not mark me iii 1 32
Kneel with me? Do, then, dear heart; for heaven shall hear our prayers iii 1 211
O heavens, can you hear a good man groan, And not relent? iv 1 123
I'll show thee wondrous things, That highly may advantage thee to hear v 1 56
'Twill vex thy soul to hear what I shall speak v 1 62
Villanies Ruthful to hear, yet piteously perform'd v 1 66
That was but a deed of charity To that which thou shalt hear of me anon v 1 90
Let them not speak to me; But let them hear what fearful words I utter v 2 169
Let him tell the tale; Your hearts will throb and weep to hear him speak v 3 95
Will they not hear? What, ho! you men, you beasts *Rom. and Jul.* i 1 90
And hear the sentence of your moved prince i 1 95
I would thou wert so happy by thy stay, To hear true shrift i 1 165
Hear all, all see, And like her most whose merit most shall be i 2 30
Nurse, come back again; I have remember'd me, thou's hear our counsel i 3 9

Hear. If he hear thee, thou wilt anger him.—This cannot anger him *Rom. and Jul.* ii 1 22
Shall I hear more, or shall I speak at this? ii 2 37
I hear some noise within; dear love, adieu! Anon, good nurse! ii 2 136
A gentleman, nurse, that loves to hear himself talk ii 4 155
That it would do you good to hear it ii 4 227
An thou make minstrels of us, look to hear nothing but discords iii 1 50
O Lord, I could have stay'd here all the night To hear good counsel iii 3 160
I must hear from thee every day in the hour iii 5 44
O, how my heart abhors To hear him named, and cannot come to him! iii 5 101
I hear thou must, and nothing may prorogue it, On Thursday next be married iv 1 48
Things that, to hear them told, have made me tremble iv 1 86
The county will be here with music straight, For so he said he would: I hear him near iv 4 22
So shall no foot upon the churchyard tread, Being loose, unfirm, with digging up of graves, But thou shalt hear it v 3 7
I hear some noise. Lady, come from that nest Of death v 3 151
I thank you; you shall hear from me anon: Go not away *T. of Athens* i 1 153
It does concern you near.—Near! why then, another time I'll hear thee i 2 184
What shall be done? he will not hear, till feel: I must be round with him ii 2 7
Though you hear now, too late—yet now's a time ii 2 152
I can tell you one thing, my lord, and which I hear from common rumours iii 2 5
In like manner was I in debt to my importunate business, but he would not hear my excuse iii 6 16
Alcibiades is banished: hear you of it? iii 6 60
You'll swear, terribly swear Into strong shudders and to heavenly agues The immortal gods that hear you iv 3 138
Ay, and you hear him cog, see him dissemble, Know his gross patchery v 1 98
That Tiber trembled underneath her banks, To hear the replication of your sounds Made in her concave shores *J. Cæsar* i 1 51
I hear a tongue, shriller than all the music, Cry 'Cæsar!' Speak; Cæsar is turn'd to hear i 2 16
Be prepared to hear: And since you know you cannot see yourself i 2 66
And that same eye whose bend doth awe the world Did lose his lustre: I did hear him groan i 2 124
What you have to say I will with patience hear i 2 169
A time Both meet to hear and answer such high things i 2 170
He hears no music; Seldom he smiles, and smiles in such a sort i 2 204
Such an exploit have I in hand, Ligarius, Had you a healthful ear to hear of it ii 1 319
Hark, boy! what noise is that?—I hear none, madam.—Prithee, listen well ii 4 17
Those that will hear me speak, let 'em stay here iii 2 5
I will hear Brutus speak.—I will hear Cassius; and compare their reasons iii 2 8
Let us hear Mark Antony.—Let him go up into the public chair; We'll hear him iii 2 67
Let us hear what Antony can say.—You gentle Romans,— Peace, ho! let us hear him iii 2 76
'Tis his will: Let but the commons hear this testament iii 2 135
We'll hear the will: read it, Mark Antony.—The will, the will! we will hear Cæsar's will iii 2 143
Read the will; we'll hear it, Antony; You shall read us the will iii 2 152
Hear the noble Antony.—We'll hear him, we'll follow him, we'll die with him iii 2 211
Let's stay and hear the will.—Here is the will, and under Cæsar's seal iii 2 244
Why ask you? hear you aught of her in yours [your letters]? iv 3 185
Didst thou not hear their shouts? Alas, thou hast misconstrued every thing! v 3 83
Thou sure and firm-set earth, Hear not my steps *Macbeth* ii 1 57
Hear it not, Duncan; for it is a knell That summons thee to heaven or to hell ii 1 63
I have done the deed. Didst thou not hear a noise? ii 2 15
I hear a knocking At the south entry: retire we to our chamber ii 2 65
O gentle lady, 'Tis not for you to hear what I can speak ii 3 89
We hear, our bloody cousins are bestow'd In England and in Ireland iii 1 30
Hark! I hear horses.—Give us a light there, ho!—Then 'tis he iii 3 8
Get thee gone: to-morrow We'll hear, ourselves, again iii 4 32
Did you send to him, sir?—I hear it by the way; but I will send iii 4 130
'Twould have anger'd any heart alive To hear the men deny't iii 6 16
I hear Macduff lives in disgrace: sir, can you tell? iii 6 22
Say, if thou'dst rather hear it from our mouths, Or from our masters? iv 1 62
He knows thy thought: Hear his speech, but say thou nought iv 1 70
Macbeth! Macbeth! Macbeth!—Had I three ears, I'ld hear thee iv 1 78
I did hear The galloping of horse: who was't came by? iv 1 139
Your royal preparation Makes us hear something v 3 58
The time has been, my senses would have cool'd To hear a night-shriek v 5 11
What is thy name?—Thou'lt be afraid to hear it v 7 5
I think I hear them. Stand, ho! Who's there? *Hamlet* i 1 14
Well, sit we down, And let us hear Bernardo speak of this i 1 34
Who, impotent and bed-rid, scarcely hears Of this his nephew's purpose i 2 29
I would not hear your enemy say so, Nor shall you do mine ear that violence i 2 170
For God's love, let me hear i 2 195
Do not sleep, But let me hear from you.—Do you doubt that? i 3 4
That looks so many fathoms to the sea And hears it roar beneath i 4 78
Speak; I am bound to hear.—So art thou to revenge, when thou shalt hear i 5 6
Now, Hamlet, hear: 'Tis given out that, sleeping in my orchard, A serpent stung me i 5 34
Come on—you hear this fellow in the cellarage—Consent to swear i 5 151
I have found The very cause of Hamlet's lunacy.—O, speak of that; that do I long to hear ii 2 50
Do you hear, let them be well used ii 2 547
Follow him, friends: we'll hear a play to-morrow. Dost thou hear me? ii 2 560
We told him; And there did seem in him a kind of joy To hear of it iii 1 19
He beseech'd me to entreat your majesties To hear and see the matter iii 1 23
It doth much content me To hear him so inclined iii 1 25
I hear him coming: let's withdraw, my lord iii 1 55
O, it offends me to the soul to hear a robustious periwig-pated fellow tear a passion to tatters, to very rags iii 2 10
How now, my lord! will the king hear this piece of work? iii 2 51
Behind the arras I'll convey myself, To hear the process iii 3 29
Fear me not: withdraw, I hear him coming iii 4 7
Do you see nothing there?—Nothing at all; yet all that is I see.—Nor did you nothing hear? iii 4 133
She speaks much of her father; says she hears There's tricks i' the world iv 5 4

Hear. Make choice of whom your wisest friends you will, And they shall hear and judge 'twixt you and me *Hamlet* iv 5 205
You shortly shall hear more: I loved your father, and we love ourself iv 7 33
I cannot live to hear the news from England v 2 365
So shall you hear Of carnal, bloody, and unnatural acts v 2 391
Let us haste to hear it, And call the noblest to the audience v 2 397
I will place you where you shall hear us confer of this *Lear* i 2 98
To my lodging, from whence I will fitly bring you to hear my lord speak i 2 185
Shall I hear from you anon?—I do serve you in this business i 2 193
He's coming, madam; I hear him i 3 11
Hear, nature, hear; dear goddess, hear! Suspend thy purpose! i 4 297
When she shall hear this of thee, with her nails She'll flay thy wolvish visage i 4 329
I hear my father coming: pardon me; In cunning I must draw my sword upon you ii 1 30
I hear that you have shown your father A child-like office ii 1 107
Ere long you are like to hear, If you dare venture in your own behalf, A mistress's command iv 2 19
Love, dear love, and our aged father's right: Soon may I hear and see him! iv 4 29
And when your mistress hears thus much from you, I pray, desire her call her wisdom to her iv 5 34
If you do chance to hear of that blind traitor, Preferment falls on him that cuts him off iv 5 37
Methinks the ground is even.—Horrible steep. Hark, do you hear the sea? iv 6 4
Go thou farther off; Bid me farewell, and let me hear thee going iv 6 31
That minces virtue, and does shake the head To hear of pleasure's name iv 6 123
Every one hears that, Which can distinguish sound iv 6 214
Far off, methinks, I hear the beaten drum iv 6 292
This I hear; the king is come to his daughter v 1 21
Laugh At gilded butterflies, and hear poor rogues Talk of court news v 3 13
Let the drum strike, and prove my title thine.—Stay yet; hear reason v 3 82
This to hear Would Desdemona seriously incline *Othello* i 3 145
Hear her speak: If she confess that she was half the wooer i 3 175
He bears the sentence well that nothing bears But the free comfort which from thence he hears i 3 213
I never yet did hear That the bruised heart was pierced through the ear i 3 218
No more of drowning, do you hear?—I am changed i 3 387
What shall we hear of this?—A segregation of the Turkish fleet ii 1 9
This is a more exquisite song than the other.—Will you hear't again? ii 3 103
But, as they say, to hear music the general does not greatly care iii 1 17
Dost thou hear, my honest friend?—No, I hear not your honest friend; I hear you iii 1 22
I am sorry to hear this iii 3 344
Within these three days let me hear thee say That Cassio's not alive iii 3 472
I will be found most cunning in my patience; But—dost thou hear?—most bloody iv 1 92
He, when he hears of her, cannot refrain From the excess of laughter iv 1 99
For Cassio, let me be his undertaker: you shall hear more by midnight iv 1 225
The bawdy wind that kisses all it meets Is hush'd within the hollow mine of earth, And will not hear it iv 2 80
I will hear further reason for this.—And you shall be satisfied iv 2 251
But so: I hear him coming.—I know his gait, 'tis he v 1 22
Did not you hear a cry?—Here, here! for heaven's sake, help me! v 1 49
Nay, if you stare, we shall hear more anon v 1 107
What did thy song bode, lady? Hark, canst thou hear me? v 2 247
News, my good lord, from Rome.—Grates me: the sum.—Nay, hear them *Ant. and Cleo.* i 1 19
Your dismission Is come from Cæsar; therefore hear it, Antony i 1 27
What sport to-night?—Hear the ambassadors i 1 48
Dear goddess, hear that prayer of the people! i 2 73
Who tells me true, though in his tale lie death, I hear him as he flatter'd i 2 103
What's your highness' pleasure?—Not now to hear thee sing i 5 9
When you hear no more words of Pompey, return it again ii 2 104
I am not married, Cæsar: let me hear Agrippa further speak ii 2 125
Will Cæsar speak?—Not till he hears how Antony is touch'd With what is spoke already ii 2 142
Let Neptune hear we bid a loud farewell To these great fellows ii 7 139
You shall hear from me still; the time shall not Out-go my thinking on you iii 2 60
Didst hear her speak? is she shrill-tongued or low? iii 3 15
Who's his lieutenant, hear you?—They say, one Taurus iii 7 78
Cæsar's will?—Hear it apart.—None but friends: say boldly iii 13 47
But it would warm his spirits, To hear from me you had left Antony iii 13 70
Tell him, from his all-obeying breath I hear The doom of Egypt iii 13 77
Where hast thou been, my heart? Dost thou hear, lady? iii 13 172
Walk; let's see if other watchmen Do hear what we do iv 3 19
How now! do you hear this?—Ay; is't not strange?—Do you hear, masters? iv 3 20
He that unbuckles this, till we do please To daff't for our repose, shall hear a storm iv 4 13
Call for Enobarbus, He shall not hear thee iv 5 8
Let's hear him, for the things he speaks May concern Cæsar iv 9 25
Awake; speak to us.—Hear you, sir?—The hand of death hath raught him iv 9 29
The business of this man looks out of him; We'll hear him what he says v 1 51
Methinks I hear Antony call; I see him rouse himself To praise my noble act; I hear him mock The luck of Cæsar v 2 286
O, couldst thou speak, That I might hear thee call great Cæsar ass! v 2 310
When shall we hear from him?—Be assured, madam, With his next vantage *Cymbeline* i 3 23
It is a recreation to be by And hear him mock the Frenchman i 6 76
Let me hear no more.—O dearest soul! your cause doth strike my heart i 6 117
Did you hear of a stranger that's come to court to-night? ii 1 35
You shall hear The legions now in Gallia sooner landed In our not-fearing Britain than have tidings Of any penny tribute paid ii 4 17
Will you hear more?—Spare your arithmetic: never count the turns ii 4 141
When we shall hear The rain and wind beat dark December iii 3 36
Thou injurious thief, Hear but my name, and tremble iv 2 87
If I do lie and do No harm by it, though the gods hear, I hope They'll pardon it iv 2 378
Your preparation can affront no less Than what you hear of iv 3 30
Nor hear I from my mistress, who did promise To yield me often tidings iv 3 38
It is not likely That when they hear the Roman horses neigh iv 4 17
Therefore, good heavens, Hear patiently my purpose v 1 22
You are made Rather to wonder at the things you hear Than to work any v 3 54
I, in mine own woe charm'd, Could not find death where I did hear him groan v 3 69
Wilt thou hear more, my lord?—All that belongs to this v 5 146
I had rather thou shouldst live while nature will Than die ere I hear more v 5 152
Peace, my lord; hear, hear— Shall's have a play of this? v 5 227

Hear. O rare instinct! When shall I hear all through? . . *Cymbeline* v 5 382
And that to hear an old man sing May to your wishes pleasure bring *Pericles* i Gower 13
Few love to hear the sins they love to act . . i 1 92
Heaven forbid That kings should let their ears hear their faults hid! . i 2 62
And to Tarsus Intend my travel, where I'll hear from thee . . . i 2 116
O, let those cities . . . hear these tears! The misery of Tarsus may be theirs . . . i 4 54
Lord governor, for so we hear you are . . . i 4 85
It grieved my heart to hear what pitiful cries they made to us to help them ii 1 22
And make us weep to hear your fate, fair creature, Rare as you seem to be iii 2 104
Shall's go hear the vestals sing?—I'll do any thing now that is virtuous iv 5 7
If thou dost Hear from me, it shall be for thy good . . iv 6 123
I'll hear you more, to the bottom of your story, And never interrupt you v 1 166
But, what music?—My lord, I hear none.—None! The music of the spheres! . . v 1 229
Rarest sounds! Do ye not hear?—My lord, I hear.—Most heavenly music! v 1 233
Now do I long to hear how you were found; How possibly preserved . v 3 56
We do our longing stay To hear the rest untold . . v 3 84
Hear further. We will hear further of it by your daughter *Much Ado* ii 3 211
And by midnight look to hear further from me . *All's Well* iii 6 82
Till you hear further from his highness . . *Hen. VIII.* iii 2 232
Wait attendance Till you hear further from me . *T. of Athens* i 1 162
Hear me. Sir, will you hear me?—No *Mer. Wives* iii 4 78
A woeful suitor to your honour, Please but your honour hear me *M. for M.* ii 2 28
Nay, but hear me. Your sense pursues not mine . . ii 4 73
You bid me seek redemption of the devil: Hear me yourself . . v 1 30
Hear me, O hear me, here!—My lord, her wits, I fear me, are not firm v 1 32
Hear me a little; for I have only been Silent so long . *Much Ado* iv 1 157
Hear me, Beatrice,— Talk with a man out at a window! . . iv 1 310
Do you hear me, and let this count kill me . . v 1 237
Hear me, dear lady; I have sworn an oath . *L. L. Lost* ii 1 97
How you storm! I would be friends with you and have your love, . . . and you'll not hear me *Mer. of Venice* i 3 142
Hear me yet, good Shylock.—I'll have my bond; speak not against my bond . . iii 3 3
Nay, but hear me: Pardon this fault, and by my soul I swear . v 1 246
Let me go, I say.—I will not, till I please: you shall hear me *As Y. L. It* i 1 69
If you be gentlemen, Do me this right; hear me with patience *T. of Shrew* i 2 239
I beseech your honour to hear me one single word . *All's Well* v 2 37
But hear me this: Since you to non-regardance cast my faith *T. Night* v 1 123
Hear me, who profess Myself your loyal servant, your physician *W. Tale* ii 3 53
O, hear me breathe my life Before this ancient sir! . . iv 4 371
Nay, but hear me.—Nay, but hear me.—Go to, then . iv 4 707
Persever not, but hear me, mighty kings . *K. John* ii 1 421
Hear me, O, hear me!—Lady Constance, peace! . iii 1 112
O husband, hear me! ay, alack, how new Is husband in my mouth! . iii 1 305
Hear me without thine ears, and make reply Without a tongue . iii 3 49
Do but hear me, sir.—Ha! I'll tell thee what; Thou'rt damn'd as black iv 3 119
Hear me, gentle liege.—Rise up, good aunt.—Not yet, I thee beseech *Richard II.* v 3 91
Dost thou hear me, Hal?—Ay, and mark thee too, Jack . 1 *Hen. IV.* ii 4 233
Didst thou hear me?—Yea, and you knew me . . 2 *Hen. IV.* ii 4 331
Hear me more plainly. I have in equal balance justly weigh'd What wrongs our arms may do, what wrongs we suffer . . iv 1 66
Then hear me, gracious sovereign, and you peers . *Hen. V.* i 2 33
Therefore exhale.—Hear me, hear me what I say . . ii 1 67
Hear me but speak, and bear me where you will 2 *Hen. VI.* iv 7 64
Hear me but one word: Let me for this my life-time reign as king 3 *Hen. VI.* i 1 170
Hear me, you wrangling pirates, that fall out In sharing that which you have pill'd from me! *Richard III.* i 3 158
And leave out thee? stay, dog, for thou shalt hear me . i 3 216
You that hear me, This from a dying man receive as certain . *Hen VIII.* ii 1 124
Let's dry our eyes: and thus far hear me, Cromwell . iii 2 431
Wast thou in prayer?—Ay: the heavens hear me! *Troi. and Cres.* ii 3 40
Hear me, my love: be thou but true of heart,— I true! how now! . iv 4 60
Fate, hear me what I say! I reck not though I end my life to-day v 6 25
Hear me profess sincerely . . *Coriolanus* i 3 23
Therefore, I beseech you, . . . before our army hear me . i 9 27
Hear me, people; peace!—Let's hear our tribune: peace! . iii 1 192
Hear me one word; Beseech you, tribunes, hear me but a word . iii 1 215
Hear me, my masters, and my common friends,— He's sentenced . iii 3 108
I think he'll hear me. Yet, to bite his lip And hum at good Cominius, much unhearts me . . v 1 48
Sweet lords, entreat her hear me but a word *T. Andron.* ii 3 138
Hear me, grave fathers! noble tribunes, stay! For pity of mine age . iii 1 1
Thou fond mad man, hear me but speak a word.—O, thou wilt speak again of banishment *Rom. and Jul.* iii 3 52
Hear me with patience but to speak a word . . iii 5 160
Thou wilt not hear me now; thou shalt not then . *T. of Athens* i 2 254
You would not hear me, At many leisures I proposed . ii 2 136
The gods confound—hear me, you good gods all—The Athenians! . iv 1 37
If it will please Cæsar To be so good to Cæsar as to hear me *J. Cæsar* ii 4 29
Hear me for my cause, and be silent, that you may hear . iii 2 13
Yet hear me, countrymen; yet hear me speak.—Peace, ho! Hear Antony iii 2 238
O royal Cæsar!—Hear me with patience.—Peace, ho! . iii 2 250
Hear me, for I will speak. Must I give way and room to your rash choler? iv 3 38
But wilt thou hear me how I did proceed?—I beseech you *Hamlet* v 2 27
Hear me, recreant! On thine allegiance, hear me! . *Lear* i 1 169
I'ld speak with them, Now, presently: bid them come forth and hear me ii 4 118
If e'er your grace had speech with man so poor, Hear me one word . v 1 39
'Sblood, but you will not hear me . . *Othello* i 1 4
Will you hear me, Roderigo?—'Faith, I have heard too much . iv 2 183
Hear me this prayer, though thou deny me a matter of more weight *Ant. and Cleo.* i 2 70
Good madam, hear me.—Well, go to, I will; But there's no goodness in thy face . . ii 5 36
Will't please you hear me?—I have a mind to strike thee ere thou speak'st ii 5 41
If for the sake of merit thou wilt hear me, Rise from thy stool . ii 7 61
Gentle, hear me: None about Cæsar trust but Proculeius . iv 15 47
Hear me, good friends,—But I will tell you at some meeter season . v 1 48
Hear me with patience.—Talk thy tongue weary; speak *Cymbeline* iii 4 115
Hear me speak. Do you not hear me speak?—I do. . *Tempest* ii 1 210
I do entreat your patience To hear me speak the message I am sent on *T. G. of Ver.* iv 4 117
Yet hear me speak. Assist me in my purpose. . *Mer. Wives* iv 6 3
Where is the duke? 'tis he should hear me speak . *Meas. for Meas.* v 1 296
Hear me speak.—I'll have my bond; I will not hear thee speak *M. of V.* iii 3 11
Dear sovereign, hear me speak.—Ay, Celia *As Y. Like It* i 3 68
Now hear me speak with a prophetic spirit . *K. John* iii 4 126
Hear me speak. When thou hast tired thyself in base comparisons, hear me speak . . 1 *Hen. IV.* ii 4 277
Hear me speak.—Thou hast spoke too much already . 3 *Hen. VI.* i 1 257
I'll prove the contrary, if you'll hear me speak.—Thou canst not . i 2 20
Sweet Clifford, hear me speak before I die. I am too mean a subject . i 3 18
Have done with words, my lords, and hear me speak . ii 2 117
King Lewis and Lady Bona, hear me speak, Before you answer Warwick iii 3 65
Hear me speak.—You speak too bitterly.—Hear me a word *Richard III.* iv 4 179
May it please your highness To hear me speak his good now? *Hen. VIII.* iv 2 47
Before we proceed any further, hear me speak.—Speak, speak *Coriolanus* i 1 2
Audience! peace, I say!—First, hear me speak.—Well, say . iii 3 41
Peace, both, and hear me speak . . v 6 111
Then hear me speak indifferently for all . *T. Andron.* i 1 430
Hear me speak.—Freely, good father . *T. of Athens* i 1 110
Madam, I'll take my leave.—Why, stay, and hear me speak *Othello* iii 3 31
Hear me speak a word.—Forbear me till anon . *Ant. and Cleo.* ii 7 44
Hear say. I had rather have my wounds to heal again Than hear say how I got them . *Coriolanus* ii 2 74
Did you ne'er hear say, Two may keep counsel, putting one away? *Rom. and Jul.* ii 4 208
I hear say you are of honourable parts . *Pericles* iv 6 86
Hear tell. She cannot endure to hear tell of a husband . *Much Ado* ii 1 362
Hear the like. Did you ever hear the like? . *Mer. Wives* ii 1 70
Did you ever hear the like?—No, nor never shall do in such a place *Per.* iv 5 1
Hear you. But hear you.—Not a word *Meas. for Meas.* iv 3 64
Hear you, my lords,— We have some haste, Leonato . *Much Ado* v 1 47
But hear you; Methought you said you neither lend nor borrow *M. of V.* i 3 69
Nay, hear you, Kate: in sooth you scape not so *T. of Shrew* ii 1 242
But hear you, my lord.—What say'st thou, my lady? . 1 *Hen. IV.* ii 3 76
But, hear you, leave behind Your son, George Stanley *Richard III.* iv 4 496
Hear you, Patroclus: We are too well acquainted with these answers *Troi. and Cres.* ii 3 121
But hear you, hear you!—Hence, broker-lackey! . v 10 32
Hear you, master steward, where's our master? . *T. of Athens* iv 2 1
Nay, but hear you, goodman delver,— Give me leave *Hamlet* v 1 14
Hear you, sir; What is the reason that you use me thus? . v 1 311
Alive or dead? Ho, you sir! friend! Hear you, sir! speak! *Lear* iv 6 46
Therefore hear you, mistress; either frame Your will to mine,—and you, sir, hear you, Either be ruled by me . *Pericles* ii 5 81
Heard. It was mine art, When I arrived and heard thee, that made gape The pine . . *Tempest* i 2 292
How? the best? What wert thou, if the King of Naples heard thee? . i 2 431
Even now, we heard a hollow burst of bellowing Like bulls . ii 1 311
I heard nothing.—O, 'twas a din to fright a monster's ear! . ii 1 313
Heard you this, Gonzalo?—Upon mine honour, sir, I heard a humming ii 1 316
This famous Duke of Milan, Of whom so often I have heard renown v 1 193
O excellent device! was there ever heard a better? *T. G. of Ver.* ii 1 145
I have heard thee say No grief did ever come so near thy heart iv 3 18
I have heard him say a thousand times His Julia gave it him iv 4 139
Be there bears i' the town?—I think there are, sir; I heard them talked of . *Mer. Wives* i 1 300
If he had been throughly moved, you should have heard him so loud . i 4 96
I never heard such a drawling, affecting rogue . . ii 1 145
You heard what this knave told me, did you not?—Yes: and you heard what the other told me? . ii 1 174
I have heard the Frenchman hath good skill in his rapier ii 1 230
I never heard a man of his place, gravity and learning, so wide of his own respect . iii 1 57
You have heard of such a spirit iv 4 35
I never heard any soldier dislike it . *Meas. for Meas.* i 2 18
You have not heard of the proclamation, have you?—What proclamation, man? . i 2 95
I have heard of the lady, and good words went with her name iii 1 219
I never heard the absent duke much detected for women . iii 2 129
I have heard it was ever his manner to do so . iv 2 138
Dishonour not your eye By throwing it on any other object Till you have heard me . v 1 24
Such a dependency of thing on thing, As e'er I heard in madness . v 1 63
I have stood by, my lord, and I have heard Your royal ear abused v 1 138
I never spake with her, saw her, nor heard from her v 1 223
Rely upon it till my tale be heard, And hold no longer out v 1 370
I have heard him swear himself there's one Whom he begot with child. v 1 516
Thus have you heard me sever'd from my bliss *Com. of Errors* i 1 119
Have you not heard men say, That Time comes stealing on? . iv 2 59
Who heard me to deny it or forswear it?—These ears of mine . v 1 25
Hear reason.—And when I have heard it, what blessing brings it? *Much Ado* i 3 7
And there heard it agreed upon that the prince should woo Hero for himself . i 3 64
How know you he loves her?—I heard him swear his affection ii 1 175
I have heard my daughter say, she hath often dreamed of unhappiness ii 1 360
I had as lief have heard the night-raven, come what plague could have come after it. ii 3 84
She will sit you, you heard my daughter tell you how . ii 3 116
And when you have seen more and heard more, proceed accordingly iii 2 125
What heard you him say else? iv 2 48
I will not hear you.—No? Come, brother; away! I will be heard v 1 108
The watch heard them talk of one Deformed v 1 317
Who accused her Upon the error that you heard debated v 4 3
This is not so well as I looked for, but the best that ever I heard *L. L. L.* i 1 283
I love thee.—So I heard you say.—And so, farewell i 2 147
At that time Was there with him, if I have heard a truth ii 1 65
I do protest I never heard of it; And if you prove it, I'll repay it back ii 1 158
I will commend you to mine own heart.—Pray you, do my commendations; I would be glad to see it.—I would you heard it groan . ii 1 183
Pray you, sir, whose daughter?—Her mother's, I have heard . ii 1 202
I heard your guilty rhymes, observed your fashion, Saw sighs reek from you iv 3 139
Oft have I heard of you, my Lord Biron, Before I saw you v 2 851
I must confess that I have heard so much *M. N. Dream* i 1 111
Once I sat upon a promontory, And heard a mermaid on a dolphin's back ii 1 150
He goes but to see a noise that he heard, and is to come again iii 1 94
I never heard So musical a discord, such sweet thunder iv 1 122
The eye of man hath not heard, the ear of man hath not seen iv 1 217
I have heard it over, And it is nothing, nothing in the world. v 1 77
It is the wittiest partition that ever I heard discourse, my lord v 1 169
O wall, full often hast thou heard my moans! v 1 190
This is the silliest stuff that ever I heard . v 1 212
A good man.—Have you heard any imputation to the contrary? *M. of V.* i 3 13
All that glisters is not gold; Often have you heard that told . ii 7 66

Heard. I never heard a passion so confused, So strange, outrageous *Mer. of Venice* ii 8 12
Antonio, as I heard in Genoa,— What, what, what? ill luck? iii 1 103
Your daughter spent in Genoa, as I heard, in one night fourscore ducats iii 1 114
I have heard him swear To Tubal and to Chus, his countrymen iii 2 286
I have heard Your grace hath ta'en great pains to qualify His rigorous course iv 1 6
Is my master yet return'd?—He is not, nor we have not heard from him v 1 35
It is the first time that ever I heard breaking of ribs was sport for ladies.—Or I, I promise thee *As Y. Like It* i 2 146
Hath heard your praises, and this night he means To burn the lodging ii 3 22
Didst thou hear these verses?—O, yes, I heard them all, and more too iii 2 173
He fell in love. I have heard him read many lectures against it iii 2 365
Not true in love?—Yes, when he is in; but I think he is not in.—You have heard him swear downright he was iii 4 31
Will you hear the letter?—So please you, for I never heard it yet; Yet heard too much of Phebe's cruelty iv 3 38
His elder brother.—O, I have heard him speak of that same brother iv 3 122
If I heard you rightly, The duke hath put on a religious life v 4 186
Out of these convertites There is much matter to be heard and learn'd v 4 191
For yet his honour never heard a play *T. of Shrew* Ind. 1 96
Have I not in my time heard lions roar? i 2 201
Have I not heard the sea puff'd up with winds Rage like an angry boar? i 2 202
Have I not heard great ordnance in the field? i 2 204
Have I not in a pitched battle heard Loud 'larums, neighing steeds? i 2 206
To make mine eye the witness Of that report which I so oft have heard ii 1 53
Well have you heard, but something hard of hearing ii 1 184
Hadst thou not crossed me, thou shouldst have heard how her horse fell and she under her horse; thou shouldst have heard in how miry a place iv 1 75
I have often heard Of your entire affection to Bianca iv 2 22
But that you are but newly come, You might have heard it else proclaim'd iv 2 87
I know him not, but I have heard of him iv 2 97
I heard not of it before.—I would it were not notorious *All's Well* i 1 40
The complaints I have heard of you I do not all believe i 3 9
The most bitter touch of sorrow that e'er I heard virgin exclaim in i 3 123
One that lies three thirds and uses a known truth to pass a thousand nothings with, should be once heard and thrice beaten ii 5 33
So that from point to point now have you heard The fundamental reasons iii 1 1
All her deserving Is a reserved honesty, and that I have not heard examined iii 5 66
And I was about to tell you, since I heard of the good lady's death iv 5 73
I have heard my father name him: He was a bachelor then *T. Night* i 2 28
Quaffing and drinking will undo you: I heard my lady talk of it yesterday i 3 15
She'll not match above her degree, . . . I have heard her swear't i 3 117
I heard you were saucy at my gates i 5 209
That piece of song, That old and antique song we heard last night ii 4 3
And I have heard herself come thus near, that, should she fancy, it should be one of my complexion ii 5 28
I have heard of some kind of men that put quarrels purposely on others iii 4 266
That for his love dares yet do more Than you have heard him brag iii 4 348
He has heard that word of some great man and now applies it to a fool iv 1 12
Ha' not you seen, Camillo,—But that's past doubt, you have, or your eyeglass Is thicker than a cuckold's horn,—or heard? *W. Tale* i 2 269
Worse than the great'st infection That e'er was heard or read! i 2 424
Shall I be heard?—Who is't that goes with me? ii 1 115
I ne'er heard yet That any of these bolder vices wanted Less impudence to gainsay what they did Than to perform it first iii 2 55
I have heard, but not believed, the spirits o' the dead May walk again iii 3 16
I have heard, sir, of such a man, who hath a daughter of most rare note iv 2 47
For I have heard it said There is an art which in their piedness shares With great creating nature iv 4 86
You have heard of my poor services, i' the love That I have borne your father? iv 4 527
I was by at the opening of the fardel, heard the old shepherd deliver the manner how he found it v 2 4
Methought I heard the shepherd say, he found the child v 2 7
They looked as they had heard of a world ransomed, or one destroyed v 2 16
I never heard of such another encounter, which lames report v 2 61
Told him I heard them talk of a fardel and I know not what v 2 125
For ere thou canst report I will be there, The thunder of my cannon shall be heard *K. John* i 1 26
Here is the strangest controversy Come from the country to be judged by you That e'er I heard i 1 46
As I have heard my father speak himself i 1 107
Who hath read or heard Of any kindred action like to this? iii 4 13
I have heard you say That we shall see and know our friends in heaven iii 4 76
Indeed we heard how near his death he was Before the child himself felt he was sick iv 2 87
This from rumour's tongue I idly heard; if true or false I know not iv 2 124
Have you beheld, Or have you read or heard? or could you think? iv 3 42
Would not my lords return to me again, After they heard young Arthur was alive? v 1 38
Have I not heard these islanders shout out 'Vive le roi!' v 2 103
Then all too late comes counsel to be heard *Richard II.* ii 1 27
Mann'd with three hundred men, as I have heard ii 3 54
I heard thee say, and vauntingly thou spakest it, That thou wert cause iv 1 36
I heard the banish'd Norfolk say That thou, Aumerle, didst send two of thy men To execute the noble duke at Calais iv 1 80
Was not he proclaim'd By Richard that dead is the next of blood?—He was; I heard the proclamation *1 Hen. IV.* i 3 147
I heard him tell it to one of his company last night at supper ii 1 61
In thy faint slumbers I by thee have watch'd, And heard thee murmur ii 3 51
And roared for mercy and still run and roared, as ever I heard bull-calf ii 4 287
He was but as the cuckoo is in June, Heard, not regarded iii 2 76
I have heard the prince tell him, I know not how oft, that that ring was copper! iii 3 96
So I told him, my lord; and I said I heard your grace say so iii 3 121
He heard him swear and vow to God He came but to be Duke of Lancaster iv 3 60
He hath heard of our confederacy, And 'tis but wisdom to make strong iv 4 38
This is the strangest tale that ever I heard v 4 158
Thus have you heard our cause and known our means *2 Hen. IV.* i 3 1
I have heard better news.—What s the news, my lord? i 1 179
He heard of your grace's coming to town: there's a letter for you ii 2 107
A good phrase.—Pardon me, sir; I have heard the word. Phrase call you it? iii 2 80
Heard. We have heard the chimes at midnight, Master Shallow *2 Hen. IV.* iii 2 228
Who hath not heard it spoken How deep you were within the books of God? iv 2 16
Heard he the good news yet? Tell it him.—He alter'd much upon the hearing it iv 5 11
I had forestall'd this dear and deep rebuke Ere you with grief had spoke and I had heard The course of it so far iv 5 142
I will be as good as my word: this that you heard was but a colour v 5 91
I heard a bird so sing, Whose music, to my thinking, pleased the king v 5 113
Let us do it with no show of fear; No, with no more than if we heard that England Were busied with a Whitsun morris-dance *Hen. V.* ii 4 24
With what great state he heard their embassy ii 4 32
For Nym, he hath heard that men of few words are the best men iii 2 38
'Wonder of nature,'— I have heard a sonnet begin so to one's mistress iii 7 44
I myself heard the king say he would not be ransomed iv 1 202
The king hath heard them; to the which as yet There is no answer made v 2 74
Ne'er heard I of a warlike enterprise More venturous *1 Hen. VI.* ii 1 44
I have heard it said, unbidden guests Are often welcomest when they are gone ii 2 55
I have heard you preach That malice was a great and grievous sin iii 1 127
But when they heard he was thine enemy, They set him free iii 3 71
A proper jest, and never heard before! *2 Hen. VI.* i 1 132
I have heard her reported to be a woman of an invincible spirit i 4 8
Many time and oft Myself have heard a voice to call him so ii 1 94
Sorry I am to hear what I have heard ii 1 193
Oft have I heard that grief softens the mind And makes it fearful iv 4 1
By my valour, the most complete champion that ever I heard! iv 10 59
That monstrous rebel Cade, Who since I heard to be discomfited v 1 63
Had he been ta'en, we should have heard the news; Had he been slain, we should have heard the news; Or had he 'scaped, methinks we should have heard The happy tidings of his good escape *3 Hen. VI.* ii 1 4
O, speak no more, for I have heard too much ii 1 48
In the marches here we heard you were, Making another head ii 1 140
Oft have I heard his praises in pursuit, But ne'er till now his scandal of retire.—Nor now my scandal ii 1 149
In the very pangs of death he cried, Like to a dismal clangor heard from far ii 3 18
Often heard him say and swear That this his love was an eternal plant iii 3 123
When I have heard your king's desert recounted, Mine ear hath tempted judgement to desire iii 3 132
But what said Henry's queen? For I have heard that she was there in place iv 1 103
The queen from France hath brought a puissant power: Even now we heard the news v 2 32
A woman of this valiant spirit Should, if a coward heard her speak these words, Infuse his breast with magnanimity v 4 40
If the rest be true which I have heard, Thou camest— I'll hear no more v 6 55
I have often heard my mother say I came into the world with my legs forward v 6 70
Heard ye not what an humble suppliant Lord Hastings was to her? *Richard III.* i 1 74
Oft have I heard of sanctuary men; But sanctuary children ne'er till now iii 1 55
We would have had you heard The traitor speak iii 5 56
Your grace's word shall serve, As well as I had seen and heard him speak iii 5 63
I have heard that fearful commenting Is leaden servitor to dull delay iv 3 51
These very words I've heard him utter to his son-in-law *Hen. VIII.* i 2 136
To this point hast thou heard him At any time speak aught? i 2 145
Having heard by fame Of this so noble and so fair assembly i 4 66
When the king once heard it, out of anger He sent command ii 1 150
Have you heard it?—Come, you are pleasant ii 3 92
Pray, do not deliver What here you've heard to her ii 3 107
And that, without delay, their arguments Be now produced and heard ii 4 68
Every thing that heard him play, Even the billows of the sea, Hung their heads iii 1 9
I have, and most unwillingly, of late Heard many grievous, I do say, my lord, Grievous complaints of you v 1 98
I should have ta'en some pains to bring together Yourself and your accusers; and to have heard you, Without indurance, further v 1 120
I would somebody had heard her talk yesterday, as I did *Troi. and Cres.* i 1 45
The gods have heard me swear.—The gods are deaf to hot and peevish vows v 3 15
I shall tell you A pretty tale: it may be you have heard it *Coriolanus* i 1 93
'Tis not four days gone Since I heard thence; these are the words i 2 7
Indeed, madam?—In earnest, it's true; I heard a senator speak it i 3 106
By interims and conveying gusts we have heard The charges of our friends i 6 5
'Tis not a mile; briefly we heard their drums i 6 16
I heard him swear, Were he to stand for consul, never would he Appear i' the market-place ii 1 247
Would pluck reproof and rebuke from every ear that heard it ii 2 38
And, being angry, does forget that ever He heard the name of death iii 1 260
If, by the tribunes' leave, and yours, good people, I may be heard iii 1 283
I have heard you say, Honour and policy, like unsever'd friends, I' the war do grow together iii 2 41
What you have seen him do and heard him speak iii 3 77
I have heard it said, the fittest time to corrupt a man's wife is when she's fallen out with her husband iv 3 33
Many an heir Of these fair edifices 'fore my wars Have I heard groan and drop iv 4 4
He was ever too hard for him; I have heard him say so himself iv 5 195
But reason with the fellow, Before you punish him, where he heard this iv 6 52
If you have heard your general talk of Rome, And of his friends there, it is lots to blanks, My name hath touch'd your ears v 2 9
Would you have heard A mother less? or granted less, Aufidius? v 3 192
The babbling echo mocks the hounds, Replying shrilly to the well-tuned horns, As if a double hunt were heard at once *T. Andron.* ii 3 19
The raven doth not hatch a lark: Yet have I heard,—O, could I find it now! ii 3 150
Or, had he heard the heavenly harmony Which that sweet tongue hath made, He would have dropp'd his knife ii 4 48
Suddenly I heard a child cry underneath a wall. I made unto the noise; when soon I heard The crying babe controll'd with this discourse v 1 24
Oft have you heard me wish for such an hour, And now I find it v 2 160
Now you have heard the truth, what say you, Romans? v 3 128
What fray was here? Yet tell me not, for I have heard it all *R. and J.* i 1 180
Else would a maiden blush bepaint my cheek For that which thou hast heard me speak to-night ii 2 87

Heard. I have heard in some sort of thy miseries . . *T. of Athens* iv 3 76
I have heard, and grieved, How cursed Athens, mindless of thy worth, Forgetting thy great deeds, . . trod upon them . . . iv 3 92
Ye've heard that I have gold; I am sure you have: speak truth . v 1 79
The enemies' drum is heard, and fearful scouring Doth choke the air . v 2 15
I have heard, Where many of the best respect in Rome . *J. Cæsar* i 2 58
O, you and I have heard our fathers say, There was a Brutus once . i 2 158
Besides the things that we have heard and seen, Recounts most horrid sights seen by the watch . . . . ii 2 15
Of all the wonders that I yet have heard, It seems to me most strange that men should fear . . . . ii 2 34
And this way have you well expounded it.—I have, when you have heard what I can say . . . . ii 2 92
Prithee, listen well; I heard a bustling rumour, like a fray . . . ii 4 18
The heavens speed thee in thine enterprise! Sure, the boy heard me . ii 4 42
I heard him say, Brutus and Cassius Are rid like madmen through the gates . . . . iii 2 273
The moon is down; I have not heard the clock . . *Macbeth* ii 1 2
Didst thou not hear a noise?—I heard the owl scream and the crickets cry . . . . ii 2 16
I stood and heard them: But they did say their prayers, and address'd them Again to sleep . . . . ii 2 24
Our chimneys were blown down; and, as they say, Lamentings heard i' the air . . . . ii 3 61
Which shall possess them with the heaviest sound That ever yet they heard . . . . iv 3 203
What, at any time, have you heard her say?—That, sir, which I will not report after her . . . . v 1 14
That struts and frets his hour upon the stage And then is heard no more v 5 26
I have heard, The cock, that is the trumpet to the morn . *Hamlet* i 1 149
So have I heard and do in part believe it . . . . . . i 1 165
I think it lacks of twelve.—No, it is struck.—Indeed? I heard it not . i 4 5
Never to speak of this that you have heard, Swear by my sword . . i 5 159
Something have you heard Of Hamlet's transformation . . . ii 2 4
I heard thee speak me a speech once, but it was never acted . . . ii 2 454
I have heard That guilty creatures sitting at a play Have by the very cunning of the scene Been struck so to the soul that presently They have proclaim'd their malefactions . . . . ii 2 617
I have heard of your paintings too, well enough . . . . iii 1 148
You need not tell us what Lord Hamlet said; We heard it all . . iii 1 188
O, there be players that I have seen play, and heard others praise . iii 2 33
Have you heard the argument? Is there no offence in't? . . . iii 2 242
His means of death, his obscure funeral . . . Cry to be heard . . iv 5 216
Sith you have heard, and with a knowing ear . . . . . iv 7 3
This presence knows, And you must needs have heard, how I am punish'd . . . . v 2 240
But I have heard him oft maintain it to be fit . . . . *Lear* i 2 76
I have told you what I have seen and heard; but faintly . . . i 2 191
You have heard of the news abroad; I mean the whispered ones? . . ii 1 7
Have you heard of no likely wars toward? . . . . . . ii 1 11
Since I came hither, Which I can call but now, I have heard strange news . . . . ii 1 89
I heard myself proclaim'd; And by the happy hollow of a tree Escaped ii 3 1
Such groans of roaring wind and rain I never Remember to have heard . iii 2 48
And yet my mind Was then scarce friends with him: I have heard more since . . . . iv 1 37
Of Albany's and Cornwall's powers you heard not?—'Tis so, they are afoot . . . . iv 3 50
The murmuring surge, That on the unnumber'd idle pebbles chafes, Cannot be heard so high . . . . iv 6 22
The shrill-gorged lark so far Cannot be seen or heard . . . . iv 6 59
In honest plainness thou hast heard me say My daughter is not for thee *Othello* i 1 97
Neither my place nor aught I heard of business Hath raised me from my bed . . . . i 3 53
Whereof by parcels she had something heard, But not intentively . . i 3 154
'Twas pitiful, 'twas wondrous pitiful: She wish'd she had not heard it . i 3 162
I heard the clink and fall of swords, And Cassio high in oath . . . ii 3 234
If you have any music that may not be heard, to't again . . . iii 1 17
Thou dost mean something: I heard thee say even now, thou likedst not that . . . . iii 3 109
In sleep I heard him say, 'Sweet Desdemona, Let us be wary' . . iii 3 419
What, If I had said I had seen him do you wrong? Or heard him say . iv 1 25
You have seen nothing then?—Nor ever heard, nor ever did suspect . iv 2 2
And then I heard Each syllable that breath made up between them . iv 2 4
I have heard too much, for your words and performances are no kin together . . . . iv 2 184
'Tis neither here nor there.—I have heard it said so. O, these men! . iv 3 60
You heard her say herself, it was not I.—She said so . . . v 2 127
What's amiss, May it be gently heard . . . *Ant. and Cleo.* ii 2 20
If Cleopatra heard you, your reproof Were well deserved of rashness . ii 2 123
And did find Her welcome friendly.—I have heard it . . . ii 6 47
I have heard that Julius Cæsar Grew fat with feasting there.—You have heard much . . . . ii 6 65
So much have I heard: And I have heard, Apollodorus carried— No more of that . . . . ii 6 68
Certainly, I have heard the Ptolemies' pyramises are very goodly things; without contradiction, I have heard that . . . . . . ii 7 39
Is she shrill-tongued or low?—Madam, I heard her speak; she is low-voiced . . . . iii 3 16
Is it not strange . . . He could so quickly cut the Ionian sea, And take in Toryne? You have heard on't, sweet? . . . . . iii 7 24
Heard you of nothing strange about the streets?—Nothing. What news? iv 3 3
Most noble empress, you have heard of me?—I cannot tell . . . v 2 71
Assuredly you know me.—No matter, sir, what I have heard or known v 2 73
I heard of one of them no longer than yesterday . . . . v 2 251
Rather shunned to go even with what I heard than in my every action to be guided by others' experiences . . . . *Cymbeline* i 4 48
By this, your king Hath heard of great Augustus . . . . ii 4 11
I have heard of riding wagers, Where horses have been nimbler than the sands . . . . iii 2 73
Honest men being heard, like false Æneas, Were in his time thought false iii 4 60
I have heard I am a strumpet; and mine ear, Therein false struck, can take no greater wound . . . . iii 4 116
I have heard you say, Love's reason's without reason . . . iv 2 21
What lies I have heard! Our courtiers say all's savage but at court . iv 2 32
Some villain mountaineers? I have heard of such . . . . iv 2 72
Perhaps It may be heard at court that such as we Cave here . . . iv 2 137
I heard no letter from my master since I wrote him . . . iv 3 36
Heard you all this, her women?—We did, so please your highness . v 5 61

Heard. Mine eyes Were not in fault, for she was beautiful; Mine ears, that heard her flattery . . . . *Cymbeline* v 5 64
We have heard your miseries as far as Tyre . . . . *Pericles* i 4 88
And I have heard, you knights of Tyre Are excellent in making ladies trip ii 3 102
I heard of an Egyptian That had nine hours lien dead . . . iii 2 84
O, you have heard something of my power, and so stand aloof . . iv 6 94
You have heard me say . . . I left behind an ancient substitute . . v 3 50
In Antiochus and his daughter you have heard Of monstrous lust the due and just reward . . . . v 3 Gower 85
Heard of. He cannot be heard of . . . . . *M. N. Dream* iv 2 3
News, old news, and such news as you never heard of! . *T. of Shrew* iii 2 31
My father was that Sebastian of Messaline, whom I know you have heard of . . . . *T. Night* ii 1 19
There is a thing, Harry, which thou hast often heard of and it is known to many in our land by the name of pitch . . *1 Hen. IV.* ii 4 454
He will still be doing.—He never did harm, that I heard of . *Hen. V.* iii 7 109
You did devise Strange tortures for offenders never heard of *2 Hen. VI.* iii 1 122
'Tis wondrous strange, the like yet never heard of . . *3 Hen. VI.* ii 1 33
The most merciless that e'er was heard of! . . . *Richard III.* i 3 184
Where no mention Of me more must be heard of . . *Hen. VIII.* iii 2 434
The noblest hateful love that e'er I heard of . . . *Troi. and Cres.* iv 1 33
Battles thrice six I have seen and heard of . . . *Coriolanus* ii 3 136
This is true; And this you might have heard of here, by me . *Cymbeline* ii 4 77
Heard on. Such whales have I heard on o' the land . . . *Pericles* ii 1 36
Heard say. How does your fallow greyhound, sir? I heard say he was outrun on Cotsall . . . . *Mer. Wives* i 1 92
Painting, sir, I have heard say, is a mystery . . *Meas. for Meas.* iv 2 38
I heard say your lordship was sick . . . . . *2 Hen. IV.* i 2 108
Heard speak. Have you not heard speak of Mariana? . *Meas. for Meas.* iii 1 216
Our courteous Antony, Whom ne'er the word of 'No' woman heard speak . . . . *Ant. and Cleo.* ii 2 228
Heard the like. Was ever heard the like? . . . . *T. Andron* ii 3 276
Heardest. Which thou heard'st cry, which thou saw'st sink . *Tempest* i 2 32
The blackest news that ever thou heardest . . . . *T. G. of Ver.* iii 1 286
Hearer. Thou wilt be like a lover presently And tire the hearer with a book of words . . . . *Much Ado* i 1 309
I say my prayers aloud.—I love you the better: the hearers may cry, Amen . . . . ii 1 109
Shall be lamented, pitied, and excused Of every hearer . . . iv 1 219
That loose grace Which shallow laughing hearers give to fools . *L. L. Lost* v 2 870
Wearying thy hearer in thy mistress' praise . . . *As Y. Like It* ii 4 38
He that speaks doth gripe the hearer's wrist . . . . *K. John* iv 2 190
And send the hearers weeping to their beds . . . *Richard II.* v 1 45
Every third word a lie, duer paid to the hearer than the Turk's tribute *2 Hen. IV.* iii 2 330
Go boast of this: And if thou tell'st the heavy story right, Upon my soul, the hearers will shed tears . . . . *3 Hen. VI.* i 4 161
For, gentle hearers, know, To rank our chosen truth . *Hen. VIII.* Prol. 17
You are known The first and happiest hearers of the town . . Prol. 24
Who play they to?—To the hearers, sir . . . *Troi. and Cres.* iii 1 24
Filling their hearers With strange invention . . . *Macbeth* iii 1 32
Hark you, Guildenstern; and you too: at each ear a hearer *Hamlet* ii 2 400
Her speech is nothing, Yet the unshaped use of it doth move The hearers to collection . . . . iv 5 9
And makes them stand Like wonder-wounded hearers . . . v 1 280
Hearest thou, Biondello?—I cannot tarry . . . *T. of Shrew* iv 4 98
O my gentle cousin, Hear'st thou the news abroad, who are arrived? *K. John* iv 2 160
What, standest thou still, and hearest such a calling? . . *1 Hen. IV.* ii 4 90
Stain to thy countrymen, thou hear'st thy doom! Be packing, therefore *1 Hen. VI.* iv 1 45
Hear'st thou, Mars?—Name not the god, thou boy of tears! . *Coriolanus* v 6 100
Tell me not, friar, that thou hear'st of this, Unless thou tell me how I may prevent it . . . . *Rom. and Jul.* iv 1 50
Whistle then to me, As signal that thou hear'st something approach . v 3 8
Whate'er thou hear'st or seest, stand all aloof, And do not interrupt me v 3 26
Or what purgative drug Would scour these English hence? Hear'st thou of them? . . . . *Macbeth* v 3 56
Hear'st thou, Pisanio? He is at Milford-Haven: read . . *Cymbeline* iii 2 50
Heareth. He heareth not, he stirreth not, he moveth not *Rom. and Jul.* ii 1 15
Hearing. Sorceries terrible To enter human hearing . . . *Tempest* i 2 265
Out o' your wits and hearing too? . . . . ii 2 87
She is not within hearing, sir . . . . . . *T. G. of Ver.* ii 1 8
I'll vouchsafe thee the hearing . . . . . . *Mer. Wives* ii 2 44
I will tell you, sir, if you will give me the hearing.—Speak . . ii 2 183
I'll take my leave, And leave you to the hearing of the cause *Meas. for Meas.* ii 1 141
He's hearing of a cause; he will come straight . . . . ii 2 1
Whilst my invention, hearing not my tongue, Anchors on Isabel . . ii 4 3
If peradventure he shall ever return to have hearing of this business . iii 1 210
Hearing how hastily you are to depart, I am come to advise you . . iv 3 53
In her bosom I'll unclasp my heart And take her hearing prisoner *M. Ado* i 1 326
Did you hear the proclamation?—I do confess much of the hearing it *L. L. Lost* i 1 287
And younger hearings are quite ravished . . . . . . ii 1 75
Warble, child; make passionate my sense of hearing . . . iii 1 2
Sweet royalty, bestow on me the sense of hearing . . . . v 2 670
What, out of hearing? gone? no sound, no word? . *M. N. Dream* ii 2 152
Wherein it doth impair the seeing sense, It pays the hearing double recompense . . . . iii 2 180
And, hearing our intent, Came here in grace of our solemnity . . iv 1 138
If they should speak, would almost damn those ears Which, hearing them, would call their brothers fools . . . *Mer. of Venice* i 1 99
Hearing applause and universal shout, Giddy in spirit . . . iii 2 144
In the hearing of these many friends, I swear to thee . . . v 1 241
Here was he merry, hearing of a song . . . *As Y. Like It* ii 7 4
Hearing how that every day Men of great worth resorted to this forest v 4 160
Players, hearing your amendment, Are come to play . *T. of Shrew* Ind. 2 131
Hearing of her beauty and her wit, Her affability . . . . ii 1 48
Well have you heard, but something hard of hearing . . . ii 1 184
Hearing thy mildness praised in every town, Thy virtues spoke of . ii 1 192
'Tis a good hearing when children are toward.—But a harsh hearing when women are froward . . . . v 2 182
Hearing your high majesty is touch'd With that malignant cause wherein the honour Of my dear father's gift stands chief in power *All's Well* ii 1 113
And hope I may that she, Hearing so much, will speed her foot again . iii 4 37
Let the garden door be shut, and leave me to my hearing *T. Night* iii 1 104
No hearing, no feeling, but my sir's song . . . *W. Tale* iv 4 625
The princess hearing of her mother's statue . . . . . v 2 102

Hearing. The Welshmen, hearing thou wert dead, Are gone to Bolingbroke . . . . *Richard II.* iii 2 73
Speak to his gentle hearing kind commends . . . . iii 3 126
Hearing how our plaints and prayers do pierce, pity may move thee . v 3 127
I come with gracious offers from the king, If you vouchsafe me hearing 1 *Hen. IV.* iv 3 31
Which of you will stop The vent of hearing when loud Rumour speaks? 2 *Hen. IV.* Ind. 2
My master is deaf.—I am sure he is, to the hearing of any thing good . i 2 80
I did not think thou wast within hearing . . . . ii 4 337
Heard he the good news yet? Tell it him.—He alter'd much upon the hearing it . . . . iv 5 13
The hour, I think, is come To give him hearing . . . *Hen. V.* i 1 93
For, hearing this, I must perforce compound With mistful eyes . iv 6 33
'Twas time, I trow, to wake and leave our beds, Hearing alarums at our chamber-doors . . . . . . 1 *Hen. VI.* ii 1 42
Vouchsafe To give me hearing what I shall reply . . . iii 1 28
Hearing of your arrival in this realm, I have awhile given truce . . iii 4 2
Sweet madam, give me hearing in a cause . . . . v 3 106
What news with you?—None good, my lord, to please you with the hearing; Nor none so bad . . . . *Richard III.* iv 4 458
They are Most pestilent to the hearing . . . *Hen. VIII.* i 2 49
May bring his plain-song And have an hour of hearing . . i 3 46
Please you to declare, in hearing Of all these ears . . . ii 4 145
Killing care and grief of heart Fall asleep, or hearing, die . . iii 1 14
I sprang not more in joy at first hearing he was a man-child than now in first seeing he had proved himself a man . *Coriolanus* i 3 17
You wear out a good wholesome forenoon in hearing a cause between an orange-wife and a fosset-seller . . . . . . ii 1 78
When you are hearing a matter between party and party . ii 1 81
Dismiss the controversy bleeding, the more entangled by your hearing ii 1 87
Hear me, my masters, and my common friends,— He's sentenced; no more hearing . . . . iii 3 109
Who, hearing of our Marcius' banishment, Thrusts forth his horns again iv 6 43
His last offences to us Shall have judicious hearing . . . v 6 128
As any mortal body hearing it Should straight fall mad . *T. Andron.* ii 3 103
It did me good . . To brave the tribune in his brother's hearing . iv 2 36
And shrieks like mandrakes' torn out of the earth, That living mortals, hearing them, run mad . . . . . *Rom. and Jul.* iv 3 48
Did I dream it so? Or am I mad, hearing him talk of Juliet? . v 3 80
I have Deserved this hearing . . . . *T. of Athens* ii 2 207
How fare you?—Ever at the best, hearing well of your lordship . iii 6 29
And we, poor mates, stand on the dying deck, Hearing the surges threat iv 2 21
Hearing you were retired, your friends fall'n off . . . v 1 62
And, being men, hearing the will of Cæsar, It will inflame you *J. Cæsar* iii 2 148
And make joyful The hearing of my wife with your approach *Macbeth* i 4 46
I have words That would be howl'd out in the desert air, Where hearing should not latch them . . . . iv 3 195
Pity me not, but lend thy serious hearing To what I shall unfold *Hamlet* i 5 5
We beg your hearing patiently . . . . . . iii 2 161
Behind the arras hearing something stir, Whips out his rapier . iv 1 9
You have been talk'd of since your travel much, And that in Hamlet's hearing . . . . iv 7 73
The ears are senseless that should give us hearing . . . v 2 380
I am almost ready to dissolve, Hearing of this . . . . *Lear* v 3 204
Mark Antony, Hearing that you prepared for war, acquainted My grieved ear withal . . . . . . *Ant. and Cleo.* iii 6 58
You lie, up to the hearing of the gods . . . . . v 2 95
He had two sons: if this be worth your hearing, Mark it . *Cymbeline* i 1 57
How worthy he is I will leave to appear hereafter, rather than story him in his own hearing . . . . i 4 35
Julius Cæsar, whose remembrance yet Lives in men's eyes and will to ears and tongues Be theme and hearing ever . . . . iii 1 4
What false Italian, As poisonous-tongued as handed, hath prevail'd On thy too ready hearing? . . . . iii 2 6
Love's counsellor should fill the bores of hearing, To the smothering of the sense . . . . iii 2 59
The which he hearing—As it is like him—might break out . . iv 2 139
No more, you petty spirits of region low, Offend our hearing . . v 4 94
I'll tell you, sir, in private, if you please To give me hearing . . v 5 116
Sitting sadly, Hearing us praise our loves of Italy . . . v 5 161
Who, hearing of your melancholy state, Did come to see you . *Pericles* v 1 222
Hearken. Being an enemy To me inveterate, hearkens my brother's suit *Tempest* i 2 122
Wilt thou be pleased to hearken once again to the suit I made to thee? iii 2 44
'Tis dinner-time.—I have dined.—Ay, but hearken, sir . *T. G. of Ver.* ii 1 178
Hearken after their offence, my lord.—Officers, what offence? *Much Ado* v 1 216
Such is the simplicity of man to hearken after the flesh . . *L. L. Lost* i 1 219
The youngest daughter whom you harken for . . . *T. of Shrew* i 2 260
Well, hearken at the end . . . . . . 2 *Hen. IV.* ii 4 303
As I can learn, He hearkens after prophecies and dreams *Richard III.* i 1 54
Would draw heaven down, and all the gods, to hearken . . *Pericles* i 1 83
Hearkened. O God! they did me too much injury That ever said I hearken'd for your death . . . . 1 *Hen. IV.* v 4 52
'Faith, they listen'd to me as they would have hearkened to their father's testament . . . . *Pericles* iv 2 107
Hearkening. Old Gremio is hearkening still . . *T. of Shrew* iv 4 53
Hearsay. Of this matter Is little Cupid's crafty arrow made, That only wounds by hearsay . . . . *Much Ado* iii 1 23
Hearse. Let all the tears that should bedew my hearse Be drops of balm to sanctify thy head . . . . . . 2 *Hen. IV.* iv 5 114
To add to your laments, Wherewith you now bedew King Henry's hearse 1 *Hen. VI.* i 1 104
If honour may be shrouded in a hearse . . . . *Richard III.* i 2 2
Stand from the hearse, stand from the body . . . *J. Cæsar* iii 2 169
We wept after her hearse, And yet we mourn . . . *Pericles* iv 3 41
Hearsed. Would she were hearsed at my foot, and the ducats in her coffin! . . . . *Mer. of Venice* iii 1 93
Tell Why thy canonized bones, hearsed in death, Have burst their cerements . . . . *Hamlet* i 4 47
Heart. Heigh, my hearts! cheerly, cheerly, my hearts! . . *Tempest* i 1 6
O, the cry did knock Against my very heart! . . . . i 2 9
Tell your piteous heart There's no harm done . . . . i 2 14
O, my heart bleeds To think o' the teen that I have turn'd you to! . i 2 63
Set all hearts i' the state To what tune pleased his ear . . i 2 84
Awake, dear heart, awake! thou hast slept well; Awake! . . i 2 305
I could find in my heart to beat him . . . . . ii 2 160
The very instant that I saw you, did My heart fly to your service . iii 1 65
With a heart as willing As bondage e'er of freedom . . . iii 1 88
Here's my hand.—And mine, with my heart in't . . . iii 1 90
Heart. The white cold virgin snow upon my heart Abates the ardour of my liver . . . . *Tempest* iv 1 55
Let grief and sorrow still embrace his heart That doth not wish you joy! v 1 214
Made wit with musing weak, heart sick with thought . *T. G. of Ver.* i 1 69
I taught my brow to frown, When inward joy enforced my heart to smile i 2 63
Sweet lines! sweet life! Here is her hand, the agent of her heart . i 3 46
My heart accords thereto, And yet a thousand times it answers 'no' . i 3 90
His thoughts immaculate, His tears pure messengers sent from his heart, His heart as far from fraud as heaven from earth . . . ii 7 77
Blessing of your heart, you brew good ale . . . . iii 1 306
Say that upon the altar of her beauty You sacrifice your tears, your sighs, your heart . . . . iii 2 74
A gentleman, Who, in my mood, I stabb'd unto the heart . . iv 1 51
You have a quick ear.—Ay, I would I were deaf; it makes me have a slow heart . . . . iv 2 65
If your heart be so obdurate, Vouchsafe me yet your picture for my love iv 2 120
I have heard thee say No grief did ever come so near thy heart . iv 3 19
A heart As full of sorrows as the sea of sands . . . . iv 3 32
Why do I pity him That with his very heart despiseth me? . . iv 4 99
Read over Julia's heart, thy first best love . . . . v 4 46
Behold her that gave aim to all thy oaths, And entertain'd 'em deeply in her heart . . . . v 4 102
I am glad to see you: much good do it your good heart! . *Mer. Wives* i 1 83
I thank you always with my heart, la! with my heart . . . i 1 86
'Tis the heart, Master Page; 'tis here, 'tis here . . . i 1 235
The best and the fairest, that would have won any woman's heart . ii 2 71
She leads a very frampold life with him, good heart . . . ii 2 94
Blessing on your heart for't! . . . . ii 2 112
Now, Sir John, here is the heart of my purpose . . . ii 2 233
My heart is ready to crack with impatience . . . . ii 2 301
And what they think in their hearts they may effect, they will break their hearts but they will effect . . . . ii 2 322
Got's will, and his passion of my heart! . . . . . iii 1 63
Your hearts are mighty, your skins are whole . . . . iii 1 111
Farewell, my hearts: I will to my honest knight Falstaff . . iii 2 88
A kind heart he hath: a woman would run through fire and water for such a kind heart . . . . iii 4 106
Alas the day! good heart, that was not her fault . . . iii 5 39
Well, she laments, sir, for it, that it would yearn your heart to see it . iii 5 45
Master Slender is let the boys leave to play.—Blessing of his heart! . iv 1 13
Good hearts, devise something: any extremity rather than a mischief . iv 2 75
You must pray, and not follow the imaginations of your own heart . iv 2 163
If they can find in their hearts the poor unvirtuous fat knight shall be any further afflicted . . . . iv 2 232
Mistress Ford, good heart, is beaten black and blue . . . iv 5 115
Good hearts, what ado here is to bring you together! . . . iv 5 128
In the lawful name of marrying, To give our hearts united ceremony . iv 6 51
But if he start, It is the flesh of a corrupted heart . . . v 5 91
Lust is but a bloody fire, Kindled with unchaste desire, Fed in heart . v 5 101
Though we would have thrust virtue out of our hearts by the head and shoulders . . . . v 5 156
My heart misgives me . . . . v 5 226
Mortality and mercy in Vienna Live in thy tongue and heart *Meas. for Meas.* i 1 46
And to jest, Tongue far from heart . . . . . . i 4 33
The valiant heart's not whipt out of his trade . . . . . ii 1 270
But might you do't, and do the world no wrong, If so your heart were touch'd with that remorse As mine is to him? . . . . ii 2 54
Go to your bosom; Knock there, and ask your heart what it doth know ii 2 137
And in my heart the strong and swelling evil Of my conception . . ii 4 6
O heavens! Why does my blood thus muster to my heart? . . ii 4 20
Such remedy as, to save a head, To cleave a heart in twain . . iii 1 63
Unfit to live or die: O gravel heart! . . . . . . iv 3 68
Revenges to your heart, And general honour . . . . iv 3 140
Command these fretting waters from your eyes With a light heart . iv 3 152
I am pale at mine heart to see thine eyes so red: thou must be patient iv 3 158
Let me have way, my lord, To find this practice out.—Ay, with my heart v 1 239
Not changing heart with habit, I am still Attorney'd at your service . v 1 389
Your brother's death, I know, sits at your heart . . . v 1 394
So deep sticks it in my penitent heart That I crave death . . v 1 480
Better cheer may you have, but not with better heart . *Com. of Errors* iii 1 29
Bear a fair presence, though your heart be tainted . . . iii 2 13
Mine eye's clear eye, my dear heart's dearer heart, My food, my fortune iii 2 62
If my breast had not been made of faith and my heart of steel . iii 2 150
My tongue, though not my heart, shall have his will . . . iv 2 18
My heart prays for him, though my tongue do curse . . . iv 2 28
One whose hard heart is button'd up with steel; A fiend, a fury . iv 2 34
Heart and good-will you might; But surely, master, not a rag of money iv 4 88
I could find in my heart to stay here still and turn witch . . iv 4 160
I would I could find in my heart that I had not a hard heart. *M. Ado* i 1 127
I dare swear he is no hypocrite, but prays from his heart . . i 1 153
In her bosom I'll unclasp my heart And take her hearing prisoner . i 1 325
Therefore all hearts in love use their own tongues . . . ii 1 184
You have lost the heart of Signior Benedick.—Indeed, my lord, he lent it me awhile; and I gave him use for it, a double heart for his single one . . . . ii 1 286
Lady, you have a merry heart.—Yea, my lord; I thank it, poor fool . ii 1 325
My cousin tells him in his ear that he is in her heart . . . ii 1 328
Then down upon her knees she falls, weeps, sobs, beats her heart . ii 3 153
Nay, that's impossible: she may wear her heart out first . . ii 3 210
Nature never framed a woman's heart Of prouder stuff . . . iii 1 49
I will requite thee, Taming my wild heart to thy loving hand . . iii 1 112
He hath a heart as sound as a bell and his tongue is the clapper, for what his heart thinks his tongue speaks . . . . . iii 2 12
I think he holds you well, and in dearness of heart . . . iii 2 101
God give me joy to wear it! for my heart is exceeding heavy . . iii 4 25
Lay it to your heart: it is the only thing for a qualm . . . iii 4 74
Indeed I cannot think, if I would think my heart out of thinking . iii 4 85
In despite of his heart, he eats his meat without grudging . . iii 4 89
If I were as tedious as a king, I could find it in my heart to bestow it all of your worship . . . . iii 5 24
What a Hero hadst thou been, If half thy outward graces had been placed About thy thoughts and counsels of thy heart! . . . iv 1 103
I was about to protest I loved you.—And do it with all thy heart.—I love you with so much of my heart that none is left to protest . iv 1 287
O God, that I were a man! I would eat his heart in the market-place . iv 1 309
Thy slander hath gone through and through her heart . . . v 1 68
We will not wake your patience. My heart is sorry for your daughter's death . . . . v 1 103
But, soft you, let me be: pluck up, my heart, and be sad . . v 1 208

Heart. I love thee against my will.—In spite of your heart, I think; alas, poor heart! *Much Ado* v 2 69

I will live in thy heart, die in thy lap and be buried in thy eyes v 2 104

I shall desire your help.—My heart is with your liking v 4 32

A miracle! here's our own hands against our hearts v 4 92

That we may lighten our own hearts and our wives' heels v 4 121

So received As you shall deem yourself lodged in my heart *L. L. Lost* ii 1 174

Lady, I will commend you to mine own heart ii 1 180

Is the fool sick?—Sick at the heart ii 1 185

By the heart's still rhetoric disclosed with eyes, Deceive me not now ii 1 229

His heart, like an agate, with your print impress'd ii 1 236

Negligent student! learn her by heart.—By heart and in heart, boy.—And out of heart iii 1 36

By heart you love her, because your heart cannot come by her; in heart you love her, because your heart is in love with her; and out of heart you love her, being out of heart that you cannot enjoy her iii 1 42

Sole imperator and great general Of trotting 'paritors:—O my little heart! iii 1 188

When, for fame's sake, for praise, an outward part, We bend to that the working of the heart iv 1 33

As I for praise alone now seek to spill The poor deer's blood, that my heart means no ill iv 1 35

I profane my lips on thy foot, my eyes on thy picture, and my heart on thy every part iv 1 87

Did not . . . thine eye . . . Persuade my heart to this false perjury? iv 3 62

Never lay his wreathed arms athwart His loving bosom to keep down his heart iv 3 136

Good heart, what grace hast thou, thus to reprove These worms for loving? iv 3 153

But, sweet heart, let that pass v 1 110

The very all of all is,—but, sweet heart, I do implore secrecy v 1 115

Sweet hearts, we shall be rich ere we depart v 2 1

For a light heart lives long v 2 18

Dost thou not wish in heart The chain were longer and the letter short? v 2 55

A pretty knavish page, That well by heart hath conn'd his embassage v 2 98

Why, that contempt will kill the speaker's heart v 2 149

Why take we hands, then?—Only to part friends: Curtsy, sweet hearts v 2 221

Lord Longaville said, I came o'er his heart v 2 278

A blister on his sweet tongue, with my heart! v 2 335

They are infected; in their hearts it lies; They have the plague v 2 420

And that a' wears next his heart for a favour v 2 721

A heavy heart bears not a nimble tongue v 2 747

Let our hands part, Neither intitled in the other's heart v 2 822

Hence ever then my heart is in thy breast v 2 826

Look on me; Behold the window of my heart, mine eye v 2 848

With cunning hast thou filch'd my daughter's heart *M. N. Dream* i 1 36

O, teach me how you look, and with what art You sway the motion of Demetrius' heart i 1 193

Set your heart at rest ii 1 121

And loosed his love-shaft smartly from his bow, As it should pierce a hundred thousand hearts ii 1 160

But yet you draw not iron, for my heart Is true as steel ii 1 196

The wildest hath not such a heart as you ii 1 229

One turf shall serve as pillow for us both; One heart, one bed ii 2 42

My heart unto yours is knit So that but one heart we can make of it ii 2 47

Nature shows art, That through thy bosom makes me see thy heart ii 2 105

Methought a serpent eat my heart away, And you sat smiling at his cruel prey ii 2 149

Pierced through the heart with your stern cruelty iii 2 59

And superpraise my parts, When I am sure you hate me with your hearts iii 2 154

My heart to her but as guest-wise sojourn'd iii 2 171

So, with two seeming bodies, but one heart iii 2 212

What, have you come by night And stolen my love's heart from him? iii 2 284

Who is't that hinders you?—A foolish heart, that I leave here behind iii 2 319

The virtue of my heart, The object and the pleasure of mine eye iv 1 174

Man's hand is not able to taste, his tongue to conceive, nor his heart to report, what my dream was iv 1 219

Where are these lads? where are these hearts? iv 2 26

Joy and fresh days of love Accompany your hearts! v 1 30

Whose gentle hearts do fear The smallest monstrous mouse v 1 222

That left pap, Where heart doth hop v 1 304

And let my liver rather heat with wine Than my heart cool with mortifying groans *Mer. of Venice* i 1 82

If I could bid the fifth welcome with so good a heart as I can bid the other four farewell, I should be glad i 2 141

Like a villain with a smiling cheek, A goodly apple rotten at the heart i 3 102

I would outstare the sternest eyes that look, Outbrave the heart most daring ii 1 28

My conscience, hanging about the neck of my heart, says very wisely ii 2 14

I have too grieved a heart To take a tedious leave ii 7 76

I will have the heart of him, if he forfeit iii 1 132

Tell me where is fancy bred, Or in the heart or in the head? iii 2 64

How many cowards, whose hearts are all as false As stairs of sand, wear yet upon their chins The beards of Hercules! iii 2 83

Hath woven A golden mesh to entrap the hearts of men iii 2 122

From brassy bosoms and rough hearts of flint iv 1 31

You may as well do any thing most hard, As seek to soften that—than which what's harder?—His Jewish heart iv 1 80

It is enthroned in the hearts of kings, It is an attribute to God himself iv 1 194

Bound to pay it ten times o'er, On forfeit of my hands, my head, my heart iv 1 212

A pound of flesh, to be by him cut off Nearest the merchant's heart iv 1 233

'Nearest his heart:' those are the very words.—It is so iv 1 254

Since you do take it, love, so much at heart v 1 145

I could not for my heart deny it him v 1 165

Even so void is your false heart of truth v 1 189

Beloved, and indeed so much in the heart of the world *As Y. Like It* i 1 175

My father's rough and envious disposition Sticks me at heart i 2 254

I could shake them off my coat: these burs are in my heart i 3 17

A boar-spear in my hand; and—in my heart Lie there what hidden woman's fear there will i 3 120

I could find in my heart to disgrace my man's apparel and to cry ii 4 4

Why, how now, Adam! no greater heart in thee? ii 6 4

O that your highness knew my heart in this! I never loved my brother iii 1 13

Helen's cheek, but not her heart, Cleopatra's majesty iii 2 153

Thus Rosalind of many parts By heavenly synod was devised, Of many faces, eyes, and hearts iii 2 159

That tripp'd up the wrestler's heels and your heart both in an instant iii 2 225

He was furnished like a hunter.—O, ominous! he comes to kill my heart iii 2 260

What stature is she of?—Just as high as my heart iii 2 286

Heart. I take upon me to wash your liver as clean as a sound sheep's heart *As Y. Like It* iii 2 444

A man may, if he were of a fearful heart, stagger in this attempt iii 3 49

Swears brave oaths and breaks them bravely, quite traverse, athwart the heart of his lover iii 4 46

Whose heart the accustom'd sight of death makes hard iii 5 4

Now I do frown on thee with all my heart iii 5 15

I'll write it straight; The matter's in my head and in my heart iii 5 137

Art thou god to shepherd turn'd, That a maiden's heart hath burn'd? iv 3 41

Why, thy godhead laid apart, Warr'st thou with a woman's heart? iv 3 45

And, after some small space, being strong at heart, He sent me hither iv 3 152

Be of good cheer, youth: you a man! you lack a man's heart iv 3 165

Well then, take a good heart and counterfeit to be a man iv 3 174

How it grieves me to see thee wear thy heart in a scarf! v 2 23

I thought thy heart had been wounded with the claws of a lion v 2 25

If you do love Rosalind so near the heart as your gesture cries it out v 2 69

To-morrow will we be married.—I do desire it with all my heart v 3 3

Join her hand with his Whose heart within his bosom is v 4 121

You and you no cross shall part: You and you are heart in heart v 4 138

I wis it is not half way to her heart *T. of Shrew* i 1 62

Affection is not rated from the heart i 1 165

And could not get him for my heart to do it i 2 38

I must, forsooth, be forced To give my hand opposed against my heart iii 2 9

My very lips might freeze to my teeth, my tongue to the roof of my mouth, my heart in my belly iv 1 8

And may you prove, sir, master of your art!—While you, sweet dear, prove mistress of my heart! iv 2 10

Much good do it unto thy gentle heart! iv 3 51

My tongue will tell the anger of my heart, Or else my heart concealing it will break iv 3 77

This has put me in heart iv 5 77

Our soft conditions and our hearts Should well agree with our external parts v 2 167

My heart as great, my reason haply more, To bandy word for word v 2 171

The remembrance of her father never approaches her heart but the tyranny of her sorrows takes all livelihood from her cheek *All's Well* i 1 57

Heart too capable Of every line and trick of his sweet favour i 1 106

Howsome'er their hearts are severed in religion, their heads are both one i 3 57

A man may draw his heart out, ere a' pluck one i 3 93

It will wear the surplice of humility over the black gown of a big heart i 3 100

My heart Will not confess he owes the malady That doth my life besiege ii 1 8

Our hearts receive your warnings ii 1 22

My state that way is dangerous, since I cannot yet find in my heart to repent ii 5 13

But the boldness of his hand, haply, which his heart was not consenting to iii 2 80

My heart is heavy and mine age is weak; Grief would have tears iii 4 41

I warrant, good creature, wheresoe'er she is, Her heart weighs sadly iii 5 70

My tongue is too foolhardy; but my heart hath the fear of Mars before it iv 1 33

My mother told me just how he would woo, As if she sat in's heart iv 2 70

If my heart were great, 'Twould burst at this iv 3 366

Whose dear perfection hearts that scorn'd to serve Humbly call'd mistress v 3 18

At first I stuck my choice upon her, ere my heart Durst make too bold a herald of my tongue v 3 45

Your gentle hands lend us, and take our hearts Epil. 340

O, she that hath a heart of that fine frame To pay this debt of love but to a brother, How will she love! *T. Night* i 1 33

Liver, brain and heart, These sovereign thrones i 1 37

Taurus! That's sides and heart.—No, sir; it is legs and thighs i 3 148

Are you a comedian?—No, my profound heart i 5 195

I will on with my speech in your praise, and then show you the heart of my message i 5 203

In what chapter of his bosom?—To answer by the method, in the first of his heart i 5 245

Love make his heart of flint that you shall love! i 5 305

How easy is it for the proper-false In women's waxen hearts to set their forms! ii 2 31

How now, my hearts! did you never see the picture of 'we three'? ii 3 16

Farewell, dear heart, since I must needs be gone ii 3 109

So wears she to him, So sways she level in her husband's heart ii 4 32

Say that some lady, as perhaps there is, Hath for your love as great a pang of heart As you have for Olivia ii 4 93

There is no woman's sides Can bide the beating of so strong a passion As love doth give my heart; no woman's heart So big, to hold so much ii 4 98

What dost thou know?—Too well what love women to men may owe: In faith, they are as true of heart as we ii 4 109

Silence, like a Lucrece knife, With bloodless stroke my heart doth gore ii 5 117

With all the unmuzzled thoughts That tyrannous heart can think iii 1 131

A cypress, not a bosom, Hideth my heart iii 1 133

I have one heart, one bosom and one truth, And that no woman has iii 1 170

Thou perhaps mayst move That heart, which now abhors, to like his love iii 1 176

To put fire in your heart, and brimstone in your liver iii 2 21

An you speak ill of the devil, how he takes it at heart! iii 4 112

I have said too much unto a heart of stone And laid mine honour too unchary out iii 4 221

Beshrew his soul for me, He started one poor heart of mine in thee iv 1 63

Why should I not, had I the heart to do it? v 1 120

To spite a raven's heart within a dove v 1 134

One that indeed physics the subject, makes old hearts fresh *W. Tale* i 1 43

My heart dances; but not for joy; not joy i 2 110

Next to thyself and my young rover, he's Apparent to my heart i 2 177

I have trusted thee, Camillo, With all the nearest things to my heart i 2 236

Do't and thou hast the one half of my heart; Do't not, thou split'st thine own i 2 348

I saw his heart in's face i 2 447

The justice of your hearts will thereto add, 'Tis pity she's not honest' ii 1 67

Even thou, that hast A heart so tender o'er it, take it hence ii 3 133

While she lives My heart will be a burthen to me ii 3 206

This sessions, to our great grief we pronounce, Even pushes 'gainst our heart iii 2 2

Harden'd be the hearts Of all that hear me! iii 2 53

Take her hence: Her heart is but o'ercharged; she will recover iii 2 151

Woe the while! O, cut my lace, lest my heart, cracking it, Break too! iii 2 174

Whose honourable thoughts, Thoughts high for one so tender, cleft the heart iii 2 197

He is touch'd To the noble heart iii 2 223

I am glad at heart To be so rid o' the business iii 3 14

Heart. Weep I cannot, But my heart bleeds *W. Tale* iii 3 52
I am no fighter: I am false of heart that way iv 3 116
A merry heart goes all the day, Your sad tires in a mile-a iv 3 134
And sung this ballad against the hard hearts of maids iv 4 282
Your heart is full of something that does take Your mind from feasting iv 4 357
The gifts she looks from me are pack'd and lock'd Up in my heart iv 4 370
O, my heart! iv 4 435
That he shall not perceive But that you have your father's bosom there And speak his very heart iv 4 575
Whose fresh complexion and whose heart together Affliction alters iv 4 585
The tortures he shall feel will break the back of man, the heart of monster iv 4 797
So locks her in embracing, as if she would pin her to her heart v 2 85
I would fain say, bleed tears, for I am sure my heart wept blood v 2 97
Needs must you lay your heart at his dispose *K. John* i 1 263
The aweless lion could not wage the fight, Nor keep his princely heart from Richard's hand i 1 267
He that perforce robs lions of their hearts May easily win a woman's i 1 268
Ay, my mother, With all my heart I thank thee for my father! i 1 270
Richard, that robb'd the lion of his heart And fought the holy wars ii 1 3
Welcome with a powerless hand, But with a heart full of unstained love ii 1 16
I bring you witnesses, Twice fifteen thousand hearts of England's breed ii 1 275
Hang'd in the frowning wrinkle of her brow! And quarter'd in her heart! ii 1 506
This act so evilly born shall cool the hearts Of all his people iii 4 149
And then the hearts Of all his people shall revolt from him iii 4 164
And will you?—And I will.—Have you the heart? iv 1 41
I then have chid away my friend! He hath a stern look, but a gentle heart iv 1 88
To sound the purposes of all their hearts, Both for myself and them iv 2 48
Didst let thy heart consent, And consequently thy rude hand to act iv 2 239
My heart hath melted at a lady's tears, Being an ordinary inundation v 2 47
And with a great heart heave away this storm v 2 55
You taught me how . . . , Yea, thrust this enterprise into my heart v 2 90
And their gentle hearts To fierce and bloody inclination v 2 157
O, my heart is sick! v 3 4
Beshrew thy very heart! I did not think to be so sad to-night v 5 14
The tackle of my heart is crack'd and burn'd v 7 52
My heart hath one poor string to stay it by v 7 55
Then, Bolingbroke, as low as to thy heart, Through the false passage of thy throat, thou liest *Richard II.* i 1 124
Never did captive with a freer heart Cast off his chains of bondage i 3 88
Even in the glasses of thine eyes I see thy grieved heart i 3 209
When the tongue's office should be prodigal To breathe the abundant dolour of the heart i 3 257
Call it a travel that thou takest for pleasure.—My heart will sigh when I miscall it so i 3 263
My heart disdained that my tongue Should so profane the word i 4 12
How he did seem to dive into their hearts With humble and familiar courtesy i 4 25
You lose a thousand well-disposed hearts And prick my tender patience ii 1 206
My heart is great; but it must break with silence, Ere't be disburden'd ii 1 228
The commons hath he pill'd with grievous taxes, And quite lost their hearts ii 1 247
The nobles hath he fined For ancient quarrels, and quite lost their hearts ii 1 248
Their love Lies in their purses, and whoso empties them By so much fills their hearts with deadly hate ii 2 131
My heart this covenant makes, my hand thus seals it ii 3 50
Show me thy humble heart, and not thy knee ii 3 83
Mine ear is open and my heart prepared: The worst is worldly loss iii 2 93
With hard bright steel and hearts harder than steel iii 2 111
Snakes, in my heart-blood warm'd, that sting my heart! iii 2 131
And sends allegiance and true faith of heart iii 3 37
His glittering arms he will commend to rust, His barbed steeds to stables, and his heart To faithful service of your majesty iii 3 117
Swell'st thou, proud heart? I'll give thee scope to beat iii 3 140
Where subjects' feet May hourly trample on their sovereign's head; For on my heart they tread now whilst I live iii 3 158
Sorrow and grief of heart Makes him speak fondly, like a frantic man iii 3 184
Me rather had my heart might feel your love Than my unpleased eye see your courtesy iii 3 192
Your heart is up, I know, Thus high at least, although your knee be low iii 3 194
My legs can keep no measure in delight, When my poor heart no measure keeps in grief iii 4 8
I will turn thy falsehood to thy heart, Where it was forged iv 1 39
I give this heavy weight from off my head And this unwieldy sceptre from my hand, The pride of kingly sway from out my heart iv 1 206
Your brows are full of discontent, Your hearts of sorrow iv 1 332
Hath Bolingbroke deposed Thine intellect? hath he been in thy heart? v 1 28
Must we part?—Ay, hand from hand, my love, and heart from heart v 1 82
Twice for one step I'll groan, the way being short, And piece the way out with a heavy heart v 1 92
One kiss shall stop our mouths, and dumbly part; Thus give I mine, and thus take I thy heart v 1 96
'Twere no good part To take on me to keep and kill thy heart v 1 98
Had not God, for some strong purpose, steel'd The hearts of men, they must perforce have melted v 2 35
Read not my name there; My heart is not confederate with my hand v 3 53
Lest thy pity prove A serpent that will sting thee to the heart v 3 58
He prays but faintly and would be denied; We pray with heart and soul v 3 104
Thine eye begins to speak; set thy tongue there; Or in thy piteous heart plant thou thine ear v 3 126
I would thou wert the man That would divorce this terror from my heart v 4 9
The sound that tells what hour it is Are clamorous groans, which strike upon my heart, Which is the bell v 5 56
Yet blessing on his heart that gives it me! For 'tis a sign of love v 5 64
O, how it yearn'd my heart when I beheld In London streets! v 5 76
What my tongue dares not, that my heart shall say v 5 97
I will ease my heart, Albeit I make a hazard of my head *1 Hen. IV.* i 3 127
You shall see now in very sincerity of fear and cold heart, will he to the king and lay open all our proceedings ii 3 33
I'll be sworn upon all the books in England, I could find in my heart ii 4 56
I am glad of it with all my heart iii 1 128; *Pericles* ii 5 74
Loseth men's hearts and leaves behind a stain Upon the beauty of all parts *1 Hen. IV.* iii 1 187
Heart! you swear like a comfit-maker's wife iii 1 252
And hold their level with thy princely heart iii 2 17
And art almost an alien to the hearts Of all the court iii 2 34
In such humility That I did pluck allegiance from men's hearts iii 2 52
Or I will tear the reckoning from his heart iii 2 152
I shall be out of heart shortly, and then I shall have no strength to repent iii 3 6

Heart. With hearts in their bellies no bigger than pins' heads *1 Hen. IV.* iv 2 23
You do not counsel well: You speak it out of fear and cold heart iv 3 7
My father, in kind heart and pity moved, Swore him assistance iv 3 64
By this face . . . did he win The hearts of all that he did angle for iv 3 84
The king himself; who, Douglas, grieves at heart v 4 29
Fare thee well, great heart! Ill-weaved ambition, how much art thou shrunk! v 4 87
Each heart being set On bloody courses, the rude scene may end *2 Hen. IV.* i 1 158
An habitation giddy and unsure Hath he that buildeth on the vulgar heart i 3 90
But I tell thee, my heart bleeds inwardly that my father is so sick ii 2 51
It angered him to the heart: but he hath forgot that ii 4 9
Your pulsidge beats as extraordinarily as heart would desire ii 4 26
Why, that's well said; a good heart's worth gold ii 4 34
I will toss the rogue in a blanket.—Do, an thou darest for thy heart ii 4 242
By my troth, I kiss thee with a most constant heart ii 4 293
God's blessing of your good heart! ii 4 329
If my heart be not ready to burst,—well, sweet Jack, have a care of thyself ii 4 409
What rank diseases grow, And with what danger, near the heart of it iii 1 40
It would have done a man's heart good to see iii 2 54
By the mass, I could anger her to the heart iii 2 217
Our cause the best; Then reason will our hearts should be as good iv 1 157
That man that sits within a monarch's heart iv 2 11
And then the vital commoners and inland petty spirits muster me all to their captain, the heart iv 3 120
The blood weeps from my heart when I do shape In forms imaginary iv 4 58
Thou hidest a thousand daggers in thy thoughts, Which thou hast whetted on thy stony heart, To stab at half an hour of my life iv 5 108
When I here came in, And found no course of breath within your majesty, How cold it struck my heart! iv 5 152
I thank thee with all my heart v 1 64
I will deeply put the fashion on And wear it in my heart v 2 53
There's a merry heart! v 3 24
What you want in meat, we'll have in drink: but you must bear; the heart's all v 3 32
And drink unto the leman mine; And a merry heart lives long-a v 3 50
My king! my Jove! I speak to thee, my heart! v 5 50
We will hear, note, and believe in heart That what you speak *Hen. V.* i 2 30
Whose hearts have left their bodies here in England i 2 128
Model to thy inward greatness, Like little body with a mighty heart ii Prol. 17
The king has killed his heart ii 1 93
Ah, poor heart! he is so shaked of a burning quotidian tertian ii 1 123
Thou hast spoke the right; His heart is fracted and corroborate ii 1 130
We carry not a heart with us from hence That grows not in a fair consent ii 2 21
And do serve you With hearts create of duty and of zeal ii 2 31
Let me bring thee to Staines.—No; for my manly heart doth yearn ii 3 3
For if you hide the crown Even in your hearts, there will he rake for it ii 4 98
The flesh'd soldier, rough and hard of heart iii 3 11
When he shall see our army, He'll drop his heart into the sink of fear iii 5 59
A man that I love and honour with my soul, and my heart, and my duty iii 6 8
A soldier, firm and sound of heart, And of buxom valour iii 6 26
God-a-mercy, old heart! thou speak'st cheerfully iv 1 34
O God of battles! steel my soldiers' hearts; Possess them not with fear; take from them now The sense of reckoning, if the opposed numbers Pluck their hearts from them iv 1 306
Time hath worn us into slovenry: But, by the mass, our hearts are in the trim iv 3 115
I did never know so full a voice issue from so empty a heart iv 4 72
Doo's me as great honours as can be desired in the hearts of his subjects iv 7 168
All offences, my lord, come from the heart: never came any from mine iv 8 50
Her vine, the merry cheerer of the heart, Unpruned dies v 2 41
Will you vouchsafe to teach a soldier terms Such as will enter at a lady's ear And plead his love-suit to her gentle heart? v 2 101
If you will love me soundly with your French heart, I will be glad to hear you confess it brokenly with your English tongue v 2 105
A good heart, Kate, is the sun and the moon; or rather the sun v 2 171
Dispraise those parts in me that you love with your heart v 2 214
Put off your maiden blushes; avouch the thoughts of your heart v 2 254
Having neither the voice nor the heart of flattery about me v 2 315
God, the best maker of all marriages, Combine your hearts in one! v 2 388
My heart and hands thou hast at once subdued *1 Hen. VI.* i 2 109
But, O! the treacherous Fastolfe wounds my heart i 4 35
Ready they were to shoot me to the heart i 4 56
How dying Salisbury doth groan! It irks his heart he cannot be revenged i 4 105
Your hearts I'll stamp out with my horse's heels i 4 108
He bears him on the place's privilege, Or durst not, for his craven heart, say thus ii 4 87
Is not quite exempt From envious malice of thy swelling heart iii 1 26
I would prevail, if prayers might prevail, To join your hearts in love iii 1 68
I would see his heart out, ere the priest Should ever get that privilege iii 1 120
And hand for hand I give.—Ay, but, I fear me, with a hollow heart iii 1 136
In this late-betrayed town Great Cœur-de-lion's heart was buried iii 2 83
Methinks I should revive the soldiers' hearts iii 2 97
Burgundy Enshrines thee in his heart and there erects Thy noble deeds iii 2 119
A gentle heart did never sway in court iii 2 135
With submissive loyalty of heart Ascribes the glory . . . First to my God iii 4 10
In heart desiring still You may behold confusion of your foes iv 1 76
The paleness of this flower Bewray'd the faintness of my master's heart iv 1 107
For, had the passions of thy heart burst out, I fear we should have seen decipher'd there More rancorous spite iv 1 183
Somerset, who in proud heart Doth stop my cornets iv 3 24
It warm'd thy father's heart with proud desire Of bold-faced victory iv 6 11
These words of yours draw life-blood from my heart iv 6 43
Dizzy-eyed fury and great rage of heart Suddenly made him from my side to start iv 7 11
My hand would free her, but my heart says no v 3 61
A pure unspotted heart, Never yet taint with love v 3 182
Ah, Joan, this kills thy father's heart outright! v 4 2
Will nothing turn your unrelenting hearts? v 4 59
Do breed love's settled passions in my heart v 5 4
O Lord, that lends me life, Lend me a heart replete with thankfulness! *2 Hen. VI.* i 1 20
Such as my wit affords And over-joy of heart doth minister i 1 31
Some sudden qualm hath struck me at the heart And dimm'd mine eyes i 1 54
France should have torn and rent my very heart, Before I would have yielded i 1 126
Let not his smoothing words Bewitch your hearts; be wise i 1 157
As did the fatal brand Althæa burn'd Unto the prince's heart of Calydon i 1 235
And stolest away the ladies' hearts of France i 3 55

Heart. She bears a duke's revenues on her back, And in her heart she scorns our poverty . . . . 2 *Hen. VI.* i 3 84
I shall never be able to fight a blow. O Lord, my heart! . . . . i 3 221
Thine eyes and thoughts Beat on a crown, the treasure of thy heart . ii 1 20
How irksome is this music to my heart! . . . . . . ii 1 56
What tidings . . . ?—Such as my heart doth tremble to unfold . . ii 1 166
Ambitious churchman, leave to afflict my heart . . . . . ii 1 182
My heart assures me that the Earl of Warwick Shall one day make the Duke of York a king . . . . ii 2 78
Mine eyes are full of tears, my heart of grief . . . . . ii 3 17
Sort thy heart to patience; These few days' wonder will be quickly worn ii 4 68
By flattery hath he won the commons' hearts . . . . . . iii 1 28
A heart unspotted is not easily daunted . . . . iii 1 100
Unburthens with his tongue The envious load that lies upon his heart . iii 1 157
My heart is drown'd with grief, Whose flood begins to flow within mine eyes . . . . iii 1 198
My heart accordeth with my tongue, Seeing the deed is meritorious . iii 1 269
Let pale-faced fear keep with the mean-born man, And find no harbour in a royal heart . . . . iii 1 336
The starved snake, Who, cherish'd in your breasts, will sting your hearts iii 1 344
I took a costly jewel from my neck, A heart it was, bound in with diamonds . . . . iii 2 107
The sea received it, And so I wish'd thy body might my heart . . iii 2 109
And bid mine eyes be packing with my heart . . . . . . iii 2 111
Meagre, pale and bloodless, Being all descended to the labouring heart. iii 2 163
With the heart there cools and ne'er returneth To blush and beautify the cheek again . . . . iii 2 166
But here's a vengeful sword, rusted with ease, That shall be scoured in his rancorous heart . . . . iii 2 199
What stronger breastplate than a heart untainted! . . . . . iii 2 232
Even now my burthen'd heart would break, Should I not curse them . iii 2 320
I go.—And take my heart with thee . . . . iii 2 408
Like ambitious Sylla, overgorged With gobbets of thy mother's bleeding heart . . . . iv 1 85
His brother's death Hath given them heart and courage to proceed . iv 4 35
Then, York, unloose thy long-imprison'd thoughts, And let thy tongue be equal with thy heart . . . . v 1 89
Even at this sight My heart is turn'd to stone . . . . . . v 2 50
Sword, hold thy temper; heart, be wrathful still . . . . . v 2 70
But that my heart's on future mischief set, I would speak blasphemy . v 2 84
Uncurable discomfit Reigns in the hearts of all our present parts . . v 2 87
My heart for anger burns; I cannot brook it . . . . 3 *Hen. VI.* i 1 60
Far be the thought of this from Henry's heart! . . . . . i 1 70
Often borne in France, And now in England to our heart's great sorrow i 1 128
O Clifford, how thy words revive my heart! . . . . . . i 1 163
The loss of those three lords torments my heart: I'll write unto them . i 1 270
I cannot rest Until the white rose that I wear be dyed Even in the lukewarm blood of Henry's heart . . . . i 2 34
It could not slake mine ire, nor ease my heart . . . . . . i 3 29
Do not honour him so much To prick thy finger, though to wound his heart . . . . i 4 55
Hath thy fiery heart so parch'd thine entrails That not a tear can fall? . i 4 87
O tiger's heart wrapt in a woman's hide! . . . . i 4 137
All my body's moisture Scarce serves to quench my furnace-burning heart . . . . ii 1 80
Nor can my tongue unload my heart's great burthen . . . . ii 1 81
They had no heart to fight, And we in them no hope to win the day . ii 1 135
Were thy heart as hard as steel, As thou hast shown it flinty by thy deeds, I come to pierce it . . . . ii 1 201
Doth not the object cheer your heart, my lord? . . . . . ii 2 4
Steel thy melting heart To hold thine own . . . . . . ii 2 41
For scarce I can refrain The execution of my big-swoln heart . . ii 2 111
Shamest thou not, knowing whence thou art extraught, To let thy tongue detect thy base-born heart? . . . . ii 2 143
I throw my hands, mine eyes, my heart to thee . . . . . ii 3 36
And here's the heart that triumphs in their death . . . . . ii 4 8
Let our hearts and eyes, like civil war, Be blind with tears . . . ii 5 77
See what showers arise, Blown with the windy tempest of my heart, Upon thy wounds, that kill mine eye and heart! . . . . . ii 5 86
These arms of mine shall be thy winding-sheet; My heart, sweet boy, shall be thy sepulchre, For from my heart thine image ne'er shall go ii 5 115
Her tears will pierce into a marble heart . . . . iii 1 38
My crown is in my heart, not on my head; Not deck'd with diamonds . iii 1 62
My eye's too quick, my heart o'erweens too much . . . . . iii 2 144
And murder whiles I smile, And cry 'Content' to that which grieves my heart . . . . iii 2 183
And stops my tongue, while heart is drown'd in cares . . . . iii 3 14
And with my tongue To tell the passion of my sovereign's heart . . iii 3 62
Mine [my news], such as fill my heart with unhoped joys . . . iii 3 172
I hold it cowardice To rest mistrustful where a noble heart Hath pawn'd an open hand in sign of love . . . . iv 2 8
Now join your hands, and with your hands your hearts . . . . iv 6 39
Henry's late presaging prophecy Did glad my heart with hope . . iv 6 93
So doth my heart misgive me, in these conflicts What may befall him . iv 6 94
My sick heart shows That I must yield my body to the earth . . . v 2 8
We are in readiness.—This cheers my heart, to see your forwardness . v 4 65
No, no, my heart will burst, an if I speak: And I will speak, that so my heart may burst . . . . v 5 60
Cursed be the heart that had the heart to do it! . . *Richard III.* i 2 15
My proud heart sues and prompts my tongue to speak . . . . i 2 171
If thy revengeful heart cannot forgive, Lo, here I lend thee this . . i 2 174
I would I knew thy heart.—'Tis figured in my tongue . . . . i 2 193
Look, how this ring encompasseth thy finger, Even so thy breast encloseth my poor heart . . . . i 2 205
To take her in her heart's extremest hate, With curses in her mouth . i 2 232
I would to God my heart were flint, like Edward's . . . . . i 3 140
I had rather be a pedlar; Far be it from my heart, the thought of it! . i 3 150
Remember this another day, When he shall split thy very heart with sorrow! . . . . i 3 300; v 1 26
Perhaps May move your hearts to pity, if you mark him . . . i 3 349
You scarcely have the hearts to tell me so, And therefore cannot have the hearts to do it . . . . i 4 180
By heaven, my heart is purged from grudging hate . . . . . ii 1 9
As I swear perfect love!—And I, as I love Hastings with my heart! . ii 1 17
A pleasing cordial . . . Is this thy vow unto my sickly heart . . ii 1 42
Your high-swoln hearts, But lately splinter'd, knit, and join'd together ii 2 117
Give your censures in this weighty business?—With all our hearts . ii 2 145
I long with all my heart to see the prince: I hope he is much grown . ii 4 4
His outward show; which, God he knows, Seldom or never jumpeth with the heart . . . . iii 1 11

Heart. Attended to their sugar'd words, But look not on the poison of their hearts . . . . *Richard III.* iii 1 14
And with a heavy heart, Thinking on them, go I unto the Tower . . iii 1 149
We know each other's faces, But for our hearts, he knows no more of mine Than I of yours . . . . iii 4 11
For by his face straight shall you know his heart.—What of his heart perceive you in his face By any likelihood he show'd to-day? . . iii 4 55
Even where his lustful eye or savage heart, Without control, listed to make his prey . . . . iii 5 83
O, cut my lace in sunder, that my pent heart May have some scope to beat! . . . . iv 1 34
My woman's heart Grossly grew captive to his honey words . . . iv 1 79
Poor heart, adieu! I pity thy complaining . . . . . . iv 1 88
Though what they do impart Help not at all, yet do they ease the heart iv 4 131
Whose hand soever lanced their tender hearts, Thy head, all indirectly, gave direction . . . . iv 4 224
No doubt the murderous knife was dull and blunt Till it was whetted on thy stone-hard heart . . . . iv 4 227
Send to her, by the man that slew her brothers, A pair of bleeding hearts iv 4 272
Put in her tender heart the aspiring flame Of golden sovereignty . . iv 4 328
Why look you so sad?—My heart is ten times lighter than my looks . v 3 3
Cheer thy heart, and be thou not dismay'd: God and good angels fight v 3 174
A thousand hearts are great within my bosom . . . . . . v 3 347
And take it from a heart that wishes towards you Honour . *Hen. VIII.* i 1 103
My life itself, and the best heart of it, Thanks you . . . . . i 2 1
Which hath flaw'd the heart Of all their loyalties . . . . . i 2 21
Tongues spit their duties out, and cold hearts freeze Allegiance in them i 2 61
If ever any malice in your heart Were hid against me, now to forgive me ii 1 80
For those you make friends And give your hearts to, when they once perceive The least rub in your fortunes, fall away . . . . ii 1 128
Every tongue speaks 'em, And every true heart weeps for't . . . ii 2 40
Has always loved her So dear in heart . . . . ii 2 111
Hearts of most hard temper Melt and lament for her . . . . ii 3 11
You, that have so fair parts of woman on you, Have too a woman's heart ii 3 28
Your heart Is cramm'd with arrogancy, spleen, and pride . . . ii 4 109
In sweet music in such art, Killing care and grief of heart . . . iii 1 13
But cardinal sins and hollow hearts I fear ye . . . . . . iii 1 104
Ye have angels' faces, but heaven knows your hearts . . . . iii 1 145
The hearts of princes kiss obedience, So much they love it . . . iii 1 162
He has my heart yet; and shall have my prayers While I shall have my life . . . . iii 1 180
He is vex'd at something.—I would 'twere something that would fret the string, The master-cord on's heart! . . . . iii 2 106
Since I had my office, I have kept you next my heart . . . . iii 2 157
As my hand has open'd bounty to you, My heart dropp'd love . . iii 2 185
So your hand and heart, Your brain, and every function of your power, Should, notwithstanding that your bond of duty, As 'twere in love's particular, be more To me, your friend, than any . . . . iii 2 186
My heart weeps to see him So little of his great self . . . . iii 2 335
Vain pomp and glory of this world, I hate ye: I feel my heart new open'd . . . . iii 2 366
Bear witness, all that have not hearts of iron, With what a sorrow Cromwell leaves his lord . . . . iii 2 424
Love thyself last: cherish those hearts that hate thee . . . . iii 2 443
This is of purpose laid by some that hate me—God turn their hearts! . v 2 15
I speak it with a single heart . . . . v 3 38
Pray heaven, the king may never find a heart With less allegiance in it! v 3 42
With a true heart And brother-love I do it . . . . v 3 172
Those joyful tears show thy true heart . . . . v 3 175
Each Trojan that is master of his heart, Let him to field *Troi. and Cres.* i 1 4
When my heart, As wedged with a sigh, would rive in twain . . . i 1 34
Pour'st in the open ulcer of my heart Her eyes, her hair, her cheek . i 1 53
Well, Troilus, well: I would my heart were in her body . . . . i 2 85
He's not hurt: why, this will do Helen's heart good now, ha! . . i 2 234
Nerve and bone of Greece, Heart of our numbers, soul and only spirit . i 3 56
Nothing so full of heart . . . . i 3 239
Who miscarrying, What heart receives from hence the conquering part? i 3 352
Without a heart to dare or sword to draw When Helen is defended . ii 2 157
My heart beats thicker than a feverous pulse . . . . . . iii 2 38
Nay, you shall fight your hearts out ere I part you . . . . . iii 2 55
Boldness comes to me now, and brings me heart . . . . . . iii 2 121
'Yea,' let them say, to stick the heart of falsehood, 'As false as Cressid' iii 2 202
Crack my clear voice with sobs and break my heart With sounding Troilus . . . . iv 2 114
Think it an altar, and thy brother Troilus A priest there offering to it his own heart . . . . iv 3 9
'O heart,' as the goodly saying is, '——O heart, heavy heart, Why sigh'st thou without breaking?' . . . . iv 4 15
Where are my tears? rain, to lay this wind, or my heart will be blown up by the root . . . . iv 4 56
Be thou but true of heart,— I true! how now! what wicked deem is this? . . . . iv 4 60
For I will throw my glove to Death himself, That there's no maculation in thy heart . . . . iv 4 66
Half heart, half hand, half Hector comes to seek This blended knight . iv 5 85
His heart and hand both open and both free; For what he has he gives iv 5 100
From heart of very heart, great Hector, welcome . . . . . iv 5 171
Do not snatch it from me; He that takes that doth take my heart withal v 2 82
One eye yet looks on thee; But with my heart the other eye doth see . v 2 108
Yet there is a credence in my heart, An esperance so obstinately strong v 2 120
In characters as red as Mars his heart Inflamed with Venus . . . v 2 164
Words, words, mere words, no matter from the heart . . . . v 3 108
Now, Troy, sink down! Here lies thy heart, thy sinews, and thy bone v 8 12
The vigilant eye, The counsellor heart, the arm our soldier . *Coriolanus* i 1 120
Through the rivers of your blood, Even to the court, the heart . . i 1 140
To break the heart of generosity, And make bold power look pale . . i 1 215
Now put your shields before your hearts, and fight With hearts more proof than shields . . . . i 4 24
In heart As merry as when our nuptial day was done . . . . i 6 30
O'er them Aufidius, Their very heart of hope . . . . . . i 6 55
Shall say against their hearts 'We thank the gods' . . . . . i 9 8
But cannot make my heart consent to take A bribe to pay my sword . i 9 37
Against the hospitable canon, would I Wash my fierce hand in's heart . i 10 27
No more of this; it does offend my heart . . . . ii 1 185
A curse begin at very root on's heart, That is not glad to see thee! . ii 1 202
And carry with us ears and eyes for the time, But hearts for the event ii 1 286
So planted his honours in their eyes, and his actions in their hearts . ii 2 34
Convented Upon a pleasing treaty, and have hearts Inclinable to honour ii 2 59
The wisdom of their choice is rather to have my hat than my heart . ii 3 106
He has it now, and by his looks methinks 'Tis warm at's heart . . ii 3 160

Heart. With a proud heart he wore his humble weeds . *Coriolanus* ii 3 161
Why, had your bodies No heart among you? . . . . ii 3 212
His heart's his mouth: What his breast forges, that his tongue must vent . . . . iii 1 257
I have a heart as little apt as yours, But yet a brain that leads my use of anger To better vantage . . . . iii 2 29
Nor by the matter which your heart prompts you . . . . iii 2 54
Correcting thy stout heart, Now humble as the ripest mulberry . iii 2 78
This but done, Even as she speaks, why, their hearts were yours . . iii 2 87
Must I with base tongue give my noble heart A lie that it must bear? . iii 2 100
I mock at death With as big heart as thou . . . . . . iii 2 128
Chide me no more. I'll mountebank their loves, Cog their hearts from them . . . . iii 2 133
Being once chafed, . . . then he speaks What's in his heart . . . iii 3 29
Remain with your uncertainty! Let every feeble rumour shake your hearts! . . . . iii 3 125
With precepts that would make invincible The heart that conn'd them. iv 1 11
It would unclog my heart Of what lies heavy to't . . . . . iv 2 47
The nobles receive so to heart the banishment of that worthy Coriolanus iv 3 22
Friends now fast sworn, Whose double bosoms seem to wear one heart. iv 4 13
A heart of wreak in thee, that wilt revenge Thine own particular wrongs iv 5 91
Each word thou hast spoke hath weeded from my heart A root of ancient envy. . . . . iv 5 108
More dances my rapt heart Than when I first my wedded mistress saw iv 5 122
This last old man, Whom with a crack'd heart I have sent to Rome v 3 9
Make our eyes flow with joy, hearts dance with comforts . . . v 3 99
Pages blush'd at him and men of heart Look'd wondering each at other v 6 99
Measureless liar, thou hast made my heart Too great for what contains it v 6 103
Reserved The cordial of mine age to glad my heart . . . *T. Andron.* i 1 166
Would thou wert shipp'd to hell, Rather than rob me of the people's hearts! . . . . i 1 207
Content thee, prince; I will restore to thee The people's hearts . . i 1 211
I make my empress, Rome's royal mistress, mistress of my heart . . i 1 241
These words are razors to my wounded heart . . . . . . i 1 314
Nor with sour looks afflict his gentle heart . . . . . . i 1 441
And cheer the heart That dies in tempest of thy angry frown . . i 1 457
I will not be denied: sweet heart, look back . . . . . i 1 481
Arm thy heart, and fit thy thoughts, To mount aloft . . . . ii 1 12
Vengeance is in my heart, death in my hand . . . . . ii 3 38
But be your heart to them As unrelenting flint to drops of rain . ii 3 140
O, be to me, though thy hard heart say no, Nothing so kind, but something pitiful! . . . . ii 3 155
Ne'er let my heart know merry cheer indeed, Till all the Andronici be made away . . . . ii 3 188
With the dismall'st object hurt That ever eye with sight made heart lament! . . . . ii 3 205
My heart suspects more than mine eye can see . . . . . ii 3 213
My compassionate heart Will not permit mine eyes once to behold The thing whereat it trembles by surmise . . . . ii 3 217
Shall I speak for thee? shall I say 'tis so? O, that I knew thy heart! . ii 4 34
Sorrow conceal'd, like an oven stopp'd, Doth burn the heart to cinders ii 4 37
In the dust I write My heart's deep languor and my soul's sad tears iii 1 13
Prepare thy aged eyes to weep; Or, if not so, thy noble heart to break iii 1 60
Wilt thou kneel with me? Do, then, dear heart; for heaven shall hear our prayers . . . . iii 1 211
Now let hot Ætna cool in Sicily, And be my heart an ever-burning hell! iii 1 243
Alas, poor heart, that kiss is comfortless As frozen water . . . iii 1 251
When my heart, all mad with misery, Beats in this hollow prison of my flesh . . . . iii 2 9
When thy poor heart beats with outrageous beating, Thou canst not strike it thus to make it still . . . . iii 2 13
Or get some little knife between thy teeth, And just against thy heart make thou a hole . . . . iii 2 17
Out on thee, murderer! thou kill'st my heart . . . . . . iii 2 54
Cursed be that heart that forced us to this shift! . . . . . iv 1 72
That hath more scars of sorrow in his heart Than foemen's marks upon his batter'd shield . . . . iv 1 126
Fie, treacherous hue, that will betray with blushing The close enacts and counsels of the heart! . . . . iv 2 118
Whose loss hath pierced him deep and scarr'd his heart . . . . iv 4 31
That, were his heart Almost impregnable, his old ears deaf, Yet should both ear and heart obey my tongue . . . . iv 4 97
And almost broke my heart with extreme laughter . . . . . v 1 113
Shall they stoop and kneel, And on them shalt thou ease thy angry heart v 2 119
That my tongue may utter forth The venomous malice of my swelling heart! . . . . v 3 13
We are beholding to you, good Andronicus.—An if your highness knew my heart, you were . . . . v 3 34
My heart is not compact of flint nor steel. . . . . v 3 88
Your hearts will throb and weep to hear him speak . . . . . v 3 95
Even with all my heart Would I were dead, so you did live again! . v 3 172
I rather weep.—Good heart, at what?—At thy good heart's oppression.—Why, such is love's transgression . . . . . *Rom. and Jul.* i 1 190
Get her heart, My will to her consent is but a part . . . . . i 2 16
Let wantons light of heart Tickle the senseless rushes with their heels i 4 35
Did my heart love till now? forswear it, sight! . . . . . . i 5 54
You must contrary me! marry, 'tis time. Well said, my hearts! . . i 5 88
For shame! I'll make you quiet. What, cheerly, my hearts! . . . i 5 90
Can I go forward when my heart is here? Turn back, dull earth . . ii 1 1
As sweet repose and rest Come to thy heart as that within my breast! . ii 2 124
Being tasted, slays all senses with the heart . . . . . . ii 3 26
Young men's love then lies Not truly in their hearts, but in their eyes . ii 3 68
The very pin of his heart cleft with the blind bow-boy's butt-shaft . ii 4 16
O, break, my heart! poor bankrupt, break at once! . . . . . iii 2 57
O serpent heart, hid with a flowering face! . . . . iii 2 73
How hast thou the heart, Being a divine, a ghostly confessor? . . . iii 3 48
God pardon him! I do, with all my heart; And yet no man like he doth grieve my heart . . . . iii 5 83
Is my poor heart so for a kinsman vex'd . . . . iii 5 96
O, how my heart abhors To hear him named, and cannot come to him! . iii 5 100
Thursday is near; lay hand on heart, advise . . . . . . iii 5 192
Beshrew my very heart, I think you are happy in this second match . iii 5 223
Speakest thou from thy heart?—And from my soul too . . . . iii 5 228
God join'd my heart and Romeo's, thou our hands; And ere this hand, by thee to Romeo seal'd, Shall be the label to another deed, Or my true heart with treacherous revolt Turn to another, this shall slay them both . . . . iv 1 55
My heart is wondrous light, Since this same wayward girl is so reclaim'd iv 2 46
My heart is full of woe: O, play me some merry dump, to comfort me . iv 5 107
When griping grief the heart doth wound . . . . iv 5 128

Heart. Properties to his love and tendance All sorts of hearts *T. of Athens* i 1 58
What wouldst do then, Apemantus?—E'en as Apemantus does now; hate a lord with my heart . . . . i 1 237
He outgoes The very heart of kindness . . . . i 1 286
In grateful virtue I am bound To your free heart . . . . . . i 2 6
My lord, in heart; and let the health go round.—Let it flow this way . i 2 54
Much good dich thy good heart, Apemantus! . . . . i 2 73
Your heart's in the field now.—My heart is ever at your service . . i 2 74
That you would once use our hearts, whereby we might express some part of our zeals . . . . i 2 88
How had you been my friends else? why have you that charitable title from thousands, did not you chiefly belong to my heart? . . . i 2 96
What a beggar his heart is, Being of no power to make his wishes good i 2 201
I take all and your several visitations So kind to heart . . . . i 2 225
Methinks, false hearts should never have sound legs . . . . i 2 240
What heart, head, sword, force, means, but is Lord Timon's? . . . ii 2 176
Sermon me no further: No villanous bounty yet hath pass'd my heart . ii 2 182
To think I shall lack friends? Secure thy heart . . . . . ii 2 185
And try the argument of hearts by borrowing . . . . . . ii 2 187
Has friendship such a faint and milky heart, It turns in less than two nights? . . . . iii 1 57
The best half should have return'd to him, So much I love his heart . iii 2 92
I wait for money.—It is against my heart . . . . iii 4 21
The place which I have feasted, does it now, Like all mankind, show me an iron heart? . . . . iii 4 84
Cut my heart in sums.—Mine, fifty talents.—Tell out my blood . . iii 4 93
And ne'er prefer his injuries to his heart, To bring it into danger . iii 5 34
I'll cheer up My discontented troops, and lay for hearts . . . iii 5 115
Yet do our hearts wear Timon's livery; That see I by our faces . . iv 2 17
Brought low by his own heart, Undone by goodness! . . . . . iv 2 37
The canker gnaw thy heart, For showing me again the eyes of man! . iv 3 49
The mouths, the tongues, the eyes and hearts of men At duty . . iv 3 261
O thou touch of hearts [gold]! Think, thy slave man rebels . . . iv 3 390
Lend me a fool's heart and a woman's eyes, And I'll beweep these comforts . . . . v 1 160
Shame that they wanted cunning, in excess Hath broke their hearts . v 4 29
So thou wilt send thy gentle heart before, To say thou'lt enter friendly v 4 48
You worse than senseless things! O you hard hearts! . . *J. Cæsar* i 1 41
We did buffet it With lusty sinews, throwing it aside And stemming it with hearts of controversy . . . . i 2 109
Cried 'Alas, good soul!' and forgave him with all their hearts . . . i 2 276
He sits high in all the people's hearts . . . . i 3 157
Let our hearts, as subtle masters do, Stir up their servants . . . ii 1 175
As dear to me as are the ruddy drops That visit my sad heart . . . ii 1 290
By and by thy bosom shall partake The secrets of my heart . . . ii 1 306
Set on your foot, And with a heart new-fired I follow you . . . ii 1 332
They could not find a heart within the beast . . . . . . ii 2 40
Cæsar should be a beast without a heart, If he should stay at home to-day ii 2 42
That every like is not the same, O Cæsar, The heart of Brutus yearns to think upon! . . . . ii 2 129
My heart laments that virtue cannot live Out of the teeth of emulation ii 3 13
Be strong upon my side, Set a huge mountain 'tween my heart and tongue! . . . . ii 4 7
Ay me, how weak a thing The heart of woman is! . . . . . ii 4 40
Metellus Cimber throws before thy seat An humble heart . . . . iii 1 35
We will grace his heels With the most boldest and best hearts of Rome iii 1 121
Our hearts you see not; they are pitiful . . . . iii 1 169
Our hearts Of brothers' temper do receive you in With all kind love . iii 1 174
O world, thou wast the forest to this hart; And this, indeed, O world, the heart of thee . . . . iii 1 208
Thy heart is big, get thee apart and weep. Passion, I see, is catching iii 1 282
Bear with me; My heart is in the coffin there with Cæsar . . . iii 2 111
O masters, if I were disposed to stir Your hearts and minds to mutiny. iii 2 127
Ingratitude, more strong than traitors' arms, Quite vanquish'd him: then burst his mighty heart . . . . iii 2 190
I come not, friends, to steal away your hearts: I am no orator . . iii 2 220
Pluck but his name out of his heart, and turn him going . . . . iii 3 38
Some that smile have in their hearts, I fear, Millions of mischiefs . . iv 1 50
Must I endure all this?—All this! ay, more: fret till your proud heart break . . . . iv 3 42
I had rather coin my heart, And drop my blood for drachmas . . iv 3 72
Brutus hath rived my heart: A friend should bear his friend's infirmities iv 3 85
A heart Dearer than Plutus' mine, richer than gold . . . . . iv 3 101
I, that denied thee gold, will give my heart . . . . iv 3 104
Do you confess so much? Give me your hand.—And my heart too . . iv 3 118
My heart is thirsty for that noble pledge . . . . iv 3 160
Now I have taken heart thou vanishest . . . . iv 3 288
Witness the hole you made in Cæsar's heart, Crying 'Long live!' . . v 1 31
He lies not like the living. O my heart! . . . . v 3 58
This is a Roman's part: Come, Cassius' sword, and find Titinius' heart v 3 90
My heart doth joy that yet in all my life I found no man but he was true to me . . . . v 5 34
My seated heart knock at my ribs, Against the use of nature. *Macbeth* i 3 136
Let us speak Our free hearts each to other . . . . i 3 155
Let me infold thee And hold thee to my heart . . . . . . i 4 32
Lay it to thy heart, and farewell . . . . i 5 15
False face must hide what the false heart doth know . . . . . i 7 82
My hands are of your colour; but I shame To wear a heart so white . ii 2 65
O horror, horror, horror! Tongue nor heart Cannot conceive nor name thee! . . . . ii 3 69
Who could refrain, That had a heart to love, and in that heart Courage to make's love known? . . . . ii 3 123
Takes your enemy off, Grapples you to the heart and love of us . . iii 1 106
Make our faces vizards to our hearts, Disguising what they are . . iii 2 34
My heart speaks they are welcome.—See, they encounter thee with their hearts' thanks . . . . iii 4 8
'Twould have anger'd any heart alive To hear the men deny't . . . iii 6 15
My heart Throbs to know one thing: tell me, if your art Can tell so much iv 1 100
Show his eyes, and grieve his heart; Come like shadows, so depart! . iv 1 110
The very firstlings of my heart shall be The firstlings of my hand . . iv 1 147
The grief that does not speak Whispers the o'er-fraught heart . . iv 3 210
Let grief Convert to anger; blunt not the heart, enrage it . . . iv 3 229
What a sigh is there! The heart is sorely charged . . . . . v 1 59
I would not have such a heart in my bosom for the dignity of the whole body . . . . v 1 61
The heart I bear Shall never sag with doubt nor shake with fear . . v 3 9
Seyton!—I am sick at heart, When I behold—Seyton, I say! . . . v 3 19
Which the poor heart would fain deny, and dare not . . . . . v 3 28
Cleanse the stuff'd bosom of that perilous stuff Which weighs upon the heart . . . . v 3 45

Heart. None serve with him but constrained things Whose hearts are absent too *Macbeth* v 4 14
For this relief much thanks; 'tis bitter cold, And I am sick at heart *Ham.* i 1 9
And that it us befitted To bear our hearts in grief i 2 3
The head is not more native to the heart i 2 47
It shows a will most incorrect to heaven, A heart unfortified i 2 96
Why should we in our peevish opposition Take it to heart? i 2 101
This gentle and unforced accord of Hamlet Sits smiling to my heart i 2 124
It cannot come to good: But break, my heart; for I must hold my tongue i 2 159
Or lose your heart, or your chaste treasure open i 3 31
I shall the effect of this good lesson keep, As watchman to my heart i 3 46
Hold, hold, my heart; And you, my sinews, grow not instant old i 5 93
How say you, then; would heart of man once think it? i 5 121
Or given my heart a winking, mute and dumb ii 2 137
Unpack my heart with words, And fall a-cursing ii 2 614
Variable objects shall expel This something-settled matter in his heart iii 1 181
Since love our hearts and Hymen did our hands Unite commutual iii 2 169
You would pluck out the heart of my mystery iii 2 382
O heart, lose not thy nature; let not ever The soul of Nero enter this firm bosom iii 2 411
Bow, stubborn knees; and, heart with strings of steel, Be soft as sinews of the new-born babe! iii 3 70
Let me wring your heart; for so I shall, If it be made of penetrable stuff iii 4 35
Thou hast cleft my heart in twain.—O, throw away the worser part iii 4 156
Hems, and beats her heart; Spurns enviously at straws iv 5 5
You must put me in your heart for friend iv 7 2
It warms the very sickness in my heart, That I shall live and tell him iv 7 56
Or are you like the painting of a sorrow, A face without a heart? iv 7 110
In my heart there was a kind of fighting, That would not let me sleep v 2 4
Thou wouldst not think how ill all's here about my heart v 2 223
If thou didst ever hold me in thy heart, Absent thee from felicity awhile v 2 357
Now cracks a noble heart. Good night, sweet prince v 2 370
In my true heart I find she names my very deed of love *Lear* i 1 72
Unhappy that I am, I cannot heave My heart into my mouth i 1 94
But goes thy heart with this?—Ay, good my lord.—So young, and so untender? i 1 107
And as a stranger to my heart and me Hold thee, from this, for ever i 1 117
So be my grave my peace, as here I give Her father's heart from her! i 1 128
Let it fall rather, though the fork invade The region of my heart i 1 147
Had he a hand to write this? a heart and brain to breed it in? i 2 60
It is his hand, my lord; but I hope his heart is not in the contents i 2 73
And shake in pieces the heart of his obedience i 2 92
Drew from my heart all love, And added to the gall i 4 291
Let me still take away the harms I fear, Not fear still to be taken: I know his heart i 4 353
O, madam, my old heart is crack'd, is crack'd! ii 1 92
O, how this mother swells up toward my heart! ii 4 56
O me, my heart, my rising heart! but, down! ii 4 122
Struck me with her tongue, Most serpent-like, upon the very heart ii 4 163
If it be you that stir these daughters' hearts Against their father, fool me not so much To bear it tamely ii 4 277
This heart Shall break into a hundred thousand flaws, Or ere I'll weep ii 4 287
The man that makes his toe What he his heart should make Shall of a corn cry woe iii 2 32
I have one part in my heart That's sorry yet for thee iii 2 72
Wilt break my heart?—I had rather break mine own iii 4 4
Your old kind father, whose frank heart gave all,—O, that way madness lies iii 4 20
Proud of heart, to ride on a bay trotting-horse over four-inched bridges iii 4 56
Set not thy sweet heart on proud array iii 4 85
A serving-man, proud in heart and mind; that curled my hair iii 4 87
Served the lust of my mistress' heart, and did the act of darkness iii 4 89
False of heart, light of ear, bloody of hand: hog in sloth iii 4 95
Let not the creaking of shoes nor the rustling of silks betray thy poor heart to woman iii 4 99
Like an old lecher's heart; a small spark, all the rest on's body cold iii 4 117
In the fury of his heart, when the foul fiend rages, eats cow-dung for sallets iii 4 136
Whose warp'd looks proclaim What store her heart is made on iii 6 57
Then let them anatomize Regan; see what breeds about her heart iii 6 81
Is there any cause in nature that makes these hard hearts? iii 6 82
Came from one that's of a neutral heart, And not from one opposed iii 7 48
Yet, poor old heart, he holp the heavens to rain iii 7 62
She heaved the name of 'father' Pantingly forth, as if it press'd her heart iv 3 28
Where he arrives he moves All hearts against us iv 5 11
I would not take this from report; it is, And my heart breaks at it iv 6 145
To know our enemies' minds, we'ld rip their hearts iv 6 265
I'll prove it on thy heart, Ere I taste bread v 3 93
If my speech offend a noble heart, Thy arm may do thee justice v 3 127
Despite thy victor sword and fire-new fortune, Thy valour and thy heart, thou art a traitor v 3 133
My best spirits are bent To prove upon thy heart, whereto I speak v 3 140
With the hell-hated lie o'erwhelm thy heart v 3 147
Let sorrow split my heart, if ever I Did hate thee or thy father! v 3 177
List a brief tale; And when 'tis told, O, that my heart would burst! v 3 182
But his flaw'd heart, Alack, too weak the conflict to support! 'Twixt two extremes of passion, joy and grief, Burst smilingly v 3 196
What means that bloody knife?—'Tis hot, it smokes; It came even from the heart of—O, she's dead! v 3 224
Break, heart; I prithee, break! v 3 312
Who, trimm'd in forms and visages of duty, Keep yet their hearts attending on themselves *Othello* i 1 51
When my outward action doth demonstrate The native act and figure of my heart In compliment extern, 'tis not long after But I will wear my heart upon my sleeve For daws to peck at i 1 62
Your heart is burst, you have lost half your soul i 1 87
Found good means To draw from her a prayer of earnest heart i 3 152
I here do give thee that with all my heart Which, but thou hast already, with all my heart I would keep from thee i 3 193
I never yet did hear That the bruised heart was pierced through the ear i 3 219
My heart's subdued Even to the very quality of my lord i 3 251
What say'st thou, noble heart?—What will I do, thinkest thou? i 3 303
She puts her tongue a little in her heart, And chides with thinking ii 1 107
This, and this, the greatest discords be That e'er our hearts shall make! ii 1 201
Let not thy discreet heart think it ii 1 227
In a town of war, Yet wild, the people's hearts brimful of fear ii 3 214
Close delations, working from the heart That passion cannot rule iii 3 123
I'll know thy thoughts.—You cannot, if my heart were in your hand iii 3 163

Heart. The execution of his wit, hands, heart, To wrong'd Othello's service! *Othello* iii 3 466
This argues fruitfulness and liberal heart: Hot, hot, and moist iii 4 38
'Tis a good hand, A frank one.—You may, indeed, say so; For 'twas that hand that gave away my heart iii 4 45
The hearts of old gave hands; But our new heraldry is hands, not hearts iii 4 46
It was dyed in mummy which the skilful Conserved of maidens' hearts iii 4 75
Whom I with all the office of my heart Entirely honour iii 4 113
No, my heart is turned to stone; I strike it, and it hurts my hand iv 1 193
But there, where I have garner'd up my heart, Where either I must live, or bear no life iv 2 57
Thrown such despite and heavy terms upon her, As true hearts cannot bear iv 2 117
Forth of my heart those charms, thine eyes, are blotted v 1 35
Thou dost stone my heart, And makest me call what I intend to do A murder v 2 63
He lies to the heart: She was too fond of her most filthy bargain v 2 156
Speak, for my heart is full.—I told him what I thought, and told no more v 2 175
This did I fear, but thought he had no weapon; For he was great of heart v 2 361
To the state This heavy act with heavy heart relate v 2 371
His captain's heart, Which in the scuffles of great fights hath burst The buckles on his breast *Ant. and Cleo.* i 1 6
I would I had thy inches; thou shouldst know There were a heart in Egypt i 3 41
But my full heart Remains in use with you i 3 43
Creeps apace Into the hearts of such as have not thrived i 3 51
'Tis sweating labour To bear such idleness so near the heart i 3 94
His speech sticks in my heart.—Mine ear must pluck it thence i 5 41
Cæsar gets money where He loses hearts: Lepidus flatters both ii 1 14
To make you brothers, and to knit your hearts With an unslipping knot ii 2 128
The heart of brothers govern in our loves And sway our great designs! ii 2 150
Let her live To join our kingdoms and our hearts ii 2 154
Welcome from Egypt, sir.—Half the heart of Cæsar, worthy Mecænas! ii 2 175
When she first met Mark Antony, she pursed up his heart ii 2 192
And for his ordinary pays his heart For what his eyes eat only ii 2 230
If beauty, wisdom, modesty, can settle The heart of Antony ii 2 247
In my bosom shall she never come, To make my heart her vassal ii 6 57
Never a fair woman has a true face.—No slander; they steal hearts ii 6 106
Hearts, tongues, figures, scribes, bards, poets, cannot Think, speak, cast iii 2 16
So, the gods keep you, And make the hearts of Romans serve your ends! iii 2 37
Her tongue will not obey her heart, nor can Her heart inform her tongue iii 2 48
Command what cost Your heart has mind to iii 4 38
Ay me, most wretched, That have my heart parted betwixt two friends! iii 6 77
Cheer your heart: Be you not troubled with the time iii 6 81
Welcome, dear madam. Each heart in Rome does love and pity you iii 6 92
Take from his heart, take from his brain, from's time, What should not then be spared iii 7 12
Thou knew'st too well My heart was to thy rudder tied by the strings iii 11 57
Your hand; this kingly seal And plighter of high hearts iii 13 126
If I be so, From my cold heart let heaven engender hail iii 13 159
Where hast thou been, my heart? iii 13 172
A diminution in our captain's brain Restores his heart iii 13 199
Know, my hearts, I hope well of to-morrow iv 2 41
What's this for?—Ah, let be, let be! thou art The armourer of my heart iv 4 7
This blows my heart: If swift thought break it not, a swifter mean Shall outstrike thought iv 6 34
Leap thou, attire and all, Through proof of harness to my heart, and there Ride on the pants triumphing! iv 8 15
Throw my heart Against the flint and hardness of my fault iv 9 15
Thou Hast sold me to this novice; and my heart Makes only wars on thee iv 12 14
The hearts That spaniel'd me at heels, to whom I gave Their wishes iv 12 20
Hath, at fast and loose, Beguiled me to the very heart of loss iv 12 29
Whose heart I thought I had, for she had mine; Which whilst it was mine had annex'd unto't A million more, now lost iv 14 16
The name of Antony; it was divided Between her heart and lips iv 14 33
The seven-fold shield of Ajax cannot keep The battery from my heart iv 14 39
Heart, once be stronger than thy continent, Crack thy frail case! iv 14 40
Our lamp is spent, it's out! Good sirs, take heart iv 15 85
That self hand, Which writ his honour in the acts it did, Hath, with the courage which the heart did lend it, Splitted the heart v 1 24
Let me lament, With tears as sovereign as the blood of hearts v 1 41
The arm of mine own body, and the heart Where mine his thoughts did kindle v 1 45
Bid her have good heart: She soon shall know of us v 1 56
I do feel, By the rebound of yours, a grief that smites My very heart at root v 2 105
All Is outward sorrow; though I think the king Be touch'd at very heart.—None but the king? *Cymbeline* i 1 10
Not a courtier . . . Hath a heart that is not Glad at the thing they scowl at i 1 14
This diamond was my mother's: take it, heart i 1 112
Your highness Shall from this practice but make hard your heart i 5 24
Even the very middle of my heart Is warm'd by the rest i 6 27
Your cause doth strike my heart With pity, that doth make me sick i 6 118
As I have such a heart that both mine ears Must not in haste abuse i 6 130
He enchants societies into him; Half all men's hearts are his i 6 168
Cannot take two from twenty, for his heart, And leave eighteen ii 1 60
Learn now, for all, That I, which know my heart, do here pronounce, By the very truth of it, I care not for you ii 3 112
Let her beauty Look through a casement to allure false hearts ii 4 34
Take it, and hit The innocent mansion of my love, my heart iii 4 70
Come, here's my heart. Something's afore't. Soft, soft! we'll no defence iii 4 80
Corrupters of my faith! you shall no more Be stomachers to my heart iii 4 86
Exposing it—but, O, the harder heart! Alack, no remedy! iii 4 164
I'll have this secret from thy heart, or rip Thy heart to find it iii 5 86
The bitterness of it I now belch from my heart iii 5 138
Have not I An arm as big as thine? a heart as big? iv 2 77
Pisanio might have kill'd thee at the heart, And left this head on iv 2 322
Having found the back-door open Of the unguarded hearts v 3 46
To taint his nobler heart and brain With needless jealousy v 4 65
Woe is my heart That the poor soldier . . . cannot be found v 5 2
To you, the liver, heart and brain of Britain v 5 14
Nor my heart, That thought her like her seeming v 5 64
Sufficeth A Roman with a Roman's heart can suffer v 5 81
That paragon, thy daughter,—For whom my heart drops blood v 5 148
Till Pericles be dead, My heart can lend no succour to my head *Pericles* i 1 171

Heart. It grieved my heart to hear what pitiful cries they made to us to help them . . . . *Pericles* ii 1 22
That neither in our hearts nor outward eyes Envy the great . . ii 3 25
Thou hast a heart That even cracks for woe! . . . . . iii 2 76
You, and your lady, Take from my heart all thankfulness! . . iii 3 4
All the grace, Which makes her both the heart and place Of general wonder . . . . iv Gower 10
I love the king your father, and yourself, With more than foreign heart iv 1 34
You are well favour'd, and your looks foreshow You have a gentle heart iv 1 87
My heart Leaps to be gone into my mother's bosom . . . v 3 44
Beshrew my heart . . . . *M. N. Dream* v 1 295; *W. Tale* i 2 281
Beshrew thy (your) heart 2 *Hen. IV.* ii 3; v 3; *Troi. and Cres.* iv 2; *Rom. and Jul.* ii 5
Do a man's heart good *M. N. Dream* i 2; 2 *Hen. IV.* iii 2; *Troi. and Cres.* i 2
With all my heart *Mer. Wives* iii 1; iii 3; *Com. of Errors* v 1; *M. N. Dream* iii 2; *Mer. of Venice* iii 2; iii 4; iv 1; *As Y. Like It* iii 2; iii 5; *T. of Shrew* Ind. 1; iv 4; *All's Well* ii 3; iii 6; *K. John* iv 2; 1 *Hen. IV.* iii 1; v 5; 1 *Hen. VI.* ii 3; *Richard III.* i 2; iii 1; iii 2; iii 4; iv 4; *Troi. and Cres.* iii 3; *T. Andron.* iii 1; *T. of Athens* iii 6; *Hamlet* iii 1; *Lear* iv 6; *Othello* iv 1; v 2; *Cymbeline* i 4; ii 4; v 5; *Pericles* v 1
Heart-ache. And by a sleep to say we end The heart-ache . *Hamlet* iii 1 62
Heart-blood. Which no balm can cure but his heart-blood . *Richard II.* i 1 172
Snakes, in my heart-blood warm'd, that sting my heart! . . . iii 2 131
And will maintain what thou hast said is false In thy heart-blood . . iv 1 28
Thy heart-blood I will have for this day's work . . 1 *Hen. VI.* i 3 83
My sword be stain'd With heart-blood of the house of Lancaster 2 *Hen. VI.* ii 2 66
Thou wouldst have left thy dearest heart-blood there . . 3 *Hen. VI.* i 1 223
The mortal Venus, the heart-blood of beauty . . *Troi. and Cres.* iii 1 34
Heart-break. But 'tis no matter; better a little chiding than a great deal of heart-break . . . . *Mer. Wives* v 3 11
Heart-breaking. It is a heart-breaking to see a handsome man loose-wived . . . . *Ant. and Cleo.* i 2 74
Heart-burned. I never can see him but I am heart-burned an hour after *Much Ado* ii 1 4
So should I be sure to be heart-burned . . . . . 1 *Hen. IV.* iii 3 59
Heart-burning. Thine, in all compliments of devoted and heart-burning heat of duty . . . . *L. L. Lost* i 1 280
Heart can think. Yet all our joints are whole.—As heart can think 1 *Hen. IV.* iv 1 84
Fouler than heart can think thee, thou canst make No excuse *Richard III.* i 2 83
As black defiance As heart can think or courage execute *Troi. and Cres.* iv 1 13
Heart can wish. As good as heart can wish . . . 2 *Hen. IV.* i 1 13
Be as free as heart can wish or tongue can tell . . . 2 *Hen. VI.* iv 7 133
Heart-grief. A subject That sits in heart-grief and uneasiness *Hen. V.* ii 2 27
Heart-hardening. Oft beheld Heart-hardening spectacles *Coriolanus* iv 1 25
Heart-heaviness. By so much the more shall I to-morrow be at the height of heart-heaviness . . . . *As Y. Like It* v 2 50
Heart of elder. What says my Æsculapius? my Galen? my heart of elder? . . . . *Mer. Wives* ii 3 30
Heart of France. Thy late exploits done in the heart of France 2 *Hen. VI.* i 1 196
Will he conduct you through the heart of France, And make the meanest of you earls and dukes? . . . . iv 8 38
His father revell'd in the heart of France, And tamed the king 3 *Hen. VI.* ii 2 150
Heart of gold. Gallants, lads, boys, hearts of gold . . 1 *Hen. IV.* ii 4 307
The king's a bawcock, and a heart of gold, A lad of life . . *Hen. V.* iv 1 44
Heart of heart. Give me that man That is not passion's slave, and I will wear him In my heart's core, ay, in my heart of heart *Hamlet* iii 2 78
Heart-offending groans Or blood-consuming sighs . . 2 *Hen. VI.* iii 2 60
Heart's content. I wish your ladyship all heart's content *Mer. of Venice* iii 4 42
Such is the fulness of my heart's content . . . . 2 *Hen. VI.* i 1 35
Though my heart's content firm love doth bear, Nothing of that shall from mine eyes appear. . . . . . . *Troi. and Cres.* i 2 320
Heart's core. I will wear him In my heart's core . . . *Hamlet* iii 2 78
Heart's dear. My heart's dear Harry . . . . . 2 *Hen. IV.* ii 3 12
If my heart's dear love— Well, do not swear . . *Rom. and Jul.* ii 2 115
My heart's dear love is set On the fair daughter of rich Capulet . ii 3 57
Heart's desire. God send every one their heart's desire! . *Much Ado* iii 4 61
Your heart's desires be with you! . . . . . . *As Y. Like It* i 2 211
Heart's discontent and sour affliction Be playfellows to keep you company! . . . . 2 *Hen. VI.* iii 2 301
Mine, full of sorrow and heart's discontent . . . 3 *Hen. VI.* iii 3 173
Heart's ease. What infinite heart's-ease Must kings neglect, that private men enjoy! . . . . *Hen. V.* iv 1 253
'Heart's ease, Heart's ease:' O, an you will have me live, play 'Heart's ease.'—Why 'Heart's ease'?—O, musicians, because my heart itself plays 'My heart is full of woe' . . . . . *Rom. and Jul.* iv 5 102
Such men as he be never at heart's ease Whiles they behold a greater than themselves . . . . *J. Cæsar* i 2 208
Heart's hope. Fortune now To my heart's hope! . . *Mer. of Venice* ii 9 20
Heart's love. A braver place In my heart's love hath no man than yourself . . . . 1 *Hen. IV.* iv 1 8
And with my hand I seal my true heart's love . . . *Richard III.* ii 1 10
To the Tower, On pure heart's love to greet the tender princes . . iv 1 4
And from my heart's love I do thank thee for it . . . . . iv 4 260
With pure heart's love, Immaculate devotion, holy thoughts . . iv 4 403
Heart's malice. Beaufort's red sparkling eyes blab his heart's malice 2 *Hen. VI.* iii 1 154
Heart's meteors. What observation madest thou in this case Of his heart's meteors tilting in his face? . . . . *Com. of Errors* iv 2 6
Heart's presages. If heart's presages be not vain, We three here part that ne'er shall meet again . . . . *Richard II.* ii 2 142
Heart's sorrow. Love hath chased sleep from my enthralled eyes And made them watchers of mine own heart's sorrow . *T. G. of Ver.* ii 4 135
Heart's table. To sit and draw His arched brows, his hawking eye, his curls, In our heart's table . . . . *All's Well* i 1 106
Hearts' thanks. They encounter thee with their hearts' thanks *Macbeth* iii 4 9
Heart's truth. If you knew his pure heart's truth . *T. G. of Ver.* iv 2 88
Heart-sick. Unless the breath of heart-sick groans, Mist-like, infold me from the search of eyes . . . . *Rom. and Jul.* iii 3 72
I am sick still; heart-sick . . . . *Cymbeline* iv 2 37
Heart-sore. Where scorn is bought with groans; Coy looks with heart-sore sighs . . . . *T. G. of Ver.* i 1 30
With penitential groans, With nightly tears and daily heart-sore sighs . ii 4 132
Heart-sorrow. Nothing but heart-sorrow And a clear life ensuing *Tempest* iii 3 81
Heart-sorrowing. You cloudy princes and heart-sorrowing peers, That bear this mutual heavy load of moan . . . . *Richard III.* ii 2 112
Heart-string. So false that he grieves my very heart-strings *T. G. of Ver.* iv 2 62
I kiss his dirty shoe, and from heart-string I love the lovely bully *Hen. V.* iv 1 47
Heart-string. Harp on it still shall I till heart-strings break *Richard III.* iv 4 365
Though that her jesses were my dear heart-strings, I'ld whistle her off and let her down the wind, To prey at fortune . . . *Othello* iii 3 261
Heart-struck. Who is with him?—None but the fool; who labours to out-jest His heart-struck injuries . . . . . . *Lear* iii 1 17
Heart-whole. Cupid hath clapped him o' the shoulder, but I'll warrant him heart-whole . . . . *As Y. Like It* iv 1 49
Hearted. My cause is hearted; thine hath no less reason . *Othello* i 3 373
Yield up, O love, thy crown and hearted throne To tyrannous hate! . iii 3 448
I will be treble-sinew'd, hearted, breathed . . . *Ant. and Cleo.* iii 13 178
Hearten those that fight in your defence . . . 3 *Hen. VI.* ii 2 79
Hearth. Where fires thou find'st unrak'd and hearths unswept *Mer. Wives* v 5 48
Let me but stand; I will not hurt your hearth . . *Coriolanus* iv 5 27
This extremity Hath brought me to thy hearth . . . . iv 5 85
He came unto my hearth; Presented to my knife his throat . . . v 6 30
Heartily. I thank you, forsooth, heartily . . . . *Mer. Wives* i 1 277
I beseech you heartily, some of you go home with me to dinner . . iii 2 80
I pray you, pardon me; pray heartily, pardon me . . . . . iii 3 243
And he heartily prays some occasion may detain us longer . *Much Ado* i 1 151
For the which she wept heartily and said she cared not . . . v 1 175
I cry your worships mercy, heartily . . . . *M. N. Dream* iii 1 182
Beshrew me but I love her heartily; For she is wise *Mer. of Venice* ii 6 52
Most heartily I do beseech the court To give the judgement . . iv 1 243
I am heartily glad I came hither to you . . . *As Y. Like It* i 1 165
O, thou didst then ne'er love so heartily! . . . . . . ii 4 33
When a man thanks me heartily, methinks I have given him a penny . ii 5 28
Come, Kate, and wash, and welcome heartily . . . *T. of Shrew* iv 1 157
I am heartily sorry that he'll be glad of this . . . *All's Well* iv 3 74
Are not you grieved that Arthur is his prisoner?—As heartily as he is glad he hath him . . . . *K. John* iii 4 124
Heartily request The enfranchisement of Arthur . . . . iv 2 51
Most heartily I pray Your highness to assign our trial day . *Richard II.* i 1 150
Which I in sufferance heartily will rejoice . . . *Hen. V.* ii 2 159
I peseech you heartily, scurvy, lousy knave, at my desires . . v 1 23
Thou dost see I eat.—Much good do you, scauld knave, heartily . . v 1 55
We heartily solicit Your gracious self to take on you the charge *Rich. III.* iii 7 130
Commend me to him: Tell him the queen hath heartily consented . iv 5 17
I say, take heed; Yes, heartily beseech you.—Let him on *Hen. VIII.* i 2 176
Be what they will, I heartily forgive 'em . . . . . . ii 1 65
We had need pray, And heartily, for our deliverance . . . ii 2 46
And heartily entreats you take good comfort . . . . . iv 2 119
The fruit she goes with I pray for heartily, that it may find Good time. v 1 21
And desired your highness Most heartily to pray for her . . v 1 66
Ye have been too prodigal: I thank ye heartily . . . . v 5 14
We hope to find you our friend; and therefore give you our voices heartily . . . . *Coriolanus* ii 3 112
The gods give you joy, sir, heartily!—Most sweet voices! . . . ii 3 118
Heartily well met, and most glad of your company . . . . iv 3 53
And laugh'd so heartily, That both mine eyes were rainy *T. Andron.* v 1 116
Nothing grieves me heartily indeed But that I cannot do ten thousand more . . . . v 1 143
Will we show our duty.—We doubt it nothing: heartily farewell *Hamlet* i 2 41
I'm sorry they offend you, heartily; Yes, 'faith, heartily . . . i 5 135
I could heartily wish this had not befallen . . . *Othello* ii 3 303
What do you pity, sir?—Two creatures heartily . . . *Cymbeline* i 6 83
Heartiness. This entertainment May a free face put on, derive a liberty From heartiness . . . . *W. Tale* i 2 113
Heartless. Art thou drawn among these heartless hinds? *Rom. and Jul.* i 1 73
Heartlings. 'Od's heartlings, that's a pretty jest indeed! *Mer. Wives* iii 4 59
Hearty. To thee and thy company I bid A hearty welcome . *Tempest* v 1 111
If hearty sorrow Be a sufficient ransom for offence . *T. G. of Ver.* v 4 74
Mistress Page hath her hearty commendations to you too *Mer. Wives* ii 2 99
Many and hearty thankings to you both . . . . *Meas. for Meas.* v 1 4
In hearty prayers That your attempts may overlive the hazard 2 *Hen. IV.* iv 1 14
And, lords, accept this hearty kind embrace . . . 1 *Hen. VI.* iii 3 82
Sit down: at first And last the hearty welcome . . . *Macbeth* iii 4 2
Hearty thanks: The bounty and the benison of heaven To boot, and boot! . . . . *Lear* iv 6 228
My hearty friends, You take me in too dolorous a sense . *Ant. and Cleo.* iv. 2 38
Heat. Even as one heat another heat expels . . *T. G. of Ver.* ii 4 192
As a figure Trenched in ice, which with an hour's heat Dissolves to water . . . . iii 2 7
As subject to heat as butter; a man of continual dissolution *Mer. Wives* iii 5 117
Thou hast neither heat, affection, limb, nor beauty . *Meas. for Meas.* iii 1 37
Both in the heat of blood, And lack of temper'd judgement afterward . v 1 477
When I am cold, he heats me with beating . . . *Com. of Errors* iv 4 34
She knows the heat of a luxurious bed; Her blush is guiltiness *M. Ado* iv 1 42
In all compliments of devoted and heart-burning heat of duty *L. L. Lost* i 1 280
If this austere insociable life Change not your offer made in heat of blood . . . . v 2 810
And when this hail some heat from Hermia felt, So he dissolved *M. N. D.* i 1 244
And let my liver rather heat with wine Than my heart cool with mortifying groans . . . . *Mer. of Venice* i 1 81
Cold, indeed; and labour lost: Then, farewell, heat, and welcome, frost! . . . . ii 7 75
The element itself, till seven years' heat, Shall not behold her face *T. N.* i 1 26
One draught above heat makes him a fool; the second mads him . . i 5 140
You may ride's With one soft kiss a thousand furlongs ere With spur we heat an acre . . . . *W. Tale* i 2 96
If you can bring Tincture or lustre in her lip, her eye, Heat outwardly or breath within . . . . iii 2 207
A rage whose heat hath this condition, That nothing can allay *K. John* iii 1 341
Heat me these irons hot; and look thou stand Within the arras . iv 1 1
The iron of itself, though heat red-hot, Approaching near these eyes, would drink my tears . . . . iv 1 61
The instrument is cold And would not harm me.—I can heat it, boy . iv 1 105
Or wallow naked in December snow By thinking on fantastic summer's heat . . . . *Richard II.* i 3 299
In the very heat And pride of their contention . . 1 *Hen. IV.* i 1 59
Who struck this heat up after I was gone? . . . . . . i 3 139
It hath the excuse of youth and heat of blood . . . . . v 2 17
Took fire and heat away From the best-temper'd courage in his troops 2 *Hen. IV.* i 1 114
You do measure the heat of our livers with the bitterness of your galls i 2 198
He will drive you out of your revenge and turn all to a merriment, if you take not the heat . . . . ii 4 325
The heat is past; follow no further now . . . . . . iv 3 27
Like a rich armour worn in heat of day, That scalds with safety . . iv 5 30
Can sodden water, A drench for sur-rein'd jades, their barley-broth, Decoct their cold blood to such valiant heat? . . . *Hen. V.* iii 5 20

Heat. He's of the colour of the nutmeg.—And of the heat of the ginger *Hen. V.* iii 7 21
And to sun's parching heat display'd my cheeks . . 1 *Hen. VI.* i 2 77
In open field, In winter's cold and summer's parching heat . 2 *Hen. VI.* i 1 81
Nay, we shall heat you thoroughly anon.—Take heed, lest by your heat you burn yourselves . . . . v 1 160
Went all afoot in summer's scalding heat . . . 3 *Hen. VI.* v 7 18
Heat not a furnace for your foe so hot That it do singe yourself *Hen. VIII.* i 1 140
His virtues shining upon others Heat them and they retort that heat again To the first giver . . . . *Troi. and Cres.* iii 3 101
Or, like a gate of steel Fronting the sun, receives and renders back His figure and his heat . . . . iii 3 123
But he in heat of action Is more vindicative than jealous love . iv 5 106
I'll heat his blood with Greekish wine to-night, Which with my scimitar I'll cool to-morrow . . . . v 1 1
Not now.—Not in this heat, sir, now.—Now, as I live . *Coriolanus* iii 1 63
And hope to come upon them in the heat of their division . iv 3 19
Sit fas aut nefas, till I find the stream To cool this heat . *T. Andron.* ii 1 134
I have a faint cold fear thrills through my veins, That almost freezes up the heat of life . . . . . *Rom. and Jul.* iv 3 16
To see meat fill knaves and wine heat fools . . . *T. of Athens* i 2 271
Words to the heat of deeds too cold breath gives . . *Macbeth* ii 1 61
These blazes, daughter, Giving more light than heat, extinct in both *Ham.* i 3 118
Your grace hath screen'd and stood between Much heat and him . iii 4 4
Upon the heat and flame of thy distemper Sprinkle cool patience . iii 4 123
O heat, dry up my brains! tears seven times salt, Burn out the sense and virtue of mine eye! . . . . iv 5 154
We shall further think on't.—We must do something, and i' the heat *Lear* i 1 312
Till some little time hath qualified the heat of his displeasure . i 2 177
The best quarrels, in the heat, are cursed By those that feel their sharpness . . . . v 3 56
It is a business of some heat . . . . . . *Othello* i 2 40
Nor to comply with heat—the young affects In me defunct . . i 3 264
I know not where is that Promethean heat That can thy light relume . v 2 12
I had rather heat my liver with drinking . . . *Ant. and Cleo.* i 2 23
You'll heat my blood: no more.—You can do better yet; but this is meetly . . . . i 3 80
Fear no more the heat o' the sun, Nor the furious winter's rages *Cymb.* iv 2 258
But a spark, To which that blast gives heat and stronger glowing *Pericles* i 2 41
My veins are chill, And have no more of life than may suffice To give my tongue that heat to ask your help . . . . . . ii 1 79
Pray, walk softly, do not heat your blood . . . . . iv 1 49
Heated. Cooled my friends, heated mine enemies . . *Mer. of Venice* iii 1 60
That robb'd my soldiers of their heated spleen . . 3 *Hen. VI.* ii 1 124
Or bathed thy growing with our heated bloods . . . . ii 2 169
Your grace, I fear, with dancing is a little heated . . *Hen. VIII.* i 4 100
Heatest. Thou art quick in answers: thou heatest my blood . *L. L. Lost* i 2 32
Heath. For an acre of barren ground, long heath, brown furze, any thing *Tempest* i 1 72
Where the place?—Upon the heath . . . . . *Macbeth* i 1 6
Why Upon this blasted heath you stop our way With such prophetic greeting? . . . . i 3 77
Heathen. The heathen philosopher, when he had a desire to eat a grape, would open his lips . . . . . . *As Y. Like It* v 1 36
Yond gull Malvolio is turned heathen, a very renegado . *T. Night* iii 2 74
All clinquant, all in gold, like heathen gods . . . *Hen. VIII.* i 1 19
What, art a heathen? How dost thou understand the Scripture? *Hamlet* v 1 40
At Rhodes, at Cyprus and on other grounds Christian and heathen *Oth.* i 1 30
Heathenish. O villain!—Most heathenish and most gross! . . . v 2 313
Heating. The making of the cake, the heating of the oven *Troi. and Cres.* i 1 24
Heat-oppressed. A false creation, Proceeding from the heat-oppressed brain . . . . *Macbeth* ii 1 39
Heave. Do as I do? when didst thou see me heave up my leg? *T. G. of V.* iv 4 40
With a great heart heave away this storm . . . *K. John* v 2 55
Heave him away upon your winged thoughts Athwart the sea *Hen. V.* v Prol. 8
To heave the traitor Somerset from hence . . . . 2 *Hen. VI.* v 1 61
This shoulder was ordain'd so thick to heave; And heave it shall 3 *Hen. VI.* v 7 23
Or else to heaven she heaves them for revenge . . *T. Andron.* iii 1 40
There's matter in these sighs, these profound heaves . . *Hamlet* iv 1 1
Unhappy that I am, I cannot heave My heart into my mouth . *Lear* i 1 93
Begin to heave the gorge, disrelish and abhor . . . . *Othello* ii 1 236
I had as lief have a reed that will do me no service as a partisan I could not heave . . . . *Ant. and Cleo.* ii 7 15
Heaved. By foul play, as thou say'st, were we heaved thence . *Tempest* i 2 62
I escaped upon a butt of sack which the sailors heaved o'erboard . ii 2 127
The wretched animal heaved forth such groans . *As Y. Like It* ii 1 36
And, having both together heaved it up, We'll both together lift our heads to heaven . . . . 2 *Hen. VI.* i 2 13
And if mine arm be heaved in the air, Thy grave is digg'd already . iv 10 54
One heaved a-high, to be hurl'd down below . . . *Richard III.* iv 4 86
Once or twice she heaved the name of 'father' Pantingly forth . *Lear* iv 3 27
'Twas at a feast,—O, would Our viands had been poison'd, or at least Those which I heaved to head! . . . . . . *Cymbeline* v 5 157
Heaven. O the heavens! . . . . *Tempest* i 2 59; 116
Thou didst smile, Infused with a fortitude from heaven . . . i 2 154
Heavens thank you for't! . . . . i 2 175
My language! heavens! I am the best of them that speak this speech . i 2 428
Let's make further search For my poor son.—Heavens keep him from these beasts! . . . . ii 1 324
Hast thou not dropp'd from heaven?—Out o' the moon, I do assure thee . . . . ii 2 140
Do you love me?—O heaven, O earth, bear witness to this sound! . iii 1 68
Heavens rain grace On that which breeds between 'em! . . . iii 1 75
Give us kind keepers, heavens! . . . . iii 3 20
Here, afore Heaven, I ratify this my rich gift . . . . . iv 1 7
No sweet aspersion shall the heavens let fall To make this contract grow . . . . iv 1 18
O heavens, that they were living both in Naples, The king and queen there! . . . . v 1 149
And Silvia—witness Heaven, that made her fair!—Shows Julia but a swarthy Ethiope . . . . *T. G. of Ver.* ii 6 25
His heart as far from fraud as heaven from earth.—Pray heaven he prove so! . . . . ii 7 78
By heaven! my wrath shall far exceed the love I ever bore my daughter iii 1 166
The heaven such grace did lend her, That she might admired be . iv 2 42
A most unholy match, Which heaven and fortune still rewards with plagues . . . . iv 3 31
Yet so coldly As, heaven it knows, I would not have him speed . . iv 4 112
O, Heaven be judge how I love Valentine! . . . . . . v 4 36
Who by repentance is not satisfied Is nor of heaven nor earth . . v 4 80
Heaven. O heaven! were man But constant, he were perfect *T. G. of Ver.* v 4 110
Bear witness, Heaven, I have my wish for ever.—And I mine . v 4 119
O heaven! this is Mistress Anne Page . . . . *Mer. Wives* i 1 197
If there be no great love in the beginning, yet heaven may decrease it upon better acquaintance . . . . i 1 255
Well, heaven send Anne Page no worse fortune! . . . . i 4 33
Nor can do more than I do with her, I thank heaven . . . i 4 138
Your friend, I can tell you that by the way; I praise heaven for it . i 4 150
I was then frugal of my mirth: Heaven forgive me! . . . ii 1 28
Well, heaven forgive you and all of us, I pray! . . . . ii 2 57
Heaven prosper the right! What weapons is he? . . . . iii 1 30
Well, heaven knows how I love you; and you shall one day find it . iii 3 87
Pray heaven it be not so, that you have such a man here! . . iii 3 119
Heaven make you better than your thoughts! . . . . . iii 3 218
Heaven forgive my sins at the day of judgement!—By gar, nor I too . iii 3 226
May be he tells you true.—No, heaven so speed me in my time to come! iii 4 12
I ne'er made my will yet, I thank heaven; I am not such a sickly creature, I give heaven praise . . . . iii 4 61
There's for thy pains.—Now heaven send thee good fortune! . . iii 4 105
Heaven guide him to thy husband's cudgel, and the devil guide his cudgel afterwards! . . . . iv 2 90
Come, come, take it up.—Pray heaven it be not full of knight again . iv 2 115
I suspect without cause, mistress, do I?—Heaven be my witness you do iv 2 139
Sure, one of you does not serve heaven well, that you are so crossed . iv 5 130
Light and spirits will become it well. Heaven prosper our sport! . v 2 14
Alas, what noise?—Heaven forgive our sins!—What should this be? . v 5 35
Heavens defend me from that Welsh fairy, lest he transform me to a piece of cheese! . . . . v 5 85
In love the heavens themselves do guide the state . . . . v 5 245
Heaven give thee joy! What cannot be eschew'd must be embraced . v 5 250
Heaven give you many, many merry days! . . . . . . v 5 254
Heaven doth with us as we with torches do . . . *Meas. for Meas.* i 1 33
The heavens give safety to your purposes! . . . . . . i 1 74
Heaven grant us its peace, but not the King of Hungary's! . . i 2 4
Thus can the demigod Authority Make us pay down for our offence by weight The words of heaven . . . . i 2 126
Well, heaven forgive him! and forgive us all! . . . . . ii 1 37
My wife, sir, whom I detest before heaven and your honour,— How? thy wife?—Ay, sir; whom, I thank heaven, is an honest woman . ii 1 69
Heaven give thee moving graces! . . . . ii 2 36
O just but severe law! I had a brother, then. Heaven keep your honour! . . . . ii 2 42
You might pardon him, And neither heaven nor man grieve at the mercy . . . . ii 2 50
I would to heaven I had your potency! . . . . ii 2 67
Shall we serve heaven With less respect than we do minister To our gross selves? Good, good my lord, bethink you . . . . . ii 2 85
Every pelting, petty officer Would use his heaven for thunder . . ii 2 113
Merciful Heaven, Thou rather with thy sharp and sulphurous bolt Split'st the unwedgeable and gnarled oak Than the soft myrtle . ii 2 114
Plays such fantastic tricks before high heaven As make the angels weep ii 2 121
He's coming; I perceive't.—Pray heaven she win him! . . . ii 2 125
With such gifts that heaven shall share with you . . . . ii 2 147
True prayers That shall be up at heaven and enter there Ere sun-rise ii 2 152
Heaven keep your honour safe!—Amen: For I am that way going to temptation, Where prayers cross . . . . ii 2 157
Which sorrow is always toward ourselves, not heaven, Showing we would not spare heaven as we love it, But as we stand in fear . ii 3 32
I think and pray To several subjects. Heaven hath my empty words . ii 4 2
Heaven in my mouth, As if I did but only chew his name . . ii 4 4
O heavens! Why does my blood thus muster to my heart? . . . ii 4 19
Your brother cannot live.—Even so. Heaven keep your honour! . . ii 4 34
'Tis set down so in heaven, but not in earth . . . . . ii 4 50
That I do beg his life, if it be sin, Heaven let me bear it! . . ii 4 70
Women! Help Heaven! men their creation mar In profiting by them ii 4 127
Angelo, having affairs to heaven, Intends you for his swift ambassador iii 1 57
O heavens! it cannot be . . . . iii 1 99
What should I think? Heaven shield my mother play'd my father fair! iii 1 141
O heavens! what stuff is here? . . . . iii 2 5
You have paid the heavens your function . . . . . . iii 2 263
He who the sword of heaven will bear Should be as holy as severe . iii 2 275
Heaven give your spirits comfort! . . . . iv 2 73
'Tis an accident that heaven provides! Dispatch it presently . . iv 3 81
This nor hurts him nor profits you a jot; Forbear it therefore; give your cause to heaven . . . . iv 3 129
Pray heaven his wisdom be not tainted! . . . . iv 4 5
When you have A business for yourself, pray heaven you then Be perfect v 1 81
By heaven, fond wretch, thou know'st not what thou speak'st . v 1 105
Heaven shield your grace from woe, As I, thus wrong'd, hence unbelieved go! . . . . v 1 118
O heaven, the vanity of wretched fools! Give us some seats . . v 1 164
As there comes light from heaven and words from breath . . . v 1 225
For what obscured light the heavens did grant Did but convey unto our fearful minds A doubtful warrant of immediate death *Com. of Er.* i 1 67
Am I in earth, in heaven, or in hell? Sleeping or waking? . . ii 2 214
My sweet hope's aim, My sole earth's heaven and my heaven's claim . iii 2 64
And to thy state of darkness hie thee straight: I conjure thee by all the saints in heaven! . . . . iv 4 60
I never saw the chain, so help me Heaven! . . . . . . v 1 267
'Get you to heaven, Beatrice, get you to heaven; here's no place for you maids:' so deliver I up my apes, and away to Saint Peter for the heavens . . . . *Much Ado* ii 1 47
Study is like the heaven's glorious sun . . . . *L. L. Lost* i 1 84
A high hope for a low heaven: God grant us patience! . . . i 1 196
Ay, and, by heaven, one that will do the deed . . . . . iii 1 200
By heaven, that thou art fair, is most infallible . . . . iv 1 60
That handful of wit! Ah, heavens, it is a most pathetical wit! . iv 1 150
Like a jewel in the ear of caelo, the sky, the welkin, the heaven . iv 2 6
By heaven, I do love: and it hath taught me to rhyme and to be melancholy . . . . iv 3 13
Shot, by heaven! Proceed, sweet Cupid . . . . . . iv 3 22
More sacks to the mill! O heavens, I have my wish! Dumain transform'd . . . . iv 3 81
By heaven, the wonder in a mortal eye!—By earth, she is not, corporal iv 3 85
The sea will ebb and flow, heaven show his face . . . . iv 3 216
What peremptory eagle-sighted eye Dares look upon the heaven of her brow? . . . . iv 3 227
By heaven, thy love is black as ebony.—Is ebony like her? . . iv 3 247
And beauty's crest becomes the heavens well . . . . . iv 3 256
The voice of all the gods Make heaven drowsy with the harmony . iv 3 345

Heaven. O, an the heavens were so pleased that thou wert but my bastard! . . . . *L. L. Lost* v 1 78
Break off, break off.—By heaven, all dry-beaten with pure scoff! . . v 2 263
When we greet, With eyes best seeing, heaven's fiery eye . . . v 2 375
I never swore this lady such an oath.—By heaven, you did . . . v 2 452
The moon, like to a silver bow New-bent in heaven *M. N. Dream* i 1 11
Brief as the lightning in the collied night, That, in a spleen, unfolds both heaven and earth . . . . i 1 146
What graces in my love do dwell, That he hath turn'd a heaven unto a hell! i 1 207
And make a heaven of hell, To die upon the hand I love so well . ii 1 243
Heavens shield Lysander, if they mean a fray! . . . . . iii 2 447
The poet's eye, in a fine frenzy rolling, Doth glance from heaven to earth, from earth to heaven . . . . v 1 13
But sway'd and fashion'd by the hand of heaven . *Mer. of Venice* i 3 94
'For the heavens, rouse up a brave mind,' says the fiend, 'and run' . ii 2 12
O heavens, this is my true-begotten father! . . . . ii 2 36
Deceased, or, as you would say in plain terms, gone to heaven . . ii 2 68
If e'er the Jew her father come to heaven, It will be for his gentle daughter's sake . . . . ii 4 34
Whether I am yours?—Heaven and thy thoughts are witness that thou art ii 6 32
The watery kingdom, whose ambitious head Spits in the face of heaven ii 7 45
I have toward heaven breathed a secret vow To live in prayer . . iii 4 27
He tells me flatly, there is no mercy for me in heaven . . . . iii 5 35
Having such a blessing in his lady, He finds the joys of heaven here on earth; And if on earth he do not mean it, then In reason he should never come to heaven . . . . iii 5 81
You may as well forbid the mountain pines To wag their high tops and to make no noise, When they are fretten with the gusts of heaven . iv 1 77
The quality of mercy is not strain'd, It droppeth as the gentle rain from heaven Upon the place beneath . . . . iv 1 185
An oath, I have an oath in heaven: Shall I lay perjury upon my soul?. iv 1 228
I have a wife, whom, I protest, I love: I would she were in heaven iv 1 291
Look how the floor of heaven Is thick inlaid with patines of bright gold v 1 58
By heaven, I will ne'er come in your bed Until I see the ring . . v 1 190
Swear to keep this ring.—By heaven, it is the same I gave the doctor!. v 1 257
Fare you well: pray heaven I be deceived in you! . . *As Y. Like It* i 2 209
By this heaven, now at our sorrows pale . . . . i 3 106
Little recks to find the way to heaven By doing deeds of hospitality . ii 4 81
I give heaven thanks and make no boast of them . . . . . ii 5 37
Call me not fool till heaven hath sent me fortune . . . . . ii 7 19
Heaven Nature charged That one body should be fill'd With all graces. iii 2 149
Heaven would that she these gifts should have, And I to live and die her slave . . . . iii 2 161
Down on your knees, And thank heaven, fasting, for a good man's love iii 5 58
Then is there mirth in heaven, When earthly things made even Atone together . . . . v 4 114
Receive thy daughter: Hymen from heaven brought her . . . v 4 118
Heaven cease this idle humour in your honour! . . *T. of Shrew* Ind. 2 14
O heavens! Spake you not these words plain? . . . . . . i 2 39
What stars do spangle heaven with such beauty, As those two eyes become that heavenly face? . . . . iv 5 31
What heaven more will, That thee may furnish and my prayers pluck down, Fall on thy head! . . . . *All's Well* i 1 77
Heaven bless him! Farewell . . . . i 1 83
Our remedies oft in ourselves do lie, Which we ascribe to heaven . . i 1 232
I care no more for than I do for heaven, So I were not his sister . . i 3 170
I charge thee, As heaven shall work in me for thine avail, To tell me truly i 3 190
I confess, Here on my knee, before high heaven and you, That before you, and next unto high heaven, I love your son . . . . . . i 3 198
Shall for my legacy be sanctified By the luckiest stars in heaven . . i 3 252
By heaven, I'll steal away.—There's honour in the theft . . . ii 1 33
But most it is presumption in us when The help of heaven we count the act of men . . . . ii 1 155
Give consent; Of heaven, not me, make an experiment . . . . ii 1 157
But will you make it even?—Ay, by my sceptre and my hopes of heaven ii 1 195
He's of a most facinerious spirit that will not acknowledge it to be the —Very hand of heaven . . . . ii 3 37
Gentlemen, Heaven hath through me restored the king to health . . ii 3 70
We understand it, and thank heaven for you . . . . ii 3 71
She's very well indeed, but for two things.—What two things?—One, that she's not in heaven, whither God send her quickly! the other, that she's in earth . . . . ii 4 11
He cannot thrive, Unless her prayers, whom heaven delights to hear And loves to grant, reprieve him . . . . iii 4 27
A heaven on earth I have won by wooing thee.—For which live long to thank both heaven and me! . . . . iv 2 66
Made a groan of her last breath, and now she sings in heaven . . iv 3 63
Heaven aiding, And by the leave of my good lord the king . . . iv 4 12
Doubt not but heaven Hath brought me up to be your daughter's dower iv 4 18
O dear heaven, bless! Or, ere they meet, in me, O nature, cesse! . v 3 71
The heavens have thought well on thee . . . . v 3 150
I think his soul is in hell, madonna.—I know his soul is in heaven, fool.—The more fool, madonna, to mourn for your brother's soul being in heaven . . . . *T. Night* i 5 75
If the heavens had been pleased, would we have so ended! . . . ii 1 21
What years, i' faith?—About your years, my lord.—Too old, by heaven ii 4 30
Most excellent accomplished lady, the heavens rain odours on you! . iii 1 95
And some have greatness thrust upon them.—Heaven restore thee! . iii 4 51
O heavens themselves!—Come, sir, I pray you, go . . . . . iii 4 391
Thy wits the heavens restore! . . . . iv 2 103
And heavens so shine, That they may fairly note this act of mine! . iv 3 34
Here comes the countess: now heaven walks on earth . . . . v 1 100
Whom I know you love, And whom, by heaven I swear, I tender dearly v 1 129
The heavens continue their loves! . . . . *W. Tale* i 1 34
We should have answer'd heaven Boldly 'not guilty' . . . . . i 2 73
Plainly as heaven sees earth and earth sees heaven . . . . . i 2 315
Swear his thought over By each particular star in heaven . . . i 2 425
I must be patient till the heavens look With an aspect more favourable ii 1 106
The queen is spotless I' the eyes of heaven and to you . . . . ii 1 132
The heavens themselves Do strike at my injustice . . . . . iii 2 147
The heavens with that we have in hand are angry And frown upon's . iii 3 5
I never saw The heavens so dim by day. A savage clamour! . . . iii 3 56
And he, and more Than he, and men, the earth, the heavens, and all iv 4 382
There's no disjunction to be made, but by—As heavens forfend!—your ruin . . . . iv 4 541
Do as the heavens have done, forget your evil; With them forgive yourself v 1 5
'Tis your counsel My lord should to the heavens be contrary . . . v 1 45
I lost a couple, that 'twixt heaven and earth Might thus have stood . v 1 132
For which the heavens, taking angry note, Have left me issueless . . v 1 173
Your father's blest, As he from heaven merits it, with you . . . v 1 175

Heaven. The heaven sets spies upon us, will not have Our contract celebrated . . . . *W. Tale* v 1 203
Who, heavens directing, Is troth-plight to your daughter . . . v 3 150
Whispers in your ear, Which none but heaven and you and I shall hear *K. John* i 1 43
But for the certain knowledge of that truth I put you o'er to heaven and to my mother . . . . i 1 62
Heaven guard my mother's honour and my land! . . . . . . i 1 70
On my knee I give heaven thanks I was not like to thee! . . . i 1 83
Why, what a madcap hath heaven lent us here! . . . . . . i 1 84
Heaven lay not my transgression to my charge! . . . . . . i 1 256
The peace of heaven is theirs that lift their swords In such a just and charitable war . . . . ii 1 35
Bleed France, and peace ascend to heaven, Whiles we, God's wrathful agent, do correct Their proud contempt that beats His peace to heaven . . . . ii 1 86
His mother's shames Draws those heaven-moving pearls from his poor eyes, Which heaven shall take in nature of a fee . . . . . ii 1 170
With these crystal beads heaven shall be bribed To do him justice . ii 1 171
Thou monstrous slanderer of heaven and earth!—Thou monstrous injurer of heaven and earth! . . . . ii 1 173
Our cannons' malice vainly shall be spent Against the invulnerable clouds of heaven . . . . ii 1 252
By heaven, these scroyles of Angiers flout you, kings . . . . ii 1 373
And pell-mell Make work upon ourselves, for heaven or hell . . ii 1 407
By heaven, lady, you shall have no cause To curse the fair proceedings iii 1 96
Arm, arm, you heavens, against these perjured kings! A widow cries; be husband to me, heavens! . . . . iii 1 107
Hail, you anointed deputies of heaven! To thee, King John . . iii 1 136
But as we, under heaven, are supreme head, So under Him that great supremacy, Where we do reign, we will alone uphold . . . . iii 1 155
Heaven knows, they were besmear'd and overstain'd With slaughter's pencil . . . . iii 1 236
Play fast and loose with faith? so jest with heaven? . . . . iii 1 242
O, let thy vow, First made to heaven, first be to heaven perform'd . iii 1 266
Alter not the doom Forethought by heaven! . . . . iii 1 312
By heaven, Hubert, I am almost ashamed To say what good respect I have of thee . . . . iii 3 27
I had a thing to say, but let it go: The sun is in the heaven . . iii 3 34
Though that my death were adjunct to my act, By heaven, I would do it iii 3 58
I am not mad: I would to heaven I were! . . . . iii 4 48
You say That we shall see and know our friends in heaven . . iii 4 77
When I shall meet him in the court of heaven I shall not know him iii 4 87
Prodigies and signs, Abortives, presages and tongues of heaven . . iii 4 158
I would to heaven I were your son, so you would love me . . . iv 1 23
If heaven be pleased that you must use me ill, Why then you must iv 1 55
To lose your eyes.—O heaven, that there were but a mote in yours! . iv 1 92
The breath of heaven hath blown his spirit out And strew'd repentant ashes on his head . . . . iv 1 110
With taper-light To seek the beauteous eye of heaven to garnish, Is wasteful . . . . iv 2 15
When the last account 'twixt heaven and earth Is to be made . . iv 2 216
Heaven take my soul, and England keep my bones! . . . . . iv 3 10
Stand back, I say; By heaven, I think my sword's as sharp as yours . iv 3 82
The life, the right and truth of all this realm Is fled to heaven . . iv 3 145
And heaven itself doth frown upon the land . . . . iv 3 159
But, heaven be thank'd, it is but voluntary . . . . v 1 29
The vaulty top of heaven Figured quite o'er with burning meteors . v 2 52
The holy legate comes apace, To give us warrant from the hand of heaven v 2 66
The sun of heaven methought was loath to set, But stay'd . . . v 5 1
Withhold thine indignation, mighty heaven, And tempt us not to bear above our power! . . . . v 6 37
Where heaven He knows how we shall answer him . . . . . v 7 60
My soul shall wait on thee to heaven, As it on earth hath been thy servant v 7 72
Until the heavens, envying earth's good hap, Add an immortal title to your crown . . . . *Richard II.* i 1 23
Heaven be the record to my speech! . . . . i 1 30
What I speak My body shall make good upon this earth, Or my divine soul answer it in heaven . . . . i 1 38
Put we our quarrel to the will of heaven . . . . i 2 6
The which if wrongfully, Let heaven revenge . . . . i 2 40
As so defend thee heaven and thy valour! . . . . i 3 15
And as I truly fight, defend me heaven! . . . . i 3 25; 41
What's thy quarrel? Speak like a true knight, so defend thee heaven! i 3 34
He is a traitor, foul and dangerous, To God of heaven, King Richard . i 3 40
If ever I were traitor, My name be blotted from the book of life, And I from heaven banish'd! . . . . i 3 203
All places that the eye of heaven visits Are to a wise man ports . . i 3 275
Plain well-meaning soul, Whom fair befal in heaven 'mongst happy souls! ii 1 129
Now God in heaven forbid!—Ah, madam, 'tis too true . . . . ii 2 51
Comfort's in heaven; and we are on the earth, Where nothing lives but crosses, cares and grief . . . . ii 2 78
And meteors fright the fixed stars of heaven . . . . ii 4 9
My comfort is that heaven will take our souls And plague injustice . iii 1 33
The means that heaven yields must be embraced, And not neglected; else, if heaven would, And we will not, heaven's offer we refuse . iii 2 29
When the searching eye of heaven is hid . . . . iii 2 37
If angels fight, Weak men must fall, for heaven still guards the right . iii 2 62
By heaven, I'll hate him everlastingly That bids me be of comfort any more . . . . iii 2 207
Lest you mistake the heavens are o'er our heads . . . . . . iii 3 17
Their thundering shock At meeting tears the cloudy cheeks of heaven . iii 3 57
The king of heaven forbid our lord the king Should so with civil and uncivil arms Be rush'd upon! . . . . iii 3 101
Who sets me else? by heaven, I'll throw at all . . . . . . iv 1 57
This is true.—As false, by heaven, as heaven itself is true . . . iv 1 64
God save the king! although I be not he; And yet, amen, if heaven do think him me . . . . iv 1 175
Mark'd with a blot, damn'd in the book of heaven . . . . . iv 1 236
But heaven hath a hand in these events, To whose high will we bound our calm contents . . . . v 2 37
Like the meteors of a troubled heaven, All of one nature . . *1 Hen. IV.* i 1 10
By heaven, methinks it were an easy leap . . . . i 3 201
Shall the blessed sun of heaven prove a micher and eat blackberries? . ii 4 450
His cheek looks pale and with A rising sigh he wisheth you in heaven . iii 1 10
At my nativity The front of heaven was full of fiery shapes . . . iii 1 14
The heavens were all on fire, the earth did tremble . . . . . iii 1 24
That pretty Welsh Which thou pour'st down from these swelling heavens iii 1 202
Mark'd For the hot vengeance and the rod of heaven . . . . . iii 2 10
I stole all courtesy from heaven, And dress'd myself in such humility . iii 2 50

Heaven. Heaven to earth, some of us never shall A second time do such a courtesy . . . *1 Hen. IV.* v 2 100
Take thy praise with thee to heaven! Thy ignominy sleep with thee! v 4 99
Let heaven kiss earth! now let not Nature's hand Keep the wild flood confined! let order die! . *2 Hen. IV.* i 1 153
Derives from heaven his quarrel and his cause . i 1 206
O thou fond many, with what loud applause Didst thou beat heaven! i 3 92
For yours [your honour], the God of heaven brighten it! For his, it stuck upon him as the sun In the grey vault of heaven ii 3 19
To rain upon remembrance with mine eyes, That it may grow and sprout as high as heaven ii 3 60
Begin to patch up thine old body for heaven ii 4 253
By heaven, Poins, I feel me much to blame ii 4 390
A tall gentleman, by heaven, and a most gallant leader iii 2 68
The very opener and intelligencer Between the grace, the sanctities of heaven And our dull workings iv 2 21
Employ the countenance and grace of heaven, As a false favourite doth his prince's name, In deeds dishonourable iv 2 24
Both against the peace of heaven and him Have here up-swarm'd them iv 2 29
From enemies heaven keep your majesty! iv 4 94
By heaven, I bid you be assured, I'll be your father and your brother too v 2 56
The heavens thee guard and keep, most royal imp of fame! v 5 45
A Muse of fire, that would ascend The brightest heaven of invention *Hen. V.* Prol. 2
Therefore doth heaven divide The state of man in divers functions i 2 183
Would I were with him, wheresome'er he is, either in heaven or in hell! ii 3 8
By gift of heaven, By law of nature and of nations ii 4 79
The Lord in heaven bless thee, noble Harry!—God-a-mercy, old heart! iv 1 33
Who twice a-day their wither'd hands hold up Toward heaven, to pardon blood iv 1 317
If we no more meet till we meet in heaven, Then, joyfully, . . . adieu! iv 3 7
The sun shall greet them, And draw their honours reeking up to heaven iv 3 101
My soul shall thine keep company to heaven; Tarry, sweet soul, for mine iv 6 16
Hung be the heavens with black, yield day to night! *1 Hen. VI.* i 1 1
Combat with adverse planets in the heavens! i 1 54
Mars his true moving, even as in the heavens, So in the earth, to this day is not known i 2 1
By a vision sent to her from heaven Ordained is to raise this tedious siege i 2 52
Heaven and our Lady gracious hath it pleased To shine on my contemptible estate i 2 74
Though thy speech doth fail, One eye thou hast, to look to heaven for grace i 4 83
Heaven, be thou gracious to none alive, If Salisbury wants mercy! i 4 85
What tumult's in the heavens? Whence cometh this alarum? i 4 98
Heavens, can you suffer hell so to prevail? i 5 9
I think this Talbot be a fiend of hell.—If not of hell, the heavens, sure, favour him ii 1 47
Heavens keep old Bedford safe! And now no more ado iii 2 100
Now, quiet soul, depart when heaven please iii 2 110
A double honour, Burgundy: Yet heavens have glory for this victory! iii 2 117
Together live and die; And soul with soul from France to heaven fly iv 5 55
Will cry for vengeance at the gates of heaven v 4 53
Now heaven forfend! the holy maid with child! v 4 65
We'll both together lift our heads to heaven *2 Hen. VI.* i 2 14
Were it not good your grace could fly to heaven?—The treasury of everlasting joy.—Thy heaven is on earth ii 1 17
For myself, to heaven I do appeal, How I have loved my king ii 1 190
Some black storm Shall blow ten thousand souls to heaven or hell iii 1 350
Nor let the rain of heaven wet this place iii 2 341
Eternal Mover of the heavens, Look with a gentle eye upon this wretch! iii 3 19
Rather let my head Stoop to the block than these knees bow to any Save to the God of heaven and to my king iv 1 126
Ignorance is the curse of God, Knowledge the wing wherewith we fly to heaven iv 7 79
And heavens and honour be witness iv 8 64
Then, heaven, set ope thy everlasting gates, To entertain my vows! iv 9 13
How much thou wrong'st me, heaven be my judge iv 10 82
By heaven, thou shalt rule no more O'er him whom heaven created for thy ruler v 1 104
Canst thou dispense with heaven for such an oath? v 1 181
If not in heaven, you'll surely sup in hell v 1 216
Peace with his soul, heaven, if it be thy will! v 2 30
O war, thou son of hell, Whom angry heavens do make their minister! v 2 34
And the premised flames of the last day Knit earth and heaven together! v 2 42
You are slow; for shame, away!—Can we outrun the heavens v 2 73
I vow by heaven these eyes shall never close *3 Hen. VI.* i 1 24
If I be not, heavens be revenged on me! i 1 57
In that hope I throw mine eyes to heaven i 4 37
Take me from the world: My soul to heaven, my blood upon your heads! i 4 168
In this the heaven figures some event.—'Tis wondrous strange ii 1 32
God forbid the hour!—Must Edward fall, which peril heaven forfend! ii 1 191
Smile, gentle heaven! or strike, ungentle death! For this world frowns ii 3 6
Yet that thy brazen gates of heaven may ope, And give sweet passage to my sinful soul! ii 3 40
Take leave until we meet again, Where'er it be, in heaven or in earth ii 3 43
O, pity, pity, gentle heaven, pity! ii 5 96
I'll make my heaven in a lady's lap, And deck my body in gay ornaments iii 2 148
I'll make my heaven to dream upon the crown iii 2 168
Though usurpers sway the rule awhile, Yet heavens are just iii 3 77
Heavens grant that Warwick's words bewitch him not! iii 3 112
I here protest, in sight of heaven, And by the hope I have of heavenly bliss iii 3 181
To whom the heavens in thy nativity Adjudged an olive branch iv 6 33
Save yourselves; For Warwick bids you all farewell, to meet in heaven v 2 49
By heaven, brat, I'll plague ye for that word v 5 27
Do it thou.—By heaven, I will not do thee so much ease v 5 72
Since the heavens have shaped my body so, Let hell make crook'd my mind v 6 78
By heaven, I think there's no man is secure *Richard III.* i 1 71
I will shortly send thy soul to heaven, If heaven will take the present i 1 120
And must not die Till George be pack'd with post-horse up to heaven i 1 146
Either heaven with lightning strike the murderer dead, Or earth, gape open wide and eat him quick! i 2 64
O, he was gentle, mild, and virtuous!—The fitter for the King of heaven i 2 105
He is in heaven, where thou shalt never come.—Let him thank me i 2 106
The heavens have bless'd you with a goodly son, To be your comforter i 3 9
By heaven, I will acquaint his majesty With those gross taunts i 3 105
Did York's dread curse prevail so much with heaven? i 3 191
Can curses pierce the clouds and enter heaven? i 3 195
If heaven have any grievous plague in store Exceeding those that I can wish upon thee, O, let them keep it till thy sins be ripe! i 3 217

Heaven. Now he delivers thee From this world's thraldom to the joys of heaven *Richard III.* i 4 255
By heavens, the duke shall know how slack thou art! i 4 282
And now in peace my soul shall part to heaven, Since I have set my friends at peace on earth ii 1 5
By heaven, my heart is purged from grudging hate ii 1 9
All-seeing heaven, what a world is this! ii 1 82
Much more to be thus opposite with heaven, For it requires the royal debt it lent you ii 2 94
God in heaven forbid We should infringe the holy privilege! iii 1 40
Let us all embrace: And take our leave, until we meet in heaven iii 3 25
By heaven, I come in perfect love to him iii 7 90
Let not the heavens hear these tell-tale women Rail on the Lord's anointed iv 4 149
What good is cover'd with the face of heaven, To be discover'd? iv 4 239
So long as heaven and nature lengthens it iv 4 353
Heaven and fortune bar me happy hours! Day, yield me not thy light! iv 4 400
The selfsame heaven That frowns on me looks sadly upon him v 3 286
Let us to't pell-mell; If not to heaven, then hand in hand to hell v 3 313
Make much of it.—Great God of heaven, say Amen to all! v 5 8
Smile heaven upon this fair conjunction, That long have frown'd! v 5 21
A gift that heaven gives for him *Hen. VIII.* i 1 65
I cannot tell What heaven hath given him,—let some graver eye Pierce into that i 1 67
The will of heaven Be done in this and all things! i 1 209
The will of heaven be done, and the king's pleasure By me obey'd! i 1 215
Yet the king our master—Whose honour heaven shield from soil! i 2 26
Heaven bear witness, And if I have a conscience, let it sink me! ii 1 59
Make of your prayers one sweet sacrifice, And lift my soul to heaven ii 1 78
Tell him You met him half in heaven ii 1 88
Heaven has an end in all: yet, you that hear me, This from a dying man receive as certain ii 1 124
Is not this course pious?—Heaven keep me from such counsel! ii 2 38
Heaven will one day open The king's eyes, that so long have slept ii 2 42
You would not be a queen?—No, not for all the riches under heaven ii 3 35
Heaven witness, I have been to you a true and humble wife ii 4 22
First, methought I stood not in the smile of heaven ii 4 187
Heaven is above all yet; there sits a judge That no king can corrupt iii 1 100
Loved him next heaven? obey'd him? Been, out of fondness, superstitious? iii 1 130
Ye have angels' faces, but heaven knows your hearts iii 1 145
Heaven forgive me! Ever God bless your highness! iii 2 135
I Can nothing render but allegiant thanks, My prayers to heaven for you iii 2 177
'Tis a burthen [honour] Too heavy for a man that hopes for heaven! iii 2 385
My robe, And my integrity to heaven, is all I dare now call mine own iii 2 453
Farewell The hopes of court! my hopes in heaven do dwell iii 2 459
Heaven bless thee! Thou hast the sweetest face I ever look'd on iv 1 42
And saint-like Cast her fair eyes to heaven and pray'd devoutly iv 1 84
He gave his honours to the world again, His blessed part to heaven iv 2 30
She is going, wench: pray, pray.—Heaven comfort her! iv 2 99
The dews of heaven fall thick in blessings on her! iv 2 133
To love her for her mother's sake, that loved him, Heaven knows how dearly iv 2 138
If heaven had pleased to have given me longer life And able means iv 2 152
Do me this last right.—By heaven, I will iv 2 158
The God of heaven Both now and ever bless her! v 1 164
He cast his eyes upon me! Pray heaven, he sound not my disgrace! v 2 13
Pray heaven, the king may never find a heart With less allegiance in it! v 3 42
'Tis no counterfeit.—'Tis the right ring, by heaven v 3 103
How much are we bound to heaven In daily thanks v 3 114
And let heaven Witness, how dear I hold this confirmation v 3 173
Heaven, from thy endless goodness, send prosperous life, long, and ever happy, to the high and mighty princess of England, Elizabeth! v 5 1
All comfort, joy, in this most gracious lady, Heaven ever laid up to make parents happy, May hourly fall upon ye! v 5 8
Let me speak, sir, For heaven now bids me v 5 16
This royal infant—heaven still move about her!—Though in her cradle v 5 18
When heaven shall call her from this cloud of darkness v 5 45
Wherever the bright sun of heaven shall shine v 5 51
Our children's children Shall see this, and bless heaven v 5 56
When I am in heaven I shall desire To see what this child does v 5 68
Strong as the axletree On which heaven rides *Troi. and Cres.* i 3 67
The heavens themselves, the planets and this centre Observe degree i 3 85
Now heavens forbid such scarcity of youth! i 3 302
Heaven bless thee from a tutor, and discipline come not near thee! ii 3 32
Art thou devout? wast thou in prayer?—Ay: the heavens hear me! ii 3 40
Thank the heavens, lord, thou art of sweet composure ii 3 251
I am ashamed. O heavens! what have I done? iii 2 146
Heavens, what a man is there! a very horse iii 3 126
O heavens, what some men do, While some men leave to do! iii 3 132
As many farewells as be stars in heaven iv 4 46
But yet be true.—O heavens! 'be true' again!—Hear why I speak it, love iv 4 76
O heavens! you love me not.—Die I a villain, then! iv 4 84
The lustre in your eye, heaven in your cheek, Pleads your fair usage iv 4 120
Tell me, you heavens, in which part of his body Shall I destroy him? iv 5 242
Answer me, heavens!—It would discredit the blest gods, proud man, To answer such a question iv 5 246
Who neither looks upon the heaven nor earth iv 5 281
Cressid is mine, tied with the bonds of heaven: Instance, O instance! strong as heaven itself; The bonds of heaven are slipp'd, dissolved, and loosed v 2 154
Bid my trumpet sound!—No notes of sally, for the heavens, sweet brother v 3 14
O, 'tis fair play.—Fool's play, by heaven, Hector v 3 43
By the flame of yonder glorious heaven, He shall not carry him v 6 23
Frown on, you heavens, effect your rage with speed! v 10 6
You may as well Strike at the heaven with your staves as lift them Against the Roman state *Coriolanus* i 1 70
Heavens bless my lord from fell Aufidius! i 3 48
Or, by the fires of heaven, I'll leave the foe And make my wars on you i 4 39
O heavens! O heavens!—Nay, I prithee, woman iv 1 12
O blessed heavens! iv 2 5
Those mysteries which heaven Will not have earth to know iv 2 35
Now, by the jealous queen of heaven, that kiss I carried from thee, dear v 3 46
Behold, the heavens do ope, The gods look down, and this unnatural scene They laugh at v 3 183
He wants nothing of a god but eternity and a heaven to throne in v 4 25
And here, in sight of heaven, to Rome I swear *T. Andron.* i 1 329
His lovely bride, Sent by the heavens for Prince Saturnine i 1 335

Heaven. Whether by device or no, the heavens can tell . . *T. Andron.* i 1 395
Rome and the righteous heavens be my judge! . . . . i 1 426
We do, and vow to heaven and to his highness, That what we did was mildly as we might . . . . . i 1 474
The empress of my soul, Which never hopes more heaven than rests in thee . . . . . . ii 3 41
My hand shall go.—By heaven, it shall not go! . . . iii 1 177
I lift this one hand up to heaven, And bow this feeble ruin to the earth iii 1 207
Heaven shall hear our prayers; Or with our sighs we'll breathe the welkin dim . . . . . . iii 1 211
When heaven doth weep, doth not the earth o'erflow? . . . iii 1 222
Thou shalt not sigh, nor hold thy stumps to heaven . . iii 2 42
Till the heavens Reveal the damn'd contriver of this deed . iv 1 35
Ay, more there was; Or else to heaven she heaves them for revenge . iv 1 40
Heaven guide thy pen to print thy sorrows plain! . . . iv 1 75
O heavens, can you hear a good man groan, And not relent? . . iv 1 123
Revenge, ye heavens, for old Andronicus! . . . . iv 1 129
She is so employ'd, He thinks, with Jove in heaven, or somewhere else iv 3 40
Sith there's no justice in earth nor hell, We will solicit heaven . iv 3 50
News, news from heaven! Marcus, the post is come . . iv 3 77
Didst thou not come from heaven?—From heaven! alas, sir, I never came there . . . . . . iv 3 88
God forbid I should be so bold to press to heaven in my young days . iv 3 91
And now he writes to heaven for his redress: See, here's to Jove . iv 4 13
Earth-treading stars that make dark heaven light *Rom. and Jul.* i 2 25
Two of the fairest stars in all the heaven, Having some business . ii 2 15
Her eyes in heaven Would through the airy region stream so bright . ii 2 20
As is a winged messenger of heaven Unto the white-upturned wondering eyes Of mortals . . . . . . ii 2 28
The sun not yet thy sighs from heaven clears . . . ii 3 73
Commend me to thy mistress.—Now God in heaven bless thee! . ii 4 206
So smile the heavens upon this holy act, That after hours with sorrow chide us not!—Amen, amen! . . . . . ii 6 1
Away to heaven, respective lenity, And fire-eyed fury be my conduct now! . . . . iii 1 128
Cut him out in little stars, And he will make the face of heaven so fine iii 2 23
Can heaven be so envious?—Romeo can, Though heaven cannot . iii 2 40
Heaven is here, Where Juliet lives . . . . iii 3 29
Every unworthy thing, Live here in heaven and may look on her . iii 3 32
Why rail'st thou on thy birth, the heaven, and earth? Since birth, and heaven, and earth, all three do meet In thee at once . . iii 3 120
That is not the lark, whose notes do beat The vaulty heaven so high . iii 5 22
God in heaven bless her! You are to blame, my lord, to rate her so . iii 5 169
My husband is on earth, my faith in heaven; How shall that faith return again to earth, Unless that husband send it me from heaven By leaving earth? . . . . . . iii 5 207
Alack, that heaven should practise stratagems Upon so soft a subject! iii 5 211
I have need of many orisons To move the heavens to smile upon my state . . . . iv 3 4
Heaven and yourself Had part in this fair maid; now heaven hath all, And all the better is it for the maid: Your part in her you could not keep from death, But heaven keeps his part in eternal life . iv 5 66
'Twas your heaven she should be advanced: And weep ye now, seeing she is advanced Above the clouds, as high as heaven itself? . . iv 5 72
The heavens do lour upon you for some ill; Move them no more . iv 5 94
By heaven, I will tear thee joint by joint . . . v 3 35
By heaven, I love thee better than myself . . . v 3 64
O heavens! O wife, look how our daughter bleeds! This dagger hath mista'en . . . . v 3 202
And bear this work of heaven with patience . . . v 3 261
See, what a scourge is laid upon your hate, That heaven finds means to kill your joys with love . . . . . . v 3 293
Heavens, that I were a lord!—What wouldst do then? *T. of Athens* i 1 233
Thou wilt not hear me now; thou shalt not then: I'll lock thy heaven from thee . . . . i 2 255
Heavens, have I said, the bounty of this lord! . . . ii 2 173
No, gods, I am no idle votarist: roots, you clear heavens! . iv 3 27
With all the abhorred births below crisp heaven . . . iv 3 183
Whose naked natures live in all the spite Of wreakful heaven . iv 3 229
That which I show, heaven knows, is merely love, Duty and zeal . iv 3 522
Not all the whips of heaven are large enough . . . v 1 64
There is a civil strife in heaven . . . . *J. Cæsar* i 3 11
Who ever knew the heavens menace so? . . . . i 3 44
The cross blue lightning seem'd to open The breast of heaven . i 3 51
But wherefore did you so much tempt the heavens? . . . i 3 53
Cast yourself in wonder, To see the strange impatience of the heavens . i 3 61
Heaven hath infused them with these spirits, To make them instruments of fear and warning Unto some monstrous state . . . . i 3 69
Nor heaven nor earth have been at peace to-night . . . ii 2 1
The heavens themselves blaze forth the death of princes . . ii 2 31
O Brutus, The heavens speed thee in thine enterprise! . . ii 4 41
By heaven, I had rather coin my heart, And drop my blood for drachmas iv 3 72
Nor heaven peep through the blanket of the dark, To cry 'Hold, hold!' . . . . *Macbeth* i 5 54
There's husbandry in heaven; Their candles are all out . . ii 1 4
Hear it not, Duncan; for it is a knell That summons thee to heaven or to hell . . . . ii 1 64
Committed treason enough for God's sake, yet could not equivocate to heaven . . . . ii 3 12
The heavens, as troubled with man's act, Threaten his bloody stage . ii 4 5
Thy soul's flight, If it find heaven, must find it out to-night . iii 1 142
Had he Duncan's sons under his key—As, an't please heaven, he shall not iii 6 19
Heaven preserve you! I dare abide no longer . . . iv 2 72
New orphans cry, new sorrows Strike heaven on the face . iv 3 6
But at his touch—Such sanctity hath heaven given his hand—They presently amend . . . . iv 3 144
How he solicits heaven, Himself best knows . . . . iv 3 149
Merciful heaven! What, man! ne'er pull your hat upon your brows . iv 3 207
Did heaven look on, And would not take their part? . . iv 3 223
Heaven rest them now! . . . . . . iv 3 227
But, gentle heavens, Cut short all intermission . . . iv 3 231
If he 'scape, Heaven forgive him too! . . . . iv 3 235
She has spoke what she should not, I am sure of that: heaven knows what she has known . . . . v 1 54
When yond same star that's westward from the pole Had made his course to illume that part of heaven Where now it burns *Hamlet* i 1 37
By heaven I charge thee, speak!—It is offended . . . i 1 49
Have heaven and earth together demonstrated Unto our climatures . i 1 124
It shows a will most incorrect to heaven, A heart unfortified . i 2 95
'Tis a fault to heaven, A fault against the dead, a fault to nature . i 2 101

Heaven. The king's rouse the heavens shall bruit again, Re-speaking earthly thunder . . . . *Hamlet* i 2 127
That he might not beteem the winds of heaven Visit her face too roughly i 2 141
Heaven and earth! Must I remember? . . . . . i 2 142
Would I had met my dearest foe in heaven Or ever I had seen that day! i 2 182
Do not, as some ungracious pastors do, Show me the steep and thorny way to heaven . . . . i 3 48
With almost all the holy vows of heaven . . . . i 3 114
Bring with thee airs from heaven or blasts from hell . . i 4 41
Unhand me, gentlemen. By heaven, I'll make a ghost of him that lets me! i 4 85
Something is rotten in the state of Denmark.—Heaven will direct it . i 4 91
But virtue, as it never will be moved, Though lewdness court it in a shape of heaven . . . . i 5 54
Leave her to heaven And to those thorns that in her bosom lodge . i 5 86
O all you host of heaven! O earth! what else? And shall I couple hell? i 5 92
Yes, by heaven! O most pernicious woman! O villain, villain! . i 5 104
Lord Hamlet,— Heaven secure him!—So be it! . . . i 5 113
Tell it.—No; you'll reveal it.—Not I, my lord, by heaven.—Nor I . i 5 120
But you'll be secret?—Ay, by heaven, my lord . . . i 5 122
There are more things in heaven and earth, Horatio, Than are dreamt of in your philosophy . . . . i 5 166
As oft as any passion under heaven That does afflict our natures . ii 1 105
By heaven, it is as proper to our age To cast beyond ourselves . ii 1 114
Heavens make our presence and our practices Pleasant and helpful to him! ii 2 38
Your ladyship is nearer to heaven than when I saw you last . ii 2 445
As we often see, against some storm, A silence in the heavens . ii 2 506
Bowl the round nave down the hill of heaven, As low as to the fiends! ii 2 518
Would have made milch the burning eyes of heaven, And passion in the gods . . . . ii 2 540
The son of a dear father murder'd, Prompted to my revenge by heaven and hell . . . . ii 2 613
What should such fellows as I do crawling between earth and heaven? . iii 1 131
Farewell.—O, help him, you sweet heavens! . . . . iii 1 138
O heavens! die two months ago, and not forgotten yet? . . iii 2 138
Nor earth to me give food, nor heaven light! . . . iii 2 226
O, my offence is rank, it smells to heaven; It hath the primal eldest curse iii 3 36
Is there not rain enough in the sweet heavens To wash it white as snow? iii 3 45
And so he goes to heaven; And so am I revenged . . . iii 3 74
And for that, I, his sole son, do this same villain send To heaven . iii 3 78
And how his audit stands who knows save heaven? . . . iii 3 82
Then trip him, that his heels may kick at heaven . . . iii 3 93
My thoughts remain below: Words without thoughts never to heaven go iii 3 98
Confess yourself to heaven; Repent what's past; avoid what is to come iii 4 149
Heaven hath pleased it so, To punish me with this and this with me . iii 4 174
Where is Polonius?—In heaven; send thither to see . . . iv 3 35
By heaven, thy madness shall be paid with weight . . . iv 5 156
O heavens! is't possible, a young maid's wits Should be as mortal as an old man's life? . . . . iv 5 159
His means of death . . . Cry to be heard, as 'twere from heaven to earth iv 5 216
Why, even in that was heaven ordinant . . . . v 2 48
The cannons to the heavens, the heavens to earth, 'Now the king drinks' v 2 288
Heaven make thee free of it! I follow thee . . . . v 2 343
As thou'rt a man, Give me the cup: let go; by heaven, I'll have't . v 2 354
To his father, that so tenderly and entirely loves him. Heaven and earth! . . . . *Lear* i 2 105
O, let me not be mad, not mad, sweet heaven! Keep me in temper . i 5 50
All the stored vengeances of heaven fall On her ingrateful top! . ii 4 164
O heavens, If you do love old men, if your sweet sway Allow obedience ii 4 192
But, for true need,—You heavens, give me that patience, patience I need! ii 4 274
Thou mayst shake the superflux to them, And show the heavens more just iii 4 36
Swore as many oaths as I spake words, and broke them in the sweet face of heaven . . . . iii 4 92
O heavens! that this treason were not, or not I the detector! . iii 5 13
Yet, poor old heart, he holp the heavens to reign . . . iii 7 62
Now, heaven help him! . . . . . . iii 7 107
That I am wretched Makes thee the happier: heavens, deal so still . iv 1 69
If that the heavens do not their visible spirits Send quickly down to tame these vile offences, It will come . . . . . iv 2 46
The bounty and the benison of heaven To boot, and boot! . . iv 6 229
He that parts us shall bring a brand from heaven, And fire us hence . v 3 22
He fasten'd on my neck, and bellow'd out As he'd burst heaven . v 3 213
This judgement of the heavens, that makes us tremble, Touches us not with pity . . . . v 3 231
By heaven, I rather would have been his hangman! . . *Othello* i 1 34
Heaven is my judge, not I for love and duty, But seeming so . i 1 59
O heaven! How got she out? O treason of the blood! . . i 1 170
As truly as to heaven I do confess the vices of my blood . . i 3 122
Rough quarries, rocks and hills whose heads touch heaven . . i 3 141
Yet she wish'd That heaven had made her such a man . . i 3 163
Vouch with me, heaven, I therefore beg it not, To please the palate . i 3 262
Heaven defend your good souls, that you think I will your serious and great business scant For she is with me . . . . . i 3 267
I cannot, 'twixt the heaven and the main, Descry a sail . . ii 1 3
Yet he looks sadly, And prays the Moor be safe . . . —Pray heavens he be ii 1 34
Let the heavens Give him defence against the elements . . ii 1 44
The grace of heaven, Before, behind thee and on every hand . . ii 1 85
Let the labouring bark climb hills of seas Olympus-high and duck again as low As hell's from heaven! . . . . . . ii 1 191
The heavens forbid But that our loves and comforts should increase! . ii 1 195
Heaven bless the isle of Cyprus and our noble general Othello! . ii 2 11
And to ourselves do that Which heaven hath forbid the Ottomites? . ii 3 171
Now, by heaven, My blood begins my safer guides to rule . . ii 3 204
Are you hurt, lieutenant?—Ay, past all surgery.—Marry, heaven forbid! ii 3 261
What dost thou think?—Think, my lord?—Think, my lord! By heaven, he echoes me . . . . iii 3 106
By heaven, I'll know thy thoughts.—You cannot . . . iii 3 162
Good heaven, the souls of all my tribe defend From jealousy! . . iii 3 175
In Venice they do let heaven see the pranks They dare not show their husbands . . . . iii 3 202
If she be false, O, then heaven mocks itself! I'll not believe't! . iii 3 278
What he will do with it Heaven knows, not I . . . iii 3 298
Do deeds to make heaven weep, all earth amazed . . . iii 3 371
O grace! O heaven forgive me! Are you a man? have you a soul or sense? iii 3 373
All my fond love thus do I blow to heaven . . . . iii 3 445
Now, by yond marble heaven, In the due reverence of a sacred vow I here engage my words . . . . iii 3 460
Is it out o' the way?—Heaven bless us!—Say you?—It is not lost . iii 4 81
Pray heaven it be state-matters, as you think . . . . iii 4 155
Heaven keep that monster [jealousy] from Othello's mind! . . iii 4 163
The devil their virtue tempts, and they tempt heaven . . iv 1 8

Heaven. But, for the handkerchief,— By heaven, I would most gladly have forgot it . . . . *Othello* iv 1 19
Dost thou mock me?—I mock you! no, by heaven . . . . iv 1 61
By heaven, that should be my handkerchief! . . . . iv 1 164
He's that he is: I may not breathe my censure What he might be: if what he might he is not, I would to heaven he were! . . . iv 1 283
Let heaven requite it with the serpent's curse! . . . . iv 2 16
Lest, being like one of heaven, the devils themselves Should fear to seize thee . . . . iv 2 36
Swear thou art honest.—Heaven doth truly know it.—Heaven truly knows that thou art false as hell . . . . . iv 2 38
Had it pleased heaven To try me with affliction . . . . iv 2 47
Heaven stops the nose at it and the moon winks . . . . iv 2 77
Impudent strumpet!—By heaven, you do me wrong.—Are not you a strumpet? . . . . iv 2 81
O, heaven forgive us!—I cry you mercy, then . . . . . iv 2 88
Beshrew him for't! How comes this trick upon him?—Nay, heaven doth know . . . . iv 2 129
Heaven pardon him!—A halter pardon him! and hell gnaw his bones! iv 2 135
Some scurvy fellow. O heaven, that such companions thou'ldst unfold! iv 2 141
By this light of heaven, I know not how I lost him . . . iv 2 150
Heaven me such uses send, Not to pick bad from bad, but by bad mend! iv 3 105
My leg is cut in two.—Marry, heaven forbid! Light, gentlemen . v 1 72
My friend and my dear countryman Roderigo! no:—yes, sure:—O heaven! v 1 90
If you bethink yourself of any crime Unreconciled as yet to heaven . v 2 27
I would not kill thy unprepared spirit; No; heaven forfend! . . v 2 32
Talk you of killing?—Ay, I do.—Then heaven Have mercy on me! . v 2 33
But with such general warranty of heaven As I might love . . v 2 60
I never gave him token.—By heaven, I saw my handkerchief in's hand v 2 62
If heaven would make me such another world Of one entire and perfect chrysolite, I'ld not have sold her for it . . . . . . v 2 144
This deed of thine is no more worthy heaven Than thou wast worthy her v 2 160
My mistress here lies murder'd in her bed,— O heavens forfend! . v 2 186
O heaven! O heavenly powers!—Come, hold your peace . . . v 2 218
Let heaven and men and devils, let them all, All, all, cry shame . v 2 221
Filth, thou liest!—By heaven, I do not, I do not, gentlemen . . v 2 232
Are there no stones in heaven But what serve for the thunder? . . v 2 234
This look of thine will hurl my soul from heaven . . . v 2 274
Then must thou needs find out new heaven, new earth . *Ant. and Cleo.* i 1 17
Our worser thoughts heavens mend! . . . . i 2 64
None our parts so poor, But was a race of heaven . . . . i 3 37
His faults in him seem as the spots of heaven . . . . . i 4 12
The dust Should have ascended to the roof of heaven . . . iii 6 49
Sues To let him breathe between the heavens and earth, A private man iii 12 14
If I be so, From my cold heart let heaven engender hail . . . iii 13 159
That heaven and earth may strike their sounds together, Applauding . iv 8 38
His face was as the heavens; and therein stuck A sun and moon . . v 2 79
That kiss Which is my heaven to have . . . . v 2 306
Our bloods No more obey the heavens than our courtiers Still seem as does the king . . . . *Cymbeline* i 1 2
What, art thou mad?—Almost, sir: heaven restore me! . . . i 1 148
At the sixth hour of morn, at noon, at midnight, To encounter me with orisons, for then I am in heaven for him . . . . . . i 3 33
But, heavens know, Some men are much to blame . . . . i 6 76
The heavens hold firm The walls of thy dear honour! . . . . ii 1 67
White and azure laced With blue of heaven's own tinct . . . . ii 2 23
This gate Instructs you how to adore the heavens . . . . iii 3 3
Hail, thou fair heaven! We house i' the rock, yet use thee not so hardly As prouder livers do . . . . iii 3 7
Hail, heaven!—Hail, heaven!—Now for our mountain sport . . . iii 3 9
I have lived at honest freedom, paid More pious debts to heaven . . iii 3 72
Heaven and my conscience knows Thou didst unjustly banish me . . iii 3 99
Not seen of late? Grant, heavens, that which I fear Prove false! . . iii 5 52
Such a foe, good heavens! . . . . iii 6 27
If there be Yet left in heaven as small a drop of pity As a wren's eye iv 2 304
But his Jovial face—Murder in heaven?—How!—'Tis gone . . . iv 2 312
Heavens, How deeply you at once do touch me! . . . . . iv 3 3
The heavens still must work. Wherein I am false I am honest . . iv 3 41
By heavens, I'll go: If you will bless me, sir, and give me leave . . iv 4 43
Therefore, good heavens, Hear patiently my purpose . . . . v 1 21
For all was lost, But that the heavens fought . . . . . v 3 4
Heavens, how they wound! Some slain before; some dying . . . v 3 46
Open'd, in despite Of heaven and men, her purposes . . . . v 5 59
Heaven mend all! . . . . v 5 68
The benediction of these covering heavens Fall on their heads like dew! v 5 350
For they are worthy To inlay heaven with stars . . . . v 5 352
Whom heavens, in justice, both on her and hers, Have laid most heavy hand . . . . v 5 464
Blithe, and full of face, As heaven had lent her all his grace *Pericles* i Gower 24
Her face, like heaven, enticeth thee to view Her countless glory . . i 1 30
I'll make my will then, and, as sick men do Who know the world, see heaven . . . . i 1 48
O you powers That give heaven countless eyes to view men's acts . . i 1 73
Would draw heaven down, and all the gods, to hearken . . . . i 1 83
The blind mole casts Copp'd hills towards heaven, to tell the earth is throng'd By man's oppression . . . . i 1 101
Heaven, that I had thy head! he has found the meaning . . . i 1 109
How dare the plants look up to heaven? . . . . i 2 55
Heaven forbid That kings should let their ears hear their faults hid! . i 2 61
If heaven slumber while their creatures want, They may awake their helps i 4 16
But see what heaven can do! . . . . i 4 33
The curse of heaven and men succeed their evils! . . . . . i 4 104
Yet cease your ire, you angry stars of heaven! . . . . . ii 1 1
Princes are A model, which heaven makes like to itself . . . . ii 2 11
A fire from heaven came and shrivell'd up Their bodies . . . . ii 4 9
Rebuke these surges, Which wash both heaven and hell! . . . . iii 1 2
As chiding a nativity As fire, air, water, earth, and heaven can make . iii 1 33
The heavens, Through you, increase our wonder . . . . . iii 2 96
Give you up to the mask'd Neptune and The gentlest winds of heaven . iii 3 37
Of all the faults beneath the heavens, the gods Do like this worst . iv 3 20
Heavens forgive it! . . . . iv 3 39
The earth, fearing to be o'erflow'd, Hath Thetis' birth-child on the heavens bestow'd . . . . iv 4 41
I am wild in my beholding. O heavens bless my girl! . . . . v 1 225
My father's dead.—Heavens make a star of him! . . . . . v 3 79
Led on by heaven, and crown'd with joy at last . . . . v 3 Gower 90
Heaven-bred. Much is the force of heaven-bred poesy . *T. G. of Ver.* iii 2 72
Heaven-kissing. New-lighted on a heaven-kissing hill . *Hamlet* iii 4 59
Heaven-moving. His grandam's wrongs, and not his mother's shames, Draws those heaven-moving pearls from his poor eyes . *K. John* ii 1 169

Heaven of beauty. Where this heaven of beauty Shall shine at full upon them . . . . *Hen. VIII.* i 4 59
Heaven sake. For heaven sake, Hubert, let me not be bound! *K. John* iv 1 78
For heaven's sake, take heed . . . . . . *Hen. VIII.* iii 1 110
Did not you hear a cry?—Here, here! for heaven's sake, help me! *Othello* v 1 50
Heaven's artillery thunder in the skies . . . *T. of Shrew* i 2 205
Heavens' assistance. By the heavens' assistance and your strength *3 Hen. VI.* v 4 68
Heaven's benediction. Thou out of heaven's benediction comest To the warm sun! . . . . *Lear* ii 2 168
Heaven's bliss. If thou think'st on heaven's bliss, Hold up thy hand, make signal of thy hope . . . . . *2 Hen. VI.* iii 3 27
Heaven's bounty towards him might Be used more thankfully *Cymbeline* i 6 78
Heaven's breath. The heaven's breath Smells wooingly here . *Macbeth* i 6 5
That the lover, sick to death, Wish himself the heaven's breath *L. L. L.* iv 3 108
Heaven's cherubim, horsed Upon the sightless couriers of the air *Macbeth* i 7 22
Heaven's claim. My sole earth's heaven, and my heaven's claim *C. of Er.* iii 2 64
Heaven's curse. Dost thou, or dost thou not, heaven's curse upon thee! *T. of Athens* iv 3 131
Heaven's eye. There's nothing situate under heaven's eye But hath his bound, in earth, in sea, in sky . . . *Com. of Errors* ii 1 16
There serve your lusts, shadow'd from heaven's eye *T. Andron.* ii 1 130
What dost thou wrap and fumble in thine arms?—O, that which I would hide from heaven's eye! . . . . iv 2 59
Heaven's face doth glow . . . . *Hamlet* iii 4 48
Heaven's gate. Hark! the lark at heaven's gate sings . *Cymbeline* ii 3 22
Heaven's image. Their saucy sweetness that do coin heaven's image In stamps that are forbid . . . . . . *Meas. for Meas.* ii 4 45
Heaven's lights. These earthly godfathers of heaven's lights *L. L. Lost* i 1 88
Heaven's peace be with him! . . . . . . *Hen. VIII.* ii 2 130
Heavens' plagues. Thou whom the heavens' plagues Have humbled to all strokes . . . . *Lear* iv 1 67
Heaven's praise. Pardon love this wrong, That sings heaven's praise with such an earthly tongue . . . . . *L. L. Lost* iv 2 122
Heaven's shaft. His greatness was no guard To bar heaven's shaft, but sin had his reward . . . . *Pericles* ii 4 15
Heaven's vault. Had I your tongues and eyes, I'ld use them so That heaven's vault should crack . . . . *Lear* v 3 259
Heaven's vows. You give away heaven's vows, and those are mine *All's Well* v 3 171
Heaven's will. It's heaven's will: Some spirit put this paper in the packet . . . . *Hen. VIII.* iii 2 128
Heavenly. Tell me, heavenly bow, If Venus or her son, as thou dost know, Do now attend the queen? . . . . . *Tempest* iv 1 86
When I have required Some heavenly music, which even now I do . v 1 52
Some heavenly power guide us Out of this fearful country! . . v 1 105
O heavenly Julia! . . . . *T. G. of Ver.* i 3 50
Is she not a heavenly saint?—No; but she is an earthly paragon . ii 4 145
Why, Phaethon, . . . Wilt thou aspire to guide the heavenly car? . iii 1 154
I claim the promise for her heavenly picture . . . . . iv 4 92
Have I caught thee, my heavenly jewel? Why, now let me die *M. Wives* iii 3 45
To make her heavenly comforts of despair . . *Meas. for Meas.* iv 3 114
The heavenly rhetoric of thine eye . . . . . *L. L. Lost* iv 3 60
My vow was earthly, thou a heavenly love . . . . . . iv 3 66
Who sees the heavenly Rosaline, That . . . Bows not his vassal head? iv 3 221
Out of your favours, heavenly spirits, vouchsafe Not to behold . v 2 166
So much I hate a breaking cause to be Of heavenly oaths . . v 2 356
Which parti-coated presence of loose love Put on by us, if, in your heavenly eyes, Have misbecomed our oaths and gravities, Those heavenly eyes, that look into these faults, Suggested us to make . . v 2 777
One of these three contains her heavenly picture . . *Mer. of Venice* ii 7 48
If two gods should play some heavenly match . . . . . iii 5 84
But heavenly Rosalind! . . . . *As Y. Like It* i 2 301
Thus Rosalind of many parts By heavenly synod was devised . . iii 2 158
Procure me music ready when he wakes, To make a dulcet and a heavenly sound . . . . *T. of Shrew* Ind. 1 51
This is The patroness of heavenly harmony . . . . . . iii 1 5
What stars do spangle heaven with such beauty, As those two eyes become that heavenly face? . . . . iv 5 32
A showing of a heavenly effect in an earthly actor . . . *All's Well* ii 3 27
God for his Richard hath in heavenly pay A glorious angel *Richard II.* iii 2 60
By this heavenly ground I tread on . . . . . . *2 Hen. IV.* ii 1 152
O heavenly God!—How fares my gracious lord? . . . *2 Hen. VI.* iii 2 37
A wilderness is populous enough, So Suffolk had thy heavenly company iii 2 361
In sight of heaven, And by the hope I have of heavenly bliss *3 Hen. VI.* iii 3 182
But 'twas thy heavenly face that set me on . . . *Richard III.* i 2 183
Now, I pray God, amen!—You bear a gentle mind, and heavenly blessings Follow such creatures . . . . *Hen. VIII.* ii 3 57
You are full of heavenly stuff, and bear the inventory Of your best graces . . . . iii 2 137
Truth shall nurse her, Holy and heavenly thoughts still counsel her . v 5 30
Nothing but heavenly business Should rob my bed-mate of my company.—That's my mind too . . . . . . *Troi. and Cres.* iv 1 4
The heavenly harmony Which that sweet tongue hath made *T. Andron.* ii 4 48
She brings news; and every tongue that speaks But Romeo's name speaks heavenly eloquence . . . . *Rom. and Jul.* iii 2 33
I know, you'll swear, terribly swear Into strong shudders and to heavenly agues The immortal gods . . . . . *T. of Athens* iv 3 137
With this strange virtue, He hath a heavenly gift of prophecy *Macbeth* iv 3 157
O heavenly powers, restore him! . . . . *Hamlet* iii 1 147
Save me, and hover o'er me with your wings, You heavenly guards! . iii 4 104
As if we were villains by necessity; fools by heavenly compulsion *Lear* i 2 132
She shook The holy water from her heavenly eyes, And clamour moisten'd . . . . iv 3 32
When devils will the blackest sins put on, They do suggest at first with heavenly shows . . . . *Othello* ii 3 358
No, by this heavenly light!—Nor I neither by this heavenly light; I might do't as well i' the dark . . . . iv 3 65
This sorrow's heavenly; It strikes where it doth love . . . . v 2 21
O, she was heavenly true! . . . . v 2 135
O heaven! O heavenly powers!—Come, hold your peace . . . v 2 218
Whip me, ye devils, From the possession of this heavenly sight! . . v 2 278
O heavenly mingle! Be'st thou sad or merry, The violence of either thee becomes, So does it no man else . . . . *Ant. and Cleo.* i 5 59
I lodge in fear; Though this a heavenly angel, hell is here *Cymbeline* ii 2 50
Flow, flow, You heavenly blessings, on her! . . . . . iii 5 167
Behold, Her eyelids; cases to those heavenly jewels . . *Pericles* iii 2 99
Most heavenly music! It nips me unto listening . . . . . v 1 234
Heavenly-harnessed. The heavenly-harness'd team Begins his golden progress in the east . . . . *1 Hen. IV.* iii 1 221

Heavier. Then was your sin of heavier kind than his . *Meas. for Meas.* ii 3 28
A heavier task could not have been imposed . . . . *Com. of Errors* i 1 32
My heart is exceeding heavy.—'Twill be heavier soon . . *Much Ado* iii 4 26
I'll offend nobody : is there any harm in 'the heavier for a husband'? iii 4 35
So sorrow's heaviness doth heavier grow . . . *M. N. Dream* iii 2 84
Do not repent these things, for they are heavier Than all thy woes *W. T.* iii 2 209
For thee remains a heavier doom . . . . . *Richard II.* i 3 148
Woe doth the heavier sit, Where it perceives it is but faintly borne . i 3 280
My tongue hath but a heavier tale to say . . . . iii 2 197
And find our griefs heavier than our offences . . . *2 Hen. IV.* iv 1 69
Well, peace be with him that hath made us heavy!—Peace be with us, lest we be heavier! . . . . v 2 26
I weigh it lightly, were it heavier . . . . *Richard III.* iii 1 121
Nor less nor more; But he as he, the heavier for a whore *Troi. and Cres.* iv 1 66
The brain the heavier for being too light . . . *Cymbeline* v 4 167
Heaviest. It hath been the longest night That ere I watch'd and the most heaviest . . . . *T. G. of Ver.* iv 2 141
What news abroad?—The heaviest and the worst Is your displeasure with the king . . . . *Hen. VIII.* iii 2 391
Or endure Your heaviest censure . . . . *Coriolanus* v 6 143
Shall be render'd to your public laws At heaviest answer *T. of Athens* v 4 63
Let not your ears despise my tongue for ever, Which shall possess them with the heaviest sound That ever yet they heard . . *Macbeth* iv 3 202
With those hands, that grasp'd the heaviest club . . *Ant. and Cleo.* iv 12 46
Heavily. Mark how heavily this befell to the poor gentlewoman *Meas. for Meas.* iii 1 226
Help us to sigh and groan, Heavily, heavily . . . *Much Ado* v 3 18
Graves, yawn and yield your dead, Till death be uttered, Heavily, heavily . . . . v 3 21
Thou shalt be heavily punished . . . . . *L. L. Lost* i 2 155
Why looks your grace so heavily to-day? . . . *Richard III.* i 4 1
Ye cannot reason almost with a man That looks not heavily . . ii 3 40
I came hither to transport the tidings, Which I have heavily borne *Macbeth* iv 3 182
Indeed it goes so heavily with my disposition . . . *Hamlet* ii 2 309
Heaviness. The strangeness of your story put Heaviness in me *Tempest* i 2 307
Let us not burthen our remembrance with A heaviness that's gone . v 1 200
So sorrow's heaviness doth heavier grow For debt that bankrupt sleep doth sorrow owe . . . . . . *M. N. Dream* iii 2 84
Quicken his embraced heaviness With some delight or other *Mer. of Ven.* ii 8 52
Lay aside life-harming heaviness And entertain a cheerful disposition *Richard II.* ii 2 3
Charming your blood with pleasing heaviness . . *1 Hen. IV.* iii 1 218
Against ill chances men are ever merry; But heaviness foreruns the good event.—Therefore be merry . . . *2 Hen. IV.* iv 2 82
I am here, brother, full of heaviness.—How now! rain within doors! iv 5 8
The tender boy . . . Doth weep to see his grandsire's heaviness *T. An.* iii 2 49
To-night she is mew'd up to her heaviness . . *Rom. and Jul.* iii 4 11
To put thee from thy heaviness, Hath sorted out a sudden day of joy . iii 5 109
In the heaviness of his sleep We put fresh garments on him . *Lear* iv 7 21
Our strength is all gone into heaviness, That makes the weight *Ant. and Cleo.* iv 15 33
The heaviness and guilt within my bosom Takes off my manhood *Cymb.* v 2 1
The purse too light, being drawn of heaviness . . . . v 4 168
Heaving. The heaving of my lungs provokes me to ridiculous smiling *L. L. Lost* iii 1 77
'Tis such as you That creep like shadows by him and do sigh At each his needless heavings . . . . . . *W. Tale* ii 3 35
Than the performance of our heaving spleens . . *Troi. and Cres.* ii 2 196
Heavy. Will you laugh me asleep, for I am very heavy? . . *Tempest* ii 1 189
Will guard your person while you take your rest, And watch your safety.—Thank you. Wondrous heavy . . . . . ii 1 198
This my mean task Would be as heavy to me as odious . . . iii 1 5
It is too heavy for so light a tune.—Heavy! belike it hath some burden then? . . . . *T. G. of Ver.* i 2 84
She is lumpish, heavy, melancholy, And . . . will be glad of you . iii 2 62
Talk not to me; my mind is heavy . . . . *Mer. Wives* iv 6 2
This week he hath been heavy, sour, sad, And much different *Com. of Er.* v 1 45
Sing no more ditties, sing no more, Of dumps so dull and heavy *M. Ado* ii 3 73
My heart is exceeding heavy.—'Twill be heavier soon . . . iii 4 25
An it be the right husband and the right wife; otherwise 'tis light, and not heavy . . . . iii 4 37
Her death shall fall heavy on you . . . . . . v 1 151
My spirit grows heavy in love . . . . . *L. L. Lost* i 2 127
Is not lead a metal heavy, dull, and slow?—Minimè, honest master . iii 1 60
He made her melancholy, sad, and heavy; And so she died . . v 2 14
The news I bring Is heavy in my tongue . . . . . v 2 727
Be it but so much As makes it light or heavy in the substance *M. of V.* iv 1 328
Knowing no burden of heavy tedious penury . . *As Y. Like It* iii 2 342
And yet as heavy as my weight should be . . . *T. of Shrew* ii 1 206
It is A charge too heavy for my strength . . . *All's Well* iii 3 4
Let every word weigh heavy of her worth That he does weigh too light iii 4 31
My heart is heavy and mine age is weak; Grief would have tears . iii 4 41
Shall suffer what wit can make heavy and vengeance bitter . *W. Tale* iv 4 801
The peril of our curses light on thee So heavy as thou shalt not shake them off, But in despair die under their black weight *K. John* iii 1 296
This fever, that hath troubled me so long, Lies heavy on me . . v 3 4
Be Mowbray's sins so heavy in his bosom, That they may break his foaming courser's back! . . . . . . *Richard II.* i 2 50
That lie shall lie so heavy on my sword, That it shall render vengeance iv 1 66
Some strait decrees That lie too heavy on the commonwealth *1 Hen. IV.* iv 3 80
I am as hot as molten lead, and as heavy too . . . . v 3 34
As the thing that's heavy in itself Upon enforcement flies with greatest speed, So did our men, heavy in Hotspur's loss . . . *2 Hen. IV.* i 1 121
To lay a heavy and unequal hand Upon our honours . . . iv 1 102
And let desert mount.—Thine's too heavy to mount . . . iv 3 62
Our argument Is all too heavy to admit much talk . . . iv 4 101
Well, peace be with him that hath made us heavy! . . . v 2 25
A living load, Nothing so heavy as these woes of mine . *2 Hen. VI.* v 2 65
Stay by me; My soul is heavy, and I fain would sleep *Richard III.* i 4 74
Our crosses on the way Have made it tedious, wearisome, and heavy . iii 1 5
It is too heavy for your grace to wear.—I weigh it lightly . . iii 1 120
Look that my staves be sound, and not too heavy . . . v 3 65
Let me sit heavy on thy soul to-morrow! . . . v 3 118; 131; 139
'Tis a burthen [honour] Too heavy for a man that hopes for heaven! *Hen. VIII.* iii 2 385
Bid the music leave, They are harsh and heavy to me . . . iv 2 95
Thus to persist In doing wrong extenuates not wrong, But makes it much more heavy . . . . . . *Troi. and Cres.* ii 2 188
What Trojan is that same that looks so heavy? . . . . iv 5 95

Heavy. I could weep And I could laugh, I am light and heavy *Coriolanus* ii 1 201
It would unclog my heart Of what lies heavy to't . . . . iv 2 48
Griefs of mine own lie heavy in my breast . . . *Rom. and Jul.* i 1 192
I am not for this ambling; Being but heavy, I will bear the light . . i 4 12
Many feign as they were dead; Unwieldy, slow, heavy and pale as lead ii 5 17
And nature, as it grows again toward earth, Is fashion'd for the journey, dull and heavy . . . . . . *T. of Athens* ii 2 228
It pleases time and fortune to lie heavy Upon a friend of mine . . iii 5 10
Weigh them, it is as heavy; conjure with 'em, Brutus will start a spirit as soon as Cæsar . . . . *J. Cæsar* i 2 146
Unfold to me, yourself, your half, Why you are heavy . . . ii 1 275
The sin of my ingratitude even now Was heavy on me . . *Macbeth* i 4 16
Seneca cannot be too heavy, nor Plautus too light . . . *Hamlet* ii 2 420
But in our circumstance and course of thought, 'Tis heavy with him . iii 3 84
Till that her garments, heavy with their drink, Pull'd the poor wretch from her melodious lay To muddy death . . . . . . iv 7 182
This is too heavy, let me see another.—This likes me well . . v 2 275
Their ships are yare; yours, heavy . . . . *Ant. and Cleo.* iii 7 39
How heavy weighs my lord! Our strength is all gone into heaviness, That makes the weight . . . . iv 15 32
Fair youth, come in: Discourse is heavy, fasting; when we have supp'd, We'll mannerly demand thee of thy story . . . *Cymbeline* iii 6 91
'Tis like a coffin, sir.—Whate'er it be, 'Tis wondrous heavy *Pericles* iii 2 53
Heavy accent. The senseless brands will sympathize The heavy accent of thy moving tongue . . . . . . *Richard II.* v 1 47
Heavy act. To the state This heavy act with heavy heart relate *Othello* v 2 371
Heavy bier. And thou and Romeo press one heavy bier! *Rom. and Jul.* iii 2 60
Heavy burden. And till this present hour My heavy burthen ne'er delivered . . . . *Com. of Errors* v 1 402
The poor mechanic porters crowding in Their heavy burdens . *Hen. V.* i 2 201
Under love's heavy burden do I sink . . . *Rom. and Jul.* i 4 22
Than is my deed to my most painted word: O heavy burthen! *Hamlet* iii 1 54
Heavy business. Some heavy business hath my lord in hand *1 Hen. IV.* ii 3 66
Heavy case. Is not this a heavy case, To see thy noble uncle thus distract? . . . . *T. Andron.* iv 3 25
Your eyes are in a heavy case, your purse in a light . . *Lear* iv 6 150
Heavy causes. Whom, I fear, Most just and heavy causes make oppose v 1 27
Heavy chance. This's a heavy chance 'twixt him and you . *T. of Shrew* i 2 46
Heavy conscience. My heavy conscience sinks my knee . *Cymbeline* v 5 413
Heavy consequence. Trust him not in matter of heavy consequence *All's Well* ii 5 49
Heavy curse. Purchase of a heavy curse from Rome . . *K. John* iii 1 205
Now thy heavy curse Is lighted on poor Hastings' wretched head! *Richard III.* iii 4 94
Therefore take with thee my most heavy curse . . . . iv 4 187
Heavy day. Alack the heavy day! . . . . *Richard II.* iii 3 7; iv 1 257
O heavy day!—O me, O me! My child, my only life! . *Rom. and Jul.* iv 5 18
Alas the heavy day! Why do you weep? Am I the motive of these tears? *Othello* iv 2 42
Most heavy day!—Nay, good my fellows . . . . *Ant. and Cleo.* iv 14 134
Heavy deed. O heavy deed! It had been so with us . . *Hamlet* iv 1 12
Heavy descension. From a God to a bull? a heavy descension! *2 Hen. IV.* ii 2 192
Heavy eye. So may you by my dull and heavy eye . . *Richard II.* iii 2 196
Canst thou hold up thy heavy eyes awhile? . . . *J. Cæsar* iv 3 256
Take vantage, heavy eyes, not to behold This shameful lodging . *Lear* ii 2 178
Heavy fall. That they may crush down with a heavy fall The usurping helmets of our adversaries! . . . . . *Richard III.* v 3 111
Heavy gait. Hath well beguiled The heavy gait of night *M. N. Dream* v 1 375
Heavy-gaited toads lie in their way . . . . *Richard II.* iii 2 15
Heavy hand. O Fate! take not away thy heavy hand . *Much Ado* iv 1 116
A bloody work; The graceless action of a heavy hand . . *K. John* iv 3 58
Whose heavy hand hath bow'd you to the grave And beggar'd yours *Macb.* iii 1 90
Heavens, in justice, both on her and hers, Have laid most heavy hand *Cymbeline* v 5 465
Heavy haps. By whom our heavy haps had their beginning *T. Andron.* v 3 202
Heavy-headed. This heavy-headed revel east and west Makes us traduced and tax'd of other nations . . . . *Hamlet* i 4 17
Heavy head-pieces. They could never wear such heavy head-pieces *Hen. V.* iii 7 149
Heavy heart. A heavy heart bears not a nimble-tongue . *L. L. Lost* v 2 747
And piece the way out with a heavy heart . . . *Richard II.* v 1 92
With a heavy heart, Thinking on them, go I unto the Tower *Richard III.* iii 1 149
O heart, heavy heart, Why sigh'st thou without breaking? *Troi. and Cres.* iv 4 17
Heavy hour. O, insupportable! O heavy hour! . . . *Othello* v 2 98
Heavy husband. A light wife doth make a heavy husband *Mer. of Venice* v 1 130
Heavy ignorance! thou praisest the worst best . . . *Othello* ii 1 144
Heavy interim. I a heavy interim shall support By his dear absence . i 3 259
Heavy issue. Here come the heavy issue of dead Harry . *2 Hen. IV.* v 2 14
Heavy judgement. But under heavy judgement bears that life *Macbeth* i 3 110
Heavy lead. Turn'd on themselves, like dull and heavy lead . *2 Hen. IV.* i 1 118
Heavy leave. Let thy Suffolk take his heavy leave . . *2 Hen. VI.* iii 2 306
Whose soul is that which takes her heavy leave? . . . *3 Hen. VI.* ii 6 42
Heavy lightness. O heavy lightness! serious vanity! . *Rom. and Jul.* i 1 184
Heavy load. This mutual heavy load of moan . . . *Richard III.* ii 2 113
But to relieve them of their heavy load . . . . *Pericles* i 4 91
Heavy looks. Whose heavy looks foretell Some dreadful story *3 Hen. VI.* ii 1 43
Love goes toward love, as schoolboys from their books, But love from love, toward school with heavy looks . . . *Rom. and Jul.* ii 2 158
Heavy matters! heavy matters! but look thee here, boy . *W. Tale* iii 3 115
Heavy message. Go tell this heavy message to the king *2 Hen. VI.* iii 2 379
Heavy middle. Upon the heavy middle of the night . *Meas. for Meas.* iv 1 35
Heavy mind. With the eyes of heavy mind I see thy glory *Richard II.* ii 4 18
Heavy miss. O, I should have a heavy miss of thee, If I were much in love with vanity! . . . . *1 Hen. IV.* v 4 105
Heavy music. Sings heavy music to thy timorous soul . *1 Hen. VI.* iv 2 40
Heavy news. Yonder is heavy news within . . . *All's Well* iii 2 35
There came A post from Wales loaden with heavy news . *1 Hen. IV.* i 1 37
Heavy night. Witness the tiring day and heavy night . *T. Andron.* v 2 24
Two or three groan: it is a heavy night . . . . *Othello* v 1 42
Heavy nothing. Makes me with heavy nothing faint . *Richard II.* ii 2 32
Heavy offer. Do not omit the heavy offer of it [sleep] . *Tempest* ii 1 194
Heavy orisons. Your too much love and care of me Are heavy orisons 'gainst this poor wretch! . . . . *Hen. V.* ii 2 53
Heavy people. You heavy people, circle me about . . *T. Andron.* iii 1 277
Heavy Pericles. In your supposing once more put your sight Of heavy Pericles . . . . *Pericles* v Gower 22
Heavy plight. As thou seest, ourselves in heavy plight . *3 Hen. VI.* iii 3 37
Heavy ploughman. Whilst the heavy ploughman snores *M. N. Dream* v 1 380
Heavy reckoning. If the cause be not good, the king himself hath a heavy reckoning . . . . *Hen. V.* iv 1 141
A heavy reckoning for you, sir . . . . . . *Cymbeline* v 4 159

Heavy riches. Thou bear'st thy heavy riches but a journey *Meas. for Meas.* iii 1 27
Heavy sad. So heavy sad As, though on thinking on no thought I think, Makes me with heavy nothing faint and shrink . *Richard II.* ii 2 30
Heavy satisfaction. She ceased In heavy satisfaction . *All's Well* v 3 100
Heavy sense. Under whose heavy sense your brother's life Falls into forfeit . . . . *Meas. for Meas.* i 4 65
Heavy sentence. A heavy sentence, my most sovereign liege *Richard II.* i 3 154
Heavy sight. A heavy sight!—I am dying, Egypt, dying *Ant. and Cleo.* iv 15 40
Heavy son. Away from light steals home my heavy son . *Rom. and Jul.* i 1 143
Heavy sorrow. Thy due from me Is tears and heavy sorrows 2 *Hen. IV.* iv 5 38
And bid her hasten all the house to bed, Which heavy sorrow makes them apt unto . . . . . *Rom. and Jul.* iii 3 157
Heavy story. If thou tell'st the heavy story right, Upon my soul, the hearers will shed tears . . . 3 *Hen. VI.* i 4 160
Heavy substance. But thou dost breathe; Hast heavy substance *Lear* iv 6 52
Heavy summons. A heavy summons lies like lead upon me *Macbeth* ii 1 6
Heavy tale. That tells a heavy tale for him . . . *Much Ado* iii 2 63
Heavy task. And day by day I'll do this heavy task . *T. Andron.* v 2 58
Give me aim awhile, For nature puts me to a heavy task . . v 3 150
Heavy terms. Thrown such despite and heavy terms upon her *Othello* iv 2 116
Heavy-thick. That surly spirit, melancholy, Had baked thy blood and made it heavy-thick . . . . . *K. John* iii 3 43
Heavy thought. To drive away the heavy thought of care *Richard II.* iii 4 2
Heavy time. Still and anon cheer'd up the heavy time . . *K. John* iv 1 47
O heavy times, begetting such events! . . 3 *Hen. VI.* ii 5 63
Heavy toil. Scarce show a harvest of their heavy toil . *L. L. Lost* iv 3 326
Heavy weight. I would bend under any heavy weight . . *Much Ado* v 1 287
I give this heavy weight from off my head . . *Richard II.* iv 1 204
Heavy well-a-day. While our scene must play His daughter's woe and heavy well-a-day . . . . . *Pericles* iv 4 49
Heavy womb. Thou slander of thy mother's heavy womb! *Richard III.* i 3 231
Hebenon. With juice of cursed hebenon in a vial . . *Hamlet* i 5 62
Hebrew. If not, thou art an Hebrew, a Jew . . *T. G. of Ver.* ii 5 57
Tubal, a wealthy Hebrew of my tribe, Will furnish me . *Mer. of Venice* i 3 58
The Hebrew will turn Christian: he grows kind . . i 3 180
Hecate. We fairies, that do run By the triple Hecate's team *M. N. Dream* v 1 391
I speak not to that railing Hecate, But unto thee . 1 *Hen. VI.* iii 2 64
Witchcraft celebrates Pale Hecate's offerings . . *Macbeth* ii 1 52
Ere to black Hecate's summons The shard-borne beetle with his drowsy hums Hath rung night's yawning peal . . . iii 2 41
Why, how now, Hecate! you look angerly.—Have I not reason, beldams? iii 5 1
Of midnight weeds collected, With Hecate's ban thrice blasted *Hamlet* iii 2 269
By the sacred radiance of the sun, The mysteries of Hecate . . *Lear* i 1 112
Hectic. For like the hectic in my blood he rages . . *Hamlet* iv 3 68
Hector. Said I well, bully Hector? . . . *Mer. Wives* i 3 12
Thou art a Castalion-King-Urinal. Hector of Greece, my boy! . ii 3 35
I take him to be valiant.—As Hector, I assure you . . *Much Ado* ii 3 196
He presents Hector of Troy . . . . . *L. L. Lost* v 2 537
Hide thy head, Achilles: here comes Hector in arms . . v 2 636
Hector was but a Troyan in respect of this . . . . v 2 639
But is this Hector?—I think Hector was not so clean-timbered . v 2 641
His leg is too big for Hector's.—More calf, certain . . . v 2 644
This cannot be Hector.—He's a god or a painter . . . v 2 647
The armipotent Mars, of lances the almighty, Gave Hector a gift . v 2 658
Rein thy tongue.—I must rather give it the rein, for it runs against Hector.—Ay, and Hector's a greyhound . . . . v 2 664
Bestow on me the sense of hearing.—Speak, brave Hector . . v 2 671
This Hector far surmounted Hannibal,— The party is gone, fellow Hector v 2 677
Then shall Hector be whipped for Jaquenetta that is quick by him . v 2 686
Hector trembles.—Pompey is moved.—More Ates, more Ates! stir them on! . . . . v 2 693
Hector will challenge him.—Ay, if a' have no more man's blood in's belly than will sup a flea . . . . v 2 696
Was not that Hector?—The worthy knight of Troy . . . v 2 889
As valorous as Hector of Troy, worth five of Agamemnon . 2 *Hen. IV.* ii 4 237
A second Hector, for his grim aspect, And large proportion . 1 *Hen. VI.* ii 3 20
Farewell, my Hector, and my Troy's true hope . 3 *Hen. VI.* iv 8 25
Lest Hector or my father should perceive me . . *Troi. and Cres.* i 1 36
Hector, whose patience Is, as a virtue, fix'd, to-day was moved . i 2 4
Every flower Did, as a prophet, weep what it foresaw In Hector's wrath i 2 11
A lord of Trojan blood, nephew to Hector; They call him Ajax . i 2 13
But how should this man, that makes me smile, make Hector angry? . i 2 33
They say he yesterday coped Hector in the battle and struck him down, the disdain and shame whereof hath ever since kept Hector fasting and waking . . . . i 2 34
Hector's a gallant man.—As may be in the world, lady . . i 2 40
Was Hector armed and gone ere ye came to Ilium? Helen was not up, was she?—Hector was gone, but Helen was not up.—E'en so: Hector was stirring early . . . . i 2 49
O Jupiter! there's no comparison.—What, not between Troilus and Hector? . . . . i 2 66
He is not Hector.—No, nor Hector is not Troilus in some degrees . i 2 72
Hector shall not have his wit this year.—He shall not need it . i 2 92
And yet will he, within three pound, lift as much as his brother Hector i 2 127
And Hector laughed.—At what was all this laughing? . . . i 2 162
That's Hector, that, that, look you, that; there's a fellow! . . i 2 215
Go thy way, Hector! There's a brave man, niece. O brave Hector! . i 2 216
How his sword is bloodied, and his helm more hacked than Hector's! . i 2 254
The great Hector's sword had lack'd a master, But for these instances . i 3 76
We have, great Agamemnon, here in Troy A prince call'd Hector . i 3 261
Hector, in view of Trojans and of Greeks, Shall make it good . i 3 273
If any come, Hector shall honour him . . . . . i 3 280
Not in love! If then one is, or hath, or means to be, That one meets Hector i 3 290
Nestor, one that was a man When Hector's grandsire suck'd . . i 3 292
This challenge that the gallant Hector sends, However it is spread in general name, Relates in purpose only to Achilles . . . i 3 321
Ay, with celerity, find Hector's purpose Pointing on him . . i 3 330
Whom may you else oppose, That can from Hector bring his honour off, If not Achilles? . . . . i 3 334
It is supposed He that meets Hector issues from our choice . . i 3 347
Give pardon to my speech: Therefore 'tis meet Achilles meet not Hector i 3 358
Do not consent That ever Hector and Achilles meet . . . i 3 363
What glory our Achilles shares from Hector, Were he not proud, we all should share with him . . . . i 3 367
And we were better parch in Afric sun Than in the pride and salt scorn of his eyes, Should he 'scape Hector fair . . . . i 3 372
And, by device, let blockish Ajax draw The sort to fight with Hector . i 3 376
Hector shall have a great catch, if he knock out either of your brains . ii 1 109
Hector, by the fifth hour of the sun, Will with a trumpet 'twixt our tents and Troy To-morrow morning call some knight to arms . . ii 1 134
Hector. Thus once again says Nestor from the Greeks: 'Deliver Helen' . . . Hector, what say you to't? . . . . *Troi. and Cres.* ii 2 7
There is no lady of more softer bowels, . . . More ready to cry out 'Who knows what follows?' Than Hector is . . . . . ii 2 14
Why, brother Hector, We may not think the justness of each act Such ii 2 118
Hector's opinion Is this in way of truth . . . . . ii 2 188
But, worthy Hector, She is a theme of honour and renown . . ii 2 198
Brave Hector would not lose So rich advantage of a promised glory . ii 2 203
Who's a-field to-day?—Hector, Deiphobus, Helenus, Antenor . iii 1 148
Sweet Helen, I must woo you To help unarm our Hector . . . iii 1 163
You shall do more Than all the island kings,—disarm great Hector . iii 1 167
Bring word if Hector will to-morrow Be answer'd in his challenge . iii 3 34
Even already They clap the lubber Ajax on the shoulder, As if his foot were on brave Hector's breast . . . . iii 3 140
Better would it fit Achilles much To throw down Hector than Polyxena iii 3 208
And all the Greekish girls shall tripping sing, 'Great Hector's sister did Achilles win' . . . . iii 3 212
I have a woman's longing . . . To see great Hector in his weeds of peace iii 3 239
He must fight singly to-morrow with Hector . . . . . iii 3 248
If Hector break not his neck i' the combat, he'll break 't himself in vain-glory . . . . iii 3 259
Invite the most valorous Hector to come unarmed to my tent . iii 3 276
I come from the worthy Achilles,— Ha!—Who most humbly desires you to invite Hector to his tent . . . . iii 3 286
What music will be in him when Hector has knocked out his brains . iii 3 303
With a bridegroom's fresh alacrity, Let us address to tend on Hector's heels . . . . iv 4 148
Stretch thy chest, and let thy eyes spout blood; Thou blow'st for Hector iv 5 11
Hector bade ask.—Which way would Hector have it?—He cares not . iv 5 71
'Tis done like Hector; but securely done, A little proudly . . iv 5 73
Valour and pride excel themselves in Hector . . . . iv 5 79
This Ajax is half made of Hector's blood: In love whereof, half Hector stays at home; Half heart, half hand, half Hector comes to seek This blended knight . . . . iv 5 83
Manly as Hector, but more dangerous; For Hector in his blaze of wrath subscribes To tender objects . . . . iv 5 104
And on him [Troilus] erect A second hope, as fairly built as Hector . iv 5 109
Now, Ajax, hold thine own!—Hector, thou sleep'st; Awake thee! . iv 5 114
I am not warm yet; let us fight again.—As Hector pleases . . iv 5 119
Let me embrace thee, Ajax: By him that thunders, thou hast lusty arms; Hector would have them fall upon him thus . . . . . iv 5 137
I thank thee, Hector: Thou art too gentle and too free a man . . iv 5 138
Not Neoptolemus so mirable . . . could promise to himself A thought of added honour torn from Hector . . . . iv 5 145
And great Achilles Doth long to see unarm'd the valiant Hector . . iv 5 153
From heart of very heart, great Hector, welcome . . . . iv 5 171
Most gentle and most valiant Hector, welcome . . . . iv 5 227
Now, Hector, I have fed mine eyes on thee; I have with exact view perused thee, Hector, And quoted joint by joint . . . . iv 5 231
And make distinct the very breach whereout Hector's great spirit flew iv 5 246
You may have every day enough of Hector, If you have stomach . iv 5 263
Dost thou entreat me, Hector? To-morrow do I meet thee, fell as death iv 5 268
Afterwards, As Hector's leisure and your bounties shall Concur together, severally entreat him . . . . iv 5 273
Old Nestor tarries; and you too, Diomed, Keep Hector company . . v 1 88
I will rather leave to see Hector, than not to dog him . . . . v 1 103
Hector, by this, is arming him in Troy . . . . . . v 2 183
Where is my brother Hector?—Here, sister; arm'd, and bloody in intent . . . . v 3 7
But vows to every purpose must not hold: Unarm, sweet Hector . v 3 25
O, 'tis fair play.—Fool's play, by heaven, Hector.—How now! . . v 3 43
Hector, then 'tis wars.—Troilus, I would not have you fight to-day . v 3 49
Hector, come, go back: Thy wife hath dream'd; thy mother hath had visions . . . . v 3 62
O, farewell, dear Hector! Look, how thou diest! look, how thy eye turns pale! . . . . v 3 80
And all cry, Hector! Hector's dead! O Hector! . . . . v 3 87
Hector, I take my leave: Thou dost thyself and all our Troy deceive . v 3 89
Art thou for Hector's match? Art thou of blood and honour? . . v 4 28
There is a thousand Hectors in the field: Now here he fights on Galathe his horse, And there lacks work . . . . v 5 19
His mangled Myrmidons, That noseless, handless, hack'd and chipp'd, come to him, Crying on Hector . . . . v 5 35
Where is this Hector? Come, come, thou boy-queller, show thy face . v 5 44
Hector! where's Hector? I will none but Hector . . . . v 5 47
Now do I see thee, ha! have at thee, Hector!—Pause, if thou wilt . v 6 13
And when I have the bloody Hector found, Empale him with your weapons . . . . v 7 4
It is decreed Hector the great must die . . . . . . v 7 8
Look, Hector, how the sun begins to set; How ugly night comes breathing at his heels: Even with the vail and darking of the sun, To close the day up, Hector's life is done . . . . . . v 8 5
And cry you all amain, 'Achilles hath the mighty Hector slain' . . v 8 14
The bruit is, Hector's slain, and by Achilles.—If it be so, yet bragless let it be; Great Hector was a man as good as he . . . . v 9 4
Hector is slain.—Hector! the gods forbid!—He's dead . . . . v 10 3
Hector is gone: Who shall tell Priam so, or Hecuba? Let him that will a screech-owl aye be call'd, Go in to Troy, and say there, Hector's dead . . . . v 10 14
March away: Hector is dead; there is no more to say . . . v 10 22
The breasts of Hecuba, When she did suckle Hector, look'd not lovelier Than Hector's forehead when it spit forth blood At Grecian sword *Cor.* i 3 44
Wert thou the Hector That was the whip of your bragg'd progeny, Thou shouldst not scape me here . . . . i 8 11
Kneel, sweet boy, the Roman Hector's hope . . . *T. Andron.* iv 1 88
You have shown all Hectors. Enter the city, clip your wives *A. and C.* iv 8 7
Hecuba. Who were those went by?—Queen Hecuba and Helen *T. and C.* i 2 1
Queen Hecuba laughed that her eyes ran o'er . . . . . i 2 157
Here is a letter from Queen Hecuba, A token from her daughter . . v 1 44
Not Priamus and Hecuba on knees . . . should stop my way . . v 3 54
Hark, how Troy roars! how Hecuba cries out! . . . . . v 3 83
Hector is gone: Who shall tell Priam so, or Hecuba? . . . v 10 15
The breasts of Hecuba, When she did suckle Hector, look'd not lovelier Than Hector's forehead when it spit forth blood At Grecian sword *Coriolanus* i 3 43
And I have read that Hecuba of Troy Ran mad for sorrow *T. Andron.* iv 1 20
Say on: come to Hecuba.—'But who, O, who had seen the mobled queen' . . . . *Hamlet* ii 2 523
What's Hecuba to him, or he to Hecuba, That he should weep for her? ii 2 585
All curses madded Hecuba gave the Greeks, And mine to boot *Cymbeline* iv 2 313

Hedge. Am fain to shuffle, to hedge and to lurch . . *Mer. Wives* ii 2 26
I had rather be a canker in a hedge than a rose in his grace . *Much Ado* i 3 28
The white sheet bleaching on the hedge . . . . . *W. Tale* iv 3 5
I will but look upon the hedge and follow you . . . . iv 4 857
Her fruit-trees all unpruned, her hedges ruin'd . *Richard II.* iii 4 45
Thy horse stands behind the hedge : when thou needest him . 1 *Hen. IV.* ii 2 74
They'll find linen enough on every hedge . . . . . iv 2 52
Her hedges even-pleach'd, Like prisoners wildly overgrown with hair, Put forth disorder'd twigs . . . . *Hen. V.* v 2 42
Meads and hedges, Defective in their natures, grow to wildness . v 2 54
Sharp stakes pluck'd out of hedges They pitched in the ground 1 *Hen. VI.* i 1 117
Born under a hedge, for his father had never a house but the cage 2 *Hen. VI.* iv 2 55
How he coasts And hedges his own way . . . . *Hen. VIII.* iii 2 39
Nay, this shall not hedge us out : we'll hear you sing *Troi. and Cres.* iii 1 65
If you give way, Or hedge aside from the direct forthright . iii 3 158
I'll not endure it : you forget yourself, To hedge me in . . *J. Cæsar* iv 3 30
There's such divinity doth hedge a king . . . . *Hamlet* iv 5 123
Thy palate then did deign The roughest berry on the rudest hedge *A. and C.* i 4 64
Hedge-born. Like a hedge-born swain That doth presume to boast of gentle blood . . . . 1 *Hen. VI.* iv 1 43
Hedge-corner. Saw'st thou not, boy, how Silver made it good At the hedge-corner, in the coldest fault? . . . *T. of Shrew* Ind. 1 20
He can come no other way but by this hedge-corner . *All's Well* iv 1 2
Hedged. If my father had not scanted me And hedged me *Mer. of Venice* ii 1 18
England, hedged in with the main, That water-walled bulwark *K. John* ii 1 26
Hedgehog. Like hedgehogs which Lie tumbling in my barefoot way *Temp.* ii 2 10
Spotted snakes with double tongue, Thorny hedgehogs . *M. N. Dream* ii 2 10
I grant ye.—Dost grant me, hedgehog? . . . *Richard III.* i 2 102
Hedge-pig. Thrice the brinded cat hath mew'd.—Thrice and once the hedge-pig whined . . . . *Macbeth* iv 1 2
Hedge-priest. The pedant, the braggart, the hedge-priest . *L. L. Lost* v 2 545
Hedge-sparrow. The hedge-sparrow fed the cuckoo so long, That it had it head bit off by it young . . . . . . *Lear* i 4 235
Heed. I am more serious than my custom : you Must be so too, if heed me . . . . *Tempest* ii 1 220
Therefore take heed, As Hymen's lamps shall light you . . . iv 1 22
Take heed, have open eye, for thieves do foot by night . *Mer. Wives* ii 1 126
Take heed, ere summer comes or cuckoo-birds do sing . . ii 1 127
And teach your ears to list me with more heed . *Com. of Errors* iv 1 101
That eye shall be his heed And give him light . . *L. L. Lost* i 1 82
Take heed the queen come not within his sight . *M. N. Dream* ii 1 19
Take heed, honest Launcelot ; take heed, honest Gobbo . *Mer. of Venice* ii 2 7
'Hic steterat Priami,' take heed he hear us not . *T. of Shrew* iii 1 44
Take heed, Signior Baptista, lest you be cony-catched in this business . v 1 101
Those girls of Italy, take heed of them . . . *All's Well* ii 1 19
Diana, take heed of this French earl : the honour of a maid is her name iii 5 12
Take heed of the allurement of one Count Rousillon, a foolish idle boy . iv 3 241
Alas the day ! take heed of him ; he stabbed me in mine own house 2 *Hen. IV.* ii 1 14
Therefore take heed what guests you receive . . . . ii 4 101
Therefore let men take heed of their company . . . . v 1 86
Therefore take heed how you impawn our person . . *Hen. V.* i 2 21
Sit with us once more, with better heed To re-survey them . . v 2 80
Take heed, be wary how you place your words . 1 *Hen. VI.* iii 2 3
If you take not heed, you shall go near To call them both a pair of crafty knaves . . . . 2 *Hen. VI.* i 2 102
Who cannot steal a shape that means deceit? Take heed, my lord . iii 1 80
Take heed, lest by your heat you burn yourselves . . . . v 1 160
Take heed of yonder dog ! Look, when he fawns, he bites *Richard III.* i 3 289
And wilt thou, then, Spurn at his edict and fulfil a man's? Take heed i 4 204
Take heed you dally not before your king . . . . . ii 1 12
With all the heed I may . . . . iii 1 187
Take good heed You charge not in your spleen a noble person And spoil your nobler soul : I say, take heed . . . . . *Hen. VIII.* i 2 173
Thus it came ; give heed to't . . . . ii 4 169
Take heed, for heaven's sake, take heed, lest at once The burthen of my sorrows fall upon ye . . . . iii 1 110
He did it with a serious mind ; a heed Was in his countenance . . iii 2 80
Let them take heed of Troilus, I can tell them that too . *Troi. and Cres.* i 2 60
Take heed, the quarrel's most ominous to us . . . . v 7 20
Have you with heed perused What I have written to you? . *Coriolanus* v 6 62
Take heed, take heed, for such die miserable . . *Rom. and Jul.* iii 3 145
I give thee warning on't.—I take no heed of thee . *T. of Athens* i 2 34
Hath stepp'd into the law, which is past depth To those that, without heed, do plunge into't . . . . iii 5 13
But there's no heed to be taken of them . . . . *J. Cæsar* i 2 276
Cæsar, beware of Brutus ; take heed of Cassius ; come not near Casca . ii 3 1
Put on him What forgeries you please ; marry, none so rank As may dishonour him ; take heed of that . . . . . . *Hamlet* ii 1 21
I am sorry that with better heed and judgement I had not quoted him . ii 1 111
Take heed, sirrah ; the whip . . . . *Lear* i 4 123
Take heed o' the foul fiend : obey thy parents ; keep thy word justly . iii 4 82
Take heed on't ; Make it a darling like your precious eye . *Othello* iii 4 65
Sweet soul, take heed, Take heed of perjury ; thou art on thy death-bed v 2 50
Come, down into the boat.—Take heed you fall not . . *Ant. and Cleo.* ii 7 136
Heeded. Take thou no care ; it shall be heeded . . . . v 2 269
Heedful. To him one of the other twins was bound, Whilst I had been like heedful of the other . . . . . . *Com. of Errors* i 1 83
And the heedful slave Is wander'd forth, in care to seek me out . ii 2 2
Be heedful : hence, and watch . . . . . . *K. John* iv 1 5
Where fame, late entering at his heedful ears, Hath placed thy beauty's image and thy virtue . . . . . . 3 *Hen. VI.* iii 3 63
Give him heedful note ; For I mine eyes will rivet to his face. *Hamlet* iii 2 89
Heedfullest. In heedfull'st reservation to bestow them . *All's Well* i 3 231
Heedfully. Dost thou attend me?—Sir, most heedfully . *Tempest* i 2 78
Unheedful vows may heedfully be broken . . *T. G. of Ver.* ii 6 11
Sit I in the sky, And wretched fools' secrets heedfully o'er-eye *L. L. Lost* iv 3 80
Heedless. You heedless joltheads and unmanner'd slaves ! *T. of Shrew* iv 1 169
O, negligent and heedless discipline ! . . . 1 *Hen. VI.* iv 2 44
Heel. Here follow her vices.—Close at the heels of her virtues *T. G. of V.* iii 1 325
Well, sirs, I am almost out at heels . . . . . . *Mer. Wives* i 3 34
Come, take a your rapier, and come after my heel to the court . i 4 62
I shall turn your head out of my door. Follow my heels . . i 4 132
Prevent, or go thou, Like Sir Actæon he, with Ringwood at thy heels . ii 1 122
Let us wag, then.—Come at my heels, Jack Rugby . . . ii 3 103
Whether had you rather lead mine eyes, or eye your master's heels? . iii 2 4
Your husband's coming, with half Windsor at his heels . . . iii 3 122
And at his heels a rabble of his companions . . . . iii 5 76
In the circumference of a peck, hilt to point, heel to head . . iii 5 113
Hold your hands ! Nay, an you will not, sir, I'll take my heels *C. of Er.* i 2 94
Heel. You would keep from my heels and beware of an ass *Com. of Errors* iii 1 18
And at her heels a huge infectious troop Of pale distemperatures . . v 1 81
Sing it, and I'll dance it.—Ye light o' love, with your heels ! . *Much Ado* iii 4 47
I scorn that with my heels . . . . iii 4 51
Let's have a dance ere we are married, that we may lighten our own hearts and our wives' heels . . . . v 4 121
Do not run ; scorn running with thy heels . . *Mer. of Venice* ii 2 10
I will run, fiend ; my heels are at your command ; I will run. . . ii 2 33
It is young Orlando, that tripp'd up the wrestler's heels and your heart both in an instant . . . . *As Y. Like It* iii 2 225
You have a nimble wit : I think 'twas made of Atalanta's heels . . iii 2 294
Thou mayst slide from my shoulder to my heel with no greater a run but my head and my neck . . . . *T. of Shrew* iv 1 15
Melancholy oft began, On the catastrophe and heel of pastime *All's Well* i 2 57
Where death and danger dogs the heels of worth . . . . iii 4 15
His heels have deserved it, in usurping his spurs so long . . iv 3 118
You might see more detraction at your heels than fortunes before you *T. Night* ii 5 149
Pants and looks pale, as if a bear were at his heels . . . iii 4 324
What maids lack from head to heel . . . . . *W. Tale* iv 4 229
Stealing away from his father with his clog at his heels . . iv 4 695
Whom I found With many hundreds treading on his heels . *K. John* iv 2 149
Be Mercury, set feathers to thy heels, And fly like thought . . iv 2 174
The Dauphin rages at our very heels . . . . . . v 7 80
Destruction straight shall dog them at the heels . . *Richard II.* v 3 139
Show it a fair pair of heels and run from it . . . 1 *Hen. IV.* ii 4 53
Hang me up by the heels for a rabbit-sucker or a poulter's hare . ii 4 480
To dog his heels and curtsy at his frowns . . . . . iii 2 127
Pages follow'd him Even at the heels in golden multitudes . . iv 3 73
Struck his armed heels Against the panting sides of his poor jade 2 *Hen. IV.* i 1 44
Thou art fitter to be worn in my cap than to wait at my heels . . i 2 18
To punish you by the heels would amend the attention of your ears . i 2 141
He leaves his back unarm'd, the French and Welsh Baying him at the heels . . . . i 3 80
He came sighing on After the admired heels of Bolingbroke . . i 3 105
And at his heels, Leash'd in like hounds, should famine, sword and fire Crouch for employment . . . . *Hen. V.* Prol. 6
With winged heels, as English Mercuries . . . . . ii Prol. 7
Saying our grace is only in our heels . . . . . . iii 5 34
And with wild rage Yerk out their armed heels at their dead masters . iv 7 83
Brother Gloucester, Follow Fluellen closely at the heels . . . iv 7 179
Senators of the antique Rome, With the plebeians swarming at their heels . . . . v Prol. 27
Your hearts I'll stamp out with my horse's heels . . 1 *Hen. VI.* i 4 108
The bodies shall be dragged at my horse heels . . 2 *Hen. VI.* iv 3 14
My followers' base and ignominious treasons makes me betake me to my heels . . . . iv 8 67
Hence will I drag thee headlong by the heels Unto a dunghill . . iv 10 86
Get thee hence ! Death and destruction dog thee at the heels *Rich. III.* iv 1 40
I'll lay ye all By the heels, and suddenly . . . *Hen. VIII.* v 4 83
I will begin at thy heel, and tell what thou art by inches *Troi. and Cres.* ii 1 53
Set The very wings of reason to his heels And fly like chidden Mercury ii 2 44
I cannot sing, Nor heel the high lavolt, nor sweeten talk . . iv 4 88
With a bridegroom's fresh alacrity, Let us address to tend on Hector's heels . . . . iv 4 148
The sun begins to set ; How ugly night comes breathing at his heels . v 8 6
Following the fliers at the very heels, With them he enters . *Coriolanus* i 4 49
Will too late Tie leaden pounds to's heels . . . . . iii 1 314
Present me Death on the wheel or at wild horses' heels . . . iii 2 2
I'll dive into the burning lake below, And pull her out of Acheron by the heels . . . . *T. Andron.* iv 3 44
Well-apparell'd April on the heel Of limping winter treads *Rom. and Jul.* i 2 27
Let wantons light of heart Tickle the senseless rushes with their heels i 4 36
By my head, here come the Capulets.—By my heel, I care not . iii 1 39
When comes your book forth?—Upon the heels of my presentment *T. of Athens* i 1 27
I will fly, like a dog, the heels o' the ass . . . . . i 1 282
Will these moss'd trees, That have outlived the eagle, page thy heels? . iv 3 224
The throng that follows Cæsar at the heels, Of senators, of prætors, common suitors, Will crowd a feeble man almost to death *J. Cæsar* ii 4 34
We will grace his heels With the most boldest and best hearts of Rome iii 1 120
Compell'd these skipping kerns to trust their heels . . *Macbeth* i 2 30
We coursed him at the heels, and had a purpose To be his purveyor . i 6 21
But is there no sequel at the heels of this mother's admiration? *Hamlet* iii 2 341
Then trip him, that his heels may kick at heaven . . . iii 3 93
At his head a grass-green turf, At his heels a stone . . . iv 5 32
One woe doth tread upon another's heel, So fast they follow . . iv 7 164
The toe of the peasant comes so near the heel of the courtier, he galls his kibe . . . . v 1 152
If a man's brains were in's heels, were't not in danger of kibes? . *Lear* i 5 8
Is it two days ago since I tripped up thy heels, and beat thee? . . ii 2 32
A good man's fortune may grow out at heels . . . . ii 2 164
A dozen sequent messengers This very night at one another's heels *Othello* i 2 42
At thy heel Did famine follow . . . . . *Ant. and Cleo.* i 4 58
I must thank him only, Lest my remembrance suffer ill report ; At heel of that, defy him . . . . ii 2 160
The soldier That has this morning left thee would have still Follow'd thy heels.—Who's gone this morning? . . . . iv 5 6
The hearts That spaniel'd me at heels, to whom I gave Their wishes . iv 12 21
A rider like myself, who ne'er wore rowel Nor iron on his heel ! *Cymb.* iv 4 40
To-day how many would have given their honours To have saved their carcases ! took heel to do't, And yet died too ! . . . . . v 3 67
Heft. He cracks his gorge, his sides, With violent hefts . . *W. Tale* ii 1 45
Heifer. Yet the steer, the heifer and the calf Are all call'd neat . i 2 124
Even such kin as the parish heifers are to the town bull . 2 *Hen. IV.* ii 2 171
Who finds the heifer dead and bleeding fresh And sees fast by a butcher with an axe, But will suspect 'twas he that made the slaughter? 2 *Hen. VI.* iii 2 188
As fox to lamb, as wolf to heifer's calf . . . . *Troi. and Cres* iii 2 200
Heigh-ho. I may sit in a corner and cry heigh-ho for a husband ! *M. Ado* ii 1 332
By my troth, I am exceeding ill : heigh-ho ! . . . . . iii 4 54
Heigh-ho ! sing, heigh-ho ! unto the green holly . *As Y. Like It* ii 7 180
Then, heigh-ho, the holly ! This life is most jolly . . . ii 7 182
Height. Therefore I know she is about my height . *T. G. of Ver.* iv 4 169
In the height of this bath, when I was more than half stewed *M. Wives* iii 5 120
Punish them to your height of pleasure . . . *Meas. for Meas.* v 1 240
Dishonour'd me Even in the strength and height of injury *Com. of Errors* v 1 200
Is he not approved in the height a villain? . . . *Much Ado* iv 1 303
She hath urged her height ; And with her personage, her tall personage, Her height, forsooth, she hath prevail'd with him . *M. N. Dream* iii 2 291

Height. You may as well go stand upon the beach And bid the main flood bate his usual height . *Mer. of Venice* iv 1 72
At the height of heart-heaviness . . . . . . *As Y. Like It* v 2 50
I shall now put you to the height of your breeding . . . *All's Well* ii 2 2
This is the very top, The height, the crest, or crest unto the crest, Of murder's arms . . . . *K. John* iv 3 46
With pale beggar-fear impeach my height . . . . *Richard II.* i 1 189
'Tis with my mind As with the tide swell'd up unto his height *2 Hen. IV.* ii 3 63
Hold hard the breath and bend up every spirit To his full height *Hen. V.* iii 1 17
Or flourish to the height of my degree . . . . *1 Hen. VI.* ii 4 111
By Him that raised me to this careful height . . . *Richard III.* i 3 83
Seduced the pitch and height of all his thoughts To base declension . iii 7 188
The dignity and height of honour, The high imperial type of this earth's glory . . . . iv 4 243
And Richard falls in height of all his pride . . . . v 3 176
By day and night, He's traitor to the height . . . . *Hen. VIII.* i 2 214
The eastern tower, Whose height commands as subject all the vale *Troi. and Cres.* i 2 3
Let us feast him to the height . . . . v 1 3
But to your wishes' height advance you both . . . *T. Andron.* ii 1 125
My grief was at the height before thou camest, And now, like Nilus, it disdaineth bounds . . . . iii 1 70
Strangers, and more than so, Captives, to be advanced to this height? . iv 2 34
Urge it no more, On height of our displeasure . . *T. of Athens* iii 5 87
We, at the height, are ready to decline . . . *J. Cæsar* iv 3 217
It takes From our achievements, though perform'd at height, The pith and marrow of our attribute . . . . . . *Hamlet* i 4 21
They know, By the height, the lowness, or the mean, if dearth Or foison follow . . . . *Ant. and Cleo.* ii 7 22
And, like a doting mallard, Leaving the fight in height, flies after her iii 10 21
Even in the height and pride of all his glory . . . *Pericles* ii 4 6
Take you the marks of her, the colour of her hair, complexion, height, age . . . . iv 2 62

Heightened. Who being so heighten'd, He water'd his new plants with dews of flattery . . . . *Coriolanus* v 6 22

Heinous. Alack, what heinous sin is it in me To be ashamed to be my father's child! . . . . *Mer. of Venice* ii 3 16
But spoke the harm that is by others done?—Which harm within itself so heinous is As it makes harmful all that speak of it . *K. John* iii 1 40
You hold too heinous a respect of grief . . . . . iii 4 90
The image of a wicked heinous fault Lives in his eye . . iv 2 71
Prove a deadly bloodshed but a jest, Exampled by this heinous spectacle iv 3 56
O, forfend it, God, That in a Christian climate souls refined Should show so heinous, black, obscene a deed! . . . *Richard II.* iv 1 131
If thou wouldst, There shouldst thou find one heinous article . v 1 233
How heinous e'er it be, To win thy after-love I pardon thee . . v 3 34
O heinous, strong and bold conspiracy! . . . . . v 3 59
If thou delight to view thy heinous deeds, Behold this . *Richard III.* i 2 53
Ingratitude, Which Rome reputes to be a heinous sin . . *T. Andron.* i 1 448
I do remit these young men's heinous faults . . . . i 1 484
Performers of this heinous, bloody deed . . . . iv 1 80
Art thou not sorry for these heinous deeds? . . . . v 1 123
I am Revenge, sent from below To join with him and right his heinous wrongs . . . . v 2 4
That heinous tiger, Tamora . . . . v 3 195
To prove upon thy head Thy heinous, manifest, and many treasons *Lear* v 3 92
The vengeance . . . Due to this heinous capital offence . . *Pericles* ii 4 5

Heinously. I am heinously unprovided . . . *1 Hen. IV.* iii 3 213

Heir. Thy father Was Duke of Milan; and thou his only heir . *Tempest* i 2 58
O thou mine heir Of Naples and of Milan, what strange fish Hath made his meal on thee? . . . . ii 1 111
Who's the next heir of Naples?—Claribel.—She that is queen of Tunis . ii 1 245
My brother's daughter's queen of Tunis; So is she heir of Naples . ii 1 256
Banished For practising to steal away a lady, An heir *T. G. of Ver.* iv 1 49
You orphan heirs of fixed destiny, Attend your office . *Mer. Wives* v 5 43
In her forehead; armed and reverted, making war against her heir *Com. of Errors* iii 2 127
No child but Hero; she's his only heir. Dost thou affect her? *M. Ado* i 1 297
Which way looks he?—Marry, on Hero, the daughter and heir of Leonato . . . . i 3 57
And she alone is heir to both of us . . . . . . v 1 299
And make us heirs of all eternity . . . . *L. L. Lost* i 1 7
The beauteous heir Of Jaques Falconbridge . . . . ii 1 41
What lady is that same?—The heir of Alençon, Katharine her name . ii 1 195
Be not offended. She is an heir of Falconbridge.—Nay, my choler is ended . . . . ii 1 205
The armipotent Mars, of lances the almighty, Gave Hector a gift, the heir of Ilion . . . . v 2 658
Shall I say to you, Let them be free, marry them to your heirs? *M. of V.* iv 1 94
And, truly, when he dies, thou shalt be his heir . . *As Y. Like It* i 2 20
And would not change that calling, To be adopted heir to Frederick . i 2 246
Let my father seek another heir . . . . . . i 3 101
Left solely heir to all his lands and goods . . . *T. of Shrew* ii 1 118
List to me: I am my father's heir and only son: If I may have your daughter . . . . ii 1 366
He is mine only son, and heir to the lands of me . . . v 1 88
She is young, wise, fair; In these to nature she's immediate heir *All's W.* ii 3 139
The king shall live without an heir, if that which is lost be not found *W. Tale* iii 2 136
Thou a sceptre's heir, That thus affect'st a sheep-hook! . . . iv 4 430
From my succession wipe me, father; I Am heir to my affection . . iv 4 492
King Leontes shall not have an heir Till his lost child be found . v 1 39
The crown will find an heir: great Alexander Left his to the worthiest v 1 47
Has the king found his heir?—Most true, if ever truth were pregnant . v 2 32
With your crown'd brother and these your contracted Heirs of your kingdoms . . . . v 3 6
What art thou?—The son and heir to that same Faulconbridge *K. John* i 1 56
My mother's son did get your father's heir; Your father's heir must have your father's land . . . . i 1 128
And, to his shape, were heir to all this land, Would I might never stir from off this place, I would give it every foot to have this face . i 1 144
Were he my brother, nay, my kingdom's heir . . . *Richard II.* i 1 116
Did not the one deserve to have an heir? Is not his heir a well-deserving son? . . . . ii 1 193
'Gainst us, our lives, our children, and our heirs . . . ii 1 245
So, Green, thou art the midwife to my woe, And Bolingbroke my sorrow's dismal heir . . . . ii 2 63
I am too young to be your father, Though you are old enough to be my heir . . . . iii 3 205
Who with willing soul Adopts thee heir, and his high sceptre yields . iv 1 109

Heir. Did King Richard then Proclaim my brother Edmund Mortimer Heir to the crown?—He did . . . . *1 Hen. IV.* i 3 157
Proffer'd him their oaths, Gave him their heirs, as pages follow'd him . iv 3 72
For he hath found to end one doubt by death Revives two greater in the heirs of life . . . . *2 Hen. IV.* iv 1 200
And heir from heir shall hold this quarrel up . . . . iv 2 48
They do observe Unfather'd heirs and loathly births of nature . iv 4 122
Rate, rebuke, and roughly send to prison The immediate heir of England! . . . . v 2 71
As heir general, being descended Of Blithild . . . *Hen. V.* i 2 66
Sole heir male Of the true line and stock of Charles the Great . i 2 70
Convey'd himself as heir to the Lady Lingare . . . . i 2 74
Also King Lewis the Tenth, Who was sole heir to the usurper Capet . i 2 78
With your puissant arm renew their feats: You are their heir . . i 2 117
By law of nature and of nations, 'long To him and to his heirs . ii 4 81
The first-begotten and the lawful heir Of Edward king . *1 Hen. VI.* ii 5 65
Young King Richard thus removed, Leaving no heir begotten of his body ii 5 72
As in this haughty great attempt They laboured to plant the rightful heir . . . . ii 5 80
Thou art my heir; the rest I wish thee gather: But yet be wary . . ii 5 96
Saying that the Duke of York was rightful heir to the crown *2 Hen. VI.* i 3 30
That Richard Duke of York Was rightful heir unto the English crown . i 3 187
Duke of Lancaster, The eldest son and heir of John of Gaunt . . ii 2 22
For Richard, the first son's heir, being dead, The issue of the next son should have reign'd.—But William of Hatfield died without an heir ii 2 31
My mother, being heir unto the crown, Married Richard . . . ii 2 44
By her I claim the kingdom: she was heir To Roger Earl of March . ii 2 47
Reputing of his high descent, As next the king he was successive heir . iii 1 49
In time to come, I hope to reign; For I am rightful heir . . iv 2 139
And in my conscience do repute his grace The rightful heir . . v 1 178
Possess it, York; For this is thine and not King Henry's heirs' *3 Hen. VI.* i 1 27
My title's weak.—Tell me, may not a king adopt an heir? . . . i 1 135
Henry the Fourth, Whose heir my father was, and I am his . . . i 1 140
He could not so resign his crown But that the next heir should succeed i 1 146
Confirm the crown to me and to mine heirs, And thou shalt reign in quiet i 1 172
Made that savage duke thine heir And disinherited thine only son . i 1 224
To entail him and his heirs unto the crown, What is it, but to make thy sepulchre And creep into it far before thy time? . . . . . i 1 235
Now you are heir, therefore enjoy it now . . . . . i 2 12
And this is he was his adopted heir . . . . . . i 4 98
I am his king, and he should bow his knee; I was adopted heir . ii 2 88
With this my son, Prince Edward, Henry's heir, Am come to crave thy just and lawful aid . . . . iii 3 31
Lord Hastings well deserves To have the heir of the Lord Hungerford . iv 1 48
Your grace hath not done well, To give the heir and daughter of Lord Scales Unto the brother of your loving bride . . . . . iv 1 52
Bestow'd the heir Of the Lord Bonville on your new wife's son . . iv 1 56
King Edward's fruit, true heir to the English crown . . . iv 4 24
Unto the sanctuary, To save at least the heir of Edward's right . iv 4 32
Which says that G Of Edward's heirs the murderer shall be *Richard III.* i 1 40
And that be heir to his unhappiness! . . . . . . i 2 25
To bar my master's heirs in true descent, God knows I will not do it . iii 2 54
Edward put to death a citizen, Only for saying he would make his son Heir to the crown . . . . iii 5 78
What heir of York is there alive but we? . . . . . iv 4 472
Lancaster, The wronged heirs of York do pray for thee . . . v 3 137
And in record, left them the heirs of shame . . . . . v 3 335
And let their heirs, God, if thy will be so, Enrich the time to come with smooth-faced peace! . . . . v 5 32
Neither the king nor's heirs, Tell you the duke, shall prosper *Hen. VIII.* i 2 168
My kingdom, Well worthy the best heir o' the world . . . ii 4 195
God safely quit her of her burthen, and With gentle travail, to the gladding of Your highness with an heir! . . . . . . v 1 72
Her ashes new create another heir, As great in admiration as herself . v 5 42
Many an heir Of these fair edifices 'fore my wars Have I heard groan and drop . . . . *Coriolanus* iv 4 2
He is so made on here within, as if he were son and heir to Mars . iv 5 204
But the fall of either Makes the survivor heir of all . . . v 6 19
He dies upon my scimitar's sharp point That touches this my first-born son and heir! . . . . *T. Andron.* iv 2 92
Their child shall be advanced, And be received for the emperor's heir . iv 2 158
What is yond gentleman?—The son and heir of old Tiberio *Rom. and Jul.* i 5 131
Now old desire doth in his death-bed lie, And young affection gapes to be his heir . . . . ii Prol. 2
One nickname for her purblind son and heir, Young Adam Cupid . ii 1 12
Death is my son-in-law, Death is my heir; My daughter he hath wedded iv 5 38
Thou art early up, To see thy son and heir more early down . . v 3 209
My estate deserves an heir more raised Than one which holds a trencher.—Well; what further? . . . . *T. of Athens* i 1 119
I will choose Mine heir from forth the beggars of the world . . i 1 138
'Tis good you know not that you are his heirs . . *J. Cæsar* iii 2 150
He hath left them you, And to your heirs for ever, common pleasures . iii 2 255
The heart-ache and the thousand natural shocks That flesh is heir to *Hamlet* iii 1 63
Coward, pandar, and the son and heir of a mongrel bitch . . *Lear* ii 2 23
Not by old gradation, where each second Stood heir to the first . *Othello* i 1 38
For even her folly help'd her to an heir . . . . . ii 1 138
Of thee craves The circle of the Ptolemies for her heirs . *Ant. and Cleo.* iii 12 18
His daughter, and the heir of's kingdom . . . . *Cymbeline* i 1 4
This Polydore, The heir of Cymbeline and Britain . . . . iii 3 87
Those rich-left heirs that let their fathers lie Without a monument! . iv 2 226
He deserved the praise o' the world, As great Sicilius' heir . . v 4 51
To my grief, I am The heir of his reward . . . . . v 5 13
This king unto him took a fere, Who died and left a female heir *Per.* i Gower 22
One sorrow never comes but brings an heir, That may succeed . . i 4 63
Endowments greater Than nobleness and riches: careless heirs May the two latter darken and expend . . . . iii 2 28
The heir of kingdoms and another like To Pericles thy father . . v 1 209

Heir-apparent. Were it not here apparent that thou art heir apparent *1 Hen. IV.* i 2 65
Go, hang thyself in thine own heir-apparent garters! . . . . ii 2 46
Was it for me to kill the heir-apparent? . . . . . . ii 4 297
Thou being heir-apparent, could the world pick thee out three such enemies? . . . . ii 4 403
He is the next of blood, And heir apparent to the English crown *2 Hen. VI.* i 1 152
Every one with claps can sound, 'Our heir-apparent is a king!' *Per.* iii Gower 37

Heirless it hath made my kingdom . . . . . *W. Tale* v 1 10

Held. The affliction of my mind amends, with which, I fear, a madness held me . . . . *Tempest* v 1 116
What sad talk was that Wherewith my brother held you? *T. G. of Ver.* i 3 2

Held. But neither bended knees, pure hands held up, Sad sighs, deep groans . . . . *T. G. of Ver.* iii 1 229
Banish'd for so small a fault?—I was, and held me glad of such a doom iv 1 32
But fate, ordaining he should be a cuckold, held his hand *Mer. Wives* iii 5 106
Married her most shamefully, Where there was no proportion held in love v 5 235
And held in idle price to haunt assemblies . . . *Meas. for Meas.* i 3 9
The greater file of the subject held the duke to be wise . . . iii 2 145
And I, to blame, have held him here too long . . *Com. of Errors* iv 1 47
How long hath this possession held the man? . . . . . v 1 44
What secret hath held you here? . . . . . *Much Ado* i 1 206
Yourself, held precious in the world's esteem . . *L. L. Lost* ii 1 4
Wanting your father's voice, The other must be held the worthier *M. N. D.* i 1 55
Wanted the modesty To urge the thing held as a ceremony *Mer. of Venice* v 1 206
Which I held my duty speedily to acquaint you withal . *All's Well* i 3 123
Made such pestiferous reports of men very nobly held . . iv 3 341
Better known to you, when I have held familiarity with fresher clothes v 2 3
Let me be clear of thee.—Well held out, i' faith! . . . *T. Night* iv 1 5
I had thought, sir, to have held my peace until You had drawn oaths from him not to stay . . . . . . *W. Tale* i 2 28
Thou dost make possible things not so held, Communicatest with dreams i 2 139
You look As if you held a brow of much distraction: Are you moved? . i 2 149
And with my hand at midnight held your head . . *K. John* iv 1 45
The deed, which both our tongues held vile to name . . . iv 2 241
To Bristol castle, which they say is held By Bushy . *Richard II.* ii 3 164
I saw the prince, And told him of those triumphs held at Oxford . v 3 14
This stream through muddy passages Hath held his current . . v 3 63
'Twixt his finger and his thumb he held A pouncet-box . 1 *Hen. IV.* i 3 37
He held me last night at least nine hours In reckoning up . . iii 1 156
The contrarious winds that held the king So long in his unlucky Irish wars v 1 52
My cloud of dignity Is held from falling with so weak a wind 2 *Hen. IV.* iv 5 100
Then resign Your crown and kingdom, indirectly held From him *Hen. V.* ii 4 94
I think he held the right . . . . . . 1 *Hen. VI.* ii 4 38
Unless my study and my books be false, The argument you held was wrong . . . . ii 4 57
Hast thou not kiss'd thy hand and held my stirrup? 2 *Hen. VI.* iv 1 53
So will the queen, that living held him dear . . . . iv 1 147
Plantagenet, Which held thee dearly as his soul's redemption 3 *Hen. VI.* ii 1 102
Held at such a rate As brings a thousand-fold more care to keep . . ii 2 51
Because I cannot flatter . . . , I must be held a rancorous enemy *Richard III.* i 3 50
Myself disgraced, and the nobility Held in contempt . . . i 3 80
Besides, he says there are two councils held . . . iii 2 12
Hath he so long held out with me untired, And stops he now for breath? iv 2 44
And, by 'r lady, Held current music too . . . *Hen. VIII.* i 3 47
Did you not of late days hear A buzzing of a separation Between the king and Katharine?—Yes, but it held not . . . . . ii 1 149
And held for certain The king will venture at it . . . . ii 1 155
Was he not held a learned man?—Yes, surely . . . . ii 2 124
The Archbishop Of Canterbury . . . Held a late court at Dunstable . iv 1 27
To York-place, where the feast is held . . . . . iv 1 94
For an old aunt whom the Greeks held captive . *Troi. and Cres.* ii 2 77
I might have still held off, And then you would have tarried . . iv 2 17
Fame . . . can not Better be held nor more attain'd . *Coriolanus* i 1 269
Spies of the Volsces Held me in chase, that I was forced to wheel . i 6 19
Go you to the city; Learn how 'tis held . . . . . i 10 28
We must suggest the people in what hatred He still hath held them . ii 1 262
It is held That valour is the chiefest virtue . . . . ii 2 87
His gracious promise, which you might, As cause had call'd you up, have held him too . . . . ii 3 202
The thing I have forsworn to grant may never Be held by you denials . v 3 81
Give me a staff of honour for mine age, But not a sceptre to control the world: Upright he held it, lords, that held it last . *T. Andron.* i 1 200
Whom thou in triumph long Hast prisoner held, fetter'd in amorous chains ii 1 15
In bootless prayer have they been held up . . . . iii 1 75
Being held a foe, he may not have access . . *Rom. and Jul.* ii Prol. 9
It may be thought we held him carelessly, Being our kinsman . . iii 4 25
A blessed time.—As thine is now, held with a brace of harlots *T. of Athens* iv 3 79
A common slave—you know him well by sight—Held up his left hand, which did flame and burn Like twenty torches join'd *J. Cæsar* i 3 16
He is superstitious grown of late, Quite from the main opinion he held once ii 1 196
You know that I held Epicurus strong And his opinion . . . v 1 77
How died my master, Strato?—I held the sword, and he did run on it . v 5 65
It was he in the times past which held you So under fortune . *Macbeth* iii 1 77
It draws near the season Wherein the spirit held his wont to walk *Hamlet* i 4 6
He took me by the wrist and held me hard . . . . ii 1 87
My life I never held but as a pawn To wage against thy enemies . *Lear* i 1 157
King Stephen was a worthy peer, His breeches cost him but a crown; He held them sixpence all too dear . . . . *Othello* ii 3 94
I have ever held my cap off to thy fortunes . . *Ant. and Cleo.* ii 7 63
The loyalty well held to fools does make Our faith mere folly . . iii 13 42
Our force by land Hath nobly held; our sever'd navy too Have knit . iii 13 170
It is my birth-day: I had thought to have held it poor . . . iii 13 186
That she held the very garment of Posthumus in more respect *Cymbeline* iii 5 138
We are held as outlaws: hence!—He is but one . . . . iv 2 67
A city on whom plenty held full hand . . . . *Pericles* i 4 22
Whilst ours was blurted at and held a malkin Not worth the time of day iv 3 34

Helen, to you our minds we will unfold . . . . *M. N. Dream* i 1 208
And, all my powers, address your love and might To honour Helen! . ii 2 144
O Helen, goddess, nymph, perfect, divine! . . . . iii 2 137
Now to Helen is it home return'd, There to remain.—Helen, it is not so iii 2 172
Helen, I love thee; by my life, I do . . . . . iii 2 251
Fair Helen told me of their stealth, Of this their purpose hither . iv 1 165
The lover, all as frantic, Sees Helen's beauty in a brow of Egypt . . v 1 11
Like Limander, am I trusty still.—And I like Helen, till the Fates me kill v 1 199
Nature presently distill'd Helen's cheek, but not her heart *As Y. Like It* iii 2 153
Little Helen, farewell: if I can remember thee, I will think of thee at court . . . . *All's Well* i 1 202
May it please you, madam, that he bid Helen come to you . . . i 3 71
Tell my gentlewoman I would speak with her; Helen, I mean . . i 3 73
I am going, forsooth: the business is for Helen to come hither . . i 3 101
You know, Helen, I am a mother to you . . . . . i 3 143
Yes, Helen, you might be my daughter-in-law: God shield you mean it not! i 3 173
But think you, Helen, If you should tender your supposed aid, He would receive it? . . . . i 3 241
Helen, thou shalt have my leave and love, Means and attendants . . i 3 257
Give Helen this, And urge her to a present answer back . . . ii 2 66
Mort du vinaigre! is not this Helen?—'Fore God, I think so . . ii 3 50
You must not marvel, Helen, at my course . . . . . ii 5 63
Be this sweet Helen's knell, and now forget her . . . . v 3 67
Helen, that's dead, Was a sweet creature . . . . . v 3 77
Helen. This ring was mine; and, when I gave it Helen, I bade her, if her fortunes ever stood Necessitied to help, that by this token I would relieve her . . . . *All's Well* v 3 83
This ring: 'twas mine, 'twas Helen's, Whoever gave it you . . v 3 104
I am afeard the life of Helen, lady, Was foully snatch'd . . . v 3 153
Thy Doll, and Helen of thy noble thoughts, Is in base durance 2 *Hen. IV.* v 5 35
Helen, the mother of great Constantine, Nor yet Saint Philip's daughters, were like thee . . . . 1 *Hen. VI.* i 2 142
Helen of Greece was fairer far than thou . . . . 3 *Hen. VI.* ii 2 146
Within whose strong immures The ravish'd Helen, Menelaus' queen, With wanton Paris sleeps . . . *Troi. and Cres.* Prol. 9
An her hair were not somewhat darker than Helen's—well, go to . . i 1 42
Because she's kin to me, therefore she's not so fair as Helen: an she were not kin to me, she would be as fair on Friday as Helen is on Sunday . . . . i 1 77
Helen must needs be fair, When with your blood you daily paint her thus . . . . i 1 93
Who were those went by?—Queen Hecuba and Helen . . . i 2 1
Helen was not up, was she?—Hector was gone, but Helen was not up . i 2 50
Helen herself swore th' other day, that Troilus, for a brown favour . i 2 99
I had as lief Helen's golden tongue had commended Troilus for a copper nose . . . . i 2 114
I swear to you, I think Helen loves him better than Paris . . . i 2 116
But to prove to you that Helen loves him: she came and puts me her white hand to his cloven chin . . . . i 2 130
To prove to you that Helen loves Troilus,— Troilus will stand to the proof . . . . i 2 141
At the white hair that Helen spied on Troilus' chin . . . . i 2 164
And Helen so blushed, and Paris so chafed, and all the rest so laughed i 2 180
This will do Helen's heart good now, ha! . . . . . . i 2 234
Paris is dirt to him; and, I warrant, Helen, to change, would give an eye to boot . . . . i 2 259
Not so much wit . . . As will stop the eye of Helen's needle . . ii 1 87
Deliver Helen, and all damage else . . . Shall be struck off . . ii 2 3
Let Helen go: Since the first sword was drawn about this question, Every tithe soul, 'mongst many thousand dismes, Hath been as dear as Helen . . . . ii 2 17
Cry, Trojans, cry! a Helen and a woe: Cry, cry! Troy burns, or else let Helen go . . . . ii 2 111
There's not the meanest spirit on our party Without a heart to dare or sword to draw When Helen is defended, nor none so noble Whose life were ill bestow'd or death unfamed Where Helen is the subject ii 2 158
If Helen then be wife to Sparta's king, As it is known she is, these moral laws Of nature and of nations speak aloud To have her back return'd . . . . ii 2 183
I propend to you In resolution to keep Helen still . . . . ii 2 191
Helen: could you not find out that by her attributes? . . . iii 1 37
Sweet Helen, I must woo you To help unarm our Hector . . . iii 1 162
Who, in your thoughts, merits fair Helen best, Myself or Menelaus? . iv 1 53
Why then for Venus' sake, give me a kiss, When Helen is a maid again . iv 5 50
Helen and Hero hildings and harlots; Thisbe a grey eye *Rom. and Jul.* ii 4 44
Who's there? my woman Helen?—Please you, madam.—What hour is it? *Cymbeline* ii 2 1

Helena. Demetrius, I'll avouch it to his head, Made love to Nedar's daughter, Helena . . . . *M. N. Dream* i 1 107
A league without the town, Where I did meet thee once with Helena . i 1 166
Look, here comes Helena.—God speed fair Helena! whither away? . i 1 179
His folly, Helena, is no fault of mine.—None, but your beauty . . i 1 200
Helena, adieu: As you on him, Demetrius dote on you! . . . i 1 224
And run through fire I will for thy sweet sake. Transparent Helena! . ii 2 104
Not Hermia but Helena I love: Who will not change a raven for a dove? ii 2 113
About the wood go swifter than the wind, And Helena of Athens look thou find . . . . iii 2 95
Captain of our fairy band, Helena is here at hand . . . . iii 2 111
You both are rivals, and love Hermia; And now both rivals, to mock Helena . . . . iii 2 156
In Hermia's love I yield you up my part; And yours of Helena to me bequeath . . . . iii 2 166
Fair Helena, who more engilds the night Than all yon fiery oes . . iii 2 187
Stay, gentle Helena; hear my excuse: My love, my life, my soul, fair Helena!—O excellent! . . . . iii 2 245
'Tis no jest That I do hate thee and love Helena . . . . iii 2 281
Be not afraid; she shall not harm thee, Helena . . . . iii 2 321
Let her alone: speak not of Helena; Take not her part . . . iii 2 332
To try whose right, Of thine or mine, is most in Helena . . . iii 2 337
This Demetrius is; This Helena, old Nedar's Helena . . . . iv 1 135
And I in fury hither follow'd them, Fair Helena in fancy following me . iv 1 168
The object and the pleasure of mine eye Is only Helena . . . iv 1 176
No more of this, Helena; go to, no more; lest it be rather thought you affect a sorrow than have it . . . . . . *All's Well* i 1 59
Valentio and his cousin Tybalt; Lucio and the lively Helena *R. and J.* i 2 74

Helenus. Who's that?—That's Helenus . . *Troi. and Cres.* i 2 238
Can Helenus fight, uncle?—Helenus? no. Yes, he'll fight indifferent well . . . . i 2 241
Helenus is a priest . . . . i 2 244
Who marvels then, when Helenus beholds A Grecian and his sword, if he do set The very wings of reason to his heels? . . . . . ii 2 42
Who's a-field to-day?—Hector, Deiphobus, Helenus, Antenor . . iii 1 148

Helias. Priam's six-gated city, Dardan, and Tymbria, Helias, Chetas, Troien, And Antenorides . . . . Prol. 16

Helicane. Good Helicane, that stay'd at home, Not to eat honey like a drone From others' labours . . . . . *Pericles* ii Gower 17
Lord Helicane, a word.—With me? and welcome . . . . ii 4 21
Wrong not your prince you love.—Wrong not yourself, then, noble Helicane . . . . ii 4 26
Live, noble Helicane!—For honour's cause, forbear your suffrages . ii 4 40
And since Lord Helicane enjoineth us, We with our travels will endeavour us . . . . ii 4 55

Helicanus, thou Hast moved us: what seest thou in our looks? . . i 2 50
Thou speak'st like a physician, Helicanus, That minister'st a potion unto me . . . . i 2 67
The men of Tyrus on the head Of Helicanus would set on The crown iii Gower 27
Old Escanes, whom Helicanus late Advanced . . . . . iv 4 13
Bear you it in mind, Old Helicanus goes along behind . . . . iv 4 16
Where is lord Helicanus? he can resolve you. O, here he is . . . v 1 1
Ho, Helicanus!—Calls my lord?—Thou art a grave and noble counsellor v 1 182
O Helicanus, strike me, honour'd sir; Give me a gash . . . v 1 192
O Helicanus, Down on thy knees, thank the holy gods . . . v 1 199
Thou art my child. Give me fresh garments. Mine own, Helicanus . v 1 216
Tell Helicanus, my Marina, tell him O'er, point by point . . . v 1 226

Helicanus. Can you remember what I call'd the man? I have named him oft?—'Twas Helicanus then *Pericles* v 3 53
In Helicanus may you well descry A figure of truth, of faith, of loyalty v 3 Gower 91
Helicon. Shall dunghill curs confront the Helicons? *2 Hen. IV.* v 3 108
Hell. Cried, 'Hell is empty, And all the devils are here' *Tempest* i 2 214
If I would but go to hell for an eternal moment or so *Mer. Wives* ii 1 49
I am damned in hell for swearing ii 2 9
See the hell of having a false woman! ii 2 305
If the bottom were as deep as hell, I should down iii 5 14
I think the devil will not have me damned, lest the oil that's in me should set hell on fire v 5 39
And have given ourselves without scruple to hell v 5 157
His filth within being cast, he would appear A pond as deep as hell *Meas. for Meas.* iii 1 94
O, 'tis the cunning livery of hell, The damned'st body to invest! iii 1 95
Am I in earth, in heaven, or in hell? Sleeping or waking? *Com. of Errors* ii 2 214
Is he well?—No, he's in Tartar limbo, worse than hell iv 2 32
One that before the judgement carries poor souls to hell iv 2 40
And lead his apes into hell *Much Ado* ii 1 43
Well, then, go you into hell?—No, but to the gate ii 1 44
While she is here, a man may live as quiet in hell as in a sanctuary ii 1 266
Black is the badge of hell, The hue of dungeons *L. L. Lost* iv 3 254
O hell! to choose love by another's eyes *M. N. Dream* i 1 140
What graces in my love do dwell, That he hath turn'd a heaven unto a hell! i 1 207
And make a heaven of hell, To die upon the hand I love so well ii 1 243
O hell! I see you all are bent To set against me for your merriment iii 2 145
One sees more devils than vast hell can hold, That is, the madman v 1 9
Our house is hell, and thou, a merry devil, Didst rob it of some taste of tediousness. But fare thee well *Mer. of Venice* ii 3 2
O hell! what have we here? A carrion Death! ii 7 62
Prove it so, Let fortune go to hell for it, not I iii 2 21
Why will you mew her up . . . for this fiend of hell? *T. of Shrew* i 1 88
Any man is so very a fool to be married to hell i 1 129
And for your love to her lead apes in hell ii 1 34
I think his soul is in hell, madonna.—I know his soul is in heaven *T. N.* i 5 74
If all the devils of hell be drawn in little, and Legion himself possessed him iii 4 94
A fiend like thee might bear my soul to hell iii 4 237
Sayest thou that house is dark?—As hell, Sir Topas iv 2 39
This house is as dark as ignorance, though ignorance were as dark as hell iv 2 50
The one He chides to hell and bids the other grow *W. Tale* iv 4 564
Who lives and dares but say thou didst not well When I was got, I'll send his soul to hell *K. John* i 1 272
And pell-mell Make work upon ourselves, for heaven or hell ii 1 407
Lest that France repent, And by disjoining hands, hell lose a soul iii 1 197
Shall braying trumpets and loud churlish drums, Clamours of hell, be measures to our pomp? iii 1 304
That you shall think the devil is come from hell iv 3 100
There is not yet so ugly a fiend of hell As thou shalt be iv 3 123
Let hell want pains enough to torture me iv 3 138
Within me is a hell v 7 46
And plague injustice with the pains of hell *Richard II.* iii 1 34
Terrible hell make war Upon their spotted souls for this offence! iii 2 133
There is my gage, the manual seal of death, That marks thee out for hell iv 1 26
Thou art damn'd to hell for this iv 1 43
Fiend, thou torment'st me ere I come to hell! iv 1 270
Go thou, and fill another room in hell v 5 108
The devil, that told me I did well, Says that this deed is chronicled in hell v 5 117
What hole in hell were hot enough for him? *1 Hen. IV.* i 2 120
He wisheth you in heaven.—And you in hell iii 1 11
For the women?—For one of them, she is in hell already *2 Hen. IV.* ii 4 365
This grace of kings must die, If hell and treason hold their promises *Hen. V.* ii Prol. 29
Hath got the voice in hell for excellence ii 2 113
Would I were with him, wheresome'er he is, either in heaven or in hell! ii 3 8
Nay, sure, he's not in hell: he's in Arthur's bosom ii 3 9
In liberty of bloody hand shall range With conscience wide as hell iii 3 13
Never sees horrid night, the child of hell iv 1 288
All hell shall stir for this v 1 72
Hundreds he sent to hell, and none durst stand him *1 Hen. VI.* i 1 123
Heavens, can you suffer hell so to prevail? i 5 9
To join with witches and the help of hell! ii 1 18
I think this Talbot be a fiend of hell.—If not of hell, the heavens, sure, favour him ii 1 47
For prisoners ask'st thou? hell our prison is iv 7 58
And hell too strong for me to buckle with v 3 28
Consume to ashes, Thou foul accursed minister of hell! v 4 93
For what is wedlock forced but a hell, An age of discord? v 5 62
To think upon my pomp shall be my hell *2 Hen. VI.* ii 4 41
I will stir up in England some black storm Shall blow ten thousand souls to heaven or hell iii 1 350
Give thee thy hire and send thy soul to hell, Pernicious blood-sucker! iii 2 225
All the foul terrors in dark-seated hell iii 2 328
And wedded be thou to the hags of hell iv 1 79
In despite of the devils and hell, have through the very middest of you! iv 8 63
And as I thrust thy body in with my sword, So wish I, I might thrust thy soul to hell iv 10 85
If not in heaven, you'll surely sup in hell v 1 216
O war, thou son of hell, Whom angry heavens do make their minister! v 2 33
And till I root out their accursed line . . . , I live in hell *3 Hen. VI.* i 3 33
Happy always was it for that son Whose father for his hoarding went to hell ii 2 48
And, whiles I live, to account this world but hell iii 2 169
Down, down to hell; and say I sent thee thither v 6 67
Since the heavens have shaped my body so, Let hell make crook'd my mind to answer it v 6 79
Avaunt, thou dreadful minister of hell! *Richard III.* i 2 46
Thou hast made the happy earth thy hell, Fill'd it with cursing cries i 2 51
And thou unfit for any place but hell.—Yes, one place else i 2 109
Hie thee to hell for shame, and leave the world, Thou cacodemon! i 3 143
Whilst some tormenting dream Affrights thee with a hell of ugly devils i 3 227
That wast seal'd in thy nativity The slave of nature and the son of hell! i 3 230
Sin, death, and hell have set their marks on him i 3 293
And for a season after Could not believe but that I was in hell, Such terrible impression made the dream i 4 62
If thou wilt outstrip death, go cross the seas, And live with Richmond, from the reach of hell iv 1 43
Hell. Richard yet lives, hell's black intelligencer *Richard III.* iv 4 71
Earth gapes, hell burns, fiends roar, saints pray iv 4 75
Thou camest on earth to make the earth my hell iv 4 166
So long as heaven and nature lengthens it.—So long as hell and Richard likes of it iv 4 354
Let us to't pell-mell; If not to heaven, then hand in hand to hell v 3 313
Whence has he that, If not from hell? *Hen. VIII.* i 1 70
And he begins A new hell in himself i 1 72
Is become as black As if besmear'd in hell i 2 124
With such a hell of pain and world of charge *Troi. and Cres.* iv 1 57
Beshrew the witch! with venomous wights she stays As tediously as hell iv 2 13
I pray you, stay; by hell and all hell's torments, I will not speak a word! v 2 43
Pluto and hell! All hurt behind; backs red, and faces pale! *Coriolanus* i 4 36
The fires i' the lowest hell fold-in the people! Call me their traitor! iii 3 68
Would thou wert shipp'd to hell, Rather than rob me! *T. Andron.* i 1 206
Now let hot Ætna cool in Sicily, And be my heart an ever-burning hell! iii 1 243
Pluto sends you word, If you will have Revenge from hell, you shall iv 3 38
Sith there's no justice in earth nor hell, We will solicit heaven iv 3 49
Would I were a devil, To live and burn in everlasting fire, So I might have your company in hell! v 1 149
Could not all hell afford you such a devil? v 2 86
Talk of peace! I hate the word, As I hate hell *Rom. and Jul.* i 1 78
This torture should be roar'd in dismal hell iii 2 44
O nature, what hadst thou to do in hell, When thou didst bower the spirit of a fiend In mortal paradise of such sweet flesh? iii 2 80
There is no world without Verona walls, But purgatory, torture, hell itself iii 3 18
The damned use that word in hell; Howlings attend it iii 3 47
I would I might go to hell among the rogues *J. Cæsar* i 2 270
Cæsar's spirit, ranging for revenge, With Ate by his side come hot from hell iii 1 271
Come, thick night, And pall thee in the dunnest smoke of hell *Macbeth* i 5 52
Hear it not, Duncan; for it is a knell That summons thee to heaven or to hell ii 1 64
This place is too cold for hell ii 3 19
Not in the legions Of horrid hell can come a devil more damn'd iv 3 56
Had I power, I should Pour the sweet milk of concord into hell iv 3 98
Hell is murky!—Fie, my lord, fie! a soldier, and afeard? v 1 40
What is thy name?—Thou'lt be afraid to hear it.—No; though thou call'st thyself a hotter name Than any is in hell v 7 7
I'll speak to it, though hell itself should gape *Hamlet* i 2 245
Be thou a spirit of health or goblin damn'd, Bring with thee airs from heaven or blasts from hell i 4 41
O all you host of heaven! O earth! what else? And shall I couple hell? i 5 93
With a look so piteous in purport As if he had been loosed out of hell ii 1 83
The son of a dear father murder'd, Prompted to my revenge by heaven and hell ii 2 613
When churchyards yawn and hell itself breathes out Contagion iii 2 407
That his soul may be as damn'd and black As hell, whereto it goes iii 3 95
Rebellious hell, If thou canst mutine in a matron's bones iii 4 82
I'll not be juggled with: To hell, allegiance! vows, to the blackest devil! iv 5 131
Thought and affliction, passion, hell itself, She turns to favour iv 5 188
There's hell, there's darkness, there's the sulphurous pit *Lear* iv 6 130
And must be driven To find out practices of cunning hell *Othello* i 3 102
Too hard for my wits and all the tribe of hell i 3 364
Hell and night Must bring this monstrous birth to the world's light i 3 409
Let the labouring bark climb hills of seas Olympus-high and duck again as low As hell's from heaven! ii 1 191
Divinity of hell! When devils will the blackest sins put on, They do suggest at first with heavenly shows ii 3 356
O, 'tis the spite of hell, the fiend's arch-mock! iv 1 71
Heaven truly knows that thou art false as hell iv 2 39
Thou young and rose-lipp'd cherubin,—Ay, there, look grim as hell! iv 2 64
That have the office opposite to Saint Peter, And keep the gate of hell! iv 2 92
Heaven pardon him!—A halter pardon him! and hell gnaw his bones! iv 2 136
She's, like a liar, gone to burning hell: 'Twas I that kill'd her v 2 129
I were damn'd beneath all depth in hell, But that I did proceed upon just grounds To this extremity v 2 137
Shot their fires Into the abysm of hell *Ant. and Cleo.* iii 13 147
It were fit That all the plagues of hell should at one time Encounter such revolt *Cymbeline* i 6 111
I lodge in fear; Though this a heavenly angel, hell is here ii 2 50
Take thy hire; and all the fiends of hell Divide themselves between you! ii 4 129
It doth confirm Another stain, as big as hell can hold ii 4 140
All faults that may be named, nay, that hell knows ii 5 27
Hell only danceth at so harsh a chime *Pericles* i 1 85
Rebuke these surges, Which wash both heaven and hell! iii 1 2
Thou hold'st a place, for which the pained'st fiend Of hell would not in reputation change iv 6 174
Hell-black. The sea, with such a storm as his bare head In hell-black night endured, would have buoy'd up *Lear* iii 7 60
Hell-broth. Like a hell-broth boil and bubble *Macbeth* iv 1 19
Hellespont. How young Leander cross'd the Hellespont *T. G. of Ver.* i 1 22
You are over boots in love, And yet you never swum the Hellespont i 1 26
For, good youth, he went but forth to wash him in the Hellespont and being taken with the cramp was drowned *As Y. Like It* iv 1 104
Keeps due on To the Propontic and the Hellespont *Othello* iii 3 456
Hell-fire. I never see thy face but I think upon hell-fire *1 Hen. IV.* iii 3 36
A' saw a flea stick upon Bardolph's nose, and a' said it was a black soul burning in hell-fire *Hen. V.* ii 3 44
Hell-gate. Here's a knocking indeed! If a man were porter of hell-gate, he should have old turning the key *Macbeth* ii 3 2
Hell-governed. Which his hell-govern'd arm hath butchered *Richard III.* i 2 67
Hell-hated. With the hell-hated lie o'erwhelm thy heart *Lear* v 3 147
Hell-hound. A hell-hound that doth hunt us all to death *Richard III.* iv 4 48
A pair of cursed hell-hounds and their dam! *T. Andron.* v 2 144
Turn, hell-hound, turn!—Of all men else I have avoided thee *Macbeth* v 8 3
Hellish. From out the state of hellish misery *Mer. of Venice* iii 4 21
Only sin And hellish obstinacy tie thy tongue *All's Well* i 3 186
That damned sorceress Hath wrought this hellish mischief *1 Hen. VI.* iii 2 39
Have prevail'd Upon my body with their hellish charms *Richard III.* iii 4 64
No sooner had they told this hellish tale *T. Andron.* ii 3 105
I have done thy mother.—And therein, hellish dog, thou hast undone iv 2 77
The hellish Pyrrhus Old grandsire Priam seeks *Hamlet* ii 2 485
To you, lord governor, Remains the censure of this hellish villain *Othello* v 2 368
Hell-kite. Did you say all? O hell-kite! All? *Macbeth* iv 3 217
Hell-pains. I would it were hell-pains for thy sake *All's Well* ii 3 245
Though I do hate him as I do hell-pains *Othello* i 1 155

Helm. Fortune play upon thy prosperous helm! . . . *All's Well* iii 3 7
For every honour sitting on his helm, Would they were multitudes!
1 Hen. IV. iii 2 142
I plucked this glove from his helm . . . . . *Hen. V.* iv 7 163
And you yourself shall steer the happy helm . . . . *2 Hen. VI.* i 3 103
Is't meet that he Should leave the helm and like a fearful lad With
tearful eyes add water to the sea? . . . . . *3 Hen. VI.* v 4 7
We will not from the helm to sit and weep, But keep our course . v 4 21
He dreamt to-night the boar had razed his helm . . *Richard III.* iii 2 11
Stanley did dream the boar did raze his helm; But I disdain'd it . . iii 4 84
Fortune and victory sit on thy helm! . . . . v 3 79
Upon them! Victory sits on our helms . . . . v 3 351
His sword is bloodied, and his helm more hack'd than Hector's *T. and C.* i 2 253
By the forge that stithied Mars his helm, I'll kill thee every where . iv 5 255
To-morrow will I wear it on my helm, And grieve his spirit . . v 2 93
That sleeve is mine that he'll bear on his helm . . . . v 2 169
Diomed has got that same scurvy doting foolish young knave's sleeve of
Troy there in his helm . . . . v 4 5
You slander The helms o' the state, who care for you like fathers *Coriol.* i 1 79
Unbuckling helms, fisting each other's throat . . . . . iv 5 131
With plumed helm thy state begins to threat . . . *Lear* iv 2 57
To watch—poor perdu!—With this thin helm . . . . . iv 7 36
Let housewives make a skillet of my helm! . . . . *Othello* i 3 273
I did not think This amorous surfeiter would have donn'd his helm For
such a petty war . . . . *Ant. and Cleo.* ii 1 33
At the helm A seeming mermaid steers . . . . ii 2 213
Helmed. The very stream of his life and the business he hath helmed
must . . . give him a better proclamation . . *Meas. for Meas.* iii 2 151
Helmet. With unhack'd swords and helmets all unbruised . *K. John* ii 1 254
Let them lay by their helmets and their spears . . . *Richard II.* i 3 119
May my hands rot off And never brandish more revengeful steel Over
the glittering helmet of my foe! . . . . iv 1 51
From helmet to the spur all blood he was . . . . . *Hen. V.* iv 6 6
The glove which your majesty is take out of the helmet of Alençon . iv 8 28
Desire him to have borne His bruised helmet and his bended sword v Prol. 18
Or shall we on the helmets of our foes Tell our devotion? . *3 Hen. VI.* ii 1 163
That they may crush down with a heavy fall The usurping helmets of our
adversaries! . . . . *Richard. III.* v 3 112
Look you what hacks are on his helmet! . . . *Troi. and Cres.* i 2 222
Not cowardly put off my helmet to My countryman . *Ant. and Cleo.* iv 15 56
Help. She did confine thee, By help of her more potent ministers *Tempest* i 2 275
If all the wine in my bottle will recover him, I will help his ague . ii 2 97
Come, temperate nymphs, and help to celebrate A contract of true love iv 1 132
Help to bear this away where my hogshead of wine is . . . iv 1 251
I rather think You have not sought her help . . . . . v 1 142
But release me from my bands With the help of your good hands . . Epil. 10
And I will help thee to prefer her too . . . *T. G. of Ver.* ii 4 157
Cease to lament for that thou canst not help, And study help for that
which thou lament'st . . . . iii 1 241
Now, of another thing she may, and that cannot I help . . . iii 1 359
Love doth to her eyes repair, To help him of his blindness . . iv 2 47
If you will help to bear it, Sir John, take all, or half . *Mer. Wives* ii 2 178
I love thee. Help me away. Let me creep in here. I'll never . . iii 3 149
Help to cover your master, boy. Call your men, Mistress Ford . . iii 3 151
Help to search my house this one time . . . . . . iv 2 167
So play the foolish throngs with one that swoons; Come all to help him,
and so stop the air . . . . *Meas. for Meas.* ii 4 25
Women! Help heaven! men their creation mar In profiting by them . ii 4 127
Here's a fellow will help you to-morrow in your execution . . iv 2 23
What, resists he? Help him, Lucio . . . . v 1 355
I'll limit thee this day To seek thy life by beneficial help *Com. of Errors* i 1 152
So, come, help: well struck! there was blow for blow . . . iii 1 56
If a crow help us in, sirrah, we'll pluck a crow together . . . . iii 1 83
God help, poor souls, how idly do they talk! . . . . . iv 4 132
Let's call more help . . . . iv 4 149
Let him be brought forth and borne hence for help . . . . v 1 160
Unless you send some present help, Between them they will kill the
conjurer . . . . v 1 176
God help the noble Claudio! if he have caught the Benedick *Much Ado* i 1 88
I will do any modest office, my lord, to help my cousin to a good
husband . . . . ii 1 391
And I, with your two helps, will so practise on Benedick that, in despite
of his quick wit and his queasy stomach, he shall fall in love . . ii 1 397
Help to dress me, good coz, good Meg, good Ursula . . . . iii 4 98
His wits are not so blunt as, God help, I would desire they were . iii 5 12
How doth the lady?—Dead, I think. Help, uncle! . . . . iv 1 114
Midnight, assist our moan; Help us to sigh and groan . . . . v 3 17
I shall desire your help.—My heart is with your liking . . . v 4 31
Hear me, dear lady; I have sworn an oath.—Our Lady help my lord!
L. L. Lost ii 1 98
Hath wisdom's warrant and the help of school And wit's own grace . v 2 71
Help, hold his brows! he'll swoon! Why look you pale? . . . v 2 392
Help me, Lysander, help me! do thy best To pluck this crawling
serpent from my breast! . . . . *M. N. Dream* ii 2 145
He murder cries and help from Athens calls . . . . . iii 2 26
Help Cavalery Cobweb to scratch . . . . iv 1 24
With the help of a surgeon he might yet recover, and prove an ass . v 1 316
Well then, it now appears you need my help . . *Mer. of Venice* i 3 115
I would have him help to waste His borrow'd purse . . . . ii 5 50
Take upon command what help we have . . . . . *As Y. Like It* ii 7 125
I will help you, if I can: I would love you, if I could . . . v 2 120
And good plays prove the better by the help of good epilogues . . Epil. 7
Help, masters, help! my master is mad . . . . *T. of Shrew* i 2 18
I can, Petruchio, help thee to a wife With wealth enough . . . i 2 85
And I have met a gentleman Hath promised me to help me . . . i 2 173
Leave your books And help to dress your sister's chamber up . . iii 1 83
Help, help, help! here's a madman will murder me . . . . v 1 60
He and his physicians Are of a mind; he, that they cannot help him,
They, that they cannot help . . . . *All's Well* i 3 244
Be sure of this, What I can help thee to thou shalt not miss . . i 3 262
To esteem A senseless help when help past sense we deem . . . ii 1 127
Thou thought'st to help me; and such thanks I give As one near death ii 1 133
Most it is presumption in us when The help of heaven we count the act
of men . . . . ii 1 155
Not helping, death's my fee; But, if I help, what do you promise me? ii 1 193
Give me some help here, ho! . . . . ii 1 212
In such a business give me leave to use The help of mine own eyes . ii 3 115
Take this purse of gold, And let me buy your friendly help thus far . iii 7 15
But this exceeding posting day and night Must wear your spirits low;
we cannot help it . . . . v 1 2

Help. This man may help me to his majesty's ear, If he would *All's Well* v 1 7
I bade her, if her fortunes ever stood Necessitied to help, that by this
token I would relieve her . . . . v 3 85
Help me to a candle, and pen, ink and paper . . . . *T. Night* iv 2 87
Good fool, help me to some light and some paper . . . . iv 2 113
I will help you to't. But tell me true, are you not mad indeed? . iv 2 121
For the love of God, your help! I had rather than forty pound I were
at home . . . . v 1 180
I'll help you, Sir Toby, because we'll be dressed together.—Will you
help? an ass-head and a coxcomb! . . . . v 1 210
By whose gentle help I was preserved to serve this noble count . . v 1 262
Camillo was his help in this, his pandar . . . . . *W. Tale* ii 1 46
What's gone and what's past help Should be past grief . . . iii 2 223
How he cried to me for help and said his name was Antigonus . . . iii 3 98
And you shall help to put him i' the ground . . . . . iii 3 140
Help me! pluck but off these rags; and then, death, death! . . . iv 3 55
No hope to help you, But as you shake off one to take another . . iv 4 579
Till your strong hand shall help to give him strength . . *K. John* ii 1 33
Under whose warrant I impeach thy wrong And by whose help I mean
to chastise it . . . . ii 1 117
My arm shall give thee help to bear thee hence . . . . . v 4 58
This England never did, nor never shall, Lie at the proud foot of a
conqueror, But when it first did help to wound itself . . . v 7 114
You never shall, so help you truth and God! . . . *Richard II.* i 3 183
Thou canst help time to furrow me with age, But stop no wrinkle . i 3 229
Now put it, God, in the physician's mind To help him to his grave
immediately! . . . . i 4 60
Help to order several powers To Oxford, or where'er these traitors are . v 3 140
Help, help, help!—How now! what means death in this rude assault? v 5 105
I prithee, good Prince Hal, help me to my horse, good king's son
1 Hen. IV. ii 2 43
If sack and sugar be a fault, God help the wicked! . . . . ii 4 517
Nor shall we need his help these fourteen days . . . . . iii 1 88
Opinion, that did help me to the crown, Had still kept loyal . . iii 2 42
With his help We shall o'erturn it topsy-turvy down . . . . iv 1 81
What with our help, what with the absent king . . . . . v 1 49
Lead me, my lord? I do not need your help . . . . . . v 4 10
And those two things, I confess, I cannot help . . . *2 Hen. IV.* ii 2 73
If the cook help to make the gluttony, you help to make the diseases . ii 4 48
She is old, and cannot help herself . . . . iii 2 247
This part of his conjoins with my disease, And helps to end me . . iv 5 65
By God's help, And yours, the noble sinews of our power *Hen. V.* i 2 222
Next day after dawn, Doth rise and help Hyperion to his horse . iv 1 292
Thou dost not wish more help from England, coz? . . . . iv 3 73
Would you and I alone, Without more help, could fight this royal
battle! . . . . iv 3 75
Christ's mother helps me, else I were too weak.—Whoe'er helps thee,
'tis thou that must help me . . . . . *1 Hen. VI.* i 2 106
Bear hence his body; I will help to bury it . . . . . . i 4 87
Cheer up thy hungry-starved men; Help Salisbury to make his
testament . . . . i 5 17
To join with witches and the help of hell! . . . . . . ii 1 18
Strike those that hurt, and hurt not those that help . . . . iii 3 53
This shall ye do, so help you righteous God! . . . . . iv 1 8
I am lowted by a traitor villain And cannot help the noble chevalier . iv 3 14
The help of one stands me in little stead . . . . . . iv 6 31
The Frenchmen fly. Now help, ye charming spells and periapts . . v 3 2
Help me this once, that France may get the field . . . . v 3 12
In earnest of a further benefit, So you do condescend to help me now . v 3 17
You judge it straight a thing impossible To compass wonders but by
help of devils. No, misconceived! . . . . v 4 48
So God help Warwick, as he loves the land, And common profit!
2 Hen. VI. i 1 205
Come, offer at my shrine, and I will help thee . . . . . ii 1 92
Thy greatest help is quiet, gentle Nell . . . . ii 4 67
For, being green, there is great hope of help . . . . . iii 1 287
Help, lords! the king is dead.—Rear up his body; wring him by the
nose.—Run, go, help, help! . . . . iii 2 33
Ye shall have a hempen caudle then and the help of hatchet . . iv 7 96
So let it help me now against thy sword As I in justice and true right
express it . . . . v 2 24
The help of Norfolk and myself, With all the friends . . *3 Hen. VI.* i 1 178
For how can I help them, and not myself? . . . . . . iii 1 21
Scotland hath will to help, but cannot help . . . . . . iii 3 34
How shall Bona be revenged But by thy help to this distressed queen? iii 3 213
And with their helps only defend ourselves . . . . . . iv 1 45
So God help Montague as he proves true! . . . . . . iv 1 143
This is he Must help you more than you are hurt by me . . . iv 6 76
Doubtless Burgundy will yield him help, And we shall have more wars iv 6 90
Repass'd the seas And brought desired help from Burgundy . . . iv 7 6
But why come you in arms?—To help King Edward in his time of storm iv 7 43
O, welcome, Oxford! for we want thy help . . . . . . v 1 66
If any such be here—as God forbid!—Let him depart before we need
his help . . . . v 4 49
He that bereft thee, lady, of thy husband, Did it to help thee to a better
husband . . . . *Richard III.* i 2 139
She may help you to many fair preferments . . . . . . i 3 95
The time will come when thou shalt wish for me To help thee
curse . . . . i 3 246; iv 4 80
Come, Hastings, help me to my closet. Oh, poor Clarence! . . . ii 1 133
Give me no help in lamentation; I am not barren to bring forth
complaints . . . . ii 2 66
God be thanked, there's no need of me, And much I need to help you . iii 7 166
Though what they do impart Help not at all, yet do they ease the heart iv 4 131
About the mid of night come to my tent And help to arm me . . . v 3 78
One that made means to come by what he hath, And slaughter'd those
that were the means to help him . . . . v 3 249
Withdraw, my lord; I'll help you to a horse . . . . . . v 4 8
It will help me nothing To plead mine innocence . . . *Hen. VIII.* i 1 207
Sent thither, and in haste too, Lest he should help his father . . ii 1 44
Now, the Lord help, They vex me past my patience! . . . . ii 4 129
Sure, you know me?—Yes, my lord; But yet I cannot help you . . v 2 5
Sweet Helen, I must woo you To help unarm our Hector *Troi. and Cres.* iii 1 163
There is no help; The bitter disposition of the time Will have it so . iv 1 47
I know what 'tis to love; And would, as I shall pity, I could help! . iv 3 11
Help to trim my tent: This night in banqueting must all be spent . v 1 50
What he cannot help in his nature, you account a vice in him *Coriolanus* i 1 42
For the dearth, The gods, not the patricians, make it, and Your knees
to them, not arms, must help . . . . i 1 76
With other muniments and petty helps In this our fabric . . . . i 1 122

Help. With smoking swords may march from hence, To help our fielded friends *Coriolanus* i 4 12
Whilst I, with those that have the spirit, will haste To help Cominius i 5 15
Your helps are many, or else your actions would grow wondrous single ii 1 39
And to make us no better thought of, a little help will serve ii 3 16
The fourth would return for conscience sake, to help to get thee a wife ii 3 37
Help, ye citizens!—On both sides more respect iii 1 180
Those cold ways, That seem like prudent helps are very poisonous Where the disease is violent iii 1 221
Help Marcius, help, You that be noble; help him, young and old! iii 1 227
You have brought A trembling upon Rome, such as was never So incapable of help iv 6 120
I cannot help it now, Unless, by using means, I lame the foot iv 7 6
If you refuse your aid In this so never-needed help, yet do not Upbraid's with our distress v 1 34
We will meet them, And help the joy v 4 65
Take him up. Help, three o' the chiefest soldiers v 6 150
And help to set a head on headless Rome *T. Andron.* i 1 186
Help to convey her hence away, And with my sword I'll keep this door i 1 287
Help me out From this unhallowed and blood-stained hole ii 3 209
O brother, help me with thy fainting hand—If fear hath made thee faint ii 3 233
Reach me thy hand, that I may help thee out ii 3 237
Nor I no strength to climb without thy help ii 3 242
I should go hang myself.—If thou hadst hands to help thee knit the cord ii 4 10
The service I require of them Is that the one will help to cut the other iii 1 78
What a sympathy of woe is this, As far from help as Limbo is from bliss! iii 1 149
I'll send the emperor My hand: Good Aaron, wilt thou help to chop it off? iii 1 162
Help, grandsire, help! my aunt Lavinia Follows me every where iv 1 1
When I have writ my name Without the help of any hand at all iv 1 71
We are all undone! Now help, or woe betide thee evermore! iv 2 56
Unhallow'd slave! Sirs, help our uncle to convey him in v 3 15
Where's Potpan, that he helps not to take away? *Rom. and Jul.* i 5 1
Hence will I to my ghostly father's cell, His help to crave ii 2 190
Both our remedies Within thy help and holy physic lies ii 3 52
Help me into some house iii 1 110
Unless philosophy can make a Juliet, Displant a town, reverse a prince's doom, It helps not, it prevails not iii 3 60
Come weep with me; past hope, past cure, past help! iv 1 45
If, in thy wisdom, thou canst give no help, Do thou but call my resolution wise, And with this knife I'll help it presently iv 1 52
Love give me strength! and strength shall help afford iv 1 125
Go with me into my closet, To help me sort such needful ornaments iv 2 34
Go thou to Juliet, help to deck up her; I'll not to bed to-night iv 2 41
What, are you busy, ho? need you my help? iv 3 6
Help, help! my lady's dead! O, well-a-day, that ever I was born! iv 5 14
Revive, look up, or I will die with thee! Help, help! Call help iv 5 21
Then music with her silver sound With speedy help doth lend redress iv 5 146
O churl! drunk all, and left no friendly drop To help me after? v 3 164
To help to take her from her borrow'd grave v 3 248
I do know him A gentleman that well deserves a help *T. of Athens* i 1 102
'Tis not enough to help the feeble up, But to support him after i 1 107
I do return those talents, Doubled with thanks and service, from whose help I derived liberty i 2 7
The gods themselves have provided that I shall have much help from you i 2 93
Cæsar creid 'Help me, Cassius, or I sink!' *J. Cæsar* i 2 111
Thrice hath Calpurnia in her sleep cried out, 'Help, ho! they murder Cæsar!' ii 2 3
I am faint, my gashes cry for help *Macbeth* i 2 42
Did line the rebel With hidden help and vantage i 3 113
Help me hence, ho!—Look to the lady ii 3 124
By the help of these—with Him above To ratify the work—we may again Give to our tables meat iii 6 32
Now is the time of help; your eye in Scotland Would create soldiers iv 3 186
But come; Here, as before, never, so help you mercy *Hamlet* i 5 169
This not to do, So grace and mercy at your most need help you, Swear. i 5 180
He seem'd to find his way without his eyes; For out o' doors he went without their helps ii 1 99
The harlot's cheek, beautied with plastering art, Is not more ugly to the thing that helps it iii 1 52
O, help him, you sweet heavens! iii 1 138
Bid the players make haste. Will you two help to hasten them? iii 2 55
Help, angels! Make assay! Bow, stubborn knees! iii 3 69
What wilt thou do? thou wilt not murder me? Help, help, ho! iii 4 22
The bark is ready, and the wind at help iv 3 46
Father, father! Stop, stop! No help? *Lear* ii 1 38
Help, ho! murder! murder!—How now! What's the matter? ii 2 46
Here's a spirit. Help me, help me! iii 4 40
Come, help to bear thy master; Thou must not stay behind iii 6 107
He that will think to live till he be old, Give me some help! iii 7 70
I'll fetch some flax and whites of eggs To apply to his bleeding face. Now, heaven help him! iii 7 107
He that helps him take all my outward worth iv 4 10
Help, help, O, help!—What kind of help? v 3 222
We lack'd your counsel and your help to-night.—So did I yours *Othello* i 3 51
Which, as a grise or step, may help these lovers Into your favour i 3 200
Help, ho!—Lieutenant,—sir,—Montano,—sir;—Help, masters! ii 3 159
There comes a fellow crying out for help; And Cassio following him ii 3 226
Importune her help to put you in your place again ii 3 324
This may help to thicken other proofs That do demonstrate thinly iii 3 430
So help me every spirit sanctified, As I have spoken for you all my best! iii 4 126
I am maim'd for ever. Help, ho! murder! murder! v 1 27
Let's think't unsafe To come in to the cry without more help v 1 44
Here, here! for heaven's sake, help me!—What's the matter? v 1 50
Help, ho! help! O lady, speak again! Sweet Desdemona! v 2 120
Help, ho! help! The Moor hath kill'd my mistress! v 2 166
Help me away, dear Charmian; I shall fall *Ant. and Cleo.* i 3 15
For that you must But say, I could no help it ii 2 71
Nay, I'll help too. What's this for?—Ah, let be, let be! iv 4 5
Sooth, la, I'll help: thus it must be.—Well, well; We shall thrive now iv 4 8
Help me, my women! O, he is more mad Than Telamon for his shield iv 13 1
Help, Charmian, help, Iras, help; Help, friends below iv 15 12
But come, come, Antony,—Help me, my women,—we must draw thee up iv 15 30
My master rather play'd than fought And had no help of anger *Cymbeline* i 1 163
But I could then have looked on him without the help of admiration i 4 5
I should be sick, But that my resolution helps me iii 6 4
Help; Or we poor ghosts will cry To the shining synod of the rest v 4 87
Help. Help, Jupiter; or we appeal, And from thy justice fly *Cymbeline* v 4 91
A man that were to sleep your sleep, and a hangman to help him to bed v 4 179
O, gentlemen, help! Mine and your mistress! v 5 229
Be my helps, As I am son and servant to your will, To compass such a boundless happiness! *Pericles* i 1 22
That, if heaven slumber while their creatures want, They may awake their helps to comfort them i 4 17
And wanting breath to speak help me with tears i 4 19
And pride so great, The name of help grew odious to repeat i 4 31
Poor souls, it grieved my heart to hear what pitiful cries they made to us to help them, when, well-a-day, we could scarce help ourselves ii 1 23
My veins are chill, And have no more of life than may suffice To give my tongue that heat to ask your help ii 1 79
Help, master, help! here's a fish hangs in the net ii 1 122
What means the nun? she dies! help, gentlemen! v 3 15
Help me. God help me! how long have you professed apprehension? *Much Ado* iii 4 67
So God help me, la!—My love to thee is sound, sans crack or flaw *L. L. L.* v 2 414
What, art thou lame?—Ay, God Almighty help me! *2 Hen. VI.* ii 1 95
So God help me, they spake not a word *Richard III.* iii 7 24
Help me God. So help me God, as I dissemble not!—So help me God, as I intend it not! *1 Hen. VI.* iii 1 140
So help me God, as I have watch'd the night! *2 Hen. VI.* iii 1 110
I say no more than truth, so help me God! iii 1 120
Help me Heaven. I never saw the chain, so help me Heaven! *Com. of Er.* v 1 267
Help the while. God help the while! a bad world, I say *1 Hen. IV.* ii 4 145
Ay, sir, it is too true; God help the while! *Richard III.* ii 3 8
Help thee. God help thee, shallow man! *As Y. Like It* iii 2 74
Now God help thee!—To the Welsh lady's bed *1 Hen. IV.* iii 1 246
Now, God help thee, poor monkey! *Macbeth* iv 2 59
Help us. God help us! it is a world to see *Much Ado* iii 5 38
Helped. Love doth to her eyes repair, To help him of his blindness, And, being help'd, inhabits there *T. G. of Ver.* iv 2 48
Incurable,— Why, there 'tis; so say I too.—Not to be helped *All's Well* ii 3 18
Would I had been by, to have helped the old man! *W. Tale* iii 3 110
I would you had been by the ship side, to have helped her iii 3 113
The first was I that help'd thee to the crown *Richard III.* v 3 167
For even her folly help'd her to an heir *Othello* ii 1 138
Helper. Who in his office lacks a helper *Meas. for Meas.* iv 2 10
It hath fated her to be my motive And helper to a husband *All's Well* iv 4 21
You speedy helpers, that are substitutes Under the lordly monarch of the north, Appear and aid me *1 Hen. VI.* v 3 5
Helpest. What mean'st thou, that thou help'st me not? *Richard III.* i 4 281
Helpful. Our helpful ship was splitted in the midst *Com. of Errors* i 1 104
Till time lend friends and friends their helpful swords *Richard II.* iii 3 132
And gave the tongue a helpful ornament *1 Hen. IV.* iii 1 125
Heavens make our presence and our practices Pleasant and helpful to him! *Hamlet* ii 2 39
Helping. Deserve well at my hands by helping me *Much Ado* v 2 2
I am helping you to mar that which God made *As Y. Like It* i 1 35
By helping Baptista's eldest daughter to a husband we set his youngest free for a husband *T. of Shrew* i 1 141
Not helping, death's my fee; But, if I help, what? *All's Well* ii 1 192
And little look'd for at your helping hands *Richard II.* iv 1 161
And give thee half, It is too little, helping him to all v 1 61
Helpless. Hopeless and helpless doth Ægeon wend *Com. of Errors* i 1 158
Thou hast no unkind mate to grieve thee, With urging helpless patience ii 1 39
I pour the helpless balm of my poor eyes *Richard III.* i 2 13
Helter-skelter have I rode to thee, And tidings do I bring *2 Hen. IV.* v 3 98
Hem. Bid sorrow wag, cry 'hem!' when he should groan *Much Ado* v 1 16
These burs are in my heart.—Hem them away.—I would try, if I could cry 'hem' and have him *As Y. Like It* i 3 18
How do you now?—Better than I was: hem! *2 Hen. IV.* ii 4 33
Our watchword was 'Hem boys!' iii 2 232
Hem, and stroke thy beard, As he being drest to some oration *Tr. and Cr.* i 3 165
Entomb'd upon the very hem o' the sea *T. of Athens* v 4 66
Hems, and beats her heart; Spurns enviously at straws *Hamlet* iv 5 5
Cough, or cry 'hem,' if any body come *Othello* iv 2 29
Hemlock. The darnel, hemlock and rank fumitory Doth root upon *Hen. V.* v 2 45
Root of hemlock digg'd i' the dark *Macbeth* iv 1 25
With bur-docks, hemlock, nettles, cuckoo-flowers *Lear* iv 4 4
Hemmed. And hemm'd about with grim destruction *1 Hen. VI.* iv 3 21
And I have seen thee pause and take thy breath, When that a ring of Greeks have hemm'd thee in *Troi. and Cres.* iv 5 193
Hemp. Let gallows gape for dog; let man go free And let not hemp his wind-pipe suffocate *Hen. V.* iii 6 45
Hempen. What hempen home-spuns have we swaggering here? *M. N. D.* iii 1 79
Behold Upon the hempen tackle ship-boys climbing *Hen. V.* iii Prol. 8
Ye shall have a hempen caudle then and the help of hatchet *2 Hen. VI.* iv 7 95
Hemp-seed. Do, do, thou rogue! do, thou hemp-seed! *2 Hen. IV.* ii 1 64
Hen. I will be more jealous of thee than a Barbary cock-pigeon over his hen *As Y. Like It* iv 1 151
A coxcomb?—A combless cock, so Kate will be my hen *T. of Shrew* ii 1 227
Lord have mercy on thee for a hen! *All's Well* ii 3 224
I have no pheasant, cock nor hen *W. Tale* iv 4 771
How now, Dame Partlet the hen! have you inquired yet? *1 Hen. IV.* iii 3 60
He'll not swagger with a Barbary hen, if her feathers turn back *2 Hen. IV.* ii 4 108
Some pigeons, Davy, a couple of short-legged hens, a joint of mutton v 1 28
She, poor hen, fond of no second brood, Has cluck'd thee to the wars and safely home, Loaden with honour *Coriolanus* v 3 162
Hence. But now he parted hence, to embark *T. G. of Ver.* i 1 71
How churlishly I chid Lucetta hence, When willingly I would have had her here! i 2 60
In lieu thereof, dispatch me hence ii 7 88
But, fly I hence, I fly away from life iii 1 187
Thy letters may be here, though thou art hence iii 1 248
I hope, sir, that you love not here.—Sir, but I do; or else I would be hence iv 2 22
Hence hath offence his quick celerity *Meas. for Meas.* iv 2 113
Give him leave to escape hence, he would not iv 2 157
As I, thus wrong'd, hence unbelieved go! v 1 119
You spurn me hence, and he will spurn me hither *Com. of Errors* ii 1 84
Therefore 'tis high time that I were hence iii 2 162
Some blessed power deliver us from hence! iv 3 44
I will not hence and leave my husband here v 1 109
But I would have thee hence, and here again *Much Ado* ii 3 7
Hence from her! let her die v 1 156
Hence ever then my heart is in thy breast *L. L. Lost* v 2 826
You must be gone from hence immediately *Mer. of Venice* ii 9 8
Come, away! For you shall hence upon your wedding-day iii 2 313

Hence. From hence I go, To make these doubts all even . *As Y. Like It* v 4 24
I will be gone ; My being here it is that holds thee hence . *All's Well* iii 2 126
But a month ago I went from hence . . . . . *T. Night* i 2 31
Hence with her, out o' door : A most intelligencing bawd ! . *W. Tale* ii 3 67
This must be answer'd either here or hence . . *K. John* iv 2 89
Since it is true That I must die here and live hence by truth . . . v 4 29
Comest thou because the anointed king is hence? . *Richard II.* ii 3 96
All members of our cause, both here and hence . *2 Hen. IV.* iv 1 171
Make less thy body hence, and more thy grace . . . v 5 56
Therefore, living hence, did give ourself To barbarous license *Hen. V.* i 2 270
Let us now persuade you.—Not to be gone from hence . *1 Hen. VI.* iii 2 94
Forslow no longer, make we hence amain . . . *3 Hen. VI.* ii 3 56
How many ages hence Shall this our lofty scene be acted over ! *J. Cæsar* iii 1 111
Both here and hence pursue me lasting strife ! . . *Hamlet* iii 2 232
Freedom lives hence, and banishment is here . . *Lear* i 1 184
The several messengers From hence attend dispatch . . ii 1 127
And from hence I'll love no friend . . . . . *Othello* iii 3 379
Hence-banished is banish'd from the world . *Rom. and Jul.* iii 3 19
Hence departure. My people did expect my hence departure *W. Tale* ii 2 450
Henceforth carry your letters yourself . . *T. G. of Ver.* i 1 153
This babble shall not henceforth trouble me . . . i 2 98
And yet I thank you, Meaning henceforth to trouble you no more ii 1 125
Pardon me, wife. Henceforth do what thou wilt . *Mer. Wives* iv 4 6
Dispose For henceforth of poor Claudio . . . *Much Ado* v 1 304
Henceforth my wooing mind shall be express'd In russet yeas *L. L. Lost* v 2 412
Henceforth be never number'd among men ! . *M. N. Dream* iii 2 67
Be merry.—From henceforth I will, coz, and devise sports *As Y. Like It* i 2 26
Let us sit and mock the good housewife Fortune from her wheel, that her gifts may henceforth be bestowed equally . . . . i 2 36
Call it a rush-candle, Henceforth I vow it shall be so for me *T. of Shrew* iv 5 15
I will henceforth eat no fish of fortune's buttering . *All's Well* v 2 9
But direct thy feet Where thou and I henceforth may never meet *T. Night* v 1 172
If ever henceforth thou These rural latches to his entrance open *W. Tale* iv 4 448
From henceforth bear his name whose form thou bear'st *K. John* i 1 160
I will from henceforth rather be myself . . *1 Hen. IV.* i 3 5
Henceforth Let me not hear you speak of Mortimer . . i 3 118
I must not have you henceforth question me Whither I go . ii 3 106
Swearest thou, ungracious boy? henceforth ne'er look on me ii 4 490
And flow henceforth in formal majesty . . *2 Hen. IV.* v 2 133
Henceforth let a Welsh correction teach you a good English condition *Hen. V.* v 1 82
Henceforth we banish thee, on pain of death . *1 Hen. VI.* iv 1 47
Henceforth I charge you, as you love our favour, Quite to forget this . iv 1 135
I will deal with him That henceforth he shall trouble us no more *2 Hen. VI.* iii 1 324
Wither, garden ; and be henceforth a burying-place . . iv 10 67
And will that thou henceforth attend on us . . . v 1 80
Henceforth I will not have to do with pity . . . v 2 56
Never henceforth shall I joy again, Never, O never ! . *3 Hen. VI.* ii 1 77
Henceforth I am thy true servitor . . . . iii 3 196
Do not frown upon my faults, For I will henceforth be no more unconstant v 1 102
Henceforth guard thee well ; For I'll not kill thee there *Troi. and Cres.* iv 5 253
Or be ye not henceforth call'd my children . *T. Andron.* ii 3 115
I'll be new baptized ; Henceforth I never will be Romeo *Rom. and Jul.* ii 2 51
Thou and my bosom henceforth shall be twain . . . iii 5 240
Henceforth be no feast, Whereat a villain's not a welcome guest *T. of A.* iii 6 112
Henceforth hated be Of Timon man and all humanity ! . . . iii 6 114
From henceforth, When you are over-earnest with your Brutus, He'll think your mother chides . . . . *J. Cæsar* iv 3 121
My thanes and kinsmen, Henceforth be earls . . . *Macbeth* v 8 63
Henceforth I'll bear Affliction till it do cry out itself 'Enough' *Lear* iv 6 75
Henceforth know, It is not Cæsar's natural vice . *Ant. and Cleo.* i 4 1
Henceforth The white hand of a lady fever thee . . iii 13 137
To write and read Be henceforth treacherous ! . . *Cymbeline* iv 2 317
Henceforward, upon pain of death . . . *1 Hen. VI.* i 3 79
Henceforward it shall be treason for any that calls me other *2 Hen. VI.* iv 6 5
Henceforward all things shall be in common . . . iv 7 20
Henceforward will I bear Upon my target three fair-shining suns *3 Hen. VI.* ii 1 39
Henceforward do your messages yourself . . *Rom. and Jul.* ii 5 66
Henceforward I am ever ruled by you . . . . iv 2 22
Hence-going. For the gap That we shall make in time, from our hence-going And our return . . . . . *Cymbeline* iii 2 65
Henchman. A little changeling boy, To be my henchman *M. N. Dream* ii 1 121
Henri. Notre très-cher fils Henri, Roi d'Angleterre . . *Hen. V.* v 2 368
Henricus. Præclarissimus filius noster Henricus, Rex Angliæ, et Hæres Franciæ . . . . v 2 370
Henry (son of King John). The lords are all come back, And brought Prince Henry in their company . . . *K. John* v 6 34
Henry Bolingbroke (Hen. IV.) The resignation of thy state and crown To Henry Bolingbroke . . . . *Richard II.* iv 1 180
Three times hath Henry Bolingbroke made head Against my power *1 Hen. IV.* iii 1 64
Henry Bolingbroke, Duke of Lancaster, The eldest son and heir of John of Gaunt . . . . *2 Hen. VI.* ii 2 21
Henry Guildford. I was spoke to, with Sir Henry Guildford This night to be comptrollers . . . . . . *Hen. VIII.* i 3 66
Henry Hereford (Hen. IV.) Hast thou . . . Brought hither Henry Hereford thy bold son? . . . . . *Richard II.* i 1 3
Henry Lord Scroop of Masham . . . *Hen. V.* ii Prol. 24 ; ii 2 148
Henry Monmouth (Hen. V.) Since Henry Monmouth first began to reign, Before whose glory I was great . . *1 Hen. VI.* ii 5 23
Henry of Lancaster. The devil take Henry of Lancaster [Hen. IV.] and thee ! Patience is stale . . . . *Richard II.* v 5 103
Henry of Lancaster [Hen. VI.], resign thy crown. What mutter you, or what conspire you, lords . . . . *3 Hen. VI.* i 1 164
Henry Percy. His son young Henry Percy . *Richard II.* ii 2 53
Doth join with all the world In praise of Henry Percy . *1 Hen. IV.* v 1 87
Henry Pimpernell And twenty more such names . *T. of Shrew* Ind. 2 96
Henry Plantagenet (Hen. V.) England is thine, Ireland is thine, France is thine, and Henry Plantagenet is thine . . *Hen. V.* v 2 259
Henry the Eighth. Now his son, Henry the Eighth, life, honour, name and all That made me happy at one stroke has taken For ever from the world . . . . *Hen. VIII.* ii 1 116
Say, Henry King of England, come into the court . . ii 4 6
Henry the Fifth. Scourge the bad revolting stars That have consented unto Henry's death ! . . . . . *1 Hen. VI.* i 1 5
King Henry the Fifth, too famous to live long ! . . . i 1 6
Henry is dead and never shall revive . . . . i 1 18
We'll offer up our arms ; Since arms avail not now that Henry's dead . i 1 47
Henry the Fifth, thy ghost I invocate : Prosper this realm ! . . i 1 52
What say'st thou, man, before dead Henry's corse? Speak softly . i 1 62
Henry the Fifth. If Henry were recall'd to life again, These news would cause him once more yield the ghost . . . *1 Hen. VI.* i 1 66
To add to your laments, Wherewith you now bedew King Henry's hearse i 1 104
Remember, lords, your oaths to Henry sworn . . . . i 1 162
With Henry's death the English circle ends . . . . i 2 136
Since Henry's death, I fear, there is conveyance . . . . i 3 2
That haughty prelate, Whom Henry, our late sovereign, ne'er could brook i 3 24
In thirteen battles Salisbury o'ercame ; Henry the Fifth he first train'd i 4 79
When Henry the Fifth, Succeeding his father Bolingbroke, did reign . ii 5 82
I fear that fatal prophecy Which in the time of Henry named the Fifth Was in the mouth of every sucking babe ; That Henry born at Monmouth should win all And Henry born at Windsor lose all . iii 1 196
That ever living man of memory, Henry the Fifth . . . iv 3 52
Henry the Fifth did sometime prophesy, 'If once he come to be a cardinal, He'll make his cap co-equal with the crown' . . v 1 31
What ! did my brother Henry spend his youth, His valour, coin and people, in the wars? . . . . . *2 Hen. VI* i 1 78
Did my brother Bedford toil his wits, To keep by policy what Henry got? i 1 84
Shall Henry's conquest, Bedford's vigilance, . . . and all our counsel die? i 1 96
Henry the Fifth, in whose time boys went to span-counter for French crowns . . . . iv 2 165
Henry the Fifth, that made all France to quake . . . iv 8 17
Is Cade the son of Henry the Fifth, That thus you do exclaim you'll go with him? . . . . iv 8 36
The name of Henry the Fifth hales them to an hundred mischiefs . iv 8 58
I am the son of Henry the Fifth, Who made the Dauphin and the French to stoop . . . . . . *3 Hen. VI.* i 1 107
Henry the Fifth, Who by his prowess conquered all France . . iii 3 85
How haps it, in this smooth discourse, You told not how Henry the Sixth hath lost All that which Henry the Fifth had gotten? . . iii 3 90
Henry the Fourth. Long live Henry, fourth of that name ! *Richard II.* iv 1 112
I have thrown A brave defiance in King Henry's teeth . *1 Hen. IV.* v 2 43
Henry the Fourth, grandfather to this king, Deposed his nephew Richard . . . . *1 Hen. VI.* ii 5 63
The eldest son and heir of John of Gaunt, Crown'd by the name of Henry the Fourth . . . . *2 Hen. VI.* ii 2 23
Henry the Fourth by conquest got the crown.—'Twas by rebellion against his king . . . . *3 Hen. VI.* i 1 132
Richard, in the view of many lords, Resign'd the crown to Henry the Fourth . . . . i 1 139
Henry the Fourth, Whose wisdom was a mirror to the wisest . . iii 3 83
Henry the Seventh. It is young Henry, earl of Richmond.—Come hither, England's hope . . . . iv 6 67
Henry the Seventh succeeding, truly pitying My father's loss *Hen. VIII.* ii 1 112
Henry the Sixth, in infant bands crown'd King . *Hen. V.* Epil. 9
I will proclaim young Henry king.—To Eltham will I . *1 Hen. VI.* i 1 169
Now, Salisbury, for thee, and for the right Of English Henry . ii 1 36
Good lords, and virtuous Henry, Pity the city of London, pity us ! . iii 1 76
When Gloucester says the word, King Henry goes . . . iii 1 184
As sure as English Henry lives And as his father here was conqueror, . . . I swear to get the town or die . . . . . iii 2 80
To Paris to the king, For there young Henry with his nobles lie . . iii 2 129
France were no place for Henry's warriors . . . . iii 3 22
Who then but English Henry will be lord And thou be thrust out? . iii 3 66
God save King Henry, of that name the sixth ! . . . iv 1 2
Pardon me, princely Henry, and the rest . . . . iv 1 18
This is my servant : hear him, noble prince.—And this is mine : sweet Henry, favour him . . . . iv 1 81
That for a toy, a thing of no regard, King Henry's peers and chief nobility Destroy'd themselves, and lost the realm of France ! . . iv 1 146
Lord Talbot, . . . Great marshal to Henry the Sixth . . . iv 7 70
Let Henry fret and all the world repine . . . . v 2 20
Henry is youthful and will quickly yield . . . . v 3 99
I'll undertake to make thee Henry's queen . . . . v 3 117
I am unworthy to be Henry's wife.—No, gentle madam . . v 3 122
My daughter shall be Henry's, if he please.—That is her ransom . v 3 156
And I again, in Henry's royal name, . . . Give thee her hand . v 3 160
I do embrace thee, as I would embrace The Christian prince, King Henry . . . . v 3 172
Solicit Henry with her wondrous praise . . . . v 3 190
That, when thou comest to kneel at Henry's feet, Thou mayst bereave him of his wits with wonder . . . . v 3 194
That, in regard King Henry gives consent, Of mere compassion . v 4 124
Of virtuous chaste intents, To love and honour Henry as her lord.—And otherwise will Henry ne'er presume . . . . . . v 5 21
Henry is able to enrich his queen And not to seek a queen to make him rich . . . . v 5 51
Whom should we match with Henry, being a king, But Margaret, that is daughter to a king? . . . . v 5 66
For Henry, son unto a conqueror, Is likely to beget more conquerors . v 5 73
To England and be crown'd King Henry's faithful and anointed queen . v 5 91
That the said Henry shall espouse the Lady Margaret . *2 Hen. VI.* i 1 46
Henry gives away his own, To match with her that brings no vantages i 1 130
Had Henry got an empire by his marriage, And all the wealthy kingdoms of the west, There's reason he should be displeased at it i 1 153
Henry was well pleased To change two dukedoms for a duke's fair daughter . . . . i 1 218
Till Henry, surfeiting in joys of love, With his new bride and England's dear-bought queen, And Humphrey with the peers be fall'n at jars i 1 251
What seest thou there? King Henry's diadem? . . . . i 2 7
And may that thought, when I imagine ill Against my king and nephew, virtuous Henry, Be my last breathing in this mortal world ! . . i 2 20
Henry and dame Margaret kneel'd to me And on my head did set the diadem . . . . i 2 39
I thought King Henry had resembled thee In courage, courtship . i 3 56
The duke yet lives that Henry shall depose . . . . i 4 33 ; 62
Demanding of King Henry's life and death . . . . ii 1 175
Henry doth claim the crown from John of Gaunt, The fourth son . ii 2 54
Henry will to himself Protector be ; and God shall be my hope . ii 3 23
God and King Henry govern England's realm . . . . ii 3 30
Here, noble Henry, is my staff : As willingly do I the same resign As e'er thy father Henry made it mine . . . . . . ii 3 32
Why, now is Henry king, And Margaret queen . . . . ii 3 39
This staff of honour raught, there let it stand Where it best fits to be, in Henry's hand . . . . ii 3 44
Ah ! thus King Henry throws away his crutch Before his legs be firm to bear his body . . . . iii 1 189
Ah, that my fear were false ! ah, that it were ! For, good King Henry, thy decay I fear . . . . iii 1 194
Henry my lord is cold in great affairs . . . . . iii 1 224

Henry the Sixth. Humphrey being dead, as he shall be, And Henry put apart, the next for me . . . *2 Hen. VI.* iii 1 383
O Henry, ope thine eyes!—He doth revive again: madam, be patient . iii 2 35
How fares my gracious lord?—Comfort, my sovereign! gracious Henry, comfort! . . . . iii 2 38
Die, Margaret! For Henry weeps that thou dost live so long . . iii 2 121
But how he died God knows, not Henry . . . . iii 2 131
O Henry, let me plead for gentle Suffolk! . . . . . . iii 2 289
King Henry's blood, The honourable blood of Lancaster, Must not be shed by such a jaded groom . . . . iv 1 50
Henry hath money, you are strong and manly; God on our side . iv 8 53
Henry, though he be infortunate, Assure yourselves, will never be unkind . . . . iv 9 18
Thus comes York to claim his right, And pluck the crown from feeble Henry's head . . . . v 1 2
A messenger from Henry, our dread liege, To know the reason of these arms . . . . v 1 17
But I must make fair weather yet a while, Till Henry be more weak . v 1 31
And let my sovereign, virtuous Henry, Command my eldest son . . v 1 48
Thus do I hope to shake King Henry's head . . . . *3 Hen. VI.* i 1 20
Possess it, York; For this is thine and not King Henry's heirs' . i 1 27
And bashful Henry deposed, whose cowardice Hath made us by-words i 1 41
Far be the thought of this from Henry's heart, To make a shambles of the parliament-house! . . . . i 1 70
Frowns, words and threats Shall be the war that Henry means to use . i 1 73
Thou art a traitor to the crown In following this usurping Henry . . i 1 81
Peace, thou! and give King Henry leave to speak . . . . . i 1 120
My title's good, and better far than his.—Prove it, Henry . . . i 1 131
For all the claim thou lay'st, Think not that Henry shall be so deposed i 1 153
King Henry, be thy title right or wrong, Lord Clifford vows to fight in thy defence . . . . i 1 159
Base, fearful and despairing Henry! . . . . i 1 178
Turn this way, Henry, and regard them not.—They seek revenge . . i 1 189
Long live King Henry! Plantagenet, embrace him . . . . . i 1 202
I here divorce myself Both from thy table, Henry, and thy bed . . i 1 248
The crown of England, father, which is yours.—Mine, boy? not till King Henry be dead . . . . i 2 10
Henry had none, but did usurp the place . . . . i 2 25
I cannot rest Until the white rose that I wear be dyed Even in the lukewarm blood of Henry's heart . . . . i 2 34
And trust not simple Henry nor his oaths . . . . i 2 59
Now looks he like a king! Ay, this is he that took King Henry's chair i 4 97
You should not be king Till our King Henry had shook hands with death . . . . i 4 102
And will you pale your head in Henry's glory, And rob his temples? . i 4 103
Our late decree in parliament Touching King Henry's oath . . . ii 1 119
Thou shalt know this strong right hand of mine Can pluck the diadem from faint Henry's head . . . . ii 1 153
Perjured Henry! wilt thou kneel for grace, And set thy diadem upon my head? . . . . ii 2 81
What say'st thou, Henry, wilt thou yield the crown? . . . . . ii 2 101
Say, Henry, shall I have my right, or no? . . . . ii 2 126
Here burns my candle out; ay, here it dies, Which, whiles it lasted, gave King Henry light . . . . ii 6 2
Impairing Henry, strengthening misproud York, The common people swarm like summer flies . . . . ii 6 7
And who shines now but Henry's enemies? . . . . ii 6 10
And, Henry, hadst thou sway'd as kings should do, Or as thy father and his father did . . . . ii 6 14
Some troops pursue the bloody-minded queen, That led calm Henry . ii 6 34
She, on his left side, craving aid for Henry, He, on his right, asking a wife for Edward. She weeps, and says her Henry is deposed . . iii 1 43
We are true subjects to the king, King Edward.—So would you be again to Henry, If he were seated . . . . iii 1 95
Henry your foe is taken, And brought your prisoner to your palace gate iii 2 118
Between my soul's desire and me . . . Is Clarence, Henry, and his son iii 2 130
Henry, sole possessor of my love, Is of a king become a banish'd man . iii 3 24
Poor Margaret, With this my son, Prince Edward, Henry's heir . . iii 3 31
If that go forward, Henry's hope is done . . . . iii 3 58
This reason may suffice, That Henry liveth still; but were he dead, Yet here Prince Edward stands, King Henry's son . . . . . iii 3 72
Thy father Henry did usurp; And thou no more art prince than she is queen . . . . iii 3 79
From these our Henry lineally descends . . . . iii 3 87
How haps it, in this smooth discourse, You told not how Henry the Sixth hath lost All that which Henry the Fifth had gotten? . . iii 3 89
For shame! leave Henry, and call Edward king . . . . . iii 3 100
Is he gracious in the people's eye?—The more that Henry was unfortunate . . . . iii 3 118
Before thy coming Lewis was Henry's friend.—And still is friend to him iii 3 143
Henry now lives in Scotland at his ease . . . . iii 3 151
Did I put Henry from his native right? And am I guerdon'd at the last with shame? . . . . iii 3 190
I here renounce him and return to Henry . . . . iii 3 194
I will revenge his wrong to Lady Bona And replant Henry . . . iii 3 198
Quite forget old faults, And joy that thou becomest King Henry's friend . . . . iii 3 201
How shall poor Henry live, Unless thou rescue him from foul despair? iii 3 214
Not that I pity Henry's misery, But seek revenge on Edward's mockery iii 3 264
Is Lewis so brave? belike he thinks me Henry . . . . . . iv 1 96
But what said Henry's queen? For I have heard that she was there . iv 1 102
You that will follow me to this attempt, Applaud the name of Henry . iv 2 27
But Henry now shall wear the English crown, And be true king . . iv 3 49
To free King Henry from imprisonment And see him seated . . . iv 3 63
He comes towards London, To set the crown once more on Henry's head . . . . iv 4 27
We'll yoke together, like a double shadow To Henry's body . . . iv 6 50
Henry's late presaging prophecy Did glad my heart with hope . . iv 6 92
Once more I shall interchange My waned state for Henry's regal crown iv 7 4
For safety of ourselves; For now we owe allegiance unto Henry . . iv 7 19
If Henry be your king, Yet Edward at the least is Duke of York . iv 7 20
Why stand you in a doubt? Open the gates: we are King Henry's friends . . . . iv 7 28
'Tis my right, And Henry but usurps the diadem . . . . . iv 7 66
How evil it beseems thee, To flatter Henry and forsake thy brother! . iv 7 85
Seize on the shame-faced Henry, bear him hence . . . . . iv 8 53
Warwick takes his gift again; And Henry is my king, Warwick his subject . . . . v 1 38
You left poor Henry at the Bishop's palace, And, ten to one, you'll meet him in the Tower . . . . v 1 45

Henry the Sixth. Henry, your sovereign, Is prisoner to the foe; his state usurp'd . . . . *3 Hen. VI.* v 4 76
Indeed, 'tis true that Henry told me of . . . . v 6 69
King Henry and the prince his son are gone: Clarence, thy turn is next v 6 89
I'll throw thy body in another room And triumph, Henry, in thy day of doom . . . . v 6 93
Rest you, whiles I lament King Henry's corse . . . *Richard III.* i 2 32
See, see! dead Henry's wounds Open their congeal'd mouths and bleed afresh! . . . . i 2 55
Causer of the timeless deaths Of these Plantagenets, Henry and Edward i 2 118
I did kill King Henry, But 'twas thy beauty that provoked me . . i 2 180
Thou slewest my husband Henry in the Tower, And Edward, my poor son . . . . i 3 119
Henry's death, my lovely Edward's death, Their kingdom's loss . . i 3 192
When Henry the Sixth Was crown'd in Paris but at nine months old . ii 3 16
When he that is my husband now Came to me, as I follow'd Henry's corse . . . . iv 1 67
Henry the Sixth Did prophesy that Richmond should be king . . . iv 2 98
Rivers, Grey, Holy King Henry, and thy fair son Edward . . . v 1 4
King Henry's issue, Richmond, comforts thee . . . . . . v 3 123
Hent. The generous and gravest citizens Have hent the gates *M. for M.* iv 6 14
Jog on, jog on, the foot-path way, And merrily hent the stile-a *W. Tale* iv 3 133
Up, sword; and know thou a more horrid hent . . . *Hamlet* iii 3 88
Her. How she opposes her against my will . . . *T. G. of Ver.* iii 2 26
I could drive her then from the ward of her purity, her reputation, her marriage-vow, and a thousand other her defences . *Mer. Wives* ii 2 257
Hie you home, And bid Bianca make her ready straight. *T. of Shrew* iv 4 63
Then rose again and bow'd her to the people . . . *Hen. VIII.* iv 1 85
Is she not proud? doth she not count her blest? . . *Rom. and Jul.* iii 5 144
And cast From her his dearest one, Sweet Imogen . . *Cymbeline* v 4 61
Herald. My herald thoughts in thy pure bosom rest them *T. G. of Ver.* iii 1 144
Silence is the perfectest herald of joy . . . . . *Much Ado* ii 1 317
My herald is return'd . . . . *L. L. Lost* iii 1 70
Their herald is a pretty knavish page . . . . v 2 97
A herald, Kate? O, put me in thy books! . . . . *T. of Shrew* ii 1 225
Ere my heart Durst make too bold a herald of my tongue . *All's Well* v 3 46
Heralds, from off our towers we might behold, From first to last *K. John* ii 1 325
Like heralds 'twixt two dreadful battles set . . . . . . iv 2 78
Thrown over the shoulders like an herald's coat without sleeves *1 Hen. IV.* iv 2 48
Where is Montjoy the herald? speed him hence . . . *Hen. V.* iii 5 36
Herald, save thou thy labour; Come thou no more for ransom, gentle herald . . . . iv 3 121
Thou never shalt hear herald any more . . . . iv 3 127
Take a trumpet, herald; Ride thou unto the horsemen on yon hill . iv 7 59
Here comes the herald of the French, my liege.—His eyes are humbler iv 7 69
What means this, herald? know'st thou not That I have fined these bones of mine for ransom? . . . . iv 7 71
I tell thee truly, herald, I know not if the day be ours or no . . iv 7 86
Our heralds go with him: Bring me just notice of the numbers dead . iv 7 121
Now, herald, are the dead number'd? . . . . iv 8 78
Heralds, wait on us: Instead of gold, we'll offer up our arms *1 Hen. VI.* i 1 45
Herald, away; and throughout every town Proclaim them traitors *2 Hen. VI.* iv 2 186
Wear it as a herald's coat, To emblaze the honour that thy master got iv 10 75
The queen's kindred and night-walking heralds That trudge betwixt the king and Mistress Shore . . . . *Richard III.* i 1 72
Jove's Mercury, and herald for a king! . . . . iv 3 55
When these suns—For so they phrase 'em—by their heralds challenged The noble spirits to arms, they did perform Beyond thought's compass . . . . *Hen. VIII.* i 1 34
After my death I wish no other herald, No other speaker of my living actions . . . . iv 2 69
May one, that is a herald and a prince, Do a fair message to his kingly ears?—With surety . . . . *Troi. and Cres.* i 3 218
The most noble corse that ever herald Did follow to his urn . *Coriolanus* v 6 145
Love's heralds should be thoughts . . . . . *Rom. and Jul.* ii 5 4
It was the lark, the herald of the morn, No nightingale . . . iii 5 6
It is the part of men to fear and tremble, When the most mighty gods by tokens send Such dreadful heralds . . . . *J. Cæsar* i 3 56
Only to herald thee into his sight, Not pay thee . . . *Macbeth* i 3 102
Like the herald Mercury New-lighted on a heaven-kissing hill *Hamlet* iii 4 58
When time shall serve, let but the herald cry, And I'll appear again *Lear* v 1 48
A herald, ho!—A herald, ho, a herald! . . . . v 3 102
Come hither, herald,—Let the trumpet sound,—And read out this . v 3 107
Thou hast as chiding a nativity As fire, air, water, earth, and heaven can make, To herald thee from the womb . . . . . *Pericles* iii 1 34
Heraldry. Like coats in heraldry, Due but to one . . *M. N. Dream* iii 2 213
You are more saucy with lords and honourable personages than the commission of your birth and virtue gives you heraldry . *All's Well* ii 3 280
A seal'd compact, Well ratified by law and heraldry . . *Hamlet* i 1 87
This dread and black complexion smear'd With heraldry more dismal . ii 2 478
The hearts of old gave hands; But our new heraldry is hands, not hearts *Othello* iii 4 47
Herb. Fetch me that flower; the herb I shew'd thee once *M. N. Dream* ii 1 169
Fetch me this herb; and be thou here again Ere the leviathan can swim a league . . . . ii 1 173
Ere I take this charm from off her sight, As I can take it with another herb . . . . ii 1 184
Then crush this herb into Lysander's eye . . . . iii 2 366
In such a night Medea gather'd the enchanted herbs . *Mer. of Venice* v 1 13
We may pick a thousand salads ere we light on such another herb *All's Well* iv 5 16
She was the sweet-marjoram of the salad, or rather, the herb of grace . iv 5 18
They are not herbs, you knave; they are nose-herbs . . . iv 5 19
Her wholesome herbs Swarming with caterpillars . . . *Richard II.* iii 4 46
Here in this place I'll set a bank of rue, sour herb of grace . . iii 4 105
They'll o'ergrow the garden And choke the herbs . . *2 Hen. VI.* iii 1 33
Small herbs have grace, great weeds do grow apace *Richard III.* ii 4 13
Such wither'd herbs as these Are meet for plucking up . *T. Andron.* iii 1 178
O, mickle is the powerful grace that lies In herbs, plants, *Rom. and Jul.* ii 3 16
Two such opposed kings encamp them still In man as well as herbs, grace and rude will . . . . ii 3 28
Supply it with one gender of herbs, or distract it with many . *Othello* i 3 327
The herbs that have on them cold dew o' the night Are strewings fitt'st for graves . . . . *Cymbeline* iv 2 284
Herbert. Sir Walter Herbert, a renowned soldier . . *Richard III.* iv 5 9
Sir William Brandon, And you, Sir Walter Herbert, stay with me . . v 3 28
Herb-grace. We may call it herb-grace o' Sundays . . . *Hamlet* iv 5 182
Herblet. You were as flowers, now wither'd: even so These herblets shall, which we upon you strew . . . . . *Cymbeline* iv 2 287

Herb-woman. Your herb-woman ; she that sets seeds and roots of shame and iniquity *Pericles* iv 6 92
Herculean. How this Herculean Roman does become The carriage of his chafe *Ant. and Cleo.* i 3 84
Hercules. Discard, bully Hercules ; cashier : let them wag *Mer. Wives* i 3 6
She would have made Hercules have turned spit *Much Ado* ii 1 261
I will in the interim undertake one of Hercules' labours ii 1 380
Like the shaven Hercules in the smirched worm-eaten tapestry iii 3 145
He is now as valiant as Hercules that only tells a lie and swears it iv 1 324
What great men have been in love?—Hercules, master.—Most sweet Hercules! More authority, dear boy, name more *L. L. Lost* i 2 69
Cupid's butt-shaft is too hard for Hercules' club i 2 182
To see great Hercules whipping a gig, And profound Solomon to tune a jig iv 3 167
Is not Love a Hercules, Still climbing trees in the Hesperides? iv 3 340
The page, Hercules,— Pardon, sir ; error : he is not quantity enough for that Worthy's thumb v 1 136
He shall present Hercules in minority v 1 141
Well done, Hercules! now thou crushest the snake! v 1 145
Armado's page, Hercules ; the pedant, Judas Maccabæus v 2 539
Great Hercules is presented by this imp, Whose club kill'd Cerberus v 2 592
I was with Hercules and Cadmus once *M. N. Dream* iv 1 117
That have I told my love, In glory of my kinsman Hercules v 1 47
If Hercules and Lichas play at dice Which is the better man *Mer. of Ven.* ii 1 32
Go, Hercules! Live thou, I live : with much much more dismay I view the fight than thou that makest the fray iii 2 60
Wear yet upon their chins The beards of Hercules and frowning Mars iii 2 85
Now Hercules be thy speed, young man! *As Y. Like It* i 2 222
Leave that labour to great Hercules *T. of Shrew* i 2 257
He professes not keeping of oaths ; in breaking 'em he is stronger than Hercules : he will lie, sir *All's Well* iv 3 283
Thou knowest I am as valiant as Hercules 1 *Hen. IV.* ii 4 299
I thought I should have seen some Hercules, A second Hector 1 *Hen. VI.* ii 3 19
Hercules himself must yield to odds 3 *Hen. VI.* ii 1 53
You were wont to say, If you had been the wife of Hercules, Six of his labours you'ld have done, and saved Your husband so much sweat *Coriolanus* iv 1 17
As Hercules Did shake down mellow fruit iv 6 99
My father's brother, but no more like my father Than I to Hercules *Ham.* i 2 153
Do the boys carry it away?—Ay, that they do, my lord ; Hercules and his load too ii 2 378
Let Hercules himself do what he may, The cat will mew v 1 314
By Hercules, I think I am i' the right.—Soldier, thou art *Ant. and Cleo.* ii 7 68
'Tis the god Hercules, whom Antony loved, Now leaves him iv 3 16
Not Hercules Could have knock'd out his brains, for he had none *Cymb.* iv 2 114
His foot Mercurial ; his Martial thigh ; The brawns of Hercules iv 2 311
Herd. Sure, it was the roar Of a whole herd of lions *Tempest* ii 1 316
For do but note a wild and wanton herd *Mer. of Venice* v 1 71
Anon a careless herd, Full of the pasture, jumps along *As Y. Like It* ii 1 52
They may joul horns together, like any deer i' the herd *All's Well* i 3 59
He had both tune and words ; which so drew the rest of the herd to me that all their other senses stuck in ears *W. Tale* iv 4 620
The herds Were strangely clamorous to the frighted fields 1 *Hen. IV.* iii 1 39
A little herd of England's timorous deer, Mazed with a yelping kennel of French curs! 1 *Hen. VI.* iv 2 46
He bore him . . . As doth a lion in a herd of neat 3 *Hen. VI.* ii 1 14
The noise of thy cross-bow Will scare the herd, and so my shoot is lost iii 1 7
The herd hath more annoyance by the breese Than by the tiger *T. and C.* i 3 48
You herd of—Boils and plagues Plaster you o'er! *Coriolanus* i 4 31
Are these your herd? Must these have voices? iii 1 33
Before he should thus stoop to the herd iii 2 32
When he perceived the common herd was glad he refused *J. Cæsar* i 2 266
O, that I were Upon the hill of Basan, to outroar The horned herd! for I have savage cause *Ant. and Cleo.* iii 13 128
Herdsman. Pray, let's see these four threes of herdsmen *W. Tale* iv 4 344
And you, enchantment,—Worthy enough a herdsman iv 4 446
Being the herdsmen of the beastly plebeians *Coriolanus* ii 1 105
Here. Thy letters may be here, though thou art hence *T. G. of Ver.* iii 1 248
Here can I sit alone, unseen of any v 4 4
That's neither here nor there *Mer. Wives* i 4 112 ; *Othello* iv 3 59
And here, by this, is your brother saved *Meas. for Meas.* iii 1 263
Hear me, O hear me, here! v 1 32
Here! go ; the desk, the purse! sweet, now, make haste *Com. of Errors* iv 2 29
I am here already, sir.—I know that ; but I would have thee hence, and here again *Much Ado* ii 3 7
From seventeen years till now almost fourscore Here lived I *As Y. Like It* ii 3 72
Is it not past two o'clock? and here much Orlando! iv 3 2
I will be gone ; My being here it is that holds thee hence *All's Well* iii 2 126
This must be answer'd either here or hence *K. John* iv 2 89
Since it is true That I must die here and live hence by truth v 4 29
Here I lay, and thus I bore my point 1 *Hen. IV.* ii 4 215
Is here all?—Here is two more called than your number 2 *Hen. IV.* iii 2 199
All members of our cause, both here and hence iv 1 171
Here, there, and every where, enraged he flew 1 *Hen. VI.* i 1 124
We are here.—And there will we be too, ere it be long iii 2 74
This devil here shall be my substitute 2 *Hen. VI.* iii 1 371
Here, there, and every where, he leaves and takes *Troi. and Cres.* v 5 26
We cannot be here and there too *Rom. and Jul.* i 5 15
If not so, then here I hit it right i 3 41
Heaven is here, Where Juliet lives iii 3 29
Every unworthy thing Live here in heaven and may look on her iii 3 32
Go hence ; good night ; and here stands all your state iii 3 166
Here's to my love! v 3 119
Calpurnia here, my wife, stays me at home *J. Cæsar* ii 2 75
Here was a Cæsar! when comes such another? iii 2 257
That but this blow Might be the be-all and the end-all here, But here, upon this bank and shoal of time, We'ld jump the life to come. But in these cases We still have judgement here *Macbeth* i 7 5
Profit again should hardly draw me here v 3 62
Here's my drift *Hamlet* ii 1 37
Both here and hence pursue me lasting strife! iii 2 232
Freedom lives hence, and banishment is here *Lear* i 1 184
Thou losest here, a better where to find i 1 264
An extravagant and wheeling stranger Of here and every where *Othello* i 1 138
Nor here, nor here, Nor what ensues, but have a fog in them *Cymbeline* iii 2 80
Hereabout. There is no other shelter hereabout *Tempest* ii 2 41
I do remember an apothecary,—And hereabouts he dwells *R. and J.* v 1 38
I'll hide me hereabout : His looks I fear, and his intents I doubt v 3 43
Walk hereabout : If I do find him fit, I'll move your suit *Othello* iii 4 165
I think that one of them is hereabout, And cannot make away v 1 57
Hereafter. And I'll be wise hereafter And seek for grace *Tempest* v 1 294
I will hereafter make known to you why I have done this *Mer. Wives* iii 3 241
If the encounter acknowledge itself hereafter *Meas. for Meas.* iii 1 262
And to deliver us from devices hereafter iv 4 15
You may think I love you not : let that appear hereafter *Much Ado* iii 2 99
Here comes Lorenzo : more of this hereafter *Mer. of Venice* ii 6 20
Hereafter, in a better world than this *As Y. Like It* i 2 296
Praised be the gods for thy foulness! sluttishness may come hereafter iii 3 41
Not being well married, it will be a good excuse for me hereafter to leave my wife iii 3 95
The business is not ended, as fearing to hear of it hereafter *All's Well* iv 3 111
But more of this hereafter iv 4 26
What is love? 'tis not hereafter *T. Night* ii 3 48
You shall know more hereafter.—Is't possible? iii 4 138
O, father, you'll know more of that hereafter *W. Tale* iv 4 353
These words hereafter thy tormentors be! *Richard II.* ii 1 136
I shall hereafter, my thrice gracious lord, Be more myself 1 *Hen. IV.* iii 2 92
But my love to ye Shall show itself more openly hereafter 2 *Hen. IV.* iv 2 76
When you take occasions to see leeks hereafter, I pray you, mock at 'em *Hen. V.* v 1 58
'Tis hereafter to know, but now to promise v 2 226
That hereafter ages may behold What ruin happen'd 1 *Hen. VI.* ii 2 10
And long hereafter say unto his child 3 *Hen. VI.* ii 2 36
Say, then, my peace is made.—That shall you know hereafter *Richard III.* i 2 199
A holy day shall this be kept hereafter ii 1 73
You live that shall cry woe for this hereafter iii 3 7
For I myself have many tears to wash Hereafter time iv 4 390
'Tis a girl, Promises boys hereafter *Hen. VIII.* v 1 166
But here's yet in the word 'hereafter' the kneading *Troi. and Cres.* i 1 23
I will obey you in every thing hereafter *Coriolanus* i 3 115
But thou wilt frame Thyself, forsooth, hereafter theirs iii 2 85
Fresh embassies and suits, Nor from the state nor private friends, hereafter Will I lend ear to v 3 18
And, as you shall use me hereafter, dry-beat the rest *Rom. and Jul.* iii 1 82
Live, and hereafter say, A madman's mercy bade thee run away v 3 66
Dead Is noble Timon : of whose memory Hereafter more *T. of Athens* v 4 81
How I have thought of this . . . , I shall recount hereafter *J. Cæsar* i 2 165
He will live, and laugh at this hereafter ii 1 191
All hail, Macbeth, that shalt be king hereafter! *Macbeth* i 3 50
Our eldest, Malcolm, whom we name hereafter The Prince of Cumberland i 4 38
Greater than both, by the all-hail hereafter! i 5 56
She should have died hereafter ; There would have been a time v 5 17
As I perchance hereafter shall think meet *Hamlet* i 5 171
Remember him hereafter as my honourable friend *Lear* i 1 27
Away, I say ; thou shalt know more hereafter : Nay, get thee gone *Oth.* ii 3 387
My news I might have told hereafter *Ant. and Cleo.* ii 5 23
How worthy he is I will leave to appear hereafter *Cymbeline* i 4 34
Why should excuse be born or e'er begot? We'll talk of that hereafter iii 2 68
Thou . . . shalt hereafter find It is no act of common passage iii 4 93
Thus did he answer me : yet said, hereafter I might know more iv 2 41
O, never say hereafter But I am truest speaker v 5 375
On whose grace You may depend hereafter *Pericles* iii 3 41
Here-approach. Before thy here-approach *Macbeth* iv 3 133
Hereby. I will visit thee at the lodge.—That's hereby *L. L. Lost* i 2 141
Hereby, upon the edge of yonder coppice iv 1 9
I will not reason what is meant hereby *Richard III.* i 4 94
Hereditary. To ebb Hereditary sloth instructs me *Tempest* ii 1 223
The imposition clear'd Hereditary ours *W. Tale* i 2 75
Peradventure some of the best of 'em were hereditary hangmen *Coriolanus* ii 1 103
These old fellows Have their ingratitude in them hereditary *T. of Athens* ii 2 224
The senator shall bear contempt hereditary, The beggar native honour iv 3 10
Put stuff To some she beggar and compounded thee Poor rogue hereditary iv 3 274
To thee and thine hereditary ever Remain this ample third *Lear* i 1 81
Hereditary, Rather than purchased ; what he cannot change, Than what he chooses *Ant. and Cleo.* i 4 13
Hereford. Hast thou, according to thy oath and band, Brought hither Henry Hereford thy bold son? *Richard II.* i 1 3
Cousin of Hereford, what dost thou object Against the Duke of Norfolk? i 1 28
O, sit my husband's wrongs on Hereford's spear! i 2 47
A caitiff recreant to my cousin Hereford! i 2 53
My Lord Aumerle, is Harry Hereford arm'd?—Yea, at all points i 3 1
Against the Duke of Hereford that appeals me i 3 21
Harry of Hereford, Lancaster and Derby Am I i 3 35
Cousin of Hereford, as thy cause is right, So be thy fortune! i 3 55
You, cousin Hereford, upon pain of life i 3 140
How far brought you high Hereford on his way?—I brought high Hereford, if you call him so, But to the next highway i 4 2
Holds you dear As Harry Duke of Hereford, were he here.—Right, you say true : as Hereford's love, so his ; As theirs, so mine ii 1 144
Not Gloucester's death, nor Hereford's banishment, Not Gaunt's rebukes ii 1 165
Seek you to seize and gripe into your hands The royalties and rights of banish'd Hereford? Is not Gaunt dead, and doth not Hereford live? ii 1 190
Take Hereford's rights away, and take from Time His charters ii 1 195
If you do wrongfully seize Hereford's rights, Call in the letters patents ii 1 201
Tends that thou wouldst speak to the Duke of Hereford? ii 1 232
Received intelligence That Harry Duke of Hereford, . . . With eight tall ships, three thousand men of war, Are making hither ii 1 279
The commons they are cold, And will, I fear, revolt on Hereford's side ii 2 89
Is gone to Ravenspurgh, To offer service to the Duke of Hereford ii 3 32
Have you forgot the Duke of Hereford, boy?—No, my good lord ii 3 36
My Lord of Hereford, my message is to you ii 3 69
I was banish'd Hereford ; But as I come, I come for Lancaster ii 3 113
My Lord of Hereford here, whom you call king, Is a foul traitor to proud Hereford's king iv 1 134
The Earl of Hereford was reputed then In England the most valiant gentleman 2 *Hen. IV.* iv 1 131
And all their prayers and love Were set on Hereford iv 1 138
When I am king, claim thou of me The earldom of Hereford *Richard III.* iii 1 195
The earldom of Hereford and the moveables The which you promised iv 2 93
Earl Of Hereford, Stafford, and Northampton *Hen. VIII.* i 1 200
Herefordshire. Leading the men of Herefordshire 1 *Hen. IV.* i 1 39
Herein. And see our pleasure herein executed *Meas. for Meas.* v 1 527
Herein you war against your reputation *Com. of Errors* ii 1 86
And yet would herein others' eyes were worse iv 2 26
Strike his honour down That violates the smallest branch herein *L. L. Lost* i 1 21
But herein mean I to enrich my pain *M. N. Dream* i 1 250
You know me well, and herein spend but time *Mer. of Venice* i 1 153
My best endeavours shall be done herein i 2 182
For herein Fortune shows herself more kind Than is her custom iv 1 267
I had myself notice of my brother's purpose herein *As Y. Like It* i 1 146

Herein. Herein I see thou lovest me not with the full weight that I love thee . . . . *As Y. L. It* i 2 8
Before I freely speak my mind herein . . . . *Richard II.* iv 1 327
Herein all breathless lies The mightiest of thy greatest enemies v 6 31
Yet herein will I imitate the sun . . . *1 Hen. IV.* i 2 221
Thou shalt have charge and sovereign trust herein . . . iii 2 161
Pardon absolute for yourself and these Herein misled by your suggestion iv 3 51
And my consent ne'er ask'd herein before ! . . *2 Hen. VI.* ii 4 72
And yet herein I judge mine own wit good . . . . iii 1 232
Herein your highness wrongs both them and me . . *3 Hen. VI.* iii 2 75
Who knows the lord protector's mind herein ? . . *Richard III.* iii 4 7
Give me some breath, . . . Before I positively speak herein . iv 2 25
Herein I teach you How you shall bid God 'ild us for your pains *Macbeth* i 6 12
And of the truth herein This present object made probation . *Hamlet* i 1 155
Nor have we herein barr'd Your better wisdoms . . . i 2 14
To suppress His further gait herein . . . . i 2 31
With an entreaty, herein further shown . . . . . ii 2 76
Hereof. I long to know the truth hereof at large . . *Com. of Errors* iv 4 146
Come, go along, and see the truth hereof . . . *T. of Shrew* iv 5 75
What will ensue hereof, there's none can tell . . *Richard II.* ii 1 212
Hereof [from sherris] comes it that Prince Harry is valiant *2 Hen. IV.* iv 3 126
The shame hereof will make me hide my head . . *1 Hen. VI.* i 5 39
Here-remain. Often, since my here-remain in England . *Macbeth* iv 3 148
Heresies. As the heresies that men do leave Are hated most of those they did deceive . . . . . . *M. N. Dream* ii 2 139
Which are heresies, And, not reform'd, may prove pernicious *Hen. VIII.* v 3 18
Heresy. O heresy in fair, fit for these days ! . . . *L. L. Lost* iv 1 22
Learned without opinion, and strange without heresy . . v 1 6
So thou, my surfeit and my heresy, Of all be hated ! . *M. N. Dream* ii 2 141
The ancient saying is no heresy, Hanging and wiving goes by destiny *Mer. of Venice* ii 9 82
O, I have read it : it is heresy . . . . . . *T. Night* i 5 246
The scriptures of the loyal Leonatus, All turn'd to heresy . *Cymbeline* iii 4 84
Heretic. Now doth thy honour stand, In him that was of late an heretic, As firm as faith . . . . . . *Mer. Wives* iv 4 9
Thou wast ever an obstinate heretic in the despite of beauty . *Much Ado* i 1 236
It is an heretic that makes the fire, Not she which burns in't *W. Tale* ii 3 115
Blessed shall he be that doth revolt From his allegiance to an heretic *K. John* iii 1 175
Again, there is sprung up An heretic, an arch one, Cranmer *Hen. VIII.* iii 2 102
A most arch heretic, a pestilence That does infect the land . . v 1 45
Transparent heretics, be burnt for liars ! . . . . *Rom. and Jul.* i 2 96
No heretics burn'd, but wenches' suitors . . . . *Lear* iii 2 84
Hereto. If he remember A kinder value of the people than He hath hereto prized them at . . . . *Coriolanus* ii 2 64
Heretofore. Hath he never heretofore sounded you in this business? *Lear* i 2 74
Hereupon. I will hereupon confess I am in love . . *L. L. Lost* i 2 60
Heritage. Service is no heritage . . . . . . *All's Well* i 3 26
It was mine own, part of my heritage . . . . . *Pericles* ii 1 129
Hermes. His hoof is more musical than the pipe of Hermes . *Hen. V.* iii 7 19
Hermia. With complaint Against my child, my daughter Hermia *M. N. D.* i 1 23
What say you, Hermia? be advised, fair maid . . . . . . i 1 46
Therefore, fair Hermia, question your desires ; Know of your youth . i 1 67
Relent, sweet Hermia : and, Lysander, yield Thy crazed title . . i 1 91
You have her father's love, Demetrius ; Let me have Hermia's . . i 1 94
I am beloved of beauteous Hermia : Why should not I then prosecute my right? . . . . i 1 104
Fair Hermia, look you arm yourself To fit your fancies to your father's will i 1 117
There, gentle Hermia, may I marry thee . . . . . . i 1 161
Sickness is catching : O, were favour so, Yours would I catch, fair Hermia i 1 187
Keep word, Lysander . —I will, my Hermia . . . . . i 1 224
And as he errs, doting on Hermia's eyes, So I, admiring of his qualities i 1 230
For ere Demetrius look'd on Hermia's eyne, He hail'd down oaths that he was only mine ; And when this hail some heat from Hermia felt, So he dissolved, and showers of oaths did melt . . . . . i 1 242
I will go tell him of fair Hermia's flight : Then to the wood will he . i 1 246
Where is Lysander and fair Hermia? The one I'll slay, the other slayeth me ii 1 189
Here am I, and wode within this wood, Because I cannot meet my Hermia ii 1 193
I have forgot our way : We'll rest us, Hermia, if you think it good . ii 2 37
By your side no bed-room me deny ; For lying so, Hermia, I do not lie ii 2 52
Beshrew my manners and my pride, If Hermia meant to say Lysander lied ii 2 55
Happy is Hermia, wheresoe'er she lies ; For she hath blessed and attractive eyes. How came her eyes so bright? . . . . . ii 2 90
What wicked and dissembling glass of mine Made me compare with Hermia's sphery eyne? . . . . ii 2 99
What though he love your Hermia? Lord, what though? Yet Hermia still loves you . . . . ii 2 109
Content with Hermia ! No ; I do repent The tedious minutes I with her have spent. Not Hermia but Helena I love . . . . ii 2 111
Hermia, sleep thou there : And never mayst thou come Lysander near ! ii 2 135
Would he have stolen away From sleeping Hermia? . . . . iii 2 52
These vows are Hermia's : will you give her o'er? . . . . iii 2 130
You both are rivals, and love Hermia ; And now both rivals, to mock Helena . . . . iii 2 155
You are unkind, Demetrius ; be not so ; For you love Hermia . . iii 2 163
With all my heart, In Hermia's love I yield you up my part . . iii 2 165
Lysander, keep thy Hermia ; I will none . . . . . . iii 2 169
Injurious Hermia ! most ungrateful maid ! Have you conspired? . . iii 2 195
We, Hermia, like two artificial gods, Have with our needles created both one flower, Both on one sampler . . . . iii 2 203
Am not I Hermia? are not you Lysander? I am as fair now as I was erewhile . . . . iii 2 273
Good Hermia, do not be so bitter with me. I evermore did love you, Hermia . . . . iii 2 306
Is not this the day That Hermia should give answer of her choice? . iv 1 141
And now I do bethink me, so it is,—I came with Hermia hither . . iv 1 156
By some power it is,—my love to Hermia, Melted as the snow . . iv 1 170
To her, my lord, Was I bethroth'd ere I saw Hermia . . . . iv 1 177
Hermione. He's beat from his best ward.—Well said, Hermione *W. Tale* i 2 33
Hermione, my dearest, thou never spokest To better purpose . . i 2 88
Hermione, How thou lovest us, show in our brother's welcome . . i 2 173
These proclamations, So forcing faults upon Hermione, I little like . iii 1 16
Hermione, queen to the worthy Leontes, king of Sicilia . . . . iii 2 12
Thou, Hermione, contrary to the faith and allegiance of a true subject . iii 2 19
Hermione is chaste ; Polixenes blameless ; Camillo a true subject . . iii 2 133
I do believe Hermione hath suffer'd death . . . . . . iii 3 42
Good Paulina, Who hast the memory of Hermione, I know, in honour . v 1 50
Unless another, As like Hermione as is her picture, Affront his eye . v 1 74
O Hermione, As every present time doth boast itself Above a better gone, so must thy grave Give way to what's seen now ! . . . . v 1 95
Hermione. The mantle of Queen Hermione's, her jewel about the neck of it . . . . *W. Tale* v 2 36
He so near to Hermione hath done Hermione that they say one would speak to her and stand in hope of answer . . . . v 2 109
She hath privately twice or thrice a day, ever since the death of Hermione, visited that removed house . . . . v 2 115
Chide me, dear stone, that I may say indeed Thou art Hermione . . v 3 25
Hermione was not so much wrinkled, nothing So aged as this seems . v 3 28
Hermit. A wither'd hermit, five-score winters worn, Might shake off fifty, looking in her eye . . . . *L. L. Lost* iv 3 242
Who comes with her?—None but a holy hermit and her maid *M. of Ven.* v 1 33
The old hermit of Prague, that never saw pen and ink . *T. Night* iv 2 15
If I were sawed into quantities, I should make four dozen of such bearded hermits' staves . . . . *2 Hen. IV.* v 1 71
And like a hermit overpass'd thy days . . . . *1 Hen. VI.* ii 5 117
Let's leave the hermit pity with our mothers . . *Troi. and Cres.* v 3 45
I will learn thy thought ; In thy dumb action will I be as perfect As begging hermits in their holy prayers . . . . *T. Andron.* iii 2 41
For those of old, And the late dignities heap'd up to them, We rest your hermits . . . . *Macbeth* i 6 20
Hermitage. Go with speed To some forlorn and naked hermitage *L. L. Lost* v 2 805
My jewels for a set of beads, My gorgeous palace for a hermitage *Rich. II.* iii 3 148
Herne the hunter, Sometime a keeper here in Windsor forest *Mer. Wives* iv 4 28
The superstitious idle-headed eld Received and did deliver to our age This tale of Herne the hunter for a truth . . . . . . iv 4 38
There want not many that do fear In deep of night to walk by this Herne's oak . . . . iv 4 40
To-night at Herne's oak, just 'twixt twelve and one, Must my sweet Nan present the Fairy Queen . . . . iv 6 19
Be you in the Park about midnight, at Herne's oak, and you shall see wonders . . . . v 1 12
They are all couched in a pit hard by Herne's oak, with obscured lights v 3 15
Am I a woodman, ha? Speak I like Herne the hunter? . . . . v 5 31
Our dance of custom round about the oak Of Herne the hunter . . v 5 80
Will none but Herne the hunter serve your turn? . . . . . v 5 108
Hero. Would serve to scale another Hero's tower . . *T. G. of Ver.* iii 1 119
I would scarce trust myself, though I had sworn the contrary, if Hero would be my wife . . . . *Much Ado* i 1 198
Mark how short his answer is ;—With Hero, Leonato's short daughter . i 1 216
No child but Hero ; she's his only heir . . . . . . i 1 297
All prompting me how fair young Hero is . . . . . . i 1 306
If thou dost love fair Hero, cherish it, And I will break with her . . i 1 310
I will assume thy part in some disguise And tell fair Hero I am Claudio i 1 324
There heard it agreed upon that the prince should woo Hero for himself i 3 65
My brother is amorous on Hero and hath withdrawn her father to break with him about it . . . . ii 1 162
He is enamoured on Hero ; I pray you, dissuade him from her . . ii 1 170
The prince hath got your Hero.—I wish him joy of her . . . ii 1 199
Fair Hero is won : I have broke with her father, and his good will obtained . . . . ii 1 310
I am in the favour of Margaret, the waiting gentlewoman to Hero . ii 2 14
A contaminated stale, such a one as Hero . . . . . . ii 2 26
To vex Claudio, to undo Hero and kill Leonato . . . . . ii 2 29
Tell them that you know that Hero loves me . . . . . ii 2 35
Hear me call Margaret Hero, hear Margaret term me Claudio . . ii 2 44
In the meantime I will so fashion the matter that Hero shall be absent ii 2 47
There shall appear such seeming truth of Hero's disloyalty . . ii 2 49
Get us some excellent music ; for to-morrow night we would have it at the Lady Hero's chamber-window . . . . ii 3 89
Hero thinks surely she will die ; for she says she will die, if he love her not ii 3 180
They have the truth of this from Hero. They seem to pity the lady . ii 3 230
Hero and Margaret have by this played their parts with Beatrice . . iii 2 78
The lady is disloyal.—Who, Hero?—Even she ; Leonato's Hero, your Hero, every man's Hero . . . . iii 2 108
Wooed Margaret, the Lady Hero's gentlewoman, by the name of Hero . iii 3 154
And thought they Margaret was Hero?—Two of them did . . . iii 3 163
Good morrow, sweet Hero?—Why, how now? do you speak in the sick tune? . . . . iii 4 40
If either of you know any inward impediment . . . , utter it.—Know you any, Hero? . . . . iv 1 15
Is this face Hero's? are our eyes our own? . . . . . . iv 1 72
Is it not Hero? Who can blot that name With any just reproach?—Marry, that can Hero ; Hero itself can blot out Hero's virtue . . iv 1 81
O Hero, what a Hero hadst thou been, If half thy outward graces had been placed About thy thoughts and counsels of thy heart ! . iv 1 101
How doth the lady?—Dead, I think. Help, uncle ! Hero ! why, Hero ! iv 1 115
Do not live, Hero ; do not ope thine eyes . . . . . . iv 1 125
Sweet Hero ! She is wronged, she is slandered, she is undone . . iv 1 314
Think you in your soul the Count Claudio hath wronged Hero? . . iv 1 332
Received a thousand ducats of Don John for accusing the Lady Hero . iv 2 51
And that Count Claudio did mean, upon his words, to disgrace Hero . iv 2 56
Hero was in this manner accused, in this very manner refused, and upon the grief of this suddenly died . . . . iv 2 64
My soul doth tell me Hero is belied ; And that shall Claudio know . v 1 42
Your brother incensed me to slander the Lady Hero . . . . v 1 243
And saw me court Margaret in Hero's garments . . . . . v 1 245
Sweet Hero ! now thy image doth appear In the rare semblance that I loved it first . . . . v 1 259
It is proved my Lady Hero hath been falsely accused . . . . v 2 99
Done to death by slanderous tongues Was the Hero that here lies . v 3 4
Another Hero !—Nothing certainer : One Hero died defiled, but I do live v 4 62
The former Hero ! Hero that is dead !—She died, my lord, but whiles her slander lived . . . . v 4 65
After that the holy rites are ended, I'll tell you largely of fair Hero's death . . . . v 4 69
Leander, he would have lived many a fair year, though Hero had turned nun, if it had not been for a hot midsummer night *As Y. Like It* iv 1 101
And the foolish coroners of that age found it was 'Hero of Sestos' . iv 1 106
Noble heroes, my sword and yours are kin . . . . *All's Well* ii 1 40
Helen and Hero hildings and harlots ; Thisbe a grey eye or so *R. and J.* ii 4 44
Then are our beggars bodies, and our monarchs and outstretched heroes the beggars' shadows . . . . *Hamlet* ii 2 270
Herod. What a Herod of Jewry is this ! O wicked, wicked world ! *M. W.* ii 1 20
As did the wives of Jewry At Herod's bloody-hunting slaughtermen *Hen. V.* iii 3 41
It out-herods Herod : pray you, avoid it . . . . . *Hamlet* iii 2 16
Let me have a child at fifty, to whom Herod of Jewry may do homage *Ant. and Cleo.* i 2 28
Herod of Jewry dare not look upon you But when you are well pleased iii 3 3
That Herod's head I'll have : but how, wnen Antony is gone? . . iii 3 4

Herod of Jewry; Mithridates, king Of Comagene . . . *Ant. and Cleo.* iii 6 73
There did persuade Great Herod to incline himself to Cæsar, and leave his master Antony . . . iv 6 14
Heroic. Being but fourth of that heroic line . . . *1 Hen. VI.* ii 5 78
Heroical. Have commiseration on thy heroical vassal! . . . *L. L. Lost* iv 1 64
Saw his heroical seed, and smiled to see him . . . *Hen. V.* ii 4 59
'Gainst your privacy The reasons are more potent and heroical . . . *Troi. and Cres.* iii 3 192
So prophetically proud of an heroical cudgelling . . . iii 3 248
Herring. By gar, de herring is no dead so as I vill kill him . . . *Mer. Wives* ii 3 12
Fools are as like husbands as pilchards are to herrings . . . *T. Night* iii 1 40
Then am I a shotten herring . . . *1 Hen. IV.* ii 4 143
We John Cade, so termed of our supposed father,— Or rather, of stealing a cade of herrings . . . *2 Hen. VI.* iv 2 36
A toad, a lizard, an owl, a puttock, or a herring without a roe . . . *T. and C.* v 1 68
Here comes Romeo.—Without his roe, like a dried herring . . . *Rom. and Jul.* ii 4 39
Hopdance cries in Tom's belly for two white herring . . . *Lear* iii 6 33
Hers. Go to thy lady's grave and call hers thence, Or, at the least, in hers sepulchre thine . . . *T. G. of Ver.* iv 2 117
In a tomb where never scandal slept, Save this of hers . . . *Much Ado* v 1 71
What an indirect and peevish course Is this of hers! . . . *Richard III.* iii 1 32
Herself and hers are highly bound to thee . . . *T. Andron.* iv 2 171
Nor shall ever see That face of hers again . . . *Lear* i 1 267
And win this ring By hers and mine adultery . . . *Cymbeline* v 5 186
Heavens, in justice, both on her and hers, Have laid most heavy hand . . . v 5 464
Herself hath taught her love himself to write unto her lover . . . *T. G. of Ver.* ii 1 174
And Julia herself did give it me; And Julia herself hath brought it . . . v 4 98
I will rather trust a Fleming with my butter . . . than my wife with herself . . . *Mer. Wives* ii 2 320
She determines Herself the glory of a creditor . . . *Meas. for Meas.* i 1 40
And did not she herself revile me there? . . . *Com. of Errors* iv 4 75
Herself poised with herself in either eye . . . *Rom. and Jul.* i 2 100
Hesperides. For valour, is not Love a Hercules, Still climbing trees in the Hesperides? . . . *L. L. Lost* iv 3 341
Before thee stands this fair Hesperides, With golden fruit . . . *Pericles* i 1 27
Hesperus. Moist Hesperus hath quench'd his sleepy lamp . . . *All's Well* ii 1 167
Hest. Refusing her grand hests, she did confine thee . . . *Tempest* i 2 274
O my father, I have broke your hest to say so! . . . iii 1 37
Which spongy April at thy hest betrims . . . iv 1 65
And shape his service wholly to my hests . . . *L. L. Lost* v 2 65
As we see when men restrain their breath On some great sudden hest . . . *1 Hen. IV.* ii 3 65
Heure. Car ce soldat ici est disposé tout à cette heure de couper votre gorge . . . *Hen. V.* iv 4 38
Heureux. Et je m'estime heureux que je suis tombé entre les mains d'un chevalier . . . iv 4 58
Hew them to pieces, hack their bones asunder . . . *1 Hen. VI.* iv 7 47
O, I could hew up rocks and fight with flint, I am so angry . . . *2 Hen. VI.* v 1 24
And many strokes, though with a little axe, Hew down and fell the hardest-timber'd oak . . . *3 Hen. VI.* ii 1 55
I will free myself, Or hew my way out with a bloody axe . . . iii 2 181
Swims with fins of lead And hews down oaks with rushes . . . *Coriolanus* i 1 185
I had purpose Once more to hew thy target from thy brawn . . . iv 5 126
Hew his limbs, and on a pile Ad manes fratrum sacrifice his flesh . . . *T. An.* i 1 97
Upon a pile of wood, Let's hew his limbs till they be clean consumed . . . i 1 129
What thou wilt, Thou rather shalt enforce it with thy smile Than hew to't with thy sword . . . *T. of Athens* v 4 46
Let's carve him as a dish fit for the gods, Not hew him as a carcass fit for hounds . . . *J. Cæsar* ii 1 174
Let every soldier hew him down a bough And bear't before him . . . *Macbeth* v 4 4
Hewed. What stern ungentle hands Have lopp'd and hew'd and made thy body bare Of her two branches? . . . *T. Andron.* ii 4 17
Hewgh. O, well flown, bird! i' the clout, i' the clout: hewgh! . . . *Lear* iv 6 93
Hewing Rutland when his leaves put forth . . . *3 Hen. VI.* ii 6 48
Hewn. Yet, know thou, since we have begun to strike, We'll never leave till we have hewn thee down . . . ii 2 168
By the heavens' assistance and your strength, Must by the roots be hewn up . . . v 4 69
Hey, Mountain, hey!—Silver! there it goes, Silver! . . . *Tempest* iv 1 256
Converting all your sounds of woe Into Hey nonny, nonny . . . *Much Ado* ii 3 71
With a hey, and a ho, and a hey nonino . . . *As Y. Like It* v 3 18
Hey, Robin, jolly Robin, Tell me how thy lady does . . . *T. Night* iv 2 78
With hey, ho, the wind and the rain . . . v 1 399; *Lear* iii 2 75
Hey non nonny, nonny, hey nonny . . . *Hamlet* iv 5 165
Hey-day. Freedom, hey-day! hey-day, freedom! . . . *Tempest* ii 2 190
At your age The hey-day in the blood is tame, it's humble . . . *Hamlet* iii 4 69
Hibocrates. He has no more knowledge in Hibocrates and Galen,—and he is a knave besides . . . *Mer. Wives* iii 1 66
Hic, hæc, hoc.—Nominativo, hig, hag, hog . . . iv 1 43
'Hic ibat Simois; hic est Sigeia tellus; Hic steterat Priami regia celsa senis.'—Construe them.—'Hic ibat,' as I told you before *T. of Shrew* iii 1 28
'Hic ibat Simois,' I know you not, 'hic est Sigeia tellus,' I trust you not; 'Hic steterat Priami,' take heed he hear us not . . . iii 1 42
Hic et ubique? then we'll shift our ground . . . *Hamlet* i 5 156
Hic jacet. I would have that drum or another, or 'hic jacet' . . . *All's Well* iii 6 66
Hick. He teaches him to hick and to hack, which they'll do fast enough of themselves . . . *Mer. Wives* iv 1 68
Hid. He was The ivy which had hid my princely trunk . . . *Tempest* i 2 86
In the deep nook, . . . there she's hid . . . i 2 229
I hid me under the dead moon-calf's gaberdine for fear of the storm . . . ii 2 115
My cellar is in a rock by the sea-side where my wine is hid . . . ii 2 138
Yet in this life Lie hid moe thousand deaths . . . *Meas. for Meas.* iii 1 40
To make the truth appear where it seems hid, And hide the false . . . v 1 66
Though now this grained face of mine be hid In sap-consuming winter's drizzled snow . . . *Com. of Errors* v 1 311
See you where Benedick hath hid himself? . . . *Much Ado* ii 3 42
And, moreover, God saw him when he was hid in the garden . . . v 1 182
Things hid and barr'd, you mean, from common sense? . . . *L. L. Lost* i 1 57
Or study where to meet some mistress fine, When mistresses from common sense are hid . . . i 1 64
All hid, all hid; an old infant play . . . iv 3 78
That superfluous case That hid the worse and show'd the better face . . . v 2 388
As two grains of wheat hid in two bushels of chaff . . . *Mer. of Venice* i 1 115
Murder cannot be hid long . . . ii 2 84
'Tis a day, Such as the day is when the sun is hid . . . v 1 126
And Cytherea all in sedges hid . . . *T. of Shrew* Ind. 2 53
Wherefore are these things hid? wherefore have these gifts a curtain before 'em? are they like to take dust? . . . *T. Night* i 3 133
A murderous guilt shows not itself more soon Than love that would seem hid . . . iii 1 160
When the searching eye of heaven is hid . . . *Richard II.* iii 2 37
Hid. Richard not far from hence hath hid his head . . . *Richard II.* iii 3 6
And hid his crisp head in the hollow bank . . . *1 Hen. IV.* i 3 106
Be not amazed, there's nothing hid from me . . . *1 Hen. VI.* i 2 68
Five days have I hid me in these woods and durst not peep out *2 Hen. VI.* iv 10 3
Iron of Naples hid with English gilt . . . *3 Hen. VI.* ii 2 139
As I had rather hide me from my greatness . . . Than in my greatness covet to be hid . . . *Richard III.* iii 7 163
If ever any malice in your heart Were hid against me . . . *Hen. VIII.* ii 1 81
And hid the gold within the letter mention'd . . . *T. Andron.* v 1 107
Come, he hath hid himself among these trees . . . *Rom. and Jul.* ii 1 30
O serpent heart, hid with a flowering face! . . . iii 2 73
Your Romeo will be here at night: I'll to him; he is hid at Laurence' cell iii 2 141
How shall's get it?—True; for he bears it not about him, 'tis hid . . . *T. of Athens* iv 3 409
Where our fate, Hid in an auger-hole, may rush, and seize us . . . *Macbeth* ii 3 128
When we have our naked frailties hid, That suffer in exposure . . . ii 3 132
If circumstances lead me, I will find Where truth is hid, though it were hid indeed Within the centre . . . *Hamlet* ii 2 158
O sir, fly this place; Intelligence is given where you are hid . . . *Lear* ii 1 23
O, lady, lady, shame would have it hid! . . . ii 1 95
Where have you hid yourself? How have you known the miseries of your father? . . . v 3 179
This is thy work: the object poisons sight; Let it be hid . . . *Othello* v 2 365
Fill till the cup be hid . . . *Ant. and Cleo.* ii 7 93
Heaven forbid That kings should let their ears hear their faults hid! *Per.* i 2 62
Hidden. Make rash remonstrance of my hidden power . . . *Meas. for Meas.* v 1 397
In my heart Lie there what hidden woman's fear there will *As Y. Like It* i 3 121
He cared not who knew it.—He needs not; it is no hidden virtue *Hen. V.* iii 7 118
Dally not before your king; Lest he that is the supreme King of kings Confound your hidden falsehood . . . *Richard III.* ii 1 14
It is very much lamented, Brutus, That you have no such mirrors as will turn Your hidden worthiness into your eye . . . *J. Cæsar* i 2 57
Or did line the rebel With hidden help and vantage . . . *Macbeth* i 3 113
For the better compassing of his salt and most hidden loose affection *Oth.* ii 1 245
Hide. If it should thunder as it did before, I know not where to hide my head . . . *Tempest* ii 2 23
All the more it seeks to hide itself, The bigger bulk it shows . . . iii 1 80
I'll prove it. The cover of the salt hides the salt, and therefore it is more than the salt; the hair that covers the wit is more than the wit, for the greater hides the less . . . *T. G. of Ver.* iii 1 369
Hide what I have said to thee . . . iv 3 35
I'll go hide me.—Do so . . . *Mer. Wives* iii 3 36
Thou canst not hide it.—Believe me, there's no such thing in me . . . iii 3 71
Bethink you of some conveyance: in the house you cannot hide him . . . iii 3 136
From whom we thought it meet to hide our love . . . *Meas. for Meas.* i 2 156
O, what may man within him hide, Though angel on the outward side! iii 2 285
To make the truth appear where it seems hid, And hide the false seems true v 1 67
When the sun shines let foolish gnats make sport, But creep in crannies when he hides his beams . . . *Com. of Errors* ii 2 31
I cannot hide what I am: I must be sad when I have cause . . . *Much Ado* i 3 14
Do you think I do not know you by your excellent wit? can virtue hide itself? . . . ii 1 127
Ha! the prince and Monsieur Love! I will hide me in the arbour . . . ii 3 38
Knavery cannot, sure, hide himself in such reverence . . . ii 3 125
There will she hide her, To listen our purpose . . . iii 1 11
Stand in your own defence; Or hide your heads like cowards . . . *L. L. Lost* v 2 86
Hide thy head, Achilles: Here comes Hector in arms . . . v 2 635
Vouchsafe In your rich wisdom to excuse or hide The liberal opposition v 2 742
An I may hide my face, let me play Thisby too . . . *M. N. Dream* i 2 53
All their elves for fear Creep into acorn-cups and hide them there . . . ii 1 31
I'll run from thee and hide me in the brakes . . . ii 1 227
Speak! In some bush? Where dost thou hide thy head? . . . iii 2 406
Devise the fittest time and safest way To hide us from pursuit *As Y. L. It* i 3 138
In the which hope I blush, and hide my sword . . . ii 7 119
A vengeance on your crafty wither'd hide! . . . *T. of Shrew* ii 1 406
They may jest Till their own scorn return to them unnoted Ere they can hide their levity in honour . . . *All's Well* i 2 35
Do not hide mine eyes . . . iv 1 74
What dost thou mean? Is it a world to hide virtues in? . . . *T. Night* i 3 140
I love thee so, that, maugre all thy pride, Nor wit nor reason can my passion hide . . . iii 1 164
The selfsame sun that shines upon his court Hides not his visage from our cottage but Looks on alike . . . *W. Tale* iv 4 456
For all the sun sees or The close earth wombs or the profound seas hide iv 4 501
One that will play the devil, sir, with you, An a' may catch your hide and you alone . . . *K. John* ii 1 136
'Tis not the roundure of your old-faced walls Can hide you . . . ii 1 260
I would set an ox-head to your lion's hide, And make a monster of you ii 1 292
Thou wear a lion's hide! doff it for shame . . . iii 1 128
The earth had not a hole to hide this deed . . . iv 3 36
Wipe off the dust that hides our sceptre's gilt . . . *Richard II.* ii 1 294
Alack the heavy day When such a sacred king should hide his head . . . iii 3 8
What wilt thou do? Wilt thou not hide the trespass of thine own? . . . v 2 89
What starting-hole canst thou now find out to hide thee from this open and apparent shame? . . . *1 Hen. IV.* ii 4 291
Go, hide thee behind the arras: the rest walk up above . . . ii 4 549
Now, my masters, for a true face and good conscience.—Both which I have had: but their date is out, and therefore I'll hide me . . . ii 4 553
But let my favours hide thy mangled face . . . v 4 96
And, by the ground they hide, I judge their number Upon or near the rate of thirty thousand . . . *2 Hen. IV.* iv 1 21
And rather choose to hide them in a net . . . *Hen. V.* i 2 93
And hides a sword from hilts unto the point With crowns imperial ii Prol. 9
As gardeners do with ordure hide those roots That shall first spring . . . ii 4 39
If you hide the crown Even in your hearts, there will he rake for it . . . ii 4 97
Make incision in their hides, That their hot blood may spin . . . iv 2 9
Their poor jades Lob down their heads, dropping the hides and hips . . . iv 2 47
The shame hereof will make me hide my head . . . *1 Hen. VI.* i 5 39
Hide such malice; With such holiness can you do it? . . . *2 Hen. VI.* ii 1 25
Ah, Gloucester, hide thee from their hateful looks! . . . ii 4 23
Hide not thy poison with such sugar'd words . . . iii 2 45
What, dost thou turn away and hide thy face? I am no loathsome leper iii 2 74
Somerset comes with the queen: Go, bid her hide him quickly from the duke.—For thousand Yorks he shall not hide his head . . . v 1 84
'Tis Warwick calls: And if thou dost not hide thee from the bear . . . v 2 2
O tiger's heart wrapt in a woman's hide! . . . *3 Hen. VI.* i 4 137
This sharp-pointed sword; Which if thou please to hide in this true bosom, I lay it naked to the deadly stroke . . . *Richard III.* i 2 176
Now must I hide his body in some hole, Until the duke take order . . . i 4 287
And with a virtuous vizard hide foul guile! . . . ii 2 28

Hide. There's never a man in Christendom That can less hide his love or hate than he . . . . *Richard III.* iii 4 54
So many my defects, As I had rather hide me from my greatness . . iii 7 161
Then would I hide my bones, not rest them here . . . . . iv 4 33
To the mercy Of a rude stream, that must for ever hide me *Hen. VIII.* iii 2 364
They are too thin and bare to hide offences . . . . . v 3 125
I'll hide my silver beard in a gold beaver . . . . *Troi. and Cres.* i 3 296
And dreaming night will hide our joys no longer . . . . iv 2 10
This brave shall oft make thee to hide thy head . . . . iv 4 139
Wilt thou not, beast, abide? Why, then fly on, I'll hunt thee for thy hide v 6 31
With comfort go: Hope of revenge shall hide our inward woe . . v 10 31
'Twere a concealment Worse than a theft, . . . To hide your doings *Cor.* i 9 23
Show them the unaching scars which I should hide . . . . ii 2 152
This is the hole where Aaron bid us hide him . . . *T. Andron.* ii 3 186
Straying in the park, Seeking to hide herself, as doth the deer That hath received some unrecuring wound . . . . iii 1 89
My bowels cannot hide her woes, But like a drunkard must I vomit them iii 1 231
What dost thou wrap and fumble in thine arms?—O, that which I would hide from heaven's eye! . . . . iv 2 59
These happy masks that kiss fair ladies' brows Being black put us in mind they hide the fair . . . . *Rom. and Jul.* i 1 237
And 'tis much pride For fair without the fair within to hide . . i 3 90
I have night's cloak to hide me from their sight . . . . ii 2 75
That runs lolling up and down to hide his bauble in a hole . . ii 4 97
My fan, Peter.—Good Peter, to hide her face; for her fan's the fairer face ii 4 113
Arise; one knocks; good Romeo, hide thyself.—Not I . . . iii 3 71
Or bid me go into a new-made grave And hide me with a dead man . iv 1 85
For all this same, I'll hide me hereabout; His looks I fear . . v 3 43
Sun, hide thy beams! Timon hath done his reign . . *T. of Athens* v 1 226
Hide it in smiles and affability . . . . *J. Cæsar* ii 1 82
Not Erebus itself were dim enough To hide thee from prevention . . ii 1 85
Some six or seven, who did hide their faces Even from darkness . ii 1 277
If Cæsar hide himself, shall they not whisper 'Lo, Cæsar is afraid'? . ii 2 100
Brutus, this sober form of yours hides wrongs . . . . . iv 2 40
And chastisement doth therefore hide his head . . . . . iv 3 16
Mount thou my horse, and hide thy spurs in him . . . . . v 3 15
My plenteous joys, Wanton in fulness, seek to hide themselves In drops of sorrow . . . . *Macbeth* i 4 34
Stars, hide your fires; Let not light see my black and deep desires . i 4 50
False face must hide what the false heart doth know . . . . i 7 82
Avaunt! and quit my sight! let the earth hide thee! . . . . iii 4 93
This must be known; which, being kept close, might move More grief to hide than hate to utter love . . . . *Hamlet* ii 1 119
Who, that's but a queen, fair, sober, wise, Would from a paddock, from a bat, a gib, Such dear concernings hide? . . . . . . iii 4 191
Hide fox, and all after . . . . iv 2 32
Which is not tomb enough and continent To hide the slain . . . iv 4 65
His hide is so tanned with his trade, that he will keep out water a great while . . . . v 1 186
Time shall unfold what plaited cunning hides . . . . *Lear* i 1 283
The quality of nothing hath not such need to hide itself . . . . i 2 34
Hide thee, thou bloody hand . . . . iii 2 53
Thou owest the worm no silk, the beast no hide, the sheep no wool . iii 4 109
Through tatter'd clothes small vices do appear; Robes and furr'd gowns hide all . . . . iv 6 169
Let us be wary, let us hide our loves . . . . . *Othello* iii 3 420
What, To hide me from the radiant sun and solace I' the dungeon? *Cymb.* i 6 86
If Cæsar can hide the sun from us with a blanket, or put the moon in his pocket, we will pay him tribute for light . . . . . . iii 1 43
How hard it is to hide the sparks of nature! . . . . . . iii 3 79
I'll hide my master from the flies, as deep As these poor pickaxes can dig iv 2 388
'Tis strange he [death] hides him in fresh cups, soft beds, Sweet words v 3 71
Hideous. In a most hideous and dreadful manner . . *Mer. Wives* iv 4 34
Which have for long run by the hideous law . . . *Meas. for Meas.* i 4 63
Extended or contracted all proportions To a most hideous object *All's W.* v 3 52
You have some hideous matter to deliver . . . . . *T. Night* i 5 221
Into a most hideous opinion of his rage, skill, fury . . . . . iii 4 212
They have laid me here in hideous darkness . . . . . . iv 2 34
Foul imaginary eyes of blood Presented thee more hideous than thou art *K. John* iv 2 266
Have I not hideous death within my view? . . . . . . v 4 22
To look upon the hideous god of war In disadvantage . . *2 Hen. IV.* ii 3 35
Dogs howl'd, and hideous tempest shook down trees . . *3 Hen. VI.* v 6 46
And howled in mine ears Such hideous cries . . . *Richard III.* i 4 60
Every man, After the hideous storm that follow'd, was A thing inspired; and, not consulting, broke Into a general prophecy . . *Hen. VIII.* i 1 90
Environed with all these hideous fears . . . . *Rom. and Jul.* iv 3 50
All the interim is Like a phantasma, or a hideous dream . *J. Cæsar* ii 1 65
What's the business, That such a hideous trumpet calls to parley The sleepers of the house? . . . . *Macbeth* ii 3 87
Revisit'st thus the glimpses of the moon, Making night hideous *Hamlet* i 4 54
Stoops to his base, and with a hideous crash Takes prisoner Pyrrhus' ear ii 2 498
And, in thy best consideration, check This hideous rashness . *Lear* i 1 153
More hideous when thou show'st thee in a child Than the sea-monster! i 4 282
He echoes me, As if there were some monster in his thought Too hideous to be shown . . . . *Othello* iii 3 108
Hideously. Which cannot look more hideously upon me Than I have drawn it in my fantasy . . . . *2 Hen. IV.* v 2 12
Hideousness. Go anticly, show outward hideousness . . *Much Ado* v 1 96
Hidest thou that forehead with a golden crown? . . *Richard III.* iv 4 140
Hideth. A cypress, not a bosom, Hideth my heart . . . *T. Night* iii 1 133
Hiding mine honour in my necessity . . . . . *Mer. Wives* ii 2 24
There is no hiding you in the house . . . . iv 2 65
Hiding the grossness with fair ornament . . . *Mer. of Venice* iii 2 80
Obscuring and hiding from me all gentleman-like qualities *As Y. Like It* i 1 72
Hiding his bitter jests in blunt behaviour . . . . *T. of Shrew* iii 2 13
As patches set upon a little breach Discredit more in hiding of the fault Than did the fault before it was so patch'd . . . . *K. John* iv 2 33
Unless it swell past hiding, and then it's past watching *Troi. and Cres.* i 2 295
Nay, what hope Have we in hiding us? . . . . . *Cymbeline* iv 4 4
Hie. Even this: That presently you hie you home to bed *T. G. of Ver.* iv 2 94
Hie home unto my chamber, Where thou shalt find me . . . iv 4 93
And prays that you will hie you home to dinner . . *Com. of Errors* i 2 90
Go hie thee presently, post to the road . . . . . . iii 2 152
To Adriana, villain, hie thee straight: Give her this key . . . iv 1 102
My way is now to hie home to his house . . . . . . iv 3 93
To what end did I bid thee hie thee home?—To a rope's-end, sir . . iv 4 15
And to thy state of darkness hie thee straight . . . . . iv 4 59
Hie therefore, Robin, overcast the night . . . *M. N. Dream* iii 2 355
Hie thee, gentle Jew. The Hebrew will turn Christian . *Mer. of Venice* i 3 178
Hie thee, go.—My best endeavours shall be done herein . *M. of Ven.* ii 2 181
Hie you home, And bid Bianca make her ready straight . *T. of Shrew* iv 4 62
Let that go: My haste is very great: farewell; hie home . *All'sWell* ii 5 82
Write, write, that from the bloody course of war My dearest master, your dear son, may hie . . . . iii 4 9
The army breaking, My husband hies him home . . . . . iv 4 12
Run after that same peevish messenger, . . . hie thee, Malvolio *T. Night* i 5 325
Thou art in jeopardy.—No more than he that threats. To arms let's hie! *K. John* iii 1 347
Hie thee to France And cloister thee in some religious house *Richard II.* v 1 22
Hie, good Sir Michael; bear this sealed brief With winged haste *1 Hen. IV.* iv 4 1
If wishes would prevail with me, My purpose should not fail with me, But thither would I hie . . . . *Hen. V.* iii 2 18
With spirit of honour edged More sharper than your swords, hie to the field iii 5 39
Hie thee to hell for shame, and leave the world, Thou cacodemon! *Richard III.* i 3 143
The mayor towards Guildhall hies him in all post . . . . iii 5 73
Go hie thee, hie thee from this slaughter-house . . . . . iv 1 44
Hie thee to thy charge; Use careful watch, choose trusty sentinels . v 3 53
Hie you to your bands: Let us alone to guard Corioli . *Coriolanus* i 2 26
Hie to the Goths, and raise an army there . . . *T. Andron.* iii 1 286
Hie you hence to Friar Laurence' cell; There stays a husband *R. and J.* ii 5 70
Hie you to church; I must another way, To fetch a ladder . . ii 5 74
Hie you to the cell.—Hie to high fortune! Honest nurse, farewell . ii 5 79
Hie to your chamber: I'll find Romeo To comfort you . . . iii 2 138
Hie you, make haste, for it grows very late . . . . . . iii 3 164
Let's talk; it is not day.—It is, it is: hie hence, be gone, away! . iii 5 26
Well, I will hie, And so bestow these papers as you bade me *J. Cæsar* i 3 150
No Rome of safety for Octavius yet; Hie hence, and tell him so . . iii 1 290
Hie you, Messala, And I will seek for Pindarus the while . . . v 3 78
Hie thee hither, That I may pour my spirits in thine ear . *Macbeth* i 5 26
Hie you to horse: adieu, Till you return at night . . . . iii 1 35
The extravagant and erring spirit hies To his confine . . *Hamlet* i 1 154
Sing willow, willow, willow; Prithee, hie thee; he'll come anon *Othello* iv 3 50
Minion, your dear lies dead, And your unblest fate hies . . . v 1 34
But yet Hie you to Egypt again . . . . . . *Ant. and Cleo.* ii 3 15
Hie thee again: I have spoke already, and it is provided . . . v 2 194
To Dorothy my woman hie thee presently . . . . *Cymbeline* ii 3 143
Hie thee, whiles I say A priestly farewell to her: suddenly, woman *Per.* iii 1 69
And to him in his barge with fervour hies . . . . . . v Gower 20
My temple stands in Ephesus: hie thee thither . . . . . . v 1 241
Hiems. This side is Hiems, Winter, this Ver, the Spring . *L. L. Lost* v 2 901
On old Hiems' thin and icy crown . . . . . . *M. N. Dream* ii 1 109
Hig. Nominativo, hig, hag, hog; pray you, mark . . . *Mer. Wives* iv 1 44
High. No hope that way is Another way so high a hope . *Tempest* ii 1 241
Sing it.—And why not you?—I cannot reach so high . *T. G. of Ver.* i 2 87
Too low a mistress for so high a servant . . . . . . ii 4 106
For contemning Love, Whose high imperious thoughts have punish'd me ii 4 130
Ay, but her forehead's low, and mine's as high . . . . . iv 4 198
He is of too high a region; he knows too much . . . *M. Wives* iii 2 75
I thank you, princes, for my daughter's death: Record it with your high and worthy deeds . . . . *Much Ado* v 1 279
In so high a style, Margaret, that no man living shall come over it . v 2 6
The roof of this court is too high to be yours . . . *L. L. Lost* ii 1 93
O cross! too high to be enthrall'd to low . . . . *M. N. Dream* i 1 136
And are you grown so high in his esteem, Because I am so dwarfish? . iii 2 294
Only to stand high in your account . . . . . *Mer. of Venice* iii 2 157
What stature is she of?—Just as high as my heart . *As Y. Like It* iii 2 286
What power is it which mounts my love so high? . . . . *All's Well* i 1 235
If thou proceed As high as word, my deed shall match thy meed . . ii 1 213
And to imperial Love, that god most high, Do my sighs stream . . ii 3 81
I have letters sent me That set him high in fame . . . . . v 3 31
Thoughts high for one so tender . . . . *W. Tale* iii 2 197
Ha, majesty! how high thy glory towers, When the rich blood of kings is set on fire! . . . . *K. John* ii 1 350
The wall is high, and yet will I leap down . . . . . . iv 3 1
How high a pitch his resolution soars! . . . . . *Richard II.* i 1 109
These high wild hills and rough uneven ways Draws out our miles . ii 3 4
Are we not high? High be our thoughts . . . . iii 2 88
So high above his limits swells the rage Of Bolingbroke . . . iii 2 109
Your heart is up, I know, Thus high at least, although your knee be low iii 3 195
Drinking my griefs, whilst you mount up on high . . . . . iv 1 189
Mount, mount, my soul! thy seat is up on high . . . . . . v 5 112
And by and by in as high a flow as the ridge of the gallows . *1 Hen. IV.* i 2 43
But I will lift the down-trod Mortimer As high in the air as this unthankful king . . . . i 3 136
Percy stands on high; And either we or they must lower lie . . . iii 3 227
That it may grow and sprout as high as heaven, For recordation *2 Hen. IV.* ii 3 60
Wilt thou upon the high and giddy mast Seal up the ship-boy's eyes? . iii 1 18
When a' was a crack not thus high . . . . iii 2 34
And teach lavoltas high and swift corantos . . . . *Hen. V.* iii 5 33
Steed threatens steed, in high and boastful neighs . . . . . iv Prol. 10
Come, come, away! The sun is high, and we outwear the day . . iv 2 63
As by your high imperial majesty I had in charge . . . *2 Hen. VI.* i 1 1
The wind was very high; And, ten to one, old Joan had not gone out . ii 1 3
Yea, man and birds are fain of climbing high . . . . . . ii 1 8
The winds grow high; so do your stomachs, lords . . . . . ii 1 55
Women and children of so high a courage, And warriors faint! *3 Hen. VI.* v 4 50
They that stand high have many blasts to shake them . *Richard III.* i 3 259
But I was born so high, Our aery buildeth in the cedar's top . . . i 3 263
Thus high, by thy advice And thy assistance, is King Richard seated . iv 2 3
The high imperial type of this earth's glory . . . . . . iv 4 244
A serious brow, Sad, high, and working, full of state and woe *Hen. VIII.* Prol 3
Such As Agamemnon . . . Should hold up high in brass *Troi. and Cres.* i 3 64
I'ld make a quarry With thousands of these quarter'd slaves, as high As I could pick my lance . . . . *Coriolanus* i 1 203
That hath beside well in his person wrought To be set high in place . ii 3 255
Scatter'd by winds and high tempestuous gusts . . . *T. Andron.* v 3 69
The orchard walls are high and hard to climb . . . *Rom. and Jul.* ii 2 63
Whose notes do beat The vaulty heaven so high above our heads . . iii 5 22
Seeing she is advanced Above the clouds, as high as heaven itself . . iv 5 74
I have upon a high and pleasant hill Feign'd Fortune . . *T. of Athens* i 1 63
Tell Athens, in the sequence of degree From high to low throughout . v 1 212
O, he sits high in all the people's hearts . . . . *J. Cæsar* i 3 157
Most high, most mighty, and most puissant Cæsar . . . . . iii 1 33
Come, high or low; Thyself and office deftly show! . . . *Macbeth* iv 1 67
In the most high and palmy state of Rome . . . . . . *Hamlet* i 1 113
The morn, in russet mantle clad, Walks o'er the dew of yon high eastward hill . . . . i 1 167
Give order that these bodies High on a stage be placed to the view . v 2 389

High. Who have—as who have not, that their great stars Throned and set high? . . *Lear* iii 1 23
A cliff, whose high and bending head Looks fearfully in the confined deep . . iv 1 76
The murmuring surge, That on the unnumber'd idle pebbles chafes, Cannot be heard so high . . iv 6 22
The wind-shaked surge, with high and monstrous mane . *Othello* ii 1 13
I heard the clink and fall of swords, And Cassio high in oath . ii 3 235
Of so high and plenteous wit and invention . . iv 1 201
High in name and power, Higher than both in blood and life *Ant. and Cleo.* i 2 196
Who neigh'd so high, that what I would have spoke Was beastly dumb'd i 5 49
Thy spirit which keeps thee is Noble, courageous, high, unmatchable . ii 3 20
It is just so high as it is, and moves with it own organs . ii 7 48
Better to leave undone, than by our deed Acquire too high a fame . iii 1 15
Let me rail so high, That the false housewife Fortune break her wheel iv 15 43
Let's do it after the high Roman fashion, And make death proud to take us . . iv 15 87
The gates of monarchs Are arch'd so high that giants may jet through And keep their impious turbans on . *Cymbeline* iii 3 5
For by his fall my honour must keep high . *Pericles* i 1 149
Whose towers bore heads so high they kiss'd the clouds . i 4 24
That never aim'd so high to love your daughter . ii 5 47
The sea works high, the wind is loud, and will not lie . iii 1 48
High account. The princes both make high account of you *Richard III.* iii 2 71
High admiral. Lord Bourbon, our high admiral . *3 Hen. VI.* iii 3 252
High affairs. To treat of high affairs . *K. John* i 1 101
High All-Seer. That high All-Seer that I dallied with Hath turn'd my feigned prayer on my head . *Richard III.* v 1 20
High and low. And high and low beguiles the rich and poor *Mer. Wives* i 3 95
He wooes both high and low, both rich and poor, Both young and old . ii 1 117
Your true love's coming, That can sing both high and low . *T. Night* ii 3 42
The odds for high and low's alike . *W. Tale* v 1 207
For government, though high and low and lower, Put into parts, doth keep in one consent . *Hen. V.* i 2 180
His hate may grow To the whole race of mankind, high and low! *T. of Athens* iv 1 40
Yet reverence, That angel of the world, doth make distinction Of place 'tween high and low . *Cymbeline* iv 2 249
High and mighty. She shall be a high and mighty queen *Richard III.* iv 4 347
To the high and mighty princess of England, Elizabeth! *Hen. VIII.* v 5 3
Which is the high and mighty Agamemnon? . *Troi. and Cres.* i 3 232
High and mighty, You shall know I am set naked on your kingdom *Ham.* iv 7 43
High authority. Hence hath offence his quick celerity, When it is borne in high authority . *Meas. for Meas.* iv 2 114
He his high authority abused, And did deserve his change *Ant. and Cleo.* iii 6 33
High-battled Cæsar will Unstate his happiness, and be staged to the show,, Against a sworder . iii 13 29
High bent. My revenges were high bent upon him . *All's Well* v 3 10
High birth. Beauty, wit, High birth, vigour of bone *Troi. and Cres.* iii 3 172
High blood. Setting aside his high blood's royalty . *Richard II.* i 1 58
I had thought weariness durst not have attached one of so high blood *2 Hen. IV.* ii 2 3
The princes orgulous, their high blood chafed . *Troi. and Cres.* Prol. 2
High-blown. My high-blown pride At length broke under me *Hen. VIII.* iii 2 361
High-born. Relate In high-born words the worth of many a knight *L. L. Lost* i 1 173
I am too high-born to be propertied, To be a secondary . *K. John* v 2 79
High charms. My high charms work . *Tempest* iii 3 88
High-coloured. Lepidus is high-coloured . *Ant. and Cleo.* ii 7 4
High commendation. You have deserved High commendation *As Y. Like It* i 2 275
High constable. 'Tis not so, my lord high constable . *Hen. V.* ii 4 41
Charles Delabreth, high constable of France . iii 5 40; iv 8 97
My lord high constable, you talk of horse and armour? . iii 7 7
When I came hither, I was lord high constable . *Hen. VIII.* ii 1 102
High court. Now call we our high court of parliament . *2 Hen. IV.* v 2 134
High cross. To be whipped at the high cross every morning *T. of Shrew* i 1 137
High curvet Of Mars's fiery steed . *All's Well* ii 3 299
High-day. Thou wilt say anon he is some kin to thee, Thou spend'st such high-day wit in praising him . *Mer. of Venice* ii 9 98
High deeds. Whose high deeds, Whose hot incursions and great name in arms Holds from all soldiers chief majority . *1 Hen. IV.* iii 2 107
Hath taught us how to cherish such high deeds . v 5 30
High degree. Unworthily Thou wast installed in that high degree *1 Hen. VI.* iv 1 17
High descent. By reputing of his high descent . *2 Hen. VI.* iii 1 48
And made a preachment of your high descent . *3 Hen. VI.* i 4 72
High desert. And lay those honours on your high deserts *Richard III.* i 3 97
O, none of both but are of high desert . *T. Andron.* iii 1 171
High designs. O, when degree is shaked, Which is the ladder to all high designs, The enterprise is sick! . *Troi. and Cres.* i 3 102
High despite. In high despite, Laugh'd in his face . *3 Hen. VI.* ii 1 59
High disgrace. And spit it bleeding in his high disgrace *Richard II.* i 1 194
High displeasure. And urged withal Your high displeasure *Rom. and Jul.* iii 1 160
High Dunsinane. Until Great Birnam wood to high Dunsinane hill Shall come against him . *Macbeth* iv 1 93
High east. The high east Stands, as the Capitol, directly here *J. Cæsar* ii 1 110
High emperor, upon my feeble knee I beg this boon . *T. Andron.* ii 3 288
High engendered. Join'd Your high engender'd battles 'gainst a head So old and white as this . *Lear* iii 2 23
High estate. Advanced in time to great and high estate . *Pericles* iv 4 14
High esteem. Of such possessions and so high esteem . *T. of Shrew* Ind. 2 16
High events as these Strike those that make them . *Ant. and Cleo.* v 2 363
High expense. And high expense Can stead the quest . *Pericles* iii Gower 20
High exploits. Whose high exploits and honourable deeds Ingrateful Rome requites with foul contempt . *T. Andron.* v 1 11
High fantastical. So full of shapes is fancy That it alone is high fantastical . *T. Night* i 1 15
High feats. Nor call'd upon For high feats done to the crown *Hen. VIII.* i 1 61
High feeding. Contention, like a horse Full of high feeding, madly hath broke loose . *2 Hen. IV.* i 1 10
High festivals. Transported shall be at high festivals . *1 Hen. VI.* i 6 26
High fever. Go, suck the subtle blood o' the grape, Till the high fever seethe your blood to froth . *T. of Athens* iv 3 433
High forehead. By her high forehead and her scarlet lip *Rom. and Jul.* ii 1 18
High fortune. Hie you to the cell.—Hie to high fortune! . ii 5 80
High gods. And the high gods, To do you justice, make them ministers Of us and those that love you *Ant. and Cleo.* iii 6 87
The most high gods not minding longer To withhold the vengeance that they had in store . *Pericles* ii 4 3
High good turn. Is she not then beholding to the man That brought her for this high good turn so far? . *T. Andron.* i 1 397
High-gravel. Being more than sand-blind, high-gravel blind *M. of Venice* ii 2 38
High-grown. Search every acre in the high-grown field . *Lear* iv 4 7
High hatred. What his high hatred would effect wants not A minister in his power . *Hen. VIII.* i 1 107
High hearts. Plighter of high hearts . *Ant. and Cleo.* iii 13 126
High heaven. Plays such fantastic tricks before high heaven As make the angels weep . *Meas. for Meas.* ii 2 121
I confess, Here on my knee, before high heaven and you, That before you, and next unto high heaven, I love your son . *All's Well* i 3 198
High Hereford. Aumerle, How far brought you high Hereford on his way?—I brought high Hereford, if you call him so, But to the next highway . *Richard II.* i 4 2
High honour. She shall be dignified with this high honour *T. G. of Ver.* ii 4 158
Honour, high honour and renown, To Hymen, god of every town! *As Y. Like It* v 4 151
High hope. A high hope for a low heaven . *L. L. Lost* i 1 196
High-illustrious. Conspirant 'gainst this high-illustrious prince *Lear* v 3 135
High-judging. Nor tell tales of thee to high-judging Jove . ii 4 231
High lavolt. I cannot sing, Nor heel the high lavolt . *Troi. and Cres.* iv 4 88
High majesty. Hearing your high majesty is touch'd . *All's Well* ii 1 113
And make high majesty look like itself . *Richard II.* ii 1 295
Let not his report Come current for an accusation Betwixt my love and your high majesty . *1 Hen. IV.* i 3 69
High-minded. I will chastise this high-minded strumpet . *1 Hen. VI.* i 5 12
High miracle. A most high miracle! . *Tempest* v 1 177
High noises. Mark the high noises . *Lear* iii 6 118
High note's Ta'en of your many virtues . *Hen. VIII.* iii 3 59
High office. Let the high office and the honour go . *Coriolanus* ii 3 129
High Olympus. Though they do appear As huge as high Olympus *J. C.* iv 3 92
High order. See High order in this great solemnity . *Ant. and Cleo.* v 2 369
High pay. With promise of high pay and great rewards . *3 Hen. VI.* ii 1 134
High perfection. Because both they Match not the high perfection of my loss . *Richard III.* iv 4 66
High person. To your high person His will is most malignant; and it stretches Beyond you . *Hen. VIII.* i 2 140
High-placed Macbeth Shall live the lease of nature . *Macbeth* iv 1 98
High powers. Arming myself with patience To stay the providence of some high powers That govern us below . *J. Cæsar* v 1 107
High praise. She's too low for a high praise . *Much Ado* i 1 174
High presence. Desires access To your high presence . *W. Tale* v 1 88
High prince. Welcome, high prince, the mighty Duke of York! *1 Hen. VI.* iii 1 177
High profession. You tender more your person's honour than Your high profession spiritual . *Hen. VIII.* ii 4 117
High profits. Employ'd you where high profits might come home . iii 2 158
High promotion. To high promotions and great dignity . *Richard III.* iv 4 314
The high promotion of his grace of Canterbury . *Hen. VIII.* v 2 23
High-proof. We are high-proof melancholy . *Much Ado* v 1 123
High pyramides. My country's high pyramides my gibbet *Ant. and Cleo.* v 2 61
High rage. The king is in high rage . *Lear* ii 4 299
High-reaching Buckingham grows circumspect . *Richard III.* iv 2 31
High reared. The prayers of holy saints and wronged souls, Like high-rear'd bulwarks, stand before our faces . v 3 242
High renown. He was a wight of high renown . *Othello* ii 3 96
High-repented. My high-repented blames . . . pardon to me *All's Well* v 3 36
High request. Your love deserves my thanks; but my desert Unmeritable shuns your high request . *Richard III.* iii 7 155
High resolve. Is likely to beget more conquerors, If with a lady of so high resolve As is fair Margaret he be link'd in love . *1 Hen. VI.* v 5 75
High-resolved. With a power Of high-resolved men . *T. Andron.* iv 4 64
High respect. Yet a place of high respect with me . *M. N. Dream* ii 1 209
Whose high respect and rich validity Did lack a parallel. *All's Well* v 3 192
He holds your temper in a high respect . *1 Hen. IV.* iii 1 170
The malevolence of fortune nothing Takes from his high respect *Macbeth* iii 6 29
High reward. Shall have a high reward . *3 Hen. VI.* v 5 10
High royalty. You were crown'd before, And that high royalty was ne'er pluck'd off . *K. John* iv 2 5
High sceptre. Adopts thee heir, and his high sceptre yields *Richard II.* iv 1 109
High scorn. With a proud majestical high scorn, He answer'd *1 Hen. VI.* iv 7 39
High seas. Tempests themselves, high seas and howling winds *Othello* ii 1 68
High self. Your high self, The gracious mark o' the land *W. Tale* iv 4 7
High shoes. Do now wear nothing but high shoes . *2 Hen. IV.* i 2 44
High shore. Nor the tide of pomp That beats upon the high shore of this world . *Hen. V.* iv 1 282
High-sighted. So let high-sighted tyranny range on . *J. Cæsar* ii 1 118
High-soaring. She is as far high-soaring o'er thy praises As thou unworthy to be call'd her servant . *Troi. and Cres.* iv 4 126
High sparks of honour in thee have I seen . *Richard II.* v 6 29
High speech. Which on my faith deserves high speech *W. Tale* ii 1 70
High speed. He that rides at high speed and with his pistol kills a sparrow flying . *1 Hen. IV.* ii 4 379
High-steward. And claims To be high-steward . *Hen. VIII.* iv 1 18
The Duke of Suffolk?—'Tis the same: high-steward . iv 1 41
High-stomach'd are they both, and full of ire . *Richard II.* i 1 18
High strains. Do not these high strains Of divination in our sister work Some touches of remorse? . *Troi. and Cres.* ii 2 113
High supper-time. It is now high supper-time . *Othello* iv 2 249
High-swoln. The broken rancour of your high-swoln hearts *Richard III.* ii 2 117
High Taurus' snow, Fann'd with the eastern wind . *M. N. Dream* iii 2 141
High terms. Thou hast astonish'd me with thy high terms . *1 Hen. VI.* i 2 93
High things. I will with patience hear, and find a time Both meet to hear and answer such high things . *J. Cæsar* i 2 170
High tides. Set Among the high tides in the calendar . *K. John* iii 1 86
High time. Therefore 'tis high time that I were hence . *Com. of Errors* iii 2 162
High top. Vailing her high-top lower than her ribs . *Mer. of Venice* i 1 28
You may as well forbid the mountain pines To wag their high tops . iv 1 76
Whose boughs were moss'd with age And high top bald . *As Y. Like It* iv 3 106
High top-gallant. To the high top-gallant of my joy *Rom. and Jul.* ii 4 202
High treason. Accused and arraigned of high treason . *W. Tale* iii 2 14
Namely, to appeal each other of high treason . *Richard II.* i 1 27
I do arrest thee, traitor, of high treason . *2 Hen. IV.* iv 2 107
God acquit them of their practices!—I arrest thee of high treason *Hen. V.* ii 2 145
This is the man That doth accuse his master of high treason . *2 Hen. VI.* i 3 185
I do arrest thee of high treason here.—Well, Suffolk . iii 1 97
Northampton, I Arrest thee of high treason . *Hen. VIII.* i 1 201
His peers, upon this evidence, Have found him guilty of high treason . ii 1 27
High upreared. Whose high upreared and abutting fronts The perilous narrow ocean parts asunder . *Hen. V.* Prol. 21
High vaunts. And such high vaunts of his nobility . *2 Hen. VI.* iii 1 50
High-viced. Be as a planetary plague, when Jove Will o'er some high-viced city hang his poison In the sick air . *T. of Athens* iv 3 109

High wedlock then be honoured . . . . *As Y. Like It* v 4 150
High will. To whose high will we bound our calm contents *Richard II.* v 2 38
While we attend, Like humble-visaged suitors, his high will . *L. L. Lost* ii 1 34
Move them no more by crossing their high will . . *Rom. and Jul.* iv 5 95
High wish. The one is filling still, never complete; The other, at high wish . . . . *T. of Athens* iv 3 245
High-witted. Thus it shall become High-witted Tamora to gloze *T. An.* iv 4 35
High words. How low soever the matter, I hope in God for high words. —A high hope for a low heaven . . . . . . *L. L. Lost* i 1 195
High wrongs. With their high wrongs I am struck to the quick *Tempest* v 1 25
High-wrought. It is a high-wrought flood . . . . . *Othello* ii 1 2
Higher. Fed in heart, whose flames aspire As thoughts do blow them, higher and higher . . . . *Mer. Wives* v 5 102
I pray you, come, hold up the jest no higher . . . . . v 5 109
A kind of boy, a little scrubbed boy, No higher than thyself *M. of Ven.* v 1 163
Let higher Italy,—Those bated that inherit but the fall Of the last monarchy,—see that you come Not to woo honour . . *All's Well* ii 1 12
Will he travel higher, or return again into France? . . . . iv 3 50
Let me see thee caper: ha! higher: ha, ha! excellent! . . *T. Night* i 3 150
And our weak spirits ne'er been higher rear'd With stronger blood *W. T.* i 2 72
The higher powers forbid! . . . . iii 2 203
Up higher to the plain; where we'll set forth In best appointment *K. John* ii 1 295
He presently, as greatness knows itself, Steps me a little higher 1 *Hen. IV.* iv 3 75
It shall serve among wits of no higher breeding than thine . 2 *Hen. IV.* ii 2 38
We will our youth lead on to higher fields . . . . . iv 4 3
Though his affections are higher mounted than ours . . *Hen. V.* iv 1 111
Between two hawks, which flies the higher pitch . . . 1 *Hen. VI.* ii 4 11
'Tis but a base ignoble mind That mounts no higher than a bird can soar. —I thought as much . . . . 2 *Hen. VI.* ii 1 14
Shall suck them dry, And swell so much the higher by their ebb 3 *Hen. VI.* iv 8 56
Advance thy halberd higher than my breast . . . *Richard III.* i 2 40
If she praised him above, his complexion is higher than his; he having colour enough, and the other higher, is too flaming a praise *T. and C.* i 2 111
The bounded waters Should lift their bosoms higher than the shores . i 3 112
If there be one . . . That holds his honour higher than his ease . i 3 266
The sun arises. . . . Some two months hence up higher toward the north He first presents his fire . . . . *J. Cæsar* ii 1 109
Go, Pindarus, get higher on that hill; My sight was ever thick . . v 3 20
Set your entreatments at a higher rate Than a command to parley *Hamlet* i 3 122
High in name and power, Higher than both in blood and life *A. and C.* i 2 197
But let us rear The higher our opinion . . . . . . ii 1 36
Say to me, Whose fortunes shall rise higher, Cæsar's or mine? . . ii 3 16
The higher Nilus swells, The more it promises . . . . . ii 7 23
She'll prove on cats and dogs, Then afterward up higher . *Cymbeline* i 5 39
We'll higher to the mountains; there secure us . . . . iv 4 8
For who digs hills because they do aspire Throws down one mountain to cast up a higher . . . . *Pericles* i 4 6
But like to groves, being topp'd, they higher rise . . . . . i 4 9
High'st queen of state, Great Juno, comes . . . . *Tempest* iv 1 101
Thy substance, valued at the highest rate, Cannot amount unto a hundred marks; Therefore by law thou art condemn'd to die *C. of Er.* i 1 24
Which is the greatest lady, the highest?—The thickest and the tallest *L. L. Lost* iv 1 46
In the highest compulsion of base fear . . . . *All's Well* iii 6 31
What is not holy, that we swear not by, But take the High'st to witness iv 2 24
Misprision in the highest degree! . . . . . . *T. Night* i 5 61
I'll requite it in the highest degree . . . . iv 2 128
Let us to the highest of the field, To see what friends are living 1 *Hen. IV.* v 4 164
I fear our happiness is at the highest . . . . . *Richard III.* iii 3 41
Perjury, perjury, in the high'st degree; Murder, stern murder . . v 3 196
I have touch'd the highest point of all my greatness . *Hen. VIII.* iii 2 223
Disasters Grow in the veins of actions highest rear'd . *Troi. and Cres.* i 3 6
Prosperity be thy page!—Thy friend no less Than those she placeth highest! So, farewell . . . . *Coriolanus* i 5 25
For thy revenge Wrench up thy power to the highest . . . . i 8 11
Tell the traitor, in the high'st degree He hath abused your powers . v 6 85
I have dogs, my lord, Will . . . climb the highest promontory top *T. An.* ii 2 22
Nothing else: you shall see him a palm in Athens again, and flourish with the highest . . . . *T. of Athens* v 1 13
It is a massy wheel, Fix'd on the summit of the highest mount *Hamlet* iii 3 18
Highest-peering. Gallops the zodiac in his glistering coach, And over-looks the highest-peering hills . . . . *T. Andron.* ii 1 8
Highly. Three things that women highly hold in hate . *T. G. of Ver.* iii 2 33
Of credit infinite, highly beloved, Second to none . . *Com. of Errors* v 1 6
And her wit Values itself so highly that to her All matter else seems weak: she cannot love . . . . *Much Ado* iii 1 53
I will show myself highly fed and lowly taught . . . *All's Well* ii 2 3
As sweet as ditties highly penn'd, Sung by a fair queen . . 1 *Hen. IV.* iii 1 209
Divided councils, Wherein thyself shalt highly be employ'd *Richard III.* iii 1 180
Mountainous error be too highly heapt For truth to o'er-peer *Coriolanus* ii 3 127
In this match I hold me highly honour'd of your grace . . *T. Andron.* i 1 245
In zeal to you and highly moved to wrath To be controll'd . . . i 1 419
For this care of Tamora, Herself and hers are highly bound to thee . iv 2 171
It highly us concerns By day and night to attend him carefully . . iv 3 27
I'll show thee wondrous things, That highly may advantage thee to hear v 1 56
What thou wouldst highly, That wouldst thou holily . . *Macbeth* i 5 21
We love him highly, And shall continue our graces towards him . . i 6 29
O, there be players that I have seen play, and heard others praise, and that highly, not to speak it profanely . . . . . . *Hamlet* iii 2 33
Highmost. Now is the sun upon the highmost hill Of this day's journey, and from nine till twelve Is three long hours . . *Rom. and Jul.* ii 5 9
Highness. Prithee, no more: thou dost talk nothing to me.—I do well believe your highness . . . . *Tempest* ii 1 172
Were I so minded, I here could pluck his highness' frown upon you . v 1 127
I invite your highness and your train To my poor cell . . . . v 1 300
Your highness said even now, I made you a duke . . *Meas. for Meas.* v 1 521
But she tells to your highness simple truth! . . . . *Com. of Errors* v 1 211
Your highness now may do me good.—My love is thine to teach *M. Ado* i 1 292
Amazed, my lord? why looks your highness sad? . . . *L. L. Lost* v 2 391
Make choice of which your highness will see first . . *M. N. Dream* v 1 43
Never so much as in a thought unborn Did I offend your highness *As Y. Like It* i 3 54
Thou art thy father's daughter; there's enough.—So was I when your highness took his dukedom; So was I when your highness banish'd him . . . . i 3 61
O that your highness knew my heart in this! I never loved my brother iii 1 13
His highness hath promised me to do it . . . . . *All's Well* iv 5 79
His highness comes post from Marseilles, of as able body . . . iv 5 85
All that he is hath reference to your highness . . . . . . v 3 29
She told me, In a sweet verbal brief, it did concern Your highness . v 3 138
Highness. Let your highness Lay a more noble thought upon mine honour . . . . *All's Well* v 3 179
But why?—To satisfy your highness . . . . . *W. Tale* i 2 232
Provided that, when he's removed, your highness Will take again your queen . . . . i 2 335
But needful conference About some gossips for your highness . . ii 3 41
It is his highness' pleasure that the queen Appear in person here in court . . . . iii 2 9
Then, till the fury of his highness settle, Come not before him . iv 4 482
Where you shall have such receiving As shall become your highness . iv 4 538
What dangers, by his highness' fail of issue, May drop upon his kingdom v 1 27
To execute the charge my father gave me For visiting your highness . v 1 163
She is sad and passionate at your highness' tent . . . *K. John* ii 1 544
My lord, I rescued her; Her highness is in safety, fear you not . . iii 2 8
This 'once again,' but that your highness pleased, Was once superfluous iv 2 3
We breathed our counsel: but it pleased your highness To overbear it iv 2 36
Every part of what we would Doth make a stand at what your highness will . . . . iv 2 39
That, ere the next Ascension-day at noon, Your highness should deliver up your crown . . . . iv 2 152
His highness yet doth speak . . . . v 7 6
On some apparent danger seen in him Aim'd at your highness *Richard II.* i 1 14
The fair reverence of your highness curbs me From giving reins and spurs to my free speech . . . . i 1 54
Eight thousand nobles In name of lendings for your highness' soldiers . i 1 89
That receipt I had for Calais Disbursed I duly to his highness' soldiers i 1 127
Most heartily I pray Your highness to assign our trial day . . . i 1 151
The appellant in all duty greets your highness . . . . . . i 3 52
A heavy sentence, my most sovereign liege, And all unlook'd for from your highness' mouth . . . . i 3 155
A dearer merit . . . Have I deserved at your highness' hands . . i 3 158
Expedient manage must be made, my liege, Ere further leisure yield them further means For their advantage and your highness' loss . i 4 41
Glad am I that your highness is so arm'd To bear the tidings of calamity iii 2 104
Those prisoners in your highness' name demanded . . . 1 *Hen. IV.* i 3 23
Moreover, his highness is fallen into this same whoreson apoplexy 2 *Hen. IV.* i 2 122
Which once attain'd, Your highness knows, comes to no further use . iv 4 72
Here at more leisure may your highness read . . . . . . iv 4 89
These fits Are with his highness very ordinary. Stand from him . . iv 4 115
Whiles I was busy for the commonwealth, Your highness pleased to forget my place . . . . v 2 77
There is no bar To make against your highness' claim to France *Hen. V.* i 2 36
Hold up this Salique law To bar your highness claiming from the female . . . . i 2 92
They know your grace hath cause and means and might; So hath your highness . . . . i 2 126
We of the spiritualty Will raise your highness such a mighty sum As never did the clergy at one time Bring in to any of your ancestors . i 2 133
Your highness, lately sending into France, Did claim some certain dukedoms . . . . i 2 246
O, let us yet be merciful.—So may your highness, and yet punish too . ii 2 48
Your highness bade me ask for it to-day . . . . ii 2 63
I do confess my fault; And do submit me to your highness' mercy . ii 2 77
Which I beseech your highness to forgive, Although my body pay the price of it . . . . ii 2 153
If your father's highness Do not, in grant of all demands at large, Sweeten the bitter mock you sent his majesty . . . . ii 4 120
So tell your master.—I shall deliver so. Thanks to your highness . iii 6 176
What your highness suffered under that shape, I beseech you take it for your own fault and not mine . . . . iv 8 56
Shall name your highness in this form and with this addition . . v 2 366
We charge and command you, in his highness' name . . 1 *Hen. VI.* i 3 76
Lets fall his sword before your highness' feet . . . . . . iii 4 9
First be tried by fight, And then your highness shall command a peace iv 1 117
It grieves his highness: good my lords, be friends . . . . . iv 1 133
I have inform'd his highness so at large . . . . v 1 42
You know, my lord, your highness is betroth'd Unto another lady . v 5 26
And had his highness in his infancy Crowned in Paris . . 2 *Hen. VI.* i 1 93
'Tis his highness' pleasure You do prepare to ride unto Saint Alban's . i 2 56
To show your highness A spirit raised from depth of under-ground . i 2 78
As I was cause Your highness came to England, so will I In England work your grace's full content . . . . i 3 69
Here comes the townsmen on procession, To present your highness with the man . . . . ii 1 69
Bring him near the king; His highness' pleasure is to talk with him . ii 1 73
Demanding of King Henry's life and death, And other of your highness' privy-council . . . . ii 1 176
It is no policy . . . That he should come about your royal person Or be admitted to your highness' council . . . . iii 1 27
Well hath your highness seen into this duke . . . . . . iii 1 42
Stay'd the soldiers' pay; By means whereof his highness hath lost France iii 1 106
I do arrest you in his highness' name . . . . iii 1 136
Foul subornation is predominant And equity exiled your highness' land iii 1 146
What, will your highness leave the parliament? . . . . . iii 1 197
They say, in him they fear your highness' death . . . . . iii 2 249
In care of your most royal person, That if your highness should intend to sleep . . . . iii 2 255
Jack Cade hath sworn to have thy head.—Ay, but I hope your highness shall have his . . . . iv 4 20
And humbly thus, with halters on their necks, Expect your highness' doom, or life or death . . . . iv 9 12
I commend this kind submission: We twain will go into his highness' tent v 1 55
In all submission and humility York doth present himself unto your highness . . . . v 1 59
I would your highness would depart the field . . . 3 *Hen. VI.* ii 2 73
Your highness shall do well to grant her suit . . . . . . iii 2 8
So shall you bind me to your highness' service . . . . . iii 2 43
My mind will never grant what I perceive Your highness aims at . . iii 2 68
Herein your highness wrongs both them and me . . . . . . iii 2 75
In sign of truth, I kiss your highness' hand . . . . . . iv 8 26
Such like toys as these Have moved his highness to commit me now *Richard III.* i 1 61
I will not rise, unless Your highness grant.—Then speak at once . . ii 1 97
If I may counsel you, some day or two Your highness shall repose you iii 1 65
What says your highness to my just demand? . . . . . . iv 2 97
What is't your highness' pleasure I shall do At Salisbury? . . . iv 4 452
Your highness told me I should post before.—My mind is changed, sir iv 4 455
'Tis his highness' pleasure You shall to the Tower . . . *Hen. VIII.* i 1 206
I would your highness Would give it quick consideration . . . . i 2 65

Highness. Not long before your highness sped to France . *Hen. VIII.* i 2 151
After your highness had reproved the duke About Sir William Blomer i 2 189
May his highness live in freedom, And this man out of prison? . i 2 200
One of her highness' women.—By heaven, she is a dainty one . i 4 93
Cardinal Campeius; Whom once more I present unto your highness ii 2 98
To your highness' hand I tender my commission . ii 2 103
His highness having lived so long with her, and she So good a lady . ii 3 2
Vouchsafe to speak my thanks and my obedience, As from a blushing handmaid, to his highness . ii 3 72
The which before His highness shall speak in, I do beseech You, gracious madam, to unthink your speaking And to say so no more . ii 4 103
You have, by fortune and his highness' favours, Gone slightly o'er low steps . ii 4 111
I require your highness, That it shall please you to declare . ii 4 144
Whether ever I Did broach this business to your highness . ii 4 149
And did entreat your highness to this course Which you are running . ii 4 216
Peace to your highness!—Your graces find me here part of a housewife iii 1 23
Can you think, lords, That any Englishman dare give me counsel? Or be a known friend, 'gainst his highness' pleasure? . iii 1 85
Heaven forgive me! Ever God bless your highness! . iii 2 136
Ever may your highness yoke together, As I will lend you cause, my doing well With my well saying! . iii 2 150
I do profess That for your highness' good I ever labour'd . iii 2 191
To Asher House, . . . Till you hear further from his highness . iii 2 232
A league between his highness and Ferrara . iii 2 323
May he continue Long in his highness' favour! . iii 2 396
I humbly do entreat your highness' pardon; My haste made me unmannerly . iv 2 104
How does his highness?—Madam, in good health.—So may he ever do . iv 2 124
Remember me In all humility unto his highness . iv 2 161
And desired your highness Most heartily to pray for her . v 1 65
With gentle travail, to the gladding of Your highness with an heir! v 1 72
I wish your highness A quiet night; and my good mistress will Remember v 1 76
Where is he, Denny?—He attends your highness' pleasure . v 1 83
It is my duty To attend your highness' pleasure . v 1 91
I humbly thank your highness . v 1 108; *Cymbeline* i 1 175; v 5 100
I'll show your grace the strangest sight— What's that, Butts?—I think your highness saw this many a day . *Hen. VIII.* v 2 21
'Tis his highness' pleasure, And our consent . v 3 52
And vow to heaven and to his highness, That what we did was mildly as we might, Tendering our sister's honour . *T. Andron.* i 1 474
Gracious mother! Why doth your highness look so pale and wan? . ii 3 90
They shall be ready at your highness' will To answer their suspicion ii 3 297
Because I would be sure to have all well, To entertain your highness . v 3 32
We are beholding to you, Good Andronicus.—An if your highness knew my heart, you were . v 3 34
Will't please you eat? will't please your highness feed? . v 3 54
He confess'd his treasons, Implored your highness' pardon . *Macbeth* i 4 6
Your highness' part Is to receive our duties . i 4 23
What is theirs, in compt, To make their audit at your highness' pleasure i 6 27
I'll request your presence.—Let your highness Command upon me . iii 1 15
Please't your highness To grace us with your royal company . iii 4 44
Where?—Here, my good lord. What is't that moves your highness? . iii 4 48
Gentlemen, rise; his highness is not well.—Sit, worthy friends . iii 4 52
But, better look'd into, he truly found It was against your highness *Hamlet* ii 2 65
And find I am alone felicitate In your dear highness' love . *Lear* i 1 78
I crave no more than what your highness offer'd, Nor will you tender less . i 1 197
Your highness is not entertained with that ceremonious affection as you were wont . i 4 62
My duty cannot be silent when I think your highness wronged . i 4 71
I did commend your highness' letters to them . ii 4 28
The very fellow that of late Display'd so saucily against your highness ii 4 41
I am glad to see your highness.—Regan, I think you are . ii 4 130
Will't please your highness walk?—You must bear with me . iv 7 83
What's your highness' pleasure?—Not now to hear thee sing *A. and C.* i 5 8
He is married?—I crave your highness' pardon.—He is married? . ii 5 98
Here is a rural fellow That will not be denied your highness' presence . v 2 234
The queen, madam, Desires your highness' company . *Cymbeline* i 3 38
Have you brought those drugs?—Pleaseth your highness, ay . i 5 5
Your highness Shall from this practice but make hard your heart . i 5 23
Leonatus is in safety And greets your highness dearly . i 6 13
My request, which I'll make bold your highness Cannot deny . v 5 89
He is a Roman; no more kin to me Than I to your highness . v 5 113
My breeding was, sir, as Your highness knows . v 5 340
Who attends us there?—Doth your highness call? . *Pericles* i 1 150
I'll make him sure enough: so, farewell to your highness . i 1 169
Beseech your highness *Meas. for Meas.* v 1; *All's Well* ii 3; *W. Tale* ii 1; ii 3; *Hen. V.* iv 8; *Cymbeline* iv 3
May it please your highness 3 *Hen. VI.* iii 2; *Hen. VIII.* iv 2; *Macb.* iii 4
Please your highness *W. Tale* i 2; ii 3; *Hen. VIII.* i 2; *Cymb.* i 1
So please your highness 2 *Hen. VI.* ii 3; *Hen. VIII.* ii 4; *Macbeth* iii 1; *Cymbeline* v 5

Hight. This child of fancy that Armado hight . *L. L. Lost* i 1 171
Which, as I remember, hight Costard . i 1 258
This grisly beast, which Lion hight by name . *M. N. Dream* v 1 140
This maid Hight Philoten . *Pericles* iv Gower 18

Highway. It is true, without any slips of prolixity or crossing the plain highway of talk . *Mer. of Venice* iii 1 13
Like the mending of highways In summer, where the ways are fair enough . v 1 263
Should be buried in highways out of all sanctified limit . *All's Well* i 1 152
Gallows and knock are too powerful on the highway . *W. Tale* iv 3 29
I brought high Hereford . . . But to the next highway . *Richard II.* i 4 4
Or I'll be buried in the king's highway, Some way of common trade . iii 3 155
He made you for a highway to my bed . *Rom. and Jul.* iii 2 134

Hilding. For shame, thou hilding of a devilish spirit . *T. of Shrew* ii 1 26
If your lordship find him not a hilding . *All's Well* iii 6 4
He was some hilding fellow that had stolen The horse he rode on 2 *Hen. IV.* i 1 57
Were enow To purge this field of such a hilding foe . *Hen. V.* iv 2 29
Helen and Hero hildings and harlots; Thisbe a grey eye *Rom. and Jul.* ii 4 44
We have a curse in having her: Out on her, hilding! . iii 5 169
A base slave, A hilding for a livery, a squire's cloth . *Cymbeline* ii 3 128

Hill. Ye elves of hills, brooks, standing lakes and groves . *Tempest* v 1 33
Spurred his horse so hard Against the steep uprising of the hill *L. L. L.* iv 1 2
At the charge-house on the top of the mountain?—Or mons, the hill . v 1 89
Over hill, over dale, Thorough bush, thorough brier . *M. N. Dream* ii 1 2
And never, since the middle summer's spring, Met we on hill, in dale *N. N. Dream* ii 1 83
We came down a foul hill, my master riding behind my mistress *T. of S.* iv 1 69
At last I spied An ancient angel coming down the hill . iv 2 61
Halloo your name to the reverberate hills . *T. Night* i 5 291
And at the other hill Command the rest to stand . *K. John* ii 1 298
These high wild hills and rough uneven ways Draws out our miles *Richard II.* ii 3 4
Where's Poins, Hal?—He is walked up to the top of the hill 1 *Hen. IV.* ii 2 9
There's money of the king's coming down the hill . ii 2 57
The boy shall lead our horses down the hill; we'll walk afoot awhile . ii 2 83
This bed-presser, this horse-back-breaker, this huge hill of flesh . ii 4 269
That runs o' horseback up a hill perpendicular . ii 4 378
How bloodily the sun begins to peer Above yon busky hill! . v 1 2
And falling from a hill, he was so bruised That the pursuers took him . v 5 21
William Visor of Woncot against Clement Perkes of the hill . 2 *Hen. IV.* v 1 43
His most mighty father on a hill Stood smiling . *Hen. V.* i 2 108
What rein can hold licentious wickedness When down the hill he holds his fierce career? . iii 3 23
Ride thou unto the horsemen on yon hill . iv 7 60
To sit upon a hill, as I do now, To carve out dials . 3 *Hen. VI.* ii 5 23
I'll stay above the hill, so both may shoot . iii 1 5
To climb steep hills Requires slow pace at first . *Hen. VIII.* i 1 131
Or pile ten hills on the Tarpeian rock, That the precipitation might down stretch Below the beam of sight *Coriolanus* iii 2 3
Gallops the zodiac in his glistering coach, And overlooks the highest-peering hills . *T. Andron.* ii 1 8
The sun's beams, Driving back shadows over louring hills *Rom. and Jul.* ii 5 6
Now is the sun upon the highmost hill Of this day's journey . ii 5 9
Upon a high and pleasant hill Feign'd Fortune to be throned *T. of Athens* i 1 63
This throne, this Fortune, and this hill, methinks, . . . would be well express'd In our condition . i 1 73
You said the enemy would not come down, But keep the hills *J. Cæsar* v 1 3
Fly far off.—This hill is far enough . v 3 12
Go, Pindarus, get higher on that hill; My sight was ever thick . v 3 20
All disconsolate, With Pindarus his bondman, on this hill . v 3 56
Until Great Birnam wood to high Dunsinane hill Shall come. *Macbeth* iv 1 93
As I did stand my watch upon the hill, I look'd toward Birnam, and anon, methought, The wood began to move . v 5 33
But, look, the morn, in russet mantle clad, Walks o'er the dew of yon high eastward hill . *Hamlet* i 1 167
Bowl the round nave down the hill of heaven, As low as to the fiends! ii 2 518
A station like the herald Mercury New-lighted on a heaven-kissing hill iii 4 59
Let go thy hold when a great wheel runs down a hill, lest it break thy neck with following it; but the great one that goes up the hill, let him draw thee after . *Lear* ii 4 73
When shall we come to the top of that same hill?—You do climb up it now . iv 6 1
Rough quarries, rocks and hills whose heads touch heaven . *Othello* i 3 141
Let the labouring bark climb hills of seas Olympus-high! . ii 1 189
Set we our squadrons on yond side o' the hill . *Ant. and Cleo.* iii 9 1
O, that I were Upon the hill of Basan, to outroar The horned herd! . iii 13 127
Our foot Upon the hills adjoining to the city Shall stay with us . iv 10 5
Now for our mountain sport: up to yond hill; Your legs are young *Cymb.* iii 3 10
The blind mole casts Copp'd hills towards heaven . *Pericles* i 1 101
For who digs hills because they do aspire Throws down one mountain to cast up a higher . i 4 5

Hillo, ho, ho, my lord!—Hillo, ho, ho, boy! come, bird, come . *Hamlet* i 5 115
Hilloa, loa!—What, art so near? . *W. Tale* iii 3 80

Hilt to point, heel to head . *Mer. Wives* iii 5 113
An old rusty sword . . . , with a broken hilt, and chapeless *T. of Shrew* iii 2 48
Four, in buckram suits.—Seven, by these hilts . 1 *Hen. IV.* ii 4 229
And hides a sword from hilts unto the point With crowns imperial *Hen. V.* ii Prol. 9
He that strikes the first stroke, I'll run him up to the hilts . ii 1 68
With purple falchion, painted to the hilt In blood . 3 *Hen. VI.* i 4 12
Take him over the costard with the hilts of thy sword . *Richard III.* i 4 160
Take thou the hilts; And, when my face is cover'd, as 'tis now, Guide thou the sword . *J. Cæsar* v 3 43
Very responsive to the hilts, most delicate carriages . *Hamlet* v 2 159

Him. Love doth to her eyes repair, To help him of his blindness *T. G. of Ver.* iv 2 47
Better than him I am before knows me . *As Y. Like It* i 1 46
Who laid him down and bask'd him in the sun . ii 7 15
Belike, some noble gentleman that means, Travelling some journey, to repose him here . *T. of Shrew* Ind. 1 76
As he that leaves A shallow plash to plunge him in the deep . i 1 23
I am appointed him to murder you . *W. Tale* i 2 412
But as we, under heaven, are supreme head, So under Him that great supremacy, Where we do reign, we will alone uphold . *K. John* iii 1 156
Let's away; Advantage feeds him fat, while men delay . 1 *Hen. IV.* iii 2 180
He that buckles him in my belt cannot live in less . 2 *Hen. IV.* i 2 157
Between two horses, which doth bear him best . 1 *Hen. VI.* ii 4 14
Him that thou magnifiest with all these titles Stinking and fly-blown lies here at our feet . iv 7 75
Like a gallant in the brow of youth, Repairs him with occasion 2 *Hen. VI.* v 3 5
By him that made us all, I am resolved . 3 *Hen. VI.* ii 2 124
First, he commends him to your noble lordship . *Richard III.* iii 2 8
Him in eye, Still him in praise . *Hen. VIII.* i 1 31
There's in him stuff that puts him to these ends . i 1 58
He stretch'd him, and, with one hand on his dagger . i 2 204
Praise him that got thee, she that gave thee suck . *Troi. and Cres.* ii 3 252
Him I accuse The city ports by this hath enter'd . *Coriolanus* v 6 5
He bears him like a portly gentleman . *Rom. and Jul.* i 5 68
He is wise; And, on my life, hath stol'n him home to bed . ii 1 4
After this let Cæsar seat him sure; For we will shake him . *J. Cæsar* i 2 325
With Him above To ratify the work . *Macbeth* iii 6 32
Let every soldier hew him down a bough And bear't before him . v 4 4
And damn'd be him that first cries 'Hold, enough!' . v 8 34
Your party in converse, him you would sound . *Hamlet* ii 1 42
Than by our deed Acquire too high a fame when him we serve's away *Ant. and Cleo.* iii 1 15

Himself. The king's son have I landed by himself . *Tempest* i 2 221
Every man shift for all the rest, and let no man take care for himself . v 1 257
Well of his wealth; but of himself, so, so . *T. G. of Ver.* i 2 13
I am the dog: no, the dog is himself, and I am the dog . ii 3 24
Himself would lodge where senseless they are lying . iii 1 143
Purchased by such sin For which the pardoner himself is in *M. for M.* iv 2 112
He is not Hector.—No, nor Hector is not Troilus in some degrees.— 'Tis just to each of them; he is himself . *Troi. and Cres.* i 2 75

Himself! no, he's not himself: would a' were himself . *Troi. and Cres.* i 2 82
And will be led At your request a little from himself . . ii 3 191
He that hath a will to die by himself fears it not from another *Coriolanus* v 2 111
He is not with himself; let us withdraw . . . *T. Andron.* i 1 368
Let him have a table by himself, for he does neither affect company, nor is he fit for't, indeed . . . *T. of Athens* i 2 30
How he solicits heaven, Himself best knows . . *Macbeth* iv 3 150
Himself upbraids us On every trifle . . . *Lear* i 3 6

Hinc. What is your accusative case?—Accusativo, hinc . *Mer. Wives* iv 1 47

Hinckley. About the sack he lost the other day at Hinckley fair *2 Hen. IV.* v 1 26

Hind. A couple of Ford's knaves, his hinds . . . *Mer. Wives* iii 5 99
Out upon thee, hind! . . . . . *Com. of Errors* iii 1 77
The rational hind Costard . . . . *L. L. Lost* i 2 123
The mild hind Makes speed to catch the tiger . . *M. N. Dream* ii 1 232
He lets me feed with his hinds, bars me the place of a brother *As Y. L. It* i 1 20
If a hart do lack a hind, Let him seek out Rosalind . . iii 2 107
The hind that would be mated by the lion Must die for love . *All's Well* i 1 102
You are a shallow cowardly hind, and you lie . . *1 Hen. IV.* ii 3 16
'Tis like the commons, rude unpolish'd hinds . . *2 Hen. VI.* iii 2 271
Rebellious hinds, the filth and scum of Kent, Mark'd for the gallows . iv 2 130
His army is a ragged multitude Of hinds and peasants . . iv 4 33
The tiger now hath seized the gentle hind . . *Richard III.* ii 4 50
Pard to the hind, or stepdame to her son . . *Troi. and Cres.* iii 2 201
What, art thou drawn among these heartless hinds? . *Rom. and Jul.* i 1 73
He were no lion, were not Romans hinds . . . *J. Cæsar* i 3 106
Fight I will no more, But yield me to the veriest hind that shall Once touch my shoulder . . . . *Cymbeline* v 3 77

Hinder them from what this ecstasy May now provoke them to *Tempest* iii 3 108
Then let me go and hinder not my course . . *T. G. of Ver.* ii 7 33
These be the stops that hinder study quite . . *L. L. Lost* i 1 70
Why, get you gone: who is't that hinders you? . *M. N. Dream* iii 2 318
For the love of laughter, hinder not the honour of his design *All's Well* iii 6 44
Which to hinder Were in your love a whip to me . . *W. Tale* i 2 24
Despair not, madam.—Who shall hinder me? . . *Richard II.* ii 2 67
Lurking in our way To hinder our beginnings . . *Hen. V.* ii 2 187
Till then fair hope must hinder life's decay . . *3 Hen. VI.* iv 4 16
That no dissension hinder government . . . . iv 6 40
Oh, who shall hinder me to wail and weep? . . *Richard III.* ii 2 34
From your affairs I hinder you too long . . . *Hen. VIII.* v 1 54
Nor you, my brother, with your true sword drawn, Opposed to hinder me, should stop my way . . . *Troi. and Cres.* v 3 57
Let me not hinder, Cassius, your desires; I'll leave you . *J. Cæsar* i 2 30
Thyself art coming To see perform'd the dreaded act which thou So sought'st to hinder . . . . *Ant. and Cleo.* v 2 335

Hindered. The current, . . . being stopp'd, impatiently doth rage; But when his fair course is not hindered, He makes sweet music with the enamell'd stones . . . . *T. G. of Ver.* ii 7 27
Hindered by the sergeant, to tarry for the hoy Delay . *Com. of Errors* iv 3 39
I am sorry, sir, that I have hinder'd you . . . . v 1 1
It seems his sleeps were hinder'd by thy railing . . . v 1 71
Thou say'st his sports were hinder'd by thy brawls . . v 1 77
He hath disgraced me, and hindered me half a million . *Mer. of Venice* iii 1 57
If we may pass, we will; if we be hinder'd, We shall your tawny ground with your red blood Discolour . . . *Hen. V.* iii 6 169
Never desired It to be stirr'd; but oft have hinder'd, oft, The passages made toward it . . . . . *Hen. VIII.* ii 4 164

Hindering. You minimus, of hindering knot-grass made . *M. N. Dream* iii 2 329

Hindmost. 'Tis not his wont to be the hindmost man . *2 Hen. VI.* iii 1 2
They all rush by And leave you hindmost . . *Troi. and Cres.* iii 3 160

Hinge. Whose fever-weaken'd joints, Like strengthless hinges, buckle under life . . . . . . *2 Hen. IV.* i 1 141
Hinge thy knee, And let his very breath, whom thou'lt observe, Blow off thy cap . . . . . . *T. of Athens* iv 3 211
Lick absurd pomp, And crook the pregnant hinges of the knee *Hamlet* iii 2 66
That the probation bear no hinge nor loop To hang a doubt on *Othello* iii 3 365

Hint. It is a hint That wrings mine eyes to't . . *Tempest* i 2 134
Our hint of woe Is common . . . . . ii 1 3
Make them be strong and ready for this hint . *Coriolanus* iii 3 23
It was my hint to speak,—such was the process . *Othello* i 3 142
Upon this hint I spake: She loved me for the dangers I had pass'd . i 3 166
When the best hint was given him, he not took't . *Ant. and Cleo.* iii 4 9
Take the hint Which my despair proclaims . . . iii 11 18
This Posthumus, Most like a noble lord in love and one That had a royal lover, took his hint . . . . *Cymbeline* v 5 172

Hip. Which of your hips has the most profound sciatica? *Meas. for Meas.* i 2 58
An ell and three quarters will not measure her from hip to hip *C. of Er.* iii 2 113
No longer from head to foot than from hip to hip . . iii 2 116
A Spaniard from the hip upward . . . *Much Ado* iii 2 36
Hold their hips and laugh, And waxen in their mirth . *M. N. Dream* ii 1 55
If I can catch him once upon the hip, I will feed fat the ancient grudge I bear him. He hates our sacred nation . . *Mer. of Venice* i 3 47
Now, infidel, I have you on the hip . . . . iv 1 334
The beachy girdle of the ocean Too wide for Neptune's hips *2 Hen. IV.* iii 1 51
Their poor jades Lob down their heads, dropping the hides and hips *Hen. V.* iv 2 47
The oaks bear mast, the briers scarlet hips . *T. of Athens* iv 3 422
I'll have our Michael Cassio on the hip . . *Othello* ii 1 314

Hipparchus, my enfranched bondman, whom He may at pleasure whip, or hang, or torture . . . . *Ant. and Cleo.* iii 13 149

Hipped. His horse hipped with an old mothy saddle . *T. of Shrew* iii 2 49

Hippolyta. Fair Hippolyta, our nuptial hour Draws on apace *M. N. Dream* i 1 1
Hippolyta, I woo'd thee with my sword, And won thy love . i 1 16
Come, my Hippolyta: what cheer, my love? . . . i 1 122
How canst thou thus for shame, Titania, Glance at my credit with Hippolyta? . . . . ii 1 75
We'll hold a feast in great solemnity. Come, Hippolyta . iv 1 191

Hire. A ship you sent me to, to hire waftage . *Com. of Errors* iv 1 95
In such great letters as they write 'Here is good horse to hire' *M. Ado* i 1 268
Compromised That all the eanlings which were streak'd and pied Should fall as Jacob's hire . . . . . *Mer. of Venice* i 3 81
The thrifty hire I saved under your father . . *As Y. Like It* ii 3 39
May it be possible, that foreign hire Could out of thee extract one spark of evil That might annoy my finger? . . *Hen. V.* ii 2 100
Give thee thy hire and send thy soul to hell . *2 Hen. VI.* iii 2 225
Your country's fat shall pay your pains the hire . *Richard III.* v 3 258
A three-pence bow'd would hire me, Old as I am . *Hen. VIII.* ii 3 36
Like to a harvest-man that's task'd to mow Or all or lose his hire *Coriol.* i 3 40
Show them the unaching scars which I should hide, As if I had received them for the hire Of their breath only! . . . . ii 2 153

Hire. Better to starve, Than crave the hire which first we do deserve *Coriolanus* ii 3 121
Go hire me twenty cunning cooks.—You shall have none ill *R. and J.* iv 2 2
Get me ink and paper, And hire post-horses . . . v 1 26
Get thee gone, And hire those horses; I'll be with thee straight . v 1 33
O, this is hire and salary, not revenge . . *Hamlet* iii 3 79
There's earnest of thy service.—Let me hire him too . *Lear* i 4 105
With no worse nor better guard But with a knave of common hire *Othello* i 1 126
There, take thy hire; and all the fiends of hell Divide themselves between you!—Sir, be patient . . . *Cymbeline* ii 4 129

Hired. Who I believe was pack'd in all this wrong, Hired to it by your brother . . . . . . *Much Ado* v 1 309
His horses are bred better; . . . they are taught their manage, and to that end riders dearly hired . . . *As Y. Like It* i 1 14
They . . . Have hired me to undermine the duchess . *2 Hen. VI.* i 2 98
If you be hired for meed, go back again . . *Richard III.* i 4 234
Here is no use for gold.—The best and truest; For here it sleeps, and does no hired harm . . . *T. of Athens* iv 3 291
I cannot strike at wretched kerns, whose arms Are hired . *Macbeth* v 7 18
He is dead, Cæsar; Not by a public minister of justice, Nor by a hired knife . . . . . *Ant. and Cleo.* v 1 21
O slave, of no more trust Than love that's hired! . . v 2 155
To be partner'd With tomboys hired with that self exhibition Which your own coffers yield! . . . . *Cymbeline* i 6 122

Hiren. Down, down, dogs! down, faitors! Have we not Hiren here? *2 Hen. IV.* ii 4 173
Have we not Hiren here?—O' my word, captain, there's none such here ii 4 189

Hirtius. Where thou slew'st Hirtius and Pansa, consuls *Ant. and Cleo.* i 4 58

His. This mis-shapen knave, His mother was a witch . *Tempest* v 1 269
If it confess A natural guiltiness such as is his . *Meas. for Meas.* ii 2 139
In his blows Denied my house for his, me for his wife . *Com. of Errors* ii 2 161
And am arm'd To suffer, with a quietness of spirit, The very tyranny and rage of his . . . . *Mer. of Venice* iv 1 13
'Gainst the count his galleys I did some service . *T. Night* iii 3 26
One that fixes No bourn 'twixt his and mine . . *W. Tale* i 2 134
If my brother had my shape, And I had his, sir Robert's his, like him *K. John* i 1 139
That close aspect of his Does show the mood of a much troubled breast iv 2 72
Show me what a face I have, Since it is bankrupt of his majesty *Rich. II.* iv 1 267
'Tis with my mind As with the tide swell'd up unto his height *2 Hen. IV.* ii 3 63
Now in the rearward comes the duke and his . . *1 Hen. VI.* iii 3 33
And left us to the rage of France his sword . . . iv 6 3
Mars his idiot! do, rudeness; do, camel; do, do . *Troi. and Cres.* ii 1 58
By Mars his gauntlet, thanks! . . . . . iv 5 177
In characters as red as Mars his heart Inflamed with Venus . v 2 164
He does deny him, in respect of his, What charitable men afford to beggars.—Religion groans at it . . . *T. of Athens* iii 2 81
My life is run his compass . . . . . *J. Cæsar* v 3 25
Banquo smiles upon me, And points at them for his . *Macbeth* iv 1 124
They are not guilty, Since nature cannot choose his origin . *Hamlet* i 4 26
The ocean, overpeering of his list . . . . iv 5 99
And the heart Where mine his thoughts did kindle. *Ant. and Cleo.* v 1 46

Hiss. Adders who with cloven tongues Do hiss me into madness *Tempest* ii 2 14
If I do not act it, hiss me . . . . *Mer. Wives* iii 3 41
If any of the audience hiss, you may cry 'Well done, Hercules!' *L. L. L.* v 1 145
When roasted crabs hiss in the bowl. . . . . v 2 935
Whose issue Will hiss me to my grave . . . *W. Tale* i 2 189
Their music frightful as the serpent's hiss! . *2 Hen. VI.* iii 2 326
Who in contempt shall hiss at thee again. . . . iv 1 78
A most unjust knave; I will no more trust him when he leers than I will a serpent when he hisses . . . *Troi. and Cres.* v 1 98
My fear is this, Some galled goose of Winchester would hiss . v 10 55
Clap him and hiss him, according as he pleased and displeased them *J. Cæsar* i 2 261
What's the newest grief?—That of an hour's age doth hiss the speaker *Macbeth* iv 3 175

Hissed. And cut the winds, Who nothing hurt withal hiss'd him in scorn *Rom. and Jul.* i 1 119

Hissing hot,—think of that, Master Brook. *Mer. Wives* iii 5 124
A thousand hissing snakes, Ten thousand swelling toads *T. Andron.* ii 3 100
To have a thousand with red burning spits Come hissing in upon 'em *Lear* iii 6 17

Hist! Romeo, hist! O, for a falconer's voice! . *Rom. and Jul.* ii 2 159

Historical-pastoral, tragical-historical, tragical-comical-historical-pastoral, scene individable . . . . *Hamlet* ii 2 417

History. There is a kind of character in thy life, That to the observer doth thy history Fully unfold . . . *Meas. for Meas.* i 1 29
For aught that I could ever read, Could ever hear by tale or history, The course of true love never did run smooth . . *M. N. Dream* i 1 133
Last scene of all, That ends this strange eventful history *As Y. Like It* ii 7 164
It is a kind of history . . . . *T. of Shrew* Ind. 2 144
And what's her history?—A blank, my lord . . *T. Night* ii 4 112
Which is more Than history can pattern . . . *W. Tale* iii 2 37
There is a history in all men's lives . . . *2 Hen. IV.* iii 1 80
And keep no tell-tale to his memory That may repeat and history his loss iv 1 203
For the which supply, Admit me Chorus to this history . *Hen. V.* Prol. 32
Our history shall with full mouth Speak freely of our acts . . i 2 230
My breast can better brook thy dagger's point Than can my ears that tragic history . . . . . . *3 Hen. VI.* v 6 28
Wherein my soul recorded The history of all her secret thoughts *Rich. III.* iii 5 28
Brutus' tongue Hath almost ended his life's history . *J. Cæsar* v 5 40
The best actors in the world, either for tragedy, comedy, history *Hamlet* ii 2 416
Vouchsafe me a word with you.—Sir, a whole history . . iii 2 309
A tardiness in nature Which often leaves the history unspoke . *Lear* i 1 239
Of my redemption thence And portance in my travels' history . *Othello* i 3 139
An index and obscure prologue to the history of lust and foul thoughts ii 1 264
That man, who knows By history, report, or his own proof, What woman is, yea, what she cannot choose But must be . . . *Cymbeline* i 6 70
Sir, This paper is the history of my knowledge . . . iii 5 99
If I should tell my history, it would seem Like lies. . *Pericles* v 1 119

Hit. I can never hit on's name . . . . *Mer. Wives* iii 2 24
Sweet mistress,—what your name is else, I know not, Nor by what wonder you do hit of mine . . . . *Com. of Errors* iii 2 30
He that hits me, let him be clapped on the shoulder . *Much Ado* i 1 260
Blunt as the fencer's foils, which hit, but hurt not . . v 2 14
She strikes at the brow.—But she herself is hit lower: have I hit her now? . . . . *L. L. Lost* iv 1 120
Thou canst not hit it, hit it, hit it, Thou canst not hit it, my good man iv 1 127
How both did fit it!—A mark marvellous well shot, for they both did hit it . . . . iv 1 132
Indeed, a' must shoot nearer, or he'll ne'er hit the clout . . iv 1 136

Hit. Flower of this purple dye, Hit with Cupid's archery . *M. N. Dream* iii 2 103
'Twill be a hard way to hit . . . . *Mer. of Venice* ii 2 48
Have all his ventures fail'd? What, not one hit? . . . . iii 2 270
He that a fool doth very wisely hit Doth very foolishly, although he smart, Not to seem senseless . . . *As Y. Like It* ii 7 53
A join'd-stool.—Thou hast hit it: come, sit on me . *T. of Shrew* ii 1 199
This bird you aim'd at, though you hit her not . . . v 2 50
Tranio hits you now.—I thank thee for that gird . . . v 2 57
Confess, confess hath he not hit you here?—A' has a little gall'd me . v 2 59
'Twas I won the wager, though you hit the white . . . v 2 186
Oft expectation fails and most oft there Where most it promises, and oft it hits Where hope is coldest and despair most fits . *All's Well* ii 1 146
O, for a stone-bow, to hit him in the eye! . . . . *T. Night* ii 5 51
As surely as your feet hit the ground they step on . . . iii 4 306
Your father's image is so hit in you . . . *W. Tale* v 1 127
You have hit it.—So did he never the sparrow . . . *1 Hen. IV.* ii 4 381
Thou sickly quoif! Thou art a guard too wanton for the head Which princes, flesh'd with conquest, aim to hit . *2 Hen. IV.* i 1 149
Claim the crown, For that's the golden mark I seek to hit *2 Hen. VI.* i 1 243
Thou hast hit it; for there's no better sign of a brave mind than a hard hand . . . . iv 2 21
Though the edge hath something hit ourselves . . *3 Hen. VI.* ii 2 166
Therefore level not to hit their lives . . . *Richard III.* iv 4 202
I think you have hit the mark . . . . *Hen. VIII.* ii 1 165
If I spared any That had a head to hit, either young or old, He or she . v 4 24
That fire-drake did I hit three times on the head . . . . v 4 46
I missed the meteor once, and hit that woman; who cried out 'Clubs!' v 4 52
If I cannot ward what I would not have hit, I can watch you for telling how I took the blow . . . . . *Troi. and Cres.* i 2 293
As to prenominate in nice conjecture Where thou wilt hit me dead . iv 5 251
Thou hast hit it.—Would you had hit it too! . . . *T. Andron.* ii 1 97
A right fair mark, fair coz, is soonest hit.—Well, in that hit you miss: she'll not be hit With Cupid's arrow . . . . *Rom. and Jul.* i 1 213
If love be blind, love cannot hit the mark . . . . . ii 1 33
Then here I hit it right, Our Romeo hath not been in bed to-night . ii 3 41
To bow in the hams.—Meaning, to court'sy.—Thou hast most kindly hit it . . . . ii 4 59
An envious thrust from Tybalt hit the life Of stout Mercutio . . iii 1 173
Why, this hits right; I dreamt of a silver basin and ewer *T. of Athens* iii 1 5
If thou couldst please me with speaking to me, thou mightst have hit upon it here . . . . iv 3 351
My former speeches have but hit your thoughts . . *Macbeth* iii 6 1
A happiness that often madness hits on . . . . *Hamlet* ii 2 213
His poison'd shot may miss our name, And hit the woundless air . . iv 1 44
The king, sir, hath laid, that in a dozen passes between yourself and him, he shall not exceed you three hits . . . . . v 2 174
I will win for him an I can; if not, I will gain nothing but my shame and the odd hits . . . . v 2 185
If Hamlet give the first or second hit, Or quit in answer of the third exchange, Let all the battlements their ordnance fire . . . v 2 279
A hit, a very palpable hit . . . . v 2 292
Another hit; what say you?—A touch, a touch, I do confess . . v 2 296
My lord, I'll hit him now.—I do not think't . . . . . v 2 306
Pray you, let's hit together . . . . . . *Lear* i 1 308
From the barge A strange invisible perfume hits the sense Of the adjacent wharfs . . . . . . *Ant. and Cleo.* ii 2 217
Was there ever man had such luck! when I kissed the jack, upon an up-cast to be hit away! . . . . *Cymbeline* ii 1 3
Their thoughts do hit The roofs of palaces . . . . . iii 3 83
I draw the sword myself: take it, and hit The innocent mansion of my love . . . . iii 4 69
A well-experienced archer hits the mark His eye doth level at *Pericles* i 1 164
Danger, which I fear'd, is at Antioch, Whose arm seems far too short to hit me here . . . . i 2 8
A delicate odour.—As ever hit my nostril . . . . . iii 2 62
Hit it. Shall I come upon thee with an old saying, that was a man when King Pepin of France was a little boy, as touching the hit it?—So I may answer thee with one as old, that was a woman when Queen Guinover of Britain was a little wench, as touching the hit it *L. L. L.* iv 1 123
Hit or miss, Our project's life this shape of sense assumes *Troi. and Cres.* i 3 384
Hither. If opportunity and humblest suit Cannot attain it, why, then, —hark you hither! . . . . *Mer. Wives* iii 4 21
Told me of their stealth, Of this their purpose hither *M. N. Dream* iv 1 166
On a moderate pace I have since arrived but hither . *T. Night* ii 2 4
'Tis catching hither, even to our camp . . . *1 Hen. IV.* iv 1 30
Methinks I hear hither your husband's drum . . *Coriolanus* i 3 32
Hitherto. England, from Trent and Severn hitherto, By south and east is to my part assign'd . . . . . *1 Hen. IV.* iii 1 74
Your eyes, which hitherto have borne in them . . . The fatal balls *Hen V.* v 2 15
We have been guided by thee hitherto . . . . *1 Hen. VI.* iii 3 9
All hitherto goes well . . . . *3 Hen. VI.* iv 2 1
Hitherto, in all the progress Both of my life and office *Hen. VIII.* v 3 32
I pray you all, If you have hitherto conceal'd this sight, Let it be ten-able in your silence still . . . . . . *Hamlet* i 2 247
And hitherto doth love on fortune tend . . . . . iii 2 216
You are the lord of duty; I am hitherto your daughter . *Othello* i 3 185
Hitherward. The Dauphin is preparing hitherward . . *K. John* v 7 59
Westmoreland, seven thousand strong, Is marching hitherwards *1 Hen. IV.* iv 1 89
The king himself in person is set forth, Or hitherwards intended speedily . . . . iv 1 92
A mighty power Of gallowglasses and stout kerns Is marching hither-ward . . . . *2 Hen. VI.* iv 9 27
By this at Dunsmore, marching hitherward . . . *3 Hen. VI.* v 1 3
Some parcels of their power are forth already, And only hitherward *Coriolanus* i 2 33
The British powers are marching hitherward.—'Tis known before . *Lear* iv 4 21
A portly sail of ships make hitherward . . . . . *Pericles* i 4 61
Hitting. What worst, as oft, Hitting a grosser quality, is cried up For our best act . . . . *Hen. VIII.* i 2 84
Hitting Each object with a joy . . . . . *Cymbeline* v 5 395
Hive. Drones hive not with me . . . . . *Mer. of Venice* ii 5 48
Wish too, Since I nor wax nor honey can bring home, I quickly were dissolved from my hive, To give some labourers room *All's Well* i 2 66
We bring it to the hive, and, like the bees, Are murdered for our pains *2 Hen. IV.* iv 5 78
So bees with smoke and doves with noisome stench Are from their hives and houses driven away . . . . . . *1 Hen. VI.* i 5 24
Like an angry hive of bees That want their leader, scatter *2 Hen. VI.* iii 2 125
When that the general is not like the hive To whom the foragers shall all repair, What honey is expected? . . . *Troi. and Cres.* i 3 81

Ho. O ho, O ho! would't had been done! . . . . *Tempest* i 2 349
Ho, ho, ho! Coward, why comest thou not? . . . *M. N. Dream* iii 2 421
Sola, sola! wo ha, ho! sola, sola! . . . . *Mer. of Venice* v 1 39
With a hey, and a ho, and a hey nonino . . . *As Y. Like It* v 3 18
With hey, ho, the wind and the rain . . *T. Night* v 1 399; *Lear* iii 2 75
With, ho! such bugs and goblins in my life . . . . *Hamlet* v 2 22
Ho, ho, ho! Now the witch take me, if I meant it thus! *Ant. and Cleo.* iv 2 36
Hoar. No hare, sir; unless a hare, sir, in a lenten pie, that is something stale and hoar ere it be spent . . . . *Rom. and Jul.* ii 4 139
An old hare hoar, And an old hare hoar, Is very good meat in lent: But a hare that is hoar Is too much for a score, When it hoars ere it be spent . . . . ii 4 141
This yellow slave [gold] Will . . . Make the hoar leprosy adored *T. of A.* iv 3 35
Hoar the flamen, That scolds against the quality of flesh . . iv 3 155
There is a willow grows aslant a brook, That shows his hoar leaves in the glassy stream . . . . *Hamlet* iv 7 168
Hoard. A venturous fairy that shall seek The squirrel's hoard *M. N. D.* iv 1 40
To what purpose dost thou hoard thy words? . . . *Richard II.* i 3 253
And learning a mere hoard of gold kept by a devil . *2 Hen. IV.* iv 3 125
Hoarded. Or any groat I hoarded to my use . . *2 Hen. VI.* iii 1 113
The hoarded plague o' the gods Requite your love! . *Coriolanus* iv 2 11
Hoarding. See thou shake the bags Of hoarding abbots . *K. John* iii 3 8
And happy always was it for that son Whose father for his hoarding went to hell . . . . *3 Hen. VI.* ii 2 48
Hoarse. Without hawking or spitting or saying we are hoarse *As Y. L. It* v 3 13
Warwick is hoarse with calling thee to arms . . . *2 Hen. VI.* v 2 7
Bondage is hoarse, and may not speak aloud . . *Rom. and Jul.* ii 2 161
Else would I tear the cave where Echo lies, And make her airy tongue more hoarse than mine, With repetition of my Romeo's name . . ii 2 163
The raven himself is hoarse That croaks the fatal entrance of Duncan Under my battlements . . . . *Macbeth* i 5 39
Hoary-headed frosts Fall in the fresh lap of the crimson rose *M. N. Dream* ii 1 107
Hob. To beg of Hob and Dick, that do appear, Their needless vouches *Coriolanus* ii 3 123
Hobbididance, prince of dumbness; Mahu, of stealing . . *Lear* iv 1 62
Hobby-horse. Which these hobby-horses must not hear . *Much Ado* iii 2 75
But O,—but O,— 'The hobby-horse is forgot.'—Callest thou my love 'hobby-horse'?—No, master; the hobby-horse is but a colt, and your love perhaps a hackney . . . . *L. L. Lost* iii 1 30
Then say My wife's a hobby-horse, deserves a name As rank . *W. Tale* i 2 276
Else shall he suffer not thinking on, with the hobby-horse, whose epitaph is 'For, O, for, O, the hobby-horse is forgot' . . . *Hamlet* iii 2 143
There; give it your hobby-horse . . . . . *Othello* iv 1 160
Hobgoblin. Crier Hobgoblin, make the fairy oyes . *Mer. Wives* v 5 45
Those that Hobgoblin call you and sweet Puck . *M. N. Dream* ii 1 40
Hobnail. As they buy hob-nails, by the hundreds . . *1 Hen. IV.* ii 4 398
I beseech God on my knees thou mayst be turned to hobnails *2 Hen. VI.* iv 10 63
Hob, nob, is his word; give't or take't . . . . *T. Night* iii 4 262
Hoc. Singulariter, nominativo, hic, hæc, hoc . . . *Mer. Wives* iv 1 43
Hodge-pudding. What, a hodge-pudding? a bag of flax? . . . v 5 159
Hog. Nominativo, hig, hag, hog; pray you, mark: genitivo, hujus . iv 1 44
Accusativo, hung, hang, hog.—'Hang-hog' is Latin for bacon . . iv 1 49
Sometime a hound, A hog, a headless bear, sometime a fire *M. N. Dream* iii 1 112
Neigh, and bark, and grunt, and roar, and burn, Like horse, hound, hog, bear, fire, at every turn . . . . iii 1 114
This making of Christians will raise the price of hogs . *Mer. of Venice* iii 5 26
Shall I keep your hogs and eat husks with them? . . *As Y. Like It* i 1 40
Thou elvish-mark'd, abortive, rooting hog! . . . *Richard III.* i 3 228
Hog in sloth, fox in stealth, wolf in greediness, dog in madness . *Lear* iii 4 95
Hogshead. Help to bear this away where my hogshead of wine is *Tempest* iv 1 252
He that is likest to a hogshead.—Piercing a hogshead! . . *L. L. Lost* iv 2 88
Swallowed with yest and froth, as you'ld thrust a cork into a hogshead *W. Tale* iii 3 95
Three or four loggerheads amongst three or four score hogsheads *1 Hen. IV.* ii 4 5
Can a weak empty vessel bear such a huge full hogshead? . *2 Hen. IV.* ii 4 68
Hoise. We'll quickly hoise Duke Humphrey from his seat . *2 Hen. VI.* i 1 169
Hoised. He, mistrusting them, Hoised sail and made away *Richard III.* iv 4 529
Hoist. There they hoist us, To cry to the sea that roar'd to us *Tempest* i 2 148
Will you hoist sail, sir? here lies your way . . . . *T. Night* i 5 215
'Tis the sport to have the enginer Hoist with his own petar . *Hamlet* iii 4 207
The breese upon her, like a cow in June, Hoists sails and flies *A. and C.* iii 10 15
Let him take thee, And hoist thee up to the shouting plebeians . . iv 12 34
Shall they hoist me up And show me to the shouting varletry? . . v 2 55
Hoisted sail and put to sea to-day . . . . *Com. of Errors* v 1 21
Holborn. When I was last in Holborn, I saw good strawberries *Rich. III.* iii 4 33
Hold. Our garments . . . hold notwithstanding their freshness *Tempest* ii 1 62
I do now let loose my opinion; hold it no longer . . . . ii 2 36
His mistress Did hold his eyes lock'd in her crystal looks *T. G. of Ver.* ii 4 89
Nay, sure, I think she holds them prisoners still . . . . ii 4 92
Valentine I'll hold an enemy, Aiming at Silvia as a sweeter friend . ii 6 29
The good conceit I hold of thee . . . . iii 2 17
Three things that women highly hold in hate . . . . . iii 2 33
There, hold! I will not look upon your master's lines . . . iv 4 132
Do not name Silvia thine; if once again, Verona shall not hold thee . v 4 129
I care not for her, I: I hold him but a fool that will endanger His body for a girl that loves him not . . . . v 4 133
Divers philosophers hold that the lips is parcel of the mouth *Mer. Wives* i 1 236
Hold, sirrah, bear you these letters tightly . . . . . . i 3 88
For gourd and fullam holds, And high and low beguiles the rich and poor i 3 94
How Falstaff, varlet vile, His dove will prove, his gold will hold . . i 3 107
Hold, there's money for thee; let me have thy voice in my behalf . i 4 166
Well said, brazen-face! hold it out. Come forth, sirrah! . . iv 2 141
Prithee, no more prattling; go. I'll hold. This is the third time . v 1 1
Hold therefore, Angelo:—In our remove be thou at full ourself *M. for M.* i 1 43
I hold you as a thing ensky'd and sainted . . . . . . i 4 34
If this law hold in Vienna ten year, I'll rent the fairest house in it . ii 1 254
Put them in secret holds, both Barnardine and Claudio . . . iv 3 91
And hold you ever to our special drift . . . . . . iv 5 4
Rely upon it till my tale be heard, And hold no longer out . . v 1 371
No longer session hold upon my shame . . . . . . v 1 376
Hold, take thou that, and that.—Hold, sir, for God's sake! *Com. of Er.* ii 2 23
I hold your dainties cheap, sir, and your welcome dear . . . iii 1 21
I cannot, nor I will not, hold me still . . . . . . iv 2 17
Hold, hurt him not, for God's sake! he is mad. Some get within . v 1 33
Rather than hold three words' conference with this harpy . *Much Ado* ii 1 278
Pray thee, come; Or, if thou wilt hold longer argument, Do it in notes ii 3 55
He hath ta'en the infection: hold it up . . . . . . ii 3 126
The sport will be, when they hold one an opinion of another's dotage . ii 3 224
I think he holds you well, and in dearness of heart . . . . iii 2 101

Hold. And in her eye there hath appear'd a fire, To burn the errors that these princes hold . . . . *Much Ado* iv 1 165
Hold you content. What, man! I know them, yea, And what they weigh . . . . v 1 92
And hold fair friendship with his majesty . . . *L. L. Lost* ii 1 141
Do not curst wives hold that self-sovereignty Only for praise sake? . iv 1 36
The allusion holds in the exchange.—'Tis true indeed . iv 2 42; 43; 45; 46
Ah, never faith could hold, if not to beauty vow'd! . . . iv 2 110
I never knew man hold vile stuff so dear . . . . . iv 3 276
Hold, there is the very remuneration I had of thy master . . v 1 75
If you deny to dance, let's hold more chat.—In private, then . v 2 228
This field shall hold me; and so hold your vow . . . . v 2 345
Help, hold his brows! he'll swoon! Why look you pale? . . . v 2 392
Can any face of brass hold longer out? . . . . . . v 2 395
He swore that he did hold me dear As precious eyesight . . . v 2 444
Your lion, that holds his poll-axe sitting on a close-stool . . v 2 580
I have vowed to Jaquenetta to hold the plough for her sweet love three years . . . . v 2 893
At the duke's oak we meet.—Enough; hold or cut bow-strings *M. N. D.* i 2 114
Then the whole quire hold their hips and laugh, And waxen in their mirth ii 1 55
Apollo flies, and Daphne holds the chase; The dove pursues the griffin ii 1 231
Let him hold his fingers thus, and through that cranny shall Pyramus and Thisby whisper . . . . iii 1 72
Hold the sweet jest up: This sport, well carried, shall be chronicled . iii 2 239
I would I had your bond, for I perceive A weak bond holds you . iii 2 268
Now she holds me not; Now follow, if thou darest . . . . iii 2 335
Three and three, We'll hold a feast in great solemnity . . . iv 1 190
One sees more devils than vast hell can hold, That is, the madman . v 1 9
A fortnight hold we this solemnity, In nightly revels . . . v 1 376
I hold the world but as the world, Gratiano . . *Mer. of Venice* i 1 77
Had I but the means To hold a rival place with one of them! . . i 1 174
Hold here, take this: tell gentle Jessica I will not fail her . . ii 4 20
That ever holds: who riseth from a feast With that keen appetite that he sits down? . . . . ii 6 8
What, must I hold a candle to my shames? . . . . . ii 6 41
If you be well pleased with this And hold your fortune for your bliss . iii 2 137
I am sure the duke Will never grant this forfeiture to hold . . iii 3 25
I'll hold thee any wager, . . . I'll prove the prettier fellow of the two iii 4 62
Are you acquainted with the difference That holds this present question in the court? . . . . iv 1 172
The law hath yet another hold on you . . . . . . iv 1 347
Be comfortable; hold death awhile at the arm's end . *As Y. Like It* ii 6 10
We shall be flouting; we cannot hold . . . . . . v 1 14
If truth holds true contents . . . . v 4 136
You may go to the devil's dam: your gifts are so good, here's none will hold you . . . . *T. of Shrew* i 1 107
Is it possible That love should of a sudden take such hold? . . i 1 152
He hath the jewel of my life in hold . . . . . . i 2 119
She'll sooner prove a soldier: Iron may hold with her, but never lutes ii 1 147
I hold you a penny, A horse and a man Is more than one . . iii 2 85
What, no man at door To hold my stirrup nor to take my horse! . iv 1 124
Thou'rt a tall fellow: hold thee that to drink . . . . . iv 4 17
'Tis thought your deer does hold you at a bay . . . . v 2 56
He that so generally is at all times good must of necessity hold his virtue to you . . . . *All's Well* i 1 9
You must hold the credit of your father . . . . . . i 1 88
I have a desire to hold my acquaintance with thee . . . . ii 3 240
Will this capriccio hold in thee? art sure? . . . . . ii 3 310
At my course, Which holds not colour with the time . . . ii 5 64
If there be breadth enough in the world, I will hold a long distance . iii 2 27
The fellow has a deal of that too much, Which holds him much to have iii 2 93
I am the caitiff that do hold him to't . . . . . . iii 2 117
I will be gone; My being here it is that holds thee hence . . iii 2 126
If your lordship find him not a hilding, hold me no more in your respect iii 6 4
This ring he holds In most rich choice . . . . . . iii 7 25
Of that I have made a bold charter; but I thank my God it holds yet iv 5 98
I am resolved on two points.—That if one break, the other will hold *T. N.* i 5 26
Who of my people hold him in delay? . . . . . . i 5 112
I hold the olive in my hand; my words are as full of peace as matter . i 5 225
Desire him not to flatter with his lord, Nor hold him up with hopes . i 5 323
Let thy love be younger than thyself, Or thy affection cannot hold the bent . . . . ii 4 38
The parts that fortune hath bestow'd upon her, Tell her, I hold as giddily as fortune . . . . ii 4 87
No woman's heart So big, to hold so much; they lack retention . . ii 4 99
I'll no more with thee. Hold, there's expenses for thee . . . iii 1 49
Hold, sir, here's my purse. In the south suburbs, at the Elephant . iii 3 38
If you hold your life at any price, betake you to your guard . . iii 4 252
He will not now be pacified: Fabian can scarce hold him yonder . iii 4 310
Hold, sir, or I'll throw your dagger o'er the house . . . . iv 1 30
Hold, Toby; on thy life I charge thee, hold! . . . . . iv 1 47
Thou shalt hold the opinion of Pythagoras ere I will allow of thy wits . iv 2 62
O, do not swear! Hold little faith, though thou hast too much fear . v 1 174
He holds Belzebub at the staves's end as well as a man in his case may do v 1 291
And many a man there is, even at this present, Now while I speak this, holds his wife by the arm, That little thinks she has been sluiced *W. Tale* i 2 193
You had much ado to make his anchor hold . . . . . . i 2 213
If the springe hold, the cock's mine . . . . iv 3 36
Your resolution cannot hold, when 'tis Opposed, as it must be . . iv 4 36
Five justices' hands at it, and witnesses more than my pack will hold . iv 4 289
As good reason The father . . . should hold some counsel In such a business . . . . iv 4 420
We'll bar thee from succession; Not hold thee of our blood, no, not our kin . . . . iv 4 441
I am put to sea With her whom here I cannot hold on shore . . iv 4 510
What course I mean to hold Shall nothing benefit your knowledge . iv 4 513
Lo, in his right hand, whose protection Is most divinely vow'd upon the right Of him it holds, stands young Plantagenet . . *K. John* ii 1 238
For him, and in his right, we hold this town . . . . . ii 1 268
Till you compound whose right is worthiest, We for the worthiest hold the right from both . . . . ii 1 282
While they weigh so even, We hold our town for neither, yet for both ii 1 333
Why holds thine eye that lamentable rheum? . . . . . iii 1 22
My grief's so great That no supporter but the huge firm earth Can hold it up . . . . iii 1 73
He that holds his kingdom holds the law . . . . . . iii 1 188
France, thou mayst hold a serpent by the tongue, A chafed lion by the mortal paw, A fasting tiger safer by the tooth, Than keep in peace that hand which thou dost hold . . . . iii 1 258

Hold. I having hold of both, They whirl asunder and dismember me *K. John* iii 1 329
You hold too heinous a respect of grief . . . . . . iii 4 90
He that stands upon a slippery place Makes nice of no vile hold to stay him up . . . . iii 4 138
May be he will not touch young Arthur's life, But hold himself safe in his prisonment . . . . iii 4 161
If what in rest you have in right you hold . . . . . iv 2 55
We cannot hold mortality's strong hand . . . . . . iv 2 82
That blood which owed the breadth of all this isle, Three foot of it doth hold . . . . iv 2 100
We hold our time too precious to be spent With such a brabbler . v 2 161
Which, in their throng and press to that last hold, Confound themselves v 7 19
My heart hath one poor string to stay it by, Which holds but till thy news be uttered . . . . v 7 56
Who can hold a fire in his hand By thinking on the frosty Caucasus? *Richard II.* i 3 294
He loves you, on my life, and holds you dear As Harry . . . ii 1 143
Bid her send me presently a thousand pound: Hold, take my ring . ii 2 92
The weeds which his broad-spreading leaves did shelter, That seem'd in eating him to hold him up . . . . iii 4 51
King Richard, he is in the mighty hold Of Bolingbroke . . . iii 4 83
What news from Oxford? hold those justs and triumphs? . . . v 2 52
On Wednesday next our council we Will hold at Windsor . 1 *Hen. IV.* i 1 104
Thou sayest well, and it holds well too . . . . . . i 2 34
For I shall never hold that man my friend Whose tongue shall ask me for one penny cost . . . . i 3 90
Shall happily meet, To bear our fortunes in our own strong arms, Which now we hold at much uncertainty . . . . . . i 3 299
It is like, if there come a hot June and this civil buffeting hold . ii 4 397
O, the father, how he holds his countenance! . . . . . ii 4 432
Trace me in the tedious ways of art And hold me pace in deep experiments . . . . iii 1 49
Shall I tell you, cousin? He holds your temper in a high respect . iii 1 170
Could . . . Such barren pleasures . . . hold their level with thy princely heart? . . . . iii 2 17
Let me wonder, Harry, At thy affections, which do hold a wing Quite from the flight of all thy ancestors . . . . iii 2 30
Whose . . . great name in arms Holds from all soldiers chief majority iii 2 109
I hold as little counsel with weak fear As you, my lord . . . iv 3 11
I saw him hold Lord Percy at the point With lustier maintenance . v 4 21
This worm-eaten hold of ragged stone . . . . 2 *Hen. IV.* Ind. 35
Master Fang, hold him sure: good Master Snare, let him not 'scape . ii 1 27
I do allow this wen to be as familiar with me as my dog; and he holds his place . . . . ii 2 116
Never, O never, do his ghost the wrong To hold your honour more precise and nice With others than with him! . . . . . ii 3 40
But many thousand reasons hold me back . . . . . . ii 3 66
You have not seen a hulk better stuffed in the hold . . . . ii 4 70
Hold hook and line, say I. Down, down, dogs! down, faitors! . ii 4 171
Like an offensive wife That hath enraged him on to offer strokes, As he is striking, holds his infant up . . . . iv 1 212
His power, like to a fangless lion, May offer, but not hold . . iv 1 219
Crowd us and crush us to this monstrous form, To hold our safety up iv 2 35
And heir from heir shall hold this quarrel up . . . . . iv 2 48
How many nobles then should hold their places! . . . . v 2 17
Can this cockpit hold The vasty fields of France? . . . *Hen. V.* Prol. 11
All appear To hold in right and title of the female . . . . i 2 89
This grace of kings must die, If hell and treason hold their promises ii Prol. 29
I have, and I will hold, the quondam Quickly For the only she . ii 1 82
What rein can hold licentious wickedness, When down the hill he holds his fierce career? . . . . iii 3 22
And hold their manhoods cheap . . . . iv 3 66
And with his cap in hand, Like a base pandar, hold the chamber-door iv 5 14
Hold, there is twelve pence for you; and I pray you to serve God . iv 8 67
On allegiance to ourself, To hold your slaughtering hands . 1 *Hen. VI.* i 1 87
O, hold me not with silence over-long! . . . . . . v 3 13
Nor hold the sceptre in his childish fist . . . 2 *Hen. VI.* i 1 245
Thus got the house of Lancaster the crown.—Which now they hold by force . . . . ii 2 30
Hold, Peter, hold! I confess, I confess treason . . . . ii 3 96
He'll wrest the sense and hold us here all day . . . . . iii 1 186
The labouring heart; Who, in the conflict that it holds with death . iii 2 164
Thereby is England mained, and fain to go with a staff, but that my puissance holds it up . . . . iv 2 173
Men shall hold of me in capite . . . . iv 7 131
Here is a hand to hold a sceptre up . . . . v 1 102
Hold, Warwick, seek thee out some other chase . . . . . v 2 14
The queen this day here holds her parliament . . . 3 *Hen. VI.* i 1 35
Fortify your hold, my lord.—Ay, with my sword . . . . i 2 52
Hold, valiant Clifford! for a thousand causes I would prolong awhile the traitor's life . . . . i 4 51
A crown for York! and, lords, bow low to him: Hold you his hands, whilst I do set it on . . . . i 4 95
Northumberland, I hold thee reverently. Break off the parley . . ii 2 109
Away! for death doth hold us in pursuit . . . . . . ii 5 127
But if you mind to hold your true obedience, Give me assurance . iv 1 140
Both Dukes of Somerset Have sold their lives unto the house of York; And thou shalt be the third, if this sword hold . . . . . v 1 75
They do hold their course toward Tewksbury . . . . . v 3 19
Hold, Richard, hold; for we have done too much . . . . v 5 43
I can no longer hold me patient. Hear me, you wrangling pirates! *Richard III.* i 3 157
I hope my holy humour will change; 'twas wont to hold me but while one would tell twenty . . . . i 4 121
He holds vengeance in his hands, To hurl upon their heads . . i 4 204
Gloucester hates you.—O, no, he loves me, and he holds me dear . i 4 239
If any here, By false intelligence, or wrong surmise, Hold me a foe . ii 1 55
O God, I fear thy justice will take hold On me, and you, and mine, and yours for this! . . . . ii 1 131
Doth this news hold of good King Edward's death?—Ay, sir, it is too true ii 3 7
The saying did not hold In him that did object the same to thee . ii 4 16
We to-morrow hold divided councils . . . . iii 1 179
I hold my life as dear as you do yours; And never in my life, I do protest, Was it more precious to me than 'tis now . . . . iii 2 80
And I in better state than e'er I was.—God hold it, to your honour's good content! . . . . iii 2 107
You have no cause to hold my friendship doubtful . . . . iv 4 493
That in the sty of this most bloody boar My son George Stanley is frank'd up in hold . . . . iv 5 3

Hold. For when they hold em, you would swear directly Their very noses had been counsellors To Pepin . . . . . *Hen. VIII.* i 3 8
Let me have such a bowl may hold my thanks, And save me so much talking . . . i 4 39
Yot hold a fair assembly ; you do well, lord : You are a churchman i 4 87
Whom, yet once more, I hold my most malicious foe . . . . ii 4 83
And all the fellowship I hold now with him Is only my obedience . iii 1 121
His grace of Canterbury ; Who holds his state at door, 'mongst pursuivants . . . . v 2 24
Let heaven Witness, how dear I hold this confirmation . . . v 3 174
I'll find A Marshalsea shall hold ye play these two months . . . v 4 90
All the best men are ours ; for 'tis ill hap, If they hold when their ladies bid 'em clap . . . . Epil. 14
Yet hold I off. Women are angels, wooing : Things won are done ; joy's soul lies in the doing . . . . . . *Troi. and Cres.* i 2 312
If there be one . . . That holds his honour higher than his ease . i 3 266
Has not so much wit— Nay, I must hold you . . . . . ii 1 86
It holds his estimate and dignity As well wherein 'tis precious of itself As in the prizer . . . . ii 2 54
Imagined worth Holds in his blood such swoln and hot discourse . . ii 3 183
He holds you well, and will be led At your request a little from himself ii 3 190
Shall he be worshipp'd Of that we hold an idol more than he? . ii 3 199
Seal it ; I'll be the witness. Here I hold your hand, here my cousin's iii 2 205
Troy holds him very dear . . . . iii 3 19
We in silence hold this virtue well, We'll but commend what we intend to sell . . . . iv 1 77
I prithee, do not hold me to mine oath . . . . . v 2 26
Good-night.—Hold, patience !—How now, Trojan ! . . . . v 2 29
It is the purpose that makes strong the vow ; But vows to every purpose must not hold . . . . v 3 24
Lay hold upon him, Priam, hold him fast : He is thy crutch . . v 3 59
Hold thy whore, Grecian !—now for thy whore, Trojan ! . . . v 4 25
I wish no better Than have him hold that purpose . . . *Coriolanus* ii 1 256
Peace, peace, peace ! Stay, hold, peace !—What is about to be? . . iii 1 188
Humble as the ripest mulberry That will not hold the handling . . iii 2 80
If you do hold the same intent wherein You wish'd us parties, we'll deliver you Of your great danger . . . . v 6 13
Hold, hold, hold, hold !—My noble masters, hear me speak . . . v 6 132
In this match I hold me highly honour'd of your grace . . *T. Andron.* i 1 245
Thou shalt not sigh, nor hold thy stumps to heaven . . . iii 2 42
Hold, hold ; meanwhile here's money for thy charges . . . iv 3 105
Who, when he knows thou art the empress' babe, Will hold thee dearly v 1 36
For that I know An idiot holds his bauble for a god . . . . v 1 79
Whilst I at a banquet hold him sure, I'll find some cunning practice . v 2 76
Whilst that Lavinia 'tween her stumps doth hold The basin . . v 2 183
Hold me not, let me go.—Thou shalt not stir a foot *Rom. and Jul.* i 1 86
This night I hold an old accustom'd feast . . . . . i 2 20
I tell you, he that can lay hold of her Shall have the chinks . . i 5 118
For stony limits cannot hold love out . . . . . . ii 2 67
The prince expressly hath Forbidden bandying in Verona streets : Hold, Tybalt ! . . . . iii 1 93
Romeo he cries aloud, 'Hold, friends ! friends, part !' . . . iii 1 170
Hold thy desperate hand : Art thou a man? thy form cries out thou art iii 3 108
Hold, daughter : I do spy a kind of hope . . . . . iv 1 68
Hold, then ; go home, be merry, give consent To marry Paris . . iv 1 89
Hold ; get you gone, be strong and prosperous In this resolve . . iv 1 122
Hold, take these keys, and fetch more spices, nurse . . . iv 4 1
I see that thou art poor : Hold, there is forty ducats . . . v 1 59
We found him in the churchyard.—Hold him in safety . . . v 3 183
No levell'd malice Infects one comma in the course I hold *T. of Athens* i 1 48
My estate deserves an heir more raised Than one which holds a trencher i 1 120
You take us even at the best.—'Faith, for the worst is filthy ; and would not hold taking . . . . i 2 159
Still in motion Of raging waste? It cannot hold ; it will not . . ii 1 4
It cannot hold ; no reason Can found his state in safety . . . ii 1 12
Yea, 'gainst the authority of manners, pray'd you To hold your hand more close . . . . ii 2 148
Will't hold ! will't hold !—It does : but time will—and so— I do conceive iii 6 70
Does the rumour hold for true, that he's so full of gold? . . v 1 4
If you know That I profess myself in banqueting To all the rout, then hold me dangerous . . . . *J. Cæsar* i 2 78
Wherefore do you hold me here so long? What is it that you would impart? . . . . i 2 83
Dine with me to-morrow?—Ay, if I be alive and your mind hold . . i 2 295
Writings all tending to the great opinion That Rome holds of his name i 2 323
The persuasion of his augurers May hold him from the Capitol to-day . ii 1 201
And every one doth shine, But there's but one in all doth hold his place iii 1 65
I do know but one That unassailable holds on his rank . . . . iii 1 69
Thou shalt sleep again ; I will not hold thee long . . . . iv 3 265
Thou vanishest : Ill spirit, I would hold more talk with thee . . iv 3 289
I prithee, Hold thou my sword-hilts, whilst I run on it . . . v 5 28
Hold then my sword, and turn away thy face, While I do run upon it . v 5 47
Let me infold thee And hold thee to my heart . . . . *Macbeth* i 4 32
Nor heaven peep through the blanket of the dark, To cry 'Hold, hold !' i 5 55
Hold, take my sword. There's husbandry in heaven ; Their candles are all out . . . . ii 1 4
To-night we hold a solemn supper, sir, And I'll request your presence'. iii 1 14
The son of Duncan, From whom this tyrant holds the due of birth . iii 6 25
Advise him to a caution, to hold what distance His wisdom can provide iii 6 44
When we hold rumour From what we fear, yet know not what we fear iv 2 19
Lay on, Macduff, And damn'd be him that first cries 'Hold, enough !' . v 8 34
Says 'tis but our fantasy, And will not let belief take hold of him *Hamlet* i 1 24
This troubles me. Hold you the watch to-night?—We do, my lord . i 2 225
The leperous distilment ; whose effect Holds such an enmity with blood of man . . . . i 5 65
Hold, hold, my heart ; And you, my sinews, grow not instant old . i 5 93
While memory holds a seat In this distracted globe . . . . i 5 96
I hold my duty, as I hold my soul, Both to my God and to my gracious king ii 2 44
I hold ambition of so airy and light a quality that it is but a shadow's shadow . . . . ii 2 267
I have an eye of you.—If you love me, hold not off . . . . ii 2 302
Do they hold the same estimation they did when I was in the city? . ii 2 348
To hold, as 'twere, the mirror up to nature . . . . . iii 2 24
Rosencrantz and Guildenstern hold their course for England . . iv 6 29
This project Should have a back or second, that might hold, If this should blast in proof . . . . iv 7 154
If he by chance escape your venom'd stuck, Our purpose may hold there iv 7 163
Nature her custom holds, Let shame say what it will . . . iv 7 188
We have many pocky corses now-a-days, that will scarce hold the laying in v 1 182
And the king hold his purpose, I will win for him an I can . . . v 2 183
Hold. He sends to know if your pleasure hold to play with Laertes *Ham.* v 2 206
If thou didst ever hold me in thy heart, Absent thee from felicity awhile v 2 357
And as a stranger to my heart and me Hold thee, from this, for ever *Lear* i 1 118
When she was dear to us, we did hold her so ; But now her price is fall'n i 1 199
I'll write straight to my sister, To hold my very course . . . i 3 26
He may enguard his dotage with their powers, And hold our lives in mercy . . . . i 4 350
No contraries hold more antipathy Than I and such a knave . . . ii 2 93
Let go thy hold when a great wheel runs down a hill . . . ii 4 73
O sides, you are too tough ; Will you yet hold? . . . . . ii 4 201
To bar my doors, And let this tyrannous night take hold upon you . iii 4 156
Fellows, hold the chair. Upon these eyes of thine I'll set my foot . iii 7 67
But better service have I never done you Than now to bid you hold . iii 7 75
Thou rascal beadle, hold thy bloody hand ! Why dost thou lash that whore? . . . . iv 6 164
Hence ; Lest that the infection of his fortune take Like hold on thee . iv 6 238
O, look upon me, sir, And hold your hands in benediction o'er me . iv 7 58
Know of the duke if his last purpose hold . . . . . . v 1 1
They are ready . . . to appear Where you shall hold your session . . v 3 54
I hold you but a subject of this war, Not as a brother . . . v 3 60
Hold, sir ; Thou worse than any name, read thine own evil . . v 3 155
If there be more, more woeful, hold it in . . . . . . v 3 202
Thou told'st me thou didst hold him in thy hate . . . . *Othello* i 1 7
Lay hold upon him : if he do resist, Subdue him at his peril . . . i 2 80
Nor doth the general care Take hold on me . . . . . i 3 55
The trust, the office I do hold of you, Not only take away . . i 3 118
He holds me well ; The better shall my purpose work on him . . i 3 396
What ribs of oak, when mountains melt on them, Can hold the mortise? ii 1 9
Noble swelling spirits, That hold their honours in a wary distance . ii 3 58
I hold him to be unworthy of his place that does those things . ii 3 104
God's will, lieutenant, hold ! You will be shamed for ever . . ii 3 162
I am hurt to the death.—Hold, for your lives !—Hold, ho ! . . ii 3 165
Hold ! the general speaks to you ; hold, hold, for shame ! . . ii 3 168
He that stirs next to carve for his own rage Holds his soul light . ii 3 174
Yet, if you please to hold him off awhile, You shall by that perceive him and his means . . . . iii 3 248
In the mean time, Let me be thought too busy in my fears—As worthy cause I have to fear I am—And hold her free . . . . iii 3 255
But if she lost it . . . , my father's eye Should hold her loathed . iii 4 62
If there be any cunning cruelty That can torment him much and hold him long, It shall be his . . . . v 2 334
You do not hold the method to enforce The like from him *Ant. and Cleo.* i 3 7
If I knew What hoop should hold us stanch, from edge to edge O' the world I would pursue it . . . . ii 2 117
To hold you in perpetual amity, To make you brothers . . . . ii 2 127
The gods confound thee ! dost thou hold there still?—Should I lie? . ii 5 92
Let determined things to destiny Hold unbewail'd their way . . . iii 6 85
Our nineteen legions thou shalt hold by land . . . . . iii 7 59
To the vales, And hold our best advantage . . . . . . iv 11 4
Here I am Antony ; Yet cannot hold this visible shape . . . . iv 14 14
Hold, worthy lady, hold : Do not yourself such wrong . . . . v 2 39
She holds her virtue still and I my mind . . . . . *Cymbeline* i 4 69
Will this hold, think you?—Signior Iachimo will not from it . . i 4 183
The remembrancer of her to hold The hand-fast to her lord . . . i 5 77
Can my sides hold, to think that man, who knows By history, report, or his own proof, What woman is? . . . . i 6 69
Another stain, as big as hell can hold, Were there no more but it . . ii 4 140
Whose repair and franchise Shall, by the power we hold, be our good deed iii 1 58
Often, to our comfort, shall we find The sharded beetle in a safer hold Than is the full-wing'd eagle . . . . iii 3 20
'Tis some savage hold : I were best not call ; I dare not call . . iii 6 18
Beseech your highness, Hold me your loyal servant . . . . iv 3 16
Thou art my brother ; so we'll hold thee ever . . . . . v 5 399
And, spite of all the rapture of the sea, This jewel holds his building on my arm . . . . *Pericles* ii 1 162
He loves you well that holds his life of you . . . . . . ii 2 22
In your imagination hold This stage the ship . . . . iii Gower 58
Hold, here's gold for thee : Persever in that clear way thou goest . iv 6 112
Whither wilt thou have me?—To take from you the jewel you hold so dear iv 6 164
Hold you (thee) still *C. of Er.* iii 2 ; *Tr. and Cr.* v 3 ; *Macbeth* iii 2
Lay hold of (on) him *Meas. for Meas.* v 1 ; *Com. of Errors* v 1 ; *T. of Shrew* v 1 ; *Coriolanus* iii 1
Hold acquaintance. I saw him hold acquaintance with the waves So long as I could see . . . . *T. Night* i 2 16
Hold amity. How, in one house, Should many people, under two commands, Hold amity? . . . . *Lear* ii 4 245
Hold argument. 'Gainst whom the world cannot hold argument *L. L. Lost* iv 3 61
Hold belief. And holds belief That, being brought into the open air, It would allay the burning quality Of that fell poison . . . *K. John* v 7 6
Hold close. Defy them then, or else hold close thy lips . . 3 *Hen. VI.* ii 2 118
Hold companionship. How is it less or worse, That it shall hold companionship in peace With honour, as in war? . . . *Coriolanus* iii 2 49
Hold current. It holds current that I told you yesternight . 1 *Hen. IV.* ii 1 59
Hold day. We should hold day with the Antipodes, If you would walk in absence of the sun . . . . *Mer. of Venice* v 1 127
Hold dear. Look, what thy soul holds dear, imagine it To lie that way thou go'st . . . . *Richard II.* i 3 286
Life every man holds dear ; but the brave man Holds honour far more precious-dear than life . . . . *Troi. and Cres.* v 3 27
My ring I hold dear as my finger . . . . *Cymbeline* i 4 145
Hold discourse. How is't with you, That you do bend your eye on vacancy And with the incorporal air do hold discourse? . . *Hamlet* iii 4 118
Hold-door. Brethren and sisters of the hold-door trade . *Troi. and Cres.* v 10 52
Hold excused. We cite our faults, That they may hold excused our lawless lives . . . . *T. G. of Ver.* iv 1 54
Hold fashion. Nothing else holds fashion . . . . . *Troi. and Cres.* v 2 196
Hold-fast is the only dog, my duck . . . . *Hen. V.* ii 3 54
Bankrupts, hold fast ; Rather than render back . . . *T. of Athens* iv 1 8
Let us rather Hold fast the mortal sword . . . . . . *Macbeth* iv 3 3
Hold firm. The heavens hold firm The walls of thy dear honour, keep unshaked That temple ! . . . . *Cymbeline* ii 1 67
Hold friends. I will hold friends with you, lady . . . *Much Ado* i 1 91
Hold hand. As she in beauty, education, blood, Holds hand with any princess of the world . . . . *K. John* ii 1 494
Hold hard the breath and bend up every spirit To his full height *Hen. V.* iii 1 16
Hold her own. Doth she hold her own well?—Old, old . 2 *Hen. IV.* iii 2 218
Hold his tongue. Plantagenet, I see, must hold his tongue, Lest it be said 'Speak, sirrah, when you should' . . . . . 1 *Hen. VI.* iii 1 61
Hold in. Such as can hold in, such as will strike sooner than speak 1 *Hen. IV.* ii 1 85

Hold in chase. Where is he, That holds in chase mine honour up and down? . . . . *K. John* i 1 223
Hold intelligence. If with myself I hold intelligence Or have acquaintance with mine own desires . . . . *As Y. Like It* i 3 49
Hold it. We will hold it as a dream till it appear itself . *Much Ado* i 2 21
Truly, I hold it a sin to match in my kindred . . . ii 1 67
I, that hold it sin To break the vow I am engaged in . . *L. L. Lost* iv 3 177
For so your doctors hold it very meet . . . . *T. of Shrew* Ind. 2 133
I hold it the more knavery to conceal it . . . *W. Tale* iv 4 697
I hold it cowardice To rest mistrustful where a noble heart Hath pawn'd an open hand in sign of love . . . . *3 Hen. VI.* iv 2 7
To strike him dead I hold it not a sin . . . *Rom. and Jul.* i 5 61
For Hamlet and the trifling of his favour, Hold it a fashion . *Hamlet* i 3 6
Without more circumstance at all, I hold it fit that we shake hands and part . . . . i 5 128
Potently believe, yet I hold it not honesty to have it thus set down . ii 2 204
The nation holds it no sin to tarre them to controversy . . ii 2 370
If you hold it fit, after the play Let his queen mother all alone entreat him To show his grief . . . . iii 1 189
I once did hold it, as our statists do, A baseness to write fair . v 2 33
Hold it true, sir, that the Duke of Cornwall was so slain? . . *Lear* iv 7 85
I hold it very stuff o' the conscience To do no contrived murder . *Othello* i 2 2
She holds it a vice in her goodness not to do more than she is requested ii 3 326
I hold it ever, Virtue and cunning were endowments greater Than nobleness and riches . . . . *Pericles* iii 2 26
Hold my mind. I'll hold my mind, were she an Ethiope *Much Ado* v 4 38
Hold my peace. You were not bid to speak.—No, my lord; Nor wish'd to hold my peace . . . . . *Meas. for Meas.* v 1 79
Hold thy peace.—I shall never begin if I hold my peace . *T. Night* ii 3 73
Image of pride, why should I hold my peace? . . *2 Hen. VI.* i 3 179
I will hold my peace when Achilles' brach bids me, shall I? *Tr. and Cr.* ii 1 125
I'll speak to it, though hell itself should gape And bid me hold my peace *Hamlet* i 2 246
Hold my tongue. Let me not hold my tongue, let me not, Hubert *K. John* iv 1 100
Bid me hold my tongue, For in this rapture I shall surely speak The thing I shall repent . . . . . *Troi. and Cres.* iii 2 137
But break, my heart; for I must hold my tongue . . *Hamlet* i 2 159
I will hold my tongue; so your face bids me, though you say nothing *Lear* i 4 214
Hold off. You shall not go, my lord.—Hold off your hands . *Hamlet* i 4 80
Hold off the earth awhile, Till I have caught her once more in mine arms v 1 272
Hold off thy hand.—Pluck them asunder.—Hamlet, Hamlet! . v 1 286
Hold opinion. To hold opinion with Pythagoras . *Mer. of Venice* iv 1 131
Hold our tongues. Why do we hold our tongues, That most may claim this argument for ours? . . . . *Macbeth* ii 3 125
Hold out. She would not hold out enemy for ever . *Mer. of Venice* iv 1 447
Now happy he whose cloak and cincture can Hold out this tempest *K. John* iv 3 156
All Kent hath yielded; nothing there holds out But Dover castle . . v 1 30
Hold out my horse, and I will first be there . . . *Richard II.* ii 1 300
The commonwealth their boots? will she hold out water? . *1 Hen. IV.* ii 1 93
He'll straight be well.—No, no, he cannot long hold out these pangs *2 Hen. IV.* iv 4 117
I dare not fight; but I will wink and hold out mine iron . *Hen. V.* ii 1 8
Else ne'er could they hold out so as they do . . . *1 Hen. VI.* i 2 43
No way to fly, nor strength to hold out flight . . . *3 Hen. VI.* ii 6 24
Mine eyes cannot hold out water, methinks . . . *T. of Athens* i 2 111
The babe Cannot hold out to Tyrus: there I'll leave it . *Pericles* iii 1 80
Hold quantity. For women's fear and love holds quantity; In neither aught, or in extremity . . . . *Hamlet* iii 2 177
Hold sortance. With such powers As might hold sortance with his quality . . . . *2 Hen. IV.* iv 1 11
Hold thee, there's my purse . . . . . . *All's Well* iv 5 46
Yet hold thee, there's some boot.—I am a poor fellow, sir . *W. Tale* iv 4 651
But, hold thee, take this garland on thy brow . . . *J. Cæsar* v 3 85
Hold thine own. Steel thy melting heart To hold thine own . *3 Hen. VI.* ii 2 42
They are in action.—Now, Ajax, hold thine own! . *Troi. and Cres.* iv 5 114
Hold thy peace, thou knave . . . . *T. Night* ii 3 68
It begins 'Hold thy peace.'—I shall never begin if I hold my peace . ii 3 73
Hold thy peace; this is not the way: do you not see you move him? . iii 4 120
Hold thy peace; If Talbot do but thunder, rain will follow *1 Hen. VI.* iii 2 58
Enough of this; I pray thee, hold thy peace . . *Rom. and Jul.* i 3 49
Hold thy temper. Sword, hold thy temper . . . *2 Hen. VI.* v 2 70
Hold thy tongue.—Nay, rather persuade him to hold his hands *C. of Er.* iv 4 22
Enchantress, hold thy tongue!—I prithee, give me leave to curse awhile *1 Hen. VI.* v 3 42
Hold together. How fares our gracious lady?—As well as one so great and so forlorn May hold together . . . . *W. Tale* ii 2 23
Hold up. Does he not hold up his head, as it were, and strut? *Mer. Wives* i 4 30
Sirrah; hold up your head; answer your master, be not afraid . . iv 1 19
Away, I say; time wears: hold up your head, and mince . . v 1 8
I pray you, come, hold up the jest no higher . . . . v 5 109
Do yet but kneel by me; Hold up your hands, say nothing *Meas. for Meas.* v 1 443
Whose estimation do you mightily hold up . . . *Much Ado* ii 2 25
How she holds up the neb, the bill to him! . . . *W. Tale* i 2 183
What colour for my visitation shall I Hold up before him? . . iv 4 567
Know him in us, that here hold up his right . . . *K. John* ii 1 364
Hold up thy head, vile Scot, or thou art like Never to hold it up again! *1 Hen. IV.* v 4 39
Whether our present five and twenty thousand May hold up head without Northumberland . . . . . . *2 Hen. IV.* i 3 17
Howbeit they would hold up this Salique law To bar your highness claiming from the female . . . . *Hen. V.* i 2 91
Who twice a-day their wither'd hands hold up Toward heaven, to pardon blood . . . . iv 1 316
If thou think'st on heaven's bliss, Hold up thy hand . *2 Hen. VI.* iii 3 28
The proudest he that holds up Lancaster, Dares stir a wing . *3 Hen. VI.* i 1 46
Such As Agamemnon . . . Should hold up high in brass *Troi. and Cres.* i 3 64
This boy, that cannot tell what he would have, But kneels and holds up hands for fellowship . . . . *Coriolanus* v 3 175
Hold up, you sluts, Your aprons mountant . . . *T. of Athens* iv 3 134
I am much forgetful. Canst thou hold up thy heavy eyes awhile? *J. C.* iv 3 256
Yet, countrymen, O, yet hold up your heads! . . . . . v 4 1
There is no ancient gentlemen but gardeners, ditchers, and grave-makers: they hold up Adam's profession . . . . . . *Hamlet* v 1 34
Hold you there: farewell . . . . . . *Meas. for Meas.* iii 1 176
Ay, leeks is good: hold you, there is a groat to heal your pate *Hen. V.* v 1 61
Hold your hand. For God's sake, hold your hands! Nay, an you will not, sir, I'll take my heels . . . . . *Com. of Errors* i 2 93
Hold your hands; though I know his brains are forfeit to the next tile that falls . . . . *All's Well* iv 3 215
Hold your hand. If you see vengeance,— Hold your hand, my lord *Lear* iii 7 72
Hold your hands, Both you of my inclining, and the rest . . *Othello* i 2 81
Hold your hand.—Let me go, sir, Or I'll knock you o'er the mazzard . ii 3 154
Hold your own. And hold your own, in any case . . *T. of Shrew* iv 4 6
Hold your peace. But better, indeed, when you hold your peace *T. G. of Ver.* v 2 18
Every dram of woman's flesh is false, If she be.—Hold your peaces *W. T.* ii 1 139
Hold your peace.—'Twill out, 'twill out: I peace! No, I will speak as liberal as the north . . . . *Othello* v 2 219
Hold your tongue. Come, sing; and you that will not, hold your tongues *As Y. Like It* ii 5 30
Is this your promise? go to, hold your tongue . . . *K. John* iv 1 97
Hold your tongue, Good prudence; smatter with your gossips, go *Rom. and Jul.* iii 5 171
Hold your word. You yet shall hold your word . . . *Mer. Wives* v 5 258
Holden. I summon your grace to his majesty's parliament, Holden at Bury . . . . *2 Hen. VI.* ii 4 71
Holdest. High Taurus' snow, Fann'd with the eastern wind, turns to a crow When thou hold'st up thy hand . . . . *M. N. Dream* iii 2 143
Thou shakest thy head and hold'st it fear or sin To speak a truth *2 Hen. IV.* i 1 95
If my love thou hold'st at aught . . . . . . *Hamlet* iv 3 60
Thou hold'st a place, for which the pained'st fiend Of hell would not in reputation change . . . . *Pericles* iv 6 173
Holdeth. Thy wife is proud; she holdeth thee in awe . . *1 Hen. VI.* i 1 39
Holding. I trust it will grow to a most prosperous perfection.—It lies much in your holding up . . . . . *Meas. for Meas.* iii 1 273
Holding a trencher, jesting merrily . . . . . *L. L. Lost* v 2 477
Things base and vile, holding no quantity, Love can transpose *M. N. Dream* i 1 232
Then fate o'er-rules, that, one man holding troth, A million fail . iii 2 92
This has no holding, To swear by him whom I protest to love, That I will work against him . . . . *All's Well* iv 2 27
You were straited For a reply, at least if you make a care Of happy holding her . . . . *W. Tale* iv 4 367
There was casting up of eyes, holding up of hands . . . . v 2 51
Holding the eternal spirit, against her will, In the vile prison *K. John* iii 4 18
As holding of the pope Your sovereign greatness and authority . . v 1 3
Holding in disdain the German women For some dishonest manners *Hen. V.* i 2 48
For so appears this fleet majestical, Holding due course to Harfleur iii Prol. 17
Brother, she is not worth what she doth cost The holding *Troi. and Cres.* ii 2 52
Holding Corioli in the name of Rome . . . . *Coriolanus* i 6 37
The rest will serve For a short holding . . . . . . i 7 4
Holding them, In human action and capacity, Of no more soul nor fitness for the world Than camels in the war . . . . . . ii 1 264
Holding thine ear close to the hollow ground . . . *Rom. and Jul.* v 3 4
Holding a weak supposal of our worth . . . . . *Hamlet* i 2 18
And sometimes I am whipped for holding my peace . . . *Lear* i 4 202
Then the boy shall sing; The holding every man shall bear as loud As his strong sides can volley . . . . . . *Ant. and Cleo.* ii 7 117
Your Italy contains none so accomplished a courtier to convince the honour of my mistress, if, in the holding or loss of that, you term her frail . . . . *Cymbeline* i 4 105
Holding out gold that's by the touchstone tried . . . *Pericles* ii 2 37
Holding-anchor. What though the mast be now blown overboard, The cable broke, the holding-anchor lost? . . . . *3 Hen. VI.* v 4 4
Hole. This shoe, with the hole in it, is my mother . . *T. G. of Ver.* ii 3 20
There's a hole made in your best coat . . . . *Mer. Wives* i 5 143
I have seen the day of wrong through the little hole of discretion *L. L. Lost* v 2 734
A wall . . . That had in it a crannied hole or chink . *M. N. Dream* v 1 159
O, kiss me through the hole of this vile wall! . . . . . v 1 202
Spit in the hole, man, and tune again . . . . *T. of Shrew* iii 1 40
As the nail to his hole, the cuckold to his horn . . . *All's Well* ii 2 26
The earth had not a hole to hide this deed . . . . *K. John* iv 3 36
And darts his light through every guilty hole . . *Richard II.* iii 2 43
If men were to be saved by merit, what hole in hell were hot enough for him? This is the most omnipotent villain . . . *1 Hen. IV.* i 2 120
Methought he had made two holes in the ale-wife's new petticoat *2 Hen. IV.* ii 2 88
Wilt thou make as many holes in an enemy's battle as thou hast done in a woman's petticoat?—I will do my good will . . . . iii 2 165
If I find a hole in his coat, I will tell him my mind . . *Hen. V.* iii 6 88
Cursed be the hand that made these fatal holes! . . *Richard III.* i 2 14
And, in those holes Where eyes did once inhabit, there were crept, As 'twere in scorn of eyes, reflecting gems . . . . i 4 29
Now must I hide his body in some hole . . . . . . i 4 287
My anointed body By thee was punched full of deadly holes . . v 3 125
Drag hence her husband to some secret hole . . . *T. Andron.* ii 3 129
Bring thou her husband: This is the hole where Aaron bid us hide him ii 3 186
What subtle hole is this, Whose mouth is cover'd with rude-growing briers? . . . . ii 3 198
Why dost not comfort me, and help me out From this unhallow'd and blood-stained hole? . . . . ii 3 210
He doth wear A precious ring, that lightens all the hole . . . ii 3 227
I'll see what hole is here, And what he is that now is leap'd into it . ii 3 246
Or get some little knife between thy teeth, And just against thy heart make thou a hole . . . . iii 2 17
I train'd thy brethren to that guileful hole . . . . . v 1 104
Runs lolling up and down to hide his bauble in a hole . *Rom. and Jul.* ii 4 97
He loves to hear That unicorns may be betray'd with trees, And bears with glasses, elephants with holes . . . . . . *J. Cæsar* ii 1 205
In your bad strokes, Brutus, you give good words: Witness the hole you made in Cæsar's heart . . . . v 1 31
Imperious Cæsar, dead and turn'd to clay, Might stop a hole to keep the wind away . . . . *Hamlet* v 1 237
The holes where eyes should be, which pitifully disaster the cheeks *Ant. and Cleo.* ii 7 17
The cat, with eyne of burning coal, Now couches fore the mouse's hole *Pericles* iii Gower 6
Holidame. Now, by my holidame, here comes Katharina! *T. of Shrew* v 2 99
Now, by my holidame, What manner of man are you? . . *Hen. VIII.* v 1 116
And, by my holidame, The pretty wretch left crying . *Rom. and Jul.* i 3 43
Holiday. Not a holiday fool there but would give a piece of silver *Tempest* ii 2 30
Come hither from the furrow and be merry: Make holiday . . iv 1 136
He writes verses, he speaks holiday . . . . . *Mer. Wives* iii 2 69
They are but burs, cousin, thrown upon thee in holiday foolery *As Y. L. It* i 3 14
Now I am in a holiday humour and like enough to consent . . iv 1 69
The yearly course that brings this day about Shall never see it but a holiday.—A wicked day, and not a holy day! . . . *K. John* iii 1 82
Awhile to work, and after holiday . . . . . *Richard II.* iii 1 44

Holiday. If all the year were playing holidays, To sport would be as tedious as to work; But when they seldom come, they wish'd for come *1 Hen. IV.* i 2 228
With many holiday and lady terms He question'd me i 3 46
This little one shall make it holiday *Hen. VIII.* v 5 77
Being holiday, the beggar's shop is shut. What, ho! apothecary! *Rom. and Jul.* v 1 56
Home, you idle creatures, get you home: Is this a holiday? *J. Cæsar* i 1 2
We make holiday, to see Cæsar and to rejoice in his triumph i 1 35
Do you now put on your best attire? And do you now cull out a holiday? i 1 54
We'll have flesh for holidays, fish for fasting-days *Pericles* ii 1 86
Holiday-time. What, have I scaped love-letters in the holiday-time of my beauty, and am I now a subject for them? *Mer. Wives* ii 1 2
Holier. What holier than, for royalty's repair, For present comfort and for future good, To bless the bed of majesty again With a sweet fellow to't? *W. Tale* v 1 31
Yet thanks I must you con That you are thieves profess'd, that you work not In holier shapes *T. of Athens* iv 3 430
Holily. How holily he works in all his business! *Hen. VIII.* ii 2 24
What thou wouldst highly, That wouldst thou holily *Macbeth* i 5 22
Yet I have known those which have walked in their sleep who have died holily in their beds v 1 67
Holiness. In special business from his holiness *Meas. for Meas.* iii 2 233
Ill it doth beseem your holiness To separate the husband and the wife.—Be quiet and depart *Com. of Errors* v 1 110
Give a holiness, a purity, To the yet unbegotten sin of times *K. John* iv 3 53
And from his holiness use all your power To stop their marches v 1 6
Money which I promised Should be deliver'd to his holiness *1 Hen. VI.* v 1 53
All his mind is bent to holiness, To number Ave-Maries *2 Hen. VI.* i 3 58
That were a state fit for his holiness i 3 67
Good uncle, hide such malice; With such holiness can you do it? ii 1 26
Appeal unto the pope, To bring my whole cause 'fore his holiness *Hen. VIII.* ii 4 120
To call back her appeal She intends unto his holiness ii 4 235
The cardinal did entreat his holiness To stay the judgement o' the divorce iii 2 32
The letter, as I live, with all the business I writ to's holiness iii 2 222
I shall sooner rail thee into wit and holiness *Troi. and Cres.* ii 1 18
Holla. Call them forth quickly; we will do so.—Holla! approach *L. L. Lost* v 2 900
Cry 'holla' to thy tongue, I prithee *As Y. Like It* iii 2 257
Holla, within! Sirrah, lead these gentlemen To my daughters *T. of S.* ii 1 109
I will find him when he lies asleep, And in his ear I'll holla *1 Hen. IV.* i 3 222
He that first lights on him Holla the other *Lear* iii 1 55
Holla, holla! That eye that told you so look'd but a-squint v 3 71
Hollaed. A cry more tuneable Was never holla'd to *M. N. Dream* iv 1 130
Hollaing. Leave hollaing, man: here.—Sola! where? *Mer. of Venice* v 1 43
Holland of eight shillings an ell *1 Hen. IV.* iii 3 82
The rest of thy low countries have made a shift to eat up thy holland *2 Hen. IV.* ii 2 26
Hollander. With hasty Germans and blunt Hollanders *3 Hen. VI.* iv 8 2
Your Dane, your German, and your swag-bellied Hollander—Drink, ho!—are nothing to your English *Othello* ii 3 80
He gives your Hollander a vomit, ere the next pottle can be filled ii 3 86
Holloa. If I fly, Marcius, Holloa me like a hare *Coriolanus* i 8 7
Holloa! what storm is this? *T. Andron.* ii 1 25
Holloaed. And spur thee on with full as many lies As may be holloa'd in thy treacherous ear *Richard II.* iv 1 54
Hollow. We heard a hollow burst of bellowing Like bulls *Tempest* ii 1 311
As jealous as Ford, that searched a hollow walnut for his wife's leman *Mer. Wives* iv 2 171
Not as one would say, healthy; but so sound as things that are hollow: thy bones are hollow; impiety has made a feast of thee *M. for M.* i 2 56
To view with hollow eye and wrinkled brow An age of poverty *M. of V.* iv 1 270
The most pathetical break-promise and the most hollow lover *As Y. L. It* iv 1 197
And fetch shrill echoes from the hollow earth *T. of Shrew* Ind. 2 48
Lo, how hollow the fiend speaks within him! *T. Night* iii 4 101
Yea, faith itself to hollow falsehood change! *K. John* iii 1 95
He will look as hollow as a ghost, As dim and meagre as an ague's fit iii 4 84
By chance Did grace our hollow parting with a tear *Richard II.* i 4 9
Gaunt as a grave, Whose hollow womb inherits nought but bones ii 1 83
Even through the hollow eyes of death I spy life peering ii 1 270
And lie full low, graved in the hollow ground iii 2 140
Within the hollow crown That rounds the mortal temples of a king Keeps Death his court iii 2 160
And hid his crisp head in the hollow bank *1 Hen. IV.* i 3 106
Hollow whistling in the leaves Foretells a tempest v 1 5
And his coffers sound With hollow poverty and emptiness *2 Hen. IV.* i 3 75
Hollow pamper'd jades of Asia ii 4 178
His eye is hollow, and he changes much iv 5 6
France hath in thee found out A nest of hollow bosoms *Hen. V.* ii Prol. 21
A fair face will wither; a full eye will wax hollow v 2 170
Hand for hand I give.—Ay, but, I fear me, with a hollow heart *1 Hen. VI.* iii 1 136
Boiling choler chokes The hollow passage of my poison'd voice v 4 121
By crying comfort from a hollow breast *2 Hen. VI.* iii 2 43
For it is known we were but hollow friends iii 2 66
I rather wish you foes than hollow friends *3 Hen. VI.* iv 1 139
Deep, hollow, treacherous, and full of guile, Be he unto me! *Richard III.* ii 1 38
But cardinal sins and hollow hearts I fear ye *Hen. VIII.* iii 1 104
And, look, how many Grecian tents do stand Hollow upon this plain, so many hollow factions *Troi. and Cres.* i 3 80
Faith and troth, Strain'd purely from all hollow bias-drawing iv 5 169
Who art thou that lately didst descend Into this gaping hollow? *T. An.* ii 3 249
[Her tongue] Is torn from forth that pretty hollow cage iii 1 84
When my heart, all mad with misery, Beats in this hollow prison iii 2 10
There's not a hollow cave or lurking-place, No vast obscurity v 2 35
Thy dear love sworn but hollow perjury *Rom. and Jul.* iii 3 128
It was the nightingale, and not the lark, That pierced the fearful hollow of thine ear iii 5 3
Lay thee all along, Holding thine ear close to the hollow ground v 3 4
To set a gloss on faint deeds, hollow welcomes *T. of Athens* i 2 16
Consumptions sow In hollow bones of man iv 3 152
But hollow men, like horses hot at hand, Make gallant show *J. Cæsar* iv 2 23
Who in want a hollow friend doth try, Directly seasons him his enemy *Hamlet* iii 2 218
By the happy hollow of a tree Escaped *Lear* ii 3 2
Arise, black vengeance, from thy hollow cell! *Othello* iii 3 447
The bawdy wind . . . Is hush'd within the hollow mine of earth iv 2 79
Is not this true?—Our cheeks and hollow eyes do witness it *Pericles* i 4 51
Hath stuff'd these hollow vessels with their power, To beat us down i 4 67
Hollow-eyed. A needy, hollow-eyed, sharp-looking wretch *Com. of Errors* v 1 240
Hollow-hearted. Throng many doubtful hollow-hearted friends *Rich. III.* iv 4 435
Hollowly. Crown what I profess with kind event If I speak true! if hollowly, invert What best is boded me to mischief! *Tempest* iii 1 70
And try your penitence, if it be sound, Or hollowly put on *Meas. for Meas.* ii 3 23
Hollowness. Grief boundeth where it falls, Not with the empty hollowness, but weight *Richard II.* i 2 59
Nor are those empty-hearted whose low sound Reverbs no hollowness *Lear* i 1 156
We have seen the best of our time: machinations, hollowness, treachery i 2 122
Holly. Heigh-ho! sing, heigh-ho! unto the green holly *As Y. Like It* ii 7 180
Then, heigh-ho, the holly! This life is most jolly ii 7 183
Holmedon. At Holmedon met, Where they did spend a sad and bloody hour *1 Hen. IV.* i 1 55
Stain'd with the variation of each soil Betwixt that Holmedon and this seat of ours i 1 65
Balk'd in their own blood did Sir Walter see On Holmedon's plains i 1 70
Those prisoners in your highness' name demanded, Which Harry Percy here at Holmedon took i 3 24
O Douglas, hadst thou fought at Holmedon thus, I never had triumph'd v 3 14
Holofernes. Master Holofernes, the epithets are sweetly varied, like a scholar at the least *L. L. Lost* iv 2 8
Good Master Holofernes, perge; so it shall please you to abrogate scurrility iv 2 54
Holp. By foul play, as thou say'st, were we heaved thence, But blessedly holp hither *Tempest* i 2 63
A man is well holp up that trusts to you *Com. of Errors* iv 1 22
You had musty victual, and he hath holp to eat it *Much Ado* i 1 51
And in dearness of heart hath holp to effect your ensuing marriage iii 2 102
Sir Robert never holp to make this leg *K. John* i 1 240
Though it [music] have holp madmen to their wits, In me it seems it will make wise men mad *Richard II.* v 5 62
Greatness too which our own hands Have holp to make so portly *1 Hen. IV.* i 3 13
Three times to-day I holp him to his horse *2 Hen. VI.* v 3 8
Let him thank me, that holp to send him thither *Richard III.* i 2 107
How comes't that you Have holp to make this rescue? *Coriolanus* iii 1 277
You have holp to ravish your own daughters iv 6 81
Thou art my warrior; I holp to frame thee v 3 63
Holp to reap the fame Which he did end all his v 6 36
Turn giddy, and be holp by backward turning *Rom. and Jul.* i 2 48
His great love, sharp as his spur, hath holp him To his home *Macbeth* i 6 23
Yet, poor old heart, he holp the heavens to rain *Lear* iii 7 62
You holp us, sir, As you did mean indeed to be our brother *Cymbeline* v 5 422
Holpest. I had a Rutland too, thou holp'st to kill him *Richard III.* iv 4 45
Sly frantic wretch, that holp'st to make me great *T. Andron.* iv 4 59
Holy. I' the name of something holy, sir, why stand you In this strange stare? *Tempest* iii 3 94
Too true, too holy, To be corrupted with my worthless gifts *T. G. of Ver.* iv 2 5
What is she, That all our swains commend her? Holy, fair, and wise is she iv 2 41
The offence is holy that she hath committed *Mer. Wives* v 5 238
He who the sword of heaven will bear Should be as holy as severe *Meas. for Meas.* iii 2 276
Good morning to you, fair and gracious daughter.—The better, given me by so holy a man iv 3 117
I know him for a man divine and holy v 1 144
I was then Advertising and holy to your business v 1 388
So holy and so perfect is my love *As Y. Like It* iii 5 99
Holy seems the quarrel Upon your grace's part *All's Well* iii 1 4
What is not holy, that we swear not by, But take the High'st to witness iv 2 23
Love is holy; And my integrity ne'er knew the crafts That you do charge men with. Stand no more off iv 2 32
What were more holy Than to rejoice the former queen is well? *W. Tale* v 1 29
Her actions shall be holy as You hear my spell is lawful v 3 104
I will pray, If ever I remember to be holy, For your fair safety *K. John* iii 3 15
Thou art not holy to belie me so; I am not mad iii 4 44
Supposed sincere and holy in his thoughts *2 Hen. IV.* i 1 202
Virtuous and holy; chosen from above, By inspiration *1 Hen. VI.* v 4 39
When holy and devout religious men Are at their beads, 'tis hard to draw them thence, So sweet is zealous contemplation *Richard III.* iii 7 92
Virtuous and holy, be thou conqueror! v 3 128
By all that's holy, he had better starve *Hen. VIII.* v 3 132
Truth shall nurse her, Holy and heavenly thoughts still counsel her v 5 30
Do not count it holy To hurt by being just *Troi. and Cres.* v 3 19
I do love My country's good with a respect more tender, More holy and profound, than mine own life *Coriolanus* iii 3 113
Most holy and religious fear it is To keep those many many bodies safe That live and feed upon your majesty *Hamlet* iii 3 8
Octavia is of a holy, cold, and still conversation *Ant. and Cleo.* ii 6 131
For he's honourable And doubling that, most holy *Cymbeline* iii 4 180
Holy Abram. This Jacob from our holy Abram was *Mer. of Venice* i 3 73
Holy abstinence. He doth with holy abstinence subdue That in himself which he spurs on his power To qualify in others *Meas. for Meas.* iv 2 84
Holy act. So smile the heavens upon this holy act, That after hours with sorrow chide us not! *Rom. and Jul.* ii 6 1
Holy-ale. Sung at festivals, On ember-eves and holy-ales *Pericles* 1 Gower 6
Holy altars. Humbly as they used to creep To holy altars *Tr. and Cr.* iii 3 74
Holy angel. Some holy angel Fly to the court of England! *Macbeth* iii 6 45
Holy band. To bind our loves up in a holy band *Much Ado* iii 1 114
Holy bell. And have with holy bell been knoll'd to church *As Y. Like It* ii 7 121
Holy bishop. I'll send some holy bishop to entreat *2 Hen. VI.* iv 4 9
Holy bread. And his kissing is as full of sanctity as the touch of holy bread *As Y. Like It* iii 4 15
Holy breath. To give us warrant from the hand of heaven, And on our actions set the name of right With holy breath *K. John* v 2 68
Holy chase. Our elders say, The barren, touched in this holy chase, Shake off their sterile curse *J. Cæsar* i 2 8
Holy church. That so stood out against the holy church *K. John* v 2 71
A true lover of the holy church *Hen. V.* i 1 23
You shall not stay alone Till holy church incorporate two in one *R. and J.* ii 6 37
Holy churchmen. Or who should study to prefer a peace, If holy churchmen take delight in broils? *1 Hen. VI.* iii 1 111
Holy churchyard. Think Upon the wounds his body bears, which show Like graves i' the holy churchyard *Coriolanus* iii 3 51
Holy clergymen. You holy clergymen, is there no plot To rid the realm of this pernicious blot? *Richard II.* iv 1 324
Holy close. Attested by the holy close of lips *T. Night* v 1 161
Holy conclave. I bid him welcome, And thank the holy conclave for their loves *Hen. VIII.* ii 2 100
Holy confession. Where shall I meet you?—At Friar Patrick's cell, Where I intend holy confession *T. G. of Ver.* iv 3 44

Holy cords. Like rats, oft bite the holy cords a-twain . . . *Lear* ii 2 80
Holy crosses. She doth stray about By holy crosses . *Mer. of Venice* v 1 31
Holy-cruel. Be not so holy-cruel: love is holy . . *All's Well* iv 2 32
Holy day. A wicked day, and not a holy day! . . . . *K. John* iii 1 83
A holy day shall this be kept hereafter . . *Richard III.* ii 1 73
Holy descant. For on that ground I'll build a holy descant . . iii 7 49
Holy duty. One that, in all obedience, makes the church The chief aim of his honour; and, to strengthen That holy duty, out of dear respect, His royal self in judgement comes to hear . *Hen. VIII.* v 3 119
I something fear my father's wrath; but nothing—Always reserved my holy duty—what His rage can do on me . . . . *Cymbeline* i 1 87
Holy eagle. The holy eagle Stoop'd, as to foot us . . . . v 4 115
Holy edifice. Should I go to church And see the holy edifice of stone, And not bethink me straight of dangerous rocks? . *Mer. of Venice* i 1 30
Holy errand. To thee, King John, my holy errand is . . *K. John* iii 1 137
Holy exercise. In no worldly suit would he be moved, To draw him from his holy exercise . . . . *Richard III.* iii 7 64
Holy father. No, holy father; throw away that thought *Meas. for Meas.* i 3 1
Hast thou forgot thyself? is it so long? Call forth the holy father *T. N.* v 1 145
You have a holy father, A graceful gentleman . . . . *W. Tale* v 1 170
Are you at leisure, holy father, now? . . . . *Rom. and Jul.* iv 1 37
Holy feeling. Hast thou that holy feeling in thy soul, To counsel me to make my peace with God? . . . . . . *Richard III.* i 4 257
Holy fields. In those holy fields Over whose acres walk'd those blessed feet . . . . 1 *Hen. IV.* i 1 24
Holy fox. This holy fox, Or wolf, or both . . . . *Hen. VIII.* i 1 158
Holy Franciscan friar! brother, ho! . . . . *Rom. and Jul.* v 2 1
Holy friar. O holy friar, O, tell me, holy friar, Where is my lady's lord? iii 3 81
This reverend holy friar, All our whole city is much bound to him . iv 2 31
Holy gods. By the holy gods, I cannot rightly say . . . *Pericles* iii 4 7
Down on thy knees, thank the holy gods as loud As thunder threatens us v 1 200
Holy Gonzalo, honourable man . . . . *Tempest* v 1 62
Holy groves. Or is it Dian, habited like her, Who hath abandoned her holy groves? . . . . *T. Andron.* ii 3 58
Holy Harry. When didst thou sleep when such a deed was done?—When holy Harry died . . . . *Richard III.* iv 4 25
Holy hat. Out of mere ambition, you have caused Your holy hat to be stamp'd on the king's coin . . . . . . *Hen. VIII.* iii 2 325
Holy head. Between you I shall have a holy head . *Com. of Errors* ii 1 80
Holy hermit. Who comes with her?—None but a holy hermit and her maid . . . . *Mer. of Venice* v 1 33
Holy honour. This is no oath: The George, profaned, hath lost his holy honour . . . . *Richard III.* iv 4 369
Holy humour. Stay a while: I hope my holy humour will change . i 4 121
Holy innocence. Hence, bashful cunning! And prompt me, plain and holy innocence! . . . . *Tempest* iii 1 82
Holy Joan. Tut, holy Joan was his defensive guard . . 1 *Hen. VI.* ii 1 49
Holy king. Poor key-cold figure of a holy king! . . *Richard III.* i 2 5
Thither Macduff Is gone to pray the holy king . . . *Macbeth* iii 6 30
Holy kiss. And seal the bargain with a holy kiss . . *T. G. of Ver.* ii 2 7
Till then, adieu; and keep this holy kiss . . . *Rom. and Jul.* iv 1 43
Holy land. I'll make a voyage to the Holy Land, To wash this blood off from my guilty hand . . . . . . *Richard II.* v 6 49
The tidings of this broil Brake off our business for the Holy Land 1 *Hen. IV.* i 1 48
And were these inward wars once out of hand, We would, dear lords, unto the Holy Land . . . . 2 *Hen. IV.* iii 1 108
And had a purpose now To lead out many to the Holy Land . . . iv 5 211
It hath been prophesied to me many years, I should not die but in Jerusalem; Which vainly I supposed the Holy Land . . . iv 5 239
Holy Laurence. And am enjoin'd By holy Laurence to fall prostrate here, And beg your pardon . . . . . *Rom. and Jul.* iv 2 20
Holy legate. Here comes the holy legate of the pope . . *K. John* iii 1 135
The holy legate comes apace, To give us warrant from the hand of heaven v 2 65
Holy lives. Our holy lives must win a new world's crown *Richard II.* v 1 24
Holy load. Come, now towards Chertsey with your holy load *Richard III.* i 2 29
Holy looks. Both your pardons, That e'er I put between your holy looks My ill suspicion . . . . *W. Tale* v 3 148
Holy lord. My holy lord of Milan, from the king I come . *K. John* v 2 120
Holy maid. A holy maid hither with me I bring . . . 1 *Hen. VI.* i 2 51
Now heaven forfend! the holy maid with child! . . . . v 4 65
Holy man. Holy men at their death have good inspirations . *M. of Ven.* i 2 30
Now go with me and with this holy man Into the chantry by *T. Night* iv 3 23
When I met this holy man, Those men you talk of came into my mind *Richard III.* iii 2 117
A book of prayer in his hand, True ornaments to know a holy man . iii 7 99
The more shame for ye: holy men I thought ye . . *Hen. VIII.* iii 1 102
For he hath still been tried a holy man . . . *Rom. and Jul.* iv 3 29
We still have known thee for a holy man . . . . . . v 3 270
Holy marriage. And all combined, save what thou must combine By holy marriage . . . . ii 3 61
Holy Mary. By holy Mary, Butts, there's knavery . . *Hen. VIII.* v 2 33
Holy monk. 'Twould prove the verity of certain words Spoke by a holy monk . . . . i 2 160
Holy mother. Do in his name religiously demand Why thou against the church, our holy mother, So wilfully dost spurn? . . *K. John* iii 1 141
By God's holy mother, She hath had too much wrong . *Richard III.* i 3 306
By the holy mother of our Lord, The citizens are mum . . . . iii 7 2
Holy nuns. I'll dispose of thee Among a sisterhood of holy nuns *R. and J.* v 3 157
Holy oath. Now in his life, against your holy oath? O, 'tis a fault too too unpardonable! . . . . 3 *Hen. VI.* i 4 105
Perhaps thou wilt object my holy oath . . . . v 1 89
Holy office. For holy offices I have a time . . . *Hen. VIII.* iii 2 144
This gate Instructs you how to adore the heavens and bows you To a morning's holy office . . . . *Cymbeline* iii 3 4
Holy oil. She had all the royal makings of a queen; As holy oil, Edward Confessor's crown . . . . *Hen. VIII.* iv 1 88
Holy order. Trust not my holy order, If I pervert your course *M. for M.* iv 3 152
By my holy order, I thought thy disposition better temper'd *R. and J.* iii 3 114
Holy palmers. And palm to palm is holy palmers' kiss.—Have not saints lips, and holy palmers too? . . . . i 5 102
Holy parcel. A holy parcel of the fairest dames . . *L. L. Lost* v 2 160
Holy Paul. By holy Paul, they love his grace but lightly *Richard III.* i 3 45
Holy Phœbus. Were it carbuncled Like holy Phœbus' car *Ant. and Cleo.* iv 8 29
Holy physic. Both our remedies Within thy help and holy physic lies: I bear no hatred, blessed man . . . . . *Rom. and Jul.* ii 3 52
Holy pilgrim. If you will tarry, holy pilgrim, But till the troops come by, I will conduct you . . . . *All's Well* iii 5 42
Holy pity. Out of holy pity, Absolved him with an axe . *Hen. VIII.* iii 2 263
Holy place. We'll set thy statue in some holy place . 1 *Hen. VI.* iii 3 14
Holy place. We'll burn his body in the holy place . . . *J. Cæsar* iii 2 259
Holy prayers. Commend thy grievance to my holy prayers *T. G. of Ver.* i 1 17
I charge thee, Satan, housed within this man, To yield possession to my holy prayers . . . . *Com. of Errors* iv 4 58
With wholesome syrups, drugs and holy prayers . . . . . v 1 104
As perfect As begging hermits in their holy prayers . *T. Andron.* iii 2 41
Hanging a golden stamp about their necks, Put on with holy prayers *Macbeth* iv 3 154
Holy priests. Vilest things Become themselves in her; that the holy priests Bless her when she is riggish . . . . *Ant. and Cleo.* ii 2 244
Holy privilege. God in heaven forbid We should infringe the holy privilege Of blessed sanctuary! . . . . . *Richard III.* iii 1 41
Holy prophetess. A holy prophetess new risen up Is come with a great power . . . . 1 *Hen. VI.* i 4 102
Holy purpose. For this cause awhile we must neglect Our holy purpose to Jerusalem . . . . 1 *Hen. IV.* i 1 102
Holy reasons. I have other holy reasons . . . . . *All's Well* i 3 34
Holy reverence. Besides a clergyman Of holy reverence *Richard II.* iii 3 29
Holy rite. Before All sanctimonious ceremonies may With full and holy rite be minister'd . . . . *Tempest* iv 1 17
When after that the holy rites are ended, I'll tell you . . *Much Ado* v 4 68
Do we all holy rites; Let there be sung 'Non nobis' and 'Te Deum' *Hen. V.* iv 8 127
Holy rood. On Holy-rood day, the gallant Hotspur there, Young Harry Percy and brave Archibald, That ever-valiant and approved Scot, At Holmedon met . . . . 1 *Hen. IV.* i 1 52
By the holy rood, I do not like these several councils . *Richard III.* iii 2 77
By the holy rood, thou know'st it well . . . . iv 4 165
Holy Sabbath. By our holy Sabbath have I sworn . . *Mer. of Venice* iv 1 36
Holy saint. Teach sin the carriage of a holy saint . *Com. of Errors* iii 2 14
The prayers of holy saints and wronged souls, Like high-rear'd bulwarks, stand before our faces . . . . *Richard III.* v 3 241
Holy Saint Francis, what a change is here! . . . . *Rom. and Jul.* ii 3 65
Holy saws. His weapons holy saws of sacred writ . . . 2 *Hen. VI.* i 3 61
Holy seal. You have not dared to break the holy seal . . *W. Tale* iii 2 130
Holy shrine. Camest thou here by chance, Or of devotion, to this holy shrine? . . . . 2 *Hen. VI.* ii 1 88
If I profane with my unworthiest hand This holy shrine *Rom. and Jul.* i 5 96
Holy sir. My holy sir, none better knows than you . *Meas. for Meas.* i 3 7
Dear sir, ere long I'll visit you again.—Most holy sir, I thank you . iii 1 47
O, holy sir, My reverend father, let it not be so! . . . *K. John* iii 1 248
Holy sport. 'Tis holy sport to be a little vain . . *Com. of Errors* iii 2 27
Holy state. When his holy state is touch'd so near.—State holy or unhallow'd, what of that? . . . . 1 *Hen. VI.* iii 1 58
Holy strength. Disguise the holy strength of their command . *T. and C.* ii 3 136
Holy suit. Though the mourning brow of progeny Forbid the smiling courtesy of love The holy suit which fain it would convince *L. L. Lost* v 2 756
Holy sun. I am ashamed To look upon the holy sun . . *Cymbeline* iv 4 41
Holy task. Come, let us to our holy task again *Richard III.* iii 7 246
Holy tear. Sinon's weeping Did scandal many a holy tear *Cymbeline* iii 4 62
Holy text. Encircled you to hear with reverence Your exposition on the holy text . . . . 2 *Hen. IV.* iv 2 7
Holy-thistle. I have no moral meaning; I meant, plain holy-thistle *M. Ado* iii 4 80
Holy thoughts. Immaculate devotion, holy thoughts *Richard III.* iv 4 404
Holy traitors. Your virtues, gentle master, Are sanctified and holy traitors to you . . . . *As Y. Like It* ii 3 13
Holy uncle. Faith, holy uncle, would 'twere come to that! . 2 *Hen. VI.* ii 1 38
Holy undertaking. Which holy undertaking with most austere sanctimony she accomplished . . . . *All's Well* iv 3 58
Holy vestments. Nor babes, Nor sight of priests in holy vestments bleeding, Shall pierce a jot . . . . . . *T. of Athens* iv 3 125
Holy virgins. Giving our holy virgins to the stain Of contumelious, beastly, mad-brain'd war . . . . v 1 176
Holy vow. A holy vow Never to taste the pleasures of the world *K. John* iv 3 67
And hath given countenance to his speech, my lord, With almost all the holy vows of heaven . . . . *Hamlet* i 3 114
Holy wars. Richard, that robb'd the lion of his heart And fought the holy wars in Palestine . . . . *K. John* ii 1 4
Holy water. Sith priest and holy water are so near . *T. Andron.* i 1 323
Holy-water in a dry house is better than this rain-water out o' door *Lear* iii 2 10
She shook The holy water from her heavenly eyes, And clamour moisten'd iv 3 32
My tears that fall Prove holy water on thee! . . . . *Cymbeline* v 5 269
Holy wedlock. In holy wedlock bands . . . . 3 *Hen. VI.* iii 3 243
Holy wishes. Madam, I desire your holy wishes . . . *All's Well* i 1 68
Holy witch. Such a holy witch That he enchants societies into him *Cymb.* i 6 166
Holy witness. An evil soul producing holy witness Is like a villain with a smiling cheek . . . . *Mer. of Venice* i 3 100
Holy word. Now keep your holy word: go meet the French . *K. John* v 1 5
Do thou but close our hands with holy words . . *Rom. and Jul.* ii 6 6
She has here spoken holy words to the Lord Lysimachus . *Pericles* iv 6 142
Holy writ. So holy writ in babes hath judgement shown . *All's Well* ii 1 141
I clothe my naked villany With old odd ends stolen out of holy writ *Richard III.* i 3 337
Trifles light as air Are to the jealous confirmations strong As proofs of holy writ . . . . *Othello* iii 3 324
Homage. To give him annual tribute, do him homage . . *Tempest* i 2 113
In lieu o' the premises Of homage and I know not how much tribute . i 2 124
We'll do thee homage and be ruled by thee . . . *T. G. of Ver.* iv 1 66
I know his eye doth homage otherwhere . . . *Com. of Errors* ii 1 104
Your weeping sister is no wife of mine, Nor to her bed no homage do I owe iii 2 43
How my men will stay themselves from laughter When they do homage to this simple peasant . . . . *T. of Shrew* Ind. 1 135
I bring no overture of war, no taxation of homage . . . *T. Night* i 5 225
If you do wrongfully seize Hereford's rights, . . . and deny his offer'd homage, You pluck a thousand dangers on your head *Richard II.* ii 1 204
His countenance enforces homage . . . . *Hen. V.* iii 7 31
What drink'st thou oft, instead of homage sweet, But poison'd flattery? iv 1 267
Call my sovereign yours, And do him homage . . . 1 *Hen. VI.* iv 2 7
And after all this fearful homage done, Give thee thy hire and send thy soul to hell . . . . 2 *Hen. VI.* iii 2 224
Do faithful homage and receive free honours . . . . *Macbeth* iii 6 36
And thy free awe Pays homage to us . . . . . . *Hamlet* iv 3 64
And when they have lined their coats Do themselves homage . *Othello* i 1 54
Let me have a child at fifty, to whom Herod of Jewry may do homage *Ant. and Cleo.* i 2 28
Homager. That blood of thine Is Cæsar's homager . . . . . i 1 31
Home. Upon the Mediterranean flote, Bound sadly home . . . *Tempest* i 2 235
I think he will carry this island home in his pocket . . . . ii 1 90
Do not torment me, prithee; I'll bring my wood home faster. . . ii 2 75
Travellers ne'er did lie, Though fools at home condemn 'em . . . iii 3 27
I will pay thy graces Home both in word and deed . . . . . v 1 71

Home. Living dully sluggardized at home, Wear out thy youth *T. G. of Ver.* i 1 7

All happiness bechance to thee in Milan!—As much to you at home! i 1 62

He wonder'd that your lordship Would suffer him to spend his youth at home . . . . i 3 5

Your son was meet, And did request me to importune you To let him spend his time no more at home . . . . i 3 14

If you think so, then stay at home and go not . . . ii 7 62

My will is even this: That presently you hie you home to bed iv 2 94

Hie home unto my chamber, Where thou shalt find me, sad and solitary iv 4 93

I here forget all former griefs, Cancel all grudge, repeal thee home again v 4 143

I melancholy! I am not melancholy. Get you home, go *Mer. Wives* ii 1 158

Her husband will be from home. Alas! the sweet woman leads an ill life ii 2 91

She bade me tell your worship that her husband is seldom from home . ii 2 105

Master Doctor Caius, I am come to fetch you home . . ii 3 54

Is she at home?—Ay; and as idle as she may hang together, for want of company. . . . . iii 2 12

Is your wife at home indeed?—Indeed she is . . . iii 2 26

I have good cheer at home; and I pray you all go with me . iii 2 53

I beseech you heartily, some of you go home with me to dinner . iii 2 81

Who's at home besides yourself?—Why, none but mine own people . iv 2 13

We'll all present ourselves, dis-horn the spirit, And mock him home iv 4 64

Let us every one go home, And laugh this sport o'er by a country fire v 5 255

Who may, in the ambush of my name, strike home. *Meas. for Meas.* i 3 41

I pray you home to dinner with me.—I humbly thank you . ii 1 292

Whose contents Shall witness to him I am near at home . iv 3 99

The duke comes home to-morrow; nay, dry your eyes . . iv 3 132

And to the head of Angelo Accuse him home and home . . iv 3 148

If the old fantastical duke of dark corners had been at home, he had lived iv 3 165

That brought you home The head of Ragozine for Claudio's . v 1 538

Say in brief the cause Why thou departed'st from thy native home *Com. of Errors* i 1 30

She is so hot because the meat is cold; The meat is cold because you come not home; You come not home because you have no stomach. . i 2 48

Methinks your maw, like mine, should be your clock And strike you home . . . . i 2 67

My charge was but to fetch you from the mart Home to your house . i 2 75

She that doth fast till you come home to dinner And prays that you will hie you home to dinner . . . . . i 2 89

Till he come home again, I would forbear. . . . . ii 1 31

Is he coming home? It seems he hath great care to please his wife . ii 1 55

When I desired him to come home to dinner, He ask'd me for a thousand marks . . . . ii 1 60

'Will you come home?' quoth I; 'My gold!' quoth he . . ii 1 64

Whilst I at home starve for a merry look . . . . ii 1 88

But, too unruly deer, he breaks the pale And feeds from home . ii 1 101

Your mistress sent to have me home to dinner? My house was at the Phœnix? . . . . ii 2 10

I did not see you since you sent me hence, Home to the Centaur . ii 2 16

Say that I linger'd with you at your shop To see the making of her carcanet And that to-morrow you will bring it home . . iii 1 5

Get you home And fetch the chain; by this I know 'tis made . iii 1 114

Go home with it and please your wife withal . . . iii 2 178

Get thee gone; Buy thou a rope and bring it home to me . iv 1 20

There's the money, bear it straight, And bring thy master home . iv 2 64

My way is now to hie home to his house, And tell his wife . iv 3 93

To what end did I bid thee hie thee home?—To a rope's-end . iv 4 15

Driven out of doors with it when I go from home; welcomed home with it . . . . iv 4 38

O husband, God doth know you dined at home . . . iv 4 68

Dined at home! Thou villain, what sayest thou? . . . iv 4 71

Good master doctor, see him safe convey'd Home to my house . iv 4 126

Let us come in, that we may bind him fast And bear him home . v 1 41

Namely, some love that drew him oft from home.—You should for that have reprehended him . . . . v 1 56

And therefore let me have him home with me . . . . v 1 101

Once did I get him bound and sent him home . . . . v 1 145

I did obey, and sent my peasant home For certain ducats . . v 1 231

Bore me thence And in a dark and dankish vault at home There left me v 1 247

I witness with him, That he dined not at home, but was lock'd out v 1 255

A victory is twice itself when the achiever brings home full numbers *Much Ado* i 1 9

And send her home again without a husband . . . . iii 3 174

Yonder's old coil at home . . . . v 2 98

Go home, Biron: adieu.—No, my good lord; I have sworn to stay with you *L. L. Lost* i 1 110

A quick venue of wit! snip, snap, quick and home! . . v 1 63

Though my mocks come home by me, I will now be merry . v 2 637

And Tom bears logs into the hall And milk comes frozen home in pail. v 2 925

My heart to her but as guest-wise sojourn'd, And now to Helen is it home return'd, There to remain . . . *M. N. Dream* iii 2 172

Ghosts, wandering here and there, Troop home to churchyards . iii 2 382

Have you sent to Bottom's house? is he come home yet? . . iv 2 2

They have acquainted me with their determinations; which is, indeed, to return to their home . . . . . . *Mer. of Venice* i 2 112

There can be no dismay; My ships come home a month before the day i 3 182

Sir, I entreat you home with me to dinner . . . . iv 1 401

We'll away to-night And be a day before our husbands home . iv 2 3

With sweetest touches pierce your mistress' ear And draw her home with music . . . . v 1 68

Dear lady, welcome home.—We have been praying for our husbands' healths . . . . v 1 113

You are welcome home, my lord.—I thank you, madam. . . v 1 132

Lie not a night from home; watch me like Argus . . . v 1 230

He keeps me rustically at home, or, to speak more properly, stays me here at home unkept . . . . . . *As Y. Like It* i 1 8

Your praise is come too swiftly home before you . . . ii 3 9

When I was at home, I was in a better place: but travellers must be content. . . . . ii 4 17

Then sing him home; Take thou no scorn to wear the horn . . iv 2 13

I would I were at home.—We'll lead you thither . . . iv 3 162

Bethink thee of thy birth, Call home thy ancient thoughts *T. of Shrew* Ind. 2 33

That till the father rid his hands of her, Master, your love must live a maid at home . . . . i 1 187

To seek their fortunes farther than at home, Where small experience grows . . . . i 2 51

Crowns in my purse I have and goods at home . . . . i 2 57

Where be these gallants? who's at home?—You are welcome, sir . iii 2 89

And is the bride and bridegroom coming home? . . . iii 2 153

That thou and the proudest of you all shall find when he comes home iv 1 90

Welcome home, Grumio!—How now, Grumio! . . . . iv 1 109

Home. Go, hop me over every kennel home, For you shall hop without my custom . . . . *T. of Shrew* iv 3 98

Hie you home, And bid Bianca make her ready straight . . iv 4 62

They may chance to need thee at home; therefore leave us . . v 1 4

While I play the good husband at home, my son and my servant spend all at the university . . . . v 1 71

Why, then let's home again. Come, sirrah, let's away . . v 1 152

To watch the night in storms, the day in cold, Whilst thou liest warm at home . . . . v 2 151

Since I nor wax nor honey can bring home . . . *All's Well* i 2 65

I'll stay at home And pray God's blessing into thy attempt . i 3 259

He wears his honour in a box unseen, That hugs his kicky-wicky here at home . . . . ii 3 297

This drives me to entreat you That presently you take your way for home . . . . ii 5 69

My haste is very great: farewell; hie home . . . . ii 5 82

Go thou toward home; where I will never come Whilst I can shake my sword . . . . ii 5 95

No, come thou home, Rousillon, Whence honour but of danger wins a scar, As oft it loses all . . . . iii 2 123

Bless him at home in peace, whilst I from far His name with zealous fervour sanctify . . . . iii 4 10

Ten o'clock: within these three hours 'twill be time enough to go home iv 1 28

The great dignity that his valour hath here acquired for him shall at home be encountered with a shame as ample . . . iv 3 81

I am supposed dead: the army breaking, My husband hies him home . iv 4 12

Your daughter-in-law had been alive at this hour, and your son here at home . . . . iv 5 6

Since I heard of the good lady's death and that my lord your son was upon his return home . . . . iv 5 75

Your son, As mad in folly, lack'd the sense to know Her estimation home . . . . v 3 4

Send for your ring, I will return it home . . . . v 3 223

Wait on me home, I'll make sport with thee . . . . v 3 323

An I thought that, I'ld forswear it. I'll ride home to-morrow *T. Night* i 3 94

Faith, I'll home to-morrow, Sir Toby: your niece will not be seen i 3 111

Why dost thou not go to church in a galliard and come home in a coranto? . . . . i 3 137

If it be a suit from the count, I am sick, or not at home; what you will i 5 117

I will waylay thee going home . . . . iii 4 177

I had rather than forty pound I were at home . . . . v 1 181

That may blow No sneaping winds at home, to make us say 'This is put forth too truly' . . . . *W. Tale* i 2 13

If at home, sir, He's all my exercise, my mirth, my matter . i 2 165

You had much ado to make his anchor hold: When you cast out, it still came home.—Didst note it? . . . . . . i 2 214

Seest a game play'd home, the rich stake drawn, And takest it all for jest i 2 248

This is fairy gold, boy, . . . up with't, keep it close: home, home iii 3 128

Let my sheep go: come, good boy, the next way home . . iii 3 131

Let my prophecy Come home to ye! . . . . . . iv 4 663

All my services You have paid home . . . . . . v 3 4

To my home, I will no more return . . . . . *K. John* ii 1 21

Till then, fair boy, Will I not think of home . . . . ii 1 31

Have sold their fortunes at their native homes . . . ii 1 69

We will bear home that lusty blood again Which here we came to spout ii 1 255

Were I at home, At your den, sirrah, with your lioness, I would set an ox-head to your lion's hide . . . . ii 1 290

Now powers from home and discontents at home Meet in one line iv 3 151

Unthread the rude eye of rebellion And welcome home again discarded faith . . . . v 4 12

Now these her princes are come home again, Come the three corners of the world in arms, And we shall shock them . . . v 7 115

Six frozen winters spent, Return with welcome home from banishment *Richard II.* i 3 212

'Tis doubt, When time shall call him home from banishment . i 4 21

If that come short, Our substitutes at home shall have blank charters i 4 48

Renowned for their deeds as far from home, For Christian service and true chivalry, As is the sepulchre in stubborn Jewry Of the world's ransom, blessed Mary's Son . . . . ii 1 53

He is gone to save far off, Whilst others come to make him lose at home ii 2 81

Get thee home, provide some carts And bring away the armour that is there . . . . ii 2 106

Come home with me to supper . . . . iv 1 333

No joyful tongue gave him his welcome home . . . . v 2 29

If you will go, I will stuff your purses full of crowns; if you will not, tarry at home and be hanged . . . . . *1 Hen. IV.* i 2 147

Shall our coffers, then, Be emptied to redeem a traitor home? . i 3 86

For I shall never hold that man my friend Whose tongue shall ask me for one penny cost To ransom home revolted Mortimer . . i 3 92

We think ourselves unsatisfied, Till he hath found a time to pay us home i 3 288

I sent him Bootless home and weather-beaten back.—Home without boots, and in foul weather, too! How 'scapes he agues? . . iii 1 67

A rendezvous, a home to fly unto . . . . . . iv 1 57

A poor unminded outlaw sneaking home . . . . . iv 3 58

It was myself, my brother and his son, That brought you home . v 1 40

Look you pray, all you that kiss my lady Peace at home . *2 Hen. IV* i 2 233

He hath eaten me out of house and home . . . . . ii 1 81

Who then persuaded you to stay at home? . . . . . ii 3 15

For you, Mouldy, stay at home till you are past service . . iii 2 269

That all their eyes may bear those tokens home Of our restored love iv 2 64

Like a school broke up, Each hurries toward his home and sporting-place iv 2 105

I owe you a thousand pound.—Yea, marry, Sir John; which I beseech you to let me have home with me . . . . . . v 5 80

Which, if like an ill venture it come unluckily home, I break . Epil. 13

It follows then the cat must stay at home . . . . *Hen. V.* i 2 174

While that the armed hand doth fight abroad, The advised head defends itself at home . . . . i 2 179

Where some, like magistrates, correct at home, Others, like merchants, venture trade abroad . . . . i 2 191

Which pillage they with merry march bring home . . . i 2 195

If we, with thrice such powers left at home, Cannot defend our own doors from the dog, Let us be worried . . . . . i 2 217

'Tis ever common That men are merriest when they are from home . i 2 272

The king has killed his heart. Good husband, come home presently . ii 1 93

Push home . . . . ii 1 103

He that outlives this day, and comes safe home, Will stand a tip-toe . iv 3 41

The lamentation of the French Invites the King of England's stay at home v Prol. 37

I rather would have lost my life betimes Than bring a burthen of dishonour home By staying there so long . . . *2 Hen. VI.* iii 1 298

Home. And so will I and write home for it straight . *2 Hen. VI.* iv 1 24
Surprised our forts And sent the ragged soldiers wounded home . iv 1 90
Not able to travel with her furred pack, she washes bucks here at home iv 2 52
Home to your cottages, forsake this groom: The king is merciful iv 2 132
Pronounce free pardon to them all That will forsake thee and go home iv 8 10
Alas, he hath no home, no place to fly to . iv 8 40
And heap'd sedition on his crown at home . *3 Hen. VI.* ii 2 158
I know not how to get the crown, For many lives stand between me and home . iii 2 173
For how can tyrants safely govern home, Unless abroad they purchase great alliance? . iii 3 69
He that will not fight for such a hope, Go home to bed . v 4 56
What news abroad?—No news so bad abroad as this at home *Richard III.* i 1 135
Your son . . . This fair alliance quickly shall call home To high promotions . iv 4 313
March on, since we are up in arms; If not to fight with foreign enemies, Yet to beat down these rebels here at home . iv 4 532
If you do fight in safeguard of your wives, Your wives shall welcome home the conquerors . v 3 260
Only to show his pomp as well in France As here at home . *Hen. VIII.* i 1 164
You that thus far have come to pity me, Hear what I say, and then go home and lose me . ii 1 57
Have not alone Employ'd you where high profits might come home . iii 2 158
Paris is returned home and hurt.—By whom, Æneas? . *Troi. and Cres.* i 1 112
What good sport is out of town to-day!—Better at home . i 1 117
Who said he came hurt home to-day? he's not hurt . i 2 233
If none of them have soul in such a kind, We left them all at home . i 3 286
If you'll confess he brought home noble prize—As you must needs . ii 2 86
But it must grieve young Pyrrhus now at home . iii 3 209
This Ajax is half made of Hector's blood: In love whereof, half Hector stays at home . iv 5 84
Desire them home. Give me thy hand, my cousin; I will go eat with thee . iv 5 157
Ajax, your guard, stays to conduct you home.—Have with you, prince v 2 184
Stand, ho! yet are we masters of the field: Never go home . v 10 2
This is strange.—Go, get you home, you fragments! . *Coriolanus* i 1 226
Hence to your homes; be gone!—Nay, let them follow . i 1 252
Mend and charge home, Or, by the fires of heaven, I'll leave the foe And make my wars on you . i 4 38
At home, upon my brother's guard, even there, Against the hospitable canon, would I Wash my fierce hand in 's heart . i 10 25
Take my cap, Jupiter, and I thank thee. Hoo! Marcius coming home! ii 1 116
Here's a letter from him: the state hath another, his wife another; and, I think, there's one at home for you . ii 1 120
Is he not wounded? he was wont to come home wounded . ii 1 131
He comes the third time home with the oaken garland . ii 1 138
Marcius is coming home: he has more cause to be proud . ii 1 161
Wouldst thou have laugh'd had I come coffin'd home? . ii 1 193
O, welcome home: And welcome, general: and ye're welcome all. ii 1 198
Some old crab-trees here at home that will not Be grafted to your relish ii 1 205
For this last, Before and in Corioli, let me say, I cannot speak him home ii 2 107
I prithee, noble friend, home to thy house; Leave us to cure this cause iii 1 234
Masters, lay down your weapons.—Go not home.—Meet on the market-place . iii 1 331
And come home beloved Of all the trades in Rome . iii 2 133
In this point charge him home, that he affects Tyrannical power . iii 3 1
Fortune's blows, When most struck home, being gentle wounded, craves A noble cunning . iv 1 8
Bid them all home; he's gone, and we'll no further . iv 2 1
Dismiss them home. Here comes his mother . iv 2 7
You have told them home; And, by my troth, you have cause . iv 2 48
You have ended my business, and I will merrily accompany you home iv 3 42
Raised only, that the weaker sort may wish Good Marcius home again iv 6 70
Go, masters, get you home; be not dismay'd . iv 6 150
Go home, And show no sign of fear.—The gods be good to us! Come, masters, let's home . iv 6 152
Nay, if he coy'd To hear Cominius speak, I'll keep at home . v 1 7
'Tis a spell, you see, of much power: you know the way home again . v 2 103
She, poor hen, . . . Has cluck'd thee to the wars and safely home v 3 163
This is the last: so we will home to Rome, And die among our neighbours . v 3 172
If The Roman ladies bring not comfort home, They'll give him death by inches . v 4 41
Your native town you enter'd like a post, And had no welcomes home . v 6 51
You are most welcome home.—I have not deserved it . v 6 61
Our spoils we have brought home Do more than counterpoise . v 6 77
He by the senate is accited home From weary wars . *T. Andron.* i 1 27
I bring unto their latest home, With burial amongst their ancestors . i 1 83
And strike her home by force, if not by words . ii 1 118
And this for me, struck home to show my strength . ii 3 117
Go home, call for sweet water, wash thy hands . ii 4 6
Let me see your archery; Look ye draw home enough, and 'tis there straight . iv 3 3
Away from light steals home my heavy son . *Rom. and Jul.* i 1 143
He is wise; And, on my life, hath stol'n him home to bed . ii 1 4
And I'll still stay, . . . Forgetting any other home but this . ii 2 176
Where the devil should this Romeo be? Came he not home to-night? ii 4 2
What, have you dined at home? . ii 5 46
Hold, then; go home, be merry, give consent To marry Paris iv 1 89
Will you leave me there?—If Timon stay at home . *T. of Athens* ii 2 96
Women are more valiant That stay at home, if bearing carry it . iii 5 48
Home, you idle creatures, get you home: Is this a holiday? *J. Cæsar* i 1 1
Wherefore rejoice? What conquest brings he home? . i 1 37
To-morrow, if you please to speak with me, I will come home to you; or, if you will, Come home to me, and I will wait for you . i 2 309
Good even, Casca: brought you Cæsar home? Why are you breathless? i 3 1
Cæsar should be a beast without a heart, If he should stay at home to-day for fear. No, Cæsar shall not . ii 2 43
For thy humour, I will stay at home . ii 2 56
Calpurnia here, my wife, stays me at home . ii 2 75
On her knee Hath begg'd that I will stay at home to-day . ii 2 82
Bring him with triumph home unto his house . iii 2 54
He hath brought many captives home to Rome . iii 2 93
That trusted home Might yet enkindle you unto the crown . *Macbeth* i 3 120
And his great love, sharp as his spur, hath holp him To his home before us . i 6 24
To feed were best at home; From thence the sauce to meat is ceremony iii 4 35
We might have met them dareful, beard to beard, And beat them backward home . v 5 7
Calling home our exiled friends abroad That fled the snares . v 8 66

Home. At night we'll feast together: Most welcome home! . *Hamlet* ii 2 85
Where's your father?—At home, my lord.—Let the doors be shut upon him . iii 1 134
I'll warrant she'll tax him home . iii 3 29
Look you lay home to him: Tell him his pranks have been too broad iii 4 1
Hamlet return'd shall know you are come home . iv 7 131
She is allow'd her virgin crants, Her maiden strewments and the bringing home Of bell and burial . v 1 256
With his prepared sword, he charges home My unprovided body . *Lear* ii 1 53
Of differences, which I least thought it fit To answer from our home . ii 1 126
Goose, if I had you upon Sarum plain, I'ld drive ye cackling home to Camelot . ii 2 90
'Tis strange that they should so depart from home . ii 4 1
I am now from home, and out of that provision Which shall be needful ii 4 208
These injuries the king now bears will be revenged home . iii 3 13
But I will punish home: No, I will weep no more . iii 4 16
I must change arms at home, and give the distaff Into my husband's hands . iv 2 17
Lord Edmund spake not with your lord at home?—No, madam . iv 5 4
He speaks home, madam: you may relish him more in the soldier than in the scholar . *Othello* ii 1 166
No, not to-night.—To-morrow dinner, then?—I shall not dine at home iii 3 58
What make you from home? . iii 4 169
They do command him home, Deputing Cassio in his government . iv 1 247
O well-painted passion!—I am commanded home. Get you away . iv 1 269
Wear thy good rapier bare, and put it home: Quick, quick; fear nothing . v 1 2
What, are you mad? I charge you, get you home . v 2 194
'Tis proper I obey him, but not now. Perchance, Iago, I will ne'er go home . v 2 197
Be wise, and get you home.—I will not . v 2 223
Speak to me home, mince not the general tongue . *Ant. and Cleo.* i 2 109
Many our contriving friends in Rome Petition us at home . i 2 190
Had we done so at first, we had droven them home With clouts about their heads . iv 7 5
This grave charm,—Whose eye beck'd forth my wars, and call'd them home . iv 12 26
That, it seems, much loves A Gallian girl at home . *Cymbeline* i 6 66
Had I not brought The knowledge of your mistress home, I grant We were to question further . ii 4 51
Go bid my woman feign a sickness; say She'll home to her father iii 2 77
We, poor unfledged, Have never wing'd from view o' the nest, nor know not What air's from home . iii 3 29
No further halting: satisfy me home What is become of her . iii 5 92
To the court I'll knock her back, foot her home again . iii 5 149
And all this done, spurn her home to her father . iv 1 20
Is he at home?—He went hence even now.—What does he mean? . iv 2 189
Thou thy worldly task hast done, Home art gone, and ta'en thy wages iv 2 261
Have I not found it Murderous to the senses? That confirms it home iv 2 328
And if I do it not, I am sure to be hanged at home . *Pericles* i 3 3
That stay'd at home, Not to eat honey like a drone From others' labours . ii Gower 17
Thou shalt go home, and we'll have flesh for holidays, fish for fasting-days . ii 1 85
If King Pericles Come not home in twice six moons . iii Gower 31
Care not for me; I can go home alone . iv 1 43
O, take her home, mistress, take her home . iv 2 134
I'll bring home some to-night . iv 2 157
Have brought This king to Tarsus, . . . To fetch his daughter home . iv 4 20
But can you teach all this you speak of?—Prove that I cannot, take me home again . iv 6 200
Home affairs. I'll leave you to confer of home affairs . *T. G. of Ver.* ii 4 119
Home alarms. Be ready to direct these home alarms . *Richard II.* i 1 205
Home-bred. This louring tempest of your home-bred hate . i 3 187
Such alliance Would more have strengthen'd this our commonwealth 'Gainst foreign storms than any home-bred marriage *3 Hen. VI.* iv 1 38
Home-keeping youth have ever homely wits . *T. G. of Ver.* i 1 2
Home return. Made daily motions for our home return . *Com. of Errors* i 1 60
The precious jewel of thy home return . *Richard II.* i 3 267
Home-spun. What hempen home-spuns have we swaggering here? *M. N. Dream* iii 1 79
Homely. Home-keeping youth have ever homely wits . *T. G. of Ver.* i 1 2
Upon a homely object Love can wink . ii 4 98
Hath homely age the alluring beauty took From my poor cheek? *C. of Er.* ii 1 89
I think, sir, you can eat none of this homely meat . *All's Well* ii 2 49
My homely stars have fail'd To equal my great fortune . ii 5 80
He is seldom from the house of a most homely shepherd *W. Tale* iv 2 43
Here has been too much homely foolery already . iv 4 341
I'll have thy beauty scratch'd with briers, and made More homely than thy state . iv 4 437
As he whose brow with homely biggen bound Snores out the watch of night . *2 Hen. IV.* iv 5 27
Where danger was, still there I met him; And like rich hangings in a homely house, So was his will in his old feeble body . *2 Hen. VI.* v 3 12
Methinks it were a happy life, To be no better than a homely swain *3 Hen. VI.* ii 5 22
The shepherd's homely curds, His cold thin drink out of his leather bottle . ii 5 47
Be plain, good son, and homely in thy drift . *Rom. and Jul.* ii 3 55
If you will take a homely man's advice, Be not found here . *Macbeth* iv 2 68
Our stomachs Will make what's homely savoury . *Cymbeline* iii 6 33
Homeward. Therefore homeward did they bend their course *Com. of Errors* i 1 118
And, coasting homeward, came to Ephesus . i 1 135
Then homeward every man attach the hand Of his fair mistress *L. L. Lost* iv 3 375
You look paler and paler: pray you, draw homewards . *As Y. Like It* iv 3 179
My affairs Do even drag me homeward . *W. Tale* i 2 24
Here I have a pilot's thumb, Wreck'd as homeward he did come *Macbeth* i 3 29
Homicide. Salisbury is a desperate homicide; He fighteth as one weary of his life . *1 Hen. VI.* i 2 25
I am with child, ye bloody homicides . v 4 62
If I thought that, I tell thee, homicide, These nails should rend that beauty from my cheeks . *Richard III* i 2 125
Every man's conscience is a thousand swords, To fight against that bloody homicide . v 2 18
A bloody tyrant and a homicide; One raised in blood . v 3 246
Homily. O most gentle pulpiter! what tedious homily of love have you wearied your parishioners withal! . *As Y. Like It* iii 2 164
Hominem. Novi hominem tanquam te . *L. L. Lost* v 1 10
Homme. Les langues des hommes sont pleines de tromperies . *Hen. V.* v 2 118
Homo. Go to; 'homo' is a common name to all men . *1 Hen. IV.* ii 1 104

Honest. And once again I do receive thee honest . . . *T. G. of Ver.* v 4 78
I'll ne'er be drunk whilst I live again, but in honest, civil, godly company, for this trick . . . . *Mer. Wives* i 1 187
An honest, willing, kind fellow, as ever servant shall come in house . i 4 10
In truth, sir, and she is pretty, and honest, and gentle . . i 4 149
If I find her honest, I lose not my labour . . . . . ii 1 247
Though she appear honest to me, yet in other places she enlargeth her mirth . . . . ii 2 230
Your wife is as honest a 'omans as I will desires among five thousand, and five hundred too . . . . iii 3 236
Wives may be merry, and yet honest too . . . . . iv 2 107
If it be honest you have spoke, you have courage to maintain it *M. for M.* iii 2 166
Your company is fairer than honest . . . . . . iv 3 185
'Cucullus non facit monachum:' honest in nothing but in his clothes v 1 263
In faith, honest as the skin between his brows . . *Much Ado* iii 5 13
I am as honest as any man living that is an old man and no honester than I . . . . iii 5 15
I, that am honest; I, that hold it sin To break the vow . . *L. L. Lost* iv 3 177
An honest exceeding poor man, and, God be thanked, well to live *Mer. of Venice* ii 2 54
Those that she makes fair she scarce makes honest, and those that she makes honest she makes very ill-favouredly . . *As Y. Like It* i 2 41
I do not know what 'poetical' is: is it honest in deed and word? . iii 3 18
For thou swearest to me thou art honest . . . . . iii 3 26
Would you not have me honest?—No, truly, unless thou wert hard-favoured . . . . iii 3 28
I am not fair; and therefore I pray the gods make me honest . iii 3 34
Though he be merry, yet withal he's honest . . . *T. of Shrew* iii 2 25
We will unto your father's Even in these honest mean habiliments iv 3 172
My friends were poor, but honest; so's my love . . . *All's Well* i 3 201
I like him well.—'Tis pity he is not honest . . . . iii 5 85
But you say she's honest.—That's all the fault: I spoke with her but once . . . . iii 6 119
She then was honest.—So should you be.—No . . . . iv 2 11
My meaning in't, I protest, was very honest in the behalf of the maid iv 3 247
Thou art not honest, or, If thou inclinest that way, thou art a coward *W. Tale* i 2 242
The justice of your hearts will thereto add 'Tis pity she's not honest' ii 1 68
When you have said 'she's goodly,' come between Ere you can say 'she's honest' . . . . ii 1 76
With words as medicinal as true, Honest as either . . . . ii 3 38
And no less honest Than you are mad; which is enough, I'll warrant, As this world goes, to pass for honest . . . . . . ii 3 70
Though I am not naturally honest, I am so sometimes by chance . iv 4 733
If I had a mind to be honest, I see Fortune would not suffer me . iv 4 862
Thou art as honest a true fellow as any is in Bohemia . . . v 2 169
Well, be honest, be honest; and God bless your expedition! . *2 Hen. IV.* i 2 248
Before this honest, virtuous, civil gentlewoman . . . . iv 4 328
Hast thou a mark to thyself, like an honest plain-dealing man? *2 Hen. VI.* iv 2 111
Plain and not honest is too harsh a style . . . . *Richard III.* iv 4 360
Though he be grown so desperate to be honest . . . *Hen. VIII.* iii 1 86
If your grace Could but be brought to know our ends are honest, You'ld feel more comfort . . . . iii 1 154
Look, the good man weeps! He's honest, on mine honour . . . v 1 153
Would you were half so honest! Men's prayers then would seek you . v 3 82
He's one honest enough: would all the rest were so! . . *Coriolanus* i 1 54
If it be not so, Thou art not honest; and the gods will plague thee . v 3 166
If that be call'd deceit, I will be honest . . . *T. Andron.* iii 1 189
My invocation Is fair and honest . . . . . *Rom. and Jul.* ii 1 28
The man is honest.—Therefore he will be, Timon: His honesty rewards him in itself; It must not bear my daughter . . *T. of Athens* i 1 128
When thou art Timon's dog, and these knaves honest . . . . i 1 180
What time o' day is't, Apemantus?—Time to be honest . . . . i 1 266
Be not sad, Thou art true and honest; ingeniously I speak . . ii 2 230
Strike me the counterfeit matron; It is her habit only that is honest . iv 3 113
Methinks thou art more honest now than wise . . . . iv 3 509
You that are honest, by being what you are, Make them best seen and known . . . . v 1 71
Brutus is noble, wise, valiant, and honest . . . *J. Cæsar* iii 1 126
This tyrant, whose sole name blisters our tongues, Was once thought honest: you have loved him well . . . . . *Macbeth* iv 3 13
No mind that's honest But in it shares some woe . . . . iv 3 197
I would you were so honest a man.—Honest, my lord!—Ay, sir; to be honest, as this world goes, is to be one man picked out of ten thousand . . . . *Hamlet* ii 2 176
What's the news?—None, my lord, but that the world's grown honest ii 2 242
Ha, ha! are you honest?—My lord?—Are you fair?—What means your lordship?—That if you be honest and fair, your honesty should admit no discourse to your beauty . . . . iii 1 103
I am myself indifferent honest . . . . iii 1 124
To love him that is honest; to converse with him that is wise *Lear* i 4 16
Where I could not be honest, I never yet was valiant . . . v 1 23
Of a free and open nature, That thinks men honest . . . *Othello* i 3 406
But I'll set down the pegs that make this music, As honest as I am . ii 1 204
With my personal eye Will I look to't.—Iago is most honest . . ii 3 6
This advice is free I give and honest, Probal to thinking . . ii 3 343
I never knew A Florentine more kind and honest . . . . iii 1 43
Indeed! ay, indeed: discern'st thou aught in that? Is he not honest? —Honest, my lord!—Honest! ay, honest.—My lord, for aught I know . . . . iii 3 103
I dare be sworn I think that he is honest.—I think so too . . iii 3 125
I do not think but Desdemona's honest.—Long live she so! . . iii 3 225
Take note, take note, O world, To be direct and honest is not safe . iii 3 378
Thou shouldst be honest.—I should be wise, for honesty's a fool . iii 3 381
I think my wife be honest and think she is not . . . . iii 3 384
Nay, but be wise: yet we see nothing done; She may be honest yet . iii 3 433
durst, my lord, to wager she is honest, Lay down my soul at stake . iv 2 12
f she be not honest, chaste, and true, There's no man happy . . iv 2 17
Therefore be double damn'd: Swear thou art honest.—Heaven doth truly know it . . . . iv 2 38
I hope my noble lord esteems me honest.—O, ay; as summer flies are in the shambles, That quicken even with blowing . . . . iv 2 65
O brave Iago, honest and just! . . . . v 1 31
I am no strumpet; but of life as honest As you that thus abuse me . v 1 122
I can do nothing But what indeed is honest to be done . *Ant. and Cleo.* i 5 16
Though it be honest, it is never good To bring bad news . . . ii 5 85
Thou hast been rightly honest;—so hast thou;—Thou,—and thou . iv 2 11
And thou art honest too. I wish I could be made so many men . . iv 2 15
Come, fellow, be thou honest: Do thou thy master's bidding *Cymbeline* iii 4 66
But if I were as wise as honest, then My purpose would prove well . iii 4 121
Honest. He was gentle, but unfortunate; Dishonestly afflicted, but yet honest . . . . *Cymbeline* iv 2 40
Wherein I am false I am honest; not true, to be true . . . iv 3 42
Further to boast were neither true nor modest, Unless I add, we are honest . . . . v 5 19
I left out one thing which the queen confess'd, Which must approve thee honest . . . . v 5 245
Peace . . . , honest fishermen.—Honest! good fellow, what's that? *Per.* ii 1 57
Honest action. It were an honest action to say So to the Moor.—Not I, for this fair island . . . . *Othello* ii 3 146
Honest aid. For I can guess that by thy honest aid Thou kept'st a wife herself, thyself a maid . . . . *All's Well* v 3 329
Honest Antonio. The good Antonio, the honest Antonio,——O that I had a title good enough to keep his name company! *Mer. of Venice* iii 1 14
Honest Athenian. Whither art going?—To knock out an honest Athenian's brains . . . . *T. of Athens* i 1 192
Honest attribute. And for an honest attribute cry out 'She died by foul play' . . . . *Pericles* iv 3 18
Honest Bardolph, whose zeal burns in his nose . . . . *2 Hen. IV.* ii 4 356
Honest bones. To lie close by his honest bones . . . *W. Tale* iv 4 467
Honest care. I thank thee for thine honest care . . . *T. G. of Ver.* iii 1 22
Stall this in your bosom; and I thank you for your honest care *All's Well* i 3 132
Honest Casca. But you and I And honest Casca, we have the falling sickness . . . . *J. Cæsar* i 2 258
Honest Christian. Some honest Christian trust me with a gage, That Norfolk lies . . . . *Richard II.* iv 1 83
Honest chronicler. But such an honest chronicler as Griffith *Hen. VIII.* iv 2 72
Honest clothes. Behold what honest clothes you send forth to bleaching! *Mer. Wives* iv 2 126
Honest company, I thank you all, That have beheld me . *T. of Shrew* iv 2 195
Honest counsel. I can keep honest counsel, ride, run . . . *Lear* i 4 34
Honest country lord. An honest country lord, as I am, beaten A long time out of play . . . . *Hen. VIII.* i 3 44
Honest creature. This honest creature doubtless Sees and knows more, much more, than he unfolds . . . . *Othello* iii 3 242
I thought I was a cave-keeper, And cook to honest creatures *Cymbeline* iv 2 299
Honest drovier. Why, that's spoken like an honest drovier *Much Ado* ii 1 201
Honest Dull. Most dull, honest Dull! To our sport, away! *L. L. Lost* v 1 162
Honest face. If he be not one that truly loves you, That errs in ignorance and not in cunning, I have no judgement in an honest face *Othello* iii 3 50
Honest fellow. How far hence is thy lord, mine honest fellow? *3 Hen. VI.* v 1 2
An honest fellow enough, and one that loves quails *Troi. and Cres.* v 1 56
I warrant it grieves my husband . . .—O, that's an honest fellow *Othello* iii 3 5
Honest fishermen. Peace be at your labour, honest fishermen.—Honest! good fellow, what's that? . . . . *Pericles* ii 1 56
Honest fools lay out their wealth on court'sies . . *T. of Athens* i 2 241
This honest fool Plies Desdemona to repair his fortunes . . *Othello* ii 3 359
Honest freedom. This rock and these demesnes have been my world; Where I have lived at honest freedom . . . . . *Cymbeline* iii 3 71
Honest friend. You have done wrong to this my honest friend *C. of Er.* v 1 19
My honest friend Launcelot, being an honest man's son *Mer. of Venice* ii 2 16
Mine honest friend, Will you take eggs for money? . . *W. Tale* i 2 160
The knave is mine honest friend, sir . . . . . *2 Hen. IV.* v 1 55
Mine honest friend, I prithee, but repair to me next morning *T. of Athens* ii 2 24
Dost thou hear, my honest friend.—No, I hear not your honest friend; I hear you.—Prithee, keep up thy quillets . . . . *Othello* iii 1 22
Mine honest friends, I turn you not away . . . *Ant. and Cleo.* iv 2 29
Honest gentleman. Truly, an honest gentleman: but Anne loves him not; for I know Anne's mind . . . . *Mer. Wives* i 4 177
Your name, honest gentleman?—Peaseblossom . . . *M. N. Dream* iii 1 187
Well met, honest gentleman.—By my troth, well met . *As Y. Like It* v 3 7
Good morrow, honest gentlemen: I beseech you, which is Justice Shallow? . . . . *2 Hen. IV.* iii 2 61
Honest gentleman, I know not your breeding.—Why then, lament . v 3 111
I thank you all; I thank you, honest gentlemen; good night *R. and J.* i 5 126
Your love says, like an honest gentleman, and a courteous, and a kind ii 5 56; 62
The best friend I had! O courteous Tybalt! honest gentleman! . . iii 2 62
Honest gentlewoman. Desire this honest gentlewoman, your maid, to speak a good word . . . . *Mer. Wives* i 4 87
Honest ghost. It is an honest ghost, that let me tell you . . *Hamlet* i 5 138
Honest good fellows, ah, put up, put up . . . *Rom. and Jul.* iv 5 98
Honest grief. I will present My honest grief unto him . *T. of Athens* iv 3 477
Honest hand. Put in every honest hand a whip To lash the rascals naked through the world . . . . *Othello* iv 2 142
Honest-hearted. What art thou?—A very honest-hearted fellow, and as poor as the king . . . . *Lear* i 4 20
Honest house. And chances Into an honest house . . . *Pericles* v Gower 2
Honest Iago, My Desdemona must I leave to thee . . . . *Othello* i 3 295
Honest Iago, that look'st dead with grieving, Speak, who began this? . ii 3 177
Good night, honest Iago.—And what's he then that says I play the villain? . . . . ii 3 341
His mouth is stopp'd; Honest Iago hath ta'en order for't . . . v 2 72
Dost understand the word? My friend, thy husband, honest, honest Iago . . . . v 2 154
Honest kersey. In russet yeas and honest kersey noes . *L. L. Lost* v 2 413
Honest kindness. You advise me well.—I protest, in the sincerity of love and honest kindness . . . . *Othello* ii 3 334
Honest knaveries. Let us about it: it is admirable pleasures and fery honest knaveries . . . . *Mer. Wives* iv 4 81
Honest knaves. Whip me such honest knaves . . . . *Othello* i 1 49
Honest knight. I will to my honest knight Falstaff *Mer. Wives* iii 2 88
Honest lads. My honest lads, I will tell you what I am about . i 3 42
Honest Launcelot. 'Take heed, honest Launcelot; take heed, honest Gobbo,' or, as aforesaid, 'honest Launcelot Gobbo' *Mer. of Venice* ii 2 7
Honest lord, Thou hast said well . . . . *Tempest* iv 2 34
I thank you, honest lord. Remember me In all humility . *Hen. VIII.* iv 2 160
Poor honest lord, brought low by his own heart! . . *T. of Athens* iv 2 37
Honest love. His demand Springs not from Edward's well-meant honest love, But from deceit . . . . *3 Hen. VI.* iii 3 67
Honest madam. And my shape as true As honest madam's issue *Lear* i 2 9
Honest maid. An honest maid as ever broke bread . . *Mer. Wives* i 4 160
Honest man. The young man is an honest man.—What shall de honest man do in my closet? dere is no honest man dat shall come in my closet . . . . i 4 75
And truly Master Page is an honest man . . . . . . ii 2 121
Having an honest man to your husband, to give him such cause of suspicion! . . . . iii 3 107
Do not say they be fled; Germans are honest men . . . . iv 5 74
'Tis pity that thou livest To walk where any honest men resort *C. of Er.* v 1 28
Do you question me, as an honest man should do? . . . *Much Ado* i 1 167

Honest man. Though I cannot be said to be a flattering honest man *M. Ado* i 3 32
You may do the part of an honest man in it . . . . . ii 1 172
He was wont to speak plain and to the purpose, like an honest man and a soldier . . . ii 3 20
As I am an honest man, he looks pale. Art thou sick, or angry? . . v 1 130
A foolish mild man; an honest man, look you, and soon dashed *L. L. Lost* v 2 585
Being an honest man's son, or rather an honest woman's son *M. of Ven.* ii 2 16
He has every thing that an honest man should not have; what an honest man should have, he has nothing . . . . *All's Well* iv 3 290
To be said an honest man and a good housekeeper goes as fairly as to say a careful man and a great scholar . . . *T. Night* iv 2 10
Go play, Mamillius; thou'rt an honest man . . . . . *W. Tale* i 2 211
All I know of it Is that Camillo was an honest man . . . iii 2 75
Who, I may say, is no honest man, neither to his father nor to me . iv 4 719
How doth thy husband? I love him well; he is an honest man 1 *Hen. IV.* iii 3 108
I would thou shouldst know it; I am an honest man's wife . . iii 3 136
Why, sir, did I say you were an honest man? . . . 2 *Hen. IV.* i 2 92
You lie in your throat, if you say I am any other than an honest man . i 2 98
What is the gross sum that I owe thee?—Marry, if thou wert an honest man, thyself and the money too . . . . . ii 1 92
I will bar no honest man my house, nor no cheater . . . ii 4 111
An honest man, sir, is able to speak for himself, when a knave is not . v 1 50
If I cannot once or twice in a quarter bear out a knave against an honest man, I have but a very little credit with your worship . . v 1 54
I need not to be ashamed of your majesty, praised be God, so long as your majesty is an honest man . . . . *Hen. V.* iv 7 120
Do not cast away an honest man for a villain's accusation . 2 *Hen. VI.* i 3 206
To prove him a knave and myself an honest man . . . ii 3 89
He was an honest man, and a good bricklayer . . . . . iv 2 42
Spare none but such as go in clouted shoon; For they are thrifty honest men . . . . iv 2 196
And understand again like honest men . . . . *Hen. VIII.* i 3 32
And to deliver, Like free and honest men, our just opinions . . iii 1 60
Ye speak like honest men; pray God, ye prove so! . . . iii 1 69
Was it discretion, lords, to let this man, This good man,—few of you deserve that title,—This honest man, wait like a lousy footboy? . v 3 139
He has done nobly, and cannot go without any honest man's voice *Cor.* ii 3 140
I never had honest man about me, I; all I kept were knaves *T. of Athens* iv 3 484
I do proclaim One honest man—mistake me not—but one; No more, I pray . . . . iv 3 504
Thou singly honest man, Here, take: the gods out of my misery Have sent thee treasure . . . . iv 3 530
Have I once lived to see two honest men? . . . . . v 1 59
Most honest men! Why, how shall I requite you? . . . . v 1 76
Ye're honest men: ye've heard that I have gold; I am sure you have: speak truth; ye're honest men . . . . v 1 79
What night is this!—A very pleasing night to honest men *J. Cæsar* i 3 43
Who must hang them?—Why, the honest men.—Then the liars and swearers are fools, for there are liars and swearers enow to beat the honest men and hang up them . . . . . *Macbeth* iv 2 55
To speak to you like an honest man, I am most dreadfully attended *Ham.* ii 2 276
I am no honest man if there be any good meaning towards you . *Lear* i 2 189
As I am an honest man, I thought you had received some bodily wound *Othello* ii 3 266
Men should be what they seem.—Why, then, I think Cassio's an honest man . . . . iii 3 129
An honest man he is, and hates the slime That sticks on filthy deeds . v 2 148
Madam, he's well.—Well said.—And friends with Cæsar.—Thou'rt an honest man . . . . *Ant. and Cleo.* ii 5 47
O, my fortunes have Corrupted honest men! . . . . . iv 5 17
True honest men being heard, like false Æneas, Were in his time thought false . . . . *Cymbeline* iii 4 60
What villany soe'er I bid thee do, to perform it directly and truly, I would think thee an honest man . . . . . . iii 5 114
Honest master. Well, let us see honest Master Page . *Mer. Wives* i 1 67
Is not lead a metal heavy, dull, and slow?—Minimè, honest master *L. L. Lost* iii 1 61
Honest method. An honest method, as wholesome as sweet *Hamlet* ii 2 465
Honest mind. He cannot flatter, he, An honest mind and plain, he must speak truth! . . . . *Lear* ii 2 105
Honest mirth. How well this honest mirth becomes their labour! *Pericles* ii 1 99
Honest name. And give her as a prey to law and shame, That hath dishonour'd Gloucester's honest name . . . 2 *Hen. VI.* ii 1 199
Honest-natured. But, for all this, my honest-natured friends, I must needs say you have a little fault . . . *T. of Athens* v 1 89
Honest Ned. No abuse, Ned, i' the world; honest Ned, none 2 *Hen. IV.* ii 4 345
Honest neighbour. One word more, honest neighbours . *Much Ado* iii 3 97
What would you with me, honest neighbour? . . . . . iii 5 1
Pity that some honest neighbours will not make them friends *M. N. D.* iii 1 148
Mine honest neighbours, Will you undo yourselves? . *Coriolanus* i 1 63
At every putting-by mine honest neighbours shouted . *J. Cæsar* i 2 231
Honest nurse. Hie to high fortune! Honest nurse, farewell *Rom. and Jul.* ii 5 80
Honest old man. As your worship shall know by this honest old man *Mer. of Venice* ii 2 147
Honest one. An ancient soldier, An honest one, I warrant . *Cymbeline* v 3 16
Honest Ovid. The most capricious poet, honest Ovid . *As Y. Like It* iii 3 8
Honest pains. I thank thee for thy care and honest pains . *Much Ado* v 1 323
Honest plain men. Tell me, for you seem to be honest plain men *W. Tale* iv 4 824
Honest plain words best pierce the ear of grief . . *L. L. Lost* v 2 763
Honest plainness. In honest plainness thou hast heard me say My daughter is not for thee . . . . *Othello* i 1 97
Honest poor servant. I have forgot thee.—An honest poor servant of yours . . . . *T. of Athens* iv 3 482
Honest Puck. As I am an honest Puck . . . *M. N. Dream* v 1 438
Honest reason. Find me tractable to any honest reason . 1 *Hen. IV.* iii 3 195
Honest Roman. And what Made the all-honour'd, honest Roman, Brutus, With the arm'd rest . . . To drench the Capitol? *A. and C.* ii 6 16
Honest slanders. I'll devise some honest slanders To stain my cousin with . . . . *Much Ado* iii 1 84
Honest soldier. Good night.—O, farewell, honest soldier . *Hamlet* i 1 16
Honest son. And wander we to see thy honest son . *T. of Shrew* iv 5 69
Honest soul. An honest soul, i' faith, sir; by my troth he is, as ever broke bread . . . . *Much Ado* iii 5 41
Honest suit. Did he tempt thy love?—With words that in an honest suit might move . . . . *Com. of Errors* iv 2 14
'Tis most easy The inclining Desdemona to subdue In any honest suit *Oth.* ii 3 347
Honest sword. Draw that thy honest sword, which thou has worn Most useful for thy country . . . . . *Ant. and Cleo.* iv 14 79
Honest taking up. If a man is through with them in honest taking up, then they must stand upon security . . . . 2 *Hen. IV.* i 2 46
Honest tale. An honest tale speeds best being plainly told *Richard III.* iv 4 358
Honest thought. He only, in a general honest thought And common good to all, made one of them . . . . . . *J. Cæsar* v 5 71
Honest trifles. Win us with honest trifles, to betray's . *Macbeth* i 3 125
Honest Troyan. Unless you play the honest Troyan, the poor wench is cast away . . . . *L. L. Lost* v 2 681
Honest-true. As I have ever found thee honest-true, So let me find thee still. Take this same letter . . . . *Mer. of Venice* iii 4 46
Honest truth. Thou hast forced me, Out of thy honest truth, to play the woman . . . . *Hen. VIII.* iii 2 430
Honest use. Can serve the world for no honest use . . *All's Well* iv 3 341
Honest water, which ne'er left man i' the mire . . *T. of Athens* i 2 59
Honest will. Sour, And not obedient to his honest will . *T. of Shrew* v 2 158
Blest be those, How mean soe'er, that have their honest wills *Cymbeline* i 6 8
Honest witnesses. To the church; take the priest, clerk, and some sufficient honest witnesses . . . . . . *T. of Shrew* iv 4 95
Honest wives. And five or six honest wives that were present *W. Tale* iv 4 273
Honest woman. By gar, I see 'tis an honest woman *Mer. Wives* iii 3 238
Mistress Ford, the honest woman, the modest wife . . . . iv 2 136
Thy wife?—Ay, sir; whom, I thank heaven, is an honest woman *M. for M.* ii 1 73
Being an honest man's son, or rather an honest woman's son *Mer. of Venice* ii 2 17
If my gossip Report be an honest woman of her word . . . iii 1 7
If she be less than an honest woman, she is indeed more than I took her for . . . . iii 5 46
Charge an honest woman with picking thy pocket! . . 1 *Hen. IV.* iii 3 176
Says he, 'you are an honest woman, and well thought on' 2 *Hen. IV.* ii 4 99
A very honest woman, but something given to lie . *Ant. and Cleo.* v 2 252
What would you have me be, an I be not a woman?—An honest woman, or not a woman . . . . *Pericles* iv 2 90
If I can place thee, I will.—But amongst honest women . . iv 6 205
Honester. I thank God I am as honest as any man living that is an old man and no honester than I . . . . . *Much Ado* iii 5 16
If he were honester He were much goodlier . . . *All's Well* iii 5 82
But an honester and truer-hearted man,—well, fare thee well 2 *Hen. IV.* ii 4 414
Honester men than thou go in their hose and doublets 2 *Hen. VI.* iv 7 55
'Tis an honester service than to meddle with thy mistress *Coriolanus* iv 5 52
Honestest. And keeps her guard In honestest defence . *All's Well* iii 5 77
Honestly. And, as I say, paying for them very honestly *Meas. for Meas.* ii 1 106
If their singing answer your saying, by my faith, you say honestly *M. Ado* ii 1 242
Not honestly, my lord; but so covertly that no dishonesty shall appear in me . . . . ii 2 9
You have discharged this honestly; keep it to yourself . . *All's Well* i 3 127
Gentlewomen that live honestly by the prick of their needles *Hen. V.* ii 1 36
Ye say honestly: rest you merry!—Stay, fellow; I can read *Rom and Jul.* i 2 65
It will show honestly in us . . . . . . *T. of Athens* v 1 16
Honesty. By mine honesty, welcome to Milan! . . *T. G. of Ver.* ii 5 1
And translated her will out of honesty into English . *Mer. Wives* i 3 55
It makes me almost ready to wrangle with mine own honesty . . ii 1 88
Act any villany . . . that may not sully the chariness of our honesty . ii 1 103
I defy all angels, in any such sort, as they say, but in the way of honesty . . . . ii 2 75
As to lay an amiable siege to the honesty of this Ford's wife . . . ii 2 244
There is written in your brow, provost, honesty and constancy *M. for M.* iv 2 163
By mine honesty, If she be mad,—as I believe no other . . . v 1 59
I'll prove mine honour and mine honesty Against thee presently *C. of Er.* v 1 30
He is of a noble strain, of approved valour and confirmed honesty *Much Ado* ii 1 395
The less you meddle or make with them, why, the more is for your honesty iii 3 56
I would not hang a dog by my will, much more a man who hath any honesty . . . . iii 3 67
A beard, fair health, and honesty; With three-fold love I wish you all these three . . . . *L. L. Lost* v 2 834
If it stand with honesty, Buy thou the cottage . . *As Y. Like It* ii 4 91
Honesty coupled to beauty is to have honey a sauce to sugar . . iii 3 30
To cast away honesty upon a foul slut were to put good meat into an unclean dish . . . . iii 3 35
I should think my honesty ranker than my wit . . . . . iv 1 85
Rich honesty dwells like a miser, sir, in a poor house . . . v 4 62
Whose skill was almost as great as his honesty . . . *All's Well* i 1 21
She derives her honesty and achieves her goodness . . . . i 1 52
Though honesty be no puritan, yet it will do no hurt . . . i 3 97
The honour of a maid is her name; and no legacy is so rich as honesty iii 5 14
All her deserving Is a reserved honesty . . . . . . iii 5 65
What his valour, honesty, and expertness in wars . . . . iv 3 202
What is his honesty?—He will steal, sir, an egg out of a cloister . iv 3 279
I have but little more to say, sir, of his honesty . . . . iv 3 290
I begin to love him for this.—For this description of thine honesty? . iv 3 294
Let death and honesty Go with your impositions . . . . iv 4 28
Have you no wit, manners, nor honesty, but to gabble like tinkers? *T. N.* ii 3 94
Believe me, I speak as my understanding instructs me and as mine honesty puts it to utterance . . . . *W. Tale* i 1 21
Which hoxes honesty behind, restraining From course required . . i 2 244
Such allow'd infirmities that honesty Is never free of . . . . i 2 263
A note infallible Of breaking honesty . . . . i 2 288
If therefore you dare trust my honesty . . . . . . i 2 434
If it be so, We need no grave to bury honesty . . . . . ii 1 155
To lock up honesty and honour from The access of gentle visitors! . ii 2 10
But it does fulfil my vow; I needs must think it honesty . . . iv 4 498
What a fool Honesty is! and Trust, his sworn brother, a very simple gentleman! . . . . iv 4 606
If I thought it were a piece of honesty to acquaint the king withal, I would not do't . . . . iv 4 696
Whose honour and whose honesty till now Endured all weathers . . v 1 194
Whose worth and honesty Is richly noted . . . . . . v 3 144
Thou wast got i' the way of honesty . . . . . . *K. John* i 1 181
There's neither honesty, manhood, nor good fellowship in thee 1 *Hen. IV.* i 2 155
There's no room for faith, truth, nor honesty in this bosom of thine . iii 3 174
There is no honesty in such dealing . . . . . 2 *Hen. IV.* ii 1 39
Mine honesty shall be my dower . . . . . 3 *Hen. VI.* iii 2 72
This proveth Edward's love and Warwick's honesty . . . . iii 3 180
To whom in all this presence speaks your grace?—To thee, that hast nor honesty nor grace . . . . *Richard III.* i 3 55
As I belong to worship and affect In honour honesty . . *Hen. VIII.* i 1 40
I should tell you You have as little honesty as honour . . . iii 2 271
If you can blush and cry 'guilty,' cardinal, You'll show a little honesty iii 2 306
Cherish those hearts that hate thee; Corruption wins not more than honesty . . . . iii 2 444
For virtue and true beauty of the soul, For honesty and decent carriage iv 2 145
The good I stand on is my truth and honesty . . . . . v 1 122
I had thought They had parted so much honesty among 'em . . . v 2 28

Honesty. Whose honesty the devil And his disciples only envy at *Hen. VIII.* v 3 111
Upon my secrecy, to defend mine honesty . . . *Troi. and Cres.* i 2 286
Now perforce we will enjoy That nice-preserved honesty of yours *T. An.* ii 3 135
There's no trust, No faith, no honesty in men ; all perjured *R. and J.* iii 2 86
His honesty rewards him in itself . . . . . *T. of Athens* i 1 130
You would throw them off, And say, you found them in mine honesty . ii 2 144
Every man has his fault, and honesty is his . . . . iii 1 29
What other oath Than honesty to honesty engaged? . *J. Cæsar* ii 1 127
There is no terror, Cassius, in your threats, For I am arm'd so strong in honesty That they pass by me as the idle wind . . . iv 3 67
Yet I hold it not honesty to have it thus set down . *Hamlet* ii 2 204
Your honesty should admit no discourse to your beauty.—Could beauty, my lord, have better commerce than with honesty? . . . iii 1 108
The power of beauty will sooner transform honesty from what it is to a bawd than the force of honesty can translate beauty into his likeness . . . . iii 1 112
The noble and true-hearted Kent banished ! his offence, honesty ! . *Lear* i 2 127
On whose foolish honesty My practices ride easy . . . . i 2 197
That such a slave as this should wear a sword, Who wears no honesty . ii 2 79
A man he is of honesty and trust . . . . . *Othello* i 3 285
Thy honesty and love doth mince this matter, Making it light . . ii 3 247
Thou'rt full of love and honesty, And weigh'st thy words . . iii 3 118
Nor for my manhood, honesty, or wisdom, To let you know my thoughts iii 3 153
This fellow's of exceeding honesty, And knows all qualities . . iii 3 258
O wretched fool, That livest to make thine honesty a vice ! . . iii 3 376
Honesty's a fool And loses that it works for . . . . iii 3 382
I am enter'd in this cause so far, Prick'd to't by foolish honesty and love iii 3 412
It is not honesty in me to speak What I have seen and known . iv 1 288
But why should honour outlive honesty? . . . . . v 2 245
Mine honesty Shall not make poor my greatness . . *Ant. and Cleo.* ii 2 92
Mine honesty and I begin to square . . . . . . iii 13 41
Given to lie ; as a woman should not do, but in the way of honesty . v 2 254
In honesty, I bid for you as I'ld buy . . . . *Cymbeline* iii 6 70
Honey. Injurious wasps, to feed on such sweet honey And kill the bees that yield it with your stings! . . . . . *T. G. of Ver.* i 2 106
One sweet word with thee.—Honey, and milk, and sugar . *L. L. Lost* v 2 231
That is all one, my fair, sweet, honey monarch . . . . v 2 530
Honesty coupled to beauty is to have honey a sauce to sugar *As Y. L. It* iii 3 31
Now, my honey love, Will we return . . . . *T. of Shrew* iv 3 52
Since I nor wax nor honey can bring home . . . *All's Well* i 2 65
'Nointed over with honey, set on the head of a wasp's nest . *W. Tale* iv 4 813
As the honey of Hybla, my old lad of the castle . . . 1 *Hen. IV.* i 2 47
Now, my good sweet honey lord, ride with us to-morrow . . i 2 179
They surfeited with honey and began To loathe the taste of sweetness . iii 2 71
Our thighs pack'd with wax, our mouths with honey . 2 *Hen. IV.* iv 5 77
The civil citizens kneading up the honey . . . . *Hen. V.* i 2 199
Your father's enemies Have steep'd their galls in honey . . . ii 2 30
Thus may we gather honey from the weed, And make a moral of the devil . . . . iv 1 11
My woman's heart Grossly grew captive to his honey words *Richard III.* iv 1 80
Matter against him that for ever mars The honey of his language *Hen. VIII.* iii 2 22
When that the general is not like the hive To whom the foragers shall all repair, What honey is expected? . . . *Troi. and Cres.* i 3 83
You have the honey still, but these the gall . . . . . v 2 144
Sweet honey Greek, tempt me no more to folly . . . . . v 2 18
Full merrily the humble-bee doth sing, Till he hath lost his honey and his sting ; And being once subdued in armed tail, Sweet honey and sweet notes together fail . . . . v 10 43
When ye have the honey ye desire, Let not this wasp outlive *T. Andron.* ii 3 131
Coming and going with thy honey breath . . . . . . ii 4 25
O honey nurse, what news? . . . . *Rom. and Jul.* ii 5 18
The sweetest honey Is loathsome in his own deliciousness . . . ii 6 11
Death, that hath suck'd the honey of thy breath . . . . v 3 92
That suck'd the honey of his music vows . . . . *Hamlet* iii 1 164
Honey, you shall be well desired in Cyprus . . . *Othello* ii 1 206
Not to eat honey like a drone From others' labours . . *Pericles* ii Gower 18
We would purge the land of these drones, that rob the bee of her honey ii 1 51
Honey-bag. The honey-bags steal from the humble-bees . *M. N. Dream* iii 1 171
And, good mounsieur, bring me the honey-bag . . . . iv 1 13
Have a care the honey-bag break not ; I would be loath to have you overflown with a honey-bag . . . . iv 1 16
Honey-bee. For so work the honey-bees, Creatures that by a rule in nature teach The act of order . . . . . *Hen. V.* i 2 187
Honeycomb. Thou shalt be pinch'd As thick as honeycomb . *Tempest* i 2 329
Honey-dew. As doth the honey-dew Upon a gather'd lily *T. Andron.* iii 1 112
Honey-drop. Diffusest honey-drops, refreshing showers . *Tempest* iv 1 79
Honeyed. Mute wonder lurketh in men's ears, To steal his sweet and honey'd sentences . . . . *Hen. V.* i 1 50
Honey-heavy. Enjoy the honey-heavy dew of slumber . . *J. Cæsar* ii 1 230
Honeying and making love Over the nasty sty . . . *Hamlet* iii 4 93
Honeyless. But for your words, they rob the Hybla bees, And leave them honeyless . . . . *J. Cæsar* v 1 35
Honey-mouthed. If I prove honey-mouth'd, let my tongue blister *W. Tale* ii 2 33
Honey-seed rogue! thou art a honey-seed, a man-queller . 2 *Hen. IV.* ii 1 57
Honey-stalk. More sweet, and yet more dangerous Than baits to fish, or honey-stalks to sheep . . . . . . *T. Andron.* iv 4 91
Honeysuckles, ripen'd by the sun, Forbid the sun to enter . *Much Ado* iii 1 8
So doth the woodbine the sweet honeysuckle Gently entwist *M. N. D.* iv 1 47
Murder, murder! Ah, thou honey-suckle villain! . . 2 *Hen. IV.* ii 1 56
Honey-sweet husband, let me bring thee to Staines . . *Hen. V.* ii 3 1
Honey-sweet lord,— Go to, sweet queen, go to . . *Troi. and Cres.* iii 1 71
You know all, Lord Pandarus.—Not I, honey-sweet queen . . iii 1 154
Honey-tongued Boyet.—A blister on his sweet tongue! . . *L. L. Lost* v 2 334
'Honi soit qui mal y pense' write In emerald tufts . . *Mer. Wives* v 5 73
Honneur. Sauf votre honneur, en vérité, vous prononcez les mots aussi droit que les natifs d'Angleterre . . . . . . *Hen. V.* iii 4 40
De nails, de arm, de ilbow.—Sauf votre honneur, de elbow . . iii 4 51
Gros et impudique, et non pour les dames d'honneur d'user . . iii 4 57
Sauf votre honneur, me understand vell . . . . . v 2 135
Sauf votre honneur, le François que vous parlez, il est meilleur que l'Anglois lequel je parle . . . . v 2 199
Honorato. Molto honorato signor mio Petruchio . . *T. of Shrew* i 2 26
Honorificabilitudinitatibus. . . . . . *L. L. Lost* v 1 44
Honour. Confer fair Milan With all the honours on my brother *Tempest* i 2 127
Till thou didst seek to violate The honour of my child . . . i 2 348
Upon mine honour, sir, I heard a humming . . . . ii 1 317
I Beyond all limit of what else i' the world Do love, prize, honour you . iii 1 73
How does thy honour? Let me lick thy shoe . . . . iii 2 26
Honour. Shall never melt Mine honour into lust . . . *Tempest* iv 1 28
Honour, riches, marriage-blessing, Long continuance, and increasing . iv 1 106
Let me embrace thine age, whose honour cannot Be measured or confined . . . . v 1 121
He after honour hunts, I after love . . . . *T. G. of Ver.* i 1 63
Here is her oath for love, her honour's pawn . . . . . i 3 47
A son that well deserves The honour and regard of such a father . ii 4 60
She shall be dignified with this high honour—To bear my lady's train . ii 4 158
Tell me some good mean How, with my honour, I may undertake A journey to my loving Proteus . . . . ii 7 6
Upon mine honour, he shall never know . . . . . . iii 1 48
I do desire thy worthy company, Upon whose faith and honour I repose iv 3 26
Rescue you from him That would have forced your honour and your love v 4 22
Now, by the honour of my ancestry, I do applaud thy spirit . . v 4 139
If it were not for one trifling respect, I could come to such honour!—Hang the trifle, woman! take the honour . . . *Mer. Wives* ii 1 45
I took't upon mine honour thou hadst it not . . . . . ii 2 12
You'll not bear a letter for me, you rogue! you stand upon your honour! . . . . ii 2 21
It is as much as I can do to keep the terms of my honour precise . . ii 2 23
Hiding mine honour in my necessity . . . . ii 2 25
Ensconce . . your bold-beating oaths under the shelter of your honour! ii 2 29
She dwells so securely on the excellency of her honour . . . . ii 2 252
Now doth thy honour stand, In him that was of late an heretic, As firm as faith.—'Tis well, 'tis well . . . . iv 4 8
If any in Vienna be of worth To undergo such ample grace and honour, It is Lord Angelo . . . . *Meas. for Meas.* i 1 24
We have with a leaven'd and prepared choice Proceeded to you ; therefore take your honours . . . . i 1 53
Nor need you, on mine honour, have to do With any scruple . . . i 1 64
I'll wait upon your honour . . . . i 1 85
Had a most noble father! Let but your honour know . . . . ii 1 8
Where is the provost?—Here, if it like your honour . . . . ii 1 33
If it please your honour . . . . ii 1 47 ; 53
And do bring in here before your good honour two notorious benefactors ii 1 50
My wife, sir, whom I detest before heaven and your honour . . . ii 1 70
And longing, saving your honour's reverence, for stewed prunes . . ii 1 92
Your honours have seen such dishes ; they are not China dishes . . ii 1 96
Come me to what was done to her.—Sir, your honour cannot come to that yet . . . . ii 1 123
Sir, but you shall come to it, by your honour's leave . . . . ii 1 126
Look upon his honour ; 'tis for a good purpose. Doth your honour mark his face? . . . . ii 1 155
Doth your honour see any harm in his face?—Why, no . . . . ii 1 159
How could Master Froth do the constable's wife any harm? I would know that of your honour . . . . ii 1 166
I crave your honour's pardon. What shall be done, sir, with the groaning Juliet? . . . . ii 2 14
God save your honour! . . . . ii 2 25
I am a woeful suitor to your honour, Please but your honour hear me . ii 2 27
Heaven keep your honour! . . . . ii 2 157 ; ii 4 34
On mine honour, My words express my purpose.—Ha! little honour to be much believed, And most pernicious purpose! . . . . . ii 4 149
Yet hath he in him such a mind of honour . . . . . . ii 4 179
Would bark your honour from that trunk you bear, And leave you naked iii 1 72
Six or seven winters more respect Than a perpetual honour . . . iii 1 77
She, having the truth of honour in her, hath made him that gracious denial . . . . iii 1 166
By this, is your brother saved, your honour untainted . . . . iii 1 264
Be good to me ; your honour is accounted a merciful man . . . iii 2 203
May it please your honour . . . . iii 2 209 ; *T. of Athens* i 2 187 ; iii 2 33
Revenges to your heart, And general honour . . . *Meas. for Meas.* iv 3 141
I warrant your honour.—The warrant's for yourself ; take heed to't . v 1 83
After much debatement, My sisterly remorse confutes mine honour . v 1 100
Thou art suborn'd against his honour In hateful practice . . . v 1 106
I never spake with her . . . , Upon my faith and honour . . . v 1 224
Whose salt imagination yet hath wrong'd Your well defended honour . v 1 407
Consenting to the safeguard of your honour, I thought your marriage fit v 1 424
And passed sentence may not be recall'd But to our honour's great disparagement . . . . *Com. of Errors* i 1 149
And draw within the compass of suspect The unviolated honour of your wife . . . . iii 1 88
I'll prove mine honour and mine honesty Against thee presently . . v 1 30
Don Peter hath bestowed much honour on a young Florentine *Much Ado* i 1 10
Spare not to tell him that he hath wronged his honour . . . . ii 2 23
In love of your brother's honour, who hath made this match . . . ii 2 37
It would better fit your honour to change your mind . . . . iii 2 119
She's but the sign and semblance of her honour . . . . . iv 1 34
Two of them have the very bent of honour . . . . . . iv 1 188
If they wrong her honour, The proudest of them shall well hear of it . iv 1 193
Spite of cormorant devouring Time, The endeavour of this present breath may buy That honour which shall bate his scythe's keen edge *L. L. Lost* i 1 6
Now subscribe your names, That his own hand may strike his honour down . . . . i 1 20
Receive such welcome at my hand As honour without breach of honour may Make tender of . . . . ii 1 170
The best ward of mine honour is rewarding my dependents . . . iii 1 133
Some certain special honours it pleaseth his greatness to impart . . v 1 112
Now by my maiden honour, yet as pure As the unsullied lily, I protest v 2 351
Upon mine honour, no.—Peace, peace! forbear : Your oath once broke v 2 439
All my powers, address your love and might To honour Helen! *M. N. Dream* ii 2 144
If it stand, as you yourself still do, Within the eye of honour *Mer. of Ven.* i 1 137
That clear honour Were purchased by the merit of the wearer! . . ii 9 42
How much low peasantry would then be glean'd From the true seed of honour! and how much honour Pick'd from the chaff and ruin of the times! . . . . ii 9 47
When your honours mean to solemnize The bargain of your faith . . iii 2 194
And one in whom The ancient Roman honour more appears . . . iii 2 297
If you knew to whom you show this honour . . . . . . iii 4 5
O wise young judge, how I do honour thee! . . . . . . iv 1 224
If you had known the virtue of the ring, Or half her worthiness that gave the ring, Or your own honour to contain the ring, You would not then have parted with the ring . . . . v 1 201
No, by my honour, madam, by my soul, No woman had it . . . v 1 209
My honour would not let ingratitude So much besmear it . . . v 1 218
Now, by mine honour, which is yet mine own, I'll have that doctor for my bedfellow . . . . v 1 232
I would be loath to foil him, as I must, for my own honour *As Y. Like It* i 1 137

Honour. No further in sport neither than with safety of a pure blush thou mayst in honour come off again . . . *As Y. Like It* i 2 32
No, by mine honour . . .—Where learned you that oath, fool?—Of a certain knight that swore by his honour they were good pancakes and swore by his honour the mustard was naught . . . i 2 67
You are not forsworn : no more was this knight, swearing by his honour, for he never had any . . . i 2 83
My father's love is enough to honour him: enough! speak no more of him . . . i 2 89
Upon mine honour, And in the greatness of my word, you die . . . i 3 90
Bearded like the pard, Jealous in honour, sudden and quick in quarrel ii 7 151
Honour, high honour and renown, To Hymen, god of every town! . . . v 4 151
You to your former honour I bequeath . . . v 4 192
Say 'What is it your honour will command?' . . . *T. of Shrew* Ind. 1 54; 115
An't please your honour . . . Ind. 1 77; *Hen. VIII.* v 4 78
I think 'twas Soto that your honour means.—'Tis very true *T. of Shrew* Ind 1 88
For yet his honour never heard a play . . . Ind. 1 96
Will't please your honour taste of these conserves? . . . Ind. 2 3
What raiment will your honour wear to-day?—I am Christopher Sly; call not me 'honour' . . . Ind. 2 4
Heaven cease this idle humour in your honour! . . . Ind. 2 14
Your honour's players, hearing your amendment, Are come to play Ind. 2 131
So honour peereth in the meanest habit . . . iv 3 176
They may jest Till their own scorn return to them unnoted Ere they can hide their levity in honour . . . *All's Well* i 2 35
His honour, Clock to itself, knew the true minute . . . i 2 38
Whose aged honour cites a virtuous youth . . . i 3 216
Would your honour But give me leave to try success, I'ld venture . . . i 3 252
See that you come Not to woo honour, but to wed it . . . ii 1 15
Till honour be bought up and no sword worn But one to dance with! . ii 1 32
By heaven, I'll steal away.—There's honour in the theft . . . ii 1 34
By my faith and honour, If seriously I may convey my thoughts . . ii 1 83
Wherein the honour Of my dear father's gift stands chief in power . ii 1 114
The honour, sir, that flames in your fair eyes, Before I speak, too threateningly replies . . . ii 3 86
Where great additions swell's, and virtue none, It is a dropsied honour ii 3 135
In these to nature she's immediate heir, And these breed honour . . ii 3 140
That is honour's scorn, Which challenges itself as honour's born . . ii 3 140
Honours thrive, When rather from our acts we them derive Than our foregoers . . . ii 3 142
Virtue and she Is her own dower; honour and wealth from me . . ii 3 151
My honour's at the stake; which to defeat, I must produce my power ii 3 156
It is in us to plant thine honour where We please to have it grow . . ii 3 163
What great creation and what dole of honour Flies where you bid it ii 3 176
By mine honour, if I were but two hours younger, I'ld beat thee . . ii 3 268
He wears his honour in a box unseen, That hugs his kicky-wicky here at home . . . ii 3 296
And all the honours that can fly from us Shall on them settle . . iii 1 20
Will lay upon him all the honour That good convenience claims . . iii 2 74
Tell him that his sword can never win The honour that he loses . . iii 2 97
Whence honour but of danger wins a scar, As oft it loses all . . . iii 2 124
The honour of a maid is her name; and no legacy is so rich as honesty iii 5 12
Brokes with all that can in such a suit Corrupt the tender honour of a maid iii 5 75
For the love of laughter, hinder not the honour of his design . . iii 6 44
Can bring this instrument of honour again into his native quarter . iii 6 69
An honour 'longing to our house, Bequeathed down from many ancestors iv 2 42
Mine honour's such a ring: My chastity's the jewel of our house . . iv 2 45
Thus your own proper wisdom Brings in the champion Honour on my part . . . iv 2 50
My house, mine honour, yea, my life, be thine, And I'll be bid by thee iv 2 52
And this night he fleshes his will in the spoil of her honour . . . iv 3 20
He had the honour to be the officer at a place there called Mile-end . iv 3 301
I would do the man what honour I can, but of this I am not certain . iv 3 304
A scar nobly got, or a noble scar, is a good livery of honour . . . iv 5 106
I beseech your honour to hear me one single word . . . v 2 37
I could not answer in that course of honour As she had made the overture . . . v 3 98
Thou speak'st it falsely, as I love mine honour . . . v 3 113
His vows are forfeited to me, and my honour's paid to him . . . v 3 143
Whose age and honour Both suffer under this complaint we bring . . v 3 162
Lay a more noble thought upon mine honour Than for to think that I would sink it here . . . v 3 180
Fairer prove your honour Than in my thought it lies . . . v 3 183
Have you not set mine honour at the stake? . . . *T. Night* iii 1 129
By the roses of the spring, By maidhood, honour, truth and every thing iii 1 162
I have said too much unto a heart of stone And laid mine honour too unchary out . . . iii 4 222
What shall you ask of me that I'll deny, That honour saved may upon asking give?—Nothing but this; your true love . . . iii 4 232
How with mine honour may I give him that Which I have given to you? iii 4 234
The gentleman will, for his honour's sake, have one bout with you . iii 4 336
That very envy and the tongue of loss Cried fame and honour on him . v 1 62
And tell me, in the modesty of honour, Why you have given me such clear lights of favour . . . v 1 343
If I Had servants true about me, that bare eyes To see alike mine honour as their profits, Their own particular thrifts . . . *W. Tale* i 2 310
I'll give no blemish to her honour, none . . . i 2 341
I conjure thee, by all the parts of man Which honour does acknowledge i 2 401
I will tell you; Since I am charged in honour . . . i 2 407
Be not uncertain; For, by the honour of my parents, I Have utter'd truth i 2 442
More it would content me To have her honour true than your suspicion ii 1 160
A worthy lady And one whom much I honour . . . ii 2 6
To lock up honesty and honour from The access of gentle visitors! . ii 2 10
Your honour and your goodness is so evident That your free undertaking cannot miss A thriving issue . . . ii 2 43
But durst not tempt a minister of honour, Lest she should be denied . ii 2 50
Unless he take the course that you have done, Commit me for committing honour, trust it, He shall not rule me . . . ii 3 49
The sacred honour of himself, his queen's, His hopeful son's . . . ii 3 84
Standing To prate and talk for life and honour . . . iii 2 42
For honour, 'Tis a derivative from me to mine . . . iii 2 44
If one jot beyond The bound of honour, or in act or will That way . iii 2 52
I do confess I loved him as in honour he required . . . iii 2 64
No life, I prize it not a straw, but for mine honour, Which I would free iii 2 111
Your honours all, I do refer me to the oracle: Apollo be my judge! . iii 2 115
He, most humane And fill'd with honour, . . . Unclasp'd my practice iii 2 167
Quit his fortunes here, . . . and to the hazard Of all incertainties himself commended, No richer than his honour . . . iii 2 171
Nor was't much, Thou wouldst have poison'd good Camillo's honour . iii 2 189
Since my desires Run not before mine honour . . . iv 4 34

Honour. Him too, That makes himself, but for our honour therein, Unworthy thee . . . *W. Tale* iv 4 447
Save him from danger, do him love and honour . . . iv 4 521
Good Paulina, Who hast the memory of Hermione, I know, in honour . v 1 51
Whose honour and whose honesty till now Endured all weathers . . v 1 194
Your honour not o'erthrown by your desires, I am friend to them and you v 1 230
We honour you with trouble . . . v 3 9
Thou dost shame thy mother And wound her honour with this diffidence *K. John* i 1 65
Heaven guard my mother's honour and my land! . . . i 1 70
My father gave me honour, yours gave land . . . i 1 164
A foot of honour better than I was; But many a many foot of land the worse . . . i 1 182
And if his name be George, I'll call him Peter; For new-made honour doth forget men's names . . . i 1 187
Where is he, That holds in chase mine honour up and down? . . . i 1 223
That for thine own gain shouldst defend mine honour . . . i 1 242
Gild her bridal bed and make her rich In titles, honours and promotions ii 1 492
She is bound in honour still to do What you in wisdom still vouchsafe to say . . . ii 1 522
That which upholdeth him that thee upholds, His honour: O, thine honour, Lewis, thine honour! . . . iii 1 316
We will not line his thin bestained cloak With our pure honours . . iv 3 25
I, by the honour of my marriage-bed, . . . claim this land for mine . v 2 93
Such offers of our peace As we with honour and respect may take . . v 7 85
If guilty dread have left thee so much strength As to take up mine honour's pawn, then stoop . . . *Richard II.* i 1 74
Mine honour is my life; both grow in one; Take honour from me, and my life is done . . . i 1 182
Mine honour let me try; In that I live and for that will I die . . i 1 184
Ere my tongue Shall wound my honour with such feeble wrong . . i 1 191
Go, say I sent thee forth to purchase honour And not the king exiled thee i 3 282
To my bed, then to my grave: Love they to live that love and honour have ii 1 138
Those thoughts Which honour and allegiance cannot think . . . ii 1 208
'Tis not my meaning To raze one title of your honour out . . . ii 3 75
By the buried hand of warlike Gaunt, And by the worth and honour of himself . . . iii 3 110
Either I must, or have mine honour soil'd . . . iv 1 23
His honour is as true In this appeal as thou art all unjust . . . iv 1 44
There is my honour's pawn; Engage it to the trial, if thou darest . iv 1 55
Here do I throw down this, If he may be repeal'd, to try his honour . iv 1 85
Thou map of honour, thou King Richard's tomb, And not King Richard v 1 12
Whose state and honour I for aye allow . . . v 2 40
Now, by mine honour, by my life, by my troth, I will appeach the villain v 2 78
Which he . . . Takes on the point of honour to support . . . v 3 11
He shall spend mine honour with his shame . . . v 3 68
Mine honour lives when his dishonour dies . . . v 3 70
For though mine enemy thou hast ever been, High sparks of honour in thee have I seen . . . v 6 29
A son who is the theme of honour's tongue . . . *1 Hen. IV.* i 1 81
Yet time serves wherein you may redeem Your banish'd honours . . . i 3 181
Send danger from the east unto the west, So honour cross it from the north to south, And let them grapple . . . i 3 196
It were an easy leap, To pluck bright honour from the pale-faced moon i 3 202
And pluck up drowned honour by the locks . . . i 3 205
Thou hast lost much honour, that thou wert not with me in this action ii 4 22
What never-dying honour hath he got Against renowned Douglas! . . iii 2 106
This same child of honour and renown, This gallant Hotspur . . . iii 2 139
For every honour sitting on his helm, Would they were multitudes! . iii 2 142
Thou art the king of honour . . . iv 1 10
I thought your honour had already been at Shrewsbury . . . iv 2 58
If well-respected honour bid me on, I hold as little counsel with weak fear iv 3 10
Honour pricks me on. Yea, but how if honour prick me off when I come on? . . . v 1 131
Can honour set to a leg? no: or an arm? no . . . v 1 133
Honour hath no skill in surgery, then? no. What is honour? a word . v 1 135
What is in that word honour? what is that honour? air. A trim reckoning! . . . v 1 137
Honour is a mere scutcheon: and so ends my catechism . . . v 1 143
What honour dost thou seek Upon my head? . . . v 3 2
There's honour for you! here's no vanity! . . . v 3 33
I like not such grinning honour as Sir Walter hath: give me life: which if I can save, so; if not, honour comes unlooked for, and there's an end . . . v 3 62
All the budding honours on thy crest I'll crop, to make a garland . v 4 72
If your father will do me any honour, so . . . v 4 144
Please it your honour . . . *2 Hen. IV.* i 1 5; *Coriolanus* v 6 140
Divorce not wisdom from your honour . . . *2 Hen. IV.* i 1 162
My honour is at pawn; And, but my going, nothing can redeem it . . ii 3 7
There were two honours lost, yours and your son's . . . ii 3 16
Never, O never, do his ghost the wrong To hold your honour more precise and nice With others than with him! . . . ii 3 40
No abuse, Hal, o' mine honour; no abuse . . . ii 4 340
These noble lords Had not been here, to dress the ugly form Of base and bloody insurrection With your fair honours . . . iv 1 41
To lay a heavy and unequal hand Upon our honours . . . iv 1 103
What thing, in honour, had my father lost, That need to be revived and breathed in me? . . . iv 1 113
By the honour of my blood, My father's purposes have been mistook . iv 2 55
And put the world's whole strength Into one giant arm, it shall not force This lineal honour from me . . . iv 5 46
Dost thou so hunger for mine empty chair That thou wilt needs invest thee with my honours Before thy hour be ripe? . . . iv 5 96
England shall give him office, honour, might . . . iv 5 130
If I affect it more Than as your honour and as your renown . . . iv 5 146
It seem'd in me But as an honour snatch'd with boisterous hand . . iv 5 192
What I did, I did in honour, Led by the impartial conduct of my soul . v 2 35
And I do wish your honours may increase . . . v 2 104
As much as would maintain, to the king's honour, Full fifteen earls *Hen. V.* i 1 12
And honour's thought Reigns solely in the breast of every man . . ii Prol. 3
What mightst thou do, that honour would thee do! . . . ii Prol. 18
Furnish him with all appertinents Belonging to his honour . . . ii 2 88
All wide-stretched honours that pertain By custom and the ordinance of times Unto the crown of France . . . ii 4 82
These be good humours! your honour wins bad humours . . . iii 2 27
O, for honour of our land, Let us not hang like roping icicles! . . iii 5 22
By faith and honour, Our madams mock at us . . . iii 5 27
With spirit of honour edged More sharper than your swords . . . iii 5 38
A man that I love and honour with my soul, and my heart . . . iii 6 8
And 'twere more honour some were away . . . iii 7 80

Honour. Though we upon this mountain's basis by Took stand for idle speculation : But that our honours must not *Hen. V.* iv 2 32
The fewer men, the greater share of honour iv 3 22
If it be a sin to covet honour, I am the most offending soul alive iv 3 28
I would not lose so great an honour As one man more, methinks, would share from me For the best hope I have iv 3 31
The sun shall greet them, And draw their honours reeking up to heaven iv 3 101
Shame and eternal shame, nothing but shame! Let us die in honour iv 5 11
I wear it for a memorable honour iv 7 109
Your grace doo's me as great honours as can be desired iv 7 167
Wear it for an honour in thy cap Till I do challenge it iv 8 63
Old I do wax ; and from my weary limbs Honour is cudgelled v 1 90
By mine honour, in true English, I love thee v 2 237
Let not sloth dim your honours new-begot *1 Hen. VI.* i 1 79
We will rush on them. Now for the honour of the forlorn French! i 2 19
Woman, do what thou canst to save our honours ; Drive them from Orleans i 2 147
How shall I honour thee for this success? i 6 5
Will not your honours bear me company?—No, truly ii 2 53
A true-born gentleman And stands upon the honour of his birth ii 4 28
Since then hath Richard been obscured, Deprived of honour and inheritance ii 5 27
In honour of a true Plantagenet And for alliance sake ii 5 52
Your honour is the last.—True ; and thou seest that I no issue have ii 5 93
Those bitter injuries . . . I doubt not but with honour to redress ii 5 126
Vow, Burgundy, by honour of thy house iii 2 77
This is a double honour, Burgundy ; Yet heavens have glory! iii 2 116
Your honours shall perceive how I will work iii 3 27
Disgracing of these colours that I wear In honour of my noble Lord of York iii 4 30
Thy lord I honour as he is.—Why, what is he? as good a man as York iii 4 35
To Bourdeaux, York! Else, farewell Talbot, France, and England's honour iv 3 23
Lives, honours, lands and all hurry to loss iv 3 53
Hath sullied all his gloss of former honour By this . . . wild adventure iv 4 6
You, his false hopes, the trust of England's honour, Keep off aloof iv 4 20
Flight cannot stain the honour you have won ; But mine it will iv 5 26
Who art thou? say, that I may honour thee v 3 50
Consent, and for thy honour give consent, Thy daughter shall be wedded v 3 136
Command in Anjou what your honour pleases v 3 147
Of virtuous chaste intents, To love and honour Henry as her lord v 5 21
How shall we then dispense with that contract, And not deface your honour? v 5 29
And shall these labours and these honours die? *2 Hen. VI.* i 1 95
May he be suffocate, That dims the honour of this warlike isle! i 1 125
Enchased with all the honours of the world i 2 8
Tumble down thy husband and thyself From top of honour to disgrace's feet i 2 49
In the city Tours Thou ran'st a tilt in honour of my love i 3 54
Noble she is, but if she have forgot Honour and virtue ii 1 195
Salute our rightful sovereign With honour of his birthright to the crown ii 2 62
You are more nobly born, Despoiled of your honour in your life ii 3 10
This staff of honour raught, there let it stand Where it best fits to be ii 3 43
In thy face I see The map of honour, truth and loyalty iii 1 203
But all the honour Salisbury hath won Is, that he was the lord ambassador iii 2 275
Far be it we should honour such as these With humble suit iv 1 123
I am sorry for't: the man is a proper man, of mine honour iv 2 103
The lord mayor craves aid of your honour from the Tower iv 5 5
Wherein have I offended most? Have I affected wealth or honour? iv 7 104
Who hateth him and honours not his father iv 8 16
And heavens and honour be witness iv 8 64
Wear it as a herald's coat, To emblaze the honour that thy master got iv 10 76
Upon thine honour, is he prisoner?—Upon mine honour, he is prisoner v 1 42
In whose cold blood no spark of honour bides *3 Hen. VI.* i 1 184
To cease this civil war, and, whilst I live, To honour me as thy king i 1 198
But thou preferr'st thy life before thine honour i 1 246
Do not honour him so much To prick thy finger, though to wound his heart i 4 54
Now to London, To see these honours in possession ii 6 110
Thereon I pawn my credit and mine honour iii 3 116
Shame on himself! for my desert is honour : And to repair my honour lost for him, I here renounce him iii 3 192
Matching more for wanton lust than honour iii 3 210
But as this title honours me and mine, So your dislike, to whom I would be pleasing, Doth cloud my joys with danger and with sorrow iv 1 72
'Tis the more honour, because more dangerous iv 3 15
Give me worship and quietness ; I like it better than a dangerous honour iv 3 17
Courage, my masters! honour now or never! iv 3 24
While he enjoys the honour and his ease iv 6 52
Here Southam lies : The drum your honour hears marcheth from Warwick v 1 13
Set down, set down your honourable load, If honour may be shrouded in a hearse *Richard III.* i 2 2
And lay those honours on your high deserts i 3 97
Thy honour, state and seat is due to me i 3 112
Thou loathed issue of thy father's loins! Thou rag of honour! i 3 233
Your fire-new stamp of honour is scarce current i 3 256
Princes have but their titles for their glories, An outward honour for an inward toil i 4 79
Bid him not fear the separated councils : His honour and myself are at the one, And at the other is my servant Catesby iii 2 21
God hold it, to your honour's good content! iii 2 107
Well met, my lord ; I am glad to see your honour iii 2 110
Your honour hath no shriving work in hand iii 2 116
But shall we wear these honours for a day? Or shall they last? iv 2 5
My due by promise, For which your honour and your faith is pawn'd iv 2 92
To the dignity and height of honour iv 4 243
What dignity, what honour, Canst thou demise to any child of mine? iv 4 246
Under what title shall I woo for thee, That God, the law, my honour and her love, Can make seem pleasing to her tender years? iv 4 341
This is no oath : The George, profaned, hath lost his holy honour iv 4 369
As I belong to worship and affect In honour honesty *Hen. VIII.* i 1 40
To whom as great a charge as little honour He meant to lay upon i 1 77
Take it from a heart that wishes towards you Honour and plenteous safety i 1 104
And from a mouth of honour quite cry down This Ipswich fellow's insolence i 1 137
Thus the cardinal Does buy and sell his honour as he pleases i 1 192
Love yourself, and in that love Not unconsider'd leave your honour i 2 15
Whose honour heaven shield from soil! i 2 26
You shall hear . . . of him Things to strike honour sad i 2 126
Restored me to my honours, and, out of ruins, Made my name once more noble ii 1 114

Honour. Life, honour, name and all That made me happy at one stroke has taken For ever from the world *Hen. VIII.* ii 1 116
All men's honours Lie like one lump before him ii 2 48
Does purpose honour to you no less flowing Than Marchioness of Pembroke ii 3 62
Beauty and honour in her are so mingled That they have caught the king ii 3 76
Honour's train Is longer than his foreskirt ii 3 97
Against mine honour aught, My bond to wedlock ii 4 39
You tender more your person's honour than Your high profession spiritual ii 4 116
Yea, upon mine honour, I free you from't ii 4 156
To taint that honour every good tongue blesses iii 1 55
In such a point of weight, so near mine honour,—More near my life iii 1 71
'Twill be much Both for your honour better and your cause iii 1 95
When she has done most, Yet will I add an honour, a great patience iii 1 137
The honour of it Does pay the act of it iii 2 181
My heart dropp'd love, my power rain'd honour, more On you than any iii 2 185
Bade me enjoy it, with the place and honours, During my life iii 2 248
I should tell you You have as little honesty as honour iii 2 271
To-morrow blossoms, And bears his blushing honours thick upon him iii 2 354
Too much honour : O, 'tis a burthen, Cromwell, 'tis a burthen Too heavy for a man that hopes for heaven! iii 2 383
No sun shall ever usher forth mine honours, Or gild again the noble troops that waited Upon my smiles iii 2 410
Once trod the ways of glory, And sounded all the depths and shoals of honour iii 2 436
In celebration of this day with shows, Pageants and sights of honour iv 1 11
They that bear The cloth of honour over her, are four barons iv 1 48
That the great child of honour, Cardinal Wolsey, Was dead iv 2 6
He gave his honours to the world again, His blessed part to heaven iv 2 29
Undoubtedly Was fashion'd to much honour from his cradle iv 2 50
And, to add greater honours to his age Than man could give him, he died fearing God iv 2 67
I wish no other herald, No other speaker of my living actions, To keep mine honour from corruption iv 2 71
Whom I most hated living, thou hast made me, With thy religious truth and modesty, Now in his ashes honour iv 2 75
When I am dead, good wench, Let me be used with honour iv 2 168
Look, the good man weeps! He's honest, on mine honour v 1 153
Of purpose laid by some that hate me . . . To quench mine honour v 2 16
Is this the honour they do one another? 'Tis well there's one above 'em yet v 2 26
If we suffer, Out of our easiness and childish pity To one man's honour, this contagious sickness, Farewell all physic v 3 26
I cry your honour mercy ; you may, worst Of all this table, say so v 3 78
One that, in all obedience, makes the church The chief aim of his honour v 3 118
The greatest monarch now alive may glory In such an honour v 3 165
Lords, one remain ; So I grow stronger, you more honour gain v 3 182
That I was fain to draw mine honour in, and let 'em win the work v 4 61
Those about her From her shall read the perfect ways of honour v 5 38
Who from the sacred ashes of her honour Shall star-like rise v 5 46
His honour and the greatness of his name Shall be, and make new nations v 5 52
I have received much honour by your presence v 5 72
That holds his honour higher than his ease *Troi. and Cres.* i 3 266
If any come, Hector shall honour him i 3 280
Whom may you else oppose, That can from Hector bring his honour off? i 3 334
Both our honour and our shame in this Are dogg'd with two strange followers i 3 364
And all damage else—As honour, loss of time, travail, expense ii 2 4
Weigh you the worth and honour of a king So great as our dread father in a scale Of common ounces? ii 2 26
Manhood and honour Should have hare-hearts ii 2 47
There can be no evasion To blench from this and to stand firm by honour ii 2 68
The goodness of a quarrel Which hath our several honours all engaged ii 2 124
She is a theme of honour and renown ii 2 199
I hope I shall know your honour better.—I do desire it iii 1 13
You are in the state of grace.—Grace! not so, friend ; honour and lordship are my titles iii 1 16
Not a man, for being simply man, Hath any honour, but honour for those honours That are without him, as place, riches iii 3 81
Perseverance, dear my lord, Keeps honour bright iii 3 151
Honour travels in a strait so narrow, Where one but goes abreast iii 3 154
Shall Ajax fight with Hector?—Ay, and perhaps receive much honour iii 3 226
But, in mine emulous honour, let him die, With every joint a wound! iv 1 28
But that you say 'be't so,' I'll speak it in my spirit and honour, 'no' iv 4 137
Cousin, all honour to thee!—I thank thee, Hector : Thou art too gentle iv 5 138
Not Neoptolemus so mirable . . . could promise to himself A thought of added honour torn from Hector iv 5 145
As gentle tell me, of what honour was This Cressida in Troy? iv 5 287
Fail fame ; honour or go or stay ; My major vow lies here v 1 48
I'll keep you company.—Sweet sir, you honour me v 1 93
Mine honour keeps the weather of my fate : Life every man holds dear ; but the brave man Hold honour far more precious-dear than life v 3 26
Art thou of blood and honour?—No, no, I am a rascal v 4 29
Half all Cominius' honours are to Marcius, Though Marcius earn'd them not, and all his faults To Marcius shall be honours, though indeed In aught he merit not *Coriolanus* i 1 277
I leave your honours i 2 33
The gods assist you!—And keep your honours safe! i 2 37
I should freelier rejoice in that absence wherein he won honour than in the embracements of his bed i 3 4
Considering how honour would become such a person i 3 11
This is true, on mine honour ; and so, I pray, go with us i 3 113
Where the dull tribunes, That, with the fusty plebeians, hate thine honours, Shall say against their hearts 'We thank the gods' i 9 7
Mine emulation Hath not that honour in't it had i 10 13
He hath won, With fame, a name to Caius Marcius ; these In honour follows Coriolanus ii 1 182
By deed-achieving honour newly named ii 1 190
I have received not only greetings, But with them change of honours ii 1 214
He cannot temperately transport his honours ii 1 240
But they Upon their ancient malice will forget With the least cause these his new honours ii 1 245
But he hath so planted his honours in their eyes ii 2 33
Whom We met here both to thank and to remember With honours like himself ii 2 52
Convented Upon a pleasing treaty, and have hearts Inclinable to honour ii 2 60
Your honours' pardon : I had rather have my wounds to heal again Than hear say how I got them ii 2 72

Honour. He had rather venture all his limbs for honour Than one on's ears to hear it . . . *Coriolanus* ii 2 84
He cannot but with measure fit the honours Which we devise him . ii 2 127
Take to you, as your predecessors have, Your honour with your form . ii 2 148
And to our noble consul Wish we all joy and honour . ii 2 157
Every one of us has a single honour, in giving him our own voices with our own tongues . ii 3 49
Rather than fool it so, Let the high office and the honour go . ii 3 129
Honour and policy, like unsever'd friends, I' the war do grow together iii 2 42
If it be honour in your wars to seem The same you are not, which, for your best ends, You adopt your policy, how is it less or worse, That it shall hold companionship in peace With honour, as in war, since that to both It stands in like request? . iii 2 46
I would dissemble with my nature where My fortunes and my friends at stake required I should do so in honour . iii 2 64
I will not do't, Lest I surcease to honour mine own truth . iii 2 121
Let them accuse me by invention, I Will answer in mine honour . iii 2 144
He was A noble servant to them; but he could not Carry his honours even . iv 7 37
You might condemn us As poisonous of your honour . v 3 135
Thou hast affected the fine strains of honour, To imitate the graces of the gods . v 3 149
Has cluck'd thee to the wars and safely home, Loaden with honour . v 3 164
I am glad thou hast set thy mercy and thy honour At difference in thee v 3 200
I raised him, and I pawn'd Mine honour for his truth . v 6 22
Made peace With no less honour to the Antiates Than shame to the Romans . v 6 80
Then let my father's honours live in me . . . *T. Andron.* i 1 7
Laden with honour's spoils, Returns the good Andronicus to Rome . i 1 36
Let us entreat, by honour of his name . i 1 39
In the . . . senate's right, Whom you pretend to honour and adore . i 1 42
So I love and honour thee and thine, Thy noble brother Titus . i 1 49
With honour and with fortune is return'd . i 1 67
In peace and honour rest you here, my sons! . i 1 150; 156
In peace and honour live Lord Titus long! . i 1 157
And triumphs over chance in honour's bed . i 1 178
Give me a staff of honour for mine age, But not a sceptre . i 1 198
I do not flatter thee, But honour thee, and will do till I die . i 1 213
Mine honour's ensigns humbled at thy feet . i 1 252
To him that, for your honour and your state, Will use you nobly . i 1 259
Proclaim our honours, lords, with trump and drum . i 1 275
And, with these boys, mine honour thou hast wounded . i 1 365
That died in honour and Lavinia's cause . i 1 377
Lord Titus here Is in opinion and in honour wrong'd . i 1 416
On mine honour dare I undertake For good Lord Titus' innocence in all i 1 436
Let it be mine honour, good my lord, That I have reconciled your friends i 1 466
That what we did was mildly as we might, Tendering our sister's honour and our own.—That, on mine honour, here I do protest . i 1 476
Upon her wit doth earthly honour wait, And virtue stoops and trembles ii 1 10
Your swarth Cimmerian Doth make your honour of his body's hue . ii 3 73
For two and twenty sons I never wept, Because they died in honour's lofty bed . iii 1 11
With all the humbleness I may, I greet your honours . iv 2 5
Nor age nor honour shall shape privilege . iv 4 57
How stands your disposition to be married?—It is an honour that I dream not of.—An honour! . *Rom. and Jul.* i 3 66
By the stock and honour of my kin, To strike him dead I hold it not a sin i 5 60
A throne where honour may be crown'd Sole monarch of the universal earth . iii 2 93
Arbitrating that Which the commission of thy years and art Could to no issue of true honour bring . iv 1 65
Fare you well.—All happiness to your honour! . *T. of Athens* i 1 109
Pawn me to this your honour, she is his.—My hand to thee; mine honour on my promise . i 1 148
I must entreat you, honour me so much As to advance this jewel . i 2 175
And has sent your honour two brace of greyhounds . i 2 195
The best of happiness, Honour and fortunes, keep with you! . i 2 235
I love and honour him, But must not break my back to heal his finger . ii 1 23
And the detention of long-since-due debts, Against my honour . ii 2 40
To Lord Lucullus you: I hunted with his honour to-day . ii 2 198
In my lord's behalf, I come to entreat your honour . iii 1 18
This slave, Unto his honour, has my lord's meat in him . iii 1 60
Denied that honourable man! there was very little honour showed in't iii 2 20
Yonder's my lord; I have sweat to see his honour . iii 2 28
How unluckily it happened, that I should purchase the day before for a little part, and undo a great deal of honour! . iii 2 53
I hope his honour will conceive the fairest of me . iii 2 59
Who bates mine honour shall not know my coin . iii 3 26
Honour, health, and compassion to the senate! . iii 5 5
Nor did he soil the fact with cowardice—An honour in him which buys out his fault . iii 5 17
I'll pawn my victories, all My honours to you, upon his good returns . iii 5 82
'Tis honour with most lands to be at odds . iii 5 116
The senator shall bear contempt hereditary, The beggar native honour . iv 3 11
What an alteration of honour Has desperate want made! . iv 3 468
Throw thy glove, Or any token of thine honour else . v 4 50
Set honour in one eye and death i' the other, And I will look on both indifferently, For let the gods so speed me as I love The name of honour more than I fear death . *J. Cæsar* i 2 86
Well, honour is the subject of my story . i 2 92
I do believe that these applauses are For some new honours . i 2 134
Every man of them, and no man here But honours you . ii 1 91
I am not sick, if Brutus have in hand Any exploit worthy the name of honour . ii 1 317
Say I love Brutus, and I honour him; Say I fear'd Cæsar, honour'd him iii 1 128
Believe me for mine honour, and have respect to mine honour . iii 2 15
As he was fortunate, I rejoice at it: as he was valiant, I honour him . iii 2 28
There is tears for his love; joy for his fortune; honour for his valour . iii 2 30
We lay these honours on this man, To ease ourselves . iv 1 19
My noble master will appear Such as he is, full of regard and honour . iv 2 12
The name of Cassius honours this corruption . iv 3 15
And sell the mighty space of our large honours For so much trash? . iv 3 25
A peevish schoolboy, worthless of such honour, Join'd with a masker! v 1 61
A fellow of a good respect; Thy life hath had some smatch of honour in it . v 5 46
Brutus only overcame himself, And no man else hath honour by his death . v 5 57
Thy words become thee as thy wounds; They smack of honour both *Macbeth* i 2 44
For an earnest of a greater honour . i 3 104

Honour. New honours come upon him, Like our strange garments, cleave not to their mould But with the aid of use . *Macbeth* i 3 144
By doing every thing Safe toward your love and honour . i 4 27
Which honour must Not unaccompanied invest him only . i 4 39
Were poor and single business to contend Against those honours deep and broad wherewith Your majesty loads our house . i 6 17
If you shall cleave to my consent, when 'tis, It shall make honour for you ii 1 26
Unsafe the while, that we Must lave our honours in these flattering streams . iii 2 33
Here had we now our country's honour roof'd, Were the graced person of our Banquo present . iii 4 40
Do faithful homage and receive free honours . iii 6 36
I am not to you known, Though in your state of honour I am perfect . iv 2 66
Reconciled my thoughts To thy good truth and honour . iv 3 117
Honour, love, obedience, troops of friends, I must not look to have . v 3 25
Henceforth be earls, the first that ever Scotland In such an honour named . v 8 64
Our duty to your honour.—Your loves, as mine to you: farewell *Hamlet* i 2 253
Then weigh what loss your honour may sustain, If with too credent ear you list his songs . i 3 29
I must tell you, You do not understand yourself so clearly As it behoves my daughter and your honour . i 3 97
Use them after your own honour and dignity . ii 2 556
So shall I hope your virtues Will bring him to his wonted way again, To both your honours . iii 1 42
How does your honour for this many a day? . iii 1 91
Pray you, avoid it.—I warrant your honour . iii 2 17
Rightly to be great Is not to stir without great argument, But greatly to find quarrel in a straw When honour's at the stake . iv 4 56
That might your nature, honour and exception Roughly awake . v 2 242
In my terms of honour I stand aloof . v 2 257
Till by some elder masters, of known honour, I have a voice and precedent . v 2 259
I love you . . . No less than life, with grace, health, beauty, honour *Lear* i 1 59
Obey you, love you, and most honour you . i 1 100
To plainness honour's bound, When majesty stoops to folly . i 1 150
It would make a great gap in your own honour . i 2 91
He hath wrote this to feel my affection to your honour . i 2 94
If your honour judge it meet, I will place you where you shall hear . i 2 97
From her derogate body never spring A babe to honour her! . i 4 303
Fetch forth the stocks! As I have life and honour, There shall he sit ii 2 140
Who hast not in thy brows an eye discerning Thine honour from thy suffering . iv 2 53
The clearest gods, who make them honours Of men's impossibilities . iv 6 73
I will maintain My truth and honour firmly . v 3 101
It is the privilege of mine honours, My oath, and my profession . v 3 129
Such addition as your honours Have more than merited . v 3 301
Spoke such scurvy and provoking terms Against your honour . *Othello* i 2 8
Which, when I know that boasting is an honour, I shall promulgate . i 2 20
To his honours and his valiant parts Did I my soul and fortunes consecrate . i 3 254
Noble swelling spirits, That hold their honours in a wary distance . ii 3 58
I would I might entreat your honour To scan this thing no further . iii 3 244
And hold her free, I do beseech your honour . iii 3 255
Whom I with all the office of my heart Entirely honour . iii 4 114
She is protectress of her honour too: May she give that?—Her honour is an essence that's not seen; They have it very oft that have it not iv 1 14
Your honour is most welcome.—Will you walk, sir? . iv 3 4
But why should honour outlive honesty? . v 2 245
For nought I did in hate, but all in honour . v 2 295
Rich in his father's honour . *Ant. and Cleo.* i 3 50
Good now, play one scene Of excellent dissembling; and let it look Like perfect honour . i 3 80
Your honour calls you hence; Therefore be deaf to my unpitied folly . i 3 97
It wounds thine honour that I speak it now . i 4 69
That sleep and feeding may prorogue his honour Even till a Lethe'd dulness! . ii 1 26
The honour is sacred which he talks on now, Supposing that I lack'd it ii 2 85
So far ask pardon as befits mine honour To stoop in such a case . ii 2 97
'Tis not my profit that does lead mine honour; Mine honour, it . ii 7 82
When perforce he could not But pay me terms of honour, cold and sickly He vented them . iii 4 7
If I lose mine honour, I lose myself: better I were not yours . iii 4 22
Experience, manhood, honour, ne'er before Did violate so itself . iii 10 23
The scars upon your honour, therefore, he Does pity, as constrained . iii 13 58
Mine honour was not yielded, But conquer'd merely . iii 13 61
I will live, Or bathe my dying honour in the blood Shall make it live again . iv 2 6
Where rather I'll expect victorious life Than death and honour . iv 2 44
Your wife Octavia, with her modest eyes And still conclusion, shall acquire no honour Demuring upon me . iv 15 28
Of Cæsar seek your honour, with your safety. O!—They do not go together . iv 15 46
That self hand, Which writ his honour in the acts it did . v 1 22
His taints and honours Waged equal with him . v 1 30
Doing the honour of thy lordliness To one so meek . v 2 161
Sicilius, who did join his honour Against the Romans . *Cymbeline* i 1 29
I honour him Even out of your report . i 1 54
Your faithful servant: I dare lay mine honour He will remain so . i 1 174
Or I could make him swear The shes of Italy should not betray Mine interest and his honour . i 3 30
None so accomplished a courtier to convince the honour of my mistress i 4 104
I will bring from thence that honour of hers which you imagine so reserved . i 4 142
If I come off, and leave her in such honour as you have trust in . i 4 164
Thou wrong'st a gentleman, who is as far From thy report as thou from honour . i 6 146
He hath a kind of honour sets him off, More than a mortal seeming . i 6 170
And pawn mine honour for their safety . i 6 194
The heavens hold firm The walls of thy dear honour! . ii 1 68
This secret Will force him think I have pick'd the lock and ta'en The treasure of her honour . ii 2 42
We must receive him According to the honour of his sender . ii 3 63
As I am bold her honour Will remain hers . ii 4 2
I now Profess myself the winner of her honour, Together with your ring ii 4 53
The foul opinion You had of her pure honour gains or loses Your sword or mine, or masterless leaves both . ii 4 59
This is her honour! Let it be granted you have seen all this . ii 4 91
Let there be no honour Where there is beauty; truth, where semblance; love, Where there's another man . ii 4 108

Honour. Thy Cæsar knighted me; my youth I spent Much under him; of him I gather'd honour . . . *Cymbeline* iii 1 71
A pain that only seems to seek out danger I' the name of fame and honour . . . iii 3 51
Whose false oaths prevail'd Before my perfect honour . . . iii 3 67
They took thee for their mother, And every day do honour to her grave iii 3 105
You are appointed for that office; The due of honour in no point omit iii 5 11
He goes hence frowning: but it honours us That we have given him cause . . . iii 5 18
'Tis wonder That an invisible instinct should frame them To royalty unlearn'd, honour untaught . . . iv 2 178
Knighthoods and honours, borne As I wear mine, are titles but of scorn v 2 6
To-day how many would have given their honours To have saved their carcases! . . . v 3 66
Our fealty and Tenantius' right With honour to maintain . . . v 4 74
By our greatness and the grace of it, Which is our honour . . . v 5 133
He, true knight, No lesser of her honour confident Than I did truly find her . . . v 5 187
With unchaste purpose and with oath to violate My lady's honour . v 5 285
Your entertain shall be As doth befit our honour . . . *Pericles* i 1 120
This prince must die; For by his fall my honour must keep high . . i 1 149
Nor boots it me to say I honour him, If he suspect I may dishonour him i 2 20
Then honour be but a goal to my will, This day I'll rise, or else add ill to ill . . . ii 1 171
Our daughter, In honour of whose birth these triumphs are . . . ii 2 5
'Tis now your honour, daughter, to explain The labour of each knight . ii 2 14
Which, to preserve mine honour, I'll perform . . . ii 2 16
Honour we love; For who hates honour hates the gods above . . ii 3 21
Princes in this should live like gods above, Who freely give to every one that comes To honour them . . . ii 3 61
For honour's cause, forbear your suffrages . . . ii 4 41
This . . . hath she vow'd, And on her virgin honour will not break it . ii 5 12
Never aim'd so high to love your daughter, But bent all offices to honour her . . . ii 5 48
I came unto your court for honour's cause, And not to be a rebel . . ii 5 61
He that otherwise accounts of me, This sword shall prove he's honour's enemy . . . ii 5 64
O you gods! . . . We here below Recall not what we give, and therein may Use honour with you . . . iii 1 26
Doth give me A more content in course of true delight Than to be thirsty after tottering honour . . . iii 2 40
Your honour has through Ephesus pour'd forth Your charity . . iii 2 43
I believe you; Your honour and your goodness teach me to't . . iii 3 26
By bright Diana, whom we honour . . . iii 3 28
Now, the gods to bless your honour!—I am glad to see your honour in good health.—You may so . . . iv 6 23
Your honour knows what 'tis to say well enough . . . iv 6 34
Come, we will leave his honour and her together. Go thy ways . . iv 6 70
If you were born to honour, show it now . . . iv 6 99
Honourable man, Mine eyes, even sociable to the show of thine, Fall fellowly drops . . . *Tempest* v 1 62
The match Were rich and honourable . . . *T. G. of Ver.* iii 1 64
It's an honourable kind of thievery . . . iv 1 40
He bears an honourable mind, And will not use a woman lawlessly . v 3 13
My chambers are honourable: fie! privacy? fie! . . *Mer. Wives* iv 5 23
Prove it before these varlets here, thou honourable man *Meas. for Meas.* ii 1 89
Stuffed with all honourable virtues . . . *Much Ado* i 1 57
Be happy, lady; for you are like an honourable father . . . i 1 113
Is not marriage honourable in a beggar? Is not your lord honourable without marriage? . . . iii 4 30
Here stand a pair of honourable men; A third is fled . . . v 1 276
This day to be conjoin'd In the state of honourable marriage . . . v 4 30
When he plays at tables, chides the dice In honourable terms *L. L. Lost* v 2 327
Who shall go about To cozen fortune and be honourable Without the stamp of merit? . . . *Mer. of Venice* ii 9 38
And tell quaint lies, How honourable ladies sought my love . . . iii 4 70
Commend me to your honourable wife . . . iv 1 273
The world esteem'd thy father honourable . . . *As Y. Like It* i 2 238
Let us make an honourable retreat; though not with bag and baggage. iii 2 169
So is the forehead of a married man more honourable than the bare brow of a bachelor . . . iii 3 61
Tell him from me, as he will win my love, He bear himself with honourable action . . . *T. of Shrew* Ind. 1 110
I am a mother to you.—Mine honourable mistress . . . *All's Well* i 3 145
You are more saucy with lords and honourable personages . . . ii 3 278
They say the French count has done most honourable service . . . iii 5 4
You need but plead your honourable privilege . . . iv 5 95
So please your majesty, my master hath been an honourable gentleman v 3 239
The honourable lady of the house, which is she? . . . *T. Night* i 5 177
But I cannot Believe this crack to be in my dread mistress, So sovereignly being honourable . . . *W. Tale* i 2 323
Since I am charged in honour and by him That I think honourable . . i 2 408
'Tis pity she's not honest, honourable . . . ii 1 68
I have That honourable grief lodged here which burns Worse than tears drown . . . ii 1 111
Whose honourable thoughts, Thoughts high for one so tender, cleft the heart . . . iii 2 196
I'll not seek far . . . to find thee An honourable husband . . . v 3 143
An honourable conduct let him have: Pembroke, look to't . . *K. John* i 1 29
From a resolved and honourable war, To a most base . . . peace . . ii 1 585
There Where honourable rescue and defence Cries out . . . v 2 18
Let me wipe off this honourable dew, That silverly doth progress on thy cheeks . . . v 2 45
My noble Lord of Lancaster, The honourable father to my foe *Richard II.* i 1 136
And by the honourable tomb he swears, That stands upon your royal grandsire's bones . . . iii 3 105
That honourable day shall ne'er be seen . . . iv 1 91
And is not this an honourable spoil? A gallant prize? . . 1 *Hen. IV.* i 1 74
For moving such a dish of skim milk with so honourable an action! . . ii 3 36
We must all to the wars, and thy place shall be honourable . . . ii 4 596
To you This honourable bounty shall belong . . . v 5 26
You call honourable boldness impudent sauciness . . 2 *Hen. IV.* ii 1 134
I will imitate the honourable Romans in brevity . . . ii 2 134
Is this proceeding just and honourable?—Is your assembly so? . . iv 2 110
His cause being just and his quarrel honourable . . . *Hen. V.* iv 1 134
To this hour is an honourable badge of the service . . . iv 7 105
Will you mock at an ancient tradition, begun upon an honourable respect? v 1 75
My honourable lords, health to you all! Sad tidings bring I 1 *Hen. VI.* i 1 57
My gracious prince, and honourable peers . . . iii 4 1
Usurp the sacred name of knight, Profaning this most honourable order iv 1 41
Honourable. Confirm it so, mine honourable lord.—Confirm it so! 1 *Hen. VI.* iv 1 122
Whiles the honourable captain there Drops bloody sweat . . . iv 4 17
O, if you love my mother, Dishonour not her honourable name! . . iv 5 14
When I am dead and gone, May honourable peace attend thy throne 2 *Hen. VI.* ii 3 38
The honourable blood of Lancaster Must not be shed by such a jaded groom . . . iv 1 51
Am I of an honourable house.—Ay, by my faith, the field is honourable iv 2 53
And shame thine honourable age with blood? . . . v 1 170
Set down, set down your honourable load, If honour may be shrouded in a hearse . . . *Richard III.* i 2 1
And his own letter, The honourable board of council out, Must fetch him in he papers . . . *Hen. VIII.* i 1 79
With all their honourable points of ignorance Pertaining thereunto . i 3 26
But I would have the soil of her fair rape Wiped off, in honourable keeping her . . . *Troi. and Cres.* ii 2 149
Your beards deserve not so honourable a grave as to stuff a botcher's cushion, or to be entombed in an ass's pack-saddle . . *Coriolanus* ii 1 97
Think'st thou it honourable for a noble man Still to remember wrongs? v 3 154
And thanks to men Of noble minds is honourable meed . . *T. Andron.* i 1 216
To advance Thy name and honourable family . . . i 1 239
My grandsire, well advised, hath sent by me The goodliest weapons of his armoury To gratify your honourable youth . . . iv 2 12
Whose high exploits and honourable deeds Ingrateful Rome requites with foul contempt . . . v 1 11
The feast is ready, which the careful Titus Hath ordain'd to an honourable end, For peace, for love . . . v 3 22
Of honourable reckoning are you both . . . *Rom. and Jul.* i 2 4
If that thy bent of love be honourable, Thy purpose marriage . . ii 2 143
A damned saint, an honourable villain! . . . iii 2 79
More honourable state, more courtship lives In carrion-flies than Romeo iii 3 34
Nobly train'd, Stuff'd, as they say, with honourable parts . . iii 5 183
Your honourable letter he desires To those have shut him up *T. of Athens* i 1 97
That honourable gentleman, Lord Lucullus, entreats your company . i 2 192
You are honourable,—But yet they could have wish'd—they know not —Something hath been amiss . . . ii 2 215
How does that honourable, complete, free-hearted gentleman? . . iii 1 9
He is my very good friend, and an honourable gentleman . . iii 2 2
Denied that honourable man! there was very little honour showed in't iii 2 20
Commend me to thy honourable virtuous lord, my very exquisite friend iii 2 31
What a wicked beast was I to disfurnish myself against such a good time, when I might ha' shown myself honourable! . . iii 2 51
I count it one of my greatest afflictions, say, that I cannot pleasure such an honourable gentleman . . . iii 2 63
His right noble mind, illustrious virtue And honourable carriage . . iii 2 88
I think this honourable lord did but try us this other day . . iii 6 3
My most honourable lord, I am e'en sick of shame . . . iii 6 45
Thou art noble; yet, I see, Thy honourable metal may be wrought *J. C.* i 2 313
You are my true and honourable wife . . . ii 1 288
Soul of Rome! Brave son, derived from honourable loins! . . . ii 1 322
Brutus is an honourable man; So are they all, all honourable men . iii 2 87
I rather choose To wrong the dead, to wrong myself and you, Than I will wrong such honourable men . . . iii 2 132
I fear I wrong the honourable men Whose daggers have stabb'd Cæsar; I do fear it.—They were traitors: honourable men! . . . iii 2 156
They that have done this deed are honourable . . . iii 2 216
They are wise and honourable, And will, no doubt, with reasons answer you iii 2 218
O, if thou wert the noblest of thy strain, Young man, thou couldst not die more honourable . . . v 1 60
He hath importuned me with love In honourable fashion . . *Hamlet* i 3 111
What do you think of me?—As of a man faithful and honourable . . ii 2 130
My honourable lord, I will most humbly take my leave of you . . ii 2 217
Remember him hereafter as my honourable friend . . . *Lear* i 1 28
I here take my oath before this honourable assembly, she kicked the poor king . . . iii 6 49
Let's teach ourselves that honourable stop, Not to outsport discretion *Othello* ii 3 2
He knows not yet of his honourable fortune . . . iv 2 241
What shall be said to thee?—Why, any thing: An honourable murderer v 2 294
His love, which stands An honourable trial . . . *Ant. and Cleo.* i 3 75
Have entertainment, but No honourable trust . . . iv 6 18
She soon shall know . . . How honourable and how kindly we Determine for her . . . v 1 58
Though he be honourable,— He'll lead me, then, in triumph? . . v 2 108
If thou wert honourable, Thou wouldst have told this tale for virtue *Cymb.* i 6 142
Her attendants are All sworn and honourable:—they induced to steal it! ii 4 125
He will embrace you, for he's honourable And doubling that, most holy iii 4 179
Who ever but his approbation added, Though not his prime consent, he did not flow From honourable sources . . . *Pericles* iv 3 28
I would have you note, this is an honourable man.—I desire to find him so iv 6 54
But how honourable he is in that, I know not . . . iv 6 60
I hear say you are of honourable parts, and are the governor . . iv 6 87
Honourable-dangerous. An enterprise Of honourable-dangerous consequence . . . *J. Cæsar* i 3 124
Honourably. Art not ashamed?—Of what, lady? of speaking honourably? Is not marriage honourable? . . . *Much Ado* iii 4 29
The noble lord Most honourably doth uphold his word . . *L. L. Lost* v 2 449
Use her honourably.—Ay, Edward will use women honourably 3 *Hen. VI.* iii 2 123
Lodged in the abbey; where the reverend abbot, With all his covent, honourably received him . . . *Hen. VIII.* iv 2 19
Do this message honourably . . . *T. Andron.* iv 4 104
Within my tent his bones to-night shall lie, Most like a soldier, order'd honourably . . . *J. Cæsar* v 5 79
Honoured. Then was this island . . . not honour'd with A human shape *Tempest* i 2 283
Go with me To bless this twain, that they may prosperous be And honour'd in their issue . . . iv 1 105
To the sweet glances of thy honour'd love . . . *T. G. of Ver.* i 1 4
Let the devil Be sometime honour'd for his burning throne! . *M. for M.* v 1 295
Our feast shall be much honour'd in your marriage . . *Mer. of Venice* iii 2 214
High wedlock then be honoured . . . *As Y. Like It* v 4 150
I am from humble, he from honour'd name . . . *All's Well* i 3 162
Where dust and damn'd oblivion is the tomb Of honour'd bones indeed ii 3 148
My honour'd lady, I have forgiven and forgotten all . . . v 3 8
As you have ever been my father's honour'd friend . . . *W. Tale* iv 4 504
Assisted with your honour'd friends, Bring them to our embracement . v 1 113
That noble honour'd lord is fear'd and loved . . . v 1 158
I honour'd him, I loved him, and will weep My date of life out *K. John* iv 3 105
But thou, most fine, most honour'd, most renown'd . 2 *Hen. IV.* iv 5 164

Honoured. And think me honoured To feast so great a warrior 1 *Hen. VI.* ii 3 81
Thy late exploits . . . Have made thee fear'd and honour'd . 2 *Hen. VI.* i 1 198
I'll to the king, And say I spoke with you.—My honour'd lord *Hen. VIII.* ii 3 80
The honour'd number, Who lack not virtue, no, nor power *Coriolanus* iii 1 72
When he did love his country, It honour'd him . . . iii 1 306
The honour'd gods Keep Rome in safety! . . . iii 3 33
The honour'd mould Wherein this trunk was framed . . . v 3 22
And in this match I hold me highly honour'd of your grace . *T. Andron.* i 1 245
Most honour'd Timon . . . *T. of Athens* i 2 1
I have sweat to see his honour. My honoured lord . . . iii 2 28
Pity not honour'd age for his white beard; He is an usurer . . iv 3 111
Believe it, My most honour'd lord, For any benefit that points to me . iv 3 525
Say I fear'd Cæsar, honour'd him and loved him . . *Jul. Cæsar* iii 1 129
Thou diest as bravely as Titinius; And mayst be honour'd, being Cato's son v 4 11
Kill Brutus, and be honour'd in his death.—We must not . . v 4 14
See, see, our honour'd hostess! . . . *Macbeth* i 6 10
We will proceed no further in this business: He hath honour'd me of late i 7 32
As I do live, my honour'd lord, 'tis true . . . *Hamlet* i 2 221
It is a custom More honour'd in the breach than the observance . . i 4 16
My honoured lord!—My most dear lord!—My excellent good friends! . ii 2 226
I never gave you aught.—My honour'd lord, you know right well you did iii 1 97
And thou shalt live in this fair world behind, Honour'd, beloved . . iii 2 186
Royal Lear, Whom I have ever honour'd as my king, Loved as my father *Lear* i 1 142
Do you not love my sister?—In honour'd love . . . v 1 9
And kiss The honour'd gashes whole . . . *Ant. and Cleo.* iv 8 11
Which hath Honour'd with confirmation your great judgement In the election of a sir so rare . . . *Cymbeline* i 6 174
Pieces of gold 'gainst this which then he wore Upon his honour'd finger v 5 184
You ne'er kill'd Imogen till now. Help, help! Mine honour'd lady . v 5 232
He comes To an honour'd triumph strangely furnished . . *Pericles* ii 2 53
We are honour'd much by good Simonides.—Your presence glads our days ii 3 20
Most honour'd Cleon, I must needs be gone . . . iii 3 1
Strike me, honour'd sir; Give me a gash, put me to present pain . . v 1 192
When fame Had spread their cursed deed, and honour'd name Of Pericles . . . v 3 Gower 96
Honourest. As thou lovest and honourest arms, Let's fight it out and not stand cavilling thus . . . 3 *Hen. VI.* i 1 116
Honour-flawed. Be she honour-flaw'd . . . *W. Tale* ii 1 143
Honour-giving. By the honour-giving hand Of Cœur-de-lion knighted *K. John* i 1 53
Honouring. Being on shore, honouring of Neptune's triumphs *Pericles* v 1 17
Honour-owing. Yoke-fellow to his honour-owing wounds . *Hen. V.* iv 6 9
Hoo! Marcius coming home!—Nay, 'tis true . . . *Coriolanus* ii 1 116
Our enemy is banish'd! he is gone! Hoo! hoo! . . . iii 3 137
Hood. By the bare scalp of Robin Hood's fat friar . . *T. G. of Ver.* iv 1 36
Hood mine eyes Thus with my hat, and sigh, and say 'amen' *M. of Ven.* ii 2 202
Now, by my hood, a Gentile and no Jew . . . ii 6 51
And there they live like the old Robin Hood of England *As Y. Like It* i 1 122
And Robin Hood, Scarlet, and John . . . 2 *Hen. IV.* v 3 107
But all hoods make not monks . . . *Hen. VIII.* iii 1 23
Hood my unmann'd blood, bating in my cheeks, With thy black mantle *Rom. and Jul.* iii 2 14
Hooded. You must be hooded, must you? . . . *Meas. for Meas.* v 1 358
'Tis a hooded valour; and when it appears, it will bate . *Hen. V.* iii 7 121
Hoodman. Hush, hush!—Hoodman comes! Portotartarosa *All's Well* iv 3 136
Hoodman-blind. What devil was't That thus hath cozen'd you at hoodman-blind? . . . *Hamlet* iii 4 77
Hoodwink. The prize I'll bring thee to Shall hoodwink this mischance *Tempest* iv 1 206
We will bind and hoodwink him so, that he shall suppose no other but that he is carried into the leaguer of the adversaries . *All's Well* iii 6 26
The time you may so hoodwink . . . *Macbeth* iv 3 72
Hoodwink'd as thou art, will lead thee on To gather from thee *All's Well* iv 1 90
We'll have no Cupid hoodwink'd with a scarf . . *Rom. and Jul.* i 4 4
Friends kill friends, and the disorder's such As war were hoodwink'd *Cymbeline* v 2 16
Hoof. Vanish like hailstones, go; Trudge, plod away o' the hoof *Mer. Wives* i 3 91
Dear earth, I do salute thee with my hand, Though rebels wound thee with their horses' hoofs . . . *Richard II.* iii 2 7
With the armed hoofs Of hostile paces . . . 1 *Hen. IV.* i 1 8
Many a nobleman lies stark and stiff Under the hoofs of vaunting enemies . . . v 3 43
Think, when we talk of horses, that you see them Printing their proud hoofs i' the receiving earth . . . *Hen. V.* Prol. 27
The basest horn of his hoof is more musical than the pipe of Hermes . iii 7 18
Hook. To cast up, With a pair of anchoring hooks . *T. G. of Ver.* iii 1 118
That, to catch a saint, With saints dost bait thy hook . *Meas. for Meas.* ii 2 181
Bait the hook well; this fish will bite . . . *Much Ado* ii 3 114
But she I can hook to me . . . *W. Tale* ii 3 7
Swore the devil his true liegeman upon the cross of a Welsh hook 1 *Hen. IV.* ii 4 373
Go, with her, with her; hook on, hook on . . 2 *Hen. IV.* ii 1 175
And she steal love's sweet bait from fearful hooks . *Rom. and Jul.* ii Prol. 8
My bended hook shall pierce Their slimy jaws . . *Ant. and Cleo.* ii 5 12
Your diver Did hang a salt-fish on his hook, which he With fervency drew up . . . ii 5 17
Besides that hook of wiving, Fairness which strikes the eye . *Cymbeline* v 5 167
Hook and line. Hold hook and line, say I. Down, down, dogs! 2 *Hen. IV.* ii 4 171
Hooking both right and wrong to the appetite . . *Meas. for Meas.* ii 4 176
Hook-nosed. That I may justly say, with the hook-nosed fellow of Rome, 'I came, saw, and overcame' . . 2 *Hen. IV.* iv 3 45
Hoop. Who with age and envy Was grown into a hoop . . *Tempest* i 2 259
And wear his colours like a tumbler's hoop! . . *L. L. Lost* iii 1 190
What's the matter?—About a hoop of gold, a paltry ring *Mer. of Venice* v 1 147
Or hoop his body more with thy embraces . . *W. Tale* iv 4 450
A hoop of gold to bind thy brothers in . . 2 *Hen. IV.* iv 4 43
That admiration did not hoop at them . . . *Hen. V.* ii 2 108
The three-hooped pot shall have ten hoops . . 2 *Hen. VI.* iv 2 72
Those friends thou hast, and their adoption tried, Grapple them to thy soul with hoops of steel . . . *Hamlet* i 3 63
If I knew What hoop should hold us stanch, from edge to edge O' the world I would pursue it . . . *Ant. and Cleo.* ii 2 117
Hooping. Most wonderful wonderful! and yet again wonderful, and after that, out of all hooping! . . . *As Y. Like It* iii 2 203
Hoot. The clamorous owl that nightly hoots and wonders *M. N. Dream* ii 2 6
Who did hoot him out o' the city . . . *Coriolanus* iv 6 123
Hooted. Should be hooted at Like an old tale . . . *W. Tale* v 3 116
The rabblement hooted and clapped their chopped hands . *J. Cæsar* i 2 245
Hooting. The people fall a-hooting . . . *L. L. Lost* iv 2 61

Hooting. You are they That made the air unwholesome, when you cast Your stinking greasy caps in hooting at Coriolanus' exile *Coriolanus* iv 6 131
Yesterday the bird of night did sit Even at noon-day upon the market-place, Hooting and shrieking . . . *J. Cæsar* i 3 28
Hop in his walks and gambol in his eyes . . *M. N. Dream* iii 1 168
Ay, that left pap, Where heart doth hop . . . v 1 304
Every elf and fairy sprite Hop as light as bird from brier . . v 1 401
Go, hop me over every kennel home, For you shall hop without my custom, sir: I'll none of it . . . *T. of Shrew* iv 3 98
Would make thee quickly hop without thy head . . 2 *Hen. VI.* i 3 140
Who lets it hop a little from her hand, Like a poor prisoner *Rom. and Jul.* ii 2 179
I saw her once Hop forty paces through the public street *Ant. and Cleo.* ii 2 234
Hopdance cries in Tom's belly for two white herring . . *Lear* iii 6 32
Hope. I have no hope That he's undrown'd.—O, out of that 'no hope' What great hope have you! no hope that way is Another way so high a hope that even Ambition cannot pierce a wink beyond *Tempest* ii 1 238
But art thou not drowned, Stephano? I hope now thou art not drowned ii 2 114
Even here I will put off my hope and keep it No longer . . iii 3 7
I am right glad that he's so out of hope . . . iii 3 11
As I hope For quiet days, fair issue and long life . . iv 1 23
And so to Naples, Where I have hope to see the nuptial . . v 1 308
And all the fair effects of future hopes . . . *T. G. of Ver.* i 1 50
Hope is a lover's staff; walk hence with that And manage it against despairing thoughts . . . iii 1 246
All her sudden quips, The least whereof would quell a lover's hope . iv 2 13
Ay, but I hope, sir, that you love not here.—Sir, but I do . . iv 2 21
I'll do what I can.—I hope thou wilt . . . iv 4 47
I hope my master's suit will be but cold . . . iv 4 186
Treacherous man! Thou hast beguiled my hopes . . . v 4 64
Come, gentlemen, I hope we shall drink down all unkindness *Mer. Wives* i 1 203
I hope, sir, I will do as it shall become one that would do reason . i 1 241
I hope, upon familiarity will grow more contempt . . . i 1 257
I think the best way were to entertain him with hope . . ii 1 68
He's as far from jealousy as I am from giving him cause; and that I hope is an unmeasurable distance . . . ii 1 108
I hope it be not so.—Hope is a curtal dog in some affairs . . ii 1 113
Her husband is seldom from home; but she hopes there will come a time . . . ii 2 105
They have not so little grace, I hope . . . ii 2 117
I hope I have your good will, father Page.—You have, Master Slender . iii 2 61
'Tis not so, I hope.—Pray heaven it be not so! . . . iii 3 118
Give him another hope, to betray him to another punishment . . iii 3 207
I hope not; I had as lief bear so much lead . . . iv 2 117
This is the third time; I hope good luck lies in odd numbers . . v 1 2
Bid herself assay him: I have great hope in that . . *Meas. for Meas.* i 2 187
Bore many gentlemen, myself being one, In hand and hope of action . i 4 52
All hope is gone, Unless you have the grace by your fair prayer . . i 4 68
Why, very well, then; I hope here be truths . . . ii 1 131; 137
So then you hope of pardon from Lord Angelo? . . . iii 1 1
The miserable have no other medicine But only hope: I've hope to live, and am prepared to die . . . iii 1 3
Do not satisfy your resolution with hopes that are fallible . . iii 1 170
I hope, sir, your good worship will be my bail.—No, indeed, will I not . iii 2 75
O, you hope the duke will return no more . . . iii 2 174
I hope, if you have occasion to use me for your own turn, you shall find me yare . . . iv 2 59
I hope it is some pardon or reprieve For the most gentle Claudio . . iv 2 74
What comfort is for Claudio?—There's some in hope . . iv 2 81
My most gracious lord, I hope you will not mock me with a husband . v 1 422
But longer did we not retain much hope . . *Com. of Errors* i 1 66
I am invited, sir, to certain merchants, Of whom I hope to make much benefit . . . i 2 25
For which, I hope, thou felt'st I was displeased . . ii 2 19
Do you hear, you minion? you'll let us in, I hope? . . . iii 1 54
My food, my fortune and my sweet hope's aim, My sole earth's heaven . iii 2 63
Have you the chain about you?—An if I have not, sir, I hope you have iv 1 43
Did claim me for her husband: She is too big, I hope, for me to compass iv 1 111
My ring, or else the chain: I hope you do not mean to cheat me so . iv 3 79
What I told you then, I hope I shall have leisure to make good . . v 1 375
But I hope you have no intent to turn husband, have you? . *Much Ado* i 1 195
Well, niece, I hope to see you one day fitted with a husband . . ii 1 60
Methinks you are sadder.—I hope he be in love . . . iii 2 17
Do you serve God?—Yea, sir, we hope.—Write down, that they hope they serve God: and write God first . . . iv 2 19
But there are other strict observances; As, not to see a woman in that term, Which I hope well is not enrolled there . . *L. L. Lost* i 1 38
I hope in God for high words.—A high hope for a low heaven . . i 1 194
Well, sir, I hope, when I do it, I shall do it on a full stomach . . i 2 153
He comes in like a perjure, wearing papers.—In love, I hope . . iv 3 49
Not so, sir; under correction, sir; I hope it is not so . . v 2 489
I hope, sir, three times thrice, sir,— Is not nine . . . v 2 491
Great thanks, great Pompey.—'Tis not so much worth; but I hope I was perfect . . . v 2 561
You, the lion's part: and, I hope, here is a play fitted . *M. N. Dream* i 2 67
Therefore be out of hope, of question, of doubt; Be certain . . iii 2 279
I hope she will be brief . . . v 1 323
The better part of my affections would Be with my hopes abroad *Mer. of Venice* i 1 17
I hope I shall make shift to go without him . . . i 2 97
My father, being, I hope, an old man, shall frutify unto you . . ii 2 142
Lest . . . I be misconstrued in the place I go to And lose my hopes . ii 2 198
Men that hazard all Do it in hope of fair advantages . . ii 7 19
Fortune now To my heart's hope! Gold; silver; and base lead . . ii 9 20
How much unlike my hopes and my deservings! . . . ii 9 57
There is but one hope in it that can do you any good; and that is but a kind of bastard hope neither.—And what hope is that? . . iii 5 7
You may partly hope that your father got you not . . . iii 5 11
That were a kind of bastard hope, indeed . . . iii 5 14
How shalt thou hope for mercy, rendering none? . . . iv 1 88
Which speed, we hope, the better for our words . . . v 1 115
What ring gave you, my lord? Not that, I hope, which you received of me . . . v 1 185
I hope I shall see an end of him . . . *As Y. Like It* i 1 170
And broke three of his ribs, that there is little hope of life in him . i 2 136
Let gentleness my strong enforcement be: In the which hope I blush . ii 7 119
Then thou art damned.—Nay, I hope.—Truly, thou art damned . . iii 2 37
I think she means to tangle my eyes too! No, faith, proud mistress, hope not after it . . . iii 5 45
Are you not good?—I hope so.—Why then, can one desire too much of a good thing? . . . iv 1 122

Hope. I hope it is no dishonest desire to desire to be a woman of the world . . . . *As Y. Like It* v 3 4
I sometimes do believe, and sometimes do not; As those that fear they hope, and know they fear . . . . . . v 4 6
I hope this reason stands for my excuse . . . *T. of Shrew* Ind. 2 126
To serve all hopes conceived, To deck his fortune with his virtuous deeds . . . . i 1 15
My fortune lives for me; And I do hope good days and long to see . i 2 193
Lucentio shall make one, Though Paris came in hope to speed alone . i 2 247
So shall you quietly enjoy your hope . . . . . . iii 2 138
Thus have I politicly begun my reign, And 'tis my hope to end successfully . . . . iv 1 192
Why, how now, Kate! I hope thou art not mad . . . . iv 5 42
Come hither, crack-hemp.—I hope I may choose, sir . . . v 1 48
My cake is dough; but I'll in among the rest, Out of hope of all, but my share of the feast . . . . v 1 146
Pray God, sir, your wife send you not a worse.—I hope, better . v 2 85
What hope is there of his majesty's amendment?—He hath abandoned his physicians, madam; under whose practices he hath persecuted time with hope, and finds no other advantage in the process but only the losing of hope by time . . . . . . *All's Well* i 1 13
I have those hopes of her good that her education promises . . i 1 45
I hope to have friends for my wife's sake . . . . . i 3 42
I know I love in vain, strive against hope . . . . . i 3 207
'Tis our hope, sir, After well enter'd soldiers, to return And find your grace in health . . . . ii 1 5
We must not So stain our judgement, or corrupt our hope . . . ii 1 123
Oft it hits Where hope is coldest and despair most fits . . . ii 1 147
But will you make it even?—Ay, by my sceptre and my hopes of heaven ii 1 195
But never hope to know why I should marry her . . . . ii 3 117
I hope, sir, I have your good will to have mine own good fortunes . ii 4 15
But I hope your lordship thinks not him a soldier . . . . ii 5 1
We, Great in our hope, lay our best love and credence Upon thy promising fortune . . . . iii 3 2
And hope I may that she, Hearing so much, will speed her foot again . iii 4 36
I hope I need not to advise you further; but I hope your own grace will keep you where you are . . . . iii 5 26
You shall not need to fear me.—I hope so. . . . . . iii 5 32
You have won A wife of me, though there my hope be done . . iv 2 65
Answer to what I shall ask you out of a note.—And truly, as I hope to live . . . . iv 3 147
Upon my reputation and credit and as I hope to live . . . . iv 3 154
It rejoices me, that I hope I shall see him ere I die . . . . iv 5 89
Courage and hope both teaching him the practice . . . *T. Night* i 2 13
Mine own escape unfoldeth to my hope . . . The like of him . . . i 2 19
And I hope to see a housewife take thee between her legs and spin it off i 3 109
Desire him not to flatter with his lord, Nor hold him up with hopes . i 5 323
A should follow, but O does.—And O shall end, I hope . . . ii 5 144
The matter, I hope, is not great, sir, begging but a beggar . . iii 1 61
Votre serviteur.—I hope, sir, you are; and I am yours . . . . iii 1 80
Nothing that can be can come between me and the full prospect of my hopes . . . . iii 4 91
God have mercy upon one of our souls! He may have mercy upon mine; but my hope is better, and so look to thyself . . . . iii 4 185
A wreck past hope he was: His life I gave him and did thereto add My love . . . . v 1 82
Acting this in an obedient hope, Why have you suffer'd me to be imprison'd? . . . . v 1 348
In hope it shall not, Most freely I confess . . . . . v 1 366
I very well agree with you in the hopes of him . . . . *W. Tale* i 1 42
Fear not thou, man, thou shalt lose nothing here.—I hope so, sir . . iv 4 260
No hope to help you, But as you shake off one to take another . . iv 4 579
Wherein my hope is I shall so prevail To force him after . . . iv 4 678
Though my case be a pitiful one, I hope I shall not be flayed out of it . iv 4 845
The sweet'st companion that e'er man Bred his hopes out of . . . v 1 12
Fled from his father, from his hopes, and with A shepherd's daughter . v 1 184
They say one would speak to her and stand in hope of answer . . v 2 110
Knowing by Paulina that the oracle Gave hope thou wast in being . v 3 127
Good my mother, let me know my father; Some proper man, I hope *K. John* i 1 250
Pray that their burthens may not fall this day, Lest that their hopes prodigiously be cross'd . . . . iii 1 91
I hope your warrant will bear out the deed.—Uncleanly scruples . . iv 1 6
Once again crown'd, And look'd upon, I hope, with cheerful eyes . iv 2 2
I will not return Till my attempt so much be glorified As to my ample hope was promised . . . . v 2 112
What surety of the world, what hope, what stay, When this was now a king, and now is clay? . . . . v 7 68
By all my hopes, most falsely doth he lie . . . . *Richard II.* i 1 68
And exactly begg'd Your grace's pardon, and I hope I had it . . . i 1 141
God defend the right!—Strong as a tower in hope, I cry amen . . i 3 102
And he our subjects' next degree in hope . . . . . . i 4 36
I hope the king is not yet shipp'd for Ireland.—Why hopest thou so? 'tis better hope he is; For his designs crave haste, his haste good hope . . . . ii 2 42
Wherefore dost thou hope he is not shipp'd?—That he, our hope, might have retired his power, And driven into despair an enemy's hope . ii 2 45
I will despair, and be at enmity With cozening hope . . . . ii 2 69
Who gently would dissolve the bands of life, Which false hope lingers . ii 2 72
Sweetened with the hope to have The present benefit which I possess . ii 3 13
Hope to joy is little less in joy Than hope enjoy'd . . . . ii 3 15
Let them go To ear the land that hath some hope to grow, For I have none . . . . iii 2 212
I see some sparks of better hope, which elder years May happily bring forth . . . . v 3 21
By how much better than my word I am, By so much shall I falsify men's hopes . . . . *1 Hen. IV.* i 2 235
I hope I shall as soon be strangled with a halter as another . . ii 4 547
The parties sure, And our induction full of prosperous hope . . . iii 1 2
The hope and expectation of thy time Is ruin'd . . . . . iii 2 36
Therein should we read The very bottom and the soul of hope . . iv 1 50
We may boldly spend upon the hope of what Is to come in . . . iv 1 54
They shall be well opposed.—I hope no less, yet needful 'tis to fear . iv 4 34
By my hopes, This present enterprise set off his head . . . . v 1 87
If he outlive the envy of this day, England did never owe so sweet a hope . . . . v 2 68
I hope your lordship goes abroad by advice . . . . *2 Hen. IV.* i 2 109
I hope he that looks upon me will take me without weighing . . . i 2 188
I pray you all, Speak plainly your opinions of our hopes . . . . i 3 3
Our supplies live largely in the hope Of great Northumberland . . i 3 12

Hope. Who lined himself with hope, Eating the air on promise of supply *2 Hen. IV.* i 3 27
It never yet did hurt To lay down likelihoods and forms of hope . . i 3 35
A cause on foot Lives so in hope as in an early spring We see the appearing buds; which to prove fruit, Hope gives not so much warrant as despair That frosts will bite them . . . . i 3 38
Grant that our hopes, yet likely of fair birth, Should be still-born . i 3 63
I hope you'll come to supper. You'll pay me all together? . . . ii 1 172
I hope, my lord, all's well: what is the news, my lord? . . . ii 1 183
The hopes we have in him touch ground And dash themselves to pieces iv 1 17
His cares are now all ended.—I hope, not dead . . . . . v 2 4
We hope no other from your majesty . . . . v 2 62
How might a prince of my great hopes forget So great indignities? . v 2 68
I hope to see London once ere I die . . . . v 3 64
A merry message.—We hope to make the sender blush at it . *Hen. V.* i 2 299
Labour shall refresh itself with hope . . . . ii 2 37
I hope they will not come upon us now.—We are in God's hand . . iii 6 177
Some of them will fall to-morrow, I hope.—And yet my sky shall not want . . . . iii 7 77
I would not lose so great an honour As one man more, methinks, would share from me For the best hope I have . . . . . . iv 3 33
Not a piece of feather in our host—Good argument, I hope, we will not fly . . . . iv 3 113
I hope your majesty is pear me testimony and witness . . . . iv 8 37
The venom of such looks, we fairly hope, Have lost their quality . . v 2 18
Fair be all thy hopes And prosperous be thy life! . . . *1 Hen. VI.* ii 5 113
If we have entrance, as I hope we shall . . . . iii 2 6
Brave Burgundy, undoubted hope of France! . . . . . . iii 3 41
I hope ere long To be presented, by your victories, With Charles . . iv 1 171
You, his false hopes, the trust of England's honour, Keep off aloof . iv 4 20
In you all hopes are lost . . . . iv 5 25
There is no hope that ever I will stay, If the first hour I shrink . . iv 5 30
Shall all thy mother's hopes lie in one tomb? . . . . . . iv 5 34
No hope to have redress? My body shall Pay recompense, if you will grant my suit . . . . v 3 18
He goes, As did the youthful Paris once to Greece, With hope to find the like event in love . . . . v 5 105
Were there hope to conquer them again, My sword should shed hot blood, mine eyes no tears . . . . *2 Hen. VI.* i 1 117
Cold news for me; for I had hope of France . . . . . i 1 237; iii 1 87
Give me leave, my Lord of York, To be the post, in hope of his reward . i 4 81
When such strings jar, what hope of harmony? . . . . . . ii 1 57
God shall be my hope, My stay, my guide and lantern to my feet . . ii 3 24
'Tis my special hope That you will clear yourself from all suspect . iii 1 139
For, being green, there is great hope of help . . . . . . iii 1 287
And we, I hope, sir, are no murderers . . . . iii 2 181
If thou think'st on heaven's bliss, Hold up thy hand, make signal of thy hope . . . . iii 3 28
Over whom, in time to come, I hope to reign . . . . . . iv 2 138
Jack Cade hath sworn to have thy head.—Ay, but I hope your highness shall have his . . . . iv 4 20
God, our hope, will succour us.—My hope is gone, now Suffolk is deceased iv 4 55
Which makes me hope you are not void of pity . . . . . iv 7 69
Such hope have all the line of John of Gaunt! . . . . *3 Hen. VI.* i 1 19
Thus do I hope to shake King Henry's head.—And so do I . . . i 1 20
The hope thereof makes Clifford mourn in steel . . . . . i 1 58
You shall be the messenger.—And I, I hope, shall reconcile them all . i 1 273
And in that hope I throw mine eyes to heaven, Scorning whate'er you can afflict me with . . . . i 4 37
And stood against them, as the hope of Troy Against the Greeks . . ii 1 51
They had no heart to fight, And we in them no hope to win the day . ii 1 136
What hap? what hope of good?—Our hap is loss, our hope but sad despair . . . . ii 3 8
This may plant courage in their quailing breasts; For yet is hope of life ii 3 55
Thou shalt not dread The scatter'd foe that hopes to rise again . . ii 6 93
And if thou fail us, all our hope is done . . . . . . iii 3 33
If that go forward, Henry's hope is done . . . . . . iii 3 58
Mark how Lewis stamps, as he were nettled: I hope all's for the best . iii 3 170
I here protest, in sight of heaven, And by the hope I have of heavenly bliss . . . . iii 3 182
In hope he'll prove a widower shortly, I'll wear the willow garland iii 3 227; iv 1 99
Till then fair hope must hinder life's decay . . . . . . iv 6 16
And turn'd my captive state to liberty, My fear to hope . . . iv 6 4
It is young Henry, earl of Richmond.—Come hither, England's hope . iv 6 68
As Henry's late presaging prophecy Did glad my heart with hope . . iv 6 93
Farewell, my Hector, and my Troy's true hope . . . . . iv 8 25
He that will not fight for such a hope, Go home to bed . . . v 4 55
By this, I hope, she hath a son for me . . . . v 5 90
Thy mother felt more than a mother's pain, And yet brought forth less than a mother's hope . . . . v 6 50
Farewell sour annoy! For here, I hope, begins our lasting joy . . v 7 46
He cannot live, I hope; and must not die . . . *Richard III.* i 1 145
So will it, madam, till I lie with you.—I hope so.—I know so . . i 2 114
But shall I live in hope?—All men, I hope, live so . . . . i 2 200
What likelihood of his amendment, lords?—Madam, good hope . . i 3 34
And shamefully by you my hopes are butcher'd . . . . . . i 3 276
Stay a while: I hope my holy humour will change . . . . . i 4 120
I charge you, as you hope to have redemption By Christ's dear blood . i 4 194
I hope the king made peace with all of us . . . . . . ii 2 132
In him there is a hope of government . . . . ii 3 12
I hope he is much grown since last I saw him.—But I hear, no . . ii 4 5
He should be gracious.—Why, madam, so, no doubt, he is.—I hope he is ii 4 22
I fear no uncles dead.—Nor none that live, I hope.—An if they live, I hope I need not fear . . . . iii 1 147
And hopes to find you forward Upon his party for the gain thereof . iii 2 46
Who builds his hopes in air of your good looks, Lives like a drunken sailor on a mast, Ready, with every nod, to tumble down . . . iii 4 100
What is your grace's pleasure?—Even that, I hope, which pleaseth God above . . . . iii 7 109
It stands me much upon, To stop all hopes whose growth may damage me iv 2 60
True hope is swift, and flies with swallow's wings . . . . v 2 23
I died for hope ere I could lend thee aid . . . . v 3 173
Such as give Their money out of hope they may believe . *Hen. VIII.* Prol. 8
These are the limbs o' the plot: no more, I hope . . . . . i 1 220
None here, he hopes, . . . has brought with her One care abroad . . i 4 3
For further life in this world I ne'er hope . . . . . . ii 1 69
There is hope All will be well.—Now, I pray God, amen! . . . . ii 3 55
Your hopes and friends are infinite . . . . iii 1 82
Where no pity, No friends, no hope; no kindred weep for me . . . iii 1 150
To-day he puts forth The tender leaves of hopes; to-morrow blossoms . iii 2 353

Hope. And when he falls, he falls like Lucifer, Never to hope again . *Hen. VIII.* iii 2 372
'Tis a burthen [honour] Too heavy for a man that hopes for heaven ! . iii 2 385
I am glad your grace has made that right use of it.—I hope I have . iii 2 387
Fling away ambition : By that sin fell the angels ; how can man, then, The image of his Maker, hope to win by it ? . iii 2 443
Farewell The hopes of court ! my hopes in heaven do dwell . iii 2 459
She is young, and of a noble modest nature, I hope she will deserve well iv 2 136
I hope I am not too late . v 2 1
Let me ne'er hope to see a chine again . v 4 26
Forty truncheoners draw to her succour, which were the hope o' the Strand v 4 55
When I do tell thee, there my hopes lie drown'd, Reply not in how many fathoms deep They lie indrench'd . *Troi. and Cres.* i 1 49
Ourself the merchant, and this sailing Pandar Our doubtful hope . i 1 107
The ample proposition that hope makes In all designs begun on earth below Fails in the promised largeness . i 3 3
He hopes it is no other But for your health and your digestion sake . ii 3 119
I hope I shall know your honour better.—I do desire it . iii 1 13
They call him Troilus, and on him erect A second hope . iv 5 109
Hope of revenge shall hide our inward woe . v 10 31
O'er them Aufidius, Their very heart of hope . *Coriolanus* i 6 55
Sir, I hope My words disbench'd you not . ii 2 74
You must think, if we give you any thing, we hope to gain by you . ii 3 78
We hope to find you our friend ; and therefore give you our voices . ii 3 111
And hope to come upon them in the heat of their divison . iv 3 18
Not out of hope—Mistake me not—to save my life . iv 5 85
The wars for my money. I hope to see Romans as cheap as Volscians . iv 5 249
So that all hope is vain, Unless his noble mother, and his wife ; Who, as I hear, mean to solicit him For mercy to his country . v 1 70
There is some hope the ladies of Rome, especially his mother, may prevail . v 4 5
There is no hope in't : our throats are sentenced and stay upon execution v 4 7
Then, madam, stand resolved, but hope withal . *T. Andron.* i 1 135
Whose virtues will, I hope, Reflect on Rome as Titan's rays on earth . i 1 225
Rest on my word, and let not discontent Daunt all your hopes . i 1 268
Make some meaner choice : Lavinia is thine elder brother's hope . ii 1 74
This way, or not at all, stand you in hope . ii 1 119
But hope to pluck a dainty doe to ground . ii 2 26
The empress of my soul, Which never hopes more heaven than rests in thee . ii 3 41
And with that painted hope braves your mightiness . ii 3 126
Lavinia, kneel ; And kneel, sweet boy, the Roman Hector's hope . iv 1 88
To gratify your honourable youth, The hope of Rome . iv 2 13
That holp'st to make me great, In hope thyself should govern Rome and me . iv 4 60
The earth hath swallow'd all my hopes but she, She is the hopeful lady of my earth . *Rom. and Jul.* i 2 14
Be fickle, fortune ; For then, I hope, thou wilt not keep him long . iii 5 63
And then, I hope, thou wilt be satisfied.—Indeed, I never shall be satisfied . iii 5 93
Come weep with me ; past hope, past cure, past help ! . iv 1 45
A kind of hope, Which craves as desperate an execution As that is desperate which we would prevent . iv 1 68
I hope his honour will conceive the fairest of me . *T. of Athens* iii 2 59
This was my lord's best hope ; now all are fled, Save only the gods . iii 3 36
I hope it is not so low with him as he made it seem . iii 6 5
I hope it remains not unkindly with your lordship that I returned you an empty messenger . iii 6 39
I'll visit thee again.—If I hope well, I'll never see thee more . iv 3 171
For any benefit that points to me, Either in hope or present . iv 3 527
Our hope in him is dead : let us return, And strain what other means is left . v 1 229
A trade, sir, that, I hope, I may use with a safe conscience . *J. Cæsar* i 1 13
Upon this hope, that you shall give me reasons Why and wherein . iii 1 221
Our hopes are answered : You said the enemy would not come down . v 1 1
Cæsar, thou canst not die by traitors' hands . . . —So I hope . v 1 57
You greet with present grace and great prediction Of noble having and of royal hope . *Macbeth* i 3 56
Do you not hope your children shall be kings ? . i 3 118
Was the hope drunk Wherein you dress'd yourself ? . i 7 35
May they not be my oracles as well, And set me up in hope ? . iii 1 10
He shall spurn fate, scorn death, and bear His hopes 'bove wisdom . iii 5 31
Where is your husband ?—I hope, in no place so unsanctified Where such as thou mayst find him . iv 2 81
I have lost my hopes.—Perchance even there where I did find my doubts iv 3 24
O my breast, Thy hope ends here ! . iv 3 114
I hope the days are near at hand That chambers will be safe . v 4 1
'Tis his main hope . v 4 10
Thoughts speculative their unsure hopes relate . v 4 19
That keep the word of promise to our ear, And break it to our hope . v 8 22
Expend your time with us awhile, For the supply and profit of our hope *Hamlet* ii 2 24
So shall I hope your virtues Will bring him to his wonted way again . iii 1 40
I hope we have reformed that indifferently with us, sir . iii 2 40
For what advancement may I hope from thee That no revenue hast but thy good spirits, To feed and clothe thee ? . iii 2 62
Then there's hope a great man's memory may outlive his life half a year iii 2 140
To desperation turn my trust and hope ! . iii 2 228
I hope all will be well. We must be patient : but I cannot choose but weep . iv 5 68
I loved your father, and we love ourself ; and that, I hope, will teach you iv 7 35
Popp'd in between the election and my hopes . v 2 65
I hope, for my brother's justification, he wrote this but as an essay or taste of my virtue . *Lear* i 2 46
It is his hand, my lord ; but I hope his heart is not in the contents . i 2 72
Take patience : I have hope You less know how to value her desert Than she to scant her duty . ii 4 140
I have good hope Thou didst not know on't . ii 4 191
When remedies are past, the griefs are ended By seeing the worst, which late on hopes depended . *Othello* i 3 203
Wilt thou be fast to my hopes, if I depend on the issue ? . i 3 369
Therefore my hopes, not surfeited to death, Stand in bold cure . ii 1 50
My hopes do shape him for the governor . ii 1 55
I hope to be saved.—And so do I too, lieutenant . ii 3 110
I hope you will consider what is spoke Comes from my love . iii 3 216
I have moved my lord on his behalf, and hope all will be well . iii 4 20
Given to captivity me and my utmost hopes . iv 2 51
I hope my noble lord esteems me honest . iv 2 65
Rather, as it seems to me now, keepest from me all conveniency than suppliest me with the least advantage of hope . iv 2 179

Hope. Have mercy on me !—Amen, with all my heart !—If you say so, I hope you will not kill me . *Othello* v 2 35
These are portents ; but yet I hope, I hope, They do not point on me . v 2 45
But I will hope Of better deeds to-morrow. Rest you happy ! *A. and C.* i 1 61
And my auguring hope Says it will come to the full . ii 1 10
Well met here.—I hope so . ii 6 58
I and my sword will earn our chronicle : There's hope in't yet . iii 13 176
Know, my hearts, I hope well of to-morrow . iv 2 42
If to-morrow Our navy thrive, I have an absolute hope Our landsmen will stand up.—'Tis a brave army . iv 3 10
By starts, His fretted fortunes give him hope, and fear . iv 12 8
Past grace ? obedience ?—Past hope, and in despair . *Cymbeline* i 1 137
This is but a custom in your tongue ; you bear a graver purpose, I hope i 4 151
Is he disposed to mirth ? I hope he is.—Exceeding pleasant . i 6 58
Heavens know, Some men are much to blame.—Not he, I hope . i 6 77
I hope it be not gone to tell my lord That I kiss aught but he . ii 3 152
'Twill not be lost.—I hope so : go and search . ii 3 154
She's my good lady, and will conceive, I hope, But the worst of me . ii 3 158
In these sear'd hopes, I barely gratify your love . ii 4 6
I hope the briefness of your answer made The speediness of your return ii 4 30
I hope you know that we Must not continue friends . ii 4 48
Hath stol'n it from her ?—Very true ; And so, I hope, he came by't . ii 4 118
I hope I dream ; For so I thought I was a cave-keeper . iv 2 297
This forwardness Makes our hopes fair . iv 2 343
If I do lie and do No harm by it, though the gods hear, I hope They'll pardon it . iv 2 378
It strikes me, past The hope of comfort . iv 3 9
Nay, what hope Have we in hiding us ? . iv 4 3
Being thus quench'd Of hope, not longing . v 5 196
Yet hope, succeeding from so fair a tree As your fair self, doth tune us otherwise . *Pericles* i 1 114
That were to blow at fire in hope to quench it . i 4 4
Till when,—the which I hope shall ne'er be seen . i 4 105
I hope, sir, if you thrive, you'll remember from whence you had it . ii 1 157
He hopes by you his fortunes yet may flourish . ii 2 47
The day is yours ; And here, I hope, is none that envies it . ii 3 14
Lips must seal it too : And being join'd, I'll thus your hopes destroy . ii 5 86
You will not do't for all the world, I hope . iv 1 85
Let her go : There's no hope she will return. I'll swear she's dead . iv 1 99
Hoped. I had well hoped thou wouldst have denied Beatrice . *Much Ado* v 4 114
He took good rest to-night ; 'Tis hoped his sickness is discharged *W. T.* ii 3 11
Bid him a' should not think of God ; I hoped there was no need to trouble himself with any such thoughts yet . *Hen. V.* ii 3 22
I hoped thou shouldst have been my Hamlet's wife . *Hamlet* v 1 267
Hoped-for. Cold biting winter mars our hoped-for hay . 3 *Hen. VI.* iv 8 61
There's no hoped-for mercy with the brothers More than with ruthless waves . v 4 35
Hopeful. Fare you well : To the hopeful execution do I leave you Of your commissions . *Meas. for Meas.* i 1 60
The sacred honour of himself, his queen's, His hopeful son's . *W. Tale* ii 3 85
A great king's daughter, The mother to a hopeful prince . iii 2 41
Whose hopeful colours Advance our half-faced sun . 2 *Hen. VI.* iv 1 97
That from his loins no hopeful branch may spring ! . 3 *Hen. VI.* iii 2 126
Whose ugly and unnatural aspect May fright the hopeful mother *Rich III.* i 2 24
I know his noble nature—not to let Thy hopeful service perish *Hen. VIII.* iii 2 419
Here comes a parcel of our hopeful booty . *T. Andron* ii 3 49
She is the hopeful lady of my earth . *Rom. and Jul.* i 2 15
Hopeless to find, yet loath to leave unsought . *Com. of Errors* i 1 136
Hopeless and helpless doth Ægeon wend, But to procrastinate his lifeless end . i 1 158
The hopeless word of 'never to return' Breathe I against thee *Richard II.* i 3 152
So desperate thieves, all hopeless of their lives, Breathe out invectives 'gainst the officers . 3 *Hen. VI.* i 4 42
Alas, I am a woman, friendless, hopeless ! . *Hen. VIII.* iii 1 80
He would pawn his fortunes To hopeless restitution . *Coriolanus* iii 1 16
Aye hopeless To have the courtesy your cradle promised . *Cymbeline* iv 4 27
Hopest. Within what space Hopest thou my cure ? . *All's Well* ii 1 163
I hope the king is not yet shipp'd for Ireland.—Why hopest thou so ? 'tis better hope he is . *Richard II.* ii 2 43
Be that thou hopest to be, or what thou art Resign to death 2 *Hen. VI.* iii 1 333
Hoping you'll find good cause to whip them all . *Meas. for Meas.* ii 1 142
I will be a fool in question, hoping to be the wiser by your answer *All's Well* ii 2 41
Hoping the consequence Will prove as bitter, black, and tragical *Richard III.* iv 4 6
Hoping To purge himself with words . *Coriolanus* v 6 8
Withal Hoping it was but an effect of humour . *J. Cæsar* ii 1 250
Not sure, though hoping, of this good success, I ask'd his blessing *Lear* v 3 194
Hopkins. A monk o' the Chartreux.—O, Nicholas Hopkins ? . *Hen. VIII.* i 1 221
He was brought to this By a vain prophecy of Nicholas Hopkins . i 2 147
What was that Hopkins ?—Sir, a Chartreux friar . i 2 148
That devil-monk, Hopkins, that made this mischief . ii 1 22
Horace. As Horace says in his—What, my soul, verses ? . *L. L. Lost* iv 2 104
'Tis a verse in Horace ; I know it well : I read it in the grammar long ago.—Ay, just ; a verse in Horace ; right, you have it *T. Andron.* iv 2 22
Horatio. If you do meet Horatio and Marcellus, The rivals of my watch, bid them make haste . *Hamlet* i 1 12
Say, What, is Horatio there ?—A piece of him . i 1 19
Horatio says 'tis but our fantasy, And will not let belief take hold of him i 1 23
Thou art a scholar ; speak to it, Horatio.—Looks it not like the king? mark it, Horatio.—Most like . i 1 42
It would be spoke to.—Question it, Horatio . i 1 45
Horatio ! you tremble and look pale : Is not this something more than fantasy? . i 1 53
I am glad to see you well : Horatio,—or I do forget myself . i 2 161
And what make you from Wittenberg, Horatio? Marcellus? . i 2 164
Thrift, thrift, Horatio ! the funeral baked meats Did coldly furnish forth the marriage tables . i 2 180
Would I had met my dearest foe in heaven Or ever I had seen that day, Horatio ! . i 2 183
Where, my lord ?—In my mind's eye, Horatio . i 2 185
There's no offence, my lord.—Yes, by Saint Patrick, but there is, Horatio . i 5 136
There are more things in heaven and earth, Horatio, Than are dreamt of in your philosophy . i 5 166
Horatio, thou art e'en as just a man As e'er my conversation coped withal . iii 2 59
If your name be Horatio, as I am let to know it is . iv 6 11
Horatio, when thou shalt have overlooked this, give these fellows some means to the king : they have letters for him . iv 6 12

Horatio. By the Lord, Horatio, these three years I have taken note of it *Hamlet* v 1 150

Alas, poor Yorick! I knew him, Horatio: a fellow of infinite jest . v 1 203

Prithee, Horatio, tell me one thing.—What's that, my lord? . v 1 215

To what base uses we may return, Horatio! v 1 224

I pray you, good Horatio, wait upon him v 1 316

Where I found, Horatio,—O royal knavery!—an exact command v 2 18

But I am very sorry, good Horatio, That to Laertes I forgot myself v 2 75

I am dead, Horatio. Wretched queen, adieu! v 2 344

Horatio, I am dead; Thou livest; report me and my cause aright v 2 349

O good Horatio, what a wounded name, Things standing thus unknown, shall live behind me! v 2 355

O, I die, Horatio; The potent poison quite o'er-crows my spirit v 2 363

Horizon. When the morning sun shall raise his car Above the border of this horizon *3 Hen. VI.* iv 7 81

Horn. My horns are his horns, whether I wake or sleep *T. G. of Ver.* i 1 79

O, odious is the name!—What, name, sir?—The horn, I say *Mer. Wives* ii 1 125

It shall hang like a meteor o'er the cuckold's horns ii 2 293

If I have horns to make one mad, let the proverb go with me: I'll be horn-mad iii 5 154

At still midnight, Walk round about an oak, with great ragg'd horns iv 4 31

I'll do what I can to get you a pair of horns v 1 7

No man means evil but the devil, and we shall know him by his horns v 2 16

Jove, thou wast a bull for thy Europa; love set on thy horns v 5 4

My horns I bequeath your husbands v 5 30

Master Brook, Falstaff's a knave, a cuckoldly knave; here are his horns v 5 115

Let's write good angel on the devil's horn *Meas. for Meas.* ii 4 16

Pluck off the bull's horns and set them in my forehead *Much Ado* i 1 266

It is said, 'God sends a curst cow short horns;' but to a cow too curst he sends none.—So, by being too curst, God will send you no horns ii 1 25

There will the devil meet me, like an old cuckold, with horns on his head ii 1 47

Well, a horn for my money, when all's done ii 3 62

When shall we set the savage bull's horns on the sensible Benedick's head? v 1 184

I can find out no rhyme to 'lady' but 'baby,' an innocent rhyme; for 'scorn,' 'horn,' a hard rhyme v 2 38

Fear not, man; we'll tip thy horns with gold v 4 44

There is no staff more reverend than one tipped with horn v 4 126

My lady goes to kill horns; but, if thou marry, Hang me by the neck, if horns that year miscarry *L. L. Lost* iv 1 113

Who is your deer?—If we choose by the horns, yourself come not near iv 1 117

Love's feeling is more soft and sensible Than are the tender horns of cockled snails iv 3 338

What is a, b, spelt backward, with the horn on his head?—Ba, pueritia, with a horn added.—Ba, most silly sheep with a horn v 1 51

What is the figure?—Horns.—Thou disputest like an infant v 1 68

Go, whip thy gig.—Lend me your horn to make one, and I will whip about your infamy circum circa,—a gig of a cuckold's horn v 1 71

Will you give horns, chaste lady? do not so.—Then die a calf, before your horns do grow v 2 252

A cry more tuneable Was never holla'd to, nor cheer'd with horn *M. N. D.* iv 1 130

Go, bid the huntsmen wake them with their horns iv 1 143

He should have worn the horns on his head.—He is no crescent, and his horns are invisible within the circumference v 1 244

A post come from my master, with his horn full of good news *M. of Ven.* v 1 47

As horns are odious, they are necessary *As Y. Like It* iii 3 52

Many a man has good horns, and knows no end of them iii 3 54

Horns? Even so. Poor men alone? No, no; the noblest deer hath them iii 3 56

By so much is a horn more precious than to want iii 3 63

He brings his destiny with him.—What's that?—Why, horns iv 1 59

Set the deer's horns upon his head, for a branch of victory iv 2 5

What shall he have that kill'd the deer? His leather skin and horns to wear iv 2 12

Take thou no scorn to wear the horn; It was a crest ere thou wast born iv 2 14

The horn, the horn, the lusty horn Is not a thing to laugh to scorn iv 2 18

Am I but three inches? why, thy horn is a foot *T. of Shrew* iv 1 29

An hasty-witted body Would say your head and butt were head and horn v 2 41

They may joul horns together, like any deer i' the herd *All's Well* i 3 58

As the nail to his hole, the cuckold to his horn ii 2 27

You have, or your eye-glass Is thicker than a cuckold's horn *W. Tale* i 2 269

What woman-post is this? hath she no husband That will take pains to blow a horn before her? *K. John* i 1 219

He may sleep in security; for he hath the horn of abundance *2 Hen. IV.* i 2 52

The basest horn of his hoof is more musical than the pipe of Hermes *Hen. V.* iii 7 17

Paris is gored with Menelaus' horn *Troi. and Cres.* i 1 115

O deadly gall, and theme of all our scorns! For which we lose our heads to gild his horns iv 5 31

It were no match, your nail against his horn iv 5 46

Wert thou the devil, and worest it on thy horn, It should be challenged v 2 95

'Loo, Paris, 'loo! The bull has the game: ware horns, ho! v 7 12

They threw their caps As they would hang them on the horns o' the moon *Coriolanus* i 1 217

With his peremptory 'shall,' being but The horn and noise o' the monster's iii 1 95

Thrusts forth his horns again into the world iv 6 44

With horn and hound we'll give your grace bonjour *T. Andron.* i 1 494

The babbling echo mocks the hounds, Replying shrilly to the well-tuned horns ii 3 18

Hounds and horns and sweet melodious birds Be unto us as is a nurse's song ii 3 27

Had I the power that some say Dian had, Thy temples should be planted presently With horns, as was Actæon's ii 3 63

See, see, thou hast shot off one of Taurus' horns iv 3 69

The Bull, being gall'd, gave Aries such a knock That down fell both the Ram's horns in the court iv 3 72

To give it away to his daughters, and leave his horns without a case *Lear* i 5 33

March to wakes and fairs and market-towns. Poor Tom, thy horn is dry iii 6 78

He had a thousand noses, Horns whelk'd and waved like the enridged sea iv 6 71

O, that I knew this husband, which, you say, must charge his horns with garlands! *Ant. and Cleo.* i 2 5

Let me lodge Lichas on the horns o' the moon iv 12 45

Horn-beast. Here we have no temple but the wood, no assembly but horn-beasts *As Y. Like It* iii 3 51

Horn-book. He teaches boys the horn-book *L. L. Lost* v 1 49

Horned. This lanthorn doth the horned moon present *M. N. Dream* v 1 248

A horned man's a monster and a beast *Othello* iv 1 63

O, that I were Upon the hill of Basan, to outroar The horned herd! *Ant. and Cleo.* iii 13 128

Horner. Against my master, Thomas Horner, for saying that the Duke of York was rightful heir *2 Hen. VI.* i 3 29

Here, neighbour Horner, I drink to you in a cup of sack ii 3 59

Horning. 'Tis thought you have a goodly gift in horning *T. Andron.* ii 3 67

Horn-mad. Sure my master is horn-mad *Com. of Errors* ii 1 57

If he had found the young man, he would have been horn-mad *M. Wives* i 4 51

If I have horns to make one mad, let the proverb go with me: I'll be horn-mad iii 5 155

If this should ever happen, thou wouldst be horn-mad *Much Ado* i 1 272

Horn-maker. Virtue is no horn-maker *As Y. Like It* iv 1 63

Hornpipe. They are most of them means and bases; but one puritan amongst them, and he sings psalms to hornpipes *W. Tale* iv 3 47

Horn-ring. Ballad, knife, tape, glove, shoe-tie, bracelet, horn-ring iv 4 611

Horologe. He'll watch the horologe a double set, If drink rock not his cradle *Othello* ii 3 135

Horrible. And moe diversity of sounds, all horrible *Tempest* v 1 234

Or to be worse than worst Of those that lawless and incertain thought Imagine howling: 'tis too horrible *Meas. for Meas.* iii 1 128

Draw; and, as thou drawest, swear horrible *T. Night* iii 4 196

Being so horrible, so bloody, must Lead on to some foul issue *W. Tale* ii 3 152

Your vile intent must needs seem horrible *K. John* iv 1 96

News fitting to the night, Black, fearful, comfortless and horrible v 6 20

Art not thou horrible afeard? *1 Hen. IV.* ii 4 402

Bitter-searching terms, As curst, as harsh and horrible to hear *2 Hen. VI.* iii 2 312

With one hand on his dagger, Another spread on's breast, mounting his eyes, He did discharge a horrible oath *Hen. VIII.* i 2 206

The horrible conceit of death and night, Together with the terror of the place,—As in a vault *Rom. and Jul.* iv 3 37

But set them down horrible traitors *T. of Athens* iv 3 118

Present fears Are less than horrible imaginings *Macbeth* i 3 138

Hence, horrible shadow! Unreal mockery, hence! iii 4 106

Some I see That two-fold balls and treble sceptres carry: Horrible sight! iv 1 122

And there assume some other horrible form, Which might deprive your sovereignty of reason *Hamlet* i 4 72

O, horrible! most horrible! If thou hast nature in thee, bear it not i 5 80

And with this horrible object . . . Enforce their charity *Lear* ii 3 17

Then let fall Your horrible pleasure; here I stand, your slave iii 2 19

Methinks the ground is even.—Horrible steep iv 6 3

Didst contract and purse thy brow together, As if thou then hadst shut up in thy brain Some horrible conceit *Othello* iii 3 115

Let me see your eyes; Look in my face.—What horrible fancy's this? iv 2 26

I know this act shows horrible and grim v 2 203

Hence, Horrible villain! or I'll spurn thine eyes Like balls *Ant. and Cleo.* ii 5 63

Horribly. I will be horribly in love with her *Much Ado* ii 3 243

The youth's a devil.—He is as horribly conceited of him *T. Night* iii 4 322

Art thou not horribly afraid? doth not thy blood thrill at it? *1 Hen. IV.* ii 4 406

Thou wilt be horribly chid to-morrow ii 4 410

I will most horribly revenge *Hen. V.* v 1 49

My niece is horribly in love with a thing you have, sweet queen *T. and C.* iii 1 106

With a bombast circumstance Horribly stuff'd with epithets of war *Othello* i 1 14

Horrid. I will meditate the while upon some horrid message *T. Night* iii 4 220

What a beard of the general's cut and a horrid suit of the camp will do *Hen. V.* iii 6 81

Presenteth them unto the gazing moon So many horrid ghosts iv Prol. 28

Never sees horrid night, the child of hell iv 1 288

Though perils did Abound, as thick as thought could make 'em, and Appear in forms more horrid *Hen. VIII.* iii 2 196

Pursy insolence shall break his wind With fear and horrid flight *T. of A.* v 4 13

Recounts most horrid sights seen by the watch *J. Cæsar* ii 2 16

That suggestion Whose horrid image doth unfix my hair *Macbeth* i 3 135

Shall blow the horrid deed in every eye, That tears shall drown the wind i 7 24

Not in the legions Of horrid hell can come a devil more damn'd iv 3 56

And cleave the general ear with horrid speech *Hamlet* ii 2 589

Up, sword; and know thou a more horrid hent iii 3 88

Such bursts of horrid thunder, Such groans of roaring wind and rain *Lear* iii 2 46

Edmund, enkindle all the sparks of nature, To quit this horrid act iii 7 87

Proper deformity seems not in the fiend So horrid as in woman iv 2 61

A wooer More hateful than the foul expulsion is Of thy dear husband, than that horrid act Of the divorce he'ld make! *Cymbeline* ii 1 66

Horrider. O! Give colour to my pale cheek with thy blood, That we the horrider may seem iv 2 331

Horridly. So horridly to shake our disposition With thoughts *Hamlet* i 4 55

Horridly trick'd With blood of fathers, mothers, daughters, sons ii 2 479

Horror. Injurious love, That respites me a life, whose very comfort Is still a dying horror! *Meas. for Meas.* ii 3 42

Her brother's ghost his paved bed would break, And take her hence in horror v 1 441

So, indeed, all disquiet, horror and perturbation follows her *Much Ado* ii 1 268

Threaten the threatener and outface the brow Of bragging horror *K. John* v 1 50

Disorder, horror, fear and mutiny Shall here inhabit *Richard II.* iv 1 142

Frights, changes, horrors, Divert and crack, rend and deracinate The unity and married calm of states Quite from their fixure! *T. and C.* i 3 98

And take the present horror from the time, Which now suits with it *Macb.* ii 1 59

O horror, horror, horror! Tongue nor heart Cannot conceive nor name thee! ii 3 69

As from your graves rise up, and walk like sprites, To countenance this horror! ii 3 85

I have supp'd full with horrors v 5 13

As if he had been loosed out of hell To speak of horrors *Hamlet* ii 1 84

But faintly, nothing like the image and horror of it *Lear* i 2 192

Is this the promised end?—Or image of that horror? v 3 264

Abandon all remorse; On horror's head horrors accumulate *Othello* iii 3 370

Behind me The inevitable prosecution of Disgrace and horror *A. and C.* iv 14 66

You do extend These thoughts of horror further than you shall Find cause v 2 63

How ended she?—With horror, madly dying, like her life *Cymbeline* v 5 31

Horse. A team of horse shall not pluck that from me *T. G. of Ver.* iii 1 265

A horse can do no more: nay, a horse cannot fetch, but only carry iii 1 275

Till he hath pawned his horses to mine host of the Garter *Mer. Wives* ii 1 100

The Germans desire to have three of your horses iv 3 2

They shall have my horses; but I'll make them pay iv 3 10

Where be my horses? speak well of them, varletto iv 5 65

Three cozen-germans that has cozened all the hosts of Readins, of Maidenhead, of Colebrook, of horses and money iv 5 81

And twenty pounds of money, which must be paid to Master Brook; his horses are arrested for it v 5 119

The body public be A horse whereon the governor doth ride *M. for M.* i 2 164

Such claim as you would lay to your horse *Com. of Errors* iii 2 86

Let him bear it for a difference between himself and his horse *Much Ado* i 1 70

I would my horse had the speed of your tongue, and so good a continuer i 1 142

In such great letters as they write 'Here is good horse to hire' i 1 268

Horse. I am exceeding ill: heigh-ho!—For a hawk, a horse, or a husband? *Much Ado* iii 4 55

An two men ride of a horse, one must ride behind . . . iii 5 40

The dancing horse will tell you . . . *L. L. Lost* i 2 57

A horse to be ambassador for an ass . . . iii 1 52

You must send the ass upon the horse, for he is very slow-gaited . iii 1 56

Was that the king, that spurred his horse so hard? . . . iv 1 1

Imitari is nothing: so doth the hound his master, the ape his keeper, the tired horse his rider . . . iv 2 131

When I a fat and bean-fed horse beguile . . . *M. N. Dream* ii 1 45

As true as truest horse that yet would never tire . . . iii 1 98

Sometime a horse I'll be, sometime a hound, A hog, a headless bear iii 1 111

And neigh, and bark, and grunt, and roar, and burn, Like horse, hound, hog . . . iii 1 114

That's a colt indeed, for he doth nothing but talk of his horse *Mer. of Venice* i 2 45

But, he! why, he hath a horse better than the Neapolitan's . . i 2 62

Where is the horse that doth untread again His tedious measures with the unbated fire That he did pace them first? . . . ii 6 10

His horses are bred better . . . *As Y. Like It* i 1 11

As the ox hath his bow, sir, the horse his curb and the falcon her bells iii 3 80

As a puisny tilter, that spurs his horse but on one side . . iii 4 47

Both in a tune, like two gipsies on a horse . . . v 3 16

Another tell him of his hounds and horse . . . *T. of Shrew* Ind. 1 61

Thy horses shall be trapp'd, Their harness studded all with gold and pearl . . . Ind. 2 43

Would I had given him the best horse in Padua to begin his wooing! . i 1 148

Though she have as many diseases as two and fifty horses . . i 2 81

His horse hipped with an old mothy saddle and stirrups of no kindred iii 2 49

Who comes with him?—O, sir, his lackey, for all the world caparisoned like the horse . . . iii 2 67

His horse comes, with him on his back . . . iii 2 81

A horse and a man Is more than one, And yet not many . . iii 2 86

My horse.—Ay, sir, they be ready: the oats have eaten the horses . iii 2 206

She is my house, My household stuff, my field, my barn, My horse, my ox iii 2 234

First, know, my horse is tired; my master and mistress fallen out . iv 1 56

My master riding behind my mistress,— Both of one horse?—What's that to thee?—Why, a horse . . . iv 1 71

Thou shouldst have heard how her horse fell and she under her horse; . . . how she was bemoiled, how he left her with the horse upon her, how he beat me because her horse stumbled . . . iv 1 76

How I cried, how the horses ran away, how her bridle was burst . iv 1 82

What, no man at door To hold my stirrup nor to take my horse! . iv 1 124

Bring our horses unto Long-lane end; There will we mount . . iv 3 187

It shall be seven ere I go to horse . . . iv 3 193

Go on, and fetch our horses back again. Evermore cross'd and cross'd! iv 5 9

Ere twice the horses of the sun shall bring Their fiery torcher his diurnal ring . . . *All's Well* ii 1 164

I have writ my letters, casketed my treasure, Given order for our horses ii 5 27

I pray you, stay not, but in haste to horse . . . ii 5 92

The general of our horse thou art . . . iii 3 1

There was excellent command,—to charge in with our horse upon our own wings, and to rend our own soldiers! . . . iii 6 52

First demand of him how many horse the duke is strong . . iv 3 149

Five or six thousand horse, I said,—I will say true,—or thereabouts . iv 3 170

The captain of his horse, Count Rousillon . . . iv 3 327

Go thy ways: let my horses be well looked to, without any tricks . iv 5 62

We must to horse again. Go, go, provide . . . v 1 37

My purpose is, indeed, a horse of that colour.—And your horse now would make him an ass . . . *T. Night* ii 3 181

I'll give him my horse, grey Capilet . . . iii 4 315

Marry, I'll ride your horse as well as I ride you . . . iii 4 319

I have his horse to take up the quarrel . . . iii 4 320

Go: fresh horses! And gracious be the issue! . . . *W. Tale* iii 1 21

To horse, to horse! urge doubts to them that fear . . *Richard II.* ii 1 299

Hold out my horse, and I will first be there . . . ii 1 300

Dear earth, I do salute thee with my hand, Though rebels wound thee with their horses' hoofs . . . iii 2 7

How fondly dost thou spur a forward horse! . . . iv 1 72

Saddle my horse. God for his mercy, what treachery is here! . v 2 74

Give me my boots, I say; saddle my horse . . . v 2 77

When Bolingbroke rode on roan Barbary, That horse that thou so often hast bestrid, That horse that I so carefully have dress'd! . . v 5 79

Forgiveness, horse! why do I rail on thee, Since thou, created to be awed by man, Wast born to bear? . . . v 5 90

I was not made a horse; And yet I bear a burthen like an ass . v 5 92

In the very heat And pride of their contention did take horse *1 Hen. IV.* i 1 60

A true industrious friend, Sir Walter Blunt, new lighted from his horse i 1 63

I have vizards for you all; you have horses for yourselves . . i 2 143

'Tis like that they will know us by our horses . . . i 2 196

Our horses they shall not see; I'll tie them in the wood . . i 2 198

Charles' wain is over the new chimney, and yet our horse not packed ii 1 3

I have removed Falstaff's horse, and he frets like a gummed velvet . ii 2 2

The rascal hath removed my horse, and tied him I know not where . ii 2 11

Give me my horse, you rogues; give me my horse, and be hanged! . ii 2 31

Good Prince Hal, help me to my horse, good king's son . . ii 2 44

Sirrah Jack, thy horse stands behind the hedge . . . ii 2 73

The boy shall lead our horses down the hill; we'll walk afoot awhile . ii 2 83

Come, my masters, let us share, and then to horse before day . ii 2 105

Now merrily to horse: The thieves are all scatter'd and possess'd with fear . . . ii 2 111

Hath Butler brought those horses from the sheriff?—One horse, my lord, he brought even now.—What horse? a roan, a crop-ear, is it not? . . . ii 3 70

What is it carries you away?—Why, my horse, my love, my horse . ii 3 79

God's me, my horse! What say'st thou, Kate? what would'st thou have? . . . ii 3 97

Says she, 'how many hast thou killed to-day?' 'Give my roan horse a drench,' says he . . . ii 4 120

If I tell thee a lie, spit in my face, call me horse . . . ii 4 215

Fast asleep behind the arras, and snorting like a horse . . ii 4 578

He is as tedious As a tired horse, a railing wife . . . iii 1 160

We'll but seal, And then to horse immediately.—With all my heart . iii 1 271

I am a peppercorn, a brewer's horse: the inside of a church! . . iii 3 10

When thou rannest up Gadshill in the night to catch my horse . iii 3 44

I have procured thee, Jack, a charge of foot.—I would it had been of horse . . . iii 3 210

To horse, to horse; for thou and I have thirty miles to ride yet ere dinner time . . . iii 3 221

Come, let me taste my horse, Who is to bear me like a thunderbolt . iv 1 119

Horse. Harry to Harry shall, hot horse to horse, Meet and ne'er part till one drop down a corse . . . *1 Hen. IV.* iv 1 122

Certain horse Of my cousin Vernon's are not yet come up . . iv 3 19

Their courage with hard labour tame and dull, That not a horse is half the half of himself.—So are the horses of the enemy . . iv 3 24

Contention, like a horse Full of high feeding, madly hath broke loose And bears down all before him . . . *2 Hen. IV.* i 1 9

A gentleman, almost forspent with speed, That stopp'd by me to breathe his bloodied horse . . . i 1 38

He gave his able horse the head . . . i 1 43

He was some hilding fellow that had stolen The horse he rode on . i 1 58

He's gone into Smithfield to buy your worship a horse.—I bought him in Paul's, and he'll buy me a horse in Smithfield . . . i 2 57

Fifteen hundred foot, five hundred horse, Are march'd up . . ii 1 186

I'll follow you, good Master Robert Shallow. Bardolph, look to our horses . . . v 1 69

Away, Bardolph! saddle my horse . . . v 3 128

Let us take any man's horses; the laws of England are at my commandment . . . v 3 143

Think, when we talk of horses, that you see them Printing their proud hoofs i' the receiving earth . . . *Hen. V.* Prol. 26

They sell the pasture now to buy the horse . . . ii Prol. 5

Let my horse have his due.—It is the best horse of Europe . . iii 7 4

My lord high constable, you talk of horse and armour? . . iii 7 8

I will not change my horse with any that treads but on four pasterns . iii 7 12

He is indeed a horse; and all other jades you may call beasts . . iii 7 25

It is a most absolute and excellent horse . . . iii 7 28

Turn the sands into eloquent tongues, and my horse is argument for them all . . . iii 7 37

My horse is my mistress.—Your mistress bears well . . . iii 7 47

I had rather have my horse to my mistress.—I had as lief have my mistress a jade . . . iii 7 62

Thou makest use of any thing.—Yet do I not use my horse for my mistress . . . iii 7 71

Even as your horse bears your praises; who would trot as well, were some of your brags dismounted . . . iii 7 82

Next day after dawn, Doth rise and help Hyperion to his horse . iv 1 292

Montez à cheval! My horse! varlet! laquais! ha! . . . iv 2 2

What, will you have them weep our horses' blood? . . . iv 2 12

To horse, you gallant princes! straight to horse! . . . iv 2 15

Give their fasting horses provender, And after fight with them . iv 2 58

Or if I might buffet for my love, or bound my horse for her favours . v 2 146

Your hearts I'll stamp out with my horse's heels . . *1 Hen. VI.* i 4 108

Sheep run not half so treacherous from the wolf, Or horse or oxen from the leopard, As you fly from your oft-subdued slaves . . i 5 31

Between two horses, which doth bear him best . . . ii 4 14

He might have sent and had the horse; I owe him little duty, and less love . . . iv 4 33

Mount on my swiftest horse; And I'll direct thee how thou shalt escape iv 5 9

Before young Talbot from old Talbot fly, The coward horse that bears me fall and die! . . . iv 6 47

So worthless peasants bargain for their wives, As market-men for oxen, sheep, or horse . . . v 5 54

Thither go these news, as fast as horse can carry them . *2 Hen. VI.* i 4 78

Then linger not, my lord; away, take horse . . . iv 4 54

Thou oughtest not to let thy horse wear a cloak, when honester men than thou go in their hose and doublets . . . iv 7 55

Lands, goods, horse, armour, any thing I have, Is his to use . . v 1 52

Three times to-day I holp him to his horse, Three times bestrid him v 3 8

That beggars mounted run their horse to death . . *3 Hen. VI.* i 4 127

I'll kill my horse, because I will not fly . . . ii 3 24

He shall here find his friends with horse and men To set him free . iv 5 12

The time and case requireth haste: Your horse stands ready . . iv 5 19

But yet I run before my horse to market . . . *Richard III.* i 1 160

Where every horse bears his commanding rein . . . ii 2 128

He sends to know your lordship's pleasure, If presently you will take horse with him . . . iii 2 16

Three times to-day my foot-cloth horse did stumble, And startled . iii 4 86

Give me another horse: bind up my wounds . . . v 3 177

Come, bustle, bustle; caparison my horse . . . v 3 289

My foreward shall be drawn out all in length, Consisting equally of horse and foot . . . v 3 294

Thomas Earl of Surrey Shall have the leading of this foot and horse . v 3 297

We will follow In the main battle, whose puissance on either side Shall be well winged with our chiefest horse . . . v 3 300

Spur your proud horses hard, and ride in blood . . . v 3 340

His horse is slain, and all on foot he fights, Seeking for Richmond . v 4 4

A horse! a horse! my kingdom for a horse! . . . v 4 7; 13

Withdraw, my lord; I'll help you to a horse . . . v 4 8

Anger is like A full-hot horse, who being allow'd his way, Self-mettle tires him . . . *Hen. VIII.* i 1 133

The horses your lordship sent for, with all the care I had, I saw well chosen, ridden, and furnished . . . ii 2 1

Those that tame wild horses Pace 'em not in their hands to make 'em gentle . . . v 3 21

Bounding between the two moist elements, Like Perseus' horse *Troi. and Cres.* i 3 42

Let this be granted, and Achilles' horse Makes many Thetis' sons . i 3 211

Thy horse will sooner con an oration than thou learn a prayer without book . . . ii 1 18

Heavens, what a man is there! a very horse, That has he knows not what . . . iii 3 126

Or, like a gallant horse fall'n in first rank, Lie there for pavement to the abject rear . . . iii 3 161

Thou shalt bear a letter to him straight.—Let me bear another to his horse; for that's the more capable creature . . . iii 3 309

Take thou Troilus' horse; Present the fair steed to my lady Cressid v 5 1

Now here he fights on Galathe his horse, And there lacks work . v 5 20

Turn . . . thou traitor, And pay thy life thou owest me for my horse! v 6 7

Tie his body to my horse's tail: Along the field I will the Trojan trail v 8 21

He's dead; and at the murderer's horse's tail, In beastly sort, dragg'd through the shameful field . . . v 10 4

A wager they have met.—My horse to yours, no . . . *Coriolanus* i 4 2

So, the good horse is mine.—I'll buy him of you.—No, I'll nor sell nor give him: lend you him I will . . . i 4 5

Of all the horses, Whereof we have ta'en good and good store, of all The treasure in this field achieved and city, We render you the tenth i 9 31

Present me Death on the wheel or at wild horses' heels . . iii 2 2

He no more remembers his mother now than an eight-year-old horse v 4 17

Horse and chariots let us have, And to our sport . . *T. Andron.* ii 2 18

Horse. I have horse will follow where the game Makes way, and run like swallows . . . . . *T. Andron.* ii 2 23
We hunt not, we, with horse nor hound, But hope to pluck a dainty doe to ground . . . ii 2 25
That very Mab That plats the manes of horses in the night *Rom. and Jul.* i 4 89
Get thee gone, And hire those horses; I'll be with thee straight . . v 1 33
'Tis Alcibiades, and some twenty horse, All of companionship *T. of Athens* i 1 250
Where be our men?—Here, my lord, in readiness.—Our horses! . i 2 173
Hath presented to you Four milk-white horses, trapp'd in silver . i 2 189
If I would sell my horse, and buy twenty more Better than he, why, give my horse to Timon, Ask nothing, give it him, it foals me, straight, And able horses . . . . ii 1 7
Paint till a horse may mire upon your face . . . . iv 3 147
Wert thou a bear, thou wouldst be killed by the horse: wert thou a horse, thou wouldst be seized by the leopard . . . . iv 3 342
Horses did neigh, and dying men did groan, And ghosts did shriek *J. C.* ii 2 23
He's a tried and valiant soldier.—So is my horse . . . iv 1 29
But hollow men, like horses hot at hand, Make gallant show . iv 2 23
The greater part, the horse in general, Are come with Cassius . iv 2 29
Mount thou my horse, and hide thy spurs in him, Till he have brought thee up to yonder troops, And here again . . . . v 3 15
Therefore, to horse; And let us not be dainty of leave-taking *Macbeth* ii 3 149
And Duncan's horses—a thing most strange and certain—Beauteous and swift, the minions of their race, Turn'd wild in nature . . ii 4 14
Go not my horse the better, I must become a borrower of the night . iii 1 26
Hie you to horse: adieu, Till you return at night. Goes Fleance with you? . . . . iii 1 35
I wish your horses swift and sure of foot; And so I do commend you to their backs. Farewell . . . . iii 1 38
Hark! I hear horses.—Give us a light there, ho! . . . iii 3 8
His horses go about.—Almost a mile . . . . . . iii 3 11
I did hear The galloping of horse: who was't came by? . . . iv 1 140
Send out moe horses: skirr the country round; Hang those that talk of fear . . . . v 3 35
Whose sable arms, Black as his purpose, did the night resemble When he lay couched in the ominous horse . . . . *Hamlet* ii 2 476
To such wondrous doing brought his horse, As had he been incorpsed and demi-natured With the brave beast . . . . . iv 7 87
My lord such-a-one, that praised my lord such-a-one's horse, when he meant to beg it . . . . v 1 93
The king, sir, hath wagered with him six Barbary horses . . v 2 155
Six Barbary horses against six French swords, their assigns . . v 2 168
May not an ass know when the cart draws the horse? . . *Lear* i 4 245
Darkness and devils! Saddle my horses . . . . . i 4 274
O, sir, are you come? Is it your will? Speak, sir. Prepare my horses i 4 280
Take you some company, and away to horse: Inform her full . i 4 359
How now! are the horses ready?—Ready, my lord.—Come, boy . i 5 52
Where may we set our horses?—I' the mire . . . . ii 2 4
Horses are tied by the heads, dogs and bears by the neck . . ii 4 7
On whose contents, They summon'd up their meiny, straight took horse ii 4 35
'Twas her brother that, in pure kindness to his horse, buttered his hay ii 4 127
Whither is he going?—He calls to horse; but will I know not whither . ii 4 300
To ride on a bay trotting-horse over four-inched bridges . . iii 4 57
Who hath had three suits to his back, six shirts to his body, horse to ride, and weapon to wear . . . . iii 4 142
He's mad that trusts in the tameness of a wolf, a horse's health . . iii 6 20
Get horses for your mistress . . . . iii 7 20
The fitchew, nor the soiled horse, goes to't With a more riotous appetite iv 6 124
It were a delicate stratagem, to shoe A troop of horse with felt . . iv 6 189
Why should a dog, a horse, a rat, have life, And thou no breath at all? v 3 306
You'll have your daughter covered with a Barbary horse . *Othello* i 1 112
Thou didst drink The stale of horses, and the gilded puddle *Ant. and Cleo.* i 4 62
Stands he, or sits he? Or does he walk? or is he on his horse? . i 5 20
O happy horse, to bear the weight of Antony! Do bravely, horse! . i 5 21
The ne'er-yet-beaten horse of Parthia We have jaded out o' the field . iii 1 33
They are his shards, and he their beetle. So; This is to horse . . iii 2 21
He has a cloud in's face.—He were the worse for that, were he a horse iii 2 52
An army for an usher, and The neighs of horse to tell of her approach . iii 6 45
If we should serve with horse and mares together, The horse were merely lost; the mares would bear A soldier and his horse . . . iii 7 8
Our nineteen legions thou shalt hold by land, And our twelve thousand horse . . . . iii 7 60
You keep by land The legions and the horse whole, do you not? . iii 7 72
To Cæsar will I render My legions and my horse . . . . iii 10 34
That which is now a horse, even with a thought The rack dislimns . iv 14 9
O, for a horse with wings! . . . . *Cymbeline* iii 2 50
I have heard of riding wagers, Where horses have been nimbler than the sands That run i' the clock's behalf . . . . . . iii 2 74
Thou told'st me, when we came from horse, the place Was near at hand iii 4 1
Why hast thou abused So many miles with a pretence? this place? Mine action and thine own? our horses' labour? . . . . iii 4 107
My horse is tied up safe: out, sword, and to a sore purpose! . . iv 1 24
It is not likely That when they hear the Roman horses neigh, . . . That they will waste their time . . . . iv 4 17
Never bestrid a horse, save one that had A rider like myself, who ne'er wore rowel Nor iron on his heel! . . . . iv 4 38
Our ships, you happily may think Are like the Trojan horse was stuff'd within With bloody veins . . . . *Pericles* i 4 93
With all due diligence That horse and sail and high expense Can stead the quest . . . . iii Gower 20
Horseback. Sits on his horse back at mine hostess' door . . *K. John* ii 1 289
And when I am o' horseback, I will swear I love thee infinitely 1 *Hen. IV.* ii 3 104
That runs o' horseback up a hill perpendicular . . . . ii 4 378
O' horseback, ye cuckoo; but afoot he will not budge a foot . . ii 4 387
I was then present, saw them salute on horseback . . *Hen. VIII.* i 1 8
And they [the French] can well on horseback . . . *Hamlet* iv 7 85
Horse-back-breaker. This horse-back-breaker, this huge hill of flesh 1 *Hen. IV.* ii 4 268
Horsed. Being better horsed, Out-rode me . . . 2 *Hen. IV.* i 1 35
An I could get me but a wife in the stews, I were manned, horsed, and wived . . . . i 2 60
Leads fill'd, and ridges horsed With variable complexions . *Coriolanus* ii 1 227
Heaven's cherubim, horsed Upon the sightless couriers of the air *Macbeth* i 7 22
Horse-drench. Of no better report than a horse-drench . *Coriolanus* ii 1 129
Horse-hairs. Which horse-hairs and calves'-guts, nor the voice of unpaved eunuch to boot, can never amend . . . . *Cymbeline* ii 3 33
Horse heels. The bodies shall be dragged at my horse heels 2 *Hen. VI.* iv 3 14
Horse-leeches. Like horse-leeches, my boys, To suck, to suck, the very blood to suck! . . . . *Hen. V.* ii 3 57
Horseman. By a horseman, or a footman?—A footman, sweet sir *W. Tale* iv 3 67
Horseman. If this be a horseman's coat, it hath seen very hot service *W. Tale* iv 3 70
The horsemen sit like fixed candlesticks . . . . *Hen. V.* iv 2 45
Take a trumpet, herald; Ride thou unto the horsemen on yon hill . iv 7 60
For yet a many of your horsemen peer And gallop o'er the field . . iv 7 88
Sharp stakes pluck'd out of hedges They pitched in the ground confusedly, To keep the horsemen off from breaking in . . 1 *Hen. VI.* i 1 119
My Lord of Somerset, unite Your troops of horsemen with his bands of foot . . . . iv 1 165
I hear the enemy: Out, some light horsemen, and peruse their wings . iv 2 43
A plague upon that villain Somerset, That thus delays my promised supply Of horsemen! . . . . iv 3 11
I will dispatch the horsemen straight: Within six hours they will be at his aid . . . . iv 4 40
While we pursued the horsemen of the north, He slily stole away 3 *Hen. VI.* i 1 2
Titinius is enclosed round about With horsemen . . . *J. Cæsar* v 3 29
It fits us therefore ripely Our chariots and our horsemen be in readiness *Cymbeline* iii 5 23
Horsemanship. And witch the world with noble horsemanship 1 *Hen. IV.* iv 1 110
You have good judgement in horsemanship . . . . *Hen. V.* iii 7 58
Horse-piss. I do smell all horse-piss . . . . . *Tempest* iv 1 199
Horse-shoe. Cooled, glowing hot, in that surge, like a horse-shoe *M. W.* iii 5 123
Horse-stealer. He is not a pick-purse nor a horse-stealer *As Y. Like It* iii 4 25
Horse-tail. And not presume to touch a hair of my master's horse-tail till they kiss their hands . . . . *T. of Shrew* iv 1 96
Horse-way. Both stile and gate, horse-way and foot-path . . *Lear* iv 1 58
Horsing. A note infallible Of breaking honesty—horsing foot on foot? Skulking in corners? . . . . *W. Tale* i 2 288
Hortensio. There, there, Hortensio, will you any wife? . *T. of Shrew* i 1 56
If you, Hortensio, Or Signior Gremio, you, know any such, Prefer them hither . . . . i 1 95
Their love is not so great, Hortensio, but we may blow our nails together . . . . i 1 108
Thinkest thou, Hortensio, though her father be very rich, any man is so very a fool to be married to hell? . . . . i 1 127
My best beloved and approved friend, Hortensio . . . . i 2 4
Signior Hortensio, come you to part the fray? . . . . . i 2 23
Good Hortensio, I bade the rascal knock upon your gate . . . i 2 36
Signior Hortensio, 'twixt such friends as we Few words suffice . . i 2 65
Hortensio, peace! thou know'st not gold's effect . . . . i 2 93
I will not sleep, Hortensio, till I see her . . . . . i 2 103
Hortensio, have you told him all her faults? . . . . . i 2 187
That she's the chosen of Signior Hortensio . . . . . i 2 237
Hortensio, to what end are all these words? . . . . . i 2 250
Is't not Hortensio?—If you affect him, sister, here I swear I'll plead for you myself, but you shall have him . . . . ii 1 13
Yet read the gamut of Hortensio.—'Gamut' I am, the ground of all accord, 'A re,' to plead Hortensio's passion . . . . . iii 1 72
If once I find thee ranging, Hortensio will be quit with thee by changing iii 1 92
Know, sir, that I am call'd Hortensio.—Signior Hortensio, I have often heard Of your entire affection to Bianca . . . . . . iv 2 21
I have ta'en you napping, gentle love, And have forsworn you with Hortensio . . . . iv 2 47
Eat it up all, Hortensio, if thou lovest me . . . . . iv 3 50
Hortensio, say thou wilt see the tailor paid . . . . . iv 3 166
And if she be froward, Then hast thou taught Hortensio to be untoward iv 5 79
And thou, Hortensio, with thy loving widow, Feast with the best . v 2 7
Now, for my life, Hortensio fears his widow . . . . . v 2 16
Hortensio is afeard of you.—He that is giddy thinks the world turns round v 2 19
Thus I conceive by him.—Conceives by me! How likes Hortensio that? v 2 23
Where is your sister, and Hortensio's wife?—They sit conferring by the parlour fire . . . . v 2 101
Hortensius. Well met; good morrow, Titus and Hortensius *T. of Athens* iii 4 1
Horum. Genitive case!—Ay.—Genitive,—horum, harum, horum *M. W.* iv 1 63
And to call 'horum:' fie upon you!—'Oman, art thou lunatics? . iv 1 70
Hose. He, being in love, could not see to garter his hose, and you, being in love, cannot see to put on your hose . . . *T. G. of Ver.* ii 1 83
A round hose, madam, now's not worth a pin, Unless you have a codpiece ii 7 55
Youthful still! in your doublet and hose this raw rheumatic day *M. W.* iii 1 47
This secrecy of thine shall be a tailor to thee and shall make thee a new doublet and hose . . . . iii 3 35
What a pretty thing man is when he goes in his doublet and hose and leaves off his wit! . . . . *Much Ado* v 1 203
Rhymes are guards on wanton Cupid's hose . . . . *L. L. Lost* iv 3 58
He bought his doublet in Italy, his round hose in France *Mer. of Venice* i 2 80
Doublet and hose ought to show itself courageous to petticoat *As Y. L. It* ii 4 7
His youthful hose, well saved, a world too wide For his shrunk shank . ii 7 160
Dost thou think, though I am caparisoned like a man, I have a doublet and hose in my disposition? . . . . iii 2 206
Alas the day! what shall I do with my doublet and hose? . . . iii 2 232
Your hose should be ungartered, your bonnet unbanded . . . iii 2 397
We must have your doublet and hose plucked over your head . . iv 1 206
A silken doublet! a velvet hose! a scarlet cloak! . . *T. of Shrew* v 1 69
Dost make hose of thy sleeves? . . . . *All's Well* ii 3 266
I am eight times thrust through the doublet, four through the hose 1 *Hen. IV.* ii 4 185
Their points being broken,— Down fell their hose . . . . ii 4 239
Your French hose off, and in your strait strossers . . *Hen. V.* iii 7 57
Honester men than thou go in their hose and doublets . 2 *Hen. VI.* iv 7 56
Here's an English tailor come hither, for stealing out of a French hose *Macbeth* ii 3 16
I have already fit—'Tis in my cloak-bag—doublet, hat, hose, all *Cymbeline* iii 4 172
Hospitable. Being no further enemy to you Than the constraint of hospitable zeal . . . . *K. John* ii 1 244
At home, upon my brother's guard, even there, Against the hospitable canon, would I Wash my fierce hand in's heart . *Coriolanus* i 10 26
I am your host: With robbers' hands my hospitable favours You should not ruffle thus . . . . *Lear* iii 7 40
Hospital. I'll jest a twelvemonth in an hospital . . *L. L. Lost* v 2 881
Hospitality. And little recks to find the way to heaven By doing deeds of hospitality . . . . *As Y. Like It* ii 4 82
Host. You're allycholly: I pray you, why is it?—Marry, mine host, because I cannot be merry . . . . *T. G. of Ver.* iv 2 28
Host, will you go?—By my halidom, I was fast asleep . . . iv 2 135
Truly, mine host, I must turn away some of my followers *Mer. Wives* i 3 4
He shall draw, he shall tap: said I well, bully Hector?—Do so, good mine host . . . . i 3 13
How now, mine host!—How now, bully-rook! thou'rt a gentleman . ii 1 199
My merry host hath had the measuring of their weapons . . . ii 1 215
Will you go, An-heires?—Have with you, mine host . . . . ii 1 229

Host. Trust me, a mad host. Follow, gentlemen, follow . *Mer. Wives* iii 1 115
I pray you now, remembrance to-morrow on the lousy knave, mine host iii 3 256
Art thou there? it is thine host, thine Ephesian, calls.—How now, mine host! . . . iv 5 19
There was, mine host, an old fat woman even now with me . . iv 5 25
Was there a wise woman with thee?—Ay, that there was, mine host . iv 5 60
There is three cozen-germans that has cozened all the host of Readins . iv 5 80
Hark, good mine host. To-night at Herne's oak, just 'twixt twelve and one iv 6 18
Which means she to deceive, father or mother?—Both, my good host . iv 6 47
Go bear it to the Centaur, where we host . . . *Com. of Errors* i 2 9
In care to seek me out By computation and mine host's report . ii 2 4
Small cheer and great welcome makes a merry feast.—Ay to a niggardly host and more sparing guest . . . iii 1 27
Your goods that lay at host, sir, in the Centaur . . . v 1 410
I will bring you Where you shall host . *All's Well* iii 5 97
On the marriage-bed Of smiling peace to march a bloody host *K. John* iii 1 246
London hath received, Like a kind host, the Dauphin and his powers . v 1 32
God help the wicked! if to be old and merry be a sin, then many an old host that I know is damned . . . 1 *Hen. IV.* ii 4 518
The shirt, to say the truth, stolen from my host at Saint Alban's . . iv 2 50
How now, mine host Pistol!—Base tike, call'st thou me host? Now, by this hand, I swear, I scorn the term . . . *Hen. V.* ii 1 30
Rush on his host, as doth the melted snow Upon the valleys . . iii 5 50
For forth he goes and visits all his host, Bids them good morrow . iv Prol. 32
Big Mars seems bankrupt in their beggar'd host . . . iv 2 43
Proclaim it, Westmoreland, through my host, That he which hath no stomach to this fight, Let him depart . . . iv 3 34
There's not a piece of feather in our host . . . iv 3 112
And be it death proclaimed through our host To boast of this . iv 8 119
The battles of the Lord of hosts he fought . . 1 *Hen. VI.* i 1 31
Swearing that you withhold his levied host, Collected for this expedition iv 4 31
'Tis politicly done, To send me packing with an host of men 2 *Hen. VI.* iii 1 342
The queen is coming with a puissant host . . 3 *Hen. VI.* ii 1 207
Whom opinion crowns The sinew and the forehand of our host *T. and C.* i 3 143
If there be not in our Grecian host One noble man that hath one spark of fire . . . i 3 293
This, sir, is proclaim'd through all our host . . . ii 1 133
For time is like a fashionable host That slightly shakes his parting guest by the hand . . . iii 3 165
You do discomfort all the host.—You understand me not that tell me so . v 10 10
Call him, With all the applause and clamour of the host . *Coriolanus* i 9 64
I request you To give my poor host freedom.—O, well-begg'd! . . i 9 87
We will before the walls of Rome to-morrow Set down our host . v 3 2
Conduct me to mine host: we love him highly *Macbeth* i 6 29
As his host, Who should against his murderer shut the door . . i 7 14
Ourself will mingle with society, And play the humble host . . iii 4 4
Thereby shall we shadow The numbers of our host and make discovery Err v 4 6
O all you host of heaven! O earth! what else? And shall I couple hell? O, fie! Hold, hold, my heart . . . *Hamlet* i 5 92
I am your host: With robbers' hands my hospitable favours You should not ruffle thus . . . *Lear* iii 7 39
Here, father, take the shadow of this tree For your good host . v 2 2
Give to a gracious message An host of tongues; but let ill tidings tell Themselves when they be felt . . . *Ant. and Cleo.* ii 5 87
Best you safed the bringer Out of the host; I must attend mine office . iv 6 27
Had our great palace the capacity To camp this host, we all would sup together . . . iv 8 33
Which portends . . . Success to the Roman host . . . *Cymbeline* iv 2 352
Host of the Garter. And the three party is, lastly and finally, mine host of the Garter . . . *Mer. Wives* i 1 143
Mine host of the Garter!—What says my bully-rook? . . . i 3 1
I have appointed mine host of de Jarteer to measure our weapon . . i 4 124
He hath pawned his horses to mine host of the Garter . . . ii 1 100
Look where my ranting host of the Garter comes . . . ii 1 196
Good mine host o' the Garter, a word with you . . . ii 1 211
Mine host de Jarteer,—have I not stay for him to kill him? have I not? iii 1 93
I'll be judgement by mine host of the Garter . . . iii 1 98
Hear mine host of the Garter. Am I politic? am I subtle? . . iii 1 102
This same scall, scurvy, cogging companion, the host of the Garter . iii 1 124
Vere is mine host de Jarteer?—Here, master doctor . . iv 5 85
Hostage. You know now your hostages; your uncle's word *Troi. and Cres.* iii 2 115
Go you to the city; Learn how 'tis held; and what they are that must Be hostages for Rome . . . *Coriolanus* i 10 29
If he stand on hostage for his safety, Bid him demand what pledge will please him best . . . *T. Andron.* iv 4 105
He craves a parley . . . , Willing you to demand your hostages . v 1 160
Your hostages I have, so have you mine; And we shall talk before we fight.—Most meet . . . *Ant. and Cleo.* ii 6 1
I have sent Cloten's clotpoll down the stream, In embassy to his mother: his body's hostage For his return . . . *Cymbeline* iv 2 185
Hostess. A man is never undone till he be hanged, nor never welcome to a place till some certain shot be paid and the hostess say 'Welcome!' *T. G. of Ver.* ii 5 7
That chain will I bestow—Be it for nothing but to spite my wife—Upon mine hostess there . . . *Com. of Errors* iii 1 119
Yet would you say ye were beaten out of door; And rail upon the hostess of the house . . . *T. of Shrew* Ind. 2 88
I think I know your hostess As ample as myself . . *All's Well* iii 5 45
Not your gaoler, then, But your kind hostess . . *W. Tale* i 2 60
You are retired, As if you were a feasted one and not The hostess . . iv 4 64
Saint George, that swinged the dragon, and e'er since Sits on his horse back at mine hostess' door . . . *K. John* ii 1 289
And is not my hostess of the tavern a most sweet wench? . 1 *Hen. IV.* i 2 45
Why, what a pox have I to do with my hostess of the tavern? . . i 2 54
Hostess, clap to the doors: watch to-night, pray to-morrow . . ii 4 305
How now, my lady the hostess! what sayest thou to me? . . ii 4 315
The tithe of a hair was never lost in my house before.—Ye lie, hostess . iii 3 68
Thou sayest true, hostess; and he slanders thee most grossly . . iii 3 149
Hostess, I forgive thee: go, make ready breakfast . . . iii 3 192
Hostess, my breakfast, come! O, I could wish this tavern were my drum! iii 3 229
Satisfy the poor woman.—Come hither, hostess . . 2 *Hen. IV.* ii 1 144
Dost thou hear, hostess?—Pray ye, pacify yourself . . . ii 4 86
No, I'll no swaggerers.—He's no swaggerer, hostess . . . ii 4 105
Feel, masters, how I shake; look you, I warrant you.—So you do, hostess ii 4 115
I charge you with a cup of sack: do you discharge upon mine hostess . ii 4 122
Is she of the wicked? is thine hostess here of the wicked? . . ii 4 355
Farewell, hostess; farewell, Doll. You see, my good wenches, how men of merit are sought after . . . ii 4 404
Mine host Pistol, you must come to my master, and you, hostess *Hen. V.* ii 1 86
Farewell, hostess.—I cannot kiss, that is the humour of it; but, adieu . ii 3 62
Hostess. Ruminates like an hostess that hath no arithmetic but her brain to set down her reckoning . . . *Troi. and Cres.* iii 3 253
See, see, our honour'd hostess! The love that follows us sometime is our trouble, Which still we thank as love . . . *Macbeth* i 6 10
Fair and noble hostess, We are your guest to-night . . . i 6 24
And shall continue our graces towards him. By your leave, hostess . i 6 31
This diamond he greets your wife withal, By the name of most kind hostess ii 1 16
Our hostess keeps her state, but in best time We will require her welcome iii 4 5
Hostess-ship. It is my father's will I should take on me The hostess-ship o' the day . . . *W. Tale* iv 4 72
Hostile. Nor bruise her flowerets with the armed hoofs Of hostile paces 1 *Hen. IV.* i 1 9
So thrive I in my dangerous attempt Of hostile arms! . *Richard III.* iv 4 399
As now at last Given hostile strokes . . . *Coriolanus* iii 3 97
To ease them of their griefs, Their fears of hostile strokes *T. of Athens* v 1 202
With hostile forces he'll o'erspread the land . . *Pericles* i 2 24
Hostility and civil tumult reigns . . . *K. John* iv 2 247
The nature of your griefs, and whereupon You conjure from the breast of civil peace Such bold hostility . . 1 *Hen. IV.* iv 3 44
It is your policy To save your subjects from such massacre And ruthless slaughters as are daily seen By our proceeding in hostility 1 *Hen. VI.* v 4 162
And neither by treason nor hostility To seek to put me down 3 *Hen. VI.* i 1 199
Hostilius. Ancus Marcius, Numa's daughter's son, Who, after great Hostilius, here was king . . . *Coriolanus* ii 3 248
Do you observe this, Hostilius?—Ay, too well. *T. of Athens* iii 2 70
Hot. Love my wife!—With liver burning hot . . *Mer. Wives* ii 1 121
And cooled, glowing hot, in that surge, like a horse-shoe; think of that,—hissing hot,—think of that, Master Brook . . iii 5 122
Be not so hot; the duke Dare no more stretch this finger of mine than he Dare rack his own . . . *Meas. for Meas.* v 1 315
She is so hot because the meat is cold . . *Com. of Errors* i 2 47
Where Spain?—Faith, I saw it not; but I felt it hot in her breath . iii 2 134
The first suit is hot and hasty, like a Scotch jig . . *Much Ado* ii 1 78
Your wit's too hot, it speeds too fast, 'twill tire . *L. L. Lost* ii 1 120
I never did apply Hot and rebellious liquors in my blood *As Y. Like It* ii 3 49
Leander, he would have lived many a fair year, though Hero had turned nun, if it had not been for a hot midsummer night . . iv 1 102
She is not hot, but temperate as the morn . . *T. of Shrew* ii 1 296
Now, were not I a little pot and soon hot, my very lips might freeze . iv 1 6
Is she so hot a shrew as she's reported? . . . iv 1 22
The mustard is too hot a little . . . iv 3 25
Yes, by Saint Anne, and ginger shall be hot i' the mouth too *T. Night* ii 3 127
Too hot, too hot! To mingle friendship far is mingling bloods *W. Tale* i 2 108
Not so hot, good sir: I come to bring him sleep . . ii 3 32
Your purse is not hot enough to purchase your spice . . iv 3 127
And then we shall repent each drop of blood That hot rash haste so indirectly shed . . . *K. John* ii 1 49
King John . . . doth approach, Commander of this hot malicious day . ii 1 314
This day grows wondrous hot; Some airy devil hovers in the sky . . iii 2 1
So hot a speed with such advice disposed . . . iii 4 11
Heat me these irons hot; and look thou stand Within the arras . . iv 1 1
I am hot with haste in seeking you . . . iv 3 74
There is so hot a summer in my bosom, That all my bowels crumble up to dust . . . v 7 30
O that there were some virtue in my tears, That might relieve you!—The salt in them is hot. Within me is a hell . . . v 7 45
The blood is hot that must be cool'd for this . . *Richard II.* i 1 51
Mounted upon a hot and fiery steed . . . v 2 8
My liege, this haste was hot in question . . 1 *Hen. IV.* i 1 34
If men were to be saved by merit, what hole in hell were hot enough for him? . . . i 2 120
All hot and bleeding will we offer them . . . iv 1 115
I am as hot as molten lead, and as heavy too . . . v 3 34
What, is it in the case?—Ay, Hal; 'tis hot, 'tis hot . . v 3 55
The room where they supped is too hot . . . 2 *Hen. IV.* ii 4 15
Of drinking . . . fertile sherris, that he is become very hot and valiant iv 3 132
He'll call you to so hot an answer of it . . *Hen. V.* ii 4 123
The knocks are too hot . . . iii 2 4
The humour of it is too hot, that is the very plain-song of it . . iii 2 5
The day is hot, and the weather, and the wars, and the king, and the dukes iii 2 113
If your pure maidens fall into the hand Of hot and forcing violation . iii 3 21
Touch'd with choler, hot as gunpowder, And quickly will return an injury iv 7 188
Are ye so hot, sir? yet, Pucelle, hold thy peace; If Talbot do but thunder, rain will follow . . 1 *Hen. VI.* iii 2 58
You, that were so hot at sea, Disgracing of these colours . . iii 4 28
Now ye grow too hot: It was the pleasure of my lord the king 2 *Hen. VI.* i 1 137
Churchmen so hot? good uncle, hide such malice . . ii 1 25
Oft have I seen a hot o'erweening cur Run back and bite . . v 1 151
The sun shines hot; and, if we use delay, Cold biting winter mars our hoped-for hay.—Away betimes . . 3 *Hen. VI.* iv 8 60
I was too hot to do somebody good, That is too cold in thinking of it now *Richard III.* i 3 311
And finds the testy gentleman so hot, As he will lose his head . . iii 4 39
Heat not a furnace for your foe so hot That it do singe yourself *Hen. VIII.* i 1 140
And now, While it is hot, I'll put it to the issue . . v 1 176
Is your blood So madly hot that no discourse of reason, Nor fear of bad success in a bad cause, Can qualify the same? . *Troi. and Cres.* ii 2 116
I have seen thee, As hot as Perseus, spur thy Phrygian steed . . iv 5 186
The gods have heard me swear.—The gods are deaf to hot and peevish vows v 3 16
Quench the fire, the room is grown too hot . . *Rom. and Jul.* i 5 30
O God's lady dear! Are you so hot? marry, come up, I trow . . ii 5 64
Let's retire: The day is hot, the Capulets abroad, And, if we meet, we shall not scape a brawl . . . iii 1 2
Thou art as hot a Jack in thy mood as any in Italy, and as soon moved to be moody . . . iii 1 12
Who, all as hot, turns deadly point to point . . . iii 1 165
You are too hot.—God's bread! it makes me mad . . . iii 5 176
Those that under hot ardent zeal would set whole realms on fire *T. of A.* iii 3 33
With Ate by his side come hot from hell . . . *J. Cæsar* iii 1 271
But hollow men, like horses hot at hand, Make gallant show . . iv 2 23
Young Fortinbras, Of unimproved mettle hot and full . . *Hamlet* i 1 96
When in your motion you are hot and dry—As make your bouts more violent . . . iv 7 158
It is very hot.—No, believe me, 'tis very cold; the wind is northerly . v 2 97
But yet methinks it is very sultry and hot for my complexion . . v 2 102
Not so hot: In his own grace he doth exalt himself . . *Lear* v 3 66
What means that bloody knife?—'Tis hot, it smokes; It came even from the heart of—O, she's dead! . . . v 3 223
Were they as prime as goats, as hot as monkeys . . . *Othello* iii 3 403
Hot, hot, and moist: this hand of yours requires A sequester from liberty iii 4 39

Hot. Like to the time o' the year between the extremes Of hot and cold *Ant. and Cleo.* i 5 52
You are most hot and furious when you win . . *Cymbeline* ii 3 7
Not too hot: First pay me for the nursing of thy sons . . . . v 5 321
If fires be hot, knives sharp, or waters deep, Untied I still my virgin knot will keep . . . . *Pericles* iv 2 159
Hot Ætna. Now let hot Ætna cool in Sicily! . . . *T. Andron.* iii 1 242
Hot assays. Galling the gleaned land with hot assays . . *Hen. V.* i 2 151
Hot backs. When gods have hot backs, what shall poor men do? *M. W.* v 5 13
Hot beams. Cold snow melts with the sun's hot beams . 2 *Hen. VI.* iii 1 223
Hot blood. All the hot bloods between fourteen and five-and-thirty *Much Ado* iii 3 141
When rage and hot blood are his counsellors 2 *Hen. IV.* iv 4 63
Make incision in their hides, That their hot blood may spin . *Hen. V.* iv 2 10
My sword should shed hot blood, mine eyes no tears . . 2 *Hen. VI.* i 1 118
He eats nothing but doves, love, and that breeds hot blood, and hot blood begets hot thoughts, and hot thoughts beget hot deeds, and hot deeds is love . . . . . *Troi. and Cres.* iii 1 141
Who, in hot blood, Hath stepp'd into the law . . . *T. of Athens* iii 5 11
Now could I drink hot blood, And do such bitter business as the day Would quake to look on . . . . . . *Hamlet* iii 2 408
Hot-blooded. Now, the hot-blooded gods assist me! . . *Mer. Wives* v 5 2
The hot-blooded France, that dowerless took Our youngest born . *Lear* ii 4 215
Hot brain. Here is more matter for a hot brain . . . *W. Tale* iv 4 699
Hot breath. Carbuncles, sapphires, declining their rich aspect to the hot breath of Spain . . . . . . *Com. of Errors* iii 2 139
Hot coals. O war, thou son of hell, . . . Throw in the frozen bosoms of our part Hot coals of vengeance! . . . . . 2 *Hen. VI.* v 2 36
Hot colts. For young hot colts being raged do rage the more *Richard II.* ii 1 70
Hot condition. Bellowing and neighing loud, Which is the hot condition of their blood . . . . *Mer. of Venice* v 1 74
Hot day. But look you pray, all you that kiss my lady Peace at home, that our armies join not in a hot day . . . 2 *Hen. IV.* i 2 233
If it be a hot day, and I brandish any thing but a bottle, I would I might never spit white again . . . . i 2 236
For now, these hot days, is the mad blood stirring . . *Rom. and Jul.* iii 1 4
Hot deeds. And hot blood begets hot thoughts, and hot thoughts beget hot deeds, and hot deeds is love . . . . . *Troi. and Cres.* iii 1 142
Hot digestion. Consumed In hot digestion of this cormorant war . . ii 2 6
Hot discourse. Imagined worth Holds in his blood such swoln and hot discourse . . . . ii 3 183
Hot dreams. He spake of her, as Dian had hot dreams, And she alone were cold . . . . *Cymbeline* v 5 180
Hot duke. Tell the hot duke that—No, but not yet . . *Lear* ii 4 105
Hot fire. I do not seek to quench your love's hot fire *T. G. of Ver.* ii 7 21
Hot friend. Thou hast described A hot friend cooling . . *J. Cæsar* iv 2 19
Hot goats. Scarce ever look'd on blood, But that of coward hares, hot goats, and venison! . . . . *Cymbeline* iv 4 37
Hot horse. Harry to Harry shall, hot horse to horse, Meet and ne'er part till one drop down a corse . . . . 1 *Hen. IV.* iv 1 122
Hot-house. Now she professes a hot-house, which, I think, is a very ill house too . . . . *Meas. for Meas.* ii 1 66
Hot ice. That is, hot ice and wondrous strange snow . *M. N. Dream* v 1 59
Hot incursions. Whose hot incursions and great name in arms Holds from all soldiers chief majority . . . . . 1 *Hen. IV.* iii 2 108
Hot infusion. With aqua-vitæ or some other hot infusion *W. Tale* iv 4 816
Hot inroads. Many hot inroads They make in Italy . *Ant. and Cleo.* i 4 50
Hot irons. Must you with hot irons burn out both mine eyes? *K. John* iv 1 39
I have sworn to do it; And with hot irons must I burn them out . . iv 1 59
Hot January. You will never run mad, niece.—No, not till a hot January *Much Ado* i 1 94
Hot June. If there come a hot June and this civil buffeting hold, we shall buy maidenheads . . . . . . 1 *Hen. IV.* ii 4 397
Hot lavender, mints, savory, marjoram . . . *W. Tale* iv 4 104
Hot livers and cold purses . . . . . . 1 *Hen. IV.* ii 4 355
Hot Lord Percy. You are as slow As hot Lord Percy is on fire to go . iii 1 269
Hot love. When I had seen this hot love on the wing . *Hamlet* ii 2 132
Hot lover. My master is become a hot lover . . *T. G. of Ver.* ii 5 53
Hot meat. I cannot abide the smell of hot meat since . *Mer. Wives* i 1 297
Hot minion. Mars's hot minion is return'd again . . *Tempest* iv 1 98
Hot office. Thou shalt soon feel, to thy cold comfort, for being slow in thy hot office . . . . *T. of Shrew* iv 1 34
Hot passion. The reasons you allege do more conduce To the hot passion of distemper'd blood . . . . . *Troi. and Cres.* ii 2 169
Hot pursuit. Sound retreat, and cease our hot pursuit . 1 *Hen. VI.* ii 2 3
Hot questrists. Some five or six and thirty of his knights, Hot questrists after him, met him at gate . . . . . . *Lear* iii 7 17
Hot service. If this be a horseman's coat, it hath seen very hot service *W. Tale* iv 3 71
Hot sheeps. Two hot sheeps, marry.—And wherefore not ships? *L. L. Lost* ii 1 219
Hot summer. This moral ties me over to time and a hot summer *Hen. V.* v 2 340
To be still hot summer's tanlings and The shrinking slaves of winter *Cymbeline* iv 4 29
Hot tears. I am ashamed That thou hast power to shake my manhood thus; That these hot tears, which break from me perforce, Should make thee worth them . . . . *Lear* i 4 320
Hot temper. But a hot temper leaps o'er a cold decree . *Mer. of Venice* i 2 20
Hot termagant. 'Twas time to counterfeit, or that hot termagant Scot had paid me scot and lot too . . . . . 1 *Hen. IV.* v 4 114
Hot thoughts. And hot blood begets hot thoughts, and hot thoughts beget hot deeds, and hot deeds is love . . *Troi. and Cres.* iii 1 142
Hot trial. England, thou hast not saved one drop of blood, In this hot trial, more than we . . . . *K. John* ii 1 342
Hot vengeance. Who, when they see the hours ripe on earth, Will rain hot vengeance on offenders' heads . . . . *Richard II.* i 2 8
Thou art only mark'd For the hot vengeance and the rod of heaven 1 *Hen. IV.* iii 2 10
Hot venison pasty. Come, we have a hot venison pasty to dinner: come, gentlemen . . . . *Mer. Wives* i 1 202
Hot weather. Fie! this is hot weather, gentlemen . . 2 *Hen. IV.* iii 2 101
Which is not amiss to cool a man's stomach this hot weather 2 *Hen. VI.* iv 10 10
Hot wench. And the blessed sun himself a fair hot wench . 1 *Hen. IV.* i 2 10
Hot wine. One that loves a cup of hot wine with not a drop of allaying Tiber in't . . . . *Coriolanus* ii 1 52
Hot youth. Were I but now the lord of such hot youth . *Richard II.* ii 3 99
Hotly. You see this chase is hotly follow'd . . . *Hen. V.* ii 4 68
And do contest As hotly and as nobly with thy love As ever in ambitious strength I did Contend against thy valour . . . *Coriolanus* iv 5 117
Strip thine own back; Thou hotly lust'st to use her in that kind For which thou whipp'st her . . . . *Lear* iv 6 166

Hotly. You have been hotly call'd for . . . . . *Othello* i 2 44
Hotspur. The gallant Hotspur there, Young Harry Percy . 1 *Hen. IV.* i 1 52
Of prisoners, Hotspur took Mordake the Earl of Fife . . . . i 1 70
I am not yet of Percy's mind, the Hotspur of the north . . . ii 4 114
Sit, cousin Percy; sit, good cousin Hotspur, For by that name as oft as Lancaster Doth speak of you, his cheek looks pale . . . . iii 1 7
This Hotspur, Mars in swathling clothes, This infant warrior . iii 2 112
This same child of honour and renown, This gallant Hotspur . . iii 2 140
The Douglas and the Hotspur both together Are confident against the world in arms . . . . v 1 116
A hare-brain'd Hotspur, govern'd by a spleen . . . . . . v 2 19
Who in a bloody field by Shrewsbury Hath beaten down young Hotspur and his troops . . . . 2 *Hen. IV.* Ind. 25
That Harry Monmouth fell Under the wrath of noble Hotspur's sword Ind. 30
Where Hotspur's father, old Northumberland, Lies crafty-sick . . Ind. 36
Said he young Harry Percy's spur was cold? Of Hotspur Coldspur? . i 1 50
As the thing that's heavy in itself Upon enforcement flies with greatest speed, So did our men, heavy in Hotspur's loss . . . . i 1 121
Indeed It was young Hotspur's case at Shrewsbury . . . . i 3 26
A field Where nothing but the sound of Hotspur's name Did seem defensible ii 3 37
Had my sweet Harry had but half their numbers, To-day might I, hanging on Hotspur's neck, Have talk'd of Monmouth's grave . ii 3 44
Hotter. A' has an English name; but his fisnomy is more hotter in France than there . . . . *All's Well* iv 5 42
Nor my lusts Burn hotter than my faith . . . . . *W. Tale* iv 4 35
Let him be damned, like the glutton! pray God his tongue be hotter! 2 *Hen. IV.* i 2 40
Though thou call'st thyself a hotter name Than any is in hell *Macbeth* v 7 6
Besides what hotter hours, Unregister'd in vulgar fame, you have Luxuriously pick'd out . . . . *Ant. and Cleo.* iii 13 118
Hottest. And in the hottest day prognostication proclaims, shall he be set against a brick-wall . . . . *W. Tale* iv 4 817
Like stinging bees in hottest summer's day . . . *T. Andron.* v 1 14
Hound. A hound that runs counter and yet draws dry-foot well *Com. of Errors* iv 2 39
Imitari is nothing; so doth the hound his master . . . *L. L. Lost* iv 2 130
Sometime a horse I'll be, sometime a hound, A hog . *M. N. Dream* iii 1 111
Neigh, and bark, and grunt, and roar, and burn, Like horse, hound, hog iii 1 114
I had rather give his carcass to my hounds . . . . . . iii 2 64
My love shall hear the music of my hounds . . . . . . iv 1 111
Mark the musical confusion Of hounds and echo in conjunction . iv 1 116
In a wood of Crete they bay'd the bear With hounds of Sparta . . iv 1 119
My hounds are bred out of the Spartan kind, So flew'd, so sanded . iv 1 124
Huntsman, I charge thee, tender well my hounds . . *T. of Shrew* Ind. 1 16
Another tell him of his hounds and horse, And that his lady mourns Ind. 1 61
Thy hounds shall make the welkin answer them . . . . . Ind. 2 47
Twenty crowns! I'll venture so much of my hawk or hound, But twenty times so much upon my wife . . . . v 2 72
My desires, like fell and cruel hounds, E'er since pursue me . *T. Night* i 1 22
And at his heels, Leash'd in like hounds, should famine, sword and fire Crouch for employment . . . . *Hen. V.* Prol. 7
O hound of Crete, think'st thou my spouse to get? . . . . . ii 1 77
Turn on the bloody hounds with heads of steel . . . 1 *Hen. VI.* iv 2 51
He will spend his mouth, and promise, like Brabbler the hound *Troi. and Cres.* v 1 99
Boy! false hound! If you have writ your annals true, 'tis there, That, like an eagle in a dove-cote, I Flutter'd your Volscians in Corioli *Coriolanus* v 6 113
With horn and hound we'll give your grace bonjour . . *T. Andron.* i 1 494
We hunt not, we, with horse nor hound, But hope to pluck a dainty doe to ground . . . . ii 2 25
The babbling echo mocks the hounds, Replying shrilly . . . . ii 3 17
Hounds and horns and sweet melodious birds Be unto us as is a nurse's song . . . . ii 3 27
And the hounds Should drive upon thy new-transformed limbs . . ii 3 63
Jove shield your husband from his hounds to-day! 'Tis pity they should take him for a stag . . . . ii 3 70
Let's kill him boldly, but not wrathfully; Let's carve him as a dish fit for the gods, Not hew him as a carcass fit for hounds . *J. Cæsar* ii 1 174
You show'd your teeth like apes, and fawn'd like hounds . . . v 1 41
Hounds and greyhounds, mongrels, spaniels, curs, Shoughs . *Macbeth* iii 1 93
Hound or spaniel, brach or lym, Or bobtail tike or trundle-tail . *Lear* iii 6 72
I do follow here in the chase, not like a hound that hunts, but one that fills up the cry . . . . *Othello* ii 3 370
Hour. Make yourself ready in your cabin for the mischance of the hour, if it so hap . . . . *Tempest* i 1 28
The hour's now come; The very minute bids thee ope thine ear . i 2 36
Wherefore did they not That hour destroy us? . . . . . . i 2 139
Made thee more profit Than other princesses can that have more time For vainer hours and tutors not so careful . . . . . . i 2 174
Took pains to make thee speak, taught thee each hour One thing or other . . . . i 2 354
They'll tell the clock to any business that We say befits the hour . ii 1 290
Pray now, rest yourself; He's safe for these three hours . . . iii 1 21
And now farewell Till half an hour hence . . . . iii 1 91
Within this half hour will he be asleep: Wilt thou destroy him then? iii 2 122
One tree, the phœnix' throne, one phœnix At this hour reigning there iii 3 24
At this hour Lie at my mercy all mine enemies . . . . . iv 1 263
How's the day?—On the sixth hour . . . . v 1 4
Who three hours since Were wreck'd upon this shore . . . . v 1 136
Your eld'st acquaintance cannot be three hours . . . . . v 1 186
When that hour o'erslips me in the day Wherein I sigh not, Julia, for thy sake, The next ensuing hour some foul mischance Torment me for my love's forgetfulness! . . . . *T. G. of Ver.* ii 2 9
Nay, 'twill be this hour ere I have done weeping . . . . . ii 3 1
From our infancy We have conversed and spent our hours together . ii 4 63
Trenched in ice, which with an hour's heat Dissolves to water . . iii 2 7
This is the hour that Madam Silvia Entreated me to call . . . iv 3 1
And now it is about the very hour . . . . v 1 2
Lovers break not hours, Unless it be to come before their time . . v 1 4
I'll be sworn, As my mother was, the first hour I was born *Mer. Wives* ii 2 39
My wife hath sent to him; the hour is fixed; the match is made . . ii 2 303
God be praised for my jealousy! Eleven o'clock the hour . . . ii 2 325
Better three hours too soon than a minute too late . . . . . ii 2 327
'Tis past the hour, sir, that Sir Hugh promised to meet . . . . ii 3 4
Bear vitness that me have stay six or seven, two, tree hours for him . ii 3 37
This is the period of my ambition: O this blessed hour! . . . . iii 3 48
I was at her house the hour she appointed me . . . . . . iii 5 66
'Twixt eight and nine is the hour, Master Brook.—'Tis past eight already, sir . . . . iii 5 132

Hour. Did he send you both these letters at an instant?—Within a quarter of an hour *Mer. Wives* iv 4 5
Why, that hour of fairy revel, In their so sacred paths he dares to tread iv 4 58
The hour draws on. To the oak, to the oak! v 3 25
Therein she doth evitate and shun A thousand irreligious cursed hours v 5 242
He promised to meet me two hours since *Meas. for Meas.* i 2 76
What shall be done, sir, with the groaning Juliet? She's very near her hour ii 2 16
At what hour to-morrow Shall I attend your lordship? ii 2 159
Having the hour limited, and an express command, under penalty iv 2 176
Dispatch it presently; the hour draws on Prefix'd by Angelo iv 3 82
And why should we proclaim it in an hour before his entering? iv 4 10
Show your sheep-biting face, and be hanged an hour! v 1 360
How came it Claudio was beheaded At an unusual hour? v 1 463
That very hour and in the self-same inn A meaner woman was delivered Of such a burden, male twins *Com. of Errors* i 1 54
Within this hour it will be dinner-time i 2 11
These jests are out of season; Reserve them till a merrier hour than this i 2 69
When spake I such a word?—Even now, even here, not half an hour since ii 2 14
Your sauciness will jest upon my love And make a common of my serious hours ii 2 29
I know you not: In Ephesus I am but two hours old ii 2 150
You must excuse us all; My wife is shrewish when I keep not hours iii 1 2
I'll meet you at that place some hour hence iii 1 122
The hour steals on; I pray you, sir, dispatch iv 1 52
You know I gave it you half an hour since.—You gave me none iv 1 65
It was two ere I left him, and now the clock strikes one.—The hours come back! that did I never hear iv 2 55
If any hour meet a sergeant, a' turns back for very fear iv 2 56
If Time be in debt and theft, and a sergeant in the way, Hath he not reason to turn back an hour in a day? iv 2 62
Why, sir, I brought you word an hour since iv 3 38
I have served him from the hour of my nativity to this instant iv 4 32
Within this hour I was his bondman, sir v 1 288
And careful hours with time's deformed hand Have written strange defeatures in my face v 1 298
And till this present hour My heavy burthen ne'er delivered v 1 401
Well, you will temporize with the hours *Much Ado* i 1 277
I never can see him but I am heart-burned an hour after ii 1 5
Out of question, you were born in a merry hour ii 1 347
Find me a meet hour to draw Don Pedro and the Count Claudio alone ii 2 33
I talk'd with no man at that hour, my lord iv 1 87
And this grieved count Did see her, hear her, at that hour last night iv 1 91
O my father, Prove you that any man with me conversed At hours unmeet! iv 1 184
You have stayed me in a happy hour: I was about to protest I loved you iv 1 285
Thus did she, an hour together, trans-shape thy particular virtues v 1 171
An hour in clamour and a quarter in rheum v 2 84
The prince and Claudio promised by this hour To visit me v 4 13
And then, to sleep but three hours in the night *L. L. Lost* i 1 42
About the sixth hour; when beasts most graze, birds best peck i 1 238
You may do it in an hour, sir.—Impossible i 2 39
What time o' day?—The hour that fools should ask ii 1 123
For revels, dances, masks and merry hours Forerun fair Love iv 3 379
I thought to close mine eyes some half an hour; When, lo! v 2 90
Here they stay'd an hour, And talk'd apace; and in that hour, my lord, They did not bless us with one happy word v 2 369
Now, at the latest minute of the hour, Grant us your loves v 2 797
Our nuptial hour Draws on apace *M. N. Dream* i 1 1
Neeze and swear A merrier hour was never wasted there ii 1 57
While she was in her dull and sleeping hour iii 2 8
The sisters' vows, the hours that we have spent iii 2 199
O weary night, O long and tedious night, Abate thy hours! iii 2 432
Bottom! O most courageous day! O most happy hour! iv 2 28
What dances shall we have, To wear away this long age of three hours? v 1 33
Is there no play, To ease the anguish of a torturing hour? v 1 37
Disguise us at my lodging and return, All in an hour *Mer. of Venice* ii 4 3
'Tis now but four o'clock: we have two hours To furnish us ii 4 8
Meet me and Gratiano At Gratiano's lodging some hour hence ii 4 27
His hour is almost past.—And it is marvel he out-dwells his hour ii 6 2
Fair thoughts and happy hours attend on you! iii 4 41
She kneels and prays For happy wedlock hours v 1 32
Whether till the next night she had rather stay, Or go to bed now, being two hours to day v 1 303
'Tis but an hour ago since it was nine, And after one hour more 'twill be eleven; And so, from hour to hour, we ripe and ripe, And then, from hour to hour, we rot and rot *As Y. Like It* ii 7 24
And I did laugh sans intermission An hour by his dial ii 7 33
Under the shade of melancholy boughs, Lose and neglect the creeping hours of time ii 7 112
Sighing every minute and groaning every hour iii 2 322
I come within an hour of my promise.—Break an hour's promise in love! iv 1 42
For these two hours, Rosalind, I will leave thee.—Alas! dear love, I cannot lack thee two hours iv 1 180
Two o'clock is your hour?—Ay, sweet Rosalind iv 1 190
Or come one minute behind your hour iv 1 195
But at this hour the house doth keep itself; There's none within iv 3 82
He left a promise to return again Within an hour iv 3 101
This carol they began that hour, With a hey, and a ho v 3 27
That will I, should I die the hour after v 4 12
Shall I be appointed hours; as though, belike, I knew not what to take, and what to leave? *T. of Shrew* i 1 103
And when in music we have spent an hour, Your lecture shall have leisure iii 1 7
I'll not be tied to hours nor 'pointed times, But learn my lessons as I please iii 1 19
The old priest of Saint Luke's church is at your command at all hours iv 4 89
'Twas pretty, though a plague, To see him every hour *All's Well* i 1 104
I'ld venture . . . on his grace's cure By such a day and hour i 3 255
If I were but two hours younger, I'ld beat thee ii 3 268
To make the coming hour o'erflow with joy And pleasure drown the brim ii 4 47
Here he comes, to beguile two hours in a sleep iv 1 25
Ten o'clock: within these three hours 'twill be time enough to go home iv 1 27
When you have conquer'd my yet maiden bed, Remain there but an hour, nor speak to me iv 2 58
You have not given him his mother's letter?—I have delivered it an hour since iv 3 3

Hour. Not till after midnight; for he is dieted to his hour *All's Well* iv 3 35
If I were to live this present hour, I will tell true iv 3 183
Your daughter-in-law had been alive at this hour, and your son here iv 5 5
Unless thou tell'st me where thou hadst this ring, Thou diest within this hour.—I'll never tell you v 3 285
I was bred and born Not three hours' travel from this very place *T. Night* i 2 23
Your cousin, my lady, takes great exceptions to your ill hours i 3 6
He left behind him myself and a sister, both born in an hour ii 1 20
Some hour before you took me from the breach of the sea was my sister drowned ii 1 22
For women are as roses, whose fair flower Being once display'd, doth fall that very hour ii 4 40
He has been yonder i' the sun practising behaviour to his own shadow this half hour ii 5 21
I'll be your purse-bearer and leave you For an hour iii 3 48
Which I had recommended to his use Not half an hour before v 1 95
Since when, my watch hath told me, toward my grave I have travell'd but two hours v 1 166
O, he's drunk, Sir Toby, an hour agone; his eyes were set at eight v 1 204
How have the hours rack'd and tortured me, Since I have lost thee! v 1 226
Let no quarrel nor no brawl to come Taint the condition of this present hour v 1 365
Wishing clocks more swift? Hours, minutes? noon, midnight? *W. Tale* i 2 290
Please your highness To take the urgent hour. Come, sir, away i 2 465
Within this hour bring me word 'tis done, And by good testimony ii 3 136
Posts From those you sent to the oracle are come An hour since ii 3 195
And in one self-born hour To plant and o'erwhelm custom iv 1 8
If I might die within this hour, I have lived To die when I desire iv 4 472
Which he shall know within this hour, if I may come to the speech of him iv 4 785
Had our prince, Jewel of children, seen this hour v 1 116
Such a deal of wonder is broken out within this hour v 2 26
I know you are now, sir, a gentleman born.—Ay, and have been so any time these four hours v 2 148
Now blessed be the hour, by night or day, When I was got! *K. John* i 1 165
Let not the hours of this ungodly day Wear out the day in peace iii 1 109
Thou shalt rue this hour within this hour iii 1 323
It cannot be . . . The misplaced John should entertain an hour, One minute, nay, one quiet breath of rest iii 4 133
And like the watchful minutes to the hour, Still and anon cheer'd up the heavy time iv 1 46
'Tis not an hour since I left him well iv 3 104
Is't not pity, O my grieved friends, That we, the sons and children of this isle, Were born to see so sad an hour as this? v 2 26
Who was he that said King John did fly an hour or two before? v 5 17
Who half an hour since came from the Dauphin v 7 83
When they see the hours ripe on earth, Will rain hot vengeance *Rich. II.* i 2 7
The sly slow hours shall not determinate The dateless limit of thy dear exile i 3 150
What is six winters? they are quickly gone.—To men in joy; but grief makes one hour ten i 3 261
Would the word 'farewell' have lengthen'd hours And added years to his short banishment, He should have had a volume i 4 16
Even so look'd he, Accomplish'd with the number of thy hours ii 1 177
Now comes the sick hour that his surfeit made; Now shall he try his friends ii 2 84
An hour before I came, the duchess died.—God for his mercy! ii 2 97
You have in manner with your sinful hours Made a divorce iii 1 11
Had borne the crown, Which waste of idle hours hath quite thrown down iii 4 66
Thou darest not, coward, live to see that day.—Now, by my soul, I would it were this hour iv 1 42
Our holy lives must win a new world's crown, Which our profane hours here have striken down v 1 25
The time shall not be many hours of age More than it is v 1 57
The sound that tells what hour it is Are clamorous groans, which strike upon my heart, Which is the bell: so sighs and tears and groans Show minutes, times, and hours v 5 55
At Holmedon met, Where they did spend a sad and bloody hour *1 Hen. IV.* i 1 56
Unless hours were cups of sack and minutes capons i 2 7
Hand to hand, He did confound the best part of an hour i 3 100
O, let the hours be short Till fields and blows and groans applaud our sport! i 3 301
How now, Kate! I must leave you within these two hours ii 3 39
Is Gilliams with the packet gone?—He is, my lord, an hour ago ii 3 69
I am so good a proficient in one quarter of an hour ii 4 20
'Give my roan horse a drench,' says he; and answers 'Some fourteen,' an hour after ii 4 121
If I were not at half-sword with a dozen of them two hours together ii 4 183
He held me last night at least nine hours In reckoning up iii 1 156
The hour before the heavenly-harness'd team Begins his golden progress iii 1 221
An the indentures be drawn, I'll away within these two hours iii 1 266
For all the world As thou art to this hour was Richard then iii 2 94
Went to a bawdy-house not above once in a quarter—of an hour iii 3 20
To set so rich a main On the nice hazard of one doubtful hour iv 1 48
I could be well content To entertain the lag-end of my life With quiet hours v 1 25
If life did ride upon a dial's point, Still ending at the arrival of an hour v 2 85
The hour is come To end the one of us v 4 68
We rose both at an instant and fought a long hour by Shrewsbury clock v 4 151
And many a creature else Had been alive this hour v 5 8
And approach The ragged'st hour that time and spite dare bring! *2 Hen. IV.* i 1 151
How many thousand of my poorest subjects Are at this hour asleep! iii 1 5
Canst thou, O partial sleep, give thy repose To the wet sea-boy in an hour so rude? iii 1 27
These unseason'd hours perforce must add Unto your sickness iii 1 105
With our surfeiting and wanton hours Have brought ourselves into a burning fever iv 1 55
Dost thou so hunger for mine empty chair That thou wilt needs invest thee with my honours Before thy hour be ripe? iv 5 97
Thou hast stolen that which after some few hours Were thine without offence iv 5 102
Thou hidest a thousand daggers in thy thoughts, Which thou hast whetted on thy stony heart, To stab at half an hour of my life iv 5 109
What! canst thou not forbear me half an hour? iv 5 110
That shall convert those tears By number into hours of happiness v 2 61
His hours fill'd up with riots, banquets, sports *Hen. V.* i 1 56
The hour, I think, is come To give him hearing i 1 92
Omit no happy hour That may give furtherance to our expedition i 2 300

Hour. I do at this hour joy o'er myself, Prevented from a damned enterprise . . . . *Hen. V.* ii 2 163
The clocks do toll, And the third hour of drowsy morning name . iv Prol. 16
But in gross brain little wots What watch the king keeps to maintain the peace, Whose hours the peasant best advantages . . . iv 1 301
The knavish crows Fly o'er them, all impatient for their hour . iv 2 52
Thrice within this hour I saw him down ; thrice up again, and fighting iv 6 4
Which, your majesty know, to this hour is an honourable badge of the service . . . . iv 7 105
More than three hours the fight continued . . . 1 *Hen. VI.* i 1 120
Otherwhiles the famish'd English, like pale ghosts, Faintly besiege us one hour in a month . . . . i 2 8
Talbot, farewell ; thy hour is not yet come . . . . . i 5 13
Ere the glass, that now begins to run, Finish the process of his sandy hour . . . . iv 2 36
Young John, who two hours since I met in travel toward his warlike father . . . . iv 3 35
Within six hours they will be at his aid.—Too late comes rescue . iv 4 41
There is no hope that ever I will stay, If the first hour I shrink . iv 5 31
'Tis like, my lord, you will not keep your hour . . 2 *Hen. VI.* ii 1 181
Ten is the hour that was appointed me To watch the coming . . ii 4 6
Yet, good Humphrey, is the hour to come That e'er I proved thee false iii 1 204
But wherefore grieve I at an hour's poor loss? . . . . iii 2 381
Mine uncles, You are come to Sandal in a happy hour . 3 *Hen. VI.* i 2 63
And when thou fail'st—as God forbid the hour!—Must Edward fall . ii 1 190
Thereby to see the minutes how they run, How many make the hour full complete ; How many hours bring about the day . . . ii 5 26
So many hours must I tend my flock ; So many hours must I take my rest ; So many hours must I contemplate ; So many hours must I sport myself . . . . ii 5 31
So minutes, hours, days, months, and years, Pass'd over to the end they were created, Would bring white hairs unto a quiet grave . . ii 5 38
If this right hand would buy two hours' life, That I in all despite might rail at him, This hand should chop it off . . . . . ii 6 80
Let us hence ; and lose no hour, Till we meet Warwick . . . iv 1 148
If about this hour he make this way Under the colour of his usual game iv 5 10
I did leave him with his forces, And do expect him here some two hours hence . . . . v 1 10
Shall rue the hour that ever thou wast born . . . . . v 6 43
So I might live one hour in your sweet bosom . . . *Richard III.* i 2 124
And, after many lengthen'd hours of grief, Die neither mother, wife! . i 3 208
Sorrow breaks seasons and reposing hours, Makes the night morning . i 4 76
They say my uncle grew so fast That he could gnaw a crust at two hours old . . . . ii 4 28
Bid them both Meet me within this hour at Baynard's Castle . . iii 5 105
Eleven hours I spent to write it over . . . . . . iii 6 5
And yet within these five hours lived Lord Hastings, Untainted, unexamined . . . . iii 6 8
Mellow'd by the stealing hours of time . . . . . . iii 7 168
Let me but meet you, ladies, one hour hence . . . . . iv 1 29
Take all the swift advantage of the hours . . . . . . iv 1 49
Never yet one hour in his bed Have I enjoy'd the golden dew of sleep . iv 1 83
Eighty odd years of sorrow have I seen, And each hour's joy wreck'd with a week of teen . . . . iv 1 97
What comfortable hour canst thou name, That ever graced me in thy company?—Faith, none, but Humphrey Hour, that call'd your grace To breakfast once forth of my company . . . . . iv 4 173
Men shall deal unadvisedly sometimes, Which after hours give leisure to repent . . . . iv 4 293
Acquaint the princess With the sweet silent hours of marriage joys . iv 4 330
Heaven and fortune bar me happy hours! Day, yield me not thy light! iv 4 400
And every hour more competitors Flock to their aid . . . iv 4 506
If that your moody discontented souls Do through the clouds behold this present hour, Even for revenge mock my destruction! . . v 1 8
And by the second hour in the morning Desire the earl to see me . v 3 31
The silent hours steal on, And flaky darkness breaks within the east . v 3 85
That wretched Anne thy wife, That never slept a quiet hour with thee v 3 160
For by the book He [the sun] should have braved the east an hour ago v 3 279
May see away their shilling Richly in two short hours *Hen. VIII.* Prol. 13
Almost with ravish'd listening, could not find His hour of speech a minute . . . . i 2 121
A choice hour To hear from him a matter of some moment . . i 2 162
May bring his plain-song And have an hour of hearing . . . i 3 46
Crave leave to view these ladies and entreat An hour of revels with 'em i 4 72
The last hour Of my long weary life is come upon me . . . ii 1 132
Know your times of business : Is this an hour for temporal affairs? . ii 2 73
I would your grace would give us but an hour Of private conference . ii 2 80
When was the hour I ever contradicted your desire? . . . ii 4 27
I should be glad to hear such news as this Once every hour . . iii 2 24
What expense by the hour Seems to flow from him! . . . . iii 2 108
Thou liest: Within these forty hours Surrey durst better Have burnt that tongue than said so . . . . iii 2 253
While her grace sat down To rest awhile, some half an hour or so . iv 1 66
About the hour of eight, which he himself Foretold should be his last . iv 2 26
These should be hours for necessities, Not for delights . . . v 1 2
Good hour of night, Sir Thomas! Whither so late? . . . . v 1 5
Who waits there?— . . . My lord archbishop ; And has done half an hour v 3 6
Speak frankly as the wind ; It is not Agamemnon's sleeping hour *Troi. and Cres.* i 3 254
Thou grumblest and railest every hour on Achilles . . . . ii 1 35
Hector, by the fifth hour of the sun, Will . . . To-morrow morning call some knight to arms . . . . ii 1 134
After so many hours, lives, speeches spent, Thus once again says Nestor ii 2 1
The hour prefix'd Of her delivery to this valiant Greek Comes fast upon . . . . iv 3 1
And you too, Diomed, Keep Hector company an hour or two . . v 1 88
What, shall I come? the hour?—Ay, come:—O Jove!—do come . v 2 104
I have been seeking you this hour, my lord . . . . . v 2 182
When for a day of kings' entreaties a mother should not sell him an hour from her beholding . . . . *Coriolanus* i 3 10
I looked upon him o' Wednesday half an hour together . . . i 3 64
See here these movers that do prize their hours At a crack'd drachma! i 5 5
How long is't since!—Above an hour, my lord.—'Tis not a mile . . i 6 15
How couldst thou in a mile confound an hour, And bring thy news so late? . . . . i 6 17
I was forced to wheel Three or four miles about, else had I, sir, Half an hour since brought my report . . . . i 6 21
Filling the air with swords advanced and darts, We prove this very hour i 6 62
Within these three hours, Tullus, Alone I fought in your Corioli walls . i 8 7
In a better hour, Let what is meet be said it must be meet . . iii 1 169

Hour. What is the matter That being pass'd for consul with full voice, I am so dishonour'd that the very hour You take it off again? *Cor.* iii 3 60
To be on foot at an hour's warning.—I am joyful to hear of their readiness . . . . iv 3 49
Whose hours, whose bed, whose meal, and exercise, Are still together . iv 4 14
Shall within this hour, On a dissension of a doit, break out . . iv 4 16
He Hath widow'd and unchilded many a one, Which to this hour bewail v 6 154
I have been broad awake two hours and more . . *T. Andron.* ii 2 17
The unhappy son of old Andronicus ; Brought hither in a most unlucky hour . . . . ii 3 251
'Tis not an hour since I left him there . . . . . . ii 3 256
One hour's storm will drown the fragrant meads . . . . ii 4 54
I'll deceive you in another sort, And that you'll say, ere half an hour pass . . . . iii 1 192
Why dost thou laugh? it fits not with this hour . . . . iii 1 266
Oft have you heard me wish for such an hour, And now I find it? . v 2 160
Is now the two hours' traffic of our stage . . . *Rom. and Jul.* Prol. 12
An hour before the worshipp'd sun Peer'd forth the golden window of the east . . . . i 1 125
Is the day so young?—But new struck nine.—Ay me! sad hours seem long . . . . i 1 167
What sadness lengthens Romeo's hours?—Not having that, which, having, makes them short . . . . i 1 169
My daughter's of a pretty age.—Faith, I can tell her age unto an hour . i 3 11
At what o'clock to-morrow Shall I send to thee?—At the hour of nine ii 2 169
Within this hour my man shall be with thee, And bring thee cords . ii 4 200
In half an hour she promised to return . . . . . . ii 5 2
And from nine till twelve Is three long hours . . . . . ii 5 11
So smile the heavens upon this holy act, That after hours with sorrow chide us not!—Amen, Amen! . . . . ii 6 2
Any man should buy the fee-simple of my life for an hour and a quarter iii 1 36
My reputation stain'd With Tybalt's slander,—Tybalt, that an hour Hath been my kinsman! . . . . iii 1 117
Let Romeo hence in haste, Else, when he's found, that hour is his last iii 1 200
An hour but married, . . . Doting like me and like me banished . iii 3 66
But for your company, I would have been a-bed an hour ago . . iii 4 7
Husband, friend! I must hear from thee every day in the hour, For in a minute there are many days . . . . iii 5 44
Day, night, hour, tide, time, work, play, Alone, in company . . iii 5 178
Thou shalt continue two and forty hours, And then awake . . iv 1 105
Where, as they say, At some hours in the night spirits resort . . iv 3 44
Most miserable hour that e'er time saw In lasting labour of his pilgrimage! . . . . iv 5 44
Within this three hours will fair Juliet wake . . . . . v 2 24
How long hath he been there?—Full half an hour . . . . v 3 130
Ah, what an unkind hour Is guilty of this lamentable chance! . . v 3 145
At the prefixed hour of her waking, Came I to take her . . . v 3 253
Let my old life Be sacrificed, some hour before his time . . . v 3 268
Let not that part of nature Which my lord paid for, be of any power To expel sickness, but prolong his hour! . . . *T. of Athens* iii 1 66
Lord Timon's happy hours are done and past, and his estate shrinks from him . . . . iii 2 6
What do you think the hour?—Labouring for nine.—So much? . . iii 4 8
If I might beseech you, gentlemen, to repair some other hour . . iii 4 69
Think not on't, sir.—If you had sent but two hours before . . iii 6 50
Make use of thy salt hours: season the slaves For tubs and baths . iv 3 85
I have been up this hour, awake all night . . . . *J. Cæsar* ii 1 88
By the eighth hour: is that the uttermost?—Be that the uttermost . ii 1 213
And withal Hoping it was but an effect of humour, Which sometime hath his hour with every man . . . . ii 1 251
What is't o'clock?—About the ninth hour, lady.—Is Cæsar yet gone? . ii 4 23
There is no hour so fit As Cæsar's death's hour, nor no instrument Of half that worth as those your swords . . . . iii 1 153
I know my hour is come.—Not so, my lord.—Nay, I am sure it is . v 5 20
My bones would rest, That have but labour'd to attain this hour . . v 5 42
Come what come may, Time and the hour runs through the roughest day *Macbeth* i 3 147
When we can entreat an hour to serve, We would spend it in some words ii 1 22
He did command me to call timely on him: I have almost slipp'd the hour . . . . ii 3 52
Had I but died an hour before this chance, I had lived a blessed time ii 3 96
Within the volume of which time I have seen Hours dreadful . . ii 4 3
I must become a borrower of the night For a dark hour or twain . iii 1 28
Within this hour at most I will advise you where to plant yourselves . iii 1 128
Must embrace the fate Of that dark hour . . . . . . iii 1 138
Let this pernicious hour Stand aye accursed in the calendar! . . iv 1 133
What's the newest grief?—That of an hour's age doth hiss the speaker. iv 3 175
I have known her continue in this a quarter of an hour . . . v 1 34
A poor player That struts and frets his hour upon the stage . . v 5 25
You come most carefully upon your hour.—'Tis now struck twelve *Hamlet* i 1 6
Twice before, and jump at this dead hour, With martial stalk hath he gone by . . . . i 1 65
I do beseech you, give him leave to go.—Take thy fair hour, Laertes . i 2 62
What hour now?—I think it lacks of twelve.—No, it is struck . . i 4 3
My hour is almost come, When I to sulphurous and tormenting flames Must render up myself . . . . i 5 2
Upon my secure hour thy uncle stole, With juice of cursed hebenon . i 5 61
You know, sometimes he walks four hours together Here in the lobby . ii 2 160
How cheerfully my mother looks, and my father died within these two hours . . . . iii 2 135
An hour of quiet shortly shall we see; Till then, in patience . . v 1 321
In thee there is not half an hour of life . . . . . . v 2 326
We have this hour a constant will to publish Our daughters' several dowers, that future strife May be prevented now . . . *Lear* i 1 44
Spake you with him?—Ay, two hours together.—Parted you in good terms? . . . . i 2 170
Every hour He flashes into one gross crime or other . . . . i 3 3
A stone-cutter or a painter could not have made him so ill, though he had been but two hours at the trade . . . . ii 2 65
If thou shouldst dally half an hour, his life, With thine, and all that offer to defend him, Stand in assured loss . . . . . iii 6 100
These weeds are memories of those worser hours: I prithee, put them off iv 7 7
Pray, do not mock me: I am a very foolish fond old man, Fourscore and upward, not an hour more nor less . . . . iv 7 61
Which I observing, Took once a pliant hour . . . . *Othello* i 3 151
I have but an hour Of love, of worldly matters and direction, To spend with thee: we must obey the time . . . . i 3 299
There is full liberty of feasting from this present hour of five . . ii 2 11
We must to the watch.—Not this hour, lieutenant . . . . ii 3 13
Pleasure and action make the hours seem short . . . . . ii 3 385

Hour. Let me but bind it hard, within this hour It will be well *Othello* iii 3 286
What sense had I of her stol'n hours of lust? I saw 't not, thought it not, it harm'd not me . . . . iii 3 338
What, keep a week away? seven days and nights? Eight score eight hours? and lovers' absent hours, More tedious than the dial eight score times? O weary reckoning! . . . . . . iii 4 174
To be naked with her friend in bed An hour or more, not meaning any harm? . . . . iv 1 4
Nay, if you strive,— But half an hour!—Being done, there is no pause v 2 82
O heavy hour! Methinks it should be now a huge eclipse Of sun and moon . . . . v 2 98
Now, for the love of Love and her soft hours, Let's not confound the time with conference harsh . . . . . . *Ant. and Cleo.* i 1 44
Every hour, Most noble Cæsar, shalt thou have report How 'tis abroad i 4 34
Mark Antony is every hour in Rome Expected . . . . . ii 1 29
When poison'd hours had bound me up From mine own knowledge . ii 2 90
From this hour The heart of brothers govern in our loves! . . . ii 2 149
And next morn, Ere the ninth hour, I drunk him to his bed . . ii 5 21
Besides what hotter hours, Unregister'd in vulgar fame . . . iii 13 118
When mine hours Were nice and lucky, men did ransom lives Of me for jests . . . . iii 13 179
Tend me to-night two hours, I ask no more, And the gods yield you for't! . . . . iv 2 32
If we be not relieved within this hour, We must return . . . . iv 9 1
They say we shall embattle By the second hour i' the morn . . . iv 9 4
Our hour Is fully out.—Come on, then . . . . . . iv 9 32
And to this hour no guess in knowledge Which way they went *Cymbeline* i 1 60
Ere I could tell him How I would think on him at certain hours . . . , or have charged him, At the sixth hour of morn, at noon, at midnight, To encounter me with orisons . . . . . . i 3 27
To think that man . . . will his free hours languish for Assured bondage i 6 72
What hour is it?—Almost midnight, madam.—I have read three hours then . . . . ii 2 3
In an hour,—was't not?—Or less,—at first?—perchance he spoke not . ii 5 14
How many score of miles may we well ride 'Twixt hour and hour? . iii 2 70
How . . . shall we discourse The freezing hours away? . . . iii 3 39
Thy head, which now is growing upon thy shoulders, shall within this hour be off . . . . iv 1 18
'Tis the ninth hour o' the morn.—Brother, farewell.—I wish ye sport . iv 2 30
Upon a time,—unhappy was the clock That struck the hour! . . v 5 154
Not an hour, In the day's glorious walk, or peaceful night *Pericles* i 2 3
Should at these early hours Shake off the golden slumber of repose . iii 2 22
Death may usurp on nature many hours, And yet the fire of life kindle again The o'erpress'd spirits . . . . iii 2 82
I heard of an Egyptian That had nine hours lien dead, Who was by good appliance recovered . . . . iii 2 85
She hath not been entranced Above five hours . . . . . iii 2 95
Come, I know 'tis good for you. Walk half an hour, Leonine, at the least . . . . iv 1 46

Hour of act. Thou but lead'st this fashion of thy malice To the last hour of act . . . . *Mer. of Venice* iv 1 19

Hour of death. You swore to me, when I did give it you, That you would wear it till your hour of death . . . . v 1 153
Therefore my grief Stretches itself beyond the hour of death 2 *Hen. IV.* iv 4 57
Away! vexation almost stops my breath, That sunder'd friends greet in the hour of death . . . . 1 *Hen. VI.* iv 3 42
Make haste; the hour of death is expiate . . . . *Richard III.* iii 3 23

Hour's talk. We had an hour's talk of that wart . . *Mer. Wives* i 4 162
Go in with us and see: we have an hour's talk with you . . . . ii 1 172
A merrier man . . . I never spent an hour's talk withal . *L. L. Lost* ii 1 68
I have an hour's talk in store for you; Remember that you call *J. Cæsar* ii 2 121

Hour-glass. I should not see the sandy hour-glass run, But I should think of shallows and of flats . . . . *Mer. of Venice* i 1 25
Turning the accomplishment of many years Into an hour-glass *Hen. V.* Prol. 31

Hourly. Sea-nymphs hourly ring his knell: Ding-dong . . *Tempest* i 2 402
Hourly joys be still upon you! Juno sings her blessings on you . iv 1 108
That dost this habitation, where thou keep'st, Hourly afflict . *M. for M.* iii 1 11
This is an accident of hourly proof, Which I mistrusted not . *Much Ado* ii 1 188
She deserves a lord That twenty such rude boys might tend upon And call her hourly mistress . . . . *All's Well* iii 2 85
An hourly promise-breaker, the owner of no one good quality . . iii 6 11
Fortune, O, . . . She adulterates hourly with thine uncle John *K. John* iii 1 56
Where subjects' feet May hourly trample on their sovereign's head *Richard II.* iii 3 157
I have forsworn his company hourly any time this two and twenty years, and yet I am bewitched . . . . . . 1 *Hen. IV.* ii 2 16
My thoughts do hourly prophesy Mischance . . . 2 *Hen. VI.* iii 2 283
All comfort, joy, in this most gracious lady, Heaven ever laid up to make parents happy, May hourly fall upon ye! . . . . *Hen. VIII.* v 5 9
The glorious gods sit in hourly synod about thy particular prosperity! *Coriolanus* v 2 74
For all the water in the ocean Can never turn the swan's black legs to white, Although she lave them hourly in the flood *T. Andron.* iv 2 103
The terms of our estate may not endure Hazard so near us as doth hourly grow Out of his lunacies . . . . . . *Hamlet* iii 3 6
But other of your insolent retinue Do hourly carp and quarrel . *Lear* i 4 222
The main descry Stands on the hourly thought . . . . iv 6 218
That we the pain of death would hourly die Rather than die at once! . v 3 185
I hourly learn A doctrine of obedience . . . *Ant. and Cleo.* v 2 30
And I shall here abide the hourly shot Of angry eyes . . *Cymbeline* i 1 89
Join gripes with hands Made hard with hourly falsehood . . . i 6 107
A father by thy step-dame govern'd, A mother hourly coining plots . ii 1 64
Report should render him hourly to your ear As truly as he moves . iii 4 153
I leap into the seas, Where's hourly trouble for a minute's ease *Pericles* ii 4 44

House. By what? by any other house or person? Of any thing the image tell me that Hath kept with thy remembrance . . *Tempest* i 2 42
If the ill spirit have so fair a house, Good things will strive to dwell with't . . . . i 2 458
His word is more than the miraculous harp; he hath raised the wall and houses too . . . . ii 1 87
He has brave utensils,—for so he calls them,—Which, when he has a house, he'll deck withal . . . . iii 2 105
The trumpery in my house, go bring it hither . . . . . iv 1 186
And all our house in a great perplexity . . . . *T. G. of Ver.* ii 3 9
Pray you, where lies Sir Proteus?—Marry, at my house . . . iv 2 138
Our day of marriage shall be yours; One feast, one house . . . v 4 173
What, hoa! Got pless your house here!—Who's there? . . *Mer. Wives* i 1 74
Go your ways, and ask of Doctor Caius' house which is the way . i 2 2
If he do, i' faith, and find any body in the house, here will be an old abusing of God's patience . . . . i 4 4

House. An honest, willing, kind fellow, as ever servant shall come in house withal . . . . *Mer. Wives* i 4 11
I may call him my master, look you, for I keep his house . . . i 4 101
Who's there, I trow! Come near the house, I pray you . . . . i 4 141
Trust me, I was going to your house.—And, trust me, I was coming to you . . . . ii 1 34
She was in his company at Page's house; and what they made there, I know not . . . . ii 1 244
She gives you to notify that her husband will be absence from his house ii 2 86
Like a fair house built on another man's ground . . . . ii 2 224
To search for a gentleman that he says is here now in the house . . iii 3 116
I had rather than a thousand pound he were out of the house . . iii 3 132
Bethink you of some conveyance: in the house you cannot hide him . iii 3 136
If there be any pody in the house, and in the chambers, and in the coffers, and in the presses, heaven forgive my sins at the day of judgement! . . . . iii 3 224
I do invite you to-morrow morning to my house to breakfast . . . iii 3 246
You wrong me, sir, thus still to haunt my house: I told you, sir, my daughter is disposed of . . . . iii 4 73
I will not lie to you; I was at her house the hour she appointed me . iii 5 66
And at his heels a rabble of his companions, thither provoked and instigated by his distemper, and, forsooth, to search his house for his wife's love . . . . iii 5 79
He is at my house; he cannot 'scape me; 'tis impossible he should . iii 5 147
There is no hiding you in the house.—I'll go out then . . . iv 2 65
Forbade her my house and hath threatened to beat her . . . . iv 2 89
There was one conveyed out of my house yesterday in this basket . . iv 2 152
In my house I am sure he is: my intelligence is true . . . . iv 2 154
Help to search my house this one time . . . . . . iv 2 167
An old cozening quean! Have I not forbid her my house? . . . iv 2 181
They have had my house a week at command; I have turned away my other guests . . . . iv 3 12
There's his chamber, his house, his castle, his standing-bed and truckle-bed . . . . iv 5 6
Thou shalt eat a posset to-night at my house . . . . . v 5 180
All houses in the suburbs of Vienna must be plucked down *Meas. for Meas.* i 2 98
If these be good people in a commonweal that do nothing but use their abuses in common houses, I know no law . . . . . . ii 1 43
A bad woman; whose house, sir, was, as they say, plucked down . . ii 1 64
Now she professes a hot-house, which, I think, is a very ill house too . ii 1 67
This house, if it be not a bawd's house, it is pity of her life, for it is a naughty house . . . . ii 1 76
For stewed prunes; sir, we had but two in the house . . . . ii 1 93
The house is a respected house; next, this is a respected fellow . . ii 1 169
If this law hold in Vienna ten year, I'll rent the fairest house in it after three-pence a bay . . . . ii 1 255
To your worship's house, sir?—To my house. Fare you well . . . ii 1 288
Ignomy in ransom and free pardon Are of two houses . . . . ii 4 112
You will turn good husband now, Pompey; you will keep the house . iii 2 74
One would think it were Mistress Overdone's own house . . . . iv 3 2
Say, by this token, I desire his company At Mariana's house to-night . iv 3 145
Let it be proclaimed betimes i' the morn; I'll call you at your house . iv 4 18
Go call at Flavius' house, And tell him where I stay . . . . iv 5 6
My charge was but to fetch you from the mart Home to your house *Com. of Errors* i 2 75
'I know,' quoth he, 'no house, no wife, no mistress' . . . . ii 1 71
My house was at the Phœnix? Wast thou mad? . . . . . ii 2 11
And in his blows Denied my house for his, me for his wife . . . ii 2 161
A villain that would face me down . . . I did deny my wife and house . iii 1 9
What art thou that keepest me out from the house I owe? . . . iii 1 42
Bring it, I pray you, to the Porpentine; For there's the house . . iii 1 117
Pleaseth you walk with me down to his house, I will discharge my bond iv 1 12
While I go to the goldsmith's house, go thou And buy a rope's end . iv 1 15
Take the stranger to my house And with you take the chain . . . iv 1 36
My way is now to hie home to his house, And tell his wife . . . iv 3 93
He rush'd into my house and took perforce My ring away . . . iv 3 95
Did this companion with the saffron face Revel and feast it at my house to-day, Whilst upon me the guilty doors were shut And I denied to enter in my house? . . . . iv 4 65
Good master doctor, see him safe convey'd Home to my house . . iv 4 126
Your husband all in rage to-day Came to my house and took away my ring . . . . iv 4 141
Bear them to my house.—Run, master, run; for God's sake, take a house! v 1 36
Enter and lay hold on him.—No, not a creature enters in my house . v 1 92
Doing displeasure to the citizens By rushing in their houses . . v 1 143
She shut the doors upon me, While she with harlots feasted in my house v 1 205
Then fairly I bespoke the officer To go in person with me to my house . v 1 234
There is a fat friend at your master's house, That kitchen'd me for you . v 1 414
Never came trouble to my house in the likeness of your grace *Much Ado* i 1 99
From my house, if I had it,— The sixth of July . . . . i 1 284
My visor is Philemon's roof; within the house is Jove . . . ii 1 100
Didst thou not hear somebody?—No; 'twas the vane on the house . iii 3 138
To-morrow morning come you to my house . . . . . . v 1 295
Climb o'er the house to unlock the little gate . . . . *L. L. Lost* i 1 109
He rather means to lodge you in the field . . . Than seek a dispensation for his oath, To let you enter his unpeopled house . . . . ii 1 88
Lodged in my heart, Though so denied fair harbour in my house . . ii 1 175
I protest, A world of torments though I should endure, I would not yield to be your house's guest . . . . v 2 354
And till that instant shut My woeful self up in a mourning house . . v 2 818
From Athens is her house remote seven leagues . . *M. N. Dream* i 1 159
If thou lovest me then, Steal forth thy father's house to-morrow night i 1 164
Giant-like ox-beef hath devoured many a gentleman of your house . iii 1 199
And will to-morrow midnight solemnly Dance in Duke Thesus' house . iv 1 94
Have you sent to Bottom's house? is he come home yet? . . . iv 2 1
Not a mouse Shall disturb this hallow'd house . . . . . v 1 395
Through the house give glimmering light, By the dead and drowsy fire v 1 398
Now, until the break of day, Through this house each fairy stray . v 1 409
See to my house, left in the fearful guard Of an unthrifty knave *M. of V.* i 3 176
Turn of no hand, but turn down indirectly to the Jew's house . . ii 2 46
Our house is hell, and thou, a merry devil, Didst rob it of some taste of tediousness. But fare thee well . . . . ii 3 2
She hath directed How I shall take her from her father's house . . ii 4 31
Jessica, my girl, Look to my house. I am right loath to go . . . ii 5 16
Stop my house's ears, I mean my casements: Let not the sound of shallow foppery enter My sober house . . . . ii 5 34
My Master Antonio is at his house and desires to speak with you both . iii 1 78
This house, these servants and this same myself Are yours, my lord . iii 2 172
I commit into your hands The husbandry and manage of my house . . iii 4 25
What if my house be troubled with a rat? . . . . . . iv 1 44

House. 'Tis well you offer it behind her back; The wish would make else an unquiet house . . . . . *Mer of Venice* iv 1 294
You take my house when you do take the prop, That doth sustain my house . . . . . iv 1 375
Bring him, if thou canst, Unto Antonio's house: away! make haste . iv 1 454
Inquire the Jew's house out, give him this deed And let him sign it . iv 2 1
I pray you, show my youth old Shylock's house.—That will I do . . iv 2 11
Come, good sir, will you show me to this house? . . . . iv 2 19
Let us prepare Some welcome for the mistress of the house . . v 1 38
Signify, I pray you, Within the house, your mistress is at hand . v 1 52
Music! hark!—It is your music, madam, of the house . . v 1 98
You are very welcome to our house: It must appear in other ways than words . . . . v 1 139
Let not that doctor e'er come near my house . . . . v 1 223
And even but now return'd; I have not yet Enter'd my house . v 1 273
Thou shouldst have better pleased me with this deed, Hadst thou descended from another house . . . *As Y. Like It* i 2 241
This house is but a butchery: Abhor it, fear it, do not enter it . ii 3 27
Let my officers of such a nature Make an extent upon his house and lands iii 1 17
Deserves as well a dark house and a whip as madmen do . . iii 2 421
O knowledge ill-inhabited, worse than Jove in a thatched house! . . iii 3 11
If you will know my house, 'Tis at the tuft of olives here hard by . iii 5 74
I had as lief be wooed of a snail.—Of a snail?—Ay, of a snail; for though he comes slowly, he carries his house on his head . . . iv 1 55
But at this hour the house doth keep itself; There's none within . iv 3 82
Are not you The owner of the house I did enquire for? . . . iv 3 90
My father's house and all the revenue . . . will I estate upon you . v 2 12
Rich honesty dwells like a miser, sir, in a poor house . . . v 4 63
Let them want nothing that my house affords . . . *T. of Shrew* Ind. 1 104
Hence comes it that your kindred shuns your house . . . Ind. 2 30
You say ye were beaten out of door; And rail upon the hostess of the house . . . . Ind. 2 88
Ay, the woman's maid of the house.—Why, sir, you know no house Ind. 2 92
Schoolmasters will I keep within my house, Fit to instruct her youth . i 1 94
Woo her, wed her and bed her and rid the house of her! . . . i 1 150
Keep house and ply his book, welcome his friends . . . . . i 1 201
We have not yet been seen in any house, Nor can we be distinguish'd . i 1 204
In my stead, Keep house and port and servants, as I should . . i 1 208
I trow this is his house. Here, sirrah Grumio; knock, I say . . i 2 4
Which is the readiest way To the house of Signior Baptista Minola? . i 2 221
Am bold to show myself a forward guest Within your house . . . ii 1 52
My house within the city Is richly furnished with plate and gold . . ii 1 348
Pewter and brass and all things that belong To house or housekeeping . ii 1 358
If I may have your daughter to my wife, I'll leave her houses three or four . . . . ii 1 368
She is my house, My household stuff, my field, my barn . . . iii 2 232
Is supper ready, the house trimmed, rushes strewed, cobwebs swept? . iv 1 48
And in my house you shall be friendly lodged . . . . . iv 2 107
Now, my honey love, Will we return unto thy father's house . . iv 3 53
Braved in mine own house with a skein of thread? . . . . iv 3 111
We will hence forthwith, To feast and sport us at thy father's house . iv 3 185
Sir, this is the house: please it you that I call? . . . . iv 4 1
Not in my house, Lucentio; for, you know, Pitchers have ears . . iv 4 51
It shall be moon, or star, or what I list, Or ere I journey to your father's house . . . . iv 5 8
Sir, here's the door, this is Lucentio's house . . . . . v 1 9
Feast with the best, and welcome to my house . . . . . v 2 8
I'll send her to my house, Acquaint my mother with my hate to her, And wherefore I am fled . . . . . . *All's Well* ii 3 303
War is no strife To the dark house and the detested wife . . ii 3 309
The air of paradise did fan the house And angels officed all . . iii 2 128
Look, here comes a pilgrim: I know she will lie at my house . . iii 5 34
Of enjoin'd penitents There's four or five . . . Already at my house . iii 5 99
Now will I lead you to the house, and show you The lass I spoke of . iii 6 118
That downward hath succeeded in his house From son to son . . iii 7 23
It is an honour 'longing to our house, Bequeathed down from many ancestors . . . . iv 2 42
My chastity's the jewel of our house, Bequeathed down from many ancestors . . . . iv 2 46
My house, mine honour, yea, my life, be thine, And I'll be bid by thee iv 2 52
His wife some two months since fled from his house . . . iv 3 57
I am for the house with the narrow gate . . . . . . iv 5 53
Come on, my son, in whom my house's name Must be digested . . v 3 73
The honourable lady of the house, which is she? . . . *T. Night* i 5 177
I pray you, tell me if this be the lady of the house, for I never saw her i 5 183
Make me a willow cabin at your gate, And call upon my soul within the house . . . . i 5 288
My lady has a white hand, and the Myrmidons are no bottle-ale houses ii 3 29
Do ye make an alehouse of my lady's house? . . . . . ii 3 96
If you can separate yourself and your misdemeanours, you are welcome to the house . . . . ii 3 106
He is about the house.—Seek him out, and play the tune the while . ii 4 13
I am all the daughters of my father's house, And all the brothers too . ii 4 123
I do live at my house, and my house doth stand by the church . . iii 1 6
Will you encounter the house? my niece is desirous you should enter . iii 1 82
We shall make him mad indeed.—The house will be the quieter . . iii 4 147
I will return again into the house and desire some conduct of the lady . iii 4 264
Back you shall not to the house, unless you undertake that with me . iii 4 272
Hold, sir, or I'll throw your dagger o'er the house . . . . iv 1 31
Go with me to my house, And hear thou there how many fruitless pranks iv 1 58
Sayest thou that house is dark?—As hell, Sir Topas . . . . iv 2 38
I am not mad, Sir Topas: I say to you, this house is dark . . . iv 2 45
This house is as dark as ignorance, though ignorance were as dark as hell . . . . iv 2 49
Or else the lady's mad; yet, if 'twere so, She could not sway her house iv 3 17
One day shall crown the alliance on't, so please you, Here at my house v 1 327
Why have you suffer'd me to be imprison'd, Kept in a dark house? . v 1 350
He is seldom from the house of a most homely shepherd . *W. Tale* iv 2 43
There shall not at your father's house these seven years Be born another such . . . . iv 4 589
Preserver of my father, now of me, The medicine of our house . . iv 4 598
She hath privately twice or thrice a day, ever since the death of Hermione, visited that removed house . . . . v 2 116
You have vouchsafed, With your crown'd brother and these your contracted Heirs of your kingdoms, my poor house to visit . . . v 3 6
In the office of a wall Or as a moat defensive to a house . *Richard II.* ii 1 48
The queen is at your house; For God's sake, fairly let her be entreated iii 1 36
O, if you raise this house against this house, It will the woefullest division prove That ever fell upon this cursed earth . . . . iv 1 145
Hie thee to France And cloister thee in some religious house . . v 1 23
Our house, my sovereign liege, little deserves The scourge of greatness to be used on it . . . . . *1 Hen. IV.* i 3 10
This house is turned upside down since Robin Ostler died . . . ii 1 11
This be the most villanous house in all London road for fleas . . ii 1 16
My lord, I could be well contented to be there, in respect of the love I bear your house . . . . ii 3 3
He loves his own barn better than he loves our house . . . . ii 3 6
And have it; yea, and can show it you here in the house . . . ii 4 284
They are come to search the house. Shall I let them in? . . . ii 4 537
A hue and cry Hath follow'd certain men unto this house . . . ii 4 557
And so let me entreat you leave the house.—I will, my lord . . ii 4 567
He is as tedious As a tired horse, a railing wife; Worse than a smoky house . . . . iii 1 161
Do you think I keep thieves in my house? . . . . . . iii 3 64
The tithe of a hair was never lost in my house before . . . . iii 3 67
God's light, I was never called so in mine own house before . . . iii 3 72
This house is turned bawdy-house; they pick pockets . . . . iii 3 114
It pleased your majesty to turn your looks Of favour from myself and all our house . . . . v 1 31
When we see the figure of the house, Then must we rate the cost *2 Hen. IV.* i 3 43
Like one that draws the model of a house Beyond his power to build it i 3 58
He stabbed me in mine own house, and that most beastly . . . ii 1 15
I will bar no honest man my house, nor no cheater . . . . ii 4 111
I'll forswear keeping house, afore I'll be in these tirrits and frights . ii 4 220
There is another indictment upon thee, for suffering flesh to be eaten in thy house, contrary to the law . . . . ii 4 373
Let us not hang like roping icicles Upon our houses' thatch . *Hen. V.* iii 5 24
Save his life: he is a gentleman of a good house . . . . iv 4 48
Even so our houses and ourselves and children Have lost, or do not learn v 2 56
So bees with smoke and doves with noisome stench Are from their hives and houses driven away . . . . . . *1 Hen. VI.* i 5 24
And for that cause I train'd thee to my house . . . . . ii 3 35
And think me honoured To feast so great a warrior in my house . . ii 3 82
This blot that they object against your house Shall be wiped out . . ii 4 116
Those bitter injuries, Which Somerset hath offer'd to my house . . ii 5 125
Vow, Burgundy, by honour of thy house, Prick'd on by public wrongs . iii 2 77
Go, get you to my house; I will reward you . . . *2 Hen. VI.* iii 2 8
Therefore am I of an honourable house.—Ay, by my faith, the field is honourable; and there was he born, under a hedge, for his father had never a house but the cage . . . . iv 2 53
He made a chimney in my father's house, and the bricks are alive at this day to testify it . . . . iv 2 157
Jack Cade proclaims himself Lord Mortimer, Descended from the Duke of Clarence' house . . . . iv 4 29
Cade hath gotten London bridge: The citizens fly and forsake their houses . . . . iv 4 50
And then break into his son-in-law's house, Sir James Cromer . . iv 7 117
Let them break your backs with burthens, take your houses over your heads . . . . iv 8 31
Wither, garden; and be henceforth a burying-place to all that do dwell in this house . . . . iv 10 69
Come, thou new ruin of old Clifford's house . . . . . . v 2 61
Like rich hangings in a homely house, So was his will in his old feeble body . . . . v 3 12
Arm'd as we are, let's stay within this house . . . *3 Hen. VI.* i 1 38
I remember it to my grief; And, by his soul, thou and thy house shall rue it . . . . i 1 94
Or I will fill the house with armed men . . . . . . i 1 167
The red rose and the white are on his face, The fatal colours of our striving houses . . . . ii 5 98
Bring forth that fatal screech-owl to our house, That nothing sung but death to us and ours . . . . ii 6 56
I will not ruinate my father's house, Who gave his blood to lime the stones together, And set up Lancaster . . . . v 1 83
O, may such purple tears be alway shed From those that wish the downfall of our house! . . . . v 6 65
And all the clouds that lour'd upon our house In the deep bosom of the ocean buried . . . . *Richard III.* i 1 3
Now fair befal thee and thy noble house! . . . . . . i 3 282
Ay me, I see the downfall of our house! . . . . . . ii 4 49
Meaning indeed his house, Which, by the sign thereof, was termed so . iii 5 78
Your due of birth, The lineal glory of your royal house . . . iii 7 121
To the disgrace and downfall of your house . . . . . iii 7 217
Richmond and Elizabeth, The true succeeders of each royal house . . v 5 30
They have done my poor house grace . . . . . *Hen. VIII.* i 4 73
And be well contented To make your house our Tower . . . . v 1 106
This day, no man think Has business at his house . . . . v 5 76
My lord would instantly speak with you.—Where?—At your own house; there he unarms him . . . . . . *Troi. and Cres.* i 2 300
His purpose meets you: twas to bring this Greek To Calchas' house . iv 1 37
Walk into her house; I'll bring her to the Grecian presently . . iv 3 5
I sometime lay here in Corioli At a poor man's house . . *Coriolanus* i 9 83
I will make my very house reel to-night . . . . . . ii 1 121
Ere in our own house I do shade my head, The good patricians must be visited . . . . ii 1 211
And what stock he springs of, The noble house o' the Marcians . . ii 3 246
Of the same house Publius and Quintus were . . . . . ii 3 249
Go, get you to your house; be gone, away! All will be naught else . iii 1 230
I prithee, noble friend, home to thy house; Leave us to cure this cause iii 1 234
We'll hear no more. Pursue him to his house, and pluck him thence . iii 1 309
As far as doth the Capitol exceed The meanest house in Rome . . iv 2 40
And feasts the nobles of the state At his house this night . . . iv 4 10
A goodly house: the feast smells well; but I Appear not like a guest . iv 5 5
A strange one as ever I looked on: I cannot get him out o' the house . iv 5 22
What have you to do here, fellow? Pray you, avoid the house . . iv 5 25
If he were putting to my house the brand That should consume it, I have not the face To say 'Beseech you, cease' . . . . . iv 6 115
Sir, if you'ld save your life, fly to your house . . . . . v 4 38
Look to my house: Lucius and I'll go brave it at the court *T. Andron.* iv 1 120
He craves a parley at your father's house . . . . . . iv 4 159
Welcome, dread Fury, to my woful house . . . . . . v 2 82
Bid him come and banquet at thy house . . . . v 2 114
Tell him the emperor and the empress too Feast at my house . . . v 2 128
The villain is alive in Titus' house, And as he is, to witness this is true v 3 123
Beat forth our brains, And make a mutual closure of our house . . v 3 134
Go into old Titus' sorrowful house, And hither hale that misbelieving Moor . . . . v 3 142
A dog of that house shall move me to stand . . . *Rom. and Jul.* i 1 14
At my poor house look to behold this night Earth-treading stars . . i 2 24
Among fresh female buds shall you this night Inherit at my house . i 2 30

House. To them say, My house and welcome on their pleasure stay *Rom. and Jul.* i 2 37

Whither should they come?—Up.—Whither?—To supper; to our house i 2 78

I would not for the wealth of all the town Here in my house do him disparagement: Therefore be patient i 5 72

Her mother is the lady of the house, And a good lady, and a wise i 5 115

Tybalt, the kinsman of old Capulet, Hath sent a letter to his father's house ii 4 7

A gentleman of the very first house, of the first and second cause ii 4 25

A plague o' both your houses! iii 1 94; 111

Help me into some house, Benvolio, Or I shall faint iii 1 110

Bid her hasten all the house to bed, Which heavy sorrow makes them apt unto iii 3 156

Graze where you will, you shall not house with me: Look to't, think on't iii 5 190

As I remember, this should be the house v 1 55

Both were in a house Where the infectious pestilence did reign v 2 9

This dagger hath mista'en,—for, lo, his house Is empty on the back of Montague,—And it mis-sheathed in my daughter's bosom! v 3 203

This thy creature By night frequents my house *T. of Athens* i 1 117

They enter my mistress' house merrily, and go away sadly ii 2 107

A noble gentleman 'tis, if he would not keep so good a house iii 1 24

Who cannot keep his wealth must keep his house iii 3 42

Who can speak broader than he that has no house to put his head in? such may rail against great buildings iii 4 64

Have I been ever free, and must my house Be my retentive enemy, my gaol? iii 4 81

Burn, house! sink, Athens! henceforth hated be Of Timon! iii 6 114

Such a house broke! So noble a master fall'n! All gone! iv 2 5

More of our fellows.—All broken implements of a ruin'd house iv 2 16

Run to your houses, fall upon your knees, Pray to the gods *J. Cæsar* i 1 58

And he's gone To seek you at your house i 3 150

Casca, you and I will yet ere day See Brutus at his house i 3 154

Think you to walk forth? You shall not stir out of your house to-day ii 2 9

Do not go forth to-day: call it my fear That keeps you in the house ii 2 51

Which way hast thou been?—At mine own house, good lady ii 4 22

Where is Antony?—Fled to his house amazed iii 1 96

Bring him with triumph home unto his house.—Give him a statue iii 2 54

We'll bring him to his house With shouts and clamours iii 2 57

We'll burn the house of Brutus.—Away, then! come, seek the conspirators iii 2 236

We'll burn his body in the holy place, And with the brands fire the traitors' houses. Take up the body iii 2 260

He and Lepidus are at Cæsar's house.—And thither will I straight iii 2 269

Burn all: some to Decius' house, and some to Casca's iii 3 42

Go you to Cæsar's house; Fetch the will hither iv 1 7

Honours deep and broad wherewith Your majesty loads our house *Macbeth* i 6 18

Still it cried 'Sleep no more!' to all the house ii 2 41

What's the business, That such a hideous trumpet calls to parley The sleepers of the house? ii 3 88

Murder'd!—Woe, alas! What, in our house?—Too cruel any where ii 3 93

There's not a one of them but in his house I keep a servant fee'd iii 4 131

Were I king, I should cut off the nobles for their lands, Desire his jewels and this other's house iv 3 80

That he may play the fool no where but in's own house *Hamlet* iii 1 137

Unpeg the basket on the house's top, Let the birds fly iii 4 193

A grave-maker: the houses that he makes last till doomsday v 1 66

I have shot mine arrow o'er the house, And hurt my brother v 2 254

I can tell why a snail has a house.—Why?—Why, to put his head in *Lear* i 5 30

If they come to sojourn at my house, I'll not be there ii 1 105

Art of this house?—Ay.—Where may we set our horses? ii 2 2

He raised the house with loud and coward cries ii 4 43

Ask her forgiveness? Do you but mark how this becomes the house ii 4 155

How, in one house, Should many people, under two commands, Hold amity? ii 4 243

What need you five and twenty, ten, or five, To follow in a house where twice so many Have a command to tend you? ii 4 265

This house is little: the old man and his people Cannot be well bestow'd ii 4 291

Court holy-water in a dry house is better than this rain-water out o' door iii 2 11

He that has a house to put's head in has a good head-piece iii 2 25

The cod-piece that will house Before the head has any, The head and he shall louse; So beggars marry many iii 2 27

This hard house—More harder than the stones whereof 'tis raised iii 2 63

When I desired their leave that I might pity him, they took from me the use of mine own house iii 3 4

Good my lord, take his offer; go into the house iii 4 161

I will have my revenge ere I depart his house iii 5 2

Quit the house on purpose, that their punishment Might have the freer course iv 2 94

Here is her father's house; I'll call aloud *Othello* i 1 74

Thieves! thieves! Look to your house, your daughter and your bags! i 1 80

What tell'st thou me of robbing? this is Venice; My house is not a grange i 1 106

Straight satisfy yourself: If she be in her chamber or your house i 1 139

At every house I'll call; I may command at most i 1 181

I will but spend a word here in the house, And go with you i 2 48

Sweet love, I was coming to your house.—And I was going to your lodging iii 4 171

It comes o'er my memory, As doth the raven o'er the infected house iv 1 21

Do you shake at that?—He supp'd at my house; but I therefore shake not v 1 119

Keep the house, And seize upon the fortunes of the Moor v 2 365

At land, indeed, Thou dost o'er-count me of my father's house *A. and C.* ii 6 27

O Antony, You have my father's house,—But, what? we are friends ii 7 135

Look well to my husband's house; and— What, Octavia? iii 2 45

This mortal house I'll ruin, Do Cæsar what he can v 2 51

A goodly day not to keep house! *Cymbeline* iii 3 1

Hail, thou fair heaven! We house i' the rock, yet use thee not so hardly As prouder livers do iii 3 8

Now peace be here, Poor house, that keep'st thyself! iii 6 36

As houses are defiled for want of use *Pericles* i 4 37

That the ship Should house him safe is wreck'd and split ii Gower 32

Now sleep yslaked hath the rout; No din but snores the house about iii Gower 2

Pure surprise and fear Made me to quit the house iii 2 18

Why, the house you dwell in proclaims you to be a creature of sale iv 6 83

Do you know this house to be a place of such resort, and will come into't? iv 6 85

Your house, but for this virgin that doth prop it, Would sink iv 6 127

Prostitute me to the basest groom That doth frequent your house iv 6 202

Marina thus the brothel 'scapes, and chances Into an honest house v Gower 2

House. They shall be brought you to my house, Whither I invite you *Pericles* v 3 26

First go with me to my house, Where shall be shown you all v 3 65

House-affairs. But still the house-affairs would draw her thence *Othello* i 3 147

House and home. He hath eaten me out of house and home 2 *Hen. IV.* ii 1 80

House-eaves. Sparrows must not build in his house-eaves *Meas. for Meas.* iii 2 186

House of death. Then is it sin To rush into the secret house of death, Ere death dare come to us? *Ant. and Cleo.* iv 15 81

House of fame. The emperor's court is like the house of Fame, The palace full of tongues, of eyes, and ears *T. Andron.* ii 1 126

House of Lancaster. Strong-fixed is the house of Lancaster And like a mountain, not to be removed 1 *Hen. VI.* ii 5 102

Bear the arms of York, To grapple with the house of Lancaster 2 *Hen. VI.* i 1 257

Thus got the house of Lancaster the crown ii 2 29

And that my sword be stain'd With heart-blood of the house of Lancaster ii 2 66

Seated in that throne Which now the house of Lancaster usurps 3 *Hen. VI.* i 1 23

By giving the house of Lancaster leave to breathe, It will outrun you i 2 13

And yet the king not privy to my drift, Nor any of the house of Lancaster i 2 47

And what beside May make against the house of Lancaster ii 1 176

While life upholds this arm, This arm upholds the house of Lancaster iii 3 107

Pale ashes of the house of Lancaster! Thou bloodless remnant! *Rich. III.* i 2 6

You and your husband Grey Were factious for the house of Lancaster i 3 128

Thou didst receive the holy sacrament, To fight in quarrel of the house of Lancaster i 4 209

Thou offspring of the house of Lancaster, The wronged heirs of York do pray for thee: Good angels guard thy battle! v 3 136

House of life. To break within the bloody house of life *K. John* iv 2 210

House of Montague. A dog of the house of Montague moves me.—To move is to stir *Rom. and Jul.* i 1 9

Draw thy tool; here comes two of the house of the Montagues i 1 38

If you be not of the house of Montagues, I pray, come and crush a cup of wine i 2 85

House of profession. I am as well acquainted here as I was in our house of profession *Meas. for Meas.* iv 3 2

Houses of resort. But shall all our houses of resort in the suburbs be pulled down? i 2 104

House of sale. I saw him enter such a house of sale *Hamlet* ii 1 60

House of tears. Therefore have I little talk'd of love; For Venus smiles not in a house of tears *Rom. and Jul.* iv 1 8

House of York. But all the whole inheritance I give That doth belong unto the house of York 1 *Hen. VI.* iii 1 165

By this I shall perceive the commons' mind, How they affect the house and claim of York 2 *Hen. VI.* iii 1 375

The house of York, thrust from the crown By shameful murder of a guiltless king iv 1 94

Meet I an infant of the house of York, Into as many gobbets will I cut it As wild Medea young Absyrtus did v 2 57

Be thou a prey unto the house of York, And die in bands! 3 *Hen. VI.* i 1 185

Thou hast undone thyesif, thy son and me; And given unto the house of York such head As thou shalt reign but by their sufferance i 1 233

To thy foul disgrace And utter ruin of the house of York i 1 254

The sight of any of the house of York Is as a fury to torment my soul i 3 30

Giving no ground unto the house of York ii 6 16

In quarrel of the house of York The worthy gentleman did lose his life ii 2 6

This arm upholds the house of Lancaster.—And I the house of York iii 3 108

Did I forget that by the house of York My father came untimely to his death? iii 3 186

Both Dukes of Somerset Have sold their lives unto the house of York v 1 74

Housed. For slander lives upon succession, For ever housed where it gets possession *Com. of Errors* iii 1 106

I charge thee, Satan, housed within this man, To yield possession iv 4 57

Even now we housed him in the abbey here; And now he's there v 1 188

If here you housed him, here he would have been v 1 271

Household. What, household stuff?—It is a kind of history *T. of Shrew* Ind. 2 143

For I am he am born to tame you Kate, And bring you from a wild Kate to a Kate Conformable as other household Kates ii 1 280

She is my house, My household stuff, my field, my barn iii 2 233

And ring these fingers with thy household worms *K. John* iii 4 31

And all the household servants fled with him *Richard II.* ii 2 60

He hath forsook the court, Broken his staff of office and dispersed The household of the king ii 3 28

From my own windows torn my household coat, Razed out my impress iii 1 24

That every day under his household roof Did keep ten thousand men iv 1 282

But what need I thus My well-known body to anatomize Among my household? 2 *Hen. IV.* Ind. 22

To brother born an household cruelty, I make my quarrel in particular iv 1 95

Our names, Familiar in his mouth as household words *Hen. V.* iv 3 52

You of my household, leave this peevish broil 1 *Hen. VI.* iii 1 92

In thee thy mother dies, our household's name, My death's revenge iv 6 38

Might I but know thee by thy household badge 2 *Hen. VI.* v 1 201

By notes of household harmony They quite forget their loss 3 *Hen. VI.* iv 6 14

His treasure, Rich stuffs, and ornaments of household *Hen. VIII.* iii 2 126

Lavinia shall forthwith Be closed in our household's monument *T. An.* v 3 194

Two households, both alike in dignity, In fair Verona *Rom. and Jul.* Prol. 1

I'll thy assistant be; For this alliance may so happy prove, To turn your households' rancour to pure love ii 3 92

Call forth my household servants: let's to-night Be bounteous *A. and C.* iv 2 9

Shall undo a whole household *Pericles* iv 6 133

Householder. And, which is more, a householder *Much Ado* iv 2 84

I press me none but good householders, yeomen's sons 1 *Hen. IV.* iv 2 16

Housekeeper. An honest man and a good housekeeper *T. Night* iv 2 10

You are manifest house-keepers. What are you sewing here? *Coriolanus* i 3 55

The valued file Distinguishes the swift, the slow, the subtle, The house-keeper, the hunter *Macbeth* iii 1 97

Housekeeping. I hear your grace hath sworn out house-keeping *L. L. Lost* ii 1 104

And all things that belong To house or housekeeping *T. of Shrew* ii 1 358

Thy plainness and thy housekeeping Hath won the greatest favour 2 *Hen. VI.* i 1 191

Houseless. You houseless poverty,—Nay, get thee in *Lear* iii 4 26

How shall your houseless heads and unfed sides, Your loop'd and window'd raggedness, defend you From seasons such as these? iii 4 30

Housewife. Bootless make the breathless housewife churn *M. N. Dream* ii 1 37

Let us sit and mock the good housewife Fortune *As Y. Like It* i 2 34

I play the noble housewife with the time, To entertain't so merrily with a fool *All's Well* ii 2 62

I hope to see a housewife take thee between her legs and spin it off *T. N.* i 3 109

Your graces find me here part of a housewife, I would be all, against the worst may happen *Hen. VIII.* iii 1 24

Housewife. Let me alone; I'll play the housewife for this once *Rom. and Jul.* iv 2 43
The bounteous housewife, nature, on each bush Lays her full mess before you. Want! why want? . . . . . . *T. of Athens* iv 3 423
Let housewives make a skillet of my helm! . . . . *Othello* i 3 273
Players in your housewifery, and housewives in your beds . . ii 1 113
A housewife that by selling her desires Buys herself bread . . iv 1 95
Let me rail so high, That the false housewife Fortune break her wheel, Provoked by my offence . . . . *Ant. and Cleo.* iv 15 44
A riding-suit, no costlier than would fit A franklin's housewife *Cymb.* iii 2 79
Pray, be not sick, For you must be our housewife . . . iv 2 45
Housewifery. Let housewifery appear: keep close, I thee command *Hen. V.* ii 3 65
Players in your housewifery, and housewives in your beds *Othello* ii 1 113
Hovel. Hard by here is a hovel; Some friendship will it lend you . *Lear* iii 2 61
That can make vile things precious. Come, your hovel . . . iii 2 71
For the rain it raineth every day.—True, my good boy. Come, bring us to this hovel . . . . iii 2 78
In, fellow, there, into the hovel: keep thee warm.—Come, let's in all . iii 4 179
And wast thou fain, poor father, To hovel thee with swine? . . iv 7 39
Hovel-post. Do I look like a cudgel or a hovel-post? . *Mer. of Venice* ii 2 71
Hover. Some airy devil hovers in the sky . . . . *K. John* iii 2 2
Ah, my tender babes! . . . Hover about me with your airy wings And hear your mother's lamentation! . . . . . *Richard III.* iv 4 13
Hover about her; say, that right for right Hath dimm'd your infant morn to aged night . . . . iv 4 15
Why suffer'st thou thy sons, unburied yet, To hover on the dreadful shore of Styx? Make way to lay them by their brethern *T. Andron.* i 1 88
Hover through the fog and filthy air . . . . . *Macbeth* i 1 12
Save me, and hover o'er me with your wings, You heavenly guards! *Ham.* iii 4 103
Hovering. A mindless slave, Or else a hovering temporizer . *W. Tale* i 2 302
How. But how is it That this lives in thy mind? . . *Tempest* i 2 48
If thou remember'st aught ere thou camest here, How thou camest here thou mayst . . . . i 2 52
Being once perfected how to grant suits, How to deny them . . . i 2 79
How came we ashore?—By Providence divine . . . . . i 2 158
Of the king's ship The mariners say how thou hast disposed . . . i 2 225
And teach me how To name the bigger light, and how the less . . i 2 334
You taught me language; and my profit on't Is, I know how to curse . i 2 364
I am standing water.—I'll teach you how to flow . . . . ii 1 222
How camest thou hither? swear by this bottle how thou camest hither ii 2 124
How features are abroad, I am skilless of . . . . . iii 1 52
How use doth breed a habit in a man! . . . . *T. G. of Ver.* v 4 1
None better knows than you How I have ever loved the life removed *Meas. for Meas.* i 3 8
My wife, sir, whom I detest before heaven . . . ,— How? thy wife? . ii 1 71
How would you be, If He, which is the top of judgement, should But judge you as you are? . . . . ii 2 75
Ever till now, When men were fond, I smiled and wonder'd how . . ii 2 187
How if your husband start some other where? . . *Com. of Errors* ii 1 30
Teach me, dear creature, how to think and speak . . . . iii 2 33
How dost thou mean a fat marriage? . . . . . . iii 2 95
How is the man esteem'd here in the city? . . . . . v 1 4
He hath indeed better bettered expectation than you must expect of me to tell you how . . . . *Much Ado* i 1 17
I never yet saw man, How wise, how noble, young, how rarely featured, But she would spell him backward . . . . iii 1 60
He be angry indeed.—If he be, he knows how to turn his girdle . . v 1 142
O, some authority how to proceed . . . . . *L. L. Lost* iv 3 287
I could teach you How to choose right, but I am then forsworn *M. of V.* iii 2 11
But her eyes,—How could he see to do them? . . . . . iii 2 124
How sweet the moonlight sleeps upon this bank! . . . . . v 1 54
Though yet I know no wise remedy how to avoid it . . *As Y. Like It* i 1 26
You must not learn me how to remember any extraordinary pleasure . i 2 6
How speed you with my daughter?—How but well? *T. of Shrew* ii 1 283
Shall sweet Bianca practise how to bride it? . . . . . iii 2 253
I, who never knew how to entreat, Nor never needed that I should entreat . . . . iv 3 7
Might do her A shrewd turn, if she pleased.—How do you mean? *All's Well* iii 5 71
Be blamed for't how you might . . . . . . *W. Tale* ii 1 161
How shall we do? We are not furnish'd like Bohemia's son . . iv 4 598
How high a pitch his resolution soars! . . . . *Richard II.* i 1 109
Subjected thus, How can you say to me, I am a king? . . . iii 2 177
How heinous e'er it be, To win thy after-love I pardon thee . . v 3 34
Look how we can, or sad or merrily, Interpretation will misquote *1 Hen. IV.* v 2 12
How a good yoke of bullocks at Stamford fair? . . . *2 Hen. IV.* iii 2 42
How a score of ewes now?—Thereafter as they be . . . . iii 2 54
There is no note How dread an army hath enrounded him *Hen. V.* iv Prol. 36
We have French quarrels enow, if you could tell how to reckon . . iv 1 241
Soldiers, march away: And how thou pleasest, God, dispose the day! . iv 3 132
Let them obey that know not how to rule . . . *2 Hen. VI.* v 1 6
How art thou call'd? and what is thy degree? . . . . . v 1 73
Look, how this ring encompasseth thy finger, Even so thy breast encloseth my poor heart . . . . *Richard III.* i 2 204
How if it [conscience] come to thee again?—I'll not meddle with it . . i 4 136
How you do talk! . . . . *Hen. VIII.* ii 3 44
That man, how dearly ever parted, How much in having *Troi. and Cres.* iii 3 96
How now, how now! how go maidenheads? . . . . . iv 2 23
Whether his fall enraged him, or how 'twas, he did so set his teeth *Cor.* i 3 69
Good faith, I'll prove him, Speed how it will . . . . . v 1 61
Let me teach you how to knit again This scatter'd corn . . *T. Andron.* v 3 70
When and where and how We met, We woo'd . . . *Rom. and Jul.* ii 3 61
Make your own purpose, How in my strength you please . . *Lear* ii 1 114
It is not lost; but what an if it were?—How! . . . . *Othello* iii 4 84
Hast thou not learn'd me how To make perfumes? distil? . *Cymbeline* i 5 12
How and which way. I'll take the sacrament on't, how and which way you will . . . . *All's Well* iv 3 156
How far The substance of my praise doth wrong this shadow In underprizing it, so far this shadow Doth limp behind the substance *Mer. of Venice* iii 2 126
How many fond fools serve mad jealousy! . . . *Com. of Errors* ii 1 116
How many Grecian tents do stand Hollow upon this plain *Troi. and Cres.* i 3 79
How many Must murder wives much better than themselves! *Cymbeline* v 1 3
How much. Of homage and I know not how much tribute . *Tempest* i 2 124
How much unlook'd for is this expedition!—By how much unexpected, by so much We must awake endeavour for defence . . . *K. John* ii 1 79
You are the better at proverbs, by how much 'A fool's blot is soon shot' *Hen. V.* iii 7 131
How much the quantity, the weight as much, As I do love my father *Cymbeline* iv 2 17
How now? moody? What is't thou canst demand? . . . *Tempest* i 2 244
How now! what means this passion at his name? . . *T. G. of Ver.* i 2 16
How now! what is in you? why dost thou tear it? . . *L. L. Lost* iv 3 200
How now, how now! how go maidenheads? . . *Troi. and Cres.* iv 2 23
How now, how now, chop-logic! What is this? . . *Rom. and Jul.* iii 5 150
How oft the sight of means to do ill deeds Make deeds ill done! *K. John* iv 2 219
How or which way. If I know how or which way to order these affairs Thus thrust disorderly into my hands, Never believe me *Richard II.* ii 2 109
Then how or which way should they first break in?—Question, my lords, no further of the case, How or which way . . . . *1 Hen. VI.* ii 1 71
How say you by the French lord, Monsieur Le Bon? . *Mer. of Venice* i 2 58
How say you to a fat tripe finely broil'd? . . . *T. of Shrew* iv 3 20
How say you to that? . . . . *T. Night* i 5 88
How say you? My prisoner? or my guest? . . . . *W. Tale* i 2 54
Prithee, see there! behold! look! lo! how say you? . . *Macbeth* iii 4 69
How say you, then; would heart of man once think it? . . *Hamlet* i 5 121
Friend, look to't.—How say you by that? . . . . . ii 2 188
How say you by this change?—This cannot be . . . *Othello* i 3 17
How say you? *Tempest* ii 1; *Mer. Wives* i 4; *Meas. for Meas.* ii 4; *Com. of Errors* iv 2; *Hen. V.* v 2; *1 Hen. VI.* ii 3; v 3; *T. Andron.* ii 2
How so, sir? Did she change her determination? . . *Mer. Wives* iii 5 69
Ajax goes up and down the field, asking for himself.—How so? *T. and C.* iii 3 246
How's the day?—On the sixth hour . . . . . *Tempest* v 1 3
How then. Shall she marry him?—No.—How then? shall he marry her? *T. G. of Ver.* ii 5 17
How well. Look how well my garments sit upon me . . . *Tempest* ii 1 272
How well he's read, to reason against reading! . . . *L. L. Lost* i 1 94
Mark how well the sequel hangs together . . . *Richard III.* ii 6 4
Howbeit they would hold up this Salique law . . . *Hen. V.* i 2 91
Howbeit, I thank you . . . . *Coriolanus* i 9 70
The Moor, howbeit that I endure him not, Is of a . . . noble nature *Oth.* ii 1 297
However, but a folly bought with wit . . . . *T. G. of Ver.* i 1 34
There was never yet philosopher That could endure the toothache patiently, However they have writ the style of gods . *Much Ado* v 1 37
Howe'er, I charge thee, . . . To tell me truly . . . *All's Well* i 3 189
It would not seem too dear, Howe'er repented after . . . . iii 7 28
Howe'er it pleases you to take it so, The ring was never hers . . v 3 88
You would believe my saying, Howe'er you lean to the nayward *W. Tale* ii 1 64
Howe'er the business goes, you have made fault I' the boldness . . iii 2 218
Have is have, however men do catch . . . . . *K. John* i 1 173
And I am I, howe'er I was begot . . . . i 1 175
However God or fortune cast my lot . . . . . *Richard II.* i 3 85
Howe'er it be, I cannot but be sad . . . . ii 2 29
Oft have shot at them, Howe'er unfortunate I miss'd my aim . *1 Hen. VI.* i 4 4
All the land knows that: However, yet there is no great breach *Hen. VIII.* iv 1 106
This challenge that the gallant Hector sends, However it is spread in general name, Relates in purpose only to Achilles . *Troi. and Cres.* i 3 322
However these disturbers of our peace Buz in the people's ears *T. Andron.* iv 4 6
So is he now . . . , However he puts on this tardy form . . *J. Cæsar* i 2 303
Howe'er you come to know it, answer me . . . . *Macbeth* iv 1 51
Till I know 'tis done, Howe'er my haps, my joys were ne'er begun *Hamlet* iv 3 70
I shall serve you, sir, Truly, however else . . . . *Lear* ii 1 119
Howe'er thou art a fiend, A woman's shape doth shield thee . . iv 2 66
This youth, howe'er distress'd, appears he hath had Good ancestors *Cymb.* iv 2 47
Howl. Thy groans Did make wolves howl . . . . *Tempest* i 2 288
I had rather hear Lady, my brach, howl in Irish . . *1 Hen. IV.* iii 1 240
Contrary to the law; for the which I think thou wilt howl . *2 Hen. IV.* ii 4 374
Let floods o'erswell, and fiends for food howl on! . . . *Hen. V.* ii 1 97
The mad mothers with their howls confused Do break the clouds . . iii 3 39
The time when screech-owls cry and ban-dogs howl . . *2 Hen. VI.* i 4 21
Alarum'd by his sentinel, the wolf, Whose howl's his watch . *Macbeth* ii 1 54
Each new morn New widows howl, new orphans cry . . . . iv 3 5
Howl, howl, howl, howl! O, you are men of stones . . . *Lear* v 3 257
Howled. I will rend an oak And peg thee in his knotty entrails till Thou hast howl'd away twelve winters . . . . . . *Tempest* i 2 296
Thou singest well enough for a shift.—An he had been a dog that should have howled thus, they would have hanged him . . *Much Ado* ii 3 82
Dogs howl'd, and hideous tempest shook down trees . *3 Hen. VI.* v 6 46
A legion of foul fiends Environ'd me about, and howled in mine ears Such hideous cries . . . . *Richard III.* i 4 59
I have words That would be howl'd out in the desert air . *Macbeth* iv 3 194
If wolves had at thy gate howl'd that stern time, Thou shouldst have said 'Good porter, turn the key' . . . . . . *Lear* iii 7 63
Howlest. And now thou wouldst eat thy dead vomit up, And howl'st to find it . . . . *2 Hen. IV.* i 3 100
Howlet. Lizard's leg and howlet's wing . . . . *Macbeth* iv 1 17
Howling. A plague upon this howling! . . . . . *Tempest* i 1 39
A howling monster; a drunken monster! . . . . . . ii 2 183
Strange and several noises Of roaring, shrieking, howling, jingling chains v 1 233
My sister crying, our maid howling, our cat wringing her hands *T. G. of Ver.* ii 3 8
Those that lawless and incertain thought Imagine howling *M. for M.* iii 1 128
The virgin tribute paid by howling Troy To the sea-monster *Mer. of Ven.* iii 2 56
'Tis like the howling of Irish wolves against the moon . *As Y. Like It* v 2 119
It is as fat and fulsome to mine ear As howling after music . *T. Night* v 1 113
The damned use that word in hell; Howlings attend it . *Rom. and Jul.* iii 3 48
A ministering angel shall my sister be, When thou liest howling *Hamlet* v 1 265
Tempests themselves, high seas and howling winds, The gutter'd rocks and congregated sands . . . . *Othello* ii 1 68
Howsoe'er you have Been justled from your senses, know for certain *Temp.* v 1 157
And talks of the basket too, howsoever he hath had intelligence *M. Wives* iv 2 94
You are partly a bawd, Pompey, howsoever you colour it *Meas. for Meas.* ii 1 231
The man doth fear God, howsoever it seems not in him . . *Much Ado* ii 3 205
But, howsoever, strange and admirable . . . . *M. N. Dream* v 1 27
Howsoe'er thou speak'st, 'mong other things I shall digest it *M. of Ven.* iii 5 94
I am glad he's come, howsoe'er he comes . . . . *T. of Shrew* iii 2 76
Howsoever rude exteriorly, Is yet the cover of a fairer mind *K. John* iv 2 257
I dare say you love him not so ill, to wish him here alone, howsoever you speak this to feel other men's minds . . . . *Hen. V.* iv 1 130
But howsoe'er, no simple man that sees This jarring discord *1 Hen. VI.* iv 1 187
Howsoever, he shall pay for me ere he has me . . *Troi. and Cres.* iii 3 297
Howsoever you have been his liar, as you say you have . *Coriolanus* v 2 32
And gold confound you howsoe'er! . . . . . *T. of Athens* iv 3 452
Howsoever thou pursuest this act, Taint not thy mind . . *Hamlet* i 5 84
Howsoe'er 'tis strange, . . . Yet is it true, sir . . . *Cymbeline* i 1 65
Howsoe'er, My brother hath done well . . . . . iv 2 146
Howsome'er their hearts are severed in religion, their heads are both one *All's Well* i 3 56

Hoxes. A coward, Which hoxes honesty behind *W. Tale* i 2 244
Hoy. Hindered by the sergeant, to tarry for the hoy Delay *Com. of Errors* iv 3 40
Hoyday, a riddle! neither good nor bad! *Richard III.* iv 4 460
Hoy-day! spirits and fires! *Troi. and Cres.* v 1 73
Hoy-day, what a sweep of vanity comes this way! They dance! *T. of A.* i 2 137
Hubert, keep this boy. Philip, make up: My mother is assailed *K. John* iii 2 5
Come hither, Hubert. O my gentle Hubert, We owe thee much! iii 3 19
Hubert, I am almost ashamed To say what good respect I have of thee iii 3 27
Good Hubert, Hubert, Hubert, throw thine eye On yon young boy iii 3 59
Hubert, I love thee; Well, I'll not say what I intend for thee: Remember iii 3 67
Hubert shall be your man, attend on you With all true duty iii 3 72
Good morrow, Hubert.—Good morrow, little prince iv 1 9
I would to heaven I were your son, so you would love me, Hubert iv 1 24
Are you sick, Hubert? you look pale to-day: In sooth, I would you were iv 1 28
Can you not read it? is it not fair writ?—Too fairly, Hubert iv 1 38
An if an angel should have come to me And told me Hubert should put out mine eyes, I would not have believed him,—no tongue but Hubert's iv 1 69
O, save me, Hubert, save me! my eyes are out Even with the fierce looks of these bloody men iv 1 73
For heaven sake, Hubert, let me not be bound! Nay, hear me, Hubert iv 1 78
Hubert, the utterance of a brace of tongues Must needs want pleading for a pair of eyes: Let me not hold my tongue, let me not, Hubert; Or, Hubert, if you will, cut out my tongue, So I may keep mine eyes iv 1 98
You will but make it blush And glow with shame of your proceedings, Hubert iv 1 114
O, now you look like Hubert! all this while You were disguised iv 1 126
And, pretty child, sleep doubtless and secure, That Hubert, for the wealth of all the world, Will not offend thee iv 1 131
O heaven! I thank you, Hubert.—Silence; no more: go closely in with me iv 1 132
Hubert, what news with you?—This is the man should do the bloody deed iv 2 68
Hubert, away with him; imprison him iv 2 155
It is the shameful work of Hubert's hand iv 3 62
If thou didst this deed of death, Art thou damn'd, Hubert iv 3 119
That villain Hubert told me he did live.—So, on my soul, he did v 1 42
How goes the day with us? O, tell me, Hubert.—Badly, I fear v 3 1
Commend me to one Hubert with your king v 4 40
Hubert, I think?—Thou hast a perfect thought v 6 6
Hubert, half my power this night, Passing these flats, are taken v 6 39
Huddled. Glancing an eye of pity on his losses, That have of late so huddled on his back *Mer. of Venice* iv 1 28
Huddling jest upon jest with such impossible conveyance upon me *M. Ado* ii 1 252
Hue. Hue and cry, villain, go! Assist me, knight. I am undone! Fly, run, hue and cry, villain! I am undone! *Mer. Wives* iv 5 92
Black is the badge of hell, The hue of dungeons *L. L. Lost* iv 3 255
Cuckoo-buds of yellow hue Do paint the meadows with delight v 2 906
Most radiant Pyramus, most lily-white of hue *M. N. Dream* iii 1 95
The ousel cock so black of hue, With orange-tawny bill iii 1 128
O grim-look'd night! O night with hue so black! v 1 171
I would not change this hue, Except to steal your thoughts *M. of Venice* ii 1 11
What says the silver with her virgin hue? ii 7 22
As brown in hue As hazel nuts and sweeter than the kernels *T. of Shrew* ii 1 256
To smooth the ice, or add another hue Unto the rainbow *K. John* iv 2 13
A hue and cry Hath follow'd certain men unto this house 1 *Hen. IV.* ii 4 556
This palliament of white and spotless hue *T. Andron.* i 1 182
A goodly lady, trust me; of the hue That I would choose ii 1 261
Your swarth Cimmerian Doth make your honour of his body's hue ii 3 73
Is black so base a hue? Sweet blowse, you are a beauteous blossom, sure iv 2 71
Coal-black is better than another hue, In that it scorns to bear another hue iv 2 99
Fie, treacherous hue, that will betray with blushing The close enacts and counsels of the heart! iv 2 117
Did not thy hue bewray whose brat thou art v 1 28
Thus the native hue of resolution Is sicklied o'er *Hamlet* iii 1 84
Hug. If I must die, I will encounter darkness as a bride, And hug it in mine arms *Meas. for Meas.* iii 1 85
That hugs his kicky-wicky here at home *All's Well* ii 3 297
To hug with swine, to seek sweet safety out In vaults *K. John* v 2 142
And stain the sun with fog, as sometime clouds When they do hug him in their melting bosoms *T. Andron.* iii 1 214
A man, Whom this beneath world doth embrace and hug *T. of Athens* i 1 44
Wear silk, drink wine, lie soft; Hug their diseased perfumes iv 3 207
If you know That I do fawn on men and hug them hard And after scandal them *J. Cæsar* i 2 75
Huge. Yond same black cloud, yond huge one, looks like a foul bombard that would shed his liquor *Tempest* ii 2 21
That her father likes Only for his possessions are so huge *T. G. of Ver.* ii 4 175
And huge leviathans Forsake unsounded deeps to dance on sands iii 2 80
At her heels a huge infectious troop Of pale distemperatures *Com. of Errors* v 1 81
And the huge army of the world's desires *L. L. Lost* i 1 10
A huge translation of hypocrisy, Vilely compiled v 2 51
To your huge store Wise things seem foolish and rich things but poor v 2 377
Greater than great, great, great, great Pompey! Pompey the Huge! v 2 692
The patch is kind enough, but a huge feeder *Mer. of Venice* ii 5 46
Horns? Even so. Poor men alone? No, no; the noblest deer hath them as huge as the rascal *As Y. Like It* iii 3 58
This little abstract doth contain that large Which died in Geffrey, and the hand of time Shall draw this brief into as huge a volume *K. John* ii 1 103
No supporter but the huge firm earth Can hold it up iii 1 72
Far too huge to be blown out With that same weak wind which enkindled it v 2 86
This bed-presser, this horse-back-breaker, this huge hill of flesh 1 *Hen. IV.* ii 4 269
That huge bombard of sack, that stuffed cloak-bag of guts ii 4 497
The frame and huge foundation of the earth Shaked like a coward iii 1 16
And cuts me from the best of all my land A huge half-moon iii 1 100
Can a weak empty vessel bear such a huge full hogshead 2 *Hen. IV.* ii 4 68
The threaden sails, Borne with the invisible and creeping wind, Draw the huge bottoms through the furrow'd sea *Hen. V.* iii Prol. 12
Is not pig great? the pig, or the great, or the mighty, or the huge iv 7 17
Which cannot in their huge and proper life Be here presented v Prol. 5
And in that sparing makes huge waste *Rom. and Jul.* i 1 224
If I were a huge man, I should fear to drink at meals *T. of Athens* i 2 51
And we petty men Walk under his huge legs and peep about *J. Cæsar* i 2 137
Set a huge mountain 'tween my heart and tongue! ii 4 7
Though they do appear As huge as high Olympus v 3 92
To whose huge spokes ten thousand lesser things Are mortised *Hamlet* iii 3 19
I stand up, and have ingenious feeling Of my huge sorrows! *Lear* iv 6 288
The world's a huge thing: it is a great price For a small vice *Othello* iv 3 68
Methinks it should be now a huge eclipse Of sun and moon v 2 99
To be called into a huge sphere, and not to be seen to move in't *A. and C.* ii 7 16
Huge. This case of that huge spirit now is cold *Ant. and Cleo.* iv 15 89
And with the ostent of war will look so huge, Amazement shall drive courage from the state *Pericles* i 2 25
I never saw so huge a billow, sir, As toss'd it upon shore iii 2 58
Hugely. Doth it [pride] not flow as hugely as the sea? *As Y. Like It* ii 7 72
Hugeness. My mistress exceeds in goodness the hugeness of your unworthy thinking *Cymbeline* i 4 157
Hugg'd and embraced by the strumpet wind *Mer. of Venice* ii 6 16
When I parted with him, He hugg'd me in his arms *Richard III.* i 4 252
Hugger-mugger. And we have done but greenly, In hugger-mugger to inter him *Hamlet* iv 5 84
Hugh. Sir Hugh, persuade me not; I will make a Star-chamber matter of it *Mer. Wives* i 1 1
There is, as 'twere, a tender, a kind of tender, made afar off by Sir Hugh here i 1 216
Hear the truth of it: he came of an errand to me from Parson Hugh i 4 81
Sir Hugh send-a you? Rugby, baille me some paper. Tarry you i 4 92
You jack'nape, give-a this letter to Sir Hugh; by gar, it is a shallenge i 4 114
There is a fray to be fought between Sir Hugh the Welsh priest and Caius the French doctor ii 1 209
I will rather trust a Fleming with my butter, Parson Hugh the Welshman with my cheese ii 2 317
'Tis past the hour, sir, that Sir Hugh promised to meet ii 3 4
Sir Hugh hath shown himself a wise and patient churchman ii 3 56
Sir Hugh is there, is he?—He is there: see what humour he is in ii 3 79
Yonder he is coming, this way, Sir Hugh.—He's welcome iii 1 27
'Save you, good Sir Hugh!—'Pless you from his mercy sake, all of you! iii 1 41
Shall I lose my parson, my priest, my Sir Hugh? no: he gives me the proverbs and the no-verbs iii 1 106
How now, Sir Hugh! no school to-day?—No; Master Slender is let the boys leave to play iv 1 10
Sir Hugh, my husband says my son profits nothing in the world at his book iv 1 14
Where is Nan now and her troop of fairies, and the Welsh devil Hugh? v 3 13
Serve Got, and leave your desires, and fairies will not pinse you.—Well said, fairy Hugh v 5 138
Hugh Capet also, who usurp'd the crown *Hen. V.* i 2 69
King Pepin's title and Hugh Capet's claim, King Lewis his satisfaction i 2 87
Hugh Mortimer. Sir John and Sir Hugh Mortimer, mine uncles, You are come to Sandal in a happy hour 3 *Hen. VI.* i 2 62
Hugh Otecake. Who think you the most desartless man to be constable?—Hugh Otecake, sir, or George Seacole *Much Ado* iii 3 11
Hugh Rebeck. What say you, Hugh Rebeck?—I say 'silver sound,' because musicians sound for silver *Rom. and Jul.* iv 5 135
Hujus. Nominativo, hig, hag, hog; pray you, mark: genitivo, hujus *Mer. Wives* iv 1 45
Hulk. Harry Monmouth's brawn, the hulk Sir John, Is prisoner 2 *Hen. IV.* i 1 19
You have not seen a hulk better stuffed in the hold ii 4 70
And like as rigour of tempestuous gusts Provokes the mightiest hulk against the tide, So am I driven 1 *Hen. VI.* v 5 6
Light boats sail swift, though greater hulks draw deep *Troi. and Cres.* ii 3 277
Hull. I am to hull here a little longer *T. Night* i 5 217
And there they hull, expecting but the aid Of Buckingham *Richard III.* iv 4 438
Hulling. Thus hulling in The wild sea of my conscience *Hen. VIII.* ii 4 199
Hum. Sometimes a thousand twangling instruments Will hum about mine ears, and sometime voices *Tempest* iii 2 147
Hum! ha! is this a vision? is this a dream? do I sleep? *Mer. Wives* iii 5 141
The shrug, the hum or ha, these petty brands That calumny doth use *W. Tale* ii 1 71
These shrugs, these hums and ha's, When you have said 'she's goodly,' come between Ere you can say 'she's honest' ii 1 74
I cried 'hum,' and 'well, go to,' But mark'd him not a word 1 *Hen. IV.* iii 1 158
The sad-eyed justice, with his surly hum, Delivering o'er to executors pale The lazy yawning drone *Hen. V.* i 2 202
The hum of either army stilly sounds iv Prol. 5
Jove bless great Ajax!—Hum!—I come from the worthy Achilles,—Ha! *Troi. and Cres.* iii 3 282
Yet, to bite his lip And hum at good Cominius, much unhearts me *Coriol.* v 1 49
Talks like a knell, and his hum is a battery v 4 22
Lord Lucius and Lucullus? hum! *T. of Athens* ii 2 204
Must he needs trouble me in't,—hum!—'bove all others? iii 3 1
Have they denied him? . . . And does he send to me? Three? hum! iii 3 9
The shard-borne beetle with his drowsy hums *Macbeth* iii 2 42
With an absolute 'Sir, not I,' The cloudy messenger turns me his back, And hums iii 6 42
Hum! I guess at it iv 3 203
Hum! This fellow might be in's time a great buyer of land *Hamlet* v 1 112
Hum—conspiracy!—'Sleep till I waked him' *Lear* i 2 58
Hum! go to thy cold bed, and warm thee iii 4 48
If you say so, I hope you will not kill me.—Hum! *Othello* v 2 36
Hum!—I'll write to my lord she's dead *Cymbeline* iii 5 103
Hail, sir! my lord, lend ear.—Hum, ha! *Pericles* v 1 84
Human. And sorceries terrible To enter human hearing *Tempest* i 2 265
Then was this island . . . not honour'd with A human shape i 2 284
I have used thee, Filth as thou art, with human care i 2 346
Their manners are more gentle-kind than of Our human generation iii 3 33
Your affections Would become tender.—Dost thou think so, spirit?—Mine would, sir, were I human v 1 20
And now he's there, past thought of human reason *Com. of Errors* v 1 189
The human mortals want their winter here *M. N. Dream* ii 1 101
In human modesty, Such separation as may well be said Becomes a virtuous bachelor and a maid, So far be distant ii 2 57
Touching now the point of human skill, Reason becomes the marshal to my will ii 2 119
Touch'd with human gentleness and love *Mer. of Venice* iv 1 25
Thy currish spirit Govern'd a wolf, who, hang'd for human slaughter iv 1 134
To set her before your eyes to-morrow human as she is *As Y. Like It* v 2 74
If powers divine Behold our human actions, as they do *W. Tale* iii 2 30
As monstrous to our human reason As my Antigonus to break his grave v 1 41
All his senses have but human conditions *Hen. V.* iv 1 108
Valiant Talbot above human thought Enacted wonders 1 *Hen. VI.* i 1 121
Kings and mightiest potentates must die, For that's the end of human misery iii 2 137
Such a pother As if that whatsoever god who leads him Were slily crept into his human powers *Coriolanus* ii 1 236
In human action and capacity, Of no more soul nor fitness for the world ii 1 265
What may be sworn by, both divine and human, Seal what I end withal! iii 1 141
Yield him, who all thy human sons doth hate, From forth thy plenteous bosom, one poor root! *T. of Athens* iv 3 185
Though thou abhorr'dst in us our human griefs v 4 75

Human. I fear thy nature; It is too full o' the milk of human kindness *Macbeth* i 5 18
Knows all qualities, with a learned spirit, Of human dealings *Othello* iii 3 260
I will try the forces Of these thy compounds on such creatures as We count not worth the hanging, but none human . . . . *Cymbeline* i 5 20
Humane. Most humane And fill'd with honour *W. Tale* iii 2 166
If I had a thousand sons, the first humane principle I would teach them should be, to forswear thin potations . . . 2 *Hen. IV.* iv 3 133
In humane gentleness, Welcome! . . . *Troi. and Cres.* iv 1 20
It is the humane way: the other course Will prove too bloody *Coriolanus* iii 1 327
I' the olden time, Ere humane statute purged the gentle weal *Macbeth* iii 4 76
Putting on the mere form of civil and humane seeming *Othello* ii 1 243
Humanely. On whom my pains, Humanely taken, all, all lost *Tempest* iv 1 190
We might guess they relieved us humanely . . . . *Coriolanus* i 1 19
Humanity. My substance is not here; For what you see is but the smallest part And least proportion of humanity . 1 *Hen. VI.* ii 3 53
What nearer debt in all humanity Than wife is to the husband? *Troi. and Cres.* ii 2 175
He's opposite to humanity . . . . *T. of Athens* i 1 284
Henceforth hated be Of Timon man and all humanity! . . iii 6 115
The middle of humanity thou never knewest, but the extremity of both ends . . . . iv 3 300
They imitated humanity so abominably . . *Hamlet* iii 2 39
Humanity must perforce prey on itself, Like monsters of the deep *Lear* iv 2 49
I would change my humanity with a baboon . . . . *Othello* i 3 317
A rarer spirit never Did steer humanity . . *Ant. and Cleo.* v 1 32
How look I, That I should seem to lack humanity So much as this? *Cymb.* iii 2 16
Humble. My affections Are then most humble; I have no ambition To see a goodlier man . . . . *Tempest* i 2 482
My mistress, dearest; And I thus humble ever.—My husband, then? . iii 1 87
A sea of melting pearl, which some call tears: Those at her father's churlish feet she tender'd; With them, upon her knees, her humble self . . . . *T. G. of Ver.* iii 1 226
But most willingly humbles himself to the determination of justice *Meas. for Meas.* iii 2 258
That she brought me up, I likewise give her most humble thanks *M. Ado* i 1 242
This is not generous, not gentle, not humble . . *L. L. Lost* v 2 632
Behold . . . mine eye, What humble suit attends thy answer there . v 2 849
Wherein your lady and your humble wife May show her duty *T. of S.* Ind. 1 116
That made great Jove to humble him to her hand . . . . i 1 174
Yet if thy thoughts, Bianca, be so humble To cast thy wandering eyes on every stale, Seize thee that list . . . . . iii 1 89
His humble ambition, proud humility, His jarring concord *All's Well* i 1 185
I am from humble, he from honour'd name; No note upon my parents i 3 162
My low and humble name to propagate With any branch or image of thy state . . . . ii 1 200
Love make your fortunes twenty times above Her that so wishes and her humble love! . . . . ii 3 89
Some that humble themselves may; but the many will be too chill and tender . . . . iv 5 55
Cast thy humble slough and appear fresh . *T. Night* ii 5 161; iii 4 76
My duty, madam, and most humble service . . . . iii 1 106
The fire-robed god, Golden Apollo, a poor humble swain *W. Tale* iv 4 30
To dive into their hearts With humble and familiar courtesy *Richard II.* i 4 26
Show me thy humble heart, and not thy knee . . . . ii 3 83
My humble duty remembered, I will not be your suitor . 2 *Hen. IV.* ii 1 137
These humble considerations make me out of love with my greatness . ii 2 14
I will stoop and humble my intents To your well-practised wise directions v 2 120
Our humble author will continue the story . . . Epil. 28
Who prologue-like your humble patience pray . . *Hen. V.* Prol. 33
Thy humble servant vows obedience And humble service 1 *Hen. VI.* iii 1 167
Stay, let thy humble handmaid speak to thee . . . . iii 3 42
Open your city gates; Be humble to us; call my sovereign yours . iv 2 6
With as humble lowliness of mind She is content to be at your command v 5 18
I cannot go before, While Gloucester bears this base and humble mind 2 *Hen. VI.* i 2 62
Far be it we should honour such as these With humble suit . . iv 1 124
No bending knee will call thee Cæsar now, No humble suitors press to speak for right . . . . 3 *Hen. VI.* iii 1 19
I see the lady hath a thing to grant, Before the king will grant her humble suit . . . . iii 2 13
My love till death, my humble thanks, my prayers . . . iii 2 62
And to my humble seat conform myself . . . . . iii 3 11
Let me give humble thanks for all at once . . . . iii 3 221
But if an humble prayer may prevail, I then crave pardon . . iv 6 7
Heard ye not what an humble suppliant Lord Hastings was to her? *Richard III.* i 1 74
In that sad time My manly eyes did scorn an humble tear . . . i 2 165
Thy voice is thunder, but thy looks are humble . . . . i 4 173
Whose humble means match not his haughty mind . . . . iv 2 37
'Tis better to be lowly born, And range with humble livers . *Hen. VIII.* ii 3 20
Heaven witness, I have been to you a true and humble wife . . ii 4 23
Be patient yet.—I will, when you are humble; nay, before . . ii 4 74
This cardinal, Though from an humble stock, undoubtedly Was fashion'd to much honour from his cradle . . . . iv 2 49
How may I deserve it, That am a poor and humble subject to you? v 3 166
And, being born, his addition shall be humble *Troi. and Cres.* iii 2 102
With a proud heart he wore his humble weeds . *Coriolanus* ii 3 161
Forget not With what contempt he wore the humble weed . . ii 3 229
Humble as the ripest mulberry That will not hold the handling . iii 2 79
For thou hast made it like an humble suppliant . . *T. Andron.* iv 3 117
I am an humble suitor to your virtues . . . *T. of Athens* i 5 7
So did we woo . . . By humble message and by promised means . . v 4 20
To o'er-read, At your best leisure, this his humble suit . *J. Cæsar* iii 1 5
Metellus Cimber throws before thy seat An humble heart . . . iii 1 35
Ourself will mingle with society, And play the humble host . *Macbeth* iii 4 4
At your age The hey-day in the blood is tame, it's humble . *Hamlet* iii 4 69
Even so my bloody thoughts, with violent pace, Shall ne'er look back, ne'er ebb to humble love . . . . *Othello* iii 3 458
Now I must To the young man send humble treaties *Ant. and Cleo.* iii 11 62
Take my power i' the court for yours.—My humble thanks *Cymbeline* i 6 180
Humble-bee. The fox, the ape and the humble-bee . . *L. L. Lost* iii 1 96
The honey-bags steal from the humble-bees . . . *M. N. Dream* iii 1 171
Kill me a red-hipped humble-bee on the top of a thistle . . iv 1 12
That red-tailed humble-bee I speak of . . . . *All's Well* iv 5 7
Full merrily the humble-bee doth sing, Till he hath lost his honey and his sting . . . . *Troi. and Cres.* v 10 42
Humbled. And presently all humbled kiss the rod . . *T. G. of Ver.* i 2 59
Love's a mighty lord And hath so humbled me as I confess There is no woe to his correction . . . . ii 4 137
Humbled. The common executioner . . . Falls not the axe upon the humbled neck But first begs pardon . . . . *As Y. Like It* iii 5 5
Making them proud of his humility, In their poor praise he humbled *All's Well* i 2 45
Her to whom my thoughts are humbled all . . . . *T. Andron.* i 1 51
The tribute that I owe, Mine honour's ensigns humbled at thy feet . i 1 252
All humbled on your knees, You shall ask pardon of his majesty . i 1 472
Thou whom the heavens' plagues Have humbled to all strokes . *Lear* iv 1 68
So humbled That he hath left part of his grief with me . *Othello* iii 3 52
Humble-mouthed. You're meek and humble-mouth'd . . *Hen. VIII.* ii 4 107
Humbleness. With bated breath and whispering humbleness *Mer. of Venice* i 3 125
Which humbleness may drive unto a fine . . . . . . iv 1 372
All humbleness, all patience and impatience, All purity *As Y. Like It* v 2 103
I come to tender it . . . With all bound humbleness . *All's Well* ii 1 117
Who return'd her thanks In the great'st humbleness . . *Hen. VIII.* v 1 65
As suitors should, Plead your deserts in peace and humbleness *T. Andron.* i 1 45
With all the humbleness I may, I greet your honours . . . iv 2 4
Humbler. His eyes are humbler than they used to be . . *Hen. V.* iv 7 70
His lordship should be humbler; It fitteth not a prelate so to plead 1 *Hen. VI.* iii 1 56
Now we have shown our power, Let us seem humbler . *Coriolanus* iv 2 4
Humblest. If opportunity and humblest suit Cannot attain it *Mer. Wives* iii 4 20
In humblest manner I require your highness . . . to declare *Hen. VIII.* ii 4 144
Humble-visaged. We attend, Like humble-visaged suitors *L. L. Lost* ii 1 34
Humbling. The gods themselves, Humbling their deities to love, have taken The shapes of beasts upon them . . . . *W. Tale* iv 4 26
Humbly. I humbly give you leave to depart . . . *Much Ado* v 1 334
I humbly do desire your grace of pardon . . . *Mer. of Venice* iv 1 402
Sir, to your pleasure humbly I subscribe . . . *T. of Shrew* i 1 81
Humbly entreating from your royal thoughts A modest one . *All's Well* ii 1 130
Whose dear perfection hearts that scorn'd to serve Humbly call'd mistress v 3 19
Harry Bolingbroke doth humbly kiss thy hand . . *Richard II.* iii 3 104
I most humbly beseech your lordship to have a reverent care 2 *Hen. IV.* i 2 112
Most humbly on my knee I beg The leading of the vaward . *Hen. V.* iv 3 129
I humbly pray them to admit the excuse Of time . . . . v Prol. 3
They humbly sue unto your excellence To have a goodly peace 1 *Hen. VI.* v 1 4
And humbly now upon my bended knee, In sight of England 2 *Hen. VI.* i 1 10
I humbly thank your royal majesty . . . . . . i 3 215
And humbly thus, with halters on their necks, Expect your highness' doom . . . . iv 9 11
Fear it not: And thus most humbly I do take my leave . 3 *Hen. VI.* i 2 61
And what God will, that let your king perform; And what he will, I humbly yield unto . . . . iii 1 101
I am commanded, with your leave and favour, Humbly to kiss your hand iii 3 61
Speak gentle words and humbly bend thy knee . . . . . v 1 22
Humbly complaining to her deity Got my lord chamberlain his liberty *Richard III.* i 1 76
And humbly beg the death upon my knee . . . . . . i 2 179
Humbly on my knee I crave your blessing.—God bless thee! . . ii 2 105
For one being sued to, one that humbly sues . . . . . iv 4 101
The king has cured me, I humbly thank his grace . *Hen. VIII.* iii 2 381
I humbly do entreat your highness' pardon; My haste made me unmannerly . . . . iv 2 104
I most humbly pray you to deliver This to my lord the king . . iv 2 129
To come as humbly as they used to creep To holy altars *Troi. and Cres.* iii 3 73
I humbly desire the valiant Ajax to invite the most valorous Hector iii 3 274; 285
When I do weep, they humbly at my feet Receive my tears *T. Andron.* iii 1 41
I humbly thank him, and I thank you all . . . . . v 1 18
Uttered With gentle breath, calm look, knees humbly bow'd *R. and J.* iii 1 161
Humbly I thank your lordship . . . . . *T. of Athens* i 1 149
And humbly prays you That with your other noble parts you'll suit In giving him his right . . . . ii 2 22
He humbly prays your speedy payment . . . . . . ii 2 28
Most humbly do I take my leave, my lord.—The time invites you; go *Hamlet* i 3 82
Humbly I thank your grace . . . . *Othello* i 3 70
Most humbly therefore bending to your state, I crave fit disposition for my wife, Due reference of place . . . . i 3 236
I humbly do beseech you of your pardon For too much loving you . iii 3 212
I humbly thank your ladyship . . . . . iii 4 168; iv 3 3
Humbly, sir, I thank you . . . . . *Ant. and Cleo.* ii 2 250
I'll humbly signify what in his name . . . we have effected . . iii 1 30
Sir, my life is yours; I humbly set it at your will . *Cymbeline* iv 3 13
Humbly take my leave *Macbeth* i 4; *Hamlet* ii 2; *Cymbeline* i 5
I humbly beseech you *W. Tale* v 2; *Hen. VIII.* ii 4; *Othello* i 3
I humby thank you *Meas. for Meas.* i 4; ii 1; iii 1; *All's Well* iii 5; iv 3; *Hamlet* iii 1; iv 4; v 2; *Othello* iii 1
I humbly thank your highness *Hen. VIII.* v 1; *Cymbeline* i 1; v 5
Hume. By the grace of God, and Hume's advice, Your grace's title shall be multiplied . . . . 2 *Hen. VI.* i 2 72
Here, Hume, take this reward; make merry, man . . . . i 2 85
Hume must make merry with the duchess' gold . . . . i 2 87
But, how now, Sir John Hume! Seal up your lips . . . i 2 88
Hume, if you take not heed, you shall go near To call them both a pair of crafty knaves . . . . i 2 102
And thus, I fear, at last Hume's knavery will be the duchess' wreck . i 2 105
Master Hume, we are therefore provided . . . . . i 4 3
But it shall be convenient, Master Hume, that you be by her aloft . i 4 10
Humidity. This unwholesome humidity, this gross watery pumpion *Mer. Wives* iii 3 43
O blessed breeding sun, draw from the earth Rotten humidity! *T. of A.* iv 3 2
Humility. O, then his lines would ravish savage ears And plant in tyrants mild humility . . . . *L. L. Lost* iv 3 349
If a Jew wrong a Christian, what is his humility? Revenge *M. of Ven.* iii 1 72
His humble ambition, proud humility, His jarring concord . *All's Well* i 1 185
Making them proud of his humility, In their poor praise he humbled . i 2 44
It will wear the surplice of humility over the black gown of a big heart i 3 99
Kiss the rod, And fawn on rage with base humility . *Richard II.* v 1 33
I have sounded the very base-string of humility . . . 1 *Hen. IV.* ii 4 6
I stole all courtesy from heaven, And dress'd myself in such humility . iii 2 51
In peace there's nothing so becomes a man As modest stillness and humility: But when the blast of war blows . . *Hen. V.* iii 1 4
In all submission and humility York doth present himself . 2 *Hen. VI.* v 1 58
I thank my God for my humility . . . . *Richard III.* ii 1 72
Laid open all . . . Your bounty, virtue, fair humility . . . iii 7 17
You sign your place and calling, in full seeming, With meekness and humility; but your heart Is cramm'd with arrogancy *Hen. VIII.* ii 4 109
Remember me In all humility unto his highness . . . . iv 2 161
Nor on him put The napless vesture of humility . . *Coriolanus* ii 1 250
Here he comes, and in the gown of humility: mark his behaviour . ii 3 44

Humming. I heard a humming, And that a strange one too *Tempest* ii 1 317
The belching whale And humming water must o'erwhelm thy corpse *Pericles* iii 1 64
Humorous. A very beadle to a humorous sigh *L. L. Lost* iii 1 177
The duke is humorous; what he is indeed, More suits you to conceive than I to speak of *As Y. Like It* i 2 278
Why would you be so fond to overcome The bonny priser of the humorous duke? ii 3 8
My often rumination wraps me in a most humorous sadness iv 1 19
Thou Fortune's champion that dost never fight But when her humorous ladyship is by To teach thee safety! *K. John* iii 1 119
The devil understands Welsh; And 'tis no marvel he is so humorous *1 Hen. IV.* iii 1 234
Being incensed, he's flint, As humorous as winter *2 Hen. IV.* iv 4 34
A vain, giddy, shallow, humorous youth *Hen. V.* ii 4 28
Underwrite in an observing kind His humorous predominance *Troi. and Cres.* ii 3 138
I am known to be a humorous patrician *Coriolanus* ii 1 51
To be consorted with the humorous night *Rom. and Jul.* ii 1 31
The humorous man shall end his part in peace *Hamlet* ii 2 335
Humour. Slice, I say! pauca, pauca: slice! that's my humour *Mer. Wives* i 1 135
Be advised, sir, and pass good humours i 1 169
I will say 'marry trap' with you, if you run the nuthook's humour on me i 1 171
He was gotten in drink: is not the humour conceited? i 3 26
The good humour is to steal at a minute's rest.—'Convey,' the wise it call i 3 30
The anchor is deep: will that humour pass? i 3 56
The humour rises; it is good: humour me the angels i 3 63
Then did the sun on dunghill shine.—I thank thee for that humour i 3 71
I will run no base humour: here, take the humour-letter i 3 85
Falstaff will learn the humour of the age, French thrift, you rogues i 3 92
I have operations which be humours of revenge.—Wilt thou revenge?—By welkin and her star!—With wit or steel?—With both the humours, I i 3 98
I will discuss the humour of this love to Page i 3 104
My humour shall not cool: I will incense Page to deal with poison i 3 109
I will possess him with yellowness, for the revolt of mine is dangerous: that is my true humour i 3 112
I like not the humour of lying. He hath wronged me in some humours ii 1 133
I love not the humour of bread and cheese, and there's the humour of it ii 1 140
'The humour of it,' quoth a'! here's a fellow frights English out of his wits ii 1 142
See what humour he is in ii 3 80
Pray you, let us not be laughing-stocks to other men's humours iii 1 88
This is fery fantastical humours and jealousies iii 3 181
Let's obey his humour a little further: come, gentlemen iv 2 210
When I am dull with care and melancholy, Lightens my humour *C. of Er.* i 2 21
I am not in a sportive humour now: Tell me, and dally not i 2 58
How now, sir! is your merry humour alter'd? ii 2 7
Saving your merry humour, here's the note iv 1 27
Fie, now you run this humour out of breath, Come, where's the chain? iv 1 57
The fellow finds his vein, And yielding to him humours well his frenzy iv 4 84
I thank God and my cold blood, I am of your humour *Much Ado* i 1 132
Laugh when I am merry and claw no man in his humour i 3 19
I will teach you how to humour your cousin, that she shall fall in love ii 1 396
These paper bullets of the brain awe a man from the career of his humour ii 3 250
What! sigh for the toothache?—Where is but a humour or a worm iii 2 27
I will leave you now to your gossip-like humour v 1 189
A college of wit-crackers cannot flout me out of my humour v 4 102
I did commend the black-oppressing humour to the most wholesome physic of thy health-giving air *L. L. Lost* i 1 235
If drawing my sword against the humour of affection would deliver me i 2 63
They say so most that most his humours know ii 1 53
Humour it with turning up your eyelids, sigh a note and sing a note iii 1 13
These are complements, these are humours; these betray nice wenches iii 1 23
And, to humour the ignorant, call I the deer the princess killed a pricket iv 2 52
His humour is lofty, his discourse peremptory, his tongue filed v 1 10
Fashioning our humours Even to the opposed end of our intents v 2 767
My chief humour is for a tyrant: I could play Ercles rarely *M. N. Dream* i 2 30
Let it be as humours and conceits shall govern *Mer. of Venice* iii 5 68
I'll not answer that: But, say, it is my humour: is it answer'd? iv 1 43
As it is a spare life, look you, it fits my humour well *As Y. Like It* iii 2 20
I drave my suitor from his mad humour of love to a living humour of madness iii 2 439
Now I am in a holiday humour and like enough to consent iv 1 69
A poor humour of mine, sir, to take that that no man else will v 4 61
Heaven cease this idle humour in your honour! *T. of Shrew* Ind. 2 14
Let him go while the humour lasts i 2 108
Would vex a very saint, Much more a shrew of thy impatient humour iii 2 29
An old hat and 'the humour of forty fancies' pricked in't for a feather iii 2 70
'Tis some odd humour pricks him to this fashion iii 2 74
He kills her in her own humour iv 1 183
And thus I'll curb her mad and headstrong humour iv 1 212
You either fear his humour or my negligence *T. Night* i 4 5
And then to have the humour of state ii 5 58
The spirit of humours intimate reading aloud to him! ii 5 93
Purge him of that humour That presses him from sleep *W. Tale* ii 3 38
And all the unsettled humours of the land *K. John* ii 1 66
It is the curse of kings to be attended By slaves that take their humours for a warrant iv 2 209
To understand a law, to know the meaning Of dangerous majesty, when perchance it frowns More upon humour than advised respect iv 2 214
This inundation of mistemper'd humour Rests by you only to be qualified v 1 12
In humours like the people of this world *Richard II.* v 5 10
In some sort it jumps with my humour *1 Hen. IV.* i 2 78
And will awhile uphold The unyoked humour of your idleness i 2 220
I am now of all humours that have showed themselves humours since the old days of goodman Adam ii 4 105
Why dost thou converse with that trunk of humours? ii 4 495
Curbs himself even of his natural scope When you come 'cross his humour iii 1 172
You are altogether governed by humours iii 1 237
An 'twere not for thy humours, there's not a better wench in England *2 Hen. IV.* ii 1 161
Come, thou must not be in this humour with me ii 1 163
In military rules, humours of blood, He was the mark and glass ii 3 30
These be good humours, indeed! ii 4 177
What humour's the prince of?—A good shallow young fellow ii 4 256
Humour. If I had a suit to Master Shallow, I would humour his men with the imputation of being near their master *2 Hen. IV.* v 1 80
I have an humour to knock you indifferently well *Hen. V.* ii 1 58
I will cut thy throat, one time or other . . .: that is the humour of it ii 1 74
That now I will have: that's the humour of it ii 1 101
I shall have my noble?—In cash most justly paid.—Well, then, that's the humour of't ii 1 121
The king hath run bad humours on the knight; that's the even of it ii 1 127
It must be as it may; he passes some humours and careers ii 1 132
I cannot kiss, that is the humour of it ii 3 63
The humour of it is too hot, that is the very plain-song of it.—The plain-song is most just; for humours do abound: Knocks go and come iii 2 5
These be good humours! your honour wins bad humours iii 2 27
Whose church-like humours fits not for a crown *2 Hen. VI.* i 1 247
They, knowing Dame Eleanor's aspiring humour i 2 97
A bedlam and ambitious humour Makes him oppose himself against his king v 1 132
Was ever woman in this humour woo'd? Was ever woman in this humour won? I'll have her *Richard III.* i 2 228
I hope my holy humour will change; 'twas wont to hold me but while one would tell twenty i 4 121
Poor soul, I envy not thy glory; To feed my humour, wish thyself no harm iv 1 65
How canst thou woo her?—That would I learn of you, As one that are best acquainted with her humour iv 4 269
A man into whom nature hath so crowded humours *Troi. and Cres.* i 2 23
I'll let his humours blood ii 3 222
Attend him carefully, And feed his humour kindly as we may *T. Andron.* iv 3 29
A goodly humour, is it not, my lords? iv 4 19
Yield to his humour, smooth and speak him fair v 2 140
Pursued my humour not pursuing his *Rom. and Jul.* i 1 135
Black and portentous must this humour prove, Unless good counsel may the cause remove i 1 147
Nay, I'll conjure too. Romeo! humours! madman! passion! lover! ii 1 7
Presently through all thy veins shall run A cold and drowsy humour iv 1 96
Ye've got a humour there Does not become a man *T. of Athens* i 2 26
There is no crossing him in's humour; Else I should tell him i 2 166
He's but a mad lord, and nought but humour sways him iii 6 122
But he loves Brutus: If I were Brutus now and he were Cassius, He should not humour me *J. Cæsar* i 2 319
Let me work; For I can give his humour the true bent ii 1 210
And withal Hoping it was but an effect of humour, Which sometime hath his hour with every man ii 1 250
Is Brutus sick? and is it physical To walk unbraced and suck up the humours Of the dank morning? ii 1 262
For thy humour, I will stay at home ii 2 56
Must I stand and crouch Under your testy humour? iv 3 46
Be angry when you will, it shall have scope; Do what you will, dishonour shall be humour iv 3 109
That rash humour which my mother gave me Makes me forgetful iv 3 120
I'll know his humour, when he knows his time iv 3 136
I think the sun where he was born Drew all such humours from him *Oth.* iii 4 31
Nor should I know him, Were he in favour as in humour alter'd iii 4 125
I pray you, be content; 'tis but his humour iv 2 165
And which she after, Except she bend her humour, shall be assured To taste of too *Cymbeline* i 5 81
His humour Was nothing but mutation iv 2 132
Humoured. I should have borne the humoured letter to her *Mer. Wives* ii 1 134
And humour'd thus Comes at the last *Richard II.* iii 2 168
Humour-letter. Here, take the humour-letter *Mer. Wives* i 3 86
Humphrey, my son of Gloucester, Where is the prince your brother?—I think he's gone to hunt *2 Hen. IV.* iv 4 12
How now, ambitious Humphrey! what means this? *1 Hen. VI.* i 3 29
Comest thou with deep premeditated lines, With written pamphlets studiously devised, Humphrey of Gloucester? iii 1 3
Humphrey of Gloucester, thou shalt well perceive That, neither in birth or for authority, The bishop will be overborne by thee v 1 58
To you Duke Humphrey must unload his grief *2 Hen. VI.* i 1 76
What though the common people favour him, Calling him 'Humphrey, the good Duke of Gloucester' i 1 159
God preserve the good Duke Humphrey! i 1 162
We'll quickly hoise Duke Humphrey from his seat i 1 169
Though Humphrey's pride And greatness of his place be grief to us i 1 172
Thou or I, Somerset, will be protector, Despite Duke Humphrey i 1 179
I never saw but Humphrey Duke of Gloucester Did bear him like a noble gentleman i 1 183
Hath won the greatest favour of the commons, Excepting none but good Duke Humphrey i 1 193
Cherish Duke Humphrey's deeds, While they do tend the profit of the land i 1 203
I will take the Nevils' parts And make a show of love to proud Duke Humphrey i 1 241
And Humphrey with the peers be fall'n at jars i 1 253
Why doth the great Duke Humphrey knit his brows? i 2 3
But list to me, my Humphrey, my sweet duke i 2 35
I fear, at last Hume's knavery will be the duchess' wreck, And her attainture will be Humphrey's fall i 2 106
More like an empress than Duke Humphrey's wife i 3 81
Yet must we join with him and with the lords, Till we have brought Duke Humphrey in disgrace i 3 99
I will follow Eleanor, And listen after Humphrey, how he proceeds i 3 152
This is the law, and this Duke Humphrey's doom i 3 214
Duke Humphrey has done a miracle to-day.—True; made the lame to leap ii 1 161
That virtuous prince, the good Duke Humphrey: 'Tis that they seek ii 2 74
Ah, Humphrey, this dishonour in thine age Will bring thy head with sorrow to the ground! ii 3 18
Stay, Humphrey Duke of Gloucester: ere thou go, Give up thy staff ii 3 22
And go in peace, Humphrey, no less beloved Than when thou wert protector ii 3 26
Humphrey Duke of Gloucester scarce himself, That bears so shrewd a maim ii 3 40
Ah, Humphrey, can I bear this shameful yoke? ii 4 37
Sometime I'll say, I am Duke Humphrey's wife, And he a prince ii 4 42
And shall I then be used reproachfully?—Like to a duchess, and Duke Humphrey's lady ii 4 98
And Humphrey is no little man in England iii 1 20
These are petty faults to faults unknown, Which time will bring to light in smooth Duke Humphrey iii 1 65
Ah, uncle Humphrey! in thy face I see The map of honour iii 1 202

Humphrey. And yet, good Humphrey, is the hour to come That e'er I proved thee false . . . . . *2 Hen. VI.* iii 1 204
Were't not all one, an empty eagle were set To guard the chicken from a hungry kite, As place Duke Humphrey for the king's protector? iii 1 250
He is a fox, By nature proved an enemy to the flock, . . . As Humphrey, proved by reasons, to my liege . . . . . iii 1 260
But now return we to the false Duke Humphrey.—No more of him . iii 1 322
Humphrey being dead, as he shall be, And Henry put apart, the next for me . . . . iii 1 382
Good Duke Humphrey traitorously is murder'd By Suffolk . iii 2 123
Some violent hands were laid on Humphrey's life . . iii 2 138
And we, I hope, sir, are no murderers.—But both of you were vow'd Duke Humphrey's foes . . . . iii 2 182
Then you, belike, suspect these noblemen As guilty of Duke Humphrey's timeless death . . . . iii 2 187
Say, if thou darest, proud Lord of Warwickshire, That I am faulty in Duke Humphrey's death . . . . iii 2 202
I'll cope with thee And do some service to Duke Humphrey's ghost . iii 2 231
They say, by him the good Duke Humphrey died . . iii 2 248
Sometime he talks as if Duke Humphrey's ghost Were by his side . iii 2 373
And thou that smiledst at good Duke Humphrey's death Against the senseless winds shalt grin in vain . . . . . . iv 1 76
Humphrey of Buckingham, I accept thy greeting . . . . v 1 15
Humphrey Stafford. Sir Humphrey Stafford and his brother are hard by iv 2 120
Sir Humphrey Stafford and his brother's death Hath given them heart iv 4 34
Hundred. To think upon her woes I do protest That I have wept a hundred several times . . . . . *T. G. of Ver.* iv 4 150
Your wife is as honest a 'omans as I will desires among five thousand, and five hundred too . . . . *Mer. Wives* iii 3 237
A word with you.—A hundred, if they'll do you any good *Meas. for Meas.* i 2 147
Five hundred ducats, villain, for a rope?—I'll serve you, sir, five hundred at the rate . . . *Com. of Errors* iv 4 13
If sore be sore, then L to sore makes fifty sores one sorel. Of one sore I an hundred make by adding but one more L . *L. L. Lost* iv 2 63
A hundred then.—Content.—A match! 'tis done . *T. of Shrew* v 2 74
There's a simple putting off. More, more, a hundred of them *All's Well* ii 2 44
Fifteen hundred shorn, what comes the wool to? . *W. Tale* iv 3 35
Whom I found With many hundreds treading on his heels . *K. John* iv 2 149
A hundred upon poor four of us.—What, a hundred, man? . *1 Hen. IV.* ii 4 181
We shall buy maidenheads as they buy hob-nails, by the hundreds ii 4 399
Fifteen hundred foot, five hundred horse, Are march'd up . *2 Hen. IV.* ii 1 186
I beseech you, good Sir John, let me have five hundred of my thousand v 5 89
Who died within the year of our redemption Four hundred twenty-six *Hen. V.* i 2 61
Did seat the French Beyond the river Sala, in the year Eight hundred five i 2 64
Of other lords and barons, knights and squires, Full fifteen hundred . iv 8 84
And nobles bearing banners, there lie dead One hundred twenty six iv 8 88
Of knights, esquires, and gallant gentlemen, Eight thousand and four hundred; of the which, Five hundred were but yesterday dubb'd knights . . . . iv 8 90
Hundreds he sent to hell, and none durst stand him . *1 Hen. VI.* i 1 123
And thou shalt have a license to kill for a hundred lacking one *2 Hen. VI.* iv 3 9
With five thousand men?—Ay, with five hundred, father, for a need *3 Hen. VI.* i 2 68
A hundred ghastly women, Transformed with their fear . *J. Cæsar* i 3 23
Stay'd it long?—While one with moderate haste might tell a hundred *Hamlet* i 2 238
You, sir, I entertain for one of my hundred . . . . *Lear* iii 6 83
Hundreds call themselves Your creatures, who by you have been restored *Pericles* iii 2 44
Hundred almshouses. A hundred almshouses right well supplied *Hen. V.* i 1 17
Hundred and fifty. He will make you a hundred and fifty pounds jointure *Mer. Wives* iii 4 49
I will kill thee a hundred and fifty ways: therefore tremble *As Y. Like It* v 1 62
I have got, in exchange of a hundred and fifty soldiers, three hundred and odd pounds . . . . . . *1 Hen. IV.* iv 2 14
You would think that I had a hundred and fifty tattered prodigals . iv 2 37
There's not three of my hundred and fifty left alive . . v 3 38
Hundred and seven. My letters say a hundred and seven galleys.—And mine, a hundred and forty.—And mine, two hundred . *Othello* i 3 3
Hundred bastards. Ere he would have hanged a man for the getting a hundred bastards, he would have paid for the nursing a thousand *Meas. for Meas.* iii 2 125
Hundred blows. I have bought it with an hundred blows . *3 Hen. VI.* ii 5 81
Hundred compasses. A sibyl, that had number'd in the world The sun to course two hundred compasses . . . . *Othello* iii 4 71
Hundred crowns. I have five hundred crowns, The thrifty hire I saved under your father . . . . . *As Y. Like It* ii 3 38
Your duty, fair Bianca, Hath cost me an hundred crowns *T. of Shrew* v 2 128
For his ransom he will give you two hundred crowns . . *Hen. V.* iv 4 49
Hundred ducats. Five hundred ducats, villain, for a rope? *Com. of Errors* iv 4 13
What is the sum he owes?—Two hundred ducats . . . iv 4 137
And those that would make mows at him while my father lived, give twenty, forty, fifty, an hundred ducats a-piece for his picture in little *Hamlet* ii 2 383
Hundred Englishmen. Let me see, by ten We shall have each a hundred Englishmen . . . . *Hen. V.* iii 7 169
Hundred knights. Full fifteen earls and fifteen hundred knights . . i 1 13
With reservation of an hundred knights, By you to be sustain'd . *Lear* i 1 135
This man hath had good counsel:—a hundred knights! 'Tis politic and safe to let him keep At point a hundred knights . . . i 4 345
What he hath utter'd I have writ my sister: If she sustain him and his hundred knights, When I have show'd the unfitness . . i 4 355
I can stay with Regan, I and my hundred knights . . . ii 4 234
Hundred marks. Thy substance, valued at the highest rate, Cannot amount unto a hundred marks . . . *Com. of Errors* i 1 25
A hundred marks, my Kate does put her down . . *T. of Shrew* v 2 35
There's a franklin in the wild of Kent hath brought three hundred marks with him in gold . . . . . *1 Hen. IV.* ii 1 61
There are two gentlemen Have in this robbery lost three hundred marks ii 4 569
A hundred mark is a long one for a poor lone woman to bear *2 Hen. IV.* ii 1 34
Give her an hundred marks. I'll to the queen.—An hundred marks! By this light, I'll ha' more . . . . . *Hen. VIII.* v 1 170
Hundred men. There stands the castle, by yon tuft of trees, Mann'd with three hundred men . . . . *Richard II.* ii 3 54
In which assault we lost twelve hundred men . . . *1 Hen. VI.* iv 1 24
Hundred mercenaries. There are but sixteen hundred mercenaries *Hen. V.* iv 8 93
Hundred merry tales. I had my good wit out of the 'Hundred Merry Tales' . . . . *Much Ado* ii 1 135
Hundred milch-kine. I have a hundred milch-kine to the pail *T. of Shrew* ii 1 359
Hundred mischiefs. The name of Henry the Fifth hales them to an hundred mischiefs . . . . . . *2 Hen. VI.* iv 8 59
Hundred paces. The English lie within fifteen hundred paces of your tents . . . . *Hen. V.* iii 7 136
Hundred poor. Five hundred poor I have in yearly pay . . iv 1 315
Hundred pound. Seven hundred pounds of moneys, and gold and silver, is her grandsire upon his death's-bed . . give . *Mer. Wives* i 1 51
Did her grandsire leave her seven hundred pound? . . . i 1 59
Seven hundred pounds and possibilities is goot gifts . . . i 1 65
O, what a world of vile ill-favour'd faults Looks handsome in three hundred pounds a year! . . . . iii 4 33
I'll give thee A hundred pound in gold more than your loss . . iv 6 5
What if a man bring him a hundred pound or two, to make merry withal?—Keep your hundred pounds to yourself: he shall need none, so long as I live . . . . . . *T. of Shrew* v 1 22
A' pops me out At least from fair five hundred pound a year . *K. John* i 1 69
A half-faced groat five hundred pound a year! . . . . . i 1 94
Your face hath got five hundred pound a year, Yet sell your face for five pence and 'tis dear . . . . i 1 152
Hundred-pound, filthy, worsted-stocking knave . . . *Lear* ii 2 17
Hundred senators. Octavius, Antony, and Lepidus, Have put to death an hundred senators . . . . . . *J. Cæsar* iv 3 175
Hundred shivers. There it is, crack'd in a hundred shivers *Richard II.* iv 1 289
Hundred spouts. She saw my statua, Which, like a fountain with an hundred spouts, Did run pure blood . . . *J. Cæsar* ii 2 77
Hundred springs. Within this mile break forth a hundred springs; The oaks bear mast . . . . *T. of Athens* iv 3 421
Hundred thousand. Your father here doth intimate The payment of a hundred thousand crowns . . . . . *L. L. Lost* ii 1 130
Yet there remains unpaid A hundred thousand more . . . ii 1 135
For here he doth demand to have repaid A hundred thousand crowns . ii 1 144
And loosed his love-shaft smartly from his bow, As it should pierce a hundred thousand hearts . . . . . *M. N. Dream* ii 1 160
That very time, I heard you say that you had rather refuse The offer of an hundred thousand crowns . . . . . *Richard II.* iv 1 16
And I will die a hundred thousand deaths Ere break the smallest parcel of this vow . . . . *1 Hen. IV.* iii 2 158
Ye're welcome all.—A hundred thousand welcomes . . *Coriolanus* ii 1 200
With twenty hundred thousand times more joy . . *Rom. and Jul.* iii 3 153
I have full cause of weeping; but this heart Shall break into a hundred thousand flaws, Or ere I'll weep . . . . . . *Lear* ii 4 288
Hundred times. Being call'd A hundred times and oftener, in my sleep, By good Saint Alban . . . . . . *2 Hen. VI.* ii 1 90
Loather a hundred times to part than die . . . . . iii 2 355
Where against My grained ash an hundred times hath broke *Coriolanus* iv 5 114
My wayward husband hath a hundred times Woo'd me to steal it *Othello* iii 3 292
Hundred voices. I'll have five hundred voices of that sound.—I twice five hundred . . . . *Coriolanus* ii 3 219
Hundred words. My ears have not yet drunk a hundred words Of that tongue's utterance . . . . . . *Rom. and Jul.* ii 2 58
Hundred years. Ay, that I do; and have done any time these three hundred years . . . . *Mer. Wives* i 1 13
Those blessed feet Which fourteen hundred years ago were nail'd For our advantage on the bitter cross . . . *1 Hen. IV.* i 1 26
I'll buy him of you.—No, I'll nor sell nor give him: lend you him I will For half a hundred years . . . . *Coriolanus* i 4 7
This monument five hundred years hath stood . . *T. Andron.* i 1 350
Where, for these many hundred years, the bones Of all my buried ancestors are pack'd . . . . . . *Rom. and Jul.* iv 3 40
Hundredth Psalm. They do no more adhere and keep place together than the Hundredth Psalm to the tune of 'Green Sleeves' *Mer. Wives* ii 1 63
Hung. I'll have the cudgel hallowed and hung o'er the altar . iv 2 217
Which have, like unscour'd armour, hung by the wall *Meas. for Meas.* i 2 171
Though I be not so in grace as you, So hung upon with love *M. N. Dream* iii 2 233
And their heads are hung With ears that sweep away the morning dew iv 1 125
She hung about my neck; and kiss on kiss She vied so fast *T. of Shrew* ii 1 310
Many likelihoods informed me of this before, which hung so tottering in the balance that I could neither believe nor misdoubt . *All's Well* i 3 129
After our ship did split, When you and those poor number saved with you Hung on our driving boat . . . . . *T. Night* i 2 11
I could have filed keys off that hung in chains . . . *W. Tale* iv 4 624
But rather drowsed and hung their eyelids down . *1 Hen. IV.* iii 2 81
His own life hung upon the staff he threw . . *2 Hen. IV.* iv 1 126
Hung be the heavens with black, yield day to night! . *1 Hen. VI.* i 1 1
No, if I digg'd up thy forefathers' graves And hung their rotten coffins up in chains, It could not slake mine ire . . *3 Hen. VI.* i 3 28
Our bruised arms hung up for monuments . . *Richard III.* i 1 6
Never hung poison on a fouler toad. Out of my sight! . . i 2 148
That, like a jewel, has hung twenty years About his neck *Hen. VIII.* ii 2 32
Even the billows of the sea Hung their heads, and then lay by . iii 1 11
When thou hast hung thy advanced sword i' the air . *Troi. and Cres.* iv 5 188
In his needy shop a tortoise hung, An alligator stuff'd *Rom. and Jul.* v 1 42
Would most resemble sweet instruments hung up in cases *T. of Athens* i 2 103
Let no images Be hung with Cæsar's trophies . . . *J. Cæsar* i 1 74
Their bloody sign of battle is hung out, And something to be done immediately . . . . v 1 14
Here hung those lips that I have kissed I know not how oft . *Hamlet* v 1 207
Hungarian. O base Hungarian wight! wilt thou the spigot wield? *M. W.* i 3 23
Hungary. If the duke with the other dukes come not to composition with the King of Hungary, why then all the dukes fall upon the king . . . . *Meas. for Meas.* i 2 2
Heaven grant us its peace, but not the King of Hungary's! . . i 2 5
Hunger. I shall see thee, ere I die, look pale with love.—With anger, with sickness, or with hunger, my lord, not with love *Much Ado* i 1 252
Oppress'd with two weak evils, age and hunger . *As Y. Like It* ii 7 132
Better 'twere I met the ravin lion when he roar'd With sharp constraint of hunger . . . . *All's Well* iii 2 121
Dost thou so hunger for mine empty chair That thou wilt needs invest thee with my honours Before thy hour be ripe? . *2 Hen. IV.* iv 5 95
Hunger will enforce them to be more eager . . *1 Hen. VI.* i 2 38
Compell'd by hunger And lack of other means . . . *Hen. VIII.* i 2 34
I speak this in hunger for bread, not in thirst for revenge . *Coriolanus* i 1 25
Sigh'd forth proverbs, That hunger broke stone walls, that dogs must eat i 1 210
If thy revenges hunger for that food Which nature loathes *T. of Athens* v 4 32
My more-having would be as a sauce To make me hunger more *Macbeth* iv 3 82
O Spartan dog, More fell than anguish, hunger, or the sea! . *Othello* v 2 362
It gave me present hunger To feed again, though full . *Cymbeline* ii 4 137
Now I think on thee, My hunger's gone; but even before, I was At point to sink for food . . . . iii 6 16
Almost spent with hunger, I am fall'n in this offence . . . iii 6 63

Hunger. Who wanteth food, and will not say he wants it, Or can conceal his hunger till he famish? . . . . . *Pericles* i 4 12
So sharp are hunger's teeth, that man and wife Draw lots who first shall die to lengthen life . . . . i 4 45
Are stored with corn to make your needy bread, And give them life whom hunger starved half dead . . . . i 4 96
Hungerford. He lives; but is took prisoner, And Lord Scales with him and Lord Hungerford . . . . *1 Hen. VI.* i 1 146
For this one speech Lord Hastings well deserves To have the heir of the Lord Hungerford . . . . . . *3 Hen. VI.* iv 1 48
Hungerly. His beard grew thin and hungerly . . . *T. of Shrew* iii 2 177
And I feed Most hungerly on your sight . . . . *T. of Athens* i 1 262
They eat us hungerly, and when they are full, They belch us *Othello* iii 4 105
Hunger-starved. Turn back and fly, like ships before the wind Or lambs pursued by hunger-starved wolves . . . . . *3 Hen. VI.* i 4 5
Hungry. Had I been seized by a hungry lion, I would have been a breakfast to the beast . . . . *T. G. of Ver.* v 4 33
A hungry lean-faced villain, A mere anatomy . . . *Com. of Errors* v 1 237
Now the hungry lion roars, And the wolf behowls the moon *M. N. Dream* v 1 378
Did he leave him there, Food to the suck'd and hungry lioness? *As Y. L. It* iv 3 127
As hungry as the sea, And can digest as much . . . *T. Night* ii 4 103
They [bears] are never curst but when they are hungry . . *W. Tale* iii 3 135
The fat ribs of peace Must by the hungry now be fed upon . . *K. John* iii 3 10
Or cloy the hungry edge of appetite By bare imagination of a feast *Richard II.* i 3 296
The poor souls for whom this hungry war Opens his vasty jaws *Hen. V.* ii 4 104
The other lords, like lions wanting food, Do rush upon us as their hungry prey . . . . *1 Hen. VI.* i 2 28
And, like a hungry lion, did commence Rough deeds of rage . . . iv 7 7
Were't not all one, an empty eagle were set To guard the chicken from a hungry kite? . . . . *2 Hen. VI.* iii 1 249
Now am I so hungry that if I might have a lease of my life for a thousand years I could stay no longer . . . . . . iv 10 5
That face of his the hungry cannibals Would not have touch'd *3 Hen. VI.* i 4 152
I am hungry for revenge, And now I cloy me with beholding it *Rich. III.* iv 4 61
Who does the wolf love?—The lamb.—Ay, to devour him; as the hungry plebeians would the noble Marcius . . . . *Coriolanus* ii 1 10
Then let the pebbles on the hungry beach Fillip the stars . . . v 3 58
By heaven, I will tear thee joint by joint And strew this hungry churchyard with thy limbs . . . . *Rom. and Jul.* v 3 36
That nature, being sick of man's unkindness, Should yet be hungry! Common mother, thou . . . . *T. of Athens* iv 3 177
Yond Cassius has a lean and hungry look; He thinks too much *J. Cæsar* i 2 194
Other women cloy The appetites they feed; but she makes hungry Where most she satisfies . . . . *Ant. and Cleo.* ii 2 242
Who starves the ears she feeds, and makes them hungry, The more she gives them speech . . . . *Pericles* v 1 113
Hungry-starved. Go, go, cheer up thy hungry-starved men *1 Hen. VI.* i 5 16
Hunt. He after honour hunts, I after love . . . . *T. G. of Ver.* i 1 63
Let fame, that all hunt after in their lives, Live register'd upon our brazen tombs And then grace us . . . . *L. L. Lost* i 1 1
The princess comes to hunt here in the park . . . . . . iii 1 165
Her love is not the hare that I do hunt . . . *As Y. Like It* iv 3 18
Look unto them all: To-morrow I intend to hunt again *T. of Shrew* Ind. 1 29
Thou hast hawks will soar Above the morning lark: or wilt thou hunt? . . . . Ind. 2 46
Will you go hunt, my lord?—What, Curio?—The hart . . *T. Night* i 1 16
Hark you now! Would any but these boiled brains of nineteen and two-and-twenty hunt this weather? . . . . . *W. Tale* iii 3 65
Where is the prince your brother?—I think he's gone to hunt *2 Hen. IV.* iv 4 14
For I myself must hunt this deer to death . . . *2 Hen. VI.* v 2 15
For I myself will hunt this wolf to death . . . *3 Hen. VI.* ii 4 13
O momentary grace of mortal men, Which we more hunt for than the grace of God! . . . . *Richard III.* iii 4 99
From forth the kennel of thy womb hath crept A hell-hound that doth hunt us all to death . . . . iv 4 48
Thou shalt hunt a lion, that will fly With his face backward *Tr. and Cr.* iv 1 19
Wilt thou not, beast, abide? Why, then fly on, I'll hunt thee for thy hide . . . . v 6 31
He is a lion That I am proud to hunt . . . . *Coriolanus* i 1 240
Do not cry havoc, where you should but hunt With modest warrant iii 1 275
An it please your majesty To hunt the panther and the hart with me, With horn and hound we'll give your grace bonjour *T. Andron.* i 1 493
The hunt is up, the morn is bright and grey . . . . . ii 2 1
We hunt not, we, with horse nor hound, But hope to pluck a dainty doe to ground . . . . ii 2 25
Echo mocks the hounds, . . . As if a double hunt were heard at once . ii 3 19
Ay, such a place there is, where we did hunt—O, had we never, never hunted there! . . . . iv 1 55
But if you hunt these bear-whelps, then beware: The dam will wake iv 1 96
Lord Lucullus entreats your company to-morrow to hunt with him *T. of Athens* i 2 194
Or else this brain of mine Hunts not the trail of policy so sure As it hath used to do . . . . *Hamlet* ii 2 47
And by the happy hollow of a tree Escaped the hunt . . . *Lear* ii 3 3
I do follow here in the chase, not like a hound that hunts, but one that fills up the cry . . . . *Othello* ii 3 370
Should hold her loathed and his spirits should hunt After new fancies iii 4 62
Boys, we'll go dress our hunt. Fair youth, come in . . *Cymbeline* iii 6 90
It may be heard at court that such as we Cave here, hunt here . iv 2 138
I had no mind To hunt this day. . . . . iv 2 148
We'll hunt no more to-day, nor seek for danger Where there's no profit iv 2 162
Hunt counter. You hunt counter: hence! avaunt! . . *2 Hen. IV.* i 2 102
Hunted. Let them be hunted soundly . . . . . *Tempest* iv 1 263
'Tis well, sir, that you hunted for yourself . . . *T. of Shrew* v 2 55
Ay, such a place there is, where we did hunt—O, had we never, never hunted there! . . . . *T. Andron.* iv 1 56
To Lord Lucullus you: I hunted with his honour to-day *T. of Athens* ii 2 197
When one so great begins to rage, he's hunted Even to falling *A. and C.* iv 1 7
Hunter. Herne the hunter, Sometime a keeper here in Windsor forest *Mer. Wives* iv 4 28
The superstitious idle-headed eld Received and did deliver to our age This tale of Herne the hunter for a truth . . . . . . iv 4 38
Am I a woodman, ha? Speak I like Herne the hunter? . . . . v 5 31
Our dance of custom round about the oak Of Herne the hunter . . v 5 80
Will none but Herne the hunter serve your turn? . . . . . v 5 108
A poor sequester'd stag, That from the hunter's aim had ta'en a hurt *As Y. Like It* ii 1 34
He was furnished like a hunter.—O, ominous! he comes to kill my heart . . . . iii 2 259
Hunter. Full of despite, bloody as the hunter . . . . *T. Night* iii 4 243
By Jove, I'll play the hunter for thy life . . . . *Troi. and Cres.* iv 1 17
Ring a hunter's peal, That all the court may echo . . . *T. Andron.* ii 2 5
I promised your grace a hunter's peal.—And you have rung it lustily . ii 2 13
Here didst thou fall; and here thy hunters stand, Sign'd in thy spoil, and crimson'd in thy lethe . . . . *J. Cæsar* iii 1 205
The valued file Distinguishes the swift, the slow, the subtle, The housekeeper, the hunter . . . . *Macbeth* iii 1 97
But up to the mountains! This is not hunters' language . *Cymbeline* iii 3 74
And to grin like lions Upon the pikes o' the hunters . . . . v 3 39
Hunteth. And when it [study] hath the thing it hunteth most, 'Tis won as towns with fire, so won, so lost . . . . . *L. L. Lost* i 1 146
Hunting. The king he is hunting the deer; I am coursing myself . iv 3 1
And, for the morning now is something worn, Our purposed hunting shall be set aside . . . . *M. N. Dream* iv 1 188
The story of the Prodigal, or the German hunting in water-work *2 Hen. IV.* ii 1 157
The man that once did sell the lion's skin While the beast lived, was kill'd with hunting him . . . . *Hen. V.* iv 3 94
And, often but attended with weak guard, Comes hunting this way *3 Hen. VI.* iv 5 8
For hunting was his daily exercise . . . . iv 6 85
My lords, a solemn hunting is in hand; There will the lovely Roman ladies troop . . . . *T. Andron.* ii 1 112
Now shall ye see Our Roman hunting . . . . ii 2 20
Or is it Dian, habited like her, Who hath abandoned her holy groves To see the general hunting in this forest? . . . . . . ii 3 59
Hunting thee hence with hunt's-up to the day. . . *Rom. and Jul.* iii 5 34
I must be round with him, now he comes from hunting . *T. of Athens* ii 2 8
When he returns from hunting, I will not speak with him . . *Lear* i 3 7
This poor trash of Venice, whom I trash For his quick hunting *Othello* ii 1 313
Remain here in the cave; We'll come to you after hunting . *Cymbeline* iv 2 2
I am very sick.—Go you to hunting; I'll abide with him . . . iv 2 6
Huntingdon. Warwick and Huntingdon, go with the king *Hen. V.* v 2 85
Huntress. Survey With thy chaste eye, from thy pale sphere above, Thy huntress' name . . . . *As Y. Like It* iii 2 4
Huntsman. Go, bid the huntsmen wake them with their horns *M. N. D.* iv 1 143
Huntsman, I charge thee, tender well my hounds . . *T. of Shrew* Ind. 1 16
Like a jolly troop of huntsmen, come Our lusty English . *K. John* ii 1 321
This way, my lord; for this way lies the game.—Nay, this way, man: see where the huntsmen stand . . . . . . *3 Hen. VI.* iv 5 15
Huntsman, what say'st thou? wilt thou go along? . . . . . iv 5 25
He was convey'd by Richard Duke of Gloucester And the Lord Hastings, who attended him In secret ambush on the forest side And from the bishop's huntsmen rescued him . . . . iv 6 84
So looks the chafed lion Upon the daring huntsman that has gall'd him; Then makes him nothing . . . . *Hen. VIII.* iii 2 207
An if we miss to meet him handsomely—Sweet huntsman, Bassianus 'tis we mean—Do thou so much as dig the grave for him *T. Andron.* ii 3 269
Find the huntsman out That should have murder'd Bassianus here . ii 3 278
You are a young huntsman, Marcus; let it alone . . . . . iv 1 101
Hunt's-up. Arm from arm that voice doth us affray, Hunting thee hence with hunt's-up to the day . . . . *Rom. and Jul.* iii 5 34
Hurdle. Go with Paris to Saint Peter's Church, Or I will drag thee on a hurdle thither . . . . iii 5 156
Hurl. Spurn at me And hurl the name of husband in my face? *Com. of Er.* ii 2 137
And interchangeably hurl down my gage . . . . . *Richard II.* i 1 146
And with my nails digg'd stones out of the ground, To hurl at the beholders of my shame . . . . *1 Hen. VI.* i 4 46
O, let them keep it till thy sins be ripe, And then hurl down their indignation On thee! . . . . *Richard III.* i 3 220
He holds vengeance in his hands, To hurl upon their heads that break his law.—And that same vengeance doth he hurl on thee . . . i 4 205
Defiance, traitors, hurl we in your teeth . . . . . *J. Cæsar* v 1 64
When we shall meet at compt, This look of thine will hurl my soul from heaven, And fiends will snatch at it . . . . . . *Othello* v 2 274
What our contempt doth often hurl from us, We wish it ours again *Ant. and Cleo.* i 2 127
Hurl'd up their caps, And some ten voices cried . . . *Richard III.* iii 7 35
One heaved a-high, to be hurl'd down below . . . . iv 4 86
Hurling. I can hardly forbear hurling things at him . . *T. Night* iii 2 87
Hurly. Ay, and amid this hurly I intend That all is done in reverend care of her . . . . *T. of Shrew* iv 1 206
Methinks I see this hurly all on foot. . . . . . . *K. John* iii 4 169
That, with the hurly, death itself awakes . . . *2 Hen. IV.* iii 1 25
Hurlyburly. Poor discontents, Which gape and rub the elbow at the news Of hurlyburly innovation . . . . *1 Hen. IV.* v 1 78
When the hurlyburly's done, When the battle's lost and won *Macbeth* i 1 3
Hurricano. Not the dreadful spout Which shipmen do the hurricano call, Constringed in mass by the almighty sun . . *Troi. and Cres.* v 2 172
Cataracts and hurricanoes, spout Till you have drench'd our steeples! *Lear* iii 2 2
Hurried thence Me and thy crying self.—Alack, for pity! . . *Tempest* i 2 131
In few, they hurried us aboard a bark, Bore us some leagues to sea . i 2 144
Desperately he hurried through the street . . . *Com. of Errors* v 1 140
Hurried Here to this place, i' the open air, before I have got strength of limit . . . . *W. Tale* iii 2 105
Ne'er through an arch so hurried the blown tide . . . *Coriolanus* v 4 50
Hurry. Wild amazement hurries up and down . . . . . *K. John* v 1 35
Like a school broke up, Each hurries toward his home . *2 Hen. IV.* iv 2 105
Lives, honours, lands and all hurry to loss . . . *1 Hen. VI.* iv 3 53
His remedies are tame i' the present peace And quietness of the people, which before Were in wild hurry . . . . *Coriolanus* iv 6 4
As hasty powder fired Doth hurry from the fatal cannon's womb *R. and J.* v 1 65
Hurt. Thou dost me yet but little hurt; thou wilt anon . . *Tempest* ii 2 82
Sounds and sweet airs, that give delight and hurt not . . . . iii 2 145
If you could hurt, Your swords are now too massy for your strengths . iii 3 66
This nor hurts him nor profits you a jot . . . . *Meas. for Meas.* iv 2 128
Hold, hurt him not, for God's sake! he is mad . . *Com. of Errors* v 1 33
And speak off half a dozen dangerous words, How they might hurt their enemies, if they durst. . . . . *Much Ado* v 1 98
'Nay,' said I, 'a good wit:' 'Just,' said she, 'it hurts nobody' . . v 1 165
You break jests as braggarts do their blades, which, God be thanked, hurt not . . . . v 1 190
Blunt as the fencer's foils, which hit, but hurt not. . . . . . v 2 14
A most manly wit, Margaret; it will not hurt a woman . . . . . v 2 16
What, should I hurt her, strike her, kill her dead? Although I hate her, I'll not harm her so . . . . *M. N. Dream* iii 2 269
I pray you, though you mock me, gentlemen, Let her not hurt me . iii 2 300
Fed with the same food, hurt with the same weapons . *Mer. of Venice* iii 1 63
A poor sequester'd stag, That from the hunter's aim had ta'en a hurt *As Y. Like It* ii 1 34

Hurt. But now mine eyes, Which I have darted at thee, hurt thee not,
Nor, I am sure, there is no force in eyes That can do hurt *As Y. L. It* iii 5 25
That man should be at woman's command, and yet no hurt done! *All's W.* i 3 97
Though honesty be no puritan, yet it will do no hurt . . . i 3 98
It hurts not him That he is loved of me . . . . i 3 202
What I can do can do no hurt to try, Since you set up your rest 'gainst remedy . . . . ii 1 137
Why is he melancholy?—Perchance he's hurt i' the battle . . iii 5 90
I must give myself some hurts, and say I got them in exploit . iv 1 40
Hurt him in eleven places . . . . . *T. Night* iii 2 37
Draw, for the supportance of his vow; he protests he will not hurt you iii 4 330
He has promised me, as he is a gentleman and a soldier, he will not hurt you . . . . iii 4 339
Why do you speak to me? I never hurt you . . . . v 1 190
But I bespake you fair, and hurt you not.—If a bloody coxcomb be a hurt, you have hurt me . . . . v 1 192
That's all one: has hurt me, and there's the end on't . . . v 1 201
Get him to bed, and let his hurt be look'd to . . . . v 1 214
I am sorry, madam, I have hurt your kinsman . . . . v 1 216
The wall is high, and yet will I leap down: Good ground, be pitiful and hurt me not! . . . . *K. John* iv 3 2
Impatience hath his privilege.—'Tis true, to hurt his master, no man else . . . . iv 3 33
It never yet did hurt To lay down likelihoods and forms of hope *2 Hen. IV.* i 3 34
Are you not hurt i' the groin? methought a' made a shrewd thrust at your belly . . . . ii 4 227
The rascal's drunk: you have hurt him, sir, i' the shoulder . ii 4 231
He is not—God be praised and blessed!—any hurt in the world *Hen. V.* iii 6 11
Opinion shall be surgeon to my hurt . . . . *1 Hen. VI.* ii 4 53
Strike those that hurt, and hurt not those that help . . . iii 3 53
Though they cannot greatly sting to hurt, Yet look to have them buzz to offend thine ears . . . . *3 Hen. VI.* ii 6 94
I may conquer fortune's spite By living low, where fortune cannot hurt me . . . . iv 6 20
This is he Must help you more than you are hurt by me . . . iv 6 76
For goodness' sake, consider what you do; How you may hurt yourself *Hen. VIII.* iii 1 160
Paris is returned home and hurt.—By whom, Æneas? . *Troi. and Cres.* i 1 112
Who said he came hurt home to-day? he's not hurt . . . i 2 233
Good boy, tell him I come. I doubt he be hurt . . . . i 2 302
O, be persuaded! do not count it holy To hurt by being just . . v 3 20
Polyxenes is slain, Amphimachus and Thoas deadly hurt, Patroclus ta'en or slain, and Palamedes Sore hurt and bruised . . . v 5 12
All hurt behind; backs red, and faces pale With flight! . *Coriolanus* i 4 37
Seven hurts i' the body.—One i' the neck, and two i' the thigh . ii 1 166
You soothed not, therefore hurt not . . . . . . ii 2 77
Let me but stand; I will not hurt your hearth . . . . iv 5 26
Who hath done To thee particularly and to all the Volsces Great hurt . iv 5 73
Speak, brother, hast thou hurt thee with the fall?—O brother, with the dismall'st object hurt That ever eye with sight made heart lament! *T. Andron.* ii 3 203
He that wounded her Hath hurt me more than had he kill'd me dead . iii 1 92
And cut the winds, Who nothing hurt withal hiss'd him in scorn *R. and J.* i 1 119
I am hurt. A plague o' both your houses! I am sped . . iii 1 93
Art thou hurt?—Ay, ay, a scratch, a scratch; marry, 'tis enough . iii 1 95
Courage, man; the hurt cannot be much.—No, 'tis not so deep as a well, nor so wide as a church-door; but 'tis enough . . iii 1 98
Why the devil came you between us? I was hurt under your arm . iii 1 107
My very friend hath got his mortal hurt In my behalf . . . iii 1 115
While they have told their money and let out Their coin upon large interest, I myself Rich only in large hurts . *T. of Athens* iii 5 109
Then he is dead? . . . Had he his hurts before?—Ay, on the front.—Why then, God's soldier be he! . . . . . *Macbeth* v 8 46
This 'should' is like a spendthrift sigh, That hurts by easing *Hamlet* iv 7 124
I have shot mine arrow o'er the house, And hurt my brother . . v 2 255
O, yet defend me, friends; I am but hurt . . . . . v 2 335
He did bewray his practice; and received This hurt you see . *Lear* ii 1 110
This tempest will not give me leave to ponder On things would hurt me more . . . . iii 4 25
Mildews the white wheat, and hurts the poor creature of earth . iii 4 124
How is't, my lord? how look you?—I have received a hurt . . iii 7 95
Regan, I bleed apace: Untimely comes this hurt: give me your arm . iii 7 98
Thy comforts can do me no good at all; Thee they may hurt . . iv 1 18
What is the matter here?—'Zounds, I bleed still; I am hurt to the death *Othello* ii 3 164
Worthy Othello, I am hurt to danger . . . . . . ii 3 197
Sir, for your hurts, myself will be your surgeon . . . . ii 3 253
What, are you hurt, lieutenant?—Ay, past all surgery.—Marry, heaven forbid! . . . . ii 3 259
Cassio hath beaten thee, And thou, by that small hurt, hast cashier'd Cassio . . . . ii 3 381
He you hurt is of great fame in Cyprus And great affinity . . iii 1 48
Have you not hurt your head?—Dost thou mock me?—I mock you! no iv 1 60
My heart is turned to stone; I strike it, and it hurts my hand . iv 1 193
Thou hast not half that power to do me harm As I have to be hurt . v 2 163
Even but now he spake, After long seeming dead, Iago hurt him . v 2 328
He is afeard to come.—I will not hurt him . . *Ant. and Cleo.* ii 5 81
The stroke of death is as a lover's pinch, Which hurts, and is desired v 2 299
Have I hurt him?—No, 'faith; not so much as his patience . *Cymbeline* i 2 7
Hurt him! his body's a passable carcass, if he be not hurt: it is a throughfare for steel, if it be not hurt . . . . . . i 2 10
She shines not upon fools, lest the reflection should hurt her . . i 2 35
Would there had been some hurt done!—I wish not so; unless it had been the fall of an ass, which is no great hurt . . . . i 2 37
Since doubting things go ill often hurts more Than to be sure they do . i 6 95
The strait pass was damm'd With dead men hurt behind . . v 3 12
And the sore eyes see clear To stop the air would hurt them . *Pericles* i 1 100
Your shafts of fortune, though they hurt you mortally, Yet glance full wanderingly on us . . . . iii 3 6
As I can remember, by my troth, I never did her hurt in all my life . iv 1 75
Believe me, la, I never kill'd a mouse, nor hurt a fly . . . iv 1 78
I saw you lately, When you caught hurt in parting two that fought . iv 1 88

Hurt fowl. Alas, poor hurt fowl! now will he creep into sedges *M. Ado* ii 1 209

Hurt minds. Balm of hurt minds, great nature's second course *Macbeth* ii 2 39

Hurt wild-duck. A struck fowl or a hurt wild-duck . . *1 Hen. IV.* iv 2 21

Hurting. Or when she would with sharp needle wound The cambric, which she made more sound By hurting it . . . *Pericles* iv Gower 25

Hurtled. The noise of battle hurtled in the air . . . *J. Cæsar* ii 2 22

Hurtless. Plate sin with gold, And the strong lance of justice hurtless breaks . . . . *Lear* iv 6 170

Hurtling. In which hurtling From miserable slumber I awaked *As Y. L. It* iv 3 132

Husband. My husband, then?—Ay, with a heart as willing As bondage e'er of freedom: here's my hand . . . . *Tempest* iii 1 87
In one voyage Did Claribel her husband find at Tunis . . v 1 209
The report goes she has all the rule of her husband's purse . *Mer. Wives* i 3 59
That my husband saw this letter! it would give eternal food to his jealousy . . . . ii 1 103
Her husband will be absence from his house between ten and eleven . ii 2 85
Her husband will be from home. Alas! the sweet woman leads an ill life with him: he's a very jealousy man . . . . . ii 2 91
She bade me tell your worship that her husband is seldom from home . ii 2 104
Her husband has a marvellous infection to the little page . . ii 2 119
There is a gentlewoman in this town; her husband's name is Ford . ii 2 199
At that time the jealous rascally knave her husband will be forth . ii 2 276
I think, if your husbands were dead, you two would marry.—Be sure of that,—two other husbands . . . . iii 2 14
I cannot tell what the dickens his name is my husband had him of . iii 2 20
Now shall I sin in my wish: I would thy husband were dead . . iii 3 52
Having an honest man to your husband, to give him such cause of suspicion! . . . . iii 3 107
Your husband's coming, with half Windsor at his heels . . . iii 3 121
Your husband's here at hand; bethink you of some conveyance . . iii 3 134
I know not which pleases me better, that my husband is deceived, or Sir John . . . . iii 3 190
What a taking was he in when your husband asked who was in the basket! . . . . iii 3 192
I think my husband hath some special suspicion of Falstaff's being here iii 3 199
Do not marry me to yond fool.—I mean it not; I seek you a better husband . . . . iii 4 88
Her husband goes this morning a-birding . . . . . iii 5 45; 130
The peaking Cornuto her husband, Master Brook, dwelling in a continual 'larum of jealousy . . . . iii 5 72
My husband says my son profits nothing in the world at his book . iv 1 14
But are you sure of your husband now?—He's a-birding, sweet Sir John iv 2 7
Why, woman, your husband is in his old lunes again: he so takes on yonder with my husband . . . . iv 2 21
And swears he was carried out, the last time he searched for him, in a basket; protests to my husband he is now here . . . . iv 2 33
I would my husband would meet him in this shape . . . iv 2 86
Heaven guide him to thy husband's cudgel, and the devil guide his cudgel! . . . . iv 2 90
But is my husband coming?—Ay, in good sadness, is he . . . iv 2 92
The virtuous creature, that hath the jealous fool to her husband! . iv 2 137
Come you and the old woman down; my husband will come into the chamber . . . . iv 2 175
Nay, good, sweet husband! Good gentlemen, let him not strike the old woman . . . . iv 2 189
Shall we tell our husbands how we have served him? . . . iv 2 228
If it be but to scrape the figures out of your husband's brains . . iv 2 231
Though well landed, is an idiot; And he my husband best of all affects iv 4 87
Husband your device . . . . iv 6 52
Her husband hath the finest mad devil of jealousy in him . . v 1 19
My husband will not rejoice so much at the abuse of Falstaff as he will chafe at the doctor's marrying my daughter . . . . . v 3 8
My horns I bequeath your husbands . . . . . . v 5 30
See you these, husband? do not these fair yokes Become the forest better? . . . . v 5 111
Good husband, let us every one go home, And laugh this sport o'er? . v 5 255
Hath she had any more than one husband?—Nine, sir . *Meas. for Meas.* ii 1 210
Her combinate husband, this well-seeming Angelo . . . iii 1 231
You will turn good husband now, Pompey; you will keep the house . iii 2 73
He is your husband on a pre-contract: To bring you thus together, 'tis no sin . . . . iv 1 72
I will not show my face Until my husband bid me . . . . v 1 170
I have known my husband; yet my husband Knows not that ever he knew me . . . . v 1 186
In self-same manner doth accuse my husband . . . . . v 1 196
You say your husband.—Why, just, my lord, and that is Angelo . v 1 201
Let's see thy face.—My husband bids me; now I will unmask . . v 1 206
I hope you will not mock me with a husband.—It is your husband mock'd you with a husband . . . . v 1 422
We do instate and widow you withal, To buy you a better husband . v 1 430
They say, best men are moulded out of faults; And, for the most, become much more the better For being a little bad: so may my husband . . . . v 1 446
Neither my husband nor the slave return'd! . . . *Com. of Errors* ii 1 1
How if your husband start some other where? . . . . ii 1 30
Now is your husband nigh.—Say, is your tardy master now at hand? . ii 1 43
How comes it now, my husband, O, how comes it, That thou art thus estranged from thyself? Thyself I call it, being strange to me . ii 2 121
Wouldst thou not spit at me and spurn at me And hurl the name of husband in my face? . . . . ii 2 137
I will fasten on this sleeve of thine: Thou art an elm, my husband, I a vine . . . . ii 2 176
Husband, I'll dine above with you to-day . . . . . ii 2 209
And may it be that you have quite forgot A husband's office? . iii 2 2
Thee will I love and with thee lead my life: Thou hast no husband yet nor I no wife. Give me thy hand . . . . . . iii 2 68
She that doth call me husband, even my soul Doth for a wife abhor . iii 2 163
Where we dined, Where Dowsabel did claim me for her husband . iv 1 110
How say you now? is not your husband mad? . . . . iv 4 48
O husband, God doth know you dined at home . . . . iv 4 68
I did not, gentle husband, lock thee forth . . . . . iv 4 100
Say, how grows it due?—Due for a chain your husband had of him . iv 4 138
Your husband all in rage to-day Came to my house and took away my ring . . . . iv 4 140
Wherefore throng you hither?—To fetch my poor distracted husband hence . . . . v 1 39
Thy jealous fits Have scared thy husband from the use of wits . v 1 86
Then let your servants bring my husband forth . . . . v 1 93
I will attend my husband, be his nurse, Diet his sickness, for it is my office . . . . v 1 98
Leave him here with me.—I will not hence and leave my husband here v 1 109
Ill it doth beseem your holiness To separate the husband and the wife v 1 111
Until my tears and prayers Have won his grace to come in person hither And take perforce my husband . . . . v 1 117
Antipholus my husband, Whom I made lord of me and all I had . v 1 136
Long since thy husband served me in my wars . . . . v 1 161
Ay me, it is my husband! Witness you, That he is borne about invisible v 1 186
I see two husbands, or mine eyes deceive me . . . . . v 1 331

Husband. I will loose his bonds And gain a husband by his liberty *Com. of Errors* v 1 340
And are not you my husband?—No; I say nay to that.—And so do I . v 1 370
The duke, my husband and my children both, And you the calendars of their nativity, Go to a gossips' feast, and go with me . v 1 403
I hope you have no intent to turn husband, have you? . *Much Ado* i 1 196
Thou wilt never get thee a husband, if thou be so shrewd of thy tongue ii 1 20
If he send me no husband; for the which blessing I am at him upon my knees every morning and evening . ii 1 29
I could not endure a husband with a beard on his face . ii 1 32
You may light on a husband that hath no beard . ii 1 34
I hope to see you one day fitted with a husband . ii 1 61
I may sit in a corner and cry heigh-ho for a husband! . ii 1 333
Your father got excellent husbands, if a maid could come by them . ii 1 337
She cannot endure to hear tell of a husband . ii 1 363
I will do any modest office, my lord, to help my cousin to a good husband ii 1 391
Is not the unhopefullest husband that I know . ii 1 393
And send her home again without a husband . iii 3 175
I think you would have me say, 'saving your reverence, a husband' . iii 4 33
Is there any harm in 'the heavier for a husband'? None, I think, an it be the right husband and the right wife . iii 4 35
If your husband have stables enough, you'll see he shall lack no barns iii 4 48
Heigh-ho!—For a hawk, a horse, or a husband? . iii 4 55
They stay for you to give your daughter to her husband . iii 5 60
If I have known her, You will say she did embrace me as a husband . iv 1 50
I am your husband, if you like of me.—And when I lived, I was your other wife: And when you loved, you were my other husband . v 4 59
This reasoning is not in the fashion to choose me a husband *Mer. of Venice* i 2 24
If I should marry him, I should marry twenty husbands . i 2 68
Made her neighbours believe she wept for the death of a third husband iii 1 12
But if you knew to whom you show this honour, How true a gentleman you send relief, How dear a lover of my lord your husband . iii 4 7
I have toward heaven breathed a secret vow To live in prayer and contemplation, Only attended by Nerissa here, Until her husband and my lord's return . iii 4 30
We'll see our husbands Before they think of us . iii 4 58
I shall be saved by my husband; he hath made me a Christian . iii 5 21
I'll tell my husband, Launcelot, what you say: here he comes . iii 5 29
Even such a husband Hast thou of me as she is for a wife . iii 5 88
These be the Christian husbands. I have a daughter; Would any of the stock of Barrabas Had been her husband rather than a Christian! . iv 1 295
We'll away to-night And be a day before our husbands home . iv 2 3
I'll see if I can get my husband's ring, Which I did make him swear to keep for ever . iv 2 13
We have been praying for our husbands' healths, Which speed, we hope, the better for our words . v 1 114
Your husband is at hand; I hear his trumpet . v 1 122
A light wife doth make a heavy husband . v 1 130
I'll not deny him any thing I have, No, not my body nor my husband's bed . v 1 228
Which, but for him that had your husband's ring, Had quite miscarried v 1 250
I do take thee, Orlando, for my husband . *As Y. Like It* iv 1 139
O, that woman that cannot make her fault her husband's occasion! . iv 1 178
I'll have no husband, if you be not he . v 4 129
I long to hear him call the drunkard husband . *T. of Shrew* Ind. 1 133
Are you my wife and will not call me husband? . Ind. 2 106
My husband and my lord, my lord and husband; I am your wife in all obedience . Ind. 2 108
Not to bestow my youngest daughter Before I have a husband for the elder . i 1 51
What's that, I pray?—Marry, sir, to get a husband for her sister . i 1 123
A husband! a devil.—I say, a husband.—I say, a devil . i 1 125
This order hath Baptista ta'en, That none shall have access unto Bianca Till Katharine the curst have got a husband . i 2 128
Nay, now I see She is your treasure, she must have a husband . ii 1 32
And, will you, nill you, I will marry you. Now, Kate, I am a husband for your turn . ii 1 274
I pray you, husband, be not so disquiet: The meat was well . iv 1 171
While I play the good husband at home, my son and my servant spend all at the university . v 1 71
Husband, let's follow, to see the end of this ado . v 1 147
Your husband, being troubled with a shrew, Measures my husband's sorrow by his woe . v 2 28
If they deny to come, Swinge me them soundly forth unto their husbands v 2 104
Tell these headstrong women What duty they do owe their lords and husbands . v 2 131
Thy husband is thy lord, thy life, thy keeper, Thy head, thy sovereign v 2 146
Such duty as the subject owes the prince, Even such a woman oweth to her husband . v 2 156
Then vail your stomachs, for it is no boot, And place your hands below your husband's foot . v 2 177
In delivering my son from me, I bury a second husband . *All's Well* i 1 2
You shall find of the king a husband, madam . i 1 7
Get thee a good husband, and use him as he uses thee: so, farewell . i 1 229
Give me with thy kingly hand What husband in thy power I will command . ii 1 197
Then call me husband: but in such a 'then' I write a 'never' . iii 2 62
What angel shall Bless this unworthy husband? . iii 4 26
Write, write, Rinaldo, To this unworthy husband of his wife . iii 4 30
First, give me trust, the count he is my husband . iii 7 8
I am supposed dead: the army breaking, My husband hies him home . iv 4 12
Doubt not but heaven Hath brought me up to be your daughter's dower, As it hath fated her to be my motive And helper to a husband . iv 4 21
Your reputation comes too short for my daughter; you are no husband for her . v 3 177
I pray you yet; Since you lack virtue, I will lose a husband . v 3 222
Choose thou thy husband, and I'll pay thy dower . v 3 328
So wears she to him, So sways she level in her husband's heart *T. Night* ii 4 32
She will keep no fool, sir, till she be married; and fools are as like husbands as pilchards are to herrings; the husband's the bigger . iii 1 39
Cesario, husband, stay.—Husband!—Ay, husband: can he that deny? —Her husband, sirrah!—No, my lord, not I . v 1 146
I have spoke to the purpose twice: The one for ever earn'd a royal husband; The other for some while a friend . *W. Tale* i 2 107
And arms her with the boldness of a wife To her allowing husband! . i 2 185
A callat Of boundless tongue, who late hath beat her husband! . ii 3 91
Lest she suspect, as he does, Her children not her husband's . ii 3 108
Stay her tongue.—Hang all the husbands That cannot do that feat, you'll leave yourself Hardly one subject . ii 3 110

Husband. To take away the life of our sovereign lord the king, thy royal husband . *W. Tale* iii 2 17
She had one eye declined for the loss of her husband, another elevated v 2 81
Thou shouldst a husband take by my consent, As I by thine a wife . v 3 136
I'll not seek far—For him, I partly know his mind—to find thee An honourable husband . v 3 143
Which fault lies on the hazards of all husbands That marry wives *K. John* i 1 119
Hath she no husband That will take pains to blow a horn before her? . i 1 218
I was seduced To make room for him in my husband's bed . i 1 255
My bed was ever to thy son as true As thine was to thy husband . ii 1 125
Many a widow's husband grovelling lies . ii 1 305
A widow cries; be husband to me, heavens! . iii 1 108
O husband, hear me! ay, alack, how new Is husband in my mouth! . iii 1 305
Husband, I cannot pray that thou mayst win; Uncle, I needs must pray that thou mayst lose . iii 1 331
O, sit my husband's wrongs on Hereford's spear! . *Richard II.* i 2 47
Your husband, he is gone to save far off, Whilst others come to make him lose at home . ii 2 80
Sweet York, sweet husband, be not of that mind: He is as like thee . v 2 107
Ah, my sour husband, my hard-hearted lord! . v 3 121
I have inquired, so has my husband, man by man . *1 Hen. IV.* iii 3 65
How doth thy husband? I love him well; he is an honest man . iii 3 107
Love thy husband, look to thy servants, cherish thy guests . iii 3 193
To rain upon remembrance with mine eyes, That it may grow and sprout as high as heaven, For recordation to my noble husband *2 Hen. IV.* ii 3 61
Davy serves you for good uses; he is your serving-man and your husband v 3 12
Many a thousand widows Shall this his mock mock out of their dear husbands; Mock mothers from their sons . *Hen. V.* i 2 285
Good husband, come home presently . ii 1 93
Prithee, honey-sweet husband, let me bring thee to Staines . ii 3 1
The pining maidens' groans, For husbands, fathers and betrothed lovers ii 4 108
Like a new-married wife about her husband's neck . v 2 190
Slain our citizens And sent our sons and husbands captivate . *1 Hen. VI.* ii 3 42
To tumble down thy husband and thyself From top of honour *2 Hen. VI.* i 2 48
The king is now in progress towards Saint Alban's, With him the husband of this lovely lady . i 4 77
Helen of Greece was fairer far than thou, Although thy husband may be Menelaus . *3 Hen. VI* ii 2 147
At Saint Alban's field This lady's husband, Sir Richard Grey, was slain iii 2 2
To do them good, I would sustain some harm.—Then get your husband's lands, to do them good . iii 2 40
Why, then, thy husband's lands I freely give thee . iii 2 55
Why, then thou shalt not have thy husband's lands . iii 2 71
I can tell you both Her suit is granted for her husband's lands . iii 2 117
Wives for their husbands, And orphans for their parents' timeless death —Shall rue the hour that ever thou wast born . v 6 41
He that doth naught with her, excepting one, Were best he do it secretly, alone.—What one, my lord?—Her husband, knave . *Richard III.* i 1 102
What though I kill'd her husband and her father? The readiest way to make the wench amends Is to become her husband and her father . i 1 154
I did not kill your husband.—Why, then he is alive . i 2 91
He that bereft thee, lady, of thy husband, Did it to help thee to a better husband.—His better doth not breathe . i 2 138
What! I, that kill'd her husband and his father, To take her in her heart's extremest hate, With curses in her mouth! . i 2 231
Thou slewest my husband Henry in the Tower, and Edward, my poor son, at Tewksbury . i 3 119
Ere you were queen, yea, or your husband king . i 3 121
You and your husband Grey Were factious for the house of Lancaster . i 3 127
Was not your husband In Margaret's battle at Saint Alban's slain? . i 3 129
A husband and a son thou owest to me; And thou a kingdom . i 3 170
So much interest have I in thy sorrow As I had title in thy noble husband! . ii 2 48
I have bewept a worthy husband's death, And lived by looking on his images . ii 2 49
Death hath snatch'd my husband from mine arms, And pluck'd two crutches from my feeble limbs . ii 2 57
Oh for my husband, for my dear lord Edward! . ii 2 71
My husband lost his life to get the crown . ii 4 57
When he that is my husband now Came to me, as I follow'd Henry's corse, When scarce the blood was well wash'd from his hands Which issued from my other angel husband . iv 1 66
Where is thy husband now? where be thy brothers? Where are thy children? wherein dost thou joy? . iv 4 92
Bring me a constant woman to her husband . *Hen. VIII.* iii 1 134
Sure, in that I deem you an ill husband . iii 2 142
Will deserve . . . A right good husband, let him be a noble . iv 2 146
Quoth she, 'which of these hairs is Paris my husband?' *Troi. and Cres.* i 2 178
What nearer debt in all humanity Than wife is to the husband? . ii 2 176
If my son were my husband, I should freelier rejoice in that absence wherein he won honour than in the embracements of his bed *Coriolanus* i 3 3
Methinks I hear hither your husband's drum . i 3 32
Go with me; and I'll tell you excellent news of your husband . i 3 101
If you had been the wife of Hercules, Six of his labours you'ld have done, and saved Your husband so much sweat . iv 1 19
You shall stay too: I would I had the power To say so to my husband . iv 2 16
So far my son—This lady's husband here, this, do you see—Whom you have banish'd, does exceed you all . iv 2 41
I have heard it said, the fittest time to corrupt a man's wife is when she's fallen out with her husband . iv 3 35
My lord and husband!—These eyes are not the same I wore in Rome . v 3 37
Making the mother, wife and child to see The son, the husband and the father tearing His country's bowels out . v 3 102
Jove shield your husband from his hounds to-day! 'Tis pity they should take him for a stag . *T. Andron.* ii 3 70
Drag hence her husband to some secret hole, And make his dead trunk pillow to our lust . ii 3 129
Bring thou her husband: This is the hole where Aaron bid us hide him ii 3 185
My niece, that flies away so fast! Cousin, a word; where is your husband? . ii 4 12
Thy husband he is dead; and for his death Thy brothers are condemn'd iii 1 108
Perchance she weeps because they kill'd her husband . iii 1 114
If they did kill thy husband, then be joyful, Because the law hath ta'en revenge on them . iii 1 116
You kill'd her husband, and for that vile fault Two of her brothers were condemn'd to death . v 2 173
My husband—God be with his soul! A' was a merry man *Rom. and Jul.* i 3 39
'Yea,' quoth my husband, 'fall'st upon thy face? Thou wilt fall backward when thou comest to age' . i 3 55

Husband. Hence to Friar Laurence' cell; There stays a husband to make you a wife . . . . *Rom. and Jul.* ii 5 71
O prince! O cousin! husband! O, the blood is spilt Of my dear kinsman! . . . . iii 1 152
Shall I speak ill of him that is my husband? Ah, poor my lord, what tongue shall smooth thy name? . . . . iii 2 97
But, wherefore, villain, didst thou kill my cousin? That villain cousin would have kill'd my husband . . . . iii 2 101
My husband lives, that Tybalt would have slain; And Tybalt's dead, that would have slain my husband . . . . iii 2 105
Art thou gone so? love, lord, ay, husband, friend! . . . . . iii 5 43
I wonder at this haste; that I must wed Ere he, that should be husband, comes to woo . . . . iii 5 120
My husband is on earth, my faith in heaven; How shall that faith return again to earth, Unless that husband send it me from heaven By leaving earth? . . . . iii 5 207
Come, come away. Thy husband in thy bosom there lies dead . v 3 155
Romeo, there dead, was husband to that Juliet; And she, there dead, that Romeo's faithful wife . . . . v 3 231
How shall she be endow'd, If she be mated with an equal husband? *T. of Athens* i 1 140
Can I bear that with patience, And not my husband's secrets? *J. Cæsar* ii 1 302
Her husband's to Aleppo gone, master o' the Tiger . . *Macbeth* i 3 7
My husband!—I have done the deed. Didst thou not hear a noise? . ii 2 14
But for your husband, He is noble, wise, judicious, and best knows . iv 2 15
How will you do for a husband?—Why, I can buy me twenty at any market . . . . iv 2 39
Where is your husband?—I hope, in no place so unsanctified Where such as thou mayst find him . . . . iv 2 80
When she saw Pyrrhus make malicious sport In mincing with his sword her husband's limbs . . . . *Hamlet* ii 2 537
And haply one as kind For husband shalt thou— O, confound the rest! iii 2 187
In second husband let me be accurst! None wed the second but who kill'd the first.—Wormwood, wormwood . . . . . iii 2 189
A second time I kill my husband dead, When second husband kisses me in bed . . . . iii 2 194
So think thou wilt no second husband wed; But die thy thoughts when thy first lord is dead . . . . iii 2 224
Still better, and worse.—So you must take your husbands . . iii 2 262
You are the queen, your husband's brother's wife; And—would it were not so!—you are my mother . . . . iii 4 15
Here is your husband; like a mildew'd ear, Blasting his wholesome brother . . . . iii 4 64
For my means, I'll husband them so well, They shall go far with little. iv 5 138
And had, indeed, sir, a son for her cradle ere she had a husband for her bed. Do you smell a fault? . . . . . . *Lear* i 1 16
Why have my sisters husbands, if they say They love you all? . . i 1 101
I am sorry, then, you have so lost a father That you must lose a husband i 1 250
Post speedily to my lord your husband; show him this letter . . iii 7 1
I marvel our mild husband Not met us on the way . . . . iv 2 1
I must change arms at home, and give the distaff Into my husband's hands . . . . iv 2 18
I know your lady does not love her husband; I am sure of that . iv 5 23
A plot upon her virtuous husband's life; And the exchange my brother! iv 6 279
Fear me not: She and the duke her husband! . . . . . . v 1 17
And hardly shall I carry out my side, Her husband being alive . . v 1 62
He compeers the best.—That were the most, if he should husband you v 3 70
And I, her husband, contradict your bans . . . . v 3 87
Here's my husband, And so much duty as my mother show'd To you, preferring you before her father, So much I challenge that I may profess Due to the Moor my lord . . . . *Othello* i 3 185
Do not learn of him, Emilia, though he be thy husband . . . ii 1 164
I dare think he'll prove to Desdemona A most dear husband . . ii 1 300
This broken joint between you and her husband entreat her to splinter ii 3 329
I warrant it grieves my husband, As if the case were his . . iii 3 3
In Venice they do let heaven see the pranks They dare not show their husbands . . . . iii 3 203
My wayward husband hath a hundred times Woo'd me to steal it . . iii 3 292
Lay on my bed my wedding sheets: remember; And call thy husband hither . . . . iv 2 106
Dost thou in conscience think,—tell me, Emilia,—That there be women do abuse their husbands In such gross kind? . . . . . . iv 3 62
But, for the whole world,—why, who would not make her husband a cuckold to make him a monarch? . . . . iv 3 76
But I do think it is their husbands' faults If wives do fall . . iv 3 87
Let husbands know Their wives have sense like them: they see and smell And have their palates both for sweet and sour, As husbands have . . . . iv 3 94
'Las, what's the matter? what's the matter, husband? . . . . v 1 111
She was heavenly true!—Cassio did top her; ask thy husband else . v 2 136
Thy husband knew it all.—My husband!—Thy husband . . . v 2 139
My husband!—What needs this iteration, woman? I say thy husband v 2 149
My husband say that she was false!—He, woman; I say thy husband: dost understand the word? My friend, thy husband, honest, honest Iago . . . . v 2 152
That handkerchief thou speak'st of I found by fortune and did give my husband . . . . v 2 226
She give it Cassio! no, alas! I found it, And I did give't my husband . v 2 231
O, that I knew this husband, which, you say, must charge his horns with garlands! . . . . *Ant. and Cleo.* i 2 4
If you were but an inch of fortune better than I, where would you choose it?—Not in my husband's nose . . . . i 2 63
Whose beauty claims No worse a husband than the best of men . ii 2 131
Look well to my husband's house; and— What, Octavia? . iii 2 45
When I shall pray, 'O, bless my lord and husband!' Undo that prayer, by crying out as loud, 'O, bless my brother!' Husband win, win brother, Prays, and destroys the prayer . . . . . . iii 4 16
Husband, I come: Now to that name my courage prove my title! . v 2 290
She's wedded; Her husband banish'd . . . . *Cymbeline* i 1 8
My dearest husband, I something fear my father's wrath . . . i 1 85
I will remain The loyal'st husband that did e'er plight troth . . i 1 96
A foolish suitor to a wedded lady, That hath her husband banish'd;— O, that husband! My supreme crown of grief! . . . . . i 6 3
A wooer More hateful than the foul expulsion is Of thy dear husband . ii 1 66
My husband's hand! That drug-damn'd Italy hath out-craftied him . iii 4 14
All good seeming, By thy revolt, O husband, shall be thought Put on iii 4 57
In my life what comfort, when I am Dead to my husband? . . . iii 4 133
I sought a husband, in which labour I found that kindness in a father: He's father, son, and husband mild; I mother, wife, and yet his child . . . . *Pericles* i 1 66

Husband. Which pleasure fits an husband, not a father . . *Pericles* i 1 129
Husbanded. It will be pastime passing excellent, If it be husbanded with modesty . . . . *T. of Shrew* Ind. 1 68
You shall as easy Prove that I husbanded her bed in Florence *All's Well* v 3 126
Like lean, sterile and bare land, manured, husbanded and tilled *2 Hen. IV.* iv 3 130
Think you I am no stronger than my sex, Being so father'd and so husbanded? Tell me your counsels . . . . . . *J. Cæsar* ii 1 297
Husbandless, subject to fears, A woman, naturally born to fears *K. John* iii 1 14
Husbandry. Even so her plenteous womb Expresseth his full tilth and husbandry . . . . *Meas. for Meas.* i 4 44
I commit into your hands The husbandry and manage of my house *Mer. of Venice* iii 4 25
Thou prunest a rotten tree, That cannot so much as a blossom yield In lieu of all thy pains and husbandry . . . . *As Y. Like It* ii 3 65
My old dame will be undone now for one to do her husbandry *2 Hen. IV.* iii 2 124
Makes us early stirrers, Which is both healthful and good husbandry *Hen. V.* iv 1 7
All her husbandry doth lie on heaps, Corrupting in it own fertility . v 2 39
They'll o'ergrow the garden And choke the herbs for want of husbandry *2 Hen. VI.* iii 1 33
Like as there were husbandry in war, Before the sun rose he was harness'd light, And to the field goes he . . . *Troi. and Cres.* i 2 7
And shows good husbandry for the Volscian state . . *Coriolanus* iv 7 22
If you suspect my husbandry or falsehood, Call me before the exactest auditors And set me on the proof . . . . *T. of Athens* ii 2 164
There's husbandry in heaven; Their candles are all out . . *Macbeth* ii 1 4
And borrowing dulls the edge of husbandry . . . . *Hamlet* i 3 77
That is the cause we trouble you so early; 'Tis not our husbandry *Per.* iii 2 20
Hush. What! An advocate for an impostor! hush! . . *Tempest* i 2 477
There's something else to do: hush, and be mute, Or else our spell is marr'd . . . . iv 1 126
Hush, master! here's some good pastime toward . . *T. of Shrew* i 1 68
The king has done you wrong: but, hush, 'tis so . . *All's Well* ii 3 317
A plague upon him! muffled! he can say nothing of me: hush, hush! . iv 3 135
My lord would speak; my duty hushes me . . . . . *T. Night* v 1 110
My tongue shall hush again this storm of war . . . *K. John* v 1 20
May they not be my oracles as well, And set me up in hope? But hush! no more . . . . *Macbeth* iii 1 10
The bold winds speechless and the orb below As hush as death *Hamlet* ii 2 508
Vex not his prescience; be attentive.—Hush! . . . *Ant. and Cleo.* i 2 21
Hush! here comes Antony.—Not he; the queen . . . . . . i 2 83
Hush, my gentle neighbours! Lend me your hands . . *Pericles* iii 2 107
Hushed. All's hush'd as midnight yet . . . . . . *Tempest* iv 1 207
How still the evening is, As hush'd on purpose to grace harmony! *M. Ado* ii 3 41
Yet can I not of such tame patience boast As to be hush'd and nought at all to say . . . . *Richard II.* i 1 53
And hush'd with buzzing night-flies to thy slumber . . *2 Hen. IV.* iii 1 11
I am hush'd until our city be afire, And then I'll speak . *Coriolanus* v 3 181
The bawdy wind that kisses all it meets Is hush'd within the hollow mine of earth, And will not hear it . . . . . *Othello* iv 2 79
Husks Wherein the acorn cradled . . . . *Tempest* i 2 463
Shall I keep your hogs and eat husks with them? . . *As Y. Like It* i 1 40
A hundred and fifty tattered prodigals lately come from swine-keeping, from eating draff and husks . . . . . . *1 Hen. IV.* iv 2 38
Leaving them but the shales and husks of men . . . *Hen. V.* iv 2 18
What's past and what's to come is strew'd with husks . *Troi. and Cres.* iv 5 166
Huswife. She has a huswife's hand; but that's no matter *As Y. Like It* iv 3 27
And sung those tunes to the overscutched huswives that he heard the carmen whistle . . . . *2 Hen. IV.* iii 2 341
Doth Fortune play the huswife with me now? . . . . *Hen. V.* v 1 85
I must have you play the idle huswife with me this afternoon *Coriolanus* i 3 76
Hybla. As the honey of Hybla, my old lad of the castle . . *1 Hen. IV.* i 2 47
For your words, they rob the Hybla bees, And leave them honeyless *J. C.* v 1 34
Hydra. Another king! they grow like Hydra's heads . . *1 Hen. IV.* v 4 25
Whereon this Hydra son of war is born . . . . *2 Hen. IV.* iv 2 38
Have you thus Given Hydra here to choose an officer? . . *Coriolanus* iii 1 93
Had I as many mouths as Hydra, such an answer would stop them all *Othello* ii 3 308
Hydra-headed. Nor never Hydra-headed wilfulness So soon did lose his seat . . . . *Hen. V.* i 1 35
Hyen. I will laugh like a hyen, and that when thou art inclined to sleep. —But will my Rosalind do so? . . . . . *As Y. Like It* iv 1 156
Hymen. Therefore take heed, As Hymen's lamps shall light you *Tempest* iv 1 23
That no bed-right shall be paid Till Hymen's torch be lighted . . iv 1 97
And Hymen now with luckier issue speed's Than this for whom we render'd up this woe . . . . *Much Ado* v 3 32
Good duke, receive thy daughter: Hymen from heaven brought her *As Y. Like It* v 4 118
Here's eight that must take hands To join in Hymen's bands . . v 4 135
O blessed bond of board and bed! 'Tis Hymen peoples every town . v 4 149
Honour, high honour and renown, To Hymen, god of every town! . v 4 152
Thou bright defiler [gold] Of Hymen's purest bed! . . *T. of Athens* iv 3 384
Since love our hearts and Hymen did our hands Unite commutual in most sacred bands . . . . *Hamlet* iii 2 169
Hymen hath brought the bride to bed . . . . . *Pericles* iii Gower 9
Hymenæus. And tapers burn so bright and every thing In readiness for Hymenæus stand . . . . *T. Andron.* i 1 325
Hymn. Now, music, sound, and sing your solemn hymn . . *Much Ado* v 3 11
Chanting faint hymns to the cold fruitless moon . . *M. N. Dream* i 1 73
No night is now with hymn or carol blest . . . . ii 1 102
Come, ho! and wake Diana with a hymn . . . . *Mer. of Venice* v 1 66
I am the cygnet to this pale faint swan, Who chants a doleful hymn to his own death . . . . *K. John* v 7 22
Our solemn hymns to sullen dirges change . . . *Rom. and Jul.* iv 5 88
Hyperbole. Three-piled hyperboles, spruce affectation . . *L. L. Lost* v 2 407
With terms unsquared, Which, from the tongue of roaring Typhon dropp'd, Would seem hyperboles . . . . . *Troi. and Cres.* i 3 161
Hyperbolical. Out, hyperbolical fiend! . . . . . *T. Night* iv 2 29
You shout me forth In acclamations hyperbolical . . . *Coriolanus* i 9 51
Hyperion. And help Hyperion to his horse . . . . *Hen. V.* iv 1 292
That were to enlard his fat already pride And add more coals to Cancer when he burns With entertaining great Hyperion . *Troi. and Cres.* ii 3 207
All day long, Even from Hyperion's rising in the east . . *T. Andron.* v 2 56
Whereon Hyperion's quickening fire doth shine . . *T. of Athens* iv 3 184
So excellent a king; that was, to this, Hyperion to a satyr . *Hamlet* i 2 140
See, what a grace was seated on this brow; Hyperion's curls . . iii 4 56
Hypocrisy. Now step I forth to whip hypocrisy . . *L. L. Lost* iv 3 151
A huge translation of hypocrisy, Vilely compiled, profound simplicity . v 2 51
His prayers are full of false hypocrisy; Ours of true zeal *Richard II.* v 3 107

Hypocrisy. And so would you, For all this spice of your hypocrisy *Hen. VIII.* ii 3 26
It is hypocrisy against the devil *Othello* iv 1 6
Hypocrite. An adulterous thief, An hypocrite, a virgin-violator *M. for M.* v 1 41
I dare swear he is no hypocrite, but prays from his heart . *Much Ado* i 1 152
An you be a cursing hypocrite once, you must be looked to . v 1 212
What wouldst thou think of me, if I should weep?—I would think thee a most princely hypocrite . . . . . . 2 *Hen. IV.* ii 2 59
Every man would think me an hypocrite indeed . . . ii 2 64
Out, tawny coats! out, scarlet hypocrite! . . . . 1 *Hen. VI.* i 3 56
My tongue and soul in this be hypocrites . . . . *Hamlet* iii 2 415
An act That blurs the grace and blush of modesty, Calls virtue hypocrite iii 4 42
Hypocrite. How courtesy would seem to cover sin, When what is done is like an hypocrite, The which is good in nothing but in sight! *Pericles* i 1 122
Hyrcan. Approach thou like the rugged Russian bear, The arm'd rhinoceros, or the Hyrcan tiger . . . . . . *Macbeth* iii 4 101
Hyrcania. You are more inhuman, more inexorable, O, ten times more, than tigers of Hyrcania . . . . . 3 *Hen. VI.* i 4 155
Hyrcanian. The Hyrcanian deserts and the vasty wilds Of wide Arabia are as throughfares now . . . *Mer. of Venice* ii 7 41
The rugged Pyrrhus, like the Hyrcanian beast. . . *Hamlet* ii 2 472
Hyssop. Sow lettuce, set hyssop and weed up thyme . *Othello* i 3 325
Hysterica passio, down, thou climbing sorrow, Thy element's below! *Lear* ii 4 57

I

I care not for her, I . . . . *T. G. of Ver.* v 4 132
I, I, I myself sometimes . . . am fain to shuffle . . *Mer. Wives* ii 2 23
A heavier task could not have been imposed Than I to speak my griefs unspeakable . . . . *Com. of Errors* i 1 33
Poor I am but his stale.—Self-harming jealousy! . . . . ii 1 101
But if that I am I, then well I know Your weeping sister is no wife of mine . . . . iii 2 41
The third of the five vowels, if you repeat them; or the fifth, if I *L. L. L.* v 1 57
Prove it so, Let fortune go to hell for it, not I . . *Mer. of Venice* iii 2 21
All debts are cleared between you and I . . . . iii 2 321
I and my friend Have by your wisdom been this day acquitted . iv 1 408
You know my father hath no child but I . . . *As Y. Like It* i 2 18
What he is indeed, More suits you to conceive than I to speak of . i 2 279
Heaven would that she these gifts should have, And I to live and die her slave . . . . iii 2 162
And then I comes behind.—Ay, an you had any eye behind you *T. Night* ii 5 147
Poor I was slain when Bassianus died . . . *T. Andron.* ii 3 171
Say thou but 'I,' And that bare vowel 'I' shall poison more Than the death-darting eye of cockatrice: I am not I, if there be such an I; Or those eyes shut, that make thee answer 'I.' If he be slain, say 'I'; or if not, no . . . . . . *Rom. and Jul.* iii 2 45
I, to bear this, That never knew but better, is some burden *T. of Athens* iv 3 266
Poor I am stale, a garment out of fashion. . . . *Cymbeline* iii 4 53
I wis. There be fools alive, I wis, Silver'd o'er . . *Mer. of Venice* ii 9 68
I wis it is not half way to her heart . . . . *T. of Shrew* i 1 62
I wis your grandam had a worser match . . . *Richard III.* i 3 102
Here have you seen a mighty king His child, I wis, to incest bring *Pericles* ii Gower 2
I wist. An if I wist he did,—but let it rest . . 1 *Hen. VI.* iv 1 180
Iachimo. Will this hold, think you?—Signior Iachimo will not from it *Cymbeline* i 4 184
See! Iachimo!—The swiftest harts have posted you by land . . ii 4 26
O, all the devils! This yellow Iachimo, in an hour,—was't not? . . ii 5 14
Thy conscience witness: Iachimo, Thou didst accuse him of incontinency . . . . iii 4 48
And they come Under the conduct of bold Iachimo . . . . iv 2 340
Why did you suffer Iachimo . . . To taint his nobler heart? . . v 4 63
That I was he, Speak, Iachimo: I had you down . . . . v 5 411
Iago. Thou, Iago, who hast had my purse As if the strings were thine *Othello* i 1 2
It is as sure as you are Roderigo, Were I the Moor, I would not be Iago i 1 57
For know, Iago, But that I love the gentle Desdemona, I would not . i 2 24
Honest Iago, My Desdemona must I leave to thee . . . . i 3 295
Iago,— What say'st thou, noble heart?—What will I do, thinkest thou? i 3 302
How now! who has put in?—'Tis one Iago, ancient to the general . ii 1 66
The bold Iago, Whose footing here anticipates our thoughts . . ii 1 75
Let it not gall your patience, good Iago, That I extend my manners . ii 1 98
I prithee, good Iago, Go to the bay and disembark my coffers . . ii 1 209
Iago hath direction what to do; But, notwithstanding, with my personal eye Will I look to't.—Iago is most honest . . . . ii 3 4
Welcome, Iago; we must to the watch.—Not this hour, lieutenant . ii 3 12
Not to-night, good Iago: I have very poor and unhappy brains for drinking . . . . ii 3 34
Honest Iago, that look'st dead with grieving, Speak, who began this? . ii 3 177
Iago can inform you,—While I spare speech, which something now offends me . . . . ii 3 198
On the court and guard of safety! 'Tis monstrous. Iago, who began't? ii 3 217
I know, Iago, Thy honesty and love doth mince this matter . . ii 3 246
Iago, look with care about the town, And silence those whom this vile brawl distracted . . . . ii 3 255
I have lost the immortal part of myself, and what remains is bestial. My reputation, Iago, my reputation! . . . . . . ii 3 265
Good night, honest Iago.—And what's he then that says I play the villain? . . . . ii 3 341
I have made bold, Iago, To send in to your wife . . . . iii 1 35
These letters give, Iago, to the pilot; And by him do my duties to the senate . . . . iii 2 1
My noble lord,— What dost thou say, Iago? . . . . . iii 3 93
Thou dost conspire against thy friend, Iago, If thou but think'st him wrong'd and makest his ear A stranger to thy thoughts . . . iii 3 142
No, Iago; I'll see before I doubt; when I doubt, prove . . . iii 3 189
Let me know more; Set on thy wife to observe: leave me, Iago . . iii 3 240
I'll have the work ta'en out, And give't Iago: what he will do with it Heaven knows, not I . . . . iii 3 297
Look here, Iago; All my fond love thus do I blow to heaven. 'Tis gone iii 3 444
Patience, I say; your mind perhaps may change.—Never, Iago . . iii 3 453
Witness that here Iago doth give up The execution of his wit, hands, heart, To wrong'd Othello's service! . . . . . . iii 3 465
Will you think so?—Think so, Iago!—What, To kiss in private? . . iv 1 1
Naked in bed, Iago, and not mean harm! . . . . . . iv 1 5
Dost thou hear, Iago? I will be found most cunning in my patience . iv 1 90
Iago beckons me; now he begins the story . . . . . iv 1 134
How shall I murder him, Iago? . . . . iv 1 179
Did you perceive how he laughed at his vice?—O Iago! . . . . iv 1 182
But yet the pity of it, Iago! O Iago, the pity of it, Iago! . . . iv 1 207
Iago. Get me some poison, Iago; this night: I'll not expostulate with her *Othello* iv 1 216
This night, Iago.—Do it not with poison, strangle her in her bed . . iv 1 219
What's the matter, lady?—Alas, Iago, my lord hath so bewhored her . iv 2 115
Am I that name, Iago?—What name, fair lady? . . . . . iv 2 118
O good Iago, What shall I do to win my lord again? . . . . iv 2 148
Every day thou daffest me with some device, Iago . . . . . iv 2 177
O brave Iago, honest and just, That hast such noble sense of thy friend's wrong! . . . . v 1 31
Iago? O, I am spoil'd, undone by villains! Give me some help . . v 1 54
O murderous slave! O villain!—O damn'd Iago! O inhuman dog! . . v 1 62
No, his mouth is stopp'd; Honest Iago hath ta'en order for't . . v 2 72
Dost understand the word? My friend, thy husband, honest, honest Iago . . . . v 2 154
O, are you come, Iago? you have done well, That men must lay their murders on your neck . . . . v 2 169
'Tis proper I obey him, but not now. Perchance, Iago, I will ne'er go home . . . . v 2 197
'Tis pitiful; but yet Iago knows That she with Cassio hath the act of shame A thousand times committed . . . . v 2 210
Iago in the interim Came in and satisfied him . . . . . . v 2 317
There is besides in Roderigo's letter, How he upbraids Iago . . . v 2 325
He spake, After long seeming dead, Iago hurt him, Iago set him on . v 2 328
Ibat. Hic ibat Simois; hic est Sigeia tellus . . . *T. of Shrew* iii 1 28
'Hic ibat,' as I told you before, 'Simois,' I am Lucentio . . . iii 1 31
Let me see if I can construe it: 'Hic ibat Simois,' I know you not . iii 1 42
Icarus. Follow thou thy desperate sire of Crete, Thou Icarus 1 *Hen. VI.* iv 6 55
And there died, My Icarus, my blossom, in his pride . . . . iv 7 16
I, Dædalus; my poor boy, Icarus; Thy father, Minos . . 3 *Hen. VI.* v 6 21
Ice. This weak impress of love is as a figure Trenched in ice *T. G. of Ver.* iii 2 7
Some run from brakes of ice, and answer none . . *Meas. for Meas.* ii 1 39
To bathe in fiery floods, or to reside In thrilling region of thick-ribbed ice . . . . iii 1 123
His urine is congealed ice . . . . iii 2 118
Tedious and brief! That is, hot ice and wondrous strange snow *M. N. D.* v 1 59
The very ice of chastity is in them [his kisses]. . . . *As Y. Like It* iii 4 18
If you break the ice and do this feat . . . . . *T. of Shrew* i 2 267
Who is that calls so coldly?—A piece of ice . . . . . iv 1 14
These boys are boys of ice, they'll none have her . . *All's Well* ii 3 99
To smooth the ice, or add another hue Unto the rainbow . *K. John* iv 2 13
You may as well go about to turn the sun to ice with fanning *Hen. V.* iv 1 212
Thou art all ice, thy kindness freezeth . . . . *Richard III.* iv 2 22
The fool slides o'er the ice that you should break . *Troi. and Cres.* iii 3 215
You are no surer, no, Than is the coal of fire upon the ice . *Coriolanus* i 1 177
Will the cold brook, Candied with ice, caudle thy morning taste? *T. of Athens* iv 3 226
When, in an angry parle, He smote the sledded Polacks on the ice *Hamlet* i 1 63
Be thou as chaste as ice, as pure as snow, thou shalt not escape calumny . . . . iii 1 140
Ice-brook. It is a sword of Spain, the ice-brook's temper . . *Othello* v 2 253
Iceland dog! thou prick-ear'd cur of Iceland! . . . . *Hen. V.* ii 1 44
Icicle. When icicles hang by the wall . . . . . *L. L. Lost* v 2 922
Where Phœbus' fire scarce thaws the icicles . . *Mer. of Venice* ii 1 5
Where you will hang like an icicle on a Dutchman's beard . *T. Night* iii 2 29
Let us not hang like roping icicles Upon our houses' thatch *Hen. V.* iii 5 23
Chaste as the ice That's curdied by the frost from purest snow *Coriolanus* v 3 65
Icy. On old Hiems thin and icy crown An odorous chaplet of sweet summer buds Is, as in mockery, set . . . . . *M. N. Dream* ii 1 109
The icy fang And churlish chiding of the winter's wind . *As Y. Like It* ii 1 6
Dead, forsook, cast off: And none of you will bid the winter come To thrust his icy fingers in my maw . . . . . . *K. John* v 7 37
And never learn'd The icy precepts of respect . . . *T. of Athens* iv 3 258
Like to the Pontic sea, Whose icy current and compulsive course Ne'er feels retiring ebb, but keeps due on . . . . . *Othello* iii 3 454
Icy-cold. If he be leaden, icy-cold, unwilling, Be thou so too *Richard III.* iii 1 176
Idea. The idea of her life shall sweetly creep Into his study . *Much Ado* iv 1 226
Full of forms, figures, shapes, objects, ideas, apprehensions . *L. L. Lost* iv 2 69
I did infer your lineaments, Being the right idea of your father *Rich. III.* iii 7 13
Idem. 'Tis 'semper idem,' for 'obsque hoc nihil est' . . 2 *Hen. IV.* v 5 30
Iden. It shall ne'er be said . . . That Alexander Iden, an esquire of Kent, Took odds to combat a poor famish'd man . . . . 2 *Hen. VI.* iv 10 46
Iden, farewell, and be proud of thy victory . . . . . . iv 10 77
Alexander Iden, that's my name; A poor esquire of Kent . . . v 1 74
Iden, kneel down. Rise up a knight. We give thee for reward a thousand marks . . . . v 1 78
May Iden live to merit such a bounty! . . . . v 1 81
Ides. Beware the ides of March.—What man is that?—A soothsayer bids you beware the ides of March . . . . *J. Cæsar* i 2 18
Beware the ides of March.—He is a dreamer; let us leave him . . i 2 23
Is not to-morrow, boy, the ides of March?—I know not, sir . . . ii 1 40
The ides of March are come.—Ay, Cæsar; but not gone . . . . iii 1 1
Remember March, the ides of March remember . . . . . iv 3 18
This same day Must end that work the ides of March begun . . . v 1 114
Idiot. That Slender, though well landed, is an idiot . . . *Mer. Wives* iv 4 86
Mome, malt-horse, capon, coxcomb, idiot, patch! . . *Com. of Errors* iii 1 32

Idiot. What's here? the portrait of a blinking idiot! *Mer. of Venice* ii 9 54
I know this letter will make a contemplative idiot of him *T. Night* ii 5 23
Making that idiot, laughter, keep men's eyes And strain their cheeks *K. John* iii 3 45
Mars his idiot! do, rudeness; do camel; do, do *Troi. and Cres.* ii 1 58
How some men creep in skittish fortune's hall, Whiles others play the idiots in her eyes! iii 3 135
For that I know An idiot holds his bauble for a god *T. Andron.* v 1 79
It is a tale Told by an idiot, full of sound and fury *Macbeth* v 5 27
For idiots in this case of favour would Be wisely definite *Cymbeline* i 6 42
Idiot-worshipper. Thou picture of what thou seemest, and idol of idiot-worshippers *Troi. and Cres.* v 1 7
Idle. No occupation; all men idle, all; And women too, but innocent and pure *Tempest* ii 1 154
No marrying 'mong his subjects?—None, man; all idle: whores and knaves ii 1 166
Or else for want of idle time, could not again reply *T. G. of Ver.* ii 1 172
Myself have been an idle truant, Omitting the sweet benefit of time ii 4 64
As idle as she may hang together, for want of company *Mer. Wives* iii 2 13
And held in idle price to haunt assemblies *Meas. for Meas.* i 3 9
Could I with boot change for an idle plume, Which the air beats for vain ii 4 11
To draw with idle spiders' strings Most ponderous and substantial things! iii 2 289
Thousand escapes of wit Make thee the father of their idle dreams iv 1 64
It is dross, Usurping ivy, brier, or idle moss *Com. of Errors* ii 2 180
I'll dine above with you to-day And shrive you of a thousand idle pranks ii 2 210
These oaths and laws will prove an idle scorn *L. L. Lost* i 1 311
And critic Timon laugh at idle toys! iv 3 170
If sickly ears, Deaf'd with the clamours of their own dear groans, Will hear your idle scorns, continue then v 2 875
Never did mockers waste more idle breath *M. N. Dream* iii 2 168
Seems to me now As the remembrance of an idle gawd iv 1 172
And this weak and idle theme, No more yielding but a dream v 1 434
I will weary you then no longer with idle talking *As Y. Like It* v 2 57
Heaven cease this idle humour in your honour! *T. of Shrew* Ind. 2 14
Did I never speak of all that time?—O, yes, my lord, but very idle words Ind. 2 85
Virginity is peevish, proud, idle, made of self-love *All's Well* i 1 157
An idle lord, I swear.—I think so ii 5 54
Yet in his idle fire, To buy his will, it would not seem too dear iii 7 26
A foolish idle boy, but for all that very ruttish iv 3 242
And your store, I think, is not for idle markets, sir *T. Night* iii 3 46
Hang yourselves all! you are idle shallow things iii 4 136
Fancies too weak for boys, too green and idle For girls of nine *W. Tale* iii 2 182
And strain their cheeks to idle merriment *K. John* iii 3 46
Full of idle dreams, Not knowing what they fear, but full of fear iv 2 145
Thou idle dreamer, wherefore didst thou so? iv 2 153
His pure brain, Which some suppose the soul's frail dwelling-house, Doth by the idle comments that it makes Foretell the ending of mortality v 7 4
Which waste of idle hours hath quite thrown down *Richard II.* iii 4 66
What, stand'st thou idle here? lend me thy sword *1 Hen. IV.* v 3 41
Repent at idle times as thou mayest; and so, farewell *2 Hen. IV.* ii 2 140
Every idle, nice and wanton reason Shall to the king taste of this action iv 1 191
Took stand for idle speculation *Hen. V.* iv 2 31
A wonder and a pointing-stock To every idle rascal follower *2 Hen. VI.* ii 4 47
Or like an idle thresher with a flail, Fell gently down *3 Hen. VI.* ii 1 131
To prove a villain And hate the idle pleasures of these days *Richard III.* i 1 31
Idle weeds are fast in growth iii 1 103
And therefore is he idle?—O, my fair cousin, I must not say so iii 1 105
Not sleeping, to engross his idle body, But praying iii 7 76
If you love an addle egg as well as you love an idle head, you would eat chickens i' the shell *Troi. and Cres.* i 2 147
Thou idle immaterial skein of sleave-silk v 1 35
Idle and unactive, Still cupboarding the viand *Coriolanus* i 1 102
I must have you play the idle huswife with me this afternoon i 3 76
My hand hath been but idle; let it serve To ransom my two nephews *T. Andron.* iii 1 172
Dreams, Which are the children of an idle brain *Rom. and Jul.* i 4 97
A lover may bestride the gossamer That idles in the wanton summer air ii 6 19
Ladies, there is an idle banquet attends you *T. of Athens* i 2 160
No, gods, I am no idle votarist; roots, you clear heavens! iv 3 27
Hence! home, you idle creatures, get you home: Is this a holiday? *J. C.* i 1 1
Break off betimes, And every man hence to his idle bed ii 1 117
They pass by me as the idle wind, Which I respect not iv 3 68
Or look'd upon this love with idle sight *Hamlet* ii 2 138
They are coming to the play; I must be idle iii 2 95
Come, come, you answer with an idle tongue.—Go, go, you question with a wicked tongue iii 4 11
I begin to find an idle and fond bondage in the oppression of aged tyranny *Lear* i 2 51
Idle old man, That still would manage those authorities That he hath given away! i 3 16
Darnel, and all the idle weeds that grow In our sustaining corn iv 4 5
The murmuring surge, That on the unnumber'd idle pebbles chafes iv 6 21
Mine's not an idle cause *Othello* i 2 95
Antres vast and deserts idle, Rough quarries, rocks and hills i 3 140
Reputation is an idle and most false imposition; oft got without merit ii 3 269
If idle talk will once be necessary, I'll not sleep neither *Ant. and Cleo.* v 2 50
Idle-headed. The superstitious idle-headed eld *Mer. Wives* iv 4 36
Idleness. Wear out thy youth with shapeless idleness *T. G. of Ver.* i 1 8
I am helping you to mar that which God made, a poor unworthy brother of yours, with idleness *As Y. Like It* i 1 37
But see, while idly I stood looking on, I found the effect of love in idleness *T. of Shrew* i 1 156
For want of other idleness, I'll bide your proof *T. Night* i 5 70
Nor conversant with ease and idleness *K. John* iv 3 70
And will awhile uphold The unyoked humour of your idleness *1 Hen. IV.* i 2 220
Assemble now, From every region, apes of idleness! *2 Hen. IV.* iv 5 123
Conceives by idleness and nothing teems But hateful docks *Hen. V.* v 2 51
Sterile with idleness, or manured with industry *Othello* i 3 328
I must from this enchanting queen break off: Ten thousand harms, more than the ills I know, My idleness doth hatch *Ant. and Cleo.* i 2 134
But that your royalty Holds idleness your subject, I should take you For idleness itself i 3 92
'Tis sweating labour To bear such idleness so near the heart i 3 94
Assemble we immediate council: Pompey Thrives in our idleness i 4 76
Idly. God help, poor souls, how idly do they talk! *Com. of Errors* iv 4 132
Idly. But see, while idly I stood looking on, I found the effect of love in idleness *T. of Shrew* i 1 155
This from rumour's tongue I idly heard; if true or false I know not *K. John* iv 2 124
Mocking the air with colours idly spread, And find no check v 1 72
Well, well, I see I talk but idly, and you laugh at me *Richard II.* iii 3 171
As in a theatre, the eyes of men, After a well-graced actor leaves the stage, Are idly bent on him that enters next v 2 25
How ill it follows, after you have laboured so hard, you should talk so idly *2 Hen. IV.* ii 2 32
I feel me much to blame, So idly to profane the precious time ii 4 391
King Pharamond, Idly supposed the founder of this law *Hen. V.* i 2 59
She is so idly king'd, Her sceptre so fantastically borne ii 4 26
Then I will slay myself, For living idly here in pomp and ease *1 Hen. VI.* i 1 142
Let's raise the siege: why live we idly here? Talbot is taken i 2 13
Who being accused a crafty murderer, His guilt should be but idly posted over, Because his purpose is not executed *2 Hen. VI.* iii 1 255
Seals a commission to a blank of danger; And danger, like an ague, subtly taints Even then when we sit idly in the sun *Troi. and Cres.* iii 3 233
I had rather have one scratch my head i' the sun When the alarum were struck than idly sit To hear my nothings monster'd *Coriolanus* ii 2 80
A thing slipp'd idly from me. Our poesy is as a gum *T. of Athens* i 1 20
Idol. Was this the idol that you worship so?—Even she *T. G. of Ver.* ii 4 144
I am very loath to be your idol, sir iv 2 129
But O how vile an idol proves this god! *T. Night* iii 4 399
What art thou, thou idol ceremony? What kind of god art thou? *Hen. V.* iv 1 257
Shall he be worshipp'd Of that we hold an idol more than he? *T. and C.* ii 3 199
Thou picture of what thou seemest, and idol of idiot-worshippers v 1 7
To the celestial and my soul's idol, the most beautified Ophelia *Hamlet* ii 2 109
Idolatrous. My idolatrous fancy Must sanctify his reliques *All's Well* i 1 108
Idolatry. Were there sense in his idolatry, My substance should be statue in thy stead *T. G. of Ver.* iv 4 205
Pure, pure idolatry. God amend us, God amend! *L. L. Lost* iv 3 75
Dotes in idolatry Upon this spotted and inconstant man *M. N. Dream* i 1 109
'Tis mad idolatry To make the service greater than the god *Tr. and Cr.* ii 2 56
Swear by thy gracious self, Which is the god of my idolatry *R. and J.* ii 2 114
If. Vouchsafe my prayer May know if you remain upon this island *Tempest* i 2 423
My prime request . . . is, O you wonder! If you be maid or no? i 2 427
If you but knew how you the purpose cherish Whiles thus you mock it! ii 1 224
I will give him some relief, if it be but for that ii 2 70
Here if thou stay, thou canst not see thy love *T. G. of Ver.* iii 1 244
If money go before, all ways do lie open *Mer. Wives* ii 2 174
And try your penitence, if it be sound, Or hollowly put on *M. for M.* ii 3 22
Canst thou tell if Claudio die to-morrow or no? iii 2 180
Can you tell if Rosalind, the duke's daughter, be banished? *As Y. Like It* i 1 110
And you may avoid that too, with an If v 4 103
One of them thought but of an If, as, 'If you said so, then I said so' v 4 106
Your If is the only peace-maker; much virtue in If v 4 107
List if thou canst hear the tread of travellers *1 Hen. IV.* ii 2 34
If thou love me, practise an answer ii 4 411
If thou have power to raise him, bring him hither iii 1 60
Now the battle's ended, If friend or foe, let him be gently used *3 Hen. VI.* ii 6 45
If! thou protector of this damned strumpet, Tellest thou me of 'ifs'? *Richard III.* iii 4 76
How if, when I am laid into the tomb, I wake before the time? *R. and J.* iv 3 30
If thou wert the lion, the fox would beguile thee *T. of Athens* iv 3 330
If it were done when 'tis done, then 'twere well It were done quickly *Macbeth* i 7 1
If I stand here, I saw him.—Fie, for shame! iii 4 74
Ignis fatuus. If I did not think thou hadst been an ignis fatuus or a ball of wildfire *1 Hen. IV.* iii 3 45
Ignoble. To most ignoble stooping *Tempest* i 2 116
Will ignoble make you, Yea, scandalous to the world *W. Tale* ii 3 120
Perish, base prince, ignoble Duke of York! *1 Hen. VI.* iii 1 178
Decrepit miser! base ignoble wretch! I am descended of a gentler blood v 4 7
'Tis but a base ignoble mind That mounts no higher than a bird can soar.—I thought as much *2 Hen. VI.* ii 1 13
Blunt-witted lord, ignoble in demeanour! iii 2 210
You must all confess That I was not ignoble of descent *3 Hen. VI.* iv 1 70
That ignoble traitor, The dangerous and unsuspected Hastings *Rich. III.* iii 5 22
Her royal stock graft with ignoble plants iii 7 127
Ignobly. Noble uncle, thus ignobly used *1 Hen. VI.* ii 5 35
Nor should thy prowess want praise and esteem, But that 'tis shown ignobly and in treason *2 Hen. VI.* v 2 23
Unwisely, not ignobly, have I given *T. of Athens* ii 2 183
By the kind gods, 'tis most ignobly done To pluck me by the beard *Lear* iii 7 35
Ignominious. With other vile and ignominious terms *1 Hen. VI.* iv 1 97
With ignominious words, though clerkly couch'd *2 Hen. VI.* iii 1 179
My followers' base and ignominious treasons makes me betake me to my heels iv 8 66
Ignominy. Thy ignominy sleep with thee in the grave! *1 Hen. IV.* v 4 100
Ignomy in ransom and free pardon Are of two houses *Meas. for Meas.* ii 4 111
Ignomy and shame Pursue thy life, and live aye with thy name! *Troi. and Cres.* v 10 33
I blush to think upon this ignomy *T. Andron.* iv 2 115
Ignorance. Fie, what the ignorance is! *Mer. Wives* i 1 182
Ignorance itself is a plummet o'er me: use me as you will v 5 172
Were my lord so, his ignorance were wise, Where now his knowledge must prove ignorance *L. L. Lost* ii 1 102
O thou monster Ignorance, how deformed dost thou look! iv 2 24
Thrust thy sharp wit quite through my ignorance; Cut me to pieces v 2 398
Thine ignorance makes thee away *All's Well* iv 1 226
Into the staggers and the careless lapse Of youth and ignorance ii 3 171
I say, there is no darkness but ignorance *T. Night* iv 2 47
This house is as dark as ignorance, though ignorance were as dark as hell iv 2 49
To choke his days With barbarous ignorance *K. John* iv 2 59
Dull unfeeling barren ignorance Is made my gaoler *Richard II.* i 3 168
O, I am ignorance itself in this! *1 Hen. IV.* iii 1 213
O gross and miserable ignorance! *2 Hen. VI.* iv 2 178
Ignorance is the curse of God, Knowledge the wing wherewith we fly to heaven iv 7 78
You come to reprehend my ignorance *Richard III.* iii 7 113
With all their honourable points of ignorance *Hen. VIII.* i 3 26
Tamer than sleep, fonder than ignorance *Troi. and Cres.* i 1 10
Which short-armed ignorance itself knows is so abundant scarce ii 3 16
The common curse of mankind, folly and ignorance, be thine in great revenue! ii 3 31
I had rather be a tick in a sheep than such a valiant ignorance iii 3 316
If he have power, Then vail your ignorance *Coriolanus* iii 1 98

Ignorance. Cannot conclude but by the yea and no Of general ignorance *Coriolanus* iii 1 146
Your ignorance, which finds not till it feels . . . iii 3 129
Are mock'd for valiant ignorance, And perish constant fools . . iv 6 104
In a violent popular ignorance, given your enemy your shield . v 2 43
Like powder in a skilless soldier's flask, Is set a-fire by thine own ignorance, And thou dismember'd . . *Rom. and Jul.* iii 3 133
This insculpture, which With wax I brought away, whose soft impression Interprets for my poor ignorance . . *T. of Athens* v 4 69
O, answer me! Let me not burst in ignorance . . *Hamlet* i 4 46
Nick-name God's creatures, and make your wantonness your ignorance iii 1 152
In mine ignorance Your skill shall, like a star i' the darkest night, Stick fiery off indeed . . . . . v 2 266
It was great ignorance, Gloucester's eyes being out, To let him live *Lear* iv 5 9
O heavy ignorance! thou praisest the worst best . . *Othello* ii 1 144
One that truly loves you, That errs in ignorance and not in cunning . iii 3 49
As salt as wolves in pride, and fools as gross As ignorance made drunk iii 3 405
The greater cantle of the world is lost With very ignorance *A. and C.* iii 10 7
Unto us it is A cell of ignorance; travelling a-bed . *Cymbeline* iii 3 33
Ignorant. Thee, my daughter, who Art ignorant of what thou art *Tempest* i 2 18
He is not valiant.—Thou liest, most ignorant monster . . iii 2 28
Their rising senses Begin to chase the ignorant fumes that mantle Their clearer reason . . . . . v 1 67
I think your lordship is not ignorant . . .—I know it well *T. G. of Ver.* i 3 25
For being ignorant to whom it goes I writ at random, very doubtfully . ii 1 116
Thou art not ignorant How she opposes her against my will . . . iii 2 25
Thou art not ignorant what dear good will I bear . . . iv 3 14
Most ignorant of what he's most assured . . . *Meas. for Meas.* ii 2 119
Either you are ignorant, Or seem so craftily; and that's not good. . ii 4 74
Let me be ignorant, and in nothing good . . . . ii 4 76
A very superficial, ignorant, unweighing fellow . . . . iii 2 147
I will keep her ignorant of her good, To make her heavenly comforts of despair . . . . . . iv 3 113
Pretty babes, That mourn'd for fashion, ignorant what to fear *Com. of Er.* i 1 74
You are not ignorant, all-telling fame Doth noise abroad . *L. L. Lost* ii 1 21
Your ladyship is ignorant what it is.—Were my lord so, his ignorance were wise . . . . . . ii 101
And, to humour the ignorant, call I the deer the princess killed a pricket iv 2 52
All ignorant that soul that sees thee without wonder . . iv 2 117
Nor is the wide world ignorant of her worth . . *Mer. of Venice* i 1 167
Cunning in music and the mathematics, To instruct her fully in those sciences, Whereof I know she is not ignorant . *T. of Shrew* ii 1 58
Being not ignorant of the impossibility . . . *All's Well* iv 1 38
This letter, being so excellently ignorant, will breed no terror *T. Night* iii 4 207
Imprison't not In ignorant concealment . . . *W. Tale* i 2 397
Either thou art most ignorant by age, Or thou wert born a fool . ii 1 173
Whose ignorant credulity will not Come up to the truth . . ii 1 192
I am as ignorant in that as you In so entitling me . . . ii 3 69
The gods themselves, Wotting no more than I, are ignorant . . iii 2 77
That shows the ignorant a kind of fear Before not dreamt of 1 *Hen. IV.* iv 1 74
Wise bearing or ignorant carriage is caught, as men take diseases 2 *Hen. IV.* v 1 84
I am ignorant and cannot guess . . . . 1 *Hen. VI.* ii 5 60
And, ignorant of his birth and parentage, Became a bricklayer 2 *Hen. VI.* iv 2 152
I am Traduced by ignorant tongues . . . *Hen. VIII.* i 2 72
Why either were you ignorant to see't, Or, seeing it, of such childish friendliness To yield your voices? . . *Coriolanus* ii 3 182
Assemble, And on a safer judgement all revoke Your ignorant election . ii 3 227
The eyes of the ignorant More learned than the ears . . . iii 2 76
That thou mightst not lose the dues of rejoicing, by being ignorant of what greatness is promised thee . . . . *Macbeth* i 5 13
Thy letters have transported me beyond This ignorant present . i 5 58
Make mad the guilty and appal the free, Confound the ignorant *Hamlet* ii 2 591
I know you are not ignorant— I would you did, sir . . . v 2 139
You are not ignorant of what excellence Laertes is . . . . v 2 143
I am guiltless, as I am ignorant Of what hath moved you . . *Lear* i 4 295
I am mainly ignorant What place this is . . . . iv 7 65
Alas, what ignorant sin have I committed? . . . *Othello* iv 2 70
O gull! O dolt! As ignorant as dirt! thou hast done a deed . v 2 164
We, ignorant of ourselves, Beg often our own harms . *Ant. and Cleo.* ii 1 5
For which myself, the ignorant motive, do So far ask pardon . . ii 2 96
His shipping—Poor ignorant baubles!—on our terrible seas . *Cymbeline* iii 1 27
I am ignorant in what I am commanded . . . . iii 2 23
Who needs must know of her departure and Dost seem so ignorant . iv 3 11
Ilbow. De nails, de arm, de ilbow.—Sauf votre honneur, de elbow *Hen. V.* iii 4 50
'Ild. God 'ild you for your last company . . *As Y. Like It* iii 3 76
I like him very well.—God 'ild you, sir; I desire you of the like . v 4 56
Herein I teach you How you shall bid God 'ild us for your pains *Macbeth* i 6 13
How do you, pretty lady?—Well, God 'ild you! . . *Hamlet* iv 5 41
Ilion. The armipotent Mars, of lances the almighty, Gave Hector a gift, the heir of Ilion . . . . *L. L. Lost* v 2 658
Troy must not be, nor goodly Ilion stand; Our firebrand brother, Paris, burns us all. Cry, Trojans, cry! . . *Troi. and Cres.* ii 2 109
And thy life shall be as safe As Priam is in Ilion . . . iv 4 118
And with private soul Did in great Ilion thus translate him to me . iv 5 112
Since first I saw yourself and Diomed In Ilion, on your Greekish embassy . . . . iv 5 216
So, Ilion, fall thou next! now, Troy, sink down! Here lies thy heart . v 8 11
Ilium. Between our Ilium and where she resides, Let it be call'd the wild and wandering flood . . . . . . i 1 104
When were you at Ilium?—This morning, uncle . . . i 2 46
Was Hector armed and gone ere ye came to Ilium? . . . i 2 50
Shall we stand up here, and see them as they pass toward Ilium? . . i 2 194
Senseless Ilium, Seeming to feel this blow, with flaming top Stoops *Ham.* ii 2 496
Ill. Abhorred slave, Which any print of goodness wilt not take, Being capable of all ill! . . . . . *Tempest* i 2 353
There's nothing ill can dwell in such a temple . . . . i 2 457
How likes she my discourse?—Ill, when you talk of war *T. G. of Ver.* v 2 16
And, trust me, I was coming to you. You look very ill . *Mer. Wives* ii 1 36
You do ill to teach the child such words . . . . iv 1 67
Look, when I serve him so, he takes it ill . . *Com. of Errors* ii 1 12
How ill agrees it with your gravity To counterfeit thus grossly! . . ii 2 170
Ill it doth beseem your holiness To separate the husband and the wife . v 1 110
If they lead to any ill, I will leave them at the next turning . *Much Ado* ii 1 159
By my troth, I am exceeding ill: heigh-ho! . . . . iii 4 54
How doth your cousin?—Very ill.—And how do you?—Very ill too . v 2 92
I am ill at reckoning; it fitteth the spirit of a tapster . *L. L. Lost* i 2 42
Nothing becomes him ill that he would well . . . . ii 1 46
Most power to do most harm, least knowing ill . . . . ii 1 58
Now mercy goes to kill, And shooting well is then accounted ill . . iv 1 25
Ill. As I for praise alone now seek to spill The poor deer's blood, that my heart means no ill . . . . . *L. L. Lost* iv 1 35
Ill, to example ill, Would from my forehead wipe a perjured note . . iv 3 124
Jack shall have Jill; Nought shall go ill . . . *M. N. Dream* iii 2 462
There is some ill a-brewing towards my rest . . *Mer. of Venice* ii 5 17
Ill, to like him that ne'er it likes . . . . *All's Well* ii 1 165
It looks ill, it eats drily . . . . i 1 175
Would you believe my oaths, When I did love you ill? . . . iv 2 27
The web of our life is of a mingled yarn, good and ill together . . iv 3 84
La you, an you speak ill of the devil, how he takes it at heart! *T. Night* iii 4 111
Or thou goest to the grange or mill.—If to either, thou dost ill *W. Tale* iv 4 310
Where doing tends to ill, The truth is then most done not doing it *K. John* iii 1 272
What can go well, when we have run so ill? Are we not beaten? . . iii 4 5
If heaven be pleased that you must use me ill, Why then you must . iv 1 55
What doth our cousin lay to Mowbray's charge? It must be great that can inherit us So much as of a thought of ill in him . *Richard II.* i 1 86
Nor never by advised purpose meet To plot, contrive, or complot any ill i 3 189
I am in health, I breathe, and see thee ill.—Now He that made me knows I see thee ill; Ill in myself to see, and in thee seeing ill . ii 1 92
Too well, too well thou tell'st a tale so ill . . . . iii 2 121
Would not this ill do well? Well, well, I see I talk but idly, and you laugh . . . . iii 3 170
Ill mayst thou thrive, if thou grant any grace! . . . . v 3 99
Whereby I told thee they were ill for a green wound . . 2 *Hen. IV.* ii 1 106
How ill it follows, after you have laboured so hard, you should talk so idly! . . . . ii 2 31
Your majesty hath been this fortnight ill, And these unseason'd hours perforce must add Unto your sickness . . . . iii 1 104
Wherefore do you so ill translate yourself? . . . . iv 1 47
You wish me health in very happy season; For I am, on the sudden, something ill . . . . iv 2 80
O me! come near me; now I am much ill . . . . . iv 4 111
How doth the king?—Exceeding ill.—Heard he the good news yet? . iv 5 11
If the deed were ill, Be you contented, wearing now the garland . . v 2 83
How ill white hairs become a fool and jester! . . . . v 5 52
Put thy face between his sheets, and do the office of a warming-pan. Faith, he's very ill . . . . . . *Hen. V.* ii 1 89
I dare say you love him not so ill, to wish him here alone . . iv 1 129
'Tis certain, every man that dies ill, the ill upon his own head . iv 1 197
Or make my ill the advantage of my good . . . 1 *Hen. VI.* ii 5 129
And fashion'd thee that instrument of ill . . . . iii 3 65
Let him perceive how ill we brook his treason . . . . v 1 74
And may that thought, when I imagine ill Against my king and nephew, virtuous Henry, Be my last breathing in this mortal world! 2 *Hen. VI.* i 2 19
I never meant him any ill, nor the king, nor the queen . . ii 3 91
Ill can thy noble mind abrook The abject people gazing on thy face . ii 4 10
Ill blows the wind that profits nobody . . . 3 *Hen. VI.* ii 5 55
Then be your eyes the witness of this ill . . . *Richard III.* iii 4 69
And something spoke in choler, ill, and hasty . . *Hen. VIII.* ii 1 34
He fell sick suddenly, and grew so ill He could not sit his mule . iv 2 15
Of his own body he was ill, and gave The clergy ill example . . iv 2 43
Those wounds heal ill that men do give themselves *Troi. and Cres.* iii 3 229
Let me deserve so ill as you, and make me Your fellow tribune *Coriol.* iii 1 51
Not having the power to do the good it would, For the ill which doth control't . . . . iii 1 161
Ill art thou repaid For that good hand thou sent'st the emperor *T. An.* iii 1 235
I curse the day—and yet, I think, Few come within the compass of my curse—Wherein I did not some notorious ill . . . . v 1 127
Bid a sick man in sadness make his will: Ah, word ill urged to one that is so ill! . . . . . . *Rom. and Jul.* i 1 209
Shall I speak ill of him that is my husband? Ah, poor my lord . iii 2 97
Go hire me twenty cunning cooks.—You shall have none ill, sir . . iv 2 3
You love your child so ill, That you run mad, seeing that she is well . iv 5 75
The heavens do lour upon you for some ill; Move them no more . iv 5 94
How fares my Juliet? that I ask again; For nothing can be ill, if she be well.—Then she is well, and nothing can be ill . . . v 1 16
Fear comes upon me: O, much I fear some ill unlucky thing . . v 3 136
Those healths will make thee and thy state look ill . *T. of Athens* i 2 58
If wrongs be evils and enforce us kill, What folly 'tis to hazard life for ill! . . . . iii 5 37
Banishment! It comes not ill; I hate not to be banish'd . . iii 5 112
Make it known to us.—You'll take it ill . . . . . v 1 93
How ill this taper burns! . . . . . . *J. Cæsar* iv 3 275
This supernatural soliciting Cannot be ill, cannot be good . *Macbeth* i 3 131
Things bad begun make strong themselves by ill . . . iii 2 55
I am ill at these numbers; I have not art to reckon my groans *Hamlet* ii 2 120
Makes us rather bear those ills we have Than fly to others that we know not of . . . . iii 1 81
The gallows does well; but how does it well? it does well to those that do ill . . . . v 1 53
Thou dost ill to say the gallows is built stronger than the church . v 1 53
Thou wouldst not think how ill all's here about my heart . . v 2 223
A stone-cutter or a painter could not have made him so ill . *Lear* ii 2 64
The king must take it ill, That he's so slightly valued in his messenger ii 2 152
If he ask for me, I am ill, and gone to bed . . . . iii 3 18
My point and period will be throughly wrought, Or well or ill, as this day's battle's fought . . . . iv 7 98
Let them know, The ills we do, their ills instruct us so . *Othello* iv 3 104
We bring forth weeds, When our quick minds lie still; and our ills told us Is as our earing . . . . *Ant. and Cleo.* i 2 114
Ten thousand harms, more than the ills I know, My idleness doth hatch i 2 133
But let it be: I am quickly ill, and well, So Antony loves . . i 3 72
You take things ill which are not so, Or being, concern you not . ii 2 29
There's gold for thee. Thou must not take my former sharpness ill . iii 3 38
I have done ill; Of which I do accuse myself so sorely, That I will joy no more . . . . iv 6 18
I have done my work ill, friends: O, make an end Of what I have begun iv 14 105
Doubting things go ill often hurts more Than to be sure they do *Cymb.* i 6 95
Many times, Doth ill deserve by doing well . . . . iii 3 54
I am ill, but your being by me Cannot amend me . . . iv 2 11
Well or ill, I am bound to you . . . . . . iv 2 45
Ghost unlaid forbear thee!—Nothing ill come near thee! . . iv 2 279
You some permit To second ills with ills, each elder worse . . v 1 14
Fair glass of light, I loved you, and could still, Were not this glorious casket stored with ill . . . . . *Pericles* i 1 77
If Jove stray, who dares say Jove doth ill? It is enough you know . i 1 104
My shipwreck now's no ill, Since I have here my father's gift in's will. ii 1 139
Honour be but a goal to my will, This day I'll rise, or else add ill to ill ii 1 172
Unscissar'd shall this hair of mine remain, Though I show ill in't . iii 3 30

Ill advantage. To take an ill advantage of his absence . *Mer. Wives* iii 3 116
Ill affected. No marvel, then, though he were ill affected . *Lear* ii 1 100
Ill angel. You follow the young prince up and down, like his ill angel.—Not so, my lord; your ill angel is light . *2 Hen. IV.* i 2 186
Ill aspects. Corrects the ill aspects of planets evil . *Troi. and Cres.* i 3 92
Ill at ease. I am very ill at ease, Unfit for mine own purposes *Othello* iii 3 32
Ill become. For as it would ill become me to be vain, indiscreet, or a fool, So were there a patch set on learning, to see him in a school *L. L. Lost* iv 2 31
Ten thousand bloody crowns of mothers' sons Shall ill become the flower of England's face . *Richard II.* iii 3 97
Enjoy thy plainness, It nothing ill becomes thee . *Ant. and Cleo.* ii 6 81
Ill befits. It ill befits thy state And birth, that thou shouldst stand while Lewis doth sit . *3 Hen. VI.* iii 3 2
Ill beginning. This was an ill beginning of the night . *J. Cæsar* iv 3 234
Ill beseem. It ill beseems this presence to cry aim . *K. John* ii 1 196
Ill beseemeth. To teach a teacher ill beseemeth me . *L. L. Lost* ii 1 108
Ill-beseeming. In these ill-beseeming arms . *2 Hen. IV.* iv 1 84
Infamous And ill beseeming any common man . *1 Hen. VI.* iv 1 31
How ill-beseeming is it in thy sex To triumph! . *3 Hen. VI.* i 4 113
Put off these frowns, An ill-beseeming semblance for a feast *Rom. and Jul.* i 5 76
Unseemly woman in a seeming man! Or ill-beseeming beast in seeming both! . iii 3 113
Ill bestowed. Suit ill spent and labour ill bestowed . *Much Ado* iii 2 103
Whose life were ill bestow'd or death unfamed . *Troi. and Cres.* ii 2 159
Ill-boding. But, O malignant and ill-boding stars! . *1 Hen VI.* iv 5 6
And his ill-boding tongue no more shall speak . *3 Hen. VI.* ii 6 59
Ill-breeding. Strew Dangerous conjectures in ill-breeding minds *Hamlet* iv 5 15
Ill chances. Against ill chances men are ever merry *2 Hen. IV.* iv 2 81
Ill-composed. There grows In my most ill-composed affection such A stanchless avarice *Macbeth* iv 3 77
Ill conditions. Yes, and his ill conditions; and, in despite of all, dies for him . *Much Ado* iii 2 68
Ill cook. 'Tis an ill cook that cannot lick his own fingers *Rom. and Jul.* iv 2 6
Ill counsel. And the ill counsel of a desert place *M. N. Dream* ii 1 218
O, you give me ill counsel . *T. Night* v 1 34
Ill day. This ill day A most outrageous fit of madness took him *C. of Er.* v 1 138
Ill deeds are doubled with an evil word . iii 2 20
How oft the sight of means to do ill deeds Make deeds ill done! *K. John* iv 2 219
Alas! for whose sake did I that ill deed? . *Richard III.* i 4 216
Ill demeaned. If York have ill demean'd himself in France, Then let him be denay'd the regentship . *2 Hen. VI.* i 3 106
Ill digestions. Unquiet meals make ill digestions . *Com. of Errors* v 1 74
Ill-dispersing. O ill-dispersing wind of misery! . *Richard III.* iv 1 53
Ill-disposed. Right ill-disposed in brawl ridiculous . *Hen. V.* iv Prol. 51
Within his tent; but ill disposed *Troi. and Cres.* ii 3 84
Ill-divining. O God, I have an ill-divining soul! . *Rom. and Jul.* iii 5 54
Ill doctrine. He may, my lord; has wherewithal: in him Sparing would show a worse sin than ill doctrine *Hen. VIII.* i 3 60
Ill-doing. We knew not The doctrine of ill-doing, nor dream'd That any did. Had we pursued that life . *W. Tale* i 2 70
Ill done. How oft the sight of means to do ill deeds Make deeds ill done! *K. John* iv 2 220
Tish ill done: the work ish give over, the trompet sound the retreat *Hen. V.* iii 2 93
Ill employment. See now how wit may be made a Jack-a-Lent, when 'tis upon ill employment! . *Mer. Wives* v 5 135
Ill end. This day, all things begun come to ill end! . *K. John* iii 1 94
Ill-erected. This is the way To Julius Cæsar's ill-erected tower *Richard II.* v 1 2
Ill event. It doth presage some ill event . *1 Hen. VI.* iv 1 191
Ill example. As he is now, nothing: Of his own body he was ill, and gave The clergy ill example . *Hen. VIII.* iv 2 44
Ill-faced. Crooked, old and sere, Ill-faced, worse bodied *Com. of Errors* iv 2 20
Ill fare. How fares your majesty?—Poison'd,—ill fare—dead . *K. John* v 7 35
Ill fashion. Thou friend of an ill fashion! . *T. G. of Ver.* v 4 61
Ill-favoured. Out, out, Lucetta! that will be ill-favour'd . ii 7 54
They are very ill-favoured rough things . *Mer. Wives* i 1 311
O, what a world of vile ill-favour'd faults Looks handsome in three hundred pounds a-year! . iii 4 32
A properer man Than she a woman: 'tis such fools as you That makes the world full of ill-favour'd children . *As Y. Like It* iii 5 53
An ill-favoured thing, sir, but mine own . v 4 60
And wish thee to a shrewd ill-favour'd wife *T. of Shrew* i 2 60
It was a black ill-favour'd fly *T. Andron.* iii 2 66
Ill-favouredly. And sped you, sir?—Very ill-favouredly . *Mer. Wives* iii 5 68
Those that she makes honest she makes very ill-favouredly *As Y. Like It* i 2 42
Mar no moe of my verses with reading them ill-favouredly . iii 2 279
Yon island carrions . . . Ill-favouredly become the morning field *Hen. V.* iv 2 40
Ill fortune. Cowardly knight! ill fortune follow thee! . *1 Hen. VI.* iii 2 109
Ill-got. Things ill-got had ever bad success . *3 Hen. VI.* ii 2 46
Ill hap. All the best men are ours; for 'tis ill hap, If they hold when their ladies bid 'em clap *Hen. VIII.* Epil. 13
Ill-headed. If tall, a lance ill-headed . *Much Ado* iii 1 64
Ill hours. My lady takes great exceptions to your ill hours . *T. Night* i 3 6
Ill house. A hot-house, which, I think, is a very ill house too *M. for M.* ii 1 67
Ill husband. Sure, in that I deem you an ill husband . *Hen. VIII.* iii 2 142
Ill-inhabited. O knowledge ill-inhabited! . *As Y. Like It* iii 3 10
Ill intent. Be you thoughten That I came with no ill intent . *Pericles* iv 6 116
Ill killed. I wished your venison better; it was ill killed . *Mer. Wives* i 1 84
Ill laid up. O, you shall see him laugh till his face be like a wet cloak ill laid up! . *2 Hen. IV.* v 1 95
Ill layer up. Old age, that ill layer up of beauty . *Hen. V.* v 2 248
Ill left. My power is weak and all ill left . *Richard II.* ii 3 154
Ill life. The sweet woman leads an ill life with him . *Mer. Wives* ii 2 92
Ill luck. Sir John, we have had ill luck; we could never meet . v 5 120
No ill luck stirring but what lights on my shoulders . *Mer. of Venice* iii 1 98
Yes, other men have ill luck too: Antonio, as I heard in Genoa,— What, what, what? ill luck, ill luck? . iii 1 102
Said he . . . that rebellion Had met ill luck? . *2 Hen. IV.* i 1 51
Ill manner. What manner of man?—Of very ill manner . *T. Night* i 5 162
Ill men. He was too good to be Where ill men were *Cymbeline* v 5 159
Ill met by moonlight, proud Titania *M. N. Dream* ii 1 60
Ill name. You are in an ill name . *2 Hen. IV.* ii 4 98
Ill neighbourhood. England, being empty of defence, Hath shook and trembled at the ill neighbourhood *Hen. V.* i 2 154
Ill news. But hear these ill news with the ears of Claudio . *Much Ado* ii 1 180
Do not seek to stuff My head with more ill news, for it is full *K. John* iv 2 134
Show me the very wound of this ill news . v 6 21
O, pardon me for bringing these ill news, Since you did leave it for my office, sir.—Is it even so? . *Rom. and Jul.* v 1 22
Ill night. Even this ill night, your breathing shall expire . *K. John* v 4 36
Ill-nurtured. Presumptuous dame, ill-nurtured Eleanor . *2 Hen. VI.* i 2 42
Ill office. 'Tis an ill office for a gentleman . *T. G. of Ver.* iii 2 40
That never may ill office, or fell jealousy, Which troubles oft the bed of blessed marriage, Thrust in between the paction of these kingdoms *Hen. V.* v 2 391
Ill officers. Pindarus, In his own change, or by ill officers, Hath given me some worthy cause to wish Things done, undone . *J. Cæsar* iv 2 7
Ill opinion. In this mystery of ill opinions *Mer. Wives* ii 1 73
There's an ill opinion spread then Even of yourself . *Hen. VIII.* ii 2 125
And policy grows into an ill opinion *Troi. and Cres.* v 4 19
For your ill opinion and the assault you have made to her chastity you shall answer me with your sword . *Cymbeline* i 4 174
Ill phrase. That's an ill phrase, a vile phrase . *Hamlet* ii 2 111
Ill planet. There's some ill planet reigns . *W. Tale* ii 1 105
Ill qualities. I have many ill qualities . *Much Ado* ii 1 106
Ill report. If any fear Lesser his person than an ill report *Coriolanus* i 6 70
Better have a bad epitaph than their ill report while you live *Hamlet* ii 2 550
I must thank him only, Lest my remembrance suffer ill report *Ant. and Cleo.* ii 2 159
Ill request. What ill request did Brutus make to thee? . *J. Cæsar* v 5 11
Ill requited. O traitors and bawds, how earnestly are you set a-work, and how ill requited! . *Troi. and Cres.* v 10 38
Ill rest betide the chamber where thou liest! *Richard III.* i 2 112
Ill-roasted. Truly, thou art damned like an ill-roasted egg, all on one side *As Y. Like It* iii 2 38
Ill-rooted. Some o' their plants are ill-rooted already . *Ant. and Cleo.* ii 7 2
Ill-schooled. And is ill-school'd In bolted language . *Coriolanus* iii 1 321
Ill-seeming. Like a fountain troubled, Muddy, ill-seeming *T. of Shrew* v 2 143
Ill shape. For he hath wit to make an ill shape good . *L. L. Lost* ii 1 59
Ill-shaped. In his needy shop a tortoise hung, An alligator stuff'd, and other skins Of ill-shaped fishes *Rom. and Jul.* v 1 44
Ill-sheathed. The edge of war, like an ill-sheathed knife, No more shall cut his master . *1 Hen. IV.* i 1 17
Ill singer. A good song.—And an ill singer . *Much Ado* ii 3 78
Ill sorted. An excellent good word before it was ill sorted . *2 Hen. IV.* ii 4 162
Ill spent. Suit ill spent and labour ill bestowed *Much Ado* iii 2 103
Ill spirit. If the ill spirit have so fair a house, Good things will strive to dwell with't . *Tempest* i 2 458
Ill spirit, I would hold more talk with thee . *J. Cæsar* iv 3 289
Ill-spirited Worcester! did not we send grace, Pardon? . *1 Hen. IV.* v 5 2
Ill-starred. O ill-starr'd wench! Pale as thy smock! . *Othello* v 2 272
Ill suspicion. Both your pardons, That e'er I put between your holy looks My ill suspicion *W. Tale* v 3 149
Ill-taken. Part of his theme, but nothing Of his ill-ta'en suspicion . i 2 460
The duke's to blame in this; 'twill be ill taken . *Lear* ii 2 166
Ill-tempered. When grief, and blood ill-temper'd, vexeth him *J. Cæsar* iv 3 115
When I spoke that, I was ill-temper'd too.—Do you confess so much? . iv 3 116
Ill thing. An ill thing to be offered to any gentlewoman *Rom. and Jul.* ii 4 179
Ill thinking. It were enough To put him to ill thinking . *Othello* iii 4 29
Ill-thought on of her and ill-thought on of you . *Troi. and Cres.* i 1 70
What, in ill thoughts again? Men must endure Their going hence, even as their coming hither: Ripeness is all . *Lear* v 2 9
Ill tidings. Thou hast made me giddy With these ill tidings . *K. John* iv 2 132
Where, when, and how, Camest thou by this ill tidings? *Richard II.* iii 4 80
Let ill tidings tell Themselves when they be felt . *Ant. and Cleo.* ii 5 87
Ill time. We have landed in ill time . *W. Tale* iii 3 3
Ill to friend. For my thoughts, you have them ill to friend Till your deeds gain them . *All's Well* v 3 182
Ill-tuned. Be more temperate: It ill beseems this presence to cry aim To these ill-tuned repetitions . *K. John* ii 1 197
Ill turn. I never spake bad word, nor did ill turn To any *Pericles* iv 1 76
Ill urged. Ah, word ill urged to one that is so ill! . *Rom. and Jul.* i 1 209
Ill-uttering. The gold I give thee will I melt and pour Down thy ill-uttering throat *Ant. and Cleo.* ii 5 35
Ill venture. If like an ill venture it come unluckily home *2 Hen. IV.* Epil. 12
Ill-weaved ambition, how much art thou shrunk! . *1 Hen. IV.* v 4 88
Ill-well. I counterfeit him.—You could never do him so ill-well, unless you were the very man . *Much Ado* ii 1 122
Ill will. Why look you so upon me?—For no ill will *As Y. Like It* iii 5 71
Things which would derive me ill will to speak of . *All's Well* v 3 265
Ill will never said well *Hen. V.* iii 7 123
That thereby he may gather The ground of your ill-will . *Richard III.* i 3 69
Ill wind. What wind blew you hither, Pistol?—Not the ill wind which blows no man to good . *2 Hen. IV.* v 3 90
Ill word. One doth not know How much an ill word may empoison liking *Much Ado* iii 1 86

Illegitimate. O illegitimate construction! . iii 4 50
Bastard in mind, bastard in valour, in every thing illegitimate *T. and C.* v 7 18
Illiterate. O illiterate loiterer! . *T. G. of Ver.* iii 1 296
Illness. Thou wouldst be great; Art not without ambition, but without The illness should attend it . *Macbeth* i 5 21
Illume. When yond same star that's westward from the pole Had made his course to illume that part of heaven Where now it burns *Hamlet* i 1 37
Illuminate. To illuminate So vile a thing as Cæsar! . *J. Cæsar* i 3 110
Illumined. By her fair influence Foster'd, illumined . *T. G. of Ver.* iii 1 184
Illumineth. It [sherris] illumineth the face, which as a beacon gives warning to all the rest of this little kingdom *2 Hen. IV.* iv 3 116
Illusion. Here we wander in illusions: Some blessed power deliver us! *Com. of Errors* iv 3 43
By some illusion see thou bring her here . *M. N. Dream* iii 2 98
By the devil's illusions The monk might be deceived . *Hen. VIII.* i 2 178
Such artificial sprites As by the strength of their illusion Shall draw him on to his confusion *Macbeth* iii 5 28
Stay, illusion! If thou hast any sound, or use of voice, Speak to me *Ham.* i 1 127
Illustrate. The magnanimous and most illustrate king Cophetua *L. L. L.* iv 1 65
This most gallant, illustrate, and learned gentleman . v 1 128
Illustrated. A loyal and obedient subject is Therein illustrated *Hen. VIII.* iii 2 181
Illustrious. A most illustrious wight . *L. L. Lost* i 1 178
The magnanimous and most illustrious six-or-seven-times-honoured captain-general of the Grecian army . *Troi. and Cres.* iii 3 278
His right noble mind, illustrious virtue . *T. of Athens* iii 2 87
Illyria. This is Illyria, lady.—And what should I do in Illyria? My brother he is in Elysium . *T. Night* i 2 2
He's as tall a man as any's in Illyria.—What's that to the purpose? . i 3 20
I'll drink to her as long as there is a passage in my throat and drink in Illyria . i 3 42
Art thou good at these kickshawses, knight?—As any man in Illyria . i 3 124
I have the back-trick simply as strong as any man in Illyria . i 3 132
Thou wert as witty a piece of Eve's flesh as any in Illyria . i 5 31

Illyria. The most skilful, bloody and fatal opposite that you could possibly have found in any part of Illyria . *T. Night* iii 4 294
I'll have an action of battery against him, if there be any law in Illyria iv 1 37
I tell thee, I am as well in my wits as any man in Illyria . . iv 2 115
Illyrian. Threatens more Than Bargulus the strong Illyrian pirate *2 Hen. VI.* iv 1 108
Image. Of any thing the image tell me that Hath kept with thy remembrance *Tempest* i 2 43
Like a waxen image 'gainst a fire, Bears no impression . *T. G. of Ver.* ii 4 201
The image of the jest I'll show you here at large . . *Mer. Wives* iv 6 17
That do coin heaven's image In stamps that are forbid . *Meas. for Meas.* ii 4 45
What think you of it?—The image of it gives me content already . iii 1 270
Is there none of Pygmalion's images, newly made woman, to be had now? iii 2 47
Is too like an image and says nothing . . *Much Ado* ii 1 9
Now thy image doth appear In the rare semblance that I loved it first . v 1 259
More witnesseth than fancy's images . *M. N. Dream* v 1 25
Grim death, how foul and loathsome is thine image! . *T. of Shrew* Ind. 1 35
To choose from forth the royal blood of France, My low and humble name to propagate With any branch or image of thy state *All's Well* ii 1 201
Unstaid and skittish in all motions else, Save in the constant image of the creature That is beloved . *T. Night* ii 4 19
Such a dream, that when the image of it leaves him he must run mad . ii 5 212
My remembrance is very free and clear from any image of offence . iii 4 249
To his image, which methought did promise Most venerable worth, did I devotion . . . . iii 4 396
Your father's image is so hit in you . . . . *W. Tale* v 1 127
If I had thought the sight of my poor image Would thus have wrought you,—for the stone is mine—I'ld not have show'd it . . v 3 57
The image of a wicked heinous fault Lives in his eye . *K. John* iv 2 71
Glittering in golden coats, like images . . . *1 Hen. IV.* iv 1 100
No counterfeit, but the true and perfect image of life indeed . v 4 120
He, the noble image of my youth, Is overspread with them [weeds] *2 Hen. IV.* iv 4 55
The image of his power lay then in me . . . v 2 74
The majesty and power of law and justice, The image of the king whom I presented . . . . v 2 79
To spurn at your most royal image And mock your workings in a second body . . . . v 2 89
His loves Are brazen images of canonized saints . . . *2 Hen. VI.* i 3 63
Image of pride, why should I hold my peace? . . . . i 3 179
Erect his statua and worship it, And make my image but an alehouse sign iii 2 81
And to survey his dead and earthy image, What were it but to make my sorrow greater? . . . . . . iii 2 147
A brood of traitors have we here!—Look in a glass, and call thy image so v 1 142
From my heart thine image ne'er shall go . . *3 Hen. VI.* ii 5 116
Fame, late entering at his heedful ears, Hath placed thy beauty's image iii 3 64
Long mayst thou live To bear his image and renew his glories! . v 4 54
And defaced The precious image of our dear Redeemer . *Richard III.* ii 1 123
I have bewept a worthy husband's death, And lived by looking on his images . . . . ii 2 50
How can man, then, The image of his Maker, hope to win by it? *Hen. VIII.* iii 2 442
The will dotes that is attributive To what infectiously itself affects, Without some image of the affected merit . . *Troi. and Cres.* ii 2 60
I, Even like a stony image, cold and numb . *T. Andron.* iii 1 259
Whither wouldst thou convey This growing image of thy fiend-like face? v 1 45
Disrobe the images, If you do find them deck'd with ceremonies *J. Cæsar* i 1 69
Let no images Be hung with Cæsar's trophies . . . . i 1 73
Marullus and Flavius, for pulling scarfs off Cæsar's images, are put to silence i 2 289
Nothing afeard of what thyself didst make, Strange images of death *Macb.* i 3 97
Why do I yield to that suggestion Whose horrid image doth unfix my hair? i 3 135
Look on death itself! up, up, and see The great doom's image! . ii 3 83
Our last king, Whose image even but now appear'd to us *Hamlet* i 1 81
To show virtue her own feature, scorn her own image . . iii 2 26
This play is the image of a murder done in Vienna . . iii 2 248
By the image of my cause, I see The portraiture of his . . v 2 77
I have told you what I have seen and heard; but faintly, nothing like the image and horror of it . . . . . . *Lear* i 2 192
Mere fetches; The images of revolt and flying off . . ii 4 91
Behold the great image of authority: a dog's obeyed in office . iv 6 162
Is this the promised end?—Or image of that horror? . . v 3 264
Imagery. All the walls With painted imagery . . *Richard II.* v 2 16
Imaginary. Sure, these are but imaginary wiles *Com. of Errors* iv 3 10
Foul imaginary eyes of blood Presented thee more hideous than thou art *K. John* iv 2 265
Sorrow's eye, Which for things true weeps things imaginary *Richard II.* ii 2 27
When I do shape In forms imaginary the unguided days *2 Hen. IV.* iv 4 59
Let us, ciphers to this great accompt, On your imaginary forces work *Hen. V.* Prol. 18
Into a thousand parts divide one man, And make imaginary puissance Prol. 25
The imaginary relish is so sweet That it enchants my sense *Troi. and Cres.* iii 2 20
Imagination. My strong imagination sees a crown Dropping upon thy head *Tempest* ii 1 208
Nor can imagination form a shape, Besides yourself, to like of . . iii 1 56
What spirit, what devil suggests this imagination? . . *Mer. Wives* iii 3 231
You must pray, and not follow the imaginations of your own heart . iv 2 163
Whose salt imagination yet hath wrong'd Your well defended honour *Meas. for Meas.* v 1 406
Beyond imagination is the wrong . . *Com. of Errors* v 1 201
The idea of her life shall sweetly creep Into his study of imagination *Much Ado* iv 1 227
The lunatic, the lover and the poet Are of imagination all compact: One sees more devils than vast hell can hold . . *M. N. Dream* v 1 8
As imagination bodies forth The forms of things unknown, the poet's pen Turns them to shapes . . . . . . v 1 14
Such tricks hath strong imagination . . . . . . v 1 18
The best in this kind are but shadows; and the worst are no worse, if imagination amend them.—It must be your imagination then . . v 1 214
My imagination Carries no favour in't but Bertram's . . *All's Well* i 1 93
Now he's deeply in: look how imagination blows him . . *T. Night* ii 5 48
I do not now fool myself, to let imagination jade me . . ii 5 178
Prove true, imagination, O, prove true! . . . . iii 4 409
From very nothing, and beyond the imagination of his neighbours *W. T.* iv 2 45
Cloy the hungry edge of appetite By bare imagination of a feast *Richard II.* i 3 297
Imagination of some great exploit Drives him beyond the bounds of patience . . . . *1 Hen. IV.* i 3 199
With great imagination Proper to madmen, led his powers to death *2 Hen. IV.* i 3 31
For unfelt imagination, They often feel a world of restless cares *Rich. III.* i 4 80
How big imagination Moves in this lip! . . . *T. of Athens* i 1 32
He waxes desperate with imagination . . . . *Hamlet* i 4 87
Imagination. Thoughts to put them in, imagination to give them shape, or time to act them in . . . . . *Hamlet* iii 1 128
And my imaginations are as foul As Vulcan's stithy . . . iii 2 88
How abhorred in my imagination it is! my gorge rises at it . . . v 1 206
Why may not imagination trace the noble dust of Alexander, till he find it stopping a bung-hole? . . . . v 1 224
Give me an ounce of civet, good apothecary, to sweeten my imagination *Lear* iv 6 133
And woes by wrong imaginations lose The knowledge of themselves . iv 6 290
In your imagination hold This stage the ship . . . *Pericles* iii Gower 58
Making, to take your imagination, From bourn to bourn, region to region iv 4 3
Imagine. Of those that lawless and incertain thought Imagine howling *Meas. for Meas.* iii 1 128
You imagine me too unhurtful an opposite . . . . . iii 2 175
What mystery there should be in hanging, if I should be hanged, I cannot imagine . . . . iv 2 43
If we imagine no worse of them than they of themselves *M. N. Dream* v 1 218
He was to imagine me his love, his mistress . *As Y. Like It* iii 2 428
Imagine 'twere the right Vincentio.—Tut, fear not me . *T. of Shrew* iv 4 12
Imagine me, Gentle spectators, that I now may be In fair Bohemia *W. T.* iv 1 19
What thy soul holds dear, imagine it To lie that way thou go'st *Richard II.* i 3 286
And then imagine me taking your part . . . . *2 Hen. IV.* v 2 96
So swift a pace hath thought that even now You may imagine him upon Blackheath . . . . *Hen. V.* v Prol. 16
And what I do imagine let that rest . . . *1 Hen. VI.* ii 5 119
Imagine him [death] a Frenchman and thy foe . . . . iv 7 26
I did imagine what would be her refuge . . . . . v 4 69
When I imagine ill Against my king and nephew . . *2 Hen. VI.* i 2 19
Who finds the partridge in the puttock's nest, But may imagine how the bird was dead? . . . . iii 2 192
Touches me deeper than you can imagine . . . *Richard III.* i 1 112
Since you teach me how to flatter you, Imagine I have said farewell already i 2 225
Would you imagine, or almost believe, Were't not that, by great preservation, We live to tell it you? . . . . . iii 5 35
He's as like to do't as any man I can imagine . . *Coriolanus* iv 5 217
I loved your father, and we love ourself; And that, I hope, will teach you to imagine—How now! . . . . . *Hamlet* iv 7 35
To imagine An Antony, were nature's piece 'gainst fancy *Ant. and Cleo.* v 2 98
I will bring from thence that honour of hers which you imagine so reserved *Cymbeline* i 4 143
Imagine Pericles arrived at Tyre, Welcomed and settled . *Pericles* iv Gower 1
Imagined. Bring them, I pray thee, with imagined speed *Mer. of Venice* iii 4 52
And did supply thee at thy garden-house In her imagined person *M. for M.* v 1 213
To us the imagined voice of God himself . . *2 Hen. IV.* iv 2 19
Thus with imagined wing our swift scene flies . . *Hen. V.* iii Prol. 1
More furious raging broils Than yet can be imagined or supposed *1 Hen. VI.* iv 1 186
Imagined worth Holds in his blood such swoln and hot discourse *T. and C.* ii 3 182
Let rich music's tongue Unfold the imagined happiness *Rom. and Jul.* ii 6 28
When I wake, it is Without me, as within me; not imagined, felt *Cymb.* iv 2 307
Imagining some fear, How easy is a bush supposed a bear! *M. N. Dream* v 1 21
Present fears Are less than horrible imaginings . . *Macbeth* i 3 138
Imbar. And rather choose to hide them in a net Than amply to imbar their crooked titles . . . . . . *Hen. V.* i 2 94
Imbecility. Strength should be lord of imbecility . *Troi. and Cres.* i 3 114
Imbrue. Come, trusty sword; Come, blade, my breast imbrue *M. N. Dream* v 1 351
What! shall we have incision? shall we imbrue? . . . *2 Hen. IV.* ii 4 210
Imitari is nothing: so doth the hound his master . . *L. L. Lost* iv 2 129
Imitate. And therefore red, that would avoid dispraise, Paints itself black, to imitate her brow . . . . iv 3 265
Which she, with pretty and with swimming gait . . ., Would imitate *M. N. Dream* ii 1 132
He went Still in this fashion, colour, ornament, For him I imitate *T. N.* iii 4 418
Yet herein will I imitate the sun . . . . . *1 Hen. IV.* i 2 221
I will imitate the honourable Romans in brevity . *2 Hen. IV.* ii 2 134
Then imitate the action of the tiger . . . . *Hen. V.* iii 1 6
I have heard a sonnet begin so to one's mistress.—Then did they imitate that which I composed to my courser . . . . . iii 7 46
Speak to me, son: Thou hast affected the fine strains of honour, To imitate the graces of the gods . . . . *Coriolanus* v 3 150
If our betters play at that game, we must not dare To imitate them; faults that are rich are fair . . . . . *T. of Athens* i 2 13
'Tis, then, because thou dost not keep a dog, Whom I would imitate . iv 3 201
Imitated. They imitated humanity so abominably . . *Hamlet* iii 2 39
Imitation. Our tardy apish nation Limps after in base imitation *Rich. II.* ii 1 23
With ridiculous and awkward action, Which, slanderer, he imitation calls, He pageants us . . . . . *Troi. and Cres.* i 3 150
In the imitation of these twain . . . many are infect . . . i 3 185
One that feeds On abjects, orts and imitations . . . *J. Cæsar* iv 1 37
With what imitation you can borrow From youth of such a season *Cymb.* iii 4 174
Immaculate. His love sincere, his thoughts immaculate . *T. G. of Ver.* ii 7 76
My love is most immaculate white and red . . . *L. L. Lost* i 2 95
Thou sheer, immaculate and silver fountain! . . . *Richard II.* v 3 61
In my pure and immaculate valour . . . . . *2 Hen. IV.* iv 3 41
Chaste and immaculate in very thought . . . *1 Hen. VI.* v 4 51
With pure heart's love, Immaculate devotion, holy thoughts *Richard III.* iv 4 404
Immanity. It was both impious and unnatural That such immanity and bloody strife Should reign among professors of one faith *1 Hen. VI.* v 1 13
Immask. To immask our noted outward garments . . *1 Hen. IV.* i 2 201
Immaterial. Thou idle immaterial skein of sleave-silk . *Troi. and Cres.* v 1 35
Immediacy. The which immediacy may well stand up, And call itself your brother . . . . *Lear* v 3 65
Immediate sentence then and sequent death Is all . . *Meas. for Meas.* v 1 378
A doubtful warrant of immediate death . . . *Com. of Errors* i 1 69
She is young, wise, fair; In these to nature she's immediate heir *All's W.* ii 3 139
And to beg Enfranchisement immediate on his knees . *Richard II.* iii 3 114
Which, as immediate from thy place and blood, Derives itself to me *2 Hen. IV.* iv 5 42
Rate, rebuke, and roughly send to prison The immediate heir of England! v 2 71
Immediate are my needs, and my relief Must not be toss'd and turn'd to me in words, But find supply immediate . . . *T. of Athens* ii 1 27
That Publius Cimber may Have an immediate freedom of repeal *J. Cæsar* iii 1 54
Let the world take note, You are the most immediate to our throne *Hamlet* i 2 109
It would come to immediate trial, if your lordship would vouchsafe the answer . . . . v 2 175
Good name in man and woman, dear my lord, Is the immediate jewel of their souls: Who steals my purse steals trash . . *Othello* iii 3 156
To that end Assemble we immediate council . . *Ant. and Cleo.* i 4 75
That which is the strength of their amity shall prove the immediate author of their variance . . . . ii 6 137
For this immediate levy, he commends His absolute commission *Cymb.* iii 7 9

Immediately. And with him at Eton Immediately to marry *Mer. Wives* iv 6 25
Bear it straight, And bring thy master home immediately *Com. of Errors* iv 2 64
I gain'd my freedom and immediately Ran hither to your grace . . v 1 250
Immediately they will again be here In their own shapes *L. L. Lost* v 2 287
According to our law Immediately provided in that case *M. N. Dream* i 1 45
Either death or you I'll find immediately . . . . . ii 2 156
Well, Jessica, go in: Perhaps I will return immediately *Mer. of Venice* ii 5 52
Without more speech, my lord, You must be gone from hence immediately ii 9 8
If I do fail in fortune of my choice, Immediately to leave you . ii 9 16
To help him to his grave immediately . . . . . *Richard II.* i 4 60
We'll but seal, And then to horse immediately . . *1 Hen. IV.* iii 1 271
Immediately he was upon his knee . . . . . *2 Hen. VI.* iii 1 11
I will resolve your grace immediately.—The king is angry *Richard III.* iv 2 26
And apprehended here immediately The unknown Ajax . *Troi. and Cres.* iii 3 124
Demand your hostages, And they shall be immediately deliver'd *T. An.* v 1 161
For that offence Immediately we do exile him hence . *Rom. and Jul.* iii 1 192
Such a waggoner As Phaethon would whip you to the west, And bring in cloudy night immediately . . . . iii 2 4
Come yourselves, and bring Messala with you Immediately to us *J. Cæsar* iv 3 142
And something to be done immediately . . . . . v 1 15
On wholesome life usurp immediately . . . . . *Hamlet* iii 2 271
Imminence. I do not speak of flight, of fear, of death, But dare all imminence that gods and men Address their dangers in *Tr. and Cr.* v 10 13
Imminent. The imminent decay of wrested pomp . . . *K. John* iv 3 154
You have defended me from imminent death . . . *2 Hen. VI.* v 3 19
To dangers As infinite as imminent . . . . *Troi. and Cres.* iv 4 71
Warnings, and portents, And evils imminent . . . *J. Cæsar* ii 2 81
In the morn and liquid dew of youth Contagious blastments are most imminent. Be wary then . . . . *Hamlet* i 3 42
While, to my shame, I see The imminent death of twenty thousand men iv 4 60
Of hair-breadth scapes i' the imminent deadly breach . *Othello* i 3 136
Immoderate. As surfeit is the father of much fast, So every scope by the immoderate use Turns to restraint . . . *Meas. for Meas.* i 2 131
Immoderately she weeps for Tybalt's death . *Rom. and Jul.* iv 1 6
Immodest. Be thou ashamed that I have took upon me Such an immodest raiment . . . . *T. G. of Ver.* v 4 106
So immodest to write to one that she knew would flout her *Much Ado* ii 3 148
With immodest hatred The child-bed privilege denied . *W. Tale* iii 2 103
'Tis needful that the most immodest word Be look'd upon and learn'd *2 Hen. IV.* iv 4 70
Are you not ashamed With this immodest clamorous outrage? *1 Hen. VI.* iv 1 126
Immoment. I some lady trifles have reserved, Immoment toys *Ant. and Cleo.* v 2 166
Immortal. She is mortal; But by immortal Providence she's mine *Temp.* v 1 189
I hold you as a thing ensky'd and sainted, By your renouncement an immortal spirit, And to be talk'd with in sincerity *Meas. for Meas.* i 4 35
'Tis now dead midnight, and by eight to-morrow Thou must be made immortal . . . . iv 2 68
Such harmony is in immortal souls . . . . *Mer. of Venice* v 1 63
O immortal gods! O fine villain! A silken doublet! . *T. of Shrew* v 1 68
Had it stretched so far, would have made nature immortal, and death should have play for lack of work . . . . *All's Well* i 1 23
Until the heavens . . . Add an immortal title to your crown *Richard II.* i 1 24
Marry, the immortal part needs a physician . . *2 Hen. IV.* ii 2 112
And sword and shield, In bloody field, Doth win immortal fame *Hen. V.* iii 2 11
O you immortal gods! I will not go . . . *Troi. and Cres.* iv 2 100
Ah, the immortal passado! the punto reverso! the hai! *Rom. and Jul.* ii 4 26
And steal immortal blessing from her lips . . . . iii 3 37
Her body sleeps in Capel's monument, And her immortal part with angels lives . . . . v 1 19
Immortal gods, I crave no pelf; I pray for no man but myself *T. of A.* i 2 63
Terribly swear Into strong shudders and to heavenly agues The immortal gods . . . . iv 3 138
Many of the best respect in Rome, Except immortal Cæsar . *J. Cæsar* i 2 60
If thou beest not immortal, look about you . . . . ii 3 7
And died so?—Even so.—O ye immortal gods! . . . iv 3 157
For my soul, what can it do to that, Being a thing immortal as itself? *Hamlet* i 4 67
I have lost the immortal part of myself, and what remains is bestial *Oth.* ii 3 263
And, O you mortal engines, whose rude throats The immortal Jove's dread clamours counterfeit! . . . . iii 3 356
I would not . . . touch him, for his biting is immortal; those that do die of it do seldom or never recover . . . *Ant. and Cleo.* v 2 247
Give me my robe, put on my crown; I have Immortal longings in me . v 2 284
His royal bird Prunes the immortal wing . . . *Cymbeline* v 4 118
She sings like one immortal, and she dances As goddess-like *Pericles* v Gower 3
That Thaisa am I, supposed dead And drown'd.—Immortal Dian! . v 3 37
Immortality attends the former, Making a man a god . . iii 2 30
Immortalized. Drive them from Orleans and be immortalized *1 Hen. VI.* i 2 148
Immortally. And He that wears the crown immortally Long guard it yours! . . . . *2 Hen. IV.* iv 5 144
Immure. Within whose strong immures The ravish'd Helen, Menelaus' queen, With wanton Paris sleeps . . . *Troi. and Cres.* Prol. 8
Immured. Thou wert immured, restrained, captivated, bound *L. L. Lost* iii 1 126
Love, first learned in a lady's eyes, Lives not alone immured in the brain . . . . iv 3 328
Shall I think in silver she's immured? . . . *Mer. of Venice* ii 7 52
Those tender babes Whom envy hath immured within your walls *Rich. III.* iv 1 100
Imogen. Keep it till you woo another wife, When Imogen is dead *Cymb.* i 1 114
Thou divine Imogen, what thou endurest, Betwixt a father by thy step-dame govern'd, A mother hourly coining plots! . . . . ii 1 62
If I could get this foolish Imogen, I should have gold enough . ii 3 9
O Imogen, Safe mayst thou wander, safe return again! . . . iii 5 104
Imogen, The great part of my comfort, gone; my queen Upon a desperate bed . . . . iv 3 4
I heard no letter from my master since I wrote him Imogen was slain . iv 3 37
So had you saved The noble Imogen to repent, and struck Me . . v 1 10
But Imogen is your own: do your best wills, And make me blest to obey! v 1 16
So I'll die For thee, O Imogen, even for whom my life Is every breath a death . . . . v 1 26
I come to spend my breath; Which neither here I'll keep nor bear again, But end it by some means for Imogen . . . . . v 3 83
For Imogen's dear life take mine; and though 'Tis not so dear, yet 'tis a life . . . . v 4 22
O Imogen! I'll speak to thee in silence . . . . . v 4 28
Or fruitful object be In eye of Imogen, that best Could deem his dignity v 4 56
And cast From her his dearest one, Sweet Imogen . . . v 4 62
He shall be lord of lady Imogen, And happier much by his affliction made v 4 107
O Imogen! My queen, my life, my wife! O Imogen, Imogen, Imogen! v 5 225
O, my lord Posthumus! You ne'er kill'd Imogen till now . . v 5 231
Imogen. Dangerous fellow, hence! Breathe not where princes are.—The tune of Imogen! . . . . *Cymbeline* v 5 238
My tears that fall Prove holy water on thee! Imogen, Thy mother's dead v 5 269
O Imogen, Thou hast lost by this a kingdom . . . . v 5 372
Imp. Sadness is one and the self-same thing, dear imp . *L. L. Lost* i 2 5
Great Hercules is presented by this imp . . . . . . v 2 592
Imp out our drooping country's broken wing . . . *Richard II.* ii 1 292
The heavens thee guard and keep, most royal imp of fame! *2 Hen. IV.* v 5 46
A lad of life, an imp of fame; Of parents good, of fist most valiant *Hen. V.* iv 1 45
Impaint. And never yet did insurrection want Such water-colours to impaint his cause . . . . *1 Hen. IV.* v 1 80
Impair. Wherein it doth impair the seeing sense, It pays the hearing double recompense . . . . . . *M. N. Dream* iii 2 179
Nor dignifies an impair thought with breath . . *Troi. and Cres.* iv 5 103
Impaired. His speech was like a tangled chain; nothing impaired, but all disordered . . . . *M. N. Dream* v 1 126
Impairing Henry, strengthening misproud York . . *3 Hen. VI.* ii 6 7
Impale. Did I impale him with the regal crown? . . . . iii 3 189
Impaled. Until my mis-shaped trunk that bears this head Be round impaled with a glorious crown . . . . iii 2 171
Impart. Some certain special honours it pleaseth his greatness to impart *L. L. Lost* v 1 113
When I did first impart my love to you, I freely told you *Mer. of Venice* iii 2 256
Our natural goodness Imparts this . . . . . . *W. Tale* ii 1 165
Go with me; I have great matters to impart to thee . *2 Hen. VI.* iii 2 299
Thou art sworn as deeply to effect what we intend As closely to conceal what we impart . . . . *Richard III.* iii 1 159
Though what they do impart Help not at all, yet do they ease the heart iv 4 130
But wherefore do you hold me here so long? What is it that you would impart to me? . . . . *J. Cæsar* i 2 84
Let us impart what we have seen to-night . . . . *Hamlet* i 1 169
And with no less nobility of love Than that which dearest father bears his son, Do I impart toward you . . . . i 2 112
This to me In dreadful secrecy impart they did . . . . i 2 207
But is there no sequel at the heels of this mother's admiration? Impart iii 2 342
If your lordship were at leisure, I should impart a thing to you . v 2 92
Imparted. As I before imparted to your worship, I am to get a man *T. of Shrew* iii 2 132
Impartial. I'll be impartial; be you judge Of your own cause *M. for M.* v 1 166
Impartial are our eyes and ears . . . . . *Richard II.* i 1 115
I did in honour, Led by the impartial conduct of my soul *2 Hen. IV.* v 2 36
That you use the same With the like bold, just and impartial spirit . v 2 116
Impartment. As if it some impartment did desire To you alone *Hamlet* i 4 59
Impasted. Baked and impasted with the parching streets . . ii 2 481
Impatience. My heart is ready to crack with impatience *Mer. Wives* ii 2 301
Sheathe thy impatience, throw cold water on thy choler . . ii 3 88
Fie, how impatience loureth in your face! . *Com. of Errors* ii 1 86
All humbleness, all patience and impatience, All purity *As Y. Like It* v 2 103
Impatience hath his privilege.—'Tis true, to hurt his master, no man else . . . . *K. John* iv 3 32
Out of my grief and my impatience, Answer'd neglectingly *1 Hen. IV.* i 3 51
Did commence Rough deeds of rage and stern impatience *1 Hen. VI.* iv 7 8
O, but impatience waiteth on true sorrow . . . *3 Hen. VI.* iii 3 42
What means this scene of rude impatience? . . . *Richard III.* ii 2 38
Then patiently hear my impatience.—Madam, I have a touch of your condition . . . . iv 4 156
His own impatience Takes from Aufidius a great part of blame *Coriol.* v 6 146
Put on fear and cast yourself in wonder, To see the strange impatience of the heavens . . . . *J. Cæsar* i 3 61
Fearing to strengthen that impatience Which seem'd too much enkindled ii 1 248
All the power of his wits have given way to his impatience . . *Lear* iii 6 5
Her garboils, Cæsar, Made out of her impatience . . *Ant. and Cleo.* ii 2 68
But Mark Antony Put me to some impatience . . . . . ii 6 43
Patience is sottish, and impatience does Become a dog that's mad . iv 15 79
No further with your din Express impatience, lest you stir up mine *Cymbeline* v 4 112
Impatient. To it presently! I am impatient of my tarriance *T. G. of Ver.* ii 7 90
My daughter is disposed of.—Nay, Master Page, be not impatient *M. W.* iii 4 75
His tongue, all impatient to speak and not see, Did stumble with haste *L. L. Lost* ii 1 238
What, will you tear Impatient answers from my gentle tongue? *M. N. D.* iii 2 287
I tell you, sirs, If you should smile he grows impatient *T. of Shrew* Ind. 1 99
With a most impatient devilish spirit . . . . . . ii 1 152
For such an injury would vex a very saint, Much more a shrew of thy impatient humour . . . . iii 2 29
England, impatient of your just demands, Hath put himself in arms *K. John* ii 1 56
Why, what a wasp-stung and impatient fool Art thou! . *1 Hen. IV.* i 3 236
Impatient of his fit, breaks like a fire Out of his keeper's arms *2 Hen. IV.* i 1 142
You are too impatient to bear crosses . . . . . i 2 253
The knavish crows Fly o'er them, all impatient for their hour *Hen. V.* iv 2 52
Wherefore is Charles impatient with his friend? . . *1 Hen. VI.* ii 1 54
Know ye not, in Rome How furious and impatient they be, And cannot brook competitors in love? . . . . . . *T. Andron.* ii 1 76
Be, as your titles witness, Imperious and impatient of your wrongs . v 1 6
So tedious is this day As is the night before some festival To an impatient child that hath new robes . . . *Rom. and Jul.* iii 2 30
Upon what sickness?—Impatient of my absence, And grief *J. Cæsar* iv 3 152
A will most incorrect to heaven, A heart unfortified, a mind impatient *Hamlet* i 2 96
I would not there reside, To put my father in impatient thoughts *Othello* i 3 243
Impatiently. The current that with gentle murmur glides, Thou know'st, being stopp'd, impatiently doth rage . . . *T. G. of Ver.* ii 7 26
Impatiently I burn with thy desire . . . . *1 Hen. VI.* i 2 108
And too impatiently stamp'd with your foot . . . *J. Cæsar* ii 1 244
Impawn. Therefore take heed how you impawn our person . *Hen. V.* i 2 21
Impawned. This trunk which you Shall bear along impawn'd *W. Tale* i 2 436
Let there be impawn'd Some surety for a safe return again *1 Hen. IV.* iv 3 108
Impeach. Thou art a villain to impeach me thus . *Com. of Errors* v 1 29
What an intricate impeach is this! I think you all have drunk of Circe's cup . . . . v 1 269
You do impeach your modesty too much . . . *M. N. Dream* ii 1 214
Doth impeach the freedom of the state, If they deny him justice *M. of V.* iii 2 280
If it be denied, Will much impeach the justice of his state . . iii 3 29
Under whose warrant I impeach thy wrong . . . *K. John* ii 1 116
With pale beggar-fear impeach my height . . . . *Richard II.* i 1 189
Or any way impeach What then he said, so he unsay it now *1 Hen. IV.* i 3 75
And ten to one is no impeach of valour . . . *3 Hen. VI.* i 4 60
And here I stand, both to impeach and purge Myself . *Rom. and Jul.* v 3 226

Impeached. I am disgraced, impeach'd and baffled here . *Richard II.* i 1 170
Impeachment. Which would be great impeachment to his age, In having known no travel in his youth . *T. G. of Ver.* i 3 15
But could be willing to march on to Calais Without impeachment *Hen. V.* iii 6 151
Devised impeachments to imprison him . *Richard III.* ii 2 22
Impede. And chastise with the valour of my tongue All that impedes thee from the golden round . *Macbeth* i 5 29
Impediment. Any impediment will be medicinable to me . *Much Ado* ii 2 4
If there be any impediment, I pray you discover it . iii 2 96
If either of you know any inward impediment why you should not be conjoined . iv 1 13
If Don Worm, his conscience, find no impediment to the contrary . v 2 87
Like an impediment in the current, made it more violent *Meas. for Meas.* iii 1 251
Let his lack of years be no impediment . *Mer. of Venice* iv 1 162
As all impediments in fancy's course Are motives of more fancy *All's Well* v 3 214
I know not what impediment this complaint may be . *W. Tale* iv 4 729
Whose passage, vex'd with thy impediment, Shall leave his native channel . *K. John* ii 1 336
I wonder much, Being men of such great leading as you are, That you foresee not what impediments Drag back our expedition 1 *Hen. IV.* iv 3 18
But for my tears, The moist impediments unto my speech 2 *Hen. IV.* iv 5 140
What was the impediment that broke this off? . *Hen. V.* i 1 90
What rub or what impediment there is . v 2 33
Fellows in arms, . . . Thus far into the bowels of the land Have we march'd on without impediment . *Richard III.* v 2 4
Cracking ten thousand curbs Of more strong link asunder than can ever Appear in your impediment . *Coriolanus* i 1 74
No impediment between, but that you must Cast your election on him ii 3 236
All continent impediments would o'erbear That did oppose my will *Macb.* iv 3 64
The impediment most profitably removed, without the which there were no expectation of our prosperity . *Othello* ii 1 286
I have made my way through more impediments Than twenty times your stop . v 2 263
May I never To this good purpose, that so fairly shows, Dream of impediment! Let me have thy hand . *Ant. and Cleo.* ii 2 148
Impenetrable. It is the most impenetrable cur . *Mer. of Venice* iii 3 18
Imperator. Sole imperator and great general Of trotting 'paritors *L. L. L.* iii 1 187
Imperceiverant. Yet this imperceiverant thing loves him *Cymbeline* iv 1 15
Imperfect. Something imperfect in favouring the first complaint *Coriol.* ii 1 54
Stay, you imperfect speakers, tell me more . *Macbeth* i 3 70
Something he left imperfect in the state . *Lear* iv 3 3
Your other senses grow imperfect By your eyes' anguish . iv 6 5
It is a judgement maim'd and most imperfect . *Othello* i 3 100
Imperfection. I shall discover a thing to you, wherein I must very much lay open mine own imperfection . *Mer. Wives* ii 2 191
I will undo This hateful imperfection of her eyes . *M. N. Dream* iv 1 68
Piece out our imperfections with your thoughts . *Hen. V.* Prol. 23
If, Duke of Burgundy, you would the peace, Whose want gives growth to the imperfections Which you have cited, you must buy that peace With full accord to all our just demands . v 2 69
But sent to my account With all my imperfections on my head *Hamlet* i 5 79
Not alone the imperfections of long-engraffed condition . *Lear* i 1 300
Imperfectly. That your wisdom yet, From one that so imperfectly conceits, Would take no notice . *Othello* iii 3 149
Imperial. Am going with Sir Proteus to the Imperial's court *T. G. of V.* ii 3 5
The imperial votaress passed on, In maiden meditation . *M. N. Dream* ii 1 163
To imperial Love, that god most high, Do my sighs stream *All's Well* ii 3 81
Bold oxlips and The crown imperial . *W. Tale* iv 4 126
Were I crown'd the most imperial monarch, Thereof most worthy . iv 4 383
My due from thee is this imperial crown . 2 *Hen. IV.* iv 5 41
That owe yourselves, your lives and services To this imperial throne *Hen. V.* i 2 35
With crowns imperial, crowns and coronets . ii Prol. 10
Now we speak upon our cue, and our voice is imperial . iii 6 31
The sceptre and the ball, The sword, the mace, the crown imperial . iv 1 278
To bring your most imperial majesties Unto this bar and royal interview v 2 26
The world's best garden he achieved, And of it left his son imperial lord . Epil. 8
As by your high imperial majesty I had in charge . 2 *Hen. VI.* i 1 1
Suffolk's imperial tongue is stern and rough, Used to command . iv 1 121
The high imperial type of this earth's glory . *Richard III.* iv 4 244
If thou hadst fear'd to break an oath by Him, The imperial metal, circling now thy brow, Had graced the tender temples of my child iv 4 382
Opinion crowns With an imperial voice . *Troi. and Cres.* i 3 187
How may A stranger to those most imperial looks Know them from eyes of other mortals?—How! . i 3 224
That was the last That wore the imperial diadem of Rome . *T. Andron.* i 1 6
And suffer not dishonour to approach The imperial seat . i 1 14
My chariot and my prisoners; Presents well worthy Rome's imperial lord i 1 250
Fit thy thoughts, To mount aloft with thy imperial mistress . ii 1 13
As happy prologues to the swelling act Of the imperial theme *Macbeth* i 3 129
A good and virtuous nature may recoil In an imperial charge . iv 3 20
Now our queen, The imperial jointress to this warlike state . *Hamlet* i 2 9
Our princely eagle, The imperial Cæsar . *Cymbeline* v 5 474
Imperious. For contemning Love, Whose high imperious thoughts have punish'd me With bitter fasts . *T. G. of Ver.* ii 4 130
So looks the strand whereon the imperious flood Hath left a witness'd usurpation . 2 *Hen. IV.* i 1 62
And rock his brains In cradle of the rude imperious surge . iii 1 20
For what are you, I pray, But one imperious in another's throne? 1 *Hen. VI.* iii 1 44
Beside the haughty protector, have we Beaufort The imperious churchman . 2 *Hen. VI.* i 3 72
This imperious man will work us all From princes into pages *Hen. VIII.* ii 2 47
Great Hector, welcome.—I thank thee, most imperious Agamemnon *Troi. and Cres.* iv 5 172
King, be thy thoughts imperious, like thy name . *T. Andron.* iv 4 81
Be, as your titles witness, Imperious and impatient of your wrongs . v 1 6
Imperious Cæsar, dead and turn'd to clay, Might stop a hole *Hamlet* v 1 236
As one would beat his offenceless dog to affright an imperious lion *Othello* ii 3 276
Not the imperious show Of the full-fortuned Cæsar ever shall Be brooch'd with me . *Ant. and Cleo.* iv 15 23
The imperious seas breed monsters, for the dish Poor tributary rivers as sweet fish . *Cymbeline* iv 2 35
Imperiously. Who's there that knocks so imperiously? . 1 *Hen. VI.* i 3 5
Impertinency. O, matter and impertinency mix'd! Reason in madness! *Lear* iv 6 178
Impertinent. Without the which this story Were most impertinent *Temp.* i 2 138
In very brief, the suit is impertinent to myself . *Mer. of Venice* ii 2 146
Impeticos. I did impeticos thy gratillity . *T. Night* ii 3 27

Impetuosity. His youth will aptly receive it, into a most hideous opinion of his rage, skill, fury and impetuosity . *T. Night* iii 4 213
Impetuous. The ocean, overpeering of his list, Eats not the flats with more impetuous haste . *Hamlet* iv 5 100
Tears his white hair, Which the impetuous blasts, with eyeless rage, Catch in their fury, and make nothing of . *Lear* iii 1 8
Impieties. Guilty of those impieties for the which they are now visited *Hen. V.* iv 1 185
Impiety has made a feast of thee . *Meas. for Meas.* i 2 57
Most foul, most fair! farewell, Thou pure impiety and impious purity! *Much Ado* iv 1 105
To keep that oath were more impiety Than Jephthah's . 3 *Hen. VI.* v 1 90
This is impiety in you: My nephew Mutius' deeds do plead for him *T. Andron.* i 1 355
To be in anger is impiety; But who is man that is not angry? *T. of A.* iii 5 56
Impious. Farewell, Thou pure impiety and impious purity! . *Much Ado* iv 1 105
Impious war, Array'd in flames like to the prince of fiends . *Hen. V.* iii 3 15
I always thought It was both impious and unnatural . 1 *Hen. VI.* v 1 12
York and impious Beaufort, that false priest . 2 *Hen. VI.* ii 4 53
To persever In obstinate condolement is a course Of impious stubbornness; 'tis unmanly grief . *Hamlet* i 2 94
The gates of monarchs Are arch'd so high that giants may jet through And keep their impious turbans on . *Cymbeline* iii 3 6
Implacable. His incensement at this moment is so implacable *T. Night* iii 4 261
Implement. All broken implements of a ruin'd house . *T. of Athens* iv 2 16
Why such daily cast of brazen cannon, And foreign mart for implements of war; Why such impress of shipwrights? . *Hamlet* i 1 74
Implies. That seeks not to find that her search implies . *All's Well* i 3 222
Implorator. But mere implorators of unholy suits . *Hamlet* i 3 129
Implore her, in my voice, that she make friends . *Meas. for Meas.* i 2 185
There's a devilish mercy in the judge, If you'll implore it . iii 1 66
I do implore secrecy . *L. L. Lost* v 1 116
I implore so much expense of thy royal sweet breath . v 2 523
Do not say 'tis superstition, that I kneel and then implore her blessing *W. Tale* v 3 44
Spare me, till I may Be by my friends in Spain advised; whose counsel I will implore . *Hen. VIII.* ii 4 56
Implored. The states of Christendom, Moved with remorse of these outrageous broils, Have earnestly implored a general peace . 1 *Hen. VI.* v 4 98
Very frankly he confess'd his treasons, Implored your highness' pardon *Macbeth* i 4 6
Imploring. All that I can do is nothing worth, Since that my penitence comes after all, Imploring pardon . *Hen. V.* iv 1 322
Imply. How have I offended, Wherein my death might yield her any profit, Or my life imply her any danger? . *Pericles* iv 1 82
Imponed. Against the which he has imponed, as I take it, six French rapiers and poniards . *Hamlet* v 2 155
Why is this 'imponed,' as you call it? . v 2 171
Import. Be they of much import? . *T. G. of Ver.* iii 1 55
It imports no reason That with such vehemency he should pursue Faults proper to himself . *Meas. for Meas.* v 1 108
I have a motion much imports your good . v 1 541
Most serious designs, and of great import indeed . *L. L. Lost* v 1 106
What occasion of import Hath all so long detain'd you? . *T. of Shrew* iii 2 104
What the import is, I know not yet . *All's Well* ii 3 294
Your guest, then, madam: To be your prisoner should import offending *W. Tale* i 2 57
Much more general than these lines import . *K. John* iv 3 17
Unwelcome news Came from the north and thus it did import 1 *Hen. IV.* i 1 51
If you knew How much they do import, you would make haste . iv 4 5
France is revolted from the English quite, Except some petty towns of no import: The Dauphin Charles is crowned king . 1 *Hen. VI.* i 1 91
It doth import him much to speak with me . *Troi. and Cres.* iv 2 52
Your looks are pale and wild, and do import Some misadventure *Rom. and Jul.* v 1 28
The letter was not nice but full of charge Of dear import . v 2 19
Belike this show imports the argument of the play . *Hamlet* iii 2 149
Which imports at full, By letters congruing to that effect, The present death of Hamlet . iv 3 65
Alas, sweet lady, what imports this song? . iv 5 27
What imports the nomination of this gentlemen? . v 2 133
Which imports to the kingdom so much fear and danger . *Lear* iv 3 5
What might import my sister's letter to him?—I know not, lady . iv 5 6
With such things else of quality and respect As doth import you *Othello* i 3 284
If it be not for some purpose of import, Give't me again . iii 3 316
His gesture imports it . iv 1 142
Upon my knees, what doth your speech import? . iv 2 31
Imports The death of Cassio to be undertook By Roderigo . v 2 310
All great fears, which now import their dangers, Would then be nothing: truths would be tales . *Ant. and Cleo.* ii 2 135
That were excusable, that, and thousands more Of semblable import . iii 4 3
Thy name, Being Leo-natus, doth import so much . *Cymbeline* v 5 445
Importance. Maria writ The letter at Sir Toby's great importance *T. Night* v 1 371
In an act of this importance 'twere Most piteous to be wild . *W. Tale* ii 1 181
The wisest beholder, that knew no more but seeing, could not say if the importance were joy or sorrow . v 2 20
At our importance hither is he come . *K. John* ii 1 7
Upon importance of so slight and trivial a nature . *Cymbeline* i 4 45
Importancy. When we consider The importancy of Cyprus to the Turk *Othello* i 3 20
Important. At your important letters . *Com. of Errors* v 1 138
If the prince be too important, tell him there is measure in every thing *Much Ado* ii 1 74
Among other important and most serious designs . *L. L. Lost* v 1 105
His important blood will nought deny That she'll demand . *All's Well* iii 7 21
Then show you the heart of my message.—Come to what is important in't *T. Night* i 5 204
Things small as nothing, for request's sake only, He makes important *Troi. and Cres.* ii 3 180
I have important business, The tide whereof is now . v 1 89
Lets go by The important acting of your dread command . *Hamlet* iii 4 108
My mourning and important tears hath pitied . *Lear* iv 4 26
Importantly. Their eyes And ears so cloy'd importantly as now *Cymb.* iv 4 19
Imported His fellowship i' the cause against your city . *T. of Athens* v 2 11
Importeth. This letter is mistook, it importeth none here . *L. L. Lost* iv 1 57
With what else more serious Importeth thee to know . *Ant. and Cleo.* i 2 125
Importing. Her business looks in her With an importing visage *All's Well* v 3 136
Comets, importing change of times and states . 1 *Hen. VI.* i 1 2
Matters of great moment, No less importing than our general good *Richard III.* iii 7 68

Importing. An inventory, thus importing . . . . *Hen. VIII.* iii 2 124
He hath not fail'd to pester us with message, Importing the surrender of those lands *Hamlet* i 2 23
His sables and his weeds, Importing health and graveness . . . iv 7 82
Larded with many several sorts of reasons Importing Denmark's health v 2 21
Tidings now arrived, importing the mere perdition of the Turkish fleet *Othello* ii 2 3
Importless. Be't of less expect That matter needless, of importless burden, Divide thy lips . . . . . . *Troi. and Cres.* i 3 71
Importunacy. Art thou not ashamed To wrong him with thy importunacy? *T. G. of Ver.* iv 2 112
Your importunacy cease till after dinner . . . . *T. of Athens* ii 2 42
Importunate. Be no more importunate : 'tis a sickness denying thee *W. Tale* iv 2 2
Put on a most importunate aspect, A visage of demand . *T. of Athens* ii 1 28
In like manner was I in debt to my importunate business . . . iii 6 16
She is importunate, indeed distract : Her mood will needs be pitied *Ham.* iv 5 2
By their own importunate suit, Or voluntary dotage of some mistress *Othello* iv 1 26
Importune you To let him spend his time no more at home *T. G. of Ver.* i 3 13
Nor need'st thou much importune me to that Whereon this month I have been hammering . . . . i 3 17
My herald thoughts in thy pure bosom rest them; While I, their king, that hither them importune, Do curse the grace that with such grace hath bless'd them . . . iii 1 145
We shall write to you, As time and our concernings shall importune *Meas. for Meas.* i 1 57
Against all sense you do importune her . . . v 1 438
I pray you, sir, dispatch.—You hear how he importunes me *Com. of Er.* iv 1 53
On serious business . . . Importunes personal conference . *L. L. Lost* ii 1 32
He is here at the door and importunes access to you . *As Y. Like It* i 1 97
Importune me no farther, For how I firmly am resolved you know *T. of S.* i 1 48
God will revenge it; whom I will importune With daily prayers *Rich. III.* ii 2 14
Importune him for my moneys; be not ceased With slight denial *T. of A.* ii 1 16
Importune him once more to go, my lord; His wits begin to unsettle *Lear* iii 4 166
Confess yourself freely to her; importune her help. . *Othello* ii 3 324
'Tis she must do't: And, lo, the happiness! go, and importune her . iii 4 108
Now he importunes him To tell it o'er: go to; well said, well said . iv 1 115
Only I here importune death awhile, until Of many thousand kisses the poor last I lay upon thy lips . . . *Ant. and Cleo.* iv 15 19
Importuned. You were kneel'd to and importuned otherwise . *Tempest* ii 1 128
Have you importuned her to such a purpose?—Never . *Mer. Wives* ii 2 220
And importuned me That his attendant . . . Might bear him company *Com. of Errors* i 1 127
Since Pentecost the sum is due, And since I have not much importuned you . . . iv 1 2
Have you importuned him by any means?—Both by myself and many other friends . *Rom. and Jul.* i 1 151
He hath importuned me with love In honourable fashion *Hamlet* i 3 110
Very oft importuned me To temper poisons for her . *Cymbeline* v 5 249
Importunity. Comes with him, at my importunity . *Mer. of Venice* iv 1 160
Or your chaste treasure open To his unmaster'd importunity . *Hamlet* i 3 32
Note, if your lady strain his entertainment With any strong or vehement importunity . . *Othello* iii 3 251
Impose. According to your ladyship's impose, I am thus early come *T. G. of Ver.* iv 3 8
Impose me to what penance your invention Can lay upon my sin *M. Ado* v 1 283
In lieu thereof, impose on thee nothing but this . *L. L. Lost* iii 1 130
It is a plague That Cupid will impose for my neglect . iii 1 204
Impose some service on me for thy love . v 2 850
Any thing, my lord, That my ability may undergo And nobleness impose *W. Tale* ii 3 165
Out of your grace, devise, ordain, impose Some gentle order . *K. John* iii 1 250
What fates impose, that men must needs abide . 3 *Hen. VI.* iv 3 58
Yoke of sovereignty, Which fondly you would here impose on me *Richard III.* iii 7 147
Resolve me, with all modest haste, which way Thou mightst deserve, or they impose, this usage . *Lear* ii 4 26
Imposed. I have on Angelo imposed the office . *Meas. for Meas.* i 3 40
A heavier task could not have been imposed . *Com. of Errors* i 1 32
His wickedness, by your rule, should be imposed upon his father *Hen. V.* iv 1 157
Thinking it harder for our mistress to devise imposition enough than for us to undergo any difficulty imposed . *Troi. and Cres.* iii 2 87
Imposition. Which else would stand under grievous imposition *M. for M.* i 2 194
Unless you may be won by some other sort than your father's imposition depending on the caskets . *Mer. of Venice* i 2 114
I do desire you Not to deny this imposition . iii 4 33
Let death and honesty Go with your impositions . *All's Well* iv 4 29
The imposition clear'd Hereditary ours . *W. Tale* i 2 74
If black scandal . . . Attend the sequel of your imposition *Richard III.* iii 7 232
Thinking it harder for our mistress to devise imposition enough than for us to undergo any difficulty imposed . *Troi. and Cres.* iii 2 86
Reputation is an idle and most false imposition . *Othello* ii 3 269
Impossibility. And what impossibility would slay In common sense, sense saves another way . *All's Well* ii 1 180
Being not ignorant of the impossibility, and knowing I had no such purpose . iv 1 39
Flattering me with impossibilities . 3 *Hen. VI.* iii 2 143
And does so much That proof is call'd impossibility . *Troi. and Cres.* v 5 29
Murdering impossibility, to make What cannot be, slight work *Coriolanus* v 3 61
Thou visible god [gold], That solder'st close impossibilities! *T. of Athens* iv 3 388
The clearest gods, who make them honours Of men's impossibilities *Lear* iv 6 74
Impossible. What impossible matter will he make easy next? *Tempest* ii 1 88
'Tis as impossible that he's undrown'd As he that sleeps here swims ii 1 237
I'll have her: and if it be a match, as nothing is impossible *T. G. of Ver.* iii 1 379
Tells me 'tis a thing impossible I should love thee but as a property *Mer. Wives* iii 4 9
He is at my house; he cannot 'scape me; 'tis impossible he should . iii 5 148
Lest the devil that guides him should aid him, I will search impossible places . iii 5 151
It is well allied: but it is impossible to extirp it quite, friar, till eating and drinking be put down . *Meas. for Meas.* iii 2 109
Make not impossible That which but seems unlike . v 1 51
Not impossible But one, the wicked'st caitiff on the ground, May seem as shy . v 1 52
Where it is impossible you should take true root . *Much Ado* i 3 24
A very dull fool; only his gift is in devising impossible slanders . ii 1 143
Huddling jest upon jest with such impossible conveyance upon me . ii 1 252
Let her wear it out with good counsel.—Nay, that's impossible . ii 3 209
I cannot bid you bid my daughter live; That were impossible . v 1 289
Impossible. You may do it in an hour, sir.—Impossible . *L. L. Lost* i 2 40
To move wild laughter in the throat of death? It cannot be; it is impossible . v 2 866
My bond to the Jew is forfeit; and since in paying it, it is impossible I should live, all debts are cleared between you and I. *Mer. of Venice* iii 2 320
It is not impossible to me, if it appear not inconvenient to you *As Y. L. It* v 2 72
Supposing it a thing impossible . . . That ever Katharina will be woo'd *T. of Shrew* i 2 123
It were impossible I should speed amiss . ii 1 285
Curster than she? why, 'tis impossible.—Why, he's a devil, a devil, a very fiend . iii 2 156
Impossible be strange attempts to those That weigh their pains in sense and do suppose What hath been cannot be . *All's Well* i 1 239
There is no Christian, that means to be saved by believing rightly, can ever believe such impossible passages of grossness . *T. Night* iii 2 76
Est-il impossible d'échapper la force de ton bras? . *Hen. V.* iv 4 17
Because you want the grace that others have, You judge it straight a thing impossible To compass wonders but by help of devils 1 *Hen. VI.* v 4 47
We will keep it, if we can; But now it is impossible we should 2 *Hen. VI.* i 1 108
But suddenly to nominate them all, it is impossible . ii 1 130
It is impossible that I should die By such a lowly vassal as thyself . iv 1 110
I'll prove the contrary, if you'll hear me speak.—Thou canst not, son; it is impossible . 3 *Hen. VI.* i 2 21
But think you, lords, that Clifford fled with them?—No, 'tis impossible ii 6 38
Impossible—Unless we sweep 'em from the door with cannons *Hen. VIII.* v 4 12
I will strive with things impossible; Yea, get the better of them *J. C.* ii 1 325
It is impossible that ever Rome Should breed thy fellow . v 3 100
How, in one house, Should many people, under two commands, Hold amity? 'Tis hard; almost impossible . *Lear* ii 4 245
It is impossible they bear it out . *Othello* ii 1 19
It is impossible you should see this, Were they as prime as goats . iii 3 402
Fie, there is no such man; it is impossible . iv 2 134
He cannot like her long.—Like her! O Isis! 'tis impossible *A. and C.* iii 3 18
Can he be there in person? 'tis impossible; Strange that his power should be . iii 7 57
She hath so strictly tied Her to her chamber, that 'tis impossible *Pericles* ii 5 9
And make my senses credit thy relation To points that seem impossible v 1 125
Imposthume. Bladders full of imposthume, sciaticas *Troi. and Cres.* v 1 24
The imposthume of much wealth and peace, That inward breaks *Hamlet* iv 4 27
Impostor. What! An advocate for an impostor! hush! . *Tempest* i 2 477
I am not an impostor that proclaim Myself against the level of mine aim; But know I think and think I know most sure . *All's Well* ii 1 158
These flaws and starts, Impostors to true fear . *Macbeth* iii 4 64
Why do you weep? It may be, You think me an impostor . *Pericles* v 1 179
Impotence. Whereat grieved, That so his sickness, age and impotence Was falsely borne in hand . *Hamlet* ii 2 66
Impotent. To enforce the pained impotent to smile . *L. L. Lost* v 2 864
Delay leads impotent and snail-paced beggary . *Richard III.* iv 3 53
Impotent and bed-rid, scarcely hears Of this his nephew's purpose *Ham.* i 2 29
O most lame and impotent conclusion! . *Othello* ii 1 162
Impounded. Taken and impounded as a stray . *Hen. V.* i 2 160
Impregnable. With self and vain conceit, As if this flesh which walls about our life Were brass impregnable . *Richard II.* iii 2 168
Let us be back'd with God and with the seas Which He hath given for fence impregnable . 3 *Hen. VI* iv 1 44
That, were his heart Almost impregnable, his old ears deaf, Yet should both ear and heart obey my tongue . *T. Andron.* iv 4 98
Imprese. Razed out my imprese, leaving me no sign . *Richard II.* iii 1 25
Impress. This weak impress of love is as a figure Trenched in ice, which with an hour's heat Dissolves . *T. G. of Ver.* iii 2 6
Ajax was here the voluntary, and you as under an impress *Tr. and Cr.* ii 1 107
Who can impress the forest, bid the tree Unfix his earth-bound root? *Macbeth* iv 1 95
As easy mayst thou the intrenchant air With thy keen sword impress . v 8 10
Such impress of shipwrights, whose sore task Does not divide the Sunday from the week . *Hamlet* i 1 75
Muleters, reapers, people Ingross'd by swift impress . *Ant. and Cleo.* iii 7 37
Impressed. His heart, like an agate, with your print impress'd *L. L. Lost* ii 1 236
Where love's strong passion is impress'd in youth . *All's Well* i 3 139
Under whose blessed cross We are impressed and engaged to fight 1 *Hen. IV.* i 1 21
Who wears my stripes impress'd upon him . *Coriolanus* v 6 108
And turn our impress'd lances in our eyes Which do command them *Lear* v 3 50
Impression. Like a waxen image 'gainst a fire, Bears no impression of the thing it was . *T. G. of Ver.* ii 4 202
The impression of keen whips I'ld wear as rubies . *Meas. for Meas.* ii 4 101
Stolen the impression of her fantasy With bracelets of thy hair *M. N. D.* i 1 32
Where the impression of mine eye infixing . *All's Well* v 3 47
An unlick'd bear-whelp That carries no impression like the dam 3 *Hen. VI.* iii 2 162
Such terrible impression made the dream . *Richard III.* i 4 63
Of thy deep duty more impression show Than that of common sons *Cor.* v 3 51
This insculpture, which With wax I brought away, whose soft impression Interprets for my poor ignorance . *T. of Athens* v 4 68
Subscribed it, gave't the impression . *Hamlet* v 2 52
Impressure. Lean but upon a rush, The cicatrice and capable impressure Thy palm some moment keeps . *As Y. Like It* iii 5 23
By your leave, wax. Soft! and the impressure her Lucrece . *T. Night* ii 5 103
Wherein my sword had not impressure made . *Troi. and Cres.* iv 5 131
Imprimendum. Cum privilegio ad imprimendum solum . *T. of Shrew* iv 4 93
'Imprimis: She can fetch and carry.' Why, a horse can do no more *T. G. of Ver.* iii 1 274
'Imprimis: She can milk.'—Ay, that she can.—'Item: She brews good ale' iii 1 302
Now I begin: Imprimis, we came down a foul hill . *T. of Shrew* iv 1 68
'Imprimis, a loose-bodied gown:'—Master, if ever I said loose-bodied gown, sew me in the skirts of it . iv 3 135
Imprimis, It is agreed between the French king Charles . 2 *Hen. VI.* i 1 43
Imprinted. You are but as a form in wax By him imprinted *M. N. Dream* i 1 50
Imprison him: if imprisonment be the due of a bawd *Meas. for Meas.* iii 2 69
Imprison't not In ignorant concealment . *W. Tale* i 2 396
Hubert, away with him; imprison him . *K. John* iv 2 155
Provoked by the queen, Devised impeachments to imprison him *Rich. III.* ii 2 22
Imprison'd thou didst painfully remain A dozen years . *Tempest* i 2 278
To be imprison'd in the viewless winds . *Meas. for Meas.* iii 1 124
Why have you suffer'd me to be imprison'd, Kept in a dark house? *T. N.* v 1 349
Imprisoned angels Set at liberty . *K. John* iii 3 8
That cause, fair nephew, that imprison'd me . 1 *Hen. VI.* ii 5 55
Our brother is imprison'd by your means, Myself disgraced *Richard III.* i 3 78
From that womb where you imprison'd were He is enfranchised *T. An.* iv 2 124
Imprison'd is he, say you?—Ay, my good lord: five talents is his debt, His means most short . *T. of Athens* i 1 94
When he was poor, Imprison'd and in scarcity of friends, I clear'd him ii 2 234

Imprisoned. Whipped from tithing to tithing, and stock-punished, and imprisoned . . . . *Lear* iii 4 140
She's wedded; Her husband banish'd; she imprison'd . . *Cymbeline* i 1 8
Imprisoning. Oft the teeming earth Is with a kind of colic pinch'd and vex'd By the imprisoning of unruly wind . . . *1 Hen. IV.* iii 1 30
Imprisonment. I had as lief have the foppery of freedom as the morality of imprisonment . . . . *Meas. for Meas.* i 2 138
The weariest and most loathed worldly life That age, ache, penury and imprisonment Can lay on nature is a paradise To what we fear of death iii 1 130
Well, then, imprison him: if imprisonment be the due of a bawd . . iii 2 69
You shall have your full time of imprisonment . . . . . iv 2 13
Beside the charge, the shame, imprisonment, You have done wrong to this my honest friend . . . . . . *Com. of Errors* v 1 18
It was proclaimed a year's imprisonment, to be taken with a wench *L. L. L.* i 1 289
Minister the potion of imprisonment to me in respect of poverty *2 Hen. IV.* i 2 146
Let dying Mortimer here rest himself. Even like a man new haled from the rack, So fare my limbs with long imprisonment *1 Hen. VI.* ii 5 4
Her easy-held imprisonment Hath gain'd thy daughter princely liberty v 3 139
To free king Henry from imprisonment And see him seated *3 Hen. VI.* iv 3 63
I'll well requite thy kindness, For that it made my imprisonment a pleasure iv 6 11
Well, your imprisonment shall not be long . . . *Richard III.* i 1 114
Welcome to the open air. How hath your lordship brook'd imprisonment? i 1 125
I shall live, my lord, to give them thanks That were the cause of my imprisonment.—No doubt, no doubt . . . . i 1 128
Deny that you were not the cause Of my Lord Hastings' late imprisonment . . . . i 3 91
What was purposed Concerning his imprisonment, was rather, If there be faith in men, meant for his trial . . . *Hen. VIII.* v 3 150
Improbable. I could condemn it as an improbable fiction *T. Night* iii 4 141
Improper. And did him service Improper for a slave . . *Lear* v 3 221
Improve. You know, his means, If he improve them, may well stretch so far As to annoy us all . . . . *J. Cæsar* ii 1 159
Improvident. Who says this is improvident jealousy? . *Mer. Wives* ii 2 302
Improvident soldiers! had your watch been good, This sudden mischief never could have fall'n . . . . *1 Hen. VI.* ii 1 58
Impudence. Hast thou or word, or wit, or impudence, That yet can do thee office? . . . . *Meas. for Meas.* v 1 368
Tax of impudence, A strumpet's boldness, a divulged shame . *All's Well* ii 1 173
I ne'er heard yet That any of these bolder vices wanted Less impudence to gainsay what they did Than to perform it first . . *W. Tale* iii 2 57
He may my proffer take for an offence, Since men take women's gifts for impudence . . . . *Pericles* ii 3 69
Impudency. Audacious without impudency, learned without opinion *L. L. Lost* v 1 5
Impudent. You might begin an impudent nation . . *All's Well* iv 3 363
She's impudent, my lord, And was a common gamester to the camp . v 3 187
Thou whoreson, impudent, embossed rascal . . . *1 Hen. IV.* iii 3 177
Words that come with such more than impudent sauciness from you *2 Hen. IV.* ii 1 123
You call honourable boldness impudent sauciness . . . ii 1 135
Thy face . . . unchanging, Made impudent with use of evil deeds *3 Hen. VI.* i 4 117
Peace, impudent and shameless Warwick, peace! . . . . . iii 3 156
A woman impudent and mannish grown Is not more loathed than an effeminate man In time of action . . . *Troi. and Cres.* iii 3 217
What committed! Impudent strumpet!—By heaven, you do me wrong *Othello* iv 2 81
Impudently. Confess, Or else be impudently negative . . *W. Tale* i 2 274
Impudique. O Seigneur Dieu! ce sont mots de son mauvais, corruptible, gros, et impudique . . . . *Hen. V.* iii 4 57
Impugn. Yet in such rule that the Venetian law Cannot impugn you *M. of V.* iv 1 179
It skills not greatly who impugns our doom . . . *2 Hen. VI.* iii 1 281
Impure. Your mere enforcement shall acquittance me From all the impure blots and stains thereof . . . . . *Richard III.* iii 7 234
Imputation. Else imputation, For that he knew you, might reproach your life And choke your good to come . . . *Meas. for Meas.* v 1 425
Have you heard any imputation to the contrary? . . *Mer. of Venice* i 3 13
I would humour his men with the imputation of being near their master *2 Hen. IV.* v 1 81
The imputation of his wickedness, by your rule, should be imposed upon his father that sent him . . . . *Hen. V.* iv 1 156
Our imputation shall be oddly poised In this wild action *Troi. and Cres.* i 3 339
In the imputation laid on him by them, in his meed he's unfellowed *Ham.* v 2 149
If imputation and strong circumstances, Which lead directly to the door of truth, Will give you satisfaction . . . . *Othello* iii 3 406
Impute it not a crime To me or my swift passage . . . *W. Tale* iv 1 4
Impute his words To wayward sickliness and age in him *Richard II.* ii 1 141
Pardon me, And not impute this yielding to light love . *Rom. and Jul.* ii 2 105
In. Widow! a pox o' that! How came that widow in? . . *Tempest* ii 1 78
In having known no travel in his youth . . . . *T. G. of Ver.* i 3 16
He in the red face had it . . . . *Mer. Wives* i 1 173
Ill in, I'll in. Follow your friend's counsel. I'll in . . . iii 3 145
Heaven be my witness you do, if you suspect me in any dishonesty . iv 2 140
Would seem in me to affect speech and discourse . *Meas. for Meas.* i 1 4
Purchased by such sin For which the pardoner himself is in . . . iv 2 112
He's in for a commodity of brown paper and old ginger . . . . iv 3 5
But creep in crannies when he hides his beams . . *Com. of Errors* ii 2 31
Take a house! This is some priory. In, or we are spoil'd! . . . v 1 37
When the age is in, the wit is out: God help us! . . *Much Ado* iii 5 37
I would not care a pin, if the other three were in . . . *L. L. Lost* iv 3 19
Do not call it sin in me, That I am forsworn for thee . . . iv 3 115
How now! what is in you? why dost thou tear it? . . . . . iv 3 200
O that I knew he were but in by the week! . . . . . . v 2 61
I make no doubt The rest will ne'er come in, if he be out . . . v 2 152
A worthy gentleman.—So is Lysander.—In himself he is; But in this kind, wanting your father's voice, The other must be held the worthier . . . . *M. N. Dream* i 1 53
How comes this gentle concord in the world? . . . . . iv 1 148
He is every man in no man . . . . . . *Mer. of Venice* i 2 65
Father, in. I cannot get a service, no; I have ne'er a tongue . . ii 2 165
I do in birth deserve her, and in fortunes, In graces . . . . ii 7 32
Since in paying it, it is impossible I should live . . . . . iii 2 320
Serve in the meat, and we will come in to dinner . . . . . iii 5 64
There is no truth in him.—Do you think so? . . . *As Y. Like It* iii 4 22
Not true in love?—Yes, when he is in; but I think he is not in . . iii 4 28
It is in us to plant thine honour where We please to have it grow *All's W.* ii 3 163
It lies in you, my lord, to bring me in some grace . . . . . v 2 49
Her business looks in her With an importing visage . . . . v 3 135
There is a fair behaviour in thee . . . . . . *T. Night* i 2 47
Now he's deeply in: look how imagination blows him . . . . ii 5 47
In himself too mighty, And in his parties, his alliance . . *W. Tale* ii 3 20
In. A piece many years in doing and now newly performed . . *W. Tale* v 2 104
In at the window, or else o'er the hatch . . . . . *K. John* i 1 171
'Tis shame such wrongs are borne In him, a royal prince *Richard II.* ii 1 239
He, in twelve, Found truth in all but one; I, in twelve thousand, none iv 1 170
My finger . . . Is pointing still, in cleansing them from tears . . v 5 54
In the which better part I have saved my life . . . . *1 Hen. IV.* v 4 122
For Doll is in. Pistol speaks nought but truth . . . *2 Hen. IV.* v 5 40
Poor we may call them in their native lords . . . . *Hen. V.* iii 5 26
Where is the best and safest passage in? . . . . . *1 Hen. VI.* iii 2 22
Suddenly surprised By bloody hands, in sleeping on your beds . . v 3 41
In pain of your dislike or pain of death . . . . *2 Hen. VI.* iii 2 257
I'll in, to urge his hatred more to Clarence . . . *Richard III.* i 1 147
As little joy may you suppose in me, That I enjoy . . . . . i 3 153
Yet execute thy wrath in me alone, O, spare my guiltless wife! . . i 4 71
God punish me With hate in those where I expect most love! . . . ii 1 35
Wept like two children in their deaths' sad stories . . . . . iv 3 8
In to our tent; the air is raw and cold . . . . v 3 46
But all Was either pitied in him or forgotten . . . *Hen. VIII.* ii 1 29
Remove these thoughts from you: the which before His highness shall speak in . . . . ii 4 103
Troy in our weakness stands, not in her strength . . *Troi. and Cres.* i 3 137
How much in having, or without or in, Cannot make boast to have that iii 3 97
He raves in saying nothing . . . . iii 3 249
They are rising, they are rising.—In, in, in, in! . . . . *Coriolanus* iv 5 251
Enter; and no sooner in, But every man betake him to his legs *R. and J.* i 4 33
I am wealthy in my friends . . . . *T. of Athens* ii 2 193
In, and prepare: Ours is the fall, I fear; our foes the snare . . v 2 16
Wear our health but sickly in his life, Which in his death were perfect *Macbeth* iii 1 107
Round about the cauldron go; In the poison'd entrails throw . . iv 1 5
A countenance more in sorrow than in anger . . . . . *Hamlet* i 2 232
In second husband let me be accurst! . . . . iii 2 189
What, in the least, Will you require in present dower with her? . *Lear* i 1 194
Make your own purpose, How in my strength you please . . . ii 1 114
'Tis not in thee To grudge my pleasures, to cut off my train . . . ii 4 176
Good nuncle, in, and ask thy daughters' blessing . . . . . iii 2 12
In, boy; go first. You houseless poverty,—Nay, get thee in . . . iii 4 26
We'll talk with them too, Who loses and who wins; who's in, who's out v 3 15
What, in your own part, can you say to this? . . . . . *Othello* i 3 74
You may relish him more in the soldier than in the scholar . . . ii 1 167
I cannot believe that in her; she's full of most blessed condition . . ii 1 254
This gentleman Steps in to Cassio, and entreats his pause . . . . ii 3 229
That errs in ignorance and not in cunning . . . . iii 3 49
O, 'tis foul in her . . . . iv 1 213
Let's think't unsafe To come in to the cry without more help . . . v 1 44
I am not so well as I should be, but I'll ne'er out.—Not till you have slept; I fear me you'll be in till then . . . . *Ant. and Cleo.* ii 7 38
There's nothing in her yet: The fellow has good judgement . . . iii 3 27
In hac spe vivo . . . . *Pericles* ii 2 44
Make me blessed in your care In bringing up my child . . . . iii 3 31
In drink. The poor monster's in drink . . . . . *Tempest* ii 2 162
He was gotten in drink: is not the humour conceited? . . *Mer. Wives* i 3 25
If he had not been in drink, he would have tickled you othergates *T. Night* v 1 197
I do not speak to thee in drink but in tears . . . *1 Hen. IV.* ii 4 458
What you want in meat, we'll have in drink . . . *2 Hen. IV.* v 3 30
In fecks. Art thou my boy?—Ay, my good lord.—I' fecks! . *W. Tale* i 2 120
In it. There's little can be said in't: 'tis against the rule of nature *All's W.* i 1 147
There's something in't, More than my father's skill . . . . i 3 248
Which the wenches say is a gallimaufry of gambols, because they are not in't . . . . *W. Tale* iv 4 336
You witch me in it . . . . *T. of Athens* v 1 158
In so far. But I am in So far in blood that sin will pluck on sin *Rich. III.* iv 2 64
I am in blood Stepp'd in so far that, should I wade no more, Returning were as tedious as go o'er . . . . . . *Macbeth* iii 4 137
In sooth, I know not why I am so sad . . . . *Mer. of Venice* i 1 1
Sir, understand you this of me in sooth . . . . *T. of Shrew* i 2 259
In sooth you scape not so . . . . ii 1 242
You were the first that found me!—Was I, in sooth? . . *All's Well* v 2 47
In sooth, good friend, your father might have kept This calf bred from his cow from all the world; In sooth he might . . . *K. John* i 1 123
In sooth, I would you were a little sick . . . . iv 1 29
Swear me, Kate, like a lady as thou art, A good mouth-filling oath, and leave 'in sooth,' And such protest of pepper-gingerbread *1 Hen. IV.* iii 1 259
Rude, in sooth; in good sooth, very rude . . . . *Troi. and Cres.* iii 1 59
In sooth, you are to blame . . . . *Othello* iii 4 97
In that. My brother had but justice, In that he did the thing *M. for M.* v 1 454
In that thou art like to be my kinsman, live unbruised . . *Much Ado* v 4 111
In that each of you have forsworn his book, Can you still dream? *L. L. L.* iv 3 297
The courtesy of nations allows you my better, in that you are the first-born; but the same tradition takes not away my blood *As Y. Like It* i 1 50
In that it is a thing of his own search . . . . i 1 141
I love thee well, in that thou likest it not . . . . *T. of Shrew* iv 3 83
I am as ignorant in that as you In so entitling me . . . *W. Tale* ii 3 70
Thou dost consent In some large measure to thy father's death, In that thou seest thy wretched brother die . . . . . . *Richard II.* i 2 27
What's more manifest? In that thou laid'st a trap to take my life *1 Hen. VI.* iii 1 22
But yet I like it not, In that he wears the badge of Somerset . . iv 1 177
Entreat her not the worse in that I pray You use her well . *2 Hen. VI.* ii 4 81
Let him die, in that he is a fox, By nature proved an enemy to the flock iii 1 257
In that you brook it ill, it makes him worse . . . *Richard III.* i 3 3
Ye alehouse painted signs! Coal-black is better than another hue, In that it scorns to bear another hue . . . . . *T. Andron.* iv 2 100
In that the levies . . . are all made Out of his subject . . . *Hamlet* i 2 31
Happy, in that we are not over-happy . . . . il 2 232
In the crop. He that ears my land spares my team and gives me leave to in the crop . . . . *All's Well* i 3 48
In this. Come, come, elder brother, you are too young in this . *As Y. L. It* i 1 57
I am in this, Your wife, your son . . . . . . *Coriolanus* iii 2 64
How strange it shows, Timon in this should pay more than he owes *T. of A.* iii 4 22
Inaccessible. Uninhabitable and almost inaccessible . . . *Tempest* ii 1 37
In this desert inaccessible . . . . *As Y. Like It* ii 7 110
In-a-door. And keep in-a-door, And thou shalt have more . . *Lear* i 4 138
Inaidible. The congregated college have concluded That labouring art can never ransom nature From her inaidible estate . . *All's Well* ii 1 122
Inaudible. The inaudible and noiseless foot of Time . . . . v 3 41
Inauspicious. And shake the yoke of inauspicious stars . *Rom. and Jul.* v 3 111
Incaged in so small a verge, The waste is no whit lesser . *Richard II.* ii 1 102
Such a pleasure as incaged birds Conceive . . . . *3 Hen. VI.* iv 6 12
Incantation. My ancient incantations are too weak . . . *1 Hen. VI.* v 3 27

Incapable. Of temporal royalties He thinks me now incapable *Tempest* i 2 111
Is not your father grown incapable Of reasonable affairs? *W. Tale* iv 4 408
Incapable and shallow innocents *Richard III.* ii 2 18
Such as was never So incapable of help . . . . *Coriolanus* iv 6 120
She chanted snatches of old tunes; As one incapable of her own distress *Hamlet* iv 7 179
Incardinate. But he's the very devil incardinate . . . *T. Night* v 1 185
Incarnadine. This my hand will rather The multitudinous seas incarnadine, Making the green one red . . . . . *Macbeth* ii 2 62
Incarnal. Certainly the Jew is the very devil incarnal . *Mer. of Venice* ii 2 29
Incarnate. And said they were devils incarnate . . . *Hen. V.* ii 3 34
This is the incarnate devil That robb'd Andronicus . . *T. Andron.* v 1 40
Incense. I will incense Page to deal with poison . . . *Mer. Wives* i 3 109
And would incense me To murder her I married . . *W. Tale* v 1 61
Breathing to his breathless excellence The incense of a vow . *K. John* iv 3 67
I never did incense his majesty Against the Duke *Richard III.* i 3 85
To fly the boar before the boar pursues, Were to incense the boar to follow us . . . . iii 2 29
Now, God incense him, And let him cry Ha! louder . *Hen. VIII.* iii 2 61
Whose smoke, like incense, doth perfume the sky . . *T. Andron.* i 1 145
Either there is a civil strife in heaven, Or else the world, too saucy with the gods, Incenses them to send destruction . *J. Cæsar* i 3 13
And what they may incense him to, being apt To have his ear abused, wisdom bids fear . . . . *Lear* ii 4 309
Upon such sacrifices, my Cordelia, The gods themselves throw incense v 3 21
Proclaim him in the streets; incense her kinsmen . . . *Othello* i 1 69
Incensed. Incensed the seas and shores, yea, all the creatures *Tempest* iii 3 74
Your brother incensed me to slander the Lady Hero . *Much Ado* v 1 242
Let me borrow my arms again.—Room for the incensed Worthies! *L. L. Lost* v 2 703
The knight is incensed against you, even to a mortal arbitrement. *T. N.* iii 4 285
Revenge did paint The fearful difference of incensed kings . *K. John* iii 1 238
Throw this report on their incensed rage . . . . . iv 2 261
Whose bosom burns With an incensed fire of injuries . *2 Hen. IV.* i 3 14
Yet notwithstanding, being incensed, he's flint . . . iv 4 33
It is not that that hath incensed the duke . . . *1 Hen. VI.* iii 1 36
He, more incensed against your majesty Than all the rest *3 Hen. VI.* iv 1 108
Think you, my lord, this little prating York Was not incensed by his subtle mother To taunt and scorn you! . . . *Richard III.* iii 1 152
This tractable obedience is a slave To each incensed will . *Hen. VIII.* i 2 65
Sir, I may tell it you, I think I have Incensed the lords o' the council . v 1 43
If 'gainst yourself you be incensed, we'll put you, Like one that means his proper harm, in manacles . . . . *Coriolanus* i 9 56
The people are incensed against him.—Stop, Or all will fall in broil . iii 1 32
'Twas you incensed the rabble: Cats, that can judge as fitly of his worth iv 2 33
Whom the vile blows and buffets of the world Have so incensed *Macbeth* iii 1 110
Tell me, Laertes, Why thou art thus incensed . . . *Hamlet* iv 5 126
'Tis dangerous when the baser nature comes Between the pass and fell incensed points Of mighty opposites . . . . . v 2 61
Have at you now!—Part them; they are incensed . . . . . v 2 313
O, I am mock'd, And thou by some incensed god sent hither . *Pericles* v 1 144
Incensement. His incensement at this moment is so implacable *T. Night* iii 4 260
Incensing. And deeper than oblivion we do bury The incensing relics of it . . . . *All's Well* v 3 25
Incertain. Or to be worse than worst Of those that lawless and incertain thought Imagine howling . . . . . . *Meas. for Meas.* iii 1 127
Dare not Say what I think of it, since I have found Myself in my incertain grounds to fail As often as I guess'd . . . *All's Well* iii 1 15
May drop upon his kingdom and devour Incertain lookers on *W. Tale* v 1 29
Surmise Of aids incertain should not be admitted . . *2 Hen. IV.* i 3 24
Willing misery Outlives incertain pomp, is crown'd before *T. of Athens* iv 3 243
Since the affairs of men rest still incertain . . . . *J. Cæsar* v 1 96
Incertainties. And to the hazard Of all incertainties himself commended, No richer than his honour . . . . *W. Tale* iii 2 170
Incessant. The incessant weepings of my wife . . . *Com. of Errors* i 1 71
The incessant care and labour of his mind . . . *2 Hen. IV.* iv 4 118
To do your grace incessant services . . . . . *Hen. V.* ii 2 38
We will plague thee with incessant wars . . . *1 Hen. VI.* v 4 154
For raging wind blows up incessant showers . . *3 Hen. VI.* i 4 145
Incessantly. I'ld play incessantly upon these jades . *K. John* ii 1 385
Incest. Is't not a kind of incest, to take life From thine own sister's shame? . . . . *Meas. for Meas.* iii 1 139
Bear it not; Let not the royal bed of Denmark be A couch for luxury and damned incest . . . . *Hamlet* i 5 83
With whom the father liking took, And her to incest did provoke *Per.* i Gower 26
Certain you were not so bad As with foul incest to abuse your soul . i 1 126
Her face was to mine eye beyond all wonder; The rest—hark in thine ear—as black as incest . . . . i 2 76
Here have you seen a mighty king His child, I wis, to incest bring ii Gower 2
Escanes, know this of me, Antiochus from incest lived not free . . ii 4 2
Incestuous. O, most wicked speed, to post With such dexterity to incestuous sheets! . . . . *Hamlet* i 2 157
That incestuous, that adulterate beast, With witchcraft of his wit . i 5 42
When he is drunk asleep, or in his rage, Or in the incestuous pleasure of his bed . . . . iii 3 90
Here, thou incestuous, murderous, damned Dane, Drink off this potion v 2 336
Thou perjured, and thou simular man of virtue That art incestuous *Lear* iii 2 55
Inch. Whom I, with this obedient steel, three inches of it, Can lay to bed for ever . . . . *Tempest* ii 1 283
I'll show thee every fertile inch o' th' island . . . . ii 2 152
I will fetch you a tooth-picker now from the furthest inch of Asia *M. Ado* ii 1 275
Ask them how many inches Is in one mile . . . *L. L. Lost* v 2 188
The princess bids you tell How many inches doth fill up one mile . . v 2 193
One inch of delay more is a South-sea of discovery . *As Y. Like It* iii 2 206
I'll not budge an inch, boy: let him come, and kindly . *T. of Shrew* Ind. 1 14
Away, you three-inch fool! I am no beast.—Am I but three inches? . iv 1 29
For every inch of woman in the world, Ay, every dram of woman's flesh is false, If she be . . . . *W. Tale* ii 1 137
I'll queen it no inch farther, But milk my ewes and weep . . . iv 4 460
My inch of taper will be burnt and done . . . *Richard II.* i 3 223
And so far will I trust thee, gentle Kate.—How! so far?—Not an inch further. But hark you, Kate . . . . . *1 Hen. IV.* ii 3 117
That you should have an inch of any ground To build a grief on *2 Hen. IV.* iv 1 109
I have speeded hither with the very extremest inch of possibility . iv 3 39
Beldam, I think we watch'd you at an inch . . . *2 Hen. VI.* i 4 45
I will begin at thy heel, and tell what thou art by inches *Troi. and Cres.* ii 1 54
With spans and inches so diminutive As fears and reasons . . ii 2 31
One that knows the youth Even to his inches . . . . iv 5 111
They'll give him death by inches . . . . . *Coriolanus* v 4 42
That stretches from an inch narrow to an ell broad . *Rom. and Jul.* ii 4 88
Till he disbursed at Saint Colme's inch Ten thousand dollars . *Macbeth* i 2 61
Inch. Ay, every inch a king: When I do stare, see how the subject quakes *Lear* iv 6 109
Am I not an inch of fortune better than she?—Well, if you were but an inch of fortune better than I, where would you choose it? *Ant. and Cleo.* i 2 59
I would I had thy inches; thou shouldst know There were a heart in Egypt . . . . i 3 40
Gave you some ground.—As many inches as you have oceans *Cymbeline* i 2 21
Should by the minute feed on life and lingering By inches waste you . v 5 52
Her stature to an inch; as wand-like straight . . . *Pericles* v 1 110
Incharitable. You bawling, blasphemous, incharitable dog! . . *Tempest* i 1 44
Inch-meal. Make him By inch-meal a disease! . . . . . ii 2 3
Inch-thick, knee-deep, o'er head and ears a fork'd one! . . *W. Tale* i 2 186
Tell her, let her paint an inch thick, to this favour she must come *Hamlet* v 1 214
Incidency. Declare What incidency thou dost guess of harm Is creeping toward me . . . . *W. Tale* i 2 403
Incident. A malady Most incident to maids . . . . . . iv 4 125
Plagues, incident to men, Your potent and infectious fevers heap On Athens, ripe for stroke! . . . . *T. of Athens* iv 1 21
With other incident throes That nature's fragile vessel doth sustain . v 1 203
Incision. A fever in your blood! why, then incision Would let her out in saucers . . . . *L. L. Lost* iv 3 97
Let us make incision for your love, To prove whose blood is reddest *Mer. of Venice* ii 1 6
God make incision in thee! thou art raw . . . . *As Y. Like It* iii 2 75
Deep malice makes too deep incision; Forget, forgive . . *Richard II.* i 1 155
What! shall we have incision! shall we imbrue? . . *2 Hen. IV.* ii 4 210
Make incision in their hides, That their hot blood may spin . *Hen. V.* iv 2 9
Incite them to quick motion . . . . *Tempest* iv 1 39
My kindness shall incite thee To bind our loves up in a holy band *M. Ado* iii 1 113
She incites me to that in the letter . . . . . *T. Night* iii 4 75
In approbation Of what your reverence shall incite us to . . *Hen. V.* i 2 20
No blown ambition doth our arms incite, But love, dear love . *Lear* iv 4 27
We do incite The gentry to this business . . . . *Cymbeline* iii 7 6
Incivil. He was a prince.—A most incivil one . . . . . v 5 292
Incivility. How say you now? is not your husband mad?—His incivility confirms no less . . . . *Com. of Errors* iv 4 49
Inclinable. And have hearts Inclinable to honour . . . *Coriolanus* ii 2 60
Inclination. He pieces out his wife's inclination . . *Mer. Wives* iii 2 35
Ostentare, to show, as it were, his inclination . . . *L. L. Lost* iv 2 16
And their gentle hearts To fierce and bloody inclination . *K. John* v 2 158
Men judge by the complexion of the sky The state and inclination of the day: So may you by my dull and heavy eye . . *Richard II.* iii 2 195
Through vassal fear, Base inclination, and the start of spleen *1 Hen. IV.* iii 2 125
This merry inclination Accords not with the sadness of my suit *3 Hen. VI.* iii 2 76
Break off your talk, And give us notice of his inclination *Richard III.* iii 1 178
Thus to have said, As you were fore-advised, had touch'd his spirit And tried his inclination . . . . *Coriolanus* ii 3 200
Observe his inclination in yourself.—I shall, my lord . . *Hamlet* ii 1 71
Pray can I not, Though inclination be as sharp as will . . . . iii 3 39
Bid him Report the feature of Octavio, her years, Her inclination *Ant. and Cleo.* ii 5 113
Tell me, how dost thou find the inclination of the people? . *Pericles* iv 2 104
Incline. If you'll a willing ear incline, What's mine is yours *Meas. for Meas.* v 1 542
And he from forage will incline to play . . . *L. L. Lost* iv 1 93
Doth his majesty Incline to it, or no?—He seems indifferent . *Hen. V.* i 1 72
I see no reason, if I wear this rose, That any one should therefore be suspicious I more incline to Somerset than York . *1 Hen. VI.* iv 1 154
If he would incline to the people, there was never a worthier man *Coriol.* ii 3 42
We must incline to the king. I will seek him, and privily relieve him *Lear* iii 3 14
This to hear Would Desdemona seriously incline . . . *Othello* i 3 146
The swan's down-feather, That stands upon the swell at full of tide, And neither way inclines . . . . *Ant. and Cleo.* iii 2 50
There did persuade Great Herod to incline himself to Cæsar . . iv 6 14
He did incline to sadness, and oft-times Not knowing why . *Cymbeline* i 6 62
Inclined. Thou art inclined to sleep; 'tis a good dulness . . *Tempest* i 2 185
Pity move my father To be inclined my way! . . . . . . i 2 447
I wish mine eyes Would, with themselves, shut up my thoughts: I find They are inclined to do so . . . . ii 1 193
He was not inclined that way.—O, sir, you are deceived *Meas. for Meas.* iii 2 130
What if we do omit This reprobate till he were well inclined? . . iv 3 78
I will laugh like a hyen, and that when thou art inclined to sleep *As Y. Like It* iv 1 157
Do it reverently, When you perceive his blood inclined to mirth *2 Hen. IV.* iv 4 38
He's inclined as is the ravenous wolf . . . . *2 Hen. VI.* iii 1 78
But angry, wrathful, and inclined to blood, If you go forward . . iv 2 134
Men well inclined to hear what thou command'st . . *3 Hen. VI.* iv 8 16
Subject to your countenance, glad or sorry As I saw it inclined *Hen. VIII.* ii 4 27
Quickly draw out my command, Which men are best inclined *Coriolanus* i 6 85
I am a man That from my first have been inclined to thrift *T. of Athens* i 1 118
There cannot be That vulture in you, to devour so many As will to greatness dedicate themselves, Finding it so inclined . *Macbeth* iv 3 76
It doth much content me To hear him so inclined . . . *Hamlet* iii 1 25
Not I, Inclined to this intelligence, pronounce The beggary *Cymbeline* i 6 114
Inclinest. If thou inclinest that way, thou art a coward . . *W. Tale* i 2 243
Inclining. Your inclining cannot be removed . . . . *All's Well* iii 6 41
Canst with thine eyes at once see good and evil, Inclining to them both *W. Tale* i 2 304
If one jot beyond The bound of honour, or in act or will That way inclining . . . . iii 2 53
His age some fifty, or, by 'r lady, inclining to three score . *1 Hen. IV.* ii 4 467
Is it your own inclining? Is it a free visitation? . . . *Hamlet* ii 2 283
Hold your hands, Both you of my inclining, and the rest . . *Othello* i 2 82
'Tis most easy The inclining Desdemona to subdue In any honest suit ii 3 346
Inclip. Whate'er the ocean pales, or sky inclips, Is thine. *Ant. and Cleo.* ii 7 74
Include. We will include all jars With triumphs, mirth . *T. G. of Ver.* v 4 160
The loss of such a lord includes all harm . . . . *Richard III.* i 3 8
Then every thing includes itself in power, Power into will *Troi. and Cres.* i 3 119
Included. Dispersed are the glories it included . . . *1 Hen. VI.* i 2 137
Inclusive. To bestow them, As notes whose faculties inclusive were More than they were in note . . . . *All's Well* i 3 232
I would to God that the inclusive verge Of golden metal that must round my brow Were red-hot steel! . . . . . *Richard III.* iv 1 59
Incomparable. A merchant of incomparable wealth . . *T. of Shrew* iv 2 98
Her words do show her wit incomparable . . . . *3 Hen. VI.* iii 2 85
Now this masque Was cried incomparable; and the ensuing night Made it a fool and beggar . . . . *Hen. VIII.* i 1 27
A most incomparable man, breathed, as it were, To an untirable and continuate goodness . . . . *T. of Athens* i 1 10
Incomprehensible lies that this same fat rogue will tell us . *1 Hen. IV.* i 2 209

Inconsiderate. Doth the inconsiderate take salve for l'envoy? *L. L. Lost* iii 1 79
Rash, inconsiderate, fiery voluntaries, With ladies' faces . *K. John* ii 1 67
Inconstancy falls off ere it begins . . . . *T. G. of Ver.* v 4 113
More than the villanous inconstancy of man's disposition is able to bear *Mer. Wives* iv 5 111
By keeping company With men like men of inconstancy. . *L. L. Lost* iv 3 180
O foul revolt of French inconstancy! . . . . *K. John* iii 1 322
The agent of thy foul inconstancy . . . *2 Hen. VI.* iii 2 115
Inconstant. Dotes in idolatry Upon this spotted and inconstant man *M. N. D.* i 1 110
Apish, shallow, inconstant, full of tears, full of smiles . *As Y. Like It* iii 2 432
Is he inconstant, sir, in his favours? . . . . . *T. Night* i 4 7
That did but show thee, of a fool, inconstant And damnable ingrateful *W. Tale* iii 2 187
Behold A city on the inconstant billows dancing . . *Hen. V.* iii Prol. 15
That she [Fortune] is turning, and inconstant, and mutability, and variation . . . . iii 6 36
Thin of substance as the air And more inconstant than the wind *R. and J.* i 4 100
O, swear not by the moon, the inconstant moon, That monthly changes ii 2 109
If no inconstant toy, nor womanish fear, Abate thy valour in the acting it iv 1 119
Incontinency. You must not put another scandal on him, That he is open to incontinency . . . . . . *Hamlet* ii 1 30
The cognizance of her incontinency Is this . . *Cymbeline* ii 4 127
Thou didst accuse him of incontinency; Thou then look'dst like a villain iii 4 49
Incontinent. They made a pair of stairs to marriage which they will climb incontinent, or else be incontinent before marriage *As Y. Like It* v 2 42
And put on sullen black incontinent . . . *Richard II.* v 6 48
Nothing but lechery! all incontinent varlets! . . *Troi. and Cres.* v 1 106
Matrons, turn incontinent! Obedience fail in children! *T. of Athens* iv 1 3
He looks gentler than he did.—He says he will return incontinent *Othello* iv 3 12
Incontinently. I will incontinently drown myself . . . . i 3 306
Inconvenience. To intercept this inconvenience . . *1 Hen. VI.* i 4 14
Why gentle Peace Should not expel these inconveniences . *Hen. V.* v 2 66
Inconvenient. And it is not impossible to me, if it appear not inconvenient to you . . . . *As Y. Like It* v 2 73
Incony. My sweet ounce of man's flesh! my incony Jew! . *L. L. Lost* iii 1 136
O' my troth, most sweet jests! most incony vulgar wit! . . iv 1 144
Incorporal. And with the incorporal air do hold discourse *Hamlet* iii 4 118
Incorporate. That, undividable, incorporate, Am better than thy dear self's better part . . . . . . *Com. of Errors* ii 2 124
As if our hands, our sides, voices and minds, Had been incorporate *M. N. Dream* iii 2 208
To make divorce of their incorporate league . . *Hen. V.* v 2 394
'True is it, my incorporate friends,' quoth he, 'That I receive the general food at first' . . . . *Coriolanus* i 1 134
I am incorporate in Rome, A Roman now adopted happily . *T. Andron.* i 1 462
You shall not stay alone Till holy church incorporate two in one *R. and J.* ii 6 37
It is Casca; one incorporate To our attempts . . *J. Cæsar* i 3 135
That great vow Which did incorporate and make us one . . ii 1 273
At hand comes the master and main exercise, the incorporate conclusion *Othello* ii 1 269
Incorpsed. As had he been incorpsed and demi-natured With the brave beast . . . . *Hamlet* iv 7 88
Incorrect. 'Tis unmanly grief; It shows a will most incorrect to heaven i 2 95
Increase. Earth's increase, foison plenty . . . *Tempest* iv 1 110
I will pray, Pompey, to increase your bondage . *Meas. for Meas.* iii 2 78
The mazed world, By their increase, now knows not which is which *M. N. Dream* ii 1 114
Loss of virginity is rational increase . . . . . *All's Well* i 1 139
Within ten year it will make itself ten, which is a goodly increase . i 1 160
Even to the world's pleasure and the increase of laughter . . ii 4 37
The children are not in the fault; whereupon the world increases *2 Hen. IV.* ii 2 29
And I do wish your honours may increase . . . . v 2 104
Thou wilt but add increase unto my wrath . . *2 Hen. VI.* iii 2 292
And with the southern clouds contend in tears, Theirs for the earth's increase, mine for my sorrows . . . . . iii 2 385
When we saw our sunshine made thy spring, And that thy summer bred us no increase . . . . . . *3 Hen. VI.* ii 2 164
Go, hie thee, hie thee from this slaughter-house, Lest thou increase the number of the dead . . . . . *Richard III.* iv 1 45
To quicken your increase, I will beget Mine issue of your blood . . iv 4 297
Let them not live to taste this land's increase . . . . v 5 38
The Lord increase this business! . . . . *Hen. VIII.* iii 2 161
Your affections are A sick man's appetite, who desires most that Which would increase his evil . . . . *Coriolanus* i 1 183
More holy and profound than mine own life, My dear wife's estimate, her womb's increase . . . . . . iii 3 114
This peace is nothing, but to rust iron, increase tailors . . iv 5 235
For you, be that you are, long; and your misery increase with your age! v 2 113
Like to the earth swallow her own increase . . *T. Andron.* v 2 192
As if increase of appetite had grown By what it fed on . . *Hamlet* i 2 144
Dry up in her the organs of increase! . . . . *Lear* i 4 301
The heavens forbid But our loves and comforts should increase, Even as our days do grow! . . . . . . *Othello* ii 1 196
Drink thou; increase the reels . . . . *Ant. and Cleo.* ii 7 100
Make denials Increase your services . . . . *Cymbeline* ii 3 54
The heavens, Through you, increase our wonder . . *Pericles* iii 2 97
Increased. Our wealth increased By prosperous voyages . *Com. of Errors* i 1 40
Increaseth. Buckingham, back'd with the hardy Welshmen, Is in the field, and still his power increaseth . . . . *Richard III.* iv 3 48
The enemy increaseth every day; We, at the height . *J. Cæsar* iv 3 216
Increasing. Long continuance, and increasing, Hourly joys be still upon you! . . . . *Tempest* iv 1 107
God send you, sir, a speedy infirmity, for the better increasing your folly! . . . . *T. Night* i 5 85
A white beard? a decreasing leg? an increasing belly? . *2 Hen. IV.* i 2 205
What is his strength by land?—Great and increasing . *Ant. and Cleo.* ii 2 165
That remains loyal to his vow, and your, increasing in love . *Cymbeline* iii 2 48
Grow, patience! And let the stinking elder, grief, untwine His perishing root with the increasing vine! . . . . . . iv 2 60
Incredible. 'Tis incredible to believe How much she loves me *T. of Shrew* ii 1 308
Incredulous. No obstacle, no incredulous or unsafe circumstance *T. Night* iii 4 88
And never live to show the incredulous world The noble change *2 Hen. IV.* iv 5 154
Incur. In peril to incur your former malady . . *T. of Shrew* Ind. 2 124
I know not what I shall incur to pass it, Having no warrant . *W. Tale* ii 2 57
Therefore, to speak, and to avoid the first, And then, in speaking, not to incur the last, Definitely thus I answer you . . *Richard III.* iii 7 152
Would ever have, to incur a general mock, Run from her guardage *Othello* i 2 69
Is not almost a fault To incur a private check . . . . iii 3 67
I shall incur I know not How much of his displeasure . *Cymbeline* i 1 102
Incurable. That gave him out incurable,— Why, there 'tis . *All's Well* i 3 16
Incurable. Present medicine must be minister'd, Or overthrow incurable ensues . . . . *K. John* v 1 16
Borrowing only lingers and lingers it out, but the disease is incurable *2 Hen. IV.* i 2 266
Limekilns i' the palm, incurable bone-ache . . *Troi. and Cres.* v 1 25
Incurr'd The danger formerly by me rehearsed . . *Mer. of Venice* iv 1 361
He hath incurred the everlasting displeasure of the king . *All's Well* iv 3 10
I have abandon'd Troy, left my possession, Incurr'd a traitor's name *Troi. and Cres.* iii 3 6
We are not the first Who, with best meaning, have incurr'd the worst *Lear* v 3 4
Incursion. Whose hot incursions and great name in arms Holds from all soldiers chief majority . . . . . . *1 Hen. IV.* iii 2 108
When thou art forth in the incursions, thou strikest as slow as another *Troi. and Cres.* ii 1 32
Ind. Do you put tricks upon's with savages and men of Ind? . *Tempest* ii 2 61
Like a rude and savage man of Inde . . . . *L. L. Lost* iv 3 222
From the east to western Ind, No jewel is like Rosalind . *As Y. Like It* iii 2 93
Indebted. And stand indebted, over and above, In love and service to you evermore . . . . . . *Mer. of Venice* iv 1 413
The king and commonweal Are deeply indebted for this . *2 Hen. VI.* i 4 47
Indeed. He did believe He was indeed the duke . . . *Tempest* i 2 103
Thou art very Trinculo indeed! . . . . . . ii 2 109
One that takes upon him to be a dog indeed . . *T. G. of Ver.* iv 4 13
You do yourself wrong, indeed, la! . . . . *Mer. Wives* i 1 326
None but mine own people.—Indeed!—No, certainly . . . iv 2 15
Many a man would take you at your word, And go indeed *Com. of Errors* i 2 18
And that Pyramus is not killed indeed . . *M. N. Dream* iii 1 20
And there indeed let him name his name, and tell them plainly . iii 1 46
But what praise couldst thou bestow on a deserving woman indeed? *Oth.* ii 1 146
Indeed! ay, indeed: discern'st thou aught in that? Is he not honest? iii 3 102
Indent. Shall we buy treason? and indent with fears, When they have lost and forfeited themselves? . . . . . . *1 Hen. IV.* i 3 87
It shall not wind with such a deep indent, To rob me of so rich a bottom iii 1 104
Indented. With indented glides did slip away Into a bush *As Y. Like It* iv 3 113
Indenture. Upon thy cheek lay I this zealous kiss, As seal to this indenture of my love . . . . *K. John* ii 1 20
Darest thou be so valiant as to play the coward with thy indenture? *1 Hen. IV.* ii 4 53
Our indentures tripartite are drawn . . . . . iii 1 80
Are the indentures drawn? . . . . iii 1 141
An the indentures be drawn, I'll away within these two hours . iii 1 265
Than the length and breadth of a pair of indentures . . *Hamlet* v 1 119
If a king bid a man be a villain, he's bound by the indenture of his oath to be one . . . . *Pericles* i 3 9
Serve by indenture to the common hangman . . . . . iv 6 187
Index. As index to the story we late talk'd of . . . *Richard III.* ii 2 149
The flattering index of a direful pageant . . . . . iv 4 85
In such indexes, although small pricks To their subsequent volumes, there is seen The baby figure . . . . *Troi. and Cres.* i 3 343
Ay me, what act, That roars so loud, and thunders in the index? *Hamlet* iii 4 52
An index and obscure prologue to the history of lust . . *Othello* ii 1 263
India. Come from the farthest steppe of India . . *M. N. Dream* ii 1 69
What, not one hit? From Tripolis, from Mexico and England, From Lisbon, Barbary and India? . . . . *Mer. of Venice* iii 2 272
Here comes the little villain. How now, my metal of India? *T. Night* ii 5 17
Wondrous affable and as bountiful As mines of India . *1 Hen. IV.* iii 1 169
And, to-morrow, they Made Britain India . . . *Hen. VIII.* i 1 21
Her bed is India; there she lies, a pearl . . *Troi. and Cres.* i 1 103
Condition, I had gone barefoot to India . . . . . i 2 80
Indian. When they will not give a doit to relieve a lame beggar, they will lay out ten to see a dead Indian . . . . *Tempest* ii 2 34
A lovely boy, stolen from an Indian king. . . *M. N. Dream* ii 1 22
In the spiced Indian air, by night, Full often hath she gossip'd by my side . . . . ii 1 124
I'll to my queen and beg her Indian boy . . . . . iii 2 375
The beauteous scarf Veiling an Indian beauty . *Mer. of Venice* iii 2 99
Not deck'd with diamonds and Indian stones, Nor to be seen *3 Hen. VI.* iii 1 63
Or have we some strange Indian with the great tool come to court? *Hen. VIII.* v 4 34
Like the base Indian, threw a pearl away Richer than all his tribe *Othello* v 2 347
Indian-like, Religious in mine error, I adore The sun . *All's Well* i 3 210
Indict. No matter in the phrase that might indict the author of affectation; but called it an honest method . . . . *Hamlet* ii 2 464
Indicted. Now I find I had suborn'd the witness, And he's indicted falsely *Othello* iii 4 154
Indictment. Read the indictment . . . . . . *W. Tale* iii 2 11
There is another indictment upon thee . . . . . *2 Hen. IV.* ii 4 371
Then threw he down himself and all their lives That by indictment and by dint of sword Have since miscarried under Bolingbroke . . iv 1 128
This is the indictment of the good Lord Hastings . . *Richard III.* iii 6 1
Indies. They shall be my East and West Indies . . *Mer. Wives* i 3 79
Where America, the Indies?—Oh, sir, upon her nose *Com. of Errors* iii 2 136
He hath an argosy bound to Tripolis, another to the Indies *Mer. of Venice* i 3 19
More lines than is in the new map with the augmentation of the Indies *T. Night* iii 2 86
Has all the Indies in his arms, And more and richer . *Hen. VIII.* iv 1 45
Indifferency. From all indifferency, From all direction . *K. John* ii 1 579
An I had but a belly of any indifferency . . . . *2 Hen. IV.* iv 3 23
Indifferent. Therefore the office is indifferent . . *T. G. of Ver.* iii 2 44
I'll tell you news indifferent good for either . . *T. of Shrew* i 2 181
Their garters of an indifferent knit . . . . . . iv 1 94
It does indifferent well in a flame-coloured stock . . *T. Night* i 3 143
Item, two lips, indifferent red; item, two grey eyes, with lids to them i 5 265
I beseech your grace Look on my wrongs with an indifferent eye *Rich II.* ii 3 116
He seems indifferent, Or rather swaying more upon our part. *Hen. V.* i 1 72
If you mark Alexander's life well, Harry of Monmouth's life is come after it indifferent well . . . . iv 7 34
Having here No judge indifferent . . . . . *Hen. VIII.* ii 4 17
Yes, he'll fight indifferent well. . . . . *Troi. and Cres.* i 2 242
This comes off well and excellent.—Indifferent . . *T. of Athens* i 1 30
I am arm'd, And dangers are to me indifferent . . *J. Cæsar* i 3 115
How do ye both?—As the indifferent children of the earth . *Hamlet* ii 2 231
I am myself indifferent honest . . . . iii 1 123
'Tis very cold; the wind is northerly.—It is indifferent cold, my lord . v 2 100
Indifferently. I have an humour to knock you indifferently well *Hen. V.* ii 1 58
He waved indifferently 'twixt doing them neither good nor harm . *Cor.* ii 2 19
Hear me speak indifferently for all . . . . *T. Andron.* i 1 430
If it be aught toward the general good, Set honour in one eye and death i' the other, And I will look on both indifferently . *J. Cæsar* i 2 87
I hope we have reformed that indifferently with us, sir . . *Hamlet* iii 2 41

Indigent faint souls past corporal toil . *Hen. V.* i 1 16
Indigest. You are born To set a form upon that indigest . *K. John* v 7 26
Indigested lump, As crooked in thy manners as thy shape! 2 *Hen. VI.* v 1 157
An indigested and deformed lump . 3 *Hen. VI.* v 6 51
Indign. And all indign and base adversities Make head against my estimation! . *Othello* i 3 274
Indignation. At which my nose is in great indignation . *Tempest* iv 1 200
To pluck his indignation on thy head . *All's Well* iii 2 32
I'll deliver thy indignation to him by word of mouth . *T. Night* ii 3 140
His indignation derives itself out of a very competent injury . iii 4 269
And ready mounted are they to spit forth Their iron indignation *K. John* ii 1 212
And quench his fiery indignation Even in the matter of mine innocence iv 1 63
They burn in indignation . iv 2 103
Withhold thine indignation, mighty heaven! . v 6 37
Change the complexion of her maid-pale peace To scarlet indignation *Richard II.* iii 3 99
His moods, and his displeasures, and his indignations . *Hen. V.* iv 7 39
O, let them keep it till thy sins be ripe, And then hurl down their indignation On thee! . *Richard III.* i 3 220
Suspend your indignation against my brother till you can derive from him better testimony of his intent . *Lear* i 2 86
Indigne. Je ne veux point que vous abaissiez votre grandeur en baisant la main d'une de votre seigneurie indigne serviteur . *Hen. V.* v 2 276
Indignity. The poor monster's my subject and he shall not suffer indignity . *Tempest* iii 2 42
Complain unto the duke of this indignity.—Come, go *Com. of Errors* v 1 113
Whom I beseech To give me ample satisfaction For these deep shames and great indignities . v 1 253
It can never be They will digest this harsh indignity . *L. L. Lost* v 2 289
You give me most egregious indignity . *All's Well* ii 3 229
My blood hath been too cold and temperate, Unapt to stir at these indignities . 1 *Hen. IV.* i 3 2
I shall make this northern youth exchange His glorious deeds for my indignities . iii 2 146
How might a prince of my great hopes forget So great indignities? 2 *Hen. IV.* v 2 69
Nor wrong mine age with this indignity . *T. Andron.* i 1 8
Some strange indignity, Which patience could not pass . *Othello* ii 3 245
Indirect. If it be proved against an alien That by direct or indirect attempts He seek the life of any citizen . *Mer. of Venice* iv 1 350
Till he hath ta'en thy life by some indirect means or other *As Y. Like It* i 1 159
Though indirect, Yet indirection thereby grows direct . *K. John* iii 1 275
His title, the which we find Too indirect for long continuance 1 *Hen. IV.* iv 3 105
God knows, my son, By what by-paths and indirect crook'd ways I met this crown . 2 *Hen. IV.* iv 5 185
He needs no indirect nor lawless course To cut off those *Richard III.* i 4 224
Fie, what an indirect and peevish course Is this of hers! . iii 1 31
Speak: Did you by indirect and forced courses Subdue and poison this young maid's affections? . *Othello* i 3 111
Indirection. Though indirect, Yet indirection thereby grows direct *K. John* iii 1 276
Than to wring From the hard hands of peasants their vile trash By any indirection . *J. Cæsar* iv 3 75
And with assays of bias, By indirections find directions out . *Hamlet* ii 1 66
Indirectly. To speak so indirectly I am loath . *Meas. for Meas.* iv 6 1
At the very next turning, turn of no hand, but turn down indirectly to the Jew's house . *Mer. of Venice* ii 2 45
Indirectly and directly too Thou hast contrived against the very life . iv 1 359
Repent each drop of blood That hot rash haste so indirectly shed *K. John* ii 1 49
This bald unjointed chat of his, my lord, I answer'd indirectly 1 *Hen. IV.* i 3 66
He bids you then resign Your crown and kingdom, indirectly held From him the native and true challenger . *Hen. V.* ii 4 94
Thy head, all indirectly, gave direction . *Richard III.* iv 4 225
Indiscreet. It would ill become me to be vain, indiscreet, or a fool *L. L. Lost* iv 2 31
So slight, so drunken, and so indiscreet an officer . *Othello* ii 3 280
Indiscretion. Our indiscretion sometimes serves us well *Hamlet* v 2 8
All's not offence that indiscretion finds And dotage terms so . *Lear* ii 4 199
Indisposed. I'll forbear; And am fall'n out with my more headier will, To take the indisposed and sickly fit For the sound man . ii 4 112
Indisposition. Perchance some single vantages you took, When my indisposition put you back . *T. of Athens* ii 2 139
Indissoluble. With a most indissoluble tie For ever knit *Macbeth* iii 1 17
Indistinct. Even till we make the main and the aerial blue An indistinct regard . *Othello* ii 1 40
The rack dislimns, and makes it indistinct, As water is in water *Ant. and Cleo.* iv 14 10
Indistinguishable. You whoreson indistinguishable cur *Troi. and Cres.* v 1 33
Indite. She will indite him to some supper *Rom. and Jul.* ii 4 135
Indited. What plume of feathers is he that indited this letter? *L. L. Lost* iv 1 96
He is indited to dinner to the Lubber's-head in Lumbert street 2 *Hen. IV.* ii 1 30
Individable. Scene individable, or poem unlimited . *Hamlet* ii 2 418
Indrenched. When I do tell thee, there my hopes lie drown'd, Reply not in how many fathoms deep They lie indrench'd . *Troi. and Cres.* i 1 51
Indubitate. The pernicious and indubitate beggar Zenelophon *L. L. Lost* iv 1 67
Induce. Whether ever I Did broach this business to your highness; or Laid any scruple in your way, which might Induce you to the question on't? . *Hen. VIII.* ii 4 151
If my frosty signs and chaps of age . . . Cannot induce you *T. Andron.* v 3 79
Some nobler token I have kept apart For Livia and Octavia, to induce Their mediation . *Ant. and Cleo.* v 2 169
My circumstances, Being so near the truth as I will make them, Must first induce you to believe . *Cymbeline* ii 4 63
Induced by my charity . *Meas. for Meas.* iv 3 53
I have your own letter that induced me to the semblance I put on *T. N.* v 1 315
Induced by potent circumstances . *Hen. VIII.* ii 4 76
Induced As you have been; that's for my country . *Coriolanus* i 9 16
Her attendants are All sworn and honourable:—they induced to steal it! And by a stranger!—No . *Cymbeline* ii 4 125
Inducement. My son corrupts a well-derived nature With his inducement *All's Well* iii 2 91
If this inducement force her not to love, Send her a story of thy noble acts . *Richard III.* iv 4 279
Then mark the inducement. Thus it came . *Hen. VIII.* ii 4 169
Induction. And our induction full of prosperous hope . 1 *Hen. IV.* iii 1 2
Plots have I laid, inductions dangerous . *Richard III.* i 1 32
A dire induction am I witness to . iv 4 5
Indue. Then lesser is my fear, I shall indue you with . *K. John* iv 2 43
Let our finger ache, and it indues Our other healthful members even to that sense Of pain . *Othello* iii 4 146
Indued with intellectual sense and souls . *Com. of Errors* ii 1 22
He is best indued in the small . *L. L. Lost* v 2 646
To mark the full-fraught man and best indued With some suspicion *Hen. V.* ii 2 139
Or like a creature native and indued Unto that element . *Hamlet* iv 7 180
Indulgence. Let your indulgence set me free . *Tempest* Epil. 20
Thou that givest whores indulgence to sin . 1 *Hen. VI.* i 3 35
Great minds, of partial indulgence To their benumbed wills *Tr. and Cr.* ii 2 178
Indulgent. You are too indulgent . *Ant. and Cleo.* i 4 16
Indurance. And to have heard you, Without indurance, further *Hen. VIII.* v 1 121
Industrious. What, Ariel! my industrious servant, Ariel! . *Tempest* iv 1 33
They gape and point At your industrious scenes and acts of death *K. John* ii 1 376
Here is a dear, a true industrious friend . 1 *Hen. IV.* i 1 62
And put we on Industrious soldiership . *Macbeth* v 4 16
Industriously. If industriously I play'd the fool, it was my negligence, Not weighing well the end . *W. Tale* i 2 257
Industry. Experience is by industry achieved . *T. G. of Ver.* i 3 22
Thine, in the dearest design of industry . *L. L. Lost* iv 1 88
His industry is up-stairs and down-stairs . 1 *Hen. IV.* ii 4 112
Over-careful fathers Have broke their sleep with thoughts, their brains with care, Their bones with industry . 2 *Hen. IV.* iv 5 70
Which industry and courage might have saved . 3 *Hen. VI.* v 4 11
Sterile with idleness, or manured with industry . *Othello* i 3 328
If thou wouldst not be a villain, but do me true service, undergo those employments wherein I should have cause to use thee with a serious industry . *Cymbeline* iii 5 112
The sweat of industry would dry and die, But for the end it works to . iii 6 31
And with a dropping industry they skip From stem to stern . *Pericles* iv 1 63
Inequality. Nor do not banish reason For inequality . *Meas. for Meas.* v 1 65
Inestimable stones, unvalued jewels, All scatter'd in the bottom of the sea: Some lay in dead men's skulls *Richard III.* i 4 27
You all clapp'd your hands, And cried 'Inestimable!' *Troi. and Cres.* ii 2 88
He was seated in a chariot Of an inestimable value . *Pericles* ii 4 8
Inevitable. Of force Must yield to such inevitable shame *Mer. of Venice* iv 1 57
I had a pass with him, . . . and he gives me the stuck in with such a mortal motion, that it is inevitable . *T. Night* iii 4 304
'Tis fond to wail inevitable strokes, As 'tis to laugh at 'em . *Coriolanus* iv 1 26
Behind me The inevitable prosecution of Disgrace and horror *A. and C.* iv 14 65
Inexecrable. O, be thou damn'd, inexecrable dog! . *Mer. of Venice* iv 1 128
Inexorable. More inexorable, O, ten times more, than tigers 3 *Hen. VI.* i 4 154
More inexorable far Than empty tigers or the roaring sea *Rom. and Jul.* v 3 38
Inexplicable. Capable of nothing but inexplicable dumb-shows *Hamlet* iii 2 13
Infallible. And he is a motion generative; that's infallible *Meas. for Meas.* iii 2 119
By heaven, that thou art fair, is most infallible . *L. L. Lost* iv 1 61
Which is most infallible disobedience . *All's Well* i 1 150
A note infallible Of breaking honesty—horsing foot on foot . *W. Tale* i 2 287
In craving your opinion of my title, Which is infallible . 2 *Hen. VI.* ii 2 5
Infallibly. The text most infallibly concludes it . *L. L. Lost* iv 2 169
Your lordship speaks most infallibly of him . *Hamlet* v 2 126
Infamonize. Dost thou infamonize me among potentates? . *L. L. Lost* v 2 684
Infamous. This fact was infamous And ill beseeming any common man 1 *Hen. VI.* iv 1 30
O Antony, Nobler than my revolt is infamous, Forgive me *Ant. and Cleo.* iv 9 19
Infamy. Then never dream on infamy, but go . *T. G. of Ver.* ii 7 64
Smirched thus and mired with infamy . *Much Ado* iv 1 135
The supposition of the lady's death Will quench the wonder of her infamy . iv 1 241
I will whip about your infamy circum circa . *L. L. Lost* v 1 72
You live in great infamy . 2 *Hen. IV.* i 2 156
From the powdering-tub of infamy Fetch forth the lazar kite *Hen. V.* ii 1 79
Beside, what infamy will there arise, When foreign princes shall be certified That for a toy, a thing of no regard, King Henry's peers and chief nobility Destroy'd themselves! . 1 *Hen. VI.* iv 1 143
Here on my knee I beg mortality, Rather than life preserved with infamy iv 5 33
To be a queen, and crown'd with infamy! . 2 *Hen. VI.* iii 2 71
Look here, I throw my infamy at thee . 3 *Hen. VI.* v 1 82
Her face defaced with scars of infamy *Richard III.* iii 7 126
Throw over her the veil of infamy . iv 4 208
He must not live to trumpet forth my infamy . *Pericles* i 1 145
Infancy. Thy nerves are in their infancy again . *Tempest* i 2 484
From our infancy We have conversed and spent our hours together *T. G. of Ver.* ii 4 62
Sleep she as sound as careless infancy . *Mer. Wives* v 5 56
Beauty doth varnish age, as if new-born, And gives the crutch the cradle's infancy: O, 'tis the sun that maketh all things shine . *L. L. Lost* iv 3 245
For she was as tender As infancy and grace . *W. Tale* v 3 27
A virgin from her tender infancy, Chaste and immaculate . 1 *Hen. VI.* v 4 50
And had his highness in his infancy Crowned in Paris . 2 *Hen. VI.* i 1 93
Tetchy and wayward was thy infancy; Thy school-days frightful *Rich. III.* iv 4 168
And skilless as unpractised infancy . *Troi. and Cres.* i 1 12
Soft infancy, that nothing canst but cry, Add to my clamours! . ii 2 105
I am as true as truth's simplicity And simpler than the infancy of truth iii 2 177
His loving breast thy pillow; Many a matter hath he told to thee, Meet and agreeing with thine infancy . *T. Andron.* v 3 165
Infant. Like an envious sneaping frost That bites the first-born infants of the spring . *L. L. Lost* i 1 101
Define, define, well-educated infant . i 2 99
All hid, all hid; an old infant play . iv 3 78
Thou disputest like an infant: go, whip thy gig . v 1 69
At first the infant, Mewling and puking in the nurse's arms *As Y. Like It* ii 7 143
Whose love had spoke, Even since it could speak, from an infant *W. Tale* iii 2 71
Who, on my life, Did perish with the infant . v 1 44
Cut off the sequence of posterity, Out-faced infant state . *K. John* ii 1 97
Whiles warm life plays in that infant's veins . iii 4 132
Draws the sweet infant breath of gentle sleep . *Richard II.* i 3 133
Evermore thanks, the exchequer of the poor; Which, till my infant fortune comes to years, Stands for my bounty . ii 3 67
Look, 'when his infant fortune came to age,' And 'gentle Harry Percy' 1 *Hen. IV.* i 3 253
This infant warrior in his enterprizes Discomfited great Douglas . iii 2 113
As he is striking, holds his infant up And hangs resolved correction in the arm That was uprear'd to execution . 2 *Hen. IV.* iv 1 212
Mowing like grass Your fresh-fair virgins and your flowering infants *Hen. V.* iii 3 14
Your naked infants spitted upon pikes . iii 3 38
Henry the Sixth, in infant bands crown'd King . Epil. 9
As very infants prattle of thy pride . 1 *Hen. VI.* iii 1 16
Meet I an infant of the house of York, Into as many gobbets will I cut it As wild Medea young Absyrtus did . 2 *Hen. VI.* v 2 57

Infant. More than the infant that is born to-night . *Richard III.* ii 1 71
Right for right Hath dimm'd your infant morn to aged night . . iv 4 16
My reasons are too deep and dead ; Too deep and dead, poor infants . iv 4 363
This royal infant—heaven still move about her !—Though in her cradle, yet now promises Upon this land a thousand thousand blessings *Hen. VIII.* v 5 18
The servants to this chosen infant Shall then be his . . v 5 49
Give as soft attachment to thy senses As infants' ! . *Troi. and Cres.* iv 2 6
And arm the minds of infants to exclaims . *T. Andron.* iv 1 86
Within the infant rind of this small flower Poison hath residence *Rom. and Jul.* ii 3 23
Yea, to chimney-tops, Your infants in your arms . *J. Cæsar* i 1 45
That mothers shall but smile when they behold Their infants quarter'd with the hands of war. . . . . . . iii 1 268
The canker galls the infants of the spring . . . *Hamlet* i 3 39
Yet, for the love Of this poor infant, this fresh-new sea-farer, I would it would be quiet . . . . . *Pericles* iii 1 41
Here I charge your charity withal, leaving her The infant of your care . iii 3 15
Infant-like. You can do very little alone ; . . . your abilities are too infant-like for doing much alone . . *Coriolanus* ii 1 41
Infect. Who was so firm, so constant, that this coil Would not infect his reason ? . . . . *Tempest* i 2 208
For you, most wicked sir, whom to call brother Would even infect my mouth . . . . v 1 131
Who, all for want of pruning, with intrusion Infect thy sap *Com. of Errors* ii 2 182
There were no living near her ; she would infect to the north star *M. Ado* ii 1 257
This is the very false gallop of verses : why do you infect yourself with them ? . . . . . . *As Y. Like It* iii 2 120
'Twas a fear Which oft infects the wisest . . *W. Tale* i 2 262
Who does infect her ?—Why, he that wears her like her medal . i 2 306
This sickness doth infect The very life-blood of our enterprise 1 *Hen. IV.* iv 1 28
If it did infect my blood with joy, Or swell my thoughts 2 *Hen. IV.* iv 5 170
Did I but suspect a fearful man, He should have leave to go away betimes, Lest in our need he might infect another . . 3 *Hen. VI.* v 4 46
Out of my sight ! thou dost infect my eyes . *Richard III.* i 2 149
It was usual with him, every day It would infect his speech . *Hen. VIII.* i 2 133
A most arch heretic, a pestilence That does infect the land . v 1 46
As knots, by the conflux of meeting sap, Infect the sound pine *Troi. and Cres.* i 3 8
And in the imitation of these twain . . . many are infect . i 3 187
And one infect another Against the wind a mile ! . *Coriolanus* i 4 33
More of your conversation would infect my brain . . ii 1 105
No levell'd malice Infects one comma in the course I hold *T. of Athens* i 1 48
Breath infect breath, That their society, as their friendship, may Be merely poison ! . . . . iv 1 30
O blessed breeding sun, draw from the earth Rotten humidity ; below thy sister's orb Infect the air ! . . . . iv 3 3
I'll beat thee, but I should infect my hands . . iv 3 369
Whiles rank corruption, mining all within, Infects unseen *Hamlet* iii 4 149
Keeps himself in clouds, And wants not buzzers to infect his ear . iv 5 90
Infect her beauty, You fen-suck'd fogs ! . . *Lear* ii 4 168
The nature of bad news infects the teller . *Ant. and Cleo.* i 2 99
Infected. Poor worm, thou art infected ! This visitation shows it *Temp.* iii 1 31
Deceive me not now, Navarre is infected.—With what ?—With that which we lovers entitle affected . . . *L. L. Lost* ii 1 230
They are infected ; in their hearts it lies . . v 2 420
Through and through Cleanse the foul body of the infected world *As Y. Like It* ii 7 60
Infected with the fashions . . *T. of Shrew* iii 2 52
Were my wife's liver Infected as her life, she would not live . *W. Tale* i 2 305
O, then my best blood turn To an infected jelly ! . . i 2 418
Never to be infected with delight, Nor conversant with ease . *K. John* iv 3 69
Of which disease Our late king, Richard, being infected, died 2 *Hen. IV.* iv 1 58
O, how hast thou with jealousy infected The sweetness of affiance ! *Hen. V.* ii 2 126
Thine eyes, sweet lady, have infected mine . *Richard III.* i 2 150
No more infected with my country's love Than when I parted hence *Cor.* v 6 72
In thee a nature but infected ; A poor unmanly melancholy *T. of Athens* iv 3 202
Approach the fold and cull the infected forth, But kill not all together v 4 43
Infected be the air whereon they ride ! . *Macbeth* iv 1 138
Infected minds To their deaf pillows will discharge their secrets . v 1 80
With Hecate's ban thrice blasted, thrice infected *Hamlet* iii 2 269
Our court, infected with their manners, Shows like a riotous inn . *Lear* i 4 264
As doth the raven o'er the infected house, Boding to all . *Othello* iv 1 21
Thy food is such As hath been belch'd on by infected lungs . *Pericles* iv 6 179
Infecting. His mind and place Infecting one another . *Hen. VIII.* i 1 162
Infection. All the infections that the sun sucks up . *Tempest* ii 2 1
Her husband has a marvellous infection to the little page *Mer. Wives* ii 2 120
He hath ta'en the infection : hold it up . . *Much Ado* ii 3 126
He hath a great infection, sir, as one would say, to serve *Mer. of Venice* ii 2 133
His very genius hath taken the infection of the device . *T. Night* ii 4 142
To the infection of my brains And hardening of my brows . *W. Tale* i 2 145
Worse than the great'st infection That e'er was heard or read ! . i 2 423
The blessed gods Purge all infection from our air whilst you Do climate here ! . . . . v 1 169
But such is the infection of the time . . *K. John* v 2 20
This fortress built by Nature for herself Against infection *Richard II.* ii 1 44
He shall not breathe infection in this air But three days longer 2 *Hen. VI.* iii 2 287
Defused infection of a man . . . *Richard III.* i 2 78
Lest his infection, being of catching nature, Spread further *Coriolanus* iii 1 310
Take thou some new infection to thy eye . *Rom. and Jul.* i 2 50
I could not send it,—here it is again,—Nor get a messenger to bring it thee, So fearful were they of infection . . v 2 16
What is amiss plague and infection mend ! *T. of Athens* v 1 224
Hence ; Lest that the infection of his fortune take Like hold on thee *Lear* iv 6 237
What a strange infection Is fall'n into thy ear ! . *Cymbeline* iii 2 3
Infectious. A huge infectious troop Of pale distemperatures *Com. of Errors* v 1 81
From his presence I am barr'd, like one infectious . *W. Tale* iii 2 99
We both were in a house Where the infectious pestilence did reign *Rom. and Jul.* v 2 10
Plagues, incident to men, Your potent and infectious fevers heap On Athens, ripe for stroke ! . . . . *T. of Athens* iv 1 22
The most infectious pestilence upon thee !—Good madam, patience *Ant. and Cleo.* ii 5 61
The seeing these effects will be Both noisome and infectious *Cymbeline* i 5 26
Infectiously. And the will dotes that is attributive To what infectiously itself affects . . . . . *Troi. and Cres.* ii 2 59
Infer. That need must needs infer this principle . *K. John* iii 1 213
This doth infer the zeal I had to see him . 2 *Hen. IV.* v 5 14
I this infer, That many things, having full reference To one consent, may work contrariously . . . . . . *Hen. V.* i 2 204
Infer. Infer the bastardy of Edward's children . . *Richard III.* iii 5 75
Withal I did infer your lineaments, Being the right idea of your father iii 7 12
Infer fair England's peace by this alliance . . . iv 4 343
Inference. When I shall turn the business of my soul To such exsufficate and blown surmises, Matching thy inference . *Othello* iii 3 183
Inferior. And yet she is inferior to none . . *T. of Shrew* Ind. 2 69
I had that which any inferior might At market-price have bought *All's W.* v 3 218
So shall inferior eyes, That borrow their behaviours from the great, Grow great by your example . . . . . *K. John* v 1 50
And shall the figure of God's majesty . . . Be judged by subject and inferior breath, And he himself not present? . . *Richard II.* iv 1 128
And, for your royal birth, Inferior to none but to his majesty 1 *Hen. VI.* iii 1 96
Winchester will not submit, I trow, Or be inferior to the proudest peer v 1 57
Yet in marriage I may not prove inferior to yourself . 3 *Hen. VI.* iv 1 122
The strongest nerves and small inferior veins From me receive *Coriolanus* i 1 142
In such cases Men's natures wrangle with inferior things, Though great ones are their object . . . . . *Othello* iii 4 144
It is fit I should commit offence to my inferiors . *Cymbeline* ii 1 32
Infernal. You shall find her the infernal Ate in good apparel *Much Ado* ii 1 263
To the infernal deep, with Erebus and tortures vile also . 2 *Hen. IV.* ii 4 170
I am Revenge ; sent from the infernal kingdom . *T. Andron.* v 2 30
Inferred. Thus saith the duke, thus hath the duke inferr'd *Richard III.* iii 7 32
What shall I say more than I have inferr'd . . v 3 314
'Tis inferr'd to us, His days are foul and his drink dangerous *T. of Athens* iii 5 73
Inferreth arguments of mighty strength . . 3 *Hen. VI.* iii 1 49
Inferring. Full well hath Clifford play'd the orator, Inferring arguments of mighty force . . . . ii 2 44
Infest. Do not infest your mind with beating on The strangeness of this business . . . . *Tempest* v 1 246
Infidel. But who comes here ? Lorenzo and his infidel ? *Mer. of Venice* iii 2 221
Now, infidel, I have you on the hip . . . iv 1 334
Peace shall go sleep with Turks and infidels . *Richard II.* iv 1 139
What a pagan rascal is this ! an infidel ! . . 1 *Hen. IV.* ii 3 32
What, think you we are Turks or infidels ? . *Richard III.* iii 5 41
Infinite. There is not only disgrace and dishonour in that, monster, but an infinite loss . . . . . . *Tempest* iv 1 210
I mean that her beauty is exquisite, but her favour infinite *T. G. of Ver.* ii 1 60
A thousand oaths, an ocean of his tears And instances of infinite of love . ii 7 70
A jewel that I have purchased at an infinite rate . *Mer. Wives* ii 2 213
An infinite distance From his true-meant design . *Meas. for Meas.* i 4 54
Of credit infinite, highly beloved, Second to none . *Com. of Errors* v 1 6
It is past the infinite of thought . . *Much Ado* ii 3 106
We number nothing that we spend for you : Our duty is so rich, so infinite, That we may do it still without accompt . *L. L. Lost* v 2 199
Gratiano speaks an infinite deal of nothing . *Mer. of Venice* i 1 114
Needs must intimate Skill infinite or monstrous desperate . *All's Well* ii 1 187
He's a most notable coward, an infinite and endless liar . iii 6 11
In fine, Her infinite cunning, with her modern grace, Subdued me to her rate . . . . v 3 216
Among the infinite doings of the world, Sometime puts forth *W. Tale* i 2 253
Beyond the infinite and boundless reach Of mercy . *K. John* iv 3 117
Albeit considerations infinite Do make against it . 1 *Hen. IV.* v 1 102
What infinite heart's-ease Must kings neglect, that private men enjoy ! *Hen. V.* iv 1 253
These fellows of infinite tongue, that can rhyme themselves into ladies' favours . . . . v 2 163
Your hopes and friends are infinite . . *Hen. VIII.* iii 1 82
Will you with counters sum The past proportion of his infinite? *T. and C.* ii 2 29
O, you shall be exposed, my lord, to dangers As infinite as imminent ! . iv 4 71
The one almost as infinite as all, The other blank as nothing . iv 5 80
O, were the sum of these that I should pay Countless and infinite, yet would I pay them ! . . . . *T. Andron.* v 3 159
My bounty is as boundless as the sea, My love as deep ; the more I give to thee, The more I have, for both are infinite . *Rom. and Jul.* ii 2 135
Of man and beast the infinite malady Crust you quite o'er ! *T. of Athens* iii 6 108
Common mother, thou, Whose womb unmeasurable, and infinite breast, Teems, and feeds all . . . . . . iv 3 178
The infinite flatteries that follow youth and opulency . . v 1 37
Be they as pure as grace, As infinite as man may undergo *Hamlet* i 4 34
I could be bounded in a nut-shell and count myself a king of infinite space . . . . ii 2 261
What a piece of work is a man ! how noble in reason ! how infinite in faculty ! . . . . ii 2 316
I knew him, Horatio : a fellow of infinite jest, of most excellent fancy v 1 204
In nature's infinite book of secrecy A little I can read *Ant. and Cleo.* i 2 9
Age cannot wither her, nor custom stale Her infinite variety . ii 2 241
O infinite virtue, comest thou smiling from The world's great snare uncaught ? . . . . iv 8 17
She hath pursued conclusions infinite Of easy ways to die . v 2 358
As I my poor self did exchange for you, To your so infinite loss *Cymbeline* i 1 120
What an infinite mock is this ! . . . . v 4 195
Infinitely. To whom I am so infinitely bound . *Mer. of Venice* v 1 135
When I am o' horseback, I will swear I love thee infinitely 1 *Hen. IV.* ii 3 105
I will pay you some and, as most debtors do, promise you infinitely 2 *Hen. IV.* Epil. 17
So infinitely endear'd . . . . . . *T. of Athens* i 2 233
To whose kindnesses I am most infinitely tied . . *Cymbeline* i 6 23
Infinitive. He's an infinitive thing upon my score . 2 *Hen. IV.* ii 1 26
Infirm. What is infirm from your sound parts shall fly . *All's Well* ii 1 170
Infirm of purpose ! Give me the daggers . *Macbeth* ii 2 52
The unruly waywardness that infirm and choleric years bring with them . . . . *Lear* i 1 302
A poor, infirm, weak, and despised old man . . . iii 2 20
Infirmity. Be not disturb'd with my infirmity . . . *Tempest* iv 1 160
Poor soul, She speaks this in the infirmity of sense . *Meas. for Meas.* v 1 47
Will you be cured of your infirmity ?—No . . *All's Well* ii 1 71
Infirmity, that decays the wise, doth ever make the better fool *T. Night* i 5 82
God send you, sir, a speedy infirmity, for the better increasing your folly ! . . . . i 5 84
Infirmities that honesty Is never free of . . *W. Tale* i 2 263
But infirmity Which waits upon worn times hath something seized His wish'd ability . . . . v 1 141
Then, Joan, discover thine infirmity, That warranteth by law to be thy privilege . . . . 1 *Hen. VI.* v 4 60
As if you were a god to punish, not A man of their infirmity *Coriolanus* iii 1 82
He desired their worships to think it was his infirmity . *J. Cæsar* i 2 274
A friend should bear his friend's infirmities . . iv 3 86
Will you, with those infirmities she owes, Unfriended, new adopted to our hate, Dower'd with our curse, and stranger'd with our oath, Take her, or leave her? . . . . *Lear* i 1 205

Infirmity. I have a strange infirmity, which is nothing To those that know me . . . . *Macbeth* iii 4 86
'Tis the infirmity of his age . . . . *Lear* i 1 296
Infirmity doth still neglect all office Whereto our health is bound . ii 4 107
I am unfortunate in the infirmity, and dare not task my weakness *Othello* ii 3 43
On some odd time of his infirmity, Will shake this island . . ii 3 132
With one of an ingraft infirmity . . . . . . ii 3 145
With diseased ventures That play with all infirmities for gold *Cymbeline* i 6 124
Excuse her keeping close, Whereto constrain'd by her infirmity . iii 5 47
Assuming man's infirmities, To glad your ear . . . *Pericles* i Gower 3
How from the finny subject of the sea These fishers tell the infirmities of men! . . . . ii 1 53
Infixed I beheld myself Drawn in the flattering table of her eye *K. John* ii 1 502
Infixing. Where the impression of mine eye infixing . *All's Well* v 3 47
Inflame. I will inflame thy noble liver, And make thee rage . 2 *Hen. IV.* v 5 33
Being men, hearing the will of Cæsar, It will inflame you . *J. Cæsar* iii 2 149
When the blood is made dull with the act of sport, there should be, again to inflame it and to give satiety a fresh appetite, loveliness in favour, sympathy in years . . . . . . *Othello* ii 1 231
Which shows that beauty hath his power and will, Which can as well inflame as it can kill . . . . . . *Pericles* ii 2 35
Let not conscience, Which is but cold, inflaming love i' thy bosom, Inflame too nicely . . . . iv 1 6
Inflamed. To stop their marches 'fore we are inflamed . . *K. John* v 1 7
In characters as red as Mars his heart Inflamed with Venus *Tr. and Cr.* v 2 165
Gods, gods! 'tis strange that from their cold'st neglect My love should kindle to inflamed respect . . . . *Lear* i 1 258
You gods that made me man, and sway in love, That have inflamed desire in my breast . . . . *Pericles* i 1 20
Inflaming. I am burn'd up with inflaming wrath . . *K. John* iii 1 340
Never yet attaint With any passion of inflaming love . . 1 *Hen. VI.* v 5 82
Let not conscience, Which is but cold, inflaming love i' thy bosom, Inflame too nicely . . . . *Pericles* iv 1 5
Inflammation. They are generally fools and cowards; which some of us should be too, but for inflammation . . 2 *Hen. IV.* iv 3 103
Inflict. I know no pain they can inflict upon him Will make him say I moved him to those arms . . . . . . 2 *Hen. VI.* iii 1 377
Infliction. So our decrees, Dead to infliction, to themselves are dead; And liberty plucks justice by the nose . . *Meas. for Meas.* i 3 28
Influence. A most auspicious star, whose influence If now I court not but omit, my fortunes Will ever after droop . . *Tempest* i 2 182
I leave to be, If I be not by her fair influence Foster'd *T. G. of Ver.* iii 1 183
A breath thou art, Servile to all the skyey influences *Meas. for Meas.* iii 1 9
A gibing spirit, Whose influence is begot of that loose grace *L. L. Lost* v 2 869
Eat, speak, and move under the influence of the most received star *All's Well* ii 1 56
Swear his thought over By each particular star in heaven and By all their influences . . . . *W. Tale* i 2 426
What! to you, Whose star-like nobleness gave life and influence To their whole being! . . . . . . *T. of Athens* v 1 66
And the moist star Upon whose influence Neptune's empire stands *Hamlet* i 1 119
By an enforced obedience of planetary influence . . *Lear* i 2 136
Whose influence, like the wreath of radiant fire On flickering Phœbus' front . . . . ii 2 113
Infold. Gilded tombs do worms infold . . *Mer. of Venice* ii 7 69
Unless the breath of heart-sick groans, Mist-like, infold me from the search of eyes . . . . . . *Rom. and Jul.* iii 3 73
Let me infold thee And hold thee to my heart . . *Macbeth* i 4 31
Inforced. We are inforced to farm our royal realm . . *Richard II.* i 4 45
Inform. 'Tis time I should inform thee farther . . . *Tempest* i 2 23
He would be drunk too; that let me inform you *Meas. for Meas.* iii 2 136
Haply thou mayst inform Something to save thy life . *All's Well* iv 1 91
A' will betray us all unto ourselves: Inform on that . . . iv 1 103
Let him approach, A stranger, no offender; and inform him So 'tis our will he should.—I shall . . . . v 3 26
Inform yourselves We need no more of your advice . *W. Tale* ii 1 167
What they will inform, Merely in hate, 'gainst any of us all, That will the king severely prosecute . . . . . . *Richard II.* ii 1 242
Our council we Will hold at Windsor; so inform the lords . 1 *Hen. IV.* i 1 104
I must inform you of a dismal fight . . . 1 *Hen. VI.* i 1 105
He did inform the truth . . . . *Coriolanus* i 6 42
Come, we'll inform them Of our proceedings here . . . ii 2 162
Have you inform'd them sithence?—How! I inform them! . . iii 1 47
I shall inform them.—And when such time they have begun to cry, Let them not cease . . . . iii 3 18
The god of soldiers, With the consent of supreme Jove, inform Thy thoughts with nobleness! . . . . v 3 71
It is the bloody business which informs Thus to mine eyes . *Macbeth* ii 1 48
Who is 't that can inform me?—That can I . . . *Hamlet* i 1 79
How all occasions do inform against me, And spur my dull revenge! . iv 4 32
Inform her full of my particular fear . . . . *Lear* i 4 360
Iago can inform you,—While I spare speech . . . *Othello* ii 3 198
To-morrow, Cæsar, I shall be furnish'd to inform you rightly *A. and C.* i 4 77
Her tongue will not obey her heart, nor can Her heart inform her tongue iii 2 48
With what patience Your wisdom may inform you . . *Cymbeline* i 1 79
I will inform your father . . . . ii 3 157
Inform us of thy fortunes, for it seems They crave to be demanded . iv 2 361
Informal. These poor informal women are no more But instruments of some more mightier member That sets them on . *Meas. for Meas.* v 1 236
Information. This is one Lucio's information against me . . iii 2 210
My mind gave me, In seeking tales and informations Against this man Ye blew the fire that burns ye . . . . . *Hen. VIII.* v 3 110
Lest you shall chance to whip your information And beat the messenger *Coriolanus* iv 6 53
Informed. I am informed throughly of the cause . *Mer. of Venice* iv 1 173
Many likelihoods informed me of this before . . *All's Well* i 3 128
I duly am inform'd His grace is at Marseilles . . . iv 4 8
And inform'd her fully I could not answer in that course of honour . v 3 97
If you know aught which does behove my knowledge Thereof to be inform'd, imprison't not In ignorant concealment . . *W. Tale* i 2 396
The prince's espials have informed me . . 1 *Hen. VI.* i 4 8
And for the proffer of my lord your master, I have inform'd his highness v 1 42
We come to be informed by yourselves What the conditions of that league . . . . v 4 118
I am inform'd that he comes towards London . . 3 *Hen. VI.* iv 4 26
In filling The whole realm, by your teaching and your chaplains, For so we are inform'd, with new opinions . . . *Hen. VIII.* v 3 17
Have you inform'd them sithence?—How! I inform them! *Coriolanus* iii 1 47
Thou'rt mad to say it: Is not thy master with him? who, were't so, Would have inform'd for preparation . . . . *Macbeth* i 5 34
Informed. I have this present evening from my sister Been well inform'd of them . . . . *Lear* ii 1 104
Who hath most fortunately been inform'd Of my obscured course . ii 2 174
I have inform'd them so.—Inform'd them! Dost thou understand me, man? . . . . ii 4 99
Are they inform'd of this? My breath and blood! Fiery? the fiery duke? . . . . ii 4 104
When I inform'd him, then he call'd me sot . . . . iv 2 8
Knows he the wickedness?—Ay, my good lord; 'twas he inform'd against him . . . . iv 2 93
'Tis reported, so.—Let Rome be thus Inform'd . . *Ant. and Cleo.* iii 6 20
Infortunate in nothing but in thee . . . . . *K. John* ii 1 178
Continue still in this so good a mind, And Henry, though he be infortunate, Assure yourselves, will never be unkind . 2 *Hen. VI.* iv 9 18
Infringe. Those many had not dared to do that evil, If the first that did the edict infringe Had answer'd for his deed . . *Meas. for Meas.* ii 2 92
Plead no more; I am not partial to infringe our laws . *Com. of Errors* i 1 4
And Jove, for your love, would infringe an oath . . *L. L. Lost* iv 3 144
God in heaven forbid We should infringe the holy privilege Of blessed sanctuary! not for all this land . . . . . *Richard III.* iii 1 41
Shall I be tempted to infringe my vow In the same time 'tis made? *Coriolanus* v 3 20
Infringed. What will Biron say when that he shall hear Faith so infringed? . . . . *L. L. Lost* iv 3 146
'Tis not my fault, Nor wittingly have I infringed my vow . 3 *Hen. VI.* ii 2 8
Infuse. To hold opinion with Pythagoras, That souls of animals infuse themselves Into the trunks of men . . . *Mer. of Venice* iv 1 132
Infuse his breast with magnanimity . . . . 3 *Hen. VI.* v 4 41
These words, these looks, infuse new life in me . . . *T. Andron.* i 1 461
Infused. Thou didst smile, Infused with a fortitude from heaven *Tempest* i 2 154
A wolf, who, hang'd for human slaughter, Even from the gallows did his fell soul fleet, And . . . Infused itself in thee . . *Mer. of Venice* iv 1 137
O, that a mighty man of such descent, Of such possessions, and so high esteem, Should be infused with so foul a spirit! *T. of Shrew* Ind. 2 17
With those clear rays which she infused on me That beauty am I bless'd with which you see . . . . 1 *Hen. VI.* i 2 85
Heaven hath infused them with these spirits, To make them instruments of fear and warning . . . . *J. Cæsar* i 3 69
Infusing him with self and vain conceit . . . *Richard II.* iii 2 166
Infusion. With aqua-vitæ or some other hot infusion . *W. Tale* iv 4 816
His infusion of such dearth and rareness . . . . *Hamlet* v 2 122
The blest infusions That dwell in vegetives, in metals, stones *Pericles* iii 2 35
Ingener. One that excels the quirks of blazoning pens, And in the essential vesture of creation Does tire the ingener . . . *Othello* ii 1 65
Ingenious. I will praise an eel with the same praise.—What, that an eel is ingenious? . . . . *L. L. Lost* i 2 29
As swift as lead, sir.—The meaning, pretty ingenious? . . . iii 1 59
Institute A course of learning and ingenious studies . *T. of Shrew* i 1 9
He looks like a poor, decayed, ingenious, foolish, rascally knave *All's Well* v 2 25
'Tis a parlous boy; Bold, quick, ingenious, forward, capable *Richard III.* iii 1 155
Whose wicked deed thy most ingenious sense Deprived thee of *Hamlet* v 1 271
I stand up, and have ingenious feeling Of my huge sorrows . *Lear* iv 6 287
My ingenious instrument! Hark, Polydore, it sounds! . *Cymbeline* iv 2 186
Send out For torturers ingenious . . . . v 5 215
Ingeniously I speak, No blame belongs to thee . . . *T. of Athens* ii 2 230
Ingenuous. If their sons be ingenuous, they shall want no instruction; if their daughters be capable . . . . . . *L. L. Lost* iv 2 80
Inglorious. O inglorious league! . . . . . . *K. John* v 1 65
Ingot. Like an ass whose back with ingots bows . *Meas for Meas.* iii 1 26
Ingraft. With one of an ingraft infirmity . . . . *Othello* ii 3 145
Ingrafted. In the ingrafted love he bears to Cæsar . . *J. Cæsar* ii 1 184
Ingrate. Will not so graceless be to be ingrate . . *T. of Shrew* i 2 270
You uncivil lady, To whose ingrate and unauspicious altars My soul the faithfull'st offerings hath breathed out! . . . . *T. Night* v 1 116
You ingrate revolts, You bloody Neroes . . . . *K. John* v 2 151
This ingrate and canker'd Bolingbroke . . . . 1 *Hen. IV.* i 3 137
That we have been familiar, Ingrate forgetfulness shall poison *Coriolanus* v 2 92
Ingrateful. That most ingrateful boy there by your side . *T. Night* v 1 80
A fool, inconstant And damnable ingrateful . . . *W. Tale* iii 2 188
And you are so strait And so ingrateful, you deny me that . *K. John* v 7 43
Thou cruel, Ingrateful, savage and inhuman creature! . . *Hen. V.* ii 2 95
For their tongues to be silent, and not confess so much, were a kind of ingrateful injury . . . . *Coriolanus* ii 2 35
For the multitude to be ingrateful, were to make a monster of the multitude . . . . ii 3 11
Whose high exploits and honourable deeds Ingrateful Rome requites with foul contempt . . . . *T. Andron.* v 1 12
Alas, kind lord! He's flung in rage from this ingrateful seat Of monstrous friends . . . . *T. of Athens* iv 2 45
Let it no more bring out ingrateful man! Go great with tigers! . . iv 3 188
All the stored vengeances of heaven fall On her ingrateful top! . *Lear* ii 4 165
Crack nature's moulds, all germens spill at once, That make ingrateful man! . . . . iii 2 9
Ingrateful fox! 'tis he.—Bind fast his corky arms . . . . iii 7 28
Ingratitude. As in revenge of thy ingratitude, I throw thy name against the bruising stones . . . . *T. G. of Ver.* i 2 110
My honour would not let ingratitude So much besmear it *Mer. of Venice* v 1 218
Thou winter wind, Thou art not so unkind As man's ingratitude *As Y. Like It* ii 7 176
I hate ingratitude more in a man Than lying, vainness, babbling *T. Night* iii 4 388
I think had been in me Both disobedience and ingratitude . *W. Tale* iii 2 69
A great-sized monster of ingratitudes . . . . *Troi. and Cres.* iii 3 147
Should they not, Well might they fester gainst ingratitude *Coriolanus* i 9 30
Ingratitude is monstrous . . . . ii 3 10
Ingratitude, Which Rome reputes to be a heinous sin . . *T. Andron.* i 1 447
And with revengeful war Take wreak on Rome for this ingratitude . iv 3 33
These old fellows Have their ingratitude in them hereditary *T. of Athens* ii 2 224
I know my lord hath spent of Timon's wealth, And now ingratitude makes it worse than stealth . . . . iii 4 27
Cannot cover The monstrous bulk of this ingratitude With any size of words . . . . v 1 68
To wipe out our ingratitude with loves Above their quantity . . . v 4 17
Fall upon your knees, Pray to the gods to intermit the plague That needs must light on this ingratitude . . . . *J. Cæsar* i 1 60
Ingratitude, more strong than traitors' arms, Quite vanquish'd him . iii 2 189
The sin of my ingratitude even now Was heavy on me . . *Macbeth* i 4 15
Ingratitude, thou marble-hearted fiend! . . . . . *Lear* i 4 281
To take't again perforce! Monster ingratitude! . . . . i 5 44
Filial ingratitude! Is it not as this mouth should tear this hand For lifting food to't? . . . . iii 4 14

Ingratitude. With which I meant To scourge the ingratitude that despiteful Rome Cast on my noble father *Ant. and Cleo.* ii 6 22
The ingratitude of this Seleucus does Even make me wild v 2 153
Ingredient. If one present The abhorr'd ingredient to his eye *W. Tale* ii 1 43
This even-handed justice Commends the ingredients of our poison'd chalice To our own lips *Macbeth* i 7 11
Add thereto a tiger's chaudron, For the ingredients of our cauldron iv 1 34
Every inordinate cup is unblessed and the ingredient is a devil *Othello* ii 3 311
Ingrossed. Your ships are not well mann'd; Your mariners are muleters, reapers, people Ingross'd by swift impress *Ant. and Cleo.* iii 7 37
Inhabit. On this island Where man doth not inhabit *Tempest* iii 3 57
All torment, trouble, wonder and amazement Inhabits here v 1 105
So eating love Inhabits in the finest wits of all *T. G. of Ver.* i 1 44
Love doth to her eyes repair, To help him of his blindness, And, being help'd, inhabits there iv 2 48
Thou that dost inhabit in my breast, Leave not the mansion so long tenantless v 4 7
There's none but witches do inhabit here *Com. of Errors* iii 2 161
And Lapland sorcerers inhabit here iv 3 11
Or any taint of vice whose strong corruption Inhabits our frail blood *T. Night* iii 4 391
What is the opinion of Pythagoras concerning wild fowl?—That the soul of our grandam might haply inhabit a bird iv 2 57
Where is that blood That I have seen inhabit in those cheeks? *K. John* iv 2 107
Disorder, horror, fear and mutiny Shall here inhabit *Richard II.* iv 1 143
In those holes Where eyes did once inhabit *Richard III.* i 4 30
If trembling I inhabit then, protest me The baby of a girl *Macbeth* iii 4 105
Inhabitable. Were I tied to run afoot Even to the frozen ridges of the Alps, Or any other ground inhabitable *Richard II.* i 1 65
Inhabitant. O, thou wilt be a wilderness again, Peopled with wolves, thy old inhabitants! *2 Hen. IV.* iv 5 138
That look not like the inhabitants o' the earth, And yet are on't *Macbeth* i 3 41
Inhearsed in the arms Of the most bloody nurser of his harms! *1 Hen. VI.* iv 7 45
Inherent. By my body's action teach my mind A most inherent baseness *Coriolanus* iii 2 123
Inherit.* All our company else being drowned, we will inherit here *Temp.* ii 2 179
The great globe itself, Yea, all which it inherit, shall dissolve iv 1 154
This, or else nothing, will inherit her *T. G. of Ver.* iii 2 87
Here's the twin-brother of thy letter: but let thine inherit first *M. Wives* ii 1 74
But that most vain, Which with pain purchased doth inherit pain *L. L. Lost* i 1 73
Nothing but fair is that which you inherit iv 1 20
Her dispositions she inherits, which makes fair gifts fairer *All's Well* i 1 47
Thy father's moral parts Mayst thou inherit too! i 2 22
Let higher Italy,—Those bated that inherit but the fall Of the last monarchy,—see that you come Not to woo honour, but to wed it ii 1 13
What doth our cousin lay to Mowbray's charge? It must be great that can inherit us So much as of a thought of ill in him *Richard II.* i 1 85
Gaunt as a grave, Whose hollow womb inherits nought but bones ii 1 83
God knows, whether those that bawl out the ruins of thy linen shall inherit his kingdom *2 Hen. IV.* ii 2 27
The cold blood he did naturally inherit of his father iv 3 128
He that had wit would think that I had none, To bury so much gold under a tree, And never after to inherit it *T. Andron.* ii 3 3
Even such delight Among fresh female buds shall you this night Inherit at my house *Rom. and Jul.* i 2 30
But to the girdle do the gods inherit, Beneath is all the fiends' *Lear* iv 6 128
Tell me how Wales was made so happy as To inherit such a haven *Cymb.* iii 2 63
Inheritance. For a quart d'écu he will sell the fee-simple of his salvation, the inheritance of it *All's Well* iv 3 312
Why, being younger born, Doth he lay claim to thine inheritance? *K. John* i 1 72
I'll go with thee, And find the inheritance of this poor child iv 2 97
Personally I lay my claim To my inheritance of free descent *Richard II.* ii 3 136
In the book of Numbers is it writ, When the man dies, let the inheritance Descend unto the daughter *Hen. V.* i 2 99
Deprived of honour and inheritance *1 Hen. VI.* ii 5 27
Not that alone But all the whole inheritance I give iii 1 164
To conquer France, his true inheritance *2 Hen. VI.* i 1 82
This small inheritance my father left me Contenteth me iv 10 20
He made thee Duke of York.—'Twas my inheritance, as the earldom was *3 Hen. VI.* i 1 78
Than spend a fawn upon 'em, For the inheritance of their loves *Coriol.* iii 2 68
To the inheritance of Fortinbras, Had he been vanquisher *Hamlet* i 1 92
Inherited. Treason is not inherited, my lord *As Y. Like It* i 3 63
I have lived To see inherited my very wishes *Coriolanus* ii 1 215
Crimes, like lands, Are not inherited *T. of Athens* v 4 38
Inheritor. Sole inheritor Of all perfections that a man may owe *L. L. Lost* ii 1 5
As with an enemy That had before my face murder'd my father, The quarrel of a true inheritor *2 Hen. IV.* iv 5 169
Think how I may do thee good, And be inheritor of thy desire *Rich. III.* iv 3 34
Out of whorish loins Are pleased to breed out your inheritors *Tr. and Cr.* iv 1 64
The very conveyances of his lands will hardly lie in this box; and must the inheritor himself have no more? *Hamlet* v 1 121
One sorrow never comes but brings an heir, That may succeed as his inheritor; And so in ours *Pericles* i 4 64
Inheritrix. No female Should be inheritrix in Salique land *Hen. V.* i 2 51
Inhibited. Self-love, which is the most inhibited sin in the canon *All's W.* i 1 157
A practiser Of arts inhibited and out of warrant *Othello* i 2 79
Inhibition. I think their inhibition comes by the means of the late innovation *Hamlet* ii 2 346
Inhooped. His quails ever Beat mine, inhoop'd, at odds *Ant. and Cleo.* ii 3 38
Inhospitable. For Tarsus, there to strike The inhospitable Cleon *Pericles* v 1 254
Inhuman. An inhuman wretch Uncapable of pity *Mer. of Venice* iv 1 4
If it should prove That thou art so inhuman,—'twill not prove so *All's W.* v 3 116
Thou cruel, Ingrateful, savage and inhuman creature! *Hen. V.* ii 2 95
But you are more inhuman, more inexorable, O, ten times more, than tigers of Hyrcania *3 Hen. VI.* i 4 154
Thy deed, inhuman and unnatural, Provokes this deluge *Richard III.* i 2 60
Her spotless chastity, Inhuman traitors, you constrain'd *T. Andron.* v 2 178
Away, inhuman dog! unhallow'd slave! v 3 14
O murderous slave! O villain!—O damn'd Iago! O inhuman dog! *Othello* v 1 62
Iniquities. And die in many irreconciled iniquities *Hen. V.* iv 1 160
Iniquity. Which is the wiser here? Justice or Iniquity? *Meas. for Meas.* ii 1 181
The prince himself is about a piece of iniquity *W. Tale* iv 4 694
That grey iniquity, that father ruffian, that vanity in years *1 Hen. IV.* ii 4 500
Sin struck down like an ox, and iniquity's throat cut like a calf *2 Hen. VI.* iv 2 29
Like the formal vice, Iniquity, I moralize two meanings in one word *Richard III.* iii 1 82
I lack iniquity Sometimes to do me service *Othello* i 2 3
If you are so fond over her iniquity, give her patent to offend iv 1 208
Iniquity. How now. wholesome iniquity have you that a man may deal withal, and defy the surgeon? *Pericles* iv 6 28
She that sets seeds and roots of shame and iniquity iv 6 93
Initiate. My strange and self-abuse Is the initiate fear that wants hard use *Macbeth* iii 4 143
Injointed. Have there injointed them with an after fleet *Othello* i 3 35
Injunction. I must remove Some thousands of these logs and pile them up, Upon a sore injunction *Tempest* iii 1 11
And that, by great injunctions, I am bound To enter publicly *M. for M.* iv 3 100
To these injunctions every one doth swear That comes to hazard *M. of V.* ii 9 17
With a kind of injunction drives me to these habits of her liking *T. N.* ii 5 183
Though their injunction be to bar my doors, And let this tyrannous night take hold upon you *Lear* iii 4 155
Injure. I fly thee, for I would not injure thee *As Y. Like It* iii 5 9
Injured. Whom have I injured, that ye seek my death? *2 Hen. VI.* iv 7 107
How hast thou injured both thyself and us! *3 Hen. VI.* i 1 179
When have I injured thee? when done thee wrong? Or thee? or thee? *Richard III.* i 3 56
I never injured thee, But love thee better than thou canst devise *Rom. and Jul.* iii 1 71
Injurer. Thou monstrous injurer of heaven and earth! *K. John* ii 1 174
Injurious wasps, to feed on such sweet honey And kill the bees that yield it! *T. G. of Ver.* i 2 106
O injurious love, That respites me a life, whose very comfort Is still a dying horror!—'Tis pity of him *Meas. for Meas.* ii 3 40
Wretched Isabel! Injurious world! most damned Angelo! iv 3 127
Injurious Hermia! most ungrateful maid! Have you conspired? *M. N. Dream* iii 2 195
Like a false traitor and injurious villain *Richard II.* i 1 91
Injurious duke, that threatest where's no cause *2 Hen. VI.* i 4 51
Injurious Margaret!—And why not queen? *3 Hen. VI.* iii 3 78
Call him my king by whose injurious doom My elder brother, the Lord Aubrey Vere, Was done to death? iii 3 101
Injurious time now with a robber's haste Crams his rich thievery up *Troi. and Cres.* iv 4 44
Injurious tribune! Within thine eyes sat twenty thousand deaths *Cor.* iii 3 69
It were for me To throw my sceptre at the injurious gods *Ant. and Cleo.* iv 15 76
Till the injurious Romans did extort This tribute from us *Cymbeline* iii 1 48
Thou injurious thief, Hear but my name, and tremble iv 2 86
Injury. Do with your injuries as seem you best *Meas. for Meas.* v 1 256
Come, sister: I am press'd down with conceit—Conceit, my comfort and my injury *Com. of Errors* iv 2 66
Abused and dishonour'd me Even in the strength and height of injury! v 1 200
Out of all eyes, tongues, minds and injuries *Much Ado* iv 1 245
I woo'd thee with my sword, And won thy love, doing thee injuries *M. N. Dream* i 1 17
Well, go thy way: thou shalt not from this grove Till I torment thee for this injury ii 1 147
If you were civil and knew courtesy, You would not do me thus much injury iii 2 148
Though I alone do feel the injury iii 2 219
I shall do . . . the world no injury, for in it I have nothing *As Y. Like It* i 2 203
Such an injury would vex a very saint, Much more a shrew *T. of Shrew* iii 2 28
His indignation derives itself out of a very competent injury *T. Night* iii 4 270
I leave my duty a little unthought of and speak out of my injury v 1 319
If that the injuries be justly weigh'd That have on both sides pass'd v 1 375
For sealing The injury of tongues in courts and kingdoms *W. Tale* i 2 338
Her sin his injury, Her injury the beadle to her sin *K. John* ii 1 188
Have stoop'd my neck under your injuries *Richard II.* iii 1 19
If thy pocket were enriched with any other injuries but these *1 Hen. IV.* iii 3 182
The injuries of a wanton time v 1 50
O God! they did me too much injury That ever said I hearken'd for your death v 4 51
Whose bosom burns With an incensed fire of injuries *2 Hen. IV.* i 3 14
It is the time, And not the king, that doth you injuries iv 1 106
The service that I truly did his life Hath left me open to all injuries v 2 8
We thought not good to bruise an injury till it were full ripe *Hen. V.* iii 6 129
Hot as gunpowder, And quickly will return an injury iv 7 189
Those wrongs, those bitter injuries, Which Somerset hath offer'd *1 Hen. VI.* ii 5 124
But what said Warwick to these injuries?—He, more incensed *3 Hen. VI.* iv 1 107
You do me shameful injury, Falsely to draw me in these vile suspects *Richard III.* i 3 88
You do him injury to scorn his corse ii 1 80
Where injury of chance Puts back leave-taking *Troi. and Cres.* iv 4 35
To be silent, and not confess so much, were a kind of ingrateful injury *Coriolanus* ii 2 35
And his injury The gaoler to his pity v 1 64
He Hath widow'd and unchilded many a one, Which to this hour bewail the injury v 6 154
Boy, this shall not excuse the injuries That thou hast done me *R. and J.* iii 1 69
Ne'er prefer his injuries to his heart, To bring it into danger *T. of A.* iii 5 34
O, sir, to wilful men, The injuries that they themselves procure Must be their schoolmasters *Lear* ii 4 306
None but the fool; who labours to out-jest His heart-struck injuries iii 1 17
These injuries the king now bears will be revenged home iii 3 12
What cannot be preserved when fortune takes Patience her injury a mockery makes *Othello* i 3 207
Since I could distinguish betwixt a benefit and an injury i 3 314
Saints in your injuries, devils being offended ii 1 112
I do suspect this trash To be a party in this injury v 1 86
The record of what injuries you did us, Though written in our flesh, we shall remember As things but done by chance *Ant. and Cleo.* v 2 118
I never do him wrong, But he does buy my injuries, to be friends *Cymb.* i 1 105
More particulars Must justify my knowledge.—So they must, Or do your honour injury ii 4 80
Some villain . . . Hath done you both this cursed injury iii 4 125
No longer exercise Upon a valiant race thy harsh And potent injuries v 4 84
Thou said'st Thou hadst been toss'd from wrong to injury *Pericles* v 1 131
Injustice. If any crave redress of injustice *Meas. for Meas.* iv 4 11
Then to glance from him To the duke himself, to tax him with injustice? v 1 312
The heavens themselves Do strike at my injustice *W. Tale* iii 2 148
We cannot deal but with the very hand Of stern injustice *K. John* v 2 23
My comfort is that heaven will take our souls And plague injustice with the pains of hell *Richard II.* iii 1 34
Whose conscience with injustice is corrupted *2 Hen. VI.* iii 2 235
All that have miscarried By underhand corrupted foul injustice *Richard III.* v 1 6
I have no spleen against you; nor injustice For you or any *Hen. VIII.* ii 4 89
Blazoning our injustice every where *T. Andron.* iv 4 18

Ink. Why, man, how black?—Why, as black as ink . *T. G. of Ver.* iii 1 288
Write till your ink be dry, and with your tears Moist it again . iii 2 75
If the skin were parchment and the blows you gave were ink *C. of Er.* iii 1 13
Why, she, O, she is fallen Into a pit of ink! . *Much Ado* iv 1 142
That draweth from my snow-white pen the ebon-coloured ink *L. L. Lost* i 1 246
He hath not eat paper, as it were; he hath not drunk ink . iv 2 27
Never durst poet touch a pen to write Until his ink were temper'd with
Love's sighs; O, then his lines would ravish savage ears . iv 3 347
Beauteous as ink; a good conclusion.—Fair as a text B in a copy-book v 2 41
Taunt him with the license of ink . *T. Night* iii 2 48
Let there be gall enough in thy ink, though thou write with a goose-pen iii 2 53
The old hermit of Prague, that never saw pen and ink, very wittily said iv 2 15
Help me to a candle, and pen, ink and paper . iv 2 88
Good fool, some ink, paper and light . iv 2 118
Turning your books to graves, your ink to blood . 2 *Hen. IV.* iv 1 51
I dare not speak: I'll call for pen and ink, and write my mind 1 *Hen. VI.* v 3 66
Give me some ink and paper in my tent . *Richard III.* v 3 23
I will not sup to-night. Give me some ink and paper . v 3 49
Is ink and paper ready?—It is, my lord . v 3 75
Her hand, In whose comparison all whites are ink . *Troi. and Cres.* i 1 56
Meanwhile here's money for thy charges. Give me pen and ink *T. Andron.* iv 3 106
Get me ink and paper, And hire post-horses . *Rom. and Jul.* v 1 25
Ink and paper, Charmian. Welcome, my good Alexas . *Ant. and Cleo.* i 5 65
Get me ink and paper: He shall have every day a several greeting . i 5 76
I'll drink the words you send, Though ink be made of gall . *Cymbeline* i 1 101
O damn'd paper! Black as the ink that's on thee! . iii 2 20
Bid Nestor bring me spices, ink and paper, My casket and my jewels
Pericles iii 1 66

Inkhorn. Bid him bring his pen and inkhorn . *Much Ado* iii 5 63
To be disgraced by an inkhorn mate . 1 *Hen. VI.* iii 1 99
Hang him with his pen and ink-horn about his neck . 2 *Hen. VI.* iv 2 117

Inkle. What's the price of this inkle?—'One penny' . *L. L. Lost* iii 1 140
Inkles, caddisses, cambrics, lawns . *W. Tale* iv 4 208
Her inkle, silk, twin with the rubied cherry *Pericles* v Gower 8

Inkling. I can give you inkling Of an ensuing evil . *Hen. VIII.* ii 1 140
They have had inkling this fortnight what we intend to do . *Coriolanus* i 1 59

Inky. 'Tis not your inky brows, your black silk hair . *As Y. Like It* iii 5 46
Bound in with shame, With inky blots and rotten parchment bonds
Richard II. ii 1 64
'Tis not alone my inky cloak, good mother . *Hamlet* i 2 77

Inlaid. Look how the floor of heaven Is thick inlaid with patines of
bright gold . *Mer. of Venice* v 1 59

Inland. Empties itself, as doth an inland brook Into the main . v 1 96
Yet am I inland bred And know some nurture . *As Y. Like It* ii 7 96
Who was in his youth an inland man . iii 2 363
And then the vital commoners and inland petty spirits muster me all to
their captain, the heart . 2 *Hen. IV.* iv 3 119
A wall sufficient to defend Our inland from the pilfering borderers *Hen. V.* i 2 142

Inlay. They are worthy To inlay heaven with stars . *Cymbeline* v 5 352

Inly. I have inly wept, Or should have spoke ere this . *Tempest* v 1 200
Didst thou but know the inly touch of love . *T. G. of Ver.* ii 7 18
Sit patiently and inly ruminate . *Hen. V.* iv Prol. 24
Weep with him, To see how inly sorrow gripes his soul . 3 *Hen. VI.* i 4 171

Inmost. 'Tis you must dig with mattock and with spade, And pierce the
inmost centre of the earth . *T. Andron.* iv 3 12
You shall not budge; You go not till I set you up a glass Where you
may see the inmost part of you . *Hamlet* iii 4 20

Inn. In the self-same inn A meaner woman was delivered *Com. of Errors* i 1 54
I'll view the manners of the town, Peruse the traders, gaze upon the
buildings, And then return and sleep within mine inn . i 2 14
Walk with me about the town, And then go to my inn and dine with me i 2 23
Thou most beauteous inn, Why should hard-favour'd grief be lodged in
thee, When triumph is become an alehouse guest? . *Richard II.* v 1 13
Shall I not take mine ease in mine inn? . 1 *Hen. IV.* iii 3 93
A' must, then, to the inns o' court shortly. I was once of Clement's Inn
2 *Hen. IV.* iii 2 15
One Sampson Stockfish, a fruiterer, behind Gray's Inn . iii 2 36
I do remember him at Clement's Inn . iii 2 332
Now spurs the lated traveller apace To gain the timely inn *Macbeth* iii 3 7
This our court, infected with their manners, Shows like a riotous inn *Lear* i 4 265

Innkeeper. The red-nose innkeeper of Daventry . 1 *Hen. IV.* iv 2 51

Innocence. Prompt me, plain and holy innocence! . *Tempest* iii 1 82
O, take the sense, sweet, of my innocence! . *M. N. Dream* ii 2 45
O, is it all forgot? All school-days' friendship, childhood innocence? . iii 2 202
I urge this childhood proof, Because what follows is pure innocence
Mer. of Venice i 1 145
And dallies with the innocence of love, Like the old age . *T. Night* ii 4 48
By innocence I swear, and by my youth, I have one heart . iii 1 169
What we changed Was innocence for innocence . *W. Tale* i 2 69
The silence often of pure innocence Persuades when speaking fails . ii 2 41
Innocence shall make False accusation blush and tyranny Tremble . iii 2 31
Has not only his innocence, which seems much, to justify him . v 2 70
Quench his fiery indignation Even in the matter of mine innocence *K. John* iv 1 64
Whose white investments figure innocence . 2 *Hen. IV.* iv 1 45
We do perceive his guilt: And God in justice hath reveal'd to us The
truth and innocence of this poor fellow . 2 *Hen. VI.* ii 3 106
The trust I have is in mine innocence, And therefore am I bold . iv 4 59
It will help me nothing To plead mine innocence . *Hen. VIII.* ii 1 208
So much fairer And spotless shall mine innocence arise . iii 2 301
God and your majesty Protect mine innocence, or I fall into The trap! v 1 141
On mine honour dare I undertake For good Lord Titus' innocence
T. Andron i 1 437
How likest thou this picture, Apemantus?—The best, for the innocence
T. of Athens i 1 199
When all, for mine, if I may call offence, Must feel war's blow, who
spares not innocence
Pericles i 2 93

Innocency. Craft, being richer than innocency . *Meas. for Meas.* iii 2 10
Makes it seem Like rivers of remorse and innocency . *K. John* iv 3 110
Mine innocency and Saint George to thrive! . *Richard II.* i 3 84
Thou knowest in the state of innocency Adam fell . 1 *Hen. IV.* iii 3 186
With tears of innocency and terms of zeal . iv 3 63
If truth and upright innocency fail me, I'll to the king . 2 *Hen. IV.* v 2 39
God and our innocency defend and guard us! . *Richard III.* iii 5 20

Innocent. All men idle, all; And women too, but innocent and pure
Tempest ii 1 155
All foison, all abundance To feed my innocent people . ii 1 164
Exposed unto the sea, which hath requit it, Him and his innocent child iii 3 72
A thousand innocent shames In angel whiteness beat away those blushes
Much Ado iv 1 162
Thou hast so wrong'd mine innocent child and me . v 1 63

Innocent. I say thou hast belied mine innocent child . *Much Ado* v 1 67
You have among you killed a sweet and innocent lady . v 1 194
Art thou the slave that with thy breath hast kill'd Mine innocent child? v 1 274
Possess the people in Messina here How innocent she died . v 1 291
I can find out no rhyme to 'lady' but 'baby,' an innocent rhyme . v 2 38
Did I not tell you she was innocent? . v 4 1
They are as innocent as grace itself . *As Y. Like It* i 3 56
And the big round tears Coursed one another down his innocent nose . ii 1 39
A dumb innocent, that could not say him nay . *All's Well* iv 3 213
The queen receives Much comfort in't; says 'My poor prisoner, I am
as innocent as you' . *W. Tale* ii 2 29
A gracious innocent soul, More free than he is jealous . ii 3 29
I'll pawn the little blood which I have left To save the innocent . ii 3 167
The innocent milk in it most innocent mouth, Haled out to murder . iii 2 101
His innocent babe truly begotten . iii 2 135
And from Pope Innocent the legate here . *K. John* iii 1 139
This, in our foresaid holy father's name, Pope Innocent, I do demand . iii 1 146
If I talk to him, with his innocent prate He will awake my mercy . iv 1 25
This hand of mine Is yet a maiden and an innocent hand . iv 2 252
Is yet the cover of a fairer mind Than to be butcher of an innocent child iv 2 259
But yet I dare defend My innocent life against an emperor . iv 3 89
Like a traitor coward, Sluiced out his innocent soul . *Richard II.* i 1 103
The wild dog Shall flesh his tooth on every innocent . 2 *Hen. IV.* iv 5 133
Stain'd with the guiltless blood of innocents . 1 *Hen. VI.* v 4 44
As innocent From meaning treason to our royal person As is the suck-
ing lamb or harmless dove . 2 *Hen. VI.* iii 1 69
My conscience tells me you are innocent . iii 1 141
Come, basilisk, And kill the innocent gazer with thy sight . iii 2 53
That of the skin of an innocent lamb should be made parchment . iv 2 86
Ah, Clifford, murder not this innocent child, Lest thou be hated both
of God and man! . 3 *Hen. VI.* i 3 8
If murdering innocents be executing, Why, then thou art an executioner v 6 32
So just is God, to right the innocent . *Richard III.* i 3 182
Are you call'd forth from out a world of men To slay the innocent? . i 4 187
Incapable and shallow innocents, You cannot guess who caused your
father's death . ii 2 18
Insulting tyranny begins to jet Upon the innocent and aweless throne . ii 4 52
Girdling one another Within their innocent alabaster arms . iv 3 11
On England's lawful earth, Unlawfully made drunk with innocents'
blood! . iv 4 30
How innocent I was From any private malice in his end *Hen. VIII.* iii 2 267
Perchance she weeps because they kill'd her husband; Perchance be-
cause she knows them innocent . *T. Andron.* iii 1 115
A deed of death done on the innocent Becomes not Titus' brother . iii 2 56
Accuse some innocent and forswear myself . v 1 130
Look like the innocent flower, But be the serpent under't . *Macbeth* i 5 66
Innocent sleep, Sleep that knits up the ravell'd sleave of care, The death
of each day's life . ii 2 36
Which you thought had been Our innocent self . iii 1 79
Be innocent of the knowledge, dearest chuck, Till thou applaud the deed iii 2 45
To offer up a weak poor innocent lamb To appease an angry god . iv 3 16
Takes off the rose From the fair forehead of an innocent love *Hamlet* iii 4 43
Pray, innocent, and beware the foul fiend . *Lear* iii 6 8
Thou hast kill'd the sweetest innocent That e'er did lift up eye *Othello* v 2 199
Some innocents 'scape not the thunderbolt . *Ant. and Cleo.* ii 5 77
Take it, and hit The innocent mansion of my love, my heart *Cymbeline* iii 4 70
Who can cross it? Unless you play the pious innocent . *Pericles* iv 3 17

Innovation. Poor discontents, Which gape and rub the elbow at the news
Of hurlyburly innovation . 1 *Hen. IV.* v 1 78
I think their inhibition comes by the means of the late innovation *Ham.* ii 2 347
That was craftily qualified too, and, behold, what innovation it makes
Othello ii 3 42

Innovator. A traitorous innovator, A foe to the public weal *Coriolanus* iii 1 175

Inns of court. A' must, then, to the inns o' court shortly 2 *Hen. IV.* iii 2 14
You had not four such swinge-bucklers in all the inns o' court again . iii 2 25
Others to the inns of court; down with them all 2 *Hen. VI.* iv 7 2

Innumerable substance—By what means got, I leave to your own conscience . *Hen. VIII.* iii 2 326

Inoculate. For virtue cannot so inoculate our old stock but we shall
relish of it . *Hamlet* iii 1 119

Inordinate. Such inordinate and low desires . 1 *Hen. IV.* iii 2 12
Every inordinate cup is unblessed and the ingredient is a devil *Othello* ii 3 311

Inquire. Go on before; I shall inquire you forth . *T. G. of Ver.* ii 4 186
Would you buy her, that you inquire after her? . *Much Ado* i 1 181
Go, presently inquire, and so will I, Where money is . *Mer. of Venice* i 1 183
Inquire the Jew's house out, give him this deed . iv 2 1
If you will pass To where you are bound, you must inquire your way
Coriolanus iii 1 54
By whose direction found'st thou out this place?—By love, who first
did prompt me to inquire . *Rom. and Jul.* ii 2 80
As I told you, my young lady bade me inquire you out . ii 4 173
Before you visit him, to make inquire Of his behaviour . *Hamlet* ii 1 4
Can you inquire him out, and be edified by report? . *Othello* iii 4 14
My brother never Did urge me in his act: I did inquire it *Ant. and Cleo.* ii 2 46

Inquired. You have not been inquired after . *Meas. for Meas.* iv 1 19

Inquiry. Or jump the after inquiry on your own peril . *Cymbeline* v 4 189

Inquisition. You have often Begun to tell me what I am, but stopp'd
And left me to a bootless inquisition . *Tempest* i 2 35
Do this suddenly, And let not search and inquisition quail To bring
again these foolish runaways . *As Y. Like It* ii 2 20

Inquisitive. My youngest boy, and yet my eldest care, At eighteen years
became inquisitive After his brother . *Com. of Errors* i 1 126
Unseen, inquisitive, confounds himself . i 2 38

Inroad. Many hot inroads They make in Italy . *Ant. and Cleo.* i 4 50

Insane. Were such things here as we do speak about? Or have we eaten
on the insane root That takes the reason prisoner? . *Macbeth* i 3 84

Insanie. It insinuateth me of insanie: anne intelligis, domine? *L. L. Lost* v 1 28

Insatiate. Light vanity, insatiate cormorant . *Richard II.* ii 1 38
The insatiate greediness of his desires . *Richard III.* iii 7 7
O most insatiate and luxurious woman! . *T. Andron.* v 1 88

Insconce. I must get a sconce for my head and insconce it too *C. of Er.* ii 2 38

Inscribed. 'Ego et Rex meus' Was still inscribed . *Hen. VIII.* iii 2 315

Inscription. The first, of gold, who this inscription bears *Mer. of Venice* ii 7 4
Let me see; I will survey the inscriptions back again . ii 7 14

Inscrolled. Your answer had not been inscroll'd . ii 7 72

Inscrutable. O jest unseen, inscrutable, invisible! . *T. G. of Ver.* ii 1 141

Insculped. A coin that bears the figure of an angel Stamped in gold, but
that's insculp'd upon . *Mer. of Venice* ii 7 57

Insculpture. And on his grave-stone this insculpture . *T. of Athens* v 4 67

Insensible of mortality, and desperately mortal . *Meas. for Meas.* iv 2 152

Insensible. 'Tis [honour] insensible, then. Yea, to the dead . 1 *Hen. IV.* v 1 140
Peace is a very apoplexy, lethargy; mulled, deaf, sleepy, insensible *Coriolanus* iv 5 239
Inseparable. Still we went coupled and inseparable . *As Y. Like It* i 3 78
Like true, inseparable, faithful loves, Sticking together in calamity *K. John* iii 4 66
Inseparate. Of this strange nature that a thing inseparate Divides more wider than the sky and earth . . . . . *Troi. and Cres.* v 2 148
Insert. To insert again my haud credo for a deer . *L. L. Lost* iv 2 19
You could, for a need, study a speech of some dozen or sixteen lines, which I would set down and insert in't, could you not? *Hamlet* ii 2 568
Inserted. Was this inserted to make interest good? . *Mer. of Venice* i 3 95
Inset. I will inset you neither in gold nor silver, but in vile apparel 2 *Hen. IV.* i 2 19
Inshelled. Thrusts forth his horns again into the world; Which were inshell'd *Coriolanus* iv 6 45
Inshipp'd Commit them to the fortune of the sea . . 1 *Hen. VI.* v 1 49
Inside. Kissing with inside lip . . . . . *W. Tale* i 2 286
Show the inside of your purse to the outside of his hand . . iv 4 833
You look but on the outside of this work.—Outside or inside *K. John* v 2 110
An I have not forgotten what the inside of a church is made of 1 *Hen. IV.* iii 3 8
Look'd he o' the inside of the paper? . . . *Hen. VIII.* iii 2 78
Insinewed. All members of our cause, both here and hence, That are insinew'd to this action 2 *Hen. IV.* iv 1 172
Insinuate. That am neither a good epilogue nor cannot insinuate with you in the behalf of a good play . . *As Y. Like It* Epil. 9
Thinkest thou, for that I insinuate, or toaze from thee thy business, I am therefore no courtier? . . . . . *W. Tale* iv 4 760
I hardly yet have learn'd To insinuate, flatter, bow . *Richard II.* iv 1 165
He would insinuate with thee but to make thee sigh . *Richard II.* i 4 152
To see so great a lord Basely insinuate and send us gifts *T. Andron.* iv 2 38
Insinuateth. It insinuateth me of insanie . . . *L. L. Lost* v 1 27
Insinuating. Base insinuating flattery . . . 1 *Hen. VI.* ii 4 35
Abused By silken, sly, insinuating Jacks . . . *Richard III.* i 3 53
I will practise the insinuating nod . . . *Coriolanus* ii 3 106
Some busy and insinuating rogue, Some cogging, cozening slave *Othello* iv 2 131
Insinuation. Yet a kind of insinuation, as it were . *L. L. Lost* iv 2 14
Send fair-play orders and make compromise, Insinuation, parley *K. John* v 1 68
Their defeat Does by their own insinuation grow . . *Hamlet* v 2 59
Insisted. I insisted, yet you answer'd not, But, with an angry wafture of your hand, Gave sign for me to leave you *J. Cæsar* ii 1 245
Insisting on the old prerogative And power i' the truth *Coriolanus* iii 3 17
Insisture, course, proportion, season, form, Office *Troi. and Cres.* i 3 87
Insociable. Such insociable and point-devise companions *L. L. Lost* v 1 20
If this austere insociable life Change not your offer made in heat of blood v 2 809
Insolence. Whence grows this insolence? . . *T. of Shrew* ii 1 23
I'll canvass thee in thy broad cardinal's hat, If thou proceed in this thy insolence.—Nay, stand thou back . . 1 *Hen. VI.* i 3 37
His insolence is more intolerable Than all the princes in the land beside 2 *Hen. VI.* i 1 175
I am protector of the realm; And, at his pleasure, will resign my place. —Resign it then and leave thine insolence . . . . i 3 125
Why, Suffolk, England knows thine insolence.—And thy ambition . ii 1 31
Wink at the Duke of Suffolk's insolence, At Beaufort's pride . ii 2 70
I'll to the king; And from a mouth of honour quite cry down This Ipswich fellow's insolence . . . *Hen. VIII.* i 1 138
His insolence draws folly from my lips . *Troi. and Cres.* iv 5 258
I do wonder His insolence can brook to be commanded *Coriolanus* i 1 266
At some time when his soaring insolence Shall touch the people . ii 1 270
We nourish 'gainst our senate The cockle of rebellion, insolence, sedition iii 1 70
Pursy insolence shall break his wind With fear and horrid flight *T. of A.* v 4 12
The pangs of despised love, the law's delay, The insolence of office *Ham.* iii 1 73
Let Rome be thus Inform'd.—Who, queasy with his insolence Already, will their good thoughts call from him . *Ant. and Cleo.* iii 6 20
Insolent noisemaker! We are less afraid to be drowned than thou *Tempest* i 1 46
Out, insolent! thy bastard shall be king, That thou mayst be a queen! *K. John* ii 1 122
How insolent of late he is become, How proud! 2 *Hen. VI.* iii 1 7
But he already is too insolent . . . *Troi. and Cres.* i 3 369
A paltry, insolent fellow!—How he describes himself! . . ii 3 218
Insolent, O'ercome with pride, ambitious past all thinking *Coriolanus* iv 6 30
Insolent villain!—Kill, kill, kill, kill, kill him! . . . v 6 131
But other of your insolent retinue Do hourly carp and quarrel . *Lear* i 4 221
Of being taken by the insolent foe And sold to slavery . . *Othello* i 3 137
Insomuch. You are a gentleman of good conceit: I speak not this that you should bear a good opinion of my knowledge, insomuch I say I know you are . . . . . *As Y. Like It* v 2 60
Inspiration. How can she thus then call us by our names? Unless it be by inspiration . . . *Com. of Errors* ii 2 169
Holy men at their death have good inspirations . *Mer. of Venice* i 2 31
Chosen from above, By inspiration of celestial grace . 1 *Hen. VI.* v 4 40
Inspire us with the spleen of fiery dragons! Upon them! *Richard III.* v 3 350
Apollo, Pallas, Jove, or Mercury, Inspire me! . . *T. Andron.* iv 1 67
Inspired. What zeal, what fury hath inspired thee now? . *L. L. Lost* iv 3 229
Inspired merit so by breath is barr'd . . . *All's Well* ii 1 151
Methinks I am a prophet new inspired . . . *Richard II.* ii 1 31
Was Mahomet inspired with a dove? Thou with an eagle art inspired then . . . . 1 *Hen. VI.* i 2 140
Inspired with the spirit of putting down kings and princes 2 *Hen. VI.* iv 2 38
Every man, After the hideous storm that follow'd, was A thing inspired; and, not consulting, broke Into a general prophecy . *Hen. VIII.* i 1 91
But dawning day new comfort hath inspired . . *T. Andron.* ii 2 10
So seem as if You were inspired to do those duties . . *Cymbeline* ii 3 55
Installed. Levied an army, weening to redeem And have install'd me in the diadem . . . . 1 *Hen. VI.* ii 5 89
Unworthily Thou wast installed in that high degree . . . iv 1 17
What! is my Lord of Winchester install'd, And call'd unto a cardinal's degree? . . . . v 1 28
He smiles, and says his Edward is install'd . . . 3 *Hen. VI.* iii 1 46
Cranmer is return'd with welcome, Install'd lord archbishop *Hen. VIII.* iii 2 401
Instalment. Each fair instalment, coat, and several crest, With loyal blazon, evermore be blest! . . . . . . *Mer. Wives* v 5 67
For the instalment of this noble duke In the seat royal *Richard III.* iii 1 163
Instance. What seem I that I am not?—Wise.—What instance of the contrary? . . . . *T. G. of Ver.* ii 4 16
An ocean of his tears And instances of infinite of love . . . ii 7 70
My desires had instance and argument to commend themselves *M. Wives* ii 2 256
One of our covent, and his confessor, Gives me this instance *M. for M.* iv 3 134
A league from Epidamnum had we sail'd, Before the always wind-obeying deep Gave any tragic instance of our harm . . *Com. of Errors* i 1 65

Instance. Besides this present instance of his rage, Is a mad tale he told to-day . . . . *Com. of Errors* iv 3 88
They will scarcely believe this without trial: offer them instances *M. Ado* ii 2 42
An old, an old instance, Beatrice, that lived in the time of good neighbours . . . . v 2 78
Full of wise saws and modern instances . . . . *As Y. Like It* ii 7 156
Instance, briefly; come, instance . . . . iii 2 53
A more sounder instance, come . . . . iii 2 62
Mend the instance, shepherd.—You have too courtly a wit for me . iii 2 71
Great ones I dare not give. Wherefore, what's the instance? *All's Well* iv 1 44
This accident and flood of fortune So far exceed all instance *T. Night* iv 3 12
For instance, sir, That you may know you shall not want, one word *W. T.* iv 4 604
Why should that gentleman that rode by Travers Give then such instances of loss? . . . . 2 *Hen. IV.* i 1 56
I have received A certain instance that Glendower is dead . . . iii 1 103
The examples Of every minute's instance, present now . . . iv 1 83
Gave thee no instance why thou shouldst do treason . *Hen. V.* ii 2 119
What instance gives Lord Warwick for his vow? . 2 *Hen. VI.* iii 2 159
Tell him his fears are shallow, wanting instance . *Richard III.* iii 2 25
Hector's sword had lack'd a master, But for these instances *Troi. and Cres.* i 3 77
Instance, O instance! strong as Pluto's gates . . . . . v 2 153
Instance, O instance! strong as heaven itself . . . . . v 2 155
What verse for it? what instance for it? Let me see . . . . v 10 41
With respect enough; But not with such familiar instances *J. Cæsar* iv 2 16
The instances that second marriage move Are base respects of thrift *Ham.* iii 2 192
Nature is fine in love, and where't is fine, It sends some precious instance of itself After the thing it loves . . . . . . iv 5 162
Instant. The very instant that I saw you, did My heart fly to your service; there resides . . . . *Tempest* iii 1 64
Comes me in the instant of our encounter . . . *Mer. Wives* iii 5 73
Did he send you both these letters at an instant?—Within a quarter of an hour . . . . iv 4 4
At the very instant of Falstaff's and our meeting . . . . v 3 16
But at this instant he is sick, my lord, Of a strange fever *Meas. for Meas.* v 1 151
In the instant that I met with you He had of me a chain *Com. of Errors* iv 1 9
I have served him from the hour of my nativity to this instant . iv 4 32
At any unseasonable instant of the night . . . *Much Ado* ii 2 16
She dying, as it must be so maintain'd, Upon the instant that she was accused . . . . iv 1 217
And this, by, in, and without, upon the instant . . *L. L. Lost* iii 1 42
And till that instant shut My woeful self up in a mourning house . v 2 817
Wilt thou show the whole wealth of thy wit in an instant? *Mer. of Venice* iii 5 61
In the instant that your messenger came . . . . . iv 1 152
We still have slept together, Rose at an instant . . *As Y. Like It* i 3 76
That tripped up the wrestler's heels and your heart both in an instant . iii 2 225
What's his will else?—That you will take your instant leave *All's Well* ii 4 49
From the time of his remembrance to this very instant disaster . iv 3 127
Let's take the instant by the forward top; For we are old . . v 3 39
That instant was I turn'd into a hart . . . *T. Night* i 1 21
Wrecked the same instant of their master's death . . *W. Tale* v 2 75
Even in the instant of repair and health, The fit is strongest . *K. John* iii 4 113
I fear the power of Percy is too weak To wage an instant trial 1 *Hen. IV.* iv 4 20
We rose both at an instant and fought a long hour by Shrewsbury clock v 4 151
Yes, if this present quality of war, Indeed the instant action . 2 *Hen. IV.* i 3 37
The French ambassador upon that instant Craved audience . *Hen. V.* i 1 91
I was not angry since I came to France Until this instant . . iv 7 59
At this instant He bores me with some trick . . *Hen. VIII.* i 1 127
Whose figure even this instant cloud puts on, By darkening my clear sun . . . . i 1 225
Take the instant way; For honour travels in a strait so narrow *T. and C.* iii 3 153
We, Even from this instant, banish him our city . *Coriolanus* iii 3 101
Your good tongue, More than the instant army we can make, Might stop our countryman . . . . v 1 37
In the instant came The fiery Tybalt, with his sword prepared *R. and J.* i 1 115
Joy had the like conception in our eyes And at that instant like a babe sprung up . . . . *T. of Athens* i 2 116
Bid 'em send o' the instant A thousand talents to me . . . ii 2 207
Give't these fellows To whom 'tis instant due . . . . ii 2 239
Having great and instant occasion to use fifty talents . . . iii 1 18
Requesting your lordship to supply his instant use with so many talents iii 2 41
To general filths Convert o' the instant, green virginity! . . iv 1 7
I feel now The future in the instant . . . . *Macbeth* i 5 59
From this instant, There's nothing serious in mortality: All is but toys ii 3 97
And a most instant tetter bark'd about, Most lazar-like, with vile and loathsome crust, All my smooth body . . . . *Hamlet* i 5 71
And you, my sinews, grow not instant old, But bear me stiffly up . i 5 94
The instant burst of clamour that she made . . . . ii 2 538
In the grapple I boarded them: on the instant they got clear of our ship iv 6 18
His displeasure; which at this instant so rageth in him . *Lear* i 2 177
The shame itself doth speak For instant remedy . . . . i 4 268
Whose virtue and obedience doth this instant So much commend itself ii 1 115
Bestow Your needful counsel to our business, Which craves the instant use . . . . ii 1 130
I have seen better faces in my time Than stands on any shoulder that I see Before me at this instant . . . . ii 2 101
This sword of mine shall give them instant way . . . v 3 149
I was contracted to them both: all three Now marry in an instant . v 3 229
He requires your haste-post-haste appearance, Even on the instant *Othello* i 2 38
I greet thy love, Not with vain thanks, but with acceptance bounteous, And will upon the instant put thee to't . . . . . iii 3 471
Even from this instant do build on thee a better opinion than ever before . . . . iv 2 208
Get you to bed on the instant; I will be returned forthwith . . iv 3 7
Or, if you borrow one another's love for the instant, you may, when you hear no more words of Pompey, return it again *Ant. and Cleo.* ii 2 104
I'll tell thee on the instant thou art then As great as is thy master *Cymbeline* i 5 50
Speak, or thy silence on the instant is Thy condemnation and thy death iii 5 97
Swore, If I discover'd not which way she was gone, It was my instant death . . . . v 5 278
The vision . . . at this instant Is full accomplish'd . . . v 5 469
Instantly. And he may fetch him.—Go do it instantly . *Meas. for Meas.* v 1 253
Go take her hence, and marry her instantly. Do you the office, friar v 1 382
He meant to take the present time by the top and instantly break with you of it . . . . *Much Ado* i 2 16
I cannot instantly raise up the gross . . . *Mer. of Venice* i 3 56
Give me a key for this, And instantly unlock my fortunes here . ii 9 52
Led me instantly unto his cave, There stripp'd himself . *As Y. Like It* iv 3 146
Take it hence And see it instantly consumed with fire . *W. Tale* ii 3 134
Go thou away: I'll follow instantly . . . . . . iii 3 14

Instantly. Disease thee instantly,—thou must think there's a necessity in't . . . *W. Tale* iv 4 648
Show now your mended faiths, And instantly return . . . *K. John* v 7 76
A double spirit Of teaching and of learning instantly . . . *1 Hen. IV.* v 2 65
My soul and body on the action both!—A dreadful lay! Address thee instantly . . . *2 Hen. VI.* v 2 27
Whoever the king favours, The cardinal instantly will find employment, And far enough from court too . . . *Hen. VIII.* ii 1 48
Sir, my lord would instantly speak with you . . . *Troi. and Cres.* i 2 297
Some say the Genius so Cries 'come' to him that instantly must die . iv 4 53
Get you hence instantly, and tell those friends . . . *Coriolanus* ii 3 221
Good my lords, keep on; I'll wait upon you instantly . *T. of Athens* ii 2 36
Delay not, Cæsar; read it instantly.—What, is the fellow mad? *J. Cæsar* iii 1 9
I beseech you instantly to visit My too much changed son . *Hamlet* ii 2 35
This courtesy, forbid thee, shall the duke Instantly know . . *Lear* iii 3 23
Seek out the villain Gloucester.—Hang him instantly.—Pluck out his eyes . . . iii 7 4
About it; and write happy when thou hast done. Mark, I say, instantly . . . v 3 36
Cleopatra, catching but the least noise of this, dies instantly *Ant. and Cleo.* i 2 145
Instantly this prince must die; For by his fall my honour must keep high . . . *Pericles* i 1 148
Instate. We do instate and widow you withal . *Meas. for Meas.* v 1 429
Instead. I remember the wooing of a peascod instead of her *As Y. Like It* ii 4 52
Instead of bullets wrapp'd in fire, To make a shaking fever in your walls, They shoot but calm words folded up in smoke . *K. John* ii 1 227
Instead of thee, King Harry, This sword hath ended him . *1 Hen. IV.* v 3 8
Using the names of men instead of men . . . *2 Hen. IV.* i 3 57
What drink'st thou oft, instead of homage sweet, But poison'd flattery? . . . *Hen. V.* iv 1 267
Instead of gold, we'll offer up our arms . . . *1 Hen. VI.* i 1 46
Wounds will I lend the French instead of eyes, To weep . . i 1 87
Instead whereof sharp stakes pluck'd out of hedges They pitched in the ground confusedly . . . i 1 117
If York, with all his far-fet policy, Had been the regent there instead of me, He never would have stay'd in France so long . *2 Hen. VI.* iii 1 294
With these borne before us, instead of maces, will we ride . iv 7 143
Lest that, instead of words, I send thee, Warwick, such a messenger . . . *3 Hen. VI.* i 1 98
And now, instead of mounting barbed steeds To fright the souls of fearful adversaries, He capers nimbly in a lady's chamber *Rich. III.* i 1 10
There be six Richmonds in the field; Five have I slain to-day instead of him . . . v 4 12
Instead of oil and balm, Thou lay'st in every gash that love hath given me The knife that made it . . . *Troi. and Cres.* i 1 61
Instead whereof let this supply the room: Measure for measure *3 Hen. VI.* ii 6 54
Insteeped. Where in gore he lay insteep'd . . . *Hen. V.* iv 6 12
Instigate. Did instigate the bedlam brain-sick duchess . *2 Hen. VI.* iii 1 51
Instigated. Thither provoked and instigated by his distemper *M. Wives* iii 5 77
Instigation. Rather follow Our forceful instigation . *W. Tale* ii 1 163
I am come hither, as it were, upon my man's instigation . *2 Hen. VI.* ii 3 88
By their vehement instigation, In this just suit come I . *Richard III.* iii 7 139
Such instigations have been often dropp'd . . . *J. Cæsar* ii 1 49
Instinct. Beware instinct; the lion will not touch the true prince . . . *1 Hen. IV.* ii 4 299
Instinct is a great matter; I was now a coward on instinct . ii 4 300
You are lions too, you ran away upon instinct . . . ii 4 331
Upon instinct.—I grant ye, upon instinct . . . ii 4 389
Doth not thy blood thrill at it?—Not a whit, i' faith; I lack some of thy instinct . . . ii 4 409
And thou a natural coward, without instinct . . . ii 4 543
He that but fears the thing he would not know Hath by instinct knowledge from others' eyes That what he fear'd is chanced *2 Hen. IV.* i 1 86
Mere instinct of love and loyalty, Free from a stubborn opposite intent . . . *2 Hen. VI.* iii 2 250
By a divine instinct men's minds mistrust Ensuing dangers *Richard III.* ii 3 42
I'll never Be such a gosling to obey instinct . . *Coriolanus* v 3 35
'Tis wonder That an invisible instinct should frame them To royalty unlearn'd, honour untaught . . . *Cymbeline* iv 2 177
O rare instinct! When shall I hear all through? . . . v 5 381
Instinctively. The very rats Instinctively have quit it . *Tempest* i 2 148
Institute. And haply institute A course of learning . *T. of Shrew* i 1 8
We institute your grace To be our regent . . *1 Hen. VI.* iv 1 162
Institution. The nature of our people, Our city's institutions *M. for M.* i 1 11
Instruct. To ebb Hereditary sloth instructs me . . *Tempest* ii 1 223
And instruct thee how To snare the nimble marmoset . . ii 2 173
Instruct me How I may formally in person bear me Like a true friar . . . *Meas. for Meas.* i 3 46
I will instruct thee in my trade . . . iv 2 57
Schoolmasters will I keep within my house, Fit to instruct her youth . . . *T. of Shrew* i 1 95
He took some care To get her cunning schoolmasters to instruct her . i 1 192
As a schoolmaster Well seen in music, to instruct Bianca . . i 2 134
A fine musician to instruct our mistress . . . i 2 174
To instruct her fully in those sciences, Whereof I know she is not ignorant . . . ii 1 57
In all these circumstances I'll instruct you . . . iv 2 119
Instruct my daughter how she shall persever . . *All's Well* iii 7 37
He had the honour to be the officer at a place there called Mile-end, to instruct for the doubling of files . . . iv 3 302
I speak as my understanding instructs me . . *W. Tale* i 1 21
As your charities Shall best instruct you, measure me . . ii 1 114
Some powerful spirit instruct the kites and ravens To be thy nurses! . ii 3 186
I will instruct my sorrows to be proud; For grief is proud . *K. John* iii 1 68
You rascally Althæa's dream, away!—Instruct us, boy; what dream? . . . *2 Hen. IV.* ii 2 95
What, shall a child instruct you what to do? . . *1 Hen. VI.* iii 1 133
Your discretions better can persuade Than I am able to instruct or teach iv 1 159
His training such, That he may furnish and instruct great teachers . . . *Hen. VIII.* i 2 113
And with what vehemency The occasion shall instruct you . . v 1 149
Did see and hear, devise, instruct, walk, feel . . *Coriolanus* i 1 105
Indeed, I was their tutor to instruct them . . *T. Andron.* v 1 98
Our own precedent passions do instruct us What levity's in youth *T. of A.* i 1 133
She well instructs me . . . *Hamlet* v 2 218
If thou dost As this instructs thee, thou dost make thy way . *Lear* v 3 29
Very nature will instruct her in it and compel her to some second choice . . . *Othello* ii 1 237
Let them know, The ills we do, their ills instruct us so . . iv 3 104
This gate Instructs you how to adore the heavens and bows you *Cymbeline* iii 3 3
Instruct. He'll then instruct us of this body. Young one, Inform us . . . *Cymbeline* iv 2 361
Instruct her what she has to do, that she may not be raw . *Pericles* iv 2 59
Instructed. A power I have, but of what strength and nature I am not yet instructed . . . *Meas. for Meas* i 1 81
He knew the service, and that instructed him to mercy . . iii 2 128
Here's Nestor; Instructed by the antiquary times, He must, he is, he cannot but be wise . . . *Troi. and Cres.* ii 3 262
Bastard begot, bastard instructed, bastard in mind, bastard in valour v 7 17
Lay thy finger thus, and let thy soul be instructed . . *Othello* ii 1 224
I have fled myself; and have instructed cowards To run *Ant. and Cleo.* iii 11 7
Instruction. Some good instruction give How I may bear me . *Tempest* i 2 424
Of my instruction hast thou nothing bated In what thou hadst to say . iii 3 85
Must die to-morrow, And I am going with instruction to him *M. for M.* ii 3 38
Correction and instruction must both work . . . iii 2 33
Framed to himself, by the instruction of his frailty, many deceiving promises . . . iii 2 259
I would be glad to receive some instruction from my fellow partner v 2 19
If my instructions may be your guide . . . iv 2 181
Keep your instruction, And hold you ever to our special drift . iv 5 3
If their sons be ingenuous, they shall want no instruction . *L. L. Lost* iv 2 81
It is a good divine that follows his own instructions *Mer. of Venice* i 2 16
It shall go hard but I will better the instruction . . iii 1 76
See this dispatch'd with all the haste thou canst: Anon I'll give thee more instructions . . . *T. of Shrew* Ind. 1 130
My instruction shall serve to naturalize thee . . *All's Well* i 1 222
You, Diana, Under my poor instructions yet must suffer Something in my behalf . . . iv 4 27
I cannot say 'tis pity She lacks instructions, for she seems a mistress To most that teach . . . *W. Tale* iv 4 593
Their noise be our instruction . . . *Coriolanus* i 4 22
Now it lies you on to speak To the people; not by your own instruction iii 2 53
Instruction, manners, mysteries, and trades, Degrees, observances, customs, and laws . . . *T. of Athens* iv 1 18
That we but teach Bloody instructions, which, being taught, return To plague the inventor . . . *Macbeth* i 7 9
I tremble at it. Nature would not invest herself in such shadowing passion without some instruction . . . *Othello* iv 1 41
Have by their brave instruction got upon me A nobleness *Ant. and Cleo.* iv 14 98
Confined in all she has, her monument, Of thy intents desires instruction v 1 54
And let instructions enter Where folly now possesses . *Cymbeline* i 5 47
Instrument. Sometimes a thousand twangling instruments Will hum about mine ears . . . *Tempest* iii 2 146
Destiny, That hath to instrument this lower world . . iii 3 54
To their instruments Tune a deploring dump . . *T. G. of Ver.* iii 2 84
These poor informal women are no more But instruments of some more mightier member That sets them on . . *Meas. for Meas.* v 1 237
To make thee an instrument and play false strains upon thee! *As Y. L. It* iv 3 68
My books and instruments shall be my company . . *T. of Shrew* i 1 82
She taketh most delight In music, instruments and poetry . . i 1 93
Toward the education of your daughters, I here bestow a simple instrument . . . ii 1 100
She struck me on the head, And through the instrument my pate made way . . . ii 1 155
Take you your instrument, play you the whiles . . iii 1 22
Madam, my instrument's in tune.—Let's hear. O fie! the treble jars . iii 1 38
Before you touch the instrument, To learn the order of my fingering . iii 1 64
If you think your mystery in stratagem can bring this instrument of honour again into his native quarter, be magnanimous in the enterprise . . . *All's Well* iii 6 69
But loath am to produce So bad an instrument . . . v 3 202
I partly know the instrument That screws me from my true place *T. N.* v 1 125
He swears, As he had seen't or been an instrument To vice you to't *W. Tale* i 2 415
I do see't and feel't, As you feel doing thus; and see withal The instruments that feel . . . ii 1 154
We'll make an instrument of this, omit Nothing may give us aid . iv 4 637
All the instruments which aided to expose the child were even then lost v 2 77
The instrument is cold And would not harm me . . *K. John* iv 1 104
I am too high-born to be propertied, To be a secondary at control, Or useful serving-man and instrument . . . v 2 81
Or like a cunning instrument cased up . . *Richard II.* i 3 163
All is said: His tongue is now a stringless instrument . . ii 1 149
Villain, thy own hand yields thy death's instrument . . v 5 107
Sound all the lofty instruments of war . . *1 Hen. IV.* v 2 98
He now doth lack The very instruments of chastisement *2 Hen. IV.* iv 1 217
Was cursed instrument of his decease . . *1 Hen. VI.* i 5 58
And fashion'd thee that instrument of ill . . . iii 3 65
I thank God and thee; He was the author, thou the instrument *3 Hen. VI.* iv 6 18
So blunt, unnatural, To bend the fatal instruments of war Against his brother? . . . v 1 87
Ships, Fraught with the ministers and instruments Of cruel war *T. and C.* Prol. 4
Limbs are his instruments, In no less working than are swords and bows Directive by the limbs . . . i 3 354
I spy.—You spy! what do you spy? Come, give me an instrument . iii 1 104
The other instruments Did see and hear, devise, instruct, walk, feel *Cor.* i 1 104
May these same instruments, which you profane, Never sound more! . i 9 41
Our instruments to melancholy bells . . *Rom. and Jul.* iv 5 86
With instruments upon them, fit to open These dead men's tombs . v 3 200
Resemble sweet instruments hung up in cases . . *T. of Athens* i 2 102
To make them instruments of fear and warning . . *J. Cæsar* i 3 70
The Genius and the mortal instruments Are then in council . . ii 1 66
Nor no instrument Of half that worth as those your swords . . iii 1 154
Canst thou hold up thy heavy eyes awhile, And touch thy instrument a strain? . . . iv 3 257
If thou dost nod, thou break'st thy instrument; I'll take it from thee . iv 3 271
The strings, my lord, are false.—He thinks he still is at his instrument . iv 3 293
To win us to harm, The instruments of darkness tell us truths *Macbeth* i 3 124
The way that I was going; And such an instrument I was to use . ii 1 43
How you were borne in hand, how cross'd, the instruments, Who wrought with them . . . iii 1 81
Macbeth is ripe for shaking, and the powers above Put on their instruments . . . iv 3 239
Call me what instrument you will . . . *Hamlet* iii 2 387
The treacherous instrument is in thy hand, Unbated and envenom'd . v 2 327
And of our pleasant vices Make instruments to plague us . . *Lear* v 3 171
Seel with wanton dullness My speculative and officed instruments *Othello* i 3 271
Have your instruments been in Naples, that they speak i' the nose thus? iii 1 3
Senators of Venice greet you.—I kiss the instrument of their pleasures iv 1 231
If haply you my father do suspect An instrument of this your calling back, Lay not your blame on me . . . iv 2 45

Instrument. Hark, how these instruments summon to supper! *Othello* iv 2 169
What poor an instrument May do a noble deed! *Ant. and Cleo.* v 2 236
Hence, vile instrument! Thou shalt not damn my hand . *Cymbeline* iii 4 75
My ingenious instrument! Hark, Polydore, it sounds! . . iv 2 186
Give me The penitent instrument to pick that bolt, Then, free for ever! v 4 10
The pregnant instrument of wrath Prest for this blow . *Pericles* iv Gower 44
Instrumental. The head is not more native to the heart, The hand more instrumental to the mouth . . . . . . *Hamlet* i 2 48
Insubstantial. Like this insubstantial pageant faded . *Tempest* iv 1 155
Insufficience. That your senses, unintelligent of our insufficience, may, though they cannot praise us, as little accuse us . . *W. Tale* i 1 16
Insufficiency. But you must flout my insufficiency . . *M. N. Dream* ii 2 128
Insult. Who might be your mother, That you insult, exult, and all at once, Over the wretched? . . . . *As Y. Like It* iii 5 36
Hath that poor monarch taught thee to insult? . . . *3 Hen. VI.* i 4 124
One part does disdain with cause, the other Insult without all reason *Coriolanus* iii 1 144
Give me thy knife, I will insult on him . . *T. Andron.* iii 2 71
Insulted, rail'd, And put upon him such a deal of man . *Lear* ii 2 126
Insulting. No lord of thine, thou haught insulting man . *Richard II.* iv 1 254
I might have let alone The insulting hand of Douglas over you 1 *Hen. IV.* v 4 54
Now am I like that proud insulting ship Which Cæsar and his fortune bare at once . . . . . . 1 *Hen. VI.* i 2 138
From thy insulting tyranny, Coupled in bonds of perpetuity . . iv 7 19
Insulting Charles! hast thou by secret means Used intercession? . v 4 147
And so he walks, insulting o'er his prey . . *3 Hen. VI.* i 3 14
The proud insulting queen, With Clifford and the haught Northumberland ii 1 168
Proud insulting boy! Becomes it thee to be thus bold in terms? . ii 2 84
Insulting tyranny begins to jet . . . . *Richard III.* ii 4 51
Insultment. My speech of insultment ended on his dead body *Cymbeline* iii 5 145
Insupportable. You do me most insupportable vexation . *All's Well* ii 3 243
O insupportable and touching loss! Upon what sickness? . *J. Cæsar* iv 3 151
My wife! my wife! what wife? I have no wife. O, insupportable! *Oth.* v 2 98
Insuppressive. Do not stain The even virtue of our enterprise, Nor the insuppressive mettle of our spirits . . *J. Cæsar* ii 1 134
Insurrection. And never yet did insurrection want Such water-colours to impaint his cause . . . . 1 *Hen. IV.* v 1 79
But now the bishop Turns insurrection to religion . . 2 *Hen. IV.* i 1 201
To dress the ugly form Of base and bloody insurrection . . iv 1 40
And throw forth greater themes For insurrection's arguing . *Coriolanus* i 1 225
There hath been in Rome strange insurrections . . . iv 3 13
And the state of man, Like to a little kingdom, suffers then The nature of an insurrection . . . . . *J. Cæsar* ii 1 69
Integer vitæ, scelerisque purus, Non eget Mauri jaculis . *T. Andron.* iv 2 20
Integritas. Tanta est erga te mentis integritas, regina serenissima *Hen. VIII.* iii 1 40
Integrity. Frame some feeling line That may discover such integrity *T. G. of Ver.* iii 2 77
Neither my coat, integrity, nor persuasion can with ease attempt you *Meas. for Meas.* iv 2 205
His integrity Stands without blemish . . . . . . v 1 107
Heavenly oaths, vow'd with integrity . . . . *L. L. Lost* v 2 356
My integrity ne'er knew the crafts That you do charge men with *All's W.* iv 2 33
We have been Deceived in thy integrity . . . *W. Tale* i 2 240
It shall scarce boot me To say 'not guilty': mine integrity Being counted falsehood . . . . iii 2 27
His prayers are full of false hypocrisy; Ours of true zeal and deep integrity. Our prayers do out-pray his . *Richard II.* v 3 108
Reverend fathers; men Of singular integrity and learning . *Hen. VIII.* ii 4 59
I am sorry my integrity should breed . . . So deep suspicion . iii 1 51
My robe, And my integrity to heaven, is all I dare now call mine own . iii 2 453
Thy truth and thy integrity is rooted In us, thy friend . . . v 1 114
More out of malice than integrity, Would try him to the utmost, had ye mean . . . . v 3 145
That my integrity and truth to you Might be affronted with the match and weight Of such a winnow'd purity in love . *Troi. and Cres.* iii 2 172
With most divine integrity, From heart of every heart, great Hector, welcome . . . . iv 5 170
Bereaves the state Of that integrity which should become't *Coriolanus* iii 1 159
So I do affy In thy uprightness and integrity . . *T. Andron.* i 1 48
This noble passion, Child of integrity . . . *Macbeth* iv 3 115
Your daughter, whom she bore in hand to love With such integrity *Cymb.* v 5 44
Intellect. And train our intellects to vain delight . *L. L. Lost* i 1 71
His intellect is not replenished; he is only an animal . . iv 2 27
I will look again on the intellect of the letter . . . . iv 2 137
Snip, snap, quick and home! it rejoiceth my intellect: true wit! . v 1 64
Hath Bolingbroke deposed Thine intellect? . . . *Richard II.* v 1 28
Intellectual. Indued with intellectual sense and souls . *Com. of Errors* ii 1 22
For if their heads had any intellectual armour, they could never wear such heavy head-pieces . . . . . . *Hen. V.* iii 7 148
Intelligence. Comes in one Mistress Page; gives intelligence of Ford's approach . . . . *Mer. Wives* iii 5 85
And talks of the basket too, howsoever he hath had intelligence . iv 2 95
My intelligence is true; my jealousy is reasonable . . . iv 2 154
I can give you intelligence of an intended marriage . . *Much Ado* i 3 46
For this intelligence If I have thanks, it is a dear expense *M. N. Dream* i 1 248
If with myself I hold intelligence . . . *As Y. Like It* i 3 49
And deliver all the intelligence in his power against you . *All's Well* iii 6 32
Hath the count all this intelligence?—Ay, and the particular confirmations iv 3 70
Or I am deceived by him that in such intelligence hath seldom failed . iv 5 88
From whom I have this intelligence, that he is seldom from the house of a most homely shepherd . . . . . *W. Tale* iv 2 42
That's likewise part of my intelligence . . . . . iv 2 51
Where hath our intelligence been drunk? Where hath it slept? *K. John* iv 2 116
I have from Port le Blanc, a bay In Brittany, received intelligence *Richard II.* ii 1 278
By this intelligence we learn The Welshmen are dispersed . . iii 3 1
Sought to entrap me by intelligence . . . 1 *Hen. IV.* iv 3 98
Many a creature else Had been alive this hour, If like a Christian thou hadst truly borne Betwixt our armies true intelligence . . v 5 10
The French, advised by good intelligence Of this most dreadful preparation, Shake in their fear . . . . *Hen. V.* ii Prol. 12
Amongst this princely heap, if any here, By false intelligence, or wrong surmise, Hold me a foe . . . . . *Richard III.* ii 1 54
Nothing can proceed that toucheth us Whereof I shall not have intelligence . . . . iii 2 24
By intelligence, And proofs as clear as founts in July . . *Hen. VIII.* i 1 153
Patroclus will give me any thing for the intelligence of this *Tr. and Cr.* v 2 193
You will be welcome with this intelligence . . *Coriolanus* iv 3 30
Say from whence You owe this strange intelligence? . . *Macbeth* i 3 76
Intelligence. O sir, fly this place; Intelligence is given where you are hid . . . . *Lear* ii 1 23
Not I, Inclined to this intelligence, pronounce The beggary of his change *Cymbeline* i 6 114
The very gods show'd me a vision—I fast and pray'd for their intelligence iv 2 347
Intelligencer. The very opener and intelligencer Between the grace, the sanctities of heaven, And our dull workings . . 2 *Hen. IV.* iv 2 20
Richard yet lives, hell's black intelligencer . . *Richard III.* iv 4 71
Intelligencing. A most intelligencing bawd! . . . *W. Tale* ii 3 68
Intelligent. Do you know, and dare not? Be intelligent to me . . i 2 378
Are to France the spies and speculations Intelligent of our state . *Lear* iii 1 25
This is the letter he spoke of, which approves him an intelligent party . iii 5 12
Our posts shall be swift and intelligent betwixt us . . . iii 7 12
Intelligis. It insinuateth me of insanie: anne intelligis? . . *L. L. Lost* v 1 28
Intelligo. Laus Deo, bene intelligo . . . . . . v 1 30
Intemperance. May salve The long-grown wounds of my intemperance 1 *Hen. IV.* iii 2 156
Boundless intemperance In nature is a tyranny . . . *Macbeth* iv 3 66
Intemperate. To his concupiscible intemperate lust . *Meas. for Meas.* v 1 98
You are more intemperate in your blood Than Venus . *Much Ado* iv 1 60
Intend. For Thurio, he intends, shall wed his daughter . *T. G. of Ver.* ii 6 39
My friend This night intends to steal away your daughter . . iii 1 11
I despise thee for thy wrongful suit, And by and by intend to chide myself . . . . iv 2 103
At Friar Patrick's cell, Where I intend holy confession . . iv 3 44
She did intend confession At Patrick's cell this even . . . v 2 41
Un boitier vert, a box, a green-a box: do intend vat I speak? *Mer. Wives* i 4 47
If he should intend this voyage towards my wife, I would turn her loose to him . . . . ii 1 188
Lord Angelo, having affairs to heaven, Intends you for his swift ambassador, Where you shall be an everlasting leiger *Meas. for Meas.* iii 1 58
Intend a kind of zeal both to the prince and Claudio . . *Much Ado* ii 2 35
I will not have to do with you.—Nor shall not, if I do as I intend *L. L. L.* v 2 429
How long within this wood intend you stay? . . *M. N. Dream* ii 1 138
If thou dost intend Never so little show of love to her, Thou shalt aby it iii 2 333
To-morrow I intend to hunt again . . . . *T. of Shrew* Ind. 1 29
Do you intend to stay with me to-night? . . . . . Ind. 1 81
Amid this hurly I intend That all is done in reverend care of her . iv 1 206
Thither . . . are they gone, and there they intend to sup . *W. Tale* v 2 112
Well, I'll not say what I intend for thee . . . . *K. John* iii 3 68
And happy newness, that intends old right . . . . . v 4 61
As I intend to thrive in this new world . . . . *Richard II.* iv 1 78
Whose temper I intend to stain With the best blood that I can meet 1 *Hen. IV.* v 2 94
The king hath note of all that they intend, By interception . *Hen. V.* ii 2 6
The king from Eltham I intend to steal . . . . 1 *Hen. VI.* i 1 176
Guard thy head; For I intend to have it ere long . . . . i 3 88
So help me God, as I intend it not! . . . . . . iii 1 141
He doth intend she shall be England's queen . . . . v 1 45
That is good deceit Which mates him first that first intends deceit 2 *Hen. VI.* iii 1 265
Say we intend to try his grace to-day, If he be guilty . . . iii 2 16
As surely as my soul intends to live With that dread King . . . iii 2 153
In care of your most royal person, That if your highness should intend to sleep . . . . iii 2 255
All scholars, lawyers, courtiers, gentlemen, They call false caterpillars and intend their death . . . . iv 4 37
Doth York intend no harm to us, That thus he marcheth with thee? . v 1 56
Then what intends these forces thou dost bring? . . . . v 1 60
As I intend, Clifford, to thrive to-day, It grieves my soul to leave thee v 2 17
Intend here to besiege you in your castle . . . . 3 *Hen. VI.* i 2 50
Not that I fear to stay, but love to go Whither the queen intends . . ii 5 139
I swear to thee I speak no more than what my soul intends . . iii 2 94
I say not, slaughter him, For I intend but only to surprise him . iv 2 25
Thou art sworn as deeply to effect what we intend As closely to conceal what we impart . . . . *Richard III.* iii 1 158
You come too late of our intents, Yet witness what you hear we did intend . . . . iii 5 70
Intend some fear; Be not you spoke with, but by mighty suit . . iii 7 45
So thrive I . . ., As I intend more good to you and yours Than ever you or yours were by me wrong'd! . . . . iv 4 237
As I intend to prosper and repent, So thrive I in my dangerous attempt! . . . . iv 4 397
To make that only true we now intend . . . . *Hen. VIII.* Prol. 21
To call back her appeal She intends unto his holiness . . . ii 4 235
You know an enemy intends you harm . . . *Troi. and Cres.* ii 2 39
We'll but commend what we intend to sell . . . . . iv 1 78
They have had inkling this fortnight what we intend to do . *Coriolanus* i 1 60
You see how he intends to use the people.—May they perceive's intent! ii 2 159
The city ports by this hath enter'd and Intends to appear before the people . . . . v 6 7
Stand gracious to the rites that we intend! . . . . *T. Andron.* i 1 78
Our empress . . . Will we acquaint with all that we intend . . ii 1 122
Shalt carry from me to the empress' sons Presents that I intend to send them . . . . iv 1 116
But if thou, jealous, dost return to pry In what I further shall intend to do, By heaven, I will tear thee joint by joint . *Rom. and Jul.* v 3 34
I know not, gentlemen, what you intend, Who else must be let blood, who else is rank . . . . *J. Cæsar* iii 1 151
Make inquire Of his behaviour.—My lord, I did intend it . . *Hamlet* ii 1 5
Since what I well intend, I'll do't before I speak . . . *Lear* i 1 228
Which often leaves the history unspoke That it intends to do . . i 1 240
Suspend thy purpose, if thou didst intend To make this creature fruitful! . . . . i 4 298
Now, sweet lord, You know the goodness I intend upon you . . v 1 7
As for the mercy Which he intends to Lear and to Cordelia, The battle done, and they within our power, Shall never see his pardon . . v 1 66
She gives it out that you shall marry her: Do you intend it? *Othello* iv 1 119
Will you sup there?—'Faith, I intend so.—Well, I may chance to see you iv 1 173
Thou dost stone my heart, And makest me call what I intend to do A murder . . . . v 2 64
Yet, if you there Did practise on my state, your being in Egypt Might be my question.—How intend you, practised? . *Ant. and Cleo.* ii 2 40
We intend so to dispose you as Yourself shall give us counsel . . v 2 186
I tell you this: Cæsar through Syria Intends his journey . . v 2 201
I now look from thee then, and to Tarsus Intend my travel . *Pericles* i 2 116
Intended. For my duty's sake, I rather chose To cross my friend in his intended drift . . . . *T. G. of Ver.* iii 1 18
Her mother hath intended, The better to denote her to the doctor *Mer. Wives* iv 6 38

Intended. Being come to knowledge that there was complaint Intended *Meas. for Meas.* v 1 154
I can give you intelligence of an intended marriage *Much Ado* i 3 47
Bring them to see this the very night before the intended wedding ii 2 46
So shall we stay, mocking intended game *L. L. Lost* v 2 155
To rehearse a play Intended for great Theseus' nuptial-day *M. N. Dream* iii 2 12
We intended To keep in darkness what occasion now Reveals *T. Night* v 1 155
Fear not, man; here's no harm intended to thee *W. Tale* iv 4 642
Intended or committed was this fault? *Richard II.* v 3 33
The king himself in person is set forth, Or hitherwards intended *1 Hen. IV.* iv 1 92
That is intended in the general's name *2 Hen. IV.* iv 1 166
I did admit it as a motive The sooner to effect what I intended *Hen. V.* ii 2 157
Yet your good will Must have that thanks from Rome, after the measure As you intended well *Coriolanus* v 1 47
Can you think to blow out the intended fire your city is ready to flame in? v 2 49
A sleeping potion; which so took effect As I intended *Rom. and Jul.* v 3 245
Know'st thou any harm's intended towards him? *J. Cæsar* ii 4 31
There is no harm intended to your person, Nor to no Roman else iii 1 90
Intendest. If thou canst accuse, Or aught intend'st to lay unto my charge, Do it without invention *1 Hen. VI.* iii 1 4
Intendeth. Away, and glister like the god of war, When he intendeth to become the field *K. John* v 1 55
Intending other serious matters *T. of Athens* ii 2 219
Start at wagging of a straw, Intending deep suspicion *Richard III.* iii 5 8
Intendment. You might stay him from his intendment *As Y. Like It* i 1 140
But fear the main intendment of the Scot *Hen. V.* i 2 144
Ay, and said nothing but what I protest intendment of doing *Othello* iv 2 206
Intenible. Yet in this captious and intenible sieve I still pour in the waters of my love *All's Well* i 3 208
Intent. These that accuse him in his intent towards our wives *M. Wives* ii 1 181
Who knew of your intent and coming hither? *Meas. for Meas.* v 1 124
His act did not o'ertake his bad intent, And must be buried but as an intent v 1 456
Thoughts are no subjects; Intents but merely thoughts v 1 459
I hope you have no intent to turn husband, have you? *Much Ado* i 1 195
What is your intent?—The effect of my intent is to cross theirs *L. L. Lost* v 2 137
They do it but in mocking merriment; And mock for mock is only my intent v 2 140
Told our intents before; which once disclosed, The ladies did change favours v 2 467
Fashioning our humours Even to the opposed end of our intents v 2 768
Hearing our intent, Came here in grace of our solemnity *M. N. Dream* iv 1 138
Our intent Was to be gone from Athens iv 1 156
Nothing in the world; Unless you can find sport in their intents v 1 79
We do not come as minding to content you, Our true intent is v 1 114
The intent and purpose of the law Hath full relation to the penalty, Which here appeareth due *Mer. of Venice* iv 1 247
Why came I hither but to that intent? *T. of Shrew* i 2 199
My project may deceive me, But my intents are fix'd *All's Well* i 1 244
Had you not lately an intent,—speak truly,—To go to Paris? i 3 224
Had I spoke with her, I could have well diverted her intents iii 4 21
Is it not meant damnable in us, to be trumpeters of our unlawful intents? iv 3 32
'Fore whose throne 'tis needful, Ere I can perfect mine intents, to kneel iv 4 4
Such disguise as haply shall become The form of my intent *T. Night* i 2 55
That their business might be every thing and their intent every where ii 4 80
From all indifferency, From all direction, purpose, course, intent *K. John* ii 1 580
Your vile intent must needs seem horrible iv 1 96
You shall not only take the sacrament To bury mine intents, but also to effect Whatever I shall happen to devise *Richard II.* iv 1 329
The arms are fair, When the intent of bearing them is just *1 Hen. IV.* v 2 89
God knows, I had no such intent *2 Hen. IV.* iii 1 72
Letters from Northumberland; Their cold intent, tenour and substance, thus iv 1 9
I will stoop and humble my intents To your well-practised wise directions v 2 120
And, God consigning to my good intents v 2 143
He hath intent his wonted followers Shall all be very well provided for v 5 104
To-morrow shall you bear our full intent Back to our brother *Hen. V.* ii 4 114
With forged quaint conceit To set a gloss upon his bold intent *1 Hen. VI.* iv 1 103
Have you perused the letters . . .?—I have, my lord: and their intent is this v 1 3
At your command; Command, I mean, of virtuous chaste intents v 5 20
For a minister of my intent, I have seduced a headstrong Kentishman *2 Hen. VI.* iii 1 355
Mere instinct of love and loyalty, Free from a stubborn opposite intent iii 2 251
Tell him privily of our intent *3 Hen. VI.* i 2 39
That she was coming with a full intent To dash our late decree ii 1 117
Belike his majesty hath some intent That you shall be new-christen'd in the Tower *Richard III.* i 1 49
If I fail not in my deep intent, Clarence hath not another day to live i 1 149
Not all so much for love As for another secret close intent i 1 158
You come too late of our intents, Yet witness what you hear we did intend iii 5 69
Achilles shall have word of this intent; So shall each lord *Troi. and Cres.* i 3 306
Arm'd, and bloody in intent v 3 8
You see how he intends to use the people.—May they perceive's intent! *Coriolanus* ii 2 160
If you do hold the same intent wherein You wish'd us parties v 6 13
And now be it known to you my full intent *T. Andron.* iv 2 151
The time and my intents are savage-wild *Rom. and Jul.* v 3 37
I'll hide me hereabout: His looks I fear, and his intents I doubt v 3 44
Did menace me with death, If I did stay to look on his intents v 3 134
A greater power than we can contradict Hath thwarted our intents v 3 154
Tell him of an intent that's coming toward him *T. of Athens* v 1 23
I have no spur To prick the sides of my intent *Macbeth* i 7 26
For your intent In going back to school in Wittenberg, It is most retrograde to our desire *Hamlet* i 2 112
Be thy intents wicked or charitable, Thou comest in such a questionable shape That I will speak to thee i 4 42
My stronger guilt defeats my strong intent iii 3 40
'Tis our fast intent To shake all cares and business from our age *Lear* i 1 39
Suspend your indignation against my brother till you can derive from him better testimony of his intent i 2 88
My good intent May carry through itself to that full issue i 4 2
When I dissuaded him from his intent, And found him pight to do it ii 1 66
Yet to be known shortens my made intent iv 7 9
You lords and noble friends, know our intent v 3 296
Intent. General, be advised; He comes to bad intent *Othello* i 2 56
Be pleased to catch at mine intent By what did here befal me *A. and C.* ii 2 41
Confined in all she has, her monument, Of thy intents desires instruction v 1 54
If you apply yourself to our intents, Which towards you are most gentle v 2 126
The way To fool their preparation, and to conquer Their most absurd intents v 2 226
Thaliard came full bent with sin And had intent to murder him *Pericles* ii Gower 24
For me, be you thoughten That I came with no ill intent iv 6 116
And give you gold for such provision As our intents will need v 1 259
Intention. She did so course o'er my exteriors with such a greedy intention *Mer. Wives* i 3 73
Affection! thy intention stabs the centre *W. Tale* i 2 138
Intentively. Whereof by parcels she had something heard, But not intentively *Othello* i 3 155
Inter their bodies as becomes their births *Richard III.* v 5 15
Yet like A queen, and daughter to a king, inter me *Hen. VIII.* iv 2 172
Remaineth nought, but to inter our brethren *T. Andron.* i 1 146
Suffer thy brother Marcus to inter His noble nephew here in virtue's nest i 1 375
We have done but greenly, In hugger-mugger to inter him *Hamlet* iv 5 84
Intercept. Where, if it please you, you may intercept him *T. G. of Ver.* iii 1 43
To intercept this inconvenience *1 Hen. VI.* i 4 14
As I thought, March'd toward Saint Alban's to intercept the queen *3 Hen. VI.* ii 1 114
Who intercepts my expedition? *Richard III.* iv 4 136
Yet in some sort they are better than the tribunes, For that they will not intercept my tale *T. Andron.* iii 1 40
Intercepted did return To be deposed and shortly murdered *1 Hen. IV.* i 3 151
Who intercepts my expedition?—O, she that might have intercepted thee, By strangling thee in her accursed womb! *Richard III.* iv 4 137
The goodness of your intercepted packets You writ to the pope *Hen. VIII.* iii 2 286
Being intercepted in your sport, Great reason that my noble lord be rated For sauciness *T. Andron.* ii 3 80
Intercepter. Thy intercepter, full of despite, bloody as the hunter, attends thee at the orchard-end *T. Night* iii 4 242
Interception. By interception which they dream not of *Hen. V.* ii 2 7
Intercession. Besides, her intercession chafed him so *T. G. of Ver.* iii 1 233
Hast thou by secret means Used intercession to obtain a league? *1 Hen. VI.* v 4 148
Let it be noised That through our intercession this revokement And pardon comes *Hen. VIII.* i 2 106
The palsied intercession of such a decayed dotant as you *Coriolanus* v 2 47
An aspect of intercession, which Great nature cries 'Deny not' v 3 32
For, lo, My intercession likewise steads my foe *Rom. and Jul.* ii 3 54
Intercessor. A soft and dull-eyed fool, To shake the head, relent, and sigh, and yield To Christian intercessors *Mer. of Venice* iii 3 16
Interchained. Two bosoms interchained with an oath *M. N. Dream* ii 2 49
Interchange. With interchange of gifts, letters *W. Tale* i 1 30
Once more I shall interchange My waned state for Henry's regal crown *3 Hen. VI.* iv 7 3
This interchange of love, I here protest, Upon my part shall be unviolable.—And so swear I *Richard III.* ii 1 26
Ceremonious vows of love And ample interchange of sweet discourse v 3 99
Good Diomed, Furnish you fairly for this interchange *Troi. and Cres.* iii 3 33
Interchangeably hurl down my gage *Richard II.* i 1 146
And interchangeably set down their hands, To kill the king at Oxford v 2 98
Which being sealed interchangeably *1 Hen. IV.* iii 1 81
Here's 'In witness whereof the parties interchangeably' *Troi. and Cres.* iii 2 62
Interchanged. And interchanged love-tokens *M. N. Dream* i 1 29
Interchangement. Attested by the holy close of lips, Strengthen'd by interchangement of your rings *T. Night* v 1 162
Interchanging blows I quickly shed Some of his bastard blood *1 Hen. VI.* iv 6 19
While we were interchanging thrusts and blows, Came more *Rom. and Jul.* i 1 120
Interdiction. By his own interdiction stands accursed *Macbeth* iv 3 107
Interessed. To whose young love The vines of France and milk of Burgundy Strive to be interess'd *Lear* i 1 87
Interest. He should give her interest, and she gives it him *T. G. of Ver.* ii 1 108
Then shall he mourn, If ever love had interest in his liver *Much Ado* iv 1 233
My bargains and my well-won thrift, Which he calls interest *M. of Ven.* i 3 52
Did he take interest?—No, not take interest, not, as you would say, Directly interest i 3 76
Was this inserted to make interest good? i 3 95
If that the youth of my new interest here Have power to bid you welcome iii 2 224
He hath no interest in me in the world *As Y. Like It* v 1 8
To part by the teeth The unowed interest of proud-swelling state *K. John* iv 3 147
Acquainted me with interest to this land v 2 89
Let the tongue of war Plead for our interest and our being here v 2 165
He hath more worthy interest to the state Than thou *1 Hen. IV.* iii 2 98
You shall have your desires with interest And pardon absolute iv 3 49
Only reserved, you claim no interest In any of our towns *1 Hen. VI.* v 4 167
All your interest in those territories Is utterly bereft you *2 Hen. VI.* iii 1 84
Ah, so much interest have I in thy sorrow As I had title in thy noble husband! *Richard III.* ii 2 47
Advantaging their loan with interest Of ten times double gain iv 4 323
That ever death should let life bear his name, Where life hath no more interest but to breathe! *T. Andron.* iii 1 250
I have an interest in your hate's proceeding *Rom. and Jul.* iii 1 193
He is so kind that he now Pays interest for't *T. of Athens* i 2 206
Then they could smile and fawn upon his debts And take down the interest into their gluttonous maws iii 4 52
While they have told their money and let out Their coin upon large interest, I myself Rich only in large hurts iii 5 108
No more that thane of Cawdor shall deceive Our bosom interest *Macbeth* i 2 64
We will divest us, both of rule, Interest of territory, cares of state *Lear* i 1 51
For your claim, fair sister, I bar it in the interest of my wife v 3 85
Make him swear The shes of Italy should not betray Mine interest *Cymb.* i 3 30
Since My lord hath interest in them, I will keep them In my bedchamber i 6 195
What's thy interest In this sad wreck? How came it? Who is it? iv 2 365
Interim. I will in the interim undertake one of Hercules' labours *M. Ado* ii 1 380
For interim to our studies shall relate In high-born words the worth of many a knight *L. L. Lost* i 1 172
If the interim be but a se'nnight, Time's pace is so hard that it seems the length of seven year *As Y. Like It* iii 2 333
No interim, not a minute's vacancy, Both day and night did we keep company *T. Night* v 1 98
Myself have play'd The interim, by remembering you 'tis past *Hen. V.* v Prol. 43
By interims and conveying gusts we have heard *Coriolanus* i 6 5

Interim. The future comes apace: What shall defend the interim? *T. of Athens* ii 2 158
All the interim is Like a phantasma, or a hideous dream . *J. Cæsar* ii 1 64
At more time, The interim having weigh'd it, let us speak . *Macbeth* i 3 154
It will be short: the interim is mine; And a man's life's no more than to say 'One.' But I am very sorry . . . . . *Hamlet* v 2 73
I a heavy interim shall support By his dear absence . . . *Othello* i 3 259
Belike Iago in the interim Came in and satisfied him . . . v 2 317
Whereto being bound, The interim, pray you, all confound . *Pericles* v 2 279
Interior. Which pries not to the interior, but, like the martlet, Builds in the weather on the outward wall . . . *Mer. of Venice* ii 9 28
Aiming, belike, at your interior hatred . . . . . *Richard III.* i 3 65
O that you could turn your eyes toward the napes of your necks, and make but an interior survey of your good selves! . . *Coriolanus* ii 1 43
Interjection. How now! interjections? Why, then, some be of laughing, as, ah, ha, he! . . . . *Much Ado* iv 1 22
Interjoin. Grow dear friends And interjoin their issues . *Coriolanus* iv 4 22
Interlude. To play in our interlude before the duke . *M. N. Dream* i 2 6
In this same interlude it doth befall That I, one Snout by name, present a wall . . . . v 1 156
I was one, sir, in this interlude; one Sir Topas, sir. . . *T. Night* v 1 380
Make your loves to me, My lady is bespoke.—An interlude! . . *Lear* v 3 89
Intermingle. That they will not admit any good part to intermingle with them . . . . *Much Ado* v 2 64
I'll intermingle every thing he does With Cassio's suit . . *Othello* iii 3 25
Intermission. You saw the mistress, I beheld the maid; You loved, I loved for intermission . . . . . . *Mer. of Venice* iii 2 201
I did laugh sans intermission An hour by his dial . . *As Y. Like It* ii 7 32
But, gentle heavens, Cut short all intermission . . . *Macbeth* iv 3 232
Deliver'd letters, spite of intermission . . . . . *Lear* ii 4 33
Intermissive. Wounds will I lend the French instead of eyes, To weep their intermissive miseries . . . . 1 *Hen. VI.* i 1 88
Intermit. Pray to the gods to intermit the plague . . *J. Cæsar* i 1 59
Intermixed. The better sort, As thoughts of things divine, are intermix'd With scruples . . . . *Richard II.* v 5 12
Interpose. Please you to interpose, fair madam . . . *W. Tale* v 3 119
What watchful cares do interpose themselves Betwixt your eyes and night?—Shall I entreat a word? . . . . . . *J. Cæsar* ii 1 98
Interposer. No rest be interposer 'twixt us twain . *Mer. of Venice* iii 2 329
Interpret. O exceeding puppet! Now will he interpret to her *T. G. of V.* ii 1 101
I can interpret all her martyr'd signs . . . . *T. Andron.* iii 2 36
To the dumbness of the gesture One might interpret . *T. of Athens* i 1 34
This insculpture, which With wax I brought away, whose soft impression Interprets for my poor ignorance . . . . . . v 4 69
You should be women, And yet your beards forbid me to interpret That you are so . . . . *Macbeth* i 3 46
My former speeches have but hit your thoughts, Which can interpret further . . . . iii 6 2
I could interpret between you and your love, if I could see the puppets dallying . . . . *Hamlet* iii 2 256
O! my fear interprets: what, is he dead? . . . . *Othello* v 2 73
If it be true that I interpret false, Then were it certain you were not so bad . . . . *Pericles* i 1 124
Interpretation. If your lass Interpretation should abuse and call this Your lack of love . . . . *W. Tale* iv 4 364
Look how we can, or sad or merrily, Interpretation will misquote our looks . . . . 1 *Hen. IV.* v 2 13
A crown's worth of good interpretation . . . . . 2 *Hen. IV.* ii 2 99
So our virtues Lie in the interpretation of the time . *Coriolanus* iv 7 50
This is a poor epitome of yours, Which by the interpretation of full time May show like all yourself . . . . v 3 69
Interpreted. This dream is all amiss interpreted . . *J. Cæsar* ii 2 83
One, but painted thus, Would be interpreted a thing perplex'd *Cymbeline* iii 4 7
Interpreter. It will not lie where it concerns, Unless it have a false interpreter . . . . *T. G. of Ver.* i 2 78
Fie, what a question's that, If thou wert near a lewd interpreter! *Mer. of Venice* iii 4 80
Some one among us whom we must produce for an interpreter *All's Well* iv 1 6
Let me be the interpreter.—Art not acquainted with him? knows he not thy voice? . . . . iv 1 8
As for you, interpreter, you must seem very politic . . . iv 1 23
I do not know if it be it or no.—Our interpreter does it well . . iv 3 236
Are as interpreters Of my behind-hand slackness . . . *W. Tale* v 1 150
Madam my interpreter, what says she? . . . . . *Hen. V.* v 2 282
What we oft do best, By sick interpreters, once weak ones, is Not ours, or not allow'd . . . . *Hen. VIII.* i 2 82
Our captain hath in every figure skill, An aged interpreter *T. of Athens* v 3 8
Interred. At Worcester must his body be interr'd . . *K. John* v 7 99
I Richard's body have interred new . . . . . . *Hen. V.* iv 1 312
I'll erect A tomb, wherein his corpse shall be interr'd . . 1 *Hen. VI.* ii 2 13
Come, now towards Chertsey with your holy load, Taken from Paul's to be interred there . . . . *Richard III.* i 2 30
After I have solemnly interr'd At Chertsey monastery this noble king . i 2 214
Death, lie thou there, by a dead man interr'd . . . *Rom. and Jul.* v 3 87
The evil, that men do lives after them; The good is oft interred with their bones . . . . *J. Cæsar* iii 2 81
And he shall be interr'd As soldiers can . . . . . *Cymbeline* iv 2 401
Interrogatories. Let us go in; And charge us there upon inter'gatories *Mer. of Venice* v 1 298
Let me answer to the particular of the inter'gatories . . *All's Well* iv 3 207
What earthy name to interrogatories Can task the free breath of a sacred king? Thou canst not, cardinal, devise a name . . *K. John* iii 1 147
But nor the time nor place Will serve our long inter'gatories . *Cymbeline* v 5 392
Interrogatory. The first inter'gatory That my Nerissa shall be sworn on is, Whether till the next night she had rather stay, Or go to bed now *Mer. of Venice* v 1 300
Interrupt the monster one word further, and, by this hand, I'll turn my mercy out o' doors . . . . *Tempest* iii 2 77
To interrupt my purposed rest . . . . *L. L. Lost* v 2 91
For he that interrupts him shall not live . . . . 3 *Hen. VI.* i 1 123
Here is Ulysses: I'll interrupt his reading. How now, Ulysses! *Troi. and Cres.* iii 3 93
I charge thee, Whate'er thou hear'st or seest, stand all aloof, And do not interrupt me in my course . . . . . . *Rom. and Jul.* v 3 27
I'll hear you more, to the bottom of your story, And never interrupt you *Pericles* v 1 167
Interrupted. And happily we might be interrupted . . *T. of Shrew* iv 4 54
Her presence would have interrupted much . . . . *K. John* ii 1 542
Whose rage doth rend Like interrupted waters . . *Coriolanus* iii 1 249
Interrupter of the good That noble-minded Titus means to thee! *T. An.* i 1 208
Interruptest. Welcome, Mercade; But that thou interrupt'st our merriment.—I am sorry, madam . . . . *L. L. Lost* v 2 725
Interruption. The interruption of their churlish drums Cuts off more circumstance . . . . *K. John* ii 1 76
And bloody England into England gone, O'erbearing interruption, spite of France . . . . iii 4 9
Pardon us the interruption Of thy devotion . . . . *Richard III.* iii 7 102
Intertissued. The intertissued robe of gold and pearl . . *Hen. V.* iv 1 279
Intervallum. And a' shall laugh without intervallums . 2 *Hen. IV.* v 1 91
Interview. At which interview All liberal reason I will yield unto *L. L. L.* ii 1 167
I have labour'd . . . To bring your most imperial majesties Unto this bar and royal interview . . . . *Hen. V.* v 2 27
This last costly treaty, the interview, That swallow'd so much treasure *Hen. VIII.* i 1 165
His fears were, that the interview betwixt England and France might, through their amity, Breed him some prejudice . . . . i 1 180
Signify this loving interview To the expecters . . . *Troi. and Cres.* iv 5 155
Intestate. Airy succeeders of intestate joys . . . *Richard III.* iv 4 128
Intestine. The mortal and intestine jars . . . . *Com. of Errors* i 1 11
In the intestine shock And furious close of civil butchery . 1 *Hen. IV.* i 1 12
Intil. And hath shipped me intil the land . . . . . *Hamlet* v 1 81
Intimate. Your father here doth intimate The payment of a hundred thousand crowns . . . . *L. L. Lost* ii 1 129
Thou this to hazard needs must intimate Skill infinite . *All's Well* ii 1 186
The spirit of humours intimate reading aloud to him! . . *T. Night* ii 5 94
Intimation. Most barbarous intimation! yet a kind of insinuation *L. L. L.* iv 2 13
Intitle. That which in mean men we intitle patience Is pale cold cowardice in noble breasts . . . . *Richard II.* i 2 33
Intitled. Neither intitled in the other's heart . . . . *L. L. Lost* v 2 822
Intituled, nominated, or called . . . . v 1 8
Into. Who having into truth, by telling of it, Made such a sinner of his memory, To credit his own lie . . . . *Tempest* i 2 100
Put not yourself into amazement how these things should be *M. for M.* iv 2 220
That puts the world into her person, and so gives me out . *Much Ado* ii 1 216
And with declining head into his bosom . . . *T. of Shrew* Ind. 1 119
I'll stay at home And pray God's blessing into thy attempt . *All's Well* i 3 260
For his sake Did I expose myself, pure for his love, Into the danger *T. N.* v 1 87
Is grown into an unspeakable estate . . . . . . *W. Tale* iv 2 46
Look back into your mighty ancestors . . . . . *Hen. V.* i 2 102
If I could win a lady at leap-frog, . . . I should quickly leap into a wife v 2 145
Cried out amain And rush'd into the bowels of the battle . 1 *Hen. VI.* i 1 129
Thus far into the bowels of the land Have we march'd on *Richard III.* v 2 3
How far into the morning is it, lords? . . . . v 3 234
A man into whom nature hath so crowded humours that his valour is crushed into folly . . . . *Troi. and Cres.* i 2 22
Every thing includes itself in power, Power into will, will into appetite i 3 120
And here, to do you service, am become As new into the world . iii 3 12
Pouring war Into the bowels of ungrateful Rome . . *Coriolanus* iv 5 136
How if, when I am laid into the tomb, I wake before the time? *R. and J.* iv 3 30
You would have me seek into myself For that which is not in me *J. C.* i 2 64
Intolerable. An intolerable fright . . . . . . *Mer. Wives* iii 5 110
Old, cold, withered and of intolerable entrails . . . . . v 5 161
She is intolerable curst And shrewd and froward . . . *T. of Shrew* i 2 89
O vile, Intolerable, not to be endured! . . . . v 2 94
But one half-pennyworth of bread to this intolerable deal of sack! 1 *Hen. IV.* ii 4 592
A married man! that's most intolerable . . . . . 1 *Hen. VI.* v 4 79
His insolence is more intolerable Than all the princes in the land beside 2 *Hen. VI.* i 1 175
His railing is intolerable . . . . iii 1 172
Despiteful and intolerable wrongs! Shall I endure this? *T. Andron.* iv 4 50
Intoxicate. Being a little intoxicates in his prains . . . *Hen. V.* iv 7 39
Intreasured. As yet not come to life, which in their seeds And weak beginnings lie intreasured . . . . 2 *Hen. IV.* iii 1 85
Intreat. He did intreat me, past all saying nay . *Mer. of Venice* iii 2 232
Intrenchant. Thou losest labour: As easy mayst thou the intrenchant air With thy keen sword impress . . . . . *Macbeth* v 8 9
Intrenched. The English, in the suburbs close intrench'd . 1 *Hen. VI.* i 4 9
Intricate. What an intricate impeach is this! . . . *Com. of Errors* v 1 269
Intrinse. Like rats, oft bite the holy cords a-twain Which are too intrinse t'unloose . . . . *Lear* ii 2 81
Intrinsicate. This knot intrinsicate Of life at once untie . *Ant. and Cleo.* v 2 307
Intrude. Thy years want wit, thy wit wants edge, And manners, to intrude where I am graced . . . . *T. Andron.* ii 1 27
Where's that palace whereinto foul things Sometimes intrude not? *Othello* iii 3 138
Intruder. Go, base intruder! . . . . *T. G. of Ver.* iii 1 157
Unmannerly intruder as thou art! . . . . . . *T. Andron.* ii 3 65
Intruding. Thou wretched, rash, intruding fool, farewell! . *Hamlet* iii 4 31
Intrusion. Emboldened me to this unseasoned intrusion . . *Mer. Wives* ii 2 174
Who, all for want of pruning, with intrusion Infect thy sap *Com. of Er.* ii 2 181
That may with foul intrusion enter in And dwell upon your grave . iii 1 103
This intrusion shall Now seeming sweet convert to bitter gall *R. and J.* i 5 93
Inundation. This inundation of mistemper'd humour . . *K. John* v 1 12
My heart hath melted at a lady's tears, Being an ordinary inundation . v 2 48
Hastes our marriage, To stop the inundation of her tears *Rom. and Jul.* iv 1 12
Inure thyself to what thou art like to be . . . . *T. Night* ii 5 160
Inurned. Why the sepulchre, Wherein we saw thee quietly inurn'd, Hath oped his ponderous and marble jaws . . . . . . *Hamlet* i 4 49
Invade. We must not only arm to invade the French, But lay down our proportions to defend Against the Scot . . . . . *Hen. V.* i 2 136
Let it fall rather, though the fork invade The region of my heart . *Lear* i 1 146
Thou think'st 'tis much that this contentious storm Invades us to the skin: so 'tis to thee . . . . iii 4 7
For this business, It toucheth us, as France invades our land . . v 1 25
Invasion. O, let me have no subject enemies, When adverse foreigners affright my towns With dreadful pomp of stout invasion! *K. John* iv 2 173
Invasive. Insinuation, parley and base truce To arms invasive . . v 1 69
Invective. So desperate thieves, all hopeless of their lives, Breathe out invectives 'gainst the officers . . . . . . 3 *Hen. VI.* i 4 43
Invectively. Thus most invectively he pierceth through The body of the country, city, court . . . . *As Y. Like It* ii 1 58
Inveigled. Achilles hath inveigled his fool from him . *Troi. and Cres.* ii 3 99
Invent. I say she never did invent this letter . . . *As Y. Like It* iv 3 28
Man is not able to invent any thing that tends to laughter, more than I invent or is invented on me . . . . 2 *Hen. IV.* i 2 9
I would invent as bitter-searching terms, As curst, as harsh . 2 *Hen. VI.* iii 2 311
I could well wish courtesy would invent some other custom of entertainment . . . . *Othello* ii 3 36
Invented. Man is not able to invent any thing that tends to laughter, more than I invent or is invented on me . . . . 2 *Hen. IV.* i 2 10

Invented. He lies, for I invented it myself . . . . . *2 Hen. VI.* iv 2 163
Invention. In her invention and Ford's wife's distraction, they conveyed me into a buck-basket . . . . *Mer. Wives* iii 5 86
Heaven hath my empty words; Whilst my invention, hearing not my tongue, Anchors on Isabel . . . . . . *Meas. for Meas.* ii 4 3
Nor age so eat up my invention . . . . . . *Much Ado* iv 1 196
Impose me to what penance your invention Can lay upon my sin . . v 1 283
If your love Can labour aught in sad invention, Hang her an epitaph . v 1 292
Smelling out the odoriferous flowers of fancy, the jerks of invention *L. L. Lost* iv 2 129
Very unlearned, neither savouring of poetry, wit, nor invention . iv 2 166
This note that I made yesterday in despite of my invention *As Y. Like It* ii 5 49
This is a man's invention and his hand . . . . iv 3 29
Women's gentle brain Could not drop forth such giant-rude invention . iv 3 34
Both our inventions meet and jump in one.—Tell me thine first *T. of S.* i 1 195
I am not so nice, To change true rules for old inventions . . . iii 1 81
Invention is ashamed, Against the proclamation of thy passion, To say thou dost not . . . . *All's Well* i 3 179
Return with an invention and clap upon you two or three probable lies iii 6 106
It must be a very plausive invention that carries it . . . . iv 1 29
No matter how witty, so it be eloquent and full of invention . *T. Night* iii 2 47
Write from it, if you can, in hand or phrase: Or say 'tis not your seal, not your invention . . . . v 1 341
Made the most notorious geck and gull That e'er invention play'd on . v 1 352
O for a Muse of fire, that would ascend The brightest heaven of invention, A kingdom for a stage! . . . . *Hen. V.* Prol. 2
Do it without invention, suddenly . . . . . . *1 Hen. VI.* iii 1 5
What if both Lewis and Warwick be appeased By such invention as I can devise? . . . . *3 Hen. VI.* iv 1 35
Let them accuse me by invention, I Will answer in mine honour *Coriol.* iii 2 143
Filling their hearers With strange invention . . . . *Macbeth* iii 1 33
If this letter speed, And my invention thrive . . . . . *Lear* i 2 20
My invention Comes from my pate as birdlime does from frize *Othello* ii 1 126
Of so high and plenteous wit and invention . . . . . . iv 1 201
Promise, And in our name, what she requires; add more, From thine invention, offers . . . . *Ant. and Cleo.* iii 12 29
Those palates who . . . Must have inventions to delight the taste *Pericles* i 4 40
Inventor. We but teach Bloody instructions, which, being taught, return To plague the inventor . . . . *Macbeth* i 7 10
In this upshot, purposes mistook Fall'n on the inventors' heads *Hamlet* v 2 396
Inventorially. I know, to divide him inventorially would dizzy the arithmetic of memory . . . . v 2 118
Inventoried. It shall be inventoried, and every particle and utensil labelled to my will . . . . *T. Night* i 5 264
Inventory. To bear the inventory of thy shirts, as, one for superfluity, and another for use . . . . *2 Hen. IV.* ii 2 20
An inventory, thus importing; The several parcels of his plate *Hen. VIII.* iii 2 124
And bear the inventory Of your best graces in your mind . . . iii 2 137
Take an inventory of all I have, To the last penny . . . . . iii 2 451
The leanness that afflicts us, the object of our misery, is as an inventory to particularize their abundance . . . . . . *Coriolanus* i 1 21
Some natural notes about her body, Above ten thousand meaner moveables Would testify, to enrich mine inventory . . . *Cymbeline* ii 2 30
Inverness. From hence to Inverness, And bind us further to you *Macbeth* i 4 42
Invert What best is boded me to mischief! . . . . . *Tempest* iii 1 70
That doth invert the attest of eyes and ears . . . *Troi. and Cres.* v 2 122
Invest. How, in stripping it, You more invest it! . . . *Tempest* ii 1 226
The damned'st body to invest and cover In prenzie guards! *M. for M.* iii 1 96
Invest me in my motley . . . . *As Y. Like It* ii 7 58
For this they have been thoughtful to invest Their sons with arts and martial exercises . . . . *2 Hen. IV.* iv 5 73
Dost thou so hunger for mine empty chair That thou wilt needs invest thee with my honours Before thy hour be ripe? . . . . . . iv 5 96
Which honour must Not unaccompanied invest him only . *Macbeth* i 4 40
I do invest you jointly with my power, Pre-eminence . . . *Lear* i 1 132
I tremble at it. Nature would not invest herself in such shadowing passion without some instruction . . . . *Othello* iv 1 40
Invested. Our substitutes in absence well invested . . *2 Hen. IV.* iv 4 6
That, in the official marks invested, you Anon do meet the senate *Coriol.* ii 3 148
He is already named, and gone to Scone To be invested . . *Macbeth* ii 4 32
In my rights, By me invested, he compeers the best . . . *Lear* v 3 69
Investing. Their gesture sad Investing lank-lean cheeks . *Hen. V.* iv Prol. 26
Investment. Whose white investments figure innocence . *2 Hen. IV.* iv 1 45
They are brokers, Not of that dye which their investments show *Hamlet* i 3 128
Inveterate. Being an enemy To me inveterate . . . . . *Tempest* i 2 122
And heal the inveterate canker of one wound By making many *K. John* v 2 14
On some apparent danger seen in him Aim'd at your highness, no inveterate malice . . . . *Richard II.* i 1 14
He did fashion After the inveterate hate he bears you . *Coriolanus* ii 3 234
Invincible against all assaults of affection . . . . *Much Ado* ii 3 120
His dimensions to any thick sight were invincible . . *2 Hen. IV.* iii 2 337
A breathing valiant man, Of an invincible unconquer'd spirit! *1 Hen. VI.* iv 2 32
I have heard her reported to be a woman of an invincible spirit *2 Hen. VI.* i 4 9
Precepts that would make invincible The heart that conn'd them *Coriol.* iv 1 10
Inviolable. And keep our faiths firm and inviolable . . . . *K. John* v 2 7
And seem to kiss, As if they vow'd some league inviolable . *3 Hen. VI.* ii 1 30
Invisible. Be subject To no sight but thine and mine, invisible To every eyeball else . . . . *Tempest* i 2 302
This was well done, my bird. Thy shape invisible retain thou still . iv 1 185
To the king's ship, invisible as thou art: There shalt thou find the mariners asleep . . . . v 1 97
Invisible, As a nose on a man's face, or a weathercock! . *T. G. of Ver.* ii 1 141
Witness you, That he is borne about invisible . . *Com. of Errors* v 1 187
Or hang my bugle in an invisible baldrick . . . . *Much Ado* i 1 244
As keen As is the razor's edge invisible . . . . *L. L. Lost* v 2 257
I am invisible; And I will overhear their conference . *M. N. Dream* ii 1 186
He is no crescent, and his horns are invisible within the circumference v 1 246
I would I were invisible, to catch the strong fellow by the leg *As Y. L. It* i 2 223
Then shall you know the wounds invisible That love's keen arrows make . . . . iii 5 30
Methinks I feel this youth's perfections With an invisible and subtle stealth To creep in at mine eyes . . . . *T. Night* i 5 316
I do not care for you: if that be to care for nothing, sir, I would it would make you invisible . . . . iii 1 35
Death, having prey'd upon the outward parts, Leaves them invisible *K. John* v 7 16
We have the receipt of fern-seed, we walk invisible.—Nay, by my faith, I think you are more beholding to the night than to fern-seed for your walking invisible . . . . *1 Hen. IV.* ii 1 96
Borne with the invisible and creeping wind . . . *Hen. V.* iii Prol. 11
Invisible. The mortal Venus, the heart-blood of beauty, love's invisible soul . . . . *Troi. and Cres.* iii 1 35
With thy bloody and invisible hand Cancel and tear to pieces that great bond Which keeps me pale! . . . . *Macbeth* iii 2 48
With divine ambition puff'd Makes mouths at the invisible event *Hamlet* iv 4 50
O thou invisible spirit of wine, if thou hast no name to be known by, let us call thee devil! . . . . *Othello* ii 3 283
From the barge A strange invisible perfume hits the sense *Ant. and Cleo.* ii 2 217
'Tis wonder That an invisible instinct should frame them To royalty unlearn'd, honour untaught . . . . *Cymbeline* iv 2 177
Invitation. She carves, she gives the leer of invitation . *Mer. Wives* i 3 50
Invite. I invite your highness and your train To my poor cell *Tempest* v 1 300
I do invite you to-morrow morning to my house to breakfast *Mer. Wives* iii 3 245
Some invite me; Some other give me thanks for kindnesses *Com. of Er.* iv 3 4
I do invite you too; you shall not say me nay . . *L. L. Lost* iv 2 170
Let your wedding be to-morrow: thither will I invite the duke *As Y. L. It* v 2 16
He'll woo a thousand, 'point the day of marriage, Make feasts, invite friends, and proclaim the banns . . . . . . *T. of Shrew* iii 2 16
The cunning of her passion Invites me in this churlish messenger *T. N.* ii 2 24
The lamentation of the French Invites the King of England's stay at home . . . . *Hen. V.* v Prol. 37
Invite my Lords of Salisbury and Warwick To sup with me . *2 Hen. VI.* i 4 83
Saw you not, even now, a blessed troop Invite me to a banquet? *Hen. VIII.* iv 2 88
Desire him To invite the Trojan lords after the combat . *Troi. and Cres.* iii 3 236
Desire the valiant Ajax to invite the most valorous Hector to come unarmed . . . . iii 3 275
Who most humbly desires you to invite Hector to his tent . . . iii 3 285
So many guests invite as here are writ . . . . *Rom. and Jul.* iv 2 1
Methinks they should invite them without knives . . *T. of Athens* i 2 45
No porter at his gate, But rather one that smiles and still invites All that pass by . . . . ii 1 11
Invite them all: let in the tide Of knaves once more; my cook and I'll provide . . . . iii 4 118
I have a tree . . . , That mine own use invites me to cut down . v 1 209
When Duncan is asleep—Whereto the rather shall his day's hard journey Soundly invite him . . . . *Macbeth* i 7 63
I go, and it is done; the bell invites me. Hear it not, Duncan . . ii 1 62
Thanks to all at once and to each one, Whom we invite to see us crown'd . . . . v 8 75
Most humbly do I take my leave, my lord.—The time invites you; go *Hamlet* i 3 83
I have some rights of memory in this kingdom, Which now to claim my vantage doth invite me . . . . v 2 401
And do invite you to my sister's view . . . . *Ant. and Cleo.* ii 2 170
Aboard my galley I invite you all . . . . ii 6 82
Invited. I am invited, sir, to certain merchants . . *Com. of Errors* i 2 24
It is two o'clock.—Perhaps some merchant hath invited him . . . ii 1 4
My dear friend Leonato hath invited you all . . . . *Much Ado* i 1 149
Rome, the nurse of judgement, Invited by your noble self, hath sent One general tongue unto us, this good man . . . *Hen. VIII.* ii 2 95
An old accustom'd feast, Whereto I have invited many a guest *R. and J.* i 2 21
Her father loved me; oft invited me; Still question'd me . . *Othello* i 3 128
Your dinner, and the generous islanders By you invited, do attend . iii 3 281
Upon her landing, Antony sent to her, Invited her to supper *A. and C.* ii 2 225
I am a maid, My lord, that ne'er before invited eyes . . *Pericles* v 1 86
Inviting. He hath sent me an earnest inviting . . . *T. of Athens* iii 6 11
An inviting eye; and yet methinks right modest . . . *Othello* ii 3 24
The time inviting thee . . . . *Cymbeline* iii 4 108
Invitis. Under the which is writ 'Invitis nubibus' . . *2 Hen. VI.* iv 1 99
Invocate. Henry the Fifth, thy ghost I invocate . . . *1 Hen. VI.* i 1 52
Be it lawful that I invocate thy ghost! . . . . . *Richard III.* i 2 8
Invocation. Sweet invocation of a child; most pretty! . . *L. L. Lost* i 2 102
'Tis a Greek invocation, to call fools into a circle . *As Y. Like It* ii 5 61
Which scorns a modern invocation . . . . . . *K. John* iii 4 42
My invocation Is fair and honest . . . . . *Rom. and Jul.* ii 1 27
Invoke his warlike spirit . . . . *Hen. V.* i 2 104
Invulnerable. My fellow-ministers Are like invulnerable . *Tempest* iii 3 66
Against the invulnerable clouds of heaven . . . . . *K. John* ii 1 252
It is, as the air, invulnerable, And our vain blows malicious mockery *Ham.* i 1 145
Inward. Whose inward pinches therefore are most strong . *Tempest* v 1 77
How angerly I taught my brow to frown, When inward joy enforced my heart to smile! . . . . *T. G. of Ver.* i 2 63
Sir, I was an inward of his. A shy fellow was the duke *Meas. for Meas.* iii 2 138
If either of you know any inward impediment . . . . *Much Ado* iv 1 12
For what is inward between us, let it pass . . . . *L. L. Lost* v 1 102
Who, inward search'd, have livers white as milk . *Mer. of Venice* iii 2 86
But from the inward motion to deliver Sweet, sweet, sweet poison *K. John* i 1 212
And the conjunction of our inward souls Married in league . . . iii 1 227
My inward soul With nothing trembles: at some thing it grieves *Rich. II.* ii 2 11
It may be so; but yet my inward soul Persuades me it is otherwise . ii 2 28
The sovereign'st thing on earth Was parmaceti for an inward bruise *1 Hen. IV.* i 3 58
He writes me here, that inward sickness—And that his friends by deputation could not So soon be drawn . . . . iv 1 31
And were these inward wars once out of hand, We would, dear lords, unto the Holy Land . . . . *2 Hen. IV.* iii 1 107
Sherris warms it and makes it course from the inwards to the parts extreme . . . . iv 3 115
Which my most inward true and duteous spirit Teacheth . . . iv 5 148
And all-admiring with an inward wish . . . . . . *Hen. V.* i 1 39
O England! model to thy inward greatness, Like little body with a mighty heart . . . . ii Prol. 16
Princes have but their titles for their glories, An outward honour for an inward toil . . . . *Richard III.* i 4 79
Who is most inward with the noble duke? . . . . iii 4 8
Hope of revenge shall hide our inward woe . . . *Troi. and Cres.* v 10 31
But, as this temple waxes, The inward service of the mind and soul Grows wide withal . . . . *Hamlet* i 3 13
Sith nor the exterior nor the inward man Resembles that it was . . ii 2 6
That inward breaks, and shows no cause without Why the man dies . iv 4 28
The thought whereof Doth, like a poisonous mineral, gnaw my inwards *Othello* ii 1 306
And things outward Do draw the inward quality after them, To suffer all alike . . . . *Ant. and Cleo.* iii 13 33
Wherefore breaks that sigh From the inward of thee? . . *Cymbeline* iii 4 6
Opinion's but a fool, that makes us scan The outward habit by the inward man . . . . *Pericles* ii 2 57
Inwardly. Like cover'd fire, Consume away in sighs, waste inwardly *Much Ado* iii 1 78

Inwardly. My heart bleeds inwardly that my father is so sick 2 *Hen. IV.* ii 2 51
I bleed inwardly for my lord . . . . . . *T. of Athens* i 2 211
Inwardness. Though you know my inwardness and love . . *Much Ado* iv 1 247
Io. We'll show thee Io as she was a maid . *T. of Shrew* Ind. 2 56
Ionia. Extended Asia from Euphrates; His conquering banner shook from Syria To Lydia and to Ionia . . . . *Ant. and Cleo.* i 2 107
Ionian. He could so quickly cut the Ionian sea, And take in Toryne . iii 7 23
Ipse. All your writers do consent that ipse is he: now, you are not ipse, for I am he . . . . *As Y. Like It* v 1 48
Ipswich. I'll to the king; And from a mouth of honour quite cry down This Ipswich fellow's insolence . . . . *Hen. VIII.* i 1 137
Ever witness for him Those twins of learning that he raised in you, Ipswich and Oxford! . . . . iv 2 59
'Ira furor brevis est;' but yond man is ever angry . . *T. of Athens* i 2 28
Iræ. Tantæne animis cœlestibus iræ? . . . . . . 2 *Hen. VI.* ii 1 24
Iras. Nay, come, tell Iras hers.—We'll know all our fortunes *Ant. and Cleo.* i 2 43
Lead me from hence; I faint: O Iras, Charmian! 'tis no matter . ii 5 110
Help, Charmian, help, Iras, help; Help, friends below . . . iv 15 12
Royal Egypt, Empress!—Peace, peace, Iras! . . . . . iv 15 71
Nay, 'tis most certain, Iras: saucy lictors Will catch at us, like strumpets . . . . v 2 214
Sirrah Iras, go. Now, noble Charmian, we'll dispatch indeed . . v 2 229
Yare, yare, good Iras; quick. Methinks I hear Antony call . . . v 2 286
Ire. Nor heady-rash, provoked with raging ire . *Com. of Errors* v 1 216
High-stomach'd are they both, and full of ire, In rage deaf . *Richard II.* i 1 18
Mad ire and wrathful fury makes me weep . . . 1 *Hen. VI.* iv 3 28
It could not slake mine ire, nor ease my heart . . 3 *Hen. VI.* i 3 29
Yet cease your ire, you angry stars of heaven! . . . *Pericles* ii 1 1
Ireful. Each one with ireful passion, with drawn swords *Com. of Errors* v 1 151
The ireful bastard Orleans, that drew blood From thee, my boy 1 *Hen. VI.* iv 6 16
Slaughter'd by the ireful arm Of unrelenting Clifford . 3 *Hen. VI.* ii 1 57
And bloody steel grasp'd in their ireful hands . . . . . ii 5 132
Ireland. In what part of her body stands Ireland? . *Com. of Errors* iii 2 119
Plantagenet lays most lawful claim To this fair island and the territories, To Ireland, Poictiers, Anjou, Touraine, Maine . *K. John* i 1 11
England and Ireland, Anjou, Touraine, Maine, In right of Arthur do I claim . . . . ii 1 152
Now for the rebels which stand out in Ireland . . . *Richard II.* i 4 38
To supply our wants; For we will make for Ireland presently . . i 4 52
To-morrow next We will for Ireland; and 'tis time, I trow . . ii 1 218
They stay The first departing of the king for Ireland . . . ii 1 290
I hope the king is not yet shipp'd for Ireland?—Why hopest thou so? . ii 2 42
Are there no posts dispatch'd for Ireland? How shall we do for money? ii 2 103
The wind sits fair for news to go to Ireland, But none returns . ii 2 123
Will you go along with us?—No; I will to Ireland to his majesty . . ii 2 141
And you rode, like a kern of Ireland, your French hose off . *Hen. V.* iii 7 56
From Ireland coming, Bringing rebellion broached on his sword . v Prol. 31
England is thine, Ireland is thine, France is thine, and Henry Plantagenet is thine . . . . v 2 258
Thy acts in Ireland, In bringing them to civil discipline . 2 *Hen. VI.* i 1 194
The realms of England, France and Ireland Bear that proportion to my flesh and blood As did the fatal brand Althæa burn'd . . . i 1 232
From Ireland am I come amain, To signify that rebels there are up . iii 1 282
The uncivil kerns of Ireland are in arms . . . . . . iii 1 310
To Ireland will you lead a band of men, Collected choicely? . . . iii 1 312
Whiles I in Ireland nourish a mighty band, I will stir up in England some black storm . . . . iii 1 348
In Ireland have I seen this stubborn Cade Oppose himself against a troop of kerns, And fought so long . . . . . . iii 1 360
Then from Ireland come I with my strength And reap the harvest . . iii 1 380
Be advertised The Duke of York is newly come from Ireland . . iv 9 24
From Ireland thus comes York to claim his right . . . . v 1 1
By the grace of God, king of England and France, and lord of Ireland 3 *Hen. VI.* iv 7 73
A bard of Ireland told me once, I should not live long *Richard III.* iv 2 109
The cardinal is the end of this.—'Tis likely, By all conjectures: first, Kildare's attainder, Then deputy of Ireland . . . *Hen. VIII.* ii 1 42
Plague of your policy! You sent me deputy for Ireland . . . iii 2 260
I'll to England.—To Ireland, I; our separated fortune Shall keep us both the safer . . . . *Macbeth* ii 3 144
We hear, our bloody cousins are bestow'd In England and in Ireland . iii 1 31
Iris. What's the matter, That this distemper'd messenger of wet, The many-colour'd Iris, rounds thine eye? . . . . *All's Well* i 3 158
For wheresoe'er thou art in this world's globe, I'll have an Iris that shall find thee out . . . . 2 *Hen. VI.* iii 2 407
Make him fall His crest that prouder than blue Iris bends *Troi. and Cres.* i 3 380
Irish. I was never so be-rhymed since Pythagoras' time, that I was an Irish rat, which I can hardly remember . . *As Y. Like It* iii 2 188
'Tis like the howling of Irish wolves against the moon . . . v 2 119
Shall make coats To deck our soldiers for these Irish wars . *Richard II.* i 4 62
Now for our Irish wars: We must supplant those rough rug-headed kerns . . . . ii 1 155
He hath not money for these Irish wars . . . . . . ii 1 259
When the unhappy king,—Whose wrongs in us God pardon!—did set forth Upon his Irish expedition . . . . 1 *Hen. IV.* i 3 150
I had rather hear Lady, my brach, howl in Irish . . . . iii 1 241
Left behind him here, When he was personal in the Irish war . . iv 3 88
The contrarious winds that held the king So long in his unlucky Irish wars . . . . v 1 53
Irishman. I will rather trust . . . an Irishman with my aqua-vitæ bottle *Mer. Wives* ii 2 318
An Irishman, a very valiant gentleman, i' faith . . *Hen. V.* iii 2 71
Try your hap against the Irishmen . . . . 2 *Hen. VI.* iii 1 314
Irk. And yet it irks me the poor dappled fools . . . *As Y. Like It* ii 1 22
It irks his heart he cannot be revenged . . . . 1 *Hen. VI.* i 4 105
To see this sight, it irks my very soul . . . . 3 *Hen. VI.* ii 2 6
Irksome. Thy company, which erst was irksome to me, I will endure *As Y. Like It* iii 5 95
I know she is an irksome brawling scold . . . *T. of Shrew* i 2 188
How irksome is this music to my heart! . . . . 2 *Hen. VI.* ii 1 56
Iron. Go get thee gone; fetch me an iron crow . . *Com. of Errors* iii 1 84
That is stronger made Which was before barr'd up with ribs of iron *Much Ado* iv 1 153
Runs not this speech like iron through your blood? . . . . v 1 252
But yet you draw not iron, for my heart Is true as steel *M. N. Dream* ii 1 196
The iron tongue of midnight hath told twelve: Lovers, to bed . . v 1 370
Iron may hold with her, but never lutes . . . *T. of Shrew* ii 1 147
For meddle you must, that's certain, or forswear to wear iron about you *T. Night* iii 4 276
Put up your iron: you are well fleshed . . . . iv 1 42
Iron. The cannons have their bowels full of wrath, And ready mounted are they to spit forth Their iron indignation 'gainst your walls *K. John* ii 1 212
The midnight bell Did, with his iron tongue and brazen mouth, Sound on iii 3 38
Heat me these irons hot; and look thou stand Within the arras . . iv 1 1
Must you with hot irons burn out both mine eyes?—Young boy, I must . . . . iv 1 39
I have sworn to do it; And with hot irons must I burn them out.—Ah, none but in this iron age would do it! . . . . iv 1 59
The iron of itself, though heat red-hot, Approaching near these eyes, would drink my tears . . . . iv 1 61
Are you more stubborn-hard than hammer'd iron? . . . . . . iv 1 67
Give me the iron, I say, and bind him here . . . . . . iv 1 75
I will not stir, nor wince, nor speak a word, Nor look upon the iron angerly . . . . iv 1 82
Only you do lack That mercy which fierce fire and iron extends . . iv 1 120
I did purpose, boy, With this same very iron to burn them out . . iv 1 125
I saw a smith stand with his hammer, thus, The whilst his iron did on the anvil cool, With open mouth . . . . iv 2 194
And grating shock of wrathful iron arms . . . . *Richard II.* i 3 136
And heard thee murmur tales of iron wars . . . . 1 *Hen. IV.* ii 3 51
Now bind my brows with iron; and approach The ragged'st hour that time and spite dare bring! . . . . 2 *Hen. IV.* i 1 150
Than now to see you here an iron man, Cheering a rout of rebels . iv 2 8
I dare not fight; but I will wink and hold out mine iron . *Hen. V.* ii 1 8
Give them great meals of beef and iron and steel, they will eat like wolves and fight like devils . . . . iii 7 161
Therefore was I created with a stubborn outside, with an aspect of iron v 2 245
Out of a great deal of old iron I chose forth . . 1 *Hen. VI.* i 2 101
Through a secret grate of iron bars In yonder tower to overpeer the city i 4 10
In iron walls they deem'd me not secure . . . . . . i 4 49
Girdled with a waist of iron And hemm'd about with grim destruction iv 3 20
I'll make thee eat iron like an ostrich, and swallow my sword 2 *Hen. VI.* iv 10 30
Iron of Naples hid with English gilt . . . . . 3 *Hen. VI.* ii 2 139
Strike now, or else the iron cools.—I had rather chop this hand off . v 1 49
Put in their hands thy bruising irons of wrath! . . . *Richard III.* v 3 110
Bear witness, all that have not hearts of iron . . . *Hen. VIII.* iii 2 424
It will not in circumvention deliver a fly from a spider, without drawing their massy irons and cutting the web . . *Troi. and Cres.* ii 3 18
As iron to adamant, as earth to the centre . . . . . . iii 2 186
Cushions, leaden spoons, Irons of a doit, doublets . . . *Coriolanus* i 5 7
Peace is nothing, but to rust iron, increase tailors, and breed ballad-makers . . . . iv 5 235
I will dry-beat you with an iron wit, and put up my iron dagger *R. and J.* iv 5 126
Get me an iron crow, and bring it straight Unto my cell . . . v 2 21
Give me that mattock and the wrenching iron. Hold, take this letter . v 3 22
The place which I have feasted, does it now, Like all mankind, show me an iron heart? . . . . *T. of Athens* iii 4 84
The felon Loaden with irons wiser than the judge, If wisdom be in suffering . . . . iii 5 50
Nor airless dungeon, nor strong links of iron, Can be retentive to the strength of spirit . . . . *J. Cæsar* i 3 94
Mine armour, Eros! Come, good fellow, put mine iron on *Ant. and Cleo.* iv 4 3
Never bestrid a horse, save one that had A rider like myself, who ne'er wore rowel Nor iron on his heel! . . . . . . *Cymbeline* iv 4 40
Iron-witted. I will converse with iron-witted fools . . *Richard III.* iv 2 28
Irreconciled. And die in many irreconciled iniquities . . *Hen. V.* iv 1 160
Irrecoverable. The fiend hath pricked down Bardolph irrecoverable 2 *Hen. IV.* ii 4 360
Irregular. Leaving our rankness and irregular course . . *K. John* v 4 54
To fight Against the irregular and wild Glendower . . 1 *Hen. IV.* i 1 40
Wherein my youth Hath faulty wander'd and irregular . . . iii 2 27
Irregulous. Conspired with that irregulous devil, Cloten . *Cymbeline* iv 2 315
Irreligious. Since therein she doth evitate and shun A thousand irreligious cursed hours . . . . *Mer. Wives* v 5 242
O cruel, irreligious piety! . . . . *T. Andron.* i 1 130
The issue of an irreligious Moor . . . . v 3 121
Irremoveable. He's irremoveable, Resolved for flight . . *W. Tale* iv 4 518
Irreparable is the loss, and patience Says it is past her cure . *Tempest* v 1 140
Irresolute. He would outgo His father by as much as a performance Does an irresolute purpose . . . . *Hen. VIII.* i 2 209
Irrevocable. Firm and irrevocable is my doom . . . . *As Y. Like It* i 3 85
No more, I say: . . . Had I but said, I would have kept my word, But when I swear, it is irrevocable . . . . . 2 *Hen. VI.* iii 2 294
Give thy hand . . . ; And, with thy hand, thy faith irrevocable 3 *Hen. VI.* iii 3 247
Is. There's but five upon this isle: we are three of them . . *Tempest* iii 2 6
Divers philosophers hold that the lips is parcel of the mouth *Mer. Wives* i 1 237
There's many have committed it . . . . . . *Meas. for Meas.* ii 2 89
There's other of our friends Will greet us here anon . . . . iv 5 12
'Tis dinner-time,' quoth I; 'My gold!' quoth he . . *Com. of Errors* ii 1 62
There's many a man hath more hair than wit . . . . . . ii 2 83
There's none but witches do inhabit here . . . . . . ii 2 161
My way is now to hie home to his house, And tell his wife . . iv 3 93
If Hero would be my wife.—Is't come to this? . . . . *Much Ado* i 1 199
There's a double tongue; there's two tongues . . . . . v 1 170
And so to study, three years is but short . . . . *L. L. Lost* i 1 181
Ask them how many inches Is in one mile . . . . . . v 2 189
There is five in the first show.—You are deceived; 'tis not so . v 2 543
But there is two hard things . . . . . . *M. N. Dream* iii 1 48
There is two or three lords and ladies more married . . . iv 2 16
Is your gold and silver ewes and rams? . . . . *Mer. of Venice* i 3 96
If Fortune be a woman, she's a good wench for this gear . . ii 2 175
For thy three thousand ducats here is six . . . . . . iv 1 84
And yet it is not that I bear thee love . . . . *As Y. Like It* iii 5 93
Abandon,—which is in the vulgar leave,—the society,—which in the boorish is company,—of this female,—which in the common is woman; which together is, abandon the society of this female . . v 1 52
Here's eight that must take hands To join in Hymen's bands . . v 4 134
This gentleman is happily arrived . . . . . . *T. of Shrew* i 2 213
It is not so with Him that all things knows As 'tis with us . *All's Well* ii 1 152
What the import is, I know not yet . . . . ii 3 294
Towards Florence is he?—Ay, madam . . . . iii 2 71
There's four or five, to great Saint Jaques bound . . . . iii 5 98
When his disguise and he is parted . . . . iii 6 113
Yet his brother is reputed one of the best that is . . . . iv 3 322
All that he is hath reference to your highness . . . . . v 3 29
There is no woman's sides Can bide the beating of so strong a passion *T. Night* ii 4 96
I'll no more with thee. Hold, there's expenses for thee . . . iii 1 49
He does smile his face into more lines than is in the new map . . iii 2 84
Jove, not I, is the doer of this, and he is to be thanked . . . iii 4 92

Is. 'That that is is;' so I, being master Parson, am master Parson; for, what is 'that' but 'that,' and 'is' but 'is'? . . . *T. Night* iv 2 17
Is whispering nothing? Is leaning cheek to cheek? is meeting noses? *W. Tale* i 2 285
Is this nothing? Why, then the world and all that's in't is nothing; The covering sky is nothing; Bohemia nothing; My wife is nothing; nor nothing have these nothings, If this be nothing . . . i 2 292
Here's flowers for you; Hot lavender, mints, savory, marjoram . . . iv 4 103
There is three carters, three shepherds, three neat-herds . . . iv 4 331
Be pitiful and hurt me not! There's few or none do know me *K. John* iv 3 3
What is six winters? they are quickly gone . . . *Richard II.* i 3 260
Eight yards of uneven ground is threescore and ten miles afoot with me *1 Hen. IV.* ii 2 27
Is there not wars? is there not employment? . . . *2 Hen. IV.* i 2 85
He is not the man that he would gladly make show to the world he is *Hen. V.* iii 6 87
There's five to one; besides, they all are fresh . . . iv 3 4
Now where's the Bastard's braves, and Charles his gleeks? *1 Hen. VI.* iii 2 123
Is he a lamb? his skin is surely lent him . . . *2 Hen. VI.* iii 1 77
There's two of you; the devil make a third! . . . iii 2 303
When is the royal day?—Are all things fitting for that royal time?—It is, and wants but nomination . . . *Richard III.* iii 4 3
That he is, For so I know he is, they know he is . . . *Hen. VIII.* v 1 43
There is a thousand Hectors in the field . . . *Troi. and Cres.* v 5 19
Which, without note, here's many else have done . . . *Coriolanus* i 9 49
In troth, there's wondrous things spoke of him . . . ii 1 152
You Anon do meet the senate.—Is this done? . . . ii 3 149
'Tis there, That, like an eagle in a dove-cote, I Flutter'd your Volscians v 6 114
From nine till twelve Is three long hours . . . *Rom. and Jul.* ii 5 11
O thou untaught! what manners is in this? . . . v 3 214
Three parts of him Is ours already . . . *J. Cæsar* i 3 155
There is tears for his love; joy for his fortune . . . iii 2 29
Publius shall not live, Who is your sister's son . . . iv 1 5
Thine evermore, most dear lady, whilst this machine is to him *Hamlet* ii 2 124
That's a fair thought . . . —What is, my lord?—Nothing . . . iii 2 125
'Tis so concluded on.—There's letters seal'd . . . iii 4 201
If it be not now, yet it will come: the readiness is all . . . v 2 234
I would not take this from report; it is, And my heart breaks at it *Lear* iv 6 144
Our sister's man is certainly miscarried.—'Tis to be doubted . . . v 1 5
I have not seen the most precious diamond that is . . . *Cymbeline* i 4 81
As I said, there is no moe such Cæsars . . . iii 1 36
Alas! There is no more such masters . . . iv 2 371
Is arrived. Cardinal Campeius is arrived, and lately . . . *Hen. VIII.* ii 1 160
Is become. I dare say my cousin William is become a good scholar *2 Hen. IV.* iii 2 11
Is befallen. What late misfortune is befall'n King Edward? *3 Hen. VI.* iv 4 3
Is chanced. Bring us word . . . How every thing is chanced *J. Cæsar* v 4 32
Is crept. The deep of night is crept upon our talk . . . iv 3 226
Is entered. He is enter'd His radiant roof . . . *Cymbeline* v 4 120
Is fallen. His highness is fallen into this same whoreson apoplexy *2 Hen. IV.* i 2 122
Is it. How is't with you, sir? how is't with you, man? . . . *T. Night* iii 4 97
Flower of warriors, How is't with Titus Lartius? . . . *Coriolanus* i 6 33
How is it with our general? . . . v 6 10
Spakest thou of Juliet? how is it with her? . . . *Rom. and Jul.* iii 3 93
How is't with you, my lord?—Well, my good lady . . . *Othello* iii 4 33
Is like. Why, then, it is like, if there come a hot June . . . *1 Hen. IV.* ii 4 396
Is living. Douglas is living, and your brother, yet . . . *2 Hen. IV.* i 1 82
Is rode. The king himself is rode to view their battle . . . *Hen. V.* iv 3 2
Is run. There shall I end; My life is run his compass . . . *J. Cæsar* v 3 25
Is set. The king by this is set him down to sleep . . . *3 Hen. VI.* iv 3 2
Is walked. His lordship is walk'd forth into the orchard *2 Hen. IV.* i 1 4
Isabel. I would to heaven I had your potency, And you were Isabel! *Meas. for Meas.* ii 2 68
Heaven hath my empty words; Whilst my invention, hearing not my tongue, Anchors on Isabel . . . ii 4 4
How now! who's there?—One Isabel, a sister, desires access to you . ii 4 18
That he shall die for it.—He shall not, Isabel, if you give me love . ii 4 144
I'll tell the world aloud What man thou art.—Who will believe thee, Isabel? . . . ii 4 154
Then, Isabel, live chaste, and, brother, die . . . ii 4 184
O, were it but my life, I'ld throw it down for your deliverance As frankly as a pin.—Thanks, dear Isabel . . . iii 1 106
O Isabel!—What says my brother?—Death is a fearful thing . . . iii 1 115
Nay, hear me, Isabel.—O, fie, fie, fie! Thy sin's not accidental . iii 1 148
Who call'd here of late?—None, since the curfew rung.—Not Isabel? iv 2 79
Peace, ho, be here!—The tongue of Isabel . . . iv 3 111
He hath released him, Isabel, from the world . . . iv 3 119
Unhappy Claudio! wretched Isabel! Injurious world! most damned Angelo! . . . iv 3 126
By my troth, Isabel, I loved thy brother . . . iv 3 163
Who thinks he knows that he ne'er knew my body, But knows he thinks that he knows Isabel's . . . v 1 204
This is the body That took away the match from Isabel . . . v 1 211
Call that same Isabel here once again: I would speak with her . v 1 270
Come hither, Isabel. Your friar is now your prince . . . v 1 386
You are pardon'd, Isabel: And now, dear maid, be you as free to us . v 1 392
O my good lord! Sweet Isabel, take my part; Lend me your knees . v 1 435
Isabel, Sweet Isabel, do yet but kneel by me . . . v 1 441
O Isabel, will you not lend a knee?—He dies for Claudio's death . v 1 447
Dear Isabel, I have a motion much imports your good . . . v 1 540
Fair Queen Isabel, his grandmother, Was lineal of the Lady Ermengare *Hen. V.* i 2 81
Isabella. Gentle Isabella, Turn you the key . . . *Meas. for Meas.* i 4 7
Can you so stead me As bring me to the sight of Isabella? . . . i 4 18
I am that Isabella and his sister . . . i 4 23
'Tis best that thou diest quickly.—O hear me, Isabella! . . . iii 1 151
O pretty Isabella, I am pale at mine heart to see thine eyes so red . iv 3 157
Isbel. If I may have your ladyship's good will to go to the world, Isbel the woman and I will do as we may . . . *All's Well* i 3 20
I do beg your good will in this case.—In what case?—In Isbel's case and mine . . . i 3 25
I have no mind to Isbel since I was at court: our old ling and our Isbels o' the country are nothing like your old ling and your Isbels o' the court . . . iii 2 13
Iscariot. A Judas!—Not Iscariot, sir. . . . *L. L. Lost* v 2 601
Isidore. To Varro and to Isidore He owes nine thousand . . . *T. of Athens* ii 1 1
Is't not your business too?—It is: and yours too, Isidore? . . . ii 2 11
From Isidore; He humbly prays your speedy payment . . . ii 2 27
Isis. O, let him marry a woman that cannot go, sweet Isis *Ant. and Cleo.* i 2 66
Isis. Good Isis, hear me this prayer, though thou deny me a matter of more weight; good Isis, I beseech thee! . . . *Ant. and Cleo.* i 2 70
Therefore, dear Isis, keep decorum, and fortune him accordingly! . i 2 77
By Isis, I will give thee bloody teeth, If thou with Cæsar paragon again i 5 70
He cannot like her long.—Like her! O Isis! 'tis impossible . . . iii 3 18
Hath he seen majesty? Isis else defend, And serving you so long! . iii 3 46
She In the habiliments of the goddess Isis That day appear'd . . . iii 6 17
Island. Sit still, and hear the last of our sea-sorrow. Here in this island we arrived . . . *Tempest* i 2 171
Then was this island . . . not honour'd with A human shape . . . i 2 281
This island's mine, by Sycorax my mother, Which thou takest from me i 2 331
And here you sty me In this hard rock, whiles you do keep from me The rest o' the island . . . i 2 344
It sounds no more; and, sure, it waits upon Some god o' the island . i 2 389
Vouchsafe my prayer May know if you remain upon this island . . . i 2 423
And hast put thyself Upon this island as a spy . . . i 2 455
Though this island seem to be desert,— . . . Uninhabitable and almost inaccessible . . . ii 1 35
He will carry this island home in his pocket and give it his son for an apple.—And, sowing the kernels of it in the sea, bring forth more islands . . . ii 1 90
Heavens keep him from these beasts! For he is, sure, i' the island . ii 1 325
I'll show thee every fertile inch o' th' island; And I will kiss thy foot . ii 2 152
Servant-monster! the folly of this island! . . . iii 2 5
A sorcerer, that by his cunning hath cheated me of the island . . . iii 2 50
For, certes, these are people of the island . . . iii 3 30
On this island Where man doth not inhabit . . . iii 3 56
Do that good mischief which may make this island Thine own for ever iv 1 217
If this prove A vision of the Island, one dear son Shall I twice lose v 1 176
Let me not . . . dwell In this bare island by your spell . . . Epil. 8
Some to discover islands far away . . . *T. G. of Ver.* i 3 9
Arthur Plantagenet lays most lawful claim To this fair island *K. John* i 1 10
That island of England breeds very valiant creatures . . . *Hen. V.* iii 7 150
And if my death might make this island happy And prove the period of their tyranny, I would expend it with all willingness *2 Hen. VI.* iii 1 148
If thou be'st death, I'll give thee England's treasure, Enough to purchase such another island, So thou wilt let me live . . . iii 3 3
Like to his island girt in with the ocean . . . *3 Hen. VI.* iv 8 20
I fear the trust Othello puts him in, On some odd time of his infirmity, Will shake this island . . . *Othello* ii 3 133
It were an honest action to say So to the Moor.—Not I, for this fair island . . . ii 3 147
Realms and islands were As plates dropp'd from his pocket *Ant. and Cleo.* v 2 91
Upon The leafy shelter that abuts against The island's side . *Pericles* v 1 52
Islander. This is no fish, but an islander . . . *Tempest* ii 2 37
Would they believe me? If I should say, I saw such islanders . . . iii 3 29
That white-faced shore, Whose foot spurns back the ocean's roaring tides And coops from other lands her islanders . . . *K. John* ii 1 25
Have I not heard these islanders shout out 'Vive le roi!'? . . . v 2 103
Savage islanders [killed] Pompey the Great . . . *2 Hen. VI.* iv 1 137
Your dinner, and the generous islanders By you invited, do attend *Oth.* iii 3 280
Island carrions. Yon island carrions, desperate of their bones *Hen. V.* iv 2 39
Island kings. You shall do more Than all the island kings,—disarm great Hector . . . *Troi. and Cres.* iii 1 167
Isle. In troops I have dispersed them 'bout the isle . . . *Tempest* i 2 220
Whom I left cooling of the air with sighs In an odd angle of the isle . i 2 223
And show'd thee all the qualities o' the isle, The fresh springs, brine-pits i 2 337
I had peopled else This isle with Calibans.—Abhorred slave! . . . i 2 351
Had I plantation of this isle, my lord,— He'ld sow't with nettle-seed ii 1 143
This is some monster of the isle with four legs . . . ii 2 67
They say there's but five upon this isle: we are three of them . . . iii 2 6
I say, by sorcery he got this isle; From me he got it . . . iii 2 60
The isle is full of noises, Sounds and sweet airs, that give delight . iii 2 144
Whose wraths to guard you from—Which here, in this most desolate isle, else falls Upon your heads—is nothing but heart-sorrow . . . iii 3 80
You do yet taste Some subtilties o' the isle . . . v 1 124
Prospero [found] his dukedom In a poor isle . . . v 1 212
You'ld be king o' the isle, sirrah?—I should have been a sore one then . v 1 287
And the particular accidents gone by Since I came to this isle . . . v 1 306
The climate's delicate, the air most sweet, Fertile the isle *W. Tale* iii 1 2
That blood which owed the breadth of all this isle, Three foot of it doth hold: bad world the while! . . . *K. John* iv 2 99
That we, the sons and children of this isle, Were born to see so sad an hour as this . . . v 2 25
This scepter'd isle, This earth of majesty, this seat of Mars *Richard II.* ii 1 40
A slobbery and a dirty farm In that nook-shotten isle of Albion *Hen V.* iii 5 14
Our isle be made a nourish of salt tears . . . *1 Hen. VI.* i 1 50
May he be suffocate, That dims the honour of this warlike isle! *2 Hen. VI.* i 1 125
Kent, in the Commentaries Cæsar writ, Is term'd the civil'st place of all this isle: Sweet is the country . . . iv 7 66
For the instalment of this noble duke In the seat royal of this famous isle . . . *Richard III.* iii 1 164
Which pleaseth God above, And all good men of this ungovern'd isle . iii 7 110
This noble isle doth want her proper limbs . . . iii 7 125
This foul swine Lies now even in the centre of this isle . . . v 2 11
But from this lady may proceed a gem To lighten all this isle *Hen. VIII.* ii 3 79
From isles of Greece The princes orgulous, their high blood chafed, Have to the port of Athens sent their ships *Troi. and Cres.* Prol. 1
From the western isles Of kerns and gallowglasses is supplied *Macbeth* i 2 12
Thanks, you the valiant of this warlike isle . . . *Othello* ii 1 43
How does my old acquaintance of this isle? . . . ii 1 205
The very elements of this warlike isle Have I to-night fluster'd . . . ii 3 59
Am I to put our Cassio in some action That may offend the isle . . . ii 3 63
Silence that dreadful bell: it frights the isle From her propriety . . . ii 3 175
And that, having in Sicily Sextus Pompeius spoil'd, we had not rated him His part o' the isle . . . *Ant. and Cleo.* iii 6 26
Remember, sir, my liege, The kings your ancestors, together with The natural bravery of your isle . . . *Cymbeline* iii 1 18
Isle of Cyprus. Heaven bless the isle of Cyprus! . . . *Othello* ii 2 12
Isle of Man. With Sir John Stanley, in the Isle of Man . . . *2 Hen. VI.* ii 3 13
Stanley is appointed now To take her with him to the Isle of Man . ii 4 78
Only convey me where thou art commanded.—Why, madam, that is to the Isle of Man . . . ii 4 94
Isle of Rhodes. Steering with due course towards the isle of Rhodes *Oth.* i 3 34
Israel. O Jephthah, judge of Israel, what a treasure hadst thou! *Hamlet* ii 2 422
Issue. As I hope For quiet days, fair issue and long life . . . *Tempest* iv 1 24
Bless this twain, that they may prosperous be And honour'd in their issue . . . iv 1 105
Was Milan thrust from Milan, that his issue Should become kings of Naples? . . . v 1 205

Issue. Let burnt sack be the issue *Mer. Wives* iii 1 112
Nay, follow him, gentlemen; see the issue of his search iii 3 186
Ford's brothers watch the door with pistols, that none shall issue out iv 2 54
Follow; see but the issue of my jealousy iv 2 207
Spirits are not finely touch'd But to fine issues *Meas. for Meas.* i 1 37
Thou exist'st on many a thousand grains That issue out of dust iii 1 21
Look you for any other issue? *Much Ado* ii 2 30
Grow this to what adverse issue it can, I will put it in practice ii 2 52
Bear it coldly but till midnight, and let the issue show itself iii 2 133
Why had I not with charitable hand Took up a beggar's issue at my gates? iv 1 134
And Hymen now with luckier issue speed's v 3 32
And the issue there create Ever shall be fortunate *M. N. Dream* v 1 412
And the blots of Nature's hand Shall not in their issue stand v 1 417
Under this excuse, That she is issue to a faithless Jew *Mer. of Venice* ii 4 38
Dardanian wives, With bleared visages, come forth to view The issue iii 2 60
I shall never have the blessing of God till I have issue o' my body *All's W.* i 3 27
Which, as the dearest issue of his practice, And of his old experience the only darling, He bade me store up ii 1 109
That gem, Conferr'd by testament to the sequent issue v 3 197
Whose issue Will hiss me to my grave *W. Tale* i 2 188
If ever fearful To do a thing, where I the issue doubted i 2 259
I had rather glib myself than they Should not produce fair issue ii 1 150
Your free undertaking cannot miss A thriving issue ii 2 45
This brat is none of mine; It is the issue of Polixenes ii 3 93
Which being so horrible, so bloody, must Lead on to some foul issue ii 3 153
No, I'll not rear Another's issue ii 3 193
Go: fresh horses! And gracious be the issue! iii 1 22
This being indeed the issue Of King Polixenes, it should here be laid iii 3 43
Kings are no less unhappy, their issue not being gracious iv 2 30
What dangers, by his highness' fail of issue, May drop upon his kingdom v 1 27
Care not for issue; The crown will find an heir v 1 46
I would most gladly know the issue of it v 2 9
Knowing . . . that the oracle Gave hope thou wast in being, have preserved Myself to see the issue v 3 128
Two kingdoms must With fearful bloody issue arbitrate *K. John* i 1 38
Thou art the issue of my dear offence, Which was so strongly urged ii 1 257
But God hath made her sin and her the plague On this removed issue ii 1 186
Lo, now! now see the issue of your peace.—Patience, good lady! iii 4 21
His passion is so ripe, it needs must break.—And when it breaks, I fear will issue thence The foul corruption of a sweet child's death iv 2 80
It issues from the rancour of a villain *Richard II.* i 1 143
To defend my loyalty and truth To God, my king and my succeeding issue i 3 20
Well, well, I see the issue of these arms: I cannot mend it ii 3 152
Uncertain of the issue any way *1 Hen. IV.* i 1 61
What cunning match have you made with this jest of the drawer? come, what's the issue? ii 4 103
Here come the heavy issue of dead Harry *2 Hen. IV.* v 2 14
I did never know so full a voice issue from so empty a heart *Hen. V.* iv 4 72
I must perforce compound With mistful eyes, or they will issue too iv 6 34
So happy be the issue, brother England, Of this good day v 2 12
Take her, fair son, and from her blood raise up Issue to me v 2 377
Thou seest that I no issue have *1 Hen. VI.* ii 5 94
We are well fortified And strong enough to issue out and fight iv 2 20
Her valiant courage and undaunted spirit, More than in women commonly is seen, Will answer our hope in issue of a king v 5 72
Duke of Clarence, from whose line I claim the crown, had issue *2 Hen. VI.* ii 2 35
Edmund had issue, Roger Earl of March; Roger had issue, Edmund, Anne and Eleanor ii 2 37
So, if the issue of the elder son Succeed before the younger, I am king ii 2 51
Till Lionel's issue fails, his should not reign: It fails not yet ii 2 56
Set our men in order, And issue forth and bid them battle *3 Hen. VI.* i 2 71
I stain'd this napkin with the blood That valiant Clifford, with his rapier's point, Made issue from the bosom of the boy i 4 81
He, but a duke, would have his son a king, And raise his issue ii 2 22
Is Clarence, Henry, and his son young Edward, And all the unlook'd for issue of their bodies, To take their rooms, ere I can place myself iii 2 131
Stand we in good array; for they no doubt Will issue out again v 1 63
A wizard told him that by G His issue disinherited should be *Rich. III.* i 1 57
Thou loathed issue of thy father's loins! Thou rag of honour! i 3 232
By just computation of the time, Found that the issue was not his begot iii 5 90
No doubt we'll bring it to a happy issue iii 7 54
This carnal cur Preys on the issue of his mother's body iv 4 57
If I have kill'd the issue of your womb, To quicken your increase, I will beget Mine issue of your blood upon your daughter iv 4 296
King Henry's issue, Richmond, comforts thee v 3 123
But minister communication of A most poor issue *Hen. VIII.* i 1 87
Things done without example, in their issue Are to be fear'd i 2 90
That if the king Should without issue die, he'll carry it so To make the sceptre his i 2 134
For her male issue Or died where they were made, or shortly after ii 4 191
I weigh'd the danger which my realms stood in By this my issue's fail ii 4 198
Our issues, Who, if he live, will scarce be gentlemen iii 2 291
And now, While it is hot, I'll put it to the issue v 1 176
It is supposed He that meets Hector issues from our choice *Tr. and Cr.* i 3 347
Why do you now The issue of your proper wisdoms rate? ii 2 89
But I'll see some issue of my spiteful execrations ii 3 7
Stop my mouth.—And shall, albeit sweet music issues thence iii 2 142
The issue is embracement iv 5 148
But had he died . . . ?—Then his good report should have been my son; I therein would have found issue *Coriolanus* i 3 23
They fear us not, but issue forth their city i 4 23
If all our wits were to issue out of one skull, they would fly east, west ii 3 23
Shall grow dear friends And interjoin their issues iv 4 22
A joyful issue.—A joyless, dismal, black, and sorrowful issue *T. Andron.* iv 2 65
Of this was Tamora delivered; The issue of an irreligious Moor v 3 121
Which the commission of thy years and art Could to no issue of true honour bring *Rom. and Jul.* iv 1 65
Away, thou issue of a mangy dog! *T. of Athens* iv 3 371
There shall I try, In my oration, how the people take The cruel issue of these bloody men *J. Cæsar* iii 1 294
Bequeathing it as a rich legacy Unto their issue iii 2 142
For Banquo's issue have I filed my mind *Macbeth* iii 1 65
Are you so gospell'd To pray for this good man and for his issue? iii 1 88
What is this That rises like the issue of a king? iv 1 87
Shall Banquo's issue ever Reign in this kingdom? iv 1 102
The truest issue of thy throne By his own interdiction stands accursed iv 3 106
But certain issue strokes must arbitrate v 4 20
Have after. To what issue will this come? *Hamlet* i 4 89

Issue. It must be shortly known to him from England What is the issue of the business there *Hamlet* v 2 72
I cannot wish the fault undone, the issue of it being so proper *Lear* i 1 18
My mind as generous, and my shape as true, As honest Madam's issue i 2 9
My good intent May carry through itself to that full issue i 4 3
One self mate and mate could not beget Such different issues iv 3 37
Wilt thou be fast to my hopes, if I depend on the issue? *Othello* i 3 370
I think the issue will be, I shall have so much experience for my pains ii 3 372
I am to pray you not to strain my speech To grosser issues nor to larger reach Than to suspicion iii 3 219
'Gainst Cæsar; Whose better issue in the war, from Italy, Upon the first encounter, drave them *Ant. and Cleo.* i 2 97
And all the unlawful issue that their lust Since then hath made iii 6 7
For which their father, Then old and fond of issue, took such sorrow That he quit being *Cymbeline* i 1 37
You are a fool granted; therefore your issues, being foolish, do not derogate ii 1 51
They are the issue of your loins, my liege, And blood of your begetting.—How! my issue!—So sure as you your father's v 5 330
Whose issue Promises Britain peace and plenty v 5 457
From whence an issue I might propagate, Are arms to princes *Pericles* i 2 73
Issued. Thou his only heir And princess no worse issued *Tempest* i 2 59
Such a warped slip of wilderness Ne'er issued from his blood *M. for M.* iii 1 143
More contrite tears Than from it issued forced drops of blood *Hen. V.* iv 1 314
Issued from the progeny of kings *1 Hen. VI.* v 4 38
When scarce the blood was well wash'd from his hands Which issued from my other angel husband *Richard III.* iv 1 69
Thy news?—The citizens of Corioli have issued *Coriolanus* i 6 10
Issueless. I have done sin: For which the heavens, taking angry note, Have left me issueless *W. Tale* v 1 174
Issuing. Every word in it a gaping wound, Issuing life-blood *Mer. of Ven.* iii 2 269
And with the issuing blood Stifle the villain *3 Hen. VI.* ii 6 82
This loss of blood, As from a conduit with three issuing spouts *T. An.* ii 4 30
With purple fountains issuing from your veins *Rom. and Jul.* i 1 92
It. But nature should bring forth, Of it own kind, all foison *Tempest* ii 1 163
She needs not, when she knows it cowardice *T. G. of Ver.* v 2 21
Or else what lets it but he would be here? *Com. of Errors* ii 1 105
I take it, your own business calls on you *Mer. of Venice* i 1 63
It is a good divine that follows his own instructions i 2 15
It is the most impenetrable cur That ever kept with men iii 3 18
You are too blunt: go to it orderly *T. of Shrew* ii 1 45
Shall sweet Bianca practise how to bride it? iii 2 253
That's it that always makes a good voyage of nothing *T. Night* ii 4 80
For the rain it raineth every day v 1 401; *Lear* iii 2 77
Leave it, Without more mercy, to it own protection *W. Tale* ii 3 178
The innocent milk in it most innocent mouth, Haled out to murder iii 2 101
Which the wenches say is a gallimaufry of gambols, because they are not in't iv 4 336
I'll queen it no inch farther, But milk my ewes and weep iv 4 460
Go to it grandam, child; Give grandam kingdom, and it grandam will Give it a plum, a cherry, and a fig *K. John* ii 1 160
It holds current that I told you yesternight *1 Hen. IV.* ii 1 58
It hath it original from much grief, from study *2 Hen. IV.* i 2 131
Grow till you come unto it: I will none of you iii 2 270
Her husbandry doth lie on heaps, Corrupting in it own fertility *Hen. V.* v 2 40
Would he not, a naughty man, let it sleep? *Troi. and Cres.* iv 2 34
Custom calls me to't: What custom wills, in all things should we do't *Coriolanus* ii 3 124
There was it: For which my sinews shall be stretch'd upon him v 6 44
Lucius and I'll go brave it at the court *T. Andron.* iv 1 121
I warrant, it had upon it brow A bump *Rom. and Jul.* i 3 52
Feeling in itself A lack of Timon's aid, hath sense withal Of it own fail, restraining aid to Timon *T. of Athens* v 1 151
It will be rain to-night.—Let it come down *Macbeth* iii 3 16
Yet once methought It lifted up it head and did address Itself to motion, like as it would speak *Hamlet* i 2 216
The corse they follow did with desperate hand Fordo it own life v 1 244
So Guildenstern and Rosencrantz go to't v 2 56
You know, nuncle, The hedge-sparrow fed the cuckoo so long, That it had it head bit off by it young *Lear* i 4 236
I cannot daub it further iv 1 54
That nature, which contemns it origin, Cannot be border'd certain in itself iv 2 32
If it were now to die, 'Twere now to be most happy *Othello* ii 1 191
Sir, you and I must part, but that's not it: Sir, you and I have loved, but there's not it *Ant. and Cleo.* i 3 87
What manner o' thing is your crocodile?—It is shaped, sir, like itself; and it is as broad as it hath breadth: it is just so high as it is, and moves with it own organs: it lives by that which nourisheth it; and the elements once out of it, it transmigrates ii 7 47
What colour is it of?—Of it own colour too.—'Tis a strange serpent.—'Tis so. And the tears of it are wet ii 7 52
'Tis not my profit that does lead mine honour; Mine honour, it ii 7 83
Another stain, as big as hell can hold, Were there no more but it *Cymb.* ii 4 141
Fear and niceness—The handmaids of all women, or, more truly, Woman it pretty self iii 4 160
A penny cord! . . . you have no true debitor and creditor but it v 4 172
Did you go to't so young? Were you a gamester at five or at seven *Per.* iv 6 80
Italian. He hath neither Latin, French, nor Italian *Mer. of Venice* i 2 75
An old Italian fox is not so kind, my boy *T. of Shrew* ii 1 405
Those Italian fields, Where noble fellows strike *All's Well* ii 3 307
If there be here German, or Dane, low Dutch, Italian, or French, let him speak iv 1 79
That rare Italian master, Julio Romano *W. Tale* v 2 105
No Italian priest Shall tithe or toll in our dominions *K. John* iii 1 153
The story is extant, and writ in choice Italian *Hamlet* iii 2 274
There's an Italian come; and, 'tis thought, one of Leonatus' friends *Cymb.* ii 1 40
I'll go see this Italian: what I have lost to-day at bowls, I'll win to-night of him ii 1 53
What false Italian, As poisonous-tongued as handed, hath prevail'd On thy too ready hearing? iii 2 4
I am brought hither Among the Italian gentry, and to fight v 1 18
I'll disrobe me Of these Italian weeds and suit myself As does a Briton v 1 23
Mine Italian brain 'Gan in your duller Britain operate Most vilely v 5 196
Methinks, I see him now.—Ay, so thou dost, Italian fiend! v 5 210
Italy. Who is so far from Italy removed I ne'er again shall see her *Tempest* ii 1 110
He is the only man of Italy, Always excepted my dear Claudio *Much Ado* iii 1 92
For shape, for bearing, . . Goes foremost in report through Italy iii 1 97
She concluded with a sigh, thou wast the properest man in Italy v 1 174
He bought his doublet in Italy, his round hose in France *Mer. of Venice* i 2 80

Italy. If any man in Italy have a fairer table . . . . *Mer. of Venice* ii 2 167
One in whom The ancient Roman honour more appears Than any that draws breath in Italy . . . iii 2 298
Fruitful Lombardy, The pleasant garden of great Italy . *T. of Shrew* i 1 4
A man well known throughout all Italy . . . ii 1 69
Let higher Italy,—Those bated that inherit but the fall Of the last monarchy,—see that you come Not to woo honour, but to wed it *All's Well* ii 1 12
Those girls of Italy, take heed of them . . . ii 1 19
You were beaten in Italy for picking a kernel out of a pomegranate . ii 3 275
Report of fashions in proud Italy, Whose manners still our tardy apish nation Limps after in base imitation . . . . *Richard II.* ii 1 21
Retired himself To Italy; and there at Venice gave His body to that pleasant country's earth . . . . iv 1 97
Let the Volsces Plough Rome, and harrow Italy . . . *Coriolanus* v 3 34
All the swords In Italy, and her confederate arms, Could not have made this peace . . . . v 3 208
Thou art as hot a Jack in thy mood as any in Italy . . *Rom. and Jul.* iii 1 13
Mean to establish Cæsar as a king; And he shall wear his crown by sea and land, In every place, save here in Italy . . . *J. Cæsar* i 3 88
And fierce civil strife Shall cumber all the parts of Italy . . . iii 1 264
From Italy, Upon the first encounter, drave them . *Ant. and Cleo.* i 2 97
Our Italy Shines o'er with civil swords . . . i 3 44
Many hot inroads They make in Italy . . . i 4 51
O, from Italy! Ram thou thy fruitful tidings in mine ears . . ii 5 23
Our great navy's rigg'd.—For Italy and Cæsar. More, Domitius . iii 5 21
Make him swear The shes of Italy should not betray Mine interest *Cymb.* i 3 29
You must not so far prefer her 'fore ours of Italy . . . i 4 71
Your Italy contains none so accomplished a courtier to convince the honour of my mistress . . . . i 4 103
That drug-damn'd Italy hath out-craftied him . . . iii 4 15
Some jay of Italy, Whose mother was her painting, hath betray'd him . iii 4 51
I have a kinsman who Is bound for Italy; he embark'd at Milford . iii 6 62
The senate hath stirr'd up the confiners And gentlemen of Italy . . iv 2 338
We fear not What can from Italy annoy us . . . iv 3 34
Why did you suffer Iachimo, Slight thing of Italy, To taint his nobler heart? . . . . . . v 4 64
Sitting sadly, Hearing us praise our loves of Italy For beauty that made barren the swell'd boast Of him that best could speak . . v 5 161
Itch. She loved not the savour of tar nor of pitch, Yet a tailor might scratch her where'er she did itch . . . *Tempest* ii 2 55
If I see a sword out, my finger itches to make one . *Mer. Wives* iii 3 48
Do not, porpentine, do not: my fingers itch.—I would thou didst itch from head to foot and I had the scratching of thee . *Troi. and Cres.* ii 1 28
Rubbing the poor itch of your opinion, Make yourselves scabs *Coriolanus* i 1 168
Speak not, reply not, do not answer me; My fingers itch *Rom. and Jul.* iii 5 165
Itches, blains, Sow all the Athenian bosoms! . . *T. of Athens* iv 1 28
Mine eyes do itch; Doth that bode weeping?—'Tis neither here nor there *Othello* iv 3 58
Why should he follow? The itch of his affection should not then Have nick'd his captainship . . . . *Ant. and Cleo.* iii 13 7
Itched. My elbow itched; I thought there would a scab follow *Much Ado* iii 3 106
Itching. You yourself Are much condemn'd to have an itching palm; To sell and mart your offices for gold To undeservers.—I an itching palm! You know that you are Brutus that speak this . *J. Cæsar* iv 3 10
Item: She can milk; look you, a sweet virtue . . *T. G. of Ver.* iii 1 277
Item: she can sew.—That's as much as to say, Can she so? . . iii 1 307
Item, That no woman shall come within a mile of my court . *L. L. Lost* i 1 119
Item, If any man be seen to talk with a woman within the term of three years . . . . i 1 130
Item, two lips, indifferent red; item, two grey eyes, with lids to them; item, one neck, one chin, and so forth . . . *T. Night* i 5 265
Read them.—Item, A capon, 2s. 2d. Item, Sauce, 4d. . 1 *Hen. IV.* ii 4 585
Item, that the duchy of Anjou . . . shall be released . 2 *Hen. VI.* i 1 50
Item, you sent a large commission To Gregory de Cassado *Hen. VIII.* iii 2 320
Though the catalogue of his endowments had been tabled by his side and I to peruse him by items . . . . . *Cymbeline* i 4 7
Iteration. Thou hast damnable iteration and art indeed able to corrupt a saint . . . . 1 *Hen. IV.* i 2 101
Truth tired with iteration, As true as steel . . . *Troi. and Cres.* iii 2 183
My husband!—What needs this iteration, woman? I say thy husband *Othello* v 2 150
Ithaca. Hear Ulysses speak.—Speak, Prince of Ithaca *Troi. and Cres.* i 3 70
You would be another Penelope: yet, they say, all the yarn she spun in Ulysses' absence did but fill Ithaca full of moths *Coriolanus* i 3 94
Its. A falsehood in its contrary as great As my trust was . *Tempest* i 2 95
Allaying both their fury and my passion With its sweet air . . i 2 393
Heaven grant us its peace! . . . . *Meas. for Meas.* i 2 4
How sometimes nature will betray its folly, Its tenderness! . *W. Tale* 2 151
My dagger muzzled, Lest it should bite its master, and so prove, As ornaments oft do, too dangerous . . . . i 2 157
Let me know my trespass By its own visage . . . . i 2 266
It should here be laid, Either for life or death, upon the earth Of its right father . . . . iii 3 46
Gentle as the cradle-babe Dying with mother's dug between its lips 2 *Hen. VI.* iii 2 393
Each following day Became the next day's master, till the last Made former wonders its . . . . . . *Hen. VIII.* i 1 18
Itself. The solemn temples, the great globe itself, Yea, all which it inherit, shall dissolve . . . . . . *Tempest* iv 1 153
I to myself am dearer than a friend, For love is still most precious in itself . . . . *T. G. of Ver.* ii 6 24
With eggs, sir?—Simple of itself . . . . *Mer. Wives* iii 5 32
Ignorance itself is a plummet o'er me: use me as you will . . v 5 172
Hath yet a kind of medicine in itself . . . *Meas. for Meas.* ii 2 135
Making both it unable for itself, And dispossessing all my other parts . . . . ii 4 21
A victory is twice itself when the achiever brings home full numbers *Much Ado* i 1 8
Hero itself can blot out Hero's virtue . . . . iv 1 83
Knows not Montague that of itself England is safe, if true within itself?—But the safer when 'tis back'd with France . 3 *Hen. VI.* iv 1 39
Nor doth the eye itself, That most pure spirit of sense, behold itself, Not going from itself . . . . . *Troi. and Cres.* iii 3 105
For speculation turns not to itself, Till it hath travell'd and is mirror'd there Where it may see itself . . . . . . iii 3 109
'Tis [jealousy] a monster Begot upon itself, born on itself . *Othello* iii 4 162
It is shaped, sir, like itself . . . . *Ant. and Cleo.* ii 7 47
And what ensues in this fell storm Shall for itself itself perform *Pericles* iii Gower 54
Ivory. There is more difference between thy flesh and hers than between jet and ivory . . . . . . *Mer. of Venice* iii 1 42
In ivory coffers I have stuff'd my crowns . . . *T. of Shrew* ii 1 352
Whom Fortune with her ivory hand wafts to her . . *T. of Athens* i 1 70
Ivy. He was The ivy which had hid my princely trunk . . *Tempest* i 2 86
It is dross, Usurping ivy, brier, or idle moss . . *Com. of Errors* ii 2 180
The female ivy so Enrings the barky fingers of the elm . *M. N. Dream* iv 1 48
They have scared away two of my best sheep, which I fear the wolf will sooner find than the master; if any where I have them, 'tis by the seaside, browsing of ivy . . . . *W. Tale* iii 3 69

J

Jacet. I would have that drum or another, or 'hic jacet'. *All's Well* iii 6 66
Jack. Has done little better than played the Jack with us . *Tempest* iv 1 198
Sayest thou so, old Jack? go thy ways; I'll make more of thy old body *Mer. Wives* ii 2 144
Vat is de clock, Jack?—'Tis past the hour, sir, that Sir Hugh promised to meet . . . . ii 3 3
Take your rapier, Jack; I vill tell you how I vill kill him . . ii 3 13
Speak you this with a sad brow? or do you play the flouting Jack? *M. Ado* i 1 186
Boys, apes, braggarts, Jacks, milksops! . . . . v 1 91
Our wooing doth not end like an old play; Jack hath not Jill *L. L. Lost* v 2 885
Jack shall have Jill; Nought shall go ill . . *M. N. Dream* iii 2 461
A thousand raw tricks of these bragging Jacks . *Mer. of Venice* iii 4 77
She did call me rascal fiddler And twangling Jack . . *T. of Shrew* ii 1 159
A mad-cap ruffian and a swearing Jack . . . . ii 1 290
Why, 'Jack, boy! ho! boy!' and as much news as will thaw . iv 1 43
Be the jacks fair within, the jills fair without, the carpets laid? . iv 1 51
Where shall we take a purse to-morrow, Jack? . . 1 *Hen. IV.* i 2 111
Jack! how agrees the devil and thee about thy soul? . . i 2 126
Sirrah Jack, thy horse stands behind the hedge . . . ii 2 73
I am no proud Jack, like Falstaff, but a Corinthian, a lad of mettle . ii 4 12
Welcome, Jack: where hast thou been?—A plague of all cowards, I say! ii 4 126
Go thy ways, old Jack; die when thou wilt . . . ii 4 141
Four of us here have ta'en a thousand pound this day morning.—Where is it, Jack? . . . . ii 4 178
If there were not two or three and fifty upon poor old Jack . . ii 4 207
Dost thou hear me, Hal?—Ay, and mark thee too, Jack . . . ii 4 234
Come, your reason, Jack, your reason.—What, upon compulsion? . ii 4 260
Come, let's hear, Jack; what trick hast thou now? . . . ii 4 293
Shall I give him his answer?—Prithee, do, Jack.—'Faith, and I'll send him packing . . . . ii 4 327
Here comes lean Jack, here comes bare-bone. How now, my sweet creature! . . . . ii 4 358
How long is't ago, Jack, since thou sawest thine own knee? . . ii 4 360
But afoot he will not budge a foot.—Yes, Jack, upon instinct . . ii 4 389
Banish plump Jack, and banish all the world . . . . ii 4 527
How! the prince is a Jack, a sneak-cup . . . . iii 3 99
They pick pockets.—What didst thou lose, Jack? . . . iii 3 115
Jack. He called you Jack, and said he would cudgel you 1 *Hen. IV.* iii 3 158
I have procured thee, Jack, a charge of foot.—I would it had been of horse iii 3 208
Jack, meet me to-morrow in the temple hall at two o'clock in the afternoon . . . . iii 3 223
How now, blown Jack! how now, quilt!—What, Hal! how now, mad wag! . . . . iv 2 53
But tell me, Jack, whose fellows are these that come after?—Mine, Hal, mine . . . . iv 2 68
If I be not Jack Falstaff, then am I a Jack . . . . v 4 143
Come, I'll be friends with thee, Jack: thou art going to the wars 2 *Hen. IV.* ii 4 71
Give me my rapier, boy.—I pray thee, Jack, I pray thee, do not draw . ii 4 216
I pray thee, Jack, be quiet; the rascal's gone . . . ii 4 224
If my heart be not ready to burst,—well, sweet Jack, have a care of thyself . . . . ii 4 410
Abused By silken, sly, insinuating Jacks . . . *Richard III.* i 3 53
Since every Jack became a gentleman, There's many a gentle person made a Jack . . . . i 3 72
Like a Jack, thou keep'st the stroke Betwixt thy begging and my meditation . . . . iv 2 117
You shall perceive that a Jack guardant cannot office me from my son *Coriolanus* v 2 67
An a' speak any thing against me, I'll take him down, an a' were lustier than he is, and twenty such Jacks . . . *Rom. and Jul.* ii 4 160
Come, come, thou art as hot a Jack in thy mood as any in Italy . iii 1 12
What a pestilent knave is this same!—Hang him, Jack! . . iv 5 149
Take hence this Jack, and whip him . . . *Ant. and Cleo.* iii 13 93
This Jack of Cæsar's shall Bear us an errand to him . . . iii 13 103
When I kiss'd the jack, upon an up-cast to be hit away! . *Cymbeline* ii 1 2
Jack-a-Lent. You little Jack-a-Lent, have you been true to us? *Mer. Wives* iii 3 27
See now how wit may be made a Jack-a-Lent, when 'tis upon ill employment! . . . . v 5 134
Jackanape. You jack'nape, give-a this letter to Sir Hugh . . i 4 113
I will teach a scurvy jack-a-nape priest to meddle or make . . . i 4 116
He speak for a jack-an-ape to Anne Page . . . . ii 3 87
I will be like a jack-an-apes also, to burn the knight with my taber . iv 4 67
Which is he?—That jack-an-apes with scarfs . . . *All's Well* iii 5 88

Jackanape. I could lay on like a butcher and sit like a jack-an-apes, never off . . . . *Hen. V.* v 2 148
And then a whoreson jackanapes must take me up for swearing *Cymbeline* ii 1 4
Jack Cade. *See* **Cade.**
Jack-dog. Scurvy jack-dog priest! by gar, me vill cut his ears *Mer. Wives* ii 3 65
By gar, you are de coward, de Jack dog, John ape . . . . . . iii 1 85
Jack Falstaff. But for sweet Jack Falstaff, kind Jack Falstaff, true Jack Falstaff, valiant Jack Falstaff . . . . 1 *Hen. IV.* ii 4 522
What should poor Jack Falstaff do in the days of villany? . . . . iii 3 187
If I be not Jack Falstaff, then am I a Jack . . . . . . v 4 142
JACK FALSTAFF with my familiars, JOHN with my brothers and sisters 2 *Hen. IV.* ii 2 143
Then was Jack Falstaff, now Sir John, a boy . . . . . . iii 2 28
Jack o' the clock. While I stand fooling here, his Jack o' the clock *Richard II.* v 5 60
Jack out of office. For me nothing remains. But long I will not be Jack out of office . . . . 1 *Hen. VI.* i 1 175
Jack priest. By gar, I vill kill de Jack priest . . . . *Mer. Wives* i 4 123
By gar, he is de coward Jack priest of de vorld . . . . . ii 3 32
Jack Rugby. You are John Rugby, and you are Jack Rugby . . . i 4 61
By gar, Jack Rugby, he is dead already, if he be come . . . . ii 3 8
Jacksauce. His reputation is as arrant a villain and a Jacksauce *Hen. V.* iv 7 148
Jack-slave. Every Jack-slave hath his bellyful of fighting . *Cymbeline* ii 1 22
Jacob. His child is a year and a quarter old, come Philip and Jacob *Meas. for Meas.* iii 2 214
When Jacob grazed his uncle Laban's sheep—This Jacob from our holy Abram was, As his wise mother wrought in his behalf, The third *Mer. of Venice* i 3 72
Mark what Jacob did . . . . i 3 78
All the eanlings which were streak'd and pied Should fall as Jacob's hire i 3 81
Did in eaning time Fall parti-colour'd lambs, and those were Jacob's . i 3 89
This was a venture, sir, that Jacob served for . . . . . . i 3 92
By Jacob's staff, I swear, I have no mind of feasting forth to-night . ii 5 36
Jacques of Chatillon, admiral of France . . . . . *Hen. V.* iv 8 98
Jaculis. Integer vitæ, scelerisque purus, Non eget Mauri jaculis *T. An.* iv 2 21
Jade. Therefore is she better than a jade . . . . . *T. G. of Ver.* iii 1 277
Let carman whip his jade . . . . *Meas. for Meas.* ii 1 269
I have done.—You always end with a jade's trick: I know you of old *Much Ado* i 1 145
Sir, give him head: I know he'll prove a jade . . . . *T. of Shrew* i 2 249
Women are made to bear, and so are you.—No such jade as you . . ii 1 202
Fie on all tired jades, on all mad masters, and all foul ways! . . iv 1 1
To other regions France is a stable; we that dwell in't jades *All's Well* ii 3 301
If I put any tricks upon 'em, sir, they shall be jades' tricks . . iv 5 64
I do not now fool myself, to let imagination jade me *T. Night* ii 5 179
I'ld play incessantly upon these jades . . . . . . *K. John* ii 1 385
Like glistering Phaethon, Wanting the manage of unruly jades *Rich. II.* iii 3 179
That jade hath eat bread from my royal hand . . . . . . v 5 85
Poor jade, is wrung in the withers out of all cess . . 1 *Hen. IV.* ii 1 7
That is the next way to give poor jades the bots . . . . . ii 1 11
Struck his armed heels Against the panting sides of his poor jade Up to the rowel-head . . . . 2 *Hen. IV.* i 1 45
Hollow pamper'd jades of Asia, Which cannot go but thirty mile a-day ii 4 178
Sodden water, A drench for sur-rein'd jades . . . . *Hen. V.* iii 5 19
He is indeed a horse; and all other jades you may call beasts . . iii 7 26
I had as lief have my mistress a jade . . . . iii 7 63
Their poor jades Lob down their heads, dropping the hides and hips . iv 2 46
And now loud-howling wolves arouse the jades That drag the tragic melancholy night . . . . 2 *Hen. VI.* iv 1 3
A red murrain o' thy jade's tricks! . . . . . *Troi. and Cres.* ii 1 21
Fall their crests, and, like deceitful jades, Sink in the trial *J. Cæsar* iv 2 26
Let the galled jade wince, our withers are unwrung *Hamlet* iii 2 253
Jaded. The honourable blood of Lancaster Must not be shed by such a jaded groom . . . . 2 *Hen. VI.* iv 1 52
If we live thus tamely, To be thus jaded by a piece of scarlet *Hen. VIII.* iii 2 280
The ne'er-yet-beaten horse of Parthia We have jaded out o' the field *Ant. and Cleo.* iii 1 34
Jakes. I will tread this unbolted villain into mortar, and daub the walls of a jakes with him . . . . *Lear* ii 2 72
Jamany. But it is tell-a me dat you make grand preparation for a duke de Jamany . . . . *Mer. Wives* iv 5 89
James Gurney, wilt thou give us leave awhile? . . . . . *K. John* i 1 230
James, There's toys abroad: anon I'll tell thee more . . . . i 1 231
God-den to your worship, good Captain James. . . . *Hen. V.* iii 2 90
Into his son-in-law's house, Sir James Cromer . . . 2 *Hen. VI.* iv 7 117
James Tyrrel, and your most obedient subject. . . *Richard III.* iv 2 68
Sir James Blunt, And Rice ap Thomas . . . . . . iv 5 11
What say you, James Soundpost?—Faith, I know not . *Rom. and Jul.* iv 5 138
Jamy. Nay, by Saint Jamy, I hold you a penny . . *T. of Shrew* iii 2 84
The Scots captain, Captain Jamy . . . . *Hen. V.* iii 2 80
Captain Jamy is a marvellous falorous gentleman, that is certain . iii 2 81
Jane Nightwork. Ha! 'twas a merry night. And is Jane Nightwork alive? . . . . 2 *Hen. IV.* iii 2 210
Jane Smile. I broke my sword upon a stone and bid him take that for coming a-night to Jane Smile . . . . . *As Y. Like It* ii 4 48
Jangled. Like sweet bells jangled, out of tune and harsh *Hamlet* iii 1 166
Jangling. Good wits will be jangling; but, gentles, agree *L. L. Lost* ii 1 225
As this their jangling I esteem a sport . . . *M. N. Dream* iii 2 353
Kept such a jangling of the bells . . . . . . *Pericles* ii 1 45
January. You will never run mad, niece.—No, not till a hot January *Much Ado* i 1 94
You'ld be so lean, that blasts of January Would blow you through *W. T.* iv 4 111
Janus. By two-headed Janus, Nature hath framed strange fellows *Mer. of Venice* i 1 50
Is it they?—By Janus, I think no . . . . *Othello* i 2 33
Japhet. Nay, they will be kin to us, or they will fetch it from Japhet. But to the letter . . . . 2 *Hen. IV.* ii 2 128
Jaquenetta. The matter is to me, sir, as concerning Jaquenetta *L. L. L.* i 1 204
For Jaquenetta,—so is the weaker vessel called . . . . . i 1 275
I was taken with Jaquenetta, and Jaquenetta is a true girl . . i 1 314
Bear this significant to the country maid Jaquenetta . . . iii 1 132
This letter is mistook, it importeth none here; It is writ to Jaquenetta iv 1 58
Then shall Hector be whipped for Jaquenetta . . . . . v 2 686
He wore none but a dishclout of Jaquenetta's . . . . . v 2 720
I have vowed to Jaquenetta to hold the plough for her sweet love three years . . . . v 2 892
Jaques. My brother Jaques he keeps at school, and report speaks goldenly of his profit . . . . . . *As Y. Like It* i 1 5
The melancholy Jaques grieves at that . . . . . . ii 1 26
The hairy fool, Much marked of the melancholy Jaques . . . . ii 1 41

Jaques. What said Jaques? Did he not moralize this spectacle? *As Y. Like It* ii 1 43
'Ay,' quoth Jaques, 'Sweep on, you fat and greasy citizens' . . . ii 1 54
It will make you melancholy, Monsieur Jaques.—I thank it . . . ii 5 11
Another stanzo: call you 'em stanzos?—What you will, Monsieur Jaques ii 5 20
Stay, Jaques, stay.—To see no pastime I . . . . . . v 4 200
I am Saint Jaques' pilgrim, thither gone . . . . *All's Well* iii 4 4
Whither are you bound?—To Saint Jaques le Grand . . . . iii 5 37
There's four or five, to great Saint Jaques bound, Already at my house iii 5 98
Her pretence is a pilgrimage to Saint Jaques le Grand . . . iv 3 58
Sebastian, so many; Corambus, so many; Jaques, so many . . . iv 3 185
Jaques Chatillon, Rambures, Vaudemont. . . . . *Hen. V.* iii 5 43
Jar. You delight not in music.—Not a whit, when it jars so *T. G. of Ver.* iv 2 67
We will include all jars With triumphs, mirth and rare solemnity . . v 4 160
The mortal and intestine jars . . . . . . *Com. of Errors* i 1 11
Here was he merry, hearing of a song.—If he, compact of jars, grow musical, We shall have shortly discord in the spheres *As Y. Like It* ii 7 5
Madam, my instrument's in tune.—Let's hear. O fie! the treble jars *T. of Shrew* iii 1 39
The base is right; 'tis the base knave that jars . . . . . iii 1 47
I love thee not a jar o' the clock behind What lady-she her lord *W. Tale* i 2 43
And with sighs they jar Their watches on unto mine eyes . *Richard II.* v 5 51
Cease, cease these jars and rest your minds in peace . 1 *Hen. VI.* i 1 44
What a scandal is it to our crown, That two such noble peers as ye should jar! . . . . iii 1 70
And Humphrey with the peers be fall'n at jars . . . 2 *Hen. VI.* i 1 253
When such strings jar, what hope of harmony? . . . . . ii 1 57
Whilst you live at jar, The fearful French . . . Should make a start . iv 8 43
Right and wrong, between whose endless jar justice resides *Troi. and Cres.* i 3 117
For shame, be friends, and join for that you jar . . *T. Andron.* ii 1 103
Jarring. At last, though long, our jarring notes agree . *T. of Shrew* v 2 1
His jarring concord, and his discord dulcet . . . . *All's Well* i 1 186
This jarring discord of nobility, This shouldering of each other 1 *Hen. VI.* iv 1 188
The untuned and jarring senses, O, wind up! . . . . . *Lear* iv 7 16
Jarteer. Appointed mine host of de Jarteer to measure our weapon *M. W.* i 4 124
Mine host de Jarteer,—have I not stay for him to kill him? have I not? iii 1 94
Vere is mine host de Jarteer?—Here, master doctor . . . . iv 5 85
Jason. Many Jasons come in quest of her . . . . *Mer. of Venice* i 1 172
He will be glad of our success; We are the Jasons, we have won the fleece . . . . iii 2 244
Jauncing. Spurr'd, gall'd and tired by jauncing Bolingbroke *Richard II.* v 5 94
Jaundice. And creep into the jaundice By being peevish. *Mer. of Venice* i 1 85
What grief hath set the jaundice on your cheeks? . . *Troi. and Cres.* i 3 2
Jaunt. Fie, how my bones ache! what a jaunt have I had! *Rom. and Jul.* ii 5 26
Jaunting. To catch my death with jaunting up and down . . . ii 5 53
Jaw. The jaws of darkness do devour it up . . . . *M. N. Dream* i 1 148
I snatch'd one half out of the jaws of death . . . . *T. Night* iii 4 394
To win renown Even in the jaws of danger and of death. . . *K. John* v 2 116
Turns head against the lion's armed jaws . . . . 1 *Hen. IV.* iii 2 102
The poor souls for whom this hungry war Opens his vasty jaws *Hen. V.* ii 4 105
From their misty jaws Breathe foul contagious darkness . 2 *Hen. VI.* iv 1 6
When rank Thersites opes his mastic jaws, We shall hear music, wit and oracle . . . . *Troi. and Cres.* i 3 73
Thus I enforce thy rotten jaws to open . . . . *Rom. and Jul.* v 3 47
Why the sepulchre, Wherein we saw thee quietly inurn'd, Hath oped his ponderous and marble jaws . . . . *Hamlet* i 4 50
He keeps them like an ape, in the corner of his jaw . . . . iv 2 20
My bended hook shall pierce Their slimy jaws . . *Ant. and Cleo.* ii 5 13
Jaw-bone. As if it were Cain's jaw-bone, that did the first murder! *Hamlet* v 1 85
Jay. Will dig thee pig-nuts; Show thee a jay's nest. . . *Tempest* ii 2 173
We'll teach him to know turtles from jays . . . . *Mer. Wives* iii 3 44
Is the jay more precious than the lark, Because his feathers are more beautiful? Or is the adder better than the eel? . . *T. of Shrew* iv 3 177
The thrush and the jay, Are summer songs for me and my aunts *W. Tale* iv 3 10
Some jay of Italy, Whose mother was her painting, hath betray'd him *Cymbeline* iii 4 51
Jealous. Fearing lest my jealous aim might err . . . *T. G. of Ver.* iii 1 28
At that time the jealous rascally knave her husband will be forth *M. W.* ii 2 276
They say the jealous wittolly knave hath masses of money . . . ii 2 283
A secure ass: he will trust his wife; he will not be jealous . . . ii 2 316
By gar, 'tis no the fashion of France; it is not jealous in France . iii 3 184
They took me on their shoulders; met the jealous knave their master in the door . . . . iii 5 102
An intolerable fright, to be detected with a jealous rotten bell-wether . iii 5 111
The virtuous creature, that hath the jealous fool to her husband!. . iv 2 137
As jealous as Ford, that searched a hollow walnut for his wife's leman . iv 2 170
Who would be jealous then of such a one? . . . . *Com. of Errors* iv 2 23
The venom clamours of a jealous woman Poisons more deadly than a mad dog's tooth . . . . v 1 69
Thy jealous fits Have scared thy husband from the use of wits . . v 1 85
Civil as an orange, and something of that jealous complexion *Much Ado* ii 1 305
And jealous Oberon would have the child Knight of his train *M. N. D.* ii 1 24
What, jealous Oberon! Fairies, skip hence: I have forsworn his bed and company . . . . ii 1 61
I shall grow jealous of you shortly . . . . *Mer. of Venice* iii 5 31
Jealous in honour, sudden and quick in quarrel . . *As Y. Like It* ii 7 151
I will be more jealous of thee than a Barbary cock-pigeon over his hen. iv 1 150
Our first merriment hath made thee jealous . . . . *T. of Shrew* iv 5 76
That my most jealous and too doubtful soul May live at peace *T. Night* iv 3 27
A gracious innocent soul, More free than he is jealous . . *W. Tale* ii 3 30
Leontes a jealous tyrant; his innocent babe truly begotten . . . iii 2 135
Your nobles, jealous of your absence, Seek through your camp *Hen. V.* iv 1 302
The jealous o'erworn widow . . . . *Richard III.* i 1 81
Well struck in years, fair, and not jealous . . . . . . i 1 92
Go with him, And from her jealous arms pluck him perforce . . . i 1 36
He in heat of action Is more vindicative than jealous love *Troi. and Cres.* iv 5 107
By the jealous queen of heaven, that kiss I carried from thee, dear *Coriol.* v 3 46
But if thou, jealous, dost return to pry . . . . *Rom. and Jul.* v 3 33
Be not jealous on me, gentle Brutus . . . . . . *J. Cæsar* i 2 71
That you do love me, I am nothing jealous . . . . . . i 2 162
Which I have rather blamed as mine own jealous curiosity . . *Lear* i 4 75
Each jealous of the other, as the stung Are of the adder. . . . v 1 56
'Tis not to make me jealous To say my wife is fair, feeds well *Othello* iii 3 183
Wear your eye thus, not jealous nor secure . . . . . . iii 3 198
Trifles light as air Are to the jealous confirmations strong As proofs of holy writ . . . . iii 3 323
Is true of mind and made of no such baseness As jealous creatures are . iii 4 28
Is he not jealous?—Who, he? I think the sun where he was born Drew all such humours from him . . . . iii 4 29
Is not this man jealous?—I ne'er saw this before . . . . . iii 4 99

Jealous. Pray heaven it be state-matters, as you think, And no conception nor no jealous toy Concerning you . . . *Othello* iii 4 156
Alas the day! I never gave him cause.—But jealous souls will not be answer'd so; They are not ever jealous for the cause, But jealous for they are jealous . . . . iii 4 159
You are jealous now That this is from some mistress, some remembrance iii 4 185
One not easily jealous, but being wrought Perplex'd in the extreme . v 2 345
Jealous-hood. A jealous-hood, a jealous-hood! . . . *Rom. and Jul.* iv 4 13
Jealousy. For love, thou know'st, is full of jealousy . *T. G. of Ver.* ii 4 177
It would give eternal food to his jealousy . . . *Mer. Wives* ii 1 104
He's as far from jealousy as I am from giving him cause . . . ii 1 107
He's a very jealousy man: she leads a very frampold life with him . ii 2 93
Who says this is improvident jealousy? . . . . ii 2 302
God be praised for my jealousy! . . . . ii 2 324
This is fery fantastical humours and jealousies . . . . . iii 3 182
I never saw him so gross in his jealousy till now . . . . iii 3 201
Dwelling in a continual 'larum of jealousy . . . . . iii 5 73
My intelligence is true; my jealousy is reasonable . . . . . iv 2 155
Pray, and not follow the imaginations of your own heart: this is jealousies . . . . iv 2 164
I beseech you, follow; see but the issue of my jealousy . . . . iv 2 208
Ford, her husband, hath the finest mad devil of jealousy in him . v 1 20
And leave your jealousies too, I pray you.—I will never mistrust my wife again . . . . v 5 139
Self-harming jealousy! fie, beat it hence! . . . . *Com. of Errors* ii 1 102
How many fond fools serve mad jealousy! . . . . . . ii 1 116
That jealousy shall be called assurance . . . . . *Much Ado* ii 2 49
These are the forgeries of jealousy . . . . . *M. N. Dream* ii 1 81
How comes this gentle concord in the world, That hatred is so far from jealousy? . . . . iv 1 149
And shuddering fear, and green-eyed jealousy . . . *Mer. of Venice* iii 2 110
Jealousy what might befall your travel, Being skilless in these parts *T. Night* iii 3 8
Kill what I love?—a savage jealousy That sometime savours nobly . v 1 122
This jealousy Is for a precious creature . . . . . . *W. Tale* i 2 451
All proofs sleeping else But what your jealousies awake . . . . iii 2 114
Being transported by my jealousies To bloody thoughts and to revenge iii 2 159
Thy tyranny Together working with thy jealousies . . . . . iii 2 181
The effects of his fond jealousies so grieving That he shuts up himself . iv 1 18
Rumour is a pipe Blown by surmises, jealousies, conjectures . 2 *Hen. IV.* Ind. 16
O, how hast thou with jealousy infected The sweetness of affiance! *Hen. V.* ii 2 126
Fell jealousy, Which troubles oft the bed of blessed marriage . . v 2 391
A kind of godly jealousy—Which, I beseech you, call a virtuous sin—Makes me afeard . . . . *Troi. and Cres.* iv 4 82
Let not my jealousies be your dishonours, But mine own safeties *Macbeth* iv 3 29
I fear'd he did but trifle, . . . but, beshrew my jealousy! . . *Hamlet* ii 1 113
So full of artless jealousy is guilt, It spills itself in fearing to be spilt . iv 5 19
At least into a jealousy so strong That judgement cannot cure *Othello* ii 1 310
Oft my jealousy Shapes faults that are not . . . . . . iii 3 147
O, beware, my lord, of jealousy; It is the green-eyed monster . . iii 3 165
Good heaven, the souls of all my tribe defend From jealousy! . . . iii 3 176
Think'st thou I'ld make a life of jealousy? . . . . . . iii 3 177
When I doubt, prove; And on the proof, there is no more but this,—Away at once with love or jealousy! . . . . iii 3 192
His unbookish jealousy must construe Poor Cassio's smiles, gestures and light behaviour, Quite in the wrong . . . . iv 1 102
Or else break out in peevish jealousies, Throwing restraint upon us . iv 3 90
All little jealousies, which now seem great, And all great fears, which now import their dangers, Would then be nothing . *Ant. and Cleo.* ii 2 134
We'll slip you for a season; but our jealousy Does yet depend *Cymbeline* iv 3 22
To taint his nobler heart and brain With needless jealousy . . . v 4 66
Jeer. Dost thou jeer and flout me in the teeth? . . *Com. of Errors* ii 2 22
Jeering. Revenge the jeering and disdain'd contempt . . 1 *Hen. IV.* i 3 183
Jelly. Then my best blood turn To an infected jelly! . . . *W. Tale* i 2 418
They, distill'd Almost to jelly with the act of fear, Stand dumb *Hamlet* i 2 205
Out, vile jelly! Where is thy lustre now?—All dark and comfortless *Lear* iii 7 83
Jenny. Genitive case!—Ay.—Genitive,—horum, harum, horum.—Vengeance of Jenny's case! . . . . *Mer. Wives* iv 1 64
Jeopardy. Look to thyself, thou art in jeopardy . . . *K. John* iii 1 346
Jephthah. To keep that oath were more impiety Than Jephthah's, when he sacrificed his daughter . . . . 3 *Hen. VI.* v 1 91
O Jephthah, judge of Israel, what a treasure hadst thou! . . *Hamlet* ii 2 422
Am I not i' the right, old Jephthah?—If you call me Jephthah, my lord, I have a daughter that I love passing well . . . . ii 2 429
Jerk. The odoriferous flowers of fancy, the jerks of invention . *L. L. Lost* iv 2 129
Jerkin. Mistress line, is not this my jerkin? Now is the jerkin under the line; now, jerkin, you are like to lose your hair and prove a bald jerkin . . . . *Tempest* iv 1 236
And how quote you my folly?—I quote it in your jerkin.—My jerkin is a doublet.—Well, then, I'll double your folly . . *T. G. of Ver.* ii 4 19
An old cloak makes a new jerkin . . . . . . *Mer. Wives* i 3 18
In a new hat and an old jerkin . . . . *T. of Shrew* iii 2 44
Is not a buff jerkin a most sweet robe of durance? . . . 1 *Hen. IV.* i 2 48
What a plague have I to do with a buff jerkin? . . . . . i 2 52
Put on two leathern jerkins and aprons, and wait upon him . 2 *Hen. IV.* ii 2 189
They will put on two of our jerkins and aprons; and Sir John must not know of it . . . . ii 4 18
A man may wear it on both sides, like a leather jerkin . *Troi. and Cres.* iii 3 266
Jeronimy. Go by, Jeronimy: go to thy cold bed, and warm thee *T. of S.* Ind. 1 9
Jerusalem. Like the mutines of Jerusalem, Be friends awhile *K. John* ii 1 378
For this cause awhile we must neglect Our holy purpose to Jerusalem 1 *Hen. IV.* i 1 102
Doth any name particular belong Unto the lodging where I first did swoon?—'Tis call'd Jerusalem . . . . . . 2 *Hen. IV.* iv 5 235
It hath been prophesied to me many years, I should not die but in Jerusalem . . . . iv 5 238
Bear me to that chamber; there I'll lie; In that Jerusalem shall Harry die . . . . iv 5 241
Her father is a king, The King of Naples and Jerusalem . . 1 *Hen. VI.* v 5 40
Reignier King of Naples, Sicilia and Jerusalem . . . 2 *Hen. VI.* i 1 48
King of Naples, Of both the Sicils and Jerusalem . . . 3 *Hen. VI.* i 4 122
So part we sadly in this troublous world, To meet with joy in sweet Jerusalem . . . . v 5 8
Reignier, her father, to the king of France Hath pawn'd the Sicils and Jerusalem . . . . v 7 39
Jesses. If I do prove her haggard, Though that her jesses were my dear heart-strings, I'ld whistle her off . . . . . *Othello* iii 3 261
Jessica. Tell gentle Jessica I will not fail her: speak it privately *Mer. of Venice* ii 4 20
Was not that letter from fair Jessica?—I must needs tell thee all . . ii 4 29
Jessica. Peruse this as thou goest: Fair Jessica shall be my torch-bearer *Mer. of Venice* ii 4 40
What, Jessica!—thou shalt not gormandise, As thou hast done with me:—What, Jessica! . . . . ii 5 3
Why, Jessica, I say!—Why, Jessica!—Who bids thee call? I do not . ii 5 6
I am bid forth to supper, Jessica: There are my keys . . . . ii 5 11
Jessica, my girl, Look to my house. I am right loath to go . . . ii 5 15
What, are there masques? Hear you me, Jessica: Lock up my doors . ii 5 28
Well, Jessica, go in: Perhaps I will return immediately . . . . ii 5 51
That in a gondola were seen together Lorenzo and his amorous Jessica . ii 8 9
My people do already know my mind, And will acknowledge you and Jessica . . . . iii 4 38
How cheer'st thou, Jessica? And now, good sweet, say thy opinion . iii 5 75
In such a night Did Jessica steal from the wealthy Jew . . . . v 1 15
In such a night Did pretty Jessica, like a little shrew, Slander her love v 1 21
Go we in, I pray thee, Jessica, And ceremoniously let us prepare Some welcome . . . . v 1 36
Sit, Jessica. Look how the floor of heaven Is thick inlaid . . . v 1 58
I give to you and Jessica, From the rich Jew, a special deed of gift . v 1 291
Jest. I thank thee for that jest; here's a garment for't . . *Tempest* iv 1 241
O jest unseen, inscrutable, invisible, As a nose on a man's face! *T. G. of V.* ii 1 141
Why, do you not perceive the jest?—No, believe me . . . . ii 1 160
After they closed in earnest, they parted very fairly in jest . . ii 5 14
Tell him my name is Brook; only for a jest . . . *Mer. Wives* ii 1 224
That were a jest indeed! . . . . ii 2 116
Let me be your jest; I deserve it . . . . iii 3 161
My uncle can tell you good jests of him . . . . iii 4 39
Tell Mistress Anne the jest, how my father stole two geese out of a pen iii 4 40
My will! 'od's heartlings, that's a pretty jest indeed! . . . . iii 4 60
We do not act that often jest and laugh . . . . iv 2 108
There would be no period to the jest, should he not be publicly shamed iv 2 237
The image of the jest I'll show you here at large . . . . . iv 6 17
While other jests are something rank on foot . . . . . . iv 6 22
I pray you, come, hold up the jest no higher . . . . . . v 5 109
To jest, Tongue far from heart . . . . *Meas. for Meas.* i 4 32
Great men may jest with saints; 'tis wit in them . . . . . ii 2 127
Here comes your ghostly father: do we jest now, think you? . . . iv 3 52
Lightens my humour with his merry jests . . . *Com. of Errors* i 2 21
I pray you, jest, sir, as you sit at dinner . . . . i 2 62
These jests are out of season; Reserve them till a merrier hour . . i 2 68
As you love strokes, so jest with me again . . . . ii 2 8
I am glad to see you in this merry vein: What means this jest? . . ii 2 21
Dost thou jeer and flout me in the teeth? Think'st thou I jest? . . ii 2 23
Now your jest is earnest: Upon what bargain do you give it me? . . ii 2 24
Because that I familiarly sometimes Do use you for my fool and chat with you, Your sauciness will jest upon my love . . . . . . ii 2 28
If you will jest with me, know my aspect . . . . ii 2 32
Learn to jest in good time: there's a time for all things . . . ii 2 65
This jest shall cost me some expense . . . . iii 1 123
I must be sad when I have cause and smile at no man's jests *Much Ado* i 3 15
Huddling jest upon jest with such impossible conveyance upon me . ii 1 252
I remember a pretty jest your daughter told us of . . . . . ii 3 141
The man doth fear God, howsoever it seems not in him by some large jests he will make . . . . ii 3 206
Tush, tush, man; never fleer and jest at me: I speak not like a dotard v 1 58
I jest not: I will make it good how you dare, with what you dare . v 1 147
You break jests as braggarts do their blades, which, God be thanked, hurt not . . . . v 1 189
By yea and nay, sir, then I swore in jest . . . . . *L. L. Lost* i 1 54
Every object that the one doth catch The other turns to a mirth-moving jest ii 1 71
Not a word with him but a jest.—And every jest but a word . . . ii 1 216
You sheep, and I pasture: shall that finish the jest?—So you grant pasture for me . . . . ii 1 221
O' my troth, most sweet jests! most incony vulgar wit! . . . . iv 1 144
Too bitter is thy jest. Are we betray'd thus to thy over-view? . iv 3 174
A pox of that jest! and I beshrew all shrows . . . . . . v 2 46
And make him proud to make me proud that jests . . . . . v 2 66
This jest is dry to me. Fair gentle sweet, Your wit makes wise things foolish . . . . v 2 373
Let us confess and turn it to a jest . . . . v 2 390
Pleasant jest and courtesy, As bombast and as lining to the time . . v 2 790
Our letters, madam, show'd much more than jest . . . . . v 2 795
A jest's prosperity lies in the ear Of him that hears it . . . . v 2 871
Befall what will befall, I'll jest a twelvemonth in an hospital . . v 2 881
I jest to Oberon and make him smile . . . . . . *M. N. Dream* ii 1 44
Wink each at other; hold the sweet jest up . . . . . . iii 2 239
Do you not jest?—Yes, sooth; and so do you . . . . . . iii 2 265
'Tis no jest That I do hate thee . . . . iii 2 280
They'll not show their teeth in way of smile, Though Nestor swear the jest be laughable . . . . *Mer. of Venice* i 1 56
Turning these jests out of service, let us talk in good earnest *As Y. L. It* i 3 26
Then take him up and manage well the jest . . . *T. of Shrew* Ind. 1 45
'Tis no time to jest, And therefore frame your manners to the time . i 1 231
Since we are stepp'd thus far in, I will continue that I broach'd in jest i 2 84
Nay then you jest, and now I well perceive You have but jested with me all this while . . . . ii 1 19
If that be jest, then all the rest was so . . . . ii 1 22
He was a frantic fool, Hiding his bitter jests in blunt behaviour . . iii 2 13
Tranio, you jest: but have you both forsworn me?—Mistress, we have iv 2 48
Like pleasant travellers, to break a jest Upon the company you overtake iv 5 72
Since you have begun, Have at you for a bitter jest or two! . . . v 2 45
As the jest did glance away from me, 'Tis ten to one it maim'd you two outright . . . . v 2 61
She says you have some goodly jest in hand: She will not come . . v 2 91
But they may jest Till their own scorn return to them unnoted *All's Well* i 2 33
But what's your jest?—A dry jest, sir.—Are you full of them? *T. Night* i 3 80
And ask no other dowry with her but such another jest . . . . ii 5 203
He must observe their mood on whom he jests . . . . . . iii 1 69
With some excellent jests, fire-new from the mint . . . . . iii 2 23
And takest it all for jest . . . . *W. Tale* i 2 249
And though thou now confess thou didst but jest, With my vex'd spirits I cannot take a truce . . . . *K. John* iii 1 16
Play fast and loose with faith? so jest with heaven? . . . . iii 1 242
And prove a deadly bloodshed but a jest, Exampled by this heinous spectacle . . . . iv 3 55
As gentle and as jocund as to jest Go I to fight . . . *Richard II.* i 3 95
His eyes do drop no tears, his prayers are in jest . . . . . v 3 101
I have a jest to execute that I cannot manage alone . . 1 *Hen. IV.* i 2 180
The virtue of this jest will be, the incomprehensible lies that this same fat rogue will tell us when we meet . . . . i 2 208

Jest. In the reproof of this lies the jest . . . . 1 *Hen. IV.* i 2 213
When a jest is so forward, and afoot too! I hate it . . . . ii 2 50
Argument for a week, laughter for a month and a good jest for ever . ii 2 101
Do you not love me? Nay, tell me if you speak in jest or no . . ii 3 102
What cunning match have you made with this jest of the drawer? . ii 4 102
What, is it a time to jest and dally now? . . . . . . v 3 57
O, it is much that a lie with a slight oath and a jest with a sad brow will do with a fellow . . . . 2 *Hen. IV.* v 1 92
Reply not to me with a fool-born jest . . . . . . v 5 59
His jest will savour but of shallow wit, When thousands weep more than did laugh at it . . . . *Hen. V.* i 2 295
He was full of jests, and gipes, and knaveries, and mocks . . . iv 7 51
A proper jest, and never heard before! . . . . 2 *Hen. VI.* i 1 132
To die by thee were but to die in jest; From thee to die were torture . iii 2 400
As if the tragedy Were play'd in jest by counterfeiting actors 3 *Hen. VI.* ii 3 28
I am a subject fit to jest withal, But far unfit to be a sovereign . . iii 2 91
Jest on, brothers: I can tell you both Her suit is granted . . . iii 2 116
Had he none else to make a stale but me? Then none but I shall turn his jest to sorrow . . . . iii 3 261
Or did he make the jest against his will? . . . . . . v 1 30
This would have been a biting jest . . . . . *Richard III.* ii 4 30
You may jest on, but, by the holy rood, I do not like these several councils . . . . iii 2 77
And given in earnest what I begg'd in jest . . . . . . v 1 22
Upon a lazy bed the livelong day Breaks scurril jests . *Troi. and Cres.* i 3 148
Verily, I do not jest with you; there came news from him last night *Coriolanus* i 3 103
My brother dead! I know thou dost but jest . . . *T. Andron.* ii 3 253
Now, what a thing it is to be an ass! Here's no sound jest! . . iv 2 26
Whiles I go tell my lord the emperor How I have govern'd our determined jest . . . . v 2 139
Her brothers were condemn'd to death, My hand cut off and made a merry jest . . . . v 2 175
To see, now, how a jest shall come about! . . . *Rom. and Jul.* i 3 45
He jests at scars that never felt a wound . . . . . . ii 2 1
Follow me this jest now till thou hast worn out thy pump, that when the single sole of it is worn, the jest may remain after the wearing sole singular . . . . ii 4 65
O single-soled jest, solely singular for the singleness! . . . ii 4 69
I will bite thee by the ear for that jest.—Nay, good goose, bite not . ii 4 81
Look to't, think on't, I do not use to jest . . . . . iii 5 191
They do but jest, poison in jest; no offence i' the world . *Hamlet* iii 2 244
I knew him, Horatio: a fellow of infinite jest, of most excellent fancy . v 1 204
Men did ransom lives Of me for jests . . . . *Ant. and Cleo.* iii 13 181
Jested. You have but jested with me all this while . *T. of Shrew* ii 1 20
Jester. I hear the parson is no jester . . . . *Mer. Wives* ii 1 218
He is the prince's jester: a very dull fool . . . . *Much Ado* ii 1 142
She told me, not thinking I had been myself, that I was the prince's jester . . . . ii 1 251
Who was it?—Feste, the jester, my lord; a fool that the lady Olivia's father took much delight in . . . . . . *T. Night* ii 4 11
He ambled up and down With shallow jesters . . . 1 *Hen. IV.* iii 2 61
How ill white hairs become a fool and jester! . . . 2 *Hen. IV.* v 5 52
This same skull, sir, was Yorick's skull, the king's jester . *Hamlet* v 1 199
Jesters do oft prove prophets . . . . *Lear* v 3 71
Jesting. Thou liest, thou jesting monkey, thou . . *Tempest* iii 2 52
Nay, but his jesting spirit; which is now crept into a lute-string and now governed by stops . . . . *Much Ado* iii 2 60
Holding a trencher, jesting merrily . . . . . *L. L. Lost* v 2 477
Close, in the name of jesting! . . . . . . *T. Night* ii 5 24
There's no jesting; there's laying on, take't off who will *Troi. and Cres.* i 2 224
Jesu preserve thee! . . . . *Richard II.* v 2 17
O Jesu, my lord the prince!—How now, my lady the hostess! 1 *Hen. IV.* ii 4 314
O Jesu, this is excellent sport, i' faith! . . . . . . ii 4 430
O Jesu, he doth it as like one of these harlotry players as ever I see! . ii 4 436
O Jesu, I have heard the prince tell him, I know not how oft! . . iii 3 96
O Jesu, are you come from Wales? . . . . . 2 *Hen. IV.* ii 4 317
Jesu, Jesu, the mad days that I have spent! . . . . . iii 2 36
Jesu, Jesu, dead! a' drew a good bow; and dead! . . . . iii 2 48
Crying with loud voice, 'Jesu maintain your royal excellence!' 2 *Hen. VI.* i 1 161
The Lord protect him, for he's a good man! Jesu bless him! . . i 3 6
Forswore himself,—which Jesu pardon!—Which God revenge! *Rich. III.* i 3 136
Give me another horse: bind up my wounds. Have mercy, Jesu! . . v 3 178
By Jesu, a very good blade! a very tall man! . . . *Rom. and Jul.* ii 4 31
Jesu, what haste? can you not stay awhile? . . . . . . ii 5 29
Jesu Christ. Many a time hath banish'd Norfolk fought For Jesu Christ in glorious Christian field . . . . . *Richard II.* iv 1 93
Speak not in spite, For you shall sup with Jesu Christ to-night 2 *Hen. VI.* v 1 214
Jesu Maria, what a deal of brine Hath wash'd thy sallow cheeks! *Rom. and Jul.* ii 3 69
Jesus. Stand!—Jesus bless us!—Strike; down with them . 1 *Hen. IV.* ii 2 86
Jesus preserve your royal majesty! . . . . . . 2 *Hen. VI.* i 2 70
And the women cried 'O, Jesus bless us, he is born with teeth!' 3 *Hen. VI.* v 6 75
Jet. There is more difference between thy flesh and hers than between jet and ivory . . . . *Mer. of Venice* iii 1 42
How he jets under his advanced plumes! . . . . . *T. Night* ii 5 36
What colour is my gown of?—Black, forsooth: coal-black as jet 2 *Hen. VI.* ii 1 112
Insulting tyranny begins to jet Upon the innocent and aweless throne: Welcome, destruction, death! . . . . *Richard III.* ii 4 51
Think you not how dangerous It is to jet upon a prince's right? *T. An.* ii 1 64
Two proper palfreys, black as jet, To hale thy vengeful waggon swift away v 2 50
The gates of monarchs Are arch'd so high that giants may jet through And keep their impious turbans on . . . . . . *Cymbeline* iii 3 5
Jetted. Whose men and dames so jetted and adorn'd, Like one another's glass to trim them by . . . . *Pericles* i 4 26
Jew. A Jew would have wept to have seen our parting . *T. G. of Ver.* ii 3 12
Thou art an Hebrew, a Jew, and not worth the name of a Christian . ii 5 58
If I do not love her, I am a Jew . . . . . . *Much Ado* ii 3 272
My sweet ounce of man's flesh! my incony Jew! . . . *L. L. Lost* iii 1 136
Most brisky juvenal and eke most lovely Jew . . . *M. N. Dream* iii 1 97
Content, i' faith: I'll seal to such a bond And say there is much kindness in the Jew . . . . *Mer. of Venice* i 3 154
Hie thee, gentle Jew. The Hebrew will turn Christian: he grows kind i 3 178
Certainly my conscience will serve me to run from this Jew my master ii 2 2
To be ruled by my conscience, I should stay with the Jew my master . ii 2 24
To run away from the Jew, I should be ruled by the fiend . . . ii 2 26
Certainly the Jew is the very devil incarnal . . . . . ii 2 28
A kind of hard conscience, to offer to counsel me to stay with the Jew ii 2 31
Young man, you, I pray you, which is the way to master Jew's? . . ii 2 35
Turn of no hand, but turn down indirectly to the Jew's house . . ii 2 45
Jew. I am Launcelot, the Jew's man, and I am sure Margery your wife is my mother . . . . *Mer. of Venice* ii 2 94
My master's a very Jew: give him a present! give him a halter . . ii 2 112
I am a Jew, if I serve the Jew any longer . . . . . . ii 2 119
My son, sir, a poor boy,— Not a poor boy, sir, but the rich Jew's man ii 2 130
To be brief, the very truth is that the Jew, having done me wrong, doth cause me, as my father, being, I hope, an old man, shall frutify unto you . . . . ii 2 141
If it be preferment To leave a rich Jew's service, to become The follower of so poor a gentleman . . . . ii 2 156
I'll take my leave of the Jew in the twinkling of an eye . . . . ii 2 177
Adieu! tears exhibit my tongue. Most beautiful pagan, most sweet Jew! ii 3 11
To bid my old master the Jew to sup to-night with my new master the Christian . . . . ii 4 18
If e'er the Jew her father come to heaven, It will be for his gentle daughter's sake: And never dare misfortune cross her foot, Unless she do it under this excuse, That she is issue to a faithless Jew . ii 4 34
Approach; Here dwells my father Jew . . . . ii 6 25
Now, by my hood, a Gentile and no Jew . . . . . . ii 6 51
The villain Jew with outcries raised the duke, Who went with him . ii 8 4
I never heard a passion so confused, So strange, outrageous, and so variable, As the dog Jew did utter in the streets . . . . . ii 8 14
For the Jew's bond which he hath of me, Let it not enter in your mind ii 8 41
Here he comes in the likeness of a Jew . . . . . . iii 1 24
I am a Jew. Hath not a Jew eyes? hath not a Jew hands, organs? . iii 1 61
If a Jew wrong a Christian, what is his humility? Revenge. If a Christian wrong a Jew, what should his sufferance be by Christian example? Why, revenge . . . . iii 1 71
A third cannot be matched, unless the devil himself turn Jew . . iii 1 82
If he had The present money to discharge the Jew, He would not take it iii 2 276
What sum owes he the Jew?—For me three thousand ducats . . iii 2 299
My estate is very low, my bond to the Jew is forfeit . . . . iii 2 319
You may partly hope that your father got you not, that you are not the Jew's daughter . . . . iii 5 12
There is no mercy for me in heaven, because I am a Jew's daughter . iii 5 36
In converting Jews to Christians, you raise the price of pork . . iii 5 38
Go one, and call the Jew into the court.—He is ready at the door . iv 1 14
We all expect a gentle answer, Jew . . . . iv 1 34
I pray you, think you question with the Jew . . . . . iv 1 70
Let me have judgement and the Jew his will . . . . . iv 1 83
The Jew shall have my flesh, blood, bones and all, Ere thou shalt lose for me one drop of blood . . . . iv 1 112
Not on thy sole, but on thy soul, harsh Jew, Thou makest thy knife keen iv 1 123
I acquainted him with the cause in controversy between the Jew and Antonio . . . . iv 1 155
Which is the merchant here, and which the Jew? . . . . iv 1 174
Do you confess the bond?—I do.—Then must the Jew be merciful . iv 1 182
Therefore, Jew, Though justice be thy plea, consider this, That, in the course of justice, none of us Should see salvation . . . . iv 1 197
Lawfully by this the Jew may claim A pound of flesh . . . iv 1 231
If the Jew do cut but deep enough, I'll pay it presently with all my heart iv 1 280
So she could Entreat some power to change this currish Jew . . iv 1 292
O upright judge! Mark, Jew: O learned judge! . . . . . iv 1 313
O learned judge! Mark, Jew: a learned judge! . . . . . iv 1 317
The Jew shall have all justice; soft! no haste: He shall have nothing but the penalty.—O Jew! an upright judge, a learned judge! . . iv 1 321
A second Daniel, a Daniel, Jew! Now, infidel, I have you on the hip . iv 1 333
Why doth the Jew pause? take thy forfeiture.—Give me my principal . iv 1 335
A second Daniel! I thank thee, Jew, for teaching me that word . . iv 1 341
Thou shalt have nothing but the forfeiture, To be so taken at thy peril, Jew iv 1 344
Tarry, Jew: The law hath yet another hold on you . . . . iv 1 346
Art thou contented, Jew? what dost thou say?—I am content . . iv 1 393
In lieu whereof, Three thousand ducats, due unto the Jew, We freely cope your courteous pains withal . . . . iv 1 411
Inquire the Jew's house out, give him this deed And let him sign it . iv 2 1
In such a night Did Jessica steal from the wealthy Jew . . . v 1 15
I give to you and Jessica, From the rich Jew, a special deed of gift . v 1 292
I am a Jew else, an Ebrew Jew . . . . . . 1 *Hen. IV.* ii 4 198
Liver of blaspheming Jew, Gall of goat, and slips of yew . *Macbeth* iv 1 26
Jewel. By my modesty, The jewel in my dower . . . *Tempest* iii 1 54
And I as rich in having such a jewel As twenty seas . *T. G. of Ver.* ii 4 169
Dumb jewels often in their silent kind More than quick words do move a woman's mind . . . . iii 1 90
And what says she to my little jewel? . . . . iv 4 51
Unless experience be a jewel that I have purchased at an infinite rate *Mer. Wives* ii 2 213
Have I caught thee, my heavenly jewel? Why, now let me die . . iii 3 45
The jewel that we find, we stoop and take't Because we see it *M. for M.* ii 1 24
I see the jewel best enamelled Will lose his beauty . . *Com. of Errors* ii 1 109
Rushing in their houses, bearing thence Rings, jewels, any thing . . v 1 144
Can the world buy such a jewel?—Yea, and a case to put it into *Much Ado* i 1 183
All his senses were lock'd in his eye, As jewels in crystal . *L. L. Lost* ii 1 243
Hangeth like a jewel in the ear of caelo, the sky, the welkin, the heaven iv 2 5
I knew her by this jewel on her sleeve.—Pardon me, sir, this jewel did she wear . . . . v 2 455
They shall fetch thee jewels from the deep . . . *M. N. Dream* iii 1 161
I have found Demetrius like a jewel, Mine own, and not mine own . iv 1 196
She hath directed How I shall take her from her father's house, What gold and jewels she is furnish'd with . . . . *Mer. of Venice* ii 4 32
And jewels, two stones, two rich and precious stones, Stolen by my daughter! . . . . ii 8 20
Two thousand ducats in that; and other precious, precious jewels . iii 1 91
I would my daughter were dead at my foot, and the jewels in her ear! iii 1 93
Let not that doctor e'er come near my house: Since he hath got the jewel that I loved . . . . v 1 224
Let's away, And get our jewels and our wealth together *As Y. Like It* i 3 136
Like the toad, ugly and venomous, Wears yet a precious jewel in his head ii 1 14
From the east to western Ind, No jewel is like Rosalind . . . iii 2 94
He hath the jewel of my life in hold . . . . . *T. of Shrew* i 2 119
My chastity's the jewel of our house, Bequeathed down . *All's Well* iv 2 46
We lost a jewel of her; and our esteem Was made much poorer by it . v 3 1
Give her this jewel; say, My love can give no place . . *T. Night* ii 4 126
And perchance wind up my watch, or play with my—some rich jewel . ii 5 67
Here, wear this jewel for me, 'tis my picture . . . . . iii 4 228
Had our prince, Jewel of children, seen this hour . . . *W. Tale* v 1 116
The mantle of Queen Hermione's, her jewel about the neck of it . . v 2 37
The jewel of life By some damn'd hand was robb'd and ta'en away *K. John* v 1 40
A jewel in a ten-times-barr'd-up chest Is a bold spirit in a loyal breast. Mine honour is my life . . . . *Richard II.* i 1 180
As foil wherein thou art to set The precious jewel of thy home return . i 3 267

Jewel. Remember me what a deal of world I wander from the jewels that I love — *Richard II.* i 3 270
I'll give my jewels for a set of beads, My gorgeous palace for a hermitage iii 3 147
Send you back again to your master, for a jewel,—the juvenal 2 *Hen. IV.* i 2 22
Yea, joy, our chains and our jewels.—'Your brooches, pearls, and ouches' ii 4 52
Bear her this jewel, pledge of my affection — 1 *Hen. VI.* v 1 47
I took a costly jewel from my neck, A heart it was, bound in with diamonds, And threw it towards thy land — 2 *Hen. VI.* iii 2 106
A jewel, lock'd into the wofull'st cask That ever did contain a thing of worth — iii 2 409
Unvalued jewels, All scatter'd in the bottom of the sea — *Richard III.* i 4 27
That, like a jewel, has hung twenty years About his neck — *Hen. VIII.* ii 2 32
A carbuncle entire, as big as thou art, Were not so rich a jewel *Coriolanus* i 4 56
I account of them As jewels purchased at an easy price — *T. Andron.* iii 1 199
She hangs upon the cheek of night Like a rich jewel in an Ethiope's ear; Beauty too rich for use! — *Rom. and Jul.* i 5 48
I have a jewel here— O, pray, let's see't: for the Lord Timon? *T. of A.* i 1 12
Sir, your jewel Hath suffer'd under praise — i 1 164
You mend the jewel by the wearing it — i 1 172
How dost thou like this jewel, Apemantus?—Not so well as plain-dealing i 1 214
The little casket bring me hither.—Yes, my lord. More jewels yet! — i 2 165
I must entreat you, honour me so much As to advance this jewel — i 2 176
I have received some small kindnesses from him, as money, plate, jewels iii 2 23
He wears jewels now of Timon's gift, For which I wait for money — iii 4 19
E'en as if your lord should wear rich jewels, And send for money for 'em iii 4 23
He gave me a jewel th' other day, and now he has beat it out of my hat: did you see my jewel? — iii 6 122
Mine eternal jewel Given to the common enemy of man — *Macbeth* iii 1 68
Were I king, I should cut off the nobles for their lands, Desire his jewels and this other's house — iv 3 80
The jewels of our father, with wash'd eyes Cordelia leaves you — *Lear* i 1 271
A jewel Well worth a poor man's taking — iv 6 28
For your sake, jewel, I am glad at soul I have no other child — *Othello* i 3 195
Good name in man and woman, dear my lord, Is the immediate jewel of their souls: Who steals my purse steals trash — iii 3 156
The jewels you have had from me to deliver to Desdemona would half have corrupted a votarist — iv 2 188
If she will return me my jewels, I will give over my suit — iv 2 201
He calls me to a restitution large Of gold and jewels that I bobb'd from him v 1 16
This world did equal theirs Till they had stol'n our jewel *Ant. and Cleo.* iv 15 78
This is the brief of money, plate, and jewels, I am possess'd of — v 2 138
Not comforted to live, But that there is this jewel in the world That I may see again — *Cymbeline* i 1 91
She your jewel, this your jewel, and my gold are yours — i 4 165
Plate of rare device, and jewels Of rich and exquisite form — i 6 189
Bid my woman Search for a jewel that too casually Hath left mine arm ii 3 146
Then, if you can, Be pale: I beg but leave to air this jewel — ii 4 96
By villany I got this ring: 'twas Leonatus' jewel; Whom thou didst banish — v 5 143
This jewel holds his building on my arm — *Pericles* ii 1 162
As jewels lose their glory if neglected, So princes their renowns — ii 2 12
Bid Nestor bring me spices, ink and paper, My casket and my jewels — iii 1 67
Her eyelids, cases to those heavenly jewels Which Pericles hath lost — iii 2 99
This letter, and some certain jewels, Lay with you in your coffer — iii 4 1
Whither wilt thou have me?—To take from you the jewel you hold so dear iv 6 164
I oped the coffin, Found there rich jewels; recover'd her — v 3 24

Jewel-house. The king has made him master O' the jewel-house *Hen. VIII.* iv 1 111
Beside that of the jewel house, is made master O' the rolls — v 1 34

Jeweller. The jeweller that owes the ring is sent for — *All's Well* v 3 297
I know the merchant.—I know them both; th' other's a jeweller *T. of A.* i 1 8

Jewel-like. Her eyes as jewel-like And cased as richly — *Pericles* v 1 111

Jewess. Look out at window, for all this: There will come a Christian by, Will be worth a Jewess' eye — *Mer. of Venice* ii 5 43

Jewish. And spit upon my Jewish gaberdine — i 3 113
You may as well do any thing most hard, As seek to soften that—than which what's harder?—His Jewish heart — iv 1 80

Jewry. What a Herod of Jewry is this! — *Mer. Wives* ii 1 20
The sepulchre in stubborn Jewry Of the world's ransom — *Richard II.* ii 1 55
As did the wives of Jewry At Herod's bloody-hunting slaughtermen — *Hen. V.* iii 3 40
Let me have a child at fifty, to whom Herod of Jewry may do homage: find me to marry me — *Ant. and Cleo* i 2 28
Herod of Jewry dare not look upon you But when you are well pleased iii 3 3
Herod of Jewry; Mithridates, king Of Comagene — iii 6 73
Alexas did revolt; and went to Jewry on Affairs of Antony — iv 6 12

Jezebel. Fie on him, Jezebel! — *T. Night* ii 5 46

Jig. Wooing, wedding, and repenting, is as a Scotch jig — *Much Ado* ii 1 77
The first suit is hot and hasty, like a Scotch jig, and full as fantastical ii 1 78
To jig off a tune at the tongue's end, canary to it with your feet *L. L. Lost* iii 1 11
To see great Hercules whipping a gig, And profound Solomon to tune a jig iv 3 168
My very walk should be a jig — *T. Night* i 3 138
Prithee, say on: he's for a jig or a tale of bawdry, or he sleeps *Hamlet* ii 2 522
You jig, you amble, and you lisp, and nick-name God's creatures — iii 1 150

Jigging. What should the wars do with these jigging fools? — *J. Cæsar* iv 3 137

Jig-maker. O God, your only jig-maker — *Hamlet* iii 2 132

Jill. Our wooing doth not end like an old play; Jack hath not Jill *L. L. L.* v 2 885
Jack shall have Jill; Nought shall go ill — *M. N. Dream* iii 2 461
Be the jacks fair within, the jills fair without? — *T. of Shrew* iv 1 52

Jingling. Roaring, shrieking, howling, jingling chains — *Tempest* v 1 233

Joan. Some men must love my lady and some Joan — *L. L. Lost* iii 1 207
Tu-who, a merry note, While greasy Joan doth keel the pot — v 2 939
What must I call her?—Madam.—Al'ce madam, or Joan madam? *T. of S. Ind.* 2 112
Well, now can I make any Joan a lady — *K. John* i 1 184
'Tis Joan, not we, by whom the day is won — 1 *Hen. VI.* i 6 17
I marvel how he sped.—Tut, holy Joan was his defensive guard — ii 1 49
Then thus it must be; this doth Joan devise — iii 3 17
Ah, Joan, this kills thy father's heart outright! — v 4 2
Ah, Joan, sweet daughter Joan, I'll die with thee! — v 4 6
Fie, Joan, that thou wilt be so obstacle! — v 4 17
For thy sake have I shed many a tear: Deny me not, I prithee, gentle Joan v 4 20
Then, Joan, discover thine infirmity — v 4 60
The wind was very high; And, ten to one, old Joan had not gone out — 2 *Hen. VI.* ii 1 4

Joan la Pucelle. With one Joan la Pucelle join'd — 1 *Hen. VI.* i 4 101
Thus Joan la Pucelle hath perform'd her word — i 6 3
No longer on Saint Denis will we cry, But Joan la Pucelle shall be France's saint — i 6 29

Joan of Arc. His new-come champion, virtuous Joan of Arc — ii 2 20
Joan of Arc hath been A virgin from her tender infancy — v 4 49

Job. And as poor as Job?—And as wicked as his wife? — *Mer. Wives* v 5 164
I am as poor as Job, my lord, but not so patient — 2 *Hen. IV.* i 2 144

Jockey of Norfolk, be not too bold — *Richard III.* v 3 304

Jocund. I am full of pleasure: Let us be jocund — *Tempest* iii 2 126
And I, most jocund, apt and willingly, To do you rest, a thousand deaths would die — *T. Night* v 1 135
As gentle and as jocund as to jest Go I to fight — *Richard II.* i 3 95
The lords at Pomfret, when they rode from London, Were jocund *Rich. III.* iii 2 86
My soul is very jocund In the remembrance of so fair a dream — v 3 232
Jocund day Stands tiptoe on the misty mountain tops — *Rom. and Jul.* iii 5 9
There's comfort yet; they are assailable; Then be thou jocund *Macbeth* iii 2 40
No jocund health that Denmark drinks to-day, But the great cannon to the clouds shall tell — *Hamlet* i 2 125

Jog on, jog on, the foot-path way, And merrily hent the stile-a — *W. Tale* iv 3 132

Jogging. You may be jogging whiles your boots are green — *T. of Shrew* iii 2 213

John. The knight, Sir John, is there; and, I beseech you, be ruled — *Mer. Wives* i 1 71
Pauca verba, Sir John; goot worts.—Good worts! good cabbage — i 1 123
Sir John and master mine, I combat challenge of this latten bilbo — i 1 164
What say you, Scarlet and John? — i 1 177
John! what, John, I say! Go, John, go inquire for my master — i 4 41
Sir John affects thy wife.—Why, sir, my wife is not young — ii 1 115
Sir John, there's one Master Brook below would fain speak with you ii 2 150
I desire more acqaintance of you.—Good Sir John, I sue for yours — ii 2 170
But, good Sir John, as you have one eye upon my follies — ii 2 192
Now, Sir John, here is the heart of my purpose — ii 2 233
Want no money, Sir John; you shall want none.—Want no Mistress Ford, Master Brook; you shall want none — ii 2 268
As I told you before, John and Robert, be ready here hard by — iii 3 9
My master, Sir John, is come in at your back-door, Mistress Ford — iii 3 24
O sweet Sir John!—Mistress Ford, I cannot cog, I cannot prate — iii 3 49
I would make thee my lady.—I your lady, Sir John! alas, I should be a pitiful lady! — iii 3 55
A plain kerchief, Sir John: my brows become nothing else — iii 3 62
What, John! Robert! John! Go take up these clothes here quickly iii 3 154
I know not which pleases me better, that my husband is deceived, or Sir John — iii 3 190
You come to know what hath passed between me and Ford's wife?—That, indeed, Sir John, is my business — iii 5 64
But are you sure of your husband now?—He's a-birding, sweet Sir John iv 2 8
If you go out in your own semblance, you die, Sir John — iv 2 68
Run up, Sir John.—Go, go, sweet Sir John — iv 2 81
Go, Mistress Ford, Send quickly to Sir John, to know his mind — iv 4 83
Bully knight! bully Sir John! speak from thy lungs military — iv 5 17
Thou art clerkly, Sir John. Was there a wise woman with thee? — iv 5 59
Sir John! art thou there, my deer? my male deer?—My doe with the black scut! — v 5 18
Hold up the jest no higher. Now, good Sir John, how like you Windsor wives? — v 5 110
Sir John, we have had ill luck; we could never meet — v 5 120
Why, Sir John, do you think . . . that ever the devil could have made you our delight? — v 5 154
Let us every one go home, And laugh this sport o'er by a country fire; Sir John and all — v 5 257
Sir John, To Master Brook you yet shall hold your word — v 5 257
Was not Count John here at supper?—I saw him not — *Much Ado* ii 1 1
Half Signior Benedick's tongue in Count John's mouth, and half Count John's melancholy in Signior Benedick's face — ii 1 13
Bring you the length of Prester John's foot — ii 1 276
Therefore know I have earned of Don John a thousand ducats — iii 3 116
Planted and placed and possessed by my master Don John — iii 3 160
Chiefly by my villany, which did confirm any slander that Don John had made — iii 3 169
Don John, and all the gallants of the town, are come to fetch you to church — iii 4 96
The practice of it lives in John the bastard — iv 1 190
This man said, sir, that Don John, the prince's brother, was a villain iv 2 42
Received a thousand ducats of Don John for accusing the Lady Hero iv 2 50
Prince John is this morning secretly stolen away — iv 2 63
How Don John your brother incensed me to slander the Lady Hero v 1 242
And Don John is the author of all, who is fled and gone — v 2 100
Your brother John is ta'en in flight, And brought with armed men back v 4 127
To rebuke the usurpation Of thy unnatural uncle, English John *K. John* ii 1 10
Liker in feature to his father Geffrey Than thou and John in manners ii 1 127
King John, this is the very sum of all — ii 1 151
Let us hear them speak Whose title they admit, Arthur's or John's ii 1 200
King John, your king and England's, doth approach — ii 1 313
But Fortune, O, She is corrupted, changed and won from thee; She adulterates hourly with thine uncle John — iii 1 56
France is a bawd to Fortune and King John, That strumpet Fortune, that usurping John! — iii 1 60
You anointed deputies of heaven! To thee, King John, my holy errand is — iii 1 137
John hath seized Arthur; and it cannot be That, whiles warm life plays in that infant's veins, The misplaced John should entertain an hour, One minute, nay, one quiet breath of rest — iii 4 131
That John may stand, then Arthur needs must fall; So be it — iii 4 139
How green you are and fresh in this old world! John lays you plots iii 4 146
Presages and tongues of heaven, Plainly denouncing vengeance upon John iii 4 159
And pick strong matter of revolt and wrath Out of the bloody fingers' ends of John — iii 4 168
King John hath reconciled Himself to Rome — v 2 69
And come ye now to tell me John hath made His peace with Rome? v 2 91
Must I back Because that John hath made his peace with Rome? — v 2 96
Warlike John; and in his forehead sits A bare-ribb'd death — v 2 176
They say King John sore sick hath left the field — v 4 6
Seek out King John and fall before his feet — v 4 13
And calmly run on in obedience Even to our ocean, to our great King John — v 4 57
What says Sir John Sack and Sugar? — 1 *Hen. IV.* i 2 125
Sir John stands to his word, the devil shall have his bargain — i 2 130
Sir John, I prithee, leave the prince and me alone — i 2 167
If I hang, old Sir John hangs with me, and thou knowest he is no starveling — ii 1 75
What, a coward, Sir John Paunch? — ii 2 69
My lord, old Sir John, with half-a-dozen more, are at the door — ii 4 92
Sir John, you are so fretful, you cannot live long — iii 3 13
You are so fat, Sir John, that you must needs be out of all compass iii 3 24
Why, Sir John, my face does you no harm.—No, I'll be sworn — iii 3 31
Why, Sir John, what do you think, Sir John? do you think I keep thieves in my house? — iii 3 62

John. No, Sir John; you do not know me, Sir John. I know you, Sir John: you owe me money, Sir John *1 Hen. IV.* iii 3 74
You owe money here besides, Sir John, for your diet and by-drinkings. iii 3 84
What beast! why, an otter.—An otter, Sir John! why an otter? iii 3 143
Said he would cudgel you.—Did I, Bardolph?—Indeed, Sir John, you said so iii 3 161
The Earl of Westmoreland, seven thousand strong, Is marching hitherwards; with him Prince John iv 1 89
Faith, Sir John, 'tis more than time that I were there, and you too iv 2 60
Mortal men.—Ay, but, Sir John, methinks they are exceeding poor and bare iv 2 74
What, is the king encamped?—He is, Sir John iv 2 83
Before, I loved thee as a brother, John; But now, I do respect thee v 4 19
Come, brother John; full bravely hast thou flesh'd Thy maiden sword v 4 133
This is the strangest fellow, brother John v 4 159
You, son John, and my cousin Westmoreland Towards York shall bend you v 5 35
Young Prince John And Westmoreland and Stafford fled the field; And Harry Monmouth's brawn, the hulk Sir John, Is prisoner to your son *2 Hen. IV.* i 1 17
Well, the truth is, Sir John, you live in great infamy i 2 155
And will you yet call yourself young? Fie, fie, fie, Sir John! i 2 209
Sir John, I arrest you at the suit of Mistress Quickly ii 1 48
How now, Sir John! what are you brawling here? ii 1 71
How comes this, Sir John? Fie! what man of good temper would endure this? ii 1 86
Sir John, Sir John, I am well acquainted with your manner of wrenching the true cause the false way ii 1 119
Pray thee, Sir John, let it be but twenty nobles ii 1 166
I thank you, good Sir John.—Sir John, you loiter here too long ii 1 197
What foolish master taught you these manners, Sir John? ii 1 203
JOHN with my brothers and sisters, and SIR JOHN with all Europe ii 2 144
Apple-johns? thou knowest Sir John cannot endure an apple-john ii 4 2
The prince once set a dish of apple-johns before him, and told him there were five more Sir Johns ii 4 6
They will put on two of our jerkins and aprons; and Sir John must not know of it ii 4 18
Pray ye, pacify yourself, Sir John: there comes no swaggerers here ii 4 87
It is mine ancient.—Tilly-fally, Sir John, ne'er tell me ii 4 90
I will discharge upon her, Sir John, with two bullets ii 4 123
Then was Jack Falstaff, now Sir John, a boy, and page iii 2 28
Shall I prick him down, Sir John?—It were superfluous iii 2 153
Sir John, do you remember since we lay all night in the windmill? iii 2 206
Sir John, said I well?—We have heard the chimes at midnight iii 2 227
Sir John, do not yourself wrong: they are your likeliest men iii 2 272
Hath the Prince John a full commission? iv 1 162
Prince John your son doth kiss your grace's hand iv 4 83
Thou bring'st me happiness and peace, son John iv 5 228
Sir John, you shall not be excused v 1 21
Where are you, Sir John? Come, come, come, off with your boots v 1 60
Sir John, I am thy Pistol and thy friend v 3 97
And Robin Hood, Scarlet, and John v 3 107
Sir John, thy tender lambkin now is king; Harry the Fifth's the man v 3 122
That Sir John were come! he would make this a bloody day to somebody v 4 13
A colour that I fear you will die in, Sir John.—Fear no colours v 5 93
Our humble author will continue the story, with Sir John in it Epil. 29
As ever you came of women, come in quickly to Sir John *Hen. V.* ii 1 123
'How now, Sir John!' quoth I: 'what, man! be o' good cheer' ii 3 18
God take mercy on brave Talbot's soul; And on his son young John *1 Hen. VI.* iv 3 35
Art thou not weary, John? how dost thou fare? iv 6 27
O, where's young Talbot? where is valiant John? iv 7 2
Sir John! nay, fear not, man, We are alone *2 Hen. VI.* i 2 68
Must you, Sir John, protect my lady here?—So am I given in charge i 4 79
Welcome, Sir John! But why come you in arms? *3 Hen. VI.* iv 7 42
I thank thee, good Sir John, with all my heart. I am in your debt *Richard III.* iii 2 111
I am a pretty piece of flesh.—'Tis well thou art not fish; if thou hadst, thou hadst been poor John *Rom. and Jul.* i 1 37
This same should be the voice of Friar John. Welcome from Mantua v 2 2
Friar John, go hence; Get me an iron crow v 2 20
But he which bore my letter, Friar John, Was stay'd by accident v 3 250

John-a-dreams. Peak, Like John-a-dreams, unpregnant of my cause *Ham.* ii 2 595

John ape. You are de coward, de Jack dog, John ape *Mer. Wives* iii 1 86

John de la Car. The duke's confessor, John de la Car *Hen. VIII.* i 1 218
Wishing me to permit John de la Car, my chaplain, a choice hour i 2 162
Sir Gilbert Peck his chancellor; and John Car, Confessor to him ii 1 20

John Drum. If you give him not John Drum's entertainment *All's Well* iii 6 41

John Naps. Stephen Sly and old John Naps of Greece *T. of Shrew* Ind. 2 95

John of Gaunt. Old John of Gaunt, time-honour'd Lancaster *Richard II.* i 1 1
Furbish new the name of John a Gaunt, Even in the lusty haviour of his son i 3 76
Old John of Gaunt is grievous sick, my lord, Suddenly taken i 4 54
I am not John of Gaunt, your grandfather; but yet no coward *1 Hen. IV.* ii 2 70
John a Gaunt loved him well, and betted much money on his head *2 Hen. IV.* iii 2 49
Talks as familiarly of John a Gaunt as if he had been sworn brother to him iii 2 344
I saw it, and told John a Gaunt he beat his own name iii 2 349
Whereas he From John of Gaunt doth bring his pedigree *1 Hen. VI.* ii 5 77
Next to whom Was John of Gaunt, the Duke of Lancaster *2 Hen. VI.* ii 2 14; 22; 54
Such hope have all the line of John of Gaunt! *3 Hen. VI.* i 1 19
Warwick disannuls great John of Gaunt, Which did subdue the greatest part of Spain iii 3 81
After John of Gaunt, Henry the Fourth, Whose wisdom was a mirror to the wisest iii 3 83

Join. On the topmast, The yards and bowsprit, would I flame distinctly, Then meet and join *Tempest* i 2 201
As I wooed for thee to obtain her, I will join with thee to disgrace her *Much Ado* iii 2 130
Can you not hate me, as I know you do, But you must join in souls to mock me too? *M. N. Dream* iii 2 150
And will you rent our ancient love asunder, To join with men in scorning your poor friend? iii 2 216
This fellow will but join you together as they join wainscot *As Y. Like It* iii 3 88
That thou mightst join her hand with his Whose heart within his bosom is v 4 120
Here's eight that must take hands To join in Hymen's bands v 4 135
The mightiest space in fortune nature brings To join like likes *All's Well* i 1 238
O, two such silver currents, when they join, Do glorify the banks *K. John* ii 1 441
If thou be pleased withal, Command thy son and daughter to join hands ii 1 532

Join. Join with the present sickness that I have *Richard II.* ii 1 132
Join not with grief, fair woman, do not so, To make my end too sudden v 1 16
And let my soul Want mercy, if I do not join with him *1 Hen. IV.* i 3 132
And then the power of Scotland and of York, To join with Mortimer, ha? i 3 281
Many a soul Shall pay full dearly for this encounter, If once they join v 1 85
The Prince of Wales doth join with all the world In praise of Henry Percy v 1 86
But look you pray, all you that kiss my lady Peace at home, that our armies join not in a hot day *2 Hen. IV.* i 2 233
Then join you with them, like a rib of steel, To make strength stronger ii 3 54
When all those legs and arms and heads, chopped off in a battle, shall join together at the latter day *Hen. V.* iv 1 143
To join with witches and the help of hell! *1 Hen. VI.* ii 1 18
I would prevail, . . . To join your hearts in love and amity iii 1 68
Trouble us no more; But join in friendship, as your lords have done iii 1 145
On, my lords, and join our powers, And seek how we may prejudice the foe iii 3 90
Join you with me, And all together, with the Duke of Suffolk, We'll quickly hoise Duke Humphrey from his seat *2 Hen. VI.* i 1 167
Join we together, for the public good, In what we can i 1 199
Although we fancy not the cardinal, Yet must we join with him i 3 98
The rascal people, thirsting after prey, Join with the traitor iv 4 52
See, see! they join, embrace, and seem to kiss *3 Hen. VI.* ii 1 29
Each one already blazing by our meeds, Should notwithstanding join our lights ii 1 37
Norfolk and myself, In haste, poste-haste, are come to join with you ii 1 139
My quarrel and this English queen's are one.—And mine, fair lady Bona, joins with yours iii 3 217
I'll join mine eldest daughter and my joy To him forthwith iii 3 242
Now join your hands, and with your hands your hearts iv 6 39
Away betimes, before his forces join, And take the great-grown traitor unawares iv 8 62
I'll join with black despair against my soul *Richard III.* ii 2 36
Thou wouldst be gone to join with Richmond: I will not trust you, sir iv 4 491
March on, join bravely, let us to't pell-mell v 3 312
And his own notion . . . shall join To thrust the lie unto him *Coriolanus* v 6 109
For shame, be friends, and join for that you jar *T. Andron.* ii 1 103
When we join in league, I am a lamb iv 2 136
Join with the Goths; and with revengeful war Take wreak on Rome iv 3 32
And say I am Revenge, sent from below To join with him v 2 4
Revenge is come to join with him, And work confusion on his enemies v 2 7
Join with me to forbid him her resort *T. of Athens* i 1 127
But now return, And with their faint reply this answer join iii 3 25
Yet, more to move you, Take my deserts to his, and join 'em both iii 5 79
But who did bid thee join with us? *Macbeth* iii 3 1
And after we will both our judgements join In censure of his seeming *Hamlet* iii 2 91
Friends both, go join you with some further aid iv 1 33
Let witchcraft join with beauty, lust with both! *Ant. and Cleo.* ii 1 22
Let her live To join our kingdoms and our hearts ii 2 154
Sicilius, who did join his honour Against the Romans *Cymbeline* i 1 29
Join gripes with hands Made hard with hourly falsehood i 6 106
Let his virtue join With my request v 5 88
By the four opposing coigns Which the world together joins *Pericles* iii Gower 18

Joinder. Confirm'd by mutual joinder of your hands *T. Night* v 1 160

Joined. Who, with a charm join'd to their suffer'd labour, I have left asleep *Tempest* i 2 231
False blood to false blood join'd! gone to be friends! *K. John* iii 1 2
At thy birth, dear boy, Nature and Fortune join'd to make thee great iii 1 52
So lately purged of blood, So newly join'd in love iii 1 240
Have woe to woe, sorrow to sorrow join'd.—Despair not, madam *Rich. II.* ii 2 66
York is join'd with Bolingbroke, And all your northern castles yielded up iii 2 200
I am joined with no foot-land rakers *1 Hen. IV.* ii 1 81
Join'd with an enemy proclaim'd *Hen. V.* ii 2 168
The Bastard of Orleans with him is join'd *1 Hen. VI.* i 1 93
The Dauphin, with one Joan la Pucelle join'd, A holy prophetess i 4 101
Forsaken your pernicious faction And join'd with Charles iv 1 60
Two mightier troops than that the Dauphin led, Which join'd with him iv 3 8
Her peerless feature, joined with her birth, Approves her fit v 5 68
Whom I encounter'd as the battles join'd *3 Hen. VI.* i 1 15
Short tale to make, we at Saint Alban's met, Our battles join'd ii 1 121
God forbid that I should wish them sever'd Whom God hath join'd together iv 1 22
Yet, to have join'd with France in such alliance Would more have strengthen'd this our commonwealth iv 1 36
Your high-swoln hearts, But lately splinter'd, knit, and join'd *Richard III.* ii 2 118
You, my lord Cardinal of York, are join'd with me their servant In the unpartial judging of this business *Hen. VIII.* ii 2 106
Marcius, Join'd with Aufidius, leads a power 'gainst Rome *Coriolanus* iv 6 66
If Marcius should be join'd with Volscians,— If! He is their god iv 6 89
Yet I wish, sir,—I mean for your particular,—you had not Join'd in commission with him iv 7 14
God join'd my heart and Romeo's, thou our hands *Rom. and Jul.* iv 1 55
His left hand, which did flame and burn Like twenty torches join'd *J. Cæsar* i 3 17
A peevish schoolboy, worthless of such honour, Join'd with a masker! v 1 62
That have with two pernicious daughters join'd Your high engender'd battles 'gainst a head So old and white as this *Lear* iii 2 22
Yet they are not join'd: where yond pine does stand, I shall discover all: I'll bring thee word Straight *Ant. and Cleo.* iv 12 1
Are now revived, To the majestic cedar join'd *Cymbeline* v 5 457
Nay, come, your hands and lips must seal it too: And being join'd, I'll thus your hopes destroy *Pericles* ii 5 86

Joined-stool. Why, what's a moveable?—A join'd-stool *T. of Shrew* ii 1 199
Thy state is taken for a joined-stool *1 Hen. IV.* ii 4 418
Jumps upon joined-stools, and swears with a good grace *2 Hen. IV.* ii 4 269

Joiner. Snug, the joiner; you, the lion's part *M. N. Dream* i 2 66
Let him name his name, and tell them plainly he is Snug the joiner iii 1 47
Then know that I, one Snug the joiner, am A lion-fell v 1 226
Her chariot is an empty hazel-nut Made by the joiner squirrel *R. and J.* i 4 68

Joinest. Who join'st thou with but with a lordly nation? *1 Hen. VI.* iii 3 62
And join'st with them will be thy slaughter-men iii 3 75

Joineth. This is the happy wedding torch That joineth Rouen unto her countrymen iii 2 27

Joint. You That are of suppler joints, follow them swiftly *Tempest* iii 3 107
Go charge my goblins that they grind their joints With dry convulsions iv 1 259
We'll touse you Joint by joint, but we will know his purpose *M. for M.* v 1 314
This swain, because of his great limb or joint, shall pass Pompey the Great; the page, Hercules *L. L. Lost* v 1 135
And clap their female joints In stiff unwieldy arms *Richard II.* iii 2 1[illegible]

Joint. How dare thy joints forget To pay their awful duty to our presence? *Richard II.* iii 3 75
This fester'd joint cut off, the rest rest sound; This let alone will all the rest confound v 3 85
Against them both my true joints bended be v 3 98
His weary joints would gladly rise, I know v 3 105
Yet all goes well, yet all our joints are whole *1 Hen. IV.* iv 1 83
Whose fever-weaken'd joints, Like strengthless hinges, buckle under life *2 Hen. IV.* i 1 140
A scaly gauntlet now with joints of steel Must glove this hand i 1 146
What's a joint of mutton or two in a whole Lent? ii 4 375
A couple of short-legged hens, a joint of mutton v 1 28
A joint burden laid upon us all v 2 55
Thou hast drawn my shoulder out of joint v 4 3
Come thou no more for ransom, gentle herald: They shall have none, I swear, but these my joints *Hen. V.* iv 3 123
Ay, every joint should seem to curse and ban *2 Hen. VI.* iii 2 319
He hath the joints of every thing, but every thing so out of joint that he is a gouty Briareus *Troi. and Cres.* i 2 28
They have galls, Good arms, strong joints, true swords i 3 238
A cause that hath no mean dependance Upon our joint and several dignities ii 2 193
The elephant hath joints, but none for courtesy ii 3 113
Let him die, With every joint a wound, and that to-morrow! iv 1 29
Her wanton spirits look out At every joint and motive of her body iv 5 57
I have with exact view perused thee, Hector, And quoted joint by joint iv 5 233
A chilling sweat o'er-runs my trembling joints *T. Andron.* ii 3 212
But fettle your fine joints 'gainst Thursday next *Rom. and Jul.* iii 5 154
And madly play with my forefathers' joints iv 3 51
Out, alas! she's cold; Her blood is settled, and her joints are stiff iv 5 26
I will tear thee joint by joint And strew this hungry churchyard v 3 35
Aches contract and starve your supple joints! *T. of Athens* i 1 257
They answer, in a joint and corporate voice, That now they are at fall ii 2 213
The time is out of joint: O cursed spite, That ever I was born to set it right! Nay, come, let's go together *Hamlet* i 5 189
This broken joint between you and her husband entreat her to splinter *Othello* ii 3 328
If I have bargained for the joint,— Thou mayst cut a morsel off the spit *Pericles* iv 2 141
Jointed. Be jointed to the old stock and freshly grow *Cymbeline* v 4 142; v 5 440
Jointing. The time's state Made friends of them, jointing their force 'gainst Cæsar *Ant. and Cleo.* i 2 96
Joint-labourer. This sweaty haste Doth make the night joint-labourer with the day *Hamlet* i 1 78
Jointly. And they jointly swear To spoil the city *2 Hen. VI.* iv 4 52
Therewithal we shall have cause of state Craving us jointly *Macbeth* iii 1 35
We shall jointly labour with your soul To give it due content *Hamlet* iv 5 211
I do invest you jointly with my power, Pre-eminence *Lear* i 1 132
Jointress. The imperial jointress to this warlike state *Hamlet* i 2 9
Joint-ring. I would not do such a thing for a joint-ring *Othello* iv 3 73
Joint-servant. I took him; Made him joint-servant with me *Coriolanus* v 6 32
Joint-stool. Away with the joint-stools, remove the court-cupboard, look to the plate *Rom. and Jul.* i 5 7
Cry you mercy, I took you for a joint-stool *Lear* iii 6 54
Jointure. He will make you a hundred and fifty pounds jointure *Mer. Wives* iii 4 50
Though he comes slowly, he carries his house on his head; a better jointure, I think, than you make a woman *As Y. Like It* iv 1 56
Besides two thousand ducats by the year Of fruitful land, all which shall be her jointure *T. of Shrew* ii 1 372
Forthwith shall articles be drawn Touching the jointure *3 Hen. VI.* iii 3 136
This is my daughter's jointure, for no more Can I demand *Rom. and Jul.* v 3 297
Jole. I'll go with thee, cheek by jole *M. N. Dream* iii 2 338
Jollity. He loseth it in a kind of jollity *Com. of Errors* ii 2 90
Wedded, with Theseus, all in jollity *M. N. Dream* iv 1 97
A fortnight hold we this solemnity, In nightly revels and new jollity v 1 377
Apprehend Nothing but jollity *W. Tale* iv 4 25
Triumphs for nothing and lamenting toys Is jollity for apes *Cymbeline* iv 2 194
Jolly. Then, heigh-ho, the holly! This life is most jolly *As Y. Like It* ii 7 183
'Tis like you'll prove a jolly surly groom *T. of Shrew* iii 2 215
Hey, Robin, jolly Robin, Tell me how thy lady does *T. Night* iv 2 78
Like a jolly troop of huntsmen, come Our lusty English *K. John* ii 1 321
To her I go, a jolly thriving wooer *Richard III.* iv 3 43
Let us deal justly. Sleepest or wakest thou, jolly shepherd? *Lear* iii 6 43
What's else to say? Be jolly, lords *Ant. and Cleo.* ii 7 65
Through Alexandria make a jolly march iv 8 30
Whiles the jolly Briton—Your lord, I mean—laughs from's free lungs *Cymb.* i 6 67
Jolt-head. Fie on thee, jolt-head! thou canst not read *T. G. of Ver.* iii 1 290
You heedless joltheads and unmanner'd slaves! *T. of Shrew* iv 1 169
Jordan. Why, they will allow us ne'er a jordan *1 Hen. IV.* ii 1 22
'When Arthur first in court'—Empty the jordan *2 Hen. IV.* ii 4 37
Joseph. Call forth Nathaniel, Joseph, Nicholas, Philip *T. of Shrew* iv 1 91
Joshua, yourself; myself and this gallant gentleman, Judas Maccabæus *L. L. Lost* v 1 133
Jot. The one has my pity; not a jot the other *Meas. for Meas.* iv 2 64
This nor hurts him nor profits you a jot iv 3 128
This bond doth give thee here no jot of blood *Mer. of Venice* iv 1 306
If you break one jot of your promise or come one minute behind your hour *As Y. Like It* iv 1 194
And not a jot of Tranio in your mouth *T. of Shrew* i 1 241
No, faith, I'll not stay a jot longer *T. Night* iii 2 1
You do mistake me, sir.—No, sir, no jot; I know your favour well iii 4 363
If one jot beyond The bound of honour, or in act or will *W. Tale* iii 2 51
Power no jot Hath she [Fortune] to change our loves v 1 217
Nor doth he dedicate one jot of colour Unto the weary and all-watched night, But freshly looks *Hen. V.* iv Prol. 37
More care to keep Than in possession any jot of pleasure *3 Hen. VI.* ii 2 53
I do not know that Englishman alive With whom my soul is any jot at odds More than the infant that is born to-night *Richard III.* ii 1 70
Would I had no being, If this salute my blood a jot: it faints me, To think what follows *Hen. VIII.* ii 3 103
Neither will they bate One jot of ceremony *Coriolanus* ii 2 145
Nor babes, Nor sight of priests in holy vestments bleeding, Shall pierce a jot *T. of Athens* iv 3 126
No more, ha?—Not a jot more, my lord *Hamlet* v 1 122
'Twere to consider too curiously, to consider so.—No, faith, not a jot v 1 229
Let me not stay a jot for dinner; go get it ready *Lear* i 4 8
This hath a little dash'd your spirits.—Not a jot, not a jot *Othello* iii 3 215
Detain no jot, I charge the: write to him—I will subscribe *A. and C.* iv 5 13
Joul. They may joul horns together, like any deer i' the herd *All's Well* i 3 58
Jour. O seigneur! le jour est perdu, tout est perdu!—Mort de ma vie! *Hen. V.* iv 5 2
Jourdain. With Margery Jourdain, the cunning witch *2 Hen. VI.* i 2 75
Mother Jourdain, be you prostrate and grovel on the earth i 4 13
Journal. Ere twice the sun hath made his journal greeting *Meas. for Meas.* iv 3 92
Stick to your journal course: the breach of custom Is breach of all *Cymbeline* iv 2 10
Journey. Tell me some good mean How, with my honour, I may undertake A journey to my loving Proteus *T. G. of Ver.* ii 7 7
How will the world repute me For undertaking so unstaid a journey? ii 7 60
If Proteus like your journey when you come, No matter who's displeased when you are gone ii 7 65
Take a note of what I stand in need of, To furnish me upon my longing journey ii 7 85
Thou bear'st thy heavy riches but a journey, And death unloads thee *Meas. for Meas.* iii 1 27
I beseech you Look forward on the journey you shall go iv 3 61
Belike, some noble gentleman that means, Travelling some journey, to repose him here *T. of Shrew* Ind. 1 76
It shall be moon, or star, or what I list, Or ere I journey iv 5 8
Journeys end in lovers meeting, Every wise man's son doth know *T. Night* ii 3 44
If the event o' the journey Prove as successful to the queen *W. Tale* iii 1 11
'Twill be Two long days' journey, lords, or ere we meet *K. John* iv 3 20
And go we to attire you for our journey *2 Hen. VI.* ii 4 106
Whoever journeys to the prince, For God's sake, let not us two be behind; For, by the way, I'll sort occasion *Richard III.* ii 2 146
O, many Have broke their backs with laying manors on 'em For this great journey. What did this vanity? *Hen. VIII.* i 1 85
Demand What was the speech among the Londoners Concerning the French journey i 2 155
My prophecy is but half his journey yet *Troi. and Cres.* iv 5 218
Bring me word thither How the world goes, that to the pace of it I may spur on my journey *Coriolanus* i 10 33
You have well saved me a day's journey iv 3 12
Now is the sun upon the highmost hill Of this day's journey *Rom. and Jul.* ii 5 10
And nature, as it grows again toward earth, Is fashion'd for the journey, dull and heavy *T. of Athens* ii 2 228
When Duncan is asleep—Whereto the rather shall his day's hard journey Soundly invite him *Macbeth* i 7 62
So many journeys may the sun and moon Make us again count o'er ere love be done! *Hamlet* iii 2 171
I have a journey, sir, shortly to go; My master calls me *Lear* v 3 321
So shall you have a shorter journey to your desires *Othello* ii 1 284
Here is my journey's end, here is my butt, And very sea-mark v 2 267
We shall, As I conceive the journey, be at the Mount Before you *A. and C.* ii 4 6
Cæsar through Syria Intends his journey v 2 201
I'll make a journey twice as far, to enjoy A second night of such sweet shortness which Was mine *Cymbeline* ii 4 43
How you shall speed in your journey's end, I think you'll never return to tell v 4 190
How far is his court . . . ?—Marry, sir, half a day's journey *Pericles* ii 1 112
Journey-bated. So are the horses of the enemy In general, journey-bated and brought low *1 Hen. IV.* iv 3 26
Journeying. Are journeying to salute the emperor *T. G. of Ver.* i 3 41
Journeyman. Having my freedom, boast of nothing else But that I was a journeyman to grief *Richard II.* i 3 274
Journeymen. I have thought some of nature's journeymen had made men and not made them well *Hamlet* iii 2 37
Jove's lightnings, the precursors O' the dreadful thunder-claps *Tempest* i 2 201
And rifted Jove's stout oak With his own bolt v 1 45
Remember, Jove, thou wast a bull for thy Europa *Mer. Wives* v 5 3
A fault done first in the form of a beast. O Jove, a beastly fault! v 5 10
Another fault in the semblance of a fowl; think on't, Jove; a foul fault! v 5 12
Send me a cool rut-time, Jove v 5 15
Could great men thunder As Jove himself does, Jove would ne'er be quiet, For every pelting, petty officer Would use his heaven *M. for M.* ii 2 111
My visor is Philemon's roof; within the house is Jove *Much Ado* ii 1 100
As once Europa did at lusty Jove, When he would play the noble beast in love v 4 46
Bull Jove, sir, had an amiable low v 4 48
Thy eye Jove's lightning bears, thy voice his dreadful thunder *L. L. Lost* iv 2 119
Thou for whom Jove would swear Juno but an Ethiope were; And deny himself for Jove, Turning mortal for thy love iv 3 119
Ay me! says one; O Jove! the other cries iv 3 141
And Jove, for your love, would infringe an oath iv 3 144
Jove shield thee well for this! *M. N. Dream* v 1 179
I'll have no worse a name than Jove's own page *As Y. Like It* i 3 126
Jove, Jove! this shepherd's passion Is much upon my fashion ii 4 61
It may well be called Jove's tree, when it drops forth such fruit iii 2 249
O knowledge ill-inhabited, worse than Jove in a thatched house! iii 3 11
Such as the daughter of Agenor had, That made great Jove to humble him to her hand, When with his knees he kiss'd the Cretan strand *T. of Shrew* i 1 174
Thy eldest son should be a fool; whose skull Jove cram with brains! *T. N.* i 5 121
Jove knows I love: But who? ii 5 107
Jove and my stars be praised! Here is yet a postscript ii 5 187
Jove, I thank thee: I will smile; I will do everything ii 5 194
Now Jove, in his next commodity of hair, send thee a beard! iii 1 50
But it is Jove's doing, and Jove make me thankful! iii 4 83
Well, Jove, not I, is the doer of this, and he is to be thanked iii 4 91
Jove bless thee, master Parson.—Bonos dies, Sir Toby iv 2 13
Jove send her A better guiding spirit! *W. Tale* ii 3 126
The ear-deafening voice o' the oracle, Kin to Jove's thunder iii 1 10
I bless the time . . . —Now Jove afford you cause! iv 4 16
From a God to a bull? a heavy descension! it was Jove's case *2 Hen. IV.* ii 2 193
My king! my Jove! I speak to thee, my heart! v 5 50
Like a Jove, That, if requiring fail, he will compel *Hen. V.* ii 4 100
Jove sometime went disguised, and why not I?—But Jove was never slain, as thou shalt be *2 Hen. VI.* iv 1 48
Whose top-branch overpeer'd Jove's spreading tree *3 Hen. VI.* v 2 14
Fiery expedition be my wing, Jove's Mercury, and herald for a king! *Richard III.* iv 3 55
Trials of great Jove To find persistive constancy in men *Troi. and Cres.* i 3 20
And, Jove's accord, Nothing so full of heart i 3 238
Fly like chidden Mercury from Jove, Or like a star disorb'd ii 2 45
And Jove forbid there should be done amongst us Such things! ii 2 127
O thou great thunder-darter of Olympus, forget that thou art Jove! ii 3 12
Jove bless great Ajax!—Hum!—I come from the worthy Achilles,— Ha! iii 3 281
Jove, let Æneas live, If to my sword his fate be not the glory! iv 1 25
By Jove multipotent iv 5 129

Jove. What, shall I come? the hour?—Ay, come:—O Jove!—do come *Troi. and Cres.* v 2 105
The nobles bended, As to Jove's statue *Coriolanus* ii 1 282
By Jove himself! It makes the consuls base: and my soul aches iii 1 107
He would not flatter Neptune for his trident, Or Jove for's power to thunder iii 1 257
Whose gratitude Towards her deserved children is enroll'd In Jove's own book iii 1 293
The god of soldiers, With the consent of supreme Jove, inform Thy thoughts with nobleness! v 3 71
Jove shield your husband from his hounds to-day! *T. Andron.* ii 3 70
Apollo, Pallas, Jove, or Mercury, Inspire me, that I may this treason find! iv 1 66
For Justice, she is so employ'd, He thinks, with Jove in heaven iv 3 40
See, here's to Jove, and this to Mercury; This to Apollo iv 4 14
At lovers' perjuries, They say, Jove laughs *Rom. and Jul.* ii 2 93
Be as a planetary plague, when Jove Will o'er some high-viced city hang his poison In the sick air *T. of Athens* iv 3 108
Know, O Damon dear, This realm dismantled was Of Jove himself *Ham.* iii 2 294
Hyperion's curls; the front of Jove himself; An eye like Mars iii 4 56
Nor tell tales of thee to high-judging Jove *Lear* ii 4 231
Great Jove, Othello guard, And swell his sail! *Othello* ii 1 77
She is sport for Jove ii 3 17
Whose rude throats The immortal Jove's dread clamours counterfeit iii 3 356
She makes a shower of rain as well as Jove *Ant. and Cleo.* i 2 157
Thou art, if thou darest be, the earthly Jove ii 7 73
The Jove of power make me most weak, most weak, Your reconciler! iii 4 29
Favours, by Jove that thunders! What art thou, fellow? iii 13 85
Your emperor Continues still a Jove iv 6 29
Had I great Juno's power, The strong-wing'd Mercury should fetch thee up, And set thee by Jove's side iv 15 36
Jove! Once more let me behold it: is it that Which I left with her? *Cymbeline* ii 4 98
Jove! When on my three-foot stool I sit and tell The warlike feats iii 3 88
Jove knows what man thou mightst have made iv 2 207
I saw Jove's bird, the Roman eagle, wing'd From the spongy south iv 2 348
Clothed like a bride, For the embracements even of Jove himself *Pericles* i 1 7
If Jove stray, who dares say Jove doth ill? It is enough you know i 1 104
By Jove, I wonder, that is king of thoughts, These cates resist me ii 3 28
By Jove *L. L. Lost* v 2; *All's Well* v 3; *Hen. V.* iv 3; *Troi. and Cres.* iv i; v 2; *Coriolanus* iii 1
Jovem. 'Ad Jovem,' that's for you: here, 'Ad Apollinem' *T. Andron.* iv 3 53
Jovial. Be bright and jovial among your guests to-night *Macbeth* iii 2 28
What! I will be jovial: come, come; I am a king, My masters *Lear* iv 6 203
His Martial thigh; The brawns of Hercules: but his Jovial face *Cymb.* iv 2 311
Our Jovial star reign'd at his birth, and in Our temple was he married v 4 105
Jowl. How the knave jowls it to the ground, as if it were Cain's jaw-bone, that did the first murder! *Hamlet* v 1 84
Joy. Be merry; you have cause, So have we all, of joy *Tempest* ii 1 2
Hourly joys be still upon you! Juno sings her blessings on you iv 1 108
Rejoice Beyond a common joy, and set it down With gold on lasting pillars v 1 207
Let grief and sorrow still embrace his heart That doth not wish you joy! v 1 215
How angerly I taught my brow to frown, When inward joy enforced my heart to smile! *T. G. of Ver.* i 2 63
I know you joy not in a love-discourse ii 4 127
There is no woe to his correction Nor to his service no such joy on earth ii 4 139
What joy is joy, if Silvia be not by? Unless it be to think that she is by iii 1 175
Heaven give thee joy! *Mer. Wives* v 5 250
I do repent me, as it is an evil, And take the shame with joy *M. for M.* ii 3 36
Joy to you, Mariana! Love her, Angelo: I have confess'd her v 1 532
With her I lived in joy *Com. of Errors* i 1 40
There appears much joy in him; even so much that joy could not show itself modest enough without a badge of bitterness *Much Ado* i 1 21
How much better is it to weep at joy than to joy at weeping! i 1 28
I wish him joy of her i 1 200
Name the day of marriage, and God give thee joy! ii 1 312
Silence is the perfectest herald of joy ii 1 317
Cousins, God give you joy! ii 1 350
God give me joy to wear it! for my heart is exceeding heavy iii 4 24
Bring me a father that so loved his child, Whose joy of her is overwhelm'd like mine, And bid him speak of patience v 1 9
Why should I joy in any abortive birth? *L. L. Lost* i 1 104
And leap for joy, though they are lame with blows v 2 291
God give thee joy of him! v 2 448
Crowns him with flowers and makes him all her joy *M. N. Dream* iv 1 27
And you come To give their bed joy and prosperity ii 1 73
And kiss thy fair large ears, my gentle joy iv 1 4
If it would but apprehend some joy, It comprehends some bringer of that joy v 1 19
Here come the lovers, full of joy and mirth v 1 28
Joy, gentle friends! joy and fresh days of love Accompany your hearts! v 1 29
Here choose I: joy be the consequence! *Mer. of Venice* iii 2 107
Be moderate; allay thy ecstasy; In measure rein thy joy iii 2 113
Turns to a wild of nothing, save of joy, Express'd and not express'd iii 2 184
Good joy: good joy, my lord and lady! iii 2 190
I wish you all the joy that you can wish iii 2 192
Having such a blessing in his lady, He finds the joys of heaven here on earth iii 5 81
The gods give us joy!—Amen. A man may, if he were of a fearful heart, stagger in this attempt *As Y. Like It* iii 3 47
Am not I your Rosalind?—I take some joy to say you are iv 1 90
With measure heap'd in joy, to the measures fall v 4 185
O, how we joy to see your wit restored! *T. of Shrew* Ind. 2 79
I know not what to say: but give me your hands; God send you joy! ii 1 321
God give him joy!—Ay, and he'll tame her iv 2 52
Fond done, done fond, Was this King Priam's joy? *All's Well* i 3 77
Make the coming hour o'erflow with joy And pleasure drown the brim ii 4 47
I have felt so many quirks of joy and grief iii 2 51
My heart dances; But not for joy! not joy *W. Tale* i 2 111
My second joy And first-fruits of my body iii 2 97
I, that please some, try all, both joy and terror Of good and bad iv 1 1
The father, all whose joy is nothing else But fair posterity iv 4 419
It should take joy To see her in your arms v 1 80
The wisest beholder, that knew no more but seeing, could not say if the importance were joy or sorrow v 2 20
There might you have beheld one joy crown another v 2 48
It seemed sorrow wept to take leave of them, for their joy waded in tears v 2 50
Being ready to leap out of himself for joy of his found daughter v 2 54
As if that joy were now become a loss v 2 55
Joy. Scarce any joy Did ever so long live; no sorrow But kill'd itself much sooner *W. Tale* v 3 51
Lest they desire upon this push to trouble Your joys with like relation v 3 130
My fair son! My life, my joy, my food, my all the world! *K. John* iii 4 104
There's nothing in this world can make me joy iii 4 107
What have you lost by losing of this day?—All days of glory, joy iii 4 117
Joy absent, grief is present for that time *Richard II.* i 3 259
What is six winters? they are quickly gone.—To men in joy i 3 261
And hope to joy is little less in joy Than hope enjoy'd ii 3 15
Let him ne'er see joy that breaks that oath! ii 3 151
I weep for joy To stand upon my kingdom once again iii 2 4
To-day, to-day, unhappy day, too late, O'erthrows thy joys, friends, fortune and thy state iii 2 72
We'll tell tales.—Of sorrow or of joy?—Of either, madam.—Of neither, girl: For if of joy, being altogether wanting, It doth remember me the more of sorrow; Or if of grief, being altogether had, It adds more sorrow to my want of joy iii 4 11
Little joy have I To breathe this news; yet what I say is true iii 4 81
For ever will I walk upon my knees, And never see day that the happy sees, Till thou give joy; until thou bid me joy, By pardoning Rutland v 3 95
But my time Runs posting on in Bolingbroke's proud joy v 5 59
Choose out some secret place, some reverend room, More than thou hast, and with it joy thy life v 6 26
Yea, joy, our chains and our jewels.—'Your brooches, pearls' *2 Hen. IV.* ii 4 52
If he be sick with joy, he'll recover without physic iv 5 14
If it did infect my blood with joy, Or swell my thoughts iv 5 170
Helter-skelter have I rode to thee, And tidings do I bring and lucky joys v 3 99
I speak of Africa and golden joys v 3 104
I do at this hour joy o'er myself, Prevented from a damned enterprise *Hen. V.* ii 2 163
Joy and good wishes To our most fair and princely cousin Katharine! v 2 3
Talbot, my life, my joy, again return'd! How wert thou handled being prisoner? *1 Hen. VI.* i 4 23
Banquet in the open streets, To celebrate the joy that God hath given us i 6 14
All France will be replete with mirth and joy i 6 15
What joy shall noble Talbot have To bid his young son welcome to his grave? iv 3 39
Makes me from wondering fall to weeping joys *2 Hen. VI.* i 1 34
Henry, surfeiting in joys of love, With his new bride i 1 251
Fly to heaven?—The treasury of everlasting joy ii 1 18
So cares and joys abound, as seasons fleet ii 4 4
My joy is death; Death, at whose name I oft have been afear'd ii 4 88
For in the shade of death I shall find joy; In life but double death iii 2 54
Is all thy comfort shut in Gloucester's tomb? Why, then, dame Margaret was ne'er thy joy iii 2 79
Live thou to joy thy life; Myself no joy in nought but that thou livest iii 2 365
A crown; Within whose circuit is Elysium And all that poets feign of bliss and joy *3 Hen. VI.* i 2 31
I cannot joy, until I be resolved Where our right valiant father is become ii 1 9
Never henceforth shall I joy again, Never, O never, shall I see more joy! ii 1 77
And he that throws not up his cap for joy Shall for the fault make forfeit of his head ii 1 196
Since this earth affords no joy to me, But to command iii 2 165
Mine, such as fill my heart with unhoped joys.—Mine, full of sorrow iii 3 172
I . . . forget old faults, And joy that thou becomest King Henry's friend iii 3 201
I'll join mine eldest daughter and my joy To him forthwith iii 3 242
Your dislike, to whom I would be pleasing, Doth cloud my joys with danger iv 1 74
Turn'd my captive state to liberty, My fear to hope, my sorrows unto joys iv 6 4
By doubtful fear My joy of liberty is half eclipsed iv 6 63
So part we sadly in this troublous world, To meet with joy in sweet Jerusalem v 5 8
Farewell sour annoy! For here, I hope, begins our lasting joy v 7 46
Much it joys me too, To see you are become so penitent *Richard III.* i 2 220
Small joy have I in being England's queen i 3 110
As little joy, my lord, as you suppose You should enjoy, were you this country's king, As little joy may you suppose in me i 3 151
Now he delivers thee From this world's thraldom to the joys of heaven i 4 255
Drown desperate sorrow in dead Edward's grave, And plant your joys in living Edward's throne ii 2 100
And often up and down my sons were toss'd, For me to joy and weep their gain and loss ii 4 59
For joy of this good news, Give Mistress Shore one gentle kiss the more iii 1 184
Eighty odd years of sorrow have I seen, And each hour's joy wreck'd with a week of teen iv 1 97
Where are thy children? wherein dost thou joy? Who sues to thee? iv 4 93
Airy succeeders of intestate joys, Poor breathing orators of miseries! iv 4 128
The sweet silent hours of marriage joys iv 4 330
Sleep in peace, and wake in joy; Good angels guard thee! v 3 155
Give me your hand: much joy and favour to you *Hen. VIII.* ii 2 118
Bring me a constant woman to her husband, One that ne'er dream'd a joy beyond his pleasure iii 1 135
Now, all my joy Trace the conjunction! iii 2 44
That time offer'd sorrow; This, general joy iv 1 7
I am stifled With the mere rankness of their joy iv 1 59
Such joy I never saw before iv 1 75
All comfort, joy, in this most gracious lady v 5 7
Things won are done; joy's soul lies in the doing *Troi. and Cres.* i 2 313
Some joy too fine, Too subtle-potent, tuned too sharp in sweetness iii 2 24
And I do fear besides, That I shall lose distinction in my joys iii 2 28
Dreaming night will hide our joys no longer iv 2 10
I sprang not more in joy at first hearing he was a man-child *Coriolanus* i 3 17
To our noble consul Wish we all joy and honour.—To Coriolanus come all joy and honour! ii 2 157
The gods give you joy, sir, heartily!—Most sweet voices! ii 3 118
The gods give him joy, and make him good friend to the people! ii 3 142
Thy sight, which should Make our eyes flow with joy, hearts dance v 3 99
This morning for ten thousand of your throats I'ld not have given a doit. Hark, how they joy! v 4 60
We will meet them, And help the joy v 4 65
Tears of true joy for his return to Rome *T. Andron.* i 1 76
O sacred receptacle of my joys, Sweet cell of virtue and nobility, How many sons of mine hast thou in store! i 1 92
And at thy feet I kneel, with tears of joy, Shed on the earth, for thy return i 1 161
Let not young Mutius, then, that was thy joy, Be barr'd his entrance here i 1 382
God give you joy, sir, of your gallant bride! i 1 400

Joy. I pray you, let us hence, And let her joy her raven-colour'd love *T. Andron.* ii 3 83
Why do the emperor's trumpets flourish thus?—Belike, for joy the emperor hath a son . . . . iv 2 50
Why, there it goes: God give his lordship joy! . . . . iv 3 76
Although I joy in thee, I have no joy of this contract to-night *R. and J.* ii 2 116
Which to the high top-gallant of my joy Must be my convoy . . . ii 4 202
But come what sorrow can, It cannot countervail the exchange of joy That one short minute gives me in her sight . . ii 6 4
If the measure of thy joy Be heap'd like mine and that thy skill be more To blazon it . . . . ii 6 24
Your tributary drops belong to woe, Which you, mistaking, offer up to joy . . . . iii 2 104
Now I have stain'd the childhood of our joy . . . . iii 3 95
And call thee back With twenty hundred thousand times more joy Than thou went'st forth in lamentation . . . . iii 3 153
But that a joy past joy calls out on me, It were a grief, so brief to part iii 3 173
Joyful tidings, girl.—And joy comes well in such a needy time . . iii 5 106
A sudden day of joy, That thou expect'st not nor I look'd not for . . iii 5 110
What say'st thou? hast thou not a word of joy? Some comfort, nurse iii 5 213
Alack! my child is dead; And with my child my joys are buried . . iv 5 64
Ah me! how sweet is love itself possess'd, When but love's shadows are so rich in joy! . . . . v 1 11
See, what a scourge is laid upon your hate, That heaven finds means to kill your joys with love . . . . v 3 293
O joy, e'en made away ere't can be born! . . . *T. of Athens* i 2 110
Joy had the like conception in our eyes And at that instant . . . i 2 115
There is tears for his love; joy for his fortune . . . *J. Cæsar* iii 2 29
Now some light. O, he lights too. He's ta'en. And, hark! they shout for joy . . . . v 3 32
Countrymen, My heart doth joy that yet in all my life I found no man but he was true to me . . . . v 5 34
My plenteous joys, Wanton in fulness, seek to hide themselves In drops of sorrow . . . . *Macbeth* i 4 33
'Tis safer to be that which we destroy Than by destruction dwell in doubtful joy . . . . iii 2 7
Give me some wine; fill full. I drink to the general joy o' the whole table . . . . iii 4 89
With a defeated joy,—With an auspicious and a dropping eye *Hamlet* i 2 10
Whereon old Norway, overcome with joy, Gives him three thousand crowns . . . . ii 2 72
There did seem in him a kind of joy To hear of it . . . . iii 1 18
The violence of either grief or joy Their own enactures with themselves destroy: Where joy most revels, grief doth most lament; Grief joys, joy grieves, on slender accident . . . . iii 2 206
Each opposite that blanks the face of joy Meet what I would have well and it destroy! . . . . iii 2 230
Till I know 'tis done, Howe'er my haps, my joys were ne'er begun . iv 3 70
For bonny sweet Robin is all my joy . . . . iv 5 187
I profess Myself an enemy to all other joys . . . . *Lear* i 1 75
Now, our joy, Although the last, not least . . . . . i 1 84
Then they for sudden joy did weep, And I for sorrow sung . . i 4 191
'Twixt two extremes of passion, joy and grief, Burst smilingly . v 3 198
Though that his joy be joy, Yet throw such changes of vexation on't, As it may lose some colour . . . . *Othello* i 1 71
Seek thou rather to be hanged in compassing thy joy than to be drowned and go without her . . . . i 3 368
O my soul's joy! If after every tempest come such calms, May the winds blow till they have waken'd death! . . . . . ii 1 186
I cannot speak enough of this content; It stops me here; it is too much of joy . . . . ii 1 199
O God, . . . that we should, with joy, pleasance, revel and applause, transform ourselves into beasts! . . . . ii 3 293
He was not merry, Which seem'd to tell them his remembrance lay In Egypt with his joy . . . . *Ant. and Cleo.* i 5 58
Of which I do accuse myself so sorely, That I will joy no more . iv 6 20
I wish you all joy of the worm . . . . v 2 261; 281
For joy whereof The famed Cassibelan . . . Made Lud's town with rejoicing fires bright . . . . *Cymbeline* iii 1 29
With joy he will embrace you, for he's honourable . . . . iii 4 179
Madam, all joy befal your grace!—And you! . . . . . iii 5 9
Fear not slander, censure rash;—Thou hast finish'd joy and moan . iv 2 273
Briefly die their joys That place them on the truth of girls and boys . v 5 106
The gods do mean to strike me To death with mortal joy . . . v 5 235
Throws her eye . . . , hitting Each object with a joy . . . v 5 396
But, feeling woe, Gripe not at earthly joys as erst they did . *Pericles* i 1 49
This mercy shows we'll joy in such a son . . . . i 1 118
Yet neither pleasure's art can joy my spirits, Nor yet the other's distance comfort me . . . . i 2 9
Joy and all comfort in your sacred breast! . . . . . . i 2 33
From whence an issue I might propagate, Are arms to princes, and bring joys to subjects . . . . i 2 74
A courser, whose delightful steps Shall make the gazer joy to see him tread . . . . ii 1 165
And for a further grief,—God give you joy!—What, are you both pleased? . . . . ii 5 87
A vestal livery will I take me to, And never more have joy . . . iii 4 11
Lest this great sea of joys rushing upon me O'erbear the shores of my mortality, And drown me . . . . v 1 194
Led on by heaven, and crown'd with joy at last . . . . . v 3 Gower 90
So, on your patience evermore attending, New joy wait on you! . v 3 Gower 101
Joyed. Poor fellow, never joyed since the price of oats rose . 1 *Hen. IV.* ii 1 13
Was ever king that joy'd an earthly throne, And could command no more content than I? . . . . 2 *Hen. VI.* iv 9 1
Indeed to be our brother; Joy'd are we that you are . . . *Cymbeline* v 5 424
Joyful. Got deliver to a joyful resurrections! . . . . *Mer. Wives* i 1 54
A joyful mother of two goodly sons . . . . *Com. of Errors* i 1 51
What a joyful father wouldst thou make me! . . . *L. L. Lost* v 1 80
I shall find you empty of that fault, Right joyful of your reformation v 2 879
To-morrow is the joyful day . . . . . . *As Y. Like It* v 3 1
We shall be joyful of thy company . . . . . *T. of Shrew* iv 5 52
No joyful tongue gave him his welcome home . . . *Richard II.* v 2 29
Sir John Umfrevile turn'd me back With joyful tidings . . 2 *Hen. IV.* i 1 35
O joyful day! I would not take a knighthood for my fortune . . v 3 132
Peace, Dear nurse of arts, plenties and joyful births . . *Hen. V.* v 2 35
How joyful am I made by this contract! . . . . 1 *Hen. VI.* iii 1 143
God make your majesty joyful as you have been! . . . *Richard III.* i 3 19
O, make them joyful, grant their lawful suit! . . . . . . iii 7 203
God give your graces both A happy and a joyful time of day! . . iv 1 6
For joyful mother, one that wails the name; For queen, a very caitiff . iv 4 99
Joyful. I am joyful To meet the least occasion that may give me Remembrance of my father-in-law . . . . *Hen. VIII.* iii 2 6
I am most joyful, madam, such good dreams Possess your fancy . . v 2 93
Good man, those joyful tears show thy true heart . . . . v 3 175
I am joyful to hear of their readiness . . . . . *Coriolanus* iv 3 51
If they did kill thy husband, then be joyful, Because the law hath ta'en revenge on them . . . . *T. Andron.* iii 1 116
A joyful issue.—A joyless, dismal, black, and sorrowful issue . . iv 2 65
I will tell her as much: Lord, Lord, she will be a joyful woman *R. and J.* ii 4 185
But now I'll tell thee joyful tidings, girl.—And joy comes well . . iii 5 105
The County Paris, at Saint Peter's Church, Shall happily make thee there a joyful bride.—Now, by Saint Peter's Church and Peter too, He shall not make me there a joyful bride . . . . iii 5 116
My dreams presage some joyful news at hand . . . . . . v 1 2
I am joyful of your sights . . . . *T. of Athens* i 1 255
And make joyful The hearing of my wife with your approach *Macbeth* i 4 45
I know this is a joyful trouble to you; But yet 'tis one . . . ii 3 53
They with joyful tears Wash the congealment from your wounds *Ant. and Cleo.* iv 8 9
All o'erjoy'd, Save these in bonds: let them be joyful too . *Cymbeline* v 5 402
Joyfully. Then, joyfully, my noble Lord of Bedford, . . . And my kind kinsman, warriors all, adieu! . . . . *Hen. V.* iv 3 8
And so most joyfully we take our leave . . . . . *Richard III.* iii 7 245
The ambassadors from Norway, my good lord, Are joyfully return'd *Hamlet* ii 2 41
Joyless. A little joy enjoys the queen thereof; For I am she, and altogether joyless . . . . *Richard III.* i 3 155
A joyless, dismal, black, and sorrowful issue . . . *T. Andron.* iv 2 66
Joyous. And wander we to see thy honest son, Who will of thy arrival be full joyous . . . . *T. of Shrew* iv 5 70
Right joyous are we to behold your face . . . . . *Hen. V.* v 2 9
Judas. Myself and this gallant gentleman, Judas Maccabæus . *L. L. Lost* v 1 134
Judas I am,— A Judas!—Not Iscariot, sir. Judas I am, ycliped Maccabæus.—Judas Maccabæus clipt is plain Judas . . . . . . v 2 599
How art thou proved Judas?—Judas I am,— The more shame for you, Judas . . . . v 2 604
What mean you, sir?—To make Judas hang himself . . . . v 2 608
You are my elder.—Well followed: Judas was hanged on an elder . v 2 610
For the ass to the Jude; give it him:—Jud-as, away! . . . . v 2 631
A light for Monsieur Judas! it grows dark, he may stumble . . v 2 633
His very hair is of the dissembling colour.—Something browner than Judas's: marry, his kisses are Judas's own children *As Y. Like It* iii 4 9
Three Judases, each one thrice worse than Judas! . . *Richard II.* iii 2 132
Did they not sometime cry, 'all hail!' to me? So Judas did to Christ iv 1 170
So Judas kiss'd his master, And cried 'all hail!' . . 3 *Hen. VI.* v 7 33
Jude. As he is an ass, let him go. And so adieu, sweet Jude! nay, why dost thou stay?—For the latter end of his name.—For the ass to the Jude; give it him:—Jud-as, away! . . . . . *L. L. Lost* v 2 629
Judge. I see things too, although you judge I wink . . *T. G. of Ver.* i 2 139
Sure as I live, he had suffer'd for't: you shall judge . . . iv 4 18
O, Heaven be judge how I love Valentine! . . . . . . v 4 36
Let her consider his frailty, and then judge of my merit . *Mer. Wives* iii 5 52
As come to— To what, I pray?—Judge . . . . *Meas. for Meas.* i 2 49
If myself might be his judge, He should receive his punishment in thanks . . . . i 4 27
The marshal's truncheon, nor the judge's robe, Become them with one half so good a grace As mercy does . . . . ii 2 61
I would tell what 'twere to be a judge, And what a prisoner . . . ii 2 68
How would you be, If He, which is the top of judgement, should But judge you as you are? . . . . ii 2 77
Thieves for their robbery have authority When judges steal themselves ii 2 177
Whose credit with the judge, or own great place, Could fetch your brother from the manacles Of the all-building law . . . ii 4 92
There is a devilish mercy in the judge, If you'll implore it . . . iii 1 65
He professes to have received no sinister measure from his judge . iii 2 257
In this I'll be impartial; be you judge Of your own cause . . . v 1 166
Thou shalt see, thy eyes shall be thy judge . . . *Mer. of Venice* ii 5 1
I love her heartily; For she is wise, if I can judge of her . . . ii 6 53
To offend, and judge, are distinct offices And of opposed natures . ii 9 61
She is damned for it.—That's certain, if the devil may be her judge . iii 1 36
A Daniel come to judgement! yea, a Daniel! O wise young judge! . iv 1 224
It doth appear you are a worthy judge; You know the law . . . iv 1 236
O noble judge! O excellent young man! . . . . iv 1 246
O wise and upright judge! How much more elder art thou than thy looks! . . . . iv 1 250
Ay, his breast: So says the bond: doth it not, noble judge? . . . iv 1 253
Most rightful judge! . . . . iv 1 301
Most learned judge! A sentence! Come, prepare! . . . . iv 1 304
O upright judge! Mark, Jew: O learned judge! . . . . . iv 1 313
O learned judge! Mark, Jew: a learned judge! . . . . . iv 1 317
O Jew! an upright judge, a learned judge! . . . . . . iv 1 323
Had I been judge, thou shouldst have had ten more . . . . iv 1 399
I swear you do me wrong; In faith, I gave it to the judge's clerk . . v 1 143
Gave it a judge's clerk! no, God's my judge, The clerk will ne'er wear hair on's face that had it . . . . v 1 157
A little scrubbed boy, No higher than thyself, the judge's clerk . . v 1 163
My Lord Bassanio gave his ring away Unto the judge that begg'd it . v 1 180
Neither his daughter, if we judge by manners . . . *As Y. Like It* i 2 283
You have said; but whether wisely or no, let the forest judge . . iii 2 130
Let her be judge how deep I am in love . . . . . . iv 1 220
So holy writ in babes hath judgement shown, When judges have been babes; great floods have flown From simple sources . . . *All's Well* ii 1 142
Thou shalt be both the plaintiff and the judge Of thine own cause *T. Night* v 1 362
Your honours all, I do refer me to the oracle: Apollo be my judge! *W. T.* iii 2 117
Compare our faces and be judge yourself . . . . . . *K. John* i 1 79
From that supernal judge, that stirs good thoughts . . . . ii 1 112
That judge hath made me guardian to this boy . . . . . ii 1 115
Nothing do I see in you, Though churlish thoughts themselves should be your judge, That I can find should merit any hate . . . ii 1 519
You urged me as a judge; but I had rather You would have bid me argue like a father . . . . *Richard II.* i 3 237
Men judge by the complexion of the sky The state and inclination of the day . . . . iii 2 194
Would God that any in this noble presence Were enough noble to be upright judge Of noble Richard! . . . . iv 1 118
By the Lord, I'll be a brave judge.—Thou judgest false already 1 *Hen. IV.* i 2 73
Well, here I am set.—And here I stand: judge, my masters . . ii 4 483
I judge their number Upon or near the rate of thirty thousand 2 *Hen. IV.* iv 1 21
Your humble patience pray, Gently to hear, kindly to judge . *Hen. V.* Prol. 34
To do your grace incessant services.—We judge no less . . . . ii 2 39

Judge. As I judge By his blunt bearing he will keep his word *Hen. V.* iv 7 184
Judge you, my Lord of Warwick, then, between us . . . 1 *Hen. VI.* ii 4 10
Then judge, great lords, if I have done amiss . . . iv 1 27
And should, if I were worthy to be judge, Be quite degraded . . . iv 1 42
You judge it straight a thing impossible To compass wonders . . v 4 47
This doom, my lord, if I may judge . . . . 2 *Hen. VI.* i 3 208
And yet herein I judge mine own wit good . . . . iii 1 232
So bad a death argues a monstrous life.—Forbear to judge . . . iii 3 31
How much thou wrong'st me, heaven be my judge . . . iv 10 82
I cannot judge: but, to conclude with truth . . . . 3 *Hen. VI.* ii 1 128
O, that your young nobility could judge What 'twere to lose it! *Rich. III.* i 3 257
What lawful quest have given their verdict up Unto the frowning judge? . . . . i 4 190
To-morrow, then, I judge a happy day . . . . . iii 4 6
Not pass'd me but By learned approbation of the judges . *Hen. VIII.* i 2 71
You are a churchman, or, I'll tell you, cardinal, I should judge now unhappily . . . . i 4 89
Born out of your dominions; having here No judge indifferent . . ii 4 17
You are mine enemy, and make my challenge You shall not be my judge ii 4 78
I say again, I utterly abhor, yea, from my soul Refuse you for my judge ii 4 82
Heaven is above all yet; there sits a judge That no king can corrupt . iii 1 100
I shall both find your lordship judge and juror, You are so merciful . v 3 60
I take my cause Out of the gripes of cruel men, and give it To a most noble judge, the king . . . . v 3 101
Which way do you judge my wit would fly? . . . . . *Coriolanus* ii 3 28
Cats, that can judge as fitly of his worth As I can of those mysteries which heaven Will not have earth to know . . . . . . iv 2 34
Rome and the righteous heavens be my judge, How I have loved! *T. An.* i 1 426
The judges have pronounced My everlasting doom of banishment . . iii 1 50
Now judge what cause had Titus to revenge These wrongs, unspeakable v 3 125
The felon Loaden with irons wiser than the judge . . *T. of Athens* iii 5 50
And awake your senses, that you may the better judge . *J. Cæsar* iii 2 18
Judge, O you gods, how dearly Cæsar loved him! . . . . iii 2 186
Judge me, you gods! wrong I mine enemies? . . . . iv 2 38
O Jephthah, judge of Israel, what a treasure hadst thou! . *Hamlet* ii 2 422
That, seeing, unseen, We may of their encounter frankly judge . iii 1 34
Make choice of whom your wisest friends you will, And they shall hear and judge 'twixt you and me . . . . iv 5 205
Come, begin: And you, the judges, bear a wary eye . . . v 2 290
If your honour judge it meet, I will place you where you shall hear us *Lear* i 2 97
Now, sir, be judge yourself, Whether I in any just term am affined To love the Moor . . . . *Othello* i 1 38
Heaven is my judge, not I for love and duty, But seeming so . i 1 59
Judge me the world, if 'tis not gross in sense That thou hast practised on her . . . . i 2 72
Why should we be tender To let an arrogant piece of flesh threat us, Play judge and executioner all himself? . . . . . *Cymbeline* iv 2 128
Judged. This love of theirs myself have often seen, Haply when they have judged me fast asleep . . . . . . *T. G. of Ver.* iii 1 25
I heard say he was outrun on Cotsall.—It could not be judged, sir *M. W.* i 1 93
Here is the strangest controversy Come from the country to be judged by you That e'er I heard . . . . *K. John* i 1 45
Thieves are not judged but they are by to hear . *Richard II.* iv 1 123
And shall the figure of God's majesty . . . Be judged by subject and inferior breath? . . . . iv 1 128
The law, thou see'st, hath judged thee . . . . . 2 *Hen. VI.* ii 3 15
It may be judged I made the duke away . . . . . . iii 2 67
Appeal unto the pope, To bring my whole cause 'fore his holiness, And to be judged by him . . . . *Hen. VIII.* ii 4 121
Took some displeasure at him; at least he judged so . . *Pericles* i 3 21
Judgement. His head unmellow'd, but his judgement ripe *T. G. of Ver.* ii 4 70
She, in my judgement, was as fair as you . . . . . . iv 4 156
As fit, by all men's judgements, As if the garment had been made for me . . . . iv 4 167
I'll be judgement by mine host of the Garter . . *Mer. Wives* iii 1 97
Heaven forgive my sins at the day of judgement! . . . iii 3 227
Let mine own judgement pattern out my death . *Meas. for Meas.* ii 1 30
I have seen, When, after execution, judgement hath Repented . ii 2 11
How would you be, If He, which is the top of judgement, should But judge you as you are? . . . . ii 2 76
He hath made an assay of her virtue to practise his judgement . . iii 1 164
In the heat of blood, And lack of temper'd judgement afterward . v 1 478
One that before the judgement carries poor souls to hell *Com. of Errors* iv 2 40
Do you question me . . . for my simple true judgement? . *Much Ado* i 1 168
I pray thee speak in sober judgement . . . . . . i 1 171
She cannot be so much without true judgement—Having so swift and excellent a wit As she is prized to have . . . . . . iii 1 88
Beauty is bought by judgement of the eye . . . . *L. L. Lost* ii 1 15
Rather your eyes must with his judgement look . *M. N. Dream* i 1 57
Nor hath Love's mind of any judgement taste . . . . . i 1 236
I had no judgement when to her I swore.—Nor none, in my mind, now you give her o'er . . . . iii 2 134
Some god direct my judgement! . . . . *Mer. of Venice* ii 7 13
Had you been as wise as bold, Young in limbs, in judgement old . ii 7 71
Seven times tried that judgement is, That did never choose amiss . ii 9 64
With all brief and plain conveniency Let me have judgement . . iv 1 83
What judgement shall I dread, doing no wrong? . . . . . iv 1 89
I stand for judgement: answer; shall I have it? . . . . iv 1 103
A Daniel come to judgement! yea, a Daniel! O wise young judge! . iv 1 223
Proceed to judgement: by my soul I swear There is no power in the tongue of man To alter me . . . . iv 1 240
Most heartily I do beseech the court To give the judgement . . iv 1 244
If you saw yourself with your eyes or knew yourself with your judgement, the fear of your adventure would counsel you *As Y. Like It* i 2 186
Provided that you weed your better judgements Of all opinion . . ii 7 45
He disabled my judgement . . . . v 4 80
Whose judgements are Mere fathers of their garments . *All's Well* i 2 61
We must not So stain our judgement, or corrupt our hope . . ii 1 123
So holy writ in babes hath judgement shown, When judges have been babes . . . . ii 1 141
Never trust my judgement in any thing . . . . . . iii 6 34
I would gladly have him see his company anatomized, that he might take a measure of his own judgements . . . . . . iv 3 38
I will prove it legitimate, sir, upon the oaths of judgement and reason *T. Night* iii 2 16
I wish, my liege, You had only in your silent judgement tried it *W. Tale* ii 1 171
If judgement lie in them, then so do we . . . . *Richard II.* ii 2 133
If the prince put thee into my service for any other reason than to set me off, why then I have no judgement . . . 2 *Hen. IV.* i 2 16
The truth is, I am only old in judgement and understanding . . . i 2 215

Judgement. My judgement is, we should not step too far . 2 *Hen. IV.* i 3 20
And struck me in my very seat of judgement . . . . . v 2 80
Not working with the eye without the ear, And but in purged judgement trusting neither . . . . *Hen. V.* ii 2 136
You have good judgement in horsemanship . . . . . . iii 7 58
Being in his right wits and his good judgements . . . . . iv 7 50
I have perhaps some shallow spirit of judgement . . 1 *Hen. VI.* ii 4 16
God's secret judgement: I did dream to-night The duke was dumb 2 *Hen. VI.* iii 2 31
Forgive me, God, For judgement only doth belong to thee . . . iii 2 140
Mine ear hath tempted judgement to desire . . . 3 *Hen. VI.* iii 3 133
So weak of courage and in judgement That they'll take no offence . iv 1 12
In choosing for yourself, you show'd your judgement . . . iv 1 61
That word 'judgement' hath bred a kind of remorse in me *Richard III.* i 4 109
When he was brought again to the bar, to hear His knell rung out, his judgement, he was stirr'd With such an agony, he sweat extremely *Hen. VIII.* ii 1 32
I have this day received a traitor's judgement . . . . . . ii 1 58
Rome, the nurse of judgement, Invited by your noble self . . . ii 2 94
Of an excellent And unmatch'd wit and judgement . . . . ii 4 47
Hence I took a thought, This was a judgement on me . . . . ii 4 194
The cardinal did entreat his holiness To stay the judgement o' the divorce . . . . iii 2 33
His royal self in judgement comes to hear The cause . . . v 3 120
His own's better.—You have no judgement, niece . *Troi. and Cres.* i 2 99
He's one o' the soundest judgements in Troy, whosoever . . i 2 208
With great speed of judgement, Ay, with celerity . . . . i 3 329
Two traded pilots 'twixt the dangerous shores Of will and judgement . ii 2 65
In self-assumption greater Than in the note of judgement . . ii 3 134
Yet gives he not till judgement guide his bounty . . . . iv 5 102
If the son of a whore fight for a whore, he tempts judgement . . v 7 22
Had you tongues to cry Against the rectorship of judgement? *Coriolanus* ii 3 213
And on a safer judgement all revoke Your ignorant election . . ii 3 226
Your dishonour Mangles true judgement and bereaves the state . iii 1 158
Defect of judgement, To fail in the disposing of those chances . . iv 7 39
Your judgements, my grave lords, Must give this cur the lie . . v 6 106
Take our good meaning, for our judgement sits Five times in that ere once in our five wits . . . . *Rom. and Jul.* i 4 46
A gentler judgement vanish'd from his lips, Not body's death . . iii 3 10
Three? hum! It shows but little love or judgement in him: Must I be his last refuge? . . . . *T. of Athens* iii 3 10
If, after two days' shine, Athens contain thee, Attend our weightier judgement . . . . iii 5 102
Performance is a kind of will or testament which argues a great sickness in his judgement that makes it . . . . v 1 31
It shall be said, his judgement ruled our hands . . . *J. Cæsar* ii 1 147
O judgement! thou art fled to brutish beasts . . . . . iii 2 109
Under heavy judgement bears that life Which he deserves to lose *Macbeth* i 3 110
But in these cases We still have judgement here . . . . i 7 8
Take each man's censure, but reserve thy judgement . . *Hamlet* i 3 69
I am sorry that with better heed and judgement I had not quoted him ii 1 111
Others, whose judgements in such matters cried in the top of mine . ii 2 458
Blest are those Whose blood and judgement are so well commingled . iii 2 74
And after we will both our judgements join In censure of his seeming . iii 2 91
At your age The hey-day in the blood is tame, it's humble, And waits upon the judgement: and what judgement Would step from this to this? . . . . iii 4 70
The distracted multitude, Who like not in their judgement, but their eyes . . . . iv 3 5
Divided from herself and her fair judgement, Without the which we are pictures, or mere beasts . . . . iv 5 85
It shall as level to your judgement pierce As day does to your eye . iv 5 151
Come, my lord.—One.—No.—Judgement.—A hit, a very palpable hit . v 2 291
Of carnal, bloody, and unnatural acts, Of accidental judgements . . v 2 393
Answer my life my judgement . . . . *Lear* i 1 153
With what poor judgement he hath now cast her off appears too grossly i 1 294
To fear judgement; to fight when I cannot choose: and to eat no fish . i 4 17
To my judgement, your highness is not entertained with that ceremonius affection . . . . i 4 62
Beat at this gate, that let thy folly in, And thy dear judgement out! . i 4 294
This judgement of the heavens, that makes us tremble, Touches us not v 3 231
Nay, it is possible enough to judgement . . . . . . *Othello* i 3 9
It is a judgement maim'd and most imperfect . . . . . i 3 99
A jealousy so strong That judgement cannot cure . . . . ii 1 311
And passion, having my best judgement collied, Assays to lead the way ii 3 206
If he be not one that truly loves you, That errs in ignorance and not in cunning, I have no judgement in an honest face . . . . iii 3 50
Her will, recoiling to her better judgement, May fall to match you . iii 3 236
Your suspicion is not without wit and judgement . . . . . iv 2 215
Being mature in knowledge, Pawn their experience to their present pleasure, And so rebel to judgement . . . . *Ant. and Cleo.* i 4 33
My salad days, When I was green in judgement . . . . . i 5 74
You praise yourself By laying defects of judgement . . . . ii 2 55
There's nothing in her yet: The fellow has good judgement.—Excellent iii 3 28
I see men's judgements are A parcel of their fortunes . . . . iii 13 31
Cæsar, thou hast subdued His judgement too . . . . . . iii 13 37
In our own filth drop our clear judgements; make us Adore our errors iii 13 113
Be it but to fortify her judgement, which else an easy battery might lay flat, for taking a beggar . . . . *Cymbeline* i 4 22
Upon my mended judgement—if I offend not to say it is mended . . i 4 49
Is't not meet That I did amplify my judgement in Other conclusions? . i 5 17
Nor i' the judgement, For idiots in this case of favour would Be wisely definite . . . . i 6 41
Hath Honour'd with confirmation your great judgement In the election i 6 174
Slanders so her judgement That what's else rare is choked . . . iii 5 76
The effect of judgement Is oft the cause of fear . . . . . iv 2 111
Our very eyes Are sometimes like our judgements, blind . . . iv 2 302
What now ensues, to the judgement of your eye I give . *Pericles* i Gower 41
If you were born to honour, show it now; If put upon you, make the judgement good That thought you worthy of it . . . . . iv 6 100
Judgement-day. The dreadful judgement-day So dreadful will not be as was his sight . . . . 1 *Hen. VI.* i 1 29
He shall never wake till the judgement-day . . . *Richard III.* i 4 106
Judgement-place. Old Free-town, our common judgement-place *R. and J.* i 1 109
Judgest. I'll be a brave judge.—Thou judgest false already . 1 *Hen. IV.* i 2 74
O thou that judgest all things, stay my thoughts! . . 2 *Hen. VI.* ii 2 136
Judging. In the unpartial judging of this business . . *Hen. VIII.* ii 2 107
Judicious. Examined my parts with most judicious œillades . *Mer. Wives* i 3 68
His last offences to us Shall have judicious hearing. . . . *Coriolanus* v 6 128
He is noble, wise, judicious, and best knows The fits o' the season *Macb.* iv 2 16

Judicious. Now this overdone, or come tardy off, though it make the unskilful laugh, cannot but make the judicious grieve . *Hamlet* iii 2 29
Judicious punishment! 'twas this flesh begot Those pelican daughters *Lear* iii 4 76
Jug. She brought stone jugs and no seal'd quarts . . *T. of Shrew* Ind. 2 90
Whoop, Jug! I love thee . . . . . . *Lear* i 4 245
Juggle. Is't possible the spells of France should juggle Men into such strange mysteries? . . . . . . *Hen. VIII.* i 3 1
Juggled. I'll not be juggled with: To hell, allegiance! . . *Hamlet* iv 5 130
Juggler. Nimble jugglers that deceive the eye . . *Com. of Errors* i 2 98
A mere anatomy, a mountebank, A threadbare juggler . . . . v 1 239
O me! you juggler! you canker-blossom! You thief of love! *M. N. D.* iii 2 282
Away, you bottle-ale rascal! you basket-hilt stale juggler, you! 2 *Hen. IV.* ii 4 141
Juggling. This juggling witchcraft . . . . *K. John* iii 1 169
She and the Dauphin have been juggling . . . 1 *Hen. VI.* v 4 68
Here is such patchery, such juggling and such knavery . *Troi. and Cres.* ii 3 77
What would you have me do?—A juggling trick,—to be secretly open . v 2 24
And be these juggling fiends no more believed, That palter with us in a double sense . . . . *Macbeth* v 8 19
Juice. With juice of balm and every precious flower . . *Mer. Wives* v 5 66
The juice of it on sleeping eye-lids laid Will make or man or woman madly dote Upon the next live creature . . . *M. N. Dream* ii 1 170
Having once this juice, I'll watch Titania when she is asleep, And drop the liquor of it in her eyes . . . . ii 1 176
And with the juice of this I'll streak her eyes, And make her full of hateful fantasies . . . . ii 1 257
Upon my secure hour thy uncle stole, With juice of cursed hebenon *Ham.* i 5 62
Now no more The juice of Egypt's grape shall moist this lip *Ant. and Cleo.* v 2 285
Jule. 'Wilt thou not, Jule?' quoth he; And, pretty fool, it stinted and said 'Ay' . . . . . . *Rom. and Jul.* i 3 43; 47; 57
Julia. Thou, Julia, thou hast metamorphosed me . . *T. G. of Ver.* i 1 66
But, dost thou hear? gavest thou my letter to Julia? . . . i 1 100
Julia would not deign my lines, Receiving them from such a worthless post . . . . i 1 160
'To Julia.' Say, from whom?—That the contents will show . . . i 2 35
Look, here is writ 'kind Julia.' Unkind Julia! . . . . i 2 109
Poor forlorn Proteus, passionate Proteus, To the sweet Julia . . . i 2 125
O, that our fathers would applaud our loves, To seal our happiness with their consents! O heavenly Julia! . . . . i 3 50
I fear'd to show my father Julia's letter, Lest he should take exceptions i 3 80
Have patience, gentle Julia.—I must, where is no remedy . . ii 2 1
Keep this remembrance for thy Julia's sake . . . . ii 2 5
When that hour o'erslips me in the day Wherein I sigh not, Julia, for thy sake . . . . ii 2 10
Julia, farewell. What, gone without a word? Ay, so true love should do . . . . ii 2 16
She is fair; and so is Julia that I love—That I did love . . . ii 4 199
How did thy master part with Madam Julia? . . . . . ii 5 12
To leave my Julia, shall I be forsworn; To love fair Silvia, shall I be forsworn . . . . ii 6 1
Julia I lose and Valentine I lose: If I keep them, I needs must lose myself; If I lose them, thus find I by their loss For Valentine myself, for Julia Silvia . . . . ii 6 19
And Silvia—witness Heaven, that made her fair!—Shows Julia but a swarthy Ethiope . . . . ii 6 26
I will forget that Julia is alive, Remembering that my love to her is dead . . . . ii 6 27
She bids me think how I have been forsworn In breaking faith with Julia . . . . iv 2 11
Bring my picture there. Go give your master this: tell him from me, One Julia, that his changing thoughts forget, Would better fit his chamber than this shadow . . . . iv 4 124
I have heard him say a thousand times His Julia gave it him at his departure. Though his false finger have profaned the ring, Mine shall not do his Julia so much wrong . . . . iv 4 140
Got me to play the woman's part, And I was trimm'd in Madam Julia's gown . . . . iv 4 166
Read over Julia's heart, thy first best love, For whose dear sake thou didst then rend thy faith Into a thousand oaths . . . . v 4 46
This is it.—How! let me see: Why, this is the ring I gave to Julia . v 4 93
I gave this unto Julia.—And Julia herself did give it me; And Julia herself hath brought it hither.—How! Julia! . . . . . v 4 97
Juliet. Here comes Signior Claudio, led by the provost to prison; and there's Madam Juliet . . . . . *Meas. for Meas.* i 2 119
But it chances The stealth of our most mutual entertainment With character too gross is writ on Juliet . . . . i 2 159
My cousin Juliet?—Is she your cousin?—Adoptedly . . . i 4 45
What shall be done, sir, with the groaning Juliet? She's very near her hour . . . . ii 2 15
My brother did love Juliet, And you tell me that he shall die for it . ii 4 142
Where's this girl? What, Juliet!—How now! who calls?—Your mother *Rom. and Jul.* i 3 4
Tell me, daughter Juliet, How stands your disposition to be married? . i 3 64
Juliet, the county stays.—Go, girl, seek happy nights to happy days . i 3 105
That fair for which love groan'd for and would die, With tender Juliet match'd, is now not fair . . . . ii Prol. 4
What light through yonder window breaks? It is the east, and Juliet is the sun . . . . ii 2 3
Ah, Juliet, if the measure of thy joy Be heap'd like mine . . . ii 6 24
O sweet Juliet, Thy beauty hath made me effeminate! . . . iii 1 118
'Romeo is banished,' to speak that word, Is father, mother, Tybalt, Romeo, Juliet, All slain, all dead . . . . iii 2 123
Heaven is here, Where Juliet lives . . . . iii 3 30
They may seize On the white wonder of dear Juliet's hand . . . iii 3 36
Hang up philosophy! Unless philosophy can make a Juliet . . . iii 3 58
Wert thou as young as I, Juliet thy love, An hour but married, Tybalt murdered, Doting like me and like me banished . . . . iii 3 65
Let me come in, and you shall know my errand; I come from Lady Juliet . . . . iii 3 80
For Juliet's sake, for her sake, rise and stand . . . . . iii 3 89
Spakest thou of Juliet? how is it with her? Doth she not think me an old murderer? . . . . iii 3 93
Thy Juliet is alive, For whose dear sake thou wast but lately dead . iii 3 135
Come, death, and welcome! Juliet wills it so. How is't, my soul? let's talk . . . . iii 5 24
Why, how now, Juliet!—Madam, I am not well.—Evermore weeping for your cousin's death? . . . . iii 5 69
Juliet, on Thursday early will I rouse ye: Till then, adieu . . . iv 1 42
Ah, Juliet, I already know thy grief; It strains me . . . . iv 1 46
Go thou to Juliet, help to deck up her; I'll not to bed to-night . . iv 2 41
Juliet. Go waken Juliet, go and trim her up; I'll go and chat with Paris *Rom. and Jul.* iv 4 24
Juliet! fast, I warrant her, she: Why, lamb! why, lady! fie, you slug-a-bed! . . . . iv 5 1
For shame, bring Juliet forth; her lord is come.—She's dead, deceased, she's dead . . . . iv 5 22
How fares my Juliet? that I ask again; For nothing can be ill, if she be well . . . . v 1 15
Well, Juliet, I will lie with thee to-night. Let's see for means . . v 1 34
Come, cordial and not poison, go with me To Juliet's grave . . . v 1 86
Within this three hours will fair Juliet wake . . . . . v 2 24
If thou be merciful, Open the tomb, lay me with Juliet . . . . v 3 73
I think He told me Paris should have married Juliet; Said he not so? or did I dream it so? Or am I mad, hearing him talk of Juliet, To think it was so? . . . . v 3 78
Here lies Juliet, and her beauty makes This vault a feasting presence . v 3 85
Ah, dear Juliet, Why art thou yet so fair? . . . . . . v 3 101
The watch is coming; Come, go, good Juliet, I dare no longer stay . v 3 159
And Juliet bleeding, warm, and newly dead, Who here hath lain these two days buried . . . . v 3 175
The people in the street cry Romeo, Some Juliet, and some Paris . . v 3 192
Romeo dead; and Juliet, dead before, Warm and new kill'd . . . v 3 196
Romeo, there dead, was husband to that Juliet; And she, there dead, that Romeo's faithful wife . . . . v 3 231
Their stol'n marriage-day Was Tybalt's dooms-day whose untimely death Banish'd the new-made bridegroom from this city, For whom, and not for Tybalt, Juliet pined . . . . v 3 236
I brought my master news of Juliet's death; And then in post he came v 3 272
And therewithal Came to this vault to die, and lie with Juliet . . v 3 290
There shall no figure at such rate be set As that of true and faithful Juliet . . . . v 3 302
Never was a story of more woe Than this of Juliet and her Romeo . v 3 310
Julietta. It is for getting Madam Julietta with child . *Meas. for Meas.* i 2 74
Thus stands it with me: upon a true contract I got possession of Julietta's bed . . . . i 2 150
Julio Romano. That rare Italian master, Julio Romano . . *W. Tale* v 2 106
Julius. This is the way To Julius Cæsar's ill-erected tower *Richard II.* v 1 2
A far more glorious star thy soul will make Than Julius Cæsar 1 *Hen. VI.* i 1 56
Did Julius Cæsar build that place [the Tower], my lord? *Richard III.* iii 1 69
That Julius Cæsar was a famous man . . . . . . iii 1 84
Pardon me, Julius! Here wast thou bay'd, brave hart; Here didst thou fall . . . . *J. Cæsar* iii 1 204
Did not great Julius bleed for justice' sake? . . . . . iv 3 19
In the most high and palmy state of Rome, A little ere the mightiest Julius fell, The graves stood tenantless . . . . *Hamlet* i 1 114
I did enact Julius Cæsar: I was killed i' the Capitol . . . iii 2 108
Since Julius Cæsar, Who at Philippi the good Brutus ghosted *A. and C.* ii 6 12
I have heard that Julius Cæsar Grew fat with feasting there . . ii 6 65
When Antony found Julius Cæsar dead, He cried almost to roaring . iii 2 54
More order'd than when Julius Cæsar Smiled at their lack of skill *Cymb.* ii 4 21
Julius Cæsar, whose remembrance yet Lives in men's eyes . . . iii 1 2
There be many Cæsars, Ere such another Julius . . . . iii 1 12
July. He makes a July's day short as December . . . *W. Tale* i 2 169
By intelligence, And proofs as clear as founts in July . *Hen. VIII.* i 1 154
Jump. Put L to sore, then sorel jumps from thicket . . *L. L. Lost* iv 2 60
I will not jump with common spirits . . . . *Mer. of Venice* ii 9 32
Anon a careless herd, Full of the pasture, jumps along by him *As Y. L. It* ii 1 53
Both our inventions meet and jump in one . . . . *T. of Shrew* i 1 195
Till each circumstance Of place, time, fortune, do cohere and jump *T. Night* v 1 259
Such delicate burthens of dildos and fadings, 'jump her and thump her' *W. Tale* iv 4 195
Not the worst of the three but jumps twelve foot and a half by the squier . . . . iv 4 347
In some sort it jumps with my humour . . . . . 1 *Hen. IV.* i 2 78
Jumps upon joined-stools, and swears with a good grace . 2 *Hen. IV.* ii 4 269
And wish To jump a body with a dangerous physic . . *Coriolanus* iii 1 154
That but this blow Might be the be-all and the end-all here, But here, upon this bank and shoal of time, We'ld jump the life to come *Macb.* i 7 7
Thus twice before, and jump at this dead hour, With martial stalk hath he gone by our watch . . . . *Hamlet* i 1 65
But since, so jump upon this bloody question, You . . . Are here arrived . . . . v 2 386
Though they jump not on a just account . . . . . *Othello* i 3 5
And bring him jump when he may Cassio find Soliciting his wife . . ii 3 392
Our fortune lies Upon this jump . . . . . *Ant. and Cleo.* iii 8 6
Or jump the after inquiry on your own peril . . . *Cymbeline* v 4 188
Jumpeth. Seldom or never jumpeth with the heart . . *Richard III.* iii 1 11
Jumping o'er times, Turning the accomplishment of many years Into an hour-glass . . . . *Hen. V.* Prol. 29
June. It is like, if there come a hot June . . . . . 1 *Hen. IV.* ii 4 397
He was but as the cuckoo is in June, Heard, not regarded . . . iii 2 75
The breese upon her, like a cow in June, Hoist sails and flies *A. and C.* iii 10 14
Junius Brutus. One's Junius Brutus, Sicinius Velutus, and I know not *Coriolanus* i 1 220
Swear with me, as . . . Lord Junius Brutus sware for Lucrece' rape *T. Andron.* iv 1 91
Junket. You know there wants no junkets at the feast . *T. of Shrew* iii 2 250
Juno. Great Juno comes; I know her by her gait . . . *Tempest* iv 1 102
Juno sings her blessings on you . . . . iv 1 109
Sweet, now, silence! Juno and Ceres whisper seriously . . . . iv 1 125
Answer your summons; Juno does command: Come, temperate nymphs iv 1 131
Thou for whom Jove would swear Juno but an Ethiope were . *L. L. Lost* iv 3 118
Like Juno's swans, Still we went coupled and inseparable *As Y. Like It* i 3 77
Wedding is great Juno's crown: O blessed bond of board and bed! . v 4 147
I, his despiteful Juno, sent him forth From courtly friends . *All's Well* iii 4 13
Sweeter than the lids of Juno's eyes Or Cytherea's breath . *W. Tale* iv 4 121
His cloven chin— Juno have mercy! how came it cloven? *Troi. and Cres.* i 2 133
For the love of Juno, let's go . . . . . . *Coriolanus* iv 5 111
By Jupiter, I swear, no.—By Juno, I swear, ay . . . . *Lear* ii 4 22
Let me sit down. O Juno!—No, no, no, no, no . . *Ant. and Cleo.* iii 11 28
Had I great Juno's power, The strong-wing'd Mercury should fetch thee up . . . . iv 15 34
Dainty trims, wherein You made great Juno angry . . . *Cymbeline* iii 4 168
And sauced our broths, as Juno had been sick And he her dieter . . iv 2 50
With Mars fall out, with Juno chide, That thy adulteries Rates and revenges . . . . v 4 32
By Juno, that is queen of marriage, All viands that I eat do seem unsavoury, Wishing him my meat . . . . . . *Pericles* ii 3 30
Her eyes as jewel-like And cased as richly; in pace another Juno . . v 1 112

Juno-like. And lament as I do, In anger, Juno-like . . *Coriolanus* iv 2 53
Jupiter. Hail, many-colour'd messenger, that ne'er Dost disobey the wife of Jupiter . . . *Tempest* iv 1 77
You were also, Jupiter, a swan for the love of Leda . *Mer. Wives* v 5 7
O Jupiter, how weary are my spirits! . . . *As Y. Like It* ii 4 1
Jupiter Became a bull, and bellow'd . . . . *W. Tale* iv 4 27
Troilus is the better man of the two.—O Jupiter! . *Troi. and Cres.* i 2 65
'Jupiter!' quoth she, 'which of these hairs is Paris my husband?' . ii 2 177
Jupiter forbid, And say in thunder, 'Achilles go to him' . . ii 3 208
I have said to some my standers by 'Lo, Jupiter is yonder, dealing life!' . . . . iv 5 191
And the goodly transformation of Jupiter there, his brother, the bull . v 1 59
His bloody brow! O Jupiter, no blood!—Away, you fool! . *Coriolanus* i 3 41
Marcius, his name?—By Jupiter! forgot. I am weary . . . i 9 90
Take my cap, Jupiter, and I thank thee . . . . . ii 1 115
If Jupiter Should from yond cloud speak divine things, And say ''Tis true,' I'ld not believe them more Than thee . . . . iv 5 109
I aim a mile beyond the moon; Your letter is with Jupiter by this *T. Andron.* iv 3 66
Shall I have justice? what says Jupiter?—O, the gibbet-maker! . iv 3 79
Alas, sir, I know not Jupiter; I never drank with him in all my life . iv 3 84
Away! by Jupiter, This shall not be revoked . . . . *Lear* i 1 181
By Jupiter, I swear, no.—By Juno, I swear, ay . . . ii 4 21
By Jupiter, Were I the wearer of Antonius' beard, I would not shave't to-day.—'Tis not a time For private stomaching . *Ant. and Cleo.* ii 2 6
Cæsar? Why, he's the Jupiter of men.—What's Antony? The god of Jupiter . . . . iii 2 9
Wert thou the son of Jupiter and no more But what thou art besides, thou wert too base To be his groom . . *Cymbeline* ii 3 130
By Jupiter, I had it from her arm.—Hark you, he swears; by Jupiter he swears.—'Tis true . . . . ii 4 121
Where is thy lady? or, by Jupiter,—I will not ask again . . iii 5 84
By Jupiter, an angel! or, if not, An earthly paragon! . . iii 6 43
Great Jupiter be praised! Lucius is taken . . . . v 3 84
Jupiter, thou king of gods, Why hast thou thus adjourn'd The graces for his merits due? . . . . v 4 77
Since, Jupiter, our son is good, Take off his miseries . . v 4 85
Help, Jupiter; or we appeal, And from thy justice fly . . v 4 91
As I slept, methought Great Jupiter, upon his eagle back'd, Appear'd to me . . . . v 5 427
In the temple of great Jupiter Our peace we'll ratify . . v 5 482
Jure. You are grandjurors, are ye? we'll jure ye, 'faith . 1 *Hen. IV.* ii 2 97
Jurement. Encore qu'il est contre son jurement de pardonner aucun prisonnier, néanmoins, pour les écus . . . *Hen. V.* iv 4 53
Jurisdiction. Within point-blank of our jurisdiction regal 2 *Hen. VI.* iv 7 29
By which power You maim'd the jurisdiction of all bishops *Hen. VIII.* iii 2 312
Juror. If your will pass, I shall both find your lordship judge and juror, You are so merciful . . . . v 3 60
Wert thou a leopard, thou wert german to the lion and the spots of thy kindred were jurors on thy life . . . . *T. of Athens* iv 3 345
Jury. The jury, passing on the prisoner's life, May in the sworn twelve have a thief or two Guiltier than him they try . *Meas. for Meas.* ii 1 19
How innocent I was From any private malice in his end, His noble jury and foul cause can witness . . . . *Hen. VIII.* iii 2 269
Just. Every day some sailor's wife, The masters of some merchant and the merchant Have just our theme of woe . . . *Tempest* ii 1 6
In the same fashion as you gave in charge, Just as you left them . v 1 9
For all the orld, as just as you will desire . . *Mer. Wives* i 1 50
Just 'twixt twelve and one . . . . . . iv 6 19
The words of heaven; on whom it will, it will; On whom it will not, so; yet still 'tis just . . . . . *Meas. for Meas.* i 2 127
O just but severe law! I had a brother, then . . . ii 2 41
Perpetual durance?—Ay, just; perpetual durance, a restraint . iii 1 68
Were he meal'd with that Which he corrects, then were he tyrannous; But this being so, he's just. . . . . . . iv 2 88
A man of Claudio's years; his beard and head Just of his colour . iv 3 77
The wicked'st caitiff on the ground May seem as shy, as grave, as just . v 1 54
You say your husband.—Why, just, my lord, and that is Angelo . v 1 202
Even just the sum that I do owe to you Is growing to me *Com. of Errors* iv 1 7
Discover how, and thou shalt find me just . . . v 1 203
He were an excellent man that were made just in the midway between him and Benedick . . . . . . *Much Ado* ii 1 8
God will send you no horns.—Just, if he send me no husband . ii 1 29
His words are a very fantastical banquet, just so many strange dishes . ii 3 22
Just so much as you may take upon a knife's point and choke a daw withal . . . . ii 3 263
'Nay,' said I, 'a good wit:' 'Just,' said she, 'it hurts nobody' . v 1 164
But always hath been just and virtuous In any thing that I do know by her . . . . v 1 311
Much like to you, for you have just his bleat.—For this I owe you . v 4 51
Nor cut thou less nor more But just a pound of flesh . *Mer. of Venice* iv 1 326
Sweep on, you fat and greasy citizens; 'Tis just the fashion *As Y. Like It* ii 1 56
Rosalind is your love's name?—Yes, just.—I do not like her name. . iii 2 281
What stature is she of?—Just as high as my heart . . . iii 2 286
'Twas just the difference Betwixt the constant red and mingled damask iii 5 122
The gown is made Just as my master had direction. . *T. of Shrew* iv 3 117
Just like the brooch and the tooth-pick, which wear not now *All's Well* i 1 171
Uncertain life, and sure death.—Just, you say well; so would I have said . . . . ii 3 21
We marvel much our cousin France Would in so just a business shut his bosom . . . . iii 1 8
My mother told me just how he would woo, As if she sat in's heart . iv 2 69
The better for my foes and the worse for my friends.—Just the contrary *T. Night* v 1 15
So shall she have A just and open trial . . . *W. Tale* ii 3 205
Apollo be my judge!—This your request Is altogether just . . iii 2 118
The peace of heaven is theirs that left their swords In such a just and charitable war.—Well then, to work . . . *K. John* ii 1 36
Peace be to France, if France in peace permit Our just and lineal entrance to our own . . . . ii 1 85
A loyal, just and upright gentleman . . . . *Richard II.* i 3 87
For he is just and always loved us well . . . . ii 1 221
This swears he, as he is a prince, is just . . . . iii 3 119
What news from Oxford? hold those justs and triumphs? . . v 2 52
And God befriend us, as our cause is just! . . 1 *Hen. IV.* v 1 120
The arms are fair, When the intent of bearing them is just . . v 2 89
Which is an excellent thing.—It is very just . . 2 *Hen. IV.* iii 2 89
Wherein It shall appear that your demands are just, You shall enjoy them . . . . iv 1 144
May well be charm'd asleep With grant of our most just and right desires iv 2 40
Just. Is this proceeding just and honourable?—Is your assembly so? 2 *Hen. IV.* iv 2 110
With the like bold, just and impartial spirit As you have done 'gainst me . . . . v 2 116
The things I speak are just . . . . . . v 3 127
I'll live by Nym, and Nym shall live by me; Is not this just? *Hen. V.* ii 1 116
A' parted even just between twelve and one, even at the turning o' the tide . . . . ii 3 13
It is too hot, that is the very plain-song of it.—The plain-song is most just . . . . iii 2 7
A valiant flea that dare eat his breakfast on the lip of a lion.—Just, just iii 7 158
His cause being just and his quarrel honourable . . . iv 1 133
We know your grace to be a man Just and upright . . 1 *Hen. VI.* iii 1 95
Why, this is just 'Aio te, Æacida, Romanos vincere posse' . 2 *Hen. VI.* i 4 64
Thrice is he arm'd that hath his quarrel just . . . iii 2 233
The head of Cade! Great God, how just art Thou! O, let me view his visage . . . . v 1 68
Thou hast one son; for his sake pity me, Lest in revenge thereof, sith God is just, He be as miserably slain as I . . 3 *Hen. VI.* i 3 41
Am come to crave thy just and lawful aid . . . . iii 3 32
Though usurpers sway the rule awhile, Yet heavens are just . . iii 3 77
And if King Edward be as true and just As I am subtle, false and treacherous, This day should Clarence closely be mew'd up *Richard III.* i 1 36
A quarrel just and reasonable, To be revenged on him that slew my husband . . . . i 2 136
So just is God, to right the innocent. . . . . . i 3 182
O upright, just, and true-disposing God, How do I thank thee! . iv 4 55
Just as I do now, He would kiss you twenty with a breath . *Hen. VIII.* i 4 29
Must now confess, if they have any goodness, The trial just and noble . ii 2 92
Be just, and fear not: Let all the ends thou aim'st at be thy country's iii 2 446
'Tis just to each of them; he is himself . . *Troi. and Cres.* i 2 75
Cries 'Excellent! 'tis Agamemnon just. Now play me Nestor' . . i 3 164
O, be persuaded! do not count it holy To hurt by being just. . . v 3 20
Rome, be as just and gracious unto me As I am confident and kind to thee. Open the gates, and let me in . . . . *T. Andron.* i 1 60
Look you eat no more Than will preserve just so much strength in us As will revenge these bitter woes of ours . . . . . iii 2 2
Or get some little knife between thy teeth, And just against thy heart make thou a hole. . . . . iii 2 17
But yet so just that he will not revenge . . . . iv 1 128
I read it in the grammar long ago.—Ay, just; a verse in Horace . iv 2 24
My report is just and full of truth . . . . . . v 3 115
Just opposite to what thou justly seem'st . . . *Rom. and Jul.* iii 2 78
O, he is even in my mistress' case, Just in her case! O woful sympathy! . . . . iii 3 85
And just of the same piece Is every flatterer's spirit *T. of Athens* iii 2 71
To kill, I grant, is sin's extremest gust; But, in defence, by mercy, 'tis most just. To be in anger is impiety . . . . . . iii 5 55
'Tis most just That thou turn rascal . . . . . . iv 3 216
Had I a steward So true, so just, and now so comfortable? . . iv 3 498
If it be a just and true report that goes of his having . . v 1 17
'Tis just: And it is very much lamented, Brutus . . *J. Cæsar* i 2 54
He was my friend, faithful and just to me . . . . iii 2 90
He needs not our mistrust, since he delivers Our offices and what we have to do To the direction just . . . . . *Macbeth* iii 3 4
You may be rightly just, Whatever I shall think . . . iv 3 30
Thou art e'en as just a man As e'er my conversation coped withal *Ham.* iii 2 59
Expose thyself to feel what wretches feel, That thou mayst shake the superflux to them, And show the heavens more just . . *Lear* iii 4 36
How malicious is my fortune, that I must repent to be just! . . iii 5 11
With others, whom, I fear, Most just and heavy causes make oppose . v 1 27
The gods are just, and of our pleasant vices Make instruments to plague us . . . . v 3 170
In a man that's just They are close delations, working from the heart That passion cannot rule . . . . . *Othello* iii 3 122
I think that thou art just and think thou art not . . . iii 3 385
Brave Iago, honest and just, That hast such noble sense of thy friend's wrong! . . . . v 1 31
If the great gods be just, they shall assist The deeds of justest men *Ant. and Cleo.* ii 1 1
It is just so high as it is, and moves with it own organ . . ii 7 48
Come from all parts of the world to just and tourney for her love *Pericles* ii 1 116
Just account. Though they jump not on a just account. . *Othello* i 3 6
Just belief. If this but answer to my just belief . . *Pericles* v 1 239
Just-borne. Before we will lay down our just-borne arms . *K. John* ii 1 345
Just cause. I am sorry for her, as I have just cause . *Much Ado* ii 3 173
Had she such power, She had just cause . . . *W. Tale* v 1 61
Your majesty hath no just cause to hate me . . 2 *Hen. IV.* v 2 66
No prince nor peer shall have just cause to say, God shorten Harry's happy life one day! . . . . v 2 144
Just censure. How blest am I In my just censure! . . *W. Tale* ii 1 37
Let our just censures Attend the true event . . . *Macbeth* v 4 14
Just command. To perform thy just command, I here confess *Pericles* v 3 1
Just commend. He had need mean better than his outward show Can any way speak in his just commend . . . . . . ii 2 49
Just computation. And, by just computation of the time, Found that the issue was not his begot. . . . . *Richard III.* iii 5 89
Just death, kind umpire of men's miseries . . . 1 *Hen. VI.* ii 5 29
Just demand. England, impatient of your just demands, Hath put himself in arms . . . . *K. John* ii 1 56
You must buy that peace With full accord to all our just demands *Hen. V.* v 2 71
I descend To give thee answer of thy just demand . . 1 *Hen. VI.* v 3 144
What says your highness to my just demand? . . *Richard III.* iv 2 97
Just distance. Pleaseth your lordship To meet his grace just distance 'tween our armies . . . . 2 *Hen. IV.* iv 1 226
Just equinox. And do but see his vice; 'Tis to his virtue a just equinox *Othello* ii 3 129
Just exception. Thou hast taken against me a most just exception . iv 2 211
Just gods. But the just gods gainsay! . . . *Troi. and Cres.* iv 5 132
The most just gods For every graff would send a caterpillar . *Pericles* v 1 59
Just grounds. I did proceed upon just grounds To this extremity *Othello* v 2 138
Just law. Which had you rather, that the most just law Now took your brother's life; or, to redeem him, Give up your body? *Meas. for Meas.* ii 4 52
Just notice. Bring me just notice of the numbers dead . *Hen. V.* iv 7 122
Just occasion. And nature, stronger than his just occasion, Made him give battle to the lioness . . . . . *As Y. Like It* iv 3 130
Just ones. Every good servant does not all commands: No bond but to do just ones . . . . *Cymbeline* v 1 7

Just opinions. And to deliver, Like free and honest men, our just opinions And comforts to your cause . . . . *Hen. VIII.* iii 1 60
Just ordinance. Either thou wilt die, by God's just ordinance, Ere from this war thou turn a conqueror . . . . . *Richard III.* iv 4 183
Just pound. If thou cut'st more Or less than a just pound *Mer. of Venice* iv 1 327
Just proceeding. Not fearing the displeasure of your master, Which on your just proceeding I'll keep off . . . . *All's Well* v 3 236
I'll acquaint our duteous citizens With all your just proceedings *Richard III.* iii 5 66
Just proof. When false opinion, whose wrong thought defiles thee, In thy just proof, repeals and reconciles thee . . *Lear* iii 6 120
Just proportion. Upon or near the rate of thirty thousand.—The just proportion that we gave them out . . . 2 *Hen. IV.* iv 1 23
And dost thou not Usurp the just proportion of my sorrow? *Richard III.* iv 4 110
And part in just proportion our small strength . . . v 3 26
Just remove. Your son gone; and he most violent author Of his own just remove . . . . *Hamlet* iv 5 81
Just report. You shall find Some that will thank you, making just report *Lear* iii 1 37
Just reproach. Who can blot that name With any just reproach? *Much Ado* iv 1 82
Just seven-night. A just seven-night; and a time too brief, too . ii 1 375
Just suit. In this just suit come I to move your grace . *Richard III.* iii 7 140
Just survey. Upon a just survey, take Titus' part . . . *T. Andron.* i 1 446
Just term. Be judge yourself, Whether I in any just term am affined To love the Moor . . . . . . *Othello* i 1 39
Justeius. Marcus Justeius, Publicola, and Cælius, are for sea *A. and C.* iii 7 73
Justest. If the great gods be just, they shall assist The deeds of justest men . . . . ii 1 2
Justice. But think upon my grief, a lady's grief, And on the justice of my flying hence . . . . . *T. G. of Ver.* iv 3 29
Here is Got's plessing, and your friend, and Justice Shallow *Mer. Wives* i 1 77
Though we are justices and doctors and churchmen, Master Page, we have some salt of our youth in us . . . . . . ii 3 49
The terms For common justice you're as pregnant in As art and practice hath enriched any That we remember . . *Meas. for Meas.* i 1 12
Liberty plucks justice by the nose; The baby beats the nurse . i 3 29
It rested in your grace To unloose this tied-up justice when you pleased . i 3 32
What's open made to justice, That justice seizes . . . ii 1 21
My name is Elbow: I do lean upon justice, sir . . . ii 1 49
Which is the wiser here? Justice or Iniquity? . . . ii 1 180
A vice that most I do abhor, And most desire should meet the blow of justice . . . . ii 2 30
Yet show some pity.—I show it most of all when I show justice . ii 2 100
But most willingly humbles himself to the determination of justice . iii 2 258
My brother justice have I found so severe, that he hath forced me to tell him he is indeed Justice . . . . . . iii 2 267
'Tis no sin, Sith that the justice of your title to him Doth flourish the deceit . . . . iv 1 74
His life is parallel'd Even with the stroke and line of his great justice . iv 2 83
Upon the very siege of justice . . . . . . iv 2 101
You will think you have made no offence, if the duke avouch the justice of your dealing? . . . . iv 2 200
We hear Such goodness of your justice . . . . . v 1 6
Justice, O royal duke! Vail your regard Upon a wrong'd, I would fain have said, a maid! . . . . v 1 20
Justice, justice, justice!—Relate your wrongs; in what? by whom? be brief . . . . v 1 25
Here is Lord Angelo shall give you justice: Reveal yourself to him . v 1 27
She hath been a suitor to me for her brother Cut off by course of justice,— By course of justice! . . . . . . v 1 35
Now, good my lord, give me the scope of justice; My patience here is touch'd . . . . v 1 234
My brother had but justice, In that he did the thing for which he died v 1 453
Justice, most gracious duke, O, grant me justice! . *Com. of Errors* v 1 190
Justice, sweet prince, against that woman there! She whom thou gavest to me to be my wife . . . . v 1 197
Come you, sir: if justice cannot tame you, she shall ne'er weigh more reasons in her balance . . . . . . *Much Ado* v 1 210
Justice always whirls in equal measure . . . *L. L. Lost* iv 3 384
O my Christian ducats! Justice! the law! my ducats! *Mer. of Venice* ii 8 17
Justice! find the girl; She hath the stones upon her, and the ducats ii 8 21
And doth impeach the freedom of the state, If they deny him justice . iii 2 281
But none can drive him from the envious plea Of forfeiture, of justice . iii 2 285
But, since I am a dog, beware my fangs: The duke shall grant me justice . . . . iii 3 8
If it be denied, Will much impeach the justice of his state . . iii 3 29
And for thy life let justice be accused . . . . . iv 1 129
Earthly power doth then show likest God's When mercy seasons justice iv 1 197
Therefore, Jew, Though justice be thy plea, consider this, That, in the course of justice, none of us Should see salvation . . . iv 1 199
I have spoke thus much To mitigate the justice of thy plea . iv 1 203
For, as thou urgest justice, be assured Thou shalt have justice . iv 1 315
The Jew shall have all justice; soft! no haste . . . iv 1 321
He shall have merely justice and his bond . . . . iv 1 339
Then the justice, In fair round belly with good capon lined *As Y. Like It* ii 7 153
Time is the old justice that examines all such offenders, and let Time try iv 1 203
I knew when seven justices could not take up a quarrel . . v 4 103
In the name of justice, Without all terms of pity . . *All's Well* ii 3 172
Unless her prayers . . . reprieve him from the wrath Of greatest justice iii 4 29
Let the justices make you and fortune friends: I am for other business v 2 35
I follow him to his country for justice: grant it me, O king! . v 3 145
The life of Helen, lady, Was foully snatch'd.—Now, justice on the doers! . . . . v 3 154
The justice of your hearts will thereto add ''Tis pity she's not honest' *W. Tale* ii 1 67
Be certain what you do, sir, lest your justice Prove violence . . ii 1 127
I do in justice charge thee, On thy soul's peril and thy body's torture . ii 3 180
Let us be clear'd Of being tyrannous, since we so openly Proceed in justice . . . . iii 2 6
Feel our justice, in whose easiest passage Look for no less than death . iii 2 91
You here shall swear upon this sword of justice . . . iii 2 125
Five justices' hands at it, and witnesses more than my pack will hold . iv 4 288
With these crystal beads heaven shall be bribed To do him justice *K. John* ii 1 172
Cries, Even from the tongueless caverns of the earth, To me for justice and rough chastisement . . . . . . *Richard II.* i 1 106
Since we can not atone you, we shall see Justice design the victor's chivalry . . . . i 1 203
Orderly proceed To swear him in the justice of his cause . . i 3 10
Why at our justice seem'st thou then to lour? . . . . i 3 235
Justice. Barely in title, not in revenue.—Richly in both, if justice had her right . . . . *Richard II.* ii 1 227
Justice hath liquored her . . . . 1 *Hen. IV.* ii 1 94
By this face, This seeming brow of justice, did he win The hearts of all iv 3 83
As I return, I will fetch off these justices: I do see the bottom of Justice Shallow . . . . 2 *Hen. IV.* iii 2 324
This same starved justice hath done nothing but prate to me of the wildness of his youth . . . . iii 2 327
They, by observing of him, do bear themselves like foolish justices . v 1 75
The majesty and power of law and justice . . . . v 2 78
To pluck down justice from your awful bench . . . . v 2 86
You are right, justice, and you weigh this well . . . v 2 102
Happy am I, that have a man so bold, That dares do justice on my proper son; And not less happy, having such a son, That would deliver up his greatness so Into the hands of justice . . . v 2 109
Bring me to a justice.—Ay, come, you starved blood-hound . . v 4 30
The sad-eyed justice, with his surly hum . . . . *Hen. V.* i 2 202
Poise the cause in justice' equal scales, Whose beam stands sure 2 *Hen. VI.* ii 1 204
God in justice hath reveal'd to us The truth and innocence of this poor fellow . . . . ii 3 105
Justice with favour have I always done; Prayers and tears have moved me . . . . iv 7 72
As I in justice and true right express it . . . . . v 2 25
I cheer'd them up with justice of our cause . . 3 *Hen. VI.* ii 1 133
Their blood upon thy head; For York in justice puts his armour on . ii 2 130
Her suit is now to repossess those lands; Which we in justice cannot well deny . . . . iii 2 5
You fight in justice: then, in God's name, lords, Be valiant . . v 4 81
O God, I fear thy justice will take hold On me, and you, and mine, and yours for this! . . . . *Richard III.* ii 1 131
We were sent for to the justices.—And so was I: I'll bear you company ii 3 46
Thus hath the course of justice wheel'd about, And left thee but a very prey to time . . . . iv 4 105
If you fight against God's enemy, God will in justice ward you . v 3 254
The law I bear no malice for my death; 'T has done, upon the premises, but justice . . . . *Hen. VIII.* ii 1 63
I desire you do me right and justice; And to bestow your pity on me . . . . ii 4 13
Shut door upon me, and so give me up To the sharp'st kind of justice . ii 4 44
Stubborn to justice, apt to accuse it, and Disdainful to be tried by't . ii 4 122
If you have any justice, any pity; If ye be any thing but churchmen's habits . . . . iii 1 116
Sharp enough, Lord, for thy justice! . . . . . . iii 2 93
And do justice For truth's sake and his conscience . . . . iii 2 396
And not ever The justice and the truth o' the question carries The due o' the verdict with it . . . . v 1 130
I do beseech your lordships, That, in this case of justice, my accusers, Be what they will, may stand forth face to face, And freely urge against me . . . . v 3 46
Right and wrong, Between whose endless jar justice resides, Should lose their names, and so should justice too . *Troi. and Cres.* i 3 117
Your virtue is To make him worthy whose offence subdues him And curse that justice did it . . . . *Coriolanus* i 1 180
Keep Rome in safety, and the chairs of justice Supplied with worthy men! . . . . iii 3 34
Given hostile strokes, and that not in the presence Of dreaded justice . iii 3 98
If he slay me, He does fair justice . . . . . . iv 4 25
Patrons of my right, Defend the justice of my cause with arms *T. Andron.* i 1 2
The imperial seat, to virtue consecrate, To justice, continence and nobility . . . . i 1 15
The people of Rome, Whose friend in justice thou hast ever been . . i 1 180
And ripen justice in this commonweal . . . . . . i 1 227
'Suum cuique' is our Roman justice: This prince in justice seizeth but his own . . . . i 1 280
Such quarrels may be broach'd Without controlment, justice, or revenge ii 1 68
You may catch her in the sea; Yet there's as little justice as at land iv 3 9
I pray you, deliver him this petition; Tell him, it is for justice . iv 3 15
Then we may go pipe for justice . . . . iv 3 24
For Justice, she is so employ'd, He thinks, with Jove in heaven . iv 3 39
And, sith there's no justice in earth nor hell, We will solicit heaven and move the gods To send down Justice for to wreak our wrongs . iv 3 49
Shall I have justice? what says Jupiter?—O, the gibbet-maker! . iv 3 79
By me thou shalt have justice at his hands . . . . iv 3 104
And, for the extent Of egal justice, used in such contempt . . iv 4 4
As who would say, in Rome no justice were . . . . iv 4 20
But he and his shall know that justice lives In Saturninus' health . iv 4 23
See justice done on Aaron, that damn'd Moor . . . . v 3 201
I beg for justice, which thou, prince, must give . . *Rom. and Jul.* iii 1 185
Peace, justice, truth, Domestic awe, night-rest . . *T. of Athens* iv 1 16
Making your wills The scope of justice . . . . . v 4 5
Not a man Shall pass his quarter, or offend the stream Of regular justice v 4 61
Did not great Julius bleed for justice' sake? What villain touch'd his body, that did stab, And not for justice? . . . . *J. Cæsar* iv 3 21
No sooner justice had with valour arm'd Compell'd these skipping kerns to trust their heels . . . . *Macbeth* i 2 29
This even-handed justice Commends the ingredients of our poison'd chalice To our own lips . . . . i 7 10
The king-becoming graces, As justice, verity, temperance, stableness . iv 3 92
In the corrupted currents of this world Offence's gilded hand may shove by justice, And oft 'tis seen the wicked prize itself Buys out the law *Hamlet* iii 3 58
That hast within thee undivulged crimes, Unwhipp'd of justice . *Lear* iii 2 53
Bring in the evidence. Thou robed man of justice, take thy place . iii 6 38
We may not pass upon his life Without the form of justice . . iii 7 25
Look with thine ears: see how yond justice rails upon yond simple thief . . . . iv 6 155
Change places; and, handy-dandy, which is the justice, which is the thief? . . . . iv 6 157
Plate sin with gold, And the strong lance of justice hurtless breaks . iv 6 170
If my speech offend a noble heart, Thy arm may do thee justice . v 3 128
Let loose on me the justice of the state For thus deluding you *Othello* i 3 140
I am for it, lieutenant; and I'll do you justice . . . . ii 3 90
Good, good: the justice of it pleases: very good . . . iv 1 222
Ah, balmy breath, that dost almost persuade Justice to break her sword! . . . . v 2 17
And the high gods, To do you justice, make them ministers Of us and those that love you . . . . *Ant. and Cleo.* iii 6 88
He is dead, Cæsar; Not by a public minister of justice, Nor by a hired knife . . . . v 1 20

Justice. Justice, and your father's wrath, should he take me in his dominion, could not be so cruel to me, as you . *Cymbeline* iii 2 40
Help, Jupiter; or we appeal, And from thy justice fly . . v 4 92
Whom heavens, in justice, both on her and hers, Have laid most heavy hand . . . . v 5 464
And yet but justice; for though This king were great, his greatness was no guard To bar heaven's shaft, but sin had his reward . *Pericles* ii 4 13
A princess To equal any single crown o' the earth I' the justice of compare! . . . . iv 3 9
Falseness cannot come from thee; for thou look'st Modest as Justice . v 1 122
Justice-like. He, by conversing with them, is turned into a justice-like serving-man . . . . . . *2 Hen. IV.* v 1 76
Justice of peace and 'Coram' . . . . . . *Mer. Wives* i 1 5
He's a justice of peace in his country, simple though I stand here . i 1 225
A justice of peace sometime may be beholding to his friend for a man . i 1 283
A poor esquire . . . , one of the king's justices of the peace . *2 Hen. IV.* iii 2 64
Thou hast appointed justices of peace, to call poor men before them about matters they were not able to answer . *2 Hen VI.* iv 7 45
Justicer. Come, sit thou here, most learned justicer . . *Lear* iii 6 23
False justicer, why hast thou let her 'scape? . . . . iii 6 59
This shows you are above, You justicers, that these our nether crimes So speedily can venge! . . . . . . iv 2 79
O, give me cord, or knife, or poison, Some upright justicer! . *Cymbeline* v 5 214
Justification. I hope, for my brother's justification, he wrote this but as an essay or taste of my virtue . . . . . *Lear* i 2 46
Justified. How is this justified? . . . . *All's Well* iv 3 64
We will be justified in our loves . . . . *W. Tale* i 1 10
Whose worth and honesty Is richly noted and here justified . . v 3 145
You're excused: But will you be more justified? . . *Hen. VIII.* ii 4 162
Justify. Were I so minded, I here could pluck his highness' frown upon you And justify you traitors . . . *Tempest* v 1 128
To justify this worthy nobleman, So vulgarly . . accused *M. for M.* v 1 159
Say't and justify't.—I would not be a stander-by to hear My sovereign mistress clouded so . . . . . *W. Tale* i 2 278
I cannot justify whom the law condemns . . *2 Hen. VI.* ii 3 16
I'll hear him his confessions justify . . . *Hen. VIII.* i 2 6
More particulars Must justify my knowledge . . *Cymbeline* ii 4 79
To the judgement of your eye I give, my cause who best can justify *Pericles* i Gower 42
Thou shalt kneel, and justify in knowledge She is thy very princess . v 1 219
Justle. I am in case to justle a constable . . *Tempest* iii 2 29
Let not the cloud of sorrow justle it From what it purposed . *L. L. Lost* v 2 758
Justles roughly by All time of pause . . . *Troi. and Cres.* iv 4 36
Justled. Howsoe'er you have Been justled from your senses . *Tempest* v 1 158
Justling. He is grievous sick.—'Zounds! how has he the leisure to be sick In such a justling time? . . . . *1 Hen. IV.* iv 1 18
Justly. Look you speak justly.—Boldly, at least . *Meas. for Meas.* v 1 298
They are both forsworn: In this the madman justly chargeth them *Com. of Errors* v 1 213

Justly. By mine honour, I will deal in this As secretly and justly as your soul Should with your body . . . . *Much Ado* iv 1 250
If you do keep your promises in love But justly, as you have exceeded all promise, Your mistress shall be happy . . *As Y. Like It* i 2 256
I must be patient: You, that have turn'd off a first so noble wife, May justly diet me . . . . . . *All's Well* v 3 221
If that the injuries be justly weigh'd . . . *T. Night* v 1 375
Sicilia means to pay Bohemia the visitation which he justly owes him *W. Tale* i 1 8
Hear me more plainly. I have in equal balance justly weigh'd What wrongs our arms may do, what wrongs we suffer . *2 Hen. IV.* iv 1 67
I may justly say, with the hook-nosed fellow of Rome, 'I came, saw, and overcame' . . . . iv 3 44
We pray you to proceed And justly and religiously unfold . *Hen. V.* i 2 10
I shall have my noble?—In cash most justly paid . . ii 1 120
Our purposes God justly hath discover'd; And I repent my fault . ii 2 151
His grace Hath spoken well and justly . . . *Hen. VIII.* ii 4 65
By him that justly may Bear his betroth'd from all the world away *T. Andron.* i 1 285
Just opposite to what thou justly seem'st, A damned saint! *Rom. and Jul.* iii 2 78
No man Can justly praise but what he does affect . *T. of Athens* i 2 221
Come, deal justly with me . . . . . *Hamlet* ii 2 284
I am justly kill'd with mine own treachery . . . v 2 318
He is justly served; It is a poison temper'd by himself . . v 2 338
That justly think'st, and hast most rightly said . . *Lear* i 1 186
Obey thy parents; keep thy word justly; swear not . . iii 4 83
Let us deal justly . . . . iii 6 42
Justly to your grave ears I'll present How I did thrive in this fair lady's love, And she in mine . . . . . *Othello* i 3 124
In the authority of her merit, did justly put on the vouch of very malice itself . . . . ii 1 147
I do not find that thou dealest justly with me.—What in the contrary? iv 2 173
A gentlewoman's son.—That's more Than some, whose tailors are as dear as yours, Can justly boast of . . . *Cymbeline* ii 3 85
Freely will I speak. Antiochus you fear, And justly too, I think *Pericles* i 2 103
Hath endured a grief Might equal yours, if both were justly weigh'd . v 1 89
Justness. We may not think the justness of each act Such and no other than event doth form it . . . *Troi. and Cres.* ii 2 119
Jutting-out. Serving of becks and jutting-out of bums! . *T. of Athens* i 2 237
Jutty. As doth a galled rock O'erhang and jutty his confounded base *Hen. V.* iii 1 13
No jutty, frieze, Buttress, nor coign of vantage . . *Macbeth* i 6 6
Juvenal. How canst thou part sadness and melancholy, my tender juvenal?—Why tender juvenal? why tender juvenal?—I spoke it, tender juvenal, as a congruent epitheton appertaining to thy young days . . . . . . *L. L. Lost* i 2 8
A most acute juvenal; volable and free of grace! . . . iii 1 67
Most brisky juvenal and eke most lovely Jew . . *M. N. Dream* iii 1 97
The juvenal, the prince your master, whose chin is not yet fledged *2 Hen. IV.* i 2 22

K

Kam. This is clean kam . . . . . *Coriolanus* iii 1 304
Kate. But none of us cared for Kate; For she had a tongue with a tang *Tempest* ii 2 51
O most divine Kate!—O most profane coxcomb! . . *L. L. Lost* iv 3 83
I prithee, sister Kate, untie my hands . . . *T. of Shrew* ii 1 21
Will you go with us, Or shall I send my daughter Kate to you? . ii 1 168
Good morrow, Kate; for that's your name, I hear.—Well have you heard ii 1 183
You are call'd plain Kate, And bonny Kate, and sometimes Kate the curst; But Kate, the prettiest Kate in Christendom, Kate of Kate Hall, my super-dainty Kate, For dainties are all Kates, and therefore, Kate, Take this of me, Kate of my consolation . . . ii 1 186
Alas! good Kate, I will not burden thee . . . . ii 1 203
A herald, Kate? O, put me in thy books!—What is your crest? a coxcomb?—A combless cock, so Kate will be my hen . . . ii 1 225
Nay, come, Kate, come; you must not look so sour . . ii 1 229
Nay, hear you, Kate: in sooth you scape not so . . . ii 1 242
Why does the world report that Kate doth limp? O slanderous world! Kate like the hazel-twig Is straight and slender . . . ii 1 254
Did ever Dian so become a grove As Kate this chamber with her princely gait? O, be thou Dian, and let her be Kate; And then let Kate be chaste and Dian sportful! . . . . . . ii 1 261
Now, Kate, I am a husband for your turn . . . . ii 1 274
Thou must be married to no man but me; For I am he am born to tame you Kate, And bring you from a wild Kate to a Kate Conformable as other household Kates . . . . ii 1 278
'Tis incredible to believe How much she loves me: O, the kindest Kate! ii 1 309
Give me thy hand, Kate: I will unto Venice, To buy apparel . ii 1 316
And kiss me, Kate, we will be married o' Sunday . . . ii 1 326
But where is Kate? where is my lovely bride? . . . iii 2 94
But where is Kate? I stay too long from her: The morning wears . iii 2 112
Could I repair what she will wear in me, As I can change these poor accoutrements, 'Twere well for Kate and better for myself . . iii 2 122
O Kate, content thee; prithee, be not angry.—I will be angry . iii 2 217
They shall go forward, Kate, at thy command. Obey the bride . iii 2 224
But for my bonny Kate, she must with me. Nay, look not big, nor stamp iii 2 229
Fear not, sweet wench, they shall not touch thee, Kate . . iii 2 240
Where are those—Sit down, Kate, and welcome . . . iv 1 144
Why, when, I say? Nay, good sweet Kate, be merry . . iv 1 146
Bid my cousin Ferdinand come hither: One, Kate, that you must kiss iv 1 155
Shall I have some water? Come, Kate, and wash, and welcome heartily iv 1 156
Kate, sit down; I know you have a stomach. Will you give thanks, sweet Kate? . . . . iv 1 161
The meat was well, if you were so contented.—I tell thee, Kate, 'twas burnt . . . . iv 1 173
How fares my Kate? What, sweeting, all amort?—Mistress, what cheer? iv 3 36
I am sure, sweet Kate, this kindness merits thanks. What, not a word? iv 3 41
Petruchio, fie! you are to blame. Come, Mistress Kate, I'll bear you company . . . . iv 3 49

Kate. Much good do it unto thy gentle heart! Kate, eat apace *T. of S.* iv 3 52
Well, come, my Kate; we will unto your father's Even in these honest mean habiliments . . . . iv 3 171
O, no, good Kate; neither art thou the worse For this poor furniture . iv 3 181
Gentle mistress: where away? Tell me, sweet Kate, and tell me truly too, Hast thou beheld a fresher gentlewoman? . . . . iv 5 28
Sweet Kate, embrace her for her beauty's sake . . . iv 5 34
Why, how now, Kate! I hope thou art not mad: This is a man . iv 5 42
Prithee, Kate, let's stand aside and see the end of this controversy . v 1 63
Husband, let's follow, to see the end of this ado.—First kiss me, Kate . . . . v 1 148
Come, my sweet Kate: Better once than never, for never too late . v 1 154
To her, Kate!—To her, widow!—A hundred marks, my Kate does put her down . . . . v 2 33
Why, there's a wench! Come on, and kiss me, Kate . . . v 2 180
How now, Kate! I must leave you within these two hours . *1 Hen. IV.* ii 3 39
Away, you trifler! Love! I love thee not, I care not for thee, Kate . ii 3 94
God's me, my horse! What say'st thou, Kate? what would'st thou have with me? . . . . ii 3 98
But hark you, Kate; I must not have you henceforth question me . ii 3 105
And, to conclude, This evening must I leave you, gentle Kate . ii 3 109
And so far will I trust thee, gentle Kate.—How! so far? . . ii 3 115
But hark you, Kate: Whither I go, thither shall you go too . . ii 3 117
To-day will I set forth, to-morrow you. Will this content you, Kate? . ii 3 120
Come, Kate, thou art perfect in lying down: come, quick, quick . iii 1 229
Come, Kate, I'll have your song too.—Not mine, in good sooth . iii 1 250
Swear me, Kate, like a lady as thou art, A good mouth-filling oath . iii 1 258
Do you like me, Kate?—Pardonnez-moi, I cannot tell vat is 'like me.' —An angel is like you, Kate, and you are like an angel . *Hen. V.* v 2 107
I' faith, Kate, my wooing is fit for thy understanding . . v 2 125
If you would put me to verses or to dance for your sake, Kate, why you undid me . . . . v 2 138
But, before God, Kate, I cannot look greenly nor gasp out my eloquence v 2 148
If thou canst love a fellow of this temper, Kate . . . v 2 153
While thou livest, dear Kate, take a fellow of plain and uncoined constancy . . . . v 2 160
But a good heart, Kate, is the sun and the moon; or rather the sun . v 2 171
No; it is not possible you should love the enemy of France, Kate . v 2 181
And, Kate, when France is mine and I am yours, then yours is France . v 2 184
It is as easy for me, Kate, to conquer the kingdom as to speak so much more French . . . . v 2 195
But, Kate, dost thou understand thus much English, canst thou love me?—I cannot tell.—Can any of your neighbours tell, Kate? . v 2 205
But, good Kate, mock me mercifully; the rather, gentle princess, because I love thee cruelly . . . . v 2 214
Do but now promise, Kate, you will endeavour for your French part . v 2 227
By mine honour, in true English, I love thee, Kate . . . v 2 238
But, in faith, Kate, the elder I wax, the better I shall appear . v 2 246

Kate. Dat is as it sall please de roi mon père.—Nay, it will please him well, Kate; it shall please him, Kate *Hen. V.* v 2 269
Then I will kiss your lips, Kate v 2 278
O Kate, nice customs curtsy to great kings. Dear Kate, you and I cannot be confined within the weak list of a country's fashion: we are the makers of manners, Kate v 2 293
You have witchcraft in your lips, Kate v 2 302
Shall Kate be my wife?—So please you.—I am content v 2 351
Now, welcome, Kate: and bear me witness all, That here I kiss her as my sovereign queen v 2 385
Then shall I swear to Kate, and you to me; And may our oaths well kept and prosperous be! v 2 401
Go thy ways, Kate: That man i' the world who shall report he has A better wife, let him in nought be trusted *Hen. VIII.* ii 4 133
Kated. I warrant him, Petruchio is Kated *T. of Shrew* iii 2 247
Kate Hall. Kate of Kate Hall, my super-dainty Kate ii 1 189
Kate Keepdown. Mistress Kate Keepdown was with child by him *Meas. for Meas.* iii 2 211
Katharina. If either of you both love Katharina, . . . Leave shall you have to court her at your pleasure *T. of Shrew* i 1 52
Katharina, you may stay; For I have more to commune with Bianca i 1 100
Katharina Minola, Renown'd in Padua for her scolding tongue i 2 99
Supposing it a thing impossible, For those defects I have before rehearsed, That ever Katharina will be woo'd i 2 125
Have you not a daughter Call'd Katharina, fair and virtuous?—I have a daughter, sir, called Katharina ii 1 43
Brother Petruchio, sister Katharina, And thou, Hortensio v 2 6
Now, by my holidame, here comes Katharina! v 2 99
Katharine. The heir of Alençon, Katharine her name *L. L. Lost* ii 1 195
I beshrew all shrows.—But, Katharine, what was sent to you from fair Dumain? v 2 47
None shall have access unto Bianca Till Katharine the curst have got a husband.—Katharine the curst! A title for a maid of all titles the worst *T. of Shrew* i 2 128
Here is a gentleman whom by chance I met, Upon agreement from us to his liking, Will undertake to woo curst Katharine i 2 184
For my daughter Katharine, this I know, She is not for your turn ii 1 63
They call me Katharine that do talk of me ii 1 185
Keep you warm.—Marry, so I mean, sweet Katharine ii 1 269
Never make denial; I must and will have Katharine to my wife ii 1 282
How now, daughter Katharine! in your dumps?—Call you me daughter? ii 1 286
I will be sure my Katharine shall be fine ii 1 319
On Sunday next you know My daughter Katharine is to be married ii 1 396
You grow too forward, sir: Have you so soon forgot the entertainment Her sister Katharine welcomed you withal? iii 1 3
This is the 'pointed day That Katharine and Petruchio should be married iii 2 2
Now must the world point at poor Katharine, And say, 'Lo, there is mad Petruchio's wife, If it would please him come and marry her!' —Patience, good Katharine iii 2 18
Yet withal he's honest.—Would Katharine had never seen him though! iii 2 26
When the priest Should ask, if Katharine should be his wife, 'Ay, by gogs-wouns,' quoth he iii 2 161
What you will have it named, even that it is; And so it shall be so for Katharine.—Petruchio, go thy ways; the field is won iv 5 22
Katharine, that cap of yours becomes you not: Off with that bauble v 2 121
Katharine, I charge thee, tell these headstrong women What duty they do owe their lords and husbands v 2 130
And make you merry with fair Katharine of France *2 Hen. IV.* Epil. 30
Tells Harry that the king doth offer him Katharine his daughter *Hen. V.* iii Prol. 30
Joy and good wishes To our most fair and princely cousin Katharine! v 2 4
Yet leave our cousin Katharine here with us: She is our capital demand v 2 95
Fair Katharine, and most fair, Will you vouchsafe to teach a soldier terms? v 2 98
O fair Katharine, if you will love me soundly with your French heart v 2 104
I said so, dear Katharine; and I must not blush to affirm it v 2 116
La plus belle Katharine du monde, mon très cher et devin déesse v 2 231
Therefore tell me, most fair Katharine, will you have me? v 2 252
Therefore, queen of all, Katharine, break thy mind to me in broken English v 2 264
At Touraine, in Saint Katharine's churchyard *1 Hen. VI.* i 2 100
A buzzing of a separation Between the king and Katharine *Hen. VIII.* ii 1 149
Katharine Queen of England, come into the court ii 4 10
Katharine our queen, before the primest creature That's paragon'd o' the world ii 4 229
Katharine no more Shall be call'd queen, but princess dowager iii 2 69
I beseech you, what's become of Katharine, The princess dowager? iv 1 22
Kecksies. Nothing teems But hateful docks, rough thistles, kecksies, burs *Hen. V.* v 2 52
Keech. Did not goodwife Keech, the butcher's wife, come in then and call me gossip Quickly? *2 Hen. IV.* ii 1 101
I wonder That such a keech can with his very bulk Take up the rays o' the beneficial sun And keep it from the earth *Hen. VIII.* i 1 55
Keel. While greasy Joan doth keel the pot *L. L. Lost* v 2 939
Congregated sands,—Traitors ensteep'd to clog the guiltless keel *Othello* ii 1 70
Famous pirates Make the sea serve them, which they ear and wound With keels of every kind *Ant. and Cleo.* i 4 50
Half the flood Hath their keel cut: but fortune's mood Varies *Pericles* iii Gower 46
Keen. Let us be keen, and rather cut a little, Than fall *Meas. for Meas.* ii 1 5
The impression of keen whips I'ld wear as rubies ii 4 101
Which shall bate his scythe's keen edge *L. L. Lost* i 1 6
The tongues of mocking wenches are as keen As is the razor's edge v 2 256
Cut me to pieces with thy keen conceit v 2 399
Wherefore was I to this keen mockery born? *M. N. Dream* ii 2 123
O, when she's angry, she is keen and shrewd! iii 2 323
That is some satire, keen and critical v 1 54
Who riseth from a feast With that keen appetite that he sits down? *Mer. of Venice* ii 6 9
So keen and greedy to confound a man iii 2 278
Not on thy sole, but on thy soul, harsh Jew, Thou makest thy knife keen iv 1 124
Thy tooth is not so keen, Because thou art not seen *As Y. Like It* ii 7 177
Then shall you know the wounds invisible That love's keen arrows make iii 5 31
Good father cardinal, cry thou amen To my keen curses *K. John* iii 1 182
To the latter end of a fray and the beginning of a feast Fits a dull fighter and a keen guest *1 Hen. IV.* iv 2 86
To leave this keen encounter of our wits *Richard III.* i 2 115
Come, thick night, And pall thee in the dunnest smoke of hell, That my keen knife see not the wound it makes *Macbeth* i 5 53
As easy mayst thou the intrenchant air With thy keen sword impress v 8 10
You are keen.—It would cost you a groaning to take off my edge *Hamlet* iii 2 258
Although assail'd with fortune fierce and keen *Pericles* v 3 Gower 88
Keen-edged. Here is my keen-edged sword, Deck'd with five flower-de-luces on each side *1 Hen. VI.* i 2 98
Keenness. No metal can, No, not the hangman's axe, bear half the keenness Of thy sharp envy *Mer. of Venice* iv 1 125
Keep. You mar our labour: keep your cabins *Tempest* i 1 15
Dull thing, I say so; he, that Caliban Whom now I keep in service i 2 286
Here you sty me In this hard rock, whiles you do keep from me The rest o' the island i 2 343
Keep in Tunis, And let Sebastian wake ii 1 259
And sends me forth—For else his project dies—to keep them living ii 1 299
If of life you keep a care, Shake off slumber, and beware ii 1 303
My poor son.—Heavens keep him from these beasts! For he is, sure, i' the island ii 1 324
If I can recover him and keep him tame, I will not take too much for him ii 2 71; 79
Keep a good tongue in your head: if you prove a mutineer,—the next tree! iii 2 39
But, while thou livest, keep a good tongue in thy head iii 2 120
Even here I will put off my hope and keep it No longer for my flatterer iii 3 7
Where live nibbling sheep, And flat meads thatch'd with stover, them to keep iv 1 63
Keep this remembrance for thy Julia's sake *T. G. of Ver.* ii 2 5
Julia I lose and Valentine I lose: If I keep them, I needs must lose myself ii 6 20
To keep me from a most unholy match iv 3 30
O, 'tis a foul thing when a cur cannot keep himself in all companies! iv 4 11
Yet I have much to do To keep them from uncivil outrages v 4 17
I keep but three men and a boy yet, till my mother be dead *Mer. Wives* i 1 284
Here, take the humour-letter: I will keep the haviour of reputation i 3 86
I keep his house; and I wash, wring, brew, bake, scour i 4 100
'Boarding,' call you it? I'll be sure to keep him above deck ii 1 94
It is as much as I can do to keep the terms of my honour precise ii 2 22
Give me my gown: or else keep it in your arms iii 1 35
Keep a gamester from the dice, and a good student from his book iii 1 37
Keep them asunder: here comes Doctor Caius iii 1 73
Let them keep their limbs whole and hack our English iii 1 79
And you shall one day find it.—Keep in that mind; I'll deserve it iii 3 89
I will at the least keep your counsel iv 6 7
Divide me like a bribe buck, each a haunch: I will keep my sides to myself v 5 28
Where youth, and cost, and witless bravery keeps *Meas. for Meas.* i 3 10
We must not make a scarecrow of the law, Setting it up to fear the birds of prey, And let it keep one shape, till custom make it Their perch ii 1 3
Heaven keep your honour! ii 2 42; ii 4 34
If I do lose thee [life], I do lose a thing That none but fools would keep iii 1 8
Grace, being the soul of your complexion, shall keep the body of it ever fair iii 1 188
The cure of it not only saves your brother, but keeps you from dishonour iii 1 246
Allowed by order of law a furred gown to keep him warm iii 2 8
But I will keep her ignorant of her good iv 3 113
Keep your instruction, And hold you ever to our special drift iv 5 3
That outward courtesies would fain proclaim Favours that keep within v 1 16
O you blessed ministers above, Keep me in patience! v 1 116
There is your money that I had to keep *Com. of Errors* i 2 8
This servitude makes you to keep unwed ii 1 26
So he would keep fair quarter with his bed! ii 1 108
Keep then fair league and truce with thy true bed ii 2 147
My wife is shrewish when I keep not hours iii 1 2
Being at that pass, You would keep from my heels and beware of an ass iii 1 18
Who is that at the door that keeps all this noise? iii 1 61
Not that Adam that kept the Paradise, but that Adam that keeps the prison iv 3 17
If he have wit enough to keep himself warm *Much Ado* i 1 68
God keep your ladyship still in that mind! i 1 134
God keep him out of my sight when the dance is done! ii 1 113
Poor fool, it keeps on the windy side of care ii 1 327
Keep your fellows' counsels and your own; and good night iii 3 92
What pace is this that thy tongue keeps?—Not a false gallop iii 4 93
God keep your worship! v 1 332; *As Y. Like It* i 1 168
To keep those statutes That are recorded in this schedule here *L. L. Lost* i 1 17
Subscribe to your deep oaths, and keep it too i 1 23
O, these are barren tasks, too hard to keep, Not to see ladies! i 1 47
Yet confident I'll keep what I have swore i 1 114
Although I seem so loath, I am the last that will last keep his oath i 1 161
I keep her as a vessel of thy law's fury i 1 277
Sir, the duke's pleasure is, that you keep Costard safe i 2 133
For this damsel, I must keep her at the park: she is allowed for the day-woman i 2 136
'Tis deadly sin to keep that oath, my lord, And sin to break it ii 1 105
Keep not too long in one tune, but a snip and away iii 1 21
This Armado is a Spaniard, that keeps here in court iv 1 100
Then thou wilt keep My tears for glasses, and still make me weep iv 3 39
Other slow arts entirely keep the brain iv 3 324
Let us once lose our oaths to find ourselves, Or else we lose ourselves to keep our oaths iv 3 362
Despise me, when I break this oath of mine.—I will: and therefore keep it v 2 442
Ergo I come with this apology. Keep some state in thy exit, and vanish v 2 598
The king doth keep his revels here to-night *M. N. Dream* ii 1 18
Reason and love keep little company together now-a-days iii 1 147
Keep thy Hermia; I will none: If e'er I loved her, all that love is gone iii 2 169
I evermore did love you, Hermia, Did ever keep your counsels iii 2 308
My legs can keep no pace with my desires. Here will I rest me iii 2 445
O, ten times faster Venus' pigeons fly To seal love's bonds new-made, than they are wont To keep obliged faith unforfeited! *Mer. of Venice* ii 6 7
Look he keep his day, Or he shall pay for this ii 8 25
I'll keep my oath, Patiently to bear my wroth ii 9 77
O that I had a title good enough to keep his name company! iii 1 15
He hath got the jewel that I loved, And that which you did swear to keep for me v 1 225
Give him this And bid him keep it better than the other v 1 255
My brother Jaques he keeps at school *As Y. Like It* i 1 6
For my part, he keeps me rustically at home i 1 7
Shall I keep your hogs and eat husks with them? i 1 40
Nay, if I keep not my rank,— Thou losest thy old smell i 2 113
And here detain'd by her usurping uncle, To keep his daughter company i 2 287
Lean but upon a rush, The cicatrice and capable impressure Thy palm some moment keeps iii 5 24
At this hour the house doth keep itself iv 3 82
Keep you your word, O duke, to give your daughter v 4 19
Schoolmasters will I keep within my house Fit to instruct her *T. of Shrew* i 1 94
But I will charm him first to keep his tongue i 1 214
In Baptista's keep my treasure is i 2 118

Keep. The youngest daughter whom you hearken for Her father keeps from all access of suitors *T. of Shrew* i 2 261
Belike, you fancy riches more: You will have Gremio to keep your fair ii 1 17
A head-stall of sheep's leather which, being restrained to keep him from stumbling, hath been often burst iii 2 59
I'll rail and brawl And with the clamour keep her still awake iv 1 210
That I may surely keep mine oath, I will be married to a wealthy widow iv 2 36
Keep your hundred pounds to yourself: he shall need none, so long as I live v 1 24
And keep thy friend Under thy own life's key *All's Well* i 1 75
How may we barricado it against him?—Keep him out i 1 125
Keep it [virginity] not; you cannot choose but lose by't: out with't! i 1 158
Keep it to yourself: many likelihoods informed me of this before i 3 128
You had my prayers to lead them on; and to keep them on, have them still ii 4 18
I hope your own grace will keep you where you are iii 5 28
But she is arm'd for him and keeps her guard In honestest defence iii 5 76
We have caught the woodcock, and will keep him muffled iv 1 100
Till then I'll keep him dark and safely lock'd iv 1 104
The master I speak of ever keeps a good fire iv 5 51
I am not such an ass but I can keep my hand dry *T. Night* i 3 79
'Tis poetical.—It is the more like to be feigned: I pray you, keep it in i 5 209
I am no fee'd post, lady; keep your purse: My master, not myself, lacks recompense i 5 303
What a caterwauling do you keep here! ii 3 76
She will keep no fool, sir, till she be married iii 1 38
Like a pedant that keeps a school i' the church iii 2 81
A good note; that keeps you from the blow of the law iii 4 168
Still you keep o' the windy side of the law iii 4 181
Pray God, he keep his oath!—I do assure you, 'tis against my will iii 4 341
Keep me in darkness, send ministers to me, asses iv 2 99
It shall come to note, What time we will our celebration keep iv 3 30
We intended To keep in darkness what occasion now Reveals before 'tis ripe v 1 156
And all those swearings keep as true in soul As doth that orbed continent the fire That severs day from night v 1 277
Force me to keep you as a prisoner, Not like a guest *W. Tale* i 2 52
With a countenance as clear As friendship wears at feasts, keep with Bohemia i 2 344
If it prove She's otherwise, I'll keep my stables where I lodge my wife ii 1 134
This place is famous for the creatures Of prey that keep upon't iii 3 13
This is fairy gold, boy, and 'twill prove so: up with't, keep it close iii 3 128
There's rosemary and rue; these keep Seeming and savour all the winter long iv 4 74
Not a ribbon, glass, . . . to keep my pack from fasting iv 4 611
Therefore I keep it Lonely, apart. But here it is v 3 17
The aweless lion could not wage the fight, Nor keep his princely heart from Richard's hand *K. John* i 1 267
Unless thou let his silver water keep A peaceful progress to the ocean ii 1 339
Not Death himself In mortal fury half so peremptory, As we to keep this city ii 1 455
And force perforce Keep Stephen Langton, chosen archbishop Of Canterbury, from that holy see iii 1 143
Keep my need up, and faith is trodden down! iii 1 216
Thou mayst hold a serpent by the tongue, . . . A fasting tiger safer by the tooth, Than keep in peace that hand which thou dost hold iii 1 261
And most forsworn, to keep what thou dost swear iii 1 287
Hubert, keep this boy. Philip, make up: My mother is assailed in our tent iii 2 5
Making that idiot, laughter, keep men's eyes And strain their cheeks iii 3 45
Thou art his keeper.—And I'll keep him so, That he shall not offend iii 3 64
I will not keep this form upon my head, When there is such disorder in my wit iii 4 101
Or, Hubert, if you will, cut out my tongue, So I may keep mine eyes iv 1 102
Heaven take my soul, and England keep my bones! iv 3 10
Now keep your holy word: go meet the French v 1 5
Let this be copied out, And keep it safe for our remembrance v 2 2
Wherefore we took the sacrament And keep our faiths firm and inviolable v 2 7
Keep good quarter and good care to-night v 5 20
Swear by the duty that you owe to God . . . To keep the oath *Richard II.* i 3 182
I swear.—And I, to keep all this i 3 192
What stir Keeps good old York there with his men of war? ii 3 52
That Power that made you king Hath power to keep you king in spite of all iii 2 28
Within the hollow crown That rounds the mortal temples of a king Keeps Death his court iii 2 162
Madam, we'll dance.—My legs can keep no measure in delight iii 4 7
Why should we in the compass of a pale Keep law and form? iii 4 41
To serve me last, that I may longest keep Thy sorrow in my breast iii 4 95
Be it your charge To keep him safely till his day of trial iv 1 153
Was this face the face That every day under his household roof Did keep ten thousand men? iv 1 283
I am sworn brother, sweet, To grim Necessity, and he and I Will keep a league till death v 1 22
'Twere no good part To take on me to keep and kill thy heart v 1 98
We'll keep him here: then what is that to him? v 2 100
The prisoners . . . To his own use he keeps *1 Hen. IV.* i 1 94
I'll keep them all; By God, he shall not have a Scot of them; No, if a Scot would save his soul, he shall not: I'll keep them, by this hand i 3 213
Those prisoners you shall keep.—Nay, I will; that's flat i 3 218
And give it him, To keep his anger still in motion i 3 226
Peace, ye fat-kidneyed rascal! what a brawling dost thou keep! ii 2 6
There is virtue in that Falstaff: him keep with, the rest banish ii 4 473
Thus did I keep my person fresh and new; My presence, like a robe pontifical iii 2 55
Do you think I keep thieves in my house? iii 3 63
I prithee, tell me, doth he keep his bed? iv 1 21
God keep lead out of me! I need no more weight than mine own bowels v 3 35
Two stars keep not their motion in one sphere v 4 65
Now let not Nature's hand Keep the wild flood confined! *2 Hen. IV.* i 1 154
'Tis not a hair amiss yet: he may keep it still at a face-royal i 2 28
But since all is well, keep it so: wake not a sleeping wolf i 2 173
Keep them off, Bardolph.—A rescue! a rescue ii 1 60
Never a man's thought in the world keeps the road-way better than thine ii 2 62
God keep you, Master Silence: I will not use many words with you iii 2 308
Therefore will he wipe his tables clean And keep no tell-tale to his memory iv 1 202
From enemies heaven keep your majesty! iv 4 94
Let God for ever keep it from my head! iv 5 175
To keep Prince Harry in continual laughter v 1 88

Keep. The heavens thee guard and keep, most royal imp of fame! *2 Hen. IV.* v 5 45
Could not keep quiet in his conscience *Hen. V.* i 2 79
Though high and low and lower, Put into parts, doth keep in one consent i 2 181
I will keep my state, Be like a king and show my sail of greatness i 2 273
It will be thought we keep a bawdy house straight ii 1 37
Why the devil should we keep knives to cut one another's throats? ii 1 96
He hath a killing tongue and a quiet sword; by the means whereof a' breaks words, and keeps whole weapons iii 2 37
But keeps the bridge most valiantly, with excellent discipline iii 6 11
He will keep that good name still.—I know him to be valiant iii 7 111
In gross brain little wots What watch the king keeps to maintain the peace iv 1 300
But all's not done; yet keep the French the field iv 6 2
So long as your majesty is an honest man.—God keep me so! iv 7 121
Is it fit this soldier keep his oath?—He is a craven and a villain else iv 7 138
It is necessary, look your grace, that he keep his vow and his oath iv 7 146
Then keep thy vow, sirrah, when thou meetest the fellow iv 7 151
Fill this glove with crowns, And give it to this fellow. Keep it, fellow iv 8 62
I pray you to serve God, and keep you out of prawls, and prabbles iv 8 69
God b' wi' you, and keep you, and heal your pate.—All hell shall stir for this v 1 71
Or rather the sun and not the moon; for it shines bright and never changes, but keeps his course truly v 2 173
Prosper this realm, keep it from civil broils! *1 Hen. VI.* i 1 53
Sharp stakes pluck'd out of hedges They pitched in the ground confusedly, To keep the horsemen off from breaking in i 1 119
Bonfires in France forthwith I am to make, To keep our great Saint George's feast withal i 1 154
Salisbury craveth supply, And hardly keeps his men from mutiny i 1 160
Shall we disturb him, since he keeps no mean? i 2 121
Opinion shall be surgeon to my hurt And keep me on the side where still I am ii 4 54
How haps it I seek not to advance Or raise myself, but keep my wonted calling? iii 1 32
Am not I a prelate of the church?—Yes, as an outlaw in a castle keeps iii 1 47
Like peasant foot-boys do they keep the walls And dare not take up arms iii 2 69
Heavens keep old Bedford safe! And now no more ado iii 2 100
To keep them here, They would but stink, and putrefy the air iv 7 89
Keep not back your powers in dalliance v 2 5
When thou didst keep my lambs a-field, I wish some ravenous wolf had eaten thee! v 4 30
No, lord ambassador, I'll rather keep That which I have than, coveting for more, Be cast from possibility of all v 4 144
His alliance will confirm our peace And keep the Frenchmen in allegiance v 5 43
Did my brother Bedford toil his wits, To keep by policy what Henry got? *2 Hen. VI.* i 1 84
For France, 'tis ours; and we will keep it still.—Ay, uncle, we will keep it, if we can; But now it is impossible we should i 1 107
Next time I'll keep my dreams unto myself, And not be check'd i 2 53
Somerset will keep me here, Without discharge, money, or furniture i 3 171
'Tis like, my lord, you will not keep your hour ii 1 181
'Tis not his wont to be the hindmost man, Whate'er occasion keeps him from us now.—Can you not see? iii 1 3
Commit you to my lord cardinal To keep, until your further time of trial iii 1 138
Those that care to keep your royal person From treason's secret knife iii 1 173
Let pale-faced fear keep with the mean-born man iii 1 335
But both of you were vow'd Duke Humphrey's foes, And you, forsooth, had the good duke to keep iii 2 183
It is great sin to swear unto a sin, But greater sin to keep a sinful oath v 1 183
You were best to go to bed and dream again, To keep thee from the tempest v 1 197
The cedar shows That keeps his leaves in spite of any storm v 1 206
I'll to my castle.—And I'll keep London with my soldiers *3 Hen. VI.* i 1 207
Keep thou the napkin, and go boast of this i 4 159
Is held at such a rate As brings a thousand-fold more care to keep Than in possession any jot of pleasure ii 2 52
So do I wish the crown, being so far off; And so I chide the means that keeps me from it iii 2 141
Yet will I keep thee safe, And they shall feel the vengeance of my wrath iv 1 81
Why commands the king That his chief followers lodge in towns about him, While he himself keeps in the cold field? iv 3 14
I'll leave you to your fortune and be gone To keep them back iv 7 56
To keep that oath were more impiety Than Jephthah's v 1 90
I seek for thee, That Warwick's bones may keep thine company v 2 4
Thus far our fortune keeps an upward course v 3 1
We will not from the helm to sit and weep, But keep our course v 4 22
I think it is our way, If we will keep in favour with the king *Richard III.* i 1 79
I'll have her; but I will not keep her long i 2 230
O, let them keep it till thy sins be ripe, And then hurl down their indignation On thee! i 3 219
Conscience flies out.— . . . it beggars any man that keeps it i 4 145
For my part, I'll resign unto your grace The seal I keep ii 4 71
God keep you from them, and from such false friends!—God keep me from false friends! but they were none iii 1 15
God keep your lordship in that gracious mind! iii 2 56
Keep it to thyself—This day those enemies are put to death iii 2 104
God keep the prince from all the pack of you! iii 3 5
I am their mother; who should keep me from them? iv 1 22
The Earl of Pembroke keeps his regiment v 3 29
Conscience is but a word that cowards use, Devised at first to keep the strong in awe v 3 310
I wonder That such a keech can with his very bulk Take up the rays o' the beneficial sun And keep it from the earth *Hen. VIII.* i 1 57
Two women placed together makes cold weather: My Lord Sands, you are one will keep 'em waking i 4 23
Good angels keep it from us! What may it be? ii 1 142
Is not this course pious?—Heaven keep me from such counsel! i 2 38
You have scarce time To steal from spiritual leisure a brief span To keep your earthly audit iii 2 141
To keep mine honour from corruption iv 2 71
Keep comfort to you v 1 144
'Tis this fever that keeps Troy on foot, Not her own sinews *Troi. and Cres.* i 3 135
In full as proud a place As broad Achilles; keeps his tent like him i 3 190
I will keep where there is wit stirring and leave the faction of fools ii 1 129
Why keep we her? the Grecians keep our aunt: Is she worth keeping? ii 2 80
O, theft most base, That we have stol'n what we do fear to keep! ii 2 93
I propend to you In resolution to keep Helen still ii 2 191
To keep her constancy in plight and youth, Outliving beauty's outward iii 2 168
Perseverance, dear my lord, Keeps honour bright iii 3 151

Keep. For honour travels in a strait so narrow, Where one but goes abreast: keep then the path . . . . *Troi. and Cres.* iii 3 155
He merits well to have her, that doth seek her . . With such a hell of pain and world of charge, And you as well to keep her, that defend her iv 1 58
Tell me, I beseech you, In what place of the field doth Calchas keep? iv 5 278
Who keeps the tent now?—The surgeon's box, or the patient's wound v 1 11
Both taxing me and gaging me to keep An oath that I have sworn . v 1 46
And you too, Diomed, Keep Hector company an hour or two . v 1 88
Now the pledge; now, now, now!—Here, Diomed, keep this sleeve v 2 66
Strike not a stroke, but keep yourselves in breath . . . . v 7 3
You cry against the noble senate, who, Under the gods, keep you in awe *Coriolanus* i 1 191
Nor did you think it folly To keep your great pretences veil'd . i 2 20
The gods assist you!—And keep your honours safe! . . . i 2 37
Let the ports be guarded: keep your duties, As I have set them down. i 7 1
If we lose the field, We cannot keep the town.—Fear not our care, sir i 7 5
Bid them wash their faces And keep their teeth clean . . . ii 3 67
To eject him hence Were but one danger, and to keep him here Our certain death: therefore it is decreed He dies to-night . . iii 1 288
The honour'd gods Keep Rome in safety! . . . . . iii 3 34
The gods keep you! . . . . . iv 6 25; *Ant. and Cleo.* iii 2 36
You keep a constant temper . . . . . . *Coriolanus* v 2 100
That brought you forth this boy, to keep your name Living to time v 3 126
Keep then this passage to the Capitol . . . *T. Andron.* i 1 12
Convey her hence away, And with my sword I'll keep this door safe i 1 288
O, keep me from their worse than killing lust . . . ii 3 175
With warm tears I'll melt the snow, And keep eternal spring-time on thy face . . . . iii 1 21
Why, what a caterwauling dost thou keep! . . . . iv 2 57
Tell the empress from me, I am of age To keep mine own . . iv 2 105
Let us all consult. My son and I will have the wind of you: Keep there iv 2 134
I know An idiot holds his bauble for a god And keeps the oath which by that god he swears . . . . v 1 80
Knock at his study, where, they say, he keeps, To ruminate strange plots v 2 5
Care keeps his watch in every old man's eye . *Rom. and Jul.* ii 3 35
My young lady bade me inquire you out; what she bade me say, I will keep to myself . . . . ii 4 174
Did ever dragon keep so fair a cave? Beautiful tyrant! . . . iii 2 74
We'll keep no great ado,—a friend or two . . . . iii 4 23
Be fickle, fortune; For then, I hope, thou wilt not keep him long. iii 5 63
Such an unaccustom'd dram, That he shall soon keep Tybalt company. iii 5 92
On Thursday early will I rouse ye: Till then, adieu; and keep this holy kiss . . . . iv 1 43
For no pulse Shall keep his native progress, but surcease . . iv 1 97
Your part in her you could not keep from death, But heaven keeps his part in eternal life . . . . iv 5 69
I will write again to Mantua, And keep her at my cell till Romeo come v 2 28
The obsequies that I for thee will keep Nightly shall be to strew thy grave v 3 16
Shall I believe That unsubstantial death is amorous, And that the lean abhorred monster keeps Thee here in dark to be his paramour? v 3 104
Meaning to keep her closely at my cell, Till I conveniently could send to Romeo . . . . v 3 255
Flow this way! A brave fellow! he keeps his tides well *T. of Athens* i 2 57
Sweet instruments hung up in cases that keep their sounds to themselves i 2 103
The best of happiness, Honour and fortunes, keep with you! . i 2 235
A noble gentleman 'tis, if he would not keep so good a house . iii 1 24
Who cannot keep his wealth must keep his house . . . iii 3 42
He's much out of health, and keeps his chamber.—Many do keep their chambers are not sick . . . . iii 4 73
Now the gods keep you old enough; that you may live Only in bone! . iii 5 104
Here is some gold for thee.—Keep it, I cannot eat it . . iv 3 100
Men report Thou dost affect my manners, and dost use them.—'Tis, then, because thou dost not keep a dog . . . . iv 3 200
I understand thee; thou hadst some means to keep a dog . . iv 3 317
Know his gross patchery, love him, feed him, Keep in your bosom v 1 100
And keep us all in servile fearfulness . . . *J. Cæsar* i 1 80
There was a Brutus once that would have brook'd The eternal devil to keep his state in Rome As easily as a king . . . . i 2 160
It is meet That noble minds keep ever with their likes . . i 2 315
To keep with you at meals, comfort your bed, And talk to you sometimes ii 1 284
Call it my fear That keeps you in the house, and not your own . ii 2 51
I was constant Cimber should be banish'd, And constant do remain to keep him so . . . . iii 1 73
You said the enemy would not come down, But keep the hills . . v 1 3
Upon the right hand I; keep thou the left . . . . v 1 18
Come now, keep thine oath; Now be a freeman . . . v 3 40
But still keep My bosom franchised and allegiance clear *Macbeth* ii 1 27
To Ireland, I; our separated fortune Shall keep us both the safer . ii 3 145
To make society The sweeter welcome, we will keep ourself Till supper-time alone . . . . iii 1 43
Cancel and tear to pieces that great bond Which keeps me pale! . iii 2 50
Our hostess keeps her state, but in best time We will require her welcome . . . . iii 4 5
You can behold such sights, And keep the natural ruby of your cheeks iii 4 115
There's not a one of them but in his house I keep a servant fee'd . iii 4 132
If it be mine, Keep it not from me, quickly let me have it . . iv 3 200
Remove from her the means of all annoyance, And still keep eyes upon her . . . . v 1 85
She is troubled with thick-coming fancies, That keep her from her rest v 3 39
The confident tyrant Keeps still in Dunsinane . . . . v 4 9
That keep the word of promise to our ear, And break it to our hope . v 8 21
Fear it, my dear sister, And keep you in the rear of your affection *Hamlet* i 3 34
I shall the effect of this good lesson keep, As watchman to my heart . i 3 45
'Tis in my memory lock'd, And you yourself shall keep the key of it . i 3 86
What means, and where they keep, What company, at what expense . ii 1 8
Let me be no assistant for a state, But keep a farm and carters . ii 2 167
Do they grow rusty?—Nay, their endeavour keeps in the wonted pace . ii 2 353
We will have no more marriages: those that are married already, all but one, shall live; the rest shall keep as they are . . . iii 1 156
Most holy and religious fear it is To keep those many many bodies safe iii 3 9
The single and peculiar life is bound, With all the strength and armour of the mind, To keep itself from noyance . . . . . iii 3 13
But, like the owner of a foul disease, To keep it from divulging, let it feed Even on the pith of life . . . . iv 1 22
Believe what?—That I can keep your counsel and not mine own . iv 2 11
He keeps them, like an ape, in the corner of his jaw . . iv 2 19
Feeds on his wonder, keeps himself in clouds . . . . iv 5 89
Cæsar, dead and turn'd to clay, Might stop a hole to keep the wind away v 1 237
I have a voice and precedent of peace, To keep my name ungored . v 2 261
Keeps our fortunes from us till our oldness cannot relish them . *Lear* i 2 50

Keep. I can keep honest counsel, ride, run, mar a curious tale in telling it *Lear* i 4 34
If I gave them all my living, I'ld keep my coxcombs myself . . i 4 120
Prithee, nuncle, keep a schoolmaster that can teach thy fool to lie . i 4 195
He that keeps nor crust nor crum, Weary of all, shall want some . i 4 217
Here do you keep a hundred knights and squires . . . i 4 262
'Tis politic and safe to let him keep At point a hundred knights . i 4 346
Thou canst tell why one's nose stands i' the middle on's face?—No.—Why, to keep one's eyes of either side's nose . . . . i 5 22
O, let me not be mad, not mad, sweet heaven! Keep me in temper . i 5 51
And, squire-like, pension beg To keep base life afoot . . ii 4 218
The lion and the belly-pinched wolf Keep their fur dry . . iii 1 14
The wrathful skies Gallow the very wanderers of the dark, And make them keep their caves . . . . iii 2 45
Let the great gods, That keep this dreadful pother o'er our heads, Find out their enemies now . . . . iii 2 50
Keep thy foot out of brothels, thy hand out of plackets . . iii 4 99
I will keep still with my philosopher . . . . . iii 4 181
Edmund, keep you our sister company . . . . . iii 7 7
Others there are Who, trimm'd in forms and visages of duty, Keep yet their hearts attending on themselves . . . . *Othello* i 1 51
'Tis a pageant, To keep us in false gaze . . . . . i 3 19
I here do give thee that with all my heart Which, but thou hast already, with all my heart I would keep from thee . . . . . i 3 195
But some uncleanly apprehensions Keep leets and law-days . . iii 3 140
Their best conscience Is not to leave't undone, but keep't unknown . iii 3 204
I had rather be a toad, And live upon the vapour of a dungeon, Than keep a corner in the thing I love For others' uses . . . iii 3 272
But she so loves the token, For he conjured her she should ever keep it iii 3 294
Whose icy current . . . Ne'er feels retiring ebb, but keeps due on . iii 3 455
Heaven keep that monster from Othello's mind! . . . . iii 4 163
What, keep a week away? seven days and nights? . . . iii 4 173
Keep it as a cistern for foul toads To knot and gender in! . . iv 2 61
There's money for your pains: I pray you, turn the key and keep our counsel . . . . iv 2 94
Let her not say 'tis I that keep you here: I have no power upon you *Ant. and Cleo.* i 3 22
To sit And keep the turn of tippling with a slave . . . i 4 19
Tie up the libertine in a field of feasts, Keep his brain fuming . ii 1 24
Thy demon, that's thy spirit which keeps thee, is Noble, courageous ii 3 19
Keep yourself within yourself: The man is innocent . . . ii 5 75
Which is set Betwixt us as the cement of our love, To keep it builded . iii 2 30
You keep by land The legions and the horse whole, do you not? . iii 7 71
The seven-fold shield of Ajax cannot keep The battery from my heart . iv 14 38
Take it, heart; But keep it till you woo another wife . *Cymbeline* i 1 113
Remain, remain thou here While sense can keep it on . . . i 1 118
He did keep The deck, with glove, or hat, or handkerchief, Still waving i 3 10
Which the gods have given you?—Which, by their graces, I will keep . i 4 95
Since My lord hath interest in them, I will keep them In my bedchamber i 6 195
Your lady's person: is she ready?—Ay, To keep her chamber . . ii 3 87
It must be married To that your diamond; I'll keep them . . ii 4 98
'Tis true:—nay, keep the ring—'tis true: I am sure She would not lose it ii 4 123
Which he to seek of me again, perforce, Behoves me keep at utterance . iii 1 73
The gates of monarchs Are arch'd so high that giants may jet through And keep their impious turbans on . . . . iii 3 6
Such gain the cap of him that makes 'em fine, Yet keeps his book uncross'd iii 3 26
The art o' the court, As hard to leave as keep . . . . iii 3 47
If't be summer news, Smile to't before; if winterly, thou need'st But keep that countenance still . . . . iii 4 14
Bloody cloth, I'll keep thee, for I wish'd Thou shouldst be colour'd thus v 1 1
I come to spend my breath; Which neither here I'll keep nor bear again v 3 82
The action of my life is like it, which I'll keep, if but for sympathy . v 4 151
He made a law, To keep her still, and men in awe . . *Pericles* i Gower 36
Who has a book of all that monarchs do, He's more secure to keep it shut i 1 95
Those men Blush not in actions blacker than the night, Will shun no course to keep them from the light . . . . i 1 136
Lest my life be cropp'd to keep you clear, By flight I'll shun the danger i 1 141
Keep your mind, till you return to us, Peaceful and comfortable! . i 2 34
For though he strive To killen bad, keep good alive . . ii Gower 20
Keep it, my Pericles; it hath been a shield 'Twixt me and death; . . For that it saved me, keep it . . . . ii 1 132
'Twere not amiss to keep our door hatched . . . . iv 2 37
Untied I still my virgin knot will keep. Diana, aid my purpose! . iv 2 160
Proclaim that I can sing, weave, sew, and dance, With other virtues, which I'll keep from boast . . . . iv 6 195
The city strived God Neptune's annual feast to keep . . v Gower 17
Keep alone. How now, my lord! why do you keep alone? . *Macbeth* iii 2 8
Why do you keep alone? How chance my daughter is not with you? *Pericles* ii 5 22
Keep aloof. Must keep aloof from strict arbitrement . 1 *Hen. IV.* iv 1 70
With a crafty madness, keeps aloof . . . . . *Hamlet* iii 1 8
Keep at home. Nay, if he coy'd To hear Cominius speak, I'll keep at home . . . . *Coriolanus* v 1 7
Keep away. Let not your private discord keep away The levied succours that should lend him aid . . . . . . 1 *Hen. VI.* iv 4 22
Keep back The clamorous owl that nightly hoots . *M. N. Dream* ii 2 5
Keep below. Play the men.—I pray now, keep below . *Tempest* i 1 12
Why, shall I always keep below stairs? . . . . *Much Ado* v 2 10
Keep close. What there is else, keep close . . 1 *Hen. IV.* i 4 593
Let housewifery appear: keep close, I thee command . *Hen. V.* ii 3 65
Will you do this, keep close within your chamber . . *Hamlet* iv 7 130
Keep company. Both day and night did we keep company . *T. Night* v 1 99
My soul shall thine keep company to heaven . . . *Hen. V.* iv 6 16
Keep counsel. Two may keep counsel when the third's away *T. Andron.* iv 2 144
Did you ne'er hear say, Two may keep counsel, putting one away? *Rom. and Jul.* ii 4 209
How hard it is for women to keep counsel! . . . *J. Cæsar* ii 4 9
The players cannot keep counsel; they'll tell all . . *Hamlet* iii 2 152
Keep covenant. We Must not continue friends.—Good sir, we must, If you keep covenant . . . . *Cymbeline* i 4 50
Keep decorum, and fortune him accordingly! . . *Ant. and Cleo.* i 2 77
Majesty, to keep decorum, must No less beg than a kingdom . . v 2 17
Keep down. Nor never lay his wreathed arms athwart His loving bosom to keep down his heart . . . . *L. L. Lost* iv 3 136
Keep for ever. I'll see if I can get my husband's ring, Which I did make him swear to keep for ever . . . . . *Mer. of Venice* iv 2 14
Keep fresh And lasting in her sad remembrance . . . *T. Night* i 1 31
Keep her company. Who keeps her company? What place? *Othello* iv 2 137
Keep her word. The lady doth protest too much, methinks.—O, but she'll keep her word . . . . *Hamlet* iii 2 241

Keep high. For by his fall my honour must keep high *Pericles* i 1 149
Keep him company. Mercutio's soul Is but a little way above our heads, Staying for thine to keep him company *Rom. and Jul.* iii 1 133
Each man apart, all single and alone, Yet an arch-villain keeps him company *T. of Athens* v 1 111
His son, that keeps him company, Whose absence is no less material to me *Macbeth* iii 1 135
Keep his word. It is not possible, it cannot be, The king should keep his word in loving us 1 *Hen. IV.* v 2 5
I judge By his blunt bearing he will keep his word *Hen. V.* iv 7 185
The sun borrows of the moon, when Diomed keeps his word *Troi. and Cres.* v 1 102
Keep house and ply his book, welcome his friends *T. of Shrew* i 1 201
Tranio, in my stead, Keep house and port and servants, as I should i 1 208
A goodly day not to keep house, with such Whose roof's as low as ours! *Cymbeline* iii 3 1
Keep in. Nay, good master parson, keep in your weapon *Mer. Wives* iii 1 75
You will not extort from me what I am willing to keep in *T. Night* ii 1 14
Could not all this flesh Keep in a little life? 1 *Hen. IV.* v 4 103
Take my hand, And with thy lips keep in my soul awhile! 3 *Hen. VI.* v 2 35
Keep in-a-door, And thou shalt have more Than two tens to a score *Lear* i 4 138
Keep lodgers. Nor shall my Nell keep lodgers *Hen. V.* ii 1 33
Keep me company but two years moe, Thou shalt not know the sound of thine own tongue *Mer. of Venice* i 1 108
Keep my word. I will keep my word with thee.—I would I had your bond *M. N. Dream* iii 2 266
Sufficeth, I am come to keep my word *T. of Shrew* iii 2 108
'Tis past: and yet it is not; I will not keep my word *Troi. and Cres.* v 2 98
Keep off. Not fearing the displeasure of your master, Which on your just proceeding I'll keep off *All's Well* v 3 236
Keep off aloof with worthless emulation 1 *Hen. VI.* iv 4 21
I'll give thee armour to keep off that word *Rom. and Jul.* iii 3 54
These quick-sands, Lepidus, Keep off them, for you sink *Ant. and Cleo.* ii 7 66
Keep on.—Truly, I will not go first; truly, la! I will not *Mer. Wives* i 1 321
They have ta'en note of us: keep on your way *Coriolanus* iv 2 10
Good my lords, keep on; I'll wait upon you instantly *T. of Athens* v 2 35
Keep out. His hide is so tanned with his trade, that he will keep out water a great while *Hamlet* v 1 187
Nay, come not near th' old man; keep out, che vor ye *Lear* iv 6 246
Keep peace. If he do fear God, a' must necessarily keep peace *Much Ado* ii 3 202
That no compunctious visitings of nature Shake my fell purpose, nor keep peace between The effect and it *Macbeth* i 5 47
Keep peace, upon your lives: He dies that strikes again *Lear* ii 2 52
Keep place. They do no more adhere and keep place together than the Hundredth Psalm to the tune of 'Green Sleeves' *Mer. Wives* ii 1 62
The providence that's in a watchful state . . . Keeps place with thought and almost, like the gods, Does thoughts unveil *Troi. and Cres.* iii 3 199
Keep promise. Cesario, you do not keep promise with me *T. Night* v 1 106
To-morrow truly will I meet with thee.—Keep promise, love *M. N. Dream* i 1 179
If thou keep promise, I shall end this strife *Mer. of Venice* ii 3 20
Keep safe. This maugre all the world will I keep safe *T. Andron.* iv 2 110
Keep seat. Pray you, keep seat; The fit is momentary *Macbeth* iii 4 54
Keep shut. She is too liberal.—Of her tongue she cannot, for that's writ down she is slow of; of her purse she shall not, for that I'll keep shut *T. G. of Ver.* iii 1 358
Keep state. You would swear directly Their very noses had been counsellors To Pepin or Clotharius, they keep state so *Hen. VIII.* i 3 10
Keep the door close, sirrah.—What would you have me do? v 4 30
Keep the door. O thou vile king, Give me my father! *Hamlet* iv 5 115
Keep the gate. Come, sir, to dinner. Dromio, keep the gate *Com. of Er.* ii 2 208
Who keeps the gate here, ho?—Where is the earl? 2 *Hen. IV.* iii 1 1
You, mistress, That have the office opposite to Saint Peter, And keep the gate of hell! *Othello* iv 2 92
Keep the house. You will turn good husband now, Pompey; you will keep the house *Meas. for Meas.* iii 2 74
Gratiano, keep the house, And seize upon the fortunes of the Moor *Othello* v 2 365
Keep the peace. Cut him to pieces.—Keep the peace, I say *K. John* iv 3 93
What is the matter? keep the peace here, ho! 2 *Hen. IV.* ii 1 67
Hold your slaughtering hands and keep the peace 1 *Hen. VI.* iii 1 87
Clubs, clubs! these lovers will not keep the peace *T. Andron.* ii 1 37
I do but keep the peace: put up thy sword *Rom. and Jul.* i 1 75
'Tis not hard, I think, For men so old as we to keep the peace i 2 3
Keeps the weather. Hold you still, I say; Mine honour keeps the weather of my fate *Troi. and Cres.* v 3 26
Keeps the wind. He knows the game: how true he keeps the wind! 3 *Hen. VI.* iii 2 14
Keep thee warm. Why, nature needs not what thou gorgeous wear'st, Which scarcely keeps thee warm *Lear* ii 4 273
In, fellow, there, into the hovel: keep thee warm.—Come, let's in all iii 4 179
I have a gown here; come, put it on; keep thee warm *Pericles* ii 1 83
Keeps thicket. The hart Achilles Keeps thicket *Troi. and Cres.* ii 3 270
Keep thy word. I will do it, though I take thee in the king's company.—Keep thy word *Hen. V.* iv 1 238
Keep time. We did keep time, sir, in our catches. Sneck up! *T. Night* ii 3 100
Music do I hear? Ha, ha! keep time: how sour sweet music is, When time is broke and no proportion kept! *Richard II.* v 5 42
He fights as you sing prick-song, keeps time, distance *Rom. and Jul.* ii 4 21
My pulse, as yours, doth temperately keep time *Hamlet* iii 4 140
Most bloody.—That's not amiss; But yet keep time in all *Othello* iv 1 93
Keep tune there still, so you will sing it out *T. G. of Ver.* i 2 89
Keep up your bright swords, for the dew will rust them *Othello* i 2 59
Dost thou hear, my honest friend?—No, I hear not your honest friend; I hear you.—Prithee, keep up thy quillets iii 1 25
Keep us company. And all that are assembled in this place, . . . go keep us company *Com. of Errors* v 1 398
Keeps wassail, and the swaggering up-spring reels *Hamlet* i 4 9
Keep whole. Publicola, and Cælius, are for sea: But we keep whole by land *Ant. and Cleo.* iii 7 75
Strike not by land; keep whole: provoke not battle, Till we have done at sea iii 8 3
Keep word, Lysander . . . —I will, my Hermia *M. N. Dream* i 1 222
Keep you company. Heart's discontent and sour affliction Be playfellows to keep you company! 2 *Hen. VI.* iii 2 302
Follow his torch; he goes to Calchas' tent: I'll keep you company *Troi. and Cres.* v 1 93
I'll keep you company. Will you along?—We stay here for the people *Coriolanus* ii 3 157
Shall we in?—I'll keep you company *T. of Athens* i 1 294
Keep you warm. Am I not wise?—Yes; keep you warm *T. of Shrew* ii 1 268
Or feed on nourishing dishes, or keep you warm *Othello* iii 3 78
Keep your place. Nay, keep your place.—Sit, Coriolanus; never shame to hear What you have nobly done *Coriolanus* ii 2 70
Keep your promise. If you do keep your promises in love But justly, as you have exceeded all promise, Your mistress shall be happy *As Y. Like It* i 2 255
Therefore beware my censure and keep your promise iv 1 200
Keep your way. Nay, keep your way, little gallant *Mer. Wives* iii 2 1
But keep your way, i' God's name *Much Ado* i 1 143
Pray you, keep your way: When you are call'd, return *Hen. VIII.* ii 4 128
Keep your word, Phebe, that you'll marry me *As Y. Like It* v 4 21
'Tis most nobly spoken.—Descend, and keep your words *T. of Athens* v 4 64
Keepdown. Mistress Kate Keepdown was with child by him *M. for M.* iii 2 211
Keeper. Give us kind keepers, heavens! *Tempest* iii 3 20
But not kissed your keeper's daughter?—Tut, a pin! *Mer. Wives* i 1 116
Herne the hunter, Sometime a keeper here in Windsor forest iv 4 29
And Don Armado shall be your keeper *L. L. Lost* i 1 306
Imitari is nothing: so doth the hound his master, the ape his keeper iv 2 131
Another way I have to man my haggard, To make her come and know her keeper's call, That is, to watch her *T. of Shrew* iv 1 197
Thy husband is thy lord, thy life, thy keeper, Thy head v 2 146
The keeper of the prison, call to him; Let him have knowledge who I am *W. Tale* ii 2 1
Thou art his keeper.—And I'll keep him so, That he shall not offend your majesty.—Death.—My lord?—A grave *K. John* iii 3 64
A parasite, a keeper back of death *Richard II.* ii 2 70
Impatient of his fit, breaks like a fire Out of his keeper's arms 2 *Hen. IV.* i 1 143
Kind keepers of my weak decaying age 1 *Hen. VI.* ii 5 1
But tell me, keeper, will my nephew come? ii 5 17
Keepers, convey him hence, and I myself Will see his burial ii 5 120
I, then in London, keeper of the king, Muster'd my soldiers 3 *Hen. VI.* ii 1 111
Ay, here's a deer whose skin's a keeper's fee: This is the quondam king iii 1 22
I pray thee, gentle keeper, stay by me; My soul is heavy *Richard III.* i 4 73
Where art thou, keeper? give me a cup of wine.—You shall have wine enough i 4 166
What, hast not thou full often struck a doe, And borne her cleanly by the keeper's nose? *T. Andron.* ii 1 94
How oft when men are at the point of death Have they been merry! which their keepers call A lightning before death *Rom. and Jul.* v 3 89
Or a keeper with my freedom; Or my friends, if I should need 'em *T. of Athens* i 2 69
Thou'lt go, strong thief [gold], When gouty keepers of thee cannot stand iv 3 46
I leave you To the protection of the prosperous gods, As thieves to keepers v 1 187
Keepest. A breath thou art, Servile to all the skyey influences, That dost this habitation, where thou keep'st, Hourly afflict *Meas. for Meas.* iii 1 10
What art thou that keepest me out from the house I owe? *Com. of Er.* iii 1 42
Go, fool, and whom thou keep'st command *T. of Shrew* iii 1 259
This pitch, as ancient writers do report, doth defile; so doth the company thou keepest 1 *Hen. IV.* ii 4 457
It is a low ebb of linen with thee when thou keepest not racket there 2 *Hen. IV.* ii 2 23
Golden care! That keep'st the ports of slumber open wide! iv 5 24
Beware; thou keep'st me from the light 3 *Hen. VI.* v 6 84
Thou keep'st the stroke Betwixt thy begging and my meditation *Richard III.* iv 2 117
And rather . . . keepest from me all conveniency than suppliest me with the least advantage of hope *Othello* iv 2 178
Now peace be here, Poor house, that keep'st thyself! *Cymbeline* iii 6 36
Keeping. I am betray'd, by keeping company With men like men of inconstancy *L. L. Lost* iv 3 179
Then fools you were these women to forswear, Or keeping what is sworn, you will prove fools iv 3 356
I'll fear no other thing So sore as keeping safe Nerissa's ring *M. of Ven.* v 1 307
Call you that keeping for a gentleman of my birth? *As Y. Like It* i 1 9
I will never trust a man again for keeping his sword clean *All's Well* iv 3 166
He professes not keeping of oaths iv 3 282
Her mother's statue, which is in the keeping of Paulina *W. Tale* v 2 103
Then art thou damned for keeping thy word with the devil 1 *Hen. IV.* i 2 134
Keeping such vile company as thou art hath in reason taken from me all ostentation of sorrow 2 *Hen. IV.* ii 2 52
I'll forswear keeping house ii 4 220
Keeping them prisoner underneath her wings 1 *Hen. VI.* v 3 57
For keeping my house, and lands, and wife and all, from me 2 *Hen. VI.* i 3 20
Rumour it abroad That Anne, my wife, is sick and like to die: I will take order for her keeping close *Richard III.* iv 2 53
Is she worth keeping? why, she is a pearl *Troi. and Cres.* ii 2 81
I would have the soil of her fair rape Wiped off, in honourable keeping her ii 2 149
Do you hear how we are shent for keeping your greatness back? *Coriolanus* v 2 105
Never may That state or fortune fall into my keeping, Which is not owed to you! *T. of Athens* i 1 150
The worm is not to be trusted but in the keeping of wise people *Ant. and Cleo.* v 2 267
When last I went to visit her, She pray'd me to excuse her keeping close *Cymbeline* iii 5 46
Keisar. Thou'rt an emperor, Cæsar, Keisar, and Pheezar *Mer. Wives* i 3 9
Ken. I ken the wight: he is of substance good i 3 40
For, lo! within a ken our army lies 2 *Hen. IV.* iv 1 151
As far as I could ken thy chalky cliffs 2 *Hen. VI.* iii 2 101
Losing ken of Albion's wished coast iii 2 113
'Tis he, I ken the manner of his gait; He rises on the toe *Troi. and Cres.* iv 5 14
Milford, When from the mountain-top Pisanio show'd thee, Thou wast within a ken: O Jove! I think Foundations fly the wretched *Cymb.* iii 6 6
Kendal green. Three misbegotten knaves in Kendal green 1 *Hen. IV.* ii 4 246
How couldst thou know these men in Kendal green, when it was so dark thou couldst not see thy hand? come, tell us ii 4 257
Kennel. Go to kennel, Pompey; go *Meas. for Meas.* iii 2 89
Go, hop me over every kennel home *T. of Shrew* iv 3 98
Mazed with a yelping kennel of French curs 1 *Hen. VI.* iv 2 47
Pool! Sir Pool! lord! Ay, kennel, puddle, sink 2 *Hen. VI.* iv 1 71
From forth the kennel of thy womb hath crept A hell-hound *Rich. III.* iv 4 47
Truth's a dog must to kennel; he must be whipped out *Lear* i 4 124
Kent. Told of a many thousand warlike French That were embattailed and rank'd in Kent *K. John* iv 2 200
All Kent hath yielded; nothing there holds out But Dover castle v 1 30
I have to London sent The heads of Oxford, Salisbury, Blunt, and Kent *Richard II.* v 6 8
A franklin in the wild of Kent hath brought three hundred marks with him in gold 1 *Hen. IV.* ii 1 60
The commons here in Kent are up in arms 2 *Hen. VI.* iv 1 100

Kent. Rebellious hinds, the filth and scum of Kent, Mark'd for the gallows . . . . 2 *Hen. VI.* iv 2 130
You men of Kent,— What say you of Kent?—Nothing but this; 'tis 'bona terra, mala gens' . . . iv 7 59
Kent, in the Commentaries Cæsar writ, Is term'd the civil'st place of all this isle: Sweet is the country . . . iv 7 65
Alexander Iden, an esquire of Kent . . . iv 10 46
Tell Kent from me, she hath lost her best man . . . iv 10 78
Alexander Iden, that's my name; A poor esquire of Kent, that loves his king . . . v 1 75
'Tis not thy southern power, Of Essex, Norfolk, Suffolk, nor of Kent 3 *Hen. VI.* i 1 156
And thou, son Clarence, Shalt stir up in Suffolk, Norfolk and in Kent iv 8 12
My liege, in Kent the Guildfords are in arms . *Richard III.* iv 4 505
My lord of Kent: remember him hereafter as my honourable friend *Lear* i 1 27
Peace, Kent! Come not between the dragon and his wrath . . i 1 123
Be Kent unmannerly, When Lear is mad . . . i 1 147
Kent, on thy life, no more.—My life I never held but as a pawn . . i 1 156
Thus Kent, O princes, bids you all adieu . . . i 1 189
Kent banish'd thus! and France in choler parted! And the king gone! i 2 23
The noble and true-hearted Kent banished! his offence, honesty! 'Tis strange . . . i 2 126
Now, banish'd Kent, If thou canst serve where thou dost stand condemn'd, So may it come, thy master, whom thou lovest, Shall find thee full of labours . . . i 4 4
Ah, that good Kent! He said it would be thus, poor banish'd man! . iii 4 168
Cried 'Sisters! sisters! Shame of ladies! sisters! Kent! father! sisters!' iv 3 30
O thou good Kent, how shall I live and work, To match thy goodness? iv 7 1
They say Edgar, his banish'd son, is with the Earl of Kent in Germany iv 7 91
But who was this?—Kent, sir, the banish'd Kent . . . v 3 219
See'st thou this object, Kent?—Alack, why thus? . . . v 3 238
O my good master!—Prithee, away.—'Tis noble Kent, your friend . v 3 268
This is a dull sight. Are you not Kent?—The same, Your servant Kent v 3 282
Kentish. Were the Duke of Suffolk now alive, These Kentish rebels would be soon appeased! . . . 2 *Hen. VI.* iv 4 42
Trust not the Kentish rebels.—Trust nobody, for fear you be betray'd . iv 4 57
Kentishman. A headstrong Kentishman, John Cade of Ashford . . iii 1 356
With whom the Kentishmen will willingly rise . . . 3 *Hen. VI.* i 2 41
Kept. Of any thing the image tell me that Hath kept with thy remembrance.—'Tis far off And rather like a dream . . *Tempest* i 2 44
His bold head 'Bove the contentious waves he kept . . . ii 1 118
I shall think, or Phœbus' steeds are founder'd, Or Night kept chain'd below . . . iv 1 31
Fire that's closest kept burns most of all . . . *T. G. of Ver.* i 2 30
I nightly lodge her in an upper tower, The key whereof myself have ever kept . . . iii 1 36
Kept severely from resort of men, That no man hath access by day to her . . . iii 1 108
Ay, but the doors be lock'd and keys kept safe . . . iii 1 111
If I be not by her fair influence Foster'd, illumined, cherish'd, kept alive iii 1 184
These banish'd men that I have kept withal Are men endued with worthy qualities . . . v 4 152
His filching was like an unskilful singer; he kept not time . *Mer. Wives* i 3 29
The gentleman is of no having: he kept company with the wild prince and Poins . . . iii 2 73
Such a one were past cure of the thing you wot of, unless they kept very good diet . . . *Meas. for Meas.* ii 1 116
A year and a quarter old, come Philip and Jacob: I have kept it myself iii 2 214
Where have you left the money that I gave you?— . . . The saddler had it, sir; I kept it not . . . *Com. of Errors* i 2 57
Swart, like my shoe, but her face nothing like so clean kept . . iii 2 105
Not that Adam that kept the Paradise, but that Adam that keeps the prison . . . iv 3 16
Let her awhile be secretly kept in, And publish it that she is dead *M. Ado* iv 1 205
It is the most impenetrable cur That ever kept with men *Mer. of Venice* iii 3 19
Yet for your vehement oaths, You should have been respective and have kept it . . . v 1 156
Let no fair be kept in mind But the fair of Rosalind *As Y. Like It* iii 2 99
You are deceived, sir: we kept time, we lost not our time . . v 3 38
That covenants may be kept on either hand . *T. of Shrew* ii 1 128
Giddy for lack of sleep, With oaths kept waking . . . iv 3 10
Virginity by being once lost may be ten times found; by being ever kept, it is ever lost . . . *All's Well* i 1 143
The longer kept, the less worth: off with't while 'tis vendible . i 1 167
The wars have so kept you under that you must needs be born under Mars . . . i 1 209
I am commanded here, and kept a coil with 'Too young' and 'the next year' . . . ii 1 27
I have kept of them tame, and know their natures . . . ii 5 50
Would not a pair of these have bred, sir?—Yes, being kept together and put to use . . . *T. Night* iii 1 56
Why have you suffer'd me to be imprison'd, Kept in a dark house? . v 1 350
In sooth, good friend, your father might have kept This calf bred from his cow from all the world . . . *K. John* i 1 123
And this blessed day Ever in France shall be kept festival . . iii 1 76
It is religion that doth make vows kept . . . iii 1 279
What, shall our feast be kept with slaughter'd men? . . . iii 1 302
So I were out of prison and kept sheep, I should be as merry as the day is long . . . iv 1 17
Within me grief hath kept a tedious fast . . *Richard II.* ii 1 75
We have stay'd ten days, And hardly kept our countrymen together . ii 4 2
With slow but stately pace kept on his course . . . v 2 10
How sour sweet music is, When time is broke and no proportion kept! v 5 42
In Gloucestershire; 'Twas where the madcap duke his uncle kept 1 *Hen. IV.* i 3 244
Opinion, that did help me to the crown, Had still kept loyal to possession iii 2 43
A mighty and a fearful head they are, If promises be kept . . iii 2 168
Loyalty and mere dislike Of our proceedings kept the earl from hence . iv 1 65
O, that this good blossom could be kept from cankers! . . 2 *Hen. IV.* ii 2 102
And learning a mere hoard of gold kept by a devil, till sack commences it iv 3 125
You won it, wore it, kept it, gave it me . . . iv 5 222
I have turn'd away my former self; So will I those that kept me company v 5 63
Treason and murder ever kept together, As two yoke-devils . *Hen. V.* ii 2 105
The true and aunchient prerogatifes and laws of the wars is not kept . iv 1 68
In this glorious and well-foughten field We kept together in our chivalry iv 6 19
Maids, well summered and warm kept, are like flies at Bartholomew-tide v 2 335
And may our oaths well kept and prosperous be! . . . v 2 402
Had all your quarters been as safely kept As that . . . 1 *Hen. VI.* ii 1 63
Early and late debating to and fro How France and Frenchmen might be kept in awe . . . 2 *Hen. VI.* i 1 92
Kept. And would have kept so long as breath did last . . 2 *Hen. VI.* i 1 211
Away with them! let them be clapp'd up close, And kept asunder . i 4 54
Who kept him in captivity till he died . . . ii 2 42
Had I but said, I would have kept my word, But when I swear, it is irrevocable . . . iii 2 293
He might have kept that glory to this day . . . 3 *Hen. VI.* ii 2 153
And thou this day hadst kept thy chair in peace . . . ii 6 20
Overpeer'd Jove's spreading tree And kept low shrubs from winter's powerful wind . . . v 2 15
O, he hath kept an evil diet long . . . *Richard III.* i 1 139
But still the envious flood Kept in my soul, and would not let it forth i 4 38
A holy day shall this be kept hereafter . . . ii 1 73
And join'd together, Must gently be preserved, cherish'd, and kept . ii 2 119
Too late he died that might have kept that title . . . iii 1 99
Which ever since hath kept my eyes from rest . . . iv 1 82
A paltry fellow, Long kept in Bretagne at our mother's cost . . v 3 324
Fearing he would rise, he was so virtuous, Kept him a foreign man still *Hen. VIII.* ii 2 129
Since I had my office, I have kept you next my heart . . . iii 2 157
From all parts they are coming, As if we kept a fair here! . . v 4 73
The disdain and shame whereof hath ever since kept Hector fasting and waking . . . *Troi. and Cres.* i 2 36
Dogs that are as often beat for barking As therefore kept to do so *Coriol.* ii 3 225
Then have I kept it to a worthy end . . . *T. Andron.* iii 1 174
Shut up in prison, kept without my food, Whipp'd and tormented *R. and J.* i 2 56
Thou art a fool to bid me farewell twice.—Why, Apemantus?—Shouldst have kept one to thyself, for I mean to give thee none *T. of Athens* i 1 275
Timon has been this lord's father, And kept his credit with his purse . iii 2 75
I have kept back their foes, While they have told their money . . iii 5 106
I never had honest man about me, I; all I kept were knaves . . iv 3 485
And I with them the third night kept the watch . . . *Hamlet* i 2 208
This must be known; which, being kept close, might move More grief to hide . . . ii 1 118
Should have kept short, restrain'd and out of haunt, This mad young man . . . iv 1 18
O, that that earth, which kept the world in awe, Should patch a wall! v 1 238
I gave you all— And in good time you gave it.—Made you my guardians, my depositaries; But kept a reservation to be follow'd With such a number . . . *Lear* ii 4 255
She told her, while she kept it, 'Twould make her amiable . *Othello* iii 4 58
The oars were silver, Which to the tune of flutes kept stroke *A. and C.* ii 2 200
Read not my blemishes in the world's report: I have not kept my square ii 3 6
I have kept me from the cup . . . ii 7 72
He at Philippi kept His sword e'en like a dancer . . . iii 11 35
A sun and moon, which kept their course, and lighted The little O, the earth . . . v 2 80
What have I kept back?—Enough to purchase what you have made known . . . v 2 147
Some nobler token I have kept apart For Livia and Octavia . . v 2 168
Send your trunk to me; it shall safe be kept . . . *Cymbeline* i 6 209
I would have kept such a jangling of the bells . . . *Pericles* ii 1 45
It kept where I kept, I so dearly loved it . . . ii 1 136
Keptest. By thy honest aid Thou kept'st a wife herself . . *All's Well* v 3 330
Kerchief. A plain kerchief, Sir John: my brows become nothing else *Mer. Wives* iii 3 62
He might put on a hat, a muffler and a kerchief, and so escape . iv 2 74
O, what a time have you chose out, brave Caius, To wear a kerchief? *J. C.* ii 1 315
Kerelybonto, sir, betake thee to thy faith . . . *All's Well* iv 1 82
Kern. We must supplant those rough rug-headed kerns . *Richard II.* ii 1 156
You rode, like a kern of Ireland, your French hose off . *Hen. V.* iii 7 56
The uncivil kerns of Ireland are in arms . . . 2 *Hen. VI.* iii 1 310
In Ireland have I seen this stubborn Cade Oppose himself against a troop of kerns, And fought so long . . . iii 1 361
Full often, like a shag-hair'd crafty kern, Hath he conversed with the enemy . . . iii 1 367
A mighty power Of gallowglasses and stout kerns Is marching hitherward iv 9 26
From the western isles Of kerns and gallowglasses is supplied *Macbeth* i 2 13
With valour arm'd Compell'd these skipping kerns to trust their heels . i 2 30
I cannot strike at wretched kerns, whose arms Are hired to bear their staves . . . v 7 17
Kernel. And, sowing the kernels of it [the island] in the sea, bring forth more islands . . . *Tempest* ii 1 92
As brown in hue As hazel nuts and sweeter than the kernels *T. of Shrew* ii 1 257
You were beaten in Italy for picking a kernel out of a pomegranate *A. W.* ii 3 276
There can be no kernel in this light nut; the soul of this man is his clothes . . . ii 5 47
How like, methought, I then was to this kernel, This squash *W. Tale* i 2 159
Were as good crack a fusty nut with no kernel . *Troi. and Cres.* ii 1 112
Kersey. I had as lief be a list of an English kersey as be piled, as thou art piled, for a French velvet . . . *Meas. for Meas.* i 2 35
In russet yeas and honest kersey noes . . . *L. L. Lost* v 2 413
A linen stock on one leg and a kersey boot-hose on the other *T. of Shrew* iii 2 68
Ketly. Sir Richard Ketly, Davy Gam, esquire: None else of name *Hen. V.* iv 8 109
Kettle. Let the kettle to the trumpet speak . . . *Hamlet* v 2 286
Kettle-drum. As he drains his draughts of Rhenish down, The kettle-drum and trumpet thus bray out The triumph of his pledge . . i 4 11
Key. Having both the key Of officer and office, set all hearts i' the state To what tune pleased his ear . . . *Tempest* i 2 83
Knowing that tender youth is soon suggested, I nightly lodge her in an upper tower, The key whereof myself have ever kept *T. G. of Ver.* iii 1 36
Resort to her by night.—Ay, but the doors be lock'd and keys kept safe iii 1 111
I will use her as the key of the cuckoldly rogue's coffer . *Mer. Wives* ii 2 285
Here, here, here be my keys: ascend my chambers; search, seek, find out iii 3 172
Turn you the key, and know his business of him . *Meas. for Meas.* i 4 8
A planched gate, That makes his opening with this bigger key . iv 1 31
For which I do discharge you of your office: Give up your keys . v 1 467
Hie thee straight: Give her this key, and tell her, in the desk *C. of Er.* iv 1 103
My only son Knows not my feeble key of untuned cares . . v 1 310
In what key shall a man take you, to go in the song? . *Much Ado* i 1 188
They say he wears a key in his ear and a lock hanging by it . v 1 318
Take this key, give enlargement to the swain, bring him *L. L. Lost* iii 1 5
I will wed thee in another key, With pomp, with triumph *M. N. Dream* i 1 18
Sitting on one cushion, Both warbling of one song, both in one key . iii 2 206
Bend low and in a bondman's key, With bated breath . *Mer. of Venice* i 3 124
I am bid forth to supper, Jessica: There are my keys . . ii 5 12
Deliver me the key: Here do I choose, and thrive I as I may! . ii 7 59
Give me a key for this, And instantly unlock my fortunes here . ii 9 51
Keep thy friend Under thy own life's key . . . *All's Well* i 1 76
It is in mine authority to command The keys of all the posterns *W. Tale* i 2 464
I could have filed keys off that hung in chains . . . iv 4 624

Key. Then give me leave that I may turn the key, That no man enter *Richard II.* v 3 36
Wear nothing but high shoes, and bunches of keys at their girdles *2 Hen. IV.* i 2 45
Thou that didst bear the key of all my counsels . . . *Hen. V.* ii 2 96
And when you have done so, bring the keys to me . . . *1 Hen. VI.* ii 3 2
These counties were the keys of Normandy . . . *2 Hen. VI.* i 1 114
What! fear not, man, but yield me up the keys . . . *3 Hen. VI.* iv 7 37
Here are the keys, there sits the duke asleep: I'll to the king *Richard III.* i 4 96
With an accent tuned in selfsame key Retorts to chiding fortune *T. and C.* i 3 53
Take these keys, and fetch more spices, nurse . . . *Rom. and Jul.* iv 4 1
If a man were porter of hell-gate, he should have old turning the key *Macbeth* ii 3 3
Had he Duncan's sons under his key—As, an't please heaven, he shall not—they should find What 'twere to kill a father . . . iii 6 18
'Tis in my memory lock'd, And you yourself shall keep the key of it *Ham.* i 3 86
Pray ye, go; there's my key: if you do stir abroad, go armed *Lear* i 2 186
Fortune, that arrant whore, Ne'er turns the key to the poor . . . ii 4 53
If wolves had at thy gate howl'd that stern time, Thou shouldst have said 'Good porter, turn the key' . . . iii 7 64
A closet lock and key of villanous secrets: And yet she'll kneel and pray . . . *Othello* iv 2 22
There's money for your pains: I pray you, turn the key and keep our counsel . . . iv 2 94
You're my prisoner, but Your gaoler shall deliver you the keys *Cymbeline* i 1 73
The sure physician, death, who is the key To unbar these locks . . . v 4 7
Key-cold. Poor key-cold figure of a holy king! . . . *Richard III.* i 2 5
Key-hole. Shut that and 'twill out at the key-hole . . . *As Y. Like It* iv 1 164
Kibe. If 'twere a kibe, 'Twould put me to my slipper . . . *Tempest* ii 1 276
I am almost out at heels.—Why, then, let kibes ensue . . . *Mer. Wives* i 3 35
The age is grown so picked that the toe of the peasant comes so near the heel of the courtier, he galls his kibe . . . *Hamlet* v 1 153
If a man's brains were in's heels, were't not in danger of kibes? *Lear* i 5 9
Kick. I should kick, being kick'd . . . *Com. of Errors* iii 1 17
Dead though she be, she feels her young one kick . . . *All's Well* v 3 303
Then trip him, that his heels may kick at heaven . . . *Hamlet* iii 3 93
Kicked. I should kick, being kick'd . . . *Com. of Errors* iii 1 17
Our spoils he kick'd at, And look'd upon things precious as they were The common muck of the world . . . *Coriolanus* ii 2 128
I here take my oath before this honourable assembly, she kicked the poor king her father . . . *Lear* iii 6 50
Kickshaws. Any pretty little tiny kickshaws, tell William cook *2 Hen. IV.* v 1 29
Kickshawses. Art thou good at these kickshawses? . . . *T. Night* i 3 122
Kicky-wicky. That hugs his kicky-wicky here at home . . . *All's Well* ii 3 297
Kid-fox. We'll fit the kid-fox with a pennyworth . . . *Much Ado* ii 3 45
Kidney. Think of that,—a man of my kidney,—think of that *Mer. Wives* iii 5 116
Kildare. First, Kildare's attainder, Then deputy of Ireland *Hen. VIII.* ii 1 41
Kill. I will kill this man: his daughter and I will be king and queen *Tempest* iii 2 114
Wound the loud winds, or with bemock'd-at stabs Kill the still-closing waters . . . iii 3 64
Is't near dinner-time?—I would it were, That you might kill your stomach on your meat And not upon your maid . . . *T. G. of Ver.* i 2 68
Injurious wasps, to feed on such sweet honey And kill the bees that yield it! . . . i 2 107
A little time, my lord, will kill that grief . . . iii 2 15
I vill kill de Jack priest; and I have appointed mine host of de Jarteer to measure our weapon . . . *Mer. Wives* i 4 123
He is wise, sir; he knew your worship would kill him, if he came . . . ii 3 11
By gar, de herring is no dead so as I vill kill him . . . ii 3 13
Take your rapier, Jack; I vill tell you how I vill kill him . . . ii 3 14
By gar, me vill kill de priest; for he speak for a jack-an-ape to Anne Page ii 3 86
Have I not stay for him to kill him? have I not, at de place I did appoint? iii 1 94
Even for our kitchens We kill the fowl of season . . . *Meas. for Meas.* ii 2 85
Shame to him whose cruel striking Kills for faults of his own liking! . . . iii 2 282
Away! they'll kill us . . . *Com. of Errors* iv 4 150
Unless you send some present help, Between them they will kill the conjurer . . . v 1 177
To vex Claudio, to undo Hero and kill Leonato . . . *Much Ado* ii 2 29
Some Cupid kills with arrows, some with traps . . . iii 1 106
Bid me do any thing for thee.—Kill Claudio.—Ha! not for the wide world.—You kill me to deny it . . . iv 1 291
If you go on thus, you will kill yourself . . . v 1 1
If thou kill'st me, boy, thou shalt kill a man.—He shall kill two of us, and men indeed: But that's no matter; let him kill one first . . . v 1 79
What though care killed a cat, thou hast mettle enough in thee to kill care v 1 134
Do you hear me, and let this count kill me . . . v 1 238
Now mercy goes to kill, And shooting well is then accounted ill *L. L. Lost* iv 1 24
It was to show my skill, That more for praise than purpose meant to kill iv 1 29
My lady goes to kill horns . . . iv 1 113
This love is as mad as Ajax: it kills sheep; it kills me, I a sheep . . . iv 3 7
Why, that contempt will kill the speaker's heart . . . v 2 149
What is Pyramus? a lover, or a tyrant?—A lover, that kills himself most gallant for love . . . *M. N. Dream* i 2 25
Hence; Some to kill cankers in the musk-rose buds . . . ii 2 3
Stay, though thou kill me, sweet Demetrius.—I charge thee, hence . . . ii 2 84
Pyramus must draw a sword to kill himself; which the ladies cannot abide . . . iii 1 11
Being o'er shoes in blood, plunge in the deep, And kill me too . . . iii 2 49
When truth kills truth, O devilish-holy fray! . . . iii 2 129
What, should I hurt her, strike her, kill her dead? . . . iii 2 269
And threaten'd me To strike me, spurn me, nay, to kill me too . . . iii 2 313
Kill me a red-hipped humble-bee on the top of a thistle . . . iv 1 11
And tragical, my noble lord, it is; For Pyramus therein doth kill himself v 1 67
Like Limander, am I trusty still.—And I like Helen, till the Fates me kill v 1 200
Do all men kill the things they do not love?—Hates any man the thing he would not kill? . . . *Mer. of Venice* iv 1 66
Come, shall we go and kill us venison? . . . *As Y. Like It* ii 1 21
And what's worse, To fright the animals and to kill them up In their assign'd and native dwelling-place . . . ii 1 62
He was furnished like a hunter.—O, ominous! he comes to kill my heart iii 2 260
And if mine eyes can wound, now let them kill thee . . . iii 5 16
I protest, her frown might kill me.—By this hand, it will not kill a fly iv 1 110
Was't you that did so oft contrive to kill him?—'Twas I; but 'tis not I iv 3 135
Or, to wit, I kill thee, make thee away, translate thy life into death . . . v 1 58
I will kill thee a hundred and fifty ways: therefore tremble, and depart v 1 62
He kills her in her own humour . . . *T. of Shrew* iv 1 183
This is a way to kill a wife with kindness . . . iv 1 211
Though I kill him not, I am the cause His death was so effected *All's W.* iii 2 118
We are reconciled, and the first view shall kill All repetition . . . v 3 21

Kill. If you will not undo what you have done, that is, kill him whom you have recovered, desire it not . . . *T. Night* ii 1 39
Where if it be thy chance to kill me,— Good.—Thou killest me like a rogue . . . iii 4 177
This will so fright them both that they will kill one another by the look iii 4 214
Fear to kill a woodcock, lest thou dispossess the soul of thy grandam . iv 2 63
Like to the Egyptian thief at point of death, Kill what I love . . . v 1 122
Poison'd good Camillo's honour, To have him kill a king . . . *W. Tale* iii 2 190
Offer me no money, I pray you; that kills my heart . . . iv 3 88
Do not shun her Until you see her die again; for then You kill her double v 3 107
My reasonable part produces reason How I may be deliver'd of these woes, And teaches me to kill or hang myself . . . *K. John* iii 4 56
I had a mighty cause To wish him dead, but thou hadst none to kill him iv 2 206
There is not yet so ugly a fiend of hell As thou shalt be, if thou didst kill this child . . . iv 3 124
Since thou dost seek to kill my name in me, I mock my name *Richard II.* ii 1 86
A breath, a little scene, To monarchize, be fear'd, and kill with looks . iii 2 165
'Twere no good part To take on me to keep and kill thy heart. So, now I have mine own again, be gone, That I may strive to kill it with a groan . . . v 1 100
And interchangeably set down their hands, To kill the king at Oxford . v 2 99
He that kills me some six or seven dozen of Scots at a breakfast *1 Hen. IV.* ii 4 115
Was it for me to kill the heir-apparent? . . . ii 4 297
He that rides at high speed and with his pistol kills a sparrow flying . ii 4 380
I will kill all his coats; I'll murder all his wardrobe, piece by piece . v 3 26
I have made him sure.—He is, indeed; and living to kill thee . . . v 3 49
If your father will do me any honour, so; if not, let him kill the next Percy himself . . . v 4 145
Wilt thou kill God's officers and the king's . . . *2 Hen. IV.* ii 1 56
He that makes the first thrust, I'll kill him . . . *Hen. V.* ii 1 105
Lightly conspired, And sworn unto the practices of France, To kill us here . . . ii 2 91
He longs to eat the English.—I think he will eat all he kills . . . iii 7 100
Then every soldier kill his prisoners; Give the word through . . . iv 6 37
Kill the poys and the luggage! 'tis expressly against the law of arms . iv 7 1
Alexander . . . did, in his ales and his angers, look you, kill his best friend . . . iv 7 41
As that slaughterer doth Which giveth many wounds when one will kill *1 Hen. VI.* ii 5 110
Ah, Joan, this kills thy father's heart outright! . . . v 4 2
Come, basilisk, And kill the innocent gazer with thy sight *2 Hen. VI.* iii 2 53
Art thou, like the adder, waxen deaf! Be poisonous too and kill thy forlorn queen . . . iii 2 77
Wherefore should I curse them? Would curses kill, as doth the mandrake's groan . . . iii 2 310
The first thing we do, let's kill all the lawyers . . . iv 2 83
And thou shalt have a license to kill for a hundred lacking one . . . iv 3 8
Up Fish Street! down Saint Magnus' Corner! kill and knock down! . iv 8 2
Dare any be so bold to sound retreat or parley, when I command them kill? . . . iv 8 5
Whose smile and frown, like to Achilles' spear, Is able with the change to kill and cure . . . v 1 101
Heart, be wrathful still: Priests pray for enemies, but princes kill . v 2 71
Ah, gentle Clifford, kill me with thy sword, And not with such a cruel threatening look . . . *3 Hen. VI.* i 3 16
A treacherous coward, As thou didst kill our tender brother Rutland . ii 2 115
I'll kill my horse, because I will not fly . . . ii 3 24
See what showers arise, Blown with the windy tempest of my heart, Upon thy wounds, that kill mine eye and heart! . . . ii 5 87
Let them fight that will, For I have murdered where I should not kill . ii 5 122
There's for twitting me with perjury.—O, kill me too!—Marry, and shall v 5 41
Ah, kill me with thy weapon, not with words! . . . v 6 26
Hadst thou been kill'd when first thou didst presume, Thou hadst not lived to kill a son of mine . . . v 6 36
I did not kill your husband.—Why, then he is alive . . . *Richard III.* i 2 91
Didst thou not kill this king?—I grant ye.—Dost grant me, hedgehog? i 2 101
For now they kill me with a living death . . . i 2 153
I did kill King Henry, But 'twas thy beauty that provoked me . . . i 2 180
Then bid me kill myself, and I will do it.—I have already . . . i 2 187
That hand, which, for thy love, did kill thy love, Shall, for thy love, kill a far truer love . . . i 2 190
Fool, fool! thou whet'st a knife to kill thyself . . . i 3 244
What, art thou afraid?—Not to kill him, having a warrant for it . . . i 4 112
It [conscience] is even now at my elbow, persuading me not to kill the duke . . . i 4 150
Darest thou resolve to kill a friend of mine?—Ay, my lord; But I had rather kill two enemies . . . iv 2 70
How chance the prophet could not at that time Have told me, I being by, that I should kill him? . . . iv 2 104
I had a Richard too, and thou didst kill him; I had a Rutland too, thou holp'st to kill him . . . iv 4 44
Thou didst kill my children.—But in your daughter's womb I bury them iv 4 422
My loyalty, Which ever has and ever shall be growing, Till death, that winter, kill it . . . *Hen. VIII.* iii 2 179
These lovers cry Oh! oh! they die! Yet that which seems the wound to kill, Doth turn oh! oh! to ha! ha! he! . . . *Troi. and Cres.* iii 1 132
By Venus' hand I swear, No man alive can love in such a sort The thing he means to kill more excellently . . . iv 1 24
To bed, to bed: sleep kill those pretty eyes! . . . iv 2 4
I came to kill thee, cousin, and bear hence A great addition earned in thy death . . . iv 5 140
Guard thee well; For I'll not kill thee there, nor there, nor there . iv 5 254
I'll kill thee every where, yea, o'er and o'er . . . iv 5 256
Let us kill him, and we'll have corn at our own price . . . *Coriolanus* i 1 10
Insolent villain!—Kill, kill, kill, kill, kill him! . . . v 6 132
O Tamora, be call'd a gentle queen, And with thine own hands kill me in this place! . . . *T. Andron.* ii 3 169
This object kills me!—Faint-hearted boy, arise, and look upon her . iii 1 64
If they did kill thy husband, then be joyful, Because the law hath ta'en revenge on them . . . iii 1 116
Wound it with sighing, girl, kill it with groans . . . iii 2 15
We are not brought so low, But that between us we can kill a fly . . . iii 2 77
Stay, murderous villains! will you kill your brother? . . . iv 2 88
I curse the day . . . Wherein I did not some notorious ill, As kill a man v 1 128
I have done a thousand dreadful things As willingly as one would kill a fly v 1 142
Arise, fair sun, and kill the envious moon . . . *Rom. and Jul.* ii 2 4
I would I were thy bird.—Sweet, so would I: Yet I should kill thee with much cherishing . . . ii 2 184
An there were two such, we should have none shortly, for one would kill the other . . . iii 1 17

Kill. Some twenty of them fought in this black strife, And all those twenty could but kill one life . . . . . *Rom. and Jul.* iii 1 184
Mercy but murders, pardoning those that kill . . . . . iii 1 202
But, wherefore, villain, didst thou kill my cousin? That villain cousin would have kill'd my husband . . . . . iii 2 100
But 'banish'd' to kill me?—'banished'? O friar, the damned use that word in hell . . . . . iii 3 46
Tybalt would kill thee, But thou slew'st Tybalt; there art thou happy too iii 3 137
And, with wild looks, bid me devise some mean To rid her from this second marriage, Or in my cell there would she kill herself . . v 3 242
See, what a scourge is laid upon your hate, That heaven finds means to kill your joys with love . . . . . v 3 293
Parts bread with him, pledges the breath of him in a divided draught, is the readiest man to kill him . . . . *T. of Athens* i 2 50
Would all those flatterers were thine enemies then, and then thou mightst kill 'em and bid me to 'em! . . . . . i 2 84
If wrongs be evils and enforce us kill, What folly 'tis to hazard life for ill! iii 5 36
To kill, I grant, is sin's extremest gust; But, in defence, by mercy, 'tis most just. To be in anger is impiety . . . . . iii 5 54
Away, thou issue of a mangy dog! Choler does kill me that thou art alive . . . . . iv 3 372
If Alcibiades kill my countrymen, Let Alcibiades know this of Timon, That Timon cares not . . . . . v 1 172
Approach the fold and cull the infected forth, But kill not all together v 4 44
Think him as a serpent's egg Which, hatch'd, would, as his kind, grow mischievous, And kill him in the shell . . . . *J. Cæsar* ii 1 34
Gentle friends, Let's kill him boldly, but not wrathfully . . ii 1 172
Revenge! About! Seek! Burn! Fire! Kill! Slay! Let not a traitor live! iii 2 209
Only I yield to die: There is so much that thou wilt kill me straight; Kill Brutus, and be honour'd in his death . . . . . v 4 13
Peace then! no words.—I'll rather kill myself . . . . . v 5 7
What ill request did Brutus make to thee?—To kill him, Clitus . . v 5 12
O, yet I do repent me of my fury, That I did kill them . . *Macbeth* ii 3 113
How monstrous It was for Malcolm and for Donalbain To kill their gracious father? damned fact! . . . . . iii 6 10
I do think That had he Duncan's sons under his key—As, an't please heaven, he shall not—they should find What 'twere to kill a father iii 6 20
I was killed i' the Capitol; Brutus killed me.—It was a brute part of him to kill so capital a calf there . . . . . *Hamlet* iii 2 110
A second time I kill my husband dead, When second husband kisses me in bed . . . . . iii 2 194
A villain kills my father; and for that, I, his sole son, do this same villain send To heaven . . . . . iii 3 76
Almost as bad, good mother, As kill a king, and marry with his brother.—As kill a king! . . . . . iii 4 29
In this brainish apprehension, kills The unseen good old man . . iv 1 11
Kill thy physcian, and the fee bestow Upon thy foul disease . . *Lear* i 1 166
What is your study?—How to prevent the fiend, and to kill vermin . iii 4 164
As flies to wanton boys, are we to the gods, They kill us for their sport iv 1 39
And when I have stol'n upon these sons-in-law, Then, kill, kill, kill, kill kill, kill! . . . . . iv 6 191
How do you now, lieutenant?—The worser that you give me the addition Whose want even kills me . . . . *Othello* iv 1 106
Whether he kill Cassio, Or Cassio him, or each do kill the other, Every way makes my gain . . . . . v 1 12
Kill men i' the dark!—Where be these bloody thieves? . . . v 1 63
Be thus when thou art dead, and I will kill thee, And love thee after . v 2 18
I would not kill thy unprepared spirit; No; heaven forfend! I would not kill thy soul.—Talk you of killing? . . . . . v 2 31
Have mercy on me!—Amen, with all my heart!—If you say so, I hope you will not kill me.—Hum! . . . . . v 2 35
That death's unnatural that kills for loving . . . . . v 2 42
O, banish me, my lord, but kill me not! . . . . . v 2 78
Kill me to-morrow: let me live to-night!—Nay, if you strive . . v 2 80
O villany!—I thought so then:—I'll kill myself for grief . . v 2 192
Come, guard the door without; let him not pass, But kill him rather . v 2 242
If that thou be'st a devil, I cannot kill thee . . . . . v 2 287
Then, we kill all our women: we see how mortal an unkindness is to them; if they suffer our departure, death's the word *Ant. and Cleo.* i 2 137
Forgive me; Since my becomings kill me, when they do not Eye well to you i 3 96
That, on my command, Thou then wouldst kill me: do't; the time is come iv 14 67
Hast thou the pretty worm of Nilus there, That kills and pains not? v 2 244
It is a basilisk unto mine eye, Kills me to look on't . . *Cymbeline* ii 4 108
I will kill thee, if thou dost deny Thou'st made me cuckold . . ii 4 145
A tribute, Yearly three thousand pounds, which by thee lately Is left untender'd.—And, to kill the marvel, Shall be so ever . . . iii 1 10
I thought you would not back again.—Most like; Bringing me here to kill me . . . . . iii 4 120
Even there, thou villain, Posthumus, will I kill thee . . . iii 5 135
With that suit upon my back, will I ravish her: first kill him . . iii 5 142
Know, if you kill me for my fault, I should Have died had I not made it iii 6 57
For friends kill friends, and the disorder's such As war were hoodwink'd v 2 15
We hate the prince of Tyre, and thou must kill him . . *Pericles* i 1 156
Here must I kill King Pericles; and if I do it not, I am sure to be hanged i 3 2
Beauty hath his power and will, Which can as well inflame as it can kill ii 2 35
Why will you kill me?—To satisfy my lady . . . . . iv 1 71
Like one that superstitiously Doth swear to the gods that winter kills the flies . . . . . iv 3 50
Kill-courtesy. Pretty soul! she durst not lie Near this lack-love, this kill-courtesy . . . . . *M. N. Dream* ii 2 77
Killed. I took him to be killed with a thunder-stroke . . *Tempest* ii 2 112
Who, with Sebastian, Whose inward pinches therefore are most strong, Would here have kill'd your king . . . . . v 1 78
I kill'd a man, whose death I much repent . . . *T. G. of Ver.* iv 1 27
I have stood on the pillory for geese he hath killed . . . iv 4 36
I wished your venison better; it was ill killed . . *Mer. Wives* i 1 84
You have beaten my men, killed my deer, and broke open my lodge . i 1 114
Are you not ashamed? I think you have killed the poor woman . . iv 2 198
Young Drop-heir that killed lusty Pudding . . *Meas. for Meas.* iv 3 16
He that goes in the calf's skin that was killed for the Prodigal *C. of Er.* iv 3 18
How many hath he killed and eaten in these wars? . . *Much Ado* i 1 43
Thou hast kill'd my child: If thou kill'st me, boy, thou shalt kill a man v 1 78
What through care killed a cat, thou hast mettle enough in thee to kill care . . . . . v 1 133
You have killed a sweet lady, and her death shall fall heavy on you . v 1 150
You have among you killed a sweet and innocent lady . . . v 1 194
Art thou the slave that with thy breath hast kill'd Mine innocent child? v 1 273
And I say beside that, 'twas a pricket that the princess killed *L. L. Lost* iv 2 49
To humour the ignorant, call I the deer the princess killed a pricket . iv 2 53
You'll ne'er be friends with him; a' kill'd your sister . . . v 2 13

Killed. Great Hercules is presented by this imp, Whose club kill'd Cerberus, that three-headed canis . . . . . *L. L. Lost* v 2 593
Let the prologue seem to say, we will do no harm with our swords and that Pyramus is not killed indeed . . . . *M. N. Dream* iii 1 20
And hast thou kill'd him sleeping? O brave touch! . . . . iii 2 70
Then I'll repent, And wish, for all that, that I had not kill'd them *Mer. of Venice* iii 4 73
If killed, but one dead that is willing to be so . . . *As Y. Like It* i 2 200
Which is he that killed the deer?—Sir, it was I . . . . . iv 2 1
What shall he have that kill'd the deer? His leather skin and horns to wear . . . . . iv 2 11
For in a quarrel since I came ashore I kill'd a man . . . *T. of Shrew* i 1 237
Your son will not be killed so soon as I thought he would.—Why should he be killed?—So say I, madam, if he run away . . *All's Well* iii 2 39
How will she love, when the rich golden shaft Hath kill'd the flock of all affections else That live in her! . . . . . *T. Night* i 1 36
Make me not sighted like the basilisk: I have look'd on thousands, who have sped the better By my regard, but kill'd none so . *W. Tale* i 2 390
She you kill'd Would be unparallel'd.—I think so. Kill'd! She I kill'd! I did so: but thou strikest me Sorely, to say I did . . . . v 1 15
Scarce any joy Did ever so long live; no sorrow But kill'd itself much sooner . . . . . v 3 53
And others more, going to seek the grave Of Arthur, whom they say is kill'd to-night On your suggestion . . . . . *K. John* iv 2 165
Who kill'd this prince?—'Tis not an hour since I left him well . . iv 3 103
Some poison'd by their wives; some sleeping kill'd; All murder'd *Richard II.* iii 2 159
'O my sweet Harry,' says she, 'how many hast thou killed to-day?' *1 Hen. IV.* ii 4 119
Therefore I'll make him sure; yea, and I'll swear I killed him . . v 4 128
Why, Percy I killed myself and saw thee dead . . . . . v 4 147
And both the Blunts Kill'd by the hand of Douglas . . *2 Hen. IV.* i 1 17
There hath been a man or two lately killed about her . . . . v 4 7
For any thing I know, Falstaff shall die of a sweat, unless already a' be killed with your hard opinions . . . . . Epil. 32
The king has killed his heart . . . . . *Hen. V.* ii 1 92
The mercy that was quck in us but late, By your own counsel is suppress'd and kill'd . . . . . ii 2 80
The man that once did sell the lion's skin While the beast lived, was killed with hunting him . . . . . iv 3 94
Our king is not like him in that: he never killed any of his friends . iv 7 43
Alexander killed his friend Cleitus, being in his ales and his cups . . iv 7 47
Is it not lawful, an please your majesty, to tell how many is killed? . iv 8 123
'Twas you that kill'd young Rutland, was it not?—Ay, and old York, and yet not satisfied . . . . . *3 Hen. VI.* ii 2 98
O God! it is my father's face, Whom in this conflict I unwares have kill'd . . . . . ii 5 62
Where my poor young was limed, was caught and kill'd . . . v 6 17
Thy son I kill'd for his presumption.—Hadst thou been kill'd when first thou didst presume, Thou hadst not lived to kill a son of mine . v 6 34
Then I'll marry Warwick's youngest daughter. What though I kill'd her husband and her father? . . . . . *Richard III.* i 1 154
What! I, that kill'd her husband and his father, To take her in her heart's extremest hate, With curses in her mouth! . . . . . i 2 231
I had an Edward, till a Richard kill'd him; I had a Harry, till a Richard kill'd him: Thou hadst an Edward, till a Richard kill'd him; Thou hadst a Richard, till a Richard kill'd him . . . . . iv 4 40
Thou hadst a Clarence too, and Richard kill'd him . . . . iv 4 46
Thy Clarence he is dead that kill'd my Edward . . . . iv 4 67
If I have kill'd the issue of your womb, To quicken your increase, I will beget Mine issue of your blood upon your daughter . . . . iv 4 296
He killed my son. My daughter. He killed my cousin Marcus. He killed my father . . . . . *Coriolanus* v 6 122
Hath hurt me more than had he kill'd me dead . . *T. Andron.* iii 1 92
Perchance she weeps because they kill'd her husband . . . iii 1 114
What dost thou strike at, Marcus, with thy knife?—At that that I have kill'd, my lord; a fly . . . . . iii 2 53
I have but kill'd a fly.—But how, if that fly had a father and mother? . iii 2 59
Came here to make us merry! and thou hast kill'd him . . . iii 2 65
Pardon me, sir; it was a black ill-favour'd fly, Like to the empress' Moor; therefore I kill'd him . . . . . iii 2 67
You kill'd her husband, and for that vile fault Two of her brothers were condemn'd to death . . . . . v 2 173
Kill'd her, for whom my tears have made me blind . . . . v 3 49
Which way ran he that kill'd Mercutio? . . . *Rom. and Jul.* iii 1 142
We are undone! Alack the day! he's gone, he's kill'd, he's dead! . iii 2 39
Tybalt is gone, and Romeo banished; Romeo that kill'd him . . iii 2 70
Will you speak well of him that kill'd your cousin?—Shall I speak ill of him that is my husband? . . . . . iii 2 96
But, wherefore, villain, didst thou kill my cousin? That villian cousin would have kill'd my husband . . . . . iii 2 101
Despised, distressed, hated, martyr'd, kill'd! . . . . . iv 5 59
Romeo dead; and Juliet, dead before, Warm and new kill'd . . . v 3 197
Wert thou a bear, thou wouldst be killed by the horse . *T. of Athens* iv 3 341
Cæsar, thou art revenged, Even with the sword that kill'd thee *J. Cæsar* v 3 46
Cæsar, now be still: I kill'd not thee with half so good a will . . v 5 51
On Tuesday last, A falcon, towering in her pride of place, Was by a mousing owl hawk'd at and kill'd . . . . . *Macbeth* ii 4 13
We have scotch'd the snake, not kill'd it . . . . . iii 2 13
Whom, you may say, if't please you, Fleance kill'd, For Fleance fled . iii 6 6
What, you egg! Young fry of treachery!—He has kill'd me, mother . iv 2 84
And I must be from thence! My wife kill'd too?—I have said . . iv 3 213
I was killed i' the Capitol; Brutus killed me . . . . *Hamlet* iii 2 108
None wed the second but who kill'd the first . . . . . iii 2 190
Where is he gone?—To draw apart the body he hath kill'd . . . iv 1 24
How stand I then, That have a father kill'd, a mother stain'd? . . iv 4 57
He that hath kill'd my king and whored my mother . . . . v 2 64
I am justly kill'd with mine own treachery . . . . . v 2 318
The great rage, You see, is kill'd in him . . . . . *Lear* iv 7 79
I kill'd the slave that was a-hanging thee.—'Tis true, my lords, he did v 3 274
Cassio, my lord, hath kill'd a young Venetian Call'd Roderigo.—Roderigo kill'd! And Cassio kill'd!—No, Cassio is not kill'd.—Not Cassio kill'd! then murder's out of tune . . . . . *Othello* v 2 112
She's, like a liar, gone to burning hell: 'Twas I that kill'd her . v 2 130
Help, ho! help! The Moor hath kill'd my mistress! Murder! murder! v 2 167
For thou hast kill'd the sweetest innocent That e'er did lift up eye . v 2 199
The woman falls; sure, he hath kill'd his wife . . . . . v 2 236
He's gone, but his wife's kill'd.—'Tis a notorious villain . . . v 2 238
I bleed, sir; but not kill'd.—I am not sorry neither: I'ld have thee live v 2 288
I kiss'd thee ere I kill'd thee: no way but this; Killing myself . . v 2 358

Killed. 'Tis gold Which makes the true man kill'd and saves the thief *Cymbeline* ii 3 76
We'll browse on that, Whilst what we have kill'd be cook'd . . iii 6 39
Pisanio might have kill'd thee at the heart, And left this head on . iv 2 322
'Tis enough That, Britian, I have kill'd thy mistress . . . v 1 20
I am Posthumus, That kill'd thy daughter:—villain-like, I lie—That caused a lesser villain than myself, A sacrilegious thief, to do't . v 5 218
O, my lord Posthumus! You ne'er killed Imogen till now . . v 5 231
Like to gnats, Which make a sound, but kill'd are wonder'd at *Pericles* ii 3 63
Why would she have me kill'd? Now, as I can remember, by my troth, I never did her hurt . . . . iv 1 73
Believe me, la, I never kill'd a mouse, nor hurt a fly . . . iv 1 78
Killen. For though he strive To killen bad, keep good alive . ii Gower 20
Killest. If thou kill'st me, boy, thou shalt kill a man . *Much Ado* v 1 79
Thou killest me like a rogue and a villain . . . *T. Night* iii 4 179
Thou kill'st me in his life; giving him breath, The traitor lives *Richard II.* v 3 72
Out on thee, murderer! thou kill'st my heart . . *T. Andron.* iii 2 54
O error, soon conceived, Thou never comest unto a happy birth, But kill'st the mother that engender'd thee! . . . *J. Cæsar* v 3 71
Antonius dead!—If thou say so, villain, Thou kill'st thy mistress *Ant. and Cleo.* ii 5 27
Killeth. Him I forgive my death that killeth me When he sees me go back one foot or fly . . . . . . 1 *Hen VI.* i 2 20
Killing. Indeed I promised to eat all of his killing . . *Much Ado* i 1 45
I believe we must leave the killing out, when all is done *M. N. Dream* iii 1 15
I doubt not but to die a fair death for all this, if I 'scape hanging for killing that rogue . . . . 1 *Hen. IV.* ii 2 15
He hath a killing tongue and a quiet sword . . . *Hen. V.* iii 2 36
As in despite, the sun looks pale, Killing their fruit with frowns . iii 5 18
Like to the bullet's grazing, Break out into a second course of mischief, Killing in relapse of mortality . . . . iv 3 107
Their wounded steeds . . . Yerk out their armed heels at their dead masters, Killing them twice . . . . iv 7 84
They have won the bridge, killing all those that withstand them 2 *Hen. VI.* iv 5 3
Art thou afraid?—Not to kill him, having a warrant for it; but to be damned for killing him, from which no warrant can defend us *Rich. III* i 4 113
In sweet music is such art, Killing care and grief of heart *Hen. VIII.* iii 1 13
The third day comes a frost, a killing frost . . . . . iii 2 355
Killing our enemies, the blood he hath lost—Which, I dare vouch, is more than that he hath, By many an ounce . *Coriolanus* iii 1 299
With no less confidence Than boys pursuing summer butterflies, Or butchers killing flies . . . . iv 6 95
O, keep me from their worse than killing lust . *T. Andron.* ii 3 175
Where is my lord the king?—Here, Tamora, though grieved with killing grief . . . . ii 3 260
Killing that love which thou hast vow'd to cherish . *Rom. and Jul.* iii 3 129
By killing of villains, Thou wast born to conquer my country *T. of Athens* iv 3 105
How 'scaped I killing when I cross'd you so? . . *J. Cæsar* iv 3 150
Where hast thou been, sister?—Killing swine . . . *Macbeth* i 3 2
I would have him nine years a-killing . . . . *Othello* iv 1 188
Talk you of killing?—Ay, I do.—Then heaven Have mercy on me! . v 2 33
I kiss'd thee ere I kill'd thee: no way but this; Killing myself, to die upon a kiss . . . . v 2 359
In killing creatures vile, as cats and dogs, Of no esteem . *Cymbeline* v 5 252
Killingworth. Retire to Killingworth, Until a power be raised to put them down . . . . 2 *Hen. VI.* iv 4 39
The traitors hate thee; Therefore away with us to Killingworth . iv 4 44
Kiln-hole. Creep into the kiln-hole . . . . . *Mer. Wives* iv 2 59
Is there not milking-time, when you are going to bed, or kiln-hole, to whistle off these secrets? . . . . . . *W. Tale* iv 4 247
Kimbolton. Removed to Kimbolton, Where she remains now sick *Hen. VIII.* iv 1 34
Kin. Lawful mercy Is nothing kin to foul redemption . *Meas. for Meas.* ii 4 113
I am half afeard Thou wilt say anon he is some kin to thee, Thou spend'st such high-day wit in praising him . . *Mer. of Venice* ii 9 97
Noble heroes, my sword and yours are kin . . . *All's Well* ii 1 41
One of thy kin has a most weak pia mater . . . *T. Night* i 5 123
What kin are you to me? What countryman? what name? what parentage? . . . . v 1 237
The ear-deafening voice o' the oracle, Kin to Jove's thunder . *W. Tale* iii 1 10
And my near'st of kin Cry fie upon my grave! . . . . iii 2 54
Not hold thee of our blood, no, not our kin, Far than Deucalion off . iv 4 441
Come, lady, I will show thee to my kin . . . . *K. John* i 1 273
His hands were guilty of no kindred blood, But bloody with the enemies of his kin . . . . *Richard II.* ii 1 183
Tumultuous wars Shall kin with kin and kind with kind confound . iv 1 141
Not like to me, or any of my kin, And yet I love him . . . v 2 109
Even like those that are kin to the king . . . . 2 *Hen. IV.* ii 2 120
Nay, they will be kin to us, or they will fetch it from Japhet . . ii 2 127
Even such kin as the parish heifers are to the town bull . . ii 2 171
So little kin to the purpose . . . . . . *Hen. V.* iii 7 72
Had he been slaughter-man to all my kin, I should not for my life but weep with him, To see how inly sorrow gripes his soul . 3 *Hen. VI.* i 4 169
Gentle, kind, effeminate remorse, Which we have noted in you to your kin, And egally indeed to all estates . . . *Richard III.* iii 7 212
Because she's kin to me, therefore she's not so fair as Helen: an she were not kin to me, she would be as fair on Friday as Helen is on Sunday . . . . *Troi. and Cres.* i 1 76
The artist and unread, The hard and soft, seem all affined and kin . i 3 25
One touch of nature makes the whole world kin . . . . iii 3 175
No kin, no love, no blood, no soul so near me As the sweet Troilus . iv 2 104
The combatants being kin Half stints their strife before their strokes begin . . . . iv 5 92
I'll never Be such a gosling to obey instinct, but stand, As if a man were author of himself And knew no other kin . . . *Coriolanus* v 3 37
Now, by the stock and honour of my kin, To strike him dead I hold it not a sin.—Why, how now, kinsman! . . . *Rom. and Jul.* i 5 60
One only daughter have I, no kin else, On whom I may confer what I have got: The maid is fair . . . . . *T. of Athens* i 1 121
Spare thy Athenian cradle and those kin Which in the bluster of thy wrath must fall With those that have offended . . . . v 4 40
A little more than kin, and less than kind . . . *Hamlet* i 2 65
What have you done, my lord, with the dead body?—Compounded it with dust, whereto 'tis kin . . . . iv 2 6
I marvel what kin thou and thy daughters are. . . . *Lear* i 4 199
Your words and performances are no kin together . . *Othello* iv 2 185
Wilt have him live? Is he thy kin, thy friend?—He is a Roman; no more kin to me Than I to your highness . . . *Cymbeline* v 5 112
Kind. No kind of traffic Would I admit; no name of magistrate *Tempest* ii 1 148
But nature should bring forth, Of it own kind, all foison, all abundance ii 1 163

Kind. You we laughed at.—Who in this kind of merry fooling am nothing to you . . . . *Tempest* ii 1 177
A kind of not of the newest Poor-John. A strange fish! . . . . ii 2 27
Some kinds of baseness Are nobly undergone . . . . . iii 1 2
They want the use of tongue, a kind Of excellent dumb discourse . . iii 3 38
My meaner ministers Their several kinds have done . . . . iii 3 88
Myself, One of their kind, that relish all as sharply . . . v 1 23
All the kind of the Launces have this very fault . . *T. G. of Ver.* ii 3 2
He is a kind of chameleon . . . . ii 4 25
Dumb jewels often in their silent kind More than quick words do move a woman's mind . . . . iii 1 90
I have the wit to think my master is a kind of a knave . . . iii 1 262
We dare trust you in this kind . . . . iii 2 56
It's an honourable kind of thievery . . . . iv 1 40
Is she kind as she is fair? For beauty lives with kindness . . iv 2 44
There is, as 'twere, a tender, a kind of tender, made afar off . *Mer. Wives* i 1 215
Thine own true knight, By day or night, Or any kind of light . . ii 1 17
I would not ha' your distemper in this kind for the wealth of Windsor Castle . . . . iii 3 232
You may know by my size that I have a kind of alacrity in sinking . iii 5 13
There is a kind of character in thy life, That to the observer doth thy history Fully unfold . . . . . . *Meas. for Meas.* i 1 28
Authority, though it err like others, Hath yet a kind of medicine in itself . . . . ii 2 135
Mutually committed?—Mutually.—Then was your sin of heavier kind than his . . . . ii 3 28
Is't not a kind of incest, to take life From thine own sister's shame? . iii 1 139
A noble and renowned brother, in his love toward her ever most kind . iii 1 229
Double and treble admonition, and still forfeit in the same kind! . . iii 2 206
It is as dangerous to be aged in any kind of course, as it is virtuous to be constant in any undertaking . . . . iii 2 238
I am a kind of burr; I shall stick . . . . iv 3 189
The sooner lost: yet he loseth it in a kind of jollity *Com. of Errors* ii 2 90
There is a kind of merry war betwixt Signior Benedick and her *Much Ado* i 1 62
If the prince do solicit you in that kind, you know your answer . . ii 1 70
Intend a kind of zeal both to the prince and Claudio . . . . ii 2 36
For such kind of men, the less you meddle or make with them, why, the more is for your honesty . . . . iii 3 55
How am I beset! What kind of catechising call you this? . . iv 1 79
They shall find, awaked in such a kind, Both strength of limb and policy of mind . . . . iv 1 199
A kind of insinuation, as it were . . . . . *L. L. Lost* iv 2 13
In himself he is; But in this kind, wanting your father's voice, The other must be held the worthier . . . . . *M. N. Dream* i 1 54
Be kind and courteous to this gentleman; Hop in his walks . . iii 1 167
Yet but three? Come one more; Two of both kinds makes up four . iii 2 438
My hounds are bred out of the Spartan kind, So flew'd, so sanded . iv 1 124
They can do nothing in this kind . . . . v 1 88
The best in this kind are but shadows . . . . . . v 1 213
In the doing of the deed of kind . . . . *Mer. of Venice* i 3 86
This is kind I offer.—This were kindness . . . . . . i 3 143
The Hebrew will turn Christian: he grows kind . . . . i 3 179
My father did something smack, something grow to, he had a kind of taste . . . . ii 2 19
The Jew my master, who, God bless the mark, is a kind of devil . . ii 2 25
That is but a kind of bastard hope neither . . . . iii 5 8; 14
The weakest kind of fruit Drops earliest to the ground . . . iv 1 115
Herein Fortune shows herself more kind Than is her custom . . iv 1 267
A youth, A kind of boy, a little scrubbed boy, No higher than thyself . v 1 162
By this kind of chase, I should hate him . . . . *As Y. Like It* i 3 33
And with a kind of umber smirch my face . . . . . i 3 114
In that kind, swears you do more usurp Than doth your brother . . ii 1 27
To some kind of men Their graces serve them but as enemies . . ii 3 10
If you like upon report The soil, the profit, and this kind of life . . ii 4 98
Of what kind should this cock come of? . . . . . . ii 7 90
If the cat will after kind, So be sure will Rosalind . . . . iii 2 109
Whether that thy youth and kind Will the faithful offer take Of me . iv 3 59
What, household stuff?—It is a kind of history . . *T. of Shrew* Ind. 2 144
I will be very kind, and liberal To mine own children in good bringing up . . . . i 1 98
I advise You use your manners discreetly in all kind of companies . i 1 247
An old Italian fox is not so kind, my boy . . . . . . ii 1 405
Padua affords nothing but what is kind . . . . . . v 2 14
Your marriage comes by destiny, Your cuckoo sings by kind *All's Well* i 3 67
Thine eyes See it so grossly shown in thy behaviours That in their kind they speak it . . . . i 3 185
When I was like this maid, I found you wondrous kind . . . v 3 311
She will admit no kind of suit, No, not the duke's . . *T. Night* i 2 45
These wise men, that crow so at these set kind of fools . . . i 5 95
What kind o' man is he?—Why, of mankind.—What manner of man? . i 5 159
Sometimes he is a kind of puritan.—O, if I thought that, I'ld beat him! ii 3 151
What kind of woman is't?—Of your complexion.—She is not worth thee, then . . . . ii 4 27
And with a kind of injunction drives me to these habits of her liking . ii 5 183
This fellow is wise enough to play the fool; And to do that well craves a kind of wit . . . . iii 1 68
I have heard of some kind of men that put quarrels purposely on others iii 4 266
O, if it prove, Tempests are kind and salt waves fresh in love . . iii 4 419
With such a kind of love as might become A lady like me . *W. Tale* iii 2 65
Which some call nature's bastards: of that kind Our rustic garden's barren . . . . iv 4 83
And make conceive a bark of baser kind By bud of noble race . . iv 4 94
The crown imperial; lilies of all kinds, The flower-de-luce being one . iv 4 126
Thy offices, So rarely kind, are as interpreters Of my behind-hand slackness . . . . v 1 150
We had a kind of light what would ensue . . . . *K. John* iv 3 61
But in this kind to come, in braving arms, Be his own carver *Richard II.* ii 3 143
And you that do abet him in this kind Cherish rebellion . . . ii 3 146
Tumultuous wars Shall kin with kin and kind with kind confound . iv 1 141
And in this thought they find a kind of ease . . . . . v 5 28
You shall hear in such a kind from me As will displease you 1 *Hen. IV.* i 3 121
A kind of auditor; one that hath abundance of charge too, God knows what . . . . ii 1 63
Oft the teeming earth Is with a kind of colic pinch'd . . . iii 1 29
And breed a kind of question in our cause . . . . . iv 1 68
That shows the ignorant a kind of fear Before not dreamt of . . iv 1 74
The king is kind; and well we know the king Knows at what time to promise . . . . iv 3 52
This apoplexy is, as I take it, a kind of lethargy, an't please your lordship; a kind of sleeping in the blood . . . . 2 *Hen. IV.* i 2 126

Kind. It [apoplexy] is a kind of deafness . . . . . 2 *Hen. IV.* i 2 134
They fall into a kind of male green-sickness . . . . iv 3 100
Rob, murder, and commit The oldest sins the newest kind of ways . iv 5 127
I have long dream'd of such a kind of man . . . . v 5 53
What mightst thou do, that honour would thee do, Were all thy children kind and natural! But see thy fault! . *Hen. V.* ii Prol. 19
Fetch forth the lazar kite of Cressid's kind, Doll Tearsheet she by name ii 1 80
Lest example Breed, by his sufferance, more of such a kind . . ii 2 46
Thus thy fall hath left a kind of blot . . . . . ii 2 138
Still be kind, And eke out our performance with your mind . iii Prol. 34
What kind of god art thou, that suffer'st more Of mortal griefs than do thy worshippers? . . . . iv 1 258
My wit untrain'd in any kind of art . . . . 1 *Hen. VI.* i 2 73
So kind a father of the commonweal . . . . . . iii 1 98
This argues what her kind of life hath been, Wicked and vile . v 4 15
That word 'judgement' hath bred a kind of remorse in me *Richard III.* i 4 110
Do not slander him, for he is kind.—Right, As snow in harvest . i 4 247
As well we know your tenderness of heart And gentle, kind, effeminate remorse . . . . iii 7 211
More mild, but yet more harmful, kind in hatred . . . iv 4 172
Which, as I take it, is a kind of puppy To the old dam, treason *Hen. VIII.* i 1 175
In what kind, let's know, Is this exaction? . . . . i 2 53
I do not know What kind of my obedience I should tender . . iii 3 66
Give me up To the sharp'st kind of justice . . . . ii 4 44
'Tis a kind of good deed to say well: And yet words are no deeds . iii 2 153
If none of them have soul in such a kind, We left them all at home *Troi. and Cres.* i 3 285
And underwrite in an observing kind His humorous predominance . ii 3 137
I have a kind of self resides with you; But an unkind self . . iii 2 155
A kind of godly jealousy—Which, I beseech you, call a virtuous sin . iv 4 82
That mongrel cur, Ajax, against that dog of as bad a kind, Achilles . v 4 15
With a kind of smile, Which ne'er came from the lungs . *Coriolanus* i 1 111
A kind of ingrateful injury; to report otherwise, were a malice . ii 2 35
He flouted us downright.—No, 'tis his kind of speech: he did not mock us . . . . ii 3 169
This kind of service Did not deserve corn gratis . . . iii 1 124
So criminal and in such capital kind, Deserves the extremest death . iii 3 81
He had, sir, a kind of face, methought,—I cannot tell how to term it . iv 5 163
O, he is grown most kind of late . . . . . . iv 6 11
He was a kind of nothing, titleless, Till he had forged himself a name v 1 13
Rome, be as just and gracious unto me As I am confident and kind to thee. Open the gates, and let me in . . . *T. Andron.* i 1 61
Many unfrequented plots there are Fitted by kind for rape . . ii 1 116
O, be to me, though thy hard heart say no, Nothing so kind, but something pitiful!—I know not what it means . . . . ii 3 156
Two of thy whelps, fell curs of bloody kind . . . . ii 3 281
What are they call'd?—Rapine and Murder; therefore called so, Cause they take vengeance of such kind of men . . . . v 2 63
Now will he sit under a medlar tree, And wish his mistress were that kind of fruit As maids call medlars . . *Rom. and Jul.* ii 1 35
Children of divers kind We sucking on her natural bosom find . ii 3 11
It were a very gross kind of behaviour, as they say . . . ii 4 176
An honest gentleman, and a courteous, and a kind, and a handsome . ii 5 57
A kind of hope, Which craves as desperate an execution As that is desperate which we would prevent . . . . . . iv 1 68
All kind of natures That labour on the bosom of this sphere *T. of Athens* i 1 65
Set a fair fashion on our entertainment, Which was not half so beautiful and kind; You have added worth unto't . . . . . i 2 153
He owes For every word: he is so kind that he now Pays interest for't i 2 205
I take all and your several visitations So kind to heart . . . i 2 225
Never mind Was to be so unwise, to be so kind . . . ii 2 6
Their blood is caked, 'tis cold, it seldom flows; 'Tis lack of kindly warmth they are not kind . . . . ii 2 226
Conceive the fairest of me, because I have no power to be kind . iii 2 61
Who, then, dares to be half so kind again? For bounty, that makes gods, does still mar men . . . . iv 2 40
In the plainer and simpler kind of people, the deed of saying is quite out of use . . . . v 1 27
Performance is a kind of will or testament which argues a great sickness . . . . v 1 30
Why birds and beasts from quality and kind . . . *J. Cæsar* i 3 64
Think him as a serpent's egg Which, hatch'd, would, as his kind, grow mischievous . . . . ii 1 33
I'll give thee a wind.—Thou'rt kind.—And I another . *Macbeth* i 3 12
A little more than kin, and less than kind . . . *Hamlet* i 2 65
There is a kind of confession in your looks . . . . ii 2 288
There did seem in him a kind of joy To hear of it . . . iii 1 18
And haply one as kind For husband shalt thou— O, confound the rest! iii 2 186
And that shall lend a kind of easiness To the next abstinence . . iii 4 166
I must be cruel, only to be kind: Thus bad begins and worse remains behind . . . . iii 4 178
Like the kind life-rendering pelican, Repast them with my blood . iv 5 146
There lives within the very flame of love A kind of wick or snuff . iv 7 116
In my heart there was a kind of fighting, That would not let me sleep . v 2 4
A kind of yesty collection, which carries them through and through . v 2 199
It is such a kind of gain-giving, as would perhaps trouble a woman . v 2 225
I had rather be any kind o' thing than a fool . . . *Lear* i 4 203
Yet have I left a daughter, Who, I am sure, is kind and comfortable . i 4 328
I will forget my nature. So kind a father! Be my horses ready? . i 5 35
These kind of knaves I know, which in this plainness Harbour more craft . . . . ii 2 107
But fathers that bear bags Shall see their children kind . . . ii 4 51
Thou hotly lust'st to use her in that kind For which thou whipp'st her iv 6 166
Kind and dear princess! . . . . iv 7 29
Help, help, O, help!—What kind of help? . . . . v 3 222
But I, for mere suspicion in that kind, Will do as if for surety . *Othello* i 3 395
She is of so free, so kind, so apt, so blessed a disposition . . ii 3 325
I never knew A Florentine more kind and honest . . . iii 1 43
There are a kind of men so loose of soul, That in their sleeps will mutter their affairs: One of this kind is Cassio . . . iii 3 418
If my offence be of such mortal kind . . . . . iii 4 115
Had they rain'd All kinds of sores and shames on my bare head . iv 2 49
Dost thou in conscience think,—tell me, Emilia,—That there be women do abuse their husbands In such gross kind? . . . . iv 3 63
Which they ear and wound With keels of every kind *Ant. and Cleo.* i 4 50
Fare thee well: The elements be kind to thee! . . . . iii 2 40
You must think this, look you, that the worm will do his kind . v 2 264
By her election may be truly read What kind of man he is . *Cymbeline* i 1 54
As fair and as good—a kind of hand-in-hand comparison . . i 4 75
He hath a kind of honour sets him off, More than a mortal seeming . i 6 170

Kind. A kind of conquest Cæsar made here; but made not here his brag Of 'Came' and 'saw' and 'overcame' . . . *Cymbeline* iii 1 22
Long'st,—O, let me bate,—but not like me—yet long'st, But in a fainter kind . . . . iii 2 57
Never master had A page so kind, so duteous, diligent, So tender . v 5 86
In this kind hath our Cleon One daughter, and a wench full grown *Pericles* iv Gower 15
Were I well assured Came of a gentle kind and noble stock . . v 1 68
Kind admittance. Let 'em have kind admittance . *T. of Athens* i 2 134
Kind answer. We'll visit Caliban my slave, who never Yields us kind answer . . . . *Tempest* i 2 309
Kind Antonio, I can no other answer make but thanks . *T. Night* iii 3 13
Kind aunt. He was lately sent From your kind aunt . 3 *Hen. VI.* ii 1 146
My niece Plantagenet Led in the hand of her kind aunt *Richard III.* iv 1 2
Kind citizens. Which trust accordingly kind citizens . *K. John* ii 1 231
Kind commends. I send to her my kind commends . *Richard II.* iii 1 38
Speak to his gentle hearing kind commends . . . . iii 3 126
Kind commiseration. Lending your kind commiseration *T. Andron.* v 3 93
Kind cousin. And 'gentle Harry Percy,' and 'kind cousin;' O, the devil take such cozeners! . . . . . 1 *Hen. IV.* i 3 254
Kind creatures. These are kind creatures . . . *Cymbeline* iv 2 32
Kind duke. O loving uncle, kind Duke of Gloucester! . 1 *Hen. VI.* iii 1 142
Kind embrace. And, lords, accept this hearty kind embrace . iii 3 82
Kind embracements. Drew me from kind embracements of my spouse *Com. of Errors* i 1 44
Kind embracements, tempting kisses . . *T. of Shrew* Ind. 1 118
Kind enough. The patch is kind enough, but a huge feeder *Mer. of Venice* ii 5 46
Kind entreats. I am not made of stones, But penetrable to your kind entreats . . . . *Richard III.* iii 7 225
Kind event. And crown what I profess with kind event! . *Tempest* iii 1 69
Kind father. Your old kind father, whose frank heart gave all . *Lear* iii 4 20
Kind fellow. An honest, willing, kind fellow, as ever servant shall come in house withal . . . . *Mer. Wives* i 4 10
But thou, like a kind fellow, gavest thyself away gratis . 2 *Hen. IV.* iv 3 75
Kind friends. To beg of you, kind friends, this coat of worth *Pericles* ii 1 142
Kind gentleman. A good old commander and a most kind gentleman *Hen. V.* iv 1 98
Kind gentlemen, your pains Are register'd where every day I turn The leaf to read them . . . . *Macbeth* i 3 150
Kind gentlemen, let's go see poor Cassio dress'd . *Othello* v 1 124
Kind gods. By the kind gods, 'tis most ignobly done . *Lear* iii 7 35
Then Edgar was abused. Kind gods, forgive me that, and prosper him! iii 7 92
O you kind gods, Cure this great breach in his abused nature! . iv 7 14
Kind good night. A kind good night to all! . *Macbeth* iii 4 121
Kind Hastings. Where is kind Hastings, Rivers, Vaughan? *Richard III.* iv 4 147
Kind heart. A kind heart he hath: a woman would run through fire and water for such a kind heart . . . . *Mer. Wives* iii 4 106
My father, in kind heart and pity moved, Swore him assistance 1 *Hen. IV.* iv 3 64
Kind host. London hath received, Like a kind host, the Dauphin and his powers . . . . *K. John* v 1 32
Kind hostess. Not your gaoler, then, But your kind hostess . *W. Tale* i 2 60
He greets your wife withal, By the name of most kind hostess *Macbeth* ii 1 16
Kind Jack Falstaff, true Jack Falstaff . . . 1 *Hen. IV.* ii 4 522
Kind Julia. Here is writ 'kind Julia.' Unkind Julia! . *T. G. of Ver.* i 2 109
Kind keepers. Give us kind keepers, heavens! . . . *Tempest* iii 3 20
Kind keepers of my weak decaying age . . . 1 *Hen. VI.* ii 5 1
Kind king. The hard rein which both of them have borne Against the old kind king . . . . *Lear* iii 1 28
Kind kinsman, warriors all, adieu! . . . . *Hen. V.* iv 3 10
Kind kiss. I can express no kinder sign of love Than this kind kiss 2 *Hen. VI.* i 1 19
Kind Lord of Masham, And you, my gentle knight . . *Hen. V.* ii 2 13
Good luck go with thee!—Farewell, kind lord; fight valiantly to-day . iv 3 12
Once more, good night, kind lords and gentlemen *Richard III.* v 3 107
Alas, kind lord! He's flung in rage from this ingrateful seat *T. of Athens* iv 2 44
Kind love. Assist me; And even in kind love I do conjure thee *T. G. of V.* ii 7 2
With all kind love, good thoughts, and reverence . *J. Cæsar* iii 1 176
Kind maid, It was the swift celerity of his death . *Meas. for Meas.* v 1 398
Fare thee well, kind maid; Thy pains not used must by thyself be paid *All's Well* ii 1 148
Kind master. Here lie I down, and measure out my grave. Farewell, kind master . . . . *As Y. Like It* ii 6 3
Kind messenger, Say to great Cæsar this . *Ant. and Cleo.* iii 13 73
Kind my lord. Accept it and wear it, Kind my lord . *T. of Athens* i 2 177
Kind nature. Because kind nature doth require it so . *T. Andron.* v 3 168
Kind neighbours. Live, and thrive!—Farewell, kind neighbours *Coriol.* iv 6 24
Kind nursery. And thought to set my rest On her kind nursery . *Lear* i 1 126
Kind offer. Will, for my kind offer, when I make curtsy, bid me farewell *As Y. Like It* Epil. 23
My nephew must not know, Sir Richard, The liberal and kind offer of the king.—'Twere best he did . . . . 1 *Hen. IV.* v 2 2
Kind one. She is busy and she cannot come! Is that an answer?—Ay, and a kind one too . . . . *T. of Shrew* v 2 83
Kind overflow. Did he break out into tears?—In great measure.—A kind overflow of kindness . . . . *Much Ado* i 1 26
Kind pains. Lend him your kind pains To find out this abuse *M. for M.* v 1 246
Kind prince. But the kind prince, Taking thy part, hath rush'd aside the law . . . . *Rom. and Jul.* iii 3 25
Kind regreet. And shall these hands . . . Unyoke this seizure and this kind regreet? . . . . *K. John* iii 1 241
Kind Rome, that hast thus lovingly reserved The cordial of mine age to glad my heart! . . . . *T. Andron.* i 1 165
Kind service. I prithee, Lucio, do me this kind service . *Meas. for Meas.* i 2 181
Kind sister, thanks: we'll enter all together . . *Richard III.* iv 1 11
O rose of May! Dear maid, kind sister, sweet Ophelia! . *Hamlet* iv 5 158
Kind soul. I have a kind soul that would give you thanks And knows not how to do it but with tears . . . . . . *K. John* v 7 108
Kind souls, what, weep you when you but behold Our Cæsar's vesture wounded? Look you here, Here is himself . . . *J. Cæsar* iii 2 199
Kind submission. I commend this kind submission . 2 *Hen. VI.* v 1 54
Kind Tyrrel, am I happy in thy news? . . *Richard III.* iv 3 24
Kind umpire. Just death, kind umpire of men's miseries . 1 *Hen. VI.* ii 5 29
Kind uncle York, the latest news we hear . . . *Richard II.* v 6 1
A beggar, brother?—Of my kind uncle, that I know will give *Richard III.* iii 1 113
Kind virgin. Thy name, my most kind virgin? . . . *Pericles* v 1 141
Kind woman. If there be a kind woman in Windsor, she is one *Mer. Wives* ii 2 126
Kinder. The kinder we, to give them thanks for nothing *M. N. Dream* v 1 89
A kinder gentleman treads not the earth . . . *Mer. of Venice* ii 8 35
I can express no kinder sign of love Than this kind kiss . 2 *Hen. VI.* i 1 18

Kinder. If he remember A kinder value of the people . . *Coriolanus* ii 2 63
He shall find The unkindest beast more kinder than mankind *T. of Athens* iv 1 36
Gloucester's bastard son Was kinder to his father than my daughters *Lear* iv 6 117
Kindest. The kindest man, The best condition'd and unwearied spirit In doing courtesies . . . . *Mer. of Venice* iii 2 294
O, the kindest Kate! She hung about my neck . . *T. of Shrew* ii 1 309
We do request your kindest ears . . . . . . *Coriolanus* ii 2 56
If you would grant the time.—At your kind'st leisure . . *Macbeth* ii 1 24
Kindle. Thou wouldst as soon go kindle fire with snow . *T. G. of Ver.* ii 7 19
Nothing remains but that I kindle the boy thither . . *As Y. Like It* i 1 179
Ever in fear to kindle your dislike . . . . . *Hen. VIII.* ii 4 25
This, as you say, suggested At some time when his soaring insolence Shall touch the people . . . will be his fire To kindle their dry stubble . . . . *Coriolanus* ii 1 274
Fie, fie, fie! This is the way to kindle, not to quench . . . iii 1 197
Bear fire enough To kindle cowards . . . . . . *J. Cæsar* ii 1 121
Gods, gods! 'tis strange that from their cold'st neglect My love should kindle to inflamed respect . . . . *Lear* i 1 258
My mate in empire, . . . The arm of mine own body, and the heart Where mine his thoughts did kindle . . . . *Ant. and Cleo.* v 1 46
Death may usurp on nature many hours, And yet the fire of life kindle again The o'erpress'd spirits . . . . . . *Pericles* iii 2 83
Kindled. Lust is but a bloody fire, Kindled with unchaste desire *M. Wives* v 5 100
As the cony that you see dwell where she is kindled . *As Y. Like It* iii 2 358
Have I not ever said How that ambitious Constance would not cease Till she had kindled France and all the world? . . . . *K. John* i 1 33
Back to the stained field, You equal potents, fiery kindled spirits! . ii 1 358
Your breath first kindled the dead coal of wars . . . . v 2 83
Shallow jesters and rash bavin wits, Soon kindled and soon burnt 1 *Hen. IV.* iii 2 62
Kindless. Remorseless, treacherous, lecherous, kindless villain! *Hamlet* ii 2 609
Kindlier. Shall not myself, One of their kind, that relish all as sharply, Passion as they, be kindlier moved than thou art? . . *Tempest* v 1 24
Kindling. For selfsame wind that I should speak withal Is kindling coals that fires all my breast . . . . . . 3 *Hen. VI.* ii 1 83
For kindling such a combustion in the state . . . *Hen. VIII.* v 4 51
Kindly. And spends what he borrows kindly in your company *T. G. of V.* ii 4 39
I'll use thee kindly for thy mistress' sake, That used me so . . iv 4 207
Gentle and fair, your brother kindly greets you . *Meas. for Meas.* i 4 24
By that fatherly and kindly power That you have in her . *Much Ado* iv 1 75
Which thou shalt find I will most kindly requite . . *As Y. Like It* i 1 144
Therefore my age is as a lusty winter, Frosty, but kindly . . ii 3 53
Betwixt us two Tears our recountments had most kindly bathed . iv 3 141
I'll not budge an inch, boy: let him come, and kindly . *T. of Shrew* Ind. 1 15
This do and do it kindly, gentle sirs . . . . . Ind. 1 66
Myself, that have been more kindly beholding to you than any . ii 1 78
My mother greets me kindly: is she well?—She is not well . *All's Well* ii 4 1
I will bestow some precepts of this virgin Worthy the note.—We'll take your offer kindly . . . . iii 5 104
Thou comest to the lady Olivia, and in my sight she uses thee kindly *T. Night* iii 4 171
Washing with kindly tears his gentle cheeks . . . 2 *Hen. IV.* iv 5 84
Your humble patience pray, Gently to hear, kindly to judge *Hen. V.* Prol. 34
O, tell me when my lips do touch his cheeks, That I may kindly give one fainting kiss . . . . 1 *Hen. VI.* ii 5 40
The bishop hath a kindly gird. For shame, my lord of Winchester, relent! iii 1 131
'Twas men I lack'd and you will give them me: I take it kindly 2 *Hen. VI.* iii 1 346
He wept, And hugg'd me in his arm, and kindly kiss'd my cheek *Rich. III.* ii 2 24
'Tis call'd ungrateful, With dull unwillingness to repay a debt Which with a bounteous hand was kindly lent . . . . . ii 2 93
To the Tower, Where, he shall see, the boar will use us kindly . iii 2 33
Why, this is kindly done . . . . . *Troi. and Cres.* iii 1 105
We must use expostulation kindly, For it is parting from us . . iv 4 62
I sometime lay here in Corioli At a poor man's house; he used me kindly *Coriolanus* i 9 83
The price is to ask it kindly.—Kindly! Sir, I pray, let me ha't . ii 3 81
Attend him carefully, And feed his humour kindly . *T. Andron.* iv 3 29
Thou hast most kindly hit it . . . . *Rom. and Jul.* ii 4 59
'Tis lack of kindly warmth they are not kind . . *T. of Athens* ii 2 226
You are kindly met, sir. Fare thee well . . . . . iii 2 30
That this great king may kindly say, Our duties did his welcome pay *Macbeth* iv 1 131
Thy other daughter will use thee kindly . . . . . . *Lear* i 5 15
Melt Egypt into Nile! and kindly creatures Turn all to serpents! *Ant. and Cleo.* ii 5 78
She soon shall know of us, by some of ours, How honourable and how kindly we Determine for her . . . . v 1 58
Thanks, good sir: You're kindly welcome . . . . *Cymbeline* i 6 14
Without any more virginal fencing, will you use him kindly? *Pericles* iv 6 63
Kindness. Lying slave, Whom stripes may move, not kindness! *Tempest* i 2 345
Is she kind as she is fair? For beauty lives with kindness *T. G. of Ver.* iv 2 45
Truly, sir, for your kindness I owe you a good turn . *Meas. for Meas.* iv 2 62
If you did wed my sister for her wealth, Then for her wealth's sake use her with more kindness . . . *Com. of Errors* iii 2 6
Some invite me; Some other give me thanks for kindnesses . . iv 3 5
A kind overflow of kindness . . . . . . *Much Ado* i 1 26
My kindness shall incite thee To bind our loves up in a holy band . iii 1 113
This were kindness.—This kindness will I show . *Mer. of Venice* i 3 144
I'll seal to such a bond And say there is much kindness in the Jew . i 3 154
But kindness, nobler ever than revenge . . . *As Y. Like It* iv 3 129
To express the like kindness, myself, that have been more kindly beholding to you than any, freely give unto you this young scholar *T. of S.* ii 1 77
This is a way to kill a wife with kindness . . . . . . iv 1 211
Kindness in women, not their beauteous looks, Shall win my love . iv 2 41
This kindness merits thanks. What, not a word? . . . . iv 3 41
Bid my father welcome, While I with selfsame kindness welcome thine v 2 5
Nothing but sit and sit, and eat and eat!—Padua affords this kindness v 2 13
Fare ye well at once: my bosom is full of kindness . . *T. Night* ii 1 41
For the fair kindness you have show'd me here . . . . iii 4 376
Do not tempt my misery, Lest that it make me so unsound a man As to upbraid you with those kindnesses That I have done for you . . iii 4 385
He did me kindness, sir, drew on my side . . . . . . v 1 69
O'er and o'er divides him 'Twixt his unkindness and his kindness *W. Tale* iv 4 563
You might have spoken a thousand things that would Have done the time more benefit and graced Your kindness better . . . . v 1 23
He is as full of valour as of kindness; Princely in both . *Hen. V.* iv 3 15
Yet hath a woman's kindness over-ruled . . . 1 *Hen. VI.* ii 2 50
And I may live to do you kindness if You do it her . . 2 *Hen. VI.* ii 4 83
I come, in kindness and unfeigned love . . . 3 *Hen. VI.* iii 3 51
Yet shall you have all kindness at my hand That your estate requires . iii 3 149
Kindness. I'll well requite thy kindness, For that it made my imprisonment a pleasure . . . . 3 *Hen. VI.* iv 6 10
If fortune serve me, I'll requite this kindness . . . . . iv 7 78
Thou art all ice, thy kindness freezeth . . . . *Richard III.* iv 2
Be brief, lest that the process of thy kindness Last longer telling than thy kindness' date . . . . iv 4 253
I cannot make you what amends I would, Therefore accept such kindness as I can . . . . iv 4 310
Yet is the kindness but particular . . . . *Troi. and Cres.* iv 5 20
You know the very road into his kindness, And cannot lose your way *Coriolanus* v 1 59
Commit him to the grave; Do him that kindness . . *T. Andron.* v 3 171
He outgoes The very heart of kindness . . . . *T. of Athens* i 1 286
I have received some small kindnesses from him, as money, plate, jewels iii 2 22
Is not thy kindness subtle, covetous, If not a usuring kindness? . . iv 3 515
To ease them of their griefs, . . . I will some kindness do them . . v 1 205
Keep this man safe; Give him all kindness . . . *J. Cæsar* v 4 28
I fear thy nature; It is too full o' the milk of human kindness *Macbeth* i 5 18
There's a great abatement of kindness appears . . . . *Lear* i 4 65
'Twas her brother that, in pure kindness to his horse, buttered his hay ii 4 127
The gods reward your kindness! . . . . iii 6 6
I protest, in the sincerity of love and honest kindness . . *Othello* ii 3 334
You shall find A conqueror that will pray in aid for kindness *Ant. and Cleo.* v 2 27
You o'er-rate my poor kindness . . . . . . *Cymbeline* i 4 41
He is one of the noblest note, to whose kindnesses I am most infinitely tied i 6 23
I shall unfold equal discourtesy To your best kindness . . . ii 3 102
I sought a husband, in which labour I found that kindness in a father *Per.* i 1 67
If thou hadst drunk to him, 't had been a kindness Becoming well thy fact iv 3 11
It greets me as an enterprise of kindness Perform'd to your sole daughter iv 3 38
Since your kindness We have stretch'd thus far . . . . . v 1 54
This, my last boon, give me, For such kindness must relieve me . v 2 269
Your present kindness Makes my past miseries sports . . . v 3 40
Kindred. The vice is of a great kindred; it is well allied *Meas. for Meas.* iii 2 109
Truly, I hold it a sin to match in my kindred . . . *Much Ado* ii 1 68
I promise you your kindred hath made my eyes water ere now *M. N. D.* iii 1 199
May complain of good breeding or comes of a very dull kindred *As Y. L. It* iii 2 32
Hence comes it that your kindred shuns your house *T. of Shrew* Ind. 2 30
His horse hipped with an old mothy saddle and stirrups of no kindred iii 2 50
The kings and the princes, our kindred, are going to see the queen's picture.—Come, follow us . . . . *W. Tale* v 2 186
Who hath read or heard Of any kindred action like to this? *K. John* iii 4 14
I throw my gage, Disclaiming here the kindred of the king *Richard II.* i 1 70
And make us wade even in our kindred's blood . . . . i 3 138
His hands were guilty of no kindred blood, But bloody with the enemies of his kin . . . . ii 1 182
Whom conscience and my kindred bids to right . . . . ii 2 115
Be no more opposed Against acquaintance, kindred and allies 1 *Hen. IV.* i 1 16
The world increases, and kindreds are mightily strengthened 2 *Hen. IV.* ii 2 30
The kindred of him hath been flesh'd upon us . . . . *Hen. V.* ii 4 50
There's no man is secure But the queen's kindred . . *Richard III.* i 1 72
And that the queen's kindred are made gentlefolks . . . . i 1 95
Hatred, Which in your outward actions shows itself Against my kindred i 3 67
The guilty kindred of the queen Look'd pale when they did hear . ii 1 135
Good aunt, you wept not for our father's death; How can we aid you with our kindred tears? . . . . ii 2 63
To part the queen's proud kindred from the king . . . . ii 2 150
This same very day your enemies, The kindred of the queen, must die . iii 2 50
By their uncle cozen'd Of comfort, kingdom, kindred, freedom, life . iv 4 223
No kindred weep for me; Almost no grave allow'd me . *Hen. VIII.* iii 1 150
Our kindred, though they be long ere they are wooed, they are constant being won: they are burs, I can tell you . . *Troi. and Cres.* iii 2 118
That . . . vault Where all the kindred of the Capulets lie *Rom. and Jul.* iv 1 112
I saw her laid low in her kindred's vault . . . . . v 1 20
At the prefixed hour of her waking, Came I to take her from her kindred's vault . . . . v 3 254
Wert thou a leopard, thou wert german to the lion and the spots of thy kindred were jurors on thy life . . . . . *T. of Athens* iv 3 344
What said she to you? Get more tapers; Raise all my kindred . *Othello* i 1 168
Great Jupiter, upon his eagle back'd, Appear'd to me, with other spritely shows Of mine own kindred . . . . *Cymbeline* v 5 429
Kine. If to be fat be to be hated, then Pharaoh's lean kine are to be loved. No, my good lord . . . . 1 *Hen. IV.* ii 4 520
King. What cares these roarers for the name of king? . . *Tempest* i 1 18
The king and prince at prayers! let's assist them, For our case is as theirs i 1 57
Let's all sink with the king.—Let's take leave of him . . . i 1 67
I boarded the king's ship; now on the beak, Now in the waist . . i 2 196
Of the king's ship The mariners say how thou hast disposed . . i 2 224
Safely in harbour Is the king's ship; in the deep nook . . . i 2 227
Supposing that they saw the king's ship wreck'd And his great person perish . . . . i 2 236
I am all the subjects that you have, Which first was mine own king . i 2 342
Sitting on a bank, Weeping again the king my father's wreck . . i 2 390
Who with mine eyes, never since at ebb, beheld The king my father wreck'd . . . . i 2 436
In Afric, at the marriage of the king's fair daughter . . . . ii 1 70
Had I plantation of this isle, my lord,— . . . And were the king on't, what would I do? . . . . ii 1 145
No sovereignty;—Yet he would be king on't . . . . . ii 1 156
Almost persuaded,—For he's a spirit of persuasion, only Professes to persuade,—the king his son's alive . . . . ii 1 236
Draw thy sword: one stroke Shall free thee from the tribute which thou payest; And I the king shall love thee . . . . . . ii 1 294
Now, good angels Preserve the king . . . . ii 1 307
So, king, go safely on to seek thy son . . . . . . ii 1 327
The king and all our company else being drowned, we will inherit here ii 2 178
I am in my condition A prince, Miranda; I do think, a king . . iii 1 60
Prithee, my king, be quiet. See'st thou here, This is the mouth o' the cell iv 1 215
Wit shall not go unrewarded while I am king of this country . . iv 1 243
Say, my spirit, How fares the king and's followers? . . . . v 1 7
The king, His brother, and yours, abide all three distracted . . v 1 11
Would here have kill'd your king; I do forgive thee . . . . v 1 78
To the king's ship, invisible as thou art: There shalt thou find the mariners . . . . v 1 97
Behold, sir king, The wronged Duke of Milan, Prospero . . . . v 1 106
The best news is, that we have safely found Our king and company . v 1 222
You'ld be king o' the isle, sirrah?—I should have been a sore one then v 1 287
My herald thoughts in thy pure bosom rest them; While I, their king, that hither them importune, Do curse the grace that with such grace hath bless'd them . . . . *T. G. of Ver.* iii 1 145
This fellow were a king for our wild faction! . . . . . . iv 1 37

King. We'll do thee homage and be ruled by thee, Love thee as our commander and our king *T. G. of Ver.* iv 1 67
Now, Master Shallow, you'll complain of me to the king? *Mer. Wives* i 1 113
Why then all the dukes fall upon the king *Meas. for Meas.* i 2 3
Even so The general, subject to a well-wish'd king, Quit their own part ii 4 27
What king so strong Can tie the gall up in the slanderous tongue? iii 2 198
For mine own part, if I were as tedious as a king, I could find it in my heart to bestow it all of your worship *Much Ado* iii 5 23
Is there not a ballad, boy, of the King and the Beggar? *L. L. Lost* i 2 114
Consider who the king your father sends, To whom he sends ii 1 2
If then the king your father will restore But that one half ii 1 138
You do the king my father too much wrong ii 1 154
Was that the king, that spurred his horse so hard Against the steep uprising of the hill? iv 1 1
He came, one; saw, two; overcame, three. Who came? the king iv 1 72
The conclusion is victory: on whose side? the king's iv 1 76
The catastrophe is a nuptial: on whose side? the king's: no, on both iv 1 78
I am the king; for so stands the comparison: thou the beggar iv 1 80
This Biron is one of the votaries with the king iv 2 141
Deliver this paper into the royal hand of the king: it may concern much iv 2 146
The king he is hunting the deer; I am coursing myself iv 3 1
You found his mote; the king your mote did see iv 3 161
With what strict patience have I sat, To see a king transformed to a gnat! iv 3 166
God bless the king!—What present hast thou there? iv 3 189
I did converse this quondam day with a companion of the king's v 1 8
It is the king's most sweet pleasure and affection to congratulate the princess v 1 92
Sir, the king is a noble gentleman, and my familiar v 1 100
The king would have me present the princess, sweet chuck, with some delightful ostentation, or show, or pageant v 1 116
Look you what I have from the loving king v 2 4
Toward that shade I might behold addrest The king and his companions v 2 93
'For,' quoth the king, 'an angel shalt thou see' v 2 103
This favour thou shalt wear, And then the king will court thee for his dear v 2 131
All in lamentable cases! The king was weeping-ripe for a good word v 2 274
But will you hear? the king is my love sworn v 2 282
'Tis some policy To have one show worse than the king's and his company v 2 514
The king your father— Dead, for my life!—Even so; my tale is told v 2 727
And by these badges understand the king v 2 764
Come when the king doth to my lady come v 2 839
The king doth keep his revels here to-night *M. N. Dream* ii 1 18
She as her attendant hath A lovely boy, stolen from an Indian king ii 1 22
Fairy king, attend, and mark: I do hear the morning lark iv 1 98
Her gentle spirit Commits itself to yours to be directed, As from her lord, her governor, her king *Mer. of Venice* iii 2 167
The attribute to awe and majesty, Wherein doth sit the dread and fear of kings iv 1 192
It is enthroned in the hearts of kings, It is an attribute to God himself iv 1 194
A substitute shines brightly as a king Until a king be by v 1 94
That would I, were I of all kingdoms king *As Y. Like It* v 4 10
And dart not scornful glances from those eyes, To wound thy lord, thy king, thy governor *T. of Shrew* v 2 138
You shall find of the king a husband, madam; you, sir, a father *All's W.* i 1 7
Would, for the king's sake, he were living! I think it would be the death of the king's disease i 1 24
The king very lately spoke of him admiringly and mourningly i 1 33
What is it, my good lord, the king languishes of?—A fistula, my lord i 1 37
The king's disease—my project may deceive me, But my intents are fix'd i 1 243
There is a remedy, approved, set down, To cure the desperate languishings whereof The king is render'd lost i 3 236
The medicine and the king Had from the conversation of my thoughts Haply been absent i 3 239
Give us a further use to be made than alone the recovery of the king ii 3 42
Heaven hath through me restored the king to health ii 3 70
She, which late Was in my nobler thoughts most base, is now The praised of the king ii 3 179
Good fortune and the favour of the king Smile upon this contract ii 3 184
Write to the king That which I durst not speak ii 3 305
The king has done you wrong: but, hush, 'tis so ii 3 317
What's his will else?—That you will take your instant leave o' the king ii 4 49
Is she gone to the king?—She is ii 5 22
I have, sir, as I was commanded from you, Spoke with the king ii 5 60
She hath recovered the king, and undone me iii 2 22
This is not well, rash and unbridled boy, To fly the favours of so good a king iii 2 31
The king had married him Against his liking: think you it is so? iii 5 56
Especially he hath incurred the everlasting displeasure of the king iv 3 11
The duke hath offered him letters of commendations to the king iv 3 92
They cannot be too sweet for the king's tartness iv 3 96
Heaven aiding, And by the leave of my good lord the king iv 4 13
More advanced by the king than by that red-tailed humble-bee iv 5 6
I moved the king my master to speak in the behalf of my daughter iv 5 75
What's your will?—That it will please you To give this poor petition to the king v 1 19
The king's not here.—Not here, sir!—Not, indeed: He hence removed last night v 1 22
Since you are like to see the king before me, Commend the paper to his gracious hand v 1 30
The king's coming; I know by his trumpets. Sirrah, inquire further after me v 2 54
I follow him to his country for justice: grant it me, O king! v 3 145
Great king, I am no strumpet, by my life v 3 293
The king's a beggar, now the play is done Epil. 1
And fill'd Her sweet perfections with one self king *T. Night* i 1 39
Thou mayst say, the king lies by a beggar, if a beggar dwell near him iii 1 8
If the king had no son, they would desire to live on crutches till he had one *W. Tale* i 1 49
If I could find example Of thousands that had struck anointed kings And flourish'd after, I'ld not do't i 2 358
The king hath on him such a countenance As he had lost some province i 2 368
I am appointed him to murder you.—By whom, Camillo?—By the king i 2 413
Nor shall you be safer Than one condemn'd by the king's own mouth i 2 445
Measure me; and so The king's will be perform'd! ii 1 115
These dangerous unsafe lunes i' the king, beshrew them! ii 2 30
If she dares trust me with her little babe, I'll show't the king ii 2 38
Freed and enfranchised, not a party to The anger of the king ii 2 62
The harlot king Is quite beyond mine arm, out of the blank And level of my brain ii 3 4
The daughter of a king, our wife, and one Of us too much beloved iii 2 3

King. Conspiring with Camillo to take away the life of our sovereign lord the king *W. Tale* iii 2 17
The king shall live without an heir, if that which is lost be not found iii 2 136
My lord the king, the king!—What is the business?—O sir, I shall be hated to report it! iii 2 143
Thou wouldst have poison'd good Camillo's honour, To have him kill a king iii 2 190
I mentioned a son o' the king's, which Florizel I now name to you iv 1 22
The penitent king, my master, hath sent for me iv 2 7
That penitent, as thou callest him, and reconciled king, my brother iv 2 26
Kings are no less unhappy, their issue not being gracious iv 2 29
For a quart of ale is a dish for a king iv 3 8
O, but, sir, Your resolution cannot hold, when 'tis Opposed, as it must be, by the power of the king iv 4 37
One three of them, by their own report, sir, hath danc'd before the king iv 4 346
That unhappy king, my master, whom I so much thirst to see iv 4 523
Think I love the king And through him what is nearest to him iv 4 532
Sent by the king your father To greet him and to give him comforts iv 4 567
What I do next, shall be to tell the king iv 4 676
If I thought it were a piece of honesty to acquaint the king withal, I would not do't iv 4 695
There is no other way but to tell the king she's a changeling iv 4 703
Your flesh and blood has not offended the king iv 4 711
I will tell the king all, every word, yea, and his son's pranks too iv 4 717
To go about to make me the king's brother-in-law iv 4 720
My business, sir, is to the king.—What advocate hast thou to him? iv 4 765
Such secrets in this fardel and box, which none must know but the king iv 4 784
The king is not at the palace; he is gone aboard a new ship iv 4 789
Thou must know the king is full of grief iv 4 792
Tell me, for you seem to be honest plain men, what you have to the king iv 4 824
If it be in man besides the king to effect your suits, here is man shall do it iv 4 828
We must to the king and show our strange sights iv 4 849
The complaint they have to the king concerns him nothing iv 4 870
Give you all greetings that a king, at friend, Can send his brother v 1 140
Is this the daughter of a king?—She is, When once she is my wife v 1 208
The changes I perceived in the king and Camillo were very notes of admiration v 2 11
Has the king found his heir?—Most true, if ever truth were pregnant v 2 32
Our king, being ready to leap out of himself for joy of his found daughter v 2 53
He thanks the old shepherd, which stands by like a weather-bitten conduit of many kings' reigns v 2 61
The dignity of this act was worth the audience of kings and princes v 2 87
The queen's death, with the manner how she came to't bravely confessed and lamented by the king v 2 94
And then the two kings called my father brother v 2 153
The kings and the princes, our kindred, are going to see the queen's picture v 2 186
Whose worth and honesty Is richly noted and here justified By us, a pair of kings v 3 146
Son unto the king, who, heavens directing, Is troth-plight to your daughter v 3 150
Then take my king's defiance from my mouth *K. John* i 1 21
Most certain of one mother, mighty king; That is well known i 1 59
The advantage of his absence took the king And in the mean time sojourn'd at my father's i 1 102
Even till that utmost corner of the west Salute thee for her king ii 1 30
With them a bastard of the king's deceased ii 1 65
But thou from loving England art so far, That thou hast under-wrought his lawful king ii 1 95
How comes it then that thou art call'd a king? ii 1 107
Out, insolent! thy bastard shall be king, That thou mayst be a queen! ii 1 122
But on the sight of us your lawful king ii 1 222
Which trust accordingly, kind citizens, And let us in, your king ii 1 232
Son to the elder brother of this man, And king o'er him ii 1 240
Acknowledge then the king, and let me in ii 1 269
He that proves the king, To him will we prove loyal ii 1 270
Doth not the crown of England prove the king? ii 1 273
In dreadful trial of our kingdom's king ii 1 286
Proclaim Arthur of Bretagne England's king and yours ii 1 311
King John, your king and England's, doth approach ii 1 313
With slaughter coupled to the name of kings.—Ha, majesty! how high thy glory towers, When the rich blood of kings is set on fire! ii 1 349
He feasts, mousing the flesh of men, In undetermined differences of kings ii 1 355
Why stand these royal fronts amazed thus? Cry, 'havoc!' kings ii 1 357
Who's your king?—The king of England, when we know the king ii 1 362
King'd of our fears, until our fears, resolved, Be by some certain king purged and deposed ii 1 372
These scroyles of Angiers flout you, kings, And stand securely ii 1 373
Shall we knit our powers And lay this Angiers even with the ground; Then after fight who shall be king of it? ii 1 400
An if thou hast the mettle of a king ii 1 401
Hear us, great kings: vouchsafe awhile to stay ii 1 416
Two such controlling bounds shall you be, kings ii 1 444
Mad world! mad kings! mad composition! ii 1 561
He that wins of all, Of kings, of beggars, old men, young men, maids ii 1 570
Since kings break faith upon commodity, Gain, be my lord ii 1 597
I do not believe thee, man; I have a king's oath to the contrary iii 1 10
I may not go without you to the kings.—Thou mayst, thou shalt iii 1 66
To me and to the state of my great grief Let kings assemble iii 1 71
Here I and sorrows sit; Here is my throne, bid kings come bow to it iii 1 74
But, ere sunset, Set armed discord 'twixt these perjured kings! iii 1 111
What earthy name to interrogatories Can task the free breath of a sacred king? iii 1 148
All the kings of Christendom Are led so grossly by this meddling priest iii 1 162
The king is moved, and answers not to this iii 1 217
Where revenge did paint The fearful difference of incensed kings iii 1 238
Go with me to the king: 'tis wonderful What may be wrought iii 4 178
For England go: I will whet on the king iii 4 181
Let us go: If you say ay, the king will not say no iii 4 183
The colour of the king doth come and go Between his purpose and his conscience iv 2 76
It is the curse of kings to be attended By slaves that take their humours for a warrant iv 2 208
To be endeared to a king, Made it no conscience to destroy a prince iv 2 228
The king by me requests your presence straight.—The king hath dispossess'd himself of us iv 3 22
It is the shameful work of Hubert's hand; The practice and the purpose of the king iv 3 63
Arthur doth live; the king hath sent for you.—O, he is bold iv 3 75
There tell the king he may inquire us out.—Here's a good world! iv 3 115

King. I'll to the king : A thousand businesses are brief in hand *K. John* iv 3 157
From the king I come, to learn how you have dealt for him . v 2 120
Now hear our English king ; For thus his royalty doth speak in me . v 2 128
This unhair'd sauciness and boyish troops The king doth smile at . v 2 134
I did not think the king so stored with friends . v 4 1
Commend me to one Hubert with your king v 4 40
The king, I fear, is poison'd by a monk v 6 23
The king Yet speaks and peradventure may recover v 6 30
The king hath pardon'd them, And they are all about his majesty . v 6 35
Conduct me to the king ; I doubt he will be dead or ere I come v 6 43
You breathe these dead news in as dead an ear. My liege ! my lord ! but now a king, now thus v 7 66
What hope, what stay, When this was now a king, and now is clay? v 7 69
Disclaiming here the kindred of the king *Richard II.* i 1 70
In God's name and the king's, say who thou art i 3 11
To defend my loyalty and truth To God, my king and my succeeding issue i 3 20
To prove him, in defending of myself, A traitor to my God, my king, and me i 3 24
Stay, the king hath thrown his warder down i 3 118
Had the king permitted us, One of our souls had wander'd in the air i 3 194
And all too soon, I fear, the king shall rue i 3 205
Four wanton springs End in a word : such is the breath of kings . i 3 215
Thou hast many years to live.—But not a minute, king, that thou canst give i 3 226
Think not the king did banish thee, But thou the king i 3 280
Say I sent thee forth to purchase honour And not the king exiled thee . i 3 283
Will the king come, that I may breathe my last In wholesome counsel to his unstaid youth? ii 1 1
This royal throne of kings, this scepter'd isle ii 1 40
This England, This nurse, this teeming womb of royal kings ii 1 51
The king is come : deal mildly with his youth ii 1 69
I mock my name, great king, to flatter thee ii 1 87
Landlord of England art thou now, not king ii 1 113
For how art thou a king But by fair sequence and succession? ii 1 198
The king is not himself, but basely led By flatterers ii 1 241
That will the king severely prosecute 'Gainst us, our lives ii 1 244
The king's grown bankrupt, like a broken man ii 1 257
Most degenerate king ! But, lords, we hear this fearful tempest sing ii 1 262
They stay The first departing of the king for Ireland ii 1 290
You promised, when you parted with the king, To lay aside life-harming heaviness And entertain a cheerful disposition.—To please the king I did ; to please myself I cannot do it ii 2 2
I hope the king is not yet shipp'd for Ireland.—Why hopest thou so? ii 2 42
I would to God, So my untruth had not provoked him to it, The king had cut off my head with my brother's ii 2 102
The other again Is my kinsman, whom the king hath wrong'd ii 2 114
Our nearness to the king in love Is near the hate of those love not the king ii 2 127
Their love Lies in their purses, and whoso empties them By so much fills their hearts with deadly hate.—Wherein the king stands generally condemn'd ii 2 132
If judgement lie in them, then so do we, Because we ever have been near the king ii 2 134
Broken his staff of office and dispersed The household of the king. ii 3 28
Comest thou because the anointed king is hence? Why, foolish boy, the king is left behind, And in my loyal bosom lies his power ii 3 96
Wherefore was I born? If that my cousin king be King of England ii 3 123
And make you stoop Unto the sovereign mercy of the king ii 3 157
We have stay'd ten days, . . . And yet we hear no tidings from the king ii 4 3
Thou trusty Welshman : The king reposeth all his confidence in thee.—'Tis thought the king is dead ; we will not stay ii 4 6
These signs forerun the death or fall of kings ii 4 15
Our countrymen are gone and fled, As well assured Richard their king is dead ii 4 17
You have misled a prince, a royal king, A happy gentleman iii 1 8
Near to the king in blood, and near in love iii 1 17
And these stones Prove armed soldiers, ere her native king Shall falter under foul rebellion's arms iii 2 25
That Power that made you king Hath power to keep you king iii 2 27
Not all the water in the rough rude sea Can wash the balm off from an anointed king iii 2 55
I had forgot myself: am I not king? Awake, thou coward majesty ! iii 2 83
Look not to the ground, Ye favourites of a king : are we not high? iii 2 88
Let us sit upon the ground And tell sad stories of the death of kings iii 2 156
Within the hollow crown That rounds the mortal temples of a king Keeps Death his court and there the antic sits iii 2 161
[Death] Comes at the last and with a little pin Bores through his castle wall, and farewell king ! iii 2 170
Subjected thus, How can you say to me, I am a king? iii 2 177
A king, woe's slave, shall kingly woe obey iii 2 210
Gone to meet the king, who lately landed With some few private friends iii 3 3
Alack the heavy day When such a sacred king should hide his head iii 3 8
The castle royally is mann'd, my lord, Against thy entrance.—Royally ! Why, it contains no king?—Yes, my good lord iii 3 24
Yet looks he like a king : behold, his eye, As bright as is the eagle's iii 3 68
Thus long have we stood To watch the fearful bending of thy knee, Because we thought ourself thy lawful king iii 3 74
What must the king do now? must he submit? The king shall do it iii 3 143
In the base court? Base court, where kings grow base, To come at traitors' calls iii 3 180
And Bolingbroke Hath seized the wasteful king iii 4 55
What, think you then the king shall be deposed?—Depress'd he is already iii 4 67
Come, ladies, go, To meet at London London's king in woe iii 4 97
What subject can give sentence on his king? iv 1 121
A subject speaks, Stirr'd up by God, thus boldly for his king iv 1 133
Hereford here, whom you call king, Is a foul traitor to proud Hereford's king iv 1 134
Alack, why am I sent for to a king, Before I have shook off the regal thoughts Wherewith I reign'd? iv 1 162
God save the king ! Will no man say amen? iv 1 172
God save the king ! although I be not he ; And yet, amen, if heaven do think him me iv 1 174
Still my griefs are mine : You may my glories and my state depose, But not my griefs ; still am I king of those iv 1 193
One heinous article, Containing the deposing of a king iv 1 234
I have given here my soul's consent To undeck the pompous body of a king iv 1 250
Good king, great king, and yet not greatly good iv 1 263
Mark, silent king, the moral of this sport iv 1 290

King. And I thank thee, king, For thy great bounty *Richard II.* iv 1 299
I am greater than a king : For when I was a king, my flatterers Were then but subjects ; being now a subject, I have a king here to my flatterer iv 1 305
Conveyers are you all, That rise thus nimbly by a true king's fall . iv 1 318
This way the king will come ; this is the way To Julius Cæsar's ill-erected tower v 1 1
If this rebellious earth Have any resting for her true king's queen v 1 6
Some will mourn in ashes, some coal-black, For the deposing of a rightful king v 1 50
Thou, which know'st the way To plant unrightful kings, wilt know again, Being ne'er so little urged, another way To pluck him headlong v 1 63
Banish us both and send the king with me.—That were some love v 1 83
I am . . . pledge for his truth And lasting fealty to the new made king v 2 45
Bring me my boots : I will unto the king v 2 84
And interchangeably set down their hands, To kill the king at Oxford . v 2 99
Mount thee upon his horse ; Spur post, and get before him to the king v 2 112
Where is the king?—What means our cousin, that he stares and looks So wildly? v 3 23
Open the door, secure, fool-hardy king v 3 43
I tore it from the traitor's bosom, king v 3 55
A woman, and thy aunt, great king ; 'tis I. Speak with me, pity me v 3 76
Our scene is alter'd from a serious thing, And now changed to 'The Beggar and the King' v 3 80
O king, believe not this hard-hearted man ! v 3 87
Say 'pardon,' king ; let pity teach thee how v 3 116
No word like 'pardon' for kings' mouths so meet v 3 118
Didst thou not mark the king, what words he spake, 'Have I no friend will rid me of this living fear?' . . . Meaning the king at Pomfret. v 4 1
Come, let's go : I am the king's friend, and will rid his foe v 4 11
Sometimes am I king ; Then treasons make me wish myself a beggar, And so I am : then crushing penury Persuades me I was better when a king v 5 32
I was a poor groom of thy stable, king, When thou wert king v 5 72
Thy fierce hand Hath with the king's blood stain'd the king's own land v 5 111
This dead king to the living king I'll bear : Take hence the rest v 5 118
Great king, within this coffin I present Thy buried fear v 6 30
When thou art king, as, God save thy grace,—majesty I should say, for grace thou wilt have none,— What, none? *1 Hen. IV.* i 2 18
When thou art king, let not us that are squires of the night's body be called thieves of the day's beauty i 2 27
Sweet wag, shall there be gallows standing in England when thou art king? i 2 67
Do not thou, when thou art king, hang a thief i 2 70
I will lift the down-trod Mortimer As high in the air as this unthankful king i 3 136
Brother, the king hath made your nephew mad i 3 138
When the unhappy king,—Whose wrongs in us God pardon !—did set forth i 3 148
I cannot blame his cousin king, That wish'd him on the barren mountains starve i 3 158
The predicament Wherein you range under this subtle king i 3 169
Revenge the jeering and disdain'd contempt Of this proud king i 3 184
Bear ourselves as even as we can, The king will always think him in our debt i 3 286
There's money of the king's coming down the hill ; 'tis going to the king's exchequer ii 2 56
Will he to the king and lay open all our proceedings ii 3 33
Let him tell the king : we are prepared ii 3 37
Where hast thou been this month?—Dost thou speak like a king? ii 4 476
I did pluck allegiance from men's hearts, Loud shouts and salutations from their mouths, Even in the presence of the crowned king iii 2 54
The skipping king, he ambled up and down With shallow jesters iii 2 60
The king himself is to be feared as the lion iii 3 169
There is no quailing now, Because the king is certainly possess'd Of all iv 1 40
The king himself in person is set forth, Or hitherwards intended iv 1 91
What may the king's whole battle reach unto?—To thirty thousand iv 1 129
The king, I can tell you, looks for us all : we must away all night iv 2 62
The number of the king exceedeth ours iv 3 28
I come with gracious offers from the king, If you vouchsafe me hearing iv 3 30
The king hath sent to know The nature of your griefs iv 3 41
If that the king Have any way your good deserts forgot iv 3 45
The king is kind ; and well we know the king Knows at what time to promise iv 3 52
Cut me off the heads Of all the favourites that the absent king In deputation left behind him here iv 3 86
He deposed the king ; Soon after that, deprived him of his life iv 3 90
Who is, if every owner were well placed, Indeed his king iv 3 95
Shall I return this answer to the king?—Not so iv 3 106
Percy is too weak To wage an instant trial with the king iv 4 20
The king hath drawn The special head of all the land together iv 4 27
Ere the king Dismiss his power, he means to visit us iv 4 36
What with our help, what with the absent king, What with the injuries v 1 49
The contrarious winds that held the king So long in his unlucky Irish wars v 1 52
It cannot be, The king should keep his word in loving us v 2 5
Let not Harry know, In any case, the offer of the king v 2 25
The king will bid you battle presently.—Defy him v 2 31
There is no seeming mercy in the king.—Did you beg any? God forbid ! v 2 35
The Prince of Wales stepp'd forth before the king, And, nephew, challenged you v 2 46
An if we live, we live to tread on kings v 2 86
My lord, prepare ; the king comes on apace.—I thank him v 2 90
I do haunt thee in the battle thus Because some tell me that thou art a king v 3 5
And thou shalt find a king that will revenge v 3 12
All's done, all's won ; here breathless lies the king v 3 16
His name was Blunt ; Semblably furnish'd like the king himself v 3 21
A borrow'd title hast thou bought too dear : Why didst thou tell me that thou wert a king? v 3 24
The king hath many marching in his coats v 3 25
Another king ! they grow like Hydra's heads v 4 25
What art thou, That counterfeit'st the person of a king?—The king himself v 4 28
So many of his shadows thou hast met And not the very king v 4 31
I fear thou art another counterfeit ; And yet, in faith, thou bear'st thee like a king v 4 36
The king before the Douglas' rage Stoop'd his anointed head . *2 Hen. IV.* Ind. 31
The king is almost wounded to the death i 1 14
Whose well-labouring sword Had three times slain the appearance of the king i 1 128
The sum of all Is that the king hath won i 1 132

King. Is there not employment? doth not the king lack subjects? *2 Hen. IV.* i 2 86
Well, the king hath severed you and Prince Harry i 2 227
I think we are a body strong enough, Even as we are, to equal with the king i 3 67
What, is the king but five and twenty thousand?—To us no more i 3 68
So is the unfirm king In three divided i 3 73
O earth, yield us that king again, And take thou this! i 3 106
Villain! wilt thou kill God's officers and the king's? ii 1 57
Being upon hasty employment in the king's affairs ii 1 140
Even like those that are kin to the king; for they never prick their finger but they say, 'There's some of the king's blood spilt' ii 2 121
I am the king's poor cousin, sir ii 2 125
To the son of the king, nearest his father, Harry Prince of Wales ii 2 130
If they get ground and vantage of the king, Then join you with them ii 3 53
'When Arthur first in court'—Empty the jordan.—'And was a worthy king' ii 4 38
Ha! a bastard son of the king's? And art not thou Poins his brother? ii 4 307
Canst thou, O partial sleep, give thy repose To the wet sea-boy in an hour so rude, And in the calmest and most stillest night, With all appliances and means to boot, Deny it to a king? iii 1 30
A cough, sir, which I caught with ringing in the king's affairs iii 2 194
Of which disease Our late king, Richard, being infected, died iv 1 58
We offer'd to the king, And might by no suit gain our audience iv 1 75
Wherein have you been galled by the king? iv 1 89
You shall say indeed, it is the time, And not the king, that doth you injuries iv 1 106
It not appears to me Either from the king or in the present time That you should have an inch of any ground To build a grief on iv 1 108
The king that loved him, as the state stood then, Was force perforce compell'd to banish him iv 1 115
When the king did throw his warder down, His own life hung upon the staff he threw iv 1 125
Whom they doted on And bless'd and graced indeed, more than the king iv 1 139
Yea, every idle, nice and wanton reason Shall to the king taste of this action iv 1 192
The king is weary Of dainty and such picking grievances iv 1 197
Besides, the king hath wasted all his rods On late offenders iv 1 215
Would he abuse the countenance of the king, Alack, what mischiefs! iv 2 13
I hear the king my father is sore sick iv 3 83
Speak lower, princes, for the king recovers iv 4 129
How doth the king?—Exceeding ill. Heard he the good news yet? iv 5 10
Sweet prince, speak low; The king your father is disposed to sleep iv 5 17
I will sit and watch here by the king. Why doth the crown lie there? iv 5 20
A sleep That from this golden rigol hath divorced So many English kings iv 5 37
Doth the king call?—What would your majesty? How fares your grace? iv 5 49
How doth the king?—Exceeding well; his cares are now all ended v 2 2
Indeed I think the young king loves you not.—I know he doth not v 2 9
I'll to the king my master that is dead, And tell him who hath sent me v 2 40
Your highness pleased to forget my place, The majesty and power of law and justice, The image of the king whom I presented v 2 79
As you are a king, speak in your state What I have done v 2 99
Why, there spoke a king v 3 73
I am, sir, under the king, in some authority.—Under which king, Bezonian? speak, or die.—Under King Harry v 3 117
A foutre for thine office! Sir John, thy tender lambkin now is king v 3 122
What, is the old king dead?—As nail in door: the things I speak are just v 3 126
I know the young king is sick for me v 3 142
I will make the king do you grace: I will leer upon him as a' comes by v 5 6
My king! my Jove! I speak to thee, my heart!—I know thee not, old man v 5 50
I like this fair proceeding of the king's: He hath intent his wonted followers Shall all be very well provided for v 5 103
The king hath call'd his parliament, my lord v 5 109
I heard a bird so sing, Whose music, to my thinking, pleased the king v 5 114
For 'tis your thoughts that now must deck our kings *Hen. V.* Prol. 28
That self bill is urged, Which in the eleventh year of the last king's reign Was like i 1 2
As much as would maintain, to the king's honour, Full fifteen earls i 1 12
And to the coffers of the king beside, A thousand pounds by the year i 1 18
The king is full of grace and fair regard.—And a true lover of the holy church i 1 22
Nor never Hydra-headed wilfulness So soon did lose his seat and all at once As in this king i 1 37
With an inward wish You would desire the king were made a prelate i 1 40
Your brother kings and monarchs of the earth Do all expect that you should rouse yourself, As did the former lions of your blood i 2 122
To fill King Edward's fame with prisoner kings i 2 162
For so work the honey-bees, . . . They have a king and officers of sorts i 2 190
We hear Your greeting is from him, not from the king i 2 236
We are no tyrant, but a Christian king i 2 241
I will keep my state, Be like a king and show my sail of greatness i 2 274
Following the mirror of all Christian kings, With winged heels ii Prol. 6
This grace of kings must die, If hell and treason hold their promises ii Prol. 28
The sum is paid; the traitors are agreed; The king is set from London ii Prol. 34
Till the king come forth, and not till then, Unto Southampton do we shift our scene ii Prol. 41
He'll yield the crow a pudding one of these days. The king has killed his heart ii 1 92
The king hath run bad humours on the knight; that's the even of it ii 1 127
The king is a good king: but it must be as it may; he passes some humours and careers ii 1 131
The king hath note of all that they intend, By interception ii 2 6
Wherein you would have sold your king to slaughter ii 2 170
Shall we shog? the king will be gone from Southampton ii 3 47
Prince Dauphin! You are too much mistaken in this king ii 4 30
Lest that our king Come here himself to question our delay ii 4 141
Suppose that you have seen The well-appointed king at Hampton pier iii Prol. 4
Tells Harry that the king doth offer him Katharine his daughter iii Prol. 29
The day is hot, and the weather, and the wars, and the king, and the dukes iii 2 114
Hark you, the king is coming, and I must speak with him from the pridge iii 6 90
So far my king and master; so much my office iii 6 144
Turn thee back, And tell thy king I do not seek him now iii 6 149
This lodging likes me better, Since I may say 'Now lie I like a king' iv 1 17
As good a gentleman as the emperor.—Then you are a better than the king iv 1 43

King. The king's a bawcock, and a heart of gold, A lad of life *Hen. V.* iv 1 44
He hath not told his thought to the king?—No iv 1 103
For, though I speak it to you, I think the king is but a man, as I am iv 1 105
I will speak my conscience of the king iv 1 124
Methinks I could not die any where so contented as in the king's company iv 1 132
For we know enough, if we know we are the king's subjects iv 1 138
If his cause be wrong, our obedience to the king wipes the crime of it out of us.—But if the cause be not good, the king himself hath a heavy reckoning to make iv 1 139
If these men do not die well, it will be a black matter for the king iv 1 152
The king is not bound to answer the particular endings of his soldiers iv 1 163
There is no king, be his cause never so spotless, if it come to the arbitrement of swords, can try it out with all unspotted soldiers iv 1 167
Here men are punished for before-breach of the king's laws in now the king's quarrel iv 1 180
If they die unprovided, no more is the king guilty of their damnation iv 1 183
Every subject's duty is the king's; but every subject's soul is his own iv 1 186
I myself heard the king say he would not be ransomed iv 1 202
I will do it, though I take thee in the king's company iv 1 237
But it is no English treason to cut French crowns, and to-morrow the king himself will be a clipper iv 1 246
Upon the king! let us our lives, our souls, Our debts, our careful wives, Our children and our sins lay on the king! iv 1 247
What infinite heart's-ease Must kings neglect, that private men enjoy! iv 1 254
And what have kings, that privates have not too, Save ceremony? iv 1 255
Thou proud dream, That play'st so subtly with a king's repose; I am a king that find thee, and I know 'Tis not the balm, the sceptre iv 1 275
The farced title running 'fore the king, The throne he sits on iv 1 280
Such a wretch, Winding up days with toil and nights with sleep, Had the fore-hand and vantage of a king iv 1 297
In gross brain little wots What watch the king keeps to maintain the peace iv 1 300
Where is the king?—The king himself is rode to view their battle iv 3 1
Is this the king we sent to for his ransom? iv 5 9
They have burned and carried away all that was in the king's tent; wherefore the king, most worthily, hath caused every soldier to cut his prisoner's throat. O, 'tis a gallant king! iv 7 8
Our king is not like him in that: he never killed any of his friends iv 7 42
Comest thou again for ransom?—No, great king iv 7 73
O, give us leave, great king, To view the field in safety! iv 7 84
Soldier, you must come to the king iv 7 124
Come apace to the king: there is more good toward you iv 8 3
Now we bear the king Toward Calais: grant him there v Prol. 6
Out-voice the deep-mouth'd sea, Which like a mighty whiffler 'fore the king Seems to prepare his way v Prol. 12
The king hath heard them; to the which as yet There is no answer made v 2 74
And you, brother Gloucester, Warwick and Huntingdon, go with the king v 2 85
Thou wouldst find me such a plain king that thou wouldst think I had sold my farm to buy my crown v 2 128
Take me; and take me, take a soldier; take a soldier, take a king v 2 176
And for my English moiety take the word of a king and a bachelor v 2 230
If he be not fellow with the best king, thou shalt find the best king of good fellows v 2 261
Nice customs curtsy to great kings v 2 294
The king hath granted every article: His daughter first v 2 360
England ne'er lost a king of so much worth.—England ne'er had a king until his time *1 Hen. VI.* i 1 7
He was a king bless'd of the King of kings i 1 28
The Dauphin crowned king! all fly to him! O, whither shall we fly? i 1 96
And then I will proclaim young Henry king.—To Eltham will I, where the young king is i 1 169
The king from Eltham I intend to steal And sit at chiefest stern of public weal i 1 176
Thou art no friend to God or to the king i 3 25
Thou most usurping proditor, And not protector, of the king or realm i 3 32
Here's Beaufort, that regards nor God nor king i 3 60
And would have armour here out of the Tower, To crown himself king i 3 68
Assembled here in arms this day against God's peace and the king's i 3 75
Was not thy father . . . For treason executed in our late king's days? ii 4 91
The lawful heir Of Edward king, the third of that descent ii 5 66
The king, thy sovereign, is not quite exempt From envious malice iii 1 25
No one but he should be about the king iii 1 38
State holy or unhallow'd, what of that? Is not his grace protector to the king? iii 1 60
Compassion on the king commands me stoop iii 1 119
Sweet king! the bishop hath a kindly gird iii 1 131
The presence of a king engenders love Amongst his subjects and his loyal friends, As it disanimates his enemies iii 1 181
Kings and mightiest potentates must die, For that's the end of human misery iii 2 136
Governor of Paris, take your oath, That you elect no other king but him iv 1 4
No more but, plain and bluntly, 'To the king!' iv 1 51
Are you not ashamed With this immodest clamorous outrage To trouble and disturb the king and us? iv 1 127
I promise you, the king Prettily, methought, did play the orator iv 1 174
Margaret my name, and daughter to a king, The King of Naples v 3 51
I'll win this Lady Margaret. For whom? Why, for my king v 3 89
Princes should be free.—And so shall you, If happy England's royal king be free v 3 115
Give consent, Thy daughter shall be wedded to my king v 3 137
Happy for so sweet a child, Fit to be made companion with a king v 3 149
In Henry's royal name, As deputy unto that gracious king, Give thee her hand v 3 161
I give thee kingly thanks, Because this is in traffic of a king v 3 164
No princely commendations to my king?—Such commendations as becomes a maid, A virgin and his servant v 3 176
A pure unspotted heart, Never yet taint with love, I send the king v 3 183
I will not so presume To send such peevish tokens to a king v 3 186
Not me begotten of a shepherd swain, But issued from the progeny of kings v 4 38
I do greet your excellence With letters of commission from the king v 4 95
Of benefit proceeding from our king And not of any challenge of desert v 4 152
A dower, my lords! disgrace not so your king v 5 48
Whom should we match with Henry, being a king, But Margaret, that is daughter to a king? v 5 66
Approves her fit for none but for a king v 5 69
Her valiant courage and undaunted spirit, More than in women commonly is seen, Will answer our hope in issue of a king v 5 72

King. Margaret shall now be queen, and rule the king; But I will rule both her, the king and realm . . . . 1 *Hen. VI.* v 5 107
The fairest queen that ever king received . . . . . 2 *Hen. VI.* i 1 16
Makes me the bolder to salute my king With ruder terms . . . i 1 29
England's kings have had Large sums of gold and dowries with their wives . . . i 1 128
Now ye grow too hot: It was the pleasure of my lord the king . . i 1 138
An enemy unto you all, And no great friend, I fear me, to the king . i 1 150
May that thought, when I imagine ill Against my king and nephew, virtuous Henry, Be my last breathing in this mortal world! . . i 2 20
Not the least of these But can do more in England than the king . i 3 74
Because the king, forsooth, will have it so.—Madam, the king is old enough himself To give his censure: these are no women's matters i 3 118
Since thou wert king—as who is king but thou?—The commonwealth hath daily run to wreck . . . . i 3 126
Good king, look to't in time; She'll hamper thee, and dandle thee like a baby . . . . i 3 147
But God in mercy so deal with my soul, As I in duty love my king! . i 3 161
Ask what thou wilt. That I had said and done!—First of the king . i 4 32
The king and commonweal Are deeply indebted for this piece of pains . i 4 46
Good deserts.—Not half so bad as thine to England's king . . i 4 50
The king is now in progress towards Saint Alban's . . . . . i 4 76
Dangerous peer, That smooth'st it so with king and commonweal! . ii 1 22
A miracle! a miracle!—Come to the king and tell him what miracle . ii 1 62
Bring him near the king; His highness' pleasure is to talk with him . ii 1 72
To heaven I do appeal, How I have loved my king and commonweal . ii 1 191
Henry the Fourth Seized on the realm, deposed the rightful king . ii 2 24
This Edmund . . . laid claim unto the crown; And, but for Owen Glendower, had been king . . . . ii 2 41
So, if the issue of the elder son Succeed before the younger, I am king . ii 2 52
Long live our sovereign Richard, England's king!—We thank you, lords. But I am not your king . . . . ii 2 63
The Earl of Warwick Shall one day make the Duke of York a king . ii 2 79
The Earl of Warwick The greatest man in England but the king . ii 2 82
No less beloved Than when thou wert protector to thy king . . ii 3 27
I see no reason why a king of years Should be to be protected like a child . . . . ii 3 28
Give up your staff, sir, and the king his realm.—My staff? . . ii 3 31
Why, now is Henry king, and Margaret queen; And Humphrey Duke of Gloucester scarce himself . . . . ii 3 39
I never meant him any ill, nor the king, nor the queen . . . ii 3 91
Master sheriff, Let not her penance exceed the king's commission . . ii 4 75
By reputing of his high descent, As next the king he was successive heir . . . . iii 1 49
All happiness unto my lord the king! Pardon, my liege, that I have stay'd so long . . . . iii 1 93
That doit that e'er I wrested from the king, Or any groat I hoarded to my use . . . . iii 1 112
The king will labour still to save his life, The commons haply rise . iii 1 239
The king and all the peers are here at hand. Have you laid fair the bed? iii 2 10
Help, lords! the king is dead.—Rear up his body; wring him by the nose . . . . iii 2 33
As my soul intends to live With that dread King that took our state upon him . . . . iii 2 154
Sirs, stand apart; the king shall know your mind . . . . . iii 2 242
An answer from the king, or we will all break in! . . . . . iii 2 278
Thus is poor Suffolk ten times banished; Once by the king, and three times thrice by thee . . . . iii 2 358
Sometime he calls the king And whispers to his pillow as to him . iii 2 374
Go tell this heavy message to the king. Ay me! what is this world! . iii 2 379
Hence: the king, thou know'st, is coming; If thou be found by me, thou art but dead . . . . iii 2 386
For daring to affy a mighty lord Unto the daughter of a worthless king iv 1 81
Thrust from the crown By shameful murder of a guiltless king . . iv 1 95
Reproach and beggary Is crept into the palace of our king . . iv 1 102
Rather let my head Stoop to the block than these knees bow to any Save to the God of heaven and to my king . . . . . iv 1 126
Nay, more, the king's council are no good workmen . . . . iv 2 15
Inspired with the spirit of putting down kings and princes . . . iv 2 38
And when I am king, as king I will be,— God save your majesty! . iv 2 75
Sir Humphrey Stafford and his brother are hard by, with the king's forces . . . . iv 2 121
Forsake this groom: The king is merciful, if you revolt . . . . iv 2 133
Tell the king from me, that, for his father's sake, Henry the Fifth, in whose time boys went to span-counter for French crowns, I am content he shall reign . . . . iv 2 164
Fellow kings, I tell you that that Lord Say hath gelded the commonwealth . . . . iv 2 173
Seeing gentle words will not prevail, Assail them with the army of the king . . . . iv 2 185
You that be the king's friends, follow me . . . . iv 2 191
Fight for your king, your country and your lives . . . . . iv 5 12
Contrary to the king, his crown and dignity, thou hast built a paper-mill . . . . iv 7 40
When have I aught exacted at your hands, But to maintain the king? . iv 7 75
Large gifts have I bestow'd on learned clerks, Because my book preferr'd me to the king . . . . iv 7 77
This tongue hath parley'd unto foreign kings For your behoof . . iv 7 82
We come ambassadors from the king Unto the commons . . . iv 8 7
Who loves the king and will embrace his pardon, Fling up his cap . iv 8 14
God save the king! . . . . iv 8 19; iv 9 22; *Macbeth* i 2 47
A Clifford! a Clifford! we'll follow the king and Clifford . 2 *Hen. VI.* iv 8 56
He that brings his head unto the king Shall have a thousand crowns . iv 8 69
We'll devise a mean To reconcile you all unto the king . . . iv 8 72
Was ever king that joy'd an earthly throne, And could command no more content than I? No sooner was I crept out of my cradle But I was made a king, at nine months old . . . . . . iv 9 1
Was never subject long'd to be a king As I do long and wish to be a subject . . . . iv 9 5
Thou wilt betray me, and get a thousand crowns of the king . . iv 10 29
Thy most ungracious head; Which I will bear in triumph to the king iv 10 89
Burn, bonfires, clear and bright, To entertain great England's lawful king . . . . v 1 4
Whom have we here? Buckingham, to disturb me? The king hath sent him, sure . . . . v 1 13
I am far better born than is the king, More like a king, more kingly . v 1 29
Why I have brought this army hither Is to remove proud Somerset from the king . . . . v 1 36
The king hath yielded unto thy demand: The Duke of Somerset is in the Tower . . . . v 1 40

King. If one so rude and of so mean condition May pass into the presence of a king . . . . 2 *Hen. VI.* v 1 65
A poor esquire of Kent, that loves his king . . . . . v 1 75
False king! why hast thou broken faith with me? . . . . v 1 91
King did I call thee? no, thou art not king, Not fit to govern . v 1 93
I arrest thee, York, Of capital treason 'gainst the king and crown . . v 1 107
Health and all happiness to my lord the king!—I thank thee . . v 1 124
This is my king, York, I do not mistake; But thou mistakest . . v 1 129
A bedlam and ambitious humour Makes him oppose himself against his king . . . . v 1 133
I am thy king, and thou a false-heart traitor . . . . . v 1 143
The king is fled to London, To call a present court of parliament . v 3 24
I wonder how the king escaped our hands . . . . 3 *Hen. VI.* i 1 1
This is the palace of the fearful king, And this the regal seat . . i 1 25
When the king comes, offer him no violence, Unless he seek to thrust you out . . . . i 1 33
The bloody parliament shall this be call'd, Unless Plantagenet, Duke of York, be king . . . . i 1 40
Neither the king, nor he that loves him best, The proudest he that holds up Lancaster, Dares stir a wing . . . . i 1 45
He means, Back'd by the power of Warwick, that false peer, To aspire unto the crown and reign as king . . . . i 1 53
Whom should he follow but his natural king? . . . . . . i 1 82
Be Duke of Lancaster; let him be king.—He is both king and Duke . i 1 86
Sound drums and trumpets, and the king will fly . . . . . i 1 118
Why faint you, lords? My title's good, and better far than his.—Prove it, Henry, and thou shalt be king . . . . i 1 131
Henry the Fourth by conquest got the crown.—'Twas by rebellion against his king . . . . i 1 133
Tell me, may not a king adopt an heir?—What then?—An if he may, then am I lawful king . . . . i 1 135
My conscience tells me he is lawful king . . . . i 1 150
Let me for this my life-time reign as king . . . . . . i 1 171
Farewell, faint-hearted and degenerate king . . . . . . i 1 183
To cease this civil war, and, whilst I live, To honour me as thy king . i 1 198
You cannot disinherit me: If you be king, why should not I succeed? . i 1 227
Art thou king, and wilt be forced? I shame to hear thee speak . . i 1 230
Richard, enough; I will be king, or die . . . . i 2 35
And yet the king not privy to my drift, Nor any of the house of Lancaster . . . . i 2 46
Warwick, Cobham, and the rest, Whom we have left protectors of the king . . . . i 2 57
What! was it you that would be England's king? . . . . . i 4 70
Now looks he like a king! Ay, this is he that took King Henry's chair i 4 96
You should not be king Till our King Henry had shook hands with death . . . . i 4 101
I, then in London, keeper of the king, Muster'd my soldiers . . . ii 1 111
To intercept the queen, Bearing the king in my behalf along . . . ii 1 115
'Twas the coldness of the king, Who look'd full gently on his warlike queen . . . . ii 1 122
No hope to win the day; So that we fled; the king unto the queen . ii 1 137
Many moe proud birds Have wrought the easy-melting king like wax . ii 1 171
He, but a duke, would have his son a king, And raise his issue, like a loving sire; Thou, being a king, blest with a goodly son, Didst yield consent to disinherit him . . . . ii 2 21
And in the towns, as they do march along, Proclaims him king . . ii 2 71
Becomes it thee to be thus bold in terms Before thy sovereign and thy lawful king?—I am his king, and he should bow his knee . . ii 2 86
You, that are king, though he do wear the crown . . . . ii 2 90
Give no limits to my tongue: I am a king, and privileged to speak . ii 2 120
Bears the title of a king,—As if a channel should be call'd the sea . ii 2 140
And ne'er was Agamemnon's brother wrong'd By that false woman, as this king by thee . . . . ii 2 149
Tamed the king, and made the dauphin stoop . . . . . . ii 2 151
We, in pity of the gentle king, Had slipp'd our claim until another age ii 2 161
Not willing any longer conference, Since thou deniest the gentle king to speak . . . . ii 2 172
Thou setter up and plucker down of kings . . . . ii 3 37; iii 3 157
Gives not the hawthorn-bush a sweeter shade To shepherds looking on their silly sheep, Than doth a rich embroider'd canopy To kings that fear their subjects' treachery? . . . . ii 5 45
From London by the king was I press'd forth . . . . . . ii 5 64
How will the country for these woful chances Misthink the king! . . ii 5 108
Was ever king so grieved for subjects' woe? . . . . . . ii 5 111
Sad-hearted men, much overgone with care, Here sits a king more woful ii 5 124
Hadst thou sway'd as kings should do, Or as thy father and his father did . . . . ii 6 14
Some troops pursue the bloody-minded queen, That led calm Henry, though he were a king, As doth a sail, fill'd with a fretting gust, Command an argosy to stem the waves . . . . . . ii 6 34
To London with triumphant march, There to be crowned England's royal king . . . . ii 6 88
This is the quondam king; let's seize upon him . . . . . iii 1 23
Warwick Is thither gone, to crave the French king's sister . . . iii 1 30
And in conclusion wins the king from her, With promise of his sister . iii 1 50
Men may talk of kings, and why not I?—Ay, but thou talk'st as if thou wert a king.—Why, so I am, in mind; and that's enough . . iii 1 58
But, if thou be a king, where is thy crown?— . . . My crown is call'd content: A crown it is that seldom kings enjoy . . . . . iii 1 61
If you be a king crown'd with content, Your crown content and you must be contented To go along with us . . . . . . iii 1 66
As we think, You are the king King Edward hath deposed . . . iii 1 69
I was anointed king at nine months old; My father and my grandfather were kings . . . . iii 1 76
We were subjects but while you were king.—Why, am I dead? . . iii 1 81
The king shall be commanded; And be you kings, command, and I'll obey . . . . iii 1 92
We are true subjects to the king, King Edward.—So would you be again to Henry, If he were seated . . . . iii 1 94
And what God will, that let your king perform . . . . . iii 1 100
The lady hath a thing to grant, Before the king will grant her humble suit . . . . iii 2 13
Shall I not hear my task?—An easy task; 'tis but to love a king . . iii 2 53
One way or other; she is for a king; And she shall be my love, or else my queen . . . . iii 2 87
Margaret Must strike her sail and learn awhile to serve Where kings command . . . . iii 3 6
Henry, sole possessor of my love, Is of a king become a banish'd man . iii 3 25
Edward Duke of York Usurps the regal title and the seat Of England's true-anointed lawful king . . . . iii 3 29

King. Grant That virtuous Lady Bona, thy fair sister, To England's king in lawful marriage . . . *3 Hen. VI.* iii 3 57
In our king's behalf, I am commanded, with your leave and favour, Humbly to kiss your hand . . . iii 3 59
For shame! leave Henry, and call Edward king.—Call him my king? . iii 3 100
Tell me, even upon thy conscience, Is Edward your true king? . iii 3 114
When I have heard your king's desert recounted, Mine ear hath tempted judgement to desire . . . iii 3 132
Shall articles be drawn Touching the jointure that your king must make iii 3 136
Be a witness That Bona shall be wife to the English king.—To Edward, but not to the English king . . . iii 3 139
What! has your king married the Lady Grey? . . . iii 3 174
No more my king, for he dishonours me, But most himself . . . iii 3 184
Tell false Edward, thy supposed king, That Lewis of France is sending over masquers To revel it with him and his new bride . iii 3 223; iv 1 93
Go fear thy king withal.—Tell him, in hope he'll prove a widower shortly, I'll wear the willow garland for his sake . . iii 3 226
Forbear this talk; here comes the king.—And his well-chosen bride . iv 1 6
I am Edward, Your king and Warwick's, and must have my will.—And shall have your will, because our king . . . iv 1 16
Edward will be king, And not be tied into his brother's will . . . iv 1 65
Now, brother king, farewell, and sit you fast . . . iv 1 119
The king by this is set him down to sleep.—What, will he not to bed? iv 3 2
What nobleman is that That with the king here resteth in his tent?—'Tis the Lord Hastings, the king's chiefest friend . . . iv 3 10
But why commands the king That his chief followers lodge in towns about him? . . . iv 3 12
Why, Warwick, when we parted, Thou call'dst me king.—Ay, but the case is alter'd: When you disgraced me in my embassade, Then I degraded you from being king . . . iv 3 31
Edward will always bear himself as king . . . iv 3 45
Then, for his mind, be Edward England's king: But Henry now shall wear the English crown, And be true king indeed, thou but the shadow . . . iv 3 48
You know our king, my brother, Is prisoner to the bishop here . iv 5 4
If Henry be your king, Yet Edward at the least is Duke of York . iv 7 20
I will hence again: I came to serve a king and not a duke . . iv 7 49
If you'll not here proclaim yourself our king, I'll leave you to your fortune . . . iv 7 54
Speak gentle words and humbly bend thy knee, Call Edward king . v 1 23
And thou shalt still remain the Duke of York.—I thought, at least, he would have said the king . . . v 1 29
And Henry is my king, Warwick his subject.—But Warwick's king is Edward's prisoner . . . v 1 38
But, whiles he thought to steal the single ten, The king was slily finger'd from the deck! . . . v 1 44
To bend the fatal instruments of war Against his brother and his lawful king? . . . v 1 88
For who lived king, but I could dig his grave? . . . v 2 21
Excuse me to the king my brother; I'll hence to London on a serious matter . . . v 5 46
See how my sword weeps for the poor king's death! . . . v 6 63
To set my brother Clarence and the king In deadly hate *Richard III.* i 1 34
'Tis not the king that sends you to the Tower . . . i 1 63
Night-walking heralds That trudge betwixt the king and Mistress Shore i 1 73
It is our way, If we will keep in favour with the king, To be her men . i 1 79
The king Is wise and virtuous, and his noble queen Well struck in years i 1 90
The king is sickly, weak and melancholy, And his physicians fear him . i 1 136
Poor key-cold figure of a holy king! Pale ashes of the house of Lancaster! . . . i 2 5
Eat him quick, As thou dost swallow up this good king's blood! . . i 2 66
Didst thou not kill this king?—I grant ye.—Dost grant me, hedgehog? i 2 101
After I have solemnly interr'd At Chertsey monastery this noble king . i 2 215
It is determined, not concluded yet: But so it must be, if the king miscarry . . . i 3 16
Saw you the king to-day, my Lord of Derby? . . . i 3 30
Who are they that complain unto the king, That I, forsooth, am stern? i 3 43
The king, of his own royal disposition, And not provoked by any suitor i 3 63
What, marry, may she! marry with a king, A bachelor, a handsome stripling . . . i 3 100
Threat you me with telling of the king? Tell him, and spare not . . i 3 113
What I have said I will avouch in presence of the king . . . i 3 115
Ere you were queen, yea, or your husband king, I was a pack-horse . i 3 121
We follow'd then our lord, our lawful king: So should we you, if you should be our king.—If I should be! I had rather be a pedlar . i 3 147
As little joy, my lord, as you suppose You should enjoy, were you this country's king, As little joy may you suppose in me . . . i 3 152
If not by war, by surfeit die your king, As ours by murder, to make him a king! . . . i 3 197
Say it is the queen and her allies That stir the king against the duke . i 3 331
I'll to the king; and signify to him That thus I have resign'd my charge . . . i 4 97
My voice is now the king's, my looks mine own . . . i 4 174
Have I offended you?—Offended us you have not, but the king . . i 4 183
What we will do, we do upon command.—And he that hath commanded is the king . . . i 4 199
Take heed you dally not before your king . . . ii 1 12
He rescued me, And said, 'Dear brother, live, and be a king' . . ii 1 113
Clarence' death? O, they did urge it still unto the king! . . ii 1 137
You mistake me much; I do lament the sickness of the king . . ii 2 9
The king my uncle is to blame for this: God will revenge it . . ii 2 13
Peace, children, peace! the king doth love you well . . ii 2 17
The king, provoked by the queen, Devised impeachments to imprison him . . . ii 2 21
Edward, my lord, your son, our king, is dead . . . ii 2 40
If die, be brief, That our swift-winged souls may catch the king's . . ii 2 44
Though we have spent our harvest of this king, We are to reap the harvest of his son . . . ii 2 115
The young prince be fetch'd Hither to London, to be crown'd our king . ii 2 122
I hope the king made peace with all of us; And the compact is firm . ii 2 132
Hear you the news abroad?—Ay, that the king is dead.—Bad news . ii 3 3
Then the king Had virtuous uncles to protect his grace . . . ii 3 20
I'll win our ancient right in France again, Or die a soldier, as I lived a king . . . iii 1 93
And, look, when I am king, claim thou of me The earldom of Hereford, and the moveables Whereof the king my brother stood possess'd . iii 1 194
Pronounced your part,—I mean, your voice,—for crowning of the king . . . iii 4 29
Cry 'God save Richard, England's royal king!' . . . iii 7 22; 240
Accept our suit or no, Your brother's son shall never reign our king . iii 7 215

King. The king hath straitly charged the contrary.—The king! why, who's that? . . . *Richard III.* iv 1 17
I would be king.—Why, so you are, my thrice renowned liege.—Ha! am I king? . . . iv 2 12
The king is angry: see, he bites the lip . . . iv 2 27
Henry the Sixth Did prophesy that Richmond should be king, When Richmond was a little peevish boy. A king, perhaps, perhaps . iv 2 99
Made I him king for this? O, let me think on Hastings, and be gone! iv 2 124
And so I left them both, To bring this tidings to the bloody king . . iv 3 22
Then fiery expedition be my wing, Jove's Mercury, and herald for a king! . . . iv 3 55
I love thy daughter, And mean to make her queen of England.—Say then, who dost thou mean shall be her king? . . . iv 4 264
The loss you have is but a son being king, And by that loss your daughter is made queen . . . iv 4 307
The king, that calls your beauteous daughter wife, Familiarly shall call thy Dorset brother; Again shall you be mother to a king . iv 4 315
Say that the king, which may command, entreats.—That at her hands which the king's King forbids . . . iv 4 345
The unity the king thy brother made Had not been broken . . iv 4 379
Is the sword unsway'd? Is the king dead? the empire unpossess'd? . iv 4 471
And who is England's king but great York's heir? . . . iv 4 473
Kings it [hope] makes gods, and meaner creatures kings . . v 2 24
Lies half a mile at least South from the mighty power of the king . v 3 38
Harry, that prophesied thou shouldst be king, Doth comfort thee . v 3 129
Live, and beget a happy race of kings! . . . v 3 157
The king enacts more wonders than a man . . . v 4 2
The two kings, Equal in lustre, were now best, now worst . *Hen. VIII.* i 1 28
A gift that heaven gives for him, which buys A place next to the king . i 1 66
Why the devil, Upon this French going out, took he upon him, Without the privity o' the king, to appoint Who should attend on him? . i 1 74
He's gone to the king; I'll follow and outstare him . . . i 1 128
I'll to the king; And from a mouth of honour quite cry down This Ipswich fellow's insolence . . . i 1 136
To the king I'll say't; and make my vouch as strong As shore of rock i 1 157
Suggests the king our master To this last costly treaty . . i 1 164
The emperor thus desired, That he would please to alter the king's course . . . i 1 189
Let the king know, As soon he shall by me . . . i 1 190
I Arrest thee of high treason, in the name Of our most sovereign king . i 1 202
The king Is pleased you shall to the Tower, till you know . . i 1 212
The will of heaven be done, and the king's pleasure By me obey'd! . i 1 215
Here is a warrant from The king to attach Lord Montacute . . i 1 217
Yet the king our master—Whose honour heaven shield from soil!—even he escapes not Language unmannerly . . . i 2 25
Let there be letters writ to every shire, Of the king's grace and pardon i 2 104
If the king Should without issue die, he'll carry it so To make the sceptre his . . . i 2 133
Men fear'd the French would prove perfidious, To the king's danger . i 2 157
Neither the king nor's heirs, Tell you the duke, shall prosper . . i 2 168
Had the king in his last sickness fail'd, The cardinal's and Sir Thomas Lovell's heads Should have gone off . . . i 2 184
The king's attorney on the contrary Urged on the examinations . . ii 1 15
Whoever the king favours, The cardinal instantly will find employment, and far enough from court too . . . ii 1 47
Nor will I sue, although the king have mercies More than I dare make faults . . . ii 1 70
My vows and prayers Yet are the king's; and, till my soul forsake, Shall cry for blessings on him . . . ii 1 89
A buzzing of a separation Between the king and Katharine . . . ii 1 149
When the king once heard it, out of anger He sent command to the lord mayor straight To stop the rumour . . . ii 1 150
Fresher than e'er it was; and held for certain The king will venture at it . . . ii 1 156
His master would be served before a subject, if not before the king . ii 2 9
How is the king employ'd?—I left him private, Full of sad thoughts . ii 2 15
The king will know him one day.—Pray God he do! he'll never know himself else . . . ii 2 22
He dives into the king's soul, and there scatters Dangers, doubts . . ii 2 27
And out of all these to restore the king, He counsels a divorce . . ii 2 30
Of her That, when the greatest stroke of fortune falls, Will bless the king ii 2 37
All that dare Look into these affairs see this main end, The French king's sister. Heaven will one day open The king's eyes . . . ii 2 42
As I am made without him, so I'll stand, If the king please . . . ii 2 53
And with some other business put the king From these sad thoughts . ii 2 57
You'll bear us company?—Excuse me; The king has sent me otherwhere . . . ii 2 60
Who am I? ha?—A gracious king that pardons all offences . . . ii 2 68
Thou art a cure fit for a king . . . ii 2 76
Much joy and favour to you; You are the king's now . . . ii 2 119
I shall not fail to approve the fair conceit The king hath of you . . ii 3 75
Beauty and honour in her are so mingled That they have caught the king . . . ii 3 77
I'll to the king, And say I spoke with you . . . ii 3 79
The king, your father, was reputed for A prince most prudent . . ii 4 45
As well For your own quiet, as to rectify What is unsettled in the king ii 4 64
We are a queen, or long have dream'd so, certain The daughter of a king ii 4 72
The king is present: if it be known to him That I gainsay my deed, how may he wound, And worthily, my falsehood! . . . ii 4 95
He might the king his lord advertise Whether our daughter were legitimate . . . ii 4 178
How you stand minded in the weighty difference Between the king and you . . . iii 1 59
Madam, you wrong the king's love with these fears . . . iii 1 81
Put your main cause into the king's protection; He's loving and most gracious . . . iii 1 93
Heaven is above all yet; there sits a judge That no king can corrupt . iii 1 101
Have I with all my full affections Still met the king? . . . iii 1 130
You may hurt yourself, ay, utterly Grow from the king's acquaintance iii 1 161
The king loves you; Beware you lose it not . . . iii 1 171
If you cannot Bar his access to the king, never attempt Any thing on him . . . iii 2 17
He hath a witchcraft Over the king in's tongue . . . iii 2 19
The king hath found Matter against him that for ever mars The honey of his language . . . iii 2 20
The cardinal's letters to the pope miscarried, And came to the eye o' the king . . . iii 2 31
My king is tangled in affection to A creature of the queen's . . . iii 2 35
Has the king this?—Believe it.—Will this work? . . . iii 2 37
The king in this perceives him, how he coasts And hedges his own way iii 2 38

King. But, will the king Digest this letter of the cardinal's? *Hen. VIII.* iii 2 52
Hath ta'en no leave; Has left the cause o' the king unhandled . iii 2 58
The king cried Ha! at this.—Now, God incense him, And let him cry Ha! louder! iii 2 61
He is return'd in his opinions; which Have satisfied the king for his divorce . . . . iii 2 65
A worthy fellow, and hath ta'en much pain In the king's business . iii 2 73
The packet, Cromwell, Gave't you the king?—To his own hand . iii 2 77
The Duchess of Alençon, The French king's sister: he shall marry her. iii 2 86
May be, he hears the king Does whet his anger to him . . iii 2 91
And not wholesome to Our cause, that she should lie i' the bosom of Our hard-ruled king . . . . iii 2 101
Cranmer; One Hath crawl'd into the favour of the king, And is his oracle . . . . iii 2 103
What cross devil Made me put this main secret in the packet I sent the king? . . . . iii 2 216
Hear the king's pleasure, cardinal: who commands you To render up the great seal . . . . iii 2 228
Who dare cross 'em, Bearing the king's will from his mouth expressly? iii 2 235
That seal, You ask with such a violence, the king, Mine and your master, with his own hand gave me . . . . . iii 2 246
Now, who'll take it?—The king, that gave it.—It must be himself, then iii 2 251
Far from his succour, from the king, from all That might have mercy . iii 2 261
In the way of loyalty and truth Toward the king, my ever royal master iii 2 273
Your intercepted packets You writ to the pope against the king . iii 2 287
Those articles, my lord, are in the king's hand: But, thus much, they are foul . . . . iii 2 299
And spotless shall mine innocence arise, When the king knows my truth iii 2 302
Without the king's assent or knowledge, You wrought to be a legate . iii 2 310
In which you brought the king To be your servant . . . . iii 2 315
Without the knowledge Either of king or council . . . . iii 2 317
Without the king's will or the state's allowance . . . iii 2 322
And to be Out of the king's protection. This is my charge . . iii 2 344
The king shall know it, and, no doubt, shall thank you . . . iii 2 348
The king has cured me, I humbly thank his grace . . . iii 2 380
The heaviest and the worst Is your displeasure with the king . iii 2 392
Lady Anne, Whom the king hath in secrecy long married . . iii 2 403
The king has gone beyond me: all my glories In that one woman I have lost for ever . . . . iii 2 408
Seek the king; That sun, I pray, may never set! . . . iii 2 414
The king shall have my service; but my prayers For ever and for ever shall be yours . . . . iii 2 426
Serve the king; And,—prithee, lead me in: There take an inventory of all I have, To the last penny; 'tis the king's . . . iii 2 449
Had I but served my God with half the zeal I served my king . iii 2 456
For not appearance and The king's late scruple, by the main assent Of all these learned men she was divorced . . . . iv 1 31
Our king has all the Indies in his arms, And more and richer, when he strains that lady . . . . iv 1 45
You must no more call it York-place, that's past; For, since the cardinal fell, that title's lost: 'Tis now the king's, and call'd Whitehall . . . . iv 1 97
A man in much esteem with the king, and truly A worthy friend . iv 1 109
The king has made him master O' the jewel house . . . iv 1 110
There is staying A gentleman, sent from the king, to see you . iv 2 106
The king's request that I would visit you; Who grieves much . iv 2 116
I most humbly pray you to deliver This to my lord The king . iv 2 130
Stand these poor people's friend, and urge the king To do me this last right . . . . iv 2 157
Although unqueen'd, yet like A queen, and daughter to a king, inter me iv 2 172
Came you from the king, my lord?—I did, Sir Thomas; and left him at primero . . . . v 1 6
The archbishop Is the king's hand and tongue; and who dare speak One syllable against him? . . . . v 1 38
Have broken with the king; who hath so far Given ear to our complaint v 1 47
I am glad I came this way so happily: the king Shall understand it v 2 9
'Tis Butts, The king's physician . . . . . . v 2 11
Misdemean'd yourself, and not a little, Toward the king first, then his laws . . . . v 3 15
Pray heaven, the king may never find a heart With less allegiance in it! v 3 42
There to remain till the king's further pleasure Be known unto us . v 3 90
I take my cause Out of the gripes of cruel men, and give it To a most noble judge, the king my master . . . . . v 3 101
This is the king's ring.—'Tis no counterfeit.—'Tis the right ring . v 3 102
Do you think, my lords, The king will suffer but the little finger Of this man to be vex'd?—'Tis now too certain . . . . v 3 106
If the king blame me for't, I'll lay ye all By the heels . . . v 4 82
Posts, like the commandment of a king, Sans check to good and bad *Troi. and Cres.* i 3 93
Kings, princes, lords! If there be one among the fair'st of Greece . i 3 264
Weigh you the worth and honour of a king So great as our dread father in a scale Of common ounces? . . . . . . ii 2 26
And turn'd crown'd kings to merchants . . . . . ii 2 83
If Helen then be wife to Sparta's king, As it is known she is . . ii 2 183
Call together all his state of war; Fresh kings are come to Troy . ii 3 272
He desires you, that if the king call for him at supper, you will make his excuse . . . . iii 1 84
You shall do more Than all the island kings—disarm great Hector . iii 1 167
I was sent for to the king; but why, I know not . . . iv 1 35
When for a day of kings' entreaties a mother should not sell him an hour from her beholding . . . . . *Coriolanus* i 3 9
Numa's daughter's son, Who, after great Hostilius, here was king . ii 3 248
O, if to fight for king and commonweal Were piety in thine, it is in these *T. Andron.* i 1 114
King and commander of our commonweal, The wide world's emperor . i 1 247
Take it up, I pray thee, And give the king this fatal-plotted scroll . ii 3 47
The king my brother shall have note of this . . . . ii 3 85
Good king, to be so mightily abused! . . . . . . ii 3 87
Now will I fetch the king to find them here . . . . ii 3 206
Where is my lord the king?—Here, Tamora, though grieved with killing grief . . . . ii 3 259
I will entreat the king: Fear not thy sons; they shall do well enough . ii 3 304
Those sweet ornaments, Whose circling shadows kings have sought to sleep in . . . . ii 4 19
Old Titus, Or any one of you, chop off your hand, And send it to the king . . . . iii 1 154
King, be thy thoughts imperious, like thy name . . . . iv 4 81
Two such opposed kings encamp them still In man as well as herbs, grace and rude will . . . . . *Rom. and Jul.* ii 3 27
I do fear, the people Choose Cæsar for their king . *J. Cæsar* i 2 80

King. There was a Brutus once that would have brook'd The eternal devil to keep his state in Rome As easily as a king . *J. Cæsar* i 2 161
They say the senators to-morrow Mean to establish Cæsar as a king . i 3 86
My ancestors did from the streets of Rome The Tarquin drive, when he was call'd a king . . . . ii 1 54
Hail, brave friend! Say to the king the knowledge of the broil *Macbeth* i 2 6
Whence camest thou, worthy thane?—From Fife, great king . . i 2 48
That now Sweno, the Norways' king, craves composition . . i 2 59
All hail, Macbeth, that shalt be king hereafter! . . . i 3 50
Thou shalt get kings, though thou be none: So all hail, Macbeth and Banquo! . . . . i 3 67
To be king Stands not within the prospect of belief . . . i 3 73
Your children shall be kings.—You shall be king . . . . i 3 86
The king hath happily received, Macbeth, The news of thy success . i 3 89
Do you not hope your children shall be kings, When those that gave the thane of Cawdor to me Promised no less to them? . . . i 3 118
If chance will have me king, why, chance may crown me . . i 3 143
Let us toward the king. Think upon what hath chanced . . i 3 152
Whiles I stood rapt in the wonder of it, came missives from the king . i 5 7
Referred me to the coming on of time, with 'Hail, king that shalt be!' i 5 10
What is your tidings?—The king comes here to-night . . i 5 32
The king's a-bed: He hath been in unusual pleasure . . . ii 1 12
Is the king stirring, worthy thane?—Not yet . . . . ii 3 50
Goes the king hence to-day?—He does: he did appoint so . . ii 3 58
Malcolm and Donalbain, the king's two sons, Are stol'n away and fled . ii 4 25
Thou hast it now: king, Cawdor, Glamis, all, As the weird women promised . . . . iii 1 1
That myself should be the root and father Of many kings . . iii 1 6
He chid the sisters When first they put the name of king upon me . iii 1 58
Then prophet-like They hail'd him father to a line of kings . . iii 1 60
To make them kings, the seed of Banquo kings! . . . . iii 1 70
Say to the king, I would attend his leisure For a few words . . iii 2 3
Macduff Is gone to pray the holy king, upon his aid To wake Northumberland and warlike Siward . . . . iii 6 30
Hath so exasperate the king that he Prepares for some attempt of war. iii 6 38
What is this That rises like the issue of a king? . . . . iv 1 87
That this great king may kindly say, Our duties did his welcome pay . iv 1 131
The untimely emptying of the happy throne And fall of many kings . iv 3 69
Were I king, I should cut off the nobles for their lands . . . iv 3 78
It [avarice] hath been The sword of our slain kings . . . iv 3 87
Thy royal father Was a most sainted king: the queen that bore thee, Oftener upon her knees than on her feet . . . . . iv 3 109
Well; more anon.—Comes the king forth, I pray you?—Ay, sir . iv 3 140
'Tis call'd the evil: A most miraculous work in this good king . iv 3 147
This tune goes manly. Come, go we to the king; our power is ready . iv 3 236
Hail, king! for so thou art: behold, where stands The usurper's cursed head . . . . v 8 54
Stand, and unfold yourself.—Long live the king! . . *Hamlet* i 1 3
Look, where it comes again!—In the same figure, like the king that's dead . . . . i 1 41
Looks it not like the king? mark it, Horatio.—Most like . . . i 1 43
Is it not like the king?—As thou art to thyself . . . . i 1 58
Our last king, Whose image even but now appear'd to us . . i 1 80
Against the which, a moiety competent Was gaged by our king . . i 1 91
So like the king That was and is the question of these wars . . i 1 110
Giving to you no further personal power To business with the king . i 2 37
The king's rouse the heavens shall bruit again, Re-speaking earthly thunder . . . . i 2 127
So excellent a king; that was, to this, Hyperion to a satyr . . i 2 139
I saw him once; he was a goodly king . . . . . . i 2 186
My lord, I think I saw him yesternight.—Saw? who?—My lord, the king your father.—The king my father! . . . . i 2 191
The king doth wake to-night and takes his rouse, Keeps wassail . i 4 8
I'll call thee Hamlet, King, father, royal Dane: O, answer me! . i 4 45
Come, go with me: I will go seek the king . . . . ii 1 101
Come, go we to the king: This must be known . . . . ii 1 117
Your visitation shall receive such thanks As fits a king's remembrance ii 2 26
I hold my duty, as I hold my soul, Both to my God and to my gracious king . . . . ii 2 45
I could be bounded in a nutshell and count myself a king of infinite space, were it not that I have bad dreams . . . . ii 2 261
He that plays the king shall be welcome; his majesty shall have tribute ii 2 332
Can say nothing; no, not for a king, Upon whose property and most dear life A damn'd defeat was made . . . . . ii 2 596
The play's the thing Wherein I'll catch the conscience of the king ii 2 634
Will the king hear this piece of work?—And the queen too . . iii 2 51
Something too much of this.—There is a play to-night before the king . iii 2 80
This is one Lucianus, nephew to the king.—You are as good as a chorus iii 2 254
The king rises.—What, frighted with false fire!—How fares my lord? iii 2 276
If the king like not the comedy, Why then, belike, he likes it not, perdy iii 2 304
The king, sir,— Ay, sir, what of him?—Is in his retirement marvellous distempered.—With drink, sir? . . . . . . iii 2 310
I lack advancement.—How can that be, when you have the voice of the king himself for your succession in Denmark? . . . iii 2 356
Never alone Did the king sigh, but with a general groan . . iii 3 23
O me, what hast thou done?—Nay, I know not: Is it the king? . iii 4 26
Almost as bad, good mother, As kill a king, and marry with his brother.—As kill a king! . . . . iii 4 29
A vice of kings; A cutpurse of the empire and the rule . . iii 4 98
Let the bloat king tempt you again to bed; Pinch wanton on your cheek iii 4 182
What replication should be made by the son of a king?—Take you me for a sponge, my lord?—Ay, sir, that soaks up the king's countenance . . . . iv 2 14
Such officers do the king best service in the end . . . iv 2 18
You must tell us where the body is, and go with us to the king.—The body is with the king, but the king is not with the body . . iv 2 28
The king is a thing— A thing, my lord!—Of nothing . . . iv 2 30
Your fat king and your lean beggar is but variable service . . iv 3 25
A man may fish with the worm that hath eat of a king . . iv 3 29
To show you how a king may go a progress through the guts of a beggar iv 3 32
Go, captain, from me greet the Danish king . . . . iv 4 1
They cry 'Choose we: Laertes shall be king:' Caps, hands, and tongues, applaud it to the clouds: 'Laertes shall be king, Laertes king!' iv 5 106
Where is this king? Sirs, stand you all without.—No, let's come in . iv 5 112
O thou vile king, Give me my father!—Calmly, good Laertes . iv 5 115
Such divinity doth hedge a king, That treason can but peep to what it would . . . . iv 5 123
Give these fellows some means to the king: they have letters for him . iv 6 14
Let the king have the letters I have sent; and repair thou to me . iv 6 22
But soft! aside: here comes the king, The queen, the courtiers . v 1 240

King. Wilt thou know The effect of what I wrote?—Ay, good my lord.—An earnest conjuration from the king . . . *Hamlet* v 2 38
Why, what a king is this!—Does it not, thinks't thee, stand me now upon—He that hath kill'd my king . . . is't not perfect conscience, To quit him with this arm? . . . v 2 62
The king, sir, hath wagered with him six Barbary horses . v 2 154
The king, sir, hath laid, that in a dozen passes between yourself and him, he shall not exceed you three hits . . v 2 172
And the king hold his purpose, I will win for him an I can . v 2 183
I am constant to my purposes; they follow the king's pleasure . v 2 209
The king shall drink to Hamlet's better breath; And in the cup an union shall he throw, Richer than that which four successive kings In Denmark's crown have worn . . . . . v 2 282
Now the king drinks to Hamlet . . . . . v 2 289
Thy mother's poison'd: I can no more: the king, the king's to blame . v 2 331
I thought the king had more affected the Duke of Albany *Lear* i 1 1
Only we still retain The name, and all the additions to a king . i 1 138
Royal Lear, Whom I have ever honour'd as my king, Loved as my father i 1 142
Now, by Apollo,— Now, by Apollo, king, Thou swear'st thy gods in vain i 1 162
Fare thee well, king: sith thus thou wilt appear, Freedom lives hence i 1 183
Towards you, who with this king Hath rivall'd for our daughter . i 1 193
For you, great king, I would not from your love make such a stray, To match you where I hate . . . . . i 1 211
Thy dowerless daughter, king, thrown to my chance, Is queen of us, of ours . . . . i 1 259
And the king gone to-night! subscribed his power! Confined to exhibition! . . . . i 2 24
The king falls from bias of nature; there's father against child . i 2 120
Divisions in state, menaces and maledictions against king and nobles . i 2 160
A very honest-hearted fellow, and as poor as the king.—If thou be as poor for a subject as he is for a king, thou art poor enough . i 4 21
That such a king should play bo-peep, And go the fools among . i 4 193
Is it two days ago since I tripped up thy heels, and beat thee before the king? . . . . ii 2 33
Draw, you rascal: you come with letters against the king . ii 2 39
What is the matter?—The messengers from our sister and the king . ii 2 55
It pleased the king his master very late To strike at me . . ii 2 123
Got praises of the king For him attempting who was self-subdued . ii 2 128
I serve the king; On whose employment I was sent to you . ii 2 135
His fault is much, and the good king his master Will check him for't . ii 2 148
The king must take it ill, That he's so slightly valued in his messenger ii 2 152
Good king, that must approve the common saw, Thou out of heaven's benediction comest To the warm sun! . . . . ii 2 167
How chance the king comes with so small a train? . . ii 4 64
The king would speak with Cornwall; the dear father Would with his daughter speak . . . . ii 4 102
The king is in high rage.—Whither is he going?—He calls to horse . ii 4 299
I know you. Where's the king?—Contending with the fretful element . iii 1 3
The hard rein which both of them have borne Against the old kind king . . . . iii 1 28
Of how unnatural and bemadding sorrow The king hath cause to plain iii 1 39
Fie on this storm! I will go see the king . . . iii 1 50
When we have found the king,—in which your pain That way, I'll this,—he that first lights on him Holla the other . . . iii 1 53
These injuries the king now bears will be revenged home; there's part of a power already footed: we must incline to the king . iii 3 12
Though I die for it, as no less is threatened me, the king my old master must be relieved . . . . iii 3 19
Thou say'st the king grows mad; I'll tell thee, friend, I am almost mad myself . . . . iii 4 170
If I find him comforting the king, it will stuff his suspicion more fully iii 5 22
Tell me whether a madman be a gentleman or a yeoman?—A king, a king! . . . . iii 6 12
'Tis Goneril. I here take my oath before this honourable assembly, she kicked the poor king her father . . . . iii 6 50
How light and portable my pain seems now, When that which makes me bend makes the king bow! . . . . . iii 6 116
What will hap more to-night, safe 'scape the king! Lurk, lurk . iii 6 121
How now! where's the king?—My lord of Gloucester hath convey'd him hence . . . . iii 7 14
To whose hands have you sent the lunatic king? . . iii 7 46
Where hast thou sent the king?—To Dover.—Wherefore to Dover? . iii 7 50
I live To thank thee for the love thou show'dst the king . iv 2 96
It seem'd she was a queen Over her passion; who, most rebel-like, Sought to be king o'er her . . . . . iv 3 17
Was this before the king return'd?—No, since . . . iv 3 39
No, they cannot touch me for coining; I am the king himself . iv 6 84
Is't not the king?—Ay, every inch a king: When I do stare, see how the subject quakes . . . . . . iv 6 109
I will be jovial: come, come; I am a king, My masters, know you that iv 6 203
A sight most pitiful in the meanest wretch, Past speaking of in a king! iv 6 209
The king is mad: how stiff is my vile sense, That I stand up, and have ingenious feeling Of my huge sorrows! . . . . iv 6 286
How does the king?—Madam, sleeps still.—O you kind gods! . iv 7 12
So please your majesty That we may wake the king: he hath slept long iv 7 18
Sir, this I hear; the king is come to his daughter . . v 1 21
It toucheth us, as France invades our land, Not bolds the king . v 1 26
For thee, oppressed king, am I cast down; Myself could else out-frown false fortune's frown . . . . . . v 3 5
I thought it fit To send the old and miserable king To some retention . v 3 46
In disguise Follow'd his enemy king, and did him service Improper for a slave . . . . v 3 220
I am come To bid my king and master aye good night: Is he not here? v 3 235
Speak, Edmund, where's the king? and where's Cordelia? . v 3 237
Let me be married to three kings in a forenoon *Ant. and Cleo.* i 2 26
Three kings I had newly feasted, and did want Of what I was i' the morning . . . . ii 2 76
A hand that kings Have lipp'd, and trembled kissing . . ii 5 29
Who now are levying The kings o' the earth for war . . iii 6 68
To Cæsar will I render My legions and my horse: six kings already Show me the way of yielding . . . . . iii 10 34
Which had superfluous kings for messengers Not many moons gone by iii 12 5
Of late, when I cried 'Ho!' Like boys unto a muss, kings would start forth, And cry 'Your will?' . . . . . iii 13 91
You have served me well, And kings have been your fellows . iv 2 13
Hadst thou done so, The kings that have revolted, and the soldier That has this morning left thee, would have still Follow'd thy heels . iv 5 4
I'll give thee, friend, An armour all of gold; it was a king's . iv 8 27
The gods rebuke me, but it is tidings To wash the eyes of kings . v 1 28
And fitting for a princess Descended of so many royal kings . v 2 330

King. Our bloods No more obey the heavens than our courtiers Still seem as does the king . . . . . *Cymbeline* i 1 3
Though I think the king Be touch'd at very heart.—None but the king? i 1 9
Although they wear their faces to the bent Of the king's looks . i 1 14
The king he takes the babe To his protection . . . i 1 40
Is she sole child to the king?—His only child . . . i 1 56
So soon as I can win the offended king, I will be known your advocate i 1 75
Though the king Hath charged you should not speak together . i 1 82
If the king come, I shall incur I know not How much of his displeasure i 1 102
Alack, the king!—Thou basest thing, avoid! hence, from my sight! . i 1 124
Our great king himself doth woo me oft For my confections . i 5 14
It is a thing I made, which hath the king Five times redeem'd from death . . . . i 5 62
I'll move the king To any shape of thy preferment such As thou 'lt desire i 5 70
A lady So fair, and fasten'd to an empery, Would make the great'st king double . . . . i 6 121
The king my father shall be made acquainted Of thy assault . . i 6 149
You are most bound to the king, Who lets go by no vantages that may Prefer you to his daughter . . . . . ii 3 49
'Shrew me, If I would lose it for a revenue Of any king's in Europe ii 3 149
I would I were so sure To win the king as I am bold her honour Will remain hers . . . . ii 4 2
By this, your king Hath heard of great Augustus . . ii 4 10
Remember, sir, my liege, The kings your ancestors . . iii 1 17
The first of Britain which did put His brows within a golden crown and call'd Himself a king . . . . . . iii 1 62
Cæsar, that hath more kings his servants than Thyself domestic officers iii 1 64
These boys know little they are sons to the king . . iii 3 80
Polydore, The heir of Cymbeline and Britain, who The king his father call'd Guiderius . . . . iii 3 88
Kings, queens, and states, Maids, matrons, nay, the secrets of the grave This viperous slander enters . . . . . iii 4 39
Thou that didst set up My disobedience 'gainst the king my father . iii 4 91
Go in and cheer the king: he rages; none Dare come about him . iii 5 67
And falsehood Is worse in kings than beggars . . . iii 6 14
Shall find I love my country, Even to the note o' the king . . iv 3 44
There secure us. To the king's party there's no going . . iv 4 9
The king Hath not deserved my service nor your loves . . iv 4 24
The king himself Of his wings destitute, the army broken . . v 3 4
He brags his service As if he were of note: bring him to the king . v 3 94
Knock off his manacles; bring your prisoner to the king . v 4 200
Hail, great king! To sour your happiness, I must report The queen is dead . . . . v 5 25
Thou, king, send out for torturers ingenious . . . v 5 214
Stay, sir king: This man is better than the man he slew . v 5 301
Thou hadst, great king, a subject who Was call'd Belarius . v 5 316
He would have well becomed this place, and graced The thankings of a king . . . . v 5 407
This king unto him took a fere, Who died and left a female heir *Pericles* i Gower 21
Graces her subjects, and her thoughts the king Of every virtue! . . i 1 13
Great king, Few love to hear the sins they love to act . . i 1 91
Kings are earth's gods; in vice their law's their will . . i 1 103
They do abuse the king that flatter him . . . . i 2 38
Whereas reproof, obedient and in order, Fits kings, as they are men . i 2 43
Heaven forbid That kings should let their ears hear their faults hid! . i 2 62
That, being bid to ask what he would of the king, desired he might know none of his secrets . . . . . . i 3 6
If a king bid a man be a villain, he's bound by the indenture of his oath to be one . . . . i 3 8
Doth speak sufficiently he's gone to travel.—How! the king gone! . i 3 15
Here have you seen a mighty king His child, I wis, to incest bring ii Gower 1
He is a happy king, since he gains from his subjects the name of good . ii 1 109
It was sometime target to a king; I know it by this mark . ii 1 143
This wreath of victory I give, And crown you king of this day's happiness ii 3 11
Yon king's to me like to my father's picture . . . ii 3 37
The king my father, sir, has drunk to you.—I thank him . ii 3 75
Though This king were great, his greatness was no guard To bar heaven's shaft . . . . ii 4 14
Let me entreat you to Forbear the absence of your king . . ii 4 46
Even in his throat—unless it be the king—That calls me traitor, I return the lie . . . . ii 5 56
Our heir-apparent is a king! Who dream'd, who thought of such a thing? . . . . iii Gower 37
Who finds her, give her burying; She was the daughter of a king . iii 2 73
I love the king your father, and yourself, With more than foreign heart iv 1 33
Well-sailing ships and bounteous winds have brought This king to Tarsus . . . . iv 4 18
Sir, Our vessel is of Tyre, in it the king . . . . v 1 23
Sir king, all hail! the gods preserve you! Hail, royal sir! . . v 1 39
Let me entreat to know at large the cause Of your king's sorrow . v 1 63
My derivation was from ancestors Who stood equivalent with mighty kings . . . . v 1 92
Thou dost look Like Patience gazing on kings' graves . . v 1 139
The name Was given me by one that had some power, My father, and a king . . . . v 1 151
My mother was the daughter of a king; Who died the minute I was born . . . . v 1 159
The king my father did in Tarsus leave me . . . . v 1 172
And pretty din The regent made in Mytilene To greet the king . . v 2 274
At Ephesus, the temple see, Our king and all his company . . v 2 283
When we with tears parted Pentapolis, The king my father gave you such a ring . . . . v 3 39
King and queen. His daughter and I will be king and queen,—save our graces! . . . . *Tempest* iii 2 115
That they were living both in Naples, The king and queen there! . v 1 150
In that chair where kings and queens are crown'd . . *2 Hen. VI.* i 2 38
Ride unto Saint Alban's, Where as the king and queen do mean to hawk i 2 58
Say, what art thou that talk'st of kings and queens? *3 Hen. VI.* iii 1 55
Good morrow to my sovereign king and queen! . *Richard III.* ii 1 46
I know the good king and queen have sent for you . . *Hamlet* ii 2 291
Your secrecy to the king and queen moult no feather . . ii 2 306
The king and queen and all are coming down . . . v 2 212
King-becoming. The king-becoming graces, As justice, verity *Macbeth* iv 3 91
King-cardinal. This is the cardinal's doing, the king-cardinal *Hen. VIII.* ii 2 20
King Cerberus. Nay, rather damn them with King Cerberus *2 Hen. IV.* ii 4 182
King christen. Ne'er a king christen could be better bit *1 Hen. IV.* ii 1 19
King Cophetua. Let King Cophetua know the truth thereof. *2 Hen. IV.* v 3 106
King Henry the Fifth, too famous to live long! . . *1 Hen. VI.* i 1 6
King-killer. O thou sweet king-killer [gold]! . . *T. of Athens* iv 3 382

King of beasts. A lion and a king of beasts?—A king of beasts, indeed, if aught but beasts, I had been still a happy king of men *Richard II.* v 1 34
King of cats. What wouldst thou have with me?—Good king of cats, nothing but one of your nine lives . . . . *Rom. and Jul.* iii 1 80
King of codpieces, Sole imperator and great general . . *L. L. Lost* iii 1 186
King of courtesy. Yet I am the king of courtesy . . *1 Hen. IV.* ii 4 11
King of England. We are the king of England's subjects: For him, and in his right, we hold this town . . . . . *K. John* ii 1 267
Who's your king?—The king of England, when we know the king . ii 1 363
If that my cousin king be King of England, It must be granted I am Duke of Lancaster . . . . *Richard II.* ii 3 123
And when I am king of England, I shall command all the good lads in Eastcheap . . . . *1 Hen. IV.* ii 4 14
Never king of England Had nobles richer and more loyal subjects *Hen. V.* i 2 126
No king of England, if not king of France . . . . . ii 2 193
Ambassadors from Harry King of England Do crave admittance . . ii 4 65
What a wretched and peevish fellow is this king of England! . . iii 7 143
The lamentation of the French Invites the King of England's stay at home . . . . v Prol. 37
Third son to the third Edward King of England . . . *1 Hen. VI.* ii 4 84
Servant in arms to Harry King of England . . . . . iv 2 4
Great King of England and my gracious lord . . . *2 Hen. VI.* i 1 24
And she sent over of the King of England's own proper cost . . i 1 60
Where did you dwell when I was King of England? . *3 Hen. VI.* iii 1 74
King of England and France, and lord of Ireland . . . . iv 7 72
Bear him hence; And once again proclaim us king of England . iv 8 54
Henry King of England, come into the court . . . . *Hen. VIII.* ii 4 6
King of France. The daughter of the King of France, On serious business, craving quick dispatch . . . . . . *L. L. Lost* ii 1 30
So do the kings of France unto this day . . . . . *Hen. V.* i 2 90
No king of England, if not king of France . . . . . ii 2 193
My duty to you both, on equal love, Great Kings of France and England! v 2 24
The King of France, having any occasion to write for matter of grant . v 2 364
Henry the Sixth, in infant bands crown'd King Of France and England Epil. 9
Join'd with Charles, the rightful King of France . . *1 Hen. VI.* iv 1 60
In presence of the Kings of France and Sicil . . . *2 Hen. VI.* i 1 6
No, mighty King of France: now Margaret Must strike her sail *3 Hen. VI.* iii 3 4
To the king of France Hath pawn'd the Sicils and Jerusalem . . . v 7 38
Betroth'd To Bona, sister to the King of France . . *Richard III.* iii 7 182
Why the King of France is so suddenly gone back know you the reason? *Lear* iv 3 1
King of gods. Forget that thou art Jove, the king of gods *Troi. and Cres.* ii 3 12
Thou king of gods, Why hast thou thus adjourn'd The graces? *Cymbeline* v 4 77
King of heaven. The king of heaven forbid our lord the king Should so with civil and uncivil arms Be rush'd upon! . . . *Richard II.* iii 3 101
O, he was gentle, mild, and virtuous!—The fitter for the King of heaven, that hath him . . . . *Richard III.* i 2 105
King of honour. Thou art the king of honour . . . *1 Hen. IV.* iv 1 10
King of kings. He was a king bless'd of the King of kings . *1 Hen. VI.* i 1 28
The great King of kings Hath in the tables of his law commanded That thou shalt do no murder . . . . . . *Richard III.* i 4 200
Take heed you dally not before your king; Lest he that is the supreme King of kings Confound your hidden falsehood . . . . ii 1 13
His sons he there proclaim'd the kings of kings . . *Ant. and Cleo.* iii 6 13
King of men. A king of beasts, indeed; if aught but beasts, I had been still a happy king of men . . . . . . *Richard II.* v 1 36
Time's the king of men, He's both their parent, and he is their grave *Pericles* ii 3 45
King of Naples. Was Milan thrust from Milan, that his issue Should become king of Naples? . . . . . . *Tempest* v 1 206
Her father is a king, The King of Naples and Jerusalem . . *1 Hen. VI.* v 5 39
King of Naples, Of both the Sicils and Jerusalem . . *3 Hen. VI.* i 4 121
King of Scots. Not only well defended But taken and impounded as a stray The King of Scots . . . . *Hen. V.* i 2 161
King of shadows. Believe me, king of shadows, I mistook *M. N. Dream* iii 2 347
King of shreds. A king of shreds and patches . . . *Hamlet* iii 4 102
King of smiles. Where I first bow'd my knee Unto this king of smiles, this Bolingbroke . . . . *1 Hen. IV.* i 3 246
King of snow. O that I were a mockery king of snow! . *Richard II.* iv 1 260
King of thoughts. By Jove, I wonder, that is king of thoughts, These cates resist me, she but thought upon . . . . *Pericles* ii 3 28
King Stephano! O peer! O worthy Stephano! . . . *Tempest* iv 1 221
King Stephen was a worthy peer . . . . . . *Othello* ii 3 92
King's coin. You have caused Your holy hat to be stamp'd on the king's coin . . . . *Hen. VIII.* iii 2 325
King's crown. Not the king's crown, nor the deputed sword . *M. for M.* ii 2 60
King's daughter. A great king's daughter, The mother to a hopeful prince *W. Tale* iii 2 40
The oracle is fulfilled; the king's daughter is found . . . . v 2 25
Other evidences proclaim her with all certainty to be the king's daughter v 2 43
This matter of marrying his king's daughter . . . *Cymbeline* i 4 14
She was of Tyrus the king's daughter, On whom foul death hath made this slaughter . . . . *Pericles* iv 4 36
How! a king's daughter? And call'd Marina? . . . . . v 1 151
King's English. Here will be an old abusing of God's patience and the king's English . . . . *Mer. Wives* i 4 6
King's highway. Or I'll be buried in the king's highway . *Richard II.* iii 3 155
King's jester. Yorick's skull, the king's jester . . . *Hamlet* v 1 199
King's justices. One of the king's justices of the peace . *2 Hen. IV.* iii 2 64
King's King. Say that the king, which may command, entreats.—That at her hands which the king's King forbids . . *Richard III.* iv 4 346
King's majesty. The king's majesty Commends his good opinion of you *Hen. VIII.* ii 3 60
King's mess. Let a beast be lord of beasts, and his crib shall stand at the king's mess . . . . *Hamlet* v 2 89
King's name. Is not the king's name twenty thousand names? *Richard II.* iii 2 85
In God's name, lead; your king's name be obey'd . . *3 Hen. VI.* iii 1 99
Besides, the king's name is a tower of strength . . *Richard III.* v 3 12
King's press. I have misused the king's press damnably . *1 Hen. IV.* iv 2 13
King's seas. But since he's gone, the king's seas must please *Pericles* i 3 28
King's secretary. Newly preferr'd from the king's secretary *Hen. VIII.* iv 1 102
Is made master O' the rolls, and the king's secretary . . . . v 1 35
King's son. The king's son, Ferdinand, With hair up-staring . *Tempest* i 2 212
The king's son have I landed by himself . . . . i 2 221
The king's son took me by the hand, and called me brother . *W. Tale* v 2 151
I'll be damned for never a king's son in Christendom . . *1 Hen. IV.* i 2 109
I prithee, good Prince Hal, help me to my horse, good king's son . . ii 2 44
A king's son! If I do not beat thee out of thy kingdom with a dagger of lath . . . . ii 4 150
King's son. Bear the king's son's body Before our army . *Ant. and Cleo.* iii 1 3
King's tavern. 'Tis going to the king's exchequer.—You lie, ye rogue; 'tis going to the king's tavern . . . . . . *1 Hen. IV.* ii 2 58
Kingdom. This will prove a brave kingdom to me, where I shall have my music for nothing . . . . *Tempest* iii 2 153
Help to bear this away where my hogshead of wine is, or I'll turn you out of my kingdom . . . . iv 1 253
For a score of kingdoms you should wrangle, And I would call it fair play v 1 174
A true-devoted pilgrim is not weary To measure kingdoms *T. G. of Ver.* ii 7 10
Give me that boy . . .—Not for thy fairy kingdom . *M. N. Dream* ii 1 144
The watery kingdom, whose ambitious head Spits in the face of heaven, is no bar To stop the foreign spirits . . . *Mer. of Venice* ii 7 44
That would I, had I kingdoms to give with her . . . *As Y. Like It* v 4 8
That would I, were I of all kingdoms king . . . . . . v 4 10
Thereby for sealing The injury of tongues in courts and kingdoms *W. Tale* i 2 338
And so still think of The wrong I did myself; which was so much, That heirless it hath made my kingdom . . . . v 1 10
What dangers, by his highness' fail of issue, May drop upon his kingdom v 1 28
With your crown'd brother and these your contracted Heirs of your kingdoms . . . . v 3 6
The manage of two kingdoms must With fearful bloody issue arbitrate *K. John* i 1 37
Give grandam kingdom, and it grandam will Give it a plum, a cherry . ii 1 161
In dreadful trial of our kingdom's king . . . . ii 1 286
Law cannot give my child his kingdom here, For he that holds his kingdom holds the law . . . . iii 1 187
Peace, amity, true love Between our kingdoms and our royal selves . iii 1 232
The inheritance of this poor child, His little kingdom of a forced grave iv 2 98
This fleshly land, This kingdom, this confine of blood and breath . iv 2 246
Your breath first kindled the dead coal of wars Between this chastised kingdom and myself . . . . v 2 84
Nor let my kingdom's rivers take their course Through my burn'd bosom v 7 38
Were he my brother, nay, my kingdom's heir . . . . *Richard II.* i 1 116
For that our kingdom's earth should not be soil'd With that dear blood which it hath fostered . . . . i 3 125
Thy word is current with him for my death, But dead, thy kingdom cannot buy my breath . . . . i 3 232
I weep for joy To stand upon my kingdom once again . . . iii 2 5
Say, is my kingdom lost? why, 'twas my care; And what loss is it to be rid of care? . . . . iii 2 95
My large kingdom for a little grave, A little little grave, an obscure grave iii 3 153
If I do not beat thee out of thy kingdom with a dagger of lath *1 Hen. IV.* ii 4 151
Through all the kingdoms that acknowledge Christ . . . . iii 2 111
If we without his help can make a head To push against a kingdom, with his help We shall o'erturn it topsy-turvy down . . . iv 1 81
When that this body did contain a spirit, A kingdom for it was too small v 4 90
Which is almost to pluck a kingdom down And set another up *2 Hen. IV.* i 3 49
And God knows, whether those that bawl out the ruins of thy linen shall inherit his kingdom . . . . ii 2 28
Then you perceive the body of our kingdom How foul it is . . . iii 1 38
It [sherris] illumineth the face, which as a beacon gives warning to all the rest of this little kingdom, man, to arm . . . . . iv 3 118
O my poor kingdom, sick with civil blows! . . . . . . iv 5 134
A kingdom for a stage, princes to act And monarchs to behold *Hen. V.* Prol. 3
For never two such kingdoms did contend Without much fall of blood . i 2 24
The Scot on his unfurnish'd kingdom Came pouring, like the tide . i 2 148
Creatures that by a rule in nature teach The act of order to a peopled kingdom . . . . i 2 189
You would have sold your king to slaughter . . . And his whole kingdom into desolation . . . . ii 2 173
We our kingdom's safety must so tender, Whose ruin you have sought, that to her laws We do deliver you . . . . ii 2 175
For peace itself should not so dull a kingdom . . . . . ii 4 16
He bids you then resign Your crown and kingdom . . . . . ii 4 94
For when lenity and cruelty play for a kingdom, the gentler gamester is the soonest winner . . . . iii 6 119
For the effusion of our blood, the muster of his kingdom too faint a number . . . . iii 6 139
It is as easy for me, Kate, to conquer the kingdom as to speak so much more French . . . . v 2 196
That the contending kingdoms Of France and England, whose very shores look pale With envy of each other's happiness, May cease their hatred v 2 377
As man and wife, being two, are one in love, So be there 'twixt your kingdoms such a spousal, That never may ill office, or fell jealousy, Which troubles oft the bed of blessed marriage, Thrust in between the paction of these kingdoms, To make divorce of their incorporate league . . . . v 2 390
The Turk, that two and fifty kingdoms hath, Writes not so tedious a style as this . . . . *1 Hen. VI.* iv 7 73
The Frenchmen's only scourge, Your kingdom's terror and black Nemesis iv 7 78
Had Henry got an empire by his marriage, And all the wealthy kingdoms of the west, There's reason he should be displeased at it . *2 Hen. VI.* i 1 154
By her I claim the kingdom: she was heir To Roger Earl of March . ii 2 47
Richard Plantagenet, Enjoy the kingdom after my decease . *3 Hen. VI.* i 1 175
But for a kingdom any oath may be broken . . . . . . i 2 16
For chair and dukedom, throne and kingdom say; Either that is thine, or else thou wert not his . . . . ii 1 93
Well, say there is no kingdom then for Richard; What other pleasure? iii 2 146
You tell a pedigree Of threescore and two years; a silly time To make prescription for a kingdom's worth . . . . iii 3 94
Though I want a kingdom, yet in marriage I may not prove inferior to yourself . . . . iv 1 121
How should you govern any kingdom, That know not how to use ambassadors? . . . . iv 3 35
'Twas I that gave the kingdom to thy brother.—Why then 'tis mine . v 1 34
I am too childish-foolish for this world.—Hie thee to hell for shame, and leave the world, Thou cacodemon! there thy kingdom is *Richard III.* i 3 144
A husband and a son thou owest to me; And thou a kingdom . . i 3 171
That Henry's death, my lovely Edward's death, Their kingdom's loss . i 3 193
Unto the kingdom of perpetual night . . . . i 4 47
Like obedient subjects, follow him To his new kingdom of perpetual rest ii 2 46
My kingdom stands on brittle glass . . . . iv 2 62
And by their uncle cozen'd Of comfort, kingdom, kindred, freedom, life iv 4 223
If I did take the kingdom from your sons, To make amends, I'll give it to your daughter . . . . iv 4 294
A horse! a horse! my kingdom for a horse! . . . . . . v 4 7; 13
There will be The beauty of this kingdom, I'll assure you . *Hen. VIII.* i 3 54
You're welcome, Most learned reverend sir, into our kingdom: Use us and it . . . . ii 2 77

Kingdom. All the clerks, I mean the learned ones, in Christian kingdoms *Hen. VIII.* ii 2 93
This was a judgement on me; that my kingdom, Well worthy the best heir o' the world, should not Be gladded in't by me . . ii 4 194
Shipwreck'd upon a kingdom, where no pity, No friends, no hope . . iii 1 149
To the mere undoing Of all the kingdom . . . . . iii 2 330
Those things you have done of late, By your power legatine, within this kingdom . . . . . . iii 2 339
With all the choicest music of the kingdom, Together sung 'Te Deum' iv 1 91
One that, by suggestion, Tied all the kingdom . . . iv 2 36
When I shall dwell with worms, and my poor name Banish'd the kingdom iv 2 127
Now, sir, you speak of two The most remark'd i' the kingdom . v 1 33
I swear he is true-hearted; and a soul None better in my kingdom . v 1 155
I am Revenge; sent from the infernal kingdom . . *T. Andron.* v 2 30
She whom mighty kingdoms court'sy to . . . . . v 3 74
I could deal kingdoms to my friends, And ne'er be weary *T. of Athens* i 2 226
The state of man, Like to a little kingdom . . *J. Cæsar* ii 1 68
And every one did bear Thy praises in his kingdom's great defence *Macb.* i 3 99
Shall Banquo's issue ever Reign in this kingdom? . . . iv 1 103
The time is free: I see thee compass'd with thy kingdom's pearl . v 8 56
And our whole kingdom To be contracted in one brow of woe *Hamlet* i 2 3
Fortinbras Craves the conveyance of a promised march Over his kingdom . . . . iv 4 4
We will our kingdom give, Our crown, our life, and all that we call ours . . . . iv 5 207
High and mighty, You shall know I am set naked on your kingdom . iv 7 44
I have some rights of memory in this kingdom . . . v 2 400
In the division of the kingdom, it appears not which of the dukes he values most; for equalities are so weighed . . . *Lear* i 1 4
Know that we have divided In three our kingdom . . . i 1 39
To thee and thine hereditary ever Remain this ample third of our fair kingdom . . . . i 1 82
Turn thy hated back Upon our kingdom . . . . . i 1 179
His picture I will send far and near, that all the kingdom May have due note of him . . . . ii 1 84
Thy half o' the kingdom hast thou not forgot, Wherein I thee endow'd. ii 4 183
From France there comes a power Into this scatter'd kingdom . iii 1 31
I never gave you kingdom, call'd you children, You owe me no subscription . . . . iii 2 17
What confederacy have you with the traitors Late footed in the kingdom? . . . . iii 7 45
Which imports to the kingdom so much fear and danger . . iv 3 5
Am I in France?—In your own kingdom, sir.—Do not abuse me . iv 7 76
'Tis time to look about; the powers of the kingdom approach apace . iv 7 93
Do this, or this; Take in that kingdom, and enfranchise that *Ant. and Cleo.* i 1 23
Kingdoms are clay: our dungy earth alike Feeds beast as man . i 1 35
To give a kingdom for a mirth . . . . . . i 4 18
To mend the petty present, I will piece Her opulent throne with kingdoms . . . . i 5 46
Let her live To join our kingdoms and our hearts . . . ii 2 154
I grant him part; but then, in his Armenia, And other of his conquer'd kingdoms, I Demand the like . . . . . iii 6 36
A charge we bear i' the war, And, as the president of my kingdom, will Appear there for a man . . . . . . iii 7 18
We have kiss'd away Kingdoms and provinces . . . . iii 10 8
Cæsar's father oft, When he hath mused of taking kingdoms in, Bestow'd his lips on that unworthy place, As it rain'd kisses . iii 13 83
Majesty, to keep decorum, must No less beg than a kingdom . v 2 18
His daughter, and the heir of's kingdom . . . *Cymbeline* i 1 4
To be styled The under-hangman of his kingdom . . . ii 3 135
There's no more tribute to be paid: our kingdom is stronger than it was . . . . iii 1 35
I am brought hither Among the Italian gentry, and to fight Against my lady's kingdom . . . . v 1 19
Thou hast lost by this a kingdom.—No, my lord; I have got two worlds by't . . . . v 5 373
This kingdom is without a head,—Like goodly buildings left without a roof Soon fall to ruin . . . . . *Pericles* ii 4 35
When peers thus knit, a kingdom ever stands . . . . ii 4 58
The heir of kingdoms and another like To Pericles thy father . v 1 209
And ourselves Will in that kingdom spend our following days . v 3 81
Kingdom'd Achilles in commotion rages . . . *Troi. and Cres.* ii 3 185
King'd of our fears, until our fears, resolved, Be by some certain king purged and deposed . . . . . *K. John* ii 1 371
Then am I king'd again: and by and by Think that I am unking'd *Richard II.* v 5 36
She is so idly king'd, Her sceptre so fantastically borne . *Hen. V.* ii 4 26
Kingly. To see no woman; Flat treason 'gainst the kingly state of youth *L. L. Lost* iv 3 293
Then shalt thou give me with thy kingly hand What husband in thy power I will command. . . . . *All's Well* ii 1 196
To my kingly guest Unclasp'd my practice . . *W. Tale* iii 2 167
Let not the world see fear and sad distrust Govern the motion of a kingly eye: Be stirring as the time . . . *K. John* v 1 47
I'll pine away; A king, woe's slave, shall kingly woe obey *Richard II.* iii 2 210
The pride of kingly sway from out my heart . . . iv 1 206
But here is Carlisle living, to abide Thy kingly doom . . v 6 23
O thou dull god, why liest thou with the vile In loathsome beds, and leavest the kingly couch A watch-case or a common 'larum-bell? *2 Hen. IV.* iii 1 16
Ruling . . . O'er France and all her almost kingly dukedoms *Hen. V.* i 2 227
I give thee kingly thanks, Because this is in traffic of a king . *1 Hen. VI.* v 3 163
I am far better born than is the king, More like a king, more kingly in my thoughts . . . . . . *2 Hen. VI.* v 1 29
Think'st thou that I will leave my kingly throne? . . *3 Hen. VI.* i 1 124
Draw thy sword in right.—My gracious father, by your kingly leave, I'll draw it as apparent to the crown . . . . . ii 2 63
The wrinkles in my brows, now fill'd with blood, Were liken'd oft to kingly sepulchres; For who lived king, but I could dig his grave? v 2 20
Warwick and Montague, That in their chains fetter'd the kingly lion . v 7 11
We heartily solicit Your gracious self to take on you the charge And kingly government of this your land . . . *Richard III.* iii 7 132
I salute you with this kingly title: Long live Richard, England's royal king! . . . . iii 7 239
I mean the lord protector.—The Lord protect him from that kingly title! . . . . iv 1 20
The crown, usurp'd, disgraced his kingly glory . . . iv 4 371
By my life And kingly dignity, we are contented To wear our mortal state to come with her . . . . . *Hen. VIII.* ii 4 227

Kingly. May one, that is a herald and a prince, Do a fair message to his kingly ears?—With surety . . . *Troi. and Cres.* i 3 219
I thrice presented him a kingly crown, Which he did thrice refuse *J. C.* iii 2 101
To-morrow shall I beg leave to see your kingly eyes . *Hamlet* iv 7 45
This kingly seal And plighter of high hearts . . *Ant. and Cleo.* iii 13 125
Galling His kingly hands, haling ropes . . . *Pericles* iv 1 55
Fair one, all goodness that consists in bounty Expect even here, where is a kingly patient . . . . v 1 71
Kingly-crowned. The kingly-crowned head, the vigilant eye . *Coriolanus* i 1 119
Kingly-poor. O poverty in wit, kingly-poor flout! . . *L. L. Lost* v 2 269
Kinsman. My kinsman shall speak for himself. . . *Mer. Wives* iii 4 23
Were he my kinsman, brother, or my son, It should be thus . *M. for M.* ii 2 81
Dull melancholy, Kinsman to grim and comfortless despair *Com. of Errors* v 1 80
But in that thou art like to be my kinsman, live unbruised . *Much Ado* v 4 112
That have I told my love, In glory of my kinsman Hercules *M. N. Dream* v 1 47
Here comes Bassanio, your most noble kinsman . . *Mer. of Venice* i 1 57
Holla, you clown!—Peace, fool: he's not thy kinsman . *As Y. Like It* ii 4 67
Commend me to my kinsmen and my son . . . . *All's Well* ii 2 68
To speak of him as my kinsman, he's a most notable coward . . iii 6 10
Who of my people hold him in delay?—Sir Toby, madam, your kinsman *T. Night* i 5 113
Though she harbours you as her kinsman, she's nothing allied to your disorders . . . . ii 3 104
I know my place as I would they should do theirs, to ask for my kinsman . . . . ii 5 61
Be opposite with a kinsman, surly with servants . . . ii 5 162; iii 4 77
I am sorry, madam, I have hurt your kinsman . . . . v 1 216
I have a kinsman not past three quarters of a mile hence . *W. Tale* iv 3 85
Come hither, little kinsman; hark, a word . . . *K. John* iii 3 18
Gentle kinsman, go, And thrust thyself into their companies . . iv 2 166
Your valiant kinsman, Faulconbridge, Desires your majesty to leave the field . . . . v 3 5
And let him be no kinsman to my liege . . . *Richard II.* i 1 59
But 'tis doubt . . . Whether our kinsman come to see his friends . . i 4 22
By the robbing of the banish'd duke.—His noble kinsman . . . ii 1 262
Both are my kinsmen: The one is my sovereign . . . . ii 2 111
My kinsman, whom the king hath wrong'd, Whom conscience and my kindred bids to right . . . . ii 2 114
There lies Two kinsmen digg'd their graves with weeping eyes . . iii 3 169
Farewell, kinsman: I'll talk to you When you are better temper'd *1 Hen. IV.* i 3 234
His kinsman March, Who is, if every owner were well placed, Indeed his king . . . . iv 3 93
Turn our offers contrary? Misuse the tenour of thy kinsman's trust? . v 5 5
Art thou his friend?—And his kinsman too . . . *Hen. V.* iv 1 59
My good Lord Exeter, And my kind kinsman, warriors all, adieu! . iv 3 10
Both are my kinsmen, and I love them both . . *1 Hen. VI.* ii 5 155
Our kinsman Gloucester is as innocent From meaning treason *2 Hen. VI.* iii 1 69
Of thee and these thy sons, Thy kinsmen and thy friends, I'll have more lives Than drops of blood were in my father's veins *3 Hen. VI.* i 1 96
Then is he more beholding to you than I.—He may command me as my sovereign; But you have power in me as in a kinsman *Richard III.* iii 1 109
I do know Kinsmen of mine, three at the least, that have By this so sicken'd their estates, that never They shall abound as formerly *Hen. VIII.* i 1 81
And, kinsmen, then we may go pipe for justice . . *T. Andron.* iv 3 24
Kinsmen, his sorrows are past remedy. Join with the Goths . . iv 3 31
Kinsmen, shoot all your shafts into the court . . . . iv 3 61
Here comes one of my master's kinsmen . . . . *Rom. and Jul.* i 1 66
Why, how now, kinsman! wherefore storm you so? . . . . i 5 62
The place death, considering who thou art, If any of my kinsmen find thee . . . . ii 2 65
Thy kinsmen are no let to me.—If they do see thee, they will murder thee . . . . ii 2 69
Tybalt, the kinsman of old Capulet, Hath sent a letter . . . ii 4 6
My reputation stain'd With Tybalt's slander,—Tybalt, that an hour Hath been my kinsman! O sweet Juliet! . . . . . iii 1 118
There lies the man, slain by young Romeo, That slew thy kinsman . iii 1 150
O prince! O cousin! husband! O, the blood is spilt Of my dear kinsman! . . . . iii 1 153
He is a kinsman to the Montague; Affection makes him false . . iii 1 181
Did murder her; as that name's cursed hand Murder'd her kinsman . iii 3 105
She loved her kinsman Tybalt dearly, And so did I . . . iii 4 3
It may be thought we held him carelessly, Being our kinsman, if we revel much . . . . iii 4 26
I never shall be satisfied With Romeo, till I behold him—dead—Is my poor heart so for a kinsman vex'd . . . . . iii 5 96
With some great kinsman's bone, As with a club, dash out my desperate brains . . . . iv 3 53
Let me peruse this face. Mercutio's kinsman, noble County Paris! . v 3 75
And I for winking at your discords too Have lost a brace of kinsmen . v 3 295
Sons, kinsmen, thanes, And you whose places are the nearest *Macbeth* i 4 35
It is a peerless kinsman . . . . i 4 58
He's here in double trust; First, as I am his kinsman and his subject . i 7 13
My thanes and kinsmen, Henceforth be earls . . . . . v 8 62
Proclaim him in the streets; incense her kinsmen . . . *Othello* i 1 69
I have a kinsman who Is bound for Italy . . . . *Cymbeline* iii 6 61
Whose kinsmen have made suit That their good souls may be appeased with slaughter Of you their captives . . . . . . v 5 71
Kinswoman. Slandered, scorned, dishonoured my kinswoman *Much Ado* iv 1 305
A proper gentlewoman, sir, and a kinswoman of my master's *2 Hen. IV.* ii 2 169
She is my kinswoman; I would not, as they term it, praise her *T. and C.* i 1 44
Kirtle. What stuff wilt have a kirtle of? . . . . *2 Hen. IV.* ii 4 297
Kiss. I can swim like a duck, I'll be sworn.—Here, kiss the book *Tempest* ii 2 135
Swear to that; kiss the book: I will furnish it anon with new contents ii 2 145
I'll show thee every fertile inch o' th' island; And I will kiss thy foot ii 2 153
Will scratch the nurse And presently all humbled kiss the rod *T. G. of V.* i 2 59
I'll kiss each several paper for amends . . . . . . i 2 108
Till thy wound be throughly heal'd; And thus I search it with a sovereign kiss . . . . i 2 116
Thus will I fold them one upon another: Now kiss, embrace, contend . i 2 129
And seal the bargain with a holy kiss . . . . . ii 2 7
Now should I kiss my father; well, he weeps on . . . ii 3 28
My mother: O, that she could speak now like a wood woman! Well, I kiss her. . . . . ii 3 31
Lest the base earth Should from her vesture chance to steal a kiss . ii 4 160
Giving a gentle kiss to every sedge He overtaketh in his pilgrimage . ii 7 29
But my kisses bring again, bring again; Seals of love *Meas. for Meas.* iv 1 5
Stop his mouth with a kiss, and let not him speak . . . *Much Ado* ii 1 322
I will kiss your hand, and so I leave you . . . . . iv 1 336

Kiss. And thereupon I will kiss thee . . . . . . *Much Ado* v 2 51
Give him for my sake but one loving kiss . . . . *L. L. Lost* ii 1 248
To see him kiss his hand! and how most sweetly a' will swear! . . iv 1 148
So sweet a kiss the golden sun gives not To those fresh morning drops iv 3 26
Strucken blind Kisses the base ground with obedient breast . . . iv 3 225
The stairs, as he treads on them, kiss his feet . . . . . v 2 330
I will kiss thy royal finger, and take leave . . . . . v 2 891
O, let me kiss This princess of pure white, this seal of bliss! *M. N. D.* iii 2 143
Stick musk-roses in thy sleek smooth head, And kiss thy fair large ears iv 1 4
O, kiss me through the hole of this vile wall!—I kiss the wall's hole, not your lips at all . . . . v 1 202
Vailing her high-top lower than her ribs To kiss her burial *Mer. of Venice* i 1 29
From the four corners of the earth they come, To kiss this shrine . . ii 7 40
Some there be that shadows kiss; Such have but a shadow's bliss . . ii 9 66
Turn you where your lady is And claim her with a loving kiss . . iii 2 139
In such a night as this, When the sweet wind did gently kiss the trees v 1 2
You salute not at the court, but you kiss your hands *As Y. Like It* iii 2 50
Would you have us kiss tar? The courtier's hands are perfumed with civet . . . . iii 2 65
His kisses are Judas's own children . . . . iii 4 10
A nun of winter's sisterhood kisses not more religiously . . . iii 4 17
I would kiss before I spoke.—Nay, you were better speak first, and when you were gravelled for lack of matter, you might take occasion to kiss . . . . iv 1 72
For lovers lacking—God warn us!—matter, the cleanliest shift is to kiss.—How if the kiss be denied?—Then she puts you to entreaty . iv 1 78
If I were a woman I would kiss as many of you as had beards that pleased me . . . . Epil. 19
With kind embracements, tempting kisses . . . *T. of Shrew* Ind. 1 118
She hung about my neck; and kiss on kiss She vied so fast . . ii 1 310
And kiss me, Kate, we will be married o' Sunday . . . . ii 1 326
Bid good morrow to my bride, And seal the title with a lovely kiss . iii 2 125
Let them curtsy with their left legs and not presume to touch a hair of my master's horse-tail till they kiss their hands . . . iv 1 97
Bid my cousin Ferdinand come hither: One, Kate, that you must kiss iv 1 155
See, how they kiss and court! . . . . iv 2 27
First kiss me, Kate, and we will.—What, in the midst of the street?—What, art thou ashamed of me?—No, sir, God forbid; but ashamed to kiss . . . . v 1 148
Let's away.—Nay, I will give thee a kiss: now pray thee, love, stay . v 1 153
Very well mended. Kiss him for that, good widow . . . . v 2 25
Why, there's a wench! Come on, and kiss me, Kate . . . . v 2 180
To join like likes and kiss like native things . . . *All's Well* i 1 238
He that loves my flesh and blood is my friend: ergo, he that kisses my wife is my friend . . . . i 3 53
He that cannot make a leg, put off's cap, kiss his hand and say nothing, has neither leg, hands, lip, nor cap . . . . . . ii 2 10
Strangers and foes do sunder, and not kiss . . . . . ii 5 91
Men are to mell with, boys are not to kiss . . . . . iv 3 257
Come kiss me, sweet and twenty, Youth's a stuff will not endure *T. N.* ii 3 52
Why dost thou smile so and kiss thy hand so oft? . . . . iii 4 36
Conclusions to be as kisses, if your four negatives make your two affirmatives . . . . v 1 23
Our praises are our wages: you may ride's With one soft kiss a thousand furlongs ere With spur we heat an acre . . . *W. Tale* i 2 95
You'll kiss me hard and speak to me as if I were a baby still . . ii 1 5
I think there is not half a kiss to choose Who loves another best . . iv 4 175
Kisses the hands Of your fresh princess . . . . . . iv 4 561
Never saw I Wretches so quake: they kneel, they kiss the earth . . v 1 199
The stars, I see, will kiss the valleys first . . . . . v 1 206
Dear queen, that ended when I but began, Give me that hand of yours to kiss . . . . v 3 46
Let no man mock me, For I will kiss her . . . . . . v 3 80
The ruddiness upon her lip is wet; You'll mar it if you kiss it . . v 3 82
Upon thy cheek lay I this zealous kiss, As seal to this indenture *K. John* ii 1 19
And kiss him with a glorious victory . . . . . . ii 1 394
So, I kiss your hand.—Farewell, gentle cousin.—Coz, farewell . . iii 3 16
I will kiss thy detestable bones And put my eyeballs in thy vaulty brows . . . . iii 4 29
Shall revolt from him And kiss the lips of unacquainted change . . iii 4 166
Nor entreat the north To make his bleak winds kiss my parched lips . v 7 40
Let me kiss my sovereign's hand, And bow my knee . . *Richard II.* i 3 46
The appellant in all duty greets your highness, And craves to kiss your hand . . . . i 3 53
Henry Bolingbroke On both his knees doth kiss King Richard's hand . iii 3 36
Thy thrice noble cousin Harry Bolingbroke doth humbly kiss thy hand iii 3 104
Take thy correction mildly, kiss the rod . . . . . . v 1 32
Let me unkiss the oath 'twixt thee and me; And yet not so, for with a kiss 'twas made . . . . v 1 75
One kiss shall stop our mouths, and dumbly part . . . . . v 1 95
Didst thou never see Titan kiss a dish of butter? . . *1 Hen. IV.* ii 4 133
I understand thy kisses and thou mine, And that's a feeling disputation iii 1 205
And posted day and night To meet you on the way, and kiss your hand v 1 36
Let heaven kiss earth! . . . . *2 Hen. IV.* i 1 153
But look you pray, all you that kiss my lady Peace at home, that our armies join not in a hot day . . . . i 2 232
And didst thou not kiss me and bid me fetch thee thirty shillings? . ii 1 110
Sweet knight, I kiss thy neif: what! we have seen the seven stars . ii 4 200
Kiss me, Doll.—Saturn and Venus this year in conjunction! . . . ii 4 285
Flattering busses.—By my troth, I kiss thee with a most constant heart . . . . ii 4 292
Necessity so bow'd the state That I and greatness were compell'd to kiss . . . . iii 1 74
Prince John your son doth kiss your grace's hand . . . . . iv 4 83
I cannot kiss, that is the humour of it . . . . *Hen. V.* ii 3 63
I kiss his dirty shoe, and from heart-string I love the lovely bully . iv 1 47
Kisses the gashes That bloodily did yawn upon his face . . . . iv 6 13
Upon that I kiss your hand, and I call you my queen . . . . v 2 271
Then I will kiss your lips, Kate . . . . v 2 278
I cannot tell vat is baiser en Anglish.—To kiss . . . . . v 2 287
It is not a fashion for the maids in France to kiss before they are married . . . . v 2 290
Upholding the nice fashion of your country in denying me a kiss . . v 2 300
Bear me witness all, That here I kiss her as my sovereign queen . . v 2 386
O, tell me when my lips do touch his cheeks, That I may kindly give one fainting kiss . . . . *1 Hen. VI.* ii 5 40
I kiss these fingers for eternal peace . . . . v 3 48
I can express no kinder sign of love Than this kind kiss . *2 Hen. VI.* i 1 19
Fain would I go to chafe his paly lips With twenty thousand kisses . iii 2 142
O, could this kiss be printed in thy hand! . . . . . . iii 2 343

Kiss. Embrace and kiss and take ten thousand leaves . *2 Hen. VI.* iii 2 354
Let them kiss one another, for they loved well when they were alive . iv 7 138
And at every corner have them kiss . . . . iv 7 145
See, see! they join, embrace, and seem to kiss . . . *3 Hen. VI.* ii 1 29
Humbly to kiss your hand and with my tongue To tell the passion . . iii 3 61
In sign of truth, I kiss your highness' hand . . . . . iv 8 26
Come hither, Bess, and let me kiss my boy . . . . . . v 7 15
Clarence and Gloucester, love my lovely queen; And kiss your princely nephew . . . . v 7 27
And, that I love the tree from whence thou sprang'st, Witness the loving kiss I give the fruit . . . . v 7 32
I'll kiss thy hand, In sign of league and amity . . *Richard III.* i 3 280
Let him kiss your hand; And what you do, do it unfeignedly . . ii 1 21
For joy of this good news, Give Mistress Shore one gentle kiss the more iii 1 185
Bear her my true love's kiss; and so, farewell . . . . . iv 4 430
Just as I do now, He would kiss you twenty with a breath *Hen. VIII.* i 4 30
Sweetheart, I were unmannerly, to take you out, And not to kiss you . i 4 96
The hearts of princes kiss obedience, So much they love it . . . iii 1 162
With this kiss take my blessing: God protect thee! . . . . v 5 11
Rub on, and kiss the mistress. How now! a kiss in fee-farm! *T. and C.* iii 2 52
I do beseech you, pardon me; 'Twas not my purpose, thus to beg a kiss iii 2 145
As many farewells as be stars in heaven, With distinct breath and consign'd kisses to them . . . . iv 4 47
Scants us with a single famish'd kiss, Distasted with the salt of broken tears . . . . iv 4 49
Come, kiss; and let us part . . . . iv 4 100
Sweet lady.—Our general doth salute you with a kiss . . . . iv 5 19
The first was Menelaus' kiss; this, mine: Patroclus kisses you.—O, this is trim!—Paris and I kiss evermore for him.—I'll have my kiss, sir . . . . iv 5 32
The kiss you take is better than you give; Therefore no kiss . . iv 5 38
May I, sweet lady, beg a kiss of you?—You may.—I do desire it.—Why, beg, then . . . . iv 5 47
Why then for Venus' sake, give me a kiss, When Helen is a maid again iv 5 49
Claim it when 'tis due.—Never's my day, and then a kiss of you . . iv 5 52
Yond towers, whose wanton tops do buss the clouds, Must kiss their own feet . . . . iv 5 221
Takes my glove, And gives memorial dainty kisses to it, As I kiss thee v 2 81
To the wanton spoil Of Phœbus' burning kisses . . . *Coriolanus* ii 1 234
O, a kiss Long as my exile, sweet as my revenge! . . . . . v 3 44
That kiss I carried from thee, dear; and my true lip Hath virgin'd it e'er since . . . . v 3 46
Those lily hands Tremble, like aspen-leaves, upon a lute, And make the silken strings delight to kiss them . . . . *T. Andron.* ii 4 46
Let me kiss thy lips; Or make some sign how I may do thee ease . . iii 1 120
That kiss is comfortless As frozen water to a starved snake . . . iii 1 251
If you love me, as I think you do, Let's kiss and part . . . . iii 1 288
And for my tidings gave me twenty kisses . . . . . . v 1 120
O, take this warm kiss on thy pale cold lips! . . . . . . v 3 153
Tear for tear, and loving kiss for kiss . . . . . . v 3 156
These happy masks that kiss fair ladies' brows *Rom. and Jul.* i 1 236
O'er ladies' lips, who straight on kisses dream . . . . . i 4 74
Ready stand To smooth that rough touch with a tender kiss . . . i 5 98
And palm to palm is holy palmers' kiss . . . . i 5 102
Sin from my lips! O trespass sweetly urged! Give me my sin again.—You kiss by the book . . . . i 5 112
Like fire and powder, Which as they kiss consume . . . . . ii 6 11
Even in pure and vestal modesty, Still blush, as thinking their own kisses sin . . . . iii 3 39
Farewell, farewell! one kiss, and I'll descend . . . . . iii 5 42
On Thursday early will I rouse ye: Till then, adieu; and keep this holy kiss . . . . iv 1 43
Breathed such life with kisses in my lips, That I revived, and was an emperor . . . . v 1 8
And, lips, O you The doors of breath, seal with a righteous kiss A dateless bargain to engrossing death! . . . . v 3 114
Thus with a kiss I die . . . . v 3 120
I will kiss thy lips; Haply some poison yet doth hang on them . . v 3 164
Thy lips rot off!—I will not kiss thee; then the rot returns To thine own lips again . . . . *T. of Athens* iv 3 64
Thou visible god, That solder'st close impossibilities, And makest them kiss! . . . . iv 3 389
Weep your tears Into the channel, till the lowest stream Do kiss the most exalted shores of all . . . . . . *J. Cæsar* i 1 65
I kiss thy hand, but not in flattery, Cæsar . . . . . . iii 1 52
They would go and kiss dead Cæsar's wounds And dip their napkins . iii 2 137
Is't night's predominance, or the day's shame, That darkness does the face of earth entomb, When living light should kiss it? . *Macbeth* ii 4 10
I will not yield, To kiss the ground before young Malcolm's feet . . v 8 28
A second time I kill my husband dead, When second husband kisses me in bed.—I do believe you think what now you speak . *Hamlet* iii 2 195
For a pair of reechy kisses, Or paddling in your neck with his damn'd fingers . . . . iii 4 184
This kiss, if it durst speak, Would stretch thy spirits up into the air *Lear* iv 2 22
O, let me kiss that hand!—Let me wipe it first; it smells of mortality iv 6 135
Restoration hang Thy medicine on my lips; and let this kiss Repair those violent harms! . . . . iv 7 27
She reserves it evermore about her To kiss and talk to . . *Othello* iii 3 206
I found not Cassio's kisses on her lips . . . . iii 3 341
And then kiss me hard, As if he pluck'd up kisses by the roots . . iii 3 422
What, To kiss in private?—An unauthorized kiss . . . . . iv 1 2
Senators of Venice greet you.—I kiss the instrument of their pleasures iv 1 231
The bawdy wind that kisses all it meets Is hush'd . . . . . iv 2 78
I kiss'd thee ere I kill'd thee: no way but this; Killing myself, to die upon a kiss.—This did I fear . . . . v 2 359
He kiss'd,—the last of many doubled kisses,—This orient pearl *A. and C.* i 5 40
Mark Antony Will e'en but kiss Octavia, and we'll follow . . . ii 4 3
There is gold, and here My bluest veins to kiss . . . . . ii 5 29
Give me a kiss; Even this repays me . . . . iii 11 70
Say to great Cæsar this: in deputation I kiss his conquering hand . iii 13 75
Bestow'd his lips on that unworthy place, As it rain'd kisses . . iii 13 85
If from the field I shall return once more To kiss these lips, I will appear in blood . . . . iii 13 174
Fare thee well, dame, whate'er becomes of me: This is a soldier's kiss iv 4 30
Mash the congealment from your wounds, and kiss The honour'd gashes whole . . . . iv 8 10
Commend unto his lips thy favouring hand: Kiss it, my warrior . . iv 8 24
Of many thousand kisses the poor last I lay upon thy lips . . . iv 15 20
If she first meet the curled Antony, He'll make demand of her, and spend that kiss Which is my heaven to have . . . . . v 2 305

Kiss. Ere I could Give him that parting kiss which I had set Betwixt two charming words, comes in my father . . . *Cymbeline* i 3 34
But kiss; one kiss! Rubies unparagon'd, How dearly they do't! . ii 2 17
I hope it be not gone to tell my lord That I kiss aught but he . . ii 3 153
Thou know'st this, 'Tis time to fear when tyrants seem to kiss *Pericles* i 2 79
But sea-room, an the brine and cloudy billow kiss the moon, I care not iii 1 46
She would make a puritan of the devil, if he should cheapen a kiss of her iv 6 10
Kissed. Courtsied when you have and kiss'd The wild waves whist *Temp.* i 2 378
She is not to be kissed fasting, in respect of her breath . *T. G. of Ver.* iii 1 326
O thou senseless form, Thou shalt be worshipp'd, kiss'd, loved and adored! . . . . iv 4 204
You have beaten my men, killed my deer, and broke open my lodge.—But not kissed your keeper's daughter? . . . . *Mer. Wives* i 1 116
In the instant of our encounter, after we had embraced, kissed, protested iii 5 75
This is he That kiss'd his hand away in courtesy . *L. L. Lost* v 2 324
My cherry lips have often kiss'd thy stones . *M. N. Dream* v 1 192
When with his knees he kiss'd the Cretan strand . . *T. of Shrew* i 1 175
He took the bride about the neck And kiss'd her lips with such a clamorous smack That at the parting all the church did echo . iii 2 180
Over Suffolk's neck He threw his wounded arm and kiss'd his lips *Hen. V.* iv 6 25
Hast thou not kiss'd thy hand and held my stirrup? *2 Hen. VI.* iv 1 53
Thy lips that kiss'd the queen shall sweep the ground . . . iv 1 75
So Judas kiss'd his master, And cried 'all hail!' . *3 Hen. VI.* v 7 33
He wept, And hugg'd me in his arm, and kindly kiss'd my cheek *Rich. III.* ii 2 24
Their lips were four red roses on a stalk, Which in their summer beauty kiss'd each other . . . . iv 3 13
'Twere better she were kiss'd in general . *Troi. and Cres.* iv 5 21
Here hung those lips that I have kissed I know not how oft . *Hamlet* v 1 208
It had been better you had not kissed your three fingers so oft *Othello* ii 1 174
Very good; well kissed! an excellent courtesy! 'tis so, indeed . ii 1 176
Then laid his leg Over my thigh, and sigh'd, and kiss'd . . . iii 3 425
I kiss'd thee ere I kill'd thee: no way but this; Killing myself, to die upon a kiss.—This did I fear . . . . v 2 358
He kiss'd,—the last of many doubled kisses,—This orient pearl *A. and C.* i 5 40
We have kiss'd away Kingdoms and provinces . . . . . iii 10 7
Then waved his handkerchief?—And kiss'd it, madam.—Senseless linen! happier therein than I! . . . . . . *Cymbeline* i 3 6
When I kissed the jack, upon an up-cast to be hit away! . . . ii 1 2
I kiss'd it: I hope it be not gone to tell my lord That I kiss aught but he ii 3 151
Winds of all the corners kiss'd your sails, To make your vessel nimble ii 4 28
I kiss'd it; and it gave me present hunger To feed again, though full ii 4 137
Whose towers bore heads so high they kiss'd the clouds . *Pericles* i 4 24
Kissing. Beat the ground For kissing of their feet . . . *Tempest* iv 1 174
Judas Maccabæus clipt is plain Judas.—A kissing traitor *L. L. Lost* v 2 604
By this virgin palm now kissing thine, I will be thine . . . v 2 816
O, how ripe in show Thy lips, those kissing cherries, tempting grow! *M. N. Dream* iii 2 140
I remember the kissing of her batlet and the cow's dugs that her pretty chopt hands had milked . . . . . *As Y. Like It* ii 4 49
His kissing is as full of sanctity as the touch of holy bread . . iii 4 14
Kissing with inside lip . . . . *W. Tale* i 2 286
Marry, garlic, To mend her kissing with! . . . . . . iv 4 163
Fair cousin, you debase your princely knee To make the base earth proud with kissing it . . . . . . *Richard II.* iii 3 191
I will have it in a particular ballad else, with mine own picture on the top on't, Colevile kissing my foot . . . . . *2 Hen. IV.* iv 3 54
Teach not thy lips such scorn, for they were made For kissing *Richard III.* i 2 173
I'll startle you Worse than the sacring bell, when the brown wench Lay kissing in your arms, lord cardinal . . . . *Hen. VIII.* iii 2 296
I had good argument for kissing once.—But that's no argument for kissing now . . . . *Troi. and Cres.* iv 5 26
In kissing, do you render or receive?—Both take and give . . . iv 5 36
Fawn'd like hounds, And bow'd like bondmen, kissing Cæsar's feet *J. C.* v 1 42
If the sun breed maggots in a dead dog, being a god kissing carrion *Hamlet* ii 2 182
A hand that kings Have lipp'd, and trembled kissing . *Ant. and Cleo.* ii 5 30
If our eyes had authority, here they might take two thieves kissing . ii 6 101
Die where thou hast lived: Quicken with kissing . . . . . iv 15 39
By watching, weeping, tendance, kissing, to O'ercome you . *Cymbeline* v 5 53
Kissing-comfits. Hail kissing-comfits and snow eringoes . *Mer. Wives* v 5 22
Kitchen. Even for our kitchens We kill the fowl of season *Meas. for Meas.* ii 2 84
His face is Lucifer's privy-kitchen . . . . . *2 Hen. IV.* ii 4 361
Bells in your parlours, wild-cats in your kitchens . . . *Othello* ii 1 111
Kitchened. There is a fat friend at your master's house, That kitchen'd me for you to-day . . . . *Com. of Errors* v 1 415
Kitchen-maid. Did not her kitchen-maid rail, taunt, and scorn me? . iv 4 77
Kitchen malkin. The kitchen malkin pins Her richest lockram 'bout her reechy neck . . . . *Coriolanus* ii 1 224
Kitchen-trull. Either our brags Were crack'd of kitchen-trulls, or his description Proved us unspeaking sots . . . . *Cymbeline* v 5 177
Kitchen-vestal. The kitchen-vestal scorn'd you . *Com. of Errors* iv 4 78
Kitchen-wench. She's the kitchen wench and all grease . . . iii 2 96
Laura to his lady was but a kitchen-wench . . *Rom. and Jul.* ii 4 42
Kite. Watch her, as we watch these kites That bate and beat *T. of Shrew* iv 1 198
Some powerful spirit instruct the kites and ravens To be thy nurses! *W. Tale* ii 3 186
When the kite builds, look to lesser linen . . . . . . iv 3 23
Fetch forth the lazar kite of Cressid's kind . . . . *Hen. V.* ii 1 80
Were't not all one, an empty eagle were set To guard the chicken from a hungry kite? . . . . *2 Hen. VI.* iii 1 249
Who finds the partridge in the puttock's nest, But may imagine how the bird was dead, Although the kite soar with unbloodied beak? . iii 2 193
Is Beaufort term'd a kite? Where are his talons? . . . . iii 2 196
Made a prey for carrion kites and crows Even of the bonny beast he loved so well . . . . v 2 11
More pity that the eagle should be mew'd, While kites and buzzards prey at liberty.—What news abroad? . . . *Richard III.* i 1 133
I' the city of kites and crows . . . . *Coriolanus* iv 5 45; 46
In their steads do ravens, crows and kites, Fly o'er our heads *J. Cæsar* v 1 85
If charnel-houses and our graves must send Those that we bury back, our monuments Shall be the maws of kites . . . *Macbeth* iii 4 73
Ere this I should have fatted all the region kites With this slave's offal *Hamlet* ii 2 607
Detested kite! thou liest . . . . *Lear* i 4 284
Approach, there! Ah, you kite! . . . . *Ant. and Cleo.* iii 13 89
Kitten. I had rather be a kitten and cry mew . . *1 Hen. IV.* iii 1 129
Kittened. So it would have done at the same season, if your mother's cat had but kittened . . . . iii 1 19
Knack. Rings, gawds, conceits, Knacks, trifles, nosegays *M. N. Dream* i 1 34
A walnut-shell, A knack, a toy, a trick, a baby's cap . *T. of Shrew* iv 3 67
Knack. When I was young And handed love as you do, I was wont To load my she with knacks . . . . *W. Tale* iv 4 360
Thou no more shalt see this knack . . . . iv 4 439
Knapped. As lying a gossip in that as ever knapped ginger *Mer. of Venice* iii 1 10
She knapped 'em o' the coxcombs with a stick, and cried 'Down, wantons!' . . . . *Lear* ii 4 125
Knave. No marrying 'mong his subjects?—None, man; all idle: whores and knaves . . . . *Tempest* ii 1 166
This mis-shapen knave, His mother was a witch . . . . v 1 268
I have the wit to think my master is a kind of a knave: but that's all one, if he be but one knave . . . . . *T. G. of Ver.* iii 1 263
If I be drunk, I'll be drunk with those that have the fear of God, and not with drunken knaves . . . . *Mer. Wives* i 1 190
Vere is dat knave Rugby?—What, John Rugby! John! . . . i 4 57
You heard what this knave told me, did you not? . . . . ii 1 174
At that time the jealous rascally knave her husband will be forth . ii 2 276
Hang him, poor cuckoldly knave! I know him not . . . . ii 2 281
They say the jealous wittolly knave hath masses of money . . . ii 2 283
Ford's a knave, and I will aggravate his style; thou, Master Brook, shalt know him for knave and cuckold . . . . . . ii 2 296
I will knog his urinals about his knave's costard . . . . iii 1 14
And he is a knave besides; a cowardly knave as you would desires . iii 1 68
I will knog your urinals about your knave's cogscomb . . . iii 1 91
May be the knave bragged of that he could not compass . . . iii 3 211
I pray you now, remembrance to-morrow on the lousy knave, mine host iii 3 256
A lousy knave, to have his gibes and his mockeries! . . . iii 3 259
A couple of Ford's knaves, his hinds . . . . . . iii 5 99
Met the jealous knave their master in the door, who asked them once or twice what they had in their basket: I quaked for fear, lest the lunatic knave would have searched it . . . . . . iii 5 102
The knave constable had set me i' the stocks, i' the common stocks . iv 5 122
That same knave Ford, her husband, hath the finest mad devil of jealousy v 1 18
I'll tell you strange things of this knave Ford . . . . . v 1 29
Who's a cuckold now? Master Brook, Falstaff's a knave, a cuckoldly knave . . . . v 5 114
If your worship will take order for the drabs and the knaves, you need not to fear the bawds . . . . . . *Meas. for Meas.* ii 1 247
Show your knave's visage, with a pox to you! show your sheep-biting face! v 1 358
Thou art the first knave that e'er madest a duke . . . . v 1 361
Come on, sir knave, have done your foolishness *Com. of Errors* i 2 72
Take you that, sir knave.—What mean you, sir? for God's sake, hold your hands! . . . . i 2 92
Are you there, wife? you might have come before.—Your wife, sir knave! iii 1 64
If you went in pain, master, this 'knave' would go sore . . . iii 1 65
Break any breaking here, and I'll break your knave's pate . . iii 1 74
Call the rest of the watch together and thank God you are rid of a knave *Much Ado* iii 3 31
A couple of as arrant knaves as any in Messina . . . . iii 5 35
Masters, it is proved already that you are little better than false knaves iv 2 24
I say to you, it is thought you are false knaves . . . . iv 2 30
They have verified unjust things; and, to conclude, they are lying knaves v 1 224
I leave an arrant knave with your worship . . . . . v 1 330
O, my good knave Costard! exceedingly well met . . *L. L. Lost* iii 1 144
As thou wilt win my favour, good my knave, Do one thing for me . iii 1 153
See to my house, left in the fearful guard Of an unthrifty knave *M. of V.* i 3 177
If a Christian did not play the knave and get thee, I am much deceived ii 3 12
Stroke your chins, and swear by your beards that I am a knave *As Y. L. It* i 2 77
I will speak to him like a saucy lackey and under that habit play the knave . . . . iii 2 315
Ne'er a fantastical knave of them all shall flout me out of my calling iii 3 109
Score me up for the lyingest knave in Christendom . *T. of Shrew* Ind. 2 26
Knock me at this gate And rap me well, or I'll knock your knave's pate i 2 12
She may perhaps call him half a score knaves or so: why, that's nothing i 2 111
The base is right; 'tis the base knave that jars . . . . iii 1 47
Now, for my life, the knave doth court my love . . . . iii 1 49
Where be these knaves? What, no man at door To hold my stirrup! . iv 1 123
No attendance? no regard? no duty? Where is the foolish knave I sent before? . . . . iv 1 130
Meet me in the park, And bring along these rascal knaves with thee . iv 1 134
A whoreson beetle-headed, flap-ear'd knave! . . . . . iv 1 160
Call forth an officer. Carry this mad knave to the gaol . . . v 1 95
What does this knave here? Get you gone, sirrah . . *All's Well* i 3 8
The knaves come to do that for me which I am aweary of . . . i 3 46
Wilt thou ever be a foul-mouthed and calumnious knave? . . . i 3 61
You'll be gone, sir knave, and do as I command you . . . i 3 94
As a scolding quean to a wrangling knave . . . . . . ii 2 27
You are not worth another word, else I'ld call you knave . . ii 3 281
O, my knave, how does my old lady? . . . . ii 4 19
Thou'rt a knave.—You should have said, sir, before a knave thou'rt a knave; that's, before me thou'rt a knave . . . . . . ii 4 29
A good knave, i' faith, and well fed . . . . ii 4 39
I know that knave; hang him! one Parolles: a filthy officer . . iii 5 17
Has sat i' the stocks all night, poor gallant knave.—No matter . iv 3 117
They are not herbs, you knave; they are nose-herbs . . . iv 5 19
Whether dost thou profess thyself, a knave or a fool?—A fool, sir, at a woman's service, and a knave at a man's . . . . . . iv 5 24
I will subscribe for thee, thou art both knave and fool.—At your service iv 5 35
A shrewd knave and an unhappy.—So he is . . . . . . iv 5 66
He looks like a poor, decayed, ingenious, foolish, rascally knave . v 2 25
Wherein have you played the knave with fortune, that she should scratch you? . . . . v 2 32
Herself is a good lady and would not have knaves thrive long under her v 2 34
Knave! dost thou put upon me at once both the office of God and the devil? v 2 51
Though you are a fool and a knave, you shall eat; go to, follow . v 2 57
As thou art a knave, and no knave. What an equivocal companion is this! v 3 249
Let our catch be, 'Thou knave.'—'Hold thy peace, thou knave,' knight? I shall be constrained in 't to call thee knave, knight.—'Tis not the first time I have constrained one to call me knave . . *T. Night* ii 3 67
The knave counterfeits well; a good knave . . . . . iv 2 22
An ass-head and a coxcomb and a knave, a thin-faced knave, a gull! v 1 213
'Gainst knaves and thieves men shut their gate . . . . v 1 404
What means this scorn, thou most untoward knave? . . *K. John* i 1 243
What is't knave?—An hour before I came, the duchess died *Richard II.* ii 2 96
As the soldiers bore dead bodies by, He call'd them untaught knaves *1 Hen. IV.* i 3 43
Bid the ostler bring my gelding out of the stable. Farewell, you muddy knave . . . . ii 1 106
Cut the villains' throats: ah! whoreson caterpillars! bacon-fed knaves! ii 2 89
Hang ye, gorbellied knaves, are ye undone? No, ye fat chuffs . . ii 2 93
On, bacons, on! What, ye knaves! young men must live . . . ii 2 95

Knave. Three misbegotten knaves in Kendal green came at my back and let drive at me *1 Hen. IV.* ii 4 246
And, setting thy knighthood aside, thou art a knave to call me so iii 3 138
Thou art a beast to say otherwise.—Say, what beast, thou knave, thou? iii 3 141
A whoreson Achitophel! a rascally yea-forsooth knave! *2 Hen. IV.* i 2 41
What! a young knave, and begging! Is there not wars? i 2 84
Unless a woman should be made an ass and a beast, to bear every knave's wrong ii 1 41
Yonder he comes; and that arrant malmsey-nose knave ii 1 42
They are arrant knaves, and will backbite v 1 36
That Visor is an arrant knave, on my knowledge v 1 45
I grant your worship that he is a knave, sir; but yet, God forbid, sir, but a knave should have some countenance at his friend's request v 1 47
An honest man, sir, is able to speak for himself, when a knave is not v 1 51
If I cannot once or twice in a quarter bear out a knave against an honest man, I have but a very little credit v 1 53
The knave is mine honest friend, sir; . . . let him be countenanced v 1 55
The knave will stick by thee, I can assure thee that v 3 70
Arrant knave; I would to God that I might die, that I might have thee hanged v 4 1
Ish a villain, and a bastard, and a knave, and a rascal *Hen. V.* iii 2 133
What an arrant, rascally, beggarly, lousy knave it is iv 8 37
The rascally, scauld, beggarly, lousy, pragging knave, Pistol v 1 6
God pless you, Aunchient Pistol! you scurvy, lousy knave, God pless you! v 1 19
Will you be so good, scauld knave, as eat it? v 1 31
Thou dost see I eat.—Much good do you, scauld knave, heartily v 1 55
Go, go; you are a counterfeit cowardly knave v 1 74
They say 'A crafty knave does need no broker' *2 Hen. VI.* i 2 100
You shall go near To call them both a pair of crafty knaves i 2 103
A subtle knave! but yet it shall not serve ii 1 104
Sit there, the lyingest knave in Christendom ii 1 126
Follow the knave; and take this drab away ii 1 156
I am come hither, as it were, upon my man's instigation, to prove him a knave ii 3 88
Dispatch: this knave's tongue begins to double ii 3 94
What one, my lord?—Her husband, knave: wouldst thou betray me? *Richard III.* i 1 102
At what ease Might corrupt minds procure knaves as corrupt To swear against you? such things have been done *Hen. VIII.* v 1 132
Where are these porters, These lazy knaves? Ye have made a fine hand, fellows v 4 74
Ye are lazy knaves; And here ye lie baiting of bombards, when Ye should do service v 4 84
A false-hearted rogue, a most unjust knave *Troi. and Cres.* v 1 96
Diomed has got that same scurvy doting foolish young knave's sleeve of Troy v 4 4
Art thou of blood and honour?—No, no, I am a rascal; a scurvy railing knave v 4 31
You are ambitious for poor knaves' caps and legs *Coriolanus* ii 1 76
All the peace you make in their cause is, calling both the parties knaves ii 1 88
The smiles of knaves Tent in my cheeks! iii 2 115
As an ostler, that for the poorest piece Will bear the knave by the volume iii 3 33
More light, you knaves; and turn the tables up *Rom. and Jul.* i 5 29
Scurvy knave! I am none of his flirt-gills; I am none of his skains-mates ii 4 161
And thou must stand by too, and suffer every knave to use me at his pleasure? ii 4 164
I am so vexed, that every part about me quivers. Scurvy knave! ii 4 171
What a pestilent knave is this same!—Hang him, Jack! iv 5 147
When thou art Timon's dog, and these knaves honest.—Why dost thou call them knaves? thou know'st them not.—Are they not Athenians? *T. of Athens* i 1 180
That there should be small love 'mongst these sweet knaves, And all this courtesy! i 1 258
To see meat fill knaves and wine heat fools i 1 271
A knave; which notwithstanding, thou shalt be no less esteemed ii 2 111
If 'twill not serve, 'tis not so base as you; For you serve knaves iii 4 59
Let in the tide Of knaves once more; my cook and I'll provide iii 4 119
Thou gavest thine ears like tapsters that bid welcome To knaves iv 3 216
Dost please thyself in't?—Ay.—What! a knave too? iv 3 238
If thou hadst not been born the worst of men, Thou hadst been a knave iv 3 276
I never had honest man about me, I; all I kept were knaves iv 3 485
There's never a one of you but trusts a knave, That mightily deceives you v 1 96
What trade, thou knave? thou naughty knave, what trade? *J. Cæsar* i 1 16
What, thou speak'st drowsily? Poor knave, I blame thee not iv 3 241
Gentle knave, good night; I will not do thee so much wrong to wake thee iv 3 269
Ne'er a villain dwelling in all Denmark But he's an arrant knave *Hamlet* i 5 124
We are arrant knaves, all; believe none of us iii 1 131
Who was in life a foolish prating knave iii 4 215
How the knave jowls it to the ground, as if it were Cain's jaw-bone! v 1 84
Why does he suffer this rude knave now to knock him about the sconce? v 1 109
How absolute the knave is! we must speak by the card v 1 148
This knave came something saucily into the world before he was sent for *Lear* i 1 21
Knaves, thieves, and treachers, by spherical predominance i 2 133
Dinner, ho, dinner! Where's my knave? my fool? i 4 46
Who am I, sir?—My lady's father.—'My lady's father'! my lord's knave i 4 88
Now, my friendly knave, I thank thee: there's earnest of thy service i 4 103
Here's my coxcomb.—How now, my pretty knave! how dost thou? i 4 107
You, sir, more knave than fool, after your master i 4 337
A knave; a rascal; an eater of broken meats ii 2 15
Filthy, worsted-stocking knave; a lily-livered, action-taking knave ii 2 18
Art nothing but the composition of a knave, beggar, coward ii 2 22
Beastly knave, know you no reverence?—Yes, sir; but anger hath a privilege ii 2 75
No contraries hold more antipathy Than I and such a knave.—Why dost thou call him knave? What's his offence?—His countenance likes me not ii 2 94
These kind of knaves I know, which in this plainness Harbour more craft ii 2 107
He that beguiled you in a plain accent was a plain knave ii 2 118
You stubborn ancient knave, you reverend braggart, We'll teach you ii 2 133
If I were your father's dog, You should not use me so.—Sir, being his knave, I will. ii 2 144
I would have none but knaves follow it, since a fool gives it ii 4 78
The knave turns fool that runs away; The fool no knave, perdy ii 4 85
Poor fool and knave, I have one part in my heart That's sorry yet for thee iii 2 72
You shall mark Many a duteous and knee-crooking knave *Othello* i 1 45
Whip me such honest knaves i 1 49
No worse nor better guard But with a knave of common hire, a gondolier i 1 126
A knave very voluble; no further conscionable than in putting on the mere form of civil and humane seeming ii 1 241

Knave. A slipper and subtle knave, a finder of occasions *Othello* ii 1 246
A devilish knave. Besides, the knave is handsome, young ii 1 249
A pestilent complete knave; and the woman hath found him already ii 1 252
A knave teach me my duty! I'll beat the knave into a twiggen bottle ii 3 151
Such things in a false disloyal knave Are tricks of custom iii 3 121
What, If I had said I had seen him do you wrong? Or heard him say,—as knaves be such abroad iv 1 25
Some most villanous knave, Some base notorious knave iv 2 139
It is a deadly sorrow to behold a foul knave uncuckolded *Ant. and Cleo.* i 2 76
And stand the buffet With knaves that smell of sweat i 4 21
O, that his fault should make a knave of thee! ii 5 102
My good knave Eros, now thy captain is Even such a body: here I am Antony; Yet cannot hold this visible shape, my knave iv 14 12
Not being Fortune, he's but Fortune's knave, A minister of her will v 2 3
A sly and constant knave, Not to be shaked *Cymbeline* i 5 75
There are verier knaves desire to live, for all he be a Roman v 4 209
What a drunken knave was the sea to cast thee in our way! *Pericles* ii 1 61
Knavery. It is admirable pleasures and fery honest knaveries *Mer. Wives* iv 4 81
Knavery cannot, sure, hide himself in such reverence *Much Ado* ii 3 124
This is a knavery of them to make me afeard *M. N. Dream* iii 1 115
I see their knavery: this is to make an ass of me; to fright me, if they could iii 1 123
Thou mistakest, Or else committ'st thy knaveries wilfully iii 2 346
By our beards, if we had them, thou art.—By my knavery, if I had it, then I were *As Y. Like It* i 2 80
Here's no knavery! See, to beguile the old folks, how the young folks lay their heads together! *T. of Shrew* i 2 138
With amber bracelets, beads and all this knavery iv 3 58
Why, this is flat knavery, to take upon you another man's name v 1 37
But I will in, to be revenged for this villany.—And I, to sound the depth of this knavery v 1 142
And have ability enough to make such knaveries yours *All's Well* i 3 13
I would we were well rid of this knavery *T. Night* iv 2 73
I hold it the more knavery to conceal it *W. Tale* iv 4 697
'Tis as arrant a piece of knavery, mark you now, as can be offer't *Hen. V.* iv 7 3
He was full of jests, and gipes, and knaveries, and mocks iv 7 52
I fear, at last Hume's knavery will be the duchess' wreck *2 Hen. VI.* i 2 105
By holy Mary, Butts, there's knavery *Hen. VIII.* v 2 33
Here is such patchery, such juggling and such knavery! *Troi. and Cres.* ii 3 78
They must sweep my way, And marshal me to knavery *Hamlet* iii 4 205
O royal knavery! v 2 19
To get his place and to plume up my will In double knavery *Othello* i 3 400
Knavery's plain face is never seen till used ii 1 321
Knavish. Their herald is a pretty knavish page *L. L. Lost* v 2 97
You are that shrewd and knavish sprite Call'd Robin Goodfellow *M. N. D.* ii 1 33
Cupid is a knavish lad, Thus to make poor females mad iii 2 440
Having flown over many knavish professions, he settled only in rogue *W. Tale* iv 3 105
And their executors, the knavish crows, Fly o'er them *Hen. V.* iv 2 51
'Tis a knavish piece of work: but what o' that? *Hamlet* iii 2 250
A knavish speech sleeps in a foolish ear iv 2 25
Knead. I will knead him; I'll make him supple *Troi. and Cres.* ii 3 231
Kneaded. This sensible warm motion to become A kneaded clod *M. for M.* iii 1 121
Kneading. The civil citizens kneading up the honey *Hen. V.* i 2 199
The kneading, the making of the cake, the heating of the oven *T. and C.* i 1 23
Knee. Neither bended knees, pure hands held up *T. G. of Ver.* iii 1 229
Buckled below fair knighthood's bending knee *Mer. Wives* v 5 76
Go to your knees and make ready *Meas. for Meas.* iii 1 171
As this is true, Let me in safety raise me from my knees! v 1 231
Lend me your knees, and all my life to come I'll lend you all my life v 1 436
O Isabel, will you not lend a knee? v 1 447
For the which blessing I am at him upon my knees every morning *M. Ado* ii 1 30
Down upon her knees she falls, weeps, sobs, beats her heart ii 3 152
I Pompey am,— With libbard's head on knee *L. L. Lost* v 2 551
But, mistress, know yourself: down on your knees, And thank heaven, fasting, for a good man's love *As Y. Like It* iii 5 57
That made great Jove to humble him to her hand, When with his knees he kiss'd the Cretan strand *T. of Shrew* i 1 175
Then, I confess, Here on my knee, before high heaven *All's Well* i 3 198
And on our knees we beg, As recompense of our dear services *W. Tale* ii 3 149
A thousand knees Ten thousand years together, naked, fasting, Upon a barren mountain iii 2 211
Father, on my knee I give heaven thanks I was not like to thee! *K. John* i 1 82
Upon my knee I beg, go not to arms Against mine uncle iii 1 308
Upon my knee, Made hard with kneeling, I do pray to thee iii 1 309
To whom, with all submission, on my knee I do bequeath my faithful services v 7 103
Let me kiss my sovereign's hand, And bow my knee *Richard II.* i 3 47
A brace of draymen bid God speed him well And had the tribute of his supple knee, With 'Thanks, my countrymen' i 4 33
Show me thy humble heart, and not thy knee, Whose duty is deceiveable ii 3 83
Henry Bolingbroke On both his knees doth kiss King Richard's hand iii 3 36
Thus long have we stood To watch the fearful bending of thy knee iii 3 73
You debase your princely knee To make the base earth proud iii 3 190
Your heart is up, I know, Thus high at least, although your knee be low iii 3 195
For ever may my knees grow to the earth, My tongue cleave to my roof v 3 30
For ever will I walk upon my knees, And never see day that the happy sees v 3 93
Unto my mother's prayers I bend my knee v 3 97
Our knees shall kneel till to the ground they grow v 3 106
O happy vantage of a kneeling knee! v 3 132
Where I first bow'd my knee Unto this king of smiles *1 Hen. IV.* i 3 245
How long is't ago, Jack, since thou sawest thine own knee? ii 4 361
An I do, I pray God my girdle break.—O, if it should, how would thy guts fall about thy knees! iii 3 173
The more and less came in with cap and knee iv 3 68
The music is come, sir.—Let them play. Play, sirs. Sit on my knee, Doll *2 Hen. IV.* ii 4 247
Then I felt to his knees, and they were as cold as any stone *Hen. V.* ii 3 26
Canst thou, when thou command'st the beggar's knee, Command the health of it? iv 1 273
My lord, most humbly on my knee I beg The leading of the vaward iv 3 129
He gives you, upon his knees, a thousand thanks iv 4 63
Stoop then and set your knee against my foot *1 Hen. VI.* iii 1 169
These haughty words of hers Have batter'd me like roaring cannon-shot, And made me almost yield upon my knees iii 3 80
Here on my knee I beg mortality, Rather than life preserved with infamy iv 5 32
When he perceived me shrink and on my knee, His bloody sword he brandish'd over me iv 7 5
I'll either make thee stoop and bend thy knee, Or sack this country v 1 61
And humbly now upon my bended knee, In sight of England *2 Hen. VI.* i 1 10

Knee. He did vow upon his knees he would be even with me 2 *Hen. VI.* i 3 203
And if we did but glance a far-off look, Immediately he was upon his knee iii 1 11
And shows an angry eye And passeth by with stiff unbowed knee . iii 1 16
I would, false murderous coward, on thy knee Make thee beg pardon . iii 2 220
Rather let my head Stoop to the block than these knees bow to any Save to the God of heaven and to my king . . . . . iv 1 125
I beseech God on my knees thou mayst be turned to hobnails . iv 10 62
First let me ask of these, If they can brook I bow a knee to man . v 1 110
Warwick, hath thy knee forgot to bow? Old Salisbury, shame to thy silver hair! . . . . v 1 161
In duty bend thy knee to me That bows unto the grave with mickle age v 1 173
I am his king, and he should bow his knee; I was adopted heir 3 *Hen. VI.* ii 2 87
Here on my knee I vow to God above I'll never pause again . . ii 3 29
I do bend my knee with thine; And in this vow do chain my soul to thine! ii 3 33
And, ere my knee rise from the earth's cold face, I throw my hands, mine eyes, my heart to thee . . . . . . ii 3 35
No bending knee will call thee Cæsar now . . . . . iii 1 18
Speak gentle words and humbly bend thy knee . . . . v 1 22
And humbly beg the death upon my knee . . . *Richard III.* i 2 179
But when your carters or your waiting-vassals Have done a drunken slaughter, and defaced The precious image of our dear Redeemer, You straight are on your knees for pardon, pardon . . . . ii 1 124
Humbly on my knee I crave your blessing . . . . . ii 2 105
He is not lolling on a lewd day-bed, But on his knees at meditation iii 7 73
When the splitting wind Makes flexible the knees of knotted oaks *T. and C.* i 3 50
Supple knees Feed arrogance and are the proud man's fees . . iii 3 48
I beseech you, on my knees I beseech you, what's the matter? . iv 2 94
Consort with me in loud and dear petition, Pursue we him on knees . v 3 10
Not Priamus and Hecuba on knees . . . should stop my way . v 3 54
For the dearth, The gods, not the patricians, make it, and Your knees to them, not arms, must help . . . . . *Coriolanus* i 1 76
He'll beat Aufidius' head below his knee And tread upon his neck . i 3 49
Slew three opposers: Tarquin's self he met, And struck him on his knee ii 2 99
Thy knee bussing the stones—for in such business Action is eloquence iii 2 75
My arm'd knees, Who bow'd but in my stirrup, bend like his That hath received an alms! . . . . iii 2 118
Ourselves, our wives, and children, on our knees, Are bound to pray for you both . . . . iv 6 22
A mile before his tent fall down, and knee The way into his mercy . v 1 5
I prate, And the most noble mother of the world Leave unsaluted: sink, my knee, i' the earth . . . . v 3 50
What is this? Your knees to me? to your corrected son? . . v 3 57
Your knee, sirrah.—That's my brave boy! . . . . . v 3 75
Let us shame him with our knees . . . . . . v 3 169
All humbled on your knees, You shall ask pardon of his majesty *T. An.* i 1 472
Upon my feeble knee I beg this boon, with tears not lightly shed . ii 3 288
Thy grandsire loved thee well: Many a time he danced thee on his knee v 3 162
O'er courtiers' knees, that dream on court'sies straight . *Rom. and Jul.* i 4 72
All this uttered With gentle breath, calm look, knees humbly bow'd . iii 1 161
I beseech you on my knees, Hear me with patience but to speak a word iii 5 159
Even he drops down The knee before him . . . *T. of Athens* i 1 61
Which labour'd after him to the mountain's top Even on their knees and hands . . . . i 1 87
You fools of fortune, trencher-friends, time's flies, Cap and knee slaves! iii 6 107
Place thieves And give them title, knee and approbation With senators iv 3 36
Hinge thy knee, And let his very breath, whom thou'lt observe, Blow off thy cap . . . . iv 3 211
Fall upon your knees, Pray to the gods to intermit the plague *J. Cæsar* i 1 58
Upon my knees, I charm you, by my once-commended beauty, By all your vows of love . . . . ii 1 270
He shall say you are not well to-day: Let me, upon my knee, prevail in this . . . . ii 2 54
And on her knee Hath begg'd that I will stay at home to-day . . ii 2 81
Oftener upon her knees than on her feet, Died every day she lived *Macb.* iv 3 110
Pale as his shirt; his knees knocking each other . . . *Hamlet* ii 1 81
Let the candied tongue lick absurd pomp, And crook the pregnant hinges of the knee Where thrift may follow fawning . . . iii 2 66
Help, angels! Make assay! Bow, stubborn knees! . . . . iii 3 70
On my knees I beg That you'll vouchsafe me raiment, bed, and food *Lear* ii 4 157
I could as well be brought To knee his throne . . . . . ii 4 217
Ye men of Cyprus, let her have your knees. Hail to thee, lady! *Othello* ii 1 84
Upon my knees, what doth your speech import? . . . . iv 2 31
Her hand on her bosom, her head on her knee, Sing willow, willow, willow . . . . iv 3 43
Before the gods my knee shall bow my prayers To them for you *A. and C.* ii 3 3
Come on, away: apart upon our knees . . . . *Cymbeline* iv 2 288
Bow your knees. Arise my knights o' the battle . . . . . v 5 19
I am too blunt and saucy: here's my knee . . . . . v 5 325
Now my heavy conscience sinks my knee, As then your force did . v 5 413
Prince, pardon me, or strike me, if you please; I cannot be much lower than my knees . . . . *Pericles* i 2 47
She has me her quirks, her reasons, her master reasons, her prayers, her knees . . . . iv 6 9
Down on thy knees, thanks to the holy gods as loud As thunder . v 1 200

Knee-crooking. Many a duteous and knee-crooking knave . . *Othello* i 1 45

Knee-deep. Inch-thick, knee-deep, o'er head and ears a fork'd one! *W. T.* i 2 186

Kneel. A brave god and bears celestial liquor. I will kneel to him *Temp.* ii 2 123
Hearken once again to the suit I made to thee?—Marry, will I: kneel and repeat it . . . . iii 2 46
When maidens sue, Men give like gods; but when they weep and kneel, All their petitions are as freely theirs As they themselves would owe them . . . . *Meas. for Meas.* i 4 81
To him again, entreat him; Kneel down before him, hang upon his gown ii 2 44
Now is your time: speak loud and kneel before him . . . v 1 19
Should she kneel down in mercy of this fact, Her brother's ghost his paved bed would break, And take her hence in horror . . . v 1 439
Sweet Isabel, do yet but kneel by me; Hold up your hands, say nothing v 1 442
She kneels and prays For happy wedlock hours . . *Mer. of Venice* v 1 31
I am ashamed that women are so simple To offer war where they should kneel for peace . . . . *T. of Shrew* v 2 162
'Fore whose throne 'tis needful, Ere I can perfect mine intents, to kneel *All's Well* iv 4 4
We all kneel.—I am a feather for each wind that blows . . *W. Tale* ii 3 153
Shall I live on to see this bastard kneel And call me father? . . ii 3 155
Never saw I Wretches so quake: they kneel, they kiss the earth . v 1 199
Do not say 'tis superstition, that I kneel and then implore her blessing v 3 44
Please you to interpose, fair madam: kneel And pray your mother's blessing . . . . v 3 119
Kneel thou down Philip, but rise more great, Arise sir Richard *K. John* i 1 161
Our knees shall kneel till to the ground they grow . . *Richard II.* v 3 106
Kneel. Let God for ever keep it from my head And make me as the poorest vassal is That doth with awe and terror kneel to it! 2 *Hen. IV.* iv 5 177
I will bid you good night: and so kneel down before you . . Epil. 35
That, when thou comest to kneel at Henry's feet, Thou mayst bereave him of his wits with wonder . . . . . . 1 *Hen. VI.* v 3 194
Kneel down and take my blessing, good my girl. Wilt thou not stoop? v 4 25
Kneel down: We here create thee the first duke of Suffolk 2 *Hen. VI.* i 1 63
Then, father Salisbury, kneel we together . . . . . ii 2 59
Iden, kneel down. Rise up a knight. We give thee for reward a thousand marks . . . . v 1 78
Obey, audacious traitor; kneel for grace.—Wouldst have me kneel? first let me ask of these, If they can brook I bow a knee to man . v 1 109
We are thy sovereign, Clifford, kneel again . . . . . v 1 127
Kneel for grace and mercy at my feet; I am thy sovereign . 3 *Hen. VI.* i 1 75
May that ground gape and swallow me alive, Where I shall kneel to him that slew my father! . . . . i 1 162
Unsheathe your sword, and dub him presently. Edward, kneel down ii 2 60
Perjured Henry! wilt thou kneel for grace, And set thy diadem upon my head? . . . . ii 2 81
Kneel down, kneel down: Nay, when? strike now, or else the iron cools v 1 48
Kneel thou, Whilst I propose the selfsame words to thee . . v 5 19
Nay, we must longer kneel: I am a suitor.—Arise, and take place by us *Hen. VIII.* i 2 9
You are to blame, Knowing she will not lose her wonted greatness, To use so rude behaviour; go to, kneel . . . . . . iv 2 103
O, stand up blest! Whilst, with no softer cushion than the flint, I kneel before thee . . . . *Coriolanus* v 3 54
This boy, that cannot tell what he would have, But kneels and holds up hands . . . . v 3 175
At thy feet I kneel, with tears of joy, Shed on the earth, for thy return to Rome: O, bless me here! . . . . . *T. Andron.* i 1 161
And make them know what 'tis to let a queen Kneel in the streets and beg for grace in vain . . . . i 1 455
The tribune and his nephews kneel for grace; I will not be denied . i 1 480
Wilt thou kneel with me? Do, then, dear heart; for heaven shall hear our prayers . . . . iii 1 210
Nor hold thy stumps to heaven, Nor wink, nor nod, nor kneel . . iii 2 43
Kneel down with me; Lavinia, kneel; And kneel, sweet boy . . iv 1 87
At the first approach you must kneel, then kiss his foot . . iv 3 111
All thy foes; And at thy mercy shall they stoop and kneel . . v 2 118
Kneel not, gentle Portia.—I should not need, if you were gentle Brutus *J. Cæsar* ii 1 278
Doth not Brutus bootless kneel? . . . . iii 1 75
Thus, Brutus, did my master bid me kneel . . . . . iii 1 123
No, sir, you must not kneel.—Pray, do not mock me: I am a very foolish fond old man, Fourscore and upward . . . . *Lear* iv 7 59
I'll kneel down, And ask of thee forgiveness . . . . . v 3 10
A closet lock and key of villanous secrets: And yet she'll kneel and pray; I have seen her do't . . . . . . *Othello* iv 2 23
Here I kneel: If e'er my will did trespass 'gainst his love . . iv 2 151
As for Cæsar, Kneel down, kneel down, and wonder . *Ant. and Cleo.* iii 2 19
Tell him, I am prompt To lay my crown at's feet, and there to kneel iii 13 76
He gives me so much of mine own, as I Will kneel to him with thanks . v 2 21
Arise, you shall not kneel: I pray you, rise; rise, Egypt . . v 2 114
Kneel not to me: The power that I have on you is to spare you *Cymbeline* v 5 417
Thou shalt kneel, and justify in knowledge She is thy very princess *Per.* v 1 219
Look, who kneels here! Flesh of thy flesh, Thaisa . . . v 3 46

Kneeled. You were kneel'd to and importuned otherwise *Tempest* ii 1 128
How I persuaded, how I pray'd, and kneel'd, How he refell'd me *M. for M.* v 1 93
I would you had kneel'd, my lord, to ask me mercy, And that at my bidding you could so stand up . . . . . . *All's Well* ii 1 66
Fed from my trencher, kneel'd down at the board . . 2 *Hen. VI.* iv 1 57
Who, in my rage, Kneel'd at my feet, and bade me be advised? *Rich. III.* ii 1 107
She kneel'd, and saint-like Cast her fair eyes to heaven . *Hen. VIII.* iv 1 83
I kneel'd before him; 'Twas very faintly he said 'Rise' . *Coriolanus* v 1 65
See, my women! Against the blown rose may they stop their nose That kneel'd unto the buds . . . . . *Ant. and Cleo.* iii 13 40
You shall find A conqueror that will pray in aid for kindness, Where he for grace is kneel'd to . . . . v 2 28

Kneeling. Upon my knee, Made hard with kneeling, I do pray to thee *K. John* iii 1 310
Kneeling before this ruin of sweet life . . . . . iv 3 65
I pardon him, as God shall pardon me.—O happy vantage of a kneeling knee! Yet am I sick for fear . . . . . *Richard II.* v 3 132
And for our disgrace, his own person, kneeling at our feet . *Hen. V.* iii 6 140
Ere I was risen from the place that show'd My duty kneeling . *Lear* ii 4 30

Knell. Sea-nymphs hourly ring his knell . . . . *Tempest* i 2 402
Let us all ring fancy's knell: I'll begin it,—Ding, dong, bell *M. of V.* iii 2 70
Be this sweet Helen's knell, and now forget her . . . *All's Well* v 3 67
Contempt and clamour Will be my knell . . . . . *W. Tale* i 2 190
When he was brought again to the bar, to hear His knell rung out *Hen. VIII.* ii 1 32
Cause the musicians play me that sad note I named my knell . . iv 2 79
Talks like a knell, and his hum is a battery . . . *Coriolanus* v 4 21
Let's shake our heads, and say, As 'twere a knell unto our master's fortunes, 'We have seen better days' . . . . *T. of Athens* iv 2 26
For it is a knell That summons thee to heaven or to hell . *Macbeth* ii 1 63
The dead man's knell Is there scarce ask'd for who . . . iv 3 170
And so, his knell is knoll'd . . . . v 8 50

Knew. O, If you but knew how you the purpose cherish! . . *Tempest* ii 1 224
I would I knew his mind.—Peruse this paper, madam . *T. G. of Ver.* i 2 33
My master is become a notable lover.—I never knew him otherwise . ii 5 45
If you knew his pure heart's truth, You would quickly learn to know him by his voice . . . . iv 2 88
I, having been acquainted with the smell before, knew it was Crab . iv 4 26
Him he knew well, and guess'd that it was she . . . . v 2 39
I never knew a woman so dote upon a man . . . *Mer. Wives* ii 2 106
I would you knew Ford, sir, that you might avoid him if you saw him ii 2 288
He is wise, sir; he knew your worship would kill him, if he came . ii 3 10
I knew not what 'twas to be beaten till lately . . . . v 1 27
Be not angry: I knew of your purpose . . . . . . v 5 214
He knew the service, and that instructed him to mercy *Meas. for Meas.* iii 2 127
Who knew of your intent and coming hither? . . . . . v 1 124
Yet my husband Knows not that ever he knew me . . . . v 1 187
Who thinks he knows that he ne'er knew my body . . . . v 1 203
But Tuesday night last gone in's garden-house He knew me as a wife . v 1 230
Else imputation, For that he knew you, might reproach your life . v 1 426
I thought it was a fault, but knew it not; Yet did repent me . . v 1 468
That knew me for a fool, a coward, One all of luxury, an ass . . v 1 505

Knew. I knew 'twould be a bald conclusion . . . . *Com. of Errors* ii 2 110
Bear him home for his recovery.—I knew he was not in his perfect wits v 1 42
So immodest to write to one that she knew would flout her *Much Ado* ii 3 148
It were good that Benedick knew of it by some other . . . ii 3 160
It were not good She knew his love, lest she make sport at it . iii 1 58
You have: I knew it would be your answer . . . . . . iii 3 18
But the devil my master knew she was Margaret . . . . iii 3 165
Nor knew not what she did when she spoke to me . . . . v 1 310
I never knew man hold vile stuff so dear . . . . . *L. L. Lost* iv 3 276
You have a favour too: Who sent it? and what is it?—I would you knew v 2 31
O that I knew he were but in by the week! . . . . . v 2 61
I knew her by this jewel on her sleeve . . . . . . v 2 455
If you were civil and knew courtesy, You would not do me thus much injury. Can you not hate me? . . . *M. N. Dream* iii 2 147
You knew, none so well, none so well as you, of my daughter's flight *Mer. of Venice* iii 1 27
I, for my part, knew the tailor that made the wings she flew withal.—And Shylock, for his own part, knew the bird was fledged . . iii 1 29
If you knew to whom you show this honour, How true a gentleman . iii 4 5
I never knew so young a body with so old a head . . . iv 1 163
Were you the doctor and I knew you not? . . . . . v 1 280
If you saw yourself with your eyes or knew yourself with your judgement, the fear of your adventure would counsel you *As Y. Like It* i 2 186
O that your highness knew my heart in this! . . . . iii 1 13
In his youth an inland man; one that knew courtship too well . iii 2 364
Go your ways; I knew what you would prove: my friends told me as much . . . . iv 1 187
No sooner knew the reason but they sought the remedy . . . v 2 39
I knew when seven justices could not take up a quarrel . . v 4 103
O, that once more you knew but what you are! . . *T. of Shrew* Ind. 2 80
A pretty peat! it is best Put finger in the eye, an she knew why . i 1 79
As though, belike, I knew not what to take, and what to leave . i 1 104
I know her father, though I know not her; And he knew my deceased father . . . i 2 102
An she knew him as well as I do, she would think scolding would do little good . . . . i 2 108
You knew my father well, and in him me, Left solely heir . . ii 1 117
If you knew my business, You would entreat me rather go than stay . iii 2 193
I, who never knew how to entreat, Nor never needed that I should entreat . . . iv 3 7
I knew a wench married in an afternoon as she went to the garden . iv 4 99
His name! as if I knew not his name: I have brought him up . v 1 84
Knew the true minute when Exception bid him speak . *All's Well* i 2 39
I knew him.—The rather will I spare my praises towards him . ii 1 105
It were fit you knew him; lest, reposing too far in his virtue . iii 6 14
I would I knew in what particular action to try him . . iii 6 18
And my integrity ne'er knew the crafts That you do charge men with . iv 2 33
For I knew the young count to be a dangerous and lascivious boy . iv 3 247
She knew her distance and did angle for me, Madding my eagerness . v 3 212
I was in that credit with them at that time that I knew of their going to bed . . . v 3 263
By Jove, if ever I knew man, 'twas you . . . . v 3 288
I knew 'twas I; for many do call me fool . . . *T. Night* ii 5 89
To force that on you, in a shameful cunning, Which you knew none of yours . . . iii 1 128
We knew not The doctrine of ill-doing, nor dream'd That any did *W. Tale* i 2 69
Would I knew the villain, I would land-damn him . . . ii 1 142
I charged thee that she should not come about me: I knew she would ii 3 44
You knew of his departure, as you know What you have underta'en to do iii 2 78
Quit his fortunes here, Which you knew great . . . iii 2 169
I knew him once a servant of the prince . . . . iv 3 92
I am no fighter: I am false of heart that way; and that he knew . iv 3 117
The wisest beholder, that knew no more but seeing, could not say if the importance were joy or sorrow . . . v 2 19
Here's a good world! Knew you of this fair work? *K. John* iv 3 116
Hubert told me he did live.—So, on my soul, he did, for aught he knew v 1 43
I would to God thou and I knew where a commodity of good names were to be bought . . . 1 *Hen. IV.* i 2 93
Before I knew thee, Hal, I knew nothing . . . . i 2 104
By the Lord, I knew ye as well as he that made ye . . ii 4 295
If you knew How much they do import, you would make haste . iv 4 4
We all . . . Knew that we ventured on such dangerous seas 2 *Hen. IV.* i 1 181
I knew of this before; but, to speak truth, This present grief had wiped it from my mind . . . i 1 210
He might have more diseases than he knew for . . . i 2 6
Yea, and you knew me, as you did when you ran away by Gad's-hill: you knew I was at your back . . . ii 4 332
We knew where the bona-robas were and had the best of them all . iii 2 26
I knew him a good backsword man . . . iii 2 69
If you knew what pains I have bestow'd to breed this present peace, You would drink freely . . . iv 2 73
I never knew yet but rebuke and check was the reward of valour . iv 3 34
After I saw him fumble with the sheets and play with flowers and smile upon his fingers' ends, I knew there was but one way *Hen. V.* ii 3 16
I knew by that piece of service the men would carry coals . iii 2 49
He told me so himself; and he said he cared not who knew it . iii 7 117
The French might have a good prey of us, if he knew of it . iv 4 81
My mother a Plantagenet,— I knew her well; she was a midwife 2 *Hen. VI.* iv 2 45
Pardon me, God, I knew not what I did! And pardon, father, for I knew not thee! My tears shall wipe away these bloody marks 3 *Hen. VI.* ii 5 69
If Warwick knew in what estate he stands, 'Tis to be doubted he would waken him . . . iv 3 18
I would I knew thy heart.—'Tis figured in my tongue *Richard III.* i 2 193
I would he knew that I had saved his brother! Take thou the fee, and tell him . . . i 4 283
O beauty; Till now I never knew thee! . . . *Hen. VIII.* i 4 76
To whom, If I but knew him, with my love and duty I would surrender it i 4 80
I am richer than my base accusers, That never knew what truth meant iii 1 105
I knew him, and I know him; so I leave him . . . iii 2 55
By my life, She never knew harm-doing . . . . v 3 5
Which of your friends Have I not strove to love, although I knew He were mine enemy? . . . ii 4 30
The times and titles now are alter'd strangely With me since first you knew me . . . iv 2 113
Do you know a man if you see him?—Ay, if I ever saw him before and knew him . . . *Troi. and Cres.* i 2 68
That she was never yet that ever knew Love got so sweet as when desire did sue . . . i 2 316

Knew. Who shall answer him?—I know not: 'tis put to lottery; otherwise He knew his man . . . *Troi. and Cres.* ii 1 141
By my troth, I knew you not: what news with you so early? . iv 2 48
Would thou hadst ne'er been born! I knew thou wouldst be his death iv 2 90
I knew thy grandsire, And once fought with him . . iv 5 196
Nay, I knew by his face that there was something in him *Coriolanus* iv 5 162
If thy captain knew I were here, he would use me with estimation . v 2 55
As if a man were author of himself And knew no other kin . . v 3 37
I care not, I, knew she and all the world: I love Lavinia *T. Andron.* ii 1 71
O, that I knew thy heart; and knew the beast, That I might rail at him! ii 4 34
'Tis sure enough, an you knew how . . . iv 1 95
We are beholding to you, good Andronicus.—An if your highness knew my heart, you were . . . v 3 34
It is my lady, O, it is my love! O, that she knew she were! *R. and J.* ii 2 11
O, she knew well Thy love did read by rote and could not spell . ii 3 87
You know the reason of this haste.—I would I knew not why it should be slow'd . . . iv 1 16
I have been bold—For that I knew it the most general way *T. of Athens* ii 2 209
The devil knew not what he did when he made man politic . iii 3 28
I, to bear this, That never knew but better, is some burden . iv 3 267
Would poison were obedient and knew my mind!—Where wouldst thou send it? . . . iv 3 296
O you hard hearts, you cruel men of Rome, Knew you not Pompey? *J. C.* i 1 42
Who ever knew the heavens menace so? . . . i 3 44
My letters, praying on his side, Because I knew the man, were slighted off iv 3 5
I knew your father; These hands are not more like . *Hamlet* i 2 211
He knew me not at first; he said I was a fishmonger: he is far gone . ii 2 189
They knew what they did; I am to do a good turn for them . iv 6 21
I knew him, Horatio: a fellow of infinite jest, of most excellent fancy . v 1 203
I knew you must be edified by the margent ere you had done . v 2 162
I never found man that knew how to love himself *Othello* i 3 315
I never knew A Florentine more kind and honest . . iii 1 42
Look, how he laughs already!—I never knew woman love man so . iv 1 111
Yet would I knew That stroke would prove the worst! . . iv 1 284
Thy husband knew it all.—My husband!—Thy husband . v 2 139
O, that I knew this husband, which, you say, must charge his horns with garlands! . . *Ant. and Cleo.* i 2 4
Let me be partaker.—Doubt not, sir; I knew it for my bond . i 4 84
If I knew What hoop should hold us stanch, from edge to edge O' the world I would pursue it . . . ii 2 116
Had our general Been what he knew himself, it had gone well . iii 10 27
You were half blasted ere I knew you . . . iii 13 105
Harping on what I am, Not what he knew I was . . iii 13 143
I am loath to tell you what I would you knew . . v 2 107
O, learn'd indeed were that astronomer That knew the stars as I his characters; He'ld lay the future open . . *Cymbeline* iii 2 28
She alone knew this; And, but she spoke it dying, I would not Believe her v 5 40
Knewest. O Corin, that thou knew'st how I do love her! *As Y. Like It* ii 4 23
O cursed wretch, That knew'st this was the prince, and wouldst adventure To mingle faith with him! . . *W. Tale* iv 4 470
That knew'st the very bottom of my soul . . *Hen. V.* ii 2 97
The middle of humanity thou never knewest . . *T. of Athens* iv 3 301
Good.—So is it, if thou knew'st our purposes . . *Hamlet* iv 3 49
Thou knew'st too well My heart was to thy rudder tied *Ant. and Cleo.* iii 11 56
O'er my spirit Thy full supremacy thou knew'st . iii 11 59
That thou couldst see my wars to-day, and knew'st The royal occupation! iv 4 16
Knife, gun, or need of any engine, Would I not have . . *Tempest* ii 1 161
Paunch him with a stake, Or cut his wezand with thy knife . iii 2 99
A short knife and a throng! . . . *Mer. Wives* ii 2 18
Just so much as you may take upon a knife's point . *Much Ado* ii 3 264
The which if I do not carve most curiously, say my knife's naught . v 1 157
Will you prick't with your eye?—No point, with my knife *L. L. Lost* ii 1 190
Why dost thou whet thy knife so earnestly? . . *Mer. of Venice* iv 1 121
Not on thy sole, but on thy soul, harsh Jew, Thou makest thy knife keen iv 1 124
You must prepare your bosom for his knife.—O noble judge! . . iv 1 245
Whose posy was For all the world like cutler's poetry Upon a knife . v 1 150
I may command where I adore; But silence, like a Lucrece knife, With bloodless stroke my heart doth gore . . *T. Night* ii 5 116
Ballad, knife, tape, glove, shoe-tie, bracelet, horn-ring . . *W. Tale* iv 4 610
The edge of war, like an ill-sheathed knife, No more shall cut his master. Therefore, friends, As far as to the sepulchre of Christ 1 *Hen. IV.* i 1 17
I'll thrust my knife in your mouldy chaps . 2 *Hen. IV.* ii 4 138
Like a forked radish, with a head fantastically carved upon it with a knife . . . iii 2 335
Have wash'd his knife With gentle eye-drops . . iv 5 87
From treason's secret knife and traitors' rage 2 *Hen. VI.* iii 1 174
Are you the butcher, Suffolk? Where's your knife? . iii 2 195
I wear no knife to slaughter sleeping men; But here's a vengeful sword iii 2 197
But set his murdering knife unto the root . 3 *Hen. VI.* ii 6 49
So first the harmless sheep doth yield his fleece And next his throat unto the butcher's knife . . v 6 9
Fool, fool! thou whet'st a knife to kill thyself . *Richard III.* i 3 244
No doubt the murderous knife was dull and blunt Till it was whetted on thy stone-hard heart . . iv 4 226
Which if granted, As he made semblance of his duty, would Have put his knife into him.—A giant traitor! . *Hen. VIII.* i 2 199
After 'the duke his father,' with 'the knife,' He stretch'd him . i 2 203
There's his period, To sheathe his knife in us . . i 2 210
Instead of oil and balm, Thou lay'st in every gash that love hath given me The knife that made it . . *Troi. and Cres.* i 1 63
He came unto my hearth; Presented to my knife his throat *Coriolanus* v 6 31
Or, had he heard the heavenly harmony Which that sweet tongue hath made, He would have dropp'd his knife . . *T. Andron.* ii 4 50
Or get some little knife between thy teeth, And just against thy heart make thou a hole . . iii 2 16
What dost thou strike at, Marcus, with thy knife?—At that that I have kill'd, my lord; a fly . . iii 2 52
Thou hast done a charitable deed. Give me thy knife, I will insult on him . . iii 2 71
Hast thou a knife? come, let me see it. Here, Marcus, fold it in the oration . . iv 3 115
And on their skins, as on the bark of trees, Have with my knife carved in Roman letters . . v 1 139
'Tis true, 'tis true; witness my knife's sharp point . v 3 63
One Paris, that would fain lay knife aboard *Rom. and Jul.* ii 4 214
Hadst thou no poison mix'd, no sharp-ground knife, No sudden mean of death? . . iii 3 44
But call my resolution wise, And with this knife I'll help it presently iv 1 54
'Twixt my extremes and me this bloody knife Shall play thee umpire . iv 1 62

Knife. That my keen knife see not the wound it makes . . *Macbeth* i 5 53
As his host, Who should against his murderer shut the door, Not bear the knife myself . . . . i 7 16
But dip a knife in it, Where it draws blood no cataplasm so rare *Hamlet* iv 7 143
What means that bloody knife?—'Tis hot, it smokes; It came even from the heart of—O, she's dead! . . . . . . *Lear* v 3 223
If knife, drugs, serpents, have Edge, sting, or operation, I am safe *Ant. and Cleo.* iv 15 25
He is dead, Cæsar; Not by a public minister of justice, Nor by a hired knife . . . . v 1 21
Prithee, dispatch: The lamb entreats the butcher: where's thy knife? *Cymbeline* iii 4 99
O, give me cord, or knife, or poison, Some upright justicer! . . v 5 213
Marina's life Seeks to take off by treason's knife . *Pericles* iv Gower 14
Knight. A knight well-spoken, neat and fine; But, were I you, he never should be mine . . . . *T. G. of Ver.* i 2 10
The knight, Sir John, is there . . . . . . *Mer. Wives* i 1 71
Knight, you have beaten my men, killed my deer, and broke open my lodge . . . . i 1 114
Thine own true knight, By day or night, Or any kind of light . . ii 1 15
These knights will hack . . . . ii 1 52
Let's consult together against this greasy knight . . . . ii 1 112
She shall be our messenger to this paltry knight . . . . ii 1 164
I do not think the knight would offer it . . . . . . ii 1 180
Hast thou no suit against my knight, my guest-cavaleire? . . . ii 1 220
Thy name shall be Brook. It is a merry knight . . . . ii 1 227
Yet there has been knights, and lords, and gentlemen, with their coaches . . . . ii 2 65
I shall procure-a you de good guest, de earl, de knight, de lords . ii 3 96
What do you call your knight's name, sirrah?—Sir John Falstaff . iii 2 21
I will to my honest knight Falstaff, and drink canary with him . iii 2 89
Are these your letters, knight?—I love thee. Help me away . . iii 3 148
Call your men, Mistress Ford. You dissembling knight! . . . iii 3 153
I am glad the fat knight is not here.—Why, does he talk of him? . iv 2 29; 37
I am undone! The knight is here.—Why then you are utterly shamed iv 2 42
Take it up.—Pray heaven it be not full of knight again . . . iv 2 115
If they can find in their hearts the poor unvirtuous fat knight shall be any further afflicted, we two will still be the ministers . . iv 2 233
Let them all encircle him about And, fairy-like, to pinch the unclean knight . . . . iv 4 57
I will be like a jack-an-apes also, to burn the knight with my taber . iv 4 68
The knight may be robbed: I'll call. Bully knight! bully Sir John! . iv 5 16
Hue and cry, villain, go! Assist me, knight. I am undone! . . iv 5 93
Yet be cheerful, knight: thou shalt eat a posset to-night at my house . v 5 179
Pardon, goddess of the night, Those that slew thy virgin knight *M. Ado* v 3 13
Shall relate In high-born words the worth of many a knight *L. L. Lost* i 1 173
A most illustrious wight, A man of fire-new words, fashion's own knight i 1 179
Your nose smells 'no' in this, most tender-smelling knight . . v 2 569
Was not that Hector?—The worthy knight of Troy . . . v 2 890
What is Thisby? a wandering knight? . . . . *M. N. Dream* i 2 47
And jealous Oberon would have the child Knight of his train . . ii 1 25
And, all my powers, address your love and might To honour Helen and to be her knight! . . . . ii 2 144
But mark, poor knight, What dreadful dole is here! . . . . v 1 282
A certain knight that swore by his honour they were good pancakes *As Y. Like It* i 2 66
The pancakes were naught and the mustard was good, and yet was not the knight forsworn . . . . i 2 70
You are not forsworn: no more was this knight, swearing by his honour, for he never had any . . . . i 2 82
There lay he, stretched along, like a wounded knight . . . iii 2 254
Dian no queen of virgins, that would suffer her poor knight surprised, without rescue in the first assaults . . . . *All's Well* i 3 120
A foolish knight that you brought in one night here to be her wooer *T. Night* i 3 16
Good Mistress Mary Accost,— You mistake, knight: 'accost' is front her 3 59
O knight, thou lackest a cup of canary: when did I see thee so put down? . . . . i 3 85
Pourquoi, my dear knight?—What is 'pourquoi'? do or not do? . i 3 95
Art thou good at these kickshawses, knight? . . . . . i 3 123
What is thy excellence in a galliard, knight? . . . . . i 3 128
There's a testril of me too: if one knight give a . . . . ii 3 35
A mellifluous voice, as I am true knight . . . . . . ii 3 55
'Hold thy peace, thou knave,' knight? I shall be constrained in't to call thee knave, knight . . . . ii 3 68
Beshrew me, the knight's in admirable fooling . . . . . ii 3 85
Thy exquisite reason, dear knight?—I have no exquisite reason . ii 3 156
Let's to bed, knight . . . . ii 3 198
'Tis too late to go to bed now: come, knight; come, knight . . ii 3 207
You waste the treasure of your time with a foolish knight,— That's me ii 5 86
He is knight, dubbed with unhatched rapier and on carpet consideration iii 4 257
Know of the knight what my offence to him is . . . . iii 4 279
The knight is incensed against you, even to a mortal arbitrement . iii 4 285
I am one that had rather go with sir priest than sir knight . . iii 4 299
A landless knight makes thee a landed squire . . . *K. John* i 1 177
Knight, knight, good mother, Basilisco-like . . . . . . i 1 244
Engaged by my oath—Which God defend a knight should violate! *Rich. II.* i 3 18
Ask yonder knight in arms, Both who he is and why he cometh hither i 3 26
What's thy quarrel? Speak like a true knight, so defend thee heaven! i 3 34
Two and twenty knights, Balk'd in their own blood . . 1 *Hen. IV.* i 1 68
Phœbus, he, 'that wandering knight so fair.' . . . . . i 2 17
Child of honour and renown, This gallant Hotspur, this all-praised knight . . . . iii 2 140
'Tis in the nose of thee; thou art the Knight of the Burning Lamp . iii 3 30
I know this face full well: A gallant knight he was . . . v 3 20
Three knights upon our party slain to-day, A noble earl . . . v 5 6
As I am a true knight . . . . 2 *Hen. IV.* i 2 50
'John Falstaff, knight,'—every man must know that, as oft as he has occasion to name himself . . . . ii 2 118
I will now take my leave of these six dry, round, old, withered knights ii 4 9
Sweet knight, I kiss thy neif: what! we have seen the seven stars . ii 4 200
How doth the good knight? may I ask how my lady his wife doth? . iii 2 70
Ha, cousin Silence, that thou hadst seen that that this knight and I have seen! . . . . iii 2 226
I am a knight, sir; and my name is Colevile of the dale . . . iv 3 3
Colevile is your name, a knight is your degree, and your place the dale iv 3 6
Sir John Colevile of the dale, a most furious knight and valorous enemy iv 3 43
Do me right, And dub me knight: Samingo . . . . . v 3 78
Sweet knight, thou art now one of the greatest men in this realm . v 3 91
Knight. O base Assyrian knight, what is thy news? Let King Cophetua know . . . . 2 *Hen. IV.* v 3 105
God bless thy lungs, good knight . . . . v 5 9
My knight, I will inflame thy noble liver, And make thee rage . v 5 33
Fifteen hundred knights, Six thousand and two hundred good esquires *Hen. V.* i 1 13
The king hath run bad humours on the knight; that's the even of it ii 1 128
Let us condole the knight; for, lambkins, we will live . . . ii 1 133
And you, my gentle knight, give me your thoughts . . . . ii 2 14
This knight, no less for bounty bound to us Than Cambridge is . ii 2 92
High dukes, great princes, barons, lords and knights, For your great seats now quit you of great shames . . . . iii 5 46
The armourers, accomplishing the knights, With busy hammers . iv Prol. 12
Good old knight, Collect them all together at my tent . . . iv 1 303
The fat knight with the great-belly doublet: he was full of jests, and gipes iv 7 50
Lords and barons, knights and squires, Full fifteen hundred . . iv 8 83
Of knights, esquires, and gallant gentlemen, Eight thousand and four hundred . . . . iv 8 89
Great is the rumour of this dreadful knight . . . 1 *Hen. VI.* ii 3 7
Cowardly knight! ill fortune follow thee! . . . . . . iii 2 109
I vow'd, base knight, when I did meet thee next, To tear the garter from thy craven's leg . . . . iv 1 14
And ill beseeming any common man, Much more a knight . . . iv 1 32
Knights of the garter were of noble birth, Valiant and virtuous . iv 1 34
Doth but usurp the sacred name of knight . . . . . . iv 1 40
Thou hear'st thy doom! Be packing, therefore, thou that wast a knight iv 1 46
Doubtless he would have made a noble knight . . . . . iv 7 44
Knight of the noble order of Saint George, Worthy Saint Michael . iv 7 68
He seems a knight, And will not any way dishonour me . . . v 3 101
Then swear allegiance to his majesty, As thou art knight . . . v 4 170
He shall be encountered with a man as good as himself: he is but a knight, is a'?—No.—To equal him, I will make myself a knight presently . . . . 2 *Hen. VI.* iv 2 125
'Twere not amiss He were created knight for his good service . . v 1 77
Iden, kneel down. Rise up a knight . . . . v 1 78
Arise a knight; And learn this lesson, draw thy sword in right 3 *Hen. VI.* ii 2 61
Stir up in Suffolk . . . The knights and gentlemen to come with thee . iv 8 13
Lords, knights, and gentlemen, what I should say My tears gainsay . v 4 73
The late queen's gentlewoman, a knight's daughter, To be her mistress' mistress! the queen's queen! . . . . . . *Hen. VIII.* iii 2 94
Call some knight to arms That hath a stomach . . *Troi. and Cres.* ii 1 136
Here's a lord,—come knights from east to west, And cull their flower . ii 3 274
Will you the knights Shall to the edge of all extremity Pursue each other? . . . . iv 5 67
A little proudly, and great deal misprizing The knight opposed . . iv 5 75
Half Hector comes to seek This blended knight, half Trojan and half Greek . . . . iv 5 86
Go, gentle knight, Stand by our Ajax . . . . iv 5 88
A true knight, Not yet mature, yet matchless, firm of word . . . iv 5 96
I will go eat with thee and see your knights . . . . . . iv 5 158
I have chastised the amorous Trojan, And am her knight by proof . v 5 5
What lady is that, which doth enrich the hand Of yonder knight? *Rom. and Jul.* i 5 44
Give this ring to my true knight, And bid him come . . . . iii 2 142
He is very often like a knight; and, generally, in all shapes that man goes up and down in from fourscore to thirteen . *T. of Athens* ii 2 118
The adventurous knight shall use his foil and target . . *Hamlet* ii 2 334
With reservation of an hundred knights, By you to be sustain'd *Lear* i 1 135
His knights grow riotous, and himself upbraids us On every trifle . i 3 6
And let his knights have colder looks among you; What grows of it, no matter . . . . i 3 22
Here do you keep a hundred knights and squires . . . . i 4 262
'Tis politic and safe to let him keep At point a hundred knights . i 4 345
Was he not companion with the riotous knights That tend upon my father? . . . . ii 1 96
I can be patient; I can stay with Regan, I and my hundred knights . ii 4 234
When every case in law is right; No squire in debt, nor no poor knight iii 2 86
Some five or six and thirty of his knights, Hot questrists after him . iii 7 16
Bow your knees. Arise my knights o' the battle . . *Cymbeline* v 5 20
He, true knight, No lesser of her honour confident Than I did truly find her . . . . v 5 186
There are princes and knights come from all parts of the world to just and tourney for her love . . . . *Pericles* ii 1 115
Are the knights ready to begin the triumph?—They are, my liege . ii 2 1
'Tis now your honour, daughter, to explain The labour of each knight in his device . . . . ii 2 15
Who is the first that doth prefer himself?—A knight of Sparta . . ii 2 18
Upon his shield Is an arm'd knight that's conquer'd by a lady . . ii 2 26
Which the knight himself With such a graceful courtesy deliver'd . ii 2 40
But stay, the knights are coming: we will withdraw Into the gallery . ii 2 58
Knights, To say you're welcome were superfluous . . . . ii 3 1
You are princes and my guests.—But you, my knight and guest . . ii 3 9
You are right courteous knights . . . . ii 3 27
Has done no more than other knights have done; Has broken a staff or so ii 3 34
What, are you merry, knights?—Who can be other in this royal presence? ii 3 48
Yon knight doth sit too melancholy, As if the entertainment in our court Had not a show might countervail his worth . . . . ii 3 54
Alas, my father, it befits not me Unto a stranger knight to be so bold . ii 3 67
I have heard, you knights of Tyre Are excellent in making ladies trip . ii 3 102
Pages and lights, to conduct These knights unto their several lodgings! ii 3 110
She tells me here, she'll wed the stranger knight . . . . ii 5 16
That she loves the knight of Tyre! 'Tis the king's subtilty to have my life . . . . ii 5 43
But, mistress, do you know the French knight that cowers i' the hams? iv 2 113
Thwarting the wayward seas, Attended on by many a lord and knight iv 4 11
Knighted. If I would but go to hell for an eternal moment or so, I could be knighted . . . . *Mer. Wives* ii 1 50
We burn daylight: here, read, read; perceive how I might be knighted ii 1 55
By the honour-giving hand Of Cœur-de-lion knighted . . *K. John* i 1 54
And buried one and twenty valiant sons, Knighted in field *T. Andron.* i 1 196
Thy Cæsar knighted me; my youth I spent Much under him *Cymbeline* iii 1 70
Knight-errant. Come, you she knight-errant, come . 2 *Hen. IV.* v 4 25
Knighthood. Buckled below fair knighthood's bending knee *Mer. Wives* v 5 76
By that and all the rites of knighthood else . . . *Richard II.* i 1 75
By that sword I swear, Which gently laid my knighthood on my shoulder i 1 79
Speak truly, on thy knighthood and thy oath . . . . . i 3 14
Setting thy knighthood aside, thou art a knave to call me so 1 *Hen. IV.* iii 3 137
Setting my knighthood and my soldiership aside, I had lied in my throat, if I had said so.—I pray you, sir, then set your knighthood and your soldiership aside . . . . 2 *Hen. IV.* i 2 93

Knighthood. I would not take a knighthood for my fortune . 2 *Hen. IV.* v 3 133
Whether that such cowards ought to wear This ornament of knighthood
1 *Hen. VI.* iv 1 29
You promised knighthood to our forward son : Unsheathe your sword, and dub him presently. Edward, kneel down . 3 *Hen VI.* ii 2 58
What safe and nicely I might well delay By rule of knighthood, I disdain *Lear* v 3 145
Knighthoods and honours, borne As I wear mine, are titles but of scorn
Cymbeline v 2 6
Knightly. When my knightly stomach is sufficed . *K. John* i 1 191
I'll answer thee in any . . . chivalrous design of knightly trial *Rich. II.* i 1 81
Say who thou art And why thou comest thus knightly clad in arms . i 3 12
Being all too base To stain the temper of my knightly sword . iv 1 29
The garter, blemish'd, pawn'd his knightly virtue . *Richard III.* iv 4 370
Knit. Mine enemies are all knit up In their distractions . *Tempest* iii 3 89
Cut your hair.—No, girl ; I'll knit it up in silken strings *T. G. of Ver.* ii 7 45
She can knit.—What need a man care for a stock with a wench, when she can knit him a stock? iii 1 310
He shall not knit a knot in his fortunes with the finger of my substance : if he take her, let him take her simply *Mer. Wives* iii 2 76
Not to be married, Not to knit my soul to an approved wanton *M. Ado* iv 1 45
My heart unto yours is knit So that but one heart we can make of it ; Two bosoms interchained with an oath *M. N. Dream* ii 2 47
By and by, with us These couples shall eternally be knit . iv 1 186
Thy stones with lime and hair knit up in thee . v 1 193
Their garters of an indifferent knit . *T. of Shrew* iv 1 95
France, shall we knit our powers? *K. John* ii 1 398
This royal hand and mine are newly knit . iii 1 226
When your head did but ache, I knit my handkercher about your brows iv 1 42
And knit our powers to the arm of peace . 2 *Hen. IV.* iv 1 177
The Earl of Armagnac, near knit to Charles . 1 *Hen. VI.* v 1 17
Why doth the great Duke Humphrey knit his brows? . 2 *Hen. VI.* i 2 3
He knits his brow and shows an angry eye And passeth by . iii 1 15
The premised flames of the last day Knit earth and heaven together ! . v 2 42
Thou smiling while he knit his angry brows . 3 *Hen. VI.* ii 2 20
The widow likes him not, she knits her brows . iii 2 82
Your high-swoln hearts, But lately splinter'd, knit, and join'd *Rich. III.* ii 2 118
Knit all the Greekish ears To his experienced tongue . *Troi. and Cres.* i 3 67
The amity that wisdom knits not, folly may easily untie . ii 3 110
An 'twere my case, I should go hang myself.—If thou hadst hands to help thee knit the cord *T. Andron.* ii 4 10
Let me teach you how to knit again This scatter'd corn into one mutual sheaf v 3 70
I'll have this knot knit up to-morrow morning . *Rom. and Jul.* iv 2 24
This yellow slave [gold] Will knit and break religions . *T. of Athens* iv 3 34
Sleep that knits up the ravell'd sleave of care . *Macbeth* ii 2 37
To the which my duties Are with a most indissoluble tie For ever knit iii 1 18
I confess me knit to thy deserving with cables of perdurable toughness
Othello i 3 342
To knit your hearts With an unslipping knot . *Ant. and Cleo.* ii 2 128
'Tis true.—Then is Cæsar and he for ever knit together . ii 6 122
Our force by land Hath nobly held ; our sever'd navy too Have knit again iii 13 171
To knit their souls, On whom there is no more dependency But brats and beggary, in self-figured knot . *Cymbeline* ii 3 122
To glad her presence, The senate-house of planets all did sit, To knit in her their best perfections *Pericles* i 1 11
When peers thus knit, a kingdom ever stands . ii 4 58
Knitter.—The spinsters and the knitters in the sun . *T. Night* ii 4 45
Knitteth.—By that which knitteth souls and prospers loves *M. N. Dream* i 1 172
Knives.—Some say knives have edges. It must be as it may . *Hen. V.* ii 1 25
Why the devil should we keep knives to cut one another's throats? . ii 1 96
Methinks they should invite them without knives ; Good for their meat, and safer for their lives *T. of Athens* i 2 45
Bankrupts, hold fast ; Rather than render back, out with your knives ! iv 1 9
Their knives care not, While you have throats to answer . v 1 181
Free from our feasts and banquets bloody knives, Do faithful homage
Macbeth iii 6 35
Hath laid knives under his pillow, and halters in his pew . *Lear* iii 4 54
If there be cords, or knives, Poison, or fire, or suffocating streams, I'll not endure it. Would I were satisfied ! *Othello* iii 3 388
[Death] hath more ministers than we That draw his knives i' the war
Cymbeline v 3 73
If fires be hot, knives sharp, or waters deep, Untied I still my virgin knot will keep. Diana, aid my purpose ! *Pericles* iv 2 159
Knob. His face is all bubukles, and whelks, and knobs . *Hen. V.* iii 6 108
Knock. O, the cry did knock Against my very heart ! . *Tempest* i 2 8
I'll yield him thee asleep, Where thou mayst knock a nail into his head iii 2 69
Go knock and call ; he'll speak like an Anthropophaginian *Mer. Wives* iv 5 10
Go to your bosom ; Knock there, and ask your heart what it doth know
Meas. for Meas. ii 2 137
Knock the door hard.—Let him knock till it ache . *Com. of Errors* iii 1 58
I'll knock elsewhere, to see if they'll disdain me . iii 1 121
Knock at the abbey-gate And bid the lady abbess come to me . v 1 165
Whiles we shut the gates upon one wooer, another knocks at the door
Mer. of Venice i 2 147
Knock, I say.—Knock, sir ! whom should I knock? . *T. of Shrew* i 2 5
Villain, I say, knock me here soundly.—Knock you here, sir ! why, sir, what am I, sir, that I should knock you here, sir? i 2 9
Knock me at this gate And rap me well, or I'll knock your knave's pate i 2 11
I should knock you first, And then I know after who comes by the worst i 2 13
Faith, sirrah, an you'll not knock, I'll ring it . i 2 16
Now, knock when I bid you, sirrah villain ! . i 2 19
He bid me knock him and rap him soundly, sir : well, was it fit? . i 2 30
I bade the rascal knock upon your gate And could not get him for my heart to do it.—Knock at the gate ! O heavens ! Spake you not these words plain, 'Sirrah, knock me here, rap me here, knock me well, and knock me soundly'? i 2 37
This cuff was but to knock at your ear, and beseech listening . iv 1 67
They're busy within ; you were best knock louder . v 1 16
What's he that knocks as he would beat down the gate? . v 1 17
When midnight comes, knock at my chamber-window . *All's Well* iv 2 54
Gallows and knock are too powerful on the highway . *W. Tale* iv 3 29
Knock but at the gate, And he himself will answer . 2 *Hen. IV.* i 1 5
Who knocks so loud at door? Look to the door there, Francis . ii 4 381
Be merry. Look who's at door there, ho ! who knocks? . v 3 75
I have an humour to knock you indifferently well . *Hen. V.* ii 1 58
The knocks are too hot ; and, for mine own part, I have not a case of lives iii 2 3
Knocks go and come ; God's vassals drop and die . iii 2 8
I'll knock his leek about his pate Upon Saint Davy's day . iv 1 54
Do not you wear your dagger in your cap that day, lest he knock that . iv 1 57

Knock. Who's there that knocks so imperiously? . 1 *Hen. VI.* i 3 5
We'll knock.—Qui est là?—Paysans, pauvres gens de France . iii 2 12
Knock him down there . 2 *Hen. VI.* iv 6 9
Up Fish Street ! down Saint Magnus' Corner ! kill and knock down ! iv 8 2
My liege, I'll knock once more to summon them . 3 *Hen. VI.* iv 7 16
Go, go, up to the leads ; the lord mayor knocks . *Richard III.* iii 7 55
Norfolk, we must have knocks ; ha ! must we not? . v 3 5
Let the music knock it . *Hen. VIII.* i 4 108
What should you do, but knock 'em down by the dozens? . v 4 32
Hector shall have a great catch, if he knock out either of your brains : a' were as good crack a fusty nut . *Troi. and Cres.* ii 1 110
How earnestly they knock ! Pray you, come in . iv 2 41
Whether to knock against the gates of Rome, Or rudely visit them in parts remote, To fright them, ere destroy . *Coriolanus* iv 5 147
When Publius shot, The Bull, being gall'd, gave Aries such a knock That down fell both the Ram's horns in the court . *T. Andron.* iv 3 71
Knock at my door, and tell me what he says . iv 3 119
Knock at his study, where, they say, he keeps . v 2 5
A bump as big as a young cockerel's stone ; A parlous knock *Rom. and Jul.* i 3 54
Knock and enter ; and no sooner in, But every man betake him to his legs i 4 33
Who knocks so hard? whence come you? what's your will? . iii 3 78
Whither art going?—To knock out an honest Athenian's brains *T. of A.* i 1 192
All our bills.—Knock me down with 'em : cleave me to the girdle . iii 4 91
'Tis good. Go to the gate ; somebody knocks . *J. Cæsar* ii 1 60
Hark, hark ! one knocks : Portia, go in awhile . ii 1 304
Lucius, who's that knocks?—Here is a sick man . ii 1 309
Doth unfix my hair And make my seated heart knock at my ribs *Macbeth* i 3 136
Knock, knock, knock ! Who's there, i' the name of Beelzebub? . ii 3 3
Knock, knock ! Who's there, in the other devil's name . ii 3 8
Open, locks, Whoever knocks ! . iv 1 47
Why does he suffer this rude knave now to knock him about the sconce?
Hamlet v 1 110
Let me go, sir, Or I'll knock you o'er the mazzard . *Othello* ii 3 155
Hark ! who is't that knocks?—It's the wind . iv 3 53
Who's there that knocks?—A gentleman.—No more?—Yes . *Cymbeline* ii 3 82
To the court I'll knock her back, foot her home again . iii 5 148
A thing More slavish did I ne'er than answering A slave without a knock iv 2 74
Knock off his manacles ; bring your prisoner to the king . v 4 199
Knocked. 'Twere good you knocked him . *T. G. of Ver.* ii 4 7
Whom would to God I had well knock'd at first . *T. of Shrew* i 2 34
The brains of my Cupid's knocked out . *All's Well* iii 2 16
Disgraces have of late knocked too often at my door . iv 1 31
That many have their giddy brains knock'd out . 1 *Hen. VI.* iii 1 83
What music will be in him when Hector has knocked out his brains, I know not ; but, I am sure, none . *Troi. and Cres.* iii 3 303
Would he were knock'd i' the head ! Who's that at door? . iv 2 35
Mark how the blood of Cæsar follow'd it, As rushing out of doors, to be resolved If Brutus so unkindly knock'd, or no . *J. Cæsar* iii 2 184
Chapless, and knocked about the mazzard with a sexton's spade *Hamlet* v 1 97
Not Hercules Could have knock'd out his brains, for he had none *Cymb.* iv 2 115
Knocking. And come you now with, 'knocking at the gate'? *T. of Shrew* i 2 42
A dozen captains, Bare-headed, sweating, knocking at the taverns 2 *Hen. IV.* ii 4 388
More knocking at the door ! How now ! what's the matter? . ii 4 398
So there is, but it lies as coldly in him as fire in a flint, which will not show without knocking . *Troi. and Cres.* iii 3 258
Whence is that knocking? How is't with me, when every noise appals me?
Macbeth ii 2 57
I hear a knocking At the south entry : retire we to our chamber . ii 2 65
Hark ! more knocking. Get on your nightgown, lest occasion call us . ii 2 69
Wake Duncan with thy knocking ! I would thou couldst ! . ii 2 74
Here's a knocking indeed ! . ii 3 1
Is thy master stirring? Our knocking has awaked him ; here he comes ii 3 48
To bed, to bed ! there's knocking at the gate : come, come, come, come v 1 73
Pale as his shirt ; his knees knocking each other . *Hamlet* ii 1 81
By making him uncapable of Othello's place ; knocking out his brains
Othello iv 2 236
Knog. I will knog his urinals about his knave's costard . *Mer. Wives* iii 1 14 ; 90
Let us knog our prains together to be revenge . iii 1 122
Knolled.—If ever been where bells have knoll'd to church *As Y. L. It* ii 7 114
And have with holy bell been knoll'd to church . ii 7 121
And so, his knell is knoll'd . *Macbeth* v 8 50
Knot.—Sitting, His arms in this sad knot . *Tempest* i 2 224
In silken strings With twenty odd-conceited true-love knots *T. G. of Ver.* ii 7 46
Trust me, a good knot . *Mer. Wives* iii 2 52
He shall not knit a knot in his fortunes with the finger of my substance iii 2 76
There's a knot, a ging, a pack, a conspiracy against me . iv 2 123
Hath been often burst and now repaired with knots . *T. of Shrew* iii 2 60
Had the whole theoric of war in the knot of his scarf . *All's Well* iv 3 163
You are undone, captain, all but your scarf ; that has a knot on't yet . iv 3 359
O time ! thou must untangle this, not I ; It is too hard a knot for me to untie ! *T. Night* ii 2 42
For by this knot thou shalt so surely tie Thy now unsured assurance to the crown *K. John* ii 1 470
Her hedges ruin'd, Her knots disorder'd . *Richard II.* iii 4 46
Will you again unknit This churlish knot of all-abhorred war? 1 *Hen. IV.* v 1 16
The Gordian knot of it he will unloose, Familiar as his garter *Hen. V.* i 1 46
The sooner to effect And surer bind this knot of amity . 1 *Hen. VI.* v 1 16
Confirm that amity With nuptial knot . 3 *Hen. VI.* iii 3 55
His ancient knot of dangerous adversaries To-morrow are let blood
Richard III. iii 1 182
A knot you are of damned blood-suckers . iii 3 6
And, by that knot, looks proudly o'er the crown . iv 3 42
As knots, by the conflux of meeting sap, Infect the sound pine *T. and C.* i 3 7
Blunt wedges rive hard knots . i 3 316
And with another knot, five-finger-tied . v 2 157
Let grow thy sinews till their knots be strong . v 3 33
I would he had continued to his country As he began, and not unknit himself The noble knot he made . *Coriolanus* iv 2 32
Unknit that sorrow-wreathen knot . *T. Andron.* iii 2 4
I'll have this knot knit up to-morrow morning . *Rom. and Jul.* iv 2 24
May you a better feast never behold, You knot of mouth-friends !
T. of Athens iii 6 99
So oft as that shall be, So often shall the knot of us be call'd The men that gave their country liberty . *J. Cæsar* iii 1 117
Wife and child, Those precious motives, those strong knots of love *Macb.* iv 3 27
Blanket my loins ; elf all my hair in knots . *Lear* ii 3 10
Keep it as a cistern for foul toads To knot and gender in ! . *Othello* iv 2 62
To knit your hearts With an unslipping knot . *Ant. and Cleo.* ii 2 129
With thy sharp teeth this knot intrinsicate Of life at once untie . v 2 307
Come off, come off : As slippery as the Gordian knot was hard ! *Cymbeline* ii 2 34

Knot. To knit their souls, On whom there is no more dependency But brats and beggary, in self-figured knot . *Cymbeline* ii 3 124
Untied I still my virgin knot will keep. Diana, aid my purpose! *Pericles* iv 2 160
Knot-grass. You minimus, of hindering knot-grass made *M. N. Dream* iii 2 329
Knotted. When the splitting wind Makes flexible the knees of knotted oaks . . . . *Troi. and Cres.* i 3 50
Thy knotted and combined locks to part . . . . . *Hamlet* i 5 18
Knotty. I will rend an oak And peg thee in his knotty entrails *Tempest* i 2 295
I have seen tempests, when the scolding winds Have rived the knotty oaks . . . . *J. Cæsar* i 3 6
Knotty-pated. Why, thou clay-brained guts, thou knotty-pated fool *1 Hen. IV.* ii 4 251
Know. More to know Did never meddle with my thoughts . *Tempest* i 2 21
Thou must now know farther.—You have often Begun to tell me what I am . . . . i 2 33
In lieu o' the premises Of homage and I know not how much tribute . i 2 124
Your reason For raising this sea-storm?—Know thus far forth . i 2 177
'Tis a good dulness, And give it way: I know thou canst not choose . i 2 186
When thou didst not, savage, Know thine own meaning . . . . i 2 356
You taught me language; and my profit on't Is, I know how to curse . i 2 364
Vouchsafe my prayer May know if you remain upon this island . i 2 423
My lord shall know what I have done: So, king, go safely on . . ii 1 326
If it should thunder as it did before, I know not where to hide my head ii 2 23
Thou dost me yet but little hurt; thou wilt anon, I know it by thy trembling . . . . ii 2 83
I should know that voice: it should be—but he is drowned . . . ii 2 90
I do not know One of my sex; no woman's face remember . . iii 1 48
Revenge it on him,—for I know thou darest, But this thing dare not . iii 2 62
Tell me, heavenly bow, If Venus or her son, as thou dost know, Do now attend the queen? . . . . iv 1 87
High'st queen of state, Great Juno, comes; I know her by her gait iv 1 102
O, ho, monster! we know what belongs to a frippery . . . iv 1 224
Not one of them That yet looks on me, or would know me . . . v 1 83
Whether thou be'st he or no, Or some enchanted trifle to abuse me, As late I have been, I not know . . . . v 1 113
Require My dukedom of thee, which perforce, I know, Thou must restore v 1 133
Howsoe'er you have Been justled from your senses, know for certain That I am Prospero . . . . v 1 158
And—how we know not—all clapp'd under hatches . . . . v 1 231
Two of these fellows you Must know and own . . . . . v 1 275
O, they love least that let men know their love *T. G. of Ver.* i 2 32
That knows I am a maid, And would not force the letter to my view! . i 2 53
Do you know Madam Silvia?—She that your worship loves? . . ii 1 14; 44
Why, how know you that I am in love?—Marry, by these special marks ii 1 17
Why, sir, I know her not.—Dost thou know her by my gazing on her, and yet knowest her not? . . . . ii 1 50
Sir, I know that well enough.—What dost thou know? . . . . ii 1 55
I know the gentleman To be of worth and worthy estimation . . ii 4 55
You know him well?—I know him as myself . . . . . ii 4 61
I know you joy not in a love-discourse . . . . . . ii 4 127
Didst thou but know the inly touch of love, Thou wouldst as soon go kindle fire with snow . . . . ii 7 18
Know, worthy prince, Sir Valentine, my friend, This night intends to steal away your daughter . . . . iii 1 10
I know you have determined to bestow her On Thurio . . . . iii 1 13
Know, noble lord, they have devised a mean . . . . . iii 1 38
He shall never know That I had any light from thee of this . . . iii 1 48
Doth Silvia know that I am banished?—Ay, ay . . . . . iii 1 221
He lives not now that knows me to be in love; yet I am in love . iii 1 264
Bastard virtues; that, indeed, know not their fathers . . . iii 1 322
We know, on Valentine's report, You are already Love's firm votary . iii 2 57
Then know that I have little wealth to lose . . . . . iv 1 11
Know, then, that some of us are gentlemen . . . . . iv 1 44
You know that love Will creep in service where it cannot go . . iv 2 19
If you knew his pure heart's truth, You would quickly learn to know him by his voice . . . . iv 2 89
Madam Silvia Entreated me to call and know her mind . . . iv 3 2
Come to know what service It is your pleasure to command me in . iv 3 9
I pity much your grievances; Which since I know they virtuously are placed, I give consent to go along with you . . . . iv 3 38
Therefore know thou, for this I entertain thee . . . . iv 4 75
But yet so coldly As, heaven it knows, I would not have him speed . iv 4 112
I know they are stuff'd with protestations And full of new-found oaths iv 4 134
Dost thou know her?—Almost as well as I do know myself . . iv 4 147
Therefore I know she is about my height . . . . . . iv 4 169
And she shall thank you for't, if e'er you know her . . . iv 4 184
What says she to my valour?—O, sir, she makes no doubt of that.—She needs not, when she knows it cowardice . . . . . v 2 21
Know then, I here forget all former griefs, Cancel all grudge . . v 4 142
I know the young gentlewoman; she has good gifts . *Mer. Wives* i 1 63
The council shall know this.—'Twere better for you if it were known in counsel . . . . i 1 120
Let us command to know that of your mouth or of your lips . . i 1 235
When we are married and have more occasion to know one another . i 1 257
Which of you know Ford of this town?—I ken the wight . . . i 3 39
But notwithstanding that, I know Anne's mind,—that's neither here nor there . . . . i 4 111
Never a woman in Windsor knows more of Anne's mind than I do. . i 4 136
What doth he think of us?—Nay, I know not . . . . . ii 1 87
Unless he know some strain in me, that I know not myself, he would never have boarded me in this fury . . . . . . ii 1 90
You stand on distance, your passes, stoccadoes, and I know not what . ii 1 234
She was in his company at Page's house; and what they made there, I know not . . . . ii 1 245
Have a nay-word, that you may know one another's mind . . ii 2 131
'Tis not good that children should know any wickedness: old folks, you know, have discretion, as they say, and know the world . . ii 2 135
Sir, I know not how I may deserve to be your porter . . . ii 2 180
Sith you yourself know how easy it is to be such an offender . . ii 2 195
Not only bought many presents to give her, but have given largely to many to know what she would have given . . . . . ii 2 207
Believe it, for you know it. There is money; spend it, spend it . . ii 2 240
Come you to me at night; you shall know how I speed . . . ii 2 277
Do you know Ford, sir?—Hang him, poor cuckoldly knave! I know him not . . . . ii 2 280
Thou, Master Brook, shalt know him for knave and cuckold . . . ii 2 297
What is he?—I think you know him . . . . iii 1 60
He is of too high a region; he knows too much . . . . . iii 2 75
My master knows not of your being here . . . . . . iii 3 29
We'll teach him to know turtles from jays . . . . . . iii 3 44

Know. Well, heaven knows how I love you; and you shall one day find it *Mer. Wives* iii 3 87
If you know yourself clear, why, I am glad of it . . . . . iii 3 123
I know not which pleases me better, that my husband is deceived, or Sir John . . . . iii 3 189
You may know by my size that I have a kind of alacrity in sinking . iii 5 12
You come to know what hath passed between me and Ford's wife? . iii 5 62
Come to me at your convenient leisure, and you shall know how I speed iii 5 137
How might we disguise him?—Alas the day, I know not! . . . iv 2 71
We do not know what's brought to pass under the profession of fortune-telling . . . . iv 2 183
Such daubery as this is beyond our element: we know nothing . iv 2 187
Well you know The superstitious idle-headed eld Received and did deliver to our age This tale . . . . iv 4 35
Send quickly to Sir John, to know his mind . . . . . . iv 4 83
I had other things to have spoken with her too from him.—What are they? let us know . . . . iv 5 43
To know if it were my master's fortune to have her or no . . . iv 5 48
By my trot, dere is no duke dat the court is know to come . . . iv 5 90
I fear not Goliath with a weaver's beam; because I know also life is a shuttle . . . . v 1 24
We have a nay-word how to know one another: I come to her in white, and cry 'mum;' she cries 'budget;' and by that we know one another . . . . v 2 5
No man means evil but the devil, and we shall know him by his horns . v 2 16
We two must go together.—I know vat I have to do. Adieu . . . v 3 6
I'll make the best in Gloucestershire know on't . . . . v 5 191
Did not I tell you how you should know my daughter by her garments? v 5 207
I am put to know that your own science Exceeds, in that *Meas. for Meas.* i 1 5
You must know, we have with special soul Elected him . . . . i 1 18
Always obedient to your grace's will, I come to know your pleasure . i 1 27
We shall write to you, . . . and do look to know What doth befall you here . . . . i 1 58
'Tis not so.—Nay, but I know 'tis so . . . . i 2 67
You know the lady; she is fast my wife . . . . . . i 2 151
That it may know He can command, lets it straight feel the spur . . i 2 165
None better knows than you How I have ever loved the life removed . i 3 7
Turn you the key, and know his business of him; You may, I may not i 4 8
I now must make you know I am that Isabella and his sister . . i 4 22
We do learn By those that know the very nerves of state . . i 4 53
Let him learn to know, when maidens sue, Men give like gods . . i 4 80
Let but your honour know, Whom I believe to be most strait in virtue ii 1 8
What know the laws That thieves do pass on thieves? . . . . ii 1 22
If these be good people in a commonweal that do nothing but use their abuses in common houses, I know no law . . . . ii 1 43
Are they not malefactors?—If it please your honour, I know not well what they are . . . . ii 1 53
I'll know His pleasure; may be he will relent . . . . . ii 2 2
I pity those I do not know, Which a dismiss'd offence would after gall . ii 2 101
Go to your bosom; Knock there, and ask your heart what it doth know ii 2 137
Make me know The nature of their crimes, that I may minister To them ii 3 6
I am come to know your pleasure.—That you might know it, would much better please me Than to demand what 'tis . . . . ii 4 31
Let me be ignorant, and in nothing good, But graciously to know I am no better . . . . ii 4 77
I know your virtue hath a license in't . . . . ii 4 145
Let me know the point.—O, I do fear thee . . . . . iii 1 73
To die, and go we know not where; To lie in cold obstruction and to rot iii 1 118
I know this to be true; therefore prepare yourself to death . . . iii 1 168
What news, friar, of the duke?—I know none. Can you tell me of any? iii 2 92
Where is he, think you?—I know not where; but wheresoever, I wish him well . . . . iii 2 96
That I know to be true . . . . iii 2 118
And I believe I know the cause of his withdrawing . . . . iii 2 139
I know him, and I love him.—Love talks with better knowledge . . iii 2 158
I know what I know.—I can hardly believe that, since you know not what you speak . . . . iii 2 161
He shall know you better, sir, if I may live to report you . . . iii 2 171
Pattern in himself to know, Grace to stand, and virtue go . . . iii 2 277
I have made him know I have a servant comes with me along . . iv 1 45
Do you persuade yourself that I respect you?—Good friar, I know you do iv 1 54
You shall hear more ere morning.—Happily You something know . . iv 2 99
It was the desire of the penitent to be so bared before his death: you know the course is common . . . . iv 2 189
Here is the hand and seal of the duke: you know the character . . iv 2 208
Within these two days he will be here. This is a thing that Angelo knows not . . . . iv 2 215
The provost knows our purpose and our plot . . . . . . iv 5 2
To make them know That outward courtesies would fain proclaim Favours that keep within . . . . v 1 14
Know you that Friar Lodowick that she speaks of?—I know him for a man divine and holy . . . . v 1 143
To speak, as from his mouth, what he doth know Is true and false . v 1 155
I have known my husband; yet my husband Knows not that ever he knew me . . . . v 1 187
Charges she more than me?—Not that I know . . . . . v 1 200
Who thinks he knows that he ne'er knew my body, But knows he thinks that he knows Isabel's . . . . v 1 203
Know you this woman?—Carnally, she says.—Sirrah, no more! . . v 1 213
I must confess I know this woman: And five years since there was some speech of marriage Betwixt myself and her . . . . . . v 1 216
Your provost knows the place where he abides And he may fetch him . v 1 252
'Tis false.—How! know you where you are?—Respect to your great place! . . . . v 1 293
We'll touse you Joint by joint, but we will know his purpose . . v 1 314
Do you know me?—I remember you, sir, by the sound of your voice . v 1 329
Your brother's death, I know, sits at your heart . . . . . v 1 394
Love her, Angelo: I have confess'd her and I know her virtue . . v 1 533
Where we'll show What's yet behind, that's meet you all should know v 1 545
We that know what 'tis to fast and pray Are penitent *Com. of Errors* i 2 51
Hang up thy mistress! I know not thy mistress; out on thy mistress! ii 1 68
'I know,' quoth he, 'no house, no wife, no mistress' . . . . ii 1 71
I know his eye doth homage otherwhere . . . . ii 1 104
Sister, you know he promised me a chain . . . . . . ii 1 106
How now, sir! . . . You know no Centaur? you received no gold? . ii 2 9
If you will jest with me, know my aspect And fashion your demeanour ii 2 32
For know, my love, as easy mayst thou fall A drop of water in the breaking gulf . . . . ii 2 127
I know thou canst; and therefore see thou do it . . . . . ii 2 141
Plead you to me, fair dame? I know you not . . . . . . ii 2 149

Know. Until I know this sure uncertainty, I'll entertain the offer'd fallacy . . . *Com. of Errors* ii 2 187
But I should know her as well as she knows me . . . ii 2 204
Say what you will, sir, but I know what I know . . . iii 1 11
And about evening come yourself alone To know the reason . . . iii 1 97
I know a wench of excellent discourse, Pretty and witty . . . iii 1 109
Get you home And fetch the chain; by this I know 'tis made . . . iii 1 115
Sweet mistress,—what your name is else, I know not . . . iii 2 29
Then well I know Your weeping sister is no wife of mine . . . iii 2 41
What, are you mad, that you do reason so?—Not mad, but mated; how, I do not know . . . iii 2 54
Do you know me, sir? am I Dromio? am I your man? am I myself? . iii 2 73
I know not what use to put her to but to make a lamp of her . iii 2 97
If every one knows us and we know none, 'Tis time, I think, to trudge iii 2 157
You know since Pentecost the sum is due . . . iv 1 1
Come, come, you know I gave it you even now . . . iv 1 55
What is the matter?—I do not know the matter: he is 'rested on the case iv 2 42
I know not at whose suit he is arrested well; But he's in a suit of buff which 'rested him . . . iv 2 44
Let us go.—'Fly pride,' says the peacock: mistress, that you know . iv 3 81
O husband, God doth know you dined at home . . . iv 4 68
Both man and master is possess'd: I know it by their pale and deadly looks . . . iv 4 96
Do you know him?—I know the man. What is the sum he owes? . iv 4 135
Bring me where the goldsmith is: I long to know the truth . . iv 4 146
There did this perjured goldsmith swear me down That I this day of him received the chain, Which, God he knows, I saw not . . . v 1 229
Why look you strange on me? you know me well.—I never saw you in my life till now . . . v 1 295
But tell me yet, dost thou not know my voice? . . . v 1 300
That here my only son Knows not my feeble key of untuned cares . v 1 310
The duke and all that know me in the city Can witness with me . v 1 323
Stay, stand apart; I know not which is which . . . v 1 364
I know none of that name, lady: there was none such in the army *M. Ado* i 1 32
That I love her, I feel.—That she is worthy, I know.—That I neither feel how she should be loved nor know how she should be worthy, is the opinion that fire cannot melt out of me . . . i 1 231
That know love's grief by his complexion . . . i 1 315
I know we shall have revelling to-night: I will assume thy part . . i 1 322
Cousins, you know what you have to do . . . i 2 26
If the prince do solicit you in that kind, you know your answer . ii 1 71
I know you well enough; you are Signior Antonio.—At a word, I am not ii 1 116
I know you by the waggling of your head . . . ii 1 119
What's he?—I am sure you know him well enough.—Not I, believe me ii 1 138
When I know the gentleman, I'll tell him what you say . . ii 1 150
And that is Claudio: I know him by his bearing . . . ii 1 165
Are not you Signior Benedick?—You know me well; I am he . ii 1 168
How know you he loves her?—I heard him swear his affection . ii 1 174
But that my Lady Beatrice should know me, and not know me! . ii 1 211
And Benedick is not the unhopefullest husband that I know . ii 1 393
Tell them that you know that Hero loves me . . . ii 2 35
I am here already, sir.—I know that; but I would have thee hence . ii 3 6
The man, as you know all, hath a contemptible spirit . . ii 3 187
I know her spirits are as coy and wild As haggerds . . . iii 1 35
I persuaded them, if they loved Benedick, To wish him wrestle with affection, And never to let Beatrice know of it . . . iii 1 43
I know he doth deserve As much as may be yielded to a man . . iii 1 47
One doth not know How much an ill word may empoison liking . iii 1 85
Nay, but I know who loves him.—That would I know too: I warrant, one that knows him not . . . iii 2 65
You know he does.—I know not that, when he knows what I know . iii 2 93
If you dare not trust that you see, confess not that you know . iii 2 123
If we know him to be a thief, shall we not lay hands on him? . iii 3 57
With any man that knows the statues, he may stay him . . iii 3 85
Therefore know I have earned of Don John a thousand ducats . iii 3 115
Seest thou not what a deformed thief this fashion is?—I know that Deformed . . . iii 3 133
And one Deformed is one of them: I know him; a' wears a lock . iii 3 183
How you may be converted I know not, but methinks you look with your eyes as other women do . . . iii 4 91
I would fain know what you have to say . . . iii 5 32
If either of you know any inward impediment why you should not be conjoined, I charge you, on your souls, to utter it . . iv 1 12
She knows the heat of a luxurious bed; Her blush is guiltiness . iv 1 42
I know what you would say: if I have known her, You will say she did embrace me as a husband . . . iv 1 49
I am so attired in wonder, I know not what to say . . . iv 1 147
What man is he you are accused of?—They know that do accuse me; I know none . . . iv 1 179
If I know more of any man alive Than that which maiden modesty doth warrant, Let all my sins lack mercy! . . . iv 1 180
You know my inwardness and love Is very much unto the prince . iv 1 247
Is not that strange?—As strange as the thing I know not . . iv 1 271
And one that knows the law, go to; and a rich fellow enough . iv 2 86
My soul doth tell me Hero is belied; And that shall Claudio know . v 1 43
Know, Claudio, to thy head, Thou hast so wrong'd mine innocent child v 1 62
God knows I loved my niece; And she is dead, slander'd to death . v 1 87
I know them, yea, And what they weigh, even to the utmost scruple . v 1 92
I think he be angry indeed.—If he be, he knows how to turn his girdle v 1 142
Fare you well, boy: you know my mind. I will leave you now . v 1 187
If you would know your wronger, look on me.—Art thou the slave? . v 1 272
I know not how to pray your patience; Yet I must speak . . v 1 281
Always hath been just and virtuous In any thing that I do know by her v 1 312
The god of love, That sits above, And knows me, and knows me . v 2 28
You know your office, brother: You must be father . . . v 4 14
What is the end of study? let me know.—Why, that to know, which else we should not know . . . *L. L. Lost* i 1 55
I will swear to study so, To know the thing I am forbid to know . i 1 60
If study's gain be thus and this be so, Study knows that which yet it doth not know . . . i 1 68
Too much to know is to know nought but fame . . . i 1 92
For well you know here comes in embassy The French king's daughter i 1 135
Our court, you know, is haunted With a refined traveller of Spain i 1 163
How you delight, my lords, I know not, I; But, I protest, I love to hear him . . . i 1 175
I am sure, you know how much the gross sum of deuce-ace amounts to i 2 48
Then if she fear, or be to blame, By this you shall not know . i 2 109
That's hereby.—I know where it is situate.—Lord, how wise you are! i 2 142
A needful course, Before we enter his forbidden gates, To know his pleasure . . . ii 1 27
Know. Know you the man?—I know him, madam . . . *L. L. Lost* ii 1 39
Is't so?—They say so most that most his humours know . . ii 1 53
I know you did.—How needless was it then to ask the question! . ii 1 116
Made a mouth of his eye, By adding a tongue which I know will not lie ii 1 252
I shall know, sir, when I have done it.—Why, villain, thou must know first . . . iii 1 159
I know not; but I think it was not he . . . iv 1 3
Which is the head lady?—Thou shalt know her, fellow, by the rest that have no heads . . . iv 1 44
Who is the suitor?—Shall I teach you to know?—Ay, my continent of beauty . . . iv 1 110
The deer was, as you know, sanguis, in blood . . . iv 2 3
If knowledge be the mark, to know thee shall suffice . . iv 2 115
How shall she know my griefs? I'll drop the paper . . . iv 3 43
Am I the first that have been perjured so?—I could put thee in comfort. Not by two that I know . . . iv 3 52
But I should blush, I know, To be o'erheard and taken napping so . iv 3 129
For all the wealth that ever I did see, I would not have him know so much by me . . . iv 3 150
They'll know By favours several which they did bestow . . v 2 124
What would these strangers? know their minds, Boyet . . . v 2 174
'Tis our will That some plain man recount their purposes: Know what they would . . . v 2 177
I know the reason, lady, why you ask.—O for your reason! quickly, sir v 2 243
Will they return?—They will, they will, Gods knows, And leap for joy v 2 290
I will; and so will she, I know, my lord . . . v 2 314
We that sell by gross, the Lord doth know, Have not the grace to grace it v 2 319
And I here protest, By this white glove,—how white the hand, God knows! . . . v 2 411
That smiles his cheek in years and knows the trick To make my lady laugh . . . v 2 465
Do not you know my lady's foot by the squier . . . v 2 474
O Lord, sir, they would know . . . v 2 485
You cannot beg us, sir, I can assure you, sir; we know what we know v 2 490
Under correction, sir, we know whereuntil it doth amount . . v 2 493
I know not the degree of the Worthy, but I am to stand for him . v 2 507
Let me o'errule you now: That sport best pleases that doth least know how . . . v 2 517
I know not by what power I am made bold . . *M. N. Dream* i 1 59
I beseech your grace that I may know The worst that may befall me in this case . . . i 1 62
Question your desires; Know of your youth, examine well your blood . i 1 68
He will not know what all but he do know . . . i 1 229
But I know When thou hast stolen away from fairy land . . ii 1 64
How canst thou thus for shame, Titania, Glance at my credit with Hippolyta, Knowing I know thy love to Theseus? . . . ii 1 76
The childing autumn, angry winter, change Their wonted liveries, and the mazed world, By their increase, now knows not which is which ii 1 114
I know a bank where the wild thyme blows . . . ii 1 249
Thou shalt know the man By the Athenian garments he hath on . ii 1 263
For, you know, Pyramus and Thisby meet by moonlight . . iii 1 50
I know your patience well . . . iii 1 196
Can you not hate me, as I know you do, But you must join in souls to mock me? . . . iii 2 149
For you love Hermia; this you know I know . . . iii 2 163
Disparage not the faith thou dost not know . . . iii 2 174
Could not this make thee know, The hate I bear thee made me leave thee so? . . . iii 2 189
I am amazed, and know not what to say . . . iii 2 344
Did not you tell me I should know the man By the Athenian garments? iii 2 348
I pray you all, stand up. I know you two are rival enemies . iv 1 147
You shall know all that you are like to know . . . v 1 117
He hath rid his prologue like a rough colt; he knows not the stop . v 1 120
This man is Pyramus, if you would know; This beauteous lady Thisby v 1 130
For, if you will know, By moonshine did these lovers think no scorn To meet . . . v 1 137
Then know that I, one Snug the joiner, am A lion-fell . . . v 1 226
In sooth, I know not why I am so sad . . *Mer. of Venice* i 1 1
Such a want-wit sadness makes of me, That I have much ado to know myself . . . i 1 7
I should be still Plucking the grass, to know where sits the wind . i 1 18
I know, Antonio Is sad to think upon his merchandise . . i 1 39
I do know of these That therefore only are reputed wise For saying nothing . . . i 1 95
Well, keep me company but two years moe, Thou shalt not know the sound of thine own tongue . . . i 1 109
You know me well, and herein spend but time To wind about my love with circumstance . . . i 1 153
If to do were as easy as to know what were good to do . . i 2 13
In truth, I know it is a sin to be a mocker . . . i 2 61
You know I say nothing to him, for he understands not me, nor I him i 2 73
If the devil be within and that temptation without, I know he will choose it . . . i 2 106
May you stead me? will you pleasure me? shall I know your answer? . i 3 8
This is my true-begotten father! who, being more than sand-blind, high-gravel blind, knows me not . . . ii 2 38
Do you know me, father?—Alack the day, I know you not, young gentleman . . . ii 2 72
It is a wise father that knows his own child . . . ii 2 81
I cannot think you are my son.—I know not what I shall think of that ii 2 93
The suit is impertinent to myself, as your worship shall know by this honest old man . . . ii 2 147
I know thee well; thou hast obtain'd thy suit . . . ii 2 153
I know the hand: in faith, 'tis a fair hand . . . ii 4 12
Tell me, for more certainty, Albeit I'll swear that I do know your tongue ii 6 27
And now who knows But you, Lorenzo, whether I am yours? . . ii 6 30
How shall I know if I do choose the right? . . . ii 7 10
No news of them? Why, so: and I know not what's spent in the search iii 1 95
And you know yourself, Hate counsels not in such a quality . . iii 2 5
I know he will be glad of our success . . . iii 2 243
Never did I know A creature, that did bear the shape of man, So keen iii 2 277
And I know, my lord, . . . It will go hard with poor Antonio . iii 2 290
He seeks my life; his reason well I know . . . iii 3 21
I know you would be prouder of the work Than customary bounty can enforce you . . . iii 4 8
My people do already know my mind, And will acknowledge you . . iii 4 37
I have work in hand That you yet know not of . . . iii 4 58
Will you cover then, sir?—Not so, sir, neither; I know my duty . iii 5 59
And I do know A many fools, that stand in better place . . iii 5 72
Where is he?—He attendeth here hard by, To know your answer . iv 1 146

Know. You know the law, your exposition Hath been most sound *M. of V.* iv 1 237
I pray you, know me when we meet again: I wish you well . iv 1 419
An if your wife be not a mad-woman, And know how well I have deserved . . . . iv 1 446
He knows me as the blind man knows the cuckoo, By the bad voice . v 1 112
If you did know to whom I gave the ring, If you did know for whom I gave the ring . . . . v 1 193
Know him I shall, I am well sure of it: Lie not a night from home . v 1 229
You shall not know by what strange accident I chanced on this letter . v 1 278
Know you where you are, sir?—O, sir, very well . *As Y. Like It* i 1 43
Know you before whom, sir?—Ay, better than him I am before knows me. I know you are my eldest brother; and, in the gentle condition of blood, you should so know me . . . . i 1 45
For my soul, yet I know not why, hates nothing more than he . i 1 171
So much in the heart of the world, and especially of my own people, who best know him . . . . i 1 176
You know my father hath no child but I, nor none is like to have . i 2 18
I was too young that time to value her; But now I know her . i 3 74
Know you not, master, to some kind of men Their graces serve them but as enemies? No more do yours . . . . . . ii 3 10
This I must do, or know not what to do: Yet this I will not do . ii 3 34
My voice is ragged: I know I cannot please you . . . ii 5 15
If ladies be but young and fair, They have the gift to know it . ii 7 38
Yet am I inland bred And know some nurture . . . ii 7 97
If ever from your eyelids wiped a tear And know what 'tis to pity . ii 7 117
Hast any philosophy in thee, shepherd?—No more but that I know the more one sickens the worse at ease he is . . . . iii 2 24
Teaching all that read to know The quintessence of every sprite . iii 2 146
But doth he know that I am in this forest and in man's apparel? . iii 2 242
Do you not know I am a woman? when I think, I must speak . iii 2 263
Chide no breather in the world but myself, against whom I know most faults . . . . iii 2 298
He taught me how to know a man in love . . . . iii 2 388
I do not know what 'poetical' is: is it honest in deed and word? . iii 3 17
Many a man knows no end of his goods . . . . iii 3 53
Many a man has good horns, and knows no end of them . . iii 3 54
Then shall you know the wounds invisible That love's keen arrows make iii 5 30
Know yourself: down on your knees, And thank heaven, fasting . iii 5 57
If you will know my house, 'Tis at the tuft of olives here hard by . iii 5 74
My pretty little coz, that thou didst know how many fathom deep I am in love! . . . . iv 1 210
A letter of your own device.—No, I protest, I know not the contents . iv 3 21
He that brings this love to thee Little knows this love in me . iv 3 57
Pray you, if you know, Where in the purlieus of this forest stands A sheep-cote? . . . . iv 3 76
If that an eye may profit by a tongue, Then should I know you . iv 3 85
Some of my shame; if you will know of me What man I am . . iv 3 96
And well he might so do, For well I know he was unnatural . iv 3 125
A youth here in the forest lays claim to you.—Ay, I know who 'tis . v 1 8
The fool doth think he is wise, but the wise man knows himself to be a fool . . . . v 1 35
And greater wonders than that.—O, I know where you are . . v 2 32
Know of me then, for now I speak to some purpose, that I know you are a gentleman of good conceit: I speak not this that you should bear a good opinion of my knowledge, insomuch I say I know you are . v 2 57
I know into what straits of fortune she is driven . . . v 2 71
I sometimes do believe, and sometimes do not; As those that fear they hope, and know they fear . . . . v 4 4
What you would have I'll stay to know . . . . . v 4 202
I know my remedy; I must go fetch the third-borough . *T. of Shrew* Ind. 1 11
I know the boy will well usurp the grace, Voice, gait, and action . Ind. 1 131
Ask Marian Hacket, the fat ale-wife of Wincot, if she know me not Ind. 2 23
You know no house nor no such maid, Nor no such men . Ind. 2 93
I am your wife in all obedience.—I know it well . . Ind. 2 110
Importune me no farther, For how I firmly am resolved you know . i 1 49
Because I know you well and love you well, Leave shall you have . i 1 53
I know she taketh most delight In music, instruments and poetry . i 1 92
If you, Hortensio, Or Signior Gremio, you, know any such, Prefer them hither . . . . i 1 96
Know now, upon advice, it toucheth us both . . . . i 1 117
Counsel me, Tranio, for I know thou canst; Assist me, Tranio, for I know thou wilt . . . . i 1 162
I should knock you first, And then I know after who comes by the worst . . . . i 2 14
I know her father, though I know not her; And he knew my deceased father . . . . i 2 101
I know she is an irksome brawling scold . . . . . i 2 188
For what reason, I beseech you?—For this reason, if you'll know . i 2 235
Sir, give him head: I know he'll prove a jade . . . i 2 249
So well I know my duty to my elders . . . . . ii 1 7
To instruct her fully in those sciences, Whereof I know she is not ignorant . . . . ii 1 58
But for my daughter Katharine, this I know, She is not for your turn . ii 1 62
I know him well: you are welcome for his sake . . . ii 1 70
May I be so bold to know the cause of your coming? . . . ii 1 88
A mighty man of Pisa; by report I know him well . . . ii 1 106
Who knows not where a wasp does wear his sting? In his tail . ii 1 214
I know not what to say: but give me your hands; God send you joy! . ii 1 320
As you know, my house within the city Is richly furnished . . ii 1 348
Preposterous ass, that never read so far To know the cause why music was ordain'd! . . . . iii 1 10
'Hic ibat Simois,' I know you not, 'hic est Sigeia tellus,' I trust you not iii 1 42
You know to-morrow is the wedding-day . . . . . iii 1 84
Why, sir, you know this is your wedding-day . . . . iii 2 99
I seeing this came thence for very shame; And after me, I know, the rout is coming . . . . iii 2 183
I know you think to dine with me to-day, And have prepared great store iii 2 187
You know there wants no junkets at the feast . . . iii 2 250
First, know, my horse is tired; my master and mistress fallen out . iv 1 56
Why, she hath a face of her own.—Who knows not that? . . iv 1 103
Come, Kate, sit down; I know you have a stomach . . iv 1 161
She, poor soul, Knows not which way to stand, to look, to speak . iv 1 188
Another way I have to man my haggard, To make her come and know her keeper's call . . . . iv 1 197
He that knows better how to tame a shrew, Now let him speak . iv 1 213
A mercatante, or a pedant, I know not what; but formal in apparel . iv 2 64
'Tis death for any one in Mantua To come to Padua. Know you not the cause? . . . . iv 2 82
I know him not, but I have heard of him; A merchant of incomparable wealth . . . . iv 2 97

Know. This is true that I say: an I had thee in place where, thou shouldst know it . . . . *T. of Shrew* iv 3 151
Where then do you know best We be affied? . . . . . iv 4 48
For, you know, Pitchers have ears, and I have many servants . . iv 4 51
I say it is the moon that shines so bright.—I know it is the sun . iv 5 5
I say it is the moon.—I know it is the moon.—Nay, then you lie . iv 5 16
And now you know my meaning.—A very mean meaning . . v 2 30
Say, I command her come to me.—I know her answer.—What?—She will not. . . . . v 2 97
I know him a notorious liar, Think him a great way fool *All's Well* i 1 111
Now shall he—I know not what he shall. God send him well! . i 1 190
You are loved, sir . . . —I fill a place, I know 't . . i 2 69
I know you lack not folly to commit them . . . . i 3 11
I have other holy reasons, such as they are.—May the world know them? . . . . i 3 36
I know, madam, you love your gentlewoman entirely . . . i 3 103
Sithence, in the loss that may happen, it concerns you something to know it . . . . i 3 126
Nor would I have him till I do deserve him; Yet never know how that desert should be. I know I love in vain, strive against hope . i 3 206
I adore The sun, that looks upon his worshipper, But knows of him no more . . . . i 3 213
You know my father left me some prescriptions Of rare and proved effects . . . . i 3 227
Will you see her, For that is her demand, and know her business? . ii 1 89
What at full I know, thou know'st no part, I knowing all my peril, thou no art . . . . ii 1 135
It is not so with Him that all things knows As 'tis with us that square our guess by shows . . . . ii 1 152
But know I think and think I know most sure My art is not past power ii 1 160
Such a one, thy vassal, whom I know Is free for me to ask, thee to bestow . . . . ii 1 202
Though more to know could not be more to trust . . . ii 1 209
I know my business is but to the court.—To the court! . . ii 2 4
But never hope to know why I should marry her . . . ii 3 117
I know her well: She had her breeding at my father's charge . ii 3 120
That wilt not know, It is in us to plant thine honour where We please ii 3 162
That I may say in the default, he is a man I know . . . ii 3 242
There's letters from my mother: what the import is, I know not yet . ii 3 294
To say nothing, to do nothing, to know nothing, and to have nothing . ii 4 25
O, I know him well, I, sir; he, sir, 's a good workman, a very good tailor . . . . ii 5 20
I know not how I have deserved to run into my lord's displeasure . ii 5 37
I have kept of them tame, and know their natures . . . ii 5 50
I think so.—Why, do you not know him?—Yes, I do know him well . ii 5 56
My appointments have in them a need Greater than shows itself at the first view To you that know them not . . . . . . ii 5 74
You know your places well; When better fall, for your avails they fell iii 1 21
You shall hear I am run away: know it before the report come . iii 2 25
Might you not know she would do as she has done, By sending me a letter? . . . . iii 4 2
They are gone a contrary way: hark! you may know by their trumpets iii 5 9
A gentleman his companion.—I know that knave; hang him! . iii 5 17
Look, here comes a pilgrim: I know she will lie at my house . . iii 5 33
I think I know your hostess As ample as myself . . . . iii 5 45
Know you such a one?—But by the ear, that hears most nobly of him: His face I know not . . . . iii 5 52
Think you it is so?—Ay, surely, mere the truth: I know his lady . iii 5 58
Such I will have, whom I am sure he knows not from the enemy . iii 6 25
I know not what the success will be, my lord; but the attempt I vow. —I know thou 'rt valiant . . . . iii 6 86
Is not this a strange fellow, my lord, that so confidently seems to undertake this business, which he knows is not to be done? . . . iii 6 95
You do not know him, my lord, as we do. . . . . . iii 6 97
If you misdoubt me that I am not she, I know not how I shall assure you . . . . iii 7 2
Art not acquainted with him? knows he not thy voice? . . . iv 1 11
We must every one be a man of his own fancy, not to know what we speak one to another; so we seem to know, is to know straight our purpose. . . . . iv 1 20
Is it possible he should know what he is, and be that he is? . . iv 1 48
I will confess what I know without constraint . . . . iv 3 139
What say you to this? what do you know of it? . . . . iv 3 205
I know him: a' was a botcher's 'prentice in Paris . . . iv 3 211
I know his brains are forfeit to the next tile that falls . . iv 3 216
The duke knows him for no other but a poor officer of mine . . iv 3 225
Shall I read it to you?—I do not know if it be it or no . . iv 3 235
For count of this, the count's a fool, I know it . . . iv 3 258
They know his conditions and lay him in straw . . . . iv 3 288
To belie him, I will not, and more of his soldiership I know not . iv 3 300
I'll whisper with the general, and know his pleasure . . . iv 3 330
So, look about you: know you any here? . . . . . iv 3 348
Who knows himself a braggart, Let him fear this, for it will come to pass That every braggart shall be found an ass. . . . . . iv 3 370
You must know, I am supposed dead . . . . . . iv 4 10
With a patch of velvet on 's face: whether there be a scar under 't or no, the velvet knows . . . . iv 5 101
The king's coming; I know by his trumpets . . . . v 2 55
Your son, As mad in folly, lack'd the sense to know Her estimation home v 3 3
Our rash faults Make trivial price of serious things we have, Not knowing them until we know their grave . . . . v 3 62
Plutus himself, That knows the tinct and multiplying medicine . . v 3 102
If it should prove That thou art so inhuman,—'twill not prove so;— And yet I know not: thou didst hate her deadly . . . . v 3 117
Whether I have been to blame or no, I know not . . . . v 3 129
The poor suppliant, who by this I know Is here attending . . v 3 134
My suit . . . you know, And therefore know how far I may be pitied . v 3 160
Do you know these women?—My lord, I neither can nor will deny But that I know them . . . . v 3 165
Know you this ring? this ring was his of late.—And this was it I gave him . . . . v 3 227
By him and by this woman here what know you? . . . . v 3 237
Do you know he promised me marriage?—Faith, I know more than I'll speak . . . . v 3 255
And talked of Satan and of Limbo and of Furies and I know not what . v 3 262
And things which would derive me ill will to speak of; therefore I will not speak what I know . . . . v 3 267
It might be yours or hers, for aught I know . . . . v 3 281
He knows I am no maid, and he'll swear to't; I'll swear I am a maid, and he knows not . . . . v 3 291

Know. Who hath abused me, as he knows himself, Though yet he never harm'd me . . . *All's Well* v 3 299
If she, my liege, can make me know this clearly, I'll love her dearly . v 3 316
Let us from point to point this story know . . . . v 3 325
As, you know, What great ones do the less will prattle of . *T. Night* i 2 32
I know thy constellation is right apt For this affair . . i 4 35
Your lord does know my mind; I cannot love him: Yet I suppose him virtuous, know him noble . . . . i 5 276
I do I know not what, and fear to find Mine eye too great a flatterer . i 5 327
Let me yet know of you whither you are bound.—No, sooth, sir . ii 1 9
You must know of me then, Antonio, my name is Sebastian . . ii 1 16
Whom I know you have heard of. He left behind him myself and a sister . . . . ii 1 19
Nay, by my troth, I know not: but I know, to be up late is to be up late . . . . ii 3 4
Journeys end in lovers meeting, Every wise man's son doth know . . ii 3 45
She shall know of it, by this hand.—Go shake your ears . . ii 3 133
Do not think I have wit enough to lie straight in my bed: I know I can do it . . . . ii 3 148
Sport royal, I warrant you: I know my physic will work with him . ii 3 187
Ay, but I know— What dost thou know?—Too well what love women to men may owe . . . . ii 4 106
I am all the daughters of my father's house, And all the brothers too: and yet I know not . . . . ii 4 124
I know this letter will make a contemplative idiot of him . . . ii 5 22
Telling them I know my place as I would they should do theirs . ii 5 60
Jove knows I love: But who? Lips, do not move; No man must know ii 5 107
Thou canst not choose but know who I am . . . . . ii 5 189
I know my lady will strike him: if she do, he'll smile . . . iii 2 88
I think we do know the sweet Roman hand . . . . . iii 4 30
Consider, he's an enemy to mankind.—Do you know what you say? . iii 4 110
I am not of your element: you shall know more hereafter . . iii 4 138
I know his youth will aptly receive it, into a most hideous opinion . iii 4 211
Of what nature the wrongs are thou hast done him, I know not . iii 4 242
Do me this courteous office, as to know of the knight what my offence to him is . . . . iii 4 278
Do you know of this matter?—I know the knight is incensed against you . . . . iii 4 285
I am one that had rather go with sir priest than sir knight: I care not who knows so much of my mettle . . . . . . iii 4 299
You do mistake me, sir.—No, sir, no jot; I know your favour well . iii 4 363
Take him away: he knows I know him well.—I must obey . . iii 4 365
Those kindnesses That I have done for you.—I know of none; Nor know I you by voice or any feature . . . . iii 4 386
I my brother know Yet living in my glass . . . . . iii 4 414
No, I do not know you; nor I am not sent to you by my lady . iv 1 6
I know thee well: how dost thou, my good fellow? . . . v 1 11
If you will let your lady know I am here to speak with her . . v 1 45
Put strange speech upon me: I know not what 'twas but distraction . v 1 71
I partly know the instrument That screws me from my true place . v 1 125
This your minion, whom I know you love . . . . . v 1 128
What thou dost know Hath newly pass'd between this youth and me . v 1 157
By the Lord, madam, you wrong me, and the world shall know it . v 1 311
But when we know the grounds and authors of it, Thou shalt be both the plaintiff and the judge Of thine own cause . . . . v 1 361
We cannot with such magnificence—in so rare—I know not what to say *W. Tale* i 1 14
Be it concluded, No barricado for a belly; know't . . . . . i 2 204
Be plainer with me; let me know my trespass By its own visage . . i 2 265
I dare not know, my lord.—How! dare not! do not. Do you know, and dare not? . . . . i 2 376
How should this grow?—I know not . . . . . . i 2 432
I know't too well. Give me the boy: I am glad you did not nurse him ii 1 55
One that knows What she should shame to know herself . . ii 1 91
When you shall know your mistress Has deserved prison, then abound in tears . . . . ii 1 119
Whom you know Of stuff'd sufficiency . . . . . . ii 1 184
I am satisfied and need no more Than what I know. . . . ii 1 190
You know me, do you not?—For a worthy lady . . . . ii 2 5
We do not know How he may soften at the sight o' the child. . . ii 2 39
I know not what I shall incur to pass it, Having no warrant . . ii 2 57
Were I a tyrant, Where were her life? she durst not call me so, If she did know me one . . . . ii 3 124
You, my lord, best know, Who least will seem to do so . . . . iii 2 33
For conspiracy, I know not how it tastes; though it be dish'd For me . iii 2 73
You knew of his departure, as you know What you have underta'en to do in's absence . . . . iii 2 78
I do give lost; for I do feel it gone, But know not how it went . . iii 2 97
All faults I make, when I shall come to know them, I do repent . . iii 2 220
I know this man well: he hath been since an ape-bearer . . . iv 3 100
I can bear my part; you must know 'tis my occupation. . . . iv 4 301
Get you hence, for I must go Where it fits not you to know . . iv 4 304
If it be not too rough for some that know little but bowling . . iv 4 338
I know, sir, we weary you.—You weary those that refresh us . . iv 4 341
O, father, you'll know more of that hereafter . . . . . iv 4 353
Old sir, I know She prizes not such trifles as these are . . . iv 4 367
What of him?—Knows he of this?—He neither does nor shall . . iv 4 404
Can he speak? hear? Know man from man? dispute his own estate? . iv 4 411
For some other reasons, my grave sir, Which 'tis not fit you know, I not acquaint My father of this business.—Let him know't . . iv 4 423
Who of force must know The royal fool thou copest with . . . iv 4 434
I cannot speak, nor think, Nor dare to know that which I know . . iv 4 463
You know your father's temper: at this time He will allow no speech . iv 4 478
Besides you know Prosperity 's the very bond of love . . . iv 4 583
I think you know my fortunes Do all lie there. . . . . . iv 4 601
For instance, sir, That you may know you shall not want, one word . iv 4 605
I am a poor fellow, sir. I know ye well enough . . . . iv 4 652
Then your blood had been the dearer by I know how much an ounce . iv 4 724
I know not what impediment this complaint may be . . . . iv 4 729
A great man, I'll warrant; I know by the picking on's teeth . . iv 4 779
Which none must know but the king; and which he shall know . . iv 4 784
If thou beest capable of things serious, thou must know the king is full of grief . . . . iv 4 792
He must know 'tis none of your daughter nor my sister. . . . iv 4 849
Which who knows how that may turn back to my advancement? . . iv 4 866
Good Paulina, Who hast the memory of Hermione, I know, in honour . v 1 51
I would most gladly know the issue of it. . . . . . . v 2 9
The letters of Antigonus found with it which they know to be his character . . . . v 2 38
A handkerchief and rings of his that Paulina knows . . . . v 2 72

Know. Told him I heard them talk of a fardel and I know not what *W. T.* v 2 126
I know you are now, sir, a gentleman born . . . . . v 2 146
I know thou art no tall fellow of thy hands and that thou wilt be drunk v 2 179
I'll not seek far—For him, I partly know his mind. . . . . v 3 142
I know not why, except to get the land . . . . *K. John* i 1 73
And so, ere answer knows what question would . . . . i 1 200
Sir Robert could not do it: We know his handiwork . . . . i 1 238
Then, good my mother, let me know my father; Some proper man, I hope . . . . i 1 249
Who's your king?—The king of England, when we know the king.—Know him in us . . . . ii 1 363
Is not the Lady Constance in this troop? I know she is not . . ii 1 541
In her right we came; Which we, God knows, have turn'd another way ii 1 549
Heaven knows, they were besmear'd and over-stain'd With slaughter's pencil . . . . iii 1 236
Then know The peril of our curses light on thee . . . . iii 1 294
I have heard you say That we shall see and know our friends in heaven iii 4 77
When I shall meet him in the court of heaven I shall not know him . iii 4 88
Your uncle must not know but you are dead . . . . . iv 1 128
This from rumour's tongue I idly heard; if true or false I know not . iv 2 124
To know the meaning Of dangerous majesty . . . . . iv 2 212
Good ground, be pitiful and hurt me not! There's few or none do know me . . . . iv 3 3
We know the worst.—Whate'er you think, good words, I think, were best . . . . iv 3 27
Yet, I know, Our party may well meet a prouder foe . . . . v 1 78
Perusing o'er these notes, May know wherefore we took the sacrament v 2 6
You taught me how to know the face of right . . . . . v 2 88
I do know the scope And warrant limited unto my tongue . . . v 2 122
Know the gallant monarch is in arms . . . . . . v 2 148
Why, know you not? the lords are all come back . . . . v 6 33
Where heaven He knows how we shall answer him . . . . v 7 60
It seems you know not, then, so much as we . . . . . v 7 81
I have a kind soul that would give you thanks And knows not how to do it . . . . v 7 109
Like a cunning instrument cased up, Or, being open, put into his hands That knows no touch to tune the harmony . . . *Richard II.* i 3 165
But what thou art, God, thou, and I do know. . . . . i 3 204
What presence must not know, From where you do remain let paper show . . . . i 3 249
When they shall know what men are rich, They shall subscribe them . i 4 49
Now He that made me knows I see thee ill; Ill in myself to see . . ii 1 93
Yet I know no cause Why I should welcome such a guest as grief . . ii 2 6
What a tide of woes Comes rushing on this woeful land at once! I know not what to do . . . . ii 2 100
If I know how or which way to order these affairs Thus thrust disorderly into my hands, Never believe me . . . . . ii 2 109
I never in my life did look on him.—Then learn to know him now . ii 3 40
To know what pricks you on To take advantage of the absent time . ii 3 78
Let me know my fault: On what condition stands it and wherein? . ii 3 106
I know it, uncle, and oppose not myself Against their will . . iii 3 18
For well we know, no hand of blood and bone Can gripe the sacred handle of our sceptre . . . . iii 3 79
Yet know, my master, God omnipotent, Is mustering in his clouds . iii 3 85
Your heart is up, I know, Thus high at least, although your knee be low iii 3 194
They well deserve to have, That know the strong'st and surest way to get . . . . iii 3 201
You will find it so; I speak no more than every one doth know . . iii 4 91
Doth not thy embassage belong to me, And am I last that knows it? . iii 4 94
Freely speak thy mind; What thou dost know of noble Gloucester's death . . . . iv 1 3
I know your daring tongue Scorns to unsay what once it hath deliver'd iv 1 8
Thou, which know'st the way To plant unrightful kings, wilt know again, Being ne'er so little urged, another way To pluck him headlong . v 1 63
Upon a hot and fiery steed Which his aspiring rider seem'd to know . v 2 9
I know not, nor I greatly care not: God knows I had as lief be none as one . . . . v 2 48
Hold those justs and triumphs?—For aught I know, my lord, they do. v 2 53
But now I know thy mind; thou dost suspect That I have been disloyal v 2 104
Peruse this writing here, and thou shalt know The treason . . v 3 49
Let your mother in: I know she is come to pray for your foul sin . v 3 82
They shall not live within this world, I swear, But I will have them, if I once know where . . . . v 3 143
Thou hast forgotten to demand that truly which thou wouldst truly know . . . . *1 Hen. IV.* i 2 6
'Tis like that they will know us by our horses, by our habits . . i 2 195
I know them to be as true-bred cowards as ever turned back . . . i 2 205
Out of my grief and my impatience, Answer'd neglectingly I know not what . . . . i 3 52
I speak not this in estimation, As what I think might be, but what I know . . . . i 3 273
I know a trick worth two of that, i' faith . . . . . . ii 1 40
One that hath abundance of charge too, God knows what . . . ii 1 64
I know thou worshippest Saint Nicholas as truly as a man of falsehood may . . . . ii 1 70
The rascal hath removed my horse, and tied him I know not where . ii 2 12
The stony-hearted villains know it well enough . . . . . ii 2 28
O, 'tis our setter: I know his voice . . . . ii 2 53
Some heavy business hath my lord in hand, And I must know it . . ii 3 67
In faith, I'll know your business, Harry, that I will . . . . ii 3 83
I know you wise, but yet no farther wise Than Harry Percy's wife . ii 3 110
I well believe Thou wilt not utter what Thou dost not know . . ii 3 114
Fought you with them all?—All! I know not what you call all . . ii 4 204
How couldst thou know these men in Kendal green, when it was so dark? ii 4 256
There is a virtuous man whom I have often noted in thy company, but I know not his name . . . . ii 4 461
The man I know.—I know thou dost.—But to say I know more harm in him than in myself, were to say more than I know . . . ii 4 510
I know his death will be a march of twelve-score . . . . ii 4 598
I know not whether God will have it so, For some displeasing service . iii 2 4
I know you well enough.—No, Sir John; you do not know me . . iii 3 73
O Jesu, I have heard the prince tell him, I know not how oft! . . iii 3 97
I am no thing to thank God on, I would thou shouldst know it . . iii 3 136
She's neither fish nor flesh; a man knows not where to have her . iii 3 147
There shalt thou know thy charge; and there receive Money . . iii 3 225
It will be thought By some, that know not why he is away . . iv 1 63
For well you know we of the offering side Must keep aloof . . iv 1 69
'Faith, for their poverty, I know not where they had that . . iv 2 76
The king hath sent to know The nature of your griefs . . . iv 3 41
And well we know the king Knows at what time to promise, when to pay iv 3 52

Know. He presently, as greatness knows itself, Steps me a little higher than his vow 1 *Hen. IV.* iv 3 74
My nephew must not know, Sir Richard, The liberal and kind offer v 2 1
Let not Harry know, In any case, the offer of the king v 2 24
I know this face full well: A gallant knight he was v 3 19
He that but fears the thing he would not know Hath by instinct knowledge from others' eyes That what he fear'd is chanced 2 *Hen. IV.* i 1 85
About it: you know where to find me i 2 271
Question surveyors, know our own estate, How able such a work to undergo i 3 53
Dost not know me? come, come, I know thou wast set on to this ii 1 164
What a disgrace is it to me to remember thy name! or to know thy face! ii 2 16
The tennis-court-keeper knows better than I ii 2 22
God knows, whether those that bawl out the ruins of thy linen shall inherit his kingdom ii 2 26
Every man must know that, as oft as he has occasion to name himself ii 2 119
Know we not Galloway nags? ii 4 204
Confess the wilful abuse; and then I know how to handle you ii 4 339
Call me pantler and bread-chipper and I know not what ii 4 342
I owe her money; and whether she be damned for that, I know not ii 4 368
Though then, God knows, I had no such intent iii 1 72
Phrase call you it? by this good day, I know not the phrase iii 2 81
Peace, fellow, peace; stand aside: know you where you are? iii 2 130
Send discoverers forth To know the numbers of our enemies iv 1 4
You speak, Lord Mowbray, now you know not what iv 1 130
Who knows on whom fortune would then have smiled? iv 1 133
Here come I from our princely general To know your griefs iv 1 142
Full well he knows He cannot so precisely weed this land iv 1 204
Let them have pay, and part: I know it will well please them iv 2 71
They know their duties iv 2 101
It was more of his courtesy than your deserving.—I know not iv 3 49
I know not how they sold themselves iv 3 74
And how accompanied?—I do not know, my lord iv 4 15
God knows, my son, By what by-paths and indirect crook'd ways I met this crown; and I myself know well How troublesome it sat upon my head iv 5 184
The young king loves you not.—I know he doth not v 2 10
What is thy news? Let King Cophetua know the truth thereof v 3 106
Honest gentleman, I know not your breeding.—Why then, lament therefore v 3 111
Boot, boot, Master Shallow: I know the young king is sick for me v 3 141
I know thee not, old man: fall to thy prayers v 5 51
Know the grave doth gape For thee thrice wider than for other men v 5 57
For God doth know, so shall the world perceive, That I have turn'd away my former self v 5 61
For any thing I know, Falstaff shall die of a sweat Epil. 31
Then go we in, to know his embassy *Hen. V.* i 1 95
For God doth know how many now in health Shall drop their blood i 2 18
They know your grace hath cause and means and might i 2 125
Now are we well prepared to know the pleasure Of our fair cousin i 2 234
This same is yours: Read them; and know, I know your worthiness ii 2 69
You know how apt our love was to accord To furnish him ii 2 86
And let them know Of what a monarchy you are the head ii 4 72
That you may know 'Tis no sinister nor no awkward claim ii 4 84
To-morrow shall you know our mind at full ii 4 140
I do not know you so good a man as myself iii 2 143
We send To know what willing ransom he will give iii 5 63
You must learn to know such slanders of the age iii 6 84
If your majesty know the man: his face is all bubukles iii 6 107
You know me by my habit.—Well then I know thee: what shall I know of thee? iii 6 121
What is thy name? I know thy quality iii 6 146
I know him to be valiant.—I was told that by one that knows him better than you iii 7 112
That's more than we know.—Ay, or more than we should seek after; for we know enough, if we know we are the king's subjects iv 1 135
How shall I know thee again?—Give me any gage of thine iv 1 222
And I know 'Tis not the balm, the sceptre and the ball iv 1 276
I know thy errand, I will go with thee iv 1 324
You know your places: God be with you all! iv 3 78
I come to know of thee, King Harry, If for thy ransom thou wilt now compound iv 3 79
I do not know the French for fer, and ferret, and firk iv 4 32
I did never know so full a voice issue from so empty a heart iv 4 71
Alexander, God knows, and you know, in his rages, and his furies, and his wraths, . . . did, in his ales and his angers, look you, kill his best friend, Cleitus iv 7 36
I tell thee truly, herald, I know not if the day be ours or no iv 7 87
Which, your majesty know, to this hour is an honourable badge of the service iv 7 105
I wear it for a memorable honour; For I am Welsh, you know iv 7 110
I am your majesty's countryman, I care not who know it iv 7 117
I do know Fluellen valiant And, touch'd with choler, hot as gunpowder iv 7 187
Sir, know you this glove?—Know the glove! I know the glove is a glove iv 8 6
Which you and yourself and all the world know to be no petter v 1 7
And my speech entreats That I may know the let v 2 65
I know no ways to mince it in love, but directly to say 'I love you' v 2 129
Come, I know thou lovest me: and at night, when you come into your closet, you'll question this gentlewoman about me; and I know, Kate, you will to her dispraise those parts in me that you love v 2 209
I do not know dat.—No; 'tis hereafter to know, but now to promise v 2 225
I will wink on her to consent, my lord, if you will teach her to know my meaning v 2 334
Hunger will enforce them to be more eager: Of old I know them 1 *Hen. VI.* i 2 39
Come, come from behind; I know thee well, though never seen before i 2 67
He may mean more than we poor men do know i 2 122
I know; and oft have shot at them i 4 3
My thoughts are whirled like a potter's wheel; I know not where I am i 5 20
My lady craves To know the cause of your abrupt departure ii 3 30
And know us by these colours for thy foes ii 4 105
But he shall know I am as good— As good! Thou bastard! iii 1 41
My lord should be religious And know the office that belongs to such iii 1 55
My lord, we know your grace to be a man Just and upright iii 1 94
What is that wrong whereof you both complain? First let me know iv 1 88
Yet know, my lord, I was provoked by him iv 1 104
To know who hath obtain'd the glory of the day iv 7 52
I come to know what prisoners thou hast ta'en And to survey the bodies iv 7 56
Fair Margaret knows That Suffolk does not flatter, face, or feign v 3 141
I did beget her, all the parish knows: Her mother liveth yet v 4 11

Know. God knows thou art a collop of my flesh 1 *Hen. VI.* v 4 18
I think she knows not well, There were so many, whom she may accuse v 4 80
I know it will excuse This sudden execution of my will v 5 98
I know your mind; 'Tis not my speeches that you do mislike 2 *Hen. VI.* i 1 139
Patience, good lady; wizards know their times i 4 18
They know their master loves to be aloft ii 1 11
Why, Suffolk, England knows thine insolence.—And thy ambition ii 1 31
Camest thou here by chance, Or of devotion, to this holy shrine?—God knows, of pure devotion ii 1 89
What's my name?—Alas, master, I know not.—What's his name?—I know not ii 1 118
For my wife, I know not how it stands; Sorry I am to hear what I have heard ii 1 192
Where, as all you know, Harmless Richard was murder'd traitorously ii 2 26
My lord, break we off; we know your mind at full ii 2 77
We know the time since he was mild and affable iii 1 9
Know that thou art come too soon, Unless thou wert more loyal iii 1 95
I know their complot is to have my life iii 1 147
I know no pain they can inflict upon him Will make him say I moved him iii 1 377
Let him know We have dispatch'd the duke, as he commanded iii 2 1
What know I how the world may deem of me? iii 2 65
That he is dead, good Warwick, 'tis too true; But how he died God knows iii 2 131
Sirs, stand apart; the king shall know your mind iii 2 242
So, get thee gone, that I may know my grief iii 2 346
What is my ransom, master? let me know iv 1 15
Will you credit this base drudge's words, That speaks he knows not what? iv 2 160
O graceless men! they know not what they do iv 4 38
Nor knows he how to live but by the spoil, Unless by robbing iv 8 41
Why, rude companion, whatsoe'er thou be, I know thee not iv 10 34
Let them obey that know not how to rule v 1 6
A messenger from Henry, our dread liege, To know the reason of these arms v 1 18
I'll write upon thy burgonet, Might I but know thee by thy household badge v 1 201
God knows how long it is I have to live v 3 17
I know our safety is to follow them v 3 23
Ah, know you not the city favours them? 3 *Hen. VI.* i 1 67
I know not what to say; my title's weak i 1 134
My sons, God knows what hath bechanced them: But this I know, they have demean'd themselves Like men i 4 6
'Tis beauty that doth oft make women proud; But, God he knows, thy share thereof is small i 4 129
Would thy best friends did know How it doth grieve me! ii 2 54
A wisp of straw were worth a thousand crowns, To make this shameless callet know herself ii 2 145
Yet, know thou, since we have begun to strike, We'll never leave ii 2 167
Speak, Clifford, dost thou know who speaks to thee? ii 6 61
The world goes hard When Clifford cannot spare his friends an oath. I know by that he's dead ii 6 79
Ah, simple men, you know not what you swear! iii 1 83
He knows the game: how true he keeps the wind! iii 2 14
We will consider of your suit; And come some other time to know our mind iii 2 17
I know I am too mean to be your queen, And yet too good to be your concubine iii 2 97
And yet I know not how to get the crown, For many lives stand between iii 2 172
And, madam, these for you; from whom I know not iii 3 166
Alas, you know, 'tis far from hence to France iv 1 4
Knows not Montague that of itself England is safe, if true within itself? iv 1 39
How should you govern any kingdom, That know not how to use ambassadors? iv 3 36
You know our king, my brother, Is prisoner to the bishop here iv 5 4
At the least is Duke of York.—True, my good lord; I know you for no less iv 7 22
Belike unlook'd-for friends.—They are at hand, and you shall quickly know v 1 15
Know you what this means? Look here, I throw my infamy at thee v 1 81
Thou art too malapert.—I know my duty; you are all undutiful v 5 33
May I know?—Yea, Richard, when I know *Richard III.* i 1 51
I know it pleaseth neither of us well i 1 113
You know no rules of charity, Which renders good for bad i 2 68
No beast so fierce but knows some touch of pity.—But I know none i 2 71
I hope so.—I know so i 2 114
Say, then, my peace is made.—That shall you know hereafter i 2 199
There's many a gentle person made a Jack.—Come, come, we know your meaning i 3 74
She may, my lord, for— She may, Lord Rivers! why, who knows not so? i 3 93
If God will be revenged for this deed, O, know you yet, he doth it publicly i 4 222
I do not know that Englishman alive With whom my soul is any jot at odds ii 1 69
Who knows not that the noble duke is dead? You do him injury ii 1 79
Who knows not he is dead! who knows he is?—All-seeing heaven! ii 1 81
I promise you, I scarcely know myself: Hear you the news abroad? ii 3 2
Nor more can you distinguish of a man Than of his outward show; which, God he knows, Seldom or never jumpeth with the heart iii 1 10
On what occasion, God he knows, not I, The queen your mother, and your brother York, Have taken sanctuary iii 1 26
A beggar, brother?—Of my kind uncle, that I know will give iii 1 113
He sends to know your lordship's pleasure, If presently you will take horse iii 2 15
To bar my master's heirs in true descent, God knows I will not do it iii 2 55
Think you, but that I know our state secure, I would be so triumphant? iii 2 83
Who knows the lord protector's mind herein? iii 4 7
We know each other's faces, But for our hearts, he knows no more of mine Than I of yours iii 4 10
No man might be bolder; His lordship knows me well, and loves me well iii 4 31
For by his face straight shall you know his heart iii 4 55
Because you know, my lord, my mother lives iii 5 94
A book of prayer in his hand, True ornaments to know a holy man iii 7 99
Then know, it is your fault that you resign The supreme seat iii 7 117
We know your tenderness of heart And gentle, kind, effeminate remorse iii 7 210
For God he knows, and you may partly see, How far I am from the desire iii 7 235
I know a discontented gentleman, Whose humble means match not his haughty mind iv 2 36
I partly know the man: go, call him hither iv 2 41
Hath buried them; But how or in what place I do not know iv 3 30
Then know, that from my soul I love thy daughter iv 4 255
I know not, mighty sovereign, but by guess iv 4 466
And he himself wander'd away alone, No man knows whither iv 4 515
I do know Kinsmen of mine, three at the least, that have By this so sicken'd their estates *Hen. VIII.* i 1 80

Know. You know his nature, That he's revengeful, and I know his sword Hath a sharp edge: it's long . . . *Hen. VIII.* i 1 108
Ready?—Ay, please your grace.—Well, we shall then know more . i 1 118
Know you not, The fire that mounts the liquor till't run o'er, In seeming to augment it wastes it? . . . . i 1 143
But this top-proud fellow . . . I do know To be corrupt and treasonous . i 1 155
Let the king know, As soon he shall by me . . . . . . i 1 190
I know but of a single part, in aught Pertains to the state . . . i 2 41
You know no more than others; but you frame Things that are known alike; which are not wholesome To those which would not know them i 2 44
The nature of it? in what kind, let's know, Is this exaction? . . . i 2 53
Traduced by ignorant tongues, which neither know My faculties nor person . . . . i 2 72
If I know you well, You were the duke's surveyor . . . . . i 2 171
The king will know him one day.—Pray God he do! he'll never know himself else . . . . ii 2 22
I knew him, and I know him; so I leave him . . . . . . ii 2 55
I'll make ye know your times of business . . . . . . ii 2 72
I know your majesty has always loved her So dear in heart . . . ii 2 110
What were't worth to know The secret of your conference? . . . ii 3 50
I do not know What kind of my obedience I should tender . . . ii 3 65
Who knows yet But from this lady may proceed a gem? . . . . ii 3 77
If he know That I am free of your report, he knows I am not of your wrong . . . . ii 4 98
That you have many enemies, that know not Why they are so . . . ii 4 158
Cranmer, Prithee, return: with thy approach, I know, My comfort comes along . . . . ii 4 239
I care not . . . if my actions Were tried by every tongue, every eye saw 'em, . . . I know my life so even . . . . iii 1 37
I am not such a truant since my coming, As not to know the language iii 1 44
To know How you stand minded in the weighty difference . . . iii 1 57
Full little, God knows, looking Either for such men or such business . iii 1 75
Ye have angels' faces, but heaven knows your hearts . . . . iii 1 145
If your grace Could but be brought to know our ends are honest, You'ld feel more comfort . . . . iii 1 154
You know I am a woman, lacking wit To make a seemly answer . . iii 1 177
What he deserves of you and me I know . . . . iii 2 14
What though I know her virtuous And well deserving? yet I know her for A spleeny Lutheran . . . . iii 2 97
I know 'twill stir him strongly; yet I know A way, if it take right, in spite of fortune Will bring me off again . . . . iii 2 218
Spotless shall mine innocence arise, When the king knows my truth . iii 2 302
The king shall know it, and, no doubt, shall thank you . . . . iii 2 348
Never so truly happy, my good Cromwell. I know myself now . . . iii 2 378
Some little memory of me will stir him—I know his noble nature . . iii 2 418
These I know: Who's that that bears the sceptre? . . . . . iv 1 37
'Tis now the king's, and call'd Whitehall.—I know it . . . . iv 1 97
All the land knows that: However, yet there is no great breach . . iv 1 105
Love her for her mother's sake, that loved him, Heaven knows how dearly iv 2 138
That all the world may know I was a chaste wife to my grave . . iv 2 169
You're a gentleman Of mine own way; I know you wise, religious . v 1 28
That he is, For so I know he is, they know he is, A most arch heretic . v 1 44
My lord! you do desire to know Wherefore I sent for you . . . v 1 89
Know you not How your state stands i' the world, with the whole world? v 1 126
Sure, you know me?—Yes, my lord; But yet I cannot help you . . v 2 4
You shall know many dare accuse you boldly . . . . . . v 3 56
Do not I know you for a favourer Of this new sect? . . . . . v 3 80
But know, I come not To hear such flattery now, and in my presence . v 3 123
How got they in, and be hang'd?—Alas, I know not . . . . v 4 18
I know, within a while All the best men are ours . . . . . Epil. 12
I know the cause too: he'll lay about him to-day . . *Troi. and Cres.* i 2 57
Do you know a man if you see him?—Ay, if I ever saw him before . . i 2 67
You know, he has not past three or four hairs on his chin . . . i 2 121
Have you any discretion? have you any eyes? do you know what a man is? . . . . i 2 274
You are such a woman! one knows not at what ward you lie . . . i 2 282
Joy's soul lies in the doing. That she beloved knows nought that knows not this . . . . i 2 314
And know by measure Of their observant toil the enemies' weight . . i 3 202
How may A stranger to those most imperial looks Know them? . . . i 3 225
That thou shalt know, Trojan, he is awake, He tells thee so himself . i 3 255
And every Greek of mettle, let him know, What Troy means fairly . . i 3 258
That knows his valour, and knows not his fear . . . . . . i 3 268
Were his brain as barren As banks of Libya,—though, Apollo knows, 'Tis dry enough . . . . i 3 328
I know that, fool.—Ay, but that fool knows not himself . . . . ii 1 71
And such a one that dare Maintain—I know not what: 'tis trash . . ii 1 138
Who shall answer him?—I know not: 'tis put to lottery . . . . ii 1 140
There is no lady . . . More ready to cry out 'Who knows what follows?' ii 2 13
Here are your reasons: You know an enemy intends you harm; You know a sword employ'd is perilous . . . . ii 2 39
What shriek is this?—'Tis our mad sister, I do know her voice . . ii 2 98
Well may we fight for her whom, we know well, The world's large spaces cannot parallel . . . . ii 2 161
Which short-armed ignorance itself knows is so abundant scarce . . ii 3 16
Lest perchance he think We dare not move the question of our place, Or know not what we are . . . . ii 3 90
How doth pride grow? I know not what pride is . . . . . ii 3 162
Not emulous, as Achilles is.—Know the whole world, he is as valiant . ii 3 243
You know me, do you not?—Faith, sir, superficially.—Friend, know me better . . . . iii 1 9
I hope I shall know your honour better.—I do desire it . . . . iii 1 13
What music is this?—I do but partly know, sir: it is music in parts . iii 1 19
Know you the musicians?—Wholly, sir.—Who play they to? . . . iii 1 21
You must not know where he sups.—I'll lay my life, with my disposer iii 1 93
He hangs the lip at something: you know all . . . . . . iii 1 153
You know now your hostages; your uncle's word . . . . . iii 2 115
I know not what I speak.—Well know they what they speak that speak so wisely . . . . iii 2 158
This Antenor, I know, is such a wrest in their affairs . . . . iii 3 23
You know my mind, I'll fight no more 'gainst Troy . . . . . iii 3 56
What mean these fellows? Know they not Achilles? . . . . . iii 3 70
The beauty that is borne here in the face The bearer knows not . . iii 3 104
Nor doth he of himself know them for aught Till he behold them . . iii 3 118
What a man is there! a very horse, That has he knows not what . . iii 3 127
Is that a wonder? The providence that's in a watchful state Knows almost every grain of Plutus' gold . . . . iii 3 197
He knows not me: I said 'Good morrow, Ajax' . . . . . . iii 3 261
What music will be in him when Hector has knocked out his brains, I know not . . . . iii 3 304

Know. We know each other well.—We do; and long to know each other worse . . . . *Troi. and Cres.* iv 1 30
I was sent for to the king; but why, I know not . . . . . iv 1 35
Is he here, say you? 'tis more than I know, I'll be sworn . . . iv 2 54
Do not you know of him, but yet go fetch him hither . . . . iv 2 58
I know what 'tis to love; And would, as I shall pity, I could help! . iv 3 10
Injurious time now with a robber's haste Crams his rich thievery up, he knows not how . . . . iv 4 45
And know you, lord, I'll nothing do on charge . . . . . iv 4 134
For you know 'tis true, That you are odd, and he is even with you . iv 5 43
One that knows the youth Even to his inches . . . . . . iv 5 110
I know your favour, Lord Ulysses, well . . . . iv 5 213
Let the trumpets blow, That this great soldier may his welcome know iv 5 276
I must not break my faith. You know me dutiful . . . . . v 3 72
Thou boy-queller, show thy face; Know what it is to meet Achilles angry v 5 46
First, you know Caius Marcius is chief enemy to the people.—We know't, we know't.—Let us kill him . . . . . *Coriolanus* i 1 9
The gods know I speak this in hunger for bread, not in thirst for revenge i 1 24
Poor suitors have strong breaths: they shall know we have strong arms too i 1 62
They'll sit by the fire, and presume to know What's done i' the Capitol i 1 195
One's Junius Brutus, Sicinius Velutus, and I know not—'Sdeath! . i 1 221
To the Capitol; where, I know, Our greatest friends attend us . . i 1 248
They of Rome are enter'd in our counsels And know how we proceed . i 2 3
Call thither all the officers o' the town, Where they shall know our mind i 5 29
The shepherd knows not thunder from a tabor More than I know the sound of Marcius' tongue From every meaner man . . . . i 6 26
Know you on which side They have placed their men of trust? . . i 6 51
Rome must know The value of her own . . . . i 9 20
Nature teaches beasts to know their friends . . . . . . ii 1 6
Do you two know how you are censured here in the city? . . . ii 1 24
I know you can do very little alone; for your helps are many . . ii 1 38
We know you well enough.—You know neither me, yourselves, nor any thing . . . . ii 1 75
Seven hurts i' the body.—One i' the neck, and two i' the thigh,—there's nine that I know . . . . ii 1 168
Know, Rome, that all alone Marcius did fight Within Corioli gates . ii 1 179
O, You have, I know, petition'd all the gods For my prosperity! . . ii 1 187
I know not where to turn: O, welcome home . . . . . . ii 1 198
There be many that they have loved, they know not wherefore . . ii 2 11
If they love they know not why, they hate upon no better a ground . ii 2 12
On the market-place, I know, they do attend us . . . . . ii 2 164
You know the cause, sir, of my standing here.—We do, sir . . . ii 3 68
'Twere well We let the people know't.—What, what? his choler? . . iii 1 83
It makes the consuls base: and my soul aches To know . . . . iii 1 109
They know the corn Was not our recompense . . . . . . iii 1 120
He shall well know The noble tribunes are the people's mouths . . iii 1 270
As I do know the consul's worthiness, So can I name his faults . . iii 1 278
I know thou hadst rather Follow thine enemy in a fiery gulf Than flatter him . . . . iii 2 90
What do you prate of service?—I talk of that, that know it . . . iii 3 84
Know, I pray you,— I'll know no further . . . . iii 3 87
Then if I would Speak that,— We know your drift: speak what? . . iii 3 116
Those mysteries which heaven Will not have earth to know . . . iv 2 36
I know you well, sir, and you know me: your name, I think, is Adrian iv 3 1
I am a Roman; and my services are, as you are, against 'em: know you me yet? . . . . iv 3 5
Then know me not, Lest that thy wives with spits and boys with stones In puny battle slay me . . . . iv 4 4
Know'st thou me yet?—I know thee not: thy name? . . . . . iv 5 70
Know thou first, I loved the maid I married . . . . . . iv 5 119
Tell not me: I know this cannot be.—Not possible . . . . . iv 6 56
It is spoke freely out of many mouths—How probable I do not know . iv 6 65
I do not know what witchcraft's in him . . . . iv 7 2
When he shall come to his account, he knows not What I can urge against him . . . . iv 7 18
I'll keep at home.—He would not seem to know me . . . . . v 1 8
You know the very road into his kindness, And cannot lose your way . v 1 59
I'll say an errand for you: you shall know now that I am in estimation v 2 66
Wife, mother, child, I know not. My affairs Are servanted to others . v 2 88
You know the way home again.—Do you hear how we are shent? . . v 2 103
Thou art my warrior; I holp to frame thee. Do you know this lady? . v 3 63
Is it most certain?—As certain as I know the sun is fire . . . v 4 48
The fall of either Makes the survivor heir of all.—I know it . . . v 6 19
You are to know That prosperously I have attempted . . . . v 6 74
When you shall know—as in this rage, Provoked by him, you cannot—the great danger Which this man's life did owe you . . . . . v 6 137
I know not, Marcus; but I know it is: Whether by device or no, the heavens can tell . . . . *T. Andron.* i 1 394
Only thus much I give your grace to know . . . . i 1 413
And make them know what 'tis to let a queen Kneel in the streets . i 1 454
Have your lath glued within your sheath Till you know better how to handle it . . . . ii 1 42
Should the empress know This discord's ground, the music would not please . . . . ii 1 69
Easy it is Of a cut loaf to steal a shive, we know . . . . . ii 1 87
Then why should he despair that knows to court it With words, fair looks? ii 1 91
Know that this gold must coin a stratagem . . . . ii 3 5
You shall know, my boys, Your mother's hand shall right your mother's wrong . . . . ii 3 120
But something pitiful!—I know not what it means; away with her! . ii 3 157
Ne'er let my heart know merry cheer indeed . . . . ii 3 188
For ne'er till now Was I a child to fear I know not what . . . ii 3 221
If it be dark, how dost thou know 'tis he? . . . . . . ii 3 225
My brother dead! I know thou dost but jest . . . . . . ii 3 253
We know not where you left him all alive; But, out, alas! here have we found him dead . . . . ii 3 257
Perchance she weeps because they kill'd her husband; Perchance because she knows them innocent . . . . iii 1 115
And by still practice learn to know thy meaning . . . . . iii 2 45
My aunt Lavinia Follows me every where, I know not why . . . iv 1 2
See how swift she comes. Alas, sweet aunt, I know not what you mean iv 1 4
I know not, I, nor can I guess, Unless some fit or frenzy do possess her iv 1 16
I know my noble aunt Loves me as dear as e'er my mother did . . iv 1 22
Heaven guide thy pen to print thy sorrows plain, That we may know the traitors! . . . . iv 1 76
I know There is enough written upon this earth To stir a mutiny . . iv 1 83
'Tis a verse in Horace; I know it well: I read it in the grammar long ago iv 2 22
My lords, you know, as know the mightful gods . . . . . iv 4 5
But he and his shall know that justice lives In Saturninus' health . iv 4 23
Who, when he knows thou art the empress' babe, Will hold thee dearly v 1 35

Know. I know thou art religious And hast a thing within thee called conscience . . . . *T. Andron.* v 1 74
For that I know An idiot holds his bauble for a god . . . v 1 78
If thou didst know me, thou wouldest talk with me.—I am not mad; I know thee well enough . . . . v 2 20
Know, thou sad man, I am not Tamora; She is thy enemy . . . v 2 28
Well mayst thou know her by thy own proportion . . . . v 2 106
I know them all, though they suppose me mad, And will o'erreach them v 2 142
What is your will?—Know you these two? . . . . . v 2 153
You know your mother means to feast with me . . . . v 2 185
Alas, you know I am no vaunter, I . . . . . . v 3 113
For well I know The common voice do cry it shall be so . . . v 3 139
Part, fools! Put up your swords; you know not what you do *R. and J.* i 1 72
Come you this afternoon, To know our further pleasure in this case . i 1 108
Do you know the cause?—I neither know it nor can learn of him . i 1 150
Could we but learn from whence his sorrows grow, We would as willingly give cure as know . . . . i 1 161
So please you, step aside; I'll know his grievance, or be much denied . i 1 163
Can you read any thing you see?—Ay, if I know the letters and the language . . . . i 2 64
This trick may chance to scathe you, I know what: You must contrary me! i 5 86
What's he that follows there, that would not dance?—I know not . i 5 135
By a name I know not how to tell thee who I am . . . ii 2 54
My ears have not yet drunk a hundred words Of that tongue's utterance, yet I know the sound . . . . ii 2 59
Know my heart's dear love is set On the fair daughter of rich Capulet . ii 3 57
R is for the— No; I know it begins with some other letter . . ii 4 224
You have made a simple choice; you know not how to choose a man . ii 5 39
All this did I know before. What says he of our marriage? what of that? ii 5 47
Love thee better than thou canst devise, Till thou shalt know the reason iii 1 73
What sorrow craves acquaintance at my hand, That I yet know not? . iii 3 6
Let me come in, and you shall know my errand . . . . iii 3 79
Commend me to your daughter.—I will, and know her mind early to-morrow . . . . iii 4 10
Yon light is not day-light, I know it, I . . . . . iii 5 12
When I do [marry], I swear, It shall be Romeo, whom you know I hate iii 5 123
I'll to the friar, to know his remedy . . . . . iii 5 241
You say you do not know the lady's mind: Uneven is the course . iv 1 4
Now do you know the reason of this haste . . . . . iv 1 15
I already know thy grief; It strains me past the compass of my wits . iv 1 46
Against thou shalt awake, Shall Romeo by my letters know our drift . iv 1 114
Farewell! God knows when we shall meet again . . . . iv 3 14
What's there?—Things for the cook, sir; but I know not what . iv 4 14
Put up, put up; For, well you know, this is a pitiful case . . iv 5 99
What say you, James Soundpost?—Faith, I know not what to say . iv 5 140
Here's one, a friend, and one that knows you well . . . v 3 123
My master knows not but I am gone hence . . . . . v 3 132
Search, seek, and know how this foul murder comes . . . v 3 198
Till we can clear these ambiguities, And know their spring . . v 3 218
Then say at once what thou dost know in this . . . . v 3 228
I know the merchant.—I know them both . . . *T. of Athens* i 1 7
I do know him A gentleman that well deserves a help . . . i 1 101
You well know, Things of like value differing in the owners Are prized by their masters . . . . i 1 169
You know me, Apemantus?—Thou know'st I do: I call'd thee by thy name i 1 185
Let's be provided to show them entertainment.—I scarce know how . i 2 186
Nor will he know his purse, or yield me this, To show him what a beggar his heart is . . . . i 2 200
I know, no man Can justly praise but what he does affect . . i 2 220
So senseless of expense, That he will neither know how to maintain it, Nor cease his flow of riot . . . . ii 2 2
If you did know, my lord, my master's wants . . . . ii 2 29
You ask me what you are, and do not know yourselves . . . ii 2 67
Read me the superscription of these letters: I know not which is which ii 2 82
They could have wish'd—they know not—Something hath been amiss . ii 2 216
One that knows what belongs to reason; and canst use the time well . iii 1 38
An honourable gentleman.—We know him for no less . . . iii 2 3
I know his lordship is but merry with me . . . . . iii 2 42
Who bates mine honour shall not know my coin . . . . iii 3 26
I know my lord hath spent of Timon's wealth . . . . iii 4 26
I need not tell him that; he knows you are too diligent . . . iii 4 39
O, here's Servilius; now we shall know some answer . . . iii 4 66
For I know your reverend ages love Security . . . . iii 5 80
Must it be so? it must not be. My lords, I do beseech you, know me . iii 5 90
Know you the quality of Lord Timon's fury? . . . . . iii 6 117
I know thee well; But in thy fortunes am unlearn'd and strange . iv 3 55
I know thee too; and more than that I know thee, I not desire to know iv 3 57
What man didst thou ever know unthrift that was beloved after his means?—Who, without those means thou talkest of, didst thou ever know beloved? . . . . iv 3 311
When I know not what else to do, I'll see thee again . . . iv 3 358
Is not this he?—Where?—'Tis his description.—He; I know him . iv 3 413
An honest poor servant of yours.—Then I know thee not . . iv 3 483
I beg of you to know me, good my lord . . . . . iv 3 494
That which I show, heaven knows, is merely love, Duty and zeal . iv 3 522
You hear him cog, see him dissemble, Know his gross patchery . . v 1 99
Remain assured That he's a made-up villain.—I know none such . v 1 102
Name them, my lord, let's know them . . . . . . v 1 108
Let Alcibiades know this of Timon, That Timon cares not . . v 1 173
Then let him know, and tell him Timon speaks it . . . . v 1 178
Know you not, Being mechanical, you ought not walk Upon a labouring day without the sign Of your profession? . . . *J. Cæsar* i 1 2
You know it is the feast of Lupercal.—It is no matter . . . i 1 72
Since you know you cannot see yourself So well as by reflection, I, your glass, Will modestly discover to yourself That of yourself which you yet know not of . . . . i 2 67
If you know That I do fawn on men and hug them hard . . . i 2 74
Or if you know That I profess myself in banqueting To all the rout . i 2 76
I know that virtue to be in you, Brutus, As well as I do know your outward favour . . . . i 2 90
I do not know the man I should avoid So soon as that spare Cassius . i 2 200
We have the falling sickness.—I know not what you mean by that . i 2 259
A common slave—you know him well by sight . . . . i 3 15
I know where I will wear this dagger then . . . . . i 3 89
If I know this, know all the world besides, That part of tyranny that I do bear I can shake off at pleasure . . . . . . i 3 98
I know he would not be a wolf, But that he sees the Romans are but sheep i 3 104
I perhaps speak this Before a willing bondman; then I know My answer must be made . . . . i 3 113
And I do know, by this, they stay for me In Pompey's porch . . i 3 125
Know. 'Tis Cinna; I do know him by his gait . . . . . *J. Cæsar* i 3 132
I know no personal cause to spurn at him, But for the general . ii 1 11
Is not to-morrow, boy, the ides of March?—I know not, sir . . ii 1 41
Do you know them?—No, sir; their hats are pluck'd about their ears . ii 1 72
Know I these men that come along with you?—Yes, every man of them ii 1 89
You know, his means, If he improve them, may well stretch so far As to annoy us all . . . . ii 1 158
Could it work so much upon your shape As it hath much prevail'd on your condition, I should not know you . . . . . . ii 1 255
Is it excepted I should know no secrets That appertain to you? . ii 1 281
If this were true, then should I know this secret. I grant I am a woman ii 1 291
With a heart new-fired I follow you, To do I know not what . . ii 1 333
Danger knows full well That Cæsar is more dangerous than he . . ii 2 44
Let me know some cause, Lest I be laugh'd at when I tell them so . ii 2 69
For your private satisfaction, Because I love you, I will let you know . ii 2 74
Know it now: the senate have concluded To give this day a crown to mighty Cæsar . . . . ii 2 93
Why dost thou stay?—To know my errand, madam . . . . ii 4 3
None that I know will be, much that I fear may chance . . . ii 4 32
Trebonius knows his time . . . . iii 1 25
Know, Cæsar doth not wrong, nor without cause Will he be satisfied . iii 1 47
I do know but one That unassailable holds on his rank . . . iii 1 68
Fates, we will know your pleasures: That we shall die, we know . . iii 1 98
I know that we shall have him well to friend.—I wish we may . . iii 1 143
I know not, gentlemen, what you intend, Who else must be let blood . iii 1 151
A word with you. You know not what you do . . . . iii 1 232
Know you how much the people may be moved By that which he will utter? . . . . iii 1 234
I know not what may fall; I like it not . . . . . iii 1 243
I speak not to disprove what Brutus spoke, But here I am to speak what I do know. You all did love him once . . . . iii 2 106
Who, you all know, are honourable men . . . . . iii 2 129
I must not read it; It is not meet you know how Cæsar loved you . iii 2 146
'Tis good you know not that you are his heirs . . . . iii 2 150
If you have tears, prepare to shed them now. You all do know this mantle . . . . iii 2 174
For Brutus, as you know, was Cæsar's angel . . . . iii 2 185
What private griefs they have, alas, I know not . . . . iii 2 217
I am no orator, as Brutus is; But, as you know me all, a plain blunt man, That love my friend; and that they know full well . . iii 2 222
I only speak right on; I tell you that which you yourselves do know . iii 2 228
You go to do you know not what: Wherein hath Cæsar thus deserved your loves? Alas, you know not . . . . iii 2 240
Be content; Speak your griefs softly: I do know you well . . iv 2 42
I an itching palm! You know that you are Brutus that speak this . iv 3 13
For, I know, When thou didst hate him worst, thou lovedst him better Than ever thou lovedst Cassius . . . . . . iv 3 105
I'll know his humour, when he knows his time . . . . iv 3 136
I know young bloods look for a time of rest . . . . iv 3 262
I do not know that I did cry.—Yes, that thou didst . . . iv 3 297
I am in their bosoms, and I know Wherefore they do it . . . v 1 7
I know not how, But I do find it cowardly and vile . . . v 1 103
And whether we shall meet again I know not . . . . . v 1 115
O, that a man might know The end of this day's business ere it come! v 1 123
Marcus Brutus, I; Brutus, my country's friend; know me for Brutus! v 4 8
I know my hour is come.—Not so, my lord.—Nay, I am sure it is . v 5 20
And the very ports they blow, All the quarters that they know *Macbeth* i 3 16
Tell me more: By Sinel's death I know I am thane of Glamis . . i 3 71
Hath he ask'd for me?—Know you not he has? . . . . i 7 30
I have given suck, and know How tender 'tis to love the babe that milks me . . . . i 7 54
False face must hide what the false heart doth know . . . i 7 82
To know my deed, 'twere best not know myself . . . . ii 2 73
I know this is a joyful trouble to you; But yet 'tis one . . ii 3 53
What is amiss?—You are, and do not know't . . . . ii 3 102
And question this most bloody piece of work, To know it further . ii 3 135
Know That it was he in the times past which held you So under fortune iii 1 76
Both of you Know Banquo was your enemy.—True, my lord . . iii 1 115
You know your own degrees; sit down: at first And last the hearty welcome . . . . iii 4 1
I have a strange infirmity, which is nothing To those that know me . iii 4 87
For now I am bent to know, By the worst means, the worst . . iii 4 134
At the pit of Acheron Meet me i' the morning: thither he Will come to know his destiny . . . . iii 5 17
And you all know, security Is mortals' chiefest enemy . . . iii 5 32
By that which you profess, Howe'er you come to know it, answer me . iv 1 51
He knows thy thought: Hear his speech, but say thou nought . . iv 1 69
Yet my heart Throbs to know one thing: tell me, if your art Can tell so much . . . . iv 1 101
Seek to know no more.—I will be satisfied . . . . . iv 1 103
Let me know. Why sinks that cauldron? and what noise is this? . iv 1 105
You know not Whether it was his wisdom or his fear . . . iv 2 4
He is noble, wise, judicious, and best knows The fits o' the season . iv 2 16
Cruel are the times, when we are traitors And do not know ourselves . iv 2 19
What I believe I'll wail, What know believe . . . . iv 3 9
It is myself I mean: in whom I know All the particulars of vice . iv 3 50
How he solicits heaven, Himself best knows . . . . . iv 3 150
My countryman; but yet I know him not . . . . . iv 3 160
Stands Scotland where it did?—Alas, poor country! Almost afraid to know itself . . . . iv 3 165
Where nothing, But who knows nothing, is once seen to smile . . iv 3 167
What need we fear who knows it, when none can call our power to account? . . . . v 1 42
She has spoke what she should not, I am sure of that: heaven knows what she has known . . . . v 1 54
Who knows if Donalbain be with his brother?—For certain, sir, he is not . . . . v 2 7
The spirits that know All mortal consequences have pronounced me thus . . . . v 3 4
The time approaches That will with due decision make us know . . v 4 17
I should report that which I say I saw, But know not how to do it . v 5 32
In what particular thought to work I know not . . . *Hamlet* i 1 67
Good now, sit down, and tell me, he that knows . . . . i 1 70
I this morning know Where we shall find him most conveniently . . i 1 174
For all, our thanks. Now follows, that you know . . . . i 2 17
Seems, madam! nay, it is; I know not 'seems' . . . . . i 2 76
But, you must know, your father lost a father; That father lost, lost his . . . . i 2 89
What we know must be and is as common As any the most vulgar thing i 2 98
I know you are no truant. But what is your affair in Elsinore? . . i 2 173

Know. And we did think it writ down in our duty To let you know of it *Hamlet* i 2 223
I do not know, my lord, what I should think.—Marry, I'll teach you: think yourself a baby i 3 104
I do know, When the blood burns, how prodigal the soul Lends the tongue vows i 3 115
Haste me to know't i 5 29
But know, thou noble youth, The serpent that did sting thy father's life Now wears his crown i 5 38
For your desire to know what is between us, O'ermaster't as you may i 5 139
Some doubtful phrase, As 'Well, well, we know' i 5 176
Finding By this encompassment and drift of question That they do know my son, come you more nearer ii 1 11
As thus, 'I know his father and his friends, And in part him' ii 1 14
Wherefore should you do this?—Ay, my lord, I would know that ii 1 37
He closes thus: 'I know the gentleman; I saw him yesterday, or t'other day' ii 1 55
Mad for thy love?—My lord, I do not know; But truly, I do fear it ii 1 85
Hath there been such a time—I'd fain know that—That I have positively said ''Tis so,' When it proved otherwise?—Not that I know ii 2 153
You know, sometimes he walks four hours together Here in the lobby ii 2 160
Do you know me, my lord?—Excellent well; you are a fishmonger ii 2 173
I know the good king and queen have sent for you ii 2 290
I have of late—but wherefore I know not—lost all my mirth ii 2 307
When the wind is southerly I know a hawk from a handsaw ii 2 397
'As by lot, God wot,' and then, you know, 'It came to pass' ii 2 435
I'll tent him to the quick: if he but blench, I know my course ii 2 627
Rather bear those ills we have Than fly to others that we know not of iii 1 82
I never gave you aught.—My honour'd lord, you know right well you did iii 1 97
For wise men know well enough what monsters you make of them iii 1 144
This show imports the argument of the play.—We shall know by this fellow iii 2 151
Now, what my love is, proof hath made you know iii 2 179
I know no touch of it, my lord.—'Tis as easy as lying iii 2 371
You would play upon me; you would seem to know my stops iii 2 381
I'll call upon you ere you go to bed, And tell you what I know iii 3 35
And how his audit stands who knows save heaven? iii 3 82
Up, sword; and know thou a more horrid hent iii 3 88
O me, what hast thou done?—Nay, I know not: Is it the king? iii 4 25
'Twere good you let him know; For who, that's but a queen, fair, sober, wise, Would from a paddock, from a bat, a gib, Such dear concernings hide? iii 4 188
I must to England; you know that?—Alack, I had forgot iii 4 200
But where is he?—Without, my lord; guarded, to know your pleasure iv 3 14
Till I know 'tis done, Howe'er my haps, my joys were ne'er begun iv 3 69
You know the rendezvous iv 4 4
We shall express our duty in his eye; And let him know so iv 4 7
I do not know Why yet I live to say 'This thing's to do' iv 4 43
How should I your true love know From another one? iv 5 23
Lord, we know what we are, but know not what we may be iv 5 42
My brother shall know of it: and so I thank you for your good counsel iv 5 71
If you desire to know the certainty Of your dear father's death iv 5 140
None but his enemies.—Will you know them then? iv 5 144
I do not know from what part of the world I should be greeted iv 6 4
If your name be Horatio, as I am let to know it is iv 6 11
High and mighty, You shall know I am set naked on your kingdom iv 7 43
Know you the hand?—'Tis Hamlet's character iv 7 52
I know him well: he is the brooch indeed And gem of all the nation iv 7 94
Why ask you this?—Not that I think you did not love your father; But that I know love is begun by time iv 7 112
Hamlet return'd shall know you are come home iv 7 131
Whose [skull] do you think it was?—Nay, I know not v 1 195
Here hung those lips that I have kissed I know not how oft v 1 208
Let us know, Our indiscretion sometimes serves us well v 2 7
Wilt thou know The effect of what I wrote?—Ay, good my lord v 2 36
Dost know this water-fly?—No, my good lord.—Thy state is the more gracious; for 'tis a vice to know him v 2 83
I know you are not ignorant— I would you did, sir v 2 139
But, to know a man well, were to know himself v 2 147
He sends to know if your pleasure hold to play v 2 205
This presence knows, And you must needs have heard, how I am punish'd With sore distraction v 2 239
Cousin Hamlet, You know the wager?—Very well, my lord v 2 271
Do you know this noble gentleman? *Lear* i 1 25
I must love you, and sue to know you better.—Sir, I shall study deserving i 1 30
Know that we have divided In three our kingdom i 1 38
She's there, and she is yours.—I know no answer i 1 204
I know you what you are; And like a sister am most loath to call Your faults as they are named i 1 272
I know no news, my lord.—What paper were you reading? i 2 29
You know the character to be your brother's? i 2 66
Where is he?—I do not well know, my lord i 2 85
Dissipation of cohorts, nuptial breaches, and I know not what i 2 162
Let him to our sister, Whose mind and mine, I know, in that are one i 3 15
Who wouldst thou serve?—You.—Dost thou know me, fellow? i 4 28
He would not.—My lord, I know not what the matter is i 4 61
Dost thou know the difference, my boy, between a bitter fool and a sweet fool? i 4 151
For wise men are grown foppish, They know not how their wits to wear i 4 183
Make use of that good wisdom, Whereof I know you are fraught i 4 241
May not an ass know when the cart draws the horse? i 4 244
Doth any here know me? This is not Lear: Doth Lear walk thus? speak thus? i 4 246
Such men as may besort your age, And know themselves and you i 4 273
Men of choice and rarest parts, That all particulars of duty know i 4 286
Whereof comes this?—Never afflict yourself to know the cause i 4 313
I know his heart. What he hath utter'd I have writ my sister i 4 353
Acquaint my daughter no further with any thing you know i 5 3
How comes that?—Nay, I know not ii 1 7
Hark, the duke's trumpets! I know not why he comes ii 1 81
You know not why we came to visit you ii 1 120
I know thee not.—Fellow, I know thee.—What dost thou know me for? ii 2 11
One that is neither known of thee nor knows thee ii 2 29
Know you no reverence?—Yes, sir; but anger hath a privilege ii 2 75
These kind of knaves I know, which in this plainness Harbour more craft ii 2 107
I know, sir, I am no flatterer ii 2 116
Whose disposition, all the world well knows, Will not be rubb'd nor stopp'd ii 2 160

Know. You know the fiery quality of the duke; How unremoveable *Lear* ii 4 93
I think you are; I know what reason I have to think so ii 4 131
You less know how to value her desert Than she to scant her duty ii 4 141
What trumpet's that?—I know't, my sister's: this approves her letter ii 4 186
I have good hope Thou didst not know on't ii 4 192
But she knows what she does.—Is this well spoken? ii 4 239
I will do such things,—What they are, yet I know not ii 4 284
Whither is he going?—He calls to horse; but will I know not whither ii 4 300
I do know you; And dare, upon the warrant of my note, Commend a dear thing to you iii 1 17
She will tell you who your fellow is That yet you do not know iii 1 49
This courtesy, forbid thee, shall the duke Instantly know iii 3 23
Be simple answerer, for we know the truth iii 7 43
Dost thou know Dover?—Ay, master iv 1 74
Knows he the wickedness?—Ay, my good lord iv 2 92
Why the King of France is so suddenly gone back know you the reason? iv 3 2
Those happy smilets, That play'd on her ripe lip, seem'd not to know What guests were in her eyes iv 3 22
What might import my sister's letter to him?—I know not iv 5 7
Might not you Transport her purposes by word? Belike, Something—I know not what iv 5 21
I know your lady does not love her husband iv 5 23
I know you are of her bosom.—I, madam?—I speak in understanding; you are, I know't iv 5 26
And yet I know not how conceit may rob The treasury of life iv 6 42
Give the word.—Sweet marjoram.—Pass.—I know that voice iv 6 96
Dost thou know me?—I remember thine eyes well enough iv 6 138
I am a king, My masters, know you that.—You are a royal one iv 6 204
I know thee well: a serviceable villain iv 6 257
To know our enemies' minds, we'ld rip their hearts iv 6 265
My boon I make it, that you know me not Till time and I think meet iv 7 10
Sir, do you know me?—You are a spirit, I know: when did you die? iv 7 48
I should e'en die with pity, To see another thus. I know not what to say iv 7 54
Methinks I should know you, and know this man; Yet I am doubtful iv 7 64
And all the skill I have Remembers not these garments; nor I know not Where I did lodge last night iv 7 67
I know you do not love me; for your sisters Have, as I do remember, done me wrong: You have some cause iv 7 73
Know of the duke if his last purpose hold v 1 1
Now, sweet lord, You know the goodness I intend upon you v 1 7
Go with us.—O, ho, I know the riddle.—I will go v 1 37
Know thou this, that men Are as the time is v 3 30
Know, my name is lost; By treason's tooth bare-gnawn and canker-bit v 3 121
Read thine own evil: No tearing, lady; I perceive you know it v 3 157
Know'st thou this paper?—Ask me not what I know v 3 160
If ever I Did hate thee or thy father!—Worthy prince, I know't v 3 178
I know when one is dead, and when one lives; She's dead as earth v 3 260
He knows not what he says: and vain it is That we present us to him v 3 293
You lords and noble friends, know our intent v 3 296
I take it much unkindly That thou . . . shouldst know of this *Othello* i 1 3
By the faith of man, I know my price, I am worth no worse a place i 1 11
Nor the division of a battle knows More than a spinster i 1 23
Do you know my voice?—Not I: what are you? i 1 93
If you know not this, my manners tell me We have your wrong rebuke i 1 130
I do know, the state, However this may gall him with some check, Cannot with safety cast him i 1 148
How didst thou know 'twas she? O, she deceives me Past thought! i 1 166
Do you know Where we may apprehend her and the Moor? i 1 177
'Tis yet to know,—Which, when I know that boasting is an honour, I shall promulgate i 2 20
For know, Iago, But that I love the gentle Desdemona, I would not i 2 24
Fetch Desdemona hither.—Ancient, conduct them; you best know the place i 3 121
I know not if't be true; But I, for mere suspicion in that kind, Will do as if for surety i 3 394
He is not yet arrived: nor know I aught But that he's well ii 1 89
The Moor! I know his trumpet.—'Tis truly so.—Let's meet him ii 1 180
Cassio knows you not. I'll not be far from you ii 1 273
Speak, who began this? on thy love, I charge thee.—I do not know ii 3 179
Iago can inform you,—While I spare speech, which something now offends me,—Of all that I do know: nor know I aught By me that's said or done amiss this night ii 3 200
Give me to know How this foul rout began, who set it on ii 3 209
I know, Iago, Thy honesty and love doth mince this matter ii 3 246
What had he done to you?—I know not.—Is't possible? ii 3 287
Away, I say; thou shalt know more hereafter: Nay, get thee gone ii 3 387
Whereby hangs a tale, sir?—Marry, sir, by many a wind-instrument that I know iii 1 11
He's never any thing but your true servant.—I know't; I thank you iii 3 10
What dost thou say?—Nothing, my lord: or if—I know not what iii 3 36
Did Michael Cassio, When you woo'd my lady, Know of your love? iii 3 95
Is he not honest?—Honest, my lord!—Honest! ay, honest.—My lord, for aught I know iii 3 104
My lord, you know I love you.—I think thou dost iii 3 117
I know thou'rt full of love and honesty, And weigh'st thy words iii 3 118
It were not for your quiet nor your good, Nor for my manhood, honesty, or wisdom, To let you know my thoughts iii 3 154
I'll know thy thoughts.—You cannot, if my heart were in your hand iii 3 162
Look to't: I know our country disposition well iii 3 201
Farewell, farewell: If more thou dost perceive, let me know more iii 3 239
This honest creature doubtless Sees and knows more, much more, than he unfolds iii 3 243
And knows all qualities, with a learned spirit, Of human dealings iii 3 259
And give't Iago: what he will do with it Heaven knows, not I iii 3 298
I swear 'tis better to be much abused Than but to know't a little iii 3 337
He that is robb'd, not wanting what is stol'n, Let him not know't, and he's not robb'd at all iii 3 343
Do you know, sirrah, where Lieutenant Cassio lies? iii 4 1
I know not where he lodges iii 4 11
Where should I lose that handkerchief, Emilia?—I know not iii 4 24
But to know so must be my benefit iii 4 119
Nor should I know him, Were he in favour as in humour alter'd iii 4 124
Whose is it?—I know not, sweet: I found it in my chamber iii 4 188
What hath he said?—'Faith, that he did—I know not what he did iv 1 32
No, let me know; And knowing what I am, I know what she shall be iv 1 73
A likely piece of work, that you should find it in your chamber, and not know who left it there! iv 1 158
Heaven doth truly know it.—Heaven truly knows that thou art false as hell iv 2 38

Know. Why did he so?—I do not know; I am sure I am none such *Othello* iv 2 123
How comes this trick upon him?—Nay, heaven doth know . . . iv 2 129
By this light of heaven, I know not how I lost him . . . . iv 2 151
He knows not yet of his honourable fortune . . . . . iv 2 240
I know a lady in Venice would have walk'd barefoot to Palestine for a touch of his nether lip . . . . iv 3 38
Let husbands know Their wives have sense like them . . . . iv 3 94
But so: I hear him coming.—I know his gait, 'tis he . . . v 1 23
Whose noise is this that cries on murder?—We do not know . . . v 1 49
Know we this face or no? Alas, my friend and my dear countryman! . v 1 88
Roderigo.—What, of Venice?—Even he, sir: did you know him?—Know him! ay . . . . v 1 92
What malice was between you?—None in the world; nor do I know the man . . . . v 1 103
Go know of Cassio where he supp'd to-night . . . . . . v 1 117
I know not where is that Promethean heat That can thy light relume . v 2 12
Why I should fear I know not, Since guiltiness I know not . . . v 2 38
Why, how should she be murder'd?—Alas, who knows? . . . . v 2 126
He says thou told'st him that his wife was false: I know thou didst not v 2 174
I scarce did know you, uncle: there lies your niece . . . . v 2 201
I know this act shows horrible and grim . . . . v 2 203
But yet Iago knows That she with Cassio hath the act of shame A thousand times committed . . . . v 2 210
Demand me nothing: what you know, you know . . . . . v 2 303
You shall understand what hath befall'n, Which, as I think, you know not v 2 308
I have done the state some service, and they know't . . . v 2 339
Who knows If the scarce-bearded Cæsar have not sent His powerful mandate to you, 'Do this, or this' . . . *Ant. and Cleo.* i 1 20
Is't you, sir, that know things?—In nature's infinite book of secrecy A little I can read . . . . i 2 8
We'll know all our fortunes.—Mine, and most of our fortunes, to-night, shall be—drunk to bed . . . . i 2 44
Her length of sickness, with what else more serious Importeth thee to know . . . . i 2 125
Ten thousand harms, more than the ills I know, My idleness doth hatch i 2 133
What's the matter?—I know, by that same eye, there's some good news i 3 19
I have no power upon you; hers you are.—The gods best know . i 3 24
I would I had thy inches; thou shouldst know There were a heart in Egypt . . . . i 3 40
Quarrel no more, but be prepared to know The purposes I bear . i 3 66
Sir, you and I have loved, but there's not it; That you know well . i 3 89
Know, It is not Cæsar's natural vice to hate Our great competitor . i 4 1
Know, worthy Pompey, That what they do delay, they not deny . ii 1 2
I know they are in Rome together, Looking for Antony . . . . ii 1 19
I know not, Menas, How lesser enmities may give way to greater . ii 1 42
But how the fear of us May cement their divisions and bind up The petty difference, we yet not know . . . . ii 1 49
Not so, not so; I know you could not lack, I am certain on't . . ii 2 57
If thou hast consider'd, let us know If 'twill tie up thy discontented sword . . . . ii 6 5
I do not know Wherefore my father should revengers want . . . ii 6 10
Know, then, I came before you here a man prepared To take this offer . ii 6 40
You must know, When Cæsar and your brother were at blows . . ii 6 44
Well, I know not What counts harsh fortune casts upon my face . . ii 6 54
I know thee now: how farest thou, soldier?—Well; And well am like to do . . . . ii 6 72
They know, By the height, the lowness, or the mean, if dearth Or foison follow . . . . ii 7 21
Thou must know, 'Tis not my profit that does lead mine honour . . ii 7 81
The man hath seen some majesty, and should know . . . . iii 3 45
The people know it; and have now received His accusations . . . iii 6 22
You did know How much you were my conqueror . . . . . iii 11 65
Fortune knows We scorn her most when most she offers blows . . iii 11 73
Let him appear that's come from Antony. Know you him? . . . iii 12 2
For us, you know Whose he is we are, and that is, Cæsar's . . . iii 13 51
He knows that you embrace not Antony As you did love . . . iii 13 56
He is a god, and knows What is most right: mine honour was not yielded . . . . iii 13 60
Though you can guess what temperance should be, You know not what it is . . . . iii 13 122
Not know me yet?—Cold-hearted toward me?—Ah, dear, if I be so . iii 13 157
Let the old ruffian know I have many other ways to die . . . . iv 1 4
Let our best heads Know, that to-morrow the last of many battles We mean to fight . . . . iv 1 11
Know, my hearts, I hope well of to-morrow . . . . . . iv 2 41
Welcome: Thou look'st like him that knows a warlike charge . . iv 4 19
Run one before, And let the queen know of our gests . . . . iv 8 2
The augurers Say they know not, they cannot tell . . . . . iv 12 5
She soon shall know of us, by some of ours, How honourable and how kindly we Determine for her . . . . v 1 57
Have comfort, for I know your plight is pitied Of him that caused it . v 2 33
Know, sir, that I Will not wait pinion'd at your master's court . . v 2 52
What thou hast done thy master Cæsar knows, And he hath sent for thee . . . . v 2 65
You have heard of me?—I cannot tell.—Assuredly you know me . . v 2 72
Know you what Cæsar means to do with me?—I am loath to tell you . v 2 106
He'll lead me, then, in triumph?—Madam, he will; I know't . . v 2 110
Cleopatra, know, We will extenuate rather than enforce . . . v 2 124
I know the devil himself will not eat a woman: I know that a woman is a dish for the gods . . . . v 2 274
I will from hence to-day.—You know the peril . . . *Cymbeline* i 1 80
I shall incur I know not How much of his displeasure . . . . i 1 102
But, you know, strange fowl light upon neighbouring ponds . . . i 4 97
I do know her spirit, And will not trust one of her malice . . . i 5 34
I do not know What is more cordial . . . . i 5 63
But, heavens know, Some men are much to blame . . . . . i 6 76
You do seem to know Something of me, or what concerns me . . i 6 93
I have spoke this, to know if your affiance Were deeply rooted . . i 6 163
It is not fit your lordship should undertake every companion that you give offence to.—No, I know that . . . . ii 1 31
A stranger, and I not know on't!—He's a strange fellow himself, and knows it not . . . . ii 1 39
I know her women are about her: what If I do line one of their hands? ii 3 71
And learn now, for all, That I, which know my heart, do here pronounce, By the very truth of it, I care not for you . . . . ii 3 112
I hope you know that we Must not continue friends.—Good sir, we must . . . . ii 4 48
Who knows if one of her women, being corrupted, Hath stol'n it from her? . . . . ii 4 116

Know. That most venerable man which I Did call my father, was I know not where When I was stamp'd . . . . *Cymbeline* ii 5 4
All faults that may be named, nay, that hell knows, Why, hers, in part or all; but rather all . . . . ii 5 27
I know your master's pleasure and he mine: All the remain is 'Welcome!' . . . . iii 1 86
We, poor unfledged, Have never wing'd from view o' the nest, nor know not What air's from home . . . . iii 3 28
Did you but know the city's usuries And felt them knowingly . . iii 3 45
These boys know little they are sons to the king . . . . . iii 3 80
Heaven and my conscience knows Thou didst unjustly banish me . iii 3 99
Know, if you kill me for my fault, I should Have died had I not made it . . . . iii 6 57
I know not why I love this youth; and I have heard you say, Love's reason's without reason . . . . iv 2 20
Thus did he answer me: yet said, hereafter I might know more . . iv 2 42
I partly know him: 'tis Cloten, the son o' the queen . . . . iv 2 64
I saw him not these many years, and yet I know 'tis he . . . . iv 2 67
To thy mere confusion, thou shalt know I am son to the queen . . iv 2 92
Thou blessed thing! Jove knows what man thou mightst have made . iv 2 207
I know the shape of 's leg: this is his hand; His foot Mercurial . iv 2 309
Who needs must know of her departure and Dost seem so ignorant . iv 3 10
I nothing know where she remains, why gone . . . . . . iv 3 14
Neither know I What is betid to Cloten; but remain Perplex'd in all . iv 3 39
They will waste their time upon our note, To know from whence we are iv 4 21
Let me make men know More valour in me than my habits show . . v 1 29
If he'll do as he is made to do, I know he'll quickly fly my friendship too . . . . v 3 62
I know you are more clement than vile men . . . . . . v 4 18
Whose bolt, you know, Sky-planted batters all rebelling coasts . . v 4 95
No care of yours it is; you know 'tis ours. Whom best I love I cross . v 4 100
I, That have this golden chance and know not why . . . . v 4 132
You know not which way you shall go.—Yes, indeed do I, fellow . . v 4 181
You must either be directed by some that take upon them to know, or to take upon yourself that which I am sure you do not know . . v 4 187
I know not why, wherefore, To say 'live, boy:' ne'er thank thy master; live . . . . v 5 95
I do not bid thee beg my life, good lad; And yet I know thou wilt . v 5 102
Her son Is gone, we know not how nor where . . . . . . v 5 273
What became of him I further know not . . . . v 5 286
Indeed a banish'd man; I know not how a traitor . . . . . v 5 320
I know not how to wish A pair of worthier sons . . . . . v 5 355
I know not how much more should be demanded . . . . . v 5 389
Who hath taught My frail mortality to know itself . . . *Pericles* i 1 42
As sick men do Who know the world, see heaven, but, feeling woe . i 1 48
If Jove stray, who dares say Jove doth ill? It is enough you know . i 1 105
One sin, I know, another doth provoke . . . . i 1 137
That, being bid to ask what he would of the king, desired he might know none of his secrets . . . . i 3 7
Antiochus—on what cause I know not—Took some displeasure at him . i 3 20
To know for what he comes, and whence he comes, And what he craves i 4 80
What I have been I have forgot to know . . . . ii 1 75
Hark you, sir, do you know where ye are?—Not well.—Why, I'll tell you . . . . ii 1 100
It was sometime target to a king; I know it by this mark . . . ii 1 144
We desire to know of him, Of whence he is, his name and parentage . ii 3 73
It is too late to talk of love; And that's the mark I know you level at. ii 3 114
No, Escanes, know this of me, Antiochus from incest lived not free . ii 4 1
Know that our griefs are risen to the top . . . . ii 4 23
Let us salute him, Or know what ground's made happy by his breath . ii 4 28
Your noble self, That best know how to rule and how to reign . . ii 4 38
Knights, from my daughter this I let you know . . . . . ii 5 2
Who, for aught I know, May be, nor can I think the contrary, As great in blood as I myself . . . . ii 5 78
Know you the character?—It is my lord's . . . . iii 4 3
Come, come, I know 'tis good for you. Walk half an hour . . . iv 1 45
Do you know the French knight that cowers i' the hams? . . . I know he will come in our shadow, to scatter his crowns in the sun . . iv 2 113
Yet none does know, but you, how she came dead, Nor none can know iv 3 29
But yet I know you'll do as I advise . . . . iv 3 51
You honour knows what 'tis to say well enough . . . . . . iv 6 34
But how honourable he is in that, I know not . . . . . . iv 6 61
Do you know this house to be a place of such resort, and will come into't? . . . . iv 6 85
Seeing this goodly vessel ride before us, I made to it, to know of whence you are . . . . v 1 19
Let me entreat to know at large the cause Of your king's sorrow . . v 1 62
If you did know my parentage, You would not do me violence . . v 1 100
Now I know you better . . . . v 3 37
Hail, madam, and my queen!—I know you not . . . . . . v 3 49
I know it well *T. G. of Ver.* i 3; ii 4; iii 1; *Com. of Errors* iii 2; *3 Hen. VI.* ii 1

Know you of old. You always end with a jade's trick: I know you of old . . . . *Much Ado* i 1 146

Knower. What's thyself?—Thy knower, Patroclus . . *Troi. and Cres.* ii 3 51

Knowest. Sycorax . . . from Argier, Thou know'st, was banish'd *Tempest* i 2 266
Thou best know'st What torment I did find thee in . . . . i 2 286
Dost thou know her by my gazing on her, and yet knowest her not? *T. G. of Ver.* ii 1 52
And I must after, For love, thou know'st, is full of jealousy . . ii 4 177
O, know'st thou not his looks are my soul's food? . . . . . ii 7 15
The current that with gentle murmur glides, Thou know'st, being stopp'd, impatiently doth rage . . . . ii 7 26
Thou know'st how willingly I would effect The match . . . . iii 2 22
Dispose of them as thou know'st their deserts. . . . . . v 4 159
Let him continue in his courses till thou knowest what they are *Meas. for Meas.* ii 1 197
Friar, thou knowest not the duke so well as I do . . . . . iv 3 169
By heaven, fond wretch, thou know'st not what thou speak'st . . v 1 105
Say, didst thou speak with him? know'st thou his mind? *Com. of Errors* ii 1 47
These ears of mine, thou know'st, did hear thee . . . . . v 1 26
But seven years since, in Syracusa, boy, Thou know'st we parted . . v 1 321
Thou knowest that the fashion of a doublet, or a hat, or a cloak, is nothing to a man.—Yes, it is apparel . . . . . *Much Ado* iii 3 125
Thou knowest not what it is.—I shall know, sir, when I have done it *L. L. Lost* iii 1 158
Thou know'st that all my fortunes are at sea . . *Mer. of Venice* i 1 177
Away! make haste: thou know'st where I will tarry . . . . iv 2 18
Know'st thou not, the duke Hath banish'd me, his daughter? *As Y. L. It* i 3 96
Know'st thou the youth that spoke to me erewhile? . . . . iii 5 105

Knowest. I would not wed her for a mine of gold.—Hortensio, peace! thou know'st not gold's effect *T. of Shrew* i 2 93
But, thou knowest, winter tames man, woman, and beast iv 1 24
But what at full I know, thou know'st no part *All's Well* ii 1 135
Know'st thou not, Bertram, What she has done for me? ii 3 115
Thou know'st she has raised me from my sickly bed ii 3 118
I know more than I'll speak.—But wilt thou not speak all thou knowest? v 3 257
Know'st thou this country?—Ay, madam, well *T. Night* i 2 21
Thou know'st no less but all i 4 13
And 'diluculo surgere,' thou know'st.—Nay, by my troth, I know not. ii 3 3
I prithee, vent thy folly somewhere else; Thou know'st not me iv 1 11
Be that thou know'st thou art, and then thou art As great as that thou fear'st v 1 152
No more; cease; thou know'st He dies to me again when talk'd of *W. T.* v 1 119
Thou art my friend, that know'st my tongue so well *K. John* v 6 8
Know'st thou not That when the searching eye of heaven is hid, . . . Then thieves and robbers range abroad? *Richard II.* iii 2 36
Thou, which know'st the way To plant unrightful kings v 1 62
Thou knowest he is no starveling *1 Hen. IV.* ii 1 76
Thou knowest my old ward; here I lay, and thus I bore my point ii 4 215
Why, thou knowest I am as valiant as Hercules ii 4 298
Why, Hal, thou knowest, as thou art but man, I dare iii 3 165
Apple-johns? thou knowest Sir John cannot endure an apple-john *2 Hen. IV.* ii 4 2
I am a Welshman.—Know'st thou Fluellen?—Yes *Hen. V.* iv 1 52
Know'st thou not That I have fined these bones of mine for ransom? iv 7 71
Knowest thou Gower?—He is my dear friend, an please you iv 7 173
Thou know'st little of my wrongs *1 Hen. VI.* i 3 59
Villain, thou know'st the law of arms is such iii 4 38
Coal-black as jet.—Why, then, thou know'st what colour jet is of? *2 Hen. VI.* ii 1 113
Now get thee hence: the king, thou know'st, is coming iii 2 386
Villain, thou know'st no law of God nor man *Richard III.* i 2 70
Thou know'st our reasons urged upon the way; What think'st thou? iii 1 160
I stay dinner there.—And supper too, although thou know'st it not iii 2 123
Our true blood, Which, as thou know'st, unjustly must be spilt iii 3 22
Know'st thou not any whom corrupting gold Would tempt? iv 2 34
Thou know'st it well, Thou camest on earth to make the earth my hell iv 4 165
What art thou?—Thou mayst tell that knowest.—O, tell, tell *T. and C.* ii 3 53
What's thy name?—If, Tullus, Not yet thou knowest me *Coriolanus* iv 5 61
Prepare thy brow to frown: know'st thou me yet?—I know thee not iv 5 69
Thou art experienced, since thou know'st Thy country's strength iv 5 145
Thou know'st, great son, The end of war's uncertain v 3 140
And may, for aught thou know'st, affected be *T. Andron.* ii 1 28
Dig the grave for him: Thou know'st our meaning ii 3 271
Thou know'st my daughter's of a pretty age *Rom. and Jul.* i 3 10
Thou know'st the mask of night is on my face ii 2 85
Villain am I none; Therefore farewell; I see thou know'st me not iii 1 68
To smile upon my state, Which, well thou know'st, is cross and full of sin iv 3 5
Thou know'st my lodging: get me ink and paper, And hire post-horses v 1 25
Why dost thou call them knaves? thou know'st them not *T. of Athens* i 1 181
You know me, Apemantus?—Thou know'st I do: I call'd thee by thy name i 1 186
Thou knowest well enough, although thou comest to me, that this is no time to lend money iii 1 43
In thy rags thou knowest none, but art despised for the contrary iv 3 304
Know'st thou any harm's intended towards him? *J. Cæsar* ii 4 31
Thou know'st that we two went to school together v 5 26
Thou know'st that Banquo, and his Fleance, lives *Macbeth* iii 2 37
Thou know'st 'tis common; all that lives must die *Hamlet* i 2 72
Farewell. He that thou knowest thine, HAMLET iv 6 31
And what to this was sequent Thou know'st already v 2 55
Have more than thou showest, Speak less than thou knowest *Lear* i 4 132
What a brazen-faced varlet art thou, to deny thou knowest me! ii 2 31
Thou better know'st The offices of nature, bond of childhood ii 4 180
Know'st thou the way to Dover?—Both stile and gate, horse-way and foot-path iv 1 57
That not know'st Fools do those villains pity who are punish'd Ere they have done their mischief iv 2 53
Come hither, friend: Tell me what more thou know'st iv 2 98
Thou know'st, the first time that we smell the air, We wawl and cry iv 6 183
Know'st thou this paper?—Ask me not what I know v 3 160
Thou know'st we work by wit, and not by witchcraft *Othello* ii 3 378
That thrust had been mine enemy indeed, But that my coat is better than thou know'st: I will make proof of thine v 1 25
Thou know'st How much we do o'er-count thee *Ant. and Cleo.* ii 6 25
Thou takest up Thou know'st not what; but take it for thy labour *Cymb.* i 5 61
Thou villain base, Know'st me not by my clothes? iv 2 81
Know'st him thou look'st on? speak, Wilt have him live? v 5 110
Thou know'st I have power To take thy life from thee *Pericles* i 2 56
Where, as thou know'st, against the face of death, I sought the purchase of a glorious beauty i 2 71
Nay, I'll be patient. Thou little know'st how thou dost startle me v 1 147

Knowing. Thee, my daughter, who Art ignorant of what thou art, nought knowing Of whence I am *Tempest* i 2 18
Knowing I loved my books, he furnish'd me From mine own library i 2 166
Knowing that tender youth is soon suggested *T. G. of Ver.* iii 1 34
Knowing my mind, you wrong me, Master Fenton *Mer. Wives* iii 4 80
Knowing whom it was their hap to save, Gave healthful welcome *C. of Er.* i 1 114
And, knowing how the debt grows, I will pay it iv 4 124
What men may do! what men daily do, not knowing what they do! *Much Ado* iv 1 20
Let me go with that I came; which is, with knowing what hath passed between you v 2 48
Most power to do most harm, least knowing ill *L. L. Lost* ii 1 58
Here was a consent, Knowing aforehand of our merriment, To dash it v 2 461
If you had your eyes, you might fail of the knowing me *Mer. of Venice* ii 2 80
Knowing no burden of heavy tedious penury *As Y. Like It* iii 2 342
Knowing thee to be but young and light *T. of Shrew* ii 1 204
I knew him.—The rather will I spare my praises towards him; Knowing him is enough *All's Well* ii 1 107
What at full I know, thou know'st no part, I knowing all my peril ii 1 136
Being not ignorant of the impossibility, and knowing I had no such purpose iv 1 39
Our rash faults Make trivial price of serious things we have, Not knowing them until we know their grave v 3 62
He shall not need to grieve At knowing of thy choice *W. Tale* iv 4 427
Knowing by Paulina that the oracle Gave hope thou wast in being v 3 126
Knowing. Full of idle dreams, Not knowing what they fear, but full of fear *K. John* iv 2 146
Knowing Dame Eleanor's aspiring humour, Have hired me *2 Hen. VI.* i 2 97
The pretty-vaulting sea refused to drown me, Knowing that thou wouldst have me drown'd on shore iii 2 95
Why hast thou broken faith with me, Knowing how hardly I can brook abuse? v 1 92
Shamest thou not, knowing whence thou art extraught, To let thy tongue detect thy base-born heart? *3 Hen. VI.* ii 2 142
Not knowing how to find the open air, But toiling desperately to find it out iii 2 177
You are to blame, Knowing she will not lose her wonted greatness, To use so rude behaviour *Hen. VIII.* iv 2 102
May I change these garments?—You may, sir.—That I'll straight do; and, knowing myself again, Repair to the senate-house *Coriolanus* ii 3 155
The eagle suffers little birds to sing, . . . Knowing that with the shadow of his wings He can at pleasure stint their melody *T. Andron.* iv 4 85
In My knowing, Timon has been this lord's father *T. of Athens* iii 2 74
This sore night Hath trifled former knowings *Macbeth* ii 4 4
Sith you have heard, and with a knowing ear *Hamlet* iv 7 3
On the view and knowing of these contents v 2 44
Knowing nought, like dogs, but following *Lear* ii 2 86
And knowing what I am, I know what she shall be *Othello* iv 1 74
He's very knowing; I do perceive't *Ant. and Cleo.* iii 3 26
That he should dream, Knowing all measures, the full Cæsar will Answer his emptiness! iii 13 35
Let him be so entertained amongst you as suits, with gentlemen of your knowing, to a stranger of his quality *Cymbeline* i 4 30
He did incline to sadness, and oft-times Not knowing why i 6 63
Certainties Either are past remedies, or, timely knowing, The remedy then born i 6 97
One of your great knowing Should learn, being taught, forbearance ii 3 102
Will poor folks lie, That have afflictions on them, knowing 'tis A punishment? iii 6 10
For he's no man on whom perfections wait That, knowing sin within, will touch the gate *Pericles* i 1 80
Knowing this kingdom is without a head ii 4 35

Knowingly. Dost thou believe't?—Ay, madam, knowingly *All's Well* i 3 256
Did you but know the city's usuries And felt them knowingly *Cymbeline* iii 3 46

Knowledge. Some oracle Must rectify our knowledge *Tempest* v 1 245
He has no more knowledge in Hibocrates and Galen *Mer. Wives* iii 1 66
If your knowledge be more it is much darkened in your malice *M. for M.* iii 2 156
Love talks with better knowledge, and knowledge with dearer love iii 2 159
But shall you on your knowledge find this way? iv 1 37
Being come to knowledge that there was complaint Intended v 1 153
Less in your knowledge and your grace you show not Than our earth's wonder, more than earth divine *Com. of Errors* iii 2 31
And though I have for barbarism spoke more Than for that angel knowledge you can say *L. L. Lost* i 1 113
His ignorance were wise, Where now his knowledge must prove ignorance ii 1 103
If knowledge be the mark, to know thee shall suffice iv 2 115
Do but say to me what I should do That in your knowledge may by me be done, And I am prest unto it *Mer. of Venice* i 1 159
How prove you that, in the great heap of your knowledge? *As Y. Like It* i 2 73
In a better world than this, I shall desire more love and knowledge of you i 2 297
Let me the knowledge of my fault bear with me i 3 48
Let me stay the growth of his beard, if thou delay me not the knowledge of his chin iii 2 222
O knowledge ill-inhabited, worse than Jove in a thatched house! iii 3 10
I speak not this that you should bear a good opinion of my knowledge v 2 60
That, upon knowledge of my parentage, I may have welcome *T. of Shrew* ii 1 96
He was skilful enough to have lived still, if knowledge could be set up against mortality *All's Well* i 1 35
We make trifles of terrors, ensconcing ourselves into seeming knowledge ii 3 5
I have a desire to hold my acquaintance with thee, or rather my knowledge ii 3 241
He is very great in knowledge and accordingly valiant ii 5 9
In mine own direct knowledge, without any malice iii 6 9
Upon my knowledge, he is, and lousy iv 3 220
I will bespeak our diet, Whiles you beguile the time and feed your knowledge With viewing of the town *T. Night* iii 3 41
By my foes, sir, I profit in the knowledge of myself v 1 21
Verily, I speak it in the freedom of my knowledge *W. Tale* i 1 13
If you know aught which does behove my knowledge Thereof to be inform'd, imprison't not i 2 395
Alack, for lesser knowledge! how accursed In being so blest! ii 1 38
There may be in the cup A spider steep'd, and one may drink, depart, And yet partake no venom, for his knowledge Is not infected ii 1 41
How will this grieve you, When you shall come to clearer knowledge! ii 1 97
Let him have knowledge who I am ii 2 2
Something rare Even then will rush to knowledge iii 1 21
Were I the fairest youth That ever made eye swerve, had force and knowledge More than was ever man's iv 4 385
What course I mean to hold Shall nothing benefit your knowledge iv 4 514
Our absence makes us unthrifty to our knowledge v 2 121
But for the certain knowledge of that truth I put you o'er to heaven and to my mother *K. John* i 1 61
That Neptune's arms, who clippeth thee about, Would bear thee from the knowledge of thyself! v 2 35
To my knowledge, I never in my life did look on him *Richard II.* ii 3 38
He that but fears the thing he would not know Hath by instinct knowledge from others' eyes That what he fear'd is chanced *2 Hen. IV.* i 1 86
An arrant knave, on my knowledge.—I grant your worship v 1 46
Of great expedition and knowledge in th' aunchient wars, upon my particular knowledge of his directions *Hen. V.* iii 2 83
To mope with his fat-brained followers so far out of his knowledge! iii 7 144
Is a good captain, and is good knowledge and literatured in the wars iv 7 157
There is more good toward you peradventure than is in your knowledge to dream of iv 8 4
By some apparent sign Let us have knowledge at the court of guard *1 Hen. VI.* ii 1 4
Seeing ignorance is the curse of God, Knowledge the wing wherewith we fly to heaven *2 Hen. VI.* iv 7 79
I never did her any [wrong], to my knowledge *Richard III.* i 3 309
Without the king's assent or knowledge, You wrought to be a legate *Hen. VIII.* iii 2 310
Without the knowledge Either of king or council, when you went Ambassador to the emperor, you made bold To carry into Flanders the great seal iii 2 316

Knowledge. Has he had knowledge of it?—Yes . . . *Hen. VIII.* v 3 4
I constantly do think—Or rather, call my thought a certain knowledge *Troi. and Cres.* iv 1 41
Neither to care whether they love or hate him manifests the true knowledge he has in their disposition . . . *Coriolanus* ii 2 15
You have received many wounds for your country.—I will not seal your knowledge with showing them . . . . ii 3 115
I shall ere long have knowledge Of my success . . . . . v 1 61
Say to the king the knowledge of the broil As thou didst leave it *Macbeth* i 2 6
They have more in them than mortal knowledge . . . . . i 5 3
Be innocent of the knowledge, dearest chuck, Till thou applaud the deed . . . . iii 2 45
Take you, as 'twere, some distant knowledge of him . . *Hamlet* ii 1 13
For, by the marks of sovereignty, knowledge, and reason, I should be false persuaded I had daughters . . . . *Lear* i 4 253
And, from some knowledge and assurance, offer This office to you . iii 1 41
And woes by wrong imaginations lose The knowledge of themselves . iv 6 291
Be govern'd by your knowledge, and proceed I' the sway of your own will . . . . iv 7 19
I mine own gain'd knowledge should profane, If I would time expend with such a snipe, But for my sport . . . . . . *Othello* i 3 390
As we rate boys, who, being mature in knowledge, Pawn their experience to their present pleasure . . . . *Ant. and Cleo.* i 4 31
When poison'd hours had bound me up From mine own knowledge . ii 2 91
Leave unexecuted Your own renowned knowledge . . . . iii 7 46
They cannot tell; look grimly, And dare not speak their knowledge iv 12 6
And to this hour no guess in knowledge Which way they went *Cymbeline* i 1 60
Had I not brought The knowledge of your mistress home, I grant We were to question further . . . . ii 4 51
More particulars Must justify my knowledge . . . . . . ii 4 79
This paper is the history of my knowledge . . . . . . iii 5 99
The satisfaction of her knowledge only In killing creatures vile . v 5 251
Which by my knowledge found, the sinful father Seem'd not to strike *Pericles* i 2 77
And not your knowledge, your personal pain, but even Your purse, still open . . . . iii 2 46
Thou shalt kneel, and justify in knowledge She is thy very princess . v 1 219

Known. I endow'd thy purposes With words that made them known *Temp.* i 2 358
Letters should not be known; riches, poverty, And use of service, none ii 1 150
Which would be great impeachment to his age, In having known no travel in his youth . . . . . . *T. G. of Ver.* i 3 16
And that thou mayst perceive how well I like it The execution of it shall make known . . . . i 3 36
'Twere better for you if it were known in counsel . . *Mer. Wives* i 1 121
You have been a man long known to me . . . . ii 2 188
I will hereafter make known to you why I have done this . . . iii 3 241
The truth being known, We'll all present ourselves, dis-horn the spirit iv 4 62
The matter will be known to-night, or never. Be you in the Park . v 1 11
Well known to the duke.—He shall know you better, sir *Meas. for Meas.* iii 2 169
I have not yet made known to Mariana A word of this . . . . iv 1 49
All difficulties are but easy when they are known . . . . iv 2 221
To save me from the danger that might come If he were known alive . iv 3 90
I have known my husband; yet my husband Knows not that ever he knew me . . . . v 1 186
Known unto these, and to myself disguised! . . . *Com. of Errors* ii 2 216
It is all the wealth that he hath left, to be known a reasonable creature *Much Ado* i 1 71
I have known when there was no music with him but the drum . . ii 3 13
I have known when he would have walked ten mile a-foot to see a good armour . . . . ii 3 16
Hath she made her affection known to Benedick?—No; and swears she never will . . . . ii 3 127
The most dangerous piece of lechery that ever was known in the commonwealth . . . . iii 3 180
If I have known her, You will say she did embrace me as a husband . iv 1 49
If she be made of white and red, Her faults will ne'er be known *L. L. Lost* i 2 105
If by me you'll be advised, Let's mock them still, as well known as disguised . . . . v 2 301
We shall be dogged with company, and our devices known *M. N. Dream* i 2 107
And the country proverb known, That every man should take his own iii 2 458
Some ten words long, Which is as brief as I have known a play . . v 1 62
In such eyes as ours appear not faults; But where thou art not known, why, there they show Something too liberal . . *Mer. of Venice* ii 2 193
Golden locks . . . , often known To be the dowry of a second head . iii 2 94
If you had known the virtue of the ring, Or half her worthiness . . v 1 199
With bills on their necks, 'Be it known unto all men by these presents' *As Y. Like It* i 2 131
Had I before known this young man his son, I should have given him tears unto entreaties . . . . i 2 249
Your humble wife May show her duty and make known her love *T. of Shrew* Ind. 1 117
A man well known throughout all Italy . . . . ii 1 69
'Tis known my father hath no less Than three great argosies . . . ii 1 379
And withal make known Which way thou travellest . . . . iv 5 50
But if thou be'st not an ass, I am a youth of fourteen; I have known thee already . . . . *All's Well* ii 3 107
What the import is, I know not yet.—Ay, that would be known . . ii 3 295
And uses a known truth to pass a thousand nothings with . . . ii 5 32
A servant only, and a gentleman Which I have sometime known . . iii 2 87
There were no further danger known but the modesty which is so lost iii 5 29
That red-tailed humble-bee I speak of.—I would I had not known him iv 5 8
I have ere now, sir, been better known to you . . . . . v 2 3
You give away myself, which is known mine . . . . . . v 3 172
He hath known you but three days, and already you are no stranger *T. Night* i 4 3
There is no slander in an allowed fool, though he do nothing but rail; nor no railing in a known discreet man . . . . i 5 103
When that is known and golden time convents . . . . . v 1 391
In courts and kingdoms Known and allied to yours . . . *W. Tale* i 2 339
But if one present The abhorr'd ingredient to his eye, make known How he hath drunk, he cracks his gorge . . . . ii 1 43
But be't known, From him that has most cause to grieve it should be, She's an adulteress . . . . ii 1 76
This business Will raise us all.—To laughter, as I take it, If the good truth were known . . . . ii 1 199
But let Time's news Be known when 'tis brought forth . . . . iv 1 27
A fellow, sir, that I have known to go about with troll-my-dames . iv 3 91
It is A way to make us better friends, more known . . . . iv 4 66
How often said, my dignity would last But till 'twere known! . . iv 4 487
And any thing that is fitting to be known, discover . . . . iv 4 742

Known. With countenance of such distraction that they were to be known by garment, not by favour . . . . . . *W. Tale* v 2 53
Most certain of one mother, mighty king; That is well known *K. John* i 1 60
That you might The better arm you to the sudden time, Than if you had at leisure known of this . . . . v 6 27
On some known ground of treachery in him . . . . *Richard II.* i 1 11
But what it is, that is not yet known; what I cannot name . . . ii 2 39
But since I cannot, be it known to you I do remain as neuter . . ii 3 158
Which thou hast often heard of and it is known to many . 1 *Hen. IV.* ii 4 454
The tree may be known by the fruit, as the fruit by the tree . . ii 4 471
What men?—One of them is well known, my gracious lord, A gross fat man . . . . ii 4 559
This oily rascal is known as well as Paul's.—Go, call him forth . . ii 4 575
Thus have you heard our cause and known our means . . 2 *Hen. IV.* i 3 1
Since my exion is entered and my case so openly known to the world ii 1 33
I have known thee these twenty nine years, come peascod-time . . ii 4 412
'Tis needful that the most immodest word Be look'd upon and learn'd; which once attain'd, Your highness knows, comes to no further use But to be known and hated . . . . iv 4 73
Be it known to you, as it is very well, I was lately here . . . . Epil. 8
For peace itself should not so dull a kingdom, Though war nor no known quarrel were in question . . . . *Hen. V.* ii 4 17
Was ever known so great and little loss On one part and on the other? iv 8 115
Mars his true moving, even as in the heavens So in the earth, to this day is not known . . . . 1 *Hen. VI.* i 2 2
My worth unknown, no loss is known in me . . . . . . iv 5 23
'Tis known already that I am possess'd With more than half . . v 4 138
'Tis known to you he is mine enemy, Nay, more . . 2 *Hen. VI.* i 1 148
If they were known, as the suspect is great, Would make thee quickly hop without thy head . . . . i 3 139
If thou hadst been born blind, thou mightst as well have known all our names as thus to name the several colours we do wear . . . ii 1 127
'Tis well known that, whiles I was protector, Pity was all the fault that was in me . . . . iii 1 124
For it is known we were but hollow friends . . . . . . iii 2 66
Be it known unto thee by these presence, even the presence of Lord Mortimer . . . . iv 7 32
How many years a mortal man may live. When this is known, then to divide the times . . . . 3 *Hen. VI.* ii 5 30
Vouchsafe, defused infection of a man, For these known evils, but to give me leave, By circumstance, to curse thy cursed self *Richard III.* i 2 79
You are known The first and happiest hearers of the town *Hen. VIII.* Prol. 23
You know no more than others; but you frame Things that are known alike . . . . i 2 45
Much better She ne'er had known pomp: though 't be temporal . . ii 3 13
If it be known to him That I gainsay my deed, how may he wound, And worthily, my falsehood! . . . . ii 4 95
Can you think, lords, That any Englishman dare give me counsel? Or be a known friend? . . . . iii 1 85
Had I not known those customs, I should have been beholding to your paper . . . . iv 1 20
There to remain till the king's further pleasure Be known unto us . v 3 91
God shall be truly known . . . . v 5 37
Would I had known no more! but she must die, She must . . . v 5 60
If Helen then be wife to Sparta's king, As it is known she is *T. and C.* ii 2 184
Let it be known to him that we are here. He shent our messengers . ii 3 85
'Tis known, Achilles, that you are in love . . . —Ha! known! . . iii 3 193
Do you purpose A victor shall be known? . . . . . . iv 5 67
They have press'd a power, but it is not known Whether for east or west *Coriolanus* i 2 9
Therefore, be it known, As to us, to all the world . . . . i 9 58
In token of the which, My noble steed, known to the camp, I give him i 9 61
You are known well enough too.—I am known to be a humorous patrician . . . . ii 1 49
If you see this in the map of my microcosm, follows it that I am known well enough too? . . . . ii 1 69
Have you not known The worthiest men have done't? . . . . ii 3 54
Why, this was known before.—Not to them all . . . . . iii 1 46
He bow'd his nature, never known before But to be rough, unswayable . v 6 25
I wot the ground of all this grudge: I would not for a million of gold The cause were known to them it most concerns . . *T. Andron.* ii 1 50
And now be it known to you my full intent . . . . . iv 2 151
Then, noble auditory, be it known to you . . . . . . v 3 96
I am the turned forth, be it known to you, That have preserved her welfare . . . . v 3 109
'Tis known I am a pretty piece of flesh . . . . *Rom. and Jul.* i 1 34
Too early seen unknown, and known too late! . . . . . . i 5 141
We still have known thee for a holy man . . . . v 3 270
How goes the world?—It wears, sir, as it grows.—Ay, that's well known: But what particular rarity? . . . . . *T. of Athens* i 1 3
I'm angry at him, That might have known my place . . . . iii 3 14
He has been known to commit outrages, And cherish factions . . iii 5 72
You that are honest, by being what you are, Make them best seen and known . . . . v 1 72
Beseech your honour To make it known to us.—You'll take it ill . . v 1 93
Who ever knew the heavens menace so?—Those that have known the earth so full of faults . . . . *J. Cæsar* i 3 45
I have not known when his affections sway'd More than his reason . ii 1 20
If this be known, Cassius or Cæsar never shall turn back . . . iii 1 20
But it sufficeth that the day will end, And then the end is known . v 1 126
That hast no less deserved, nor must be known No less to have done so *Macbeth* i 4 30
Who could refrain, That had a heart to love, and in that heart Courage to make's love known? . . . . ii 3 124
Is't known who did this more than bloody deed? . . . . . ii 4 22
You made it known to us.—I did so, and went further . . . . iii 1 84
Stones have been known to move and trees to speak . . . . iii 4 123
I am not to you known, Though in your state of honour I am perfect . iv 2 65
I have known her continue in this a quarter of an hour . . . . v 1 33
You have known what you should not.—She has spoke what she should not . . . . v 1 51
Heaven knows what she has known . . . . v 1 55
I have known those which have walked in their sleep who have died holily in their beds . . . . v 1 66
Our valiant Hamlet—For so this side of our known world esteem'd him *Hamlet* i 1 85
Never make known what you have seen to-night . . . . . i 5 144
As are companions noted and most known To youth and liberty . . ii 1 23
This must be known; which, being kept close, might move More grief to hide . . . . ii 1 118

Known. As the world were now but to begin, Antiquity forgot, custom not known *Hamlet* iv 5 104
Gave 't the impression, placed it safely, The changeling never known v 2 53
It must be shortly known to him from England What is the issue v 2 71
And will no reconcilement, Till by some elder masters, of known honour, I have a voice and precedent of peace v 2 259
Make known It is no vicious blot, murder, or foulness *Lear* i 1 229
'Tis the infirmity of his age: yet he hath ever but slenderly known himself i 1 297
I had thought, by making this well known unto you, To have found a safe redress i 4 224
What a monstrous fellow art thou, thus to rail on one that is neither known of thee nor knows thee! ii 2 28
Yet better thus, and known to be contemn'd, Than still contemn'd and flatter'd iv 1 1
When I am known aright, you shall not grieve Lending me this acquaintance iv 3 55
The British powers are marching hitherward.—'Tis known before iv 4 22
Who, by the art of known and feeling sorrows, Am pregnant to good pity iv 6 226
Yet to be known shortens my made intent iv 7 9
Good guard, Until their greater pleasures first be known v 3 2
How have you known the miseries of your father?—By nursing them v 3 180
If this be known to you and your allowance, We then have done you bold and saucy wrongs *Othello* i 1 128
Were it my cue to fight, I should have known it Without a prompter i 2 83
The fortitude of the place is best known to you i 3 223
O thou invisible spirit of wine, if thou hast no name to be known by, let us call thee devil! ii 3 284
You do love my lord: You have known him long iii 3 11
I had been happy, if the general camp, Pioners and all, had tasted her sweet body, So I had nothing known iii 3 347
This hand is moist, my lady.—It yet hath felt no age nor known no sorrow iii 4 37
Alas! It is not honesty in me to speak What I have seen and known iv 1 289
I tell you 'tis not very well. I will make myself known to Desdemona iv 2 200
Known. I care not for thy sword; I'll make thee known, Though I lost twenty lives *Othello* v 2 165
You shall close prisoner rest, Till that the nature of your fault be known v 2 336
I should have known no less. It hath been taught us from the primal state, That he which is was wish'd until he were *Ant. and Cleo.* i 4 40
You and I have known, sir.—At sea, I think.—We have, sir ii 6 86
Sister, welcome: pray you, Be ever known to patience: my dear'st sister! iii 6 98
Our will is Antony be took alive; Make it so known iv 6 3
Assuredly you know me.—No matter, sir, what I have heard or known v 2 73
What have I kept back?—Enough to purchase what you have made known v 2 148
Be it known, that we, the greatest, are misthought For things that others do v 2 176
I will be known your advocate *Cymbeline* i 1 76
Who to my father was a friend, to me Known but by letter i 1 99
I beseech you all, be better known to this gentleman i 4 31
Sir, we have known together in Orleans.—Since when I have been debtor to you i 4 36
Haply this life is best, If quiet life be best; sweeter to you That have a sharper known iii 3 31
This She wish'd me to make known iii 5 50
We being not known, not muster'd Among the bands iv 4 10
O, I am known Of many in the army iv 4 21
Pray, sir, to the army: I and my brother are not known iv 4 32
It is fit, What being more known grows worse, to smother it *Pericles* i 1 106
And what may make him blush in being known, He'll stop the course by which it might be known i 2 22
She'll not undertake A married life. Her reason to herself is only known ii 5 5
'Tis known, I ever Have studied physic iii 2 31
'Tis but a blow, which never shall be known iv 1 2
Hath your principal made known unto you who I am?—Who is my principal? iv 6 89
By her own most clear remembrance, she Made known herself my daughter v 3 13

L

L. Put L to sore, then sorel jumps from thicket *L. L. Lost* iv 2 60
If sore be sore, then L to sore makes fifty sores one sorel. Of one sore I an hundred make by adding but one more L iv 2 62
La. I thank you always with my heart, la! with my heart *Mer. Wives* i 1 86
Ut, re, sol, la, mi, fa *L. L. Lost* iv 2 102
So God help me, la!—My love to thee is sound, sans crack or flaw v 2 414
One clef, two notes have I: 'E la mi,' show pity, or I die *T. of Shrew* iii 1 78
La you, an you speak ill of the devil, how he takes it at heart! *T. Night* iii 4 111
He shall not rule me.—La you now, you hear *W. Tale* ii 3 50
La, la, la, la! 'nothing doubting,' says he? *T. of Athens* iii 1 22
O, these eclipses do portend these divisions! fa, sol, la, mi *Lear* i 2 149
Sooth, la, I'll help: thus it must be *Ant. and Cleo.* iv 4 8
Laban. When Jacob grazed his uncle Laban's sheep *Mer. of Venice* i 3 72
When Laban and himself were compromised i 3 79
Label. Ere this hand, by thee to Romeo seal'd, Shall be the label to another deed *Rom. and Jul.* iv 1 57
When I waked, I found This label on my bosom *Cymbeline* v 5 430
Labelled. It shall be inventoried, and every particle and utensil labelled to my will *T. Night* i 5 265
Labeo and Flavius, set our battles on *J. Cæsar* v 3 108
Labienus—This is stiff news—hath, with his Parthian force, Extended Asia from Euphrates *Ant. and Cleo.* i 2 103
Labour. You mar our labour: keep your cabins: you do assist the storm *Tempest* i 1 15
Who, with a charm join'd to their suffer'd labour, I have left asleep i 2 231
There be some sports are painful, and their labour Delight in them sets off iii 1 1
The mistress which I serve quickens what's dead And makes my labours pleasures iii 1 7
These sweet thoughts do even refresh my labours iii 1 14
I will fetch off my bottle, though I be o'er ears for my labour iv 1 214
Shortly shall all my labours end, and thou Shalt have the air at freedom iv 1 265
If lost, why then a grievous labour won *T. G. of Ver.* i 1 33
And she, a laced mutton, gave me, a lost mutton, nothing for my labour i 1 104
If it please me, madam, what then?—Why, if it please you, take it for your labour ii 1 139
If I find her honest, I lose not my labour; if she be otherwise, 'tis labour well bestowed *Mer. Wives* ii 1 247
As fast lock'd up in sleep as guiltless labour *Meas. for Meas.* iv 2 69
You do but lose your labour. Away with him to death! v 1 433
Against my soul's pure truth why labour you? *Com. of Errors* iii 2 37
That labour may you save: see where he comes iv 1 14
Till I have brought him to his wits again, Or lose my labour in assaying it v 1 97
I will in the interim undertake one of Hercules' labours *Much Ado* ii 1 380
Surely suit ill spent and labour ill bestowed iii 2 103
If your love Can labour aught in sad invention, Hang her an epitaph v 1 292
Skim milk, and sometimes labour in the quern *M. N. Dream* ii 1 36
Your suit is cold.—Cold, indeed; and labour lost *Mer. of Venice* ii 7 74
If thou diest before I come, thou art a mocker of my labour *As Y. Like It* ii 6 14
He saves my labour by his own approach ii 7 8
Neither do I labour for a greater esteem v 2 62
To labour and effect one thing specially *T. of Shrew* i 1 120
Leave that labour to great Hercules; And let it be more than Alcides' twelve i 2 257
For thy maintenance commits his body To painful labour v 2 149
His taken labours bid him me forgive *All's Well* iii 4 12
We have lost our labour; they are gone a contrary way iii 5 8
Ever a friend whose thoughts more truly labour To recompense your love iv 4 17
This is a practice As full of labour as a wise man's art *T. Night* iii 1 73
Labour. Her face o' fire With labour and the thing she took to quench it, She would to each one sip *W. Tale* iv 4 61
Age, thou hast lost thy labour iv 4 787
Very little pains Will bring this labour to an happy end *K. John* iii 2 10
All my treasury Is yet but unfelt thanks, which more enrich'd Shall be your love and labour's recompense *Richard II.* ii 3 62
Your presence makes us rich, most noble lord.—And far surmounts our labour ii 3 64
The guilt of conscience take thou for thy labour v 6 41
'Tis no sin for a man to labour in his vocation *1 Hen. IV.* i 2 117
O, I do not like that paying back; 'tis a double labour iii 3 202
This bottle makes an angel.—An if it do, take it for thy labour iv 2 7
Their courage with hard labour tame and dull iv 3 23
And saved the treacherous labour of your son v 4 57
The incessant care and labour of his mind Hath wrought the mure that should confine it in So thin that life looks through *2 Hen. IV.* iv 4 118
And labour shall refresh itself with hope *Hen. V.* ii 2 37
There's for thy labour, Montjoy iii 6 167
Follows so the ever-running year, With profitable labour, to his grave iv 1 294
Herald, save thou thy labour; Come thou no more for ransom, gentle herald iv 3 121
And shall these labours and these honours die? *2 Hen. VI.* i 1 95
While these do labour for their own preferment, Behoves it us to labour for the realm i 1 182
The king will labour still to save his life, The commons haply rise iii 1 239
Stay my thoughts, My thoughts, that labour to persuade my soul! iii 2 137
And yet it is said, labour in thy vocation iv 2 17
I have seen a swan With bootless labour swim against the tide *3 Hen. VI.* i 4 20
And of our labours thou shalt reap the gain v 7 20
And swore, with sobs, That he would labour my delivery *Richard III.* i 4 253
A blessed labour, my most sovereign liege ii 1 52
That their very labour Was to them as a painting *Hen. VIII.* i 1 25
I'll save you That labour, sir.—All's now done ii 1 4
The queen's in labour, They say, in great extremity; and fear'd She'll with the labour end v 1 18
I have had my labour for my travail *Troi. and Cres.* i 1 70
Gone between and between, but small thanks for my labour i 1 73
A labour saved! iii 3 241
Cupboarding the viand, never bearing Like labour with the rest *Coriol.* i 1 104
I cannot go thither.—Why, I pray you?—'Tis not to save labour i 3 90
If you had been the wife of Hercules, Six of his labours you'ld have done iv 1 18
He sold the blood and labour Of our great action v 6 47
Unhappy, wretched, hateful day! Most miserable hour that e'er time saw In lasting labour of his pilgrimage! *Rom. and Jul.* iv 5 45
All kind of natures, That labour on the bosom of this sphere *T. of Athens* i 1 66
Vouchsafe my labour, and long live your lordship!—I thank you i 1 152
A lascivious apprehension.—So thou apprehendest it: take it for thy labour i 1 213
He is worthy of thee, and to pay thee for thy labour i 1 232
Welcome hither: I have begun to plant thee, and will labour To make thee full of growing *Macbeth* i 4 28
The rest is labour, which is not used for you i 4 44
The death of each day's life, sore labour's bath, Balm of hurt minds ii 2 38
The labour we delight in physics pain ii 3 55
Thou losest labour: As easy mayst thou the intrenchant air With thy keen sword impress as make me bleed v 8 8
We thank you for your well-took labour: Go to your rest *Hamlet* ii 2 83
We shall jointly labour with your soul To give it due content iv 5 211
Thy master, whom thou lovest, Shall find thee full of labours *Lear* i 4 7
None but the fool; who labours to out-jest His heart-struck injuries iii 1 16

Labour. From the loathed warmth whereof deliver me, and supply the place for your labour *Lear* iv 6 274
My Muse labours, And thus she is deliver'd *Othello* ii 1 128
Confessions—handkerchief!—To confess, and be hanged for his labour . iv 1 38
Having the world for your labour, 'tis a wrong in your own world . iv 3 81
I'll fetch the general's surgeon. For you, mistress, Save you your labour v 1 101
'Tis sweating labour To bear such idleness so near the heart *Ant. and Cleo.* i 3 93
It's monstrous labour, when I wash my brain, And it grows fouler ii 7 105
With news the time's with labour, and throes forth, Each minute, some iii 7 81
That thou depart'st hence safe, Does pay thy labour richly . iv 14 37
Now all labour Mars what it does; yea, very force entangles Itself with strength iv 14 47
Thou takest up Thou know'st not what; but take it for thy labour *Cymb.* i 5 61
Hands Made hard with hourly falsehood—falsehood, as With labour . i 6 108
Why hast thou abused So many miles with a pretence? this place? Mine action and thine own? our horses' labour? iii 4 107
This fool's speed Be cross'd with slowness; labour be his meed! . iii 5 168
I sought a husband, in which labour I found that kindness in a father *Per.* i 1 66
Not to eat honey like a drone From others' labours ii Gower 19
How well this honest mirth becomes their labour! ii 1 99
'Tis now your honour, daughter, to explain The labour of each knight in his device ii 2 15
Laboured. I have laboured for the poor gentleman to the extremest shore of my modesty *Meas. for Meas.* iii 2 265
In the quest of him: Whom whilst I labour'd of a love to see, I hazarded the loss of whom I loved *Com. of Errors* i 1 131
Which never labour'd in their minds till now *M. N. Dream* v 1 73
And have by underhand means laboured to dissuade him *As Y. Like It* i 1 146
Whose labour'd spirits, Forwearied in this action of swift speed *K. John* ii 1 232
And laboured all I could to do him right *Richard II.* ii 3 142
How ill it follows, after you have laboured so hard, you should talk so idly! *2 Hen. IV.* ii 2 32
I have labour'd, With all my wits, my pains *Hen. V.* v 2 24
They laboured to plant the rightful heir, I lost my liberty . *1 Hen. VI.* ii 5 80
For your highness' good I ever labour'd More than mine own *Hen. VIII.* iii 2 191
In all the progress Both of my life and office, I have labour'd v 3 33
We labour'd, No impediment between, but that you must Cast your election on him *Coriolanus* ii 3 235
All his dependants Which labour'd after him to the mountain's top *T. of A.* i 1 86
Your words have took such pains as if they labour'd iii 5 26
My bones would rest, That have but labour'd to attain this hour *J. Cæsar* v 5 42
Or that with both He labour'd in his country's wreck *Macbeth* i 3 114
I once did hold it, as our statists do, A baseness to write fair and labour'd much How to forget that learning *Hamlet* v 2 34
Art hath thus decreed, To make some good, but others to exceed; And you are her labour'd scholar *Pericles* ii 3 17
Labourer. I am a true labourer: I earn that I eat *As Y. Like It* iii 2 77
Since I nor wax nor honey can bring home, I quickly were dissolved from my hive, To give some labourers room *All's Well* i 2 67
Labourest. Thou art death's fool; For him thou labour'st by thy flight to shun And yet runn'st toward him still *Meas. for Meas.* iii 1 12
Labouring. I obscured myself, Labouring to save his life v 1 396
When great things labouring perish in their birth *L. L. Lost* v 2 521
Labouring art can never ransom nature From her inaidible estate *All's W.* ii 1 121
Thou variest no more from picking of purses than giving direction doth from labouring; thou layest the plot how *1 Hen. IV.* ii 1 57
My brain more busy than the labouring spider Weaves tedious snares *2 Hen. VI.* iii 1 339
Oft have I seen a timely-parted ghost, Of ashy semblance, meagre pale and bloodless, Being all descended to the labouring heart . iii 2 163
Which is as much to say as, let the magistrates be labouring men . iv 2 19
Even in the birth of our own labouring breath *Troi. and Cres.* iv 4 40
I have, thou gallant Trojan, seen thee oft Labouring for destiny . iv 5 184
What do you think the hour?—Labouring for nine *T. of Athens* iii 4 8
Being mechanical, you ought not walk Upon a labouring day without the sign Of your profession *J. Cæsar* i 1 4
We'll set thee to school to an ant, to teach thee there's no labouring i' the winter *Lear* ii 4 69
Let the labouring bark climb hills of seas Olympus-high! *Othello* ii 1 189
Since Julius Cæsar, Who at Philippi the good Brutus ghosted, There saw you labouring for him *Ant. and Cleo.* ii 6 14
Laboursome. He hath, my lord, wrung from me my slow leave By laboursome petition *Hamlet* i 2 59
Your laboursome and dainty trims, wherein You made great Juno angry *Cymbeline* iii 4 167
Labras. Word of denial in thy labras here! *Mer. Wives* i 1 166
Labyrinth. Thou mayst not wander in that labyrinth; There Minotaurs and ugly treasons lurk *1 Hen. VI.* v 3 188
What, lost in the labyrinth of thy fury! *Troi. and Cres.* ii 3 2
Lace. O, cut my lace, lest my heart, cracking it, Break too! *W. Tale* iii 2 174
Will you buy any tape, Or lace for your cape, My dainty duck, my dear-a? iv 4 323
A pedler's daughter, and sold many laces *2 Hen. VI.* iv 2 49
O, cut my lace in sunder, that my pent heart May have some scope to beat, or else I swoon! *Richard III.* iv 1 34
Envious streaks Do lace the severing clouds in yonder east *Rom. and Jul.* iii 5 8
Cut my lace, Charmian, come; But let it be: I am quickly ill, and well, So Antony loves *Ant. and Cleo.* i 3 71
Laced. I, a lost mutton, gave your letter to her, a laced mutton, and she, a laced mutton, gave me, a lost mutton, nothing *T. G. of Ver.* i 1 102
Cloth o' gold, and cuts, and laced with silver, set with pearls *Much Ado* iii 4 20
A pair of boots that have been candlecases, one buckled, another laced, an old rusty sword *T. of Shrew* iii 2 46
Here lay Duncan, His silver skin laced with his golden blood *Macbeth* ii 3 118
White and azure laced With blue of heaven's own tinct *Cymbeline* ii 2 22
Lacedæmon. To Lacedæmon did my land extend *T. of Athens* ii 2 160
His service done At Lacedæmon and Byzantium Were a sufficient briber iii 5 60
Lacies. My wife descended of the Lacies,— She was, indeed, a pedler's daughter, and sold many laces *2 Hen. VI.* iv 2 47
Lack. The truth you speak doth lack some gentleness *Tempest* ii 1 137
Tester I'll have in pouch when thou shalt lack, Base Phrygian Turk! *M. W.* i 3 96
They lack no direction iii 3 19
You shall not lack a priest iv 6 53
Come; fear not you: good counsellors lack no clients *Meas. for Meas.* i 2 110
My wife, Save that we do the denunciation lack Of outward order i 2 152
A common executioner, who in his office lacks a helper iv 2 10
Many that are not mad Have, sure, more lack of reason v 1 68
In the heat of blood, And lack of temper'd judgement afterward v 1 478
If your husband have stables enough, you'll see he shall lack no barns *Much Ado* iii 4 49

Lack. Let all my sins lack mercy! *Much Ado* iv 1 182
I fear these stubborn lines lack power to move *L. L. Lost* iv 3 55
Beauty doth beauty lack, If that she learn not of her eye to look . iv 3 251
And the quaint mazes in the wanton green For lack of tread are undistinguishable *M. N. Dream* ii 1 100
Nor doth this wood lack worlds of company, For you in my respect are all the world: Then how can it be said I am alone? ii 1 223
Shall I have the thought To think on this, and shall I lack the thought That such a thing bechanced would make me sad? *Mer. of Venice* i 1 37
They shall think we are accomplished With that we lack iii 4 62
Let his lack of years be no impediment to let him lack a reverend estimation iv 1 162
That could give more, but that her hand lacks means *As Y. Like It* i 2 259
Rosalind lacks then the love Which teacheth thee that thou and I am one i 3 98
Thou shalt not die for lack of a dinner ii 6 17
And that a great cause of the night is lack of the sun iii 2 29
If a hart do lack a hind, Let him seek out Rosalind iii 2 107
Who ambles Time withal?—With a priest that lacks Latin iii 2 337
When you were gravelled for lack of matter, you might take occasion to kiss iv 1 74
Alas! dear love, I cannot lack thee two hours iv 1 182
She says I am not fair, that I lack manners; She calls me proud . iv 3 15
Be of good cheer, youth: you a man! you lack a man's heart iv 3 165
Giddy for lack of sleep *T. of Shrew* iv 3 9
And death should have play for lack of work *All's Well* i 1 23
'Let me not live,' quoth he, 'After my flame lacks oil' i 2 59
They that least lend it you shall lack you first i 2 68
You lack not folly to commit them, and have ability enough i 3 11
I still pour in the waters of my love And lack not to lose still i 3 210
They say, our French lack language to deny, If they demand ii 1 20
You did never lack advice so much iii 4 19
Behold this ring, Whose high respect and rich validity Did lack a parallel v 3 193
Since you lack virtue, I will lose a husband; Send for your ring v 3 222
And I, that am sure I lack thee [wit], may pass for a wise man *T. Night* i 5 38
Keep your purse: My master, not myself, lacks recompense i 5 304
No woman's heart So big, to hold so much; they lack retention ii 4 99
A little thing would make me tell them how much I lack of a man . iii 4 332
Is't possible that my deserts to you Can lack persuasion? iii 4 383
What! lack I credit?—I had rather you did lack than I *W. Tale* ii 1 157
Dost lack any money? I have a little money for thee iv 3 82
O, these I lack, To make you garlands of! iv 4 127
Pins and poking-sticks of steel, What maids lack from head to heel iv 4 229
If your lass Interpretation should abuse and call this Your lack of love iv 4 365
I cannot say 'tis pity She lacks instructions, for she seems a mistress iv 4 593
Saying, 'What lack you?' and 'Where lies your grief?' *K. John* iv 1 48
You do lack That mercy which fierce fire and iron extends iv 1 119
I lack some of thy instinct *1 Hen. IV.* ii 4 408
Is there not employment? doth not the king lack subjects? *2 Hen. IV.* i 2 86
Things that are mouldy lack use iii 2 119
He now doth lack The very instruments of chastisement iv 1 216
Lack nothing: be merry v 3 73
For competence of life I will allow you, That lack of means enforce you not to evil v 5 71
And sheathed their swords for lack of argument *Hen. V.* iii 1 21
If the English had any apprehension, they would run away.—That they lack iii 7 147
Compell'd by hunger And lack of other means *Hen. VIII.* i 2 35
Then will Ajax lack matter, if he have lost his argument *Troi. and Cres.* ii 3 103
Now here he fights on Galathe his horse, And there lacks work v 5 21
Though abundantly they lack discretion, Yet are they passing cowardly *Coriolanus* i 1 206
Such eyes the widows in Corioli wear, And mothers that lack sons ii 1 196
I shall lack voice: the deeds of Coriolanus Should not be utter'd feebly ii 2 86
Who lack not virtue, no, nor power, but that Which they have given to beggars iii 1 73
When he did stand for consul, which he lost By lack of stooping . v 6 29
Here lacks but your mother for to say amen *T. Andron.* iv 2 44
This unbound lover, To beautify him, only lacks a cover *Rom. and Jul.* i 3 88
The greatest of your having lacks a half To pay your present debts *T. of Athens* ii 2 153
Canst thou the conscience lack, To think I shall lack friends? ii 2 184
'Tis lack of kindly warmth they are not kind ii 2 226
Mend my company, take away thyself.—So I shall mend mine own, by the lack of thine iv 3 284
Feeling in itself A lack of Timon's aid, hath sense withal Of it own fail, restraining aid to Timon v 1 150
I do lack some part Of that quick spirit that is in Antony *J. Cæsar* i 2 28
Life, being weary of these worldly bars, Never lacks power to dismiss itself i 3 97
Your noble friends do lack you.—I do forget *Macbeth* iii 4 84
You lack the season of all natures, sleep.—Come, we'll to sleep . iii 4 141
Our power is ready; Our lack is nothing but our leave v 3 237
What hour now?—I think it lacks of twelve.—No, it is struck *Hamlet* i 4 3
What so poor a man as Hamlet is May do, to express his love and friending to you, God willing, shall not lack i 5 187
It is as proper to our age To cast beyond ourselves in our opinions As it is common for the younger sort To lack discretion ii 1 117
They have a plentiful lack of wit, together with most weak hams . ii 2 202
I am pigeon-liver'd and lack gall To make oppression bitter ii 2 605
For who not needs shall never lack a friend iii 2 217
Sir, I lack advancement.—How can that be, when you have the voice of the king? iii 2 354
Our foster-nurse of nature is repose, The which he lacks *Lear* iv 4 13
To't, luxury, pell-mell! for I lack soldiers iv 6 119
I lack iniquity Sometimes to do me service *Othello* i 2 3
But altogether lacks the abilities That Rhodes is dress'd in i 3 25
If virtue no delighted beauty lack, Your son-in-law is far more fair than black i 3 290
Give't me again: poor lady, she'll run mad When she shall lack it . iii 3 318
The borders maritime Lack blood to think on't *Ant. and Cleo.* i 4 52
Not so; I know you could not lack, I am certain on't ii 2 57
Let us, Lepidus, Not lack your company ii 2 172
These hands do lack nobility, that they strike A meaner than myself ii 5 82
Condemn myself to lack The courage of a woman iv 14 59
I care not for you, And am so near the lack of charity *Cymbeline* ii 3 114
Our countrymen Are men more order'd than when Julius Cæsar Smiled at their lack of skill ii 4 22
How look I, That I should seem to lack humanity? iii 2 16
Thou shalt not lack The flower that's like thy face, pale primrose . iv 2 220
That pupils lacks she none of noble race *Pericles* v Gower 9

'Lack, good youth! Thou movest no less with thy complaining *Cymbeline* iv 2 374
Nay, be not angry, sir.—'Lack, to what end? . . . v 3 59
Lackbeard. For my Lord Lackbeard there, he and I shall meet *M. Ado* v 1 195
Lack-brain. What a lack-brain is this! . . . . . . 1 *Hen. IV.* ii 3 17
Lacked. But being lack'd and lost, Why, then we rack the value *M. Ado* iv 1 221
You three fools lack'd me fool to make up the mess . *L. L. Lost* iv 3 207
But your son, As mad in folly, lack'd the sense to know Her estimation home.—'Tis past, my liege . . . . . . *All's Well* v 3 3
That lack'd sight only, nought for approbation But only seeing *W. Tale* ii 1 177
There your charity would have lacked footing . . . . . iii 3 114
'Twas men I lack'd and you will give them me . . . 2 *Hen. VI.* iii 1 345
And the great Hector's sword had lack'd a master . . *Troi. and Cres.* i 3 76
If You had not show'd them how ye were disposed Ere they lack'd power to cross you . . . . *Coriolanus* iii 2 23
What, what, what! I shall be loved when I am lack'd . . . iv 1 15
What he spake, though it lack'd form a little, Was not like madness *Hamlet* iii 1 171
We lack'd your counsel and your help to-night.—So did I yours . *Othello* i 3 51
Never lack'd gold and yet went never gay, Fled from her wish . ii 1 151
He which is was wish'd until he were; And the ebb'd man, ne'er loved till ne'er worth love, Comes dear'd by being lack'd . *Ant. and Cleo.* i 4 44
The honour is sacred which he talks on now, Supposing that I lack'd it ii 2 86
Lackest. Thou lackest a cup of canary . . . . . *T. Night* i 3 85
'Tis breath thou lack'st, and that breath wilt thou lose . *Richard II.* ii 1 30
As much foolery as I have, so much wit thou lackest . *T. of Athens* ii 2 124
Lackey. I will speak to him like a saucy lackey . . *As Y. Like It* iii 2 314
His lackey, for all the world caparisoned like the horse . *T. of Shrew* iii 2 66
And not like a Christian footboy or a gentleman's lackey . . . iii 2 73
In a retreat he outruns any lackey . . . . . *All's Well* iv 3 323
He held me last night at least nine hours In reckoning up the several devils' names That were his lackeys . . . . 1 *Hen. IV.* iii 1 158
Never any body saw it but his lackey: 'tis a hooded valour . *Hen. V.* iii 7 121
But, like a lackey, from the rise to set Sweats in the eye of Phœbus . iv 1 289
Our superfluous lackeys and our peasants, Who in unnecessary action swarm . . . . iv 2 26
I must stay with the lackeys, with the luggage of our camp . . iv 4 79
A scum of Bretons, and base lackey peasants . . . *Richard III.* v 3 317
A fellow-counsellor, 'Mong boys, grooms, and lackeys . . *Hen. VIII.* v 2 18
Lackeying. Goes to and back, lackeying the varying tide *Ant. and Cleo.* i 4 46
Lacking. Proud, disobedient, stubborn, lacking duty . *T. G. of Ver.* iii 1 69
Lacking the burden of lean and wasteful learning . . *As Y. Like It* iii 2 341
For lovers lacking—God warn us!—matter, the cleanliest shift is to kiss iv 1 77
Thou shalt have a license to kill for a hundred lacking one 2 *Hen. VI.* iv 3 9
You know I am a woman, lacking wit To make a seemly answer *Hen. VIII.* iii 1 177
Lack-linen. Rascally, cheating, lack-linen mate! . . 2 *Hen. IV.* ii 4 134
Lack-love. She durst not lie Near this lack-love . . *M. N. Dream* ii 2 77
Lack-lustre. Looking on it with lack-lustre eye . . *As Y. Like It* ii 7 21
Lad. There are yet missing of your company Some few odd lads *Tempest* v 1 255
My honest lads, I will tell you what I am about . . *Mer. Wives* i 3 42
We will thrive, lads, we will thrive . . . . i 3 82
Follow me, lads of peace . . . . iii 1 113
Cupid is a knavish lad, Thus to make poor females mad . *M. N. Dream* iii 2 440
Where are these lads? where are these hearts? . . . . . iv 2 25
How now, old lad? . . . . *T. of Shrew* iv 1 113
Spoke like an officer: ha' to thee, lad! . . . . . . v 2 37
Well, go thy ways, old lad: for thou shalt ha't . . . . v 2 181
Dear lad, believe it; For they shall yet belie thy happy years, That say thou art a man: Diana's lip Is not more smooth . . *T. Night* i 4 29
I have been dear to him, lad, some two thousand strong, or so . . iii 2 58
Like a mad lad, Pare thy nails, dad . . . . iv 2 139
Two lads that thought there was no more behind But such a day to-morrow as to-day, And to be boy eternal . . . *W. Tale* i 2 63
Golden quoifs and stomachers, For my lads to give their dears . . iv 4 227
Come buy, come buy; Buy, lads, or else your lasses cry . . . iv 4 231
Young lad, come forth; I have to say with you . . . *K. John* iv 1 8
My old lad of the castle . . . . 1 *Hen. IV.* i 2 47
My lads, my lads, to-morrow morning, by four o'clock, early at Gadshill! i 2 138
A Corinthian, a lad of mettle, a good boy . . . . . . ii 4 13
When I am king of England, I shall command all the good lads in Eastcheap . . . . ii 4 15
Shall we be merry?—As merry as crickets, my lad . . . . . ii 4 100
Gallants, lads, boys, hearts of gold, all the titles of good fellowship . ii 4 306
How now, lad! is the wind in that door, i' faith? must we all march? . iii 3 102
When flesh is cheap and females dear, And lusty lads roam here and there 2 *Hen. IV.* v 3 21
A lad of life, an imp of fame; Of parents good, of fist most valiant *Hen. V.* iv 1 45
This pretty lad will prove our country's bliss . . . 3 *Hen. VI.* iv 6 70
Is't meet that he Should leave the helm and like a fearful lad With tearful eyes add water to the sea? . . . . v 4 7
Untutor'd lad, thou art too malapert . . . . v 5 32
I like you, lads; about your business straight; Go, go, dispatch *Rich. III.* i 3 355
Cut me to pieces, Volsces; men and lads, Stain all your edges on me *Cor.* v 6 112
Thy counsel, lad, smells of no cowardice . . . . *T. Andron.* ii 1 132
Here's a young lad framed of another leer . . . . . . iv 2 119
Old lad, I am thine own . . . . iv 2 121
Good lads, how do ye both? . . . . *Hamlet* ii 2 230
Three lads of Cyprus, noble swelling spirits . . . . . *Othello* ii 3 57
Golden lads and girls all must, As chimney-sweepers, come to dust *Cymb.* iv 2 262
If in your country wars you chance to die, That is my bed too, lads . iv 4 52
Lads more like to run The country base than to commit such slaughter v 3 19
I do not bid thee beg my life, good lad; And yet I know thou wilt . v 5 101
One sand another Not more resembles that sweet rosy lad Who died . v 5 121
Ladder. I must climb her window, The ladder made of cords *T. G. of Ver.* ii 4 182
He meaneth with a corded ladder To climb celestial Silvia's chamber-window . . . . ii 6 33
He her chamber-window will ascend And with a corded ladder fetch her down . . . . iii 1 40
A ladder quaintly made of cords, To cast up . . . . . . iii 1 117
Advise me where I may have such a ladder . . . . . . iii 1 122
I will go to her alone: How shall I best convey the ladder thither? . iii 1 128
'Silvia, this night I will enfranchise thee.' 'Tis so; and here's the ladder iii 1 152
Northumberland, thou ladder wherewithal The mounting Bolingbroke ascends my throne . . . . *Richard II.* v 1 55; 2 *Hen. IV.* iii 1 70
Now in as low an ebb as the foot of the ladder . . 1 *Hen. IV.* i 2 42
Being the agents, or base second means, The cords, the ladder . . i 3 166
When degree is shaked, Which is the ladder to all high designs *Tr. and Cr.* i 3 102
O, they are at it!—Their noise be our instruction. Ladders, ho! *Coriol.* i 4 22
A sight to vex the father's soul withal. Get me a ladder . *T. Andron.* v 1 53
I must another way, To fetch a ladder, by the which your love Must climb a bird's nest . . . . *Rom. and Jul.* ii 5 75
Ladder. Lowliness is young ambition's ladder, Whereto the climber-upward turns his face; But when he once attains the upmost round, He then unto the ladder turns his back . . . *J. Cæsar* ii 1 22
Ladder-tackle. From the ladder-tackle washes off A canvas-climber *Per.* iv 1 61
Lade. Chides the sea that sunders him from thence, Saying, he'll lade it dry to have his way . . . . 3 *Hen. VI.* iii 2 139
Laden with honour's spoils, Returns the good Andronicus *T. Andron.* i 1 36
I have a ship Laden with gold; take that, divide it; fly *Ant. and Cleo.* iii 11 5
Laden with like frailties which before Have often shamed our sex . v 2 123
Ladies. The old saying is, Black men are pearls in beauteous ladies' eyes.—'Tis true; such pearls as put out ladies' eyes . *T. G. of Ver.* v 2 12
Nay, Got's lords and his ladies! you must speak possitable *Mer. Wives* i 1 243
It is certain I am loved of all ladies, only you excepted . . *Much Ado* i 1 126
Sigh no more, ladies, sigh no more, Men were deceivers ever . . . ii 3 64
O, these are barren tasks, too hard too keep, Not to see ladies! *L. L. Lost* i 1 48
God bless my ladies! are they all in love? . . . . . . ii 1 77
Lord, Lord, how the ladies and I have put him down! . . . . iv 1 143
Then when ourselves we see in ladies' eyes, Do we not likewise see our learning there? . . . . iv 3 316
The gallants shall be task'd; For, ladies, we will every one be mask'd . v 2 127
Fair ladies mask'd are roses in their bud . . . . . . v 2 295
Ladies, withdraw: the gallants are at hand . . . . . . v 2 308
The ladies call him sweet; The stairs, as he treads on them, kiss his feet v 2 329
Which once disclosed, The ladies did change favours . . . . v 2 468
Your beauty, ladies, Hath much deform'd us . . . . . . v 2 766
Ladies, Our love being yours, the error that love makes Is likewise yours v 2 780
We to ourselves prove false, By being once false for ever to be true To those that make us both,—fair ladies, you . . . . . v 2 784
These ladies' courtesy Might well have made our sport a comedy . . v 2 885
You would fright the duchess and the ladies, that they would shriek *M. N. Dream* i 2 77
If that you should fright the ladies out of their wits, they would have no more discretion but to hang us . . . . i 2 82
Pyramus must draw a sword to kill himself; which the ladies cannot abide . . . . iii 1 12
Will not the ladies be afeard of the lion?—I fear it, I promise you . iii 1 28
To bring in—God shield us!—a lion among ladies, is a most dreadful thing iii 1 32
'Ladies,'—or 'Fair ladies,—I would wish you,'—or 'I would request you' iii 1 40
And there is two or three lords and ladies more married . . . iv 2 16
Ladies, you, whose gentle hearts do fear The smallest monstrous mouse v 1 222
And tell quaint lies, How honourable ladies sought my love *Mer. of Venice* iii 4 70
Fair ladies, you drop manna in the way Of starved people . . . v 1 294
And never two ladies loved as they do . . . . *As Y. Like It* i 1 117
But what is the sport, monsieur, that the ladies have lost? . . . i 2 143
It is the first time that ever I heard breaking of ribs was sport for ladies i 2 147
Speak to him, ladies; see if you can move him . . . . . i 2 172
I confess me much guilty, to deny so fair and excellent ladies any thing i 2 197
The ladies, her attendants of her chamber, Saw her a-bed . . . ii 2 5
If ladies be but young and fair, They have the gift to know it . . ii 7 37
Such as he hath observed in noble ladies Unto their lords *T. of Shrew* Ind. 1 111
'Madam,' and nothing else: so lords call ladies . . . . . Ind. 2 113
'Tis age that nourisheth.—But youth in ladies' eyes that flourisheth . ii 1 342
How vexest thou this man! talkest thou nothing but of ladies? *T. Night* iv 2 30
Fiery voluntaries, With ladies' faces and fierce dragons' spleens *K. John* ii 1 68
Your own ladies and pale-visaged maids Like Amazons come tripping after drums . . . . v 2 154
The flowers fair ladies . . . . *Richard II.* i 3 290
Come, ladies, go, To meet at London London's king in woe . . . iii 4 96
And in my conduct shall your ladies come; From whom you now must steal and take no leave . . . . 1 *Hen. IV.* iii 1 92
These fellows of infinite tongue, that can rhyme themselves into ladies' favours, they do always reason themselves out again . *Hen. V.* v 2 165
With an aspect of iron, that, when I come to woo ladies, I fright them v 2 245
Dat it is not be de fashion pour les ladies of France,—I cannot tell vat is baiser en Anglish . . . . v 2 285
I see our wars Will turn unto a peaceful comic sport, When ladies crave to be encounter'd with . . . . 1 *Hen. VI.* ii 2 46
And stolest away the ladies' hearts of France . . . . 2 *Hen. VI.* i 3 55
She sweeps it through the court with troops of ladies . . . . i 3 80
And witch sweet ladies with my words and looks . . 3 *Hen. VI.* iii 2 150
Let me but meet you, ladies, one hour hence . . . . *Richard III.* iv 1 29
What a loss our ladies Will have of these trim vanities! . . *Hen. VIII.* i 3 37
The sly whoresons Have got a speeding trick to lay down ladies . . i 3 40
This night he makes a supper, and a great one, To many lords and ladies i 3 53
Ladies, a general welcome from his grace Salutes ye all . . . . i 4 1
Sweet ladies, will it please you sit? Sir Harry, Place you that side . i 4 19
My Lord Sands, you are one will keep 'em waking; Pray, sit between these ladies . . . . i 4 24
By your leave, sweet ladies: If I chance to talk a little wild, forgive me i 4 25
Gentlemen, the penance lies on you, if these fair ladies Pass away frowning . . . . i 4 32
Ladies, you are not merry: gentlemen, Whose fault is this? . . . i 4 42
Nay, ladies, fear not; By all the laws of war you're privileged . . i 4 51
And, under your fair conduct, Crave leave to view these ladies . . i 4 71
Lead in your ladies, every one: sweet partner, I must not yet forsake you i 4 103
I have half a dozen healths To drink to these fair ladies . . . . i 4 106
Good morrow, ladies. What were't worth to know The secret of your conference? . . . . ii 3 50
The rich stream Of lords and ladies . . . . iv 1 63
We shall have Great store of room, no doubt, left for the ladies . . v 4 77
All the best men are ours; for 'tis ill hap, If they hold when their ladies bid 'em clap . . . . Epil. 14
My ladies both, good day to you.—Sweet madam . . . *Coriolanus* i 3 51
Where ladies shall be frighted, And, gladly quaked, hear more . . . i 9 5
My as fair as noble ladies,—and the moon, were she earthly, no nobler ii 1 107
Good ladies, let's go. Yes, yes, yes; the senate has letters from the general . . . . ii 1 147
Matrons flung gloves, Ladies and maids their scarfs and handkerchers, Upon him . . . . ii 1 280
He turns away: Down, ladies; let us shame him with our knees . . v 3 169
Ladies, you deserve To have a temple built you . . . . . . v 3 206
There is some hope the ladies of Rome, especially his mother, may prevail with him . . . . v 4 6
If The Roman ladies bring not comfort home, They'll give him death by inches . . . . v 4 41
The ladies have prevail'd, The Volscians are dislodged . . . . v 4 43
This is good news: I will go meet the ladies . . . . . . v 4 55
Cry 'Welcome, ladies, welcome!'—Welcome, ladies, Welcome! . . v 5 6
My lords, a solemn hunting is in hand; There will the lovely Roman ladies troop: The forest walks are wide . . . *T. Andron.* ii 1 113

Ladies. Somewhat too early for new-married ladies *T. Andron.* ii 2 15
Then let the ladies tattle what they please iv 2 168
These happy masks that kiss fair ladies' brows *Rom. and Jul.* i 1 236
Younger than you, Here in Verona, ladies of esteem, Are made already mothers i 3 70
Bearing a Tartar's painted bow of lath, Scaring the ladies like a crow-keeper i 4 6
O'er ladies' lips, who straight on kisses dream i 4 74
Ladies that have their toes Unplagued with corns will have a bout with you i 5 18
Wilt dine with me, Apemantus?—No; I eat not lords.—An thou shouldst, thou 'ldst anger ladies *T. of Athens* i 1 208
There are certain ladies most desirous of admittance.—Ladies! i 2 122
You have done our pleasures much grace, fair ladies i 2 151
Ladies, there is an idle banquet attends you: Please you to dispose yourselves i 2 160
And I, of ladies most deject and wretched, That suck'd the honey of his music vows *Hamlet* iii 1 163
Good night, ladies; good night, sweet ladies; good night, good night iv 5 73
And ladies too, they will not let me have all fool to myself *Lear* i 4 168
Cried 'Sisters! sisters! Shame of ladies! sisters! Kent! father! sisters!' iv 3 29
Less attemptable than any the rarest of our ladies in France *Cymbeline* i 4 66
If you buy ladies' flesh at a million a dram, you cannot preserve it from tainting i 4 147
Not born where't grows, But worn a bait for ladies iii 4 59
She hath all courtly parts more exquisite Than lady, ladies, woman iii 5 72
Lords and ladies in their lives Have read it for restoratives *Pericles* 1 Gower 7
I will not have excuse, with saying this Loud music is too harsh for ladies' heads, Since they love men in arms ii 3 97
I have heard, you knights of Tyre Are excellent in making ladies trip ii 3 103
Lading. A ship of rich lading wrecked *Mer. of Venice* iii 1 3
As the bark . . . Returns with precious lading to the bay *T. Andron* i 1 72
Let your cares o'erlook What shipping and what lading's in our haven *Pericles* i 2 49
Lady. Bountiful Fortune, Now my dear lady, hath mine enemies Brought to this shore *Tempest* i 2 179
Full many a lady I have eyed with best regard iii 1 39
Ceres, most bounteous lady, thy rich leas Of wheat, rye, barley iv 1 60
And second father This lady makes him to me v 1 196
How does your lady? and how thrives your love? *T. G. of Ver.* ii 4 125
She shall be dignified with this high honour—To bear my lady's train ii 4 159
I love his lady too too much, And that's the reason I love him so little ii 4 205
There is a lady in Verona here Whom I affect iii 1 81
Visit by night your lady's chamber-window With some sweet concert iii 2 83
Myself was from Verona banished For practising to steal away a lady iv 1 48
Gone to seek his dog; which to-morrow, by his master's command, he must carry for a present to his lady iv 2 80
I grant, sweet love, that I did love a lady; But she is dead iv 2 105
Go to thy lady's grave and call hers thence iv 2 117
A thousand times good morrow.—As many, worthy lady, to yourself iv 3 7
I have heard thee say No grief did ever come so near thy heart As when thy lady and thy true love died iv 3 20
Think upon my grief, a lady's grief, And on the justice of my flying hence iv 3 28
Tell my lady I claim the promise for her heavenly picture iv 4 91
Alas, poor lady, desolate and left! I weep myself to think upon thy words iv 4 179
I would make thee my lady.—I your lady, Sir John! alas, I should be a pitiful lady! *Mer. Wives* iii 3 54
You know the lady; she is fast my wife *Meas. for Meas.* i 2 151
You may most uprighteously do a poor wronged lady a merited benefit iii 1 206
I have heard of the lady, and good words went with her name iii 1 219
She is a virtuous and a reverend lady *Com. of Errors* v 1 134
And a good soldier too, lady.—And a good soldier to a lady: but what is he to a lord?—A lord to a lord *Much Ado* i 1 53
The lady fathers herself. Be happy, lady; for you are like an honourable father i 1 112
Is she not a modest young lady?—Do you question me, as an honest man? i 1 166
In mine eye she is the sweetest lady that ever I looked on i 1 189
Amen, if you love her; for the lady is very well worthy i 1 224
The other too like my lady's eldest son, evermore tattling ii 1 10
I think I told him true, that your grace had got the good will of this young lady ii 1 224
You have put him down, lady, you have put him down ii 1 292
I' faith, lady, I think your blazon to be true ii 1 307
In faith, lady, you have a merry heart ii 1 324
Will you have me, lady?—No, my lord, unless I might have another for working-days ii 1 339
A pleasant-spirited lady.—There's little of the melancholy element in her ii 1 356
Appoint her to look out at her lady's chamber window ii 2 17
I did never think that lady would have loved any man ii 3 96
He would make but a sport of it and torment the poor lady worse ii 3 163
She's an excellent sweet lady ii 3 165
I could wish he would modestly examine himself, to see how much he is unworthy so good a lady ii 3 216
They seem to pity the lady: it seems her affections have their full bent ii 3 231
They say the lady is fair; 'tis a truth, I can bear them witness; and virtuous ii 3 239
By this day! she's a fair lady: I do spy some marks of love in her ii 3 254
You come hither, my lord, to marry this lady.—No.—To be married to her iv 1 5
Thus, pretty lady, I am sorry for thy much misgovernment iv 1 99
How doth the lady?—Dead, I think iv 1 114
By noting of the lady I have mark'd A thousand blushing apparitions To start into her face iv 1 160
If this sweet lady lie not guiltless here Under some biting error iv 1 171
The supposition of the lady's death Will quench the wonder of her infamy iv 1 240
You have killed a sweet lady, and her death shall fall heavy on you v 1 150
You have among you killed a sweet and innocent lady v 1 194
Secondarily, they are slanders; sixth and lastly, they have belied a lady v 1 222
The lady is dead upon mine and my master's false accusation v 1 248
I can find out no rhyme to 'lady' but 'baby,' an innocent rhyme v 2 37
Which is the lady I must seize upon?—This same is she v 4 53
Hear me, dear lady; I have sworn an oath.—Our Lady help my lord! *L. L. Lost* ii 1 97
What lady is that same?—The heir of Alencon, Katharine her name.—A gallant lady ii 1 194
She is a most sweet lady.—Not unlike, sir, that may be ii 1 207
A gentle lady; When tongues speak sweetly, then they name her name iii 1 166
Some men must love my lady and some Joan iii 1 207
And praise we may afford To any lady that subdues a lord iv 1 40
Lady. Which is the head lady?—Thou shalt know her, fellow, by the rest that have no heads *L. L. Lost* iv 1 43
Which is the greatest lady, the highest?—The thickest and the tallest iv 1 46
From my lord to my lady.—From which lord to which lady? iv 1 104
My lady goes to kill horns; but, if thou marry, Hang me by the neck iv 1 113
To see him walk before a lady and to bear her fan! To see him kiss his hand! iv 1 147
The clown bore it, the fool sent it, and the lady hath it: sweet clown, sweeter fool, sweetest lady! iv 3 17
O, if in black my lady's brows be deck'd iv 3 258
Love, first learned in a lady's eyes, Lives not alone immured in the brain iv 3 327
A lady wall'd about with diamonds! v 2 3
Not a man of them shall have the grace, Despite of suit, to see a lady's face v 2 129
Fair lady,— Say you so? Fair lord,—Take that for your fair lady v 2 239
My lady, to the manner of the days, In courtesy gives undeserving praise v 2 365
When you then were here, What did you whisper in your lady's ear? v 2 436
By my life, my troth, I never swore this lady such an oath v 2 451
And knows the trick To make my lady laugh when she's disposed v 2 466
Do not you know my lady's foot by the squier? v 2 474
Come when the king doth to my lady come v 2 839
Studies my lady? mistress, look on me; Behold the window of my heart v 2 847
And she, sweet lady, dotes, Devoutly dotes, dotes in idolatry, Upon this spotted and inconstant man *M. N. Dream* i 1 108
What is Thisby? a wandering knight?—It is the lady that Pyramus must love i 2 48
Ah Pyramus, my lover dear! thy Thisby dear, and lady dear! i 2 56
Tarry, rash wanton: am not I thy lord?—Then I must be thy lady ii 1 64
A sweet Athenian lady is in love With a disdainful youth ii 1 260
Anoint his eyes; But do it when the next thing he espies May be the lady ii 1 263
Never harm, Nor spell, nor charm, Come our lovely lady nigh ii 2 18
O, that a lady, of one man refused, Should of another therefore be abused! ii 2 133
If you were men, as men you are in show, You would not use a gentle lady so iii 2 152
Thou takest True delight In the sight Of thy former lady's eye iii 2 457
What lady is the same To whom you swore a secret pilgrimage? *M. of V.* i 1 119
In Belmont is a lady richly left; And she is fair i 1 161
I am much afeard my lady his mother played false with a smith i 2 47
He, of all the men that ever my foolish eyes looked upon, was the best deserving a fair lady i 2 131
Yea, mock the lion when he roars for prey, To win thee, lady ii 1 31
If you choose wrong Never to speak to lady afterward In way of marriage ii 1 41
Thou dost deserve enough; and yet enough May not extend so far as to the lady ii 7 28
As much as I deserve! Why, that's the lady: I do in birth deserve her ii 7 31
'Who chooseth me shall gain what many men desire.' Why, that's the lady ii 7 38
Where is my lady?—Here: what would my lord? ii 9 85
Here is a letter, lady; The paper as the body of my friend iii 2 266
Having such a blessing in his lady, He finds the joys of heaven here on earth iii 5 80
Sweet lady, you have given me life and living v 1 286
His malice 'gainst the lady Will suddenly break forth *As Y. Like It* i 2 294
I have neither the scholar's melancholy, which is emulation, . . . nor the lady's, which is nice iv 1 14
I thought thy heart had been wounded with the claws of a lion.—Wounded it is, but with the eyes of a lady v 2 27
I have flattered a lady; I have been politic with my friend v 4 46
It is not the fashion to see the lady the epilogue Epil. 1
Another tell him of his hounds and horse, And that his lady mourns at his disease *T. of Shrew* Ind. 1 62
Go you to Barthol'mew my page, And see him dress'd in all suits like a lady Ind. 1 106
What is't your honour will command, Wherein your lady and your humble wife May show her duty? Ind. 1 116
I am not bestraught: here's— O, this it is that makes your lady mourn! Ind. 2 28
A lady far more beautiful Than any woman in this waning age Ind. 2 64
Am I a lord? and have I such a lady? Or do I dream? Ind. 2 70
Bring our lady hither to our sight; And once again, a pot o' the smallest ale Ind. 2 76
'Tis a very excellent piece of work, madam lady: would 'twere done! i 1 259
Bless you, my fortunate lady! *All's Well* ii 4 14
How does my old lady?—So that you had her wrinkles and I her money, I would she did as you say ii 4 19
Yonder is heavy news within between two soldiers and my young lady! iii 2 36
Think you it is so?—Ay, surely, mere the truth: I know his lady iii 5 58
Alas, poor lady! 'Tis a hard bondage to become the wife Of a detesting lord iii 5 66
Were I his lady, I would poison that vile rascal iii 5 86
He has much worthy blame laid upon him for shaking off so good a wife and so sweet a lady iv 3 9
A good lady: we may pick a thousand salads ere we light on such another herb iv 5 14
I was about to tell you, since I heard of the good lady's death iv 5 74
Wherein have you played the knave with fortune, that she should scratch you, who of herself is a good lady? v 2 33
The young lord Did to his majesty, his mother, and his lady Offence of mighty note; but to himself The greatest wrong v 3 13
O that I served that lady And might not be delivered to the world! *T. N.* i 2 41
That quaffing and drinking will undo you: I heard my lady talk of it i 3 15
Fair lady, do you think you have fools in hand?—Sir, I have not you by the hand i 3 68
I'll do my best To woo your lady: yet, a barful strife! i 4 41
My lady will hang thee for thy absence i 5 3
Here comes my lady: make your excuse wisely, you were best i 5 33
Take the fool away.—Do you not hear, fellows? Take away the lady i 5 44
The lady bade take away the fool; therefore, I say again, take her away i 5 57
A lady, sir, though it was said she much resembled me, was yet of many accounted beautiful ii 1 26
What means this lady? Fortune forbid my outside have not charm'd her! ii 2 18
If it be so, as 'tis, Poor lady, she were better love a dream ii 2 27
My lady has a white hand ii 3 28
If my lady have not called up her steward Malvolio and bid him turn you out of doors, never trust me.—My lady's a Cataian ii 3 77
There dwelt a man in Babylon, lady, lady! ii 3 84
Do ye make an alehouse of my lady's house? ii 3 96
If you prized my lady's favour at any thing more than contempt ii 3 130
Since the youth of the count's was to-day with my lady, she is much out of quiet ii 3 144

Lady. I can write very like my lady your niece *T. Night* ii 3 173
Say that some lady, as perhaps there is, Hath for your love as great a pang of heart As you have ii 4 92
He brought me out o' favour with my lady about a bear-baiting here ii 5 9
The lady of the Strachy married the yeoman of the wardrobe ii 5 44
This is my lady's hand: these be her very C's, her U's, and her T's ii 5 95
And the impressure her Lucrece, with which she uses to seal: 'tis my lady ii 5 105
'I may command where I adore.' Why, she may command me: I serve her; she is my lady ii 5 128
Every reason excites to this, that my lady loves me ii 5 180
Mark his first approach before my lady ii 5 218
My lady is within, sir. I will construe to them whence you come iii 1 63
Most excellent accomplished lady, the heavens rain odours on you! iii 1 95
You are now sailed into the north of my lady's opinion iii 2 28
I know my lady will strike him: if she do, he'll smile iii 2 88
Why appear you with this ridiculous boldness before my lady? iii 4 41
My lady prays you to have a care of him.—Ah, ha! does she so? iii 4 102
My lady would not lose him for more than I'll say iii 4 116
He is now in some commerce with my lady, and will by and by depart iii 4 191
I will return again into the house and desire some conduct of the lady. iii 4 265
I do not know you; nor I am not sent to you by my lady iv 1 6
Ungird thy strangeness and tell me what I shall vent to my lady iv 1 17
This will I tell my lady straight: I would not be in some of your coats for two pence iv 1 32
Tell me how thy lady does.—Fool!—My lady is unkind, perdy iv 2 79
Some ink, paper, and light; and convey what I will set down to my lady iv 2 119
I am mad Or else the lady's mad iv 3 16
There's something in't That is deceiveable. But here the lady comes. iv 3 21
Let your lady know I am here to speak with her, and bring her along v 1 45
Still so constant, lord.—What, to perverseness? you uncivil lady! v 1 115
All the occurrence of my fortune since Hath been between this lady and this lord.—So comes it, lady, you have been mistook v 1 265
A gentleman, and follower of my lady's v 1 284
Verily, You shall not go: a lady's 'Verily' 's As potent as a lord's *W. Tale* i 2 50
O my most sacred lady! Temptations have since then been born to's i 2 76
O miserable lady! But, for me, What case stand I in? i 2 351
I have seen a lady's nose That has been blue, but not her eyebrows ii 1 14
Say, 'she is a goodly lady,' and The justice of your hearts will thereto add ''Tis pity she's not honest' ii 1 66
Good lady, No court in Europe is too good for thee ii 2 2
You know me, do you not?—For a worthy lady ii 2 5
How fares our gracious lady?—As well as one so great and so forlorn May hold together ii 2 21
Her frights and griefs, Which never tender lady hath borne greater ii 2 24
There is no lady living So meet for this great errand ii 2 45
Away with that audacious lady! Antigonus, I charged thee that she should not come about me: I knew she would ii 3 42
Summon a session, that we may arraign Our most disloyal lady ii 3 203
With such a kind of love as might become A lady like me iii 2 66
Meets he on the way The father of this seeming lady v 1 191
Well, now can I make any Joan a lady *K. John* i 1 184
What say'st thou, boy? look in the lady's face ii 1 495
Can you love this lady?—Nay, ask me if I can refrain from love ii 1 524
How may we content This widow lady? ii 1 548
Rouse from sleep that fell anatomy Which cannot hear a lady's feeble voice iii 4 41
My heart hath melted at a lady's tears, Being an ordinary inundation v 2 47
An I were now by this rascal, I could brain him with his lady's fan *1 Hen IV.* ii 3 25
Constant you are, But yet a woman: and for secrecy, No lady closer ii 3 113
My lord the prince!—How now, my lady the hostess! what sayest thou? ii 4 315
Lie still, ye thief, and hear the lady sing in Welsh.—I had rather hear Lady, my brach, howl in Irish iii 1 238
Now God help thee!—To the Welsh lady's bed iii 1 247
Swear me, Kate, like a lady as thou art, A good mouth-filling oath iii 1 258
Why, my skin hangs about me like an old lady's loose gown iii 3 4
Thou didst swear to me then, as I was washing thy wound, to marry me and make me my lady thy wife *2 Hen. IV.* ii 1 100
How doth the good knight? may I ask how my lady his wife doth? iii 2 71
By the white hand of my lady, he's a gallant prince *Hen. V.* iii 7 101
Will you vouchsafe to teach a soldier terms Such as will enter at a lady's ear? v 2 100
If I could win a lady at leap-frog, or by vaulting into my saddle v 2 142
The virtuous lady, Countess of Auvergne *1 Hen. VI.* ii 2 38
Well then, alone, since there's no remedy, I mean to prove this lady's courtesy ii 2 58
My lady craves To know the cause of your abrupt departure ii 3 29
As liking of the lady's virtuous gifts, Her beauty and the value of her dower v 1 43
Is likely to beget more conquerors, If with a lady of so high resolve As is fair Margaret he be link'd in love v 5 75
With him the husband of this lovely lady *2 Hen. VI.* i 4 77
By this means Your lady is forthcoming yet at London ii 1 179
Two pulls at once; His lady banish'd, and a limb lopp'd off ii 3 42
Must you, Sir John, protect my lady here? ii 4 79
And shall I then be used reproachfully?—Like to a duchess, and Duke Humphrey's lady; According to that state ii 4 98
My sovereign lady, with the rest, Causeless have laid disgraces on my head iii 1 161
Hath he not twit our sovereign lady here With ignominious words? iii 1 178
If ever lady wrong'd her lord so much, Thy mother took into her blameful bed Some stern untutor'd churl iii 2 211
This lady's husband, Sir Richard Grey, was slain *3 Hen. VI.* iii 2 2
I see the lady hath a thing to grant, Before the king will grant her humble suit iii 2 12
I'll make my heaven in a lady's lap, And deck my body in gay ornaments iii 2 148
Teach not thy lips such scorn, for they were made For kissing, lady *Richard III.* i 2 173
Welcome, my fair guests: that noble lady, Or gentleman, that is not freely merry, Is not my friend *Hen. VIII.* i 4 35
Prithee, come hither: what fair lady's that? i 4 91
His conscience Has crept too near another lady ii 2 19
So good a lady that no tongue could ever Pronounce dishonour of her ii 3 3
Alas, poor lady! She's a stranger now again ii 3 16
Who knows yet But from this lady may proceed a gem? ii 3 78
There was a lady once, 'tis an old story, That would not be a queen ii 3 90
With thanks to God for such A royal lady ii 4 153
That my lady's womb, If it conceived a male child by me, should Do no more ii 4 188

Lady. A wretched lady, A woman lost among ye, laugh'd at, scorn'd *Hen. VIII.* iii 1 106
What will become of me now, wretched lady! I am the most unhappy woman living iii 1 146
The king already Hath married the fair lady iii 2 42
Our king has all the Indies in his arms, And more and richer, when he strains that lady iv 1 46
She that carries up the train Is that old noble lady, Duchess of Norfolk iv 1 52
Alas, good lady!—God safely quit her of her burthen! v 1 69
All comfort, joy, in this most gracious lady v 5 7
I thank ye heartily; so shall this lady, When she has so much English v 5 14
Shall make it good . . . , He hath a lady, wiser, fairer, truer, Than ever Greek did compass in his arms *Troi. and Cres.* i 3 275
My lady Was fairer than his grandam and as chaste As may be i 3 298
There is no lady of more softer bowels, More spongy to suck in the sense of fear ii 2 11
To make sweet lady sad is a sour offence iii 1 79
What too curious dreg espies my sweet lady in the fountain of our love? iii 2 71
O, let my lady apprehend no fear: in all Cupid's pageant there is presented no monster.—Nor nothing monstrous neither? iii 2 80
Tell you the lady what she is to do, And haste her to the purpose iv 3 4
My lord, is the lady ready?—Hark! you are call'd iv 4 51
Here is the lady Which for Antenor we deliver you iv 4 111
May I, sweet lady, beg a kiss of you?—You may.—I do desire it.—Why, beg iv 5 47
Come, you must go visit the good lady that lies in *Coriolanus* i 3 85
Noble lady! Come, go with us; speak fair iii 2 69
This lady's husband here, this, do you see—Whom you have banish'd, does exceed you all iv 2 41
Thou art my warrior; I holp to frame thee. Do you know this lady? v 3 63
Even he, your wife, this lady, and myself, Are suitors to you v 3 77
A goodly lady, trust me; of the hue That I would choose *T. Andron.* i 1 261
He and his lady both are at the lodge ii 3 254
She is the hopeful lady of my earth *Rom. and Jul.* i 2 15
Let there be weigh'd Your lady's love against some other maid i 2 102
A man, young lady! lady, such a man As all the world—why, he's a man of wax i 3 75
The guests are come, supper served up, you called, my young lady asked for i 3 101
And could tell A whispering tale in a fair lady's ear, Such as would please i 5 25
What lady is that, which doth enrich the hand Of yonder knight? i 5 43
So shows a snowy dove trooping with crows, As yonder lady o'er her fellows shows i 5 51
It is my lady, O, it is my love! O, that she knew she were! ii 2 10
Laura to his lady was but a kitchen-wench ii 4 42
Farewell, ancient lady; farewell, 'lady, lady, lady.'—Marry, farewell! ii 4 150
As I told you, my young lady bade me inquire you out ii 4 173
Nurse, commend me to thy lady and mistress ii 4 182
My mistress is the sweetest lady—Lord, Lord! when 'twas a little prating thing ii 4 212
Commend me to thy lady.—Ay, a thousand times ii 4 228
O God's lady dear! Are you so hot? marry, come up, I trow ii 5 63
Here comes the lady: O, so light a foot Will ne'er wear out the everlasting flint ii 6 16
O, tell me, holy friar, Where is my lady's lord, where's Romeo? iii 3 82
How doth she? and what says My conceal'd lady to our cancell'd love? iii 3 98
Wilt thou slay thyself? And slay thy lady too that lives in thee? iii 3 117
Commend me to thy lady; And bid her hasten all the house to bed iii 3 155
I'll tell my lady you will come.—Do so, and bid my sweet prepare to chide iii 3 161
Tell my lady I am gone, Having displeased my father iii 5 231
You say you do not know the lady's mind: Uneven is the course iv 1 4
Look, sir, here comes the lady towards my cell iv 1 17
Happily met, my lady and my wife!—That may be, sir, when I may be a wife iv 1 18
I dreamt my lady came and found me dead—Strange dream! v 1 6
How doth my lady? Is my father well? How fares my Juliet? that I ask again v 1 14
Why I descend into this bed of death, Is partly to behold my lady's face v 3 29
Ah, what an unkind hour Is guilty of this lamentable chance! The lady stirs v 3 147
Lady, come from that nest Of death, contagion, and unnatural sleep v 3 151
He came with flowers to strew his lady's grave v 3 281
As rich shall Romeo's by his lady's lie; Poor sacrifices of our enmity! v 3 303
Whose eyes are on this sovereign lady [Fortune] fix'd *T. of Athens* i 1 68
O gentle lady, 'Tis not for you to hear what I can speak *Macbeth* ii 3 88
Help me hence, ho!—Look to the lady ii 3 125
Thine evermore, most dear lady, whilst this machine is to him *Hamlet* ii 2 123
The lady shall say her mind freely, or the blank verse shall halt for't ii 2 338
What, my young lady and mistress! ii 2 444
The lady doth protest too much, methinks.—O, but she'll keep her word iii 2 240
Speak to her, Hamlet.—How is it with you, lady?—Alas, how is't with you? iii 4 115
One word more, good lady.—What shall I do?—Not this, by no means iii 4 180
Of all these bounds, even from this line to this, . . . We make thee lady *Lear* i 1 67
My lord of Burgundy, What say you to the lady? i 1 241
Since my young lady's going into France, sir, the fool hath much pined away i 4 79
Who am I, sir?—My lady's father.—'My lady's father'! my lord's knave i 4 87
He must be whipped out, when Lady the brach may stand by the fire i 4 125
Thou art a lady; If only to go warm were gorgeous, Why, nature needs not what thou gorgeous wear'st, Which scarcely keeps thee warm ii 4 270
O filthy traitor!—Unmerciful lady as you are, I'm none iii 7 33
Naughty lady, These hairs, which thou dost ravish from my chin, Will quicken, and accuse thee iii 7 37
Where was his son when they did take his eyes?—Come with my lady hither iv 2 90
My lady charged my duty in this business iv 5 18
I know your lady does not love her husband; I am sure of that iv 5 23
And more convenient is he for my hand Than for your lady's iv 5 32
Do not laugh at me; For, as I am a man, I think this lady To be my child Cordelia iv 7 69
If you will marry, make your loves to me, My lady is bespoke v 3 89
Who dead? speak, man.—Your lady, sir, your lady: and her sister v 3 226
Send for the lady to the Sagittary, And let her speak of me *Othello* i 3 115
Justly to your grave ears I'll present How I did thrive in this fair lady's love i 3 125

Lady. This only is the witchcraft I have used: Here comes the lady; let her witness it . . . . *Othello* i 3 170
She's a most exquisite lady . . . . ii 3 18
Did Michael Cassio, when you woo'd my lady, Know of your love? . iii 3 94
Note, if your lady strain his entertainment With any strong or vehement importunity; Much will be seen in that . . . . . . iii 3 250
Give't me again; poor lady, she'll run mad When she shall lack it . iii 3 317
I will not stay to offend you.—Truly, an obedient lady . . . iv 1 259
I know a lady in Venice would have walked barefoot to Palestine for a touch of his nether lip . . . . iv 3 38
Run you to the citadel, And tell my lord and lady what hath happ'd . v 1 127
Alas! that was my lady's voice. Help! help, ho! help! O lady, speak again! . . . . v 2 119
You shall outlive the lady whom you serve . . . *Ant. and Cleo.* i 2 31
She's a most triumphant lady, if report be square to her . . . ii 2 189
A more unhappy lady, If this division chance, ne'er stood between, Praying for both parts . . . . iii 4 12
Henceforth The white hand of a lady fever thee, Shake thou to look on't iii 13 138
O, thy vile lady! She has robb'd me of my sword . . . . iv 14 22
His gentle lady, Big of this gentleman our theme, deceased As he was born . . . . *Cymbeline* i 1 38
That lady is not now living, or this gentleman's opinion by this worn out . . . . i 4 67
Something too fair and too good for any lady in Britain . . . . i 4 77
I have not seen the most precious diamond that is, nor you the lady . i 4 82
I durst attempt it against any lady in the world . . . . . i 4 123
What lady would you choose to assail?—Yours; whom in constancy you think stands so safe . . . . i 4 136
Commend me to the court where your lady is . . . . . . i 4 140
A foolish suitor to a wedded lady, That hath her husband banish'd . i 6 2
A lady So fair, and fasten'd to an empery, Would make the great'st king double . . . . i 6 119
A lady that disdains Thee and the devil alike . . . . . . i 6 147
The credit that thy lady hath of thee Deserves thy trust . . . i 6 157
A lady to the worthiest sir that ever Country call'd his! . . . i 6 160
With every thing that pretty is, My lady sweet, arise: Arise, arise . ii 3 29
What's your lordship's pleasure?—Your lady's person: is she ready? . ii 3 86
I am much sorry, sir, You put me to forget a lady's manners, By being so verbal . . . . ii 3 110
She's my good lady, and will conceive, I hope, But the worst of me . ii 3 158
Your lady Is one of the fairest that I have look'd upon . . . . ii 4 31
The stone's too hard to come by.—Not a whit, Your lady being so easy ii 4 47
A lady So tender of rebukes that words are strokes And strokes death to her . . . . iii 5 39
She hath all courtly parts more exquisite Than lady, ladies, woman . iii 5 72
Where is thy lady? or, by Jupiter,—I will not ask again . . . iii 5 84
The same suit he wore when he took leave of my lady . . . . iii 5 128
I am brought hither . . . to fight Against my lady's kingdom . . v 1 19
I have belied a lady, The princess of this country, and the air on't Revengingly enfeebles me . . . . v 2 2
Help, help! Mine honour'd lady! . . . . v 5 232
Why did you throw your wedded lady from you? . . . . . v 5 261
Cloten, Upon my lady's missing, came to me With his sword drawn . v 5 275
With unchaste purpose and with oath to violate My lady's honour . v 5 285
Here stands a lord, and there a lady weeping . . . . *Pericles* i 4 47
Wilt thou tourney for the lady?—I'll show the virtue I have borne in arms . . . . ii 1 150
Upon his shield Is an arm'd knight that's conquer'd by a lady . . ii 2 26
Come, sir; Here is a lady that wants breathing too . . . . ii 3 101
The lady shrieks, and well-a-near Does fall in travail with her fear iii Gower 51
You, and your lady, Take from my heart all thankfulness! . . . iii 3 3
Why will you kill me?—To satisfy my lady.—Why should she have me kill'd? . . . . iv 1 72
Your lady seeks my life; come you between, And save poor me, the weaker . . . . iv 1 90
O lady, Much less in blood than virtue, yet a princess To equal any single crown o' the earth! . . . . iv 3 6
O, here is The lady that I sent for. Welcome, fair one! Is't not a goodly presence?—She's a gallant lady . . . . v 1 65
Look to the lady; O, she's but o'erjoy'd . . . . v 3 21
Early in blustering morn this lady was Thrown upon this shore . . v 3 22
By'r lady *Mer. Wives* i 1; *Much Ado* iii 3; iii 4; *T. Night* ii 3; 1 *Hen. IV.* ii 4; iii 1; 2 *Hen. IV.* v 3; *Richard III.* ii 3; *Hen. VIII.* i 3; *T. Andron.* iv 4; *Rom. and Jul.* i 5; *Hamlet* ii 2; iii 2

Lady-bird. What, lamb! what, lady-bird! God forbid! *Rom. and Jul.* i 3 3

Lady daughter. Peace, Dear lady daughter, peace! . . . *Cymbeline* i 1 154

Lady Disdain. My dear Lady Disdain! are you yet living? . *Much Ado* i 1 119

Lady Fortune. O lady Fortune, Stand you auspicious! . *W. Tale* iv 4 51

Lady gracious. Heaven and our Lady gracious hath it pleased To shine on my contemptible estate . . . . 1 *Hen. VI.* i 2 74

Lady mother. I have . . . writ to my lady mother . . *All's Well* iv 3 102
Your lady mother is coming to your chamber . . . *Rom. and Jul.* iii 5 39
Ho, daughter! are you up?—Who is't that calls? is it my lady mother? iii 5 66

Lady of esteem. You know, my lord, your highness is betroth'd Unto another lady of esteem . . . . 1 *Hen. VI.* v 5 27

Lady of the house. The honourable lady of the house, which is she?—Speak to me . . . . *T. Night* i 5 177
Tell me if this be the lady of the house . . . . i 5 183
Her mother is the lady of the house, And a good lady . *Rom. and Jul.* i 5 115

Lady Peace. But look you pray, all you that kiss my lady Peace at home, that our armies join not in a hot day . . . . 2 *Hen. IV.* i 2 232

Lady's chamber. Perfume for a lady's chamber . . . *W. Tale* iv 4 225
He capers nimbly in a lady's chamber . . . . *Richard III.* i 1 12
Now get you to my lady's chamber, and tell her, let her paint an inch thick, to this favour she must come . . . . . *Hamlet* v 1 213

Lady-she. I love thee not a jar o' the clock behind What lady-she her lord *W. Tale* i 2 44

Lady-smocks all silver-white And cuckoo-buds . . . *L. L. Lost* v 2 905

Lady terms. With many holiday and lady terms He question'd me 1 *Hen. IV.* i 3 46

Lady Tongue. I cannot endure my Lady Tongue . . . *Much Ado* ii 1 284

Lady trifles. I some lady trifles have reserved, Immoment toys, things of such dignity As we greet modern friends withal . *Ant. and Cleo.* v 2 165

Lady widow. The lady widow of Vitruvio . . . . *Rom. and Jul.* i 2 69

Lady wisdom. You are to blame, my lord, to rate her so.—And why, my lady wisdom? hold your tongue . . . . iii 5 171

Ladyship. What would your ladyship?—Is't near dinner-time? *T. G. of V.* i 2 66
Give me a note: your ladyship can set.—As little by such toys . . i 2 81
Which I was much unwilling to proceed in But for my duty to your ladyship . . . . ii 1 113

Ladyship. What means your ladyship? do you not like it?—Yes, yes *T. G. of Ver.* ii 1 127
I'll write your ladyship another.—And when it's writ, for my sake read it . . . . ii 1 135
Borrows his wit from your ladyship's looks, and spends what he borrows ii 4 38
This is the gentleman I told your ladyship Had come along with me . ii 4 87
Entertain him To be my fellow-servant to your ladyship . . . ii 4 105
We'll both attend upon your ladyship . . . . ii 4 121
Why, then, your ladyship must cut your hair . . . . . . ii 7 44
Good even to your ladyship.—I thank you for your music, gentlemen . iv 2 85
Your servant and your friend; One that attends your ladyship's command iv 3 5
According to your ladyship's impose, I am thus early come . . . iv 3 8
I will not fail your ladyship. Good morrow, gentle lady . . . iv 3 45
This is the letter to your ladyship.—I pray thee, let me look on that again . . . . iv 4 129
He sends your ladyship this ring.—The more shame for him . . . iv 4 137
God keep your ladyship still in that mind! . . . . *Much Ado* i 1 134
Your ladyship is ignorant what it is.—Were my lord so, his ignorance were wise . . . . *L. L. Lost* ii 1 101
Your ladyship's in all desired employment . . . . . . iv 2 139
If your ladyship would say, 'Thanks, Pompey,' I had done . . . v 2 559
I wish your ladyship all heart's content . . . . *Mer. of Venice* iii 4 42
I will tell you the beginning; and, if it please your ladyships, you may see the end; for the best is yet to do . . . . *As Y. Like It* i 2 120
If I may have your ladyship's good will to go to the world . *All's Well* i 3 19
How does your ladyship like it?—With very much content . . . iv 5 82
I marvel your ladyship takes delight in such a barren rascal . *T. Night* i 5 89
Good disposition Attend your ladyship! . . . . iii 1 147
Your ladyship were best to have some guard about you, if he come . iii 4 12
He attends your ladyship's pleasure.—I'll come to him . . . iii 4 64
An your ladyship will have it as it ought to be, you must allow Vox . v 1 303
Yet have I the benefit of my senses as well as your ladyship . . v 1 314
Please your ladyship To visit the next room . . . . *W. Tale* ii 2 46
Thou Fortune's champion that dost never fight But when her humorous ladyship is by To teach thee safety! . . . . . . *K. John* iii 1 119
According as your ladyship desired, By message craved . . 1 *Hen. VI.* ii 3 12
Since your ladyship is not at leisure, I'll sort some other time to visit you . . . . ii 3 26
I laugh to see your ladyship so fond . . . . ii 3 45
Will her ladyship behold and hear our exorcisms? . . . 2 *Hen. VI.* i 4 4
Here's to your ladyship: and pledge it, madam . . . *Hen. VIII.* i 4 47
Good day to you.—Sweet madam.—I am glad to see your ladyship *Coriol.* i 3 53
How does your little son?—I thank your ladyship; well . . . i 3 58
Joyful tidings, girl.—And joy comes well in such a needy time: What are they, I beseech your ladyship? . . . . *Rom. and Jul.* iii 5 107
Your ladyship is nearer to heaven than when I saw you last . *Hamlet* ii 2 445
Before your ladyship, I grant, She puts her tongue a little in her heart *Othello* ii 1 106
I humbly thank your ladyship . . . . iii 4 168; iv 3 3

Laertes. Wise Laertes' son Did graciously plead for his funerals *T. An.* i 1 380
Now, Laertes, what's the news with you? You told us of some suit *Ham.* i 2 42
What is't, Laertes? You cannot speak of reason to the Dane, And lose your voice . . . . i 2 43
What wouldst thou beg, Laertes, That shall not be my offer, not thy asking? . . . . i 2 45
What wouldst thou have, Laertes?—My dread lord, Your leave and favour to return to France . . . . i 2 50
Take thy fair hour, Laertes; time be thine! . . . . . . i 2 62
Laertes! aboard, aboard, for shame! The wind sits in the shoulder of your sail . . . . i 3 55
Young Laertes, in a riotous head, O'erbears your officers . . . iv 5 101
They cry 'Choose we: Laertes shall be king:' Caps, hands, and tongues, applaud it to the clouds: 'Laertes shall be king, Laertes king!' iv 5 106
Calmly, good Laertes.—That drop of blood that's calm proclaims me bastard . . . . iv 5 116
What is the cause, Laertes, That thy rebellion looks so giant-like? . iv 5 120
Tell me, Laertes, Why thou art thus incensed . . . . . . iv 5 125
Laertes, I must commune with your grief, Or you deny me right . . iv 5 202
If it be so, Laertes—As how should it be so? how otherwise? . . . iv 7 58
Laertes, was your father dear to you? . . . . iv 7 108
But, good Laertes, Will you do this, keep close within your chamber . iv 7 129
Your sister's drown'd, Laertes.—Drown'd! O, where? . . . . iv 7 165
O, he is mad, Laertes.—For love of God, forbear him . . . . v 1 295
But I am very sorry, good Horatio, That to Laertes I forgot myself . v 2 76
Here is newly come to court Laertes; believe me, an absolute gentleman v 2 111
Of Laertes?—His purse is empty already; all's golden words are spent v 2 135
You are not ignorant of what excellence Laertes is . . . . . v 2 144
The queen desires you to use some gentle entertainment to Laertes . v 2 216
Was't Hamlet wrong'd Laertes? Never Hamlet: If Hamlet from himself be ta'en away, And when he's not himself does wrong Laertes, Then Hamlet does it not, Hamlet denies it . . . . . . v 2 244
Give us the foils. Come on.—Come, one for me.—I'll be your foil, Laertes . . . . v 2 266
Come, for the third, Laertes: you but dally . . . . . . v 2 308
How is't, Laertes?—Why, as a woodcock to mine own springe . . v 2 316

Lafeu. Good Lafeu, Bring in the admiration; that we with thee May spend our wonder too . . . . *All's Well* ii 1 90
He was first smoked by the old lord Lafeu . . . . . . iii 6 112
Captain, what greeting will you to my Lord Lafeu? I am for France . iv 3 353
Good Monsieur Lavache, give my Lord Lafeu this letter . . . v 2 2
The heavens have thought well on thee, Lafeu, To bring forth this discovery . . . . v 3 150

Lag. Fortune in favour makes him lag behind . . . 1 *Hen. VI.* iii 3 34
Came too lag to see him buried . . . . . . *Richard III.* ii 1 90
The senators of Athens, together with the common lag of people *T. of Athens* iii 6 90
I am some twelve or fourteen moonshines Lag of a brother . . *Lear* i 2 6

Lag-end. I could be well content To entertain the lag-end of my life With quiet hours . . . . 1 *Hen. IV.* v 1 24
Wear away The lag end of their lewdness and be laugh'd at . *Hen. VIII.* i 3 35

Lagging. Four lagging winters and four wanton springs . *Richard II.* i 3 214

Laid. Good plots, they are laid . . . . *Mer. Wives* iii 2 39
Have I laid my brain in the sun and dried it? . . . . . . v 5 143
They must be bound and laid in some dark room . . *Com. of Errors* iv 4 97
The juice of it on sleeping eye-lids laid Will make or man or woman madly dote Upon the next live creature that it sees . *M. N. Dream* ii 1 170
Thou hast mistaken quite And laid the love-juice on some true-love's sight . . . . iii 2 89
The sins of the father are to be laid upon the children . *Mer. of Venice* iii 5 2
I met a fool; Who laid him down and bask'd him in the sun *A. Y. L. It* ii 7 15

Laid. Can you remember any of the principal evils that he laid to the charge of women? . . . . *As Y. Like It* iii 2 370
Be the jacks fair within, the jills fair without, the carpets laid? *T. of S.* iv 1 52
He has much worthy blame laid upon him . . . *All's Well* iv 3 7
Come away, death, And in sad cypress let me be laid . . *T. Night* ii 4 53
I have said too much unto a heart of stone And laid mine honour too unchary out . . . . iii 4 222
They have laid me here in hideous darkness . . . . . iv 2 34
Nor is 't directly laid to thee, the death Of the young prince . *W. Tale* iii 2 195
This is not, no, Laid to thy answer . . . . iii 2 200
It should here be laid, Either for life or death, upon the earth Of its right father . . . . iii 3 44
I would that I were low laid in my grave: I am not worth this coil that's made for me . . . . *K. John* ii 1 164
Thy sins are visited in this poor child; The canon of the law is laid on him . . . . ii 1 180
By that sword I swear, Which gently laid my knighthood on my shoulder *Richard II.* i 1 79
From forth thy reach he would have laid thy shame . . . . . ii 1 106
That e'er this tongue of mine, That laid the sentence of dread banishment On yon proud man, should take it off again! . . . . . iii 3 134
Therein laid,—there lies Two kinsmen digg'd their graves with weeping eyes . . . . iii 3 168
Our plot is a good plot as ever was laid; our friends true . 1 *Hen. IV.* ii 3 18
Attended him on bridges, stood in lanes, Laid gifts before him . . iv 3 71
And laid his love and life under my foot . . . . 2 *Hen. IV.* iii 1 63
A joint burden laid upon us all . . . . v 2 55
How might a prince of my great hopes forget So great indignities you laid upon me? . . . . v 2 69
Not all these, laid in bed majestical, Can sleep so soundly . *Hen. V.* iv 1 284
The plot is laid: if all things fall out right . . . . 1 *Hen. VI.* ii 3 4
But mightier crimes are laid unto your charge . . 2 *Hen. VI.* iii 1 134
My sovereign lady, with the rest, Causeless have laid disgraces on my head . . . . iii 1 162
All of you have laid your heads together . . . . iii 1 165
Have you laid fair the bed? Is all things well, According as I gave directions? . . . . iii 2 11
Some violent hands were laid on Humphrey's life . . . . . iii 2 138
I do believe that violent hands were laid Upon the life . . . . iii 2 156
All the country is laid for me . . . . iv 10 4
And with dishonour laid me on the ground . . . 3 *Hen. VI.* iii 3 9
I'll blast his harvest, if your head were laid . . . . . v 7 21
Plots have I laid, inductions dangerous, By drunken prophecies *Rich. III.* i 1 32
Her slanderous tongue, Which laid their guilt upon my guiltless shoulders . . . . i 2 98
The curse my noble father laid on thee . . . . i 3 174
Clarence, whom I, indeed, have laid in darkness, I do beweep . . i 3 327
Is my beaver easier than it was? And all my armour laid into my tent? v 3 51
Or Laid any scruple in your way . . . . *Hen. VIII.* ii 4 150
The rod, and bird of peace, and all such emblems Laid nobly on her . iv 1 90
Foreseeing those fell mischiefs Our reasons laid before him . . . v 1 50
Protect mine innocence, or I fall into The trap is laid for me! . . v 1 142
This is of purpose laid by some that hate me . . . . . v 2 14
Nor has Coriolanus Deserved this so dishonour'd rub, laid falsely I' the plain way of his merit . . . . *Coriolanus* iii 1 60
I had then laid wormwood to my dug, Sitting in the sun *Rom. and Jul.* i 3 26
Letting it there stand Till she had laid it and conjured it down . . ii 1 26
How if, when I am laid into the tomb, I wake before the time? . iv 3 30
See, what a scourge is laid upon your hate . . . . . . v 3 292
Wherefore ere this time Had you not fully laid my state before me? *T. of Athens* ii 2 134
At many times I brought in my accounts, Laid them before you . . ii 2 143
When I have laid proud Athens on a heap,— Warr'st thou 'gainst Athens? iv 3 101
Hark! I laid their daggers ready; He could not miss 'em . *Macbeth* ii 2 12
Here abjure The taints and blames I laid upon myself, For strangers to my nature . . . . iv 3 124
Alas, how shall this bloody deed be answer'd? It will be laid to us *Ham.* iv 1 17
He has laid a great wager on your head . . . . v 2 105
In the imputation laid on him by them, in his meed he's unfellowed . v 2 149
The king, sir, hath laid, that in a dozen passes between yourself and him, he shall not exceed you three hits . . . . v 2 172
He hath laid on twelve for nine . . . . v 2 174
Your grace hath laid the odds o' the weaker side . . . . . v 2 272
Then laid his leg Over my thigh, and sigh'd . . . . *Othello* iii 3 424
I shifted him away, And laid good 'scuse upon your ecstasy . . . iv 1 80
A beggar in his drink Could not have laid such terms upon his callat . iv 2 121
I have laid those sheets you bade me on the bed . . . . . iv 3 22
He hath laid strange courtesies and great Of late upon me *Ant. and Cleo.* ii 2 157
Nothing saves The wager you have laid . . . . . *Cymbeline* ii 4 95
Malice and lucre in them Have laid this woe here . . . . . iv 2 325
Laid apart. Why, thy godhead laid apart, Warr'st thou with a woman's heart? . . . . *As Y. Like It* iv 3 44
Laid aside. And harmful pity must be laid aside . . . 3 *Hen. VI.* ii 2 10
Tell him, my mourning weeds are laid aside . . . . . . iii 3 229
Laid by. For that I have laid by my majesty . . . . . *Hen. V.* i 2 276
His ceremonies laid by, in his nakedness he appears but a man . . iv 1 109
Laid claim. This drudge, or diviner, laid claim to me . *Com. of Errors* iii 2 144
As I have read, laid claim unto the crown . . . . 2 *Hen. VI.* ii 2 40
Laid low. I saw her laid low in her kindred's vault . *Rom. and Jul.* v 1 20
Laid on. Well said: that was laid on with a trowel . *As Y. Like It* i 2 112
Whose red and white Nature's own sweet and cunning hand laid on *T. N.* i 5 258
Your sorrow was too sore laid on . . . . *W. Tale* v 3 49
Laid open. The pretence whereof being by circumstances partly laid open . . . . iii 2 19
Laid open all your victories in Scotland . . . . *Richard III.* iii 7 15
Laid up. The gold I gave to Dromio is laid up Safe at the Centaur *Com. of Errors* ii 2 1
Then there were two cousins laid up . . . . . . *As Y. Like It* i 3 7
See him laugh till his face be like a wet cloak ill laid up! . 2 *Hen. IV.* v 1 95
All comfort, joy, in this most gracious lady, Heaven ever laid up to make parents happy, May hourly fall upon ye! . . . . *Hen. VIII.* v 5 8
Laidest. Thou laid'st a trap to take my life . . . 1 *Hen. VI.* iii 1 22
Lain. Because he hath wakened thy dog that hath lain asleep in the sun *Rom. and Jul.* iii 1 28
O son! the night before thy wedding-day Hath Death lain with thy wife . . . . iv 5 36
And Juliet bleeding, warm, and newly dead, Who here hath lain these two days buried . . . . v 3 176
This skull has lain in the earth three and twenty years . . . *Hamlet* v 1 190
Laissez, mon seigneur, laissez, laissez . . . . . *Hen. V.* v 2 273
Lake. The foul lake O'erstunk their feet . . . . . . *Tempest* iv 1 183
Ye elves of hills, brooks, standing lakes and groves . . . . v 1 33
I'll see her damned first; to Pluto's damned lake . . 2 *Hen. IV.* ii 4 170
Descend to darkness and the burning lake! . . . . 2 *Hen. VI.* i 4 42
I'll dive into the burning lake below, And pull her out of Acheron by the heels . . . . *T. Andron.* iv 3 43
Nero is an angler in the lake of darkness . . . . . . *Lear* iii 6 8
Lakin. By'r lakin, I can go no further . . . . . . *Tempest* iii 3 1
By'r lakin, a parlous fear . . . . *M. N. Dream* iii 1 14
Lamb. Thou hast entertain'd A fox to be the shepherd of thy lambs *T. G. of Ver.* iv 4 97
O, poor souls, Come you to seek the lamb here of the fox? *Meas. for Meas.* v 1 300
Doing, in the figure of a lamb, the feats of a lion . . . *Much Ado* i 1 15
The ewe that will not hear her lamb when it baes will never answer a calf iii 3 75
No sheep, sweet lamb, unless we feed on your lips . . . *L. L. Lost* ii 1 220
Thus dost thou hear the Nemean lion roar 'Gainst thee, thou lamb . iv 1 91
Did in eaning time Fall parti-colour'd lambs . . . *Mer. of Venice* i 3 89
As well use question with the wolf Why he hath made the ewe bleat for the lamb . . . . iv 1 74
The greatest of my pride is to see my ewes graze and my lambs suck.—That is another simple sin in you . . . . . *As Y. Like It* iii 2 81
Tut, she's a lamb, a dove, a fool to him! . . . . *T. of Shrew* iii 2 159
I'll sacrifice the lamb that I do love, To spite a raven's heart *T. Night* v 1 133
We were as twinn'd lambs that did frisk i' the sun . . . *W. Tale* i 2 67
I will sit as quiet as a lamb; I will not stir, nor wince . *K. John* iv 1 80
In peace was never gentle lamb more mild . . . . *Richard II.* ii 1 174
From the rising of the lark to the lodging of the lamb . . *Hen. V.* iii 7 35
Whilst I waited on my tender lambs, And to sun's parching heat display'd my cheeks, God's mother deigned to appear to me 1 *Hen. VI.* i 2 76
Or else, when thou didst keep my lambs a-field, I wish some ravenous wolf had eaten thee! . . . . v 4 30
The fox barks not when he would steal the lamb . . 2 *Hen. VI.* iii 1 55
As innocent . . . As is the sucking lamb or harmless dove . . . . iii 1 71
Is he a lamb? his skin is surely lent him . . . . iii 1 77
Is not this a lamentable thing, that of the skin of an innocent lamb should be made parchment? . . . . iv 2 87
Such safety finds The trembling lamb environed with wolves 3 *Hen. VI.* i 1 242
Fly, like ships before the wind Or lambs pursued by hunger-starved wolves . . . . i 4 5
O bloody times! Whiles lions war and battle for their dens, Poor harmless lambs abide their enmity . . . . ii 5 75
When the lion fawns upon the lamb, The lamb will never cease to follow him . . . . iv 8 50
Wilt thou, O God, fly from such gentle lambs, And throw them in the entrails of the wolf? . . . . *Richard III.* iv 4 22
That dog, that had his teeth before his eyes, To worry lambs . . iv 4 50
It was whetted on thy stone-hard heart, To revel in the entrails of my lambs . . . . iv 4 228
As fox to lamb, as wolf to heifer's calf, Paid to the hind *Troi. and Cres.* iii 2 200
We see it, we see it. How now, lambs? . . . . iv 4 25
Pray you, who does the wolf love?—The lamb.—Ay, to devour him *Cor.* ii 1 9
He's a lamb indeed, that baes like a bear.—He's a bear indeed, that lives like a lamb . . . . ii 1 12
All on a heap, like to a slaughter'd lamb . . . . *T. Andron.* ii 3 223
When we join in league, I am a lamb . . . . iv 2 137
What, lamb! what, lady-bird! God forbid! Where's this girl? *R. and J.* i 3 3
He is not the flower of courtesy, but, I'll warrant him, as gentle as a lamb . . . . ii 5 45
Fiend angelical! Dove-feather'd raven! wolvish-ravening lamb! . . iii 2 76
Why, lamb! why, lady! fie, you slug-a-bed! Why, love, I say! . . iv 5 2
If thou wert the lamb, the fox would eat thee . . . *T. of Athens* iv 3 331
You are yoked with a lamb That carries anger as the flint bears fire *J. C.* iv 3 110
To offer up a weak poor innocent lamb To appease an angry god *Macbeth* iv 3 16
Macbeth Will seem as pure as snow, and the poor state Esteem him as a lamb . . . . iv 3 54
Ravening first the lamb Longs after for the garbage . . *Cymbeline* i 6 49
Prithee, dispatch: The lamb entreats the butcher . . . . iii 4 99
Lambert. At Coventry, upon Saint Lambert's day . . *Richard II.* i 1 199
Lambkin. Thy tender lambkin now is king . . . 2 *Hen. IV.* v 3 122
For, lambkins, we will live . . . . *Hen. V.* ii 1 133
Lamb-skin. Furred with fox and lamb-skins . . . *Meas. for Meas.* iii 2 9
Lame. When they will not give a doit to relieve a lame beggar, they will lay out ten to see a dead Indian . . . . *Tempest* ii 2 33
Leap for joy, though they are lame with blows . . *L. L. Lost* v 2 291
Throw some of them at me; come, lame me with reasons *As Y. Like It* i 3 6
When service should in my old limbs lie lame . . . . . ii 3 41
The feet were lame and could not bear themselves without the verse . iii 2 178
Which lames report to follow it and undoes description to do it *W. Tale* v 2 62
Lame, foolish, crooked, swart, prodigious . . . . *K. John* iii 1 46
What, art thou lame?—Ay, God Almighty help me!—How camest thou so?—A fall off of a tree . . . . 2 *Hen. VI.* ii 1 95
Made the lame to leap and fly away . . . . ii 1 162
They have all new legs, and lame ones . . . . . *Hen. VIII.* i 3 11
Unless, by using means, I lame the foot Of our design . *Coriolanus* iv 7 7
O, she is lame! love's heralds should be thoughts . *Rom. and Jul.* ii 5 4
For nature so preposterously to err, Being not deficient, blind, or lame of sense, Sans witchcraft could not . . . . *Othello* i 3 63
O most lame and impotent conclusion! . . . . ii 1 162
Only I carry winged time Post on the lame feet of my rhyme *Pericles* iv Gower 48
Lamed. And, I think, when he hath lamed me, I shall beg with it from door to door . . . . *Com. of Errors* iv 4 41
One should be lamed with reasons and the other mad without any *As Y. Like It* i 3 8
Lamely. Are they not lamely writ?—No, boy . . . *T. G. of Ver.* ii 1 97
Ay, but the feet were lame and could not bear themselves without the verse and therefore stood lamely in the verse . . *As Y. Like It* iii 2 180
Scarce half made up, And that so lamely and unfashionable That dogs bark at me as I halt by them . . . . *Richard III.* i 1 22
Thou cold sciatica, Cripple our senators, that their limbs may halt As lamely as their manners! . . . . *T. of Athens* iv 1 25
Lameness. Strike her young bones, You taking airs, with lameness! *Lear* ii 4 166
Lament. Cease to lament for that thou canst not help . *T. G. of Ver.* iii 1 241
She laments, sir, for it, that it would yearn your heart to see it *M. Wives* iii 5 44
I shall do my friends no wrong, for I have none to lament me *As Y. L. It* i 2 202
I, an old turtle, Will wing me to some wither'd bough and there My mate, that's never to be found again, Lament till I am lost *W. Tale* v 3 135
Lament we may, but not revenge thee dead . . . . *Richard II.* i 3 58
These external manners of laments Are merely shadows to the unseen . iv 1 296
Thy great bounty, that not only givest Me cause to wail but teachest me the way How to lament the cause . . . . iv 1 392

Lament. Mourn with me for that I do lament, And put on sullen black incontinent. *Richard II.* v 6 47
I know not your breeding.—Why then, lament therefore . 2 *Hen. IV.* v 3 113
To add to your laments, Wherewith you now bedew King Henry's hearse, I must inform you of a dismal fight . 1 *Hen. VI.* i 1 103
Although the duke was enemy to him, Yet he most Christian-like laments his death . 2 *Hen. VI.* iii 2 58
But that I hate thee deadly, I should lament thy miserable state 3 *Hen. VI.* i 4 85
What cannot be avoided 'Twere childish weakness to lament or fear . v 4 38
Whilst I awhile obsequiously lament . *Richard III.* i 2 3
And still, as you are weary of the weight, Rest you, whiles I lament . i 2 32
You mistake me much; I do lament the sickness of the king . ii 2 9
If you will live, lament; if die, be brief . ii 2 43
Hearts of most hard temper Melt and lament for her . *Hen. VIII.* ii 3 12
Leave this faint puling and lament as I do, In anger, Juno-like *Coriolanus* iv 2 52
That ever eye with sight made heart lament . *T. Andron.* ii 3 205
O noble father, you lament in vain: The tribunes hear you not . iii 1 27
But yet let reason govern thy lament . iii 1 219
Good grandsire, leave these bitter deep laments . iii 2 46
Bear her to church: For though fond nature bids us all lament, Yet nature's tears are reason's merriment . *Rom. and Jul.* iv 5 82
My heart laments that virtue cannot live Out of the teeth of emulation *J. Cæsar* ii 3 13
Where joy most revels, grief doth most lament . *Hamlet* iii 2 208
The miserable change now at my end Lament nor sorrow at *A. and C.* iv 15 52
Strange it is, That nature must compel us to lament Our most persisted deeds . v 1 29
But yet let me lament, With tears as sovereign as the blood of hearts . v 1 40
Why lament you, pretty one?—That I am pretty . *Pericles* iv 2 72
Lamentable. I did play a lamentable part . *T. G. of Ver.* iv 4 171
O, they were all in lamentable cases! . *L. L. Lost* v 2 273
The most lamentable comedy . *M. N. Dream* i 2 11
Why holds thine eye that lamentable rheum? . *K. John* iii 1 22
To quit their griefs, Tell thou the lamentable tale of me . *Richard II.* v 1 44
Ah, poor heart! he is so shaked of a burning quotidian tertian, that it is most lamentable to behold . *Hen. V.* ii 1 125
Is not this a lamentable thing, that of the skin of an innocent lamb should be made parchment? . 2 *Hen. VI.* iv 2 86
Is not this a lamentable thing, grandsire, that we should be thus afflicted with these strange flies? . *Rom. and Jul.* ii 4 32
O lamentable day!—O woful time! . iv 5 17; 30
Most lamentable day, most woful day, That ever, ever, I did yet behold! iv 5 50
Ah, what an unkind hour Is guilty of this lamentable chance! . v 3 146
The lamentable change is from the best; The worst returns to laughter *Lear* iv 1 5
The approbation of those that weep this lamentable divorce . *Cymbeline* i 4 20
What wreck discern you in me Deserves your pity?—Lamentable! . i 6 85
Lamentably. A very pleasant thing indeed and sung lamentably *W. Tale* iv 4 190
Our fortune on the sea is out of breath, And sinks most lamentably *Ant. and Cleo.* iii 10 26
Lamentation. In few, bestowed her on her own lamentation *M. for M.* iii 1 237
Raining the tears of lamentation . *L. L. Lost* v 2 819
Moderate lamentation is the right of the dead . *All's Well* i 1 64
As yet the lamentation of the French Invites the King of England's stay at home . *Hen. V.* v Prol. 36
I invocate thy ghost, To hear the lamentations of poor Anne! *Richard III.* i 2 9
Give me no help in lamentation; I am not barren to bring forth complaints . ii 2 66
I am your sorrow's nurse, And I will pamper it with lamentations . ii 2 88
Hover about me with your airy wings And hear your mother's lamentation! . iv 4 14
We should by this, to all our lamentation, If he had gone forth consul, found it so.—The gods have well prevented it . *Coriolanus* iv 6 34
Which modern lamentation might have moved . *Rom. and Jul.* iii 2 120
And call thee back With twenty hundred thousand times more joy Than thou went'st forth in lamentation . iii 3 154
Lamented. Shall be lamented, pitied, and excused Of every hearer *Much Ado* iv 1 218
Whose loss of his most precious queen and children are even now to be afresh lamented . *W. Tale* iv 2 28
How she came to't bravely confessed and lamented by the king . v 2 93
It is very much lamented, Brutus, That you have no such mirrors as will turn Your hidden worthiness into your eye . *J. Cæsar* i 2 55
If there were no more women but Fulvia, then had you indeed a cut, and the case to be lamented . *Ant. and Cleo.* i 2 174
No less in pity than his glory which Brought them to be lamented . v 2 366
Lamentest. Cease to lament for that thou canst not help, And study help for that which thou lament'st . *T. G. of Ver.* iii 1 242
Lamenting some enforced chastity . *M. N. Dream* iii 1 205
With new lamenting ancient oversights . 2 *Hen. IV.* ii 3 47
How now, madam! Still lamenting and mourning for Suffolk's death? 2 *Hen. VI.* iv 4 22
But first I'll turn yon fellow in his grave; And then return lamenting to my love. Shine out, fair sun . *Richard III.* i 2 262
Drown the lamenting fool in sea-salt tears . *T. Andron.* iii 2 20
Hang his slender gilded wings, And buzz lamenting doings in the air . iii 2 62
Lamentings heard i' the air; strange screams of death . *Macbeth* ii 3 61
Triumphs for nothing and lamenting toys Is jollity for apes . *Cymbeline* iv 2 193
Laming. For feature, laming The shrine of Venus, or straight-pight Minerva . v 5 163
Lammas-tide. How long is it now To Lammas-tide?—A fortnight and odd days . *Rom. and Jul.* i 3 15
Lammas-eve. Come Lammas-eve at night shall she be fourteen . i 3 17; 21
Lamond. A Norman was't?—A Norman.—Upon my life, Lamond *Hamlet* iv 7 93
Lamp. Therefore take heed, As Hymen's lamps shall light you *Tempest* iv 1 23
I know not what use to put her to but to make a lamp of her *C. of Er.* iii 2 98
My wasting lamps some fading glimmer left, My dull deaf ears a little use . v 1 315
Ere twice in murk and occidental damp Moist Hesperus hath quench'd his sleepy lamp . *All's Well* ii 1 167
My oil-dried lamp and time-bewasted light Shall be extinct with age *Richard II.* i 3 221
Thou art the Knight of the Burning Lamp . 1 *Hen. IV.* iii 3 30
These eyes, like lamps whose wasting oil is spent, Wax dim . 1 *Hen. VI.* ii 5 8
Now are they but one lamp, one light, one sun . 3 *Hen. VI.* ii 1 31
To feed for aye her lamp and flames of love . *Troi. and Cres.* iii 2 167
In delay We waste our lights in vain, like lamps by day. *Rom. and Jul.* i 4 45
Her cheek would shame those stars, As daylight doth a lamp . ii 2 20
'Tis day, And yet dark night strangles the travelling lamp . *Macbeth* ii 4 7
He fishes, drinks, and wastes The lamps of night in revel *Ant. and Cleo.* i 4 5
Lamp. Ah, women, women, look, Our lamp is spent, it's out! Good sirs, take heart . *Ant. and Cleo.* iv 15 85
For a monument upon thy bones, And e'er-remaining lamps, the belching whale And humming water must o'erwhelm thy corpse *Pericles* iii 1 63
Lampass. Troubled with the lampass, infected with the fashions *T. of S.* iii 2 52
Lancaster. Old John of Gaunt, time-honour'd Lancaster . *Richard II.* i 1 1
My noble Lord of Lancaster, The honourable father to my foe . i 1 135
Harry of Hereford, Lancaster and Derby Am I . i 3 35; 100
How fares our noble uncle, Lancaster?—What comfort, man? . ii 1 71
Words, life and all, old Lancaster hath spent . ii 1 150
The Duke of Lancaster is dead.—And living too; for now his son is duke . ii 1 224
My message is to you.—My lord, my answer is—to Lancaster . ii 3 70
I was banish'd Hereford; But as I come, I come for Lancaster . ii 3 114
If that my cousin king be King of England, It must be granted I am Duke of Lancaster . ii 3 124
The devil take Henry of Lancaster and thee! Patience is stale . v 5 103
As oft as Lancaster Doth speak of you, his cheek looks pale . 1 *Hen. IV.* iii 1 8
Westmoreland set forth to-day; With him my son, Lord John of Lancaster . iii 2 171
Go bear this letter to Lord John of Lancaster, to my brother John . iii 3 219
He heard him swear and vow to God He came but to be Duke of Lancaster . iv 3 61
Nor claim no further than your new-fall'n right, The seat of Gaunt, dukedom of Lancaster: To this we swore our aid . v 1 45
Harry, withdraw thyself; thou bleed'st too much. Lord John of Lancaster, go you with him . v 4 3
Thou hast deceived me, Lancaster; I did not think thee lord of such a spirit . v 4 17
Then, brother John of Lancaster, to you This honourable bounty shall belong . v 5 25
The king hath won, and hath sent out A speedy power to encounter you, my lord, Under the conduct of young Lancaster . 2 *Hen. IV.* i 1 134
And, as I hear, is now going with some charge to the Lord John of Lancaster . i 2 73
Go bear this letter to my Lord of Lancaster; this to the prince . i 2 267
Five hundred horse Are march'd up to my lord of Lancaster . ii 1 187
Good my Lord of Lancaster, I am not here against your father's peace . iv 2 30
Look, look, here comes my John of Lancaster . v 5 226
Strong-fixed is the house of Lancaster And like a mountain . 1 *Hen. VI.* ii 5 102
Nor shall proud Lancaster usurp my right . 2 *Hen. VI.* i 1 244
Bear the arms of York, To grapple with the house of Lancaster . i 1 257
Duke of Clarence; next to whom Was John of Gaunt, the Duke of Lancaster . ii 2 14
Bolingbroke, Duke of Lancaster, The eldest son and heir of John of Gaunt . ii 2 21
The duke hath told the truth; Thus got the house of Lancaster the crown . ii 2 29
But I am not your king Till I be crown'd and that my sword be stain'd With heart-blood of the house of Lancaster . ii 2 66
The honourable blood of Lancaster Must not be shed by such a jaded groom . iv 1 51
That throne Which now the house of Lancaster usurps . 3 *Hen. VI.* i 1 23
Nor . . . The proudest he that holds up Lancaster Dares stir a wing . i 1 46
Be duke of Lancaster; let him be king.—He is both king and Duke of Lancaster . i 1 86
Henry of Lancaster, resign thy crown. What mutter you? . i 1 164
York and Lancaster are reconciled.—Accursed be he that seeks to make them foes! . i 1 204
By giving the house of Lancaster leave to breathe, It will outrun you, father . i 2 13
The king not privy to my drift, Nor any of the house of Lancaster . i 2 47
And now to London all the crew are gone, To frustrate both his oath and what beside May make against the house of Lancaster . ii 1 176
O Lancaster, I fear thy overthrow More than my body's parting with my soul! . ii 6 3
While life upholds this arm, This arm upholds the house of Lancaster . iii 3 107
O cheerful colours! see where Oxford comes!—Oxford, Oxford, for Lancaster! . v 1 59
I will not ruinate my father's house, Who gave his blood to lime the stones together, And set up Lancaster . v 1 85
That you might still have worn the petticoat, And ne'er have stol'n the breech from Lancaster . v 5 24
What, will the aspiring blood of Lancaster Sink in the ground? . v 6 61
Whilst I awhile obsequiously lament The untimely fall of virtuous Lancaster: Poor key-cold figure of a holy king! *Richard III.* i 2 4
Pale ashes of the house of Lancaster! Thou bloodless remnant! . i 2 6
You and your husband Grey Were factious for the house of Lancaster . i 3 128
Cited up a thousand fearful times, During the wars of York and Lancaster . i 4 15
Thou didst receive the holy sacrament, To fight in quarrel of the house of Lancaster . i 4 209
Thou offspring of the house of Lancaster, The wronged heirs of York do pray for thee: Good angels guard thy battle! . v 3 136
All this divided York and Lancaster, Divided in their dire division . v 5 27
Lance. If tall, a lance ill-headed . *Much Ado* iii 1 64
The armipotent Mars, of lances the almighty . *L. L. Lost* v 2 657
Now I see our lances are but straws, Our strength as weak *T. of Shrew* v 2 173
Their thimbles into armed gauntlets change, Their needles to lances *K. John* v 2 157
There shall your swords and lances arbitrate The swelling difference of your settled hate . *Richard II.* i 1 200
And with thy blessings steel my lance's point . i 3 74
Receive thy lance; and God defend the right! . i 3 101
Go bear this lance to Thomas, Duke of Norfolk . i 3 103
Turning your books to graves, your ink to blood, Your pens to lances 2 *Hen. IV.* iv 1 51
Above human thought Enacted wonders with his sword and lance 1 *Hen. VI.* i 1 122
Break a lance, And run a tilt at death within a chair . iii 2 50
A braver soldier never couched lance, A gentler heart did never sway . iii 2 134
Broach'd with the steely point of Clifford's lance . 3 *Hen. VI.* ii 3 16
Let fall thy lance: despair, and die! . *Richard III.* v 3 143
He'll say in Troy when he retires, The Grecian dames are sunburnt and not worth The splinter of a lance . *Troi. and Cres.* i 3 283
I'ld make a quarry With thousands of these quarter'd slaves, as high As I could pick my lance . *Coriolanus* i 1 204
Plate sin with gold, And the strong lance of justice hurtless breaks *Lear* iv 6 170
And turn our impress'd lances in our eyes Which do command them . v 3 50
But we do lance Diseases in our bodies . *Ant. and Cleo.* v 1 36

Lance. More charming With their own nobleness, which could have turn'd A distaff to a lance, gilded pale looks *Cymbeline* v 3 34
He appears To have practised more the whipstock than the lance *Pericles* ii 2 51
Lanced. Whose hand soever lanced their tender hearts, Thy head, all indirectly, gave direction *Richard III.* iv 4 224
He charges home My unprovided body, lanced mine arm *Lear* ii 1 54
Lanceth. Fell sorrow's tooth doth never rankle more Than when he bites, but lanceth not the sore *Richard II.* i 3 303
Land. I not doubt He came alive to land. No, no, he's gone *Tempest* ii 1 122
Contract, succession, Bourn, bound of land, tilth, vineyard ii 1 152
The sea mocks Our frustrate search on land iii 3 10
Leave your crisp channels and on this green land Answer your summons iv 1 130
I prophesied, if a gallows were on land, This fellow could not drown v 1 217
Now, blasphemy, That swear'st grace o'erboard, not an oath on shore? Hast thou no mouth by land? v 1 220
All that is mine I leave at thy dispose, My goods, my lands *T. G. of Ver.* ii 7 87
Money buys lands, and wives are sold by fate *Mer. Wives* v 5 246
This is the fairy land: O spite of spites! We talk with goblins, owls and sprites *Com. of Errors* ii 2 191
The ship is in her trim; the merry wind Blows fair from land iv 1 91
One that countermands The passages of alleys, creeks and narrow lands iv 2 38
Falleth like a crab on the face of terra, the soil, the land, the earth *L. L. Lost* iv 2 7
The gallants are at hand.—Whip to our tents, as roes run o'er land v 2 309
But I know When thou hast stolen away from fairy land *M. N. Dream* ii 1 65
Fogs; which falling in the land Have every pelting river made so proud ii 1 90
The fairy land buys not the child of me ii 1 122
And sail upon the land, To fetch me trifles, and return again ii 1 132
She gave me, and her fairy sent To bear him to my bower in fairy land iv 1 66
If thou dost shed One drop of Christian blood, thy lands and goods Are, by the laws of Venice, confiscate *Mer. of Venice* iv 1 310
Whose lands and revenues enrich the new duke *As Y. Like It* i 1 107
Thy lands and all things that thou dost call thine Worth seizure do we seize into our hands iii 1 9
Let my officers of such a nature Make an extent upon his house and lands iii 1 17
I fear you have sold your own lands to see other men's iv 1 23
And all their lands restored to them again That were with him exiled v 4 170
To one his lands withheld, and to the other A land itself at large v 4 174
You to your land and love and great allies v 4 195
Solely heir to all his lands and goods, Which I have better'd *T. of Shrew* ii 1 118
What dowry shall I have . . . ?—After my death the one half of my lands ii 1 122
For that dowry, I'll assure her of Her widowhood, be it that she survive me, In all my lands and leases whatsoever ii 1 126
Besides two thousand ducats by the year Of fruitful land ii 1 372
Two thousand ducats by the year of land! My land amounts not to so much in all ii 1 374
He is mine only son, and heir to the lands of me v 1 89
Commits his body To painful labour both by sea and land v 2 149
He that ears my land spares my team *All's Well* i 3 47
My love, more noble than the world, Prizes not quantity of dirty lands *T. Night* ii 4 85
Make your best haste, and go not Too far i' the land *W. Tale* iii 3 11
What ailest thou, man?—I have seen two such sights, by sea and by land! iii 3 85
And married a tinker's wife within a mile where my land and living lies iv 3 104
Your high self, The gracious mark o' the land, you have obscured iv 4 8
The lands and waters 'twixt your throne and his Measured to look upon you v 1 144
Heaven guard my mother's honour and my land! *K. John* i 1 70
Why, being younger born, Doth he lay claim to thine inheritance?—I know not why, except to get the land i 1 73
Sirrah, speak, What doth move you to claim your brother's land? i 1 91
Because he hath a half-face, like my father. With half that face would he have all my land i 1 93
Your brother did employ my father much,— Well, sir, by this you cannot get my land i 1 97
Upon his death-bed he by will bequeath'd His lands to me i 1 110
Let me have what is mine, My father's land, as was my father's will i 1 115
Your father's heir must have your father's land i 1 129
Hadst thou rather be a Faulconbridge And like thy brother, to enjoy thy land, Or the reputed son of Cœur-de-lion? i 1 135
Lord of thy presence and no land beside i 1 137
And, to his shape, were heir to all this land, Would I might never stir from off this place, I would give it every foot to have this face i 1 144
Wilt thou forsake thy fortune, Bequeath thy land to him, and follow me? i 1 149
Brother, take you my land, I'll take my chance i 1 151
My father gave me honour, yours gave land i 1 164
A foot of honour better than I was; But many a many foot of land the worse i 1 183
I have disclaim'd sir Robert and my land; Legitimation, name and all is gone i 1 247
That white-faced shore, Whose foot spurns back the ocean's roaring tides And coops from other lands her islanders ii 1 25
The adverse winds, . . . have given him time To land his legions ii 1 59
And all the unsettled humours of the land, Rash, inconsiderate ii 1 66
Fresh expectation troubled not the land With any long'd-for change iv 2 7
Never such a power For any foreign preparation Was levied in the body of a land iv 2 112
As I travell'd hither through the land, I find the people strangely fantasied iv 2 143
In the body of this fleshly land, This kingdom, this confine of blood iv 2 245
And heaven itself doth frown upon the land iv 3 159
And make fair weather in your blustering land v 1 21
Shall we, upon the footing of our land, Send fair-play orders? v 1 66
To grace the gentry of a land remote v 2 31
Acquainted me with interest to this land v 2 89
I, by the honour of my marriage-bed, After young Arthur, claim this land v 2 94
Happily may your sweet self put on The lineal state and glory of the land! v 7 102
That all the treasons for these eighteen years Complotted and contrived in this land Fetch from false Mowbray their first head and spring *Richard II.* i 1 96
Nor never by advised purpose meet To plot, contrive, or complot any ill 'Gainst us, our state, our subjects, or our land i 3 190
One of our souls had wander'd in the air, Banish'd this frail sepulchre of our flesh, As now our flesh is banish'd from this land i 3 197
For I will ride, As far as land will let me, by your side i 3 252
Or as a moat defensive to a house, Against the envy of less happier lands ii 1 49
This land of such dear souls, this dear dear land, Dear for her reputation ii 1 57
Incaged in so small a verge, The waste is no whit lesser than thy land ii 1 103
Land. Wert thou regent of the world, It were a shame to let this land by lease *Richard II.* ii 1 110
We seize into our hands His plate, his goods, his money and his lands ii 1 210
'Tis shame such wrongs are borne In him, a royal prince, and many moe Of noble blood in this declining land ii 1 240
Driven into despair an enemy's hope, Who strongly hath set footing in this land ii 2 48
Here am I left to underprop his land, Who, weak with age, cannot support myself ii 2 82
What a tide of woes Comes rushing on this woeful land at once! ii 2 99
I come, what lord you will, From the most gracious regent of this land ii 3 77
Covering your fearful land With hard bright steel and hearts harder iii 2 110
Our lands, our lives and all are Bolingbroke's, And nothing can we call our own but death iii 2 151
Let them go To ear the land that hath some hope to grow iii 2 212
Provided that my banishment repeal'd And lands restored again be freely granted iii 3 41
Such crimson tempest should bedrench The fresh green lap of fair King Richard's land iii 3 47
Every stride he makes upon my land Is dangerous treason iii 3 92
Our sighs and they shall lodge the summer corn, And make a dearth in this revolting land iii 3 163
When our sea-walled garden, the whole land, Is full of weeds iii 4 43
O, what pity is it That he had not so trimm'd and dress'd his land As we this garden! iii 4 56
Adding withal, how blest this land would be In this your cousin's death iv 1 18
And, though mine enemy, restored again To all his lands iv 1 89
And this land be call'd The field of Golgotha and dead men's skulls iv 1 143
Grievous crimes Committed by your person and your followers Against the state and profit of this land iv 1 225
Speak 'pardon' as 'tis current in our land v 3 123
Thy fierce hand Hath with the king's blood stain'd the king's own land v 5 111
Thou hast wrought A deed of slander with thy fatal hand Upon my head and all this famous land v 6 36
I'll make a voyage to the Holy Land, To wash this blood off v 6 49
This broil Brake off our business for the Holy Land *1 Hen. IV.* i 1 48
You may buy land now as cheap as stinking mackerel ii 4 394
It is known to many in our land by the name of pitch ii 4 454
Beyond the Severn shore, And all the fertile land within that bound iii 1 77
This river comes me cranking in, And cuts me from the best of all my land iii 1 99
I'll give thrice so much land To any well-deserving friend iii 1 137
The land is burning; Percy stands on high iii 3 227
Teaching his duteous land Audacious cruelty iv 3 44
The king hath drawn The special head of all the land together iv 4 28
Rebellion in this land shall lose his sway, Meeting the check of such another day v 5 41
He doth bestride a bleeding land, Gasping for life *2 Hen. IV.* i 1 207
And were these inward wars once out of hand, We would, dear lords, unto the Holy Land iii 1 108
And now has he land and beefs iii 2 352
He cannot so precisely weed this land As his misdoubts present occasion iv 1 205
This land, like an offensive wife That hath enraged him on to offer strokes iv 1 210
He hath, like lean, sterile and bare land, manured iv 3 129
And had a purpose now To lead out many to the Holy Land iv 5 211
It hath been prophesied to me many years, I should not die but in Jerusalem; Which vainly I supposed the Holy Land iv 5 239
Choose what office thou wilt in the land, 'tis thine v 3 130
For all the temporal lands which men devout By testament have given to the church Would they strip from us *Hen. V.* i 1 9
'No woman shall succeed in Salique land:' Which Salique land the French unjustly gloze To be the realm of France i 2 39
Faithfully affirm That the land Salique is in Germany i 2 44
Galling the gleaned land with hot assays i 2 151
For he is footed in this land already ii 4 143
O, for honour of our land, Let us not hang like roping icicles Upon our houses' thatch! iii 5 22
Bar Harry England, that sweeps through our land iii 5 48
So let him land, And solemnly see him set on to London v Prol 13
Lives, honours, lands and all hurry to loss *1 Hen. VI.* iv 3 53
Your grief, the common grief of all the land *2 Hen. VI.* i 1 77
His insolence is more intolerable Than all the princes in the land beside i 1 176
And, as we may, cherish Duke Humphrey's deeds, While they do tend the profit of the land.—So God help Warwick, as he loves the land! i 1 204
So York must sit and fret and bite his tongue, While his own lands are bargain'd for and sold i 1 231
For keeping my house, and lands, and wife and all, from me i 3 20
She vaunted 'mongst her minions t'other day, The very train of her worst wearing gown Was better worth than all my father's lands i 3 89
A fouler fact Did never traitor in the land commit i 3 177
I think I am thy married wife And thou a prince, protector of this land ii 4 29
I am Duke Humphrey's wife, And he a prince and ruler of the land ii 4 43
And equity exiled your highness' land iii 1 146
When the dusky sky began to rob My earnest-gaping sight of thy land's view, I took a costly jewel from my neck, A heart it was, bound in with diamonds, And threw it towards thy land iii 2 105
'Tis not the land I care for, wert thou thence iii 2 359
Lands, goods, horse, armour, any thing I have, Is his to use v 1 52
And ask the Lady Bona for thy queen: So shalt thou sinew both these lands together *3 Hen. VI.* ii 6 91
From Scotland am I stol'n, even of pure love, To greet mine own land with my wishful sight. No, Harry, Harry, 'tis no land of thine iii 1 14
Sir Richard Grey was slain, His lands then seized on by the conqueror: Her suit is now to repossess those lands iii 2 3
I'll warrant you all your lands, An if what pleases him shall pleasure you iii 2 21
'Twere pity they should lose their father's lands iii 2 31
To do them good, I would sustain some harm.—Then get your husband's lands iii 2 40
I'll tell you how these lands are to be got iii 2 42
Why, then, thy husband's lands I freely give thee iii 2 55
I'll undertake to land them on our coast iii 3 205
And that the people of this blessed land May not be punish'd with my thwarting stars iv 6 21
I make you both protectors of this land iv 6 41
It is more than needful Forthwith that Edward be pronounced a traitor, And all his lands and goods be confiscate iv 6 55
Of all my lands Is nothing left me but my body's length v 2 25
Woe to that land that's govern'd by a child! *Richard III.* ii 3 11
Then this land was famously enrich'd With politic grave counsel ii 3 19

Land. Were they to be ruled, and not to rule, This sickly land might solace as before . . . . *Richard III.* ii 3 30
Not for all this land Would I be guilty of so deep a sin . . . . iii 1 42
Amend that fault!—Else wherefore breathe I in a Christian land? iii 7 116
We heartily solicit Your gracious self to take on you the charge And kingly government of this your land . . . . . . iii 7 132
If not to bless us and the land withal, Yet to draw forth your noble ancestry From the corruption of abusing times . . . . . iii 7 197
Do, good my lord, lest all the land do rue it . . . . . . iii 7 222
The most arch act of piteous massacre That ever yet this land was guilty of . . . . iv 3 3
Without her, follows to this land and me, To thee, herself, and many a Christian soul, Death, desolation, ruin and decay . . . . iv 4 407
Thus far into the bowels of the land Have we march'd on . . v 2 3
You having lands, and blest with beauteous wives, They would restrain the one, distain the other . . . . v 3 321
Bretons; whom our fathers Have in their own land beaten, bobb'd v 3 334
Shall these enjoy our lands? lie with our wives? Ravish our daughters? v 3 336
Let them not live to taste this land's increase That would with treason wound this fair land's peace! . . . . v 5 38
A hand as fruitful as the land that feeds us . . . . *Hen. VIII.* i 3 56
Men Of singular integrity and learning, Yea, the elect o' the land . ii 4 60
By all the reverend fathers of the land And doctors learn'd . . ii 4 205
I persuade me, from her Will fall some blessing to this land . . iii 2 51
Thy ambition, Thou scarlet sin, robb'd this bewailing land . . . iii 2 255
Yes, that goodness Of gleaning all the land's wealth into one . . iii 2 284
To forfeit all your goods, lands, tenements, Chattels, and whatsoever iii 2 342
All the land knows that: However, yet there is no great breach . iv 1 105
A most arch heretic, a pestilence That does infect the land . . . v 1 46
Now promises Upon this land a thousand thousand blessings . . v 5 20
Beggar the estimation which you prized Richer than sea and land *T. and C.* ii 2 92
This Volumnia Is worth of consuls, senators, patricians, A city full; of tribunes, such as you, A sea and land full . . . *Coriolanus* v 4 58
Cast your nets; Happily you may catch her in the sea; Yet there's as little justice as at land . . . . *T. Andron.* iv 3 9
His land's put to their books . . . . *T. of Athens* i 2 206
All the lands thou hast Lie in a pitch'd field.—Ay, defiled land . i 2 231
Let all my land be sold.—'Tis all engaged, some forfeited and gone . ii 2 154
How goes our reckoning?—To Lacedæmon did my land extend . . ii 2 160
'Tis honour with most lands to be at odds . . . . . . iii 5 116
Crimes, like lands, Are not inherited . . . . v 4 37
He shall wear his crown by sea and land, In every place, save here *J. C.* i 3 87
The weird sisters, hand in hand, Posters of the sea and land . *Macbeth* i 3 33
What had he done, to make him fly the land? . . . . . . iv 2 1
Were I king, I should cut off the nobles for their lands . . . . iv 3 79
If thou couldst, doctor, cast The water of my land, find her disease . v 3 51
Tell me, he that knows, Why this same strict and most observant watch So nightly toils the subject of the land . . . . . *Hamlet* i 1 72
Did forfeit, with his life, all those his lands Which he stood seized of . i 1 88
To recover of us, by strong hand And terms compulsatory, those foresaid lands . . . . i 1 103
And the chief head Of this post-haste and romage in the land . . i 1 107
Importing the surrender of those lands Lost by his father . . . i 2 23
And hath shipped me intil the land, As if I had never been such . v 1 81
This fellow might be in's time a great buyer of land . . . . v 1 113
The very conveyances of his lands will hardly lie in this box . . . v 1 120
He hath much land, and fertile . . . . v 2 87
Legitimate Edgar, I must have your land . . . . . . *Lear* i 2 16
Let me, if not by birth, have lands by wit; All with me's meet . . i 2 199
Tell him, so much the rent of his land comes to: he will not believe a fool . . . . i 4 148
That lord that counsell'd thee To give away thy land, Come place him here by me . . . . i 4 155
Not in this land shall he remain uncaught; And found—dispatch. . ii 1 59
Of my land, Loyal and natural boy, I'll work the means To make thee capable . . . . ii 1 85
France spreads his banners in our noiseless land . . . . . . iv 2 56
For this business, It toucheth us, as France invades our land . . v 1 25
I am changed: I'll go sell all my land . . . . . . *Othello* i 3 388
Methinks the wind hath spoke aloud at land . . . . . . ii 1 5
I shall be furnish'd to inform you rightly Both what by sea and land I can be able To front this present time . . . *Ant. and Cleo.* i 4 78
What is his strength by land?—Great and increasing . . . . ii 2 164
We'll speak with thee at sea: at land, thou know'st How much we do o'er-count thee.—At land, indeed, Thou dost o'er-count me of my father's house . . . . ii 6 25
You have done well by water.—And you by land . . . . . . ii 6 90
It cannot be denied what I have done by land.—Nor what I have done by water . . . . ii 6 93
You have been a great thief by sea.—And you by land . . . . ii 6 97
We should have met you By sea and land; supplying every stage With an augmented greeting . . . . iii 6 54
No disgrace Shall fall you for refusing him at sea, Being prepared for land . . . . iii 7 41
Most worthy sir, you therein throw away The absolute soldiership you have by land . . . . iii 7 43
But if we fail, We then can do't at land . . . . iii 7 54
Canidius, Our nineteen legions thou shalt hold by land . . . . iii 7 59
You keep by land The legions and the horse whole, do you not? . . iii 7 71
Strike not by land; keep whole: provoke not battle, Till we have done at sea . . . . iii 8 3
The land bids me tread no more upon't; It is ashamed to bear me! . iii 11 1
Our force by land Hath nobly held; our sever'd navy too Have knit again iii 13 169
To-morrow, soldier, By sea and land I'll fight. . . . . . . iv 2 5
Would thou and those thy scars had once prevail'd To make me fight at land! . . . . iv 5 3
Their preparation is to-day by sea; We please them not by land . iv 10 2
Being charged, we will be still by land, Which, as I take't, we shall . iv 11 1
You have land enough of your own: but he added to your having; gave you some ground . . . . *Cymbeline* i 2 18
Hath nature given them eyes To see this vaulted arch, and the rich crop Of sea and land? . . . . i 6 34
That thou mayst stand, To enjoy thy banish'd lord and this great land! ii 1 70
The swiftest harts have posted you by land . . . . . . ii 4 27
Thinking to bar thee of succession, as Thou reft'st me of my lands . iii 3 103
If you are sick at sea, Or stomach-qualm'd at land, a dram of this Will drive away distemper . . . . iii 4 193
With hostile forces he'll o'erspread the land . . . . *Pericles* i 2 24
He'll fill this land with arms, And make pretence of wrong . . . i 2 90
He 'scaped the land, to perish at the sea . . . . i 3 29

Land. I marvel how the fishes live in the sea.—Why, as men do a-land *Pericles* ii 1 31
Such whales have I heard on o' the land, who never leave gaping till they've swallowed the whole parish . . . . ii 1 36
We would purge the land of these drones, that rob the bee of her honey ii 1 50
Land carack. He to-night hath boarded a land carack . . . *Othello* i 2 50
Land-damn. Would I knew the villain, I would land-damn him *W. Tale* ii 1 143
Landed. The king's son have I landed by himself . . . *Tempest* i 2 221
Who most strangely Upon this shore, where you were wreck'd, was landed . . . . v 1 161
Slender, though well landed, is an idiot . . . . . *Mer. Wives* iv 4 86
Cleomenes and Dion . . . are both landed, Hasting to the court *W. Tale* ii 3 196
We have landed in ill time: the skies look grimly And threaten present blusters . . . . iii 3 3
A landless knight makes thee a landed squire . . . . *K. John* i 1 177
Under whose conduct came those powers of France That thou for truth givest out are landed here? . . . . iv 2 130
Salisbury Is gone to meet the king, who lately landed . *Richard II.* iii 3 3
They are already, or quickly will be landed . . . . *3 Hen. VI.* iv 1 132
Richmond Is with a mighty power landed at Milford *Richard III.* iv 4 535
They've left their barge and landed; And hither make . *Hen. VIII.* i 4 54
Show him this letter: the army of France is landed . . . *Lear* iii 7 3
I told him of the army that was landed; He smiled at it . . . iv 2 4
You shall hear The legions now in Gallia sooner landed In our not-fearing Britain than have tidings Of any penny tribute paid . *Cymbeline* ii 4 18
The Roman legions, all from Gallia drawn, Are landed on your coast . iv 3 25
Land-fish. He's grown a very land-fish, languageless *Troi. and Cres.* iii 3 264
Landing. Upon her landing, Antony sent to her . . *Ant. and Cleo.* ii 2 224
Since my landing I have understood Your lord has betook himself to unknown travels, My message must return . . . . *Pericles* i 3 34
Landless. A landless knight makes thee a landed squire . . *K. John* i 1 177
Landlord of England art thou now, not king . . . *Richard II.* ii 1 113
Put yourself under his shrowd, The universal landlord . *Ant. and Cleo.* iii 13 72
Landmen. If to-morrow Our navy thrive, I have an absolute hope Our landmen will stand up . . . . iv 3 11
Land-rat. There be land-rats and water-rats . . . *Mer. of Venice* i 3 23
Land-service. And then for the land-service, to see how the bear tore out his shoulder-bone . . . . *W. Tale* iii 3 96
Advised by my learned counsel in the laws of this land-service *2 Hen. IV.* i 2 153
You have been a great thief by sea.—And you by land.—There I deny my land service . . . . *Ant. and Cleo.* ii 6 98
Land-thieves. There be land-rats and water-rats, water-thieves and land-thieves, I mean pirates . . . . *Mer. of Venice* i 3 24
Lane. Even such, they say, as stand in narrow lanes . *Richard II.* v 3 8
You four shall front them in the narrow lane . . . . *1 Hen. IV.* ii 2 63
Attended him on bridges, stood in lanes, Laid gifts before him . . iv 3 70
Three times did Richard make a lane to me . . . . *3 Hen. VI.* i 4 9
We have the advantage of the ground; The lane is guarded . *Cymbeline* v 2 12
And but the backs of Britons seen, all flying Through a strait lane . v 3 7
Where was this lane?—Close by the battle, ditch'd, and wall'd with turf v 3 13
Athwart the lane, He, with two striplings . . . . v 3 18
This was strange chance: A narrow lane, an old man, and two boys . v 3 52
Two boys, an old man twice a boy, a lane, Preserved the Britons . . v 3 57
Lane's end. I'll go with thee to the lane's end . . *Meas. for Meas.* iv 3 188
Every lane's end, every shop, . . . yields a careful man work *W. Tale* iv 4 700
Langage. Tu as été en Angleterre, et tu parles bien le langage *Hen. V.* iii 4 2
Langley. Famous Edmund Langley, Duke of York . . *1 Hen. VI.* ii 5 85
Son To Edmund Langley, Edward the Third's fifth son . *2 Hen. VI.* ii 2 46
Langton. Keep Stephen Langton, chosen archbishop Of Canterbury, from that holy see . . . . *K. John* iii 1 143
Language. You taught me language; and my profit on't Is, I know how to curse. The red plague rid you For learning me your language! *Tempest* i 2 363
My language! heavens! I am the best of them that speak this speech i 2 428
It is a sleepy language and thou speak'st Out of thy sleep . . . ii 1 211
Where the devil should he learn our language? . . . . . . ii 2 69
Open your mouth; here is that which will give language to you, cat ii 2 86
What, in metre?—In any proportion or in any language. *Meas. for Meas.* i 2 23
I have no tongue but one: gentle my lord, Let me entreat you speak the former language . . . . ii 4 140
There is not chastity enough in language Without offence to utter them *Much Ado* iv 1 98
They have been at a great feast of languages, and stolen the scraps *L. L. Lost* v 1 40
If they do speak our language, 'tis our will That some plain man recount their purposes . . . . v 2 175
Cunning in Greek, Latin, and other languages . . . *T. of Shrew* ii 1 82
They say, our French lack language to deny, If they demand *All's Well* ii 1 20
Is it not a language I speak?—A most harsh one . . . . . ii 3 197
When you sally upon him, speak what terrible language you will . . iv 1 3
Now he hath a smack of all neighbouring languages . . . . iv 1 18
Choughs' language, gabble enough, and good enough . . . . iv 1 22
And I shall lose my life for want of language . . . . . iv 1 77
Speaks three or four languages word for word without book . *T. Night* i 3 27
O thou thing! Which I'll not call a creature of thy place, Lest barbarism, making me the precedent, Should a like language use to all degrees . . . . *W. Tale* ii 1 85
You speak a language that I understand not . . . . iii 2 81
There was speech in their dumbness, language in their very gesture . v 2 15
The language I have learn'd these forty years, My native English, now I must forego . . . . *Richard II.* i 3 159
I can drink with any tinker in his own language during my life *1 Hen. IV.* ii 4 21
I will never be a truant, love, Till I have learn'd thy language . . iii 1 208
Upon my tongues continual slanders ride, The which in every language I pronounce, Stuffing the ears of men . . . . *2 Hen. IV.* Ind. 7
To gain the language, 'Tis needful that the most immodest word Be look'd upon and learn'd . . . . iv 4 69
None of the French upbraided or abused in disdainful language *Hen. V.* iii 6 118
For he is fierce and cannot brook hard language . . *2 Hen. VI.* iv 9 45
Even he escapes not Such a Language unmannerly . . . *Hen. VIII.* i 2 27
No Latin; I am not such a truant since my coming, As not to know the language I have lived in . . . . iii 1 44
Matter against him that for ever mars The honey of his language . . iii 2 22
He has strangled His language in his tears . . . . v 1 157
I shall remember this bold language.—Do. Remember your bold life too v 3 84
There's language in her eye, her cheek, her lip, Nay, her foot *T. and C.* iv 5 55
And is ill school'd In bolted language . . . . . *Coriolanus* iii 1 322
I pray, can you read any thing you see?—Ay, if I know the letters and the language. . . . . *Rom. and Jul.* i 2 64
Lips, let sour words go by and language end! . . . *T. of Athens* v 1 223

Language. But up to the mountains! This is not hunters' language *Cymbeline* iii 3 74
He did provoke me With language that would make me spurn the sea, If it could so roar to me . . . v 5 294
We commit no crime To use one language in each several clime *Pericles* iv 4 6
Languageless. He's grown a very land-fish, languageless *Troi. and Cres.* iii 3 264
Langues. O bon Dieu! les langues des hommes sont pleines de tromperies *Hen. V.* v 2 118
Languish. What thou seest when thou dost wake, Do it for thy true-love take, Love and languish for his sake *M. N. Dream* ii 2 29
To the which place a poor sequester'd stag, That from the hunter's aim had ta'en a hurt, Did come to languish *As Y. Like It* ii 1 35
What is it, my good lord, the king languishes of?—A fistula *All's Well* i 1 37
One desperate grief cures with another's languish *Rom. and Jul.* i 2 49
A suitor here, A man that languishes in your displeasure *Othello* iii 3 43
What, of death too, That rids our dogs of languish? *Ant. and Cleo.* v 2 42
Let her languish A drop of blood a day! *Cymbeline* i 1 156
To think that man, who knows By history, report, or his own proof, What woman is, yea, what she cannot choose But must be, will his free hours languish for Assured bondage? . . . i 6 72
Makes both my body pine and soul to languish *Pericles* i 2 31
Languished. Threw off his spirit, his appetite, his sleep, And downright languish'd *W. Tale* ii 3 17
Languishing. There is a remedy, approved, set down, To cure the desperate languishings whereof The king is render'd lost. *All's Well* i 3 235
Poisonous compounds, Which are the movers of a languishing death *Cymbeline* i 5 9
Languishment. A speedier course than lingering languishment Must we pursue, and I have found the path *T. Andron.* ii 1 110
Languor. In the dust I write My heart's deep languor . . . iii 1 13
Lank. The clergy's bags Are lank and lean with thy extortions 2 *Hen. VI.* i 3 132
About her lank and all o'er-teemed loins, A blanket *Hamlet* ii 2 531
Lanked. All this . . . Was borne so like a soldier, that thy cheek So much as lank'd not *Ant. and Cleo.* i 4 71
Lank-lean cheeks and war-worn coats *Hen. V.* iv Prol. 26
Lantern. And twenty glow-worms shall our lanterns be *Mer. Wives* v 5 82
Therefore bear you the lantern *Much Ado* iii 3 25
Lend me thy lantern, to see my gelding in the stable 1 *Hen. IV.* ii 1 38
Thou art our admiral, thou bearest the lantern in the poop . . . iii 3 29
God shall be my hope, My stay, my guide, and lantern to my feet 2 *Hen. VI.* ii 3 25
I'll bury thee in a triumphant grave; A grave? O, no! a lantern *Rom. and Jul.* v 3 84
Lanthorn. One must come in with a bush of thorns and a lanthorn, and say he comes to disfigure, or to present, the person of Moonshine *M. N. Dream* iii 1 61
This man, with lanthorn, dog, and bush of thorn, Presenteth Moonshine . . . v 1 136
This lanthorn doth the horned moon present; Myself the man i' the moon . . . v 1 248
The man should be put into the lanthorn. How is it else the man i' the moon? . . . v 1 251
All that I have to say, is, to tell you that the lanthorn is the moon . . . v 1 262
All these should be in the lanthorn; for all these are in the moon . . . v 1 265
Yet cannot he see, though he have his own lanthorn to light him 2 *Hen. IV.* i 2 55
Lap. They'll take suggestion as a cat laps milk *Tempest* ii 1 288
I will live in thy heart, die in thy lap, and be buried in thy eyes *Much Ado* v 2 104
Hoary-headed frosts Fall in the fresh lap of the crimson rose *M. N. Dream* ii 1 108
Such crimson tempest should bedrench The fresh green lap of fair King Richard's land *Richard II.* iii 3 47
Who are the violets now That strew the green lap of the new come spring? . . . v 2 47
And rest your gentle head upon her lap 1 *Hen. IV.* iii 1 215
Come, quick, quick, that I may lay my head in thy lap . . . iii 1 231
Then, Pistol, lay thy head in Furies' lap 2 *Hen. IV.* v 3 110
Now the time is come That France must vail her lofty-plumed crest And let her head fall into England's lap 1 *Hen. VI.* v 3 26
If I depart from thee, I cannot live; And in thy sight to die, what were it else But like a pleasant slumber in thy lap? 2 *Hen. VI.* iii 2 390
I'll make my heaven in a lady's lap 3 *Hen. VI.* iii 2 148
Frozen almost to death, how he did lap me Even in his own garments *Richard III.* ii 1 115
That dog, that had his teeth before his eyes, To worry lambs and lap their gentle blood . . . iv 4 50
Draw. O, well said, Lucius! Good boy, in Virgo's lap *T. Andron.* iv 3 64
Nor ope her lap to saint-seducing gold *Rom. and Jul.* i 1 220
Uncover, dogs, and lap *T. of Athens* iii 6 95
Whose blush doth thaw the consecrated snow That lies on Dian's lap! iv 3 387
A sailor's wife had chesnuts in her lap, And munch'd *Macbeth* i 3 4
Shall I lie in your lap?—No, my lord.—I mean, my head upon your lap? —Ay, my lord *Hamlet* iii 2 121
And pour our treasures into foreign laps *Othello* iv 3 89
That our stirring Can from the lap of Egypt's widow pluck The ne'er-lust-wearied Antony *Ant. and Cleo.* ii 1 37
Lapis. What is 'lapis,' William?—A stone.—And what is 'a stone,' William? —A pebble.—No, it is 'lapis' *Mer. Wives* iv 1 32
Lapland. And Lapland sorcerers inhabit here *Com. of Errors* iv 3 11
Lapped. Bellona's bridegroom, lapp'd in proof, Confronted him *Macbeth* i 2 54
He, sir, was lapp'd In a most curious mantle *Cymbeline* v 5 360
Lapse. Into the staggers and the careless lapse Of youth and ignorance *All's Well* ii 3 170
To lapse in fulness Is sorer than to lie for need *Cymbeline* iii 6 12
Lapsed. If I be lapsed in this place, I shall pay dear *T. Night* iii 3 36
Lapsed in time and passion, lets go by The important acting. *Hamlet* iii 4 107
Lapsing. All the size that verity Would without lapsing suffer *Coriolanus* v 2 19
Lapwing. With maids to seem the lapwing and to jest *Meas. for Meas.* i 4 32
Far from her nest the lapwing cries away *Com. of Errors* iv 2 27
Like a lapwing, runs Close by the ground *Much Ado* iii 1 24
This lapwing runs away with the shell on his head *Hamlet* v 2 193
Lard. Falstaff sweats to death, And lards the lean earth as he walks along 1 *Hen. IV.* ii 2 116
It is the pasture lards the rother's sides *T. of Athens* iv 3 12
Larded. The mirth whereof so larded with my matter *Mer. Wives* iv 6 14
Wit larded with malice and malice forced with wit *Troi. and Cres.* v 1 63
Larded with sweet flowers *Hamlet* iv 5 37
An exact command, Larded with many several sorts of reasons . . . v 2 20
Larder. Good master porter, I belong to the larder *Hen. VIII.* v 4 5
Larding. In which array, brave soldier, doth he lie, Larding the plain *Hen. V.* iv 6 8

Large. Confer at large Of all that may concern thy love-affairs *T. G. of V.* iii 1 253
Shall you have access Where you with Silvia may confer at large . . . iii 2 61
The image of the jest I'll show you here at large *Mer. Wives* iv 6 18
I long to know the truth hereof at large *Com. of Errors* iv 4 146
Go with us into the abbey here And hear at large discoursed all our fortunes . . . v 1 395
The man doth fear God, howsoever it seems not in him by some large jests he will make *Much Ado* ii 3 206
I never tempted her with any word too large . . . iv 1 53
So to the laws at large I write my name *L. L. Lost* i 1 156
The world's large tongue Proclaims you for a man replete with mocks . v 2 852
And kiss thy fair large ears, my gentle joy *M. N. Dream* iv 1 4
Let Lion, Moonshine, Wall, and lovers twain At large discourse . . . v 1 152
I must have liberty Withal, as large a charter as the wind *As Y. Like It* ii 7 48
A land itself at large, a potent dukedom . . . v 4 175
Your praises are too large *W. Tale* iv 4 147
Do you not read some tokens of my son In the large composition of this man? *K. John* i 1 88
Large lengths of seas and shores Between my father and my mother lay i 1 105
This little abstract doth contain that large Which died in Geffrey . . ii 1 101
Here's a large mouth, indeed, That spits forth death and mountains, rocks and seas! . . . ii 1 457
Thou dost consent In some large measure to thy father's death *Richard II.* i 2 26
They shall subscribe them for large sums of gold . . . i 4 50
I have dispatch'd With letters of your love to her at large . . . iii 1 41
And my large kingdom for a little grave, A little little grave . . . iii 3 153
The manner of their taking may appear At large discoursed in this paper v 6 10
If we can make our peace Upon such large terms and so absolute 2 *Hen. IV.* iv 1 186
The manner and true order of the fight This packet, please it you, contains at large . . . iv 4 101
Causes now in hand, Which I have open'd to his grace at large *Hen. V.* i 1 78
There we'll sit, Ruling in large and ample empery . . . i 2 226
Do not, in grant of all demands at large, Sweeten the bitter mock . . ii 4 121
The circumstance I'll tell you more at large 1 *Hen. VI.* i 1 109
O'ercharging your free purses with large fines . . . i 3 64
But we shall meet, and break our minds at large . . . i 3 81
His grim aspect, And large proportion of his strong-knit limbs . . . ii 3 21
Discover more at large what cause that was, For I am ignorant . . . ii 5 59
Proffers his only daughter . . . , with a large and sumptuous dowry . v 1 20
I have inform'd his highness so at large . . . v 1 42
Whose large style Agrees not with the leanness of his purse 2 *Hen. VI.* i 1 111
England's kings have had Large sums of gold and dowries with their wives i 1 129
As more at large your grace shall understand . . . ii 1 177
Large gifts have I bestow'd on learned clerks . . . iv 7 76
Doubt not of the day, And, that once gotten, doubt not of large pay 3 *Hen. VI.* iv 7 88
You sent a large commission To Gregory de Cassado *Hen. VIII.* iii 2 320
The large Achilles, on his press'd bed lolling *Troi. and Cres.* i 3 162
Fair leave and large security . . . i 3 223
The baby figure of the giant mass Of things to come at large . . . i 3 346
Whom, we know well, The world's large spaces cannot parallel . . . ii 2 162
And fell so roundly to a large confession, To angle for your thoughts . iii 2 161
Mine own searching eyes Shall find him by his large and portly size . iv 5 162
There will be large cicatrices to show the people *Coriolanus* ii 1 164
Throng our large temples with the shows of peace, And not our streets with war! . . . iii 3 36
Thou wouldst else have made thy tale large *Rom. and Jul.* ii 4 102
His large fortune Upon his good and gracious nature hanging *T. of Athens* i 1 55
While they have told their money and let out Their coin upon large interest, I myself Rich only in large hurts . . . iii 5 109
There's gold to pay thy soldiers: Make large confusion . . . iv 3 127
Sell the mighty space of our large honours For so much trash? *J. Cæsar* iv 3 25
Be large in mirth; anon we'll drink a measure The table round *Macbeth* iii 4 11
We shall not spend a large expense of time Before we reckon . . . v 8 60
He that made us with such large discourse *Hamlet* iv 4 36
Pre-eminence, and all the large effects That troop with majesty *Lear* i 1 133
Your large speeches may your deeds approve . . . i 1 187
He calls me to a restitution large Of gold and jewels *Othello* v 1 15
Most large In his abominations *Ant. and Cleo.* iii 6 93
You have at large received The danger of the task *Pericles* i 1 1
Let me entreat to know at large the cause Of your king's sorrow . . v 1 62
Large enough. My library Was dukedom large enough *Tempest* i 2 110
Have you nuns no farther privileges?—Are not these large enough? *Meas. for Meas.* i 4 2
Make this match; Give with our niece a dowry large enough *K. John* ii 1 469
Not all the whips of heaven are large enough *T. of Athens* v 1 64
Large-handed robbers your grave masters are, And pill by law . . . iv 1 11
Largely. Have given largely to many to know what she would have given *Mer. Wives* ii 2 207
I'll tell you largely of fair Hero's death *Much Ado* v 4 69
Our supplies live largely in the hope Of great Northumberland 2 *Hen. IV.* i 3 12
O, let those cities that of plenty's cup And her prosperities so largely taste, With their superfluous riots, hear these tears! *Pericles* i 4 53
Largeness. The ample proposition that hope makes In all designs begun on earth below Fails in the promised largeness *Troi. and Cres.* i 3 5
Larger. It lends . . . A larger dare to our great enterprise 1 *Hen. IV.* iv 1 78
And with a larger tether may he walk Than may be given you *Hamlet* i 3 125
I am to pray you not to strain my speech To grosser issues nor to larger reach Than to suspicion *Othello* iii 3 219
And what may follow, To try a larger fortune *Ant. and Cleo.* ii 6 34
The kings of Mede and Lycaonia, With a more larger list of sceptres . iii 6 76
Largess. I'll mend it with a largess *T. of Shrew* i 2 151
For our coffers, with too great a court And liberal largess, are grown somewhat light *Richard II.* i 4 44
A largess universal like the sun His liberal eye doth give to every one *Hen. V.* iv Prol. 43
The king's a-bed: He hath been in unusual pleasure, and Sent forth great largess to your offices *Macbeth* ii 1 14
Largest. That we our largest bounty may extend Where nature doth with merit challenge *Lear* i 1 53
Lark. And merry larks are ploughmen's clocks *L. L. Lost* v 2 914
More tuneable than lark to shepherd's ear *M. N. Dream* i 1 184
The finch, the sparrow, and the lark, The plain-song cuckoo gray . . iii 1 133
Attend, and mark: I do hear the morning lark . . . iv 1 99
The crow doth sing as sweetly as the lark When neither is attended *Mer. of Venice* v 1 102
Thou hast hawks will soar Above the morning lark *T. of Shrew* Ind. 2 46
Is the jay more precious than the lark, Because his feathers are more beautiful? Or is the adder better than the eel? . . . iv 3 177

Lark. My dial goes not true: I took this lark for a bunting . *All's Well* ii 5 7
The lark, that tirra-lyra chants . *W. Tale* iv 3 9
Night-owls shriek where mounting larks should sing . *Richard II.* iii 3 183
From the rising of the lark to the lodging of the lamb . *Hen. V.* iii 7 34
Stir with the lark to-morrow, gentle Norfolk . *Richard III.* v 3 56
With your theme, I could O'ermount the lark . *Hen. VIII.* ii 3 94
Let his grace go forward, And dare us with his cap like larks . iii 2 282
The busy day, Waked by the lark, hath roused the ribald crows *Troi. and Cres.* iv 2 9
'Tis true; the raven doth not hatch a lark . *T. Andron.* ii 3 149
Did ever raven sing so like a lark? . iii 1 158
It is not yet near day: It was the nightingale, and not the lark *R. and J.* iii 5 2
It was the lark, the herald of the morn, No nightingale . iii 5 6
That is not the lark, whose notes do beat The vaulty heaven so high . iii 5 21
It is the lark that sings so out of tune, Straining harsh discords . iii 5 27
Some say the lark makes sweet division; This doth not so, for she divideth us . iii 5 29
Some say the lark and loathed toad change eyes . iii 5 31
The shrill-gorged lark so far Cannot be seen or heard . *Lear* iv 6 58
The lark at heaven's gate sings, And Phœbus 'gins arise . *Cymbeline* ii 3 21
The night to the owl and morn to the lark less welcome . iii 6 94
Larron. O diable, diable! vat is in my closet? Villain! larron! *M. Wives* i 4 71
Lartius. Titus Lartius, thou Shalt see me once more strike at Tullus' face. What, art thou stiff? . *Coriolanus* i 1 243
Titus Lartius, a most valiant Roman . i 2 14
Your lord and Titus Lartius are set down before their city Corioli . i 3 110
The citizens of Corioli have issued, And given to Lartius and to Marcius battle . i 6 11
Flower of warriors, How is't with Titus Lartius? . i 6 33
You, Titus Lartius, Must to Corioli back: send us to Rome The best . i 9 75
Titus Lartius writes, they fought together, but Aufidius got off . ii 1 140
Having determined of the Volsces and To send for Titus Lartius . ii 2 42
'Larum. Dwelling in a continual 'larum of jealousy . *Mer. Wives* iii 5 73
Have I not in a pitched battle heard Loud 'larums? . *T. of Shrew* i 2 207
Then shall we hear their 'larum, and they ours . *Coriolanus* i 4 9
And with loud 'larums welcome them to Rome . *T. Andron.* i 1 147
'Larum-bell. And leavest the kingly couch A watch-case or a common 'larum-bell . 2 *Hen. IV.* iii 1 17
Lascivious. The loose encounters of lascivious men . *T. G. of Ver.* ii 7 41
I will find you twenty lascivious turtles ere one chaste man *Mer. Wives.* ii 1 82
I knew the young count to be a dangerous and lascivious boy *All's Well* iv 3 248
To beguile the supposition of that lascivious young boy the count . iv 3 333
Lascivious metres, to whose venom sound The open ear of youth doth always listen; Report of fashions *Richard II.* ii 1 19
Lascivious, wanton, more than well beseems A man of thy profession 1 *Hen. VI.* iii 1 19
Lascivious Edward, and thou perjured George. . 3 *Hen. VI.* v 5 34
He capers nimbly in a lady's chamber To the lascivious pleasing of a lute *Richard III.* i 1 13
And then they call'd me foul adulteress, Lascivious Goth *T. Andron.* ii 3 110
That's a lascivious apprehension *T. of Athens* i 1 211
Sound to this coward and lascivious town Our terrible approach . v 4 1
To the gross clasps of a lascivious Moor . *Othello* i 1 127
Antony, Leave thy lascivious wassails . *Ant. and Cleo.* i 4 56
Lash hence these overweening rags of France . *Richard III.* v 3 328
Her whip of cricket's bone, the lash of film *Rom. and Jul.* i 4 63
How smart a lash that speech doth give my conscience! *Hamlet* iii 1 50
Rascal beadle, hold thy bloody hand! Why dost thou lash that whore? *Lear* iv 6 165
Put in every honest hand a whip To lash the rascals naked through the world Even from the east to the west! *Othello* iv 2 143
Lashed. Headstrong liberty is lash'd with woe. . *Com. of Errors* ii 1 15
Lass. Is it so brave a lass? . *Tempest* iii 2 111
And lay my arms before the legs of this sweet lass of France . *L. L. Lost* v 2 558
It was a lover and his lass, With a hey, and a ho *As Y. Like It* v 3 17
Now will I lead you to the house, and show you The lass I spoke of *All's Well* iii 6 119
This is the prettiest low-born lass that ever Ran on the green-sward *W. T.* iv 4 156
Come buy, come buy; Buy, lads, or else your lasses cry iv 4 231
If your lass Interpretation should abuse and call this Your lack of love iv 4 363
Now boast thee, death, in thy possession lies A lass unparallel'd *A. and C.* v 2 319
Lass-lorn. Broom-groves, Whose shadow the dismissed bachelor loves, Being lass-lorn . *Tempest* iv 1 68
Last. Sit still, and hear the last of our sea-sorrow . i 2 170
My prime request, Which I do last pronounce, is, O you wonder! If you be maid? . i 2 426
I will stand to and feed, Although my last . iii 3 50
I have been in such a pickle since I saw you last . v 1 283
Too forward.—And yet I was last chidden for being too slow *T G. of Ver.* ii 1 12
Upon All-hallowmas last, a fortnight afore Michaelmas . *Mer. Wives* i 1 211
And last, as I am a gentleman, you shall, if you will, enjoy Ford's wife. ii 2 264
Mistress Overdone.—Hath she had any more than one husband?—Nine, sir; Overdone by the last.—Nine! *Meas. for Meas.* ii 1 212
O,—sixpence, that I had o' Wednesday last To pay the saddler *Com. of Er.* i 2 55
If I last in this service, you must case me in leather . ii 1 85
Belike you thought our love would last too long, If it were chain'd together . iv 1 25
Which of these sorrows is he subject to?—To none of these, except it be the last . v 1 55
O, grief hath changed me since you saw me last . v 1 297
Nay, then, give him another staff: this last was broke cross . *Much Ado* v 1 139
Although I seem so loath, I am the last that will last keep his oath *L. L. L.* i 1 161
That last is Biron, the merry mad-cap lord . ii 1 215
If frosts and fasts, hard lodging and thin weeds Nip not the gaudy blossoms of your love, But that it bear this trial and last love . v 2 813
It was play'd When I from Thebes came last a conqueror *M. N. Dream* v 1 51
You spit on me on Wednesday last . *Mer. of Venice* i 3 127
He had more hair of his tail than I have of my face when I last saw him ii 2 105
My nose fell a-bleeding on Black-Monday last at six o'clock . ii 5 25
At last, if promise last, I got a promise of this fair one here . iii 2 207
When last the young Orlando parted from you He left a promise to return again . *As Y. Like It* iv 3 99
When from the first to last betwixt us two Tears our recountments had most kindly bathed . iv 3 140
I pray you, sir, let him go while the humour lasts . *T. of Shrew* i 2 108
Where left we last?—Here, madam . iii 1 26
Happily I have arrived at the last Unto the wished haven of my bliss . v 1 130
At last, though long, our jarring notes agree . v 2 1
The last was the greatest, but that I have not ended yet *All's Well* iv 3 105
Such a ring as this, The last that e'er I took her leave at court, I saw . v 3 79

Last. That face of his I do remember well; Yet, when I saw it last, it was besmear'd As black as Vulcan in the smoke of war . *T. Night* v 1 55
'Tis far gone, When I shall gust it last . *W. Tale* i 2 219
This is not, no, Laid to thy answer: but the last,—O lords . iii 2 200
How often said, my dignity would last But till 'twere known! . iv 4 486
At the last, Do as the heavens have done, forget your evil . v 1 4
It is a surplus of your grace, which never My life may last to answer . v 3 8
We might behold, From first to last, the onset and retire . *K. John* ii 1 326
Last in the field, and almost lords of it! . v 5 8
Since last I went to France to fetch his queen . *Richard II.* i 1 131
But ere I last received the sacrament I did confess it . i 1 139
So I regreet The daintiest last, to make the end most sweet . i 3 68
Will the king come, that I may breathe my last In wholesome counsel? ii 1 1
His rash fierce blaze of riot cannot last, For violent fires soon burn out themselves; Small showers last long, but sudden storms are short ii 1 33
I am the last of noble Edward's sons . ii 1 171
Comes at the last and with a little pin Bores through his castle wall . iii 2 169
Doth not thy embassage belong to me, And am I last that knows it? O, thou think'st To serve me last, that I may longest keep Thy sorrow iii 4 94
Even here thou takest, As from my death-bed, thy last living leave . v 1 39
'Tis full three months since I did see him last . v 3 2
Thoughts tending to content flatter themselves That they are not the first of fortune's slaves, Nor shall not be the last . v 5 25
That thou soldest him on Good-Friday last for a cup of Madeira 1 *Hen. IV.* i 2 128
O villain! thy lips are scarce wiped since thou drunkest last. . ii 4 171
Whom I sent On Tuesday last to listen after news . 2 *Hen. IV.* i 1 29
But I am thrust upon it: well, I cannot last ever . i 2 240
As he said to me, 'twas no longer ago than Wednesday last . ii 4 94
First my fear; then my courtesy; last my speech . Epil. 1
The tenth of August last this dreadful lord, Retiring from the siege 1 *Hen. VI.* i 1 110
Of which, my lord, your honour is the last . ii 5 93
This late dissension . . . will at last break out into a flame . iii 1 191
Shall we at last conclude effeminate peace? . v 4 107
Ay, grief, I fear me, both at first and last . v 5 102
And would have kept so long as breath did last . 2 *Hen. VI.* i 1 211
We'll weed them all at last, And you yourself shall steer the happy helm i 3 102
The day of combat shall be the last of the next month . i 3 224
William of Windsor was the seventh and last . ii 2 17
If for the last, say ay, and to it, lords . 3 *Hen. VI.* ii 1 165
When you and I met at Saint Alban's last, Your legs did better service ii 2 103
Ten days' wonder at the least.—That's a day longer than a wonder lasts iii 2 114
And am I guerdon'd at the last with shame? . iii 3 191
Therefore at last I firmly am resolved You shall have aid . iii 3 219
At last by notes of household harmony They quite forget their loss of liberty . iv 6 14
Montague hath breathed his last; And to the latest gasp cried out for Warwick . v 2 40
I hope he is much grown since last I saw him . *Richard III.* ii 4 5
I tell thee, man, 'tis better with me now Than when I met thee last . iii 2 101
When I was last in Holborn, I saw good strawberries in your garden . iii 4 33
To speak, and to avoid the first, And then, in speaking, not to incur the last . iii 7 152
Shall they last, and we rejoice in them?—Still live they and for ever may they last! . iv 2 6
When last I was at Exeter, The mayor in courtesy show'd me the castle iv 2 106
And came I not at last to comfort you?—No, by the holy rood . iv 4 164
Be brief, lest that the process of thy kindness Last longer telling than thy kindness' date . iv 4 254
Say, I will love her everlastingly.—But how long shall that title 'ever' last?—Sweetly in force unto her fair life's end.—But how long fairly shall her sweet life last? . iv 4 350
The first was I that help'd thee to the crown; The last was I that felt thy tyranny . v 3 168
How have ye done Since last we saw in France? . *Hen. VIII.* i 1 2
Each following day Became the next day's master, till the last Made former wonders its . i 1 17
This last costly treaty, the interview, That swallow'd so much treasure i 1 165
Love thyself last: cherish those hearts that hate thee . iii 2 443
About the hour of eight, which he himself Foretold should be his last . iv 2 27
The last [petition] is, for my men; they are the poorest . iv 2 148
Make perforce an universal prey, And last eat up himself *Troi. and Cres.* i 3 124
Princes all, Lay negligent and loose regard upon him: I will come last iii 3 42
For this last, . . . let me say, I cannot speak him home *Coriolanus* ii 2 105
You had more beard when I last saw you . iv 3 8
This is the last: so we will home to Rome, And die among our neighbours v 3 172
Till, at the last, I seem'd his follower, not partner . v 6 38
The army marvell'd at it, and, in the last, When he had carried Rome . v 6 42
What faults he made before the last, I think Might have found easy fines v 6 64
I am his first-born son, That was the last that wore the imperial diadem of Rome . *T. Andron.* i 1 5
Upright he held it, lords, that held it last . i 1 200
And here display, at last, What God will have discover'd for revenge . iv 1 73
The last true duties of thy noble son . v 3 155
It is written, that the shoemaker should meddle with his yard, and the tailor with his last . *Rom. and Jul.* i 2 40
How long is't now since last yourself and I Were in a mask? . i 5 34
Our Romeo hath not been in bed to-night.—That last is true . ii 3 43
Let Romeo hence in haste, Else, when he's found, that hour is his last iii 1 200
Eyes, look your last! Arms, take your last embrace! . v 3 112
Where's the fool now?—He last asked the question . *T. of Athens* ii 2 60
I was the first man That e'er received gift from him: And does he think so backwardly of me now, That I'll requite it last? . iii 3 19
This is Timon's last . iii 6 100
And whilst this poor wealth lasts To entertain me as your steward . iv 3 495
Be Alcibiades your plague, you his, And last so long enough! . v 1 193
Though last, not least in love . *J. Cæsar* iii 1 189
Be patient till the last . iii 2 12
You know that you are Brutus that speak this, Or, by the gods, this speech were else your last . iv 3 14
The last of all the Romans, fare thee well! . v 3 99
On Tuesday last, A falcon, towering in her pride of place *Macbeth* ii 4 11
At first And last the hearty welcome . iii 4 2
When was it she last walked? . v 1 3
Yet I will try the last . v 8 32
And, to the last, bended their light on me *Hamlet* ii 1 100
My old friend! thy face is valanced since I saw thee last . ii 2 443
By'r lady, your ladyship is nearer to heaven than when I saw you last ii 2 446
Last, and as much containing as all these, Her brother is in secret come iv 5 87
A grave-maker: the houses that he makes last till doomsday . v 1 67

Last. He will last you some eight year or nine year: a tanner will last you nine year . . . . *Hamlet* v 1 183
Now, our joy, Although the last, not least . . . . . . *Lear* i 1 85
Who cover faults, at last shame them derides . . . . . . i 1 284
When saw you my father last?—Why, the night gone by . . . i 2 167
I ask'd his blessing, and from first to last Told him my pilgrimage . v 3 195
That policy may either last so long, Or feed upon such nice and waterish diet, Or breed itself so out of circumstance . . . *Othello* iii 3 14
Did Michael Cassio . . . Know of your love?—He did, from first to last iii 3 96
One more, and this the last: So sweet was ne'er so fatal . . . v 2 19
At the last, best . . . . *Ant. and Cleo.* i 3 61
Since I saw you last, There is a change upon you . . . . ii 6 53
But, first Or last, your fine Egyptian cookery Shall have the fame . ii 6 64
Know, that to-morrow the last of many battles We mean to fight . . iv 1 11
Go tell him I have slain myself; Say, that the last I spoke was 'Antony' iv 13 8
What thou wouldst do Is done unto thy hand: the last she spake Was 'Antony!' . . . . iv 14 29
I here importune death awhile, until Of many thousand kisses the poor last I lay upon thy lips . . . . iv 15 20
Bravest at the last, She levell'd at our purposes . . . . . v 2 338
Who was last with them?—A simple countryman . . . . . v 2 341
What was the last That he spake to thee?—It was his queen, his queen! *Cymbeline* i 3 4
A cunning thief, or a that way accomplished courtier, would hazard the winning both of first and last . . . . i 4 102
When last I went to visit her, She pray'd me to excuse her keeping close iii 5 45
Whilst summer lasts and I live here, Fidele, I'll sweeten thy sad grave iv 2 219
Sharp physic is the last . . . . *Pericles* i 1 72
The purple violets, and marigolds, Shall as a carpet hang upon thy grave, While summer-days do last . . . . iv 1 18
This man, Through whom the gods have shown their power; that can From first to last resolve you . . . . v 3 61
Led on by heaven, and crown'd with joy at last . . . . v 3 Gower 90
At last *Tempest* iv 1; *M. Ado* v 1; *Mer. of Ven.* iii 2: *T. of S.* iv 2; *Richard II.* iv 1; 2 *Hen. IV.* ii 2; 2 *Hen. VI.* i 2; 3 *Hen. VI.* v 2; *Hen. VIII.* iv 2; *Coriolanus* iii 3; *T. Andron.* i 1; *Hamlet* i 2; ii 1; *Pericles* ii 1; iii Gower
Last account. O, when the last account 'twixt heaven and earth Is to be made, then shall this hand and seal Witness against us to damnation! . . . . *K. John* iv 2 216
Last action. Am I not fallen away vilely since this last action? 1 *Hen. IV.* iii 3 2
Last article. She was mine, and not mine, twice or thrice in that last article . . . . *T. G. of Ver.* iii 1 365
If I do vow a friendship, I'll perform it To the last article . *Othello* iii 3 22
Last attempt. The man was noble, But with his last attempt he wiped it out . . . . *Coriolanus* v 3 146
Last boon. This, my last boon, give me . . . . . *Pericles* v 2 268
Last breath. In fine, made a groan of her last breath . . *All's Well* iv 3 62
Last breathing. My last breathing in this mortal world . 2 *Hen. VI.* i 2 21
Last company. God 'ild you for your last company . *As Y. Like It* iii 3 76
Last conference. This I made good to you In our last conference *Macbeth* iii 1 80
Last conflict. In our last conflict four of his five wits went halting off *Much Ado* i 1 66
How full of valour did he bear himself In the last conflict! *T. of Athens* iii 5 66
Last cry. They shouted thrice: what was the last cry for? . *J. Cæsar* i 2 226
Last day. Let the vile world end, And the premised flames of the last day Knit earth and heaven together! . . . . 2 *Hen. VI.* v 2 41
This last day was A shrewd one to's . . . . . . *Ant. and Cleo.* iv 9 4
Last draught. I think I have taken my last draught in this world 2 *Hen. VI.* ii 3 73
Last embrace. Arms, take your last embrace! . . . *Rom. and Jul.* v 3 113
Last enchantment. After the last enchantment you did here *T. Night* iii 1 123
Last encounter. At our last encounter, The Duke of Buckingham came from his trial . . . . *Hen. VIII.* iv 1 4
Last exercise. I am in your debt for your last excercise *Richard III.* iii 2 112
Last expedition. He had, before this last expedition, twenty-five wounds upon him . . . . *Coriolanus* ii 1 169
Last farewell. Bid him come to take his last farewell . *Rom. and Jul.* iii 2 143
Last fit. For I feel The last fit of my greatness . . *Hen. VIII.* iii 1 78
Last gasp. I will follow thee, To the last gasp, with truth and loyalty *As Y. Like It* ii 3 70
Fight till the last gasp . . . . 1 *Hen. VI.* i 2 127
His fortunes all lie speechless and his name Is at last gasp . *Cymbeline* i 5 53
Last general. The present consul, and last general . . . *Coriolanus* ii 2 47
Last gone. But Tuesday night last gone in 's garden-house He knew me as a wife . . . . *Meas. for Meas.* v 1 229
Last good deed. My last good deed was to entreat his stay . *W. Tale* i 2 97
Last hold. Legions of strange fantasies, Which, in their throng and press to that last hold, Confound themselves . . . . *K. John* v 7 19
Last hour. Thou but lead'st this fashion of thy malice To the last hour of act . . . . *Mer. of Venice* iv 1 19
The last hour Of my long weary life is come upon me . *Hen. VIII.* ii 1 132
Last king. That self bill is urged, Which in the eleventh year of the last king's reign Was like . . . . *Hen. V.* i 1 2
Our last king, Whose image even but now appear'd to us . *Hamlet* i 1 80
That day that our last king Hamlet overcame Fortinbras . . v 1 156
Last leave. The last leave of thee takes my weeping eye . *Richard II.* i 2 74
Last man. Your worship was the last man in our mouths *Mer. of Venice* i 3 61
We ready are to try our fortunes To the last man . 2 *Hen. IV.* iv 2 44
Last monarchy. Let higher Italy,—Those bated that inherit but the fall Of the last monarchy . . . . *All's Well* ii 1 14
Last morning you could not see to wipe my shoes . *T. G. of Ver.* ii 1 86
Last night she enjoined me to write some lines to one she loves . ii 1 93
Did see her, hear her, at that hour last night Talk with a ruffian *M. Ado* iv 1 91
Lady, were you her bedfellow last night?—No, truly not; although, until last night, I have this twelvemonth been her bedfellow . . . iv 1 149
The doctor's clerk, In lieu of this last night did lie with me *Mer. of Venice* v 1 262
Last night she slept not, nor to-night she shall not . *T. of Shrew* iv 1 201
He hence removed last night and with more haste Than is his use *All's W.* v 1 23
Inquire further after me; I had talk of you last night . . . v 2 56
In sooth, thou wast in very gracious fooling last night . *T. Night* ii 3 23
That old and antique song we heard last night . . . . ii 4 3
O, fellow, come, the song we had last night . . . . . ii 4 43
If such thing be, thy mother Appear'd to me last night . *W. Tale* iii 3 18
Letters came last night To a dear friend of the good Duke of York's *Richard II.* iii 4 69
I heard him tell it to one of his company last night at supper 1 *Hen. IV.* ii 1 62
He held me last night at least nine hours In reckoning up the several devils' names That were his lackeys . . . . iii 1 156
Where lay the king last night?—At Basingstoke . . . 2 *Hen. IV.* ii 1 181
Last night. A rascal that swaggered with me last night . . *Hen. V.* iv 7 131
Last night, I hear, they lay at Northampton . . . *Richard III.* ii 4 1
I do not jest with you; there came news from him last night *Coriolanus* i 3 104
You gave us the counterfeit fairly last night . . . *Rom. and Jul.* ii 4 48
The ghost of Cæsar hath appear'd to me Two several times by night; at Sardis once, And, this last night, here in Philippi fields . *J. Cæsar* v 5 19
I dreamt last night of the three weird sisters . . . . *Macbeth* ii 1 20
I believe drink gave thee the lie last night.—That it did, sir . . ii 3 41
Last night of all, When yond same star that's westward from the pole Had made his course . . . . *Hamlet* i 1 35
Strengthen your patience in our last night's speech . . . . v 1 317
I' the last night's storm I such a fellow saw . . . . *Lear* iv 1 34
Nor I know not Where I did lodge last night . . . . . iv 7 68
It was much like an argument that fell out last night . *Cymbeline* i 4 61
I do think I saw't this morning: confident I am Last night 'twas on mine arm . . . . ii 3 151
Last night the very gods show'd me a vision—I fast and pray'd . . iv 2 346
I am beholding to you For your sweet music this last night . *Pericles* ii 5 26
Last of December. Exceeds her as much in beauty as the first of May doth the last of December . . . . *Much Ado* i 1 194
Last offences. His last offences to us Shall have judicious hearing *Cor.* v 6 127
Last old man. This last old man, Whom with a crack'd heart I have sent to Rome, Loved me . . . . v 3 8
Last out. This will last out a night in Russia . . . *Meas. for Meas.* ii 1 139
Last penny. Take an inventory of all I have, To the last penny *Hen. VIII.* iii 2 452
Last purpose. Know of the duke if his last purpose hold . . *Lear* v 1 1
Last rain. Is't not drowned i' the last rain? . . *Meas. for Meas.* iii 2 51
Last refuge. Must I be his last refuge? . . . . *T. of Athens* iii 3 11
Last repeating. This act is as an ancient tale new told, And in the last repeating troublesome . . . . *K. John* iv 2 19
Last right. Urge the king To do me this last right . . *Hen. VIII.* iv 2 158
Last scene of all, That ends this strange eventful history *As Y. Like It* ii 7 163
Last served. What touches us ourself shall be last served . *J. Cæsar* iii 1 8
Last service. Your last service Did worthily perform . . *Tempest* iv 1 35
I serve here voluntary.—Your last service was sufferance *Troi. and Cres.* ii 1 104
'Tis the last service that I shall command you . *Ant. and Cleo.* iv 14 132
Last sickness. Had the king in his last sickness fail'd, The cardinal's and Sir Thomas Lovell's heads Should have gone off *Hen. VIII.* i 2 184
Last step. Till the last step have brought me to my love *T. G. of Ver.* ii 7 36
Last subsidy. He that made us pay one and twenty fifteens, and one shilling to the pound, the last subsidy . . . 2 *Hen. VI.* iv 7 25
Last surrender. This last surrender of his will but offend us . *Lear* i 1 309
Last swallowed. First mouthed, to be last swallowed . . *Hamlet* iv 2 20
Last syllable. To the last syllable of recorded time . . *Macbeth* v 5 21
Last taste. As the last taste of sweets, is sweetest last *Richard II.* ii 1 13
Last tempest. When did you lose your daughter?—In this last tempest *Tempest* v 1 153
Last thing he did, dear queen, He kiss'd,—the last of many doubled kisses,—This orient pearl . . . . . . *Ant. and Cleo.* i 5 39
Last time. And swears he was carried out, the last time he searched for him, in a basket . . . . *Mer. Wives* iv 2 32
I'll appoint my men to carry the basket again, to meet him at the door with it, as they did last time . . . . iv 2 98
Last time, I danced attendance on his will Till Paris was besieged 2 *Hen. VI.* i 3 174
Then is this The very last time we shall speak together . . *J. Cæsar* v 1 99
Last trumpet. She should in ground unsanctified have lodged Till the last trumpet . . . . *Hamlet* v 1 253
Last warmth. Take the last warmth of my lips . . *Ant. and Cleo.* v 2 294
Last work. Thou liest: look in thy last work . . . *T. of Athens* i 1 228
Last year. We will eat a last year's pippin . . . 2 *Hen. IV.* v 3 2
Lasted. He lasted long; But on us both did haggish age steal on And wore us out of act . . . . *All's Well* i 2 28
Here burns my candle out; ay, here it dies, Which, whiles it lasted, gave King Henry light . . . . 3 *Hen. VI.* ii 6 2
Lasting. And set it down With gold on lasting pillars . . *Tempest* v 1 208
Which she would keep fresh And lasting in her sad remembrance *T. Night* i 1 32
Might bespice a cup, To give mine enemy a lasting wink . *W. Tale* i 2 317
Arise forth from the couch of lasting night . . . . *K. John* iii 4 27
From the organ-pipe of frailty sings His soul and body to their lasting rest . . . . v 7 24
I am in parliament pledge for his truth And lasting fealty *Richard II.* v 2 45
Farewell sour annoy! For here, I hope, begins our lasting joy 3 *Hen. VI.* v 7 46
Which she shall purchase with still lasting war . . *Richard III.* iv 4 344
As sun and showers There had made a lasting spring . . *Hen. VIII.* iii 1 8
Do this, and purchase us thy lasting friends . . . *T. Andron.* ii 3 275
Unhappy, wretched, hateful day! Most miserable hour that e'er time saw In lasting labour of his pilgrimage! . . . *Rom. and Jul.* iv 5 45
Forward, not permanent, sweet, not lasting . . . . . *Hamlet* i 3 8
Both here and hence pursue me lasting strife, If, once a widow, ever I be wife! . . . . iii 2 232
This world to me is like a lasting storm, Whirring me from my friends *Pericles* iv 1 20
Lastly and finally . . . . *Mer. Wives* i 1 142
Sixth and lastly, they have belied a lady; thirdly, they have verified unjust things; and, to conclude, they are lying knaves . *Much Ado* v 1 221
Sixth and lastly, why they are committed . . . . . . v 1 227
Latch. If ever henceforth thou These rural latches to his entrance open *W. Tale* iv 4 449
I have words That would be howl'd out in the desert air, Where hearing should not latch them . . . . *Macbeth* iv 3 195
Latched. But hast thou yet latch'd the Athenian's eyes With the love-juice? . . . . *M. N. Dream* iii 2 36
Late. Help to celebrate A contract of true love; be not too late *Tempest* iv 1 133
Whether thou be'st he or no, Or some enchanted trifle to abuse me, As late I have been, I not know . . . . v 1 113
You the like loss!—As great to me as late . . . . . . v 1 145
Which of you saw Sir Eglamour of late? . . . . *T. G. of Ver.* v 2 32
To be up early and down late . . . . *Mer. Wives* i 4 108
Better three hours too soon than a minute too late . . . . . ii 2 328
Now doth thy honour stand, In him that was of late an heretic, As firm as faith . . . . iv 4 9
He's sentenced; 'tis too late . . .—Too late? why, no; I, that do speak a word, May call it back again . . . . *Meas. for Meas.* ii 2 57
You seem'd of late to make the law a tyrant . . . . . ii 4 114
I am a brother Of gracious order, late come from the See . . . iii 2 232
Who call'd here of late?—None, since the curfew rung . . . iv 2 77
Discord which of late Sprung from the rancorous outrage *Com. of Errors* i 1 5
Return'd so soon! rather approach'd too late . . . . . i 2 43

Late. Come, come, Antipholus, we dine too late *Com. of Errors* ii 2 221

Let my master in, Luce.—Faith, no; he comes too late iii 1 49

You have of late stood out against your brother *Much Ado* i 3 22

So you, to study now it is too late, Climb o'er the house to unlock the little gate.—Well, sit you out *L. L. Lost* i 1 108

A mess of Russians left us but of late v 2 361

Meeting her of late behind the wood, Seeking sweet favours *M. N. Dream* iv 1 53

He came too late, the ship was under sail *Mer. of Venice* ii 8 6

His losses, That have of late so huddled on his back iv 1 28

I do recant The pardon that I late pronounced here iv 1 392

Of late this duke Hath ta'en displeasure 'gainst his gentle niece *As Y. Like It* i 2 289

But at fourscore it is too late a week ii 3 74

Where is the life that late I led? *T. of Shrew* iv 1 143; *2 Hen. IV.* v 3 147

Better once than never, for never too late *T. of Shrew* v 1 155

I was very late more near her than I think she wished me *All's Well* i 3 110

I find that she, which late Was in my nobler thoughts most base, is now The praised of the king ii 3 177

Disgraces have of late knocked too often at my door iv 1 31

What would you have me to do? 'Tis too late to pare her nails now v 2 31

But love that comes too late, Like a remorseful pardon slowly carried, To the great sender turns a sour offence v 3 57

This ring was his of late.—And this was it I gave him v 3 227

He was a bachelor then.—And so is now, or was so very late *T. Night* i 2 30

I know not: but I know, to be up late is to be up late ii 3 5

I'll go burn some sack; 'tis too late to go to bed now ii 3 207

She did commend my yellow stockings of late ii 5 181

I saw thee late at the Count Orsino's iii 1 42

She is spread of late Into a goodly bulk *W. Tale* ii 1 19

A callat Of boundless tongue, who late hath beat her husband! ii 3 91

I have missingly noted, he is of late much retired from court iv 2 36

I was promised them against the feast; but they come not too late now iv 4 238

It is too late: the life of all his blood Is touch'd corruptibly *K. John* v 7 1

After our sentence plaining comes too late *Richard II.* i 3 175

Let's all go visit him: Pray God we may make haste, and come too late! i 4 64

That late broke from the Duke of Exeter ii 1 281

One day too late, I fear me, noble lord, Hath clouded all thy happy days on earth iii 2 67

To-day, to-day, unhappy day, too late, O'erthrows thy joys, friends iii 2 71

Be quiet; 'tis very late, i' faith *2 Hen. IV.* ii 4 175

It grows late; we'll to bed. Thou'lt forget me when I am gone ii 4 299

The mercy that was quick in us but late, By your own counsel is suppress'd *Hen. V.* ii 2 79

Late did he shine upon the English side; Now we are victors *1 Hen. VI.* i 2 3

Why didst thou say, of late thou wert despised? ii 5 42

The Duke of Gloucester's men, Forbidden late to carry any weapon iii 1 79

They that of late were daring with their scoffs Are glad and fain by flight to save themselves iii 2 113

It is too late; I cannot send them now iv 4 1

Within six hours they will be at his aid.—Too late comes rescue iv 4 42

Sat in the council-house Early and late, debating to and fro *2 Hen. VI.* i 1 91

How insolent of late he is become! iii 1 7

But now of late, not able to travel with her furred pack iv 2 50

The fearful French, whom you late vanquished, Should make a start iv 8 44

O boy, thy father gave thee life too soon, And hath bereft thee of thy life too late! *3 Hen. VI.* ii 5 93

Reason that I be released From giving aid which late I promised iii 3 148

Henry's late presaging prophecy Did glad my heart with hope iv 6 92

I'll sort occasion, As index to the story we late talk'd of *Richard III.* ii 2 149

Too late he died that might have kept that title iii 1 99

You come too late of our intents iii 5 69

We shall be late else; which I would not be, For I was spoke to *Hen. VIII.* i 3 65

Nor could Come pat betwixt too early and too late For any suit of pounds ii 3 84

All those things you have done of late, By your power legatine iii 2 338

That comfort comes too late iv 2 120

Good hour of night, Sir Thomas! Whither so late? v 1 6

Of late Heard many grievous, I do say, my lord, Grievous complaints of you v 1 97

I hope I am not too late; and yet the gentleman, That was sent to me from the council, pray'd me To make great haste v 2 1

What, am I poor of late? *Troi. and Cres.* iii 3 74

But in these fields of late, Made emulous missions 'mongst the gods themselves iii 3 188

For my own part, I came in late iv 2 55

How couldst thou in a mile confound an hour, And bring thy news so late? *Coriolanus* i 6 18

Come I too late?—Ay, if you come not in the blood of others i 6 27

And of late, When corn was given them gratis, you repined iii 1 42

Marcius, Whom late you have named for consul iii 1 196

This tiger-footed rage, when it shall find The harm of unscann'd swiftness, will too late Tie leaden pounds to's heels iii 1 313

Is this Menenius?—'Tis he, 'tis he: O, he is grown most kind of late iv 6 11

Then all too late I bring this fatal writ *T. Andron.* ii 3 264

Supper is done, and we shall come too late *Rom. and Jul.* i 4 105

Come on then, let's to bed. Ah, sirrah, by my fay, it waxes late i 5 128

Too early seen unknown, and known too late! i 5 141

Take the villain back again, That late thou gavest me iii 1 131

Hie you, make haste, for it grows very late iii 3 164

Give me thy hand; 'tis late: farewell; good night iii 3 172

'Tis very late, she'll not come down to-night iii 4 5

Tybalt being slain so late, It may be thought we held him carelessly iii 4 24

It is so very very late, That we may call it early by and by iii 4 34

Is it my lady mother? Is she not down so late, or up so early? iii 5 67

And hereabouts he dwells,—which late I noted In tatter'd weeds v 1 38

All those which were his fellows but of late *T. of Athens* i 1 78

And late, five thousand: to Varro and to Isidore He owes nine thousand ii 1 1

Though you hear now, too late—yet now's a time ii 2 152

I have but little gold of late iv 3 90

In whose breast Doubt and suspect, alas, are placed too late iv 3 519

We sin against our own estate, When we may profit meet, and come too late v 1 45

Hail, worthy Timon!—Our late noble master! v 1 58

I do observe you now of late *J. Cæsar* i 2 32

Vexed I am Of late with passions of some difference i 2 40

He is superstitious grown of late ii 1 195

He hath honour'd me of late; and I have bought Golden opinions *Macb.* i 7 32

Was it so late, friend, ere you went to bed, That you do lie so late? ii 3 24

Late. The right-valiant Banquo walk'd too late *Macbeth* iii 6 5

Men must not walk too late iii 6 7

Thinking by our late dear brother's death Our state to be disjoint *Hamlet* i 2 19

He hath very oft of late Given private time to you i 3 91

He hath, my lord, of late made many tenders Of his affection to me i 3 99

Have you given him any hard words of late? ii 1 107

I have of late—but wherefore I know not—lost all my mirth ii 2 307

A clout upon that head Where late the diadem stood ii 2 530

But, woe is me, you are so sick of late iii 2 173

It is the poison'd cup: it is too late v 2 303

The sight is dismal; And our affairs from England come too late v 2 379

I have perceived a most faint neglect of late *Lear* i 4 74

Methinks you are too much of late i' the frown i 4 208

Put away These dispositions, that of late transform you i 4 242

Woe, that too late repents,—O, sir, are you come? Is it your will? i 4 279

It pleased the king his master very late To strike at me ii 2 123

The very fellow that of late Display'd so saucily ii 4 40

He sought my life, But lately, very late iii 4 173

Come, sir, what letters had you late from France? iii 7 42

At her late being here She gave strange œillades and most speaking looks iv 5 24

When remedies are past, the griefs are ended By seeing the worst, which late on hopes depended *Othello* i 3 203

Being done, there is no pause.—But while I say one prayer!—It is too late v 2 83

He hath laid strange courtesies and great Of late upon me *Ant. and Cleo.* ii 2 158

I was of late as petty to his ends As is the morn-dew on the myrtle-leaf iii 12 8

Of late, when I cried 'Ho!' Like boys unto a muss, kings would start forth iii 13 90

There are, Of those that served Mark Antony but late, Enough to fetch him iv 1 13

I am come, I dread, too late iv 14 127

He purposed to his wife's sole son—a widow That late he married *Cymb.* i 1 6

She hath been reading late The tale of Tereus ii 2 44

I am glad I was up so late; for that's the reason I was up so early ii 3 37

Her doors lock'd? Not seen of late? iii 5 52

Now, sir, What have you dream'd of late of this war's purpose? iv 2 345

These mouths, who but of late, earth, sea, and air, Were all too little to content and please *Pericles* i 4 34

It is too late to talk of love; And that's the mark I know you level at ii 3 113

Late Advanced in time to great and high estate iv 4 13

Late ago. Pardon me, sweet one, even for the vows We made each other but so late ago *T. Night* v 1 222

Late ambassadors. Question your grace the late ambassadors *Hen. V.* ii 4 31

Late appeal. Here to make good the boisterous late appeal, Which then our leisure would not let us hear *Richard II.* i 1 4

Late-betrayed. In this late-betrayed town Great Cœur-de-lion's heart was buried *1 Hen. VI.* iii 2 82

Late business. If there be No great offence belongs to't, give your friend Some touch of your late business *Hen. VIII.* v 1 13

Late censure. Forgetting, like a good man, your late censure iii 1 64

Late commissioners. Who are the late commissioners? *Hen. V.* ii 2 61

Late court. Held a late court at Dunstable *Hen. VIII.* iv 1 27

Late days. Did you not of late days hear A buzzing of a separation? ii 1 147

As, of late days, our neighbours, The upper Germany, can dearly witness v 3 29

Late deceased. The thrice three Muses mourning for the death Of Learning, late deceased in beggary *M. N. Dream* v 1 53

The noble Duke of Bedford late deceased *1 Hen. VI.* iii 2 132

Our late-deceased emperor's sons *T. Andron.* i 1 184

Late decree. To dash our late decree in parliament *3 Hen. VI.* ii 1 118

Late demand. I have consider'd in my mind The late demand that you did sound me in *Richard III.* iv 2 87

Late despised. Your nephew, late despised Richard, comes *1 Hen. VI.* ii 5 36

Late dignities. For those of old, And the late dignities heap'd up to them, We rest your hermits *Macbeth* i 6 19

Late dissension. This late dissension grown betwixt the peers Burns under feigned ashes of forged love *1 Hen. VI.* iii 1 189

Late-disturbed. Like bubbles in a late-disturbed stream *1 Hen. IV.* ii 3 62

Late eclipses. These late eclipses in the sun and moon portend no good to us *Lear* i 2 112

Late edict. Our late edict shall strongly stand in force *L. L. Lost* i 1 11

Late entering. Where fame, late entering at his heedful ears, Hath placed thy beauty's image *3 Hen. VI.* iii 3 63

Late escape. And privy To this their late escape *W. Tale* ii 1 95

Late examples. It fits us then to be as provident As fear may teach us out of late examples *Hen. V.* ii 4 12

Late exploits. Thy late exploits done in the heart of France *2 Hen. VI.* i 1 196

Late footed. And what confederacy have you with the traitors Late footed in the kingdom? *Lear* iii 7 45

Late imprisonment. You were not the cause Of my Lord Hastings' late imprisonment *Richard III.* i 3 91

Late innovation. Their inhibition comes by the means of the late innovation *Hamlet* ii 2 347

Late king. Our late king, Richard, being infected, died *2 Hen. IV.* iv 1 58

For treason executed in our late king's days *1 Hen. VI.* ii 4 91

Late marriage. And the late marriage made of none effect *Hen. VIII.* iv 1 33

Late master. Hast any of thy late master's garments? *Cymbeline* iii 5 125

Late misfortune. Are you yet to learn What late misfortune is befall'n King Edward? *3 Hen. VI.* iv 4 3

Late offenders. Besides, the king hath wasted all his rods On late offenders *2 Hen. IV.* iv 1 216

Late overthrow. Hath the late overthrow wrought this offence? *1 Hen. VI.* i 2 49

Late queen. The late queen's gentlewoman, a knight's daughter *Hen. VIII.* iii 2 94

Late sovereign. That haughty prelate, Whom Henry, our late sovereign, ne'er could brook *1 Hen. VI.* i 3 24

Late tossing. How brooks your grace the air, After your late tossing on the breaking seas? *Richard II.* iii 2 3

Late voyage. All the good our English Have got by the late voyage is but merely A fit or two o' the face *Hen. VIII.* i 3 6

Late-walking. This is enough to be the decay of lust and late-walking *Mer. Wives* v 5 153

Lated. Now spurs the lated traveller apace To gain the timely inn *Macb.* iii 3 6

I am so lated in the world, that I Have lost my way for ever *A. and C.* iii 11 3

Lately. An islander, that hath lately suffered by a thunderbolt *Tempest* ii 2 38

I knew not what 'twas to be beaten till lately *Mer. Wives* v 1 28

For lately we were bound, as you are now *Com. of Errors* v 1 293

The gentleman That lately stole his daughter *Mer. of Venice* iv 1 385

Lately. That did but lately foil the sinewy Charles . . *As Y. Like It* ii 2 14
The king very lately spoke of him admiringly and mourningly *All's Well* i 1 33
Had you not lately an intent,—speak truly,—To go to Paris? . . . i 3 224
You were lately whipped, sir, as I think . . . . . . ii 2 52
Though lately we intended To keep in darkness what occasion now Reveals before 'tis ripe . . . . *T. Night* v 1 155
These hands, so lately purged of blood, So newly join'd in love *K. John* iii 1 239
Salisbury Is gone to meet the king, who lately landed . *Richard II.* iii 3 3
Did lately meet in the intestine shock . . . . *1 Hen. IV.* i 1 12
Whose daughter, as we hear, the Earl of March Hath lately married . i 3 85
Baited like eagles having lately bathed . . . . . . iv 1 99
A hundred and fifty tattered prodigals lately come from swine-keeping iv 2 37
There hath been a man or two lately killed about her . . *2 Hen. IV.* v 4 7
Be it known to you, as it is very well, I was lately here . . Epil. 9 124
Lately sending into France, Did claim some certain dukedoms *Hen. V.* i 2 246
For your brother, he was lately sent From your kind aunt . *3 Hen. VI.* ii 1 145
A riotous gentleman Lately attendant on the Duke of Norfolk *Rich. III.* ii 1 101
Your high-swoln hearts, But lately splinter'd, knit, and join'd together ii 2 118
Cardinal Campeius is arrived, and lately . . . . . *Hen. VIII.* ii 1 160
'Tis so lately alter'd, that the old name Is fresh about me . . iv 1 98
'Tis true that you have lately told us . . . . . *Coriolanus* i 1 231
Who art thou that lately didst descend Into this gaping hollow? *T. An.* ii 3 248
Juliet is alive, For whose dear sake thou wast but lately dead *R. and J.* iii 3 136
Ventidius lately Buried his father . . . . . *T. of Athens* ii 2 231
He sought my life, But lately, very late . . . . . *Lear* iii 4 173
I lay with Cassio lately . . . . *Othello* iii 3 413
Three thousand pounds, which by thee lately Is left untender'd *Cymb.* iii 1 9
I saw you lately, When you caught hurt in parting two that fought *Pericles* iv 1 87

Later. Therefore thy later vows against thy first Is in thyself rebellion to thyself . . . . *K. John* iii 1 288
And she goes down at twelve.—I take't, 'tis later, sir . . *Macbeth* ii 1 3

Latest. At the latest minute of the hour . . . *L. L. Lost* v 2 797
The latest breath that gave the sound of words Was deep-sworn faith *K. John* iii 1 230
The latest news we hear Is that the rebels have consumed with fire Our town of Cicester . . . . *Richard II.* v 6 1
Hear, I think, the very latest counsel That ever I shall breathe *2 Hen. IV.* iv 5 183
This is the latest parle we will admit . . . . . *Hen. V.* iii 3 2
This is the latest glory of thy praise . . . . *1 Hen. VI.* iv 2 33
Where your brave father breathed his latest gasp . . *3 Hen. VI.* ii 1 108
To the latest gasp cried out for Warwick . . . . . . v 2 41
Great Agamemnon, Nestor shall apply Thy latest words *Troi. and Cres.* i 3 33
Their latest refuge Was to send him . . . . . *Coriolanus* v 3 11
These that I bring unto their latest home, With burial . *T. Andron.* i 1 83
And let Andronicus Make this his latest farewell to their souls . i 1 149
Good fellows all, The latest of my wealth I'll share amongst you *T. of Athens* iv 2 23
Take him to follow thee, That did the latest service to my master *J. C.* v 5 67
To leave that latest which concerns him first . . . . *Othello* i 3 28

Lath. Who, with dagger of lath, In his rage and his wrath, Cries, ah, ha! to the devil . . . . *T. Night* iv 2 136
If I do not beat thee out of thy kingdom with a dagger of lath *1 Hen. IV.* ii 4 151
Come, and get thee a sword, though made of a lath . . *2 Hen. VI.* iv 2 2
Go to; have your lath glued within your sheath Till you know better how to handle it . . . . *T. Andron.* ii 1 41
We'll have no Cupid hoodwink'd with a scarf, Bearing a Tartar's painted bow of lath, Scaring the ladies . . . . . . *Rom. and Jul.* i 4 5

Latin. Ay, you spake in Latin then too . . . . *Mer. Wives* i 1 185
'Hang-hog' is Latin for bacon, I warrant you . . . . . iv 1 50
Remuneration! O, that's the Latin word for three farthings *L. L. Lost* iii 1 138
I smell false Latin; dunghill for unguem . . . . . . v 1 83
He hath neither Latin, French, nor Italian . . . *Mer. of Venice* i 2 75
Who ambles Time withal?—With a priest that lacks Latin *As Y. Like It* iii 2 337
Nay, 'tis no matter, sir, what he 'leges in Latin . . *T. of Shrew* i 2 29
Cunning in Greek, Latin, and other languages . . . . . ii 1 81
And thus in Latin, Præclarissimus filius noster Henricus . *Hen. V.* v 2 369
Away with him! he speaks Latin . . . . . *2 Hen. VI.* iv 7 63
O, good my lord, no Latin . . . . . . *Hen. VIII.* iii 1 42

Latten. I combat challenge of this latten bilbo . . *Mer. Wives* i 1 165

Latter. The latter end of his commonwealth forgets the beginning *Temp.* ii 1 157
At the latter end of a sea-coal fire . . . . . *Mer. Wives* i 4 9
Sweet Jude! nay, why dost thou stay?—For the latter end of his name *L. L. Lost* v 2 630
I will sing it in the latter end of a play . . . *M. N. Dream* iv 1 223
Bring your latter hazard back again . . . . *Mer. of Venice* i 1 151
The rarest argument of wonder that hath shot out in our latter times *All's Well* ii 3 8
A good traveller is something at the latter end of a dinner . . ii 5 31
Farewell, thou latter spring! farewell, All-hallown summer! *1 Hen. IV.* i 2 177
To the latter end of a fray and the beginning of a feast Fits a dull fighter and a keen guest . . . . iv 2 85
Is now alive To grace this latter age with noble deeds . . . . v 1 92
All those legs and arms and heads, chopped off in a battle, shall join together at the latter day . . . . *Hen. V.* iv 1 143
I shall catch the fly, your cousin, in the latter end. . . . . v 2 341
And in his bosom spend my latter gasp . . . . *1 Hen. VI.* ii 5 38
And in devotion spend my latter days, To sin's rebuke . *3 Hen. VI.* iv 6 43
These well express in thee thy latter spirits . . *T. of Athens* v 4 74
I will go seek Some ditch wherein to die; the fouls't best fits My latter part of life . . . . *Ant. and Cleo.* iv 6 39
You, born in these latter times, When wit's more ripe . *Pericles* 1 Gower 11
Virtue and cunning were endowments greater Than nobleness and riches: careless heirs May the two latter darken and expend . . iii 2 29

Latter-born. My wife, more careful for the latter-born *Com. of Errors* i 1 79

Lattice. So, my good window of lattice, fare thee well: thy casement I need not open . . . . *All's Well* ii 3 225

Laud. I laud them, I praise them . . . . . *1 Hen. IV.* iii 3 215
Laud be to God! even there my life must end . . . *2 Hen. IV.* iv 5 236
Give to dust that is a little gilt More laud than gilt o'er-dusted *T. and C.* iii 3 179
Laud we the gods . . . . *Cymbeline* v 5 476

Laudable. Redeem it by some laudable attempt . . *T. Night* iii 2 31
In this earthly world; where to do harm Is often laudable *Macbeth* iv 2 76

Laudis. Di faciant laudis summa sit ista tuæ! . . . *3 Hen. VI.* i 3 48

Laugh. Of such sensible and nimble lungs that they always use to laugh at nothing . . . . *Tempest* ii 1 175
So you may continue and laugh at nothing still.—What a blow! . . ii 1 178
Will you laugh me asleep, for I am very heavy? . . . . ii 1 188
I shall laugh myself to death at this puppy-headed monster . . ii 2 158

Laugh. I shall never laugh but in that maid's company! . *Mer. Wives* i 4 162
Detect my wife, be revenged on Falstaff, and laugh at Page . . . ii 2 326
We do not act that often jest and laugh . . . . . . iv 2 108
I will desire thee to laugh at my wife, that now laughs at thee . v 5 181
Let us every one go home, And laugh this sport o'er by a country fire . v 5 256
Angels weep; who, with our spleens, Would all themselves laugh mortal . . . . *Meas. for Meas.* ii 2 123
No longer will I be a fool, To put the finger in the eye and weep, Whilst man and master laugh my woes to scorn . *Com. of Errors* ii 2 207
O Lord, I must laugh! . . . . iii 1 50
Laugh when I am merry and claw no man in his humour . *Much Ado* i 3 18
Did he never make you laugh?—I pray you, what is he? . . ii 1 140
He both pleases men and angers them, and then they laugh at him and beat him . . . . ii 1 147
She would laugh me Out of myself, press me to death with wit . . iii 1 75
To hear meekly, sir, and to laugh moderately; or to forbear both *L. L. Lost* i 1 199
How will he triumph, leap and laugh at it! . . . . . iv 3 148
Nestor play at push-pin with the boys, And critic Timon laugh at idle toys! . . . . iv 3 170
That smiles his cheek in years and knows the trick To make my lady laugh . . . . v 2 466
And laugh upon the apple of her eye . . . . v 2 475
'Twere as easy For you to laugh and leap and say you are merry, Because you are not sad . . . . . . *Mer. of Venice* i 1 49
Peep through their eyes And laugh like parrots at a bag-piper . . i 1 53
When shall we laugh? say, when? You grow exceeding strange: must it be so? . . . . i 1 66
If you prick us, do we not bleed? if you tickle us, do we not laugh? . iii 1 68
The roynish clown, at whom so oft Your grace was wont to laugh *As Y. Like It* ii 2 9
I did laugh sans intermission An hour by his dial . . . . ii 7 32
And they that are most galled with my folly, They most must laugh . ii 7 51
I will laugh like a hyen, and that when thou art inclined to sleep . iv 1 156
The lusty horn Is not a thing to laugh to scorn . . . . . iv 2 19
You saw my master wink and laugh upon you? . . *T. of Shrew* iv 4 75
Will you . . . know her business? That done, laugh well at me *All's W.* ii 1 90
Unless you laugh and minister occasion to him, he is gagged *T. Night* i 5 93
If you desire the spleen, and will laugh yourselves into stitches, follow me iii 2 72
Madam, why laugh you at such a barren rascal? . . . . . v 1 383
Laugh at me, make their pastime at my sorrow: They should not laugh if I could reach them, nor Shall she within my power . *W. Tale* ii 3 24
Well, well, I see I talk but idly, and you laugh at me . *Richard II.* iii 3 171
Come out of that fat room, and lend me thy hand to laugh a little *1 Hen. IV.* ii 4 2
And gave his countenance, against his name, To laugh at gibing boys . iii 2 66
A man cannot make him laugh; but that's no marvel, he drinks no wine . . . . *2 Hen. IV.* iv 3 95
And a' shall laugh without intervallums . . . . . . v 1 90
You shall see him laugh till his face be like a wet cloak ill laid up! . v 1 94
His jest will savour but of shallow wit, When thousands weep more than did laugh at it . . . . *Hen. V.* i 2 296
I shall never move thee in French, unless it be to laugh at me . v 2 198
I laugh to see your ladyship so fond . . . . . *1 Hen. VI.* ii 3 45
It made me laugh to see the villain run . . . . *2 Hen. VI.* ii 1 155
The ruthless flint doth cut my tender feet, And when I start, the envious people laugh And bid me be advised how I tread . . . ii 4 35
The world may laugh again; And I may live to do you kindness . ii 4 82
I shall laugh at this a twelve-month hence . . . *Richard III.* iii 2 57
I come no more to make you laugh . . . . . *Hen. VIII.* Prol. 1
I cannot choose but laugh, to think how she tickled his chin *T. and C.* i 2 149
From his deep chest laughs out a loud applause . . . . i 3 163
I think they have swallowed one another: I would laugh at that miracle v 4 37
I could weep And I could laugh, I am light and heavy . *Coriolanus* ii 1 201
'Tis fond to wail inevitable strokes, As 'tis to laugh at 'em . . iv 1 27
The gods look down, and this unnatural scene They laugh at . . v 3 185
Why dost thou laugh? it fits not with this hour . . *T. Andron.* iii 1 266
Dost thou not laugh?—No, coz, I rather weep. . *Rom. and Jul.* i 1 189
I cannot choose but laugh, To think it should leave crying and say 'Ay' i 3 50
That kind of fruit As maids call medlars, when they laugh alone . ii 1 30
At lovers' perjuries, They say, Jove laughs . . . . . ii 2 93
That death in me at others' lives may laugh . . *T. of Athens* iv 3 381
For mine own part, I durst not laugh, for fear of opening my lips and receiving the bad air . . . . *J. Cæsar* i 2 251
He will live, and laugh at this hereafter . . . . . . ii 1 191
There's one did laugh in's sleep, and one cried 'Murder!' . *Macbeth* ii 2 23
Be bloody, bold, and resolute; laugh to scorn The power of man . . iv 1 79
Our castle's strength Will laugh a siege to scorn . . . . . v 5 3
But swords I smile at, weapons laugh to scorn . . . . . v 7 12
There was no such stuff in my thoughts.—Why did you laugh then? *Ham.* ii 2 326
The clown shall make those laugh whose lungs are tickle o' the sere . ii 2 337
Though it make the unskilful laugh, cannot but make the judicious grieve iii 2 29
Themselves laugh, to set on some quantity of barren spectators to laugh too . . . . iii 2 45
Paint an inch thick, to this favour she must come; make her laugh at that v 1 215
She that's a maid now, and laughs at my departure, Shall not be a maid long, unless things be cut shorter . . . . *Lear* i 5 55
Do not laugh at me; For, as I am a man, I think this lady To be my child Cordelia . . . . iv 7 68
Laugh At gilded butterflies, and hear poor rogues Talk of court news . v 3 12
These are old fond paradoxes to make fools laugh i' the alehouse *Othello* ii 1 140
Look, how he laughs already!—I never knew woman love man so . iv 1 110
Now he denies it faintly, and laughs it out . . . . . iv 1 113
Ha, ha, ha!—So, so, so, so: they laugh that win . . . . iv 1 125
Whom every thing becomes, to chide, to laugh, To weep *Ant. and Cleo.* i 1 49
Pompey doth this day laugh away his fortune.—If he do, sure, he cannot weep't back again . . . . ii 6 109
Make us Adore our errors; laugh at's, while we strut To our confusion iii 13 114
I have many other ways to die; meantime Laugh at his challenge . iv 1 6
You laugh when boys or women tell their dreams; Is't not your trick? v 2 74
He furnaces The thick sighs from him, whiles the jolly Briton—Your lord, I mean—laughs from's free lungs . . . . . *Cymbeline* i 6 68
Those that I reverence those I fear, the wise: At fools I laugh, not fear them . . . . iv 2 96
O, I am mock'd, And thou by some incensed god sent hither To make the world to laugh at me . . . . *Pericles* v 1 145

Laughable. Though Nestor swear the jest be laughable . *Mer. of Venice* i 1 56

Laughed. Use to laugh at nothing.—'Twas you we laughed at *Tempest* ii 1 176
You were wont, when you laughed, to crow like a cock . *T. G. of Ver.* ii 1 27
Better for you if it were known in counsel: you'll be laughed at *Mer. W.* i 1 122
Not marked or not laughed at, strikes him into melancholy *Much Ado* ii 1 154

Laughed. After he hath laughed at such shallow follies in others *M. Ado* ii 3 10
With that, all laugh'd and clapp'd him on the shoulder . . *L. L. Lost* v 2 107
We have laugh'd to see the sails conceive . . . *M. N. Dream* ii 1 128
Laughed at my losses, mocked at my gains, scorned my nation *M. of V.* iii 1 57
He asked me of what parentage I was; I told him, of as good as he; so he laughed and let me go . . . . *As Y. Like It* iii 4 41
A fond and desperate creature, Whom sometime I have laugh'd with *All's Well* v 3 179
Crown'd the gracious duke in high despite, Laugh'd in his face *3 Hen. VI.* ii 1 60
Wear away The lag end of their lewdness and be laugh'd at . *Hen. VIII.* i 3 35
Is this your comfort? The cordial that ye bring a wretched lady, A woman lost among ye, laugh'd at, scorn'd? . . . iii 1 107
Queen Hecuba laughed that her eyes ran o'er . *Troi. and Cres.* i 2 157
And Cassandra laughed.—But there was more temperate fire . . i 2 159
And Hector laughed.—At what was all this laughing? . . . i 2 162
An't had been a green hair, I should have laughed too.—They laughed not so much at the hair as at his pretty answer . . . i 2 167
And Paris so chafed, and all the rest so laughed, that it passed . . i 2 181
Wouldst thou have laugh'd had I come coffin'd home, That weep'st to see me triumph? . . . . . . *Coriolanus* ii 1 193
She laugh'd, and told the Moor he should not choose . *T. Andron.* iv 3 74
Laugh'd so heartily, That both mine eyes were rainy . . . v 1 116
Let me know some cause, Lest I be laugh'd at . . . *J. Cæsar* ii 2 70
Did you perceive how he laughed at his vice? . . . . *Othello* iv 1 180
I must be laugh'd at, If, or for nothing or a little, I Should say myself offended, and with you Chiefly i' the world; more laugh'd at, that I should Once name you derogately . . . . *Ant. and Cleo.* ii 2 30
That time,—O times!—I laughed him out of patience; and that night I laugh'd him into patience . . . . . . ii 5 19
Howsoe'er 'tis strange, Or that the negligence may well be laugh'd at, Yet is it true, sir.—I do well believe you . . . . *Cymbeline* i 1 66
Thus smiling, as some fly had tickled slumber, Not as death's dart, being laugh'd at . . . . iv 2 211
Laugher. Were I a common laugher, or did use To stale with ordinary oaths my love To every new protester . . . *J. Cæsar* i 2 72
Laughest thou, wretch? thy mirth shall turn to moan . . *1 Hen. VI.* ii 3 44
Thou antic death, which laugh'st us here to scorn . . . . iv 7 18
Laughing. And waked herself with laughing . . . . *Much Ado* ii 1 361
How now! interjections? Why, then, some be of laughing, as, ah, ha, he! iv 1 23
That loose grace Which shallow laughing hearers give to fools *L. L. Lost* v 2 870
Mislead night-wanderers, laughing at their harm . *M. N. Dream* ii 1 39
They say you are a melancholy fellow.—I am so; I do love it better than laughing . . . . . . *As Y. Like It* iv 1 4
Went they not quickly, I should die with laughing . . *T. of Shrew* iii 2 243
Were't not for laughing, I should pity him . . . *1 Hen. IV.* ii 2 117
And let another half stand laughing by, All out of work . *Hen. V.* i 2 113
With envious looks, laughing at thy shame . . . *2 Hen. VI.* ii 4 12
But there was such laughing! . . . . *Troi. and Cres.* i 2 156; 180
At what was all this laughing?—Marry, at the white hair that Helen spied on Troilus' chin . . . . i 2 163
Strange times, that weep with laughing, not with weeping! *T. of Athens* iv 3 493
Till the worst of all follow him laughing to his grave! *Ant. and Cleo.* i 2 69
Laughing-stock. Pray you, let us not be laughing-stocks to other men's humours . . . . *Mer. Wives* iii 1 88
Laughter. Done. The wager?—A laughter.—A match! . . *Tempest* ii 1 33
By virtue, thou enforcest laughter . . . . *L. L. Lost* iii 1 76
O, I am stabb'd with laughter! . . . . v 2 80
They all did tumble on the ground, With such a zealous laughter . . v 2 116
To move wild laughter in the throat of death? It cannot be . . v 2 865
More merry tears The passion of loud laughter never shed *M. N. Dream* v 1 70
With mirth and laughter let old wrinkles come . *Mer. of Venice* i 1 80
How my men will stay themselves from laughter When they do homage to this simple peasant . . . . . . *T. of Shrew* Ind. 1 134
Even to the world's pleasure and the increase of laughter . *All's Well* ii 4 38
For the love of laughter, hinder not the honour of his design . . iii 6 44
What is love? 'tis not hereafter; Present mirth hath present laughter *T. N.* ii 3 49
May rather pluck on laughter than revenge . . . . v 1 374
Stopping the career Of laughter with a sigh . . . *W. Tale* i 2 287
This business Will raise us all.—To laughter, as I take it . . ii 1 198
Making that idiot, laughter, keep men's eyes And strain their cheeks *K. John* iii 3 45
It would be argument for a week, laughter for a month . . *1 Hen. IV.* ii 2 101
The brain of this foolish-compounded clay, man, is not able to invent any thing that tends to laughter . . . . . . *2 Hen. IV.* i 2 10
In continual laughter the wearing out of six fashions, which is four terms v 1 89
Scratches with briers, Scars to move laughter only. . *Coriolanus* iii 3 52
And almost broke my heart with extreme laughter . . *T. Andron.* v 1 113
It may prove an argument of laughter To the rest . *T. of Athens* iii 3 20
Thou art a woman, and disclaim'st Flinty mankind; whose eyes do never give But thorough lust and laughter . . . . . iv 3 492
I'll use you for my mirth, yea, for my laughter, When you are waspish *J. Cæsar* iv 3 49
Hath Cassius lived To be but mirth and laughter to his Brutus? . . iv 3 114
Turn all her mother's pains and benefits To laughter and contempt *Lear* i 4 309
The lamentable change is from the best; The worst returns to laughter iv 1 6
He, when he hears of her, cannot refrain From the excess of laughter *Oth.* iv 1 100
With his eyes in flood with laughter . . . . . *Cymbeline* i 6 74
Launce. All the kind of the Launces have this very fault *T. G. of Ver.* ii 3 2
Launce, away, away, aboard! thy master is shipped and thou art to post after . . . . ii 3 36
Launce! by mine honesty, welcome to Milan!—Forswear not thyself . ii 5 1
Launce, how sayest thou, that my master is become a notable lover? . ii 5 42
Signior Launce! what news with your mastership?—With my master's ship? . . . . iii 1 279
I tell you what Launce, his man, told me: he loved her out of all nick iv 2 75
Where is Launce?—Gone to seek his dog . . . . . . iv 2 77
Launcelot. The fiend is at mine elbow and tempts me saying to me, 'Gobbo, Launcelot Gobbo, good Launcelot' . . *Mer. of Venice* ii 2 4
'Honest Gobbo,' or, as aforesaid, 'honest Launcelot Gobbo; do not run' ii 2 9
My honest friend Launcelot, being an honest man's son . . . . ii 2 15
My conscience says 'Launcelot, budge not.' 'Budge,' says the fiend ii 2 19
Can you tell me whether one Launcelot, that dwells with him, dwell with him or no? . . . . ii 2 48
Let his father be what a' will, we talk of young Master Launcelot . ii 2 57
Ergo, old man, ergo, I beseech you, talk you of young Master Launcelot? ii 2 60
I am sure you are not Launcelot, my boy . . . . . ii 2 87
I am Launcelot, your boy that was, your son that is . . . ii 2 89
I am Launcelot, the Jew's man, and I am sure Margery your wife is my mother.—Her name is Margery, indeed . . . . . ii 2 94
If thou be Launcelot, thou art mine own flesh and blood . . . ii 2 97
Launcelot. And, Launcelot, soon at supper shalt thou see Lorenzo *Mer. of Venice* ii 3 5
I'll tell my husband, Launcelot, what you say: here he comes.—I shall grow jealous of you shortly, Launcelot, if you thus get my wife into corners . . . . iii 5 32
Launcelot and I are out. He tells me flatly, there is no mercy for me . iii 5 34
Launched. Why, she is a pearl, Whose price hath launch'd above a thousand ships . . . . . . *Troi. and Cres.* ii 2 82
Laund. Through this laund anon the deer will come . *3 Hen. VI.* iii 1 2
Laundress. Carry them to the laundress in Datchet-mead *Mer. Wives* iii 3 157
Whither bear you this?—To the laundress, forsooth . . . . iii 3 163
Laundry. His cook, or his laundry, his washer, and his wringer . . i 2 5
Laura to his lady was but a kitchen-wench . . . *Rom. and Jul.* ii 4 41
Laurel. To whom the heavens in thy nativity Adjudged an olive branch and laurel crown . . . . *3 Hen. VI.* iv 6 34
Crowns, sceptres, laurels, But by degree, stand in authentic place *T. and C.* i 3 107
Cometh Andronicus, bound with laurel boughs . . . *T. Andron.* i 1 74
Upon your sword Sit laurel victory! . . . . *Ant. and Cleo.* i 3 100
Laurence. Friar Laurence met them both, As he in penance wander'd through the forest . . . . *T. G. of Ver.* v 2 37
She shall at Friar Laurence' cell Be shrived and married *Rom. and Jul.* ii 4 193
Hie you hence to Friar Laurence' cell; There stays a husband . . ii 5 70
Romeo will be here at night: I'll to him; he is hid at Laurence' cell . iii 2 141
Tell my lady I am gone, Having displeased my father, to Laurence' cell iii 5 232
What, is my daughter gone to Friar Laurence? . . . . iv 2 11
And am enjoin'd By holy Laurence to fall prostrate here . . . iv 2 20
I met the youthful lord at Laurence' cell. . . . . . iv 2 25
Laus Deo, bene intelligo . . . . *L. L. Lost* v 1 30
Lavache. Monsieur Lavache, give my Lord Lafeu this letter . *All's Well* v 2 1
Lave. Basins and ewers to lave her dainty hands . . *T. of Shrew* ii 1 350
For all the water in the ocean Can never turn the swan's black legs to white, Although she lave them hourly in the flood . *T. Andron.* iv 2 103
Unsafe the while, that we Must lave our honours in these flattering streams . . . . *Macbeth* iii 2 33
Lavée. Le chien est retourné à son propre vomissement, et la truie lavée au bourbier . . . . *Hen. V.* iii 7 69
Lavender. Here's flowers for you; Hot lavender, mints . . *W. Tale* iv 4 104
Lavinia. Gracious Lavinia, Rome's rich ornament . . *T. Andron.* i 1 52
Lavinia, live; outlive thy father's days, And fame's eternal date! . . i 1 167
Lavinia will I make my empress, Rome's royal mistress, mistress of my heart . . . . i 1 240
Lavinia, you are not displeased with this?—Not I, my lord . . . i 1 270
Treason, my lord! Lavinia is surprised!—Surprised! by whom? . . i 1 284
Restore Lavinia to the emperor.—Dead, if you will; but not to be his wife . . . . i 1 296
His noble nephew here . . . , That died in honour and Lavinia's cause . i 1 377
In the rescue of Lavinia With his own hand did slay his youngest son . i 1 417
Fear not, lords, and you, Lavinia . . . . i 1 471
Lavinia, though you left me like a churl, I found a friend . . . i 1 486
You are my guest, Lavinia, and your friends . . . . . i 1 490
And plead my passions for Lavinia's love . . . . . . ii 1 36
What, is Lavinia then become so loose, Or Bassianus so degenerate? . ii 1 65
I love Lavinia more than all the world . . . . . . ii 1 72
Make some meaner choice: Lavinia is thine elder brother's hope . . ii 1 74
She is a woman, therefore may be won; She is Lavinia, therefore must be loved . . . . ii 1 84
Lucrece was not more chaste Than this Lavinia, Bassianus' love . . ii 1 109
Serve your lusts, shadow'd from heaven's eye, And revel in Lavinia's treasury . . . . ii 1 131
Somewhat too early for new-married ladies.—Lavinia, how say you? . ii 2 16
Speak, Lavinia, What accursed hand Hath made thee handless? . . iii 1 66
'Tis well, Lavinia, that thou hast no hands; For hands, to do Rome service, are but vain . . . . iii 1 79
But that which gives my soul the greatest spurn, Is dear Lavinia . . iii 1 102
Gentle Lavinia, let me kiss thy lips; Or make some sign . . . iii 1 120
Ah, my Lavinia, I will wipe thy cheeks . . . . . . iii 1 142
Lavinia, thou shalt be employ'd: these arms! Bear thou my hand, sweet wench, between thy teeth . . . . iii 1 282
Farewell, Lavinia, my noble sister; O, would thou wert as thou tofore hast been! But now nor Lucius nor Lavinia lives But in oblivion and hateful griefs . . . . iii 1 293
Lavinia, go with me: I'll to thy closet; and go read with thee . . iii 2 81
Grandsire, help! my aunt Lavinia Follows me every where, I know not why . . . . iv 1 1
What means my niece Lavinia by these signs?—Fear her not . . . iv 1 8
Lavinia, shall I read? This is the tragic tale of Philomel . . . iv 1 46
Lavinia, wert thou thus surprised, sweet girl, Ravish'd and wrong'd? . iv 1 51
Look here, Lavinia: This sandy plot is plain; guide, if thou canst, This after me, when I have writ my name. . . . . . . iv 1 68
Lavinia, kneel; And kneel, sweet boy, the Roman Hector's hope . . iv 1 87
Come, come, Lavinia; look, thy foes are bound. Sirs, stop their mouths v 2 167
Whilst that Lavinia 'tween her stumps doth hold The basin that receives your guilty blood . . . . v 2 183
Die, die, Lavinia, and thy shame with thee; And, with thy shame, thy father's sorrow die! . . . . v 3 46
My father and Lavinia shall forthwith Be closed in our household's monument . . . . v 3 193
Lavish.—Let her have needful, but not lavish, means . *Meas. for Meas.* ii 2 24
Had I so lavish of my presence been, So common-hackney'd *1 Hen. IV.* iii 2 39
When means and lavish manners meet together . . *2 Hen. IV.* iv 4 64
Among which terms he used his lavish tongue . . . *1 Hen. VI.* ii 5 47
Arm 'gainst arm, Curbing his lavish spirit . . . . *Macbeth* i 2 57
Lavishly. Some about him have too lavishly Wrested his meaning *2 Hen. IV.* iv 2 57
Lavolt. I cannot sing, Nor heel the high lavolt. . *Troi. and Cres.* iv 4 88
Lavolta.—And teach lavoltas high and swift corantos . . *Hen. V.* iii 5 33
Law. That make their wills their law . . . . . *T. G. of Ver.* v 4 14
Your scope is as mine own, So to enforce or qualify the laws *Meas. for Meas.* i 1 66
We have strict statutes and most biting laws . . . . . i 3 19
Which have for long run by the hideous law, As mice by lions . . i 4 63
We must not make a scarecrow of the law . . . . . . ii 1 1
What know the laws That thieves do pass on thieves? . . . . ii 1 22
If these be good people in a commonweal that do nothing but use their abuses in common houses, I know no law . . . . ii 1 43
Is it a lawful trade?—If the law would allow it, sir.—But the law will not allow it . . . . ii 1 239
If this law hold in Vienna ten year, I'll rent the fairest house in it after three-pence a bay . . . . ii 1 254
O just but severe law! I had a brother, then . . . . . . ii 2 41
Your brother is a forfeit of the law, And you but waste your words . ii 2 71
Be you content, fair maid: It is the law, not I condemn your brother . ii 2 80

Law. The law hath not been dead, though it hath slept *Meas. for Meas.* ii 2 90
Which had you rather, that the most just law Now took your brother's life; or, to redeem him, Give up your body? ii 4 52
I, now the voice of the recorded law, Pronounce a sentence ii 4 61
His offence is so, as it appears, Accountant to the law upon that pain ii 4 86
From the manacles Of the all-building law ii 4 94
You seem'd of late to make the law a tyrant ii 4 114
Bidding the law make court'sy to their will ii 4 175
Has he affections in him, That thus can make him bite the law by the nose? iii 1 109
I had rather my brother die by the law than my son should be unlawfully born iii 1 195
Redeem your brother from the angry law iii 1 208
Allowed by order of law a furred gown to keep him warm iii 2 8
He hath offended the law: and, sir, we take him to be a thief too iii 2 16
Claudio, whom here you have warrant to execute, is no greater forfeit to the law than Angelo who hath sentenced him iv 2 168
A deflower'd maid! And by an eminent body that enforced The law against it! iv 4 26
Laws for all faults, But faults so countenanced, that the strong statutes Stand like the forfeits in a barber's shop v 1 321
The very mercy of the law cries out Most audible v 1 412
I am not partial to infringe our laws *Com. of Errors* i 1 4
Therefore by law thou art condemn'd to die i 1 26
Were it not against our laws, Against my crown, my oath, my dignity i 1 143
I shall have law in Ephesus, To your notorious shame iv 1 83
Put unluckily into this bay Against the laws and statutes of this town v 1 126
One that knows the law, go to; and a rich fellow enough, go to *M. Ado* iv 2 86
A dangerous law against gentility! *L. L. Lost* i 1 129
So to the laws at large I write my name i 1 156
I keep her as a vessel of thy law's fury i 1 278
These oaths and laws will prove an idle scorn i 1 311
For charity itself fulfils the law, And who can sever love from charity? iv 3 364
According to our law Immediately provided in that case *M. N. Dream* i 1 44
Arm yourself To fit your fancies to your father's will; Or else the law of Athens yields you up i 1 119
And to that place the sharp Athenian law Cannot pursue us i 1 162
Our intent Was to be gone from Athens, where we might, Without the peril of the Athenian law iv 1 158
I beg the law, the law, upon his head iv 1 160
The brain may devise laws for the blood, but a hot temper leaps o'er a cold decree *Mer. of Venice* i 2 19
Justice! the law! my ducats, and my daughter! ii 8 17
In law, what plea so tainted and corrupt But, being season'd with a gracious voice, Obscures the show of evil? iii 2 75
If law, authority and power deny not, It will go hard with poor Antonio iii 2 291
The duke cannot deny the course of law iii 3 26
'Tis mine and I will have it. If you deny me, fie upon your law! iv 1 101
I stand here for law iv 1 142
Yet in such rule that the Venetian law Cannot impugn you iv 1 178
I crave the law, The penalty and forfeit of my bond iv 1 206
Wrest once the law to your authority: To do a great right, do a little wrong iv 1 215
You know the law, your exposition Hath been most sound iv 1 237
I charge you by the law, Whereof you are a well-deserving pillar iv 1 238
The intent and purpose of the law Hath full relation to the penalty iv 1 247
A pound of that same merchant's flesh is thine: The court awards it, and the law doth give it iv 1 300
Cut this flesh from off his breast: The law allows it, and the court awards it iv 1 303
Thy lands and goods Are, by the laws of Venice, confiscate iv 1 311
Is that the law?—Thyself shalt see the act iv 1 314
The law hath yet another hold on you iv 1 347
It is enacted in the laws of Venice, If it be proved against an alien iv 1 348
Third, or fourth, or fifth borough, I'll answer him by law *T. of Shrew* Ind. 1 14
Since this bar in law makes us friends i 1 140
Do as adversaries do in law, Strive mightily, but eat and drink as friends i 2 278
By law, as well as reverend age, I may entitle thee my loving father iv 5 60
Most fain would steal What law does vouch mine own *All's Well* ii 5 87
A good note; that keeps you from the blow of the law *T. Night* iii 4 169
Still you keep o' the windy side of the law iii 4 182
I'll have an action of battery against him, if there be any law iv 1 37
By law and process of great nature *W. Tale* ii 2 60
I tell you 'Tis rigour and not law iii 2 115
To o'erthrow law and in one self-born hour To plant and o'erwhelm custom iv 1 8
This being done, let the law go whistle iv 4 715
The canon of the law is laid on him *K. John* ii 1 180
There's law and warrant, lady, for my curse iii 1 184
When law can do no right, Let it be lawful that law bar no wrong iii 1 185
Law cannot give my child his kingdom here, For he that holds his kingdom holds the law; Therefore, since law itself is perfect wrong, How can the law forbid my tongue to curse? iii 1 187
On the winking of authority To understand a law iv 2 212
Must I rob the law? iv 3 78
And formally, according to our law, Depose him *Richard II.* i 3 29
Thy state of law is bondslave to the law ii 1 114
I am a subject, And I challenge law: attorneys are denied me ii 3 134
But yet I'll pause; For I am loath to break our country's laws ii 3 169
Why should we in the compass of a pale Keep law and form? iii 4 41
Fobbed as it is with the rusty curb of old father antic the law 1 *Hen. IV.* i 2 69
I was then advised by my learned counsel in the laws 2 *Hen. IV.* i 2 154
For suffering flesh to be eaten in thy house, contrary to the law ii 4 373
Hastings and all Are brought to the correction of your law iv 4 85
In the administration of his law, Whiles I was busy for the commonwealth v 2 75
The majesty and power of law and justice v 2 78
To pluck down justice from your awful bench, To trip the course of law v 2 87
See your most dreadful laws so loosely slighted v 2 94
The laws of England are at my commandment v 3 143
Unfold Why the law Salique that they have in France Or should, or should not, bar us in our claim *Hen. V.* i 2 11
And Pharamond The founder of this law and female bar i 2 42
This law; to wit, no female Should be inheritrix in Salique land i 2 50
The Salique law Was not devised for the realm of France i 2 54
King Pharamond, Idly supposed the founder of this law i 2 59
Hold up this Salique law To bar your highness claiming from the female i 2 91
Their faults are open: Arrest them to the answer of the law ii 2 143
But we our kingdom's safety must so tender, Whose ruin you have sought, that to her laws We do deliver you ii 2 176

Law. It is the greatest admiration in the universal world, when the true and aunchient prerogatifes and laws of the wars is not kept *Hen. V.* iv 1 68
If these men have defeated the law and outrun native punishment, though they can outstrip men, they have no wings to fly from God iv 1 176
Men are punished for before-breach of the king's laws in now the king's quarrel iv 1 180
Let his neck answer for it, if there is any martial law in the world iv 8 46
I'll be no breaker of the law: But we shall meet, and break our minds at large.—Gloucester, we will meet 1 *Hen. VI.* i 3 80
I have been a truant in the law, And never yet could frame my will to it; And therefore frame the law unto my will ii 4 7
In these nice sharp quillets of the law, Good faith, I am no wiser than a daw ii 4 17
Stubbornly he did repugn the truth About a certain question in the law iv 1 95
Discover thine infirmity, That warranteth by law to be thy privilege v 4 61
Thy cruelty in execution Upon offenders hath exceeded law And left thee to the mercy of the law 2 *Hen. VI.* i 3 136
As for your spiteful false objections, Prove them, and I lie open to the law i 3 159
Let him have all the rigour of the law i 3 199
What shall we say to this in law? i 3 207
This is the law, and this Duke Humphrey's doom i 3 214
I banish her my bed and company And give her as a prey to law ii 1 198
Your guilt is great: Receive the sentence of the law for sins Such as by God's book are adjudged to death ii 3 3
The law, thou see'st, hath judged thee: I cannot justify whom the law condemns ii 3 15
Yet thy scandal were not wiped away, But I in danger for the breach of law ii 4 66
Did he not, contrary to form of law, Devise strange deaths for small offences? iii 1 58
'Tis meet he be condemn'd by course of law iii 1 237
Only that the laws of England may come out of your mouth.—Mass, 'twill be sore law, then; for he was thrust in the mouth with a spear iv 7 7
It will be stinking law; for his breath stinks with eating toasted cheese iv 7 13
A hand to hold a sceptre up And with the same to act controlling laws v 1 103
And, for I should not deal in her [love's] soft laws, She did corrupt frail nature with some bribe 3 *Hen. VI.* iii 2 154
For this once my will shall stand for law iv 1 50
Villain, thou know'st no law of God nor man *Richard III.* i 2 70
Before I be convict by course of law, To threaten me with death is most unlawful i 4 192
Erroneous vassal! the great King of kings Hath in the tables of his law commanded That thou shalt do no murder i 4 201
He holds vengeance in his hands, To hurl upon their heads that break his law i 4 205
How canst thou urge God's dreadful law to us, When thou hast broke it? i 4 214
Think you we are Turks or infidels? Or that we would, against the form of law, Proceed thus rashly? iii 5 42
Their aunt I am in law, in love their mother iv 1 24
Under what title shall I woo for thee, That God, the law, my honour and her love, Can make seem pleasing to her tender years? iv 4 341
Our strong arms be our conscience, swords our law v 3 311
Have you a precedent Of this commission? . . . We must not rend our subjects from our laws, And stick them in our will *Hen. VIII.* i 2 93
If he may Find mercy in the law, 'tis his; if none, Let him not seek 't of us i 2 212
He pleaded still not guilty and alleged Many sharp reasons to defeat the law ii 1 14
The law I bear no malice for my death ii 1 62
Not to deny her that A woman of less place might ask by law ii 2 112
If the trial of the law o'ertake ye, You'll part away disgraced iii 1 96
The duke by law Found his deserts iii 2 266
His faults lie open to the laws; let them, Not you, correct him iii 2 334
His own opinion was his law: i' the presence He would say untruths iv 2 37
You, that best should teach us, Have misdemean'd yourself, and not a little, Toward the king first, then his laws v 3 15
There is a law in each well-order'd nation To curb those raging appetites that are Most disobedient and refractory *Troi. and Cres.* ii 2 180
In a rebellion, When what's not meet, but what must be, was law *Cor.* iii 1 168
He hath resisted law, And therefore law shall scorn him further trial iii 1 267
Beating your officers, cursing yourselves, Opposing laws with strokes iii 3 79
Traitor, if Rome have law or we have power, Thou and thy faction shall repent this rape *T. Andron.* i 1 403
Let the laws of Rome determine all; Meanwhile I am possess'd of that is mine i 1 407
If they did kill thy husband, then be joyful, Because the law hath ta'en revenge on them iii 1 117
There nought hath pass'd, But even with law iv 4 8
His traitorous sons, That died by law for murder of our brother iv 4 54
Let us take the law of our sides; let them begin *Rom. and Jul.* i 1 44
Do you bite your thumb at us, sir?—Is the law of our side, if I say ay? i 1 54
I dare draw as soon as another man, if I see occasion in a good quarrel, and the law on my side ii 4 169
His fault concludes but what the law should end iii 1 190
O rude unthankfulness! Thy fault our law calls death iii 3 25
The kind prince, Taking thy part, hath rush'd aside the law iii 3 26
The law that threaten'd death becomes thy friend And turns it to exile iii 3 139
Mortal drugs I have; but Mantua's law Is death to any he that utters them v 1 66
The world is not thy friend nor the world's law; The world affords no law to make thee rich; Then be not poor, but break it, and take this v 1 72
Let my old life Be sacrificed, some hour before his time, Unto the rigour of severest law v 3 269
That's a deed thou 'lt die for.—Right, if doing nothing be death by the law *T. of Athens* i 1 196
Nothing emboldens sin so much as mercy.—Most true; the law shall bruise him iii 5 4
For pity is the virtue of the law, And none but tyrants use it cruelly iii 5 8
In hot blood, Hath stepp'd into the law, which is past depth To those that, without heed, do plunge into 't iii 5 12
If by this crime he owes the law his life, Why, let the war receive 't in valiant gore; For law is strict, and war is nothing more iii 5 83
We are for law: he dies; urge it no more, On height of our displeasure iii 5 86
Large-handed robbers your grave masters are, And pill by law iv 1 12
Degrees, observances, customs, and laws, Decline to your confounding contraries, And let confusion live! iv 1 19
Religious canons, civil laws are cruel; Then what should war be? iv 3 60
The laws, your curb and whip, in their rough power Have uncheck'd theft iv 3 446
Shall be render'd to your public laws At heaviest answer v 4 62
A seal'd compact, Well ratified by law and heraldry *Hamlet* i 1 87
Importing the surrender of those lands . . . with all bonds of law i 2 24
The proud man's contumely, The pangs of despised love, the law's delay iii 1 72

Law. Oft 'tis seen the wicked prize itself Buys out the law . *Hamlet* iii 3 60
How dangerous is it that this man goes loose! Yet must not we put the strong law on him: He's loved . . . . iv 3 3
But is this law?—Ay, marry, is't; crowner's quest law . . . . v 1 23
I have, sir, a son by order of law, some year elder than this . *Lear* i 1 19
Thou, nature, art my goddess; to thy law My services are bound . . i 2 1
When every case in law is right; No squire in debt, nor no poor knight iii 2 85
The laws are mine, not thine: Who can arraign me for't? . . v 3 158
Put upon you what restraint and grievance The law, with all his might to enforce it on, Will give him cable . . . . . *Othello* i 2 16
To prison, till fit time Of law and course of direct session Call thee . i 2 86
The bloody book of law You shall yourself read in the bitter letter . i 3 67
Try thy cunning, Thyreus; Make thine own edict for thy pains, which we Will answer as a law . . . . . . *Ant. and Cleo.* iii 12 33
Here's a voucher, Stronger than ever law could make . *Cymbeline* ii 2 40
Our ancestor was that Mulmutius which Ordain'd our laws . . iii 1 56; 59
The law Protects not us: then why should we be tender To let an arrogant piece of flesh threat us, Play judge and executioner all himself, For we do fear the law? . . . . iv 2 125
I died whilst in the womb he stay'd Attending nature's law . . . v 4 38
By thine own tongue thou art condemn'd, and must Endure our law . v 5 299
Which to prevent he made a law, To keep her still . *Pericles* 1 Gower 35
Touch not, upon thy life, For that's an article within our law . . i 1 88
Kings are earth's gods; in vice their law's their will . . . i 1 103
Here's a fish hangs in the net, like a poor man's right in the law . ii 1 124
Law-breaker. Thou art a robber, A law-breaker, a villain . *Cymbeline* iv 2 75
Law-day. Who has a breast so pure, But some uncleanly apprehensions Keep leets and law-days? . . . . *Othello* iii 3 140
Law of arms. 'Tis expressly against the law of arms . . *Hen. V.* iv 7 2
The law of arms is such That whoso draws a sword, 'tis present death 1 *Hen. VI.* iii 4 38
In defence of my lord's worthiness, I crave the benefit of law of arms . iv 1 100
By the law of arms thou wast not bound to answer An unknown opposite *Lear* v 3 152
Law of children. Might fire the blood of ordinary men, And turn preordinance and first decree Into the law of children . *J. Cæsar* iii 1 39
Law of friendship. That which I would discover The law of friendship bids me to conceal . . . . . *T. G. of Ver.* iii 1 5
Law of nature. Their own right by the law of nature . *All's Well* iv 5 65
I see no reason in the law of nature but I may snap at him 2 *Hen. IV.* iii 2 357
By gift of heaven, By law of nature and of nations . . *Hen. V.* ii 4 80
If this law Of nature be corrupted through affection *Troi. and Cres.* ii 2 176
These moral laws Of nature and of nations speak aloud . . ii 2 184
Laws of war. Nay, ladies, fear not; By all the laws of war you're privileged.—How now! what is't? . . . . *Hen. VIII.* i 4 52
Law of writ. For the law of writ and the liberty, these are the only men *Hamlet* ii 2 420
Lawful. In the lawful name of marrying . . . *Mer. Wives* iv 6 50
Is it a lawful trade?—If the law would allow it . . *Meas. for Meas.* ii 1 238
Lawful mercy Is nothing kin to foul redemption . . . . ii 4 112
But yet I will be content to be a lawful hangman . . . . iv 2 18
Now prove Our loving lawful, and our faith not torn . *L. L. Lost.* iv 3 285
No lawful means can carry me Out of his envy's reach . *Mer. of Venice* iv 1 9
Truly, she must be given, or the marriage is not lawful . *As Y. Like It* iii 3 71
If this be not a lawful cause for me to leave his service . *T. of Shrew* i 2 29
Now I see The bottom of your purpose.—You see it lawful, then *All's Well* iii 7 30
That time and place with this deceit so lawful May prove coherent . iii 7 38
Is wicked meaning in a lawful deed And lawful meaning in a lawful act iii 7 45
Is't lawful, pray you, To see her women? any of them? Emilia? *W. Tale* ii 2 11
Her actions shall be holy as You hear my spell is lawful . . . v 3 105
If this be magic, let it be an art Lawful as eating . . . . v 3 111
Arthur Plantagenet lays most lawful claim To this fair island *K. John* i 1 9
But thou from loving England art so far, That thou hast under-wrought his lawful king . . . . ii 1 95
On the sight of us your lawful king . . . . ii 1 222
By the lawful power that I have, Thou shalt stand cursed . . . iii 1 172
O, lawful let it be That I have room with Rome to curse awhile! . iii 1 179
Long have we stood To watch the fearful bending of thy knee, Because we thought ourself thy lawful king . . . . *Richard II.* iii 3 74
Is it not lawful, an please your majesty, to tell how many is killed? *Hen. V.* iv 8 122
The first-begotten and the lawful heir Of Edward king . 1 *Hen. VI.* ii 5 65
And France exclaims on thee, Doubting thy birth and lawful progeny . iii 3 61
I am possess'd With more than half the Gallian territories, And therein reverenced for their lawful king . . . . v 4 140
Ring, bells, aloud; burn, bonfires, clear and bright, To entertain great England's lawful king . . . . 2 *Hen. VI.* v 1 4
Tell me, may not a king adopt an heir?—What then?—And if he may, then am I lawful king . . . . 3 *Hen. VI.* i 1 137
My conscience tells me he is lawful king . . . . i 1 150
An oath is of no moment, being not took Before a true and lawful magistrate . . . . i 2 23
Becomes it thee to be thus bold in terms Before thy sovereign and thy lawful king?—I am his king . . . . ii 2 86
Usurps the regal title and the seat Of England's true-anointed lawful king . . . . iii 3 29
Am come to crave thy just and lawful aid . . . . iii 3 32
Vouchsafe to grant That virtuous Lady Bona, thy fair sister, To England's king in lawful marriage . . . . iii 3 57
I were loath To link with him that were not lawful chosen . . iii 3 115
So blunt, unnatural, To bend the fatal instruments of war Against his brother and his lawful king? . . . . v 1 88
Be it lawful that I invocate thy ghost! . . . . *Richard III.* i 2 8
We follow'd then our lord, our lawful king: So should we you . i 3 147
What lawful quest have given their verdict up Unto the frowning judge? i 4 189
O, make them joyful, grant their lawful suit! . . . . iii 7 203
Rest thy unrest on England's lawful earth . . . . iv 4 29
They had gather'd a wise council to them Of every realm, that did debate this business, Who deem'd our marriage lawful . . *Hen. VIII.* ii 4 53
Prove but our marriage lawful, by my life And kingly dignity, we are contented To wear our mortal state to come with her . . . . ii 4 226
It is as lawful, For we would give much, to use violent thefts, And rob in the behalf of charity . . . . . . *Troi. and Cres.* v 3 20
He shall answer, by a lawful form, In peace, to his utmost peril *Coriol.* iii 1 325
To suffer lawful censure for such faults As shall be proved upon you . iii 3 46
O that I had him, With six Aufidiuses, . . . To use my lawful sword . v 6 131
Not to be his wife, That is another's lawful promised love *T. Andron.* i 1 298
Cæsar shall Have all true rites and lawful ceremonies . *J. Cæsar* iii 1 241
Her father and myself, lawful espials . . . . . . *Hamlet* iii 1 32
Be it lawful I take up what's cast away . . . . . . *Lear* i 1 256

Lawful. Gloucester's bastard son Was kinder to his father than my daughters Got 'tween the lawful sheets . . . . . . *Lear* iv 6 118
To know our enemies' minds, we'ld rip their hearts; Their papers, is more lawful . . . . iv 6 266
If it prove lawful prize, he's made for ever . . . . . *Othello* i 2 51
But some uncleanly apprehensions Keep leets and law-days and in session sit With meditations lawful . . . . iii 3 140
Forborne the getting of a lawful race, And by a gem of women *A. and C.* iii 13 107
We will have these things set down by lawful counsel . . *Cymbeline* i 4 178
Me of my lawful pleasure she restrain'd And pray'd me oft forbearance ii 5 9
Who, finger'd to make man his lawful music, Would draw heaven down and all the gods, to hearken . . . . *Pericles* i 1 82
Lawfully by this the Jew may claim A pound of flesh *Mer. of Venice* iv 1 231
May lawfully make title to as much love as she finds . *All's Well* i 3 107
What a man cannot get, he may lawfully deal for—his wife's soul *Pericles* ii 1 120
Lawless. But to the purpose—for we cite our faults, That they may hold excused our lawless lives . . . . *T. G. of Ver.* iv 1 54
Of those that lawless and incertain thought Imagine howling *M. for M.* iii 1 127
This lawless bloody book Of forged rebellion . . . 2 *Hen. IV.* iv 1 91
Take not the quarrel from his powerful arm; He needs no indirect nor lawless course To cut off those that have offended him *Richard III.* i 4 224
One fit to bandy with thy lawless sons . . . . *T. Andron.* i 1 312
Here and there Shark'd up a list of lawless resolutes . . *Hamlet* i 1 98
In his lawless fit, Behind the arras hearing something stir . . iv 1 8
Lawlessly. And will not use a woman lawlessly . . *T. G. of Ver.* v 3 14
Lawn. Inkles, caddisses, cambrics, lawns . . . . . *W. Tale* iv 4 209
Lawn as white as driven snow; Cyprus black as e'er was crow . . iv 4 220
I would not do such a thing for a joint-ring, nor for measures of lawn *Othello* iv 3 73
Lawyer. Who stays it [Time] still withal?—With lawyers in the vacation; for they sleep between term and term . . . *As Y. Like It* iii 2 349
I have neither the scholar's melancholy, which is emulation, . . . nor the lawyer's, which is politic . . . . iv 1 13
Points more than all the lawyers in Bohemia can learnedly handle *W. T.* iv 4 206
The first thing we do, let's kill all the lawyers . . 2 *Hen. VI.* iv 2 84
All scholars, lawyers, courtiers, gentlemen, They call false caterpillars iv 4 36
O'er lawyers' fingers, who straight dream on fees . *Rom. and Jul.* i 4 73
Sometime, 't appears like a lord; sometime like a lawyer *T. of Athens* ii 2 116
Crack the lawyer's voice, That he may never more false title plead . iv 3 153
Why may not that be the skull of a lawyer? Where be his quiddities now? . . . . *Hamlet* v 1 107
'Tis like the breath of an unfee'd lawyer; you gave me nothing for't *Lear* i 4 143
I will make One of her women lawyer to me . . . *Cymbeline* ii 3 79
Lay her a-hold, a-hold! . . . . *Tempest* i 1 52
Set her two courses off to sea again; lay her off . . . . . i 1 53
It was a torment To lay upon the damn'd . . . . i 2 290
Whom I, with this obedient steel, three inches of it, Can lay to bed for ever . . . . ii 1 284
I have been content, sir, you should lay my countenance to pawn *M. W.* ii 2 5
The best courtier of them all, when the court lay at Windsor . . ii 2 63
To lay an amiable siege to the honesty of this Ford's wife . . ii 2 243
Come, lay their swords to pawn. Follow me, lads of peace . . iii 1 112
I never saw him so gross in his jealousy till now.—I will lay a plot to try that . . . . iii 3 202
Besides these, other bars he lays before me, My riots past . . . iii 4 7
And how long lay you there?—Nay, you shall hear . . . . iii 5 95
The weariest and most loathed worldly life That age, ache, penury and imprisonment Can lay on nature is a paradise To what we fear of death . . . . *Meas. for Meas.* iii 1 131
In the boldness of my cunning, I will lay myself in hazard . . iv 2 165
Had he been lay, my lord, For certain words he spake against your grace In your retirement, I had swinged him soundly . . . . . v 1 128
Lay bolts enough upon him . . . . v 1 350
One that will have me.—What claim lays she to thee?—Marry, sir, such claim as you would lay to your horse . . . *Com. of Errors* iii 2 84
What stuff of mine hast thou embark'd?—Your goods that lay at host . v 1 410
The false sweet bait that we lay for it . . . . . *Much Ado* iii 1 33
And lay it to your heart: it is the only thing for a qualm . . iii 4 74
Doubt not but success Will fashion the event in better shape Than I can lay it down in likelihood . . . . iv 1 238
Nay, never lay thy hand upon thy sword; I fear thee not . . . v 1 54
I am forced to lay my reverence by . . . . v 1 64
Why they are committed; and, to conclude, what you lay to their charge . . . . v 1 228
Impose me to what penance your invention Can lay upon my sin . . v 1 284
Nor never lay his wreathed arms athwart His loving bosom . *L. L. Lost* iv 3 135
Now to plain-dealing; lay these glozes by . . . . . . iv 3 370
And lay my arms before the legs of this sweet lass . . . . v 2 558
Lay breath so bitter on your bitter foe . . . . *M. N. Dream* iii 2 44
Lay them in gore, Since you have shore With shears his thread of silk v 1 346
Which my love and some necessity Now lays upon you . *Mer. of Venice* iii 4 35
And on the wager lay two earthly women . . . . iii 5 85
I have an oath in heaven: Shall I lay perjury upon my soul? . . iv 1 229
Sigh'd his soul toward the Grecian tents, Where Cressid lay that night v 1 6
For, by this ring, the doctor lay with me . . . . v 1 259
There lay he, stretched along, like a wounded knight . *As Y. Like It* iii 2 253
A wretched ragged man, o'ergrown with hair, Lay sleeping on his back iv 3 108
A lioness, with udders all drawn dry, Lay couching . . . . iv 3 116
Though you lay here in this goodly chamber, Yet would you say ye were beaten out of door . . . . *T. of Shrew* Ind. 2 86
'Twas a commodity lay fretting by you: 'Twill bring you gain, or perish ii 1 330
If thou account'st it shame, lay it on me . . . . iv 3 183
Lay upon him all the honour That good convenience claims . *All's Well* iii 2 74
Lay our best love and credence Upon thy promising fortune . . iii 3 2
It nothing steads us To chide him from our eaves; for he persists As if his life lay on't . . . . iii 7 43
But they know his conditions and lay him in straw . . . . iv 3 288
Goaded with most sharp occasions, Which lay nice manners by . . v 1 15
Let your highness Lay a more noble thought upon mine honour . . v 3 180
I shall crave of you your leave that I may bear my evils alone: it were a bad recompense for your love, to lay any of them on you *T. Night* ii 1 7
Lay me, O, where Sad true lover never find my grave, To weep there! ii 4 65
I dare lay any money 'twill be nothing yet . . . . . . ii 4 432
Might we lay the old proverb to your charge, So like you, 'tis the worse *W. Tale* ii 3 96
Like very sanctity, she did approach My cabin where I lay . . iii 3 24
I desire to lay my bones there . . . . iv 2 6
Thou hast need of more rags to lay on thee, rather than have these off . iv 3 58
Come on, lay it by: and let's first see moe ballads . . . . iv 4 277
Put on my shroud and lay me Where no priest shovels in dust . . iv 4 468

Lay. Lay 't so to his charge . . . *W. Tale* v 1 195
Arthur Plantagenet lays most lawful claim To this fair island *K. John* i 1 9
Whether I be as true begot or no, That still I lay upon my mother's head i 1 76
Large lengths of seas and shores Between my father and my mother lay i 1 106
Heaven lay not my transgression to my charge! . . . i 1 256
Needs must you lay your heart at his dispose . . . i 1 263
Upon thy cheek lay I this zealous kiss, As seal to this indenture . ii 1 19
We'll lay before this town our royal bones, Wade to the market-place . ii 1 41
But, ass, I'll take that burthen from your back, Or lay on that shall make your shoulders crack . . . ii 1 146
Shall we knit our powers And lay this Angiers even with the ground? ii 1 399
How green you are and fresh in this old world! John lays you plots . iii 4 146
Murder, as hating what himself hath done, Doth lay it open . iv 3 38
What doth our cousin lay to Mowbray's charge? *Richard II.* i 1 84
Once did I lay an ambush for your life . . . i 1 137
Lay on our royal sword your banish'd hands . . . i 3 179
I lay my claim To my inheritance of free descent . . . ii 3 135
Even at his feet to lay my arms and power . . . iii 3 39
And lay the summer's dust with showers of blood . . . iii 3 43
I'll lay A plot shall show us all a merry day . . . iv 1 333
O that it could be proved That some night-tripping fairy had exchanged In cradle-clothes our children where they lay! . . 1 *Hen. IV.* i 1 88
I will lay him down such reasons for this adventure that he shall go . i 2 168
Lay thine ear close to the ground and list if thou canst hear the tread of travellers . . . ii 2 33
Thou knowest my old ward; here I lay, and thus I bore my point . ii 4 216
She bids you on the wanton rushes lay you down . . . iii 1 214
Come, quick, quick, that I may lay my head in thy lap . . . iii 1 230
Nor did he think it meet To lay so dangerous and dear a trust On any soul removed but on his own . . . iv 1 34
Rebellion lay in his way, and he found it . . . v 1 28
O, would the quarrel lay upon our heads! . . . v 2 48
Where lay the king last night?—At Basingstoke 2 *Hen. IV.* ii 1 181
Do you remember since we lay all night in the windmill? . iii 2 207
I remember at Mile-end Green, when I lay at Clement's Inn . iii 2 299
And suffer the condition of these times To lay a heavy and unequal hand Upon our honours . . . iv 1 102
The image of his power lay then in me . . . v 2 74
And shall good news be baffled? Then, Pistol, lay thy head in Furies' lap v 3 110
Or lay these bones in an unworthy urn, Tombless *Hen. V.* i 2 228
So a' bade me lay more clothes on his feet . . . ii 3 24
The French may lay twenty French crowns to one, they will beat us . iv 1 242
Let us our lives, our souls, Our debts, our careful wives, Our children and our sins lay on the king! . . . iv 1 249
York, all haggled over, Comes to him, where in gore he lay insteep'd . iv 6 12
Sleeping or waking must I still prevail, Or will you blame and lay the fault on me? . . 1 *Hen. VI.* ii 1 57
Gather our soldiers, scatter'd and dispersed, And lay new platforms . ii 1 77
If thou canst accuse, Or aught intend'st to lay unto my charge, Do it . iii 1 4
Even with the earth Shall lay your stately and air-braving towers . iv 2 13
Come, come and lay him in his father's arms . . . iv 7 29
I kiss these fingers for eternal peace, And lay them gently on thy tender side . . . v 3 49
She will light to listen to the lays, And never mount . 2 *Hen. VI.* i 3 93
Lay not thy hands on me; forbear, I say; Their touch affrights me . iii 2 46
O, beat away the busy meddling fiend That lays strong siege unto this wretch's soul And from his bosom purge this black despair! . iii 3 22
Lay your weapons down; Home to your cottages, forsake this groom . iv 2 131
My soul and body on the action both!—A dreadful lay! . . v 2 27
I lay me down a little while to breathe . 3 *Hen. VI.* ii 3 2
I lay it naked to the deadly stroke, And humbly beg the death *Rich. III.* i 2 178
And lay those honours on your high deserts . . . i 3 97
Mischiefs that I set abroach I lay unto the grievous charge of others . i 3 326
Inestimable stones, unvalued jewels, All scatter'd in the bottom of the sea: Some lay in dead men's skulls . . . i 4 29
And mock'd the dead bones that lay scatter'd by . . . i 4 33
Lay no hands on me: The deed you undertake is damnable . . i 4 196
When we both lay in the field Frozen almost to death . . ii 1 114
Last night, I hear, they lay at Northampton . . . ii 4 1
On him I lay what you would lay on me . . . iii 7 171
'Lo, thus,' quoth Dighton, 'lay those tender babes' . . iv 3 9
A book of prayers on their pillow lay . . . iv 3 14
To whom as great a charge as little honour He meant to lay upon *Hen. VIII.* i 1 78
Stops on a sudden, looks upon the ground, Then lays his finger on his temple . . . iii 2 115
This, and all else This talking lord can lay upon my credit . . iii 2 265
When the brown wench Lay kissing in your arms . . . iii 2 296
Six miles off From Ampthill where the princess lay . . iv 1 28
Believe me, sir, she is the goodliest woman That ever lay by man . iv 1 70
O, father abbot, An old man, broken with the storms of state, Is come to lay his weary bones among ye . . . iv 2 22
Embalm me, Then lay me forth . . . iv 2 171
I shall clear myself, Lay all the weight ye can upon my patience . v 3 66
If the king blame me for't, I'll lay ye all By the heels, and suddenly . v 4 82
But peace, Æneas, Peace, Trojan; lay thy finger on thy lips! *Tr. and Cr.* i 3 240
If she that lays thee out says thou art a fair corse . . ii 3 34
And, princes all, Lay negligent and loose regard upon him . . iii 3 41
Rain, to lay this wind, or my heart will be blown up by the root . iv 4 55
I sometime lay here in Corioli At a poor man's house *Coriolanus* i 9 82
Lay A fault on us, your tribunes; that we labour'd, No impediment between . . . ii 3 234
Lay the fault on us.—Ay, spare us not . . . ii 3 242
The way to kindle, not to quench.—To unbuild the city and to lay all flat . . . iii 1 198
That is the way to lay the city flat; To bring the roof to the foundation iii 1 204
O'erborne their way, consumed with fire, and took What lay before them . . . iv 6 78
Why suffer'st thou thy sons, unburied yet, To hover on the dreadful shore of Styx? Make way to lay them by their brethren *T. Andron.* i 1 89
When he by night lay bathed in maiden blood . . . ii 3 232
Teach her not thus to lay Such violent hands upon her tender life . iii 2 21
What violent hands can she lay on her life? . . . iii 2 25
And with a gad of steel will write these words, And lay it by . iv 1 104
Revenge now goes To lay a complot to betray thy foes . . v 2 147
In fair Verona, where we lay our scene . . . *Rom. and Jul.* Prol. 2
She's not fourteen.—I'll lay fourteen of my teeth,—And yet, to my teen be it spoken, I have but four,—She is not fourteen . . i 3 12
And all my fortunes at thy foot I'll lay And follow thee my lord . ii 2 147
Bad'st me bury love.—Not in a grave, To lay one in, another out to have ii 3 84

Lay. There is a nobleman in town, one Paris, that would fain lay knife aboard . . . *Rom. and Jul.* ii 4 214
Then will I lay the serving-creature's dagger on your pate . . iv 5 119
Lay thee all along, Holding thine ear close to the hollow ground . . v 3 3
If thou be merciful, Open the tomb, lay me with Juliet . . . v 3 73
I'll cheer up My discontented troops, and lay for hearts *T. of Athens* iii 5 115
What wouldst thou do with the world, Apemantus, if it lay in thy power? . . . iv 3 322
The bounteous housewife, nature, on each bush Lays her full mess . iv 3 424
Under these hard conditions as this time Is like to lay upon us *J. Cæsar* i 2 175
He was very loath to lay his fingers off it . . . i 2 243
Take this paper, And look you lay it in the prætor's chair . . i 3 143
We lay these honours on this man, To ease ourselves . . iv 1 19
Lay it to thy heart, and farewell . . . *Macbeth* i 5 14
The night has been unruly: where we lay, Our chimneys were blown down . . . ii 3 59
Here lay Duncan, His silver skin laced with his golden blood . ii 3 117
His absence, sir, Lays blame upon his promise . . . iii 4 44
Great tyranny! lay thou thy basis sure, For goodness dare not check thee . . . iv 3 32
Come hither, gentlemen, And lay your hands again upon my sword *Ham.* i 5 158
In the full bent To lay our service freely at your feet . . ii 2 31
When he lay couched in the ominous horse . . . ii 2 476
Lay not that flattering unction to your soul . . . iii 4 145
I cannot choose but weep, to think they should lay him i' the cold ground . . . iv 5 70
Her garments, heavy with their drink, Pull'd the poor wretch from her melodious lay To muddy death . . . iv 7 183
Lay her i' the earth: And from her fair and unpolluted flesh May violets spring! . . . v 1 261
Methought I lay Worse than the mutines in the bilboes . . v 2 5
An admirable evasion of whoremaster man, to lay his goatish disposition to the charge of a star! . . . *Lear* i 2 138
Our good old friend, Lay comforts to your bosom . . . ii 1 128
Thou'ldst shun a bear; But if thy flight lay toward the raging sea, Thou'ldst meet the bear i' the mouth . . . iii 4 10
I will lay trust upon thee . . . iii 5 25
There is a litter ready; lay him in't, And drive towards Dover . iii 6 97
To lay the blame upon her own despair, That she fordid herself . v 3 254
Let me speak like yourself, and lay a sentence, Which, as a grise or step, may help these lovers Into your favour . . . *Othello* i 3 199
Lay thy finger thus, and let thy soul be instructed . . ii 1 223
For the command, I'll lay't upon you . . . ii 1 272
My fortunes against any lay worth naming . . . ii 3 330
I lay with Cassio lately . . . iii 3 413
Lay not your blame on me . . . iv 2 46
Prithee, to-night Lay on my bed my wedding sheets . . iv 2 105
Her salt tears fell from her, and soften'd the stones;—Lay by these . iv 3 48
You have done well, That men must lay their murders on your neck . v 2 170
Nay, lay thee down and roar; For thou hast kill'd the sweetest innocent . . . v 2 198
O, lay me by my mistress' side . . . v 2 237
Lo, now, if it lay in their hands to make me a cuckold *Ant. and Cleo.* i 2 80
He was not merry, Which seem'd to tell them his remembrance lay In Egypt . . . i 5 57
Royal wench! She made great Cæsar lay his sword to bed . . ii 2 232
I dare him therefore To lay his gay comparisons apart . . iii 13 26
Tell him, I am prompt To lay my crown at's feet, and there to kneel . iii 13 76
Give me grace to lay My duty on your hand . . . iii 13 81
Until Of many thousand kisses the poor last I lay upon thy lips . iv 15 21
In the name lay A moiety of the world . . . v 1 18
Rather on Nilus' mud Lay me stark naked! . . . v 2 59
If you seek To lay on me a cruelty, by taking Antony's course . . v 2 129
I dare lay mine honour He will remain so . . . *Cymbeline* i 1 174
I will lay you ten thousand ducats to your ring . . . i 4 138
I will have it no lay.—By the gods, it is one . . . i 4 159
Learn'd indeed were that astronomer That knew the stars as I his characters; He'ld lay the future open . . . iii 2 29
Wilt lay the leaven on all proper men . . . iii 4 64
To the grave!—Say, where shall's lay him? . . . iv 2 233
We must lay his head to the east; My father hath a reason for't . iv 2 255
We have done our obsequies: come, lay him down.—Here's a few flowers . . . iv 2 282
This tablet lay upon his breast . . . v 4 109
Bear with patience Such griefs as you yourself do lay upon yourself *Per.* i 2 66
The care I had and have of subjects' good On thee I lay . . i 2 119
Lay the babe Upon the pillow: hie thee, whiles I say A priestly farewell . . . iii 1 68
Madam, this letter, and some certain jewels, Lay with you in your coffer iii 4 2
She sings like one immortal, and she dances As goddess-like to her admired lays . . . v Gower 4
Lay about. He'll lay about him to-day, I can tell them . *Troi. and Cres.* i 2 58
Lay along. As he lay along Under an oak . . . *As Y. Like It* ii 1 30
Lay apart. Divest yourself, and lay apart The borrow'd glories *Hen. V.* ii 4 78
To lay apart their particular functions and wonder at him . . . iii 7 41
Lay aside the thoughts of Sicilia.—I willingly obey . . . *W. Tale* iv 2 58
Desiring thee to lay aside the sword . . . *K. John* i 1 12
And lay aside my high blood's royalty . . . *Richard II.* i 1 71
Lay aside life-harming heaviness And entertain a cheerful disposition . ii 2 3
I lay aside that which grows to me! . . . 2 *Hen. IV.* i 2 99
Would the nobility lay aside their ruth, And let me use my sword *Coriol.* i 1 201
Come, lay aside your stitchery . . . i 3 75
Lay bare. Therefore lay bare your bosom . . . *Mer. of Venice* iv 1 252
Lay by all nicety and prolixious blushes . . . *Meas. for Meas.* ii 4 162
Let them lay by their helmets and their spears . . . *Richard II.* i 3 119
Got with swearing 'Lay by' and spent with crying 'Bring in' 1 *Hen. IV.* i 2 40
Even the billows of the sea Hung their heads, and then lay by *Hen. VIII.* iii 1 11
We lay by Our appertainments, visiting of him . *Troi. and Cres.* ii 3 86
Lay claim. A very beastly creature lays claim to me . *Com. of Errors* iii 2 89
There is a youth here in the forest lays claim to you *As Y. Like It* v 1 7
Why, being younger born, Doth he lay claim to thine inheritance? *K. John* i 1 72
Lay down. Either You must lay down the treasures of your body To this supposed, or else to let him suffer . . . *Meas. for Meas.* ii 4 96
He wooes your daughter, Lays down his wanton siege before her beauty *All's Well* iii 7 18
I dare my life lay down and will do't, sir . . . *W. Tale* ii 1 130
My life stands in the level of your dreams, Which I'll lay down . iii 2 83
Wilt thou resign them and lay down thy arms? . . . *K. John* ii 1 154
Before we will lay down our just-borne arms, We'll put thee down . ii 1 345
Go I to make the French lay down their arms . . . v 1 24

Lay down. He flatly says he'll not lay down his arms *K. John* v 2 126
It never yet did hurt To lay down likelihoods and forms of hope *2 Hen. IV.* i 3 35
We must not only arm to invade the French, But lay down our proportions to defend Against the Scot *Hen. V.* i 2 137
A thousand crowns, or else lay down your head *2 Hen. VI.* iv 1 16
The sly whoresons Have got a speeding trick to lay down ladies *Hen. VIII.* i 3 40
Masters, lay down your weapons.—Go not home *Coriolanus* iii 1 331
I durst, my lord, to wager she is honest, Lay down my soul at stake *Oth.* iv 2 13
Lay flat. Be it but to fortify her judgement, which else an easy battery might lay flat *Cymbeline* i 4 23
Lay forth. Let us see these ornaments; Lay forth the gown *T. of Shrew* iv 3 62
Lay hands. If we know him to be a thief, shall we not lay hands on him? *Much Ado* iii 3 58
Wilt thou lay hands on me, villain? *As Y. Like It* i 1 58
Lay hands on the villain: I believe a' means to cozen somebody *T. of S.* v 1 39
Lay hands upon these traitors and their trash *2 Hen. VI.* i 4 44
Why linger we? let us lay hands upon him.—Forbear awhile *3 Hen. VI.* iii 1 26
Lay hands on them. Oft have you heard me wish for such an hour *T. An.* v 2 159
Lay hand on heart, advise: An you be mine, I'll give you to my friend *Rom. and Jul.* iii 5 192
O, here he is: lay hand upon him *Lear* iv 6 192
Lay hands on him; a dog! *Cymbeline* v 3 91
Lay hold on him.—This may prove worse than hanging *Meas. for Meas.* v 1 394
Lay hold on him.—No, not a creature enters in my house *Com. of Errors* v 1 91
He hath murdered his master! Lay hold on him *T. of Shrew* v 1 91
Lay hold upon him, Priam, hold him fast: He is thy crutch *T. and C.* v 3 59
Lay hold of him; Bear him to the rock Tarpeian *Coriolanus* iii 1 212
He that can lay hold of her Shall have the chinks *Rom. and Jul.* i 5 118
Lay hold upon him: if he do resist, Subdue him at his peril *Othello* i 2 80
Lay home. Look you lay home to him *Hamlet* iii 4 1
Lays it on. I would I could see this taborer; he lays it on *Tempest* iii 2 160
My father hath made her mistress of the feast, and she lays it on *W. Tale* iv 3 43
Lay lime to tangle her desires By wailful sonnets *T. G. of Ver.* iii 2 68
Lay my head. I'll lay my head to any good man's hat, These oaths and laws will prove an idle scorn *L. L. Lost* i 1 310
Lay my life. I'll lay my life, with my disposer *Troi. and Cres.* iii 1 95
Lay odds. I will lay odds that, ere this year expire, We bear our civil swords *2 Hen. IV.* v 5 111
Lay on. I could lay on like a butcher *Hen. V.* v 2 147
Lay on, Macduff, And damn'd be him that first cries 'Hold, enough!' *Macbeth* v 8 33
Lay open. Wherein I must very much lay open mine own imperfection *Mer. Wives* ii 2 191
Lay open to my earthy-gross conceit, Smother'd in errors, feeble, shallow, weak, The folded meaning of your words' deceit *Com. of Errors* iii 2 34
Will he to the king and lay open all our proceedings *1 Hen. IV.* ii 3 34
Lay out. When they will not give a doit to relieve a lame beggar, they will lay out ten to see a dead Indian *Tempest* ii 2 34
Will you give me money, captain?—Lay out, lay out *1 Hen. IV.* iv 2 5
Thus honest fools lay out their wealth on court'sies *T. of Athens* i 2 241
You lay out too much pains For purchasing but trouble *Cymbeline* ii 3 92
Lay siege. Or, if there were a sympathy in choice, War, death, or sickness did lay siege to it *M. N. Dream* i 1 142
Not nature, To whom all sores lay siege, can bear great fortune, But by contempt of nature *T. of Athens* iv 3 7
Lay the dust. But see how I lay the dust with my tears *T. G. of Ver.* ii 3 35
Lay their heads together. See, how to beguile the old folks, how the young folks lay their heads together! *T. of Shrew* i 2 139
I see them lay their heads together to surprise me *2 Hen. VI.* iv 8 60
Lay thoughts. Had the cardinal But half my lay thoughts in him, some of these Should find a running banquet *Hen. VIII.* i 4 11
Lay-to your fingers: help to bear this away *Tempest* iv 1 251
Layer up. Old age, that ill layer up of beauty *Hen. V.* v 2 248
Layest. Even from the gallows did his fell soul fleet, And, whilst thou lay'st in thy unhallow'd dam, Infused itself in thee *Mer. of Venice* iv 1 136
Thou variest no more from picking of purses than giving direction doth from labouring; thou layest the plot how *1 Hen. IV.* ii 1 57
For all the claim thou lay'st, Think not that Henry shall be so deposed.—Deposed he shall be *3 Hen. VI.* i 1 152
Instead of oil and balm, Thou lay'st in every gash that love hath given me The knife that made it *Troi. and Cres.* i 1 62
O murderous slumber, Lay'st thou thy leaden mace upon my boy? *J. C.* iv 3 268
Laying. I was taken up for laying them down *T. G. of Ver.* i 2 135
The more fool you, for laying on my duty *T. of Shrew* v 2 129
I lost mine eye in laying the prize aboard *2 Hen. VI.* iv 1 25
O, many Have broke their backs with laying manors on 'em *Hen. VIII.* i 1 84
You seem to understand me, By each at once her choppy finger laying Upon her skinny lips *Macbeth* i 3 44
You laying these slight sullies on my son *Hamlet* ii 1 39
To use his eyes for garden water-pots, Ay, and laying autumn's dust *Lear* iv 6 201
You praise yourself By laying defects of judgement to me *Ant. and Cleo.* ii 2 55
Laying by That nothing-gift of differing multitudes *Cymbeline* iii 6 85
Laying in. That will scarce hold the laying in *Hamlet* v 1 182
Laying on. There's laying on, take't off who will *Troi. and Cres.* i 2 224
Lazar. To relief of lazars and weak age *Hen. V.* i 1 15
I'll be sworn and sworn upon't she never shrouded any but lazars *T. and C.* ii 3 36
For I care not to be the louse of a lazar v 1 72
Lazar-kite. Fetch forth the lazar kite of Cressid's kind *Hen. V.* ii 1 80
Lazar-like. A most instant tetter bark'd about, Most lazar-like, with vile and loathsome crust, All my smooth body *Hamlet* i 5 72
Lazarus. As ragged as Lazarus in the painted cloth *1 Hen. IV.* iv 2 27
Lazy. While I sit lazy by *Tempest* iii 1 28
How shall we beguile The lazy time, if not with some delight? *M. N. D.* v 1 41
The lazy foot of Time . . . —And why not the swift foot *As Y. Like It* iii 2 322
Delivering o'er to executors pale The lazy yawning drone *Hen. V.* i 2 204
Like the night-owl's lazy flight *3 Hen. VI.* ii 1 130
Where are these porters, These lazy knaves? *Hen. VIII.* v 4 74
Ye are lazy knaves; And here ye lie baiting of bombards, when Ye should do service. Hark! the trumpets sound v 4 84
Upon a lazy bed the livelong day Breaks scurril jests *Troi. and Cres.* i 3 147
Trumpet, blow loud, Send thy brass voice through all these lazy tents i 3 257
A round little worm Prick'd from the lazy finger of a maid *Rom. and Jul.* i 4 66
Lazy-pacing. When he bestrides the lazy-pacing clouds ii 2 31
Lea. Rich leas Of wheat, rye, barley, vetches, oats and pease *Tempest* iv 1 60
Her fallow leas The darnel, hemlock and rank fumitory Doth root upon *Hen. V.* v 2 44
Dry up thy marrows, vines, and plough-torn leas! *T. of Athens* iv 3 193
Lead off this ground *Tempest* ii 1 323
Nor lead me, like a firebrand, in the dark Out of my way ii 2 6
I prithee now, lead the way without any more talking ii 2 177
Lead. Upon the rising of the mountain-foot That leads towards Mantua *T. G. of Ver.* v 2 47
Lead him on with a fine-baited delay *Mer. Wives* ii 1 98
The sweet woman leads an ill life with him ii 2 92
She leads a very frampold life with him, good heart ii 2 93
Never a wife in Windsor leads a better life than she does ii 2 122
Had you rather lead mine eyes, or eye your master's heels? iii 2 3
I had as lief bear so much lead iv 2 118
The heavens give safety to your purposes!—Lead forth and bring you back in happiness! *Meas. for Meas.* i 1 75
A little door Which from the vineyard to the garden leads iv 1 33
Thee will I love and with thee lead my life *Com. of Errors* iii 2 67
We'll draw cuts for the senior: till then lead thou first v 1 422
Please it your grace lead on?— . . . We will go together *Much Ado* i 1 160
And lead his apes into hell ii 1 43
If they lead to any ill, I will leave them at the next turning ii 1 159
Being that I flow in grief, The smallest twine may lead me iv 1 252
Away!—As swift as lead, sir *L. L. Lost* iii 1 58
Is not lead a metal heavy, dull, and slow? iii 1 60
I say lead is slow.—You are too swift, sir, to say so: Is that lead slow which is fired from a gun? iii 1 62
We came to visit you, and purpose now To lead you to our court v 2 344
In a brooch of lead v 2 621
Didst thou not lead him through the glimmering night? *M. N. Dream* ii 1 77
Reason becomes the marshal to my will And leads me to your eyes ii 2 121
I'll follow you, I'll lead you about a round iii 1 109
Come, wait upon him; lead him to my bower iii 1 202
Lead these testy rivals so astray As one come not within another's way iii 2 358
And from each other look thou lead them thus iii 2 363
Up and down, up and down, I will lead them up and down iii 2 397
Goblin, lead them up and down iii 2 399
These three chests of gold, silver and lead, whereof who chooses his meaning chooses you *Mer. of Venice* i 2 33
I pray you, lead me to the caskets To try my fortune ii 1 23
Dull lead, with warning all as blunt ii 7 8
Must give: for what? for lead? hazard for lead? This casket threatens ii 7 17
I'll then nor give nor hazard aught for lead ii 7 21
Is't like that lead contains her? ii 7 49
Fortune now To my heart's hope! Gold; silver; and base lead ii 9 20
Thou meagre lead, Which rather threatenest than dost promise aught iii 2 104
We'll lead you thither. I pray you, will you take him by the arm? *As Y. Like It* iv 3 162
And for your love to her lead apes in hell *T. of Shrew* ii 1 34
Lead these gentlemen To my daughters ii 1 109
Though the devil lead the measure, such are to be followed *All's Well* ii 1 57
Why, he's able to lead her a coranto ii 3 49
You had my prayers to lead them on ii 4 17
Yond's that same knave That leads him to these places iii 5 86
Now will I lead you to the house, and show you The lass I spoke of iii 6 118
And, hoodwink'd as thou art, will lead thee on To gather from thee iv 1 90
The flowery way that leads to the broad gate and the great fire iv 5 57
You are the cruell'st she alive, If you will lead these graces to the grave And leave the world no copy *T. Night* i 5 260
Must Lead on to some foul issue *W. Tale* ii 3 153
Boiling? In leads or oils? iii 2 178
Come and lead me Unto these sorrows iii 2 243
Lead us from hence, where we may leisurely Each one demand and answer v 3 152
The path which shall directly lead Thy foot to England's throne *K. John* iii 4 129
Lead me to the revolts of England here v 4 7
Thou hast said enough. Beshrew thee, cousin, which didst lead me forth Of that sweet way I was in to despair! *Richard II.* iii 2 204
Wilfully betray'd The lives of those that he did lead to fight *1 Hen. IV.* i 3 82
The boy shall lead our horses down the hill; we'll walk afoot awhile ii 2 83
O esperance! Bid Butler lead him forth into the park ii 3 75
Ere I lead this life long, I'll sew nether stocks ii 4 129
Leads ancient lords and reverend bishops on To bloody battles iii 2 104
Who leads his power? Under whose government come they along? iv 1 18
I am as hot as molten lead, and as heavy too: God keep lead out of me! I need no more weight than mine own bowels v 3 34
I'll lead you to your tent.—Lead me, my lord? I do not need your help v 4 9
The rest Turn'd on themselves, like dull and heavy lead *2 Hen. IV.* i 1 118
Who is it like should lead his forces hither? i 3 81
What a life dost thou lead!—A better than thou ii 4 310
Lead him hence; and see you guard him sure iv 3 81
We will our youth lead on to higher fields iv 5 3
And had a purpose now To lead out many to the Holy Land iv 5 211
Will make him burst his lead and rise from death *1 Hen. VI.* i 1 64
Use no entreaty, for it is in vain.—Then lead me hence iv 4 86
To Ireland will you lead a band of men? *2 Hen. VI.* iii 1 312
Yield to mercy whilst 'tis offer'd you; Or let a rebel lead you to your deaths iv 8 13
In God's name, lead; your king's name be obey'd *3 Hen. VI.* iii 1 99
I myself will lead a private life And in devotion spend my latter days iv 6 42
If thou darest.—Yes, Warwick, Edward dares, and leads the way v 1 112
Come, lead me to the block; bear him my head *Richard III.* iii 4 108
Go, go, up to the leads; the lord mayor knocks iii 7 55
Delay leads impotent and snail-paced beggary iv 3 53
That with a fearful soul Leads discontented steps in foreign soil iv 4 312
Will I come And lead thy daughter to a conqueror's bed iv 4 334
Let us be lead within thy bosom, Richard, And weigh thee down to ruin! v 3 152
I will lead forth my soldiers to the plain, And thus my battle shall be ordered v 3 291
And who doth lead them but a paltry fellow? v 3 323
Lead in your ladies, every one *Hen. VIII.* i 4 103
I have half a dozen healths To drink to these fair ladies, and a measure To lead 'em once again i 4 107
Lead on, o' God's name ii 1 78
When old time shall lead him to his end, Goodness and he fill up one monument! ii 1 93
Lead me in: There take an inventory of all I have, To the last penny iii 2 450
To our pavilion shall I lead you, sir *Troi. and Cres.* i 3 305
Blind fear, that seeing reason leads, finds safer footing than blind reason stumbling without fear iii 2 76
What error leads must err v 2 111
He that depends Upon your favours swims with fins of lead *Coriolanus* i 1 184
These three lead on this preparation Whither 'tis bent i 2 15
Ye Roman gods! Lead their successes as we wish our own i 6 7
Stalls, bulks, windows, Are smother'd up, leads fill'd ii 1 227

Lead. Such a pother As if that whatsoever god who leads him Were slily crept into his human powers . *Coriolanus* ii 1 235
But yet a brain that leads my use of anger To better vantage . iii 2 30
That Marcius, Join'd with Aufidius, leads a power 'gainst Rome . iv 6 66
To melt the city leads upon your pates . . . . . iv 6 82
He leads them like a thing Made by some other deity than nature . iv 6 90
From forth this place I lead espoused my bride along with me *T. Andron.* i 1 325
Who leads towards Rome a band of warlike Goths . . . . v 2 113
Feather of lead, bright smoke, cold fire, sick health! . . *Rom. and Jul.* i 1 186
I have a soul of lead So stakes me to the ground I cannot move . i 4 15
If ye should lead her into a fool's paradise, as they say . . . ii 4 175
But old folks, many feign as they were dead; Unwieldy, slow, heavy and pale as lead . . . . ii 5 17
Then will I be general of your woes, And lead you even to death . v 3 220
Why dost thou lead these men about the streets? . . . *J. Cæsar* i 1 32
Into what dangers would you lead me, Cassius? . . . . i 2 63
I follow you, To do I know not what: but it sufficeth That Brutus leads me on . . . . ii 1 334
Brutus shall lead; and we will grace his heels With the most boldest and best hearts of Rome . . . . iii 1 120
I have no will to wander forth of doors, Yet something leads me forth . iii 3 4
Bid our commanders lead their charges off A little from this ground . iv 2 48
There is a tide in the affairs of men, Which, taken at the flood, leads on to fortune . . . . iv 3 219
Lead your battle softly on . . . . v 1 16
That we may, Lovers in peace, lead on our days to age! . . . v 1 95
A heavy summons lies like lead upon me, And yet I would not sleep *Macbeth* ii 1 6
You, worthy uncle, Shall . . . Lead our first battle . . . . v 6 4
Where wilt thou lead me? speak; I'll go no further . . *Hamlet* i 5 1
And leads the will to desperate undertakings As oft as any passion . ii 1 104
If circumstances lead me, I will find Where truth is hid . . . ii 2 157
'Tis a question left us yet to prove, Whether love lead fortune, or else fortune love . . . . iii 2 213
To follow him thither with modesty enough, and likelihood to lead it . v 1 231
'Tis best to give him way; he leads himself . . . . *Lear* ii 4 301
Let's follow the old earl, and get the Bedlam To lead him where he would iii 7 104
Bring some covering for this naked soul, Who I'll entreat to lead me . iv 1 47
'Tis the times' plague, when madmen lead the blind . . . . iv 1 48
Give me thy arm: Poor Tom shall lead thee . . . . . iv 1 82
Lest his ungovern'd rage dissolve the life That wants the means to lead it iv 4 20
Give me your hand, I'll lead you to some biding . . . . iv 6 228
Mine own tears Do scald like molten lead . . . . . . iv 7 48
Another of his fathom they have none, To lead their business . *Othello* i 1 154
Lead to the Sagittary the raised search; And there will I be with him . i 1 159
Each man to what sport and revels his addiction leads him . . . ii 2 6
And passion, having my best judgement collied, Assays to lead the way ii 3 207
Sir, for your hurts, myself will be your surgeon: Lead him off . . ii 3 254
Strong circumstances, Which lead directly to the door of truth . . iii 3 407
Do invite you to my sister's view, Whither straight I'll lead you *A. and C.* ii 2 171
Lead me from hence; I faint: O Iras, Charmian! 'tis no matter . ii 5 109
Pity me, Charmian, But do not speak to me. Lead me to my chamber ii 5 119
'Tis not my profit that does lead mine honour; Mine honour, it . . ii 7 82
Love, I am full of lead. Some wine, within there, and our viands! . iii 11 72
Lead you Where rather I'll expect victorious life Than death and honour iv 2 42
He'll lead me, then, in triumph?—Madam, he will . . . . v 2 109
That is my bed too, lads, and there I'll lie: Lead, lead . *Cymbeline* iv 4 53
We do our longing stay To hear the rest untold: sir, lead's the way *Per.* v 3 84
Lead the way *Tempest* ii 2; *Mer. Wives* i 1; *T. of Shrew* iv 4; *T. Night* iv 3; *2 Hen. VI.* ii 4; *Hen. VIII.* v 5; *Troi. and Cres.* iii 3

Leaden. In leaden contemplation have found out Such fiery numbers *L. L. Lost* iv 3 321
There's an eye Wounds like a leaden sword . . . . . . v 2 481
Death-counterfeiting sleep With leaden legs and batty wings *M. N. Dream* iii 2 365
What says this leaden casket? 'Who chooseth me must give and hazard all he hath.' Must give: for what? . . . *Mer. of Venice* ii 7 15
O you leaden messengers, That ride upon the violent speed of fire *All's W.* iii 2 111
Thy golden sceptre for a leaden dagger . . . *1 Hen. IV.* ii 4 419
Leaden age, Quicken'd with youthful spleen and warlike rage *1 Hen. VI.* iv 6 12
If he be leaden, icy-cold, unwilling, Be thou so too *Richard III.* iii 1 176
Fearful commenting Is leaden servitor to dull delay . . . . iv 3 52
To take a nap, Lest leaden slumber peise me down to-morrow . . v 3 105
Leaden spoons, Irons of a doit . . . . . . *Coriolanus* i 5 6
Will too late Tie leaden pounds to's heels . . . . . iii 1 314
To you our swords have leaden points, Mark Antony . *J. Cæsar* iii 1 173
O murderous slumber, Lay'st thou thy leaden mace upon my boy? . iv 3 268
I have this while with leaden thoughts been press'd *Othello* iii 4 177

Leader. You were wont to be a follower, but now you are a leader *M. W.* iii 2 3
We must follow the leaders.—In every good thing . . . *Much Ado* ii 1 157
Hence, therefore, every leader to his charge . . . *1 Hen. IV.* v 1 118
A tall gentleman, by heaven, and a most gallant leader . *2 Hen. IV.* iii 2 68
I cannot put him to a private soldier that is the leader of so many thousands . . . . iii 2 178
What well-appointed leader fronts us here? . . . . . iv 1 25
The leaders, having charge from you to stand, Will not go off . . iv 2 99
Living idly here in pomp and ease, Whilst such a worthy leader, wanting aid, Unto his dastard foemen is betray'd . . . *1 Hen. VI.* i 1 143
Ill beseeming any common man, Much more a knight, a captain and a leader . . . . iv 1 32
Thou princely leader of our English strength, Never so needful . . iv 3 17
Like an angry hive of bees That want their leader . . *2 Hen. VI.* iii 2 126
Applaud the name of Henry with your leader . . . *3 Hen. VI.* iv 2 27
Limit each leader to his several charge . . . . *Richard III.* v 3 25
They have a leader, Tullus Aufidius, that will put you to't *Coriolanus* i 1 232
So our leader's led, And we are women's men . . . *Ant. and Cleo.* iii 7 70

Leadest. Thou but lead'st this fashion of thy malice To the last hour of act *Mer. of Venice* iv 1 18
Thou rascal, that art worst in blood to run, Lead'st first to win *Coriolanus* i 1 164
We'll follow where thou lead'st, Like stinging bees . . *T. Andron.* v 1 13

Leading. And so may I, blind fortune leading me, Miss that which one unworthier may attain . . . . *Mer. of Venice* ii 1 36
Mortimer, Leading the men of Herefordshire to fight . . *1 Hen. IV.* i 1 39
I wonder much, Being men of such great leading as you are . . iv 3 17
Most humbly on my knee I beg The leading of the vaward . *Hen. V.* iv 3 130
Earl of Surrey Shall have the leading of this foot and horse *Richard III.* v 3 297
If thou wilt have The leading of thine own revenges . . *Coriolanus* iv 5 143
From that place I shall no leading need . . . . . *Lear* iv 1 81

Leaf. An oak but with one green leaf on it would have answered her *Much Ado* ii 1 247
Writ o' both sides the leaf, margent and all . . . *L. L. Lost* v 2 8
Leaf. He that hath suffer'd this disorder'd spring Hath now himself met with the fall of leaf . . . . *Richard II.* iii 4 49
Do I? yea, in very truth, do I, an 'twere an aspen leaf . . *2 Hen. IV.* ii 4 117
I will go get a leaf of brass, And with a gad of steel will write these words, And lay it by . . . . *T. Andron.* iv 1 102
Are not within the leaf of pity writ . . . . *T. of Athens* iv 3 117
Let me see; is not the leaf turn'd down Where I left reading? *J. Cæsar* iv 3 273
Your pains Are register'd where every day I turn The leaf to read them *Macbeth* i 3 152
My way of life Is fall'n into the sear, the yellow leaf . . . . v 3 23
Fold down the leaf where I have left: to bed . . . . *Cymbeline* ii 2 4
The tale of Tereus; here the leaf's turn'd down Where Philomel gave up ii 2 45
Leaf of eglantine, whom not to slander, Out-sweeten'd not thy breath . iv 2 223

Leafy. *See* **Leavy**

League. They hurried us aboard a bark, Bore us some leagues to sea *Temp.* i 2 145
She that dwells Ten leagues beyond man's life . . . . . . ii 1 247
I swam . . . five and thirty leagues off and on . . . . . iii 2 17
The forest is not three leagues off . . . . . *T. G. of Ver.* v 1 11
There is such a league between my good man and he! . *Mer. Wives* iii 2 25
Meet me at the consecrated fount A league below the city *Meas. for Meas.* iv 3 103
A league from Epidamnum had we sail'd . . . . *Com. of Errors* i 1 63
Ere the ships could meet by twice five leagues . . . . . i 1 101
Keep then fair league and truce with thy true bed . . . . ii 2 147
He was not three leagues off when I left him . . . . *Much Ado* i 1 4
From Athens is her house remote seven leagues . . . *M. N. Dream* i 1 159
In the wood, a league without the town, Where I did meet thee once . i 1 165
Be thou here again Ere the leviathan can swim a league . . . ii 1 174
With league whose date till death shall never end . . . . iii 2 373
I shall show you peace and fair-faced league . . . . *K. John* ii 1 417
This league that we have made Will give her sadness very little cure . ii 1 545
Our oppression hath made up this league . . . . . . iii 1 106
And the conjunction of our inward souls Married in league . . . iii 1 228
Withhold thy speed, dreadful occasion! O, make a league with me! . iv 2 126
O inglorious league! . . . . v 1 65
These two Christian armies might combine The blood of malice in a vein of league . . . . v 2 38
I am sworn brother, sweet, To grim Necessity, and he and I Will keep a league till death . . . . *Richard II.* v 1 22
And those musicians that shall play to you Hang in the air a thousand leagues from hence . . . . *1 Hen. IV.* iii 1 227
Bardolph stole a lute-case, bore it twelve leagues, and sold it. *Hen. V.* iii 2 46
To make divorce of their incorporate league . . . . . v 2 394
We'll take your oath, And all the peers', for surety of our leagues . . v 2 400
We come to be informed by yourselves What the conditions of that league must be . . . . *1 Hen. VI.* v 4 119
Hast thou by secret means Used intercession to obtain a league? . . v 4 148
Shameful is this league! Fatal this marriage! . . . *2 Hen. VI.* i 1 98
France should have torn and rent my very heart, Before I would have yielded to this league . . . . i 1 127
And seem to kiss, As if they vow'd some league inviolable . *3 Hen. VI.* ii 1 30
First, to do greetings to thy royal person; And then to crave a league of amity . . . . iii 3 53
Look, therefore, Lewis, that by this league and marriage Thou draw not on thy danger . . . . iii 3 74
I'll kiss thy hand, In sign of league and amity with thee *Richard III.* i 3 281
You peers, continue this united league . . . . ii 1 2
Seal thou this league With thy embracements to my wife's allies . . ii 1 29
France hath flaw'd the league . . . . *Hen. VIII.* i 1 95
From this league Peep'd harms that menaced him . . . . . i 1 182
Now he has crack'd the league Between us and the emperor . . . ii 2 25
To conclude . . . A league between his highness and Ferrara . . . iii 2 323
She's with the lion deeply still in league . . . . *T. Andron.* iv 1 98
When we join in league, I am a lamb . . . . iv 2 136
For peace, for love, for league, and good to Rome . . . . v 3 23
He lies to-night within seven leagues of Rome . . . *J. Cæsar* iii 1 286
Thus time we waste, and longest leagues make short . . *Pericles* iv 4 1

Leagued. If partially affined, or leagued in office, Thou dost deliver more or less than truth, Thou art no soldier . . . . . *Othello* ii 3 218
His arms thus leagued: I thought he slept . . . *Cymbeline* iv 2 213

Leaguer. He shall suppose no other but that he is carried into the leaguer of the adversaries . . . . *All's Well* iii 6 27

Leah. It was my turquoise; I had it of Leah when I was a bachelor *Mer. of Venice* iii 1 126

Leak. They will allow us ne'er a jordan, and then we leak in your chimney *1 Hen. IV.* ii 1 22
That the united vessel of their blood . . . Shall never leak *2 Hen. IV.* iv 4 47
Her boat hath a leak, And she must not speak . . . *Lear* iii 6 28

Leak'd is our bark, And we, poor mates, stand on the dying deck *T. of A.* iv 2 19

Leaky. As leaky as an unstanched wench . . . . . . *Tempest* i 1 51
Thou art so leaky, That we must leave thee to thy sinking *Ant. and Cleo.* iii 13 63

Lean. Look thee, I'll but lean, and my staff understands me *T. G. of Ver.* ii 5 31
My name is Elbow: I do lean upon justice, sir . . *Meas. for Meas.* ii 1 49
I have but lean luck in the match . . . . . *Com. of Errors* iii 2 93
She leans me out at her mistress' chamber-window . . *Much Ado* iii 3 155
Fat paunches have lean pates . . . . *L. L. Lost* i 1 26
It will please his grace, by the world, sometime to lean upon my poor shoulder . . . . v 1 108
Ragged sails, Lean, rent and beggar'd by the strumpet wind *Mer. of Ven.* ii 6 19
The sixth age shifts Into the lean and slipper'd pantaloon *As Y. Like It* ii 7 158
Lacking the burden of lean and wasteful learning . . . . . iii 2 341
A lean cheek, which you have not, a blue eye and sunken . . . iii 2 392
Lean but upon a rush, The cicatrice and capable impressure Thy palm some moment keeps . . . . iii 5 22
Out of my lean and low ability I'll lend you something . . *T. Night* iii 4 378
Nor lean enough to be thought a good student . . . . . iv 2 8
You would believe my saying, Howe'er you lean to the nayward *W. Tale* ii 1 64
So lean, that blasts of January Would blow you through and through . iv 4 111
Another lean unwash'd artificer Cuts off his tale . . . *K. John* iv 2 201
For obtaining of suits, whereof the hangman hath no lean wardrobe *1 Hen. IV.* i 2 82
Falstaff sweats to death, And lards the lean earth as he walks along . ii 2 116
Here comes lean Jack, here comes bare-bone . . . . . ii 4 358
If to be fat be to be hated, then Pharaoh's lean kine are to be loved . ii 4 520
Northumberland did lean to him, The more and less came in . . iv 3 67
The lives of all your loving complices Lean on your health *2 Hen. IV.* i 1 164
O, give me always a little, lean, old, chapt, bald shot . . . iii 2 294
He hath, like lean, sterile and bare land, manured, husbanded . iv 3 129
I'll turn, And something lean to cutpurse of quick hand . *Hen. V.* v 1 91
Lean raw-boned rascals! who would e'er suppose They had such courage? *1 Hen. VI.* i 2 35

Lean. Lean thine aged back against mine arm — *1 Hen. VI.* ii 5 43
My three attendants, Lean famine, quartering steel, and climbing fire — iv 2 11
The clergy's bags Are lank and lean with thy extortions — *2 Hen. VI.* i 3 132
Sweet Duke of York, our prop to lean upon, Now thou art gone *3 Hen. VI.* ii 1 68
On thy shoulder will I lean; And when thou fail'st . . . Must Edward fall ii 1 189
I'll lean upon one crutch and fight with t'other, Ere stay behind *Coriol.* i 1 246
The trees, though summer, yet forlorn and lean — *T. Andron.* ii 3 94
See, how she leans her cheek upon her hand! — *Rom. and Jul.* ii 2 23
The lean abhorred monster keeps Thee here in dark to be his paramour v 3 104
My lord leans wondrously to discontent — *T. of Athens* iii 4 70
It is the pasture lards the rother's sides, The want that makes him lean iv 3 13
Yond Cassius has a lean and hungry look; He thinks too much *J. Cæsar* i 2 194
Cæsar was ne'er so much your enemy As that same ague which hath made you lean — ii 2 113
Your fat king and your lean beggar is but variable service — *Hamlet* iv 3 25
For every thing is seal'd and done That else leans on the affair — iv 3 59
I struck The lean and wrinkled Cassius — *Ant. and Cleo.* iii 11 37
It much would please him, That of his fortunes you should make a staff To lean upon — iii 13 69
What shalt thou expect, To be depender on a thing that leans? *Cymbeline* i 5 58
Leander. How young Leander cross'd the Hellespont — *T. G. of Ver.* i 1 22
Would serve to scale another Hero's tower, So bold Leander would adventure it — iii 1 120
Leander the good swimmer — *Much Ado* v 2 30
Leander, he would have lived many a fair year, though Hero had turned nun, if it had not been for a hot midsummer night — *As Y. Like It* iv 1 100
Leaned. The love that lean'd on them as slippery too — *Troi. and Cres.* iii 3 85
'Twere good You lean'd unto his sentence with what patience Your wisdom may inform you — *Cymbeline* i 1 78
Leaner. That which combined us was most great, and let not A leaner action rend us — *Ant. and Cleo.* ii 2 19
Lean-faced. A hungry lean-faced villain, A mere anatomy *Com. of Errors* v 1 237
With full as many signs of deadly hate As lean-faced Envy — *2 Hen. VI.* iii 2 315
Leaning cheek to cheek — *W. Tale* i 2 285
Thus, leaning on mine elbow, I begin — *K. John* i 1 194
Breathless and faint, leaning upon my sword — *1 Hen. IV.* i 3 32
He is thy crutch; now if thou lose thy stay, Thou on him leaning, and all Troy on thee, Fall all together — *Troi. and Cres.* v 3 61
Lean-look'd prophets, whisper fearful change — *Richard II.* ii 4 11
Leanness. Watching breeds leanness, leanness is all gaunt *Richard II.* ii 1 78
Whose large style Agrees not with the leanness of his purse *2 Hen. VI.* i 1 112
The leanness that afflicts us, the object of our misery, is as an inventory to particularize their abundance — *Coriolanus* i 1 20
Lean-witted fool. A lunatic lean-witted fool — *Richard II.* ii 1 115
Leap. Cricket, to Windsor chimneys shalt thou leap — *Mer. Wives* v 5 47
How will he triumph, leap and laugh at it! — *L. L. Lost* iv 3 148
Leap for joy, though they are lame with blows — v 2 291
And 'twere as easy For you to laugh and leap and say you are merry, Because you are not sad — *Mer. of Venice* i 1 49
A hot temper leaps o'er a cold decree: such a hare is madness the youth i 2 20
Be clamorous and leap all civil bounds — *T. Night* i 4 21
Being ready to leap out of himself for joy — *W. Tale* v 2 54
The wall is high, and yet will I leap down: Good ground, be pitiful! *K. John* iv 3 1
Rich men look sad and ruffians dance and leap — *Richard II.* ii 4 12
An easy leap, To pluck bright honour from the pale-faced moon *1 Hen. IV.* i 3 201
I should quickly leap into a wife — *Hen. V.* v 2 145
Leap o'er the walls for refuge in the field — *1 Hen. VI.* ii 2 25
If you mean to save yourself from whipping, leap me over this stool *2 Hen. VI.* ii 1 144
Sirrah beadle, whip him till he leap over that same stool — ii 1 148
Made the lame to leap and fly away — ii 1 162
You take a precipice for no leap of danger — *Hen. VIII.* v 1 139
Our play Leaps o'er the vaunt and firstlings of those broils *Tr. and Cr.* Prol. 27
And Romeo Leap to these arms, untalk'd of and unseen *Rom. and Jul.* iii 2 7
O, bid me leap, rather than marry Paris, From off the battlements iv 1 77
Darest thou, Cassius, now Leap in with me into this angry flood? *J. Cæsar* i 2 103
It is more worthy to leap in ourselves, Than tarry till they push us v 5 24
Dogs leap the hatch, and all are fled. Do de, de, de. Sessa! *Lear* iii 6 76
For all beneath the moon Would I not leap upright — iv 6 27
If Cæsar please, our master Will leap to be his friend *Ant. and Cleo.* iii 13 51
Leap thou, attire and all, Through proof of harness to my heart! iv 8 14
I leap into the seas, Where's hourly trouble for a minute's ease *Pericles* ii 4 43
My heart Leaps to be gone into my mother's bosom — v 3 45
Leaped. Ferdinand, With hair up-staring,—then like reeds, not hair,—Was the first man that leap'd — *Tempest* i 2 214
And some such strange bull leap'd your father's cow *Much Ado* v 4 49
Like him that leaped into the custard — *All's Well* ii 5 40
Though I swore I leaped from the window of the citadel— How deep? iv 1 60
And winking leap'd into destruction — *2 Hen. IV.* i 3 33
As the year Had found some months asleep and leap'd them over iv 4 124
He parted frowning from me, as if ruin Leap'd from his eyes *Hen. VIII.* iii 2 206
See what hole is here, And what he is that now is leap'd into it *T. Andron.* ii 3 247
He ran this way, and leap'd this orchard wall — *Rom. and Jul.* ii 1 5
I do suspect the lusty Moor Hath leap'd into my seat — *Othello* ii 1 305
Leap-frog. If I could win a lady at leap-frog — *Hen. V.* v 2 142
Leaping. To outface me with leaping in her grave — *Hamlet* v 1 301
Leaping-house. And dials the signs of leaping-houses — *1 Hen. IV.* i 2 9
Leaping-time. I had rather Have skipp'd from sixteen years of age to sixty, To have turn'd my leaping-time into a crutch, Than have seen this — *Cymbeline* iv 2 200
Lear. Royal Lear, Whom I have ever honour'd as my king — *Lear* i 1 141
Be Kent unmannerly, When Lear is mad — i 1 148
See better, Lear; and let me still remain The true blank of thine eye i 1 160
Royal Lear, Give but that portion which yourself proposed — i 1 244
This is not Lear: Doth Lear walk thus? speak thus? Where are his eyes? — i 4 246
Who is it that can tell me who I am?—Lear's shadow — i 4 251
O Lear, Lear, Lear! Beat at this gate, that let thy folly in, And thy dear judgement out! — i 4 292
Nuncle Lear, nuncle Lear, tarry and take the fool with thee — i 4 338
The poor distressed Lear's i' the town; Who sometime, in his better tune, remembers What we are come about — iv 3 40
I'll bring you to our master Lear, And leave you to attend him — iv 3 52
As for the mercy Which he intends to Lear and to Cordelia, The battle done, and they within our power, Shall never see his pardon — v 1 66
Give me thy hand; away! King Lear hath lost, he and his daughter ta'en v 2 6
Told the most piteous tale of Lear and him That ever ear received v 3 214
Quickly send, Be brief in it, to the castle; for my writ Is on the life of Lear and on Cordelia — v 3 246

Learn. But thy vile race, Though thou didst learn, had that in't which good natures Could not abide to be with — *Tempest* i 2 359
Where the devil should he learn our language? — ii 2 69
And he wants wit that wants resolved will To learn his wit to exchange the bad for better — *T. G. of Ver.* ii 6 13
You would quickly learn to know him by his voice — iv 2 89
Seek shelter, pack! Falstaff will learn the humour of the age *Mer. Wives* i 3 92
I will, out of thine own confession, learn to begin thy health. *M. for M.* i 2 39
Away! let's go learn the truth of it — i 2 82
But we do learn By those that know the very nerves of state — i 4 52
Let him learn to know, when maidens sue, Men give like gods — i 4 80
I'll gladly learn — ii 3 23
I will instruct thee in my trade: follow.—I do desire to learn, sir — iv 2 59
Ere I learn love, I'll practise to obey — *Com. of Errors* ii 1 29
Learn to jest in good time: there's a time for all things — ii 2 65
See how apt it is to learn Any hard lesson that may do thee good *M. Ado* i 1 294
I will presently go learn their day of marriage — ii 2 57
Sweet prince, you learn me noble thankfulness — iv 1 31
He is Cupid's grandfather and learns news of him — *L. L. Lost* ii 1 254
Learn her by heart.—By heart and in heart, boy.—And out of heart — iii 1 36
If that she learn not of her eye to look — iv 3 252
How I caught it, found it, or came by it, What stuff 'tis made of, whereof it is born, I am to learn — *Mer. of Venice* i 1 5
Happy in this, she is not yet so old But she may learn — iii 2 163
Happier than this, She is not bred so dull but she can learn — iii 2 164
You must not learn me how to remember — *As Y. Like It* i 2 6
Learn of the wise, and perpend — iii 2 68
Then learn this of me: to have, is to have — v 1 44
She's apt to learn and thankful for good turns — *T. of Shrew* ii 1 166
I'll not be tied to hours nor 'pointed times, But learn my lessons as I please — iii 1 20
To learn the order of my fingering, I must begin with rudiments of art iii 1 65
It shall do you no harm to learn — *All's Well* ii 2 39
I will not practise to deceive, Yet, to avoid deceit, I mean to learn *K. John* i 1 215
From the king I come, to learn how you have dealt for him — v 2 121
Learn to know him now — *Richard II.* ii 3 40
Thy very beadsmen learn to bend their bows Of double-fatal yew — iii 2 116
My father hath a power; inquire of him, And learn to make a body of a limb — iii 2 187
So that by this intelligence we learn The Welshmen are dispersed — iii 3 1
A clergyman Of holy reverence; who, I cannot learn — iii 3 29
True noblesse would Learn him forbearance from so foul a wrong — iv 1 120
Learn, good soul, To think our former state a happy dream — v 1 17
You must needs learn, lord, to amend this fault — *1 Hen. IV.* iii 1 180
Learn this, Thomas, And thou shalt prove a shelter to thy friends *2 Hen. IV.* iv 4 41
They will learn you by rote where services were done — *Hen. V.* iii 6 74
You must learn to know such slanders of the age — iii 6 84
Have lost, or do not learn for want of time, The sciences — v 2 57
I would have her learn, my fair cousin, how perfectly I love her — v 2 309
Come, wife, let's in, and learn to govern better — *2 Hen. VI.* iv 9 48
Arise a knight; And learn this lesson, draw thy sword in right *3 Hen. VI.* ii 2 62
Now Margaret Must strike her sail and learn awhile to serve — iii 3 5
Are you yet to learn What late misfortune is befall'n King Edward? iv 4 2
As I can learn, He hearkens after prophecies and dreams *Richard III.* i 1 53
These, as I learn, and such like toys as these Have moved his highness i 1 60
My tongue could never learn sweet smoothing words — i 2 169
Good counsel, marry: learn it, learn it — i 3 261
How canst thou woo her?—That would I learn of you — iv 4 268
And wilt thou learn of me?—Madam, with all my heart — iv 4 270
Learn this, brother, We live not to be grip'd by meaner persons *Hen. VIII.* ii 2 135
Thy horse will sooner con an oration than thou learn a prayer *T. and C.* ii 1 19
Toadstool, learn me the proclamation — ii 1 22
I bade the vile owl go learn me the tenour of the proclamation — ii 1 99
He knew his man.—O, meaning you. I will go learn more of it — ii 1 142
I'll learn to conjure and raise devils, but I'll see some issue — ii 3 6
Go you to the city; Learn how 'tis held — *Coriolanus* i 10 28
Youngling, learn thou to make some meaner choice — *T. Andron.* ii 1 73
When did the tiger's young ones teach the dam? O, do not learn her wrath — ii 3 143
Speechless complainer, I will learn thy thought — iii 2 39
And by still practice learn to know thy meaning — iii 2 45
Come hither, boy; come, come, and learn of us To melt in showers v 3 160
Do you know the cause?—I neither know it nor can learn of him *R. and J.* i 1 150
Could we but learn from whence his sorrows grow, We would as willingly give cure as know — i 1 160
This is the hag, when maids lie on their backs, That presses them and learns them first to bear — i 4 93
Come, civil night, . . . And learn me how to lose a winning match — iii 2 12
Men must learn now with pity to dispense — *T. of Athens* iii 2 93
For mine own part, I shall be glad to learn of noble men — *J. Cæsar* iv 3 54
We learn no other but the confident tyrant Keeps still in Dunsinane *Macbeth* v 4 8
Learn more than thou trowest, Set less than thou throwest — *Lear* i 4 135
Keep a schoolmaster that can teach thy fool to lie: I would fain learn to lie — i 4 196
Who is it that can tell me who I am?—Lear's shadow.—I would learn that — i 4 252
Sir, I am too old to learn — ii 2 134
My life and education both do learn me How to respect you — *Othello* i 3 183
Do not learn of him, Emilia, though he be thy husband — ii 1 163
I learn, you take things ill which are not so — *Ant. and Cleo.* ii 2 29
I hourly learn A doctrine of obedience — v 2 30
One of your great knowing Should learn, being taught, forbearance *Cymbeline* ii 3 103
Learn now, for all, That I, which know my heart, do here pronounce, By the very truth of it, I care not for you — ii 3 111
What he learns by this May prove his travel, not her danger — iii 5 102
We'll learn our freeness of a son-in-law; Pardon's the word to all — v 5 421
I do beseech you To learn of me, who stand i' the gaps to teach you *Per.* iv 4 8
Learned. You have learned, like Sir Proteus, to wreathe your arms *T. G. of Ver.* ii 1 19
A thousand more mischances than this one Have learn'd me how to brook this patiently — v 3 4
Allowed for your many war-like, court-like, and learned preparations *Mer. Wives* ii 2 237
One that hath taught me more wit than ever I learned before in my life iv 5 61
I am sorry, one so learned and so wise As you . . . Should slip *M. for M.* v 1 475
Get the learned writer to set down our excommunication — *Much Ado* iii 5 68

Learned. This learned constable is too cunning to be understood : what's your offence? . . . . . *Much Ado* v 1 234
What, my soul, verses?—Ay, sir, and very learned . . . *L. L. Lost* iv 2 106
Well learned is that tongue that well can thee commend . . . iv 2 116
Love, first learned in a lady's eyes, Lives not alone immured in the brain . . . . iv 3 327
Learned without opinion, and strange without heresy . . . . v 1 5
This most gallant, illustrate, and learned gentleman . . . . v 1 129
And wit's own grace to grace a learned fool . . . . . v 2 72
Will you hear the dialogue that the two learned men have compiled? . v 2 895
Bellario, a learned doctor . . . . *Mer. of Venice* iv 1 105
This letter from Bellario doth commend A young and learned doctor . iv 1 144
You hear the learn'd Bellario, what he writes : And here, I take it, is the doctor . . . . iv 1 167
The law allows it, and the court awards it.—Most learned judge! . . iv 1 304
O learned judge! Mark, Jew : a learned judge! . . . . iv 1 317
He's gentle, never schooled and yet learned . . . *As Y. Like It* i 1 173
Where learned you that oath, fool?—Of a certain knight . . . i 2 65
We still have slept together, Rose at an instant, learn'd, play'd, eat together . . . . i 3 76
He that hath learned no wit by nature nor art may complain of good breeding . . . . iii 2 30
Art thou learned?—No, sir.—Then learn this of me . . . . v 1 42
Out of these convertites There is much matter to be heard and learn'd v 4 191
When our most learned doctors leave us . . . . . *All's Well* ii 1 119
But a trifle neither, in good faith, if the learned should speak truth of it ii 2 37
Of all the learned and authentic fellows . . . . ii 3 14
Yet you began rudely . . . —The rudeness that hath appeared in me have I learned from my entertainment . . . . *T. Night* i 5 231
In voices well divulged, free, learn'd, and valiant . . . . i 5 279
The copy of your speed is learn'd by them . . . . *K. John* iv 2 113
The language I have learn'd these forty years, My native English, now I must forego . . . . *Richard II.* i 3 159
I had thought, my lord, to have learn'd his health of you . . . ii 3 24
I hardly yet have learn'd To insinuate, flatter, bow, and bend my limbs iv 1 164
I will never be a truant, love, Till I have learn'd thy language 1 *Hen. IV.* iii 1 208
And further, I have learn'd, The king himself in person is set forth . iv 1 90
And for their bareness, I am sure they never learned that of me . . iv 2 78
Not a man of them brings other news Than they have learn'd of me 2 *Hen. IV.* Ind. 39
I was then advised by my learned counsel in the laws . . . . i 2 152
Wherein, to gain the language, 'Tis needful that the most immodest word Be look'd upon and learn'd . . . . iv 4 71
My learned lord, we pray you to proceed . . . . . *Hen. V.* i 2 9
Seem they grave and learned? Why, so didst thou . . . . ii 2 128
With all the learned council of the realm . . . . . 2 *Hen. VI.* i 1 89
Large gifts have I bestow'd on learned clerks . . . . . . iv 7 76
By learned approbation of the judges . . . . . *Hen. VIII.* i 2 71
The gentleman is learn'd, and a most rare speaker ; To nature none more bound . . . . i 2 111
My learn'd lord cardinal, Deliver all with charity . . . . . i 2 142
You're welcome, Most learned reverend sir, into our kingdom . . . ii 2 77
All the clerks, I mean the learned ones, in Christian kingdoms . . ii 2 93
This good man, This just and learned priest . . . . . ii 2 97
Was he not held a learned man?—Yes, surely . . . . . ii 2 124
By all the reverend fathers of the land And doctors learn'd . . . ii 4 206
My learn'd and well-beloved servant, Cranmer . . . . . ii 4 238
He's a learned man. May he continue Long in his highness' favour! . iii 2 395
Accompanied with other Learned and reverend fathers of his order . iv 1 26
By the main assent Of all these learned men she was divorced . . iv 1 32
If you are learn'd, Be not as common fools . . . . *Coriolanus* iii 1 99
Action is eloquence, and the eyes of the ignorant More learned than the ears . . . . iii 2 77
That bloody mind, I think, they learn'd of me . . . . *T. Andron* v 1 101
And can never find what names the writing person hath here writ. I must to the learned . . . . *Rom. and Jul.* i 2 45
Perhaps you have learned it without book : but, I pray, can you read any thing you see? . . . . i 2 61
What's this?—A rhyme I learn'd even now Of one I danced withal . i 5 144
Where I have learn'd me to repent the sin Of disobedient opposition To you and your behests . . . . iv 2 17
The learned pate Ducks to the golden fool : all is oblique *T. of Athens* iv 3 17
And never learn'd The icy precepts of respect . . . . . . iv 3 257
All his faults observed, Set in a note-book, learn'd . . . *J. Cæsar* iv 3 98
I have learned by the perfectest report . . . . . . *Macbeth* i 5 2
I learn'd, The night before there was no purpose in them Of this *Lear* ii 4 2
Where learned you this, fool?—Not i' the stocks, fool . . . ii 4 87
I'll talk a word with this same learned Theban. What is your study? . iii 4 162
Come, sit thou here, most learned justicer; Thou, sapient sir, sit here . iii 6 23
'Fore God, an excellent song.—I learned it in England . . *Othello* ii 3 78
Knows all qualities, with a learned spirit, Of human dealings . . iii 3 259
Thy master dies thy scholar : to do thus I learn'd of thee *Ant. and Cleo.* iv 14 103
Hast thou not learn'd me how To make perfumes? distil? preserve? *Cymbeline* i 5 12
Learn'd indeed were that astronomer That knew the stars as I his characters . . . . iii 2 27
The worth that learned charity aye wears . . . . *Pericles* v 3 Gower 94
Learnedly. Temperance was a delicate wench.—Ay, and a subtle ; as he most learnedly delivered . . . . *Tempest* ii 1 44
Points more than all the lawyers in Bohemia can learnedly handle *W. Tale* iv 4 207
Much He spoke, and learnedly, for life . . . . *Hen. VIII.* ii 1 28
Learning. The red plague rid you For learning me your language! *Tempest* i 2 365
I have lived fourscore years and upward ; I never heard a man of his place, gravity and learning, so wide of his own respect *Mer. Wives* iii 1 58
I paid nothing for it neither, but was paid for my learning . . . iv 5 63
So were there a patch set on learning, to see him in a school *L. L. Lost* iv 2 32
Learning is but an adjunct to ourself And where we are our learning likewise is : Then when ourselves we see in ladies' eyes, Do we not likewise see our learning there? . . . . iv 3 314
Ba, most silly sheep with a horn. You hear his learning . . . v 1 54
The thrice three Muses mourning for the death Of Learning *M. N. Dream* v 1 53
The Sisters Three and such branches of learning . . *Mer. of Venice* ii 2 67
That choose by show, Not learning more than the fond eye doth teach ii 9 27
Bettered with his own learning, the greatness whereof I cannot enough commend . . . . iv 1 158
Lacking the burden of lean and wasteful learning . . . *As Y. Like It* iii 2 341
Institute A course of learning and ingenious studies . . *T. of Shrew* i 1 9
O this learning, what a thing it is!—O this woodcock, what an ass it is! i 2 160
This young man, for learning and behaviour Fit for her turn . . . i 2 169
Learning. A double spirit Of teaching and of learning instantly 1 *Hen. IV.* v 2 65
Whose learning and good letters peace hath tutor'd . . 2 *Hen. IV.* iv 1 44
Learning a mere hoard of gold kept by a devil, till sack commences it . iv 3 124
The most convenient place that I can think of For such receipt of learning is Black-Friars ; There ye shall meet . . . *Hen. VIII.* ii 2 139
Reverend fathers ; men Of singular integrity and learning . . . ii 4 59
With my weak wit, And to such men of gravity and learning . . iii 1 73
Ever witness for him Those twins of learning that he raised in you, Ipswich and Oxford! one of which fell with him . . . . iv 2 58
Learning, gentleness, virtue, youth, liberality, and such like *Tr. and Cr.* i 2 276
O Lord, I could have stay'd here all the night To hear good counsel : O, what learning is! . . . . *Rom. and Jul.* iii 3 160
There will little learning die then, that day thou art hanged *T. of Athens* ii 2 86
I once did hold it, as our statists do, A baseness to write fair and labour'd much How to forget that learning . . . . *Hamlet* v 2 35
I did inquire it ; And have my learning from some true reports *A. and C.* ii 2 47
All the learnings that his time Could make him the receiver of *Cymbeline* i 1 43
The sceptre, learning, physic, must All follow this, and come to dust . iv 2 268
Learning place. The court's a learning place . . . . *All's Well* i 1 191
Learnt. Thus much I have learnt : He rather means to lodge you in the field . . . . *L. L. Lost* ii 1 84
Who taught you this?—I learnt it out of women's faces . . *W. Tale* ii 1 12
I am never able to deal with my master, he hath learnt so much fence 2 *Hen. VI.* ii 3 79
Lease. That they are out by lease . . . . . *T. G. of Ver.* v 2 29
I'll assure her of Her widowhood, be it that she survive me, In all my lands and leases whatsoever . . . . . . *T. of Shrew* ii 1 126
It were a shame to let this land by lease . . . . *Richard II.* ii 1 110
Five year! by'r lady, a long lease for the clinking of pewter . 1 *Hen. IV.* ii 4 50
Now am I so hungry that if I might have a lease of my life for a thousand years I could stay no longer . . . . . . 2 *Hen. VI.* iv 10 6
Shall live the lease of nature, pay his breath To time . . *Macbeth* iv 1 99
Leased. This dear dear land, Dear for her reputation through the world, Is now leased out . . . . *Richard II.* ii 1 59
Leash. More straining on for plucking back, not following My leash unwillingly . . . . *W. Tale* iv 4 477
I am sworn brother to a leash of drawers . . . . . 1 *Hen. IV.* ii 4 7
Even like a fawning greyhound in the leash . . . . *Coriolanus* i 6 38
Leashed. At his heels, Leash'd in like hounds, should famine, sword and fire Crouch for employment . . . . *Hen. V.* Prol. 7
Leasing. Now Mercury endue thee with leasing! . . . . *T. Night* i 5 105
And in his praise Have almost stamp'd the leasing . . . *Coriolanus* v 2 22
Least. Past the mid season.—At least two glasses . . . . *Tempest* i 2 240
Where she at least is banish'd from your eye . . . . . . ii 1 126
She as far surpasseth Sycorax As great'st does least . . . . iii 2 111
O, they love least that let men know their love . . . *T. G. of Ver.* i 2 32
He will scarce be pleased withal.—That is the least, Lucetta, of my fear . . . . ii 7 68
Her sudden quips, The least whereof would quell a lover's hope . . iv 2 13
Go to thy lady's grave and call hers thence, Or, at the least, in hers sepulchre thine . . . . iv 2 118
Let it suffice thee, Mistress Page,—at the least, if the love of soldier can suffice,—that I love thee . . . . . . *Mer. Wives* ii 1 11
I will at the least keep your counsel . . . . iv 6 7
A dozen times at least . . . . *Meas. for Meas.* i 2 21
It is no sin ; Or of the deadly seven it is the least.—Which is the least? iii 1 111
Look you speak justly.—Boldly, at least . . . . v 1 299
I tell him we shall stay here at the least a month . . . *Much Ado* i 1 150
If not a present remedy, at least a patient sufferance . . . . i 3 9
At the least of thy sweet notice, bring her to trial . . . *L. L. Lost* i 1 278
Most power to do most harm, least knowing ill . . . . . ii 1 58
The epithets are sweetly varied, like a scholar at the least . . . iv 2 9
That sport best pleases that doth least know how . . . . . v 2 517
Love, therefore, and tongue-tied simplicity In least speak most *M. N. D.* v 1 105
So may the outward shows be least themselves . . *Mer. of Venice* iii 2 73
She moves me not, or not removes, at least, Affection's edge in me *T. of S.* i 2 72
I may, by this device, at least Have leave and leisure to make love . i 2 135
Am I but three inches? why, thy horn is a foot ; and so long am I at the least . . . . iv 1 30
That seeming to be most which we indeed least are . . . . v 2 175
You are loved, sir ; They that least lend it you shall lack you first *All's W.* i 2 68
Your oaths Are words and poor conditions, but unseal'd, At least in my opinion . . . . iv 2 31
I myself am best When least in company . . . . . *T. Night* i 4 38
Whereof the least Is not this suit of mine . . . . . *W. Tale* i 2 401
At least thus much : I'll pawn the little blood which I have left . . ii 3 165
You, my lord, best know, Who least will seem to do so . . . . iii 2 34
Straited For a reply, at least if you make a care Of happy holding her . iv 4 366
To the fearful usage, At least ungentle, of the dreadful Neptune . . v 1 154
Pops me out At least from fair five hundred pound a year . . *K. John* i 1 69
Let it at least be said They saw we had a purpose of defence . . . v 1 75
Your heart is up, I know, Thus high at least . . . . *Richard II.* iii 3 195
How thirty, at least, he fought with . . . . . . 1 *Hen. IV.* i 2 212
Redeeming time when men think least I will . . . . . . i 2 241
We four set upon some dozen— Sixteen at least, my lord . . . ii 4 194
He held me last night at least nine hours In reckoning up . . . iii 1 156
The least of which haunting a nobleman Loseth men's hearts . . . iii 1 186
Speak, Salisbury ; at least, if thou canst speak . . . 1 *Hen. VI.* i 4 73
For every drop of blood was drawn from him There hath at least five Frenchmen died to-night . . . . ii 2 9
Not the least of these But can do more in England than the king 2 *Hen. VI.* i 3 73
The least of all these signs were probable . . . . iii 2 178
A man at least, for less I should not be . . . . 3 *Hen. VI.* iii 1 57
That would be ten days' wonder at the least . . . . . . iii 2 113
Unto the sanctuary, To save at least the heir of Edward's right . . iv 4 32
If Henry be your king, Yet Edward at the least is Duke of York . . iv 7 21
I thought, at least, he would have said the king . . . . . v 1 29
His regiment lies half a mile at least South from the mighty power *Richard III.* v 3 37
The least of you shall share his part thereof . . . . . . v 3 268
Three at the least, that have By this so sicken'd their estates *Hen. VIII.* i 1 81
Have uncontemn'd gone by him, or at least Strangely neglected . . iii 2 10
They had parted so much honesty among 'em, At least, good manners . v 2 29
Be angry at your pleasures ; at the least, if you take it as a pleasure *Coriolanus* ii 1 34
When I do forget The least of these unspeakable deserts . *T. Andron.* i 1 256
Or, at the least, make them his enemies . . . . v 2 79
I am the greatest, able to do least, Yet most suspected . *Rom. and Jul.* v 3 223
Suspect still comes where an estate is least . . . *T. of Athens* iv 3 521

Least. Are his files As full as thy report?—I have spoke the least *T. of Athens* v 2 2
Though last, not least in love . . . . *J. Cæsar* iii 1 189
Twenty trenched gashes on his head ; The least a death to nature *Macb.* iii 4 28
Blow, wind ! come, wrack ! At least we'll die with harness on our back v 5 52
At least, the whisper goes so . . . . *Hamlet* i 1 80
I set it down, That one may smile, and smile, and be a villain ; At least I'm sure it may be so in Denmark . . . . i 5 109
Now, our joy, Although the last, not least . . . . . *Lear* i 1 85
Answer my life my judgement, Thy youngest daughter does not love thee least . . . . i 1 154
What, in the least, Will you require in present dower with her? . . i 1 194
I cannot think my sister in the least Would fail her obligation . . ii 4 143
They do discharge their shot of courtesy : Our friends at least *Othello* ii 1 57
Yet that I put the Moor At least into a jealousy so strong . . ii 1 310
Make me to see't ; or, at the least, so prove it . . . . . iii 3 364
You shall at least Go see my lord aboard . . . . *Cymbeline* i 1 177
Haply, near The residence of Posthumus ; so nigh at least . . iii 4 151
Would Our viands had been poison'd, or at least Those which I heaved to head ! . . . . v 5 156
Took some displeasure at him ; at least he judged so *Pericles* i 3 21
Walk half an hour, Leonine, at the least : Remember what I have said . iv 1 46
Least advantage. With the least advantage of hope . . *Othello* iv 2 179
Least affection. With the least affection of a welcome . *2 Hen. IV.* iv 5 173
Least cause. But they Upon their ancient malice will forget With the least cause these his new honours . . . . . *Coriolanus* ii 1 245
You shall not find, Though you be therein curious, the least cause For what you seem to fear . . . . *Ant. and Cleo.* iii 2 35
Least degree. And he that breaks them in the least degree Stands in attainder of eternal shame . . . . *L. L. Lost* i 1 157
Least expected. To make her heavenly comforts of despair, When it is least expected . . . . *Meas. for Meas.* iv 3 115
Least fear. No glory's got to overcome.—That's the least fear *Pericles* i 4 71
Least misuse. How have I been behaved, that he might stick The small'st opinion on my least misuse? . . . . . . *Othello* iv 2 109
Least noise. Cleopatra, catching but the least noise of this, dies instantly *Ant. and Cleo.* i 2 145
Least occasion. Upon the least occasion more mine eyes will tell tales of me . . . . *T. Night* ii 1 42
I am joyful To meet the least occasion that may give me Remembrance of my father-in-law . . . . *Hen. VIII.* iii 2 7
Least proportion. For what you see is but the smallest part And least proportion of humanity . . . . *1 Hen. VI.* ii 3 53
Least rub. When they once perceive The least rub in your fortunes, fall away . . . . *Hen. VIII.* ii 1 129
Least sinister. I am very comptible, even to the least sinister usage *T. N.* i 5 187
Least syllable. If thou deniest the least syllable of thy addition *Lear* ii 2 25
Least wind. The least wind i' the world will blow them down *A. and C.* ii 7 2
Least word. Spake one the least word that might Be to the prejudice of her present state . . . . *Hen. VIII.* ii 4 153
Leather. A present for any emperor that ever trod on neat's-leather *Temp.* ii 2 73
If I last in this service, you must case me in leather . *Com. of Errors* ii 1 85
He that went, like a bass-viol, in a case of leather . . . . . iv 3 23
What shall he have that kill'd the deer? His leather skin and horns to wear. Then sing him home . . . . . . *As Y. Like It* iv 2 12
A head-stall of sheep's leather . . . . . . *T. of Shrew* iii 2 58
The nobility think scorn to go in leather aprons . . *2 Hen. VI.* iv 2 13
His cold thin drink out of his leather bottle . . . *3 Hen. VI.* ii 5 48
A plague of opinion ! a man may wear it on both sides, like a leather jerkin . . . . *Troi. and Cres.* iii 3 266
Where is thy leather apron and thy rule? . . . . . *J. Cæsar* i 1 7
As proper men as ever trod upon neat's leather . . . . . i 1 29
Leather-coats. There's a dish of leather-coats for you . *2 Hen. IV.* v 3 44
Leathern. Some war with rere-mice for their leathern wings *M. N. Dream* ii 2 4
The wretched animal heaved forth such groans That their discharge did stretch his leathern coat . . . . . . *As Y. Like It* ii 1 37
She has a leathern hand, A freestone-colour'd hand . . . . iv 3 24
Wilt thou rob this leathern jerkin? . . . . . *1 Hen. IV.* ii 4 77
Put on two leathern jerkins and aprons, and wait upon him . *2 Hen. IV.* ii 2 189
Leave. Let's all sink with the king.—Let's take leave of him. *Tempest* i 1 68
This is a devil, and no monster : I will leave him ; I have no long spoon ii 2 103
They now are in my power ; And in these fits I leave them . . . iii 3 91
The queen o' the sky . . . Bids thee leave these . . . . iv 1 72
Leave your crisp channels and on this green land Answer your summons iv 1 130
And, like this insubstantial pageant faded, Leave not a rack behind . iv 1 156
Say again, where didst thou leave these varlets? . . . . . iv 1 170
Now let us take our leave. To Milan let me hear from thee *T. G. of Ver.* i 1 56
He leaves his friends to dignify them more ; I leave myself, my friends and all, for love . . . . i 1 64
Do you change colour?—Give him leave, madam ; he is a kind of chameleon . . . . ii 4 25
I'll leave you to confer of home affairs . . . . ii 4 119
To leave my Julia, shall I be forsworn . . . . ii 6 1
I cannot leave to love, and yet I do ; But there I leave to love where I should love. Julia I lose and Valentine I lose . . . . . ii 6 18
All that is mine I leave at thy dispose, My goods, my lands, my reputation . . . . ii 7 86
Longer than swiftest expedition Will give thee time to leave . . . iii 1 165
And I leave to be, If I be not by her fair influence Foster'd . . iii 1 182
I remember the trick you served me when I took my leave of Madam Silvia . . . . iv 4 38
It seems you loved not her, to leave her token. She is dead, belike? . iv 4 79
Leave not the mansion so long tenantless, Lest, growing ruinous, the building fall And leave no memory of what it was ! . . . . . v 4 8
The more degenerate and base art thou, To make such means for her as thou hast done And leave her on such slight conditions . . . . v 4 138
It were a goot motion if we leave our pribbles and prabbles . *Mer. Wives* i 1 56
Did her grandsire leave her seven hundred pound? . . . . . i 1 59
Qu'ai-j'oublie ! dere is some simples in my closet, dat I vill not for the varld I shall leave behind . . . . i 4 66
We must give folks leave to prate : what, the good-jer ! . . . . i 4 128
I will be thrown into Etna, as I have been into Thames, ere I will leave her thus . . . . iii 5 130
Master Slender is let the boys leave to play.—Blessing of his heart ! . iv 1 12
'Hang-hog' is Latin for bacon, I warrant you.—Leave your prabbles, 'oman . . . . iv 1 52
We'll leave a proof, by that which we will do, Wives may be merry, and yet honest too . . . . iv 2 106
Serve Got, and leave your desires, and fairies will not pinse you . . v 5 137
And leave your jealousies too, I pray you . . . . v 5 139

Leave. Our haste from hence is of so quick condition That it prefers itself and leaves unquestion'd Matters of needful value . *Meas. for Meas.* i 1 55
To the hopeful execution do I leave you Of your commissions . . i 1 60
Yet give leave, my lord, That we may bring you something on the way i 1 61
I shall desire you, sir, to give me leave To have free speech with you . i 1 77
I take my leave of you.—Good sir, adieu . . . . i 4 90
I mean it not.—Sir, but you shall come to it, by your honour's leave . ii 1 126
I'll take my leave, And leave you to the hearing of the cause . . ii 1 140
Would bark your honour from that trunk you bear, And leave you naked iii 1 73
Leave me awhile with the maid : my mind promises with my habit no loss shall touch her by my company . . . . iii 1 180
Did Angelo so leave her?—Left her in her tears, and dried not one of them . . . . iii 1 233
But leave we him to his events . . . . iii 2 252
Give him leave to escape hence, he would not . . . . . . iv 2 156
I for a while will leave you ; But stir not you . . . . . v 1 257
Give me leave to question ; you shall see how I'll handle her. . . v 1 272
Advise him ; I leave him to your hand . . . . v 1 491
I'll utter what my sorrow gives me leave . . . . *Com. of Errors* i 1 36
Hopeless to find, yet loath to leave unsought . . . . . . i 1 136
Sconce call you it? so you would leave battering, I had rather have it a head . . . . ii 2 35
Say whether you'll answer me or no : If not, I'll leave him to the officer iv 1 61
Thou art, as you are all, a sorceress : I conjure thee to leave me . iv 3 68
I'll give thee, ere I leave thee, so much money, To warrant thee . . iv 4 2
Leave him here with me.—I will not hence and leave my husband here v 1 108
When you depart from me, sorrow abides and happiness takes his leave *Much Ado* i 1 102
And so I leave you . . . . . i 1 291 ; *T. Andron.* iv 2 17
Nay, if they lead to any ill, I will leave them at the next turning *M. Ado* ii 1 159
I pray you, leave me.—Ho ! now you strike like the blind man . . ii 1 204
If it will not be, I'll leave you.—Alas, poor hurt fowl ! . . . . ii 1 208
This is thy office ; Bear thee well in it and leave us alone . . . iii 1 13
I must leave you . . . . iii 5 48 ; *Othello* i 1 145
I will challenge him. I will kiss your hand, and so I leave you *M. Ado* iv 1 336
I will leave you now to your gossip-like humour . . . . . v 1 188
To-morrow then I will expect your coming ; To-night I take my leave . v 1 306
I leave an arrant knave with your worship . . . . . . v 1 330
God restore you to health ! I humbly give you leave to depart . . v 1 334
There will I leave you too, for here comes one in haste . . . . v 2 96
Thanks to you all, and leave us : fare you well . . . . . v 3 28
Your wit's too hot, it speeds too fast, 'twill tire.—Not till it leave the rider in the mire . . . . *L. L. Lost* ii 1 121
Study his bias leaves and makes his book thine eyes . . . . iv 2 113
Then leave this chat ; and, good Biron, now prove Our loving lawful . iv 3 284
Construe my speeches better, if you may.—Then wish me better ; I will give you leave . . . . v 2 342
Bear with me, I am sick ; I'll leave it by degrees . . . . . . v 2 418
I will kiss thy royal finger, and take leave . . . . v 2 892
You are but as a form in wax By him imprinted and within his power To leave the figure or disfigure it . . . . . . *M. N. Dream* i 1 51
Leave you your power to draw, And I shall have no power to follow you ii 1 197
Only give me leave, Unworthy as I am, to follow you . . . . ii 1 206
You do impeach your modesty too much, To leave the city . . . ii 1 215
I'll run from thee . . . , And leave thee to the mercy of wild beasts . ii 1 228
Ere he do leave this grove, Thou shalt fly him and he shall seek thy love ii 1 245
Hence, and do not haunt me thus.—O, wilt thou darkling leave me? . ii 2 86
The heresies that men do leave Are hated most of those they did deceive . . . . ii 2 139
I believe we must leave the killing out, when all is done . . . iii 1 15
Leave a casement of the great chamber window, where we play, open . iii 1 57
But why unkindly didst thou leave me so?—Why should he stay? . . iii 2 183
Could not this make thee know, The hate I bear thee made me leave thee so? . . . . iii 2 190
Who is't that hinders you?—A foolish heart, that I leave here behind . iii 2 319
Pray you, leave your courtesy, good mounsieur.—What's your will? . iv 1 21
Leave it to his discretion, and let us listen to the moon . . . v 1 241
Fare ye well : We leave you now with better company . *Mer. of Venice* i 1 59
We two will leave you : but at dinner-time, I pray you, have in mind where we must meet . . . . i 1 70
Well, we will leave you then till dinner-time . . . . . . i 1 105
The four strangers seek for you, madam, to take their leave . . . i 2 136
Hath preferr'd thee, if it be preferment To leave a rich Jew's service . ii 2 156
Take leave of thy old master and inquire My lodging out . . . ii 2 162
I'll take my leave of the Jew in the twinkling of an eye . . . ii 2 176
I am sorry thou wilt leave my father so : Our house is hell . . . ii 3 1
I have too grieved a heart To take a tedious leave . . . . ii 7 77
If I do fail in fortune of my choice, Immediately to leave you . . ii 9 16
The bird was fledged ; and then it is the complexion of them all to leave the dam . . . . iii 1 33
But her eyes,—How could he see to do them? having made one, Methinks it should have power to steal both his And leave itself unfurnish'd . . . . iii 2 126
Fair lady, by your leave ; I come by note, to give and to receive . iii 2 140
By your leave, I bid my very friends and countrymen, Sweet Portia, welcome . . . . iii 2 225
With leave, Bassanio ; I am half yourself . . . . iii 2 251
Since I have your good leave to go away, I will make haste . . . iii 2 326
I leave him to your gracious acceptance . . . . iv 1 164
Beg that thou mayst have leave to hang thyself . . . . . iv 1 364
I pray you, give me leave to go from hence ; I am not well . . . iv 1 395
Master Lorenzo, sola, sola !—Leave hollaing, man : here.—Sola ! where? v 1 43
Like cutler's poetry Upon a knife, 'Love me, and leave me not' . . v 1 150
I dare be sworn for him he would not leave it . . . . . . v 1 172
Therefore be well advised How you do leave me to mine own protection v 1 235
I pray you, leave me.—I will no further offend you . . *As Y. Like It* i 1 82
Therefore he gives them good leave to wander . . . . . . i 1 109
And never leave thee till he hath ta'en thy life by some indirect means i 1 158
So please you give us leave.—You will take little delight in it . . i 2 167
Good sir, I do in friendship counsel you To leave this place . . . i 2 274
Do not seek . . . To bear your griefs yourself and leave me out . . i 3 105
He'll go along o'er the wide world with me ; Leave me alone to woo him i 3 135
And did you leave him in this contemplation?—We did, my lord . . ii 1 64
If I bring thee not something to eat, I will give thee leave to die . . ii 6 12
Invest me in my motley ; give me leave To speak my mind . . . ii 7 58
And not being well married, it will be a good excuse for me hereafter to leave my wife . . . . iii 3 95
O sweet Oliver, O brave Oliver, Leave me not behind thee . . . iii 3 103
For these two hours, Rosalind, I will leave thee.—Alas ! dear love, I cannot lack thee two hours . . . . iv 1 181

Leave. Did he leave him there, Food to the suck'd and hungry lioness? *As Y. Like It* iv 3 126
Therefore, you clown, abandon,—which is in the vulgar leave,—the society . . . v 1 53
Servants, leave me and her alone. Madam, undress you *T. of Shrew* Ind. 2 118
By my father's love and leave am arm'd With his good will . . . i 1 5
As he that leaves A shallow plash to plunge him in the deep . . . i 1 22
Leave shall you have to court her at your pleasure . . . i 1 54
As though, belike, I knew not what to take, and what to leave, ha? . i 1 105
Verona, for a while I take my leave, To see my friends in Padua . i 2 1
If this be not a lawful cause for me to leave his service, look you, sir . i 2 30
I may, by this device, at least Have leave and leisure to make love to her . . . i 2 136
Yea, leave that labour to great Hercules . . . i 2 257
You wrong me, Signior Gremio: give me leave . . . ii 1 46
If I may have your daughter to my wife, I'll leave her houses three or four . . . ii 1 368
Then give me leave to have prerogative . . . iii 1 6
Give me leave to read philosophy, And while I pause, serve in your harmony . . . iii 1 13
You'll leave his lecture when I am in tune?—That will be never . iii 1 24
Give me leave a while: My lessons make no music in three parts . iii 1 59
Leave your books And help to dress your sister's chamber up . iii 1 82
My haste doth call me hence, And therefore here I mean to take my leave . . . iii 2 190
Such a one as leaves a gentleman, And makes a god of such a cullion . iv 2 19
I trust I may have leave to speak; And speak I will . . . iv 3 73
They may chance to need thee at home; therefore leave us . . . v 1 4
Here I leave you, sir.—You shall not choose but drink before you go . v 1 11
'Tis a wonder, by your leave, she will be tamed so . . . v 2 189
But my intents are fix'd and will not leave me . . . *All's Well* i 1 244
Freely have they leave To stand on either part . . . i 2 14
He that ears my land spares my team and gives me leave to in the crop i 3 48
Pray you, leave me: stall this in your bosom . . . i 3 131
But give me leave to try success, I'ld venture The well-lost life of mine i 3 253
Thou shalt have my leave and love, Means and attendants . . . i 3 257
I am Cressid's uncle, That dare leave two together; fare you well . ii 1 101
May not be so credulous of cure, When our most learned doctors leave us . . . ii 1 119
In such a business give me leave to use The help of mine own eyes . ii 3 114
For doing I am past; as I will by thee, in what motion age will give me leave . . . ii 3 248
You are not worth another word, else I'ld call you knave. I leave you ii 3 281
A young man married is a man that's marr'd: Therefore away, and leave her . . . ii 3 316
What's his will else?—That you will take your instant leave o' the king ii 4 49
And have procured his leave For present parting . . . ii 5 60
'Twill be two days ere I shall see you, so I leave you to your wisdom . ii 5 76
As't please your lordship: I'll leave you . . . iii 6 117
When you have our roses, You barely leave our thorns to prick ourselves . . . iv 2 19
He met the duke in the street, sir, of whom he hath taken a solemn leave . . . iv 3 90
Nay, by your leave, hold your hands . . . iv 3 215
That shall you, and take your leave of all your friends . . . iv 3 347
Heaven aiding, And by the leave of my good lord the king . . . iv 4 13
I do pity his distress in my similes of comfort and leave him to your lordship . . . v 2 26
Such a ring as this, The last that e'er I took her leave at court, I saw . v 3 79
He stole from Florence, taking no leave, and I follow him to his country v 3 144
If Sir Toby would leave drinking, thou wert as witty a piece of Eve's flesh as any in Illyria . . . *T. Night* i 5 29
Give me leave to prove you a fool.—Can you do it? . . . i 5 64
You are the cruell'st she alive, If you will lead these graces to the grave And leave the world no copy . . . i 5 261
I shall crave of you your leave that I may bear my evils alone . . ii 1 6
Please you to take leave of her, she is very willing to bid you farewell . ii 3 107
Give me now leave to leave thee.—Now, the melancholy god protect thee . . . ii 4 74
When the image of it leaves him he must run mad . . . ii 5 212
Let the garden door be shut, and leave me to my hearing . . . iii 1 103
O, by your leave, I pray you, I bade you never speak again of him . iii 1 117
I'll be your purse-bearer and leave you For an hour . . . iii 3 47
Give them way till he take leave, and presently after him . . . iii 4 217
Endeavour thyself to sleep, and leave thy vain bibble babble . . iv 2 104
I leave my duty a little unthought of and speak out of my injury . v 1 318
We two will walk, my lord, And leave you to your graver steps *W. Tale* i 2 173
So leaves me to consider what is breeding That changeth thus his manners . . . i 2 374
My women, come; you have leave.—Go, do our bidding; hence! . . ii 1 124
Leave me solely: go, See how he fares. Fie, fie! no thought of him . ii 3 17
Stay her tongue.—Hang all the husbands That cannot do that feat, you'll leave yourself Hardly one subject . . . ii 3 111
There thou leave it, Without more mercy, to it own protection . . ii 3 177
Leave me, And think upon my bidding . . . ii 3 206
Places remote enough are in Bohemia, There weep and leave it crying . iii 3 32
I slide O'er sixteen years and leave the growth untried Of that wide gap iv 1 6
If tinkers may have leave to live, And bear the sow-skin budget . . iv 3 19
I will even take my leave of you, and pace softly towards my kinsman's iv 3 120
I should leave grazing, were I of your flock, And only live by gazing . iv 4 109
Leave your prating: since these good men are pleased, let them come in iv 4 349
I'll make it as much more and leave this young man in pawn till I bring it iv 4 838
Will you swear Never to marry but by my free leave? . . . v 1 70
It seemed sorrow wept to take leave of them, for their joy waded in tears v 2 50
And give me leave, And do not say 'tis superstition . . . v 3 42
Wilt thou give us leave awhile?—Good leave, good Philip . *K. John* i 1 230
And leave your children, wives and you in peace . . . ii 1 257
Whose passage, vex'd with thy impediment, Shall leave his native channel ii 1 337
Till unfenced desolation Leave them as naked as the vulgar air . . ii 1 387
Leave those woes alone which I alone Am bound to under-bear . . iii 1 64
I leave your highness. Grandam, I will pray . . . iii 3 14
Evils that take leave, On their departure most of all show evil . . iii 4 114
My nobles leave me; and my state is braved, Even at my gates . . iv 2 243
Nor attend the foot That leaves the print of blood where'er it walks . iv 3 26
Give me leave to speak.—No, I will speak.—We will attend to neither . v 2 162
Faulconbridge Desires your majesty to leave the field . . . v 3 6
Who didst thou leave to tend his majesty?—Why, know you not? . . v 6 32
Death, having prey'd upon the outward parts, Leaves them invisible . v 7 16
With purpose presently to leave this war . . . v 7 86
I take my leave before I have begun . . . *Richard II.* i 2 60

Leave. Desolate, will I hence and die: The last leave of thee takes my weeping eye . . . *Richard II.* i 2 74
Let us take a ceremonious leave And loving farewell of our several friends i 3 50
Greets your highness, And craves to kiss your hand and take his leave i 3 53
But you gave leave to my unwilling tongue Against my will . . . i 3 245
No leave take I; for I will ride, As far as land will let me . . . i 3 251
No greeting to thy friends?—I have too few to take my leave of you . i 3 255
I am denied to sue my livery here, And yet my letters-patents give me leave . . . ii 3 130
Will his majesty Give Richard leave to live till Richard die? . . iii 3 174
Give sorrow leave awhile to tutor me To this submission . . . iv 1 166
Then give me leave to go.—Whither?—Whither you will . . . iv 1 313
Even here thou takest, As from my death-bed, thy last living leave . v 1 39
Take leave and part; for you must part forthwith . . . v 1 70
Where did I leave?—At that sad stop, my lord . . . v 2 4
As in a theatre, the eyes of men, After a well-graced actor leaves the stage, Are idly bent on him that enters next . . . v 2 24
Withdraw yourselves, and leave us here alone . . . v 3 28
Give me leave that I may turn the key, That no man enter . . . v 3 36
With much ado at length have gotten leave To look upon my sometimes royal master's face . . . v 5 74
Leave the prince and me alone . . . *1 Hen. IV.* i 2 167
Our vizards we will change after we leave them . . . i 2 200
You have good leave to leave us: when we need Your use and counsel, we shall send for you . . . i 3 20
As good a deed as drink, to turn true man and to leave these rogues . ii 2 24
But yet no coward, Hal.—Well, we leave that to the proof . . ii 2 72
How now, Kate! I must leave you within these two hours . . . ii 3 39
Whither I must, I must; and, to conclude, This evening must I leave you ii 3 109
And do thou never leave calling 'Francis' . . . ii 4 34
And so let me entreat you leave the house.—I will, my lord . . ii 4 567
Give me leave To tell you once again . . . iii 1 36
From whom you now must steal and take no leave . . . iii 1 93
And leaves behind a stain Upon the beauty of all parts besides . iii 1 187
Good manners be your speed! Here come our wives, and let us take our leave . . . iii 1 191
Swear me, Kate, like a lady as thou art, A good mouth-filling oath, and leave 'in sooth,' And such protest of pepper-gingerbread . . iii 1 259
O Hal, I prithee, give me leave to breathe awhile . . . v 3 45
If thou embowel me to-day, I'll give you leave to powder me . . v 4 112
I'll purge, and leave sack, and live cleanly as a nobleman should do . v 4 168
Let us not leave till all our own be won . . . v 5 44
Give me leave to tell you, you lie in your throat . . . *2 Hen. IV.* i 2 97
I give thee leave to tell me so! I lay aside that which grows to me! If thou gettest any leave of me, hang me; if thou takest leave, thou wert better be hanged . . . i 2 99
Who, half through, Gives o'er and leaves his part-created cost . . i 3 60
If he should do so, He leaves his back unarm'd . . . i 3 79
I commend me to thee, I commend thee, and I leave thee . . . ii 2 137
Him did you leave, Second to none, unseconded by you . . . ii 3 33
I will now take my leave of these six dry, round, old, withered knights ii 4 8
When wilt thou leave fighting o' days and foining o' nights? . . ii 4 251
Now comes in the sweetest morsel of the night, and we must hence and leave it unpicked . . . ii 4 397
I beseech you, give me leave to go Through Gloucestershire . . iv 3 87
'Tis seldom when the bee doth leave her comb In the dead carrion . iv 4 79
This from thee Will I to mine leave, as 'tis left to me . . . iv 5 47
Why did you leave me here alone, my lords? . . . iv 5 51
Come hither to me, Harry. Depart the chamber, leave us here alone . iv 5 91
Make less thy body hence, and more thy grace; Leave gormandizing . v 5 57
Give us leave Freely to render what we have in charge . . *Hen. V.* i 2 237
Leave not one behind that doth not wish Success and conquest to attend on us . . . ii 2 23
And leave your England, as dead midnight still! . . . iii Prol. 19
I must leave them, and seek some better service . . . iii 2 55
I will not leave the half-achieved Harfleur Till in her ashes she lie buried . . . iii 3 8
And those that leave their valiant bones in France, Dying like men . iv 3 98
They shall have none, I swear, but these my joints; Which if they have as I will leave 'em them, Shall yield them little . . . iv 3 124
O, give us leave, great king, To view the field in safety! . . . iv 7 84
Yet leave our cousin Katharine here with us . . . —She hath good leave v 2 95
And here take my leave, To go about my preparation . . *1 Hen. VI.* i 1 165
Let's leave this town; for they are hare-brained slaves . . . i 2 37
Stand back, you lords, and give us leave awhile . . . i 2 70
And in a vision full of majesty Will'd me to leave my base vocation . i 2 80
Whilst any trump did sound, or drum struck up, His sword did ne'er leave striking in the field . . . i 4 81
'Twas time, I trow, to wake and leave our beds . . . ii 1 41
Leave this peevish broil And set this unaccustom'd fight aside . . iii 1 92
What! will you fly, and leave Lord Talbot? . . . iii 2 107
We will entice the Duke of Burgundy To leave the Talbot . . . iii 3 20
Give them leave to speak. Say, gentlemen, what makes you thus exclaim? . . . iv 1 82
Then both fly.—And leave my followers here to fight and die? . . iv 5 45
I take my leave of thee, fair son, Born to eclipse thy life this afternoon iv 5 52
How dost thou fare? Wilt thou yet leave the battle, boy, and fly? . iv 6 28
Give me leave to curse awhile.—Curse, miscreant . . . v 3 43
I were best to leave him, for he will not hear . . . v 3 82
O, give me leave, I have deluded you . . . v 4 76
Then lead me hence; with whom I leave my curse . . . v 4 86
Will resign my place.—Resign it then and leave thine insolence *2 Hen. VI.* i 3 125
Give me leave To show some reason, of no little force . . . i 3 165
And so, I pray you, go, in God's name, and leave us . . . i 4 12
Your grace shall give me leave, my Lord of York, To be the post . . i 4 80
Yet, by your leave, the wind was very high . . . ii 1 3
Ambitious churchman, leave to afflict my heart . . . ii 1 182
Give me leave In this close walk to satisfy myself . . . ii 2 2
Give me leave to go; Sorrow would solace and mine age would ease . ii 3 20
As willingly at thy feet I leave it As others would ambitiously receive it ii 3 35
Come, leave your drinking, and fall to blows . . . ii 3 80
Well, I will be there. My Nell, I take my leave . . . ii 4 74
But I can give the loser leave to chide.—Far truer spoke than meant . iii 1 182
They play'd me false! And well such losers may have leave to speak . iii 1 185
What, will your highness leave the parliament? . . . iii 1 197
Let thy Suffolk take his heavy leave . . . iii 2 306
You bade me ban, and will you bid me leave? . . . iii 2 333
Embrace and kiss and take ten thousand leaves . . . iii 2 354
Thou shalt have cause to fear before I leave thee. What, are ye daunted now? . . . iv 1 118

Leave. We will not leave one lord, one gentleman *2 Hen. VI.* iv 2 194

Hath my sword therefore broke through London gates, that you should leave me at the White Hart? iv 8 25

The name of Henry the Fifth hales them to an hundred mischiefs and makes them leave me desolate iv 8 60

Come to seize me for a stray, for entering his fee-simple without leave iv 10 28

If I do not leave you all as dead as a door-nail iv 10 43

Or why thou . . . Should raise so great a power without his leave v 1 21

It grieves my soul to leave thee unassail'd v 2 18

Leave me not, my lords; be resolute; I mean to take possession *3 Hen. VI.* i 1 43

Give King Henry leave to speak.—Plantagenet shall speak first i 1 120

Think'st thou that I will leave my kingly throne? i 1 124

Thus do I leave thee. Come, son, let's away i 1 255

Brother, though I be youngest, give me leave.—No, I can better play the orator i 2 1

By giving the house of Lancaster leave to breathe, It will outrun you i 2 13

I'll win them, fear it not: And thus most humbly I do take my leave i 2 61

And till I root out their accursed line And leave not one alive, I live in hell i 3 33

By your leave I speak it, You love the breeder better than the male ii 1 41

Steel thy melting heart To hold thine own and leave thine own with him ii 2 42

I'll leave my son my virtuous deeds behind; And would my father had left me no more! ii 2 49

Draw thy sword in right.—My gracious father, by your kingly leave, I'll draw it as apparent to the crown ii 2 63

Leave us to our fortune.—Why, that's my fortune too; therefore I'll stay ii 2 75

Since we have begun to strike, We'll never leave till we have hewn thee down ii 2 168

Take leave until we meet again, Where'er it be, in heaven or in earth ii 3 42

Give them leave to fly that will not stay ii 3 50

Whose soul is that which takes her heavy leave? ii 6 42

Lords, give us leave: I'll try this widow's wit.—Ay, good leave have you; for you will have leave, Till youth take leave and leave you to the crutch iii 2 34

I take my leave with many thousand thanks iii 2 56

And give my tongue-tied sorrows leave to speak iii 3 22

I am commanded, with your leave and favour, Humbly to kiss your hand iii 3 60

For shame! leave Henry, and call Edward king iii 3 100

And leave your brothers to go speed elsewhere iv 1 58

You shall give me leave To play the broker in mine own behalf iv 1 62

And to that end I shortly mind to leave you.—Leave me, or tarry iv 1 64

If you'll not here proclaim yourself our king, I'll leave you to your fortune iv 7 55

Fair lords, take leave and stand not to reply iv 8 23

How nigh is Clarence now?—At Southam I did leave him with his forces v 1 9

Is't meet that he Should leave the helm and like a fearful lad With tearful eyes add water to the sea? v 4 7

Did I but suspect a fearful man, He should have leave to go away betimes v 4 45

Sirrah, leave us to ourselves: we must confer v 6 6

And leave the world for me to bustle in *Richard III.* i 1 152

Give me leave, By circumstance, but to acquit myself i 2 76

Give me leave, By circumstance, to curse thy cursed self i 2 79

Leave this keen encounter of our wits, And fall somewhat into a slower method i 2 115

Leave these sad designs To him that hath more cause to be a mourner i 2 211

Hie thee to hell for shame, and leave the world, Thou cacodemon! i 3 143

That is the butt-end of a mother's blessing: I marvel why her grace did leave it out ii 2 111

We see The waters swell before a boisterous storm. But leave it all to God ii 3 45

And in this resolution here we leave you iii 7 218

We will attend your grace: And so most joyfully we take our leave iii 7 245

Pray you, by your leave, How doth the prince? iv 1 13

I may not leave it so: I am bound by oath, and therefore pardon me iv 1 27

Adieu, poor soul, that takest thy leave of it [glory]! iv 1 91

Even here I slip my weary neck, And leave the burthen of it all on thee iv 4 113

Please it your majesty to give me leave, I'll muster up my friends iv 4 488

But, hear you, leave behind Your son, George Stanley iv 4 496

Will leave us never an understanding friend *Hen. VIII.* Prol. 22

Love yourself, and in that love Not unconsider'd leave your honour i 2 15

And, though we leave it with a root, thus hack'd, The air will drink the sap i 2 97

Leave those remnants Of fool and feather that they got in France i 3 24

They could do no less, Out of the great respect they bear to beauty, But leave their flocks; and, under your fair conduct, Crave leave to view these ladies i 4 70

By all your good leaves, gentlemen; here I'll make My royal choice i 4 85

His noble friends and fellows, whom to leave Is only bitter to him, only dying ii 1 73

I know him; so I leave him To him that made him proud, the pope ii 2 55

Would it not grieve an able man to leave So sweet a bedfellow? But, conscience, conscience! O, 'tis a tender place; and I must leave her ii 2 142

To leave a thousand-fold more bitter than 'Tis sweet at first to acquire ii 3 8

Make yourself mirth with your particular fancy, And leave me out on't ii 3 102

And got your leave To make this present summons ii 4 218

My soul grows sad with troubles; Sing, and disperse 'em, if thou canst: leave working iii 1 2

I would your grace Would leave your griefs, and take my counsel iii 1 92

Campeius Is stol'n away to Rome; hath ta'en no leave iii 2 57

Is he ready To come abroad?—I think, by this he is.—Leave me awhile iii 2 84

Innumerable substance—By what means got, I leave to your own conscience iii 2 327

We'll leave you to your meditations How to live better iii 2 345

Must I, then, leave you? must I needs forgo So good, so noble and so true a master? Bear witness, all that have not hearts of iron, With what a sorrow Cromwell leaves his lord iii 2 425

My legs, like loaden branches, bow to the earth, Willing to leave their burthen iv 2 3

Yet thus far, Griffith, give me leave to speak him, And yet with charity iv 2 32

Are ye all gone, And leave me here in wretchedness behind ye? iv 2 84

Bid the music leave, They are harsh and heavy to me iv 2 94

Nay, Patience, You must not leave me yet: I must to bed iv 2 166

I must to him too, Before he go to bed. I'll take my leave v 1 9

Leave me alone; For I must think of that which company Would not be friendly to v 1 74

You'll leave your noise anon, ye rascals: do you take the court for Paris-garden? ye rude slaves, leave your gaping v 4 1

So shall she leave her blessedness to one, When heaven shall call her v 5 44

Leave. I will leave all as I found it, and there an end *Troi. and Cres.* i 1 91

Fair leave and large security i 3 223

I will keep where there is wit stirring and leave the faction of fools ii 1 130

For this time will I take my leave, my lord.—Your leave, sweet Cressid!—Leave! an you take leave till to-morrow morning iii 2 147

I have a kind of self resides with you; But an unkind self, that itself will leave, To be another's fool iii 2 156

O heavens, what some men do, While some men leave to do! iii 3 133

Like to an enter'd tide, they all rush by And leave you hindmost iii 3 160

Make Cressid's name the very crown of falsehood, If ever she leave Troilus! iv 2 107

Time Will one day end it.—So to him we leave it iv 5 226

I will rather leave to see Hector, than not to dog him v 1 103

For the love of all the gods, Let's leave the hermit pity with our mothers v 3 45

Give me leave To take that course by your consent and voice v 3 73

Hector, I take my leave: Thou dost thyself and all our Troy deceive v 3 89

And what one thing, what another, that I shall leave you one o' these days v 3 104

Here, there, and every where, he leaves and takes v 5 26

Yet I can make my audit up, that all From me do back receive the flour of all, And leave me but the bran *Coriolanus* i 1 150

Beseech you, give me leave to retire myself i 3 30

I would your cambric were sensible as your finger, that you might leave pricking it for pity i 3 96

Mend and charge home, Or, by the fires of heaven, I'll leave the foe i 4 39

I will be bold to take my leave of you ii 1 106

Before him he carries noise, and behind him he leaves tears ii 1 175

Leaves nothing undone that may fully discover him their opposite ii 2 22

Leave nothing out for length ii 2 53

You'll mar all: I'll leave you: pray you, speak to 'em ii 3 65

I prithee, noble friend, home to thy house; Leave us to cure this cause iii 1 235

If, by the tribunes' leave, and yours, good people, I may be heard iii 1 282

Give me leave, I'll go to him, and undertake to bring him iii 1 323

Come, leave your tears: a brief farewell iv 1 1

We'll leave you.—Why stay we to be baited With one that wants her wits? iv 2 43

Leave this faint puling and lament as I do, In anger, Juno-like iv 2 52

Come, go in, And take our friendly senators by the hands; Who now are here, taking their leaves of me iv 5 139

He will mow all down before him, and leave his passage polled iv 5 215

He said 'twas folly, For one poor grain or two, to leave unburnt v 1 27

But, by your leave, I am an officer of state v 2 2

Therefore, fellow, I must have leave to pass v 2 23

I prate, And the most noble mother of the world Leave unsaluted v 3 50

Here Goths have given me leave to sheathe my sword *T. Andron.* i 1 85

Leave to plead my deeds: 'Tis thou and those that have dishonour'd me i 1 424

They told me they would bind me here Unto the body of a dismal yew, And leave me to this miserable death ii 3 108

Were't not for shame, Well could I leave our sport to sleep awhile ii 3 197

She hath no tongue to call, nor hands to wash; And so let's leave her ii 4 8

Then give me leave, for losers will have leave To ease their stomachs with their bitter tongues iii 1 233

He leaves his pledges dearer than his life iii 1 292

Good grandsire, leave these bitter deep laments: Make my aunt merry iii 2 46

Pray be careful all, And leave you not a man-of-war unsearch'd iv 3 22

Madam, depart at pleasure; leave us here v 2 145

Commit him to the grave; Do him that kindness, and take leave of him v 3 171

Soft! I will go along; An if you leave me so, you do me wrong *R. and J.* i 1 202

What is your will?—This is the matter:—Nurse, give leave awhile i 3 7

I cannot choose but laugh, To think it should leave crying and say 'Ay' i 3 51

O, wilt thou leave me so unsatisfied?—What satisfaction canst thou have to-night? ii 2 125

By and by, I come:—To cease thy suit, and leave me to my grief ii 2 153

I am a-weary, give me leave awhile: Fie, how my bones ache! ii 5 25

Have you got leave to go to shrift to-day?—I have ii 5 68

By your leaves, you shall not stay alone Till holy church incorporate two in one ii 6 36

Gentle nurse, I pray thee, leave me to myself to-night iv 3 2

Death is my heir; My daughter he hath wedded: I will die, And leave him all iv 5 40

I dreamt my lady came and found me dead—Strange dream, that gives a dead man leave to think! v 1 7

Pardon me for bringing these ill news, Since you did leave it for my office v 1 23

Leave me, and do the thing I bid thee do v 1 30

Good gentle youth, tempt not a desperate man; Fly hence, and leave me v 3 60

I will go with you to Lord Timon's.—Will you leave me there? *T. of Athens* ii 2 95

That I might so have rated my expense, As I had leave of means ii 2 136

The swallow follows not summer more willing than we your lordship.—Nor more willingly leaves winter iii 6 33

Leave their false vows with him, Like empty purses pick'd iv 2 11

Were all the wealth I have shut up in thee, I'ld give thee leave to hang it iv 3 280

I leave you To the protection of the prosperous gods, As thieves to keepers v 1 185

Then, dear countryman, Bring in thy ranks, but leave without thy rage v 4 39

Set on; and leave no ceremony out *J. Cæsar* i 2 11

Beware the ides of March.—He is a dreamer; let us leave him i 2 24

Let me not hinder, Cassius, your desires; I'll leave you i 2 31

For this time I will leave you: To-morrow, if you please to speak with me i 2 307

I think he will stand very strong with us.—Let us not leave him out ii 1 143

Then leave him out.—Indeed he is not fit ii 1 152

The morning comes upon's: we'll leave you, Brutus ii 1 221

With an angry wafture of your hand, Gave sign for me to leave you ii 1 247

Leave me with haste. Lucius, who's that knocks? ii 1 309

Leave us, Publius; lest that the people . . . do your age some mischief iii 1 92

What Antony shall speak, I will protest He speaks by leave iii 1 239

Here, under leave of Brutus and the rest iii 2 86

Let me show you him that made the will. Shall I descend? and will you give me leave?— . . . You shall have leave iii 2 164

You know me all, a plain blunt man, That love my friend; and that they know full well That gave me public leave to speak of him iii 2 224

When you are over-earnest with your Brutus, He'll think your mother chides, and leave you so iv 3 123

But for your words, they rob the Hybla bees, And leave them honeyless v 1 35

Where did you leave him?—All disconsolate, With Pindarus his bondman v 3 55

By your leave, gods:—this is a Roman's part v 3 89

Say to the king the knowledge of the broil As thou didst leave it *Macbeth* i 2 7

Only look up clear; To alter favour ever is to fear: Leave all the rest to me i 5 74

Equivocates him in a sleep, and, giving him the lie, leaves him ii 3 40

And with him—To leave no rubs nor botches in the work—Fleance his son iii 1 134

Leave. You must leave this.—O, full of scorpions is my mind, dear wife! *Macbeth* iii 2 35
Wisdom! to leave his wife, to leave his babes, His mansion and his titles in a place From whence himself does fly? . . . . . iv 2 6
I take my leave of you: Shall not be long but I'll be here again . . iv 2 22
To the succeeding royalty he leaves The healing benediction . . . iv 3 155
They were well at peace when I did leave 'em . . . . . . iv 3 179
Our power is ready; Our lack is nothing but our leave . . . iv 3 237
What wouldst thou have, Laertes?—My dread lord, Your leave and favour to return to France . . . . *Hamlet* i 2 51
My thoughts and wishes bend again toward France And bow them to your gracious leave and pardon.—Have you your father's leave? . i 2 56
He hath, my lord, wrung from me my slow leave By laboursome petition . . . . i 2 58
I do beseech you, give him leave to go.—Take thy fair hour, Laertes . i 2 61
A double blessing is a double grace; Occasion smiles upon a second leave . . . . i 3 54
Most humbly do I take my leave, my lord.—The time invites you; go . i 3 82
Leave her to heaven And to those thorns that in her bosom lodge . i 5 86
I was about to say something: where did I leave? . . . . ii 1 51
O, give me leave: How does my good Lord Hamlet?—Well, God-a-mercy . . . . ii 2 170
I will leave him, and suddenly contrive the means of meeting . . ii 2 215
My honourable lord, I will most humbly take my leave of you . . ii 2 218
My good friends, I'll leave you till night . . . . . . ii 2 572
Sweet Gertrude, leave us too; For we have closely sent for Hamlet hither . . . . iii 1 28
'Faith, I must leave thee, love, and shortly too; My operant powers their functions leave to do . . . . iii 2 184
Sweet, leave me here awhile; My spirits grow dull . . . . iii 2 235
Begin, murderer; pox, leave thy damnable faces, and begin . . . iii 2 263
By and by is easily said. Leave me, friends . . . . . iii 2 405
Leave wringing of your hands: peace! sit you down, And let me wring your heart . . . . iii 4 34
Could you on this fair mountain leave to feed, And batten on this moor? iii 4 66
There I see such black and grained spots As will not leave their tinct . iii 4 91
In the fatness of these pursy times Virtue itself of vice must pardon beg, Yea, curb and woo for leave to do him good . . . . . iii 4 155
Sirs, stand you all without.—No, let's come in.—I pray you, give me leave . . . . iv 5 113
To-morrow shall I beg leave to see your kingly eyes . . . . iv 7 45
Give me leave. Here lies the water; good: here stands the man; good v 1 16
Since no man has aught of what he leaves, what is't to leave betimes? v 2 235
Take her, or leave her?—Pardon me, royal sir; Election makes not up on such conditions.—Then leave her, sir . . . . . . *Lear* i 1 208
Which often leaves the history unspoke That it intends to do . . i 1 239
The jewels of our father, with wash'd eyes Cordelia leaves you . . i 1 272
Leave thy drink and thy whore, And keep in-a-door . . . . i 4 137
Not to give it away to his daughters, and leave his horns without a case i 5 33
If you will give me leave, I will tread this unbolted villain into mortar ii 2 70
Will pack when it begins to rain, And leave thee in the storm . ii 4 82
When I desired their leave that I might pity him, they took from me the use of mine own house . . . . iii 3 2
This tempest will not give me leave to ponder On things would hurt me more . . . . iii 4 24
Pluck out his eyes.—Leave him to my displeasure . . . . iii 7 6
I'll bring you to our master Lear, And leave you to attend him . iv 3 53
Leave, gentle wax; and, manners, blame us not . . . . iv 6 264
Your daughter, if you have not given her leave, I say again, hath made a gross revolt . . . . *Othello* i 1 134
We must not think the Turk is so unskilful To leave that latest which concerns him first . . . . i 3 28
Leave some officer behind, And he shall our commission bring to you . i 3 281
Honest Iago, My Desdemona must I leave to thee . . . . . i 3 296
Madam, I'll take my leave.—Why, stay, and hear me speak . . . iii 3 30
I do beseech thee, grant me this, To leave me but a little to myself . iii 3 85
Their best conscience Is not to leave't undone, but keep't unknown . iii 3 204
Set on thy wife to observe: leave me, Iago.—My lord, I take my leave. iii 3 240
Scan this thing no further; leave it to time . . . . . iii 3 245
I once more take my leave.—This fellow's of exceeding honesty . . iii 3 257
I will not leave him now till Cassio Be call'd to him . . . . iii 4 32
Leave me for this time.—Leave you! wherefore? . . . . . iii 4 191
Well, I must leave her company . . . . iv 1 148
Leave procreants alone and shut the door . . . . . . iv 2 28
Let me have leave to speak: 'Tis proper I obey him, but not now . . v 2 195
Would she had never given you leave to come! . . *Ant. and Cleo.* i 3 21
I'll leave you, lady.—Courteous lord, one word . . . . . i 3 86
Antony, Leave thy lascivious wassails . . . . i 4 56
Give me leave, Cæsar.—Speak, Agrippa . . . . ii 2 118
Now Antony must leave her utterly.—Never; he will not . . . ii 2 238
Better to leave undone, than by our deed Acquire too high a fame when him we serve's away . . . . iii 1 14
Leave unexecuted Your own renowned knowledge . . . . . iii 7 45
Take the hint Which my despair proclaims; let that be left Which leaves itself . . . . iii 11 20
Leave me, I pray, a little: pray you now: Nay, do so; for, indeed, I have lost command . . . . iii 11 22
'Twas a shame no less Than was his loss, to course your flying flags, And leave his navy gazing . . . . iii 13 12
Thou art so leaky, That we must leave thee to thy sinking . . . iii 13 64
I will seek Some way to leave him . . . . iii 13 201
Perchance to-morrow You'll serve another master. I look on you As one that takes his leave . . . . iv 2 29
'Tis the god Hercules, whom Antony loved, Now leaves him . . . iv 3 17
I'll leave thee Now, like a man of steel . . . . iv 4 32
I'll take my leave.—And may, through all the world: 'tis yours . . v 2 133
When thou hast done this chare, I'll give thee leave To play till doomsday . . . . v 2 231
This is the man.—Avoid, and leave him . . . . v 2 242
These fig-leaves Have slime upon them, such as the aspic leaves . . v 2 355
Should we be taking leave As long a term as yet we have to live, The loathness to depart would grow . . . . . . *Cymbeline* i 1 106
Leave us to ourselves; and make yourself some comfort Out of your best advice . . . . i 1 155
You shall at least Go see my lord aboard: for this time leave me . . i 1 178
I did not take my leave of him, but had Most pretty things to say . i 3 25
How worthy he is I will leave to appear hereafter . . . . . i 4 33
Let us leave here, gentlemen.—Sir, with all my heart . . . . i 4 109
If I come off, and leave her in such honour as you have trust in, she your jewel, this your jewel, and my gold are yours . . . . i 4 164

Leave. No further service, doctor, Until I send for thee.—I humbly take my leave . . . . *Cymbeline* i 5 45
Desire My man's abode where I did leave him: he Is strange and peevish . . . . i 6 53
Her son Cannot take two from twenty, for his heart, And leave eighteen . . . . ii 1 61
To bed; Take not away the taper, leave it burning . . . . . ii 2 5
To leave you in your madness, 'twere my sin: I will not . . . ii 3 104
So, I leave you, sir, To the worst of discontent . . . . . ii 3 159
The foul opinion You had of her pure honour gains or loses Your sword or mine, or masterless leaves both To who shall find them . . ii 4 60
You'll give me leave to spare, when you shall find You need it not . ii 4 65
Then, if you can, Be pale: I beg but leave to air this jewel . . . ii 4 96
Good wax, thy leave. Blest be You bees that make these locks of counsel! . . . . iii 2 35
The art o' the court, As hard to leave as keep . . . . . iii 3 47
Constrain'd by her infirmity, She should that duty leave unpaid to you iii 5 48
The same suit he wore when he took leave of my lady and mistress . iii 5 128
So please you, leave me; Stick to your journal course . . . . iv 2 9
We'll leave you for this time: go in and rest.—We'll not be long away iv 2 43
If you will bless me, sir, and give me leave, I'll take the better care . iv 4 44
The boy disdains me, He leaves me, scorns me . . . . . v 5 106
Thou'lt torture me to leave unspoken that Which, to be spoke, would torture thee . . . . v 5 139
Give me leave; I faint . . . . v 5 149
Your danger's ours.—And our good his.—Have at it then, by leave . v 5 315
All love the womb that their first being bred, Then give my tongue like leave to love my head . . . . *Pericles* i 1 108
All leave us else; but let your cares o'erlook What shipping and what lading's in our haven, And then return . . . . . . i 2 48
My lord, since you have given me leave to speak, Freely will I speak . i 2 101
Who never leave gaping till they've swallowed the whole parish . . ii 1 37
Give's cause to mourn his funeral, And leave us to our free election . ii 4 33
Loath to bid farewell, we take our leaves . . . . . . ii 5 13
There I'll leave it At careful nursing . . . . iii 1 80
His woeful queen we leave at Ephesus, Unto Diana there a votaress iv Gower 3
I'll leave you, my sweet lady, for a while: Pray, walk softly . . . iv 1 48
Well, there's for you: leave us.—I beseech your honour, give me leave: a word . . . . iv 6 50
Come, we will leave his honour and her together. Go thy ways . . iv 6 70
Come, let us leave her; And the gods make her prosperous! . . . v 1 79
Yet, give me leave: How came you in these parts? where were you bred? . . . . v 1 170
Let me rest.—A pillow for his head: So, leave him all . . . . v 1 238
By your leave *Mer. Wives* i 1; iii 2; iii 5; *Meas. for Meas.* iv 3; v 1; *Much Ado* iv 1; *Mer. of Venice* ii 4; *T. of Shrew* iv 4; v 2; *T. Night* ii 5; *2 Hen. IV.* i 3; *Hen. VIII.* i 4; *Troi. and Cres.* iv 5; *T. Andron.* i 1; *T. of Athens* iii 4; *Macbeth* i 6; *Othello* ii 3; *Cymbeline* ii 3
Give us leave *T. G. of Ver.* iii 1; *Mer. Wives* ii 2; *1 Hen. IV.* iii 2; *3 Hen. VI.* iii 2
So I take my leave *L. L. Lost* v 2; *Mer. of Venice* iv 1; *T. of Shrew* ii 1; *All's Well* ii 3; *3 Hen. VI.* iv 8; *T. Andron.* i 1; *Pericles* iii 3

Leave off discourse of disability: Sweet lady, entertain him *T. G. of Ver.* ii 4 109
What a pretty thing man is when he goes in his doublet and hose and leaves off his wit! . . . . *Much Ado* v 1 203
Leave off delays, and let us raise the siege . . . . *1 Hen. VI.* i 2 146
Leave off to wonder why I drew you hither . . . . *3 Hen. VI.* iv 5 2

Leave out. And mannerly distinguishment leave out Betwixt the prince and beggar . . . . *W. Tale* ii 1 86
I am so fraught with curious business that I leave out ceremony . iv 4 526
And leave out thee? stay, dog, for thou shalt hear me . *Richard III.* i 3 216
Let him not leave out The colour of her hair . . *Ant. and Cleo.* ii 5 113

Leaven. Speak then, thou vinewedst leaven, speak . *Troi. and Cres.* ii 1 15
Wilt lay the leaven on all proper men; Goodly and gallant shall be false and perjured From thy great fail . . . . *Cymbeline* iii 4 64

Leavened. No more evasion: We have with a leaven'd and prepared choice Proceeded to you . . . . . . *Meas. for Meas.* i 1 52

Leavening. Have I not tarried?—Ay, the bolting, but you must tarry the leavening.—Still have I tarried.—Ay, to the leavening *T. and C.* i 1 20

Leaves. I'll drop the paper: Sweet leaves, shade folly . *L. L. Lost* iv 3 44
Through the velvet leaves the wind, All unseen, can passage find . . iv 3 105
When briers shall have leaves as well as thorns . . . *All's Well* iv 4 32
Is hack'd down, and his summer leaves all faded . . . *Richard II.* i 2 20
The weeds which his broad-spreading leaves did shelter . . . . iii 4 50
Hollow whistling in the leaves Foretells a tempest . . . *1 Hen. IV.* v 1 5
Upbraided me about the rose I wear; Saying, the sanguine colour of the leaves Did represent my master's blushing cheeks *1 Hen. VI.* iv 1 92
My blossoms blasted in the bud And caterpillars eat my leaves away *2 Hen. VI.* iii 1 90
As on a mountain top the cedar shows That keeps his leaves in spite of any storm . . . . v 1 206
In hewing Rutland when his leaves put forth . . . . *3 Hen. VI.* i 6 48
The leaves and fruit maintain'd with beauty's sun, Exempt from envy . ii 3 126
Why wither not the leaves the sap being gone? . . . *Richard III.* ii 2 42
When great leaves fall, the winter is at hand . . . . . ii 3 33
To-day he puts forth The tender leaves of hopes; to-morrow blossoms *Hen. VIII.* iii 2 353
The green leaves quiver with the cooling wind . . . *T. Andron.* ii 3 14
Rude-growing briers, Upon whose leaves are drops of new-shed blood . ii 3 200
See, brother, see; note how she quotes the leaves . . . . iv 1 50
The angry northern wind Will blow these sands, like Sibyl's leaves, abroad . . . . iv 1 105
As is the bud bit with an envious worm, Ere he can spread his sweet leaves to the air, Or dedicate his beauty to the sun . *Rom. and Jul.* i 1 158
That numberless upon me stuck as leaves Do on the oak *T. of Athens* iv 3 263
Drown'd! O, where?—There is a willow grows aslant a brook, That shows his hoar leaves in the glassy stream . . . . *Hamlet* iv 7 168
Shook down my mellow hangings, nay, my leaves, And left me bare *Cymbeline* iii 3 63

Leavest. O thou dull god, why liest thou with the vile In loathsome beds, and leavest the kingly couch? . . . . . *2 Hen. IV.* iii 1 16

Leave-taking. Where injury of chance Puts back leave-taking *Troi. and Cres.* iv 4 36
Let us not be dainty of leave-taking, But shift away . . . *Macbeth* ii 3 150
Why in that rawness left you wife and child, Those precious motives, those strong knots of love, Without leave-taking? . . . . . iv 3 28
There is further compliment of leave-taking . . . . . *Lear* i 1 306
Dost thou lie still? If thus thou vanishest, thou tell'st the world It is not worth leave-taking . . . . *Ant. and Cleo.* v 2 301

Leaving the fear of God on the left hand *Mer. Wives* ii 2 23
Leaving his wealth and ease, A stubborn will to please *As Y. Like It* ii 5 54
Leaving her In the protection of his son, her brother *T. Night* i 2 37
His dishonesty appears in leaving his friend here in necessity iii 4 422
Leontes leaving, The effects of his fond jealousies so grieving *W. Tale* iv 1 17
Wipe not out the rest of thy services by leaving me now iv 2 12
Like a bated and retired flood, Leaving our rankness *K. John* v 4 54
Leaving me no sign, Save men's opinions and my living blood *Rich. II.* iii 1 25
Leaving his body as a paradise, To envelope and contain celestial spirits *Hen. V.* i 1 30
The men do sympathize with the mastiffs in robustious and rough coming on, leaving their wits with their wives iii 7 160
Shall suck away their souls, Leaving them but the shales and husks of men iv 2 18
Leaving their earthly parts to choke your clime iv 3 102
Leaving no heir begotten of his body—I was the next by birth 1 *Hen. VI.* ii 5 72
Leaving thy trunk for crows to feed upon 2 *Hen. VI.* iv 10 90
But, leaving this, what is your grace's pleasure? *Richard III.* iii 7 108
My husband is on earth, my faith in heaven; How shall that faith return again to earth, Unless that husband send it me from heaven By leaving earth? *Rom. and Jul.* iii 5 210
Flies an eagle flight, bold and forth on, Leaving no tract behind *T. of A.* i 1 50
Give them diseases, leaving with thee their lust iv 3 84
Nothing in his life Became him like the leaving it *Macbeth* i 4 8
Who alone suffers suffers most i' the mind, Leaving free things and happy shows behind *Lear* iii 6 112
Antony Claps on his sea-wing, and, like a doting mallard, Leaving the fight in height, flies after her *Ant. and Cleo.* iii 10 21
I'll weep and sigh; And leaving so his service, follow you *Cymbeline* iv 2 393
I charge your charity withal, leaving her The infant of your care *Pericles* iii 3 14
Leavy. The fraud of men was ever so, Since summer first was leavy *Much Ado* ii 3 75
Now near enough: your leavy screens throw down *Macbeth* v 6 1
Upon The leafy shelter that abuts against The island's side *Pericles* v 1 51
Le Beau. Here comes Monsieur Le Beau *As Y. Like It* i 2 97
Le Bon. How say you by the French lord, Monsieur Le Bon? *Mer. of Ven.* i 2 59
Lecher. I will now take the lecher; he is at my house *Mer. Wives* iii 5 147
You, like a lecher, out of whorish loins Are pleased to breed out your inheritors *Troi. and Cres.* iv 1 63
Like an old lecher's heart; a small spark, all the rest on's body cold *Lear* iii 4 117
The wren goes to't, and the small gilded fly Does lecher in my sight iv 6 115
The post unsanctified Of murderous lechers iv 6 282
Lecherous. Sparrows must not build in his house-eaves, because they are lecherous *Meas. for Meas.* iii 2 186
A' was the very genius of famine; yet lecherous as a monkey 2 *Hen. IV.* iii 2 338
Remorseless, treacherous, lecherous, kindless villain! *Hamlet* ii 2 609
My nativity was under Ursa major; so that it follows, I am rough and lecherous. Tut, I should have been that I am *Lear* i 2 142
Lechery. Against such lewdsters and their lechery Those that betray them do no treachery *Mer. Wives* v 3 23
What, is't murder?—No.—Lechery?—Call it so *Meas. for Meas.* i 2 143
Is lechery so look'd after? i 2 148
A little more lenity to lechery would do no harm in him iii 2 103
The most dangerous piece of lechery that ever was known *Much Ado* iii 3 180
How have you come so early by this lethargy?—Lechery! I defy lechery *T. Night* i 5 133
A man can no more separate age and covetousness than a' can part young limbs and lechery: but the gout galls the one 2 *Hen. IV.* i 2 257
War and lechery confound all! *Troi. and Cres.* ii 3 81
Nothing but lechery! all incontinent varlets! v 1 106
How the devil Luxury, with his fat rump and potato-finger, tickles these together! Fry, lechery, fry! v 2 57
Lechery, lechery; still, wars and lechery; nothing else holds fashion v 2 195
Yet, in a sort, lechery eats itself v 4 37
Lechery, sir, it [drink] provokes, and unprovokes *Macbeth* ii 3 32
Therefore, much drink may be said to be an equivocator with lechery ii 3 35
But that was but courtesy.—Lechery, by this hand *Othello* ii 1 263
Leçon. Je reciterai une autre fois ma leçon ensemble *Hen. V.* iii 4 61
Lecture. I have heard him read many lectures against it [love] *As Y. L. It* iii 2 365
And see you read no other lectures to her *T. of Shrew* i 2 148
When in music we have spent an hour, Your lecture shall have leisure iii 1 8
His lecture will be done ere you have tuned.—You'll leave his lecture when I am in tune?—That will be never iii 1 23
If thy offences were upon record, Would it not shame thee in so fair a troop To read a lecture of them? *Richard II.* iv 1 232
Say we read lectures to you, How youngly he began to serve his country *Coriolanus* ii 3 243
So by my former lecture and advice, Shall you my son *Hamlet* ii 1 67
Led. Here comes Signior Claudio, led by the provost to prison *M. for M.* i 2 118
What, at the wheels of Cæsar? art thou led in triumph? iii 2 46
I led them on in this distracted fear *M. N. Dream* iii 2 31
I am not solely led By nice direction of a maiden's eyes *Mer. of Venice* ii 1 13
Who led me instantly unto his cave, There stripp'd himself *As Y. Like It* iv 3 146
Where is the life that late I led? *T. of Shrew* iv 1 143; 2 *Hen. IV.* v 3 147
Led hither by pure love *All's Well* iii 4 38
Faith, sir, has led the drum before the English tragedians iv 3 298
The kings of Christendom Are led so grossly by this meddling priest *K. John* iii 1 163
He hath promised to dismiss the powers Led by the Dauphin v 1 65
The king is not himself, but basely led By flatterers *Richard II.* ii 1 241
I have led my ragamuffins where they are peppered 1 *Hen. IV.* v 3 36
With great imagination Proper to madmen, led his powers to death 2 *Hen. IV.* i 3 32
In base and abject routs, Led on by bloody youth, guarded with rags iv 1 34
I am, my lord, but as my betters are That led me hither iv 3 72
What I did, I did in honour, Led by the impartial conduct of my soul v 2 36
Now, if these men do not die well, it will be a black matter for the king that led them to it *Hen. V.* iv 1 152
Then broke I from the officers that led me 1 *Hen. VI.* i 4 44
Discovered Two mightier troops than that the Dauphin led iv 3 7
Methinks I should not thus be led along 2 *Hen. VI.* ii 4 30
Thrice I led him off, Persuaded him from any further act v 3 9
Some troops pursue the bloody-minded queen, That led calm Henry 3 *Hen. VI.* ii 6 34
My niece Plantagenet Led in the hand of her kind aunt *Richard III.* iv 1 2
Ten thousand soldiers Armed in proof, and led by shallow Richmond v 3 219
My election Is led on in the conduct of my will *Troi. and Cres.* ii 2 62
He holds you well, and will be led At your request a little from himself ii 3 190
A fearful army, led by Caius Marcius Associated with Aufidius *Coriol.* iv 6 75
Our raiment And state of bodies would bewray what life We have led v 3 96
Led. As a foreign recreant, be led With manacles thorough our streets *Coriolanus* v 3 114
And With bloody passage led your wars even to The gates of Rome v 6 76
Rome, I have been thy soldier forty years, And led my country's strength successfully *T. Andron.* i 1 194
Was't not a happy star Led us to Rome? iv 2 33
Like stinging bees in hottest summer's day Led by their master v 1 15
But who comes here, led by a lusty Goth? v 1 19
But, O grief, Where hast thou led me? *J. Cæsar* i 3 112
Either led or driven, as we point the way iv 1 23
Then, if we lose this battle, You are contented to be led in triumph? v 1 109
This is the air-drawn dagger which, you said, Led you to Duncan *Macb.* iii 4 63
The English power is near, led on by Malcolm, His uncle Siward v 2 1
This army of such mass and charge Led by a delicate and tender prince *Hamlet* iv 4 48
All that follow their noses are led by their eyes but blind men *Lear* ii 4 70
You should be ruled and led By some discretion, that discerns your state ii 4 150
Poor Tom? whom the foul fiend hath led through fire and through flame iii 4 52
But who comes here? My father, poorly led? World, world, O world! iv 1 10
Often 'twould say 'The fiend, the fiend:' he led me to that place iv 6 79
You have shown to-day your valiant strain, And fortune led you well v 3 41
He led our powers; Bore the commission of my place and person v 3 63
Became his guide, Led him, begg'd for him, saved him from despair v 3 191
But partly led to diet my revenge *Othello* ii 1 303
And saw her led Between her brother and Mark Antony *Ant. and Cleo.* iii 3 12
We perceived, both how you were wrong led, And we in negligent danger iii 6 80
So our leader's led, And we are women's men iii 7 70
O, whither hast thou led me, Egypt? iii 11 51
Take me up: I have led you oft: carry me now, good friends, And have my thanks iv 14 139
Led on by heaven, and crown'd with joy at last *Pericles* v 3 Gower 90
Led by the nose. He is oft led by the nose with gold *W. Tale* iv 4 832
And will as tenderly be led by the nose As asses are *Othello* i 3 407
Leda. You were also, Jupiter, a swan for the love of Leda *Mer. Wives* v 5 7
Fair Leda's daughter had a thousand wooers *T. of Shrew* i 2 244
Ledest. Didst thou not tell me, Griffith, as thou led'st me, That the great child of honour, Cardinal Wolsey, Was dead? *Hen. VIII.* iv 2 5
Leech. Make war breed peace, make peace stint war, make each Prescribe to other as each other's leech *T. of Athens* v 4 84
Leek. His eyes were green as leeks *M. N. Dream* v 1 342
I'll knock his leek about his pate Upon Saint Davy's day *Hen. V.* iv 1 54
The Welshmen did good service in a garden where leeks did grow, wearing leeks in their Monmouth caps iv 7 103
I do believe your majesty takes no scorn to wear the leek upon Saint Tavy's day iv 7 107
But why wear you your leek to-day? Saint Davy's day is past v 1 2
And prings me pread and salt yesterday, look you, and bid me eat my leek v 1 10
Hence! I am qualmish at the smell of leek v 1 22
Eat, look you, this leek: because, look you, you do not love it v 1 25
I pray you, fall to: if you can mock a leek, you can eat a leek v 1 39
I will make him eat some part of my leek, or I will peat his pate four days v 1 43
By this leek, I will most horribly revenge v 1 49
Have some more sauce to your leek? there is not enough leek to swear by v 1 52
When you take occasions to see leeks hereafter, I pray you, mock at 'em v 1 58
Leer. She discourses, she carves, she gives the leer of invitation *Mer. W.* i 3 50
You leer upon me, do you? *L. L. Lost* v 2 480
He hath a Rosalind of a better leer than you *As Y. Like It* iv 1 67
I will leer upon him as a' comes by 2 *Hen. IV.* v 5 7
A most unjust knave; I will no more trust him when he leers than I will a serpent when he hisses *Troi. and Cres.* v 1 97
Here's a young lad framed of another leer *T. Andron.* iv 2 119
Lees. Drink up The lees and dregs of a flat tamed piece *Troi. and Cres.* iv 1 62
The wine of life is drawn, and the mere lees Is left this vault to brag of *Macbeth* ii 3 100
Leet. And rail upon the hostess of the house; And say you would present her at the leet *T. of Shrew* Ind. 2 89
Some uncleanly apprehensions Keep leets and law-days *Othello* iii 3 140
Left. But stopp'd And left me to a bootless inquisition *Tempest* i 2 35
Whom I left cooling of the air with sighs In an odd angle of the isle i 2 222
Who, with a charm join'd to their suffer'd labour, I have left asleep i 2 232
This blue-eyed hag was hither brought with child And here was left i 2 270
Within which space she died And left thee there i 2 280
No matter, since They have left their viands behind; for we have stomachs iii 3 41
At last I left them I' the filthy-mantled pool beyond your cell iv 1 181
In the same fashion as you gave in charge, Just as you left them v 1 9
I left them all in health *T. G. of Ver.* ii 4 124
Alas, poor lady, desolate and left! iv 4 179
Thou hast no faith left now, unless thou'dst two; And that's far worse than none v 4 50
Left her in her tears, and dried not one of them *Meas. for Meas.* iii 1 234
My factor's death And the great care of goods at random left *Com. of Er.* i 1 43
The sailors sought for safety by our boat, And left the ship i 1 78
Fortune had left to both of us alike What to delight in, what to sorrow for i 1 106
Tell me this, I pray: Where have you left the money that I gave you? i 2 54
But, if thou live to see like right bereft, This fool-begg'd patience in thee will be left ii 1 41
Since that my beauty cannot please his eye, I'll weep what's left away ii 1 115
It was two ere I left him, and now the clock strikes one iv 2 54
In a dark and dankish vault at home There left me and my man v 1 248
My wasting lamps some fading glimmer left v 1 315
By force took Dromio and my son from them And me they left v 1 353
He is very near by this: he was not three leagues off when I left him *Much Ado* i 1 4
It is all the wealth that he hath left, to be known a reasonable creature i 1 71
War-thoughts Have left their places vacant, in their rooms Come thronging soft and delicate desires i 1 304
I would not marry her, though she were endowed with all that Adam had left him before he transgressed ii 1 259
How long have you professed apprehension?—Ever since you left it iii 4 69
All the grace that she hath left Is that she will not add to her damnation A sin of perjury iv 1 173
Your daughter here the princes left for dead iv 1 204
I love you with so much of my heart that none is left to protest iv 1 289
A mess of Russians left us but of late.—How, madam! Russians! *L. L. Lost* v 2 361
And left sweet Pyramus translated there *M. N. Dream* iii 2 32

Left. Since night you loved me; yet since night you left me: Why, then you left me—O, the gods forbid!—In earnest, shall I say? *M. N. Dream* iii 2 275
Starveling! God's my life, stolen hence, and left me asleep! . iv 1 209
Moonshine and Lion are left to bury the dead.—Ay, and Wall too . . v 1 355
My chief care Is to come fairly off from the great debts Wherein my time something too prodigal Hath left me gaged . *Mer. of Venice* i 1 130
In Belmont is a lady richly left; And she is fair . . . i 1 161
My house, left in the fearful guard Of an unthrifty knave . . . i 3 176
Turn up on your right hand at the next turning, but, at the next turning of all, on your left . . . . ii 2 44
Thy wealth being forfeit to the state, Thou hast not left the value of a cord . . . . iv 1 366
Conceive for what I gave the ring And how unwillingly I left the ring . v 1 196
Give me the poor allottery my father left me by testament *As Y. Like It* i 1 77
Being there alone, Left and abandon'd of his velvet friends . . . ii 1 50
Left on your right hand brings you to the place . . . . iv 3 81
He left a promise to return again Within an hour . . . . iv 3 100
Fare you well: I have left you commands.—I'll not fail, if I live . . v 2 131
For I have Pisa left And am to Padua come . . . *T. of Shrew* i 1 21
You knew my father well, and in him me, Left solely heir to all his lands ii 1 118
Where left we last?—Here, madam . . . . iii 1 26
How he left her with the horse upon her, how he beat me . . . iv 1 78
Has left me here behind, to expound the meaning or moral of his signs iv 4 78
My father left me some prescriptions Of rare and proved effects *All's Well* i 3 227
He left this ring behind him, Would I or not . . . . *T. Night* i 5 320
I left no ring with her: what means this lady? . . . . ii 2 18
Having come from a day-bed, where I have left Olivia sleeping . . ii 5 55
Since we have left our throne Without a burthen . . . *W. Tale* i 2 2
Lest that the treachery of the two fled hence Be left her to perform . ii 1 196
I'll pawn the little blood which I have left To save the innocent . . ii 3 166
Why he left your court, the gods themselves, Wotting no more than I, are ignorant . . . . iii 2 76
If there be any of him left, I'll bury it . . . . . iii 3 136
If thou mayest discern by that which is left of him what he is, fetch me to the sight of him . . . . iii 3 138
Indeed, he should be a footman by the garments he has left with thee . iv 3 70
Is there no manners left among maids? . . . . . . iv 4 244
I had not left a purse alive in the whole army . . . . . iv 4 631
The crown will find an heir: great Alexander Left his to the worthiest v 1 48
And left them More rich for what they yielded . . . . v 1 54
For which the heavens, taking angry note, Have left me issueless . . v 1 174
The half part of a blessed man, Left to be finished by such as she *K. John* ii 1 438
'Tis not an hour since I left him well . . . . . . iv 3 104
And England now is left To tug and scamble . . . . . iv 3 145
They say King John sore sick hath left the field . . . . v 4 6
The king, I fear, is poison'd by a monk: I left him almost speechless . v 6 24
He is more patient Than when you left him; even now he sung . . v 7 12
To set a form upon that indigest Which he hath left so shapeless . . v 7 27
There I left him.—And say, what store of parting tears were shed? *Richard II.* i 4 4
Here am I left to underprop his land, Who, weak with age, cannot support myself . . . . ii 2 82
All is uneven, And every thing is left at six and seven . . . ii 2 122
I see the issue of these arms: I cannot mend it, I must needs confess, Because my power is weak and all ill left . . . . . . ii 3 154
Your grace mistakes; only to be brief, Left I his title out . . . iii 3 10
And left me in reputeless banishment . . . . *1 Hen. IV.* iii 2 44
Whereon the imperious flood Hath left a witness'd usurpation *2 Hen. IV.* i 1 63
So you left him. Never, O never, do his ghost the wrong! . . . ii 3 38
Now, have you left pursuit?—Retreat is made and execution stay'd . iv 3 77
Left the liver white and pale, which is the badge of pusillanimity . iv 3 113
This from thee Will I to mine leave, as 'tis left to me . . . . iv 5 47
We left the prince my brother here, my liege, Who undertook to sit and watch by you . . . . iv 5 52
Who took it from my pillow?—When we withdrew, my liege, we left it here . . . . iv 5 59
The service that I truly did his life Hath left me open to all injuries . v 2 8
The breath no sooner left his father's body, But that his wildness, mortified in him, Seem'd to die too . . . . . *Hen. V.* i 1 25
Whose hearts have left their bodies here in England . . . . i 2 128
If we, with thrice such powers left at home, Cannot defend our own doors i 2 217
Thus thy fall hath left a kind of blot, To mark the full-fraught man . ii 2 138
As fear may teach us out of late examples Left by the fatal and neglected English Upon our fields . . . . ii 4 13
Some crying for a surgeon, some upon their wives left poor behind them, some upon the debts they owe, some upon their children rawly left iv 1 146
The world's best garden he achieved, And of it left his son imperial lord Epil. 8
And none but women left to wail the dead . . . . *1 Hen. VI.* i 1 51
I would ne'er have fled, But that they left me 'midst my enemies . . i 2 24
I'll be so bold to take what they have left . . . . . . ii 1 78
Will not this malice, Somerset, be left? . . . . . . iv 1 108
Broke his word And left us to the rage of France his sword . . . iv 6 3
He left me proudly, as unworthy fight . . . . iv 7 43
Were but his picture left amongst you here, It would amaze the proudest iv 7 83
Thy cruelty in execution Upon offenders hath exceeded law And left thee to the mercy of the law . . . . . . *2 Hen. VI.* i 3 137
For purposely therefore Left I the court, to see this quarrel tried . . iii 1 53
Yet Æolus would not be a murderer, But left that hateful office unto thee iii 2 93
This small inheritance my father left me Contenteth me. . . . . iv 10 20
He slily stole away and left his men . . . . . *3 Hen. VI.* i 1 3
Thou wouldst have left thy dearest heart-blood there . . . . i 1 223
Whom we have left protectors of the king . . . . . . i 2 57
His name that valiant duke hath left with thee; His dukedom and his chair with me is left . . . . ii 1 89
I'll leave my son my virtuous deeds behind; And would my father had left me no more! . . . . ii 2 50
Ah, boy, if any life be left in thee, Throw up thine eye! . . . ii 5 84
I and ten thousand in this luckless realm Had left no mourning widows ii 6 19
You left poor Henry at the Bishop's palace, And, ten to one, you'll meet him in the Tower.—'Tis even so . . . . v 1 45
Of all my lands Is nothing left me but my body's length . . . . v 2 26
Thou art a mother, And hast the comfort of thy children left thee *Rich III.* ii 2 56
Our fatherless distress was left unmoan'd; Your widow-dolour likewise be! ii 2 64
Left nothing fitting for the purpose Untouch'd, or slightly handled, in discourse . . . . iii 7 18
The royal tree hath left us royal fruit . . . . iii 7 167
They could not speak; and so I left them both, To bring this tidings . iv 3 21
Thus hath the course of justice wheel'd about, And left thee but a very prey to time; Having no more but thought of what thou wert . . iv 4 106

Left. And in record, left them the heirs of shame . . . . *Richard III.* v 3 335
They've left their barge and landed; And hither make . . *Hen. VIII.* i 4 54
I left him private, Full of sad thoughts and troubles . . . ii 2 15
Unsolicited I left no reverend person in this court . . . . ii 4 220
This is yet but young, and may be left To some ears unrecounted . . iii 2 47
Hath ta'en no leave; Has left the cause o' the king unhandled . . iii 2 58
Left me, Weary and old with service, to the mercy Of a rude stream . iii 2 362
He would not in mine age Have left me naked to mine enemies . . iii 2 457
And left him at primero With the Duke of Suffolk . . . . v 1 7
We shall have Great store of room, no doubt, left for the ladies . . v 4 77
If none of them have soul in such a kind, We left them all at home *Troi. and Cres.* i 3 286
I have abandon'd Troy, left my possession, Incurr'd a traitor's name . iii 3 5
Thou art left, Marcius . . . . *Coriolanus* i 4 54
Now you have left your voices, I have no further with you . . ii 3 180
The blood he hath lost . . . he dropp'd it for his country; And what is left, to lose it by his country, Were to us all . . . A brand to the end o' the world . . . . iii 1 302
Either Had borne the action of yourself, or else To him had left it solely iv 7 16
He hath left undone That which shall break his neck or hazard mine . iv 7 24
Though you left me like a churl, I found a friend . . . *T. Andron.* i 1 486
'Tis not an hour since I left him there.—We know not where you left him all alive; But, out, alas! here have we found him dead . . . ii 3 257
As meadows, yet not dry, With miry slime left on them by a flood . iii 1 126
This poor right hand of mine Is left to tyrannize upon my breast . . iii 2 8
As Tarquin erst, That left the camp to sin in Lucrece' bed . . iv 1 64
There's not a god left unsolicited . . . . iv 3 60
This one hand yet is left to cut your throats . . . . . v 2 182
By my holidame, The pretty wretch left crying and said 'Ay' *Rom. and Jul.* i 3 44
Threaten'd me with death, going in the vault, If I departed not and left him v 3 277
He is gone happy, and has left me rich . . . . *T. of Athens* i 2 4
Honest water, which ne'er left man i' the mire . . . . . i 2 60
If I should be bribed too, there would be none left to rail upon thee . i 2 245
Lord Timon will be left a naked gull, Which flashes now a phœnix . ii 1 31
There is not so much left, to furnish out A moderate table . . . iii 4 116
Left me open, bare For every storm that blows . . . . . iv 3 265
Let us return, And strain what other means is left unto us . . . v 1 230
Seek not my name: a plague consume you wicked caitiffs left! . . v 4 71
He hath left you all his walks, His private arbours . . . *J. Cæsar* iii 2 252
He hath left them you, And to your heirs for ever . . . . iii 2 254
Let me see; is not the leaf turn'd down Where I left reading? . . iv 3 274
Only I have left to say, More is thy due than more than all can pay *Macb.* i 4 20
He has almost supp'd: why have you left the chamber? . . . i 7 29
Your constancy Hath left you unattended . . . . . . ii 2 69
The wine of life is drawn, and the mere lees Is left this vault to brag of ii 3 101
There's warrant in that theft Which steals itself, when there's no mercy left . . . . ii 3 152
Why in that rawness left your wife and child, Those precious motives? iv 3 26
Ere yet the salt of most unrighteous tears Had left the flushing in her galled eyes, She married . . . . *Hamlet* i 2 155
For 'tis a question left us yet to prove, Whether love lead fortune, or else fortune love . . . . iii 2 212
I am more an antique Roman than a Dane: Here's yet some liquor left v 2 353
Thou hast pared thy wit o' both sides, and left nothing i' the middle *Lear* i 4 205
So, out went the candle, and we were left darkling . . . . i 4 237
I'll not trouble thee: Yet have I left a daughter . . . . i 4 276
Yet have I left a daughter, Who, I am sure, is kind and comfortable . i 4 327
You have one eye left To see some mischief on him . . . . iii 7 81
Know you the reason?—Something he left imperfect in the state . . iv 3 3
Twice then the trumpets sounded, And there I left him tranced . . iv 6 218
Our great captain's captain, Left in the conduct of the bold Iago *Othello* ii 1 75
So humbled That he hath left part of his grief with me, To suffer with him iii 3 53
I heard thee say even now, thou likedst not that, When Cassio left my wife . . . . iii 3 110
That you should find it in your chamber, and not know who left it there! iv 1 158
Would I had never seen her!—O, sir, you had then left unseen a wonderful piece of work . . . . *Ant. and Cleo.* i 2 159
The ostentation of our love, which, left unshown, Is often left unloved iii 6 52
Take the hint Which my despair proclaims; let that be left Which leaves itself . . . . iii 11 19
But it would warm his spirits, To hear from me you had left Antony . iii 13 70
Have I my pillow left unpress'd in Rome? . . . . . . iii 13 106
My good stars, that were my former guides, Have empty left their orbs iii 13 146
The soldier That has this morning left thee, would have still Follow'd . iv 5 5
Nay, weep not, gentle Eros; there is left us Ourselves to end ourselves iv 14 21
And there is nothing left remarkable Beneath the visiting moon . . iv 15 67
Left these notes Of what commands I should be subject to . *Cymbeline* i 1 171
Thou shouldst have made him As little as a crow, or less, ere left To after-eye him.—Madam, so I did . . . . i 3 15
Fold down the leaf where I have left: to bed: Take not away the taper ii 2 4
Search for a jewel that too casually Hath left mine arm . . . ii 3 147
Jove! Once more let me behold it: is it that Which I left with her? . ii 4 100
Yearly three thousand pounds, which by thee lately Is left untender'd . iii 1 10
Shook down my mellow hangings, nay, my leaves, And left me bare to weather . . . . iii 3 64
Here's money for my meat: I would have léft it on the board . . iii 6 51
In this place we left them: I wish my brother make good time with him iv 2 107
If there be Yet left in heaven as small a drop of pity As a wren's eye . iv 2 304
Pisanio might have kill'd thee at the heart, And left this head on . . iv 2 323
Who died and left a female heir . . . . . . *Pericles* i Gower 22
Yet those which see them fall Have scarce strength left to give them burial . . . . i 4 49
Left me breath Nothing to think on but ensuing death . . . . ii 1 6
He should never have left, till he cast bells, steeple, church, . . . up again ii 1 46
Did bequeath to me With this strict charge, even as he left his life . ii 1 131
Like goodly buildings left without a roof Soon fall to ruin . . . ii 4 36
Here's all that is left living of your queen, A little daughter . . . iii 1 20
Old Escanes . . . Is left to govern . . . . iv 4 15
To her father turn our thoughts again, Where we left him, on the sea v Gower 13

Left alive. There's not three of my hundred and fifty left alive *1 Hen. IV.* v 3 38
There's not a boy left alive; and the cowardly rascals that ran from the battle ha' done this slaughter . . . . . . *Hen. V.* iv 7 5

Left alone. If she do chide, 'tis not to have you gone; For why, the fools are mad, if left alone . . . . . . *T. G. of Ver.* iii 1 99
If I be left alone, Now, by mine honour, which is yet mine own, I'll have that doctor for my bedfellow . . . . . *Mer. of Venice* v 1 231
So please you, let me now be left alone . . . *Rom. and Jul.* iv 3 9

Left arm. The great wart on my left arm . . . . *Com. of Errors* iii 2 148
Where is he wounded?—I' the shoulder and i' the left arm . *Coriolanus* ii 1 163

Left behind. He left behind him myself and a sister . . *T. Night* ii 1 19
Comest thou because the anointed king is hence? Why, foolish boy, the king is left behind . . . *Richard II.* ii 3 97
Cut me off the heads Of all the favourites that the absent king In deputation left behind him here . . . . . . 1 *Hen. IV.* iv 3 87
Having subdued the Saxons, There left behind and settled certain French *Hen. V.* i 2 47
Edward the Black Prince died before his father And left behind him Richard, his only son . . . . . . 2 *Hen. VI.* ii 2 19
Who hath he left behind him general? . . . . . *Lear* iv 3 8
If I be left behind, A moth of peace, and he go to the war, The rites for which I love him are bereft me . . . . *Othello* i 3 256
See, How I convey my shame out of thine eyes By looking back what I have left behind . . . . . . *Ant. and Cleo.* iii 11 53
When I did fly from Tyre, I left behind an ancient substitute *Pericles* v 3 51
Left breast. On her left breast A mole cinque-spotted . *Cymbeline* ii 2 37
Left cheek. His left cheek is a cheek of two pile and a half *All's Well* iv 5 102
Left hand. Leaving the fear of God on the left hand . *Mer. Wives* ii 2 24
Why, I were best to cut my left hand off And swear I lost the ring defending it . . . . . . *Mer. of Venice* v 1 177
Lead your battle softly on, Upon the left hand of the even field.—Upon the right hand I; keep thou the left . . . *J. Cæsar* v 1 17
This is my right hand, and this is my left: I am not drunk now *Othello* ii 3 119
Left in trust. His seal'd commission, left in trust with me . *Pericles* i 3 13
Left legs. Let them curtsy with their left legs . *T. of Shrew* iv 1 95
Left off. When the schools, Embowell'd of their doctrine, have left off The danger to itself . . . . *All's Well* i 3 247
Left out. I am left out; for me nothing remains . . . 1 *Hen. VI.* i 1 174
The cutter Was as another nature, dumb; outwent her, Motion and breath left out . . . . *Cymbeline* ii 4 85
I left out one thing which the queen confess'd, Which must approve thee honest . . . . v 5 244
Left pap. Thumped him with thy bird-bolt under the left pap *L. L. Lost* iv 3 24
Out, sword, and wound The pap of Pyramus; Ay, that left pap, Where heart doth hop: Thus die I, thus . . . *M. N. Dream* v 1 303
Left shoe. This shoe is my father: no, this left shoe is my father: no, no, this left shoe is my mother . . . *T. G. of Ver.* ii 3 16
Left side. She, on his left side, craving aid for Henry, He, on his right, asking a wife for Edward . . . . 3 *Hen. VI.* iii 1 43
Leg. I have not 'scaped drowning to be afeard now of your four legs *Temp.* ii 2 62
As proper a man as ever went on four legs cannot make him give ground ii 2 63
This is some monster of the isle with four legs . . . ii 2 68
Four legs and two voices: a most delicate monster! . . . ii 2 93
I'll pull thee by the lesser legs: if any be Trinculo's legs, these are they ii 2 108
He steps me to her trencher and steals her capon's leg . *T. G. of Ver.* iv 4 10
When didst thou see me heave up my leg? . . . . . iv 4 41
And yet she takes exceptions at your person.—What, that my leg is too long? . . . . v 2 4
Pinch them, arms, legs, backs, shoulders, sides and shins . *Mer. Wives* v 5 58
With a good leg and a good foot, uncle, and money enough . *Much Ado* ii 1 15
Then comes repentance and, with his bad legs, falls into the cinque pace ii 1 81
I will call Beatrice to you, who I think hath legs.—And therefore will come . . . . v 2 24
When shall you hear that I Will praise a hand, a foot, . . . A leg? *L. L. L.* iv 3 186
The music plays; vouchsafe some motion to it.—Our ears vouchsafe it.—But your legs should do it . . . . . v 2 217
And lay my arms before the legs of this sweet lass of France . . v 2 558
His leg is too big for Hector's.—More calf, certain . . . v 2 644
Your hands than mine are quicker for a fray, My legs are longer though, to run away . . . . *M. N. Dream* iii 2 343
Death-counterfeiting sleep With leaden legs and batty wings doth creep iii 2 365
My legs can keep no pace with my desires. Here will I rest me . iii 2 445
Use your legs, take the start, run away . . *Mer. of Venice* ii 2 6
I would I were invisible, to catch the strong fellow by the leg *As Y. L. It* i 2 224
I care not for my spirits, if my legs were not weary . . . ii 4 2
For his years he's tall: His leg is but so so; and yet 'tis well . iii 5 119
No more stockings than legs, nor no more shoes than feet *T. of Shrew* Ind. 2 10
Or Daphne roaming through a thorny wood, Scratching her legs . Ind. 2 60
A linen stock on one leg and a kersey boot-hose on the other . . iii 2 68
Let them curtsy with their left legs . . . . . . iv 1 95
He that cannot make a leg, put off's cap, kiss his hand, and say nothing, has neither leg, hands, lip, nor cap . . . . . *All's Well* ii 2 10
I am there before my legs . . . . ii 2 73
It hangs like flax on a distaff; and I hope to see a housewife take thee between her legs and spin it off . . . . . *T. Night* i 3 110
I did think, by the excellent constitution of thy leg, it was formed under the star of a galliard . . . . i 3 141
Taurus! That's sides and heart.—No, sir; it is legs and thighs . i 3 149
I had rather than forty shillings I had such a leg . . . . ii 3 21
By the colour of his beard, the shape of his leg, the manner of his gait . ii 3 170
She did commend my yellow stockings of late, she did praise my leg . ii 5 182
Taste your legs, sir; put them to motion.—My legs do better understand me, sir, than I understand what you mean by bidding me taste my legs iii 1 87
Not black in my mind, though yellow in my legs . . . . iii 4 29
If this letter move him not, his legs cannot: I'll give't him . . iii 4 188
He that did the Tiger board, When your young nephew Titus lost his leg v 1 66
If my legs were two such riding-rods, My arms such eel-skins *K. John* i 1 140
Sir Robert never holp to make this leg . . . . . . i 1 240
Why have those banish'd and forbidden legs Dared once to touch a dust of England's ground? . . . . . . *Richard II.* ii 3 90
You make a leg, and Bolingbroke says ay . . . . . iii 3 175
My legs can keep no measure in delight, When my poor heart no measure keeps in grief . . . . iii 4 7
A cup of Madeira and a cold capon's leg . . . . 1 *Hen. IV.* i 2 129
We'll walk afoot awhile, and ease our legs . . . . . ii 2 84
Well, here is my leg.—And here is my speech . . . . ii 4 427
The villains march wide betwixt the legs, as if they had gyves on . iv 2 44
Can honour set to a leg? no: or an arm? . . . . . v 1 133
A white beard? a decreasing leg? an increasing belly? . 2 *Hen. IV.* i 2 205
He had no legs that practised not his gait . . . . . ii 3 23
Why does the prince love him so, then?—Because their legs are both of a bigness . . . . ii 4 265
And wears his boots very smooth, like unto the sign of the leg . ii 4 271
If my tongue cannot entreat you to acquit me, will you command me to use my legs? . . . . Epil. 19
My tongue is weary; when my legs are too, I will bid you good night . Epil. 34
I thought upon one pair of English legs Did march three Frenchmen *Hen. V.* iii 6 158
When all those legs and arms and heads, chopped off in a battle, shall join together at the latter day . . . . iv 1 142
Leg. I would fain see the man, that has but two legs, that shall find himself aggriefed at this glove . . . . . *Hen. V.* iv 7 169
A good leg will fall; a straight back will stoop . . . . v 2 167
And I will chain these legs and arms of thine . . . . 1 *Hen. VI.* ii 3 39
I vow'd, base knight, when I did meet thee next, To tear the garter from thy craven's leg, Which I have done . . . . . iv 1 15
Would ye not think his cunning to be great, that could restore this cripple to his legs again? . . . . . . 2 *Hen. VI.* ii 1 133
Well, sir, we must have you find your legs . . . . . ii 1 148
Throws away his crutch Before his legs be firm to bear his body . iii 1 190
Thy hand is but a finger to my fist, Thy leg a stick compared with this truncheon . . . . iv 10 52
Hath clapp'd his tail between his legs and cried . . . . v 1 154
Your legs did better service than your hands . . . 3 *Hen. VI.* ii 2 104
Where sits deformity to mock my body; To shape my legs of an unequal size . . . . iii 2 159
I have often heard my mother say I came into the world with my legs forward . . . . v 6 71
I came hither on my legs . . . . . . *Richard III.* i 4 87
They have all new legs, and lame ones . . . . *Hen. VIII.* i 3 11
My legs, like loaden branches, bow to the earth . . . . iv 2 2
Stands alone.—So do all men, unless they are drunk, sick, or have no legs *Troi. and Cres.* i 2 18
His legs are legs for necessity, not for flexure . . . . . ii 3 114
The sinews of this leg All Greek, and this all Troy . . . iv 5 126
A thrifty shoeing-horn in a chain, hanging at his brother's leg . v 1 62
The counsellor heart, the arm our soldier, Our steed the leg . *Coriolanus* i 1 121
You are ambitious for poor knaves' caps and legs . . . . ii 1 77
If I could shake off but one seven years From these old arms and legs . iv 1 56
For all the water in the ocean Can never turn the swan's black legs to white, Although she lave them hourly . . . *T. Andron.* iv 2 102
And no sooner in, But every man betake him to his legs *Rom. and Jul.* i 4 34
Her waggon-spokes made of long spinners' legs . . . . . i 4 59
By her fine foot, straight leg and quivering thigh . . . . ii 1 19
Though his face be better than any man's, yet his leg excels all men's . ii 5 41
I doubt whether their legs be worth the sums That are given for 'em *T. of Athens* i 2 238
Methinks, false hearts should never have sound legs . . . i 2 240
We petty men Walk under his huge legs and peep about . *J. Cæsar* i 2 137
He took up my legs sometime, yet I made a shift to cast him *Macbeth* ii 3 45
Adder's fork and blind-worm's sting, Lizard's leg and howlet's wing . iv 1 17
That's a fair thought to lie between maids' legs.—What is, my lord? *Hamlet* iii 2 126
Bring away the stocks! . . . Put in his legs . . . . *Lear* ii 2 157
Horses are tied by the heads, dogs and bears by the neck, monkeys by the loins, and men by the legs . . . . ii 4 9
When a man's over-lusty at legs, then he wears wooden nether-stocks . ii 4 10
Give me your arm: Up: so. How is't? Feel you your legs? You stand iv 6 65
Would in action glorious I had lost Those legs that brought me! *Othello* ii 3 187
Then laid his leg Over my thigh, and sigh'd, and kiss'd . . . iii 3 424
My leg is cut in two.—Marry, heaven forbid! Light, gentlemen: I'll bind it . . . . v 1 72
His legs bestrid the ocean: his rear'd arm Crested the world *A. and C.* v 2 82
Up to yond hill; Your legs are young; I'll tread these flats *Cymbeline* iii 3 11
I know the shape of's leg: this is his hand; His foot Mercurial . iv 2 309
A leg of Rome shall not return to tell What crows have peck'd them here . . . . v 3 92
'Tis the better for you that your resorters stand upon sound legs *Pericles* iv 6 27
Where a man may serve seven years for the loss of a leg, and have not money enough in the end to buy him a wooden one . . . . iv 6 182
Legacy. It was Eve's legacy, and cannot be ta'en from her *T. G. of Ver.* iii 1 343
His good receipt Shall for my legacy be sanctified . . *All's Well* i 3 251
No legacy is so rich as honesty . . . . iii 5 13
Bequeathing it as a rich legacy Unto their issue . . *J. Cæsar* iii 2 141
Fetch the will hither, and we shall determine How to cut off some charge in legacies . . . . iv 1 9
Legate. Here comes the holy legate of the pope . . . *K. John* iii 1 135
I Pandulph, of fair Milan cardinal, And from Pope Innocent the legate iii 1 139
The legate of the pope hath been with me, And I have made a happy peace . . . . v 1 62
The holy legate comes apace, To give us warrant from the hand of heaven v 2 65
Not trusting to this halting legate here . . . . . v 2 174
Stay, my lord legate: you shall first receive The sum of money 1 *Hen. VI.* v 1 51
Without the king's assent or knowledge, You wrought to be a legate; by which power You maim'd the jurisdiction of all bishops *Hen. VIII.* iii 2 311
Legatine. All those things you have done of late, By your power legatine iii 2 339
Lege. Let me here a staff, a stanze, a verse; lege, domine . *L. L. Lost* iv 2 108
'Lege. 'Tis no matter, sir, what he 'leges in Latin . . *T. of Shrew* i 2 28
Legerity. Newly move, With casted slough and fresh legerity *Hen. V.* iv 1 23
Legged like a man! and his fins like arms! . . . *Tempest* ii 2 35
Legion. But one fiend at a time, I'll fight their legions o'er . . iii 3 103
He hath a legion of angels.—As many devils entertain . *Mer. Wives* i 3 59
If all the devils of hell be drawn in little, and Legion himself possessed him, yet I'll speak to him . . . . *T. Night* iii 4 95
The adverse winds . . . have given him time To land his legions *K. John* ii 1 59
With many legions of strange fantasies . . . . . . v 7 18
He might return to vasty Tartar back, And tell the legions 'I can never win A soul so easy as that Englishman's' . . . . *Hen. V.* ii 2 124
To beat assailing death from his weak legions . . . 1 *Hen. VI.* iv 4 16
Methoughts, a legion of foul fiends Environ'd me about . *Richard III.* i 4 58
I did send To you for gold to pay my legions, Which you denied *J. Cæsar* iv 3 76
We have tried the utmost of our friends, Our legions are brim-full . iv 3 215
Ride, and give these bills Unto the legions on the other side . . v 2 2
For Octavius Is overthrown by noble Brutus' power, As Cassius' legions are by Antony . . . . v 3 53
Not in the legions Of horrid hell can come a devil more damn'd *Macbeth* iv 3 55
Canidius, Our nineteen legions thou shalt hold by land . *Ant. and Cleo.* iii 7 59
You keep by land The legions and the horse whole, do you not? . . iii 7 72
To Cæsar will I render My legions and my horse . . . . iii 10 34
His coin, ships, legions, May be a coward's . . . . . iii 13 22
You shall hear The legions now in Gallia sooner landed In our not-fearing Britain than have tidings Of any penny tribute paid *Cymb.* ii 4 18
The legions now in Gallia are Full weak to undertake our wars . iii 7 4
Those legions Which I have spoke of, whereunto your levy Must be supplyant . . . . iii 7 12
The legions garrison'd in Gallia, After your will, have cross'd the sea . iv 2 333
The Roman legions, all from Gallia drawn, Are landed on your coast . iv 3 24
Legitimate. I will prove it legitimate, sir, upon the oaths of judgement and reason . . . . *T. Night* iii 2 15
Sirrah, your brother is legitimate . . . . . . *K. John* i 1 116

Legitimate. Wherein he might the king his lord advertise Whether our daughter were legitimate, Respecting this our marriage . *Hen. VIII.* ii 4 179
Legitimate Edgar, I must have your land: Our father's love is to the bastard Edmund As to the legitimate . . . . . . *Lear* i 2 16
Fine word,—legitimate! Well, my legitimate, if this letter speed, And my invention thrive, Edmund the base Shall top the legitimate . i 2 18
Legitimation, name and all is gone . . . . . . *K. John* i 1 248
Leicester. This foul swine Lies now even in the centre of this isle, Near to the town of Leicester . . . . . . *Richard III.* v 2 12
Is young George Stanley living?—He is, my lord, and safe in Leicester town . . . . v 5 10
At last, with easy roads, he came to Leicester, Lodged in the abbey *Hen. VIII.* iv 2 17
Leicestershire. Thou, brother Montague, in Buckingham, Northampton and in Leicestershire, shalt find Men . . . . *3 Hen. VI.* iv 8 15
Leiger. *See* **Lieger**
Leisure. At pick'd leisure Which shall be shortly . . . *Tempest* v 1 247
Come to me at your convenient leisure . . . *Mer. Wives* iii 5 137
Moe reasons for this action At our more leisure shall I render *M. for M.* i 3 49
Might you dispense with your leisure, I would by and by have some speech . . . . iii 1 154
I have no superfluous leisure; my stay must be stolen out of other affairs . . . . iii 1 158
Which I by my good leisure have discredited to him . . . iii 2 261
I shall attend your leisure: but make haste . . . . iv 1 57
Haste still pays haste, and leisure answers leisure; Like doth quit like v 1 415
I will debate this matter at more leisure . . . *Com. of Errors* iv 1 100
What I told you then, I hope I shall have leisure to make good . v 1 375
Eat when I have stomach and wait for no man's leisure . . *Much Ado* i 3 17
If your leisure served, I would speak with you . . . . iii 2 84
We'll make our leisures to attend on yours . . . *Mer. of Venice* i 1 68
I am sorry that your leisure serves you not . . . . iv 1 405
Here is a letter; read it at your leisure . . . . . v 1 267
At least Have leave and leisure to make love to her. . . *T. of Shrew* i 2 136
When in music we have spent an hour, Your lecture shall have leisure. iii 1 8
Who woo'd in haste and means to wed at leisure . . . iii 2 11
Which, at more leisure, I will so excuse As you shall well be satisfied . iii 2 110
What hast thou to do? Father, be quiet: he shall stay my leisure . iii 2 219
The tailor stays thy leisure, To deck thy body with his ruffling treasure iv 3 59
When thou hast leisure, say thy prayers . . . . *All's Well* i 1 227
Nature and sickness Debate it at their leisure . . . . . i 2 75
I thank you, and will stay upon your leisure . . . . iii 5 48
All the progress, more and less, Resolvedly more leisure shall express . v 3 332
The adverse winds, Whose leisure I have stay'd, have given him time To land his legions . . . . *K. John* ii 1 58
That you might The better arm you to the sudden time, Than if you had at leisure known of this . . . . v 6 27
Which then our leisure would not let us hear . . . *Richard II.* i 1 5
Ere further leisure yield them further means . . . . . i 4 40
We will stay your leisure.—I have done, i' faith . . . *1 Hen. IV.* i 3 258
How has he the leisure to be sick In such a justling time? . . iv 1 17
Here at more leisure may your highness read . . *2 Hen. IV.* iv 4 89
No leisure had he to enrank his men . . . . *1 Hen. VI.* i 1 115
Since your ladyship is not at leisure, I'll sort some other time to visit you . . . . ii 3 26
I will attend upon your lordship's leisure . . . . . v 1 55
Are you not at leisure? . . . . v 3 97
Let me have Some patient leisure to excuse myself . . *Richard III.* i 2 82
Had you such leisure in the time of death To gaze upon the secrets of the deep?—Methought I had . . . . i 4 34
Men shall deal unadvisedly sometimes, Which after hours give leisure to repent . . . . iv 4 293
The leisure and the fearful time Cuts off the ceremonious vows of love . v 3 97
God give us leisure for these rites of love! . . . . . v 3 101
More than I have said, loving countrymen, The leisure and enforcement of the time Forbids to dwell upon . . . . v 3 238
You have scarce time To steal from spiritual leisure a brief span To keep your earthly audit . . . . . . *Hen. VIII.* iii 2 140
I scarce have leisure to salute you, My matter is so rash *Troi. and Cres.* iv 2 61
As Hector's leisure and your bounties shall Concur together . . iv 5 273
I'll trust, by leisure, him that mocks me once. . . *T. Andron.* i 1 301
Are you at leisure, holy father, now? . . . *Rom. and Jul.* iv 1 37
My leisure serves me, pensive daughter, now . . . . . iv 1 39
You would not hear me, At many leisures I proposed . . *T. of Athens* ii 2 137
O'er-read, At your best leisure, this his humble suit . . *J. Cæsar* iii 1 5
Worthy Macbeth, we stay upon your leisure.—Give me your favour *Macb.* i 3 148
If you would grant the time.—At your kind'st leisure . . . ii 1 24
Say to the king, I would attend his leisure For a few words . . iii 2 3
This is for all: I would not, in plain terms, from this time forth, Have you so slander any moment leisure . . . . . *Hamlet* i 3 133
No leisure bated, No, not to stay the grinding of the axe . . v 2 23
Here's the commission: read it at more leisure . . . . v 2 26
If your lordship were at leisure, I should impart a thing to you . v 2 91
Commanded me to follow, and attend The leisure of their answer . *Lear* ii 4 37
Mend when thou canst; be better at thy leisure: I can be patient . ii 4 232
At thy sovereign leisure read The garboils she awaked . *Ant. and Cleo.* i 3 60
Leisurely. Lead us from hence, where we may leisurely Each one demand and answer to his part. . . . . *W. Tale* v 3 152
He was the wretched'st thing when he was young, So long a-growing and so leisurely . . . . *Richard III.* ii 4 19
Leman. That searched a hollow walnut for his wife's leman *Mer. Wives* iv 2 172
I sent thee sixpence for thy leman: hadst it? . . . *T. Night* ii 3 26
And drink unto the leman mine . . . . . *2 Hen. IV.* v 3 49
Lemon. A gilt nutmeg.—A lemon.—Stuck with cloves . *L. L. Lost* v 2 653
Lena. What said Popilius Lena!—He wish'd to-day our enterprise might thrive. I fear our purpose is discovered . . . *J. Cæsar* iii 1 15
Cassius, be constant: Popilius Lena speaks not of our purposes . iii 1 23
Lend thy hand, And pluck my magic garment from me . . *Tempest* i 2 23
Lend me the letter; let me see what news . . . *T. G. of Ver.* i 3 55
Love, lend me wings to make my purpose swift! . . . . ii 6 42
Heaven such grace did lend her, That she might admired be . . iv 2 42
Love, lend me patience to forbear awhile . . . . . v 4 27
Book of Riddles! why, did you not lend it to Alice Shortcake? *M. Wives* i 1 210
I will not lend thee a penny . . . . ii 2 1
What is he, William, that does lend articles?—Articles are borrowed of the pronoun . . . . iv 1 40
Nature never lends The smallest scruple of her excellence *Meas. for Meas.* i 1 37
Lend him your kind pains To find out this abuse, whence 'tis derived . v 1 246
Lend me your knees, and all my life to come I'll lend you all my life . v 1 436
O Isabel, will you not lend a knee?—He dies for Claudio's death . v 1 447
Lend. Men grow hard-hearted and will lend nothing for God's sake *Much Ado* v 1 321
Lend me the flourish of all gentle tongues . . . . *L. L. Lost* iv 3 238
Go, whip thy gig.—Lend me your horn to make one . . . . v 1 71
He lends out money gratis and brings down The rate of usance *M. of Ven.* i 3 45
Although I neither lend nor borrow By taking nor by giving of excess . i 3 62
Methought you said you neither lend nor borrow Upon advantage . i 3 70
Is it possible A cur can lend three thousand ducats? . . . . i 3 123
You call'd me dog; and for these courtesies I'll lend you thus much moneys . . . . i 3 130
If thou wilt lend this money, lend it not As to thy friends; . . . But lend it rather to thine enemy, Who, if he break, thou mayst with better face Exact the penalty . . . . i 3 133
He was wont to lend money for a Christian courtesy . . . . iii 1 51
I once did lend my body for his wealth . . . . . . v 1 249
Lend thine ear.—Here.—There.—This is to feel a tale . *T. of Shrew* iv 1 62
As far as Rome; And so to Tripoli, if God lend me life . . . iv 2 76
You are loved, sir; They that least lend it you shall lack you first *All's W.* i 2 68
Lend me an arm; the rest have worn me out With several applications i 2 73
Give me that ring.—I'll lend it thee, my dear . . . . . iv 2 40
Contempt his scornful perspective did lend me . . . . . v 3 48
Good Tom Drum, lend me a handkercher . . . . . . v 3 322
Your gentle hands lend us, and take our hearts . . . . . Epil. 340
Out of my lean and low ability I'll lend you something . *T. Night* iii 4 379
Lend me thy hand, I'll help thee: come, lend me thy hand . *W. Tale* iv 3 71
And pluck nights from me, but not lend a morrow . . *Richard II.* i 3 228
Let's fight with gentle words Till time lend friends . . . iii 3 132
You start away And lend no ear unto my purposes . . . *1 Hen. IV.* i 3 217
I prithee, lend me thy lantern, to see my gelding in the stable . . ii 1 38
Lend me thy hand to laugh a little . . . . ii 4 2
It lends a lustre and more great opinion, A larger dare . . . iv 1 77
What, stand'st thou idle here? lend me thy sword . . . . v 3 41
O, this boy Lends mettle to us all! . . . . v 4 24
So did our men, heavy in Hotspur's loss, Lend to this weight such lightness with their fear . . . . *2 Hen. IV.* i 1 122
He that will caper with me for a thousand marks, let him lend me the money . . . . i 2 217
Will your lordship lend me a thousand pound to furnish me forth? . i 2 250
Then lend the eye a terrible aspect . . . . . *Hen. V.* iii 1 9
Wounds will I lend the French instead of eyes . . . *1 Hen. VI.* i 1 87
Let not your private discord keep away The levied succours that should lend him aid . . . . iv 4 23
O Lord, that lends me life, Lend me a heart replete with thankfulness! *2 Hen. VI.* i 1 20
If thy revengeful heart cannot forgive, Lo, here I lend thee this sharp-pointed sword . . . . *Richard III.* i 2 175
Lend favourable ears to our request . . . . iii 7 101
Rise, and lend thine ear . . . . iv 2 80
I died for hope ere I could lend thee aid . . . . . . v 3 173
Ever may your highness yoke together, As I will lend you cause, my doing well With my well saying! . . . . . *Hen. VIII.* iii 2 151
Lend me ten thousand eyes, And I will fill them with prophetic tears *Troi. and Cres.* ii 2 101
I'll nor sell nor give him: lend you him I will . . . *Coriolanus* i 4 6
Suits, Nor from the state nor private friends, hereafter Will I lend ear to v 3 19
Lend me thy hand, and I will give thee mine . . . *T. Andron.* iii 1 188
Read o'er the volume of young Paris' face . . .; Examine every married lineament And see how one another lends content . *Rom. and Jul.* i 3 84
But passion lends them power, time means, to meet . . . ii Prol. 13
Then music with her silver sound With speedy help doth lend redress . iv 5 146
What torch is yond, that vainly lends his light To grubs? . . . v 3 125
This is no time to lend money, especially upon bare friendship *T. Athens* iii 1 44
Lend to each man enough, that one need not lend to another . . iii 6 82
Stay, I will lend thee money, borrow none . . . . . iii 6 111
Lend me a fool's heart and a woman's eyes, And I'll beweep these comforts . . . . v 1 160
Friends, Romans, countrymen, lend me your ears . . . *J. Cæsar* iii 2 78
When the blood burns, how prodigal the soul Lends the tongue vows *Hamlet* i 3 117
Pity me not, but lend thy serious hearing To what I shall unfold . i 5 5
The parching streets, That lend a tyrannous and damned light . . ii 2 482
Refrain to-night, And that shall lend a kind of easiness To the next abstinence . . . . iii 4 166
Be you content to lend your patience to us, And we shall jointly labour with your soul To give it due content . . . . iv 5 210
Lend less than thou owest, Ride more than thou goest . . . *Lear* i 4 133
Hard by here is a hovel; Some friendship will it lend you 'gainst the tempest. . . . . iii 2 62
Lend me a looking-glass; If that her breath will mist or stain the stone, Why, then she lives . . . . v 3 261
To my unfolding lend your prosperous ear . . . . *Othello* i 3 245
Lend me thy handkerchief.—Here, my lord . . . . . iii 4 52
Lend me a garter. So. O, for a chair, To bear him easily hence! . v 1 82
Come, come; Lend me a light. Know we this face or no? . . . v 1 88
To lend me arms and aid when I required them; The which you both denied.—Neglected, rather . . . . . . *Ant. and Cleo.* ii 2 88
But that self hand, Which writ his honour in the acts it did, Hath, with the courage which the heart did lend it, Splitted the heart . v 1 23
I shall but lend my diamond till your return . . . *Cymbeline* i 4 154
That play with all infirmities for gold Which rottenness can lend nature! i 6 125
Who's here? If any thing that's civil, speak; if savage, Take or lend . iii 6 24
And lend my best attention . . . . v 5 117
Till Pericles be dead, My heart can lend no succour to my head *Pericles* i 1 171
Feast here awhile, Until our stars that frown lend us a smile . . i 4 108
Hush, my gentle neighbours! Lend me your hands; to the next chamber bear her. . . . . iii 2 108
She will speak to him.—Hail, sir! my lord, lend ear.—Hum, ha! . . v 1 83
Sir, lend me your arm . . . . v 1 264
Lender. I think myself in better plight for a lender than you are *M. W.* ii 2 172
Neither a borrower nor a lender be . . . . . . *Hamlet* i 3 75
Keep . . . thy hand out of plackets, thy pen from lenders' books *Lear* iii 4 100
Lending. The great'st grace lending grace. . . . . . *All's Well* ii 1 163
Mowbray hath received eight thousand nobles In name of lendings *Richard II.* i 1 89
Lending your kind commiseration . . . . . *T. Andron.* v 3 93
Off, off, you lendings! come, unbutton here . . . . . *Lear* iii 4 113
You shall not grieve Lending me this acquaintance. . . . . iv 3 56
Length. Under a cloak that is of any length . . . . *T. G. of Ver.* iii 1 130
Then let me see thy cloak: I'll get me one of such another length . iii 1 133
And how I replied,—For this was of much length . . *Meas. for Meas.* v 1 95

Length. At length the sun, gazing upon the earth, Dispersed those vapours *Com. of Errors* i 1 89
At length, another ship had seized on us . . . i 1 113
Bring you the length of Prester John's foot . . . . *Much Ado* ii 1 276
Measure his woe the length and breadth of mine . . . v 1 11
Faintness constraineth me To measure out my length on this cold bed. By day's approach look to be visited . . . . *M. N. Dream* iii 2 429
But at the length truth will out . . . *Mer. of Venice* ii 2 85
'Tis to peize the time, To eke it and to draw it out in length . . iii 2 23
Time's pace is so hard that it seems the length of seven year *As Y. Like It* iii 2 334
I have to-night dispatched sixteen businesses, a month's length a-piece *All's Well* iv 3 99
Large lengths of seas and shores Between my father and my mother lay *K. John* i 1 105
The time hath been, Would you have been so brief with him, he would Have been so brief with you, to shorten you, For taking so the head, your whole head's length . . . . *Richard II.* iii 3 13
Is not my arm of length? . . . . iv 1 11
Come, come, in wooing sorrow let's be brief, Since, wedding it, there is such length in grief . . . . v 1 94
With much ado at length have gotten leave . . . . . v 5 74
So came I a widow; And never shall have length of life enough To rain upon remembrance with mine eyes . . *2 Hen. IV.* ii 3 58
Of all my lands Is nothing left me but my body's length *3 Hen. VI.* v 2 26
My foreward shall be drawn out all in length . . *Richard III.* v 3 293
My high-blown pride At length broke under me . . *Hen. VIII.* iii 2 362
At length her grace rose, and with modest paces Came to the altar . iv 1 82
They fell on; I made good my place: at length they came to the broom-staff to me . . . . v 4 57
To end a tale of length, Troy in our weakness stands . *Troi. and Cres.* i 3 136
Speak, good Cominius: Leave nothing out for length . *Coriolanus* ii 2 53
Till at length Your ignorance, which finds not till it feels . . iii 3 128
And at length How goes our reckoning? . . . . *T. of Athens* ii 2 158
Within my sword's length set him . . . . . *Macbeth* iv 3 234
Thrice he walk'd By their oppress'd and fear-surprised eyes, Within his truncheon's length . . . . *Hamlet* i 2 204
Then goes he to the length of all his arm . . . . . . ii 1 88
The length and breadth of a pair of indentures . . . . . v 1 118
This likes me well. These foils have all a length? . . . . v 2 276
If you will measure your lubber's length again, tarry . . . *Lear* i 4 101
Her length of sickness, with what else more serious Importeth thee to know, this bears . . . . *Ant. and Cleo.* i 2 124
All length is torture: since the torch is out, Lie down, and stray no farther . . . . iv 14 46
If I can get him within my pistol's length, I'll make him sure enough *Pericles* i 1 168
Our griefs are risen to the top, And now at length they overflow . . ii 4 24

Lengthen. Frame your mind to mirth and merriment, Which bars a thousand harms and lengthens life . . . . . *T. of Shrew* Ind. 2 138
By small and small To lengthen out the worst that must be spoken *Richard II.* iii 2 199
Put forth thy hand, reach at the glorious gold. What, is't too short? I'll lengthen it with mine . . . . *2 Hen. VI.* i 2 12
But how long fairly shall her sweet life last?—So long as heaven and nature lengthens it . . . . . . *Richard III.* iv 4 353
What sadness lengthens Romeo's hours?—Not having that, which, having, makes them short.—In love? . . . . *Rom. and Jul.* i 1 169
That man and wife Draw lots who first shall die to lengthen life *Pericles* i 4 46

Lengthened. Would the word 'farewell' have lengthen'd hours *Richard II.* i 4 16
After many lengthen'd hours of grief, Die neither mother, wife! *Rich. III.* i 3 208
My dream was lengthen'd after life . . . . i 4 43
Cowards living To die with lengthen'd shame . . . . *Cymbeline* v 3 13

Lengthening. I shall short my word By lengthening my return . . i 6 201

Lenity. A little more lenity to lechery would do no harm *Meas. for Meas.* iii 2 103
Use lenity, sweet chuck! . . . . *Hen V.* iii 2 26
For when lenity and cruelty play for a kingdom, the gentler gamester is the soonest winner . . . . iii 6 118
Gives consent, Of mere compassion and of lenity . . *1 Hen. VI.* v 4 125
This too much lenity And harmful pity must be laid aside *3 Hen. VI.* ii 2 9
And what makes robbers bold but too much lenity? . . . . ii 6 22
Awake Your dangerous lenity . . . . . . *Coriolanus* iii 1 99
Away to heaven, respective lenity, And fire-eyed fury be my conduct now! . . . . *Rom. and Jul.* iii 1 128

Lent. Love, lend me wings to make my purpose swift, As thou hast lent me wit to plot this drift! . . . . . *T. G. of Ver.* ii 6 43
Elected him our absence to supply, Lent him our terror *Meas. for Meas.* i 1 20
I am made to understand that you have lent him visitation . . . iii 2 255
Come, lady, come; you have lost the heart of Signior Benedick.—Indeed, my lord, he lent it me awhile . . . . . . *Much Ado* ii 1 287
Your niece regards me with an eye of favour.—That eye my daughter lent her . . . . v 4 23
Rather had depart withal And have the money by our father lent *L. L. L.* ii 1 148
This is the fool that lent out money gratis . . . *Mer. of Venice* iii 3 2
If God have lent a man any manners, he may easily put it off at court: he that cannot make a leg . . . . *All's Well* ii 2 8
Who lent it you?—It was not lent me neither . . . . . . v 3 274
Why, what a madcap hath heaven lent us here! . . . . *K. John* i 1 84
That sun that warms you here shall shine on me; And those his golden beams to you here lent Shall point on me and gild my banishment *Richard II.* i 3 146
You owe money here besides, Sir John, for your diet and by-drinkings, and money lent you, four and twenty pound . . *1 Hen. IV.* iii 3 85
Whose spirit lent a fire Even to the dullest peasant in his camp *2 Hen. IV.* i 1 112
What's a joint of mutton or two in a whole Lent? . . . . . ii 4 376
Is he a lamb? his skin is surely lent him . . . . *2 Hen. VI.* iii 1 77
Thus will I reward thee, the Lent shall be as long again as it is . iv 3 7
'Tis call'd ungrateful, With dull unwillingness to repay a debt Which with a bounteous hand was kindly lent; Much more to be thus opposite with heaven, For it requires the royal debt it lent you *Richard III.* ii 2 93
Had nature lent thee but thy mother's look, Villain, thou mightst have been an emperor . . . . *T. Andron.* v 1 29
He lent me counsel and I lent him eyes . . . *Rom. and Jul.* ii 2 81
An old hare hoar, And an old hare hoar, Is very good meat in Lent . ii 4 143
We scarce thought us blest That God had lent us but this only child . iii 5 166
Gracious England hath Lent us good Siward and ten thousand men *Macb.* iv 3 190
Cold and sickly He vented them; most narrow measure lent me *A. and C.* iii 4 8
Then does he say, he lent me Some shipping unrestored . . . . iii 6 26
Lucina lent not me her aid, But took me in my throes . . *Cymbeline* v 4 43
Blithe, and full of face, As heaven had lent her all his grace *Pericles* 1 Gower 24

Lenten. A good lenten answer . . . . *T. Night* i 5 9
No hare, sir; unless a hare, sir, in a lenten pie . *Rom. and Jul.* ii 4 139
What lenten entertainment the players shall receive from you *Hamlet* ii 2 329

Lentus. Magni Dominator poli, Tam lentus audis scelera? tam lentus vides?—O, calm thee, gentle lord . . . . . . *T. Andron* iv 1 82

L'envoy. No egma, no riddle, no l'envoy; no salve in the mail, sir *L. L. Lost* iii 1 73
No l'envoy; no salve, sir, but a plantain! . . . . iii 1 75
Doth the inconsiderate take salve for l'envoy, and the word l'envoy for a salve?—Do the wise think them other? is not l'envoy a salve? . iii 1 80
Let me see; a fat l'envoy; ay, that's a fat goose . . . . iii 1 105; 110

Leonardo. I pray thee, good Leonardo, think on this . . *Mer. of Venice* ii 2 178

Leonati. Gods, put the strength o' the Leonati in me! . . *Cymbeline* v 1 31
Thrown From Leonati seat, and cast From her his dearest one, Sweet Imogen . . . . v 4 60

Leonato. Good Signior Leonato, you are come to meet your trouble *Much Ado* i 1 96
If Signior Leonato be her father, she would not have his head on her shoulders . . . . i 1 114
My dear friend Leonato hath invited you all . . . . . . i 1 149
Didst thou note the daughter of Signior Leonato?—I noted her not . i 1 164
What secret hath held you here, that you followed not to Leonato's? . i 1 207
Mark how short his answer is;—With Hero, Leonato's short daughter . i 1 216
Hath Leonato any son, my lord?—No child but Hero . . . . i 1 296
Your brother is royally entertained by Leonato . . . . . i 3 46
To vex Claudio, to undo Hero and kill Leonato . . . . . ii 2 29
Even she; Leonato's Hero, your Hero, every man's Hero . . . iii 2 109
One word more, honest neighbours. I pray you, watch about Signior Leonato's door . . . . iii 3 98
There, Leonato, take her back again: Give not this rotten orange to your friend . . . . iv 1 32
Leonato, stand I here? Is this the prince? is this the prince's brother? iv 1 70
Let these men be bound, and brought to Leonato's . . . . iv 2 67
Our sexton hath reformed Signior Leonato of the matter . . . v 1 262
Is this the monument of Leonato?—It is, my lord . . . . . v 3 1
Put on other weeds; And then to Leonato's we will go . . . v 3 31
Signior Leonato, . . . Your niece regards me with an eye of favour . v 4 21

Leonatus. He served with glory and admired success, So gain'd the sur-addition Leonatus . . . . *Cymbeline* i 1 33
The king he takes the babe To his protection, calls him Posthumus Leonatus . . . . i 1 41
Would I were A neat-herd's daughter, and my Leonatus Our neighbour shepherd's son!—Thou foolish thing! . . . . i 1 149
The worthy Leonatus is in safety And greets your highness dearly . i 6 12
O happy Leonatus! I may say . . . . i 6 156
There's an Italian come; and, 'tis thought, one of Leonatus' friends . ii 1 41
Leonatus! a banished rascal; and he's another, whatsoever he be . ii 1 42
Leonatus! O master! what a strange infection Is fall'n into thy ear! . iii 2 2
That remains loyal to his vow, and your, increasing in love, LEONATUS iii 2 49
What is here? The scriptures of the loyal Leonatus, All turn'd to heresy? iii 4 83
I'ld change my sex to be companion with them, Since Leonatus's false iii 6 89
By villany I got this ring: 'twas Leonatus' jewel . . . . v 5 143
I return'd with simular proof enough To make the noble Leonatus mad v 5 201
Thou, Leonatus, art the lion's whelp; The fit and apt construction of thy name, Being Leo-natus, doth import so much . . . . . v 5 443

Leonine. Dionyza does appear, With Leonine, a murderer *Pericles* iv Gower 52
Walk with Leonine; the air is quick there . . . . . . iv 1 28
Walk half an hour, Leonine, at the least: Remember what I have said iv 1 46
Alack that Leonine was so slack, so slow! He should have struck, not spoke . . . . iv 2 68
O villain Leonine! Whom thou hast poison'd too . . . . . iv 3 9
Yet none does know, but you, how she came dead, Nor none can know, Leonine being gone . . . . iv 3 30

Leontes. Yet, good deed, Leontes, I love thee not a jar o' the clock behind What lady-she her lord . . . . . . *W. Tale* i 2 42
You have mistook, my lady, Polixenes for Leontes . . . . ii 1 82
Hermione, queen to the worthy Leontes, king of Sicilia . . . . iii 2 13
Leontes a jealous tyrant; his innocent babe truly begotten . . iii 2 134
Leontes leaving, The effects of his fond jealousies so grieving . . iv 1 17
There present yourself and your fair princess . . . 'fore Leontes . iv 4 556
Methinks I see Leontes opening his free arms and weeping His welcomes iv 4 559
King Leontes shall not have an heir Till his lost child be found . v 1 39

Leopard. Lions make leopards tame.—Yea, but not change his spots *Richard II.* i 1 174
Sheep run not half so treacherous from the wolf, Or horse or oxen from the leopard, As you fly . . . . *1 Hen. VI.* i 5 31
Wert thou a horse, thou wouldst be seized by the leopard: wert thou a leopard, thou wert german to the lion and the spots of thy kindred were jurors on thy life . . . . *T. of Athens* iv 3 343

Leper. What, dost thou turn away and hide thy face? I am no loath-some leper; look on me . . . . *2 Hen. VI.* iii 2 75

Leperous. In the porches of my ears did pour The leperous distilment *Ham.* i 5 64

Lepidus. He and Lepidus are at Cæsar's house . . . *J. Cæsar* iii 2 269
Your brother too must die; consent you, Lepidus?—I do consent . iv 1 2
But, Lepidus, go you to Cæsar's house; Fetch the will hither . . iv 1 7
His corporal motion govern'd by my spirit. And, in some taste, is Lepidus but so . . . . iv 1 34
Octavius, Antony, and Lepidus, Have put to death an hundred senators iv 3 174
You may see, Lepidus, and henceforth know, It is not Cæsar's natural vice to hate Our great competitor . . . . *Ant. and Cleo.* i 4 1
Lepidus flatters both, Of both is flatter'd; but he neither loves . . ii 1 14
Cæsar and Lepidus Are in the field: a mighty strength they carry . ii 1 16
Let us, Lepidus, Not lack your company.—Noble Antony, Not sickness should detain me . . . . ii 2 171
Lepidus is high-coloured.—They have made him drink alms-drink . ii 7 4
A health to Lepidus!—I am not so well as I should be, but I'll ne'er out ii 7 33
These quick-sands, Lepidus, Keep off them, for you sink . . . ii 7 66
This health to Lepidus!—Bear him ashore. I'll pledge it for him . ii 7 90
Lepidus, Since Pompey's feast, as Menas says, is troubled With the green sickness.—'Tis a noble Lepidus.—A very fine one . . . iii 2 4
Cæsar and Lepidus have made wars upon Pompey.—This is old . . iii 5 4
Cries, 'Fool Lepidus!' And threats the throat of that his officer . iii 5 18
He frets that Lepidus of the triumvirate Should be deposed . . . iii 6 28
I have told him, Lepidus was grown too cruel . . . . . . iii 6 32

Leprosy. Itches, blains, Sow all the Athenian bosoms; and their crop Be general leprosy! . . . . *T. of Athens* iv 1 30
This yellow slave [gold] Will knit and break religions, bless the accursed, Make the hoar leprosy adored . . . . iv 3 35
There is no leprosy but what thou speak'st.—If I name thee . . iv 3 367
Yon ribaudred nag of Egypt,—Whom leprosy o'ertake! *Ant. and Cleo.* iii 10 11

Less. Teach me how To name the bigger light, and how the less *Tempest* i 2 335

That dare not offer What I desire to give, and much less take What I shall die to want iii 1 78

Less than a pound shall serve me for carrying your letter *T. G. of Ver.* i 1 111

Much less shall she that hath Love's wings to fly ii 7 11

For the greater hides the less iii 1 372

But one fair look; A smaller boon than this I cannot beg And less than this, I am sure, you cannot give v 4 25

Hail, virgin, if you be, as those cheek-roses Proclaim you are no less! Can you so stead me? *Meas. for Meas.* i 4 17

Hoping you'll find good cause to whip them all.—I think no less ii 1 143

Great men may jest with saints; 'tis wit in them, But in the less foul profanation.—Thou 'rt i' the right ii 2 128

More nor less to others paying Than by self-offences weighing iii 2 279

If he be less, he's nothing; but he's more, Had I more name for badness v 1 58

Who is as free from touch or soil with her As she from one ungot.—We did believe no less v 1 142

Less in your knowledge and your grace you show not Than our earth's wonder, more than earth divine *Com. of Errors* iii 2 31

Is not your husband mad?—His incivility confirms no less iv 4 49

He is no less than a stuffed man: but for the stuffing *Much Ado* i 1 58

He that hath a beard is more than a youth, and he that hath no beard is less than a man: and he that is more than a youth is not for me, and he that is less than a man, I am not for him ii 1 39

The less you meddle or make with them, why, the more is for your honesty iii 3 55

The letter is too long by half a mile.—I think no less *L. L. Lost* v 2 55

O, I am yours, and all that I possess!—All the fool mine?—I cannot give you less v 2 384

Less than an ace, man; for he is dead; he is nothing *M. N. Dream* v 1 314

Scant this excess. I feel too much thy blessing: make it less *M. of V.* iii 2 114

If she be less than an honest woman, she is indeed more than I took her for iii 5 45

Nor cut thou less nor more But just a pound of flesh: if thou cut'st more Or less than a just pound, . . Thou diest iv 1 325

So doth the greater glory dim the less v 1 93

My friends told me as much, and I thought no less *As Y. Like It* iv 1 188

He is no less than what we say he is *T. of Shrew* Ind. 1 71

Let it not displease thee, good Bianca, For I will love thee ne'er the less i 1 77

'Tis known my father hath no less Than three great argosies ii 1 379

I cannot give thee less, to be call'd grateful *All's Well* ii 1 132

All the progress, more and less, Resolvedly more leisure shall express v 3 331

What great ones do the less will prattle of *T. Night* i 2 33

Thou know'st no less but all i 4 13

His employment between his lord and my niece confirms no less iii 4 206

I must have done no less with wit and safety v 1 218

You never spoke what did become you less Than this *W. Tale* i 2 282

Which no less adorns Our gentry than our parents' noble names i 2 392

His great authority; Which often hath no less prevail'd than so ii 1 54

Your most obedient counsellor, yet that dare Less appear so ii 3 56

In whose easiest passage Look for no less than death iii 2 92

To greet a man not worth her pains, much less The adventure of her person v 1 155

'Tis nothing but conceit, my gracious lady.—'Tis nothing less *Rich. II.* ii 2 34

And hope to joy is little less in joy Than hope enjoy'd ii 3 15

If they speak more or less than truth, they are villains *1 Hen. IV.* ii 4 190

The more and less came in with cap and knee iv 3 68

They shall be well opposed.—I hope no less, yet needful 'tis to fear iv 4 34

If I do grow great, I'll grow less; for I'll purge, and leave sack v 4 168

And more and less do flock to follow him *2 Hen. IV.* i 1 209

He that buckles him in my belt cannot live in less i 2 158

Make less thy body hence, and more thy grace v 5 56

To do your grace incessant services.—We judge no less *Hen. V.* ii 2 39

This knight, no less for bounty bound to us Than Cambridge is ii 2 92

I find thou art no less than fame hath bruited *1 Hen. VI.* ii 3 68

Methinks, my father's execution Was nothing less than bloody tyranny ii 5 100

Much less to take occasion from their mouths To raise a mutiny iv 1 130

To speak truth, thou deservest no less *2 Hen. VI.* iv 3 12

To weep is to make less the depth of grief *3 Hen. VI.* ii 1 85

What art thou . . . ?—More than I seem, and less than I was born to: A man at least, for less I should not be iii 1 56

It were dishonour to deny it her.—It were no less iii 2 10

I blame not her, she could say little less; She had the wrong iv 1 101

I know you for no less iv 7 22

Edward is at hand, Ready to fight; therefore be resolute.—I thought no less v 4 62

Thy mother felt more than a mother's pain, And yet brought forth less than a mother's hope v 6 50

There's never a man in Christendom That can less hide his love or hate *Richard III.* iii 4 54

Matters of great moment, No less importing than our general good iii 7 68

A grandam's name is little less in love Than is the doting title of a mother iv 4 299

They could do no less, Out of the great respect they bear to beauty *Hen. VIII.* i 4 68

Limbs are his instruments, In no less working than are swords and bows Directive by the limbs *Troi. and Cres.* i 3 355

Take not that little little less than little wit from them that they have! ii 3 14

Vowing more than the perfection of ten and discharging less than the tenth part of one iii 2 94

What they do in present, Though less than yours in past, must o'ertop yours iii 3 164

Both merits poised, each weighs nor less nor more iv 1 65

I thank thee, most imperious Agamemnon.—My well-famed lord of Troy, no less to you iv 5 173

Nor a man that fears you less than he, That's lesser than a little *Coriol.* i 4 14

'Twere a concealment Worse than a theft, no less than a traducement i 9 22

He covets less Than misery itself would give ii 2 130

For your voices have Done many things, some less, some more ii 3 137

As his worthy deeds did claim no less Than what he stood for ii 3 194

You are plebeians, If they be senators: and they are no less iii 1 102

You might have been enough the man you are, With striving less to be so iii 2 20

How is it less or worse, That it shall hold companionship in peace With honour, as in war? iii 2 48

It [peace] makes men hate one another.—Reason; because they then less need one another iv 5 247

Very well: Could he say less? v 1 22

Were you in my stead, would you have heard A mother less? or granted less? v 3 193

Less. I say no more, Nor wish no less; and so, I take my leave *T. Andron.* i 1 402

More or less, or ne'er a whit at all iv 2 53

So shall you share all that he doth possess, By having him, making yourself no less.—No less! nay, bigger *Rom. and Jul.* i 3 94

She as much in love, her means much less To meet her new-beloved any where ii Prol. 11

Is it good den?—'Tis no less, I tell you ii 4 118

Thou wilt quarrel with a man that hath a hair more, or a hair less iii 1 19

What less than dooms-day is the prince's doom? iii 3 9

Many a time and often I ha' dined with him, and told him on't, and come again to supper to him, of purpose to have him spend less *T. of Athens* iii 1 27

Has friendship such a faint and milky heart, It turns in less than two nights? iii 1 58

My very good friend, and an honourable gentleman.—We know him for no less iii 2 3

He cannot want fifty-five hundred talents.—But in the mean time he wants less iii 2 44

Steal no less for this I give you; and gold confound you howsoe'er! iv 3 451

If Cæsar had stabb'd their mothers, they would have done no less *J. C.* i 2 278

I say, that Brutus' love to Cæsar was no less than his iii 2 20

Not that I loved Cæsar less, but that I loved Rome more iii 2 23

This is not Brutus, friend; but, I assure you, A prize no less in worth v 4 27

Do you not hope your children shall be kings, When those that gave the thane of Cawdor to me Promised no less to them? *Macbeth* i 3 120

Present fears Are less than horrible imaginings i 3 138

Would thou hadst less deserved, That the proportion both of thanks and payment Might have been mine! i 4 18

That hast no less deserved, nor must be known No less to have done so i 4 30

And delight No less in truth than life iv 3 130

Both more and less have given him the revolt v 4 12

A little more than kin, and less than kind *Hamlet* i 2 65

The less they deserve, the more merit is in your bounty ii 2 557

For youth no less becomes The light and careless livery that it wears Than settled age his sables and his weeds iv 7 79

Without debatement further, more or less v 2 45

So tell him, with the occurrents, more and less, Which have solicited v 2 368

No less than life, with grace, health, beauty, honour *Lear* i 1 59

No less in space, validity, and pleasure, Than that conferr'd on Goneril i 1 83

I love your majesty According to my bond; nor more nor less i 1 95

I crave no more than what your highness offer'd, Nor will you tender less i 1 198

I do profess to be no less than I seem i 4 14

Speak less than thou knowest, Lend less than thou owest i 4 132

Learn more than thou trowest, Set less than thou throwest i 4 136

You less know how to value her desert Than she to scant her duty ii 4 141

Servants, who seem no less, Which are to France the spies iii 1 23

Though I die for it, as no less is threatened me iii 3 19

No less than all: The younger rises when the old doth fall iii 3 25

A very foolish fond old man, Fourscore and upward, not an hour more nor less iv 7 61

Thou art in nothing less Than I have here proclaim'd thee v 3 94

I am no less in blood than thou art v 3 167

If partially affined, or leagued in office, Thou dost deliver more or less than truth, Thou art no soldier *Othello* ii 3 219

'Tis the plague of great ones; Prerogatived are they less than the base iii 3 274

I should have known no less. It hath been taught us *Ant. and Cleo.* i 4 40

'Twas a shame no less Than was his loss, to course your flying flags iii 13 10

Majesty, to keep decorum, must No less beg than a kingdom v 2 18

And their story is No less in pity than his glory v 2 365

Thou shouldst have made him As little as a crow, or less *Cymbeline* i 3 15

To whom I have been often bound for no less than my life i 4 27

This yellow Iachimo, in an hour,—was't not?—Or less,—at first? ii 5 15

Famous in Cæsar's praises, no whit less Than in his feats deserving it iii 1 6

If brothers. Would it had been so, that they Had been my father's sons! then had my prize Been less iii 6 78

Great griefs, I see, medicine the less iv 2 243

Thou movest no less with thy complaining than Thy master in bleeding iv 2 375

Your preparation can affront no less Than what you hear of iv 3 29

To shame the guise o' the world, I will begin The fashion, less without and more within v 1 33

And Be villany less than 'twas! v 5 225

It pleaseth you, my royal father, to express My commendations great, whose merit's less *Pericles* ii 2 9

O lady, Much less in blood than virtue, yet a princess! iv 3 7

I can be modest.—That dignifies the renown of a bawd, no less than it gives a good report to a number to be chaste iv 6 43

Less account. And his achievements of no less account *1 Hen. VI.* ii 3 8

Less advancement. His own disorders Deserved much less advancement *Lear* ii 4 203

Less afraid. We are less afraid to be drowned than thou art *Tempest* i 1 47

Less allegiance. Pray heaven, the king may never find a heart With less allegiance in it! *Hen. VIII.* v 3 43

Less apparent. And is no less apparent To the vulgar eye *Coriolanus* iv 7 20

Less art. But let that go.—More matter, with less art *Hamlet* ii 2 95

Less attemptable than any the rarest of our ladies in France *Cymbeline* i 4 65

Less beloved. No less beloved of her uncle than his own daughter *As Y. Like It* i 1 116

No less beloved Than when thou wert protector to thy king *2 Hen. VI.* ii 3 26

Wilt take thy chance with me? I will not say Thou shalt be so well master'd, but, be sure, No less beloved *Cymbeline* iv 2 384

Less celerity. In motion of no less celerity Than that of thought *Hen. V.* iii Prol. 2

Less confidence. With no less confidence Than boys pursuing summer butterflies, Or butchers killing flies *Coriolanus* iv 6 93

Less dear. Had I a dozen sons, each in my love alike and none less dear than thine i 3 25

Less degree. Even daughter, welcome, in no less degree *As Y. Like It* v 4 154

Less easy. Which is for me less easy to commit Than you to punish *W. T.* i 2 58

Less esteemed. And a knave; which notwithstanding, thou shalt be no less esteemed *T. of Athens* ii 2 112

Less expect. And be't of less expect That matter needless, of importless burden, Divide thy lips *Troi. and Cres.* i 3 70

Less expected. I minded him how royal 'twas to pardon When it was less expected *Coriolanus* v 1 19

Less fear. Put thyself Into a haviour of less fear *Cymbeline* iii 4 9

Less fearful. You that will be less fearful than discreet *Coriolanus* iii 1 150

Less fine. Other, less fine in carat, is more precious *2 Hen. IV.* iv 5 162

Less flowing. Does purpose honour to you no less flowing Than Marchioness of Pembroke *Hen. VIII.* ii 3 62

Less frequent to his princely exercises than formerly . . . *W. Tale* iv 2 36
Less furnished. You speak of him when he was less furnished than now he is . . . . *Cymbeline* i 4 8
Less gracious. 'Tis not the difference of a year or two Makes me less gracious or thee more fortunate . . . . . *T. Andron.* ii 1 32
Less happier. Against the envy of less happier lands . *Richard II.* ii 1 49
Less happy. And not less happy, having such a son . 2 *Hen. IV.* v 2 110
Wherein thou art less happy being fear'd Than they in fearing *Hen. V.* iv 1 265
Less honest. And no less honest Than you are mad . *W. Tale* ii 3 70
Less honour. We have made peace With no less honour to the Antiates Than shame to the Romans . . . . . *Coriolanus* v 6 80
Less impudence. I ne'er heard yet That any of these bolder vices wanted Less impudence to gainsay what they did Than to perform it first *W. Tale* iii 2 57
Less likelihood. Which shall bear no less likelihood than to see me at her chamber-window . . . . *Much Ado* ii 2 42
Less love. I owe him little duty, and less love . 1 *Hen. VI.* iv 4 34
Less loving. And you, our no less loving son of Albany . *Lear* i 1 43
Less material. Whose absence is no less material to me . *Macbeth* iii 1 136
Less matter. I could have given less matter A better ear *Ant. and Cleo.* ii 1 31
Less nobility. With no less nobility of love Than that which dearest father bears his son . . . . . . *Hamlet* i 2 110
Less noble. God grant that some, less noble and less loyal, Nearer in bloody thoughts, but not in blood, Deserve not worse ! *Richard III.* ii 1 91
You are as strong, as valiant, as wise, no less noble . *Troi. and Cres.* ii 3 159
Less noble mind Than she which by her death our Cæsar tells 'I am conqueror of myself' . . . . . *Ant. and Cleo.* iv 14 60
Less noise. He changes much.—Less noise, less noise ! . 2 *Hen. IV.* iv 5 7
Less place. So dear in heart, not to deny her that A woman of less place might ask by law . . . . . . *Hen. VIII.* ii 2 112
Less power. Gnarling sorrow hath less power to bite The man that mocks at it and sets it light . . . . . *Richard II.* i 3 292
Less presence. Now he goes, With no less presence, but with much more love . . . . . . *Mer. of Venice* iii 2 54
Less proud. I am less proud to hear you tell my worth Than you *L. L. L.* ii 1 17
Less quality. For taking a beggar without less quality . *Cymbeline* i 4 23
Less reason. My cause is hearted ; thine hath no less reason . *Othello* i 3 374
Less religion. Keep your promise.—With no less religion than if thou wert indeed my Rosalind . . . . *As Y. Like It* iv 1 201
Less remorse. And never did the Cyclops' hammers fall On Mars's armour forged for proof eterne With less remorse . . *Hamlet* ii 2 513
Less respect. Shall we serve heaven With less respect than we do minister To our gross selves? . . . *Meas. for Meas.* ii 2 86
Less sovereignty. And for ourself To show less sovereignty than they, must needs Appear unkinglike . . . . . *Cymbeline* iii 5 6
Less spirit. Though far more cause, yet much less spirit to curse Abides in me . . . . *Richard III.* iv 4 196
Less spoil. We look'd For no less spoil than glory . . *Coriolanus* v 6 44
Less terror. Should meet With no less terror than the elements Of fire and water . . . . *Richard II.* iii 3 55
Less unhappy. Kings are no less unhappy, their issue not being gracious, than they are in losing them . . . . *W. Tale* iv 2 29
Less valiant than the virgin in the night . . . *Troi. and Cres.* i 1 11
Less value. Of much less value is my company Than your good words. But who comes here? . . . . . . *Richard II.* ii 3 19
Less weight. The plea of no less weight . . . . *L. L. Lost* ii 1 7
Less welcome. Pray, draw near.—The night to the owl and morn to the lark less welcome . . . . . . *Cymbeline* iii 6 94
Less wit. Fools had ne'er less wit in a year . . . . *Lear* i 4 181
Less worth. [Virginity] the longer kept, the less worth . *All's Well* i 1 167
Less young. No less young, more strong . . . *Cymbeline* iv 1 11
Lessen. I shall lessen God's sending that way . . . *Much Ado* ii 1 24
And Buckingham Shall lessen this big look . . . *Hen. VIII.* i 1 119
Which not granted, He lessens his requests . . *Ant. and Cleo.* iii 12 13
Consider, When you above perceive me like a crow, That it is place which lessens and sets off . . . . . *Cymbeline* iii 3 13
Lessened. My people are with sickness much enfeebled, My numbers lessened . . . . *Hen. V.* iii 6 155
And lessen'd be that small, God, I beseech thee ! . *Richard III.* i 3 111
One pain is lessen'd by another's anguish . . *Rom. and Jul.* i 2 47
The Roman eagle, From south to west on wing soaring aloft, Lessen'd herself, and in the beams o' the sun So vanish'd . . *Cymbeline* v 5 472
Lesser. I'll pull thee by the lesser legs . . . *Tempest* ii 2 108
It is the lesser blot, modesty finds, Women to change their shapes than men their minds.—Than men their minds ! . *T. G. of Ver.* v 4 108
Burdened With lesser weight but not with lesser woe *Com. of Errors* i 1 109
The more my prayer, the lesser is my grace . . *M. N. Dream* ii 2 89
Alack, for lesser knowledge ! how accursed In being so blest ! *W. Tale* ii 1 38
My traffic is sheets ; when the kite builds, look to lesser linen . iv 3 24
And more, more strong, then lesser is my fear, I shall indue you with *K. John* iv 2 42
Thy death-bed is no lesser than thy land . . . . *Richard II.* ii 1 95
The waste is no whit lesser than thy land . . . . . ii 1 103
O that I were as great As is my grief, or lesser than my name ! . iii 3 137
Set limb to limb, and thou art far the lesser . . 2 *Hen. VI.* iv 10 50
You may chance to burn your lips.—Patience herself, what goddess e'er she be, Doth lesser blench at sufferance than I do . *Troi. and Cres.* i 1 28
No man lesser fears the Greeks than I As far as toucheth my particular ii 2 8
Nor a man that fears you less than he, That's lesser than a little *Coriol.* i 4 15
If any fear Lesser his person than an ill report . . . . i 6 70
Lesser had been The thwartings of your dispositions . . . iii 2 20
I have watch'd ere now All night for lesser cause . *Rom. and Jul.* iv 3 10
The greater scorns the lesser . . . . . *T. of Athens* iv 3 6
Lesser than Macbeth, and greater.—Not so happy, yet much happier *Macbeth* i 3 65
Some say he's mad ; others that lesser hate him Do call it valiant fury v 2 13
A massy wheel, Fix'd on the summit of the highest mount, To whose huge spokes ten thousand lesser things Are mortised . *Hamlet* iii 3 19
Where the greater malady is fix'd, The lesser is scarce felt . *Lear* iii 4 9
I know not, Menas, How lesser enmities may give way to greater *A. and C.* ii 1 43
No lesser of her honour confident Than I did truly find her *Cymbeline* v 5 187
I am Posthumus, That kill'd thy daughter :—villain-like, I lie—That caused a lesser villain than myself, A sacrilegious thief, to do't . v 5 219
Like lesser lights, Did vail their crowns to his supremacy . *Pericles* ii 3 41
Lesson. To lesson me and tell me some good mean . *T. G. of Ver.* ii 7 5
See how apt it is to learn Any hard lesson that may do thee good *M. Ado* i 1 295
I'll not be tied to hours nor 'pointed times, But learn my lessons as I please myself . . . . *T. of Shrew* iii 1 20
My lessons make no music in three parts . . . . . iii 1 60
And learn this lesson, draw thy sword in right . . 3 *Hen. VI.* ii 2 62

Lesson. The angry northern wind Will blow these sands, like Sibyl's leaves, abroad, And where's your lesson, then? . . *T. Andron.* iv 1 106
I shall the effect of this good lesson keep, As watchman to my heart *Hamlet* i 3 45
Lessoned. He will weep.—Ay, millstones ; as he lesson'd us to weep *Richard III.* i 4 246
Could you not have told him As you were lesson'd? . . *Coriolanus* ii 3 185
Well hast thou lesson'd us ; this shall we do . . *T. Andron.* v 2 110
Lest too light winning Make the prize light . . . *Tempest* i 2 451
These sweet thoughts do even refresh my labours, Most busy lest, when I do it . . . . iii 1 15
I thought to have told thee of it, but I fear'd Lest I might anger thee . iv 1 169
Lest he should take exceptions to my love . . *T. G. of Ver.* i 3 81
Lest the base earth Should from her vesture chance to steal a kiss ii 4 159
Qualify the fire's extreme rage, Lest it should burn above the bounds of reason . . . . ii 7 23
Fearing lest my jealous aim might err . . . . . iii 1 28
As you unwind her love from him, Lest it should ravel and be good to none, You must provide to bottom it on me . . . . . iii 2 52
Lest, growing ruinous, the building fall And leave no memory . v 4 9
I quaked for fear, lest the lunatic knave would have searched it *M. Wives* iii 5 105
Lest the devil that guides him should aid him, I will search . . iii 5 150
Lest the oil that's in me should set hell on fire . . . v 5 39
Defend me from that Welsh fairy, lest he transform me ! . . v 5 86
Why dost thou ask again?—Lest I might be too rash . *Meas. for Meas.* ii 2 9
But lest you do repent, As that the sin hath brought you to this shame ii 3 30
I quake, Lest thou a feverous life shouldst entertain . . . iii 1 75
Lest that your goods too soon be confiscate . . *Com. of Errors* i 2 2
Your reason?—Lest it make you choleric . . . . . . ii 2 63
And let none enter, lest I break your pate . . . . . ii 2 220
Let him walk from whence he came, lest he catch cold on's feet . iii 1 37
Lest myself be guilty to self-wrong, I'll stop mine ears . . iii 2 168
Bear it with you, lest I come not time enough . . . . iv 1 41
Lest my liking might too sudden seem, I would have salved it *Much Ado* i 1 316
Lest I should prove the mother of fools . . . . . ii 1 295
It were not good She knew his love, lest she make sport at it . iii 1 58
Lest, to thy peril, thou aby it dear . . . . *M. N. Dream* iii 2 175
For fear lest day should look their shames upon . . . . iii 2 385
Lest through thy wild behaviour I be misconstrued . *Mer. of Venice* ii 2 196
Let me say 'amen' betimes, lest the devil cross my prayer . . iii 1 22
Lest you should not understand me well . . . . . iii 2 7
Stop his wounds, lest he do bleed to death . . . . iv 1 258
Lest you be cony-catched in this business . . . *T. of Shrew* v 1 101
My dagger muzzled, Lest it should bite its master . . *W. Tale* i 2 157
Lest barbarism, making me the precedent, Should a like language use . ii 1 84
Durst not tempt a minister of honour, Lest she should be denied . ii 2 51
He scorns to say his prayers, lest a' should be thought a coward *Hen. V.* iii 2 40
Lest bleeding you do paint the white rose red . . 1 *Hen. VI.* ii 4 50
Lest it be said 'Speak, sirrah, when you should' . . . iii 1 62
It were but necessary you were waked, Lest, being suffer'd in that harmful slumber . . . . 2 *Hen. VI.* iii 2 262
Take heed, lest by your heat you burn yourselves . . . v 1 160
Urge it no more ; lest that, instead of words, I send thee, Warwick, such a messenger As shall revenge . . . . 3 *Hen. VI.* i 1 98
Lest thou be hated both of God and man ! . . . . . i 3 9
Dally not before your king ; Lest he that is the supreme King of kings Confound your hidden falsehood . . . . *Richard III.* ii 1 13
Lest, by a multitude, The new-heal'd wound of malice should break out ii 2 124
Then fly. What, from myself? Great reason why : Lest I revenge . v 3 186
Back, I say, go ; lest I let forth your half-pint of blood . . *Coriolanus* v 2 60
So Cæsar may. Then, lest he may, prevent . . . . *J. Cæsar* ii 1 28
Hence ; Lest that the infection of his fortune take Like hold on thee *Lear* iv 6 237
Doubting lest that he had err'd or sinn'd . . . . *Pericles* i 3 22
Lestrale. Fauconberg, Foix, Lestrale, Bouciqualt . *Hen. V.* iii 5 45 ; iv 8 105
Let's assist them, For our case is as theirs . . . *Tempest* i 1 57
Let's all sink with the king.—Let's take leave of him . . . i 1 67
Let me remember thee what thou hast promised . . . . i 2 243
That made gape The pine and let thee out . . . . . i 2 293
All corners else o' the earth Let liberty make use of . . . i 2 492
Let's draw our weapons.—Lead off this ground ; and let's make further search . . . . ii 1 322
Lo, how he mocks me ! wilt thou let him? . . . . . iii 2 34
Every man shift for all the rest, and let no man take care for himself . v 1 256
Let us take our leave. To Milan let me hear from thee *T. G. of Ver.* i 1 56
Let it lie for those that it concerns . . . . . . i 2 76
Let me have What thou thinkest meet and is most mannerly . . ii 7 57
What lets but one may enter at her window? . . . . . iii 1 113
Let me see thy cloak : I'll get me one of such another length . iii 1 132
Longer than I prove loyal to your grace Let me not live . . iii 2 21
Let us into the city presently To sort some gentlemen . . . iii 2 91
What he gets more of her than sharp words, let it lie on my head *Mer. Wives* ii 1 191
Let but your honour know, Whom I believe to be most strait *M. for M.* ii 1 8
There he must stay until the officer Arise to let him in . . . iv 2 94
I know his eye doth homage otherwhere ; Or else what lets it but he would be here? . . . . *Com. of Errors* ii 1 105
Let none enter, lest I break your pate . . . . . . ii 2 220
Depart in patience, And let us to the Tiger all to dinner . . iii 1 95
Not rough enough.—As roughly as my modesty would let me . . v 1 59
Let us thither : this may prove food to my displeasure . *Much Ado* i 3 67
Let us to the great supper : their cheer is the greater that I am subdued i 3 73
Let every eye negotiate for itself And trust no agent . . . ii 1 185
Let wonder seem familiar, And to the chapel let us presently . . v 4 70
Is the fool sick?—Sick at the heart.—Alack, let it blood *L. L. Lost* ii 1 186
You will be my purgation and let me loose . . . . . iii 1 128
A fever in your blood ! why, then incision Would let her out in saucers iv 3 98
I beseech your grace, let this letter be read . . . . iv 3 193
Let's have the tongs and the bones . . . . *M. N. Dream* iv 1 32
But let me to my fortune and the caskets . . *Mer. of Venice* ii 2 39
Let us go in ; And charge us there upon inter'gatories . . . v 1 297
Let's away, And get our jewels and our wealth together *As Y. Like It* i 3 135
If nothing lets to make us happy both But this . . . *T. Night* v 1 256
I'll give him my commission To let him there a month . . *W. Tale* i 2 41
Let me pocket up my pedlar's excrement . . . . . iv 4 733
Let me have no lying : it becomes none but tradesmen . . . iv 4 744
And let him be no kinsman to my liege, I do defy him . *Richard II.* i 1 59
Wert thou regent of the world, It were a shame to let this land by lease ii 1 110
But let him from my thoughts . . . . . . 1 *Hen. IV.* i 1 91
Let us to the highest of the field, To see what friends are living . . v 4 164

Let. Let heaven kiss earth! now let not Nature's hand Keep the wild flood confined! let order die! And let this world no longer be a stage To feed contention in a lingering act; But let one spirit of the first-born Cain Reign in all bosoms! . . . . *2 Hen. IV.* i 1 153
Which I beseech you to let me have home with me— That can hardly be v 5 80
My speech entreats That I may know the let . . . *Hen. V.* v 2 65
By my consent, we'll even let them alone.—Be it so . . *1 Hen. VI.* i 2 44
Presently we'll try: come, let's away about it . . . i 2 149
Let us four to dinner: I dare say This quarrel will drink blood another day ii 4 133
Let's stand close: my lord protector will come this way . *2 Hen. VI.* i 3 1
Close up his eyes and draw the curtain close; And let us all to meditation iii 3 33
Let him to the Tower, And chop away that factious pate of his . v 1 134
Let us all together to our troops . . . . . . *3 Hen. VI.* ii 3 49
Let's on our way in silent sort: For Warwick and his friends! . . iv 2 28
Come, therefore, let's about it speedily . . . . . iv 6 102
Cursed the blood that let this blood from hence! . . *Richard III.* i 2 16
Let the soul forth that adoreth thee, I lay it naked to the deadly stroke i 2 177
The envious flood Kept in my soul, and would not let it forth . i 4 38
Come, let us to our holy task again . . . . . . iii 7 246
Let us to't pell-mell; If not to heaven, then hand in hand to hell . v 3 312
Let him on. Go forward.—On my soul, I'll speak but truth. *Hen. VIII.* i 2 176
A right good husband, let him be a noble . . . . iv 2 146
Each Trojan that is master of his heart, Let him to field *Troi. and Cres.* i 1 5
I'll let his humours blood . . . . ii 3 222
Let us make ready straight . . . . iv 4 146
Let us address to tend on Hector's heels . . . . iv 4 148
Let me have war, say I; it exceeds peace. . . . *Coriolanus* iv 5 236
And what love can do that dares love attempt; Therefore thy kinsmen are no let to me . . . . . . *Rom. and Jul.* ii 2 69
Let me have men about me that are fat: Sleek-headed men . *J. Cæsar* i 2 192
For your private satisfaction, Because I love you, I will let you know . ii 2 74
Unhand me, gentlemen. By heaven, I'll make a ghost of him that lets me! *Hamlet* i 4 85
Let us see: Leave, gentle wax; and, manners, blame us not . . *Lear* iv 6 263
I'ld whistle her off and let her down the wind . . . *Othello* iii 3 262
Let me know; And knowing what I am, I know what she shall be . iv 1 73
Let's do it after the high Roman fashion . . . *Ant. and Cleo.* iv 15 87
I'll throw't into the creek Behind our rock; and let it to the sea *Cymb.* iv 2 152
I'ld let a parish of such Clotens blood, And praise myself for charity . iv 2 168
The noise is round about us.—Let us from it . . . . . iv 4 1
Heaven forbid That kings should let their ears hear their faults hid! *Per.* i 2 62
Let-alone. Mean you to enjoy him?—The let-alone lies not in your good will . . . . *Lear* v 3 79
Let be, let be. Would I were dead . . . . . *W. Tale* v 3 61
And they were ratified As he cried 'Thus let be' . . *Hen. VIII.* i 1 171
Ah, let be, let be! thou art The armourer of my heart *Ant. and Cleo.* iv 4 6
Let blood. His ancient knot of dangerous adversaries To-morrow are let blood at Pomfret-castle . . . . . *Richard III.* iii 1 183
I know not, gentlemen, what you intend, Who else must be let blood, who else is rank . . . . . . *J. Cæsar* iii 1 152
Let drive. Four rogues in buckram let drive at me . . *1 Hen. IV.* ii 4 217
Three misbegotten knaves in Kendal green came at my back and let drive at me . . . . ii 4 247
Let forth. Every one lets forth his sprite . . . *M. N. Dream* v 1 388
Whose great decision hath much blood let forth . . . *All's Well* iii 1 3
In these windows that let forth thy life . . . . *Richard. III.* i 2 12
Back, I say, go; lest I let forth your half-pint of blood . *Coriolanus* v 2 60
Let go thy hold when a great wheel runs down a hill . . *Lear* ii 4 72
Let her go hang. Then to sea, boys, and let her go hang! . *Tempest* ii 2 56
Let in. It will let in and out the enemy With bag and baggage *W. Tale* i 2 205
Whoe'er he be, you may not be let in . . . *1 Hen. VI.* i 3 7
I have express commandment That thou nor none of thine shall be let in i 3 21
Ye have made a fine hand, fellows: There's a trim rabble let in *Hen. VIII.* v 4 75
Let in the maid, that out a maid Never departed more . *Hamlet* iv 5 54
Let it alone, thou fool; it is but trash . . . *Tempest* iv 1 223
Let it alone; I'll make other shift . . . . *2 Hen. IV.* ii 1 169
Let it alone; my state now will but mock me . . . *Hen. VIII.* ii 1 101
Let it alone; And, come, I will go get a leaf of brass *T. Andron.* iv 1 101
Your napkin is too little: Let it alone . . . . *Othello* iii 3 288
Let it alone; let's to billiards . . . . . *Ant. and Cleo.* ii 5 3
Let it be. 'Twill be naught: But let it be . . . . . iii 5 24
Let it be so; thy truth, then, be thy dower . . . . *Lear* i 1 110
Yea, is it come to this? Let it be so . . . . . . i 4 327
Let it go. Must he lose The name of king? o' God's name, let it go *Richard II.* iii 3 146
Tempest ii 2 36
Let loose. I do now let loose my opinion . . . . .
Let loose, Or I will shake thee from me like a serpent! . *M. N. Dream* iii 2 260
Their ragged curtains poorly are let loose . . . . *Hen. V.* iv 2 41
That excellent grand tyrant of the earth . . . Thy womb let loose *Richard III.* iv 4 54
Let loose on me the justice of the state For thus deluding you *Othello* i 1 140
Let me be that I am and seek not to alter me . . *Much Ado* i 3 38
Let me be: pluck up, my heart, and be sad . . . . . v 1 207
Let out. Break open the gaols and let out the prisoners . *2 Hen. VI.* iv 3 18
And let out Their coin upon large interest . . *T. of Athens* iii 5 107
Let to know. If your name be Horatio, as I am let to know . *Hamlet* iv 6 11
Let us hence, and put on other weeds . . . . *Much Ado* v 3 30
Now therefore let us hence; and lose no hour . . *3 Hen. VI.* iv 1 148
Let us hence, my sovereign, to provide A salve for any sore that may betide . . . . iv 6 87
Let us in. But, soft! my door is lock'd. Go bid them let us in *C. of Er.* iii 1 30
Let's in, and there expect their coming . . . *Mer. of Venice* v 1 49
Which trust accordingly, kind citizens, And let us in . . *K. John* ii 1 232
Let us in, and with all speed provide To see her coronation . *2 Hen. VI.* i 1 73
Come, wife, let's in, and learn to govern better . . . . iv 9 48
Let us in, To comfort Edward with our company . *Richard III.* ii 1 138
Let us on, And publish the occasion of our arms . . *2 Hen. IV.* i 3 85
Now let us on, my lords, and join our powers . . *1 Hen. VI.* iii 3 90
Why, then, let's on our way in silent sort . . . *3 Hen. VI.* iv 2 28
Letest. Thou let'st thy fortune sleep—die, rather . . *Tempest* ii 1 216
O Proserpina, For the flowers now, that frighted thou let'st fall From Dis's waggon! . . . . *W. Tale* iv 4 117
Before the game is afoot, thou still let'st slip . . . *1 Hen. IV.* i 3 278
Lethargied. His notion weakens, his discernings Are lethargied . *Lear* i 4 249
Lethargy. How have you come so early by this lethargy? . *T. Night* i 5 132
In this time of lethargy I picked and cut most of their festival purses *W. T.* iv 4 627
This apoplexy is, as I take it, a kind of lethargy . . . *2 Hen. IV.* i 2 127
Loads o' gravel i' the back, lethargies . . . *Troi. and Cres.* v 1 23
Peace is a very apoplexy, lethargy; mulled, deaf, sleepy *Coriolanus* iv 5 234
The lethargy must have his quiet course: If not, he foams at mouth *Oth.* iv 1 59

Lethe. Let fancy still my sense in Lethe steep . . . . *T. Night* iv 1 66
Was this easy? May this be wash'd in Lethe, and forgotten? *2 Hen. IV.* v 2 72
So in the Lethe of thy angry soul Thou drown the sad remembrance of those wrongs . . . . *Richard III.* iv 4 250
Sign'd in thy spoil, and crimson'd in thy lethe . . . *J. Cæsar* iii 1 206
And duller shouldst thou be than the fat weed That roots itself in ease on Lethe wharf, Wouldst thou not stir in this . . . *Hamlet* i 5 33
Let's all take hands, Till that the conquering wine hath steep'd our sense In soft and delicate Lethe . . . . . *Ant. and Cleo.* ii 7 114
Lethe'd. That sleep and feeding may prorogue his honour Even till a Lethe'd dulness! . . . . ii 1 27
Letters should not be known . . . . *Tempest* ii 1 150
Let me hear from thee by letters . . . . . *T. G. of Ver.* i 1 57
Gavest thou my letter to Julia?—Ay, sir: I, a lost mutton, gave your letter to her . . . . i 1 100
Nay, sir, less than a pound shall serve me for carrying your letter . i 1 112
'Tis threefold too little for carrying a letter to your lover . . i 1 116
Nothing at all from her; no, not so much as a ducat for delivering your letter . . . . i 1 146
In requital whereof, henceforth carry your letters yourself . . . i 1 154
And yet I would I had o'erlooked the letter . . . . . i 2 50
What a fool is she, that knows I am a maid, And would not force the letter to my view! Since maids, in modesty, say 'no' . . . i 2 54
But she would be best pleased To be so anger'd with another letter . i 2 103
Good wind, blow not a word away Till I have found each letter in the letter . . . . i 2 119
How now! what letter are you reading there? . . . . . i 3 51
Lend me the letter; let me see what news.—There is no news, my lord i 3 55
I fear'd to show my father Julia's letter, Lest he should take exceptions i 3 80
I have writ your letter Unto the secret nameless friend of yours . . ii 1 110
That my master, being scribe, to himself should write the letter . ii 1 146
She wooes you by a figure.—What figure?—By a letter, I should say . ii 1 156
She hath given you a letter.—That's the letter I writ to her friend.—And that letter hath she delivered, and there an end . . . ii 1 165
What say you to a letter from your friends Of much good news? . ii 4 51
There is a messenger That stays to bear my letters to my friends . iii 1 53
What letter is this same? What's here? 'To Silvia'! . . . iii 1 137
Thy letters may be here, though thou art hence . . . . iii 1 248
Now will he be swinged for reading my letter . . . . . iii 1 393
Well, give her that ring and therewithal This letter . . . iv 4 91
Peruse this letter.—Pardon me, madam; I have unadvised Deliver'd you a paper that I should not: This is the letter to your ladyship . iv 4 126
The letter is, to desire and require her to solicit your master's desires to Mistress Anne Page . . . . *Mer. Wives* i 2 10
I have writ me here a letter to her: and here another to Page's wife . i 3 65
Here's another letter to her: she bears the purse too . . . i 3 75
Go bear thou this letter to Mistress Page; and thou this to Mistress Ford i 3 80
Bear you these letters tightly; Sail like my pinnace to these golden shores . . . . i 3 88
Give-a this letter to Sir Hugh; by gar, it is a shallenge . . . i 4 113
Letter for letter, but that the name of Page and Ford differs! . . ii 1 71
Here's the twin-brother of thy letter: but let thine inherit first . ii 1 74
I warrant he hath a thousand of these letters, writ with blank space for different names,—sure, more . . . . ii 1 76
O, that my husband saw this letter! it would give eternal food to his jealousy . . . . ii 1 104
I should have borne the humoured letter to her . . . . . ii 1 135
You'll not bear a letter for me, you rogue! you stand upon your honour! ii 2 20
Coach after coach, letter after letter, gift after gift . . . . ii 2 66
She hath received your letter, for the which she thanks you a thousand times . . . . ii 2 83
This boy will carry a letter twenty mile, as easy as a cannon will shoot point-blank twelve score . . . . iii 2 33
What, Sir John Falstaff! Are these your letters, knight? . . . iii 3 148
And did he send you both these letters at an instant? . . . iv 4 3
Here is a letter will say somewhat. Good hearts, what ado here is! . iv 5 127
I have a letter from her Of such contents as you will wonder at . iv 6 12
He this very day receives letters of strange tenour . *Meas. for Meas.* iv 2 215
Now will I write letters to Angelo,—The provost, he shall bear them . iv 3 97
This letter, then, to Friar Peter give; 'Tis that he sent me . . iv 3 142
Wend you with this letter: Command these fretting waters from your eyes . . . . iv 3 150
Every letter he hath writ hath disvouched other . . . . iv 4 1
These letters at fit time deliver me: The provost knows our purpose . iv 5 1
Whom I made lord of me and all I had, At your important letters *C. of E.* v 1 138
I have already delivered him letters, and there appears much joy in him *Much Ado* i 1 20
In such great letters as they write 'Here is good horse to hire' . . i 1 267
O, she tore the letter into a thousand halfpence . . . . ii 3 146
For a hawk, a horse, or a husband?—For the letter that begins them all iii 4 56
There's villany abroad: this letter will tell you more . . *L. L. Lost* i 1 189
A letter from the magnificent Armado . . . . . . i 1 193
Will you hear this letter with attention?—As we would hear an oracle . i 1 217
Bring him festinately hither: I must employ him in a letter to my love iii 1 7
Fetch hither the swain: he must carry me a letter . . . . iii 1 51
A letter from Monsieur Biron to one Lady Rosaline.—O, thy letter, thy letter! . . . . iv 1 53
This letter is mistook, it importeth none here; It is writ to Jaquenetta iv 1 57
What plume of feathers is he that indited this letter? . . . iv 1 96
Thou fellow, a word: Who gave thee this letter?—I told you; my lord iv 1 103
Thou hast mistaken his letter. Come, lords, away . . . iv 1 108
I will something affect the letter, for it argues facility . . . iv 2 56
Good Master Parson, be so good as read me this letter . . . iv 2 93
I will look again on the intellect of the letter . . . . iv 2 138
And here he hath framed a letter to a sequent of the stranger queen's . iv 2 142
Let this letter be read: Our parson misdoubts it; 'twas treason, he said iv 3 193
O, he hath drawn my picture in his letter!—Any thing like?—Much in the letters; nothing in the praise . . . . v 2 38
Let me not die your debtor, My red dominical, my golden letter . v 2 44
The letter is too long by half a mile . . . . . . v 2 54
Dost thou not wish in heart The chain were longer and the letter short? v 2 56
We have received your letters full of love; Your favours . . v 2 787
Our letters, madam, show'd much more than jest.—So did our looks . v 2 795
See these letters delivered; put the liveries to making *Mer. of Venice* ii 2 123
Give him this letter; do it secretly; And so farewell . . . ii 3 7
Was not that letter from fair Jessica?—I must needs tell thee all . ii 4 29
Ere I ope his letter, I pray you, tell me how my good friend doth . iii 2 235
His letter there Will show you his estate . . . . . . iii 2 238
Here is a letter, lady; The paper as the body of my friend . . iii 2 266
But let me hear the letter of your friend . . . . . . iii 2 316

Letter. If your love do not persuade you to come, let not my letter *Mer. of Venice* iii 2 324
Take this same letter, And use thou all the endeavour of a man In speed iii 4 47
A messenger with letters from the doctor, New come from Padua.—Bring us the letters; call the messenger . iv 1 108
This letter from Bellario doth commend A young and learned doctor . iv 1 143
Meantime the court shall hear Bellario's letter . . . iv 1 149
Understand that at the receipt of your letter I am very sick . iv 1 151
Here is a letter; read it at your leisure; It comes from Padua v 1 267
Better news in store for you Than you expect: unseal this letter soon v 1 275
You shall not know by what strange accident I chanced on this letter v 1 279
I'll write to him a very taunting letter . . . . *As Y. Like It* iii 5 134
Patience herself would startle at this letter And play the swaggerer . iv 3 13
This is a letter of your own device.—No, I protest, I know not the contents . . . . iv 3 20
I say she never did invent this letter; This is a man's invention . iv 3 28
Will you hear the letter?—So please you, for I never heard it yet . iv 3 36
You have done me much ungentleness, To show the letter that I writ to you . . . . v 2 84
Which hath two letters for her name fairly set down in studs *T. of Shrew* iii 2 62
Letters from my mother: what the import is, I know not yet *All's Well* ii 3 293
I have writ my letters, casketed my treasure, Given order for our horses ii 5 26
Look on his letter, madam; here's my passport . . iii 2 58
Brought you this letter, gentlemen?—Ay, madam . . . iii 2 65
Would you take the letter of her? Might you not know she would do as she has done, By sending me a letter? . . . . iii 4 1
I sent to her . . . Tokens and letters which she did re-send . iii 6 123
You have not given him his mother's letter?—I have delivered it . iv 3 2
How is this justified?—The stronger part of it by her own letters . iv 3 66
The duke hath offered him letters of commendations to the king . iv 3 92
I think I have his letter in my pocket.—Marry, we'll search . iv 3 228
Either it is there, or it is upon a file with the duke's other letters iv 3 232
That is not the duke's letter, sir; that is an advertisement . iv 3 239
I have letters that my son will be here to-night . . . iv 5 90
I have letters sent me That set him high in fame . . . v 3 30
There is your ring; And, look you, here's your letter . . v 3 312
He shall think, by the letters that thou wilt drop, that they come from my neice, and that she's in love with him . . *T. Night* ii 3 178
I will plant you two . . . where he shall find the letter . . ii 3 190
This letter will make a contemplative idiot of him . . . ii 5 22
For every one of these letters are in my name . . . ii 5 153
We shall have a rare letter from him: but you'll not deliver't? iii 2 60
He does obey every point of the letter that I dropped to betray him iii 2 83
This concurs directly with the letter: she sends him on purpose, that I may appear stubborn to him; for she incites me to that in the letter . . . . iii 4 73
If this letter move him not, his legs cannot . . . iii 4 188
Now will not I deliver his letter . . . . . iii 4 202
This letter, being so excellently ignorant, will breed no terror in the youth . . . . iii 4 206
It shall advantage thee more Than ever the bearing of letter did . iv 2 120
As thou lovest me, let me see his letter.—Good Master Fabian, grant me another request.—Any thing.—Do not desire to see this letter . v 1 2
I have your own letter that induced me to the semblance I put on v 1 315
Pray you, peruse that letter. You must not now deny it is your hand v 1 338
And in such forms which here were presupposed Upon thee in the letter v 1 359
Maria writ The letter at Sir Toby's great importance . . v 1 371
With interchange of gifts, letters, loving embassies . *W. Tale* i 1 31
Nay, but my letters, by this means being there So soon as you arrive, shall clear that doubt . . . . iv 4 632
The letters of Antigonus found with it which they know to be his character . . . . v 2 37
What hath it done, That it in golden letters should be set? *K. John* iii 1 85
Who brought that letter from the cardinal?—The Count Melun . iv 3 14
With letters of your love to her at large . . . *Richard II.* iii 1 41
Letters came last night To a dear friend of the good Duke of York's, That tell black tidings . . . . iii 4 69
No further go in this Than I by letters shall direct your course *1 Hen. IV.* i 3 293
Have I not all their letters to meet me in arms by the ninth of the next month? . . . . ii 3 28
Go bear this letter to Lord John of Lancaster, to my brother John . iii 3 218
What letters hast thou there?—I can but thank you.—These letters come from your father.—Letters from him! . . . . iv 1 13
His letters bear his mind, not I, my lord . . . . iv 1 20
My lord, here are letters for you.—I cannot read them now . v 2 80
Get posts and letters, and make friends with speed . *2 Hen. IV.* i 1 214
Go bear this letter to my Lord of Lancaster; this to the prince . i 2 267
You shall have letters of me presently . . . . ii 1 190
He heard of your grace's coming to town: there's a letter for you . ii 2 108
I'll steep this letter in sack and make him eat it . . ii 2 147
Bid them o'er-read these letters, And well consider of them . iii 1 2
Have you read o'er the letters that I sent you?—We have, my liege . iii 1 36
I have received New-dated letters from Northumberland . . iii 1 8
Whose learning and good letters peace hath tutor'd . . iv 1 44
Will Fortune never come with both hands full, But write her fair words still in foulest letters? . . . . iv 4 104
Lords, view these letters full of bad mischance . . *1 Hen. VI.* i 1 89
A letter was deliver'd to my hands, Writ to your grace . . iv 1 11
View the letter Sent from our uncle Duke of Burgundy . . iv 1 48
Is that the worst this letter doth contain?—It is the worst . iv 1 66
Have you perused the letters from the pope? . . . v 1 1
I do greet your excellence With letters of commission . . v 4 95
A villain!—Has a book in his pocket with red letters in't *2 Hen. VI.* iv 2 98
What is thy name?—Emmanuel.—They use to write it on the top of letters . . . . iv 2 107
These letters are for you, Sent from your brother . *3 Hen. VI.* iii 3 163
As my letters tell me, He's very likely now to fall from him . iii 3 208
Now, messenger, what letters or what news From France? . . iv 1 84
What answer makes King Lewis unto our letters? . . . iv 1 91
And from the cross-row plucks the letter G . . *Richard III.* i 1 55
You shall have letters from me to my son To meet you on the way . iv 1 50
Look to your wife: if she convey Letters to Richmond, you shall answer it . . . . iv 2 96
These letters will resolve him of my mind . . . . iv 5 19
And his own letter, the honourable board of council out, Must fetch him in the papers . . . . *Hen. VIII.* i 1 78
Send our letters, with Free pardon to each man . . . i 2 99
Let there be letters writ to every shire, Of the king's grace and pardon i 2 103
The cardinal's letters to the pope miscarried, And came to the eye o' the king . . . . iii 2 30

Letter. But, will the king Digest this letter of the cardinal's? *Hen. VIII.* iii 2 53
The letter, as I live, with all the business I writ to's holiness . iii 2 221
Patience, is that letter, I caused you write, yet sent away? . . iv 2 127
Thou shalt bear a letter to him straight.—Let me bear another to his horse; for that's the more capable creature . *Troi. and Cres.* iii 3 307
Here's a letter for thee.—From whence, fragment? . . . v 1 7
Here is a letter from Queen Hecuba, A token from her daughter . v 1 44
What now?—Here's a letter come from yond poor girl . . v 3 99
These are the words: I think I have the letter here . *Coriolanus* i 2 8
Look, here's a letter from him: the state hath another . . ii 1 118
I will make my very house reel to-night: a letter for me! . . ii 1 122
A letter for me! it gives me an estate of seven years' health . ii 1 125
The senate has letters from the general . . . . ii 1 148
Seest thou this letter? take it up, I pray thee . . *T. Andron.* ii 3 46
Who found this letter? Tamora, was it you? . . . ii 3 293
I aim a mile beyond the moon; Your letter is with Jupiter by this . iv 3 66
News, news from heaven! Marcus, the post is come. Sirrah, what tidings? have you any letters? . . . . . . iv 3 78
I have brought you a letter and a couple of pigeons here . . iv 4 43
My faithful friends, I have received letters from great Rome . v 1 2
I wrote the letter that thy father found And hid the gold within the letter mention'd . . . . v 1 107
And on their skins, as on the bark of trees, Have with my knife carved in Roman letters, 'Let not your sorrow die' . . . . v 1 139
Can you read any thing you see?—Ay, if I know the letters *Rom. and Jul.* i 2 64
The kinsman of old Capulet Hath sent a letter to his father's house ii 4 7
Any man that can write may answer a letter.—Nay, he will answer the letter's master, how he dares, being dared . . . . ii 4 11
Doth not rosemary and Romeo begin both with a letter? . . ii 4 220
Against thou shalt awake, Shall Romeo by my letters know our drift iv 1 114
I'll send a friar with speed To Mantua, with my letters to thy lord iv 1 124
Dost thou not bring me letters from the friar? How doth my lady? v 1 13
Hast thou no letters to me from the friar?—No, my good lord . v 1 31
What says Romeo? Or, if his mind be writ, give me his letter . v 2 4
Who bare my letter, then, to Romeo?—I could not send it,—here it is again . . . . v 2 13
The letter was not nice but full of charge Of dear import, and the neglecting it May do much danger . . . . . . v 2 18
Hold, take this letter; early in the morning See thou deliver it . v 3 23
But he which bore my letter, Friar John, Was stay'd by accident, and yesternight Return'd my letter back . . . . . . v 3 250
This letter he early bid me give his father . . . . v 3 275
Give me the letter; I will look on it . . . . . v 3 278
This letter doth make good the friar's words . . . . v 3 286
Your honourable letter he desires To those have shut him up *T. of Athens* i 1 97
Read me the superscription of these letters: I know not which is which ii 2 82
With letters of entreaty, which imported His fellowship i' the cause . v 2 11
He did receive his letters, and is coming . . . *J. Cæsar* iii 1 279
My letters, praying on his side, Because I knew the man, were slighted off . . . . iv 3 4
I have here received letters, That young Octavius and Mark Antony Come down upon us . . . . iv 3 167
Myself have letters of the selfsame tenour . . . . iv 3 171
Therein our letters do not well agree . . . . . iv 3 176
Had you your letters from your wife, my lord?—No, Messala.—Nor nothing in your letters writ of her? . . . . . . iv 3 181
Thy letters have transported me beyond This ignorant present *Macbeth* i 5 57
I did repel his letters and denied His access to me . . *Hamlet* ii 1 109
There's letters seal'd: and my two schoolfellows, Whom I will trust as I will adders fang'd, They bear the mandate . . . iii 4 202
Imports at full, By letters congruing to that effect, The present death iv 3 66
Sailors, sir: they say they have letters for you . . . iv 6 2
Give these fellows some means to the king: they have letters for him . iv 6 14
Come, I will make you way for these your letters . . . iv 6 32
How now! what news?—Letters, my lord, from Hamlet . . iv 7 36
If this letter speed, And my invention thrive . . . *Lear* i 2 19
Why so earnestly seek you to put up that letter? . . . i 2 28
It is a letter from my brother, that I have not all o'er-read . i 2 38
Give me the letter, sir.—I shall offend, either to detain or give it . i 2 41
O villain, villain! His very opinion in the letter! . . . i 2 81
How now, Oswald! What, have you writ that letter to my sister? . i 4 357
Go you before to Gloucester with these letters. Acquaint my daughter no further with any thing you know than comes from her demand out of the letter . . . . i 5 2
I will not sleep, my lord, till I have delivered your letter . . i 5 7
Strong and fasten'd villain! Would he deny his letter? . . ii 1 80
Draw, you rascal: you come with letters against the king . . ii 2 38
Thou whoreson zed! thou unnecessary letter! . . . . ii 2 70
Approach, thou beacon to this under globe, That by thy comfortable beams I may Peruse this letter! . . . . . . ii 2 172
When at their home I did commend your highness letters to them . ii 4 28
Deliver'd letters, spite of intermission, Which presently they read . ii 4 33
This approves her letter, That she would soon be here . . ii 4 186
I have received a letter this night; 'tis dangerous to be spoken; I have locked the letter in my closet . . . . iii 3 10
This courtesy, forbid thee, shall the duke Instantly know; and of that letter too . . . . iii 3 23
This is the letter he spoke of, which approves him an intelligent party to the advantages of France . . . . iii 5 11
Post speedily to my lord your husband; show him this letter . . iii 7 2
Come, sir, what letters had you late from France? . . . iii 7 42
I have a letter guessingly set down . . . . . . iii 7 47
This letter, madam, craves a speedy answer; 'Tis from your sister . iv 2 82
Did your letters pierce the queen to any demonstration of grief? . iv 3 11
What might import my sister's letter to him?—I know not, lady . iv 5 6
I must needs after him, madam, with my letter . . . iv 5 15
Something—I know not what: I'll love thee much, Let me unseal the letter . . . . iv 5 22
Were all the letters suns, I could not see one . . . iv 6 143
Give the letters which thou find'st about me To Edmund earl of Gloucester iv 6 254
Let's see these pockets: the letters that he speaks of May be my friends iv 6 261
Before you fight the battle, ope this letter . . . . v 1 40
Stay till I have read the letter.—I was forbid it . . . v 1 47
Preferment goes by letter and affection, And not by old gradation *Othello* i 1 36
They are disproportion'd; My letters say a hundred and seven galleys i 3 3
You shall yourself read in the bitter letter After your own sense . i 3 68
These letters give, Iago, to the pilot; And by him do my duties . iii 2 1
Are you wise?—What, is he angry?—May be the letter moved him . iv 1 246
Is it his use? Or did the letters work upon his blood? . . iv 1 286

Letter. Here is a letter Found in the pocket of the slain Roderigo; And here another *Othello* v 2 308
There is besides in Roderigo's letter, How he upbraids Iago . . v 2 324
I pray you, in your letters, When you shall these unlucky deeds relate, Speak of me as I am . . . v 2 340
But the letters too Of many our contriving friends in Rome Petition us at home . . . . *Ant. and Cleo.* i 2 188
Of this my letters Before did satisfy you . . . ii 2 51
You Did pocket up my letters, and with taunts Did gibe my missive . ii 2 73
Go make thee ready; Our letters are prepared . . . iii 3 41
Not resting here, accuses him of letters he had formerly wrote to Pompey iii 5 11
Welcome hither: Your letters did withhold our breaking forth . iii 6 79
You shall Have letters from me to some friends that will Sweep your way iii 11 16
Who to my father was a friend, to me Known but by letter . *Cymbeline* i 1 99
A noble gentleman of Rome, Comes from my lord with letters . . i 6 11
Here are letters for you.—Their tenour good, I trust.—'Tis very like . ii 4 35
Do't: the letter That I have sent her, by her own command Shall give thee opportunity . . . . iii 2 17
Madam, here is a letter from my lord.—Who? thy lord? that is my lord iii 2 25
She hath my letter for the purpose . . . iii 4 30
Sirrah, is this letter true?—Sir, as I think . . . iii 5 106
Damn'd Pisanio Hath with his forged letters . . . From this most bravest vessel of the world Struck the main-top! . . . iv 2 318
The Roman emperor's letters, Sent by a consul to me, should not sooner Than thine own worth prefer thee . . . iv 2 384
I heard no letter from my master since I wrote him . . . iv 3 36
By accident, I had a feigned letter of my master's Then in my pocket . v 5 279
Answering the letter of the oracle . . . v 5 450
Where I'll hear from thee; And by whose letters I'll dispose myself *Per.* i 2 117
Now to my daughter's letter: She tells me here, she'll wed the stranger knight . . . . ii 5 15
What's here? A letter, that she loves the knight of Tyre! . . ii 5 43
To the court of King Simonides Are letters brought . . iii Gower 24
This letter, and some certain jewels, Lay with you in your coffer . iii 4 1
Train'd In music, letters; who hath gain'd Of education all the grace iv Gower 8
Lettered. Are you not lettered? . . . . *L. L. Lost* v 1 48
Letters-patents. Call in the letters-patents that he hath By his attorneys-general to sue His livery . . . *Richard II.* ii 1 202
I am denied to sue my livery here, And yet my letters-patents give me leave . . . . ii 3 130
And, to confirm his goodness, Tied it by letters-patents *Hen. VIII.* iii 2 250
Letting. You did never lack advice so much, As letting her pass so *All's Well* iii 4 20
Let's purge this choler without letting blood . . *Richard II.* i 1 153
When thou hast hung thy advanced sword i' the air, Not letting it decline on the declined . . . *Troi. and Cres.* iv 5 189
Letting it there stand Till she had laid it and conjured it down *R. and J.* ii 1 25
Letting 'I dare not' wait upon 'I would,' Like the poor cat *Macbeth* i 7 44
Letting go safely by The divine Desdemona . . *Othello* ii 1 72
Who of their broken debtors take a third, A sixth, a tenth, letting them thrive again On their abatement . . *Cymbeline* v 4 20
Lettuce. If we will plant nettles, or sow lettuce . . . *Othello* i 3 325
Leve. And I sall quit you with gud leve, as I may pick occasion *Hen. V.* iii 2 110
Level. We steal by line and level, an't like your grace . *Tempest* iv 1 239
'Steal by line and level' is an excellent pass of pate . . iv 1 243
According to my description, level at my affection . *Mer. of Venice* i 2 41
Love no god, that would not extend his might, only where qualities were level; Dian no queen of virgins . . *All's Well* i 3 118
I am not an impostor that proclaim Myself against the level of mine arm ii 1 159
So wears she to him, So sways she level in her husband's heart *T. Night* ii 4 32
Out of the blank And level of my brain, plot-proof . *W. Tale* ii 3 6
My life stands in the level of your dreams, Which I'll lay down . iii 2 82
And hold their level with thy princely heart . . *1 Hen. IV.* iii 2 17
From a level consideration . . . *2 Hen. IV.* ii 1 124
And see the revolution of the times Make mountains level . . iii 1 47
The foeman may with as great aim level at the edge of a penknife . iii 2 286
Every thing lies level to our wish: Only, we want a little personal strength . . . . iv 4 7
By false accuse doth level at my life . . . *2 Hen. VI.* iii 1 160
Ambitious York did level at thy crown . . *3 Hen. VI.* ii 2 19
Therefore level not to hit their lives . . *Richard III.* iv 4 202
I stood i' the level Of a full-charged confederacy . *Hen. VIII.* i 2 2
As if that name, Shot from the deadly level of a gun *Rom. and Jul.* iii 3 103
There's nothing level in our cursed natures, But direct villany *T. of A.* iv 3 19
As level as the cannon to his blank, Transports his poison'd shot *Hamlet* iv 1 42
It shall as level to your judgement pierce, As day does to your eye iv 5 151
Such accommodation and besort As levels with her breeding . *Othello* i 3 240
Young boys and girls Are level now with men . . *Ant. and Cleo.* iv 15 66
A well-experienced archer hits the mark His eye doth level at *Pericles* i 1 165
It is too late to talk of love; And that's the mark I know you level at. ii 3 114
Levelled. If all aim but this be levell'd false . . *Much Ado* iv 1 239
No levell'd malice Infects one comma in the course I hold *T. of Athens* i 1 47
Bravest at the last, She levell'd at our purposes . *Ant. and Cleo.* v 2 339
'Leven. Every 'leven wether tods; every tod yields pound and odd shilling . . . . *W. Tale* iv 3 33
Lever. Have you any levers to lift me up again, being down? *1 Hen. IV.* ii 2 36
Leviathan. Make tigers tame and huge leviathans Forsake unsounded deeps to dance on sands . . . *T. G. of Ver.* iii 2 80
Be thou here again Ere the leviathan can swim a league . *M. N. Dream* ii 1 174
As send precepts to the leviathan To come ashore . . *Hen. V.* iii 3 26
Levied. A treacherous army levied, one midnight . . *Tempest* i 2 128
His goods confiscate . . . , Unless a thousand marks be levied *C. of Er.* i 1 22
Never such a power For any foreign preparation Was levied . *K. John* iv 2 112
To discover What power the Duke of York had levied *Richard II.* ii 3 34
If they do this, . . . my ransom then Will soon be levied . *Hen. V.* iv 3 121
Again in pity of my hard distress Levied an army . . *1 Hen. VI.* ii 5 88
A plague upon that villain Somerset, That thus delays my promised supply Of horsemen, that were levied for this siege! . . iv 3 11
Let not your private discord keep away The levied succours . . iv 4 23
Swearing that you withhold his levied host, Collected for this expedition . . . . iv 4 31
Why stay we now? These soldiers shall be levied . *3 Hen. VI.* iii 3 251
The sixth part of his substance, to be levied Without delay . *Hen. VIII.* i 2 58
To employ those soldiers, So levied as before, against the Polack *Hamlet* ii 2 75
Trust to thy single virtue; for thy soldiers, All levied in my name, have in my name Took their discharge . . . *Lear* v 3 104
Levity. Her reputation was disvalued In levity . *Meas. for Meas.* v 1 222
Ere they can hide their levity in honour . . *All's Well* i 2 35
Else might the world convince of levity As well my undertakings *Troi. and Cres.* ii 2 130
Levity. Our own precedent passions do instruct us What levity's in youth *T. of Athens* i 1 134
Our graver business Frowns at this levity . . . *Ant. and Cleo.* ii 7 128
He is already Traduced for levity . . . . ii 7 14
Levy. To levy power Proportionable to the enemy Is all unpossible *Richard II.* ii 2 124
Forthwith a power of English shall we levy . . *1 Hen. IV.* i 1 22
With such powers As might hold sortance with his quality, The which he could not levy; whereupon He is retired . . *2 Hen. IV.* iv 1 12
Did he not, in his protectorship, Levy great sums of money? *2 Hen. VI.* iii 1 61
In our behalf Go levy men, and make prepare for war . *3 Hen. VI.* iv 1 131
Let's levy men, and beat him back again . . . . iv 8 6
Bid him levy straight The greatest strength and power he can make *Richard III.* iv 4 448
And give away The benefit of our levies . . . *Coriolanus* v 6 67
Malice domestic, foreign levy, nothing, Can touch him further *Macbeth* iii 2 25
In that the levies, The lists and full proportions, are all made Out of his subject . . . . . *Hamlet* i 2 31
Upon our first, he sent out to suppress His nephew's levies . . ii 2 62
For this immediate levy, he commends His absolute commission *Cymb.* iii 7 9
Whereunto your levy Must be supplyant . . . . iii 7 13
Never did thought of mine levy offence . . . *Pericles* ii 5 52
Levying. Brutus and Cassius Are levying powers . . *J. Cæsar* iv 1 42
Who now are levying The kings o' the earth for war . *Ant. and Cleo.* iii 6 67
Lewd. Is any woman wrong'd by this lewd fellow, . . . let her appear *Meas. for Meas.* v 1 515
How her acquaintance grew with this lewd fellow . . *Much Ado* v 1 341
Fie, what a question's that, If thou wert near a lewd interpreter! *Mer. of Venice* iii 4 80
A velvet dish: fie, fie! 'tis lewd and filthy . . *T. of Shrew* iv 3 65
The which he hath detain'd for lewd employments . . *Richard II.* i 1 90
Such poor, such bare, such lewd, such mean attempts . *1 Hen. IV.* iii 2 13
Because you have been so lewd and so much engraffed to Falstaff *2 Hen. IV.* ii 2 66
Thy lewd, pestiferous, and dissentious pranks . . *1 Hen. VI.* iii 1 15
But you must trouble him with lewd complaints . . *Richard III.* i 3 61
He is not lolling on a lewd day-bed, But on his knees at meditation . iii 7 72
Damn her, lewd minx! O, damn her! . . . *Othello* iii 3 475
Lewdly. If that man should be lewdly given, he deceiveth me *1 Hen. IV.* ii 4 469
A sort of naughty persons, lewdly bent . . *2 Hen. VI.* ii 1 167
Lewdly-inclined. Thunder shall not so awake the beds of eels as my giving out her beauty stir up the lewdly-inclined . *Pericles* iv 2 156
Lewdness. They may, 'cum privilegio,' wear away The lag end of their lewdness and be laugh'd at . . . *Hen. VIII.* i 3 35
But virtue, as it never will be moved, Though lewdness court it in a shape of heaven . . . . *Hamlet* i 5 54
Lewdster. Against such lewdsters and their lechery Those that betray them do no treachery . . . *Mer. Wives* v 3 23
Lewd-tongued. Thy lewd-tongued wife . . . *W. Tale* ii 3 172
Lewis, determine what we shall do straight . . *K. John* ii 1 149
Look upon the years Of Lewis the Dauphin and that lovely maid . . ii 1 425
Shall Lewis have Blanch, and Blanch those provinces? It is not so . iii 1 3
Lewis marry Blanch! O boy, then where art thou? . . . iii 1 34
O Lewis, stand fast! the devil tempts thee here In likeness of a new untrimmed bride . . . . . iii 1 208
That which upholdeth him that thee upholds, His honour: O, thine honour, Lewis, thine honour! . . . . iii 1 316
Thou shalt thrust thy hand as deep Into the purse of rich prosperity As Lewis himself . . . . . v 2 62
If Lewis do win the day, He is forsworn . . . . v 4 30
A treacherous fine of all your lives, If Lewis by your assistance win . v 4 39
Lewis the emperor, and Lewis the son Of Charles the Great. Also King Lewis the Tenth, Who was sole heir to the usurper Capet *Hen. V.* i 2 76
King Pepin's title and Hugh Capet's claim, King Lewis his satisfaction, all appear To hold in right and title of the female . . . i 2 88
And Lewis a prince soon won with moving words . *3 Hen. VI.* iii 1 34
Sit down with us: it ill befits thy state And birth, that thou shouldst stand while Lewis doth sit . . . . iii 3 3
Now, therefore, be it known to noble Lewis, That Henry, sole possessor of my love, Is of a king become a banish'd man . . iii 3 23
King Lewis and Lady Bona, hear me speak, Before you answer Warwick iii 3 65
Look, therefore, Lewis, that by this league and marriage Thou draw not on thy danger and dishonour . . . . iii 3 74
Before thy coming Lewis was Henry's friend.—And still is friend to him iii 3 143
I will not hence, till, with my talk and tears, Both full of truth, I make King Lewis behold Thy sly conveyance and thy lord's false love . iii 3 159
Mark how Lewis stamps, as he were nettled: I hope all's for the best . iii 3 169
King Lewis, I here protest, in sight of heaven, And by the hope I have of heavenly bliss, That I am clear from this misdeed of Edward's . iii 3 181
If King Lewis vouchsafe to furnish us With some few bands . . iii 3 203
And tell false Edward, thy supposed king, That Lewis of France is sending over masquers To revel it with him and his new bride iii 3 224; iv 1 94
How like you our choice . . . ?—As well as Lewis of France . . iv 1 11
They are but Lewis and Warwick: I am Edward, Your king and Warwick's . . . . . . iv 1 15
King Lewis Becomes your enemy, for mocking him About the marriage iv 1 29
What if both Lewis and Warwick be appeased By such invention as I can devise? . . . . . iv 1 34
What answer makes King Lewis unto our letters? . . . . iv 1 91
Is Lewis so brave? belike he thinks me Henry . . . . iv 1 96
I'll follow you, and tell what answer Lewis and the Lady Bona send . iv 3 56
Liable, congruent and measurable for the afternoon . . *L. L. Lost* v 1 97
Find liable to our crown and dignity . . . *K. John* ii 1 490
Fit for bloody villany, Apt, liable to be employ'd in danger . . iv 2 226
Who else but I, And such as to my claim are liable, Sweat in this business? . . . . . . v 2 101
If my name were liable to fear, I do not know the man I should avoid So soon as that spare Cassius . . . *J. Cæsar* i 2 199
My dear dear love To your proceeding bids me tell you this; And reason to my love is liable . . . . . ii 2 104
To the choleric fisting of every rogue Thy ear is liable . *Pericles* iv 6 178
Liar. I do despise a liar as I do despise one that is false . *Mer. Wives* i 1 69
We will make amends ere long; Else the Puck a liar call *M. N. Dream* v 1 442
Now I find report a very liar . . . . *T. of Shrew* ii 1 246
I know him a notorious liar, Think him a great way fool . *All's Well* i 1 111
An infinite and endless liar, an hourly promise-breaker . . iii 6 11
He is not guilty of her coming hither.—You're liars all . *W. Tale* ii 3 146
He hath promised you more than that, or there be liars . . . iv 4 240

Liar. How God and good men hate so foul a liar *Richard II.* i 1 114
Your wit, too, lies in your sinews, or else there be liars *Troi. and Cres.* ii 1 109
Howsoever you have been his liar, as you say you have *Coriolanus* v 2 32
Measureless liar, thou hast made my heart Too great for what contains it v 6 103
Transparent heretics, be burnt for liars! *Rom. and Jul.* i 2 96
Who must hang them?—Why, the honest men.—Then the liars and swearers are fools, for there are liars and swearers enow to beat the honest men and hang up them *Macbeth* iv 2 56
Liar and slave!—Let me endure your wrath, if't be not so v 5 35
Doubt truth to be a liar; But never doubt I love *Hamlet* ii 2 118
Liars, and adulterers, by an enforced obedience of planetary influence *Lear* i 2 134
She's, like a liar, gone to burning hell *Othello* v 2 129
I am full sorry That he approves the common liar *Ant. and Cleo.* i 1 60
Thou, the greatest soldier of the world, Art turn'd the greatest liar i 3 39
Libbard. With libbard's head on knee *L. L. Lost* v 2 551
Libel. By drunken prophecies, libels, and dreams *Richard III.* i 1 33
Libelling. What's this but libelling against the senate? *T. Andron.* iv 4 17
Liberal. She is too liberal.—Of her tongue she cannot *T. G. of Ver.* iii 1 355
Who hath indeed, most like a liberal villain, Confess'd *Much Ado* iv 1 93
All liberal reason I will yield unto *L. L. Lost* ii 1 168
To excuse or hide The liberal opposition of our spirits v 2 743
In such eyes as ours appear not faults; But where thou art not known, why, there they show Something too liberal *Mer. of Venice* ii 2 194
You are liberal in offers: You taught me first to beg iv 1 438
I will become as liberal as you; I'll not deny him any thing v 1 226
And liberal To mine own children in good bringing up *T. of Shrew* i 1 98
For our coffers, with too great a court And liberal largess, are grown somewhat light *Richard II.* i 4 44
My heart is great; but it must break with silence, Ere't be disburden'd with a liberal tongue.—Nay, speak thy mind ii 1 229
O, no, my nephew must not know, Sir Richard, The liberal and kind offer of the king *1 Hen. IV.* v 2 2
His liberal eye doth give to every one, Thawing cold fear *Hen. V.* iv Prol. 44
It's sign she hath been liberal and free *1 Hen. VI.* v 4 82
Beside, his wealth doth warrant a liberal dower v 5 46
The people liberal, valiant, active, wealthy *2 Hen. VI.* iv 7 68
Witty, courteous, liberal, full of spirit *3 Hen. VI.* i 2 43
A liberal rewarder of his friends *Richard III.* i 3 124
Men of his way should be most liberal *Hen. VIII.* i 3 61
Where you are liberal of your loves and counsels Be sure you be not loose ii 1 126
And this is all a liberal course allows; Who cannot keep his wealth must keep his house *T. of Athens* iii 3 41
And long purples That liberal shepherds give a grosser name *Hamlet* iv 7 171
Most delicate carriages, and of very liberal conceit v 2 160
Is he not a most profane and liberal counsellor?—He speaks home *Othello* ii 1 165
This argues fruitfulness and liberal heart: Hot, hot, and moist iii 4 38
'Twas that hand that gave away my heart.—A liberal hand iii 4 46
I will speak as liberal as the north v 2 220
Am well studied for a liberal thanks Which I do owe you *Ant. and Cleo.* ii 6 48
Liberal arts. For the liberal arts Without a parallel *Tempest* i 2 73
Liberal-conceited. Against six French swords, their assigns, and three liberal-conceited carriages *Hamlet* v 2 169
Liberality. Over and beside Signior Baptista's liberality, I'll mend it with a largess *T. of Shrew* i 2 150
Liberality, and such like, the spice and salt that season a man *T. and C.* i 2 277
Then why should he despair that knows to court it With words, fair looks, and liberality? *T. Andron.* ii 1 92
Liberté. Il est content de vous donner la liberté *Hen. V.* iv 4 56
Libertine. None but libertines delight in him *Much Ado* ii 1 144
Thyself hast been a libertine, As sensual as the brutish sting *As Y. L. It* ii 7 65
Never did I hear Of any prince so wild a libertine *1 Hen. IV.* v 2 72
When he speaks, The air, a charter'd libertine, is still *Hen. V.* i 1 48
Like a puff'd and reckless libertine, Himself the primrose path of dalliance treads, And recks not his own rede *Hamlet* i 3 49
Tie up the libertine in a field of feasts *Ant. and Cleo.* ii 1 23
Liberty. What is't thou canst demand?—My liberty *Tempest* i 2 245
All corners else o' the earth Let liberty make use of i 2 492
We were awaked; straightway, at liberty v 1 235
Threatened to put me into everlasting liberty *Mer. Wives* iii 3 31
Whence comes this restraint?—From too much liberty *Meas. for Meas.* i 2 129
Liberty plucks justice by the nose; The baby beats the nurse i 3 29
To give fear to use and liberty, Which have for long run by the hideous law i 4 62
How came it that the absent duke had not either delivered him to his liberty or executed him? iv 2 137
He hath evermore had the liberty of the prison iv 2 156
And many such-like liberties of sin *Com. of Errors* i 2 102
A man is master of his liberty ii 1 7
Why should their [men's] liberty than ours be more?—Because their business still lies out o' door ii 1 10
Why, headstrong liberty is lash'd with woe ii 1 15
He that came behind you, sir, like an evil angel, and bid you forsake your liberty iv 3 20
A sin prevailing much in youthful men, Who give their eyes the liberty of gazing v 1 53
I will loose his bonds And gain a husband by his liberty v 1 340
If I had my liberty, I would do my liking *Much Ado* i 3 37
I mean setting thee at liberty, enfreedoming thy person *L. L. Lost* iii 1 125
Let me loose.—I give thee thy liberty, set thee from durance iii 1 129
Now go we in content To liberty and not to banishment *As Y. Like It* i 3 140
I must have liberty Withal, as large a charter as the wind ii 7 47
Translate thy life into death, thy liberty into bondage v 1 59
This liberty is all that I request *T. of Shrew* ii 1 95
I do; and will repute you ever The patron of my life and liberty iv 2 113
Derive a liberty From heartiness, from bounty *W. Tale* i 2 112
See thou shake the bags Of hoarding abbots; imprisoned angels Set at liberty *K. John* iii 3 9
O that these hands could so redeem my son, As they have given these hairs their liberty! But now I envy at their liberty iii 4 72
Let it be our suit That you have bid us ask his liberty iv 2 63
Our weal, on you depending, Counts it your weal he have his liberty iv 2 66
In liberty of bloody hand shall range With conscience wide as hell *Hen. V.* iii 3 12
The liberty that follows our places stops the mouth of all find-faults v 2 297
I lost my liberty and they their lives *1 Hen. VI.* ii 5 81
And crave I may have liberty to venge this wrong iii 4 42
To wall thee from the liberty of flight iv 2 24

Liberty. I think I have you fast: Unchain your spirits now with spelling charms And try if they can gain your liberty v 3 32
This her easy-held imprisonment Hath gain'd thy daughter princely liberty v 3 140
Now show yourselves men; 'tis for liberty *2 Hen. VI.* iv 2 193
Is Somerset at liberty? Then, York, unloose thy long-imprison'd thoughts v 1 87
At whose hands He hath good usage and great liberty *3 Hen. VI.* iv 5 6
And turn'd my captive state to liberty, My fear to hope iv 6 3
After many moody thoughts At last by notes of household harmony They quite forget their loss of liberty iv 6 15
By doubtful fear My joy of liberty is half eclipsed iv 6 63
Humbly complaining to her deity Got my lord chamberlain his liberty *Richard III.* i 1 77
Pity that the eagle should be mew'd, While kites and buzzards prey at liberty i 1 133
I muse why she's at liberty i 3 305
A prince's son, Being pent from liberty i 4 267
And yet within these five hours lived Lord Hastings, Untainted, unexamined, free, at liberty. Here's a good world! iii 6 9
I am sorry To see you ta'en from liberty *Hen. VIII.* i 1 205
[Your wit], 'tis strongly wedged up in a block-head, but if it were at liberty, 'twould, sure, southward *Coriolanus* ii 3 31
He was your enemy, ever spake against Your liberties ii 3 188
They have chose a consul that will from them take Their liberties ii 3 223
You are at point to lose your liberties iii 1 194
By giving liberty unto thine eyes; Examine other beauties *Rom. and Jul.* i 1 233
With a silk thread plucks it back again, So loving-jealous of his liberty ii 2 182
To prison, eyes, ne'er look on liberty! Vile earth, to earth resign! iii 2 58
I do return those talents, Doubled with thanks and service, from whose help I derived liberty.—O, by no means *T. of Athens* i 2 8
Lust and liberty Creep in the minds and marrows of our youth! iv 1 25
Liberty! Freedom! Tyranny is dead! *J. Cæsar* iii 1 78
Some to the common pulpits, and cry out 'Liberty, freedom!' iii 1 81
And, waving our red weapons o'er our heads, Let's all cry 'Peace, freedom and liberty!' iii 1 110
Shall the knot of us be call'd The men that gave their country liberty iii 1 118
Am I compell'd to set Upon one battle all our liberties v 1 76
As are companions noted and most known To youth and liberty *Hamlet* ii 1 24
But breathe his faults so quaintly That they may seem the taints of liberty ii 1 32
For the law of writ and the liberty, these are the only men ii 2 421
You do, surely, bar the door upon your own liberty, if you deny your griefs to your friend iii 2 352
His liberty is full of threats to all; To you yourself, to us, to every one iv 1 14
Dearer than eye-sight, space, and liberty *Lear* i 1 57
There is full liberty of feasting from this present hour of five *Othello* ii 2 10
This hand of yours requires A sequester from liberty, fasting and prayer iii 4 40
What poor an instrument May do a noble deed! he brings me liberty *Ant. and Cleo.* v 2 237
The Pannonians and Dalmatians for Their liberties are now in arms *Cymbeline* iii 1 75
Most welcome, bondage! for thou art a way, I think, to liberty v 4 4
But should he wrong my liberties in my absence? *Pericles* i 2 112
Library. Me, poor man, my library Was dukedom large enough *Tempest* i 2 109
He furnish'd me From mine own library with volumes that I prize i 2 167
Take choice of all my library, And so beguile thy sorrow *T. Andron.* iv 1 34
Libya. She came from Libya.—Where the warlike Smalus, That noble honour'd lord, is fear'd and loved? *W. Tale* v 1 157
To signify Not only my success in Libya, sir, But my arrival v 1 166
Were his brain as barren As banks of Libya *Troi. and Cres.* i 3 328
He hath assembled Bocchus, the king of Libya *Ant. and Cleo.* iii 6 69
License. Your virtue hath a license in't *Meas. for Meas.* ii 4 145
That fellow is a fellow of much license iii 2 216
Evils, That thou with license of free foot hast caught *As Y. Like It* ii 7 68
Taunt him with the license of ink *T. Night* iii 2 48
We license your departure with your son *1 Hen. IV.* i 3 123
The fifth Harry from curb'd license plucks The muzzle of restraint *2 Hen. IV.* iv 5 131
And therefore, living hence, did give ourself To barbarous license *Hen. V.* i 2 271
I come to thee for charitable license v 7 74
Thou shalt have a license to kill for a hundred lacking one *2 Hen. VI.* iv 3 8
Tell him that, by his license, Fortinbras Craves the conveyance of a promised march Over his kingdom *Hamlet* iv 4 2
And taunt my faults With such full license as both truth and malice Have power to utter *Ant. and Cleo.* i 2 112
Licentious. How dearly would it touch thee to the quick, Shouldst thou but hear I were licentious! *Com. of Errors* ii 2 133
What rein can hold licentious wickedness? *Hen. V.* iii 3 22
You have gone on and fill'd the time With all licentious measure *T. of A.* v 4 4
My sanctity Will to my sense bend no licentious ear *Pericles* v 3 30
Lichas. If Hercules and Lichas play at dice *Mer. of Venice* ii 1 32
Let me lodge Lichas on the horns o' the moon *Ant. and Cleo.* iv 12 45
Licio. His name is Licio, born in Mantua.—You're welcome, sir *T. of S.* ii 1 60
The narrow-prying father, Minola, The quaint musician, amorous Licio iii 2 149
Is't possible, friend Licio, that Mistress Bianca Doth fancy any other? iv 2 1
Mistake no more: I am not Licio, Nor a musician, as I seem to be iv 2 16
Then we are rid of Licio iv 2 49
Lick. Let me lick thy shoe. I'll not serve him *Tempest* iii 2 26
Whose hand is that the forest bear doth lick? *3 Hen. VI.* ii 2 13
Let them not lick The sweet which is their poison *Coriolanus* iii 1 156
I'll try if they can lick their fingers.—How canst thou try them so?—Marry, sir, 'tis an ill cook that cannot lick his own fingers: therefore he that cannot lick his fingers goes not with me *Rom. and Jul.* iv 2 4
And may diseases lick up their false bloods! *T. of Athens* iv 3 539
Let the candied tongue lick absurd pomp *Hamlet* iii 2 65
A gracious aged man, Whose reverence even the head-lugg'd bear would lick *Lear* iv 2 42
Licked. As ragged as Lazarus in the painted cloth, where the glutton's dogs licked his sores *1 Hen. IV.* iv 2 28
Lictor. Saucy lictors Will catch at us, like strumpets *Ant. and Cleo.* v 2 214
Lid. Two grey eyes, with lids to them *T. Night* i 5 266
Violets dim, But sweeter than the lids of Juno's eyes *W. Tale* iv 4 121
By God's lid, it does one's heart good *Troi. and Cres.* i 2 228
Sleep shall neither night nor day Hang upon his pent-house lid *Macbeth* i 3 20
Do not for ever with thy vailed lids Seek for thy noble father *Hamlet* i 2 70
The flame o' the taper Bows toward her, and would under-peep her lids, to see the enclosed lights *Cymbeline* ii 2 20
Lie there, my art. Wipe thou thine eyes; have comfort *Tempest* i 2 25
Made such a sinner of his memory, To credit his own lie i 2 102

Lie. Told thee no lies, made thee no mistakings . . . *Tempest* i 2 248
Full fathom five thy father lies; Of his bones are coral made . i 2 396
If but one of his pockets could speak, would it not say he lies? . ii 1 66
But, for your conscience?—Ay, sir; where lies that? . . . ii 1 276
Here lies your brother, No better than the earth he lies upon . ii 1 280
While you here do snoring lie, Open-eyed conspiracy His time doth take ii 1 300
Like hedgehogs which Lie tumbling in my barefoot way . . . ii 2 11
You'll lie like dogs and yet say nothing neither . . . iii 2 22
Wilt thou tell a monstrous lie, being but half a fish and half a monster? iii 2 32
Thou liest.—Thou liest, thou jesting monkey, thou: . . . I do not lie . iii 2 54
As you like this, give me the lie another time.—I did not give the lie . iii 2 85
Travellers ne'er did lie, Though fools at home condemn 'em . . iii 3 26
At this hour Lie at my mercy all mine enemies . . . . iv 1 264
Where the bee sucks, there suck I: In a cowslip's bell I lie . . v 1 89
I wish Myself were mudded in that oozy bed Where my son lies . v 1 152
Let it lie for those that it concerns.—Madam, it will not lie where it concerns, Unless it have a false interpreter . . *T. G. of Ver.* i 2 76
What, shall these papers lie like tell-tales here? . . . . i 2 133
Yet here they shall not lie, for catching cold . . . . i 2 136
My face?—She says it is a fair one. Nay then, the wanton lies . v 2 10
Shall I tell you a lie? I do despise a liar . . . *Mer. Wives* i 1 69
I had rather be a giantess, and lie under Mount Pelion . . . ii 1 81
Does he lie at the Garter?—Ay, marry, does he . . . . ii 1 187
And what he gets more of her than sharp words, let it lie on my head . ii 1 191
I would have nothing lie on my head . . . . . ii 1 194
I will predominate over the peasant, and thou shalt lie with his wife . ii 2 295
I will not lie to you: I was at her house the hour she appointed me . iii 5 65
This is the third time; I hope good luck lies in odd numbers . . v 1 2
To Master Brook you yet shall hold your word; For he to-night shall lie with Mistress Ford . . . . v 5 259
To die, and go we know not where; To lie in cold obstruction *M. for M.* iii 1 119
It lies much in your holding up . . . . iii 1 273
With Angelo to-night shall lie His old betrothed but despised . . iii 2 292
Because their [men's] business still lies out o' door . *Com. of Errors* ii 1 11
Spread o'er the silver waves thy golden hairs, And as a bed I'll take them and there lie . . . . iii 2 49
I could not endure a husband with a beard on his face: I had rather lie in the woollen . . . . *Much Ado* ii 1 33
The poison of that lies in you to temper . . . . . ii 2 21
In my chamber-window lies a book: bring it hither . . . ii 3 3
Now will he lie ten nights awake, carving the fashion of a new doublet ii 3 18
Would the two princes lie, and Claudio lie, Who loved her so? . . iv 1 154
If this sweet lady lie not guiltless here Under some biting error . iv 1 171
Believe me not; and yet I lie not; I confess nothing, nor I deny nothing . . . . iv 1 273
He is now as valiant as Hercules that only tells a lie and swears it . iv 1 324
Fashion-monging boys, That lie and cog and flout, deprave and slander . . . . v 1 95
Done to death by slanderous tongues Was the Hero that here lies . . v 3 4
Ere you find where light in darkness lies, Your light grows dark *L. L. Lost* i 1 78
She must lie here on mere necessity . . . . . . i 1 149
I love to hear him lie And I will use him for my minstrelsy . . i 1 176
If my observation, which very seldom lies, . . . Deceive me not now . ii 1 228
Made a mouth of his eye, By adding a tongue which I know will not lie ii 1 252
I do nothing in the world but lie, and lie in my throat . . . iv 3 12
By heaven, the wonder in a mortal eye!—By earth, she is not, corporal, there you lie . . . . iv 3 86
Where lies thy grief, O, tell me? . . . . . . iv 3 171
Where lies thy pain? And where my liege's? all about the breast . . iv 3 172
What upward lies The street should see as she walk'd overhead . . iv 3 280
They are infected; in their hearts it lies; They have the plague . . v 2 420
I Pompey am,— You lie, you are not he.—I Pompey am . . . v 2 550
You on all estates will execute That lie within the mercy of your wit . v 2 856
A jest's prosperity lies in the ear Of him that hears it . . . v 2 871
Where often you and I Upon faint primrose-beds were wont to lie *M. N. Dream* i 1 215
Do you amend it then; it lies in you . . . . . . ii 1 118
For my sake, my dear, Lie further off yet, do not lie so near . . ii 2 44
For lying so, Hermia, I do not lie . . . . . . ii 2 52
Pretty soul! she durst not lie Near this lack-love, this kill-courtesy . ii 2 76
Happy is Hermia, wheresoe'er she lies . . . . . ii 2 90
Who would give a bird the lie, though he cry 'cuckoo' never so? . . iii 1 138
There lies your love.—How came these things to pass? . . . iv 1 83
Puts the wretch that lies in woe In remembrance of a shroud . . v 1 384
My extremest means Lie all unlock'd to your occasions . *Mer. of Venice* i 1 139
But here an angel in a golden bed Lies all within . . . . ii 7 59
Take it, prince; and if my form lie there, Then I am yours . . ii 7 61
And fancy dies In the cradle where it lies . . . . . iii 2 69
For never shall you lie by Portia's side With an unquiet soul . . iii 2 307
Speak of frays Like a fine bragging youth, and tell quaint lies . . iii 4 69
And twenty of these puny lies I'll tell . . . . . iii 4 74
And the offender's life lies in the mercy Of the duke only . . . iv 1 355
You swore to me, when I did give it you, That you would wear it till your hour of death And that it should lie with you in your grave . v 1 154
If I could add a lie unto a fault, I would deny it . . . . v 1 186
Lie not a night from home; watch me like Argus . . . . v 1 230
The doctor's clerk In lieu of this last night did lie with me . . v 1 262
You shall be my bedfellow: When I am absent, then lie with my wife . v 1 285
And, as much as in him lies, mines my gentility . . *As Y. Like It* i 1 21
Yonder they lie; the poor old man, their father, making such pitiful dole over them . . . . i 2 138
Where is this young gallant that is so desirous to lie with his mother earth? . . . . i 2 213
And—in my heart Lie there what hidden woman's fear there will . . i 3 121
This night he means To burn the lodging where you use to lie . . ii 3 23
Under the greenwood tree Who loves to lie with me . . . . ii 5 2
O, I die for food! Here lie I down, and measure out my grave . . ii 6 2
In the which women still give the lie to their consciences . . . iii 2 410
O, for shame, for shame, Lie not, to say mine eyes are murderers! . iii 5 19
But these are all lies: men have died from time to time and worms have eaten them, but not for love . . . . iv 1 107
With a hey, and a ho, and a hey nonino, These pretty country folks would lie . . . . v 3 25
Upon a lie seven times removed . . . . v 4 71
So to the Lie Circumstantial and the Lie Direct . . . . . v 4 85
I durst go no further than the Lie Circumstantial, nor he durst not give me the Lie Direct . . . . v 4 89
Can you nominate in order now the degrees of the lie? . . . . v 4 93
The sixth, the Lie with Circumstance; the seventh, the Lie Direct. All these you may avoid but the Lie Direct . . . . v 4 100

Lie. O monstrous beast! how like a swine he lies . . *T. of Shrew* Ind. 1 34
They call me Katharine that do talk of me.—You lie, in faith . . ii 1 186
Best beware my sting.—My remedy is then, to pluck it out.—Ay, if the fool could find it where it lies . . . . ii 1 213
The door is open, sir; there lies your way; You may be jogging . . iii 2 212
The note lies in's throat, if he say I said so . . . . . iv 3 133
Then at my lodging, an it like you: There doth my father lie . . iv 4 56
I know it is the moon.—Nay, then you lie: it is the blessed sun . . iv 5 17
Our remedies oft in ourselves do lie, Which we ascribe to heaven *All's W.* i 1 231
His good remembrance, sir, Lies richer in your thoughts than on his tomb i 2 49
One that lies three thirds . . . . ii 5 31
Look, here comes a pilgrim: I know she will lie at my house . . iii 5 34
Return with an invention and clap upon you two or three probable lies iii 6 107
Here he comes, to beguile two hours in a sleep, and then to return and swear the lies he forges . . . . iv 1 26
He had sworn to marry me When his wife's dead; therefore I'll lie with him When I am buried . . . . iv 2 72
He will lie, sir, with such volubility, that you would think truth were a fool . . . . iv 3 283
It lies in you, my lord, to bring me in some grace, for you did bring me out v 2 49
For justice: grant it me, O king! in you it best lies . . . v 3 146
Fairer prove your honour Than in my thought it lies . . . . v 3 184
Will you hoist sail, sir? here lies your way.—No, good swabber *T. Night* i 5 215
Where lies your text?—In Orsino's bosom.—In his bosom! . . . i 5 240
There it lies in your eye; if not, be it his that finds it . . . ii 2 16
In delay there lies no plenty; Then come kiss me, sweet and twenty . ii 3 51
Thou mayst say, the king lies by a beggar, if a beggar dwell near him . iii 1 8
There lies your way, due west.—Then westward-ho! . . . . iii 1 145
And as many lies as will lie in thy sheet of paper . . . . iii 2 49
I'll bring you to a captain in this town, Where lie my maiden weeds . v 1 262
It is; you lie, you lie: I say thou liest, Camillo, and I hate thee *W. Tale* i 2 299
If therefore you dare trust my honesty, That lies enclosed in this trunk i 2 435
Once a day I'll visit The chapel where they lie . . . . . iii 2 240
Speed thee well! There lie, and there thy character . . . . iii 3 47
While we lie tumbling in the hay . . . . iv 3 12
And married a tinker's wife within a mile where my land and living lies iv 3 105
What, like a corse?—No, like a bank for love to lie and play on . . iv 4 130
Why should I carry lies abroad? . . . . iv 4 274
Lies he not bed-rid? . . . . iv 4 412
To die upon the bed my father died, To lie close by his honest bones . iv 4 467
I think you know my fortunes Do all lie there . . . . . iv 4 602
I see the play so lies That I must bear a part . . . . . iv 4 669
We are but plain fellows, sir.—A lie; you are rough and hairy . . iv 4 744
Let me have no lying: it becomes none but tradesmen, and they often give us soldiers the lie . . . . iv 4 746
They do not give us the lie.—Your worship had like to have given us one iv 4 749
There lies such secrets in this fardel and box, which none must know . iv 4 783
Give me the lie, do, and try whether I am not now a gentleman born . v 2 144
Which fault lies on the hazards of all husbands That marry wives *K. John* i 1 119
Who says it was, he lies; I say 'twas not . . . . . . i 1 276
It lies as sightly on the back of him As great Alcides' shows upon an ass ii 1 143
Whose sons lie scattered on the bleeding ground; Many a widow's husband grovelling lies, Coldly embracing the discolour'd earth . . ii 1 304
And she a fair divided excellence, Whose fulness of perfection lies in him ii 1 440
Lady, with me, with me thy fortune lies . . . . . . iii 1 337
Austria's head lie there, While Philip breathes . . . . . iii 2 3
And wheresoe'er this foot of mine doth tread, He lies before me . . iii 3 63
Lies in his bed, walks up and down with me, Puts on his pretty looks . iii 4 94
Saying, 'What lack you?' and 'Where lies your grief?' . . . iv 1 48
This is the prison. What is he lies here? . . . . . . iv 3 34
Whose tongue soe'er speaks false, Not truly speaks; who speaks not truly, lies . . . . iv 3 92
To lie like pawns lock'd up in chests and trunks . . . . . v 2 141
England never did, nor never shall, Lie at the proud foot of a conqueror v 7 113
By all my hopes, most falsely doth he lie. . . . . *Richard II.* i 1 68
Now swallow down that lie . . . . i 1 132
How long a time lies in one little word! . . . . i 3 213
What thy soul holds dear, imagine it To lie that way thou go'st . . i 3 287
Where lies he?—At Ely House . . . . i 4 57
Their love Lies in their purses . . . . ii 2 130
If judgement lie in them, then so do we . . . . ii 2 133
The king is left behind, And in my loyal bosom lies his power . . ii 3 98
And heavy-gaited toads lie in their way . . . . iii 2 15
How far off lies your power?—Nor near nor farther off, my gracious lord, Than this weak arm . . . . iii 2 63
Have felt the worst of death's destroying wound And lie full low . . iii 2 140
Say, Scroop, where lies our uncle with his power? Speak sweetly, man iii 2 192
King Richard lies Within the limits of yon lime and stone . . . iii 3 25
There lies Two kinsmen digg'd their graves with weeping eyes . . iii 3 168
And spur thee on with full as many lies As may be holloa'd in thy treacherous ear From sun to sun . . . . iv 1 53
That lie shall lie so heavy on my sword, That it shall render vengeance and revenge Till thou the lie-giver and that lie do lie In earth as quiet as thy father's skull . . . . iv 1 66
And spit upon him, whilst I say he lies, And lies, and lies . . . iv 1 75
Some honest Christian trust me with a gage, That Norfolk lies . . iv 1 84
Long mayst thou live in Richard's seat to sit, And soon lie Richard in an earthy pit! God save King Harry! . . . . iv 1 219
'Tis very true, my grief lies all within . . . . . . iv 1 295
There lies the substance: and I thank thee, king, For thy great bounty iv 1 299
My shamed life in his dishonour lies . . . . v 3 71
Herein all breathless lies The mightiest of thy greatest enemies . . v 6 31
Gadshill lies to-night in Rochester . . . . . . *1 Hen. IV.* i 2 143
The virtue of this jest will be, the incomprehensible lies that this same fat rogue will tell us when we meet . . . . i 2 209
And in the reproof of this lies the jest . . . . . . i 2 213
And yet, 'zounds, I lie; for they pray continually to their saint . . ii 1 88
'Tis going to the king's exchequer.—You lie, ye rogue . . . ii 2 58
I say unto you again, you are a shallow cowardly hind, and you lie . ii 3 17
If I tell thee a lie, spit in my face, call me horse . . . . ii 4 214
These lies are like their father that begets them; gross as a mountain . ii 4 249
Here lies the point; why, being son to me, art thou so pointed at? . ii 4 448
The tithe of a hair was never lost in my house before.—Ye lie, hostess . iii 3 68
Percy stands on high; And either we or they must lower lie . . . iii 3 228
Some strait decrees That lie too heavy on the commonwealth . . iv 3 80
All's done, all's won; here breathless lies the king . . . . v 3 16
Where stain'd nobility lies trodden on, And rebels' arms triumph . . v 4 13
Come, cousin Westmoreland, Our duty this way lies . . . . v 4 16
The earthy and cold hand of death Lies on my tongue . . . . v 4 85
Embowell'd will I see thee by and by: Till then in blood by noble Percy lie v 4 110

Lie. Counterfeit? I lie, I am no counterfeit: to die, is to be a counterfeit . . 1 *Hen. IV.* v 4 115
If a lie may do thee grace, I'll gild it with the happiest terms I have . v 4 161
Hotspur's father, old Northumberland, Lies crafty-sick 2 *Hen. IV.* Ind. 37
Tell thou an earl his divination lies, And I will take it as a sweet disgrace i 1 88
You lie in your throat, if you say I am any other than an honest man . i 2 97
Give me some sack: and, sweetheart, lie thou there . . . ii 4 197
Uneasy lies the head that wears a crown . . . . . iii 1 31
Every third word a lie, duer paid to the hearer than the Turk's tribute iii 2 330
Lo! within a ken our army lies, Upon mine honour, all too confident . iv 1 151
I trust, lords, we shall lie to-night together . . . . iv 2 97
Why doth the crown lie there upon his pillow, Being so troublesome? . iv 5 21
By his gates of breath There lies a downy feather which stirs not . . iv 5 32
Bear me to that chamber; there I'll lie; In that Jerusalem shall Harry die iv 5 240
O, it is much that a lie with a slight oath and a jest with a sad brow will do! . . . . v 1 91
My father is gone wild into his grave, For in his tomb lie my affections . v 2 124
I speak the truth: When Pistol lies, do this . . . . . v 3 124
A man or two lately killed about her.—Nut-hook, nut-hook, you lie . v 4 8
But this lies all within the will of God, To whom I do appeal *Hen. V.* i 2 289
And silken dalliance in the wardrobe lies . . . . . ii Prol. 2
The English lie within fifteen hundred paces of your tents . . iii 7 135
This lodging likes me better, Since I may say 'Now lie I like a king' . iv 1 17
These fields, where, wretches, their poor bodies Must lie and fester . iv 3 88
In which array, brave soldier, doth he lie, Larding the plain . . iv 6 7
Yoke-fellow to his honour-owing wounds, The noble Earl of Suffolk also lies . . . . iv 6 10
I am no traitor.—That's a lie in thy throat . . . . . iv 8 17
All her husbandry doth lie on heaps, Corrupting in it own fertility . v 2 39
The peace, Which you before so urged, lies in his answer . . . v 2 76
At pleasure here we lie near Orleans . . . . 1 *Hen. VI.* i 2 6
Vouchsafe To visit her poor castle where she lies . . . . ii 2 41
To Paris to the king, For there young Henry with his nobles lie . . iii 2 129
York lies; he might have sent and had the horse . . . . iv 4 33
Shall all thy mother's hopes lie in one tomb? . . . . . iv 5 34
He lies inhearsed in the arms Of the most bloody nurser of his harms! . iv 7 45
Him that thou magnifiest with all these titles Stinking and fly-blown lies here at our feet . . . . iv 7 76
There all is marr'd; there lies a cooling card . . . . v 3 83
Sharp Buckingham unburthens with his tongue The envious load that lies upon his heart . . . . . 2 *Hen. VI.* iii 1 157
There let his head and lifeless body lie, Until the queen his mistress bury it . . . . iv 1 142
Here may his head lie on my throbbing breast . . . . . iv 4 5
So, lie thou there . . . . v 2 66
I am resolved That Clifford's manhood lies upon his tongue . 3 *Hen. VI.* ii 2 125
To tell thee plain, I aim to lie with thee.—To tell you plain, I had rather lie in prison . . . . iii 2 69
In them and in ourselves our safety lies . . . . . . iv 1 46
He hath made a solemn vow Never to lie and take his natural rest . . iv 3 5
This way, my lord; for this way lies the game . . . . . iv 5 14
Here Southam lies: The drum your honour hears marcheth from Warwick v 1 12
So, lie thou there: die thou, and die our fear . . . . . v 2 1
I will deliver you, or else lie for you . . . . *Richard III.* i 1 115
With lies well steel'd with weighty arguments . . . . . i 1 148
Ill rest betide the chamber where thou liest!—So will it, madam, till I lie with you.—I hope so . . . . i 2 113
He cannot lie with his neighbour's wife, but it [conscience] detects him i 4 140
I to my grave, where peace and rest lie with me! . . . . iv 1 95
This foul swine Lies now even in the centre of this isle . . . v 2 11
Here will I lie to-night; But where to-morrow? Well, all's one for that v 3 7
His regiment lies half a mile at least South from the mighty power . v 3 37
I am a villain: yet I lie, I am not. Fool, of thyself speak well . . v 3 191
Shall these enjoy our lands? lie with our wives? Ravish our daughters? v 3 336
Gentlemen, The penance lies on you, if these fair ladies Pass away frowning.—For my little cure, Let me alone . . *Hen. VIII.* i 4 32
All men's honours Lie like one lump before him . . . . . ii 2 49
Therefore in him It lies to cure me . . . . ii 4 101
A spleeny Lutheran; and not wholesome to Our cause, that she should lie i' the bosom of Our hard-ruled king . . . . . . iii 2 100
I dare avow, And now I should not lie . . . . . . iv 2 143
And here ye lie baiting of bombards, when Ye should do service . . v 4 85
In Troy, there lies the scene . . . . *Troi. and Cres.* Prol. 1
Her bed is India; there she lies, a pearl . . . . . . i 1 103
You are such a woman! one knows not at what ward you lie . . . i 2 283
And at all these wards I lie, at a thousand watches . . . . i 2 288
Women are angels, wooing: Things won are done; joy's soul lies in the doing . . . . i 2 313
In the reproof of chance Lies the true proof of men . . . . i 3 34
Grows dainty of his worth and in his tent Lies mocking our designs . i 3 146
Like a strutting player, whose conceit Lies in his hamstring . . . i 3 154
A great deal of your wit, too, lies in your sinews . . . . ii 1 109
But let him, like an engine Not portable, lie under this report . . ii 3 144
I love you now; but not, till now, so much But I might master it: in faith, I lie; My thoughts were like unbridled children . . . iii 2 129
Or, like a gallant horse fall'n in first rank, Lie there for pavement to the abject rear . . . . iii 3 162
It lies as coldly in him as fire in a flint . . . . . . iii 3 256
Had I so good occasion to lie long As you . . . . . . iv 1 3
Here lies our way . . . . iv 1 79
The glory of our Troy doth this day lie On his fair worth . . . iv 4 149
My major vow lies here, this I'll obey . . . . . . v 1 49
Thy master now lies thinking in his bed Of thee and me . . . v 2 78
If I tell how these two did co-act, Shall I not lie in publishing a truth? v 2 119
Now, Troy, sink down! Here lies thy heart, thy sinews, and thy bone v 8 12
They lie in view; but have not spoke as yet . . . *Coriolanus* i 4 4
How far off lie these armies?—Within this mile and half . . . i 4 8
How lies their battle? know you on which side They have placed their men of trust? . . . . i 6 51
As if I loved my little should be dieted In praises sauced with lies . i 9 53
Yet they lie deadly that tell you you have good faces . . . . ii 1 67
Death, that dark spirit, in's nervy arm doth lie . . . . . ii 1 177
That, giving itself the lie, would pluck reproof and rebuke from every ear ii 2 37
Why force you this?—Because that now it lies you on to speak . . iii 2 52
Must I with base tongue give my noble heart A lie that it must bear? . iii 2 101
He has, As much as in him lies, from time to time Envied . . . iii 3 94
Direct me, if it be your will, Where great Aufidius lies . . . iv 4 8
And with the deepest malice of the war Destroy what lies before 'em . iv 6 42
Would half my wealth Would buy this for a lie! . . . . . iv 6 161
So our virtues Lie in the interpretation of the time . . . . iv 7 50

Lie. If you had told as many lies in his behalf as you have uttered words in your own, you should not pass here; no, though it were as virtuous to lie as to live chastely . . . . *Coriolanus* v 2 25
My remission lies In Volscian breasts . . . . v 2 90
At a few drops of women's rheum, which are As cheap as lies . . v 6 47
Your judgements, my grave lords, Must give this cur the lie . . v 6 107
Shall join To thrust the lie unto him . . . . v 6 110
There lie thy bones, sweet Mutius, with thy friends . . *T. Andron.* i 1 387
The snake lies rolled in the cheerful sun . . . . . . ii 3 13
You lie.—Draw, if you be men . . . . . *Rom. and Jul.* i 1 68
An she agree, within her scope of choice Lies my consent . . . i 2 19
What obscured in this fair volume lies Find written in the margent of his eyes . . . . i 3 85
Dreamers often lie.—In bed asleep, while they do dream things true . i 4 51
This is the hag, when maids lie on their backs, That presses them . i 4 92
When good manners shall lie all in one or two men's hands and they unwashed too, 'tis a foul thing . . . . i 5 4
Now old desire doth in his death-bed lie . . . . . . ii Prol. 1
By her fine foot, straight leg and quivering thigh And the demesnes that there adjacent lie . . . . ii 1 20
Alack, there lies more peril in thine eye Than twenty of their swords . ii 2 71
Else would I tear the cave where Echo lies . . . . . ii 2 162
O, mickle is the powerful grace that lies In herbs, plants, stones . . ii 3 15
And where care lodges, sleep will never lie . . . . . . ii 3 36
Both our remedies Within thy help and holy physic lies . . . ii 3 52
Young men's love then lies Not truly in their hearts, but in their eyes ii 3 67
There lies the man, slain by young Romeo, That slew thy kinsman . iii 1 149
My blood for your rude brawls doth lie a-bleeding . . . . iii 1 194
Thou wilt lie upon the wings of night Whiter than new snow on a raven's back . . . . iii 2 18
Even so lies she, Blubbering and weeping, weeping and blubbering . iii 3 86
Make the bridal bed In that dim monument where Tybalt lies . . iii 5 203
To-morrow night look that thou lie alone; Let not thy nurse lie with thee . . . . iv 1 91
That same ancient vault Where all the kindred of the Capulets lie . iv 1 112
No, no: this shall forbid it: lie thou there . . . . . iv 3 23
Death lies on her like an untimely frost Upon the sweetest flower . iv 5 28
There she lies, Flower as she was, deflowered by him. Death is my son-in-law, Death is my heir . . . . iv 5 36
Well, Juliet, I will lie with thee to-night. Let's see for means . . v 1 34
Here lies Juliet, and her beauty makes This vault a feasting presence full of light. Death, lie thou there, by a dead man interr'd . . v 3 85
What mean these masterless and gory swords To lie discolour'd by this place of peace? . . . . v 3 143
Here lies the county slain; And Juliet bleeding, warm, and newly dead . . . . v 3 174; 195
We see the ground whereon these woes do lie; But the true ground of all these piteous woes We cannot without circumstance descry . . v 3 179
And therewithal Came to this vault to die, and lie with Juliet . . v 3 290
As rich shall Romeo's by his lady's lie; Poor sacrifices of our enmity! . v 3 303
Philosopher!—Thou liest.—Art not one?—Yes.—Then I lie not *T. of A.* i 1 225
All the lands thou hast Lie in a pitch'd field . . . . . i 2 231
Did you see my cap?—Here 'tis.—Here lies my gown . . . . iii 6 127
Lie where the light foam of the sea may beat Thy grave-stone daily . iv 3 379
Whose blush doth thaw the consecrated snow That lies on Dian's lap! . iv 3 387
On special dignities, which vacant lie For thy best use and wearing . v 1 145
Here lies a wretched corse, of wretched soul bereft: Seek not my name v 4 70
Here lie I, Timon; who, alive, all living men did hate . . . v 4 72
I am sure, It did not lie there when I went to bed . . *J. Cæsar* ii 1 38
Here lies the east: doth not the day break here?—No.—O, pardon, sir, it doth . . . . ii 1 101
Say he is sick.—Shall Cæsar send a lie? . . . . . . ii 2 65
And he resolved How Cæsar hath deserved to lie in death . . . iii 1 132
O mighty Cæsar! dost thou lie so low? . . . . iii 1 148
How like a deer, strucken by many princes, Dost thou here lie! . . iii 1 210
He lies to-night within seven leagues of Rome . . . . . iii 1 286
Now lies he there, And none so poor to do him reverence . . . iii 2 124
I pray you, sirs, lie in my tent and sleep . . . . . . iv 3 246
Their shadows seem A canopy most fatal, under which Our army lies . v 1 89
Is not that he that lies upon the ground?—He lies not like the living . v 3 57
Where, where, Messala, doth his body lie?—Lo, yonder . . . v 3 91
Within my tent his bones to-night shall lie, Most like a soldier . . v 5 78
That is a step On which I must fall down, or else o'erleap, For in my way it lies . . . . *Macbeth* i 4 50
When in swinish sleep Their drenched natures lie as in a death . . i 7 68
A heavy summons lies like lead upon me, And yet I would not sleep . ii 1 6
Hark! Who lies i' the second chamber?—Donalbain . . . . ii 2 20
Why did you bring these daggers from the place? They must lie there . ii 2 49
Was it so late, friend, ere you went to bed, That you do lie so late? . ii 3 25
Equivocates him in a sleep, and, giving him the lie, leaves him . . ii 3 40
Drink gave thee the lie last night.—That it did, sir, i' the very throat on me: but I requited him for his lie . . . . ii 3 41
Better be with the dead, Whom we, to gain our peace, have sent to peace, Than on the torture of the mind to lie In restless ecstasy . . iii 2 21
There the grown serpent lies . . . . iii 4 29
That I may tell pale-hearted fear it lies, And sleep in spite of thunder . iv 1 85
What is a traitor?—Why, one that swears and lies . . . . iv 2 47
And must they all be hanged that swear and lie?—Every one . . iv 2 52
Here let them lie Till famine and the ague eat them up . . . v 5 3
And begin To doubt the equivocation of the fiend That lies like truth . v 5 44
Thou liest, abhorred tyrant; with my sword I'll prove the lie thou speak'st . . . . v 7 11
Be wary then; best safety lies in fear . . . . . . *Hamlet* i 3 43
Whether aught, to us unknown, afflicts him thus, That, open'd, lies within our remedy . . . . ii 2 18
His antique sword, Rebellious to his arm, lies where it falls . . ii 2 492
Tweaks me by the nose? gives me the lie i' the throat, As deep as to the lungs? . . . . ii 2 601
Shall I lie in your lap?—No, my lord.—I mean, my head upon your lap? iii 2 119
That's a fair thought to lie between maids' legs . . . . . iii 2 125
There is no shuffling, there the action lies In his true nature . . iii 3 61
For here lies the point: if I drown myself wittingly, it argues an act . v 1 10
Here lies the water; good: here stands the man; good . . . . v 1 16
The very conveyances of his lands will hardly lie in this box . . v 1 120
I think it be thine, indeed; for thou liest in't.—You lie out on't, sir, and therefore it is not yours: for my part, I do not lie in't, and yet it is mine.—Thou dost lie in't, to be in't and say it is thine . . v 1 133
'Tis for the dead, not for the quick; therefore thou liest.—'Tis a quick lie, sir . . . . v 1 139
How long will a man lie i' the earth ere he rot? . . . . . v 1 178

Lie. Lo, here I lie, Never to rise again . . . . . *Hamlet* v 2 329
Keep a schoolmaster that can teach thy fool to lie: I would fain learn to lie.—An you lie, sirrah, we'll have you whipped . . . . *Lear* i 4 196
O, that way madness lies; let me shun that; No more of that . . iii 4 21
Lie here and rest awhile.—Make no noise, make no noise; draw the curtains . . . . . iii 6 87
They told me I was every thing; 'tis a lie, I am not ague-proof . iv 6 107
Mean you to enjoy him?—The let-alone lies not in your good will . v 3 79
What in the world he is That names me traitor, villain-like he lies . v 3 98
With the hell-hated lie o'erwhelm thy heart . . . . . v 3 147
The power and corrigible authority of this lies in our wills . *Othello* i 3 330
Bragging and telling her fantastical lies . . . . . ii 1 226
Do you know, sirrah, where Lieutenant Cassio lies?—I dare not say he lies any where.—Why, man?—He's a soldier, and for one to say a soldier lies, is stabbing . . . . . iii 4 2
Where lodges he?—To tell you where he lodges, is to tell you where I lie iii 4 9
For me to devise a lodging and say he lies here or he lies there, were to lie in mine own throat . . . . . iii 4 12
Lie with her! lie on her! We say lie on her, when they belie her . iv 1 35
There's millions now alive That nightly lie in those unproper beds . iv 1 69
She might lie by an emperor's side and command him tasks . . iv 1 195
He lies to the heart: She was too fond of her most filthy bargain . . v 2 156
You told a lie; an odious, damned lie; Upon my soul, a lie, a wicked lie v 2 180
There lies your niece, Whose breath, indeed, these hands have newly stopp'd . . . . . v 2 201
'Tis thus; Who tells me true, though in his tale lie death, I hear him as he flatter'd . . . . . *Ant. and Cleo.* i 2 102
Where lies he?—About the mount Misenum . . . . ii 2 162
She did lie In her pavilion—cloth-of-gold of tissue . . . ii 2 203
I' the east my pleasure lies . . . . . ii 3 40
Should I lie, madam?—O, I would thou didst! . . . ii 5 93
Lie they upon thy hand, And be undone by 'em! . . . ii 5 105
He's walking in the garden—thus; and spurns The rush that lies before him . . . . . iii 5 18
Our fortune lies Upon this jump . . . . . iii 8 5
That noble countenance, Wherein the worship of the whole world lies . iv 14 86
You lie, up to the hearing of the gods . . . . . v 2 95
A very honest woman, but something given to lie; as a woman should not do, but in the way of honesty . . . . . v 2 253
Now boast thee, death, in thy possession lies A lass unparallel'd . . v 2 318
His steeds to water at those springs On chaliced flowers that lies *Cymb.* ii 3 24
Under her breast—Worthy the pressing—lies a mole . . . ii 4 135
I'll be sworn— No swearing. If you will swear you have not done't, you lie . . . . . ii 4 144
What is it to be false? To lie in watch there and to think on him? . iii 4 43
Will poor folks lie, That have afflictions on them? . . . iii 6 9
To lapse in fulness Is sorer than to lie for need . . . iii 6 13
What lies I have heard! Our courtiers say all's savage but at court . iv 2 32
Those rich-left heirs that let their fathers lie Without a monument! . iv 2 226
For notes of sorrow out of tune are worse Than priests and fanes that lie iv 2 242
If I do lie and do No harm by it, though the gods hear, I hope They'll pardon it . . . . . iv 2 377
That is my bed too, lads, and there I'll lie . . . . iv 4 52
That kill'd thy daughter:—villain-like, I lie—That caused a lesser villain v 5 218
Shall's have a play of this? Thou scornful page, There lie thy part . v 5 229
Traitor, thou liest.—Traitor!—Ay, traitor.—Even in his throat—unless it be the king—That calls me traitor, I return the lie . *Pericles* ii 5 57
The wind is loud, and will not lie till the ship be cleared of the dead . iii 1 49
Most wretched queen!—Here she lies, sir . . . . . iii 1 56
Could I rage and roar As doth the sea she lies in, yet the end Must be as 'tis . . . . . iii 3 11
The fairest, sweet'st, and best lies here, Who wither'd in her spring of year iv 4 34
Amongst honest women.—'Faith, my acquaintance lies little amongst them iv 6 206
I am the governor of this place you lie before . . . . v 1 21
If I should tell my history, it would seem Like lies disdain'd . . v 1 120
Lie along. When he lies along, After your way his tale pronounced shall bury His reasons with his body . . . *Coriolanus* v 6 57
That now on Pompey's basis lies along No worthier than the dust! *J. C.* iii 1 115
Lie asleep. Athwart men's noses as they lie asleep . . *Rom. and Jul.* i 4 58
Tickling a parson's nose as a' lies asleep . . . . . i 4 80
I will find him when he lies asleep, And in his ear I'll holla . 1 *Hen. IV.* i 3 221
Lie bleeding. The testimonies whereof lie bleeding in me . *Cymbeline* iii 4 23
Lie buried. And she lies buried with her ancestors . . . *Much Ado* v 1 69
Where the carcases of many a tall ship lie buried . . *Mer. of Venice* iii 1 6
If I begin the battery once again, I will not leave the half-achieved Harfleur Till in her ashes she lie buried . . . . *Hen. V.* iii 3 9
Lie dead. If I talk to him, with his innocent prate He will awake my mercy which lies dead . . . . . *K. John* iv 1 26
And nobles bearing banners, there lie dead One hundred twenty sir *Hen. V.* iv 8 87
The names of those their nobles that lie dead . . . . iv 8 96
Thy husband in thy bosom there lies dead . . . *Rom. and Jul.* v 3 155
Minion, your dear lies dead, And your unblest fate hies . . *Othello* v 1 33
Lie down; lay thine ear close to the ground and list . . 1 *Hen IV.* ii 2 33
Then happy low, lie down! Uneasy lies the head that wears a crown 2 *Hen. IV.* iii 1 30
We will stand and watch your pleasure.—I will not have it so: lie down *J. Cæsar* iv 3 250
Will you lie down and rest upon the cushions? . . . *Lear* iii 6 36
Since the torch is out, Lie down, and stray no farther . *Ant. and Cleo.* iv 14 47
'Faith, I'll lie down and sleep. But, soft! no bedfellow! . *Cymbeline* iv 2 294
Lie drown'd and soak'd in mercenary blood . . . *Hen. V.* iv 7 79
When I do tell thee, there my hopes lie drown'd, Reply not in how many fathoms deep They lie indrench'd . . . . *Troi. and Cres.* i 1 49
Lie drowning. Would thou mightst lie drowning! . . . *Tempest* i 1 60
Lie dull. O sleep, thou ape of death, lie dull upon her! . . *Cymbeline* ii 2 31
Lie embrewed. Lies embrewed here, All on a heap . . *T. Andron.* ii 3 222
Lie forfeited. There without ransom to lie forfeited . 1 *Hen. IV.* iv 3 96
Lie foul. The approaching tide Will shortly fill the reasonable shore That now lies foul and muddy . . . . . *Tempest* v 1 82
The gimmal bit Lies foul with chew'd grass . . . . *Hen. V.* iv 2 50
Lie gently. It may lie gently at the foot of peace . . *K. John* v 2 76
So may he rest; his faults lie gently on him! . . . *Hen. VIII.* iv 2 31
Lie-giver. Till thou the lie-giver and that lie do lie In earth as quiet as thy father's skull . . . . . *Richard II.* iv 1 68
Lie glowing. This lies glowing, I can tell you . . . *Coriolanus* iv 3 26
Lie graveless. My brave Egyptians all, By the discandying of this pelleted storm, Lie graveless . . . . *Ant. and Cleo.* iii 13 166
Lie heavy. This fever, that hath troubled me so long, Lies heavy on me *K. John* v 3 4
Lie heavy. It would unclog my heart Of what lies heavy to't *Coriolanus* iv 2 48
Griefs of mine own lie heavy in my breast . . . *Rom. and Jul.* i 1 192
It pleases time and fortune to lie heavy Upon a friend of mine *T. of A.* iii 5 10
Lie hid. Yet in this life Lie hid moe thousand deaths *Meas. for Meas.* iii 1 40
Lie in. Come, you must go visit the good lady that lies in . *Coriolanus* i 3 86
Lie intreasured. Which in their seeds And weak beginnings lie intreasured . . . . . 2 *Hen. IV.* iii 1 85
Lie lame. When service should in my old limbs lie lame *As Y. Like It* ii 3 41
Lie level. And every thing lies level to our wish . . 2 *Hen. IV.* iv 4 7
Lie low. If he could right himself with quarreling, Some of us would lie low . . . . . *Much Ado* v 1 52
Lie mudded. I'll seek him deeper than e'er plummet sounded And with him there lie mudded . . . . . *Tempest* iii 3 102
Lie murdered. Poor Bassianus here lies murdered . . *T. Andron.* ii 3 263
My mistress here lies murder'd in her bed . . . *Othello* v 2 185
Lie open. If money go before, all ways do lie open . . *Mer. Wives* ii 2 175
Prove them, and I lie open to the law . . . 2 *Hen. VI.* i 3 159
His faults lie open to the laws; let them, Not you, correct him *Hen. VIII.* iii 2 334
Lie pavilion'd in the fields of France . . . . . *Hen. V.* i 2 129
Lie rich. Love-thoughts lie rich when canopied with bowers *T. Night* i 1 41
What hath mass or matter, by itself Lies rich in virtue . *Troi. and Cres.* i 3 30
Lie slain. This note doth tell me of ten thousand French That in the field lie slain . . . . . *Hen. V.* iv 8 86
He that lies slain here, Cassio, Was my dear friend . . *Othello* v 1 101
A very valiant Briton . . . , That here by mountaineers lies slain *Cymb.* iv 2 370
Lie soft. Thy flatterers yet wear silk, drink wine, lie soft *T. of Athens* iv 3 206
Lie speechless. His fortunes all lie speechless . . . *Cymbeline* i 5 52
Lie stark. Many a nobleman lies stark and stiff . . . 1 *Hen. IV.* v 3 42
Lie starkly. As fast lock'd up in sleep as guiltless labour When it lies starkly in the traveller's bones . . . *Meas. for Meas.* iv 2 70
Lie still, ye thief, and hear the lady sing in Welsh . . 1 *Hen. IV.* iii 1 238
Then we bring forth weeds, When our quick minds lie still *Ant. and Cleo.* i 2 114
Dost thou lie still? If thus thou vanishest, thou tell'st the world It is not worth leave-taking . . . . . v 2 299
If she be up, I'll speak with her; if not, Let her lie still and dream *Cymbeline* ii 3 70
Lie straight. Do not think I have wit enough to lie straight in my bed *T. Night* ii 3 147
Lie unswept. The dust on antique time would lie unswept . *Coriolanus* ii 3 126
Lied. Didst thou not say he lied?—Thou liest.—Do I so? . *Tempest* iii 2 82
Lysander riddles very prettily: Now much beshrew my manners and my pride, If Hermia meant to say Lysander lied . *M. N. Dream* ii 2 55
I had lied in my throat, if I had said so . . . 2 *Hen. IV.* i 2 94
Lief. I had as lief you would tell me of a mess of porridge *Mer. Wives* iii 1 63
I had as lief bear so much lead . . . . . iv 2 117
I had as lief be a list of an English kersey . . . *Meas. for Meas.* i 2 34
I had as lief have the foppery of freedom as the morality of imprisonment . . . . . i 2 137
I had as lief have heard the night-raven . . . *Much Ado* ii 3 84
I had as lief thou didst break his neck as his finger . *As Y. Like It* i 1 152
I had as lief have been myself alone . . . . . iii 2 269
I had as lief be wooed of a snail . . . . . iv 1 52
I had as lief take her dowry with this condition, to be whipped at the high cross every morning . . . . *T. of Shrew* i 1 135
Policy I hate: I had as lief be a Brownist as a politician . *T. Night* iii 2 33
God knows I had as lief be none as one . . . *Richard II.* v 2 49
I had as lief they would put ratsbane in my mouth . 2 *Hen. IV.* i 2 47
I had as lief be hanged, sir, as go . . . . . iii 2 238
I had as lief have my mistress a jade . . . . *Hen. V.* iii 7 63
Too flaming a praise for a good complexion. I had as lief Helen's golden tongue had commended Troilus for a copper nose *Tr. and Cr.* i 2 114
She, good soul, had as lief see a toad, a very toad, as see him *R. and J.* ii 4 215
I had as lief not be as live to be In awe of such a thing as I myself *J. C.* i 2 95
I had as lief the town-crier spoke my lines . . . *Hamlet* iii 2 4
I had as lief have a reed that will do me no service as a partisan I could not heave . . . . . *Ant. and Cleo.* ii 7 13
Liefest. Stirr'd up My liefest liege to be mine enemy . 2 *Hen. VI.* iii 1 164
Liege. Sir, my liege, Do not infest your mind with beating . *Tempest* v 1 245
Gentle my liege,— You do but lose your labour . *Meas. for Meas.* v 1 433
My liege, I am advised what I say . . . *Com. of Errors* v 1 214
'Tis true, my liege; this ring I had of her . . . . v 1 277
As sure, my liege, as I do see your grace . . . . v 1 279
My liege, your highness now may do me good . . . *Much Ado* i 1 292
So much, dear liege, I have already sworn . . . *L. L. Lost* i 1 34
Let me say no, my liege, an if you please . . . . i 1 50
This article, my liege, yourself must break . . . . i 1 134
Liege of all loiterers and malcontents, Dread prince of plackets . . iii 1 185
Where lies thy pain? And where my liege's? all about the breast . iv 3 173
My royal liege, He is not guilty of her coming hither . . *W. Tale* ii 3 143
My gracious sovereign, my most loving liege! . . . *Richard II.* i 1 21
And let him be no kinsman to my liege, I do defy him . . . i 1 59
For that my sovereign liege was in my debt . . . . i 1 129
Most mighty liege, and my companion peers . . . . i 3 93
My liege, old Gaunt commends him to your majesty . . . ii 1 147
O my liege, Pardon me, if you please . . . . . ii 1 186
Comfort, my liege; remember who you are.—I had forgot myself . . iii 2 82
More health and happiness betide my liege Than can my care-tuned tongue deliver him! . . . . . iii 2 91
Sweet York, be patient. Hear me, gentle liege . . . . v 3 91
Thus, my most royal liege, Accusing it, I put it on my head 2 *Hen. IV.* iv 5 165
That misbecame my place, My person, or my liege's sovereignty . . v 2 101
My thrice-puissant liege Is in the very May-morn of his youth *Hen. V.* i 2 119
My good liege, she is so idly king'd . . . That fear attends her not . ii 4 26
Yes, if it please your majesty, my liege . . . 1 *Hen. VI.* iii 4 15
Pardon, my liege, that I have stay'd so long . . 2 *Hen. VI.* ii 1 94
Stirr'd up My liefest liege to be mine enemy . . . . iii 1 164
An enemy to the flock, . . . As Humphrey, proved by reasons, to my liege . . . . . iii 1 260
I'll provide his executioner, I tender so the safety of my liege . . iii 1 277
A messenger from Henry, our dread liege . . . . . v 1 17
May Iden live to merit such a bounty, And never live but true unto his liege! . . . . . v 1 82
The fruits of love I mean, my loving liege . . . 3 *Hen. VI.* iii 2 59
Canst thou speak against thy liege? . . . . . iii 3 95
I would be king.—Why, so you are, my thrice renowned liege *Rich. III.* iv 2 13
Most dread liege, The good I stand on is my truth and honesty *Hen. VIII.* v 1 121
We are men, my liege.—Ay, in the catalogue ye go for men . *Macbeth* iii 1 91
I assure my good liege, I hold my duty, as I hold my soul, Both to my God and to my gracious king . . . . *Hamlet* ii 2 43

Liege. Remember, sir, my liege, The kings your ancestors . *Cymbeline* iii 1 16
Good my liege *L. L. Lost* iv 3; *As Y. Like It* i 3; *W. Tale* ii 3; iii 2; *K. John* i 1; *Lear* i 1; *Cymbeline* iv 3
My gracious liege *K. John* i 1; 2 *Hen. IV.* iv 5; 3 *Hen. VI.* ii 2
My sovereign liege *Richard II.* i 1; 1 *Hen. IV.* i 3; 3 *Hen. VI.* iv 1

Liegeman. We enjoin thee, As thou art liege-man to us . *W. Tale* ii 3 174
Swore the devil his true liegeman upon the cross of a Welsh hook 1 *Hen. IV.* ii 4 372
You shall become true liegemen to his crown . . . . 1 *Hen. VI.* v 4 128
Who's there?—Friends to this ground.—And liegemen to the Dane *Hamlet* i 1 15

Lieger. Where you shall be an everlasting lieger *Meas. for Meas.* iii 1 59
Which, if he take, shall quite unpeople her Of liegers for her sweet *Cymb.* i 5 80

Lien. Many a poor man's son would have lien still And ne'er have spoke a loving word to you . . . . *K. John* iv 1 50
I heard of an Egyptian That had nine hours lien dead, Who was by good appliance recovered . . . . *Pericles* iii 2 85

Liest. Thou liest, malignant thing! . . . . . . *Tempest* i 2 257
He is not valiant.—Thou liest, most ignorant monster . . . iii 2 28
Thou liest.—Thou liest, thou jesting monkey, thou. . . . iii 2 51
Jolt-head! thou canst not read.—Thou liest; I can . *T. G. of Ver.* iii 1 292
Word of denial: froth and scum, thou liest! . . *Mer. Wives* i 1 167
I could be knighted.—What? thou liest! Sir Alice Ford! . . . ii 1 51
Varlet, thou liest; thou liest, wicked varlet! . . . *Meas. for Meas.* ii 1 174
I never saw her till this time.—Villain, thou liest . *Com. of Errors* ii 2 165
Yet thou liest in the bleak air: come, I will bear thee . *As Y. Like It* ii 6 15
I never yet beheld that special face Which I could fancy more than any other.—Minion, thou liest . . . *T. of Shrew* ii 1 13
Thou liest, thou thread, thou thimble, Thou yard, three-quarters! . iv 3 107
But I did not bid him cut it to pieces: ergo, thou liest . . . iv 3 129
His father is come from Pisa . . . —Thou liest: his father is come from Padua . . . . v 1 31
Watch the night in storms, the day in cold, Whilst thou liest warm at home . . . . v 2 151
But thou liest in thy throat; that is not the matter . . *T. Night* iii 4 172
You lie, you lie: I say thou liest, Camillo, and I hate thee . *W. Tale* i 2 300
Through the false passage of thy throat, thou liest . . . *Richard II.* i 1 125
Thy death-bed is no lesser than thy land Wherein thou liest in reputation sick . . . . ii 1 96
I say, thou liest, And will maintain what thou hast said is false . . iv 1 26
Fitzwater, thou art damn'd to hell for this.—Aumerle, thou liest . . iv 1 44
Mean ye to colt me thus?—Thou liest; thou art not colted . 1 *Hen. IV.* ii 2 41
Why rather, sleep, liest thou in smoky cribs, Upon uneasy pallets? 2 *Hen. IV.* iii 1 9
O thou dull god, why liest thou with the vile In loathsome beds? . . iii 1 15
Slain by Edward's hand.—In thy foul throat thou liest . *Richard III.* i 2 93
Ill rest betide the chamber where thou liest! . . . . . . i 2 112
Thou art a proud traitor, priest.—Proud lord, thou liest *Hen. VIII.* iii 2 252
I would say 'Thou liest' unto thee with a voice as free As I do pray the gods.—Mark you this, people? . . . . . *Coriolanus* iii 3 73
Tybalt, liest thou there in thy bloody sheet? . . . . *Rom. and Jul.* v 3 97
Philosopher!—Thou liest.—Art not one?—Yes.—Then I lie not.—Art not a poet?—Yes.—Then thou liest . . . *T of Athens* i 1 222
Where liest o' nights, Timon?—Under that's above me . . . iv 3 292
Thou liest, thou shag-hair'd villain!—What, you egg! . *Macbeth* iv 2 83
Thou liest, abhorred tyrant; with my sword I'll prove the lie . . v 7 10
Whose grave's this, sirrah?—Mine, sir . . . —I think it be thine, indeed; for thou liest in't . . . . . . *Hamlet* v 1 132
'Tis for the dead, not for the quick; therefore thou liest . . v 1 138
A ministering angel shall my sister be, When thou liest howling . . v 1 265
Thou liest: My train are men of choice and rarest parts . . . . *Lear* i 4 284
My best spirits are bent To prove upon thy heart, whereto I speak, Thou liest . . . . v 3 141
Filth, thou liest!—By heaven, I do not, I do not, gentlemen *Othello* v 2 231
Traitor, thou liest.—Traitor!—Ay, traitor *Pericles* ii 5 55

Lieth. Correction lieth in those hands Which made the fault . *Richard II.* i 2 4

Lieu. In lieu o' the premises Of homage . . . . . *Tempest* i 2 123
Only, in lieu thereof, dispatch me hence . . . . *T. G. of Ver.* ii 7 88
And, in lieu thereof, impose on thee nothing but this . . *L. L. Lost* iii 1 130
In lieu whereof, Three thousand ducats . . . . *Mer. of Venice* iv 1 410
The doctor's clerk In lieu of this last night did lie with me . . . v 1 262
In lieu of all thy pains and husbandry . . . . *As Y. Like It* ii 3 65
In lieu whereof, I pray you, bear me hence From forth the noise *K. John* v 4 44
In lieu of this, Desires you let the dukedoms that you claim Hear no more of you. This the Dauphin speaks . . . . *Hen. V.* i 2 255

Lieutenant. Thou shalt be my lieutenant, monster, or my standard.—Your lieutenant, if you list; he's no standard . . *Tempest* iii 2 18
Under your arm, like a lieutenant's scarf. . . . . *Much Ado* ii 1 197
Bid my lieutenant Peto meet me at town's end . . 1 *Hen. IV.* iv 2 9
My whole charge consists of ancients, corporals, lieutenants . . . iv 2 26
There is an aunchient lieutenant there at the pridge . . *Hen. V.* iii 6 13
Lieutenant, is it you whose voice I hear? Open the gates . 1 *Hen. VI.* i 3 16
Master lieutenant, . . . what are thy due fees? 3 *Hen. VI.* iv 6 1
I then crave pardon of your majesty.—For what, lieutenant? for well using me? . . . . iv 6 9
Here the lieutenant comes. Master lieutenant, pray you, by your leave *Richard III.* iv 1 12
Three great ones of the city, In personal suit to make me his lieutenant, Off-capp'd to him . . . . *Othello* i 1 9
This counter-caster, He, in good time, must his lieutenant be . . i 1 32
Servants of the duke, and my lieutenant. The goodness of the night upon you! . . . . i 2 34
Michael Cassio, Lieutenant to the warlike Moor Othello . . . ii 1 27
But, good lieutenant, is your general wived?—Most fortunately . . ii 1 60
The lieutenant to-night watches on the court of guard . . . . ii 1 219
We must to the watch.—Not this hour, lieutenant; tis not yet ten . ii 3 13
Come, lieutenant, I have a stoup of wine . . . . . . ii 3 30
To the health of our general!—I am for it, lieutenant . . . . ii 3 89
And there be souls must be saved, and there be souls must not be saved.—It's true, good lieutenant . . . . ii 3 108
Not before me; the lieutenant is to be saved before the ancient . . ii 3 114
How now, Roderigo! I pray you, after the lieutenant; go . . . ii 3 142
You rascal!—What's the matter, lieutenant?—A knave teach me my duty! . . . . ii 3 150
Nay, good lieutenant,—alas, gentlemen;—Help, ho!—Lieutenant,—sir ii 3 158
What, are you hurt, lieutenant?—Ay, past all surgery . . . ii 3 259
Good lieutenant, I think you think I love you.—I have well approved it ii 3 315
Good night, lieutenant; I must to the watch.—Good night, honest Iago ii 3 340
Good morrow, good lieutenant: I am sorry For your displeasure . . iii 1 44
A man that languishes in your displeasure.—Who is't you mean?—Why, your lieutenant, Cassio . . . . iii 3 45
Now art thou my lieutenant.—I am your own for ever *Othello* iii 3 478
How do you now, lieutenant?—The worser that you give me the addition Whose want even kills me . . . . iv 1 104
O me, lieutenant! what villains have done this? . . . . . . v 1 56
Sossius, One of my place in Syria, his lieutenant . . *Ant. and Cleo.* iii 1 18
Who's his lieutenant, hear you?—They say, one Taurus . . . . iii 7 78

Lieutenantry. If such tricks as these strip you out of your lieutenantry, it had been better you had not kissed your three fingers so oft *Oth.* ii 1 173
He alone Dealt on lieutenantry, and no practice had In the brave squares of war: yet now—No matter . . . *Ant. and Cleo.* iii 11 39

Lieve. Had as lieve hear the devil as a drum . . 1 *Hen. IV.* iv 2 19
I would not be a Roman, of all nations; I had as lieve be a condemned man.—Wherefore? wherefore? . . . . . *Coriolanus* iv 5 186

Life. For one thing she did They would not take her life . *Tempest* i 2 267
Here is every thing advantageous to life.—True; save means to live . ii 1 49
She that dwells Ten leagues beyond man's life . . . . . . ii 1 247
If of life you keep a care, Shake off slumber, and beware . . . ii 1 303
Speak once in thy life, if thou beest a good moon-calf . . . . iii 2 24
Nothing but heart-sorrow And a clear life ensuing . . . . . iii 3 82
So, with good life And observation strange . . . . . . iii 3 86
I Have given you here a thrid of mine own life, Or that for which I live iv 1 3
As I hope For quiet days, fair issue and long life . . . . iv 1 24
I had forgot that foul conspiracy . . . Against my life . . . . iv 1 141
We are such stuff As dreams are made on, and our little life Is rounded with a sleep . . . . iv 1 157
Of whom I have Received a second life . . . . v 1 195
And this demi-devil . . . had plotted with them To take my life . . v 1 274
I'll waste With such discourse as, I not doubt, shall make it Go quick away; the story of my life . . . . v 1 304
I long To hear the story of your life, which must Take the ear strangely v 1 312
Sweet love! sweet lines! sweet life! Here is her hand . . *T. G. of Ver.* i 3 45
But that life is alter'd now . . . . ii 4 128
So shelving that one cannot climb it Without apparent hazard of his life iii 1 116
As thou lovest thy life, make speed from hence . . . . . iii 1 169
Tarry I here, I but attend on death: But, fly I hence, I fly away from life iii 1 187
No more; unless the next word that thou speak'st Have some malignant power upon my life: If so, I pray thee, breathe it . . . . iii 1 238
Thou canst not see thy love; Besides, thy staying will abridge thy life iii 1 245
This service I have done for you, . . . To hazard life and rescue you . v 4 21
How I love Valentine, Whose life's as tender to me as my soul! . . v 4 37
It is a life that I have desired: I will thrive . . . *Mer. Wives* i 3 21
Alas! the sweet woman leads an ill life with him . . . . . ii 2 92
She leads a very frampold life with him, good heart . . . . ii 2 94
Never a wife in Windsor leads a better life than she does . . . ii 2 122
Defend your reputation, or bid farewell to your good life for ever . . iii 3 127
Taught me more wit than ever I learned before in my life . . . iv 5 62
I fear not Goliath with a weaver's beam; because I know also life is a shuttle . . . . v 1 24
There is a kind of character in thy life, That to the observer doth thy history Fully unfold . . . . *Meas. for Meas.* i 1 28
Thy life, who I would be sorry should be thus foolishly lost . . i 2 195
None better knows than you How I have ever loved the life removed . i 3 8
Under whose heavy sense your brother's life Falls into forfeit . . i 4 65
Doth he so seek his life?—Has censured him Already . . . . i 4 72
Whether you had not sometime in your life Err'd in this point . . ii 1 14
If it be not a bawd's house, it is pity of her life, for it is a naughty house ii 1 77
Let it not sound a thought upon your tongue Against my brother's life ii 2 141
O injurious love, That respites me a life, whose very comfort Is still a dying horror! . . . . ii 3 41
'Tis all as easy Falsely to take away a life true made As to put metal in restrained means To make a false one . . . . ii 4 47
Which had you rather, that the most just law Now took your brother's life; or, to redeem him, Give up your body? . . . . . . ii 4 53
I . . . Pronounce a sentence on your brother's life . . . . . ii 4 62
Might there not be a charity in sin To save this brother's life? . . ii 4 64
That I do beg his life, if it be sin, Heaven let me bear it! . . . ii 4 69
Admit no other way to save his life . . . . ii 4 88
My unsoil'd name, the austereness of my life . . . . . . ii 4 155
Be absolute for death; either death or life Shall thereby be the sweeter iii 1 5
Reason thus with life: If I do lose thee, I do lose a thing That none but fools would keep: a breath thou art . . . . iii 1 6
[Life], merely, thou art death's fool . . . . iii 1 11
What's yet in this That bears the name of life? Yet in this life Lie hid moe thousand deaths: yet death we fear, That makes these odds all even . . . . iii 1 39
To sue to live, I find I seek to die; And, seeking death, find life . . iii 1 43
That will free your life, But fetter you till death . . . . . iii 1 66
And I quake, Lest thou a feverous life shouldst entertain . . . iii 1 75
Thou art too noble to conserve a life In base appliances . . . . iii 1 88
Were it but my life, I'ld throw it down for your deliverance As frankly as a pin . . . . iii 1 104
Death is a fearful thing.—And shamed life a hateful . . . . iii 1 117
The weariest and most loathed worldly life That age, ache, penury and imprisonment Can lay on nature is a paradise To what we fear of death iii 1 129
What sin you do to save a brother's life, Nature dispenses with the deed so far That it becomes a virtue . . . . iii 1 134
Is't not a kind of incest, to take life From thine own sister's shame? . iii 1 139
I am so out of love with life that I will sue to be rid of it . . . iii 1 174
What corruption in this life, that it will let this man live! . . . iii 1 242
Canst thou believe thy living is a life, So stinkingly depending? . . iii 2 27
For the rebellion of a codpiece to take away the life of a man! . . iii 2 123
The very stream of his life and the business he hath helmed must upon a warranted need give him a better proclamation . . . . . iii 2 150
Yet had he framed to himself, by the instruction of his frailty, many deceiving promises of life . . . . iii 2 260
If his own life answer the straitness of his proceeding, it shall become him iii 2 269
His life is parallel'd Even with the stroke and line of his great justice . iv 2 82
By the saint whom I profess, I will plead against it with my life . . iv 2 193
By so receiving a dishonour'd life With ransom of such shame . . iv 4 34
You may marvel why I obscured myself, Labouring to save his life . v 1 396
That life is better life, past fearing death, Than that which lives to fear v 1 402
In double violation Of sacred chastity and of promise-breach Thereon dependent, for your brother's life . . . . v 1 411
Might reproach your life And choke your good to come . . . . v 1 426
All my life to come I'll lend you all my life to do you service . . v 1 436
That apprehends no further than this world, And squarest thy life according . . . . v 1 487
By misfortunes was my life prolong'd, To tell sad stories *Com. of Errors* i 1 120
Here must end the story of my life; And happy were I in my timely death i 1 138

Life. I'll limit thee this day To seek thy life by beneficial help *Com. of Errors* i 1 152
Not being able to buy out his life According to the statute of the town i 2 5
I never spake with her in all my life ii 2 167
Thee will I love and with thee lead my life iii 2 67
As from a bear a man would run for life, So fly I from her iii 2 159
A huge infectious troop Of pale distemperatures and foes to life v 1 82
When I bestrid thee in the wars and took Deep scars to save thy life v 1 193
Haply I see a friend will save my life And pay the sum v 1 283
You know me well.—I never saw you in my life till now v 1 296
Yet hath my night of life some memory v 1 314
Thou art my son Antipholus.—I never saw my father in my life v 1 319
I ne'er saw Syracusa in my life v 1 325
These ducats pawn I for my father here.—It shall not need; thy father hath his life v 1 390
To make an account of her life to a clod of wayward marl *Much Ado* ii 1 65
My very visor began to assume life and scold with her ii 1 249
What life is in that, to be the death of this marriage? ii 2 19
There was never counterfeit of passion came so near the life of passion ii 3 110
Myself would, on the rearward of reproaches, Strike at thy life iv 1 129
Nor my bad life reft me so much of friends iv 1 198
The idea of her life shall sweetly creep Into his study of imagination iv 1 226
Every lovely organ of her life Shall come apparell'd in more precious habit, More moving-delicate and full of life iv 1 228
In some reclusive and religious life, Out of all eyes, tongues, minds iv 1 244
So the life that died with shame Lives in death with glorious fame v 3 7
I yield upon great persuasion; and partly to save your life v 4 96
I might have cudgelled thee out of thy single life v 4 116
Now, God save thy life!—And yours from long living! *L. L. Lost* ii 1 191
Sir, God save your life!—Have with thee, my girl iv 2 150
Society, saith the text, is the happiness of life iv 2 168
If this austere insociable life Change not your offer made in heat of blood v 2 809
To live a barren sister all your life *M. N. Dream* i 1 72
On Diana's altar to protest For aye austerity and single life i 1 90
To death, or to a vow of single life i 1 121
Good night, sweet friend: Thy love ne'er alter till thy sweet life end!—Amen, amen, to that fair prayer, say I; And then end life when I end loyalty! ii 2 61
I would entreat you,—not to fear, not to tremble: my life for yours. If you think I come hither as a lion, it were pity of my life iii 1 43
Stay, gentle Helena; hear my excuse: My love, my life, my soul! iii 2 246
Thus hath he lost sixpence a day during his life iv 2 20
'Tide life, 'tide death, I come without delay v 1 205
If I should as lion come in strife Into this place, 'twere pity on my life v 1 229
Here's a simple line of life: here's a small trifle of wives *Mer. of Venice* ii 2 169
To be in peril of my life with the edge of a feather-bed ii 2 173
Many a man his life hath sold But my outside to behold ii 7 67
Next, if I fail Of the right casket, never in my life To woo a maid ii 9 12
There may as well be amity and life 'Tween snow and fire iii 2 30
Promise me life, and I'll confess the truth.—Well then, confess and live iii 2 34
But when this ring Parts from this finger, then parts life from hence iii 2 186
I'll follow him no more with bootless prayers. He seeks my life iii 3 21
It is very meet The Lord Bassanio live an upright life iii 5 79
O, be thou damn'd, inexecrable dog! And for thy life let justice be accused iv 1 129
I am married to a wife Which is as dear to me as life itself; But life itself, my wife, and all the world, Are not with me esteem'd above thy life iv 1 283
If it be proved against an alien That by direct or indirect attempts He seek the life of any citizen, The party 'gainst the which he doth contrive Shall seize one half his goods iv 1 351
And the offender's life lies in the mercy Of the duke only iv 1 355
Thou hast contrived against the very life Of the defendant iv 1 360
I pardon thee thy life before thou ask it iv 1 369
You take my life When you do take the means whereby I live iv 1 376
Even he that did uphold the very life Of my dear friend v 1 214
Sweet lady, you have given me life and living v 1 286
And never leave thee till he hath ta'en thy life *As Y. Like It* i 1 158
And broke three of his ribs, that there is little hope of life in him i 2 136
Hath not old custom made this life more sweet Than that of painted pomp? ii 1 2
And this our life exempt from public haunt Finds tongues in trees ii 1 15
Thus most invectively he pierceth through The body of the country, city, court, Yea, and of this our life ii 1 60
If you like upon report The soil, the profit, and this kind of life ii 4 98
What a life is this, That your poor friends must woo your company? ii 7 9
Then, heigh-ho, the holly! This life is most jolly ii 7 183
I never loved my brother in my life.—More villain thou iii 1 14
In respect of itself, it is a good life; but in respect that it is a shepherd's life, it is naught iii 2 14
In respect that it is private, it is a very vile life iii 2 17
As it is a spare life, look you, it fits my humour well iii 2 20
How brief the life of man Runs his erring pilgrimage iii 2 137
'Od's my little life, I think she means to tangle my eyes too! iii 5 43
Translate thy life into death, thy liberty into bondage v 1 58
How that a life was but a flower In spring time v 3 29
This to be true, I do engage my life v 4 172
The duke hath put on a religious life v 4 187
I ne'er drank sack in my life *T. of Shrew* Ind. 2 7
Mirth and merriment, Which bars a thousand harms and lengthens life Ind. 2 138
To save my life, Puts my apparel and my countenance on i 1 233
While I make way from hence to save my life: You understand me? i 1 239
He hath the jewel of my life in hold i 2 119
O sir, such a life, with such a wife, were strange! i 2 194
Where is the life that late I led? iv 1 143; 2 *Hen. IV.* v 3 147
As far as Rome; And so to Tripoli, if God lend me life *T. of Shrew* iv 2 76
What countryman, I pray?—Of Mantua.—Of Mantua, sir? marry, God forbid! And come to Padua, careless of your life? iv 2 79
To save your life in this extremity, This favour will I do you iv 2 102
Will repute you ever The patron of my life and liberty iv 2 113
I dare not for my life.—The more my wrong, the more his spite appears iv 3 1
Go, take it up unto thy master's use.—Villain, not for thy life iv 3 160
I could not forget you, for I never saw you before in all my life v 1 53
Peace it bodes, and love, and quiet life, And awful rule v 2 108
Thy husband is thy lord, thy life, thy keeper, Thy head, thy sovereign v 2 146
I'ld venture The well-lost life of mine on his grace's cure *All's Well* i 3 254
My heart Will not confess he owes the malady That doth my life besiege ii 1 10
I have seen a medicine That's able to breathe life into a stone ii 1 76
Nay, worse—if worse—extended With vilest torture let my life be ended ii 1 177
Thy life is dear; for all that life can rate Worth name of life in thee hath estimate, Youth, beauty, wisdom, courage ii 1 182

Life. I ne'er had worse luck in my life in my 'O Lord, sir!' *All's Well* ii 2 59
As 'twere, a man assured of a— Uncertain life, and sure death ii 3 20
I had rather be in this choice than throw ames-ace for my life ii 3 85
It nothing steads us To chide him from our eaves; for he persists As if his life lay on't iii 7 43
And I shall lose my life for want of language iv 1 77
Haply thou mayst inform Something to save thy life iv 1 92
My house, mine honour, yea, my life, be thine, And I'll be bid by thee iv 2 52
The web of our life is of a mingled yarn, good and ill together iv 3 83
We shall be fain to hang you.—My life, sir, in any case iv 3 270
If your life be saved, will you undertake to betray the Florentine? iv 3 325
Time was, I did him a desired office, Dear almost as his life iv 4 6
I am afeard the life of Helen, lady, Was foully snatch'd v 3 153
I am sure care's an enemy to life *T. Night* i 3 3
When did I see thee so put down?—Never in your life, I think i 3 87
Tut, there's life in't, man i 3 118
If I did love you in my master's flame, With such a suffering, such a deadly life, In your denial I would find no sense i 5 284
Does not our life consist of the four elements? ii 3 10
Would you have a love-song, or a song of good life?—A love-song, a love-song.—Ay, ay: I care not for good life ii 3 37
My life upon't, young though thou art, thine eye Hath stay'd upon some favour that it loves ii 4 24
M, O, A, I, doth sway my life.—A fustian riddle! ii 5 118
If you hold your life at any price, betake you to your guard iii 4 252
Hold, Toby; on thy life I charge thee, hold! iv 1 49
His life I gave him and did thereto add My love v 1 83
More than I love these eyes, more than my life, More, by all mores v 1 138
If I do feign, you witnesses above Punish my life for tainting of my love! v 1 141
They that went on crutches ere he was born desire yet their life to see him a man.—Would they else be content to die? *W. Tale* i 1 45
Had we pursued that life, And our weak spirits ne'er been higher rear'd i 2 71
Were my wife's liver Infected as her life, she would not live The running of one glass.—Who does infect her? i 2 305
I will respect thee as a father if Thou bear'st my life off hence i 2 462
There is a plot against my life, my crown; All's true that is mistrusted ii 1 47
For her, my lord, I dare my life lay down and will do't, sir ii 1 130
Fear you his tyrannous passion more, alas, Than the queen's life? ii 3 29
Were I a tyrant, Where were her life? she durst not call me so ii 3 123
You that have been so tenderly officious With Lady Margery, your midwife there, To save this bastard's life ii 3 161
What will you adventure To save this brat's life?—Any thing, my lord ii 3 163
Conspiring with Camillo to take away the life of our sovereign lord iii 2 16
My past life Hath been as continent, as chaste, as true, As I am now unhappy iii 2 34
To prate and talk for life and honour 'fore Who please to come and hear iii 2 42
For life, I prize it As I weigh grief, which I would spare iii 2 43
My life stands in the level of your dreams, Which I'll lay down iii 2 82
To me can life be no commodity: The crown and comfort of my life, your favour, I do give lost iii 2 94
No life, I prize it not a straw, but for mine honour, Which I would free iii 2 110
Beseech you, tenderly apply to her Some remedies for life iii 2 154
Laid, Either for life or death, upon the earth Of its right father iii 3 45
These your unusual weeds to each part of you Do give a life iv 4 2
You must change this purpose, Or I my life iv 4 40
I love a ballad in print o' life, for then we are sure they are true iv 4 264
O, hear me breathe my life Before this ancient sir! iv 4 371
I am sorry that by hanging thee I can But shorten thy life one week iv 4 433
Though bearing misery, I desire my life Once more to look on him v 1 137
Now, had I not the dash of my former life in me, would preferment drop on my head v 2 123
Thou wilt amend thy life?—Ay, an it like your good worship v 2 166
It is a surplus of your grace, which never My life may last to answer v 3 8
Prepare To see the life as lively mock'd as ever Still sleep mock'd death v 3 19
She stood, Even with such life of majesty, warm life, As now it coldly stands v 3 35
Masterly done: The very life seems warm upon her lip v 3 66
Bequeath to death your numbness, for from him Dear life redeems you v 3 103
She hangs about his neck: If she pertain to life let her speak too v 3 113
God shall forgive you Cœur-de-lion's death The rather that you give his offspring life *K. John* ii 1 13
Wilt thou resign them and lay down thy arms?—My life as soon ii 1 155
Let belief and life encounter so As doth the fury of two desperate men iii 1 31
Thou darest not say so, villain, for thy life iii 1 132
And meritorious shall that hand be call'd, Canonized and worshipp'd as a saint, That takes away by any secret course Thy hateful life iii 1 179
There where my fortune lives, there my life dies iii 1 338
My fair son! My life, my joy, my food, my all the world! iii 4 104
Life is as tedious as a twice-told tale Vexing the dull ear of a drowsy man iii 4 108
Whiles warm life plays in that infant's veins iii 4 132
And lose it, life and all, as Arthur did iii 4 144
May be he will not touch young Arthur's life iii 4 160
Have I commandment on the pulse of life? iv 2 92
No sure foundation set on blood, No certain life achieved by others' death iv 2 105
It is the curse of kings to be attended By slaves that take their humours for a warrant To break within the bloody house of life iv 2 210
Kneeling before this ruin of sweet life iv 3 65
Not for my life: but yet I dare defend My innocent life against an emperor iv 3 89
I loved him, and will weep My date of life out for his sweet life's loss iv 3 106
The life, the right and truth of all this realm Is fled to heaven iv 3 145
An empty casket, where the jewel of life By some damn'd hand was robb'd v 1 40
Retaining but a quantity of life, Which bleeds away, even as a form of wax v 4 23
It is too late: the life of all his blood Is touch'd corruptibly v 7 1
And all the shrouds wherewith my life should sail Are turned to one thread v 7 53
Look, what I speak, my life shall prove it true *Richard II.* i 1 87
I say and further will maintain Upon his bad life to make all this good i 1 99
This arm shall do it, or this life be spent i 1 108
Once did I lay an ambush for your life i 1 137
My life thou shalt command, but not my shame: The one my duty owes i 1 166
Mine honour is my life; both grow in one; Take honour from me, and my life is done: Then, dear my liege, mine honour let me try i 1 182
More solicit me than your exclaims, To stir against the butchers of his life i 2 3
But Thomas, my dear lord, my life, my Gloucester i 2 16
Thou seest thy wretched brother die, Who was the model of thy father's life i 2 28

Life. Thou showest the naked pathway to thy life . . . . *Richard II.* i 2 31
To safeguard thine own life, The best way is to venge my Gloucester's death . . . . i 2 35
Thy sometimes brother's wife With her companion grief must end her life . . . . i 2 55
We banish you our territories : You, cousin Hereford, upon pain of life i 3 140
If ever I were traitor, My name be blotted from the book of life ! i 3 202
I should have been more mild : A partial slander sought I to avoid, And in the sentence my own life destroy'd . . . . . . i 3 242
Would the scandal vanish with my life, How happy then were my ensuing death ! . . . . ii 1 67
Words, life and all, old Lancaster hath spent . . . . ii 1 150
Even through the hollow eyes of death I spy life peering . . ii 1 271
Who gently would dissolve the bands of life, Which false hope lingers . ii 2 71
To my knowledge, I never in my life did look on him . . ii 3 39
If I could, by Him that gave me life, I would attach you all . . ii 3 155
As if this flesh which walls about our life Were brass impregnable iii 2 167
It is no more Than my poor life must answer.—Thy life answer ! . . v 2 83
My shamed life in his dishonour lies : Thou kill'st me in his life . . v 3 71
Choose out some secret place, some reverend room, More than thou hast, and with it joy thy life . . . . v 6 26
I must give over this life, and I will give it over . 1 *Hen. IV.* i 2 107
I see a good amendment of life in thee ; from praying to purse-taking . i 2 114
I can drink with any tinker in his own language during my life . . ii 4 21
One that never spake other English in his life than 'Eight shillings' . ii 4 27
And says to his wife 'Fie upon this quiet life ! I want work' . ii 4 117
Ere I lead this life long, I'll sew nether stocks and mend them . . ii 4 129
I shall think the better of myself and thee during my life . . ii 4 303
Do thou stand for my father, and examine me upon the particulars of my life . . . . ii 4 414
All the courses of my life do show I am not in the roll of common men iii 1 42
But thou dost in thy passages of life Make me believe that thou art only mark'd For the hot vengeance and the rod of heaven . . . . iii 2 8
The end of life cancels all bands . . . . iii 2 157
Do thou amend thy face, and I'll amend my life . . . . . iii 3 28
By my life, And I dare well maintain it with my life . . . . iv 3 8
He deposed the king ; Soon after that, deprived him of his life . . iv 3 91
I could be well content To entertain the lag-end of my life With quiet hours . . . . v 1 24
I never in my life Did hear a challenge urged more modestly . . . v 2 52
O gentlemen, the time of life is short ! To spend that shortness basely were too long, If life did ride upon a dial's point . . . . v 2 82
And they are for the town's end, to beg during life . . . . v 3 39
Give me life : which if I can save, so ; if not, honour comes unlooked for v 3 63
And show'd thou makest some tender of my life, In this fair rescue . v 4 49
I better brook the loss of brittle life Than those proud titles . . v 4 78
But thought's the slave of life, and life time's fool . . . . v 4 81
What, old acquaintance ! could not all this flesh Keep in a little life? . v 4 103
For he is but the counterfeit of a man who hath not the life of a man . v 4 118
No counterfeit, but the true and perfect image of life indeed . . v 4 121
The better part of valour is discretion ; in the which better part I have saved my life . . . . v 4 123
To the earth, From whence with life he never more sprung up 2 *Hen. IV.* i 1 111
Whose fever-weaken'd joints, Like strengthless hinges, buckle under life i 1 141
Knew that we ventured on such dangerous seas That if we wrought out life 'twas ten to one ; And yet we ventured . . . . . . i 1 182
He doth bestride a bleeding land, Gasping for life under great Bolingbroke . . . . i 1 208
I sent for you, when there were matters against you for your life . . i 2 151
Never shall have length of life enough To rain upon remembrance . . ii 3 58
Why, thou globe of sinful continents, what a life dost thou lead ! . . ii 4 310
Like a brother toil'd in my affairs And laid his love and life under my foot . . . . iii 1 63
A man may prophesy, With a near aim, of the main chance of things As yet not come to life . . . . iii 1 84
And purge the obstructions which begin to stop Our very veins of life . iv 1 66
O, when the king did throw his warder down, His own life hung upon the staff . . . . iv 1 126
To end one doubt by death Revives two greater in the heirs of life . iv 1 200
Turning the word to sword and life to death . . . . . iv 2 10
So thin that life looks through and will break out . . . . iv 4 120
Thy life did manifest thou lovedst me not, And thou wilt have me die assured . . . . iv 5 105
Thou hast whetted on thy stony heart, To stab at half an hour of my life iv 5 109
Give that which gave thee life unto the worms . . . . . iv 5 117
More precious, Preserving life in medicine potable . . . . iv 5 163
Laud be to God ! even there my life must end . . . . . iv 5 236
The service that I truly did his life Hath left me open to all injuries . v 2 7
No prince nor peer shall have just cause to say, God shorten Harry's happy life one day ! . . . . v 2 145
Health and long life to you, Master Silence.—Fill the cup . . v 3 54
For competence of life I will allow you . . . . . . v 5 70
The art and practic part of life Must be the mistress to this theoric *Hen. V.* i 1 51
Holding in disdain the German women For some dishonest manners of their life . . . . i 2 49
That he should, for a foreign purse, so sell His sovereign's life to death ii 2 11
You show great mercy, if you give him life . . . . . . ii 2 50
That I love and honour with my soul, and my heart, and my duty, and my life . . . . iii 6 9
Speak, captain, for his life, and I will thee requite . . . . iii 6 51
The king's a bawcock, and a heart of gold, A lad of life, an imp of fame iv 1 45
Where they feared the death, they have borne life away . . . iv 1 181
To demonstrate the life of such a battle In life so lifeless as it shows itself . . . . iv 2 54
What are his words?—He prays you to save his life . . . . iv 4 47
Let life be short ; else shame will be too long . . . . . iv 5 23
If you mark Alexander's life well, Harry of Monmouth's life is come after it . . . . iv 7 33
Things, Which cannot in their huge and proper life Be here presented v Prol. 5
Had not churchmen pray'd, His thread of life had not so soon decay'd 1 *Hen. VI.* i 1 34
If Henry were recall'd to life again, These news would cause him once more yield the ghost . . . . i 1 66
He fighteth as one weary of his life. The other lords, like lions . . i 2 26
Talbot, my life, my joy, again return'd ! How wert thou handled? . i 4 23
Hast thou any life? Speak unto Talbot ; nay, look up to him . . i 4 88
Fair be all thy hopes And prosperous be thy life ! . . . . ii 5 114
Convey him hence, and I myself Will see his burial better than his life ii 5 121
What's more manifest? In that thou laid'st a trap to take my life . iii 1 22
Thou art reverent Touching thy spiritual function, not thy life . . iii 1 50

Life. What ! will you fly, and leave Lord Talbot?—Ay, All the Talbots in the world, to save my life . . . . . 1 *Hen. VI.* iii 2 108
Sell every man his life as dear as mine, And they shall find dear deer of us iv 2 53
He, renowned noble gentleman, Yields up his life unto a world of odds iv 4 25
Never to England shall he bear his life ; But dies, betray'd to fortune . iv 4 38
I beg mortality, Rather than life preserved with infamy . . iv 5 33
I take my leave of thee, fair son, Born to eclipse thy life this afternoon iv 5 53
I gave thee life and rescued thee from death . . . . . iv 6 5
The life thou gavest me first was lost and done . . . . . iv 6 7
'Tis but the shortening of my life one day . . . . . . iv 6 37
To save a paltry life and slay bright fame . . . . . . iv 6 45
Thy life to me is sweet : If thou wilt fight, fight by thy father's side . iv 6 55
Where is my other life? mine own is gone ; O, where's young Talbot? . iv 7 1
Hack their bones asunder, Whose life was England's glory, Gallia's wonder . . . . iv 7 48
That which we have fled During the life, let us not wrong it dead . . iv 7 50
O, that I could but call these dead to life ! . . . . . iv 7 81
This argues what her kind of life hath been, Wicked and vile . . v 4 15
O Lord, that lends me life, Lend me a heart replete with thankfulness ! 2 *Hen. VI.* i 1 19
A man that ne'er saw in his life before . . . . . . ii 1 65
Wouldst climb a tree?—But that in all my life, when I was a youth . ii 1 99
My wife desired some damsons, And made me climb, with danger of my life . . . . ii 1 103
I think, jet did he never see.—But cloaks and gowns, before this day, a many.—Never, before this day, in all his life . . . . ii 1 116
Raising up wicked spirits from under ground, Demanding of King Henry's life and death . . . . ii 1 175
You are more nobly born, Despoiled of your honour in your life . . ii 3 10
I know their complot is to have my life . . . . . . iii 1 147
And dogged York . . . By false accuse doth level at my life . . . iii 1 160
Laid your heads together . . . And all to make away my guiltless life . iii 1 167
These great lords . . . Do seek subversion of thy harmless life . . iii 1 208
That were no policy : The king will labour still to save his life, The commons haply rise, to save his life . . . . iii 1 239
I rather would have lost my life betimes Than bring a burthen of dishonour home . . . . iii 1 297
For in the shade of death I shall find joy ; In life but double death . iii 2 55
Might liquid tears or heart-offending groans Or blood-consuming sighs recall his life, I would be blind with weeping . . . . . iii 2 61
Some violent hands were laid on Humphrey's life . . . . iii 2 138
For seeing him I see my life in death . . . . iii 2 152
Violent hands were laid Upon the life of this thrice-famed duke . . iii 2 157
His hands abroad display'd, as one that grasp'd And tugg'd for life . iii 2 173
Your loving uncle, . . . They say, is shamefully bereft of life . . iii 2 269
The world shall not be ransom for thy life . . . . . . iii 2 297
Yet now farewell ; and farewell life with thee ! . . . . . iii 2 356
Live thou to joy thy life ; Myself no joy in nought but that thou livest iii 2 365
Ah, what a sign it is of evil life, Where death's approach is seen so terrible ! . . . . iii 3 5
O God, forgive him !—So bad a death argues a monstrous life . . iii 3 30
Such a petty sum !—I'll give it, sir ; and therefore spare my life . . iv 1 23
Argo, their thread of life is spun . . . . iv 2 31
I lost not Normandy, Yet, to recover them, would lose my life . . iv 7 71
He shall die, an it be but for pleading so well for his life . . . iv 7 113
And therefore yet relent, and save my life.—Away with him ! . . iv 7 124
With halters on their necks, Expect your highness' doom, of life or death iv 9 12
If I might have a lease of my life for a thousand years I could stay no longer . . . . iv 10 6
But thou preferr'st thy life before thine honour . . . 3 *Hen. VI.* i 1 246
Your right depends not on his life or death . . . . . . i 2 11
Chaplain, away ! thy priesthood saves thy life . . . . . i 3 3
They have demean'd themselves Like men born to renown by life or death i 4 8
The sands are number'd that make up my life ; Here must I stay, and here my life must end . . . . i 4 25
For a thousand causes I would prolong awhile the traitor's life . . i 4 52
And will you pale your head in Henry's glory, And rob his temples of the diadem, Now in his life? . . . . i 4 105
I should not for my life but weep with him . . . . . i 4 170
This may plant courage in their quailing breasts; For yet is hope of life ii 3 55
O God ! methinks it were a happy life, To be no better than a homely swain . . . . ii 5 21
Ah, what a life were this ! how sweet ! how lovely ! . . . . ii 5 41
Some store of crowns ; And I, that haply take them from him now, May yet ere night yield both my life and them To some man else . . ii 5 59
I, who at his hands received my life, Have by my hands of life bereaved him . . . . ii 5 67
Ah, boy, if any life be left in thee, Throw up thine eye ! . . . O boy, thy father gave thee life too soon, And hath bereft thee of thy life too late . . . . ii 5 84
A deadly groan, like life and death's departing . . . . . ii 6 43
Dark cloudy death o'ershades his beams of life, And he nor sees nor hears ii 6 62
If this right hand would buy two hours' life, That I in all despite might rail at him, This hand should chop it off . . . . . . ii 6 80
In quarrel of the house of York The worthy gentleman did lose his life iii 2 7
While life upholds this arm, This arm upholds the house of Lancaster . iii 3 106
I myself will lead a private life And in devotion spend my latter days . iv 6 42
Who finds Edward Shall have a reward, and he his life . . . v 5 10
Thyself the sea Whose envious gulf did swallow up his life . . . v 6 25
But wherefore dost thou come? is't for my life? . . . . v 6 29
If any spark of life be yet remaining, Down, down to hell . . v 6 66
I will buz abroad such prophecies That Edward shall be fearful of his life . . . . v 6 87
Lo, in these windows that let forth thy life, I pour the helpless balm of my poor eyes . . . . *Richard III.* i 2 12
As all the world is cheered by the sun, So I by that ; it is my day, my life . . . . i 2 130
Black night o'ershade thy day, and death thy life !—Curse not thyself . i 2 131
My charity is outrage, life my shame . . . . i 3 277
My dream was lengthen'd after life ; O, then began the tempest to my soul . . . . i 4 43
To my brother Gloucester, Who shall reward you better for my life . i 4 236
Which of you, . . . If two such murderers as yourselves came to you, Would not entreat for life? . . . . i 4 269
What is it thou demand'st?—The forfeit, sovereign, of my servant's life ii 1 99
The proudest of you all Have been beholding to him in his life ; Yet none of you would once plead for his life . . . . ii 1 129
My husband lost his life to get the crown . . . . . . ii 4 57
Death makes no conquest of this conqueror ; For now he lives in fame, though not in life . . . . iii 1 88

Life. My lord, I hold my life as dear as you do yours; And never in my life, I do protest, Was it more precious to me than 'tis now . . . *Richard III.* iii 2 80
And be thy wife—if any be so mad—As miserable by the life of thee As thou hast made me by my dear lord's death! . . . iv 1 76
Blind sight, dead life, poor mortal living ghost, Woe's scene, world's shame, grave's due by life usurp'd! . . . iv 4 26
Cancel his bond of life, dear God, I pray . . . iv 4 77
Bloody will be thy end; Shame serves thy life and doth thy death attend . . . iv 4 195
She is of royal blood.—To save her life, I'll say she is not so.—Her life is only safest in her birth . . . iv 4 212
My babes were destined to a fairer death, If grace had bless'd thee with a fairer life . . . iv 4 220
By their uncle cozen'd Of comfort, kingdom, kindred, freedom, life . iv 4 223
Sweetly in force unto her fair life's end.—But how long fairly shall her sweet life last? . . . iv 4 351
My father's death— Thy life hath that dishonour'd . . . iv 4 375
One that never in his life Felt so much cold as over shoes in snow . v 3 325
I have set my life upon a cast, And I will stand the hazard of the die . v 4 9
The tract of every thing Would by a good discourser lose some life *Hen. VIII.* i 1 41
My life is spann'd already: I am the shadow of poor Buckingham . i 1 223
My life itself, and the best heart of it, Thanks you for this great care . i 2 1
Unfit for other life, compell'd by hunger And lack of other means . i 2 34
Much He spoke, and learnedly, for life . . . ii 1 28
For further life in this world I ne'er hope, Nor will I sue . . . ii 1 69
Life, honour, name, and all That made me happy at one stroke has taken For ever from the world . . . ii 1 116
The last hour Of my long weary life is come upon me . . . ii 1 133
Should Do no more offices of life to't than The grave does to the dead . ii 4 190
So much I am happy Above a number, . . . I know my life so even . iii 1 37
In such a point of weight, so near mine honour,—More near my life . iii 1 72
He has my heart yet; and shall have my prayers While I shall have my life . . . iii 1 181
Bade me enjoy it, with the place and honours, During my life . . iii 2 249
Produce the grand sum of his sins, the articles Collected from his life . iii 2 294
If heaven had pleased to have given me longer life And able means, we had not parted thus . . . iv 2 152
In all the progress Both of my life and office, I have labour'd . . v 3 33
I shall remember this bold language.—Do. Remember your bold life too . . . v 3 85
'Tis now too certain: How much more is his life in value with him? . v 3 108
Send prosperous life, long, and ever happy! . . . v 5 2
God protect thee! Into whose hand I give thy life . . . v 5 12
And thou most reverend for thy stretch'd-out life . . *Troi. and Cres.* i 3 61
Our project's life this shape of sense assumes . . . i 3 385
None so noble Whose life were ill bestow'd or death unfamed . . ii 2 159
There you touch'd the life of our design . . . ii 2 194
You must not know where he sups.—I'll lay my life, with my disposer iii 1 95
I'll play the hunter for thy life With all my force, pursuit, and policy . iv 1 17
Welcome to Troy! now, by Anchises' life, Welcome, indeed! . . iv 1 21
For every false drop in her bawdy veins A Grecian's life hath sunk . iv 1 70
I shall have such a life! . . . iv 2 22
Name Cressid, and thy life shall be as safe As Priam is in Ilion . . iv 4 117
Lo, Jupiter is yonder, dealing life! . . . iv 5 191
Think'st thou to catch my life so pleasantly As to prenominate in nice conjecture Where thou wilt hit me dead? . . . iv 5 249
Life every man holds dear; but the brave man Holds honour far more precious-dear than life . . . v 3 27
Turn thy false face, thou traitor, And pay thy life thou owest me for my horse! . . . v 6 7
Fate, hear me what I say! I reck not though I end my life to-day . v 6 26
Most putrefied core, so fair without, Thy goodly armour thus hath cost thy life . . . v 8 2
How ugly night comes breathing at his heels: Even with the vail and darking of the sun, To close the day up, Hector's life is done . . v 8 8
Ignomy and shame Pursue thy life, and live aye with thy name! . . v 10 34
If any think brave death outweighs bad life . . . *Coriolanus* i 6 71
I do owe them still My life and services . . . ii 2 138
That prefer A noble life before a long . . . iii 1 153
You have put me now to such a part which never I shall discharge to the life . . . iii 2 106
I do love My country's good with a respect more tender, More holy and profound, than mine own life . . . iii 3 113
Not out of hope—Mistake me not—to save my life . . . iv 5 86
Our raiment And state of bodies would bewray what life We have led . v 3 95
Thou hast never in thy life Show'd thy dear mother any courtesy . . v 3 160
Sir, if you'ld save your life, fly to your house . . . v 4 38
Behold our patroness, the life of Rome! . . . v 5 1
When you shall know . . . the great danger Which this man's life did owe you, you'll rejoice That he is thus cut off . . . v 6 139
To-morrow yield up rule, resign my life . . . *T. Andron.* i 1 191
Thanks, noble Titus, father of my life! . . . i 1 253
What I have done, as best I may, Answer I must and shall do with my life . . . i 1 412
His traitorous sons, To whom I sued for my dear son's life . . . i 1 453
These words, these looks, infuse new life in me . . . i 1 461
Ah, my sweet Moor, sweeter to me than life! . . . ii 3 51
Revenge it, as you love your mother's life . . . ii 3 114
For my father's sake, That gave thee life, when well he might have slain thee . . . ii 3 159
Kill me in this place! For 'tis not life that I have begg'd so long . ii 3 170
Fell curs of bloody kind, Have here bereft my brother of his life . . ii 3 282
He would not then have touch'd them for his life . . . ii 4 47
And they have nursed this woe, in feeding life . . . iii 1 74
Ah, that this sight should make so deep a wound, And yet detested life not shrink thereat! That ever death should let life bear his name, Where life hath no more interest but to breathe! . . . iii 1 248
He leaves his pledges dearer than his life . . . iii 1 292
Teach her not thus to lay Such violent hands upon her tender life.— . . . What violent hands can she lay on her life? . . . iii 2 22
Thou art made of tears, And tears will quickly melt thy life away . iii 2 51
He is your brother, lords, sensibly fed Of that self-blood that first gave life to you . . . iv 2 123
Alas, sir, I know not Jupiter; I never drank with him in all my life . iv 3 85
Nay, truly, sir, I could never say grace in all my life . . . iv 3 101
Lord of my life, commander of my thoughts, Calm thee . . . iv 4 28
This do thou for my love; and so let him, As he regards his aged father's life . . . v 2 130

Life. Some direful slaughtering death, As punishment for his most wicked life . . . *T. Andron.* v 3 145
If one good deed in all my life I did, I do repent it from my very soul . v 3 189
Her life was beast-like, and devoid of pity . . . v 3 199
From forth the fatal loins of these two foes A pair of star-cross'd lovers take their life . . . *Rom. and Jul.* Prol. 6
And expire the term Of a despised life closed in my breast . . i 4 110
Is she a Capulet? O dear account! my life is my foe's debt . . i 5 120
Let them find me here: My life were better ended by their hate, Than death prorogued, wanting of thy love . . . ii 2 77
An I were so apt to quarrel as thou art, any man should buy the fee-simple of my life for an hour and a quarter . . . iii 1 35
An envious thrust from Tybalt hit the life Of stout Mercutio . . iii 1 173
And all those twenty could but kill one life . . . iii 1 184
His fault concludes but what the law should end, The life of Tybalt . iii 1 191
The day is broke; be wary, look about.—Then, window, let day in, and let life out . . . iii 5 41
Thy eyes' windows fall, Like death, when he shuts up the day of life . iv 1 101
I have a faint cold fear thrills through my veins, That almost freezes up the heat of life . . . iv 3 16
O me, O me! My child, my only life, Revive, look up! . . . iv 5 19
Her joints are stiff; Life and these lips have long been separated . iv 5 27
I will die, And leave him all; life, living, all is Death's . . . iv 5 40
O love! O life! not life, but love in death! . . . iv 5 58
Your part in her you could not keep from death, But heaven keeps his part in eternal life . . . iv 5 70
And breathed such life with kisses in my lips, That I revived . . v 1 8
Let my old life Be sacrificed, some hour before his time . . . v 3 267
It is a pretty mocking of the life . . . *T. of Athens* i 1 35
Artificial strife Lives in these touches, livelier than life . . . i 1 38
Like madness is the glory of this life, As this pomp shows to a little oil i 2 139
I never tasted Timon in my life, Nor came any of his bounties over me iii 2 84
If wrongs be evils and enforce us kill, What folly 'tis to hazard life for ill! . . . iii 5 37
His service done At Lacedæmon . . . Were a sufficient briber for his life iii 5 61
If by this crime he owes the law his life, Why, let the war receive't . iii 5 83
Nor has he with him to Supply his life, or that which can command it . iv 2 47
That the whole life of Athens were in this! Thus would I eat it . . iv 3 281
If thou wert the wolf, thy greediness would afflict thee, and oft thou shouldst hazard thy life for thy dinner . . . iv 3 338
Wert thou a leopard, thou wert german to the lion and the spots of thy kindred were jurors on thy life . . . iv 3 345
And, as my lord, Still serve him with my life . . . iv 3 478
Whose star-like nobleness gave life and influence To their whole being! v 1 66
I cannot tell what you and other men Think of this life . . *J. Cæsar* i 2 94
And those sparks of life That should be in a Roman you do want . i 3 57
Life, being weary of these worldly bars, Never lacks power to dismiss itself . . . i 3 96
He that cuts off twenty years of life Cuts off so many years of fearing death . . . iii 1 101
What, durst not tempt him!—For your life you durst not . . iv 3 62
All the voyage of their life Is bound in shallows and in miseries . . iv 3 220
For fear of what might fall, so to prevent The time of life . . v 1 106
Where I did begin, there shall I end; My life is run his compass . . v 3 25
Then I swore thee, saving of thy life, That whatsoever I did bid thee do, Thou shouldst attempt it . . . v 3 38
Yet in all my life I found no man but he was true to me . . . v 5 34
Thy life hath had some smatch of honour in it . . . v 5 46
His life was gentle, and the elements So mix'd in him that Nature might stand up And say to all the world 'This was a man!' . . . v 5 73
The thane lives yet; But under heavy judgement bears that life *Macbeth* i 3 110
Nothing in his life Became him like the leaving it . . . i 4 7
Wouldst thou have that Which thou esteem'st the ornament of life? . i 7 42
Sleep that knits up the ravell'd sleave of care, The death of each day's life? . . . ii 2 38
Most sacrilegious murder hath broke ope The lord's anointed temple, and stole thence The life o' the building!—What is't you say? the life? . . . ii 3 74
The wine of life is drawn, and the mere lees Is left this vault to brag of ii 3 100
They stared, and were distracted; no man's life Was to be trusted with them . . . ii 3 110
Who wear our health but sickly in his life, Which in his death were perfect . . . iii 1 107
I would set my life on any chance, To mend it, or be rid on't . . iii 1 113
Every minute of his being thrusts Against my near'st of life . . . iii 1 118
And delight No less in truth than life . . . iv 3 130
My way of life Is fall'n into the sear, the yellow leaf . . . v 3 22
My fell of hair Would at a dismal treatise rouse and stir As life were in't v 5 13
Out, out, brief candle! Life's but a walking shadow, a poor player . v 5 24
I bear a charm'd life, which must not yield To one of woman born . v 8 12
Did forfeit, with his life, all those his lands . . . *Hamlet* i 1 88
Or if thou hast uphoarded in thy life Extorted treasure . . . i 1 136
His beard was grizzled,—no?—It was, as I have seen it in his life . . i 2 241
Why, what should be the fear? I do not set my life at a pin's fee . . i 4 65
The serpent that did sting thy father's life Now wears his crown . . i 5 39
By a brother's hand Of life, of crown, of queen, at once dispatch'd . i 5 75
I will most humbly take my leave of you.—You cannot, sir, take from me any thing that I will more willingly part withal: except my life, except my life, except my life . . . ii 2 221
Upon whose property and most dear life A damn'd defeat was made . ii 2 597
There's the respect That makes calamity of so long life . . . iii 1 69
Who would fardels bear, To grunt and sweat under a weary life? . . iii 1 77
Then there's hope a great man's memory may outlive his life half a year iii 2 141
Thy natural magic and dire property, On wholesome life usurp immediately . . . iii 2 271
The single and peculiar life is bound, With all the strength and armour of the mind, To keep itself from noyance . . . iii 3 11
Your bedded hair, like life in excrements, Start up, and stand an end . iii 4 121
Be thou assured, if words be made of breath, And breath of life, I have no life to breathe What thou hast said to me . . . iii 4 198
Who was in life a foolish prating knave . . . iii 4 215
To keep it from divulging, let it feed Even on the pith of life . . iv 1 23
Is't possible, a young maid's wits Should be as mortal as an old man's life? . . . iv 5 160
We will our kingdom give, Our crown, our life, and all that we call ours iv 5 208
He which hath your noble father slain Pursued my life . . . iv 7 5
She's so conjunctive to my life and soul . . . iv 7 14
He that is not guilty of his own death shortens not his own life . . v 1 22
The corse they follow did with desperate hand Fordo it own life . . v 1 244
With, ho! such bugs and goblins in my life . . . v 2 22

Life. Thrown out his angle for my proper life . . . . . *Hamlet* v 2 66
And a man's life's no more than to say 'One' . . . . . v 2 74
Thou art slain; No medicine in the world can do thee good; In thee there is not half an hour of life . . . . . v 2 326
Where should we have our thanks?—Not from his mouth, Had it the ability of life to thank you . . . . . v 2 384
I love you . . . No less than life, with grace, health, beauty, honour *Lear* i 1 59
Answer my life my judgement, Thy youngest daughter does not love thee least . . . . . i 1 153
On thy life, no more.—My life I never held but as a pawn To wage against thy enemies; nor fear to lose it . . . . . i 1 156
I dare pawn down my life for him . . . . . i 2 93
Life and death! I am ashamed That thou hast power to shake my manhood thus . . . . . i 4 318
What, did my father's godson seek your life? . . . . . ii 1 93
This ancient ruffian, sir, whose life I have spared at suit of his gray beard . . . . . ii 2 67
Fetch forth the stocks! As I have life and honour, There shall he sit till noon . . . . . ii 2 140
Squire-like, pension beg To keep base life afoot . . . . . ii 4 218
Allow not nature more than nature needs, Man's life's as cheap as beast's . . . . . ii 4 270
That under covert and convenient seeming Hast practised on man's life iii 2 57
He sought my life, But lately, very late: I loved him, friend . . . iii 4 172
If thou shouldst dally half an hour, his life, With thine, and all that offer to defend him, Stand in assured loss . . . . . iii 6 100
Though well we may not pass upon his life Without the form of justice iii 7 24
World, world, O world! But that thy strange mutations make us hate thee, Life would not yield to age . . . . . iv 1 12
May all the building in my fancy pluck Upon my hateful life . . . iv 2 87
Lest his ungovern'd rage dissolve the life That wants the means to lead it . . . . . iv 4 19
Gone, In pity of his misery, to dispatch His nighted life . . . . iv 5 13
And yet I know not how conceit may rob The treasury of life, when life itself Yields to the theft . . . . . iv 6 43
Thy life's a miracle. Speak yet again . . . . . iv 6 55
I pardon that man's life. What was thy cause? Adultery? Thou shalt not die . . . . . iv 6 111
Then there's life in't. Nay, if you get it, you shall get it with running iv 6 206
An chud ha' bin zwaggered out of my life, 'twould not ha' bin zo long as 'tis . . . . . iv 6 244
A plot upon her virtuous husband's life! . . . . . iv 6 279
How shall I live and work, To match thy goodness? My life will be too short . . . . . iv 7 2
'Tis wonder that thy life and wits at once Had not concluded all . . iv 7 41
His life grew puissant, and the strings of life Began to crack . . v 3 216
I pant for life: some good I mean to do, Despite of mine own nature v 3 243
To the castle; for my writ Is on the life of Lear and on Cordelia . . v 3 246
Take my sword, Give it the captain.—Haste thee, for thy life . . v 3 251
For us, we will resign, During the life of this old majesty . . . v 3 299
And my poor fool is hang'd! No, no, no life! Why should a dog, a horse, a rat, have life, And thou no breath at all? . . . . . v 3 306
The wonder is, he hath endured so long: He but usurp'd his life . . v 3 317
For necessity of present life, I must show out a flag and sign of love *Othello* i 1 156
I fetch my life and being From men of royal siege . . . . . i 2 21
The trust, the office I do hold of you, Not only take away, but let your sentence Even fall upon my life . . . . . i 3 120
Still question'd me the story of my life, From year to year . . . . i 3 129
I do perceive here a divided duty: To you I am bound for life and education; My life and education both do learn me How to respect you . . . . . i 3 182
A soldier's a man; A life's but a span; Why, then, let a soldier drink . ii 3 74
'Tis the soldiers' life To have their balmy slumbers waked with strife . ii 3 257
Why is this? Think'st thou I'ld make a life of jealousy? . . . . iii 3 177
So prove it, That the probation bear no hinge nor loop To hang a doubt on; or woe upon thy life! . . . . . iii 3 366
Where I have garner'd up my heart, Where either I must live, or bear no life . . . . . iv 2 58
His unkindness may defeat my life, But never taint my love . . . . iv 2 160
Take me from this world with treachery and devise engines for my life iv 2 222
He hath a daily beauty in his life That makes me ugly . . . . . v 1 19
I am no strumpet; but of life as honest As you that thus abuse me . v 1 122
No, by my life and soul! Send for the man, and ask him . . . . v 2 49
And have you mercy too! I never did Offend you in my life . . . v 2 59
The nobleness of life Is to do thus . . . . . *Ant. and Cleo.* i 1 36
O excellent! I love long life better than figs . . . . . i 2 32
Who, high in name and power, Higher than both in blood and life . . i 2 197
Like the courser's hair, hath yet but life, And not a serpent's poison . i 2 200
There would he anchor his aspect and die With looking on his life . . i 5 34
She shows a body rather than a life, A statue than a breather . . . iii 3 23
So she From Egypt drive her all-disgraced friend, Or take his life there iii 12 23
The first stone Drop in my neck: as it determines, so Dissolve my life! iii 13 162
Lead you Where rather I'll expect victorious life Than death and honour iv 2 43
No: I will go seek Some ditch wherein to die; the foul'st best fits My latter part of life . . . . . iv 6 39
That life, a very rebel to my will, May hang no longer on me . . . iv 9 14
She render'd life, Thy name so buried in her . . . . . iv 14 33
He was my master; and I wore my life To spend upon his haters . . v 1 8
If thou please To take me to thee, as I was to him I'll be to Cæsar; if thou pleasest not, I yield thee up my life . . . . . v 1 12
Her life in Rome Would be eternal in our triumph . . . . . v 1 65
My desolation does begin to make A better life . . . . . v 2 2
I am fire and air; my other elements I give to baser life . . . . v 2 293
With thy sharp teeth this knot intrinsicate Of life at once untie . . v 2 308
To whom I have been often bound for no less than my life . *Cymbeline* i 4 28
So rarely and exactly wrought, Since the true life on't was— This is true . . . . . ii 4 76
O, this life Is nobler than attending for a check . . . . . iii 3 21
No life to ours.—Out of your proof you speak . . . . . iii 3 26
Haply this life is best, If quiet life be best; sweeter to you . . . iii 3 29
Strikes life into my speech and shows much more His own conceiving . iii 3 97
Let thine own hands take away her life: I shall give thee opportunity . iii 4 28
In my life what comfort, when I am Dead to my husband? . . . . iii 4 132
Since the exile of Posthumus, most retired Hath her life been . . . iii 5 37
I see a man's life is a tedious one: I have tired myself . . . . iii 6 1
And though you took his life, as being our foe, Yet bury him as a prince iv 2 250
A fever with the absence of her son, A madness, of which her life's in danger . . . . . iv 3 3
Sir, my life is yours; I humbly set it at your will . . . . . iv 3 12

Life. What pleasure, sir, find we in life, to lock it From action and adventure? . . . . . *Cymbeline* iv 4 2
Find in my exile the want of breeding, The certainty of this hard life . iv 4 27
So I'll die For thee, O Imogen, even for whom my life Is every breath a death . . . . . v 1 26
Our cowards, Like fragments in hard voyages became The life o' the need v 3 45
For Imogen's dear life take mine; and though 'Tis not so dear, yet 'tis a life . . . . . v 4 22
If you will take this audit, take this life, And cancel these cold bonds . v 4 27
Be what it is, The action of my life is like it, which I'll keep . . . v 4 150
By medicine life may be prolong'd, yet death Will seize the doctor too . v 5 29
How ended she?—With horror, madly dying, like her life . . . . v 5 31
Whose life, But that her flight prevented it, she had Ta'en off by poison v 5 45
Should by the minute feed on life and lingering By inches waste you . v 5 51
I do not bid thee beg my life, good lad; And yet I know thou wilt . . v 5 101
Your life, good master, Must shuffle for itself.—The boy disdains me . v 5 104
O Imogen! My queen, my life, my wife! O Imogen, Imogen! . . . . v 5 226
A certain stuff, which, being ta'en, would cease The present power of life v 5 256
I life would wish, and that I might Waste it for you, like taper-light *Pericles* i Gower 15
That whoso ask'd her for his wife, His riddle told not, lost his life i Gower 38
Death remember'd should be like a mirror, Who tells us life's but breath i 1 46
Thus ready for the way of life or death, I wait the sharpest blow . . i 1 54
Touch not, upon thy life, For that's an article within our law . . . i 1 87
Lest my life be cropp'd to keep you clear, By flight I'll shun the danger i 1 141
The passions of the mind, That have their first conception by mis-dread, Have after-nourishment and life by care . . . . . i 2 13
When Signior Sooth here does proclaim a peace, He flatters you, makes war upon your life . . . . . i 2 45
Thou know'st I have power To take thy life from thee . . . . . i 2 57
Who either by public war or private treason Will take away your life . i 2 105
Or till the Destinies do cut his thread of life . . . . . i 2 108
Unto the shipman's toil, With whom each minute threatens life or death i 3 25
So sharp are hunger's teeth, that man and wife Draw lots who first shall die to lengthen life . . . . . i 4 46
To make your needy bread, And give them life whom hunger starved half dead . . . . . i 4 96
My veins are chill, And have no more of life than may suffice To give my tongue that heat to ask your help . . . . . ii 1 78
With this strict charge, even as he left his life, 'Keep it, my Pericles' . ii 1 131
He loves you well that holds his life of you . . . . . ii 2 22
The king my father, sir, has drunk to you.—I thank him.—Wishing it so much blood unto your life . . . . . ii 3 77
For this twelvemonth she'll not undertake A married life . . . . ii 5 4
'Tis the king's subtilty to have my life. O, seek not to entrap me . . ii 5 44
If you love me, sir.—Even as my life my blood that fosters it . . . ii 5 89
That, as a duck for life that dives, So up and down the poor ship drives . . . . . iii Gower 49
Now, mild may be thy life! For a more blustrous birth had never babe iii 1 27
Death may usurp on nature many hours, And yet the fire of life kindle again The o'erpress'd spirits . . . . . iii 2 83
Marina's life Seeks to take off by treason's knife . . . . . iv Gower 13
I never did her hurt in all my life: I never spake bad word . . . . iv 1 75
How have I offended, Wherein my death might yield her any profit, Or my life imply her any danger? . . . . . iv 1 82
Your lady seeks my life; come you between, And save poor me, the weaker . . . . . iv 1 90
Call And give them repetition to the life . . . . . v 1 247
By my life *L. L. Lost* v 2; *M. N. Dream* iii 2; *As Y. Like It* iv 1; v 2; *All's Well* ii 3; v 3; *T. Night* ii 5; v 1; *W. Tale* ii 1; *K. John* iii 2; *Richard II.* v 2; 1 *Hen. IV.* iv 3; *Hen. VIII.* i 2; i 4; ii 3; ii 4; *Troi. and Cres.* iii 1; *Lear* i 3; *Cymbeline* ii 4
For my life *Much Ado* iii 2; *L. L. Lost* v 2; *T. of Shrew* iii 1; v 2; *W. Tale* iv 3; *Richard III.* iv 1
God's my life . . . . . *Much Ado* iv 2 72; *M. N. Dream* iv 1 209
On my life *Mer. Wives* i 1; *As Y. Like It* i 2; *All's Well* iii 6; v 3; *W. Tale* v 1; *Richard II.* ii 1; 1 *Hen. IV.* v 1; 2 *Hen. IV.* iv 3; *Richard III.* iii 2; *Rom. and Jul.* ii 1; ii 4; *Cymbeline* iii 4
Upon my life *Mer. Wives* v 5; *Com. of Errors* i 2; v 1; *T. of Shrew* Ind. 2 iii 2; *All's Well* iv 3; 1 *Hen. IV.* i 3; 2 *Hen. IV.* i 1; 2 *Hen. VI.* iii 1; *Richard III.* i 2; v 3; *Macbeth* v 1; *Hamlet* i 1; iv 7
Life's counsel. Though Richard my life's counsel would not hear, My death's sad tale may yet undeaf his ear . . . . . *Richard II.* ii 1 15
Life's decay. Till then fair hope must hinder life's decay . 3 *Hen. VI.* iv 4 16
Life's delight. To see his daughter, all his life's delight . *Pericles* iv 4 12
Life's end. Sweetly in force unto her fair life's end . *Richard III.* iv 4 351
Life's feast. Balm of hurt minds, great nature's second course, Chief nourisher in life's feast . . . . . *Macbeth* ii 2 40
Life's fitful fever. After life's fitful fever he sleeps well . . . iii 2 23
Life's flower. She gins to blow Into life's flower again! . *Pericles* iii 2 96
Life's history. Brutus' tongue Hath almost ended his life's history *J. C.* v 5 40
Life's key. Keep thy friend Under thy own life's key . . *All's Well* i 1 76
Life's means. Thriftless ambition, that wilt ravin up Thine own life's means! . . . . . *Macbeth* ii 4 29
Life's rate. She reckon'd it At her life's rate . . . . . *All's Well* v 3 91
Life's uncertain voyage. With other incident throes That nature's fragile vessel doth sustain In life's uncertain voyage . *T. of Athens* v 1 205
Life to come. All my life to come I'll lend you all my life to do you service *Meas. for Meas.* v 1 437
For the life to come, I sleep out the thought of it . . . . *W. Tale* iv 3 30
That but this blow Might be the be-all and the end-all here, But here, upon this bank and shoal of time, We'ld jump the life to come *Macb.* i 7 7
Life-blood. Every word in it a gaping wound, Issuing life-blood *M. of V.* iii 2 269
This sickness doth infect The very life-blood of our enterprise 1 *Hen. IV.* iv 1 29
These words of yours draw life-blood from my heart . 1 *Hen. VI.* iv 6 43
How couldst thou drain the life-blood of the child, To bid the father wipe his eyes withal? . . . . . 3 *Hen. VI.* i 4 138
By my soul, Your long coat, priest, protects you; thou shouldst feel My sword i' the life-blood of thee else . . . . . *Hen. VIII.* iii 2 277
I have touch'd thee to the quick, Thy life-blood out . *T. Andron.* iv 4 37
Life-harming. Lay aside life-harming heaviness . . *Richard II.* ii 2 3
Lifeless. But to procrastinate his lifeless end . . *Com. of Errors* i 1 159
Is but a quintain, a mere lifeless block . . . . . *As Y. Like It* i 2 263
In life so lifeless as it shows itself . . . . . *Hen. V.* iv 2 55
There lest his head and lifeless body lie . . . . . 2 *Hen. VI.* iv 1 142
Lifelings. 'Od's lifelings, here he is! . . . . . *T. Night* v 1 187
Life-preserving. In sport and life-preserving rest . . *Com. of Errors* v 1 83
Life-rendering. And like the kind life-rendering pelican, Repast them with my blood . . . . . *Hamlet* iv 5 146
Life-time. Let me for this my life-time reign as king . . 3 *Hen. VI.* i 1 171

Life-weary. That the life-weary taker may fall dead . *Rom. and Jul.* v 1 62
Lift. You would lift the moon out of her sphere . . . *Tempest* ii 1 183
Lift up your countenance . . . . *W. Tale* iv 4 49
Lift up thy looks . . . . iv 4 490
The peace of heaven is theirs that lift their swords In such a just and charitable war.—Well then, to work . . . . . . *K. John* ii 1 35
Lift up thy brow, renowned Salisbury . . . . . . v 2 54
The which if wrongfully, Let heaven revenge; for I may never lift An angry arm against His minister . . . . . *Richard II.* i 2 40
Whose youthful spirit . . . Doth with a twofold vigour lift me up . i 3 71
To lift shrewd steel against our golden crown . . . . iii 2 59
And they shall strike Your children yet unborn and unbegot, That lift your vassal hands against my head . . . . . . iii 3 89
I'll empty all these veins . . . , But I will lift the down-trod Mortimer As high in the air as this unthankful king. . . . . 1 *Hen. IV.* i 3 135
Have you any levers to lift me up again, being down? . . . ii 2 36
Better consider what you have to do Than I, that have not well the gift of tongue, Can lift your blood up with persuasion . . . . v 2 79
His forward spirit Would lift him where most trade of danger ranged 2 *Hen. IV.* i 1 174
He ne'er lift up his hand but conquered . . . . 1 *Hen. VI.* i 1 16
We'll both together lift our heads to heaven . . . 2 *Hen. VI.* i 2 14
As the long divorce of steel falls on me, Make of your prayers one sweet sacrifice, And lift my soul to heaven . . . *Hen. VIII.* ii 1 78
Will he, within three pound, lift as much as his brother Hector *T. and C.* i 2 126
The bounded waters Should lift their bosoms higher than the shores . i 3 112
That spirit of his In aspiration lifts him from the earth . . . iv 5 16
You may as well Strike at the heaven with your staves as lift them Against the Roman state . . . . . *Coriolanus* i 1 70
Shall lift up Their rotten privilege and custom 'gainst My hate . . i 10 22
O, here I lift this one hand up to heaven, And bow this feeble ruin to the earth: If any power pities wretched tears . . *T. Andron.* iii 1 207
Why lifts she up her arms in sequence thus? . . . . iv 1 37
And all this day an unaccustom'd spirit Lifts me above the ground with cheerful thoughts . . . . . *Rom. and Jul.* v 1 5
Hence! wilt thou lift up Olympus? . . . . *J. Cæsar* iii 1 74
If I once stir, Or do but lift this arm, the best of you Shall sink in my rebuke . . . . *Othello* ii 3 208
For thou hast kill'd the sweetest innocent That e'er did lift up eye . v 2 200
So; lift there.—What is that? . . . . . *Pericles* iii 2 49
Lifted. Advanced their eyelids, lifted up their noses . *Tempest* iv 1 177
She lifted the princess from the earth, and so locks her in embracing *W. T.* v 2 83
It lifted up it head and did address Itself to motion . . *Hamlet* i 2 216
Lifter. Is he so young a man and so old a lifter? . *Troi. and Cres.* i 2 129
Lifting. A summer bird, Which ever in the haunch of winter sings The lifting up of day . . . . 2 *Hen. IV.* iv 4 93
It is not as this mouth should tear this hand For lifting food to 't *Lear* iii 4 16
Lig. Ay'll de gud service, or ay'll lig i' the grund for it . *Hen. V.* iii 2 124
Ligarius. Caius Ligarius doth bear Cæsar hard . . . *J. Cæsar* ii 1 215
Here is a sick man that would speak with you.—Caius Ligarius . ii 1 311
Such an exploit have I in hand, Ligarius, Had you a healthful ear to hear ii 1 318
Caius Ligarius, Cæsar was ne'er so much your enemy As that same ague ii 2 111
Decius Brutus loves thee not: thou hast wronged Caius Ligarius . ii 3 5
Liggens. By God's liggens, I thank thee . . . . 2 *Hen. IV.* v 3 69
Light. Teach me how To name the bigger light, and how the less *Tempest* i 2 335
All the charms Of Sycorax, toads, beetles, bats, light on you! . i 2 340
This man's threats, To whom I am subdued, are but light to me . i 2 489
By this good light, this is a very shallow monster! . . . ii 2 147
By this light, a most perfidious and drunken monster! . . . ii 2 153
By this light, thou shalt be my lieutenant, monster, or my standard . iii 2 17
Therefore take heed, As Hymen's lamps shall light you . . . iv 1 23
It is too heavy for so light a tune . . . *T. G. of Ver.* i 2 84
Love is blind. O, that you had mine eyes; or your own eyes had the lights they were wont to have! . . . . . . ii 1 77
But her picture I have yet beheld, And that hath dazzled my reason's light . . . . ii 4 210
He shall never know That I had any light from thee of this . . iii 1 49
How shall I best convey the ladder thither?—It will be light, my lord iii 1 129
What light is light, if Silvia be not seen? What joy is joy? . . iii 1 174
Thine own true knight, By day or night, Or any kind of light *Mer. Wives* ii 1 17
We'll couch i' the castle ditch till we see the light of our fairies . v 2 2
The night is dark; light and spirits will become it well . . . v 2 13
They are all couched in a pit hard by Herne's oak, with obscured lights v 3 15
Heaven doth with us as we with torches do, Not light them for themselves; for if our virtues Did not go forth of us . *Meas. for Meas.* i 1 34
The duke yet would have dark deeds darkly answered; he would never bring them to light . . . . iii 2 189
And those eyes, the break of day, Lights that do mislead the morn . iv 1 4
As there comes light from heaven and words from breath . . . v 1 225
That's the way; for women are light at midnight . . . . v 1 280
For what obscured light the heavens did grant Did but convey unto our fearful minds A doubtful warrant of immediate death *Com. of Er.* i 1 67
By the benefit of his wished light, The seas wax'd calm . . . i 1 91
Let Love, being light, be drowned if she sink! . . . . iii 2 52
I know not what use to put her to but to make a lamp of her and run from her by her own light . . . . iii 2 99
It is written, they appear to men like angels of light . . . iv 3 56
Light is an effect of fire, and fire will burn . . . . iv 3 56
It seems his sleeps were hinder'd by thy railing, And thereof comes it that his head is light . . . . v 1 72
You may light on a husband that hath no beard . . . *Much Ado* ii 1 34
An it be the right husband and the right wife; otherwise 'tis light, and not heavy . . . . iii 4 37
These things, come thus to light, Smother her spirits up . . iv 1 112
By this light, he changes more and more: I think he be angry indeed . v 1 140
What your wisdoms could not discover, these shallow fools have brought to light . . . . v 1 240
Come, I will have thee; but, by this light, I take thee for pity . v 4 93
Light seeking light doth light of light beguile . . . *L. L. Lost* i 1 77
So, ere you find where light in darkness lies, Your light grows dark by losing of your eyes . . . . i 1 79
That eye shall be his heed And give him light that it was blinded by . i 1 83
Earthly godfathers of heaven's lights That give a name to every fixed star i 1 88
What is she in the white?—A woman sometimes, an you saw her in the light.—Perchance light in the light . . . . . . ii 1 198
By this light, but for her eye, I would not love her . . . iv 3 10
As doth thy face through tears of mine give light . . . . iv 3 32
Her mistress is a gracious moon; She an attending star, scarce seen a light iv 3 231
Devils soonest tempt, resembling spirits of light . . . . iv 3 257
Dark needs no candles now, for dark is light . . . . . iv 3 269
Light. Had she been light, like you, Of such a merry, nimble, stirring spirit, She might ha' been a grandam ere she died . *L. L. Lost* v 2 15
We need more light to find your meaning out.—You'll mar the light by taking it in snuff; Therefore I'll darkly end the argument . . v 2 21
When we greet, With eyes best seeing, heaven's fiery eye, By light we lose light . . . . v 2 376
A light for Monsieur Judas! it grows dark, he may stumble . . . v 2 633
The honey-bags steal from the humble-bees, And for night tapers crop their waxen thighs And light them at the fiery glow-worm's eyes *M. N. Dream* iii 1 173
Who more engilds the night Than all yon fiery oes and eyes of light . iii 2 188
They wilfully themselves exile from light . . . . . iii 2 386
Come, thou gentle day! For if but once thou show me thy grey light, I'll find Demetrius . . . . iii 2 419
My soul is in the sky: Tongue, lose thy light; Moon, take thy flight . v 1 309
Through the house give glimmering light, By the dead and drowsy fire v 1 398
Every elf and fairy sprite Hop as light as bird from brier . . v 1 401
Truth will come to light; murder cannot be hid long . *Mer. of Venice* ii 2 83
What, must I hold a candle to my shames? They in themselves, good sooth, are too too light . . . . ii 6 42
Nor no ill luck stirring but what lights on my shoulders . . . iii 1 99
Let the danger light Upon your charter and your city's freedom . . iv 1 38
Be it but so much As makes it light or heavy in the substance . . iv 1 328
That light we see is burning in my hall . . . . . . v 1 89
Let me give light, but let me not be light . . . . . v 1 129
We'll light upon some settled low content . . . *As Y. Like It* ii 3 68
If I can by any means light on a fit man to teach her . *T. of Shrew* i 1 112
There be good fellows in the world, an a man could light on them . . i 1 133
Knowing thee to be but young and light— Too light for such a swain as you to catch . . . . ii 1 204
By this light, whereby I see thy beauty . . . . . ii 1 275
In his bright radiance and collateral light Must I be comforted *All's Well* i 1 99
Let every word weigh heavy of her worth That he does weigh too light iii 4 32
If the quick fire of youth light not your mind, You are no maiden . iv 2 5
We may pick a thousand salads ere we light on such another herb . iv 5 15
Haply your eye shall light upon some toy You have desire to purchase *T. Night* iii 3 44
Help me to some light and some paper . . . . . . iv 2 113
Good fool, some ink, paper and light . . . . iv 2 118
I will fetch you light and paper and ink . . . . . . iv 2 126
A nest of traitors!—I am none, by this good light . . . *W. Tale* ii 3 82
If young Doricles Do light upon her, she shall bring him that Which he not dreams of . . . . iv 4 179
By this light, . . . I would not wish a better father . . *K. John* i 1 259
Our curses light on thee So heavy as thou shalt not shake them off . iii 1 295
We had a kind of light what would ensue . . . . . iv 3 61
And when I mount, alive may I not light, If I be traitor! *Richard II.* i 1 82
I turn me from my country's light, To dwell in solemn shades of endless night . . . . i 3 176
My oil-dried lamp and time-bewasted light Shall be extinct with age . i 3 221
For gnarling sorrow hath less power to bite The man that mocks at it and sets it light . . . . i 3 293
Our coffers, with too great a court . . . , are grown somewhat light . i 4 44
When the searching eye of heaven is hid, Behind the globe, that lights the lower world, Then thieves and robbers range abroad . . . iii 2 38
And darts his light through every guilty hole . . . . . iii 2 43
Nothing but himself, And some few vanities that make him light . . iii 4 86
And never show thy head by day nor light . . . . . . v 6 44
If they 'scape from your encounter, then they light on us . 1 *Hen. IV.* ii 2 65
Your whole plot too light for the counterpoise of so great an opposition ii 3 14
And that shall be the day, whene'er it lights . . . . . iii 2 138
And wert indeed, but for the light in thy face, the son of utter darkness iii 3 41
The sack that thou hast drunk me would have bought me lights . . iii 3 51
God's light, I was never called so in mine own house before . . . iii 3 71
Move in that obedient orb again Where you did give a fair and natural light . . . . v 1 18
Yet cannot he see, though he have his own lanthorn to light him 2 *Hen. IV.* i 2 55
Not so, my lord; your ill angel is light; but I hope he that looks upon me will take me without weighing . . . . i 2 187
By this light, I am well spoke on . . . . ii 2 69
By his light Did all the chivalry of England move To do brave acts . ii 3 19
Believe me, I am passing light in spirit . . . . . . iv 2 85
By his gates of breath There lies a downy feather which stirs not: Did he suspire, that light and weightless down Perforce must move . iv 5 33
Since God so graciously hath brought to light This dangerous treason *Hen. V.* ii 2 185
A most contagious treason come to light, look you . . . . iv 8 23
By this day and this light, the fellow has mettle enough . . . iv 8 66
A plaguing mischief light on Charles and thee! . . . 1 *Hen. VI.* v 3 39
She will light to listen to the lays, And never mount . . 2 *Hen. VI.* i 3 93
That to believing souls Gives light in darkness, comfort in despair! . ii 1 67
Dark shall be my light and night my day . . . . . . ii 4 40
These are petty faults to faults unknown, Which time will bring to light iii 1 65
And so, God's curse light upon you all! . . . . . . iv 8 33
Now are they but one lamp, one light, one sun . . . 3 *Hen. VI.* ii 1 31
Notwithstanding join our lights together And over-shine the earth . ii 1 37
Like to the morning's war, When dying clouds contend with growing light ii 5 2
Here burns my candle out; ay, here it dies, Which, whiles it lasted, gave King Henry light . . . . ii 6 2
Thou keep'st me from the light: But I will sort a pitchy day for thee . v 6 84
Prodigious, and untimely brought to light . . . . *Richard III.* i 2 22
Day, yield me not thy light; nor, night, thy rest! . . . . iv 4 401
The lights burn blue. It is now dead midnight . . . . . v 3 180
How came His practices to light?—Most strangely . . . *Hen. VIII.* iii 2 29
An hundred marks! By this light, I'll ha' more . . . . . v 1 171
Lest Hector or my father should perceive me, I have, as when the sun doth light a storm, Buried this sigh in wrinkle of a smile *T. and C.* i 1 37
As there were husbandry in war, Before the sun rose he was harness'd light . . . . i 2 8
Distinction, with a broad and powerful fan, Puffing at all, winnows the light away . . . . i 3 28
We go wrong.—No, yonder 'tis; There, where we see the lights . . v 1 75
All the contagion of the south light on you, You shames of Rome! *Coriol.* i 4 30
I could weep And I could laugh, I am light and heavy . . . . ii 1 201
From that womb . . . He is enfranchised and come to light *T. Andron.* iv 2 125
Come down, and welcome me to this world's light; Confer with me of murder . . . . v 2 33
Away from light steals home my heavy son . . . *Rom. and Jul.* i 1 143
Look to behold this night Earth-treading stars that make dark heaven light . . . . i 2 25

Light. I am not for this ambling; Being but heavy, I will bear the light *Rom. and Jul.* i 4 12
In delay We waste our lights in vain, like lamps by day . i 4 45
More light, you knaves; and turn the tables up, And quench the fire . i 5 29
You are a princox; go: Be quiet, or—More light, more light! . . i 5 89
What light through yonder window breaks? It is the east, and Juliet is the sun . . . . ii 2 2
I am too fond, And therefore thou mayst think my 'haviour light. . ii 2 99
A thousand times good night!—A thousand times the worse, to want thy light . . . . ii 2 156
Chequering the eastern clouds with streaks of light . . . . ii 3 2
O, so light a foot Will ne'er wear out the everlasting flint . . ii 6 16
A lover may bestride the gossamer That idles in the wanton summer air, And yet not fall; so light is vanity . . . . ii 6 20
A pack of blessings lights upon thy back; Happiness courts thee . . iii 3 141
Light to my chamber, ho! Afore me! it is so very very late . . iii 4 33
Yon light is not day-light, I know it, I: It is some meteor that the sun exhales, To be to thee this night a torch-bearer, And light thee on thy way to Mantua . . . . iii 5 12
O, now be gone; more light and light it grows.—More light and light; more dark and dark our woes! . . . . iii 5 35
My heart is wondrous light . . . . iv 2 46
Give me the light: upon thy life, I charge thee, Whate'er thou hear'st or seest, stand all aloof . . . . v 3 25
Her beauty makes This vault a feasting presence full of light . . v 3 86
What torch is yond, that vainly lends his light To grubs and eyeless skulls? . . . . v 3 125
Anon comes one with light to ope the tomb . . . . . v 3 283
Lights, more lights! . . . . *T. of Athens* i 2 234
When every room Hath blazed with lights and bray'd with minstrelsy . ii 2 170
How came the noble Timon to this change?—As the moon does, by wanting light to give . . . . iv 3 67
Yonder comes a poet and a painter: the plague of company light upon thee! . . . . iv 3 357
When the day serves, before black-corner'd night, Find what thou want'st by free and offer'd light . . . . v 1 48
Fall upon your knees, Pray to the gods to intermit the plague That needs must light on this ingratitude . . . . . *J. Cæsar* i 1 60
The exhalations whizzing in the air Give so much light that I may read by them . . . . ii 1 45
A curse shall light upon the limbs of men . . . . . . iii 1 262
Now some light. O, he lights too. He's ta'en . . . . v 3 31
Stars, hide your fires; Let not light see my black and deep desires *Macb.* i 4 51
Darkness does the face of earth entomb, When living light should kiss it . . . . ii 4 10
Light thickens; and the crow Makes wing to the rooky wood . . iii 2 50
Hark! I hear horses.—Give us a light there, ho!—Then 'tis he . . iii 3 9
Who did strike out the light?—Was't not the way? . . . . iii 3 19
How came she by that light?—Why, it stood by her: she has light by her continually . . . . v 1 25
These blazes, daughter, Giving more light than heat . . *Hamlet* i 3 118
He seem'd to find his way without his eyes; For out o' doors he went without their helps, And, to the last, bended their light on me . ii 1 100
And I hold ambition of so airy and light a quality that it is but a shadow's shadow . . . . ii 2 268
Seneca cannot be too heavy, nor Plautus too light . . . . ii 2 420
Baked and impasted with the parching streets, That lend a tyrannous and damned light To their lord's murder . . . . . . ii 2 482
Nor earth to me give food, nor heaven light! . . . . . iii 2 226
Give me some light: away!—Lights, lights, lights! . . . . iii 2 280
Yet are they much too light for the bore of the matter . . . iv 6 26
Youth no less becomes The light and careless livery that it wears Than settled age his sables and his weeds . . . . iv 7 80
But I do prophesy the election lights On Fortinbras . . . . v 2 366
Light, ho, here! Fly, brother. Torches, torches! So, farewell . *Lear* ii 1 33
That way, I'll this,—he that first lights on him Holla the other . iii 1 54
Now, all the plagues that in the pendulous air Hang fated o'er men's faults light on thy daughters! . . . . iii 4 70
How light and portable my pain seems now, When that which makes me bend makes the king bow! . . . . iii 6 115
Your eyes are in a heavy case, your purse in a light . . . iv 6 151
This accident is not unlike my dream: Belief of it oppresses me already. Light, I say! light! . . . . *Othello* i 1 145
What lights come yond?—Those are the raised father and his friends . i 2 28
Destruction on my head, if my bad blame Light on the man! . . i 3 178
Hell and night Must bring this monstrous birth to the world's light . i 3 410
He that stirs next to carve for his own rage Holds his soul light . ii 3 174
Thy honesty and love doth mince this matter, Making it light to Cassio ii 3 248
Witness, you ever-burning lights above, You elements that clip us round about . . . . iii 3 463
No, by this heavenly light!—Nor I neither by this heavenly light; I might do't as well i' the dark . . . . iv 3 65
O, help, ho! light! a surgeon! . . . . v 1 30
Here's one comes in his shirt, with light and weapons . . . v 1 47
My leg is cut in two.—Marry, heaven forbid! Light, gentlemen: I'll bind it . . . . v 1 73
Lend me a light.—Know we this face or no? . . . . . v 1 88
Put out the light, and then put out the light: If I quench thee, thou flaming minister, I can again thy former light restore, Should I repent me: but once put out thy light, Thou cunning'st pattern of excelling nature, I know not where is that Promethean heat That can thy light relume . . . . v 2 7
And made the night light with drinking . . . *Ant. and Cleo.* ii 2 182
Let all the number of the stars give light To thy fair way! . . iii 2 65
But, you know, strange fowl light upon neighbouring ponds . *Cymbeline* i 4 97
Base and unlustrous as the smoky light That's fed with stinking tallow i 6 109
The flame o' the taper Bows toward her, and would under-peep her lids, To see the enclosed lights . . . . ii 2 21
If Cæsar can hide the sun from us with a blanket, or put the moon in his pocket, we will pay him tribute for light . . . . . iii 1 45
Though light, take pieces for the figure's sake . . . . . v 4 25
Purse and brain both empty; the brain the heavier for being too light, the purse too light, being drawn of heaviness . . . . . v 4 167
Fair glass of light, I loved you, and could still, Were not this glorious casket stored with ill . . . . *Pericles* i 1 76
Those men Blush not in actions blacker than the night, Will shun no course to keep them from the light . . . . i 1 136
Day serves not light more faithful than I'll be . . . . . i 2 110
Why . . . He would depart, I'll give some light unto you . . . i 3 18
Like lesser lights, Did vail their crowns to his supremacy . . . ii 3 41

Light. Like a glow-worm in the night, The which hath fire in darkness, none in light . . . . *Pericles* ii 3 44
Pages and lights, to conduct These knights unto their several lodgings! ii 3 109
She'll wed the stranger knight, Or never more to view nor day nor light . . . . ii 5 17
No light, no fire: the unfriendly elements Forgot thee utterly . . iii 1 58
You are light into my hands, where you are like to live . . . iv 2 77
Light airs. It did relieve my passion much, More than light airs *T. Night* ii 4 5
Light answers. No more light answers . . . . *Ant. and Cleo.* i 2 183
Light as air. Trifles light as air Are to the jealous confirmations strong As proofs of holy writ . . . . *Othello* iii 3 322
Light as chaff. Even our corn shall seem as light as chaff . 2 *Hen. IV.* iv 1 195
Light as tales. Put in two scales, Will even weigh, and both as light as tales . . . . *M. N. Dream* iii 2 133
Light behaviour. His unbookish jealousy must construe Poor Cassio's smiles, gestures, and light behaviour, Quite in the wrong *Othello* iv 1 103
Light boats sail swift, though greater hulks draw deep . *Troi. and Cres.* ii 3 277
Light condition. A light condition in a beauty dark . . *L. L. Lost* v 2 20
Light crowns. Hath, for a few light crowns, lightly conspired *Hen. V.* ii 2 89
Light deliverance. If seriously I may convey my thoughts In this my light deliverance . . . . *All's Well* ii 1 85
Light enough. Ay, gentle cousin, were it light enough . *Richard III.* iii 1 117
Light feathers. I am too sore enpierced with his [Cupid's] shaft To soar with his light feathers . . . . *Rom. and Jul.* i 4 20
Light flesh. By this light flesh and corrupt blood . . 2 *Hen. IV.* ii 4 320
Light foam. Prepare thy grave; Lie where the light foam of the sea may beat Thy grave-stone daily . . . . . *T. of Athens* iv 3 379
Light-foot. Some light-foot friend post to the Duke . *Richard III.* iv 4 440
Light gifts. O, then, I see, you will part but with light gifts . . iii 1 118
Light heart. Command these fretting waters from your eyes With a light heart . . . . *Meas. for Meas.* iv 3 152
A light heart lives long . . . . *L. L. Lost* v 2 18
Light horsemen. I hear the enemy: Out, some light horsemen 1 *Hen. VI.* iv 2 43
Light loss. The difference Is purchase of a heavy curse from Rome, Or the light loss of England for a friend . . . . . *K. John* iii 1 206
Light love. Pardon me, And not impute this yielding to light love, Which the dark night hath so discovered . . . *Rom. and Jul.* ii 2 105
Light nut. There can be no kernel in this light nut . . . *All's Well* ii 5 48
Light of brain. Are his wits safe? is he not light of brain? . *Othello* iv 1 280
Light of discretion. It appears, by his small light of discretion, that he is in the wane . . . . *M. N. Dream* v 1 257
Light of ear. False of heart, light of ear, bloody of hand . . *Lear* iii 4 95
Lights of favour. You have given me such clear lights of favour *T. Night* v 1 344
Light of foot. Nimble mischance, that art so light of foot *Richard II.* iii 4 92
Light of heart. Let wantons light of heart Tickle the senseless rushes with their heels . . . . *Rom. and Jul.* i 4 35
Light of heaven. By this light of heaven, I know not how I lost him *Oth.* iv 2 150
Light of love. Best sing it to the tune of 'Light o' love.'—It is too heavy for so light a tune . . . . *T. G. of Ver.* i 2 83
Clap's into 'Light o' love;' that goes without a burden . *Much Ado* iii 4 44
Ye light o' love, with your heels! . . . . iii 4 47
Lights of men. Those suns of glory, those two lights of men . *Hen. VIII.* i 1 6
Light of truth. As, painfully to pore upon a book To seek the light of truth . . . . *L. L. Lost* i 1 75
Light payment. And yet that were but light payment . 2 *Hen. IV.* Epil. 20
Light skirmishes. Or with light skirmishes enfeebled . 1 *Hen. VI.* i 4 69
Light vanity, insatiate cormorant, Consuming means, soon preys upon itself . . . . *Richard II.* ii 1 38
Light wench. She is the devil's dam; and here she comes in the habit of a light wench . . . . *Com. of Errors* iv 3 52
'God damn me;' that's as much to say 'God make me a light wench' iv 3 55
Light is an effect of fire, and fire will burn; ergo, light wenches will burn . . . . iv 3 57
Sing, boy; my spirit grows heavy in love.—And that's great marvel, loving a light wench . . . . *L. L. Lost* i 2 128
Light wenches may prove plagues to men forsworn. . . . . iv 3 385
You are a light wench.—Indeed I weigh not you, and therefore light . v 2 25
Light wife. A light wife doth make a heavy husband . *Mer. of Venice* v 1 130
Light wings. With love's light wings did I o'er-perch these walls *Rom. and Jul.* ii 2 66
Light-wing'd toys Of feather'd Cupid . . . . *Othello* i 3 269
Light winning. Lest too light winning Make the prize light . *Tempest* i 2 451
Light word. What's your dark meaning, mouse, of this light word? *L. L. L.* v 2 19
Lighted. No bed-right shall be paid Till Hymen's torch be lighted *Temp.* iv 1 97
By good fortune I have lighted well On this young man . *T. of Shrew* i 2 168
New lighted from his horse, Stain'd with the variation of each soil 1 *Hen. IV.* i 1 63
Now thy heavy curse Is lighted on poor Hastings' wretched head! *Richard III.* iii 4 95
When they lighted, how they clung In their embracement . *Hen. VIII.* i 1 9
A taper in my study, Lucius: When it is lighted, come and call me *J. C.* ii 1 8
This murderous shaft that's shot Hath not yet lighted . . *Macbeth* ii 3 148
And all our yesterdays have lighted fools The way to dusty death. . . v 5 22
His face was as the heavens; and therein stuck A sun and moon, which kept their course, and lighted The little O, the earth *Ant. and Cleo.* v 2 80
Lighten. Very oft . . . Lightens my humour with his merry jests *C. of Er.* i 2 21
Let's have a dance ere we are married, that we may lighten our own hearts and our wives' heels . . . . *Much Ado* v 4 120
Yet looks he like a king: behold, his eye, As bright as is the eagle's, lightens forth Controlling majesty . . . . . *Richard II.* iii 3 69
Now the Lord lighten thee! thou art a great fool . . 2 *Hen. IV.* ii 1 208
A gem To lighten all this isle . . . . *Hen. VIII.* ii 3 79
He doth wear A precious ring, that lightens all the hole *T. Andron.* ii 3 227
Too unadvised, too sudden; Too like the lightning, which doth cease to be Ere one can say 'It lightens' . . . . . *Rom. and Jul.* ii 2 120
This dreadful night, That thunders, lightens, opens graves, and roars *J. Cæsar* i 3 74
Lighter. To frown Upon Sir Toby and the lighter people . *T. Night* v 1 347
My heart is ten times lighter than my looks . . *Richard III.* v 3 3
Lighter-heeled. The villain is much lighter-heel'd than I *M. N. Dream* iii 2 415
Lightest. Making them lightest that wear most of it . *Mer. of Venice* iii 2 91
I could a tale unfold whose lightest word Would harrow up thy soul *Ham.* i 5 15
Lightly. O, could their master come and go as lightly! . *T. G. of Ver.* iii 1 142
And will not lightly trust the messenger . . . *Com. of Errors* iv 4 5
They are but lightly rewarded . . . . *L. L. Lost* i 2 157
This man Hath, for a few light crowns, lightly conspired . *Hen. V* ii 2 89
Was ever feather so lightly blown to and fro as this multitude? 2 *Hen. VI.* iv 8 57
By holy Paul, they love his grace but lightly That fill his ears with such dissentious rumours . . . . *Richard III.* i 3 45
Short summers lightly have a forward spring . . . . . . iii 1 94
I weigh it lightly, were it heavier . . . . iii 1 121

Lightly. Believe't not lightly — *Coriolanus* iv 1 29
I beg this boon, with tears not lightly shed — *T. Andron.* ii 3 289
My bosom's lord sits lightly in his throne — *Rom. and Jul.* v 1 3
Bid that welcome Which comes to punish us, and we punish it Seeming to bear it lightly — *Ant. and Cleo.* iv 14 138

Lightness. Can it be That modesty may more betray our sense Than woman's lightness? — *Meas. for Meas.* ii 2 170
Since mine eyes are witness of her lightness, . . . Forswear Bianca — *T. of S.* iv 2 24
So did our men, heavy in Hotspur's loss, Lend to this weight such lightness with their fear That arrows fled not swifter — *2 Hen. IV.* i 1 122
He hath the horn of abundance, and the lightness of his wife shines through it — i 2 53
Such is the lightness of you common men — *3 Hen. VI.* iii 1 89
O heavy lightness! serious vanity! Mis-shapen chaos! — *Rom. and Jul.* i 1 184
Thence to a watch, thence into a weakness, Thence to a lightness — *Hamlet* ii 2 149
When we do bear So great weight in his lightness — *Ant. and Cleo.* i 4 25

Lightning. Jove's lightnings, the precursors O' the dreadful thunder-claps, more momentary And sight-outrunning were not — *Tempest* i 2 201
I would the lightning had Burnt up those logs that you are enjoin'd to pile! — iii 1 16
Thy eye Jove's lightning bears, thy voice his dreadful thunder — *L. L. Lost* iv 2 119
Brief as the lightning in the collied night — *M. N. Dream* i 1 145
Be thou as lightning in the eyes of France — *K. John* i 1 24
Be swift like lightning in the execution — *Richard II.* i 3 79
Their weapons like to lightning came and went — *3 Hen. VI.* ii 1 129
Either heaven with lightning strike the murderer dead, Or earth, gape open wide and eat him quick! — *Richard III.* i 2 64
Too unadvised, too sudden; Too like the lightning, which doth cease to be Ere one can say 'It lightens' — *Rom. and Jul.* ii 2 119
And to't they go like lightning — iii 1 177
A lightning before death: O, how may I Call this a lightning? — v 3 90
The cross blue lightning seem'd to open The breast of heaven — *J. Cæsar* i 3 50
When shall we three meet again In thunder, lightning, or in rain? — *Macb.* i 1 2
You nimble lightnings, dart your blinding flames Into her scornful eyes! — *Lear* ii 4 167
In the most terrible and nimble stroke Of quick, cross lightning — iv 7 35
Now he'll outstare the lightning — *Ant. and Cleo.* iii 13 195
And she, like harmless lightning, throws her eye On him — *Cymbeline* v 5 394

Lightning-flash. And sits aloft, Secure of thunder's crack or lightning-flash — *T. Andron.* ii 1 3
Fear no more the lightning-flash,—Nor the all-dreaded thunder-stone — *Cymbeline* iv 2 271

Like. 'Tis far off And rather like a dream — *Tempest* i 2 45
And my trust, Like a good parent, did beget of him A falsehood in its contrary as great As my trust was — i 2 94
Like one Who having into truth, by telling of it, Made such a sinner of his memory, To credit his own lie — i 2 99
Go make thyself like a nymph o' the sea — i 2 301
No better than the earth he lies upon, If he were that which now he's like, that's dead — ii 1 282
Draw together; And when I rear my hand, do you the like — ii 1 295
Take thou that. As you like this, give me the lie another time — iii 2 85
Dost thou like the plot, Trinculo?—Excellent — iii 2 117
Will money buy 'em?—Very like; one of them is a plain fish — v 1 265
And yet methinks I do not like this tune — *T. G. of Ver.* i 2 90
I like thy counsel; well hast thou advised: And that thou mayst perceive how well I like it The execution of it shall make known — i 3 35
Like Sir Proteus, to wreathe your arms, like a malecontent; to relish a love-song, like a robin-redbreast; to walk alone, like one that had the pestilence; . . . to weep, like a young wench that had buried her grandam; to fast, like one that takes diet; to watch, like one that fears robbing; . . . You were wont, when you laughed, to crow like a cock; when you walked, to walk like one of the lions — ii 1 19
To sigh, like a school-boy that had lost his A B C — ii 1 22
To speak puling, like a beggar at Hallowmas — ii 1 26
What means your ladyship? do you not like it?—Yes, yes — ii 1 127
O, be not like your mistress; be moved, be moved — ii 1 181
When I was sick, you gave me bitter pills, And I must minister the like to you — ii 4 150
My foolish rival, that her father likes Only for his possessions — ii 4 174
If Proteus like your journey when you come, No matter who's displeased — ii 7 65
For such like petty crimes as these — iv 1 52
The music likes you not.—You mistake; the musician likes me not — iv 2 56
How likes she my discourse?—Ill, when you talk of war — v 2 15
How like a dream is this I see and hear! — v 4 26
Vat is you sing? I do not like des toys — *Mer. Wives* i 4 45
Did you ever hear the like? — ii 1 70
I like it never the better for that — ii 1 186
Like a fair house built on another man's ground — ii 2 224
I like his money well. O, here he comes — iii 5 59
May I be bold to say so, sir?—Ay, sir; like who more bold — iv 5 55
Now, good Sir John, how like you Windsor wives? — v 5 110
But, like a thrifty goddess, she determines Herself the glory of a creditor, Both thanks and use — *Meas. for Meas.* i 1 39
I love the people, But do not like to stage me to their eyes — i 1 69
She can persuade.—I pray she may; as well for the encouragement of the like — i 2 193
Where is the provost?—Here, if it like your honour — ii 1 33
An it like you, the house is a respected house — ii 1 169
She comes to do you good.—I do desire the like — iv 1 52
'Tis a meddling friar; I do not like the man — v 1 128
Like doth quit like, and MEASURE still FOR MEASURE — v 1 416
As like almost to Claudio as himself — v 1 494
If he be like your brother, for his sake Is he pardon'd — v 1 495
The one so like the other As could not be distinguish'd but by names — *Com. of Errors* i 1 52
His attendant—so his case was like, Reft of his brother — i 1 128
If you like elsewhere, do it by stealth — iii 2 7
What complexion is she of?—Swart, like my shoe — iii 2 104
Bearing thence Rings, jewels, any thing his rage did like — v 1 144
These two Antipholuses, these two so like, And these two Dromios — v 1 357
Be happy, lady; for you are like an honourable father — *Much Ado* i 1 113
She would not have his head on her shoulders for all Messina, as like him as she is — i 1 116
Being no other but as she is, I do not like her — i 1 178
Thou wilt be like a lover presently And tire the hearer with a book of words — i 1 308
And when please you to say so?—When I like your favour; for God defend the lute should be like the case! — ii 1 98
I would you did like me.—So would not I, for your own sake — *Much Ado* ii 1 104
Hath your grace ne'er a brother like you? — ii 1 336
I like the new tire within excellently, if the hair were a thought browner — iii 4 13
Pray thee, fellow, peace: I do not like thy look, I promise thee — iv 2 46
But no man's virtue nor sufficiency To be so moral when he shall endure The like himself — v 1 31
Let me see his eyes, That, when I note another man like him, I may avoid him — v 1 270
Then was Venus like her mother, for her father is but grim — *L. L. Lost* ii 1 255
Thy love is black as ebony.—Is ebony like her? O wood divine! — iv 3 248
To look like her are chimney-sweepers black — iv 3 266
He hath drawn my picture in his letter.—Any thing like? — v 2 39
How like you the young German? — *Mer. of Venice* i 2 90
Is't like that lead contains her? — ii 7 49
If we are like you in the rest, we will resemble you in that — iii 1 70
Antonio, Being the bosom lover of my lord, Must needs be like my lord — iii 4 18
Say thy opinion, How dost thou like the Lord Bassanio's wife? — iii 5 77
For affection, Mistress of passion, sways it to the mood Of what it likes or loathes — iv 1 52
And with a kind of umber smirch my face; The like do you — *As Y. Like It* i 3 115
I like this place, And willingly could waste my time in it — ii 4 94
If you like upon report The soil, the profit and this kind of life — ii 4 97
And how like you this shepherd's life, Master Touchstone? — iii 2 11
In respect that it is solitary, I like it very well — iii 2 16
I do not like her name.—There was no thought of pleasing you when she was christened — iii 2 282
They were all like one another as half-pence are — iii 2 372
Would now like him, now loathe him — iii 2 436
Do not fall in love with me, For I am falser than vows made in wine: Besides, I like you not — iii 5 74
Is't possible that on so little acquaintance you should like her? — v 2 2
Like this fellow.—I like him very well.—God 'ild you, sir; I desire you of the like — v 4 54
I am not furnished like a beggar — Epil. 10
I charge you, O women, for the love you bear to men, to like as much of this play as please you — Epil. 14
I see thy beauty, Thy beauty, that doth make me like thee well — *T. of S.* ii 1 276
If you like me, she shall have me and mine — ii 1 385
'Tis like you'll prove a jolly surly groom — iii 2 215
Of all mad matches never was the like — iii 2 244
Peter, didst ever see the like? — iv 1 182
Here I take the like unfeigned oath, Never to marry with her — iv 2 32
I like the cap; And it I will have, or I will have none — iv 3 84
If you please to like No worse than I, upon some agreement Me shall you find ready and willing — iv 4 32
Then at my lodging, an it like you: There doth my father lie — iv 4 55
Conceives by me! How likes Hortensio that? — v 2 23
How likes Gremio these quick-witted folks? — v 2 38
What was he like? I have forgot him — *All's Well* i 1 92
Let me see: marry, ill, to like him that ne'er it likes — i 1 165
Is a virtue of a good wing, and I like the wear well — i 1 219
The mightiest space in fortune nature brings To join like likes and kiss like native things — i 1 238
I'll like a maid the better, whilst I have a tooth in my head — ii 3 47
If thou canst like this creature as a maid, I can create the rest — ii 3 149
Our old ling and our Isbels o' the country are nothing like your old ling and your Isbels o' the court — iii 2 15
Great Mars, I put myself into thy file: Make me but like my thoughts — iii 3 10
How does your ladyship like it?—With very much content — iv 5 82
Take her away; I do not like her now; To prison with her — v 3 282
When I was like this maid, I found you wondrous kind — v 3 310
And my desires, like fell and cruel hounds, E'er since pursue me — *T. Night* i 1 22
Mine own escape unfoldeth to my hope, Whereto thy speech serves for authority, The like of him — i 2 21
What's a drunken man like, fool?—Like a drowned man, a fool, and a mad man — i 5 138
O, if I thought that, I'ld beat him like a dog! — ii 3 154
I can write very like my lady your niece — ii 3 173
How dost thou like this tune?—It gives a very echo to the seat Where Love is throned — ii 4 20
Thou perhaps mayst move That heart, which now abhors, to like his love — iii 1 176
Fare thee well: A fiend like thee might bear my soul to hell — iii 4 237
This is not my writing, Though, I confess, much like the character — v 1 354
Thou want'st a rough pash and the shoots that I have, To be full like me — *W. Tale* i 2 129
Yet were it true To say this boy were like me — i 2 135
How like, methought, I then was to this kernel, This squash — i 2 159
How now, boy!—I am like you, they say.—Why, that's some comfort — i 2 208
And, might we lay the old proverb to your charge, So like you, 'tis the worse — ii 3 97
These proclamations, So forcing faults upon Hermione, I little like — iii 1 17
Say you the like to him?—I cannot speak So well, nothing so well — iv 4 391
Are you a courtier, an't like you, sir?—Whether it like me or no, I am a courtier — iv 4 750
What advocate hast thou to him?—I know not, an't like you — iv 4 767
This news which is called true is so like an old tale — v 2 30
Like an old tale still, which will have matter to rehearse — v 2 66
Thou wilt amend thy life?—Ay, an it like your good worship — v 2 167
I like your silence, it the more shows off Your wonder — v 3 21
Were it but told you, should be hooted at Like an old tale — v 3 117
If old sir Robert did beget us both And were our father and this son like him, O old sir Robert, father, on my knee I give heaven thanks I was not like to thee! — *K. John* i 1 81
Both are alike; and both alike we like. One must prove greatest — ii 1 331
How like you this wild counsel, mighty states? — ii 1 395
If he see aught in you that makes him like, That any thing he sees, which moves his liking, I can with ease translate it to my will — ii 1 511
It likes us well; young princes, close your hands — ii 1 533
For then, 'tis like I should forget myself — iii 4 49
Yet looks he like a king — *Richard II.* iii 3 68
I task the earth to the like — iv 1 52
Is he not like thee? is he not thine own? — v 2 94
He is as like thee as a man may be, Not like to me, or any of my kin — v 2 108
In this thought they find a kind of ease, Bearing their own misfortunes on the back Of such as have before endured the like — v 5 30
Yea, but 'tis like that they will know us by our horses — *1 Hen. IV.* i 2 195
These lies are like their father that begets them — ii 4 249

Like. O for breath to utter what is like thee! you tailor's-yard, you sheath . . . . 1 *Hen. IV.* ii 4 272
Make you believe that it was done in fight, and persuaded us to do the like . . . . ii 4 339
It is like, if there come a hot June and this civil buffeting hold . ii 4 396
It is like we shall have good trading that way . . . . . ii 4 401
O, I do not like that paying back; 'tis a double labour . . iii 3 201
Thrown over the shoulders like an herald's coat without sleeves . iv 2 48
Hold up thy head, vile Scot, or thou art like Never to hold it up again! v 4 39
Like a sow that hath overwhelmed all her litter but one . 2 *Hen. IV.* i 2 13
Who is it like should lead his forces hither? . . . . . i 3 81
She says up and down the town that her eldest son is like you . . ii 1 115
Even like those that are kin to the king . . . . . . ii 2 120
Put not you on the visage of the times And be like them . . ii 3 4
Would turn their own perfection to abuse, To seem like him . . ii 3 28
Do you like him, Sir John?—Shadow will serve for summer . . iii 2 143
Answer them directly How far forth you do like their articles.—I like them all, and do allow them well . . . . iv 2 53
With the like bold, just and impartial spirit As you have done . . v 2 116
I like this fair proceeding of the king's . . . . . . v 5 103
That self bill is urged, Which in the eleventh year of the last king's reign Was like, and had indeed against us pass'd . *Hen. V.* i 1 3
I may say 'Now lie I like a king' . . . . iv 1 17
Our king is not like him in that: he never killed any of his friends . iv 7 42
Do you like me, Kate?—Pardonnez-moi, I cannot tell vat is 'like me.'—An angel is like you, Kate, and you are like an angel . . v 2 107
None do you like but an effeminate prince, Whom, like a school-boy, you may over-awe.—Gloucester, whate'er we like, thou art protector 1 *Hen. VI.* i 1 35
Who ever saw the like? what men have I! . . . . . i 2 22
Helen, the mother of great Constantine, Nor yet Saint Philip's daughters, were like thee . . . . i 2 143
And like thee, Nero, Play on the lute, beholding the towns burn . . i 4 95
But now the substance shall endure the like . . . . . ii 3 38
Even like a man new haled from the rack . . . . . . ii 5 3
Which obloquy set bars before my tongue, Else with the like I had requited him . . . . ii 5 50
'Twas full of darnel; do you like the taste? . . . . . iii 2 44
Do what you will, the like do I; For live I will not, if my father die . iv 5 50
And like me to the peasant boys of France, To be shame's scorn! . . iv 6 48
Why, as you, my lord, An't like your lordly lord-protectorship 2 *Hen. VI.* ii 1 30
'Tis like, my lord, you will not keep your hour . . . . ii 1 181
Say that he thrive, as 'tis great like he will . . . . . iii 1 379
Am I not witch'd like her? or thou not false like him? . . . iii 2 119
'Tis like you would not feast him like a friend; And 'tis well seen he found an enemy . . . . iii 2 184
Like ambitious Sylla, overgorged With gobbets of thy mother's bleeding heart . . . . iv 1 84
'Tis wondrous strange, the like yet never heard of . . . 3 *Hen. VI.* ii 1 33
Thou hast thy mother's tongue.—But thou art neither like thy sire nor dam . . . . ii 2 135
And cheers these hands that slew thy sire and brother To execute the like upon thyself . . . . ii 4 10
The widow likes him not, she knits her brows . . . . . iii 2 82
How like you our choice, That you stand pensive, as half malcontent? iv 1 9
Give me worship and quietness; I like it better than a dangerous honour iv 3 17
'Tis like that Richmond with the rest shall down . . . . iv 6 100
An indigested and deformed lump, Not like the fruit of such a goodly tree v 6 52
I have no brother, I am like no brother; And this word 'love,' which greybeards call divine, Be resident in men like one another And not in me . . . . v 6 80
Die in his youth by like untimely violence! . . *Richard III.* i 3 201
I like you, lads; about your business straight; Go, go, dispatch . . i 3 355
I seal my true heart's love.—So thrive I, as I truly swear the like! . ii 1 11
I do not like the Tower, of any place. Did Julius Cæsar build that place? iii 1 68
You may jest on, but, by the holy rood, I do not like these several councils . . . . iii 2 78
Being nothing like the noble duke my father . . . . . iii 5 92
Like it your grace, The state takes notice of the private difference Betwixt you and the cardinal . . . . . . *Hen. VIII.* i 1 100
Not a man in England Can advise me like you . . . . . i 1 135
What can be their business With me, a poor weak woman, fall'n from favour? I do not like their coming . . . . iii 1 21
'Tis as like you As cherry is to cherry . . . . . . v 1 168
Like or find fault; do as your pleasures are . . *Troi. and Cres.* Prol. 30
Youth, liberality, and such like, the spice and salt that season a man . i 2 277
'Tis like he'll question me Why such unplausive eyes are bent on him . iii 3 42
A soldier good; But, by great Mars, the captain of us all, Never like thee iv 5 199
I do not like this fooling.—Nor I, by Pluto: but that that likes not you pleases me best . . . . v 2 101
I like thy armour well; I'll frush it and unlock the rivets all . . v 6 28
Hark! a retire upon our Grecian part.—The Trojan trumpets sound the like . . . . v 8 16
What would you have, you curs, That like nor peace nor war? *Coriolanus* i 1 173
Mark me, and do the like.—Fool-hardiness; not I.—Nor I . . . i 4 45
He's a lamb indeed, that baes like a bear . . . . . . ii 1 12
He's a bear indeed, that lives like a lamb . . . . . . ii 1 14
I wish no better Than have him hold that purpose and to put it in execution.—'Tis most like he will . . . . ii 1 257
I never saw the like . . . . ii 1 284
Hear from me still, and never of me aught But what is like me formerly iv 1 53
Three examples of the like have been Within my age . . . iv 6 50
I do not like this news.—Nor I . . . . iv 6 158
This is a poor epitome of yours, Which by the interpretation of full time May show like all yourself . . . . v 3 70
His wife is in Corioli and his child Like him by chance . . . v 3 180
Or is it Dian, habited like her? . . . . . *T. Andron.* ii 3 57
Was ever heard the like? . . . . ii 3 276
Thy father hath full oft For his ungrateful country done the like . . iv 1 111
Good Lord, how like the empress' sons they are! And you, the empress! . . . . v 2 64; 84
A . . . lively warrant, For me, most wretched, to perform the like . v 3 45
Hear all, all see, And like her most whose merit most shall be *R. and J.* i 2 31
I'll look to like, if looking liking move: But no more deep . . i 3 97
If the measure of thy joy Be heap'd like mine . . . . . ii 6 25
Am I like such a fellow?—Come, come, thou art as hot a Jack in thy mood as any in Italy . . . . iii 1 11
It presses to my memory, Like damned guilty deeds to sinners' minds . iii 2 111
An hour but married, . . . Doting like me, and like me banished . . iii 3 67
Will you be ready? do you like this haste? We'll keep no great ado . iii 4 22

Like. And yet no man like he doth grieve my heart . . *Rom. and Jul.* iii 5 84
Or, if I live, is it not very like, . . . if I wake, shall I not be distraught? . . . . iv 3 36
I like your work; And you shall find I like it . . . *T. of Athens* i 1 160
How dost thou like this jewel, Apemantus?—Not so well as plain-dealing i 1 214
So they were bleeding-new, my lord, there's no meat like 'em . . i 2 81
Joy had the like conception in our eyes And at that instant like a babe sprung up . . . . i 2 115
A fool in good clothes, and something like thee. 'Tis a spirit: sometime't appears like a lord; sometime like a lawyer; sometime like a philosopher, with two stones more than's artificial one: he is very often like a knight . . . . ii 2 115
Good morrow, Titus and Hortensius.—The like to you . . . . iii 4 2
Does it now, Like all mankind, show me an iron heart? . . . . iii 4 84
Were I like thee, I'ld throw away myself . . . . . . iv 3 219
Dost hate a medlar?—Ay, though it look like thee . . . . iv 3 308
I like this well; he will return again . . . . v 1 207
'Tis very like: he hath the falling sickness . . . . *J. Cæsar* i 2 256
It is meet That noble minds keep ever with their likes . . . . i 2 315
Now could I, Casca, name to thee a man Most like this dreadful night . i 3 73
We, like friends, will straightway go together.—That every like is not the same, O Cæsar, The heart of Brutus yearns to think upon! . . ii 2 128
Lead their charges off A little from this ground.—Lucilius, do you the like . . . . iv 2 50
I do not like your faults.—A friendly eye could never see such faults . iv 3 89
That look not like the inhabitants o' the earth, And yet are on't *Macbeth* i 3 41
To beguile the time, Look like the time; bear welcome in your eye . i 5 65
Look like the innocent flower, But be the serpent under't . . . i 5 66
Good repose the while!—Thanks, sir: the like to you! . . . . ii 1 30
Then 'tis most like The sovereignty will fall upon Macbeth . . . ii 4 29
Thou art the best o' the cut-throats: yet he's good That did the like . iii 4 18
Thou art too like the spirit of Banquo; down! . . . . . iv 1 112
Thou other gold-bound brow, is like the first. A third is like the former iv 1 114
Would I could answer This comfort with the like! . . . . iv 3 193
Your leavy screens throw down, And show like those you are . . v 6 2
In the same figure, like the king that's dead . . . . *Hamlet* i 1 41
Looks it not like the king? mark it, Horatio.—Most like . . . i 1 43
So like the king That was and is the question of these wars . . i 1 110
My father's brother, but no more like my father Than I to Hercules . i 2 152
He was a man, take him for all in all, I shall not look upon his like again i 2 188
A figure like your father, Armed at point exactly, cap-a-pe . . . i 2 199
I knew your father; These hands are not more like . . . . i 2 212
It would have much amazed you.—Very like, very like . . . . i 2 237
It likes us well; And at our more consider'd time we'll read . . ii 2 80
If they should grow themselves to common players—as it is most like . ii 2 365
And then, you know, 'It came to pass, as most like it was' . . . ii 2 437
Play something like the murder of my father Before mine uncle . . ii 2 624
Madam, how like you this play?—The lady doth protest too much, methinks . . . . iii 2 239
'Tis like a camel, indeed.—Methinks it is like a weasel.—It is backed like a weasel.—Or like a whale?—Very like a whale . . . . iii 2 395
I like him not, nor stands it safe with us To let his madness range . iii 3 1
The distracted multitude, Who like not in their judgement, but their eyes . . . . iv 3 5
I like thy wit well, in good faith: the gallows does well . . . v 1 51
If I like thee no worse after dinner, I will not part from thee yet *Lear* i 4 44
Though she's as like this as a crab's like an apple, yet I can tell what I can tell.—Why, what canst thou tell, my boy?—She will taste as like this as a crab does to a crab . . . . i 5 15
Only I do not like the fashion of your garments . . . . . iii 6 84
Advise the duke, where you are going, to a most festinate preparation: we are bound to the like . . . . iii 7 11
What most he should dislike seems pleasant to him; What like, offensive iv 2 11
One way I like this well . . . . iv 2 84
You have seen Sunshine and rain at once: her smiles and tears Were like a better way . . . . iv 3 21
With like timorous accent and dire yell As when, by night and negligence, the fire Is spied in populous cities . . . . *Othello* i 1 75
And the general so likes your music, that he desires you, for love's sake, to make no more noise with it . . . . iii 1 12
Thou likedst not that, When Cassio left my wife: what didst not like? iii 3 110
I like the work well: ere it be demanded—As like enough it will—I'ld have it copied . . . . iii 4 189
Lest, being like one of heaven, the devils themselves Should fear to seize thee . . . . iv 2 36
'Tis like she comes to speak of Cassio's death . . . . . v 2 92
Cold, cold, my girl! Even like thy chastity . . . . . . v 2 276
Like the base Indian, threw a pearl away Richer than all his tribe . v 2 347
Perchance! nay, and most like: You must not stay here longer *A. and C.* i 1 25
Madam, methinks, if you did love him dearly, You do not hold the method to enforce The like from him . . . . i 3 8
But yet, madam,— I do not like 'But yet,' it does allay The good precedence . . . . ii 5 50
He cannot like her long.—Like her! O Isis! 'tis impossible . . . iii 3 17
I grant him part; but then, in his Armenia, And other of his conquer'd kingdoms, I demand the like . . . . iii 6 37
You come not Like Cæsar's sister . . . . iii 6 43
He may at pleasure whip, or hang, or torture, As he shall like, to quit me iii 13 151
Welcome: Thou look'st like him that knows a warlike charge . . iv 4 19
Here, on her breast, There is a vent of blood and something blown: The like is on her arm . . . . v 2 353
To seek through the regions of the earth For one his like, there would be something failing In him that should compare . . *Cymbeline* i 1 21
I do not like her. She doth think she has Strange lingering poisons . i 5 33
So like you, sir, ambassadors from Rome . . . . ii 3 59
Here are letters for you.—Their tenour good, I trust.—'Tis very like . ii 4 36
Who long'st, like me, to see thy lord; who long'st,—O, let me bate,—but not like me—yet long'st, But in a fainter kind:—O, not like me iii 2 55
In as like a figure, Strikes life into my speech . . . . . iii 3 96
I thought you would not back again.—Most like; Bringing me here to kill me . . . . iii 4 119
And am almost A man already.—First, make yourself but like one . iii 4 170
She looks us like A thing more made of malice than of duty . . . iii 5 32
The which he hearing—As it is like him—might break out, and swear . iv 2 140
Thou shalt not lack The flower that's like thy face, pale primrose . iv 2 221
Have you ta'en of it?—Most like I did, for I was dead . . . v 5 259
For vice repeated is like the wandering wind, Blows dust in others' eyes, to spread itself . . . . *Pericles* i 1 96
Thou speak'st like him's untutor'd to repeat . . . . . . i 4 74
Your choice agrees with mine; I like that well . . . . . ii 5 19

Like. If you like her, so; if not, I have lost my earnest . . *Pericles* iv 2 48
Come, young one, I like the manner of your garments well . . iv 2 145
Of all the faults beneath the heavens, the gods Do like this worst . iv 3 21
Did you ever hear the like?—No, nor never shall do in such a place . iv 5 1
But there never came her like in Mytilene . . . . . iv 6 31
My dearest wife was like this maid, and such a one My daughter . v 1 108
Thou look'st Like one I loved indeed . . . . . v 1 126
I Have suffer'd like a girl . . . . v 1 138
Are you not Pericles? Like him you spake, Like him you are . . v 3 32
The gods can have no mortal officer More like a god than you . . v 3 63
Like advantage. He bears his course, and runs me up With like advantage on the other side . . . . *1 Hen. IV.* iii 1 109
Like allayment. The like allayment could I give my grief *Troi. and Cres.* iv 4 8
Like as. Most likely!—O, that it were as like as it is true! *Meas. for Meas.* v 1 104
Yet they say we are Almost as like as eggs . . . . *W. Tale* i 2 130
Being as like As rain to water, or devil to his dam . . *K. John* ii 1 127
Like as there were husbandry in war, Before the sun rose he was harness'd light, And to the field goes he . . . *Troi. and Cres.* i 2 7
As like as Vulcan and his wife . . . . i 3 168
And did address Itself to motion, like as it would speak . *Hamlet* i 2 217
Like attempts. To warn false traitors from the like attempts *Rich. III.* iii 5 49
Like Brutus. When you do find him, or alive or dead, He will be found like Brutus, like himself . . . . *J. Cæsar* v 4 25
Like Cassius. Was that done like Cassius? . . . . . iv 3 77
Like conception. Joy had the like conception in our eyes *T. of Athens* i 2 115
Like conditions. In like conditions as our argument *Troi. and Cres.* Prol. 25
Which we, On like conditions, will have counter-seal'd . *Coriolanus* v 3 205
Like Demetrius. And sometime rail thou like Demetrius *M. N. Dream* iii 2 362
Like devotion. Upon the like devotion as yourselves . *Richard III.* iv 1 9
Like elves and fairies in a ring, Enchanting all that you put in *Macbeth* iv 1 42
Like enough. May be she doth but counterfeit.—Faith, like enough *Much Ado* ii 3 108
Now I am in a holiday humour and like enough to consent *As Y. Like It* iv 1 69
Like enough, through vassal fear, . . . To fight against me *1 Hen. IV.* iii 2 124
I guess their tenour.—Like enough you do . . . . . iv 4 7
Thy mother's son! like enough, and thy father's shadow *2 Hen. IV.* iii 2 139
I shall return before your lordship thence.—'Tis like enough *Rich. III.* iii 2 122
Ere it be demanded—As like enough it will—I'ld have it copied *Othello* iii 4 190
Like enough, high-battled Cæsar will Unstate his happiness! *A. and C.* iii 13 29
Like event. With hope to find the like event in love . *1 Hen. VI.* v 5 105
To order well the state, That like events may ne'er it ruinate *T. Andron.* v 3 204
Like evil. Or, shedding, breed a nursery of like evil . *Troi. and Cres.* i 3 319
Like executor. Such baseness Had never like executor . . *Tempest* iii 1 13
Like exhibition. What maintenance he from his friends receives, Like exhibition thou shalt have from me . . . *T. G. of Ver.* i 3 69
Like fortune. And meaner than myself have had like fortune *3 Hen. VI.* iv 1 71
Like friends. We, like friends, will straightway go together . *J. Cæsar* ii 2 127
Like glorious. The enterprise whereof Shall be to you, as us, like glorious . . . . *Hen. V.* ii 2 183
Like goodness. And nothing is at a like goodness still . . *Hamlet* iv 7 117
Like grief. Each substance of a grief hath twenty shadows, Which shows like grief itself . . . . . . *Richard II.* ii 2 15
Like hardiment Posthumus hath To Cymbeline perform'd . *Cymbeline* v 4 75
Like haste. We do condemn thee to the very block Where Claudio stoop'd to death, and with like haste . . . . *Meas. for Meas.* v 1 420
Like heedful. To him one of the other twins was bound, Whilst I had been like heedful of the other . . *Com. of Errors* i 1 83
Like Hermione. Unless another, As like Hermione as is her picture, Affront his eye . . . . *W. Tale* v 1 74
Like Herne. Speak I like Herne the hunter? . . . *Mer. Wives* v 5 31
Like him well. Is't not a handsome gentleman?—I like him well *All's Well* iii 5 84
He has no pace, but runs where he will.—I like him well . . iv 5 72
There's some conceit or other likes him well . . *Richard III.* iii 4 51
Like himself. As may beseem a monarch like himself . *3 Hen. VI.* iii 3 122
Now my sovereign speaketh like himself . . . . . . iv 7 67
Both to thank and to remember With honours like himself . *Coriolanus* ii 2 52
When you do find him, or alive or dead, He will be found like Brutus, like himself.—This is not Brutus . . . *J. Cæsar* v 4 25
Like hold. Hence; Lest that the infection of his fortune take Like hold on thee . . . . *Lear* iv 6 238
Like Hubert. O, now you look like Hubert! . . . *K. John* iv 1 126
Like husbands. Fools are as like husbands as pilchards are to herrings; the husband's the bigger . . . . . *T. Night* iii 1 39
Like invulnerable. My fellow-ministers Are like invulnerable *Tempest* iii 3 66
Like it not. Call you this gamut? tut, I like it not . . *T. of Shrew* iii 1 79
But yet I like it not, In that he wears the badge of Somerset *1 Hen. VI.* iv 1 176
The widow likes it not, for she looks very sad . . *3 Hen. VI.* iii 2 110
Uneven is the course, I like it not . . . . *Rom. and Jul.* iv 1 5
I know not what may fall; I like it not . . . *J. Cæsar* iii 1 243
Like it well. A fat tripe finely broil'd?—I like it well . *T. of Shrew* iv 3 21
Now, by the sky that hangs above our heads, I like it well . *K. John* ii 1 398
Needs must I like it well: I weep for joy . . . *Richard II.* iii 2 4
I like it well that our fair queen and mistress Smiles at her news *3 Hen. VI.* iii 3 167
Like itself. And make high majesty look like itself . . *Richard II.* ii 1 295
If that rebellion Came like itself, in base and abject routs *2 Hen. IV.* iv 1 33
What manner o' thing is your crocodile?—It is shaped, sir, like itself; and it is as broad as it hath breadth . . . *Ant. and Cleo.* ii 7 47
Like kindness. To express the like kindness, myself, that have been more kindly beholding to you than any . . . *T. of Shrew* ii 1 77
Like labour. Never bearing Like labour with the rest . *Coriolanus* i 1 104
Like lamps. These eyes, like lamps whose wasting oil is spent, Wax dim *1 Hen. VI.* ii 5 8
Like language. Lest barbarism, making me the precedent, Should a like language use to all degrees . . . . . . *W. Tale* ii 1 85
Like leave. All love the womb that their first being bred, Then give my tongue like leave to love my head . . . . *Pericles* i 1 108
Like lies. If I should tell my history, it would seem Like lies . v 1 120
Like loss. For the like loss I have her sovereign aid And rest myself content.—You the like loss! . . . . . . *Tempest* v 1 143
Like madness is the glory of this life . . . *T. of Athens* i 2 139
Like man. Moe things like men! Eat, Timon, and abhor them . iv 3 398
Nothing but himself which looks like man Is friendly with him . v 1 121
Like manner. In like manner was I in debt to my importunate business iii 6 15
Likes me better. This lodging likes me better . . . *Hen. V.* iv 1 16
Which likes me better than to wish us one . . . . iv 3 77
Likes me not. The music likes you not.—You mistake; the musician likes me not . . . . *T. G. of Ver.* iv 2 57
His countenance likes me not . . . . *Lear* ii 2 96

Likes me well. You are like to have a thin and slender pittance.—It likes me well . . . . *T. of Shrew* iv 4 62
This likes me well. These foils have all a length? . . *Hamlet* v 2 276
Like molestation. I never did like molestation view On the enchafed flood . . . . *Othello* ii 1 16
Like Muscovites. Disguised like Muscovites . . . *L. L. Lost* v 2 303
Like myself. If I speak like myself in this, let him be whipped that first finds it so . . . . *Lear* i 4 179
Never bestrid a horse, save one that had A rider like myself . *Cymbeline* iv 4 39
Like necessity. It saved me, keep it; in like necessity—The which the gods protect thee from!—may defend thee . . . *Pericles* ii 1 134
Like nobles. Go search like nobles, like noble subjects . . ii 4 50
Like not. And this is true; I like not the humour of lying . *Mer. Wives* ii 1 132
I like not when a 'oman has a great peard . . . . iv 2 203
He grows kind.—I like not fair terms and a villain's mind *Mer. of Venice* i 3 181
Or else you like not of my company . . . . *T. of Shrew* ii 1 65
O, that is entertainment My bosom likes not, nor my brows! *W. Tale* i 2 119
We like not this; thou dost forget thyself . . . *K. John* iii 1 134
I like not such grinning honour as Sir Walter hath . . *1 Hen. IV.* v 3 62
The offer likes not . . . . *Hen. V.* iii Prol. 32
I like not of this flight of Edward's . . . . *3 Hen. VI.* iv 6 89
The gates made fast! Brother, I like not this . . . . iv 7 10
That that likes not you pleases me best . . . *Troi. and Cres.* v 2 102
For if the king like not the comedy, Why then, belike, he likes it not, perdy . . . . *Hamlet* iii 2 304
Alack, alack, Edmund, I like not this unnatural dealing . *Lear* iii 3 1
Ha! I like not that.—What dost thou say?—Nothing, my lord *Othello* iii 3 35
Like note. Sing him to the ground, As once our mother; use like note and words . . . . *Cymbeline* iv 2 237
Like notice. Give the like notice To Valentinus . . *Meas. for Meas.* iv 5 7
Like oaths. All men Have the like oaths . . . . *All's Well* iv 2 71
Like occasion. On the like occasion whereon my services are now on foot, you shall see . . . . *W. Tale* i 1 2
Like of. Nor can imagination form a shape, Besides yourself, to like of *Tempest* iii 1 57
I am your husband, if you like of me . . . . *Much Ado* v 4 59
But like of each thing that in season grows . . . *L. L. Lost* i 1 107
Tush, none but minstrels like of sonneting! But are you not ashamed? iv 3 158
So long as hell and Richard likes of it . . . . *Richard III.* iv 4 354
Speak briefly, can you like of Paris' love?—I'll look to like *Rom. and Jul.* i 3 96
Like offices. Wolves and bears, they say, Casting their savageness aside have done Like offices of pity . . . . . . *W. Tale* ii 3 189
Like opportunity. We shall not find like opportunity . *1 Hen. VI.* v 4 158
Like precurse. And even the like precurse of fierce events . *Hamlet* i 1 121
Like proportion. There must be needs a like proportion Of lineaments, of manners and of spirit . . . . . *Mer. of Venice* iii 4 14
Like relation. To trouble Your joys with like relation . *W. Tale* v 3 130
Like request. Since that to both It stands in like request *Coriolanus* iii 2 51
Like right. But, if thou live to see like right bereft, This fool-begg'd patience in thee will be left . . . . *Com. of Errors* ii 1 40
Like seat. Where I must take like seat unto my fortune *3 Hen. VI.* iii 3 10
Like something. You are like something that—What countrywoman? *Pericles* v 1 103
Like sorrow. I never saw a vessel of like sorrow, So fill'd *W. Tale* iii 3 21
Of your very blood; Of all one pain, save for a night of groans Endured of her, for whom you bid like sorrow . . . . *Richard III.* iv 4 304
Like spirit. Lest in our need he might infect another And make him of like spirit to himself . . . . *3 Hen. VI.* v 4 47
Like success. Why should I not now have the like success? . . i 2 76
Like syllable. That it resounds As if it felt with Scotland and yell'd out Like syllable of dolour . . . . *Macbeth* iv 3 8
Like the lightning. Too sudden; Too like the lightning *Rom. and Jul.* ii 2 119
Like the office. I do not like the office . . . . *Othello* iii 3 410
Like the sire. Too like the sire for ever being good . *T. Andron.* v 1 50
Like thee well. I like thee well And will employ thee . *T. G. of Ver.* iv 4 44
I like thee well: wilt thou forsake thy fortune? . . *K. John* ii 1 148
Like thyself. Whate'er it be, be thou still like thyself . *3 Hen. VI.* iii 3 15
When thou find'st a man that's like thyself, Good Murder, stab him *T. Andron.* v 2 99
Were I like thee, I'ld throw away myself.—Thou hast cast away thyself, being like thyself . . . . *T. of Athens* iv 3 220
Like Timon. Thou art proud, Apemantus.—Of nothing so much as that I am not like Timon . . . . i 1 190
Like to. The visage Of Ragozine, more like to Claudio *Meas. for Meas.* iv 3 80
His actions show much like to madness . . . . . . iv 4 4
Much like to you, for you have just his bleat . . . *Much Ado* v 4 51
So we grew together, Like to a double cherry . . *M. N. Dream* iii 2 209
Like to Lysander sometime frame thy tongue . . . . . iii 2 360
But if thy love were ever like to mine—As sure I think did never man love so—How many actions most ridiculous? . . *As Y. Like It* ii 4 28
Possessed with the glanders and like to mose in the chine *T. of Shrew* iii 2 51
Not the worst of all your fortunes That you are like to Sir Vincentio . iv 2 105
I'll be with you again, In a trice, Like to the old Vice . *T. Night* iv 2 134
Boy, thou hast said to me a thousand times Thou never shouldst love woman like to me . . . . v 1 275
Good goddess Nature, which hast made it So like to him that got it *W. T.* ii 3 105
Thy brat hath been cast out, like to itself, No father owning it . . iii 2 88
He comes not Like to his father's greatness . . . . . v 1 89
On my knee I give heaven thanks I was not like to thee! . *K. John* i 1 83
Not like to me, or any of my kin, And yet I love him *Richard II.* v 2 109
This man's brow, like to a title-leaf, Foretells the nature of a tragic volume: So looks the strand . . . . . *2 Hen. IV.* i 1 60
Like to a pair of loving turtle-doves That could not live asunder *1 Hen. VI.* ii 2 30
Before . . . a stroke was given, Like to a trusty squire did run away . iv 1 23
Like to a ship that, having 'scaped a tempest, Is straightway calm'd *2 Hen. VI.* iv 9 32
Like to Achilles' spear, Is able with the change to kill and cure . . v 1 100
Their weapons like to lightning came and went . . *3 Hen. VI.* ii 1 129
Said I for this, the girl was like to him? I will have more *Hen. VIII.* v 1 174
Rome could afford no tribune like to these . . . *T. Andron.* iii 1 44
His child is like to her, fair as you are . . . . . iv 2 154
And when it is thy hap To find another that is like to thee, Good Rapine, stab him; he's a ravisher . . . . v 2 102
That not another comfort like to this Succeeds in unknown fate *Othello* ii 1 194
For princes are A model, which heaven makes like to itself . *Pericles* ii 2 11
The heir of kingdoms and another like To Pericles thy father . . v 1 209
Like to be. I was like to be apprehended for the witch . *Mer. Wives* iv 5 119
Who is thus like to be cozened with the semblance of a maid *Much Ado* ii 2 39
But in that thou art like to be my kinsman, live unbruised . . v 4 112
Here is like to be a good presence of Worthies . . . *L. L. Lost* v 2 536

Like to be. She's like to be Lucentio's wife.—I pray the gods she may! *T. of Shrew* iv 4 66
Welcome! one mess is like to be your cheer . . . . . iv 4 70
You are like to be much advanced . . . . *T. Night* i 4 2
'Tis poetical.—It is the more like to be feigned: I pray you, keep it in i 5 208
To inure thyself to what thou art like to be, cast thy humble slough ii 5 161
Go not Too far i' the land: 'tis like to be loud weather . . *W. Tale* iii 3 11
So his successor Was like to be the best . . . . . . v 1 49
You are married?—We are not, sir, nor are we like to be . . . v 1 205
What hath then befallen, Or what hath this bold enterprise brought forth, More than that being which was like to be? . *2 Hen. IV.* i 1 179
Simon Shadow!—Yea, marry, . . . he's like to be a cold soldier . . iii 2 134
One that is like to be executed for robbing a church . *Hen. V.* iii 6 106
Let deeds express What's like to be their words . . *Coriolanus* iii 1 133
If he be married, My grave is like to be my wedding bed *Rom. and Jul.* i 5 137
The arbitrement is like to be bloody . . . . *Lear* iv 7 95
I do believe, Statist though I am none, nor like to be . . *Cymbeline* ii 4 16
Tell me, if thou canst, What this maid is, or what is like to be? *Pericles* v 1 186
Like to call. I am as like to call thee so again *Mer. of Venice* i 3 131
Like to dance. I have some of 'em in Limbo Patrum, and there they are like to dance these three days . . . . . . *Hen. VIII.* v 4 68
Like to die. Rumour it abroad That Anne, my wife, is sick and like to die *Richard III.* iv 2 52
I say again, give out That Anne my wife is sick and like to die . iv 2 58
You are light into my hands, where you are like to live.—The more my fault To scape his hands where I was like to die . *Pericles* iv 2 80
Like to do. It forged him some design, which, being believed, It was much like to do . . . . *Hen. VIII.* i 2 182
You are like to do such business . . . *Coriolanus* iii 1 48
You so remain.—And so are like to do . . . . . . iii 1 203
He's as like to do't as any man I can imagine . . . . . iv 5 216
How farest thou, soldier?—Well; And well am like to do *Ant. and Cleo.* ii 6 74
Here is a thing too young for such a place, Who, if it had conceit, would die, as I Am like to do . . . . *Pericles* iii 1 17
Like to find. Nothing of that wonderful promise, to read him by his form, as you are like to find him . . . . *T. Night* iii 4 291
Was pleased to let him seek danger where he was like to find fame *Cor.* i 3 14
Like to go. I'll bring thee word Straight, how 'tis like to go *Ant. and Cleo.* iv 12 3
Like to have. We had like to have had our two noses snapped off *M. Ado* v 1 115
My father hath no child but I, nor none is like to have . *As Y. Like It* i 2 19
I have had four quarrels, and like to have fought one . . . v 4 48
I see she's like to have neither cap nor gown . *T. of Shrew* iv 3 93
You are like to have a thin and slender pittance.—It likes me well . iv 4 61
Thou'rt like to have A lullaby too rough . . . *W. Tale* iii 3 54
Your worship had like to have given us one . . . . . iv 4 750
Have we more sons? or are we like to have? . . *Richard II.* v 2 90
We are like to have the overthrow again . . . *1 Hen. VI.* iii 2 106
Then we are like to have biting statutes . . . *2 Hen. VI.* iv 7 18
Like to hear. All the expected good we're like to hear *Hen. VIII.* Epil. 8
Ere long you are like to hear, If you dare venture in your own behalf, A mistress's command . . . . *Lear* iv 2 19
Like to know. By their show You shall know all that you are like to know . . . . *M. N. Dream* v 1 117
Like to lay. Under these hard conditions as this time Is like to lay upon us . . . . *J. Cæsar* i 2 175
Like to live. A goodly babe, Lusty and like to live . . *W. Tale* ii 2 27
You are light into my hands, where you are like to live . . *Pericles* iv 2 78
Like to lose. You are like to lose your hair . . *Tempest* iv 1 237
Like to marry. I were better to be married of him than of another: for he is not like to marry me well . . . . *As Y. L. It* iii 3 93
Like to prove. We are like to prove a goodly commodity . *Much Ado* iii 3 190
Worthy fellows; and like to prove most sinewy sword-men . *All's Well* ii 1 61
Like to reap. Your wife is like to reap a proper man . *T. Night* iii 1 144
Like to rise. Who's like to rise, Who thrives and who declines *Coriolanus* i 1 196
Like to rot. Like fair fruit in an unwholesome dish, Are like to rot untasted . . . . . . *Troi. and Cres.* ii 3 130
Like to run. Lads more like to run The country base than to commit such slaughter . . . . *Cymbeline* v 3 19
Like to see. Since you are like to see the king before me, Commend the paper to his gracious hand . . . . . *All's Well* v 1 30
Like to take. Wherefore have these gifts a curtain before 'em? are they like to take dust? . . . . *T. Night* i 3 135
Like toys. Such like toys as these Have moved his highness to commit me now . . . . *Richard III.* i 1 60
Like us. Few in millions Can speak like us . . . *Tempest* ii 1 8
If th' other two be brained like us, the state totters . . . iii 2 8
Like value. Things of like value differing in the owners Are prized by their masters . . . . *T. of Athens* i 1 170
Like want. Her life was beast-like, and devoid of pity; And, being so, shall have like want of pity . . . . *T. Andron.* v 3 200
Like warlike as the wolf for what we eat . . . *Cymbeline* iii 3 41
Like weight. But were we burden'd with like weight of pain, As much or more we should ourselves complain . . *Com. of Errors* ii 1 36
Like well. You like well and bear your years very well . *2 Hen. IV.* iii 2 92
Like wing. When they stoop, they stoop with the like wing . *Hen. V.* iv 1 112
Like wit. He doth indeed show some sparks that are like wit *Much Ado* ii 3 194
Like your grace. We steal by line and level, an't like your grace *Tempest* iv 1 240
That's I, an't like your grace . . . . *Meas. for Meas.* v 1 74
An't like your grace,— You are a saucy fellow *Hen. VIII.* iv 2 100
May it like your grace To let my tongue excuse all . . . v 3 148
If aught within that little seeming substance . . . may fitly like your grace, She's there, and she is yours . . . . *Lear* i 1 203
Like your majesty. What manner of man, an it like your majesty? *1 Hen. IV.* ii 4 462
No marvel, an it like your majesty . . . *2 Hen. VI.* ii 1 9
Art thou the man that slew him?—I was, an't like your majesty . v 1 72
Like your worship. Whither are you bound?—To the palace, an it like your worship . . . . *W. Tale* iv 4 737
What woman is this?—His wife, an't like your worship. . *2 Hen. VI.* ii 1 80
Like yourself. Your majesty came not like yourself: you appeared to me but as a common man . . . . . . *Hen. V.* iv 8 53
I do profess You speak not like yourself . . . *Hen. VIII.* ii 4 85
Let me speak like yourself, and lay a sentence . . *Othello* i 3 199
Liked. For several virtues Have I liked several women . *Tempest* iii 1 43
I look'd upon her with a soldier's eye, That liked, but had a rougher task in hand Than to drive liking to the name of love *Much Ado* i 1 301
I liked her ere I went to wars.—Thou wilt be like a lover presently . i 1 307
The fairest dame That lived, that loved, that liked . . *M. N. Dream* v 1 299
Complexions that liked me and breaths that I defied not *As Y. Like It* Epil. 20
I liked her, And boarded her i' the wanton way of youth . *All's Well* v 3 210
He would not take his band and yours; he liked not the security *2 Hen. IV.* i 2 37
Liked. A' could never abide carnation; 'twas a colour he never liked *Hen. V.* ii 3 36
You gave Good words the other day of a bay courser I rode on: it is yours, because you liked it . . . . *T. of Athens* i 2 218
Likedst. Thou dost mean something: I heard thee say even now, thou likedst not that, When Cassio left my wife . . . . *Othello* iii 3 109
Likeliest. They are your likeliest men . . *2 Hen. IV.* iii 2 273
Likelihood. These likelihoods confirm her flight from hence *T. G. of Ver.* v 2 43
But what likelihood is in that? . . . . . *Meas. for Meas.* iv 2 202
No less likelihood than to see me at her chamber-window . *Much Ado* ii 2 42
Doubt not but success Will fashion the event in better shape Than I can lay it down in likelihood . . . . iv 1 238
Tell me whereon the likelihood depends . . . . *As Y. Like It* i 3 59
By all likelihood, some cheer is toward . . . *T. of Shrew* v 1 14
Many likelihoods informed me of this before . . . *All's Well* i 3 128
A sad and bloody hour; As by discharge of their artillery, And shape of likelihood, the news was told . . . . . *1 Hen. IV.* i 1 58
A fellow of no mark nor likelihood . . . . . . iii 2 45
It never yet did hurt To lay down likelihoods and forms of hope *2 Hen. IV.* i 3 35
By a lower but loving likelihood . . . . . *Hen. V.* v Prol. 29
What likelihood of his amendment? . . . . *Richard III.* i 3 33
It should be put To no apparent likelihood of breach . . . ii 2 136
What of his heart perceive you in his face By any likelihood he show'd to-day? . . . . iii 4 57
Follow him thither with modesty enough, and likelihood to lead it *Hamlet* v 1 230
These thin habits and poor likelihoods Of modern seeming . . *Othello* i 3 108
What place? what time? what form? what likelihood? . . . iv 2 138
Two that would by all likelihood have confounded one the other *Cymbeline* i 4 54
Likely. Most likely!—O, that it were as like as it is true! *Meas. for Meas.* v 1 103
I have not seen So likely an ambassador of love . *Mer. of Venice* ii 9 92
I never thought it possible or likely . . . . . *T. of Shrew* i 1 154
More likely to fall in than to get o'er . . . . *2 Hen. IV.* i 1 171
We ventured, for the gain proposed Choked the respect of likely peril fear'd . . . . i 1 184
Grant that our hopes, yet likely of fair birth, Should be still-born . i 3 63
'Fore God, a likely fellow! . . . . iii 2 186
Not seeing what is likely to ensue . . . . *1 Hen. VI.* iii 1 188
For Henry, son unto a conqueror, Is likely to beget more conquerors . v 5 74
Is Jack Cade slain?—No, my lord, nor likely to be slain. *2 Hen. VI.* iv 5 2
He's very likely now to fall from him . . . *3 Hen. VI.* iii 3 209
An olive branch and laurel crown, As likely to be blest in peace and war iv 6 35
And himself Likely in time to bless a regal throne . . . . iv 6 74
'Tis likely, By all conjectures . . . . . *Hen. VIII.* ii 1 40
These three lead on this preparation Whither 'tis bent: most likely 'tis for you: Consider of it. . . . . . . *Coriolanus* i 2 16
This is most likely! . . . . iv 6 68
He thereby may give a likely guess . . . . . *T. Andron.* ii 3 207
Then is it likely thou wilt undertake A thing like death *Rom. and Jul.* iv 1 73
Is very likely to load our purposes with what they travail for *T. of Athens* v 1 16
Do you think 'tis this?—It may be, very likely . . *Hamlet* ii 2 152
He was likely, had he been put on, To have proved most royally . . v 2 408
Have you heard of no likely wars toward? . . . . . *Lear* ii 1 11
A likely piece of work! . . . . *Othello* iv 1 156
Never saw I figures So likely to report themselves . . *Cymbeline* ii 4 83
It is not likely . . . That they will waste their time upon our note . iv 4 16
This chanced to-night.—Most likely, sir.—Nay, certainly to-night *Pericles* iii 2 78
I said, and said no more but what my thoughts Did warrant me was likely . . . . v 1 135
Likened. The wrinkles in my brows, now fill'd with blood, Were liken'd oft to kingly sepulchres . . . . *3 Hen. VI.* v 2 20
Likeness. If thou beest a man, show thyself in thy likeness . *Tempest* iii 2 138
How may likeness made in crimes, Making practice on the times, To draw with idle spiders' strings Most ponderous and substantial things! *Meas. for Meas.* iii 2 287
Never came trouble to my house in the likeness of your grace *Much Ado* i 1 100
Now, in thy likeness, one more fool appear! . . . . *L. L. Lost* iv 3 46
Neighing in likeness of a filly foal . . . . *M. N. Dream* ii 1 46
Sometime lurk I in a gossip's bowl, In very likeness of a roasted crab . ii 1 48
Here he comes in the likeness of a Jew . . . *Mer. of Venice* iii 1 24
Her dead likeness, I do well believe, Excels whatever yet you look'd upon, Or hand of man hath done . . . . . *W. Tale* v 3 15
The devil tempts thee here In likeness of a new untrimmed bride *K. John* iii 1 209
Thou, old Adam's likeness, set to dress this garden . *Richard II.* iii 4 73
There is a devil haunts thee in the likeness of an old fat man *1 Hen. IV.* ii 4 493
The Lord of Stafford dear to-day hath bought Thy likeness . . . v 3 8
I cannot so conjure up the spirit of love in her, that he will appear in his true likeness . . . . *Hen. V.* v 2 317
If you would conjure in her, you must make a circle: if conjure up love in her in his true likeness, he must appear naked and blind . . v 2 321
Take that, thou likeness of this railer here . . . *3 Hen. VI.* v 5 38
We can kill a fly That comes in likeness of a coal-black Moor *T. Andron.* iii 2 78
Lover! Appear thou in the likeness of a sigh . . *Rom. and Jul.* ii 1 8
I conjure thee by Rosaline's bright eyes . . . That in thy likeness thou appear to us! . . . . ii 1 21
And in this borrow'd likeness of shrunk death Thou shalt continue two and forty hours, And then awake . . . . iv 1 104
Do not assume my likeness.—Were I like thee, I'ld throw away myself *T. of Athens* iv 3 218
The power of beauty will sooner transform honesty from what it is to a bawd than the force of honesty can translate beauty into his likeness *Hamlet* iii 1 114
My good intent May carry through itself to that full issue For which I razed my likeness . . . . *Lear* i 4 4
Liker. The time is long.—The liker you; few taller are so young *L. L. Lost* v 2 846
And this boy Liker in feature to his father Geffrey Than thou and John in manners . . . . *K. John* ii 1 126
Likest. 'What compass will you wear your farthingale?' Why even what fashion thou best likest . . . . . . *T. G. of Ver.* ii 7 52
I pray thee tell me truly how thou likest her . . . . *Much Ado* i 1 180
Marry, master schoolmaster, he that is likest to a hogshead . *L. L. Lost* iv 2 88
It is an attribute to God himself; And earthly power doth then show likest God's When mercy seasons justice . . *Mer. of Venice* iv 1 196
A paltry cap, . . . I love thee well, in that thou likest it not *T. of Shrew* iv 3 83
How likest thou this picture, Apemantus?—The best, for the innocence *T. of Athens* i 1 197
Likewise. Let me hear from thee by letters . . . ; And I likewise will visit thee with mine . . . . *T. G. of Ver.* i 1 60
I likewise hear that Valentine is dead.—And so suppose am I . . iv 2 113
That likewise have we thought upon . . . *Mer. Wives* iv 4 46
Hath appointed That he shall likewise shuffle her away . . . . iv 6 29

Likewise. To this her mother's plot She seemingly obedient likewise hath Made promise . . . . *Mer. Wives* iv 6 33
The satisfaction I would require is likewise your own benefit *M. for M.* iii 1 156
My woes end likewise with the evening sun . . . *Com. of Errors* i 1 28
That she brought me up, I likewise give her most humble thanks *M. Ado* i 1 241
Where we are our learning likewise is: Then when ourselves we see in ladies' eyes, Do we not likewise see our learning there? . *L. L. Lost* iv 3 317
Our love being yours, the error that love makes Is likewise yours . . v 2 782
That 's likewise part of my intelligence . . . . . *W. Tale* iv 2 51
My father . . . was likewise a snapper-up of unconsidered trifles . iv 3 26
And liquor likewise will I give to thee . . . . . *Hen. V.* ii 1 113
This knight, no less for bounty bound to us . . . , hath likewise sworn ii 2 93
Most of the rest slaughter'd or took likewise . . . 1 *Hen. VI.* i 1 147
I would his troubles likewise were expired, That so he might recover . ii 5 31
Our fatherless distress was left unmoan'd ; Your widow-dolour likewise be unwept!—Give me no help in lamentation . . *Richard III.* ii 2 65
O, swear not by the moon, the inconstant moon, . . . Lest that thy love prove likewise variable . . . . *Rom. and Jul.* ii 2 111
For, lo, My intercession likewise steads my foe . . . . ii 3 54
Had gold of him : he likewise enriched poor straggling soldiers *T. of A.* v 1 6
He likewise gives a frock or livery, That aptly is put on . . *Hamlet* iii 4 164
They give their greeting to the citadel : This likewise is a friend *Othello* ii 1 96
This is a thing Which you might from relation likewise reap . *Cymbeline* ii 4 86
Liking. If matters grow to your likings . . . . . . *Mer. Wives* i 1 79
As long as I have an eye to make difference of men's liking . . . ii 1 57
Shame to him whose cruel striking Kills for faults of his own liking! Twice treble shame on Angelo! . . . . . *Meas. for Meas.* iii 2 282
A rougher task in hand Than to drive liking to the name of love *Much Ado* i 1 302
Lest my liking might too sudden seem, I would have salved it with a longer treatise.—What need the bridge much broader than the flood? i 1 316
If I had my liberty, I would do my liking . . . . . . i 3 38
One doth not know How much an ill word may empoison liking . . iii 1 86
I shall desire your help.—My heart is with your liking.—And my help . v 4 32
Let us talk in good earnest : is it possible, on such a sudden, you should fall into so strong a liking? . . . . *As Y. Like It* i 3 28
Grieve, be effeminate, changeable, longing and liking . . . . iii 2 431
Upon agreement from us to his liking . . . . . *T. of Shrew* i 2 183
But to her love concerneth us to add Her father's liking . . . iii 2 131
How might one do, sir, to lose it [virginity] to her own liking? *All's Well* i 1 164
In so true a flame of liking Wish chastely and love dearly . . . i 3 217
The king had married him Against his liking . . . . . . iii 5 57
With a kind of injunction drives me to these habits of her liking *T. Night* ii 5 184
And bring him up to liking . . . . . . *W. Tale* iv 4 544
Most sorry, you have broken from his liking Where you were tied in duty v 1 212
If he see aught in you that makes him like, That any thing he sees, which moves his liking, I can with ease translate it to my will . *K. John* ii 1 512
Well, I'll repent, and that suddenly, while I am in some liking 1 *Hen. IV.* iii 3 6
When the prince broke thy head for liking his father to a singing-man 2 *Hen. IV.* ii 1 97
As liking of the lady's virtuous gifts, Her beauty . . . 1 *Hen. VI.* v 1 43
As being thought to contradict your liking . . . 2 *Hen. VI.* iii 2 252
What friend of mine That had to him derived your anger, did I Continue in my liking? . . . . *Hen. VIII.* ii 4 33
Feebling such as stand not in their liking Below their cobbled shoes *Coriol.* i 1 199
I 'll look to like, if looking liking move : But no more deep *Rom. and Jul.* i 3 97
Avert your liking a more worthier way . . . . . *Lear* i 1 214
And such a tongue As I am glad I have not, though not to have it Hath lost me in your liking . . . . i 1 236
He protests he loves you And needs no other suitor but his likings *Othello* iii 1 51
With whom the father liking took, And her to incest did provoke *Per.* i Gower 25
Lily. She is as white as a lily and as small as a wand . *T. G. of Ver.* ii 3 22
By my maiden honour, yet as pure As the unsullied lily . . *L. L. Lost* v 2 352
These lily lips, This cherry nose, These yellow cowslip cheeks *M. N. D.* v 1 337
Lilies of all kinds, The flower-de-luce being one . . . *W. Tale* iv 4 126
Of Nature's gifts thou mayst with lilies boast . . . *K. John* iii 1 53
To paint the lily, To throw a perfume on the violet . . . . iv 2 11
Like the lily, That once was mistress of the field and flourish'd *Hen. VIII* iii 1 151
A most unspotted lily shall she pass To the ground . . . . v 5 62
Those lily hands Tremble, like aspen-leaves, upon a lute . *T. Andron.* ii 4 44
As doth the honey-dew Upon a gather'd lily almost wither'd . . . iii 1 113
How bravely thou becomest thy bed, fresh lily! . . . *Cymbeline* ii 2 15
O sweetest, fairest lily! My brother wears thee not the one half so well As when thou grew'st thyself . . . . iv 2 201
Lily-bed. And give me swift transportance to those fields Where I may wallow in the lily-beds . . . . *Troi. and Cres.* iii 2 13
Lily-livered. Go prick thy face, and over-red thy fear, Thou lily-liver'd boy . . . . *Macbeth* v 3 15
A lily-livered, action-taking knave . . . . *Lear* ii 2 18
Lily-tincture. Pinch'd the lily-tincture of her face . . *T. G. of Ver.* iv 4 160
Lily-white. Most lily-white of hue . . . . . *M. N. Dream* iii 1 95
Limander. And, like Limander, am I trusty still . . . . . v 1 198
Limb. Let them keep their limbs whole and hack our English *Mer. Wives* iii 1 79
Thou hast neither heat, affection, limb, nor beauty *Meas. for Meas.* iii 1 37
Both strength of limb and policy of mind, Ability in means . *Much Ado* iv 1 200
When shall you hear that I Will praise a hand, . . . A leg, a limb! *L. L. L.* iv 3 186
This swain, because of his great limb or joint, shall pass Pompey the Great v 1 135
Had you been as wise as bold, Young in limbs, in judgement old *M. of V.* ii 7 71
I wrestle for my credit ; and he that escapes me without some broken limb shall acquit him well . . . . . . *As Y. Like It* i 1 134
To be my foster-nurse When service should in my old limbs lie lame . ii 3 41
Is 't I That chase thee from thy country and expose Those tender limbs of thine to the event Of the none-sparing war? . . . *All's Well* iii 2 107
Made the days and nights as one, To wear your gentle limbs in my affairs v 1 4
Thy limbs, actions and spirit, Do give thee five-fold blazon . *T. Night* i 5 311
Therefore, good mother, To whom am I beholding for these limbs? *K. John* i 1 239
And hang a calf's-skin on those recreant limbs . . . iii 1 129 ; 131 ; 133 ; 199
Yet I 'll venture it. If I get down, and do not break my limbs, I 'll find a thousand shifts to get away . . . . iv 3 6
Inquire of him, And learn to make a body of a limb . *Richard II.* iii 2 187
I hardly yet have learn'd To insinuate, flatter, bow, and bend my limbs iv 1 165
Your father's sickness is a maim to us.—A perilous gash, a very limb lopp'd off : And yet, in faith, it is not . . . . 1 *Hen. IV.* iv 1 43
To crush our old limbs in ungentle steel . . . . . . v 1 13
Even so my limbs, Weaken'd with grief, being now enraged with grief, Are thrice themselves . . . . . . 2 *Hen. IV.* i 1 143
A man can no more separate age and covetousness than a' can part young limbs and lechery . . . . i 2 257
Care I for the limb, the thewes, the stature, bulk, and big assemblance of a man! . . . . iii 2 276
Like a broken limb united, Grow stronger for the breaking . . . iv 1 222
Limb. Let us choose such limbs of noble counsel . . . 2 *Hen. IV.* v 2 135
And you, good yeomen, Whose limbs were made in England . *Hen. V.* iii 1 26
So do our vulgar drench their peasant limbs In blood of princes . . iv 7 80
Old I do wax ; and from my weary limbs Honour is cudgelled . . v 1 89
Some Hercules, A second Hector, for his grim aspect, And large proportion of his strong-knit limbs . . . . . 1 *Hen. VI.* ii 3 21
Even like a man new haled from the rack, So fare my limbs . . . ii 5 4
Drops bloody sweat from his war-wearied limbs . . . . . iv 4 18
In thee revived When sapless age and weak unable limbs Should bring thy father to his drooping chair . . . . iv 5 4
Two pulls at once ; His lady banish'd, and a limb lopp'd off . 2 *Hen. VI.* ii 3 42
Outface me with thy looks : Set limb to limb, and thou art far the lesser iv 10 50
And so he comes, to rend his limbs asunder . . . . 3 *Hen. VI.* i 3 15
But death hath snatch'd my husband from mine arms, And pluck'd two crutches from my feeble limbs . . . . . . *Richard III.* ii 2 58
This noble isle doth want her proper limbs ; Her face defaced . . iii 7 125
Who set the body and the limbs Of this great sport together? *Hen. VIII.* i 1 46
So, so ; These are the limbs o' the plot : no more, I hope . . . i 1 220
Have you limbs To bear that load of title? . . . . . . ii 3 38
No audience, but the tribulation of Tower-hill, or the limbs of Limehouse v 4 66
Limbs are his instruments, In no less working than are swords and bows Directive by the limbs . . . . . . *Troi. and Cres.* i 3 356
I will the second time, As I would buy thee, view thee limb by limb . iv 5 238
When you now see He had rather venture all his limbs for honour Than one on's ears to hear it . . . . *Coriolanus* ii 2 84
He 's a limb that has but a disease : Mortal, to cut it off ; to cure it, easy iii 1 296
Hew his limbs, and on a pile Ad manes fratrum sacrifice his flesh *T. An.* i 1 97
Upon a pile of wood, Let 's hew his limbs till they be clean consumed . i 1 129
Alarbus' limbs are lopp'd, And entrails feed the sacrificing fire . . i 1 143
And the hounds Should drive upon thy new-transformed limbs . . ii 3 64
O, let me teach you how to knit again This scatter'd corn into one mutual sheaf, These broken limbs again into one body . . . . v 3 72
Where unbruised youth with unstuff'd brain Doth couch his limbs *Rom. and Jul.* ii 3 38
I will tear thee joint by joint And strew this hungry churchyard with thy limbs . . . . v 3 36
Thou cold sciatica, Cripple our senators, that their limbs may halt As lamely as their manners! . . . . *T. of Athens* iv 1 24
For Romans now Have thews and limbs like to their ancestors *J. Cæsar* i 3 81
Our course will seem too bloody, Caius Cassius, To cut the head off and then hack the limbs, . . . For Antony is but a limb of Cæsar . ii 1 163
A curse shall light upon the limbs of men . . . . . . iii 1 262
Brevity is the soul of wit, And tediousness the limbs . . *Hamlet* ii 2 91
When she saw Pyrrhus make malicious sport In mincing with his sword her husband's limbs . . . . ii 2 537
Limbeck. And the receipt of reason A limbeck only . . . *Macbeth* i 7 67
Limber vows. You put me off with limber vows . . . *W. Tale* i 2 47
Limb-meal. O, that I had her here, to tear her limb-meal! . *Cymbeline* ii 4 147
Limbo. Is he well?—No, he 's in Tartar limbo, worse than hell *C. of Er.* iv 2 32
Talked of Satan and of Limbo and of Furies and I know not what *All's W.* v 3 261
I have some of 'em in Limbo Patrum . . . . . *Hen. VIII.* v 4 67
As far from help as Limbo is from bliss! . . . . *T. Andron.* iii 1 149
Lime. Come, put some lime upon your fingers . . . . *Tempest* iv 1 246
You must lay lime to tangle her desires By wailful sonnets *T. G. of Ver.* iii 2 68
Let me see thee froth and lime : I am at a word ; follow . *Mer. Wives* i 3 15
This man, with lime and rough-cast, doth present Wall . *M. N. Dream* v 1 132
Would you desire lime and hair to speak better? . . . . . v 1 166
My cherry lips have often kiss'd thy stones, Thy stones with lime and hair knit up in thee . . . . v 1 193
By this time from their fixed beds of lime Had been dishabited *K. John* ii 1 219
King Richard lies Within the limits of yon lime and stone *Richard II.* iii 3 26
You rogue, here 's lime in this sack too . . . . 1 *Hen. IV.* ii 4 137
Yet a coward is worse than a cup of sack with lime in it . . ii 4 140
I throw my infamy at thee : I will not ruinate my father's house, Who gave his blood to lime the stones together . . 3 *Hen. VI.* v 1 84
Thou 'ldst never fear the net nor lime, The pitfall nor the gin *Macbeth* iv 2 34
Limed. She 's limed, I warrant you . . . . . . *Much Ado* iii 1 104
But that they are limed with the twigs that threaten them . *All's Well* iii 5 26
I have limed her ; but it is Jove's doing . . . . *T. Night* iii 4 82
Madam, myself have limed a bush for her, And placed a quire of such enticing birds, That she will light to listen to the lays . 2 *Hen. VI.* i 3 91
York and impious Beaufort . . . Have all limed bushes to betray thy wings ii 4 54
The bird that hath been limed in a bush, With trembling wings misdoubteth every bush . . . . 3 *Hen. VI.* v 6 13
Where my poor young was limed, was caught and kill'd . . . . v 6 17
O limed soul, that, struggling to be free, Art more engaged! . *Hamlet* iii 3 68
Limehouse. No audience, but the tribulation of Tower-hill, or the limbs of Limehouse . . . . *Hen. VIII.* v 4 66
Lime-kiln. Which is as hateful to me as the reek of a lime-kiln *Mer. Wives* iii 3 86
Limekilns i' the palm, incurable bone-ache . . . *Troi. and Cres.* v 1 25
Lime-twig. Comb down his hair ; look, look! it stands upright, Like lime-twigs set to catch my winged soul . . . 2 *Hen. VI.* iii 3 16
Limit. Which had indeed no limit, A confidence sans bound . *Tempest* i 2 96
I Beyond all limit of what else i' the world Do love, prize, honour you iii 1 72
Between which time of the contract and limit of the solemnity *M. for M.* iii 1 224
I 'll limit thee this day To seek thy life by beneficial help *Com. of Errors* i 1 151
The sadness is without limit . . . . *Much Ado* i 3 5
A merrier man, Within the limit of becoming mirth . . *L. L. Lost* ii 1 67
Should be buried in highways out of all sanctified limit . . *All's Well* i 1 152
You must confine yourself within the modest limits of order . *T. Night* i 3 9
I' the open air, before I have got strength of limit . . *W. Tale* iii 2 107
The farthest limit of my embassy . . . . *K. John* i 1 22
The sly slow hours shall not determinate The dateless limit of thy dear exile ; The hopeless word of 'never to return' Breathe I *Richard II.* i 3 151
So high above his limits swells the rage Of Bolingbroke . . . . iii 2 109
King Richard lies Within the limits of yon lime and stone . . . iii 3 26
And many limits of the charge set down But yesternight . 1 *Hen. IV.* i 1 35
The archdeacon hath divided it Into three limits very equally . . iii 1 73
Out of limit and true rule You stand against anointed majesty . iv 3 39
I prithee, give no limits to my tongue : I am a king . . 3 *Hen. VI.* ii 2 119
Dispatch ; the limit of your lives is out . . . . *Richard III.* iii 3 8
For reverence to some alive, I give a sparing limit to my tongue . . iii 7 194
Limit each leader to his several charge . . . . . . v 3 25
The desire is boundless and the act a slave to limit . *Troi. and Cres.* iii 2 90
Let reason govern thy lament.—If there were reason for these miseries, Then into limits could I bind my woes . . . *T. Andron.* iii 1 221
Stony limits cannot hold love out . . . . *Rom. and Jul.* ii 2 67
'Banished!' There is no end, no limit, measure, bound, In that word's death . . . . iii 2 125
A prison for a debtor, that not dares To stride a limit . . *Cymbeline* iii 3 35

Limitation. You have stood your limitation . . . . Coriolanus ii 3 146
Am I yourself But, as it were, in sort or limitation? . . . J. Cæsar ii 1 283
Limited. Alack, how may I do it, having the hour limited? Meas. for Meas. iv 2 176
I do know the scope And warrant limited unto my tongue . K. John v 2 123
There is boundless theft In limited professions . . T. of Athens iv 3 431
I'll make so bold to call, For 'tis my limited service . . Macbeth ii 3 57
Limned. Most truly limn'd and living in your face . As Y. Like It ii 7 194
Limp. So far this shadow Doth limp behind the substance Mer. of Venice iii 2 130
Why does the world report that Kate doth limp? . . T. of Shrew ii 1 254
Our tardy apish nation Limps after in base imitation . Richard II. ii 1 23
Who, like a foul and ugly witch, doth limp So tediously away Hen. V. iv Prol. 21
Limped. After me hath many a weary step Limp'd in pure love As Y. L. It ii 7 131
Limping. When well-apparell'd April on the heel Of limping winter treads, even such delight . . . . . . Rom. and Jul. i 2 28
Son of sixteen, Pluck the lined crutch from thy old limping sire T. of A. iv 1 14
Lincoln. First I began in private With you, my Lord of Lincoln Hen. VIII. ii 4 207
Lincolnshire. Or the drone of a Lincolnshire bagpipe . 1 Hen. IV. i 2 85
Lincoln Washes. These Lincoln Washes have devoured them K. John v 6 41
Line. Come, hang them on this line . . . . . . Tempest iv 1 193
Mistress line, is not this my jerkin? Now is the jerkin under the line iv 1 235
We steal by line and level, an't like your grace . . . iv 1 239
'Steal by line and level' is an excellent pass of pate . . . . iv 1 243
I must go send some better messenger: I fear my Julia would not deign my lines, Receiving them from such a worthless post T. G. of Ver. i 1 160
Dare you presume to harbour wanton lines? To whisper and conspire? i 2 42
Here in one line is his name twice writ, 'Poor forlorn Proteus' . . i 2 123
Sweet love! sweet lines! sweet life! Here is her hand . . . i 3 45
Last night she enjoined me to write some lines to one she loves . . ii 1 94
The lines are very quaintly writ; But since unwillingly, take them again ii 1 128
And frame some feeling line . . . . iii 2 76
I will not look upon your master's lines: I know they are stuff'd with protestations And full of new-found oaths . . . . . . iv 4 133
With full line of his authority . . . . . Meas. for Meas. i 4 56
His life is parallel'd Even with the stroke and line of his great justice . iv 2 83
I fear these stubborn lines lack power to move . . L. L. Lost iv 3 55
What, did these rent lines show some love of thine? . . . . iv 3 220
His lines would ravish savage ears And plant in tyrants mild humility iv 3 348
Here's a simple line of life: here's a small trifle of wives Mer. of Venice ii 2 169
Heart too capable Of every line and trick of his sweet favour All's Well i 1 107
Which warp'd the line of every other favour . . . . . v 3 49
He does smile his face into more lines than is the new map . T. Night iii 2 84
Looking on the lines Of my boy's face, methoughts I did recoil Twenty-three years, and saw myself unbreech'd . . . . W. Tale i 2 153
I am angling now, Though you perceive me not how I give line . i 2 181
O, now doth Death line his dead chaps with steel . . . K. John ii 1 352
Whose private with me . . . Is much more general than these lines import iv 3 17
We will not line his thin bestained cloak With our pure honours . iv 3 24
Now powers from home and discontents at home Meet in one line . iv 3 152
To show the line and the predicament Wherein you range . 1 Hen. IV. i 3 168
And hath sent for you To line his enterprize . . . . . ii 3 86
And in that very line, Harry, standest thou . . . . . iii 2 85
Hold hook and line, say I . . . . 2 Hen. IV. ii 4 172
But, being moody, give him line and scope . . . . . iv 4 39
Of the true line and stock of Charles the Great . . . Hen. V. i 2 71
By the which marriage the line of Charles the Great Was re-united . i 2 84
As many lines close in the dial's centre . . . . . . i 2 210
To line and new repair our towns of war With men of courage . . ii 4 7
He sends you this most memorable line, In every branch truly demonstrative . . . . ii 4 88
From John of Gaunt . . . , Being but fourth of that heroic line 1 Hen. VI. ii 5 78
Comest thou with deep premeditated lines, With written pamphlets? . iii 1 1
Would make a volume of enticing lines, Able to ravish any dull conceit v 5 14
Duke of Clarence, from whose line I claim the crown . . 2 Hen. VI. ii 2 34
Such hope have all the line of John of Gaunt! . . . 3 Hen. VI. i 1 19
Till I root out their accursed line And leave not one alive, I live in hell i 3 32
Lines of fair comfort and encouragement . . . Richard III. v 2 6
All that stand about him are under the line . . . Hen. VIII. v 4 44
Season, form, Office and custom, in all line of order . Troi. and Cres. i 3 88
And sends them weapons wrapp'd about with lines, That wound, beyond their feeling, to the quick . . . . T. Andron. iv 2 27
What I mean to do See here in bloody lines I have set down . . . v 2 14
Witness this wretched stump, witness these crimson lines . . . v 2 22
Yon gray lines That fret the clouds are messengers of day . J. Cæsar ii 1 103
Or did line the rebel With hidden help and vantage . . Macbeth i 3 112
Then prophet-like They hail'd him father to a line of kings . . iii 1 60
What, will the line stretch out to the crack of doom? . . . . iv 1 117
His wife, his babes, and all unfortunate souls That trace him in his line iv 1 153
There were no sallets in the lines to make the matter savoury Hamlet ii 2 462
If it live in your memory, begin at this line . . . . . . ii 2 470
You could, for a need, study a speech of some dozen or sixteen lines? . ii 2 567
I had as lief the town-crier spoke my lines . . . . . . iii 2 4
O, 'tis most sweet, When in one line two crafts directly meet . . iii 4 210
Of all these bounds, even from this line to this . . . . Lear i 1 64
What If I do line one of their hands? 'Tis gold Which buys admittance; oft it doth . . . . Cymbeline ii 3 72
The lines of my body are as well drawn as his; no less young . . iv 1 10
Time hath nothing blurr'd those lines of favour Which then he wore . iv 2 104
Will you use him kindly? He will line your apron with gold Pericles iv 6 63
Lineal. Peace be to France, if France in peace permit Our just and lineal entrance to our own . . . . K. John ii 1 85
Happily may your sweet self put on The lineal state and glory of the land! . . . . v 7 102
His coming hither hath no further scope Than for his lineal royalties and to beg Enfranchisement . . . . . . Richard II. iii 3 113
It shall not force This lineal honour from me . . . 2 Hen. IV. iv 5 46
Queen Isabel, his grandmother, Was lineal of the Lady Ermengare Hen. V. i 2 82
From whence you spring by lineal descent . . . 1 Hen. VI. iii 1 166
Your due of birth, The lineal glory of your royal house . Richard III. iii 7 121
Yet to draw forth your noble ancestry From the corruption of abusing times, Unto a lineal true-derived course . . . . . . iii 7 200
Lineally. From these our Henry lineally descends . 3 Hen. VI. iii 3 87
Lineament. In every lineament, branch, shape, and form . Much Ado v 1 14
There must be needs a like proportion Of lineaments, of manners M. of V. iii 4 15
Now thou goest from Fortune's office to Nature's: Fortune reigns in gifts of the world, not in the lineaments of Nature . As Y. Like It i 2 45
'Tis not her glass, but you, that flatters her; And out of you she sees herself more proper Than any of her lineaments can show her . iii 5 56
A happy gentleman in blood and lineaments . . . Richard II. iii 1 9
The issue was not his begot; Which well appeared in his lineaments Richard III. iii 5 91

Lineament. I did infer your lineaments, Being the right idea of your father . . . . Richard III. iii 7 12
Find delight writ there with beauty's pen; Examine every married lineament And see how one another lends content . Rom and Jul. i 3 83
Lined. The justice, In fair round belly with good capon lined As Y. Like It ii 7 154
All the pictures fairest lined Are but black to Rosalind . . . . iii 2 97
Winter garments must be lined, So must slender Rosalind . . . iii 2 111
Who lined himself with hope, Eating the air on promise of supply 2 Hen. IV. i 3 27
Pluck the lined crutch from thy old limping sire! . . T. of Athens iv 1 14
And when they have lined their coats Do themselves homage . Othello i 1 53
Line-grove. In the line-grove which weather-fends your cell . Tempest v 1 10
Linen. Rich garments, linen, stuffs and necessaries . . . . . i 2 164
Throw foul linen upon him, as if it were going to bucking Mer. Wives iii 3 139
This 'tis to have linen and buck-baskets! . . . . . . iii 5 145
Mistress Page and I will look some linen for your head . . . iv 2 83
Go up; I'll bring linen for him straight . . . . . . iv 2 102
My jealousy is reasonable. Pluck me out all the linen . . . iv 2 156
It was enjoined him in Rome for want of linen . . L. L. Lost v 2 719
Let Thisby have clean linen . . . . . M. N. Dream iv 2 40
Fine linen, Turkey cushions boss'd with pearl . . . T. of Shrew ii 1 355
A linen stock on one leg and a kersey boot-hose on the other . . iii 2 67
When the kite builds, look to lesser linen . . . . W. Tale iv 3 24
They'll find linen enough on every hedge . . . . 1 Hen. IV. iv 2 52
For it is a low ebb of linen with thee . . . . . 2 Hen. IV. ii 2 22
And God knows, whether those that bawl out the ruins of thy linen shall inherit his kingdom . . . . ii 2 27
No worse than they are backbitten, sir; for they have marvellous foul linen . . . . v 1 38
Those linen cheeks of thine Are counsellors to fear . . . Macbeth v 3 16
Then waved his handkerchief?—And kiss'd it, madam.—Senseless linen! happier therein than I! . . . . Cymbeline i 3 7
Get linen: now this matter must be look'd to, For her relapse is mortal Pericles iii 2 109
Ling. Our old ling and our Isbels o' the country are nothing like your old ling and your Isbels o' the court . . . . . All's Well iii 2 14
Lingare. Heir to the Lady Lingare, Daughter to Charlemain . Hen. V. i 2 74
Linger. If thou linger in my territories Longer than swiftest expedition Will give thee time to leave . . . . . T. G. of Ver. iii 1 163
She lingers my desires, Like to a step-dame or a dowager M. N. Dream i 1 4
Still more fool I shall appear By the time I linger here . Mer. of Venice ii 9 74
Gently would dissolve the bands of life, Which false hope lingers Rich. II. ii 2 72
Borrowing only lingers and lingers it out . . . . 2 Hen. IV. i 2 265
Linger your patience on . . . . Hen. V. ii Prol. 31
Then linger not, my lord; away, take horse.—Come, Margaret 2 Hen. VI. iv 4 54
I'll follow her.—Come, son, away; we may not linger thus . 3 Hen. VI. i 1 263
Why do we linger thus? I cannot rest . . . . . . i 2 32
Why linger we? let us lay hands upon him.—Forbear awhile . . . iii 1 26
I say, at once let your brief plagues be mercy, And linger not our sure destructions on! . . . . Troi. and Cres. v 10 9
Vagabond exile, flaying, pent to linger But with a grain a day Coriolanus iii 3 89
I would not have thee linger in thy pain . . . . Othello v 2 87
Lingered. We have lingered about a match . . . Mer. Wives iii 2 58
Say that I linger'd with you at your shop . . . Com. of Errors iii 1 3
Unless his abode be lingered here by some accident . . Othello iv 2 231
Lingering perdition, worse than any death Can be at once . Tempest iii 3 77
His death draw out To lingering sufferance . . . Meas. for Meas. ii 4 167
From which lingering penance Of such misery doth she cut me off M. of V. iv 1 271
With a lingering dram that should not work Maliciously like poison W. T. i 2 320
Let order die! And let this world no longer be a stage To feed contention in a lingering act! . . . . 2 Hen. IV. i 1 156
One would have lingering wars with little cost . . 1 Hen. VI. i 1 74
And, in advantage lingering, looks for rescue . . . . . iv 4 19
And torture him with grievous lingering death . . 2 Hen. VI. iii 2 247
A speedier course than lingering languishment Must we pursue T. An. ii 1 110
Stew'd in brine, Smarting in lingering pickle . . Ant. and Cleo. ii 5 66
She doth think she has Strange lingering poisons . . . Cymbeline i 5 34
Should by the minute feed on life and lingering By inches waste you . v 5 51
Linguist. A linguist and a man of such perfection As we do in our quality much want . . . . T. G. of Ver. iv 1 57
The manifold linguist and the armipotent soldier . . . All's Well iv 3 265
Lining. Pleasant jest and courtesy, As bombast and as lining to the time L. L. Lost v 2 791
The lining of his coffers shall make coats . . . . . Richard II i 4 61
Link. To link my dear friend to a common stale . . . Much Ado iv 1 66
There was no link to colour Peter's hat . . . T. of Shrew iv 1 137
Thou hast saved me a thousand marks in links and torches 1 Hen. IV. iii 3 48
Now, sir, a new link to the bucket must needs be had . 2 Hen. IV. v 1 23
I were loath To link with him that were not lawful chosen 3 Hen. VI. iii 3 115
Cracking ten thousand curbs Of more strong link asunder . Coriolanus i 1 73
No airless dungeon, nor strong links of iron, Can be retentive to the strength of spirit . . . . J. Cæsar i 3 94
Link'd together With all religious strength of sacred vows . K. John iii 1 228
Is likely to beget more conquerors, If with a lady of so high resolve As is fair Margaret he be link'd in love . . . . . 1 Hen. VI. v 5 76
They are so link'd in friendship, That young Prince Edward marries Warwick's daughter.—Belike the elder . . . 3 Hen. VI. iv 1 116
So lust, though to a radiant angel link'd, Will sate itself in a celestial bed, And prey on garbage . . . . Hamlet i 5 55
Our slippery people, Whose love is never link'd to the deserver Till his deserts are past . . . . Ant. and Cleo. i 2 193
Linsey-woolsey. But what linsey-woolsey hast thou to speak to us again? —E'en such as you speak to me . . . . All's Well iv 1 13
Linstock. With linstock now the devilish cannon touches Hen. V. iii Prol. 33
Lion. A hollow burst of bellowing Like bulls, or rather lions . Tempest ii 1 312
Sure, it was the roar Of a whole herd of lions . . . . . ii 1 316
To walk like one of the lions . . . . . . T. G. of Ver. ii 1 29
Had I been seized by a hungry lion, I would have been a breakfast . v 4 33
Like an o'ergrown lion in a cave, That goes not out to prey Meas. for Meas. i 3 22
Which have for long run by the hideous law, As mice by lions . . i 4 64
Doing, in the figure of a lamb, the feats of a lion . . . Much Ado i 1 15
Thus dost thou hear the Nemean lion roar 'Gainst thee, thou lamb L. L. Lost iv 1 90
Your lion, that holds his poll-axe sitting on a close-stool . . v 2 580
But you have out-faced them all.—An thou wert a lion, we would do so v 2 627
You, the lion's part: and, I hope, here is a play fitted . M. N. Dream i 2 66
Have you the lion's part written? . . . . i 2 68
Let me play the lion too: I will roar, that I will do any man's heart good i 2 72
Be it on lion, bear, or wolf, or bull, On meddling monkey . . . ii 1 180
Will not the ladies be afeard of the lion?—I fear it, I promise you . iii 1 28

Lion. To bring in—God shield us!—a lion among ladies, is a most dreadful thing . . . . *M. N. Dream* iii 1 31
There is not a more fearful wild-fowl than your lion living . . . iii 1 33
Therefore another prologue must tell he is not a lion . . . . iii 1 36
Name his name, and half his face must be seen through the lion's neck iii 1 38
If you think I come hither as a lion, it were pity of my life . . . iii 1 44
Let not him that plays the lion pare his nails, for they shall hang out for the lion's claws . . . . iv 2 41
This grisly beast, which Lion hight by name . . . . . . v 1 140
Her mantle she did fall, Which Lion vile with bloody mouth did stain . v 1 144
Let Lion, Moonshine, Wall, and lovers twain At large discourse . . v 1 151
I wonder if the lion be to speak.—No wonder, my lord: one lion may, when many asses do . . . . v 1 153
Here come two noble beasts in, a man and a lion . . . . . v 1 221
Both quake and tremble here, When lion rough in wildest rage doth roar v 1 225
I, one Snug the joiner, am A lion-fell, nor else no lion's dam . . . v 1 227
If I should as lion come in strife Into this place, 'twere pity on my life v 1 228
This lion is a very fox for his valour.—True; and a goose for his discretion v 1 234
Oh—— Well roared, Lion.—Well run, Thisbe.—Well shone, Moon v 1 270
Well moused, Lion.—And so the lion vanished.—And then came Pyramus v 1 274
O wherefore, Nature, didst thou lions frame? Since lion vile hath here deflower'd my dear . . . . v 1 296
Moonshine and Lion are left to bury the dead.—Ay, and Wall too . . v 1 355
Now the hungry lion roars, And the wolf behowls the moon . . . v 1 378
Yea, mock the lion when he roars for prey . . . *Mer. of Venice* ii 1 30
In such a night Did Thisbe fearfully o'ertrip the dew And saw the lion's shadow ere himself And ran dismay'd away . . . . . . v 1 8
I thought thy heart had been wounded with the claws of a lion *As Y. L. It* v 2 26
Have I not in my time heard lions roar? . . . . *T. of Shrew* i 2 201
The hind that would be mated by the lion Must die for love . *All's Well* i 1 102
Better 'twere I met the ravin lion when he roar'd . . . . iii 2 120
How much the better To fall before the lion than the wolf! . *T. Night* iii 1 140
Against whose fury . . . The aweless lion could not wage the fight *K. John* i 1 266
He that perforce robs lions of their hearts May easily win a woman's . i 1 268
Richard, that robb'd the lion of his heart . . . . . . ii 1 3
You are the hare of whom the proverb goes, Whose valour plucks dead lions by the beard . . . . ii 1 138
Well did he become that lion's robe That did disrobe the lion of that robe! . . . . ii 1 141
I would set an ox-head to your lion's hide, And make a monster of you ii 1 292
Peace! no more.—O, tremble, for you hear the lion roar . . . ii 1 294
The sea enraged is not half so deaf, Lions more confident . . . ii 1 452
Talks as familiarly of roaring lions As maids of thirteen do of puppy-dogs! . . . . ii 1 459
Thou wear a lion's hide! doff it for shame, And hang a calf's-skin on . iii 1 128
Thou mayst hold a serpent by the tongue, A chafed lion by the mortal paw . . . . iii 1 259
What, shall they seek the lion in his den, And fright him there? . . v 1 57
Like a lion foster'd up at hand, It may lie gently at the foot of peace . v 2 75
Lions make leopards tame . . . . *Richard II.* i 1 174
In war was never lion raged more fierce . . . . . . ii 1 173
The lion dying thrusteth forth his paw, And wounds the earth . . v 1 29
A lion and a king of beasts?—A king of beasts, indeed . . . v 1 34
I am as melancholy as a gib cat or a lugged bear.—Or an old lion 1 *Hen. IV.* i 2 84
O, the blood more stirs To rouse a lion than to start a hare! . . i 3 198
The lion will not touch the true prince. Instinct is a great matter . ii 4 300
I for a valiant lion, and thou for a true prince . . . . . ii 4 303
You are lions too, you ran away upon instinct . . . . . ii 4 331
A clip-wing'd griffin and a moulten raven, A couching lion . . . iii 1 153
Valiant as a lion And wondrous affable and as bountiful As mines of India . . . . iii 1 167
Turns head against the lion's armed jaws . . . . . . iii 2 102
I fear thee as I fear the roaring of the lion's whelp.—And why not as the lion?—The king himself is to be feared as the lion . . . iii 3 167
The young lion repents; marry, not in ashes and sackcloth . 2 *Hen. IV.* i 2 221
His power, like to a fangless lion, May offer, but not hold . . iv 1 218
Rouse yourself, As did the former lions of your blood . . *Hen. V.* i 2 124
If that same demon that hath gull'd thee thus Should with his lion gait walk the whole world, He might return to vasty Tartar back . . ii 2 122
That's a valiant flea that dare eat his breakfast on the lip of a lion . iii 7 157
The man that once did sell the lion's skin While the beast lived, was killed with hunting him . . . . iv 3 93
Like lions wanting food, Do rush upon us as their hungrey prey 1 *Hen. VI.* i 2 27
Either renew the fight, Or tear the lion's out of England's coat; Renounce your soil, give sheep in lions' stead . . . . . i 5 28
Like a hungry lion, did commence Rough deeds of rage . . . . iv 7 7
Small curs are not regarded when they grin; But great men tremble when the lions roars . . . . 2 *Hen. VI.* iii 1 19
That winter lion, who in rage forgets Aged contusions . . . . v 3 2
So looks the pent-up lion o'er the wretch That trembles under his devouring paws; And so he walks . . . . . 3 *Hen. VI.* i 3 12
He bore him in the thickest troop As doth a lion in a herd of neat . ii 1 14
To whom do lions cast their gentle looks? Not to the beast that would usurp their den . . . . ii 2 11
O bloody times! Whiles lions war and battle for their dens, Poor harmless lambs abide their enmity . . . . ii 5 74
When the lion fawns upon the lamb, The lamb will never cease to follow him . . . . iv 8 49
Under whose shade the ramping lion slept . . . . . . v 2 13
The two brave bears, . . . That in their chains fetter'd the kingly lion v 7 11
So looks the chafed lion Upon the daring huntsman . *Hen. VIII.* iii 2 206
Valiant as the lion, churlish as the bear . . . . *Troi. and Cres.* i 2 21
They that have the voice of lions and the act of hares, are they not monsters? . . . . iii 2 96
And, like a dew-drop from the lion's mane, Be shook to air . . . iii 3 224
And thou shalt hunt a lion, that will fly With his face backward . . iv 1 19
You have a vice of mercy in you, Which better fits a lion than a man . v 3 38
He that trusts to you, Where he should find you lions, finds you hares *Coriolanus* i 1 175
He is a lion That I am proud to hunt . . . . i 1 239
Yet have I heard,—O could I find it now!—The lion moved with pity did endure To have his princely paws pared all away . *T. Andron.* ii 3 151
She's with the lion deeply still in league . . . . . . iv 1 98
The ass more captain than the lion . . . . . *T. of Athens* iii 5 49
If thou wert the lion, the fox would beguile thee . . . . . iv 3 330
If thou wert the fox, the lion would suspect thee . . . . . iv 3 333
Wert thou a leopard, thou wert german to the lion and the spots of thy kindred were jurors on thy life . . . . iv 3 344
I met a lion, Who glared upon me, and went surly by . . *J. Cæsar* i 3 20
Thunders, lightens, opens graves, and roars As doth the lion in the Capitol i 3 75

Lion. He were no lion, were not Romans hinds . . . *J. Cæsar* i 3 106
Unicorns may be betray'd with trees, And bears with glasses, elephants with holes, Lions with toils and men with flatterers . . . . ii 1 206
We are two lions litter'd in one day, And I the elder and more terrible ii 2 46
Dismay'd not this Our captains, Macbeth and Banquo?—Yes; As sparrows eagles, or the hare the lion . . . . . . *Macbeth* i 2 35
Each petty artery in this body As hardy as the Nemean lion's nerve *Ham.* i 4 83
The lion and the belly-pinched wolf Keep their fur dry . . . *Lear* iii 1 13
Wolf in greediness, dog in madness, lion in prey . . . . . iii 4 97
As one would beat his offenceless dog to affright an imperious lion *Othello* ii 3 276
A vapour sometime like a bear or lion . . . . *Ant. and Cleo.* iv 14 3
The round world Should have shook lions into civil streets . . . v 1 16
And to grin like lions Upon the pikes o' the hunters . . *Cymbeline* v 3 38
Lionel. His grandfather was Lionel Duke of Clarence . . 1 *Hen. VI.* ii 4 83
Lionel Duke of Clarence, the third son To King Edward the Third . ii 5 75
Lionel Duke of Clarence; next to whom Was John of Gaunt . 2 *Hen. VI.* ii 2 13
Lioness. A lioness, with udders all drawn dry, Lay couching *As Y. Like It* iv 3 115
Did he leave him there, Food to the suck'd and hungry lioness? . . iv 3 127
Nature, stronger than his just occasion, Made him give battle to the lioness . . . . iv 3 131
And here upon his arm The lioness had torn some flesh away . . iv 3 148
Were I at home, At your den, sirrah, with your lioness . . *K. John* ii 1 291
The mountain lioness, The ocean swells not so as Aaron storms *T. An.* iv 2 138
A lioness hath whelped in the streets; And graves have yawn'd *J. Cæsar* ii 2 17
Lion-fell. A lion-fell, nor else no lion's dam . . . *M. N. Dream* v 1 227
Lion-mettled. Be lion-mettled, proud . . . . . . *Macbeth* iv 1 90
Lion-sick. He is not sick.—Yes, lion-sick, sick of proud heart *Tr. and Cr.* ii 3 93
Lion's whelp. I fear thee as I fear the roaring of the lion's whelp.—And why not as the lion? . . . . 1 *Hen. IV.* iii 3 167
Stood smiling to behold his lion's whelp Forage in blood . . *Hen. V.* i 2 109
'Tis better playing with a lion's whelp Than with an old one dying *Ant. and Cleo.* iii 13 94
When as a lion's whelp shall, to himself unknown, without seeking find *Cymbeline* v 4 138; v 5 435
Thou, Leonatus, art the lion's whelp . . . . v 5 443
Lip. Let us command to know that of your mouth or of your lips; for divers philosophers hold that the lips is parcel of the mouth *M. Wives* i 1 236
O, think on that; And mercy then will breathe within your lips *M. for M.* ii 2 78
I will open my lips in vain, or discover his government . . . . iii 1 199
'Tis a secret must be locked within the teeth and the lips . . . iii 2 143
Take, O, take those lips away, That so sweetly were forsworn . . iv 1 1
No sheep, sweet lamb, unless we feed on your lips . . . *L. L. Lost* ii 1 220
My lips are no common, though several they be . . . . . ii 1 223
I profane my lips on thy foot, my eyes on thy picture . . . . iv 1 86
And when she drinks, against her lips I bob . . . . *M. N. Dream* ii 1 49
O, how ripe in show Thy lips, those kissing cherries, tempting grow! . iii 2 140
My cherry lips have often kiss'd thy stones . . . . . . v 1 192
O, kiss me through the hole of this vile wall!—I kiss the wall's hole, not your lip's at all . . . . v 1 203
These lily lips, This cherry nose, These yellow cowslip cheeks . . v 1 337
I am Sir Oracle, And when I ope my lips let no dog bark! *Mer. of Venice* i 1 94
Here are sever'd lips, Parted with sugar breath . . . . . iii 2 118
Then open not thy lips: Firm and irrevocable is my doom *As Y. Like It* i 3 84
Our hands are hard.—Your lips will feel them the sooner . . . iii 2 61
He hath bought a pair of cast lips of Diana . . . . . . iii 4 16
There was a pretty redness in his lip, A little riper and more lusty . iii 5 120
When he had a desire to eat a grape, would open his lips when he put it into his mouth; meaning thereby that grapes were made to eat and lips to open . . . . v 1 37
I saw her coral lips to move . . . . . . *T. of Shrew* i 1 179
Thou canst not frown, thou canst not look askance, Nor bite the lip . ii 1 250
Kiss'd her lips with such a clamorous smack . . . . . . iii 2 180
My very lips might freeze to my teeth, my tongue to the roof of my mouth . . . . iv 1 6
Has neither leg, hands, lip, nor cap . . . . . . *All's Well* ii 2 11
As the nun's lip to the friar's mouth, nay, as the pudding to his skin . ii 2 28
Diana's lip Is not more smooth and rubious . . . . . *T. Night* i 4 31
I will not open my lips so wide as a bristle may enter . . . . i 5 2
Item, two lips, indifferent red; item, two grey eyes, with lids to them i 5 265
Does not Toby take you a blow o' the lips then? . . . . . ii 5 76
Lips, do not move; No man must know . . . . ii 5 109
O, what a deal of scorn looks beautiful In the contempt and anger of his lip! . . . . iii 1 158
Attested by the holy close of lips . . . . v 1 161
Meeting noses? Kissing with inside lip? . . . . . . *W. Tale* i 2 286
Wafting his eyes to the contrary and falling A lip of much contempt . i 2 373
The whole matter And copy of the father, eye, nose, lip . . . . ii 3 99
Go and see: if you can bring Tincture or lustre in her lip . . . iii 2 206
Taken treasure from her lips— And left them More rich for what they yielded . . . . v 1 54
Masterly done: The very life seems warm upon her lip . . . . v 3 66
The ruddiness upon her lip is wet; You'll mar it if you kiss it . . v 3 81
Young princes, close your hands.—And your lips too . . *K. John* ii 1 534
His people shall revolt from him And kiss the lips of unacquainted change iii 4 166
Whose restraint Doth move the murmuring lips of discontent . . iv 2 53
Entreat the north To make his bleak winds kiss my parched lips . . v 7 40
Within my mouth you have engaol'd my tongue, Doubly portcullis'd with my teeth and lips . . . . *Richard II.* i 3 167
Or have mine honour soil'd With the attainder of his slanderous lips . iv 1 24
No more the thirsty entrance of this soil Shall daub her lips with her own children's blood . . . . 1 *Hen. IV.* i 1 6
This is no world To play with mammets and to tilt with lips . . . ii 3 95
Thy lips are scarce wiped since thou drunkest last . . . . . ii 4 170
A villanous trick of thine eye and a foolish hanging of thy nether lip . ii 4 447
My love, give me thy lips. Look to my chattels and my movables *Hen. V.* ii 3 49
And his lips blows at his nose, and it is like a coal of fire . . . iii 6 109
That's a valiant flea that dare eat his breakfast on the lip of a lion . iii 7 157
Over Suffolk's neck He threw his wounded arm and kiss'd his lips . iv 6 25
I will kiss your lips, Kate.—Les dames et demoiselles pour être baisées devant leur noces, il n'est pas la coutume . . . . . . v 2 278
You have witchcraft in your lips . . . . v 2 302
O, tell me when my lips do touch his cheeks, That I may kindly give one fainting kiss . . . . 1 *Hen. VI.* ii 5 39
Seal up your lips, and give no words but mum . . . 2 *Hen. VI.* i 2 89
Fain would I go to chafe his paly lips With twenty thousand kisses . iii 2 141
Gentle as the cradle-babe Dying with mother's dug between its lips . iii 2 393
To have thee with thy lips to stop my mouth . . . . . . iii 2 396
Thy lips that kiss'd the queen shall sweep the ground . . . . iv 1 75
Defy them then, or else hold close thy lips . . . . 3 *Hen. VI.* ii 2 118
Take my hand, And with thy lips keep in my soul awhile! . . . . v 2 35

Lip. Thy tears would wash this cold congealed blood That glues my lips *3 Hen. VI.* v 2 38
The duty that I owe unto your majesty I seal upon the lips of this sweet babe v 7 29
A cherry lip, a bonny eye, a passing pleasing tongue *Richard III.* i 1 94
Teach not thy lips such scorn, for they were made For kissing i 2 172
Curses never pass The lips of those that breathe them in the air i 3 286
The king is angry: see, he bites the lip iv 2 27
Their lips were four red roses on a stalk iv 3 12
He bites his lip, and starts; Stops on a sudden *Hen. VIII.* iii 2 113
Stay the cooling too, or you may chance to burn your lips *Troi. and Cres.* i 1 26
That matter needless, of importless burden, Divide thy lips i 3 72
Peace, Trojan; lay thy finger on thy lips! i 3 240
With truant vows to her own lips he loves i 3 270
He hangs the lip at something iii 1 152
Bites his lip with a politic regard iii 3 254
More bright in zeal than the devotion which Cold lips blow to their deities iv 4 29
Rudely beguiles our lips Of all rejoindure iv 4 37
I'll take that winter from your lips, fair lady iv 5 24
There's language in her eye, her cheek, her lip, Nay, her foot speaks iv 5 55
Pardon me this brag; His insolence draws folly from my lips iv 5 258
Mark'd you his lip and eyes?—Nay, but his taunts *Coriolanus* i 1 259
A letter for me! it gives me an estate of seven years' health; in which time I will make a lip at the physician ii 1 127
When with his Amazonian chin he drove The bristled lips before him ii 2 96
A beggar's tongue Make motion through my lips! iii 2 118
A parcel of their feast, and to be executed ere they wipe their lips iv 5 232
Yet, to bite his lip And hum at good Cominius, much unhearts me v 1 48
By the jealous queen of heaven, that kiss I carried from thee, dear; and my true lip Hath virgin'd it e'er since v 3 47
A crimson river of warm blood, Like to a bubbling fountain stirr'd with wind, Doth rise and fall between thy rosed lips *T. Andron.* ii 4 24
Let me kiss thy lips; Or make some sign how I may do thee ease iii 1 120
O, take this warm kiss on thy pale cold lips! v 3 153
And loving kiss for kiss Thy brother Marcus tenders on thy lips v 3 157
O'er ladies' lips, who straight on kisses dream *Rom. and Jul.* i 4 74
My lips, two blushing pilgrims, ready stand To smooth that rough touch with a tender kiss i 5 97
Have not saints lips, and holy palmers too?—Ay, pilgrim, lips that they must use in prayer.—O, then, dear saint, let lips do what hands do; They pray, grant thou, lest faith turn to despair i 5 103
Thus from my lips, by yours, my sin is purged.—Then have my lips the sin that they have took.—Sin from my lips? O trespass sweetly urged! Give me my sin again i 5 109
By her high forehead and her scarlet lip, By her fine foot ii 1 18
A gentler judgement vanish'd from his lips iii 3 10
And steal immortal blessing from her lips iii 3 37
The roses in thy lips and cheeks shall fade To paly ashes iv 1 99
Her joints are stiff; Life and these lips have long been separated iv 5 27
And breathed such life with kisses in my lips, That I revived v 1 8
Beauty's ensign yet Is crimson in thy lips and in thy cheeks v 3 95
And, lips, O you The doors of breath, seal with a righteous kiss A dateless bargain to engrossing death! v 3 113
I will kiss thy lips; Haply some poison yet doth hang on them, To make me die with a restorative. Thy lips are warm v 3 164
How big imagination Moves in this lip! *T. of Athens* i 1 33
He ne'er drinks, But Timon's silver treads upon his lip iii 2 78
Each man to his stool, with that spur as he would to the lip of his mistress iii 6 74
Thy lips rot off!—I will not kiss thee; then the rot returns To thine own lips again iv 3 63
These words become your lips as they pass thorough them v 1 198
Lips, let sour words go by and language end v 1 223
This god did shake: His coward lips did from their colour fly *J. Cæsar* i 2 122
I durst not laugh, for fear of opening my lips and receiving the bad air i 2 251
Over thy wounds now do I prophesy,—Which, like dumb mouths, do ope their ruby lips iii 1 260
Each at once her choppy finger laying Upon her skinny lips *Macbeth* i 3 45
Commends the ingredients of our poison'd chalice To our own lips i 7 12
Sliver'd in the moon's eclipse, Nose of Turk and Tartar's lips iv 1 29
Let us go in together; And still your fingers on your lips, I pray *Hamlet* i 5 188
Here hung those lips that I have kissed I know not how oft v 1 207
Those happy smilets, That play'd on her ripe lip *Lear* iv 3 22
Take that of me, my friend, who have the power To seal the accuser's lips iv 6 174
O my dear father! Restoration hang Thy medicine on my lips! iv 7 27
Do you see this? Look on her, look, her lips, Look there, look there! v 3 310
Would she give you so much of her lips As of her tongue she oft bestows on me, You'ld have enough *Othello* ii 1 101
Yet again your fingers to your lips? would they were clyster-pipes! ii 1 178
They met so near with their lips that their breaths embraced together ii 1 265
I found not Cassio's kisses on her lips iii 3 341
As if he pluck'd up kisses by the roots That grew upon my lips iii 3 424
Pish! Noses, ears, and lips.—Is't possible?—Confess—handkerchief! iv 1 43
O, 'tis the spite of hell, the fiend's arch-mock, To lip a wanton in a secure couch, And to suppose her chaste! iv 1 72
Steep'd me in poverty to the very lips iv 2 50
Would have walked barefoot to Palestine for a touch of his nether lip iv 3 40
Alas, why gnaw you so your nether lip? v 2 43
I never will speak word.—What, not to pray?—Torments will ope your lips v 2 305
Eternity was in our lips and eyes, Bliss in our brows' bent *Ant. and Cleo.* i 3 35
But all the charms of love, Salt Cleopatra, soften thy waned lip! ii 1 21
Bestow'd his lips on that unworthy place, As it rain'd kisses iii 13 84
If from the field I shall return once more To kiss these lips iii 13 174
Behold this man; Commend unto his lips thy favouring hand iv 8 23
The name of Antony; it was divided Between her heart and lips iv 14 33
Only I here importune death awhile, until Of many thousand kisses the poor last I lay upon thy lips iv 15 21
Quicken with kissing: had my lips that power, Thus would I wear them out iv 15 39
I had rather seal my lips, than, to my peril, Speak that which is not v 2 146
Now no more The juice of Egypt's grape shall moist this lip v 2 285
Have you done? Come then, and take the last warmth of my lips v 2 294
Have I the aspic in my lips? Dost fall? v 2 296
Had I this cheek To bathe my lips upon *Cymbeline* i 6 100
Slaver with lips as common as the stairs That mount the Capitol i 6 105
Let me my service tender on your lips i 6 140
But she spoke it dying, I would not Believe her lips in opening it v 5 42

Lip. I would not thy good deeds should from my lips Pluck a hard sentence *Cymbeline* v 5 288
As you do love, fill to your mistress' lips *Pericles* ii 3 51
Come, your hands and lips must seal it too ii 5 85
That on the touching of her lips I may Melt and no more be seen v 3 42
Lipped. A hand that kings Have lipp'd, and trembled kissing *A. and C.* ii 5 30
Lipsbury pinfold. If I had thee in Lipsbury pinfold, I would make thee care for me *Lear* ii 2 9
Liquid. Decking with liquid pearl the bladed grass *M. N. Dream* i 1 211
Liquid tears or heart-offending groans Or blood-consuming sighs *2 Hen. VI.* iii 2 60
The liquid drops of tears that you have shed Shall come again, transform'd to orient pearl *Richard III.* iv 4 321
The strong-ribb'd bark through liquid mountains cut *Troi. and Cres.* i 3 40
Put this in any liquid thing you will, And drink it off *Rom. and Jul.* v 1 77
The sea's a thief, whose liquid surge resolves The moon into salt tears: the earth's a thief *T. of Athens* iv 3 442
In the morn and liquid dew of youth *Hamlet* i 3 41
Roast me in sulphur! Wash me in steep-down gulfs of liquid fire! *Othello* v 2 280
Liquor. Looks like a foul bombard that would shed his liquor *Tempest* ii 2 22
That's a brave god and bears celestial liquor ii 2 122
I'll swear upon that bottle to be thy true subject; for the liquor is not earthly ii 2 131
Where should they Find this grand liquor that hath gilded 'em? v 1 280
She will often praise her liquor.—If her liquor be good, she shall *T. G. of Ver.* iii 1 351
There is either liquor in his pate or money in his purse when he looks so merrily *Mer. Wives* ii 1 197
Such Brooks are welcome to me, that o'erflow such liquor ii 2 158
Melt me out of my fat drop by drop and liquor fishermen's boots with me iv 5 100
And drop the liquor of it in her eyes *M. N. Dream* ii 1 178
Whose liquor hath this virtuous property iii 2 367
I never did apply Hot and rebellious liquors in my blood *As Y. Like It* ii 3 49
Is crack'd, and all the precious liquor spilt *Richard II.* i 2 19
And changes fill the cup of alteration With divers liquors *2 Hen. IV.* iii 1 53
Liquor likewise will I give to thee, And friendship shall combine *Hen. V.* ii 1 113
Know you not, The fire that mounts the liquor till't run o'er, In seeming to augment it wastes it? *Hen. VIII.* i 1 144
And with this hateful liquor temper it *T. Andron.* v 2 200
Being then in bed, And this distilled liquor drink thou off *R. and J.* iv 1 94
Fetch me a stoup of liquor *Hamlet* v 1 68
Here's yet some liquor left.—As thou'rt a man, Give me the cup v 2 353
Liquored. Justice hath liquored her *1 Hen. IV.* ii 1 94
Liquorish. With liquorish draughts And morsels unctuous *T. of Athens* iv 3 194
Lisbon. From Lisbon, Barbary and India *Mer. of Venice* iii 2 272
Lisp. A' can carve too, and lisp *L. L. Lost* v 2 323
Look you lisp and wear strange suits *As Y. Like It* iv 1 34
You jig, you amble, and you lisp, and nick-name God's creatures *Hamlet* iii 1 151
Lisping. These lisping hawthorn-buds *Mer. Wives* iii 3 77
Lisping to his master's old tables, his note-book *2 Hen. IV.* ii 4 289
The pox of such antic, lisping, affecting fantasticoes! *Rom. and Jul.* ii 4 29
List. Your lieutenant, if you list; he's no standard *Tempest* iii 2 19
If thou beest a devil, take't as thou list iii 2 138
Go to bed when she list, rise when she list, all is as she will *Mer. Wives* ii 2 124
Elves, list your names; silence, you airy toys v 5 46
Your own science Exceeds, in that, the lists of all advice *Meas. for Meas.* i 1 6
There went but a pair of shears between us.—I grant; as there may between the lists and the velvet. Thou art the list.—And thou the velvet i 2 31
I had as lief be a list of an English kersey as be piled, as thou art piled, for a French velvet i 2 34
And teach your ears to list me with more heed *Com. of Errors* iv 1 101
I am not such a fool to think what I list, nor I list not to think what I can, nor indeed I cannot think *Much Ado* iii 4 83
Sir, list to me: I am my father's heir and only son *T. of Shrew* ii 1 365
Yet if thy thoughts, Bianca, be so humble . . . , Seize thee that list iii 1 91
Gartered with a red and blue list iii 2 69
'Now take them up,' quoth he, 'if any list' iii 2 167
It shall be moon, or star, or what I list, Or ere I journey iv 5 7
You have restrained yourself within the list of too cold an adieu *All's W.* ii 1 53
I am bound to your niece, sir; I mean, she is the list of my voyage *T. N.* iii 1 86
What of her ensues I list not prophesy *W. Tale* iv 1 26
Then list to me: This follows, if you will not change your purpose iv 4 552
Son, list to this conjunction, make this match *K. John* ii 1 468
And throw the rider headlong in the lists *Richard II.* i 2 52
Wherefore comest thou hither, Before King Richard in his royal lists? i 3 32
To prove, by God's grace and my body's valour, In lists i 3 38
No person be so bold Or daring-hardy as to touch the lists i 3 43
Draw near, And list what with our council we have done i 3 124
Lie down; lay thine ear close to the ground and list if thou canst hear the tread of travellers *1 Hen. IV.* ii 2 34
Prithee, let her alone, and list to me.—What sayest thou, Jack? iii 3 110
The very list, the very utmost bound Of all our fortunes iv 1 51
List his discourse of war, and you shall hear A fearful battle render'd you in music: Turn him to any cause of policy *Hen. V.* i 1 43
I cannot be confined within the weak list of a country's fashion v 2 295
A witch, by fear, not force, like Hannibal, Drives back our troops and conquers as she lists *1 Hen. VI.* i 5 22
Forsaketh yet the lists By reason of his adversary's odds v 5 32
But list to me, my Humphrey, my sweet duke *2 Hen. VI.* i 2 35
List to me; For I am bold to counsel you in this i 3 95
And ready are the appellant and defendant . . . to enter the lists ii 3 50
See the lists and all things fit: Here let them end it ii 3 54
That blind priest, like the eldest son of fortune, Turns what he list *Hen. VIII.* ii 2 22
The list Of those that claim their offices this day iv 1 14
What should she remember?—List *Troi. and Cres.* v 2 17
List, what work he makes Amongst your cloven army *Coriolanus* i 4 20
Do as thou list. Thy valiantness was mine, thou suck'dst it from me, But owe thy pride thyself iii 2 128
Draw near, ye people.—List to your tribunes. Audience! iii 3 40
And when he sleeps will she do what she list *T. Andron.* iv 1 100
I will frown as I pass by, and let them take it as they list *Rom. and Jul.* i 1 47
List a word.—What says my lord? *J. Cæsar* v 5 15
Rather than so, come fate into the list, And champion me! *Macbeth* iii 1 71
Here and there Shark'd up a list of lawless resolutes *Hamlet* i 1 98
The lists and full proportions are all made Out of his subject i 2 32
What loss your honour may sustain, If with too credent ear you list his songs i 3 30
List, list, O, list! If thou didst ever thy dear father love i 5 22
Or 'If we list to speak,' or 'There be, an if they might,' Or such i 5 177

List. Save yourself, my lord: The ocean, overpeering of his list, Eats not the flats with more impetuous haste *Hamlet* iv 5 99
Not as a brother.—That's as we list to grace him *Lear* v 3 61
If any man of quality or degree within the lists of the army v 3 111
List a brief tale; And when 'tis told, O, that my heart would burst! v 3 181
Alas, she has no speech.—In faith, too much; I find it still, when I have list to sleep *Othello* ii 1 105
List me. The lieutenant to-night watches on the court of guard ii 1 219
She may make, unmake, do what she list, Even as her appetite shall play the god With his weak function ii 3 352
Stand you awhile apart; Confine yourself but in a patient list iv 1 76
Mede and Lycaonia, With a more larger list of sceptres *Ant. and Cleo.* iii 6 76
Peace! what noise?—List, list!—Hark!—Music i' the air iv 3 13
What man is this?—Stand close, and list him iv 9 6
Like a bold champion, I assume the lists *Pericles* i 1 61
The music of the spheres! List, my Marina v 1 231

Listed. Even where his lustful eye or savage heart, Without control, listed to make his prey *Richard III.* iii 5 84

Listen. There will she hide her, To listen our purpose *Much Ado* iii 1 12
What, Longaville! and reading! listen, ear *L. L. Lost* iv 3 45
Listen to the moon.—This lanthorn doth the horned moon present *M. N. Dream* v 1 241
Listen to me, and if you speak me fair, I'll tell you news *T. of Shrew* i 2 180
King Philip, listen to the cardinal *K. John* iii 1 198
To whose venom sound The open ear of youth doth always listen *Rich II.* ii 1 20
Whom I sent On Tuesday last to listen after news *2 Hen. IV.* i 1 29
Lady, vouchsafe to listen what I say *1 Hen. VI.* v 3 103
Such enticing birds, That she will light to listen to the lays *2 Hen. VI.* i 3 93
I will follow Eleanor, And listen after Humphrey, how he proceeds i 3 152
Sweet lords, entreat her hear me but a word.—Listen, fair madam *T. An.* ii 3 139
What noise is that?—I hear none, madam.—Prithee, listen well *J. Cæsar* ii 4 17
And now, Octavius, Listen great things iv 1 41
Listen, but speak not to't.—Be lion-mettled, proud *Macbeth* iv 1 89

Listened. He that no more must say is listen'd more *Richard II.* ii 1 9
'Faith, they listened to me as they would have hearkened to their father's testament *Pericles* iv 2 106

Listening. 'Tis called a sensible tale: and this cuff was but to knock at your ear, and beseech listening *T. of Shrew* iv 1 68
It is worth the listening to *1 Hen. IV.* ii 4 235
It is the disease of not listening, the malady of not marking *2 Hen. IV.* i 2 138
When we, Almost with ravish'd listening, could not find His hour of speech a minute *Hen. VIII.* i 2 120
Listening their fear, I could not say 'Amen' *Macbeth* ii 2 29
That I should open to the listening air *Pericles* i 2 87
It nips me unto listening, and thick slumber Hangs upon mine eyes v 1 235

Literatured. Is good knowledge and literatured in the wars *Hen. V.* iv 7 157

Lither. Two Talbots, winged through the lither sky *1 Hen. VI.* iv 7 21

Litigious. Tyrus stands In a litigious peace *Pericles* iii 3 3

Litter. Save for the son that she did litter here *Tempest* i 2 282
With as little remorse as they would have drowned a blind bitch's puppies, fifteen i' the litter *Mer. Wives* iii 5 12
To crouch in litter of your stable planks *K. John* v 2 140
To my litter straight; Weakness possesseth me, and I am faint v 3 16
Like a sow that hath overwhelmed all her litter but one *2 Hen. IV.* i 2 14
I read That stout Pendragon in his litter sick Came to the field and vanquished his foes *1 Hen. VI.* iii 2 95
There is a litter ready; lay him in't *Lear* iii 6 97

Littered. Being, as I am, littered under Mercury *W. Tale* iv 3 25
I would they were barbarians—as they are, Though in Rome litter'd *Coriolanus* iii 1 239
We are two lions litter'd in one day, And I the elder *J. Cæsar* ii 2 46

Little. Of that there's none, or little *Tempest* i 2 51
For a little Follow, and do me service iv 1 266
'Tis threefold too little for carrying a letter to your lover *T. G. of Ver.* i 1 116
Your ladyship can set.—As little by such toys as may be possible i 2 82
I love his lady too much, And that's the reason I love him so little ii 4 206
Recking as little what betideth me As much I wish all good befortune you iv 3 40
Yet the painter flatter'd her a little, Unless I flatter with myself iv 4 192
She takes exceptions at your person.—What, that my leg is too long?—No; that it is too little v 2 5
And rather cut a little, Than fall, and bruise to death *Meas. for Meas.* ii 1 5
But man, proud man, Drest in a little brief authority ii 2 118
The time is come even now. I shall crave your forbearance a little iv 1 23
Little have you to say When you depart from him, but, soft and low iv 1 68
If it be too little for your thief, your true man thinks it big enough; if it be too big for your thief, your thief thinks it little enough iv 2 47
If bawdy talk offend you, we'll have very little of it v 3 189
Too little for a great praise *Much Ado* i 1 175
A pleasant-spirited lady.—There's little of the melancholy element in her ii 1 357
And salt too little which may season give To her foul-tainted flesh! iv 1 144
Hear me a little; for I have only been Silent so long iv 1 157
I do confess much of the hearing it, but little of the marking of it *L. L. L.* i 1 288
Pretty, because little.—Little pretty, because little i 2 22
Much too little of that good I saw Is my report to his great worthiness ii 1 62
It fell upon a little western flower, Before milk-white *M. N. Dream* ii 1 166
And though she be but little, she is fierce.—'Little' again! nothing but 'low' and 'little'! iii 2 325
How little is the cost I have bestow'd In purchasing the semblance of my soul From out the state of hellish misery! *Mer. of Venice* iii 4 19
Have you any thing to say?—But little: I am arm'd and well prepared iv 1 264
Tarry a little; there is something else iv 1 305
How now, Adam! no greater heart in thee? Live a little; comfort a little; cheer thyself a little *As Y. Like It* ii 6 5
The quintessence of every sprite Heaven would in little show iii 2 148
How now! back, friends! Shepherd, go off a little iii 2 168
Let's meet as little as we can.—I do desire we may be better strangers iii 2 273
Go hence a little and I shall conduct you, If you will mark it iii 4 58
Thou 'ldst thank me but a little for my counsel *T. of Shrew* i 2 61
An she stand him but a little, he will throw a figure in her face i 2 113
We will go walk a little in the orchard, And then to dinner ii 1 112
Ay, but the mustard is too hot a little iv 3 25
Confess, hath he not hit you here?—A' has a little gall'd me v 2 60
I will stand for't a little, though therefore I die a virgin *All's Well* i 1 145
There's little can be said in't; 'tis against the rule of nature i 1 147
Which is within a very little of nothing ii 4 27
My greatest grief, Though little he do feel it, set down sharply iii 4 33
Slight ones will not carry it; they will say, 'Came you off with so little?' iv 1 43

Little. I am for the house with the narrow gate, which I take to be too little for pomp to enter *All's Well* iv 5 54
Having vainly fear'd too little v 3 123
Thine eye Hath stay'd upon some favour that it loves: Hath it not, boy?—A little, by your favour *T. Night* ii 4 26
For still we prove Much in our vows, but little in our love ii 4 121
And yet, to crush this a little, it would bow to me ii 5 152
If all the devils of hell be drawn in little iii 4 95
Come, sir, I pray you, go.—Let me speak a little iii 4 393
May, though they cannot praise us, as little accuse us *W. Tale* i 1 17
Although the print be little, the whole matter And copy of the father ii 3 98
Poor trespasses, More monstrous standing by: whereof I reckon The casting forth to crows thy baby-daughter To be or none or little iii 2 193
If it be not too rough for some that know little but bowling iv 4 338
It is my father's music To speak your deeds, not little of his care To have them recompensed as thought on iv 4 530
Consider little What dangers, by his highness' fail of issue, May drop v 1 26
What though? Something about, a little from the right *K. John* i 1 170
Little are we beholding to your love, And little looked for at your helping hands *Richard II.* iv 1 160
Though he divide the realm and give thee half, It is too little v 1 61
Come out of that fat room, and lend me thy hand to laugh a little *1 Hen. IV.* ii 4 2
Whereof a little More than a little is by much too much iii 2 73
Virtuous enough; swore little; diced not above seven times a week iii 3 18
Your day's service at Shrewsbury hath a little gilded over your night's exploit on Gad's-hill *2 Hen. IV.* i 2 169
Thou whoreson little tidy Bartholomew boar-pig ii 4 250
O, give me always a little, lean, old, chapt, bald shot iii 2 294
There was a little quiver fellow, and a' would manage you his piece thus iii 2 300
Only, we want a little personal strength iv 4 8
Stay but a little; for my cloud of dignity Is held from falling with so weak a wind That it will quickly drop iv 5 99
For my part, I care not: I say little *Hen. V.* ii 1 5
If you would walk off, I would prick your guts a little ii 1 62
A very little little let us do, And all is done iv 2 33
Which if they have as I will leave 'em them, Shall yield them little iv 3 125
Thou know'st little of my wrongs *1 Hen. VI.* i 3 59
Upon my death the French can little boast; In yours they will iv 5 24
Such . . . severe covenants As little shall the Frenchmen gain thereby v 4 115
This late complaint Will make but little for his benefit *2 Hen. VI.* i 3 101
Because that I am little, like an ape, He thinks that you should bear me on your shoulders *Richard III.* iii 1 130
Think you, my lord, this little prating York Was not incensed by his subtle mother? iii 1 151
Rough cradle for such little pretty ones! Rude ragged nurse! iv 1 101
When Richmond was a little peevish boy iv 2 100
Whereof We cannot feel too little, hear too much *Hen. VIII.* i 2 128
Pray, how pass'd it?—I'll tell you in a little ii 1 11
He never was so womanish; the cause He may a little grieve at ii 1 39
Pluck off a little; I would not be a young count in your way ii 3 40
Full little, God knows, looking Either for such men or such business iii 1 75
Your hopes and friends are infinite.—In England But little for my profit iii 1 83
My heart weeps to see him So little of his great self iii 2 336
I have ventured, Like little wanton boys that swim on bladders iii 2 359
Not till then, he felt himself, And found the blessedness of being little iv 2 66
I hope she will deserve well,—and a little To love her for her mother's sake iv 2 136
Sir, I did never win of you before.—But little, Charles v 1 59
You, that best should teach us, Have misdemean'd yourself, and not a little v 3 14
You are a little, By your good favour, too sharp v 3 73
Stay, good my lords, I have a little yet to say v 3 98
And will be led At your request a little from himself *Troi. and Cres.* ii 3 191
In the extremity of great and little, Valour and pride excel themselves in Hector iv 5 78
I will tell you; If you'll bestow a small—of what you have little—Patience awhile, you'll hear *Coriolanus* i 1 129
Nor a man that fears you less than he, That's lesser than a little i 4 15
As if I loved my little should be dieted In praises sauced with lies i 9 52
I know you can do very little alone; for your helps are many ii 1 38
To report A little of that worthy work perform'd ii 2 49
I'll try whether my old wit be in request With those that have but little iii 1 252
A very little I have yielded to v 3 16
I am hush'd until our city be afire, And then I'll speak a little v 3 182
Be true. Stay but a little, I will come again *Rom. and Jul.* ii 2 138
I would have thee gone: And yet no further than a wanton's bird; Who lets it hop a little from her hand ii 2 179
The sweetest lady—Lord, Lord! when 'twas a little prating thing ii 4 212
With blood removed but little from her own iii 3 96
She weeps for Tybalt's death, And therefore have I little talk'd of love iv 1 7
The County Paris hath set up his rest, That you shall rest but little iv 5 7
To build his fortune I will strain a little *T. of Athens* i 1 143
That is, one may reach deep enough, and yet Find little iii 4 16
And that I am he, Let me a little show it, even in this *J. Cæsar* iii 1 71
Bid our commanders lead their charges off A little from this ground iv 2 49
As little is the wisdom, where the flight So runs against all reason *Mac.* iv 2 13
The day almost itself professes yours, And little is to do v 7 28
A little ere the mightiest Julius fell, The graves stood tenantless *Hamlet* i 1 114
Give twenty, forty, fifty, an hundred ducats a-piece for his picture in little ii 2 384
What he spake, though it lack'd form a little, Was not like madness iii 1 171
There's such divinity doth hedge a king, That treason can but peep to what it would, Acts little of his will iv 5 125
For my means, I'll husband them so well, They shall go far with little iv 5 139
Mend your speech a little, Lest it may mar your fortunes *Lear* i 1 96
If aught within that little seeming substance, Or all of it, . . . may fitly like your grace, She's there, and she is yours i 1 201
It is not a little I have to say of what most nearly appertains to us both i 1 286
The observation we have made of it hath not been little i 1 293
To love him that is honest; to converse with him that is wise, and says little i 4 17
Be then desired By her . . . A little to disquantity your train i 4 270
This house is little: the old man and his people Cannot be well bestow'd ii 4 291
I might have saved her; now she's gone for ever! Cordelia, Cordelia! stay a little v 3 271
Little of this great world can I speak, More than pertains to feats of broil and battle, And therefore little shall I grace my cause In speaking for myself *Othello* i 3 86
She puts her tongue a little in her heart, And chides with thinking ii 1 107
With as little a web as this will I ensnare as great a fly as Cassio ii 1 169
I do beseech thee, grant me this, To leave me but a little to myself iii 3 85

Little. I see this hath a little dash'd your spirits.—Not a jot . *Othello* iii 3 214
Your napkin is too little: Let it alone. Come, I'll go in with you . iii 3 287
'Tis better to be much abused Than but to know't a little . . iii 3 337
Bring me on the way a little, And say if I shall see you soon at night . iii 4 197
In nature's infinite book of secrecy A little I can read *Ant. and Cleo.* i 2 10
I must be laugh'd at, If, or for nothing or a little, I Should say myself offended, and with you Chiefly i' the world . . . . ii 2 31
Leave me, I pray, a little: pray you now: Nay, do so . . . iii 11 22
Sleep a little.—No, my chuck. Eros, come; mine armour, Eros! . iv 4 1
Yet come a little,—Wishers were ever fools,—O, come, come, come! . iv 15 36
I am dying, Egypt, dying: Give me some wine, and let me speak a little iv 15 42
Nay, stay a little: Were you but riding forth to air yourself, Such parting were too petty . . . . *Cymbeline* i 1 109
Thou shouldst have made him As little as a crow, or less . . i 3 15
These boys know little they are sons to the king . . . iii 3 80
When thou see'st him, A little witness my obedience . . . iii 4 68
Murder wives much better than themselves For wrying but a little! . v 1 5
'Gainst whom I am too little to contend, Since he's so great *Pericles* i 2 17
Who but of late, earth, sea, and air, Were all too little to content . i 4 35
Faith, my acquaintance lies little amongst them . . . . iv 6 206
O, stop there a little! . . . . v 1 162
Now our sands are almost run: More a little, and then dumb . v 2 267
Little abstract. This little abstract doth contain that large Which died in Geffrey . . . . *K. John* ii 1 101
Little Academe. Our court shall be a little Academe . *L. L. Lost* i 1 13
Little acquaintance. Is't possible that on so little acquaintance you should like her? . . . . . *As Y. Like It* v 2 1
Little act. But with a little act upon the blood, Burn like the mines of sulphur . . . . *Othello* iii 3 328
Little advantage. Make the rope of his destiny our cable, for our own doth little advantage . . . . . *Tempest* i 1 34
Little amazedness. After a little amazedness, we were all commanded out of the chamber . . . . . *W. Tale* v 2 5
Little angry. A little angry for my so rough usage . . *Cymbeline* iv 1 21
Little apt. I have a heart as little apt as yours . *Coriolanus* iii 2 29
Little arm. With this little arm and this good sword, I have made my way through more impediments . . . . *Othello* v 2 262
Little atomies. Drawn with a team of little atomies *Rom. and Jul.* i 4 57
Little axe. Many strokes, though with a little axe, Hew down and fell the hardest-timber'd oak . . . . . *3 Hen. VI.* ii 1 54
Little babe. If she dares trust me with her little babe . *W. Tale* ii 2 37
Little bad. Best men are moulded out of faults; And, for the most, become much more the better For being a little bad *Meas. for Meas.* v 1 446
Little baggage. That lay with the little baggage . . *Pericles* iv 2 24
Little beard. He hath but a little beard.—Why, God will send more, if the man will be thankful . . . . *As Y. Like It* iii 2 219
I'ld give bay Curtal and his furniture, My mouth no more were broken than these boys', And writ as little beard . . *All's Well* ii 3 67
Little before. I'll be with you straight. Go a little before *Hamlet* iv 4 31
Little beholding. The duke is marvellous little beholding to your reports . . . . *Meas. for Meas.* iv 3 166
Little benefit. Give me now a little benefit . . *Troi. and Cres.* iii 3 14
Little better. Has done little better than played the Jack with us *Temp.* iv 1 197
It is proved already that you are little better than false knaves *Much Ado* iv 2 23
When he is worst, he is little better than a beast . *Mer. of Venice* i 2 95
Who began to be much sea-sick, and himself little better . *W. Tale* v 2 129
Darest thou, thou little better thing than earth, Divine his downfal? *Richard II.* iii 4 78
Now am I, if a man should speak truly, little better than one of the wicked. I must give over this life . . . *1 Hen. IV.* i 2 106
My good lord:—my lord, I should say rather; 'Tis sin to flatter; 'good' was little better . . . . *3 Hen. VI.* v 6 3
Little birds. The eagle suffers little birds to sing . *T. Andron.* iv 4 83
Little bless'd with the soft phrase of peace . . *Othello* i 3 82
Little blood. I'll pawn the little blood which I have left . *W. Tale* ii 3 166
These two may run mad; but, if with too much brain and too little blood they do, I'll be a curer of madmen *Troi. and Cres.* v 1 55
Little body. My little body is aweary of this great world *Mer. of Venice* i 2 1
Like little body with a mighty heart . . . *Hen. V.* ii Prol. 17
In one little body Thou counterfeit'st a bark, a sea, a wind *Rom. and Jul.* iii 5 131
Little boy. An old saying, that was a man when King Pepin of France was a little boy . . . . *L. L. Lost* iv 1 123
Little brain. With too much blood and too little brain, these two may run mad . . . . *Troi. and Cres.* v 1 53
Little breach. As patches set upon a little breach Discredit more in hiding of the fault . . . . . . *K. John* iv 2 32
Little candle. How far that little candle throws his beams! *Mer. of Ven.* v 1 90
Little care. That little cares for buying any thing . *As Y. Like It* ii 4 90
O, I have ta'en Too little care of this! Take physic, pomp . *Lear* iii 4 33
He hath a court He little cares for and a daughter . *Cymbeline* i 6 154
Little casket. The little casket bring me hither . *T. of Athens* i 2 164
Little cause. You have little cause to say so . . . *Othello* ii 1 109
Little changeling. I do but beg a little changeling boy . *M. N. Dream* ii 1 120
Little characters. Perspicuous even as substance, Whose grossness little characters sum up . . . . . *Troi. and Cres.* i 3 325
Little charge. But a little charge will trench him here . *1 Hen. IV.* iii 1 112
Little chiding. But 'tis no matter; better a little chiding than a great deal of heart-break . . . . . . *Mer. Wives* v 3 11
Little cloth. Spoil his coat with scanting A little cloth . *Hen. V.* ii 4 48
Little comfort. Finding little comfort to relieve them . *Pericles* i 2 99
Little company. To say the truth, reason and love keep little company together now-a-days . . . . . *M. N. Dream* iii 1 147
Little cost. One would have lingering wars with little cost *1 Hen. VI.* i 1 74
To study fashions to adorn my body: Since I am crept in favour with myself, I will maintain it with some little cost . *Richard III.* i 2 260
Little counsel. I hold as little counsel with weak fear As you *1 Hen. IV.* iv 3 11
Little cousin. Give me this dagger.—My dagger, little cousin? *Rich. III.* iii 1 111
Little coz. My pretty little coz, that thou didst know how many fathom deep I am in love! . . . . . *As Y. Like It* iv 1 209
Little credit. I have but a very little credit . . . *2 Hen. IV.* v 1 54
Little Cupid. Of this matter Is little Cupid's crafty arrow made *M. Ado* iii 1 22
Little cure. For my little cure, Let me alone . . *Hen. VIII.* i 4 33
This league . . . Will give her sadness very little cure . *K. John* ii 1 546
Little darlings. Are ready now To eat those little darlings . *Pericles* i 4 44
Little daughter. Here's all that is left living of your queen, A little daughter . . . . iii 1 21
Little delight. You will take little delight in it . . *As Y. Like It* i 2 168
Little deserves. Our house, my sovereign liege, little deserves The scourge of greatness to be used on it . . . . *1 Hen. IV.* i 3 10
Little din. Think you a little din can daunt mine ears? . *T. of Shrew* i 2 200
Little dogs. The little dogs and all, Tray, Blanch, and Sweet-heart, see, they bark at me . . . . *Lear* iii 6 65
Little door. Doth command a little door Which from the vineyard to the garden leads . . . . *Meas. for Meas.* iv 1 32
Little doubt. I make as little doubt, as you do conscience In doing daily wrongs . . . . *Hen. VIII.* v 3 67
Little duty. I owe him little duty, and less love . . *1 Hen. VI.* iv 4 34
Little earth. Give him a little earth for charity! . *Hen. VIII.* iv 2 23
Little ease. Reach a chair: So; now, methinks, I feel a little ease . iv 2 4
Little employment. 'Tis e'en so: the hand of little employment hath the daintier sense . . . . *Hamlet* v 1 77
Little England. I would not be a queen For all the world.—In faith, for little England You'ld venture an emballing . *Hen. VIII.* ii 3 46
Little eyases. An aery of children, little eyases . . *Hamlet* ii 2 355
Little faith. Hold little faith, though thou hast too much fear *T. Night* v 1 174
Little fault. I hope I was perfect: I made a little fault in 'Great' *L. L. L.* v 2 562
If little faults, proceeding on distemper, Shall not be wink'd at, how shall we stretch our eye When capital crimes, chew'd, swallow'd, and digested, Appear before us? . . . . . . *Hen. V.* ii 2 54
For all this . . . , I must needs say you have a little fault *T. of Athens* v 1 90
But, alack, You snatch some hence for little faults . *Cymbeline* v 1 12
Little favour. Entreats her a little favour of speech . *Othello* iii 1 28
Little fears. Where love is great, the littlest doubts are fear; Where little fears grow great, great love grows there . . *Hamlet* iii 2 182
Little finger. That I'll prove upon thee, though thy little finger be armed in a thimble . . . . *T. of Shrew* iv 3 149
I'll break thy little finger, Harry, An if thou wilt not tell me *1 Hen. IV.* ii 3 90
Do you think, my lords, The king will suffer but the little finger Of this man to be vex'd?—'Tis now too certain . . *Hen. VIII.* v 3 106
What of that?—If it be possible for you to displace it with your little finger, there is some hope . . . . . *Coriolanus* v 4 5
Little fire. Though little fire grows great with little wind, Yet extreme gusts will blow out fire and all . . . . *T. of Shrew* ii 1 135
A little fire is quickly trodden out; Which, being suffer'd, rivers cannot quench . . . . *3 Hen. VI.* iv 8 7
A little fire in a wild field were like an old lecher's heart . *Lear* iii 4 116
Little flower. When she weeps, weeps every little flower *M. N. Dream* iii 1 204
Little foolery. Since the little wit that fools have was silenced, the little foolery that wise men have makes a great show *As Y. Like It* i 2 206
Little force. To show some reason, of no little force . *2 Hen. VI.* i 3 96
Little fouler. I know your virtue hath a license in't, Which seems a little fouler than it is . . . . . *Meas. for Meas.* ii 4 146
Little further. Hear a little further . . . . *Tempest* i 2 135
Let's obey his humour a little further . . . . *Mer. Wives* iv 2 210
Little gain. Didst thou at first, to flatter us withal, Make us partakers of a little gain? . . . . *1 Hen. VI.* ii 1 52
Little gale. A little gale will soon disperse that cloud . *3 Hen. VI.* v 3 10
Little gallant. Keep your way, little gallant . . *Mer. Wives* iii 2 1
Little gate. Climb o'er the house to unlock the little gate . *L. L. Lost* i 1 109
Little gilt. And give to dust that is a little gilt More laud than gilt o'er-dusted . . . . *Troi. and Cres.* iii 3 178
Little godliness. With the little godliness I have, I did full hard forbear him . . . . *Othello* i 2 9
Little gold. I have but little gold of late . . . *T. of Athens* iv 3 90
Little good. An she knew him as well as I do, she would think scolding would do little good upon him . . . . *T. of Shrew* i 2 110
So fare you well, my little good lord cardinal.—So farewell to the little good you bear me. Farewell! . . . *Hen. VIII.* iii 2 349
Little grace. They have not so little grace, I hope . *Mer. Wives* ii 2 117
Little grave. My large kingdom for a little grave, A little little grave, an obscure grave . . . . . . *Richard II.* iii 3 153
Little hair. And all the shrouds wherewith my life should sail Are turned to one thread, one little hair . . . . *K. John* v 7 54
Little hand. All the perfumes of Arabia will not sweeten this little hand. Oh, oh, oh! . . . . *Macbeth* v 1 58
Little hangman. He hath twice or thrice cut Cupid's bow-string and the little hangman dare not shoot at him . . . *Much Ado* iii 2 11
Little happier. A little happier than my wretched father *Hen. VIII.* ii 1 120
Little happy. I were but little happy, if I could say how much *M. Ado* ii 1 318
Little harm. But indeed I can do you little harm *Meas. for Meas.* iii 2 176
And in his sleep he does little harm, save to his bed-clothes *All's Well* iv 3 287
Little heart. O my little heart! . . . . . *L. L. Lost* iii 1 188
Little heated. With dancing is a little heated . . . *Hen. VIII.* i 4 100
Little Helen, farewell: if I can remember thee, I will think of thee at court . . . . *All's Well* i 1 202
Little help. A little help will serve . . . . *Coriolanus* ii 3 16
Little herd. A little herd of England's timorous deer . *1 Hen. VI.* iv 2 46
Little higher. Steps me a little higher than his vow . *1 Hen. IV.* iv 3 75
Little hole. I have seen the day of wrong through the little hole of discretion, and I will right myself . . . *L. L. Lost* v 2 734
Little honesty. You have as little honesty as honour . *Hen. VIII.* iii 2 271
Now, if you can blush and cry 'guilty,' cardinal, You'll show a little honesty . . . . iii 2 306
Little honour. Ha! little honour to be much believed! *Meas. for Meas.* ii 4 149
As great a charge as little honour He meant to lay upon . *Hen. VIII.* i 1 77
There was very little honour showed in't . . . *T. of Athens* iii 2 20
Little hope. That there is little hope of life in him . *As Y. Like It* i 2 136
Little hurt. Thou dost me yet but little hurt . . *Tempest* ii 2 82
Little intoxicates. Being a little intoxicates in his prains . *Hen. V.* iv 7 39
Little Jack-a-Lent, have you been true to us? . . *Mer. Wives* iii 3 27
Little jealousies. All little jealousies, which now seem great, And all great fears, which now import their dangers . . *Ant. and Cleo.* ii 2 134
Little jewel. And what says she to my little jewel? . *T. G. of Ver.* iv 4 51
Little John Doit of Staffordshire . . . . . *2 Hen. IV.* iii 2 21
Little joy have I To breathe this news . . . *Richard II.* iii 4 81
As little joy, my lord, as you suppose You should enjoy, were you this country's king, As little joy may you suppose in me, That I enjoy, being the queen thereof . . . . *Richard III.* i 3 151
Little justice. Happily you may catch her in the sea; Yet there's as little justice as at land . . . . . . *T. Andron.* iv 3 9
Little kin. Or any such proverb so little kin to the purpose . *Hen. V.* iii 7 72
Little kingdom. His little kingdom of a forced grave . *K. John* iv 2 98
Gives warning to all the rest of this little kingdom, man, to arm *2 Hen. IV.* iv 3 118
And the state of man, Like to a little kingdom, suffers then The nature of an insurrection . . . . *J. Cæsar* ii 1 68
Little kinsman. Come hither, little kinsman; hark, a word *K. John* iii 3 18
Little knife. Or get some little knife between thy teeth *T. Andron.* iii 2 16
Little knows. He that brings this love to thee Little knows this love in me . . . . *As Y. Like It* iv 3 57

Little knowest. Thou little know'st how thou dost startle me *Pericles* v 1 147
Little learning. Canst not read?—No.—There will little learning die then, that day thou art hanged . . . . . *T. of Athens* ii 2 86
Little less. And hope to joy is little less in joy Than hope enjoy'd *Richard II.* ii 3 15
I blame not her, she could say little less; She had the wrong *3 Hen. VI.* iv 1 101
A grandam's name is little less in love Than is the doting title of a mother; They are as children but one step below *Richard III.* iv 4 299
Take not that little little less than little wit from them! *Troi. and Cres.* ii 3 14
Little life. And our little life Is rounded with a sleep . *Tempest* iv 1 157
'Od's my little life, I think she means to tangle my eyes too! *As Y. L. It* iii 5 43
Could not all this flesh Keep in a little life? . . . . . *1 Hen. IV.* v 4 103
Little like. These proclamations, So forcing faults upon Hermione, I little like . . . . *W. Tale* iii 1 17
Little longer. I am to hull here a little longer . . . *T. Night* i 5 218
Little look'd for at your helping hands . . . *Richard II.* iv 1 161
Little lord. What, would you have my weapon, little lord?—I would, that I might thank you as you call me.—How?—Little . *Richard III.* iii 1 122
Little loss. And victory, with little loss, doth play Upon the dancing banners of the French . . . . *K. John* ii 1 307
Was ever known so great and little loss? . . . . . *Hen. V.* iv 8 115
Little love. It shows but little love or judgement . . *T. of Athens* iii 3 10
Little man. Humphrey is no little man in England . . *2 Hen. VI.* iii 1 20
Little measure. Neither do I labour for a greater esteem than may in some little measure draw a belief from you . . . *As Y. Like It* v 2 63
O mighty Cæsar! dost thou lie so low? Are all thy conquests, glories, triumphs, spoils, Shrunk to this little measure? . *J. Cæsar* iii 1 150
Little medicine. To his former strength may be restored With good advice and little medicine . . . . . . *2 Hen. IV.* iii 1 43
Little memory. Of as little memory When he is earth'd . . *Tempest* ii 1 233
Some little memory of me will stir him . . . . *Hen. VIII.* iii 2 417
Little mercy. Is it the fashion, that discarded fathers Should have thus little mercy on their flesh? . . . . *Lear* iii 4 75
Little might. It is a plague That Cupid will impose for my neglect Of his almighty dreadful little might . . . . . *L. L. Lost* iii 1 205
Little mistress. Look to your little mistress . . . *Pericles* iii 3 40
Little money. Dost lack any money? I have a little money . *W. Tale* iv 3 82
Little month. A little month, or ere those shoes were old . *Hamlet* i 2 147
Little more. A little more lenity to lechery would do no harm in him: something too crabbed that way . . . . . *Meas. for Meas.* iii 2 103
I have but little more to say, sir, of his honesty . . . *All's Well* iv 3 289
I can say little more than I have studied . . . . *T. Night* i 5 190
Whereof a little More than a little is by much too much *1 Hen. IV.* iii 2 72
Lay hands upon him.—Forbear awhile; we'll hear a little more *3 Hen. VI.* iii 1 27
Since it serves my purpose, I will venture To stale't a little more *Coriol.* i 1 95
A little more than kin, and less than kind . . . . *Hamlet* i 2 65
And so, with no money at all and a little more wit . . . *Othello* ii 3 374
Little mouse. Every cat and dog And little mouse, every unworthy thing, Live here in heaven . . . . . . *Rom. and Jul.* iii 3 31
Little nearer. Come a little nearer this ways . . *Mer. Wives* ii 2 46; 50
Little Ned Plantagenet. Where is thy brother Clarence? And little Ned Plantagenet? . . . . *Richard III.* iv 4 146
Little number. Wild amazement hurries up and down The little number of your doubtful friends . . . . . . *K. John* v 1 36
Little O. A sun and moon, which kept their course, and lighted The little O, the earth . . . . *Ant. and Cleo.* v 2 81
Little overparted. You see how 'tis,—a little o'erparted . *L. L. Lost* v 2 588
Little off. Goodman Verges, sir, speaks a little off the matter *Much Ado* iii 5 10
Little office The hateful commons will perform for us . *Richard II.* ii 2 137
Little oil. Like madness is the glory of this life, As this pomp shows to a little oil and root . . . . *T. of Athens* i 2 140
Little one. I said, thou hadst a fine wit: 'True,' said she, 'a fine little one' . . . . *Much Ado* v 1 162
Come, little ones . . . . *Richard II.* v 5 15
For all shall stay: This little one shall make it holiday . *Hen. VIII.* v 5 77
Hence, with your little ones . . . . *Macbeth* iv 2 69
They have given me a rouse already.—Good faith, a little one *Othello* ii 3 68
Why, as men do a-land; the great ones eat up the little ones *Pericles* ii 1 32
Little or nothing. I would little or nothing with you . *Mer. Wives* iii 4 65
Little organ. Excellent voice in this little organ . . . *Hamlet* iii 2 385
Little out of fashion. Though it appear a little out of fashion *Hen. V.* iv 1 85
Little page. Send her your little page, of all loves . . *Mer. Wives* ii 2 119
Little pains. But on, my liege; for very little pains Will bring this labour to an happy end . . . . *K. John* iii 2 9
Little paler. This night methinks is but the daylight sick; It looks a little paler . . . . *Mer. of Venice* v 1 125
Little part. That I should purchase the day before for a little part, and undo a great deal of honour! . . . . . *T. of Athens* iii 2 53
Little patch. We go to gain a little patch of ground That hath in it no profit but the name . . . . *Hamlet* iv 4 18
Little patience. I will say nothing: I thank God I have as little patience as another man . . . . *L. L. Lost* i 2 170
Little pause. A night is but small breath and little pause To answer matters of this consequence . . . . . . *Hen. V.* ii 4 145
They shall die?—Give me some breath, some little pause, my lord, Before I positively speak herein . . . . *Richard III.* iv 2 24
Little payment. Too little payment for so great a debt . *T. of Shrew* v 2 154
Little piece. I will tell him a little piece of my desires . *Hen. V.* v 1 14
Little pin. With a little pin Bores through his castle wall *Richard II.* iii 2 169
Little place. A crooked figure may Attest in little place a million *Hen. V.* Prol. 16
Little policy. That were some love but little policy . *Richard II.* v 1 84
Little pot. Were not I a little pot and soon hot . *T. of Shrew* iv 1 6
Little preparation. I make bold to press with so little preparation upon you.—You're welcome . . . . . . *Mer. Wives* ii 2 162
Little pretty, because little . . . . . . *L. L. Lost* i 2 23
Little price. But Exeter hath given the doom of death For pax of little price . . . . *Hen. V.* iii 6 47
Little prince. Good morrow, little prince.—As little prince, having so great a title To be more prince, as may be . . . *K. John* iv 1 10
Little proudly. But securely done, A little proudly . *Troi. and Cres.* iv 5 74
Little purpose. For they have pardons, being ask'd, as free As words to little purpose . . . . *Coriolanus* iii 2 89
Little purposeth. That, it seems, he little purposeth . *L. L. Lost* ii 1 142
Little question. Which That he will give them make I as little question As he is proud to do't . . . . *Coriolanus* ii 1 246
Little quill. The wren with little quill . . . *M. N. Dream* iii 1 131
Little ratsbane. I would the milk Thy mother gave thee when thou suck'dst her breast Had been a little ratsbane! *1 Hen. VI.* v 4 29

Little reason. I love thee.—Methinks, mistress, you should have little reason for that . . . . *M. N. Dream* iii 1 146
There is little reason in your grief . . . . . *K. John* iv 3 30
'Tis no little reason bids us speed, To save our heads . . *1 Hen. IV.* i 3 283
Little recks. And little recks to find the way to heaven By doing deeds of hospitality . . . . *As Y. Like It* ii 4 81
Little regard. I cannot tell. Virtue is of so little regard in these costermonger times . . . . *2 Hen. IV.* i 2 191
Little remorse. With as little remorse as they would have drowned a blind bitch's puppies . . . . *Mer. Wives* iii 5 10
Little rest. And nature must obey necessity; Which we will niggard with a little rest . . . . *J. Cæsar* iv 3 228
Little riper. A little riper and more lusty red . . . *As Y. Like It* iii 5 121
Little Robin. Here comes little Robin.—How now! . *Mer. Wives* iii 3 21
Little rogue. Ah, you sweet little rogue, you! . . . *2 Hen. IV.* ii 4 233
Little room. It strikes a man more dead than a great reckoning in a little room . . . . *As Y. Like It* iii 3 15
In little room confining mighty men . . . . . . *Hen. V.* Epil. 3
Little rub. What I mean to speak Shall blow each dust, each straw, each little rub, Out of the path . . . . . . *K. John* iii 4 128
Little scene. Allowing him a breath, a little scene, To monarchize, be fear'd and kill with looks . . . . . . *Richard II.* iii 2 164
Little scratched. A little scratched, 'twill serve . . *L. L. Lost* v 1 31
Little scrubbed. A kind of boy, a little scrubbed boy . *Mer. of Venice* v 1 162
Little shaking. At last, a little shaking of mine arm . . *Hamlet* ii 1 92
Little show. If thou dost intend Never so little show of love to her, Thou shalt aby it . . . . *M. N. Dream* iii 2 334
Little shrew. Pretty Jessica, like a little shrew . *Mer. of Venice* v 1 21
Little sick. I would you were a little sick, That I might sit all night and watch with you . . . . *K. John* iv 1 29
Little skill. With the little skill I have, Full well shalt thou perceive how much I dare . . . . *T. Andron.* ii 1 43
Little snow. Or as a little snow, tumbled about, Anon becomes a mountain . . . . *K. John* iii 4 176
Little soiled. A thing a little soil'd i' the working . . . *Hamlet* ii 1 40
Little soldier. My little soldier there, be merry . . *2 Hen. IV.* v 3 34
Little son. My daughter and my little son And three or four more *Mer. Wives* iv 4 47
How does your little son?—I thank your ladyship; well, good madam *Coriolanus* i 3 56
Little souls. And there the little souls of Edward's children Whisper the spirits of thine enemies . . . . . . *Richard III.* iv 4 191
Little space. If you require a little space for prayer, I grant it *Pericles* iv 1 68
Little speaking. His little speaking shows his love but small.—Fire that's closest kept burns most of all . . . *T. G. of Ver.* i 2 29
Little spirit. My little spirit, see, Sits in a foggy cloud . . *Macbeth* iii 5 34
Little stars. Take him and cut him out in little stars *Rom. and Jul.* iii 2 22
Little stead. The help of one stands me in little stead *1 Hen. VI.* iv 6 31
Little stomach. They think my little stomach to the war And your great love to me restrains you thus . . . *Troi. and Cres.* iii 3 220
Little strength. The little strength that I have, I would it were with you.—And mine, to eke out hers . . . *As Y. Like It* i 2 206
Little study. I have labour'd, And with no little study . *Hen. VIII.* v 3 34
Little taste. Have of their puissance made a little taste . *2 Hen. IV.* ii 3 52
Little thanks. Your wife would give you little thanks for that *M. of V.* iv 1 288
Little thief. For a very little thief of occasion will rob you of a great deal of patience . . . . *Coriolanus* ii 1 32
Little thing. A little thing would make me tell . . *T. Night* iii 4 331
It is no little thing to make Mine eyes to sweat compassion *Coriolanus* v 3 195
Little thinks she has been sluiced in's absence . . . *W. Tale* i 2 194
But little thinks we shall be of her council . . *3 Hen. VI.* i 1 36
Little thought. He little thought of this divided friendship *Richard III.* i 4 244
She now begs, That little thought, when she set footing here, She should have bought her dignities so dear . . *Hen. VIII.* iii 1 183
Forgive my fearful sails! I little thought You would have follow'd *Ant. and Cleo.* iii 11 55
Little time. After a little time I'll beat him too . . . *Tempest* iii 2 93
A little time will melt her frozen thoughts . . *T. G. of Ver.* iii 2 9
A little time, my lord, will kill that grief.—So I believe . . iii 2 15
A little time before That our great-grandsire, Edward, sick'd *2 Hen. IV.* iv 4 127
Vouchsafe your rest here in our court Some little time . *Hamlet* ii 2 14
Till some little time hath qualified the heat of his displeasure *Lear* i 2 176
Little tiny. When that I was and a little tiny boy . . *T. Night* v 1 398
A joint of mutton, and any pretty little tiny kickshaws . *2 Hen. IV.* v 1 29
Welcome, my little tiny thief, and welcome indeed too . . v 3 60
Little touch. A little touch of Harry in the night . *Hen. V.* iv Prol. 47
Little train. With some little train, Forthwith from Ludlow the young prince be fetched . . .—Why with some little train? *Richard III.* ii 2 120
Little unthought of. I leave my duty a little unthought of and speak out of my injury . . . . *T. Night* v 1 318
Little urged. Wilt know again, Being ne'er so little urged *Richard II.* v 1 64
Little use. My dull deaf ears a little use to hear . *Com. of Errors* v 1 316
Little vain. 'Tis holy sport to be a little vain . . . . . iii 2 27
Little valiant. Thou little valiant, great in villany! . . *K. John* iii 1 116
Ah, you whoreson little valiant villain, you! . . . *2 Hen. IV.* ii 4 225
Little vanity. Shall tax my fears of little vanity . . . *All's Well* v 3 122
Little variations. Save the phrase is a little variations . *Hen. V.* iv 7 19
Little villain. Here comes the little villain . . . *T. Night* ii 5 16
Little voice. I'll speak in a monstrous little voice . . *M. N. Dream* i 2 54
Little water. Put but a little water in a spoon, And it shall be as all the ocean, Enough to stifle such a villain up . . . *K. John* iv 3 131
A little water clears us of this deed: How easy is it, then! . *Macbeth* ii 2 67
Little way. 'Tis but a little way that I can bring you . . *Othello* iii 4 199
Mercutio's soul Is but a little way above our heads . *Rom. and Jul.* iii 1 132
Little wealth. I have little wealth to lose . . . *T. G. of Ver.* iv 1 11
Little wee. A little wee face, with a little yellow beard . *Mer. Wives* i 4 22
Little wench. That was a woman when Queen Guinover of Britain was a little wench . . . . *L. L. Lost* iv 1 126
Little while. Tarry you a little-a while . . . . *Mer. Wives* i 4 93
Stay a little while. You're welcome: what's your will? *Meas. for Meas.* ii 2 26
Then but forbear your food a little while . . . *As Y. Like It* ii 7 127
She lives, Though yet she speak not. Mark a little while . *W. Tale* v 3 118
Bid his ears a little while be deaf, Till I have told this slander *Richard II.* i 1 112
As runners with a race, I lay me down a little while to breathe *3 Hen. VI.* ii 3 2
Nay, stay; . . . stay a little while . . . . *Troi. and Cres.* v 2 54
Bestow this place on us a little while . . . . . . *Hamlet* iv 1 4
Do you withdraw yourself a little while, He will recover straight *Othello* iv 1 57
Little wild. If I chance to talk a little wild, forgive me . . *Hen. VIII.* i 4 26
Little wit. Since the little wit that fools have was silenced, the little foolery that wise men have makes a great show . . *As Y. Like It* i 2 95

Little wit. Take not that little little less than little wit from them! *Troi. and Cres.* ii 3 15
Thou hadst little wit in thy bald crown, when thou gavest thy golden one away . . . . *Lear* i 4 177
Little word. How long a time lies in one little word! . *Richard II.* i 3 213
Little world. This little world, This precious stone set in the silver sea ii 1 45
And these same thoughts people this little world . . . v 5 9
Strives in his little world of man to out-scorn The to-and-fro-conflicting wind and rain . . . . *Lear* iii 1 10
Little worm. Not half so big as a round little worm *Rom. and Jul.* i 4 65
Little worse. When he is best, he is a little worse than a man *M. of Ven.* i 2 94
Little worth. Since thou dost deign to woo her little worth . 1 *Hen. VI.* v 3 151
Little wots What watch the king keeps to maintain the peace *Hen. V.* iv 1 299
Little wrong. To do a great right, do a little wrong *Mer. of Venice* iv 1 216
Soldiers should brook as little wrongs as gods. . *T. of Athens* iii 5 117
Cassio did some little wrong to him . . . *Othello* ii 3 242
Littlest. Where love is great, the littlest doubts are fear . *Hamlet* iii 2 181
Live. But how is it That this lives in thy mind? . . . *Tempest* i 2 49
Here is every thing advantageous to life.—True; save means to live . ii 1 50
Sir, he may live: I saw him beat the surges under him . . ii 1 113
You 'mongst men Being most unfit to live . . . iii 3 58
I Have given you here a thrid of mine own life, Or that for which I live iv 1 4
Thy turfy mountains, where live nibbling sheep . . . iv 1 62
Let me live here ever . . . . iv 1 122
Merrily shall I live now Under the blossom that hangs on the bough . v 1 93
He writes How happily he lives, how well beloved . *T. G. of Ver.* i 3 57
I think Crab my dog be the sourest-natured dog that lives . ii 3 6
That hath more mind to feed on your blood than live in your air . ii 4 28
It appears, by their bare liveries, that they live by your bare words ii 4 46
Which to requite, command me while I live . . . iii 1 23
He lives not now that knows me to be in love . . . iii 1 264
Longer than I prove loyal to your grace Let me not live . . iii 2 21
Make a virtue of necessity And live, as we do, in this wilderness . iv 1 63
Thou shalt not live to brag what we have offer'd . . iv 1 69
I take your offer and will live with you . . . . iv 1 70
Is she kind as she is fair? For beauty lives with kindness . . iv 2 45
Sure as I live, he had suffered for 't . . . . iv 4 17
She is dead, belike?—Not so; I think she lives . . iv 4 80
Be thou ashamed . . ., if shame live In a disguise of love . v 4 106
I'll ne'er be drunk whilst I live again . . . *Mer. Wives* i 1 186
Yet I live like a poor gentleman born . . . . i 1 286
Mortality and mercy in Vienna Live in thy tongue and heart *M. for M.* i 1 46
But, whilst I live, forget to drink after thee . . . i 2 40
Truly, sir, I am a poor fellow that would live.—How would you live? . ii 1 235
If you live to see this come to pass . . . . ii 1 256
Are now to have no successive degrees, But, ere they live, to end . ii 2 99
Do him right that, answering one foul wrong, Lives not to act another ii 2 104
O, let her brother live: Thieves for their robbery have authority When judges steal themselves . . . . ii 2 175
Your brother cannot live.—Even so. Heaven keep your honour!—Yet may he live awhile; and, it may be, As long as you or I . . ii 4 33
Then, Isabel, live chaste, and, brother, die . . . ii 4 184
I've hope to live, and am prepared to die . . . iii 1 4
To sue to live, I find I seek to die; And, seeking death, find life . iii 1 42
Yes, brother, you may live: There is a devilish mercy in the judge . iii 1 64
Sweet sister, let me live: What sin you do to save a brother's life, Nature dispenses with the deed so far . . . . . iii 1 133
What corruption in this life, that it will let this man live! . . iii 1 242
The evil that thou causest to be done, That is thy means to live . iii 2 22
From their . . . beastly touches I drink, I eat, array myself, and live iii 2 26
He shall know you better, sir, if I may live to report you . iii 2 172
Unfit to live or die: O gravel heart! After him, fellows . iv 3 68
The duke is marvellous little beholding to your reports; but the best is, he lives not in them . . . . iv 3 167
That life is better life, past fearing death, Than that which lives to fear v 1 403
Here must end the story of my life; And happy were I in my timely death, Could all my travels warrant me they live *Com. of Errors* i 1 140
Beg thou, or borrow, to make up the sum, And live . . i 1 155
If thou live to see like right bereft . . . . ii 1 40
I live unstain'd, thou undishonoured . . . . ii 2 148
With intrusion Infect thy sap and live on thy confusion . . ii 2 182
If she lives till doomsday, she'll burn a week longer than the whole world . . . . iii 2 101
I see a man here needs not live by shifts, When in the streets he meets such golden gifts . . . . iii 2 187
Highly beloved, Second to none that lives here in the city . . v 1 7
The fine is, for the which I may go the finer, I will live a bachelor *M. Ado* i 1 248
And there live we as merry as the day is long . . . ii 1 51
While she is here, a man may live as quiet in hell as in a sanctuary ii 1 265
I did not think I should live till I were married . . ii 3 253
Maiden pride, adieu! No glory lives behind the back of such . iii 1 110
Do not live, Hero; do not ope thine eyes . . . iv 1 125
The practice of it lives in John the bastard . . . iv 1 190
Come, lady, die to live: this wedding-day Perhaps is but prolong'd . iv 1 255
I cannot bid you bid my daughter live; That were impossible . v 1 288
He shall live no longer in monument than the bell rings and the widow weeps . . . . v 2 81
I will live in thy heart, die in thy lap and be buried in thy eyes . v 2 104
So the life that died with shame Lives in death with glorious fame v 3 8
One Hero died defiled, but I do live, And surely as I live, I am a maid v 4 63
But in that thou art like to be my kinsman, live unbruised . . v 4 112
Have sworn for three years' term to live with me My fellow-scholars *L. L. Lost* i 1 16
I have already sworn, That is, to live and study here three years . i 1 35
On payment of a hundred thousand crowns, To have his title live . ii 1 146
What wilt thou prove?—A man, if I live . . . . iii 1 41
Where all those pleasures live that art would comprehend . . iv 2 114
Love, first learned in a lady's eyes, Lives not alone immured in the brain iv 3 328
For a light heart lives long . . . . . . v 2 18
To live a barren sister all your life, Chanting faint hymns *M. N. Dream* i 1 72
Grows, lives and dies in single blessedness.—So will I grow, so live, so die i 1 78
Those be rubies, fairy favours, In those freckles live their savours . ii 1 13
If you live, good sir, awake.—And run through fire I will . . ii 2 102
Superfluity comes sooner by white hairs, but competency lives longer.—Good sentences and well pronounced . . . *Mer. of Venice* i 2 10
If I live to be as old as Sibylla, I will die as chaste as Diana . . i 2 116
An honest exceeding poor man and, God be thanked, well to live . ii 2 55
It lives there unchecked that Antonio hath a ship of rich lading wrecked iii 1 2
Let me choose; For as I am, I live upon the rack . . . iii 2 25
Promise me life, and I'll confess the truth.—Well then, confess and live iii 2 35
Live. Live thou, I live: with much much more dismay I view the fight than thou . . . . *Mer. of Venice* iii 2 61
Nerissa and myself meantime Will live as maids and widows . . iii 2 312
My bond to the Jew is forfeit; and since in paying it, it is impossible I should live, all debts are cleared between you and I . . . iii 2 321
Breathed a secret vow To live in prayer and contemplation . . iii 4 28
We were Christians enow before; e'en as many as could well live . iii 5 25
It is very meet The Lord Bassanio live an upright life . . iii 5 79
So let me: You cannot better be employ'd, Bassanio, Than to live still and write mine epitaph . . . . iv 1 118
You take my life When you do take the means whereby I live . iv 1 377
He will, an if he live to be a man.—Ay, if a woman live to be a man . v 1 159
While I live I'll fear no other thing So sore as keeping safe Nerissa's ring v 1 306
Where will the old duke live? . . . . . *As Y. Like It* i 1 119
And there they live like the old Robin Hood of England . . i 1 122
I cannot live out of her company.—You are a fool . . . i 3 88
Within this roof The enemy of all your graces lives . . . ii 3 18
From seventeen years till now almost fourscore Here lived I, but now live here no more. At seventeen years many their fortunes seek . ii 3 72
Who doth ambition shun And loves to live i' the sun . . . ii 5 41
How now, Adam? no greater heart in thee? Live a little; comfort a little . . . . ii 6 5
Thou shalt not die for lack of a dinner, if there live any thing in this desert . . . . ii 6 18
As I do live by food, I met a fool . . . . . ii 7 14
Heaven would that she these gifts should have, And I to live and die her slave . . . . iii 2 162
Lives merrily because he feels no pain . . . . . iii 2 340
To forswear the full stream of the world and to live in a nook merely monastic . . . . iii 2 441
And by the way you shall tell me where in the forest you live . . iii 2 453
We must be married, or we must live in bawdry . . . iii 3 99
Will you sterner be Than he that dies and lives by bloody drops? . iii 5 7
Loose now and then A scatter'd smile, and that I'll live upon . iii 5 104
And here live and die a shepherd . . . . . . v 2 14
I can live no longer by thinking . . . . . . v 2 55
I have left you commands.—I'll not fail, if I live . . . v 2 132
Master, your love must live a maid at home . . . *T. of Shrew* i 1 187
My father dead, my fortune lives for me . . . . i 2 192
But will you woo this wild-cat?—Will I live? . . . . i 2 197
If I die to-morrow, this is hers, If whilst I live she will be only mine ii 1 364
But one that scorn to live in this disguise . . . . iv 2 18
He shall need none, so long as I live . . . . . v 1 25
Pardon, sweet father.—Lives my sweet son? . . . . v 1 115
So in approof lives not his epitaph As in your royal speech *All's Well* i 2 50
'Let me not live,'—This his good melancholy oft began, . . . 'Let me not live,' quoth he, 'After my flame lacks oil, to be the snuff Of younger spirits' . . . . i 2 55
And I His servant live, and will his vassal die . . . . i 3 165
But riddle-like lives sweetly where she dies . . . . i 3 223
Whether I live or die, be you the sons Of worthy Frenchmen . . ii 1 11
Say to him, I live; and observe his reports for me . . . ii 1 46
And such thanks I give As one near death to those that wish him live . ii 1 134
What is infirm from your sound parts shall fly, Health shall live free . ii 1 171
I give Me and my service, ever whilst I live, Into your guiding power . ii 3 110
Sent him forth From courtly friends, with camping foes to live . iii 4 14
O, let me live! And all the secrets of our camp I'll show . . iv 1 92
For which live long to thank both heaven and me! . . . iv 2 67
Since Frenchmen are so braid, Marry that will, I live and die a maid iv 2 74
Answer to what I shall ask you out of a note.—And truly, as I hope to live . . . . iv 3 147
If I were to live this present hour, I will tell true . . . iv 3 182
Let me live, sir, in a dungeon, i' the stocks, or any where, so I may live iv 3 273
O Lord, sir, let me live, or let me see my death! . . . . iv 3 344
Simply the thing I am Shall make me live . . . . iv 3 370
When the rich golden shaft Hath kill'd the flock of all affections else That live in her . . . . *T. Night* i 1 37
Prosper well in this, And thou shalt live as freely as thy lord . . i 4 39
Shall this fellow live? . . . . i 5 69
Dost thou live by thy tabor?—No, sir, I live by the church . . iii 1 2
I do live by the church; for I do live at my house, and my house doth stand by the church . . . . iii 1 5
It shall be done to-morrow morning, if I live . . . . iii 4 116
I will live to be thankful to thee for't . . . . . iv 2 89
Live you the marble-breasted tyrant still . . . . . v 1 127
If there were no other excuse why they should desire to live *W. Tale* i 1 48
If the king had no son, they would desire to live on crutches till he had one . . . . i 1 50
Were my wife's liver Infected as her life, she would not live The running of one glass.—Who does infect her? . . . . i 2 305
A daughter, and a goodly babe, Lusty and like to live . . . ii 2 27
Shall I live on to see this bastard kneel And call me father? . . ii 3 155
Better burn it now Than curse it then. But be it; let it live . . ii 3 157
While she lives My heart will be a burthen to me . . . . ii 3 205
The king shall live without an heir, if that which is lost be not found . iii 2 136
If the sins of your youth are forgiven you, you're well to live . . iii 3 125
If tinkers may have leave to live, And bear the sow-skin budget . iv 3 19
I should leave grazing, were I of your flock, And only live by gazing . iv 4 110
There was the first gentleman-like tears that ever we shed.—We may live, son, to shed many more . . . . v 2 157
Scarce any joy Did ever so long live . . . . . . v 3 52
My lord's almost so far transported that He'll think anon it lives . v 3 70
But it appears she lives, Though yet she speak not . . . v 3 117
Who lives and dares but say thou didst not well When I was got, I'll send his soul to hell . . . . *K. John* i 1 271
O, if thou grant my need, Which only lives but by the death of faith, That need must needs infer this principle, That faith would live again by death of need . . . . iii 1 212
There where my fortune lives, there my life dies . . . . iii 1 338
My good friend, thy voluntary oath Lives in this bosom, dearly cherished iii 3 24
Death.—My lord?—A grave.—He shall not live.—Enough . . iii 3 66
Well, see to live; I will not touch thine eye . . . . iv 1 122
The image of a wicked heinous fault Lives in his eye . . . iv 2 72
Doth Arthur live? O, haste thee to the peers! . . . . iv 2 260
Lords, I am hot with haste in seeking you: Arthur doth live . . iv 3 75
Hubert told me he did live.—So, on my soul, he did, for aught he knew v 1 42
Since it is true That I must die here and live hence by truth . v 4 29
A miscreant, Too good to be so and too bad to live . . *Richard II.* i 1 40
My fair name, Despite of death that lives upon my grave, To dark dishonour's use thou shalt not have . . . . i 1 168

Live. Mine honour let me try; In that I live and for that will I die *Richard II.* i 1 185
Rouse up thy youthful blood, be valiant and live . . . . . i 3 83
However God or fortune cast my lot, There lives or dies, true to King Richard's throne, A loyal, just, and upright gentleman . . i 3 86
Thou hast many years to live.—But not a minute, king, that thou canst give . . . i 3 225
Should dying men flatter with those that live?—No, no, men living flatter those that die . . . . ii 1 88
Live in thy shame, but die not shame with thee! . . . . ii 1 135
Love they to live that love and honour have . . . . ii 1 138
Those rough rug-headed kerns, Which live like venom where no venom else But only they have privilege to live . . . . . . ii 1 158
Is not Gaunt dead, and doth not Hereford live? Was not Gaunt just? ii 1 191
We are on the earth, Where nothing lives but crosses, cares, and grief . ii 2 79
I live with bread like you, feel want, Taste grief, need friends . . iii 2 175
For on my heart they tread now whilst I live . . . . . iii 3 158
Will his majesty Give Richard leave to live till Richard die? . . . iii 3 174
Superfluous branches We lop away, that bearing boughs may live . . iii 4 64
Thou darest not, coward, live to see that day . . . . . iv 1 41
If I dare eat, or drink, or breathe, or live, I dare meet Surrey in a wilderness . . . . iv 1 73
Is Norfolk dead?—As surely as I live, my lord . . . . iv 1 102
And long live Henry, fourth of that name! . . . . . iv 1 112
Long mayst thou live in Richard's seat to sit . . . . . iv 1 218
Mine honour lives when his dishonour dies . . . . . v 3 70
Giving him breath, The traitor lives, the true man's put to death . . v 3 73
They shall not live within this world, I swear, But I will have them . v 3 142
Studying how I may compare This prison where I live unto the world . v 5 2
Where no man never comes but that sad dog That brings me food to make misfortune live . . . . v 5 71
For whose death we in the world's wide mouth Live scandalized *1 Hen. IV.* i 3 154
On, bacons, on! What, ye knaves! young men must live . . . ii 2 96
There live not three good men unhanged in England . . . ii 4 144
O, while you live, tell truth and shame the devil! . . . . iii 1 62
I had rather live With cheese and garlic in a windmill . . . . iii 1 161
And 'as true as I live,' and 'as God shall mend me,' and 'as sure as day' iii 1 254
You are so fretful, you cannot live long . . . . . iii 3 14
And now I live out of all order, out of all compass . . . . iii 3 22
A comfort of retirement lives in this . . . . . . iv 1 56
If well-respected honour bid me on, I hold as little counsel with weak fear As you, my lord, or any Scot that this day lives . . . . iv 3 12
But will it [honour] not live with the living? no. Why? . . . . v 1 141
All his offences live upon my head And on his father's . . . . v 2 20
An if we live, we live to tread on kings; If die, brave death! . . v 2 86
I'll purge, and leave sack, and live cleanly as a nobleman should do . v 4 169
The truth is, Sir John, you live in great infamy.—He that buckles him in my belt cannot live in less . . . *2 Hen. IV.* i 2 156
Our supplies live largely in the hope Of great Northumberland . . i 3 12
Lives so in hope as in an early spring We see the appearing buds . . i 3 38
You'll pay me all together?—Will I live? . . . . . . ii 1 174
I must live among my neighbours; I'll no swaggerers . . . ii 4 80
Hang him, rogue! he lives upon mouldy stewed prunes and dried cakes ii 4 158
And is Jane Nightwork alive?—She lives, Master Shallow . . . iii 2 212
And their memory Shall as a pattern or a measure live . . . iv 4 76
Let me in my present wildness die And never live to show the incredulous world The noble change that I have purposed! . . . iv 5 154
How I came by the crown, O God forgive; And grant it may with thee in true peace live! . . . . iv 5 220
He's walk'd the way of nature; And to our purposes he lives no more . v 2 5
But Harry lives, that shall convert those tears By number into hours of happiness.—We hope no other . . . . . . v 2 60
And I do wish your honours may increase, Till you do live to see a son of mine Offend you and obey you, as I did . . . . v 2 105
So shall I live to speak my father's words . . . . . v 2 107
And drink unto the leman mine; And a merry heart lives long-a . . v 3 50
Faith, I will live so long as I may, that's the certain of it; and when I cannot live any longer, I will do as I may . . . *Hen. V.* ii 1 15
Gentlewomen that live honestly by the prick of their needles . . ii 1 36
I'll live by Nym, and Nym shall live by me; Is not this just? . . ii 1 115
Let us condole the knight; for, lambkins, we will live . . . ii 1 133
And if he be not fought withal, my lord, Let us not live in France . iii 5 3
If I live to see it, I will never trust his word after . . . . iv 1 207
Let it be a quarrel between us, if you live.—I embrace it . . . iv 1 220
If ever I live to see it, I will challenge it . . . . . iv 1 233
And if to live, The fewer men, the greater share of honour . . iv 3 21
He that shall live this day, and see old age . . . . . iv 3 44
Lives he, good uncle? thrice within this hour I saw him down . . iv 6 4
Then keep thy vow, sirrah . . . —So I will, my liege, as I live . . iv 7 153
I will desire you to live in the mean time, and eat your victuals . . v 1 34
King Henry the Fifth, too famous to live long! . . . *1 Hen. VI.* i 1 6
O no, he lives; but is took prisoner . . . . i 1 145
Why live we idly here? Talbot is taken, whom we wont to fear . . i 2 13
I fear no woman.—And while I live, I'll ne'er fly from a man . . i 2 103
A pair of loving turtle-doves That could not live asunder day or night ii 2 31
His trespass yet lives guilty in thy blood . . . . . . ii 4 94
If thou be not then created York, I will not live to be accounted Warwick . . . . ii 4 120
As sure as English Henry lives And as his father here was conqueror . iii 2 80
His fame lives in the world, his shame in you . . . . . iv 4 46
Do what you will, the like do I; For live I will not, if my father die . iv 5 51
Come, side by side together live and die . . . . . . iv 5 54
Well, go to; we'll have no bastards live . . . . . . v 4 70
Long live Queen Margaret, England's happiness! . . . *2 Hen. VI.* i 1 37
She scorns our poverty: Shall I not live to be avenged on her? . . i 3 85
Thy betters, Warwick.—Warwick may live to be the best of all . . i 3 115
The duke yet lives that Henry shall depose; But him outlive . . i 4 33; 62
Long live our sovereign Richard, England's king! . . . . ii 2 63
Richard shall live to make the Earl of Warwick The greatest man in England but the king . . . . ii 2 81
Live in your country here in banishment . . . . . . iii 3 12
The world may laugh again; And I may live to do you kindness . . ii 4 83
Die, Margaret! For Henry weeps that thou dost live so long . . iii 2 121
As surely as my soul intends to live With that dread King . . . iii 2 153
Live thou to joy thy life; Myself no joy in nought but that thou livest iii 2 365
If I depart from thee, I cannot live . . . . iii 2 388
If thou be'st death, I'll give thee England's treasure, Enough to purchase such another island, So thou wilt let me live . . . iii 3 4
Can I make men live, whether they will or no? . . . . . iii 3 10
Be not so rash; take ransom, let him live . . . . . . iv 1 28

Live. And because they could not read, thou hast hanged them; when, indeed, only for that cause they have been most worthy to live *2 Hen. VI.* iv 7 51
O, let me live!—I feel remorse in myself with his words; but I'll bridle it . . . . iv 7 110
You are all recreants and dastards, and delight to live in slavery . . iv 8 29
Nor knows he how to live but by the spoil, Unless by robbing . . iv 8 41
Who would live turmoiled in the court, And may enjoy such quiet walks? . . . . iv 10 18
I'll send them all as willing as I live: Lands, goods, horse, armour . v 1 51
May Iden live to merit such a bounty, And never live but true unto his liege! . . . . v 1 81
We will live To see their day and them our fortune give . . . v 2 88
God knows how long it is I have to live . . . . . . v 3 17
For he that interrupts him shall not live . . . . *3 Hen. VI.* i 1 123
To cease this civil war, and, whilst I live, To honour me as thy king . i 1 197
Long live King Henry! Plantagenet, embrace him.—And long live thou! . . . . i 1 202
Be thou revenged on men, and let me live . . . . . . i 3 20
Till I root out their accursed line And leave not one alive, I live in hell . . . . i 3 33
Ah, let me live in prison all my days; And when I give occasion of offence, Then let me die, for now thou hast no cause . . . . i 3 43
Ne'er may he live to see a sunshine day, That cries 'Retire' . . . ii 1 187
How many years a mortal man may live . . . . ii 5 29
And, whiles I live, to account this world but hell . . . . iii 2 169
A banish'd man, And forced to live in Scotland a forlorn . . . iii 3 26
Lives in Scotland at his ease, Where having nothing, nothing can he lose iii 3 151
How shall poor Henry live, Unless thou rescue him from foul despair? iii 3 214
Long live Edward the Fourth!—Thanks, brave Montgomery . . . iv 7 76
Live we how we can, yet die we must . . . . v 2 28
And half our sailors swallow'd in the flood? Yet lives our pilot still . v 4 6
Thy famous grandfather Doth live again in thee: long mayst thou live To bear his image and renew his glories! . . . . v 4 53
Why should she live, to fill the world with words? . . . . . v 5 44
I shall live, my lord, to give them thanks That were the cause *Rich. III.* i 1 127
He cannot live, I hope; and must not die . . . . . . i 1 145
If I fail not in my deep intent, Clarence hath not another day to live . i 1 150
Clarence still breathes; Edward still lives and reigns . . . . i 1 161
Adders, spiders, toads, Or any creeping venom'd thing that lives! . . i 2 20
Your beauty which did haunt me in my sleep To undertake the death of all the world, So I might live one hour in your sweet bosom . . i 2 124
He lives that loves thee better than he could . . . . . i 2 141
But shall I live in hope?—All men, I hope, live so . . . . i 2 200
Cannot a plain man live and think no harm? . . . . . . i 3 51
Long mayst thou live to wail thy children's loss! . . . . . i 3 204
God, I pray him, That none of you may live your natural age! . . i 3 213
Life my shame; And in that shame still live my sorrow's rage! . . i 3 278
Live each of you the subjects to his hate, And he to yours, and all of you to God's!—My hair doth stand on end . . . . . . i 3 302
I thought thou hadst been resolute.—So I am, to let him live . . i 4 117
Every man that means to live well endeavours to trust to himself and to live without it [conscience] . . . . i 4 147
He rescued me, And said, 'Dear brother, live, and be a king' . . ii 1 113
If you will live, lament; if die, be brief . . . . . . ii 2 43
Send straight for him; Let him be crown'd; in him your comfort lives ii 2 98
The truth should live from age to age, As 'twere retail'd to all posterity iii 1 76
So wise so young, they say, do never live long . . . . . iii 1 79
I say, without characters, fame lives long . . . . . . iii 1 81
With what his valour did enrich his wit, His wit set down to make his valour live: Death makes no conquest of this conqueror; For now he lives in fame, though not in life . . . . iii 1 86
An if I live until I be a man, I'll win our ancient right in France again iii 1 91
I fear no uncles dead.—Nor none that live, I hope.—An if they live, I hope I need not fear . . . . iii 1 147
They who brought me in my master's hate, I live to look upon their tragedy . . . . iii 2 59
You live that shall cry woe for this hereafter . . . . . iii 3 7
Lives like a drunken sailor on a mast, Ready, with every nod, to tumble iii 4 101
By great preservation, We live to tell it you . . . . . iii 5 37
But touch this sparingly, as 'twere far off; Because you know, my lord, my mother lives . . . . iii 5 94
For first he was contract to Lady Lucy—Your mother lives a witness . iii 7 180
Go cross the seas, And live with Richmond, from the reach of hell . iv 1 43
Still live they and for ever may they last! . . . . . . iv 2 7
Young Edward lives: think now what I would say.—Say on, my loving lord . . . . iv 2 10
Ha! am I king? 'tis so: but Edward lives.—True, noble prince.—O bitter consequence, That Edward still should live! . . . . iv 2 14
A bard of Ireland told me once, I should not live long after I saw Richmond . . . . iv 2 110
Richard yet lives, hell's black intelligencer . . . . . iv 4 71
Dear God, I pray, That I may live to say, The dog is dead! . . iv 4 78
O, let her live, And I'll corrupt her manners, stain her beauty . . iv 4 205
So she may live unscarr'd of bleeding slaughter . . . . iv 4 209
The children live, whose parents thou hast slaughter'd, Ungovern'd youth, to wail it in their age; The parents live, whose children thou hast butcher'd . . . . iv 4 391
Harry, that prophesied thou shouldst be king, Doth comfort thee in thy sleep: live, and flourish! . . . . v 3 130
Good angels guard thy battle! live, and flourish! . . . . . v 3 138
Live, and beget a happy race of kings! . . . . v 3 157
Let them not live to taste this land's increase That would with treason wound this fair land's peace! . . . . v 5 38
Peace lives again: That she may long live here, God say amen! . . v 5 41
Their curses now Live where their prayers did . . . *Hen. VIII.* i 2 63
May his highness live in freedom, And this man out of prison? . . i 2 200
May he live Longer than I have time to tell his years! . . . ii 1 90
Learn this, brother, We live not to be grip'd by meaner persons . . ii 2 136
Though he be grown so desperate to be honest, And live a subject . iii 1 87
They that my trust must grow to, live not here . . . . . iii 1 89
The letter, as I live, with all the business I writ to's holiness . . iii 2 221
If we live thus tamely, To be thus jaded by a piece of scarlet . . iii 2 279
Our issues, Who, if he live, will scarce be gentlemen . . . . iii 2 292
We'll leave you to your meditations How to live better . . . . iii 2 346
And fear'd She'll with the labour end.—The fruit she goes with I pray for heartily, that it may find Good time, and live . . . . v 1 22
More out of malice than integrity, Would try him to the utmost, had ye mean; Which ye shall never have while I live . . . . v 3 147
As I live, If the king blame me for't, I'll lay ye all By the heels . v 4 81

Live. I could live and die i' the eyes of Troilus . . . *Troi. and Cres.* i 2 263
Doth turn oh! oh! to ha! ha! he! So dying love lives still . . . iii 1 134
We vow to weep seas, live in fire, eat rocks, tame tigers . . . iii 2 84
Which, you say, live to come in my behalf . . . iii 3 16
Jove, let Æneas live, If to my sword his fate be not the glory! . . . iv 1 25
Let us cast away nothing, for we may live to have need . . . iv 4 23
I'll make my match to live, The kiss you take is better than you give . iv 5 37
Even in the fan and wind of your fair sword, You bid them rise, and live . . . v 3 42
A very filthy rogue.—I do believe thee: live . . . v 4 32
Ignomy and shame Pursue thy life, and live aye with thy name! . . . v 10 34
I receive the general food at first, Which you do live upon . *Coriolanus* i 1 136
From me receive that natural competency Whereby they live . . . i 1 144
He's a bear indeed, that lives like a lamb . . . ii 1 14
And live you yet? O my sweet lady, pardon . . . ii 1 197
At Antium lives he?—At Antium . . . iii 1 17
Suffer't, and live with such as cannot rule Nor ever will be ruled . iii 1 40
Not in this heat, sir, now.—Now, as I live, I will . . . iii 1 64
Thou'rt tired, then, in a word, I also am Longer to live most weary . iv 5 101
And cannot live but to thy shame, unless It be to do thee service . iv 5 106
Live, and thrive!—Farewell, kind neighbours . . . iv 6 23
No, though it were as virtuous to lie as to live chastely . . . v 2 27
Let my father's honours live in me . . . *T. Andron.* i 1 7
A nobler man, a braver warrior, Lives not this day within the city walls i 1 26
Live Lord Titus long; My noble lord and father, live in fame! . . i 1 157
Lavinia, live; outlive thy father's days, And fame's eternal date! . i 1 167
Crown him, and say, 'Long live our emperor!' . . . i 1 229
Seizeth but his own.—And that he will, and shall, if Lucius live . . i 1 282
He lives in fame that died in virtue's cause . . . i 1 390
You are very short with us; But, if we live, we'll be as sharp with you i 1 410
I will be honest, And never, whilst I live, deceive men so . . . iii 1 190
But now nor Lucius nor Lavinia lives But in oblivion and hateful griefs. If Lucius live, he will requite your wrongs . . . iii 1 295
Thy father hath . . . done the like.—And, uncle, so will I, an if I live iv 1 112
It shall not live.—It shall not die . . . iv 2 80
Shall she live to betray this guilt of ours, A long-tongued babbling gossip? . . . iv 2 149
Not far, one Muli lives, my countryman . . . iv 2 152
But if I live, his feigned ecstasies Shall be no shelter to these outrages iv 4 21
But he and his shall know that justice lives In Saturninus' health . iv 4 23
As she in fury shall Cut off the proud'st conspirator that lives . . iv 4 26
Thy child shall live, and I will see it nourish'd.—An if it please thee! . v 1 60
Tell on thy mind; I say thy child shall live . . . v 1 69
Would I were a devil, To live and burn in everlasting fire! . . . v 1 148
Even with all my heart Would I were dead, so you did live again! . v 3 173
Ay, while you live, draw your neck out o' the collar . *Rom. and Jul.* i 1 5
From love's weak childish bow she lives unharm'd . . . i 1 217
Then she hath sworn that she will still live chaste?—She hath . . i 1 223
She hath forsworn to love, and in that vow Do I live dead that live to tell it now . . . i 1 230
I warrant, an I should live a thousand years, I never should forget it . i 3 46
An I might live to see thee married once, I have my wish . . . i 3 61
The fish lives in the sea, and 'tis much pride For fair without the fair within to hide . . . i 3 89
For nought so vile that on the earth doth live But to the earth some special good doth give . . . ii 3 17
Romeo slew Tybalt, Romeo must not live . . . iii 1 186
Honest gentleman! That ever I should live to see thee dead! . . . iii 2 63
My husband lives, That Tybalt would have slain; And Tybalt's dead, that would have slain my husband . . . iii 2 105
Heaven is here, Where Juliet lives; and every cat and dog And little mouse, every unworthy thing, Live here in heaven . . . iii 3 30
More honourable state, more courtship lives In carrion-flies than Romeo iii 3 34
Wilt thou slay thyself? And slay thy lady too that lives in thee? . iii 3 117
Where thou shalt live, till we can find a time To blaze your marriage . iii 3 150
I must be gone and live, or stay and die . . . iii 5 11
Wilt thou wash him from his grave with tears? An if thou couldst, thou couldst not make him live . . . iii 5 72
Thou weep'st not so much for his death, As that the villain lives which slaughter'd him . . . iii 5 80
He doth grieve my heart.—That is, because the traitor murderer lives . iii 5 85
I'll send to one in Mantua, Where that same banish'd runagate doth live iii 5 90
And I will do it without fear or doubt, To live an unstain'd wife . . iv 1 88
Or, if I live, is it not very like, The horrible conceit of death and night, Together with the terror of the place? . . . iv 3 36
For shame! confusion's cure lives not In these confusions . . . iv 5 65
She's not well married that lives married long . . . iv 5 77
O, an you will have me live, play 'Heart's ease' . . . iv 5 103
Her body sleeps in Capel's monument, And her immortal part with angels lives . . . v 1 19
If a man did need a poison now, Whose sale is present death in Mantua, Here lives a caitiff wretch would sell it him . . . v 1 52
Take thou that: Live, and be prosperous: and farewell, good fellow . v 3 42
Live, and hereafter say, A madman's mercy bade thee run away . . v 3 66
Artificial strife Lives in these touches, livelier than life . *T. of Athens* i 1 38
Vouchsafe my labour, and long live your lordship!—I thank you . . i 1 152
Long may he live in fortunes! . . . i 1 293
Who lives that's not depraved or depraves? . . . i 2 145
Now the gods keep you old enough; that you may live Only in bone! . iii 5 104
Live loathed and long, Most smiling, smooth, detested parasites! . . iii 6 103
And let confusion live! . . . iv 1 21
Who would be so mock'd with glory? or to live But in a dream of friendship? . . . iv 2 33
Creatures Whose naked natures live in all the spite Of wreakful heaven iv 3 228
Live, and love thy misery.—Long live so, and so die . . . iv 3 396
We cannot live on grass, on berries, water, As beasts and birds and fishes . . . iv 3 425
Go, live rich and happy; But thus condition'd: thou shalt build from men . . . iv 3 532
Allow'd with absolute power and thy good name Live with authority . v 1 166
Go, live still; Be Alcibiades your plague, you his! . . . v 1 191
Some beast rear'd this; there does not live a man . . . v 3 4
Truly, sir, all that I live by is with the awl . . . *J. Cæsar* i 1 24
I had as lief not be as live to be In awe of such a thing as I myself . i 2 95
Let him not die; For he will live, and laugh at this hereafter . . ii 1 191
My heart laments that virtue cannot live Out of the teeth of emulation ii 3 13
If thou read this, O Cæsar, thou mayst live . . . ii 3 15
Live a thousand years, I shall not find myself so apt to die . . . iii 1 159
Had you rather Cæsar were living and die all slaves, than that Cæsar were dead, to live all free men? . . . iii 2 25

Live. Live, Brutus! live, live!—Bring him with triumph home *J. Cæsar* iii 2 53
The evil that men do lives after them . . . iii 2 80
About! Seek! Burn! Fire! Kill! Slay! Let not a traitor live! . iii 2 209
Prick him down, Antony.—Upon condition Publius shall not live . iv 1 4
He shall not live; look, with a spot I damn him . . . iv 1 6
If I do live, I will be good to thee . . . iv 3 265
Witness the hole you made in Cæsar's heart, Crying 'Long live! hail, Cæsar!' . . . v 1 32
O, coward that I am, to live so long, To see my best friend ta'en! . v 3 34
He shall live a man forbid . . . *Macbeth* i 3 21
Live you? or are you aught That man may question? . . . i 3 42
The thane of Cawdor lives: why do you dress me In borrow'd robes?—Who was the thane lives yet; But under heavy judgement bears that life . . . i 3 108
Wouldst thou have that Which thou esteem'st the ornament of life, And live a coward in thine own esteem? . . . i 7 43
Whiles I threat, he lives: Words to the heat of deeds too cold breath gives ii 1 60
That death and nature do contend about them, Whether they live or die ii 2 8
Dear wife! Thou know'st that Banquo, and his Fleance, lives . . iii 2 37
I hear Macduff lives in disgrace: sir, can you tell Where he bestows himself? . . . iii 6 23
The son of Duncan . . . Lives in the English court . . . iii 6 26
For none of woman born Shall harm Macbeth.—Then live, Macduff . iv 1 82
I'll make assurance double sure, And take a bond of fate: thou shalt not live . . . iv 1 84
Shall live the lease of nature, pay his breath To time and mortal custom iv 1 99
How will you live?—As birds do, mother.—What, with worms and flies? iv 2 31
Fit to govern! No, not to live. O nation miserable! . . . iv 3 103
Then yield thee, coward, And live to be the show and gaze o' the time . v 8 24
Stand, and unfold yourself.—Long live the king! . . . *Hamlet* i 1 3
All that lives must die, Passing through nature to eternity . . . i 2 72
'Tis very strange.—As I do live, my honour'd lord, 'tis true . . . i 2 221
All alone shall live Within the book and volume of my brain . . . i 5 102
On fortune's cap we are not the very button. Nor the soles of her shoe?—Neither, my lord.—Then you live about her waist? . . . ii 2 236
If it live in your memory, begin at this line . . . ii 2 470
You were better have a bad epitaph than their ill report while you live ii 2 551
Those that are married already, all but one, shall live . . . iii 1 155
And thou shalt live in this fair world behind, Honour'd, beloved . . iii 2 185
To keep those many many bodies safe That live and feed upon your majesty . . . iii 3 10
Nay, but to live In the rank sweat of an enseamed bed . . . iii 4 91
O, throw away the worser part of it, And live the purer with the other half . . . iii 4 158
I do not know Why yet I live to say 'This thing's to do;' Sith I have cause and will and strength and means To do't . . . iv 4 44
The queen his mother Lives almost by his looks . . . iv 7 12
It warms the very sickness in my heart, That I shall live and tell him iv 7 57
There lives within the very flame of love A kind of wick or snuff . iv 7 115
What a wounded name, Things standing thus unknown, shall live behind me! . . . v 2 356
I cannot live to hear the news from England . . . v 2 365
Freedom lives hence, and banishment is here . . . *Lear* i 1 184
And live the beloved of your brother . . . i 2 57
If she must teem, Create her child of spleen; that it may live, And be a thwart disnatured torment to her! . . . i 4 304
When slanders do not live in tongues; Nor cutpurses come not to throngs iii 2 87
He that will think to live till he be old, Give me some help! . . . iii 7 69
If she live long, And in the end meet the old course of death, Women will all turn monsters . . . iii 7 100
To be worst, The lowest and most dejected thing of fortune, Stands still in esperance, lives not in fear . . . iv 1 4
Might I but live to see thee in my touch, I'ld say I had eyes again! . iv 1 25
I live To thank thee for the love thou show'dst the king . . . iv 2 95
It was great ignorance, Gloucester's eyes being out, To let him live . iv 5 10
If Edgar live, O, bless him! Now, fellow, fare thee well . . . iv 6 40
How shall I live and work, To match thy goodness? . . . iv 7 1
So we'll live, And pray, and sing, and tell old tales, and laugh . . v 3 11
I know when one is dead, and when one lives . . . v 3 260
If that her breath will mist or stain the stone, Why, then she lives . v 3 263
This feather stirs: she lives! if it be so, It is a chance which does redeem all sorrows That ever I have felt . . . v 3 265
We that are young Shall never see so much, nor live so long . . . v 3 326
That I did love the Moor to live with him, My downright violence and storm of fortunes May trumpet to the world . . . *Othello* i 3 249
It is silliness to live when to live is torment . . . i 3 309
Long live she so! and long live you to think so! . . . iii 3 226
I had rather be a toad, And live upon the vapour of a dungeon . . iii 3 271
My friend is dead; 'tis done at your request: But let her live . . iii 3 475
Ay, let her rot, and perish, and be damned to-night; for she shall not live iv 1 192
How does Lieutenant Cassio?—Lives, sir . . . iv 1 235
But there, where I have garner'd up my heart, Where either I must live, or bear no life . . . iv 2 58
Live Roderigo, He calls me to a restitution large . . . v 1 14
Kill me to-morrow: let me live to-night!—Nay, if you strive . . v 2 80
Did he live now, This sight would make him do a desperate turn . . v 2 206
I'ld have thee live; For, in my sense, 'tis happiness to die . . . v 2 289
The tears live in an onion that should water this sorrow *Ant. and Cleo.* i 2 176
Let her live To join our kingdoms and our hearts . . . ii 2 153
If thou say Antony lives, is well, Or friends with Cæsar, or not captive to him, I'll set thee in a shower of gold . . . ii 5 43
It lives by that which nourisheth it; and the elements once out of it, it transmigrates . . . ii 7 49
Lord of his fortunes he salutes thee, and Requires to live in Egypt . iii 12 12
If that thy father live, let him repent Thou wast not made his daughter iii 13 134
I will live, Or bathe my dying honour in the blood Shall make it live again . . . iv 2 5
'Tis well thou'rt gone, If it be well to live . . . iv 12 40
Lives he? Wilt thou not answer, man? . . . iv 14 114
Woe, woe are we, sir, you may not live to wear All your true followers out . . . iv 14 133
Cæsar cannot live To be ungentle . . . v 1 59
Not comforted to live, But that there is this jewel in the world That I may see again . . . *Cymbeline* i 1 90
Should we be taking leave As long a term as yet we have to live, The loathness to depart would grow . . . i 1 107
Should he make me Live, like Diana's priest, betwixt cold sheets? . . i 6 133
Blessed live you long! A lady to the worthiest sir! . . . i 6 159
Julius Cæsar, whose remembrance yet Lives in men's eyes . . . iii 1 3
Why, good fellow, What shall I do the while? where bide? how live? . iii 4 131

Live. Nor measure our good minds By this rude place we live in *Cymb.* iii 6 66
Long live Cæsar! . . . . iii 7 10
Whilst summer lasts and I live here, Fidele, I'll sweeten thy sad grave iv 2 219
I am merrier to die than thou art to live . . . . . . v 4 176
Yet, on my conscience, there are verier knaves desire to live . . . v 4 209
The liver, heart and brain of Britain, By whom I grant she lives . v 5 15
A Roman with a Roman's heart can suffer: Augustus lives to think on't v 5 82
I know not why, wherefore, To say 'live, boy:' ne'er thank thy master; live . . . . v 5 96
Speak, Wilt have him live? Is he thy kin? thy friend? . . . v 5 111
I had rather thou shouldst live while nature will Than die ere I hear more v 5 151
Live, And deal with others better.—Nobly doom'd! . . . . v 5 419
How they may be, and yet in two, As you will live, resolve it you *Pericles* i 1 71
He must not live to trumpet forth my infamy . . . . . i 1 145
Prince Pericles is fled.—As thou Wilt live, fly after . . . . i 1 163
In our orbs we'll live so sound and safe . . . . . . i 2 122
I marvel how the fishes live in the sea.—Why, as men do a-land . ii 1 29
Princes in this should live like gods above, Who freely give to every one ii 3 59
If the prince do live, let us salute him . . . . . . ii 4 27
If in the world he live, we'll seek him out; If in his grave he rest, we'll find him there; And be resolved he lives to govern us, Or dead, give's cause to mourn his funeral . . . . ii 4 29
Live, noble Helicane!—For honour's cause, forbear your suffrages . ii 4 40
Live, And make us weep to hear your fate, fair creature . . iii 2 103
Three or four thousand chequins were as pretty a proportion to live quietly iv 2 29
You are light in my hands, where you are like to live . . . . iv 2 78
Ay, and you shall live in pleasure . . . . iv 2 81
To weep that you live as ye do makes pity in your lovers . . iv 2 129
To use one language in each several clime Where our scenes seem to live iv 4 7
Where do you live?—Where I am but a stranger . . . . v 1 114
Live alone. And live alone as secret as I may . . *2 Hen. VI.* iv 4 48
Live at jar. Were't not a shame, that whilst you live at jar, The fearful French, whom you late vanquished, Should make a start o'er seas and vanquish you? . . . . iv 8 43
Live at peace. That my most jealous and too doubtful soul May live at peace . . . . *T. Night* iv 3 28
Live creature. Will make or man or woman madly dote Upon the next live creature that it sees . . . . . . *M. N. Dream* ii 1 172
Live in bliss. That cuckold lives in bliss Who, certain of his fate, loves not his wronger . . . . *Othello* iii 3 167
Live in brass. Shall witness live in brass of this day's work . *Hen. V.* iv 3 97
Men's evil manners live in brass; their virtues We write in water *Hen. VIII.* iv 2 45
Live in hope. But shall I live in hope?—All men, I hope, live so *Rich. III.* i 2 200
Live in peace. Peace be to England, if that war return From France to England, there to live in peace . . . . . . *K. John* ii 1 90
But ere the crown he looks for live in peace, Ten thousand bloody crowns of mothers' sons . . . . *Richard II.* iii 3 95
In dreadful war mayst thou be overcome, Or live in peace abandon'd! *3 Hen. VI.* i 1 188
Lived. Give thanks you have lived so long . . . . *Tempest* i 1 27
I have lived fourscore years and upward . . . *Mer. Wives* iii 1 56
Now let me die, for I have lived long enough: this is the period of my ambition . . . . iii 3 46
Have I lived to be carried in a basket, like a barrow of butcher's offal . iii 5 4
Have I lived to stand at the taunt of one that makes fritters of English? v 5 150
I loved thy brother: if the old fantastical duke of dark corners had been at home, he had lived . . . . . . *Meas. for Meas.* iv 3 165
He should have lived, Save that his riotous youth, with dangerous sense, Might in the times to come have ta'en revenge . . . . iv 4 31
Would yet he had lived! Alack, when once our grace we have forgot, Nothing goes right: we would, and we would not . . . iv 4 35
Look, if it please you, on this man condemn'd, As if my brother lived . v 1 450
With her I lived in joy; our wealth increased . . . *Com. of Errors* i 1 40
More moving-delicate and full of life, Into the eye and prospect of his soul, Than when she lived indeed . . . . . *Much Ado* iv 1 232
An old instance, Beatrice, that lived in the time of good neighbours . v 2 79
And when I lived, I was your other wife . . . . . . v 4 60
She died, my lord, but whiles her slander lived . . . . . v 4 66
O, they have lived long on the alms-basket of words . . *L. L. Lost* v 1 41
You have lived in desolation here, Unseen, unvisited, much to our shame v 2 357
When in the world I lived, I was the world's commander . . v 2 565
The fairest dame That lived, that loved, that liked . . *M. N. Dream* v 1 299
From seventeen years till now almost fourscore Here lived I, but now live here no more . . . . *As Y. Like It* ii 3 72
Leander, he would have lived many a fair year, though Hero had turned nun, if it had not been for a hot midsummer night . . . . iv 1 101
And he did render him the most unnatural That lived amongst men . iv 3 124
He was skilful enough to have lived still, if knowledge could be set up against mortality . . . . *All's Well* i 1 34
To a strong mast that lived upon the sea . . . . . *T. Night* i 2 14
When my old wife lived, upon This day she was both pantler, butler, cook . . . . *W. Tale* iv 4 55
If I might die within this hour, I have lived To die when I desire . . iv 4 472
As she lived peerless, So her dead likeness, I do well believe, Excels . v 3 14
Which lets go by some sixteen years and makes her As she lived now . v 3 32
Make't manifest where she has lived, Or how stolen from the dead . v 3 114
Tell me, mine own, Where hast thou been preserved? where lived? . v 3 124
When that my father lived, Your brother did employ my father much *K. John* i 1 95
They might have lived to bear and he to taste Their fruits of duty *Richard II.* iii 4 62
Lived well and in good compass . . . . . *1 Hen. IV.* iii 3 21
I never see thy face but I think upon hell-fire and Dives that lived in purple . . . . iii 3 36
They that, when Richard lived, would have him die, Are now become enamour'd on his grave . . . . *2 Hen. IV.* i 3 101
I have not lived all this while, to have swaggering now . . . . ii 4 84
The man that once did sell the lion's skin While the beast lived, was killed with hunting him . . . . *Hen. V.* iv 3 94
Small time, but in that small most greatly lived This star of England Epil. 5
She hath lived too long, To fill the world with vicious qualities *1 Hen. VI.* v 4 34
His eye-balls further out than when he lived . . *2 Hen. VI.* iii 2 169
And then it lived in sweet Elysium . . . . iii 2 399
He durst not sit there, had your father lived . . . . *3 Hen. VI.* i 1 63
For who lived king, but I could dig his grave? . . . . . v 2 21
Hadst thou been kill'd when first thou didst presume, Thou hadst not lived to kill a son of mine . . . . v 6 36
I have bewept a worthy husband's death, And lived by looking on his images: But now two mirrors of his princely semblance Are crack'd *Richard III.* ii 2 50
Lived. I'll win our ancient right in France again, Or die a soldier, as I lived a king . . . . *Richard III.* iii 1 93
He lived from all attainder of suspect . . . . iii 5 32
He was the covert'st shelter'd traitor That ever lived . . . . iii 5 34
Yet within these five hours lived Lord Hastings, Untainted, unexamined iii 6 8
His highness having lived so long with her, and she So good a lady *Hen. VIII.* ii 3 2
No Latin; I am not such a truant since my coming, As not to know the language I have lived in . . . . iii 1 44
Have I lived thus long . . . a wife, a true one? . . . . . . iii 1 125
Whiles here he lived Upon this naughty earth . . . . . v 1 137
I have lived To see inherited my very wishes . . . . *Coriolanus* ii 1 214
My noble father, The wofull'st man that ever lived in Rome *T. Andron.* iii 1 290
And pity 'tis you lived at odds so long . . . . *Rom. and Jul.* i 2 5
Is't possible the world should so much differ, And we alive that lived? Fly, damned baseness, To him that worships thee! . *T. of Athens* iii 1 50
Have I once lived to see two honest men? . . . . . . v 1 59
Thou art the ruins of the noblest man That ever lived . . *J. Cæsar* iii 1 257
When Cæsar lived, he durst not thus have moved me . . . iv 3 58
Hath Cassius lived To be but mirth and laughter to his Brutus? . . iv 3 113
Had I but died an hour before this chance, I had lived a blessed time *Macb.* ii 3 97
Oftener upon her knees than on her feet, Died every day she lived . iv 3 111
I have lived long enough: my way of life Is fall'n into the sear, the yellow leaf . . . . v 3 22
Has paid a soldier's debt: He only lived but till he was a man . . v 8 40
And those that would make mows at him while my father lived, give twenty, forty, fifty, an hundred ducats a-piece for his picture in little . . . . *Hamlet* ii 2 382
Look, how it steals away! My father, in his habit as he lived! . . . iii 4 135
Rogue, thou hast lived too long . . . . . . *Ant. and Cleo.* ii 5 73
I have lived in such dishonour, that the gods Detest my baseness . iv 14 56
Welcome, welcome! die where thou hast lived: Quicken with kissing iv 15 38
My former fortunes Wherein I lived, the greatest prince o' the world . iv 15 54
His delights Were dolphin-like; they show'd his back above The element they lived in . . . . v 2 90
O Cæsar, This Charmian lived but now; she stood and spake . . v 2 344
Lived in court—Which rare it is to do—most praised, most loved *Cymbeline* i 1 46
Where I have lived at honest freedom, paid More pious debts to heaven iii 3 71
May drive us to a render Where we have lived . . . . . iv 4 12
Gods! if you should have ta'en vengeance on my faults, I never Had lived to put on this . . . . v 1 9
A nobler sir ne'er lived 'Twixt sky and ground . . . . . v 5 145
Know this of me, Antiochus from incest lived not free . . *Pericles* ii 4 2
Livedst. If thou wert the ass, thy dulness would torment thee, and still thou livedst but as a breakfast to the wolf . . . *T. of Athens* iv 3 335
Livelier. Artificial strife Lives in these touches, livelier than life . . i 1 38
Livelihood. The tyranny of her sorrows takes all livelihood from her cheek. No more of this, Helena . . . . *All's Well* i 1 58
Livelong. Upon a lazy bed the livelong day . . . *Troi. and Cres.* i 3 147
There have sat The livelong day, with patient expectation . *J. Cæsar* i 1 46
The obscure bird Clamour'd the livelong night . . . *Macbeth* ii 3 65
Lively. Which I so lively acted with my tears . . . *T. G. of Ver* iv 4 174
Some lively touches of my daughter's favour . . . *As Y. Like It* v 4 27
As lively painted as the deed was done . . . *T. of Shrew* Ind. 2 58
O, that record is lively in my soul! . . . . *T. Night* v 1 253
Prepare To see the life as lively mock'd as ever Still sleep mock'd death *W. Tale* v 3 19
What shall I do Now I behold thy lively body so? . . *T. Andron.* iii 1 105
A pattern, precedent, and lively warrant . . . . . . v 3 44
His cousin Tybalt; Lucio and the lively Helena . . *Rom. and Jul.* i 2 73
Thou counterfeit'st most lively . . . . *T. of Athens* v 1 85
Liver. I warrant you, sir; The white cold virgin snow upon my heart Abates the ardour of my liver . . . . *Tempest* iv 1 56
Love my wife!—With liver burning hot . . . . *Mer. Wives* ii 1 121
Then shall he mourn, If ever love had interest in his liver *Much Ado* iv 1 233
Let my liver rather heat with wine Than my heart cool . *Mer. of Venice* i 1 81
Who, inward search'd, have livers white as milk . . . . . iii 2 86
To wash your liver as clean as a sound sheep's heart . *As Y. Like It* iii 2 443
Liver, brain and heart, These sovereign thrones . . . *T. Night* i 1 37
Their love may be call'd appetite, No motion of the liver, but the palate ii 4 101
This wins him, liver and all . . . . ii 5 106
To put fire in your heart, and brimstone in your liver . . . . iii 2 22
If . . . you find so much blood in his liver as will clog the foot of a flea iii 2 66
Were my wife's liver Infected as her life, she would not live The running of one glass.—Who does infect her? . . . . . . *W. Tale* i 2 304
What think you they portend?—Hot livers and cold purses . *1 Hen. IV.* ii 4 355
You do measure the heat of our livers with the bitterness of your galls *2 Hen. IV.* i 2 198
Left the liver white and pale, which is the badge of pusillanimity . iv 3 113
I will inflame thy noble liver, And make thee rage . . . . . v 5 33
'Tis better to be lowly born, And range with humble livers in content *Hen. VIII.* ii 3 20
Reason and respect Make livers pale and lustihood deject *Troi. and Cres.* ii 2 50
Dirt-rotten livers, wheezing lungs . . . . v 1 24
More abhorr'd Than spotted livers in the sacrifice . . . . . v 3 18
Cheerly, boys; be brisk awhile, and the longer liver take all . *R. and J.* i 5 17
Liver of blaspheming Jew, Gall of goat, and slips of yew . . *Macbeth* iv 1 26
I had rather heat my liver with drinking . . . *Ant. and Cleo.* i 2 23
Hail, thou fair heaven! We house i' the rock, yet use thee not so hardly As prouder livers do . . . . *Cymbeline* iii 3 9
Prithee, think There's livers out of Britain . . . . . . iii 4 143
Which I will add To you, the liver, heart and brain of Britain . . v 5 14
Liver-vein. This is the liver-vein, which makes flesh a deity . *L. L. Lost* iv 3 74
Livery. It appears, by their bare liveries, that they live by your bare words . . . . *T. G. of Ver.* ii 4 46
Show it now, By putting on the destined livery . . *Meas. for Meas.* ii 4 138
'Tis the cunning livery of hell, The damned'st body to invest and cover iii 1 95
Endure the livery of a nun, For aye to be in shady cloister *M. N. Dream* i 1 70
The childing autumn, angry winter, change Their wonted liveries . . ii 1 113
Mislike me not for my complexion, The shadow'd livery of the burnish'd sun, To whom I am a neighbour . . . . . . *Mer. of Venice* ii 1 2
Master Bassanio, who, indeed, gives rare new liveries . . . . ii 2 117
See these letters delivered; put the liveries to making . . . . ii 2 124
Give him a livery More guarded than his fellows' . . . . . ii 2 163
A noble scar is a good livery of honour . . . . . *All's Well* iv 5 106
By his attorneys-general to sue His livery . . . . *Richard II.* ii 1 204
I am denied to sue my livery here, And yet my letters-patents give me leave . . . . ii 3 129
To sue his livery and beg his peace . . . . . *1 Hen. IV.* iv 3 62
If I had had time to have made new liveries, I would have bestowed the thousand pound I borrowed of you . . . . . *2 Hen. IV.* v 5 11

Livery. I will apparel them all in one livery . . . . 2 *Hen. VI.* iv 2 80
And to achieve The silver livery of advised age . . . . v 2 47
It is our way, If we will keep in favour with the king, To be her men and wear her livery . . . . *Richard III.* i 1 80
Her vestal livery is but sick and green . . . *Rom. and Jul.* ii 2 8
Here comes my man.—But I'll be hang'd, sir, if he wear your livery . iii 1 60
Yet do our hearts wear Timon's livery . . . *T. of Athens* iv 2 17
The stamp of one defect, Being nature's livery, or fortune's star *Hamlet* i 4 32
To the use of actions fair and good He likewise gives a frock or livery . . . . iii 4 164
For youth no less becomes The light and careless livery that it wears . iv 7 80
In his livery Walk'd crowns and crownets . . . *Ant. and Cleo.* v 2 90
A base slave, A hilding for a livery, a squire's cloth . *Cymbeline* ii 3 128
One twelve moons more she'll wear Diana's livery . . *Pericles* ii 5 10
A vestal livery will I take me to, And never more have joy . . iii 4 10
A maid-child call'd Marina; who, O goddess, Wears yet thy silver livery . . . . v 3 7
Lives. We are merely cheated of our lives by drunkards . . *Tempest* i 1 59
We cite our faults, That they may hold excused our lawless lives *T. G. of Ver.* iv 1 54
Wanting guilders to redeem their lives . . *Com. of Errors* i 1 8
Let fame, that all hunt after in their lives, Live register'd upon our brazen tombs And then grace us . . . . . *L. L. Lost* i 1 1
An we do not, it is pity of our lives . . . *T. Night* ii 5 15
Bastards, and else.—To verify our title with their lives . . *K. John* ii 1 277
Rescue those breathing lives to die in beds . . . . ii 1 419
Even with a treacherous fine of all your lives . . . . v 4 38
Be ready, as your lives shall answer it . . . *Richard II.* i 1 198
More are men's ends mark'd than their lives before . . . ii 1 11
That will the king severely prosecute 'Gainst us, our lives, our children ii 1 245
I will not vex your souls—Since presently your souls must part your bodies—With too much urging your pernicious lives . . . iii 1 4
Our lands, our lives, and all are Bolingbroke's, And nothing can we call our own but death . . . . iii 2 151
Our holy lives must win a new world's crown . . . . v 1 24
How sour sweet music is, When time is broke and no proportion kept! So is it in the music of men's lives . . . . . v 5 44
Wilfully betray'd The lives of those that he did lead to fight . 1 *Hen. IV.* i 3 82
Suspicion all our lives shall be stuck full of eyes . . . v 2 8
The lives of all your loving complices Lean on your health . 2 *Hen. IV.* i 1 163
It may chance cost some of us our lives, for he will stab . . ii 1 13
There is a history in all men's lives, Figuring the nature of the times deceased . . . . iii 1 80
Then threw he down himself and all their lives . . . iv 1 127
And their memory Shall as a pattern or a measure live, By which his grace must mete the lives of others . . . . . iv 4 77
That owe yourselves, your lives and services To this imperial throne *Hen. V.* i 2 34
The knocks are too hot; and, for mine own part, I have not a case of lives . . . . iii 2 5
Therefore, great king, We yield our town and lives to thy soft mercy . iii 3 48
So should he be sure to be ransomed, and a many poor men's lives saved iv 1 128
Let us our lives, our souls, Our debts, our careful wives, Our children and our sins lay on the king! We must bear all . . . iv 1 247
Let us on heaps go offer up our lives . . . . . iv 5 18
I lost my liberty and they their lives . . . . 1 *Hen. VI.* ii 5 81
This seven years did not Talbot see his son; And now they meet where both their lives are done . . . . . . iv 3 38
Whiles they each other cross, Lives, honours, lands and all hurry to loss . . . . iv 3 53
Too much folly is it, well I wot, To hazard all our lives in one small boat! . . . . iv 6 33
It dies, an if it had a thousand lives . . . . . v 4 75
We'll take her from the sheriff.—No, stir not, for your lives . 2 *Hen. VI.* ii 4 18
Die you shall: The lives of those which we have lost in fight, Be counter-poised with such a petty sum! . . . . . . iv 1 21
Fight for your king, your country and your lives . . . iv 5 12
Soldiers, this day have you redeem'd your lives . . . iv 9 15
I'll have more lives Than drops of blood were in my father's veins 3 *Hen. VI.* i 1 96
Had I thy brethren here, their lives and thine Were not revenge sufficient . . . . i 3 25
So desperate thieves, all hopeless of their lives, Breathe out invectives i 4 42
Offering their own lives in their young's defence . . . ii 2 32
These words will cost ten thousand lives this day . . . ii 2 177
If you contend, a thousand lives must wither . . . . ii 5 102
And yet I know not how to get the crown, For many lives stand between . . . . iii 2 173
Both Dukes of Somerset Have sold their lives unto the house of York . v 1 74
Dispatch; the limit of your lives is out . . . *Richard III.* iii 3 8
Therefore level not to hit their lives . . . . . iv 4 202
Lo, at their births good stars were opposite.—No, to their lives bad friends were contrary . . . . iv 4 216
These famish'd beggars, weary of their lives . . . . v 3 329
After so many hours, lives, speeches spent . . *Troi. and Cres.* ii 2 1
Where he did Run reeking o'er the lives of men . . *Coriolanus* ii 2 123
Here comes a parcel of our hopeful booty, Which dreads not yet their lives' destruction . . . . . . *T. Andron.* ii 3 50
Ready at your highness' will To answer their suspicion with their lives ii 3 298
My youth can better spare my blood than you; And therefore mine shall save my brothers' lives . . . . iii 1 167
Your lives shall pay the forfeit of the peace . . *Rom. and Jul.* i 1 104
What wouldst thou have with me?—Good king of cats, nothing but one of your nine lives . . . . iii 1 81
Methinks they should invite them without knives; Good for their meat, and safer for their lives . . . . . *T. of Athens* i 2 46
Make thine epitaph, That death in me at others' lives may laugh . iv 3 381
Take wealth and lives together; Do villany, do, since you protest to do't . . . . iv 3 436
We shall, my lord, Perform what you command us.—Though our lives—Your spirits shine through you . . . . *Macbeth* iii 1 127
And good men's lives Expire before the flowers in their caps . . iv 3 171
Whiles I see lives, the gashes Do better upon them . . . . v 8 2
That spirit upon whose weal depend and rest The lives of many *Hamlet* iii 3 15
He may enguard his dotage with their powers, And hold our lives in mercy . . . . *Lear* i 4 350
Keep peace, upon your lives: He dies that strikes again . . ii 2 52
O, our lives' sweetness! That we the pain of death would hourly die Rather than die at once! . . . . v 3 184
If the balance of our lives had not one scale of reason . . . *Othello* i 3 330
Lives. 'Zounds, I bleed still; I am hurt to the death.—Hold, for your lives! . . . . *Othello* ii 3 165
O, that the slave had forty thousand lives! One is too poor, too weak for my revenge . . . . iii 3 442
Had all his hairs been lives, my great revenge Had stomach for them all v 2 74
I care not for thy sword; I'll make thee known, Though I lost twenty lives . . . . v 2 166
Not a minute of our lives should stretch Without some pleasure now *Ant. and Cleo.* i 1 46
It only stands Our lives upon to use our strongest hands . . ii 1 51
When mine hours Were nice and lucky, men did ransom lives Of me for jests . . . . iii 13 180
What have we to lose, But that he swore to take, our lives? . *Cymbeline* iv 2 125
No reason I, since of your lives you set So slight a valuation, should reserve My crack'd one to more care . . . . . iv 4 48
Since the gods Will have it thus, that nothing but our lives May be call'd ransom, let it come . . . . v 5 79
Lords and ladies in their lives Have read it for restoratives *Pericles* i Gower 7
Livest. But, while thou livest, keep a good tongue in thy head *Tempest* iii 2 120
'Tis pity that thou livest To walk where any honest men resort *C. of Er.* v 1 27
As thou shalt think on prating whilst thou livest! . . *T. of Shrew* iv 3 114
Though thou livest and breathest, Yet art thou slain in him *Richard II.* i 2 24
So as thou livest in peace, die free from strife . . . . v 6 27
Whilst thou livest, dear Kate, take a fellow of plain and uncoined constancy . . . . *Hen. V.* v 2 160
Yet livest thou, Salisbury? though thy speech doth fail . 1 *Hen. VI.* i 4 82
Myself no joy in nought but that thou livest . . . 2 *Hen. VI.* iii 2 366
Confirm the crown to me and to mine heirs, And thou shalt reign in quiet while thou livest.—I am content . . . . 3 *Hen. VI.* i 1 173
Thy friends suspect for traitors while thou livest! . . *Richard III.* i 3 223
No warmth, no breath, shall testify thou livest . . *Rom. and Jul.* iv 1 98
Horatio, I am dead; Thou livest; report me and my cause aright *Hamlet* v 2 350
O wretched fool, That livest to make thine honesty a vice! . *Othello* iii 3 376
If thou livest, Pericles, thou hast a heart That even cracks for woe! *Pericles* iii 2 76
Perform my bidding, or thou livest in woe; Do it, and happy . . v 1 248
Liveth. But to counterfeit dying, when a man thereby liveth, is to be no counterfeit . . . . 1 *Hen. IV.* v 4 119
Her mother liveth yet, can testify She was the first fruit . 1 *Hen. VI.* v 4 12
To prove him tyrant this reason may suffice, That Henry liveth still 3 *Hen. VI.* iii 3 72
Livia. My fair niece Rosaline; Livia; Signior Valentio . *Rom. and Jul.* i 2 72
Some nobler token I have kept apart For Livia and Octavia *Ant. and Cleo.* v 2 169
Living. Sends me forth—For else his project dies—to keep them living *Tempest* ii 1 299
And art thou living, Stephano? O Stephano, two Neapolitans 'scaped! ii 2 117
But how should Prospero Be living and be here? . . . . v 1 120
That they were living both in Naples, The king and queen there! . . v 1 149
Living dully sluggardized at home, Wear out thy youth . *T. G. of Ver.* i 1 7
Then may I set the world on wheels, when she can spin for her living . iii 1 318
Canst thou believe thy living is a life, So stinkingly depending? *M. for M.* iii 2 27
Are you yet living?—Is it possible disdain should die while she hath such meet food to feed it? . . . . . . *Much Ado* i 1 120
There were no living near her; she would infect to the north star . . ii 1 257
I am as honest as any man living that is an old man and no honester iii 5 16
In so high a style, Margaret, that no man living shall come over it . v 2 7
I pine and die; With all these living in philosophy . . *L. L. Lost* i 1 32
Now, God save thy life!—And yours from long living! . . . ii 1 192
It were pity you should get your living by reckoning . . . v 2 498
There is not a more fearful wild-fowl than your lion living *M. N. Dream* iii 1 34
That only to stand high in your account, I might in virtues, beauties, livings, friends, Exceed account . . . . *Mer. of Venice* iii 2 158
Sweet lady, you have given me life and living . . . . v 1 286
There is not one so young and so villanous this day living *As Y. Like It* i 1 161
Enforce A thievish living on the common road . . . . ii 3 33
His effigies witness Most truly limn'd and living in your face . ii 7 194
Bring him dead or living . . . . iii 1 6
Turn thou no more To seek a living in our territory . . . iii 1 8
To get your living by the copulation of cattle . . . . iii 2 84
Would, for the king's sake, he were living! I think it would be the death of the king's disease . . . . . *All's Well* i 1 24
Moderate lamentation is the right of the dead, excessive grief the enemy to the living.—If the living be enemy to the grief, the excess makes it soon mortal . . . . i 1 65
There is no living, none, If Bertram be away . . . . i 1 95
If he were living, I would try him yet. Lend me an arm . . i 2 72
O my dear mother, do I see you living?—Mine eyes smell onions . v 3 320
I my brother know Yet living in my glass . . . *T. Night* iii 4 415
There is no lady living So meet for this great errand . *W. Tale* ii 2 45
Within a mile where my land and living lies . . . . iv 3 104
Whom he loves—He bade me say so—more than all the sceptres And those that bear them living . . . . v 1 147
That she is living, Were it but told you, should be hooted at . . v 3 115
Good lords, although my will to give is living, The suit which you demand is gone and dead . . . . . *K. John* iv 2 83
Should dying men flatter with those that live?—No, no, men living flatter those that die . . . . . . *Richard II.* ii 1 89
The Duke of Lancaster is dead.—And living too; for now his son is duke . . . . ii 1 225
But here is Carlisle living, to abide Thy kingly doom . . . v 6 22
Where is he living, clipp'd in with the sea? . . 1 *Hen. IV.* iii 1 44
But will it [honour] not live with the living? no. Why? . . . v 1 141
I have made him sure.—He is, indeed; and living to kill thee . . v 3 49
Let us to the highest of the field, To see what friends are living . v 4 165
Douglas is living, and your brother, yet; But, for my lord your son,—Why, he is dead . . . . . . 2 *Hen. IV.* i 1 82
Death is certain. Is old Double of your town living yet?—Dead, sir . iii 2 46
And I had many living to upbraid My gain of it by their assistances iv 5 193
Therefore, living hence, did give ourself To barbarous license *Hen. V.* i 2 270
And my life, and my living, and my uttermost power . . iii 6 9
We are enow yet living in the field To smother up the English . iv 5 19
Is Talbot slain? then I will slay myself, For living idly here 1 *Hen. VI.* i 1 142
If he revenge it not, yet will his friends; So will the queen, that living held him dear . . . . . . 2 *Hen. VI.* iv 1 147
Great God, how just art Thou! O, let me view his visage, being dead, That living wrought me such exceeding trouble . . . . v 1 70
I may conquer fortune's spite By living low . . . 3 *Hen. VI.* iv 6 20
But, tell me, is young George Stanley living?—He is, my lord *Rich. III.* v 5 9
Think ye see The very persons of our noble story As they were living; think you see them great . . . . . . *Hen. VIII.* Prol. 27

Living. That what he spoke My chaplain to no creature living, but To me, should utter . . . . *Hen. VIII.* i 2 166
Wretched lady! I am the most unhappy woman living . . . . iii 1 147
No man living Could say 'This is my wife' there . . . . iv 1 79
Whom I most hated living, thou hast made me, With thy religious truth and modesty, Now in his ashes honour . . . . . iv 2 73
Nor is there living, I speak it with a single heart, my lords, A man that more detests, . . . Defacers of a public peace . . . . . v 3 37
Few now living can behold that goodness—A pattern to all princes living . . . . v 5 23
That brought you forth this boy, to keep your name Living to time *Cor.* v 3 127
Then, dreadful trumpet, sound the general doom! For who is living, if those two are gone? . . . . . . *Rom. and Jul.* iii 2 68
Is dead; or 'twere as good he were, As living here and you no use of him iii 5 227
I will die, And leave him all; life, living, all is Death's . . . iv 5 40
The most needless creatures living, should we ne'er have use for 'em *T. of Athens* i 2 101
All thy living Is 'mongst the dead . . . . i 2 229
When there is nothing living but thee, thou shalt be welcome . . iv 3 360
Duty and zeal to your unmatched mind, Care of your food and living . iv 3 524
My long sickness Of health and living now begins to mend . . . v 1 190
Nor are they living Who were the motives that you first went out . v 4 26
Mark Antony shall not love Cæsar dead So well as Brutus living *J. C.* iii 1 134
Had you rather Cæsar were living and die all slaves, than that Cæsar were dead, to live all free men? . . . . iii 2 24
Is not that he that lies upon the ground?—He lies not like the living . v 3 58
Are yet two Romans living such as these? . . . . . . v 3 98
Sure I am two men there are not living To whom he more adheres *Hamlet* ii 2 20
If I gave them all my living, I'ld keep my coxcombs myself . . *Lear* i 4 120
You or any man living may be drunk at a time, man . . *Othello* ii 3 318
That lady is not now living, or this gentleman's opinion by this worn out.—She holds her virtue still . . . . . *Cymbeline* i 4 67
And cowards living To die with lengthen'd shame . . . . . v 3 12
He hath been search'd among the dead and living, But no trace of him v 5 11
Since she is living, let the time run on To good or bad . . . v 5 128
Here's all that is left living of your queen, A little daughter . *Pericles* iii 1 20
Living actions. After my death I wish no other herald, No other speaker of my living actions . . . . *Hen. VIII.* iv 2 70
Living art. Still and contemplative in living art . . . *L. L. Lost* i 1 14
Living blood. How comes it then that thou art call'd a king, When living blood doth in these temples beat? . . . . . . *K. John* ii 1 108
Leaving me no sign, Save men's opinions and my living blood *Rich. II.* iii 1 26
Living corse. Poor living corse, closed in a dead man's tomb! *R. and J.* v 2 30
Living creature. Nor did ill turn To any living creature . *Pericles* iv 1 77
Living daughter. So is the will of a living daughter curbed by the will of a dead father . . . . *Mer. of Venice* i 2 26
Living-dead. A fortune-teller, A needy, hollow-eyed, sharp-looking wretch, A living-dead man . . . . . *Com. of Errors* v 1 241
Living death. They kill me with a living death . . . *Richard III.* i 2 153
Living drollery. What were these?—A living drollery . . *Tempest* iii 3 21
Living Edward. Drown desperate sorrow in dead Edward's grave, And plant your joys in living Edward's throne . . . . *Richard III.* ii 2 100
Living fear. Have I no friend will rid me of this living fear? *Richard II.* v 4 2
Living fire. Hath love in thy old blood no living fire? . . . . i 2 10
Living ghost. Dead life, poor mortal living ghost . . *Richard III.* iv 4 26
Living Harry. Here come the heavy issue of dead Harry: O that the living Harry had the temper Of him! . . . . . *2 Hen. IV.* v 2 15
Living humour. To a living humour of madness . . *As Y. Like It* iii 2 439
Living king. This dead king to the living king I'll bear . *Richard II.* v 5 118
Living leave. Thou takest, As from my death-bed, thy last living leave v 1 39
Living light. Darkness does the face of earth entomb, When living light should kiss it . . . . *Macbeth* ii 4 10
Living load. Æneas bare a living load, Nothing so heavy . *2 Hen. VI.* v 2 64
Living man. That ever living man of memory, Henry the Fifth *1 Hen. VI.* iv 3 51
Past patience, Or more than any living man could bear . *T. Andron.* v 3 127
Here lie I, Timon; who, alive, all living men did hate . *T. of Athens* v 4 72
Living monument. This grave shall have a living monument. *Hamlet* v 1 320
Living mortals. And shrieks like mandrakes' torn out of the earth, That living mortals, hearing them, run mad . . . . *Rom. and Jul.* iv 3 48
Living murmurers. For living murmurers There's places of rebuke. He was a fool . . . . *Hen. VIII.* ii 2 131
Living prince. For more assurance that a living prince Does now speak to thee, I embrace thy body . . . . *Tempest* v 1 108
Living reason. Give me a living reason she's disloyal . . *Othello* iii 3 409
Living torment. Why not death rather than living torment? *T. G. of V.* iii 1 170
Living woe. Compare dead happiness with living woe . *Richard III.* iv 4 119
Living women. More unfortunate than all living women . *Coriolanus* v 3 97
Lizard. Their softest touch as smart as lizards' stings! *2 Hen. VI.* iii 2 325
To be avoided, As venom toads, or lizards' dreadful stings! *3 Hen. VI.* ii 2 138
To be . . . a toad, a lizard, an owl, . . . I would not care *Troi. and Cres.* v 1 67
Adder's fork and blind-worm's sting, Lizard's leg and howlet's wing *Macb.* iv 1 17
Lo, now, lo! Here comes a spirit of his . . . . . . *Tempest* ii 2 14
Lo, how he mocks me! . . . . iii 2 34
Lo, how hollow the fiend speaks within him! . . . . *T. Night* iv 2 101
Why, lo you now, I have spoke to the purpose twice . . *W. Tale* i 2 106
Lo, now my glory smear'd in dust and blood! . . . . *3 Hen. VI.* v 2 23
Lo, you, my lord, The net has fall'n upon me! . . . *Hen. VIII.* i 1 202
But soft, behold! lo, where it comes again! . . . . . *Hamlet* i 1 126
Lo thee!—My sword is drawn.—Then let it do at once . *Ant. and Cleo.* iv 14 87
Loach. Your chamber-lie breeds fleas like a loach . . *1 Hen. IV.* ii 1 23
Load. 'Tis all men's office to speak patience To those that wring under the load of sorrow . . . . *Much Ado* v 1 28
Sooth, when I was young And handed love as you do, I was wont To load my she with knacks . . . . *W. Tale* iv 4 360
Would I were able to load him with his desert! . . . *Hen. V.* iii 7 85
Like over-ripen'd corn, Hanging the head at Ceres' plenteous load *2 Hen. VI.* i 2 2
Unburthens with his tongue The envious load that lies upon his heart . iii 1 157
But then Æneas bare a living load, Nothing so heavy as these woes of mine . . . . v 2 64
Set down, set down your honourable load . . . *Richard III.* i 2 1
Come, now towards Chertsey with your holy load . . . . . i 2 29
Heart-sorrowing peers, That bear this mutual heavy load of moan . ii 2 113
Whether I will or no, I must have patience to endure the load . . iii 7 230
And, to bear 'em, The back is sacrifice to the load . . *Hen. VIII.* i 2 50
Have you limbs To bear that load of title? . . . . . . ii 3 39
Out of pity, taken A load would sink a navy, too much honour . . iii 2 383
In the gap and trade of moe preferments, With which the time will load him . . . . v 1 37
'Tis a cruelty To load a falling man . . . . v 3 77
Load. Loads o' gravel i' the back, lethargies, cold palsies *Troi. and Cres.* v 1 22
You were used to load me With precepts . . . . . *Coriolanus* iv 1 9
Is very likely to load our purposes with what they travail for *T. of Athens* v 1 16
We lay these honours on this man, To ease ourselves of divers slanderous loads, . . . And having brought our treasure where we will, Then take we down his load, and turn him off, Like to the empty ass *J. C.* iv 1 20
Those honours deep and broad wherewith Your majesty loads our house *Macbeth* i 6 18
Hercules and his load too . . . . *Hamlet* ii 2 379
I chiefly . . . am bound To load thy merit richly . . . *Cymbeline* i 5 74
We have heard your miseries . . . : Nor come we to add sorrow to your tears, But to relieve them of their heavy load . . . . *Pericles* i 4 91
Loaden. There came A post from Wales loaden with heavy news *1 Hen. IV.* i 1 37
I have loaden me with many spoils . . . . . . *1 Hen. VI.* ii 1 80
My legs, like loaden branches, bow to the earth . . *Hen. VIII.* iv 2 2
Has cluck'd thee to the wars and safely home, Loaden with honour *Cor.* v 3 164
And when thy car is loaden with their heads, I will dismount *T. Andron.* v 2 53
The felon Loaden with irons wiser than the judge . . *T. of Athens* iii 5 50
Loading. Look on the tragic loading of this bed . . . . *Othello* v 2 363
Loaf. Easy it is Of a cut loaf to steal a shive, we know . *T. Andron.* ii 1 87
Loam. Let him have some plaster, or some loam . . . *M. N. Dream* iii 1 70
Men are but gilded loam or painted clay . . . . . *Richard II.* i 1 179
Of earth we make loam; and why of that loam, whereto he was converted, might they not stop a beer-barrel? . . . . . *Hamlet* v 1 233
Loan. Advantaging their loan with interest . . . *Richard III.* iv 4 323
For loan oft loses both itself and friend . . . . . *Hamlet* i 3 76
Loath. That, my lord, I shall be loath to do . . . *T. G. of Ver.* iii 2 39
I am very loath to be your idol, sir . . . . iv 2 129
I would be loath to turn them together . . . . *Mer. Wives* ii 1 193
To speak so indirectly I am loath . . . . . *Meas. for Meas.* iv 6 1
Hopeless to find, yet loath to leave unsought . . . *Com. of Errors* i 1 136
Although I seem so loath, I am the last that will last keep his oath *L. L. L.* i 1 160
I would be loath to have you overflown with a honey-bag *M. N. Dream* iv 1 16
I am right loath to go: There is some ill a-brewing . . *Mer. of Venice* ii 5 16
And, for your love, I would be loath to foil him . . *As Y. Like It* i 1 136
I would be loath to fall into my dreams again . . . *T. of Shrew* Ind. 2 128
But loath am to produce So bad an instrument . . . *All's Well* v 3 201
I would be loath to cast away my speech . . . . . *T. Night* i 5 184
Words are grown so false, I am loath to prove reason with them . iii 1 28
If they can but stay you Where you'll be loath to be . . *W. Tale* iv 4 583
The sun of heaven methought was loath to set . . . . *K. John* v 5 1
I'll pause; For I am loath to break our country's laws . *Richard II.* ii 3 169
I would be loath to pay him before his day . . . . *1 Hen. IV.* v 1 128
I am loath to gall a new-healed wound . . . . . *2 Hen. IV.* i 2 166
I' faith, I am loath to pawn my plate, so God save me, la! . . . ii 1 167
Since you are tongue-tied and so loath to speak, In dumb significants proclaim your thoughts . . . . *1 Hen. VI.* ii 4 25
I were loath To link with him that were not lawful chosen *3 Hen. VI.* iii 3 114
Why, then, though loath, yet must I be content . . . . . iv 6 48
I do lament the sickness of the king, As loath to lose him *Richard III.* ii 2 10
My foot-cloth horse did stumble, And startled, when he look'd upon the Tower, As loath to bear me to the slaughter-house . . . . iii 4 88
If you refuse it,—as, in love and zeal, Loath to depose the child . iii 7 209
Alas the day, how loath you are to offend daylight! . *Troi. and Cres.* iii 2 50
To my thinking, he was very loath to lay his fingers off it . *J. Cæsar* i 2 243
Like a sister am most loath to call Your faults as they are named . *Lear* i 1 273
I am loath to tell you what I would you knew . . *Ant. and Cleo.* v 2 107
Thou art some fool; I am loath to beat thee . . . *Cymbeline* iv 2 86
Loath to bid farewell, we take our leaves . . . . . *Pericles* ii 5 13
Loathe. But love will not be spurr'd to what it loathes . *T. G. of Ver.* v 2 7
O, how mine eyes do loathe his visage now! . . . *M. N. Dream* iv 1 84
But, like in sickness, did I loathe this food . . . . . . iv 1 178
For affection, Mistress of passion, sways it to the mood Of what it likes or loathes . . . . *Mer. of Venice* iv 1 52
Would now like him, now loathe him; then entertain him *As Y. Like It* iii 2 436
So lust doth play With what it loathes for that which is away *All's W.* iv 4 25
Surfeited with honey and began To loathe the taste of sweetness *1 Hen. IV.* iii 2 72
Say, I, her sovereign, am her subject love.—But she, your subject, loathes such sovereignty . . . . *Richard III.* iv 4 356
If thy revenges hunger for that food Which nature loathes *T. of Athens* v 4 33
I am abused; and my relief Must be to loathe her . . . *Othello* iii 3 268
Loathed. The weariest and most loathed worldly life . *Meas. for Meas.* iii 1 129
Thy love! out, tawny Tartar, out! Out, loathed medicine! *M. N. Dream* iii 2 264
Thou loathed issue of thy father's loins! . . . . *Richard III.* i 3 232
Seduced . . . his thoughts To base declension and loathed bigamy . iii 7 189
A woman impudent and mannish grown Is not more loathed than an effeminate man In time of action. . . . . . *Troi. and Cres.* iii 3 218
Why should our endeavour be so loved and the performance so loathed? v 10 40
Woe to her chance, and damn'd her loathed choice! . . *T. Andron.* iv 2 78
Prodigious birth of love it is to me, That I must love a loathed enemy.—What's this? what's this? . . . . *Rom. and Jul.* i 5 143
Some say the lark and loathed toad change eyes . . . . . iii 5 31
Live loathed and long, Most smiling, smooth, detested parasites! *T. of A.* iii 6 103
My snuff and loathed part of nature should Burn itself out . . *Lear* iv 6 39
His bed my goal; from the loathed warmth whereof deliver me . . iv 6 272
My father's eye Should hold her loathed and his spirits . . *Othello* iii 4 62
Nor tell the world Antiochus doth sin In such a loathed manner *Pericles* i 1 147
Loather a hundred times to part than die . . . *2 Hen. VI.* iii 2 355
Loathing. For as a surfeit of the sweetest things The deepest loathing to the stomach brings . . . . *M. N. Dream* ii 2 138
More than a lodged hate and a certain loathing . . *Mer. of Venice* iv 1 60
And shrivell'd up Their bodies, even to loathing . . . *Pericles* ii 4 10
Loathly. Sour-eyed disdain and discord shall bestrew The union of your bed with weeds so loathly That you shall hate it both . *Tempest* iv 1 21
Unfather'd heirs and loathly births of nature . . . *2 Hen. IV.* iv 4 122
Seeing how loathly opposite I stood To his unnatural purpose . *Lear* ii 1 51
Loathness. Weigh'd between loathness and obedience . . *Tempest* ii 1 130
Pray you, look not sad, Nor make replies of loathness *Ant. and Cleo.* iii 11 18
Should we be taking leave As long a term as yet we have to live, The loathness to depart would grow . . . . *Cymbeline* i 1 108
Loathsome. To make a loathsome abject scorn of me *Com. of Errors* iv 4 106
Grim death, how foul and loathsome is thine image! *T. of Shrew* Ind. 1 35
Hath esteemed him No better than a poor and loathsome beggar . Ind. 1 123
O thou dull god [sleep], why liest thou with the vile In loathsome beds? *2 Hen. IV.* iii 1 16
This loathsome sequestration have I had . . . . *1 Hen. VI.* ii 5 25
All my flowering youth Within a loathsome dungeon, there to pine . ii 5 57
Dost thou turn away and hide thy face? I am no loathsome leper *2 Hen. VI.* iii 2 75

Loathsome. As many signs of deadly hate, As lean-faced Envy in her loathsome cave . . . . . . 2 *Hen. VI.* iii 2 315
Tumble me into some loathsome pit . . . . . *T. Andron.* ii 3 176
Straight will I bring you to the loathsome pit Where I espied the panther ii 3 193
Here is the babe, as loathsome as a toad . . . . iv 2 67
The sweetest honey Is loathsome in his own deliciousness *Rom. and Jul.* ii 6 12
What with loathsome smells, And shrieks like mandrakes' . . iv 3 46
There is thy gold, worse poison to men's souls, Doing more murders in this loathsome world, Than these poor compounds . . . v 1 81
Bark'd about, Most lazar-like, with vile and loathsome crust *Hamlet* i 5 72
Loathsomeness. The loathsomeness of them offends me more *W. Tale* iv 3 59
Loathsomest. I would make thee the loathsomest scab in Greece *T. and C.* ii 1 31
Loaves. In England seven halfpenny loaves sold for a penny 2 *Hen. VI.* iv 2 71
Lob. Farewell, thou lob of spirits; I'll be gone *M. N. Dream* ii 1 16
Their poor jades Lob down their heads, dropping the hides and hips *Hen. V.* iv 2 47
Lobby. How in our voiding lobby hast thou stood? . . 2 *Hen. VI.* iv 1 61
His lobbies fill with tendance . . . . . *T. of Athens* i 1 80
Sometimes he walks four hours together Here in the lobby *Hamlet* ii 2 161
You shall nose him as you go up the stairs into the lobby . iv 3 39
Local. Gives to airy nothing A local habitation and a name *M. N. Dream* v 1 17
That I may give the local wound a name . *Troi. and Cres.* iv 5 244
Lock. Pray you, lock hand in hand . . . . *Mer. Wives* v 5 81
I should wrong it, To lock it in the wards of covert bosom *Meas. for Meas.* v 1 10
Say, wherefore didst thou lock me forth to-day? . . .—I did not, gentle husband, lock thee forth . . . *Com. of Errors* iv 4 98
I know him; a' wears a lock . . . . *Much Ado* iii 3 183
For thee I'll lock up all the gates of love . . . . iv 1 106
They say he wears a key in his ear and a lock hanging by it . . v 1 318
And shivering shocks Shall break the locks Of prison gates *M. N. Dream* i 2 35
Her sunny locks Hang on her temples like a golden fleece *Mer. of Venice* i 1 169
What, are there masques? Hear you me, Jessica: Lock up my doors . ii 5 29
Crisped snaky golden locks Which make such wanton gambols with the wind . . . . iii 2 92
Here's ado, To lock up honesty and honour! . . . *W. Tale* ii 2 10
And so locks her in embracing, as if she would pin her to her heart . v 2 83
We do lock Our former scruple in our strong-barr'd gates . *K. John* ii 1 369
And pluck up drowned honour by the locks . . 1 *Hen. IV.* i 3 205
Since we have locks to safeguard necessaries . . *Hen. V.* i 2 176
With foul hand Defile the locks of your shrill-shrieking daughters . iii 3 35
These grey locks, the pursuivants of death . . 1 *Hen. VI.* ii 5 5
Well, I will lock his counsel in my breast . . . . ii 5 118
Which will in time Break ope the locks o' the senate . *Coriolanus* iii 1 138
Locks fair daylight out And makes himself an artificial night *Rom. and Jul.* i 1 145
That book in many's eyes doth share the glory, That in gold clasps locks in the golden story . . . . i 3 92
I'll lock thy heaven from thee . . . . *T. of Athens* i 2 255
So covetous, To lock such rascal counters from his friends . *J. Cæsar* iv 3 80
Thou canst not say I did it: never shake Thy gory locks at me *Macbeth* iii 4 51
Open, locks, Whoever knocks! . . . . . . iv 1 46
Thy knotted and combined locks to part . . . . *Hamlet* i 5 18
Then I prescripts gave her, That she should lock herself from his resort ii 2 143
Sport and repose lock from me day and night! . . . . iii 2 227
A closet lock and key of villanous secrets . . *Othello* iv 2 22
There lock yourself, and send him word you are dead . *Ant. and Cleo.* iv 13 4
You're my prisoner, but Your gaoler shall deliver you the keys That lock up your restraint . . . . . *Cymbeline* i 1 74
This secret Will force him think I have pick'd the lock . . . ii 2 41
Good wax, thy leave. Blest be You bees that make these locks of counsel! . . . . iii 2 36
What pleasure, sir, find we in life, to lock it From action and adventure? . . . . iv 4 2
You shall not now be stol'n, you have locks upon you . . . v 4 1
Cured by the sure physician, death, who is the key To unbar these locks v 4 8
Locked. Did hold his eyes lock'd in her crystal looks *T. G. of Ver.* ii 4 89
Ay, but the doors be lock'd and keys kept safe . . . iii 1 111
'Tis a secret must be locked within the teeth and the lips *Meas. for Meas.* iii 2 143
As fast lock'd up in sleep as guiltless labour . . . iv 2 69
But, soft! my door is lock'd. Go bid them let us in *Com. of Errors* iii 1 30
Were not my doors lock'd up and I shut out?—Perdie, your doors were lock'd . . . . iv 4 73
We were lock'd out.—Dissembling villain, thou speak'st false . iv 4 102
This woman lock'd me out this day from dinner . . . v 1 218
Thus far I witness with him, That he dined not at home, but was lock'd out . . . . v 1 255
All his senses were lock'd in his eye, As jewels in crystal *L. L. Lost* ii 1 242
I am lock'd in one of them: If you do love me, you will find me out *Mer. of Venice* iii 2 40
Till then I'll keep him dark and safely lock'd . . *All's Well* iv 1 105
The gifts she looks from me are pack'd and lock'd Up in my heart *W. T.* iv 4 369
To lie like pawns lock'd up in chests and trunks . *K. John* v 2 141
Like the fox, Who, ne er so tame, so cherish'd and lock'd up, Will have a wild trick of his ancestors . . . . 1 *Hen. IV.* v 2 10
And he but naked, though lock'd up in steel, Whose conscience with injustice is corrupted . . . . . 2 *Hen. VI.* iii 2 234
A jewel, lock'd into the wofull'st cask . . . . iii 2 409
Forcibly prevents Our lock'd embrasures . . *Troi. and Cres.* iv 4 39
But this thy countenance, still lock'd in steel, I never saw till now . iv 5 195
'Tis in my memory lock'd, And you yourself shall keep the key of it *Hamlet* i 3 85
O villany! Ho! let the door be lock'd: Treachery! Seek it out. . v 2 322
I have locked the letter in my closet . . . *Lear* iii 3 11
Signior, is all your family within?—Are your doors lock'd? . *Othello* i 1 85
Where is she?—Lock'd in her monument . . . *Ant. and Cleo.* iv 14 120
Her chambers are all lock'd; and there's no answer That will be given *Cymbeline* iii 5 43
Her doors lock'd? Not seen of late? Grant, heavens, that which I fear Prove false!—Son, I say, follow . . . . . . iii 5 51
Locking. Buy a rope's end: that will I bestow Among my wife and her confederates, For locking me out of my doors by day *Com. of Errors* iv 1 18
Locking-up. No danger in what show of death it makes, More than the locking-up the spirits a time . . . . . *Cymbeline* i 5 41
Lockram. The kitchen malkin pins Her richest lockram 'bout her reechy neck, Clambering the walls to eye him . . . *Coriolanus* ii 1 225
Locust. The food that to him now is as luscious as locusts, shall be to him shortly as bitter as coloquintida . . . . . *Othello* i 3 354
Lode-star. O happy fair! Your eyes are lode-stars . . *M. N. Dream* i 1 183
Lodge. My bosom as a bed Shall lodge thee . . *T. G. of Ver.* i 2 115
I nightly lodge her in an upper tower . . . . iii 1 35
Himself would lodge where senseless they are lying! . . . iii 1 143

Lodge. You have beaten my men, killed my deer, and broke open my lodge . . . . *Mer. Wives* i 1 115
I found him here as melancholy as a lodge in a warren . *Much Ado* ii 1 222
I will visit thee at the lodge.—That's hereby . *L. L. Lost* i 2 140
Thus much I have learnt: He rather means to lodge you in the field . ii 1 85
Where do the palmers lodge, I do beseech you. . . *All's Well* iii 5 38
In the south suburbs, at the Elephant, Is best to lodge . . *T. Night* iii 3 40
I'll keep my stables where I lodge my wife . . . *W. Tale* ii 1 135
Our sighs and they shall lodge the summer corn . *Richard II.* iii 3 162
By whose power I well might lodge a fear To be again displaced 2 *Hen. IV.* iv 5 208
We cannot lodge and board a dozen or fourteen gentlewomen *Hen. V.* ii 1 35
Did he so often lodge in open field, In winter's cold? . . 2 *Hen. VI.* i 1 80
Stay by me, my lords; And, soldiers, stay and lodge by me this night 3 *Hen. VI.* i 1 32
But why commands the king That his chief followers lodge in towns about him? . . . . iv 3 13
A certain knowledge—My brother Troilus lodges there to-night *Troi. and Cres.* iv 1 42
At the lodge Upon the north side of this pleasant chase. *T. Andron.* ii 3 254
And where care lodges, sleep will never lie . . *Rom. and Jul.* ii 3 36
In what vile part of this anatomy Doth my name lodge? . . iii 3 107
Bid the commanders Prepare to lodge their companies to-night *J. Cæsar* iv 3 140
Leave her to heaven And to those thorns that in her bosom lodge *Hamlet* i 5 87
I know not Where I did lodge last night . . . . *Lear* iv 7 68
Where lodges he?—To tell you where he lodges, is to tell you where I lie . . . I know not where he lodges, and for me to devise a lodging and say he lies here or he lies there, were to lie in mine own throat . . . . *Othello* iii 4 7
Let me lodge Lichas on the horns o' the moon . *Ant. and Cleo.* iv 12 45
I lodge in fear; Though this a heavenly angel, hell is here . *Cymbeline* ii 2 49
If we had of every nation a traveller, we should lodge them with this sign . . . . *Pericles* iv 2 124
Lodged thee In mine own cell . . . . . . *Tempest* i 2 346
So received As you shall deem yourself lodged in my heart . *L. L. Lost* ii 1 174
I give no reason, nor I will not, More than a lodged hate *Mer. of Venice* iv 1 60
And in my house you shall be friendly lodged . . *T. of Shrew* iv 2 107
I will conduct you where you shall be lodged . . . *All's Well* iii 5 44
I have That honourable grief lodged here which burns Worse than tears drown . . . . *W. Tale* ii 1 111
Why should hard-favour'd grief be lodged in thee? . . *Richard II.* v 1 14
Rough and rugged, Like to the summer's corn by tempest lodged 2 *Hen. VI.* iii 2 176
If ever any grudge were lodged between us . . *Richard III.* ii 1 65
With easy roads, he came to Leicester, Lodged in the abbey *Hen. VIII.* iv 2 18
There are two lodged together.—One cried 'Good bless us!' . *Macbeth* ii 2 26
Though bladed corn be lodged and trees blown down . . . iv 1 55
She should in ground unsanctified have lodged Till the last trumpet *Hamlet* v 1 252
Lodger. In Genoa, Where we were lodgers at the Pegasus *T. of Shrew* iv 4 5
Nor shall my Nell keep lodgers . . . . . *Hen. V.* ii 1 33
Lodging. If frosts and fasts, hard lodging and thin weeds Nip not the gaudy blossoms of your love . . . . *L. L. Lost* v 2 811
Desire Gratiano to come anon to my lodging.—To him, father *M. of Ven.* ii 2 125
Take leave of thy old master and inquire My lodging out . . ii 2 163
We will slink away in supper-time, Disguise us at my lodging and return . . . . ii 4 2
Meet me and Gratiano At Gratiano's lodging some hour hence . . ii 4 27
This night he means To burn the lodging where you use to lie *As Y. L. It* ii 3 23
And burn sweet wood to make the lodging sweet . *T. of Shrew* Ind. 1 49
We could at once put us in readiness, And take a lodging . . . i 1 44
Happily we might be interrupted.—Then at my lodging, an it like you iv 4 55
Best first go see your lodging . . . . . *T. Night* iii 3 20
But empty lodgings and unfurnish'd walls, Unpeopled offices *Richard II.* i 2 68
Doth any name particular belong Unto the lodging? . 2 *Hen. IV.* iv 5 234
From the rising of the lark to the lodging of the lamb . *Hen. V.* iii 7 34
This lodging likes me better, Since I may say 'Now lie I like a king' . iv 1 16
Gallop apace, you fiery-footed steeds, Towards Phœbus' lodging *Rom. and Jul.* iii 2 2
Thou know'st my lodging: get me ink and paper, And hire post-horses v 1 25
Retire with me to my lodging, from whence I will fitly bring you. *Lear* i 2 184
Take vantage, heavy eyes, not to behold This shameful lodging . . ii 2 179
Being not at your lodging to be found, The senate hath sent about three several quests To search you out . . . . *Othello* i 2 45
Where shall we meet i' the morning?—At my lodging . . . i 3 382
I will in Cassio's lodging lose this napkin, And let him find it . iii 3 321
For me to devise a lodging and say he lies here or he lies there, were to lie in mine own throat . . . . iii 4 12
Sweet love, I was coming to your house.—And I was going to your lodging . . . . iii 4 172
Under her breast—Worthy the pressing—lies a mole, right proud Of that most delicate lodging . . . . . *Cymbeline* ii 4 136
I have, my lord, at my lodging, the same suit he wore when he took leave of my lady . . . . iii 5 127
Pages and lights, to conduct These knights unto their several lodgings! *Pericles* ii 3 110
Our lodgings, standing bleak upon the sea, Shook as the earth did quake . . . . iii 2 14
Lodovico. Something from Venice, sure. 'Tis Lodovico . . *Othello* iv 1 227
And what's the news, good cousin Lodovico? . . . . iv 1 232
This Lodovico is a proper man.—A very handsome man . . iv 3 35
Lodowick. Who knows that Lodowick?—My lord, I know him; 'tis a meddling friar . . . . *Meas. for Meas.* v 1 126
Know you that Friar Lodowick that she speaks of?—I know him for a man divine and holy . . . . v 1 143
Did not you say you knew that Friar Lodowick to be a dishonest person? . . . . v 1 262
Cosmo, Lodowick, and Gratii, two hundred and fifty each . *All's Well* iv 3 186
Lofty. His humour is lofty, his discourse peremptory . . *L. L. Lost* v 1 11
This was lofty! . . . . *M. N. Dream* i 2 41
Cut off the heads of too fast growing sprays, That look too lofty in our commonwealth: All must be even in our government *Richard II.* iii 4 35
Sound all the lofty instruments of war . . . 1 *Hen. IV.* v 2 98
Breasting the lofty surge . . . . . *Hen. V.* iii Prol. 13
Saying our grace is only in our heels, And that we are most lofty runaways . . . . iii 5 35
Of such a spacious lofty pitch, Your roof were not sufficient 1 *Hen. VI.* ii 3 55
Thus droops this lofty pine and hangs his sprays . 2 *Hen. VI.* ii 3 45
By shameful murder of a guiltless king And lofty proud encroaching tyranny . . . . iv 1 96

Lofty and sour to them that loved him not . . . . *Hen. VIII.* iv 2 53
I never wept, Because they died in honour's lofty bed . *T. Andron.* iii 1 11
How many ages hence Shall this our lofty scene be acted over! *J. Cæsar* iii 1 112
Doth with his lofty and shrill-sounding throat Awake the god of day *Hamlet* i 1 151
The lofty cedar, royal Cymbeline, Personates thee . . . *Cymbeline* v 5 453
Lofty-plumed. France must vail her lofty-plumed crest . . 1 *Hen. VI.* v 3 25
Log. I must remove Some thousands of these logs and pile them up *Tempest* iii 1 10
I would the lightning had Burnt up those logs that you are enjoin'd to pile! . . . . iii 1 17
If you'll sit down, I'll bear your logs the while . . . . iii 1 24
With a log Batter his skull, or paunch him with a stake . . iii 2 97
Tom bears logs into the hall And milk comes frozen home in pail *L. L. L.* v 2 924
Sirrah, fetch drier logs: Call Peter, he will show thee where they are.—I have a head, sir, that will find out logs, And never trouble Peter for the matter . . . . *Rom. and Jul.* iv 4 15
Loggats. Did these bones cost no more the breeding, but to play at loggats with 'em? mine ache to think on't . . . *Hamlet* v 1 100
Loggerhead. Ah, you whoreson loggerhead! . . . *L. L. Lost* iv 3 204
Three or four loggerheads amongst three or four score hogsheads 1 *Hen. IV.* ii 4 4
Well said; a merry whoreson, ha! Thou shalt be logger-head *R. and J.* iv 4 20
Logger-headed. You logger-headed and unpolish'd grooms! *T. of Shrew* iv 1 128
Logic. Balk logic with acquaintance that you have . . . . i 1 34
Log-man. For your sake Am I this patient log-man . . . *Tempest* iii 1 67
Loins. Thine own bowels, which do call thee sire, The mere effusion of thy proper loins, Do curse the gout . . . . *Meas. for Meas.* iii 1 30
This shame derives itself from unknown loins . . . *Much Ado* iv 1 137
That from his loins no hopeful branch may spring, To cross me! 3 *Hen. VI.* iii 2 126
Thou loathed issue of thy father's loins! . . . *Richard III.* i 3 232
Out of whorish loins Are pleased to breed out your inheritors *T. and C.* iv 1 63
My dear wife's estimate, her womb's increase, And treasure of my loins *Coriolanus* iii 3 115
From forth the fatal loins of these two foes A pair of star-cross'd lovers take their life . . . . *Rom. and Jul.* Prol. 5
Brave son, derived from honourable loins! . . . *J. Cæsar* ii 1 322
About her lank and all o'er-teemed loins, A blanket . . *Hamlet* ii 2 531
My face I'll grime with filth; Blanket my loins; elf all my hair . *Lear* ii 3 10
Horses are tied by the heads, dogs and bears by the neck, monkeys by the loins, and men by the legs . . . . ii 4 9
They are the issue of your loins, my liege . . . . *Cymbeline* v 5 330
Loiter. Sir John, you loiter here too long . . . . 2 *Hen. IV.* ii 1 198
Loiterer. O illiterate loiterer! . . . . . . *T. G. of Ver.* iii 1 296
Liege of all loiterers and malcontents, Dread prince of plackets *L. L. L.* iii 1 185
Loitering. Where have you been these two days loitering? *T. G. of Ver.* iv 4 48
Loll. So hangs, and lolls, and weeps upon me; so hales, and pulls me *Othello* iv 1 143
Lolling. He is not lolling on a lewd day-bed, But on his knees at meditation . . . . *Richard III.* iii 7 72
The large Achilles, on his press'd bed lolling . . *Troi. and Cres.* i 3 162
Like a great natural, that runs lolling up and down to hide his bauble in a hole . . . . *Rom. and Jul.* ii 4 96
The enemy full-hearted, Lolling the tongue with slaughtering *Cymbeline* v 3 8
Lombardy, The pleasant garden of great Italy . . . *T. of Shrew* i 1 3
London hath received, Like a kind host, the Dauphin . . *K. John* v 1 31
For do we must what force will have us do. Set on towards London *Richard II.* iii 3 208
Post you to London, and you will find it so . . . . . iii 4 90
Come, ladies, go, To meet at London London's king in woe . . . iii 4 97
Weeping made you break the story off, Of our two cousins coming into London . . . . v 2 3
Inquire at London, 'mongst the taverns there . . . . . v 3 5
I have to London sent The heads of Oxford, Salisbury, Blunt, and Kent v 6 7
I have . . . sent to London The heads of Brocas and Sir Bennet Seely . v 6 13
And traders riding to London with fat purses . . 1 *Hen. IV.* i 2 141
What time do you mean to come to London?—Time enough to go to bed . . . . ii 1 47
Now could thou and I rob the thieves and go merrily to London . . ii 2 100
Though I could 'scape shot-free at London, I fear the shot here . . v 3 30
When through proud London he came sighing on . 2 *Hen. IV.* i 3 104
Is your master here in London?—Yea, my lord.—Where sups he? . ii 2 157
As common as the way between Saint Alban's and London . . . ii 2 185
Welcome to London. Now, the Lord bless that sweet face of thine! . ii 4 316
He dines in London.—And how accompanied? canst thou tell that? . iv 4 51
I hope to see London once ere I die . . . . v 3 64
Would I were in an alehouse in London! . . . . *Hen. V.* iii 2 12
Goes to the wars, to grace himself at his return into London. . . iii 6 72
So let him land, And solemnly see him set on to London . . v Prol. 14
How London doth pour out her citizens! . . . . . v Prol. 24
Now in London place him . . . . v Prol. 35
Pity the city of London, pity us! . . . . . 1 *Hen. VI.* iii 1 77
By this means Your lady is forthcoming yet at London . . 2 *Hen. VI.* ii 1 179
For this night we will repose us here: To-morrow toward London . ii 1 201
The bodies shall be dragged at my horse heels till I do come to London iv 3 15
If not through your neglect, We shall to London get, where you are loved . . . . v 2 81
The king is fled to London, To call a present court of parliament . v 3 24
Sound drums and trumpets, and to London all . . . . . v 3 32
I'll to my castle.—And I'll keep London with my soldiers . 3 *Hen. VI.* i 1 207
Thou shalt to London presently, And whet on Warwick . . . . i 2 36
You shall stay with me; My brother Montague shall post to London . i 2 55
I, then in London, keeper of the king, Muster'd my soldiers . . . ii 1 111
And now to London all the crew are gone, To frustrate both his oath . ii 1 174
Why, Via! to London will we march amain . . . . . . ii 1 182
From London by the king was I press'd forth . . . . . ii 5 64
And now to London with triumphant march, There to be crowned . ii 6 87
Now to London, To see these honours in possession . . . . ii 6 109
What now remains, my lords, for us to do But march to London? . iv 3 61
He comes towards London, To set the crown once more on Henry's head iv 4 26
Doth march amain to London; And many giddy people flock to him . iv 8 4
My sovereign . . . Shall rest in London till we come to him . . . iv 8 22
I'll hence to London on a serious matter . . . . v 5 47
Where's Richard gone?—To London, all in post . . . . . v 5 84
Let's away to London And see our gentle queen how well she fares . v 5 88
Fetch'd Hither to London, to be crown'd our king . . *Richard III.* ii 2 122
Welcome, sweet prince, to London, to your chamber . . . . iii 1 1
My lord, the mayor of London comes to greet you . . . . . iii 1 17
The lords at Pomfret, when they rode from London, Were jocund . iii 2 85
London. Towards London they do bend their course . *Richard III.* iv 5 14
When they were ready to set out for London . . . *Hen. VIII.* ii 2 5
Stokesly and Gardiner; the one of Winchester, . . . The other, London iv 1 103
London bridge. In that thou laid'st a trap to take my life, As well at London bridge as at the Tower . . . . . . 1 *Hen. VI.* iii 1 23
Jack Cade hath gotten London bridge: The citizens fly . 2 *Hen. VI.* iv 4 49
But first, go and set London bridge on fire . . . . . iv 6 16
Londoner. Did of me demand What was the speech among the Londoners Concerning the French journey . . . . . . *Hen. VIII.* i 2 154
London gates. Hath my sword therefore broke through London gates? 2 *Hen. VI.* iv 8 24
London road. I think this be the most villanous house in all London road for fleas . . . . 1 *Hen. IV.* ii 1 16
London-stone. Here, sitting upon London-stone . . . 2 *Hen. VI.* iv 6 2
London streets. In London streets, that coronation-day *Richard II.* v 5 77
Already in this civil broil I see them lording it in London streets 2 *Hen. VI.* iv 8 47
Lone woman. A hundred mark is a long one for a poor lone woman to bear . . . . 2 *Hen. IV.* ii 1 35
Loneliness. Now I see The mystery of your loneliness . . *All's Well* i 3 177
That show of such an exercise may colour Your loneliness . *Hamlet* iii 1 46
Lonely. Therefore I keep it Lonely, apart . . . . . *W. Tale* v 3 18
Like to a lonely dragon, that his fen Makes fear'd and talk'd of *Coriol.* iv 1 30
Long. Give thanks you have lived so long . . . . . *Tempest* i 1 27
Quickly, spirit; Thou shalt ere long be free . . . . . . v 1 87
How long hath she been deformed?—Ever since you loved her *T. G. of V.* ii 1 70
Alas, the way is wearisome and long! . . . . ii 7 8
Pity the dearth that I have pined in, By longing for that food so long a time . . . . ii 7 17
Run to him, for thou hast stayed so long that going will scarce serve . iii 1 388
Have you long sojourned there?—Some sixteen months . . . iv 1 20
She takes exceptions at your person.—What, that my leg is too long? . v 2 4
Leave not the mansion so long tenantless . . . . . . v 4 8
'Twere pity two such friends should be long foes . . . . . v 4 118
Go into this closet: he will not stay long . . . . *Mer. Wives* i 4 40
By my trot, I tarry too long. Od's me! . . . . i 4 64
He loves your wife; there's the short and the long . . . . ii 1 137
This is the short and the long of it . . . . ii 2 60
And how long lay you there?—Nay, you shall hear, Master Brook . iii 5 95
Come, come home, boy. Come, we stay too long . . . . . iv 1 87
So long that nineteen zodiacs have gone round . . *Meas. for Meas.* i 2 172
To give fear to use and liberty, Which have for long run by the hideous law i 4 63
How long have you been in this place of constable?—Seven year and a half ii 1 272
Ere long I'll visit you again.—Most holy sir, I thank you . . . iii 1 46
Only refer yourself to this advantage, first, that your stay with him may not be long . . . . iii 1 256
They will, then, ere't be long . . . . iv 2 79
There had she not been long but she became A joyful mother *Com. of Errors* i 1 50
An you use these blows long, I must get a sconce for my head . . ii 2 37
The chain unfinish'd made me stay thus long . . . . . . iii 2 173
Belike you thought our love would last too long, If it were chain'd together . . . . iv 1 25
Both wind and tide stays for this gentleman, And I, to blame, have held him here too long . . . . iv 1 47
I long that we were safe and sound aboard . . . . iv 4 154
How long hath this possession held the man?—This week . . . v 1 44
And there live we as merry as the day is long . . . . *Much Ado* ii 1 52
You shake the head at so long a breathing . . . . . . ii 1 378
I have railed so long against marriage: but doth not the appetite alter? ii 3 246
She has been too long a talking of . . . . iii 2 106
How long have you professed apprehension?—Ever since you left it . iii 4 68
Hear me a little; for I have only been Silent so long . . . . iv 1 158
Borrows money in God's name, the which he hath used so long and never paid . . . . v 1 320
How long is that, think you?—Question: why, an hour in clamour . v 2 83
And keep not too long in one tune, but a snip and away . *L. L. Lost* iii 1 21
O, they have lived long on the alms-basket of words . . . . v 1 41
Thou art not so long by the head as honorificabilitudinitatibus . . v 1 43
For a light heart lives long . . . . v 2 18
The letter is too long by half a mile.—I think no less . . . v 2 54
O for your reason! quickly, sir; I long . . . . v 2 244
I'll stay with patience; but the time is long.—The liker you . . v 2 845
A twelvemonth and a day, And then 'twill end.—That's too long for a play v 2 888
How long within this wood intend you stay? . . . *M. N. Dream* ii 1 138
O weary night, O long and tedious night, Abate thy hours! . . . iii 2 431
For the short and the long is, our play is preferred . . . . iv 2 39
A play there is, my lord, some ten words long, . . . But by ten words, my lord, it is too long, Which makes it tedious . . . . . v 1 61
Now to 'scape the serpent's tongue, We will make amends ere long . v 1 441
Murder cannot be hid long; a man's son may . . . *Mer. of Venice* ii 2 84
The short and the long is, I serve the Jew . . . . . . ii 2 135
When you shall please to play the thieves for wives, I'll watch as long for you . . . . ii 6 24
Too long a pause for that which you find there . . . . . ii 9 53
I speak too long; but 'tis to peize the time, To eke it and to draw it out iii 2 22
Get you in: I will not long be troubled with you . . *As Y. Like It* i 1 80
That I am altogether misprised: but it shall not be so long . . . i 1 178
Tell me how long you would have her after you have possessed her.—For ever and a day.—Say 'a day,' without the 'ever' . . . . iv 1 143
You to a long and well-deserved bed: And you to wrangling . . v 4 196
Ay, it stands so that I may hardly tarry so long . . *T. of Shrew* Ind. 2 128
And I do hope good days and long to see . . . . i 2 193
This young scholar, that hath been long studying at Rheims . . ii 1 80
How I long to have some chat with her!—Well, go with me . . . ii 1 163
Now is the day we long have looked for . . . . ii 1 335
What occasion of import Hath all so long detain'd you from your wife? iii 2 105
I stay too long from her: The morning wears, 'tis time we were at church iii 2 112
Why, thy horn is a foot; and so long am I at the least . . . iv 1 30
That teacheth tricks eleven and twenty long, To tame a shrew . . iv 2 57
I have watch'd so long That I am dog-weary . . . . . . iv 2 59
To stay him not too long, I am content, in a good father's care, To have him match'd; and if you please to like No worse . . . . . iv 4 30
To Padua; there to visit A son of mine, which long I have not seen . iv 5 57
At last, though long, our jarring notes agree: And time it is . . v 2 1
He lasted long; But on us both did haggish age steal on . *All's Well* i 2 28
How long is't, count, Since the physician at your father's died? . . i 2 69
I see things may serve long, but not serve ever . . . . . ii 2 60
For which live long to thank both heaven and me! . . . . . ii 2 67
His heels have deserved it, in usurping his spurs so long . . . iv 3 119
A good lady and would not have knaves thrive long under her . . v 2 34

Long. I am not weary, and 'tis long to night . . . *T. Night* iii 3 21
Who does do you wrong?—Hast thou forgot thyself? is it so long? . v 1 144
And since you call'd me master for so long, Here is my hand . v 1 332
But once before I spoke to the purpose: when? Nay, let me have't; I long . . . . *W. Tale* i 2 101
Rosemary and rue; these keep Seeming and savour all the winter long iv 4 75
Scarce any joy Did ever so long live . . . . . v 3 52
Not these twenty years.—So long could I Stand by, a looker on . v 3 84
By long and vehement suit I was seduced . . . *K. John* i 1 254
I should be as merry as the day is long . . . . iv 1 18
This will break out To all our sorrows, and ere long I doubt . . iv 2 102
This fever, that hath troubled me so long, Lies heavy on me . . v 3 3
Your supply, which you have wish'd so long, Are cast away . . v 5 12
Is Harry Hereford arm'd?—Yea, at all points; and longs to enter *Richard II.* i 3 2
Like two men That vow a long and weary pilgrimage . . . i 3 49
How long a time lies in one little word! . . . . . . i 3 213
Small showers last long, but sudden storms are short . . . ii 1 35
How long shall I be patient? ah, how long? . . . . ii 1 163
Thus long have we stood To watch the fearful bending of thy knee iii 3 72
His captain Christ, Under whose colours he had fought so long . iv 1 100
Long mayst thou live in Richard's seat to sit! . . . . iv 1 218
How long hast thou to serve, Francis?—Forsooth, five years 1 *Hen. IV.* ii 4 45
Ere I lead this life long, I'll sew nether stocks and mend them . ii 4 129
How long is't ago, Jack, since thou sawest thine own knee? . . ii 4 360
You are so fretful, you cannot live long.—Why, there is it . . iii 3 14
Is the king encamped?—He is, Sir John: I fear we shall stay too long iv 2 83
Contrarious winds that held the king So long in his unlucky Irish wars v 1 53
The time of life is short! To spend that shortness basely were too long v 2 83
We breathe too long: come, cousin Westmoreland, Our duty this way lies v 4 15
Saying that ere long they should call me madam . . 2 *Hen. IV.* ii 1 109
Sir John, you loiter here too long . . . . . . ii 1 198
Harry Threw many a northward look to see his father Bring up his powers; but he did long in vain . . . . ii 3 14
He'll straight be well.—No, no, he cannot long hold out these pangs . iv 4 117
Now, where is he that will not stay so long Till his friend sickness hath determined me? . . . . iv 5 81
I stay too long by thee, I weary thee . . . . . iv 5 94
And He that wears the crown immortally Long guard it yours! . iv 5 145
And a merry heart lives long-a . . . . . . v 3 50
Nor shall my Nell keep lodgers.—No, by my troth, not long . *Hen. V.* ii 1 34
That sall I suerly do, that is the breff and the long . . . iii 2 126
Why do you stay so long, my lords of France? . . . . iii 5 38
I'll to the throng: Let life be short; else shame will be too long . iv 5 23
Dear nurse of arts, . . . Alas, she hath from France too long been chased v 2 38
King Henry the Fifth, too famous to live long! . . . 1 *Hen. VI.* i 1 6
But long I will not be Jack out of office . . . . . i 1 175
Gloucester, guard thy head; For I intend to have it ere long . . i 3 88
A maid! and be so martial!—Pray God she prove not masculine ere long ii 1 22
I trust ere long to choke thee with thine own . . . . iii 2 46
We are here.—And there will we be too, ere it be long . . . iii 2 75
Is this the Lord Talbot, . . . That hath so long been resident in France? iii 4 14
Thence to England; where I hope ere long To be presented . . iv 1 171
She hath lived too long, To fill the world with vicious qualities . v 4 34
Studied so long, sat in the council-house Early and late . 2 *Hen. VI.* i 1 90
And say, when I am gone, I prophesied France will be lost ere long i 1 146
How long hast thou been blind?—O, born so, master . . . ii 1 97
O God, seest Thou this, and bearest so long? . . . . ii 1 154
I will remedy this gear ere long, Or sell my title for a glorious grave iii 1 91
Pardon, my liege, that I have stay'd so long . . . . iii 1 94
He never would have stay'd in France so long.—No, not to lose it all . iii 1 295
I rather would have lost my life betimes Than bring a burthen of dishonour home By staying there so long . . . . . . iii 1 299
And fought so long, till that his thighs with darts Were almost like a sharp-quill'd porpentine . . . . iii 1 362
Die, Margaret! For Henry weeps that thou dost live so long . . iii 2 121
Never subject long'd to be a king As I do long and wish to be a subject iv 9 6
God knows how long it is I have to live . . . . . v 3 17
Tell him from me that he hath done me wrong, And therefore I'll uncrown him ere't be long . . . 3 *Hen. VI.* iii 3 232; iv 1 111
I long till Edward fall by war's mischance, For mocking marriage . iii 3 254
And we shall have more wars before't be long . . . . iv 6 91
Long mayst thou live To bear his image and renew his glories! . v 4 53
Your imprisonment shall not be long; I will deliver you *Richard III.* i 1 114
He hath kept an evil diet long, And overmuch consumed his royal person i 1 139
I'll have her; but I will not keep her long . . . . i 2 230
I have too long borne Your blunt upbraidings and your bitter scoffs . i 3 103
Long mayst thou live to wail thy children's loss! . . . . i 3 204
Long die thy happy days before thy death! . . . . . i 3 207
I long with all my heart to see the prince: I hope he is much grown . ii 4 4
So long a-growing and so leisurely . . . . . . ii 4 19
So wise so young, they say, do never live long . . . . iii 1 79
What say you, uncle?—I say, without characters, fame lives long . iii 1 81
Go you toward the Tower?—I do, my lord; but long I shall not stay . iii 2 120
Good morrow. I have been long a sleeper . . . . . iii 4 24
The precedent was full as long a-doing . . . . . iii 6 7
Hath he so long held out with me untired, And stops he now for breath? iv 2 44
How long shall that title 'ever' last?—Sweetly in force unto her fair life's end.—But how long fairly shall her sweet life last? . . . iv 4 350
Smile heaven upon this fair conjunction, That long have frown'd! . v 5 21
England hath long been mad, and scarr'd herself . . . v 5 23
His sword Hath a sharp edge: it's long . . . *Hen. VIII.* i 1 110
Heaven will one day open The king's eyes, that so long have slept upon This bold bad man . . . . ii 2 43
Having lived so long with her, and she So good a lady . . . ii 3 2
We are a queen, or long have dream'd so, certain The daughter of a king ii 4 71
I have spoke long: be pleased yourself to say How far you satisfied me ii 4 210
Have I lived thus long . . . a wife, a true one? . . . . iii 1 125
Patience, be near me still; and set me lower: I have not long to trouble thee . . . . iv 2 77
How much her grace is alter'd on the sudden? How long her face is drawn? . . . . iv 2 97
My wretched women, that so long Have follow'd both my fortunes faithfully . . . . iv 2 140
From your affairs I hinder you too long: good night . . . v 1 54
I long To have this young one made a Christian . . . . v 3 179
Heaven, from thy endless goodness, send prosperous life, long, and ever happy! . . . . v 5 2
His evasions have ears thus long . . . . *Troi. and Cres.* ii 1 75
Though they be long ere they are wooed, they are constant being won iii 2 118

Long. Had I so good occasion to lie long As you . . *Troi. and Cres.* iv 1 5
Our bloods are now in calm; and, so long, health! . . . . iv 1 15
Good old chronicle, That hast so long walk'd hand in hand with time . iv 5 203
You'll hear the belly's answer.—Ye're long about it . . *Coriolanus* i 1 131
How long is't since?—Above an hour, my lord . . . . i 6 14
That prefer A noble life before a long . . . . . iii 1 153
I shall ere long have knowledge Of my success . . . . v 1 61
I' the state of hanging, or of some death more long in spectatorship v 2 71
For you, be that you are, long; and your misery increase with your age! v 2 113
I have sat too long, Nay, go not from us thus . . . . v 3 131
That shall our poor city find: and all this is long of you . . v 4 32
In peace and honour live Lord Titus long! . . . *T. Andron.* i 1 157
Whom thou in triumph long Hast prisoner held, fetter'd in amorous chains ii 1 14
For these slips have made him noted long . . . . . ii 3 86
Kill me in this place! For 'tis not life that I have begg'd so long . ii 3 170
Away! for thou hast stay'd us here too long . . . . ii 3 181
And in the fountain shall we gaze so long Till the fresh taste be taken from that clearness, And made a brine-pit . . . . . iii 1 127
Trot, like a servile footman, all day long . . . . . v 2 55
Long have I been forlorn, and all for thee . . . . . v 2 81
But new struck nine.—Ay me! sad hours seem long . *Rom. and Jul.* i 1 167
And pity 'tis you lived at odds so long . . . . . i 2 5
How long is it now To Lammas-tide?—A fortnight and odd days . . i 3 14
Be fickle, fortune; For then, I hope, thou wilt not keep him long . iii 5 63
Be not so long to speak; I long to die . . . . . iv 1 66
Her joints are stiff; Life and these lips have long been separated . . iv 5 27
Have I thought long to see this morning's face, And doth it give me such a sight as this? . . . . iv 5 41
She's not well married that lives married long . . . . iv 5 77
How long hath he been there?—Full half an hour . . . . v 3 130
I have not seen you long: how goes the world? . . *T. of Athens* i 1 2
This gentleman of mine hath served me long: To build his fortune I will strain a little . . . . i 1 142
Long may he live in fortunes! . . . . i 1 293
Thou givest so long, Timon, I fear me thou wilt give away thyself . i 2 247
Live loathed and long, Most smiling, smooth, detested parasites! . iii 6 103
A madman so long, now a fool . . . . iv 3 221
But wherefore do you hold me here so long? What is it? . *J. Cæsar* i 2 83
See! Antony, that revels long o' nights, Is notwithstanding up . ii 2 116
Thou shalt sleep again; I will not hold thee long . . . iv 3 265
O, coward that I am, to live so long, To see my best friend ta'en! . v 3 34
I take my leave of you: Shall not be long but I'll be here again *Macbeth* iv 2 23
Receive what cheer you may: The night is long that never finds the day iv 3 240
The bird of dawning singeth all night long . . . *Hamlet* i 1 160
Stay'd it long?—While one with moderate haste might tell a hundred . i 2 237
O, fear me not. I stay too long: but here my father comes . . i 3 52
This is too long.—It shall to the barber's, with your beard . . ii 2 520
I have remembrances of yours, That I have longed long to re-deliver . iii 1 94
And my father died within these two hours.—Nay, 'tis twice two months, my lord.—So long? . . . . iii 2 137
How long hath she been thus?—I hope all will be well . . . iv 5 67
But long it could not be Till that her garments, heavy with their drink, Pull'd the poor wretch from her melodious lay To muddy death . iv 7 181
How long hast thou been a grave-maker? . . . . . v 1 153
How long is that since?—Cannot you tell that? every fool can tell that v 1 158
How long will a man lie i' the earth ere he rot? . . . . v 1 178
Long in our court have made their amorous sojourn . . . *Lear* i 1 48
How long have you been a sectary astronomical? . . . . i 2 164
For, you know, nuncle, The hedge-sparrow fed the cuckoo so long, That it had it head bit off by it young . . . . i 4 235
She that's a maid now, and laughs at my departure, Shall not be a maid long i 5 56
I will not be long from you . . . . iii 6 3
If she live long, And in the end meet the old course of death, Women will all turn monsters . . . . iii 7 100
Ere long you are like to hear, If you dare venture in your own behalf . iv 2 19
Wake the king: he hath slept long . . . . . . iv 7 18
The wonder is, he hath endured so long: He but usurp'd his life . v 3 316
We that are young Shall never see so much, nor live so long . . v 3 326
You do love my lord: You have known him long . . *Othello* iii 3 11
Policy may either last so long, Or feed upon such nice and waterish diet iii 3 14
And even but now he spake, After long seeming dead, Iago hurt him . v 2 328
If there be any cunning cruelty That can torment him much and hold him long, It shall be his . . . . v 2 334
It cannot be thus long, the sides of nature Will not sustain it *A. and C.* i 3 16
Rogue, thou hast lived too long.—Nay, then I'll run . . . ii 5 73
He cannot like her long.—Like her! O Isis! 'tis impossible . . iii 3 17
Bear'st thou her face in mind? is't long or round?—Round even to faultiness . . . . iii 3 32
Hath he seen majesty? Isis else defend, And serving you so long! . iii 3 47
How long is this ago?—Some twenty years . . . *Cymbeline* i 1 61
Should we be taking leave As long a term as yet we have to live . . i 1 107
Till you had measured how long a fool you were upon the ground . . i 2 25
Have I not been Thy pupil long? Hast thou not learn'd me? . . i 5 12
Ravening first the lamb Longs after for the garbage . . . i 6 50
I do condemn mine ears that have So long attended thee . . . i 6 142
Blessed live you long! A lady to the worthiest sir! . . . . i 6 159
How long is't since she went to Milford-Haven? . . . . iii 5 153
Long is it since I saw him, But time hath nothing blurr'd those lines of favour . . . . iv 2 103
The want is but to put those powers in motion That long to move . iv 3 32
I am ashamed To look upon the holy sun, to have The benefit of his blest beams, remaining So long a poor unknown . . . . . iv 4 43
The time seems long; their blood thinks scorn, Till it fly out . . iv 4 53
Who deserved So long a breeding . . . . v 3 17
Long of her it was That we meet here so strangely . . . . v 5 271
Pardon old Gower,—this longs the text . . . *Pericles* ii Gower 40
Come, gentlemen, we sit too long on trifles . . . . . ii 3 92
When she weaved the sleided silk With fingers long . . . iv Gower 21
Now, pretty one, how long have you been at this trade?—What trade? iv 6 72
How long have you been of this profession?—E'er since I can remember iv 6 78

Long abode. Your patience for my long abode. . *Mer. of Venice* ii 6 21

Long absence. And we forgetful In our long absence . *Hen. VIII.* ii 3 106
Such a welcome as I'd give to him After long absence . . *Cymbeline* iii 6 74

Long absent. You will be hanged for being so long absent . *T. Night* i 5 18

Long after this, when Henry the Fifth . . . did reign . 1 *Hen. VI.* i 5 82
Told me once, I should not live long after I saw Richmond *Richard III.* iv 2 110
'Tis not long after But I will wear my heart upon my sleeve . *Othello* i 1 63

Long again. Time as long again Would be fill'd up . . *W. Tale* i 2 3
Thus will I reward thee, the Lent shall be as long again as it is 2 *Hen. VI.* iv 3 7

Long age. To wear away this long age of three hours . *M. N. Dream* v 1 33

Long ago. Why, I am past my gamut long ago . . . . *T. of Shrew* iii 1 71
He might have took his answer long ago . . . . . *T. Night* i 5 282
Of woeful ages long ago betid . . . . *Richard II.* v 1 42
Alas, has banish'd me his bed already, His love, too long ago! *Hen. VIII.* iii 1 120
I read it in the grammar long ago . . . . *T. Andron.* iv 2 23
Not long ago, one of his men was with the Lord Lucullus *T. of Athens* iii 2 12
I will make him tell the tale anew, Where, how, how oft, how long ago, and when He hath, and is again to cope your wife . . *Othello* iv 1 86
Are you ready for death?—Over-roasted rather; ready long ago *Cymbeline* v 4 154
Long agone. For long agone I have forgot to court . . *T. G. of Ver.* iii 1 85
Long apprenticehood. Must I not serve a long apprenticehood To foreign passages? . . . . . . *Richard II.* i 3 271
Long as. A cloak as long as thine will serve the turn? . . *T. G. of Ver.* iii 1 131
As long as I have an eye to make difference of men's liking *Mer. Wives* ii 1 56
Yet may he live awhile; and, it may be, As long as you or I *M. for M.* ii 4 36
I saw him hold acquaintance with the waves So long as I could see *T. N.* i 2 17
I'll drink to her as long as there is a passage in my throat . . i 3 41
Tears shed there Shall be my recreation: so long as nature Will bear up with this exercise, so long I daily vow to use it . . . *W. Tale* iii 2 241
So long as out of limit and true rule You stand . . 1 *Hen. IV.* iv 3 39
I will live so long as I may, that's the certain of it . . . *Hen. V.* ii 1 15
God pless it and preserve it, as long as it pleases his grace! . . iv 7 113
I need not to be ashamed of your majesty, praised be God, so long as your majesty is an honest man . . . . . . iv 7 119
And would have kept so long as breath did last . . . 2 *Hen. VI.* i 1 211
All these could not procure me any scathe, So long as I am loyal . . ii 4 63
What danger or what sorrow can befall thee, So long as Edward is thy constant friend, And their true sovereign? . . . 3 *Hen. VI.* iv 1 77
So long as heaven and nature lengthens it.—So long as hell and Richard likes of it . . . . *Richard III.* iv 4 353
O, a kiss Long as my exile, sweet as my revenge! . . *Coriolanus* v 3 45
My short date of breath Is not so long as is a tedious tale *Rom. and Jul.* v 3 230
The worst is not So long as we can say 'This is the worst' . . *Lear* iv 1 30
'Twould not ha' bin zo long as 'tis by a vortnight . . . . iv 6 244
We lose it not, so long as we can smile . . . . *Othello* i 3 211
See his vice; 'Tis to his virtue a just equinox, The one as long as the other ii 3 130
So long As he could make me with this eye or ear Distinguish him *Cymb.* i 3 8
Long as I live. Keep your hundred pounds to yourself: he shall need none, so long as I live . . . . *T. of Shrew* v 1 25
Long away. Go in and rest.—We'll not be long away . . *Cymbeline* iv 2 44
Long become it. God and his angels guard your sacred throne And make you long become it! . . . . *Hen. V.* i 2 8
Long before. I'll not be long before I call upon thee . . *W. Tale* iii 3 8
Not long before your highness sped to France . . *Hen. VIII.* i 2 151
Long behind. I'll not be long behind; though I be old . *Richard II.* v 2 114
Long blind. Hast thou been long blind and now restored? . 2 *Hen. VI.* ii 1 76
Long-boat. And on our long-boat's side Strike off his head . . iv 1 68
Long coat. Your long coat, priest, protects you . . *Hen. VIII.* iii 2 276
Long continuance, and increasing, Hourly joys be still upon you! *Tempest* iv 1 107
Which we find Too indirect for long continuance . . 1 *Hen. IV.* iv 3 105
When they are cloy'd With long continuance in a settled place 1 *Hen. VI.* ii 5 106
Long continue. She shall not long continue love to him . *T. G. of Ver.* iii 2 48
It cannot be that Desdemona should long continue her love to the Moor *Othello* i 3 348
Long-continued. Who in this dull and long-continued truce Is rusty grown . . . . *Troi. and Cres.* i 3 262
How youngly he began to serve his country, How long continued *Coriol.* ii 3 245
Long day. 'Twill be Two long days' journey, lords, or ere we meet *K. John* iv 3 20
The long day's task is done, And we must sleep . . *Ant. and Cleo.* iv 14 35
Long divorce. As the long divorce of steel falls on me . *Hen. VIII.* ii 1 76
Long dreamed. I have long dream'd of such a kind of man . 2 *Hen. IV.* v 5 53
Long-during action tires The sinewy vigour of the traveller . *L. L. Lost* iv 3 307
Long ears. I am an ass, indeed; you may prove it by my long ears *C. of E.* iv 4 31
Long-engraffed. The imperfections of long-engraffed condition . *Lear* i 1 300
Long enough. Now let me die, for I have lived long enough *Mer. Wives* iii 3 46
If my wind were but long enough to say my prayers, I would repent . iv 5 105
Be Alcibiades your plague, you his, And last so long enough! *T. of Athens* v 1 193
I have lived long enough . . . . *Macbeth* v 3 22
Long ere. Which long ere this we offer'd to the king . 2 *Hen. IV.* iv 1 75
I thought my mother . . . Would long ere this have met us *Richard III.* iii 1 21
The neighs of horse to tell of her approach Long ere she did appear *Ant. and Cleo.* iii 6 46
Long-experienced. Therefore, out of thy long-experienced time, Give me some present counsel . . . . . . *Rom. and Jul.* iv 1 60
Long farewell. Farewell! a long farewell, to all my greatness! *Hen. VIII.* iii 2 351
Farewell, kind Charmian; Iras, long farewell . . *Ant. and Cleo.* v 2 295
Long for. For Love is like a child, That longs for every thing that he can come by . . . . *T. G. of Ver.* iii 1 125
She rides me and I long for grass. 'Tis so, I am an ass . *Com. of Errors* ii 2 202
Now I do wish it, love it, long for it . . . . *M. N. Dream* iv 1 180
The Dauphin longs for morning.—He longs to eat the English *Hen. V.* iii 7 99
Alas, poor Harry of England! he longs not for the dawning as we do . iii 7 141
Long forth. I had no mind To hunt this day: the boy Fidele's sickness Did make my way long forth . . . . . *Cymbeline* iv 2 149
Long grief. After so long grief, such festivity! . . *Com. of Errors* v 1 406
Long-grown. I do beseech your majesty may salve The long-grown wounds of my intemperance . . . . . . 1 *Hen. IV.* iii 2 156
Long heath. Now would I give a thousand furlongs of sea for an acre of barren ground, long heath, brown furze, any thing . . *Tempest* i 1 70
Long hereafter say unto his child, 'What my great-grandfather and grandsire got My careless father fondly gave away' . . 3 *Hen. VI.* ii 2 36
Long hour. And fought a long hour by Shrewsbury clock . 1 *Hen. IV.* v 4 151
From nine till twelve Is three long hours, yet she is not come *R. and J.* ii 5 11
Long-imprisoned. Unloose thy long-imprison'd thoughts . 2 *Hen. VI.* v 1 88
Long imprisonment. Even like a man new haled from the rack, So fare my limbs with long imprisonment . . . . . 1 *Hen. VI.* ii 5 4
Long in talk. My lord, methinks, is very long in talk . . . i 2 118
Long kept in Bretagne at our mother's cost . . . *Richard III.* v 3 324
Long known. You have been a man long known to me . . *Mer. Wives* ii 2 188
Long-lane end. Bring our horses unto Long-lane end . *T. of Shrew* iv 3 187
Long lease. Five year! by'r lady, a long lease . . . 1 *Hen. IV.* ii 4 50
Long-legged. Hence, you long-legg'd spinners, hence! . *M. N. Dream* ii 2 21
Long life. As I hope For quiet days, fair issue, and long life . *Tempest* iv 1 24
Health and long life to you, Master Silence.—Fill the cup . 2 *Hen. IV.* v 3 54
There's the respect That makes calamity of so long life . . *Hamlet* iii 1 69
O excellent! I love long life better than figs . . . *Ant. and Cleo.* i 2 32
Long live. God save his majesty!—Long live Gonzalo! . . *Tempest* ii 1 169
And long live Henry, fourth of that name! . . . *Richard II.* iv 1 112
Long live Queen Margaret, England's happiness! . . . 2 *Hen. VI.* i 1 37
Long live. Long live our sovereign Richard, England's king! 2 *Hen. VI.* ii 2 63
Long live King Henry! Plantagenet, embrace him.—And long live thou! 3 *Hen. VI.* i 1 202
Long live Edward the Fourth!—Thanks, brave Montgomery . . . iv 7 76
Peace lives again; That she may long live here, God say amen! *Rich. III.* v 5 41
Long live Lord Titus, my beloved brother! . . . . *T. Andron.* i 1 169
Vouchsafe my labour, and long live your lordship! . . . *T. of Athens* i 1 152
Live, and love thy misery.—Long live so, and so die . . . . iv 3 397
Witness the hole you made in Cæsar's heart, Crying 'Long live!' *J. Cæsar* v 1 32
Stand, and unfold yourself.—Long live the king! . . . . *Hamlet* i 1 3
Long live she so! and long live you to think so! . . . . *Othello* iii 3 226
Long live Cæsar! . . . . *Cymbeline* iii 7 10
Long living. God save thy life!—And yours from long living! *L. L. Lost* ii 1 192
Long lost. Carouse together Like friends long lost . . *Ant. and Cleo.* iv 12 13
Long love. Love moderately; long love doth so . . *Rom. and Jul.* ii 6 14
Long loved. I have long loved her . . . . . . *Mer. Wives* ii 2 201
As long loved me As I have loved this proud disdainful haggard *T. of S.* iv 2 38
Long married. The Lady Anne, Whom the king hath in secrecy long married, This day was view'd in open as his queen . . *Hen. VIII.* iii 2 403
Long motley coat. A fellow In a long motley coat . . . . Prol. 16
Long nails. And I with my long nails will dig thee pig-nuts . *Tempest* ii 2 172
Long night. What a long night is this! . . . . . *Hen. V.* iii 7 11
Long one. Her passion ends the play.—Methinks she should not use a long one for such a Pyramus . . . . . . *M. N. Dream* v 1 322
A hundred mark is a long one for a poor lone woman to bear . 2 *Hen. IV.* ii 1 35
Long-parted. As a long-parted mother with her child Plays fondly with her tears and smiles in meeting . . . . . *Richard II.* iii 2 8
Long past. Writ in remembrance more than things long past . . ii 1 14
Long peace. The cankers of a calm world and a long peace 1 *Hen. IV.* iv 2 33
It hath pleased the gods to remember my father's age, And call him to long peace. He is gone happy . . . . . . *T. of Athens* i 2 3
Long process. And often at his very loose decides That which long process could not arbitrate . . . . *L. L. Lost* v 2 753
Long purples That liberal shepherds give a grosser name . . *Hamlet* iv 7 170
Long sickness. My long sickness Of health and living now begins to mend, And nothing brings me all things . . . *T. of Athens* v 1 189
Long since. She and I, long since contracted, Are now so sure that nothing can dissolve us . . . . *Mer. Wives* v 5 236
Long since thy husband served me in my wars . . *Com. of Errors* v 1 161
O, grant me justice! Even for the service that long since I did thee . v 1 191
Long since we were resolved of your truth . . . 1 *Hen. VI.* iii 4 20
Long-since-due. With clamorous demands of date-broke bonds, And the detention of long-since-due debts . . . . . . *T. of Athens* ii 2 39
Long sitting to determine poor men's causes Hath made me full of sickness and diseases . . . . 2 *Hen. VI.* iv 7 93
Long sleep. That, if I then had waked after long sleep, Will make me sleep again . . . . *Tempest* iii 2 148
Long spinners' legs. Her waggon-spokes made of long spinners' legs *Rom. and Jul.* i 4 59
Long spoon. I will leave him; I have no long spoon . . *Tempest* ii 2 103
Bespeak a long spoon.—Why, Dromio?—Marry, he must have a long spoon that must eat with the devil . . . . *Com. of Errors* iv 3 62
Long-staff. I am joined with no foot-land rakers, no long-staff sixpenny strikers . . . . 1 *Hen. IV.* ii 1 82
Long stay. Our dinner will not recompense this long stay *T. of Athens* iii 6 35
Long stayed. He falls to such perusal of my face As he would draw it. Long stay'd he so . . . . *Hamlet* ii 1 91
Long sundered. And ample interchange of sweet discourse, Which so long sunder'd friends should dwell upon . . . *Richard III.* v 3 100
Long sword. With my long sword I would have made you four tall fellows skip like rats . . . . *Mer. Wives* ii 1 236
Give me my long sword, ho!—A crutch, a crutch! . . *Rom. and Jul.* i 1 82
Long-tail. Ay, that I will, come cut and long-tail . . *Mer. Wives* iii 4 47
Long time. For sleeping England long time have I watch'd *Richard II.* ii 1 77
Long time thy shadow hath been thrall to me . . . 1 *Hen. VI.* ii 3 36
Beaten A long time out of play . . . . . . *Hen. VIII.* i 3 45
O, from Italy! Ram thou thy fruitful tidings in mine ears, That long time have been barren . . . . *Ant. and Cleo.* ii 5 25
Long to hear. I long To hear the story of your life . . . *Tempest* v 1 311
I long to hear him call the drunkard husband . . . *T. of Shrew* Ind. 1 133
I'll wait upon you, and I long to hear it . . . . . *Hen. V.* i 1 98
My lord, I long to hear it at full . . . . . 2 *Hen. VI.* ii 2 6
What was your dream? I long to hear you tell it . . *Richard III.* i 4 8
I long to hear how they sped to-day . . . . *Troi. and Cres.* iii 1 154
O, speak of that; that do I long to hear . . . . *Hamlet* ii 2 50
Now do I long to hear how you were found . . . . *Pericles* v 3 56
Long to know. I long to know the truth hereof at large *Com. of Errors* iv 4 146
We know each other well.—We do; and long to know each other worse *Troi. and Cres.* iv 1 31
Long to see. I long to see Quick Cupid's post . . . *Mer. of Venice* ii 9 99
Is there any else longs to see this broken music in his sides? *As Y. L. It* i 2 149
To tell, he longs to see his son, were strong . . . . *W. Tale* i 2 34
Go, lead the way; I long to see my prison . . . 2 *Hen. VI.* ii 4 110
Make a short shrift; he longs to see your head . . *Richard III.* iii 4 97
Achilles Doth long to see unarm'd the valiant Hector . *Troi. and Cres.* iv 5 153
Moreover that we much did long to see you . . . . *Hamlet* ii 2 2
Long to talk. I long to talk with the young noble soldier . *All's Well* iv 5 109
Long-tongued Warwick! dare you speak? . . . . 3 *Hen. VI.* ii 2 102
'Tis a deed of policy: Shall she live to betray this guilt of ours, A long-tongued babbling gossip? . . . . *T. Andron.* iv 2 150
Long traded. And he, long traded in it, makes it seem Like rivers of remorse and innocency . . . . *K. John* iv 3 109
Long travel. With long travel I am stiff and weary . . *Com. of Errors* i 2 15
Long trouble. Say his long trouble now is passing Out of this world; tell him, in death I bless'd him . . . . . . *Hen. VIII.* iv 2 162
Long use. But custom what they did begin Was with long use account no sin . . . . *Pericles* i Gower 30
Long-usurped. This long-usurped royalty From the dead temples of this bloody wretch Have I pluck'd off . . . . *Richard III.* v 5 4
Long-vanished. Pick'd from the worm-holes of long-vanish'd days *Hen. V.* ii 4 86
Long voyage. She would serve after a long voyage at sea . *Pericles* iv 6 48
Long weary life. The last hour Of my long weary life is come upon me *Hen. VIII.* ii 1 133
Long-winded. And one poor penny-worth of sugar-candy to make thee long-winded . . . . 1 *Hen. IV.* iii 3 181
Long withered. To crop at once a too long wither'd flower *Richard II.* ii 1 134
Long withering out. Like to a step-dame or a dowager Long withering out a young man's revenue . . . . . . *M. N. Dream* i 1 6
Long year. But mice and rats, and such small deer, Have been Tom's food for seven long year . . . . *Lear* iii 4 145

'Long. No ceremony that to great ones 'longs, Not the king's crown *Meas. for Meas.* ii 2 59
'Tis 'long of you that spur me with such questions . . . *L. L. Lost* ii 1 119
Mistress, all this coil is 'long of you . . . *M. N. Dream* iii 2 339
The child-bed privilege denied, which 'longs To women of all fashion *W. Tale* iii 2 104
The borrow'd glories that by gift of heaven, By law of nature and of nations, 'long To him and to his heirs . . . . *Hen. V.* ii 4 80
We lose, they daily get; All 'long of this vile traitor 1 *Hen. VI.* iv 3 33
Poictiers and Tours are won away, 'Long all of Somerset and his delay iv 3 46
Would fain that all were well, So 'twere not 'long of him 3 *Hen. VI.* iv 7 32
To his surname Coriolanus 'longs more pride Than pity to our prayers *Coriolanus* v 3 170
Longaville. Biron, Dumain, and Longaville, Have sworn *L. L. Lost* i 1 15
In Normandy, saw I this Longaville: A man of sovereign parts he is esteem'd . . . . . . ii 1 43
Who is he comes here? What, Longaville! and reading! listen, ear iv 3 45
O, would the king, Biron, and Longaville, Were lovers too! . iv 3 123
Longaville Did never sonnet for her sake compile . . iv 3 133
And, gentle Longaville, where lies thy pain? And where my liege's? iv 3 172
This and these pearls to me sent Longaville . . . v 2 53
Lord Longaville said, I came o'er his heart; And trow you what he call'd me? . . . . . . v 2 278
Biron hath plighted faith to me.—And Longaville was for my service born . . . . . . v 2 284
Sweet Lord Longaville, rein thy tongue.—I must rather give it the rein v 2 662
Longed. And how she longed to eat adders heads and toads carbonadoed *W. Tale* iv 4 267
I never long'd to hear a word till now . *Richard II.* v 3 115
Was never subject long'd to be a king As I do long and wish to be a subject . . . . . . 2 *Hen. VI.* iv 9 5
I have remembrances of yours, That I have longed long to re-deliver *Hamlet* iii 1 94
Ne'er long'd my mother so To see me first, as I have now . *Cymbeline* iii 4 2
'Longed. I myself Would for Carnarvonshire, although there 'long'd No more to the crown but that . . *Hen. VIII.* ii 3 48
Longed-for. Fresh expectation troubled not the land With any long'd-for change . . . . *K. John* iv 2 8
Longer. I do now let loose my opinion; hold it no longer . *Tempest* ii 2 37
Even here I will put off my hope and keep it No longer for my flatterer iii 3 8
The tide is now: nay, not thy tide of tears; That tide will stay me longer than I should . . . *T. G. of Ver.* ii 2 15
Away, ass! you'll lose the tide, if you tarry any longer . . ii 3 40
Longer than swiftest expedition Will give thee time to leave . . iii 1 164
Longer than I prove loyal to your grace Let me not live . . iii 2 20
Have you long sojourned there?—Some sixteen months, and longer might have stay'd . . . . . . iv 1 21
You are not to go loose any longer; you must be pinioned *Mer. Wives* iv 2 128
No longer staying but to give the mother Notice of my affair *M. for M.* i 4 86
That in his reprieve, Longer or shorter, he may be so fitted . ii 4 40
Rely upon it till my tale be heard, And hold no longer out . v 1 371
No longer session hold upon my shame . . . . v 1 376
But longer did we not retain much hope . *Com. of Errors* i 1 66
No longer will I be a fool, To put the finger in the eye and weep . ii 2 205
If she lives till doomsday, she'll burn a week longer than the whole world . . . . . . iii 2 101
No longer from head to foot than from hip to hip . . . iii 2 115
And he heartily prays some occasion may detain us longer *Much Ado* i 1 151
But lest my liking might too sudden seem, I would have salved it with a longer treatise . . . . . . i 1 317
Cupid is no longer an archer: his glory shall be ours . ii 1 401
If thou wilt hold longer argument, Do it in notes . . ii 3 55
Have you wept all this while?—Yea, and I will weep a while longer iv 1 258
If a man do not erect in this age his own tomb ere he dies, he shall live no longer in monument than the bell rings . . v 2 81
Dost thou not wish in heart The chain were longer and the letter short? *L. L. Lost* v 2 56
Can any face of brass hold longer out? Here stand I . v 2 395
Fairies, away! We shall chide downright, if I longer stay *M. N. Dream* ii 1 145
I will not trust you, I, Nor longer stay in your curst company . iii 2 341
Your hands than mine are quicker for a fray, My legs are longer though iii 2 343
Superfluity comes sooner by white hairs, but competency lives longer. —Good sentences and well pronounced *Mer. of Venice* i 2 10
For I am a Jew, if I serve the Jew any longer . . . ii 2 120
Why, then the devil give him good of it! I'll stay no longer question iv 1 346
I will no longer endure it . . . *As Y. Like It* i 1 25; 74
No longer Celia, but Aliena . . . . . . i 3 130
I'll tarry no longer with you: farewell, good Signior Love . iii 2 309
I can live no longer by thinking.—I will weary you then no longer with idle talking . . . . v 2 55
[Virginity], the longer kept, the less worth . *All's Well* i 1 167
I'll stay a month longer. I am a fellow o' the strangest mind *T. Night* i 3 119
Bid the dishonest man mend himself; if he mend, he is no longer dishonest . . . . i 5 50
Here lies your way.—No, good swabber; I am to hull here a little longer . . . . i 5 218
Will you stay no longer? nor will you not that I go with you? . ii 1 1
I'll not stay a jot longer.—Thy reason, dear venom, give thy reason . iii 2 1
Though so much As might have drawn one to a longer voyage . iii 3 7
There's money for thee: if you tarry longer, I shall give worse payment iv 1 20
No longer stay.—One seven-night longer.—Very sooth, to-morrow *W. Tale* i 2 16
This great sir will yet stay longer.—You had much ado . . i 2 212
Bohemia stays here longer.—Ha!—Stays here longer.—Ay, but why? i 2 230
Do not draw the curtain.—No longer shall you gaze on't . . v 3 60
No longer than we well could wash our hands . *K. John* iii 1 234
Here is no longer stay.—If thou love me, 'tis time thou wert away *Richard II.* v 5 95
If he fight longer than he sees reason, I'll forswear arms . 1 *Hen. IV.* i 2 207
I'll be no longer guilty of this sin . . . . . ii 4 267
I can no longer brook thy vanities . . . . . v 4 74
He seem'd in running to devour the way, Staying no longer question 2 *Hen. IV.* i 1 48
Let this world no longer be a stage To feed contention in a lingering act! . . . . i 1 155
'Twas no longer ago than Wednesday last . . . . ii 4 93
And when I cannot live any longer, I will do as I may . *Hen. V.* ii 1 17
Enter our gates; dispose of us and ours; For we no longer are defensible . . . . iii 3 50
Now do thou watch, for I can stay no longer . . 1 *Hen. VI.* i 4 18
No longer on Saint Denis will we cry, But Joan la Pucelle . . i 6 28
Longer. So farewell, Talbot; I'll no longer trust thee.—Done like a Frenchman . . . . 1 *Hen. VI.* iii 3 84
My spirit can no longer bear these harms . . . . . iv 7 30
If I longer stay, We shall begin our ancient bickerings . 2 *Hen. VI.* i 1 143
He shall not breathe infection in this air But three days longer . iii 2 288
If I might have a lease of my life for a thousand years I could stay no longer . . . . iv 10 7
No longer Earl of March, but Duke of York . . . 3 *Hen. VI.* ii 1 192
Stay we no longer, dreaming of renown, But sound the trumpets . ii 1 199
In this resolution, I defy thee; Not willing any longer conference . ii 2 171
We'll no longer stay: These words will cost ten thousand lives this day ii 2 176
Forslow no longer, make we hence amain . . . . ii 3 56
Ten days' wonder at the least.—That's a day longer than a wonder lasts . . . . iii 2 114
Altogether joyless. I can no longer hold me patient *Richard III.* i 3 157
Be brief, lest that the process of thy kindness Last longer telling than thy kindness' date . . . . . . iv 4 254
Nay, we must longer kneel: I am a suitor.—Arise . . *Hen. VIII.* i 2 9
May he live Longer than I have time to tell his years! . . ii 1 91
That promises moe thousands: honour's train Is longer than his foreskirt . . . . ii 3 98
It shall be therefore bootless That longer you desire the court . ii 4 62
If heaven had pleased to have given me longer life And able means iv 2 152
Dreaming night will hide our joys no longer *Troi. and Cres.* iv 2 10
Then, in a word, I also am Longer to live most weary . *Coriolanus* iv 5 101
This done, see that you take no longer days . *T. Andron.* iv 2 165
Cheerly, boys; be brisk awhile, and the longer liver take all *Rom. and Jul.* i 5 16
Be but sworn my love, And I'll no longer be a Capulet . . ii 2 36
And meant, indeed, to occupy the argument no longer . . ii 4 106
The excuse that thou dost make in this delay Is longer than the tale thou dost excuse. Is thy news good, or bad? . . . . ii 5 34
I dare no longer stay.—Go, get thee hence . . . . v 3 159
Should I stay longer, It would be my disgrace and your discomfort *Macbeth* iv 2 28
Heaven preserve you! I dare abide no longer.—Whither should I fly? iv 2 73
A beast, that wants discourse of reason, Would have mourn'd longer *Hamlet* i 2 151
While one with moderate haste might tell a hundred.—Longer, longer. i 2 239
Will they pursue the quality no longer than they can sing? . ii 2 363
I will fight with him upon this theme Until my eyelids will no longer wag . . . . v 1 290
O you mighty gods! . . . If I could bear it longer, and not fall To quarrel with your great opposeless wills . . . *Lear* iv 6 37
He hates him much That would upon the rack of this tough world Stretch him out longer . . . . v 3 315
I will indeed no longer endure it . . . . *Othello* iv 2 180
You must not stay here longer, your dismission Is come *Ant. and Cleo.* i 1 26
Naught, naught, all naught! I can behold no longer . . iii 10 1
That life, a very rebel to my will, May hang no longer on me . iv 9 15
I heard of one of them no longer than yesterday: A very honest woman v 2 251
Make pastime with us a day or two, or longer . . *Cymbeline* iii 1 79
No longer exercise Upon a valiant race thy harsh And potent injuries . v 4 82
Forty days longer we do respite you . . . . *Pericles* i 1 116
And that in Tarsus was not best Longer for him to make his rest ii Gower 26
The most high gods not minding longer To withhold the vengeance . ii 4 3
It shall no longer grieve without reproof . . . . ii 4 19
A twelvemonth longer, let me entreat you to Forbear . . ii 4 45
I do commend her choice; And will no longer have it be delay'd . ii 5 22
Longest. It hath been the longest night That e'er I watch'd *T. G. of Ver.* v 2 140
This will last out a night in Russia, When nights are longest there *Meas. for Meas.* ii 1 140
Am I last that knows it? O, thou think'st To serve me last, that I may longest keep Thy sorrow in my breast . . *Richard II.* iii 4 95
So longest way shall have the longest moans . . . . v 1 90
Who long'st, like me, to see thy lord; who long'st,—O, let me bate,—but not like me—yet long'st, But in a fainter kind . *Cymbeline* iii 2 55
Thus time we waste, and longest leagues make short *Pericles* iv 4 1
'Longeth. Such grace As 'longeth to a lover's blessed case! *T. of Shrew* iv 2 45
Hold your own, in any case, With such austerity as 'longeth to a father iv 4 7
Longing. Pity the dearth that I have pined in, By longing for that food so long a time . . . . . . *T. G. of Ver.* ii 7 17
What I stand in need of, To furnish me upon my longing journey . ii 7 85
Longing, saving your honour's reverence, for stewed prunes *Meas. for Meas.* ii 1 92; 102
And strip myself to death, as to a bed That longing have been sick for ii 4 103
Changeable, longing and liking, proud, fantastical . *As Y. Like It* iii 2 431
More longing, wavering, sooner lost and worn, Than women's are *T. N.* ii 4 35
For whose sight I have a woman's longing . . *W. Tale* iv 4 681
But benefit no further Than vainly longing . . . *Hen. VIII.* i 2 81
I have a woman's longing, An appetite that I am sick withal *Troi. and Cres.* iii 3 237
You have saved my longing, and I feed Most hungerly on your sight *T. of Athens* i 1 261
Expectation fainted, Longing for what it had not . . *Ant. and Cleo.* ii 6 48
I have Immortal longings in me . . . . . . v 2 284
Ambitions, covetings, change of prides, disdain, Nice longing *Cymbeline* ii 5 26
Being thus quench'd Of hope, not longing . . . . v 5 196
Lord Cerimon, we do our longing stay To hear the rest untold *Pericles* v 3 83
'Longing. It is an honour 'longing to our house . . *All's Well* iv 2 42
The clothiers all, not able to maintain The many to them 'longing, have put off The spinsters, carders, fullers, weavers . . . *Hen. VIII.* i 2 32
Longly. You look'd so longly on the maid . . . *T. of Shrew* i 1 170
'Loo, Paris, 'loo! now my double-henned sparrow! 'loo, Paris, 'loo! *Troi. and Cres.* v 7 10
Pillicock sat on Pillicock-hill: Halloo, halloo, loo, loo! . *Lear* iii 4 79
Loofed. She once being loof'd, The noble ruin of her magic, Antony, Claps on his sea-wing . . . . . . *Ant. and Cleo.* iii 10 18
Look. How lush and lusty the grass looks! how green! . *Tempest* ii 1 52
You look wearily.—No, noble mistress; 'tis fresh morning with me . iii 1 32
Look thou be true; do not give dalliance Too much the rein . . iv 1 51
Naiads of the windring brooks, With your sedged crowns and ever-harmless looks . . . . iv 1 129
You do look, my son, in a moved sort . . . . . iv 1 146
O, look, sir, look, sir! here is more of us . . . . v 1 216
Scorn is bought with groans; Coy looks with heart-sore sighs *T. G. of Ver.* i 1 30
Borrows his wit from your ladyship's looks, and spends what he borrows . . . . ii 4 39
His mistress Did hold his eyes lock'd in her crystal looks . . ii 4 89
But too mean a servant To have a look of such a worthy mistress . ii 4 108
O, know'st thou not his looks are my soul's food? . . . . ii 7 15

Look. I gave him gentle looks, thereby to find That which thyself hast now disclosed to me . . . . *T. G. of Ver.* iii 1 31
Vouchsafe me, for my meed, but one fair look . . . . . v 4 23
What dangerous action, stood it next to death, Would I not undergo for one calm look! O, 'tis the curse in love! . . . . . v 4 42
I was coming to you. You look very ill . . . . *Mer. Wives* ii 1 36
Look where my ranting host of the Garter comes . . . . ii 1 196
There is either liquor in his pate or money in his purse when he looks so merrily . . . . ii 1 198
Your cat-a-mountain looks, your red-lattice phrases . . . . ii 2 27
By gar, me do look he shall clapper-de-claw me . . . . ii 3 71
I most fehemently desire you you will also look that way . . . iii 1 9
What a world of vile ill-favour'd faults Looks handsome in three hundred pounds a-year! . . . . iii 4 33
Mistress Page and I will look some linen for your head . . . iv 2 83
Mercy is not itself, that oft looks so . . . . *Meas. for Meas.* ii 1 297
Look, what I will not, that I cannot do . . . . . ii 2 52
Sir, a good favour you have, but that you have a hanging look . iv 2 35
Look, if it please you, on this man condemn'd, As if my brother lived . v 1 449
Your evil quits you well: Look that you love your wife . . . v 1 502
Excludes all pity from our threatening looks . . *Com. of Errors* i 1 10
Whilst I at home starve for a merry look . . . . . ii 1 88
My decayed fair A sunny look of his would soon repair . . . ii 1 99
Know my aspect And fashion your demeanour to my looks . . . ii 2 33
Look strange and frown: Some other mistress hath thy sweet aspects . ii 2 112
Look sweet, speak fair, become disloyalty . . . . . iii 2 11
'Tis double wrong, to truant with your bed And let her read it in thy looks . . . . iii 2 18
Where stood Belgia, the Netherlands?—Oh, sir, I did not look so low . iii 2 143
Alas, how fiery and how sharp he looks! . . . . . . iv 4 53
I know it by their pale and deadly looks . . . . . iv 4 96
Ay me, poor man, how pale and wan he looks! . . . . . iv 4 111
Why look you strange on me? you know me well . . . . v 1 295
Look, what will serve is fit: 'tis once, thou lovest . . *Much Ado* i 1 320
A proper squire! And who, and who? which way looks he? . . i 3 55
How tartly that gentleman looks! . . . . ii 1 3
So you walk softly and look sweetly and say nothing, I am yours for the walk . . . . ii 1 91
Look you for any other issue?—Only to despite them . . . . ii 2 30
For look where Beatrice, like a lapwing, runs Close by the ground . iii 1 24
Indeed, he looks younger than he did, by the loss of a beard . . iii 2 48
Methinks, you look with your eyes as other women do . . . iii 4 92
This looks not like a nuptial . . . . iv 1 69
Pray thee, fellow, peace: I do not like thy look, I promise thee . iv 2 47
Thou wilt be, if my cousin do not look exceeding narrowly to thee . v 4 118
While truth the while Doth falsely blind the eyesight of his look *L. L. L.* i 1 76
Study is like the heaven's glorious sun, That will not be deep-search'd with saucy looks . . . . i 1 85
O thou monster Ignorance, how deformed dost thou look! . . . iv 2 24
I will look again on the intellect of the letter . . . . iv 2 137
Beauty doth beauty lack, If that she learn not of her eye to look . iv 3 252
In that each of you have forsworn his book, Can you still dream and pore and thereon look? . . . . iv 3 298
Why looks your highness sad?—Help, hold his brows! he'll swoon! Why look you pale? Sea-sick, I think . . . . . v 2 391
Our letters, madam, show'd much more than jest.—So did our looks . v 2 796
Rather your eyes must with his judgement look . . *M. N. Dream* i 1 57
O, teach me how you look . . . . i 1 192
Love looks not with the eyes, but with the mind . . . . i 1 234
And look thou meet me ere the first cock crow . . . . ii 1 267
I did never, no, nor never can, Deserve a sweet look from Demetrius' eye ii 2 127
The moon methinks looks with a watery eye . . . . . iii 1 203
So should a murderer look, so dead, so grim.—So should the murder'd look . . . . iii 2 57
Yet you, the murderer, look as bright, as clear, As yonder Venus . . iii 2 60
Go swifter than the wind, And Helena of Athens look thou find . . iii 2 95
Counterfeit sad looks, Make mouths upon me when I turn my back . iii 2 237
And from each other look thou lead them thus . . . . iii 2 363
For fear lest day should look their shames upon . . . . iii 2 385
And darest not stand, nor look me in the face . . . . iii 2 424
You look not well, Signior Antonio . . . . *Mer. of Venice* i 1 73
How like a fawning publican he looks! . . . . . . i 3 42
I would outstare the sternest eyes that look . . . . . ii 1 27
Wear prayer-books in my pocket, look demurely . . . . ii 2 201
Let good Antonio look he keep his day, Or he shall pay for this . . ii 8 25
You shall look fairer, ere I give or hazard . . . . . ii 9 22
My eyes, my lord, can look as swift as yours . . . . iii 2 199
Look, what notes and garments he doth give thee, Bring them, I pray thee . . . . iii 4 51
O wise and upright judge! How much more elder art thou than thy looks! . . . . iv 1 251
This night methinks is but the daylight sick; It looks a little paler . v 1 125
Alas, he is too young! yet he looks successfully . . *As Y. Like It* i 2 162
He hath been all this day to look you . . . . . . ii 5 34
What, you look merrily! . . . . ii 7 11
Every eye which in this forest looks Shall see thy virtue witness'd every where . . . . iii 2 7
Looks he as freshly as he did? . . . . iii 2 243
He is drowned in the brook: look but in, and you shall see him . . iii 2 305
Fast as she answers thee with frowning looks, I'll sauce her . . . iii 5 68
Why look you so upon me?—For no ill will I bear you . . . iii 5 69
My books and instruments shall be my company, On them to look *T. of S.* i 1 83
How now, my friend! why dost thou look so pale? . . . . ii 1 143
I'll say she looks as clear As morning roses newly wash'd with dew . ii 1 173
You must not look so sour.—It is my fashion, when I see a crab . . ii 1 229
Nay, look not big, nor stamp, nor stare, nor fret; I will be master . iii 2 230
She, poor soul, Knows not which way to stand, to look, to speak . . iv 1 188
Kindness in women, not their beauteous looks, Shall win my love . iv 2 41
Pluck up thy spirits; look cheerfully upon me . . . . . iv 3 38
Look not pale, Bianca; thy father will not frown . . . . v 1 143
Craves no other tribute at thy hands But love, fair looks . . . v 2 153
When virtue's steely bones Look bleak i' the cold wind . . *All's Well* i 1 115
He did look far Into the service of the time . . . . . i 2 26
'Tis so; for, look, thy cheeks Confess it, th' one to th' other . . i 3 182
I must go look my twigs; he shall be caught . . . . . iii 6 115
Nay, look not so upon me; we shall hear of your lordship anon . . iv 3 221
I perceive, sir, by the general's looks, we shall be fain to hang you . iv 3 269
He looks well on't . . . . v 3 31
Her business looks in her With an importing visage . . . . v 3 135
Why do you look so strange upon your wife?—She's none of mine . . v 3 168

Look. Now I am your fool.—O, what a deal of scorn looks beautiful In the contempt and anger of his lip! . . . . . . *T. Night* iii 1 157
They will kill one another by the look, like cockatrices . . . . iii 4 215
Look then to be well edified when the fool delivers the madman . . v 1 298
I must be patient till the heavens look With an aspect more favourable *W. Tale* ii 1 106
A thousand knees Ten thousand years together . . could not move the gods To look that way thou wert . . . . iii 2 215
The skies look grimly And threaten present blusters . . . . iii 3 3
How would he look, to see his work so noble Vilely bound up? . . iv 4 21
The gifts she looks from me are pack'd and lock'd Up in my heart . iv 4 369
Why look you so upon me? I am but sorry, not afeard . . . . iv 4 473
Lift up thy looks: From my succession wipe me, father . . . iv 4 490
I thought of her, Even in these looks I made . . . . . v 1 228
Look upon my brother: both your pardons, That e'er put between your holy looks My ill suspicion . . . . v 3 148
Lest men should say 'Look, where three-farthings goes!' . . *K. John* i 1 143
I see a yielding in the looks of France; Mark, how they whisper . . ii 1 474
Why dost thou look so sadly on my son? What means that hand? . . iii 1 20
Cousin, look not sad: Thy grandam loves thee . . . . . iii 3 2
He will look as hollow as a ghost, As dim and meagre as an ague's fit . iii 4 84
Walks up and down with me, Puts on his pretty looks . . . . iii 4 95
Heat me these irons hot; and look thou stand Within the arras . . iv 1 1
Save me! my eyes are out Even with the fierce looks of these bloody men iv 1 74
He hath a stern look, but a gentle heart . . . . . . iv 1 88
Why look you sad? Be great in act, as you have been in thought . . v 1 44
You look but on the outside of this work . . . . . . v 2 109
Look, what I speak, my life shall prove it true . . . *Richard II.* i 1 87
The pleasure that some fathers feed upon, Is my strict fast; I mean, my children's looks . . . . ii 1 80
O, full of careful business are his looks! . . . . . . ii 2 75
The pale-faced moon looks bloody on the earth . . . . . ii 4 10
Comfort, my liege: why looks your grace so pale? . . . . iii 2 75
Look not to the ground, Ye favourites of a king: are we not high? . iii 2 87
Allowing him a breath, a little scene, To monarchize, be fear'd, and kill with looks . . . . iii 2 165
Speak sweetly, man, although thy looks be sour . . . . . iii 2 193
March on, and mark King Richard how he looks . . . . . iii 3 61
Yet looks he like a king: behold, his eye, As bright as is the eagle's . iii 3 68
We do debase ourselves, cousin, do we not, To look so poorly? . . iii 3 128
Cut off the heads of too fast growing sprays, That look too lofty . . iii 4 35
That my sad look Should grace the triumph of great Bolingbroke . . iii 4 98
You would have thought the very windows spake, So many greedy looks v 2 13
What means our cousin, that he stares and looks So wildly? . . . v 3 24
Who then, affrighted with their bloody looks, Ran fearfully . 1 *Hen. IV.* i 3 104
See already how he doth begin To make us strangers to his looks of love i 3 290
A cheerful look, a pleasing eye and a most noble carriage . . . ii 4 465
I see virtue in his looks . . . . ii 4 470
I understand thy looks: that pretty Welsh Which thou pour'st down from these swelling heavens I am too perfect in . . . . . iii 1 201
Thy looks are full of speed.—So hath the business that I come to speak of . . . . iii 2 162
Why say you so? looks he not for supply?—So do we . . . . iv 3 3
It pleased your majesty to turn your looks Of favour from myself . . v 1 30
Look how we can, or sad or merrily, Interpretation will misquote our looks . . . . v 2 13
Yea, this man's brow . . . : So looks the strand whereon the imperious flood Hath left a witness'd usurpation . . . . 2 *Hen. IV.* i 1 62
Even such a man, so faint, so spiritless, So dull, so dead in look . . i 1 71
We should advance ourselves To look with forehead bold and big enough . ii 3 8
Dear Harry Threw many a northward look to see his father . . . ii 3 13
And, look, whether the fiery Trigon, his man, be not lisping . . ii 4 288
Lest rest and lying still might make them look Too near unto my state iv 5 212
Which cannot look more hideously upon me Than I have drawn it . . v 2 12
You all look strangely on me . . . . v 2 63
Look who's at door there, ho! who knocks? . . . . . . v 3 74
Freshly looks and over-bears attaint With cheerful semblance *Hen. V.* iv Prol. 39
That every wretch, pining and pale before, Beholding him, plucks comfort from his looks . . . . iv Prol. 42
That we may wander o'er this bloody field To look our dead . . . iv 7 76
The venom of such looks, we fairly hope, Have lost their quality . . v 2 18
Grow like savages,—as soldiers will That nothing do but meditate on blood,—To swearing and stern looks . . . . v 2 61
I cannot look greenly nor gasp out my eloquence . . . . . v 2 149
Avouch the thoughts of your heart with the looks of an empress . . v 2 254
Whom all France with their chief assembled strength Durst not presume to look once in the face . . . . . . 1 *Hen. VI.* i 1 140
Or piteous they will look, like drowned mice . . . . . i 2 12
Methinks your looks are sad, your cheer appall'd . . . . i 2 48
Let thy looks be stern: By this means shall we sound what skill she hath . . . . i 2 62
Meantime look gracious on thy prostrate thrall . . . . . i 2 117
Though thy speech doth fail, One eye thou hast, to look to heaven for grace . . . . i 4 83
This was your default, That, being captain of the watch to-night, Did look no better to that weighty charge . . . . . . ii 1 62
For pale they look with fear, as witnessing The truth on our side . . ii 4 63
Why look you still so stern and tragical? . . . . . . iii 1 125
Let's get us from the walls; For Talbot means no goodness by his looks iii 2 72
As looks the mother on her lowly babe When death doth close his tender dying eyes, See, see the pining malady of France . . . . iii 3 47
If they perceive dissension in our looks . . . . . . iv 1 139
See here the tainture of thy nest, And look thyself be faultless 2 *Hen. VI.* ii 1 189
The abject people gazing on thy face, With envious looks . . . ii 4 12
Hide thee from their hateful looks, And, in thy closet pent up, rue my shame . . . . ii 4 23
If we did but glance a far-off look, Immediately he was upon his knee . iii 1 10
Look not upon me, for thine eyes are wounding . . . . . iii 2 51
Look, on the sheets his hair, you see, is sticking . . . . iii 2 174
Eternal Mover of the heavens, Look with a gentle eye upon this wretch! iii 3 20
See if thou canst outface me with thy looks . . . . . . iv 10 49
Nay, do not fright us with an angry look . . . . . . v 1 126
Here comes the queen, whose looks bewray her anger . . 3 *Hen. VI.* i 1 211
So looks the pent-up lion o'er the wretch That trembles under his devouring paws; And so he walks . . . . i 3 12
Kill me with thy sword, And not with such a cruel threatening look . i 3 17
Now looks he like a king! Ay, this is he that took King Henry's chair . i 4 96
What art thou, whose heavy looks foretell Some dreadful story? . . ii 1 43
To whom do lions cast their gentle looks? Not to the beast that would usurp their den . . . . ii 2 11

Look. And smooth the frowns of war with peaceful looks . *3 Hen. VI.* ii 6 32
Her looks do argue her replete with modesty; Her words do show her wit iii 2 84
The widow likes it not, for she looks very sad . iii 2 110
And witch sweet ladies with my words and looks . iii 2 150
Look, therefore, Lewis, that by this league and marriage Thou draw not on thy danger and dishonour iii 3 74
His looks are full of peaceful majesty iv 6 71
If you ever chance to have a child, Look in his youth to have him so cut off . v 5 66
And I nothing to back my suit at all, But the plain devil and dissembling looks, And yet to win her! *Richard III.* i 2 237
Take heed of yonder dog! Look, when he fawns, he bites i 3 290
Why looks your grace so heavily to-day? i 4 1
Thy voice is thunder, but thy looks are humble.—My voice is now the king's, my looks mine own i 4 173
Why look you pale? Who sent you hither? Wherefore do you come? i 4 176
My friend, I spy some pity in thy looks i 4 270
Look I so pale, Lord Dorset, as the rest?—Ay, my good lord ii 1 83
Ye cannot reason almost with a man That looks not heavily and full of fear ii 3 40
And, look, when I am king, claim thou of me The earldom of Hereford iii 1 194
'Tis a vile thing to die, my gracious lord, When men are unprepared and look not for it.—O monstrous, monstrous! iii 2 65
His grace looks cheerfully and smooth to-day iii 4 50
With no man here he is offended; For, were he, he had shown it in his looks iii 4 59
Look that it be done iii 4 80
Who builds his hopes in air of your good looks, Lives like a drunken sailor on a mast, Ready, with every nod, to tumble down iii 4 100
Ghastly looks Are at my service, like enforced smiles iii 5 8
And, by that knot, looks proudly o'er the crown iv 3 42
Look, what is done cannot be now amended iv 4 291
Look your faith be firm, Or else his head's assurance is but frail iv 4 497
Why look you so sad?—My heart is ten times lighter than my looks v 3 3
Look that my staves be sound, and not too heavy v 3 65
And Buckingham Shall lessen this big look *Hen. VIII.* i 1 119
I read in's looks Matter against me; and his eye reviled Me i 1 125
Yet let 'em look they glory not in mischief ii 1 66
How sad he looks! sure, he is much afflicted ii 2 63
So looks the chafed lion Upon the daring huntsman that has gall'd him iii 2 206
How long her face is drawn? how pale she looks, And of an earthy cold? iv 2 97
Now, by thy looks I guess thy message. Is the queen deliver'd? v 1 161
She looked yesternight fairer than ever I saw her look *Troi. and Cres.* i 1 33
Look you what hacks are on his helmet! look you yonder, do you see? look you there: there's no jesting i 2 222
Look ye yonder, niece; is't not a gallant man too, is't not? i 2 231
Look well upon him, niece: look you how his sword is bloodied! i 2 252
And how he looks, and how he goes! O admirable youth! i 2 254
Ne'er look, ne'er look; the eagles are gone: crows and daws! i 2 264
How may A stranger to those most imperial looks Know them from eyes of other mortals? i 3 224
Regard him well.—'Well!' why, I do so.—But yet you look not well upon him ii 1 69
I do enjoy At ample point all that I did possess, Save these men's looks iii 3 90
Neither gave to me Good word nor look: what, are my deeds forgot? iii 3 144
What Trojan is that same that looks so heavy? iv 5 95
With thy grim looks and The thunder-like percussion of thy sounds, Thou madest thine enemies shake *Coriolanus* i 4 58
By his looks methinks 'Tis warm at's heart ii 3 159
And that is there which looks With us to break his neck iii 3 29
We survive To tremble under Titus' threatening looks *T. Andron.* i 1 134
Look graciously on him; Lose not so noble a friend on vain suppose, Nor with sour looks afflict his gentle heart i 1 439
These words, these looks, infuse new life in me i 1 461
Why should he despair that knows to court it With words, fair looks? ii 1 92
Why doth your highness look so pale and wan? ii 3 90
Look, sirs, if you can find the huntsman out ii 3 278
And for thy hand Look by and by to have thy sons with thee iii 1 202
Look ye draw home enough, and 'tis there straight. iv 3 3
Had nature lent thee but thy mother's look, Villain, thou mightst have been an emperor v 1 29
Look round about the wicked streets of Rome v 2 98
I'll look to like, if looking liking move *Rom. and Jul.* i 3 97
Romeo is beloved and loves again, Alike bewitched by the charm of looks ii Prol. 6
Look thou but sweet, And I am proof against their enmity ii 2 72
Love goes toward love, as schoolboys from their books, But love from love, toward school with heavy looks ii 2 158
I'll warrant you, when I say so, she looks as pale as any clout ii 4 218
Here all eyes gaze on us.—Men's eyes were made to look, and let them gaze iii 1 57
All this uttered With gentle breath, calm look, knees humbly bow'd iii 1 161
For exile hath more terror in his look, Much more than death iii 3 13
Get thee to church o' Thursday, Or never after look me in the face iii 5 163
To-morrow night look that thou lie alone; Let not thy nurse lie with thee iv 1 91
See where she comes from shrift with merry look iv 2 15
What is the matter?—Look, look! O heavy day!—O me, O me! iv 5 18
I do beseech you, sir, have patience: Your looks are pale and wild v 1 28
Meagre were his looks, Sharp misery had worn him to the bones v 1 40
I'll hide me hereabout: His looks I fear, and his intents I doubt v 3 44
Eyes, look your last! Arms, take your last embrace! v 3 112
What further woe conspires against mine age?—Look, and thou shalt see v 3 213
With wild looks, bid me devise some mean To rid her from this second marriage v 3 240
After distasteful looks and these hard fractions *T. of Athens* ii 2 220
They froze me into silence.—You gods, reward them! Prithee, man, look cheerly ii 2 223
I'll look you out a good turn iii 2 67
You undergo too strict a paradox, Striving to make an ugly deed look fair iii 5 25
You cannot make gross sins look clear: To revenge is no valour iii 5 38
Hath in her more destruction than thy sword, For all her cherubin look iv 3 63
Why this spade? this place? This slave-like habit? and these looks of care? iv 3 205
Be not deceived: if I have veil'd my look, I turn the trouble of my countenance Merely upon myself *J. Cæsar* i 2 37
Cicero Looks with such ferret and such fiery eyes i 2 186
Yond Cassius has a lean and hungry look; He thinks too much i 2 194
He is a great observer and he looks Quite through the deeds of men i 2 202
Tell us what hath chanced to-day, That Cæsar looks so sad i 2 217
An I tell you that, I'll ne'er look you i' the face again i 2 284

Look. Look fresh and merrily; Let not our looks put on our purposes *J. Cæsar* ii 1 225
When I ask'd you what the matter was, You stared upon me with ungentle looks ii 1 242
And look where Publius is come to fetch me ii 2 108
Yes, bring me word, boy, if thy lord look well, For he went sickly forth ii 4 13
So should he look That seems to speak things strange *Macbeth* i 2 46
Look what I have.—Show me, show me i 3 26
That look not like the inhabitants o' the earth, And yet are on't i 3 41
And wakes it now, to look so green and pale At what it did so freely? i 7 37
Sleek o'er your rugged looks; Be bright and jovial among your guests iii 2 27
Why do you make such faces? When all's done, You look but on a stool iii 4 68
Prithee, see there! behold! look! lo! how say you? Why, what care I? iii 4 69
Why, how now, Hecate! you look angerly.—Have I not reason? iii 5 1
Though all things foul would wear the brows of grace, Yet grace must still look so iv 3 24
Wash your hands, put on your nightgown; look not so pale v 1 69
Thou cream-faced loon! Where got'st thou that goose look? v 3 12
Peace, break thee off; look, where it comes again! *Hamlet* i 1 40
Looks it not like the king? mark it, Horatio.—Most like i 1 43
The very place puts toys of desperation, Without more motive, into every brain That looks so many fathoms to the sea i 4 77
With a look so piteous in purport As if he had been loosed out of hell ii 1 82
But, look, where sadly the poor wretch comes reading ii 2 168
There is a kind of confession in your looks ii 2 289
I'll observe his looks; I'll tent him to the quick: if he but blench, I know my course ii 2 625
How cheerfully my mother looks, and my father died within these two hours iii 2 133
Whereon do you look?—On him, on him! Look you, how pale he glares! iii 4 124
Thy cicatrice looks raw and red After the Danish sword iv 3 62
What is the cause, Laertes, That thy rebellion looks so giant-like? iv 5 121
The queen his mother Lives almost by his looks iv 7 12
And let his knights have colder looks among you *Lear* i 3 22
Do you bandy looks with me, you rascal? i 4 92
Commanded me to follow, . . . gave me cold looks ii 4 37
Those wicked creatures yet do look well-favour'd, When others are more wicked ii 4 259
Whose warp'd looks proclaim What store her heart is made on iii 6 56
How is't, my lord? how look you?—I have received a hurt iii 7 94
A cliff, whose high and bending head Looks fearfully in the confined deep iv 1 77
She gave strange œillades and most speaking looks iv 5 25
I'll look no more; Lest my brain turn, and the deficient sight Topple down iv 6 22
Look with thine ears: see how yond justice rails upon yond simple thief iv 6 154
Since thy outside looks so fair and warlike v 3 142
Good Michael, look you to the guard to-night *Othello* ii 3 1
Perhaps he sees it not; or his good nature Prizes the virtue that appears in Cassio, And looks not on his evils ii 3 140
Look with care about the town, And silence those whom this vile brawl distracted ii 3 255
And when she seem'd to shake and fear your looks, She loved them most iii 3 207
Patience, thou young and rose-lipp'd cherubin,—Ay, there, look grim as hell! iv 2 64
Dismiss your attendant there: look it be done.—I will, my lord iv 3 9
How goes it now? he looks gentler than he did.—He says he will return iv 3 11
What, look you pale? O, bear him out o' the air v 1 104
Look you pale, mistress? Do you perceive the gastness of her eye? v 1 105
Now, how dost thou look now? O ill-starr'd wench! Pale as thy smock! v 2 272
When we shall meet at compt, This look of thine will hurl my soul from heaven v 2 274
He was not sad, for he would shine on those That make their looks by his; he was not merry *Ant. and Cleo.* i 5 56
Look well to my husband's house; and— What, Octavia?—I'll tell you in your ear iii 2 45
Pray you, look not sad, Nor make replies of loathness iii 11 17
Look, thou say He makes me angry with him iii 13 140
They cannot tell; look grimly, And dare not speak their knowledge iv 12 5
Look you sad, friends? The gods rebuke me, but it is tidings To wash the eyes of kings.—And strange it is v 1 26
And would gladly Look him i' the face.—This I'll report v 2 32
Although they wear their faces to the bent Of the king's looks *Cymbeline* i 1 14
How look I, That I should seem to lack humanity So much as this fact comes to? iii 2 15
Why tender'st thou that paper to me, with A look untender? iii 4 12
She looks us like A thing more made of malice than of duty iii 5 32
Gilded pale looks, Part shame, part spirit renew'd v 3 34
Some turn'd coward But by example . . . gan to look The way that they did v 3 37
Such precious deeds in one that promised nought But beggary and poor looks v 5 10
So for her many a wight did die, As yon grim looks do testify *Pericles* 1 Gower 40
He'll o'erspread the land, And with the ostent of war will look so huge, Amazement shall drive courage from the state i 2 25
Thou Hast moved us: what seest thou in our looks?—An angry brow i 2 51
Tyre, I now look from thee then, and to Tarsus Intend my travel i 2 115
You are well favour'd, and your looks foreshow You have a gentle heart iv 1 86
My authority shall not see thee, or else look friendly upon thee iv 6 97
Look, Thaisa is Recovered.—O, let me look! v 3 28
And now, This ornament Makes me look dismal will I clip to form v 3 74
Look about. What is't? a spirit? Lord, how it looks about! *Tempest* i 2 410
Master, master, look about you: who goes there? *T. of Shrew* i 2 141
So, look about you: know you any here? *All's Well* iv 3 348
Look about, Davy. Where are you, Sir John? Come, come, come *2 Hen. IV.* v 1 59
The day is broke; be wary, look about *Rom. and Jul.* iii 5 40
If thou beest not immortal, look about you *J. Cæsar* ii 3 7
Report is changeable. 'Tis time to look about *Lear* iv 7 93
Look after. Will they yet look after thee? *Mer. Wives* ii 2 146
Go, look after him.—He is but mad yet, madonna *T. Night* i 5 144
With dimm'd eyes Look after him and cannot do him good *2 Hen. VI.* iii 1 219
Look after her; Remove from her the means of all annoyance *Macbeth* v 1 83
All those requisites in him that folly and green minds look after *Othello* ii 1 251
Honest! good fellow, what's that? If it be a day fits you, search out of the calendar, and nobody look after it *Pericles* ii 1 59
Look as. You look as you had something more to say *Lear* v 3 201
Look as if. You look As if you held a brow of much distraction *W. Tale* i 2 148
Look as though. Methinks he looks as though he were in love *T. of S.* iii 1 88
Look askance. Thou canst not frown, thou canst not look askance ii 1 249
Look back into your mighty ancestors *Hen. V.* i 2 102

Look back. Speak and look back, and pry on every side . *Richard III.* iii 5 6
Look back, defend thee, here are enemies . . . . iii 5 19
Stay, yet look back with me unto the Tower . . . . . . iv 1 98
I will not be denied : sweet heart, look back . . . . . *T. Andron.* i 1 481
Let me look back upon thee. O thou wall! . . . . *T. of Athens* iv 1 1
Even so my bloody thoughts, with violent pace, Shall ne'er look back *Othello* iii 3 458
And may save, But to look back in frown . . . . *Cymbeline* v 3 28
Look behind you, my lord.—Take that, and that . . *Richard III.* i 4 275
See suitors following and not look behind . . . . *Othello* ii 1 158
Look beyond. You look beyond him quite . . . *2 Hen. IV.* iv 4 67
Look big. A rendezvous, a home to fly unto, If that the devil and mischance look big . . . . *1 Hen. IV.* iv 1 58
Look down, you gods, And on this couple drop a blessed crown ! *Tempest* v 1 201
Look down And see what death is doing . . . . . *W. Tale* iii 2 149
You gods, look down And from your sacred vials pour your graces Upon my daughter's head ! . . . . v 3 121
Look down into the Pomgarnet, Ralph . . . . . *1 Hen. IV.* ii 4 41
The gods look down, and this unnatural scene They laugh at *Coriolanus* v 3 184
Look down into this den, And see a fearful sight of blood *T. Andron.* ii 3 215
I look down towards his feet ; but that's a fable. If that thou be'st a devil, I cannot kill thee . . . . *Othello* v 2 286
Look for. I will proclaim thee, Angelo ; look for't . . *Meas. for Meas.* ii 4 151
I look for an earthquake too, then . . . . . . *Much Ado* i 1 275
But on this travail look for greater birth . . . . . . iv 1 215
We look for you to-morrow.—We will not fail . . . . . . v 1 338
Do not look for further recompense Than thine own gladness *As Y. L. It* iii 5 97
If this be not that you look for, I have no more to say . *T. of Shrew* iv 4 96
In whose easiest passage Look for no less than death . . *W. Tale* iii 2 92
Ere the crown he looks for live in peace . . . . *Richard II.* iii 3 95
The king, I can tell you, looks for us all : we must away . *1 Hen. IV.* iv 2 63
With lustier maintenance than I did look for Of such an ungrown warrier v 4 22
If you look for a good speech now, you undo me . . *2 Hen. IV.* Epil. 4
And, in advantage lingering, looks for rescue . . . . *1 Hen. VI.* iv 4 19
To cross me from the golden time I look for ! . . . . *3 Hen. VI.* iii 2 127
When the sun sets, who doth not look for night? . . *Richard III.* ii 3 34
Towards three or four o'clock Look for the news that the Guildhall affords . . . . iii 5 102
Do you look for ale and cakes here? . . . . . *Hen. VIII.* v 4 10
Look for thy reward Among the nettles at the elder-tree *T. Andron.* ii 3 271
Deliver up your pigeons, and then look for your reward . . . iv 3 112
I know young bloods look for a time of rest . . . *J. Cæsar* iv 3 262
We must think men are not gods, Nor of them look for such observances As fit the bridal . . . . *Othello* iii 4 149
Look For fury not to be resisted. Thus defied, I thank thee *Cymbeline* iii 1 67
We do not look for reverence, but for love . . . . *Pericles* i 4 99
We sit too long on trifles, And waste the time, which looks for other revels . . . . ii 3 93
Look forward on the journey you shall go . . . . . *Meas. for Meas.* iv 3 61
Look further. I know not. Well, I will look further into't *Mer. Wives* ii 1 245
A very pretence and purpose of unkindness : I will look further into't *Lear* i 4 76
Look here what I found on a palm-tree . . . . *As Y. Like It* iii 2 185
Look here upon thy brother Geffrey's face ; These eyes, these brows *K. John* ii 1 99
Look here, I throw my infamy at thee . . . . . *3 Hen. VI.* v 1 82
My lord, look here : look here, Lavinia : This sandy plot is plain *T. Andron.* iv 1 68
Look here, upon this picture, and on this . . . . *Hamlet* iii 4 53
Look here, and at thy sovereign leisure read . . . *Ant. and Cleo.* i 3 60
Look here, love ; This diamond was my mother's : take it, heart . *Cymb.* i 1 111
Look how he claws him with a talent . . . . . *L. L. Lost* iv 2 65
I go, I go ; look how I go, Swifter than arrow . . . *M. N. Dream* iii 2 100
Look, how far The substance of my praise doth wrong this shadow *M. of V.* iii 2 126
Look how the floor of heaven Is thick inlaid with patines of bright gold v 1 58
Look how we can, or sad or merrily, Interpretation will misquote *1 Hen. IV.* v 2 12
Look how he looks ! there's a countenance ! . . . . *Troi. and Cres.* i 2 218
O heavens ! O wife, look how our daughter bleeds ! . . *Rom. and Jul.* v 3 202
What is it she does now? Look, how she rubs her hands . *Macbeth* v 1 30
Look how thou stirrest now ! come away, or I'll fetch thee . *Pericles* ii 1 16
Look how fresh she looks ! They were too rough That threw her in the sea . . . . iii 2 79
Look ill. It looks ill, it eats drily . . . . . . *All's Well* i 1 175
Those healths will make thee and thy state look ill . . *T. of Athens* i 2 58
Look in. This cell's my court : . . . pray you, look in . . *Tempest* v 1 167
I beseech you, sir, look in this gentleman's face . . *Meas. for Meas.* ii 1 153
Like a prophet, Looks in a glass, that shows what future evils . . ii 2 95
A calendar ! look in the almanac ; find out moonshine . . *M. N. Dream* iii 1 54
The Slys are no rogues ; look in the chronicles . . . *T. of Shrew* Ind. 1 4
What say'st thou, boy? look in the lady's face.—I do, my lord *K. John* ii 1 495
If you look in the maps of the 'orld, I warrant you sall find . *Hen. V.* iv 7 24
Never looks in his glass for love of any thing he sees there . . . v 2 154
Let us look in ; the sight will much delight thee . . . *1 Hen. VI.* i 4 62
Look in a glass, and call thy image so . . . . . *2 Hen. VI.* v 1 142
Thou liest : look in thy last work . . . . . . *T. of Athens* v 1 228
He then unto the ladder turns his back, Looks in the clouds *J. Cæsar* ii 1 26
Is not to-morrow, boy, the ides of March?—I know not, sir.—Look in the calendar, and bring me word . . . . ii 1 42
Let me see your eyes ; Look in my face . . . . . *Othello* iv 2 26
Look in upon me then and speak with me . . . . . . v 2 257
Look into. It concerns me To look into the bottom of my place *M. for M.* i 1 79
Look into Master Froth here, sir ; a man of fourscore pound a year . ii 1 126
Those heavenly eyes, that look into these faults, Suggested us *L. L. Lost* v 2 779
But, O, how bitter a thing it is to look into happiness through another man's eyes ! . . . . *As Y. Like It* v 2 48
That by degrees we mean to look into, And watch our vantage *T. of Shrew* iii 2 145
To look into the blots and stains of right. . . . . *K. John* ii 1 114
Toward London back again, To look into this business thoroughly *2 Hen. VI.* ii 1 202
None are for me That look into me with considerate eyes *Richard III.* iv 2 30
All that dare Look into these affairs see this main end . *Hen. VIII.* ii 2 41
If you can look into the seeds of time, And say which grain will grow and which will not, Speak then to me . . . . . *Macbeth* i 3 58
Look like. Yond same black cloud, yond huge one, looks like a foul bombard . . . . *Tempest* ii 2 21
To look like her are chimney-sweepers black . . . . *L. L. Lost.* iv 3 266
Do I look like a cudgel or a hovel-post, a staff or a prop? *Mer. of Venice* ii 2 71
A traitor you do look like ; but such traitors His majesty seldom fears *All's Well* ii 1 99
He looks like a poor, decayed, ingenious, foolish, rascally knave . v 2 24
He looks like sooth. He says he loves my daughter : I think so too *W. T.* iv 4 171
O, now you look like Hubert ! all this while You were disguised *K. John* iv 1 126
And make high majesty look like itself . . . . *Richard II.* ii 1 295
Weigh him well, And that which looks like pride is courtesy *T. and C.* iv 5 82
Look like. Dost hate a medlar?—Ay, though it look like thee *T. of A.* iv 3 308
That nothing but himself which looks like man Is friendly with him . v 1 121
And all the rest look like a chidden train . . . . *J. Cæsar* i 2 184
To beguile the time, Look like the time ; bear welcome in your eye *Macbeth* i 5 65
Look like the innocent flower, But be the serpent under't . . . i 5 66
And let thine eye look like a friend on Denmark . . . *Hamlet* i 2 69
Play one scene Of excellent dissembling ; and let it look Like perfect honour.—You'll heat my blood : no more . . . *Ant. and Cleo.* i 3 79
She looks like sleep, As she would catch another Antony In her strong toil . . . . v 2 349
You look like Romans, And not o' the court of Britain . . *Cymbeline* v 5 24
Thou dost look Like Patience gazing on kings' graves . . *Pericles* v 1 138
Look old. Though I look old, yet I am strong and lusty . *As Y. Like It* ii 3 47
Look on. 'Tis a villain, sir, I do not love to look on. . . *Tempest* i 2 310
That hath dazzled my reason's light ; But when I look on her perfections, There is no reason but I shall be blind . . . *T. G. of Ver.* ii 4 211
Unless I look on Silvia in the day, There is no day for me to look upon iii 1 180
Let me look on that again.—It may not be ; good madam, pardon me . iv 4 130
I had rather wink than look on them . . . . v 2 14
'Nay,' said I, 'will you cast away your child on a fool, and a physician? Look on Master Fenton' . . . . *Mer. Wives* iii 4 101
As good to wink, sweet love, as look on night . . . *Com. of Errors* iii 2 58
Ne'er may I look on day, nor sleep on night, But she tells to your highness simple truth ! . . . . v 1 210
Disdain and scorn ride sparkling in her eyes, Misprising what they look on, and her wit Values itself so highly . . . *Much Ado* iii 1 52
For I am sick when I do look on thee.—And I am sick when I look not on you . . . . *M. N. Dream* ii 1 212
Look on beauty, And you shall see 'tis purchased by the weight *M. of V.* iii 2 88
Many will swoon when they do look on blood . . . *As Y. Like It* iv 3 159
So bedazzled with the sun That everything I look on seemeth green *T. of S.* iv 5 47
Look on his letter, madam ; here's my passport . . . *All's Well* iii 2 58
The selfsame sun that shines upon his court Hides not his visage from our cottage but Looks on alike . . . . *W. Tale* iv 4 457
She was more worth such gazes Than what you look on now . . . v 1 227
What you can make her do, I am content to look on . . . . v 3 92
I beseech your grace Look on my wrongs with an indifferent eye *Rich. II.* ii 3 116
Yea, strike the Dauphin blind to look on us . . . . *Hen. V.* i 2 280
Look on thy country, look on fertile France, And see the cities and the towns defaced By wasting ruin . . . . . *1 Hen. VI.* iii 3 44
Look on my George ; I am a gentleman : Rate me at what thou wilt *2 Hen. VI.* iv 1 29
But who can cease to weep and look on this? . . . . . . iv 4 4
Look on the boy ; And let his manly face, which promiseth Successful fortune, steel thy melting heart. . . . . *3 Hen. VI.* ii 2 39
End thy damned spleen ; Or let me die, to look on death no more ! *Rich. III.* ii 4 65
O Thou, whose captain I account myself, Look on my forces with a gracious eye ! . . . . v 3 109
I am sorry To see you ta'en from liberty, to look on The business present : 'tis his highness' pleasure . . . . *Hen. VIII.* i 1 205
Stand fair, I pray thee : let me look on thee.—Behold thy fill *Tr. and Cr.* iv 5 235
One eye yet looks on thee ; But with my heart the other eye doth see . v 2 107
Now they are clapper-clawing one another ; I'll go look on . . . v 4 2
I'll be a candle-holder, and look on . . . . . *Rom. and Jul.* i 4 38
To prison, eyes, ne'er look on liberty ! Vile earth, to earth resign ! . iii 2 58
Fearfully did menace me with death, If I did stay to look on his intents v 3 134
If it be aught toward the general good, Set honour in one eye and death i' the other, And I will look on both indifferently . . *J. Cæsar* i 2 87
Ravens, crows and kites, Fly o'er our heads and downward look on us v 1 86
Look on death itself ! up, up, and see The great doom's image ! *Macbeth* ii 3 82
A bold one, that dare look on that Which might appal the devil . . iii 4 59
Did heaven look on, And would not take their part? . . . . iv 3 223
And do such bitter business as the day Would quake to look on *Hamlet* iii 2 410
To fall in love with what she fear'd to look on ! . . . . *Othello* i 3 98
Her eye must be fed ; and what delight shall she have to look on the devil? . . . . ii 1 229
Look on the tragic loading of this bed ; This is thy work . . . v 2 363
Thou didst eat strange flesh, Which some did die to look on *Ant. and Cleo.* i 4 68
To be abused By one that looks on feeders . . . . . . iii 13 109
Where their appointment we may best discover, And look on their endeavour . . . . iv 10 9
I must perforce Have shown to thee such a declining day, Or look on thine v 1 39
Look on her. Fair, or I'll never look on her . . . . *Much Ado* ii 3 34
You, my lords, Look on her, mark her well . . . . *W. Tale* ii 1 65
Every cat and dog And little mouse, every unworthy thing, Live here in heaven and may look on her . . . . . *Rom. and Jul.* iii 3 32
Do you see this? Look on her, look, her lips, Look there, look there ! *Lear* v 3 310
She did distain my child, and stood between Her and her fortunes : none would look on her . . . . *Pericles* iv 3 32
Look on him better, And be not proud . . . . *As Y. Like It* iii 5 78
It is his grounds of faith that all that look on him love him . *T. Night* ii 3 164
Though bearing misery, I desire my life Once more to look on him *W. Tale* v 1 138
To my knowledge, I never in my life did look on him . *Richard II.* ii 3 39
Look on it. Give me the letter ; I will look on it . . *Rom. and Jul.* v 3 278
I am afraid to think what I have done ; Look on't again I dare not *Macb.* ii 2 52
The white hand of a lady fever thee, Shake thou to look on't *A. and C.* iii 13 139
It is a basilisk unto mine eye, Kills me to look on't . . *Cymbeline* ii 4 108
If mine enemy But fear the sword like me, he'll scarcely look on't . iii 6 26
Look on me. Not one of them That yet looks on me, or would know me *Tempest* v 1 83
A due sincerity govern'd his deeds, Till he did look on me *Meas. for Meas.* v 1 452
If you would know your wronger, look on me.—Art thou the slave? *M. Ado* v 1 272
Mistress, look on me ; Behold the window of my heart, mine eye *L. L. L.* v 2 847
Alone, When all the world is here to look on me? . . . *M. N. Dream* ii 1 226
I am glad 'tis night, you do not look on me . . . *Mer. of Venice* ii 6 34
Why, what means this? Why do you look on me? . . *As Y. Like It* iii 5 41
Come, sir page, Look on me with your welkin eye . . . *W. Tale* i 2 136
Swearest thou, ungracious boy? henceforth ne'er look on me *1 Hen. IV.* ii 4 491
I am no loathsome leper ; look on me . . . . . *2 Hen. VI.* iii 2 75
Look on me well : I have eat no meat these five days . . . . iv 10 40
Which of you trembles not that looks on me? . . . *Richard III.* i 3 160
You look on me : what wreck discern you in me Deserves your pity? *Cymb.* i 6 84
Look on you. You are metamorphosed with a mistress, that, when I look on you, I can hardly think you my master . . . *T. G. of Ver.* ii 1 33
O, spare mine eyes, Though to no use but still to look on you ! *K. John* iv 1 103
Coming to look on you, thinking you dead . . . . *2 Hen. IV.* iv 5 156
That you may live Only in bone, that none may look on you ! *T. of Athens* iii 5 105
I look on you As one that takes his leave. . . . . *Ant. and Cleo.* iv 2 28
Look out. Appoint her to look out at her lady's chamber window *M. Ado* ii 2 17
Look out at window, for all this . . . . . . *Mer. of Venice* ii 5 40

Look out. See where he looks out of the window.—Is't so, indeed? T. of Shrew v 1 57
He tells her something That makes her blood look out . . W. Tale iv 4 160
Look out there, some of ye.—What warlike voice . . . is this? Hen. VIII. i 4 50
Her wanton spirits look out At every joint and motive of her body Troi. and Cres. iv 5 56
And yet—O, see the monstrousness of man When he looks out in an ungrateful shape! . . . . T. of Athens iii 2 80
Look out, and speak to friends . . . . v 1 131
Look out o' the other side your monument . . . Ant. and Cleo. iv 15 8
The business of this man looks out of him . . . . . v 1 50
Thy crystal window ope; look out . . . . . . Cymbeline v 4 81
Look over. Every man look o'er his part . . . M. N. Dream iv 2 38
If Cæsar move him, Let Antony look over Cæsar's head . Ant. and Cleo. ii 2 5
Look pale. I shall see thee, ere I die, look pale with love . Much Ado i 1 249
He looks pale. Art thou sick, or angry? . . . . . v 1 130
You may look pale, but I should blush, I know, To be o'erheard L. L. L. iv 3 129
Where I have seen them shiver and look pale . . . M. N. Dream v 1 95
I must blush and weep and thou must look pale and wonder As Y. Like It i 1 164
How now, my friend! why dost thou look so pale?—For fear, I promise you, if I look pale . . . . . . T. of Shrew ii 1 143
And pants and looks pale, as if a bear were at his heels . . T. Night iii 4 323
Are you sick, Hubert? you look pale to-day . . . K. John iv 1 28
Till so much blood thither come again, Have I not reason to look pale? Richard II. iii 2 79
As oft as Lancaster Doth speak of you, his cheek looks pale 1 Hen. IV. iii 1 9
How bloodily the sun begins to peer Above yon busky hill! the day looks pale . . . . v 1 2
On whom, as in despite, the sun looks pale . . . Hen. V. iii 5 17
Whose very shores look pale With envy of each other's happiness . v 2 378
Look pale as primrose with blood-drinking sighs . . 2 Hen. VI. iii 2 63
To break the heart of generosity, And make bold power look pale Coriol. i 1 216
But is this true, sir?—Ay; and you'll look pale Before you find it other iv 6 101
You look pale and gaze And put on fear . . . J. Cæsar i 3 59
You tremble and look pale: Is not this something more than fantasy? Hamlet i 1 53
You that look pale and tremble at this chance . . . . v 2 345
Look paler. Come, you look paler and paler . . . As Y. Like It iv 3 178
Look red. And Marian's nose looks red and raw . . L. L. Lost v 2 934
Give me a cup of sack to make my eyes look red . 1 Hen. IV. ii 4 423
Yet do thy cheeks look red as Titan's face . . T. Andron. ii 4 31
Look sad. What sign is it when a man of great spirit grows melancholy?—A great sign, sir, that he will look sad . . . L. L. Lost i 2 3
The death of a dear friend would go near to make a man look sad M. N. D. v 1 294
Rich men look sad and ruffians dance and leap . . Richard II. ii 4 12
Look sadly. For the selfsame heaven That frowns on me looks sadly upon him . . . . Richard III. v 3 287
Yet he looks sadly, And prays the Moor be safe . . . Othello ii 1 32
Look thee, I'll but lean, and my staff understands me . T. G. of Ver. ii 5 30
Here's a sight for thee; look thee . . . W. Tale iii 3 118
Thou art preparing fire for us; look thee, here's water to quench it Coriolanus v 2 77
Look there, my lords; By virtue of that ring, I take my cause Out of the gripes of cruel men . . . . . . Hen. VIII. v 3 98
Look on her, look, her lips, Look there, look there! . . . Lear v 3 311
Look through. Such shoes as my toes look through the over-leather T. of Shrew Ind. 2 12
Thy casement I need not open, for I look through thee . All's Well ii 3 226
So thin that life looks through and will break out . . 2 Hen. IV. iv 4 120
What a haste looks through his eyes! . . . . . Macbeth i 2 46
If this should fail, And that our drift look through our bad performance, 'Twere better not assay'd . . . . Hamlet iv 7 152
Let her beauty Look through a casement to allure false hearts Cymbeline ii 4 34
Have a fog in them, That I cannot look through . . . iii 2 82
Look to the boy.—Why, boy! why, wag! how now! . T. G. of Ver. v 4 85
We'll look to that anon . . . . . . Com. of Errors v 1 412
Niece, will you look to those things I told you of? . . Much Ado ii 1 351
Now will I look to his remuneration. Remuneration! . . L. L. Lost iii 1 137
If I do it, let the audience look to their eyes . . . M. N. Dream i 2 28
Look to my house. I am right loath to go . . . Mer. of Venice ii 5 16
Let him look to his bond . . . . iii 1 52
Look to him: tell not me of mercy; This is the fool that lent out money gratis: Gaoler, look to him . . . . iii 3 1
The fool shall look to the madman . . . . . T. Night i 5 146
Do you come near me now? no worse man than Sir Toby to look to me! iii 4 72
Look to your babe, my lord; 'tis yours . . . W. Tale ii 3 126
Go, get aboard; Look to thy bark: I'll not be long . . . iii 3 8
My traffic is sheets; when the kite builds, look to lesser linen . iv 3 23
Look to that, devil; lest that France repent . . . K. John iii 1 196
Standest thou still, and hearest such a calling? Look to the guests 1 Hen. IV. ii 4 91
Love thy husband, look to thy servants, cherish thy guests . . . iii 3 193
Who knocks so loud at door? Look to the door there, Francis 2 Hen. IV. ii 4 381
My love, give me thy lips. Look to my chattels and my movables Hen. V. ii 3 50
Look to the drawbridge there!—Hark! a drum . . Richard III. iii 5 15
Look to your wife: if she convey Letters to Richmond, you shall answer it . . . . iv 2 95
Look to my house: Lucius and I'll go brave it at the court T. Andron. iv 1 120
Remove the court-cupboard, look to the plate . . Rom. and Jul. i 5 8
Look to the baked meats, good Angelica: Spare not for cost . . iv 4 5
Help me hence, ho!—Look to the lady . . . . . Macbeth ii 3 125
Look to the queen there, ho! . . . . Hamlet v 2 314
Look to your house, your daughter and your bags! Thieves! thieves! Othello i 1 80
Look to her, Moor, if thou hast eyes to see: She has deceived her father i 3 293
Gentlemen, let's look to our business. Do not think, gentlemen, I am drunk . . . . ii 3 116
Look to your wife; observe her well with Cassio; Wear your eye thus iii 3 197
Look to your little mistress, on whose grace You may depend hereafter Pericles iii 3 40
Look to the lady; O, she's but o'erjoy'd . . . . . . v 3 21
Look to be. By day's approach look to be visited . . M. N. Dream iii 2 430
I look to be either earl or duke, I can assure you . . 1 Hen. IV. v 4 145
As men wrecked upon a sand, that look to be washed off the next tide Hen. V. iv 1 101
A plague on them, they ne'er come but I look to be washed . Pericles ii 1 28
Look to behold this night Earth-treading stars . . Rom. and Jul. i 2 24
Look to have. As you look To have my pardon, trim it handsomely Temp. v 1 292
Yet look to have them buzz to offend thine ears . . 3 Hen. VI. ii 6 95

Look to have. I'll claim that promise at your grace's hands.—And look to have it yielded with all willingness . . . . Richard III. iii 1 198
Honour, love, obedience, troops of friends, I must not look to have Macb. v 3 26
Look to hear. When you have done, we look to hear from you T. G. of Ver. ii 4 120
By midnight look to hear further from me . . . All's Well iii 6 82
An thou make minstrels of us, look to hear nothing but discords Rom. and Jul. iii 1 50
Look to it. There is not a more fearful wild-fowl than your lion living; and we ought to look to 't . . . . . . M. N. Dream iii 1 34
Thou wert best look to 't . . . . As Y. Like It i 1 154
But look to it: Find out thy brother, wheresoe'er he is . . . . . iii 1 4
An honourable conduct let him have: Pembroke, look to 't . K. John i 1 30
I'll smoke your skin-coat, an I catch you right; Sirrah, look to 't . ii 1 140
Uncleanly scruples! fear not you: look to 't . . . . . . iv 1 7
Therefore captains had need look to 't . . . . 2 Hen. IV. ii 4 163
Look to it well and say you are well warn'd . . . 1 Hen. VI. ii 4 103
Look to it, lords; let not his smoothing words Bewitch your hearts 2 Hen. VI. i 1 156
Look to 't in time; She'll hamper thee, and dandle thee like a baby . i 3 147
He is your wife's son: well, look to it . . . . Richard III. iv 2 90
Pray, look to 't; I put it to your care . . . . . Hen. VIII. i 2 101
I'll leave the foe And make my wars on you: look to 't . . Coriolanus i 4 40
Look to 't, think on 't, I do not use to jest . . . Rom. and Jul. iii 5 191
Look to 't, I charge you: come your ways.—I shall obey . . Hamlet i 3 135
Conception is a blessing: but not as your daughter may conceive. Friend, look to 't . . . . ii 2 187
But, notwithstanding, with my personal eye Will I look to 't . Othello ii 3 6
Look to 't: I know our country disposition well . . . . . iii 3 200
Indeed! is 't true?—Most veritable; therefore look to 't well . . iii 4 76
Command our present numbers Be muster'd; bid the captains look to 't Cymbeline iv 2 344
She will be your scholar: therefore look to it . . . . Pericles ii 5 39
Look to know. Do look to know What doth befall you . Meas. for Meas. i 1 58
Look to receive. Then must we look to receive from his age, not alone the imperfections of long-engraffed condition . . . . . Lear i 1 299
Look to see. In a moment look to see The blind and bloody soldier Hen. V. iii 3 33
Then, masters, look to see a troublous world . . . Richard III. ii 3 9
Look to taste the due Meet for rebellion . . . . 2 Hen. IV. iv 2 116
Look to thyself. Thy friend, as thou usest him . . T. Night iii 4 186
Look to thyself, thou art in jeopardy.—No more than he that threats K. John iii 1 346
Look to thyself; Thou hast a traitor in thy presence there Richard II. v 3 39
Look unto. Sup them well and look unto them all . . T. of Shrew Ind. 1 28
Look unto the main.—Unto the main! O father, Maine is lost 2 Hen. VI. i 1 208
Look up. Why, boy! why, wag! how now! what's the matter? Look up T. G. of Ver. v 4 87
Dost thou look up?—Yea, wherefore should she not? . . Much Ado iv 1 120
Dear, look up: Though Fortune, visible an enemy, Should chase us with my father, power no jot Hath she to change our loves . W. Tale v 1 215
Yet look up, behold, That you in pity may dissolve to dew Richard II. v 1 8
My sovereign lord, cheer up yourself, look up . . 2 Hen. IV. iv 4 113
Hast thou any life? Speak unto Talbot; nay, look up to him 1 Hen VI. i 4 89
My child, my only life, Revive, look up, or I will die with thee! R. and J. iv 5 20
Only look up clear; To alter favour ever is to fear . . . Macbeth i 5 72
Then I'll look up; My fault is past . . . . . Hamlet iii 3 50
Look up a-height; the shrill-gorged lark so far Cannot be seen or heard: do but look up.—Alack, I have no eyes . . . . . Lear iv 6 59
Break, heart; I prithee, break!—Look up, my lord.—Vex not his ghost v 3 312
How dare the plants look up to heaven? . . . . . Pericles i 2 55
Look upon. Unless I look on Silvia in the day, There is no day for me to look upon . . . . T. G. of Ver. iii 1 181
Longer than I prove loyal to your grace Let me not live to look upon your grace . . . . iii 2 21
I will not look upon your master's lines . . . . iv 4 133
'Tis one of the best discretions of a 'oman as ever I did look upon M. W. iv 4 2
Look upon his honour; 'tis for a good purpose . . Meas. for Meas. ii 1 154
Go fetch him hither; let me look upon him . . . . . v 1 474
Some shall see.—What shall some see?—Nay, nothing, Master Moth, but what they look upon . . . . L. L. Lost i 2 168
What peremptory eagle-sighted eye Dares look upon the heaven of her brow? . . . . iv 3 227
The next thing then she waking looks upon, . . She shall pursue it with the soul of love . . . . M. N. Dream ii 1 179
I pray you, let me look upon the bond.—Here 'tis . . Mer. of Venice iv 1 225
Wherefore do you look Upon that poor and broken bankrupt? As Y. Like It ii 1 56
You are there followed by a faithful shepherd; Look upon him, love him v 2 88
And till she stoop she must not be full-gorged, For then she never looks upon her lure . . . . T. of Shrew iv 1 195
I adore The sun, that looks upon his worshipper . . . All's Well i 3 212
He will look upon his boot and sing; mend the ruff and sing . . iii 2 6
I have eyes under my service which look upon his removedness W. Tale iv 2 41
Go on the right hand: I will but look upon the hedge and follow you . iv 4 857
He had himself The lands and waters 'twixt your throne and his Measured to look upon you . . . . v 1 145
But we saw not That which my daughter came to look upon . . v 3 13
Be stone no more; approach; Strike all that look upon with marvel . v 3 100
Let's from this place. What! look upon my brother . . . v 3 147
Look upon the years Of Lewis the Dauphin and that lovely maid K. John ii 1 424
No, no; when Fortune means to men most good, She looks upon them with a threatening eye . . . . iii 4 120
I will not stir, nor wince, nor speak a word, Nor look upon the iron angerly . . . . iv 1 82
Nor never look upon each other's face . . . . . Richard II. i 3 185
Cousin, stand forth, and look upon that man . . . . . iv 1 7
Nay, all of you that stand and look upon, Whilst that my wretchedness doth bait myself . . . . iv 1 237
Look upon his face; His eyes do drop no tears, his prayers are in jest . v 3 100
At length have gotten leave To look upon my sometimes royal master's face . . . . v 5 75
How! poor? look upon his face; what call you rich? . 1 Hen. IV. iii 3 89
I hope he that looks upon me will take me without weighing 2 Hen. IV. i 2 188
To look upon the hideous god of war In disadvantage . . . . ii 3 35
The unguided days And rotten times that you shall look upon . . iv 4 60
Trow'st thou that e'er I'll look upon the world? . . . 2 Hen. VI. ii 4 38
I'll give a thousand pound to look upon him . . . . . iii 3 13
And look upon, as if the tragedy Were play'd in jest . . 3 Hen. VI. ii 3 27
I live to look upon their tragedy . . . . . . Richard III. iii 2 59
I with grief and extreme age shall perish And never look upon thy face again . . . . iv 4 186

Look upon. Stops on a sudden, looks upon the ground . *Hen. VIII.* iii 2 114
What's the matter?—Nay, look upon him.—So I do . *Troi. and Cres.* ii 1 65
Who neither looks upon the heaven nor earth . . . . . iv 5 281
You look upon that sleeve; behold it well . . . . . v 2 69
I'll fight with him alone: stand, Diomed.—He is my prize; I will not look upon . . . . v 6 10
He had rather see the swords, and hear a drum, than look upon his schoolmaster.—O' my word, the father's son . *Coriolanus* i 3 61
Faint-hearted boy, arise, and look upon her . . *T. Andron.* iii 1 65
Turn thee, Benvolio, look upon thy death . . *Rom. and Jul.* i 1 74
Let me see his face.—Fellow, come from the throng; look upon Cæsar *J. Cæsar* i 2 21
If then thy spirit look upon us now; Shall it not grieve thee? . iii 1 195
Take him for all in all, I shall not look upon his like again . *Hamlet* i 2 188
Do not look upon me; Lest with this piteous action you convert My stern effects: then what I have to do Will want true colour . . iii 4 127
Art not ashamed to look upon this beard? . . . . *Lear* ii 4 196
O, look upon me, sir, And hold your hands in benediction o'er me . iv 7 57
Look upon her: Do you see, gentlemen? nay, guiltiness will speak *Othello* v 1 108
My lord approaches.—We will not look upon him . . *Ant. and Cleo.* i 2 91
Herod of Jewry dare not look upon you But when you are well pleased iii 3 3
I follow'd that I blush to look upon: My very hairs do mutiny . . iii 11 12
I would have broke mine eye-strings; crack'd them, but To look upon him, till the diminution Of space had pointed him sharp *Cymbeline* i 3 18
Is it fit I went to look upon him? is there no derogation in't? . ii 1 46
He'll grant the tribute, send the arrearages, Or look upon our Romans ii 4 14
I am ashamed To look upon the holy sun . . . . . . iv 4 41
Set't down, let's look upon't.—'Tis like a coffin, sir . . *Pericles* iii 2 51
Look you. If I should take a displeasure against you, look you *Tempest* iv 1 202
For, look you, she is as white as a lily . . . . *T. G. of Ver.* ii 3 22
The several chairs of order look you scour With juice of balm *Mer. Wives* v 5 65
Meadow-fairies, look you sing, Like to the Garter's compass, in a ring . v 5 69
We will hear you speak: Look you speak justly . . *Meas. for Meas.* v 1 298
She, Claudio, that you wrong'd, look you restore . . . . . v 1 531
Look you arm yourself To fit your fancies to your father's will *M. N. D.* i 1 117
Why, look you, how you storm! . . . . *Mer. of Venice* i 3 138
Look you call me Ganymede. But what will you be call'd? *As Y. Like It* i 3 127
Look you lisp and wear strange suits . . . . iv 1 33
Go you and prepare Aliena; for look you, here comes my Rosalind . v 2 18
Look you, sir, he tells you flatly what his mind is . . *T. of Shrew* i 2 77
Why, look you, I am whipp'd and scourged with rods . . *1 Hen. IV.* i 3 239
But look you pray, all you that kiss my lady Peace at home . *2 Hen. IV.* i 2 232
And, princes, look you strongly arm to meet him . . . *Hen. V.* ii 4 49
And look you get a prayer-book in your hand . . . *Richard III.* iii 7 47
Look you, she loved her kinsman Tybalt dearly . . *Rom. and Jul.* iii 4 3
Take this paper, And look you lay it in the prætor's chair . *J. Cæsar* i 3 143
For mine own poor part, Look you, I'll go pray . . . *Hamlet* i 5 132
Why, look you now, how unworthy a thing you make of me! . . iii 2 379
Look you lay home to him: Tell him his pranks have been too broad . iii 4 1
This was your husband. Look you now, what follows . . . . iii 4 63
Look you here. Here is himself, marr'd, as you see, with traitors *J. Cæsar* iii 2 200
Look you there. He there: that he: look you there . *Troi. and Cres.* ii 1 91
Look you there! look, how it steals away! . . . . *Hamlet* iii 4 134
Look your grace. It is necessary, look your grace, that he keep his vow and his oath . . . . *Hen. V.* iv 7 146
Looked. This is a strange thing as e'er I look'd on . . . *Tempest* v 1 289
When you looked sadly, it was for want of money . *T. G. of Ver.* ii 1 30
Looked through the grate, like a geminy of baboons . *Mer. Wives* ii 2 8
She is too bright to be looked against . . . . ii 2 254
Have you looked for Master Caius, that calls himself doctor of physic? iii 1 3
Is lechery so look'd after?—Thus stands it with me . *Meas. for Meas.* i 2 148
Your grace, like power divine, Hath look'd upon my passes . . . v 1 375
Never object pleasing in thine eye, . . . Unless I spake, or look'd, or touch'd, or carved to thee . . . . *Com. of Errors* ii 2 120
I looked for the chalky cliffs, but I could find no whiteness in them . iii 2 129
Look'd he or red or pale, or sad or merrily? . . . . . iv 2 4
I noted her not; but I looked on her . . . . *Much Ado* i 1 165
In mine eye she is the sweetest lady that ever I look'd on . . . i 1 190
I look'd upon her with a soldier's eye, That liked . . . . i 1 300
An you be a cursing hypocrite once, you must be looked to . . . v 1 213
This is not so well as I looked for, but the best that ever I heard *L. L. L.* i 1 281
I would my father look'd but with my eyes . . *M. N. Dream* i 1 56
For ere Demetrius look'd on Hermia's eyne, He hail'd down oaths that he was only mine . . . . i 1 242
Durst thou have look'd upon him being awake, And hast thou kill'd him sleeping? O brave touch! . . . . iii 2 69
The fairest dame That lived, that loved, that liked, that look'd with cheer v 1 299
He, of all the men that ever my foolish eyes looked upon, was the best deserving a fair lady . . . . . *Mer. of Venice* i 2 130
Yourself . . . then stood as fair As any comer I have look'd on yet . ii 1 21
If ever you have look'd on better days . . . *As Y. Like It* ii 7 113
What said he? How looked he? Wherein went he? What makes he here? iii 2 233
Your brother and my sister no sooner met but they looked, no sooner looked but they loved, no sooner loved but they sighed . . . v 2 36
You look'd so longly on the maid, Perhaps you mark'd not . *T. of Shrew* i 1 170
Now is the day we long have looked for . . . . . . ii 1 335
My father is here look'd for every day . . . . . . iv 2 116
And that you look'd for him this day in Padua . . . . . iv 4 16
Go thy ways: let my horses be well look'd to, without any tricks *All's W.* iv 5 62
This was looked for at your hand, and this was balked . . *T. Night* iii 2 25
Good Maria, let this fellow be looked to . . . . . iii 4 67; 85
Get him to bed, and let his hurt be look'd to . . . . . v 1 214
I have look'd on thousands, who have sped the better By my regard *W. T.* i 2 389
If you had but looked big and spit at him, he'ld have run . . iv 3 113
Then, even now, I might have look'd upon my queen's full eyes . . v 1 53
What might I have been, Might I a son and daughter now have look'd on! v 1 177
They looked as they had heard of a world ransomed, or one destroyed . v 2 16
Excels whatever yet you look'd upon Or hand of man hath done . . v 3 16
Once again crown'd, And look'd upon, I hope, with cheerful eyes *K. John* iv 2 2
I look'd when some of you should say, I was too strict . . *Richard II.* i 3 243
Even so look'd he, Accomplish'd with the number of thy hours . . ii 1 176
Which, look'd on as it is, is nought but shadows Of what it is not . ii 2 23
And little look'd for at your helping hands . . . . . iv 1 161
He wistly look'd on me; As who should say, 'I would thou wert the man' v 4 7
His cheek look'd pale, And on my face he turn'd an eye of death *1 Hen. IV.* i 3 142
Matters should be look'd into, for their own credit sake . . . ii 1 80
I looked a' should have sent me two and twenty yards of satin *2 Hen. IV.* i 2 49
'Tis needful that the most immodest word Be look'd upon and learn'd . iv 4 71
Who look'd full gently on his warlike queen . . . *3 Hen. VI.* ii 1 123
For yet I am not look'd on in the world . . . . . . v 7 22
Looked. I had thought That thou hadst call'd me all these bitter names. —Why, so I did; but look'd for no reply . . . *Richard III.* i 3 237
Thence we look'd toward England, And cited up a thousand fearful times i 4 13
Mark'd you not How that the guilty kindred of the queen Look'd pale? ii 1 136
Attended to their sugar'd words, But look'd not on the poison of their hearts . . . . iii 1 14
Did stumble, And startled, when he look'd upon the Tower . . . iii 4 87
Miserable England! I prophesy the fearfull'st time to thee That ever wretched age hath look'd upon . . . . iii 4 107
I never look'd for better at his hands . . . . iii 5 50
Gazed each on other, and look'd deadly pale . . . . . . iii 7 26
O, when, I say, I look'd on Richard's face, This was my wish . . iv 1 71
Look'd he o' the inside of the paper?—Presently . . *Hen. VIII.* iii 2 78
Thou hast the sweetest face I ever look'd on . . . . . . iv 1 43
I look'd You would have given me your petition . . . . . v 1 117
She looked yesternight fairer than ever I saw her look . *Troi. and Cres.* i 1 32
Either greet him not, Or else disdainfully, which shall shake him more Than if not look'd on . . . . iii 3 54
The breasts of Hecuba, When she did suckle Hector, look'd not lovelier *Coriolanus* i 3 44
I looked upon him o' Wednesday half an hour together . . . . i 3 63
The blood upon your visage dries; 'tis time It should be look'd to . i 9 94
Look'd upon things precious as they were The common muck of the world ii 2 129
What fellow's this?—A strange one as ever I looked on . . . iv 5 21
When he had carried Rome and that we look'd For no less spoil than glory v 6 43
Pages blush'd at him and men of heart Look'd wondering each at other v 6 100
You are looked for and called for, asked for and sought for *Rom. and Jul.* i 5 13
A sudden day of joy, That thou expect'st not nor I look'd not for . iii 5 111
The things that threaten'd me Ne'er look'd but on my back . *J. Cæsar* ii 2 11
And his gash'd stabs look'd like a breach in nature . . *Macbeth* ii 3 119
To the amazement of mine eyes That look'd upon't . . . . ii 4 20
I look'd toward Birnam, and anon, methought, The wood began to move v 5 34
Look'd he frowningly?—A countenance more in sorrow than in anger *Hamlet* i 2 231
Appear'd To be a preparation 'gainst the Polack; But, better look'd into, he truly found It was against your highness . . . . . ii 2 64
Or look'd upon this love with idle sight . . . . . . ii 2 138
Dost thou think Alexander looked o' this fashion i' the earth?—E'en so v 1 218
Look'd black upon me; struck me with her tongue, Most serpent-like, upon the very heart . . . . *Lear* ii 4 162
I look'd not for you yet, nor am provided For your fit welcome . . ii 4 235
That eye that told you so look'd but a-squint . . . . . . v 3 72
I have looked upon the world for four times seven years . *Othello* i 3 312
We looked not for Mark Antony here: pray you, is he married? *A. and C.* ii 6 113
Didst thou behold Octavia? . . . —I look'd her in the face . . iii 3 12
I could then have looked on him without the help of admiration *Cymbeline* i 4 4
Your lady Is one of the fairest that I have look'd upon . . . ii 4 32
Found no opposition But what he look'd for should oppose . . . ii 5 18
'Tis not sleepy business; But must be look'd to speedily and strongly . iii 5 27
I never Did see man die! scarce ever look'd on blood! . . . . iv 4 36
Thou hast look'd thyself into my grace, And art mine own . . . v 5 94
This matter must be look'd to, For her relapse is mortal . . *Pericles* iii 2 109
Such a piece of slaughter The sun and moon ne'er look'd upon! . . iv 3 3
Mark'd he your music?—No, nor look'd on us . . . . . . v 1 81
Lookedst. What majesty is in her gait? Remember, If e'er thou look'dst on majesty . . . . *Ant. and Cleo.* iii 3 21
Thou then look'dst like a villain; now methinks Thy favour's good enough . . . . *Cymbeline* iii 4 50
Looker on. My business in this state Made me a looker on here in Vienna *Meas. for Meas.* v 1 319
What dangers, by his highness' fail of issue, May drop upon his kingdom and devour Incertain lookers on . . . . . . *W. Tale* v 1 29
So long could I Stand by, a looker on . . . . v 3 85
A woful looker-on When as the noble Duke of York was slain *3 Hen. VI.* ii 1 45
As mother, And reverend looker on, of two fair queens . *Richard III.* iv 1 31
Lookest. Telling the bushes that thou look'st for wars . *M. N. Dream* iii 2 408
Thou lookest cheerly, and I'll be with thee quickly . *As Y. Like It* ii 6 14
Look'st thou pale, France? do not let go thy hand . . *K. John* iii 1 195
Yea, look'st thou pale? let me see the writing . . . *Richard II.* v 2 57
Thou art protector And lookest to command the prince and realm *1 Hen. VI.* i 1 38
How now! why look'st thou pale? why tremblest thou? *2 Hen. VI.* iii 2 27
Wherefore look'st thou sad, When every thing doth make a gleeful boast? The birds chant melody . . . . *T. Andron.* ii 3 10
Why look'st thou sad? Though news be sad, yet tell them merrily *Rom. and Jul.* ii 5 21
Either my eyesight fails, or thou look'st pale . . . . . iii 5 57
Honest Iago, that look'st dead with grieving, Speak, who began this? *Othello* ii 3 177
Welcome: Thou look'st like him that knows a warlike charge *A. and C.* iv 4 19
Art thou a feodary for this act, and look'st So virgin-like? *Cymbeline* iii 2 21
Know'st him thou look'st on? speak, Wilt have him live? Is he thy kin? v 5 110
Thou look'st Modest as Justice . . . . *Pericles* v 1 121
Thou look'st Like one I loved indeed . . . . v 1 125
Looking. Wherefore this ghastly looking?—What's the matter? *Tempest* ii 1 309
Sweating and blowing and looking wildly . . . . *Mer. Wives* iii 3 94
Which once thou sworest was worth the looking on . *Meas. for Meas.* v 1 208
All senses to that sense did make their repair, To feel only looking on fairest of fair . . . . *L. L. Lost* ii 1 241
A wither'd hermit . . . Might shake off fifty, looking in her eye . . iv 3 243
Now, for not looking on a woman's face, You have in that forsworn the use of eyes . . . . iv 3 309
Looking on it with lack-lustre eye . . . . . *As Y. Like It* ii 7 21
While idly I stood looking on . . . . . . *T. of Shrew* i 1 155
I stood amazed for a while, As on a pillory, looking through the lute . ii 1 157
His father is come from Padua and here looking out at the window . v 1 32
Looking on the lines Of my boy's face, methoughts I did recoil Twenty-three years, and saw myself . . . . *W. Tale* i 2 153
The sun looking with a southward eye upon him . . . . . iv 4 819
Looking awry upon your lord's departure, Find shapes of grief *Richard II.* ii 2 21
Whilst I, by looking on the praise of him, See riot and dishonour stain the brow Of my young Harry . . . . *1 Hen. IV.* i 1 84
Then they will endure handling, which before would not abide looking on . . . . *Hen. V.* v 2 338
As the dam runs lowing up and down, Looking the way her harmless young one went, And can do nought but wail . . *2 Hen. VI.* iii 1 215
Gives not the hawthorn-bush a sweeter shade To shepherds looking on their silly sheep? . . . . *3 Hen. VI.* ii 5 43
I have bewept a worthy husband's death, And lived by looking on his images: But now two mirrors of his princely semblance Are crack'd *Richard III.* ii 2 50

Looking. Full little, God knows, looking Either for such men or such business . . . *Hen. VIII.* iii 1 75
Looking as it were—would I were hanged, but I thought there was more in him than I could think . . . . . . *Coriolanus* iv 5 165
Sit round about some fountain, Looking all downwards . *T. Andron.* iii 1 124
I'll look to like, if looking liking move : But no more deep *Rom. and Jul.* i 3 97
But was, indeed, Sway'd from the point, by looking down on Cæsar *J. Cæsar* iii 1 219
He that made us with such large discourse, Looking before and after *Ham.* iv 4 37
There would he anchor his aspect and die With looking on his life *A. and C.* i 5 34
I know they are in Rome together, Looking for Antony . . . . ii 1 20
See, How I convey my shame out of thine eyes By looking back what I have left behind 'Stroy'd in dishonour . . . iii 11 53
Who, looking for adventures in the world, Was by the rough seas reft of ships and men . . . . *Pericles* ii 3 83
Looking-glass. Since she did neglect her looking-glass . *T. G. of Ver.* iv 4 157
Making practised smiles, As in a looking-glass . . *W. Tale* i 2 117
Go some of you and fetch a looking-glass . . . . *Richard II.* iv 1 268
Nor made to court an amorous looking-glass . . *Richard III.* i 1 15
I'll be at charges for a looking-glass . . . . . . i 2 256
She's dead as earth. Lend me a looking-glass ; If that her breath will mist or stain the stone, Why, then she lives . . *Lear* v 3 261
Loon. The devil damn thee black, thou cream-faced loon ! *Macbeth* v 3 11
Loop. Stop all sight-holes, every loop . . . . . *1 Hen. IV.* iv 1 71
At the least, so prove it, That the probation bear no hinge nor loop To hang a doubt on . . . . *Othello* iii 3 365
Looped. Your loop'd and window'd raggedness . . . . *Lear* iii 4 31
Loose. I do now let loose my opinion ; hold it no longer . . *Tempest* ii 2 36
I would prevent The loose encounters of lascivious men . *T. G. of Ver.* ii 7 41
You are afraid, if you see the bear loose, are you not ? . *Mer. Wives* i 1 304
I have seen Sackerson loose twenty times, and have taken him by the chain . . . . i 1 307
If he should intend this voyage towards my wife, I would turn her loose to him . . . . ii 1 190
You are not to go loose any longer ; you must be pinioned . . . iv 2 128
Quaint in green she shall be loose enrobed, With ribands pendent . . iv 6 41
They are loose again.—And come with naked swords . *Com. of Errors* iv 4 147
My master and his man are both broke loose, Beaten the maids a-row v 1 169
I will loose his bonds And gain a husband by his liberty . . . v 1 339
I will fast, being loose.—No, sir ; that were fast and loose . *L. L. Lost* i 2 161
To sell a bargain well is as cunning as fast and loose . . . iii 1 104
And now you will be my purgation and let me loose . . . iii 1 128
Often at his very loose decides That which long process could not arbitrate . . . . v 2 752
Which parti-coated presence of loose love Put on by us . . . . v 2 776
That loose grace Which shallow laughing hearers give to fools . . v 2 869
Away, you Ethiope !—No, no ; he'll . . . Seem to break loose *M. N. D.* iii 2 258
Vile thing, let loose, Or I will shake thee from me like a serpent ! . . iii 2 260
Not only loose the forfeiture, But, touch'd with human gentleness and love, Forgive a moiety of the principal . . *Mer. of Venice* iv 1 24
Loose now and then A scatter'd smile, and that I'll live upon *As Y. L. It* iii 5 103
Play fast and loose with faith . . . . . *K. John* iii 1 242
Arm thy constant and thy nobler parts Against these giddy loose suggestions . . . . iii 1 292
He daily doth frequent, With unrestrained loose companions *Richard II.* v 3 7
This loose behaviour I throw off . . . . . . *1 Hen. IV.* i 2 232
My skin hangs about me like an old lady's loose gown . . . iii 3 4
Contention, like a horse Full of high feeding, madly hath broke loose And bears down all before him . . . . . *2 Hen. IV.* i 1 10
Their ragged curtains poorly are let loose . . . . *Hen. V.* iv 2 41
That excellent grand tyrant of the earth, That reigns in galled eyes of weeping souls, Thy womb let loose . . . . *Richard III.* iv 4 54
This from a dying man receive as certain : Where you are liberal of your loves and counsels Be sure you be not loose . *Hen. VIII.* ii 1 127
Had their faces Been loose, this day they had been lost . . . iv 1 75
A file of boys behind 'em, loose shot, delivered such a shower of pebbles v 4 59
Lay negligent and loose regard upon him . . . *Troi. and Cres.* iii 3 41
He fumbles up into a loose adieu . . . . . . iv 4 48
What, is Lavinia then become so loose ? . . . *T. Andron.* ii 1 65
Thy hand once more ; I will not loose again, Till thou art here aloft . ii 3 243
As good to shoot against the wind. To it, boy ! Marcus, loose when I bid iv 3 58
So shall no foot upon the churchyard tread, Being loose, unfirm, with digging up of graves, But thou shalt hear it . . *Rom. and Jul.* v 3 6
Now does he feel his title Hang loose about him, like a giant's robe Upon a dwarfish thief . . . . *Macbeth* v 2 21
I'll loose my daughter to him : Be you and I behind an arras then *Ham.* ii 2 162
How dangerous is it that this man goes loose ! Yet must not we put the strong law on him : He's loved . . . . iv 3 2
Let loose on me the justice of the state For thus deluding you . *Othello* i 3 140
For the better compassing of his salt and most hidden loose affection . ii 1 245
There are a kind of men so loose of soul, That in their sleeps will mutter iii 3 416
Like a right gipsy, hath, at fast and loose, Beguiled me . *Ant. and Cleo.* iv 12 28
Loose-bodied. 'Imprimis, a loose-bodied gown :'—Master, if ever I said loose-bodied gown, sew me in the skirts of it . . *T. of Shrew* iv 3 135
Loosed his love-shaft smartly from his bow . . *M. N. Dream* ii 1 159
As many arrows, loosed several ways, Come to one mark . *Hen. V.* i 2 207
Cursed the gentle gusts And he that loosed them forth . *2 Hen. VI.* iii 2 89
The bonds of heaven are slipp'd, dissolved, and loosed . *Troi. and Cres.* v 2 156
With a look so piteous in purport As if he had been loosed out of hell To speak of horrors . . . . *Hamlet* ii 1 83
Loosely. A prince should not be so loosely studied as to remember so weak a composition . . . . *2 Hen. IV.* ii 2 9
See your most dreadful laws so loosely slighted . . . . v 2 94
Loosen. I had rather lose the battle than that sister Should loosen him and me . . . . *Lear* v 1 19
Loose-wived. It is a heart-breaking to see a handsome man loose-wived *Ant. and Cleo.* i 2 75
Loosing. Both my revenge and hate Loosing upon thee . . *All's Well* ii 3 172
Lop. Superfluous branches We lop away . . . . *Richard II.* iii 4 64
I'll lop a member off and give it you . . . . *1 Hen. VI.* v 3 15
We take From every tree lop, bark, and part o' the timber . *Hen. VIII.* i 2 96
To lop that doubt, he'll fill this land with arms . . *Pericles* i 2 90
Lopped. A perilous gash, a very limb lopp'd off . . *1 Hen. IV.* iv 1 43
Two pulls at once ; His lady banish'd, and a limb lopp'd off *2 Hen. VI.* ii 3 42
Not contented that he lopp'd the branch In hewing Rutland . *3 Hen. VI.* i 6 47
Alarbus' limbs are lopp'd, And entrails feed the sacrificing fire *T. Andron.* i 1 143
Have lopp'd and hew'd and made thy body bare Of her two branches . ii 4 17
Lopped branches, which, being dead many years, shall after revive *Cymbeline* v 4 141 ; v 5 438
Thy lopp'd branches point Thy two sons forth . . . . . v 5 454

Loquitur. Vir sapit qui pauca loquitur . . . . . . *L. L. Lost* iv 2 83
Lord. What is't ? a spirit ? Lord, how it looks about ! . . . *Tempest* i 2 410
My father wreck'd.—Alack, for mercy !—Yes, faith, and all his lords . i 2 437
Put thyself Upon this island as a spy, to win it From me, the lord on't i 2 456
Good Lord, how you take it ! . . . . ii 1 80
This lord of weak remembrance, this, Who shall be of as little memory When he is earth'd . . . . ii 1 232
Lords that can prate As amply and unnecessarily . . . . . ii 1 263
Prospero my lord shall know what I have done . . . . . ii 1 326
He shall not suffer indignity.—I thank my noble lord . . . . iii 2 43
Thou shalt be lord of it and I'll serve thee . . . . . . iii 2 65
Him that you term'd, sir, 'The good old lord' . . . . . . v 1 15
But you, my brace of lords, were I so minded, I here could pluck his highness' frown upon you . . . . v 1 126
These lords At this encounter do so much admire . . . . . v 1 153
Upon this shore, where you were wreck'd, was landed, To be the lord on't v 1 162
Lord, Lord ! to see what folly reigns in us ! . . . . *T. G. of Ver.* i 2 15
Love's a mighty lord And hath so humbled me . . . . . . ii 4 136
They are sent by me, That they should harbour where their lord would be iii 1 149
Nay, Got's lords and his ladies ! you must speak possitable . *Mer. Wives* i 1 243
Why, sir, she's a good creature. Lord, Lord ! your worship's a wanton ! ii 2 56
Yet there has been knights, and lords, and gentlemen, with their coaches ii 2 65
I shall procure-a you de good guest, de earl, de knight, de lords . . ii 3 96
I'll speak it before the best lord . . . . iii 3 53
A buck-basket !—By the Lord, a buck-basket ! . . . . . . iii 5 90
My lord hath sent you this note . . . . . . *Meas. for Meas.* iv 2 105
Lords of the wide world and wild watery seas . . . *Com. of Errors* ii 1 21
Men, more divine, . . . Are masters to their females, and their lords . ii 1 24
My husband, Whom I made lord of me and all I had . . . . v 1 137
But what is he to a lord ?—A lord to a lord, a man to a man . *Much Ado* i 1 55
O Lord, he will hang upon him like a disease . . . . . . i 1 86
Lord, I could not endure a husband with a beard on his face . . . ii 1 31
Good Lord, for alliance ! Thus goes every one to the world but I . . ii 1 330
O Lord, my lord, if they were but a week married . . . . . ii 1 368
So entirely ?—So says the prince and my new-trothed lord . . . iii 1 38
Is not your lord honourable without marriage ? . . . . . iii 4 31
Is my lord well, that he doth speak so wide ? . . . . . . iv 1 63
Lord, how wise you are !—I will tell thee wonders . . . . *L. L. Lost* i 2 143
Some merry mocking lord, belike ; is't so ? . . . . . . ii 1 52
Our Lady help my lord ! he'll be forsworn . . . . . . ii 1 98
Your ladyship is ignorant what it is.—Were my lord so, his ignorance were wise . . . . ii 1 102
That last is Biron, the merry mad-cap lord . . . . . . ii 1 215
Dan Cupid ; Regent of love-rhymes, lord of folded arms . . . . iii 1 183
When they strive to be Lords o'er their lords ?—Only for praise : and praise we may afford To any lady that subdues a lord . . . . iv 1 38
From my lord to my lady.—From which lord to which lady ? . . . iv 1 104
Lord, Lord, how the ladies and I have put him down ! . . . . iv 1 143
Sir, I praise the Lord for you : and so may my parishioners . . . iv 2 75
From one Monsieur Biron, one of the strange queen's lords . . . iv 2 134
By the Lord, this love is as mad as Ajax : it kills sheep . . . . iv 3 6
O that I had my wish !—And I had mine !—And I mine too, good Lord ! iv 3 93
Fair lady,— Say you so ? Fair lord,—Take that for your fair lady . v 2 239
We that sell by gross, the Lord doth know, Have not the grace to grace it v 2 319
Write, 'Lord have mercy on us' on those three . . . . . v 2 419
These lords are visited ; you are not free, For the Lord's tokens on you do I see.—No, they are free . . . . v 2 422
The noble lord Most honourably doth uphold his word . . . . . v 2 448
O Lord, sir, it were pity you should get your living by reckoning . . v 2 497
Tarry, rash wanton : am not I thy lord ?—Then I must be thy lady *M. N. Dream* ii 1 63
I thought you lord of more true gentleness . . . . . . iii 2 132
Lord, what fools these mortals be ! . . . . iii 2 115
My fairy lord, this must be done with haste . . . . . . iii 2 378
Come, my lord, and in our flight Tell me how it came this night . . iv 1 104
There is two or three lords and ladies more married . . . . . iv 2 16
How say you by the French lord, Monsieur Le Bon ? . *Mer. of Venice* i 2 58
What think you of the Scottish lord ? . . . . i 2 83
You need not fear, lady, the having any of these lords . . . . i 2 110
Lord worshipped might he be ! what a beard hast thou got ! . . . . ii 2 98
Lord, how art thou changed ! How dost thou and thy master agree ? . ii 2 106
Where is my lady ?—Here : what would my lord ? . . . . . ii 9 85
One that comes before To signify the approaching of his lord . . . ii 9 88
A day in April never came so sweet, To show how costly summer was at hand, As this fore-spurrer comes before his lord . . . . . ii 9 95
Her gentle spirit Commits itself to yours to be directed, As from her lord iii 2 167
But now I was the lord Of this fair mansion . . . . . . iii 2 169
Which appears most strongly In bearing thus the absence of your lord iii 4 4
How dear a lover of my lord your husband . . . . . . iii 4 7
Antonio, Being the bosom lover of my lord, Must needs be like my lord iii 4 17
I commit into your hands The husbandry and manage of my house Until my lord's return . . . . iii 4 26
Only attended by Nerissa here, Until her husband and my lord's return iii 4 30
Goodly Lord, what a wit-snapper are you ! . . . . iii 5 55
Your lord Will never more break faith advisedly . . . . . v 1 252
Three or four loving lords have put themselves into voluntary exile with him, whose lands and revenues enrich the new duke *As Y. L. It* i 1 106
O Lord, Lord ! it is a hard matter for friends to meet . . . . iii 2 194
Doth my simple feature content you ?—Your features ! Lord warrant us ! what features ? . . . . iii 3 5
You to his love must accord, Or have a woman to your lord . . . v 4 140
It is not the fashion to see the lady the epilogue ; but it is no more unhandsome than to see the lord the prologue . . . . . . Epil. 3
Say that he dreams, For he is nothing but a mighty lord *T. of Shrew* Ind. 1 65
There is a lord will hear you play to-night . . . . . . Ind. 1 93
Such as he hath observed in noble ladies Unto their lords . . . Ind. 1 112
Bid him shed tears, as being overjoy'd To see her noble lord restored Ind. 1 121
Thou art a lord and nothing but a lord : Thou hast a lady . . . Ind. 2 63
Am I a lord ? and have I such a lady ? Or do I dream ? . . . . Ind. 2 70
I am a lord indeed And not a tinker nor Christophero Sly . . . Ind. 2 74
Now Lord be thanked for my good amends ! . . . . Ind. 2 99
How fares my noble lord ?—Marry, I fare well ; for here is cheer enough . . . . Ind. 2 102
Are you my wife and will not call me husband ? My men should call me 'lord' . . . . Ind. 2 107
My husband and my lord, my lord and husband ; I am your wife in all obedience . . . . Ind. 2 108
What must I call her ?—Madam.—Al'ce madam, or Joan madam ?— 'Madam,' and nothing else : so lords call ladies . . . . . Ind. 2 113
From all such devils, good Lord deliver us !—And me too, good Lord ! i 1 66

Lord. 'B mi,' Bianca, take him for thy lord, 'C fa ut,' that loves with all affection . . . *T. of Shrew* iii 1 75
Good Lord, how bright and goodly shines the moon! . . . iv 5 2
Lord, let me never have a cause to sigh! . . . v 2 123
Tell these headstrong women What duty they do owe their lords and husbands . . . v 2 131
And dart not scornful glances from those eyes, To wound thy lord . . . v 2 138
Thy husband is thy lord, thy life, thy keeper, Thy head, thy sovereign . . . v 2 146
A foul contending rebel And graceless traitor to her loving lord . . . v 2 160
In his youth He had the wit which I can well observe To-day in our young lords . . . *All's Well* i 2 33
My master, my dear lord he is; and I His servant live . . . i 3 164
So that my lord your son were not my brother,—Indeed my mother! . . . i 3 168
My lord your son made me to think of this . . . i 3 238
Use a more spacious ceremony to the noble lords . . . ii 1 52
Call before me all the lords in court.—Sit, my preserver . . . ii 3 52
Your lord and master did well to make his recantation.—Recantation! My lord! . . . ii 3 194
Which if—Lord have mercy on thee for a hen! . . . ii 3 223
Scurvy, old, filthy, scurvy lord! Well, I must be patient . . . ii 3 250
I'll beat him, . . . an he were double and double a lord . . . ii 3 254
Your lord and master's married; there's news for you . . . ii 3 257
He is my good lord: whom I serve above is my master . . . ii 3 261
You are more saucy with lords and honourable personages . . . ii 3 278
My lord will go away to-night; A very serious business calls on him . . . ii 4 40
Is there any unkindness between my lord and you, monsieur?—I know not how I have deserved to run into my lord's displeasure . . . ii 5 36
I take my young lord to be a very melancholy man . . . iii 2 3
Madam, my lord is gone, for ever gone.—Do not say so . . . iii 2 48
She deserves a lord That twenty such rude boys might tend upon . . . iii 2 83
Poor lord! is't I That chase thee from thy country? . . . iii 2 105
Do not touch my lord. Whoever shoots at him, I set him there . . . iii 2 114
Poor lady! 'Tis a hard bondage to become the wife Of a detesting lord . . . iii 5 68
O Lord, sir, let me live, or let me see my death! . . . iv 3 344
Heaven aiding, And by the leave of my good lord the king . . . iv 4 13
My lord that's gone made himself much sport out of him . . . iv 5 67
I heard . . . that my lord your son was upon his return home . . . iv 5 74
Yonder's my lord your son with a patch of velvet on's face . . . iv 5 99
Lord, how we lose our pains! . . . v 1 24
The young lord Did to his majesty, his mother and his lady Offence . . . v 3 12
You remember The daughter of this lord?—Admiringly . . . v 3 43
But for this lord, Who hath abused me, as he knows himself . . . v 3 298
Thou shalt live as freely as thy lord, To call his fortunes thine . . . *T. Night* i 4 39
Have you any commission from your lord to negotiate with my face? . . . i 5 249
But, if you were the devil, you are fair. My lord and master loves you . . . i 5 271
Your lord does know my mind; I cannot love him: Yet I suppose him virtuous . . . i 5 276
Get you to your lord; I cannot love him: let him send no more . . . i 5 298
Desire him not to flatter with his lord, Nor hold him up with hopes . . . i 5 322
You should put your lord into a desperate assurance she will none of him . . . ii 2 8
Be never so hardy to come again in his affairs, unless it be to report your lord's taking of this . . . ii 2 11
None of my lord's ring! why, he sent her none . . . ii 2 25
Attend your ladyship! You'll nothing, madam, to my lord by me? . . . iii 1 148
O Lord!—Prithee, hold thy peace; this is not the way . . . iii 4 119
His employment between his lord and my niece confirms no less . . . iii 4 205
What would my lord, but that he may not have? . . . v 1 104
Good my lord,— My lord would speak; my duty hushes me . . . v 1 109
What shall I do?—Even what it please my lord, that shall become him . . . v 1 119
My fortune since Hath been between this lady and this lord . . . v 1 265
By the Lord, madam, you wrong me, and the world shall know it . . . v 1 310
When at Bohemia You take my lord, I'll give him my commission . . . *W. T.* i 2 40
I love thee not a jar o' the clock behind What lady-she her lord . . . i 2 44
You shall not go: a lady's 'Verily''s As potent as a lord's . . . i 2 51
I'll question you Of my lord's tricks and yours when you were boys . . . i 2 61
Was not my lord The verier wag o' the two? . . . i 2 65
A most unworthy and unnatural lord Can do no more . . . ii 3 113
These lords, my noble fellows, if they please, Can clear me in't . . . ii 3 142
To take away the life of our sovereign lord the king, thy royal husband . . . iii 2 17
My lord the king, the king!—What is the business? . . . iii 2 143
I'll not remember you of my own lord, Who is lost too . . . iii 2 231
For this ungentle business, Put on thee by my lord, thou ne'er shalt see Thy wife Paulina more . . . iii 3 35
'Tis your counsel My lord should to the heavens be contrary . . . v 1 45
Yet, if my lord will marry,—if you will, sir, No remedy, but you will,—give me the office To choose you a queen . . . v 1 76
Had our prince, Jewel of children, seen this hour, he had pair'd Well with this lord: there was not full a month Between their births . . . v 1 117
That noble honour'd lord is fear'd and loved . . . v 1 158
My lord's almost so far transported that He'll think anon it lives . . . v 3 69
Lord of thy presence and no land beside . . . *K. John* i 1 137
Shall your city call us lord, In that behalf which we have challenged it? . . . ii 1 263
Lord of our presence, Angiers, and of you . . . ii 1 367
This rich fair town We make him lord of . . . ii 1 553
Since kings break faith upon commodity, Gain, be my lord . . . ii 1 598
O Lord! my boy, my Arthur, my fair son! My life, my joy! . . . iii 4 103
To my closet bring The angry lords with all expedient haste . . . iv 2 268
Would not my lords return to me again, After they heard young Arthur was alive?—They found him dead . . . v 1 37
Return the precedent to these lords again . . . v 2 3
My holy lord of Milan, from the king I come . . . v 2 120
If the French be lords of this loud day . . . v 4 14
Last in the field, and almost lords of it! . . . v 5 8
Melun is slain; the English lords By his persuasion are again fall'n off . . . v 5 10
The lords are all come back, And brought Prince Henry . . . v 6 33
Myself and other lords, If you think meet, this afternoon will post . . . v 7 93
At some thing it grieves, More than with parting from my lord . . . *Rich. II.* ii 2 13
So your sweet majesty, Looking awry upon your lord's departure, Find shapes of grief, more than himself, to wail . . . ii 2 21
Then, thrice-gracious queen, More than your lord's departure weep not . . . ii 2 25
By this the weary lords Shall make their way seem short . . . ii 3 16
Were I but now the lord of such hot youth . . . ii 3 99
My lords of England, let me tell you this: I have had feeling of my cousin's wrongs . . . ii 3 140
The breath of worldly men cannot depose The deputy elected by the Lord . . . iii 2 57
The king of heaven forbid our lord the king Should so with civil and uncivil arms Be rush'd upon! . . . iii 3 101

Lord. In your lord's scale is nothing but himself, And some few vanities that make him light . . . *Richard II.* iii 4 85
Princes and noble lords, What answer shall I make to this base man? . . . iv 1 19
My lord,— No lord of thine, thou haught insulting man, Nor no man's lord . . . iv 1 254
To whose flint bosom my condemned lord Is doom'd a prisoner . . . v 1 3
Ah, my sour husband, my hard-hearted lord! . . . v 3 121
Our council we Will hold at Windsor; so inform the lords . . . *1 Hen. IV.* i 1 104
By the Lord, thou sayest true, lad . . . i 2 44
By the Lord, I'll be a brave judge.—Thou judgest false already . . . i 2 72
An old lord of the council rated me the other day in the street . . . i 2 94
By the Lord, an I do not, I am a villain . . . i 2 108
By the Lord, I'll be a traitor then, when thou art king . . . i 2 164
Now, my good sweet honey lord, ride with us to-morrow . . . i 2 179
A certain lord, neat, and trimly dress'd, Fresh as a bridegroom . . . i 3 33
By the Lord, our plot is a good plot as ever was laid . . . ii 3 17
Some heavy business hath my lord in hand, And I must know it . . . ii 3 66
Ye fat paunch, an ye call me coward, by the Lord, I'll stab thee . . . ii 4 160
By the Lord, I knew ye as well as he that made ye . . . ii 4 295
But, by the Lord, lads, I am glad you have the money . . . ii 4 304
Leads ancient lords and reverend bishops on To bloody battles . . . iii 2 104
When the lords and barons of the realm Perceived Northumberland did lean to him, The more and less came in . . . iv 3 66
I did not think thee lord of such a spirit . . . v 4 18
Lord, lord, how this world is given to lying! . . . v 4 148
In the fortune of my lord your son, Prince Harry slain outright . . . *2 Hen. IV.* i 1 15
But, for my lord your son,— Why, he is dead . . . i 1 83
My lord your son had only but . . . the shows of men to fight . . . i 1 192
Sir, my lord would speak with you.—Sir John Falstaff, a word . . . i 2 104
He gave it like a rude prince, and you took it like a sensible lord . . . i 2 220
Now the Lord lighten thee! thou art a great fool . . . ii 1 208
O, the Lord preserve thy good grace! by my troth, welcome to London . . . ii 4 315
O Lord! good my lord captain,— What, dost thou roar? . . . iii 2 188
O Lord, sir! I am a diseased man . . . iii 2 191
Lord, Lord, how subject we old men are to this vice of lying! . . . iii 2 325
You, reverend father, and these noble lords Had not been here . . . iv 1 38
By the Lord, I will have it in a particular ballad else . . . iv 3 51
When you come to court, Stand my good lord, pray, in your good report . . . iv 3 89
O the Lord, that Sir John were come! he would make this a bloody day to somebody . . . v 4 13
And bids you, in the bowels of the Lord, Deliver up the crown . . . *Hen. V.* ii 4 102
Poor we may call them in their native lords . . . iii 5 26
To my lords of England: I and my bosom must debate a while . . . iv 1 30
The Lord in heaven bless thee, noble Harry!—God-a-mercy, old heart! . . . iv 1 33
Not to-day, O Lord, O, not to-day, think not upon the fault My father made! . . . iv 1 309
My sovereign lord, bestow yourself with speed . . . iv 3 68
Sixteen hundred mercenaries; The rest are princes, barons, lords . . . iv 8 94
Where that his lords desire him to have borne His bruised helmet . . . v Prol. 17
To say to thee that I shall die, is true; but for thy love, by the Lord, no . . . v 2 159
Is't so, my lords of England?—The king hath granted every article . . . v 2 359
The world's best garden he achieved, And of it left his son imperial lord . . . Epil. 8
This dreadful lord, Retiring from the siege of Orleans . . . *1 Hen. VI.* i 1 110
Four of their lords I'll change for one of ours . . . i 1 151
He fighteth as one weary of his life. The other lords, like lions wanting food . . . i 2 27
Answer you so the lord protector?—The Lord protect him! so we answer him . . . i 3 9
Thou manifest conspirator, Thou that contrivedst to murder our dead lord . . . i 3 34
I think, at the north gate; for there stand lords . . . i 4 66
O Lord, have mercy on us, wretched sinners!—O Lord, have mercy on me, woful man! . . . i 4 70
Prisoner! to whom?—To me, blood-thirsty lord . . . ii 3 34
The reason moved these warlike lords to this Was, for that . . . I was the next by birth and parentage . . . ii 5 70
My lord should be religious And know the office that belongs to such . . . iii 1 54
Must your bold verdict enter talk with lords? . . . iii 1 63
Trouble us no more; But join in friendship, as your lords have done . . . iii 1 145
Our sacks shall be a mean to sack the city, And we be lords and rulers . . . iii 2 11
Henry will be lord And thou be thrust out like a fugitive . . . iii 3 66
Return, thou wandering lord; Charles and the rest will take thee in their arms . . . iii 3 76
Welcome, brave captain and victorious lord! . . . iii 4 16
Thy lord I honour as he is.—Why, what is he? as good a man as York . . . iii 4 35
In defence of my lord's worthiness, I crave the benefit of law of arms . . . iv 1 99
Good Lord, what madness rules in brainsick men! . . . iv 1 111
O, send some succour to the distress'd lord!—He dies, we lose . . . iv 3 30
For the proffer of my lord your master, I have inform'd his highness . . . v 1 41
Of virtuous chaste intents, To love and honour Henry as her lord . . . v 5 21
O Lord, that lends me life, Lend me a heart replete with thankfulness! . . . *2 Hen. VI.* i 1 19
Now ye grow too hot: It was the pleasure of my lord the king . . . i 1 138
Still revelling like lords till all be gone . . . i 1 224
Why droops my lord, like over-ripen'd corn? . . . i 2 1
If thou dost love thy lord, Banish the canker of ambitious thoughts . . . i 2 17
My troublous dream this night doth make me sad.—What dream'd my lord? . . . i 2 23
Marry, the Lord protect him, for he's a good man! . . . i 3 5
Not all these lords do vex me half so much As that proud dame . . . i 3 78
Yet must we join with him and with the lords, Till we have brought Duke Humphrey in disgrace . . . i 3 98
O Lord, have mercy upon me! I shall never be able to fight a blow. O Lord, my heart! . . . i 3 219
Tell us here the circumstance, That we for thee may glorify the Lord . . . ii 1 75
God's goodness hath been great to thee: Let never day nor night unhallow'd pass, But still remember what the Lord hath done . . . ii 1 86
O Lord bless me! I pray God! for I am never able to deal with my master . . . ii 3 77
All happiness unto my lord the king! . . . iii 1 93
These great lords . . . Do seek subversion of thy harmless life . . . iii 1 207
Free lords, cold snow melts with the sun's hot beams. Henry my lord is cold in great affairs . . . iii 1 223
Here comes my lord.—Now, sirs, have you dispatch'd this thing? . . . iii 2 5
Blunt-witted lord, ignoble in demeanour! If ever lady wrong'd her lord so much, Thy mother took into her blameful bed Some stern untutor'd churl . . . iii 2 210
How fares my lord? speak, Beaufort, to thy sovereign . . . iii 3 1

Lord. Pool! Sir Pool! lord! Ay, kennel, puddle, sink . *2 Hen. VI.* iv 1 70
And wedded be thou to the hags of hell, For daring to affy a mighty lord Unto the daughter of a worthless king . iv 1 80
The false revolting Normans thorough thee Disdain to call us lord . iv 1 88
I will apparel them all in one livery, that they may agree like brothers and worship me their lord . iv 2 82
'Tis for liberty. We will not leave one lord, one gentleman . iv 2 194
Now is Mortimer lord of this city . iv 6 1
Ah, thou say, thou serge, nay, thou buckram lord! . iv 7 28
Lord, who would live turmoiled in the court? . iv 10 18
Here's the lord of the soil come to seize me for a stray . iv 10 26
Health and all happiness to my lord the king!—I thank thee, Clifford . v 1 124
Proud northern lord, Clifford of Cumberland, Warwick is hoarse with calling thee to arms. How now, my noble lord! . v 2 6
The northern lords that have forsworn thy colours Will follow mine, if once they see them spread . *3 Hen. VI.* i 1 251
The loss of those three lords torments my heart: I'll write unto them . i 1 270
The queen with all the northern earls and lords Intend here to besiege you in your castle . i 2 49
A crown for York! and, lords, bow low to him: Hold you his hands . i 4 94
York was slain, Your princely father and my loving lord! . ii 1 47
Cheer these noble lords And hearten those that fight in your defence . ii 2 78
I'll cross the sea, To effect this marriage, so it please my lord . ii 6 98
Why stops my lord? shall I not hear my task?—An easy task . iii 2 52
My lord and sovereign, and thy vowed friend . iii 3 50
I make King Lewis behold Thy sly conveyance and thy lord's false love iii 3 160
How far hence is thy lord, mine honest fellow? . v 1 2
Good day, my lord. What, at your book so hard?—Ay, my good lord: —my lord, I should say rather: 'Tis sin to flatter . v 6 1
Good time of day unto my gracious lord! . *Richard III.* i 1 122
Let her be made As miserable by the death of him As I am made by my poor lord and thee! . i 2 28
Hath she forgot already that brave prince, Edward, her lord? . i 2 241
What would betide of me?—No other harm but loss of such a lord.— The loss of such a lord includes all harm . i 3 7
And for his meed, poor lord, he is mew'd up . i 3 139
We follow'd then our lord, our lawful king: So should we you . i 3 147
Lord, Lord! methought, what pain it was to drown! . i 4 21
Dukes, earls, lords, gentlemen; indeed, of all . ii 1 68
Edward, my lord, your son, our king, is dead . ii 2 40
And, in good time, here comes the sweating lord.—Welcome, my lord . iii 1 24
Go, effect this business soundly.—My good lords both, with all the heed I may . iii 1 187
Return unto thy lord; Bid him not fear the separated councils . iii 2 19
Many good morrows to my noble lord!—Good morrow, Catesby . iii 2 35
The lords at Pomfret, when they rode from London, Were jocund . iii 2 85
Now, by the holy mother of our Lord, The citizens are mum . iii 7 2
I mean the lord protector.—The Lord protect him from that kingly title! iv 1 19
And be thy wife—if any be so mad—As miserable by the life of thee As thou hast made me by my dear lord's death! . iv 1 77
What were I best to say? her father's brother Would be her lord? . iv 4 338
Return unto thy lord; commend me to him . iv 5 16
An honest country lord, as I am, beaten A long time out of play *Hen. VIII.* i 3 44
This night he makes a supper, and a great one, To many lords and ladies i 3 53
For it is you Have blown this coal betwixt my lord and me . ii 4 79
Now, the Lord help, They vex me past my patience! . ii 4 129
He might the king his lord advertise Whether our daughter were legitimate . ii 4 178
The Lord increase this business! . iii 2 161
All else This talking lord can lay upon my credit, I answer is most false iii 2 265
I am a poor fall'n man, unworthy now To be thy lord and master . iii 2 414
Bear witness, all that have not hearts of iron, With what a sorrow Cromwell leaves his lord . iii 2 425
The rich stream Of lords and ladies . iv 1 63
There is among the Greeks A lord of Trojan blood . *Troi. and Cres.* i 2 13
My lord would instantly speak with you.—Where?—At your own house i 2 297
Strength should be lord of imbecility . i 3 114
Kings, princes, lords! If there be one among the fair'st of Greece . i 3 264
Achilles shall have word of this intent; So shall each lord of Greece . i 3 307
The plague of Greece upon thee, thou mongrel beef-witted lord! . ii 1 14
Thou sodden-witted lord! thou hast no more brain than I have in mine elbows . ii 1 47
You dog!—You scurvy lord!—You cur! . ii 1 56
This lord, Achilles, Ajax, who wears his wit in his belly . ii 1 79
What's Achilles?—Thy lord, Thersites . ii 3 49
Agamemnon commands Achilles; Achilles is my lord . ii 3 57
Shall the proud lord . . . be worshipp'd Of that we hold an idol more than he? . ii 3 194
No, this thrice worthy and right valiant lord Must not so stale his palm ii 3 200
This lord go to him! Jupiter forbid, And say in thunder 'Achilles go to him' . ii 3 208
Here's a lord,—come knights from east to west, And cull their flower . ii 3 274
I do depend upon the lord.—You depend upon a noble gentleman . iii 1 5
I must needs praise him.—The Lord be praised! . iii 1 8
At the request of Paris my lord, who's there in person . iii 1 33
I have business to my lord, dear queen. My lord, will you vouchsafe me a word? . iii 1 63
If my lord get a boy of you, you'll give him me. Be true to my lord . iii 2 112
So do each lord, and either greet him not, Or else disdainfully . iii 3 52
Expressly proves That no man is the lord of any thing . iii 3 115
To see these Grecian lords!—why, even already They clap the lubber Ajax on the shoulder . iii 3 138
Invite the Trojan lords after the combat To see us here unarm'd . iii 3 236
Why sigh you so profoundly? where's my lord? gone! . iv 2 84
I tell thee, lord of Greece, She is as far high-soaring o'er thy praises iv 4 125
My well-famed lord of Troy, no less to you . iv 5 173
When was my lord so much ungently temper'd, To stop his ears? . v 3 1
I'll not over the threshold till my lord return from the wars . *Coriolanus* i 3 82
Your lord and Titus Lartius are set down before their city Corioli . i 3 110
Are you lords o' the field? If not, why cease you till you are so? . i 6 47
Translate his malice towards you into love, Standing your friendly lord ii 3 198
I'ld have beaten him like a dog, but for disturbing the lords within . iv 5 57
To fail in the disposing of those chances Which he was lord of . iv 7 41
Report to the Volscian lords, how plainly I have borne this business . v 3 3
My lord and husband!—These eyes are not the same I wore in Rome . v 3 37
Go tell the lords o' the city I am here: Deliver them this paper . v 6 1
Say no more: Here come the lords . v 6 60
But, worthy lords, have you with heed perused What I have written to you? . v 6 62

Lord. You lords and heads o' the state, perfidiously He has betray'd your business . *Coriolanus* v 6 91
See, lord and father, how we have perform'd Our Roman rites *T. Andron.* i 1 142
In peace and honour live Lord Titus long; My noble lord and father! . i 1 158
Presents well worthy Rome's imperial lord . i 1 250
My lord the emperor Sends thee this word . iii 1 150
Give signs, sweet girl, for here are none but friends, What Roman lord it was durst do the deed . iv 1 62
To see so great a lord Basely insinuate and send us gifts . iv 2 37
Lord of my life, commander of my thoughts . iv 4 28
My lord and you were then at Mantua . *Rom. and Jul.* i 3 28
And follow thee my lord throughout the world . ii 2 148
Lord, Lord, she will be a joyful woman . ii 4 185
The sweetest lady—Lord, Lord! when 'twas a little prating thing . ii 4 212
Good sweet nurse,—O Lord, why look'st thou sad? . ii 5 21
Lord, how my head aches! what a head have I! . ii 5 49
Is Romeo slaughter'd, and is Tybalt dead? My dear-loved cousin, and my dearer lord? . iii 2 66
Ah, poor my lord, what tongue shall smooth thy name? . iii 2 98
Where is my lady's lord, where's Romeo? . iii 3 82
O Lord, I could have stay'd here all the night To hear good counsel . iii 3 159
Art thou gone so? love, lord, ay, husband, friend! . iii 5 43
I pray you, tell my lord and father, madam, I will not marry yet . iii 5 121
Is it more sin to wish me thus forsworn, Or to dispraise my lord? . iii 5 237
I'll send a friar with speed To Mantua, with my letters to thy lord . iv 1 124
I met the youthful lord at Lawrence' cell . iv 2 25
For shame, bring Juliet forth; her lord is come . iv 5 22
My bosom's lord sits lightly in his throne . v 1 3
Take this letter; . . . See thou deliver it to my lord and father . v 3 24
O Lord, they fight! I will go call the watch . v 3 71
O comfortable friar! where is my lord? . v 3 148
O, 'tis a worthy lord.—Nay, that's most fix'd . *T. of Athens* i 1 9
You are rapt, sir, in some work, some dedication To the great lord . i 1 20
How this lord is follow'd!—The senators of Athens: happy man! . i 1 39
Wilt dine with me, Apemantus?—No; I eat not lords.—An thou shouldst, thou'ldst anger ladies.—O, they eat lords . i 1 207
That I were a lord!—What wouldst do then, Apemantus?—E'en as Apemantus does now; hate a lord with my heart . i 1 234
That I had no angry wit to be a lord. Art not thou a merchant? . i 1 241
I bleed inwardly for my lord.—You do yourselves Much wrong . i 2 211
Sometime 't appears like a lord; sometime like a lawyer . ii 2 116
Heavens, have I said, the bounty of this lord! . ii 2 173
I have told my lord of you; he is coming down to you . iii 1 1
How does that honourable, complete, free-hearted gentleman of Athens, thy very bountiful good lord and master? . iii 1 11
Which, in my lord's behalf, I come to entreat your honour to supply . iii 1 17
Alas, good lord! a noble gentleman 'tis, if he would not keep so good a house . iii 1 23
Thy lord's a bountiful gentleman: but thou art wise . iii 1 42
This slave, Unto his honour, has my lord's meat in him . iii 1 60
Let not that part of nature Which my lord paid for, be of any power To expel sickness, but prolong his hour? . iii 1 65
By good hap, yonder's my lord; I have sweat to see his honour . iii 2 27
Commend me to thy honourable virtuous lord, my very exquisite friend iii 2 32
Please your honour, my lord hath sent— Ha! what has he sent? . iii 2 33
I am so much endeared to that lord; he's ever sending . iii 2 36
Timon has been this lord's father, And kept his credit with his purse . iii 2 74
It may prove an argument of laughter To the rest, and 'mongst lords I be thought a fool . iii 3 21
How fairly this lord strives to appear foul! . iii 3 31
This was my lord's best hope; now all are fled, Save only the gods . iii 3 36
Is not my lord seen yet?—Not yet.—I wonder on't . iii 4 9
Your lord sends now for money.—Most true, he does . iii 4 18
E'en as if your lord should wear rich jewels, And send for money for 'em iii 4 23
I know my lord hath spent of Timon's wealth . iii 4 26
Pray, is my lord ready to come forth?—No, indeed, he is not . iii 4 35
Why then preferr'd you not your sums and bills, When your false masters eat of my lord's meat? . iii 4 50
My lord and I have made an end; I have no more to reckon, he to spend iii 4 55
Take 't of my soul, my lord leans wondrously to discontent . iii 4 70
I think this honourable lord did but try us this other day . iii 6 3
He's but a mad lord, and nought but humour sways him . iii 6 121
Poor honest lord, brought low by his own heart, Undone by goodness! iv 2 37
Alas, kind lord! He's flung in rage from this ingrateful seat . iv 2 44
Raise me this beggar, and deny 't that lord . iv 3 9
Is yond despised and ruinous man my lord? Full of decay and failing? iv 3 465
And, as my lord, Still serve him with my life . iv 3 477
Ne'er did poor steward wear a truer grief For his undone lord . iv 3 488
For many so arrive at second masters, Upon their first lord's neck . iv 3 513
Bring me word, boy, if thy lord look well, For he went sickly forth *J. C.* ii 4 13
Commend me to my lord; Say I am merry . ii 4 44
Calls my lord?—I pray you, sirs, lie in my tent and sleep . iv 3 245
Stay thou by thy lord: Thou art a fellow of a good respect . v 5 44
The Norweyan lord surveying vantage, With furbish'd arms . *Macbeth* i 2 31
Sit, worthy friends: my lord is often thus, And hath been from his youth . iii 4 53
Streets, That lend a tyrannous and damned light To their lord's murder *Hamlet* ii 2 483
Follow that lord; and look you mock him not . ii 2 570
No second husband wed; But die thy thoughts when thy first lord is dead . iii 2 225
How fares my lord?—Give o'er the play.—Give me some light: away! . iii 2 278
A slave that is not twentieth part the tithe Of your precedent lord . iii 4 98
For this same lord, I do repent: but heaven hath pleased it so . iii 4 172
Ah, mine own lord, what have I seen to-night! . iv 1 5
Bring him before us.—Ho, Guildenstern! bring in my lord . iv 3 16
Lord, we know what we are, but know not what we may be . iv 5 42
The rabble call him lord . iv 5 102
That lord whose hand must take my plight shall carry Half my love *Lear* i 1 103
Prescribe not us our duties.—Let your study Be to content your lord . i 1 280
To my lodging, from whence I will fitly bring you to hear my lord speak i 2 185
'My lady's father'! my lord's knave: you whoreson dog! you slave! . i 4 88
That lord that counsell'd thee To give away thy land, Come place him here . i 4 154
Not altogether fool, my lord.—No, faith, lords and great men will not let me . i 4 165
Smooth every passion That in the natures of their lords rebel . ii 2 82
Post speedily to my lord your husband; show him this letter . iii 7 1
Lord Edmund spake not with your lord at home?—No, madam . iv 5 4
My lord is dead; Edmund and I have talk'd . iv 5 30

Lord. How does my royal lord? How fares your majesty? . . . *Lear* iv 7 44
Witness the world, that I create thee here My lord and master . . . v 3 78
She is sub-contracted to this lord, And I, her husband, contradict your bans . . . . v 3 86
Throwing but shows of service on their lords . . . . . *Othello* i 1 52
My heart's subdued Even to the very quality of my lord . . . i 3 252
What tidings can you tell me of my lord?—He is not yet arrived . . ii 1 88
I will have my lord and you again As friendly as you were . . . iii 3 6
You do love my lord: You have known him long . . . . . . iii 3 10
My lord shall never rest; I'll watch him tame and talk him out of patience . . . . iii 3 22
Here comes my lord.—Madam, I'll take my leave.—Why, stay . . iii 3 29
Tell him I have moved my lord on his behalf, and hope all will be well iii 4 19
My advocation is not now in tune; My lord is not my lord . . . iii 4 124
Is my lord angry?—He went hence but now . . . . . . iii 4 132
My lord is fall'n into an epilepsy: This is his second fit . . . iv 1 51
Is there division 'twixt my lord and Cassio?—A most unhappy one . iv 1 242
I hope my noble lord esteems me honest . . . . iv 2 65
If to preserve this vessel for my lord From any other foul unlawful touch Be not to be a strumpet, I am none . . . . . . iv 2 83
What's the matter with my lord?—With who?—Why, with my lord, madam.—Who is thy lord?—He that is yours . . . . . . iv 2 98
Alas, Iago, my lord hath so bewhored her . . . . iv 2 115
Am I that name, Iago?—What name, fair lady?—Such as she says my lord did say I was . . . . iv 2 119
O good Iago, What shall I do to win my lord again? . . . . iv 2 149
Run you to the citadel, And tell my lord and lady what hath happ'd . v 1 127
Thou art to die.—Then Lord have mercy on me! . . . . . v 2 57
Farewell: Commend me to my kind lord: O, farewell! . . . . v 2 125
Saw you my lord!—No, lady.—Was he not here? . . *Ant. and Cleo.* i 2 84
My lord approaches.—We will not look upon him: go with us . . i 2 90
What say'st thou?—Wilt thou be lord of the whole world? . . . ii 7 68
When I shall pray, 'O, bless my lord and husband!' Undo that prayer, by crying out as loud, 'O, bless my brother!' . . . . . iii 4 16
So your desires are yours.—Thanks to my lord . . . . . iii 4 28
My lord desires you presently: my news I might have told hereafter . iii 5 22
Hail, Cæsar, and my lord! hail, most dear Cæsar! . . . . . iii 6 39
Why will my lord do so?—For that he dares us to 't.—So hath my lord dared him to single fight . . . . iii 7 30
Lord of his fortunes he salutes thee, and Requires to live in Egypt . iii 12 11
That would make his will Lord of his reason . . . . . . iii 13 4
He that can endure To follow with allegiance a fall'n lord Does conquer him that did his master conquer . . . . iii 13 44
There's hope in 't yet.—That's my brave lord! . . . . . iii 13 177
But, since my lord Is Antony again, I will be Cleopatra . . . iii 13 186
Call all his noble captains to my lord.—Do so, we'll speak to them . iii 13 188
Ah, thou spell! Avaunt!—Why is my lord enraged against his love? . iv 12 31
What would my lord?—Since Cleopatra died, I have lived in such dishonour . . . . iv 14 55
Come, your lord calls!—Bear me, good friends, where Cleopatra bides . iv 14 130
How heavy weighs my lord! Our strength is all gone into heaviness . iv 15 32
Make your full reference freely to my lord, Who is so full of grace . v 2 23
The gods Will have it thus; my master and my lord I must obey . . v 2 116
My lord your son drew on my master.—Ha! No harm, I trust? *Cymbeline* i 1 160
You shall at least Go see my lord aboard: for this time leave me . . i 1 178
The remembrancer of her to hold The hand-fast to her lord . . . i 5 78
When to my good lord I prove untrue, I'll choke myself . . . . i 5 86
A noble gentleman of Rome, Comes from my lord with letters . . . i 6 11
Continues well my lord? His health, beseech you?—Well, madam . . i 6 56
Whiles the jolly Briton—Your lord, I mean—laughs from's free lungs . i 6 68
Will my lord say so?—Ay, madam, with his eyes in flood with laughter i 6 73
My lord, I fear, Has forgot Britain.—And himself . . . . . i 6 112
I have spoke this, to know if your affiance Were deeply rooted; and shall make your lord, That which he is, new o'er . . . . . i 6 164
A small request, And yet of moment too, for it concerns Your lord . i 6 183
Some dozen Romans of us and your lord—The best feather of our wing—have mingled sums To buy a present . . . . i 6 185
Since My lord hath interest in them, I will keep them In my bedchamber i 6 195
If you please To greet your lord with writing, do't to-night . . i 6 206
That thou mayst stand, To enjoy thy banish'd lord and this great land! ii 1 70
And this will witness outwardly, As strongly as the conscience does within, To the madding of her lord . . . . ii 2 37
I hope it be not gone to tell my lord That I kiss aught but he . . ii 3 152
Here is a letter from my lord.—Who? thy lord? that is my lord! . . iii 2 25
Let what is here contain'd relish of love, Of my lord's health . . iii 2 31
Who long'st, like me, to see thy lord; who long'st,—O, let me bate . iii 2 55
He that strikes The venison first shall be the lord o' the feast . . iii 3 75
O, my all-worthy lord!—All-worthy villain! Discover where thy mistress is at once, At the next word: no more of 'worthy lord!' . iii 5 94
I'll write to my lord she's dead. O Imogen, Safe mayst thou wander! iii 5 104
My dear lord! Thou art one o' the false ones. Now I think on thee, My hunger's gone . . . . iii 6 14
Conspired with that irregulous devil, Cloten, Hast here cut off my lord iv 2 316
If that thy gentry, Britain, go before This lout as he exceeds our lords, the odds Is that we scare are men and you are gods . . . . v 2 9
This is a lord! O noble misery, To be i' the field, and ask 'what news?' of me! . . . . v 3 64
He shall be lord of lady Imogen, And happier much by his affliction made . . . . v 4 107
Like a noble lord in love and one That had a royal lover, took his hint v 5 171
That headless man I thought had been my lord . . . . . . v 5 300
Lords and ladies in their lives Have read it for restoratives *Pericles* i Gower 7
Peace to the lords of Tyre! . . . . i 3 30
I have understood Your lord has betook himself to unknown travels . i 3 35
O my distressed lord, even such our griefs are . . . . . . i 4 7
Here stands a lord, and there a lady weeping . . . . . . i 4 47
Doth my lord call?—Get fire and meat for these poor men . . . iii 2 2
Where am I? Where's my lord? What world is this? . . . . iii 2 106
Know you the character?—It is my lord's . . . . iii 4 4
My wedded lord I ne'er shall see again . . . . iii 4 9
Blame both my lord and me, that we have taken No care to your best courses . . . . iv 1 38
Were I chief lord of all this spacious world, I'ld give it to undo the deed . . . . iv 3 5
Thwarting the wayward seas, Attended on by many a lord and knight iv 4 11
We should have both lord and lown . . . . iv 6 19
Lord calf. A calf, fair lady!—No, a fair lord calf . . . *L. L. Lost* v 2 248
Lord captain. O Lord! good my lord captain . . . . 2 *Hen. IV.* iii 2 188
Lord fool. But I tell you, my lord fool, out of this nettle, danger, we pluck this flower, safety . . . . 1 *Hen. IV.* ii 3 10
Lord governor. We create, in absence of ourself, Our uncle York lord governor of England . . . . *Richard II.* ii 1 220
Lord Love, if thy will it be! . . . . *Mer. of Venice* ii 9 101
Lord mayor. Up to the leads; the lord mayor knocks . *Richard III.* iii 7 55
Lord of all. As stout and proud as he were lord of all . 2 *Hen. VI.* i 1 187
Lord of beasts. Let a beast be lord of beasts, and his crib shall stand at the king's mess . . . . *Hamlet* v 2 88
Lord of duty. You are the lord of duty . . . . . . *Othello* i 3 184
Lord of hosts. The battles of the Lord of hosts he fought . 1 *Hen. VI.* i 1 31
Lord of lords! O infinite virtue, comest thou smiling from The world's great snare uncaught? . . . . *Ant. and Cleo.* iv 8 16
Lord protector. Answer you so the lord protector?—The Lord protect him! so we answer him . . . . 1 *Hen. VI.* i 3 8
Lord protector, give consent That Margaret may be England's royal queen . . . . v 5 23
Stand close: my lord protector will come this way by and by 2 *Hen. VI.* i 3 2
I pray, my lord, pardon me; I took ye for my lord protector . . i 3 14
The lord protector lost it, and not I . . . . . 3 *Hen. VI.* i 1 111
I mean the lord protector.—The Lord protect him from that kingly title! . . . . *Richard III.* iv 1 19
Lord-protectorship. An't like your lordly lord-protectorship 2 *Hen. VI.* ii 1 30
Lorded. Being thus lorded, Not only with what my revenue yielded, But what my power might else exact . . . . . . *Tempest* i 2 97
Lording. You were pretty lordings then? . . . . . *W. Tale* i 2 62
We shall begin our ancient bickerings. Lordings, farewell . 2 *Hen. VI.* i 1 145
I see them lording it in London streets . . . . iv 8 47
Lordliness. Vouchsafing here to visit me, Doing the honour of thy lordliness To one so meek . . . . *Ant. and Cleo.* v 2 161
Lordly. Ay, lordly sir; for what are you, I pray? . . 1 *Hen. VI.* iii 1 43
A lordly nation That will not trust thee but for profit's sake . . iii 3 62
That are substitutes Under the lordly monarch of the north . . . v 3 6
In sight of England and her lordly peers . . . . . 2 *Hen. VI.* i 1 11
An't like your lordly lord-protectorship . . . . ii 1 30
Lord's anointed. Let not the heavens hear these tell-tale women Rail on the Lord's anointed . . . . *Richard III.* iv 4 150
Sacrilegious murder hath broke ope The Lord's anointed temple! *Macb.* ii 3 73
Lords appellants, Your differences shall all rest under gage *Richard II.* iv 1 104
Lords dependants. With some other of the lords dependants . *Lear* iii 7 18
Lord's sake. And are now 'for the Lord's sake' . *Meas. for Meas.* iv 3 21
Lordship. He wonder'd that your lordship Would suffer him to spend his youth at home . . . . *T. G. of Ver.* i 3 4
Whither were I best to send him?—I think your lordship is not ignorant i 3 25
'Twere good, I think, your lordship sent him thither . . . i 3 29
May't please your lordship, 'tis a word or two Of commendations . i 3 52
Relying on your lordship's will And not depending on his friendly wish . . . . i 3 61
Good morrow to your lordship . . . . . . *Meas. for Meas.* ii 1 143
At what hour to-morrow Shall I attend your lordship? . . . . ii 2 160
This is his lordship's man.—And here comes Claudio's pardon . . iv 2 103
Shall we go prove what's to be done?—We'll wait upon your lordship *Much Ado* i 3 77
I told your lordship a year since, how much I am in the favour of Margaret . . . . ii 2 12
Means your lordship to be married to-morrow?—You know he does . iii 2 91
Ere I will yield my virgin patent up Unto his lordship . *M. N. Dream* i 1 81
Get a wife.—I thank your lordship, you have got me one *Mer. of Venice* iii 2 198
And say 'Will't please your lordship cool your hands?' *T. of Shrew* Ind. 1 58
Please your honour, players That offer service to your lordship . . Ind. 1 78
So please your lordship to accept our duty . . . . . . Ind. 1 82
Will't please your lordship drink a cup of sack? . . . . . Ind. 2 2
I am Christophero Sly; call not me 'honour' nor 'lordship' . . Ind. 2 6
I most unfeignedly beseech your lordship to make some reservation *All's Well* ii 3 259
But I hope your lordship thinks not him a soldier . . . . . . ii 5 1
If your lordship find him not a hilding, hold me no more in your respect . . . . iii 6 3
The owner of no one good quality worthy your lordship's entertainment iii 6 13
Be but your lordship present at his examination . . . . . iii 6 29
When your lordship sees the bottom of his success in't . . . iii 6 38
You shall see his fall to-night; for indeed he is not for your lordship's respect . . . . iii 6 109
As't please your lordship: I'll leave you . . . . iii 6 117
His lordship will next morning for France . . . . iv 3 90
Here's his lordship now.—How now, my lord! is't not after midnight? iv 3 96
It requires haste of your lordship . . . . iv 3 109
I have told your lordship already, the stocks carry him . . . . iv 3 121
If your lordship be in't, . . . you must have the patience to hear it . iv 3 131
Look not so upon me; we shall hear of your lordship anon . . . iv 3 222
I shall beseech your lordship to remain with me . . . . . iv 5 91
I do pity his distress . . . and leave him to your lordship . . . v 2 27
Sith wives are monsters to you, And that you fly them as you swear them lordship . . . . v 3 156
He is not here, so please your lordship, that should sing it . *T. Night* ii 4 8
My father had a daughter loved a man, As it might be, perhaps, were I a woman, I should your lordship . . . . ii 4 112
I had forgot to tell your lordship, To-day, as I came by, I called *Rich. II.* ii 2 93
He was not so resolved when last we spake together.—Because your lordship was proclaimed traitor . . . . ii 3 30
His lordship is walk'd forth into the orchard . . . . 2 *Hen. IV.* i 1 4
God give your lordship good time of day. I am glad to see your lordship abroad: I heard say your lordship was sick: I hope your lordship goes abroad by advice. Your lordship, though not clean past your youth, hath yet some smack of age in you . . . . . . i 2 106
I most humbly beseech your lordship to have a reverent care of your health . . . . i 2 113
Your lordship may minister the potion of imprisonment to me . . i 2 145
Will your lordship lend me a thousand pound to furnish me forth? . i 2 250
Pleaseth your lordship To meet his grace just distance 'tween our armies . . . . iv 1 225
His lordship should be humbler; It fitteth not a prelate . 1 *Hen. VI.* iii 1 56
Belike your lordship takes us then for fools . . . . . . iii 2 62
I will attend upon your lordship's leisure . . . . v 1 55
Are your supplications to his lordship? Let me see them . 2 *Hen. VI.* i 3 16
I have a suit unto your lordship.—Be it a lordship, thou shalt have it for that word . . . . iv 7 5
Cousin of Exeter, what thinks your lordship? . . . . 3 *Hen. VI.* iv 8 34
How hath your lordship brook'd imprisonment?—With patience *Rich. III.* i 1 125
He sends to know your lordship's pleasure, If presently you will take horse . . . . iii 2 15
God keep your lordship in that gracious mind! . . . . . . iii 2 56

Lordship. How goes the world with thee?—The better that your lordship please to ask . . . *Richard III.* iii 2 99
But long I shall not stay: I shall return before your lordship thence . iii 2 121
Come, will you go?—I'll wait upon your lordship . . . iii 2 125
His lordship knows me well, and loves me well . . . iii 4 31
Yet had not we determined he should die Until your lordship came . iii 5 53
And to that end we wish'd your lordship here. . . . iii 5 67
Your lordship is a guest too.—O, 'tis true . . . *Hen. VIII.* i 3 51
My barge stays; Your lordship shall along . . . —I am your lordship's i 3 64
O, that your lordship were but now confessor To one or two of these! . i 4 15
Sit between these ladies.—By my faith, And thank your lordship . i 4 25
The horses your lordship sent for, with all the care I had, I saw well chosen . . . ii 2 1
Beseech your lordship, Vouchsafe to speak my thanks . . . ii 3 70
To dance attendance on their lordship's pleasures . . . v 2 31
I do beseech your lordships, That, in this case of justice, my accusers, Be what they will, may stand forth face to face . . . v 3 45
If your will pass, I shall both find your lordship judge and juror . v 3 60
You are in the state of grace.—Grace! not so, friend; honour and lordship are my titles . . . *Troi. and Cres.* iii 1 16
And so I do, and with his gifts present Your lordships *T. Andron.* iv 2 15
God give his lordship joy! News, news from heaven! . iv 3 76
I'll pay the debt, and free him.—Your lordship ever binds him *T. of A.* i 1 104
Attends he here, or no? Lucilius!—Here, at your lordship's service . i 1 115
Humbly I thank your lordship . . . i 1 149
Vouchsafe my labour, and long live your lordship! . i 1 152
A piece of painting, which I do beseech Your lordship to accept . i 1 156
Will you be chid?—We'll bear, with your lordship . . i 1 177
Please it your lordship, he hath put me off To the succession of new days . . . ii 2 19
Your steward puts me off, my lord; And I am sent expressly to your lordship . . . ii 2 33
Cease till after dinner, That I may make his lordship understand . ii 2 43
Hath sent to your lordship to furnish him, nothing doubting . iii 1 20
Please your lordship, here is the wine . . . iii 1 32
Here's to thee.—Your lordship speaks your pleasure . iii 1 35
Requesting your lordship to supply his instant use with so many talents. —I know his lordship is but merry with me . iii 2 40
Commend me bountifully to his good lordship . iii 2 59
Your lordship's a goodly villain . iii 3 27
We attend his lordship; pray, signify so much.—I need not tell him that . iii 4 37
How fare you?—Ever at the best, hearing well of your lordship . iii 6 30
The swallow follows not summer more willing than we your lordship . iii 6 32
I hope it remains not unkindly with your lordship . iii 6 40
When your lordship this other day sent to me, I was so unfortunate . iii 6 46
Uncover, dogs, and lap.—What does his lordship mean?—I know not . iii 6 96
I was sure your lordship did not give it me *J. Cæsar* iv 3 254
Hail to your lordship!—I am glad to see you well . *Hamlet* i 2 160
Are you honest?—My lord?—Are you fair?—What means your lordship? . iii 1 106
Your lordship is right welcome back to Denmark.—I humbly thank you v 2 81
If your lordship were at leisure, I should impart a thing to you . v 2 91
I thank your lordship, it is very hot.—No, believe me, 'tis very cold . v 2 97
Your lordship speaks most infallibly of him . v 2 126
It would come to immediate trial, if your lordship would vouchsafe the answer . v 2 176
I commend my duty to your lordship.—Yours, yours . v 2 189
My services to your lordship.—I must love you *Lear* i 1 29
How now! what news?—So please your lordship, none . i 2 27
By no means what?—Persuade me to the murder of your lordship ii 1 46
Gentlemen, shall we see't?—We'll wait upon your lordship *Othello* iii 2 6
I do beseech your lordship, call her back. . iv 1 260
I'll attend your lordship.—Nay, come, let's go together *Cymbeline* i 2 41
It is not fit your lordship should undertake every companion . ii 1 28
It is fit I should commit offence to my inferiors.—Ay, it is fit for your lordship only . ii 1 33
Who told you of this stranger?—One of your lordship's pages . ii 1 45
Your lordship is the most patient man in loss . ii 3 1
Not every man patient after the noble temper of your lordship . ii 3 6
What's your lordship's pleasure?—Your lady's person: is she ready? . ii 3 85
But I much marvel that your lordship, having Rich tire about you, should at these early hours Shake off the golden slumber of repose *Pericles* iii 2 21
Lorenzo. Here comes . . . Gratiano and Lorenzo. Fare ye well *M. of V.* i 1 58
I must to Lorenzo and the rest: But we will visit you at supper-time . ii 2 214
Soon at supper shalt thou see Lorenzo, who is thy new master's guest . ii 3 6
O Lorenzo, If thou keep promise, I shall end this strife . ii 3 19
This is the pent-house under which Lorenzo Desired us to make stand . ii 6 1
Lorenzo, and thy love.—Lorenzo, certain, and my love indeed, For who love I so much? And now who knows But you, Lorenzo, whether I am yours? . ii 6 28
In their ship I am sure Lorenzo is not . ii 8 3
In a gondola were seen together Lorenzo and his amorous Jessica . ii 8 9
But who comes here? Lorenzo and his infidel? . iii 2 221
Lorenzo, I commit into your hands The husbandry and manage of my house . iii 4 24
Nay, you need not fear us, Lorenzo: Launcelot and I are out . iii 5 33
That he do record a gift, Here in the court, of all he dies possess'd, Unto his son Lorenzo and his daughter . iv 1 390
This deed will be well welcome to Lorenzo . iv 2 4
In such a night Did young Lorenzo swear he loved her well . v 1 18
Sola! did you see Master Lorenzo? Master Lorenzo, sola, sola! . v 1 41
Lorenzo here Shall witness I set forth as soon as you . v 1 270
How now, Lorenzo! My clerk hath some good comforts too for you . v 1 288
Lorraine. Duke of Lorraine, sole heir male Of the true line and stock of Charles the Great *Hen. V.* i 2 70
Lady Ermengare, Daughter to Charles the foresaid duke of Lorraine . i 2 83
Lose. That would not bless our Europe with your daughter, But rather lose her to an African *Tempest* ii 1 125
But to lose our bottles in the pool,— There is not only disgrace and dishonour in that, monster, but an infinite loss . iv 1 208
Now, jerkin, you are like to lose your hair and prove a bald jerkin . iv 1 237
We shall lose our time, And all be turn'd to barnacles, or to apes . iv 1 248
When did you lose your daughter?—In this last tempest . v 1 152
If this prove A vision of the Island, one dear son Shall I twice lose . v 1 177
Made me neglect my studies, lose my time *T. G. of Ver.* i 1 67
Thou'lt lose the flood, and, in losing the flood, lose thy voyage, and, in losing thy voyage, lose thy master, and, in losing thy master, lose thy service . ii 3 46
Lose. Why dost thou stop my mouth?—For fear thou shouldst lose thy tongue.—Where should I lose my tongue?—In thy tale *T. G. of Ver.* ii 3 52
Lose the tide, and the voyage, and the master, and the service, and the tied! . ii 3 56
Julia I lose and Valentine I lose: If I keep them, I needs must lose myself; If I lose them, thus find I by their loss, For Valentine myself, for Julia Silvia . ii 6 19
With an hour's heat Dissolves to water and doth lose his form . iii 2 8
Then know that I have little wealth to lose . iv 1 11
Shall I do any good, think'st thou? shall I not lose my suit? *Mer. Wives* i 4 153
If I find her honest, I lose not my labour. . ii 1 247
Shall I lose my doctor? no; he gives me the potions and the motions . iii 1 104
Shall I lose my parson, my priest, my Sir Hugh? . iii 1 106
And this deceit loses the name of craft, Of disobedience . v 5 239
Alas, I doubt— Our doubts are traitors And make us lose the good we oft might win By fearing to attempt *Meas. for Meas.* i 4 78
If I do lose thee [life], I do lose a thing That none but fools would keep iii 1 7
Condemn'd upon the act of fornication To lose his head . v 1 71
You do but lose your labour. Away with him to death! . v 1 433
I will go lose myself And wander up and down to view the city *C. of Er.* i 2 30
I, to find a mother and a brother, In quest of them, unhappy, lose myself . i 2 40
I see the jewel best enamelled Will lose his beauty . ii 1 110
Not a man of those but he hath the wit to lose his hair . ii 2 86
This course I fittest choose; For forty ducats is too much to lose. iv 3 97
Till I have brought him to his wits again, Or lose my labour in assaying it . v 1 97
Not with love: prove that ever I lose more blood with love than I will get again with drinking *Much Ado* i 1 253
Then go we near her, that her ear lose nothing Of the false sweet bait . iii 1 32
What fool is not so wise To lose an oath to win a paradise? *L. L. Lost* iv 3 73
Let us once lose our oaths to find ourselves, Or else we lose ourselves to keep our oaths . iv 3 361
When we greet, With eyes best seeing, heaven's fiery eye, By light we lose light . v 2 376
What mean you? You will lose your reputation . v 2 708
But, being over-full of self-affairs, My mind did lose it *M. N. Dream* i 1 114
Use me but as your spaniel, spurn me, strike me, Neglect me, lose me. ii 1 206
I love thee; by my life, I do: I swear by that which I will lose for thee iii 2 252
Tongue, lose thy light; Moon, take thy flight: Now die, die . v 1 309
They lose it that do buy it with much care *Mer. of Venice* i 1 75
Lest . . I be misconstrued in the place I go to And lose my hopes . ii 2 198
When they do choose, They have the wisdom by their wit to lose . ii 9 81
I pray you, tarry: pause a day or two Before you hazard; for, in choosing wrong, I lose your company . iii 2 3
There's something tells me, but it is not love, I would not lose you . iii 2 5
Then, if he lose, he makes a swan-like end, Fading in music . iii 2 44
I give them with this ring; Which when you part from, lose, or give away, Let it presage the ruin of your love . iii 2 174
Treble that, Before a friend of this description Shall lose a hair . iii 2 304
Courage yet! The Jew shall have my flesh, blood, bones and all, Ere thou shalt lose for me one drop of blood . iv 1 113
Repent but you that you shall lose your friend, And he repents not that he pays your debt . iv 1 278
I would lose all, ay, sacrifice them all Here to this devil, to deliver you iv 1 286
She made me vow That I should neither sell nor give nor lose it . iv 1 443
Lose and neglect the creeping hours of time *As Y. Like It* ii 7 112
I would not lose the dog for twenty pound *T. of Shrew* Ind. 1 21
I thank thee: thou shalt not lose by it . Ind. 2 101
I'll cuff you, if you strike again.—So may you lose your arms . ii 1 222
With the breach yourselves made, you lose your city *All's Well* i 1 137
Keep it [virginity] not; you cannot choose but lose by't: out with't! . i 1 159
How might one do, sir, to lose it to her own liking? . i 1 163
'Tis a commodity will lose the gloss with lying . i 1 166
I still pour in the waters of my love And lack not to lose still . i 3 210
That cannot choose But lend and give where she is sure to lose . i 3 221
I have now found thee; when I lose thee again, I care not . ii 3 217
Tell him that his sword can never win The honour that he loses . iii 2 97
Whence honour but of danger wins a scar, As oft it loses all . iii 2 125
Come; for if they do approach the city, we shall lose all the sight . iii 5 2
Lose our drum! well.—He's shrewdly vexed at something . iii 5 91
But I shall lose the grounds I work upon . iii 7 3
And I shall lose my life for want of language . iv 1 77
Which were the greatest obloquy i' the world In me to lose . iv 2 45
Lord, how we lose our pains!—ALL'S WELL THAT ENDS WELL yet . v 1 24
Since you lack virtue, I will lose a husband . v 3 222
If I lose a scruple of this sport, let me be boiled to death *T. Night* ii 5 2
My lady would not lose him for more than I'll say. . iii 4 116
Fear not thou, man, thou shalt lose nothing here *W. Tale* iv 4 258
Having no external thing to lose But the word 'maid' *K. John* ii 1 571
Lest that France repent, And by disjoining hands, hell lose a soul . iii 1 197
Husband, I cannot pray that thou mayst win; Uncle, I needs must pray that thou mayst lose . iii 1 332
Whoever wins, on that side shall I lose . iii 1 335
Your wife May then make all the claim that Arthur did.—And lose it, life and all, as Arthur did . iii 4 144
Is there no remedy?—None, but to lose your eyes . iv 1 91
And lose my way Among the thorns and dangers of this world . iv 3 140
What in the world should make me now deceive, Since I must lose the use of all deceit? . v 4 27
'Tis breath thou lack'st, and that breath wilt thou lose . *Richard II.* ii 1 30
You lose a thousand well-disposed hearts . ii 1 206
He is gone to save far off, Whilst others come to make him lose at home . ii 2 81
One in fear to lose what they enjoy, The other to enjoy by rage and war ii 4 13
Must he lose The name of king? o' God's name, let it go . iii 3 145
They pick pockets.—What didst thou lose, Jack? . *1 Hen. IV.* iii 3 115
Rebellion in this land shall lose his sway. . v 5 41
Blunt not his love, Nor lose the good advantage of his grace *2 Hen. IV.* iv 4 28
I break, and you, my gentle creditors, lose . Epil. 14
If it pass against us, We lose the better half of our possession *Hen. V.* i 1 8
Nor never Hydra-headed wilfulness So soon did lose his seat . i 1 36
Let us be worried and our nation lose The name of hardiness and policy i 2 219
What see you in those papers that you lose So much complexion? . ii 2 72
I would not lose so great an honour . . . For the best hope I have . iv 3 31
That fatal prophecy . . . That Henry born at Monmouth should win all And Henry born at Windsor lose all . *1 Hen. VI.* iii 1 199
He dies, we lose; I break my warlike word; We mourn, France smiles; we lose, they daily get . iv 3 32
Thou never hadst renown, nor canst not lose it . iv 5 40

Lose. He that breaks a stick of Gloucester's grove Shall lose his head for his presumption . . . 2 *Hen. VI.* i 2 34
I lose, indeed; Beshrew the winners, for they play'd me false! . iii 1 183
He never would have stay'd in France so long.—No, not to lose it all . iii 1 296
I lost not Normandy, Yet, to recover them, would lose my life . iv 7 71
Wast thou ordain'd, dear father, To lose thy youth in peace? . v 2 46
You are old enough now, and yet, methinks, you lose . 3 *Hen. VI.* i 1 113
Hath he deserved to lose his birthright thus? . i 1 219
Pity that this goodly boy Should lose his birthright by his father's fault . ii 2 35
In quarrel of the house of York The worthy gentleman did lose his life ii 2 7
'Twere pity they should lose their father's lands . iii 2 31
At his ease, Where having nothing, nothing can he lose . iii 3 152
Therefore let us hence; and lose no hour . iv 1 148
Warwick may lose, that now hath won the day . iv 4 15
O, that your young nobility could judge What 'twere to lose it! *Rich. III.* i 3 258
I do lament the sickness of the king, As loath to lose him . ii 2 10
As he will lose his head ere give consent His master's son, as worshipful he terms it, Shall lose the royalty of England's throne . iii 4 40
Up to some scaffold, there to lose their heads . iv 4 242
Every thing Would by a good discourser lose some life . *Hen. VIII.* i 1 41
We may outrun, By violent swiftness, that which we run at, And lose by over-running . i 1 143
All good people, You that thus far have come to pity me, Hear what I say, and then go home and lose me . ii 1 57
The king loves you; Beware you lose it not . iii 1 172
You are to blame, Knowing she will not lose her wonted greatness . iv 2 102
Do me this last right.—By heaven, I will, Or let me lose the fashion of a man! . iv 2 159
Should lose their names, and so should justice too . *Troi. and Cres.* i 3 118
Brave Hector would not lose So rich advantage of a promised glory . ii 2 203
And, Mercury, lose all the serpentine craft of thy caduceus! . ii 3 13
Yet all his virtues . . . Do in our eyes begin to lose their gloss . ii 3 128
And I do fear besides, That I shall lose distinction in my joys . iii 2 28
And all my powers do their bestowing lose . iii 2 39
For which we lose our heads to gild his horns . iv 5 31
He is thy crutch; now if thou lose thy stay, Thou on him leaning, and all Troy on thee, Fall all together . v 3 60
Believe, I come to lose my arm, or win my sleeve . v 3 96
Like to a harvest-man that's task'd to mow Or all or lose his hire *Coriol.* i 3 40
If we lose the field, We cannot keep the town . i 7 4
He cannot temperately transport his honours From where he should begin and end, but will Lose those he hath won . ii 1 242
To lose itself in a fog . ii 3 34
They would forget me, like the virtues Which our divines lose by 'em . ii 3 64
Speak, speak.—You are at point to lose your liberties . iii 1 194
Let us stand to our authority, Or let us lose it . iii 1 209
The blood he hath lost— . . . he dropp'd it for his country; And what is left, to lose it by his country, Were to us all . . . A brand . iii 1 302
Grant that, and tell me, In peace what each of them by the other lose . iii 2 44
Yet, were there but this single plot to lose, This mould of Marcius . iii 2 102
Send O'er the vast world to seek a single man, And lose advantage . iv 1 43
Once more to hew thy target from thy brawn, Or lose mine arm for't . iv 5 127
You know the very road into his kindness, And cannot lose your way . v 1 60
Alack, or we must lose The country, our dear nurse, or else thy person v 3 109
Lose not so noble a friend on vain suppose . *T. Andron.* i 1 440
His Philomel must lose her tongue to-day . ii 3 43
Come, civil night, Thou sober-suited matron, all in black, And learn me how to lose a winning match . *Rom. and Jul.* iii 2 12
Since birth, and heaven, and earth, all three do meet In thee at once; which thou at once wouldst lose . iii 3 121
Thou tedious rogue! I am sorry I shall lose A stone by thee *T. of Athens* iv 3 374
Break open shops; nothing can you steal, But thieves do lose it . iv 3 451
That same eye whose bend doth awe the world Did lose his lustre *J. C.* i 2 124
And we must take the current when it serves, Or lose our ventures . iv 3 224
If we do lose this battle, then is this The very last time we shall speak together: What are you then determined to do? . v 1 98
Then, if we lose this battle, You are contented to be led in triumph? . v 1 108
But under heavy judgement bears that life Which he deserves to lose *Macbeth* i 3 111
That thou mightst not lose the dues of rejoicing, by being ignorant . i 5 13
It shall make honour for you.—So I lose none In seeking to augment it ii 1 26
You cannot speak of reason to the Dane, And lose your voice *Hamlet* i 2 45
Let not thy mother lose her prayers, Hamlet: I pray thee, stay with us i 2 118
Or lose your heart, or your chaste treasure open . i 3 31
For loan oft loses both itself and friend . i 3 76
What to ourselves in passion we propose, The passion ending, doth the purpose lose . iii 2 205
O heart, lose not thy nature . iii 2 411
You will lose this wager, my lord.—I do not think so . v 2 219
My life I never held but as a pawn To wage against thy enemies; nor fear to lose it, Thy safety being the motive . *Lear* i 1 158
I am sorry, then, you have so lost a father That you must lose a husband . i 1 250
It shall lose thee nothing . i 2 125
Old fond eyes, Beweep this cause again, I'll pluck ye out, And cast you, with the waters that you lose, To temper clay . i 4 325
This seems a fair deserving, and must draw me That which my father loses . iii 3 25
And woes by wrong imaginations lose The knowledge of themselves . iv 6 290
I had rather lose the battle than that sister Should loosen him and me v 1 18
We'll talk with them too, Who loses and who wins . v 3 15
Though that his joy be joy, Yet throw such changes of vexation on't, As it may lose some colour . *Othello* i 1 73
So let the Turk of Cyprus us beguile; We lose it not, so long as we can smile . i 3 211
Though he had twinn'd with me, both at a birth, Shall lose me . ii 3 213
I will in Cassio's lodging lose this napkin, And let him find it . iii 3 321
I should be wise, for honesty's a fool And loses that it works for . iii 3 383
Where should I lose that handkerchief, Emilia?—I know not, madam . iii 4 23
To lose't or give't away were such perdition As nothing else could match . iii 4 67
Or lose myself in dotage . *Ant. and Cleo.* i 2 121
Cross him in nothing.—Thou teachest like a fool; the way to lose him . i 3 10
Cæsar gets money where He loses hearts: Lepidus flatters both . ii 1 14
If thou dost play with him at any game, Thou art sure to lose . ii 3 26
Though I lose The praise of it by telling, you must know . ii 6 43
If I lose mine honour, I lose myself: better I were not yours Than yours so branchless . iii 4 23
It would make any man cold to lose . *Cymbeline* ii 3 4

Lose. 'Shrew me, If I would lose it for a revenue Of any king's in Europe *Cymbeline* ii 3 148
Gains or loses Your sword or mine, or masterless leaves both . ii 4 59
Nay, keep the ring—'tis true: I am sure She would not lose it . ii 4 124
But to win time To lose so bad employment . iii 4 113
What have we to lose, But that he swore to take, our lives? . iv 2 124
And I must lose Two of the sweet'st companions in the world . v 5 348
As jewels lose their glory if neglected, So princes their renowns *Pericles* ii 2 12
Report what a sojourner we have; you'll lose nothing by custom . iv 2 149
Before the people all, Reveal how thou at sea didst lose thy wife . v 1 245

Loser. I have too grieved a heart To take a tedious leave: thus losers part *Mer. of Venice* ii 7 77
A blustering day.—Then with the losers let it sympathise . 1 *Hen. IV.* v 1 7
Both parties nobly are subdued, And neither party loser 2 *Hen. IV.* iv 2 91
I can give the loser leave to chide . 2 *Hen. VI.* iii 1 182
They play'd me false! And well such losers may have leave to speak . iii 1 185
Then give me leave, for losers will have leave To ease their stomachs with their bitter tongues . *T. Andron.* iii 1 233
Is't writ in your revenge, That, swoopstake, you will draw both friend and foe, Winner and loser? . *Hamlet* iv 5 143
Reputation is an idle and most false imposition; . . . you have lost no reputation at all, unless you repute yourself such a loser *Othello* ii 3 272

Losest. If I keep not my rank,— Thou losest thy old smell *As Y. Like It* i 2 114
Thou losest labour: As easy mayst thou the intrenchant air With thy keen sword impress as make me bleed . *Macbeth* v 8 8
Thou losest here, a better where to find . *Lear* i 1 264

Loseth. Yet he loseth it in a kind of jollity . *Com. of Errors* ii 2 90
Loseth men's hearts and leaves behind a stain . 1 *Hen. IV.* iii 1 187

Losing his verdure even in the prime . *T. G. of Ver.* i 1 49
And I have play'd the sheep in losing him . i 1 73
I mean thou'lt lose the flood, and, in losing the flood, lose thy voyage, and, in losing thy voyage, lose thy master, and, in losing thy master, lose thy service, and, in losing thy service,—Why dost thou stop my mouth? . ii 3 47
Your light grows dark by losing of your eyes . *L. L. Lost* i 1 79
Let's see the penalty. 'On pain of losing her tongue' . i 1 124
I follow thus A losing suit against him . *Mer. of Venice* iv 1 62
No other advantage . . . but only the losing of hope by time *All's Well* i 1 18
Kings are no less unhappy, their issue not being gracious, than they are in losing them when they have approved their virtues *W. Tale* iv 2 31
And so locks her in embracing, as if she would pin her to her heart that she might no more be in danger of losing . v 2 85
What have you lost by losing of this day?—All days of glory *K. John* iii 4 116
The first bringer of unwelcome news Hath but a losing office . 2 *Hen. IV.* i 1 101
The even mead, . . . Losing both beauty and utility . *Hen. V.* v 2 53
For losing ken of Albion's wished coast . 2 *Hen. VI.* iii 2 113
I shall have glory by this losing day More than Octavius and Mark Antony By this vile conquest shall attain unto . *J. Cæsar* v 5 36
How came he mad? . . . —Faith, e'en with losing his wits . *Hamlet* v 1 174
So find we profit By losing of our prayers . *Ant. and Cleo.* ii 1 8
Losing a mite, a mountain gain . *Pericles* ii Gower 8

Loss. My father's loss, the weakness which I feel . *Tempest* i 2 487
For our escape Is much beyond our loss . ii 1 3
Sir, you may thank yourself for this great loss . ii 1 123
The fault's your own.—So is the dear'st o' the loss . ii 1 135
Not only disgrace and dishonour in that, monster, but an infinite loss . iv 1 210
Irreparable is the loss, and patience Says it is past her cure . v 1 140
For the like loss I have her sovereign aid And rest myself content.—You the like loss!—As great to me as late . v 1 143
Supportable To make the dear loss, have I means much weaker Than you . v 1 146
I have consider'd well his loss of time . *T. G. of Ver.* i 3 19
If I lose them, thus find I by their loss For Valentine myself . ii 6 21
I'll give thee A hundred pound in gold more than your loss *Mer. Wives* iv 6 5
I subscribe not that, nor any other, But in the loss of question *M. for M.* ii 4 90
My mind promises with my habit no loss shall touch her by my company . iii 1 181
But that her tender shame Will not proclaim against her maiden loss . iv 4 27
I hazarded the loss of whom I loved . *Com. of Errors* i 1 132
Indeed, he looks younger than he did, by the loss of a beard . *Much Ado* iii 2 49
A fellow that hath had losses, and one that hath two gowns . iv 2 87
I would it might prove the end of his losses . *Mer. of Venice* iii 1 21
Do you hear whether Antonio have had any loss at sea or no? . iii 1 45
Laughed at my losses, mocked at my gains, scorned my nation . iii 1 58
Loss upon loss! the thief gone with so much, and so much to find the thief . iii 1 96
These griefs and losses have so bated me . iii 3 32
Forgive a moiety of the principal; Glancing an eye of pity on his losses iv 1 27
He cried upon it at the merest loss . *T. of Shrew* Ind. 1 23
And I will add Unto their losses twenty thousand crowns . v 2 113
Loss of virginity is rational increase . *All's Well* i 1 138
In the loss that may happen, it concerns you something to know it . i 3 125
That's the loss of men, though it be the getting of children . iii 2 44
Some dishonour we had in the loss of that drum . iii 6 59
How mightily sometimes we make us comforts of our losses! . iv 3 77
Very envy and the tongue of loss Cried fame and honour on him *T. Night* v 1 61
The loss, the gain, the ordering on't, is all Properly ours . *W. Tale* ii 1 169
Poor thing, condemn'd to loss! . ii 3 192
Poor wretch, That for thy mother's fault art thus exposed To loss! . iii 3 51
My brother; whose loss of his most precious queen and children are even now to be afresh lamented . iv 2 26
She had one eye declined for the loss of her husband, another elevated . v 2 81
Victory, with little loss, doth play Upon the dancing banners *K. John* ii 1 307
Gracing the scroll that tells of this war's loss . ii 1 348
A heavy curse from Rome, Or the light loss of England for a friend . iii 1 206
Whoever wins, on that side shall I lose; Assured loss before the match be play'd . iii 1 336
Had you such a loss as I, I could give better comfort than you do . iii 4 99
I loved him, and will weep My date of life out for his sweet life's loss . iv 3 106
Ere further leisure yield them further means For their advantage and your highness' loss . *Richard II.* i 4 41
The worst is worldly loss thou canst unfold . iii 2 94
Why, 'twas my care; And what loss is it to be rid of care? . iii 2 96
My care is loss of care, by old care done; Your care is gain of care . iv 1 196
I better brook the loss of brittle life Than those proud titles . 1 *Hen. IV.* v 4 78
Why should that gentleman that rode by Travers Give then such instances of loss? . 2 *Hen. IV.* i 1 56
Flies with greatest speed, So did our men, heavy in Hotspur's loss . i 1 121
We all that are engaged to this loss Knew that we ventured . i 1 180
Keep no tell-tale to his memory That may repeat and history his loss . iv 1 203

Loss. Now he weighs time Even to the utmost grain: that you shall read In your own losses . . . *Hen. V.* ii 4 139
Consider of his ransom; which must proportion the losses we have borne . . . iii 6 134
For our losses, his exchequer is too poor . . . iii 6 137
If we are mark'd to die, we are enow To do our country loss . . . iv 3 21
Was ever known so great and little loss On one part and on the other? . iv 8 115
Sad tidings bring I to you out of France, Of loss, of slaughter *1 Hen. VI.* i 1 59
The loss of those great towns Will make him burst his lead . . . i 1 63
Didst thou at first, to flatter us withal, Make us partakers of a little gain, That now our loss might be ten times so much? . . . ii 1 53
Sleeping neglection doth betray to loss The conquest . . . iv 3 49
Whiles they each other cross, Lives, honours, lands and all hurry to loss iv 3 53
Do you fly: Your loss is great, so your regard should be; My worth unknown, no loss is known in me . . . iv 5 23
I foresee with grief The utter loss of all the realm of France . . . v 4 112
And can do nought but wail her darling's loss . . . *2 Hen. VI.* iii 1 216
But wherefore grieve I at an hour's poor loss? . . . iii 2 381
The loss of those three lords torments my heart . . . *3 Hen. VI.* i 1 270
Tidings, as swiftly as the posts could run, Were brought me of your loss ii 1 110
What hap? what hope of good?—Our hap is loss . . . ii 3 9
Why stand we like soft-hearted women here, Wailing our losses? . . . ii 3 26
And so obsequious will thy father be, Even for the loss of thee, having no more, As Priam was for all his valiant sons . . . ii 5 119
By that loss I will not purchase them . . . iii 2 73
What! loss of some pitch'd battle against Warwick?—No, but the loss of his own royal person . . . iv 4 4
By notes of household harmony They quite forget their loss of liberty . iv 6 15
Wert thou as we are, We might recover all our loss again . . . v 2 30
Wise men ne'er sit and wail their loss, But cheerly seek how to redress v 4 1
What would betide of me?—No other harm but loss of such a lord.—The loss of such a lord includes all harm . . . *Richard III.* i 3 7
Henry's death, my lovely Edward's death, Their kingdom's loss . . . i 3 193
Long mayst thou live to wail thy children's loss! . . . i 3 204
Was never widow had so dear a loss!—Were never orphans had so dear a loss!—Was never mother had so dear a loss! . . . ii 2 77
Up and down my sons were toss'd, For me to joy and weep their gain and loss . . . ii 4 59
Both they Match not the high perfection of my loss . . . iv 4 66
Bettering thy loss makes the bad causer worse . . . iv 4 122
The loss you have is but a son being king, And by that loss your daughter is made queen . . . iv 4 307
What a loss our ladies Will have of these trim vanities! . *Hen. VIII.* i 3 37
Truly pitying My father's loss, like a most royal prince, Restored me . ii 1 113
A loss of her That, like a jewel, has hung twenty years About his neck ii 2 31
And in this fashion, . . . Success or loss, what is or is not, serves As stuff for these two to make paradoxes . . . *Troi. and Cres.* i 3 183
And all damage else—As honour, loss of time, travail, expense . . . ii 2 4
With such a costly loss of wealth and friends . . . iv 1 60
My love admits no qualifying dross; No more my grief, in such a precious loss . . . iv 4 10
And loss assume all reason Without revolt . . . v 2 145
No further harm Than so much loss of time . . . *Coriolanus* iii 1 285
You may salve so, Not what is dangerous present, but the loss Of what is past . . . iii 2 71
Notwithstanding all this loss of blood . . . *T. Andron.* ii 4 29
Whose loss hath pierced him deep and scarr'd his heart . . . iv 4 31
So strong a fine That you shall all repent the loss of mine *Rom. and Jul.* iii 1 196
Yet let me weep for such a feeling loss.—So shall you feel the loss, but not the friend Which you weep for.—Feeling so the loss, I cannot choose but ever weep the friend . . . iii 5 75
What a beast art thou already, that seest not thy loss in transformation! *T. of Athens* iv 3 349
To ease them of their griefs, Their fears of hostile strokes, their aches, losses, Their pangs of love . . . v 1 202
O insupportable and touching loss! Upon what sickness? . *J. Cæsar* iv 3 151
Even so great men great losses should endure . . . iv 3 193
Then weigh what loss your honour may sustain . . . *Hamlet* i 3 29
Seeking to give Losses their remedies . . . *Lear* ii 2 177
If thou shouldst dally half an hour, his life, With thine, and all that offer to defend him, Stand in assured loss . . . iii 6 102
Though he speak of comfort Touching the Turkish loss, yet he looks sadly *Othello* ii 1 32
There's some wonder in this handkerchief: I am most unhappy in the loss of it . . . iii 4 102
Rather makes choice of loss, Than gain which darkens him *Ant. and Cleo.* iii 1 23
'Twas a shame no less Than was his loss, to course your flying flags . iii 13 11
Hath, at fast and loose, Beguiled me to the very heart of loss . iv 12 29
Your loss is as yourself, great; and you bear it As answering to the weight . . . v 2 101
As I my poor self did exchange for you, To your so infinite loss *Cymbeline* i 1 120
If, in the holding or loss of that [her honour], you term her frail . . . i 4 105
The most patient man in loss, the most coldest that ever turned up ace ii 3 2
Make not, sir, Your loss your sport . . . ii 4 48
Come, and be true.—Thou bid'st me to my loss . . . iii 5 163
That The Britons have razed out, though with the loss Of many a bold one v 5 70
Their dear loss, The more of you 'twas felt, the more it shaped Unto my end . . . v 5 345
Where, by the loss of maidenhead, A babe is moulded . *Pericles* iii Gower 10
Even at the first Thy loss is more than can thy portage quit . . . iii 1 35
Go to the wars, would you? where a man may serve seven years for the loss of a leg? . . . iv 6 182
The main grief springs from the loss Of a beloved daughter and a wife . v 1 29
Lost. All lost! to prayers, to prayers! all lost! . . . *Tempest* i 1 54
He hath lost his fellows And strays about to find 'em . . . i 2 416
Would I had never Married my daughter there! for, coming thence, My son is lost and, in my rate, she too . . . ii 1 109
We have lost your son, I fear, for ever . . . ii 1 131
On whom my pains, Humanely taken, all, all lost, quite lost . . . iv 1 190
I have lost—How sharp the point of this remembrance is!—My dear son v 1 137
I Have lost my daughter.—A daughter? O heavens! . . . v 1 148
Ferdinand, her brother, found a wife Where he himself was lost . . . v 1 211
If lost, why then a grievous labour won . . . *T. G. of Ver.* i 1 33
To sigh, like a school-boy that had lost his A B C . . . ii 1 23
It is no matter if the tied were lost; for it is the unkindest tied . ii 3 41
When Mistress Bridget lost the handle of her fan, I took't upon mine honour thou hadst it not . . . *Mer. Wives* ii 2 11
So that I have lost my edifice by mistaking the place where I erected it ii 2 225
Thus foolishly lost at a game of tick-tack . . . *Meas. for Meas.* i 2 196
There she lost a noble and renowned brother . . . iii 1 228
Lost. Rather Make rash remonstrance of my hidden power Than let him so be lost . . . *Meas. for Meas.* v 1 398
That I saved, Who should have died when Claudio lost his head . . . v 1 493
Thou didst conclude hairy men plain dealers without wit.—The plainer dealer, the sooner lost . . . *Com. of Errors* ii 2 89
No time to recover hair lost by nature . . . ii 2 104
No evil lost is wail'd when it is gone . . . iv 2 24
How hast thou lost thy breath?—By running fast . . . iv 2 30
Hath he not lost much wealth by wreck of sea? . . . v 1 49
Even for the blood That then I lost for thee, now grant me justice . v 1 194
How many gentlemen have you lost in this action? . . . *Much Ado* i 1 5
You have lost the heart of Signior Benedick.—Indeed, my lord, he lent it me . . . ii 1 285
Once before he won it of me with false dice, therefore your grace may well say I have lost it . . . ii 1 291
What we have we prize not to the worth Whiles we enjoy it, but being lack'd and lost, Why, then we rack the value . . . iv 1 221
'Tis won as towns with fire, so won, so lost . . . *L. L. Lost* i 1 147
The worth of many a knight From tawny Spain lost in the world's debate i 1 174
Since, to wail friends lost Is not by much so wholesome-profitable As to rejoice at friends but newly found . . . v 2 759
The ploughman lost his sweat . . . *M. N. Dream* ii 1 94
Their sense thus weak, lost with their fears thus strong . . . iii 2 27
Thus hath he lost sixpence a day during his life . . . iv 2 20
When I had lost one shaft, I shot his fellow of the self-same flight The self-same way with more advised watch . . . *Mer. of Venice* i 1 140
I owe you much, and, like a wilful youth, That which I owe is lost . i 1 147
If my fortune be not crost, I have a father, you a daughter, lost . . ii 5 57
Cold, indeed; and labour lost: Then, farewell, heat, and welcome, frost! ii 7 74
Ha! what sayest thou? Why, the end is, he hath lost a ship . . . iii 1 19
I would you had won the fleece that he hath lost . . . iii 2 245
I were best to cut my left hand off And swear I lost the ring defending it v 1 178
Most true, I have lost my teeth in your service . . . *As Y. Like It* i 1 87
You have lost much good sport . . . i 2 105
Good wrestling, which you have lost the sight of . . . i 2 117
But what is the sport, monsieur, that the ladies have lost? . . . i 2 143
You are deceived, sir: we kept time, we lost not our time . . . v 3 39
I count it but time lost to hear such a foolish song . . . v 3 41
How her bridle was burst, how I lost my crupper . . . *T. of Shrew* iv 1 83
And there was never virgin got till virginity was first lost . *All's Well* i 1 140
Virginity by being once lost may be ten times found; by being ever kept, it is ever lost . . . i 1 142
To cure the desperate languishings whereof The king is render'd lost . . i 3 236
We have lost our labour; they are gone a contrary way . . . iii 5 8
There were no further danger known but the modesty which is so lost . iii 5 30
'But a drum'! is't 'but a drum'? A drum so lost! . . . iii 6 51
O my good lord, you were the first that found me!—Was I, in sooth? and I was the first that lost thee . . . v 2 48
We lost a jewel of her; and our esteem Was made much poorer by it . v 3 1
He lost a wife Whose beauty did astonish the survey Of richest eyes . v 3 15
Praising what is lost Makes the remembrance dear . . . v 3 19
She whom all men praised and whom myself, Since I have lost, have loved . . . v 3 54
Methought her eyes had lost her tongue . . . *T. Night* ii 2 21
Our fancies are more giddy and unfirm, More longing, wavering, sooner lost and worn, Than women's are . . . ii 4 35
When your young nephew Titus lost his leg . . . v 1 66
How have the hours rack'd and tortured me, Since I have lost thee! . v 1 227
The king hath on him such a countenance As he had lost some province *W. Tale* i 2 369
Or both yourself and me Cry lost, and so good night! . . . i 2 411
I'll put My fortunes to your service, which are here By this discovery lost . . . i 2 441
The crown and comfort of my life, your favour, I do give lost . . iii 2 96
The king shall live without an heir, if that which is lost be not found . iii 2 137
I'll not remember you of my own lord, Who is lost too . . . iii 2 232
And, for the babe Is counted lost for ever, Perdita, I prithee, call't . iii 3 33
Have I not told thee how I was cozened by the way and lost all my money? . . . iv 4 255
Age, thou hast lost thy labour . . . iv 4 787
I lost a couple, that 'twixt heaven and earth Might thus have stood . v 1 132
I lost—All mine own folly—the society, Amity too, of your brave father v 1 134
Then have you lost a sight, which was to be seen, cannot be spoken of . v 2 46
So that all the instruments which aided to expose the child were even then lost when it was found . . . v 2 78
My mate, that's never to be found again, Lament till I am lost . . v 3 135
England, thou hast not saved one drop of blood, In this hot trial, more than we of France; Rather, lost more . . . *K. John* ii 1 343
Is not Angiers lost? Arthur ta'en prisoner? divers dear friends slain? iii 4 6
I was Geffrey's wife; Young Arthur is my son, and he is lost . . . iii 4 47
What have you lost by losing of this day?—All days of glory, joy . . iii 4 116
How much King John hath lost In this which he accounts so clearly won iii 4 121
And quite lost their hearts . . . *Richard II.* ii 1 248
Say, is my kingdom lost? why, 'twas my care . . . iii 2 95
Ay, all of them at Bristol lost their heads . . . iii 2 142
Aumerle that was; But that is lost for being Richard's friend . . . v 2 42
And therefore lost that title of respect Which the proud soul ne'er pays but to the proud . . . *1 Hen. IV.* i 3 8
And indent with fears, When they have lost and forfeited themselves? . i 3 88
Why hast thou lost the fresh blood in thy cheeks? . . . ii 3 47
Thou hast lost much honour, that thou wert not with me in this action ii 4 22
There are two gentlemen Have in this robbery lost three hundred marks ii 4 569
Thy place in council thou hast rudely lost . . . iii 2 32
For thou hast lost thy princely privilege With vile participation . . iii 2 86
Bardolph was shaved and lost many a hair . . . iii 3 69
I have lost a seal-ring of my grandfather's worth forty mark . . . iii 3 94
For my voice, I have lost it with halloing and singing of anthems *2 Hen. IV.* i 2 213
There were two honours lost, yours and your son's . . . ii 3 16
What thing, in honour, had my father lost, That need to be revived and breathed in me? . . . iv 1 113
Do you mean to stop any of William's wages, about the sack he lost? . v 1 25
O, good my lord, you have lost a friend indeed . . . v 2 27
What men have you lost, Fluellen?—The perdition of th' athversary hath been very great, reasonable great . . . *Hen. V.* iii 6 102
Lost never a man, but one that is like to be executed for robbing a church iii 6 105
Which must proportion the losses we have borne, the subjects we have lost . . . iii 6 135
The time was blessedly lost wherein such preparation was gained . . iv 1 191
In these ten thousand they have lost, There are but sixteen hundred mercenaries . . . iv 8 92

Lost. The venom of such looks, we fairly hope, Have lost their quality *Hen. V.* v 2 19
Ourselves and children Have lost, or do not learn for want of time . v 2 57
So many had the managing, That they lost France . . . Epil. 12
England ne'er lost a king of so much worth . . . . 1 *Hen. VI.* i 1 7
Orleans, Paris, Guysors, Poictiers, are all quite lost . . . . i 1 61
Is Paris lost? is Rouen yielded up? . . . . i 1 65
How were they lost? what treachery was used?—No treachery . . i 1 68
I would his troubles likewise were expired, That so he might recover what was lost . . . . ii 5 32
Declare the cause My father, Earl of Cambridge, lost his head . . ii 5 54
I lost my liberty and they their lives . . . . . . ii 5 81
Lost, and recover'd in a day again! This is a double honour . . . iii 2 115
In which assault we lost twelve hundred men . . . . . iv 1 24
Destroy'd themselves, and lost the realm of France . . . . iv 1 147
In you all hopes are lost . . . . iv 5 25
Twice am I thy son! The life thou gavest me first was lost and done . iv 6 7
Have we not lost most part of all the towns, By treason, falsehood? . v 4 108
Say, when I am gone, I prophesied France will be lost ere long 2 *Hen. VI.* i 1 146
O father, Maine is lost; That Maine which by main force Warwick did win . . . . i 1 209
Anjou and Maine are given to the French; Paris is lost . . . . i 1 215
I danced attendance on his will Till Paris was besieged, famish'd, and lost . . . . i 3 175
All your interest in those territories Is utterly bereft you; all is lost . iii 1 85
By means whereof his highness hath lost France . . . . iii 1 106
I rather would have lost my life betimes Than bring a burthen of dishonour home By staying there so long till all were lost . . iii 1 299
And even with this I lost fair England's view . . . . iii 2 110
Die you shall: The lives of those which we have lost in fight Be counterpoised with such a petty sum! . . . . iv 1 21
I lost mine eye in laying the prize aboard . . . . . iv 1 25
I sold not Maine, I lost not Normandy . . . . . . iv 7 70
To France, to France, and get what you have lost . . . . iv 8 51
Give me but the ten meals I have lost, and I'ld defy them all . . iv 10 66
Tell Kent from me, she hath lost her best man . . . . iv 10 78
Nor have we won one foot, If Salisbury be lost . . . . v 3 7
Talk not of France, sith thou hast lost it all.—The lord protector lost it, and not I . . . . 3 *Hen. VI.* i 1 110
The noise of thy cross-bow Will scare the herd, and so my shoot is lost iii 1 7
If this news be true, Poor queen and son, your labour is but lost . iii 1 32
Like one lost in a thorny wood, That rends the thorns and is rent . . iii 2 174
How Henry the Sixth hath lost All that which Henry the Fifth had gotten . . . . iii 3 89
And to repair my honour lost for him, I here renounce him . . . iii 3 193
The cable broke, the holding-anchor lost . . . . . . v 4 4
As it was won with blood, lost be it so! . . . . *Richard III.* i 3 272
It were lost sorrow to wail one that's lost . . . . . ii 2 11
My husband lost his life to get the crown . . . . . ii 4 57
That title, Which by his death hath lost much majesty . . . . iii 1 100
This is no oath: The George, profaned, hath lost his holy honour . . iv 4 369
While we reason here, A royal battle might be won and lost . . iv 4 538
Rescue, fair lord, or else the day is lost! . . . . . v 4 6
I was my chamber's prisoner.—Then you lost The view . . *Hen. VIII.* i 1 13
The duke's surveyor, and lost your office On the complaint o' the tenants i 2 172
Like a jewel, has hung twenty years About his neck, yet never lost her lustre . . . . ii 2 33
A woman lost among ye, laugh'd at, scorn'd . . . . . iii 1 107
All my glories In that one woman I have lost for ever . . . iii 2 409
Had their faces Been loose, this day they had been lost . . . iv 1 75
No more call it York-place, that's past; For, since the cardinal fell, that title's lost . . . . iv 1 96
If we have lost so many tenths of ours, To guard a thing not ours *Troi. and Cres.* ii 2 21
How now, Thersites! what, lost in the labyrinth of thy fury! . . ii 3 1
Then will Ajax lack matter, if he have lost his argument . . . . ii 3 104
Is't possible? no sooner got but lost? . . . . . . iv 2 76
Ajax hath lost a friend And foams at mouth, and he is arm'd and at it . v 5 35
Full merrily the humble-bee doth sing, Till he hath lost his honey . v 10 43
The blood he hath lost—Which, I dare vouch, is more than that he hath, By many an ounce . . . . *Coriolanus* iii 1 299
When he did stand for consul, which he lost By lack of stooping . . v 6 28
Fair Philomela, she but lost her tongue . . . . *T. Andron.* ii 4 38
Tut, I have lost myself; I am not here; This is not Romeo . *R. and J.* i 1 203
Cannot forget The precious treasure of his eyesight lost . . . i 1 239
And I for winking at your discords too Have lost a brace of kinsmen . v 3 295
Did you see my cap?—I have lost my gown . . . *T. of Athens* iii 6 120
His wits Are drown'd and lost in his calamities . . . . . v 3 89
Rome, thou hast lost the breed of noble bloods! . . . *J. Cæsar* i 2 151
O judgement! thou art fled to brutish beasts, And men have lost their reason . . . . iii 2 110
When the battle's lost and won . . . . . . *Macbeth* i 1 4
What he hath lost noble Macbeth hath won . . . . . . i 2 67
Though his bark cannot be lost, Yet it shall be tempest-tost . . . i 3 24
Be not lost So poorly in your thoughts . . . . . . ii 2 71
We have lost Best half of our affair . . . . iii 3 20
I have lost my hopes.—Perchance even there where I did find my doubts iv 3 24
Those foresaid lands So by his father lost . . . . . *Hamlet* i 1 104
Importing the surrender of those lands Lost by his father . . . i 2 24
But, you must know, your father lost a father; That father lost, lost his i 2 89
I have of late—but wherefore I know not—lost all my mirth . . . ii 2 307
Their perfume lost, Take these again; for to the noble mind Rich gifts wax poor when givers prove unkind . . . . iii 1 99
And so have I a noble father lost; A sister driven into desperate terms iv 7 25
Can you advise me?—I'm lost in it . . . . iv 7 55
And such a tongue As I am glad I have not, though not to have it Hath lost me in your liking . . . . *Lear* i 1 236
I am sorry, then, you have so lost a father That you must lose a husband i 1 250
But, O poor Gloucester! Lost he his other eye?—Both, both, my lord iv 2 81
And yet it is danger To make him even o'er the time he has lost . iv 7 80
King Lear hath lost, he and his daughter ta'en . . . . v 2 6
At this time We sweat and bleed: the friend hath lost his friend . . v 3 55
My name is lost; By treason's tooth bare-gnawn and canker-bit . . v 3 121
Met I my father with his bleeding rings, Their precious stones new lost v 3 190
Your heart is burst, you have lost half your soul . . *Othello* i 1 87
What, have you lost your wits? . . . . i 1 92
For I have lost him on a dangerous sea.—Is he well shipp'd? . . ii 1 46
How lost you company?—The great contention of the sea and skies Parted our fellowship . . . . ii 1 91
Would in action glorious I had lost Those legs that brought me! . . ii 3 186
Lost. I have lost my reputation! I have lost the immortal part of myself *Othello* ii 3 263
Reputation is an idle and most false imposition; oft got without merit, and lost without deserving: you have lost no reputation at all, unless you repute yourself such a loser . . . . ii 3 270
Believe me, I had rather have lost my purse Full of crusadoes . . iii 4 25
If she lost it Or made a gift of it, my father's eye Should hold her loathed . . . . iii 4 60
Is't lost? is't gone? speak, is it out o' the way?—Heaven bless us!—Say you?—It is not lost; but what an if it were?—How!—I say, it is not lost . . . . iii 4 80
Lay not your blame on me: if you have lost him, Why, I have lost him too . . . . iv 2 46
By this light of heaven, I know not how I lost him . . . . iv 2 151
I care not for thy sword; I'll make thee known, Though I lost twenty lives . . . . v 2 166
And having lost her breath, she spoke, and panted . *Ant. and Cleo.* ii 2 235
His lieutenant, For quick accumulation of renown, . . . lost his favour iii 1 20
If we should serve with horse and mares together, The horse were merely lost . . . . iii 7 9
The greater cantle of the world is lost With very ignorance . . . iii 10 6
I am so lated in the world, that I Have lost my way for ever . . iii 11 4
Leave me, I pray, a little: pray you now: Nay, do so; for, indeed, I have lost command, Therefore I pray you . . . . iii 11 23
Fall not a tear, I say; one of them rates All that is won and lost . . iii 11 70
All is lost; This foul Egyptian hath betrayed me . . . . iv 12 9
They cast their caps up and carouse together Like friends long lost . iv 12 13
Whose heart I thought I had, for she had mine; Which whilst it was mine had annex'd unto't A million more, now lost . . . . iv 14 18
The gods withhold me! Shall I do that which all the Parthian darts, Though enemy, lost aim, and could not? . . . . . . iv 14 71
I think the king Be touch'd at very heart.—None but the king?—He that hath lost her too . . . . *Cymbeline* i 1 11
If he should write, And I not have it, 'twere a paper lost, As offer'd mercy is . . . . i 3 3
She is alone the Arabian bird, and I Have lost the wager . . . i 6 18
What I have lost to-day at bowls I'll win to-night of him . . . ii 1 54
'Twill not be lost.—I hope so: go and search . . . . . ii 3 153
If I had lost it, I should have lost the worth of it in gold . . . ii 4 41
Take your ring again; 'tis not yet won: It may be probable she lost it ii 4 115
No blame be to you, sir; for all was lost, But that the heavens fought v 3 3
I lost my children: If these be they, I know not how to wish A pair of worthier sons . . . . v 5 354
Whoso ask'd her for his wife, His riddle told not, lost his life *Pericles* i Gower 38
He, good prince, having all lost, By waves from coast to coast is tost ii Gower 33
I, King Pericles, have lost This queen, worth all our mundane cost . iii 2 70
Her eyelids, cases to those heavenly jewels Which Pericles hath lost . iii 2 100
We lost too much money this mart by being too wenchless . . . iv 2 4
If you like her, so; if not, I have lost my earnest . . . . iv 2 49
Where we left him, on the sea. We there him lost . . . . v Gower 13
What were thy friends? How lost thou them? . . . . . v 1 141
Lost child. That King Leontes shall not have an heir Till his lost child be found . . . . *W. Tale* v 1 40
Lost fear. Do you go back dismay'd? 'tis a lost fear . . *Othello* v 2 269
Lost hair. To pay a fine for a periwig and recover the lost hair of another man . . . . *Com. of Errors* ii 2 77
Lost monster. Thou wert but a lost monster . . . . *Tempest* iv 1 203
Lost mutton. I, a lost mutton, gave your letter to her, a laced mutton, and she, a laced mutton, gave me, a lost mutton, nothing for my labour . . . . *T. G. of Ver.* i 1 101
Lost opinion. Thou hast redeem'd thy lost opinion . . . 1 *Hen. IV.* v 4 48
Lost sorrow. It were lost sorrow to wail one that's lost . *Richard III.* ii 2 11
Lot. However God or fortune cast my lot . . . . *Richard II.* i 3 85
That hot termagant Scot had paid me scot and lot too . . 1 *Hen. IV.* v 4 115
It is lots to blanks, My name hath touch'd your ears . . *Coriolanus* v 2 10
Why, 'As by lot, God wot,' and then, you know . . . . *Hamlet* ii 2 435
If we draw lots, he speeds . . . . *Ant. and Cleo.* ii 3 35
We'll feast each other ere we part; and let's Draw lots who shall begin.—That will I, Pompey.—No, Antony, take the lot . . . . ii 6 62
That man and wife Draw lots who first shall die to lengthen life *Pericles* i 4 46
Lottery. The lottery, that he hath devised in these three chests of gold, silver and lead . . . . *Mer. of Venice* i 2 32
The lottery of my destiny Bars me the right of voluntary choosing . ii 1 15
An we might have a good woman born but one every blazing star, or at an earthquake, 'twould mend the lottery well . . . *All's Well* i 3 92
Make a lottery; And, by device, let blockish Ajax draw The sort to fight with Hector . . . . *Troi. and Cres.* i 3 374
Who shall answer him?—I know not: 'tis put to lottery . . . ii 1 140
Let high-sighted tyranny range on, Till each man drop by lottery *J. Cæsar* ii 1 119
If beauty, wisdom, modesty, can settle The heart of Antony, Octavia is A blessed lottery to him . . . . *Ant. and Cleo.* ii 2 248
Loud. May as well Wound the loud winds . . . . *Tempest* iii 3 63
You should have heard him so loud and so melancholy . *Mer. Wives* i 4 96
I do not relish well Their loud applause and Aves vehement . *M. for M.* i 1 71
Your desert speaks loud . . . . v 1 9
Now is your time: speak loud and kneel before him . . . . v 1 19
But more merry tears The passion of loud laughter never shed *M. N. D.* v 1 70
Whilst the screech-owl, screeching loud . . . . . . v 1 383
Thou but offend'st thy lungs to speak so loud . . . *Mer. of Venice* iv 1 140
Unhandled colts, Fetching mad bounds, bellowing and neighing loud . v 1 73
Though it pass your patience and mine to endure her loud alarums *T. of S.* i 1 131
I will board her, though she chide as loud As thunder . . . i 2 95
Have I not in a pitched battle heard Loud 'larums, neighing steeds? . i 2 207
And swore so loud, That, all-amazed, the priest let fall the book . . iii 2 162
Find what you seek, That fame may cry you loud . . . *All's Well* ii 1 17
And sing them loud even in the dead of night . . . . *T. Night* i 5 290
I speak too loud . . . . iii 4 4
'Tis like to be loud weather . . . . *W. Tale* iii 3 11
Braying trumpets and loud churlish drums, Clamours of hell *K. John* iii 1 303
At hand a drum is ready braced That shall reverberate all as loud as thine v 2 170
If the French be lords of this loud day . . . . . . v 4 14
As to o'er-walk a current roaring loud . . . . . 1 *Hen. IV.* i 3 192
That I did pluck allegiance from men's hearts, Loud shouts and salutations from their mouths . . . . iii 2 53
Which of you will stop The vent of hearing when loud Rumour speaks? 2 *Hen. IV.* Ind. 2
O thou fond many, with what loud applause Didst thou beat heaven! . i 3 91
Who knocks so loud at door? Look to the door there . . . ii 4 381
Turning . . . your tongue divine To a loud trumpet and a point of war iv 1 52
And the loud trumpet blowing them together . . . . . iv 1 122

Loud. The enemy is loud; you hear him all night *Hen. V.* iv 1 76
Make open proclamation: Come, officer; as loud as e'er thou canst *1 Hen. VI.* i 3 72
She hath beheld the man Whose glory fills the world with loud report ii 2 43
Within the Temple-hall we were too loud; The garden here is more convenient ii 4 3
Clapping their hands, and crying with loud voice *2 Hen. VI.* i 1 160
Breaks The sides of loyalty, and almost appears In loud rebellion *Hen. VIII.* i 2 29
Such a noise arose As the shrouds make at sea in a stiff tempest, As loud iv 1 73
But mark Troilus above the rest.—Speak not so loud *Troi. and Cres.* i 2 201
From his deep chest laughs out a loud applause i 3 163
Trumpet, blow loud, Send thy brass voice through all these lazy tents i 3 256
That will physic the great Myrmidon Who broils in loud applause i 3 379
Give with thy trumpet a loud note to Troy, Thou dreadful Ajax iv 5 3
Beat loud the tabourines, let the trumpets blow iv 5 275
Consort with me in loud and dear petition, Pursue we him on knees v 3 9
Peace, peace; be not so loud *Coriolanus* iv 2 12
And with loud 'larums welcome them to Rome *T. Andron.* i 1 147
What, ho! apothecary!—Who calls so loud? *Rom. and Jul.* v 1 57
Curses, not loud but deep, mouth-honour, breath *Macbeth* v 3 27
But even then the morning cock crew loud *Hamlet* i 2 218
Ay me, what act, That roars so loud, and thunders in the index? iii 4 52
My arrows, Too slightly timber'd for so loud a wind iv 7 22
He raised the house with loud and coward cries *Lear* ii 4 43
He s embark'd With such loud reason to the Cyprus wars *Othello* i 1 151
Had tongue at will and yet was never loud ii 1 150
Find some occasion to anger Cassio, either by speaking too loud, or tainting his discipline ii 1 275
And speaks as loud As his own state and ours *Ant. and Cleo.* i 4 29
Let Antony look over Cæsar's head And speak as loud as Mars ii 2 6
When we debate Our trivial difference loud, we do commit Murder ii 2 21
All take hands. Make battery to our ears with the loud music ii 7 115
The holding every man shall bear as loud As his strong sides can volley ii 7 117
Let Neptune hear we bid a loud farewell To these great fellows ii 7 139
Undo that prayer, by crying out as loud, 'O, bless my brother!' iii 4 17
And put My clouted brogues from off my feet, whose rudeness Answer'd my steps too loud *Cymbeline* iv 2 215
Loud music is too harsh for ladies' heads *Pericles* ii 3 97
The wind is loud, and will not lie till the ship be cleared of the dead iii 1 48
Down on thy knees, thank the holy gods as loud As thunder threatens us v 1 200
Louder. A plague upon this howling! they are louder than the weather *Tempest* i 1 40
Speak louder.—Truly, I am so glad you have nobody here *Mer. Wives* iv 2 17
As these black masks Proclaim an enshield beauty ten times louder Than beauty could, display'd *Meas. for Meas.* ii 4 80
My griefs cry louder than advertisement *Much Ado* v 1 32
They're busy within; you were best knock louder *T. of Shrew* v 1 16
Both roaring louder than the sea or weather *W. Tale* iii 3 103
Tell him I am deaf.—You must speak louder *2 Hen. IV.* i 2 78
Now, God incense him, And let him cry Ha! louder! *Hen. VIII.* iii 2 62
Please you, draw near. Louder the music there! *Lear* iv 7 25
Weep, Till tongues fetch breath that may proclaim them louder *Pericles* i 4 15
No din but snores the house about, Made louder by the o'er-fed breast iii Gower 3
Loudest. And undertake to be Her advocate to the loud'st *W. Tale* ii 2 39
On whose bright crest Fame with her loud'st Oyes Cries *Troi. and Cres.* iv 5 143
There s no answer That will be given to the loudest noise we make *Cymb.* iii 5 44
Loud-howling. Now loud-howling wolves arouse the jades *2 Hen. VI.* iv 1 3
Loudly. The soldiers' music and the rites of war Speak loudly for him *Hamlet* v 2 411
Lour. Why at our justice seem'st thou then to lour? *Richard II.* i 3 235
The heavens do lour upon you for some ill; Move them no more *R. and J.* iv 5 94
Loured. All the clouds that lour'd upon our house In the deep bosom of the ocean buried *Richard III.* i 1 3
Loureth. Fie, how impatience loureth in your face! *Com. of Errors* ii 1 86
Louring. Nor reconcile This louring tempest of your home-bred hate *Richard II.* i 3 187
What louring star now envies thy estate? *2 Hen. VI.* iii 1 206
Driving back shadows over louring hills *Rom. and Jul.* ii 5 6
Louse. The dozen white louses do become an old coat well *Mer. Wives* i 1 19
For I care not to be the louse of a lazar *Troi. and Cres.* v 1 72
The cod-piece that will house Before the head has any, The head and he shall louse; So beggars marry many *Lear* iii 2 29
Lousy I pray you now, remembrance to-morrow on the lousy knave *M. W.* iii 3 256
A lousy knave, to have his gibes and his mockeries! iii 3 259
Upon my knowledge, he is, and lousy *All's Well* iv 3 220
What an arrant, rascally, beggarly, lousy knave it is *Hen. V.* iv 8 37
The rascally, scauld, beggarly, lousy, pragging knave v 1 6
You scurvy, lousy knave, God pless you! v 1 19
Wait like a lousy footboy At chamber-door *Hen. VIII.* v 3 139
Lout. 'Tis no trusting to yond foolish lout *T. G. of Ver.* iv 4 71
I hate thee, Pronounce thee a gross lout *W. Tale* i 2 301
That . . . there should be In such a love so vile a lout as he *K. John* ii 1 509
Hang nothing but a calf's-skin, most sweet lout iii 1 220
And you will rather show our general louts How you can frown *Coriolanus* iii 2 66
If that thy gentry, Britain, go before This lout as he exceeds our lords, the odds Is that we scarce are men and you are gods *Cymbeline* v 2 9
Louvre. He'll make your Paris Louvre shake for it *Hen. V.* ii 4 132
An English courtier may be wise, And never see the Louvre *Hen. VIII.* i 3 23
Love. None that I more love than myself *Tempest* i 1 22
So dear the love my people bore me i 2 141
'Tis a villain, sir, I do not love to look on i 2 310
Draw thy sword: one stroke Shall free thee from the tribute which thou payest; And I the king shall love thee ii 1 294
Do you love me?—O heaven, O earth, bear witness! iii 1 67
I Beyond all limit of what else i' the world Do love, prize, honour you iii 1 73
All thy vexations Were but my trials of thy love iv 1 6
With such love as 'tis now, . . . shall never melt Mine honour into lust iv 1 24
Do you love me, master? no?—Dearly, my delicate Ariel iv 1 48
Broom-groves, Whose shadow the dismissed bachelor loves, Being lass-lorn iv 1 67
A contract of true love to celebrate iv 1 84; 133
Sweet lord, you play me false.—No, my dear'st love v 1 172
Were't not affection chains thy tender days To the sweet glances of thy honour'd love *T. G. of Ver.* i 1 4
Love still and thrive therein, Even as I would when I to love begin i 1 10
On a love-book pray for my success?—Upon some book I love I'll pray i 1 20
Some shallow story of deep love: How young Leander cross'd the Hellespont.—That's a deep story of a deeper love; For he was more than over shoes in love i 1 21
Love. You are over boots in love, And yet you never swum the Hellespont *T. G. of Ver.* i 1 25
To be in love, where scorn is bought with groans i 1 29
'Tis love you cavil at: I am not Love.—Love is your master i 1 38
So eating love Inhabits in the finest wits of all i 1 43
Even so by love the young and tender wit Is turn'd to folly i 1 47
Let me hear from thee by letters Of thy success in love i 1 58
He after honour hunts, I after love: He leaves his friends to dignify them more; I leave myself, my friends and all, for love i 1 63
Now we are alone, Wouldst thou then counsel me to fall in love? i 2 2
Of all the fair resort of gentlemen That every day with parle encounter me, In thy opinion which is worthiest love? i 2 6
Wouldst thou have me cast my love on him?—Ay, if you thought your love not cast away i 2 25
He, of all the rest, hath never moved me.—Yet he, of all the rest, I think, best loves ye i 2 28
His little speaking shows his love but small i 2 29
They do not love that do not show their love.—O, they love least that let men know their love i 2 31
To plead for love deserves more fee than hate i 2 48
Fie, fie, how wayward is this foolish love That, like a testy babe, will scratch the nurse And presently all humbled kiss the rod! i 2 57
Some love of yours hath writ to you in rhyme.—That I might sing it, madam i 2 79
Best sing it to the tune of 'Light o' love.'—It is too heavy i 2 83
Sweet love! sweet lines! sweet life! Here is her hand, the agent of her heart; Here is her oath for love, her honour's pawn i 3 45
O, that our fathers would applaud our loves, To seal our happiness! i 3 48
I fear'd to show my father Julia's letter, Lest he should take exceptions to my love; And with the vantage of mine own excuse Hath he excepted most against my love i 3 81
How this spring of love resembleth The uncertain glory of an April day! i 3 84
Do you know Madam Silvia?—She that your worship loves? ii 1 16
How know you that I am in love?—Marry, by these special marks ii 1 17
If you love her, you cannot see her.—Why?—Because Love is blind ii 1 74
He, being in love, could not see to garter his hose, and you, being in love, cannot see to put on your hose ii 1 83
You are in love; for last morning you could not see to wipe my shoes ii 1 85
I was in love with my bed: I thank you, you swinged me for my love, which makes me the bolder to chide you for yours ii 1 87
Last night she enjoined me to write some lines to one she loves ii 1 94
Herself hath taught her love himself to write unto her lover ii 1 174
Though the chameleon Love can feed on the air, I am one that am nourished by my victuals ii 1 179
What, gone without a word?—Ay, so true love should do: it cannot speak ii 2 17
Sir Thurio frowns on you.—Ay, boy, it's for love.—Not of you ii 4 4
He is as worthy for an empress' love As meet to be an emperor's counsellor ii 4 76
Love hath twenty pair of eyes.—They say that Love hath not an eye at all ii 4 95
Upon a homely object Love can wink ii 4 98
How does your lady? and how thrives your love? ii 4 125
My tales of love were wont to weary you ii 4 126
I have done penance for contemning Love ii 4 129
In revenge of my contempt of love, Love hath chased sleep from my enthralled eyes ii 4 133
Love's a mighty lord And hath so humbled me ii 4 136
Now no discourse, except it be of love; Now can I break my fast, dine, sup and sleep, Upon the very naked name of love ii 4 142
O, flatter me; for love delights in praises ii 4 148
Except not any; Except thou wilt except against my love ii 4 155
I do not dream on thee, Because thou see'st me dote upon my love ii 4 173
I must after, For love, thou know'st, is full of jealousy ii 4 177
But she loves you?—Ay, and we are betroth'd ii 4 178
The remembrance of my former love Is by a newer object quite forgotten ii 4 194
She is fair; and so is Julia that I love—That I did love, for now my love is thaw'd; Which, like a waxen image 'gainst a fire ii 4 199
Methinks my zeal to Valentine is cold, And that I love him not as I was wont. O, but I love his lady too too much, And that's the reason I love him so little ii 4 204
How shall I dote on her with more advice, That thus without advice begin to love her! ii 4 208
If I can check my erring love, I will; If not, to compass her I'll use my skill ii 4 213
I tell thee, I care not though he burn himself in love ii 5 56
To love fair Silvia, shall I be forsworn ii 6 2
Love bade me swear and Love bids me forswear ii 6 6
O sweet-suggesting Love, if thou hast sinn'd, Teach me, thy tempted subject, to excuse it! ii 6 7
I cannot leave to love, and yet I do; But there I leave to love where I should love ii 6 17
I to myself am dearer than a friend, For love is still most precious in itself ii 6 24
I will forget that Julia is alive, Remembering that my love to her is dead ii 6 28
Love, lend me wings to make my purpose swift! ii 6 42
Gentle girl, assist me; And even in kind love I do conjure thee ii 7 2
Didst thou but know the inly touch of love, Thou wouldst as soon go kindle fire with snow As seek to quench the fire of love with words ii 7 20
I do not seek to quench your love's hot fire, But qualify the fire's extreme rage, Lest it should burn above the bounds of reason ii 7 21
And make a pastime of each weary step, Till the last step have brought me to my love; And there I'll rest ii 7 36
A thousand oaths, an ocean of his tears And instances of infinite of love ii 7 70
His oaths are oracles, His love sincere, his thoughts immaculate ii 7 76
Only deserve my love by loving him ii 7 82
This love of theirs myself have often seen iii 1 24
For love of you, not hate unto my friend, Hath made me publisher of this pretence iii 1 46
This pride of hers, Upon advice, hath drawn my love from her iii 1 73
If she do frown, 'tis not in hate of you, But rather to beget more love iii 1 97
Love is like a child, That longs for every thing that he can come by iii 1 124
My wrath shall far exceed the love I ever bore my daughter or thyself iii 1 166
Here if thou stay, thou canst not see thy love iii 1 244
Shall be deliver'd Even in the milk-white bosom of thy love iii 1 250
He lives not now that knows me to be in love; yet I am in love; but a team of horse shall not pluck that from me; nor who 'tis I love iii 1 264
She hath no teeth.—I care not for that neither, because I love crusts iii 1 346

Love. Fear not but that she will love you *T. G. of Ver.* iii 2 1
This weak impress of love is as a figure Trenched in ice iii 2 6
What might we do to make the girl forget The love of Valentine and love Sir Thurio?—The best way is to slander Valentine iii 2 30
She shall not long continue love to him iii 2 48
But say this weed her love from Valentine, It follows not that she will love Sir Thurio iii 2 49
Therefore, as you unwind her love from him, Lest it should ravel and be good to none, You must provide to bottom it on me iii 2 51
You are already Love's firm votary, And cannot soon revolt iii 2 58
Temper her by your persuasion To hate young Valentine and love my friend iii 2 65
This discipline shows thou hast been in love iii 2 88
We'll do thee homage and be ruled by thee, Love thee as our commander iv 1 67
Under the colour of commending him, I have access my own love to prefer iv 2 4
The more she spurns my love, The more it grows and fawneth on her still iv 2 14
You know that love Will creep in service where it cannot go iv 2 19
I hope, sir, that you love not here.—Sir, but I do iv 2 21
Love doth to her eyes repair, To help him of his blindness iv 2 46
Return, return, and make thy love amends iv 2 99
I grant, sweet love, that I did love a lady; But she is dead iv 2 105
In his grave Assure thyself my love is buried iv 2 115
If your heart be so obdurate, Vouchsafe me yet your picture for my love iv 2 121
I am but a shadow; And to your shadow will I make true love iv 2 126
I have heard thee say No grief did ever come so near thy heart As when thy lady and thy true love died iv 3 20
Methinks that she loved you as well As you do love your lady Silvia iv 4 85
She dreams on him that has forgot her love; You dote on her that cares not for your love. 'Tis pity love should be so contrary iv 4 86
Because he loves her, he despiseth me; Because I love him, I must pity him iv 4 100
I am my master's true-confirmed love iv 4 108
I hope my master's suit will be but cold, Since she respects my mistress' love so much. Alas, how love can trifle with itself! iv 4 187
If that be all the difference in his love, I'll get me such a colour'd periwig iv 4 195
If this fond Love were not a blinded god iv 4 201
Scratch'd out your unseeing eyes, To make my master out of love with thee! iv 4 210
But love will not be spurr'd to what it loathes v 2 7
How likes she my discourse?—Ill, when you talk of war.—But well, when I discourse of love and peace? v 2 17
More to be revenged on Eglamour Than for the love of reckless Silvia v 2 52
And I will follow, more for Silvia's love Than hate of Eglamour v 2 53
I will follow, more to cross that love Than hate for Silvia that is gone for love v 2 55
They love me well; yet I have much to do To keep them from uncivil outrages v 4 16
From him That would have forced your honour and your love v 4 22
Love, lend me patience to forbear awhile v 4 27
O, Heaven be judge how I love Valentine! v 4 36
'Tis the curse in love, and still approved, When women cannot love where they're beloved!—When Proteus cannot love where he's beloved v 4 43
Read over Julia's heart, thy first best love v 4 46
And all those oaths Descended into perjury, to love me v 4 49
In love Who respects friend?—All men but Proteus v 4 53
I'll woo you like a soldier, at arms' end, And love you 'gainst the nature of love v 4 58
Thou common friend, that's without faith or love, For such is a friend now v 4 62
That my love may appear plain and free v 4 82
If shame live In a disguise of love v 4 107
I dare thee but to breathe upon my love v 4 131
I care not for her, I: I hold him but a fool that will endanger His body for a girl that loves him not v 4 134
And think thee worthy of an empress' love v 4 141
'Tis your penance but to hear The story of your loves discovered v 4 171
It is a familiar beast to man, and signifies love *Mer. Wives* i 1 21
Can you love her?—I hope, sir, I will do as it shall become one that would do reason i 1 239
Can you love the maid?—I will marry her, sir, at your request: but if there be no great love in the beginning, yet heaven may decrease it i 1 252
I love the sport well; but I shall as soon quarrel at it as any man i 1 302
I do mean to make love to Ford's wife: I spy entertainment in her i 3 48
I will discuss the humour of this love to Page i 3 104
I would have no words of it,—my master himself is in love i 4 110
Sir, the maid loves you, and all shall be well i 4 127
I'll be sworn on a book, she loves you i 4 156
Truly, an honest gentleman: but Anne loves him not i 4 178
Ask me no reason why I love you; for though Love use Reason for his physician, he admits him not for his counsellor ii 1 4
You love sack, and so do I; would you desire better sympathy? ii 1 9
Let it suffice thee, Mistress Page,—at the least, if the love of soldier can suffice,—that I love thee ii 1 11
I will not say, pity me; 'tis not a soldier-like phrase: but I say, love me ii 1 14
He loves the gallimaufry: Ford, perpend.—Love my wife! ii 1 119
He loves your wife; there's the short and the long ii 1 136
Falstaff loves your wife. Adieu. I love not the humour of bread and cheese ii 1 139
Has Ford's wife and Page's wife acquainted each other how they love me? ii 2 115
Mistress Page would desire you to send her your little page, of all loves ii 2 119
I have pursued her as love hath pursued me ii 2 208
Love like a shadow flies when substance love pursues ii 2 215
Of what quality was your love, then?—Like a fair house built on another man's ground ii 2 223
By gar, me dank you vor dat: by gar, I love you ii 3 95
Be-gar; and de maid is love-a me: my nursh-a Quickly tell me so mush iii 2 65
What made me love thee? let that persuade thee there's something extraordinary in thee. Come, I cannot cog iii 3 74
But I love thee; none but thee; and thou deservest it iii 3 80
I fear you love Mistress Page.—Thou mightst as well say I love to walk by the Counter-gate iii 3 83
Well, heaven knows how I love you; and you shall one day find it iii 3 87

Love. I love thee. Help me away. Let me creep in here *Mer. Wives* iii 3 149
I see I cannot get thy father's love; Therefore no more turn me to him iii 4 1
'Tis a thing impossible I should love thee but as a property iii 4 10
Gentle Master Fenton, Yet seek my father's love; still seek it, sir iii 4 19
My cousin loves you.—Ay, that I do; as well as I love any woman iii 4 42
Now, Master Slender: love him, daughter Anne iii 4 71
For that I love your daughter In such a righteous fashion as I do, . . . I must advance the colours of my love And not retire iii 4 82
And, forsooth, to search his house for his wife's love iii 5 79
I see you are obsequious in your love, and I profess requital iv 2 3
Not only, Mistress Ford, in the simple office of love, but in all the accoutrement, complement, and ceremony of it iv 2 5
I have acquainted you With the dear love I bear to fair Anne Page iv 6 9
Remember, Jove, thou wast a bull for thy Europa; love set on thy horns v 5 4
O powerful love! that, in some respects, makes a beast a man v 5 5
You were also, Jupiter, a swan for the love of Leda v 5 7
O omnipotent Love! how near the god drew to the complexion of a goose! v 5 8
I will never take you for my love again; but I will always count you my deer v 5 122
Hear the truth of it. You would have married her most shamefully, Where there was no proportion held in love v 5 235
In love the heavens themselves do guide the state v 5 245
Lent him our terror, dress'd him with our love *Meas. for Meas.* i 1 20
I love the people, But do not like to stage me to their eyes i 1 68
We thought it meet to hide our love Till time had made them for us i 2 156
And thy head stands so tickle on thy shoulders that a milkmaid, if she be in love, may sigh it off i 2 178
Believe not that the dribbling dart of love Can pierce a complete bosom i 3 2
What, do I love her, That I desire to hear her speak again? ii 2 177
Love you the man that wrong'd you?—Yes, as I love the woman that wrong'd him ii 3 24
Showing we would not spare heaven as we love it, But as we stand in fear ii 3 33
O injurious love, That respites me a life, whose very comfort Is still a dying horror!—'Tis pity of him ii 3 40
Their untaught love Must needs appear offence ii 4 29
I something do excuse the thing I hate, For his advantage that I dearly love ii 4 120
I love you.—My brother did love Juliet, And you tell me that he shall die for it.—He shall not, Isabel, if you give me love ii 4 142
I am so out of love with life that I will sue to be rid of it iii 1 174
To the love I have in doing good a remedy presents itself iii 1 203
In his love toward her ever most kind and natural iii 1 228
His unjust unkindness, that in all reason should have quenched her love, hath, like an impediment in the current, made it more violent and unruly iii 1 251
Sir, I know him, and I love him.—Love talks with better knowledge, and knowledge with dearer love iii 2 159
My kisses bring again, bring again; Seals of love, but seal'd in vain iv 1 6
Mercy's so extended, That for the fault's love is the offender friended iv 2 116
I'll depose I had him in mine arms With all the effect of love v 1 199
I protest I love the duke as I love myself v 1 344
Look that you love your wife; her worth worth yours v 1 502
Love her, Angelo: I have confess'd her and I know her virtue v 1 532
In the quest of him: Whom whilst I labour'd of a love to see, I hazarded the loss of whom I loved *Com. of Errors* i 1 131
Ere I learn love, I'll practise to obey ii 1 29
As you love strokes, so jest with me again ii 2 8
Your sauciness will jest upon my love ii 2 28
My love, as easy mayst thou fall A drop of water in the breaking gulf ii 2 127
Shall, Antipholus, Even in the spring of love, thy love-springs rot? Shall love, in building, grow so ruinous? iii 2 3
Do it by stealth; Muffle your false love with some show of blindness iii 2 8
Alas, poor women! make us but believe, Being compact of credit, that you love us; Though others have the arm, show us the sleeve iii 2 22
Let Love, being light, be drowned if she sink! iii 2 52
As good to wink, sweet love, as look on night.—Why call you me love? iii 2 58
Thee will I love and with thee lead my life iii 2 67
Belike you thought our love would last too long, If it were chain'd together iv 1 25
That love I begg'd for you he begg'd of me iv 2 12
With what persuasion did he tempt thy love? iv 2 13
Hath not else his eye Stray'd his affection in unlawful love? v 1 51
Some love that drew him oft from home v 1 56
Truly, I love none.—A dear happiness to women *Much Ado* i 1 128
I had rather hear my dog bark at a crow than a man swear he loves me i 1 133
Mark you this, on my allegiance. He is in love. With who? i 1 214
Amen, if you love her; for the lady is very well worthy i 1 223
That I love her, I feel.—That she is worthy, I know i 1 230
I shall see thee, ere I die, look pale with love.—With anger, with sickness, or with hunger, my lord, not with love i 1 250
Prove that ever I lose more blood with love than I will get again with drinking i 1 253
My love is thine to teach i 1 293
Had a rougher task in hand Than to drive liking to the name of love i 1 302
If thou dost love fair Hero, cherish it, And I will break with her i 1 310
How sweetly you do minister to love, That know love's grief by his complexion! i 1 314
It better fits my blood to be disdained of all than to fashion a carriage to rob love from any i 3 31
Speak low, if you speak love ii 1 103
I say my prayers aloud.—I love you the better ii 1 109
You are very near my brother in his love ii 1 170
How know you he loves her?—I heard him swear his affection ii 1 174
Friendship is constant in all other things Save in the office and affairs of love: Therefore all hearts in love use their own tongues ii 1 183
O God, sir, here's a dish I love not: I cannot endure my Lady Tongue ii 1 283
Time goes on crutches till love have all his rites ii 1 373
I will teach you how to humour your cousin, that she shall fall in love ii 1 397
In despite of his quick wit and his queasy stomach, he shall fall in love ii 1 400
Tell them that you know that Hero loves me ii 2 35
In love of your brother's honour, who hath made this match ii 2 37
That one man, seeing how much another man is a fool when he dedicates his behaviours to love, will, after he hath laughed at such shallow follies in others, become the argument of his own scorn by falling in love ii 3 10
I will not be sworn but love may transform me to an oyster ii 3 25
Ha! the prince and Monsieur Love! I will hide me in the arbour ii 3 38

Love. Yet he wooes, Yet will he swear he loves . . . *Much Ado* ii 3 54
That your niece Beatrice was in love with Signior Benedick . ii 3 93
She loves him with an enraged affection ; it is past the infinite of thought ii 3 105
'Shall I,' says she, 'that have so oft encountered him with scorn, write to him that I love him?' . ii 3 134
I should flout him, if he writ to me ; yea, though I love him, I should . ii 3 151
She says she will die, if he love her not, and she will die, ere she make her love known . ii 3 181
If she should make tender of her love, 'tis very possible he'll scorn it . ii 3 186
Shall we go seek Benedick, and tell him of her love? . ii 3 208
I love Benedick well ; and I could wish he would modestly examine himself . ii 3 212
Love me! why, it must be requited. I hear how I am censured : they say I will bear myself proudly, if I perceive the love come from her ii 3 232
I will be horribly in love with her . ii 3 244
A man loves the meat in his youth that he cannot endure in his age . ii 3 247
She's a fair lady : I do spy some marks of love in her . ii 3 255
If I do not take pity of her, I am a villain ; if I do not love her, I am a Jew . ii 3 272
My talk to thee must be how Benedick Is sick in love with Beatrice . iii 1 21
But are you sure That Benedick loves Beatrice so entirely? . iii 1 37
O god of love! I know he doth deserve As much as may be yielded to a man . iii 1 47
She cannot love, Nor take no shape nor project of affection . iii 1 54
Certainly it were not good She knew his love, lest she make sport at it iii 1 58
And, Benedick, love on ; I will requite thee . iii 1 111
If thou dost love, my kindness shall incite thee To bind our loves up in a holy band . iii 1 113
Methinks you are sadder.—I hope he be in love . iii 2 17
There's no true drop of blood in him, to be truly touched with love . iii 2 20
Yet say I, he is in love.—There is no appearance of fancy in him . iii 2 30
If he be not in love with some woman, there is no believing old signs . iii 2 40
That's as much as to say, the sweet youth's in love . iii 2 53
Conclude he is in love.—Nay, but I know who loves him . iii 2 64
You may think I love you not : let that appear hereafter . iii 2 98
If you love her then, to-morrow wed her . iii 2 118
Clap's into 'Light o' love ;' that goes without a burden . iii 4 44
I'll dance it.—Ye light o' love, with your heels! . iii 4 47
You may think perchance that I think you are in love . iii 4 82
Nor indeed I cannot think, if I would think my heart out of thinking, that you are in love or that you will be in love or that you can be in love . iii 4 85
As a brother to his sister, show'd Bashful sincerity and comely love . iv 1 55
For thee I'll lock up all the gates of love . iv 1 106
Then shall he mourn, If ever love had interest in his liver . iv 1 233
Though you know my inwardness and love Is very much unto the prince iv 1 247
I do love nothing in the world so well as you : is not that strange? . iv 1 269
By my sword, Beatrice, thou lovest me.—Do not swear, and eat it.—I will swear by it that you love me ; and I will make him eat it that says I love not you . iv 1 278
I protest I love thee.—Why, then, God forgive me! . iv 1 282
I love you with so much of my heart that none is left to protest . iv 1 288
Tarry, sweet Beatrice.—I am gone, though I am here : there is no love in you . iv 1 296
By this hand, I love thee.—Use it for my love some other way than swearing by it . iv 1 328
If she did not hate him deadly, she would love him dearly . v 1 179
In most profound earnest ; and, I'll warrant you, for the love of Beatrice . v 1 199
If your love Can labour aught in sad invention . v 1 291
The god of love, That sits above, And knows me, and knows me . v 2 26
They were never so truly turned over and over as my poor self in love . v 2 35
For which of my bad parts didst thou first fall in love with me? . v 2 61
For which of my good parts did you first suffer love for me?—Suffer love! a good epithet! I do suffer love indeed, for I love thee against my will . v 2 65
I will never love that which my friend hates . v 2 71
Serve God, love me and mend. There will I leave you . v 2 95
And I do with an eye of love requite her . v 4 24
As once Europa did at lusty Jove, When he would play the noble beast in love . v 4 47
What is your will?—Do not you love me?—Why, no ; no more than reason . v 4 74
Then you do not love me?—No, truly, but in friendly recompense . v 4 82
I am sure you love the gentleman.—And I'll be sworn upon't that he loves her . v 4 84
In that thou art like to be my kinsman, live unbruised and love my cousin . v 4 112
To love, to wealth, to pomp, I pine and die . *L. L. Lost* i 1 31
I love to hear him lie And I will use him for my minstrelsy . i 1 176
I love not to be crossed.—He speaks the mere contrary ; crosses love not him . i 2 34
I will hereupon confess I am in love : and as it is base for a soldier to love, so am I in love with a base wench . i 2 60
Comfort me, boy : what great men have been in love? . i 2 68
He was in love.—O well-knit Samson! strong-jointed Samson! . i 2 76
I am in love too. Who was Samson's love, my dear Moth?—A woman . i 2 80
But to have a love of that colour, methinks Samson had small reason . i 2 91
My love is most immaculate white and red . i 2 95
Boy, I do love that country girl that I took in the park . i 2 122
She deserves well.—To be whipped ; and yet a better love than my master i 2 126
Sing, boy ; my spirit grows heavy in love . i 2 127
I will tell thee wonders.—With that face?—I love thee.—So I heard you say . i 2 145
I shall be forsworn, which is a great argument of falsehood, if I love. And how can that be true love which is falsely attempted? . i 2 176
Love is a familiar ; Love is a devil : there is no evil angel but Love . i 2 177
Adieu! valour! rust, rapier! be still, drum! for your manager is in love i 2 188
A well-accomplish'd youth, Of all that virtue love for virtue loved . ii 1 57
God bless my ladies! are they all in love? . ii 1 77
I must employ him in a letter to my love.—Master, will you win your love with a French brawl? . iii 1 7
Through the throat, as if you swallowed love with singing love . iii 1 15
Through the nose, as if you snuffed up love by smelling love . iii 1 17
Callest thou my love 'hobby-horse'?—No, master ; the hobby-horse is but a colt, and your love perhaps a hackney . iii 1 31
But have you forgot your love?—Almost I had . iii 1 34
By heart you love her, because your heart cannot come by her . iii 1 42
In heart you love her, because your heart is in love with her . iii 1 44
Out of heart you love her, being out of heart that you cannot enjoy her iii 1 45

Love. And I, forsooth, in love! I, that have been love's whip! *L. L. Lost* iii 1 175
What, I! I love! I sue! I seek a wife! A woman, that is like a German clock! . iii 1 191
And, among three, to love the worst of all ; A wightly wanton . iii 1 197
Well, I will love, write, sigh, pray, sue and groan : Some men must love my lady and some Joan . iii 1 206
Shall I command thy love? I may : shall I enforce thy love? I could : shall I entreat thy love? I will . iv 1 82
Many can brook the weather that love not the wind . iv 2 34
Old Mantuan! who understandeth thee not, loves thee not . iv 2 102
If love make me forsworn, how shall I swear to love? . iv 2 109
Celestial as thou art, O, pardon love this wrong, That sings heaven's praise with such an earthly tongue . iv 2 121
By the Lord, this love is as mad as Ajax . iv 3 6
I will not love : if I do, hang me ; i' faith, I will not . iv 3 9
O, but her eye,—by this light, but for her eye, I would not love her . iv 3 11
I do love : and it hath taught me to rhyme and to be melancholy . iv 3 13
But do not love thyself ; then thou wilt keep My tears for glasses . iv 3 39
In love, I hope : sweet fellowship in shame!—One drunkard loves another . iv 3 49
O sweet Maria, empress of my love! . iv 3 56
My vow was earthly, thou a heavenly love . iv 3 66
Once more I'll mark how love can vary wit . iv 3 100
Love, whose month is ever May, Spied a blossom passing fair . iv 3 102
And deny himself for Jove, Turning mortal for thy love . iv 3 120
Something else more plain, That shall express my true love's fasting pain . iv 3 122
Thy love is far from charity, That in love's grief desirest society . iv 3 128
You chide at him, offending twice as much ; You do not love Maria . iv 3 133
And Jove, for your love, would infringe an oath . iv 3 144
Good heart, what grace hast thou, thus to reprove These worms for loving, that art most in love? . iv 3 154
When shall you see me write a thing in rhyme? Or groan for love? . iv 3 182
I post from love : good lover, let me go . iv 3 188
He, he, and you, and you, my liege, and I, Are pick-purses in love . iv 3 209
What, did these rent lines show some love of thine? . iv 3 220
My love, her mistress, is a gracious moon ; She an attending star . iv 3 230
O, but for my love, day would turn to night! . iv 3 233
Thy love is black as ebony.—Is ebony like her? O wood divine! . iv 3 247
Look, here's thy love : my foot and her face see . iv 3 277
Are we not all in love?—Nothing so sure . iv 3 282
Love, first learned in a lady's eyes, Lives not alone immured in the brain . iv 3 327
For valour, is not Love a Hercules, Still climbing trees in the Hesperides? . iv 3 340
When Love speaks, the voice of all the gods Make heaven drowsy with the harmony . iv 3 344
For wisdom's sake, a word that all men love, Or for love's sake, a word that loves all men . iv 3 357
Charity itself fulfils the law, And who can sever love from charity? . iv 3 365
For revels, dances, masks and merry hours Forerun fair Love . iv 3 380
As much love in rhyme As would be cramm'd up in a sheet of paper . v 2 6
Love doth approach disguised, Armed in arguments . v 2 83
And change you favours too ; so shall your loves Woo contrary . v 2 134
Their several counsels they unbosom shall To loves mistook . v 2 142
But will you hear? the king is my love sworn . v 2 282
My love to thee is sound, sans crack or flaw . v 2 415
I do adore thy sweet grace's slipper.—Loves her by the foot . v 2 673
Though the mourning brow of progeny Forbid the smiling courtesy of love . v 2 755
Love is full of unbefitting strains, All wanton as a child, skipping and vain . v 2 770
Which parti-coated presence of loose love Put on by us . v 2 776
Ladies, Our love being yours, the error that love makes Is likewise yours v 2 781
Received your letters full of love ; Your favours, the ambassadors of love . v 2 787
And therefore met your loves In their own fashion, like a merriment . v 2 793
Now, at the latest minute of the hour, Grant us your loves . v 2 798
If for my love, as there is no such cause, You will do aught, this shall you do . v 2 802
If frosts and fasts, hard lodging and thin weeds, Nip not the gaudy blossoms of your love, But that it bear this trial and last love . v 2 812
And what to me, my love? and what to me?—You must be purged too v 2 827
But what to me, my love? but what to me? A wife?—A beard, fair health, and honesty ; With three-fold love I wish you all these three v 2 833
Come when the king doth to my lady come ; Then, if I have much love, I'll give you some . v 2 840
Impose some service on me for thy love . v 2 850
I have vowed to Jaquenetta to hold the plough for her sweet love three years . v 2 893
And won thy love, doing thee injuries . *M. N. Dream* i 1 17
At her window sung With feigning voice verses of feigning love . i 1 31
By the next new moon—The sealing-day betwixt my love and me . i 1 84
You have her father's love, Demetrius ; Let me have Hermia's . i 1 93
True, he hath my love, And what is mine my love shall render him . i 1 96
My love is more than his ; My fortunes every way as fairly rank'd . i 1 100
Demetrius, I'll avouch it to his head, Made love to Nedar's daughter . i 1 107
Come, my Hippolyta : what cheer, my love? . i 1 122
How now, my love! why is your cheek so pale? . i 1 128
The course of true love never did run smooth . i 1 134
O hell! to choose love by another's eyes . i 1 140
As due to love as thoughts and dreams and sighs, Wishes and tears . i 1 154
By that which knitteth souls and prospers loves . i 1 172
To-morrow truly will I meet with thee.—Keep promise, love . i 1 179
Demetrius loves your fair : O happy fair! Your eyes are lode-stars . i 1 182
I frown upon him, yet he loves me still.—O that your frowns would teach my smiles such skill! . i 1 194
I give him curses, yet he gives me love.—O that my prayers could such affection move! . i 1 196
The more I hate, the more he follows me.—The more I love, the more he hateth me . i 1 199
What graces in my love do dwell, That he hath turn'd a heaven unto a hell! . i 1 206
Things base and vile, holding no quantity, Love can transpose to form i 1 233
Love looks not with the eyes, but with the mind ; And therefore is wing'd Cupid painted blind . i 1 234
Therefore is Love said to be a child, Because in choice he is so oft beguiled . i 1 238
As waggish boys in game themselves forswear, So the boy Love is perjured every where . i 1 241

Love. A lover, that kills himself most gallant for love *M. N. Dream* i 2 26
Thisby? a wandering knight?—It is the lady that Pyramus must love i 2 48
Playing on pipes of corn and versing love To amorous Phillida ii 1 67
Your buskin'd mistress and your warrior love ii 1 71
How canst thou thus for shame, Titania, Glance at my credit with Hippolyta, Knowing I know thy love to Theseus? ii 1 76
On meddling monkey, or on busy ape, She shall pursue it with the soul of love ii 1 182
I love thee not, therefore pursue me not ii 1 188
Do I not in plainest truth Tell you, I do not, nor I cannot love you?—And even for that do I love you the more ii 1 201
What worser place can I beg in your love,—And yet a place of high respect with me,—Than to be used as you use your dog? ii 1 208
You do impeach your modesty too much, To leave the city and commit yourself Into the hands of one that loves you not ii 1 216
We cannot fight for love, as men may do; We should be woo'd ii 1 241
And make a heaven of hell, To die upon the hand I love so well ii 1 244
Ere he do leave this grove, Thou shalt fly him and he shall seek thy love ii 1 246
A sweet Athenian lady is in love With a disdainful youth ii 1 260
That he may prove More fond on her than she upon her love ii 1 266
What thou seest when thou dost wake, Do it for thy true-love take, Love and languish for his sake ii 2 28
Fair love, you faint with wandering in the wood ii 2 35
Love takes the meaning in love's conference ii 2 46
But, gentle friend, for love and courtesy Lie further off ii 2 56
Good night, sweet friend: Thy love ne'er alter till thy sweet life end! ii 2 61
On whose eyes I might approve This flower's force in stirring love ii 2 69
Let love forbid Sleep his seat on thy eyelid ii 2 80
What though he love your Hermia? Lord, what though? Yet Hermia still loves you: then be content ii 2 109
Not Hermia but Helena I love: Who will not change a raven for a dove? ii 2 113
And, all my powers, address your love and might To honour Helen! ii 2 143
Alack, where are you? speak, an if you hear; Speak, of all loves! ii 2 154
And thy fair virtue's force perforce doth move me On the first view to say, to swear, I love thee iii 1 144
Reason and love keep little company together now-a-days iii 1 147
I do love thee: therefore, go with me; I'll give thee fairies to attend iii 1 159
Light them at the fiery glow-worm's eyes, To have my love to bed and to arise iii 1 174
My mistress with a monster is in love iii 2 6
O, why rebuke you him that loves you so? iii 2 43
Of thy misprision must perforce ensue Some true love turn'd iii 2 91
All fancy-sick she is and pale of cheer, With sighs of love iii 2 97
When his love he doth espy, Let her shine as gloriously As the Venus of the sky iii 2 105
Demetrius loves her, and he loves not you iii 2 136
To what, my love, shall I compare thine eyne? Crystal is muddy iii 2 138
You both are rivals, and love Hermia iii 2 155
You are unkind, Demetrius; be not so; For you love Hermia iii 2 163
With all my heart, In Hermia's love I yield you up my part iii 2 165
Whom I do love and will do till my death iii 2 167
If e'er I loved her, all that love is gone iii 2 170
Look, where thy love comes; yonder is thy dear iii 2 176
Why should he stay, whom love doth press to go? iii 2 184
What love could press Lysander from my side?—Lysander's love iii 2 185
And will you rent our ancient love asunder? iii 2 215
And made your other love, Demetrius, Who even but now did spurn me with his foot, To call me goddess iii 2 224
Wherefore doth Lysander Deny your love, so rich within his soul? iii 2 229
So hung upon with love, so fortunate, But miserable most, to love unloved iii 2 233
Hear my excuse: My love, my life, my soul, fair Helena! iii 2 246
I love thee; by my life, I do: I swear by that which I will lose for thee, To prove him false that says I love thee not iii 2 251
I love thee more than he can do.—If thou say so, withdraw; and prove it iii 2 254
What change is this? Sweet love,— Thy love! out, tawny Tartar, out! iii 2 263
Hate me! wherefore? O me! what news, my love! Am not I Hermia? iii 2 272
'Tis no jest That I do hate thee and love Helena.—O me! you juggler! iii 2 281
You thief of love! what, have you come by night And stolen my love's heart? iii 2 283
I evermore did love you, Hermia, Did ever keep your counsels iii 2 307
In love unto Demetrius, I told him of your stealth unto this wood iii 2 309
He follow'd you; for love I follow'd him; But he hath chid me hence iii 2 311
If thou dost intend Never so little show of love to her, Thou shalt aby it iii 2 334
I with the morning's love have oft made sport iii 2 389
What, wilt thou hear some music, my sweet love? iv 1 30
Or say, sweet love, what thou desirest to eat.—Truly, a peck of provender iv 1 33
O, how I love thee! how I dote on thee! iv 1 50
There lies your love.—How came these things to pass? iv 1 83
My love shall hear the music of my hounds. Uncouple in the western valley iv 1 111
My love to Hermia, Melted as the snow iv 1 170
Now I do wish it, love it, long for it, And will for evermore be true to it iv 1 180
Joy, gentle friends! joy and fresh days of love Accompany your hearts! v 1 29
That have I told my love, In glory of my kinsman Hercules v 1 46
A tedious brief scene of young Pyramus And his love Thisbe v 1 57
I love not to see wretchedness o'ercharged v 1 85
Love, therefore, and tongue-tied simplicity In least speak most v 1 104
My love thou art, my love I think.—Think what thou wilt v 1 196
This is old Ninny's tomb. Where is my love?—Oh—— Well roared, Lion v 1 268
Asleep, my love? What, dead, my dove? O Pyramus, arise! v 1 331
My merchandise makes me not sad.—Why, then you are in love.—Fie, fie!—Not in love neither? *Mer. of Venice* i 1 46
I tell thee what, Antonio—I love thee, and it is my love that speaks i 1 87
I owe the most, in money and in love, And from your love I have a warranty i 1 131
And herein spend but time To wind about my love with circumstance i 1 154
Will, no doubt, never be chosen by any rightly but one who shall rightly love i 2 36
If he love me to madness, I shall never requite him i 2 69
I would be friends with you and have your love i 3 139
Let us make incision for your love, To prove whose blood is reddest ii 1 6
By my love, I swear The best-regarded virgins of our clime Have loved it ii 1 9
I am not bid for love; they flatter me: But yet I'll go in hate ii 5 13
Who are you? . . . Lorenzo, and thy love.—Lorenzo, certain, and my love indeed, For who love I so much? ii 6 28
Love is blind and lovers cannot see The pretty follies that themselves commit ii 6 36
Why, 'tis an office of discovery, love; And I should be obscured ii 6 43

Love. Beshrew me but I love her heartily; For she is wise *Mer. of Venice* ii 8 52
But more than these, in love I do deserve ii 7 34
Let it not enter in your mind of love ii 8 42
Employ your chiefest thoughts To courtship and such fair ostents of love ii 8 44
I think he only loves the world for him ii 8 50
Yet I have not seen So likely an ambassador of love ii 9 92
Bassanio, lord Love, if thy will it be! ii 9 101
There's something tells me, but it is not love, I would not lose you iii 2 4
Confess What treason there is mingled with your love.—None but that ugly treason of mistrust, Which makes me fear the enjoying of my love iii 2 27
As well be amity and life 'Tween snow and fire, as treason and my love iii 2 31
'Confess' and 'love' Had been the very sum of my confession iii 2 35
If you do love me, you will find me out iii 2 41
With no less presence, but with much more love, Than young Alcides iii 2 54
O love, Be moderate; allay thy ecstasy; In measure reign thy joy iii 2 111
I give them with this ring; Which when you part from, lose, or give away, Let it presage the ruin of your love iii 2 175
And swearing till my very roof was dry With oaths of love iii 2 207
I got a promise of this fair one here To have her love iii 2 209
When I did first impart my love to you, I freely told you, all the wealth I had Ran in my veins iii 2 256
Since you are dear bought, I will love you dear iii 2 315
If your love do not persuade you to come, let not my letter iii 2 323
O love, dispatch all business, and be gone! iii 2 325
Whose souls do bear an equal yoke of love iii 4 13
The which my love and some necessity Now lays upon you iii 4 34
Honourable ladies sought my love, Which I denying, they fell sick and died iii 4 70
Touch'd with human gentleness and love, Forgive a moiety iv 1 25
Some men there are love not a gaping pig iv 1 47
Do all men kill the things they do not love? iv 1 66
Bid her be judge Whether Bassanio had not once a love iv 1 277
I have a wife, whom, I protest, I love iv 1 290
And stand indebted, over and above, In love and service to you evermore iv 1 414
And, for your love, I'll take this ring from you iv 1 427
I'll take no more; And you in love shall not deny me this iv 1 429
And my love withal Be valued 'gainst your wife's commandment iv 1 450
In such a night Stood Dido with a willow in her hand Upon the wild sea banks and waft her love To come again to Carthage v 1 11
And with an unthrift love did run from Venice As far as Belmont v 1 16
In such a night Did pretty Jessica, like a little shrew, Slander her love v 1 22
Would he were gelt that had it, for my part, Since you do take it, love, so much at heart v 1 145
Like cutler's poetry Upon a knife, 'Love me, and leave me not' v 1 150
I gave my love a ring and made him swear Never to part with it v 1 170
So loves her, being ever from their cradles bred together *As Y. Like It* i 1 113
And, for your love, I would be loath to foil him i 1 136
Out of my love to you, I came hither to acquaint you withal i 1 138
I thank thee for thy love to me i 1 143
Herein I see thou lovest me not with the full weight that I love thee i 2 9
I could have taught my love to take thy father for mine: so wouldst thou, if the truth of thy love to me were so righteously tempered as mine is to thee i 2 12
Devise sports. Let me see; what think you of falling in love? i 2 28
Love no man in good earnest; nor no further in sport neither than with safety of a pure blush thou mayst in honour come off again i 2 30
My father's love is enough to honour him: enough! speak no more i 2 89
If you do keep your promises in love But justly, as you have exceeded all promise, Your mistress shall be happy i 2 255
You have deserved High commendation, true applause and love i 2 275
Whose loves Are dearer than the natural bond of sisters i 2 287
In a better world than this, I shall desire more love and knowledge of you i 2 297
The duke my father loved his father dearly.—Doth it therefore ensue that you should love his son dearly? i 3 33
Let me love him for that, and do you love him because I do i 3 40
The love Which teacheth thee that thou and I am one i 3 98
I love to cope him in these sullen fits, For then he's full of matter ii 1 67
Why do people love you? And wherefore are you gentle, strong and valiant? ii 3 5
O Corin, that thou knew'st how I do love her!—I partly guess ii 4 23
If thy love were ever like to mine—As sure I think did never man love so ii 4 28
O, thou didst then ne'er love so heartily! If thou remember'st not the slightest folly That ever love did make thee run into, Thou hast not loved ii 4 33
I remember, when I was in love I broke my sword upon a stone ii 4 47
As all is mortal in nature, so is all nature in love mortal in folly ii 4 56
If that love or gold Can in this desert place buy entertainment ii 4 71
Under the greenwood tree Who loves to lie with me ii 5 2
Who doth ambition shun And loves to live i' the sun ii 5 41
Who after me hath many a weary step Limp'd in pure love ii 7 131
Hang there, my verse, in witness of my love iii 2 1
What tedious homily of love have you wearied your parishioners withal! iii 2 164
Rosalind is your love's name?—Yes, just.—I do not like her name iii 2 280
The worst fault you have is to be in love.—'Tis a fault I will not change iii 2 300
Farewell, good Signior Love.—I am glad of your departure iii 2 310
One that knew courtship too well, for there he fell in love iii 2 364
He seems to have the quotidian of love upon him iii 2 384
He taught me how to know a man in love iii 2 388
Fair youth, I would I could make thee believe I love.—Me believe it! you may as soon make her that you love believe it iii 2 405
But are you so much in love as your rhymes speak? iii 2 416
Love is merely a madness, and, I tell you, deserves as well a dark house iii 2 420
The lunacy is so ordinary that the whippers are in love too iii 2 424
He was to imagine me his love, his mistress; and I set him every day to woo me iii 2 428
I drave my suitor from his mad humour of love to a living humour of madness iii 2 439
There shall not be one spot of love in't iii 2 445
Come every day to my cote and woo me.—Now, by the faith of my love, I will iii 2 449
For his verity in love, I do think him as concave as a covered goblet iii 4 25
Not true in love?—Yes, when he is in; but I think he is not in iii 4 28
You have oft inquired After the shepherd that complain'd of love iii 4 51
Between the pale complexion of true love And the red glow of scorn iii 4 56
The sight of lovers feedeth those in love iii 4 60
Say that you love me not, but say not so In bitterness iii 5 2
Then shall you know the wounds invisible That love's keen arrows make iii 5 31
Down on your knees, And thank heaven, fasting, for a good man's love iii 5 58
Cry the man mercy; love him; take his offer iii 5 61

Love. He's fallen in love with your foulness and she'll fall in love with my anger . . . . *As Y. Like It* iii 5 66
Do not fall in love with me, For I am falser than vows made in wine . iii 5 72
If you do sorrow at my grief in love, By giving love your sorrow and my grief Were both extermined . . . . iii 5 88
Thou hast my love: is not that neighbourly?—I would have you . iii 5 90
The time was that I hated thee, And yet it is not that I bear thee love; But since that thou canst talk of love so well, Thy company, which erst was irksome to me, I will endure . . . . iii 5 93
So holy and so perfect is my love, And I in such a poverty of grace . iii 5 99
Think not I love him, though I ask for him; 'Tis but a peevish boy . iii 5 109
There be some women, Silvius, had they mark'd him In parcels as I did, would have gone near To fall in love with him . . . . iii 5 126
For my part, I love him not nor hate him not; and yet I have more cause to hate him than to love him . . . . . iii 5 127
You are a melancholy fellow.—I am so; I do love it better than laughing iv 1 4
Be out of love with your nativity and almost chide God . . iv 1 35
Break an hour's promise in love! He that will divide a minute into a thousand parts and break but a part of the thousandth part of a minute in the affairs of love . . . . iv 1 44
He [Troilus] is one of the patterns of love . . . . . iv 1 100
Men have died from time to time and worms have eaten them, but not for love . . . . iv 1 108
Then love me, Rosalind.—Yes, faith, will I, Fridays and Saturdays and all iv 1 115
Rosalind, I will leave thee.—Alas! dear love, I cannot lack thee two hours . . . . iv 1 182
My pretty little coz, that thou didst know how many fathom deep I am in love! . . . . iv 1 211
Let him be judge how deep I am in love . . . . . . iv 1 220
With pure love and troubled brain, he hath ta'en his bow and arrows . iv 3 3
And that she could not love me, Were man as rare as phœnix . . iv 3 16
Her love is not the hare that I do hunt . . . . . . iv 3 18
Come, come, you are a fool And turn'd into the extremity of love . iv 3 23
If the scorn of your bright eyne Have power to raise such love in mine iv 3 51
Whiles you chid me, I did love; How then might your prayers move! iv 3 54
He that brings this love to thee Little knows this love in me . . iv 3 56
Or else by him my love deny, And then I'll study how to die . . iv 3 62
He deserves no pity. Wilt thou love such a woman? . . . iv 3 67
I see love hath made thee a tame snake . . . . . . iv 3 70
Say this to her: that if she love me, I charge her to love thee . iv 3 71
Committing me unto my brother's love . . . . . . iv 3 145
You do love this maid?—I do, sir.—Give me your hand . . . v 1 40
That but seeing you should love her? and loving woo? . . . v 2 3
I love Aliena; say with her that she loves me . . . . v 2 9
They are in the very wrath of love and they will together . . v 2 44
If you do love Rosalind so near the heart as your gesture cries it out . v 2 68
Look upon him, love him; he worships you . . . . . v 2 88
Tell this youth what 'tis to love.—It is to be all made of sighs and tears v 2 89
If this be so, why blame you me to love you? . . . . . v 2 110
I would love you, if I could . . . . v 2 121
As you love Rosalind, meet: as you love Phebe, meet: and as I love no woman, I'll meet . . . . v 2 128
When birds do sing, hey ding a ding, ding: Sweet lovers love the spring v 3 22
For love is crowned with the prime In spring time . . . . v 3 33
If sight and shape be true, Why then, my love adieu! . . . . v 4 127
You to his love must accord, Or have a woman to your lord . . . v 4 139
You to a love that your true faith doth merit: You to your land and love v 4 194
I charge you, O women, for the love you bear to men . . . . Epil. 13
I charge you, O men, for the love you bear to women . . . . Epil. 15
Tell him from me, as he will win my love, He bear himself with honourable action . . . . *T. of Shrew* Ind. 1 109
Command Wherein your lady and your humble wife May show her duty and make known her love . . . . Ind. 1 117
Dost thou love hawking? thou hast hawks will soar . . . . Ind. 2 45
Dost thou love pictures? we will fetch thee straight Adonis painted Ind. 2 51
By my father's love and leave am arm'd With his good will . . i 1 5
If either of you both love Katharina, Because I know you well and love you well, Leave shall you have to court her at your pleasure . . i 1 52
Let it not displease thee, good Bianca, For I will love thee ne'er the less . . . . i 1 77
Their love is not so great, Hortensio, but we may blow our nails together . . . . i 1 108
Yet, for the love I bear my sweet Bianca . . . . i 1 111
Have access to our fair mistress and be happy rivals in Bianca's love . i 1 120
Is it possible That love should of a sudden take such hold? . . i 1 152
If love have touch'd you, nought remains but so, 'Redime te captum quam queas minimo' . . . . i 1 166
If you love the maid, Bend thoughts and wits to achieve her . . i 1 183
Your love must live a maid at home . . . . i 1 187
I am content to be Lucentio, Because so well I love Lucentio.—Tranio, be so, because Lucentio loves . . . . i 1 222
Be she as foul as was Florentius' love, As old as Sibyl . . . i 2 69
Suitors to her and rivals in my love . . . . i 2 122
So I may, by this device, at least Have leave and leisure to make love to her . . . . i 2 136
Who goes there, ha?—Peace, Grumio! it is the rival of my love . . i 2 142
I'll have them very fairly bound: All books of love, see that at any hand . . . . i 2 147
'Tis now no time to vent our love: Listen to me . . . . . i 2 179
Not her that chides, sir, at any hand, I pray.—I love no chiders . i 2 228
For this reason, if you'll know, That she's the choice love of Signior Gremio . . . . i 2 236
And for your love to her lead apes in hell . . . . . . ii 1 34
If I get your daughter's love, What dowry shall I have with her to wife? ii 1 120
Ay, when the special thing is well obtain'd, That is, her love . . ii 1 130
It is a lusty wench; I love her ten times more than e'er I did . . ii 1 162
I tell you, 'tis incredible to believe How much she loves me . . . ii 1 309
So fast, protesting oath on oath, That in a twink she won me to her love . . . . ii 1 312
And I am one that love Bianca more Than words can witness . . ii 1 337
Youngling, thou canst not love so dear as I.—Greybeard, thy love doth freeze . . . . ii 1 339
And he of both That can assure my daughter greatest dower Shall have my Bianca's love . . . . ii 1 346
'Sigeia tellus,' disguised thus to get your love . . . . . iii 1 34
Now, for my life, the knave doth court my love . . . . . iii 1 49
'B mi,' Bianca, take him for thy lord, 'C fa ut,' that loves with all affection . . . . iii 1 76
Methinks he looks as though he were in love . . . . . . iii 1 88
But to her love concerneth us to add Her father's liking . . . iii 2 130

Love. But yet not stay, entreat me how you can.—Now, if you love me, stay . . . . *T. of Shrew* iii 2 205
Where is the rascal cook?—How durst you, villains, bring it from the dresser, And serve it thus to me that love it not? . . . . . iv 1 167
I read that I profess, the Art to Love.—And may you prove, sir, master of your art! . . . . iv 2 8
O despiteful love! unconstant womankind! . . . . . . iv 2 14
I will with you, if you be so contented, Forswear Bianca and her love for ever . . . . iv 2 26
Kindness in women, not their beauteous looks, Shall win my love . iv 2 42
Nay, I have ta'en you napping, gentle love . . . . . . iv 2 46
Take in your love, and then let me alone . . . . . . iv 2 71
He does it under name of perfect love . . . . iv 3 12
What say you to a piece of beef and mustard?—A dish that I do love . iv 3 24
Here, love; thou see'st how diligent I am To dress thy meat myself . iv 3 39
And now, my honey love, Will we return unto thy father's house . . iv 3 52
I love thee well, in that thou likest it not.—Love me or love me not, I like the cap; And it I will have . . . . iv 3 83
Made me acquainted with a weighty cause Of love . . . . . iv 4 27
For the love he beareth to your daughter And she to him . . . iv 4 29
Your son Lucentio here Doth love my daughter and she loveth him . iv 4 41
Love wrought these miracles . . . . v 1 127
Nay, I will give thee a kiss: now pray thee, love, stay . . . . v 1 153
Peace it bodes, and love and quiet life, And awful rule . . . . v 2 108
Craves no other tribute at thy hands But love, fair looks . . . v 2 153
When they are bound to serve, love and obey . . . . . . v 2 164
Love all, trust a few, Do wrong to none . . . . *All's Well* i 1 73
He cannot want the best That shall attend his love . . . . i 1 82
'Twere all one That I should love a bright particular star . . . i 1 97
The ambition in my love thus plagues itself . . . . . . i 1 101
The hind that would be mated by the lion Must die for love . . . i 1 103
I love him for his sake; And yet I know him a notorious liar . . i 1 110
There shall your master have a thousand loves . . . . . i 1 180
What power is it which mounts my love so high? . . . . . i 1 235
Who ever strove To show her merit, that did miss her love? . . . i 1 242
His love and wisdom, Approved so to your majesty, may plead . . i 2 9
He that cherishes my flesh and blood loves my flesh and blood; he that loves my flesh and blood is my friend . . . . i 3 51
I know, madam, you love your gentlewoman entirely . . . . i 3 103
And she herself, without other advantage, may lawfully make title to as much love as she finds . . . . i 3 107
Love no god, that would not extend his might, only where qualities were level . . . . i 3 117
It is the show and seal of nature's truth, Where love's strong passion is impress'd in youth . . . . i 3 139
Now to all sense 'tis gross You love my son . . . . . . i 3 179
Tell me truly.—Good madam, pardon me!—Do you love my son? . . i 3 192
Love you my son?—Do not you love him, madam?—Go not about; my love hath in't a bond, Whereof the world takes note . . . . i 3 193
I love your son. My friends were poor, but honest; so's my love . . i 3 200
I know I love in vain, strive against hope . . . . . . i 3 207
In this captious and intenible sieve I still pour in the waters of my love i 3 209
Let not your hate encounter with my love For loving where you do . i 3 214
Wish chastely and love dearly, that your Dian Was both herself and love i 3 219
Thou shalt have my leave and love, Means and attendants . . . i 3 257
Sir, I am a poor friend of yours, that loves you . . . . . ii 2 46
To each of you one fair and virtuous mistress Fall, when Love please! ii 3 64
Who shuns thy love shuns all his love in me . . . . . . ii 3 79
Now, Dian, from thy altar do I fly, And to imperial Love, that god most high, Do my sighs stream . . . . ii 3 81
Love make your fortunes twenty times above Her that so wishes and her humble love!—No better, if you please . . . . . . ii 3 88
My wish receive, Which great Love grant! . . . . ii 3 91
I cannot love her, nor will strive to do't . . . . . . ii 3 152
Unworthy this good gift; That dost in vile misprision shackle up My love . . . . ii 3 160
As thou lovest her, Thy love's to me religious . . . . . . ii 3 190
The great prerogative and rite of love, Which, as your due, time claims ii 4 42
I begin to love, as an old man loves money, with no stomach . . iii 2 17
Lay our best love and credence Upon thy promising fortune . . iii 3 2
Make me but like my thoughts, and I shall prove A lover of thy drum, hater of love . . . . iii 3 11
Ambitious love hath so in me offended, That barefoot plod I the cold ground upon, With sainted vow . . . . iii 4 5
Unless her prayers, whom heaven delights to hear And loves to grant . iii 4 28
She, Hearing so much, will speed her foot again, Led hither by pure love . . . . iii 4 38
For the love of laughter, hinder not the honour of his design . . iii 6 43
I love not many words.—No more than a fish loves water . . . iii 6 91
But, fair soul, In your fine frame hath love no quality? . . . iv 2 4
But I love thee By love's own sweet constraint . . . . . iv 2 15
If I should swear by God's great attributes, I loved you dearly, would you believe my oaths, When I did love you ill? . . . . . iv 2 27
This has no holding, To swear by him whom I protest to love, That I will work against him . . . . iv 2 28
Be not so holy-cruel: love is holy . . . . iv 2 32
Say thou art mine, and ever My love as it begins shall so persever . iv 2 37
I begin to love him for this.—For this description of thine honesty? . iv 3 293
A friend whose thoughts more truly labour To recompense your love . iv 4 18
If she had . . . cost me the dearest groans of a mother, I could not have owed her a more rooted love . . . . iv 5 13
That thou didst love her, strikes some scores away From the great compt: but love that comes too late, Like a remorseful pardon slowly carried, To the great sender turns a sour offence . . . . v 3 56
Our own love waking cries to see what's done . . . . . . v 3 65
Thou speak'st it falsely, as I love mine honour . . . . . v 3 113
Come, to the purpose: did he love this woman?—Faith, sir, he did love her . . . . v 3 242
He did love her, sir, as a gentleman loves a woman . . . . v 3 245
If she, my liege, can make me know this clearly, I'll love her dearly . v 3 317
If music be the food of love, play on; Give me excess of it . *T. Night* i 1 1
O spirit of love! how quick and fresh art thou . . . . . i 1 9
All this to season A brother's dead love . . . . i 1 31
O, she that hath a heart of that fine frame To pay this debt of love but to a brother, How will she love, when the rich golden shaft Hath kill'd the flock of all affections else That live in her! . . . . i 1 34
Then 'twas fresh in murmur,—as, you know, What great ones do the less will prattle of,—That he did seek the love of fair Olivia . . i 2 34
For whose dear love, They say, she hath abjured the company And sight of men . . . . i 2 39

Love. That you call in question the continuance of his love . *T. Night* i 4 7
Unfold the passion of my love, Surprise her with discourse of my dear faith . i 4 24
My lord and master loves you: O, such love Could be but recompensed, though you were crown'd The nonpareil of beauty! . i 5 271
How does he love me?—With adorations, fertile tears, With groans that thunder love, with sighs of fire . i 5 273
I cannot love him: Yet I suppose him virtuous, know him noble . i 5 276
But yet I cannot love him; He might have took his answer long ago . i 5 281
If I did love you in my master's flame, With such a suffering . i 5 283
Write loyal cantons of contemned love And sing them loud . i 5 289
Get you to your lord; I cannot love him: let him send no more . i 5 299
Love make his heart of flint that you shall love! . i 5 305
It were a bad recompense for your love, to lay any of them on you . ii 1 7
If you will not murder me for my love, let me be your servant . ii 1 36
She loves me, sure; the cunning of her passion Invites me in this . ii 2 23
Poor lady, she were better love a dream . ii 2 27
My master loves her dearly; And I, poor monster, fond as much on him ii 2 34
As I am man, My state is desperate for my master's love . ii 2 38
Your true love's coming, That can sing both high and low . ii 3 41
What is love? 'tis not hereafter; Present mirth hath present laughter . ii 3 48
Shall we do that?—An you love me, let's do't: I am dog at a catch . ii 3 63
For the love o' God, peace! . ii 3 92
It is his grounds of faith that all that look on him love him . ii 3 165
I will drop in his way some obscure epistles of love . ii 3 169
He shall think, by the letters that thou wilt drop, that they come from my niece, and that she's in love with him . ii 3 180
If ever thou shalt love, In the sweet pangs of it remember me . ii 4 15
It gives a very echo to the seat Where Love is throned . ii 4 22
Young though thou art, thine eye Hath stay'd upon some favour that it loves . ii 4 25
Let thy love be younger than thyself, Or thy affection cannot hold the bent . ii 4 37
And dallies with the innocence of love, Like the old age . ii 4 48
My love, more noble than the world, Prizes not quantity of dirty lands ii 4 84
But if she cannot love you, sir?—I cannot be so answer'd . ii 4 90
Say that some lady, as perhaps there is, Hath for your love as great a pang of heart As you have for Olivia: you cannot love her; You tell her so; must she not then be answer'd? . ii 4 93
There is no woman's sides Can bide the beating of so strong a passion As love doth give my heart . ii 4 98
Their love may be call'd appetite, No motion of the liver, but the palate ii 4 100
Make no compare Between that love a woman can bear me And that I owe . ii 4 105
What dost thou know?—Too well what love women to men may owe . ii 4 108
She never told her love, But let concealment, like a worm i' the bud, Feed on her damask cheek . ii 4 113
Was not this love indeed? We men may say more, swear more: but indeed Our shows are more than will; for still we prove Much in our vows, but little in our love . ii 4 118
But died thy sister of her love, my boy? . ii 4 122
Say, My love can give no place, bide no denay . ii 4 127
Observe him, for the love of mockery . ii 5 21
Jove knows I love: But who? Lips, do not move; No man must know ii 5 107
For every reason excites to this, that my lady loves me . ii 5 180
And in this she manifests herself to my love . ii 5 183
If thou entertainest my love, let it appear in thy smiling . ii 5 190
I pity you.—That's a degree to love.—No, not a grize . iii 1 134
A murderous guilt shows not itself more soon Than love that would seem hid: love's night is noon . iii 1 160
By maidhood, honour, truth and every thing, I love thee so, that, maugre all thy pride, Nor wit nor reason can my passion hide . iii 1 163
Love sought is good, but given unsought is better . iii 1 168
Thou perhaps mayst move That heart, which now abhors, to like his love . iii 1 176
This was a great argument of love in her toward you . iii 2 12
My desire, More sharp than filed steel, did spur me forth; And not all love to see you . iii 3 6
My willing love . . . Set forth in your pursuit . iii 3 11
Nothing but this; your true love for my master.—How with mine honour may I give him that Which I have given to you? . iii 4 233
For his love dares yet do more Than you have heard him brag to you . iii 4 347
Relieved him with such sanctity of love . iii 4 395
O, if it prove, Tempests are kind and salt waves fresh in love . iii 4 419
My lady is unkind, perdy.—Fool!—Alas, why is she so?—Fool, I say!—She loves another . iv 2 85
And did thereto add My love, without retention or restraint . v 1 84
For his sake Did I expose myself, pure for his love . v 1 86
Like to the Egyptian thief at point of death, Kill what I love . v 1 122
Your minion, whom I know you love . v 1 128
I'll sacrifice the lamb that I do love, To spite a raven's heart within a dove . v 1 133
After him I love More than I love these eyes, more than my life, More, by all mores, than e'er I shall love wife . v 1 137
If I do feign, you witnesses above Punish my life for tainting of my love! . v 1 141
Eternal bond of love, Confirm'd by mutual joinder of your hands . v 1 159
For the love of God, a surgeon! . v 1 175
For the love of God, your help! . v 1 180
Thou hast said to me a thousand times Thou never shouldst love woman like to me . v 1 275
Wherein our entertainment shall shame us we will be justified in our loves . *W. Tale* i 1 10
The heavens continue their loves! . i 1 35
Which to hinder Were in your love a whip to me . i 2 25
I love thee not a jar o' the clock behind What lady-she her lord . i 2 43
Ere I could make thee open thy white hand And clap thyself my love . i 2 104
The prince my son, Who I do think is mine and love as mine . i 2 331
As he had lost some province and a region Loved as he loves himself . i 2 370
You'll . . . speak to me as if I were a baby still. I love you better ii 1 6
With such a kind of love as might become A lady like me, with a love even such, So and no other, as yourself commanded . iii 2 65
Whose love had spoke, Even since it could speak, from an infant, freely That it was yours . iii 2 70
Sir, royal sir, forgive a foolish woman: The love I bore your queen . iii 2 229
The gods themselves, Humbling their deities to love, have taken The shapes of beasts upon them . iv 4 26
Like a bank for love to lie and play on; Not like a corse . iv 4 130
He says he loves my daughter: I think so too. . iv 4 171
I think there is not half a kiss to choose Who loves another best . iv 4 176

Love. I love a ballad but even too well, if it be doleful matter *W. Tale* iv 4 188
If I were not in love with Mopsa, thou shouldst take no money of me . iv 4 233
I love a ballad in print o' life, for then we are sure they are true . iv 4 263
Thou hast sworn my love to be.—Thou hast sworn it more to me . iv 4 312
When I was young And handed love as you do . iv 4 359
If your lass Interpretation should abuse and call this Your lack of love iv 4 365
I would not prize them Without her love; for her employ them all . iv 4 387
Save him from danger, do him love and honour . iv 4 521
You have heard of my poor services, i' the love That I have borne your father? . iv 4 527
I love the king And through him what is nearest to him . iv 4 532
Besides you know Prosperity's the very bond of love . iv 4 584
Grew so in love with the wenches' song, that he would not stir . iv 4 618
Women will love her, that she is a woman More worth than any man . v 1 110
Whom he loves—He bade me say so—more than all the sceptres . v 1 145
Though Fortune, visible an enemy, Should chase us with my father, power no jot Hath she to change our loves . v 1 218
And made whole With very easy arguments of love. . *K. John* i 1 36
Subjected tribute to commanding love . i 1 264
Welcome with a powerless hand, But with a heart full of unstained love ii 1 16
Lay I this zealous kiss, As seal to this indenture of my love . ii 1 20
To give him strength To make a more requital to your love . ii 1 34
England we love; and for that England's sake With burden of our armour here we sweat . ii 1 91
Yield thee to my hand; And out of my dear love I'll give thee more ii 1 157
If lusty love should go in quest of beauty, Where should he find it fairer? . ii 1 426
If zealous love should go in search of virtue, Where should he find it purer? . ii 1 428
If love ambitious sought a match of birth, Whose veins bound richer blood? . ii 1 430
If . . . thy princely son Can in this book of beauty read 'I love' . ii 1 485
That . . . there should be In such a love so vile a lout as he . ii 1 509
To speak more properly, I will enforce it easily to my love . ii 1 515
I will not flatter you, my lord, That all I see in you is worthy love . ii 1 517
Can you love this lady?—Nay, ask me if I can refrain from love; For I do love her most unfeignedly . ii 1 524
I then would be content, For then I should not love thee . iii 1 49
Deep-sworn faith, peace, amity, true love Between our kingdoms . iii 1 231
These hands, so lately purged of blood, So newly join'd in love . iii 1 240
All form is formless, order orderless, Save what is opposite to England's love . iii 1 254
Now shall I see thy love: what motive may Be stronger with thee than the name of wife? . iii 1 313
Cousin, look not sad: Thy grandam loves thee . iii 3 3
Counts thee her creditor And with advantage means to pay thy love . iii 3 22
Yet I love thee well; And, by my troth, I think thou lovest me well . iii 3 54
Hubert, I love thee; Well, I'll not say what I intend for thee . iii 3 67
Misery's love, O, come to me!—O fair affliction, peace! . iii 4 35
O, what love I note In the fair multitude of those her hairs! . iii 4 61
Like true, inseparable, faithful loves, Sticking together in calamity . iii 4 66
I would to heaven I were your son, so you would love me . iv 1 24
I warrant I love you more than you do me . iv 1 31
Where lies your grief? Or What good love may I perform for you? . iv 1 49
You may think my love was crafty love And call it cunning . iv 1 53
I have a way to win their loves again . iv 2 168
Whose private with me of the Dauphin's love Is much more general . iv 3 16
Swearing allegiance and the love of soul To stranger blood . v 1 10
On that altar where we swore to you Dear amity and everlasting love . v 4 20
The love of him, and this respect besides, . . . Awakes my conscience v 4 41
Beshrew my soul But I do love the favour and the form . v 4 50
The like tender of our love we make, To rest without a spot for evermore v 7 106
In the devotion of a subject's love . *Richard II.* i 1 31
Hath love in thy old blood no living fire? . i 2 10
You never shall . . . Embrace each other's love in banishment . i 3 184
Every tedious stride I make Will but remember me what a deal of world I wander from the jewels that I love . i 3 270
Love they to live that love and honour have . ii 1 138
He loves you, on my life, and holds you dear . ii 1 143
As Hereford's love, so his; As theirs, so mine; and all be as it is . ii 1 145
Our nearness to the king in love Is near the hate of those love not the king . ii 2 127
Their love Lies in their purses, and whoso empties them By so much fills their hearts with deadly hate . ii 2 129
As my fortune ripens with thy love, It shall be still thy true love's recompense . ii 3 48
I wot your love pursues A banish'd traitor: all my treasury Is yet but unfelt thanks, which more enrich'd Shall be your love and labour's recompense . ii 3 59
Near to the king in blood, and near in love . iii 1 17
A gentleman of mine I have dispatch'd With letters of your love to her iii 1 41
Sweet love, I see, changing his property, Turns to the sourest and most deadly hate . iii 2 135
Me rather had my heart might feel your love Than my unpleased eye see your courtesy . iii 3 192
So far be mine . . . As my true service shall deserve your love . iii 3 199
Nay, dry your eyes; Tears show their love, but want their remedies . iii 3 203
Little are we beholding to your love . iv 1 160
The love of wicked men converts to fear; That fear to hate . v 1 66
Must we part?—Ay, hand from hand, my love, and heart from heart . v 1 82
Send the king with me.—That were some love but little policy . v 1 84
Not like to me, or any of my kin, And yet I love him . v 2 110
Foolhardy king: Shall I for love speak treason to thy face? . v 3 44
Fear, and not love, begets his penitence . v 3 56
Love loving not itself none other can . v 3 88
For 'tis a sign of love; and love to Richard Is a strange brooch in this all-hating world . v 5 65
If thou love me, 'tis time thou wert away . v 5 96
They love not poison that do poison need, Nor do I thee: though I did wish him dead, I hate the murderer, love him murdered . v 6 38
Let not his report Come current for an accusation Betwixt my love and your high majesty . *1 Hen. IV.* i 3 69
His father loves him not And would be glad he met with some mischance . i 3 231
See already how he doth begin To make us stangers to his looks of love i 3 290
If the rascal have not given me medicines to make me love him . ii 2 20
Well contented to be there, in respect of the love I bear your house . ii 3 3
He shows in this, he loves his own barn better than he loves our house ii 3 5
Some heavy business hath my lord in hand, And I must know it, else he loves me not . ii 3 67

Love. What is it carries you away?—Why, my horse, my love, my horse 1 *Hen. IV.* ii 3 79
But if you go,— So far afoot, I shall be weary, love ii 3 87
Away, Away, you trifler! Love! I love thee not, I care not for thee . ii 3 93
Do you not love me? do you not, indeed? Well, do not then; for since you love me not, I will not love myself. Do you not love me? Nay, tell me if you speak in jest or no ii 3 99
When I am o' horseback, I will swear I love thee infinitely ii 3 105
If thou love me, practise an answer ii 4 411
But I will never be a truant, love, Till I have learn'd thy language iii 1 207
How doth thy husband! I love him well; he is an honest man iii 3 107
A million: thy love is worth a million: thou owest me thy love iii 3 156
Love thy husband, look to thy servants, cherish thy guests iii 3 193
But a braver place In my heart's love hath no man than yourself iv 1 8
Some of us love you well; and even those some Envy your great deservings iv 3 34
I would you would accept of grace and love.—And may be so we shall. iv 3 112
That even our love durst not come near your sight For fear of swallowing v 1 63
We love our people well; even those we love That are misled v 1 104
O, I should have a heavy miss of thee, If I were much in love with vanity! v 4 106
Did not we send grace, Pardon and terms of love to all of you? v 5 3
Sick of their own choice; Their over-greedy love hath surfeited 2 *Hen. IV.* i 3 88
These humble considerations make me out of love with my greatness ii 2 14
But, for all our loves, First let them try themselves ii 3 55
I do not love swaggering, by my troth ii 4 112
I' faith, I love thee: thou art as valorous as Hector of Troy ii 4 236
Why does the prince love him so, then?—Because their legs are both of a bigness, and a' plays at quoits well ii 4 264
I love thee better than I love e'er a scurvy young boy of them all. ii 4 295
I dispraised him before the wicked, that the wicked might not fall in love with him ii 4 347
Toil'd in my affairs And laid his love and life under my foot iii 1 63
All their prayers and love Were set on Hereford, whom they doted on. iv 1 137
Forced us to compel this offer; And it proceeds from policy, not love. iv 1 148
That, were our royal faiths martyrs in love, We shall be winnow'd iv 1 193
That all their eyes may bear those tokens home Of our restored love iv 2 65
But my love to ye Shall show itself more openly hereafter iv 2 75
This same young sober-blooded boy doth not love me iv 3 94
He loves thee, and thou dost neglect him iv 4 21
Blunt not his love, Nor lose the good advantage of his grace iv 4 27
I shall observe him with all care and love iv 4 49
Love, and filial tenderness, Shall, O dear father, pay thee plenteously iv 5 39
That thou mightst win the more thy father's love, Pleading so wisely iv 5 180
I think the young king loves you not.—I know he doth not v 2 9
Let me but bear you love, I'll bear your cares v 2 58
You are, I think, assured I love you not.—I am assured v 2 64
Alas, your too much love and care of me Are heavy orisons 'gainst this poor wretch! *Hen. V.* ii 2 52
You know how apt our love was to accord To furnish him ii 2 86
My love, give me thy lips. Look to my chattels and my movables ii 3 49
A man that I love and honour with my soul, and my heart, and my duty iii 6 7
Exeter doth love thee well.—Ay, I praise God; and I have merited some love at his hands iii 6 26
'Tis good for men to love their present pains Upon example iv 1 18
I kiss his dirty shoe, and from heart-string I love the lovely bully iv 1 48
I dare say you love him not so ill, to wish him here alone iv 1 129
With blood he seal'd A testament of noble-ending love iv 6 27
If thou encounter any such, apprehend him, an thou dost me love iv 7 166
You do not love it, nor your affections and your appetites and your digestions doo's not agree with it v 1 26
And that this day Shall change all griefs and quarrels into love v 2 20
My duty to you both, on equal love, Great Kings! v 2 23
If you will love me soundly with your French heart v 2 104
I know no ways to mince it in love, but directly to say 'I love you' v 2 130
Or if I might buffet for my love, or bound my horse for her favours v 2 146
If thou canst love a fellow of this temper, Kate v 2 152
That never looks in his glass for love of any thing he sees there v 2 155
If thou canst love me for this, take me; if not, to say to thee that I shall die, is true; but for thy love, by the Lord, no; yet I love thee too v 2 157
What sayest thou then to my love? speak, my fair, and fairly, I pray thee v 2 176
Is it possible dat I sould love de enemy of France?—No; it is not possible you should love the enemy of France, Kate: but, in loving me, you should love the friend of France; for I love France v 2 178
Canst thou love me?—I cannot tell.—Can any of your neighbours tell? v 2 206
You will to her dispraise those parts in me that you love with your heart v 2 213
Mock me mercifully; the rather, gentle princess, because I love thee cruelly v 2 215
By mine honour, in true English, I love thee, Kate v 2 237
I would have her learn, my fair cousin, how perfectly I love her v 2 310
I cannot so conjure up the spirit of love in her, that he will appear in his true likeness.— . . . If conjure up love in her in his true likeness, he must appear naked and blind v 2 316
Yet they do wink and yield, as love is blind and enforces v 2 327
You may, some of you, thank love for my blindness v 2 344
In love and dear alliance, Let that one article rank with the rest v 2 373
As man and wife, being two, are one in love v 2 389
I must not yield to any rites of love, For my profession's sacred 1 *Hen. VI.* i 2 113
Pluck a red rose from off this thorn with me.—I love no colours ii 4 34
In signal of my love to thee, . . Will I upon thy party wear this rose ii 4 121
I would prevail, if prayers might prevail, To join your hearts in love iii 1 68
If you love me, as you say you do, Let me persuade you to forbear awhile iii 1 104
I will yield to thee; Love for thy love and hand for hand I give iii 1 135
The presence of a king engenders love Amongst his subjects iii 1 181
Burns under feigned ashes of forged love And will at last break out iii 1 190
I charge you, as you love our favour, Quite to forget this quarrel iv 1 135
Both are my kinsmen, and I love them both iv 1 155
As we hither came in peace, So let us still continue peace and love iv 1 161
Even with the earth Shall lay your stately and air-braving towers, If you forsake the offer of their love iv 2 14
I owe him little duty, and less love iv 4 34
O, if you love my mother, Dishonour not her honourable name! iv 5 13

Love. How canst thou tell she will deny thy suit, Before thou make a trial of her love? 1 *Hen. VI.* v 3 76
If thou wilt condescend to be my— What?—His love.—I am unworthy v 3 121
A pure unspotted heart, Never yet taint with love v 3 183
My child is none of his: It was Alençon that enjoy'd my love v 4 73
Her virtues graced with external gifts Do breed love's settled passions v 5 4
Either to suffer shipwreck or arrive Where I may have fruition of her love v 5 9
Of virtuous chaste intents, To love and honour Henry as her lord v 5 21
So abject, base and poor, To choose for wealth and not for perfect love v 5 50
If with a lady of so high resolve As is fair Margaret he be link'd in love v 5 76
My tender youth was never yet attaint With any passion of inflaming love v 5 82
As did the youthful Paris once to Greece, With hope to find the like event in love, But prosper better v 5 105
I can express no kinder sign of love Than this kind kiss. 2 *Hen. VI.* i 1 18
In this beauteous face A world of earthly blessings to my soul, If sympathy of love unite our thoughts i 1 23
Lords, with one cheerful voice welcome my love i 1 36
So God help Warwick, as he loves the land, And common profit! i 1 205
I will take the Nevils' parts And make a show of love i 1 241
Surfeiting in joys of love, With his new bride i 1 251
If thou dost love thy lord, Banish the canker of ambitious thoughts i 2 17
You, that love to be protected Under the wings of our protector's grace i 3 40
When in the city Tours Thou ran'st a tilt in honour of my love i 3 54
His loves Are brazen images of canonized saints i 3 62
God in mercy so deal with my soul, As I in duty love my king and country! i 3 161
They know their master loves to be aloft ii 1 11
To tell my love unto his dumb deaf trunk iii 2 144
Mere instinct of love and loyalty iii 2 250
And you that love the commons, follow me. Now show yourselves men iv 2 192
I fear me, love, if that I had been dead, Thou wouldest not have mourn'd so much for me.—No, my love, I should not mourn, but die for thee iv 4 23
Who loves the king and will embrace his pardon, Fling up his cap iv 8 14
This day have you . . . show'd how well you love your prince iv 9 16
Command my eldest son, nay, all my sons, As pledges of my fealty and love v 1 50
A poor esquire of Kent, that loves his king v 1 75
Why dost thou pause?—With thy brave bearing should I be in love v 2 20
Nor he that loves himself Hath not essentially but by circumstance The name of valour v 2 38
Neither the king, nor he that loves him best, . . . Dares stir 3 *Hen. VI.* i 1 45
How love to me and to her son Hath made her break out into terms of rage! i 1 264
Trimm'd like a younker prancing to his love! ii 1 24
By your leave I speak it, You love the breeder better than the male ii 1 42
Blame me not: 'Tis love I bear thy glories makes me speak ii 1 158
Not that I fear to stay, but love to go Whither the queen intends ii 5 138
My love and fear glued many friends to thee ii 6 5
Thou didst love York, and I am son to York ii 6 73
From Scotland am I stol'n, even of pure love, To greet mine own land iii 1 13
Madam, do you love your children?—Ay, full as dearly as I love myself iii 2 36
Shall I not hear my task?—An easy task: 'tis but to love a king iii 2 53
'Tis the fruits of love I mean.—The fruits of love I mean iii 2 58
What love, think'st thou, I sue so much to get?—My love till death, my humble thanks, my prayers; That love which virtue begs and virtue grants iii 2 61
I did not mean such love.—Why, then you mean not as I thought you did iii 2 64
And she shall be my love, or else my queen iii 2 88
I swear to thee I speak no more than what my soul intends; And that is, to enjoy thee for my love iii 2 95
Why, love forswore me in my mother's womb iii 2 153
Henry, sole possessor of my love, Is of a king become a banish'd man iii 3 24
I come, in kindness and unfeigned love, First, to do greetings iii 3 51
His demand Springs not from Edward's well-meant honest love iii 3 67
All dissembling set aside, Tell me for truth the measure of his love iii 3 120
His love was an eternal plant, Whereof the root was fix'd in virtue's ground iii 3 124
Till, with my talk and tears, Both full of truth, I make King Lewis behold Thy sly conveyance and thy lord's false love iii 3 160
This proveth Edward's love and Warwick's honesty iii 3 180
These words have turn'd my hate to love; And I forgive and quite forget iii 3 199
My love, forbear to fawn upon their frowns iv 1 75
Nay, whom they shall obey, and love thee too iv 1 79
You that love me and Warwick, follow me iv 1 123
I Stay not for the love of Edward, but the crown iv 1 126
Tell me if you love Warwick more than me? If it be so, then both depart iv 1 137
I hold it cowardice To rest mistrustful where a noble heart Hath pawn'd an open hand in sign of love iv 2 9
I the rather wean me from despair For love of Edward's offspring iv 4 18
Then why should they love Edward more than me? iv 8 47
An upright zeal to right prevails More than the nature of a brother's love v 1 79
To hell; and say I sent thee thither: I, that have neither pity, love, nor fear v 6 68
This word 'love,' which greybeards call divine, Be resident in men like one another And not in me: I am myself alone v 6 81
Clarence and Gloucester, love my lovely queen v 7 26
That I love the tree . . . , Witness the loving kiss I give the fruit v 7 31
Now am I seated as my soul delights, Having my country's peace and brothers' loves v 7 36
I do love thee so, That I will shortly send thy soul to heaven *Richard III.* i 1 118
Not all so much for love As for another secret close intent i 1 157
He lives that loves thee better than he could i 2 141
That hand, which, for thy love, did kill thy love, Shall, for thy love, kill a far truer love i 2 191
I'll turn yon fellow in his grave; And then return lamenting to my love i 2 262
A man that loves not me, nor none of you i 3 13
Notwithstanding she's your wife, And loves not me i 3 23
Who are they that complain unto the king, That I, forsooth, am stern and love them not? By holy Paul, they love his grace but lightly i 3 44
My brother's love, the devil, and my rage.—Thy brother's love, our duty, and thy fault, Provoke us hither now to slaughter thee i 4 229
Oh, if you love my brother, hate not me; I am his brother, and I love him i 4 232
Gloucester hates you.—O, no, he loves me, and he holds me dear i 4 239
And charged us from his soul to love each other i 4 243
Take each other's hand; Dissemble not your hatred, swear your love ii 1 8
And with my hand I seal my true heart's love ii 1 10
So prosper I, as I swear perfect love!—And I, as I love Hastings! ii 1 16
Wife, love Lord Hastings, let him kiss your hand ii 1 21
This interchange of love, I here protest, Upon my part shall be unviolable ii 1 26

Love. But with all duteous love Doth cherish you and yours *Richard III.* ii 1 33
God punish me With hate in those where I expect most love! ii 1 35
We have done deeds of charity; Made peace of enmity, fair love of hate ii 1 50
'Tis death to me to be at enmity; I hate it, and desire all good men's love ii 1 61
Have I offer'd love for this, To be so flouted in this royal presence? ii 1 77
Who spake of brotherhood? who spake of love? ii 1 108
Peace, children, peace! the king doth love you well ii 2 17
Bade me rely on him as on my father, And he would love me dearly ii 2 26
Put meekness in thy mind, Love, charity, obedience, and true duty! ii 2 108
Now cheer each other in each other's love ii 2 114
He for his father's sake so loves the prince, That he will not be won iii 1 165
You and he are near in love.—I thank his grace, I know he loves me well iii 4 14
His lordship knows me well, and loves me well iii 4 31
There's never a man in Christendom That can less hide his love or hate iii 4 54
The tender love I bear your grace, my lord, Makes me most forward iii 4 65
The rest, that love me, rise and follow me iii 4 81
I bid them that did love their country's good Cry 'God save Richard!' iii 7 21
This general applause and loving shout Argues your wisdoms and your love iii 7 40
By heaven, I come in perfect love to him iii 7 90
This suit of yours, So season'd with your faithful love to me iii 7 149
Definitively thus I answer you. Your love deserves my thanks iii 7 154
Refuse not, mighty lord, this proffer'd love iii 7 202
If you refuse it,—as, in love and zeal, Loath to depose the child iii 7 208
On pure heart's love to greet the tender princes iv 1 4
Hath he set bounds betwixt their love and me? I am their mother iv 1 21
Their aunt I am in law, in love their mother: Then bring me to their sights iv 1 24
Say it is done, And I will love thee, and prefer thee too iv 2 82
Then know, that from my soul I love thy daughter iv 4 255
That thou dost love my daughter from thy soul: So from thy soul's love didst thou love her brothers; And from my heart's love I do thank thee for it iv 4 258
I mean, that with my soul I love thy daughter, And mean to make her queen iv 4 262
If this inducement force her not to love, Send her a story of thy noble acts iv 4 279
Say that I did all this for love of her.—Nay, then indeed she cannot choose but hate thee, Having bought love with such a bloody spoil iv 4 288
A grandam's name is little less in love Than is the doting title of a mother iv 4 299
Under what title shall I woo for thee, That God, the law, my honour and her love, Can make seem pleasing to her tender years? iv 4 341
I will love her everlastingly.—But how long shall that title 'ever' last? iv 4 349
Say, I, her sovereign, am her subject love iv 4 355
With pure heart's love, Immaculate devotion, holy thoughts iv 4 403
Good mother,—I must call you so—Be the attorney of my love to her iv 4 413
The fearful time Cuts off the ceremonious vows of love v 3 98
God give us leisure for these rites of love! v 3 101
Richard loves Richard; that is, I am I. Is there a murderer here? No. Yes, I am: Then fly. What, from myself? Great reason why: Lest I revenge. What, myself upon myself? Alack, I love myself v 3 183
There is no creature loves me; And if I die, no soul shall pity me v 3 200
That you would love yourself, and in that love Not unconsider'd leave your honour, nor The dignity of your office *Hen. VIII.* i 2 14
Bid him strive To gain the love o' the commonalty i 2 170
Was he mad, sir?—O, very mad, exceeding mad, in love too i 4 28
To whom, If I but knew him, with my love and duty I would surrender it i 4 80
All the commons Hate him perniciously, and, o' my conscience, Wish him ten fathom deep: this duke as much They love and dote on ii 1 52
Where you are liberal of your loves and counsels Be sure you be not loose ii 1 126
Loves him with that excellence That angels love good men with ii 2 34
I love him not, nor fear him; there's my creed ii 2 51
I bid him welcome, And thank the holy conclave for their loves ii 2 100
Your grace must needs deserve all strangers' loves, You are so noble ii 2 102
Which of your friends Have I not strove to love? ii 4 30
Against mine honour aught, My bond to wedlock, or my love and duty ii 4 40
Out with it boldly: truth loves open dealing iii 1 39
Madam, you wrong the king's love with these fears iii 1 81
Alas, has banish'd me his bed already, His love, too long ago! iii 1 120
The hearts of princes kiss obedience, So much they love it iii 1 163
The king loves you; Beware you lose it not iii 1 171
As my hand has open'd bounty to you, My heart dropp'd love iii 2 185
Dare mate a sounder man than Surrey can be, And all that love his follies iii 2 275
Love thyself last: cherish those hearts that hate thee iii 2 443
I have commended to his goodness The model of our chaste loves iv 2 132
And a little To love her for her mother's sake, that loved him iv 2 137
By that you love the dearest in this world iv 2 155
I love you; And durst commend a secret to your ear Much weightier v 1 16
Love and meekness, lord, Become a churchman better than ambition v 3 62
If a prince May be beholding to a subject, I Am, for his love and service v 3 158
I charge you, Embrace and love this man v 3 172
Peace, plenty, love, truth, terror, That were the servants to this chosen infant v 5 48
I tell thee I am mad In Cressid's love: thou answer'st 'she is fair' *Troi. and Cres.* i 1 52
This thou tell'st me, As true thou tell'st me, when I say I love her i 1 60
Thou lay'st in every gash that love hath given me The knife that made it i 1 62
Tell me, Apollo, for thy Daphne's love, What Cressid is, what Pandar? i 1 101
I swear to you, I think Helen loves him better than Paris i 2 116
But to prove to you that Helen loves him: she came and puts me her white hand to his cloven chin i 2 130
If you love an addle egg as well as you love an idle head, you would eat chickens i' the shell i 2 146
Words, vows, gifts, tears, and love's full sacrifice, He offers i 2 308
That she was never yet that ever knew Love got so sweet as when desire did sue. Therefore this maxim out of love I teach: Achievement is command; ungain'd, beseech i 2 317
Then though my heart's content firm love doth bear, Nothing of that shall from mine eyes appear i 2 320
The fineness of which metal is not found In fortune's love i 3 23
That loves his mistress more than in confession, With truant vows to her own lips he loves i 3 269
To rouse a Grecian that is true in love i 3 279
But we are soldiers; And may that soldier a mere recreant prove, That means not, hath not, or is not in love! i 3 288
If there be not in our Grecian host One noble man that hath one spark of fire, To answer for his love i 3 295
I do hate a proud man, as I hate the engendering of toads.—Yet he loves himself ii 3 171
At whose pleasure, friend?—At mine, sir, and theirs that love music iii 1 26
The mortal Venus, the heart-blood of beauty, love's invisible soul iii 1 35
Love. My niece is horribly in love with a thing you have, sweet queen *Troi. and Cres.* iii 1 106
Let thy song be love: this love will undo us all. O Cupid, Cupid, Cupid! iii 1 110
Love! ay, that it shall, i' faith.—Ay, good now, love, love, nothing but love iii 1 121
Love, love, nothing but love, still more! For, O, love's bow Shoots buck and doe iii 1 125
Yet that which seems the wound to kill, Doth turn oh! oh! to ha! ha! he! So dying love lives still iii 1 134
In love, i' faith, to the very tip of the nose iii 1 138
He eats nothing but doves, love, and that breeds hot blood iii 1 140
Hot thoughts beget hot deeds, and hot deeds is love.—Is this the generation of love? hot blood, hot thoughts, and hot deeds? Why, they are vipers: is love a generation of vipers? iii 1 143
Sweet, above thought I love thee iii 1 172
Love's thrice repured nectar iii 2 23
What too curious dreg espies my sweet lady in the fountain of our love? iii 2 71
This is the monstruosity in love, lady, that the will is infinite and the execution confined, that the desire is boundless and the act a slave iii 2 88
I love you now; but not, till now, so much But I might master it iii 2 128
Perchance, my lord, I show more craft than love iii 2 160
But you are wise, Or else you love not, for to be wise and love Exceeds man's might; that dwells with gods above iii 2 163
O that I thought it could be in a woman ... To feed for aye her lamp and flames of love; To keep her constancy! iii 2 167
Be affronted with the match and weight Of such a winnow'd purity in love iii 2 174
True swains in love shall in the world to come Approve their truths by Troilus iii 2 180
Let memory, From false to false, among false maids in love, Upraid my falsehood! iii 2 197
That, through the sight I bear in things to love, I have abandon'd Troy iii 3 4
Being slippery standers, The love that lean'd on them as slippery too iii 3 85
Love, friendship, charity, are subjects all To envious and culumniating time iii 3 173
'Tis known, Achilles, that you are in love With one of Priam's daughters iii 3 193
They think my little stomach to the war And your great love to me restrains you iii 3 221
By Venus' hand I swear, No man alive can love in such a sort The thing he means to kill more excellently iv 1 23
This is the most despiteful gentle greeting, The noblest hateful love iv 1 33
Flies the grasps of love With wings more momentary-swift than thought iv 2 13
No kin, no love, no blood, no soul so near me As the sweet Troilus iv 2 104
The strong base and building of my love Is as the very centre of the earth iv 2 109
I know what 'tis to love; And would, as I shall pity, I could help! iv 3 10
My love admits no qualifying dross iv 4 9
I love thee in so strain'd a purity iv 4 26
Hear me, my love: be thou but true of heart,— I true! how now! iv 4 60
But yet be true.—O heavens! 'be true' again!—Hear why I speak it, love iv 4 77
O heavens! you love me not.—Die I a villain, then! iv 4 84
This Ajax is half made of Hector's blood: In love whereof, half Hector stays at home iv 5 84
He in heat of action Is more vindicative than jealous love iv 5 107
But still sweet love is food for fortune's tooth iv 5 293
A letter from Queen Hecuba, A token from her daughter, my fair love v 1 45
An honest fellow enough, and one that loves quails v 1 57
The fractions of her faith, orts of her love, The fragments, scraps v 2 158
As much as I do Cressid love, So much by weight hate I her Diomed v 2 167
For the love of all the gods, Let's leave the hermit pity with our mothers v 3 44
I am offended with you: Upon the love you bear me, get you in v 3 78
My love with words and errors still she feeds; But edifies another with her deeds v 3 111
I love bastards: I am a bastard begot, bastard instructed, bastard in mind v 7 16
If the wars eat us not up, they will; and there's all the love they bear us *Coriolanus* i 1 88
I should freelier rejoice in that absence wherein he won honour than in the embracements of his bed where he would show most love i 3 6
Had I a dozen sons, each in my love alike and none less dear than thine i 3 25
I cannot go thither.—Why, I pray you?—'Tis not to save labour, nor that I want love i 3 91
Now the fair goddess, Fortune, Fall deep in love with thee! i 5 22
If any such be here—As it were sin to doubt—that love this painting i 6 68
Pray you, who does the wolf love?—The lamb.—Ay, to devour him ii 1 8
One that loves a cup of hot wine with not a drop of allaying Tiber in't ii 1 52
My boy Marcius approaches; for the love of Juno, let's go ii 1 111
He's vengeance proud, and loves not the common people ii 2 6
If they love they know not why, they hate upon no better a ground ii 2 12
Therefore, for Coriolanus neither to care whether they love or hate him manifests the true knowledge he has in their disposition ii 2 14
He did not care whether he had their love or no ii 2 19
To seem to affect the malice and displeasure of the people is as bad as that which he dislikes, to flatter them for their love ii 2 26
He loves your people; But tie him not to be their bedfellow ii 2 68
But your people, I love them as they weigh ii 2 78
Account me the more virtuous that I have not been common in my love ii 3 101
We pray the gods he may deserve your loves ii 3 165
Translate his malice towards you into love, Standing your friendly lord ii 3 197
He did solicit you in free contempt When he did need your loves ii 3 209
Your loves, Thinking upon his services, took from you The apprehension ii 3 230
That love the fundamental part of state More than you doubt the change on't iii 1 151
When he did love his country, It honour'd him iii 1 305
And you will rather show our general louts How you can frown than spend a fawn upon 'em, For the inheritance of their loves iii 2 68
Hast not the soft way which, thou dost confess, Were fit for thee to use as they to claim, In asking their good loves iii 2 84
I'll mountebank their loves, Cog their hearts from them iii 2 132
Plant love among's! Throng our large temples with the shows of peace! iii 3 35
I do love My country's good with a respect more tender, More holy and profound, than mine own life iii 3 111
Whose loves I prize As the dead carcasses of unburied men iii 3 121
The hoarded plague o' the gods Requite your love! iv 2 12
Who twin, as 'twere, in love Unseparable iv 4 15
My birth-place hate I, and my love's upon This enemy town iv 4 23
And do contest As hotly and as nobly with thy love As ever in ambitious strength I did Contend against thy valour iv 5 117
The nobility of Rome are his: The senators and patricians love him too iv 7 30
What should I do?—Only make trial what your love can do For Rome v 1 40
And love thee no worse than thy old father Menenius does! v 2 75

Love. For whose old love I have, Though I show'd sourly to him, once more offer'd The first conditions . . . *Coriolanus* v 3 12
No more infected with my country's love Than when I parted hence . v 6 72
So I love and honour thee and thine, Thy noble brother . *T. Andron.* i 1 49
And to the love and favour of my country Commit myself, my person . i 1 58
These that survive let Rome reward with love . . . . . i 1 82
But not to be his wife, That is another's lawful promised love . . i 1 298
My true-betrothed love and now my wife . . . . . i 1 406
My sword upon thee shall approve, And plead my passions for Lavinia's love . . . . ii 1 36
Is Lavinia then become so loose, Or Bassianus so degenerate, That for her love such quarrels may be broach'd? . . . . ii 1 67
I love Lavinia more than all the world . . . . . ii 1 72
Know ye not, in Rome How furious and impatient they be, And cannot brook competitors in love? . . . . ii 1 77
A thousand deaths Would I propose to achieve her whom I love . ii 1 80
Let us hence, And let her joy her raven-colour'd love . . ii 3 83
Revenge it, as you love your mother's life . . . . ii 3 114
And might not gain so great a happiness As have thy love . ii 4 21
If thou love thy sons, Let Marcus, Lucius, or thyself, old Titus, Or any one of you, chop off your hand . . . . . . iii 1 151
Now let me show a brother's love to thee . . . . . iii 1 183
If you love me, as I think you do, Let's kiss and part . . iii 1 287
She loves thee, boy, too well to do thee harm . . . . iv 1 6
I know my noble aunt Loves me as dear as e'er my mother did . iv 1 23
For love of her that's gone, Perhaps she cull'd it from among the rest . iv 1 43
A charitable wish and full of love . . . . . . iv 2 43
'Tis he the common people love so much . . . . . iv 4 73
This do thou for my love; and so let him, As he regards his aged father's life . . . . v 2 129
Ordain'd to an honourable end, For peace, for love, for league . v 3 23
The fearful passage of their death-mark'd love . . *Rom. and Jul.* Prol. 9
In love?—Out— Of love?—Out of her favour, where I am in love . i 1 171
Alas, that love, so gentle in his view, Should be so tyrannous and rough in proof!—Alas, that love, whose view is muffled still, Should, without eyes, see pathways to his will! . . . . . . i 1 175
Here's much to do with hate, but more with love . . . i 1 180
O brawling love! O loving hate! O any thing, of nothing first create! . i 1 182
This love feel I, that feel no love in this . . . . i 1 188
This love that thou hast shown Doth add more grief to too much of mine own . . . . i 1 194
Love is a smoke raised with the fume of sighs . . . . i 1 196
Tell me in sadness, who is that you love.—What, shall I groan and tell thee? . . . . i 1 205
I do love a woman.—I aim'd so near, when I supposed you loved . i 1 210
And she's fair I love.—A right fair mark, fair coz, is soonest hit . i 1 212
From love's weak childish bow she lives unharm'd . . . i 1 217
She hath forsworn to love, and in that vow Do I live dead . . i 1 229
Whereto I have invited many a guest, Such as I love . . i 2 22
One fairer than my love! the all-seeing sun Ne'er saw her match . i 2 97
Let there be weigh'd Your lady's love against some other maid . i 2 102
Thus then in brief: The valiant Paris seeks you for his love . i 3 74
Can you love the gentleman? This night you shall behold him at our feast . . . . i 3 79
This precious book of love, this unbound lover, To beautify him, only lacks a cover . . . . i 3 87
Can you like of Paris' love?—I'll look to like, if looking liking move . i 3 96
Under love's heavy burden do I sink.—And, to sink in it, should you burden love . . . . i 4 22
Is love a tender thing? it is too rough, Too rude, too boisterous . i 4 25
If love be rough with you, be rough with love; Prick love for pricking, and you beat love down . . . . i 4 27
We'll draw thee from the mire Of this sir-reverence love, wherein thou stick'st Up to the ears . . . . i 4 42
She gallops night by night Through lovers' brains, and then they dream of love . . . . i 4 71
Did my heart love till now? forswear it, sight! For I ne'er saw true beauty till this night . . . . i 5 54
My only love sprung from my only hate! Too early seen unknown! . i 5 140
Prodigious birth of love it is to me, That I must love a loathed enemy . i 5 142
That fair for which love groan'd for and would die, With tender Juliet match'd, is now not fair . . . . ii Prol. 3
Romeo is beloved and loves again, Alike bewitched by the charm of looks . . . . ii Prol. 5
And she steal love's sweet bait from fearful hooks . . ii Prol. 8
And she as much in love, her means much less To meet her new-beloved . . . . ii Prol. 11
Cry but 'Ay me!' pronounce but 'love' and 'dove' . . ii 1 10
Blind is his love and best befits the dark.—If love be blind, love cannot hit the mark . . . . ii 1 32
O, it is my love! O, that she knew she were! . . . . ii 2 10
Be but sworn my love, And I'll no longer be a Capulet . . ii 2 35
Call me but love, and I'll be new baptized . . . . ii 2 50
With love's light wings did I o'er-perch these walls; For stony limits cannot hold love out, And what love can do that dares love attempt ii 2 66
And but thou love me, let them find me here: My life were better ended by their hate, Than death prorogued, wanting of thy love . . ii 2 76
Love, who first did prompt me to inquire; He lent me counsel . ii 2 80
But farewell compliment! Dost thou love me? I know thou wilt say 'Ay' . . . . ii 2 90
O gentle Romeo, If thou dost love, pronounce it faithfully . . ii 2 94
Pardon me, And not impute this yielding to light love . . ii 2 105
O, swear not by the moon, the inconstant moon, That monthly changes in her circled orb, Lest that thy love prove likewise variable . ii 2 111
If my heart's dear love.—Well, do not swear: although I joy in thee . ii 2 115
This bud of love, by summer's ripening breath, May prove a beauteous flower . . . . ii 2 121
What satisfaction canst thou have to-night?—The exchange of thy love's faithful vow for mine . . . . ii 2 127
Wouldst thou withdraw it? for what purpose, love?—But to be frank . ii 2 130
My bounty is as boundless as the sea, My love as deep . . ii 2 134
I hear some noise within; dear love, adieu! Anon, good nurse! . ii 2 136
If that thy bent of love be honourable, Thy purpose marriage . ii 2 143
Love goes toward love, as schoolboys from their books, But love from love, toward school with heavy looks . . . . . . ii 2 157
I shall forget, to have thee still stand there, Remembering how I love thy company.—And I'll still stay . . . . . . ii 2 174
My heart's dear love is set On the fair daughter of rich Capulet . ii 3 57
Is Rosaline, whom thou didst love so dear, So soon forsaken? young men's love then lies Not truly in their hearts, but in their eyes . ii 3 66
Love. How much salt water thrown away in waste, To season love! *Rom. and Jul.* ii 3 72
Bad'st me bury love.—Not in a grave, To lay one in, another out to have ii 3 83
Chide not: she whom I love now Doth grace for grace and love for love allow . . . . ii 3 85
O, she knew well Thy love did read by rote and could not spell . ii 3 88
May so happy prove, To turn your households' rancour to pure love . ii 3 92
She had a better love to be-rhyme her . . . . . . ii 4 43
Why, is not this better now than groaning for love? . . . ii 4 93
This drivelling love is like a great natural, that runs lolling up and down ii 4 95
A gentleman, nurse, that loves to hear himself talk . . . ii 4 155
Therefore do nimble-pinion'd doves draw love . . . . ii 5 7
My words would bandy her to my sweet love, And his to me . . ii 5 14
What says my love?—Your love says, like an honest gentleman . ii 5 55
To fetch a ladder, by the which your love Must climb a bird's nest soon ii 5 75
Love moderately; long love doth so; Too swift arrives as tardy as too slow . . . . ii 6 14
My true love is grown to such excess I cannot sum up sum of half my wealth . . . . ii 6 33
The reason that I have to love thee Doth much excuse the appertaining rage . . . . iii 1 65
I never injured thee, But love thee better than thou canst devise, Till thou shalt know the reason of my love . . . . . iii 1 72
If love be blind, It best agrees with night. Come, civil night . iii 2 9
Till strange love, grown bold, Think true love acted simple modesty . iii 2 15
That all the world will be in love with night . . . . iii 2 24
O, I have bought the mansion of a love, But not possess'd it . . iii 2 26
Thou canst not speak of that thou dost not feel: Wert thou as young as I, Juliet thy love, An hour but married, Tybalt murdered, Doting like me and like me banished, Then mightst thou speak . . iii 3 65
How doth she? and what says My conceal'd lady to our cancell'd love? iii 3 98
Thou shamest thy shape, thy love, thy wit; . . . And usest none in that true use indeed Which should bedeck thy shape, thy love, thy wit iii 3 122
Thy dear love sworn but hollow perjury, Killing that love which thou hast vow'd to cherish . . . . iii 3 128
Thy wit, that ornament to shape and love . . . . . iii 3 130
Thou pout'st upon thy fortune and thy love: Take heed, take heed iii 3 144
Go, get thee to thy love, as was decreed, Ascend her chamber . iii 3 146
I will make a desperate tender Of my child's love: I think she will be ruled . . . . iii 4 13
Go you to her ere you go to bed; Acquaint her here of my son Paris' love . . . . iii 4 16
Believe me, love, it was the nightingale.—It was the lark . . iii 5 5
Look, love, what envious streaks Do lace the severing clouds in yonder east . . . . iii 5 7
Art thou gone so? love, lord, ay, husband, friend! . . . . iii 5 43
I will omit no opportunity That may convey my greetings, love, to thee iii 5 50
Thou look'st pale.—And trust me, love, in my eye so do you . . iii 5 58
Some grief shows much of love; But much of grief shows still some want of wit . . . . iii 5 73
To wreak the love I bore my cousin Upon his body . . . . iii 5 102
But thankful even for hate, that is meant love . . . . iii 5 149
To answer 'I'll not wed; I cannot love, I am too young' . . iii 5 187
I little talk'd of love; For Venus smiles not in a house of tears . iv 1 7
That may be, sir, when I may be a wife.—That may be must be, love . iv 1 20
Do not deny to him that you love me.—I will confess to you that I love him.—So will ye, I am sure, that you love me . . . . iv 1 24
Without fear or doubt, To live an unstain'd wife to my sweet love . iv 1 88
Love give me strength! and strength shall help afford . . iv 1 125
Gave him what becomed love I might, Not stepping o'er the bounds of modesty . . . . iv 2 26
Why, love, I say! madam! sweet-heart! why, bride! What, not a word? iv 5 3
O love! O life! not life, but love in death! . . . . iv 5 58
O, in this love, you love your child so ill, That you run mad, seeing that she is well . . . . iv 5 75
How sweet is love itself possess'd, When but love's shadows are so rich! v 1 10
That banish'd haughty Montague, That murder'd my love's cousin . v 3 50
I love thee better than myself; For I come hither arm'd against myself v 3 64
O my love! my wife! Death, that hath suck'd the honey of thy breath, Hath had no power yet upon thy beauty . . . . . v 3 91
Here's to my love! O true apothecary! Thy drugs are quick . . v 3 119
And there's my master, One that you love . . . . . v 3 129
What's here? a cup, closed in my true love's hand? . . . v 3 161
This letter doth make good the friar's words, Their course of love . v 3 287
See, what a scourge is laid upon your hate, That heaven finds means to kill your joys with love . . . . v 3 293
Properties to his love and tendance All sorts of hearts . *T. of Athens* i 1 57
That few things loves better Than to abhor himself . . . i 1 59
This man of thine Attempts her love: I prithee, noble lord, Join with me to forbid him her resort . . . . i 1 126
Does she love him?—She is young and apt . . . . . i 1 131
Love you the maid?—Ay, my good lord, and she accepts of it . i 1 134
He that loves to be flattered is worthy o' the flatterer . . i 1 232
Small love 'mongst these sweet knaves, And all this courtesy! . . i 1 258
You mistake my love: I gave it freely ever . . . . . i 2 9
Out of his free love, hath presented to you Four milk-white horses . i 2 188
A trifle of our love.—With more than common thanks I will receive it . i 2 213
I love and honour him, But must not break my back to heal his finger ii 1 23
Secure thy heart; If I would broach the vessels of my love, And try the argument of hearts by borrowing . . . . ii 2 186
Commend me to their loves, and, I am proud, say, that my occasions have found time to use 'em . . . . ii 2 199
The best half should have return'd to him, So much I love his heart . iii 2 92
It shows but little love or judgement in him: Must I be his last refuge? iii 3 10
Of such a nature is his politic love . . . . . . iii 3 35
And, for I know your reverend ages love Security, I'll pawn my victories iii 5 80
I do wish thou wert a dog, That I might love thee something . iv 3 55
They love thee not that use thee; Give them diseases . . iv 3 83
I love thee better now than e'er I did.—I hate thee worse . . iv 3 233
I am sick of this false world, and will love nought But even the mere necessities upon't . . . . iv 3 376
Live, and love thy misery.—Long live so, and so die . . iv 3 396
Love not yourselves: away, Rob one another . . . . iv 3 447
How rarely does it meet with this time's guise, When man was wish'd to love his enemies! Grant I may ever love, and rather woo Those that would mischief me than those that do! . . . . . iv 3 474
I love thee, Because thou art a woman, and disclaim'st Flinty mankind iv 3 489
That which I show, heaven knows, is merely love, Duty and zeal . iv 3 522
Tis not amiss we tender our loves to him, in this supposed distress of his . . . . v 1 14

Love. See him dissemble, Know his gross patchery, love him, feed him *T. of Athens* v 1 99
Look you, I love you well; I'll give you gold v 1 103
The senators with one consent of love Entreat thee back to Athens v 1 143
Even such heaps and sums of love and wealth As shall to thee blot out what wrongs were theirs And write in thee the figures of their love v 1 155
I do prize it at my love before The reverend'st throat in Athens v 1 184
I love my country, and am not One that rejoices in the common wreck v 1 194
Their fears of hostile strokes, their aches, losses, Their pangs of love v 1 203
Our old love made a particular force, And made us speak like friends v 2 8
To wipe out our ingratitude with loves Above their quantity v 4 17
So did we woo Transformed Timon to our city's love By humble message v 4 19
I do observe you now of late: I have not from your eyes that gentleness And show of love as I was wont to have *J. Cæsar* i 2 34
You bear too stubborn and too strange a hand Over your friend that loves you i 2 36
Poor Brutus, with himself at war, Forgets the shows of love to other men i 2 47
Or did use To stale with ordinary oaths my love To every new protester i 2 73
I think you would not have it so.—I would not, Cassius, yet I love him i 2 82
I love The name of honour more than I fear death i 2 88
That you do love me, I am nothing jealous i 2 162
I would not, so with love I might entreat you, Be any further moved i 2 166
He loves no plays, As thou dost, Antony; he hears no music i 2 203
Cæsar doth bear me hard; but he loves Brutus i 2 317
Yet I fear him; For in the ingrafted love he bears to Cæsar ii 1 184
If he love Cæsar, all that he can do Is to himself ii 1 186
For he loves to hear That unicorns may be betray'd with trees ii 1 203
He loves me well, and I have given him reasons; Send him but hither ii 1 219
By my once-commended beauty, By all your vows of love and that great vow Which did incorporate and make us one ii 1 272
For your private satisfaction, Because I love you, I will let you know ii 2 74
For my dear dear love To your proceeding bids me tell you this; And reason to my love is liable ii 2 104
Mark well Metellus Cimber: Decius Brutus loves thee not ii 3 4
Say I love Brutus, and I honour him; Say I fear'd Cæsar iii 1 128
Mark Antony shall not love Cæsar dead So well as Brutus living iii 1 133
Do receive you in With all kind love, good thoughts, and reverence iii 1 176
Why I, that did love Cæsar when I struck him, Have thus proceeded iii 1 182
Though last, not least in love iii 1 189
That I did love thee, Cæsar, O, 'tis true iii 1 194
Friends am I with you all and love you all iii 1 220
To him I say, that Brutus' love to Cæsar was no less than his iii 2 20
There is tears for his love; joy for his fortune; honour for his valour iii 2 29
Who is here so vile that will not love his country? If any, speak iii 2 35
You all did love him once, not without cause: What cause withholds you then, to mourn for him? iii 2 107
But, as you know me all, a plain blunt man, That love my friend iii 2 223
Wherein hath Cæsar thus deserved your loves? Alas, you know not iii 2 241
When love begins to sicken and decay, It useth an enforced ceremony iv 2 20
Before the eyes of both our armies here, Which should perceive nothing but love iv 2 44
Do not presume too much upon my love; I may do that I shall be sorry for iv 3 63
You love me not.—I do not like your faults iv 3 89
Hated by one he loves; braved by his brother; Check'd like a bondman iv 3 96
Have not you love enough to bear with me? iv 3 119
Love, and be friends, as two such men should be iv 3 131
Till the wine o'erswell the cup; I cannot drink too much of Brutus' love iv 3 162
Words before blows: is it so, countrymen?—Not that we love words better, as you do v 1 28
Even for that our love of old, I prithee, Hold thou my sword-hilts v 5 27
Doing every thing Safe toward your love and honour *Macbeth* i 4 27
My dearest love, Duncan comes here to-night i 5 59
The love that follows us sometime is our trouble, Which still we thank as love i 6 12
His great love, sharp as his spur, hath holp him To his home before us i 6 23
We love him highly, And shall continue our graces towards him i 6 29
From this time Such I account thy love i 7 39
I have given suck, and know How tender 'tis to love the babe that milks me i 7 55
The expedition of my violent love Outrun the pauser, reason ii 3 116
Who could refrain, That had a heart to love, and in that heart Courage to make's love known? ii 3 123
Takes your enemy off, Grapples you to the heart and love of us iii 1 106
Certain friends that are both his and mine, Whose loves I may not drop iii 1 122
Thence it is, That I to your assistance do make love iii 1 124
Be bright and jovial among your guests to-night.—So shall I, love iii 2 29
Come, love and health to all; Then I'll sit down. Give me some wine iii 4 87
Spiteful and wrathful, who, as others do, Loves for his own ends iii 5 13
He loves us not; He wants the natural touch iv 2 8
All is the fear and nothing is the love; As little is the wisdom iv 2 12
Wife and child, Those precious motives, those strong knots of love iv 3 27
Those he commands move only in command, Nothing in love v 2 20
That which should accompany old age, As honour, love, obedience v 3 25
Before we reckon with your several loves, And make us even with you v 8 61
Do you consent we shall acquaint him with it, As needful in our loves, fitting our duty? *Hamlet* i 1 173
With no less nobility of love Than that which dearest father bears his son i 2 110
For God's love, let me hear i 2 195
I will requite your loves. So, fare you well i 2 251
Our duty to your honour.—Your loves, as mine to you: farewell i 2 254
Perhaps he loves you now, And now no soil nor cautel doth besmirch The virtue of his will: but you must fear i 3 14
If he says he loves you, It fits your wisdom so far to believe it i 3 24
He hath importuned me with love In honourable fashion i 3 110
List, list, O, list! If thou didst ever thy dear father love i 5 23
With wings as swift As meditation or the thoughts of love i 5 30
Whose love was of that dignity That it went hand in hand even with the vow I made to her in marriage i 5 48
So, gentlemen, With all my love I do commend me to you i 5 184
What so poor a man as Hamlet is May do, to express his love and friending i 5 186
Mad for thy love?—My lord, I do not know; But truly, I do fear it ii 1 85
This is the very ecstasy of love, Whose violent property fordoes itself ii 1 102
Being kept close, might move More grief to hide than hate to utter love ii 1 119
Doubt truth to be a liar; But never doubt I love ii 2 119
But that I love thee best, O most best, believe it ii 2 121
But how hath she Received his love?—What do you think of me? ii 2 129
Love. But what might you think, When I had seen this hot love on the wing . . . , If I had . . . look'd upon this love with idle sight? *Ham.* ii 2 132
If he love her not And be not from his reason fall'n thereon, Let me be no assistant for a state ii 2 164
Truly in my youth I suffered much extremity for love; very near this ii 2 192
By the obligation of our ever-preserved love ii 2 296
I have an eye of you.—If you love me, hold not off ii 2 302
I have a daughter that I love passing well ii 2 431
If't be the affliction of his love or no That thus he suffers for iii 1 36
The pangs of despised love, the law's delay, The insolence of office iii 1 72
I did love you once.—Indeed, my lord, you made me believe so iii 1 116
Love! his affections do not that way tend iii 1 170
The origin and commencement of his grief Sprung from neglected love iii 1 186
'Tis brief, my lord.—As woman's love iii 2 164
Since love our hearts and Hymen did our hands Unite commutual iii 2 169
So many journeys may the sun and moon Make us again count o'er ere love be done! iii 2 172
Women's fear and love holds quantity; In neither aught, or in extremity iii 2 177
What my love is, proof hath made you know; And as my love is sized, my fear is so: Where love is great, the littlest doubts are fear; Where little fears grow great, great love grows there iii 2 179
O, confound the rest! Such love must needs be treason in my breast iii 2 188
The instances that second marriage move Are base respects of thrift, but none of love iii 2 193
'Tis not strange That even our loves should with our fortunes change iii 2 211
For 'tis a question left us yet to prove, Whether love lead fortune, or else fortune love iii 2 213
Hitherto doth love on fortune tend; For who not needs shall never lack a friend iii 2 216
I could interpret between you and your love, if I could see the puppets dallying.—You are keen, my lord iii 2 257
You shall see anon how the murderer gets the love of Gonzago's wife iii 2 275
My lord, you once did love me.—So I do still iii 2 347
O, my lord, if my duty be too bold, my love is too unmannerly iii 2 364
Takes off the rose From the fair forehead of an innocent love iii 4 43
You cannot call it love; for at your age The hey-day in the blood is tame iii 4 68
Honeying and making love Over the nasty sty iii 4 93
For love of grace, Lay not that flattering unction to your soul iii 4 144
So much was our love, We would not understand what was most fit iv 1 19
If my love thou hold'st at aught—As my great power thereof may give thee sense iv 3 60
How should I your true love know From another one? iv 5 23
Nature is fine in love, and where 'tis fine, It sends some precious instance of itself After the thing it loves iv 5 163
Pray, love, remember: and there is pansies, that's for thoughts iv 5 176
The great love the general gender bear him iv 7 18
I loved your father, and we love ourself; And that, I hope, will teach you iv 7 34
Not that I think you did not love your father; But that I know love is begun by time; And that I see, in passages of proof, Time qualifies the spark and fire of it iv 7 111
There lives within the very flame of love A kind of wick or snuff iv 7 115
In youth, when I did love, did love, Methought it was very sweet v 1 69
Forty thousand brothers Could not, with all their quantity of love, Make up my sum v 1 293
O, he is mad, Laertes.—For love of God, forbear him v 1 296
As love between them like the palm might flourish v 2 40
Why, man, they did make love to this employment v 2 57
I do receive your offer'd love like love, And will not wrong it v 2 262
I must love you, and sue to know you better *Lear* i 1 30
Great rivals in our youngest daughter's love i 1 47
Tell me, my daughters, . . . Which of you shall we say doth love us most? i 1 52
I love you more than words can wield the matter; Dearer than eyesight i 1 56
A love that makes breath poor, and speech unable; Beyond all manner of so much I love you i 1 61
What shall Cordelia do? Love, and be silent i 1 63
I find she names my very deed of love; Only she comes too short i 1 73
And find I am alone felicitate In your dear highness' love i 1 78
I am sure, my love's More richer than my tongue i 1 79
To whose young love The vines of France and milk of Burgundy Strive to be interess'd i 1 85
I love your majesty According to my bond; nor more nor less i 1 94
I Return those duties back as are right fit, Obey you, love you i 1 100
Why have my sisters husbands, if they say They love you all? i 1 102
That lord whose hand must take my plight shall carry Half my love with him i 1 104
Sure, I shall never marry like my sisters, To love my father all i 1 106
Answer my life my judgement, Thy youngest daughter does not love thee least i 1 154
May your deeds approve, That good effects may spring from words of love i 1 188
What, in the least, Will you require in present dower with her, Or cease your quest of love? i 1 196
I would not from your love make such a stray, To match you where I hate i 1 212
Love's not love When it is mingled with regards that stand Aloof from the entire point i 1 241
Since that respects of fortune are his love, I shall not be his wife i 1 251
Gods, gods! 'tis strange that from their cold'st neglect My love should kindle to inflamed respect i 1 258
Therefore be gone Without our grace, our love, our benison i 1 268
Our father's love is to the bastard Edmund As to the legitimate i 2 17
To his father, that so tenderly and entirely loves him. Heaven and earth! i 2 105
Love cools, friendship falls off, brothers divide: in cities, mutinies i 2 115
To love him that is honest; to converse with him that is wise i 4 16
Not so young, sir, to love a woman for singing, nor so old to dote on her i 4 40
I thank thee, fellow; thou servest me, and I'll love thee i 4 98
May not an ass know when the cart draws the horse? Whoop, Jug! I love thee i 4 245
Drew from my heart all love, And added to the gall i 4 291
I cannot be so partial, Goneril, To the great love I bear you i 4 335
I love thee not.—Why, then, I care not for thee ii 2 7
O heavens, If you do love old men, if your sweet sway Allow obedience ii 4 193
Thy fifty yet doth double five-and-twenty, And thou art twice her love ii 4 263
Are you here? things that love night Love not such nights as these iii 2 42
I will lay trust upon thee; and thou shalt find a dearer father in my love iii 5 26
He's mad that trusts in the tameness of a wolf, a horse's health, a boy's love iii 6 20
Do it for ancient love iv 1 45
I live To thank thee for the love thou show'dst the king iv 2 96
No blown ambition doth our arms incite, But love, dear love iv 4 28
I know not what: I'll love thee much, Let me unseal the letter iv 5 21

Love. I know your lady does not love her husband; I am sure of that *Lear* iv 5 23
No, do thy worst, blind Cupid; I'll not love . . . iv 6 141
I know you do not love me; for your sisters Have, as I do remember, done me wrong: You have some cause, they have not . iv 7 73
Speak the truth, Do you not love my sister?—In honour'd love . v 1 9
Fortune love you! . . . v 1 46
To both these sisters have I sworn my love . . . v 1 55
If you will marry, make your loves to me, My lady is bespoke . v 3 88
This would have seem'd a period To such as love not sorrow . v 3 205
Be judge yourself, Whether I in any just term am affined To love the Moor.—I would not follow him then . *Othello* i 1 40
Not I for love and duty, But seeming so, for my peculiar end . i 1 59
For necessity of present life, I must show out a flag and sign of love . i 1 157
But that I love the gentle Desdemona, I would not my unhoused free condition Put into circumscription and confine . i 2 25
I will a round unvarnish'd tale deliver Of my whole course of love . i 3 91
To fall in love with what she fear'd to look on! . . . i 3 98
I'll present How I did thrive in this fair lady's love, And she in mine . i 3 125
That I did love the Moor to live with him, My downright violence and storm of fortunes May trumpet to the world . . . i 3 249
The rites for which I love him are bereft me . . . i 3 258
I have but an hour Of love, of worldly matters and direction, To spend i 3 300
I will . . . drown myself.—If thou dost, I shall never love thee after . i 3 307
I never found man that knew how to love himself . . i 3 315
Ere I would say, I would drown myself for the love of a guinea-hen . i 3 317
Our unbitted lusts, whereof I take this that you call love to be a sect . i 3 336
It cannot be that Desdemona should long continue her love to the Moor i 3 348
Make love's quick pants in Desdemona's arms . . . ii 1 80
Our loves and comforts should increase, Even as our days do grow . ii 1 196
Honey, you shall be well desired in Cyprus; I have found great love . ii 1 207
They say, base men being in love have then a nobility in their natures more than is native to them . . . ii 1 217
I must tell thee this—Desdemona is directly in love with him . ii 1 221
Will she love him still for prating? let not thy discreet heart think it . ii 1 226
That Cassio loves her, I do well believe it; That she loves him, 'tis apt ii 1 295
Now, I do love her too; Not out of absolute lust . . ii 1 300
Thank me, love me and reward me, For making him egregiously an ass ii 1 317
Come, my dear love, The purchase made, the fruits are to ensue . ii 3 8
Our general cast us thus early for the love of his Desdemona . ii 3 15
When she speaks, is it not an alarum to love? . . . ii 3 27
My sick fool Roderigo, Whom love hath turn'd almost the wrong side out ii 3 54
I do love Cassio well; and would do much To cure him of this evil . ii 3 148
Speak, who began this? on thy love, I charge thee.—I do not know . ii 3 178
Thy honesty and love doth mince this matter, Making it light . ii 3 247
Cassio, I love thee; But never more be officer of mine . ii 3 248
Look, if my gentle love be not raised up! I'll make thee an example . ii 3 250
I think you think I love you.—I have well approved it, sir . ii 3 316
This crack of your love shall grow stronger than it was before . ii 3 331
I protest, in the sincerity of love and honest kindness . ii 3 333
His soul is so enfetter'd to her love, That she may make, unmake . ii 3 351
He protests he loves you And needs no other suitor but his likings . iii 1 50
You do love my lord: You have known him long . . iii 3 10
I being absent and my place supplied, My general will forget my love . iii 3 18
If he be not one that truly loves you, That errs in ignorance . iii 3 48
Good love, call him back.—Not now, sweet Desdemona; some other time iii 3 54
When I have a suit Wherein I mean to touch your love indeed, It shall be full of poise and difficult weight . . . iii 3 81
I do love thee! and when I love thee not, Chaos is come again . iii 3 91
Did Michael Cassio, when you woo'd my lady, Know of your love? . iii 3 95
If thou dost love me, Show me thy thought.—My lord, you know I love you iii 3 115
I know thou 'rt full of love and honesty, And weigh'st thy words . iii 3 118
That cuckold lives in bliss Who, certain of his fate, loves not his wronger; But, O, what damned minutes tells he o'er Who dotes, yet doubts, suspects, yet strongly loves! . . . iii 3 168
'Tis not to make me jealous To say my wife is fair, feeds well, loves company . . . iii 3 184
When I doubt, prove; And on the proof, there is no more but this,—Away at once with love or jealousy! . . . iii 3 192
Now I shall have reason To show the love and duty that I bear you . iii 3 194
I hope you will consider what is spoke Comes from my love . iii 3 217
Than keep a corner in the thing I love For others' uses . iii 3 272
But she so loves the token . . . That she reserves it evermore about her iii 3 293
Villain, be sure thou prove my love a whore, Be sure of it . iii 3 359
And from hence I'll love no friend, sith love breeds such offence . iii 3 380
Sith I am enter'd in this cause so far, Prick'd to't by foolish honesty and love, I will go on . . . iii 3 412
I heard him say 'Sweet Desdemona, Let us be wary, let us hide our loves' . . . iii 3 420
All my fond love thus do I blow to heaven . . . iii 3 445
Yield up, O love, thy crown and hearted throne To tyrannous hate! . iii 3 448
My bloody thoughts . . . Shall ne'er look back, ne'er ebb to humble love iii 3 458
I greet thy love, Not with vain thanks, but with acceptance bounteous iii 3 469
'Twould make her amiable and subdue my father Entirely to her love . iii 4 60
A man that all his time Hath founded his good fortunes on your love . iii 4 94
I may again Exist, and be a member of his love . . iii 4 112
Nor purposed merit in futurity, Can ransom me into his love again . iii 4 118
I' faith, sweet love, I was coming to your house . . iii 4 171
Not that I love you not.—But that you do not love me . . iii 4 196
I never knew woman love man so.—Alas, poor rogue! I think, i' faith, she loves me . . . iv 1 111
She is persuaded I will marry her, out of her own love and flattery . iv 1 133
I would do much To atone them, for the love I bear to Cassio . iv 1 244
Here I kneel: If e'er my will did trespass 'gainst his love . iv 2 152
Ever did, And ever will—though he do shake me off To beggarly divorcement—love him dearly . . . iv 2 158
His unkindness may defeat my life, But never taint my love . iv 2 161
I would you had never seen him!—So would not I: my love doth so approve him . . . iv 3 19
She was in love, and he she loved proved mad And did forsake her . iv 3 27
I call'd my love false love; but what said he then? . . iv 3 55
Be thus when thou art dead, and I will kill thee, And love thee after . v 2 19
This sorrow's heavenly; It strikes where it doth love . . v 2 22
Think on thy sins.—They are loves I bear to you . . v 2 40
Never loved Cassio But with such general warranty of heaven As I might love . . . v 2 61
O mistress, villany hath made mocks with love! . . . v 2 151
She did gratify his amorous works With that recognizance and pledge of love Which I first gave her . . . v 2 214
If it be love indeed, tell me how much.—There's beggary in the love that can be reckon'd . . . *Ant. and Cleo.* i 1 14

Love. How, my love!—Perchance! nay, and most like: You must not stay here longer . . . *Ant. and Cleo.* i 1 24
Excellent falsehood! Why did he marry Fulvia, and not love her? . i 1 41
Now, for the love of Love and her soft hours, Let's not confound the time with conference harsh . . . i 1 44
O excellent! I love long life better than figs . . . i 2 32
Her passions are made of nothing but the finest part of pure love . i 2 152
Whose love is never link'd to the deserver Till his deserts are past . i 2 193
If you did love him dearly, You do not hold the method to enforce The like from him.—What should I do, I do not? . i 3 6
The hated, grown to strength, Are newly grown to love . i 3 49
O most false love! Where be the sacred vials thou shouldst fill With sorrowful water? . . . i 3 62
I am quickly ill, and well, So Antony loves . . . i 3 73
And give true evidence to his love, which stands An honourable trial . i 3 74
The ebb'd man, ne'er loved till ne'er worth love . . i 4 43
Did I, Charmian, Ever love Cæsar so?—O that brave Cæsar! . i 5 67
The people love me, and the sea is mine; My powers are crescent . ii 1 9
Lepidus flatters both, Of both is flatter'd; but he neither loves . ii 1 15
But all the charms of love, Salt Cleopatra, soften thy waned lip! . ii 1 20
Or, if you borrow one another's love for the instant, you may . . . return it . . . ii 2 103
Her love to both Would, each to other and all loves to both, Draw after her . . . ii 2 137
From this hour The heart of brothers govern in our loves! . ii 2 150
A sister I bequeath you, whom no brother Did ever love so dearly . ii 2 153
And never Fly off our loves again!—Happily, amen! . . ii 2 155
Give me some music; music, moody food Of us that trade in love . ii 5 2
The policy of that purpose made more in the marriage than the love . ii 6 127
O, how he loves Cæsar!—Nay, but how dearly he adores Mark Antony! iii 2 7
He loves Cæsar best; yet he loves Antony: Ho! hearts, tongues, figures, scribes, bards, poets, cannot Think, speak, cast, write, sing, number, ho! His love to Antony . . . iii 2 15
Both he loves.—They are his shards, and he their beetle . . iii 2 19
Let not the piece of virtue, which is set Betwixt us as the cement of our love, To keep it builded, be the ram to batter The fortress of it iii 2 29
I'll wrestle with you in my strength of love: Look, here I have you . iii 2 62
Let your best love draw to that point, which seeks Best to preserve it iii 4 21
Our faults Can never be so equal, that your love Can equally move with them . . . iii 4 35
The ostentation of our love, which, left unshown, Is often left unloved iii 6 52
You are abused Beyond the mark of thought: and the high gods, To do you justice, make them ministers Of us and those that love you . iii 6 89
Welcome, dear madam. Each heart in Rome does love and pity you . iii 6 92
Love, I am full of lead. Some wine, within there, and our viands! . iii 11 72
You embrace not Antony As you did love, but as you fear'd him . iii 13 57
The next time I do fight, I'll make death love me . . iii 13 193
O love, That thou couldst see my wars to-day! . . iv 4 15
To business that we love we rise betime, And go to't with delight . iv 4 20
Ah, thou spell! Avaunt!—Why is my lord enraged against his love? . iv 12 31
Let him that loves me strike me dead.—Not I.—Nor I.—Nor any one . iv 14 108
O slave, of no more trust Than love that's hired! . . v 2 155
Thereto sworn by your command, Which my love makes religion to obey v 2 199
Look here, love; This diamond was my mother's: take it, heart . *Cymb.* i 1 111
For my sake wear this; It is a manacle of love . . i 1 122
And that she should love this fellow and refuse me! . . i 2 27
When thou shalt bring me word she loves my son, I'll tell thee . i 5 49
An eminent monsieur, that, it seems, much loves A Gallian girl at home i 6 65
The love I bear him Made me to fan you thus . . i 6 176
Still, I swear I love you.—If you but said so, 'twere as deep with me ii 3 95
In these sear'd hopes, I barely gratify your love . . ii 4 7
Let there be no honour Where there is beauty; truth, where semblance; love, Where there's another man . . . ii 4 109
Murder her? Upon the love and truth and vows which I Have made? iii 2 12
Let what is here contain'd relish of love, Of my lord's health . iii 2 30
Some griefs are med'cinable; that is one of them, For it doth physic love iii 2 34
What your own love will out of this advise you, follow . iii 2 45
That remains loyal to his vow, and your, increasing in love . iii 2 48
Take it, and hit The innocent mansion of my love, my heart . iii 4 70
Haply, despair hath seized her, Or, wing'd with fervour of her love, she's flown . . . iii 5 61
I love and hate her: for she's fair and royal . . iii 5 70
And she, of all compounded, Outsells them all; I love her therefore . iii 5 74
I'll make't my comfort He is a man; I'll love him as my brother . iii 6 72
Yet this imperceiverant thing loves him in my despite . iv 1 15
I love thee; I have spoke it: How much the quantity, the weight as much, As I do love my father . . . iv 2 16
I know not why I love this youth; and I have heard you say, Love's reason's without reason . . . iv 2 21
I love thee brotherly, but envy much Thou hast robb'd me of this deed iv 2 158
These present wars shall find I love my country . . iv 3 43
The king Hath not deserved my service nor your loves . . iv 4 25
You snatch some hence for little faults; that's love, To have them fall no more . . . v 1 12
Whom best I love I cross; to make my gift, The more delay'd, delighted v 4 101
Your daughter, whom she bore in hand to love With such integrity . v 5 43
I love thee more and more: think more and more What's best to ask . v 5 109
Sitting sadly, Hearing us praise our loves of Italy . . v 5 161
A shop of all the qualities that man Loves woman for . . v 5 167
Like a noble lord in love and one That had a royal lover, took his hint v 5 171
Though you did love this youth, I blame ye not; You had a motive for't v 5 267
You gods that made me man, and sway in love . . *Pericles* i 1 19
My riches to the earth . . . ; my unspotted fire of love to you . i 1 53
Few love to hear the sins they love to act . . . i 1 92
All love the womb that their first being bred, Then give my tongue like leave to love my head . . . i 1 107
Which love to all, of which thyself art one, Who now reprovest me for it i 2 94
Why, as it were unlicensed of your loves, He would depart . i 3 17
We do not look for reverence, but for love, And harbourage for ourself i 4 99
Knights come from all parts of the world to just and tourney for her love ii 1 116
He loves you well that holds his life of you . . . ii 2 22
Honour we love; For who hates honour hates the gods above . ii 3 21
As you do love, fill to your mistress' lips . . . ii 3 51
Since they love men in arms as well as beds . . . ii 3 98
It is too late to talk of love; And that's the mark I know you level at ii 3 113
Your griefs! for what? wrong not your prince you love . . ii 4 25
Forbear your suffrages: If that you love Prince Pericles, forbear . ii 4 42
If I cannot win you to this love, Go search like nobles . ii 4 49
Then you love us, we you, and we'll clasp hands . . ii 4 57
That she loves the knight of Tyre! 'Tis the king's subtilty . ii 5 43

Love. Never aim'd so high to love your daughter, But bent all offices to honour her . . . . *Pericles* ii 5 47
Never did my actions yet commence A deed might gain her love . . ii 5 54
Resolve your angry father, if my tongue Did e'er solicit, or my hand subscribe To any syllable that made love to you . . . . ii 5 70
Will you . . . Bestow your love and your affections Upon a stranger? . ii 5 77
If you love me, sir.—Even as my life my blood that fosters it . . ii 5 88
Why do you make us love your goodly gifts, And snatch them straight away? . . . . iii 1 23
For the love Of this poor infant, this fresh-new sea-farer, I would it would be quiet . . . . iii 1 40
Let not conscience, Which is but cold, inflaming love i' thy bosom, Inflame too nicely . . . . iv 1 5
Love-affair. Of all that may concern thy love-affairs . *T. G. of Ver.* iii 1 254
Love-book. And on a love-book pray for my success . . . i 1 19
Love-broker. There is no love-broker in the world can more prevail in man's commendation with woman than report of valour . *T. Night* iii 2 39
Love-cause. In all this time there was not any man died in his own person, videlicet, in a love-cause . . . *As Y. Like It* iv 1 97
Love-day. This day shall be a love-day . . . . . *T. Andron.* i 1 491
Love-devouring. Do thou but close our hands with holy words, Then love-devouring death do what he dare . . *Rom. and Jul.* ii 6 7
Love-discourse. I know you joy not in a love-discourse . *T. G. of Ver.* ii 4 127
Love-feat. And every one his love-feat will advance . . *L. L. Lost* v 2 123
Love-God. Cupid is no longer an archer : his glory shall be ours, for we are the only love-gods . . . . *Much Ado* ii 1 402
Love-in-idleness. Maidens call it love-in-idleness . . *M. N. Dream* ii 1 168
While idly I stood looking on, I found the effect of love in idleness *T. of Shrew* i 1 156
Love-juice. But hast thou yet latch'd the Athenian's eyes With the love-juice, as I did bid thee do? . . . . . *M. N. Dream* iii 2 37
Thou hast mistaken quite And laid the love-juice on some true-love's sight . . . . iii 2 89
Love-letter. Pox of your love-letters ! . . . . . *T. G. of Ver.* iii 1 391
What, have I scaped love-letters in the holiday-time of my beauty? *Mer. Wives* ii 1 1
Love-line. And write to her a love-line . . . . . *All's Well* ii 1 81
Love-monger. Thou art an old love-monger . . . . *L. L. Lost* ii 1 253
Love-news, in faith . . . . *Mer. of Venice* ii 4 14
Love-performing. Spread thy close curtain, love-performing night, That runaways' eyes may wink . . . . . . *Rom. and Jul.* iii 2 5
Love-prate. Misused our sex in your love-prate . . *As Y. Like It* iv 1 206
Love-rhyme. Dan Cupid ; Regent of love-rhymes . . . *L. L. Lost* iii 1 183
Love-shaft. Loosed his love-shaft smartly from his bow . *M. N. Dream* ii 1 159
Love-shaked. I am he that is so love-shaked . . *As Y. Like It* iii 2 385
Love-sick. To love-sick Dido's sad attending ear . . *T. Andron.* v 3 82
So perfumed that The winds were love-sick with them . *Ant. and Cleo.* ii 2 199
Love-song. To relish a love-song, like a robin-redbreast . *T. G. of Ver.* ii 1 20
Mar no more trees with writing love-songs in their barks *As Y. Like It* iii 2 277
Would you have a love-song, or a song of good life?—A love-song, a love-song.—Ay, ay : I care not for good life . . . *T. Night* ii 3 36
He has the prettiest love-songs for maids . . . . *W. Tale* iv 4 193
Shot thorough the ear with a love-song . . . . *Rom. and Jul.* ii 4 15
Love-spring. Shall, Antipholus, Even in the spring of love, thy love-springs rot? . . . . *Com. of Errors* iii 2 3
Love-suit. And plead his love-suit to her gentle heart . . *Hen. V.* v 2 101
Whose love-suit hath been to me As fearful as a siege . . *Cymbeline* iii 4 136
Love-thoughts lie rich when canopied with bowers . . *T. Night* i 1 41
Love-token. Given her rhymes And interchanged love-tokens *M. N. D.* i 1 29
'Love-wounded Proteus.' Poor wounded name ! . . *T. G. of Ver.* i 2 113
Love's argument. Yet, since love's argument was first on foot, Let not the cloud of sorrow justle it . . . . . . *L. L. Lost* v 2 757
Love's bonds. O, ten times faster Venus' pigeons fly To seal love's bonds new-made ! . . . . *Mer. of Venice* ii 6 6
Love's bow. For, O, love's bow Shoots buck and doe . *Troi. and Cres.* iii 1 126
Love's conference. Love takes the meaning in love's conference *M. N. D.* ii 2 46
Love's counsellor should fill the bores of hearing . . *Cymbeline* iii 2 59
Love's feeling is more soft and sensible Than are the tender horns of cockled snails . . . . *L. L. Lost* iv 3 337
Love's forgetfulness. Some foul mischance Torment me for my love's forgetfulness ! . . . . *T. G. of Ver.* ii 2 12
Love's grief. How sweetly you do minister to love, That know love's grief by his complexion ! . . . . *Much Ado* i 1 315
Thy love is far from charity, That in love's grief desirest society *L. L. L.* iv 3 128
Love's heralds should be thoughts . . . . . *Rom. and Jul.* ii 5 4
Love's kiss. Bear her my true love's kiss . . . . *Richard III.* iv 4 430
Love's majesty. I, that am rudely stamp'd, and want love's majesty . i 1 16
Love's mind. Nor hath Love's mind of any judgement taste *M. N. Dream* i 1 236
Love's night is noon . . . . *T. Night* iii 1 160
Love's particular. And every function of your power, Should, notwithstanding that your bond of duty, As 'twere in love's particular, be more To me, your friend, than any . . . . *Hen. VIII.* iii 2 189
Love's passion. Thou overheard'st, ere I was ware, My true love's passion *Rom. and Jul.* ii 2 104
Love's prick. He that sweetest rose will find Must find love's prick and Rosalind . . . . *As Y. Like It* iii 2 118
Love's reason's without reason . . . . . . *Cymbeline* iv 2 22
Love's recompense. As my fortune ripens with thy love, It shall be still thy true love's recompense . . . . *Richard II.* ii 3 49
Love's sake. Or for love's sake, a word that loves all men . *L. L. Lost* iv 3 358
He desires you, for love's sake, to make no more noise with it *Othello* iii 1 13
Love's shadows. How sweet is love itself possess'd, When but love's shadows are so rich in joy ! . . . . . . *Rom. and Jul.* v 1 11
Love's sighs. Never durst poet touch a pen to write Until his ink were temper'd with Love's sighs . . . . *L. L. Lost* iv 3 347
Love's spring. The April's in her eyes : it is love's spring *Ant. and Cleo.* iii 2 43
Love's stories written in love's richest book . . . *M. N. Dream* ii 2 122
Love's tongue proves dainty Bacchus gross in taste . . *L. L. Lost* iv 3 339
Tie up my love's tongue, bring him silently . . . *M. N. Dream* iii 1 206
Love's traitor. He doth espy Himself love's traitor . . *K. John* ii 1 507
Love's transgression. At thy good heart's oppression.—Why, such is love's transgression . . . . *Rom. and Jul.* i 1 191
Love's Tyburn. The shape of Love's Tyburn that hangs up simplicity *L. L. Lost* iv 3 54
Love's whip. I, forsooth, in love ! I, that have been love's whip ! . iii 1 176
Love's wings. Much less shall she that hath Love's wings to fly *T. G. of V.* ii 7 11
Love's wound. A little western flower, Before milk-white, now purple with love's wound . . . . *M. N. Dream* ii 1 167
Loved. He whom next thyself Of all the world I loved . . *Tempest* i 2 69
Knowing I loved my books, he furnish'd me From mine own library . i 2 166

Loved. And then I loved thee And show'd thee all the qualities o' the isle *Tempest* i 2 336
The gunner and his mate Loved Mall, Meg and Marian and Margery . ii 2 50
She loved not the savour of tar nor of pitch . . . . . ii 2 54
And his and mine loved darling. . . . . iii 3 93
How long hath she been deformed?—Ever since you loved her.—I have loved her ever since I saw her . . . . *T. G. of Ver.* ii 1 71
I have been forsworn In breaking faith with Julia whom I loved . . iv 2 11
His man told me he loved her out of all nick . . . . . iv 2 76
Thyself hast loved ; and I have heard thee say No grief did ever come so near thy heart As when thy lady and thy true love died . . iv 3 18
She loved me well deliver'd it to me.—It seems you loved not her . iv 4 78
Methinks that she loved you as well As you do love your lady Silvia . iv 4 84
When she did think my master loved her well, She, in my judgement, was as fair as you . . . . iv 4 155
O thou senseless form, Thou shalt be worshipp'd, kiss'd, loved and adored ! . . . . iv 4 204
I have long loved her, and, I protest to you, bestowed much on her *Mer. Wives* ii 2 201
How I have ever loved the life removed . . . *Meas. for Meas.* i 3 8
I loved thy brother : if the old fantastical duke of dark corners had been at home, he had lived . . . . iv 3 163
In the quest of him : Whom whilst I labour'd of a love to see, I hazarded the loss of whom I loved . . . *Com. of Errors* i 1 132
It is certain I am loved of all ladies, only you excepted . . *Much Ado* i 1 126
I neither feel how she should be loved nor know how she should be worthy . . . . i 1 233
He loved my niece your daughter and meant to acknowledge it this night i 2 12
I did never think that lady would have loved any man . . . ii 3 97
I persuaded them, if they loved Benedick, To wish him wrestle with affection . . . . iii 1 41
Mine I loved and mine I praised And mine that I was proud on . . iv 1 138
Would the two princes lie, and Claudio lie, Who loved her so? . iv 1 155
It were as possible for me to say I loved nothing so well as you . iv 1 272
You have stayed me in a happy hour : I was about to protest I loved you iv 1 286
Bring me a father that so loved his child, Whose joy of her is overwhelm'd like mine . . . . v 1 8
God knows I loved my niece ; And she is dead, slander'd to death . v 1 87
Now thy image doth appear In the rare semblance that I loved it first . v 1 260
And when you loved, you were my other husband . . . . v 4 61
A well-accomplish'd youth, Of all that virtue love for virtue loved *L. L. L.* ii 1 57
But she perforce withholds the loved boy . . . *M. N. Dream* ii 1 26
So it came to pass, Titania waked and straightway loved an ass . iii 2 34
If e'er I loved her, all that love is gone . . . . . iii 2 170
Since night you loved me ; yet since night you left me . . . iii 2 275
The fairest dame That lived, that loved, that liked, that look'd with cheer v 1 299
The best-regarded virgins of our clime Have loved it too *Mer. of Venice* ii 1 11
You saw the mistress, I beheld the maid ; You loved, I loved for intermission . . . . iii 2 201
Say how I loved you, speak me fair in death . . . . . iv 1 275
In such a night Did young Lorenzo swear he loved her well . . . v 1 18
Since he hath got the jewel that I loved . . . . . . v 1 224
And never two ladies loved as they do . . . . *As Y. Like It* i 1 117
My father loved Sir Rowland as his soul . . . . . i 2 247
The duke my father loved his father dearly . . . . . i 3 30
That thou knew'st how I do love her !—I partly guess ; for I have loved ere now . . . . ii 4 24
If thou remember'st not the slightest folly That ever love did make thee run into, Thou hast not loved . . . . . . ii 4 36
If thou hast not sat as I do now, Wearying thy hearer in thy mistress' praise, Thou hast not loved . . . . ii 4 39
If thou hast not broke from company Abruptly, as my passion now makes me, Thou hast not loved . . . . ii 4 42
Be truly welcome hither : I am the duke That loved your father . ii 7 196
I never loved my brother in my life.—More villain thou. . . iii 1 14
Who ever loved that loved not at first sight? . . . . . iii 5 83
No sooner looked but they loved, no sooner loved but they sighed . v 2 37
You that durst swear that your mistress Bianca Loved none in the world so well as Lucentio . . . . . *T. of Shrew* iv 2 13
I will be married to a wealthy widow, Ere three days pass, which hath as long loved me As I have loved this proud disdainful haggard . iv 2 38
You are loved, sir ; They that least lend it you shall lack you first *All's W.* i 2 67
Her matter was, she loved your son . . . . . . i 3 115
Be not offended ; for it hurts not him That he is loved of me . . i 3 203
I would he loved his wife : if he were honester He were much goodlier iii 5 82
If I should swear by God's great attributes, I loved you dearly, would you believe my oaths, When I did love you ill? . . . . iv 2 26
I am a woodland fellow, sir, that always loved a great fire . . iv 5 50
She whom all men praised and whom myself, Since I have lost, have loved . . . . v 3 54
He loved her, sir, and loved her not . . . . . . v 3 248
But more than that, he loved her : for indeed he was mad for her . v 3 260
My father had a daughter loved a man, As it might be, perhaps, were I a woman, I should your lordship . . . . *T. Night* ii 4 110
I have loved thee,— Make that thy question, and go rot ! . *W. Tale* i 2 324
As he had lost some province and a region Loved as he loves himself . i 2 370
I do confess I loved him as in honour he required . . . iii 2 64
She was a woman and was turned into a cold fish for she would not exchange flesh with one that loved her . . . . . iv 4 285
O, hear me breathe my life Before this ancient sir, who, it should seem, Hath sometime loved ! . . . . iv 4 373
That noble honour'd lord is fear'd and loved . . . . v 1 158
I do protest I never loved myself Till now . . . . *K. John* ii 1 501
I honour'd him, I loved him, and will weep My date of life out . iv 3 105
For he is just and always loved us well . . . . *Richard II.* ii 1 221
If to be fat be to be hated, then Pharaoh's lean kine are to be loved *1 Hen. IV.* ii 4 520
Before, I loved thee as a brother, John ; But now, I do respect thee . v 4 19
John a Gaunt loved him well, and betted much money on his head *2 Hen. IV.* iii 2 50
The king that loved him . . . Was force perforce compell'd to banish him iv 1 115
Never was monarch better fear'd and loved Than is your majesty *Hen. V.* ii 2 25
To heaven I do appeal, How I have loved my king and commonweal *2 Hen. VI.* ii 1 191
They loved well when they were alive . . . . . . iv 7 139
Made a prey for carrion kites and crows Even of the bonny beast he loved so well . . . . v 2 12
We shall to London get, where you are loved . . . . . v 2 81
Hadst thou but loved him half so well as I, Or felt that pain which I did for him once, Or nourish'd him as I did . . *3 Hen. VI.* i 1 220

Loved. So dear I loved the man, that I must weep . . *Richard III.* iii 5 24
You few that loved me, . . . Go with me, like good angels, to my end *Hen. VIII.* ii 1 71
Both Fell by our servants, by those men we loved most . . ii 1 122
I know your majesty has always loved her So dear in heart . . ii 2 110
Loved him next heaven? obey'd him? Been, out of fondness, superstitious to him? . . . . iii 1 130
My father loved you: He said he did; and with his deed did crown His word . . . . iii 2 154
If I loved many words, lord, I should tell you You have as little honesty iii 2 270
Lofty and sour to them that loved him not . . . iv 2 53
For her mother's sake, that loved him, Heaven knows how dearly . iv 2 137
She shall be loved and fear'd: her own shall bless her . . v 5 31
I have loved you night and day For many weary months *Troi. and Cres.* iii 2 122
But, though I loved you well, I woo'd you not . . . iii 2 134
She was beloved, she loved; she is, and doth . . . iv 5 292
You look upon that sleeve; behold it well. He loved me—O false wench! v 2 70
Tell me whose it was.—'Twas one's that loved me better than you will v 2 89
Why should our endeavour be so loved and the performance so loathed? v 10 39
One that hath always loved the people . . . *Coriolanus* i 1 53
As if I loved my little should be dieted In praises sauced with lies . i 9 52
There have been many great men that have flattered the people, who ne'er loved them; and there be many that they have loved, they know not wherefore . . . . ii 2 10
You have not indeed loved the common people . . . ii 3 99
I shall be loved when I am lack'd . . . . . iv 1 15
I loved the maid I married; never man Sigh'd truer breath . . iv 5 120
Kind neighbours: we wish'd Coriolanus Had loved you as we did . iv 6 25
We loved him; but, like beasts And cowardly nobles, gave way . iv 6 121
Who loved him In a most dear particular. He call'd me father . . v 1 2
Yet, for I loved thee, Take this along; I writ it for thy sake . . v 2 95
Loved me above the measure of a father; Nay, godded me, indeed . v 3 10
He loved his mother dearly.—So did he me . . . v 4 15
Rome and the righteous heavens be my judge, How I have loved! *T. An.* i 1 427
She is Lavinia, therefore must be loved . . . . ii 1 84
Use her as you will, The worse to her, the better loved of me . . ii 3 167
Thy grandsire loved thee well: Many a time he danced thee on his knee v 3 161
I do love a woman.—I aim'd so near, when I supposed you loved *R. and J.* i 1 211
He that shot so trim, When King Cophetua loved the beggar-maid! . ii 1 14
Look you, she loved her kinsman Tybalt dearly, And so did I . . iii 4 3
An thou hadst hated meddlers sooner, thou shouldst have loved thyself better now . . . . *T. of Athens* iv 3 310
Thou valiant Mars! Thou ever young, fresh, loved and delicate wooer! iv 3 385
Say I fear'd Cæsar, honour'd him and loved him . . *J. Cæsar* iii 1 129
Not that I loved Cæsar less, but that I loved Rome more . . iii 2 23
As Cæsar loved me, I weep for him; as he was fortunate, I rejoice at it iii 2 26
It is not meet you know how Cæsar loved you . . . iii 2 146
Judge, O you gods, how dearly Cæsar loved him! . . . iii 2 186
The temple-haunting martlet does approve, By his loved mansionry *Macb.* i 6 5
You have loved him well: He hath not touch'd you yet . . . iv 3 13
One fair daughter, and no more, The which he loved passing well *Hamlet* ii 2 427
One speech in it I chiefly loved: 'twas Æneas' tale to Dido . ii 2 467
I loved you not.—I was the more deceived . . . iii 1 120
He 's loved of the distracted multitude, Who like not in their judgement iv 3 4
I loved your father, and we love ourself . . . . iv 7 34
I loved Ophelia: forty thousand brothers Could not, with all their quantity of love, Make up my sum . . . . . . v 1 292
What is the reason that you use me thus? I loved you ever . . v 1 313
As much as child e'er loved, or father found . . . *Lear* i 1 60
You have begot me, bred me, loved me: I Return those duties back . i 1 98
I loved her most, and thought to set my rest On her kind nursery . i 1 125
Royal Lear, Whom I have ever honour'd as my king, Loved as my father i 1 143
Most rich, being poor; Most choice, forsaken; and most loved, despised! i 1 254
He always loved our sister most; and with what poor judgement he hath now cast her off appears too grossly . . . . . i 1 293
Wine loved I deeply, dice dearly; and in woman out-paramoured the Turk iii 4 93
I loved him, friend; No father his son dearer: truth to tell thee, The grief hath crazed my wits . . . . iii 4 173
If fortune brag of two she loved and hated, One of them we behold . v 3 280
Her father loved me; oft invited me; Still question'd me . *Othello* i 3 128
Bade me, if I had a friend that loved her, I should but teach him how to tell my story, And that would woo her . . . . i 3 164
She loved me for the dangers I had pass'd, And I loved her that she did pity them. This only is the witchcraft I have used . . . i 3 167
Mark me with what violence she first loved the Moor, but for bragging ii 1 225
If she had been blessed, she would never have loved the Moor. Blessed pudding! . . . . ii 1 258
And when she seem'd to shake and fear your looks, She loved them most iii 3 208
She was in love, and he she loved proved mad And did forsake her . iv 3 27
That handkerchief which I so loved and gave thee Thou gavest to Cassio v 2 48
Never loved Cassio But with such general warranty of heaven As I might love . . . . v 2 59
She loved thee, cruel Moor; So come my soul to bliss, as I speak true . v 2 249
Of one that loved not wisely but too well; Of one not easily jealous . v 2 344
Sir, you and I have loved, but there's not it . . *Ant. and Cleo.* i 3 88
The ebb'd man, ne'er loved till ne'er worth love, Comes dear'd by being lack'd . . . . i 4 43
Sir, I never loved you much; but I ha' praised ye . . . ii 6 78
For better might we Have loved without this mean, if on both parts This be not cherish'd . . . . iii 2 32
'Tis the god Hercules, whom Antony loved, Now leaves him . . iv 3 16
My mistress loved thee, and her fortunes mingled With thine entirely . iv 14 24
Most praised, most loved, A sample to the youngest . . *Cymbeline* i 1 47
It is your fault that I have loved Posthumus: You bred him as my playfellow . . . . i 1 144
My report was once First with the best of note: Cymbeline loved me . iii 3 58
Yet who this should be, Doth miracle itself, loved before me . . iv 2 29
She confess'd she never loved you, only Affected greatness got by you . v 5 37
Did you e'er meet?—Ay, my good lord.—And at first meeting loved . v 5 379
Fair glass of light, I loved you, and could still, Were not this glorious casket stored with ill . . . . *Pericles* i 1 76
Are ready now To eat those little darlings whom they loved . . i 4 44
It kept where I kept, I so dearly loved it . . . . ii 1 136
He loved me dearly, And for his sake I wish the having of it . . ii 1 144
Thou look'st Like one I loved indeed . . . . . v 1 126
Lovedst. Thy life did manifest thou lovedst me not, And thou wilt have me die assured of it . . . . *2 Hen. IV.* iv 5 105
Mass, thou lovedst plums well, that wouldst venture so . *2 Hen. VI.* ii 1 101
I know, When thou didst hate him worst, thou lovedst him better Than ever thou lovedst Cassius . . . . . . *J. Cæsar* iv 3 106

Lovel and Ratcliff, look that it be done . . . . *Richard III.* iii 4 80
Go, Lovel, with all speed to Doctor Shaw; Go thou to Friar Penker . iii 5 103
Sir Thomas Lovel and Lord Marquis Dorset, 'Tis said, my liege, in Yorkshire are in arms . . . . iv 4 520
That, had the king in his last sickness fail'd, The cardinal's and Sir Thomas Lovell's heads Should have gone off . . *Hen. VIII.* i 2 185
Sir Thomas Lovell, I as free forgive you As I would be forgiven . ii 1 82
I'll take my leave.—Not yet, Sir Thomas Lovell. What's the matter? v 1 10
Now, Lovell, from the queen what is the news? . . . . v 1 61
Lovelier. A sweeter and a lovelier gentleman . . *Richard III.* i 2 243
The breasts of Hecuba, When she did suckle Hector, look'd not lovelier Than Hector's forehead when it spit forth blood . *Coriolanus* i 3 44
Loveliness in favour, sympathy in years, manners and beauties *Othello* ii 1 232
Lovely. 'Tis a passing shame That I, unworthy body as I am, Should censure thus on lovely gentlemen . . . . *T. G. of Ver.* i 2 19
If I had such a tire, this face of mine Were full as lovely as is this of hers iv 4 191
For your lovely sake, Give me your hand and say you will be mine *M. for M.* v 1 496
Why ever wast thou lovely in my eyes? . . . . *Much Ado* iv 1 132
Every lovely organ of her life Shall come apparell'd in more precious habit . . . . iv 1 228
True, that thou art beauteous; truth itself, that thou art lovely *L. L. L.* iv 1 62
A most lovely gentleman-like man . . . . *M. N. Dream* i 2 89
A lovely boy, stolen from an Indian king . . . . ii 1 22
Never harm, Nor spell nor charm, Come our lovely lady nigh . . ii 2 18
Most brisky juvenal and eke most lovely Jew . . . . iii 1 97
Two lovely berries moulded on one stem . . . . . iii 2 211
O wall, O sweet, O lovely wall! . . . . . . v 1 175
Even in the lovely garnish of a boy . . . *Mer. of Venice* ii 6 45
The tears . . . Like envious floods o'er-run her lovely face *T. of Shrew* Ind. 2 67
But where is Kate? where is my lovely bride? . . . . iii 2 94
And seal the title with a lovely kiss . . . . . iii 2 125
Fair lovely maid, once more good day to thee . . . . iv 5 33
Happier the man, whom favourable stars Allot thee for his lovely bed-fellow! . . . . iv 5 41
Look upon the years Of Lewis the Dauphin and that lovely maid *K. John* ii 1 425
O amiable lovely death! Thou odoriferous stench! . . . . iii 4 25
That sweet lovely rose . . . . . . *1 Hen. IV.* i 3 175
I framed to the harp Many an English ditty lovely well . . . iii 1 124
And from heart-string I love the lovely bully . . . *Hen. V.* iv 1 48
Why . . . Peace . . . Should not in this best garden of the world, Our fertile France, put up her lovely visage? . . . . . . v 2 37
The chief perfections of that lovely dame, Had I sufficient skill to utter them, Would make a volume of enticing lines . . . *1 Hen. VI.* v 5 12
With him the husband of this lovely lady . . . *2 Hen. VI.* i 4 77
Hath this lovely face Ruled, like a wandering planet, over me? . . iv 4 15
Ah, what a life were this! how sweet! how lovely! . . *3 Hen. VI.* ii 5 41
Love my lovely queen; And kiss your princely nephew, brothers both v 7 26
Henry's death, my lovely Edward's death, Their kingdom's loss *Rich. III.* i 3 192
A lovely boy: the God of heaven Both now and ever bless her! *Hen. VIII.* v 1 164
Lovely Tamora, queen of Goths . . . . . *T. Andron.* i 1 315
Lords, accompany Your noble emperor and his lovely bride . . . i 1 334
At my lovely Tamora's entreats, I do remit these . . . . i 1 483
A solemn hunting is in hand; There will the lovely Roman ladies troop ii 1 113
And wake the emperor and his lovely bride . . . . ii 2 4
My lovely Aaron, wherefore look'st thou sad? . . . . ii 3 10
Now will I hence to seek my lovely Moor . . . . ii 3 190
But, lovely niece, that mean is cut from thee . . . . ii 4 40
Gramercy, lovely Lucius: what's the news? . . . . iv 2 7
My lovely Saturnine, Lord of my life . . . . . iv 4 27
Signior Placentio and his lovely nieces . . . *Rom. and Jul.* i 2 70
O, he's a lovely gentleman! . . . . iii 5 220
O thou weed, Who art so lovely fair and smell'st so sweet! . *Othello* iv 2 68
Lover. Some donation freely to estate On the blest lovers . *Tempest* iv 1 86
'Tis threefold too little for carrying a letter to your lover *T. G. of Ver.* i 1 116
Herself hath taught her love himself to write unto her lover . . ii 1 174
Alas! this parting strikes poor lovers dumb . . . . ii 2 21
They say that Love hath not an eye at all.—To see such lovers . ii 4 97
My master is become a notable lover?—I never knew him otherwise.—Than how?—A notable lubber . . . . ii 5 44
A hot lover.—Why, I tell thee, I care not though he burn himself in love ii 5 54
With a corded ladder fetch her down; For which the youthful lover now is gone . . . . iii 1 41
Hope is a lover's staff; walk hence with that . . . . iii 1 246
Her sudden quips, The least whereof would quell a lover's hope . iv 2 13
Lovers break not hours, Unless it be to come before their time . v 1 4
Your brother and his lover have embraced . . *Meas. for Meas.* i 4 40
Thou wilt be like a lover presently And tire the hearer . *Much Ado* i 1 308
Green indeed is the colour of lovers . . . . *L. L. Lost* i 2 90
And send you many lovers!—Amen, so you be none . . . ii 1 126
Is infected.—With what?—With that which we lovers entitle affected . ii 1 232
That the lover, sick to death, Wish himself the heaven's breath . iv 3 107
O, would the king, Biron, and Longaville, Were lovers too! . . iv 3 124
I post from love: good lover, let me go . . . . . iv 3 188
Sweet lovers, O, let us embrace! As true we are as flesh and blood can be iv 3 214
A lover's eyes will gaze an eagle blind; A lover's ear will hear the lowest sound . . . . iv 3 334
Some thousand verses of a faithful lover, A huge translation of hypocrisy v 2 50
We are wise girls to mock our lovers so.—They are worse fools . v 2 58
Adding thereto moreover That he would wed me, or else die my lover . v 2 447
If then true lovers have been ever cross'd, It stands as an edict in destiny: Then let us teach our trial patience . . *M. N. Dream* i 1 150
A time that lovers' flights doth still conceal . . . . i 1 212
We must starve our sight From lovers' food till morrow deep midnight i 1 223
What is Pyramus? a lover, or a tyrant?—A lover, that kills himself most gallant . . . . i 2 24
This is Ercles' vein, a tyrant's vein; a lover is more condoling . . i 2 43
Ah Pyramus, my lover dear! thy Thisby dear, and lady dear! . . i 2 55
And the youth, mistook by me, Pleading for a lover's fee . . iii 2 113
Thou see'st these lovers seek a place to fight . . . . iii 2 354
And back to Athens shall the lovers wend, With league whose date till death shall never end . . . . iii 2 372
I'll apply To your eye, Gentle lover, remedy . . . . iii 2 452
There shall the pairs of faithful lovers be Wedded, with Theseus . iv 1 96
Fair lovers, you are fortunately met . . . . . iv 1 182
'Tis strange, my Theseus, that these lovers speak of . . . v 1 1
Lovers and madmen have such seething brains, Such shaping fantasies v 1 4
The lunatic, the lover and the poet Are of imagination all compact . v 1 7
The lover, all as frantic, Sees Helen's beauty in a brow of Egypt . v 1 10
Here come the lovers, full of joy and mirth . . . . . v 1 28
Wall, that vile Wall which did these lovers sunder . . . . v 1 133

Lover. By moonshine did these lovers think no scorn To meet at Ninus' tomb *M. N. Dream* v 1 138
Let Lion, Moonshine, Wall, and lovers twain At large discourse v 1 151
Through which the lovers, Pyramus and Thisby, Did whisper often v 1 160
And this the cranny is, right and sinister, Through which the fearful lovers are to whisper v 1 165
Think what thou wilt, I am thy lover's grace v 1 197
How chance Moonshine is gone before Thisbe comes back and finds her lover? v 1 319
These yellow cowslip cheeks, Are gone, are gone: Lovers, make moan. v 1 341
The iron tongue of midnight hath told twelve: Lovers, to bed v 1 371
For lovers ever run before the clock *Mer. of Venice* ii 6 4
Love is blind and lovers cannot see The pretty follies that themselves commit ii 6 36
How dear a lover of my lord your husband iii 4 7
Antonio, Being the bosom lover of my lord, Must needs be like my lord iii 4 17
As true a lover As ever sigh'd upon a midnight pillow *As Y. Like It* ii 4 26
We that are true lovers run into strange capers ii 4 55
And then the lover, Sighing like furnace, with a woeful ballad ii 7 147
It is as easy to count atomies as to resolve the propositions of a lover iii 2 246
There's no clock in the forest.—Then there is no true lover in the forest iii 2 320
As loving yourself than seeming the lover of any other iii 2 403
The truest poetry is the most feigning; and lovers are given to poetry, and what they swear in poetry may be said as lovers they do feign iii 3 20
The oath of a lover is no stronger than the word of a tapster iii 4 34
Swears brave oaths and breaks them bravely, quite traverse, athwart the heart of his lover iii 4 46
The sight of lovers feedeth those in love iii 4 60
I have neither the scholar's melancholy . . . nor the lover's iv 1 15
You a lover! An you serve me such another trick, never come in my sight more iv 1 40
For lovers lacking—God warn us!—matter, the cleanliest shift is to kiss iv 1 76
The most pathetical break-promise and the most hollow lover iv 1 197
If you be a true lover, hence, and not a word iv 3 74
Here comes a lover of mine and a lover of hers v 2 82
It was a lover and his lass, With a hey, and a ho, and a hey nonino v 3 17
Hey ding a ding, ding: Sweet lovers love the spring v 3 22
Bless you with such grace As 'longeth to a lover's blessed case! *T. of S.* iv 2 45
And I shall prove A lover of thy drum, hater of love *All's Well* iii 3 11
Journeys end in lovers meeting, Every wise man's son doth know *T. N.* ii 3 44
As I am all true lovers are, Unstaid and skittish in all motions else ii 4 17
Lay me, O, where Sad true lover never find my grave, To weep there! ii 4 66
I am as melancholy as . . . an old lion, or a lover's lute 1 *Hen. IV.* i 2 84
If I do sweat, they are the drops of thy lovers 2 *Hen. IV.* iv 3 14
And a true lover of the holy church *Hen. V.* i 1 23
The pining maidens' groans, For husbands, fathers and betrothed lovers ii 4 108
Since I cannot prove a lover, To entertain these fair well-spoken days, I am determined to prove a villain *Richard III.* i 1 28
He of Winchester Is held no great good lover of the archbishop's *Hen. VIII.* iv 1 104
The Grecian dames are sunburnt and not worth The splinter of a lance. Even so much.—This shall be told our lovers *Troi. and Cres.* i 3 284
These lovers cry Oh! oh! they die! iii 1 131
They say all lovers swear more performance than they are able iii 2 91
I as your lover speak; The fool slides o'er the ice that you should break iii 3 214
Had she no lover there That wails her absence? iv 5 288
I tell thee, fellow, Thy general is my lover *Coriolanus* v 2 14
These lovers will not keep the peace. *T. Andron.* ii 1 37
From forth the fatal loins of these two foes A pair of star-cross'd lovers take their life *Rom. and Jul.* Prol. 6
Love is a smoke raised with the fume of sighs; Being purged, a fire sparkling in lovers' eyes; Being vex'd, a sea nourish'd with lovers' tears i 1 197
This unbound lover, To beautify him, only lacks a cover i 3 87
You are a lover; borrow Cupid's wings, And soar with them. i 4 17
In this state she gallops night by night Through lovers' brains i 4 71
To breathe such vows as lovers use to swear ii Prol. 10
At lovers' perjuries, They say, Jove laughs ii 2 92
How silver-sweet sound lovers' tongues by night, Like softest music! ii 2 166
A lover may bestride the gossamer That idles in the wanton summer air ii 6 18
Lovers can see to do their amorous rites By their own beauties iii 2 8
I do not always follow lover, elder brother and woman *T. of Athens* ii 2 130
The mighty gods defend thee! Thy lover, ARTEMIDORUS *J. Cæsar* ii 3 9
Romans, countrymen, and lovers! hear me for my cause iii 2 13
I slew my best lover for the good of Rome, I have the same dagger for myself iii 2 49
That we may, Lovers in peace, lead on our days to age! v 1 95
The lover shall not sigh gratis *Hamlet* ii 2 335
Which, as a grise or step, may help these lovers Into your favour *Othello* i 3 200
And lovers' absent hours, More tedious than the dial eight score times iii 4 174
But I will be A bridegroom in my death, and run into't As to a lover's bed. Come, then *Ant. and Cleo.* iv 14 101
The stroke of death is as a lover's pinch, Which hurts, and is desired v 2 298
Lovers And men in dangerous bonds pray not alike *Cymbeline* iii 2 36
All lovers young, all lovers must Consign to thee, and come to dust iv 2 274
Like a noble lord in love and one That had a royal lover, took his hint v 5 172
To weep that you live as ye do makes pity in your lovers *Pericles* iv 2 130

Lovest. Since thou lovest, love still and thrive therein *T. G. of Ver.* i 1 9
As thou lovest me, let me have What thou thinkest meet ii 7 57
Now, as thou lovest me, do him not that wrong ii 7 80
But, as thou lovest thy life, make speed from hence iii 1 169
As thou lovest Silvia, though not for thyself, Regard thy danger iii 1 255
I give thee this for Thy sweet mistress' sake, because thou lovest her iv 4 182
'Tis once, thou lovest, And I will fit thee with the remedy *Much Ado* i 1 320
By my sword, Beatrice, thou lovest me.—Do not swear, and eat it iv 1 276
If thou lovest me then, Steal forth thy father's house *M. N. Dream* i 1 163
I see thou lovest me not with the full weight that I love thee *As Y. L. It* i 2 8
Of all thy suitors, here I charge thee, tell Whom thou lovest best *T. of S.* ii 1 9
This kindness merits thanks. What, not a word? Nay, then thou lovest it not iv 3 42
Eat it up all, Hortensio, if thou lovest me iv 3 50
As thou lovest her, Thy love's to me religious; else, does err *All's Well* ii 3 189
Now, as thou lovest me, let me see his letter *T. Night* v 1 1
How thou lovest us, show in our brother's welcome *W. Tale* i 2 174
As thou lovest me, Camillo, wipe not out the rest of thy services by leaving me iv 2 11
I love thee well; And, by my troth, I think thou lovest me well *K. John* iii 3 55
Ah, no more of that, Hal, an thou lovest me! 1 *Hen. IV.* ii 4 312
Come, I know thou lovest me *Hen. V.* v 2 210

Lovest. I dare not swear thou lovest me; yet my blood begins to flatter me that thou dost *Hen. V.* v 2 239
Name not religion, for thou lovest the flesh 1 *Hen. VI.* i 1 41
As thou lovest and honourest arms, Let's fight it out 3 *Hen. VI.* i 1 116
Thou lovest me not; for, brother, if thou didst, Thy tears would wash this cold congealed blood v 2 36
Sups the fair Rosaline whom thou so lovest *Rom. and Jul.* i 2 88
And, as thou lovest me, let the porter let in Susan Grindstone and Nell i 5 10
If thou lovest me, Mount thou my horse *J. Cæsar* v 3 14
Thy master, whom thou lovest, Shall find thee full of labours *Lear* i 4 6
If thou lovest me, tell me.—I love thee not ii 2 6

Loveth. Be still, drum! for your manager is in love; yea, he loveth *L. L. Lost* i 2 189
Lucentio here Doth love my daughter and she loveth him *T. of Shrew* iv 4 41
Most unnatural, To be revenged on him that loveth you *Richard III.* i 2 135

Loving. Whose pity, sighing back again, Did us but loving wrong *Tempest* i 2 151
Cease to persuade, my loving Proteus *T. G. of Ver.* i 1 1
O hateful hands, to tear such loving words! i 2 105
How, with my honour, I may undertake A journey to my loving Proteus ii 7 7
Only deserve my love by loving him ii 7 82
What is't I dream on? . . . Most dangerous Is that temptation that doth goad us on To sin in loving virtue *Meas. for Meas.* ii 2 183
The sixth of July: Your loving friend, Benedick *Much Ado* i 1 285
She is exceeding wise.—In every thing but in loving Benedick ii 3 168
And virtuous; 'tis so, I cannot reprove it; and wise, but for loving me ii 3 241
If it proves so, then loving goes by haps iii 1 105
I will requite thee, Taming my wild heart to thy loving hand iii 1 112
But in loving, . . . why, they were never so truly turned over and over as my poor self in love v 2 30
My loving lord, Dumain is mortified *L. L. Lost* i 1 28
My spirit grows heavy in love.—And that's great marvel, loving a light wench i 2 128
Who are the votaries, my loving lords, That are vow-fellows? ii 1 37
I'll give you Aquitaine and all that is his, An you give him for my sake but one loving kiss ii 1 248
Lay his wreathed arms athwart His loving bosom to keep down his heart iv 3 136
What grace hast thou, thus to reprove These worms for loving? iv 3 154
Now prove Our loving lawful, and our faith not torn iv 3 285
Look you what I have from the loving king v 2 4
So shall all the couples three Ever true in loving be *M. N. Dream* v 1 415
Become a Christian and thy loving wife *Mer. of Venice* ii 3 21
Turn you where your lady is And claim her with a loving kiss iii 2 139
In loving visitation was with me a young doctor of Rome iv 1 153
The old duke is banished . . . ; and three or four loving lords have put themselves into voluntary exile with him *As Y. Like It* i 1 106
Most friendship is feigning, most loving mere folly ii 7 181
As loving yourself than seeming the lover of any other iii 2 402
That but seeing you should love her? and loving woo? v 2 3
Thy loving voyage Is but for two months victuall'd v 4 197
And now by law . . . I may entitle thee my loving father *T. of Shrew* iv 5 61
With thy loving widow, Feast with the best, and welcome v 2 7
A foul contending rebel And graceless traitor to her loving lord v 2 160
Let not your hate encounter with my love For loving where you do *All's Well* i 3 215
Have my leave and love, Means and attendants and my loving greetings i 3 258
Attorneyed with interchange of gifts, letters, loving embassies *W. Tale* i 1 31
But thou from loving England art so far *K. John* ii 1 94
You men of Angiers, and my loving subjects,— You loving men of Angiers ii 1 203
Many a poor man's son would have lien still And ne'er have spoke a loving word iv 1 51
Happy days befal My gracious sovereign, my most loving liege! *Rich. II.* i 1 21
Then let us take a ceremonious leave And loving farewell i 3 51
My loving lord, I take my leave of you; Of you, my noble cousin i 3 63
Thanks, my countrymen, my loving friends i 4 34
Hard-hearted man! Love loving not itself none other can v 3 88
It cannot be, The king should keep his word in loving us 1 *Hen. IV.* v 2 5
The lives of all your loving complices Lean on your health 2 *Hen. IV.* i 1 163
Loving wife, and gentle daughter, Give even way unto my rough affairs ii 3 1
As, by a lower but loving likelihood *Hen. V.* v Prol. 29
But, in loving me, you should love the friend of France v 2 181
Like to a pair of loving turtle-doves 1 *Hen. VI.* ii 2 30
My lord, your loving nephew now is come ii 5 33
My friends and loving countrymen, This token serveth for a flag of truce iii 1 137
O loving uncle, kind Duke of Gloucester, How joyful am I made by this! iii 1 142
My loving lords, our pleasure is That Richard be restored to his blood iii 1 158
No loving token to his majesty?—Yes, my good lord, a pure unspotted heart v 3 181
Your loving uncle, . . . They say, is shamefully bereft of life 2 *Hen. VI.* iii 2 268
And tell them all from me, I thank them for their tender loving care iii 2 280
Your princely father and my loving lord! 3 *Hen. VI.* ii 1 47
Thou, brave Earl of March, Amongst the loving Welshmen ii 1 180
Would have his son a king, And raise his issue, like a loving sire ii 2 22
To give the heir and daughter of Lord Scales Unto the brother of your loving bride iv 1 53
My sovereign, with the loving citizens, . . . Shall rest in London iv 8 19
Sweet Oxford, and my loving Montague, And all at once, once more a happy farewell iv 8 30
What says my loving son? And, by thy guess, how nigh is Clarence now? v 1 7
We are advertised by our loving friends v 3 18
That I love the tree . . ., Witness the loving kiss I give the fruit v 7 32
How fares our loving brother?—Well, my dread lord *Richard III.* iii 1 96
Which now the loving haste of these our friends, Somewhat against our meaning, have prevented iii 5 54
Your very worshipful and loving friends iii 7 138
Think now what I would say.—Say on, my loving lord iv 2 11
Then in plain terms tell her my loving tale iv 4 359
Fellows in arms, and my most loving friends v 2 1
Noble father-in-law! Tell me, how fares our loving mother? v 3 82
More than I have said, loving countrymen, The leisure and enforcement of the time Forbids to dwell upon v 3 237
Ever beloved and loving may his rule be! *Hen. VIII.* ii 1 92
Put your main cause into the king's protection; He's loving iii 1 94
They're loving, well composed with gifts of nature. *Troi. and Cres.* iv 4 79
Call my brother Troilus to me, And signify this loving interview iv 5 155
We do request your kindest ears, and after, Your loving motion *Coriol.* ii 2 57
My loving followers, Plead my successive title with your swords *T. An.* i 1 3

Loving. That I will here dismiss my loving friends . . . *T. Andron.* i 1 53
She will a handmaid be to his desires, A loving nurse . . . i 1 332
Tear for tear, and loving kiss for kiss . . . v 3 156
He danced thee on his knee, Sung thee asleep, his loving breast thy pillow . . . v 3 163
Like a loving child, Shed yet some small drops from thy tender spring v 3 166
Some loving friends convey the emperor hence . . . v 3 191
O brawling love! O loving hate! . . . *Rom. and Jul.* i 1 182
She will not stay the siege of loving terms . . . i 1 218
Thou chid'st me oft for loving Rosaline.—For doting, not for loving . ii 3 81
Come, loving, black-brow'd night, Give me my Romeo . . . iii 2 20
But one, poor one, one poor and loving child . . . iv 5 46
Commend me to my loving countrymen . . . *T. of Athens* v 1 197
Cæsar was mighty, bold, royal, and loving . . . *J. Cæsar* iii 1 127
Why, 'tis a loving and a fair reply . . . *Hamlet* i 2 121
So loving to my mother That he might not beteem the winds of heaven Visit her face too roughly . . . i 2 140
Farewell, dear mother.—Thy loving father, Hamlet.—My mother . iv 3 52
Our son of Cornwall, And you, our no less loving son of Albany . *Lear* i 1 43
Our very loving sister, well be-met . . . v 1 20
He, as loving his own pride and purposes, Evades them . . . *Othello* i 1 12
Howbeit that I endure him not, Is of a constant, loving, noble nature . ii 1 298
I humbly do beseech you of your pardon For too much loving you . iii 3 213
That death's unnatural that kills for loving . . . v 2 42
There is mettle in death, which commits some loving act upon her, she hath such a celerity in dying . . . *Ant. and Cleo.* i 2 148
You call my course unnatural, You not your child well loving *Pericles* iv 3 37
Loving-jealous. And with a silk thread plucks it back again, So loving-jealous of his liberty . . . *Rom. and Jul.* ii 2 182
Lovingly. Kind Rome, that hast thus lovingly reserved The cordial of mine age to glad my heart! . . . *T. Andron.* i 1 165
Low. Turn'd to barnacles, or to apes With foreheads villanous low *Temp.* iv 1 250
Too low a mistress for so high a servant . . . *T. G. of Ver.* ii 4 106
Her eyes are grey as glass, and so are mine: Ay, but her forehead's low iv 4 198
And high and low beguiles the rich and poor . . . *Mer. Wives* i 3 95
He wooes both high and low, both rich and poor, Both young and old ii 1 117
Little have you to say When you depart from him, but, soft and low *Meas. for Meas.* iv 1 69
Oh, sir, I did not look so low . . . *Com. of Errors* iii 2 143
She's too low for a high praise, too brown for a fair praise *Much Ado* i 1 173
Speak low, if you speak love . . . ii 1 103
If low, an agate very vilely cut . . . iii 1 65
If he could right himself with quarrelling, Some of us would lie low v 1 52
Bull Jove, sir, had an amiable low . . . v 4 48
How low soever the matter, I hope in God for high words.—A high hope for a low heaven: God grant us patience! . . . *L. L. Lost* i 1 194
O cross! too high to be enthrall'd to low . . . *M. N. Dream* i 1 136
And are you grown so high in his esteem, Because I am so dwarfish and so low? How low am I, thou painted maypole? speak; How low am I? I am not yet so low But that my nails can reach unto thine eyes . . . iii 2 295
Nothing but 'low' and 'little'! Why will you suffer her to flout me thus? . . . iii 2 326
In low simplicity He lends out money gratis . . . *Mer. of Venice* i 3 44
Bend low and in a bondman's key, With bated breath . . . i 3 124
How much low peasantry would then be glean'd From the true seed of honour! . . . ii 9 46
My creditors grow cruel, my estate is very low . . . iii 2 319
We'll light upon some settled low content . . . *As Y. Like It* ii 3 68
The woman low And browner than her brother . . . iv 3 88
And with a low submissive reverence Say 'What is it?' *T. of Shrew* Ind. 1 53
Such duty to the drunkard let him do With soft low tongue . . Ind. 1 114
And bow'd his eminent top to their low ranks . . . *All's Well* i 2 43
My low and humble name to propagate . . . ii 1 200
If there be here German, or Dane, low Dutch, Italian, or French . iv 1 78
This exceeding posting day and night Must wear your spirits low . v 1 2
Falls into abatement and low price, Even in a minute . . . *T. Night* i 1 13
Your true love's coming, That can sing both high and low . . . ii 3 42
Out of my lean and low ability I'll lend you something . . . iii 4 378
The odds for high and low's alike . . . *W. Tale* v 1 207
Stoop low within those bounds we have o'erlook'd . . . *K. John* v 4 55
Then, Bolingbroke, as low as to thy heart, Through the false passage of thy throat, thou liest . . . *Richard II.* i 1 124
And lie full low, graved in the hollow ground . . . iii 2 140
Your heart is up, I know, Thus high at least, although your knee be low iii 3 195
Now in as low an ebb as the foot of the ladder . . . 1 *Hen. IV.* i 2 41
O, pardon me that I descend so low . . . i 3 167
Such inordinate and low desires . . . iii 2 12
So are the horses of the enemy In general, journey-bated and brought low iv 3 26
Sick in the world's regard, wretched and low, A poor unminded outlaw iv 3 57
Stoop'd his anointed head as low as death . . . 2 *Hen. IV.* Ind. 32
It is a low ebb of linen with thee when thou keepest not racket there . ii 2 22
The rest of thy low countries have made a shift to eat up thy holland . ii 2 25
From a prince to a prentice? a low transformation! . . . ii 2 194
For those that could speak low and tardily Would turn their own perfection to abuse, To seem like him . . . ii 3 26
Then happy low, lie down! Uneasy lies the head that wears a crown . iii 1 30
Not so much noise, my lords: sweet prince, speak low . . . iv 5 16
For government, though high and low and lower, Put into parts, doth keep in one consent . . . *Hen. V.* i 2 180
Whose low vassal seat The Alps doth spit and void his rheum upon . iii 5 51
Will it give place to flexure and low bending? . . . iv 1 272
A squire of low degree . . . v 1 38
And never more abase our sight so low . . . 2 *Hen. VI.* i 2 15
A crown for York! and, lords, bow low to him . . . 3 *Hen. VI.* i 4 94
I may conquer fortune's spite By living low, where fortune cannot hurt me . . . iv 6 20
I had rather chop this hand off at a blow, And with the other fling it at thy face, Than bear so low a sail, to strike to thee . . . v 1 52
And kept low shrubs from winter's powerful wind . . . v 2 15
So that, betwixt their titles and low names, There's nothing differs but the outward fame . . . *Richard III.* i 4 82
Gone slightly o'er low steps and now are mounted . . . *Hen. VIII.* ii 4 112
We are not brought so low, But that between us we can kill a fly *T. An.* iii 2 76
I saw her laid low in her kindred's vault . . . *Rom. and Jul.* v 1 20
I hope it is not so low with him as he made it seem . . . *T. of Athens* iii 6 6
As Timon grows, his hate may grow To the whole race of mankind, high and low! . . . iv 1 40
Poor honest lord, brought low by his own heart, Undone by goodness! iv 2 37
Tell Athens, in the sequence of degree From high to low throughout . v 1 212

Low. Taught thee to make vast Neptune weep for aye On thy low grave *T. of Athens* v 4 79
As low as to thy foot doth Cassius fall, To beg enfranchisement *J. Cæsar* iii 1 56
O mighty Cæsar! dost thou lie so low? . . . iii 1 148
Come, high or low; Thyself and office deftly show! . . . *Macbeth* iv 1 67
Bowl the round nave down the hill of heaven, As low as to the fiends! *Hamlet* ii 2 519
Nor are those empty-hearted whose low sound Reverbs no hollowness *Lear* i 1 155
Your purposed low correction . . . ii 2 149
Low farms, Poor pelting villages, sheep-cotes, and mills . . . ii 3 17
How fearful And dizzy 'tis, to cast one's eyes so low! . . . iv 6 12
Her voice was ever soft, Gentle, and low, an excellent thing in woman v 3 273
Let the labouring bark climb hills of seas Olympus-high and duck again as low As hell's from heaven! . . . *Othello* ii 1 190
He was a wight of high renown, And thou art but of low degree . . ii 3 97
Didst hear her speak? is she shrill-tongued or low? *Ant. and Cleo.* iii 3 15
Her hair, what colour?—Brown, madam: and her forehead As low as she would wish it . . . iii 3 37
Thy mind to her is now as low as were Thy fortunes . . . *Cymbeline* iii 2 10
A goodly day not to keep house, with such Whose roof's as low as ours! . iii 3 2
And nature prompts them In simple and low things to prince it much . iii 3 85
Throwing favours on The low Posthumus slanders so her judgement . iii 5 76
Yet reverence, That angel of the world, doth make distinction Of place 'tween high and low . . . iv 2 249
No more, you petty spirits of region low, Offend our hearing . . . v 4 93
If that ever my low fortune's better, I'll pay your bounties *Pericles* ii 1 148
We are gentlemen That neither in our hearts nor outward eyes Envy the great nor do the low despise . . . ii 3 26
Low-born. This is the prettiest low-born lass that ever Ran on the green-sward . . . *W. Tale* iv 4 156
Low-crooked court'sies and base spaniel-fawning . . . *J. Cæsar* iii 1 43
Lower. Down with the topmast! yare! lower, lower! . . . *Tempest* i 1 37
Destiny, That hath to instrument this lower world . . . iii 3 54
He, sir, sitting, as I say, in a lower chair, sir . . . *Meas. for Meas.* ii 1 132
But she herself is hit lower: have I hit her now? . . . *L. L. Lost* iv 1 120
Master, let me take you a button-hole lower . . . v 2 707
Dock'd in sand, Vailing her high-top lower than her ribs *Mer. of Venice* i 1 28
Thou wert best set thy lower part where thy nose stands *All's Well* ii 3 267
Lower messes Perchance are to this business purblind? say . *W. Tale* i 2 227
When the searching eye of heaven is hid, Behind the globe, that lights the lower world, Then thieves and robbers range abroad *Richard II.* iii 2 38
Bareheaded, lower than his proud steed's neck . . . v 2 19
Ned Poins and I will walk lower: if they 'scape from your encounter, then they light on us . . . 1 *Hen. IV.* ii 2 63
Percy stands on high; And either we or they must lower lie . . . iii 3 228
Speak lower, princes, for the king recovers . . . 2 *Hen. IV.* iv 4 129
For government, though high and low and lower, Put into parts, doth keep in one consent . . . *Hen. V.* i 2 180
So! in the name of Jesu Christ, speak lower . . . iv 1 66
I will speak lower.—I pray you and beseech you that you will . . iv 1 82
As, by a lower but loving likelihood . . . v Prol. 29
Some followers of mine own, At the lower end of the hall *Richard III.* iii 7 35
Set me lower: I have not long to trouble thee . . . *Hen. VIII.* iv 2 76
A lower place, note well, May make too great an act *Ant. and Cleo.* iii 1 12
Made her Of lower Syria, Cyprus, Lydia, Absolute queen . . . iii 6 10
Strike me, if you please; I cannot be much lower than my knees *Pericles* i 2 47
Lowering. Present pleasure, By revolution lowering, does become The opposite of itself . . . *Ant. and Cleo.* i 2 129
Lowest. A lover's ear will hear the lowest sound . . . *L. L. Lost* iv 3 335
From lowest place when virtuous things proceed, The place is dignified by the doer's deed . . . *All's Well* ii 3 132
For that, being one o' the lowest, basest, poorest, Of this most wise rebellion, thou go'st foremost . . . *Coriolanus* i 1 161
The fires i' the lowest hell fold-in the people! Call me their traitor! . iii 3 68
Till the lowest stream Do kiss the most exalted shores of all . *J. Cæsar* i 1 64
You would sound me from my lowest note to the top of my compass *Hamlet* iii 2 383
To be worst, The lowest and most dejected thing of fortune, Stands still in esperance, lives not in fear . . . *Lear* iv 1 3
What need we fear? The ground's the lowest, and we are half way there . . . *Pericles* i 4 78
Lowing. That calf-like they my lowing follow'd . . . *Tempest* iv 1 179
As the dam runs lowing up and down . . . 2 *Hen. VI.* iii 1 214
Low-laid. I would that I were low laid in my grave . . . *K. John* ii 1 164
Be content; Your low-laid son our godhead will uplift . . *Cymbeline* v 4 103
Lowliness. For so witnesseth thy lowliness . . . *L. L. Lost* iv 1 81
Witness the night, your garments, your lowliness . . . *Hen. V.* iv 8 55
But with as humble lowliness of mind She is content to be at your command; Command, I mean, of virtuous chaste intents 1 *Hen. VI.* v 5 18
Lowliness is young ambition's ladder . . . *J. Cæsar* ii 1 22
The king-becoming graces, As . . . perseverance, mercy, lowliness *Macb.* iv 3 93
Lowly. With soft low tongue and lowly courtesy . . . *T. of Shrew* Ind. 1 114
And banish hence these abject lowly dreams . . . Ind. 2 34
I will show myself highly fed and lowly taught . . . *All's Well* ii 2 3
'Twas never merry world Since lowly feigning was call'd compliment *T. Night* iii 1 110
And me, poor lowly maid, Most goddess-like prank'd up . . . *W. Tale* iv 4 9
Thy sun sets weeping in the lowly west, Witnessing storms to come *Richard II.* ii 4 21
As looks the mother on her lowly babe . . . 1 *Hen. VI.* iii 3 47
And lowly words were ransom for their fault . . . 2 *Hen. VI.* iii 1 127
Obscure and lowly swain . . . iv 1 50
It is impossible that I should die By such a lowly vassal as thyself . iv 1 111
Steward, substitute, Or lowly factor for another's gain . *Richard III.* iii 7 134
'Tis better to be lowly born, And range with humble livers *Hen. VIII.* ii 3 19
These lowly courtesies Might fire the blood of ordinary men *J. Cæsar* iii 1 36
Lown. With that he call'd the tailor lown . . . *Othello* ii 3 95
We should have both lord and lown . . . *Pericles* iv 6 19
Lowness. Nothing could have subdued nature To such a lowness but his unkind daughters . . . *Lear* iii 4 73
They know, By the height, the lowness, or the mean, if dearth Or foison follow: the higher Nilus swells, The more it promises *A. and C.* ii 7 22
Send humble treaties, dodge And palter in the shifts of lowness . . iii 11 63
Low-rated. Do the low-rated English play at dice . . . *Hen. V.* iv Prol. 19
Low-spirited. That low-spirited swain, that base minnow . . *L. L. Lost* i 1 250
Lowted. And I am lowted by a traitor villain . . . 1 *Hen. VI.* iv 3 13
Low-voiced. Madam, I heard her speak; she is low-voiced *Ant. and Cleo.* iii 3 16
Loyal. And a loyal sir To him thou follow'st! . . . *Tempest* v 1 69
Longer than I prove loyal to your grace Let me not live *T. G. of Ver.* ii 2 20
With loyal blazon, evermore be blest! . . . *Mer. Wives* v 5 68

Loyal. Write loyal cantons of contemned love And sing them loud *T. Night* i 5 289
Hear me, who profess Myself your loyal servant, your physician *W. Tale* ii 3 54
But he that proves the king, To him will we prove loyal . *K. John* ii 1 271
To prove myself a loyal gentleman Even in the best blood *Richard II.* i 1 148
A jewel in a ten-times-barr'd-up chest Is a bold spirit in a loyal breast i 1 181
A loyal, just and upright gentleman . . . . . . i 3 87
The king is left behind, And in my loyal bosom lies his power . ii 3 98
Strong and bold conspiracy! O loyal father of a treacherous son! . v 3 60
Opinion, that did help me to the crown, Had still kept loyal to possession And left me in reputeless banishment . . 1 *Hen. IV.* iii 2 43
Never king of England Had nobles richer and more loyal subjects *Hen. V.* i 2 127
The presence of a king engenders love Amongst his subjects and his loyal friends, As it disanimates his enemies . . 1 *Hen. VI.* iii 1 182
These could not procure me any scathe, So long as I am loyal 2 *Hen. VI.* ii 4 63
Thou art come too soon, Unless thou wert more loyal than thou art . iii 1 96
But why come you in arms?—To help King Edward in his time of storm, As every loyal subject ought to do . . 3 *Hen. VI.* iv 7 44
In God's name, what art thou?—A man, as you are.—But not, as I am, royal.—Nor you, as we are, loyal . . *Richard III.* i 4 172
Less noble and less loyal, Nearer in bloody thoughts, but not in blood ii 1 91
A loyal and obedient subject is Therein illustrated . *Hen. VIII.* iii 2 180
He has a loyal breast, For you have seen him open 't . . iii 2 200
Call me to your senate, I'll deliver Myself your loyal servant *Coriolanus* v 6 142
Who can be wise, amazed, temperate and furious, Loyal and neutral, in a moment? No man . . . . . *Macbeth* ii 3 115
I should forge Quarrels unjust against the good and loyal . . iv 3 83
Loyal and natural boy, I'll work the means To make thee capable *Lear* ii 1 86
Of Gloucester's treachery, And of the loyal service of his son . iv 2 7
What art thou?—Your wife, my lord; your true And loyal wife *Othello* iv 2 35
So he wishes you all happiness, that remains loyal to his vow *Cymbeline* iii 2 47
What is here? The scriptures of the loyal Leonatus, All turn'd to heresy? iii 4 83
Beseech your highness, Hold me your loyal servant . . . . iv 3 16

Loyalest. The loyal'st husband that did e'er plight troth . . i 1 96

Loyally. He's true and shall perform All parts of his subjection loyally iv 3 19

Loyalty. When I protest true loyalty to her, She twits me with my falsehood to my friend . . . . . . *T. G. of Ver.* iv 2 7
And then end life when I end loyalty! . . . *M. N. Dream* ii 2 63
I will follow thee, To the last gasp, with truth and loyalty *As Y. Like It* ii 3 70
Mean time let this defend my loyalty . . . . *Richard II.* i 1 67
To defend my loyalty and truth To God, my king and my succeeding issue . . . . i 3 19
Wisdom, loyalty, and mere dislike Of our proceedings . 1 *Hen. IV.* iv 1 64
Crowned with faith and constant loyalty . . . *Hen. V.* ii 2 5
With submissive loyalty of heart . . . . 1 *Hen. VI.* iii 4 10
In thy face I see The map of honour, truth and loyalty . 2 *Hen. VI.* iii 1 203
Mere instinct of love and loyalty . . . . . . iii 2 250
O, where is loyalty? If it be banish'd from the frosty head . . v 1 166
Answer me one doubt, What pledge have we of thy firm loyalty?—This shall assure my constant loyalty . . 3 *Hen. VI.* iii 3 240
Behold a subject die For truth, for duty, and for loyalty *Richard III.* iii 3 4
Hath flaw'd the heart Of all their loyalties . . *Hen. VIII.* i 2 22
Language unmannerly, yea, such which breaks The sides of loyalty *Hen. VIII.* i 2 28
My loyalty, Which ever has and ever shall be growing . . . iii 2 177
In the way of loyalty and truth Toward the king . . . iii 2 272
Stood upon her chastity, Upon her nuptial vow, her loyalty *T. Andron.* ii 3 125
The service and the loyalty I owe, In doing it, pays itself *Macbeth* i 4 22
How, my lord, I may be censured, that nature thus gives way to loyalty *Lear* iii 5 4
I will persevere in my course of loyalty, though the conflict be sore iii 5 23
The loyalty well held to fools does make Our faith mere folly *Ant. and Cleo.* iii 13 42
This hand, whose touch, Whose every touch, would force the feeler's soul To the oath of loyalty . . . . . *Cymbeline* i 6 102
Beaten for loyalty Excited me to treason . . . . . v 5 344
In Helicanus may you well descry A figure of truth, of faith, of loyalty *Pericles* v 3 92

Lozel. A gross hag! And, lozel, thou art worthy to be hang'd *W. Tale* ii 3 109

Lubber. A notable lubber, as thou reportest him to be . *T. G. of Ver.* ii 5 47
I am afraid this great lubber, the world, will prove a cockney *T. Night* iv 1 14
Why, even already They clap the lubber Ajax on the shoulder *T. and C.* iii 3 139
If you will measure your lubber's length again, tarry . . *Lear* i 4 101

Lubberly. And she's a great lubberly boy . . . *Mer. Wives* v 5 195

Lubber's-head. He is indited to dinner to the Lubber's-head in Lumbert street . . . . 2 *Hen. IV.* ii 1 30

Luccicos. Marcus Luccicos, is not he in town? . . . *Othello* i 3 44

Luce. They may give the dozen white luces in their coat . *Mer. Wives* i 1 16
The luce is the fresh fish; the salt fish is an old coat . . . i 1 22
Let my master in, Luce.—Faith, no; he comes too late . *Com. of Errors* iii 1 49
If thy name be call'd Luce,—Luce, thou hast answer'd him well . iii 1 53

Lucentio. I am content to be Lucentio, Because so well I love Lucentio *T. of Shrew* i 1 221
Tranio is changed into Lucentio.—The better for him . . . i 1 242
Wish after, That Lucentio indeed had Baptista's youngest daughter . i 1 245
Then I am Tranio; But in all places else your master Lucentio . i 1 249
Lucentio shall make one, Though Paris came in hope to speed alone . i 2 246
Lucentio is your name; of whence, I pray?—Of Pisa, sir . . ii 1 103
Supposed Lucentio Must get a father, call'd 'supposed Vincentio' . ii 1 409
'Simois,' I am Lucentio, 'hic est,' son unto Vincentio of Pisa . iii 1 32
That Lucentio that comes a-wooing, 'Priami,' is my man Tranio . iii 1 34
What says Lucentio to this shame of ours?—No shame but mine . iii 2 7
Lucentio, you shall supply the bridegroom's place . . . iii 2 251
Is't possible, friend Licio, that Mistress Bianca Doth fancy any other but Lucentio? . . . . iv 2 2
You that durst swear that your mistress Bianca Loved none in the world so well as Lucentio . . . . iv 2 13
Your son Lucentio here Doth love my daughter and she loveth him . iv 4 40
Tell what hath happened, Lucentio's father is arrived in Padua, And how she's like to be Lucentio's wife . . . . . iv 4 66
Here's the door, this is Lucentio's house . . . . . v 1 9
I pray you, tell Signior Lucentio that his father is come from Pisa . v 1 29
Away, mad ass! his name is Lucentio; and he is mine only son . v 1 87
Then thou wert best say that I am not Lucentio . . . v 1 107
Where is Lucentio?—Here's Lucentio, Right son to the right Vincentio v 1 117
Tell me, is not this my Cambio?—Cambio is changed into Lucentio . v 1 126
Lucentio slipp'd me like his greyhound . . . . . v 2 52
'Tis since the nuptial of Lucentio, Come pentecost . . *Rom. and Jul.* i 5 37

Lucetta. How churlishly I chid Lucetta hence! . . *T. G. of Ver.* i 2 60
My penance is to call Lucetta back And ask remission . . . i 2 64
Counsel, Lucetta; gentle girl, assist me . . . . . ii 7 1

Luciana. Sure, Luciana, it is two o'clock . . . *Com. of Errors* ii 1 3
Ah, Luciana, did he tempt thee so? . . . . . . iv 2 1

Lucianus. This is one Lucianus, nephew to the king . . *Hamlet* iii 2 254

Lucifer. Shall I Sir Pandarus of Troy become, And by my side wear steel? then, Lucifer take all! . . . . . *Mer. Wives* i 3 84
Thou art more deep damn'd than Prince Lucifer . . *K. John* iv 3 122
Made Lucifer cuckold and swore the devil his true liegeman . 1 *Hen. IV.* ii 4 371
His face is Lucifer's privy-kitchen . . . . . 2 *Hen. IV.* ii 4 360
As good a gentleman as the devil is, as Lucifer and Belzebub himself *Hen. V.* iv 7 145
And when he falls, he falls like Lucifer, Never to hope again *Hen. VIII.* iii 2 371

Lucilius. Thou hast a servant named Lucilius.—I have so: what of him? *T. of Athens* i 1 111
A word, Lucilius; How he received you, let me be resolved . *J. Cæsar* iv 2 13
Ever note, Lucilius, When love begins to sicken and decay, It useth an enforced ceremony . . . . iv 2 19
Lucilius, come; And come, young Cato; let us to the field . . v 3 106
I thank thee, Brutus, That thou hast proved Lucilius' saying true . v 5 59

Lucina lent not me her aid, But took me in my throes . . *Cymbeline* v 4 43
At whose conception, till Lucina reign'd, Nature this dowry gave *Pericles* i 1 8
Lucina, O Divinest patroness, and midwife gentle! . . . iii 1 10

Lucio. Whence comes this restraint?—From too much liberty, my Lucio, liberty . . . . *Meas. for Meas.* i 2 129
Lucio, a word with you.—A hundred, if they'll do you any good . i 2 146
I prithee, Lucio, do me this kind service . . . . . i 2 181
My name is Lucio; well known to the duke.—He shall know you better iii 2 169
My lord, this is one Lucio's information against me . . . iii 2 210
Was sent to by my brother; one Lucio As then the messenger . . v 1 73
Signior Lucio? Is this the man that you did tell us of? . . . v 1 326
His cousin Tybalt; Lucio and the lively Helena . . *Rom. and Jul.* i 2 73

Lucius. This prince in justice seizeth but his own.—And that he will, and shall, if Lucius live . . . . . . *T. Andron.* i 1 282
Ah, Lucius, for thy brothers let me plead . . . . . iii 1 30
Foolish Lucius, dost thou not perceive That Rome is but a wilderness of tigers? . . . . iii 1 53
Thy brother Lucius, And thou, and I, sit round about some fountain . iii 1 122
Till Lucius come again, He leaves his pledges dearer than his life . iii 1 291
But now nor Lucius nor Lavinia lives But in oblivion . . . iii 1 295
If Lucius live, he will requite your wrongs . . . . . iii 1 297
Stand by me, Lucius; do not fear thine aunt.—She loves thee, boy . iv 1 5
Look to my house: Lucius and I'll go brave it at the court . . iv 1 121
They hither march amain, under conduct Of Lucius . . . iv 4 66
Is warlike Lucius general of the Goths? These tidings nip me . iv 4 69
That Lucius' banishment was wrongfully, And they have wish'd that Lucius were their emperor . . . . iv 4 76
Ay, but the citizens favour Lucius, And will revolt from me . . iv 4 79
Say that the emperor requests a parley Of warlike Lucius . . iv 4 102
Now will I to that old Andronicus, And temper him with all the art I have, To pluck proud Lucius from the warlike Goths . . iv 4 110
Lucius, and you princes of the Goths, The Roman emperor greets you v 1 156
In this mad thought, I'll make him send for Lucius his son . . v 2 75
Marcus, to thy nephew Lucius; Thou shalt inquire him out among the Goths . . . . v 2 122
I'll call my brother back again, And cleave to no revenge but Lucius v 2 136
And if you say we shall, Lo, hand in hand, Lucius and I will fall . v 3 136
And bring our emperor gently in thy hand, Lucius our emperor . v 3 139
Lucius, all hail, Rome's royal emperor! . . . . . . v 3 141
Lord Lucius, Out of his free love, hath presented to you Four milk-white horses, trapp'd in silver . . . . *T. of Athens* i 2 187
I will dispatch you severally; you to Lord Lucius . . . ii 2 197
Lord Lucius and Lucullus? hum!—Go you, sir . . . . ii 2 204
He might have tried Lord Lucius or Lucullus . . . . iii 3 2
Go, bid all my friends again, Lucius, Lucullus, and Sempronius . iii 4 112
What, Lucius, ho! I cannot, by the progress of the stars, Give guess how near to day. Lucius, I say! . . . . *J. Cæsar* ii 1 1
When, Lucius, when? awake, I say! what, Lucius! . . . ii 1 5
Get me a taper in my study, Lucius: When it is lighted, come and call me . . . . ii 1 7
Boy! Lucius! Fast asleep? It is no matter . . . . ii 1 229
Let Lucius and Titinius guard our door . . . . . iv 2 52
You have condemn'd and noted Lucius Pella For taking bribes . . iv 3 2
Fill, Lucius, till the wine o'erswell the cup . . . . iv 3 161
Lucius, here's the book I sought for so; I put it in the pocket . iv 3 252
Lucius, awake!—My lord?—Didst thou dream, Lucius, that thou so criedst out? . . . . iv 3 294
Fulvia thy wife first came into the field.—Against my brother Lucius? —Ay: But soon that war had end . . . *Ant. and Cleo.* i 2 93
Ambassadors from Rome; The one is Caius Lucius . . *Cymbeline* ii 3 60
Caius Lucius Will do's commission throughly . . . . . iii 4 11
Lucius the Roman comes to Milford-Haven To-morrow . . . iii 4 145
'Fore noble Lucius Present yourself, desire his service . . . iii 4 175
Leave not the worthy Lucius, good my lords, Till he have cross'd the Severn . . . . iii 5 16
Lucius hath wrote already to the emperor How it goes here . . iii 5 21
Is Lucius general of the forces?—Ay.—Remaining now in Gallia? . iii 7 11
Great Jupiter be praised! Lucius is taken . . . . . v 3 84

Luck. If it be my luck, so; if not, happy man be his dole! *Mer. Wives* iii 4 67
As good luck would have it . . . . iii 5 84
I hope good luck lies in odd numbers . . . . . . v 1 2
Strew good luck, ouphes, on every sacred room . . . . v 5 61
We have had ill luck; we could never meet . . . . . v 5 120
I have but lean luck in the match . . . . *Com. of Errors* iii 2 93
And good luck grant thee thy Demetrius! . . . *M. N. Dream* i 1 221
Sweet Puck, You do their work, and they shall have good luck . ii 1 41
If we have unearned luck . . . . v 1 439
Nor no ill luck stirring but what lights on my shoulders *Mer. of Venice* iii 1 99
Yes, other men have ill luck too: Antonio, as I heard in Genoa,— What, what, what? ill luck, ill luck?—Hath an argosy cast away iii 1 102
I ne'er had worse luck in my life . . . . . *All's Well* ii 2 59
Good luck, an't be thy will! what have we here? . . *W. Tale* iii 3 69
Else 'twere hard luck, being in so preposterous estate as we are . v 2 158
He told me that rebellion had bad luck . . . . 2 *Hen. IV.* i 1 41
Farewell, good Salisbury; and good luck go with thee! . *Hen. V.* iv 3 11
Be opposite all planets of good luck To my proceedings! *Richard III.* iv 4 402
Ween you of better luck, I mean, in perjured witness? . *Hen. VIII.* v 1 135
As if that luck, in very spite of cunning, Bade him win all *Troi. and Cres.* v 5 41
Of that natural luck, He beats thee 'gainst the odds . *Ant. and Cleo.* ii 3 26
I hear Antony call; I see him rouse himself To praise my noble act; I hear him mock The luck of Cæsar . . . . v 2 289
Was there ever man had such luck! . . . . . *Cymbeline* ii 1 1

Luckier. And Hymen now with luckier issue speeds . . *Much Ado* v 3 32
Luckiest. Sanctified By the luckiest stars in heaven *All's Well* i 3 252
Luckily. Seeing thou fall'st on me so luckily, I will assay thee 1 *Hen. IV.* v 4 33
Luckless. I and ten thousand in this luckless realm Had left no mourning widows for our death . . . 3 *Hen. VI.* ii 6 18
The night-crow cried, aboding luckless time . . . v 6 45
Lucky. We are lucky, boy; and to be so still requires nothing but secrecy . . . . *W. Tale* iii 3 129
'Tis a lucky day, boy, and we'll do good deeds on't . . iii 3 142
Tidings do I bring and lucky joys And golden times . 2 *Hen. IV.* v 3 99
We doubt not of a fair and lucky war . . *Hen. V.* ii 2 184
'Tis meet that lucky ruler be employ'd . 2 *Hen. VI.* iii 1 291
When mine hours Were nice and lucky, men did ransom lives Of me for jests; but now I'll set my teeth . *Ant. and Cleo.* iii 13 180
Lucre. Shall I, for lucre of the rest unvanquish'd, Detract so much from that prerogative? . . . . 1 *Hen. VI.* v 4 141
Malice and lucre in them Have laid this woe here . . *Cymbeline* iv 2 324
Lucrece. And Roman Lucrece for her chastity . . *T. of Shrew* ii 1 298
And the impressure her Lucrece, with which she uses to seal *T. Night* ii 5 104
Silence, like a Lucrece knife, With bloodless stroke my heart doth gore ii 5 116
Lucrece was not more chaste Than this Lavinia . *T. Andron.* ii 1 108
As Tarquin erst, That left the camp to sin in Lucrece' bed . iv 1 64
Lucretia. Atalanta's better part, Sad Lucretia's modesty *As Y. Like It* iii 2 156
Lucullus entreats your company to-morrow to hunt . . *T. of Athens* i 2 193
I will dispatch you severally; you to Lord Lucius; to Lord Lucullus you . . . . ii 2 197
As you have said, my lord.—Lord Lucius and Lucullus? hum! . ii 2 204
One of his men was with the Lord Lucullus to borrow so many talents iii 2 13
Hum!—'bove all others? He might have tried Lord Lucius or Lucullus iii 3 2
Has Ventidius and Lucullus denied him? And does he send to me? . iii 3 8
Go, bid all my friends again, Lucius, Lucullus, and Sempronius . iii 4 112
Lucy, farewell: no more my fortune can, But curse the cause 1 *Hen. VI.* iv 3 43
Sir William Lucy, who with me Set from our o'ermatch'd forces forth for aid . . . . iv 4 10
Touch'd you the bastardy of Edward's children?—I did; with his contract with Lady Lucy . . . . *Richard III.* iii 7 5
He was contract to Lady Lucy—Your mother lives a witness to that vow . . . . iii 7 179
Ludlow. Forthwith from Ludlow the young prince be fetch'd . ii 2 121
Go we to determine Who they shall be that straight shall post to Ludlow . . . . ii 2 142
Towards Ludlow then, for we'll not stay behind . . ii 2 154
Lud's-town. Made Lud's town with rejoicing fires bright . *Cymbeline* iii 1 32
On the gates of Lud's-town set your heads . . . iv 2 99
Lug. This [gold] Will lug your priests and servants from your sides *T. of Athens* iv 3 31
I'll lug the guts into the neighbour room . . . *Hamlet* iii 4 212
Luggage. What do you mean To dote thus on such luggage? . *Tempest* iv 1 231
Hence, and bestow your luggage where you found it . . v 1 299
Come, bring your luggage nobly on your back . . 1 *Hen. IV.* v 4 160
I must stay with the lackeys, with the luggage of our camp *Hen. V.* iv 4 80
Kill the poys and the luggage! 'tis expressly against the law of arms . iv 7 1
Lugged. I am as melancholy as a gib cat or a lugged bear . 1 *Hen. IV.* i 2 83
Luke. I will presently to Saint Luke's . . *Meas. for Meas.* iii 1 276
The old priest of Saint Luke's church is at your command *T. of Shrew* iv 4 88
My master hath appointed me to go to Saint Luke's, to bid the priest be ready . . . . iv 4 103
Lukewarm. I cannot rest Until the white rose that I wear be dyed Even in the lukewarm blood of Henry's heart . . 3 *Hen. VI.* i 2 34
Smoke and luke-warm water Is your perfection . *T. of Athens* iii 6 99
Lull. Or the virgin voice That babies lulls asleep . *Coriolanus* iii 2 115
And lulls him whilst she playeth on her back . . *T. Andron.* iv 1 99
Lullaby. Sing in our sweet lullaby; Lulla, lulla, lullaby *M. N. Dream* ii 2 14
So, good night, with lullaby . . . . . ii 2 19
Marry, sir, lullaby to your bounty till I come again . *T. Night* v 1 48
The day frowns more and more: thou'rt like to have A lullaby too rough . . . . *W. Tale* iii 3 55
As is a nurse's song Of lullaby to bring her babe asleep . *T. Andron.* ii 3 29
Lull'd in these flowers with dances and delight . *M. N. Dream* ii 1 254
And lull'd with sound of sweetest melody . . 2 *Hen. IV.* iii 1 14
Lumbert. He is indited to dinner to the Lubber's-head in Lumbert street ii 1 31
Lump. To what metal this counterfeit lump of ore will be melted *All's Well* iii 6 40
This lump of clay, Swift-winged with desire to get a grave . 1 *Hen. VI.* ii 5 14
Foul indigested lump, As crooked in thy manners as thy shape! 2 *Hen. VI.* v 1 157
An indigested and deformed lump . . . . 3 *Hen. VI.* v 6 51
Blush, blush, thou lump of foul deformity! . . *Richard III.* i 2 57
All men's honours Lie like one lump before him . *Hen. VIII.* ii 2 49
Lumpish. She is lumpish, heavy, melancholy . . *T. G. of Ver.* iii 2 62
Luna. What is Dictynna?—A title to Phœbe, to Luna, to the moon *L. L. Lost* iv 2 39
Lunacy. This closing with him fits his lunacy . . *T. Andron.* v 2 70
The lunacy is so ordinary that the whippers are in love too *As Y. Like It* iii 2 423
Shuns your house, As beaten hence by your strange lunacy *T. of Shrew* Ind. 2 31
I have found The very cause of Hamlet's lunacy . . *Hamlet* ii 2 49
Grating so harshly all his days of quiet With turbulent and dangerous lunacy . . . . iii 1 4
The terms of our estate may not endure Hazard so near us as doth hourly grow Out of his lunacies . . . . . iii 3 7
Lunatic. I quaked for fear, lest the lunatic knave would have searched it *Mer. Wives* iii 5 105
'Oman, art thou lunatics? hast thou no understandings? . . iv 1 71
Why, this is lunatics! this is mad as a mad dog! . . iv 2 130
Tell his wife that, being lunatic, He rush'd into my house *Com. of Errors* iv 3 94
Abbominable: it insinuateth me of insanie: anne intelligis, domine? to make frantic, lunatic . . . . . *L. L. Lost* v 1 29
The lunatic, the lover and the poet Are of imagination all compact: One sees more devils than vast hell can hold . *M. N. Dream* v 1 7
Persuade him that he hath been lunatic . . *T. of Shrew* Ind. 1 63
To wish me wed to one half lunatic; A mad-cap ruffian . . ii 1 289
What, is the man lunatic? . . . . . . v 1 74
Sir Topas the curate, who comes to visit Malvolio the lunatic *T. Night* iv 2 26
A lunatic lean-witted fool, Presuming on an ague's privilege *Richard II.* ii 1 115
Dispute not with her; she is lunatic . . *Richard III.* i 3 254
Sometime with lunatic bans, sometime with prayers, Enforce their charity . . . . *Lear* ii 3 19
To whose hands have you sent the lunatic king? . . iii 7 46
Lune. Why, woman, your husband is in his old lunes again *Mer. Wives* iv 2 22
These dangerous unsafe lunes i' the king, beshrew them! . *W. Tale* ii 2 30
Yea, watch His pettish lunes, his ebbs, his flows . *Troi. and Cres* ii 3 139

Lung. The air breathes upon us here most sweetly.—As if it had lungs and rotten ones . . . . . *Tempest* ii 1 47
Gentlemen, who are of such sensible and nimble lungs . . . ii 1 174
Speak from thy lungs military . . . . *Mer. Wives* iv 5 18
The heaving of my lungs provokes me to ridiculous smiling . *L. L. Lost* iii 1 77
Thou but offend'st thy lungs to speak so loud . *Mer. of Venice* iv 1 140
My lungs began to crow like chanticleer . . . *As Y. Like It* ii 7 30
My lungs are wasted so That strength of speech is utterly denied me 2 *Hen. IV.* iv 5 217
Let vultures vile seize on his lungs also! . . . . v 3 146
God bless thy lungs, good knight . . . . . v 5 9
The 'solus' in thy teeth, and in thy throat, And in thy hateful lungs! *Hen. V.* ii 1 52
Now crack thy lungs, and split thy brazen pipe . *Troi. and Cres.* iv 5 7
Dirt-rotten livers, wheezing lungs, bladders full of imposthume . . v 1 24
With a kind of smile, Which ne'er came from the lungs . . *Coriolanus* i 1 112
So shall my lungs Coin words till their decay against those measles . iii 1 77
The clown shall make those laugh whose lungs are tickle o' the sere *Ham.* ii 2 337
Tweaks me by the nose? gives me the lie i' the throat, As deep as to the lungs? . . . . ii 2 602
The jolly Briton—Your lord, I mean—laughs from's free lungs *Cymbeline* i 6 68
Thy food is such As hath been belch'd on by infected lungs . *Pericles* iv 6 179
Lupercal. You know it is the feast of Lupercal . . *J. Cæsar* i 1 72
You all did see that on the Lupercal I thrice presented him a kingly crown . . . . iii 2 100
Lurch. Am fain to shuffle, to hedge and to lurch . *Mer. Wives* ii 2 26
Lurched. And in the brunt of seventeen battles since He lurch'd all swords of the garland . . . . *Coriolanus* ii 2 105
Lure. And till she stoop she must not be full-gorged, For then she never looks upon her lure . . . *T. of Shrew* iv 1 195
O, for a falconer's voice, To lure this tassel-gentle back again! *Rom. and Jul.* ii 2 160
Lurk. And sometime lurk I in a gossip's bowl . . *M. N. Dream* ii 1 47
There Minotaurs and ugly treasons lurk . . 1 *Hen. VI.* v 3 189
I like not this; For many men that stumble at the threshold Are well foretold that danger lurks within . . . 3 *Hen. VI.* iv 7 12
In each grace of these There lurks a still and dumb-discoursive devil That tempts most cunningly . . . *Troi. and Cres.* iv 4 92
Here lurks no treason, here no envy swells . . *T. Andron.* i 1 153
Or bid me lurk Where serpents are; chain me with roaring bears *Rom. and Jul.* iv 1 79
What will hap more to-night, safe 'scape the king! Lurk, lurk . *Lear* iii 6 122
Lurked. Here in these confines slily have I lurk'd . *Richard III.* iv 4 3
Where have you lurk'd, that you make doubt of it? . *Coriolanus* v 4 49
Lurketh. Mute wonder lurketh in men's ears . . *Hen. V.* i 1 49
Lurking. Guard it, I pray thee, with a lurking adder . *Richard II.* iii 2 20
Since God so graciously hath brought to light This dangerous treason lurking in our way . . . . *Hen. V.* ii 2 186
Who 'scapes the lurking serpent's mortal sting? . 3 *Hen. VI.* ii 2 15
His soldiers lurking in the towns about . . . . iv 2 15
Lurking-place. There's not a hollow cave or lurking-place, No vast obscurity or misty vale, Where bloody murder or detested rape Can couch for fear, but I will find them out . . . *T. Andron.* v 2 35
Luscious. Quite over-canopied with luscious woodbine . *M. N. Dream* ii 1 251
The food that to him now is as luscious as locusts, shall be to him shortly as bitter as coloquintida . . . . *Othello* i 3 354
Lush. How lush and lusty the grass looks! how green! . *Tempest* ii 1 52
Lust. Shall never melt Mine honour into lust . . . iv 1 28
Till the wicked fire of lust have melted him in his own grease *Mer. Wives* ii 1 69
Fie on sinful fantasy! Fie on lust and luxury! . . . v 5 98
Lust is but a bloody fire, Kindled with unchaste desire . . v 5 99
This is enough to be the decay of lust and late-walking through the realm v 5 152
To his concupiscible intemperate lust . . *Meas. for Meas.* v 1 98
By ruffian lust should be contaminate . . *Com. of Errors* ii 2 135
My blood is mingled with the crime of lust . . . ii 2 143
Enticements, oaths, tokens, and all these engines of lust . *All's Well* iii 5 21
So lust doth play With what it loathes for that which is away . iv 4 24
Nor my lusts Burn hotter than my faith . . *W. Tale* iv 4 34
And they will give Their bodies to the lust of English youth *Hen. V.* iii 5 30
You, that are polluted with your lusts . . 1 *Hen. VI.* v 4 43
Matching more for wanton lust than honour . 3 *Hen. VI.* iii 3 210
Urge his hateful luxury, And bestial appetite in change of lust *Rich. III.* iii 5 81
When I am hence, I'll answer to my lust . . *Troi. and Cres.* iv 4 134
There serve your lusts, shadow'd from heaven's eye *T. Andron.* ii 1 130
Drag hence her husband to some secret hole, And make his dead trunk pillow to our lust . . . . ii 3 130
O, keep me from their worse than killing lust . . . ii 3 175
No, let them satisfy their lust on thee . . . . ii 3 180
I would we had a thousand Roman dames At such a bay, by turn to serve our lust.—A charitable wish and full of love . . iv 2 42
And here's the base fruit of his burning lust . . . v 1 43
Lust and liberty Creep in the minds and marrows of our youth! *T. of A.* iv 1 25
Give them diseases, leaving with thee their lust . . . iv 3 84
Melted down thy youth In different beds of lust . . . iv 3 257
Thou art a woman, and disclaim'st Flinty mankind; whose eyes do never give But thorough lust and laughter . . . . iv 3 492
Your wives, your daughters, Your matrons and your maids, could not fill up The cistern of my lust . . . . *Macbeth* iv 3 63
This avarice Sticks deeper, grows with more pernicious root Than summer-seeming lust . . . . iv 3 86
Won to his shameful lust The will of my most seeming-virtuous queen *Hamlet* i 5 45
So lust, though to a radiant angel link'd, Will sate itself in a celestial bed i 5 55
Epicurism and lust Make it more like a tavern or a brothel . *Lear* i 4 265
Wore gloves in my cap; served the lust of my mistress' heart . iii 4 89
One that slept in the contriving of lust, and waked to do it . . iii 4 92
Five fiends have been in poor Tom at once; of lust, as Obidicut . iv 1 62
We have reason to cool our raging motions, our carnal stings, our unbitted lusts, whereof I take this that you call love to be a sect *Othello* i 3 335
It is merely a lust of the blood and a permission of the will . i 3 339
An index and obscure prologue to the history of lust and foul thoughts ii 1 264
Now, I do love her too; Not out of absolute lust, though peradventure ii 1 301
I'll pour this pestilence into his ear, That she repeals him for her body's lust . . . . ii 3 363
What sense had I of her stol'n hours of lust? I saw't not, thought it not iii 3 338
Thy bed, lust-stain'd, shall with lust's blood be spotted . . v 1 36
Is become the bellows and the fan To cool a gipsy's lust *Ant. and Cleo.* i 1 10
Let witchcraft join with beauty, lust with both! . . . ii 1 22
All the unlawful issue that their lust Since then hath made between them iii 6 7

Lust. I begg'd His pardon for return.—Which soon he granted, Being an obstruct 'tween his lust and him . . . . *Ant. and Cleo.* iii 6 61
Be it lying, note it, The woman's; flattering, hers; deceiving, hers; Lust and rank thoughts, hers, hers . . . . . . *Cymbeline* ii 5 24
When my lust hath dined . . . . iii 5 146
Murder's as near to lust as flame to smoke . . . *Pericles* i 1 138
You have heard Of monstrous lust the due and just reward . . v 3 86
Lust-dieted. The superfluous and lust-dieted man . . *Lear* iv 1 70
Lustest. Strip thine own back; Thou hotly lust'st to use her in that kind For which thou whipp'st her . . . . . iv 6 166
Lustful. Softer and sweeter than the lustful bed On purpose trimm'd up for Semiramis . . . . . . *T. of Shrew* Ind. 2 40
Hag of all despite, Encompass'd with thy lustful paramours! 1 *Hen. VI.* iii 2 53
The lustful Edward's title buried . . . . 3 *Hen. VI.* iii 2 129
His lustful eye or savage heart, Without control . *Richard III.* iii 5 83
What! the lustful sons of Tamora Performers of this? . *T. Andron.* iv 1 79
Lustier. Why, your dolphin is not lustier . . . *All's Well* ii 3 31
With lustier maintenance than I did look for . . . 1 *Hen. IV.* v 4 22
I'll take him down, an a' were lustier than he is . . *Rom. and Jul.* ii 4 159
Lustiest. He would unhorse the lustiest challenger . . *Richard II.* v 3 19
Lustig, as the Dutchman says: I'll like a maid the better . *All's Well* ii 3 47
Lustihood. His May of youth and bloom of lustihood . . *Much Ado* v 1 76
Reason and respect Make livers pale and lustihood deject *Troi. and Cres.* ii 2 50
Lustily. Let's tune, and to it lustily awhile . . . *T. G. of Ver.* iv 2 25
I determine to fight lustily for him . . . . . *Hen. V.* iv 1 201
You have rung it lustily . . . . *T. Andron.* ii 2 14
Lustre. A good lustre of conceit in a turf of earth . . *L. L. Lost* iv 2 89
If you can bring Tincture or lustre in her lip, her eye . *W. Tale* iii 2 206
It lends a lustre and more great opinion, A larger dare . 1 *Hen. IV.* iv 1 77
I doubt not; For there is none of you so mean and base, That hath not noble lustre in your eyes . . . . . . *Hen. V.* iii 1 30
The two kings, Equal in lustre, were now best, now worst . *Hen. VIII.* i 1 29
Like a jewel, has hung twenty years About his neck, yet never lost her lustre . . . . ii 2 33
The lustre of the better yet to show, Shall show the better *Troi. and Cres.* i 3 361
The lustre in your eye, heaven in your cheek, Pleads your fair usage . iv 4 120
You have added worth unto't and lustre . . . *T. of Athens* i 2 154
That same eye whose bend doth awe the world Did lose his lustre *J. C.* i 2 124
Out, vile jelly! Where is thy lustre now?—All dark . . *Lear* iii 7 84
Thy lustre thickens, When he shines by . . . . *Ant. and Cleo.* ii 3 27
No; I rather added A lustre to it . . . . . *Cymbeline* i 1 143
Lustrous. Good sparks and lustrous . . . . *All's Well* ii 1 41
As lustrous as ebony . . . . *T. Night* iv 2 42
Lust-stained. Thy bed, lust-stain'd . . . . . *Othello* v 1 36
Lust-wearied. The ne'er-lust-wearied Antony . . . *Ant. and Cleo.* ii 1 38
Lusty. How lush and lusty the grass looks! how green! . *Tempest* ii 1 52
And oar'd Himself with his good arms in lusty stroke To the shore . ii 1 119
Young Drop-heir that killed lusty Pudding . . . *Meas. for Meas.* iv 3 17
All Europa shall rejoice at thee, As once Europa did at lusty Jove *M. Ado* v 4 46
Though I look old, yet I am strong and lusty . . *As Y. Like It* ii 3 47
Therefore my age is as a lusty winter, Frosty, but kindly . . ii 3 52
A little riper and more lusty red Than that mix'd in his cheek . . iii 5 121
The horn, the horn, the lusty horn Is not a thing to laugh to scorn . iv 2 18
It is a lusty wench; I love her ten times more than e'er I did *T. of Shrew* ii 1 161
He'll have a lusty widow now, That shall be woo'd and wedded in a day iv 2 50
A daughter, and a goodly babe, Lusty and like to live . . *W. Tale* ii 2 27
When this same lusty gentleman was got . . . . *K. John* i 1 108
We will bear home that lusty blood again Which here we came to spout ii 1 255
And, like a jolly troop of huntsmen, come Our lusty English . . ii 1 322
If lusty love should go in quest of beauty, Where should he find it fairer? ii 1 426
What cannoneer begot this lusty blood? He speaks plain cannon fire . ii 1 461
What lusty trumpet thus doth summon us? . . . . . v 2 117
But lusty, young, and cheerly drawing breath . . *Richard II.* i 3 66
Furbish new the name of John a Gaunt, Even in the lusty haviour of his son i 3 77
Where's your yoeman? Is't a lusty yoeman? will a' stand to't? 2 *Hen. IV.* ii 1 4
They will talk of mad Shallow yet.—You were called 'lusty Shallow' then iii 2 17
When flesh is cheap and females dear, And lusty lads roam here and there v 3 21
Of lusty earls, Grandpré and Roussi, Fauconberg and Foix . *Hen. V.* iv 8 103
Where are your mess of sons to back you now? The wanton Edward, and the lusty George? . . . . 3 *Hen. VI.* i 4 74
By him that thunders, thou hast lusty arms . . *Troi. and Cres.* iv 5 136
But who comes here, led by a lusty Goth? . . . *T. Andron.* v 1 19
Such comfort as do lusty young men feel . . . *Rom. and Jul.* i 2 26
He, that hath the steerage of my course, Direct my sail! On, lusty gentlemen . . . . i 4 113
The torrent roar'd, and we did buffet it With lusty sinews . *J. Cæsar* i 2 108
Many lusty Romans Came smiling, and did bathe their hands in it . ii 2 78
Who, in the lusty stealth of nature, take More composition . . *Lear* i 2 11
I do suspect the lusty Moor Hath leap'd into my seat . . *Othello* ii 1 304
Lute. For Orpheus' lute was strung with poets' sinews . *T. G. of Ver.* iii 2 78
God defend the lute should be like the case! . . . *Much Ado* ii 1 98
As sweet and musical As bright Apollo's lute, strung with his hair *L. L. L.* iv 3 343
Take you the lute, and you the set of books . . *T. of Shrew* ii 1 107
Iron may hold with her, but never lutes.—Why, then thou canst not break her to the lute?—Why, no; for she hath broke the lute to me ii 1 147
There I stood amazed for a while, As on a pillory, looking through the lute ii 1 157
I am as melancholy as . . an old lion, or a lover's lute . 1 *Hen. IV.* i 2 84
Sung by a fair queen in a summer's bower, With ravishing division, to her lute . . . . iii 1 211
Like thee, Nero, Play on the lute, beholding the towns burn 1 *Hen. VI.* i 4 96
Capers nimbly in a lady's chamber To the lascivious pleasing of a lute *Richard III.* i 1 13
Take thy lute, wench: my soul grows sad with troubles *Hen. VIII.* iii 1 1
Orpheus with his lute made trees, And the mountain tops that freeze, Bow themselves when he did sing . . . . iii 1 3
O, had the monster seen those lily hands Tremble, like aspen-leaves, upon a lute, And make the silken strings delight to kiss them! *T. An.* ii 4 45
When to the lute She sung, and made the night-bird mute *Pericles* iv Gower 25
Lute-case. Bardolph stole a lute-case, bore it twelve leagues . *Hen. V.* iii 2 45
Lute-string. Nay, but his jesting spirit; which is now crept into a lute-string and now governed by stops . . . . *Much Ado* iii 2 61
Lutheran. Yet I know her for A spleeny Lutheran . . *Hen. VIII.* iii 2 99
'Lux tua vita mihi.'—He loves you well that holds his life of you *Pericles* ii 2 21
Luxurious. She knows the heat of a luxurious bed . . *Much Ado* iv 1 42
Thou damned and luxurious mountain goat, Offer'st me brass? *Hen. V.* iv 4 20
The dissembling luxurious drab . . . . . *Troi. and Cres.* v 4 9
O most insatiate and luxurious woman! . . . . *T. Andron.* v 1 88
Luxurious, avaricious, false, deceitful, Sudden, malicious . *Macbeth* iv 3 58
Luxuriously. Besides what hotter hours, Unregister'd in vulgar fame, you have Luxuriously pick'd out . . . *Ant. and Cleo.* iii 13 120
Luxury. Fie on lust and luxury . . . . . . *Mer. Wives* v 5 98
One all of luxury, an ass, a madman . . . . *Meas. for Meas.* v 1 506
A few sprays of us, The emptying of our fathers' luxury . *Hen. V.* iii 5 6
Moreover, urge his hateful luxury, And bestial appetite . *Richard III.* iii 5 80
How the devil Luxury, with his fat rump and potato-finger, tickles these together! Fry, lechery, fry! . . . . *Troi. and Cres.* v 2 55
Let not the royal bed of Denmark be A couch for luxury . . *Hamlet* i 5 83
To't, luxury, pell-mell! for I lack soldiers . . . . *Lear* iv 6 119
Lycaonia. The kings of Mede and Lycaonia, With a more larger list of sceptres . . . . *Ant. and Cleo.* iii 6 75
Lychorida, her nurse, she takes, And so to sea . . . *Pericles* iii Gower 43
O, how, Lychorida, How does my queen? . . . . . . iii 1 6
Lychorida!—Lucina, O Divinest patroness, and midwife gentle! . . iii 1 10
Now, Lychorida!—Here is a thing too young for such a place . . iii 1 14
O Lychorida, Bid Nestor bring me spices, ink and paper . . . iii 1 65
O, no tears, Lychorida, no tears: Look to your little mistress . . iii 3 39
My mother was the daughter of a king; Who died the minute I was born, As my good nurse Lychorida hath oft Deliver'd weeping . v 1 161
Lycurguses. Meeting two such wealsmen as you are—I cannot call you Lycurguses . . . . *Coriolanus* ii 1 60
Lydia. His conquering banner shook from Syria To Lydia *Ant. and Cleo.* i 2 107
Made her Of lower Syria, Cyprus, Lydia, Absolute queen . . . iii 6 10
Lying. Thou most lying slave, Whom stripes may move, not kindness! *Tempest* i 2 344
Himself would lodge where senseless they are lying! . *T. G. of Ver.* iii 1 143
And this is true; I like not the humour of lying . . *Mer. Wives* ii 1 133
But it is I That, lying by the violet in the sun, Do as the carrion does, not as the flower, Corrupt with virtuous season . *Meas. for Meas.* ii 2 166
You bald-pated, lying rascal, you must be hooded, must you? . v 1 357
They have verified unjust things; and, to conclude, they are lying knaves *Much Ado* v 1 224
No bed-room me deny; For lying so, Hermia, I do not lie *M. N. Dream* ii 2 52
I would she were as lying a gossip in that as ever knapped ginger *Mer. of Venice* iii 1 9
An argosy That now is lying in Marseilles' road . . *T. of Shrew* ii 1 377
'Tis [virginity] a commodity will lose the gloss with lying . *All's Well* i 1 167
Debosh'd on every tomb, on every grave A lying trophy . . . ii 3 146
I hate ingratitude more in a man Than lying . . . . *T. Night* iii 4 389
Let me have no lying: it becomes none but tradesmen . . *W. Tale* iv 4 745
To you The remnant northward, lying off from Trent . . 1 *Hen. IV.* iii 1 79
Thou art perfect in lying down: come, quick, quick . . . iii 1 229
Lord, Lord, how this world is given to lying! . . . . . v 4 149
Lord, Lord, how subject we old men are to this vice of lying! 2 *Hen. IV.* iii 2 326
Lest rest and lying still might make them look Too near unto my state iv 5 212
Within thine eyes sat twenty thousand deaths, In thy hands clutch'd as many millions, In Thy lying tongue both numbers, I would say 'Thou liest' . . . . *Coriolanus* iii 3 72
Whilst we, lying still, Are full of rest, defence . . . *J. Cæsar* iv 3 201
'Tis as easy as lying . . . . *Hamlet* iii 2 372
They'll have me whipped for speaking true, thou'lt have me whipped for lying . . . . *Lear* i 4 201
O sleep, thou ape of death, lie dull upon her! And be her sense but as a monument, Thus in a chapel lying! . . . . . *Cymbeline* ii 2 33
Be it lying, note it, The woman's; flattering, hers; deceiving, hers . ii 5 22
Humming water must o'erwhelm thy corpse, Lying with simple shells *Pericles* iii 1 65
Lyingest. The lyingest knave in Christendom *T. of Shrew* Ind. 2 25; 2 *Hen. VI.* ii 1 125
Lym. Hound or spaniel, brach or lym, Or bobtail tike . . . *Lear* iii 6 72
Lymoges. O Lymoges! O Austria! thou dost shame That bloody spoil *K. John* iii 1 114
Lynn. Whither shall we then?—To Lynn, my lord, And ship from thence 3 *Hen. VI.* iv 5 20
Lysander. Stand forth, Lysander: and, my gracious duke, This man hath bewitch'd the bosom of my child . . . . *M. N. Dream* i 1 26
Thou, Lysander, thou hast given her rhymes . . . . . . i 1 28
Demetrius is a worthy gentleman.—So is Lysander.—In himself he is . i 1 53
Lysander, yield Thy crazed title to my certain right . . . . i 1 91
Do you marry him.—Scornful Lysander! true, he hath my love . . i 1 95
There will I stay for thee.—My good Lysander! . . . . . i 1 168
Lysander and myself will fly this place. Before the time I did Lysander see, Seem'd Athens as a paradise to me . . . . . . i 1 203
There my Lysander and myself shall meet . . . . . . i 1 217
Keep word, Lysander: we must starve our sight From lovers' food . i 1 222
Where is Lysander and fair Hermia? The one I'll slay, the other slayeth me . . . . ii 1 189
For lying so, Hermia, I do not lie.—Lysander riddles very prettily . ii 2 53
Beshrew my manners and my pride, If Hermia meant to say Lysander lied ii 2 55
But who is here? Lysander! on the ground! Dead? or asleep? . . ii 2 100
Lysander, if you live, good sir, awake.—And run through fire I will . ii 2 102
Hermia, sleep thou there: And never mayst thou come Lysander near! ii 2 136
Lysander, help me! do thy best To pluck this crawling serpent from my breast! . . . . ii 2 145
What a dream was here! Lysander, look how I do quake with fear . ii 2 148
Lysander! what, removed? Lysander! lord! What, out of hearing? . ii 2 151
If thou hast slain Lysander in his sleep, Being o'er shoes in blood, plunge in the deep, And kill me too . . . . iii 2 47
What's this to my Lysander? where is he? . . . . . . iii 2 62
I am not guilty of Lysander's blood; Nor is he dead, for aught that I can tell . . . . iii 2 75
Lysander, keep thy Hermia; I will none . . . . . . iii 2 169
Thou art not by mine eye, Lysander, found; Mine ear, I thank it, brought me to thy sound . . . . iii 2 181
What love could press Lysander from my side?—Lysander's love, that would not let him bide, Fair Helena . . . . . . iii 2 185
Have you not set Lysander, as in scorn, To follow me? . . . iii 2 222
And wherefore doth Lysander Deny your love, so rich within his soul? iii 2 228
Lysander, whereto tends all this?—Away, you Ethiope! . . . iii 2 256
O me! what news, my love! Am not I Hermia? are not you Lysander? iii 2 273
A foolish heart, that I leave here behind.—What, with Lysander? . iii 2 320
Like to Lysander sometime frame thy tongue, Then stir Demetrius up . iii 2 360
Then crush this herb into Lysander's eye . . . . . . iii 2 366
Lysander! speak again: Thou runaway, thou coward, art thou fled? . iii 2 404
Heavens shield Lysander, if they mean a fray! . . . . . iii 2 447
This is my daughter here asleep; And this, Lysander; this Demetrius is iv 1 134
Lysimachus. Here comes the Lord Lysimachus disguised . . *Pericles* iv 6 18
She has here spoken holy words to the Lord Lysimachus . . . iv 6 142
From whence Lysimachus our Tyrian ship espies . . . . v Gower 18
There's a barge put off from Mytilene, And in it is Lysimachus the governor . . . . v 1 4

M

Mab. O, then, I see Queen Mab hath been with you . *Rom. and Jul.* i 4 53
Which oft the angry Mab with blisters plagues, Because their breaths with sweetmeats tainted are . . . i 4 75
This is that very Mab That plats the manes of horses in the night . i 4 88

Macbeth. Upon the heath.—There to meet with Macbeth . *Macbeth* i 1 7
Brave Macbeth—well he deserves that name . . . i 2 16
Dismay'd not this Our captains, Macbeth and Banquo? . . i 2 34
Go pronounce his present death, And with his former title greet Macbeth i 2 65
What he hath lost noble Macbeth hath won . . . i 2 67
A drum, a drum! Macbeth doth come . . . . i 3 31
All hail, Macbeth! hail to thee, thane of Glamis! . . . i 3 48
All hail, Macbeth! hail to thee, thane of Cawdor! . . . i 3 49
All hail, Macbeth, that shalt be king hereafter! . . . i 3 50
Lesser than Macbeth, and greater.—Not so happy, yet much happier . i 3 65
So all hail, Macbeth and Banquo!—Banquo and Macbeth, all hail! . i 3 68
The king hath happily received, Macbeth, The news of thy success . i 3 89
Worthy Macbeth, we stay upon your leisure.—Give me your favour . i 3 148
I heard a voice cry 'Sleep no more! Macbeth does murder sleep' . ii 2 36
Cawdor Shall sleep no more; Macbeth shall sleep no more . . ii 2 43
Who did this more than bloody deed?—Those that Macbeth hath slain. ii 4 23
Most like The sovereignty will fall upon Macbeth.—He is already named ii 4 30
If there come truth from them—As upon thee, Macbeth, their speeches shine . . . . iii 1 7
But who did bid thee join with us?—Macbeth.—He needs not our mistrust . . . . iii 3 1
How did you dare To trade and traffic with Macbeth In riddles and affairs of death? . . . . iii 5 4
The gracious Duncan Was pitied of Macbeth: marry, he was dead . iii 6 4
Damned fact! How it did grieve Macbeth! did he not straight In pious rage the two delinquents tear? . . . . . iii 6 11
Macbeth! Macbeth! Macbeth! beware Macduff; Beware the thane of Fife . . . . iv 1 71
Macbeth! Macbeth! Macbeth!—Had I three ears, I'ld hear thee . iv 1 77
For none of woman born Shall harm Macbeth . . . . iv 1 81
Macbeth shall never vanquish'd be until Great Birnam wood to high Dunsinane hill Shall come against him . . . . iv 1 92
Our high-placed Macbeth Shall live the lease of nature . . iv 1 98
Why Stands Macbeth thus amazedly? Come, sisters, cheer we up his sprites . . . . iv 1 126
I am not treacherous.—But Macbeth is . . . . . iv 3 18
When they shall be open'd, black Macbeth Will seem as pure as snow . iv 3 52
Not in the legions Of horrid hell can come a devil more damn'd In evils to top Macbeth . . . . iv 3 57
Better Macbeth Than such an one to reign . . . . iv 3 65
Devilish Macbeth By many of these trains hath sought to win me Into his power . . . . iv 3 117
Macbeth Is ripe for shaking, and the powers above Put on their instruments . . . . iv 3 237
Fear not, Macbeth; no man that's born of woman Shall e'er have power upon thee . . . . v 3 6
My name's Macbeth.—The devil himself could not pronounce a title More hateful to mine ear . . . . v 7 7
Either thou, Macbeth, Or else my sword with an unbatter'd edge I sheathe again undeeded . . . . v 7 18

Maccabæus. This gallant gentleman, Judas Maccabæus . *L. L. Lost* v 1 134
Judas I am, ycliped Maccabæus.—Judas Maccabæus clipt is plain Judas v 2 602
Alas, poor Maccabæus, how hath he been baited! . . . . v 2 634

Macdonwald. The merciless Macdonwald—Worthy to be a rebel *Macbeth* i 2 9

Macduff. Here comes the good Macduff. How goes the world, sir, now? ii 4 20
How say'st thou, that Macduff denies his person At our great bidding? iii 4 128
From broad words and 'cause he fail'd His presence at the tyrant's feast, I hear Macduff lives in disgrace . . . . . iii 6 23
Macduff Is gone to pray the holy king, upon his aid . . . iii 6 29
Sent he to Macduff?—He did: and with an absolute 'Sir, not I,' The cloudy messenger turns me his back . . . . . iii 6 39
Macbeth! Macbeth! Macbeth! beware Macduff; Beware the thane of Fife . . . . iv 1 71
None of woman born Shall harm Macbeth.—Then live, Macduff . . iv 1 81
'Tis two or three, my lord, that bring you word Macduff is fled to England . . . . iv 1 142
The castle of Macduff I will surprise; Seize upon Fife; give to the edge o' the sword His wife, his babes . . . . . . iv 1 150
Macduff, this noble passion, Child of integrity, hath from my soul Wiped the black scruples . . . . iv 3 114
Sinful Macduff, They were all struck for thee! naught that I am . iv 3 224
The English power is near, led on by Malcolm, His uncle Siward and the good Macduff . . . . v 2 2
Worthy Macduff and we Shall take upon's what else remains to do . v 6 4
Macduff was from his mother's womb Untimely ripp'd . . . v 8 15
Lay on, Macduff, And damn'd be him that first cries 'Hold enough!' . v 8 33
Macduff is missing, and your noble son . . . . . v 8 38

Mace. To do more exploits with his mace than a morris-pike *Com. of Errors* iv 3 28
I must have saffron to colour the warden pies; mace; dates? *W. Tale* iv 3 49
The sceptre and the ball, The sword, the mace . *Hen. V.* iv 1 278
With these borne before us, instead of maces, will we ride *2 Hen. VI.* iv 7 144
O murderous slumber, Lay'st thou thy leaden mace upon my boy? *J. C.* iv 3 268

Macedon. I think Alexander the Great was born in Macedon: his father was called Philip of Macedon . . . . *Hen. V.* iv 7 21
I think it is in Macedon where Alexander is porn . . . iv 7 24
You sall find, in the comparisons between Macedon and Monmouth, that the situations, look you, is both alike . . . . iv 7 26
A river in Macedon; and there is also moreover a river at Monmouth . iv 7 28
Who is the second that presents himself?—A prince of Macedon *Pericles* ii 2 24

Machiavel. Am I politic? am I subtle? am I a Machiavel? *Mer. Wives* iii 1 104
Alençon! that notorious Machiavel! . . . *1 Hen. VI.* v 4 74
And set the murderous Machiavel to school . *3 Hen. VI.* iii 2 193

Machinations, hollowness, treachery . . . . *Lear* i 2 122
Your business of the world hath so an end, And machination ceases . v 1 46

Machine. Adieu. 'Thine evermore, most dear lady, whilst this machine is to him, Hamlet' . . . . . . *Hamlet* ii 2 124

Mackerel. You may buy land now as cheap as stinking mackerel *1 Hen. IV.* ii 4 395

Macmorris. Captain Macmorris, is it not?—I think it be. *Hen. V.* iii 2 72
How now, Captain Macmorris! have you quit the mines? . . iii 2 91
Captain Macmorris, I beseech you now, will you voutsafe me, look you, a few disputations? . . . . iii 2 100
If you take the matter otherwise than is meant, Captain Macmorris . iii 2 137

Maculate. Immaculate white and red.—Most maculate thoughts, master, are masked under such colours . . . *L. L. Lost* i 2 97

Maculation. I will throw my glove to Death himself, That there's no maculation in thy heart . . . . *Troi. and Cres.* iv 4 66

Mad. Not a soul But felt a fever of the mad . . *Tempest* i 2 209
I have made you mad; And even with such-like valour men hang and drown Their proper selves . . . . iii 3 58
The fools [women] are mad, if left alone . . *T. G. of Ver.* iii 1 99
Ay me, he'll find the young man there, and be mad! *Mer. Wives* iii 4 69
If I have horns to make one mad, let the proverb go with me . ii 5 154
He is very courageous mad about his throwing into the water . iv 1 4
It was a mad fantastical trick of him . . *Meas. for Meas.* iii 2 98
If she be mad,—as I believe no other,—Her madness hath the oddest frame of sense, Such a dependency of thing on thing . . . v 1 60
Many that are not mad Have, sure, some lack of reason . . . v 1 67
But, sure, he is stark mad . . . . *Com. of Errors* ii 1 59
Wast thou mad, That thus so madly thou didst answer me? . . ii 2 11
Am I in earth . . . ? Sleeping or waking? mad or well-advised? . ii 2 215
It would make a man mad as a buck, to be so bought and sold . iii 1 72
What, are you mad, that you do reason so?—Not mad, but mated . iii 2 53
Antipholus is mad, Else would he never so demean himself . . iv 3 82
The reason that I gather he is mad, Besides this present instance of his rage, Is a mad tale he told to-day at dinner . . . . iv 3 87
Is not your husband mad?—His incivility confirms no less . . iv 4 48
I am not mad.—O, that thou wert not, poor distressed soul! . . iv 4 61
Wherefore dost thou mad me?—Will you be bound for nothing? be mad iv 4 129
Hold, hurt him not, for God's sake! he is mad . . . . v 1 33
Still did I tell him it was vile and bad.—And thereof came it that the man was mad . . . . v 1 68
To be disturb'd, would mad or man or beast . . . . v 1 84
He hurried through the street,—With him his bondman, all as mad as he . . . . v 1 141
Provoked with raging ire, Albeit my wrongs might make one wiser mad v 1 217
If he were mad, he would not plead so coldly . . . . v 1 272
I think you are all mated or stark mad . . . . . v 1 281
He is sooner caught than the pestilence, and the taker runs presently mad . . . . *Much Ado* i 1 88
You will never run mad, niece.—No, not till a hot January . . i 1 93
If they were but a week married, they would talk themselves mad . ii 1 369
By the Lord, this love is as mad as Ajax: it kills sheep. *L. L. Lost* iv 3 7
Cupid is a knavish lad, Thus to make poor females mad. *M. N. Dream* iii 2 441
Some, that are mad if they behold a cat . . *Mer. of Venice* iv 1 48
An 'twere to me, I should be mad at it . . . . . v 1 176
One . . . lamed with reasons and the other mad without any *As Y. L. It* i 3 9
What, would you make me mad? . . . *T. of Shrew* Ind. 2 18
That wench is stark mad or wonderful froward . . . . i 1 69
Help, masters, help! my master is mad . . . . . i 2 18
Be mad and merry, or go hang yourselves . . . . . iii 2 228
That, being mad herself, she's madly mated . . . . iii 2 246
And thus I'll curb her mad and headstrong humour . . . iv 1 212
A' will make the man mad, to make a woman of him . . . iv 5 35
Why, how now, Kate! I hope thou art not mad . . . . iv 5 42
As mad in folly, lack'd the sense to know . . . *All's Well* v 3 3
He loved her: for indeed he was mad for her . . . . v 3 260
One draught above heat makes him a fool; the second mads him *T. Night* i 5 141
He is but mad yet, madonna; and the fool shall look to the madman . i 5 145
If you be not mad, be gone; if you have reason, be brief . . i 5 211
My masters, are you mad? or what are you? Have you no wit? . ii 3 93
Such a dream, that when the image of it leaves him he must run mad . ii 5 213
I am as mad as he, If sad and merry madness equal be . . . iii 4 15
Why, we shall make him mad indeed.—The house will be the quieter . iii 4 146
My niece is already in the belief that he's mad . . . . iii 4 150
The man grows mad: away with him! Come, come, sir . . . iii 4 405
Why, there's for thee, and there, and there. Are all the people mad? iv 1 29
Or I am mad, or else this is a dream . . . . . iv 1 65
Do not think I am mad: they have laid me here in hideous darkness . iv 2 33
I am not mad, Sir Topas: I say to you, this house is dark . . iv 2 44
I am no more mad than you are: make the trial of it . . . iv 2 52
Then you are mad indeed, if you be no better in your wits than a fool . iv 2 97
But tell me true, are you not mad indeed? or do you but counterfeit? . iv 2 122
I am ready to distrust mine eyes And wrangle with my reason that persuades me To any other trust but that I am mad Or else the lady's mad . . . . iv 3 15
How now! art thou mad?—No, madam, I do but read madness . v 1 301
Now I do bethink me, it was she First told me thou wast mad . . v 1 357
But that's all one. By the Lord, fool, I am not mad . . . v 1 382
I am . . . no less honest Than you are mad; which is enough *W. Tale* ii 3 71
O, think what they have done And then run mad indeed, stark mad! . iii 2 184
I am not mad: this hair I tear is mine . . . *K. John* iii 4 45
I am not mad: I would to heaven I were! . . . . iii 4 48
Preach some philosophy to make me mad, And thou shalt be canonized iii 4 51
Being not mad but sensible of grief, My reasonable part produces reason . . . . iii 4 53
If I were mad, I should forget my son, Or madly think a babe of clouts were he: I am not mad . . . . iii 4 57
This music mads me; let it sound no more; For though it have holp madmen to their wits, In me it seems it will make wise men mad *Richard II.* v 5 61
He made me mad To see him shine so brisk and smell so sweet *1 Hen. IV.* i 3 53
Brother, the king hath made your nephew mad . . . . i 3 138
None of these mad mustachio purple-hued malt-worms . . . ii 1 82
What, art thou mad? art thou mad? is not the truth the truth? . . ii 4 254
Thou art essentially mad, without seeming so . . . . ii 4 541
Peace, cousin Percy; you will make him mad . . . . iii 1 51
I am afraid my daughter will run mad, So much she doteth . . iii 1 145
Nay, if you melt, then will she run mad . . . . . iii 1 212
He talks at random; sure, the man is mad . . . *1 Hen. VI.* v 3 84
From thy sight, I should be raging mad . . . *2 Hen. VI.* iii 2 394

Mad. To Bedlam with him! is the man grown mad? *2 Hen. VI.* v 1 131
Why art thou patient, man? thou shouldst be mad; And I, to make thee mad, do mock thee thus *3 Hen. VI.* i 4 90
Begin again, and stop again, As if thou wert distraught and mad with terror *Richard III.* iii 5 4
And be thy wife—if any be so mad—As miserable by the life of thee As thou hast made me by my dear lord's death! iv 1 75
England hath long been mad, and scarr'd herself v 5 23
Was he mad, sir?—O, very mad, exceeding mad, in love too *Hen. VIII.* i 4 27
Which so grieved him, That he ran mad and died ii 2 130
I tell thee I am mad In Cressid's love *Troi. and Cres.* i 1 51
Nor once deject the courage of our minds, Because Cassandra's mad ii 2 122
The young prince will go mad: a plague upon Antenor! iv 2 78
With too much blood and too little brain, these two may run mad v 1 54
Who hath done to-day Mad and fantastic execution v 5 38
Let's not meet her.—Why?—They say she's mad *Coriolanus* iv 2 9
Why, are ye mad? or know ye not? *T. Andron.* ii 1 75
Any mortal body hearing it Should straight fall mad, or else die suddenly ii 3 104
If the winds rage, doth not the sea wax mad, Threatening the welkin? iii 1 223
When my heart, all mad with misery, Beats in this hollow prison of my flesh iii 2 9
Why, Marcus, no man should be mad but I iii 2 24
I have heard my grandsire say full oft, Extremity of griefs would make men mad iv 1 19
And I have read that Hecuba of Troy Ran mad for sorrow iv 1 21
I am not mad; I know thee well enough v 2 21
But we worldly men Have miserable, mad, mistaking eyes v 2 66
I know them all, though they suppose me mad, And will o'erreach them v 2 142
You know your mother means to feast with me, And calls herself Revenge, and thinks me mad v 2 186
Why, Romeo, art thou mad?—Not mad, but bound more *Rom. and Jul.* i 2 54
That Rosaline Torments him so, that he will sure run mad ii 4 5
Out, you baggage! You tallow-face!—Fie, fie! what, are you mad? iii 5 158
You are too hot.—God's bread! it makes me mad iii 5 177
That living mortals, hearing them, run mad iv 3 48
You love your child so ill, That you run mad, seeing that she is well iv 5 76
Said he not so? or did I dream it so? Or am I mad? v 3 80
I'm worse than mad: I have kept back their foes *T. of Athens* iii 5 106
Let's make no stay.—Lord Timon's mad.—I feel't upon my bones iii 6 129
Delay not, Cæsar; read it instantly.—What, is the fellow mad? *J. C.* iii 1 10
Hearing the will of Cæsar, It will inflame you, it will make you mad iii 2 149
The king comes here to-night.—Thou'rt mad to say it *Macbeth* i 5 32
These deeds must not be thought After these ways; so, it will make us mad ii 2 34
Some say he's mad; others that lesser hate him Do call it valiant fury v 2 13
Mad for thy love?—My lord, I do not know; But truly, I do fear it *Ham.* ii 1 85
And denied His access to me.—That hath made him mad ii 1 110
Your noble son is mad: Mad call I it; for, to define true madness, What is't but to be nothing else but mad? ii 2 92
That he is mad, 'tis true: 'tis true 'tis pity; And pity 'tis 'tis true ii 2 97
I am but mad north-north-west: when the wind is southerly I know a hawk from a handsaw ii 2 396
Make mad the guilty and appal the free, Confound the ignorant ii 2 590
It hath made me mad. I say, we will have no more marriages iii 1 153
What would your gracious figure?—Alas, he's mad! iii 4 105
That I essentially am not in madness, But mad in craft iii 4 188
Mad as the sea and wind, when both contend Which is the mightier iv 1 7
He that is mad, and sent into England v 1 161
Why was he sent into England?—Why, because he was mad v 1 165
'Twill not be seen in him there; there the men are as mad as he v 1 170
How came he mad?—Very strangely, they say.—How strangely?—Faith, e'en with losing his wits v 1 171
O, he is mad Laertes.—For love of God, forbear him v 1 295
Be Kent unmannerly, When Lear is mad *Lear* i 1 148
O, let me not be mad, not mad, sweet heaven! Keep me in temper: I would not be mad! i 5 50
What, art thou mad, old fellow?—How fell you out? say that ii 2 91
I prithee, daughter, do not make me mad: I will not trouble thee ii 4 221
This heart Shall break into a hundred thousand flaws, Or ere I'll weep. O fool, I shall go mad! ii 4 289
The king grows mad; I'll tell thee, friend, I am almost mad myself iii 4 170
He's mad that trusts in the tameness of a wolf, a horse's health iii 6 19
Alack, sir, he is mad.—'Tis the times' plague, when madmen lead the blind iv 1 47
He was met even now As mad as the vex'd sea iv 4 2
What, art mad? A man may see how this world goes with no eyes iv 6 153
The king is mad: how stiff is my vile sense, That I stand up! iv 6 286
To take the widow Exasperates, makes mad her sister Goneril v 1 60
Poor lady, she'll run mad When she shall lack it *Othello* iii 3 317
Here he comes: As he shall smile, Othello shall go mad iv 1 101
I am glad to see you mad.—Why, sweet Othello,— Devil! iv 1 250
She was in love, and he she loved proved mad And did forsake her iv 3 27
It is the very error of the moon; She comes more nearer earth than she was wont, And makes men mad v 2 111
O villany, villany!—What, are you mad? I charge you, get you home v 2 194
Call the slave again: Though I am mad, I will not bite him *Ant. and Cleo.* ii 5 80
I think thou'rt mad. The matter? ii 7 62
O, he is more mad Than Telamon for his shield iv 13 1
Patience is sottish, and impatience does Become a dog that's mad iv 15 80
What, art thou mad?—Almost, sir: heaven restore me! *Cymbeline* i 1 147
What, are men mad? Hath nature given them eyes To see this vaulted arch? i 6 32
Fools are not mad folks.—Do you call me fool?—As I am mad, I do ii 3 105
If you'll be patient, I'll no more be mad; That cures us both iii 3 109
Is Cadwal mad?—Look, here he comes iv 2 195
I return'd with simular proof enough To make the noble Leonatus mad v 5 201
Mad ass. Away, away, mad ass! *T. of Shrew* v 1 87
Mad attendant. His mad attendant and himself *Com. of Errors* v 1 150
Mad attire. He hath some meaning in his mad attire *T. of Shrew* iii 2 126
Mad blood. These hot days, is the mad blood stirring *Rom. and Jul.* iii 1 4
Mad bounds. Unhandled colts, Fetching mad bounds *Mer. of Venice* v 1 73
Mad-brain. A mad-brain rudesby full of spleen *T. of Shrew* iii 2 10
Mad-brained. This mad-brain'd bridegroom took him such a cuff iii 2 165
Remaineth none but mad-brain'd Salisbury *1 Hen. VI.* i 2 15
To the stain Of contumelious, beastly, mad-brain'd war *T. of Athens* v 1 177
Mad-bred. The fury of this mad-bred flaw *2 Hen. VI.* iii 1 354
Mad Brutus. 'Twas I That the mad Brutus ended *Ant. and Cleo.* iii 11 38
Mad composition. Mad kings! mad composition! *K. John* ii 1 561
Mad compound. Thou whoreson mad compound of majesty *2 Hen. IV.* ii 4 319
Mad days. The mad days that I have spent! *2 Hen. IV.* iii 2 37
Mad devil. The finest mad devil of jealousy in him *Mer. Wives* v 1 19
Mad dog. Why, this is lunatics! this is mad as a mad dog! iv 2 131
A jealous woman Poisons more deadly than a mad dog's tooth *Com. of Er.* v 1 70
Mad fellow. That same mad fellow of the north, Percy *1 Hen. IV.* ii 4 369
A mad fellow met me on the way and told me I had unloaded all the gibbets iv 2 39
A whoreson mad fellow's it was: whose do you think it was? *Hamlet* v 1 193
Mad flesh. But for the mountain of mad flesh that claims marriage of me, I could find in my heart to stay here *Com. of Errors* iv 4 158
Mad folks. Fools are not mad folks *Cymbeline* ii 3 106
Mad grandfather. He hath some message to deliver us.—Ay, some mad message from his mad grandfather *T. Andron.* iv 2 3
Mad-headed. Out, you mad-headed ape! *1 Hen. IV.* ii 3 80
Mad host. Trust me, a mad host *Mer. Wives* iii 1 115
Mad humour. I drave my suitor from his mad humour of love to a living humour of madness *As Y. Like It* iii 2 438
Mad idolatry. 'Tis mad idolatry To make the service greater than the god *Troi. and Cres.* ii 2 56
Mad ire and wrathful fury makes me weep *1 Hen. VI.* iv 3 28
Mad jealousy. How many fond fools serve mad jealousy! *Com. of Errors* ii 1 116
Mad kings. Mad world! mad kings! mad composition! *K. John* ii 1 561
Mad knave. Carry this mad knave to the gaol *T. of Shrew* v 1 95
Mad lad. Like a mad lad, Pare thy nails, dad *T. Night* iv 2 139
Mad lord. A mad lord, and nought but humour sways him *T. of Athens* iii 6 121
Mad man. Thou fond mad man, hear me but speak a word *Rom. and Jul.* iii 3 52
Mad marriage. Such a mad marriage never was before *T. of Shrew* iii 2 184
Mad masters. Fie, fie on all tired jades, on all mad masters iv 1 1
Mad matches. Of all mad matches never was the like iii 2 244
Mad message. He hath some message to deliver us.—Ay, some mad message from his mad grandfather *T. Andron.* iv 2 3
Mad misleader of thy brain-sick son! *2 Hen. VI.* v 1 163
Mad mistaking. I perceive thou art a reverend father; Pardon, I pray thee, for my mad mistaking *T. of Shrew* iv 5 49
Mad mothers. Whiles the mad mothers with their howls confused Do break the clouds *Hen. V.* iii 3 39
Mad Petruchio. There is mad Petruchio's wife *T. of Shrew* iii 2 19
Mad rogue. A pestilence on him for a mad rogue! *Hamlet* v 1 196
Mad Shallow. I was once of Clement's Inn, where I think they will talk of mad Shallow yet *2 Hen. IV.* iii 2 16
Mad sister. What shriek is this?—'Tis our mad sister *Troi. and Cres.* ii 2 98
Mad soul. My lord, this is a poor mad soul *2 Hen. IV.* ii 1 113
Mad spirit. How now, mad spirit! What night-rule now? *M. N. Dream* iii 2 4
Mad tale. A mad tale he told to-day at dinner *Com. of Errors* iv 3 89
Mad thought. Being credulous in this mad thought *T. Andron.* v 2 74
Mad Tom. I am worse than e'er I was.—'Tis poor mad Tom *Lear* iv 1 28
Mad wag. How now, mad wag! what, in thy quips? *1 Hen. IV.* i 2 50
How now, mad wag! what a devil dost thou in Warwickshire? iv 2 55
Mad wenches. Do you hear, my mad wenches?—No *L. L. Lost* ii 1 256
Farewell, mad wenches; you have simple wits v 2 264
Mad woman. If your wife be not a mad-woman, . . . She would not hold out enemy for ever *Mer. of Venice* iv 1 445
Thou fond mad woman, Wilt thou conceal this dark conspiracy? *Rich. II.* v 2 95
They dance! they are mad women *T. of Athens* i 2 138
Mad world! mad kings! mad composition! *K. John* ii 1 561
Mad yeoman. For he's a mad yeoman that sees his son a gentleman before him *Lear* iii 6 14
Mad young man. Whose providence Should have kept short, restrained, and out of haunt, This mad young man *Hamlet* iv 1 19
Madam, and pretty mistresses, give ear *L. L. Lost* v 2 286
All hail, sweet madam, and fair time of day! v 2 339
Teach us, sweet madam, for our rude transgression Some fair excuse v 2 431
What must I call her?—Madam.—Al'ce madam, or Joan madam?—'Madam,' and nothing else: so lords call ladies.—Madam wife, they say that I have dream'd *T. of Shrew* Ind. 2 111
'Tis a very excellent piece of work, madam lady: would 'twere done! i 1 259
Please you to interpose, fair madam *W. Tale* v 3 119
Saying that ere long they should call me madam *2 Hen. IV.* ii 1 109
Our madams mock at us, and plainly say Our mettle is bred out *Hen. V.* iii 5 28
Madam my interpreter, what says she? v 2 282
The madams too, Not used to toil, did almost sweat *Hen. VIII.* i 1 23
Sweet lords, entreat her hear me but a word.—Listen, fair madam *T. An.* ii 3 139
And my shape as true As honest madam's issue *Lear* i 2 9
Madcap. Come on, you madcap, I'll to the alehouse *T. G. of Ver.* i 5 8
That last is Biron, the merry mad-cap lord *L. L. Lost* ii 1 215
One half lunatic; A mad-cap ruffian and a swearing Jack *T. of Shrew* ii 1 290
Why, what a madcap hath heaven lent us here! *K. John* i 1 84
Well then, once in my days I'll be a madcap *1 Hen. IV.* i 2 160
'Twas where the madcap duke his uncle kept i 3 244
The nimble-footed madcap Prince of Wales iv 1 95
Madded. Had I but seen thy picture in this plight, It would have madded me: what shall I do Now? *T. Andron.* iii 1 104
A father, and a gracious aged man, . . . have you madded *Lear* iv 2 43
All curses madded Hecuba gave the Greeks, And mine to boot *Cymbeline* iv 2 313
Madding my eagerness with her restraint *All's Well* v 3 213
When he to madding Dido would unfold His father's acts *2 Hen. VI.* iii 2 117
This will witness outwardly, As strongly as the conscience does within, To the madding of her lord *Cymbeline* ii 2 37
Made such a sinner of his memory, To credit his own lie *Tempest* i 2 101
I, thy schoolmaster, made thee more profit Than other princesses can i 2 172
Told thee no lies, made thee no mistakings i 2 248
It was mine art . . . that made gape The pine and let thee out i 2 292
Thou shalt be pinch'd As thick as honeycomb, each pinch more stinging Than bees that made 'em i 2 330
I endow'd thy purposes With words that made them known i 2 358
Of his bones are coral made i 2 397
What strange fish Hath made his meal on thee? ii 1 113
By this bottle! which I made of the bark of a tree with mine own hands ii 2 128
Though thou canst swim like a duck, thou art made like a goose ii 2 136
Be pleased to hearken once again to the suit I made to thee iii 2 44
I have made you mad iii 3 58
We are such stuff As dreams are made on iv 1 157
Made me neglect my studies, lose my time *T. G. of Ver.* i 1 67
Made wit with musing weak, heart sick with thought i 1 69
What need she, when she hath made you write to yourself? ii 1 158
Made use and fair advantage of his days ii 4 68
Love hath chased sleep from my enthralled eyes And made them watchers ii 4 135
The ladder made of cords, and all the means Plotted ii 4 182
And Silvia—witness Heaven, that made her fair! ii 6 25

Made. When the flight is made to one so dear, Of such divine perfection *T. G. of Ver.* ii 7 12
Myself am one made privy to the plot . iii 1 12
Love of you, not hate unto my friend, Hath made me publisher of this iii 1 47
A ladder quaintly made of cords . iii 1 117
My youthful travel therein made me happy . iv 1 34
As if the garment had been made for me . iv 4 168
I made her weep agood, For I did play a lamentable part . iv 4 170
But by my coming I have made you happy . v 4 30
I thank your grace; the gift hath made me happy . v 4 148
I cannot remember what I did when you made me drunk *Mer. Wives* i 1 175
There is, as 'twere, a tender, a kind of tender, made afar off . i 1 215
Revenged I will be, as sure as his guts are made of puddings . ii 1 32
I would have made you four tall fellows skip like rats . ii 1 237
What they made there, I know not . ii 1 244
So far that there is shrewd construction made of her . ii 2 232
The hour is fixed; the match is made. Would any man have thought this? . ii 2 304
He has made us his vlouting-stog. I desire you that we may be friends iii 1 120
What made me love thee? let that persuade thee there's something extraordinary in thee . iii 3 74
I ne'er made my will yet, I thank heaven . iii 4 60
Your father and my uncle hath made motions: if it be my luck, so . iii 4 67
There's a hole made in your best coat, Master Ford . iii 5 143
She seemingly obedient likewise hath Made promise to the doctor . iv 6 34
I do begin to perceive that I am made an ass . v 5 124
See now how wit may be made a Jack-a-Lent! . v 5 134
Do you think . . . that ever the devil could have made you our delight? v 5 158
Let there be some more test made of my metal . *Meas. for Meas.* i 1 49
Thy bones are hollow; impiety has made a feast of thee . i 2 57
We thought it meet to hide our love Till time had made them for us . i 2 157
What's open made to justice, That justice seizes . ii 1 21
And mercy then will breathe within your lips, Like man new made . ii 2 79
As good To pardon him that hath from nature stolen A man already made ii 4 44
'Tis all as easy Falsely to take away a life true made . ii 4 47
We are made to be no stronger Than faults may shake our frames . ii 4 132
Dishonest wretch! Wilt thou be made a man out of my vice? . iii 1 138
He hath made an assay of her virtue to practise his judgement . iii 1 163
She, having the truth of honour in her, hath made him that gracious denial . iii 1 166
The hand that hath made you fair hath made you good . iii 1 184
He will avoid your accusation; he made trial of you only . iii 1 202
Like an impediment in the current, made it more violent . iii 1 252
What offence hath this man made you? . iii 2 15
Is there none of Pygmalion's images, newly made woman, to be had now? iii 2 48
They say this Angelo was not made by man and woman after this downright way of creation . . . —How should he be made, then? . iii 2 111
I am made to understand . iii 2 254
How may likeness made in crimes, Making practice on the times, To draw with idle spiders' strings Most ponderous and substantial things! . iii 2 287
I made my promise Upon the heavy middle of the night To call upon him iv 1 34
I have made him know I have a servant comes with me along . iv 1 45
I have not yet made known to Mariana A word of this . iv 1 49
By eight to-morrow Thou must be made immortal . iv 2 68
You will think you have made no offence . iv 2 199
Of which he made five marks, ready money . iv 3 7
Ere twice the sun hath made his journal greeting To the under generation iv 3 92
Thou hast made good haste: Come, we will walk . iv 5 11
We have made inquiry of you . v 1 5
My business in this state Made me a looker on here in Vienna . v 1 319
Your highness said even now, I made you a duke . v 1 522
Our wealth increased By prosperous voyages I often made *Com. of Errors* i 1 41
Had made provision for her following me . i 1 48
Made daily motions for our home return: Unwilling I agreed . i 1 60
The clock hath strucken twelve upon the bell; My mistress made it one upon my cheek . i 2 46
What patch is made our porter? My master stays in the street . iii 1 36
She will well excuse Why at this time the doors are made against you . iii 1 93
In the stirring passage of the day, A vulgar comment will be made of it iii 1 100
Get you home And fetch the chain; by this I know 'tis made . iii 1 115
If my breast had not been made of faith and my heart of steel, She had transform'd me to a curtal dog and made me turn i' the wheel . iii 2 150
Hath almost made me traitor to myself . iii 2 167
The chain unfinish'd made me stay thus long . iii 2 173
I have made it for you.—Made it for me, sir! I bespoke it not . iii 2 175
My husband, Whom I made lord of me and all I had . v 1 137
Indeed he hath made great preparation . *Much Ado* i 1 280
He were an excellent man that were made just in the midway . ii 1 8
Yet it had not been amiss the rod had been made . ii 1 235
She would have made Hercules have turned spit . ii 1 260
His grace hath made the match, and all grace say Amen to it . ii 1 314
Till he have made an oyster of me, he shall never make me such a fool . ii 3 27
Hath she made her affection known to Benedick? . ii 3 127
I would have daffed all other respects and made her half myself . ii 3 177
Like favourites, Made proud by princes . iii 1 10
Of this matter Is little Cupid's crafty arrow made . iii 1 22
If black, why, Nature, drawing of an antique, Made a foul blot . iii 1 64
You'll be made bring Deformed forth, I warrant you . iii 3 185
And made defeat of her virginity . iv 1 48
O, that is stronger made Which was before barr'd up with ribs of iron! iv 1 152
Nor fortune made such havoc of my means . iv 1 197
And made a push at chance and sufferance . v 1 38
This article is made in vain . *L. L. Lost* i 1 140
If she be made of white and red, Her faults will ne'er be known . i 2 104
All-telling fame Doth noise abroad, Navarre hath made a vow . ii 1 22
I only have made a mouth of his eye, By adding a tongue . ii 1 251
Some say a sore; but not a sore, till now made sore with shooting . iv 2 59
O, we have made a vow to study, lords . iv 3 318
He made her melancholy, sad, and heavy; And so she died . v 2 14
Ever and anon they made a doubt Presence majestical would put him out v 2 101
What, was your vizard made without a tongue? . v 2 242
I hope I was perfect: I made a little fault in 'Great' . v 2 562
Change not your offer made in heat of blood . v 2 810
These ladies' courtesy Might well have made our sport a comedy . v 2 886
I know not by what power I am made bold . *M. N. Dream* i 1 59
Demetrius, I'll avouch it to his head, Made love to Nedar's daughter . i 1 107
Falling in the land Have every pelting river made so proud . ii 1 91
We should be woo'd and were not made to woo . ii 1 242
I promise you your kindred hath made my eyes water ere now . iii 1 199

Made. Made senseless things begin to do them wrong *M. N. Dream* iii 2 28
The hate I bear thee made me leave thee so . iii 2 190
And made you other love, Demetrius, . . . To call me goddess . iii 2 224
Now I perceive that she hath made compare Between our statures . iii 2 290
You dwarf; You minimus, of hindering knot-grass made . iii 2 329
I with the morning's love have oft made sport . iii 2 389
If our sport had gone forward, we had all been made men . iv 2 18
When I saw rehearsed, I must confess, Made mine eyes water . v 1 69
What stuff 'tis made of, whereof it is born, I am to learn *Mer. of Venice* i 1 4
I would have stay'd till I had made you merry . i 1 60
Than if you had made waste of all I have . i 1 157
God made him, and therefore let him pass for a man . i 2 60
After dinner Your hazard shall be made . ii 1 45
Return, All in an hour.—We have not made good preparation . ii 4 4
Not I, but my affairs, have made you wait . ii 6 22
Made her neighbours believe she wept for the death of a third husband iii 1 10
I, for my part, knew the tailor that made the wings she flew withal . iii 1 30
But her eyes,—How could he see to do them? having made one, Methinks it should have power to steal both his . iii 2 124
I'll not be made a soft and dull-eyed fool, To shake the head, relent . iii 3 14
Deliver'd from his forfeitures Many that have at times made moan to me . iii 3 23
I shall be saved by my husband; he hath made me a Christian . iii 5 22
As well use question with the wolf Why he hath made the ewe bleat . iv 1 74
Let their [your slaves'] beds Be made as soft as yours . iv 1 96
She made me vow That I should neither sell nor give nor lose it . iv 1 442
I gave my love a ring and made him swear Never to part with it . v 1 170
I am helping you to mar that which God made . *As Y. Like It* i 1 36
When Nature hath made a fair creature, may she not by Fortune fall into the fire? . i 2 46
You must come away to your father.—Were you made the messenger? . i 2 62
I fill up a place, which may be better supplied when I have made it empty . i 2 205
Safest way To hide us from pursuit that will be made After my flight . i 3 138
Hath not old custom made this life more sweet Than that of painted pomp? . ii 1 2
I'll give you a verse to this note that I made yesterday . ii 5 49
With a woeful ballad Made to his mistress' eyebrow . ii 7 149
Were I not the better part made mercy . iii 1 2
You have a nimble wit: I think 'twas made of Atalanta's heels . iii 2 294
I would the gods had made thee poetical . iii 3 16
Now show the wound mine eye hath made in thee . iii 5 20
Do not fall in love with me, For I am falser than vows made in wine . iii 5 73
Go your way to her, for I see love hath made thee a tame snake . iv 3 70
Made him give battle to the lioness, Who quickly fell before him . iv 3 131
Meaning thereby that grapes were made to eat and lips to open . v 1 39
And in these degrees have they made a pair of stairs to marriage . v 2 41
Tell this youth what 'tis to love.—It is to be all made of sighs and tears v 2 90
It is to be all made of faith and service . v 2 95
All made of fantasy, All made of passion, and all made of wishes . v 2 100
Mirth in heaven, When earthly things made even Atone together . v 4 115
Saw'st thou not, boy, how Silver made it good? . *T. of Shrew* Ind. 1 19
As the daughter of Agenor had, That made great Jove to humble him . i 1 174
She struck me on the head, And through the instrument my pate made way . ii 1 155
Asses are made to bear, and so are you.—Women are made to bear . ii 1 200
I see a woman may be made a fool, If she had not a spirit to resist . iii 2 222
Nathaniel's coat, sir, was not fully made . iv 1 135
The gown is made Just as my master had direction . iv 3 116
How did you desire it should be made?—Marry, sir, with needle and thread . iv 3 120
My son Lucentio Made me acquainted with a weighty cause . iv 4 26
And pass my daughter a sufficient dower, The match is made . iv 4 46
See the truth hereof; For our first merriment hath made thee jealous . iv 5 76
That have by marrige made thy daughter mine . v 1 119
Bianca's love Made me exchange my state with Tranio . v 1 128
Whose skill . . . would have made nature immortal . *All's Well* i 1 22
With the breach yourselves made, you lose your city . i 1 136
That you were made of is metal to make virgins . i 1 141
Besides, virginity is peevish, proud, idle, made of self-love . i 1 157
My lord your son made me to think of this . i 3 238
A further use to be made than alone the recovery of the king . ii 3 41
You have made shift to run into't, boots and spurs and all . iii 5 39
And thinks himself made in the unchaste composition . iv 3 21
Made a groan of her last breath, and now she sings in heaven . iv 3 62
Half won is match well made; match, and well make it . iv 3 254
Whose villanous saffron would have made all the unbaked and doughy youth of a nation in his colour . iv 5 3
My lord that's gone made himself much sport out of him . iv 5 67
Of that I have made a bold charter; but I thank my God it holds yet . iv 5 97
Since you have made the days and nights as one . v 1 3
We lost a jewel of her; and our esteem Was made much poorer by it . v 3 2
I could not answer in that course of honour As she had made the overture v 3 99
Till I had made mine own occasion mellow . *T. Night* i 2 43
Fortune forbid my outside have not charm'd her! She made good view of me . ii 2 20
Our frailty is the cause, not we! For such as we are made of, such we be ii 2 33
Go to, thou art made, if thou desirest to be so . ii 5 168; iii 4 57
Am I made?—'If not, let me see thee a servant still' . iii 4 59
Whom thou, in terms so bloody and so dear, Hast made thine enemies . v 1 75
Away with him! Who hath made this havoc with them? . v 1 208
Pardon me, sweet one, even for the vows We made each other but so late v 1 222
How have you made division of yourself? . v 1 229
That day that made my sister thirteen years . v 1 255
Made the most notorious geck and gull That e'er invention play'd on . v 1 351
A solemn combination shall be made Of our dear souls . v 1 392
Royal necessities made separation of their society . *W. Tale* i 1 28
The offences we have made you do we'll answer . i 2 83
He would not stay at your petitions; made His business more material . i 2 215
Why, his revenges must In that be made more bitter . i 2 457
In a semicircle, Or a half-moon made with a pen . ii 1 11
All other circumstances Made up to the deed, doth push on this . ii 1 179
Good goddess Nature, which hast made it So like to him that got it . ii 3 104
You have made fault I' the boldness of your speech . iii 2 218
Since fate, against thy better disposition, Hath made thy person for the thrower-out Of my poor babe . iii 3 29
You're a made old man: if the sins of your youth are forgiven you . iii 3 124
The need I have of thee thine own goodness hath made . iv 2 14
Having made me businesses which none without thee can sufficiently manage . iv 2 15

Made. But my father hath made her mistress of the feast, and she lays it on. She hath made me four and twenty nosegays for the shearers *W. Tale* iv 3 42
Yet nature is made better by no mean But nature makes that mean . iv 4 89
Swine-herds, that have made themselves all men of hair . . . iv 4 333
Were I the fairest youth That ever made eye swerve . . . iv 4 385
I'll have thy beauty scratch'd with briers, and made More homely iv 4 436
From the whom, I see, There's no disjunction to be made . . iv 4 540
Yet nature might have made me as these are, Therefore I will not disdain iv 4 773
He'll be made an example . . . . iv 4 847
Heirless it hath made my kingdom and Destroy'd the sweet'st companion v 1 10
I thought of her, Even in these looks I made . . . . v 1 228
This is a match, And made between's by vows . . . . v 3 138
This might have been prevented and made whole . . *K. John* i 1 35
That judge hath made me guardian to this boy . . . . ii 1 115
I am not worth this coil that's made for me . . . . ii 1 165
God hath made her sin and her the plague On this removed issue . ii 1 185
And wide havoc made For bloody power to rush upon your peace . ii 1 220
This day hath made Much work for tears in many an English mother . ii 1 302
And two such shores to two such streams made one . . . ii 1 443
Ope your gates, Let in that amity which you have made . . ii 1 537
This match made up Her presence would have interrupted much . ii 1 541
This league that we have made Will give her sadness very little cure . ii 1 545
Who of itself is peised well, Made to run even upon even ground . ii 1 576
I cannot brook thy sight: This news hath made thee a most ugly man . iii 1 37
And made his majesty the bawd to theirs . . . . . iii 1 59
No bargains break that are not this day made! . . . . iii 1 93
And our oppression hath made up this league . . . . iii 1 106
O, let thy vow First made to heaven, first be to heaven perform'd! . iii 1 266
Upon my knee, Made hard with kneeling, I do pray to thee . . iii 1 310
Melancholy Had baked thy blood and made it heavy-thick . . iii 3 43
Thou hast made me giddy With these ill tidings . . . . iv 2 131
O, when the last account 'twixt heaven and earth Is to be made! . iv 2 217
To be endeared to a king, Made it no conscience to destroy a prince . iv 2 229
Hadst thou but shook thy head or made a pause When I spake darkly . iv 2 231
Deep shame had struck me dumb, made me break off . . . iv 2 235
Forgive the comment that my passion made Upon thy feature . . iv 2 263
O death, made proud with pure and princely beauty! . . . iv 3 35
The legate of the pope hath been with me, And I have made a happy peace . . . . v 1 63
And come ye now to tell me John hath made His peace with Rome? . v 2 91
The sun of heaven methought was loath to set, But stay'd and made the western welkin blush . . . . v 5 2
I did not think to be so sad to-night As this hath made me . . v 5 16
Since correction lieth in those hands Which made the fault *Richard II.* i 2 5
That metal, that self mould, that fashion'd thee Made him a man . i 2 24
Expedient manage must be made . . . . i 4 39
That England, that was wont to conquer others, Hath made a shameful conquest of itself . . . . ii 1 66
And therein fasting, hast thou made me gaunt . . . . ii 1 81
Now He that made me knows I see thee ill . . . . . ii 1 93
Have ever made me sour my patient cheek . . . . . ii 1 169
Now comes the sick hour that his surfeit made . . . . ii 2 84
Base men by his endowments are made great . . . . . ii 3 139
With your sinful hours Made a divorce betwixt his queen and him . iii 1 12
That Power that made you king Hath power to keep you king . . iii 2 27
Peace have they made with him indeed, my lord . . . . iii 2 128
Their peace is made With heads, and not with hands . . . iii 2 137
Made glory base and sovereignty a slave, Proud majesty a subject . iv 1 251
Hath sorrow struck So many blows upon this face of mine, And made no deeper wounds? . . . . iv 1 279
Let me unkiss the oath 'twixt thee and me; And yet not so, for with a kiss 'twas made . . . . v 1 75
When weeping made you break the story off . . . . . v 2 2
For now hath time made me his numbering clock . . . . v 5 50
This hand hath made him proud with clapping him . . . . v 5 86
I was not made a horse; And yet I bear a burthen like an ass . . v 5 92
He made me mad To see him shine so brisk . . . *1 Hen. IV.* i 3 53
Brother, the king hath made your nephew mad . . . . i 3 138
An I have not ballads made on you all and sung to filthy tunes . ii 2 48
What cunning match have you made with this jest of the drawer? . ii 4 101
I made me no more ado but took all their seven points in my target . ii 4 223
I knew ye as well as he that made ye . . . . . . ii 4 296
Three times hath Henry Bolingbroke made head Against my power . iii 1 64
Made a friend of him, To fill the mouth of deep defiance up . . iii 2 115
An I have not forgotten what the inside of a church is made of . iii 3 9
Given them away to bakers' wives, and they have made bolters of them iii 3 80
To steal cream indeed, for thy theft hath already made thee butter . iv 2 67
Steps me a little higher than his vow Made to my father . . iv 3 76
You have deceived our trust, And made us doff our easy robes of peace . v 1 12
He made a blushing cital of himself . . . . . . v 2 62
I have paid Percy, I have made him sure.—He is, indeed . . v 3 48
These news, Having been well, that would have made me sick, Being sick, have in some measure made me well . . . *2 Hen. IV.* i 1 138
Pregnancy is made a tapster, and hath his quick wit wasted . . i 2 192
Unless a woman should be made an ass and a beast, to bear every knave's wrong . . . . ii 1 40
And made her serve your uses both in purse and in person . . ii 1 126
The rest of thy low countries have made a shift to eat up thy holland . ii 2 25
Methought he had made two holes in the ale-wife's new petticoat . ii 2 88
Speaking thick, which nature made his blemish . . . . ii 3 24
The armed commons Have of their puissance made a little taste . ii 3 52
Methought a' made a shrewd thrust at your belly . . . . ii 4 228
A' would have made a good pantler, a' would ha' chipped bread well . ii 4 258
Like a man made after supper of a cheese-paring . . . . iii 2 332
Now, have you left pursuit?—Retreat is made . . . . iv 3 78
Let there be no noise made, my gentle friends . . . . iv 5 1
Peace be with him that hath made us heavy!—Peace be with us! . v 2 25
If I had had time to have made new liveries . . . . . v 5 11
Never was such a sudden scholar made . . . . *Hen. V.* i 1 32
With an inward wish You would desire the king were made a prelate . i 1 40
I have made an offer to his majesty, Upon our spiritual convocation . i 1 75
He hath made a match with such a wrangler . . . . . i 2 264
How he comes o'er us with our wilder days, Not measuring what use we made of them . . . . i 2 268
A' made a finer end and went away an it had been any christom child ii 3 11
That by God and by French fathers Had twenty years been made . ii 4 62
Good yeomen, Whose limbs were made in England, show us here The mettle of your pasture . . . . iii 1 26
Think not upon the fault My father made in compassing the crown! . iv 1 311

Made. His passport shall be made And crowns for convoy put into his purse . . . . *Hen. V.* iv 3 36
It is not well done, mark you now, to take the tales out of my mouth, ere it is made and finished . . . . iv 7 45
For had you been as I took you for, I made no offence . . . iv 8 58
To the which as yet There is no answer made . . . . . v 2 75
Fortune made his sword; By which the world's best garden he achieved Epil. 6
They lost France and made his England bleed . . . . . Epil. 12
The church's prayers made him so prosperous.—The church! *1 Hen. VI.* i 1 32
Our isle be made a nourish of salt tears, And none but women left to wail . . . . i 1 50
My grisly countenance made others fly; None durst come near . . i 4 47
They found some place But weakly guarded, where the breach was made ii 1 74
By him that made me, I'll maintain my words . . . . . ii 4 88
These haughty words of hers Have batter'd me like roaring cannon-shot, And made me almost yield upon my knees . . . . . iii 3 80
The sword of Orleans hath not made me smart . . . . . iv 6 42
Great rage of heart Suddenly made him from my side to start . . iv 7 12
Doubtless he would have made a noble knight . . . . . iv 7 44
Would you not suppose Your bondage happy, to be made a queen? . v 3 111
Happy for so sweet a child, Fit to be made companion with a king . v 3 149
Thy late exploits . . . Have made thee fear'd and honour'd . *2 Hen. VI.* i 1 198
Am I a queen in title and in style, And must be made a subject to a duke? . . . . i 3 52
What a point, my lord, your falcon made, And what a pitch she flew! . ii 1 5
My wife desired some damsons, And made me climb . . . . ii 1 103
It made me laugh to see the villain run . . . . . . ii 1 155
Made the lame to leap and fly away.—But you have done more miracles than I; You made in a day, my lord, whole towns to fly . . . ii 1 162
As willingly do I the same resign As e'er thy father Henry made it mine ii 3 34
Whilst I, his forlorn duchess, Was made a wonder and a pointing-stock ii 4 46
The reverent care I bear unto my lord Made me collect these dangers . iii 1 35
But mine is made the prologue to their play . . . . . iii 1 151
It may be judged I made the duke away . . . . . . iii 2 67
View this body.—That is to see how deep my grave is made . . iii 2 150
His well-proportion'd beard made rough and rugged . . . . iii 2 175
Who . . . But will suspect 'twas he that made the slaughter? . . iii 2 190
Come, and get thee a sword, though made of a lath . . . . iv 2 2
That of the skin of an innocent lamb should be made parchment . . iv 2 87
He made a chimney in my father's house, and the bricks are alive . iv 2 156
Lord Say hath gelded the commonwealth, and made it an eunuch . . iv 2 175
He that made us pay one and twenty fifteens . . . . . iv 7 24
Long sitting to determine poor men's causes Hath made me full of sickness . . . . iv 7 94
Henry the Fifth, that made all France to quake . . . . iv 8 17
No sooner was I crept out of my cradle But I was made a king . iv 9 4
This hand was made to handle nought but gold . . . . . v 1 7
Made a prey for carrion kites and crows Even of the bonny beast he loved so well . . . . v 2 11
Somerset Hath made the wizard famous in his death . . . . v 2 69
What are you made of? you'll nor fight nor fly . . . . v 2 74
And where this breach now in our fortunes made May readily be stopp'd v 2 82
Whose cowardice Hath made us by-words to our enemies . *3 Hen. VI.* i 1 42
He made thee Duke of York.—'Twas my inheritance . . . . i 1 77
Henry the Fifth, Who made the Dauphin and the French to stoop . i 1 108
He rose against him . . . And made him to resign his crown perforce . i 1 142
Rather than have made that savage duke thine heir . . . . i 1 224
How love to me and to her son Hath made her break out into terms of rage! . . . . i 1 265
Seeing 'twas he that made you to depose, Your oath, my lord, is vain . i 2 26
And made an evening at the noontide prick . . . . . i 4 34
Whose frown hath made thee faint and fly ere this . . . . i 4 48
And made a preachment of your high descent . . . . . i 4 72
With his rapier's point, Made issue from the bosom of the boy . . i 4 81
Made impudent with use of evil deeds . . . . i 4 117
Having pinch'd a few and made them cry, The rest stand all aloof . ii 1 16
Unsheathe thy sword: By him that made us all, I am resolved . . ii 2 124
And tamed the king, and made the dauphin stoop . . . . ii 2 151
When we saw our sunshine made thy spring . . . . . ii 2 163
The match is made; she seals it with a curtsy . . . . iii 2 57
When he was made a shriver, 'twas for shift . . . . . iii 2 108
Hath not our brother made a worthy choice? . . . . . iv 1 3
How could he stay till Warwick made return? . . . . . iv 1 5
He hath made a solemn vow Never to lie and take his natural rest . iv 3 4
I'll well requite thy kindness, For that it made my imprisonment a pleasure . . . . iv 6 11
Unsavoury news! but how made he escape? . . . . . . iv 6 80
The gates made fast! Brother, I like not this . . . . . iv 7 10
I am so sorry for my trespass made . . . . v 1 92
Is proclamation made, that who finds Edward Shall have a high reward? v 5 9
And made the forest tremble when they roar'd . . . . . v 7 12
We swept suspicion from our seat And made our footstool of security . v 7 14
Now is the winter of our discontent Made glorious summer *Richard III.* i 1 2
Nor made to court an amorous looking-glass . . . . . i 1 15
Sent before my time Into this breathing world, scarce half made up . i 1 21
Was it not she . . . That made him send Lord Hastings to the Tower? i 1 68
And that the queen's kindred are made gentlefolks . . . . i 1 95
Stabb'd by the selfsame hand that made these wounds! . . . i 2 11
Cursed be the hand that made these fatal holes! . . . . i 2 14
If ever he have wife, let her be made As miserable by the death of him As I am made! . . . . i 2 26; iv 1 77
Thou hast made the happy earth thy hell, Fill'd it with cursing cries . i 2 51
Edward wept, To hear the piteous moan that Rutland made . . i 2 158
And twenty times made pause to sob and weep . . . . . i 2 162
And made them blind with weeping . . . . i 2 167
Teach not thy lips such scorn, for they were made For kissing, lady . i 2 172
Say, then, my peace is made.—That shall you know hereafter . . i 2 198
That cropp'd the golden prime of this sweet prince, And made her widow . . . . i 2 249
There's many a gentle person made a Jack . . . . . . i 3 73
Such terrible impression made the dream . . . . . . i 4 63
It [conscience] made me once restore a purse of gold that I found . i 4 143
Who made thee, then, a bloody minister? . . . . . . i 4 226
We have done deeds of charity; Made peace of enmity . . . ii 1 50
I hope the king made peace with all of us . . . . . . ii 2 132
The weary way hath made you melancholy . . . . . . iii 1 3
Our crosses on the way Have made it tedious, wearisome . . . iii 1 5
I loved the man, . . . Made him my book, wherein my soul recorded The history of all her secret thoughts . . . . iii 5 27
Made prize and purchase of his lustful eye . . . . . . iii 7 187

Made. I am not made of stones, But penetrable to your kind entreats *Richard III.* iii 7 224
Made I him king for this? O, let me think on Hastings, and be gone! iv 2 124
England's lawful earth, Unlawfully made drunk with innocents' blood! iv 4 30
The loss you have is but a son being king, And by that loss your daughter is made queen iv 4 308
Thy broken faith hath made a prey for worms iv 4 386
He, mistrusting them, Hoised sail and made away for Brittany iv 4 529
The weary sun hath made a golden set v 3 19
One that made means to come by what he hath v 3 248
A base foul stone, made precious by the foil Of England's chair v 3 250
Till the last [day] Made former wonders its *Hen. VIII.* i 1 18
They Made Britain India: every man that stood Show'd like a mine i 1 21
This masque Was cried incomparable; and the ensuing night Made it a fool i 1 28
When the way was made, And paved with gold i 1 187
Made suit to come in 's presence; which if granted, As he made semblance of his duty, would Have put his knife into him i 2 197
With that devil-monk, Hopkins, that made this mischief ii 1 22
And, out of ruins, Made my name once more noble ii 1 115
Life, honour, name and all That made me happy at one stroke has taken for ever from the world ii 1 117
As I am made without him, So I'll stand ii 2 52
So I leave him To him that made him proud, the pope ii 2 56
Then you are weakly made ii 3 40
When was the hour I ever contradicted your desire, Or made it not mine? ii 4 29
But oft have hinder'd, oft, The passages made toward it ii 4 165
With a splitting power, and made to tremble The region of my breast ii 4 183
Or died where they were made, or shortly after This world had air'd them ii 4 192
Meanwhile must be an earnest motion Made to the queen ii 4 234
Orpheus with his lute made trees, And the mountain tops that freeze, Bow themselves when he did sing iii 1 3
As sun and showers There had made a lasting spring iii 1 8
Have I not made you The prime man of the state? iii 2 161
What cross devil Made me put this main secret in the packet? iii 2 215
You made bold To carry into Flanders the great seal iii 2 318
I am glad your grace has made that right use of it iii 2 386
And the late marriage made of none effect iv 1 33
The king has made him master O' the jewel house iv 1 110
Whom I most hated living, thou hast made me, With thy religious truth and modesty, Now in his ashes honour iv 2 73
Your highness' pardon; My haste made me unmannerly iv 2 105
Beside that of the jewel house, is made master O' the rolls v 1 34
Her sufferance made Almost each pang a death v 1 68
I long To have this young one made a Christian. As I have made ye one, lords, one remain v 3 180
I made no spare, sir.—You did nothing, sir v 4 21
They fell on; I made good my place v 4 56
Ye have made a fine hand, fellows: There's a trim rabble let in v 4 74
Thou hast made me now a man! v 5 65
And their vow is made To ransack Troy *Troi. and Cres.* Prol. 7
Either to harbour fled, Or made a toast for Neptune i 3 45
The ram that batters down the wall, for the great swing and rudeness of his poise, They place before his hand that made the engine i 3 208
You must be watched ere you be made tame, must you? iii 2 46
Go to, a bargain made: seal it, seal it; I'll be the witness iii 2 204
Made tame and most familiar to my nature iii 3 10
Which are devour'd As fast as they are made, forgot as soon As done iii 3 149
Though they are made and moulded of things past iii 3 177
Made emulous missions 'mongst the gods themselves iii 3 189
This Ajax is half made of Hector's blood iv 5 83
Wherein my sword had not impressure made Of our rank feud iv 5 131
Some two months hence my will shall here be made v 10 53
Well, sir, what answer made the belly? *Coriolanus* i 1 110
That dogs must eat, That meat was made for mouths i 1 211
Let's hence, and hear How the dispatch is made i 1 281
We never yet made doubt but Rome was ready To answer us i 2 18
No better than picture-like to hang by the wall, if renown made it not stir i 3 13
By the vows We have made to endure friends i 6 58
Alone I fought in your Corioli walls, And made what work I pleased i 8 9
Let courts and cities be Made all of false-faced soothing! i 9 44
Let him be made a coverture for the wars! i 9 46
He still hath held them; that to 's power he would Have made them mules ii 1 263
The commons made A shower and thunder with their caps and shouts ii 1 282
When blows have made me stay, I fled from words ii 2 76
When Tarquin made a head for Rome, he fought ii 2 92
And by his rare example made the coward turn terror into sport ii 2 108
Made you against the grain To voice him consul ii 3 241
Tullus Aufidius then had made new head!—He had, my lord iii 1 1
The accusation Which they have often made against the senate iii 1 128
As thou hast said My praises made thee first a soldier iii 2 108
Is this the promise that you made your mother? iii 3 86
I would he had continued to his country As he began, and not unknit himself The noble knot he made iv 2 32
A goodly city is this Antium. City, 'Tis I that made thy widows iv 4 2
And yet my mind gave me his clothes made a false report of him iv 5 157
Why, he is so made on here within, as if he were son and heir to Mars iv 5 203
O, you have made good work!—What news? what news? iv 6 80
You have made fair work, I fear me iv 6 88
He leads them like a thing Made by some other deity than nature iv 6 91
You have made fair hands, You and your crafts! you have crafted fair! iv 6 117
You are they That made the air unwholesome iv 6 130
Made him fear'd, So hated, and so banish'd: but he has a merit iv 7 47
You have made good work! A pair of tribunes that have rack'd for Rome, to make coals cheap v 1 15
Shall I be tempted to infringe my vow In the same time 'tis made? v 3 21
All the swords In Italy, Could not have made this peace v 3 209
He sits in his state, as a thing made for Alexander v 4 23
Made him joint-servant with me; gave him way In all his own desires v 6 32
What faults he made before the last, I think Might have found easy fines v 6 64
Made peace With no less honour to the Antiates Than shame to the Romans v 6 79
Measureless liar, thou hast made my heart Too great for what contains it v 6 103
Thou comest not to be made a scorn in Rome *T. Andron.* i 1 265
These slips have made him noted long ii 3 86

Made. See that you make her sure. Ne'er let my heart know merry cheer indeed, Till all the Andronici be made away *T. Andron.* ii 3 189
With the dismall'st object hurt That ever eye with sight made heart lament! ii 3 205
How these were they that made away his brother ii 3 208
Help me with thy fainting hand—If fear hath made thee faint ii 3 234
What stern ungentle hands Have lopp'd and hew'd and made thy body bare? ii 4 17
Had he heard the heavenly harmony Which that sweet tongue hath made! ii 4 49
What accursed hand Hath made thee handless in thy father's sight? iii 1 67
And made a brine-pit with our bitter tears iii 1 129
How now! has sorrow made thee dote already? iii 2 23
How Troy was burnt and he made miserable iii 2 28
Thou art made of tears, And tears will quickly melt thy life away iii 2 50
Ran mad for sorrow: that made me to fear iv 1 21
Which made me down to throw my books, and fly,—Causeless, perhaps iv 1 25
Such a place there is, . . . By nature made for murders and for rapes iv 1 58
The midwife and the nurse well made away, Then let the ladies tattle iv 2 167
I made thee miserable What time I threw the people's suffrages On him iv 3 18
I heard a child cry underneath a wall. I made unto the noise v 1 25
Witness these trenches made by grief and care v 2 23
My hand cut off and made a merry jest v 2 175
Kill'd her, for whom my tears have made me blind v 3 49
And made Verona's ancient citizens Cast by their grave beseeming ornaments, To wield old partisans *Rom. and Jul.* i 1 99
Towards him I made, but he was ware of me And stole into the covert i 1 131
Younger than she are happy mothers made.—And too soon marr'd are those so early made i 2 12
Younger than you, . . . ladies of esteem, Are made already mothers i 3 71
Her waggon-spokes made of long spinners' legs i 4 59
Her chariot is an empty hazel-nut Made by the joiner squirrel i 4 68
When and where and how We met, we woo'd, and made exchange of vow ii 3 62
Thou wouldst else have made thy tale large.—O, thou art deceived; I would have made it short ii 4 101
One, gentlewoman, that God hath made for himself to mar ii 4 121
My man shall be with thee, And bring thee cords made like a tackled stair ii 4 201
You have made a simple choice; you know not how to choose a man ii 5 38
Men's eyes were made to look, and let them gaze; I will not budge iii 1 57
They have made worms' meat of me: I have it, And soundly too iii 1 112
Thy beauty hath made me effeminate iii 1 119
He made you for a highway to my bed iii 2 134
Where's Romeo?—There on the ground, with his own tears made drunk iii 3 83
Things that, to hear them told, have made me tremble iv 1 86
What made your master in this place?—He came with flowers v 3 280
He wrought better that made the painter *T. of Athens* i 1 201
O joy, e'en made away ere't can be born! i 2 110
And that unaptness made your minister, Thus to excuse yourself i 2 140
When the means are gone that buy this praise, The breath is gone whereof this praise is made ii 2 179
Had his necessity made use of me, I would have put my wealth into donation iii 2 89
The devil knew not what he did when he made man politic iii 3 29
Believe't, my lord and I have made an end iii 4 55
And made plenteous wounds!—He has made too much plenty with 'em iii 5 66
I hope it is not so low with him as he made it seem iii 6 6
Thy great fortunes Are made thy chief afflictions iv 2 44
Thy nature did commence in sufferance, time Hath made thee hard in't iv 3 269
What an alteration of honour Has desperate want made! iv 3 469
Made his everlasting mansion Upon the beached verge of the salt flood v 1 218
Yet our old love made a particular force, And made us speak like friends v 2 8
Have you not made an universal shout? *J. Cæsar* i 1 49
To hear the replication of your sounds Made in her concave shores i 1 52
Then I know My answer must be made i 3 114
There's a bargain made i 3 120
I have made strong proof of my constancy ii 1 299
Ne'er so much your enemy As that same ague which hath made you lean ii 2 113
Your swords, made rich With the most noble blood of all this world iii 1 155
Ambition should be made of sterner stuff iii 2 97
Let me show you him that made the will. Shall I descend? iii 2 163
What private griefs they have, alas, I know not, That made them do it iii 2 218
Let our alliance be combined, Our best friends made iv 1 44
That young Octavius with Mark Antony Have made themselves so strong iv 3 154
You give good words: Witness the hole you made in Cæsar's heart v 1 31
If we do meet again, why, we shall smile; If not, why then, this parting was well made v 1 119
He only, in a general honest thought And common good to all, made one v 5 72
They made themselves air, into which they vanished *Macbeth* i 5 5
This bird Hath made his pendent bed and procreant cradle i 6 8
What beast was't, then, That made you break this enterprise to me? i 7 48
They have made themselves, and that their fitness now Does unmake you i 7 53
Mine eyes are made the fools o' the other senses ii 1 44
That which hath made them drunk hath made me bold ii 2 1
Yet I made a shift to cast him ii 3 46
What's the matter?—Confusion now hath made his masterpiece! ii 3 71
By the verities on thee made good, May they not be my oracles as well? iii 1 8
This I made good to you In our last conference iii 1 79
You made it known to us.—I did so, and went further iii 1 84
Where sighs and groans and shrieks that rend the air Are made, not mark'd iv 3 169
And of the truth herein This present object made probation *Hamlet* i 1 156
The lists and full proportions are all made Out of his subject i 2 32
Both in time, Form of the thing, each word made true and good i 2 210
Did you not speak to it?—My lord, I did; But answer made it none i 2 215
He hath, my lord, of late made many tenders Of his affection to me i 3 99
It went hand in hand even with the vow I made to her in marriage i 5 50
No reckoning made, but sent to my account With all my imperfections i 5 78
And denied His access to me.—That hath made him mad ii 1 110
The instant burst of clamour that she made ii 2 538
Upon whose property and most dear life A damn'd defeat was made ii 2 598
With them, words of so sweet breath composed As made the things more rich iii 1 99
I did love you once.—Indeed, my lord, you made me believe so iii 1 117
I'll no more on't; it hath made me mad iii 1 153
I have thought some of nature's journeymen had made men and not made them well iii 2 38
Now, what my love is, proof hath made you know iii 2 179
Let me wring your heart; for so I shall, If it be made of penetrable stuff iii 4 36
What replication should be made by the son of a king? iv 2 13
He that made us with such large discourse, Looking before and after iv 4 36

Made. They withered all when my father died: they say he made a good end . . . . . . *Hamlet* iv 5 186
You must not think That we are made of stuff so flat and dull . iv 7 31
He made confession of you, And gave you such a masterly report . . iv 7 96
Custom hath made it in him a property of easiness . . . v 1 75
O, a pit of clay for to be made For such a guest is meet . . v 1 104
Is not parchment made of sheep-skins?—Ay, my lord, and of calf-skins v 1 123
Till of this flat a mountain you have made, To o'ertop old Pelion . v 1 275
Long in our court have made their amorous sojourn . *Lear* i 1 48
I am made Of the self-same metal that my sister is . . . i 1 70
Our potency made good, take thy reward . . . . i 1 175
By the power that made me, I tell you all her wealth . . i 1 210
The observation we have made of it hath not been little . . i 1 292
Can you make no use of nothing, nuncle?—Why, no, boy; nothing can be made out of nothing . . . . . . i 4 145
Gasted by the noise I made, Full suddenly he fled . . . ii 1 57
You cowardly rascal, nature disclaims in thee: a tailor made thee ii 2 60
A stone-cutter or a painter could not have made him so ill . ii 2 64
Made you no more offence but what you speak of?—None . . ii 4 61
Made you my guardians, my depositaries; But kept a reservation ii 4 254
For there was never yet fair woman but she made mouths in a glass iii 2 35
Made him proud of heart, to ride on a bay trotting-horse . iii 4 56
Your brother's evil disposition made him seek his death . . iii 5 7
True or false, it hath made thee earl of Gloucester . . iii 5 18
Whose warp'd looks proclaim What store her heart is made on . iii 6 57
It was he That made the overture of thy treasons to us . . iii 7 89
I such a fellow saw; Which made me think a man a worm . . iv 1 35
Made she no verbal question?—'Faith, once or twice . . iv 3 26
What are you?—A most poor man, made tame to fortune's blows . iv 6 225
Pardon me, dear madam; Yet to be known shortens my made intent iv 7 9
Those violent harms that my two sisters Have in thy reverence made iv 7 29
With my good biting falchion I would have made them skip . v 3 277
Your daughter, . . . I say again, hath made a gross revolt . . *Othello* i 1 135
If it prove lawful prize, he's made for ever . . . . i 2 51
She wish'd That heaven had made her such a man . . . i 3 163
The tyrant custom, most grave senators, Hath made the flinty and steel couch of war My thrice-driven bed of down . . . . i 3 231
When the blood is made dull with the act of sport . . . ii 1 229
Blessed fig's-end! the wine she drinks is made of grapes . . ii 1 257
The purchase made, the fruits are to ensue . . . . ii 3 9
He hath not yet made wanton the night with her . . . ii 3 16
I have made bold, Iago, To send in to your wife . . . iii 1 35
As salt as wolves in pride, and fools as gross As ignorance made drunk iii 3 405
Can any thing be made of this? . . . . . . iii 4 10
Is true of mind and made of no such baseness As jealous creatures are . iii 4 27
But if she lost it Or made a gift of it . . . . . iii 4 61
Some unhatch'd practice Made demonstrable here . . . iii 4 142
And then I heard Each syllable that breath made up between them . iv 2 5
Was this fair paper, this most goodly book, Made to write 'whore' upon? iv 2 72
And made you to suspect me with the Moor . . . . iv 2 147
O mistress, villany hath made mocks with love! . . . v 2 151
I have made my way through more impediments . . . v 2 263
He upbraids Iago, that he made him Brave me upon the watch . v 2 325
And the time's state Made friends of them . . *Ant. and Cleo.* i 2 96
Her passions are made of nothing but the finest part of pure love . i 2 151
Your wife and brother Made wars upon me . . . . ii 2 43
So much uncurbable, her garboils, Cæsar, Made out of her impatience . ii 2 68
Truth is, that Fulvia, To have me out of Egypt made wars here . ii 2 95
And made the night light with drinking . . . . . ii 2 182
The oars were silver, Which to the tune of flutes kept stroke, and made The water which they beat to follow faster . . . . ii 2 200
So many mermaids, tended her i' the eyes, And made their bends adornings . . . . ii 2 213
The air; which, but for vacancy Had gone to gaze on Cleopatra too And made a gap in nature . . . . ii 2 223
Royal wench! She made great Cæsar lay his sword to bed . . ii 2 232
I made no such report . . . . ii 5 57
Gracious madam, I that do bring the news made not the match . ii 5 67
What mean you, madam? I have made no fault . . . . ii 5 74
So half my Egypt were submerged and made A cistern for scaled snakes! ii 5 94
And what Made the all-honour'd, honest Roman, Brutus, With the arm'd rest, . . . To drench the Capitol? . . . . . ii 6 16
Have one man but a man? And that is it Hath made me rig my navy . ii 6 20
You have made me offer Of Sicily, Sardinia . . . . ii 6 34
Thy father, Pompey, would ne'er have made this treaty . . . ii 6 85
The policy of that purpose made more in the marriage than the love . ii 6 126
Lepidus is high-coloured.—They have made him drink alms-drink . ii 7 5
He hath waged New wars 'gainst Pompey; made his will . . iii 4 4
Cæsar and Lepidus have made wars upon Pompey.—This is old . . iii 5 4
Having made use of him in the wars . . . , presently denied him rivalry iii 5 7
My sword, made weak by my affection, would Obey it . . . iii 11 67
If that thy father live, let him repent Thou wast not made his daughter iii 13 135
Never anger Made good guard for itself . . . . . iv 1 10
I wish I could be made so many men . . . . . iv 2 16
I had a wound here that was like a T, But now 'tis made an H . . iv 7 8
I made these wars for Egypt: and the queen . . . . iv 14 15
And o'er green Neptune's back With ships made cities . . . iv 14 59
What have I kept back?—Enough to purchase what you have made known . . . . v 2 148
I'll drink the words you send, Though ink be made of gall . *Cymbeline* i 1 101
Thou took'st a beggar; wouldst have made my throne A seat for baseness i 1 141
The violence of action hath made you reek as a sacrifice . . . i 2 2
Made him As little as a crow, or less, ere left To after-eye him . . i 3 14
The assault you have made to her chastity you shall answer me . i 4 175
It is a thing I made, which hath the king Five times redeem'd from death i 5 62
Hands Made hard with hourly falsehood—falsehood, as With labour . i 6 107
The king my father shall be made acquainted Of thy assault . . i 6 149
The love I bear him Made me to fan you thus, but the gods made you, Unlike all others, chaffless . . . . i 6 177
Thou wert dignified enough, Even to the point of envy, if 'twere made Comparative for your virtues . . . . ii 3 133
His meanest garment . . . is dearer In my respect than all the hairs above thee, Were they all made such men . . . . . . ii 3 141
I hope the briefness of your answer made The speediness of your return ii 4 30
The vows of women Of no more bondage be, to where they are made, Than they are to their virtues . . . . ii 4 111
And I will kill thee, if thou dost deny Thou'st made me cuckold . . ii 4 146
Some coiner with his tools Made me a counterfeit . . . . ii 5 6
A kind of conquest Cæsar made here; but made not here his brag . . iii 1 23
Made Lud's town with rejoicing fires bright And Britons strut . . iii 1 32

Made. Upon the love and truth and vows which I Have made to thy command . . . . *Cymbeline* iii 2 13
Tell me how Wales was made so happy as To inherit such a haven . iii 2 62
Dainty trims, wherein You made great Juno angry . . . . iii 4 168
Our expectation that it would be thus Hath made us forward . . iii 5 29
She looks us like A thing more made of malice than of duty . . iii 5 33
But our great court Made me to blame in memory . . . . iii 5 51
For two nights together Have made the ground my bed . . . iii 6 3
I would have left it [money] on the board so soon As I had made my meal . . . . iii 6 52
Know, if you kill me for my fault, I should Have died had I not made it iii 6 58
How fit his garments serve me! Why should his mistress, who was made by him that made the tailor, not be fit too? . . . . iv 1 4
He made those clothes, Which, as it seems, make thee.—Thou precious varlet, My tailor made them not . . . . iv 2 82
Being scarce made up, I mean, to man, he had not apprehension . . iv 2 109
The bird is dead That we have made so much on . . . . iv 2 198
Thou blessed thing! Jove knows what man thou mightst have made . iv 2 207
Camest thou from where they made the stand?—I did . . . v 3 1
He, with two striplings, . . . Made good the passage . . . v 3 23
Forthwith they fly . . . slaves, The strides they victors made . . v 3 43
You are made Rather to wonder at the things you hear Than to work any v 3 53
If he'll do as he is made to do, I know he'll quickly fly my friendship too v 3 61
Great the slaughter is Here made by the Roman . . . . v 3 79
And happier much by his affliction made . . . . . v 4 108
I am called to be made free.—I'll be hang'd then . . . v 4 202
You whom the gods have made Preservers of my throne . . . v 5 1
Whose kinsmen have made suit That their good souls may be appeased v 5 71
Beauty that made barren the swell'd boast Of him that best could speak v 5 162
He began His mistress' picture; which by his tongue being made . . v 5 175
Whereat I, wretch, Made scruple of his praise . . . . v 5 182
I had you down and might Have made you finish . . . . v 5 412
The beauty of this sinful dame Made many princes thither frame *Per.* i Gower 32
Which to prevent he made a law, To keep her still, and men in awe i Gower 35
You gods that made me man, and sway in love . . . . i 1 19
It grieved my heart to hear what pitiful cries they made to us to help them . . . . ii 1 22
A man whom both the waters and the wind, In that vast tennis-court, have made the ball For them to play upon . . . . . ii 1 64
'Twas we that made up this garment through the rough seams of the waters . . . . ii 1 155
Let us salute him, Or know what ground's made happy by his breath . ii 4 28
No din but snores the house about, Made louder by the o'er-fed breast . . . . iii Gower 3
The careful search . . . Is made with all due diligence . . iii Gower 19
Pure surprise and fear Made me to quit the house . . . . iii 2 18
I have, Together with my practice, made familiar . . . . iii 2 34
She would with sharp needle wound The cambric, which she made more sound By hurting it; or when to the lute She sung, and made the night-bird mute . . . . iv Gower 24
She quickly pooped him; she made him roast-meat for worms . . iv 2 25
But he made a groan at it, and swore he would see her to-morrow . iv 2 117
On whom foul death hath made this slaughter . . . . iv 4 37
Why, hath your principal made known unto you who I am? . . . iv 6 89
Seeing this goodly vessel ride before us, I made to it . . . v 1 19
Tell me, if thou canst, What this maid is, or what is like to be, That thus hath made me weep? . . . . v 1 187
What minstrelsy, and pretty din, The regent made in Mytilene . . v 2 273
By her own most clear remembrance, she Made known herself . . v 3 22
Madeira. A cup of Madeira and a cold capon's leg . . . 1 *Hen. IV.* i 2 128
Madest. Thou strokedst me and madest much of me . . . *Tempest* i 2 333
Thou art the first knave that e'er madest a duke . . *Meas. for Meas.* v 1 361
What observation madest thou in this case? . . *Com. of Errors* iv 2 5
O God, which this blood madest, revenge his death! . . *Richard III.* i 2 62
Tell her thou madest away her uncle Clarence, Her uncle Rivers; yea, and, for her sake, Madest quick conveyance with her good aunt Anne . . . . iv 4 281
Thou madest thine enemies shake . . . . . *Coriolanus* i 4 60
Ever since thou madest thy daughters thy mother . . . *Lear* i 4 188
Made-up. Remain assured That he's a made-up villain . . *T. of Athens* v 1 101
Madly. That's somewhat madly spoken . . . *Meas. for Meas.* v 1 89
Wast thou mad, That thus so madly thou didst answer me? *Com. of Errors* ii 2 11
Met us again and madly bent on us Chased us away . . . v 1 152
And certain stars shot madly from their spheres . . *M. N. Dream* ii 1 153
Will make or man or woman madly dote Upon the next live creature . ii 1 171
At the gun's report, Sever themselves and madly sweep the sky . . iii 2 23
I play a merchant's part, And venture madly on a desperate mart *T. of S.* ii 1 329
That, being mad herself, she's madly mated . . . . iii 2 246
If I were mad, I should forget my son, Or madly think a babe of clouts were he: I am not mad . . . . *K. John* iii 4 58
Like a horse Full of high feeding, madly hath broke loose . 2 *Hen. IV.* i 1 10
So madly hot that no discourse of reason . . . Can qualify *Troi. and Cres.* ii 2 116
And madly play with my forefathers' joints . . . *Rom. and Jul.* iv 3 51
How ended she?—With horror, madly dying, like her life . *Cymbeline* v 5 31
Madly-used. The madly-used Malvolio . . . . *T. Night* v 1 319
Madman. One all of luxury, an ass, a madman . . *Meas. for Meas.* v 1 506
A madman! Why, thou peevish sheep, What ship? . *Com. of Errors* iv 1 93
In this the madman justly chargeth them . . . . . v 1 213
Behaviour, what wert thou Till this madman show'd thee? . *L. L. Lost* v 2 338
One sees more devils than vast hell can hold, That is, the madman: the lover, all as frantic . . . . . . *M. N. Dream* v 1 10
Help, help! here's a madman will murder me . . . *T. of Shrew* v 1 60
A sober ancient gentleman by your habit, but your words show you a madman . . . . v 1 76
He speaks nothing but madman . . . . . . *T. Night* i 5 115
What's a drunken man like, fool?—Like a drowned man, a fool and a mad man . . . . i 5 139
He is but mad yet, madonna; and the fool shall look to the madman . i 5 146
Madman, thou errest: I say, there is no darkness but ignorance . . iv 2 46
I'll ne'er believe a madman till I see his brains . . . . iv 2 125
A madman's epistles are no gospels . . . . . . v 1 294
Look then to be well edified when the fool delivers the madman . . v 1 299
Is this the madman?—Ay, my lord, this same . . . . v 1 335
Yet be well assured You put sharp weapons in a madman's hands 2 *Hen. VI.* iii 1 347
Art thou mad?—Not mad, but bound more than a madman is *R. and J.* i 2 55
Romeo! humours! madman! passion! lover! Appear thou . . ii 1 7
Live, and hereafter say, A madman's mercy bade thee run away . . v 3 67
Our masters may throw their caps at their money: these debts may well be called desperate ones, for a madman owes 'em *T. of Athens* iii 4 103

Madman. A madman so long, now a fool . . . . . *T. of Athens* iv 3 221
Shall I be frighted when a madman stares? . . . . *J. Cæsar* iv 3 40
Tell me whether a madman be a gentleman or a yeoman?—A king! *Lear* iii 6 10
Is it a beggar-man?—Madman and beggar too . . . . iv 1 32
Taught me to shift Into a madman's rags; to assume a semblance That very dogs disdain'd . . . . v 3 187

Madmen. Lovers and madmen have such seething brains *M. N. Dream* v 1 4
Love is merely a madness, and, I tell you, deserves as well a dark house and a whip as madmen do . . . *As Y. Like It* iii 2 422
And crown thee for a finder of madmen . . . *T. Night* iii 4 154
For though it [music] have holp madmen to their wits, In me it seems it will make wise men mad . . . *Richard II.* v 5 62
With great imagination Proper to madmen . . . *2 Hen. IV.* i 3 32
These two may run mad; but, if with too much brain and too little blood they do, I'll be a curer of madmen . *Troi. and Cres.* v 1 56
O, then I see that madmen have no ears . . *Rom. and Jul.* iii 3 61
Brutus and Cassius Are rid like madmen through the gates *J. Cæsar* iii 2 274
This cold night will turn us all to fools and madmen . *Lear* iii 4 81
'Tis the times' plague, when madmen lead the blind . iv 1 49
A dream, or else such stuff as madmen Tongue and brain not *Cymbeline* v 4 146

Madness. All wound with adders who with cloven tongues Do hiss me into madness . . . . . . *Tempest* ii 2 14
The affliction of my mind amends, with which, I fear, a madness held me v 1 116
Any madness I ever yet beheld seemed but tameness, civility and patience, to this his distemper . . . *Mer. Wives* iv 2 27
His actions show much like to madness . . *Meas. for Meas.* iv 4 4
Neglect me not, with that opinion That I am touch'd with madness! . v 1 51
Her madness hath the oddest frame of sense, Such a dependency of thing on thing, As e'er I heard in madness . . . v 1 61
And what's a fever but a fit of madness? . . . *Com. of Errors* v 1 76
This ill day A most outrageous fit of madness took him . . . v 1 139
Fetter strong madness in a silken thread, Charm ache with air *Much Ado* v 1 25
Such a hare is madness the youth . . . *Mer. of Venice* i 2 21
If he love me to madness, I shall never requite him . . . i 2 69
Love is merely a madness . . . . . *As Y. Like It* iii 2 420
I drave my suitor from his mad humour of love to a living humour of madness . . . . iii 2 439
Begot of thought, conceived of spleen, and born of madness . . iv 1 218
I am as mad as he, If sad and merry madness equal be . *T. Night* iii 4 16
Why, this is very midsummer madness . . . . . iii 4 61
Though 'tis wonder that enwraps me thus, Yet 'tis not madness . iv 3 4
This may be some error, but no madness . . . . . iv 3 10
Fellow, thy words are madness . . . . v 1 101
Art thou mad?—No, madam, I do but read madness . . . v 1 302
If not, my senses, better pleased with madness, Do bid it welcome *W. T.* iv 4 495
No settled senses of the world can match The pleasure of that madness v 3 73
Lady, you utter madness, and not sorrow . . . *K. John* iii 4 43
Of this madness cured, Stoop tamely to the foot of majesty *2 Hen. IV.* iv 2 41
What madness rules in brainsick men! . . . *1 Hen. VI.* iv 1 111
Were't not madness, then, To make the fox surveyor of the fold? *2 Hen. VI.* iii 1 252
One word in your ear.—O plague and madness! . *Troi. and Cres.* v 2 35
Why, my negation hath no taste of madness . . . . . v 2 127
O madness of discourse, That cause sets up with and against itself! . v 2 142
A madness most discreet, A choking gall . . . *Rom. and Jul.* i 1 199
And all the madness is, he cheers them up too . . *T. of Athens* i 2 42
Like madness is the glory of this life, As this pomp shows . . i 2 139
His flight was madness . . . . *Macbeth* iv 2 3
Might deprive your sovereignty of reason And draw you into madness *Hamlet* i 4 74
To define true madness, What is't but to be nothing else but mad? . . ii 2 93
And, by this declension, Into the madness wherein now he raves . ii 2 150
Though this be madness, yet there is method in't . . . . ii 2 207
A happiness that often madness hits on . . . . . ii 2 213
But, with a crafty madness, keeps aloof . . . . . iii 1 8
What he spake, though it lack'd form a little, Was not like madness . iii 1 172
It shall be so: Madness in great ones must not unwatch'd go . . iii 1 196
I like him not, nor stands it safe with us To let his madness range . iii 3 2
For madness would not err, Nor sense to ecstasy was ne'er so thrall'd . iii 4 73
It is not madness That I have utter'd: bring me to the test, And I the matter will re-word; which madness Would gambol from . . iii 4 141
Lay not that flattering unction to your soul, That not your trespass, but my madness speaks . . . . iii 4 146
That I essentially am not in madness, But mad in craft . . . iii 4 187
O'er whom his very madness, like some ore Among a mineral of metals base, Shows itself pure . . . . iv 1 25
Hamlet in madness hath Polonius slain . . . . . iv 1 34
By heaven, thy madness shall be paid with weight . . . . iv 5 156
A document in madness, thoughts and remembrance fitted . . iv 5 178
This is mere madness: And thus awhile the fit will work on him . . v 1 307
What I have done, That might your nature, honour and exception Roughly awake, I here proclaim was madness . . . . . v 2 243
Then Hamlet does it not, Hamlet denies it. Who does it, then? His madness . . . . v 2 248
Hamlet is of the faction that is wrong'd; His madness is poor Hamlet's enemy . . . . v 2 250
O, that way madness lies; let me shun that; No more of that . *Lear* iii 4 21
Hog in sloth, fox in stealth, wolf in greediness, dog in madness . . iii 4 97
His roguish madness Allows itself to any thing . . . . iii 7 104
O, matter and impertinency mix'd! Reason in madness! . . . iv 6 179
In madness, Being full of supper and distempering draughts . . *Othello* i 1 98
Practising upon his peace and quiet Even to madness . . . ii 1 320
If not, he foams at mouth and by and by Breaks out to savage madness iv 1 56
Riotous madness, To be entangled with those mouth-made vows! *A. and C.* i 3 29
To leave you in your madness, 'twere my sin: I will not . *Cymbeline* ii 3 104
Not frenzy, not Absolute madness could so far have raved . . iv 2 135
A fever with the absence of her son, A madness . . . . iv 3 3

Madonna, that drink and good counsel will amend . . *T. Night* i 5 47
Good madonna, give me leave to prove you a fool . . . . i 5 64
Make your proof.—I must catechize you for it, madonna . . . i 5 68
Good madonna, why mournest thou?—Good fool, for my brother's death i 5 72
I think his soul is in hell, madonna.—I know his soul is in heaven, fool i 5 74
The more fool, madonna, to mourn for your brother's soul being in heaven i 5 76
Thou hast spoke for us, madonna, as if thy eldest son should be a fool i 5 120
He is but mad yet, madonna; and the fool shall look to the madman i 5 145
Prithee, read i' thy right wits.—So I do, madonna . . . . v 1 306

Madrigal. To whose falls Melodious birds sings madrigals *M r. Wives* iii 1 18

Maggot. Have blown me full of maggot ostentation . . *L. L. Lost* v 2 409
If the sun breed maggots in a dead dog . . . . *Hamlet* ii 2 181
We fat all creatures else to fat us, and we fat ourselves for maggots iv 3 24

Magic. Lend thy hand, And pluck my magic garment from me *Tempest* i 2 24
But this rough magic I here abjure . . . . v 1 50
There's magic in thy majesty . . . . . . *W. Tale* v 3 39
If this be magic, let it be an art Lawful as eating . . . . v 3 110
By magic verses have contrived his end . . . *1 Hen. VI.* i 1 27
Magic of bounty! all these spirits thy power Hath conjured *T. of Athens* i 1 6
Distill'd by magic sleights Shall raise such artificial sprites *Macbeth* iii 5 26
Thy natural magic and dire property, On wholesome life usurp *Hamlet* iii 2 270
If she in chains of magic were not bound . . . . *Othello* i 2 65
What charms, What conjuration and what mighty magic . . . i 3 92
Is't possible?—'Tis true: there's magic in the web of it . . . iii 4 69
The noble ruin of her magic, Antony . . . *Ant. and Cleo.* iii 10 19

Magical. What in his name, That magical word of war, we have effected iii 1 31

Magician. A magician, most profound in his art . . *As Y. Like It* v 2 67
I am a magician. Therefore, put you in your best array . . . v 2 78
His uncle, Whom he reports to be a great magician . . . . v 4 33
That great magician, damn'd Glendower . . . . *1 Hen. IV.* i 3 83
What black magician conjures up this fiend? . . . *Richard III.* i 2 34

Magistrate. Some, like magistrates, correct at home . . . *Hen. V.* i 2 191
No kind of traffic Would I admit; no name of magistrate . *Tempest* ii 1 149
Fie, lords! that you, being supreme magistrates, Thus contumeliously should break the peace! . . . . . . *1 Hen. VI.* i 3 57
Labour in thy vocation; which is as much to say as, let the magistrates be labouring men; and therefore should we be magistrates *2 Hen. VI.* iv 2 19
An oath is of no moment, being not took Before a true and lawful magistrate, That hath authority over him that swears . *3 Hen. VI.* i 2 23
Proud, violent, testy magistrates, alias fools . . . *Coriolanus* ii 1 47
They choose their magistrate, And such a one as he . . . iii 1 104
By the consent of all, we were establish'd The people's magistrates . iii 1 202

Magnanimity. Infuse his breast with magnanimity . . *3 Hen. VI.* v 4 41

Magnanimous. The magnanimous and most illustrate king *L. L. Lost* iv 1 65
Be magnanimous in the enterprise and go on . . . *All's Well* iii 6 70
As valiant as the wrathful dove or most magnanimous mouse *2 Hen. IV.* iii 2 171
As magnanimous as Agamemnon . . . . . . *Hen. V.* iii 6 6
The mighty, or the huge, or the magnanimous, are all one reckonings . iv 7 18
She is . . . A spur to valiant and magnanimous deeds *Troi. and Cres.* ii 2 200
Magnanimous and most illustrious six-or-seven-times-honoured captain-general . . . . iii 3 277

Magni Dominator poli, Tam lentus audis scelera? . . . *T. Andron.* iv 1 81

Magnificence. We cannot with such magnificence—in so rare—I know not what to say . . . . *W. Tale* i 1 13

Magnificent. A letter from the magnificent Armado . . *L. L. Lost* i 1 193
A domineering pedant o'er the boy; Than whom no mortal so magnificent! iii 1 180

Magnifico. The magnifico is much beloved . . . . *Othello* i 2 12
The magnificoes Of greatest port have all persuaded with him *Mer. of Venice* iii 2 282

Magnifiest. Him that thou magnifiest with all these titles Stinking and fly-blown lies here at our feet . . . . . *1 Hen. VI.* iv 7 75

Magnus. Up Fish Street! down Saint Magnus' Corner! . *2 Hen. VI.* iv 8 1

Magot-pies. Have By magot-pies and choughs and rooks brought forth The secret'st man of blood . . . . *Macbeth* iii 4 125

Mahomet. Was Mahomet inspired with a dove? . . . *1 Hen. VI.* i 2 140

Mahu. No better company?—The prince of darkness is a gentleman: Modo he's called, and Mahu . . . . *Lear* iii 4 149
Hobbididance, prince of dumbness; Mahu, of stealing; Modo, of murder iv 1 63

Maid. If you be maid or no?—No wonder, sir; But certainly a maid *Temp.* i 2 428
Might I but through my prison once a day Behold this maid . . . i 2 491
I am your wife, if you will marry me; If not, I'll die your maid . . iii 1 84
Here thought they to have done Some wanton charm upon this man and maid . . . . iv 1 95
What is this maid with whom thou wast at play? . . . . v 1 185
What a fool is she, that knows I am a maid, And would not force the letter to my view! Since maids, in modesty, say 'no' *T. G. of Ver.* i 2 53
You might kill your stomach on your meat And not upon your maid . i 2 69
My sister crying, our maid howling, our cat wringing her hands . ii 3 8
This hat is Nan, our maid: I am the dog: no, the dog is himself . ii 3 24
'Tis a milkmaid; yet 'tis not a maid, for she hath had gossips; yet 'tis a maid, for she is her master's maid, and serves for wages . . iii 1 269
She can milk; look you, a sweet virtue in a maid with clean hands . iii 1 278
Therefore, precisely, can you carry your good will to the maid? *Mer. Wives* i 1 238
Can you love the maid?—I will marry her, sir, at your request . . i 1 252
Desire this honest gentlewoman, your maid, to speak a good word . i 4 88
Sir, the maid loves you, and all shall be well . . . . . i 4 127
It is such another Nan; but, I detest, an honest maid as ever broke bread i 4 161
I shall never laugh but in that maid's company! . . . . i 4 163
Good morrow, good wife.—Not so, an't please your worship.—Good maid, then . . . . ii 2 37
De maid is love-a me: my nursh-a Quickly tell me so mush . . ii 2 65
My maid's aunt, the fat woman of Brentford, has a gown above . iv 2 77
What old woman's that?—Why, it is my maid's aunt of Brentford . iv 2 178
On that token, The maid hath given consent to go with him . . . iv 6 45
I'll to the vicar: Bring you the maid, you shall not lack a priest . iv 6 53
There pinch the maids as blue as bilberry . . . . . . v 5 49
Where you find a maid That, ere she sleep, has thrice her prayers said v 5 53
Why went you not with master doctor, maid?—You do amaze her . v 5 232
What, is there a maid with child by him?—No, but there's a woman with maid by him . . . . *Meas. for Meas.* i 2 92
'Tis my familiar sin With maids to seem the lapwing and to jest . . i 4 32
A very virtuous maid, And to be shortly of a sisterhood . . . ii 2 20
Be you content, fair maid; It is the law, not I condemn your brother . ii 2 79
Fasting maids whose minds are dedicate To nothing temporal . . ii 2 154
But this virtuous maid Subdues me quite . . . . . . ii 2 185
Be gone. Leave me awhile with the maid . . . . . . iii 1 180
What a merit were it in death to take this poor maid from the world! . iii 1 241
This forenamed maid hath yet in her the continuance of her first affection iii 1 248
We shall advise this wronged maid to stead up your appointment . iii 1 260
The maid will I frame and make fit for his attempt . . . . iii 1 266
Be acquainted with this maid; She comes to do you good . . . iv 1 51
A deflower'd maid! And by an eminent body that enforced The law against it! . . . . iv 4 24
Vail your regard Upon a wrong'd, I would fain have said, a maid! . v 1 21
Are you a maid?—No, my lord.—A widow, then?—Neither, my lord . v 1 173
You are nothing then: neither maid, widow, nor wife? . . . v 1 178
She may be a punk; for many of them are neither maid, widow, nor wife v 1 180
I ne'er was married; And I confess besides I am no maid . . . v 1 185
You are pardon'd, Isabel: And now, dear maid, be you as free to us . v 1 393
O most kind maid, It was the swift celerity of his death . . . v 1 398
Are both broke loose, Beaten the maids a-row. . . *Com. of Errors* v 1 170
Get you to heaven; here's no place for you maids . . . *Much Ado* ii 1 49
Your father got excellent husbands, if a maid could come by them . ii 1 338

Maid. Who is thus like to be cozened with the semblance of a maid *Much Ado* ii 2 40
A maid, and stuffed! there's goodly catching of cold iii 4 65
Will you with free and unconstrained soul Give me this maid? iv 1 26
Behold how like a maid she blushes here! iv 1 35
Would you not swear, All you that see her, that she were a maid? iv 1 40
Now, if you are a maid, answer to this iv 1 86
They are dangerous weapons for maids v 2 22
But I do live, And surely as I live, I am a maid v 4 64
A maid of grace and complete majesty *L. L. Lost* i 1 137
I was taken with a maid.—This maid will not serve your turn, sir.—This maid will serve my turn, sir i 1 299
Maid!—Man?—I will visit thee at the lodge i 2 138
Bear this significant to the country maid Jaquenetta iii 1 132
One o' these maids' girdles for your waist should be fit iv 1 50
Not one word more, my maids; break off, break off v 2 262
Be advised, fair maid: To you your father should be as a god *M. N. Dream* i 1 46
Such separation as may well be said Becomes a virtuous bachelor and a maid ii 2 59
This is he, my master said, Despised the Athenian maid ii 2 73
Man is by his reason sway'd; And reason says you are the worthier maid ii 2 116
A manly enterprise, To conjure tears up in a poor maid's eyes! iii 2 158
Most ungrateful maid! Have you conspired, have you with these contrived? iii 2 195
I am a right maid for my cowardice: Let her not strike me iii 2 302
Thanks, i' faith, for silence is only commendable In a neat's tongue dried and a maid not vendible *Mer. of Venice* i 1 112
Eleven widows and nine maids is a simple coming-in for one man ii 2 171
If I fail Of the right casket, never in my life To woo a maid ii 9 13
You saw the mistress, I beheld the maid iii 2 200
My maid Nerissa and myself meantime Will live as maids and widows iii 2 312
Who comes with her?—None but a holy hermit and her maid v 1 33
Alas, what danger will it be to us, Maids as we are, to travel forth so far! Beauty provoketh thieves sooner than gold *As Y. Like It* i 3 111
Here's a young maid with travel much oppress'd And faints for succour ii 4 74
But the devil take mocking: speak, sad brow and true maid iii 2 227
He [Time] trots hard with a young maid between the contract of her marriage and the day it is solemnized iii 2 331
Maids are May when they are maids, but the sky changes when they are wives iv 1 149
You do love this maid?—I do, sir.—Give me your hand v 1 40
We'll show thee Io as she was a maid *T. of Shrew* Ind. 2 56
Cicely Hacket.—Ay, the woman's maid of the house.—Why, sir, you know no house nor no such maid Ind. 2 92
Mates, maid! how mean you that? no mates for you i 1 59
In the other's silence do I see Maid's mild behaviour and sobriety i 1 71
You look'd so longly on the maid, Perhaps you mark'd not what's the pith of all i 1 170
If you love the maid, Bend thoughts and wits to achieve her i 1 183
Till the father rid his hands of her, Master, your love must live a maid i 1 187
You will be schoolmaster And undertake the teaching of the maid i 1 197
To achieve that maid Whose sudden sight hath thrall'd my wounded eye i 1 224
Katharine the curst! A title for a maid of all titles the worst i 2 130
A word ere you go; Are you a suitor to the maid you talk of, yea or no? i 2 230
Why, then the maid is mine from all the world, By your firm promise ii 1 386
Fair lovely maid, once more good day to thee iv 5 33
I must not hear thee; fare thee well, kind maid *All's Well* ii 1 148
I'll like a maid the better, whilst I have a tooth in my head ii 3 48
Fair maid, send forth thine eye: this youthful parcel Of noble bachelors stand at my bestowing ii 3 58
I am a simple maid, and therein wealthiest, That I protest I simply am a maid ii 3 72
If thou canst like this creature as a maid, I can create the rest ii 3 149
By the misprising of a maid too virtuous For the contempt of empire iii 2 33
The honour of a maid is her name; and no legacy is so rich as honesty iii 5 13
Oaths, tokens, and all these engines of lust are not the things they go under: many a maid hath been seduced by them iii 5 22
This young maid might do her A shrewd turn, if she pleased iii 5 70
Brokes with all that can in such a suit Corrupt the tender honour of a maid iii 5 75
Please it this matron and this gentle maid To eat with us to-night iii 5 100
Since Frenchmen are so braid, Marry that will, I live and die a maid iv 2 74
That is an advertisement to a proper maid in Florence iv 3 240
My meaning in't, I protest, was very honest in the behalf of the maid iv 3 247
Otherwise a seducer flourishes, and a poor maid is undone iv 3 147
He knows I am no maid, and he'll swear to't; I'll swear I am a maid v 3 291
I am either maid, or else this old man's wife v 3 294
O my good lord, when I was like this maid, I found you wondrous kind v 3 310
By thy honest aid Thou kept'st a wife herself, thyself a maid v 3 330
A virtuous maid, the daughter of a count *T. Night* i 2 36
The free maids that weave their thread with bones Do use to chant it ii 4 46
I am slain by a fair cruel maid ii 4 55
You would have been contracted to a maid; Nor are you therein, by my life, deceived, You are betroth'd both to a maid and man v 1 268
The captain that did bring me first on shore Hath my maid's garments v 1 282
And me, poor lowly maid, Most goddess-like prank'd up *W. Tale* iv 4 9
You see, sweet maid, we marry A gentler scion to the wildest stock iv 4 92
A malady Most incident to maids iv 4 125
He has the prettiest love-songs for maids; so without bawdry iv 4 193
He makes the maid to answer 'Whoop, do me no harm, good man' iv 4 199
Pins and poking-sticks of steel, What maids lack from head to heel iv 4 229
Is there no manners left among maids? iv 4 244
And sung this ballad against the hard hearts of maids iv 4 283
Goes to the tune of 'Two maids wooing a man:' there's scarce a maid westward but she sings it iv 4 295
Look upon the years Of Lewis the Dauphin and that lovely maid *K. John* ii 1 425
Talks as familiarly of roaring lions As maids of thirteen do of puppy-dogs! ii 1 460
Maids, Who, having no external thing to lose But the word 'maid,' cheats the poor maid of that ii 1 572
Ladies and pale-visaged maids Like Amazons come tripping after drums v 2 154
To the fire-eyed maid of smoky war *1 Hen. IV.* iv 1 114
It is not a fashion for the maids in France to kiss before they are married, would she say? *Hen. V.* v 2 289
A maid yet rosed over with the virgin crimson of modesty v 2 323
It were, my lord, a hard condition for a maid to consign to v 2 326
Maids, well summered and warm kept, are like flies at Bartholomew-tide v 2 335
Cannot see many a fair French city for one fair French maid v 2 345
Maid. You see them perspectively, the cities turned into a maid *Hen. V.* v 2 348
The maid that stood in the way for my wish shall show me the way to my will v 2 354
Succour is at hand: A holy maid hither with me I bring *1 Hen. VI.* i 2 51
Fair maid, is't thou wilt do these wondrous feats? i 2 64
What's that Pucelle whom they term so pure?—A maid, they say.—A maid! and be so martial!—Pray God she prove not masculine ii 1 21
And thus I said: 'Thou maiden youth, be vanquish'd by a maid' iv 7 38
Such commendations as becomes a maid, A virgin v 3 177
Because she is a maid, Spare for no faggots, let there be enow v 4 55
Now heaven forfend! the holy maid with child! v 4 65
Not a maid be married, but she shall pay to me her maidenhead *2 Hen. VI.* iv 7 129
Wretched man! would I had died a maid, And never seen thee! *3 Hen. VI.* i 1 216
Play the maid's part, still answer nay, and take it *Richard III.* iii 7 51
I was set at work Among my maids *Hen. VIII.* iii 1 75
A fair young maid that yet wants baptism, You must be godfather v 3 162
Yet let memory, From false to false, among false maids in love, Upbraid my falsehood! *Troi. and Cres.* iii 2 197
How go maidenheads? Here, you maid! where's my cousin Cressid? iv 2 24
Give me a kiss, When Helen is a maid again, and his iv 5 50
Make wells and Niobes of the maids and wives, Cold statues of the youth v 10 19
Matrons flung gloves, Ladies and maids their scarfs *Coriolanus* ii 1 280
I loved the maid I married; never man Sigh'd truer breath iv 5 120
Lord Titus, by your leave, this maid is mine *T. Andron.* i 1 276
Ravish a maid, or plot the way to do it v 1 129
I will take the wall of any man or maid of Montague's *Rom. and Jul.* i 1 15
I will push Montague's men from the wall, and thrust his maids to the wall i 1 22
When I have fought with the men, I will be cruel with the maids, and cut off their heads.—The heads of the maids? i 1 27
Let there be weigh'd Your lady's love against some other maid i 2 102
I was your mother much upon these years That you are now a maid i 3 73
A round little worm Prick'd from the lazy finger of a maid i 4 66
This is the hag, when maids lie on their backs, That presses them i 4 92
That kind of fruit As maids call medlars, when they laugh alone ii 1 36
Who is already sick and pale with grief, That thou her maid art far more fair than she: Be not her maid, since she is envious ii 2 6
But I, a maid, die maiden-widowed iii 2 135
Now heaven hath all, And all the better is it for the maid iv 5 68
The maid is fair, o' the youngest for a bride *T. of Athens* i 1 123
Love you the maid?—Ay, my good lord, and she accepts of it i 1 134
Maid, to thy master's bed; Thy mistress is o' the brothel! iv 1 12
Nor yells of mothers, maids, nor babes . . . Shall pierce a jot iv 3 124
Your wives, your daughters, Your matrons and your maids, could not fill up The cistern of my lust *Macbeth* iv 3 62
The chariest maid is prodigal enough, If she unmask her beauty to the moon: Virtue itself 'scapes not calumnious strokes *Hamlet* i 3 36
That's a fair thought to lie between maids' legs iii 2 126
And I a maid at your window, To be your Valentine iv 5 50
Let in the maid, that out a maid Never departed more iv 5 54
O rose of May! Dear maid, kind sister, sweet Ophelia! iv 5 158
Is't possible, a young maid's wits Should be as mortal as an old man's life? iv 5 159
Our cold maids do dead men's fingers call them iv 7 172
I thought thy bride-bed to have deck'd, sweet maid v 1 268
The gods to their dear shelter take thee, maid! *Lear* i 1 185
Not all the dukes of waterish Burgundy Can buy this unprized precious maid i 1 262
She that's a maid now, and laughs at my departure, Shall not be a maid long i 5 55
A maid so tender, fair and happy, So opposite to marriage *Othello* i 2 66
Did you . . . Subdue and poison this young maid's affections? i 3 112
He hath achieved a maid That paragons description and wild fame ii 1 61
My mother had a maid call'd Barbara: She was in love iv 3 26
'Tis said in Rome That Photinus an eunuch and your maids Manage this war.—Sink Rome, and their tongues rot! *Ant. and Cleo.* iii 7 15
E'en a woman, and commanded By such poor passion as the maid that milks iv 15 74
Maids, matrons . . . This viperous slander enters *Cymbeline* iii 4 40
Ripe for marriage-rite; this maid Hight Philoten *Pericles* iv Gower 17
Ay me! poor maid, Born in a tempest, when my mother died iv 1 18
A maid, though most ungentle fortune Have placed me in this sty iv 6 104
We have a maid in Mytilene, I durst wager, Would win some words of him v 1 43
With her fellow maids, is now upon The leafy shelter that abuts v 1 50
I am a maid, My lord, that ne'er before invited eyes v 1 85
My dearest wife was like this maid v 1 108
Tell me, if thou canst, What this maid is, or what is like to be? v 1 186
Her fortunes brought the maid aboard us v 3 11
Maid-child. But brought forth A maid-child call'd Marina v 3 6
Maiden. When maidens sue, Men give like gods *Meas. for Meas.* i 4 80
Must he needs die?—Maiden, no remedy ii 2 48
If you are a maid, answer to this.—I talk'd with no man at that hour, my lord.—Why, then are you no maiden *Much Ado* iv 1 88
And maidens bleach their summer smocks *L. L. Lost* v 2 916
Are not you he That frights the maidens of the villagery? *M. N. Dream* ii 1 35
And maidens call it love-in-idleness ii 1 168
And here the maiden, sleeping sound, On the dank and dirty ground ii 2 74
Thou drivest me past the bounds Of maiden's patience iii 2 66
I am not solely led By nice direction of a maiden's eyes *Mer. of Venice* ii 1 14
Yet a maiden hath no tongue but thought iii 2 8
Mark how the tyrant writes. Art thou god to shepherd turn'd, That a maiden's heart hath burn'd? *As Y. Like It* iv 3 41
This is a man, old, wrinkled, faded, wither'd, And not a maiden, as thou say'st he is *T. of Shrew* iv 5 44
'Tis the best brine a maiden can season her praise in *All's Well* i 1 55
God's mercy, maiden! does it curd thy blood To say I am thy mother? i 3 155
We thank you, maiden; But may not be so credulous of cure ii 1 117
My maiden's name Sear'd otherwise; nay, worse—if worse ii 1 175
You are no maiden, but a monument iv 2 6
Thy small pipe Is as the maiden's organ, shrill and sound *T. Night* i 4 33
Wherefore, gentle maiden, Do you neglect them? *W. Tale* iv 4 85
This hand of mine Is yet a maiden and an innocent hand *K. John* iv 2 252
The pining maidens' groans For . . . fathers and betrothed lovers *Hen. V.* ii 4 107
You yourselves are cause, If your pure maidens fall into the hand Of hot and forcing violation iii 3 20
And Cupid grant all tongue-tied maidens here Bed, chamber, Pandar to provide this gear! *Troi. and Cres.* iii 2 219
A maiden never bold; Of spirit so still and quiet *Othello* i 3 94
It was dyed in mummy which the skilful Conserved of maidens' hearts iii 4 75

Maiden battle. A maiden battle, then? . . . *Troi. and Cres.* iv 5 87
Maiden bed. When you have conquer'd my yet maiden bed, Remain there but an hour . . . . *All's Well* iv 2 57
Maiden blood. Whose maiden blood, thus rigorously effused, Will cry for vengeance at the gates of heaven . . *1 Hen. VI.* v 4 52
So pale did shine the moon on Pyramus When he by night lay bathed in maiden blood . . . . *T. Andron.* ii 3 232
Maiden blossom. For the truth and plainness of the case, I pluck this pale and maiden blossom here . . *1 Hen. VI.* ii 4 47
Now, by this maiden blossom in my hand, I scorn thee . . ii 4 75
Maiden blush. Put off your maiden blushes . *Hen. V.* v 2 253
Else would a maiden blush bepaint my cheek . *Rom. and Jul.* ii 2 86
Maiden cities. I am content; so the maiden cities you talk of may wait on her . . . . *Hen. V.* v 2 353
Maiden council. In our maiden council, rated them At courtship, pleasant jest and courtesy . . . *L. L. Lost* v 2 789
Maiden flowers. Strew me over With maiden flowers, that all the world may know I was a chaste wife to my grave . *Hen. VIII.* iv 2 169
Maiden honour. Now by my maiden honour, yet as pure As the unsullied lily, I protest . . . *L. L. Lost* v 2 351
Maiden loss. But that her tender shame Will not proclaim against her maiden loss, How might she tongue me! . *Meas. for Meas.* iv 4 27
Maiden meditation. In maiden meditation, fancy-free . *M. N. Dream* ii 1 164
Maiden modesty. If I know more of any man alive Than that which maiden modesty doth warrant . . . . *Much Ado* iv 1 181
Maiden phœnix. But as when The bird of wonder dies, the maiden phœnix, Her ashes new create another heir . *Hen. VIII.* v 5 41
Maiden pilgrimage. To undergo such maiden pilgrimage *M. N. Dream* i 1 75
Maiden presence. From this time Be somewhat scanter of your maiden presence . . . . *Hamlet* i 3 121
Maiden pride. Contempt, farewell! and maiden pride, adieu! *Much Ado* iii 1 109
Maiden priests. There, when my maiden priests are met . *Pericles* v 1 243
Maiden shame. Have you no modesty, no maiden shame? *M. N. Dream* iii 2 285
Maiden strewments. Yet here she is allow'd her virgin crants, Her maiden strewments . . . . . . *Hamlet* v 1 256
Maiden sword. Bravely hast thou flesh'd Thy maiden sword *1 Hen. IV.* v 4 134
Maiden truth. Against her maiden truth . . . *Much Ado* iv 1 166
Maiden virtue. Out-faced infant state and done a rape Upon the maiden virtue of the crown . . . . . *K. John* ii 98
Maiden walls. They are all girdled with maiden walls . *Hen. V.* v 2 349
Maiden weeds. Where lie my maiden weeds . . *T. Night* v 1 262
Maiden-widowed. But I, a maid, die maiden-widowed . *Rom. and Jul.* iii 2 135
Maiden youth, be vanquish'd by a maid . . *1 Hen. VI.* iv 7 38
Maidenhead. All the hosts of Readins, of Maidenhead *Mer. Wives* iv 5 80
Carouse full measure to her maidenhead . . *T. of Shrew* iii 2 227
What I am, and what I would, are as secret as maidenhead *T. Night* i 5 232
Wear upon your virgin branches yet Your maidenheads growing *W. Tale* iv 4 116
We shall buy maidenheads as they buy hob-nails, by the hundreds *1 Hen. IV.* ii 4 398
A rendezvous, a home to fly unto, If that the devil and mischance look big Upon the maidenhead of our affairs . . . iv 1 59
Is't such a matter to get a pottle-pot's maidenhead? *2 Hen. IV.* ii 2 84
Not a maid be married, but she shall pay to me her maidenhead *2 Hen. VI.* iv 7 130
By my troth and maidenhead, I would not be a queen.—Beshrew me, I would, And venture maidenhead for 't; and so would you *Hen. VIII.* ii 3 25
How now, how now! how go maidenheads? . *Troi. and Cres.* iv 2 23
Ay, the heads of the maids, or their maidenheads *Rom. and Jul.* i 1 31
Now, by my maidenhead, at twelve year old, I bade her come . i 3 2
I'll to my wedding-bed; And death, not Romeo, take my maidenhead! iii 2 137
Where, by the loss of maidenhead, A babe is moulded . *Pericles* iii Gower 10
Such a maidenhead were no cheap thing, if men were as they have been iv 2 64
I must have your maidenhead taken off, or the common hangman shall execute it . . . . iv 6 136
Maidenhood. And the misery is, example, that so terrible shows in the wreck of maidenhood . . . . . *All's Well* iii 5 24
And had the maidenhood Of thy first fight . . . *1 Hen. VI.* iv 6 17
And learn me how to lose a winning match, Play'd for a pair of stainless maidenhoods . . . . *Rom. and Jul.* iii 2 13
Maidenliest. I should have been that I am, had the maidenliest star in the firmament twinkled on my bastardizing . . *Lear* i 2 143
Maidenly. It is not friendly, 'tis not maidenly . *M. N. Dream* iii 2 217
What a maidenly man-at-arms are you become! . . *2 Hen. IV.* ii 2 82
Maidhood. By maidhood, honour, truth and every thing *T. Night* iii 1 162
Is there not charms By which the property of youth and maidhood May be abused? Have you not read? . . . *Othello* i 1 173
Maid-pale. Change the complexion of her maid-pale peace To scarlet indignation . . . . *Richard II.* iii 3 98
Mail. No egma, no riddle, no l'envoy; no salve in the mail, sir *L. L. Lost* iii 1 74
Quite out of fashion, like a rusty mail In monumental mockery *Troi. and Cres.* iii 3 152
Mailed. The mailed Mars shall on his altar sit . . *1 Hen. IV.* iv 1 116
Methinks I should not thus be led along, Mail'd up in shame *2 Hen. VI.* ii 4 31
His bloody brow With his mail'd hand then wiping . *Coriolanus* i 3 38
Maim. Not so deep a maim As to be cast forth in the common air *Rich. II.* i 3 156
Your father's sickness is a maim to us . . . *1 Hen. IV.* iv 1 42
That bears so shrewd a maim; two pulls at once . *2 Hen. VI.* ii 3 41
And stop those maims Of shame seen through thy country *Coriolanus* iv 5 92
Maimed. As the jest did glance away from me, 'Tis ten to one it maim'd you two outright . . . . *T. of Shrew* v 2 62
By which power You maim'd the jurisdiction of all bishops *Hen. VIII.* iii 2 312
Who is this they follow? And with such maimed rites? *Hamlet* v 1 242
It is a judgement maim'd and most imperfect . . *Othello* i 3 99
I am maim'd for ever. Help, ho! murder! murder! . . v 1 27
Main. As doth an inland brook Into the main of waters . *Mer. of Venice* v 1 97
That England, hedged in with the main . . . *K. John* ii 1 26
To set so rich a main On the nice hazard of one doubtful hour *1 Hen. IV.* iv 1 47
Comment appelez-vous la main en Anglois?—La main? . . *Hen. V.* iii 4 6
La main, de hand; les doigts, de fingres . . . . iii 4 12
Et je m'estime heureux que je suis tombé entre les mains d'un chevalier iv 4 59
Je ne veux point que vous abaissiez votre grandeur en baisant la main v 2 275
Look unto the main.—Unto the main! . . . *2 Hen. VI.* i 1 208
Overboard, Into the tumbling billows of the main . . *Richard III.* i 4 20
We must with all our main of power stand fast . *Troi. and Cres.* ii 3 273
I doubt it is no other but the main; His father's death *Hamlet* ii 2 56
Goes it against the main of Poland, sir, Or for some frontier? . iv 4 15
Or swell the curled waters 'bove the main . . . *Lear* iii 1 6
I cannot, 'twixt the heaven and the main, Descry a sail . *Othello* ii 1 3
Till we make the main and the aerial blue An indistinct regard . ii 1 39

Main article. But the main article I do approve . . *Othello* i 3 11
Main assent. By the main assent Of all these learned men she was divorced . . . . *Hen. VIII.* iv 1 31
Main battle. Charged our main battle's front . . *3 Hen. VI.* i 1 8
We will follow In the main battle . . . *Richard III.* v 3 299
Main blaze. The main blaze of it is past . . *Coriolanus* iv 3 20
Main cause. Put your main cause into the king's protection; He's loving and most gracious . . . . *Hen. VIII.* iii 1 93
Main chance. A man may prophesy, With a near aim, of the main chance of things As yet not come to life . *2 Hen. IV.* iii 1 83
Main chance, father, you meant; but I meant Maine . *2 Hen. VI.* i 1 212
Main consents. The main consents are had . . *All's Well* v 3 69
Main-course. Bring her to try with main-course . *Tempest* i 1 38
Main danger. He might at some great and trusty business in a main danger fail you . . . . . . *All's Well* iii 6 17
Main descry. The main descry Stands on the hourly thought *Lear* iv 6 217
Main end. All that dare Look into these affairs see this main end, The French king's sister . . . . *Hen. VIII.* ii 2 41
Main exercise. At hand comes the master and main exercise *Othello* ii 1 269
Main force. That Maine which by main force Warwick did win *2 Hen. VI.* i 1 210
Main flood. You may as well go stand upon the beach And bid the main flood bate his usual height . . . *Mer. of Venice* iv 1 72
Main grief. The main grief springs from the loss Of a beloved daughter and a wife . . . . *Pericles* v 1 29
Main harvest. To glean the broken ears after the man That the main harvest reaps . . . . . . *As Y. Like It* iii 5 103
Main hope. 'Tis his main hope . . . . *Macbeth* v 4 10
Main intendment. Fear the main intendment of the Scot . *Hen. V.* i 2 144
Main-mast. The ship boring the moon with her main-mast *W. Tale* iii 3 94
Main motive. This, I take it, Is the main motive . . *Hamlet* i 1 105
Main opinion. We did our main opinion crush In taint of our best man *Troi. and Cres.* i 3 373
Quite from the main opinion he held once Of fantasy . *J. Cæsar* ii 1 196
Main parcels. And between these main parcels of dispatch effected many nicer needs . . . . . . *All's Well* iv 3 104
Main part. Though the main part Pertains to you alone . *Macbeth* iv 3 198
To satisfy, If of my freedom 'tis the main part . . *Cymbeline* v 4 16
Main point. As the main point of this our after-meeting *Coriolanus* ii 2 43
Main power. By commission and main power . . *Hen. VIII.* ii 2 7
Main secret. What cross devil Made me put this main secret in the packet I sent the king? . . . . iii 2 215
Main soldier. Stands up For the main soldier . *Ant. and Cleo.* i 2 198
Main-top. From this most bravest vessel of the world Struck the main-top! O Posthumus! alas, Where is thy head? . *Cymbeline* iv 2 320
Main voice. No further Than the main voice of Denmark goes *Hamlet* i 3 28
Maine. Poictiers, Anjou, Touraine, Maine . . . *K. John* i 1 11
Ireland, Anjou, Touraine, Maine, In right of Arthur do I claim . ii 1 152
I give Volquessen, Touraine, Maine, Poictiers and Anjou . . . With her ii 1 527
Maine, Blois, Poictiers, and Tours, are won away . *1 Hen. VI.* iv 3 45
King of Naples, Duke of Anjou and Maine, yet is he poor . . v 3 95
Upon condition I may quietly Enjoy mine own, the country Maine and Anjou . . . . v 3 154
The duchy of Anjou and the county of Maine shall be released *2 Hen. VI.* i 1 51
Hath given the duchy of Anjou and Maine Unto the poor King Reignier i 1 110
Anjou and Maine! myself did win them both . . . . i 1 119
Maine is lost; That Maine which by main force Warwick did win . i 1 209
Main chance, father, you meant; but I meant Maine, Which I will win i 1 212
Anjou and Maine are given to the French; Paris is lost . . i 1 214
By thee Anjou and Maine were sold to France . . . iv 1 86
We'll have the Lord Say's head for selling the dukedom of Maine . iv 2 170
I sold not Maine, I lost not Normandy . . . . iv 7 70
Mained. Thereby is England mained, and fain to go with a staff . iv 2 172
Mainly. These four came all a-front, and mainly thrust at me *1 Hen. IV.* ii 4 222
I do not call your faith in question So mainly as my merit *Troi. and Cres.* iv 4 87
You mainly were stirr'd up . . . . . *Hamlet* iv 7 9
I am mainly ignorant What place this is . . . . *Lear* iv 7 65
Maintain. He will maintain you like a gentlewoman . *Mer. Wives* iii 4 45
If it be honest you have spoke, you have courage to maintain it *Meas. for Meas.* iii 2 167
Never could maintain his part but in the force of his will *Much Ado* i 1 238
Publish it that she is dead indeed; Maintain a mourning ostentation . iv 1 207
I thank my good father, I am able to maintain it . . *T. of Shrew* v 1 79
Maintain no words with him, good fellow . . . *T. Night* iv 2 107
Who else but I, And such as to my claim are liable, Sweat in this business and maintain this war? . . . . . *K. John* v 2 102
Which to maintain I would allow him odds . . . *Richard II.* i 1 62
Further I say and further will maintain . . . . . i 1 98
And will maintain what thou hast said is false In thy heart-blood . i 1 27
And I dare well maintain it with my life . . . *1 Hen. IV.* iv 3 9
I will maintain the word with my sword to be a soldier-like word *2 Hen. IV.* iii 2 82
I give it you, and will maintain my word . . . . . iv 2 67
'Gainst all the world will rightfully maintain . . . . iv 5 225
As much as would maintain . . . Full fifteen earls . . *Hen V.* i 1 12
He will maintain his argument as well as any military man in the world . . . . iii 2 85
In gross brain little wots What watch the king keeps to maintain the peace . . . . iv 1 300
This is muttered, That here you maintain several factions . *1 Hen. VI.* i 1 71
No coward nor no flatterer, But dare maintain the party of the truth . ii 4 32
Sharp and piercing, to maintain his truth . . . . . ii 4 70
I'll find friends . . . That shall maintain what I have said is true . ii 4 73
I'll maintain my words On any plot of ground in Christendom . . ii 4 88
Will not you maintain the thing you teach, But prove a chief offender? iii 1 129
Darest thou maintain the former words thou spakest? . . . iii 4 31
Crying with loud voice, 'Jesu maintain your royal excellence!' *2 Hen. VI.* i 1 161
When have I aught exacted at your hands, But to maintain the king? iv 7 75
That I have maintains my state And sends the poor well pleased from my gate . . . . iv 10 24
Westmoreland shall maintain.—And Warwick shall disprove it *3 Hen. VI.* i 1 88
You have a father able to maintain you . . . . iii 3 154
I will maintain it with some little cost . . . *Richard III.* i 2 260
The clothiers all, not able to maintain The many to them longing, have put off The spinsters, carders, fullers, weavers . . *Hen. VIII.* i 2 31
One that dare Maintain—I know not what: 'tis trash *Troi. and Cres.* ii 1 138
Such things as might offend the weakest spleen To fight for and maintain ii 2 129
Dare you draw, And maintain such a quarrel openly? *T. Andron.* ii 1 47
Whate'er I forge to feed his brain-sick fits, Do you uphold and maintain v 2 72
When the devout religion of mine eye Maintains such falsehood, then turn tears to fires! . . . . *Rom. and Jul.* i 2 94

Maintain. No stop! so senseless of expense, That he will neither know how to maintain it, Nor cease his flow of riot . *T. of Athens* ii 2 2
What friendship may I do thee?—None, but to Maintain my opinion . iv 3 71
What, are they children? who maintains 'em? *Hamlet* ii 2 361
I have heard him oft maintain it to be fit, that, sons at perfect age, and fathers declining, the father should be as ward to the son *Lear* i 2 77
Maintain talk with the duke, that my charity be not of him perceived . iii 3 16
I will maintain My truth and honour firmly . . . . v 3 100
If any man . . . will maintain upon Edmund, supposed Earl of Gloucester, that he is a manifold traitor, let him appear . . v 3 111
Our fealty and Tenantius' right With honour to maintain . *Cymbeline* v 4 74
Maintained the change of words with any creature . . . *Much Ado* iv 1 185
She dying, as it must be so maintain'd, Upon the instant . . iv 1 216
Maintained so politic a state of evil that they will not admit any good part v 2 62
The one maintained by the owl, the other by the cuckoo . *L. L. Lost* v 2 902
It shall be so far forth friendly maintained . . *T. of Shrew* i 1 141
Must be as boisterously maintain'd as gain'd . . *K. John* iii 4 136
I have maintained that salamander of yours with fire . 1 *Hen. IV.* iii 3 53
Whose see is by a civil peace maintain'd . . 2 *Hen. IV.* iv 1 42
The fuel is gone that maintained that fire . . *Hen. V.* ii 3 45
But that defences, musters, preparations, Should be maintain'd . ii 4 19
The Duke of Exeter has very gallantly maintained the pridge . iii 6 95
Then say at once if I maintain'd the truth . . 1 *Hen. VI.* ii 4 5
The leaves and fruit maintain'd with beauty's sun . 3 *Hen. VI.* iii 3 126
Maintenance. What maintenance he from his friends receives, Like exhibition thou shalt have from me . . . *T. G. of Ver.* i 3 68
For thy maintenance commits his body To painful labour *T. of Shrew* v 2 148
With lustier maintenance than I did look for . . 1 *Hen. IV.* v 4 22
Maison. Je suis gentilhomme de bonne maison . . *Hen. V.* iv 4 44
Majestas. Ah! sancta majestas, who would not buy thee dear? 2 *Hen. VI.* v 1 5
Majestee. Your majestee ave fausse French enough to deceive de most sage demoiselle . . . . . . *Hen. V.* v 2 233
Majestic. This is a most majestic vision . . *Tempest* iv 1 118
So get the start of the majestic world And bear the palm alone *J. Cæsar* i 2 130
Are now revived, To the majestic cedar join'd . *Cymbeline* v 5 457
Majestical. His eye ambitious, his gait majestical . . *L. L. Lost* v 1 12
They made a doubt Presence majestical would put him out . v 2 102
So appears this fleet majestical, Holding due course . *Hen. V.* iii Prol. 16
Not all these, laid in bed majestical, Can sleep so soundly . iv 1 284
But, with a proud majestical high scorn, He answer'd thus 1 *Hen. VI.* iv 7 39
The throne majestical, The sceptr'd office of your ancestors *Richard III.* iii 7 118
We do it wrong, being so majestical, To offer it the show of violence; For it is, as the air, invulnerable . . . *Hamlet* i 1 143
This brave o'erhanging firmament, this majestical roof . ii 2 313
Majestically. If thou dost it half so gravely, so majestically, both in word and matter, hang me up by the heels . 1 *Hen. IV.* ii 4 479
Majesty. A maid of grace and complete majesty . *L. L. Lost* i 1 137
Give up our right in Aquitaine, And hold fair friendship with his majesty ii 1 141
What peremptory eagle-sighted eye Dares look upon the heaven of her brow, That is not blinded by her majesty? . . iv 3 228
The attribute to awe and majesty . . . *Mer. of Venice* iv 1 191
Cleopatra's majesty, Atalanta's better part . . *As Y. Like It* iii 2 154
I must attend his majesty's command . . . *All's Well* i 1 4
What hope is there of his majesty's amendment? . . . i 1 13
His love and wisdom, Approved so to your majesty, may plead . i 2 10
My thanks and duty are your majesty's . . . . i 2 23
Health, at your bidding, serve your majesty! . . . ii 1 18
This is his majesty; say your mind to him: A traitor you do look like; but such traitors His majesty seldom fears . . . ii 1 98
Hearing your high majesty is touch'd With that malignant cause . ii 1 113
His majesty, out of a self-gracious remembrance, did first propose iv 5 77
This man may help me to his majesty's ear, If he would spend his power . . . . v 1 7
Did to his majesty, his mother and his lady Offence of mighty note v 3 13
I am a poor man, and at your majesty's command . . v 3 251
To bless the bed of majesty again With a sweet fellow to't . *W. Tale* v 1 33
The majesty of the creature in resemblance of the mother . v 2 39
O, thus she stood, Even with such life of majesty! . . v 3 35
There's magic in thy majesty . . . . . v 3 39
In my behaviour to the majesty, The borrow'd majesty, of England here.—A strange beginning: 'borrow'd majesty!' . *K. John* i 1 3
Ha, majesty! how high thy glory towers, When the rich blood of kings is set on fire! . . . . ii 1 350
Why answer not the double majesties? . . . . ii 1 480
Have I not pawn'd to you my majesty?—You have beguiled me with a counterfeit Resembling majesty . . . . iii 1 100
I muse your majesty doth seem so cold . . . iii 1 317
O fair return of banish'd majesty! . . . . iii 1 321
I am much bounden to your majesty.—Good friend, thou hast no cause iii 3 29
And I'll keep him so, That he shall not offend your majesty . iii 3 65
I'll send those powers o'er to your majesty.—My blessing go with thee! iii 3 70
To know the meaning Of dangerous majesty, when perchance it frowns iv 2 213
For the bare-pick'd bone of majesty Doth dogged war bristle his angry crest . . . . iv 3 148
Faulconbridge Desires your majesty to leave the field . . v 3 6
Who didst thou leave to tend his majesty?—Why, know you not? . v 6 32
The king hath pardon'd them, And they are all about his majesty . v 6 36
O, I am scalded with my violent motion, . . . to see your majesty! . v 7 50
And stay For nothing but his majesty's approach . *Richard II.* i 3 6
Let me kiss my sovereign's hand, And bow my knee before his majesty i 3 47
And hath sent post haste To entreat your majesty to visit him . i 4 56
This earth of majesty, this seat of Mars, This other Eden . ii 1 41
By my seat's right royal majesty . . . . ii 1 120
My liege, old Gaunt commends him to your majesty . . ii 1 147
Wipe off the dust that hides our sceptre's gilt And make high majesty look like itself . . . . ii 1 295
Madam, your majesty is too much sad . . . . ii 2 1
So your sweet majesty, Looking awry upon your lord's departure . ii 2 20
Will you go along with us?—No; I will to Ireland to his majesty . ii 2 141
Am I not king? Awake, thou coward majesty! thou sleepest . iii 2 84
White-beards have arm'd their thin and hairless scalps Against thy majesty . . . . iii 2 113
His eye, As bright as is the eagle's, lightens forth Controlling majesty iii 3 70
And his heart To faithful service of your majesty . . iii 3 118
Will his majesty Give Richard leave to live till Richard die? . iii 3 173
What says his majesty?—Sorrow and grief of heart Makes him speak fondly . . . . iii 3 184
Stand all apart, And show fair duty to his majesty . . iii 3 188
To do that office of thine own good will Which tired majesty did make thee offer, The resignation of thy state . . . . iv 1 178

Majesty. All pomp and majesty I do forswear . . *Richard II.* iv 1 211
Made glory base and sovereignty a slave, Proud majesty a subject . iv 1 252
Command a mirror hither straight, That it may show me what a face I have, Since it is bankrupt of his majesty . . . . iv 1 267
God save thy grace,—majesty I should say . . . 1 *Hen. IV.* i 2 19
Majesty might never yet endure The moody frontier of a servant brow i 3 18
Not with such strength denied As is delivered to your majesty . i 3 26
Amongst the rest, demanded My prisoners in your majesty's behalf . i 3 48
Let not his report Come current for an accusation Betwixt my love and your high majesty . . . . i 3 69
No extraordinary gaze, Such as is bent on sun-like majesty . . iii 2 79
And God forgive them that so much have sway'd Your majesty's good thoughts away from me! . . . . . . iii 2 131
So long as out of limit and true rule You stand against anointed majesty iv 3 40
It pleased your majesty to turn your looks Of favour from myself . v 1 30
Yet this before my father's majesty . . . . v 1 96
I hear his majesty is returned with some discomfort from Wales 2 *Hen. IV.* i 2 118
Thou whoreson mad compound of majesty . . . . ii 4 319
Many good morrows to your majesty!—Is it good morrow, lords? . iii 1 32
Your majesty hath been this fortnight ill . . . . iii 1 104
Of this madness cured, Stoop tamely to the foot of majesty . iv 2 42
Our news shall go before us to his majesty . . . iv 3 84
Both which we doubt not but your majesty Shall soon enjoy . iv 4 11
From enemies heaven keep your majesty! . . . . iv 4 94
O me! come near me; now I am much ill.—Comfort, your majesty! . iv 4 112
O majesty! When thou dost pinch thy bearer . . . iv 5 28
When I here came in, And found no course of breath within your majesty, How cold it struck my heart! . . . . . . iv 5 151
I would his majesty had call'd me with him . . . v 2 6
This new and gorgeous garment, majesty, Sits not so easy on me as you think . . . . v 2 43
We hope no other from your majesty.—You all look strangely on me v 2 62
If I be measured rightly, Your majesty hath no just cause to hate me . v 2 66
The majesty and power of law and justice . . . . v 2 78
And flow henceforth in formal majesty . . . . v 2 133
Doth his majesty Incline to it, or no?—He seems indifferent *Hen. V.* i 1 71
I have made an offer to his majesty, Upon our spiritual convocation . i 1 75
How . . . received, my lord?—With good acceptance of his majesty . i 1 83
Who, busied in his majesty, surveys The singing masons . . i 2 197
I have laid by my majesty And plodded like a man for working-days . i 2 276
Never was monarch better fear'd and loved Than is your majesty . ii 2 26
Ambassadors . . . Do crave admittance to your majesty . . ii 4 66
Sweeten the bitter mock you sent his majesty . . . ii 4 122
I can tell your majesty, the duke is a prave man . . iii 6 101
If your majesty know the man: his face is all bubukles, and whelks . iii 6 107
And over-bears attaint With cheerful semblance and sweet majesty iv Prol. 40
The Duke of York commends him to your majesty.—Lives he? . iv 6 3
Your majesty says very true: if your majesties is remembered of it iv 7 101
Which, your majesty know, to this hour is an honourable badge . iv 7 105
Your majesty takes no scorn to wear the leek upon Saint Tavy's day iv 7 106
All the water in Wye cannot wash your majesty's Welsh plood out of your pody . . . . iv 7 112
God pless it and preserve it, as long as it pleases his grace, and his majesty too! . . . . iv 7 114
I am your majesty's countryman, I care not who know it . . iv 7 116
I need not to be ashamed of your majesty, praised be God, so long as your majesty is an honest man . . . . . iv 7 119
I charge you in his majesty's name, apprehend him . . iv 8 18
Your majesty hear now, saving your majesty's manhood, what an arrant, rascally, beggarly, lousy knave it is . . . . . iv 8 35
I hope your majesty is pear me testimony and witness . . iv 8 37
Never came any from mine that might offend your majesty . . iv 8 51
Your majesty came not like yourself: you appeared to me but as a common man . . . . iv 8 53
To bring your most imperial majesties Unto this bar . . v 2 26
Your majesty shall mock at me; I cannot speak your England . v 2 102
Your majesty entendre bettre que moi . . . . v 2 288
God's mother . . . in a vision full of majesty . . 1 *Hen. VI.* i 2 79
And, for your royal birth, Inferior to none but to his majesty . iii 1 96
So perish they That grudge one thought against your majesty! . iii 1 176
Now will it best avail your majesty To cross the seas . . iii 1 179
I'll unto his majesty, and crave I may have liberty to venge this wrong iii 4 41
Beauty's princely majesty is such, Confounds the tongue . . v 3 70
I must trouble you again; No loving token to his majesty? . v 3 181
Then swear allegiance to his majesty, As thou art knight . . v 4 169
As by your high imperial majesty I had in charge . . 2 *Hen. VI.* i 1 1
Her grace in speech, Her words y-clad with wisdom's majesty . i 1 33
Methought I sat in seat of majesty In the cathedral church . i 2 36
Your royal majesty!—What say'st thou? majesty! I am but grace . i 2 70
That your majesty was an usurper.—Say, man, were these thy words? . i 3 188
I humbly thank your royal majesty.—And I accept the combat . i 3 215
I summon your grace to his majesty's parliament . . . ii 4 70
With what a majesty he bears himself, How insolent of late he is become! . . . . iii 1 6
Upon thy eye-balls murderous tyranny Sits in grim majesty . . iii 2 50
Were there a serpent seen, with forked tongue, That slily glided towards your majesty, It were but necessary you were waked . . iii 2 260
Tell his majesty That even now he cries aloud for him . . iii 2 377
What canst thou answer to my majesty for giving up of Normandy? . iv 7 30
Health and glad tidings to your majesty! . . . . iv 9 7
Get your husband's lands . . —Therefore I came unto your majesty 3 *Hen. VI.* iii 2 41
Scorn us in this manner?—I told your majesty as much before . iii 3 179
Before it pleased his majesty To raise my state to title of a queen . iv 1 67
He, more incensed against your majesty Than all the rest, discharged me . . . . iv 1 108
But if an humble prayer may prevail, I then crave pardon of your majesty . . . . iv 6 8
His looks are full of peaceful majesty . . . . iv 6 71
The duty that I owe unto your majesty I seal upon the lips of this sweet babe . . . . v 7 28
I, that am rudely stamp'd, and want love's majesty . *Richard III.* i 1 16
His majesty, Tendering my person's safety, hath appointed This conduct i 1 43
Belike his majesty hath some intent That you shall be new-christen'd . i 1 49
His majesty hath straitly given in charge . . . . i 1 85
There's no doubt his majesty Will soon recover his accustom'd health . i 3 1
God make your majesty joyful as you have been! . . . i 3 19
Buckingham and I Are come from visiting his majesty . . i 3 32
I never did incense his majesty Against the Duke of Clarence . i 3 85
I will acquaint his majesty With those gross taunts I often have endured i 3 105

Majesty. Too late he died that might have kept that title, Which by his death hath lost much majesty . . . *Richard III.* iii 1 100
Will well become the seat of majesty, And make, no doubt, us happy . iii 7 169
Why would you heap these cares on me? I am unfit for state and majesty . . . . iii 7 205
And meet your grace Where and what time your majesty shall please . iv 4 490
I know your majesty has always loved her . . *Hen. VIII.* ii 2 110
After So many courses of the sun enthroned, Still growing in a majesty ii 3 7
The king's majesty Commends his good opinion of you . . . ii 3 60
I am sorry my integrity should breed, And service to his majesty and you, So deep suspicion . . . . . . iii 1 52
Pray, do my service to his majesty: He has my heart yet . . iii 1 179
God and your majesty Protect mine innocence! . . . v 1 140
Like vassalage at unawares encountering The eye of majesty *Troi. and Cres.* iii 2 41
Many good morrows to your majesty; Madam, to you as many *T. An.* ii 2 11
Give his majesty my hand: Tell him it was a hand that warded him From thousand dangers . . . . . iii 1 194
Honours deep and broad wherewith Your majesty loads our house *Macb.* i 6 18
What is't you say? the life?—Mean you his majesty? . . ii 3 75
Thanks to your majesty . . . . . . iii 4 2
Good night; and better health Attend his majesty! . . iii 4 121
When was it she last walked?—Since his majesty went into the field v 1 4
In which the majesty of buried Denmark Did sometimes march *Hamlet* i 1 48
Both your majesties Might, by the sovereign power you have of us, Put your dread pleasures more into command Than to entreaty *Hamlet* ii 2 26
Never more To give the assay of arms against your majesty . ii 2 71
To expostulate What majesty should be, what duty is . . ii 2 87
What might you, Or my dear majesty your queen here, think? . ii 2 135
He that plays the king shall be welcome; his majesty shall have tribute of me . . . . ii 2 333
And he beseech'd me to entreat your majesties To hear and see the matter iii 1 22
Your majesty and we that have free souls, it touches us not . . iii 2 251
Most holy and religious fear it is To keep those many many bodies safe That live and feed upon your majesty . . . iii 3 10
The cease of majesty Dies not alone; but, like a gulf, doth draw What's near it with it . . . . . . iii 3 15
We must, with all our majesty and skill, Both countenance and excuse iv 1 31
If that his majesty would aught with us, We shall express our duty . iv 4 5
Where is the beauteous majesty of Denmark? . . . iv 5 21
I should impart a thing to you from his majesty . . . v 2 93
I love your majesty According to my bond; nor more nor less *Lear* i 1 94
Power, Pre-eminence, and all the large effects That troop with majesty i 1 134
To plainness honour's bound, When majesty stoops to folly . i 1 151
We will resign, During the life of this old majesty, To him . v 3 299
Good majesty, Herod of Jewry dare not look upon you *Ant. and Cleo.* iii 3 2
What majesty is in her gait? Remember, If e'er thou look'dst on majesty . . . . iii 3 20
The man hath seen some majesty, and should know.—Hath he seen majesty? . . . . iii 3 45
Majesty, to keep decorum, must No less beg than a kingdom . . v 2 17
An it like your majesty 1 *Hen. IV.* ii 4; 2 *Hen. VI.* ii 1; v 1
God save your (his) majesty! *Tempest* ii 1; *Richard II.* ii 2; 2 *Hen. IV.* v 2; *Hen. V.* v 2; 2 *Hen. VI.* iv 2; iv 8
How fares your majesty? *L. L. Lost* v 2; *K. John* v 3; v 7; *Lear* iv 7
I [do] beseech your majesty *All's Well* v 3; *Richard II.* ii 1; v 3; 1 *Hen. IV.* iii 2; v 4; *Hen. V.* iii 5; 2 *Hen. VI.* ii 3; *Cymbeline* iii 5
Please it your majesty *L. L. Lost* v 2; *All's Well* ii 3; 2 *Hen. VI.* i 3; ii 3; *Richard III.* iv 4
Please your (his) majesty *All's Well* v 3; 1 *Hen. IV.* iii 2; *Hen. V.* i 2; iii 6; iv 7; iv 8; 1 *Hen. VI.* iii 4; 2 *Hen. VI.* iii 1; *T. Andron.* i 1; *Hamlet* v 2; *Lear* iv 7; *Cymbeline* iv 3; *Pericles* ii 5
Thank your majesty *All's Well* i 2 76; *Hen. VIII.* i 2 13

Major. A natural coward, without instinct.—I deny your major 1 *Hen. IV.* ii 4 544
My major vow lies here, this I'll obey *Troi. and Cres.* v 1 49
I find the ass in compound with the major part of your syllables *Coriol.* ii 1 64
My nativity was under Ursa major *Lear* i 2 141

Majority. Holds from all soldiers chief majority 1 *Hen. IV.* iii 2 109

Make yourself ready in your cabin for the mischance *Tempest* i 1 27
Make the rope of his destiny our cable . . . . . i 1 33
Thy groans Did make wolves howl . . . . . i 2 288
Go make thyself like a nymph o' the sea . . . . i 2 301
He does make our fire, Fetch in our wood . . . . i 2 311
I pitied thee, Took pains to make thee speak . . . i 2 354
I'll rack thee with old cramps, Fill all thy bones with aches, make thee roar . . . . i 2 370
It would control my dam's god, Setebos, And make a vassal of him i 2 374
I'll make you The queen of Naples.—Soft, sir! one word more . i 2 448
This swift business I must uneasy make, lest too light winning Make the prize light . . . . i 2 451
Make not too rash a trial of him, for He's gentle . . . i 2 467
I can here disarm thee with this stick And make thy weapon drop i 2 473
Silence! one word more Shall make me chide thee, if not hate thee . i 2 476
All corners else o' the earth Let liberty make use of . . . i 2 492
'Widow Dido' said you? you make me study of that . . ii 1 81
What impossible matter will he make easy next? . . . ii 1 88
I myself could make A chough of as deep chat . . . ii 1 265
O, 'twas a din to fright a monster's ear, To make an earthquake! . ii 1 315
And let's make further search For my poor son . . . ii 1 323
On Prosper fall and make him By inch-meal a disease! . . ii 2 2
Were I in England now, . . . there would this monster make a man; any strange beast there makes a man . . . . ii 2 31
As proper a man as ever went on four legs cannot make him give ground . . . . ii 2 64
A most ridiculous monster, to make a wonder of a poor drunkard! . ii 2 169
No more dams I'll make for fish; Nor fetch in firing . . ii 2 184
The mistress which I serve . . . makes my labours pleasures . iii 1 7
Did My heart fly to your service; there resides, To make me slave to it iii 1 66
I'll turn my mercy out o' doors and make a stock-fish of thee . iii 2 79
Voices That, if I then had waked after long sleep, Will make me sleep again . . . . iii 2 149
If I have too austerely punish'd you, Your compensation makes amends iv 1 1
She will outstrip all praise And make it halt behind her . . iv 1 11
No sweet aspersion shall the heavens let fall To make this contract grow iv 1 19
Spongy April at thy hest betrims, To make cold nymphs chaste crowns iv 1 66
So rare a wonder'd father and a wife Makes this place Paradise . iv 1 124
Come hither from the furrow and be merry: Make holiday . . iv 1 136
Do that good mischief which may make this island Thine own for ever iv 1 217
He'll fill our skins with pinches, Make us strange stuff . . iv 1 234
And more pinch-spotted make them Than pard or cat o' mountain . iv 1 261

Make. You demi-puppets that By moonshine do the green sour ringlets make . . . . *Tempest* v 1 37
And you whose pastime Is to make midnight mushrooms . . . v 1 39
Supportable To make the dear loss, have I means much weaker Than you v 1 146
And second father This lady makes him to me . . . . v 1 196
One so strong That could control the moon, make flows and ebbs . v 1 270
With such discourse as, I not doubt, shall make it Go quick away . v 1 303
Thou art a sheep.—Such another proof will make me cry 'baa' *T. G. of V.* i 1 97
She makes it strange; but she would be best pleased To be so anger'd . i 2 102
How well I like it The execution of it shall make known . . i 3 36
So painted, to make her fair, that no man counts of her beauty . ii 1 64
You swinged me for my love, which makes me the bolder to chide you . ii 1 89
We'll make exchange; here, take you this . . . . ii 2 6
Now come I to my sister; mark the moan she makes . . . ii 3 33
If he make this good, He is as worthy for an empress' love . . ii 4 75
And make rough winter everlastingly . . . . . . ii 4 163
All I can is nothing To her whose worth makes other worthies nothing ii 4 166
Love, lend me wings to make my purpose swift! . . . ii 6 42
Better forbear till Proteus make return . . . . . ii 7 14
He makes sweet music with the enamell'd stones . . . ii 7 28
And make a pastime of each weary step . . . . . ii 7 35
What fashion, madam, shall I make your breeches? . . . ii 7 49
I fear me, it will make me scandalized . . . . . ii 7 61
But, as thou lovest thy life, make speed from hence . . . iii 1 169
I have fed upon this woe already, And now excess of it will make me surfeit . . . . iii 1 220
She hath a sweet mouth.—That makes amends for her sour breath . iii 1 331
More wealth than faults.—Why, that word makes the faults gracious . iii 1 377
The good conceit I hold of thee—For thou hast shown some sign of good desert—Makes me the better to confer with thee . . . iii 2 19
What might we do to make the girl forget? . . . . iii 2 29
Make tigers tame and huge leviathans Forsake unsounded deeps . iii 2 80
Throw us that you have about ye: If not, we'll make you sit and rifle you . . . . iv 1 4
Are you content to be our general? To make a virtue of necessity? . iv 1 62
Ay, I would I were deaf; it makes me have a slow heart . . iv 2 64
Return, return, and make thy love amends . . . . iv 2 99
I am but a shadow; And to your shadow will I make true love.—If 'twere a substance, you would, sure, deceive it, And make it but a shadow . . . . iv 2 126
Where I hear he makes abode . . . . . . iv 3 23
He makes me no more ado, but whips me out of the chamber . . iv 4 30
And make water against a gentlewoman's farthingale . . . iv 4 41
Pity love should be so contrary; And thinking on it makes me cry 'alas!' . . . . iv 4 89
What should it be that he respects in her But I can make respective? . iv 4 200
I should have scratch'd out your unseeing eyes, To make my master out of love with thee! . . . . iv 4 210
It is too little.—I'll wear a boot, to make it somewhat rounder . v 2 6
What says she to my valour?—O, sir, she makes no doubt of that. . v 2 20
These are my mates, that make their wills their law . . . v 4 14
O Proteus, let this habit make thee blush! . . . . . v 4 104
That one error Fills him with faults; makes him run through all the sins . . . . v 4 112
Let me be blest to make this happy close . . . . . v 4 117
The more degenerate and base art thou, To make such means for her . v 4 137
I dare be bold With our discourse to make your grace to smile . v 4 163
I will make a Star-chamber matter of it . . . *Mer. Wives* i 1 2
And will be glad to do my benevolence to make atonements . . i 1 33
Seven hundred pound?—Ay, and her father is make her a petter penny i 1 61
Fery goot: I will make a prief of it in my note-book . . . i 1 146
I will make an end of my dinner; there's pippins and cheese to come . i 2 12
An old cloak makes a new jerkin . . . . . . i 3 18
I do mean to make love to Ford's wife: I spy entertainment in her . i 3 48
I wash, wring, brew, bake, scour, dress meat and drink, make the beds i 4 102
And I will teach a scurvy jack-a-nape priest to meddle or make . i 4 116
As long as I have an eye to make difference of men's liking . . ii 1 57
It makes me almost ready to wrangle with mine own honesty . . ii 1 87
God bless them and make them his servants! . . . . ii 2 54
I'll make more of thy old body than I have done . . . ii 2 145
I make bold to press with so little preparation upon you . . ii 2 162
I had never so good means, as desire, to make myself acquainted with you . . . . ii 2 189
I will first make bold with your money; next, give me your hand . ii 2 262
If I see a sword out, my finger itches to make one . . . ii 3 48
Clapper-de-claw! vat is dat?—That is, he will make thee amends . ii 3 70
There will we make our peds of roses, And a thousand fragrant posies iii 1 19
I desire you in friendship, and I will one way or other make you amends iii 1 90
Ha, do I perceive dat? have you make-a de sot of us, ha, ha? . iii 1 118
I think I shall drink in pipe-wine first with him; I'll make him dance . iii 2 91
This secrecy of thine shall be a tailor to thee and shall make thee a new doublet and hose . . . . iii 3 35
I'll speak it before the best lord; I would make thee my lady . iii 3 53
Thou art a traitor to say so: thou wouldst make an absolute courtier . iii 3 66
If I suspect without cause, why then make sport at me . . iii 3 160
Heaven make you better than your thoughts! . . . . iii 3 218
I will hereafter make known to you why I have done this . . iii 3 241
If there is one, I shall make two in the company.—If dere be one or two, I shall make-a the turd . . . . iii 3 250
I'll make a shaft or a bolt on't: 'slid, 'tis but venturing . . iii 4 24
He will make you a hundred and fifty pounds jointure . . . iii 4 49
She'll make you amends, I warrant you . . . . . iii 5 48
Yet to be what I would not shall not make me tame . . . iii 5 153
If I have horns to make one mad, let the proverb go with me . iii 5 154
To make another experiment of his suspicion . . . . iv 2 35
But what make you here? . . . . iv 2 55
They shall have my horses; but I'll make them pay; I'll sauce them . iv 3 10
To make us public sport, Appoint a meeting with this old fat fellow . iv 4 14
He blasts the tree and takes the cattle And makes milch-kine yield blood . . . . iv 4 33
O powerful love! that, in some respects, makes a beast a man . v 5 5
Now is Cupid a child of conscience; he makes restitution . . v 5 32
Make the fairy oyes.—Elves, list your names . . . . v 5 45
Have I lived to stand at the taunt of one that makes fritters of English? v 5 151
I'll make the best in Gloucestershire know on't . . . v 5 190
Thus can the demigod Authority Make us pay down *Meas. for Meas.* i 2 125
Implore her, in my voice, that she make friends . . . i 2 185
I now must make you know I am that Isabella and his sister . i 4 22
He hath got his friend with child.—Sir, make me not your story . i 4 30
And follows close the rigour of the statute, To make him an example . i 4 68

Make. Our doubts are traitors And make us lose the good we oft might win By fearing to attempt *Meas. for Meas.* i 4 78
We must not make a scarecrow of the law ii 1 1
Let it keep one shape, till custom make it Their perch and not their terror ii 1 3
Plays such fantastic tricks before high heaven As make the angels weep ii 2 122
Dost thou desire her foully for those things That make her good? ii 2 175
Make me know The nature of their crimes, that I may minister To them ii 3 6
'Tis all as easy Falsely to take away a life true made As to put metal in restrained means To make a false one ii 4 49
I'll make it my morn prayer To have it added to the faults of mine ii 4 71
You seem'd of late to make the law a tyrant ii 4 114
Women are frail too.—Ay, as the glasses where they view themselves; Which are as easy broke as they make forms ii 4 126
Bidding the law make court'sy to their will ii 4 175
Neither heat, affection, limb, nor beauty, To make thy riches pleasant iii 1 38
Yet death we fear, That makes these odds all even iii 1 41
Therefore your best appointment make with speed iii 1 60
Has he affections in him, That thus can make him bite the law by the nose? iii 1 109
You must die; go to your knees and make ready iii 1 172
The goodness that is cheap in beauty makes beauty brief in goodness iii 1 186
I do make myself believe that you may iii 1 205
The maid will I frame and make fit for his attempt iii 1 266
It is certain that when he makes water his urine is congealed ice iii 2 117
Let me desire you to make your answer before him iii 2 165
This would make mercy swear and play the tyrant iii 2 206
There is scarce truth enough alive to make societies secure; but security enough to make fellowships accurst iii 2 240
Rather rejoicing to see another merry, than merry at any thing which professed to make him rejoice iii 2 250
Though music oft hath such a charm To make bad good iv 1 15
A planched gate, That makes his opening with this bigger key iv 1 31
Thousand escapes of wit Make thee the father of their idle dreams iv 1 64
When vice makes mercy, mercy's so extended, That for the fault's love is the offender friended iv 2 115
To make you understand this in a manifested effect iv 2 169
I may make my case as Claudio's, to cross this in the smallest iv 2 178
A pox o' your throats! Who makes that noise there? What are you? iv 3 27
Make a swift return; For I would commune with you of such things That want no ear but yours.—I'll make all speed iv 3 109
To make her heavenly comforts of despair, When it is least expected iv 3 114
This deed unshapes me quite, makes me unpregnant And dull iv 4 23
You make my bonds still greater.—O, your desert speaks loud v 1 8
To make them know That outward courtesies would fain proclaim Favours that keep within v 1 14
Make not impossible That which but seems unlike v 1 51
Let your reason serve To make the truth appear where it seems hid v 1 66
What he with his oath And all probation will make up full clear v 1 157
I am affianced this man's wife as strongly As words could make up vows v 1 228
You must, sir, change persons with me, ere you make that my report v 1 340
And would not rather Make rash remonstrance of my hidden power v 1 397
Make it your comfort, So happy is your brother v 1 403
Beg thou, or borrow, to make up the sum *Com. of Errors* i 1 154
Certain merchants, Of whom I hope to make much benefit i 2 25
This servitude makes you to keep unwed ii 1 26
Will jest upon my love And make a common of my serious hours ii 2 29
When the sun shines let foolish gnats make sport ii 2 30
I'll make you amends next, to give you nothing for something ii 2 54
Eat none of it.—Your reason?—Lest it make you choleric ii 2 63
Married to thy stronger state Makes me with thy strength to communicate ii 2 178
A table full of welcome makes scarce one dainty dish iii 1 23
Small cheer and great welcome makes a merry feast iii 1 26
It would make a man mad as a buck, to be so bought and sold iii 1 72
Poor women! make us but believe, Being compact of credit, that you love us iii 2 21
Why labour you To make it wander in an unknown field? iii 2 38
I know not what use to put her to but to make a lamp of her iii 2 98
Therefore make present satisfaction, Or I'll attach you by this officer iv 1 5
'God damn me;' that's as much to say, 'God make me a light wench' iv 3 55
Confederate with a damned pack To make a loathsome abject scorn of me iv 4 106
I am thy prisoner: wilt thou suffer them To make a rescue? iv 4 114
Unquiet meals make ill digestions v 1 74
With . . . drugs and holy prayers, To make of him a formal man again v 1 105
Engaged a prince's word, When thou didst make him master of thy bed v 1 163
Unless the fear of death doth make me dote v 1 195
Albeit my wrongs might make one wiser mad v 1 217
I see thy age and dangers make thee dote v 1 329
What I told you then, I hope I shall have leisure to make good v 1 375
And we shall make full satisfaction v 1 399
That will make a voyage with him to the devil *Much Ado* i 1 82
Scratching could not make it worse, an 'twere such a face as yours i 1 137
But you must not make the full show of this i 3 20
Where it is impossible you should take true root but by the fair weather that you make yourself i 3 25
Can you make no use of your discontent?—I make all use of it i 3 40
Dress him in my apparel and make him my waiting-gentlewoman ii 1 37
It is my cousin's duty to make curtsy and say 'Father, as it please you' ii 1 56
Else make another curtsy and say 'Father, as it please me' ii 1 58
Not till God make men of some other metal than earth ii 1 62
To make an account of her life to a clod of wayward marl ii 1 65
The revellers are entering, brother: make good room ii 1 88
Did he never make you laugh?—I pray you, what is he? ii 1 140
Either to make him a garland, as being forsaken, or to bind him up a rod ii 1 225
Wilt thou make a trust a transgression? ii 1 232
She would have made Hercules have turned spit, yea, and have cleft his club to make the fire too ii 1 262
Till he have made an oyster of me, he shall never make me such a fool ii 3 27
He would make but a sport of it and torment the poor lady worse ii 3 162
She will die, ere she make her love known ii 3 182
If she should make tender of her love, 'tis very possible he'll scorn it ii 3 185
The man doth fear God, howsoever it seems not in him by some large jests he will make ii 3 206
I'll make her come, I warrant you, presently iii 1 14
It were not good She knew his love, lest she make sport at it iii 1 58
For your favour, sir, why, give God thanks, and make no boast of it iii 3 20
You shall also make no noise in the streets iii 3 35
Make. If they make you not then the better answer, you may say they are not the men you took them for *Much Ado* iii 3 49
The less you meddle or make with them, why, the more is for your honesty iii 3 56
For when rich villains have need of poor ones, poor ones may make what price they will iii 3 122
I dare make his answer, none.—O, what men dare do! iv 1 18
What kind of catechising call you this?—To make you answer truly iv 1 80
I will make him eat it that says I love not you iv 1 279
Patch grief with proverbs, make misfortune drunk With candle-wasters v 1 17
Make those that do offend you suffer too v 1 40
I will make it good how you dare, with what you dare, and when you dare v 1 147
Cudgelled thee out of thy single life, to make thee a double-dealer v 4 116
And make us heirs of all eternity *L. L. Lost* i 1 7
Fat paunches have lean pates, and dainty bits Make rich the ribs i 1 27
And make a dark night too of half the day i 1 45
Necessity will make us all forsworn Three thousand times i 1 150
He hath wit to make an ill shape good, And shape to win grace ii 1 59
For you'll prove perjured if you make me stay ii 1 113
Your fair self should make A yielding 'gainst some reason in my breast ii 1 151
As honour without breach of honour may Make tender of ii 1 171
All his behaviours did make their retire To the court of his eye ii 1 234
All senses to that sense did make their repair ii 1 240
Warble, child; make passionate my sense of hearing iii 1 1
And make them men of note—do you note me? iii 1 25
It is an epilogue or discourse, to make plain Some obscure precedence iii 1 82
A Monarcho, and one that makes sport To the prince and his bookmates iv 1 101
If sore be sore, then L to sore makes fifty sores one sorel iv 2 62
If love make me forsworn, how shall I swear to love? iv 2 109
Study his bias leaves and makes his book thine eyes iv 2 113
Then thou wilt keep My tears for glasses, and still make me weep iv 3 40
This is the liver-vein, which makes flesh a deity, A green goose a goddess iv 3 74
Your eyes do make no coaches; in your tears There is no certain princess iv 3 155
What makes treason here?—Nay, it makes nothing, sir iv 3 190
What?—That you three fools lack'd me fool to make up the mess iv 3 207
In her fair cheek, Where several worthies make one dignity iv 3 236
Therefore is she born to make black fair iv 3 261
The voice of all the gods Make heaven drowsy with the harmony iv 3 345
Anne intelligis, domine? to make frantic, lunatic v 1 28
What a joyful father wouldst thou make me! v 1 80
That is the way to make an offence gracious v 1 147
I'll make one in a dance, or so; or I will play On the tabor v 1 160
Fain to seal on Cupid's name.—That was the way to make his godhead wax v 2 10
How I would make him fawn and beg and seek! v 2 62
And make him proud to make me proud that jests v 2 66
I make no doubt The rest will ne'er come in, if he be out v 2 151
To make theirs ours and ours none but our own v 2 154
Fair gentle sweet, Your wit makes wise things foolish v 2 374
That smiles his cheek in years and knows the trick To make my lady laugh v 2 466
And might not you Forestall our sport, to make us thus untrue? v 2 473
Their form confounded makes most form in mirth v 2 520
That oft in field, with targe and shield, did make my foe to sweat v 2 556
He's a god or a painter; for he makes faces v 2 648
Those heavenly eyes, that look into these faults, Suggested us to make v 2 780
Our love being yours, the error that love makes Is likewise yours v 2 781
Once false for ever to be true To those that make us both,—fair ladies v 2 784
A time, methinks, too short To make a world-without-end bargain in v 2 799
A jest's prosperity lies in the ear Of him that hears it, never in the tongue Of him that makes it v 2 873
Or a part to tear a cat in, to make all split *M. N. Dream* i 2 32
Phibbus' car Shall shine from far And make and mar The foolish Fates i 2 39
I will roar, that I will make the duke say 'Let him roar again' i 2 74
Crowns him with flowers and makes him all her joy ii 1 27
And bootless make the breathless housewife churn; And sometime make the drink to bear no barm ii 1 37
I jest to Oberon and make him smile ii 1 44
On sleeping eye-lids laid Will make or man or woman madly dote ii 1 171
I'll make her render up her page to me ii 1 185
The mild hind Makes speed to catch the tiger ii 1 233
And make a heaven of hell, To die upon the hand I love so well ii 1 243
I'll streak her eyes, And make her full of hateful fantasies ii 1 258
War with rere-mice for their leathern wings, To make my small elves coats ii 2 5
My heart unto yours is knit So that but one heart we can make of it ii 2 48
Nature shows art, That through thy bosom makes me see thy heart ii 2 105
Not a whit: I have a device to make all well iii 1 17
It shall be written in eight and six.—No, make it two more iii 1 26
Why do they run away? this is a knavery of them to make me afeard iii 1 116
This is to make an ass of me; to fright me, if they could iii 1 123
More the pity that some honest neighbours will not make them friends iii 1 149
Master Cobweb: if I cut my finger, I shall make bold with you iii 1 187
It will pay, If for his tender here I make some stay iii 2 87
Stand aside: the noise they make Will cause Demetrius to awake iii 2 116
And extort A poor soul's patience, all to make you sport iii 2 161
Dark night, that from the eye his function takes, The ear more quick of apprehension makes iii 2 178
Could not this make thee know, The hate I bear thee made me leave thee so? iii 2 189
Persever, counterfeit sad looks, Make mouths upon me iii 2 238
If you have any pity . . . , You would not make me such an argument iii 2 242
And make his eyeballs roll with wonted sight iii 2 369
Haste; make no delay: We may effect this business yet ere day iii 2 394
Yet but three? Come one more; Two of both kinds makes up four iii 2 438
Cupid is a knavish lad, Thus to make poor females mad iii 2 441
To make it the more gracious, I shall sing it at her death iv 1 224
Make choice of which your highness will see first v 1 43
But by ten words, my lord, it is too long, Which makes it tedious v 1 64
Shiver and look pale, Make periods in the midst of sentences v 1 96
You wonder at this show; But wonder on, till truth make all things plain v 1 129
The death of a dear friend would go near to make a man look sad v 1 294
These yellow cowslip cheeks Are gone, are gone: Lovers, make moan v 1 341
Trip away; make no stay; Meet me all by break of day v 1 428
We will make amends ere long; Else the Puck a liar call v 1 441
Such a want-wit sadness makes of me *Mer. of Venice* i 1 6
And every object that might make me fear Misfortune to my ventures i 1 20
Shall I lack the thought That such a thing bechanced would make me sad? i 1 38
We'll make our leisures to attend on yours i 1 68

Make. Nor do I now make moan to be abridged From such a noble rate *Mer. of Venice* i 1 126
Which makes her seat of Belmont Colchos' strand, And many Jasons come . . . . i 1 171
I no question make To have it of my trust or for my sake . i 1 184
He makes it a great appropriation to his own good parts . i 2 45
I hope I shall make shift to go without him . . . . . . i 2 97
Was this inserted to make interest good? . . . . i 3 95
Is your gold and silver ewes and rams?—I cannot tell; I make it breed as fast . . . . i 3 97
Let us make incision for your love, To prove whose blood is reddest ii 1 6
Good fortune then! To make me blest or cursed'st among men ii 1 46
This is the pent-house under which Lorenzo Desired us to make stand. ii 6 2
I will make fast the doors, and gild myself With some more ducats ii 6 49
Bassanio told him he would make some speed Of his return . ii 8 37
Were he out of Venice, I can make what merchandise I will . iii 1 133
But if you do, you'll make me wish a sin, That I had been forsworn iii 2 13
Ugly treason of mistrust, Which makes me fear the enjoying of my love iii 2 29
Let music sound while he doth make his choice; Then, if he lose, he makes a swan-like end . . . . iii 2 43
Golden locks Which make such wanton gambols with the wind . . iii 2 93
I feel too much thy blessing: make it less, For fear I surfeit . . iii 2 114
Which makes me think that this Antonio, Being the bosom lover of my lord, Must needs be like my lord . . . . iii 4 16
Make room, and let him stand before our face . . . . . iv 1 16
As well forbid the mountain pines To wag their high tops and to make no noise . . . . iv 1 76
I do beseech you, Make no more offers, use no farther means . iv 1 81
Can no prayers pierce thee?—No, none that thou hast wit enough to make . . . . iv 1 127
Your wife would give you little thanks for that, If she were by, to hear you make the offer . . . . iv 1 289
You offer it behind her back; The wish would make else an unquiet house iv 1 294
Be it but so much As makes it light or heavy in the substance . iv 1 328
The sweet wind did gently kiss the trees And they did make no noise . v 1 3
Music touch their ears, You shall perceive them make a mutual stand . v 1 77
But let me not be light; For a light wife doth make a heavy husband . v 1 130
Were you the clerk that is to make me cuckold? . . . . . v 1 281
What make you here?—Nothing: I am not taught to make any thing *As Y. Like It* i 1 31
I prithee, do, to make sport withal: but love no man in good earnest . i 2 29
Those that she [Fortune] makes fair she scarce makes honest, and those that she makes honest she makes very ill-favouredly . . . i 2 40
When Fortune makes Nature's natural the cutter-off of Nature's wit . i 2 52
The little foolery that wise men have makes a great show . . i 2 96
Yet your mistrust cannot make me a traitor . . . . . . i 3 58
Why, what make you here? Why are you virtuous? why do people love you? . . . . ii 3 4
That is the way to make her scorn you still . . . . . . ii 4 22
If thou remember'st not the slightest folly That ever love did make thee run into, Thou hast not loved . . . . ii 4 35
Or if thou hast not broke from company Abruptly, as my passion now makes me, Thou hast not loved . . . . ii 4 41
More, I prithee, more.—It will make you melancholy . . . . ii 5 10
But I give heaven thanks and make no boast of them . . . . ii 5 38
Let my officers of such a nature Make an extent upon his house and lands iii 1 17
That good pasture makes fat sheep . . . . iii 2 28
God make incision in thee! thou art raw . . . . iii 2 75
Let us make an honourable retreat; though not with bag and baggage . iii 2 169
What makes he here? Did he ask for me? Where remains he? . . iii 2 234
Fair youth, I would I could make thee believe I love.—Me believe it! you may as soon make her that you love believe it . . . . . iii 2 404
Well, I am not fair; and therefore I pray the gods make me honest . iii 3 34
The common executioner, Whose heart the accustom'd sight of death makes hard . . . . iii 5 4
Then shall you know the wounds invisible That love's keen arrows make iii 5 31
'Tis such fools as you That makes the world full of ill-favour'd children iii 5 53
And faster than his tongue Did make offence his eye did heal it up iii 5 117
And your experience makes you sad: I had rather have a fool to make me merry than experience to make me sad . . . . iv 1 27
A better jointure, I think, than you make a woman . . . . iv 1 56
Make the doors upon a woman's wit and it will out at the casement . iv 1 162
That woman that cannot make her fault her husband's occasion . . iv 1 177
No matter how it be in tune, so it make noise enough . . . . iv 2 10
Will the faithful offer take Of me and all that I can make . . . iv 3 61
What, to make thee an instrument and play false strains upon thee! . iv 3 68
I kill thee, make thee away, translate thy life into death . . . v 1 58
I have promised to make all this matter even . . . . . . v 4 18
From hence I go, To make these doubts all even . . . . . v 4 25
'Tis I must make conclusion Of these most strange events . . . v 4 132
Will, for my kind offer, when I make curtsy, bid me farewell . . Epil. 23
And burn sweet wood to make the lodging sweet . . *T. of Shrew* Ind. 1 49
Music ready when he wakes, To make a dulcet and a heavenly sound Ind. 1 51
And your humble wife May show her duty and make known her love Ind. 1 117
What, would you make me mad? Am not I Christopher Sly? . Ind. 2 18
O, this it is that makes your lady mourn!—O, this is it that makes your servants droop! . . . . Ind. 2 28
Wilt thou hunt? Thy hounds shall make the welkin answer them Ind. 2 47
Is it your will To make a stale of me amongst these mates? . . i 1 58
That I may soon make good What I have said, Bianca, get you in . i 1 74
And make her bear the penance of her tongue . . . . . . i 1 89
But come; since this bar in law makes us friends, it shall be so far forth friendly maintained . . . . i 1 140
While I make way from hence to save my life . . . . . . i 1 239
That thyself execute, to make one among these wooers . . . . i 1 251
To make love to her And unsuspected court her by herself . . . i 2 136
Lucentio shall make one, Though Paris came in hope to speed alone . i 2 246
Wrong me not, nor wrong yourself, To make a bondmaid and a slave of me . . . . ii 1 2
Do make myself a suitor to your daughter . . . . ii 1 91
I see thy beauty, Thy beauty, that doth make me like thee well . ii 1 276
Never make denial; I must and will have Katharine to my wife . . ii 1 281
A meacock wretch can make the curstest shrew . . . . . . ii 1 315
And, let your father make her the assurance, She is your own . . ii 1 389
Shall Bianca Be bride to you, if you make this assurance . . . ii 1 398
My lessons make no music in three parts . . . . iii 1 60
'Point the day of marriage, Make feasts, invite friends . . . iii 2 16
Make assurance here in Padua Of greater sums than I have promised iii 2 136
I must away to-day, before night come: Make it no wonder . . iii 2 193
I am sent before to make a fire, and they are coming after . . iv 1 4

Make. But wilt thou make a fire, or shall I complain on thee to our mistress? . . . . *T. of Shrew* iv 1 31
Another way I have to man my haggard, To make her come . . . iv 1 197
Leaves a gentleman, And makes a god of such a cullion . . . iv 2 20
Then go with me to make the matter good . . . . . . iv 2 114
You bid me make it orderly and well, According to the fashion . iv 3 94
I'll none of it: hence! make your best of it . . . . . iv 3 100
You mean to make a puppet of me.—Why, true; he means to make a puppet of thee . . . . iv 3 103
Our garments poor; For 'tis the mind that makes the body rich . iv 3 174
Hie you home, And bid Bianca make her ready straight . . . iv 4 63
A' will make the man mad, to make a woman of him . . . . iv 5 35
And withal make known Which way thou travellest . . . . iv 5 50
A hundred pound or two, to make merry withal . . . . . v 1 23
Her dispositions she inherits, which makes fair gifts fairer *All's Well* i 1 47
If the living be enemy to the grief, the excess makes it soon mortal . i 1 67
Be comfortable to my mother, your mistress, and make much of her . i 1 87
That you were made of is metal to make virgins . . . . . i 1 141
Within ten year it will make itself ten, which is a goodly increase . i 1 160
But the composition that your valour and fear makes in you is a virtue i 1 218
Thou diest in thine unthankfulness, and thine ignorance makes thee away . . . . i 1 226
Mounts my love so high, That makes me see, and cannot feed mine eye i 1 236
Prejudicates the business and would seem To have us make denial . i 2 9
We wound our modesty and make foul the clearness of our deservings . i 3 6
And have ability enough to make such knaveries yours . . . . i 3 12
May lawfully make title to as much love as she finds . . . . i 3 107
To breathe life into a stone, Quicken a rock, and make you dance canary ii 1 77
Of heaven, not me, make an experiment . . . . ii 1 157
Make thy demand.—But will you make it even? . . . . . ii 1 194
So make the choice of thy own time . . . . ii 1 206
What place make you special, when you put off that with such contempt? . . . . ii 2 5
He that cannot make a leg, put off's cap, kiss his hand and say nothing ii 2 10
To make modern and familiar, things supernatural and causeless . . ii 3 2
Thy frank election make; Thou hast power to choose . . . . ii 3 61
Make choice; and, see, Who shuns thy love shuns all his love in me . ii 3 78
Love make your fortunes twenty times above Her that so wishes! . ii 3 88
I would send them to the Turk, to make eunuchs of . . . . ii 3 94
Your lord and master did well to make his recantation . . . . ii 3 194
Thou didst make tolerable vent of thy travel; it might pass . . ii 3 212
Dost make hose of thy sleeves? do other servants so? . . . . ii 3 266
To make the coming hour o'erflow with joy And pleasure drown the brim ii 4 47
And make this haste as your own good proceeding . . . . . ii 4 50
Strengthen'd with what apology you think May make it probable need ii 4 52
I pray you, make us friends; I will pursue the amity . . . . ii 5 14
I have wedded her, not bedded her; and sworn to make the 'not' eternal . . . . iii 2 24
Make me but like my thoughts, and I shall prove A lover of thy drum iii 3 10
I have no skill in sense To make distinction . . . . . . iii 4 40
Do you think he will make no deed at all of this? . . . . . iii 6 102
We'll make you some sport with the fox ere we case him . . . iii 6 110
Three great oaths would scarce make that be believed . . . . iv 1 65
'Tis not the many oaths that makes the truth, But the plain single vow iv 2 21
Men make ropes in such a scarre That we'll forsake ourselves . . iv 2 38
Which makes her story true, even to the point of her death . . . iv 3 66
How mightily sometimes we make us comforts of our losses! . . . iv 3 77
Half won is match well made; match, and well make it . . . iv 3 254
Simply the thing I am Shall make me live . . . . iv 3 370
But, O strange men! That can such sweet use make of what they hate iv 4 22
Shall render you no blame But rather make you thank your pains for it v 1 33
With what good speed Our means will make us means . . . . v 1 35
Let the justices make you and fortune friends . . . . . . v 2 35
Make it Natural rebellion, done i' the blaze of youth . . . . v 3 5
Praising what is lost Makes the remembrance dear . . . . . v 3 20
Ere my heart Durst make too bold a herald of my tongue . . . v 3 46
Our rash faults Make trivial price of serious things we have . . v 3 61
If she, my liege, can make me know this clearly, I'll love her dearly v 3 316
Wait on me home, I'll make sport with thee: Let thy courtesies alone v 3 323
This story know, To make the even truth in pleasure flow . . v 3 326
I would not so much as make water but in a sink-a-pace . *T. Night* i 3 139
Leap all civil bounds Rather than make unprofited return . . . i 4 22
Needs to fear no colours.—Make that good . . . . i 5 7
Here comes my lady: make your excuse wisely, you were best . . i 5 33
Make your proof.—I must catechize you for it . . . . . . i 5 67
Infirmity, that decays the wise, doth ever make the better fool . . i 5 83
One draught above heat makes him a fool; the second mads him . . i 5 140
'Tis not that time of moon with me to make one in so skipping a dialogue . . . . i 5 213
What would you?—Make me a willow cabin at your gate . . . i 5 287
And make the babbling gossip of the air Cry out . . . . . i 5 292
Love make his heart of flint that you shall love! . . . . . i 5 305
But shall we make the welkin dance indeed? . . . . . . ii 3 59
Do ye make an alehouse of my lady's house? . . . . . . ii 3 96
And then to break promise with him and make a fool of him . . . ii 3 138
If I do not gull him into a nayword, and make him a common recreation ii 3 146
On a forgotten matter we can hardly make distinction of our hands ii 3 174
And your horse now would make him an ass . . . . ii 3 183
I will plant you two, and let the fool make a third . . . . . ii 3 189
And the tailor make thy doublet of changeable taffeta . . . . ii 4 76
For that's it that always makes a good voyage of nothing . . . ii 4 81
Make no compare Between that love a woman can bear me And that I owe . . . . ii 4 104
I know this letter will make a contemplative idiot of him . . . ii 5 22
Contemplation makes a rare turkey-cock of him . . . . . . ii 5 35
Seven of my people, with an obedient start, make out for him . . ii 5 65
And thus makes she her great P's . . . . ii 5 97
If I could make that resemble something in me,—Softly! M, O, A, I,— O, ay, make up that . . . . ii 5 131
And O shall end, I hope.—Ay, or I'll cudgel him, and make him cry O! ii 5 145
Follow me.—To the gates of Tartar . . . !—I'll make one too . . ii 5 228
They that dally nicely with words may quickly make them wanton . iii 1 17
If that be to care for nothing, sir, I would it would make you invisible iii 1 35
'Slight, will you make an ass o' me? . . . . iii 2 14
Since you make your pleasure of your pains, I will no further chide you iii 3 2
I can no other answer make but thanks, And thanks; and ever . . iii 3 14
This does make some obstruction in the blood, this cross-gartering . iii 4 22
But it is Jove's doing, and Jove make me thankful! . . . . . iii 4 83
Why, we shall make him mad indeed.—The house will be the quieter . iii 4 146
I will make your peace with him if I can . . . . iii 4 295

Make. I'll make the motion : stand here, make a good show . *T. Night* iii 4 316
A little thing would make me tell them how much I lack of a man iii 4 332
What will you do, now my necessity Makes me to ask you for my purse? iii 4 369
My having is not much ; I'll make division of my present with you iii 4 380
Do not tempt my misery, Lest that it make me so unsound a man iii 4 384
Will you make me believe that I am not sent for you? iv 1 1
Put on this gown and this beard ; make him believe thou art Sir Topas iv 2 2
I am no more mad than you are : make the trial of it iv 2 52
Marry, sir, they praise me and make an ass of me v 1 19
If your four negatives make your two affirmatives, why then v 1 24
Such scathful grapple did he make With the most noble bottom of our fleet v 1 59
It is the baseness of thy fear That makes thee strangle thy propriety v 1 150
If nothing lets to make us happy both But this v 1 256
One that indeed physics the subject, makes old hearts fresh *W. Tale* i 1 43
No sneaping winds at home, to make us say 'This is put forth too truly' i 2 13
Of this make no conclusion, lest you say Your queen and I are devils i 2 81
Tell me ; cram's with praise, and make's As fat as tame things i 2 91
Ere I could make thee open thy white hand And clap thyself my love i 2 103
Thou dost make possible things not so held, Communicatest with dreams i 2 139
How sometimes nature will betray its folly, Its tenderness, and make itself a pastime To harder bosoms! i 2 152
He makes a July's day short as December i 2 169
You had much ado to make his anchor hold i 2 213
I have loved thee,— Make that thy question, and go rot! i 2 324
How! caught of me! Make me not sighted like the basilisk i 2 388
Make known How he hath drunk, he cracks his gorge ii 1 43
Here's such ado to make no stain a stain As passes colouring ii 2 19
Laugh at me, make their pastime at my sorrow ii 3 24
I say good queen ; And would by combat make her good, so were I A man ii 3 60
Let him that makes but trifles of his eyes First hand me ii 3 62
It is an heretic that makes the fire, Not she which burns in't ii 3 115
This most cruel usage of your queen . . . will ignoble make you ii 3 120
I doubt not then but innocence shall make False accusation blush iii 2 31
And how his piety Does my deeds make the blacker! iii 2 173
All faults I make, when I shall come to know them, I do repent iii 2 220
Make your best haste, and go not Too far i' the land iii 3 10
But to make an end of the ship, to see how the sea flap-dragoned it iii 3 99
Both joy and terror Of good and bad, that makes and unfolds error iv 1 2
And make stale The glistering of this present iv 1 13
There's no virtue whipped out of the court : they cherish it to make it stay there iv 3 98
If I make not this cheat bring out another iv 3 129
It is A way to make us better friends, more known iv 4 66
Yet nature is made better by no mean But nature makes that mean iv 4 90
Over that art Which you say adds to nature, is an art That nature makes iv 4 92
And make conceive a bark of baser kind By bud of nobler race iv 4 94
Make your garden rich in gillyvors, And do not call them bastards iv 4 98
O, these I lack, To make you garlands of iv 4 128
He tells her something That makes her blood look out iv 4 160
He makes the maid to answer 'Whoop, do me no harm' iv 4 198
Straited For a reply, at least if you make a care Of happy holding her iv 4 366
I give my daughter to him, and will make Her portion equal his iv 4 396
That makes himself, but for our honour therein, Unworthy thee iv 4 447
Make for Sicilia, And there present yourself and your fair princess iv 4 554
We'll make an instrument of this, omit Nothing may give us aid iv 4 637
For the outside of thy poverty we must make an exchange iv 4 647
Is no honest man, neither to his father nor to me, to go about to make me the king's brother-in-law iv 4 720
There is that in this fardel will make him scratch his beard iv 4 728
Not he alone shall suffer what wit can make heavy and vengeance bitter iv 4 801
Here is that gold I have : I'll make it as much more iv 4 838
No fault could you make, Which you have not redeem'd v 1 2
Would make her sainted spirit Again possess her corpse v 1 57
Make proselytes Of who she but bid follow v 1 108
Therefore follow me And mark what way I make v 1 233
I make a broken delivery of the business v 2 10
Our absence makes us unthrifty to our knowledge v 2 120
Which lets go by some sixteen years and makes her As she lived now v 3 31
Methinks, already—What was he that did make it? v 3 63
O sweet Paulina, Make me to think so twenty years together! v 3 71
If you can behold it, I'll make the statue move indeed v 3 88
What you can make her do, I am content to look on : what to speak, I am content to hear ; for 'tis as easy To make her speak as move v 3 91
Make't manifest where she has lived, Or how stolen from the dead v 3 114
A landless knight makes thee a landed squire *K. John* i 1 177
Well, now can I make any Joan a lady. 'Good den, sir Richard!' i 1 184
Sir Robert never holp to make this leg i 1 240
I was seduced To make room for him in my husband's bed i 1 255
Wade to the market-place in Frenchmen's blood, But we will make it subject to this boy ii 1 43
To make a hazard of new fortunes here ii 1 71
Who is it thou dost call usurper, France?—Let me make answer ii 1 121
Or lay on that shall make your shoulders crack ii 1 146
Instead of bullets wrapp'd in fire, To make a shaking fever in your walls ii 1 228
When I have said, make answer to us both ii 1 235
I would set an ox-head to your lion's hide, And make a monster of you ii 1 293
And pell-mell Make work upon ourselves, for heaven or hell ii 1 407
Son, list to this conjunction, make this match ii 1 468
And make her rich In titles, honours and promotions ii 1 491
Becomes a sun and makes your son a shadow ii 1 500
If he see aught in you that makes him like ii 1 511
And this rich fair town We make him lord of ii 1 553
This Commodity Makes it take head from all indifferency ii 1 579
Teach thou this sorrow how to make me die iii 1 30
At thy birth, dear boy, Nature and Fortune join'd to make thee great iii 1 52
For grief is proud and makes his owner stoop iii 1 69
Make my person yours, And tell me how you would bestow yourself iii 1 224
So jest with heaven, Make such unconstant children of ourselves iii 1 243
It is religion that doth make vows kept iii 1 279
And better conquest never canst thou make iii 1 290
Make up : My mother is assailed in our tent, And ta'en, I fear iii 2 5
O, this will make my mother die with grief! iii 3 5
Hear me without thine ears, and make reply Without a tongue iii 3 49
Preach some philosophy to make me mad, And thou shalt be canonized iii 4 51
There's nothing in this world can make me joy iii 4 107

Make. Makes nice of no vile hold to stay him up *K. John* iii 4 138
Your wife May then make all the claim that Arthur did iii 4 143
Strong reasons make strong actions iii 4 182
You will but make it blush And glow with shame of your proceedings iv 1 113
It makes the course of thoughts to fetch about iv 2 24
And oftentimes excusing of a fault Doth make the fault the worse iv 2 31
What we would Doth make a stand at what your highness will iv 2 39
O, make a league with me, till I have pleased My discontented peers! iv 2 126
Whilst he that hears makes fearful action, With wrinkled brows iv 2 191
How oft the sight of means to do ill deeds Make deeds ill done! iv 2 220
I'll make a peace between your soul and you iv 2 250
And make them tame to their obedience iv 2 262
He, long traded in it, makes it seem Like rivers of remorse and innocency iv 3 109
And make fair weather in your blustering land v 1 21
Go I to make the French lay down their arms v 1 24
What, shall they seek the lion in his den, And fright him there? and make him tremble there? v 1 58
Send fair-play orders and make compromise v 1 67
My liege, to arms : Perchance the cardinal cannot make your peace v 1 74
Great affections wrestling in thy bosom Doth make an earthquake of nobility v 2 42
Makes me more amazed Than had I seen the vaulty top of heaven v 2 51
Even at your door, To cudgel you and make you take the hatch v 2 138
What in the world should make me now deceive? v 4 26
Doth by the idle comments that it makes Foretell the ending of mortality v 7 4
Nor entreat the north To make his bleak winds kiss my parched lips v 7 40
The like tender of our love we make, To rest without a spot for evermore v 7 106
Nought shall make us rue, If England to itself do rest but true v 7 117
What I speak My body shall make good upon this earth *Richard II.* i 1 37
Which fear, not reverence, makes thee to except i 1 72
Will I make good against thee, arm to arm, What I have spoke i 1 76
Now, by my sceptre's awe, I make a vow i 1 118
Deep malice makes too deep incision ; Forget, forgive i 1 155
Lions make leopards tame.—Yea, but not change his spots i 1 174
Since we cannot do to make you friends, Be ready i 1 197
So I regreet The daintiest last, to make the end most sweet i 3 68
God in thy good cause make thee prosperous! Be swift like lightning i 3 78
Fright fair peace And make us wade even in our kindred's blood i 3 138
Some of you should say, I was too strict to make mine own away i 3 244
They are quickly gone.—To men in joy ; but grief makes one hour ten i 3 261
Every tedious stride I make Will but remember me i 3 268
The lining of his coffers shall make coats To deck our soldiers i 4 61
Let's all go visit him : Pray God we may make haste, and come too late! i 4 64
No, misery makes sport to mock itself ii 1 85
Darest with thy frozen admonition Make pale our cheek ii 1 118
Ah, how long Shall tender duty make me suffer wrong? ii 1 164
And make high majesty look like itself ii 1 295
Makes me with heavy nothing faint and shrink ii 2 32
He is gone to save far off, Whilst others come to make him lose at home ii 2 81
Rough uneven ways Draws out our miles, and makes them wearisome ii 3 5
By this the weary lords Shall make their way seem short, as mine hath ii 3 17
My heart this covenant makes, my hand thus seals it ii 3 50
Your presence makes us rich, most noble lord ii 3 63
And I must find that title in your tongue, Before I make reply ii 3 73
I would attach you all and make you stoop ii 3 156
And near in love Till you did make him misinterpret me iii 1 18
Stormy day, Which makes the silver rivers drown their shores iii 2 107
Would they make peace? terrible hell make war Upon their spotted souls! iii 2 133
Make dust our paper and with rainy eyes Write sorrow on the bosom of the earth, Let's choose executors iii 2 146
Inquire of him, And learn to make a body of a limb iii 2 187
That every stride he makes upon my land Is dangerous treason iii 3 92
We'll make foul weather with despised tears iii 3 161
And make some pretty match with shedding tears iii 3 165
Sorrow and grief of heart Makes him speak fondly, like a frantic man iii 3 185
You debase your princely knee To make the base earth proud iii 3 191
We'll play at bowls.—'Twill make me think the world is full of rubs iii 4 4
Which, like unruly children, make their sire Stoop with oppression iii 4 30
What serpent hath suggested thee To make a second fall of cursed man? iii 4 76
Some few vanities that make him light iii 4 86
Princes and noble lords, What answer shall I make to this base man? iv 1 20
To do that office of thine own good will Which tired majesty did make thee offer, The resignation of thy state iv 1 178
Make me, that nothing have, with nothing grieved iv 1 216
Was this the face That, like the sun, did make beholders wink? iv 1 284
Join not with grief, fair woman, do not so, To make my end too sudden v 1 17
And so two, together weeping, make one woe v 1 86
We make woe wanton with this fond delay v 1 101
Villain, I'll make thee safe.—Stay thy revengeful hand v 3 41
What shrill-voiced suppliant makes this eager cry?—A woman v 3 75
Thou frantic woman, what dost thou make here? v 3 89
Twice saying 'pardon' doth not pardon twain, But makes one pardon strong v 3 135
Come, my old son : I pray God make thee new v 3 146
For though it [music] have holp madmen to their wits, In me it seems it will make wise men mad v 5 63
Where no man never comes but that sad dog That brings me food to make misfortune live v 5 71
My soul is full of woe, That blood should sprinkle me to make me grow v 6 46
I'll make a voyage to the Holy Land, To wash this blood off v 6 49
Makes him prune himself, and bristle up The crest of youth *1 Hen. IV.* i 1 98
I'll make one ; an I do not, call me villain i 2 112
Wilt thou make one?—Who, I rob? I a thief? not I i 2 152
I'll so offend, to make offence a skill i 2 240
Greatness too which our own hands Have holp to make so portly i 3 13
Make the Douglas' son your only mean For powers in Scotland i 3 261
See already how he doth begin To make us strangers to his looks of love i 3 290
If I hang, I'll make a fat pair of gallows ii 1 74
That would, if matters should be looked into, for their own credit sake, make all whole ii 1 80
They ride up and down on her and make her their boots ii 1 91
If the rascal have not given me medicines to make me love him ii 2 19
There's enough to make us all.—To be hanged ii 2 60
Give him as much as will make him a royal man ii 4 320
But he would make you believe it was done in fight ii 4 338
To tickle our noses with spear-grass to make them bleed ii 4 341
Give me a cup of sack to make my eyes look red ii 4 423
Peace, cousin Percy ; you will make him mad iii 1 51
Thy tongue Makes Welsh as sweet as ditties highly penn'd iii 1 200

Make. Thy passages of life Make me believe that thou art only mark'd For the hot vengeance and the rod of heaven — *1 Hen. IV.* iii 2 9
Make blind itself with foolish tenderness — iii 2 91
I shall make this northern youth exchange His glorious deeds — iii 2 145
Come sing me a bawdy song ; make me merry — iii 3 16
I make as good use of it as many a man doth of a Death's-head — iii 3 33
What, will you make a younker of me? — iii 3 92
One poor penny-worth of sugar-candy to make thee long-winded — iii 3 180
You strain too far. I rather of his absence make this use — iv 1 76
If we without his help can make a head — iv 1 80
This bottle makes an angel.—An if it do, take it for thy labour — iv 2 6
If you knew How much they do import, you would make haste — iv 4 5
'Tis but wisdom to make strong against him : Therefore make haste — iv 4 40
Albeit considerations infinite Do make against it — v 1 103
If I come in his [way] willingly, let him make a carbonado of me — v 3 61
Your majesty, make up, Lest your retirement do amaze your friends — v 4 5
Would to God Thy name in arms were now as great as mine!—I'll make it greater ere I part from thee — v 4 71
All the budding honours on thy crest I'll crop, to make a garland — v 4 73
If thou wert sensible of courtesy, I should not make so dear a show of zeal — v 4 95
He would prove the better counterfeit. Therefore I'll make him sure — v 4 127
'Zounds, I would make him eat a peace of my sword — v 4 157
Who but Rumour, who but only I, Make fearful musters? — *2 Hen. IV.* Ind. 12
And make thee rich for doing me such wrong — i 1 90
Summ'd the account of chance, before you said 'Let us make head' — i 1 168
Make friends with speed : Never so few, and never yet more need — i 1 214
The wise may make some dram of a scruple, or indeed a scruple itself — i 2 148
It was alway yet the trick of our English nation, if they have a good thing, to make it too common — i 2 242
A good wit will make use of any thing — i 2 277
Thou didst swear to me then, as I was washing thy wound, to marry me and make me my lady thy wife — ii 1 100
If a man will make courtesy and say nothing, he is virtuous — ii 1 135
Let it alone ; I'll make other shift — ii 1 169
These humble considerations make me out of love with my greatness — ii 2 14
An you do not make him hanged among you, the gallows shall have wrong — ii 2 104
I'll steep this letter in sack and make him eat it.—That's to make him eat twenty of his words — ii 2 147
Then join you with them, like a rib of steel, To make strength stronger — ii 3 55
As with the tide swell'd up unto his height, That makes a still-stand — ii 3 64
You make fat rascals, Mistress Doll.—I make them! gluttony and diseases make them ; I make them not — ii 4 45
A captain! God's light, these villains will make the word as odious — ii 4 160
See now, whether pure fear and entire cowardice doth not make thee wrong this virtuous gentlewoman to close with us? — ii 4 353
Bid them o'er-read these letters, And well consider of them : make good speed — iii 1 3
Make mountains level, and the continent, Weary of solid firmness, melt — iii 1 47
Wilt thou make as many holes in an enemy's battle as thou hast done in a woman's petticoat? — iii 2 164
Mend him and make him fit to go — iii 2 176
It shall go hard but I will make him a philosopher's two stones to me — iii 2 354
To brother born an household cruelty, I make my quarrel in particular — iv 1 96
I muse you make so slight a question — iv 1 167
Fear you not that : if we can make our peace Upon such large terms — iv 1 185
If we do now make our atonement well — iv 1 221
A man cannot make him laugh ; but that's no marvel, he drinks no wine — iv 3 95
But the sherris warms it and makes it course from the inwards — iv 3 115
And wherefore should these good news make me sick? — iv 4 102
God for ever keep it from my head And make me as the poorest vassal is! — iv 5 176
All my friends, which thou must make thy friends — iv 5 205
Lest rest and lying still might make them look Too near — iv 5 212
Upon thy sight My worldly business makes a period — iv 5 231
I should make four dozen of such bearded hermits' staves — v 1 70
Question your royal thoughts, make the case yours — v 2 91
Quoth-a, we shall Do nothing but eat, and make good cheer — v 3 18
He would make this a bloody day to somebody — v 4 14
I will make the king do you grace : I will leer upon him — v 5 6
My knight, I will inflame thy noble liver, And make thee rage — v 5 34
Make less thy body hence, and more thy grace ; Leave gormandizing — v 5 56
I will be the man yet that shall make you great — v 5 85
A good conscience will make any possible satisfaction, and so would I. Epil. 21
And make imaginary puissance — *Hen. V.* Prol. 25
God and his angels guard your sacred throne And make you long become it! — i 2 8
Give edge unto the swords That make such waste in brief mortality — i 2 28
There is no bar To make against your highness' claim to France — i 2 35
May I with right and conscience make this claim? — i 2 96
To defend Against the Scot, who will make road upon us — i 2 138
Armed in their stings, Make boot upon the summer's velvet buds — i 2 194
And you withal shall make all Gallia shake — i 2 216
A merry message.—We hope to make the sender blush at it — i 2 299
I will bestow a breakfast to make you friends — ii 1 12
Come, shall I make you two friends? We must to France together — ii 1 94
By this sword, he that makes the first thrust, I'll kill him — ii 1 104
His approaches makes as fierce As waters to the sucking of a gulf — ii 4 9
He'll make your Paris Louvre shake for it — ii 4 132
Which makes much against my manhood — iii 2 52
The poet makes a most excellent description of it [Fortune] — iii 6 32
He is not the man that he would gladly make show to the world he is — iii 6 88
I could make as true a boast as that, if I had a sow to my mistress — iii 7 66
Our bad neighbour makes us early stirrers — iv 1 6
We gather honey from the weed, And make a moral of the devil himself — iv 1 12
If the cause be not good, the king himself hath a heavy reckoning to make — iv 1 141
Ay, he said so, to make us fight cheerfully — iv 1 204
If ever thou darest acknowledge it, I will make it my quarrel — iv 1 225
Mount them, and make incision in their hides — iv 2 9
That their souls May make a peaceful and a sweet retire — iv 3 86
The saying is true, 'The empty vessel makes the greatest sound' — iv 4 73
We will come to them, And make them skirr away — iv 7 64
How canst thou make me satisfaction? — iv 8 48
But I will make you to-day a squire of low degree — v 1 37
I will make him eat some part of my leek — v 1 42
If you would conjure in her, you must make a circle — v 2 320
But your request shall make me let it pass — v 2 372

Make. Thrust in between the paction of these kingdoms, To make divorce of their incorporate league — *Hen. V.* v 2 394
A far more glorious star thy soul will make Than Julius Cæsar — *1 Hen. VI.* i 1 55
Speak softly, or the loss of those great towns Will make him burst his lead — i 1 64
To my task will I ; Bonfires in France forthwith I am to make — i 1 153
Whose bloody deeds shall make all Europe quake — i 1 156
Nor men nor money hath he to make war — i 2 17
Only this proof I'll of thy valour make — i 2 94
Nought rests for me in this tumultuous strife But to make open proclamation — i 3 71
Express opinions Where is best place to make our battery next — i 4 65
And make a quagmire of your mingled brains — i 4 109
Help Salisbury to make his testament : This day is ours — i 5 17
The shame hereof will make me hide my head — i 5 39
Command the citizens make bonfires And feast and banquet — i 6 12
Better far, I guess, That we do make our entrance several ways — ii 1 30
And here will Talbot mount, or make his grave — ii 1 34
Arm! arm! the enemy doth make assault! — ii 1 38
Didst thou at first, to flatter us withal, Make us partakers of a little gain? — ii 1 52
To be restored to my blood, Or make my ill the advantage of my good — ii 5 129
That engenders thunder in his breast And makes him roar these accusations — iii 1 40
The gates of Rouen, Through which our policy must make a breach — iii 2 2
And make thee curse the harvest of that corn — iii 2 47
And we will make thee famous through the world — iii 3 13
Fortune in favour makes him lag behind. Summon a parley — iii 3 34
She hath bewitch'd me with her words, Or nature makes me suddenly relent — iii 3 59
Thy friendship makes us fresh.—And doth beget new courage — iii 3 86
Say, gentlemen, what makes you thus exclaim? — iv 1 83
And make the cowards stand aloof at bay — iv 2 52
Mad ire and wrathful fury makes me weep, That thus we die — iv 3 28
Dishonour not her honourable name, To make a bastard and a slave of me! — iv 5 15
A phœnix that shall make all France afeard — iv 7 93
I'll either make thee stoop and bend thy knee, Or sack this country — v 1 61
Confounds the tongue and makes the senses rough — v 3 71
How canst thou tell she will deny thy suit, Before thou make a trial? — v 3 76
I'll undertake to make thee Henry's queen — v 3 117
What answer makes your grace unto my suit? — v 3 150
To England with this news, And make this marriage to be solemnized — v 3 168
Never glorious sun reflex his beams Upon the country where you make abode! — v 4 88
Would make a volume of enticing lines, Able to ravish — v 5 14
Is able to enrich his queen And not to seek a queen to make him rich — v 5 52
Makes me the bolder to salute my king With ruder terms — *2 Hen. VI.* i 1 29
Makes me from wondering fall to weeping joys — i 1 34
Then let's make haste away, and look unto the main — i 1 208
Pirates may make cheap pennyworths of their pillage — i 1 222
Therefore I will take the Nevils' parts And make a show of love — i 1 241
And, force perforce, I'll make him yield the crown — i 1 258
My troublous dream this night doth make me sad — i 2 22
A spirit raised from depth of under-ground, That shall make answer — i 2 80
When from Saint Alban's we do make return, We'll see these things — i 2 83
Take this reward ; make merry, man, With thy confederates — i 2 85
Hume must make merry with the duchess' gold — i 2 87
This late complaint Will make but little for his benefit — i 3 101
Would make thee quickly hop without thy head — i 3 140
Before we make election, give me leave To show some reason — i 3 165
Whom we raise, We will make fast within a hallow'd verge — i 4 25
Let me be blessed for the peace I make! — ii 1 36
Make up no factious numbers for the matter — ii 1 40
When he please to make commotion, 'Tis to be fear'd they all will follow — iii 1 29
If my death might make this island happy, I would expend it — iii 1 148
And all to make away my guiltless life — iii 1 167
'Twill make them cool in zeal unto your grace — iii 1 177
And were't not madness, then, To make the fox surveyor of the fold? — iii 1 253
I have seduced a headstrong Kentishman. To make commotion — iii 1 358
I know no pain they can inflict upon him Will make him say I moved him — iii 1 378
Erect his statua and worship it, And make my image but an alehouse sign — iii 2 81
The mortal worm might make the sleep eternal — iii 2 263
There's two of you ; the devil make a third! — iii 2 303
And boding screech-owls make the concert full! — iii 2 327
A grievous sickness took him, That makes him gasp and stare — iii 2 371
Where should he die? Can I make men live, whether they will or no? — iii 3 10
See, how the pangs of death do make him grin! — iii 3 24
Hold up thy hand, make signal of thy hope. He dies, and makes no sign — iii 3 28
Here shall they make their ransom on the sand — iv 1 10
And thou that art his mate, make boot of this — iv 1 13
Yet let not this make thee be bloody-minded — iv 1 36
Remember it and let it make thee crest-fall'n — iv 1 59
Small things make base men proud — iv 1 106
He shall have the skin of our enemies, to make dog's-leather of — iv 2 26
I will make it felony to drink small beer — iv 2 73
He is a conjurer.—Nay, he can make obligations — iv 2 100
To equal him, I will make myself a knight presently — iv 2 127
Oft have I heard that grief softens the mind And makes it fearful — iv 4 2
What answer makes your grace to the rebels' supplication? — iv 4 8
Which makes me hope you are not void of pity — iv 7 69
Give him a box o' the ear and that will make 'em red again — iv 7 92
If when you make your prayers, God should be so obdurate as yourselves — iv 7 121
For me, I will make shift for one ; and so, God's curse light upon you — iv 8 32
Should make a start o'er seas and vanquish you — iv 8 45
And makes them leave me desolate — iv 8 60
My sword make way for me, for here is no staying — iv 8 62
Only my followers' . . . treasons makes me betake me to my heels — iv 8 67
Is the traitor Cade surprised? Or is he but retired to make him strong? — iv 9 9
But I'll make thee eat iron like an ostrich — iv 10 30
See where they come : I'll warrant they'll make it good — v 1 122
A bedlam and ambitious humour Makes him oppose himself against his king — v 1 133
O war, thou son of hell, Whom angry heavens do make their minister! — v 2 34
The hope thereof makes Clifford mourn in steel — *3 Hen. VI.* i 1 58
To make a shambles of the parliament-house! — i 1 71
Which makes thee thus presumptuous and proud — i 1 157
Accursed be he that seeks to make them foes! — i 1 205
What is it, but to make thy sepulchre And creep into it? — i 1 236
Is he dead already? or is it fear That makes him close his eyes? — i 3 11

Make. Thy son's blood cleaving to my blade . . . till thy blood, Congeal'd with this, do make me wipe off both *3 Hen. VI.* i 3 52
Three times did Richard make a lane to me i 4 9
The sands are number'd that make up my life i 4 25
Wrath makes him deaf: speak thou, Northumberland i 4 53
Come, make him stand upon this molehill here i 4 67
I prithee, grieve, to make me merry, York i 4 86
Thou shouldst be mad; And I, to make thee mad, do mock thee thus i 4 90
Thou wouldst be fee'd, I see, to make me sport i 4 92
Nay, stay; let's hear the orisons he makes i 4 110
I would assay, proud queen, to make thee blush i 4 118
'Tis beauty that doth oft make women proud; But, God he knows, thy share thereof is small: 'Tis virtue that doth make them most admired; The contrary doth make thee wonder'd at: 'Tis government that makes them seem divine; The want thereof makes thee abominable i 4 128
To weep is to make less the depth of grief: Tears then for babes ii 1 85
Short tale to make, we at Saint Alban's met, Our battles join'd ii 1 120
Blame me not: 'Tis love I bear thy glories makes me speak ii 1 158
To frustrate both his oath and what beside May make against the house ii 1 176
Shall for the fault make forfeit of his head ii 1 197
Even with those wings Which sometime they have used with fearful flight, Make war with him that climb'd unto their nest ii 2 31
For shame, my liege, make them your precedent! ii 2 33
This soft courage makes your followers faint ii 2 57
'Twas not your valour, Clifford, drove me thence.—No, nor your manhood that durst make you stay ii 2 108
Ere sunset I'll make thee curse the deed.—Have done with words ii 2 116
To make this shameless callet know herself ii 2 145
Forslow no longer, make we hence amain ii 3 56
See the minutes how they run, How many make the hour full complete ii 5 26
Nay, stay not to expostulate, make speed; Or else come after ii 5 135
And what makes robbers bold but too much lenity? ii 6 22
And much effuse of blood doth make me faint ii 6 28
In this covert will we make our stand iii 1 3
Her sighs will make a battery in his breast iii 1 37
For of that sin My mild entreaty shall not make you guilty iii 1 91
Dishonour to deny it her.—It were no less; but yet I'll make a pause iii 2 10
I'll make my heaven in a lady's lap iii 2 148
To make an envious mountain on my back, Where sits deformity iii 2 157
I'll make my heaven to dream upon the crown iii 2 168
It was thy device By this alliance to make void my suit iii 3 142
Had he none else to make a stale but me? iii 3 260
What answer makes King Lewis unto our letters? iv 1 91
Go levy men, and make prepare for war iv 1 131
Madam, what makes you in this sudden change? iv 4 1
This is it that makes me bridle passion And bear with mildness iv 4 19
If about this hour he make this way Under the colour of his usual game iv 5 10
I make you both protectors of this land iv 6 41
Make much of him, my lords, for this is he Must help you iv 6 75
But when the fox hath once got in his nose, He'll soon find means to make the body follow iv 7 26
When we grow stronger, then we'll make our claim iv 7 59
Come, fellow-soldier, make thou proclamation iv 7 70
You are the fount that makes small brooks to flow iv 8 55
Or did he make the jest against his will? v 1 30
Pardon me, Edward, I will make amends v 1 100
And make him, naked, foil a man at arms v 4 42
He might infect another And make him of like spirit to himself v 4 47
And yonder is the wolf that makes this spoil v 4 80
What satisfaction canst thou make For bearing arms? v 5 14
And, as I guess, To make a bloody supper in the Tower v 5 85
Had I not reason, think ye, to make haste, And seek their ruin? v 6 72
Since the heavens have shaped my body so, Let hell make crook'd my mind to answer it v 6 79
The readiest way to make the wench amends *Richard III.* i 1 155
More direful hap betide that hated wretch, That makes us wretched! i 2 18
Set down the corse; or, by Saint Paul, I'll make a corse of him that disobeys i 2 37
Thou canst make No excuse current, but to hang thyself i 2 83
In that you brook it ill, it makes him worse i 3 3
God make your majesty joyful as you have been! i 3 19
He desires to make atonement i 3 36
That wrens make prey where eagles dare not perch i 3 71
What makest thou in my sight?—But repetition of what thou hast marr'd; That will I make before I let thee go i 3 166
By surfeit die your king, As ours by murder, to make him a king! i 3 198
O, let me make the period to my curse!—'Tis done by me i 3 238
Sorrow breaks seasons and reposing hours, Makes the night morning i 4 77
It [conscience] is a dangerous thing: it makes a man a coward i 4 138
Believe him not: he would insinuate with thee but to make thee sigh i 4 153
O excellent device! make a sop of him! i 4 162
Make peace with God, for you must die, my lord.—Hast thou that holy feeling in thy soul, To counsel me to make my peace with God? i 4 256
And make me happy in your unity ii 1 31
To make the perfect period of this peace ii 1 44
To make an act of tragic violence ii 2 39
Make me die a good old man! That is the butt-end of a mother's blessing ii 2 109
Untimely storms make men expect a dearth ii 3 35
Because sweet flowers are slow and weeds make haste ii 4 15
The conquerors Make war upon themselves; blood against blood ii 4 62
I go, my lord.—Good lords, make all the speedy haste you may iii 1 60
His wit set down to make his valour live iii 1 86
Death makes no conquest of this conqueror; For now he lives in fame iii 1 87
And that may be determined at the one [council] Which may make you and him to rue at the other iii 2 14
And make pursuit where he did mean no chase iii 2 30
Ere a fortnight make me elder, I'll send some packing iii 2 62
The princes both make high account of you iii 2 71
The tender love I bear your grace, my lord, Makes me most forward iii 4 66
Make a short shrift; he longs to see your head iii 4 97
Put to death a citizen, Only for saying he would make his son Heir iii 5 77
Where his lustful eye . . . Without control, listed to make his prey iii 5 84
And make, no doubt, us happy by his reign iii 7 170
O, make them joyful, grant their lawful suit! iii 7 203
And make me die the thrall of Margaret's curse, Nor mother, wife iv 1 46
And makes her pew-fellow with others' moan iv 4 58
These English woes will make me smile in France iv 4 115
Bettering thy loss makes the bad causer worse iv 4 122
Thy woes will make them [thy words] sharp iv 4 125

Make. Thou camest on earth to make the earth my hell *Richard III.* iv 4 166
Unavoided is the doom of destiny.—True, when avoided grace makes destiny iv 4 218
But that still use of grief makes wild grief tame iv 4 229
I love thy daughter, And mean to make her queen of England iv 4 263
Who dost thou mean shall be her king?—Even he that makes her queen iv 4 265
To make amends, I'll give it to your daughter iv 4 295
I cannot make you what amends I would iv 4 309
Make bold her bashful years with your experience iv 4 326
Under what title shall I woo for thee, That God, the law, my honour and her love, Can make seem pleasing to her tender years? iv 4 342
Bid him levy straight The greatest strength and power he can make iv 4 449
He makes for England, there to claim the crown iv 4 469
And makes his trough In your embowell'd bosoms v 2 9
Kings it [hope] makes gods, and meaner creatures kings v 2 24
Let's want no discipline, make no delay v 3 17
Make us thy ministers of chastisement, That we may praise thee! v 3 113
Wear it, enjoy it, and make much of it v 5 7
And make poor England weep in streams of blood! v 5 37
I come no more to make you laugh *Hen. VIII.* Prol. 1
To make that only true we now intend Prol. 21
The first and happiest hearers of the town, Be sad, as we would make ye Prol. 25
The force of his own merit makes his way i 1 64
He makes up the file Of all the gentry i 1 75
To the king I'll say't; and make my vouch as strong As shore of rock i 1 157
But he came To whisper Wolsey,—here makes visitation i 1 179
That dye is on me Which makes my whitest part black i 1 209
This makes bold mouths: Tongues spit their duties out i 2 60
If the king Should without issue die, he'll carry it so To make the sceptre his i 2 135
This night he makes a supper, and a great one i 3 52
As merry As . . . good company . . . Can make good people i 4 7
You must not freeze; Two women placed together makes cold weather i 4 22
You are a merry gamester, My Lord Sands.—Yes, if I make my play i 4 46
They've left their barge and landed; And hither make i 4 55
By all your good leaves, gentlemen; here I'll make My royal choice i 4 85
Although the king have mercies More than I dare make faults ii 1 71
Make of your prayers one sweet sacrifice, And lift my soul to heaven ii 1 77
I now seal it; And with that blood will make 'em one day groan for't ii 1 106
I had my trial, And, must needs say, a noble one; which makes me A little happier than my wretched father ii 1 119
Those you make friends And give your hearts to ii 1 127
I'll make ye know your times of business ii 2 72
Make yourself mirth with your particular fancy, And leave me out on't ii 3 101
You are mine enemy, and make my challenge You shall not be my judge ii 4 77
Nor ever more Upon this business my appearance make ii 4 132
But all hoods make not monks iii 1 23
A strange tongue makes my cause more strange, suspicious iii 1 45
But how to make ye suddenly an answer, In such a point of weight iii 1 70
All your studies Make me a curse like this.—Your fears are worse iii 1 124
I dare not make myself so guilty, To give up willingly that noble title iii 1 139
I am a woman, lacking wit To make a seemly answer to such persons iii 1 178
Moe wasps that buzz about his nose Will make this sting the sooner iii 2 56
Though perils did Abound, as thick as thought could make 'em iii 2 195
So looks the chafed lion Upon the daring huntsman that has gall'd him; Then makes him nothing iii 2 208
Make use now, and provide For thine own future safety iii 2 420
Such a noise arose As the shrouds make at sea in a stiff tempest iv 1 72
Like rams In the old time of war, would shake the press, And make 'em reel iv 1 79
And be well contented To make your house our Tower v 1 106
This ring Deliver them, and your appeal to us There make before them v 1 152
The tidings that I bring Will make my boldness manners v 1 159
The gentleman . . . pray'd me To make great haste v 2 3
They would shame to make me Wait else at door v 2 16
Those that tame wild horses Pace 'em not in their hands to make 'em gentle v 3 22
Men that make Envy and crooked malice nourishment Dare bite the best v 3 43
That I shall clear myself, . . . I make as little doubt v 3 67
I could say more, But reverence to your calling makes me modest v 3 69
One that, in all obedience, makes the church The chief aim of his honour v 3 117
Make me no more ado, but all embrace him v 3 159
Make way there for the princess.—You great fellow, Stand close up, or I'll make your head ache v 4 91
All comfort, joy, . . . Heaven ever laid up to make parents happy v 5 8
His honour and the greatness of his name Shall be, and make new nations v 5 53
All shall stay: This little one shall make it holiday v 5 77
For my part, I'll not meddle nor make no further *Troi. and Cres.* i 1 14
I'll meddle nor make no more i' the matter i 1 85
But how should this man, that makes me smile, make Hector angry? i 2 32
That's true; make no question of that i 2 174
The ample proposition that hope makes In all designs begun on earth i 3 3
The splitting wind Makes flexible the knees of knotted oaks i 3 50
And make a sop of all this solid globe i 3 113
Makes factious feasts; rails on our state of war, Bold as an oracle i 3 191
Let this be granted, and Achilles' horse Makes many Thetis' sons i 3 212
Shall make it good, or do his best to do it i 3 274
And, in the publication, make no strain i 3 326
And choice, being mutual act of all our souls, Makes merit her election i 3 349
Make a lottery; And, by device, let blockish Ajax draw The sort i 3 374
And make him fall His crest that prouder than blue Iris bends i 3 379
I would make thee the loathsomest scab in Greece ii 1 31
Yoke you like draught-oxen and make you plough up the wars ii 1 116
Reason and respect Make livers pale and lustihood deject ii 2 50
'Tis mad idolatry To make the service greater than the god ii 2 57
Whose . . . freshness Wrinkles Apollo's, and makes stale the morning ii 2 79
Which hath our several honours all engaged To make it gracious ii 2 125
To make up a free determination 'Twixt right and wrong ii 2 170
To persist In doing wrong extenuates not wrong, But makes it much more heavy ii 2 188
Why am I a fool?—Make that demand of the prover ii 3 72
Things small as nothing, for request's sake only, He makes important ii 3 180
We'll consecrate the steps that Ajax makes When they go from Achilles ii 3 193
I will knead him; I'll make him supple.—He's not yet through warm ii 3 231
I will make a complimental assault upon him, for my business seethes iii 1 41
You have broke it, cousin: and, by my life, you shall make it whole again iii 1 54
To make a sweet lady sad is a sour offence iii 1 79
That if the king call for him at supper, you will make his excuse iii 1 85
Falling in, after falling out, may make them three iii 1 112
Disarm great Hector.—'Twill make us proud to be his servant iii 1 168

Make. What should they grant? what makes this pretty abruption? *Troi. and Cres.* iii 2 69
Fears make devils of cherubins; they never see truly iii 2 74
What wouldst thou of us, Trojan? make demand iii 3 17
Cannot make boast to have that which he hath, Nor feels not what he owes iii 3 98
One touch of nature makes the whole world kin iii 3 175
Let Patroclus make demands to me, you shall see the pageant of Ajax iii 3 272
Unless the fiddler Apollo get his sinews to make catlings on iii 3 305
O you gods divine! Make Cressid's name the very crown of falsehood! iv 2 106
Alas, a kind of godly jealousy . . . Makes me afeard iv 4 84
This brave shall oft make thee to hide thy head iv 4 139
Let us make ready straight.—Yea, with a bridegroom's fresh alacrity iv 4 146
I'll make my match to live, The kiss you take is better than you give iv 5 37
Labouring for destiny make cruel way Through ranks of Greekish youth iv 5 184
And make distinct the very breach whereout Hector's great spirit flew iv 5 245
To make a recordation to my soul Of every syllable v 2 116
It is the purpose that makes strong the vow v 3 23
This foolish, dreaming, superstitious girl Makes all these bodements v 3 80
Make wells and Niobes of the maids and wives, Cold statues of the youth v 10 19
For the dearth, The gods, not the patricians, make it *Coriolanus* i 1 75
Make edicts for usury, to support usurers i 1 83
For, look you, I may make the belly smile As well as speak i 1 113
Yet I can make my audit up, that all From me do back receive the flour i 1 148
Make you ready your stiff bats and clubs i 1 165
That, rubbing the poor itch of your opinion, Make yourselves scabs i 1 169
Like nor peace nor war? the one affrights you, The other makes you proud i 1 174
Your virtue is To make him worthy whose offence subdues him i 1 179
I'ld make a quarry With thousands of these quarter'd slaves i 1 202
To break the heart of generosity, And make bold power look pale i 1 216
I'ld revolt, to make Only my wars with him i 1 238
They nothing doubt prevailing and to make it brief wars i 3 112
List, what work he makes Amongst your cloven army i 4 20
Disdain us much beyond our thoughts, Which makes me sweat with wrath i 4 26
By the fires of heaven, I'll leave the foe And make my wars on you i 4 40
Let's fetch him off, or make remain alike i 4 62
Down with them! And hark, what noise the general makes! To him! i 5 10
Take Convenient numbers to make good the city i 5 13
Follow Marcius. O, me alone! make you a sword of me? i 6 76
Make good this ostentation, and you shall Divide in all with us i 6 86
I thank you, general; But cannot make my heart consent to take A bribe i 9 37
O that you could . . . make but an interior survey of your good selves! ii 1 43
If you chance to be pinched with the colic, you make faces like mummers ii 1 83
All the peace you make in their cause is, calling both the parties knaves ii 1 87
I will make my very house reel to-night: a letter for me! ii 1 121
Seven years' health; in which time I will make a lip at the physician ii 1 126
That he will give them make I as little question As he is proud to do't ii 1 246
No more of him; he's a worthy man: make way, they are coming ii 2 40
And make us think Rather our state's defective for requital ii 2 53
The senate, Coriolanus, are well pleased To make thee consul ii 2 137
For the multitude to be ingrateful, were to make a monster of the multitude ii 3 11
To make us no better thought of, a little help will serve ii 3 15
He's to make his requests by particulars ii 3 47
I will make much of your voices, and so trouble you no further ii 3 116
The gods give him joy, and make him good friend to the people! ii 3 142
Make them of no more voice Than dogs that are as often beat for barking ii 3 223
Ready, when time shall prompt them, to make road Upon's again iii 1 5
It will be dangerous to go on: no further.—What makes this change? iii 1 27
Let me deserve so ill as you, and make me Your fellow tribune iii 1 51
He'll turn your current in a ditch, And make your channel his iii 1 97
By Jove himself! It makes the consuls base iii 1 108
We debase The nature of our seats and make the rabble Call our cares fears iii 1 136
'Tis fit You make strong party, or defend yourself By calmness iii 2 94
A beggar's tongue Make motion through my lips! iii 2 118
Make them be strong and ready for this hint, When we shall hap to give't iii 3 24
With precepts that would make invincible The heart that conn'd them iv 1 10
A lonely dragon, that his fen Makes fear'd and talk'd of more than seen iv 1 31
He'ld make an end of thy posterity.—Bastards and all iv 2 26
The main blaze of it is past, but a small thing would make it flame again iv 3 21
Speed thee straight, And make my misery serve thy turn iv 5 94
Our general himself makes a mistress of him iv 5 207
Ay, and it [peace] makes men hate one another iv 5 245
Here do we make his friends Blush that the world goes well iv 6 4
Desperation Is all the policy, strength and defence, That Rome can make iv 6 128
A pair of tribunes that have rack'd for Rome, To make coals cheap v 1 17
Your good tongue, More than the instant army we can make, Might stop our countryman v 1 37
Only make trial what your love can do For Rome v 1 40
Those doves' eyes, Which can make gods forsworn v 3 28
The sorrow that delivers us thus changed Makes you think so v 3 40
Murdering impossibility, to make What cannot be, slight work v 3 61
Make our eyes flow with joy, hearts dance with comforts v 3 99
It is no little thing to make Mine eyes to sweat compassion v 3 195
Where have you lurk'd, that you make doubt of it? v 4 49
Tabors and cymbals and the shouting Romans Make the sun dance v 4 54
Call all your tribes together, praise the gods, And make triumphant fires v 5 3
But the fall of either Makes the survivor heir of all v 6 19
Let's make the best of it.—My rage is gone v 6 148
Make way to lay them by their brethren *T. Andron.* i 1 89
Away with him! and make a fire straight i 1 127
And this suit I make, That you create your emperor's eldest son i 1 223
Lavinia will I make my empress, Rome's royal mistress i 1 240
He comforts you Can make you greater than the Queen of Goths i 1 269
Was there none else in Rome to make a stale, But Saturnine? i 304
And make them know what 'tis to let a queen Kneel in the streets i 1 454
'Tis not the difference of a year or two Makes me less gracious ii 1 32
Youngling, learn thou to make some meaner choice ii 1 73
Uncouple here and let us make a bay And wake the emperor ii 2 3
I have horse will follow where the game Makes way ii 2 24
Wherefore look'st thou sad, When every thing doth make a gleeful boast? ii 3 11
And make a chequer'd shadow on the ground ii 3 15
Thy sons make pillage of her chastity ii 3 44
Your swarth Cimmerian Doth make your honour of his body's hue ii 3 73
And make his dead trunk pillow to our lust ii 3 130
I warrant you, madam, we will make that sure ii 3 133
Farewell, my sons: see that you make her sure ii 3 187
And make the silken strings delight to kiss them [her hands] ii 4 46

Make. Come, let us go, and make thy father blind *T. Andron.* ii 4 52
Witness the sorrow that their sister makes iii 1 119
Let me kiss thy lips; Or make some sign how I may do thee ease iii 1 121
Plot some device of further misery, To make us wonder'd at iii 1 135
Ah, that this sight should make so deep a wound! iii 1 247
Usurp upon my watery eyes, And make them blind with tributary tears iii 1 270
When thy poor heart beats with outrageous beating, Thou canst not strike it thus to make it still iii 2 14
Or get some little knife between thy teeth, And just against thy heart make thou a hole iii 2 17
Nor wink, nor nod, nor kneel, nor make a sign iii 2 43
Leave these bitter deep laments: Make my aunt merry iii 2 47
That, with his pretty buzzing melody, Came here to make us merry iii 2 65
See how much she makes of thee: Somewhither would she have thee go iv 1 10
Heard my grandsire say full oft, Extremity of griefs would make men mad iv 1 19
I'll make you feed on berries and on roots, And feed on curds and whey iv 2 177
Make no more ado, But give your pigeons to the emperor iv 3 102
That holp'st to make me great, In hope thyself should govern Rome and me iv 4 59
Wherein Rome hath done you any scath, Let him make treble satisfaction v 1 8
Make poor men's cattle break their necks; Set fire on barns v 1 132
Is it your trick to make me ope the door? v 2 10
My dreadful name, Revenge, which makes the foul offender quake v 2 40
I will grind your bones to dust And with your blood and it I'll make a paste, And of the paste a coffin I will rear And make two pasties of your shameful heads v 2 188
Where civil blood makes civil hands unclean *Rom. and Jul.* Prol. 4
Locks fair daylight out And makes himself an artificial night i 1 146
What sadness lengthens Romeo's hours?—Not having that, which, having, makes them short i 1 170
Bid a sick man in sadness make his will: Ah, word ill urged! i 1 208
And in that sparing makes huge waste i 1 224
One more, most welcome, makes my number more i 2 23
Earth-treading stars that make dark heaven light i 2 25
I will make thee think thy swan a crow i 2 92
But no more deep will I endart mine eye Than your consent gives strength to make it fly i 3 99
She that makes dainty, She, I'll swear, hath corns i 5 21
And, touching hers, make blessed my rude hand i 5 53
God shall mend my soul! You'll make a mutiny among my guests! i 5 82
More light, more light! For shame! I'll make you quiet i 5 91
Patience perforce with wilful choler meeting Makes my flesh tremble i 5 92
And make her [Echo's] airy tongue more hoarse than mine ii 2 163
The excuse that thou dost make in this delay Is longer than the tale ii 5 33
There stays a husband to make you a wife ii 5 71
Come with me, and we will make short work ii 6 35
Make it a word and a blow.—You shall find me apt enough to that iii 1 43
An thou make minstrels of us, look to hear nothing but discords: here's my fiddlestick; here's that shall make you dance iii 1 50
Nothing but one of your nine lives; that I mean to make bold withal iii 1 81
Affection makes him false; he speaks not true iii 1 182
Cut him out in little stars, And he will make the face of heaven so fine iii 2 23
Or those eyes shut, that make thee answer 'I' iii 2 49
These griefs, these woes, these sorrows make me old iii 2 89
Hang up philosophy! Unless philosophy can make a Juliet iii 3 58
Hasten all the house to bed, Which heavy sorrow makes them apt unto iii 3 157
I will make a desperate tender Of my child's love iii 4 12
Some say the lark makes sweet division; This doth not so iii 5 29
Wilt thou wash him from his grave with tears? An if thou couldst, thou couldst not make him live iii 5 72
The County Paris, at Saint Peter's Church, Shall happily make thee there a joyful bride.—Now, by Saint Peter's Church and Peter too, He shall not make me there a joyful bride iii 5 116
You are too hot.—God's bread! it makes me mad iii 5 177
Make the bridal bed In that dim monument where Tybalt lies iii 5 202
To make confession and to be absolved iii 5 233
Come you to make confession to this father? iv 1 22
Death, that hath ta'en her hence to make me wail, Ties up my tongue iv 5 31
And old cakes of roses Were thinly scatter'd, to make up a show v 1 48
The world affords no law to make thee rich; Then be not poor, but break it v 1 73
Her beauty makes This vault a feasting presence full of light v 3 85
I will kiss thy lips; Haply some poison yet doth hang on them, To make me die with a restorative v 3 166
Yet most suspected, as the time and place Doth make against me v 3 225
This letter doth make good the friar's words v 3 286
Make sacred even his stirrup *T. of Athens* i 1 82
What you bestow, in him I'll counterpoise, And make him weigh with her i 1 146
I will do nothing at thy bidding: make thy requests to thy friend i 1 279
You shall not make me welcome: I come to have thee thrust me out of doors i 2 24
Let my meat make thee silent.—I scorn thy meat i 2 36
Those healths will make thee and thy state look ill i 2 57
I drink to you.—Thou weepest to make them drink i 2 113
Let 'em have kind admittance: Music, make their welcome! i 2 135
We make ourselves fools, to disport ourselves i 2 141
What a beggar his heart is, Being of no power to make his wishes good i 2 202
Nine thousand; besides my former sum, Which makes it five and twenty ii 1 3
That I may make his lordship understand Wherefore you are not paid ii 2 43
You make me marvel ii 2 133
And now ingratitude makes it worse than stealth iii 4 27
He should the sooner pay his debts, And make a clear way to the gods iii 4 77
You undergo too strict a paradox, Striving to make an ugly deed look fair iii 5 25
And make his wrongs His outsides, to wear them like his raiment iii 5 32
You cannot make gross sins look clear: To revenge is no valour iii 5 38
If there be Such valour in the bearing, what make we Abroad? iii 5 46
Banish your dotage; banish usury, That makes the senate ugly iii 5 100
Make not a city feast of it, to let the meat cool ere we can agree iii 6 75
For your own gifts, make yourselves praised: but reserve still to give iii 6 80
Make the meat be beloved more than the man that gives it iii 6 85
Let's make no stay.—Lord Timon's mad.—I feel't upon my bones iii 6 128
For bounty, that makes gods, does still mar men iv 2 41
It is the pasture lards the rother's sides, The want that makes him lean iv 3 13
Thus much of this [gold] will make black white, foul fair, Wrong right iv 3 28
This yellow slave [gold] Will . . . Make the hoar leprosy adored iv 3 35
This [gold] is it That makes the wappen'd widow wed again iv 3 38
I will make thee Do thy right nature iv 3 43
Make use of thy salt hours: season the slaves For tubs and baths iv 3 85
Little gold of late, brave Timon, The want whereof doth daily make revolt iv 3 91
Let not the virgin's cheek Make soft thy trenchant sword iv 3 115
Make large confusion; and, thy fury spent, Confounded be thyself! iv 3 127

Make. Enough to make a whore forswear her trade, And to make whores, a bawd *T. of Athens* iv 3 133
Make curl'd-pate ruffians bald iv 3 160
And make thine own self the conquest of thy fury iv 3 340
Make thine epitaph, That death in me at others' lives may laugh iv 3 380
Let us make the assay upon him: if he care not for't, he will supply us iv 3 406
Performance is a kind of will or testament which argues a great sickness in his judgement that makes it v 1 31
You that are honest, by being what you are, Make them best seen and known v 1 72
Make it known to us.—You'll take it ill.—Most thankfully, my lord v 1 93
You are an alchemist; make gold of that v 1 117
Offering the fortunes of his former days, The former man may make him v 1 128
And send forth us, to make their sorrow'd render v 1 152
All thy powers Shall make their harbour in our town v 4 53
Taught thee to make vast Neptune weep for aye On thy low grave v 4 78
Make war breed peace, make peace stint war, make each Prescribe to other as each other's leech v 4 83
But, indeed, sir, we make holiday, to see Cæsar *J. Cæsar* i 1 35
Feathers pluck'd from Cæsar's wing Will make him fly an ordinary pitch i 1 78
Heaven hath infused them with these spirits, To make them instruments of fear i 3 70
Therein, ye gods, you make the weak most strong i 3 91
Those that with haste will make a mighty fire Begin it with weak straws i 3 107
Am I entreated To speak and strike? O Rome, I make thee promise! ii 1 56
This shall make Our purpose necessary and not envious ii 1 177
Dear my lord, Make me acquainted with your cause of grief ii 1 256
That great vow Which did incorporate and make us one ii 1 273
Make sick men whole.—But are not some whole that we must make sick? ii 1 327
I fear our purpose is discovered.—Look, how he makes to Cæsar iii 1 18
It will inflame you, it will make you mad iii 2 149
Make a ring about the corpse of Cæsar, And let me show you him iii 2 162
We must straight make head: Therefore let our alliance be combined iv 1 42
Hollow men, like horses hot at hand, Make gallant show and promise iv 2 24
Older in practice, abler than yourself To make conditions iv 3 32
Go show your slaves how choleric you are, And make your bondmen tremble iv 3 44
Make your vaunting true, And it shall please me well iv 3 52
A friend should bear his friend's infirmities, But Brutus makes mine greater than they are iv 3 87
That rash humour which my mother gave me Makes me forgetful iv 3 121
Of your philosophy you make no use, If you give place to accidental evils iv 3 145
The enemy, marching along by them, By them shall make a fuller number up iv 3 208
Make forth; the generals would have some words v 1 25
If arguing make us sweat, The proof of it will turn to redder drops v 1 48
Enclosed round about With horsemen, that make to him on the spur v 3 29
What ill request did Brutus make to thee?—To kill him, Clitus v 5 11
The conquerors can but make a fire of him v 5 55
And thrice again, to make up nine *Macbeth* i 3 36
Nothing afeard of what thyself didst make, Strange images of death i 3 96
Doth unfix my hair And make my seated heart knock at my ribs i 3 136
And make joyful The hearing of my wife with your approach i 4 45
Almost dead for breath, had scarcely more Than would make up his message i 5 38
Make thick my blood; Stop up the access and passage to remorse! i 5 44
Have theirs, themselves and what is theirs, in compt, To make their audit i 6 27
Nor time nor place Did then adhere, and yet you would make both i 7 52
Who dares receive it other, As we shall make our griefs and clamour roar? i 7 78
If you shall cleave to my consent, when 'tis, It shall make honour for you ii 1 26
These deeds must not be thought After these ways; so, it will make us mad ii 2 34
It [drink] makes him, and it mars him; . . . makes him stand to, and not stand to ii 3 35
This is the door.—I'll make so bold to call ii 3 56
Who could refrain, That had a heart to love, and in that heart Courage to make 's love known? ii 3 124
Contending 'gainst obedience, as they would make War with mankind ii 4 17
God's benison go with you; and with those That would make good of bad, and friends of foes! ii 4 40
To make society The sweeter welcome, we will keep . . . alone iii 1 42
Mine eternal jewel Given to the common enemy of man, To make them kings! iii 1 70
And thence it is, That I to your assistance do make love iii 1 124
And make our faces vizards to our hearts, Disguising what they are iii 2 34
Light thickens; and the crow Makes wing to the rooky wood iii 2 51
But hold thee still: Things bad begun make strong themselves by ill iii 2 55
So all men do, from hence to the palace gate Make it their walk iii 3 14
Why do you make such faces? iii 4 67
You make me strange Even to the disposition that I owe iii 4 112
Make the gruel thick and slab: Add thereto a tiger's chaudron iv 1 32
But yet I'll make assurance double sure, And take a bond of fate iv 1 83
What had he done, to make him fly the land? iv 2 1
When our actions do not, Our fears do make us traitors iv 2 4
And my more-having would be as a sauce To make me hunger more iv 3 82
Good God, betimes remove The means that makes us strangers! iv 3 163
Your eye in Scotland Would create soldiers, make our women fight iv 3 187
Let's make us medicines of our great revenge, To cure this deadly grief iv 3 214
Your royal preparation Makes us hear something v 3 58
Shadow The numbers of our host and make discovery Err in report of us v 4 6
The time approaches That will with due decision make us know v 4 17
Make all our trumpets speak; give them all breath v 6 9
Thou losest labour: As easy mayst thou the intrenchant air With thy keen sword impress as make me bleed v 8 10
Doth make the night joint-labourer with the day *Hamlet* i 1 78
And what make you from Wittenberg, Horatio? Marcellus? i 2 164
Do mine ear that violence, To make it truster of your own report i 2 172
This heavy-headed revel east and west Makes us traduced i 4 18
Makes each petty artery in this body As hardy as the Nemean lion's nerve i 4 82
Unhand me, gentlemen. By heaven, I'll make a ghost of him that lets me! i 4 85
Make thy two eyes, like stars, start from their spheres i 5 17
Never make known what you have seen to-night i 5 144
Make inquire Of his behaviour.—My lord, I did intend it ii 1 4
Heavens make our presence and our practices Pleasant and helpful to him! ii 2 38
Makes vow before his uncle never more To give the assay of arms ii 2 70
A short tale to make—Fell into a sadness, then into a fast ii 2 146

Make. There is nothing either good or bad, but thinking makes it so *Hamlet* ii 2 256
To me it is a prison.—Why then, your ambition makes it one ii 2 258
But, in the beaten way of friendship, what make you at Elsinore? ii 2 277
The clown shall make those laugh whose lungs are tickle o' the sere ii 2 336
Their writers do them wrong, to make them exclaim against their own succession ii 2 367
One said there were no sallets in the lines to make the matter savoury ii 2 462
Make mad the guilty and appal the free, Confound the ignorant ii 2 590
But I am pigeon-liver'd and lack gall To make oppression bitter ii 2 606
There's the respect That makes calamity of so long life iii 1 69
When he himself might his quietus make With a bare bodkin iii 1 75
Thus conscience does make cowards of us all iii 1 83
For wise men know well enough what monsters you make of them iii 1 144
God has given you one face, and you make yourselves another iii 1 150
Nick-name God's creatures, and make your wantonness your ignorance iii 1 152
Though it make the unskilful laugh, cannot but make the judicious grieve iii 2 29
Make you ready. How now, my lord! will the king hear this piece? iii 2 50
Bid the players make haste. Will you two help to hasten them? iii 2 54
So many journeys may the sun and moon Make us again count o'er! iii 2 172
The poor advanced makes friends of enemies iii 2 215
If it shall please you to make me a wholesome answer iii 2 327
I cannot.—What, my lord?—Make you a wholesome answer iii 2 333
Such answer as I can make, you shall command iii 2 335
Why, look you now, how unworthy a thing you make of me! iii 2 380
Some more audience than a mother, Since nature makes them partial iii 3 32
Help, angels! Make assay! Bow, stubborn knees! iii 3 69
Makes marriage-vows As false as dicers' oaths iii 4 44
And sweet religion makes A rhapsody of words iii 4 47
Preaching to stones, Would make them capable iii 4 127
For a pair of reechy kisses, . . . Make you to ravel all this matter out iii 4 186
Makes mouths at the invisible event iv 4 50
Indeed would make one think there might be thought, Though nothing sure iv 5 12
Indeed, la, without an oath, I'll make an end on't iv 5 57
Make choice of whom your wisest friends you will, And they shall hear iv 5 204
I have words to speak in thine ear will make thee dumb iv 6 25
Let me see: We'll make a solemn wager on your cunnings iv 7 156
Make your bouts more violent to that end iv 7 159
Make her grave straight: the crowner hath sat on her v 1 4
Say 'a grave-maker:' the houses that he makes last till doomsday v 1 67
Let her paint an inch thick, to this favour she must come; make her laugh at that v 1 215
The dust is earth; of earth we make loam v 1 233
Whose phrase of sorrow Conjures the wandering stars, and makes them stand like wonder-wounded hearers v 1 279
Could not, with all their quantity of love, Make up my sum v 1 294
Ere I could make a prologue to my brains, They had begun the play v 2 30
They did make love to this employment; They are not near my conscience v 2 57
As, to make true diction of him, his semblable is his mirror v 2 123
Pass with your best violence; I am afeard you make a wanton of me v 2 310
Heaven make thee free of it! v 2 343
That curiosity in neither can make choice of either's moiety *Lear* i 1 6
A love that makes breath poor, and speech unable i 1 61
Of all these bounds, even from this line to this, . . . We make thee lady i 1 67
Or he that makes his generation messes To gorge his appetite i 1 119
By you to be sustain'd, shall our abode Make with you by due turns i 1 137
The bow is bent and drawn, make from the shaft i 1 145
Election makes not up on such conditions i 1 209
I would not from your love make such a stray, To match you where I hate i 1 212
Make known It is no vicious blot, murder, or foulness i 1 229
Reverence of age makes the world bitter to the best of our times i 2 49
It would make a great gap in your own honour i 2 90
We make guilty of our disasters the sun, the moon, and the stars i 2 130
Can you make no use of nothing, nuncle?—Why, no, boy i 4 144
How now, daughter! what makes that frontlet on? i 4 207
Make use of that good wisdom, Whereof I know you are fraught i 4 240
Epicurism and lust Make it more like a tavern or a brothel i 4 266
Your disorder'd rabble Make servants of their betters i 4 278
Dear goddess hear! Suspend thy purpose, if thou didst intend To make this creature fruitful! i 4 299
I am ashamed . . .; That these hot tears, which break from me perforce, Should make thee worth them i 4 321
Canst tell how an oyster makes his shell?—No.—Nor I neither i 5 26
Thou wouldst make a good fool i 5 41
Would the reposal Of any trust . . . in thee Make thy words faith'd? ii 1 72
And thou must make a dullard of the world ii 1 76
Very pregnant and potential spurs To make thee seek it [my death] ii 1 79
Of my land, Loyal and natural boy, I'll work the means To make thee capable ii 1 87
Make your own purpose, How in my strength you please ii 1 113
If I had thee in Lipsbury pinfold, I would make thee care for me ii 2 10
Yet the moon shines; I'll make a sop o' the moonshine of you ii 2 34
A tailor made thee.—Thou art a strange fellow: a tailor make a man? ii 2 62
Fathers that wear rags Do make their children blind ii 4 49
Therefore, I pray you, That to our sister you do make return ii 4 153
O heavens, If you do love old men, if your sweet sway Allow obedience, if yourselves are old, Make it your cause! ii 4 195
I prithee, daughter, do not make me mad: I will not trouble thee ii 4 221
Tears his white hair, Which the impetuous blasts, with eyeless rage, Catch in their fury, and make nothing of iii 1 9
Make your speed to Dover, you shall find Some that will thank you iii 1 36
Crack nature's moulds, all germens spill at once, That make ingrateful man! iii 2 9
The man that makes his toe What he his heart should make iii 2 31
Gallow the very wanderers of the dark, And make them keep their caves iii 2 45
The art of our necessities is strange, That can make vile things precious iii 2 71
Must make content with his fortunes fit, For the rain it raineth every day iii 2 76
This prophecy Merlin shall make; for I live before his time iii 2 95
Is there any cause in nature that makes these hard hearts? iii 6 82
Make no noise, make no noise; draw the curtains: so, so, so. iii 6 89
How light and portable my pain seems now, When that which makes me bend makes the king bow! iii 6 116
O world! But that thy strange mutations make us hate thee iv 1 11
That I am wretched Makes thee the happier: heavens, deal so still! iv 1 69
Ten masts at each make not the altitude iv 6 53
The clearest gods, who make them honours Of men's impossibilities iv 6 73

Make. When the rain came to wet me once, and the wind to make me chatter . . . *Lear* iv 6 103
Why, this would make a man a man of salt . . . iv 6 199
My boon I make it, that you know me not Till time and I think meet . . . iv 7 10
And yet it is danger To make him even o'er the time he has lost . . . iv 7 80
With others, whom, I fear, Most just and heavy causes make oppose . . . v 1 27
To take the widow Exasperates, makes mad her sister Goneril . . . v 1 60
Ere they shall make us weep: we'll see 'em starve first . . . v 3 25
If thou dost As this instructs thee, thou dost make thy way . . . v 3 29
If you will marry, make your loves to me, My lady is bespoke . . . v 3 88
The gods are just, and of our pleasant vices Make instruments to plague us . . . v 3 171
To amplify too much, would make much more, And top extremity . . . v 3 206
This judgement of the heavens, that makes us tremble, Touches us not with pity . . . v 3 231
In personal suit to make me his lieutenant . . . *Othello* i 1 9
Make after him, poison his delight, Proclaim him in the streets . . . i 1 68
Or else the devil will make a grandsire of you . . . i 1 91
What makes he here?—'Faith, he to-night hath boarded a land carack . . . i 2 49
What's the business?—The Turkish preparation makes for Rhodes . . . i 3 14
If we make thought of this, We must not think the Turk is so unskilful . . . i 3 26
Patience her injury a mockery makes . . . i 3 207
The Turk with a most mighty preparation makes for Cyprus . . . i 3 222
Let housewives make a skillet of my helm, And all indign and base adversities Make head against my estimation! . . . i 3 273
Make all the money thou canst . . . i 3 361
Therefore make money. A pox of drowning thyself! . . . i 3 365
Framed to make women false . . . i 3 404
Even till we make the main and the aerial blue An indistinct regard . . . ii 1 39
Make love's quick pants in Desdemona's arms . . . ii 1 80
These are old fond paradoxes to make fools laugh i' the alehouse . . . ii 1 139
This, and this, the greatest discords be That e'er our hearts shall make! . . . ii 1 201
But I'll set down the pegs that make this music, As honest as I am . . . ii 1 203
Make the Moor thank me, love me and reward me, For making him egregiously an ass . . . ii 1 317
Some to dance, some to make bonfires . . . ii 2 5
That was craftily qualified too, and, behold, what innovation it makes . . . ii 3 42
Look, if my gentle love be not raised up! I'll make thee an example . . . ii 3 251
One unperfectness shows me another, to make me frankly despise myself . . . ii 3 299
She may make, unmake, do what she list . . . ii 3 352
Out of her own goodness make the net That shall enmesh them all . . . ii 3 367
'Tis morning; Pleasure and action make the hours seem short . . . ii 3 385
They say the wars must make examples Out of their best . . . iii 3 65
Robs me of that which not enriches him And makes me poor indeed . . . iii 3 161
Think'st thou I'ld make a life of jealousy? . . . iii 3 177
'Tis not to make me jealous To say my wife is fair, feeds well . . . iii 3 183
Farewell the plumed troop, and the big wars, That make ambition virtue! . . . iii 3 350
Make me to see't; or, at the least, so prove it . . . iii 3 364
Do deeds to make heaven weep, all earth amazed . . . iii 3 371
O wretched fool, That livest to make thine honesty a vice! . . . iii 3 376
Catechize the world for him; that is, make questions, and by them answer . . . iii 4 17
She told her, while she kept it, 'Twould make her amiable . . . iii 4 59
Make it a darling like your precious eye . . . iii 4 66
What make you from home? . . . iii 4 169
I will make him tell the tale anew, Where, how, how oft . . . iv 1 85
There's fall'n between him and my lord An unkind breach: but you shall make all well . . . iv 1 237
'Tis very much: Make her amends; she weeps . . . iv 1 255
You did wish that I would make her turn: Sir, she can turn, and turn . . . iv 1 263
But, alas, to make me A fixed figure for the time of scorn! . . . iv 2 53
I should make very forges of my cheeks . . . iv 2 74
Would it not make one weep?—It is my wretched fortune . . . iv 2 127
To do the act . . . Not the world's mass of vanity could make me . . . iv 2 164
'Tis not very well. I will make myself known to Desdemona . . . iv 2 200
Who would not make her husband a cuckold to make him a monarch? . . . iv 3 76
'Tis a wrong in your own world, and you might quickly make it right . . . iv 3 83
It makes us, or it mars us; think on that . . . v 1 4
Every way makes my gain . . . v 1 14
He hath a daily beauty in his life That makes me ugly . . . v 1 20
My coat is better than thou know'st: I will make proof of thine . . . v 1 26
I think that one of them is hereabout, And cannot make away . . . v 1 58
This is the night That either makes me or fordoes me quite . . . v 1 129
She comes more nearer earth than she was wont, And makes men mad . . . v 2 111
If heaven would make me such another world Of one entire and perfect chrysolite, I'ld not have sold her for it . . . v 2 144
I'll make thee known, Though I lost twenty lives . . . v 2 165
Did he live now, This sight would make him do a desperate turn . . . v 2 207
Every passion fully strives To make itself, in thee, fair . . . *Ant. and Cleo.* i 1 51
Give me good fortune.—I make not, but foresee . . . i 2 14
If it lay in their hands to make me a cuckold, they would make themselves whores, but they'ld do't! . . . i 2 80
She makes a shower of rain as well as Jove . . . i 2 156
That when old robes are worn out, there are members to make new . . . i 2 172
Sextus Pompeius Makes his approaches to the port of Rome . . . i 3 46
Famous pirates Make the sea serve them . . . i 4 49
Many hot inroads They make in Italy . . . i 4 51
And great Pompey Would stand and make his eyes grow in my brow . . . i 5 32
He was not sad, for he would shine on those That make their looks by his . . . i 5 56
Antony In Egypt sits at dinner, and will make No wars without doors . . . ii 1 12
If you'll patch a quarrel, As matter whole you have not to make it with . . . ii 2 53
But mine honesty Shall not make poor my greatness . . . ii 2 93
To make you brothers, and to knit your hearts With an unslipping knot . . . ii 2 128
What power is in Agrippa . . . To make this good? . . . ii 2 145
She did make defect perfection, And, breathless, power breathe forth . . . ii 2 236
But she makes hungry Where most she satisfies . . . ii 2 242
Make yourself my guest Whilst you abide here . . . ii 2 249
Therefore Make space enough between you . . . ii 3 23
Though I make this marriage for my peace, I' the east my pleasure lies . . . ii 3 39
Make thee a fortune from me.—But yet, madam,— I do not like 'But yet' . . . ii 5 49
Say 'tis not so, a province I will give thee, And make thy fortunes proud . . . ii 5 69
The blow thou hadst Shall make thy peace for moving me to rage . . . ii 5 70
To punish me for what you make me do Seems much unequal . . . ii 5 100
O, that his fault should make a knave of thee! . . . ii 5 102
But in my bosom shall she never come, To make my heart her vassal . . . ii 6 57
Possess it, I'll make answer . . . ii 7 107

Make. Make battery to our ears with the loud music . . . *Ant. and Cleo.* ii 7 115
Now Pleased fortune does of Marcus Crassus' death Make me revenger . . . iii 1 3
I have done enough; a lower place, note well, May make too great an act . . . iii 1 13
Rather makes choice of loss, Than gain which darkens him . . . iii 1 23
Sister, prove such a wife As my thoughts make thee . . . iii 2 26
Make me not offended In your distrust . . . iii 2 33
So, the gods keep you, And make the hearts of Romans serve your ends! . . . iii 2 37
The elements be kind to thee, and make Thy spirits all of comfort! . . . iii 2 40
Three in Egypt Cannot make better note.—He's very knowing . . . iii 3 26
I find thee Most fit for business: go make thee ready . . . iii 3 40
Make your soonest haste; So your desires are yours . . . iii 4 27
The Jove of power make me most weak, most weak, Your reconciler! . . . iii 4 29
And the high gods, To do you justice, make them ministers Of us . . . iii 6 88
Fly, And make your peace with Cæsar.—Fly! not we . . . iii 11 6
Pray you, look not sad, Nor make replies of loathness . . . iii 11 18
And death will seize her, but Your comfort makes the rescue . . . iii 11 48
Make thine own edict for thy pains, which we Will answer as a law . . . iii 12 32
That would make his will Lord of his reason . . . iii 13 3
The loyalty well held to fools does make Our faith mere folly . . . iii 13 42
It much would please him, That of his fortunes you should make a staff . . . iii 13 68
Make us Adore our errors; laugh at's, while we strut To our confusion . . . iii 13 113
Say He makes me angry with him; for he seems Proud . . . iii 13 141
He makes me angry; And at this time most easy 'tis to do't . . . iii 13 143
The next time I do fight, I'll make death love me . . . iii 13 193
Give him no breath, but now Make boot of his distraction . . . iv 1 9
I will live, Or bathe my dying honour in the blood Shall make it live again . . . iv 2 7
Make as much of me As when mine empire was your fellow too . . . iv 2 21
What does he mean?—To make his followers weep . . . iv 2 24
The gods make this a happy day to Antony! . . . iv 5 1
Would thou . . . had once prevail'd To make me fight at land! . . . iv 5 3
Our will is Antony be took alive; Make it so known . . . iv 6 3
To this great fairy I'll commend thy acts, Make her thanks bless thee . . . iv 8 13
Give me thy hand: Through Alexandria make a jolly march . . . iv 8 30
Make mingle with our rattling tabourines . . . iv 8 37
Thou Hast sold me to this novice; and my heart Makes only wars on thee . . . iv 12 15
The rack dislimns, and makes it indistinct, As water is in water . . . iv 14 10
We'll hand in hand, And with our sprightly port make the ghosts gaze . . . iv 14 52
When I did make thee free, sworest thou not then To do this? . . . iv 14 81
I have done my work ill, friends: O, make an end Of what I have begun . . . iv 14 105
Our size of sorrow, Proportion'd to our cause, must be as great As that which makes it . . . iv 15 6
Our strength is all gone into heaviness, That makes the weight . . . iv 15 34
Let's do it after the high Roman fashion, And make death proud to take us . . . iv 15 88
Being so frustrate, tell him he mocks The pauses that he makes . . . v 1 3
But you, gods, will give us Some faults to make us men . . . v 1 33
My desolation does begin to make A better life . . . v 2 1
Make your full reference freely to my lord, Who is so full of grace . . . v 2 23
Rather make My country's high pyramides my gibbet! . . . v 2 60
I cannot project mine own cause so well To make it clear . . . v 2 122
The ingratitude of this Seleucus does Even make me wild . . . v 2 154
Cæsar's no merchant, to make prize with you . . . v 2 183
Therefore be cheer'd; Make not your thoughts your prisons . . . v 2 185
By your command, Which my love makes religion to obey . . . v 2 199
Make your best use of this: I have perform'd Your pleasure . . . v 2 203
Truly, she makes a very good report o' the worm . . . v 2 255
He'll make demand of her, and spend that kiss Which is my heaven to have . . . v 2 305
High events as these Strike those that make them . . . v 2 364
Breeds him and makes him of his bed-chamber . . . *Cymbeline* i 1 42
All the learnings that his time Could make him the receiver of . . . i 1 44
Make yourself some comfort Out of your best advice . . . i 1 155
If it be a sin to make a true election, she is damned . . . i 2 29
So long As he could make me with this eye or ear Distinguish him . . . i 3 9
Or I could make him swear The shes of Italy should not betray Mine interest . . . i 3 28
When he was less furnished than now he is with that which makes him both without and within . . . i 4 9
This worthy signior, I thank him, makes no stranger of me . . . i 4 111
I should get ground of your fair mistress, make her go back . . . i 4 114
I make my wager rather against your confidence than her reputation . . . i 4 120
Hast thou not learn'd me how To make perfumes? distil? preserve? . . . i 5 13
Your highness Shall from this practice but make hard your heart . . . i 5 24
But there is No danger in what show of death it makes . . . i 5 40
Can we not Partition make with spectacles so precious 'Twixt fair and foul? . . . i 6 37
What makes your admiration? . . . i 6 38
To such neat excellence opposed Should make desire vomit emptiness . . . i 6 45
Your cause doth strike my heart With pity, that doth make me sick . . . i 6 119
A lady So fair . . . Would make the great'st king double . . . i 6 121
Should he make me Live, like Diana's priest, betwixt cold sheets? . . . i 6 132
And shall make your lord, That which he is, new o'er . . . i 6 164
You make amends.—He sits 'mongst men like a descended god . . . i 6 168
I will make bold To send them to you, only for this night . . . i 6 197
Here's a voucher, Stronger than ever law could make . . . ii 2 40
It would make any man cold to lose.—But not every man patient . . . ii 3 4
Make denials Increase your services . . . ii 3 53
Yea, and [gold] makes Diana's rangers false themselves . . . ii 3 73
'Tis gold Which makes the true man kill'd and saves the thief . . . ii 3 76
I will make One of her women lawyer to me . . . ii 3 78
I hate you; which I had rather You felt than make't my boast . . . ii 3 116
Ay, I said so, sir: If you will make't an action, call witness to't . . . ii 3 156
What means do you make to him? . . . ii 4 3
Winds of all the corners kiss'd your sails, To make your vessel nimble . . . ii 4 29
I'll make a journey twice as far, to enjoy A second night . . . ii 4 43
Make not, sir, Your loss your sport . . . ii 4 47
If you can make't apparent That you have tasted her in bed . . . ii 4 56
My circumstances, Being so near the truth as I will make them . . . ii 4 62
Make pastime with us a day or two, or longer . . . iii 1 78
Blest be You bees that make these locks of counsel! . . . iii 2 36
And for the gap That we shall make in time, from our hence-going And our return, to excuse . . . iii 2 65
Such gain the cap of him that makes 'em fine . . . iii 3 25
Our cage We make a quire, as doth the prison'd bird . . . iii 3 43
What is in thy mind, That makes thee stare thus? . . . iii 4 5
If thou fear to strike and to make me certain it is done, thou art the pandar to her dishonour . . . iii 4 31

Make. And make me put into contempt the suits Of princely fellows *Cymbeline* iii 4 92
Tell him Wherein you're happy,—which you'll make him know iii 4 177
And there's no answer That will be given to the loudest noise we make iii 5 44
This She wished me to make known; but our great court Made me to blame iii 5 50
To death or to dishonour; and my end Can make good use of either iii 5 64
Yet famine, Ere clean it o'erthrow nature, makes it valiant iii 6 20
Come; our stomachs Will make what's homely savoury iii 6 33
I'll make't my comfort He is a man; I'll love him as my brother iii 6 71
Thy tailor, rascal, Who is thy grandfather: he made those clothes, Which, as it seems, make thee iv 2 82
I wish my brother make good time with him, You say he is so fell iv 2 108
The boy Fidele's sickness Did make my way long forth iv 2 149
The rudest wind, That by the top doth take the mountain pine, And make him stoop to the vale iv 2 176
He but sleeps: If he be gone, he'll make his grave a bed iv 2 216
Doth make distinction Of place 'tweeen high and low iv 2 248
But a bolt of nothing, shot at nothing, Which the brain makes of fumes iv 2 301
This forwardness Makes our hopes fair iv 2 343
For nature doth abhor to make his bed With the defunct iv 2 357
And make him with our pikes and partisans A grave iv 2 399
You some permit To second ills with ills, ... And make them dread it v 1 15
Do your best wills, And make me blest to obey! v 1 17
Let me make men know More valour in me than my habits show v 1 29
Whom best I love I cross; to make my gift, The more delay'd, delighted v 4 101
He shall be happy that can find him, if Our grace can make him so v 5 7
With my request, which I'll make bold your highness Cannot deny v 5 89
Stand thou by our side; Make thy demand aloud. Sir, step you forth v 5 130
I return'd with simular proof enough To make the noble Leonatus mad v 5 201
With language that would make me spurn the sea, If it could so roar to me v 5 294
Is so from sense in hardness, that I can Make no collection of it v 5 432
The purchase is to make men glorious *Pericles* i Gower 9
I'll make my will then, and, as sick men do Who know the world, see heaven, but, feeling woe i 1 47
If this be true, which makes me pale to read it i 1 75
Who, finger'd to make man his lawful music, Would draw heaven down i 1 82
If I can get him within my pistol's length, I'll make him sure enough i 1 169
Since he's so great can make his will his act i 2 18
And what may make him blush in being known, He'll stop the course by which it might be known i 2 22
Makes both my body pine and soul to languish i 2 31
He flatters you, makes war upon your life i 2 45
And make pretence of wrong that I have done him i 2 91
Upon our neighbouring shore, A portly sail of ships make hitherward i 4 61
And make a conquest of unhappy me, Whereas no glory's got to overcome i 4 69
Who makes the fairest show means most deceit i 4 75
Are stored with corn to make your needy bread i 4 95
To remember what he does, Build his statue to make him glorious ii Gower 14
And that in Tarsus was not best Longer for him to make his rest ii Gower 26
I could wish to make one there ii 1 118
Whose delightful steps Shall make the gazer joy to see him tread ii 1 165
Thou shalt have my best gown to make thee a pair ii 1 169
For princes are A model, which heaven makes like to itself ii 2 11
That makes us scan The outward habit by the inward man ii 2 56
Art hath thus decreed, To make some good, but others to exceed ii 3 16
Like to gnats, Which make a sound, but kill'd are wonder'd at ii 3 63
To make his entrance more sweet, Here, say we drink this ii 3 64
Say if you had, Who takes offence at that would make me glad? ii 5 72
Either be ruled by me, or I will make you—Man and wife ii 5 83
His queen with child makes her desire—Which who shall cross? iii Gower 40
Make swift the pangs Of my queen's travails! iii 1 13
Why do you make us love your goodly gifts, And snatch them straight away? iii 1 23
As chiding a nativity As fire, air, water, earth, and heaven can make iii 1 33
O, make for Tarsus! There will I visit Cleon iii 1 78
Make a fire within: Fetch hither all my boxes in my closet iii 2 80
Do appear, to make the world twice rich iii 2 103
Live, And make us weep to hear your fate, fair creature iii 2 104
Take from my heart all thankfulness! The gods Make up the rest upon you! iii 3 5
If neglection Should therein make me vile iii 3 21
Make me blessed in your care In bringing up my child iii 3 31
Which makes her both the heart and place Of general wonder iv Gower 10
There's no further necessity of qualities can make her be refused iv 2 53
To weep that you live as ye do makes pity in your lovers iv 2 130
Thus time we waste, and longest leagues make short iv 4 1
And swears she'll never stint, Make raging battery upon shores of flint iv 4 43
She would make a puritan of the devil, if he should cheapen a kiss of her iv 6 9
She'll disfurnish us of all our cavaliers, and make our swearers priests iv 6 12
Make the judgement good That thought you worthy of it iv 6 100
She makes our profession as it were to stink afore the face of the gods iv 6 144
Therefore I will make them acquainted with your purpose iv 6 209
Would allure, And make a battery through his deafen'd parts v 1 47
Come, let us leave her; And the gods make her prosperous! v 1 80
Who starves the ears she feeds, and makes them hungry v 1 113
How achieved you these endowments, which You make more rich to owe? v 1 118
I will believe thee, And make my senses credit thy relation v 1 124
Thou by some incensed god sent hither To make the world to laugh at me v 1 145
You gods! your present kindness Makes my past miseries sports v 3 41
This ornament Makes me look dismal will I clip to form v 3 74
My father's dead.—Heavens make a star of him! v 3 79

Make haste. *T. G. of Ver.* ii 4; iii 1; *Meas. for Meas.* iv 1; *Com. of Errors* iii 1; *Mer. of Venice* iii 2; iv 1; iv 2; *K. John* iv 2; *1 Hen. IV.* iv 2; *Richard III.* iii 3; *Rom. and Jul.* iii 1; iii 3; iv 4; *Macbeth* iii 5; *Hamlet* i 1; iv 3; *Cymbeline* i 5

Make-peace. To be a make-peace shall become my age *Richard II.* i 1 160

Maker. We are the makers of manners *Hen. V.* v 2 296
God, the best maker of all marriages, Combine your hearts in one! v 2 387
How can man, then, The image of his Maker, hope to win by it? *Hen. VIII.* iii 2 442
That when I am in heaven I shall desire To see what this child does, and praise my Maker v 5 69
It cannot be denied but peace is a great maker of cuckolds *Coriolanus* iv 5 244

Makest. Who makest a show but darest not strike *Tempest* i 2 470
Thou makest me merry; I am full of pleasure: Let us be jocund iii 2 125
By thy approach thou makest me most unhappy *T. G. of Ver.* v 4 31
Thou makest the triumviry, the corner-cap of society *L. L. Lost* iv 3 53

Makest. Live thou, I live: with much much more dismay I view the fight than thou that makest the fray *Mer. of Venice* iii 2 62
Not on thy sole, but on thy soul, harsh Jew, Thou makest thy knife keen iv 1 124
Thou almost makest me waver in my faith iv 1 130
Thou makest a testament As worldlings do *As Y. Like It* ii 1 47
And makest conjectural fears to come into me *All's Well* v 3 114
I may disjoin my hand, but not my faith.—So makest thou faith an enemy to faith *K. John* iii 1 263
And makest an oath the surety for thy truth Against an oath iii 1 282
There thou makest me sad and makest me sin In envy *1 Hen. IV.* i 1 78
And show'd thou makest some tender of my life v 4 49
Thou makest use of any thing *Hen. V.* iii 7 70
What makest thou in my sight? *Richard III.* i 3 164
To achieve her! how?—Why makest thou it so strange? *T. Andron.* ii 1 81
That solder'st close impossibilities, And makest them kiss! *T. of Athens* iv 3 389
That makest my blood cold and my hair to stare *J. Cæsar* iv 3 280
Makest thou this shame thy pastime? *Lear* ii 4 6
If thou but think'st him wrong'd and makest his ear A stranger *Othello* iii 3 143
Thou dost stone my heart, And makest me call what I intend to do A murder v 2 64
Who is this Thou makest thy bloody pillow? *Cymbeline* iv 2 363
My child! What, makest thou me a dullard in this act? v 5 265
Who by thy wisdom makest a prince thy servant *Pericles* i 2 64

Maketh. O, 'tis the sun that maketh all things shine *L. L. Lost* iv 3 246
Yet thus far fortune maketh us amends *3 Hen. VI.* iv 7 2

Making. Have Moe widows in them of this business' making *Tempest* ii 1 133
Making both it unable for itself, And dispossessing all my other parts Of necessary fitness *Meas. for Meas.* ii 4 21
Likeness made in crimes, Making practice on the times iii 2 288
Good my lord, do not recompense me in making me a cuckold v 1 523
We discovered Two ships from far making amain to us *Com. of Errors* i 1 93
Say that I linger'd with you at your shop To see the making of her carcanet iii 1 4
Armed and reverted, making war against her heir iii 2 127
Foolish, blunt, unkind, Stigmatical in making, worse in mind iv 2 22
As prodigal of all dear grace As Nature was in making graces dear *L. L. L.* ii 1 10
Making the bold wag by their praises bolder v 2 108
He speaks not like a man of God's making v 2 529
Making it momentany as a sound, Swift as a shadow *M. N. Dream* i 1 143
Either I mistake your shape and making quite ii 1 32
You do me now more wrong In making question of my uttermost *Mer. of Venice* i 1 156
Put the liveries to making ii 2 124
Works a miracle in nature, Making them lightest that wear most of it iii 2 91
This making of Christians will raise the price of hogs iii 5 25
The poor old man, their father, making such pitiful dole *As Y. Like It* i 2 138
Is he of God's making? What manner of man? iii 2 216
Almost chide God for making you that countenance you are iv 1 36
In her chamber, making a sermon of continency to her *T. of Shrew* iv 1 185
Some undeserved fault I'll find about the making of the bed iv 1 203
Making practised smiles, As in a looking-glass *W. Tale* i 2 116
Lest barbarism, making me the precedent, Should a like language use to all ii 1 84
Making that idiot, laughter, keep men's eyes *K. John* iii 3 45
And heal the inveterate canker of one wound By making many v 2 15
Three thousand men of war Are making hither *Richard II.* ii 1 287
Your fair discourse hath been as sugar, Making the hard way sweet ii 3 7
Making such difference 'twixt wake and sleep *1 Hen. IV.* iii 1 219
Making you ever better than his praise v 2 59
Making the wind my post-horse *2 Hen. IV.* Ind. 4
Making many fish-meals, that they fall into a kind of male green-sickness iv 3 99
What I have to say is of mine own making Epil. 6
Making defeat on the full power of France *Hen. V.* i 2 107
Some, making the wars their bulwark iv 1 173
It were not sin to think that, making God so free an offer iv 1 193
In the marches here we heard you were, Making another head *3 Hen. VI.* ii 1 141
Accursed, For making me, so young, so old a widow! *Richard III.* iv 1 73
She had all the royal makings of a queen; As holy oil *Hen. VIII.* iv 1 87
The making of the cake, the heating of the oven *Troi. and Cres.* i 1 23
How many shallow bauble boats dare sail Upon her patient breast, making their way With those of nobler bulk! i 3 36
She's making her ready, she'll come straight iii 2 31
That doth seek her, Not making any scruple of her soilure iv 1 56
Making parties strong And feebling such as stand not in their liking Below their cobbled shoes *Coriolanus* i 1 198
Making not reservation of yourselves, Still your own foes iii 3 130
Making the mother, wife and child to see The son, the husband and the father tearing His country's bowels out v 3 101
Give the all-hail to thee, and cry 'Be blest For making up this peace!' v 3 140
Wisely too fair, To merit bliss by making me despair *Rom. and Jul.* i 1 228
You share all that he doth possess, By having him, making yourself no less i 3 94
Making them women of good carriage i 4 94
I'ld exchange For this one wish, that you had power and wealth To requite me, by making rich yourself *T. of Athens* iv 3 529
Making your wills The scope of justice v 4 4
To see thy Antony making his peace *J. Cæsar* iii 1 197
The multitudinous seas incarnadine, Making the green one red *Macbeth* ii 2 63
Why do you keep alone, Of sorriest fancies your companions making? iii 2 9
The feast is sold That is not often vouch'd, while 'tis a-making iii 4 34
Extinct in both, Even in their promise, as it is a-making *Hamlet* i 3 119
Revisit'st thus the glimpses of the moon, Making night hideous i 4 54
Stew'd in corruption, honeying and making love Over the nasty sty iii 4 93
Making so bold, My fears forgetting manners v 2 16
Yet was his mother fair; there was good sport at his making *Lear* i 1 24
Thought, by making this well known unto you, To have found a safe redress i 4 224
Making just report Of how unnatural and bemadding sorrow iii 1 37
Are now making the beast with two backs *Othello* i 1 117
Make the Moor thank me, love me and reward me, For making him egregiously an ass ii 1 318
Thy honesty and love doth mince this matter, Making it light to Cassio ii 3 248
How do you mean, removing of him?—Why, by making him uncapable iv 2 235
Making peace or war As thou affect'st *Ant. and Cleo.* i 3 70
Who With half the bulk o' the world play'd as I pleased, Making and marring fortunes iii 11 65
If she remain unseduced, you not making it appear otherwise *Cymbeline* i 4 174
You knights of Tyre Are excellent in making ladies trip *Pericles* ii 3 103
But immortality attends the former [virtue], Making a man a god iii 2 31

Mala. Nothing but this; 'tis 'bona terra, mala gens' *2 Hen. VI.* iv 7 61

Maladies. And abstinence engenders maladies *L. L. Lost* iv 3 295

Malady. Not an eye that sees you but is a physician to comment on your malady . . . *T. G. of Ver.* ii 1 42
In peril to incur your former malady . *T. of Shrew* Ind. 2 124
And yet my heart Will not confess he owes the malady . *All's Well* i 1 9
To prostitute our past-cure malady To empirics . . ii 1 124
A malady Most incident to maids . . *W. Tale* iv 4 124
It is the disease of not listening, the malady of not marking . *2 Hen. IV.* i 2 139
My Nell is dead i' the spital Of malady of France . *Hen. V.* v 1 87
See, see the pining malady of France; Behold the wounds *1 Hen. VI.* iii 3 49
Of man and beast the infinite malady Crust you quite o'er! *T. of Athens* iii 6 108
Their malady convinces The great assay of art . *Macbeth* iv 3 142
Where the greater malady is fix'd, The lesser is scarce felt *Lear* iii 4 8
Malapert. Untutor'd lad, thou art too malapert . . *3 Hen. VI.* v 5 32
I must have an ounce or two of this malapert blood from you *T. Night* iv 1 47
Peace, master marquess, you are malapert . *Richard III.* i 3 255
Malchus. King Malchus of Arabia . . *Ant. and Cleo.* iii 6 72
Malcolm. We will establish our estate upon Our eldest, Malcolm *Macbeth* i 4 38
Banquo and Donalbain! Malcolm! awake! Shake off this downy sleep! ii 3 80
Malcolm! Banquo! As from your graves rise up, and walk like sprites! ii 3 83
Malcolm and Donalbain, the king's two sons, Are stol'n away and fled . ii 4 25
How monstrous it was for Malcolm and for Donalbain To kill their gracious father? damned fact! . . . iii 6 9
The English power is near, led on by Malcolm, His uncle Siward . . v 2 1
What's the boy Malcolm? Was he not born of woman? . . v 3 3
I will not yield, To kiss the ground before young Malcolm's feet v 8 28
Malcontent. To wreathe your arms, like a malecontent . *T. G. of Ver.* ii 1 20
Thou art the Mars of malecontents . . *Mer. Wives* i 3 113
Liege of all loiterers and malcontents . . . *L. L. Lost* iii 1 185
You stand pensive, as half malcontent . *3 Hen. VI.* iv 1 10
Is it for a wife that thou art malcontent? I will provide thee . iv 1 60
Male. Sir John! art thou there, my deer? my male deer? *Mer. Wives* v 5 19
A meaner woman was delivered Of such a burden, male twins *Com. of Er.* i 1 56
The beasts, the fishes and the winged fowls Are their males' subjects . ii 1 19
For since the birth of Cain, the first male child, To him that did but yesterday suspire, There was not such a gracious creature born *K. John* iii 4 79
So the son of the female is the shadow of the male . *2 Hen. IV.* iii 2 141
Making many fish-meals, that they fall into a kind of male green-sickness iv 3 100
Sole heir male Of the true line and stock of Charles the Great *Hen. V.* i 2 70
You love the breeder better than the male . *3 Hen. VI.* ii 1 42
And I, the hapless male to one sweet bird . . v 6 15
That my lady's womb, If it conceived a male child by me, should Do no more offices of life to't than The grave does to the dead; for her male issue Or died where they were made, or shortly after *Hen. VIII.* ii 4 189
Male varlet, you rogue! what's that?—Why, his masculine whore *Troi. and Cres.* v 1 19
No more mercy in him than there is milk in a male tiger *Coriolanus* v 4 30
For thy undaunted mettle should compose Nothing but males *Macbeth* i 7 74
Malediction. Menaces and maledictions against king and nobles *Lear* i 2 160
Malefaction. Been struck so to the soul that presently They have proclaim'd their malefactions . . . *Hamlet* ii 2 621
Malefactor. Benefactors? Well; what benefactors are they? are they not malefactors? . . . . . . *Meas. for Meas.* ii 1 52
Which be the malefactors?—Marry, that am I and my partner *Much Ado* iv 2 3
Fie upon 'But yet!' 'But yet' is as a gaoler to bring forth Some monstrous malefactor . . . *Ant. and Cleo.* ii 5 53
Malevolence. That the malevolence of fortune nothing Takes from his high respect . . . . *Macbeth* iii 6 28
Malevolent to you in all aspects . . . . *1 Hen. IV.* i 1 97
Malice. Shrug'st thou, malice? . . . . *Tempest* i 2 367
If your knowledge be more it is much darkened in your malice *M. for M.* iii 2 157
Lead'st this fashion of thy malice To the last hour of act *Mer. of Venice* iv 1 18
If this will not suffice, it must appear That malice bears down truth . iv 1 214
His malice 'gainst the lady Will suddenly break forth *As Y. Like It* i 2 294
I rather will subject me to the malice Of a diverted blood . ii 3 36
In mine own direct knowledge, without any malice . *All's Well* iii 6 9
By the very fangs of malice I swear, I am not that I play *T. Night* i 5 196
How with a sportful malice it was follow'd, May rather pluck on laughter v 1 373
There is not in the world either malice or matter to alter it . *W. Tale* i 1 37
Our cannons' malice vainly shall be spent . *K. John* ii 1 251
And both conjointly bend Your sharpest deeds of malice on this town . ii 1 380
There is no malice in this burning coal . . iv 1 109
These . . . armies might combine The blood of malice in a vein of league v 2 38
Hast thou sounded him, If he appeal the duke on ancient malice? *Rich. II.* i 1 9
No inveterate malice . . . . . . i 1 14
Deep malice makes too deep incision; Forget, forgive . . i 1 155
As the malice of this age shapes them . *2 Hen. IV.* i 2 195
Is not quite exempt From envious malice of thy swelling heart *1 Hen. VI.* iii 1 26
An uproar, I dare warrant, Begun through malice of the bishop's men . iii 1 75
I have heard you preach That malice was a great and grievous sin . iii 1 128
Will not this malice, Somerset, be left? . . . iv 1 108
For he hath witness of his servant's malice . *2 Hen. VI.* i 3 213
Churchmen so hot? good uncle, hide such malice . . ii 1 25
No malice, sir; no more than well becomes So good a quarrel . ii 1 27
Beaufort's red sparkling eyes blab his heart's malice . . iii 1 154
God forbid any malice should prevail, That faultless may condemn a nobleman! . . . . . . iii 2 23
Though fortune's malice overthrow my state, My mind exceeds *3 Hen. VI.* iv 3 46
May seem as wise as virtuous, By spying and avoiding fortune's malice iv 6 28
Proceeds From wayward sickness, and no grounded malice *Richard III.* i 3 29
Lest, by a multitude, The new-heal'd wound of malice should break out ii 2 125
Read The cardinal's malice and his potency Together . *Hen. VIII.* i 1 105
The law I bear no malice for my death . . . ii 1 62
If ever any malice in your heart Were hid against me . . ii 1 80
Have, out of malice To the good queen, possess'd him with a scruple . ii 1 157
A gracious king that pardons all offences Malice ne'er meant . ii 2 69
Till I find more than will or words to do it, I mean your malice, know, officious lords, I dare and must deny it . . . iii 2 237
Follow your envious courses, men of malice . . . iii 2 243
How innocent I was From any private malice in his end . iii 2 268
You are potently opposed; and with a malice Of as great size . v 1 134
This is a piece of malice . . . . . v 2 8
God turn their hearts! I never sought their malice . . v 2 15
Men that make Envy and crooked malice nourishment Dare bite the best v 3 44
More out of malice than integrity, Would try him to the utmost . v 3 145
Was rather, If there be faith in men, meant for his trial, And fair purgation to the world, than malice . . . . v 3 152
Wit larded with malice and malice forced with wit . *Troi. and Cres.* v 1 63
What I think I utter, and spend my malice in my breath . *Coriolanus* ii 1 58
But they Upon their ancient malice will forget . . . his new honours . ii 1 244
Malice. To seem to affect the malice and displeasure of the people is as bad as that which he dislikes, to flatter them for their love *Coriol.* ii 2 24
To report otherwise, were a malice . . . . ii 2 36
And Translate his malice towards you into love . . . ii 3 197
And witness of the malice and displeasure Which thou shouldst bear me iv 5 78
And present My throat to thee and to thy ancient malice . . iv 5 102
And with the deepest malice of the war Destroy what lies before 'em . iv 6 41
The venomous malice of my swelling heart . *T. Andron.* v 3 13
No levell'd malice Infects one comma in the course I hold *T. of Athens* i 1 47
'Tis in the malice of mankind that he thus advises us . . iv 3 456
Our arms, in strength of malice, and our hearts Of brothers' temper, do receive you in . . . . . . *J. Cæsar* iii 1 174
Against the undivulged pretence I fight Of treasonous malice *Macbeth* ii 3 138
Whilst our poor malice Remains in danger of her former tooth . iii 2 14
Malice domestic, foreign levy, nothing, Can touch him further . iii 2 25
You shall do small respect, show too bold malice . . *Lear* ii 2 137
One that, in the authority of her merit, did justly put on the vouch of very malice itself . . . . . *Othello* ii 1 148
A punishment more in policy than in malice . . . ii 3 275
What malice was between you?—None in the world; nor do I know the man . . . . v 1 102
Speak of me as I am; nothing extenuate, Nor set down aught in malice v 2 343
And taunt my faults With such full license as both truth and malice Have power to utter . . . *Ant. and Cleo.* i 2 112
Will not trust one of her malice with A drug of such damn'd nature *Cymb.* i 5 35
She looks us like A thing more made of malice than of duty . . iii 5 33
Malice and lucre in them Have laid this woe here . . iv 2 324
Kneel not to me: The power that I have on you is to spare you; The malice towards you to forgive you . . . . v 5 419
Malicious. This hot malicious day . . . *K. John* ii 1 314
And none your foes but such as shall pretend Malicious practices *1 Hen. VI.* iv 1 7
We must not stint Our necessary actions, in the fear To cope malicious censurers . . . . . . *Hen. VIII.* i 2 78
Whom, yet once more, I hold my most malicious foe . . ii 4 83
Hear me speak his good now?—Yes, good Griffith; I were malicious else iv 2 48
Confess yourselves wondrous malicious, Or be accused of folly *Coriolanus* i 1 91
Do not take His rougher accents for malicious sounds . . iii 3 55
Sudden, malicious, smacking of every sin That has a name . *Macbeth* iv 3 59
Invulnerable, And our vain blows malicious mockery . *Hamlet* i 1 146
When she saw Pyrrhus make malicious sport In mincing with his sword her husband's limbs . . . . ii 2 536
How malicious is my fortune, that I must repent to be just! . *Lear* iii 5 10
Upon malicious bravery, dost thou come To start my quiet . *Othello* i 1 100
Maliciously. Nay, but speak not maliciously . . . *Coriolanus* i 1 35
A lingering dram that should not work Maliciously like poison *W. Tale* i 2 321
I will be treble-sinew'd . . . And fight maliciously *Ant. and Cleo.* iii 13 179
Malign. You malign our senators for that They are not such as you *Cor.* i 1 117
Though wayward fortune did malign my state . . *Pericles* v 1 90
Malignancy. My stars shine darkly over me: the malignancy of my fate might perhaps distemper yours . . . *T. Night* ii 1 4
Malignant. Thou liest, malignant thing! . . . *Tempest* i 2 257
No more; unless the next word that thou speak'st Have some malignant power upon my life . . . *T. G. of Ver.* iii 1 238
Hearing your high majesty is touch'd With that malignant cause *All's W.* ii 1 114
But, O malignant and ill-boding stars . . *1 Hen. VI.* iv 5 6
Are crack'd in pieces by malignant death . *Richard III.* ii 2 52
To your high person His will is most malignant . *Hen. VIII.* i 2 141
Where a malignant and a turban'd Turk Beat a Venetian . *Othello* v 2 353
Malignantly. If he should still malignantly remain Fast foe . *Coriolanus* iii 3 191
Malkin. The kitchen malkin pins Her richest lockram 'bout her reechy neck . . . . ii 1 224
Blurted at and held a malkin Not worth the time of day . *Pericles* iv 3 34
Mall. The gunner and his mate Loved Mall, Meg and Marian . *Tempest* ii 2 50
Are they like to take dust, like Mistress Mall's picture? . *T. Night* i 3 135
Mallard. Like a doting mallard . . . *Ant. and Cleo.* iii 10 20
Malleable. And make the rest malleable . . *Pericles* iv 6 152
Mallecho. This is miching mallecho; it means mischief . *Hamlet* iii 2 147
Mallet. There's no more conceit in him than is in a mallet . *2 Hen. IV.* ii 4 263
Mallow. He'ld sow't with nettle-seed.—Or docks, or mallows *Tempest* ii 1 144
Malmsey. Metheglin, wort, and malmsey . . *L. L. Lost* v 2 233
Malmsey-butt. We will chop him in the malmsey-butt . *Richard III.* i 4 161
If all this will not do, I'll drown you in the malmsey-butt . i 4 277
Malmsey-nose. That arrant malmsey-nose knave . *2 Hen. IV.* ii 1 42
Malt. When brewers mar their malt with water . . *Lear* iii 2 82
Malt-horse. Mome, malt-horse, capon, coxcomb, idiot! . *Com. of Errors* iii 1 32
You whoreson malt-horse drudge! . . . *T. of Shrew* iv 1 132
Malt-worm. Mad mustachio purple-hued malt-worms . *1 Hen. IV.* ii 1 83
And his face is Lucifer's privy-kitchen, where he doth nothing but roast malt-worms . . . . . *2 Hen. IV.* ii 4 361
Malvolio. What think you of this fool, Malvolio? . . *T. Night* i 5 79
You are sick of self-love, Malvolio, and taste with a distempered appetite i 5 97
I did impeticos thy gratillity; for Malvolio's nose is no whipstock . ii 3 27
Called up her steward Malvolio and bid him turn you out of doors . ii 3 77
My lady's a Cataian, we are politicians, Malvolio's a Peg-a-Ramsey . ii 3 81
For Monsieur Malvolio, let me alone with him: if I do not gull him . ii 3 145
Get ye all three into the box-tree: Malvolio's coming down this walk . ii 5 18
To be Count Malvolio!—Ah, rogue!—Pistol him, pistol him . . ii 5 40
'No man must know:' if this should be thee, Malvolio? . . ii 5 113
M,—Malvolio; M,—why, that begins my name.—Did not I say he would work it out? . . . . ii 5 137
Yond gull Malvolio is turned heathen, a very renegado . . iii 2 74
Where is Malvolio? he is sad and civil, And suits well for a servant . iii 4 5
How now, Malvolio!—Sweet lady, ho, ho.—Smilest thou? . . iii 4 17
Wilt thou go to bed, Malvolio?—To bed! ay, sweetheart . . iii 4 32
Fellow! not Malvolio, nor after my degree, but fellow . . iii 4 85
Sir Topas the curate, who comes to visit Malvolio the lunatic . iv 2 26
Malvolio, Malvolio, thy wits the heavens restore! . . . iv 2 103
He upon some action Is now in durance, at Malvolio's suit . v 1 283
And speak out of my injury. THE MADLY-USED MALVOLIO . . v 1 319
How now, Malvolio!—Madam, you have done me wrong, Notorious wrong v 1 336
Alas, Malvolio, this is not my writing, Though, I confess, much like . v 1 353
I confess, myself and Toby Set this device against Malvolio here . v 1 368
Mamillius. Your young prince Mamillius . . . *W. Tale* i 1 38
Mamillius, Art thou my boy?—Ay, my good lord . . . i 2 119
Go play, Mamillius; thou'rt an honest man . . . i 2 211
Mammering. I wonder in my soul, What you would ask me, that I should deny, Or stand so mammering on . . . *Othello* iii 3 70
Mammet. This is no world To play with mammets . . *1 Hen. IV.* ii 3 95
A wretched puling fool, A whining mammet . . *Rom. and Jul.* iii 5 186

Mammocked.—O, I warrant, how he mammocked it! . . . *Coriolanus* i 3 71
Man. Me, poor man, my library Was dukedom large enough *Tempest* i 2 109
Would I might But ever see that man! . . . i 2 169
Ferdinand, With hair up-staring, . . . Was the first man that leap'd . i 2 214
This is the third man that e'er I saw, the first That e'er I sigh'd for . i 2 445
And hast put thyself Upon this island as a spy . —No, as I am a man i 2 456
I have no ambition To see a goodlier man . . . i 2 483
This man's threats, To whom I am subdued, are but light to me . . i 2 488
No marrying 'mong his subjects?—None, man; all idle . . ii 1 166
She that dwells Ten leagues beyond man's life . . . ii 1 247
What have we here? a man or a fish! dead or alive? . . ii 2 25
There would this monster make a man; any strange beast there makes a man . . . ii 2 32
Legged like a man! and his fins like arms? . . . ii 2 35
Misery acquaints a man with strange bed-fellows . . ii 2 41
This is a very scurvy tune to sing at a man's funeral . . ii 2 46
As proper a man as ever went on four legs cannot make him give ground ii 2 63
Swum ashore, man, like a duck: I can swim like a duck . ii 2 133
Hast any more of this?—The whole butt, man . . . ii 2 137
I'll bear him no more sticks, but follow thee, Thou wondrous man . ii 2 168
'Ban, 'Ban, Cacaliban Has a new master: get a new man . . ii 2 189
Was there ever man a coward that hath drunk so much sack as I to-day? iii 2 30
Monster, I will kill this man: his daughter and I will be king and queen iii 2 114
If thou beest a man, show thyself in thy likeness . . iii 2 137
On this island Where man doth not inhabit . . . iii 3 57
Here thought they to have done Some wanton charm upon this man and maid . . . iv 1 95
Holy Gonzalo, honourable man . . . v 1 62
Ferdinand . . . found a wife Where he himself was lost, . . . and all of us ourselves When no man was his own . . v 1 213
Every man shift for all the rest, and let no man take care for himself . v 1 256
He cannot be a perfect man, Not being tried and tutor'd *T. G. of Ver.* i 3 20
So painted, to make her fair, that no man counts of her beauty . ii 1 65
O jest unseen, inscrutable, invisible, As a nose on a man's face . ii 1 142
What's the matter? why weepest thou, man? Away, ass! . ii 3 38
It is the unkindest tied that ever any man tied . . ii 3 42
Why, man, if the river were dry, I am able to fill it with my tears . ii 3 58
Come away, man; I was sent to call thee.—Sir, call me what thou darest ii 3 61
Let her alone.—Not for the world: why, man, she is mine own . ii 4 168
I reckon this always, that a man is never undone till he be hanged . ii 5 5
Fearing lest my jealous aim might err And so unworthily disgrace the man iii 1 29
That man that hath a tongue, I say, is no man, If with his tongue he cannot win a woman . . . iii 1 104
Kept severely from resort of men, That no man hath access by day to her iii 1 109
And keys kept safe, That no man hath recourse to her by night . iii 1 112
She can knit.—What need a man care for a stock with a wench, when she can knit him a stock? . . . iii 1 311
For thee! ay, who art thou? he hath stayed for a better man than thee iii 1 385
We'll hear him.—Ay, by my beard, will we, for he's a proper man . iv 1 10
I have little wealth to lose: A man I am cross'd with adversity . iv 1 12
I kill'd a man, whose death I much repent; But yet I slew him manfully iv 1 27
A man of such perfection As we do in our quality much want . iv 1 57
Because you are a banish'd man, Therefore, above the rest, we parley to you . . . iv 1 59
How now! are you sadder than you were before? How do you, man? . iv 2 55
I tell you what Launce, his man, told me: he loved her out of all nick iv 2 75
Thou subtle, perjured, false, disloyal man! Think'st thou I am so shallow? . . . iv 2 95
When a man's servant shall play the cur with him, look you, it goes hard iv 4 1
How use doth breed a habit in a man! . . . v 4 1
Treacherous man! Thou hast beguiled my hopes . . v 4 63
O heaven! were man But constant, he were perfect . . v 4 110
Your grace is welcome to a man disgraced . . . v 4 123
It is a familiar beast to man, and signifies love . . *Mer. Wives* i 1 21
Where's Simple, my man? Can you tell, cousin?—Peace, I pray you . i 1 136
Go, sirrah, for all you are my man, go wait upon my cousin Shallow . i 1 281
A justice of peace sometime may be beholding to his friend for a man . i 1 284
But I shall as soon quarrel at it as any man in England . . . i 2 303
A softly-sprighted man, is he not?—Ay, forsooth: but he is as tall a man of his hands as any is between this and his head . . . i 4 26
Run in here, good young man; go into this closet: he will not stay long i 4 39
If he had found the young man, he would have been horn-mad . . i 4 51
Ay me, he'll find the young man there, and be mad! . . . i 4 68
The young man is an honest man.—What shall de honest man do in my closet? dere is no honest man dat shall come in my closet . . i 4 75
But notwithstanding, man, I'll do you your master what good I can . i 4 97
I will find you twenty lascivious turtles ere one chaste man . . . ii 1 83
My good man too; he's as far from jealousy as I am from giving him cause ii 1 107
Though the priest o' the town commended him for a true man . . ii 1 150
A man may be too confident: I would have nothing lie on my head . ii 1 193
I do relent: what would thou more of man? . . . ii 2 31
He's a very jealousy man: she leads a very frampold life with him . ii 2 93
I never knew a woman so dote upon a man: surely I think you have charms . . . ii 2 107
Page is an honest man. Never a wife in Windsor leads a better life than she ii 2 121
You have been a man long known to me . . . ii 2 187
Like a fair house built on another man's ground . . . ii 2 224
If any man may, you may as soon as any . . . ii 2 245
Would any man have thought this? See the hell of having a false woman! ii 2 304
He is no come.—He is the wiser man, master doctor . . ii 3 39
You have yourself been a great fighter, though now a man of peace . ii 3 44
A man of his place, gravity and learning, so wide of his own respect . iii 1 57
I warrant you, he's the man should fight with him . . iii 1 70
I had rather, forsooth, go before you like a man than follow him like a dwarf . . . iii 2 6
There is such a league between my good man and he! . . iii 2 26
A man may hear this shower sing in the wind . . . iii 2 37
Having an honest man to your husband, to give him such cause of suspicion! . . . iii 3 107
Pray heaven it be not so, that you have such a man here! . . iii 3 120
If it be my luck, so; if not, happy man be his dole! . . iii 4 68
A death that I abhor; for the water swells a man . . iii 5 16
Bid her think what a man is: let her consider his frailty . . iii 5 51
Think of that,—a man of my kidney,—think of that,—that am as subject to heat as butter; a man of continual dissolution and thaw iii 5 116
I'll but bring my young man here to school . . . iv 1 8
Why then you are utterly shamed, and he's but a dead man . . iv 2 44
As I am a man, there was one conveyed out of my house yesterday . iv 2 151
If you find a man there, he shall die a flea's death.—Here's no man iv 2 157
The very same man that beguiled Master Slender of his chain cozened him iv 5 37

Man. More than the villanous inconstancy of man's disposition is able to bear . . . *Mer. Wives* iv 5 111
I went to her, Master Brook, as you see, like a poor old man; but I came from her, Master Brook, like a poor old woman . . v 1 17
In the shape of man, Master Brook, I fear not Goliath with a weaver's beam . . . v 1 23
No man means evil but the devil, and we shall know him by his horns v 2 15
O powerful love! that, in some respects, makes a beast a man, in some other, a man a beast . . . v 5 6
I'll wink and couch: no man their works must eye . . v 5 52
Round about the tree. But, stay; I smell a man of middle-earth . v 5 84
Nor do I think the man of safe discretion That does affect it *M. for M.* i 1 72
Yonder man is carried to prison.—Well; what has he done?—A woman i 2 87
A man of stricture and firm abstinence . . . i 3 12
It is a man's voice . . . i 4 7
A man whose blood Is very snow-broth . . . i 4 57
Prove it before these varlets here, thou honourable man; prove it . ii 1 89
This very man, having eaten the rest [of the prunes], as I said . ii 1 104
A man of fourscore pound a year; whose father died at Hallowmas . ii 1 127
Ask him what this man did to my wife.—I beseech your honour, ask me ii 1 149
The time is yet to come that she was ever respected with man, woman, or child . . . ii 1 176
Here is the sister of the man condemn'd Desires access to you . ii 2 18
You might pardon him, And neither heaven nor man grieve at the mercy . . . ii 2 50
Mercy then will breathe within your lips, Like man new made . . ii 2 79
But man, proud man, Drest in a little brief authority, Most ignorant of what he's most assured . . . ii 2 117
A young man More fit to do another such offence Than die for this . ii 3 13
Love you the man that wrong'd you?—Yes, as I love the woman that wrong'd him . . . ii 3 24
My gravity, Wherein—let no man hear me—I take pride . . ii 4 10
It were as good To pardon him that hath from nature stolen A man already made, as to remit Their saucy sweetness that do coin heaven's image In stamps that are forbid . . . ii 4 44
With an outstretch'd throat I'll tell the world aloud What man thou art ii 4 154
O dishonest wretch! Wilt thou be made a man out of my vice? . iii 1 138
What corruption in this life, that it will let this man live! . . iii 1 242
What offence hath this man made you, sir? . . . iii 2 15
Is the world as it was, man? Which is the way? Is it sad, and few words? . . . iii 2 53
Not made by man and woman after this downright way of creation . iii 2 112
For the rebellion of a codpiece to take away the life of a man! . iii 2 123
Ere he would have hanged a man for the getting a hundred bastards, he would have paid for the nursing a thousand . . iii 2 125
Be good to me; your honour is accounted a merciful man . . iii 2 203
O, what may man within him hide, Though angel on the outward side! iii 2 285
Here comes a man of comfort . . . iv 1 8
Can you cut off a man's head?—If the man be a bachelor, sir, I can; but if he be a married man, he's his wife's head . . iv 2 2
Every true man's apparel fits your thief: if it be too little for your thief, your true man thinks it big enough . . . iv 2 48
This is his lordship's man.—And here comes Claudio's pardon . iv 2 103
A man that apprehends death no more dreadfully but as a drunken sleep . . . iv 2 149
Master Starve-lackey the rapier and dagger man . . iv 3 16
I will not die to-day for any man's persuasion . . . iv 3 63
A man of Claudio's years; his beard and head Just of his colour . iv 3 76
Good morning to you, fair and gracious daughter.—The better, given me by so holy a man . . . iv 3 117
I know him; 'tis a meddling friar; I do not like the man . . v 1 128
I know him for a man divine and holy; Not scurvy . . v 1 144
A man that never yet Did, as he vouches, misreport your grace . v 1 147
I am affianced this man's wife as strongly As words could make up vows v 1 227
Is't not enough thou hast suborn'd these women To accuse this worthy man? . . . v 1 309
Is this the man that you did tell us of?—'Tis he, my lord . . v 1 327
For this new-married man approaching here, . . . you must pardon . v 1 405
I crave no other, nor no better man . . . v 1 431
Look, if it please you, on this man condemn'd, As if my brother lived . v 1 449
There was a friar told me of this man . . . v 1 484
Nay, forward, old man; do not break off so . *Com. of Errors* i 1 97
Many a man would take you at your word, And go indeed . . i 2 17
Let us dine and never fret: A man is master of his liberty . . ii 1 7
Here comes your man; now is your husband nigh . . ii 1 43
No man that hath a name, By falsehood and corruption doth it shame . ii 1 112
Was there ever any man thus beaten out of season? . . ii 2 48
There's no time for a man to recover his hair that grows bald by nature ii 2 73
To pay a fine for a periwig and recover the lost hair of another man . ii 2 77
There's many a man hath more hair than wit.—Not a man of those but he hath the wit to lose his hair . . . ii 2 83
Whilst man and master laugh my woes to scorn . . . ii 2 207
It would make a man mad as a buck, to be so bought and sold . iii 1 72
A man may break a word with you, sir, and words are but wind . iii 1 75
Am I your man? am I myself?—Thou art Dromio, thou art my man . iii 2 74
I am an ass, I am a woman's man and besides myself.—What woman's man? . . . iii 2 77
Such a one as a man may not speak of without he say 'Sir-reverence' . iii 2 92
A man may go over shoes in the grime of it . . . iii 2 106
As from a bear a man would run for life, So fly I from her . . iii 2 159
You are a merry man, sir: fare you well . . . iii 2 183
There's no man is so vain That would refuse so fair an offer'd chain . iii 2 185
I see a man here needs not live by shifts . . . iii 2 187
A man is well holp up that trusts to you . . . iv 1 22
Why, man, what is the matter?—I do not know the matter . . iv 2 41
There's not a man I meet but doth salute me . . . iv 3 1
The man, sir, that, when gentlemen are tired, gives them a sob and 'rests them . . . iv 3 24
The sergeant of the band; he that brings any man to answer it . . iv 3 31
One that thinks a man always going to bed . . . iv 3 32
Your man and you are marvellous merry, sir . . . iv 3 59
Fear me not, man; I will not break away . . . iv 4 1
Here comes my man; I think he brings the money . . . iv 4 8
I charge thee, Satan, housed within this man, To yield possession . iv 4 57
Both man and master is possess'd . . . iv 4 95
Ay me, poor man, how pale and wan he looks! . . . iv 4 111
Go bind this man, for he is frantic too.—What wilt thou do? . iv 4 116
Hast thou delight to see a wretched man Do outrage . . . to himself? . iv 4 118
Do you know him?—I know the man. What is the sum he owes? . iv 4 136
How is the man esteem'd here in the city?—Of very reverend reputation v 1 4

Man. How long hath this possession held the man?—This week he hath been heavy, sour, sad, And much different from the man he was *Com. of Errors* v 1 44
And thereof came it that the man was mad v 1 68
To be disturb'd, would mad or man or beast v 1 84
With . . . drugs and holy prayers, To make of him a formal man again v 1 105
My master and his man are both broke loose, Beaten the maids a-row v 1 169
And the while His man with scissors nicks him like a fool v 1 175
Thy master and his man are here, And that is false thou dost report to us v 1 178
A needy, hollow-eyed, sharp-looking wretch, A living-dead man v 1 241
In a dark and dankish vault at home There left me and my man v 1 248
I was his bondman, sir, But he, I thank him, gnaw'd in two my cords: Now am I Dromio and his man unbound v 1 290
Whatsoever a man denies, you are now bound to believe him v 1 305
Most mighty duke, behold a man much wrong'd v 1 330
Which is the natural man, And which the spirit? v 1 333
If thou be'st the man That hadst a wife once call'd Æmilia v 1 341
This purse of ducats I received from you And Dromio my man did bring them me v 1 386
We still did meet each other's man, And I was ta'en for him, and he for me v 1 387
What is he to a lord?—A lord to a lord, a man to a man *Much Ado* i 1 56
A stuffed man: but for the stuffing,—well, we are all mortal i 1 59
In our last conflict four of his five wits went halting off, and now is the whole man governed with one i 1 67
We may guess by this what you are, being a man i 1 111
I had rather hear my dog bark at a crow than a man swear he loves me i 1 133
Do you question me, as an honest man should do? i 1 167
Come, in what key shall a man take you, to go in the song? i 1 188
Hath not the world one man but he will wear his cap with suspicion? i 1 200
I can be secret as a dumb man; I would have you think so i 1 212
Here you may see Benedick the married man i 1 270; v 1 186; v 4 100
In mine orchard, were thus much overheard by a man of mine i 2 11
I must be sad when I have cause and smile at no man's jests i 3 15
Eat when I have stomach and wait for no man's leisure i 3 16
Sleep when I am drowsy and tend on no man's business i 3 18
Laugh when I am merry and claw no man in his humour i 3 19
Though I cannot be said to be a flattering honest man i 3 32
He were an excellent man that were made just in the midway ii 1 7
Such a man would win any woman in the world, if a' could get her good-will ii 1 16
He that hath a beard is more than a youth, and he that hath no beard is less than a man: and he that is more than a youth is not for me, and he that is less than a man, I am not for him ii 1 40
You could never do him so ill-well, unless you were the very man ii 1 123
You may do the part of an honest man in it ii 1 173
Now you strike like the blind man: 'twas the boy that stole your meat ii 1 205
I stood like a man at a mark, with a whole army shooting at me ii 1 254
While she is here, a man may live as quiet in hell as in a sanctuary ii 1 265
I do much wonder that one man, seeing how much another man is a fool when he dedicates his behaviours to love, will, after he hath laughed at such shallow follies in others, become the argument of his own scorn by falling in love: and such a man is Claudio ii 3 8
To speak plain and to the purpose, like an honest man and a soldier ii 3 20
I did never think that lady would have loved any man ii 3 97
He'll scorn it; for the man, as you know all, hath a contemptible spirit.—He is a very proper man ii 3 187
The man doth fear God, howsoever it seems not in him by some large jests he will make ii 3 204
A man loves the meat in his youth that he cannot endure in his age ii 3 247
Shall quips and sentences and these paper bullets of the brain awe a man from the career of his humour? ii 3 250
Let it be thy part To praise him more than ever man did merit iii 1 19
He doth deserve As much as may be yielded to a man iii 1 48
I never yet saw man, How wise, how noble, young, how rarely featured, But she would spell him backward iii 1 59
So turns she every man the wrong side out iii 1 68
He is the only man of Italy, Always excepted my dear Claudio iii 1 92
Hath any man seen him at the barber's?—No, but the barber's man hath been seen with him iii 2 43
Who, Hero?—Even she; Leonato's Hero, your Hero, every man's Hero iii 2 110
Who think you the most desartless man to be constable? iii 3 10
To be a well-favoured man is the gift of fortune iii 3 15
The most senseless and fit man for the constable of the watch iii 3 23
You are to bid any man stand, in the prince's name iii 3 26
If you meet a thief, you may suspect him by virtue of your office, to be no true man iii 3 54
You have been always called a merciful man, partner iii 3 65
I would not hang a dog by my will, much more a man who hath any honesty in him iii 3 67
With any man that knows the statues, he may stay him iii 3 84
The watch ought to offend no man; and it is an offence to stay a man iii 3 87
Here, man; I am at thy elbow.—Mass, and my elbow itched; I thought there would a scab follow iii 3 105
The fashion of a doublet, or a hat, or a cloak, is nothing to a man iii 3 126
I see that the fashion wears out more apparel than the man iii 3 149
My heart is exceeding heavy.—'Twill be heavier soon by the weight of a man iii 4 27
Yet Benedick was such another, and now is he become a man iii 4 88
An old man, sir, and his wits are not so blunt as, God help, I would desire iii 5 11
I am as honest as any man living that is an old man and no honester iii 5 16
I hear as good exclamation on your worship as of any man in the city; and though I be but a poor man, I am glad to hear it iii 5 29
A good old man, sir; he will be talking iii 5 36
Well, God's a good man; an two men ride of a horse, one must ride behind iii 5 40
What man was he talk'd with you yesternight Out at your window? iv 1 84
I talk'd with no man at that hour, my lord iv 1 87
Hath no man's dagger here a point for me? iv 1 110
Lady, what man is he you are accused of?—They know that do accuse me iv 1 178
If I know more of any man alive Than that which maiden modesty doth warrant iv 1 180
Prove you that any man with me conversed At hours unmeet iv 1 183
Ah, how much might the man deserve of me that would right her iv 1 263
May a man do it?—It is a man's office, but not yours iv 1 267
That I were a man! I would eat his heart in the market-place iv 1 308
Talk with a man out at a window! A proper saying! iv 1 311

Man. O that I were a man for his sake! or that I had any friend would be a man for my sake! *Much Ado* iv 1 319
I cannot be a man with wishing, therefore I will die a woman with grieving iv 1 325
And I of him will gather patience. But there is no such man v 1 20
'Tis all men's office to speak patience . . . But no man's virtue nor sufficiency To be so moral when he shall endure The like himself v 1 29
Nay, do not quarrel with us, good old man v 1 50
Tush, tush, man; never fleer and jest at me v 1 58
Do challenge thee to trial of a man v 1 66
My villany?—Thine, Claudio; thine, I say.—You say not right, old man v 1 73
Thou hast kill'd my child: If thou kill'st me, boy, thou shalt kill a man v 1 79
Dare as well answer a man indeed As I dare take a serpent by the tongue v 1 89
What, man! I know them, yea, And what they weigh v 1 92
See, see; here comes the man we went to seek v 1 110
As I am an honest man, he looks pale. Art thou sick, or angry?—What, courage, man! What though care killed a cat v 1 130
At last she concluded with a sigh, thou wast the properest man in Italy v 1 174
She would love him dearly: the old man's daughter told us all v 1 179
What a pretty thing man is when he goes in his doublet and hose and leaves off his wit! v 1 202
He is then a giant to an ape; but then is an ape a doctor to such a man v 1 206
Who in the night overheard me confessing to this man v 1 241
Let me see his eyes, That, when I note another man like him, I may avoid him v 1 270
To satisfy this good old man, I would bend under any heavy weight v 1 286
This naughty man Shall face to face be brought to Margaret v 1 306
In so high a style, Margaret, that no man living shall come over it v 2 7
To have no man come over me! why, shall I always keep below stairs? v 2 9
There's not one wise man among twenty that will praise himself v 2 76
If a man will be beaten with brains, a' shall wear nothing handsome v 4 104
For man is a giddy thing, and this is my conclusion v 4 109
If any man be seen to talk with a woman within the term of three years, he shall endure such public shame as the rest of the court can possibly devise *L. L. Lost* i 1 130
Every man with his affects is born, Not by might master'd i 1 152
A man in all the world's new fashion planted i 1 165
A man of complements, whom right and wrong Have chose as umpire i 1 169
A most illustrious wight, A man of fire-new words, fashion's own knight i 1 179
It is the manner of a man to speak to a woman i 1 212
Such is the simplicity of man to hearken after the flesh i 1 219
Peace!—Be to me and every man that dares not fight!—No words! i 1 229
A man of good repute, carriage, bearing, and estimation i 1 271
I'll lay my head to any good man's hat i 1 310
What sign is it when a man of great spirit grows melancholy? i 2 1
They are both the varnish of a complete man i 2 47
Samson, master: he was a man of good carriage i 2 73
Maid!—Man?—I will visit thee at the lodge i 2 139
I thank God I have as little patience as another man i 2 171
The sole inheritor Of all perfections that a man may owe ii 1 6
Know you the man?—I know him, madam ii 1 39
A man of sovereign parts he is esteem'd ii 1 44
But a merrier man, Within the limit of becoming mirth, I never spent an hour's talk withal ii 1 66
Your hands in your pocket like a man after the old painting iii 1 21
What wilt thou prove?—A man, if I live; and this, by, in, and without iii 1 41
My sweet ounce of man's flesh! my incony Jew! iii 1 136
How much carnation ribbon may a man buy for a remuneration? iii 1 147
That was a man when King Pepin of France was a little boy iv 1 122
Thou canst not hit it, hit it, hit it, Thou canst not hit it, my good man iv 1 128
O, a most dainty man! To see him walk before a lady and to bear her fan! iv 1 146
Ovidius Naso was the man: and why, indeed, Naso? iv 2 127
Whither away so fast? A true man or a thief that gallops so? iv 3 187
Like a rude and savage man of Inde iv 3 222
I never knew man hold vile stuff so dear iv 3 276
Then homeward every man attach the hand Of his fair mistress iv 3 375
True wit!—Offered by a child to an old man; which is wit-old v 1 65
A soldier, a man of travel, that hath seen the world v 1 113
Not a man of them shall have the grace, Despite of suit v 2 128
'Tis our will That some plain man recount their purposes v 2 176
You took the moon at full, but now she's changed.—Yet still she is the moon, and I the man v 2 215
I am, as they say, but to parfect one man in one poor man v 2 503
Doth this man serve God?—Why ask you?—He speaks not like a man of God's making.—That is all one v 2 528
A foolish mild man; an honest man, look you, and soon dashed v 2 584
A man so breathed, that certain he would fight; yea From morn till night v 2 659
Beat not the bones of the buried: when he breathed, he was a man v 2 668
No more man's blood in's belly than will sup a flea v 2 697
I will not fight with a pole, like a northern man: I'll slash v 2 701
The world's large tongue Proclaims you for a man replete with mocks v 2 853
A dowager Long withering out a young man's revenue *M. N. Dream* i 1 7
My noble lord, This man hath my consent to marry her i 1 25
This man hath bewitch'd the bosom of my child i 1 27
Devoutly dotes, dotes in idolatry, Upon this spotted and inconstant man i 1 110
Ere a man hath power to say 'Behold!' The jaws of darkness do devour it up i 1 147
You were best to call them generally, man by man i 2 3
Here is the scroll of every man's name, which is thought fit i 2 4
I will roar, that I will do any man's heart good to hear me i 2 73
A sweet-faced man; a proper man, as one shall see in a summer's day; a most lovely gentleman-like man i 2 88
Will make or man or woman madly dote ii 1 171
Thou shalt know the man By the Athenian garments he hath on ii 1 263
The will of man is by his reason sway'd ii 2 115
Is't not enough, young man, That I did never, no, nor never can? ii 2 125
That a lady, of one man refused, Should of another therefore be abused! ii 2 133
I am no such thing; I am a man as other men are iii 1 45
Some man or other must present Wall iii 1 69
The plain-song cuckoo gray, Whose note full many a man doth mark iii 1 135
This is the same Athenian.—This is the woman, but not this the man iii 2 42
Fate o'er-rules, that, one man holding troth, A million fail iii 2 92
You are a tame man, go! iii 2 259
Did not you tell me I should know the man By the Athenian garments? iii 2 348
That every man should take his own, In your waking shall be shown iii 2 459

Man. The man shall have his mare again, and all shall be well *M. N. D.* iii 2 463
I have had a dream, past the wit of man to say what dream it was iv 1 211
Man is but an ass, if he go about to expound this dream iv 1 212
Methought I was—there is no man can tell what iv 1 213
Man is but a patched fool, if he will offer to say what methought I had iv 1 215
The eye of man hath not heard, the ear of man hath not seen, man's hand is not able to taste, his tongue to conceive, nor his heart to report iv 1 217
You have not a man in all Athens able to discharge Pyramus but he iv 2 7
He hath simply the best wit of any handicraft man in Athens iv 2 10
Every man look o'er his part iv 2 38
This man is Pyramus, if you would know v 1 130
This man, with lime and rough-cast, doth present Wall, that vile Wall v 1 132
They are content To whisper. At the which let no man wonder v 1 135
This man, with lanthorn, dog, and bush of thorn, Presenteth Moonshine v 1 136
Here come two noble beasts in, a man and a lion v 1 220
The death of a dear friend would go near to make a man look sad v 1 294
Beshrew my heart, but I pity the man v 1 295
An ace for him; for he is but one.—Less than an ace, man; for he is dead v 1 314
Which Pyramus, which Thisbe, is the better; he for a man, God warrant us; she for a woman, God bless us v 1 326
A stage where every man must play a part, And mine a sad one *M. of Ven.* i 1 78
Why should a man, whose blood is warm within, Sit like his grandsire? i 1 83
Gratiano speaks an infinite deal of nothing, more than any man i 1 114
God made him, and therefore let him pass for a man i 2 61
He is every man in no man; if a throstle sing, he falls straight a capering i 2 65
A proper man's picture, but, alas, who can converse with a dumb-show? i 2 77
When he is best, he is a little worse than a man i 2 95
My meaning in saying he is a good man is to have you understand me that he is sufficient i 3 16
The man is, notwithstanding, sufficient i 3 26
Your worship was the last man in our mouths i 3 61
A pound of man's flesh taken from a man Is not so estimable i 3 166
Play at dice Which is the better man, the greater throw May turn by fortune from the weaker hand ii 1 33
Being an honest man's son, or rather an honest woman's son ii 2 16
Master young man, you, I pray you, which is the way to master Jew's? ii 2 34
No master, sir, but a poor man's son: his father, though I say it, is an honest exceeding poor man ii 2 53
But I pray you, ergo, old man, ergo, I beseech you ii 2 59
Well, old man, I will tell you news of your son: give me your blessing ii 2 81
Murder cannot be hid long; a man's son may ii 2 84
I am Launcelot, the Jew's man ii 2 94
O rare fortune! here comes the man ii 2 119
A poor boy,— Not a poor boy, sir, but the rich Jew's man ii 2 131
As my father, being, I hope, an old man, shall frutify unto you ii 2 142
This honest old man; and, though I say it, though old man, yet poor man ii 2 148
If any man in Italy have a fairer table ii 2 167
Eleven widows and nine maids is a simple coming-in for one man ii 2 172
Many a man his life hath sold But my outside to behold ii 7 67
None of thee [silver], thou pale and common drudge 'Tween man and man iii 2 104
Nothing in the world Could turn so much the constitution Of any constant man iii 2 250
Never did I know A creature, that did bear the shape of man, So keen and greedy to confound a man iii 2 278
The kindest man, The best-condition'd and unwearied spirit iii 2 294
And use thou all the endeavour of a man In speed to Padua iii 4 48
Speak between the change of man and boy With a reed voice iii 4 66
I pray thee, understand a plain man in his plain meaning iii 5 62
This is no answer, thou unfeeling man iv 1 63
Do all men kill the things they do not love?—Hates any man the thing he would not kill? iv 1 67
Good cheer, Antonio! What, man, courage yet! iv 1 111
There is no power in the tongue of man To alter me iv 1 241
Prepare your bosom for his knife.—O noble judge! O excellent young man! iv 1 246
It is still her use To let the wretched man outlive his wealth iv 1 269
But, hark, I hear the footing of a man v 1 24
Sola, sola!—Leave hollaing, man: here.—Sola! where? where? v 1 43
The man that hath no music in himself, Nor is not moved with concord of sweet sounds, Is fit for treasons . . . : Let no such man be trusted v 1 83
He knows me as the blind man knows the cuckoo, By the bad voice v 1 112
This is the man, this is Antonio, To whom I am so infinitely bound v 1 134
He will, an if he live to be a man.—Ay, if a woman live to be a man v 1 159
And neither man nor master would take aught But the two rings v 1 183
What man is there so much unreasonable? v 1 203
The clerk that never means to do it, Unless he live until he be a man v 1 283
An envious emulator of every man's good parts *As Y. Like It* i 1 150
Love no man in good earnest; nor no further in sport neither i 2 30
There comes an old man and his three sons i 2 125
The poor old man, their father, making such pitiful dole over them i 2 138
Is yonder the man?—Even he, madam.—Alas, he is too young i 2 160
You will take little delight in it, . . . there is such odds in the man i 2 169
Young man, have you challenged Charles the wrestler?—No, fair princess i 2 178
You have seen cruel proof of this man's strength i 2 185
But come your ways.—Now Hercules be thy speed, young man! i 2 222
O excellent young man! i 2 225
Bear him away. What is thy name, young man?—Orlando, my liege i 2 233
I would thou hadst been son to some man else i 2 237
Had I before known this young man his son, I should have given him tears unto entreaties i 2 249
Were it not better, Because that I am more than common tall, That I did suit me all points like a man? i 3 118
What shall I call thee when thou art a man? i 3 125
Can it be possible that no man saw them? It cannot be ii 2 1
I'll do the service of a younger man In all your business and necessities ii 3 54
O good old man, how well in thee appears The constant service of the antique world, When service sweat for duty! ii 3 56
I could find in my heart to disgrace my man's apparel and to cry ii 4 5
Look you, who comes here; a young man and an old in solemn talk ii 4 20
As sure I think did never man love so ii 4 29
Question yond man If he for gold will give us any food ii 4 64
I am shepherd to another man And do not shear the fleeces that I graze ii 4 78

Man. Well then, if ever I thank any man, I'll thank you *As Y. Like It* ii 5 25
When a man thanks me heartily, methinks I have given him a penny ii 5 27
If it do come to pass That any man turn ass ii 5 53
I think he be transform'd into a beast; For I can no where find him like a man ii 7 2
If not, The wise man's folly is anatomized ii 7 56
Why then my taxing like a wild-goose flies, Unclaim'd of any man ii 7 87
Art thou thus bolden'd, man, by thy distress? ii 7 91
If ever sat at any good man's feast ii 7 115
An old poor man, Who after me hath many a weary step Limp'd in pure love ii 7 129
One man in his time plays many parts, His acts being seven ages ii 7 142
Blow, thou winter wind, Thou art not so unkind As man's ingratitude ii 7 176
Good old man, Thou art right welcome as thy master is ii 7 197
Is not the grease of a mutton as wholesome as the sweat of a man? iii 2 58
Most shallow man! thou worms-meat, in respect of a good piece of flesh! iii 2 67
God help thee, shallow man! God make incision in thee! thou art raw iii 2 75
I earn that I eat, get that I wear, owe no man hate, envy no man's happiness iii 2 78
How brief the life of man Runs his erring pilgrimage iii 2 137
Is it a man?—And a chain, that you once wore, about his neck iii 2 190
Dost thou think, though I am caparisoned like a man, I have a doublet and hose in my disposition? iii 2 205
That thou mightst pour this concealed man out of thy mouth iii 2 210
So you may put a man in your belly.—Is he of God's making? What manner of man? Is his head worth a hat? iii 2 215
Why, God will send more, if the man will be thankful iii 2 220
But doth he know that I am in this forest and in man's apparel? iii 2 243
Who ambles Time withal?—With a priest that lacks Latin and a rich man that hath not the gout iii 2 338
Who was in his youth an inland man iii 2 363
There is a man haunts the forest, that abuses our young plants with carving 'Rosalind' on their barks iii 2 377
He taught me how to know a man in love iii 2 388
You are no such man; you are rather point-device in your accoutrements iii 2 401
Am I the man yet? doth my simple feature content you? iii 3 3
When a man's verses cannot be understood, nor a man's good wit seconded with the forward child Understanding, it strikes a man more dead than a great reckoning in a little room iii 3 12
A man may, if he were of a fearful heart, stagger in this attempt iii 3 48
It is said, 'many a man knows no end of his goods' iii 3 53
Many a man has good horns, and knows no end of them iii 3 54
Is the single man therefore blessed? No iii 3 59
So is the forehead of a married man more honourable than the bare brow of a bachelor iii 3 61
Is there none here to give the woman?—I will not take her on gift of any man iii 3 69
As the ox hath his bow, sir, the horse his curb, and the falcon her bells, so man hath his desires iii 3 81
Being a man of your breeding, be married under a bush like a beggar? iii 3 84
Have the grace to consider that tears do not become a man iii 4 3
But what talk we of fathers, when there is such a man as Orlando? iii 4 42
O, that's a brave man! he writes brave verses, speaks brave words iii 4 43
You are a thousand times a properer man Than she a woman iii 5 51
Down on your knees, And thank heaven, fasting, for a good man's love iii 5 58
You are not for all markets: Cry the man mercy; love him; take his offer iii 5 61
Chide a year together: I had rather hear you chide than this man woo iii 5 65
I shall think it a most plenteous crop To glean the broken ears after the man That the main harvest reaps iii 5 102
He's proud, and yet his pride becomes him: He'll make a proper man iii 5 115
There was not any man died in his own person, videlicet, in a love-cause iv 1 96
A man that had a wife with such a wit, he might say 'Wit, whither wilt?' iv 1 167
And that she could not love me, Were man as rare as phœnix iv 3 17
This is a man's invention and his hand iv 3 29
Whiles the eye of man did woo me, That could do no vengeance to me iv 3 47
If you will know of me What man I am iv 3 97
A wretched ragged man, o'ergrown with hair iv 3 107
With catlike watch, When that the sleeping man should stir iv 3 117
Orlando did approach the man And found it was his brother iv 3 120
Be of good cheer, youth: you a man! you lack a man's heart iv 3 164
Well then, take a good heart and counterfeit to be a man iv 3 175
He hath no interest in me in the world: here comes the man you mean v 1 9
The fool doth think he is wise, but the wise man knows himself to be a fool v 1 35
How bitter a thing it is to look into happiness through another man's eyes! v 2 49
I will satisfy you, if ever I satisfied man, and you shall be married v 2 125
If any man doubt that, let him put me to my purgation v 4 44
A poor humour of mine, sir, to take that that no man else will v 4 62
Where meeting with an old religious man v 4 166
Welcome, young man; Thou offer'st fairly to thy brothers' wedding v 4 172
I will practise on this drunken man *T. of Shrew* Ind. 1 36
A mighty man of such descent, Of such possessions, and so high esteem Ind. 2 15
Such names and men as these Which never were nor no man ever saw Ind. 2 98
If I can by any means light on a fit man to teach her i 1 112
Any man is so very a fool to be married to hell i 1 128
Why, man, there be good fellows in the world, an a man could light on them i 1 132
Happy man be his dole! He that runs fastest gets the ring i 1 144
I will some other be, some Florentine, Some Neapolitan, or meaner man i 1 210
Since I came ashore I kill'd a man and fear I was descried i 1 237
Whom should I knock? is there any man has rebused your worship? i 2 7
And by good fortune I have lighted well On this young man i 2 169
And will not promise her to any man Until the elder sister first be wed i 2 262
You are the man Must stead us all and me amongst the rest i 2 265
I do present you with a man of mine, Cunning in music ii 1 55
A man well known throughout all Italy ii 1 69
A mighty man of Pisa; by report I know him well ii 1 105
Thou must be married to no man but me; For I am he am born to tame you ii 1 277
Was it not to refresh the mind of man After his studies or his usual pain? iii 1 11
And, to be noted for a merry man, He'll woo a thousand iii 2 14
A horse and a man Is more than one, And yet not many iii 2 86

Man. I am to get a man,—whate'er he be, It skills not much *T. of Shrew* iii 2 133
We are beset with thieves; Rescue thy mistress, if thou be a man iii 2 239
Was ever man so beaten? was ever man so rayed? was ever man so weary? . . . . iv 1 2
Considering the weather, a taller man than I will take cold . iv 1 11
But, thou knowest, winter tames man, woman and beast . iv 1 24
What, no man at door To hold my stirrup nor to take my horse! iv 1 123
Another way I have to man my haggard . . . . iv 1 196
A' will make the man mad, to make a woman of him . iv 5 35
Happier the man, whom favourable stars Allot thee for his lovely bed-fellow! . . . . iv 5 40
This is a man, old, wrinkled, faded, wither'd, And not a maiden iv 5 43
What if a man bring him a hundred pound or two, to make merry withal? . . . . v 1 22
Why, this is flat knavery, to take upon you another man's name v 1 38
How now! what's the matter?—What, is the man lunatic? v 1 74
How called you the man you speak of, madam? . . . *All's Well* i 1 27
Man is enemy to virginity; how may we barricado it against him? i 1 123
Man, sitting down before you, will undermine you and blow you up i 1 129
Virginity being blown down, man will quicklier be blown up. i 1 134
Such a man Might be a copy to these younger times . i 2 45
A man may draw his heart out, ere a' pluck one . i 3 92
That man should be at woman's command, and yet no hurt done! i 3 96
Then here's a man stands, that has brought his pardon . ii 1 65
If God have lent a man any manners, he may easily put it off at court . ii 2 8
As 'twere, a man assured of a— Uncertain life, and sure death ii 3 19
This is the man.—Why, then, young Bertram, take her; she's thy wife ii 3 111
To any count, to all counts, to what is man.—To what is count's man . ii 3 203
I write man; to which title age cannot bring thee . ii 3 208
I may say in the default, he is a man I know . . . ii 3 242
Methinks, thou art a general offence, and every man should beat thee . ii 3 270
France is a dog-hole, and it no more merits The tread of a man's foot ii 3 292
A young man married is a man that's marr'd . . ii 3 315
I say nothing.—Marry, you are the wiser man; for many a man's tongue shakes out his master's undoing . . . . . ii 4 23
The soul of this man is his clothes. Trust him not . ii 5 48
But like a common and an outward man . . . . iii 1 11
By my troth, I take my young lord to be a very melancholy man . iii 2 4
A man that had this trick of melancholy sold a goodly manor for a song iii 2 8
I begin to love, as an old man loves money, with no stomach . iii 2 17
He will steal himself into a man's favour . . . iii 6 99
Therefore we must every one be a man of his own fancy . iv 1 19
On the reading it he changed almost into another man . iv 3 6
He has every thing that an honest man should not have; what an honest man should have, he has nothing . . . . . . iv 3 290
I would do the man what honour I can, but of this I am not certain . iv 3 303
There's place and means for every man alive . . . iv 3 375
A fool, sir, at a woman's service, and a knave at a man's . iv 5 26
I would cozen the man of his wife and do his service . iv 5 28
Most courteous feathers, which bow the head and nod at every man . iv 5 112
This man may help me to his majesty's ear, If he would spend his power . . . . v 1 7
If your metaphor stink, I will stop my nose; or against any man's metaphor . . . . v 2 14
I am a man whom fortune hath cruelly scratched . . v 2 28
I saw the man to-day, if man he be.—Find him, and bring him hither . v 3 203
I am a poor man, and at your majesty's command . . v 3 251
If ever I knew man, 'twas you.—Wherefore hast thou accused him? . v 3 288
I am either maid, or else this old man's wife . . . v 3 294
I have no more wit than a Christian or an ordinary man *T. Night* i 3 90
Tut, there's life in't, man.—I'll stay a month longer . i 3 118
Art thou good at these kickshawses, knight?—As any man in Illyria . i 3 124
And yet I will not compare with an old man . . . i 3 126
I think I have the back-trick simply as strong as any man . i 3 132
They shall yet belie thy happy years, That say thou art a man . i 4 31
And I, that am sure I lack thee, may pass for a wise man . i 5 38
Bid the dishonest man mend himself; if he mend, he is no longer dishonest . . . . i 5 50
No railing in a known discreet man, though he do nothing but reprove i 5 103
A fair young man, and well attended . . . . i 5 111
What's a drunken man like, fool?—Like a drowned man, a fool, and a mad man . . . . i 5 138
What kind o' man is he?—Why, of mankind.—What manner of man? i 5 159
Not yet old enough for a man, nor young enough for a boy . i 5 165
'Tis with him in standing water, between boy and man . i 5 169
Unless the master were the man . . . . . i 5 313
Run after that same peevish messenger, The county's man . i 5 320
None of my lord's ring! why, he sent her none. I am the man . ii 2 26
As I am man, My state is desperate . . . . ii 2 37
Journeys end in lovers meeting, Every wise man's son doth know . ii 3 45
Tillyvally. Lady! 'There dwelt a man in Babylon, lady, lady!' ii 3 84
'Twere as good a deed as to drink when a man's a-hungry . ii 3 136
My father had a daughter loved a man, As it might be, perhaps, were I a woman, I should your lordship . . . . ii 4 110
Jove knows I love: But who? Lips, do not move; No man must know ii 5 110
'No man must know:' if this should be thee, Malvolio? . ii 5 112
I will be point-devise the very man . . . . ii 5 178
This is a practice As full of labour as a wise man's art . iii 1 73
Your wife is like to reap a proper man . . . . iii 1 144
No love-broker in the world can more prevail in man's commendation . iii 2 40
For, sure, the man is tainted in's wits . . . iii 4 13
Why, how dost thou, man? what is the matter with thee? . iii 4 26
No worse man than Sir Toby to look to me! . . . iii 4 72
How is't with you, man?—Go off; I discard you . . iii 4 98
What, man! defy the devil: consider, he's an enemy to mankind . iii 4 107
I am sure no man hath any quarrel to me: my remembrance is very free and clear from any image of offence done to any man . . . iii 4 247
Hath in him what youth, strength, skill and wrath can furnish man withal . . . . iii 4 255
Belike this is a man of that quirk.—Sir, no . . . iii 4 268
What manner of man is he?—Nothing of that wonderful promise . iii 4 288
Why, man, he's a very devil; I have not seen such a firago . iii 4 301
A little thing would make me tell them how much I lack of a man . iii 4 333
This is the man; do thy office.—Antonio, I arrest thee . iii 4 359
Lest that it make me so unsound a man As to upbraid you . iii 4 384
I hate ingratitude more in a man Than lying, vainness, babbling . iii 4 388
The man grows mad: away with him! Come, come, sir . iii 4 405
He has heard that word of some great man and now applies it to a fool iv 1 13
To be said an honest man and a good housekeeper goes as fairly as to say a careful man and a great scholar . . . . . . iv 2 10
Man. How vexest thou this man! talkest thou nothing but of ladies? *T. Night* iv 2 30
Never was man thus wronged: good Sir Topas, do not think I am mad iv 2 32
I say, there was never man thus abused . . . . iv 2 51
There was never man so notoriously abused . . . iv 2 94
I tell thee, I am as well in my wits as any man in Illyria . iv 2 115
Now go with me and with this holy man Into the chantry by . iv 3 23
What do you say?—I'll follow this good man, and go with you . iv 3 32
Here comes the man, sir, that did rescue me . . . v 1 53
You are betroth'd both to a maid and man . . . v 1 270
He holds Belzebub at the staves's end as well as a man in his case may do . . . . v 1 292
Cesario, come; For so you shall be, while you are a man . v 1 395
When I came to man's estate . . . . . . v 1 402
They that went on crutches ere he was born desire yet their life to see him a man . . . . *W. Tale* i 1 45
My lord, I'll fight.—You will! why, happy man be's dole! . i 2 163
And many a man there is, even at this present, Now while I speak this i 2 192
Go play, Mamillius; thou'rt an honest man . . . i 2 211
Negligent, foolish and fearful; In every one of these no man is free . i 2 251
For cogitation Resides not in that man that does not think . . i 2 272
Would I do this? Could man so blench?—I must believe you, sir . i 2 333
I conjure thee, by all the parts of man Which honour does acknowledge i 2 400
He does conceive He is dishonour'd by a man which ever Profess'd to him . . . . i 2 455
There was a man— Nay, come, sit down; then on.—Dwelt by a churchyard . . . . ii 1 29
You smell this business with a sense as cold As is a dead man's nose . ii 1 152
Would by combat make her good, so were I A man, the worst about you ii 3 61
All I know of it Is that Camillo was an honest man . iii 2 75
Whom I proclaim a man of truth, of mercy . . . iii 2 158
What ailest thou, man?—I have seen two such sights, by sea and by land! . . . . iii 3 83
Would I had been by, to have helped the old man! . . iii 3 111
You're a made old man: if the sins of your youth are forgiven you . iii 3 124
A man, they say, that from very nothing, and beyond the imagination of his neighbours, is grown into an unspeakable estate . . iv 2 44
I have heard, sir, of such a man, who hath a daughter of most rare note iv 2 47
Alas, poor man! a million of beating may come to a great matter . iv 3 62
I know this man well: he hath been since an ape-bearer . iv 3 100
He hath songs for man or woman, of all sizes . . iv 4 191
He makes the maid to answer 'Whoop, do me no harm, good man' iv 4 200
Fear not thou, man, thou shalt lose nothing here.—I hope so, sir . iv 4 258
A passing merry one and goes to the tune of 'Two maids wooing a man' iv 4 295
Had force and knowledge More than was ever man's . . iv 4 386
Can he speak? hear? Know man from man? dispute his own estate? . iv 4 411
You have undone a man of fourscore three . . . iv 4 464
That I may call thee something more than man And after that trust to thee . . . . iv 4 546
My clown, who wants but something to be a reasonable man . iv 4 617
Had not the old man come in with a whoo-bub against his daughter . iv 4 628
Why shakest thou so? Fear not, man; here's no harm intended to thee iv 4 642
I see this is the time that the unjust man doth thrive . iv 4 688
Every shop, church, session, hanging, yields a careful man work.—See, see; what a man you are now! . . . . iv 4 701
Who, I may say, is no honest man, neither to his father nor to me . iv 4 719
A great man, I'll warrant; I know by the picking on's teeth . iv 4 779
Will break the back of man, the heart of monster . . iv 4 797
Has the old man e'er a son, sir, do you hear, an't like you, sir? . iv 4 810
If it be in man besides the king to effect your suits, here is man shall do it . . . . iv 4 828
And leave this young man in pawn till I bring it you . iv 4 838
I will give you as much as this old man does when the business is performed . . . . iv 4 852
We are blest in this man, as I may say, even blest . . iv 4 858
Destroy'd the sweet'st companion that e'er man Bred his hopes out of . v 1 11
Women will love her, that she is a woman More worth than any man . v 1 111
To greet a man not worth her pains, much less The adventure of her person . . . . v 1 155
I brought the old man and his son aboard the prince . . v 2 124
Excels whatever yet you look'd upon Or hand of man hath done . v 3 17
Let no man mock me, For I will kiss her . . . . v 3 79
Out on thee, rude man! thou dost shame thy mother *K. John* i 1 64
Some tokens of my son In the large composition of this man . i 1 88
Why then I suck my teeth and catechize My picked man of countries . i 1 193
Old sir Robert's son? Colbrand the giant, that same mighty man? . i 1 225
Then, good my mother, let me know my father; Some proper man, I hope i 1 250
Young Plantagenet, Son to the elder brother of this man . ii 1 239
He is the half part of a blessed man, Left to be finished by such as she ii 1 437
For thy word Is but the vain breath of a common man . iii 1 8
This news hath made thee a most ugly man . . . iii 1 37
O, that a man should speak those words to me! . . iii 1 130
By the merit of vile gold, dross, dust, Purchase corrupted pardon of a man iii 1 166
Hubert shall be your man, attend on you With all true duty . iii 3 72
Life is as tedious as a twice-told tale Vexing the dull ear of a drowsy man iii 4 109
Many a poor man's son would have lien still . . . iv 1 50
This is the man should do the bloody deed . . . iv 2 69
Impatience hath his privilege.—'Tis true, to hurt his master, no man else iv 3 33
That self mould that fashion'd thee Made him a man . *Richard II.* i 2 24
Against what man thou comest, and what thy quarrel . i 3 13
All places that the eye of heaven visits Are to a wise man ports . i 3 276
For gnarling sorrow hath less power to bite The man that mocks at it . i 3 293
How fares our noble uncle, Lancaster?—What comfort, man? . ii 1 72
Out with it boldly, man; Quick is mine ear to hear of good towards him ii 1 233
The king's grown bankrupt, like a broken man . . . ii 1 257
Thou art a banish'd man, and here art come Before the expiration . ii 3 110
For every man that Bolingbroke hath press'd . . ., God for his Richard hath in heavenly pay A glorious angel . . . . . . iii 2 58
Dogs, easily won to fawn on any man! . . . . iii 2 130
Of comfort no man speak: Let's talk of graves, of worms . iii 2 144
Speak sweetly, man, although thy looks be sour . . iii 2 193
Let no man speak again To alter this, for counsel is but vain. . iii 2 213
That laid the sentence of dread banishment On yon proud man . iii 3 135
Sorrow and grief of heart Makes him speak fondly, like a frantic man . iii 3 185
What serpent, hath suggested thee To make a second fall of cursed man? iii 4 76
Cousin, stand forth, and look upon that man . . . iv 1 7
What answer shall I make to this base man? . . . iv 1 20
Will no man say amen? Am I both priest and clerk? well then, amen iv 1 172
No lord of thine, thou haught insulting man, Nor no man's lord . iv 1 255
No man cried 'God save him!' No joyful tongue gave him his welcome v 2 28

Man. He is as like thee as a man may be, Not like to me, or any of my kin *Richard II.* v 2 108
Can no man tell me of my unthrifty son? v 3 1
Turn the key, That no man enter till my tale be done v 3 37
The traitor lives, the true man's put to death v 3 73
Believe not this hard-hearted man! Love loving not itself none other can v 3 87
I would thou wert the man that would divorce this terror from my heart v 4 8
Nor I nor any man that but man is With nothing shall be pleased v 5 39
What art thou? and how comest thou hither, Where no man never comes? v 5 70
And break the neck Of that proud man that did usurp his back v 5 89
Thou, created to be awed by man, Wast born to bear v 5 91
For wisdom cries out in the streets, and no man regards it *1 Hen. IV.* i 2 100
Now am I, if a man should speak truly, little better than one of the wicked i 2 105
'Tis my vocation, Hal; 'tis no sin for a man to labour in his vocation i 2 117
The most omnipotent villain that ever cried 'Stand' to a true man i 2 122
I shall never hold that man my friend Whose tongue shall ask me for one penny i 3 90
You, that set the crown Upon the head of this forgetful man i 3 161
As truly as a man of falsehood may ii 1 71
Thou shalt have a share in our purchase, as I am a true man ii 1 101
As good a deed as drink, to turn true man and to leave these rogues ii 2 24
Happy man be his dole, say I: every man to his business ii 2 80
There is nothing but roguery to be found in villanous man ii 4 139
Why, you whoreson round man, what's the matter? ii 4 155
I never dealt better since I was a man: all would not do ii 4 188
They were not bound.—You rogue, they were bound, every man of them ii 4 197
I would give no man a reason upon compulsion, I ii 4 265
Give him as much as will make him a royal man, and send him back ii 4 321
What manner of man is he?—An old man ii 4 323
A plague of sighing and grief! it blows a man up like a bladder ii 4 366
There is a virtuous man whom I have often noted in thy company ii 4 460
What manner of man, an it like your majesty?—A goodly portly man ii 4 462
If that man should be lewdly given, he deceiveth me ii 4 469
A devil haunts thee in the likeness of an old fat man; a tun of man ii 4 493
My lord, the man I know.—I know thou dost ii 4 510
If I become not a cart as well as another man, a plague on my bringing up! ii 4 546
A gross fat man.—As fat as butter.—The man, I do assure you, is not here ii 4 560
I will, by to-morrow dinner-time, Send him to answer thee, or any man ii 4 565
I think there's no man speaks better Welsh iii 1 49
I can call spirits from the vasty deep.—Why, so can I, or so can any man iii 1 53
That man is not alive Might so have tempted him as you have done iii 1 173
The soul of every man Prophetically doth forethink thy fall iii 2 37
I make as good use of it as many a man doth of a Death's-head iii 3 34
Man by man, boy by boy, servant by servant iii 3 65
How doth thy husband? I love him well; he is an honest man iii 3 108
He speaks most vilely of you, like a foul-mouthed man as he is iii 3 123
I would thou shouldst know it; I am an honest man's wife iii 3 137
A man knows not where to have her.—Thou art an unjust man in saying so: thou or any man knows where to have me iii 3 144
As thou art but man, I dare: but as thou art prince, I fear thee iii 3 166
I have more flesh than another man, and therefore more frailty iii 3 188
A braver place In my heart's love hath no man than yourself iv 1 8
No man so potent breathes upon the ground But I will beard him iv 1 11
Yea, every man Shall be my friend again and I'll be his v 1 107
That no man might draw short breath to-day But I and Harry Monmouth! v 2 49
He gave you all the duties of a man; Trimm'd up your praises v 2 56
I profess not talking; only this—Let each man do his best v 2 93
Farewell! I could have better spared a better man v 4 104
He is but the counterfeit of a man who hath not the life of a man v 4 117
Did you not tell me this fat man was dead?—I did; I saw him dead v 4 135
I am not a double man; but if I be not Jack Falstaff, then am I a Jack v 4 142
If the man were alive and would deny it, 'zounds, I would make him eat a piece of my sword v 4 155
Not a man of them brings other news *2 Hen. IV.* Ind. 38
This man's brow, like to a title-leaf, Foretells the nature i 1 60
Even such a man, so faint, so spiritless, So dull, so dead in look i 1 70
He is a man Who with a double surety binds his followers i 1 190
Counsel every man The aptest way for safety and revenge i 1 212
The brain of this foolish-compounded clay, man, is not able to invent any thing that tends to laughter i 2 9
Crowing as if he had writ man ever since his father was a bachelor i 2 30
If a man is through with them in honest taking up i 2 45
You lie in your throat, if you say I am any other than an honest man i 2 98
All the other gifts appertinent to man, as the malice of this age shapes them, are not worth a gooseberry i 2 194
If ye will needs say I am an old man, you should give me rest i 2 243
A man can no more separate age and covetousness than a' can part young limbs and lechery i 2 256
And that we now possess'd The utmost man of expectation i 3 65
He will spare neither man, woman, nor child ii 1 18
What man of good temper would endure this tempest of exclamation? ii 1 87
I owe thee?—Marry, if thou wert an honest man, thyself and the money too ii 1 92
If a man will make courtesy and say nothing, he is virtuous ii 1 135
Let the end try the man ii 2 51
It would be every man's thought; and thou art a blessed fellow to think as every man thinks ii 2 60
Never a man's thought in the world keeps the road-way better than thine ii 2 62
Every man would think me an hypocrite indeed ii 2 63
Every man must know that, as oft as he has occasion to name himself ii 2 119
I will bar no honest man my house, nor no cheater ii 4 111
I'll drink no more than will do me good, for no man's pleasure, I ii 4 129
Whether the fiery Trigon, his man, be not lisping to his master's old tables ii 4 289
The undeserver may sleep, when the man of action is called on ii 4 406
But an honester and truer-hearted man,—well, fare thee well ii 4 414
It is but eight years since This Percy was the man nearest my soul iii 1 61
A man may prophesy, With a near aim, of the main chance of things iii 1 82
It would have done a man's heart good to see iii 2 54
I knew him a good backsword man. How doth the good knight? iii 2 70
That is, when a man is, as they say, accommodated; or when a man is, being, whereby a' may be thought to be accommodated iii 2 85
But if he had been a man's tailor, he'ld ha' pricked you iii 2 163
I would thou wert a man's tailor, that thou mightst mend him iii 2 175
A man can die but once: we owe God a death iii 2 250
No man is too good to serve's prince iii 2 253
How to choose a man? Care I for the limb, the thewes, the stature, bulk, and big assemblance of a man! Give me the spirit iii 2 276
Give me this man: he presents no mark to the enemy iii 2 284
Like a man made after supper of a cheese-paring iii 2 332

Man. An iron man, Cheering a rout of rebels with your drum *2 Hen. IV.* iv 2 8
That man that sits within a monarch's heart, And ripens in the sunshine iv 2 11
We ready are to try our fortunes To the last man iv 2 44
Are not you Sir John Falstaff?—As good a man as he, sir iv 3 12
Nor a man cannot make him laugh; but that's no marvel iv 3 95
This little kingdom, man iv 3 118
Doth the man of war stay all night? v 1 31
An honest man, sir, is able to speak for himself, when a knave is not v 1 50
If I cannot once or twice in a quarter bear out a knave against an honest man, I have but a very little credit v 1 54
That no man could better command his servants v 1 83
Though no man be assured what grace to find, You stand in coldest expectation v 2 30
Happy am I, that have a man so bold, That dares do justice on my proper son v 2 108
I did not think Master Silence had been a man of this mettle v 3 41
Is't so? Why then, say an old man can do somewhat v 3 82
Not the ill wind which blows no man to good v 3 90
I pray thee now, deliver them like a man of this world v 3 102
Thy tender lambkin now is king; Harry the Fifth's the man v 3 123
Let us take any man's horses; the laws of England are at my commandment v 3 142
There hath been a man or two lately killed about her v 4 7
The man is dead that you and Pistol beat amongst you v 4 19
You thin man in a censer, I will have you as soundly swinged for this v 4 20
Speak to that vain man.—Have you your wits? know you what 'tis you speak? v 5 48
I know thee not, old man: fall to thy prayers v 5 51
I have long dream'd of such a kind of man, So surfeit-swell'd, so old v 5 53
I will be the man yet that shall make you great v 5 85
For Oldcastle died a martyr, and this is not the man Epil. 34
Into a thousand parts divide one man *Hen. V.* Prol. 24
When the man dies, let the inheritance Descend unto the daughter i 2 99
Therefore doth heaven divide The state of man in divers functions i 2 184
I have laid by my majesty And plodded like a man for working-days i 2 277
Let every man now task his thought i 2 309
And honour's thought Reigns solely in the breast of every man ii Prol. 4
And it will endure cold as another man's sword will ii 1 10
Nay, but the man that was his bedfellow ii 2 8
No doubt, my liege, if each man do his best.—I doubt not that ii 2 19
Enlarge the man committed yesterday, That rail'd against our person ii 2 40
We'll yet enlarge that man ii 2 57
And this man Hath, for a few light crowns, lightly conspired ii 2 88
Thus thy fall hath left a kind of blot, To mark the full-fraught man ii 2 139
This revolt of thine, methinks, is like Another fall of man ii 2 142
He's in Arthur's bosom, if ever man went to Arthur's bosom ii 3 10
Quoth I: 'what, man! be o' good cheer.' So a' cried out 'God, God, God!' ii 3 19
In peace there's nothing so becomes a man As modest stillness iii 1 3
But all they three, though they would serve me, could not be man to me; for indeed three such antics do not amount to a man iii 2 32
A' never broke any man's head but his own, and that was against a post iii 2 43
As well as any military man in the world iii 2 86
I do not know you so good a man as myself iii 2 143
A man that I love and honour with my soul, and my heart, and my duty iii 6 7
He is a man of no estimation in the world iii 6 15
Let gallows gape for dog; let man go free iii 6 44
He is not the man that he would gladly make show to the world he is iii 6 87
I can tell your majesty, the duke is a prave man iii 6 101
I think the duke hath lost never a man, but one iii 6 105
One Bardolph, if your majesty know the man: his face is all bubukles iii 6 107
The man hath no wit that cannot, from the rising of the lark to the lodging of the lamb, vary deserved praise on my palfrey iii 7 33
Though I speak it to you, I think the king is but a man, as I am iv 1 106
His ceremonies laid by, in his nakedness he appears but a man iv 1 110
No man should possess him with any appearance of fear iv 1 115
Therefore should every soldier in the wars do as every sick man in his bed iv 1 188
'Tis certain, every man that dies ill, the ill upon his own head iv 1 197
God's will! I pray thee, wish not one man more iv 3 23
We would not die in that man's company That fears iv 3 38
This story shall the good man teach his son iv 3 56
Perish the man whose mind is backward now! iv 3 72
The man that once did sell the lion's skin While the beast lived, was kill'd with hunting him iv 3 93
I had not so much of man in me, And all my mother came into mine eyes iv 6 30
Not a man of them that we shall take Shall taste our mercy iv 7 67
I need not to be ashamed of your majesty, praised be God, so long as your majesty is an honest man iv 7 120
If any man challenge this, he is a friend to Alençon iv 7 163
I would fain see the man, that has but two legs iv 7 169
I met this man with my glove in his cap iv 8 32
You appeared to me but as a common man iv 8 54
De tongues of de mans is be full of deceits v 2 122
As man and wife, being two, are one in love v 2 389
What say'st thou, man, before dead Henry's corse? Speak softly *1 Hen VI.* i 1 62
While I live, I'll ne'er fly from a man i 2 103
A baser man of arms by far i 4 30
O Lord, have mercy on me, woful man! i 4 71
That she may boast she hath beheld the man Whose glory fills the world ii 2 42
Is this the man?—Madam, it is.—Is this the scourge of France? ii 3 14
What means this silence? Dare no man answer in a case of truth? ii 4 2
So evident That it will glimmer through a blind man's eye ii 4 24
Even like a man new haled from the rack, So fare my limbs ii 5 3
More than well beseems A man of thy profession and degree iii 1 20
We know your grace to be a man Just and upright iii 1 94
Becomes it thee to taunt his valiant age And twit with cowardice a man half dead? iii 2 55
What is the trust or strength of foolish man? iii 2 112
Why, what is he? as good a man as York.—Hark ye; not so iii 4 36
This fact was infamous And ill beseeming any common man iv 1 31
No simple man that sees This jarring discord . . . But that it doth presage some ill event iv 1 187
Lo, there thou stand'st, a breathing valiant man iv 2 31
Sell every man his life as dear as mine, And they shall find dear deer iv 2 53
No more my fortune can, But curse the cause I cannot aid the man iv 3 44
That ever living man of memory iv 3 51
A man of great authority in France v 1 18
A proper man; No shape but his can please your dainty eye v 3 37
Fond man, remember that thou hast a wife v 3 80
He talks at random; sure, the man is mad v 3 84
You have suborn'd this man, Of purpose to obscure my noble birth v 4 21

Man. A married man! that's most intolerable . . . . *1 Hen. VI.* v 4 79
Yet, in substance and authority, Retain but privilege of a private man v 4 136
More like a soldier than a man o' the church . . *2 Hen. VI.* i 1 186
Were I a man, a duke, and next of blood, I would remove these . . i 2 63
Nay, fear not, man, We are alone; here's none but thee and I . i 2 68
What say'st thou, man? hast thou as yet conferr'd With Margery Jourdain? . . . . i 2 74
Make merry, man, With thy confederates in this weighty cause . i 2 85
The Lord protect him, for he's a good man! Jesu bless him! . i 3 6
York is meetest man To be your regent in the realm of France.— . . .
York is most unmeet of any man . . . . . i 3 163
Why should I hold my peace?—Because here is a man accused of treason i 3 180
This is the man That doth accuse his master of high treason . i 3 184
Do not cast away an honest man for a villain's accusation . . i 3 206
The spite of man prevaileth against me. O Lord, have mercy upon me! i 3 218
Yea, man and birds are fain of climbing high . . . ii 1 8
Had not your man put up the fowl so suddenly, We had had more sport ii 1 45
A blind man at Saint Alban's shrine, Within this half-hour, hath received his sight; A man that ne'er saw in his life before . ii 1 63
To make the Earl of Warwick The greatest man in England but the king ii 2 82
With Sir John Stanley, in the Isle of Man . . . . ii 3 13
Ready are the appellant and defendant, The armourer and his man ii 3 50
Drink, and fear not your man.—Let it come, i' faith, and I'll pledge you ii 3 65
I am come hither, as it were, upon my man's instigation, to prove him a knave and myself an honest man . . . . . ii 3 88
Stanley is appointed now To take her with him to the Isle of Man ii 4 78
'Tis not his wont to be the hindmost man, Whate'er occasion keeps him iii 1 2
And Humphrey is no little man in England . . . . iii 1 20
Gloucester is a man Unsounded yet and full of deep deceit . iii 1 56
The welfare of us all Hangs on the cutting short that fraudful man . iii 1 81
Thou never didst them wrong nor no man wrong . . . iii 1 209
You would not have him die.—Ah, York, no man alive so fain as I! . iii 1 244
Let pale-faced fear keep with the mean-born man . . . iii 1 335
What have we done? Didst ever hear a man so penitent? . . iii 2 4
Ah, woe is me for Gloucester, wretched man! . . . . iii 2 72
Staring full ghastly like a strangled man; His hair uprear'd . . iii 2 170
And charge that no man should disturb your rest . . . iii 2 256
A cunning man did calculate my birth . . . . . iv 1 34
He was an honest man, and a good bricklayer . . . iv 2 42
That parchment, being scribbled o'er, should undo a man . . iv 2 88
I did but seal once to a thing, and I was never mine own man since . iv 2 91
I am sorry for't: the man is a proper man, of mine honour . . iv 2 102
Hast thou a mark to thyself, like an honest plain-dealing man? . iv 2 111
He shall be encountered with a man as good as himself . . iv 2 124
Why dost thou quiver, man?—The palsy, and not fear, provokes me . iv 7 97
Which is not amiss to cool a man's stomach this hot weather . . iv 10 10
Iden, an esquire of Kent, Took odds to combat a poor famish'd man . iv 10 47
Tell Kent from me, she hath lost her best man . . . iv 10 79
Art thou the man that slew him?—I was, an't like your majesty . v 1 71
First let me ask of these, If they can brook I bow a knee to man . v 1 110
To Bedlam with him! is the man grown mad? . . . . v 1 131
Who can be bound by any solemn vow . . . to rob a man? . . v 1 185
Ah, wretched man! would I had died a maid, And never seen thee! *3 Hen. VI.* i 1 216
Murder not this innocent child, Lest thou be hated both of God and man! i 3 9
He is a man, and, Clifford, cope with him . . . . i 3 24
Why art thou patient, man? thou shouldst be mad . . . i 4 89
Though man's face be fearful to their eyes . . . . ii 2 27
How many years a mortal man may live . . . . . ii 5 29
This man, whom hand to hand I slew in fight, May be possessed with some store of crowns . . . . ii 5 56
May yet ere night yield both my life and them To some man else, as this dead man doth me . . . . ii 5 60
My father, being the Earl of Warwick's man, Came on the part of York ii 5 65
Weep, wretched man, I'll aid thee tear for tear . . . ii 5 76
Here comes a man; let's stay till he be past . . . . iii 1 12
No, not a man comes for redress of thee; For how can I help them? . iii 1 20
A man at least, for less I should not be; And men may talk of kings iii 1 57
Why, am I dead? do I not breathe a man? . . . . iii 1 82
And go we, brothers, to the man that took him, To question . . iii 2 121
Am I then a man to be beloved? O monstrous fault! . . . iii 2 163
Henry, sole possessor of my love, Is of a king become a banish'd man . iii 3 25
Each man take his stand: The king by this is set him down to sleep . iv 3 1
Tush, man, abodements must not now affright us . . . iv 7 13
The good old man would fain that all were well, So 'twere not 'long of him iv 7 31
What! fear not, man, but yield me up the keys . . . iv 7 37
See how the surly Warwick mans the wall! . . . . v 1 17
Did I but suspect a fearful man, He should have leave to go away betimes v 4 44
He was a man; this, in respect, a child: And men ne'er spend their fury on a child . . . . v 5 56
Many an old man's sigh and many a widow's . . . . v 6 39
That good man of worship, Anthony Woodville . . *Richard III.* i 1 66
I think there's no man is secure But the queen's kindred . . i 1 71
Straitly given in charge That no man shall have private conference . i 1 86
You may partake of any thing we say: We speak no treason, man . i 1 90
Villain, thou know'st no law of God nor man: No beast so fierce . i 2 70
Vouchsafe, defused infection of a man, For these known evils . . i 2 78
Then never man was true.—Well, well, put up your sword . . i 2 196
She finds, although I cannot, Myself to be a marvellous proper man . i 2 255
A man that loves not me, nor none of you . . . . i 3 13
Cannot a plain man live and think no harm? . . . . i 3 51
No man but prophesied revenge for it . . . . . i 3 186
As I am a Christian faithful man, I would not spend another such a night i 4 4
It [conscience] is a dangerous thing: it makes a man a coward: a man cannot steal, but it accuseth him . . . . . . i 4 138
'Tis [conscience] a blushing shamefast spirit that mutinies in a man's bosom; . . . it beggars any man that keeps it . . . . i 4 142
Every man that means to live well endeavours to trust to himself and to live without it [conscience] . . . . . . i 4 147
And wilt thou, then, Spurn at his edict and fulfil a man's? . . i 4 203
My brother slew no man; his fault was thought . . . ii 1 104
Not a man of you Had so much grace to put it in my mind . . ii 1 119
But for my brother not a man would speak, Nor I, ungracious, speak . ii 1 126
Make me die a good old man! That is the butt-end of a mother's blessing ii 2 109
Ye cannot reason almost with a man That looks not heavily . . ii 3 39
Nor more can you distinguish of a man Than of his outward show . iii 1 9
That Julius Cæsar was a famous man . . . . . iii 1 84
If I live until I be a man, I'll win our ancient right in France again . iii 1 91
I tell thee, man, 'tis better with me now Than when I met thee last . iii 2 100
When I met this holy man, Those men you talk of came into my mind . iii 2 117

Man. Than my Lord Hastings no man might be bolder *Richard III.* iii 4 30
There's never a man in Christendom That can less hide his love or hate iii 4 53
With no man here he is offended; For, were he, he had shown it in his looks . . . . iii 4 58
So dear I loved the man, that I must weep . . . . iii 5 24
A book of prayer in his hand, True ornaments to know a holy man . iii 7 99
I partly know the man: go, call him hither . . . . iv 2 41
Send to her, by the man that slew her brothers, A pair of bleeding hearts iv 4 271
And he himself wander'd away alone, No man knows whither . iv 4 515
Every man's conscience is a thousand swords . . . . v 2 17
Every man unto his charge: Let not our babbling dreams affright our souls . . . . v 3 307
The king enacts more wonders than a man . . . . . v 4 2
I'll say A man may weep upon his wedding-day . . *Hen. VIII.* Prol. 32
Every man that stood Show'd like a mine . . . . . i 1 21
No man's pie is freed From his ambitious finger . . . . i 1 52
Every man, After the hideous storm that follow'd, was A thing inspired i 1 89
Not a man in England Can advise me like you . . . . i 1 134
Send our letters, with Free pardon to each man . . . . i 2 100
This man so complete, Who was enroll'd 'mongst wonders . . i 2 118
Ha! what, so rank? Ah ha! There's mischief in this man . . i 2 187
May his highness live in freedom, And this man out of prison? . i 2 201
See the noble ruin'd man you speak of.—Let's stand close . . ii 1 54
Yet, you that hear me, This from a dying man receive as certain . ii 1 125
A man of my lord cardinal's, by commission and main power, took 'em ii 2 6
Eyes, that so long have slept upon This bold bad man . . . ii 2 44
This imperious man will work us all From princes into pages . . ii 2 47
This good man, This just and learned priest, Cardinal Campeius . ii 2 96
They have sent me such a man I would have wish'd for . . . ii 2 101
Was not one Doctor Pace In this man's place before him? . . ii 2 123
Was he not held a learned man?—Yes, surely . . . . ii 2 124
Fearing he would rise, he was so virtuous, Kept him a foreign man still ii 2 129
Would it not grieve an able man to leave So sweet a bedfellow? . ii 2 142
That man i' the world who shall report he has A better wife, let him in nought be trusted . . . . ii 4 134
Forgetting, like a good man, your late censure . . . . iii 1 64
Have I not made you The prime man of the state? . . . iii 2 162
Which went Beyond all man's endeavours . . . . . iii 2 169
I shall fall Like a bright exhalation in the evening, And no man see me more . . . . iii 2 227
Dare mate a sounder man than Surrey can be, And all that love his follies . . . . iii 2 274
I could despise this man, But that I am bound in charity against it! . iii 2 297
Press not a falling man too far! 'tis virtue: His faults lie open . iii 2 333
This is the state of man: to-day he puts forth The tender leaves of hopes iii 2 352
When he thinks, good easy man, full surely His greatness is a-ripening iii 2 356
O, how wretched Is that poor man that hangs on princes' favours! . iii 2 367
Can thy spirit wonder A great man should decline? . . . iii 2 375
'Tis a burthen [honour] Too heavy for a man that hopes for heaven! . iii 2 385
He's a learned man. May he continue Long in his highness' favour! . iii 2 395
I am a poor fall'n man, unworthy now To be thy lord and master . iii 2 413
Fling away ambition: By that sin fell the angels; how can man, then, The image of his Maker, hope to win by it? . . . . . iii 2 441
Believe me, sir, she is the goodliest woman That ever lay by man . . iv 1 70
No man living Could say 'This is my wife' there . . . . iv 1 79
A man in much esteem with the king, and truly A worthy friend . . iv 1 109
Arrested him at York, and brought him forward, As a man sorely tainted iv 2 14
And grew so ill He could not sit his mule.—Alas, poor man! . . iv 2 16
An old man, broken with the storms of state . . . . iv 2 21
A man Of an unbounded stomach, ever ranking Himself with princes . iv 2 33
To add greater honours to his age Than man could give him, he died fearing God . . . . iv 2 68
By heaven, I will, Or let me lose the fashion of a man! . . . iv 2 159
None stands under more calumnious tongues Than I myself, poor man . v 1 113
Now, by my holidame, What manner of man are you? . . . v 1 117
Look, the good man weeps! He's honest, on mine honour . . v 1 152
Suffer A man of his place, and so near our favour, To dance attendance! v 2 30
If we suffer, Out of our easiness and childish pity To one man's honour v 3 26
A man that more detests, more stirs against, Both in his private conscience and his place, Defacers of a public peace, than I do . . v 3 39
You are a counsellor, And, by that virtue, no man dare accuse you . v 3 50
Being but a private man again, You shall know many dare accuse you boldly . . . . v 3 55
'Tis a cruelty To load a falling man . . . . . . v 3 77
Do you think, my lords, The king will suffer but the little finger Of this man to be vex'd? . . . . v 3 107
In seeking tales and informations Against this man, . . . Ye blew the fire v 3 111
Was it discretion, lords, to let this man, This good man,—few of you deserve that title,—This honest man, wait like a lousy footboy? . v 3 137
Every man shall eat in safety, Under his own vine, what he plants . v 5 34
O lord archbishop, Thou hast made me now a man! . . . v 5 65
This day, no man think Has business at his house . . . . v 5 75
They say he is a very man per se, And stands alone . *Troi. and Cres.* i 2 15
This man, lady, hath robbed many beasts of their particular additions i 2 19
A man into whom nature hath so crowded humours that his valour is crushed into folly . . . . i 2 22
There is no man hath a virtue that he hath not a glimpse of, nor any man an attaint but he carries some stain of it . . . . . i 2 25
How should this man, that makes me smile, make Hector angry? . . i 2 32
Hector's a gallant man.—As may be in the world, lady . . . i 2 40
Troilus is the better man of the two.—O Jupiter! there's no comparison i 2 64
Do you know a man if you see him?—Ay, if I ever saw him before . i 2 67
Hector is not a better man than Troilus.—Excuse me.—He is elder . i 2 86
Is he so young a man and so old a lifter? . . . . . . i 2 128
I think his smiling becomes him better than any man in all Phrygia . i 2 135
He will weep you, an 'twere a man born in April . . . . i 2 189
Is not that a brave man? he's one of the flowers of Troy, I can tell you i 2 202
He has a shrewd wit, I can tell you; and he's a man good enough . i 2 207
And a proper man of person . . . . i 2 209
There's a brave man, niece. O brave Hector! Look how he looks! there's a countenance! is't not a brave man?—O, a brave man!—Is a' not? it does a man's heart good . . . . i 2 217
Look ye yonder, niece; is't not a gallant man too, is't not? . . . i 2 231
I had rather be such a man as Troilus than Agamemnon and all Greece i 2 266
Have you any discretion? have you any eyes? do you know what a man is? i 2 275
Youth, liberality, and such like, the spice and salt that season a man . i 2 278
A minced man: and then to be baked with no date in the pie, for then the man's date's out . . . . i 2 279
Tell him of Nestor, one that was a man When Hector's grandsire suck'd i 3 291
In our Grecian host One noble man that hath one spark of fire . . i 3 294

Man. As 'twere from forth us all, a man distill'd Out of our virtues *Troi. and Cres.* i 3 350
Why then, we did our main opinion crush In taint of our best man . i 3 374
Among ourselves Give him allowance for the better man . . . i 3 377
Was sufferance, 'twas not voluntary: no man is beaten voluntary . ii 1 105
Though no man lesser fears the Greeks than I . . . . . . ii 2 8
What propugnation is in one man's valour? . . . . . . ii 2 136
Peace, fool! I have not done.—He is a privileged man. Proceed . . ii 3 61
You may call it melancholy, if you will favour the man . . . . ii 3 95
Do you not think he thinks himself a better man than I am? . . ii 3 154
Why should a man be proud? How doth pride grow? . . . . ii 3 161
I do hate a proud man, as I hate the engendering of toads . . . ii 3 169
Here is a man—but 'tis before his face; I will be silent . . . ii 3 240
I wish'd myself a man, Or that we women had men's privilege . . iii 2 135
To be wise and love Exceeds man's might; that dwells with gods . . iii 2 164
Supple knees Feed arrogance and are the proud man's fees . . . iii 3 49
Not a man, for being simply man, Hath any honour . . . . iii 3 80
That man, how dearly ever parted, How much in having, or without or in . . . . iii 3 96
Expressly proves That no man is the lord of any thing . . . iii 3 115
Heavens, what a man is there! a very horse . . . . . iii 3 126
How one man eats into another's pride, While pride is fasting . . iii 3 136
Then marvel not, thou great and complete man . . . . . iii 3 181
A woman impudent and mannish grown Is not more loathed than an effeminate man In time of action . . . . iii 3 218
The man's undone for ever; for if Hector break not his neck i' the combat, he'll break 't himself in vain-glory . . . . . . iii 3 258
What think you of this man that takes me for the general? . . . iii 3 263
A plague of opinion! a man may wear it on both sides, like a leather jerkin . . . . iii 3 265
No man alive can love in such a sort The thing he means to kill . iv 1 23
Hast not slept to-night? would he not, a naughty man, let it sleep? . iv 2 34
You're an odd man; give even, or give none.—An odd man, lady! every man is odd . . . . iv 5 41
Thou art too gentle and too free a man: I came to kill thee, cousin . iv 5 139
Let an old man embrace thee; And, worthy warrior, welcome to our tents . . . . iv 5 199
It would discredit the blest gods, proud man, To answer such a question iv 5 247
She will sing any man at first sight.—And any man may sing her . . v 2 9
Never did young man fancy With so eternal and so fix'd a soul . . v 2 165
Life every man holds dear; but the brave man Holds honour far more precious-dear than life . . . . v 3 27
How now, young man! mean'st thou to fight to-day? . . . . v 3 29
You have a vice of mercy in you, Which better fits a lion than a man . v 3 38
Unless a man were cursed, I cannot tell what to think on't . . . v 3 106
I would have been much more a fresher man, Had I expected thee . . v 6 20
Strike, fellows, strike; this is the man I seek . . . . . . v 8 10
If it be so, yet bragless let it be; Great Hector was a man as good as he v 9 6
Through the cranks and offices of man . . . . *Coriolanus* i 1 141
Your affections are A sick man's appetite . . . . i 1 182
Was ever man so proud as is this Marcius?—He has no equal . . i 1 256
Shall be the general's fault, though he perform To the utmost of a man i 1 272
I sprang not more in joy at first hearing he was a man-child than now in first seeing he had proved himself a man . . . . . . i 3 19
Away, you fool! it [blood] more becomes a man Than gilt his trophy . i 3 42
Nor a man that fears you less than he, That's lesser than a little . . i 4 14
There is the man of my soul's hate . . . . i 5 11
I know the sound of Marcius' tongue From every meaner man . . i 6 27
How is't with Titus Lartius?—As with a man busied about decrees . i 6 34
I sometime lay here in Corioli At a poor man's house . . . . i 9 83
No more of him; he's a worthy man . . . . ii 2 40
The man I speak of cannot in the world Be singly counterpoised . . ii 2 90
He proved best man i' the field . . . . ii 2 101
Worthy man!—He cannot but with measure fit the honours . . . ii 2 126
Your wit will not so soon out as another man's will . . . . ii 3 30
If he would incline to the people, there was never a worthier man . ii 3 43
I will counterfeit the bewitchment of some popular man . . . ii 3 109
He has done nobly, and cannot go without any honest man's voice . ii 3 140
How now, my masters! have you chose this man?—He has our voices, sir . . . . ii 3 163
No man saw 'em.—He said he had wounds, which he could show . . ii 3 173
As if you were a god to punish, not A man of their infirmity . . . iii 1 82
This man has marr'd his fortune.—His nature is too noble for the world iii 1 254
This viper That would depopulate the city and Be every man himself . iii 1 265
Rather say I play The man I am . . . . iii 2 16
You might have been enough the man you are, With striving less to be so . . . . iii 2 19
Thy tears are salter than a younger man's, And venomous to thine eyes iv 1 22
We shall not send O'er the vast world to seek a single man . . iv 1 42
Was not a man my father? . . . . iv 2 18
Good man, the wounds that he does bear for Rome! . . . . iv 2 28
Time to corrupt a man's wife is when she's fallen out with her husband iv 3 34
And am the man, I think, that shall set them in present action . . iv 3 52
Thy name? Why speak'st not? speak, man: what's thy name? . . iv 5 59
Not yet thou knowest me, and, seeing me, dost not Think me for the man I am . . . . iv 5 62
I loved the maid I married; never man Sigh'd truer breath . . . iv 5 120
He is simply the rarest man i' the world . . . . iv 5 169
I would not be a Roman, of all nations; I had as lieve be a condemned man . . . . iv 5 186
And he's as like to do't as any man I can imagine . . . . . iv 5 217
But when they shall see, sir, his crest up again, and the man in blood . iv 5 225
Like a thing Made by some other deity than nature, That shapes man better . . . . iv 6 92
Pride, Which out of daily fortune ever taints The happy man . . iv 7 39
This man, Aufidius, Was my beloved in Rome: yet thou behold'st! . . v 2 98
This last old man, Whom with a crack'd heart I have sent to Rome . v 3 8
As if a man were author of himself And knew no other kin . . . v 3 36
The man was noble, But with his last attempt he wiped it out . . v 3 145
Think'st thou it honourable for a noble man Still to remember wrongs? v 3 154
Is't possible that so short a time can alter the condition of a man? . v 4 10
This Marcius is grown from man to dragon: he has wings . . . v 4 13
As with a man by his own alms empoison'd, And with his charity slain v 6 11
The man is noble and his fame folds-in This orb o' the earth . . v 6 126
When you shall know . . . the great danger Which this man's life did owe you, you'll rejoice That he is thus cut off . . . . . . v 6 139
A nobler man, a braver warrior, Lives not this day . . . *T. Andron.* i 1 25
Is she not then beholding to the man That brought her? . . . . i 1 396
Take up this good old man, and cheer the heart . . . . . i 1 457
Into some loathsome pit, Where never man's eye may behold my body . ii 3 177

Man. Doth shine upon the dead man's earthy cheeks . *T. Andron.* ii 3 229
And wonder greatly that man's face can fold In pleasing smiles such murderous tyranny . . . . ii 3 266
No man is by; And you recount your sorrows to a stone . . . iii 1 28
O happy man! they have befriended thee . . . . iii 1 52
Here stands my other son, a banish'd man, And here my brother, weeping . . . . iii 1 99
For thou, poor man, hast drown'd it with thine own [tears] . . . iii 1 141
The wofull'st man that ever lived in Rome . . . . iii 1 290
Why, Marcus, no man should be mad but I . . . . iii 2 24
Alas, poor man! grief has so wrought on him . . . . . . iii 2 79
If I were a man, Their mother's bed-chamber should not be safe . . iv 1 107
O heavens, can you hear a good man groan, And not relent? . . . iv 1 123
Here's no sound jest! the old man hath found their guilt . . . iv 2 26
Then let no man but I Do execution on my flesh and blood . . . iv 2 83
For the man must not be hanged till the next week . . . . iv 3 81
Often over-heard them say, When I have walked like a private man . iv 4 75
And brought him hither, To use as you think needful of the man . . v 1 39
Wherein I did not some notorious ill, As kill a man . . . . v 1 128
Know, thou sad man, I am not Tamora; She is thy enemy . . . v 2 28
When thou find'st a man that's like thyself, Good Murder, stab him . v 2 99
Tell us, old man, how shall we be employ'd?—Tut, I have work enough v 2 149
Unspeakable, past patience, Or more than any living man could bear . v 3 127
Come, thou reverend man of Rome, And bring our emperor gently . . v 3 137
No funeral rite, nor man in mourning weeds, No mournful bell . . v 3 196
I will take the wall of any man or maid of Montague's . *Rom. and Jul.* i 1 15
I serve as good a man as you.—No better.—Well, sir.—Say 'better' . i 1 62
Bid a sick man in sadness make his will . . . . i 1 208
My husband—God be with his soul! A' was a merry man . . . i 3 40
A man, young lady! lady, such a man As all the world—why, he's a man of wax . . . . i 3 75
Knock and enter; and no sooner in, But every man betake him to his legs . . . . i 4 34
Thirty years.—What, man! 'tis not so much . . . . . . i 5 36
You will set cock-a-hoop! you'll be the man! . . . . . . i 5 83
Nor arm, nor face, nor any other part Belonging to a man . . . ii 2 42
What man art thou that thus bescreen'd in night So stumblest on my counsel? . . . . ii 2 52
Two such opposed kings encamp them still In man as well as herbs . ii 3 28
Care keeps his watch in every old man's eye . . . . ii 3 35
I bear no hatred, blessed man . . . . ii 3 53
Came he not home to-night?—Not to his father's; I spoke with his man ii 4 3
Any man that can write may answer a letter . . . . ii 4 10
Is he a man to encounter Tybalt?—Why, what is Tybalt? . . . . ii 4 17
A very good blade! a very tall man! . . . . ii 4 31
In such a case as mine a man may strain courtesy . . . . . ii 4 54
Such a case as yours constrains a man to bow in the hams . . . ii 4 57
Out upon you! what a man are you!—One, gentlewoman, that God hath made for himself to mar . . . . ii 4 120
I saw no man use you at his pleasure . . . . ii 4 165
I dare draw as soon as another man, if I see occasion . . . . ii 4 168
Within this hour my man shall be with thee, And bring thee cords . ii 4 200
Is your man secret? Did you ne'er hear say, Two may keep counsel? . ii 4 208
I warrant thee, my man's as true as steel . . . . ii 4 210
I anger her sometimes and tell her that Paris is the properer man . . ii 4 217
Send thy man away.—Peter, stay at the gate . . . . . . ii 5 19
Well, you have made a simple choice; you know not how to choose a man . . . . ii 5 39
Though his face be better than any man's, yet his leg excels all men's . ii 5 40
Thou wilt quarrel with a man that hath a hair more, or a hair less . iii 1 18
Thou wilt quarrel with a man for cracking nuts . . . . . . iii 1 20
Thou hast quarrelled with a man for coughing in the street . . . iii 1 27
An I were so apt to quarrel as thou art, any man should buy the fee-simple of my life for an hour and a quarter . . . . iii 1 35
Let them gaze; I will not budge for no man's pleasure . . . . iii 1 58
Here comes my man.—But I'll be hang'd, sir, if he wear your livery . iii 1 59
Marry, go before to field, he'll be your follower; Your worship in that sense may call him 'man' . . . . iii 1 62
Courage, man; the hurt cannot be much.—No, 'tis not so deep as a well iii 1 98
Ask for me to-morrow, and you shall find me a grave man . . . iii 1 102
'Zounds, a dog, a rat, a mouse, a cat, to scratch a man to death! . . iii 1 105
There lies the man, slain by young Romeo, That slew thy kinsman . iii 1 149
Where's my man? give me some aqua vitæ . . . . iii 2 88
Romeo, come forth; come forth, thou fearful man . . . . . iii 3 1
Thou fond mad man, hear me but speak a word . . . . . . iii 3 52
Stand up, stand up; stand, an you be a man: For Juliet's sake . . iii 3 88
Hold thy desperate hand: Art thou a man? thy form cries out thou art iii 3 109
Unseemly woman in a seeming man! Or ill-beseeming beast in seeming both! . . . . iii 3 112
Thy noble shape is but a form of wax, Digressing from the valour of a man . . . . iii 3 127
I'll find out your man, And he shall signify from time to time . . iii 3 169
And yet no man like he doth grieve my heart . . . . . . iii 5 84
If you could find out but a man To bear a poison, I would temper it . iii 5 97
Find thou the means, and I'll find such a man . . . . . . iii 5 104
Proportion'd as one's thought would wish a man . . . . . iii 5 184
Bid me go into a new-made grave And hide me with a dead man in his shroud . . . . iv 1 85
For he hath still been tried a holy man . . . . iv 3 29
Strange dream, that gives a dead man leave to think! . . . . v 1 7
If a man did need a poison now, . . . Here lives a caitiff wretch would sell it him . . . ; And this same needy man must sell it me . . v 1 50
Come hither, man. I see that thou art poor: Hold, there is forty ducats . . . . v 1 58
Poor living corse, closed in a dead man's tomb! . . . . . . v 2 30
Good gentle youth, tempt not a desperate man; Fly hence, and leave me . . . . v 3 59
What said my man, when my betossed soul Did not attend him? . . v 3 76
Death, lie thou there, by a dead man interr'd . . . . . . v 3 87
Here's Romeo's man; we found him in the churchyard . . . . v 3 182
Here is a friar, and slaughter'd Romeo's man; With instruments upon them . . . . v 3 199
We still have known thee for a holy man. Where's Romeo's man? . . v 3 270
A most incomparable man . . . . *T. of Athens* i 1 10
How this lord is follow'd!—The senators of Athens: happy man! . . i 1 40
A man, Whom this beneath world doth embrace and hug . . . . i 1 43
With one man beckon'd from the rest below, Bowing his head . . i 1 74
I am a man That from my first have been inclined to thrift . . . i 1 117
This man of thine Attempts her love: I prithee, noble lord, Join with me to forbid him her resort . . . . i 1 125

Man. The man is honest.—Therefore he will be *T. of Athens* i 1 128
Painting is welcome. The painting is almost the natural man i 1 157
For since dishonour traffics with man's nature, He is but outside i 1 158
Not so well as plain-dealing, which will not cost a man a doit i 1 217
The strain of man's bred out Into baboon and monkey i 1 259
The noblest mind he carries That ever govern'd man i 1 292
Ye've got a humour there Does not become a man; 'tis much to blame i 2 27
They say, my lords, 'ira furor brevis est;' but yond man is ever angry i 2 29
It grieves me to see so many dip their meat in one man's blood i 2 42
Parts bread with him, . . . is the readiest man to kill him i 2 50
If I were a huge man, I should fear to drink at meals i 2 51
Honest water, which ne'er left man i' the mire i 2 60
Immortal gods, I crave no pelf; I pray for no man but myself i 2 64
Grant I may never prove so fond, To trust man on his oath or bond i 2 66
'Tis pity bounty had not eyes behind, That man might ne'er be wretched i 2 170
I know, no man Can justly praise but what he does affect i 2 220
In all shapes that man goes up and down in from fourscore to thirteen ii 2 119
Thou art not altogether a fool.—Nor thou altogether a wise man ii 2 123
Prithee, man, look cheerly. These old fellows Have their ingratitude ii 2 223
Every man has his fault, and honesty is his iii 1 29
Denied that honourable man! there was very little honour showed in 't iii 2 20
O, see the monstrousness of man When he looks out in an ungrateful shape! iii 2 79
I was the first man That e'er received gift from him iii 3 16
The devil knew not what he did when he made man politic; he crossed himself by 't: and I cannot think but, in the end, the villanies of man will set him clear iii 3 29
He is a man, setting his fate aside, Of comely virtues iii 5 14
He's truly valiant that can wisely suffer The worst that man can breathe iii 5 32
To be in anger is impiety; But who is man that is not angry? iii 5 57
I am sick of that grief too . . . —Every man here's so iii 6 21
Here's a noble feast toward.—This is the old man still iii 6 69
Each man to his stool, with that spur as he would to the lip of his mistress iii 6 73
Lend to each man enough, that one need not lend to another iii 6 82
Make the meat be beloved more than the man that gives it iii 6 86
Of man and beast the infinite malady Crust you quite o'er iii 6 103
Henceforth hated be Of Timon man and all humanity! iii 6 115
Strange, unusual blood, When man's worst sin is, he does too much good! iv 2 39
Who dares . . . say 'This man's a flatterer?' if one be, So are they all iv 3 15
The canker gnaw thy heart, For showing me again the eyes of man! iv 3 50
Is man so hateful to thee, That art thyself a man? iv 3 51
With man's blood paint the ground, gules, gules iv 3 59
If thou wilt not promise, the gods plague thee, for thou art a man! if thou dost perform, confound thee, for thou art a man! iv 3 74
Consumptions sow In hollow bones of man; strike their sharp shins iv 3 152
That nature, being sick of man's unkindness, Should yet be hungry! iv 3 176
Whose self-same mettle, Whereof thy proud child, arrogant man, is puff'd, Engenders the black toad and adder blue iv 3 180
Let it no more bring out ingrateful man! Go great with tigers! iv 3 188
Whereof ingrateful man, with liquorish draughts And morsels unctuous, greases his pure mind, That from it all consideration slips! iv 3 194
More man? plague, plague! iv 3 197
What man didst thou ever know unthrift that was beloved after his means? iv 3 311
O thou touch of hearts [gold]! Think, thy slave man rebels iv 3 391
There is no time so miserable but a man may be true iv 3 462
Is yond despised and ruinous man my lord? Full of decay and failing? iv 3 465
How rarely does it meet with this time's guise, When man was wish'd to love his enemies! iv 3 473
I have forgot all men; Then, if thou grant'st thou 'rt a man, I have forgot thee iv 3 481
I never had honest man about me, I; all I kept were knaves iv 3 484
Let me behold thy face. Surely, this man Was born of woman iv 3 500
I do proclaim One honest man—mistake me not—but one iv 3 504
Thou singly honest man, Here, take iv 3 530
Fly, whilst thou art blest and free: Ne'er see thou man iv 3 543
Excellent workman! thou canst not paint a man so bad as is thyself v 1 33
Each man apart, all single and alone, Yet an arch-villain keeps him company v 1 110
Nothing but himself which looks like man Is friendly with him v 1 121
Offering the fortunes of his former days, The former man may make him v 1 128
Some beast rear'd this; there does not live a man v 3 4
Not a man Shall pass his quarter, or offend the stream Of regular justice v 4 59
What man is that?—A soothsayer *J. Cæsar* i 2 18
And this man Is now become a god, and Cassius is A wretched creature i 2 115
It doth amaze me A man of such a feeble temper should So get the start of the majestic world i 2 129
Why, man, he doth bestride the narrow world Like a Colossus i 2 135
When went there by an age, since the great flood, But it was famed with more than with one man? i 2 153
When could they say till now, that talk'd of Rome, That her wide walls encompass'd but one man? i 2 155
Rome indeed and room enough, When there is in it but one only man i 2 157
I do not know the man I should avoid So soon as that spare Cassius i 2 200
If the tag-rag people did not clap him and kiss him, . . . I am no true man i 2 263
An I had been a man of any occupation, if I would not have taken him at a word i 2 269
Now could I, Casca, name to thee a man Most like this dreadful night i 3 72
A man no mightier than thyself or me In personal action i 3 76
Poor man! I know he would not be a wolf, But that he sees the Romans are but sheep i 3 104
You speak to Casca, and to such a man That is no fleering tell-tale i 3 116
Three parts of him Is ours already, and the man entire Upon the next encounter yields him ours i 3 155
Shall Rome stand under one man's awe? What, Rome? ii 1 52
And the state of man, Like to a little kingdom, suffers then The nature of an insurrection ii 1 67
Every man of them, and no man here But honours you ii 1 90
Break off betimes, And every man hence to his idle bed ii 1 117
So let high-sighted tyranny range on, Till each man drop by lottery ii 1 119
Shall no man else be touch'd but only Cæsar? ii 1 154
But an effect of humour, Which sometime hath his hour with every man ii 1 251
Here is a sick man that would speak with you ii 1 310
I have a man's mind, but a woman's might ii 4 8
The throng that follows Cæsar at the heels, Of senators, of prætors, common suitors, Will crowd a feeble man almost to death ii 4 36
Let no man abide this deed, But we the doers iii 1 94

Man. Ay, every man away: Brutus shall lead; and we will grace his heels *J. Cæsar* iii 1 119
Your voice shall be as strong as any man's In the disposing of new dignities iii 1 177
Let each man render me his bloody hand: First, Marcus Brutus iii 1 184
Thou art the ruins of the noblest man That ever lived in the tide of times iii 1 256
I do entreat you, not a man depart, Save I alone, till Antony have spoke iii 2 65
For Brutus is an honourable man: So are they all, all honourable men iii 2 87
There's not a nobler man in Rome than Antony iii 2 121
I am no orator, as Brutus is; But, as you know me all, a plain blunt man iii 2 222
He gives To every several man seventy five drachmas iii 2 247
Are you a married man or a bachelor?—Answer every man directly iii 3 8
Then, to answer every man directly and briefly, wisely and truly iii 3 16
This is a slight unmeritable man, Meet to be sent on errands iv 1 12
We lay these honours on this man, To ease ourselves iv 1 19
And let no man Come to our tent till we have done our conference iv 2 50
My letters, praying on his side, Because I knew the man, were slighted off iv 3 5
The foremost man of all this world iv 3 22
Away, slight man!—Is't possible?—Hear me, for I will speak iv 3 37
No man bears sorrow better. Portia is dead.—Ha! Portia!—She is dead iv 3 147
If thou wert the noblest of thy strain, Young man, thou couldst not die more honourable v 1 60
O, that a man might know The end of this day's business ere it come! v 1 123
Friends, I owe more tears To this dead man than you shall see me pay v 3 102
Keep this man safe; Give him all kindness v 4 27
Yet in all my life I found no man but he was true to me v 5 35
What man is that?—My master's man v 5 52
Brutus only overcame himself, And no man else hath honour by his death v 5 57
Nature might stand up And say to all the world 'This was a man!' v 5 75
What bloody man is that? He can report *Macbeth* i 2 1
He shall live a man forbid: Weary se'nnights nine times nine i 3 21
Live you? or are you aught That man may question? i 3 43
Shakes so my single state of man that function Is smother'd in surmise i 3 140
I dare do all that may become a man; Who dares do more is none i 7 46
Then you were a man; And, to be more than what you were, you would Be so much more the man i 7 49
If a man were porter of hell-gate, he should have old turning the key ii 3 1
No man's life Was to be trusted with them ii 3 110
Who can be wise, amazed, temperate and furious, Loyal and neutral, in a moment? No man ii 3 115
To show an unfelt sorrow is an office Which the false man does easy ii 3 143
The heavens, as troubled with man's act, Threaten his bloody stage ii 4 5
Let every man be master of his time Till seven at night iii 1 41
And mine eternal jewel Given to the common enemy of man iii 1 69
Are you so gospell'd To pray for this good man and for his issue? iii 1 89
Are you a man?—Ay, and a bold one, that dare look on that iii 4 58
The time has been, That, when the brains were out, the man would die iii 4 79
What man dare, I dare: Approach thou like the rugged Russian bear iii 4 99
Unreal mockery, hence! Why, so: being gone, I am a man again iii 4 108
Brought forth The secret'st man of blood iii 4 126
Laugh to scorn The power of man, for none of woman born Shall harm Macbeth iv 1 80
If you will take a homely man's advice, Be not found here iv 2 68
The dead man's knell Is there scarce ask'd for who iv 3 170
What, man! ne'er pull your hat upon your brows; Give sorrow words iv 3 208
Dispute it like a man.—I shall do so; But I must also feel it as a man iv 3 221
Who would have thought the old man to have had so much blood in him? v 1 44
Would to the bleeding and the grim alarm Excite the mortified man v 2 5
No man that's born of woman Shall e'er have power upon thee v 3 6
Weapons laugh to scorn, Brandish'd by man that's of a woman born v 7 13
It hath cow'd my better part of man v 8 18
He only lived but till he was a man; The which no sooner had his prowess confirm'd In the unshrinking station where he fought, But like a man he died v 8 40
These indeed seem, For they are actions that a man might play *Hamlet* i 2 84
He was a man, take him for all in all, I shall not look upon his like again i 2 187
Give every man thy ear, but few thy voice; Take each man's censure, but reserve thy judgement i 3 68
Rich, not gaudy; For the apparel oft proclaims the man i 3 72
Thou canst not then be false to any man i 3 80
Be they as pure as grace, As infinite as man may undergo i 4 34
Whose effect Holds such an enmity with blood of man i 5 65
How say you, then; would heart of man once think it? i 5 121
Every man has business and desire, Such as it is i 5 130
What so poor a man as Hamlet is May do, to express his love i 5 185
According to the phrase or the addition Of man and country ii 1 48
Sith nor the exterior nor the inward man Resembles that it was ii 2 6
What do you think of me?—As of a man faithful and honourable ii 2 130
A fishmonger.—Not I, my lord.—Then I would you were so honest a man ii 2 176
To be honest, as this world goes, is to be one man picked out of ten thousand ii 2 179
To speak to you like an honest man, I am most dreadfully attended ii 2 276
What a piece of work is a man! how noble in reason! how infinite in faculty! ii 2 316
Man delights not me: no, nor woman neither ii 2 321
Why did you laugh then, when I said 'man delights not me?' ii 2 327
If you delight not in man, what lenten entertainment the players shall receive from you ii 2 329
The humorous man shall end his part in peace ii 2 335
They say an old man is twice a child ii 2 403
Use every man after his desert, and who should 'scape whipping? ii 2 555
The proud man's contumely, The pangs of despised love iii 1 71
Nor the gait of Christian, pagan, nor man iii 2 36
Thou art e'en as just a man As e'er my conversation coped withal iii 2 59
A man that fortune's buffets and rewards Hast ta'en with equal thanks iii 2 72
Give me that man That is not passion's slave iii 2 76
What should a man do but be merry? iii 2 133
Then there's hope a great man's memory may outlive his life half a year iii 2 140
The great man down, you mark his favourite flies iii 2 214
Like a man to double business bound, I stand in pause iii 3 41
Every god did seem to set his seal, To give the world assurance of a man iii 4 62
This man shall set me packing: I'll lug the guts into the neighbour room iii 4 211
In this brainish apprehension, kills The unseen good old man iv 1 12
Should have kept short, restrain'd and out of haunt, This mad young man iv 1 19
How dangerous is it that this man goes loose! iv 3 2
A man may fish with the worm that hath eat of a king iv 3 28

Man. Father and mother is man and wife; man and wife is one flesh *Hamlet* iv 3 53
That inward breaks, and shows no cause without Why the man dies iv 4 29
What is a man, If his chief good and market of his time Be but to sleep and feed? a beast, no more iv 4 33
Let him go, Gertrude. Speak, man.—Where is my father?—Dead iv 5 127
Is't possible, a young maid's wits Should be as mortal as an old man's life iv 5 160
Here lies the water; good: here stands the man; good: if the man go to this water, and drown himself, it is, will he, nill he, he goes v 1 17
What man dost thou dig it for?—For no man, sir.—What woman, then? v 1 141
I have been sexton here, man and boy, thirty years v 1 177
How long will a man lie i' the earth ere he rot? v 1 178
Why, man, they did make love to this employment v 2 57
A man's life's no more than to say 'One' v 2 74
To know a man well, were to know himself v 2 147
Since no man has aught of what he leaves, what is't to leave betimes? v 2 234
As thou'rt a man, Give me the cup: let go; by heaven, I'll have 't v 2 353
What wilt thou do, old man? . . . Reverse thy doom *Lear* i 1 148
An admirable evasion of whore-master man, to lay his goatish disposition to the charge of a star! i 2 138
I am no honest man if there be any good meaning towards you i 2 189
Idle old man, That still would manage those authorities That he hath given away! i 3 16
How now! what art thou?—A man, sir.—What dost thou profess? i 4 11
This man hath had good counsel i 4 345
If a man's brains were in's heels, were't not in danger of kibes? i 5 8
That what a man cannot smell out, he may spy into i 5 23
'Tis they have put him on the old man's death ii 1 101
A tailor made thee.—Thou art a strange fellow: a tailor make a man? ii 2 62
Insulted, rail'd, And put upon him such a deal of man, That worthied him ii 2 127
A good man's fortune may grow out at heels ii 2 164
Poorest shape That ever penury, in contempt of man, Brought near to beast ii 3 8
When a man's over-lusty at legs, then he wears wooden nether-stocks ii 4 10
Having more man than wit about me, drew: He raised the house ii 4 42
When a wise man gives thee better counsel, give me mine again ii 4 76
But I will tarry; the fool will stay, And let the wise man fly ii 4 84
To take the indisposed and sickly fit For the sound man ii 4 113
How came my man i' the stocks?—I set him there, sir ii 4 201
Allow not nature more than nature needs, Man's life's as cheap as beast's ii 4 270
You see me here, you gods, a poor old man, As full of grief as age! ii 4 275
Let not women's weapons, water-drops, Stain my man's cheeks! ii 4 281
This house is little: the old man and his people Cannot be well bestow'd ii 4 291
Where is my lord of Gloucester?—Follow'd the old man forth ii 4 298
Strives in his little world of man to out-scorn The to-and-fro-conflicting wind and rain iii 1 10
Crack nature's moulds, all germens spill at once, That make ingrateful man! iii 2 9
Here's a night pities neither wise man nor fool iii 2 13
Here I stand, your slave, A poor, infirm, weak, and despised old man iii 2 20
The man that makes his toe What he his heart should make Shall of a corn cry woe iii 2 31
Since I was man, Such sheets of fire, such bursts of horrid thunder, Such groans of roaring wind and rain, I never Remember to have heard iii 2 45
Man's nature cannot carry The affliction nor the fear iii 2 48
Thou perjured, and thou simular man of virtue That art incestuous iii 2 54
That under covert and convenient seeming Hast practised on man's life iii 2 57
I am a man More sinn'd against than sinning iii 2 59
Commit not with man's sworn spouse iii 4 84
Is man no more than this? Consider him well iii 4 107
Unaccommodated man is no more but such a poor, bare, forked animal iii 4 112
Ah, that good Kent! He said it would be thus, poor banish'd man! iii 4 169
Fie, foh, and fum, I smell the blood of a British man iii 4 189
Bring in the evidence. Thou robed man of justice, take thy place iii 6 38
I'll never care what wickedness I do, If this man come to good iii 7 100
I such a fellow saw; Which made me think a man a worm iv 1 35
Bless thee, good man's son, from the foul fiend! iv 1 60
The superfluous and lust-dieted man, That slaves your ordinance iv 1 70
So distribution should undo excess, And each man have enough iv 1 74
Where's your master?—Madam, within; but never man so changed iv 2 3
O, the difference of man and man! iv 2 26
A father, and a gracious aged man iv 2 41
Could my good brother suffer you to do it? A man, a prince! iv 2 45
Milk-liver'd man! That bear'st a cheek for blows, a head for wrongs iv 2 50
What can man's wisdom In the restoring his bereaved sense? iv 4 8
Be aidant and remediate In the good man's distress! iv 4 18
Another purse; in it a jewel Well worth a poor man's taking iv 6 29
That thing you speak of, I took it for a man iv 6 78
I pardon that man's life. What was thy cause? Adultery? Thou shalt not die iv 6 111
What, art mad? A man may see how this world goes with no eyes iv 6 153
This would make a man a man of salt, To use his eyes for garden water-pots iv 6 199
A most poor man, made tame to fortune's blows iv 6 225
Nay, come not near th' old man; keep out, che vor ye iv 6 245
Do not mock me: I am a very foolish fond old man, Fourscore and upward iv 7 60
Methinks I should know you, and know this man; Yet I am doubtful iv 7 64
Do not laugh at me; For, as I am a man, I think this lady To be my child iv 7 69
Our sister's man is certainly miscarried.—'Tis to be doubted, madam v 1 5
If e'er your grace had speech with man so poor, Hear me one word v 1 38
Away, old man; give me thy hand; away! King Lear hath lost v 2 5
No farther, sir; a man may rot even here.—What, in ill thoughts again? v 2 8
I cannot draw a cart, nor eat dried oats; If it be man's work, I'll do't v 3 39
Any man of quality or degree within the lists of the army v 3 110
A man, Who, having seen me in my worst estate, Shunn'd my abhorr'd society v 3 208
Help, help, O, help!—What kind of help?—Speak, man v 3 222
I am the very man,— I'll see that straight v 3 286
You are welcome hither.—Nor no man else: all's cheerless, dark v 3 290
By the faith of man, I know my price *Othello* i 1 10
That I have ta'en away this old man's daughter, It is most true i 3 78
Yet she wish'd That heaven had made her such a man i 3 163
If she confess that she was half the wooer, Destruction on my head, if my bad blame Light on the man! i 3 178
A man he is of honesty and trust i 3 285
I never found man that knew how to love himself i 3 315

Man. Come, be a man. Drown thyself! drown cats and blind puppies *Othello* i 3 340
Cassio's a proper man: let me see now: To get his place i 3 398
I have served him, and the man commands Like a full soldier ii 1 35
Every man put himself into triumph; some to dance, some to make bonfires, each man to what sport and revels his addiction leads him ii 2 4
What, man! 'tis a night of revels: the gallants desire it ii 3 45
A soldier's a man; A life's but a span; Why, then, let a soldier drink ii 3 73
No offence to the general, nor any man of quality ii 3 110
As I am an honest man, I thought you had received some bodily wound ii 3 266
What, man! there are ways to recover the general again ii 3 272
To be now a sensible man, by and by a fool, and presently a beast! ii 3 309
You or any man living may be drunk at a time, man ii 3 318
Talking with a suitor here, A man that languishes in your displeasure iii 3 43
In a man that's just They are close delations, working from the heart iii 3 122
Men should be what they seem.—Why, then, I think Cassio's an honest man iii 3 129
Good name in man and woman, dear my lord, Is the immediate jewel of their souls: Who steals my purse steals trash iii 3 155
By the worth of man's eternal soul iii 3 361
Are you a man? have you a soul or sense? God be wi' you iii 3 374
This is within the compass of man's wit; and therefore I will attempt iii 4 21
Come, come; You'll never meet a more sufficient man iii 4 91
A man that all his time Hath founded his good fortunes on your love iii 4 93
Is not this man jealous?—I ne'er saw this before iii 4 99
'Tis not a year or two shows us a man: They are all but stomachs iii 4 103
'Tis hers, my lord; and, being hers, She may, I think, bestow't on any man iv 1 13
Bear your fortune like a man!—A horned man's a monster iv 1 62
Be a man; Think every bearded fellow that's but yoked May draw with you iv 1 66
O'erwhelmed with your grief—A passion most unsuiting such a man iv 1 78
Patience; Or I shall say you are all in all in spleen, And nothing of a man iv 1 90
I never knew woman love man so.—Alas, poor rogue! iv 1 111
If she be not honest, chaste, and true, There's no man happy iv 2 18
There is no such man; it is impossible iv 2 134
Very well! go to! I cannot go to, man; nor 'tis not very well iv 2 195
A proper man.—A very handsome man.—He speaks well iv 3 35
And yet he hath given me satisfying reasons: 'Tis but a man gone v 1 10
Some good man bear him carefully from hence v 1 99
What malice was between you?—None in the world; nor do I know the man v 1 103
No, by my life and soul! Send for the man, and ask him v 2 50
An honest man he is, and hates the slime That sticks on filthy deeds v 2 148
Disprove this villain, if thou be'st a man v 2 172
Man but a rush against Othello's breast, And he retires v 2 270
Where is this rash and most unfortunate man?—That's he that was Othello v 2 283
Our dungy earth alike Feeds beast as man *Ant. and Cleo.* i 1 36
Is this the man? Is't you, sir, that know things? i 2 8
It is a heart-breaking to see a handsome man loose-wived i 2 75
The man from Sicyon,—is there such an one? i 2 118
She is cunning past man's thought i 2 150
When it pleaseth their deities to take the wife of a man from him, it shows to man the tailors of the earth i 2 169
A man who is the abstract of all faults That all men follow i 4 9
The ebb'd man, ne'er loved till ne'er worth love, Comes dear'd by being lack'd i 4 43
O well-divided disposition! Note him, Note him, good Charmian, 'tis the man i 5 54
Sad or merry, The violence of either thee becomes, So does it no man else i 5 61
If thou with Cæsar paragon again My man of men i 5 72
Thou shouldst come like a Fury crown'd with snakes, Not like a formal man ii 5 41
And friends with Cæsar.—Thou'rt an honest man ii 5 47
The man is innocent.—Some innocents 'scape not the thunderbolt ii 5 76
They would Have one man but a man ii 6 19
I came before you here a man prepared To take this offer ii 6 41
I will praise any man that will praise me ii 6 91
Though thou think me poor, I am the man Will give thee all the world ii 7 70
The holding every man shall bear as loud As his strong sides can volley ii 7 117
He were the worse for that, were he a horse; So is he, being a man iii 2 53
A proper man.—Indeed, he is so: I repent me much That so I harried him iii 3 41
The man hath seen some majesty, and should know.—Hath he seen majesty? iii 3 45
And, as the president of my kingdom, will Appear there for a man iii 7 19
Now I must To the young man send humble treaties iii 11 62
Sues To let him breathe between the heavens and earth, A private man iii 12 15
One that but performs The bidding of the fullest man iii 13 8
I'll leave thee Now, like a man of steel iv 4 33
Fought Not as you served the cause, but as't had been Each man's like mine iv 8 7
Behold this man; Commend unto his lips thy favouring hand iv 8 22
What man is this?—Stand close, and list him iv 9 6
His best force Is forth to man his galleys. To the vales iv 11 3
The business of this man looks out of him; We'll hear him v 1 50
O, such another sleep, that I might see But such another man! v 2 78
Think you there was, or might be, such a man As this I dream'd of? v 2 93
Wert thou a man, Thou wouldst have mercy on me v 2 174
This is the man.—Avoid, and leave him v 2 241
You do not meet a man but frowns *Cymbeline* i 1 1
That married her, alack, good man! And therefore banish'd i 1 18
I do not think So fair an outward and such stuff within Endows a man but he i 1 24
By her election may be truly read What kind of man he is i 1 54
To be suspected of more tenderness Than doth become a man i 1 95
He is A man worth any woman i 1 146
Desire My man's abode where I did leave him: he Is strange i 6 53
To think that man, who knows By history, report, or his own proof, What woman is, yea, what she cannot choose But must be, will his free hours languish for Assured bondage? i 6 69
Was there ever man had such luck! ii 1 1
Man's o'er-labour'd sense Repairs itself by rest ii 2 11
The most patient man in loss, the most coldest that ever turned up ace ii 3 2
It would make any man cold to lose.—But not every man patient ii 3 4
Winning will put any man into courage ii 3 8
'Tis gold Which makes the true man kill'd and saves the thief; Nay, sometime hangs both thief and true man ii 3 76

Man. Let there be no honour Where there is beauty; truth, where semblance; love, Where there's another man . . . . *Cymbeline* ii 4 110

That most venerable man which I Did call my father . . . ii 5 3

No motion That tends to vice in man, but I affirm It is the woman's part ii 5 21

Madam, you're best consider.—I see before me, man . . . iii 2 80

Speak, man: thy tongue May take off some extremity . . . iii 4 16

And you shall find me, wretched man, a thing The most disdain'd of fortune . . . . iii 4 19

I see into thy end, and am almost A man already . . . . iii 4 170

I see a man's life is a tedious one . . . . iii 6 1

I'll make't my comfort He is a man; I'll love him as my brother . iii 6 72

It is not vain-glory for a man and his glass to confer in his own chamber . iv 1 8

Are we not brothers?—So man and man should be . . . . iv 2 3

Hence, then, and thank The man that gave them thee . . . . iv 2 85

Being scarce made up, I mean, to man, he had not apprehension . . iv 2 110

Thou blessed thing! Jove knows what man thou mightst have made . iv 2 207

These flowers are like the pleasures of the world; This bloody man, the care . . . . iv 2 297

A headless man! The garments of Posthumus! I know the shape of's leg . . . . iv 2 308

What thing is it that I never Did see man die! . . . . . iv 4 36

This was strange chance: A narrow lane, an old man, and two boys . v 3 52

Two boys, an old man twice a boy, a lane, Preserved the Britons . . v 3 57

'Tis thought the old man and his sons were angels . . . . . v 3 85

There was a fourth man, in a silly habit, That gave the affront with them v 3 86

'Tween man and man they weigh not every stamp . . . . . v 4 24

When once he was mature for man . . . . v 4 52

But a man that were to sleep your sleep, and a hangman to help him to bed, I think he would change places with his officer . . . v 4 178

That a man should have the best use of eyes to see the way of blindness! v 4 196

Unless a man would marry a gallows and beget young gibbets . . v 4 206

A shop of all the qualities that man Loves woman for . . . v 5 166

That headless man I thought had been my lord . . . . v 5 299

This man is better than the man he slew, As well descended as thyself v 5 302

He it is that hath Assumed this age; indeed a banish'd man . . v 5 319

Assuming man's infirmities, To glad your ear . . *Pericles* i Gower 3

And that to hear an old man sing May to your wishes pleasure bring i Gower 13

You gods that made me man, and sway in love . . . . . i 1 19

He's no man on whom perfections wait That, knowing sin within, will touch the gate . . . . i 1 79

Who, finger'd to make man his lawful music, Would draw heaven down i 1 82

The earth is throng'd By man's oppression . . . . . . i 1 102

If a king bid a man be a villain, he's bound by the indenture of his oath to be one . . . . i 3 8

Man and wife Draw lots who first shall die to lengthen life . . . i 4 45

Where each man Thinks all is writ he speken can . . . . ii Gower 11

All perishen of man, of pelf, Ne aught escapen but himself . . ii Gower 35

Wind, rain, and thunder, remember, earthly man Is but a substance that must yield to you . . . . ii 1 2

A man whom both the waters and the wind, In that vast tennis-court, have made the ball . . . . ii 1 63

A man throng'd up with cold: my veins are chill . . . . . ii 1 77

When I am dead, For that I am a man, pray see me buried . . . ii 1 81

What a man cannot get, he may lawfully deal for—his wife's soul . . ii 1 120

Here's a fish hangs in the net, like a poor man's right in the law . . ii 1 123

Till the rough seas, that spare not any man, Took it in rage . . . ii 1 137

Opinion's but a fool, that makes us scan The outward habit by the inward man . . . . ii 2 57

Not a man in private conference Or council has respect with him but he ii 4 17

Be ruled by me, or I will make you—Man and wife . . . . ii 5 84

Immortality attends the former [virtue], Making a man a god . . iii 2 31

Have you that a man may deal withal, and defy the surgeon? . . iv 6 28

I would have you note, this is an honourable man . . . . iv 6 54

He's the governor of this country, and a man whom I am bound to . iv 6 58

A man may serve seven years for the loss of a leg, and have not money enough in the end to buy him a wooden one . . . . . . iv 6 181

This is the man that can, in aught you would, Resolve you . . . v 1 12

A man who for this three months hath not spoken To any one . . . v 1 24

Thou art a man, and I Have suffer'd like a girl . . . . . v 1 137

Can you remember what I call'd the man? I have named him oft . . v 3 52

This man, Through whom the gods have shown their power . . . v 3 59

Manacle. I'll manacle thy neck and feet together . . . *Tempest* i 2 461

From the manacles Of the all-building law . . . *Meas. for Meas.* ii 4 93

We'll bait thy bears to death, And manacle the bear-ward . 2 *Hen. VI.* v 1 149

We'll put you, Like one that means his proper harm, in manacles *Coriol.* i 9 57

As a foreign recreant, be led With manacles thorough our streets . . v 3 115

For my sake wear this; It is a manacle of love . . . *Cymbeline* i 1 122

Knock off his manacles; bring your prisoner . . . . . . v 4 199

Manage. I loved and to him put The manage of my state . *Tempest* i 2 70

Hope is a lover's staff; walk hence with that And manage it against despairing thoughts . . . . *T. G. of Ver.* iii 1 247

Full merrily Hath this brave manage, this career, been run . *L. L. Lost* v 2 482

I commit into your hands The husbandry and manage of my house *Mer. of Venice* iii 4 25

His horses are bred better; for, besides that they are fair with their feeding, they are taught their manage . . . . *As Y. Like It* i 1 13

Then take him up and manage well the jest . . . *T. of Shrew* Ind. 1 45

Businesses which none without thee can sufficiently manage . *W. Tale* iv 2 17

This might have been prevented . . . , Which now the manage of two kingdoms must With fearful bloody issue arbitrate . . . *K. John* i 1 37

Expedient manage must be made . . . . . . *Richard II.* i 4 39

Yea, distaff-women manage rusty bills Against thy seat . . . . iii 2 118

Like glistering Phaëthon, Wanting the manage of unruly jades . . iii 3 179

I have a jest to execute that I cannot manage alone . . 1 *Hen. IV.* i 2 181

Speak terms of manage to thy bounding steed . . . . . . ii 3 52

Come, manage me your caliver. So: very well . . 2 *Hen. IV.* iii 2 292

There was a little quiver fellow, and a' would manage you his piece thus iii 2 301

And spur 'em, Till they obey the manage . . . . *Hen. VIII.* v 3 24

Their negotiations all must slack, Wanting his manage . *Troi. and Cres.* iii 3 25

Put up thy sword, Or manage it to part these men . *Rom. and Jul.* i 1 76

I can discover all The unlucky manage of this fatal brawl . . . iii 1 148

Sons at perfect age, and fathers declining, the father should be as ward to the son, and the son manage his revenue . . . . *Lear* i 2 79

That still would manage those authorities That he hath given away! . i 3 17

What! in a town of war, Yet wild, the people's hearts brimful of fear, To manage private and domestic quarrel! . . . . . *Othello* ii 3 215

That Photinus an eunuch and your maids Manage this war *Ant. and Cleo.* iii 7 16

You must take some pains to work her to your manage . . *Pericles* iv 6 69

Managed. Shame hath a bastard fame, well managed . *Com. of Errors* iii 2 19

Other affairs must now be managed . . . . . . 1 *Hen. VI.* iv 1 181

Manager. Be still, drum! for your manager is in love . . *L. L. Lost* i 2 188

Where is our usual manager of mirth? . . . . . *M. N. Dream* v 1 35

Managing. In the managing of quarrels you may say he is wise *Much Ado* ii 3 197

Whose state so many had the managing . . . . . . *Hen. V.* Epil. 11

Manakin. This is a dear manakin to you, Sir Toby . . . *T. Night* iii 2 57

Man-at-arms. What a maidenly man-at-arms are you become! 2 *Hen. IV.* ii 2 82

And make him, naked, foil a man at arms . . . . . 3 *Hen. VI.* v 4 42

Man-child. I sprang not more in joy at first hearing he was a man-child than now in first seeing he had proved himself a man . *Coriolanus* i 3 18

Mandate. They bear the mandate; they must sweep my way *Hamlet* iii 4 204

Your special mandate for the state-affairs Hath hither brought *Othello* i 3 72

Sir, I obey the mandate, And will return to Venice . . . . iv 1 270

Who knows If the scarce-bearded Cæsar have not sent His powerful mandate to you, 'Do this, or this' . . . . . *Ant. and Cleo.* i 1 22

Mandragora. Not poppy, nor mandragora, Nor all the drowsy syrups of the world . . . . *Othello* iii 3 330

Give me to drink mandragora.—Why, madam?—That I might sleep out this great gap of time . . . . *Ant. and Cleo.* i 5 4

Mandrake. Thou whoreson mandrake, thou art fitter to be worn in my cap than to wait at my heels . . . . 2 *Hen. IV.* i 2 17

Lecherous as a monkey, and the whores called him mandrake . . . iii 2 339

Would curses kill, as doth the mandrake's groan . . 2 *Hen. VI.* iii 2 310

And shrieks like mandrakes' torn out of the earth . *Rom. and Jul.* iv 3 47

Mane. Like a dew-drop from the lion's mane, Be shook to air *T. and C.* iii 3 224

That very Mab That plats the manes of horses in the night *Rom. and Jul.* i 4 89

The wind-shaked surge, with high and monstrous mane . . *Othello* ii 1 13

Man-entered. His pupil age Man-enter'd thus, he waxed . *Coriolanus* ii 2 103

Manes. On a pile Ad manes fratrum sacrifice his flesh . . *T. Andron.* i 1 98

Till I find . . . a charm to calm these fits, Per Styga, per manes vehor ii 1 135

Manfully. Yet I slew him manfully in fight . . . . *T. G. of Ver.* iv 1 28

Knighted in field, slain manfully in arms . . . . *T. Andron.* i 1 196

Mangle. And smiled to see him Mangle the work of nature . *Hen. V.* ii 4 60

Your dishonour Mangles true judgement and bereaves the state *Coriol.* iii 1 158

To mangle me with that word 'banished' . . . . *Rom. and Jul.* iii 3 51

Mangled. The which he vents In mangled forms . . . *As Y. Like It* ii 7 42

But let my favours hide thy mangled face . . . . 1 *Hen. IV.* v 4 96

Mangled shalt thou be by this my sword . . . . . *Hen. V.* iv 4 41

The naked, poor and mangled Peace, Dear nurse of arts . . . . v 2 34

My mangled body shows, My blood, my want of strength . 3 *Hen. VI.* v 2 7

Patroclus' wounds have roused his drowsy blood, Together with his mangled Myrmidons . . . . *Troi. and Cres.* v 5 33

Thy two sons' heads, Thy warlike hand, thy mangled daughter *T. An.* iii 1 256

Ah, poor my lord, what tongue shall smooth thy name, When I, thy three-hours wife, have mangled it? . . . . . *Rom. and Jul.* iii 2 99

And pluck the mangled Tybalt from his shroud . . . . . iv 3 52

Take up this mangled matter at the best . . . . . *Othello* i 3 173

Cassio, may you suspect Who they should be that have thus mangled you? v 1 79

Haply you shall not see me more; or if, A mangled shadow *A. and C.* iv 2 27

Our laws, whose use the sword of Cæsar Hath too much mangled *Cymb.* iii 1 57

Mangling by starts the full course of their glory . . . *Hen. V.* Epil. 4

Mangy. Away, thou issue of a mangy dog! . . . . *T. of Athens* iv 3 371

Manhood is melted into courtesies, valour into compliment . *Much Ado* iv 1 321

Follow my voice: we'll try no manhood here . . . *M. N. Dream* iii 2 412

A swaggering accent sharply twanged off gives manhood more approbation than ever proof itself would have earned him . . *T. Night* iii 4 198

There's neither honesty, manhood, nor good fellowship in thee 1 *Hen. IV.* i 2 155

If manhood, good manhood, be not forgot upon the face of the earth . ii 4 141

A' comes continuantly to Pie-corner—saving your manhoods 2 *Hen. IV.* ii 1 29

That's the humour of it.—As manhood shall compound: push home *Hen. V.* ii 1 103

Which makes much against my manhood, if I should take from another's pocket to put into mine . . . . iii 2 53

And hold their manhoods cheap . . . . iv 3 66

Your majesty hear now, saving your majesty's manhood . . . . iv 8 36

Now is it manhood, wisdom and defence, To give the enemy way 2 *Hen. VI.* v 2 75

'Twas not your valour, Clifford, drove me thence.—No, nor your manhood that durst make you stay . . . . 3 *Hen. VI.* ii 2 108

I am resolved That Clifford's manhood lies upon his tongue . . . ii 2 125

And stout Diomede With sleight and manhood stole to Rhesus' tents . iv 2 20

Thy prime of manhood daring, bold, and venturous . *Richard III.* iv 4 170

Manhood, learning, gentleness, virtue, youth, liberality, and such like, the spice and salt that season a man . . . . *Troi. and Cres.* i 2 276

Manhood and honour Should have hare-hearts . . . . . . ii 2 47

Manhood is call'd foolery, when it stands Against a falling fabric *Coriol.* iii 1 246

Who dares, who dares, In purity of manhood stand upright, And say 'This man's a flatterer?' . . . . *T. of Athens* iv 3 14

If you have a station in the file, Not i' the worst rank of manhood *Macb.* iii 1 102

Many unrough youths that even now Protest their first of manhood . v 2 11

I am ashamed That thou hast power to shake my manhood thus . *Lear* i 4 319

Marry, your manhood now . . . . iv 2 68

It were not for your quiet nor your good, Nor for my manhood *Othello* iii 3 153

Experience, manhood, honour, ne'er before Did violate so itself *A. and C.* iii 10 23

To some shade, And fit you to your manhood . . . . *Cymbeline* iii 4 195

The heaviness and guilt within my bosom Takes off my manhood . . v 2 2

Manifest. It is now apparent.—Most manifest . . *Meas. for Meas.* iv 2 145

The duke's unjust, Thus to retort your manifest appeal . . . . v 1 303

Aim better at me by that I now will manifest . . . . *Much Ado* iii 2 100

It appears, by manifest proceeding . . . . . *Mer. of Venice* iv 1 358

Such as his reading And manifest experience had collected . *All's Well* i 3 229

In this she manifests herself to my love . . . . . *T. Night* ii 5 182

And make't manifest where she has lived . . . . . . *W. Tale* v 3 114

Thy life did manifest thou lovedst me not . . . 2 *Hen. IV.* iv 5 105

Stand back, thou manifest conspirator . . . . . 1 *Hen. VI.* i 3 33

And for thy treachery, what's more manifest? . . . . . . iii 1 21

You are manifest house-keepers . . . . *Coriolanus* i 3 54

Manifests the true knowledge he has in their disposition . . . ii 2 14

And throw their power i' the dust.—Manifest treason! . . . . . iii 1 172

To prove upon thy head Thy heinous, manifest, and many treasons *Lear* v 3 92

My title and my perfect soul Shall manifest me rightly . . . *Othello* i 2 32

Manifested. Neither singly can be manifested . . . *Mer. Wives* iv 6 15

To make you understand this in a manifested effect . *Meas. for Meas.* iv 2 169

You shall find Your safety manifested . . . . iv 3 94

Then, Angelo, thy fault's thus manifested . . . . v 1 417

Manifold. For mischiefs manifold and sorceries terrible . . *Tempest* i 2 264

The manifold linguist and the armipotent soldier . . . *All's Well* iv 3 265

Your good deserts forgot, Which he confesseth to be manifold 1 *Hen. IV.* iv 3 47

What strange, Which manifold record not matches? . . *T. of Athens* i 1 5

With how manifold and strong a bond The child was bound to the father *Lear* ii 1 49

That he is a manifold traitor . . . . v 3 113

Manifoldly. Did manifoldly dissuade me from believing . . *All's Well* ii 3 214
Man in the moon. Unless the sun were post—The man i' the moon's too slow . . . . *Tempest* ii 1 249
I was the man i' the moon when time was . . . . . . ii 2 142
The man i' the moon! A most poor credulous monster! . . . ii 2 149
Myself the man i' the moon do seem to be . . *M. N. Dream* v 1 249
The man should be put into the lanthorn. How is it else the man i' the moon? . . . . v 1 252
The lanthorn is the moon; I, the man in the moon . . . . v 1 262
Manka revania dulche . . . . *All's Well* iv 1 86
Mankind. How beauteous mankind is! O brave new world! *Tempest* v 1 183
So rails against all married mankind . . . . *Mer. Wives* iv 2 23
What kind o' man is he?—Why, of mankind . . . . *T. Night* i 5 160
What, man! defy the devil: consider, he's an enemy to mankind . iii 4 108
Should all despair That have revolted wives, the tenth of mankind Would hang themselves . . . . . . *W. Tale* i 2 199
Out! A mankind witch! Hence with her, out o' door . . . ii 3 67
The common curse of mankind, folly and ignorance . *Troi. and Cres.* ii 3 30
Are you mankind?—Ay, fool; is that a shame? *Coriolanus* iv 2 16
The place which I have feasted, does it now, Like all mankind, show me an iron heart? . . . . *T. of Athens* iii 4 84
He shall find The unkindest beast more kinder than mankind . iv 1 36
Grant, as Timon grows, his hate may grow To the whole race of mankind! iv 1 40
His semblable, yea, himself, Timon disdains: Destruction fang mankind! iv 3 23
Come, damned earth, Thou common whore of mankind . . . iv 3 42
I am Misanthropos, and hate mankind . . . . . . iv 3 53
'Tis in the malice of mankind that he thus advises us . . . iv 3 456
I love thee, Because thou art a woman, and disclaim'st Flinty mankind iv 3 491
How fain would I have hated all mankind! And thou redeem'st thyself iv 3 506
Contending 'gainst obedience, as they would make War with mankind *Macbeth* ii 4 18
He hath fought to-day As if a god, in hate of mankind, had Destroy'd in such a shape . . . . *Ant. and Cleo.* iv 8 25
Manlike. Is not more manlike Than Cleopatra; nor the queen of Ptolemy More womanly than he . . . . i 4 5
Manly. A most manly wit, Margaret; it will not hurt a woman *Much Ado* v 2 15
A manly enterprise, To conjure tears up in a poor maid's eyes! *M. N. D.* iii 2 157
These foolish drops do something drown my manly spirit *Mer. of Venice* ii 3 14
And turn two mincing steps Into a manly stride . . . . iii 4 68
His big manly voice, Turning again toward childish treble *As Y. Like It* ii 7 161
Spending his manly marrow in her arms . . . . *All's Well* ii 3 298
But this effusion of such manly drops, This shower . . *K. John* v 2 49
Let me bring thee to Staines.—No; for my manly heart doth yearn *Hen. V.* ii 3 3
Abate thy rage, abate thy manly rage, Abate thy rage, great duke! . iii 2 24
Henry hath money, you are strong and manly; God on our side 2 *Hen. VI.* iv 8 53
As did Æneas old Anchises bear, So bear I thee upon my manly shoulders v 2 63
His manly face, which promiseth Successful fortune . . 3 *Hen. VI.* i 2 40
In that sad time My manly eyes did scorn an humble tear *Richard III.* i 2 165
Manly as Hector, but more dangerous . . . *Troi. and Cres.* iv 5 104
I saw the wound, I saw it with mine eyes,—God save the mark!—here on his manly breast . . . . . . *Rom. and Jul.* iii 2 53
Let's briefly put on manly readiness, And meet i' the hall *Macbeth* ii 3 139
This tune goes manly. Come, go we to the king; our power is ready . iv 3 235
My friends, The boy hath taught us manly duties . . . *Cymbeline* iv 2 397
A little daughter: for the sake of it, Be manly . . *Pericles* iii 1 22
Man-monster. My man-monster hath drowned his tongue in sack *Tempest* iii 2 14
Manna. You drop manna in the way Of starved people . *Mer. of Venice* v 1 294
Mann'd with three hundred men, as I have heard . . *Richard II.* ii 3 54
The castle royally is mann'd, my lord, Against thy entrance . . . iii 3 21
I was never manned with an agate till now . . . 2 *Hen. IV.* i 2 18
An I could get me but a wife in the stews, I were manned, horsed, and wived . . . . i 2 60
Your ships are not well mann'd; Your mariners are muleters *A. and C.* iii 7 35
Manner. Yet, note, Their manners are more gentle-kind . . *Tempest* iii 3 32
He is as disproportion'd in his manners As in his shape . . . v 1 290
O, give ye good even! here's a million of manners . . *T. G. of Ver.* ii 1 105
Nay, I'll show you the manner of it . . . . ii 3 15
All the cunning manner of our flight Determined of . . . . ii 4 180
Which is in the manner of his nurse, or his dry nurse . *Mer. Wives* i 2 3
That he dares in this manner assay me . . . . . . ii 1 25
Against all checks, rebukes and manners, I must advance . . . iii 4 84
And shakes a chain In a most hideous and dreadful manner . . . iv 4 34
I have heard it was ever his manner to do so . . . *Meas. for Meas.* iv 2 138
In most uneven and distracted manner . . . . . . iv 4 3
In self-same manner doth accuse my husband . . . . . v 1 196
I'll view the manners of the town . . . *Com. of Errors* i 2 12
Hero was in this manner accused, in this very manner refused *Much Ado* iv 2 64
The grosser manner of these world's delights . . *L. L. Lost* i 1 29
The manner of it is, I was taken with the manner.—In what manner?—In manner and form following . . . . i 1 204
For the manner,—it is the manner of a man to speak to a woman . . i 1 212
My lady, to the manner of the days, In courtesy gives undeserving praise v 2 365
Now much beshrew my manners and my pride . . *M. N. Dream* ii 2 54
You do me wrong, good sooth, you do, In such disdainful manner me to woo . . . . ii 2 130
If you have any pity, grace, or manners . . . . . . iii 2 241
Unless I be obtained by the manner of my father's will . *Mer. of Venice* i 2 118
Though I am a daughter to his blood, I am not to his manners . . ii 3 19
There must be needs a like proportion Of lineaments, of manners . . iii 4 15
Yet tell us the manner of the wrestling . . . *As Y. Like It* i 2 118
Neither his daughter, if we judge by manners . . . . . i 2 283
A rude despiser of good manners . . . . ii 7 92
If thou never wast at court, thou never sawest good manners; if thou never sawest good manners, then thy manners must be wicked . iii 2 42
Those that are good manners at the court are as ridiculous in the country iii 2 47
What manner of man? Is his head worth a hat, or his chin worth a beard? iii 2 216
Did you ever cure any so?—Yes, one, and in this manner . . . iii 2 427
She says I am not fair, that I lack manners . . . . . iv 3 15
We quarrel in print, by the book; as you have books for good manners v 4 95
And therefore frame your manners to the time . . . *T. of Shrew* i 1 232
I advise You use your manners discreetly in all kind of companies . . i 1 247
Stand by and mark the manner of his teaching . . . . . iv 2 5
And succeed thy father In manners, as in shape! . . . *All's Well* i 1 71
If God have lent a man any manners, he may easily put it off at court . ii 2 9
I was thinking with what manners I might safely be admitted . . iv 5 93
Goaded with most sharp occasions, Which lay nice manners by . . v 1 15
What manner of man?—Of very ill manner . . . . *T. Night* i 5 161
It charges me in manners the rather to express myself . . . . ii 1 15
I am yet so near the manners of my mother, that upon the least occasion more mine eyes will tell tales of me . . . . ii 1 41

Manner. Have you no wit, manners, nor honesty, but to gabble like tinkers at this time of night? . . . . *T. Night* ii 3 94
By the colour of his beard, the shape of his leg, the manner of his gait ii 3 170
He's coming, madam; but in very strange manner . . . . . iii 4 9
And consequently sets down the manner how; as, a sad face . . . iii 4 80
What manner of man is he?—Nothing of that wonderful promise . . iii 4 288
Ungracious wretch, Fit for the mountains and the barbarous caves, Where manners ne'er were preach'd! . . . . iv 1 53
To consider what is breeding That changeth thus his manners *W. Tale* i 2 375
What manner of fellow was he that robbed you? . . . . . iv 3 89
Not a word, a word; we stand upon our manners . . . . . iv 4 164
Is there no manners left among maids? . . . . iv 4 244
The manner of your bearing towards him . . . I'll write you down . iv 4 569
They do not give us the lie.—Your worship had like to have given us one, if you had not taken yourself with the manner . . . . iv 4 752
Heard the old shepherd deliver the manner how he found it . . . v 2 4
So and in such manner that it seemed sorrow wept to take leave of them v 2 49
At the relation of the queen's death, with the manner how she came to't v 2 92
Our country manners give our betters way . . . . *K. John* i 1 156
Liker in feature to his father Geffrey Than thou and John in manners . ii 1 127
Our griefs, and not our manners, reason now . . . . . . iv 3 29
Nay, it is in a manner done already . . . . v 7 89
Whose manners still our tardy apish nation Limps after *Richard II.* ii 1 22
You have in manner with your sinful hours Made a divorce . . . iii 1 11
These external manners of laments Are merely shadows to the unseen grief iv 1 296
The manner of their taking may appear At large . . . . . v 6 9
What manner of man is he?—An old man . . . 1 *Hen. IV.* ii 4 323
Thou stolest a cup of sack eighteen years ago, and wert taken with the manner . . . . ii 4 347
What manner of man, an it like your majesty?—A goodly portly man . ii 4 462
Oftentimes it doth present harsh rage, Defect of manners . . . iii 1 184
Well, I am school'd: good manners be your speed! . . . . iii 1 190
Your manner of wrenching the true cause the false way . 2 *Hen. IV.* ii 1 120
What foolish master taught you these manners? . . . . ii 1 203
When means and lavish manners meet together . . . . . iv 4 64
The manner how this action hath been borne Here at more leisure may your highness read . . . . iv 4 88
The manner and true order of the fight This packet, please it you, contains . . . . iv 4 100
The seasons change their manners . . . . iv 4 123
For some dishonest manners of their life . . . . *Hen. V.* i 2 49
The pretty and sweet manner of it forced Those waters from me . . iv 6 28
We are the makers of manners . . . . v 2 296
All manner of men assembled here in arms this day . 1 *Hen. VI.* i 3 74
The treacherous manner of his mournful death . . . . . ii 2 16
Bear me company?—No, truly; it is more than manners will . . ii 2 54
In writing I preferr'd The manner of thy vile outrageous crimes . . iii 1 11
Foul indigested lump, As crooked in thy manners as thy shape! 2 *Hen. VI.* v 1 158
Dare he presume to scorn us in this manner? . . . 3 *Hen. VI.* iii 3 178
Timorously confess The manner and the purpose of his treason *Rich. III.* iii 5 58
That no manner of person At any time have recourse unto the princes . iii 5 108
This Edward, whom our manners term the prince . . . . . iii 7 191
O, let her live, And I'll corrupt her manners, stain her beauty . . iv 4 206
In desperate manner Daring the event to the teeth . . . *Hen. VIII.* i 2 35
In humblest manner I require your highness, That it shall please you . ii 4 144
If I blush, It is to see a nobleman want manners . . . . . iii 2 308
Men's evil manners live in brass; their virtues We write in water . . iv 2 45
Now, by my holidame, What manner of man are you? . . . . . v 1 117
The tidings that I bring Will make my boldness manners . . . v 1 159
I had thought They had parted so much honesty among 'em, At least, good manners . . . . v 2 29
'Tis he, I ken the manner of his gait; He rises on the toe *Troi. and Cres.* iv 5 14
In fellest manner execute your aims . . . . v 7 6
Showing, as the manner is, his wounds To the people . . *Coriolanus* ii 1 251
Speak to 'em, I pray you, In wholesome manner . . . . . . ii 3 66
Thy wit wants edge, And manners, to intrude . . . . *T. Andron.* ii 1 27
When good manners shall lie all in one or two men's hands and they unwashed too, 'tis a foul thing . . . . . . *Rom. and Jul.* i 5 4
As the manner of our country is . . . . iv 1 109
What manners is in this, To press before thy father to a grave? . . v 3 214
Yea, 'gainst the authority of manners, pray'd you . . *T. of Athens* i 2 147
In like manner was I in debt to my importunate business . . . iii 6 15
Instruction, manners, mysteries, and trades, Degrees, observances . iv 1 18
Thou cold sciatica, cripple our senators, that their limbs may halt As lamely as their manners! . . . . iv 1 25
Men report Thou dost affect my manners, and dost use them . . iv 3 199
Tell us the manner of it, gentle Casca.—I can as well be hanged as tell the manner of it: it was mere foolery . . . . . . *J. Cæsar* i 2 234
She is dead, and by strange manner . . . . iv 3 189
Savagely slaughter'd: to relate the manner, Were, on the quarry of these murder'd deer, To add the death of you . . . . *Macbeth* iv 3 205
Though I am native here And to the manner born . . . *Hamlet* i 4 15
Some habit that too much o'er-leavens The form of plausive manners . i 4 30
Making so bold, My fears forgetting manners . . . . . . v 2 17
Beyond all manner of so much I love you. . . . . . . *Lear* i 1 62
Sir, he answered me in the roundest manner, he would not . . . i 4 59
They know not how their wits to wear, Their manners are so apish . i 4 184
That this our court, infected with their manners, Shows like a riotous inn i 4 264
Leave, gentle wax; and, manners, blame us not . . . . . iv 6 264
The time will not allow the compliment Which very manners urges . v 3 234
My manners tell me We have your wrong rebuke . . . . *Othello* i 1 130
Let it not gall your patience, good Iago, That I extend my manners . ii 1 99
Loveliness in favour, sympathy in years, manners and beauties . . ii 1 232
These bloody accidents must excuse my manners, That so neglected you v 1 94
I do not much dislike the matter, but The manner of his speech *A. and C.* ii 2 114
What manner o' thing is your crocodile?—It is shaped, sir, like itself . ii 7 46
Here's the manner of't: I' the market-place, on a tribunal silver'd . iii 6 2
The manner of their deaths? I do not see them bleed . . . . v 2 340
Can we, with manners, ask what was the difference?—Safely. *Cymbeline* i 4 56
Sir, You put me to forget a lady's manners, By being so verbal . . ii 3 110
Nor tell the world Antiochus doth sin In such a loathed manner *Pericles* i 1 147
Come, young one, I like the manner of your garments well . . . iv 2 145
Mannered. He is one The truest manner'd . . . . *Cymbeline* i 6 166
Give her princely training, that she may be Manner'd as she is born *Per.* iii 3 17
Mannerly. What thou thinkest meet and is most mannerly *T. G. of Ver.* ii 7 58
I long to see Quick Cupid's post that comes so mannerly *Mer. of Venice* ii 9 100
Mannerly distinguishment leave out Betwixt the prince and beggar *W. Tale* ii 1 86
Here is a mannerly forbearance. . . . . . . 1 *Hen. VI.* ii 4 19
Which mannerly devotion shows in this . . . . *Rom. and Jul* i 5 100
When we have supp'd, We'll mannerly demand thee of thy story *Cymb.* iii 6 92

Mannerly-modest. The wedding, mannerly-modest . . . *Much Ado* ii 1 79
Manningtree ox. That roasted Manningtree ox with the pudding in his belly . . . . 1 *Hen. IV.* ii 4 498
Mannish. A martial outside, As many other mannish cowards *As Y. L. It* i 3 123
A woman impudent and mannish grown Is not more loathed than an effeminate man In time of action . *Troi. and Cres.* iii 3 217
Though now our voices Have got the mannish crack . *Cymbeline* iv 2 236
Man-of-war. Leave you not a man-of-war unsearch'd . *T. Andron.* iv 3 22
Manor. To your manor of Pickt-hatch! Go . . *Mer. Wives* ii 2 19
I know a man that . . . sold a goodly manor for a song . . *All's Well* iii 2 10
My manors, rents, revenues I forego . . *Richard II.* iv 1 212
My walks, my manors that I had, Even now forsake me . 3 *Hen. VI.* v 2 24
O, many Have broke their backs with laying manors on 'em . *Hen. VIII.* i 1 84
Manor-house. In the manor-house, sitting with her . . *L. L. Lost* i 1 208
Man-queller. A man-queller, and a woman-queller . 2 *Hen. IV.* ii 1 58
Mansion. Leave not the mansion so long tenantless . *T. G. of Ver.* v 4 8
But now I was the lord Of this fair mansion . *Mer. of Venice* iii 2 170
The case of a treble hautboy was a mansion for him, a court 2 *Hen. IV.* iii 2 351
I have bought the mansion of a love, But not possess'd it *Rom. and Jul.* iii 2 26
Tell me, that I may sack The hateful mansion . . . iii 3 108
Teem with new monsters, whom thy upward face Hath to the marbled mansion all above Never presented! . . . . *T. of Athens* iv 3 191
Made his everlasting mansion Upon the beached verge of the salt flood v 1 218
To leave his wife, to leave his babes, His mansion and his titles in a place From whence himself does fly? . . . . . *Macbeth* iv 2 7
Take it, and hit The innocent mansion of my love, my heart . *Cymbeline* iii 4 70
Peep through thy marble mansion; help; Or we poor ghosts will cry . v 4 87
It was in Rome,—accursed The mansion where!—'twas at a feast . . v 5 155
Mansionry. The temple-haunting martlet does approve, By his loved mansionry, that the heaven's breath Smells wooingly here *Macbeth* i 6 5
Manslaughter. Your words have took such pains as if they labour'd To bring manslaughter into form . . . . *T. of Athens* iii 5 27
Mantle. Their rising senses Begin to chase the ignorant fumes that mantle Their clearer reason . . . . . *Tempest* v 1 67
And, as she fled, her mantle she did fall . . . *M. N. Dream* v 1 143
Anon comes Pyramus, . . . And finds his trusty Thisby's mantle slain v 1 146
O dainty duck! O dear! Thy mantle good, What, stain'd with blood! v 1 287
Men whose visages Do cream and mantle like a standing pond *Mer. of Venice* i 1 89
Such unity in the proofs. The mantle of Queen Hermione's . *W. Tale* v 2 36
Night is fled, Whose pitchy mantle over-veil'd the earth . 1 *Hen. VI.* ii 2 2
Well cover'd with the night's black mantle . . . 3 *Hen. VI.* iv 2 22
Hood my unmann'd blood . . . With thy black mantle . *Rom. and Jul.* iii 2 15
You all do know this mantle: I remember The first time ever Cæsar put it on; 'Twas on a summer's evening . . . . *J. Cæsar* iii 2 174
And, in his mantle muffling up his face, Even at the base of Pompey's statua, Which all the while ran blood, great Cæsar fell . . iii 2 191
Look, the morn, in russet mantle clad, Walks o'er the dew *Hamlet* i 1 166
Drinks the green mantle of the standing pool . . . *Lear* iii 4 139
Put my tires and mantles on him, whilst I wore his sword *Ant. and Cleo.* ii 5 22
He, sir, was lapp'd In a most curious mantle . . *Cymbeline* v 5 361
Mantled. Come I too late?—Ay, if you come not in the blood of others, But mantled in your own . . . . . . *Coriolanus* i 6 29
Mantua. From Verona banished . . . —And I from Mantua *T. G. of Ver.* iv 1 50
I would to Valentine, To Mantua, where I hear he makes abode . iv 3 23
Upon the rising of the mountain-foot That leads toward Mantua . . v 2 47
His name is Licio, born in Mantua.—You're welcome, sir *T. of Shrew* ii 1 60
What countryman, I pray?—Of Mantua.—Of Mantua, sir? marry, God forbid! . . . . iv 2 77
'Tis death for any one in Mantua To come to Padua . . . iv 2 81
My lord and you were then at Mantua:—Nay, I do bear a brain *Rom. and Jul.* i 3 28
Stay not till the watch be set, For then thou canst not pass to Mantua iii 3 149
Sojourn in Mantua; I'll find out your man, And he shall signify . iii 3 169
It is some meteor that the sun exhales, To be to thee this night a torch-bearer, And light thee on thy way to Mantua . . . . iii 5 15
I'll send to one in Mantua, Where that same banish'd runagate doth live iii 5 89
And that very night Shall Romeo bear thee hence to Mantua . iv 1 117
I'll send a friar with speed To Mantua, with my letters to thy lord iv 1 124
An if a man did need a poison now, Whose sale is present death in Mantua, Here lives a caitiff wretch would sell it him . . v 1 51
Mortal drugs I have; but Mantua's law Is death to any he that utters them . . . . v 1 66
This same should be the voice of Friar John. Welcome from Mantua . v 2 3
And would not let us forth; So that my speed to Mantua there was stay'd . . . . v 2 12
I will write again to Mantua, And keep her at my cell till Romeo come v 2 28
In post he came from Mantua To this same place, to this same monument . . . . v 3 273
Mantuan. Ah, good old Mantuan! . . . . . *L. L. Lost* iv 2 97
Old Mantuan, old Mantuan! who understandeth thee not, loves thee not iv 2 101
Manual. There is my gage, the manual seal of death . *Richard II.* iv 1 25
Manure. The blood of English shall manure the ground . . . iv 1 137
Manured, husbanded, and tilled with excellent endeavour 2 *Hen. IV.* iv 3 129
Either to have it sterile with idleness, or manured with industry *Othello* i 3 328
Manus. Thus did he strangle serpents in his manus . *L. L. Lost* v 2 595
Many. Full many a lady I have eyed with best regard . *Tempest* iii 1 39
More gentle-kind than . . . you shall find Many, nay, almost any . iii 3 34
Of many good I think him best . . . . . *T. G. of Ver.* i 2 21
Many a man would take you at your word . *Com. of Errors* i 2 17
There's many a man hath more hair than wit . . . ii 2 83
When one is one too many . . . . iii 1 35
How many is one thrice told?—I am ill at reckoning . *L. L. Lost* i 2 41
Many a time and oft In the Rialto you have rated me . *Mer. of Venice* i 3 107
And I do know A many fools, that stand in better place . . iii 5 73
And a many merry men with him . . . . *As Y. Like It* i 1 121
A horse and a man Is more than one, And yet not many *T. of Shrew* iii 2 88
But the many will be too chill and tender, and they'll be for the flowery way that leads to the broad gate and the great fire . *All's Well* iv 5 55
Was yet of many accounted beautiful . . . *T. Night* ii 1 27
But many a many foot of land the worse . . . *K. John* i 1 183
Many a time hath banish'd Norfolk fought For Jesu Christ *Richard II.* iv 1 92
Thou hast called her to a reckoning many a time and oft 1 *Hen. IV.* i 2 56
O thou fond many, with what loud applause Didst thou beat heaven with blessing Bolingbroke! . . . . . . 2 *Hen. IV.* i 3 91
They flock together in consent, like so many wild-geese . . v 1 79
As many ways meet in one town; As many fresh streams meet in one salt sea; As many lines close in the dial's centre . *Hen. V.* i 2 208
And those few I have Almost no better than so many French . iii 6 156
A many of our bodies shall no doubt Find native graves . . iv 3 95
Many. Many a thousand, Which now mistrust no parcel of my fear, And many an old man's sigh and many a widow's, And many an orphan's water-standing eye . . . Shall rue the hour that ever thou wast born 3 *Hen. VI.* v 6 37
A care-crazed mother of a many children . . *Richard III.* iii 7 184
Not able to maintain The many to them longing . . *Hen. VIII.* i 2 32
The wisest prince that there had reign'd by many A year before . . ii 4 49
This many summers in a sea of glory, But far beyond my depth . iii 2 360
The strangest sight . . . I think your highness saw this many a day . v 2 21
What so many may do, Not being torn a-pieces, we have done . v 4 79
Let him alone, or so many so minded, Wave thus *Coriolanus* i 6 73
I know you can do very little alone; for your helps are many . ii 1 39
The mutable, rank-scented many . . . . . . iii 1 66
Many a time he danced thee on his knee . . *T. Andron.* v 3 162
That book in many's eyes doth share the glory, That in gold clasps locks in the golden story . . . . . . *Rom. and Jul.* i 3 91
Many for many virtues excellent, None but for some . . ii 3 13
Which many my near occasions did urge me to put off . *T. of Athens* iii 6 11
Many a time and oft Have you climb'd up to walls . . *J. Cæsar* i 1 42
How does your honour for this many a day? . . . *Hamlet* iii 1 91
Most holy and religious fear it is To keep those many many bodies safe That live and feed upon your majesty . . . . . iii 3 9
To beguile many and be beguiled by one . . . *Othello* iv 1 98
Many our contriving friends in Rome Petition us at home *Ant. and Cleo.* i 2 189
Many-coloured. Hail, many-colour'd messenger, that ne'er Dost disobey the wife of Jupiter . . . . . . *Tempest* iv 1 76
The many-colour'd Iris rounds thine eye . . . *All's Well* i 3 158
Many-headed. Stuck not to call us the many-headed multitude *Coriol.* ii 3 18
Map. Peering in maps for ports and piers and roads . *Mer. of Venice* i 1 19
He does smile his face into more lines than is in the new map with the augmentation of the Indies . . . . . . *T. Night* iii 2 85
Thou map of honour, thou King Richard's tomb . *Richard II.* v 1 12
A plague upon it! I have forgot the map.—No, here it is 1 *Hen. IV.* iii 1 6
Here's the map: shall we divide our right? . . . iii 1 70
If you look in the maps of the 'orld, I warrant you sall find . *Hen. V.* iv 7 25
In thy face I see The map of honour, truth and loyalty . 2 *Hen. VI.* iii 1 203
Welcome, destruction . . .! I see, as in a map, the end of all *Rich. III.* ii 4 54
If you see this in the map of my microcosm . . *Coriolanus* ii 1 68
Thou map of woe, that thus dost talk in signs! . *T. Andron.* iii 2 12
Give me the map there. Know that we have divided In three our kingdom . . . . *Lear* i 1 38
Mapped. I am near to the place where they should meet, if Pisanio have mapped it truly . . . . *Cymbeline* iv 1 2
Mappery. They call this bed-work, mappery, closet-war . *Troi. and Cres.* i 3 205
Mar. You mar our labour: keep your cabins . . . *Tempest* i 1 14
You are too flat And mar the concord . . . *T. G. of Ver.* i 2 94
Women! Help Heaven! men their creation mar In profiting by them. Nay, call us ten times frail . . . . *Meas. for Meas.* ii 4 127
Some certain treason.—What makes treason here?—Nay, it makes nothing, sir.—If it mar nothing neither . . . . *L. L. Lost* iv 3 191
You'll mar the light by taking it in snuff . . . . . v 2 22
And make and mar The foolish Fates . . . *M. N. Dream* i 2 39
I'll mar the young clerk's pen . . . . *Mer. of Venice* v 1 237
I am not taught to make any thing.—What mar you then, sir?—Marry, sir, I am helping you to mar that which God made . *As Y. Like It* i 1 34
I pray you, mar no more trees with writing love-songs in their barks . iii 2 276
I pray you, mar no moe of my verses with reading them ill-favouredly . iii 2 278
But if you be remember'd, I did not bid you mar it . *T. of Shrew* iv 3 97
And then Let nature crush the sides o' the earth together And mar the seeds within! . . . . *W. Tale* iv 4 490
The ruddiness upon her lip is wet; You'll mar it if you kiss it . v 3 82
If we use delay, Cold biting winter mars our hoped-for hay 3 *Hen. VI.* iv 8 61
His spell in that is out: the king hath found Matter against him that for ever mars The honey of his language . . . *Hen. VIII.* iii 2 21
You'll mar all: I'll leave you: pray you, speak to 'em . *Coriolanus* ii 3 64
One, gentlewoman, that God hath made for himself to mar.—By my troth, it is well said; 'for himself to mar,' quoth a'? *Rom. and Jul.* ii 4 122
For bounty, that makes gods, does still mar men . *T. of Athens* iv 2 41
Consumptions sow In hollow bones of man; strike their sharp shins, And mar men's spurring . . . . iv 3 153
It [drink] makes him, and it mars him . . . . *Macbeth* ii 3 36
No more o' that, my lord, no more o' that: you mar all with this starting . . . . v 1 50
Mend your speech a little, Lest it may mar your fortunes . . *Lear* i 1 97
Mar a curious tale in telling it, and deliver a plain message bluntly . i 4 35
Striving to better, oft we mar what's well . . . . i 4 369
When brewers mar their malt with water . . . . . iii 2 82
My tears begin to take his part so much, They'll mar my counterfeiting iii 6 64
It makes us, or it mars us; think on that . . . . *Othello* v 1 4
Stray no farther: now all labour Mars what it does . *Ant. and Cleo.* iv 14 48
These same whoreson devils do the gods great harm in their women; for in every ten that they make, the devils mar five . . . . v 2 279
Come, give me your flowers, ere the sea mar it . . . *Pericles* iv 1 27
Marble. He, a marble to her tears, is washed with them *Meas. for Meas.* iii 1 238
Or else for ever be confixed here, A marble monument! . . . v 1 233
Unkindness blunts it more than marble hard . . *Com. of Errors* ii 1 93
Who was most marble there changed colour . . . . *W. Tale* v 2 98
Her tears will pierce into a marble heart . . . 3 *Hen. VI.* iii 1 38
He plies her hard; and much rain wears the marble . . . iii 2 50
Forgotten, as I shall be, And sleep in dull cold marble . *Hen. VIII.* iii 2 433
The milk thou suck'dst from her did turn to marble . *T. Andron.* ii 3 144
I had else been perfect, Whole as the marble . . . *Macbeth* iii 4 22
Why the sepulchre, Wherein we saw thee quietly inurn'd, Hath oped his ponderous and marble jaws, To cast thee up again . . *Hamlet* i 4 50
By yond marble heaven, In the due reverence of a sacred vow *Othello* iii 3 460
Peep through thy marble mansion; help; Or we poor ghosts will cry *Cymbeline* v 4 87
The marble pavement closes, he is enter'd His radiant roof . . v 4 120
Marble-breasted. Live you the marble-breasted tyrant . . *T. Night* v 1 127
Marble-constant. I have nothing Of woman in me: now from head to foot I am marble-constant . . . . . . *Ant. and Cleo.* v 2 240
Marbled. To the marbled mansion all above Never presented! *T. of A.* iv 3 191
Marble-hearted. Ingratitude, thou marble-hearted fiend! . . . *Lear* i 4 281
Marcellus. Horatio and Marcellus, The rivals of my watch . . *Hamlet* i 1 12
Marcellus and myself, The bell then beating one,— Peace, break thee off! . . . . i 1 38
Stop it, Marcellus.—Shall I strike at it with my partisan? . . . i 1 139
Marcellus and Bernardo, on their watch, In the dead vast and middle of the night, Been thus encounter'd . . . . i 2 197
Octavia.—True, sir; she was the wife of Caius Marcellus *Ant. and Cleo.* ii 6 118

March. And take The winds of March with beauty *W. Tale* iv 4 120
His marches are expedient to this town *K. John* ii 1 60
Who painfully with much expedient march Have brought a counter-check ii 1 223
We tread In warlike march these greens before your town ii 1 242
And on the marriage-bed Of smiling peace to march a bloody host iii 1 246
Use all your power To stop their marches 'fore we are inflamed v 1 7
Wherein we step after a stranger march Upon her gentle bosom v 2 27
Why have they dared to march So many miles? *Richard II.* ii 3 92
While here we march Upon the grassy carpet of this plain iii 3 49
Let's march without the noise of threatening drum iii 3 51
March on, and mark King Richard how he looks iii 3 61
March sadly after; grace my mournings here v 6 51
In mutual well-beseeming ranks, March all one way *1 Hen. IV.* i 1 15
Whose daughter, as we hear, the Earl of March Hath lately married i 3 84
I know his death will be a march of twelve-score ii 4 598
You shall set forward; On Thursday we ourselves will march iii 2 174
How now, lad! is the wind in that door, i' faith? must we all march? iii 3 103
Worse than the sun in March, This praise doth nourish agues iv 1 111
Our soldiers shall march through; we'll to Sutton Co'fil' to-night iv 2 2
I'll not march through Coventry with them, that's flat iv 2 42
The villains march wide betwixt the legs, as if they had gyves on iv 2 43
Suffer'd his kinsman March . . . to be engaged in Wales iv 3 93
Towards Wales, To fight with Glendower and the Earl of March v 5 40
Let our trains March by us, that we may peruse the men *2 Hen. IV.* iv 2 94
They of those marches, gracious sovereign, Shall be a wall sufficient to defend Our inland from the pilfering borderers *Hen. V.* i 2 140
Which pillage they with merry march bring home i 2 195
Touch her soft mouth, and march.—Farewell, hostess ii 3 61
To-morrow for the march are we addrest iii 3 58
If they march along Unfought withal, but I will sell my dukedom iii 5 11
His soldiers sick and famish'd in their march iii 5 57
And we give express charge, that in our marches through the country, there be nothing compelled from the villages iii 6 115
I do not seek him now; But could be willing to march on to Calais iii 6 150
I thought upon one pair of English legs Did march three Frenchmen iii 6 159
March to the bridge; it now draws toward night: Beyond the river we'll encamp ourselves, And on to-morrow bid them march away iii 6 179
We may march in England or in France, Not seeing what is likely to ensue *1 Hen. VI.* iii 1 187
Gather strength and march unto him straight iv 1 73
Join'd with him and made their march for Bourdeaux iv 3 8
March to Paris, royal Charles of France, And keep not back your powers v 2 4
Philippe, a daughter, Who married Edmund Mortimer, Earl of March: Edmund had issue, Roger Earl of March *2 Hen. VI.* ii 2 36
They are all in order and march toward us iv 2 198
Come, let's march towards London iv 3 20
Thy grandfather, Roger Mortimer, Earl of March *3 Hen. VI.* i 1 106
In the marches here we heard you were, Making another head ii 1 140
With all the friends that thou, brave Earl of March, . . . canst procure ii 1 179
To London will we march amain, And once again bestride our foaming steeds ii 1 182
No longer Earl of March, but Duke of York ii 1 192
And in the towns, as they do march along, Proclaims him king ii 2 70
And now to London with triumphant march, There to be crowned ii 6 87
What now remains, my lords, for us to do But march to London? iv 3 61
Drummer, strike up, and let us march away.—Nay, stay iv 7 50
Doth march amain to London; And many giddy people flock to him iv 8 4
Have arrived our coast And, as we hear, march on to fight with us v 3 9
And, as we march, our strength will be augmented v 3 22
Now march we hence: discharge the common sort With pay and thanks v 5 87
Our dreadful marches to delightful measures *Richard III.* i 1 8
Let me march on, and not offend your grace iv 4 178
March on, march on, since we are up in arms iv 4 530
But one day's march. In God's name, cheerly on, courageous friends v 2 13
Then, in God's name, march: True hope is swift v 2 22
March on, join bravely, let us to't pell-mell v 3 312
March patiently along *Troi. and Cres.* v 9 7
March away: Hector is dead; there is no more to say v 10 21
Strike a free march to Troy! with comfort go v 10 30
That we with smoking swords may march from hence *Coriolanus* i 4 11
Please you to march; And four shall quickly draw out my command i 6 83
March on, my fellows: Make good this ostentation i 6 85
They hither march amain, under conduct Of Lucius *T. Andron.* iv 4 65
March, noble lord, Into our city with thy banners spread *T. of Athens* v 4 29
Beware the ides of March *J. Cæsar* i 2 18
A soothsayer bids you beware the ides of March.—Set him before me i 2 19
Is not to-morrow, boy, the ides of March?—I know not, sir ii 1 40
Sir, March is wasted fourteen days ii 1 59
The ides of March are come.—Ay, Cæsar; but not gone iii 1 1
Hark! he is arrived. March gently on to meet him iv 2 31
Remember March, the ides of March remember iv 3 18
This same day Must end that work the ides of March begun v 1 114
Well, march we on, To give obedience where 'tis truly owed *Macbeth* v 2 25
Make we our march towards Birnam v 2 31
In which the majesty of buried Denmark Did sometimes march *Hamlet* i 1 49
Appears before them, and with solemn march Goes slow and stately by them i 2 201
Fortinbras Craves the conveyance of a promised march Over his kingdom iv 4 3
Come, march to wakes and fairs and market-towns *Lear* iii 6 77
Through Alexandria make a jolly march *Ant. and Cleo.* iv 8 30
Let A Roman and a British ensign wave Friendly together: so through Lud's-town march *Cymbeline* v 5 481

March-chick. A very forward March-chick! *Much Ado* i 3 58

Marched. Have hither march'd to your endamagement *K. John* ii 1 209
Their armours, that march'd hence so silver-bright, Hither return all gilt with Frenchmen's blood ii 1 315
Our colours do return in those same hands That did display them when we first march'd forth ii 1 320
Fifteen hundred foot, five hundred horse, Are march'd up *2 Hen. IV.* ii 1 187
Give it out That he is march'd to Bourdeaux with his power *1 Hen. VI.* iv 3 4
As he march'd along, By your espials were discovered Two mightier troops iv 3 5
And with colours spread March'd through the city *3 Hen. VI.* i 1 92
And very well appointed, as I thought, March'd toward Saint Alban's ii 1 114
Thus far into the bowels of the land Have we march'd on *Richard III.* v 2 4

Marcheth. Doth York intend no harm to us, That thus he marcheth with thee arm in arm? *2 Hen. VI.* v 1 57
The drum your honour hears marcheth from Warwick *3 Hen. VI.* v 1 13

Marching. The Earl of Westmoreland, seven thousand strong, Is marching hitherwards *1 Hen. IV.* iv 1 89
The king hath many marching in his coats v 3 25
Our gayness and our gilt are all besmirch'd With rainy marching *Hen. V.* iv 3 111
You may perceive Their powers are marching unto Paris-ward *1 Hen. VI.* iii 3 30
What say'st thou, Charles? for I am marching hence iii 3 39
A mighty power Of gallowglasses and stout kerns Is marching hitherward in proud array *2 Hen. VI.* iv 9 27
When I have been dry and bravely marching, it hath served me instead of a quart pot to drink in iv 10 15
How far hence is thy lord, mine honest fellow?—By this at Dunsmore, marching hitherward *3 Hen. VI.* v 1 3
What do you think Of marching to Philippi presently? *J. Cæsar* iv 3 197
The enemy, marching along by them, By them shall make a fuller number up iv 3 207
The British powers are marching hitherward.—'Tis known before *Lear* iv 4 21

Marchpane. Save me a piece of marchpane *Rom. and Jul.* i 5 9

Marcians. The noble house o' the Marcians, from whence came That Ancus Marcius, Numa's daughter's son *Coriolanus* ii 3 246

Marcius. First, you know Caius Marcius is chief enemy to the people i 1 7
Would you proceed especially against Caius Marcius?—Against him first i 1 27
Was ever man so proud as is this Marcius?—He has no equal i 1 256
Giddy censure Will then cry out of Marcius 'O, if he Had borne the business!' i 1 273
Opinion that so sticks on Marcius shall Of his demerits rob Cominius i 1 275
Half all Cominius' honours are to Marcius, Though Marcius earn'd them not, and all his faults To Marcius shall be honours i 1 277
Marcius your old enemy, Who is of Rome worse hated than of you i 2 12
If we and Caius Marcius chance to meet, 'Tis sworn between us i 2 34
And none less dear than thine and my good Marcius i 3 26
What is become of Marcius?—Slain, sir, doubtless i 4 48
Thou are left, Marcius: A carbuncle entire, as big as thou art, Were not so rich a jewel i 4 54
O, 'tis Marcius! Let's fetch him off, or make remain alike i 4 61
Thou worthiest Marcius! Go sound thy trumpet in the market-place i 5 26
Have issued, And given to Lartius and to Marcius battle i 6 11
He has the stamp of Marcius; and I have Before-time seen him thus i 6 23
The shepherd knows not thunder from a tabor More than I know the sound of Marcius' tongue From every meaner man i 6 26
So many so minded, Wave thus, to express his disposition, And follow Marcius i 6 75
If I fly, Marcius, Holloa me like a hare i 8 6
Caius Marcius Wears this war's garland i 9 59
CAIUS MARCIUS CORIOLANUS! Bear The addition nobly ever! i 9 65
Deliver him, Titus.—Marcius, his name?—By Jupiter! forgot. I am weary i 9 90
Five times, Marcius, I have fought with thee; so often hast thou beat me i 10 7
Embarquements all of fury, shall lift up Their rotten privilege and custom 'gainst My hate to Marcius i 10 24
Not according to the prayer of the people, for they love not Marcius ii 1 5
Ay, to devour him; as the hungry plebeians would the noble Marcius ii 1 11
In what enormity is Marcius poor in, that you two have not in abundance? ii 1 18
You blame Marcius for being proud?—We do it not alone, sir ii 1 36
Yet you must be saying, Marcius is proud ii 1 100
My boy Marcius approaches; for the love of Juno, let's go.—Ha! Marcius coming home! ii 1 110
Marcius is coming home: he has more cause to be proud ii 1 160
These are the ushers of Marcius: before him he carries noise, and behind him he leaves tears ii 1 174
Know, Rome, that all alone Marcius did fight Within Corioli gates: where he hath won, With fame, a name to Caius Marcius ii 1 179
Nay, my good soldier, up; My gentle Marcius, worthy Caius ii 1 189
'Tis thought That Marcius shall be consul ii 1 277
The noble house o' the Marcians, from whence came That Ancus Marcius ii 3 247
You are at point to lose your liberties: Marcius would have all from you; Marcius, Whom late you have named for consul iii 1 195
Marcius is worthy Of present death.—Therefore lay hold of him iii 1 211
Ædiles, seize him!—Yield, Marcius, yield!—Hear me one word iii 1 215
Help Marcius, help, You that be noble; help him, young and old! iii 1 227
If you bring not Marcius, we'll proceed In our first way.—I'll bring him iii 1 333
Were there but this single plot to lose, This mould of Marcius, they to dust should grind it And throw't against the wind iii 2 103
My name is Caius Marcius, who hath done To thee particularly and to all the Volsces Great hurt and mischief iv 5 71
O Marcius, Marcius! Each word thou hast spoke hath weeded from my heart A root of ancient envy iv 5 107
I'ld not believe them more Than thee, all noble Marcius iv 5 112
Marcius, Had we no quarrel else to Rome, but that Thou art thence banish'd iv 5 132
And more a friend than e'er an enemy; Yet, Marcius, that was much iv 5 153
Here's he that was wont to thwack our general, Caius Marcius iv 5 189
Caius Marcius was A worthy officer i' the war; but insolent iv 6 29
'Tis Aufidius, Who, hearing of our Marcius' banishment, Thrusts forth his horns again into the world; Which were inshell'd when Marcius stood for Rome iv 6 43
Come, what talk you Of Marcius?—Go see this rumourer whipp'd iv 6 47
Marcius, Join'd with Aufidius, leads a power 'gainst Rome iv 6 65
The weaker sort may wish Good Marcius home again iv 6 70
A fearful army, led by Caius Marcius Associated with Aufidius, rages iv 6 75
If Marcius should be join'd with Volscians,— If! He is their god iv 6 89
Only make trial what your love can do For Rome, towards Marcius.—Well, and say that Marcius Return me, as Cominius is return'd, Unheard? v 1 41
This Marcius is grown from man to dragon: he has wings v 4 13
The ladies have prevail'd, The Volscians are dislodged, and Marcius gone v 4 44
Unshout the noise that banish'd Marcius, Repeal him with the welcome of his mother v 5 4
Ay, traitor, Marcius!—Marcius!—Ay, Marcius, Caius Marcius v 6 87

Marcus. He killed my son. My daughter. He killed my cousin Marcus v 6 123
Marcus Andronicus, so I do affy In thy uprightness *T. Andron.* i 1 47
Thanks, gentle tribune, noble brother Marcus.—And welcome, nephews! i 1 171
Marcus, even thou hast struck upon my crest i 1 364
Suffer thy brother Marcus to inter His noble nephew here i 1 375
Rise, Marcus, rise. The dismall'st day is this that e'er I saw i 1 383
Marcus, for thy sake and thy brother's here, And at my lovely Tamora's entreats, I do remit these young men's heinous faults i 1 482
But who comes with our brother Marcus here? iii 1 58

Marcus. Ah, Marcus, Marcus! brother, well I wot Thy napkin cannot drink a tear of mine, For thou, poor man, hast drown'd it with thine own . . . . *T. Andron.* iii 1 139
Mark, Marcus, mark! I understand her signs . . . . . . iii 1 143
Let Marcus, Lucius, or thyself, old Titus, Or any one of you, chop off your hand, And send it to the king . . . . . . iii 1 152
Marcus, unknit that sorrow-wreathen knot . . . . . . iii 2 4
Has sorrow made thee dote already? Why, Marcus, no man should be mad but I . . . . iii 2 24
As if we should forget we had no hands, If Marcus did not name the word of hands! . . . . iii 2 33
What dost thou strike at, Marcus, with thy knife?—At that that I have kill'd, my lord; a fly . . . . iii 2 52
Good uncle Marcus, see how swift she comes. Alas, sweet aunt, I know not what you mean . . . . iv 1 3
If my uncle Marcus go, I will most willingly attend your ladyship . iv 1 27
Marcus, what means this? Some book there is that she desires to see iv 1 30
You are a young huntsman, Marcus; let it alone . . . . . iv 1 101
Marcus, look to my house: Lucius and I'll go brave it at the court . iv 1 120
Marcus, attend him in his ecstasy . . . . iv 1 125
Terras Astræa reliquit: Be you remember'd, Marcus, she's gone, she's fled . . . . iv 3 5
Marcus, we are but shrubs, no cedars we, . . . But metal, Marcus . iv 3 45
Come, to this gear. You are a good archer, Marcus . . . . iv 3 52
News, news from heaven! Marcus, the post is come. Sirrah, what tidings? . . . . iv 3 77
A knife; come, let me see it. Here, Marcus, fold it in the oration . iv 3 116
Let the emperor give his pledges Unto my father and my uncle Marcus v 1 164
Marcus, my brother! 'tis sad Titus calls. Go, gentle Marcus, to thy nephew . . . . v 2 121
Uncle Marcus, since it is my father's mind That I repair to Rome, I am content.—And ours with thine . . . . v 3 1
And loving kiss for kiss Thy brother Marcus tenders on thy lips . v 3 157
Marcus Antonius. The wife of Marcus Antonius . . . *Ant. and Cleo.* ii 6 119
Marcus Brutus, will I shake with you . . . . *J. Cæsar* iii 1 185
When Marcus Brutus grows so covetous . . . . . . iv 3 79
And I am Brutus, Marcus Brutus, I; Brutus, my country's friend! . v 4 7
Marcus Cato. I am the son of Marcus Cato, ho! . . . . . v 4 6
Marcus Crassus. Pleased fortune does of Marcus Crassus' death Make me revenger . . . . *Ant. and Cleo.* iii 1 2
Thy Pacorus, Orodes, Pays this for Marcus Crassus . . . . iii 1 5
Marcus Luccicos, is not he in town? . . . . . . *Othello* i 3 44
Marcus Octavius, Marcus Justeius, Publicola, and Cælius *Ant. and Cleo.* iii 7 73
Mardian. Eunuch Mardian!—What's your highness' pleasure? . . i 5 8
Play with Mardian.—As well a woman with an eunuch play'd As with a woman . . . . ii 5 4
To the monument! Mardian, go tell him I have slain myself . . iv 13 7
Hence, Mardian, And bring me how he takes my death. To the monument! . . . . iv 13 9
Mare. The man shall have his mare again . . . *M. N. Dream* iii 2 463
How now! whose mare's dead? what's the matter? . *2 Hen. IV.* ii 1 46
Or I will ride thee o' nights like the mare.—I think I am as like to ride the mare, if I have any vantage of ground to get up . . . ii 1 83
Though patience be a tired mare, yet she will plod . . . *Hen. V.* ii 1 26
If we should serve with horse and mares together, The horse were merely lost; the mares would bear A soldier and his horse *Ant. and Cleo.* iii 7 8
Margarelon. Bastard Margarelon Hath Doreus prisoner *Troi. and Cres.* v 5 7
Margaret, the waiting gentlewoman to Hero . . . . *Much Ado* ii 2 13
Hear me call Margaret Hero, hear Margaret term me Claudio . . ii 2 44
Good Margaret, run thee to the parlour; There shalt thou find my cousin iii 1 1
Hero and Margaret have by this played their parts with Beatrice . iii 2 78
Wooed Margaret, the Lady Hero's gentlewoman, by the name of Hero iii 3 154
And thought they Margaret was Hero?—Two of them did . . . ; but the devil my master knew she was Margaret . . . . . iii 3 162
How you were brought into the orchard and saw me court Margaret . v 1 244
This naughty man Shall face to face be brought to Margaret . . v 1 307
We'll talk with Margaret, How her acquaintance grew with this lewd fellow . . . . v 1 340
Sweet Mistress Margaret, deserve well at my hands by helping me . v 2 1
In so high a style, Margaret, that no man living shall come over it . v 2 6
A most manly wit, Margaret; it will not hurt a woman . . . v 2 15
But Margaret was in some fault for this, Although against her will . v 4 4
Why, then my cousin Margaret and Urusla Are much deceived . . v 4 78
Margaret my name, and daughter to a king, The King of Naples *1 Hen. VI.* v 3 51
Remember that thou hast a wife; Then how can Margaret be thy paramour? . . . . v 3 81
I'll win this Lady Margaret. For whom? Why, for my king . . v 3 88
Fair Margaret knows That Suffolk doth not flatter, face, or feign . v 3 141
Good wishes, praise and prayers Shall Suffolk ever have of Margaret . v 3 174
But hark you, Margaret; No princely commendations to my king? . v 3 175
Your wondrous rare description, noble earl, Of beauteous Margaret hath astonish'd me . . . . v 5 2
Lord protector, give consent That Margaret may be England's royal queen . . . . v 5 24
I pray, is Margaret more than that? Her father is no better than an earl . . . . v 5 36
Whom should we match with Henry, being a king, But Margaret, that is daughter to a king? . . . . v 5 67
A lady of so high resolve As is fair Margaret . . . . . v 5 76
Margaret shall be queen, and none but she . . . . . . v 5 78
Agree to any covenants, and procure That Lady Margaret . . . v 5 89
Margaret shall now be queen, and rule the king; But I will rule both her, the king and realm . . . . v 5 107
As procurator to your excellence, To marry Princess Margaret *2 Hen. VI.* i 1 4
Welcome, Queen Margaret: I can express no kinder sign of love Than this kind kiss . . . . i 1 17
Long live Queen Margaret, England's happiness! . . . . . i 1 37
Where Henry and dame Margaret kneel'd to me . . . . . i 2 39
Why, now is Henry king, and Margaret queen . . . . . ii 3 39
Ay, Margaret; my heart is drown'd with grief . . . . . iii 1 198
And Margaret our queen Do seek subversion of thy harmless life . iii 1 207
Is all thy comfort shut in Gloucester's tomb? Why, then, dame Margaret was ne'er thy joy . . . . iii 2 79
Thy flinty heart, more hard than they, Might in thy palace perish Margaret . . . . iii 2 100
Die, Margaret! For Henry weeps that thou dost live so long . . iii 2 120
Kneel'd down at the board, When I have feasted with Queen Margaret iv 1 58
Come, Margaret; God, our hope, will succour us.—My hope is gone, now Suffolk is deceased . . . . iv 4 55
Good Margaret, stay.—What are you made of? you'll nor fight nor fly . v 2 73
Margaret. Pardon me, Margaret; pardon me, sweet son . *3 Hen. VI.* i 1 228
Stay, gentle Margaret, and hear me speak.—Thou hast spoke too much i 1 257
For Margaret my queen, and Clifford too, Have chid me from the battle ii 5 16
Where's Captain Margaret, to fence you now? . . . . . ii 6 75
Margaret may win him; For she's a woman to be pitied much . iii 1 35
O Margaret, thus 'twill be; and thou, poor soul, Art then forsaken! . iii 1 53
Fair Queen of England, worthy Margaret, Sit down with us . . . iii 3 1
Now Margaret Must strike her sail and learn awhile to serve . . iii 3 4
Be plain, Queen Margaret, and tell thy grief; It shall be eased . iii 3 19
This is the cause that I, poor Margaret, With this my son, Prince Edward, Henry's heir, Am come . . . . iii 3 30
Injurious Margaret!—And why not queen? . . . . . . iii 3 78
Queen Margaret, Prince Edward, . . . Vouchsafe . . . to stand aside . iii 3 109
Draw near, Queen Margaret, and be a witness . . . . . iii 3 138
Lewis was Henry's friend.—And still is friend to him and Margaret . iii 3 144
My quarrel . . . joins . . . with hers, and thine, and Margaret's . . iii 3 218
But say, is Warwick friends with Margaret?—Ay, gracious sovereign . iv 1 115
That Margaret your queen and my son Edward Be sent for . . . iv 6 60
What will your grace have done with Margaret? . . . . . v 7 37
Queen Margaret saw Thy murderous falchion smoking in his blood *Richard III.* i 2 93
Was not your husband In Margaret's battle at Saint Alban's slain? . i 3 130
Margaret.—Richard!—Ha!—I call thee not.—I cry thee mercy then . i 3 234
Let me make the period to my curse!—'Tis done by me, and ends in 'Margaret' . . . . i 3 239
O, but remember this another day, When he shall split thy very heart with sorrow, And say poor Margaret was a prophetess! . . . i 3 301
Now Margaret's curse is fall'n upon our heads . . . . . iii 3 15
O Margaret, Margaret, now thy heavy curse Is lighted on poor Hastings' wretched head! . . . . iii 4 94
And make me die the thrall of Margaret's curse, Nor mother, wife . iv 1 46
Withdraw thee, wretched Margaret: who comes here? . . . . iv 4 8
Present to her,—as sometime Margaret Did to thy father, steep'd in Rutland's blood,—A handkerchief . . . . iv 4 274
Now Margaret's curse is fallen upon my head; 'When he,' quoth she, 'shall split thy heart with sorrow, Remember Margaret was a prophetess' . . . . v 1 25
Margent. His face's own margent did quote such amazes . *L. L. Lost* ii 1 245
Writ o' both sides the leaf, margent and all . . . . . . v 2 8
By rushy brook, Or in the beached margent of the sea . *M. N. Dream* ii 1 85
Find written in the margent of his eyes . . . . *Rom. and Jul.* i 3 86
I knew you must be edified by the margent ere you had done *Hamlet* v 2 162
Margery. The gunner and his mate Loved Mall, Meg and Marian and Margery, But none of us cared for Kate . . . . *Tempest* ii 2 50
I am sure Margery your wife is my mother.—Her name is Margery, indeed: I'll be sworn . . . . *Mer. of Venice* ii 2 95
With Lady Margery, your midwife there . . . . . *W. Tale* ii 3 160
Margery Jourdain, the cunning witch . . . . . *2 Hen. VI.* i 2 75
Maria. O sweet Maria, empress of my love! . . . *L. L. Lost* iv 3 56
You do not love Maria; Longaville Did never sonnet for her sake compile . . . . iv 3 133
What says Maria?—At the twelvemonth's end I'll change my black gown . . . . v 2 843
Maria once told me she did affect me . . . . . *T. Night* ii 5 27
Good Maria, let this fellow be looked to . . . . . . iii 4 67
But out of question 'tis Maria's hand . . . . v 1 355
Maria writ The letter at Sir Toby's great importance . . . . v 1 370
Jesu Maria, what a deal of brine! . . . . . . *Rom. and Jul.* ii 3 69
Marian. The gunner and his mate Loved Mall, Meg and Marian and Margery . . . . *Tempest* ii 2 50
Maud, Bridget, Marian, Cicely, Gillian, Ginn! . . . *Com. of Errors* iii 1 31
And Marian's nose looks red and raw . . . . . . *L. L. Lost* v 2 934
Marian Hacket, the fat ale-wife of Wincot . . . . *T. of Shrew* Ind. 2 22
Marian, I say! a stoup of wine! . . . . *T. Night* ii 3 14
Maid Marian may be the deputy's wife of the ward to thee *1 Hen. IV.* iii 3 129
Mariana. Have you not heard speak of Mariana? . . *Meas. for Meas.* iii 1 216
Your honour untainted, the poor Mariana advantaged . . . . iii 1 265
There, at the moated grange, resides this dejected Mariana . . . iii 1 277
I have not yet made known to Mariana A word of this . . . . iv 1 49
Say, by this token, I desire his company At Mariana's house to-night . iv 3 145
Come hither, Mariana. Say, wast thou e'er contracted to this woman? v 1 379
This new-married man . . . you must pardon For Mariana's sake . . v 1 408
Joy to you, Mariana! Love her, Angelo: I have confess'd her . . v 1 532
Marigold. The marigold, that goes to bed wi' the sun . . *W. Tale* iv 4 105
The yellows, blues, The purple violets, and marigolds . . . *Pericles* iv 1 16
Marina, whom, For she was born at sea, I have named so . . . iii 3 12
Now to Marina bend your mind . . . . iv Gower 5
Marina's life Seeks to take off by treason's knife . . . . . iv Gower 13
It is said For certain in our story, she Would ever with Marina be iv Gower 20
Still This Philoten contends in skill With absolute Marina . . iv Gower 31
Marina gets All praises, which are paid as debts, And not as given iv Gower 33
A present murderer does prepare For good Marina . . . . . iv Gower 39
How now, Marina! why do you keep alone? . . . . . . iv 1 22
These roguing thieves . . . have seized Marina. Let her go . . . iv 1 98
None would look on her, But cast their gazes on Marina's face . . iv 3 33
Now please you wit The epitaph is for Marina writ By wicked Dionyza iv 4 32
Marina thus the brothel 'scapes, and chances Into an honest house v Gower 1
My name is Marina.—O, I am mock'd . . . . v 1 143
Thou little know'st how thou dost startle me, To call thyself Marina . v 1 148
How! a king's daughter? And call'd Marina? . . . . . . v 1 152
Wherefore call'd Marina?—Call'd Marina For I was born at sea . . v 1 157
This is Marina. What was thy mother's name? tell me but that . . v 1 201
Tell Helicanus, my Marina, tell him O'er, point by point . . . v 1 226
The music of the spheres! List, my Marina . . . . . . v 1 231
So he thrived, That he is promised to be wived To fair Marina . . v 2 276
At sea in childbed died she, but brought forth A maid-child call'd Marina . . . . v 3 6
Thy burden at the sea, and call'd Marina For she was yielded there . v 3 47
Mariner. Speak to the mariners: fall to't, yarely . . . . *Tempest* i 1 3
All but mariners Plunged in the foaming brine and quit the vessel . i 2 210
Of the king's ship The mariners say how thou hast disposed . . i 2 225
The mariners all under hatches stow'd . . . . i 2 230
There shalt thou find the mariners asleep Under the hatches . . v 1 98
Your ships are not well mann'd; Your mariners are muleters *Ant. and Cleo.* iii 7 36
Mariner, say what coast is this?—We are near Tarsus.—Thither, gentle mariner, Alter thy course . . . . *Pericles* iii 1 73
Maritime. The borders maritime Lack blood to think on't *Ant. and Cleo.* i 4 51
Marjoram. Hot lavender, mints, savory, marjoram . . . *W. Tale* iv 4 104
Give the word.—Sweet marjoram.—Pass.—I know that voice . *Lear* iv 6 94

Mark. Methinks he hath no drowning mark upon him . . *Tempest* i 1 31
My brother and thy uncle, call'd Antonio—I pray thee, mark me . . i 2 67
Mark his condition and the event; then tell me If this might be a brother i 2 117
Nor set A mark so bloody on the business . . . . . i 2 142
And,—do you mark me, sir?—Prithee, no more: thou dost talk nothing ii 1 169
Mark but the badges of these men, my lords, Then say if they be true . v 1 267
How know you that I am in love?—Marry, by these special marks *T. G. of Ver.* ii 1 18
Now come I to my sister; mark the moan she makes . . ii 3 33
Did not I bid thee still mark me and do as I do? . . . . iv 4 39
But mark the sequel, Master Brook . . *Mer. Wives* iii 5 108
Nominativo, hig, hag, hog; pray you, mark: genitivo, hujus . iv 1 45
Doth your honour mark his face?—Ay, sir, very well.—Nay, I beseech you, mark it well.—Well, I do so . *Meas. for Meas.* ii 1 156
But mark me; To be received plain, I'll speak more gross . ii 4 81
But mark how heavily this befell to the poor gentlewoman . iii 1 226
Of which he made five marks, ready money . . . . iv 3 7
Mark what I say, which you shall find By every syllable a faithful verity iv 3 130
Stand like the forfeits in a barber's shop, As much in mock as mark . v 1 324
His goods confiscate . . . , Unless a thousand marks be levied *Com. of Er.* i 1 22
Valued at the highest rate, Cannot amount unto a hundred marks . i 1 25
Where is the thousand marks thou hadst of me?—I have some marks of yours upon my pate, Some of my mistress' marks upon my shoulders, But not a thousand marks between you both . . i 2 81
Thy mistress' marks? what mistress, slave, hast thou? . . . i 2 87
He ask'd me for a thousand marks in gold: ''Tis dinner-time,' quoth I ii 1 61
Where is the thousand marks I gave thee, villain?—'The pig,' quoth I ii 1 65
And charged him with a thousand marks in gold . . . . iii 1 8
Told me what privy marks I had about me, as, the mark of my shoulder iii 2 146
Mark how he trembles in his ecstasy! . . . . . iv 4 54
I wonder that you will still be talking . . . nobody marks you *Much Ado* i 1 118
But, on my allegiance, mark you this, on my allegiance. He is in love i 1 213
Mark how short his answer is;—With Hero, Leonato's short daughter i 1 215
I stood like a man at a mark, with a whole army shooting at me . ii 1 254
She's a fair lady: I do spy some marks of love in her . . ii 3 255
A mark marvellous well shot . . . . *L. L. Lost* iv 1 132
A mark! O, mark but that mark! A mark, says my lady! Let the mark have a prick in't, to mete at, if it may be . . . iv 1 133
If knowledge be the mark, to know thee shall suffice . . . iv 2 115
Once more I'll mark how love can vary wit . . . . . iv 3 100
They do not mark me, and that brings me out . . . . v 2 172
I'll mark no words that smooth-faced wooers say . . . . v 2 838
Cuckoo gray, Whose note full many a man doth mark *M. N. Dream* iii 1 135
Fairy king, attend, and mark: I do hear the morning lark . . iv 1 98
And mark the musical confusion Of hounds and echo in conjunction . iv 1 115
But mark, poor knight, What dreadful dole is here! . . . v 1 282
Never mole, hare lip, nor scar, Nor mark prodigious . . . v 1 419
Mark what Jacob did. When Laban and himself were compromised *Mer. of Venice* i 3 78
Mark you this, Bassanio, The devil can cite Scripture for his purpose . i 3 98
Mark me now; now will I raise the waters . . . . ii 2 51
There is no vice so simple but assumes Some mark of virtue . . iii 2 82
O upright judge! Mark, Jew: O learned judge! . . . . iv 1 313
O learned judge! Mark, Jew: a learned judge! . . . . iv 1 317
Mark the music . . . . v 1 88
Mark you but that! In both my eyes he doubly sees himself . . v 1 243
There is none of my uncle's marks upon you . . *As Y. Like It* iii 2 387
What were his marks?—A lean cheek, which you have not . . iii 2 391
Go hence a little and I shall conduct you, If you will mark it . . iii 4 59
She Phebes me: mark how the tyrant writes . . . . . iv 3 39
He threw his eye aside, And mark what object did present itself . iv 3 104
Stand by and mark the manner of his teaching . . *T. of Shrew* iv 2 5
A hundred marks, my Kate does put her down . . . . v 2 35
To be the mark Of smoky muskets . . . . *All's Well* iii 2 110
The song we had last night. Mark it, Cesario, it is old and plain *T. N.* ii 4 44
Mark his first approach before my lady . . . . . ii 5 218
Mark my counsel, Which must be even as swiftly follow'd . *W. Tale* i 2 408
You, my lords, Look on her, mark her well . . . . . ii 1 65
Perform my bidding.—I will, my lord.—Mark and perform it, see'st thou! ii 3 170
Your high self, The gracious mark o' the land, you have obscured . iv 4 8
Mark our contract.—Mark your divorce, young sir . . . iv 4 428
Mark thou my words: Follow us to the court . . . . iv 4 442
Mark Her eye, and tell me for what dull part in't You chose her . v 1 63
Follow me And mark what way I make . . . . . . v 1 233
Mark a little while. Please you to interpose, fair madam . . v 3 118
I see a yielding in the looks of France; Mark, how they whisper *K. John* ii 1 475
And this addition more, Full thirty thousand marks of English coin . ii 1 530
Patch'd with foul moles and eye-offending marks . . . . iii 1 47
I turn to thee, And mark my greeting well . . . *Richard II.* i 1 36
March on, and mark King Richard how he looks . . . . iii 3 61
There is my gage, the manual seal of death, That marks thee out for hell iv 1 26
Now mark me, how I will undo myself . . . . . . iv 1 203
Mark, silent king, the moral of this sport . . . . . iv 1 290
Didst thou not mark the king, what words he spake? . . . v 4 1
A franklin in the wild of Kent hath brought three hundred marks *1 Hen. IV.* ii 1 61
Dost thou hear me, Hal?—Ay, and mark thee too, Jack . . ii 4 234
Mark now, how a plain tale shall put you down . . . . ii 4 281
There are two gentlemen Have in this robbery lost three hundred marks ii 4 569
Mark how he bears his course, and runs me up . . . . iii 1 108
In the way of bargain, mark ye me, I'll cavil on the ninth part of a hair iii 1 139
A fellow of no mark nor likelihood . . . . . . iii 2 45
Thou hast saved me a thousand marks in links and torches . . iii 3 48
I have lost a seal-ring of my grandfather's worth forty mark . . iii 3 95
He that will caper with me for a thousand marks . *2 Hen. IV.* i 2 217
A hundred mark is a long one for a poor lone woman to bear . . ii 1 34
He was the mark and glass, copy and book, That fashion'd others . ii 3 31
Give me this man: he presents no mark to the enemy . . . iii 2 284
Do but mark the countenance that he will give me . . . . v 5 7
As many arrows, loosed several ways, Come to one mark . *Hen. V.* i 2 208
Thy fall hath left a kind of blot, To mark the full-fraught man . ii 2 139
Mark then abounding valour in our English . . . . . iv 3 104
Perpend my words, O Signieur Dew, and mark . . . . iv 4 8
'Tis as arrant a piece of knavery, mark you now, as can be offer't . iv 7 3
If you mark Alexander's life well, Harry of Monmouth's life is come after it indifferent well . . . . iv 7 33
It is not well done, mark you now, to take the tales out of my mouth . iv 7 44
But mark: . . . I lost my liberty and they their lives . . *1 Hen. VI.* i 5 79
An if your grace mark every circumstance, You have great reason . iii 1 153
Call we to mind, and mark but this for proof . . . . iii 3 68

Mark. Claim the crown, For that's the golden mark I seek to hit *2 Hen. VI.* i 1 243
Dost thou use to write thy name? or hast thou a mark to thyself, like an honest plain-dealing man? . . . . iv 2 110
Rise up a knight. We give thee for reward a thousand marks . . iv 1 79
My tears shall wipe away these bloody marks . . *3 Hen. VI.* ii 5 71
Nay, mark how Lewis stamps, as he were nettled . . . iii 3 169
Sin, death, and hell have set their marks on him . *Richard III.* i 3 293
And perhaps May move your hearts to pity, if you mark him . . i 3 349
Mark how well the sequel hangs together . . . . . iii 6 4
No black envy Shall mark my grave . . . . *Hen. VIII.* ii 1 86
You have hit the mark: but is't not cruel That she should feel the smart? . . . . ii 1 165
I will be bold with time and your attention: Then mark the inducement ii 4 169
Mark but my fall, and that that ruin'd me . . . . iii 2 439
Mark her eyes!—She is going, wench: pray, pray . . . iv 2 98
Give her an hundred marks. I'll to the queen.—An hundred marks! . v 1 170
Mark Troilus above the rest.—Speak not so loud . *Troi. and Cres.* i 2 199
Mark him; note him. O brave Troilus! Look well upon him, niece . i 2 251
Stand, stand, thou Greek; thou art a goodly mark: No? wilt thou not? v 6 27
Mark what I say. Attend me where I wheel: Strike not a stroke . v 7 2
Mark me, and do the like.—Fool-hardiness; not I . *Coriolanus* i 4 45
When Tarquin made a head for Rome, he fought Beyond the mark of others . . . . ii 2 93
His sword, death's stamp, Where it did mark, it took . . . ii 2 112
And might well Be taken from the people.—Mark you that? . . ii 2 150
Here he comes, and in the gown of humility: mark his behaviour . ii 3 45
Remains That, in the official marks invested, you Anon do meet the senate . . . . ii 3 148
He should have show'd us His marks of merit, wounds received . ii 3 172
Hear you this Triton of the minnows? mark you His absolute 'shall'? iii 1 89
Mark you this, people?—To the rock, to the rock with him! . . iii 3 74
I have been consul, and can show for Rome Her enemies' marks upon me iii 3 111
You Volsces, mark; for we'll Hear nought from Rome in private . v 3 92
Let us sit down and mark their yelping noise . . *T. Andron.* ii 3 20
They would not mark me, or if they did mark, They would not pity me iii 1 34
Who marks the waxing tide grow wave by wave . . . . iii 1 95
Mark, Marcus, mark! I understand her signs . . . . iii 1 143
That hath more scars of sorrow in his heart Than foemen's marks upon his batter'd shield . . . . iv 1 127
A right fair mark, fair coz, is soonest hit . . *Rom. and Jul.* i 1 213
God mark thee to his grace! Thou wast the prettiest babe that e'er I nursed . . . . i 3 59
If love be blind, love cannot hit the mark . . . . ii 1 33
What wilt thou tell her, nurse? thou dost not mark me . . . ii 4 188
I never tasted Timon in my life, Nor came any of his bounties over me, To mark me for his friend . . . . *T. of Athens* iii 2 86
Mark, how strange it shows, Timon in this should pay more than he owes iii 4 2-
Whose fall the mark of his ambition is . . . . . v 3 10
When the fit was on him, I did mark How he did shake . *J. Cæsar* i 2 120
Bade the Romans Mark him and write his speeches in their books . i 2 126
It was mere foolery; I did not mark it . . . . . i 2 236
That by no means I may discover them By any mark of favour . . ii 1 76
Trust not Trebonius; mark well Metellus Cimber . . . ii 3 3
Look, how he makes to Cæsar: mark him.—Casca, be sudden . iii 1 18
Now mark him, he begins again to speak . . . . . iii 2 122
Mark how the blood of Cæsar follow'd it, As rushing out of doors . iii 2 182
Do you mark that?—The thane of Fife had a wife . . *Macbeth* v 1 46
Looks it not like the king? mark it, Horatio.—Most like . *Hamlet* i 1 43
Speak; I'll go no further.—Mark me.—I will . . . . i 5 2
As 'twere a thing a little soil'd i' the working, Mark you . . ii 1 41
Who, in her duty and obedience, mark, Hath given me this . . ii 2 107
Be you and I behind an arras then; Mark the encounter . . ii 2 164
Here's metal more attractive.—O, ho! do you mark that? . . iii 2 118
You are naught, you are naught: I'll mark the play . . . iii 2 158
The great man down, you mark his favourite flies . . . iii 2 214
Nay, but, Ophelia,— Pray you, mark. White his shroud . . iv 5 34
Will he, nill he, he goes,—mark you that . . . . . v 1 19
Couch we awhile, and mark . . . . v 1 245
Sirrah, I'll teach thee a speech.—Do.—Mark it, nuncle . . *Lear* i 4 130
By the marks of sovereignty, knowledge, and reason, I should be false persuaded I had daughters . . . . i 4 252
Do you mark that, my lord?—I cannot be so partial, Goneril . . i 4 333
Ask her forgiveness? Do you but mark how this becomes the house . ii 4 155
Tom, away! Mark the high noises . . . . . . iii 6 118
Read thou this challenge; mark but the penning of it . . . iv 6 142
I will preach to thee: mark . . . . iv 6 184
About it; and write happy when thou hast done. Mark, I say, instantly v 3 36
You shall mark Many a duteous and knee-crooking knave . . *Othello* i 1 44
Mark me with what violence she first loved the Moor . . . ii 1 224
Didst thou not see her paddle with the palm of his hand? didst not mark? ii 1 260
Given up himself to the contemplation, mark, and denotement of her parts and graces . . . . ii 3 322
And mark the fleers, the gibes, and notable scorns, That dwell in every region of his face . . . . iv 1 83
I say, but mark his gesture . . . . iv 1 88
Do but go after, And mark how he continues . . . . iv 1 292
But, sirrah, mark, we use To say the dead are well . *Ant. and Cleo.* ii 5 32
You are abused Beyond the mark of thought . . . . iii 6 87
If this be worth your hearing, Mark it . . . . *Cymbeline* i 1 58
Some marks Of secret on her person . . . . . . v 5 205
Upon his neck a mole, a sanguine star; It was a mark of wonder . v 5 365
A well-experienced archer hits the mark . . . . *Pericles* i 1 164
It was sometime target to a king; I know it by this mark . . ii 1 144
It is too late to talk of love; And that's the mark I know you level at ii 3 114
This so darks In Philoten all graceful marks . . . iv Gower 36
Take you the marks of her, the colour of her hair, complexion, height, age iv 2 61
Mark me: you must seem to do that fearfully . . . . iv 2 127
Bless the mark! . . . . *T. G. of Ver.* iv 4 21
God bless the mark! . . . . *Mer. of Venice* ii 2 25; *Othello* i 1 33
God save the mark! . . . . 1 *Hen. IV.* i 3 56; *Rom. and Jul.* iii 2 53

Marked. Hapless Ægeon, whom the fates have mark'd To bear the extremity of dire mishap! . . . . . *Com. of Errors* i 1 141
Not marked or not laughed at, strikes him into melancholy *Much Ado* ii 1 153
I have mark'd A thousand blushing apparitions To start into her face iv 1 160
I have been closely shrouded in this bush And mark'd you both *L. L. L.* iv 3 138
Yet mark'd I where the bolt of Cupid fell . . *M. N. Dream* ii 1 165
The hairy fool, Much marked of the melancholy Jaques . *As Y. Like It* ii 1 41
Had they mark'd him In parcels as I did . . . . . iii 5 124
Perhaps you mark'd not what's the pity of all . . *T. of Shrew* i 1 171

Marked. Mark'd you not how her sister Began to scold? *T. of Shrew* i 1 176
A fellow by the hand of nature mark'd, Quoted and sign'd *K. John* iv 2 221
More are men's ends mark'd than their lives before *Richard II.* ii 1 11
Mark'd with a blot, damn'd in the book of heaven iv 1 236
I marked him not; and yet he talked very wisely *1 Hen. IV.* i 2 96
These signs have mark'd me extraordinary iii 1 41
I cried 'hum,' and 'well, go to,' But mark'd him not a word iii 1 159
Mark'd For the hot vengeance and the rod of heaven iii 2 9
If we are mark'd to die, we are enow To do our country loss *Hen. V.* iv 3 20
The filth and scum of Kent, Mark'd for the gallows *2 Hen. VI.* iv 2 131
Mark'd by the destinies to be avoided *3 Hen. VI.* ii 2 137
Your brother Richard mark'd him for the grave ii 6 40
Mark'd you not How that the guilty kindred of the queen Look'd pale when they did hear of Clarence' death? *Richard III.* ii 1 134
That by their witchcraft thus have marked me iii 4 74
Mark'd you his lip and eyes?—Nay, but his taunts *Coriolanus* i 1 259
To this your son is mark'd, and die he must *T. Andron.* i 1 125
You are both decipher'd, that's the news, For villains mark'd with rape iv 2 9
Mark'd ye his words? He would not take the crown *J. Cæsar* i 2 117
Will it not be received, When we have mark'd with blood those sleepy two Of his own chamber? *Macbeth* i 7 75
Where sighs and groans and shrieks that rend the air Are made, not mark'd iv 3 169
My body's mark'd With Roman swords *Cymbeline* iii 3 56
Mark'd he your music?—No, nor look'd on us *Pericles* v 1 81
Market. And he ended the market *L. L. Lost* iii 1 111
And retails his wares At wakes and wassails, meetings, markets, fairs v 2 318
It is the right butter-women's rank to market *As Y. Like It* iii 2 104
Sell when you can: you are not for all markets iii 5 60
And your store, I think, is not for idle markets, sir *T. Night* iii 3 46
But yet I run before my horse to market *Richard III.* i 1 160
Why, I can buy me twenty [husbands] at any market *Macbeth* iv 2 40
What is a man, If his chief good and market of his time Be but to sleep and feed? a beast, no more *Hamlet* iv 4 34
Search the market narrowly *Pericles* iv 2 3
But shall I search the market?—What else, man? iv 2 18
Hast thou cried her through the market?—I have cried her almost to the number of her hairs iv 2 99
Marketable. A plain fish, and, no doubt, marketable *Tempest* v 1 266
We shall be the more marketable *As Y. Like It* i 2 103
Market bell. Go in; the market bell is rung *1 Hen. VI.* iii 2 16
Market-cross. Proclaim'd at market-crosses *1 Hen. IV.* v 1 73
Market-day. Seen him whipped three market-days together *2 Hen. VI.* iv 2 62
Market folks that come to sell their corn *1 Hen. VI.* iii 2 15
Market-maid. But you are come A market-maid to Rome *Ant. and Cleo.* iii 6 51
Market-men. Talk like the vulgar sort of market men *1 Hen. VI.* iii 2 4
So worthless peasants bargain for their wives, As market-men for oxen v 5 54
Market-place. The other squirrel was stolen from me by the hangman boys in the market-place *T. G. of Ver.* iv 4 60
I would eat his heart in the market-place *Much Ado* iv 1 309
My father's [house] bears more toward the market-place *T. of Shrew* v 1 10
Wade to the market-place in Frenchmen's blood *K. John* ii 1 42
In open market-place produced they me, To be a public spectacle *1 Hen. VI.* i 4 40
Advance it in the market-place, The middle centre of this cursed town iii 2 5
Go sound thy trumpet in the market-place *Coriolanus* i 5 27
Never would he Appear i' the market-place ii 1 249
On the market-place, I know, they do attend us ii 2 163
Tribunes, give way; he shall to the market-place iii 1 31
Go not home.—Meet on the market-place. We'll attend you there iii 1 332
I have been i' the market-place; and, sir, 'tis fit You make strong party iii 2 93
To the market-place! You have put me now to such a part iii 2 104
Be content: Mother, I am going to the market-place; chide me no more iii 2 131
Deliver them this paper: having read it, Bid them repair to the market-place v 6 3
He fell down in the market-place, and foamed at mouth *J. Cæsar* i 2 254
Yesterday the bird of night did sit Even at noon-day upon the market-place, Hooting and shrieking i 3 27
Then walk we forth, even to the market-place iii 1 108
And am moreover suitor that I may Produce his body to the market-place iii 1 228
Thou shalt not back till I have borne this corse Into the market-place. iii 1 292
Antony, Enthroned i' the market-place, did sit alone *Ant. and Cleo.* ii 2 220
I' the market-place, on a tribunal silver'd, Cleopatra and himself iii 6 3
Market-price. And I had that which any inferior might At market-price have bought *All's Well* v 3 219
Market-town. Whipped through every market-town *2 Hen. VI.* ii 1 159
Come, march to wakes and fairs and market-towns *Lear* iii 6 78
Marking. Did you hear the proclamation?—I do confess much of the hearing it, but little of the marking of it *L. L. Lost* i 1 288
Marking the embarked traders on the flood *M. N. Dream* ii 1 127
Lest I, by marking of your rage, forget Your worth *K. John* iv 3 85
It is the disease of not listening, the malady of not marking *2 Hen. IV.* i 2 139
Mark-man. A right good mark-man! *Rom. and Jul.* i 1 212
Marl. To make an account of her life to a clod of wayward marl *Much Ado* ii 1 66
Marle. Fauconberg and Foix, Beaumont and Marle *Hen. V.* iv 8 105
Marmoset. And instruct thee how To snare the nimble marmoset *Temp.* ii 2 174
Marquess. The happiest gift that ever marquess gave *2 Hen. VI.* i 1 15
Marquess of Suffolk, ambassador for Henry King of England i 1 45
Peace, master marquess, you are malapert *Richard III.* i 3 255
Good counsel, marry: learn it, learn it, marquess i 3 261
Dorset, embrace him; Hastings, love lord marquess ii 1 25
Marred. Hush, and be mute, Or else our spell is marr'd *Tempest* iv 1 127
You had marr'd all else *Meas. for Meas.* ii 2 148
If voluble and sharp discourse be marr'd, Unkindness blunts it more than marble hard *Com. of Errors* ii 1 92
If he come not, then the play is marred *M. N. Dream* iv 2 5
I tell thee, I, that thou hast marr'd her gown *T. of Shrew* iv 3 115
A young man married is a man that's marr'd *All's Well* ii 3 315
He will not hear.—There all is marr'd; there lies a cooling card *1 Hen. VI.* v 3 83
Foul wrinkled witch, what makest thou in my sight?—But repetition of what thou hast marr'd *Richard III.* i 3 165
This man has marr'd his fortune *Coriolanus* iii 1 254
Younger than she are happy mothers made.—And too soon marr'd are those so early made *Rom. and Jul.* i 2 13
Here is himself, marr'd, as you see, with traitors *J. Cæsar* iii 2 201
O bloody period!—All that's spoke is marr'd *Othello* v 2 357
Marriage. At the marriage of the king's fair daughter Claribel *Tempest* ii 1 70
'Twas a sweet marriage, and we prosper well in our return ii 1 72
Our garments seem now as fresh as when we were at Tunis at the marriage ii 1 98

Marriage. Our day of marriage shall be yours; One feast, one house *T. G. of Ver.* v 4 172
Leave our pribbles and prabbles, and desire a marriage *Mer. Wives* i 1 57
The question is concerning your marriage.—Ay, there's the point i 1 228
Speak a good word to Mistress Anne Page for my master in the way of marriage i 4 89
A thousand irreligious cursed hours, Which forced marriage would have brought upon her v 5 243
He promised her marriage: his child is a year and a quarter old *Meas. for Meas.* iii 2 213
There was some speech of marriage Betwixt myself and her v 1 217
Consenting to the safeguard of your honour, I thought your marriage fit v 1 425
I have but lean luck in the match, and yet is she a wondrous fat marriage.—How dost thou mean a fat marriage? *Com. of Errors* iii 2 94
But for the mountain of mad flesh that claims marriage of me, I could find in my heart to stay here iv 4 159
I can give you intelligence of an intended marriage *Much Ado* i 3 47
Name the day of marriage, and God give thee joy! ii 1 312
How canst thou cross this marriage?—Not honestly ii 2 8
What life is in that, to be the death of this marriage? ii 2 20
I will presently go learn their day of marriage ii 2 58
I have railed so long against marriage: but doth not the appetite alter? ii 3 246
I do but stay till your marriage be consummate. iii 2 1
A soil in the new gloss of your marriage iii 2 6
And in dearness of heart hath holp to effect your ensuing marriage iii 2 102
Is not marriage honourable in a beggar? Is not your lord honourable without marriage? iii 4 30
Be brief; only to the plain form of marriage iv 1 2
This day to be conjoin'd In the state of honourable marriage v 4 30
Swear before you choose, if you choose wrong Never to speak to lady afterward In way of marriage *Mer. of Venice* ii 1 42
If I fail . . . never in my life To woo a maid in way of marriage ii 9 13
Those dulcet sounds in break of day That creep into the dreaming bridegroom's ear And summon him to marriage iii 2 53
Our feast shall be much honour'd in your marriage iii 2 215
He [Time] trots hard with a young maid between the contract of her marriage and the day it is solemnized *As Y. Like It* iii 2 332
Truly, she must be given, or the marriage is not lawful iii 3 71
Get you to church, and have a good priest that can tell you what marriage is iii 3 87
In these degrees have they made a pair of stairs to marriage which they will climb incontinent, or else be incontinent before marriage v 2 41
According as marriage binds and blood breaks v 4 59
What mockery will it be, To want the bridegroom when the priest attends To speak the ceremonial rites of marriage! *T. of Shrew* iii 2 6
He'll woo a thousand, 'point the day of marriage iii 2 15
Steal our marriage; Which once perform'd, let all the world say no iii 2 142
Such a mad marriage never was before iii 2 184
To pass assurance of a dower in marriage iv 2 117
That have by marriage made thy daughter mine v 1 119
And, indeed, I do marry that I may repent.—Thy marriage, sooner than thy wickedness *All's Well* i 3 40
If men could be contented to be what they are, they were no fear in marriage i 3 55
Your marriage comes by destiny, Your cuckoo sings by kind i 3 66
Do you know he promised me marriage?—Faith, I know more than I'll speak v 3 255
I knew of their going to bed, and of other motions, as promising her marriage v 3 264
Many a good hanging prevents a bad marriage *T. Night* i 5 21
Presently The rites of marriage shall be solemnized *K. John* ii 1 539
The prevention of poor Bolingbroke About his marriage *Richard II.* ii 1 168
Bad men, you violate A twofold marriage v 1 72
By the which marriage the line of Charles the Great Was re-united *Hen. V.* i 2 84
God, the best maker of all marriages, Combine your hearts in one! v 2 387
Fell jealousy, Which troubles oft the bed of blessed marriage v 2 392
Prepare we for our marriage v 2 398
Proffers his only daughter to your grace In marriage *1 Hen. VI.* v 1 20
Marriage, uncle! alas, my years are young! And fitter is my study v 1 21
I'll over then to England with this news, And make this marriage to be solemnized v 3 168
Marriage is a matter of more worth Than to be dealt in by attorneyship v 5 55
Shameful is this league! Fatal this marriage! *2 Hen. VI.* i 1 99
Had Henry got an empire by his marriage, And all the wealthy kingdoms of the west, There's reason he should be displeased at it i 1 153
And then to Brittany I'll cross the sea, To effect this marriage *3 Hen. VI.* ii 6 98
Vouchsafe to grant That virtuous Lady Bona, thy fair sister, To England's king in lawful marriage iii 3 57
Look, therefore, Lewis, that by this league and marriage Thou draw not on thy danger and dishonour iii 3 74
I long till Edward fall by war's mischance, For mocking marriage with a dame of France iii 3 255
Matter of marriage was the charge he gave me iii 3 258
What think you Of this new marriage with the lady Grey? iv 1 2
Yet hasty marriage seldom proveth well iv 1 18
Your enemy, for mocking him About the marriage of the Lady Bona iv 1 31
Warwick, doing what you gave in charge, Is now dishonoured by this new marriage iv 1 33
Such alliance Would more have strengthen'd this our commonwealth 'Gainst foreign storms than any home-bred marriage iv 1 38
But what said Lady Bona to my marriage? iv 1 97
I want a kingdom, yet in marriage I may not prove inferior to yourself iv 1 121
His daughter meanly have I match'd in marriage *Richard III.* iv 3 37
The marriage with his brother's wife Has crept too near his conscience. —No, his conscience Has crept too near another lady *Hen. VIII.* ii 2 17
Dangers, doubts, wringing of the conscience, Fears, and despairs; and all these for his marriage ii 2 29
They had gather'd a wise council to them Of every realm, that did debate this business, Who deem'd our marriage lawful ii 4 53
Debating A marriage 'twixt the Duke of Orleans and Our daughter Mary ii 4 174
Respecting this our marriage with the dowager, Sometimes our brother's wife ii 4 180
Prove but our marriage lawful, by my life . . . we are contented ii 4 226
Shortly, I believe, His second marriage shall be publish'd iii 2 68
She was divorced, And the late marriage made of none effect iv 1 33
Side factions and give out Conjectural marriages *Coriolanus* i 1 198
Think of marriage now; younger than you, Here in Verona, ladies of esteem, Are made already mothers *Rom. and Jul.* i 3 69

Marriage. If that thy bent of love be honourable, Thy purpose marriage *Rom. and Jul.* ii 2 144
And all combined, save what thou must combine By holy marriage . ii 3 61
All this did I know before. What says he of our marriage? . . ii 5 48
Till we can find a time To blaze your marriage, reconcile your friends . iii 3 151
O, sweet my mother, cast me not away! Delay this marriage for a month iii 5 201
In his wisdom hastes our marriage, To stop the inundation of her tears iv 1 11
What if it be a poison, which the friar Subtly hath minister'd to have me dead, Lest in this marriage he should be dishonour'd? . . . iv 3 26
Bid me devise some mean To rid her from this second marriage . . v 3 241
All this I know; and to the marriage Her nurse is privy . . v 3 265
If in her marriage my consent be missing, I call the gods to witness, I will choose Mine heir from forth the beggars of the world *T. of Athens* i 1 136
Within the bond of marriage, tell me, Brutus, Is it excepted I should know no secrets That appertain to you? . . . . *J. Cæsar* ii 1 280
With mirth in funeral and with dirge in marriage . . *Hamlet* i 2 12
Whose love was of that dignity That it went hand in hand even with the vow I made to her in marriage . . . . . . i 5 50
No other but the main; His father's death, and our o'erhasty marriage ii 2 57
We will have no more marriages: those that are married already, all but one, shall live . . . . iii 1 154
The instances that second marriage move Are base respects of thrift . iii 2 192
A maid so tender, fair and happy, So opposite to marriage . *Othello* i 2 67
O curse of marriage, That we can call these delicate creatures ours, And not their appetites! . . . . iii 3 268
By this marriage, All little jealousies, which now seem great, And all great fears, which now import their dangers, Would then be nothing *Ant. and Cleo.* ii 2 133
Though I make this marriage for my peace, I' the east my pleasure lies ii 3 39
The policy of that purpose made more in the marriage than the love . ii 6 127
With marriage wherefore was he mock'd, To be exiled? . . *Cymbeline* v 4 58
By Juno, that is queen of marriage, All viands that I eat do seem unsavoury, Wishing him my meat . . . . . *Pericles* ii 3 30
Marriage-bed. This servitude makes you to keep unwed.—Not this, but troubles of the marriage-bed . . . *Com. of Errors* ii 1 27
On the marriage-bed Of smiling peace to march a bloody host *K. John* iii 1 245
I, by the honour of my marriage-bed, After young Arthur, claim this land . . . . v 2 93
Marriage-blessing. Honour, riches, marriage-blessing . *Tempest* iv 1 106
Marriage-day. To see our widower's second marriage-day *All's Well* v 3 70
Their stol'n marriage-day Was Tybalt's dooms-day . . *Rom. and Jul.* v 3 233
And what this fourteen years no razor touch'd, To grace thy marriage-day, I'll beautify . . . . *Pericles* v 3 76
Marriage-dowry. With him, . . . her marriage-dowry . *Meas. for Meas.* iii 1 230
Marriage-feast. At a marriage-feast, Between Lord Perigort and the beauteous heir Of Jaques Falconbridge . . . . *L. L. Lost* ii 1 40
The o'er-fed breast Of this most pompous marriage-feast *Pericles* iii Gower 4
Marriage-hour. Our marriage-hour, With all the cunning manner of our flight, Determined of . . . . *T. G. of Ver.* ii 4 179
Marriage joys. The sweet silent hours of marriage joys . *Richard III.* iv 4 330
Marriage-pleasures. In marriage-pleasures play-fellow . *Pericles* i Gower 34
Marriage-rite. A wench full grown, Even ripe for marriage-rite . iv Gower 17
Marriage tables. The funeral baked meats Did coldly furnish forth the marriage tables . . . . *Hamlet* i 2 181
Marriage-vow. I could drive her then from the ward of her purity, her reputation, her marriage-vow . . . . . *Mer. Wives* ii 2 258
Makes marriage-vows As false as dicers' oaths . . . *Hamlet* iii 4 44
Married. Would I had never Married my daughter there! *Tempest* ii 1 108
When we are married and have more occasion to know one another *M. W.* i 1 256
This 'tis to be married! this 'tis to have linen and buck-baskets! . . iii 5 144
Tell her Master Slender hath married her daughter . . . v 5 182
If I had been married to him, for all he was in woman's apparel, I would not have had him . . . . v 5 204
She is now with the doctor at the deanery, and there married . . v 5 216
I ha' married un garçon, a boy; un paysan, by gar, a boy . . v 5 218
You would have married her most shamefully . . . . v 5 234
Sir, she was respected with him before he married with her *Meas. for Meas.* ii 1 179
I respected with her before I was married to her! . . . ii 1 184
She should this Angelo have married; was affianced to her by oath . iii 1 221
They would else have married me to the rotten medlar . . iv 3 183
Are you married?—No, my lord.—Are you a maid?—No, my lord.—A widow, then?—Neither, my lord . . . . . . v 1 171
I do confess I ne'er was married; And I confess besides I am no maid . v 1 184
Whose weakness married to thy stronger state Makes me with thy strength to communicate . . . . . *Com. of Errors* ii 2 177
What, was I married to her in my dream? . . . . . ii 2 184
If they were but a week married, they would talk themselves mad *M. Ado* ii 1 369
When I said I would die a bachelor, I did not think I should live till I were married . . . . ii 3 253
When are you married, madam?—Why, every day, to-morrow . iii 1 100
Means your lordship to be married to-morrow?—You know he does . iii 2 92
To be married to her: friar, you come to marry her.—Lady, you come hither to be married to this count.—I do . . . . . iv 1 7
What do you mean, my lord?—Not to be married . . . . iv 1 44
Let's have a dance ere we are married, that we may lighten our own hearts . . . . v 4 120
And there is two or three lords and ladies more married *M. N. Dream* iv 2 17
I had rather be married to a death's-head . . *Mer. of Venice* i 2 55
I will do any thing, Nerissa, ere I'll be married to a sponge . . i 2 107
I do beseech you, Even at that time I may be married too . . iii 2 196
I am married to a wife Which is as dear to me as life itself . . iv 1 282
Will you be married, motley?—As the ox hath his bow . *As Y. Like It* iii 3 79
A man of your breeding, be married under a bush like a beggar? . iii 3 85
I am not in the mind but I were better to be married of him than of another: for he is not like to marry me well; and not being well married, it will be a good excuse for me hereafter to leave my wife iii 3 92
We must be married, or we must live in bawdry . . . . iii 3 99
They shall be married to-morrow, and I will bid the duke to the nuptial v 2 46
If you will be married to-morrow, you shall, and to Rosalind, if you will v 2 80
I will marry you, if ever I marry woman, and I'll be married to-morrow: I will satisfy you, if ever I satisfied man, and you shall be married to-morrow . . . . v 2 123
To-morrow will we be married.—I do desire it with all my heart . . v 3 2
Any man is so very a fool to be married to hell . . *T. of Shrew* i 1 129
I'll crave the day When I shall ask the banns and when be married . ii 1 181
Thou must be married to no man but me; For I am he am born to tame you . . . . ii 1 277
And kiss me, Kate, we will be married o' Sunday . . . ii 1 326
On Sunday next you know My daughter Katharine is to be married . ii 1 396
This is the 'pointed day That Katharine and Petruchio should be married iii 2 2

Married. Ha' done with words: To me she's married, not unto my clothes *T. of Shrew* iii 2 119
I will be married to a wealthy widow, Ere three days pass . . . iv 2 37
I knew a wench married in an afternoon as she went to the garden for parsley to stuff a rabbit . . . . iv 4 99
The sister to my wife, this gentlewoman, Thy son by this hath married iv 5 63
Have you married my daughter without asking my good will? . . v 1 136
We'll to bed. We three are married, but you two are sped . . v 2 185
Your lord and master's married; there's news for you . . *All's Well* ii 3 257
O my Parolles, they have married me! . . . . . . ii 3 289
A young man married is a man that's marr'd . . . . ii 3 315
He stole from France, As 'tis reported, for the king had married him . iii 5 56
Thou hast spoken all already, unless thou canst say they are married . v 3 269
The lady of the Strachy married the yeoman of the wardrobe *T. Night* ii 5 45
Having been three months married to her, sitting in my state . . ii 5 49
She will keep no fool, sir, till she be married . . . . . iii 1 38
In recompense whereof he hath married her . . . . . . v 1 372
And married a tinker's wife within a mile . . . . *W. Tale* iv 3 103
About his son, that should have married a shepherd's daughter . iv 4 794
And would incense me To murder her I married . . . . v 1 62
You are married?—We are not, sir, nor are we like to be . . v 1 204
Gone to be married! gone to swear a peace! . . . *K. John* iii 1 1
And the conjunction of our inward souls Married in league . . iii 1 228
Upon thy wedding-day? Against the blood that thou hast married? . iii 1 301
As we hear, the Earl of March Hath lately married . . *1 Hen. IV.* i 3 85
Their spirits are so married in conjunction . . . *2 Hen. IV.* v 1 77
It is certain, corporal, that he is married to Nell Quickly *Hen. V.* ii 1 19
It is not a fashion for the maids in France to kiss before they are married v 2 290
Philippe, a daughter, Who married Edmund Mortimer . . *2 Hen. VI.* ii 2 36
There shall not a maid be married, but she shall pay to me her maidenhead . . . . iv 7 129
What! has your king married the Lady Grey? . . *3 Hen. VI.* iii 3 174
I must be married to my brother's daughter, Or else my kingdom stands on brittle glass . . . . *Richard III.* iv 2 61
Men might say, Till this time pomp was single, but now married To one above itself . . . . *Hen. VIII.* i 1 15
The king already Hath married the fair lady.—Would he had! . . iii 2 42
The Lady Anne, Whom the king hath in secrecy long married . . iii 2 403
Know thou first, I loved the maid I married . . . *Coriolanus* iv 5 120
An I might live to see thee married once, I have my wish *Rom. and Jul.* i 3 61
Tell me, daughter Juliet, How stands your disposition to be married? . i 3 65
Go, ask his name: if he be married, My grave is like to be my wedding bed . . . . i 5 136
And there she shall at Friar Laurence' cell Be shrived and married . ii 4 194
An hour but married, Tybalt murdered, Doting like me and like me banished . . . . iii 3 66
O' Thursday, tell her, She shall be married to this noble earl . . iii 4 21
I would the fool were married to her grave! . . . . . iii 5 141
Then, since the case so stands as now it doth, I think it best you married iii 5 219
I hear thou must, and nothing may prorogue it, On Thursday next be married . . . . iv 1 49
What if this mixture do not work at all? Shall I be married then to-morrow morning? No, no . . . . iv 3 22
Lest . . . he should be dishonour'd, Because he married me before . iv 3 27
She's not well married that lives married long; But she's best married that dies married young . . . . iv 5 77
I think He told me Paris should have married Juliet . . . v 3 78
And she, there dead, that Romeo's faithful wife: I married them . . v 3 233
Betroth'd and would have married her perforce To County Paris . v 3 238
Within a month . . . married with my uncle, My father's brother *Hamlet* i 2 151
Ere yet the salt of most unrighteous tears Had left the flushing in her galled eyes, She married . . . . i 2 156
Those that are married already, all but one, shall live; the rest shall keep as they are . . . . iii 1 155
Are they married, think you?—Truly, I think they are . . *Othello* i 1 168
But, I pray you, sir, Are you fast married? . . . . . i 2 11
He's made for ever.—I do not understand.—He's married . . i 2 52
That I have ta'en away this old man's daughter, It is most true; true, I have married her . . . . i 3 79
I took you for that cunning whore of Venice That married with Othello iv 2 90
Let me be married to three kings in a forenoon *Ant. and Cleo.* i 2 26
I am not married, Cæsar: let me hear Agrippa further speak . . ii 2 125
Madam, he's married to Octavia.—The most infectious pestilence upon thee! . . . . ii 5 60
Is he married? I cannot hate thee worser than I do, If thou again say 'Yes.'—He's married, madam . . . . ii 5 89
Is he married to Cleopatra?—Cæsar's sister is called Octavia . . ii 6 114
Antony will use his affection where it is: he married but his occasion here . . . . ii 6 139
But, like a master Married to your good service, stay till death . iv 2 31
A widow That late he married . . . . . . *Cymbeline* i 1 6
He that hath her—I mean, that married her, alack, good man! . . i 1 18
This jewel; see! . . . it must be married To that your diamond . . ii 4 97
Our Jovial star reign'd at his birth, and in Our temple was he married . v 4 106
Married your royalty, was wife to your place; Abhorr'd your person . v 5 39
Till she be married, madam, . . . Unscissar'd shall this hair of mine remain, Though I show ill in't . . . . . . *Pericles* iii 3 27
Married calm. The unity and married calm of states . *Troi. and Cres.* i 3 100
Married ear. Cuckoo, cuckoo: O word of fear, Unpleasing to a married ear! . . . . *L. L. Lost* v 2 921
Married life. She'll not undertake A married life . . . *Pericles* ii 5 4
Married lineament. Examine every married lineament And see how one another lends content . . . . . . *Rom. and Jul.* i 3 83
Married man. If he be a married man, he's his wife's head *M. for M.* iv 2 4
Here you may see Benedick the married man . . . *Much Ado* i 1 270; v 1 186
How dost thou, Benedick, the married man? . . . . . v 4 100
The cuckoo then, on every tree, Mocks married men . . *L. L. Lost* v 2 918
So is the forehead of a married man more honourable than the bare brow of a bachelor . . . . *As Y. Like It* iii 3 61
A married man! that's most intolerable . . . . *1 Hen. VI.* v 4 79
Are you a married man or a bachelor?—Answer every man *J. Cæsar* iii 3 8
Married mankind. So rails against all married mankind *Mer. Wives* iv 2 23
Married ones. So you married ones, If each of you should take this course, how many Must murder wives much better than themselves! *Cymb.* v 1 2
Married wife. Betwixt me and my married wife . . . *Richard II.* v 1 73
I am thy married wife . . . . *2 Hen. VI.* ii 4 28
Married woman. What says the married woman? . . *Ant. and Cleo.* i 3 20
Marries. She which marries you must marry me . . . *All's Well* v 3 174
When your brother marries Aliena, shall you marry her . *As Y. Like It* v 2 70
Young Prince Edward marries Warwick's daughter . . *3 Hen. VI.* iv 1 117

Marring. It is marring indeed, if he quarter it . . . *Mer. Wives* i 1 26
What indeed I should say will, I doubt, prove mine own marring 2 *Hen. IV.* Epil. 7
Play'd as I pleased, Making and marring fortunes . . *Ant. and Cleo.* iii 11 65
Marrow. Spending his manly marrow in her arms . . *All's Well* ii 3 298
Would he were wasted, marrow, bones and all! . . 3 *Hen. VI.* iii 2 125
Lust and liberty Creep in the minds and marrows of our youth *T. of A.* iv 1 26
O, a root,—dear thanks!—Dry up thy marrows, vines, and plough-torn leas! . . . . iv 3 193
When crouching marrow in the bearer strong Cries of itself 'No more' v 4 9
It takes From our achievements, though perform'd at height, The pith and marrow of our attribute . . . . . *Hamlet* i 4 22
Marrowless. Thy bones are marrowless, thy blood is cold . *Macbeth* iii 4 94
Marry. I am your wife, if you will marry me . *Tempest* iii 1 83
But shall she marry him?—No.—How then? shall he marry her? *T. G. of Ver.* ii 5 15
My father would enforce me marry Vain Thurio, whom my very soul abhors . . . . iv 3 16
I will marry her upon any reasonable demands . . *Mer. Wives* i 1 232
Will you, upon good dowry, marry her? . . . . i 1 247
I will marry her, sir, at your request . . . . i 1 253
But if you say, 'Marry her,' I will marry her; that I am freely dissolved i 1 259
I think, if your husbands were dead, you two would marry . . iii 2 15
Good mother, do not marry me to yond fool . . . iii 4 87
In that time Shall Master Slender steal my Nan away And marry her . iv 4 75
The doctor: he hath my good will, And none but he, to marry with Nan Page . . . . iv 4 85
Her father hath commanded her to slip Away with Slender and with him at Eton Immediately to marry . . . . . . iv 6 25
And at the deanery, where a priest attends, Straight marry her . iv 6 32
She it is.—O, let him marry her.—This is the point *Meas. for Meas.* i 4 49
Go take her hence, and marry her instantly . . . . v 1 382
Whom he begot with child, let her appear, And he shall marry her . v 1 518
I beseech your highness, do not marry me to a whore . . v 1 520
Upon mine honour, thou shalt marry her. Thy slanders I forgive . v 1 524
Well, I will marry one day, but to try . . *Com. of Errors* ii 1 42
And he swore he would marry her to-night . . *Much Ado* ii 1 177
I would not marry her, though she were endowed with all that Adam had left him before he transgressed . . . . . ii 1 258
The Count Claudio shall marry the daughter of Leonato . . ii 2 2
I did never think to marry: I must not seem proud . . ii 3 237
If I see any thing to-night why I should not marry her to-morrow, in the congregation, where I should wed, there will I shame her . . iii 2 127
And now is he become a man: he swore he would never marry . iii 4 89
You come hither, my lord, to marry this lady.—No.—To be married to her: friar, you come to marry her . . . . . . iv 1 4
To disgrace Hero before the whole assembly, and not marry her . iv 2 57
How you disgraced her, when you should marry her . . . v 1 246
Are you yet determined To-day to marry with my brother's daughter? . v 4 37
Take her hand Before this friar and swear to marry her . . v 4 57
Since I do purpose to marry, I will think nothing to any purpose that the world can say against it . . . . v 4 106
I will enfranchise thee.—O, marry me to one Frances . *L. L. Lost* iii 1 122
If thou marry, Hang me by the neck, if horns that year miscarry . iv 1 113
This man hath my consent to marry her . . . *M. N. Dream* i 1 25
Be it so she will not here before your grace Consent to marry . . i 1 40
You have her father's love, Demetrius; Let me have Hermia's: do you marry him.—Scornful Lysander! . . . . . . i 1 94
There, gentle Hermia, may I marry thee; And to that place the sharp Athenian law Cannot pursue us . . . . . . i 1 161
If I should marry him, I should marry twenty husbands *Mer. of Venice* i 2 67
Shall I say to you, Let them be free, marry them to your heirs? . iv 1 94
But be it as it may be, I will marry thee . . *As Y. Like It* iii 3 42
I were better to be married of him than of another: for he is not like to marry me well . . . . iii 3 93
Come, sister, you shall be the priest and marry us . . . iv 1 125
Pray thee, marry us.—I cannot say the words . . . . iv 1 127
I am he.—Which he, sir?—He, sir, that must marry this woman . v 1 51
When your brother marries Aliena, shall you marry her . . . v 2 70
I will marry you, if ever I marry woman . . . . . v 2 122
You'll marry me, if I be willing?—That will I, should I die the hour after . . . . v 4 11
Keep your word, Phebe, that you'll marry me, Or else refusing me, to wed this shepherd: Keep your word, Silvius, that you'll marry her, If she refuse me . . . . v 4 21
Give him gold enough and marry him to a puppet . *T. of Shrew* i 2 79
To woo curst Katharine, Yea, and to marry her, if her dowry please . i 2 185
And, will you, nill you, I will marry you . . . . ii 1 273
There is mad Petruchio's wife, If it would please him come and marry her! . . . . iii 2 20
Thus I'll visit her.—But thus, I trust, you will not marry her . . iii 2 117
So shall you quietly enjoy your hope, And marry sweet Bianca . . iii 2 139
Never to marry with her though she would entreat . . . iv 2 33
What, did he marry me to famish me? . . . . . iv 3 3
Tell me thy reason why thou wilt marry.—My poor body, madam, requires it: I am driven on by the flesh . . . *All's Well* i 3 29
I do marry that I may repent.—Thy marriage, sooner than thy wickedness . . . . i 3 39
But never hope to know why I should marry her . . . ii 3 117
After this, To marry her, I'll add three thousand crowns . . iii 7 35
He had sworn to marry me When his wife's dead . . . iv 2 71
Since Frenchmen are so braid, Marry that will, I live and die a maid . iv 2 74
Upon his many protestations to marry me when his wife was dead . v 3 140
I wonder, sir, sith wives are monsters to you, And that you fly them as you swear them lordship, Yet you desire to marry . . . . v 3 157
If you shall marry, You give away this hand, and that is mine . . v 3 169
I by vow am so embodied yours, That she which marries you must marry me . . . . v 3 174
I could marry this wench for this device.—So could I too . *T. Night* ii 5 199
We marry A gentler scion to the wildest stock, And make conceive a bark of baser kind By bud of nobler race . . . *W. Tale* iv 4 92
I see, There's no disjunction to be made, but by—As heavens forfend!—your ruin; marry her . . . . iv 4 541
Will you swear Never to marry but by my free leave . . . v 1 70
Yet, if my lord will marry,—if you will, sir, No remedy, but you will,—give me the office To choose you a queen . . . . . v 1 76
We shall not marry till thou bid'st us . . . . . v 1 82
Which fault lies on the hazards of all husbands That marry wives *K. John* ii 1 120
Two such controlling bounds shall you be, kings, To these two princes, if you marry them . . . . ii 1 445
Marry. Lewis marry Blanch! O boy, then where art thou? . *K. John* iii 1 34
Whom I have weekly sworn to marry . . . . 2 *Hen. IV.* i 2 270
Thou didst swear to me then, as I was washing thy wound, to marry me ii 1 99
He misuses thy favours so much, that he swears thou art to marry his sister . . . . ii 2 139
But do you use me thus, Ned? must I marry your sister? . . . ii 2 151
And then, when they marry, they get wenches . . . . iv 3 101
As procurator to your excellence, To marry Princess Margaret 2 *Hen. VI.* i 1 4
You'ld think it strange if I should marry her.—To whom? 3 *Hen. VI.* iii 2 111
Then I'll marry Warwick's youngest daughter. What though I kill'd her husband and her father? . . . . . . *Richard III.* i 1 153
What, marry, may she! marry with a king, A bachelor, a handsome stripling . . . . i 3 100
Inquire me out some mean-born gentleman, Whom I will marry straight to Clarence' daughter . . . . iv 2 55
Murder her brothers, and then marry her! Uncertain way of gain! . iv 2 63
The French king's sister: he shall marry her. Anne Bullen! No *Hen. VIII.* iii 2 86
Marry, that 'marry' is the very theme I came to talk of *Rom. and Jul.* i 3 63
But this I pray, That thou consent to marry us to-day . . ii 3 64
I will not marry yet; and, when I do, I swear, It shall be Romeo . . iii 5 122
If, rather than to marry County Paris, Thou hast the strength of will to slay thyself . . . . iv 1 71
O, bid me leap, rather than marry Paris, From off the battlements . iv 1 77
Go home, be merry, give consent To marry Paris . . . . iv 1 90
Wisely I say, I am a bachelor.—That's as much as to say, they are fools that marry . . . . *J. Cæsar* iii 3 20
If thou dost marry, I'll give thee this plague for thy dowry . *Hamlet* iii 1 139
If thou wilt needs marry, marry a fool; for wise men know well enough what monsters you make of them . . . . iii 1 143
Almost as bad, good mother, As kill a king, and marry with his brother iii 4 29
Sure, I shall never marry like my sisters, To love my father all . *Lear* i 1 105
Let pride, which she calls plainness, marry her . . . . i 1 131
The cod-piece that will house Before the head has any, The head and he shall louse; So beggars marry many . . . . iii 2 30
If you will marry, make your loves to me, My lady is bespoke . . v 3 88
I was contracted to them both: all three Now marry in an instant . v 3 229
Why did I marry? . . . . *Othello* iii 3 242
She gives it out that you shall marry her: Do you intend it? . . iv 1 118
I marry her! what? a customer! Prithee, bear some charity to my wit iv 1 122
The cry goes that you shall marry her.—Prithee, say true . . iv 1 127
She is persuaded I will marry her, out of her own love and flattery . iv 1 132
Why did he marry Fulvia, and not love her? . . *Ant. and Cleo.* i 1 41
Find me to marry me with Octavius Cæsar . . . . . i 2 29
O, let him marry a woman that cannot go, sweet Isis, I beseech thee! . i 2 66
Unless a man would marry a gallows and beget young gibbets, I never saw one so prone . . . . *Cymbeline* v 4 206
The fair-betrothed of your daughter Shall marry her at Pentapolis *Per.* v 3 72
Marrying. No marrying 'mong his subjects?—None, man . *Tempest* ii 1 165
I may quarter, coz.—You may, by marrying.—It is marring indeed, if he quarter it . . . . *Mer. Wives* i 1 25
And, in the lawful name of marrying, To give our hearts united ceremony . . . . iv 6 50
He will chafe at the doctor's marrying my daughter . . . . v 3 9
Marrying a punk, my lord, is pressing to death, whipping *Meas. for Meas.* v 1 528
He hath wronged his honour in marrying the renowned Claudio *M. Ado* ii 2 23
Bless me from marrying a usurer! . . . . . *W. Tale* iv 4 271
Marrying my sister that thy mother was . . . . . 1 *Hen. VI.* ii 5 86
Not all so much for love As for another secret close intent, By marrying her which I must reach unto . . . . . *Richard III.* i 1 159
She did deceive her father, marrying you . . . . *Othello* iii 3 206
This matter of marrying his king's daughter, wherein he must be weighed rather by her value than his own . . . . *Cymbeline* i 4 14
Marry trap. I will say 'marry trap' with you, if you run the nuthook's humour on me . . . . *Mer. Wives* i 1 170
Mars's hot minion is return'd again . . . . . *Tempest* iv 1 98
Thou art the Mars of malecontents . . . . . *Mer. Wives* i 3 113
The armipotent Mars, of lances the almighty . . *L. L. Lost* v 2 657
Upon their chins The beards of Hercules and frowning Mars *Mer. of Ven.* iii 2 85
You were born under a charitable star.—Under Mars, I.—I especially think, under Mars.—Why under Mars?—The wars have so kept you under that you must needs be born under Mars . . . *All's Well* i 1 206
Mars dote on you for his novices! what will ye do? . . . . ii 1 48
The bound and high curvet Of Mars's fiery steed . . . . ii 3 300
This very day, Great Mars, I put myself into thy file . . . iii 3 9
My heart hath the fear of Mars before it . . . . . iv 1 33
This earth of majesty, this seat of Mars, This other Eden *Richard II.* ii 1 41
The Black Prince, that young Mars of men . . . . . ii 3 101
This Hotspur, Mars in swathling clothes, This infant warrior 1 *Hen. IV.* iii 2 112
The mailed Mars shall on his altar sit Up to the ears in blood . iv 1 116
The warlike Harry, like himself, Assume the port of Mars . *Hen. V.* Prol. 6
Big Mars seems bankrupt in their beggar'd host And faintly through a rusty beaver peeps . . . . iv 2 43
Mars his true moving, even as in the heavens So in the earth, to this day is not known . . . . 1 *Hen. VI.* i 2 1
Mars his idiot! do, rudeness; do, camel; do, do . . *Troi. and Cres.* ii 1 58
Let Mars divide eternity in twain, And give him half . . . ii 3 256
Whose glorious deeds, but in these fields of late, Made emulous missions 'mongst the gods themselves And drave great Mars to faction . . iii 3 190
By Mars his gauntlet, thanks! . . . . iv 5 177
He was a soldier good; But, by great Mars, the captain of us all, Never like thee . . . . iv 5 198
By the forge that stithied Mars his helm, I'll kill thee every where . iv 5 255
In characters as red as Mars his heart Inflamed with Venus . . v 2 164
Who should withhold me? Not fate, obedience, nor the hand of Mars . v 3 52
Now, Mars, I prithee, make us quick in work! . . . *Coriolanus* i 4 10
Why, thou Mars! I tell thee, We have a power on foot . . . iv 5 124
Why, he is so made on here within, as if he were son and heir to Mars . iv 5 204
Hear'st thou, Mars?—Name not the god, thou boy of tears! . . v 6 100
Bright defiler [gold] Of Hymen's purest bed! thou valiant Mars! *T. of A.* iv 3 384
Never did the Cyclops' hammers fall On Mars's armour forged for proof eterne With less remorse . . . . *Hamlet* ii 2 512
The front of Jove himself; An eye like Mars, to threaten and command iii 4 57
Those his goodly eyes, That o'er the files and musters of the war Have glow'd like plated Mars . . . . *Ant. and Cleo.* i 1 4
Yet have I fierce affections, and think What Venus did with Mars . . i 5 18
Let Antony look over Cæsar's head And speak as loud as Mars . . ii 2 6
Though he be painted one way like a Gorgon, The other way's a Mars . ii 5 117
With Mars fall out, with Juno chide . . . . . . *Cymbeline* v 4 32

Marseilles. An argosy That now is lying in Marseilles' road *T. of Shrew* ii 1 377
I duly am inform'd His grace is at Marseilles *All's Well* iv 4 9
His highness comes post from Marseilles iv 5 85
Marsh. My lord, the enemy is past the marsh *Richard III.* v 3 345
Marshal. The marshal's truncheon, nor the judge's robe *Meas. for Meas.* ii 2 61
Reason becomes the marshal to my will And leads me *M. N. Dream* ii 2 120
Lord marshal, command our officers at arms Be ready *Richard II.* i 1 204
Marshal, demand of yonder champion The cause of his arrival i 3 7
Marshal, ask yonder knight in arms, Both who he is and why he cometh i 3 26
Except the marshal and such officers Appointed to direct these fair designs i 3 44
Lord marshal, let me kiss my sovereign's hand, And bow my knee i 3 46
Order the trial, marshal, and begin i 3 99
Bear this sealed brief With winged haste to the lord marshal *1 Hen. IV.* iv 4 2
And first, lord marshal, what say you to it? *2 Hen. IV.* i 3 4
The marshal and the archbishop are strong ii 3 42
He burst his head for crowding among the marshal's men iii 2 348
'Tis very true: And therefore be assured, my good lord marshal iv 1 220
Great marshal to Henry the Sixth *1 Hen. VI.* iv 7 70
The Duke of Norfolk, He to be earl marshal *Hen. VIII.* iv 1 19
They must sweep my way, And marshal me to knavery *Hamlet* iii 4 205
The Marshal of France, Monsieur La Far *Lear* iv 3 9
When these mutualities so marshal the way, hard at hand comes the master and main exercise *Othello* ii 1 268
Here take your place: Marshal the rest, as they deserve their grace *Per.* ii 3 19
Marshallest. Thou marshall'st me the way that I was going *Macbeth* ii 1 42
Marshalsea. Let the troop pass fairly; or I'll find A Marshalsea shall hold ye play these two months *Hen. VIII.* v 4 90
Mart. Nay, more, If any born at Ephesus be seen At any Syracusian marts and fairs *Com. of Errors* i 1 18
I'll meet with you upon the mart And afterward consort you till bed-time i 2 27
My charge was but to fetch you from the mart Home to your house i 2 74
And from the mart he's somewhere gone to dinner ii 1 5
I could not speak with Dromio since at first I sent him from the mart ii 2 6
Even her very words Didst thou deliver to me on the mart ii 2 166
Here's a villain that would face me down He met me on the mart iii 1 7
That you beat me at the mart, I have your hand to show iii 1 12
If any bark put forth, come to the mart, Where I will walk iii 2 155
I'll to the mart and there for Dromio stay iii 2 189
These ears of mine Heard you confess you had the chain of him After you first forswore it on the mart v 1 261
A beggar, that was used to come so smug upon the mart *Mer. of Venice* iii 1 49
I play a merchant's part, And venture madly on a desperate mart *T. of Shrew* ii 1 329
To sell and mart your offices for gold To undeservers *J. Cæsar* iv 3 11
Why such daily cast of brazen cannon, And foreign mart for implements of war; Why such impress of shipwrights? *Hamlet* i 1 74
A saucy stranger in his court to mart As in a Romish stew *Cymbeline* i 6 151
We lost too much money this mart by being too wenchless *Pericles* iv 2 5
Marted. You have let him go And nothing marted with him *W. Tale* iv 4 363
Martem. Here, 'Ad Apollinem:' 'Ad Martem,' that's for myself *T. An.* iv 3 54
Martext. Sir Oliver Martext, the vicar *As Y. Like It* iii 3 43
A most wicked Sir Oliver, Audrey, a most vile Martext v 1 6
Martial. We'll have a swashing and a martial outside i 3 122
Write it in a martial hand *T. Night* iii 2 45
To invest Their sons with arts and martial exercises *2 Hen. IV.* iv 5 74
Let his neck answer for it, if there is any martial law *Hen. V.* iv 8 46
How farest thou, mirror of all martial men? *1 Hen. VI.* i 4 74
A maid! and be so martial!—Pray God she prove not masculine ere long ii 1 21
Warlike and martial Talbot, Burgundy Enshrines thee in his heart iii 2 118
With a martial scorn, with one hand beats Cold death aside *R. and J.* iii 1 166
With martial stalk hath he gone by our watch *Hamlet* i 1 66
This is his hand; His foot Mercurial; his Martial thigh *Cymbeline* iv 2 310
Martin. Expect Saint Martin's summer, halcyon days *1 Hen. VI.* i 2 131
Martino. Signior Martino and his wife and daughters *Rom. and Jul.* i 2 67
Martlemas. And how doth the martlemas, your master? *2 Hen. IV.* ii 2 110
Martlet. Like the martlet, Builds in the weather *Mer. of Venice* ii 9 28
This guest of summer, The temple-haunting martlet *Macbeth* i 6 4
Martyr. Were our royal faiths martyrs in love *2 Hen. IV.* iv 1 193
Oldcastle died a martyr, and this is not the man Epil. 33
Then if thou fall'st, O Cromwell, Thou fall'st a blessed martyr! *Hen. VIII.* iii 2 449
Hark, wretches! how I mean to martyr you *T. Andron.* v 2 181
Here they stand martyrs, slain in Cupid's wars *Pericles* i 1 38
Martyred. Speak, gentle sister, who hath martyr'd thee? *T. Andron.* iii 1 81
Thou hast no hands, to wipe away thy tears; Nor tongue, to tell me who hath martyr'd thee iii 1 107
I can interpret all her martyr'd signs iii 2 36
Despised, distressed, hated, martyr'd, kill'd! *Rom. and Jul.* iv 5 59
Marullus and Flavius, for pulling scarfs off Cæsar's images, are put to silence *J. Cæsar* i 2 288
Marvel. I marvel I hear not of Master Brook *Mer. Wives* iii 5 58
You may marvel why I obscured myself *Meas. for Meas.* v 1 395
Patience unmoved! no marvel though she pause *Com. of Errors* ii 1 32
My spirit grows heavy in love.—And that's great marvel *L. L. Lost* i 2 128
I marvel thy master hath not eaten thee for a word v 1 42
No marvel though Demetrius Do, as a monster, fly my presence *M. N. D.* ii 2 96
It is marvel he out-dwells his hour, For lovers ever run before *M. of V.* ii 6 3
I marvel why I answer'd not again *As Y. Like It* iii 5 132
'Tis marvel, but that you are but newly come, You might have heard it else proclaim'd about *T. of Shrew* iv 2 86
I marvel Cambio comes not all this while v 1 8
You must not marvel, Helen, at my course *All's Well* iv 5 63
We marvel much our cousin France Would in so just a business shut his bosom iii 1 7
I marvel your ladyship takes delight in such a barren rascal *T. Night* i 5 89
I speak amazedly; and it becomes My marvel and my message *W. Tale* v 1 187
Strike all that look upon with marvel v 3 100
I do not only marvel where thou spendest thy time *1 Hen. IV.* ii 4 439
And 'tis no marvel he is so humorous. By'r lady, he is a good musician iii 1 234
A man cannot make him laugh; but that's no marvel, he drinks no wine *2 Hen. IV.* iv 3 96
Here cometh Charles: I marvel how he sped *1 Hen. VI.* i 2 48
No marvel . . . My lord protector's hawks do tower so well *2 Hen. VI.* ii 1 9
No marvel, my lord, though it affrighted you *Richard III.* i 4 64
I marvel why her grace did leave it out ii 2 111
Who's that?—That's Helenus. I marvel where Troilus is *Troi. and Cres.* i 2 238
No marvel, though you bite so sharp at reasons, You are so empty of them ii 2 33

Marvel. Who marvels then, when Helenus beholds A Grecian and his sword, if he do set The very wings of reason to his heels? *Troi. and Cres.* ii 2 42
Then marvel not, thou great and complete man iii 3 181
You make me marvel: wherefore ere this time Had you not fully laid my state before me? *T. of Athens* ii 2 133
Till I may deliver, Upon the witness of these gentlemen, This marvel *Ham.* i 2 195
I marvel what kin thou and thy daughters are *Lear* i 4 199
No marvel, then, though he were ill affected ii 1 100
I am scarce in breath, my lord.—No marvel, you have so bestirred your valour ii 2 58
I marvel our mild husband Not met us on the way iv 2 1
And, to kill the marvel, Shall be so ever *Cymbeline* iii 1 10
I marvel how the fishes live in the sea.—Why, as men do a-land *Pericles* ii 1 29
I much marvel that your lordship, having Rich tire about you, should at these early hours Shake off the golden slumber of repose iii 2 21
Marvelled. The army marvell'd at it *Coriolanus* v 6 42
Marvellest. Thou marvell'st at my words: but hold thee still *Macbeth* iii 2 54
Marvellous sweet music! *Tempest* iii 3 19
Her husband has a marvellous infection to the little page *Mer. Wives* ii 2 120
Marvellous little beholding to your reports *Meas. for Meas.* iv 3 166
Your man and you are marvellous merry, sir *Com. of Errors* iv 3 59
A marvellous witty fellow, I assure you *Much Ado* iv 2 27
A mark marvellous well shot *L. L. Lost* iv 1 132
Marvellous well for the pen iv 2 158
He is a marvellous good neighbour v 2 586
Here's a marvellous convenient place for our rehearsal *M. N. Dream* iii 1 2
Methinks I am marvellous hairy about the face iv 1 26
You are marvellous forward *T. of Shrew* ii 1 73
The rogues are marvellous poor *All's Well* iii 3 179
Too much canaries; and that's a marvellous searching wine *2 Hen. IV.* ii 4 30
They have marvellous foul linen v 1 38
A marvellous falorous gentleman, that is certain *Hen. V.* iii 2 81
She finds, although I cannot, Myself to be a marvellous proper man *Richard III.* i 2 255
She has a marvellous white hand *Troi. and Cres.* i 2 150
What are you?—A gentleman.—A marvellous poor one *Coriolanus* iv 5 30
Well, thou hast comforted me marvellous much *Rom. and Jul.* iii 5 230
You shall do marvellous wisely, good Reynaldo *Hamlet* ii 1 3
Is in his retirement marvellous distempered.—With drink, sir? iii 2 312
Marvellously. You are marvellously changed *Mer. of Venice* i 1 76
You may be marvellously mistook *Hen. V.* iii 6 85
Mary. My name is Mary, sir.—Good Mistress Mary Accost *T. Night* i 3 57
Mistress Mary, if you prized my lady's favour at any thing ii 3 130
At Saint Mary's chapel presently The rites of marriage *K. John* ii 1 538
The world's ransom, blessed Mary's Son *Richard II.* ii 1 56
A marriage 'twixt the Duke of Orleans and Our daughter Mary *Hen. VIII.* ii 4 175
By holy Mary, Butts, there's knavery v 2 33
Mary-bud. Winking Mary-buds begin To ope their golden eyes *Cymbeline* ii 3 26
Masculine. My masculine usurp'd attire *T. Night* v 1 257
A maid! and be so martial!—Pray God she prove not masculine *1 Hen. VI.* ii 1 22
Male varlet, you rogue! what's that?—Why, his masculine whore *Troi. and Cres.* v 1 20
Masham. And the second, Henry Lord Scroop of Masham *Hen. V.* ii Prol. 24
My kind Lord of Masham, And you, my gentle knight, give me your thoughts ii 2 13
There is yours; There yours, Lord Scroop of Masham ii 2 67
I arrest thee . . . by the name of Henry Lord Scroop of Masham ii 2 148
Mask. Her sun-expelling mask *T. G. of Ver.* iv 4 158
These black masks Proclaim an enshield beauty *Meas. for Meas.* ii 4 79
Now fair befall your mask!—Fair fall the face it covers! *L. L. Lost* ii 1 124
Revels, dances, masks and merry hours Forerun fair Love iv 3 379
You have a double tongue within your mask v 2 245
That's all one: you shall play it in a mask *M. N. Dream* i 2 52
Masks for faces and for noses *W. Tale* iv 4 223
And stain my favours in a bloody mask *1 Hen. IV.* iii 2 136
Where hateful death put on his ugliest mask To fright our party *2 Hen. IV.* i 1 66
My mask, to defend my beauty *Troi. and Cres.* i 2 286
Degree being vizarded, The unworthiest shows as fairly in the mask i 3 84
These happy masks that kiss fair ladies' brows *Rom. and Jul.* i 1 236
We mean well in going to this mask; But 'tis no wit to go i 4 48
How long is't now since last yourself and I Were in the mask? i 5 35
The mask of night is on my face, Else would a maiden blush bepaint my cheek ii 2 85
O, then by day Where wilt thou find a cavern dark enough To mask thy monstrous visage? Seek none, conspiracy *J. Cæsar* ii 1 81
To fetch her fan, her gloves, her mask, nor nothing? *Othello* iv 2 9
With faces fit for masks, or rather fairer *Cymbeline* v 3 21
Masked. But, being mask'd, he was not sure of it *T. G. of Ver.* v 2 40
They must all be mask'd and vizarded *Mer. Wives* iv 6 40
When I send for you, come hither mask'd *Much Ado* v 4 12
Most maculate thoughts, master, are masked under such colours *L. L. Lost* i 2 98
The gallants shall be task'd; For, ladies, we will every one be mask'd v 2 127
The trumpet sounds: be mask'd; the maskers come v 2 157
Fair ladies mask'd are roses in their bud v 2 295
'Tis not my blood Wherein thou seest me mask'd *Coriolanus* i 8 10
Some five and twenty years; and then we mask'd *Rom. and Jul.* i 5 39
Give you up to the mask'd Neptune and The gentlest winds *Pericles* iii 3 36
Masker. Be mask'd; the maskers come *L. L. Lost* v 2 157
A peevish schoolboy, . . . Join'd with a masker and a reveller! *J. Cæsar* v 1 62
Masking the business from the common eye *Macbeth* iii 1 125
Mason. The singing masons building roofs of gold *Hen. V.* i 2 198
What is he that builds stronger than either the mason, the shipwright, or the carpenter?—The gallows-maker *Hamlet* v 1 47
Who builds stronger than a mason, a shipwright, or a carpenter? v 1 57
Masonry. Creaking my shoes on the plain masonry *All's Well* ii 1 31
Masque. What masques, what dances shall we have? *M. N. Dream* v 1 32
What masque? what music? How shall we beguile The lazy time? v 1 40
Will you prepare you for this masque to-night? *Mer. of Venice* ii 4 23
I will not say you shall see a masque ii 5 23
What, are there masques? Hear you me, Jessica: Lock up my doors ii 5 28
No masque to-night: the wind is come about ii 6 64
I delight in masques and revels sometimes altogether *T. Night* i 3 121
This harness'd masque and unadvised revel *K. John* v 2 132
Now this masque Was cried incomparable *Hen. VIII.* i 1 26
Masquer. Lewis of France is sending over masquers To revel it with him and his new bride *3 Hen. VI.* iii 3 224; iv 1 94
Masquing. Our masquing mates by this time for us stay *Mer. of Venice* ii 6 59
What masquing stuff is here? What's this? a sleeve? *T. of Shrew* iv 3 87

Mass. They say the jealous wittolly knave hath masses of money *M. Wives* ii 2 284
I am at thy elbow.—Mass, and my elbow itched *Much Ado* iii 3 106
Flat burglary as ever was committed.—Yea, by mass, that it is iv 2 53
And thy wife's attire Have cost a mass of public treasury *2 Hen. VI.* i 3 134
Mass, thou lovedst plums well, that wouldst venture so ii 1 101
Mass, 'twill be sore law, then iv 7 9
And what hath mass or matter, by itself Lies rich in virtue *Troi. and Cres.* i 3 29
The baby figure of the giant mass Of things to come at large i 3 345
Let us pay betimes A moiety of that mass of moan to come ii 2 107
The dreadful spout Which shipmen do the hurricano call, Constringed in mass by the almighty sun v 2 173
Shall I come to you at evening mass? *Rom. and Jul.* iv 1 38
Mass, and well said; a merry whoreson, ha! Thou shalt be logger-head iv 4 19
It is noised he hath a mass of treasure *T. of Athens* iv 3 404
This solidity and compound mass, With tristful visage *Hamlet* iii 4 49
Witness this army of such mass and charge Led by a delicate and tender prince iv 4 47
Marry, now I can tell.—To't.—Mass, I cannot tell v 1 62
I remember a mass of things, but nothing distinctly *Othello* ii 3 289
Not the world's mass of vanity could make me iv 2 164
By the mass *Mer. Wives* iv 2; *1 Hen. IV.* ii 1; ii 4; *2 Hen. IV.* ii 2; ii 4; iii 2; v 3; *Hen. V.* iv 3; *2 Hen. VI.* v 3; *Hamlet* ii 1; iii 2; *Othello* ii 3

Massacre. And rebels' arms triumph in massacres *1 Hen. IV.* v 4 14
Hence grew the general wreck and massacre *1 Hen. VI.* i 1 135
In all our bloody massacre, I muse we met not with the Dauphin's grace ii 2 18
It is your policy To save your subjects from such massacre v 4 160
Welcome, destruction, death, and massacre! *Richard III.* ii 4 53
The most arch act of piteous massacre That ever yet this land was guilty of iv 3 2
I'll find a day to massacre them all And raze their faction *T. Andron.* i 1 450
I must talk of murders, rapes and massacres, Acts of black night v 1 63

Massy. Your swords are now too massy for your strengths *Tempest* iii 3 67
Where his codpiece seems as massy as his club *Much Ado* iii 3 147
Massy staples And corresponsive and fulfilling bolts *Troi. and Cres.* Prol. 17
Without drawing their massy irons and cutting the web ii 3 18
It is a massy wheel, Fix'd on the summit of the highest mount *Hamlet* iii 3 17

Mast. A boat, not rigg'd, Nor tackle, sail, nor mast *Tempest* i 2 147
A small spare mast, Such as seafaring men provide for storms *Com. of Er.* i 1 80
My wife and I, Fixing our eyes on whom our care was fix'd, Fasten'd ourselves at either end the mast i 1 86
To a strong mast that lived upon the sea *T. Night* i 2 14
Upon the high and giddy mast Seal up the ship-boy's eyes *2 Hen. IV.* iii 1 18
What though the mast be now blown overboard? *3 Hen. VI.* v 4 3
Is not Oxford here another anchor? And Somerset another goodly mast? v 4 17
Lives like a drunken sailor on a mast *Richard III.* iii 4 101
The oaks bear mast, the briers scarlet hips *T. of Athens* iv 3 422
Ten masts at each make not the altitude Which thou hast perpendicularly fell: Thy life's a miracle *Lear* iv 6 53
Clasping to the mast, endured a sea That almost burst the deck *Pericles* iv 1 56

Master. Boatswain!—Here, master: what cheer? *Tempest* i 1 2
Take in the topsail. Tend to the master's whistle i 1 8
Good boatswain, have care. Where's the master? Play the men i 1 11
Where is the master, boatswain?—Do you not hear him? i 1 13
Master of a full poor cell, And thy no greater father i 2 20
Being then appointed Master of this design i 2 163
All hail, great master! grave sir, hail! i 2 189
Pardon, master; I will be correspondent to command i 2 296
That's my noble master! What shall I do? say what i 2 299
Every day some sailor's wife, The masters of some merchant and the merchant Have just our theme of woe ii 1 5
My master through his art foresees the danger That you, his friend, are in ii 1 297
The master, the swabber, the boatswain and I ii 2 48
Farewell, master; farewell, farewell!—A howling monster! ii 2 182
'Ban, 'Ban, Cacaliban Has a new master: get a new man ii 2 189
Thou jesting monkey, thou: I would my valiant master would destroy thee! iii 2 53
What would my potent master? here I am iv 1 34
Do you love me, master? no?—Dearly, my delicate Ariel iv 1 48
Weak masters though ye be, I have bedimm'd The noontide sun v 1 41
The master and the boatswain Being awake, enforce them to this place v 1 99
Beheld Our royal, good and gallant ship, our master Capering to eye her v 1 237
How fine my master is! I am afraid He will chastise me v 1 262
Love is your master, for he masters you *T. G. of Ver.* i 1 39
You conclude that my master is a shepherd then and I a sheep?—I do i 1 77
I seek my master, and my master seeks not me: therefore I am no sheep i 1 89
Thou for wages followest thy master; thy master for wages follows not thee i 1 94
When I look on you, I can hardly think you my master ii 1 33
My master sues to her, and she hath taught her suitor, He being her pupil, to become her tutor ii 1 143
That my master, being scribe, to himself should write the letter ii 1 146
Thy master is shipped and thou art to post after with oars ii 3 36
Lose thy master, and, in losing thy master, lose thy service ii 3 48
Lose the tide, and the voyage, and the master, and the service! ii 3 57
That my master is become a notable lover?—I never knew him otherwise ii 5 43
Thou mistakest me.—Why, fool, I meant not thee; I meant thy master ii 5 52
I tell thee, my master is become a hot lover.—Why, I tell thee, I care not ii 5 53
O, could their master come and go as lightly! iii 1 142
Master, shall I strike?—Who wouldst thou strike?—Nothing iii 1 199
And yet I have the wit to think my master is a kind of a knave iii 1 262
Yet 'tis a maid, for she is her master's maid, and serves for wages iii 1 270
What news with your mastership?—With my master's ship? why, it is at sea iii 1 281
Why, then will I tell thee—that thy master stays for thee at the North-gate iii 1 382
Master, be one of them; it's an honourable kind of thievery.—Peace! iv 1 39
By his master's command, he must carry for a present to his lady iv 2 79
I was sent to deliver him as a present to Mistress Silvia from my master iv 4 8
How many masters would do this for his servant? iv 4 32
I am my master's true-confirmed love; But cannot be true servant to my master, Unless I prove false traitor to myself iv 4 108
Bring my picture there. Go give your master this iv 4 123
I will not look upon your master's lines iv 4 133
Poor gentlewoman! my master wrongs her much iv 4 146
When she did think my master loved her well, She, in my judgement, was as fair as you iv 4 155
I hope my master's suit will be but cold iv 4 186
I should have scratch'd out your unseeing eyes, To make my master out of love with thee! iv 4 210
My master charged me to deliver a ring to Madam Silvia v 4 88

Master. Sir John and master mine *Mer. Wives* i 1 164
Playing at sword and dagger with a master of fence i 1 295
The letter is, to desire and require her to solicit your master's desires i 2 11
I pray thee, go to the casement, and see if you can see my master i 4 2
Tell Master Parson Evans I will do what I can for your master i 4 35
Out, alas! here comes my master.—We shall all be shent i 4 37
Go inquire for my master; I doubt he be not well, that he comes not home i 4 42
Good master, be content.—Wherefore shall I be content-a? i 4 73
Speak a good word to Mistress Anne Page for my master i 4 89
I'll do you your master what good I can: and the very yea and the no is, the French doctor, my master,—I may call him my master i 4 98
In your ear; I would have no words of it,—my master himself is in love i 4 110
There comes my master, Master Shallow, and another gentleman iii 1 32
Whether had you rather lead mine eyes, or eye your master's heels? iii 2 4
My master, Sir John, is come in at your back-door, Mistress Ford iii 3 24
My master knows not of your being here and hath threatened to put me into everlasting liberty if I tell you of it iii 3 29
Go tell thy master I am alone. Mistress Page, remember you your cue iii 3 37
Help to cover your master, boy. Call your men, Mistress Ford iii 3 151
I seek you a better husband.—That's my master, master doctor iii 4 89
But yet I would my master had Mistress Anne; or I would Master Slender had her; or, in sooth, I would Master Fenton had her iii 4 108
Met the jealous knave their master in the door, who asked them once or twice what they had in their basket iii 5 103
I'll but bring my young man here to school. Look, where his master comes iv 1 9
Hold up your head; answer your master, be not afraid iv 1 20
Take the basket again on your shoulders: your master is hard at door iv 2 111
To know if it were my master's fortune to have her or no iv 5 48
I thank your worship: I shall make my master glad with these tidings iv 5 57
Neither my husband nor the slave return'd, That in such haste I sent to seek his master! *Com. of Errors* ii 1 2
A man is master of his liberty: Time is their master ii 1 7
Men, more divine, the masters of all these, Lords of the wide world ii 1 20
Of more pre-eminence than fish and fowls, Are masters to their females ii 1 24
Say, is your tardy master now at hand?—Nay, he's at two hands with me ii 1 44
Sure my master is horn-mad.—Horn-mad, thou villain! ii 1 57
'I know not thy mistress; out on thy mistress!'—Quoth who?—Quoth my master ii 1 70
Hence, prating peasant! fetch thy master home ii 1 81
That's not my fault: he's master of my state ii 1 95
I am transformed, master, am I not?—I think thou art in mind, and so am I ii 2 197
Whilst man and master laugh my woes to scorn ii 2 207
If any ask you for your master, Say he dines forth ii 2 211
My master stays in the street.—Let him walk from whence he came iii 1 36
Let my master in, Luce.—Faith, no; he comes too late; And so tell your master iii 1 49
If you went in pain, master, this 'knave' would go sore iii 1 65
Go borrow me a crow.—A crow without feather? Master, mean you so? iii 1 81
They stay for nought at all But for their owner, master, and yourself iv 1 92
Although against my will, For servants must their masters' minds fulfil iv 1 113
Where is thy master, Dromio? is he well?—No, he's in Tartar limbo iv 2 31
There's the money, bear it straight, And bring thy master home immediately iv 2 64
Master, is this Mistress Satan?—It is the devil iv 3 49
Heart and good-will you might; But surely, master, not a rag of money iv 4 89
Both man and master is possess'd; I know it by their pale and deadly looks iv 4 95
Gentle master, I received no gold; But I confess, sir, that we were lock'd out iv 4 101
Masters, let him go: He is my prisoner, and you shall not have him iv 4 114
Will you be bound for nothing? be mad, good master: cry 'The devil!' iv 4 131
Run, master, run; for God's sake, take a house! This is some priory v 1 36
When thou didst make him master of thy bed v 1 163
My master and his man are both broke loose, Beaten the maids a-row v 1 169
My master preaches patience to him and the while His man with scissors nicks him like a fool v 1 174
O, my old master! who hath bound him here? v 1 338
He speaks to me. I am your master, Dromio v 1 411
There is a fat friend at your master's house, That kitchen'd me for you v 1 414
Every one can master a grief but he that has it *Much Ado* iii 2 28
Masters, good night: an there be any matter of weight chances, call up me iii 3 90
I will, like a true drunkard, utter all to thee.—Some treason, masters iii 3 113
But the devil my master knew she was Margaret iii 3 165
Masters, do you serve God?—Yea, sir, we hope iv 2 18
What else?—This is all.—And this is more, masters, than you can deny iv 2 62
The lady is dead upon mine and my master's false accusation v 1 249
She deserves better love than my master *L. L. Lost* i 2 126
How meanest thou? brawling in French?—No, my complete master iii 1 11
Is not lead a metal heavy, dull, and slow?—Minimè, honest master; or rather, master, no iii 1 61
A wonder, master! here's a costard broken in a shin iii 1 71
Imitari is nothing: so doth the hound his master, the ape his keeper iv 2 130
I marvel thy master hath not eaten thee for a word v 1 42
There is the very remuneration I had of thy master v 1 77
Thrice-blessed they that master so their blood *M. N. Dream* i 1 74
Masters, spread yourselves i 2 16
Masters, here are your parts i 2 101
This is he, my master said, Despised the Athenian maid ii 2 72
Masters, you ought to consider with yourselves iii 1 30
Pray, masters! fly, masters! Help! iii 1 108
My conscience will serve me to run from this Jew my master *Mer. of Ven.* ii 2 2
My master, who, God bless the mark, is a kind of devil ii 2 24
Talk you of young Master Launcelot?—No master, sir, but a poor man's son ii 2 53
How dost thou and thy master agree? I have brought him a present ii 2 107
My master's a very Jew: give him a present! give him a halter ii 2 111
His master and he, saving your worship's reverence, are scarce cater-cousins ii 2 138
Thy master spoke with me this day, And hath preferr'd thee ii 2 154
Take leave of thy old master and inquire My lodging out ii 2 162
Where is your master?—Yonder, sir, he walks ii 2 183
Soon at supper shalt thou see Lorenzo, who is thy new master's guest ii 3 6
To bid my old master the Jew to sup to-night with my new master the Christian ii 4 17
I beseech you, sir, go: my young master doth expect your reproach ii 5 20
But now I was the lord Of this fair mansion, master of my servants iii 2 170
Is my master yet return'd?—He is not, nor we have not heard from him v 1 34
There's a post come from my master, with his horn full of good news v 1 47
For the wealth That the world masters v 1 174

Master. And neither man nor master would take aught But the two rings *Mer. of Venice* v 1 183
Yonder comes my master, your brother.—Go apart, Adam *As Y. Like It* i 1 28
Sweet masters, be patient: for your father's remembrance, be at accord i 1 66
God be with my old master! he would not have spoke such a word i 1 88
Or Charles or something weaker masters thee i 2 272
What, my young master? O my gentle master! O my sweet master! ii 3 2
Your virtues, gentle master, Are sanctified and holy traitors to you ii 3 12
Master, go on, and I will follow thee, To the last gasp ii 3 69
Yet fortune cannot recompense me better Than to die well and not my master's debtor ii 3 76
My master is of churlish disposition And little recks to find the way to heaven By doing deeds of hospitality ii 4 80
Dear master, I can go no further: O, I die for food! ii 6 1
Good old man, Thou art right welcome as thy master is ii 7 198
Mistress and master, you have oft inquired After the shepherd iii 4 50
The cottage and the bounds That the old carlot once was master of iii 5 108
Our master and mistress seeks you; come, away, away! v 1 66
Gentle master mine, I am in all affected as yourself *T. of Shrew* i 1 25
Good master, while we do admire This virtue and this moral discipline, Let's be no stoics i 1 29
What company is this?—Master, some show to welcome us to town i 1 47
Peace, Tranio!—Well said, master; mum! and gaze your fill i 1 73
Master, it is no time to chide you now i 1 164
Till the father rid his hands of her, Master, your love must live a maid i 1 187
Master, for my hand, Both our inventions meet and jump in one i 1 194
Nor can we be distinguish'd by our faces For man or master i 1 206
Thou shalt be master, Tranio, in my stead, Keep house and port i 1 207
Master, has my fellow Tranio stolen your clothes? Or you stolen his? i 1 228
Not for my sake, but your master's, I advise You use your manners discreetly i 1 246
I'll knock your knave's pate.—My master is grown quarrelsome i 2 13
Help, masters, help! my master is mad.—Now, knock when I bid you i 2 18
Was it fit for a servant to use his master so? i 2 32
Master, master, look about you: who goes there, ha?—Peace, Grumio! i 2 141
Softly, my masters! if you be gentlemen, Do me this right i 2 238
'Tis in my head to do my master good ii 1 408
I must believe my master; else, I promise you, I should be arguing still iii 1 54
Good masters, take it not unkindly, pray, That I have been thus pleasant iii 1 57
Farewell, sweet masters both; I must be gone.—Faith, mistress, then I have no cause to stay iii 1 85
Master, master! news, old news, and such news as you never heard of! iii 2 30
All for my master's sake iii 2 150
I will be master of what is mine own: She is my goods, my chattels iii 2 231
Fie, fie on all tired jades, on all mad masters, and all foul ways! iv 1 2
Is my master and his wife coming? iv 1 18
Winter tames man, woman and beast; for it hath tamed my old master and my new mistress and myself iv 1 25
My master and mistress are almost frozen to death.—There's fire ready iv 1 39
My master and mistress fallen out.—How?—Out of their saddles iv 1 57
We came down a foul hill, my master riding behind my mistress iv 1 69
And not presume to touch a hair of my master's horse-tail iv 1 96
Do you hear, ho? you must meet my master to countenance my mistress iv 1 101
How near is our master?—E'en at hand, alighted by this iv 1 119
And therefore be not—Cock's passion, silence! I hear my master iv 1 122
Now, mistress, profit you in what you read?—What, master, read you? iv 2 7
And may you prove, sir, master of your art! iv 2 9
The taming-school! what, is there such a place?—Ay, mistress, and Petruchio is the master iv 2 56
O master, master, I have watch'd so long That I am dog-weary iv 2 59
The gown is made Just as my master had direction iv 3 117
I bid thy master cut out the gown; but I did not bid him cut it to pieces iv 3 127
Master, if ever I said loose-bodied gown, sew me in the skirts of it iv 3 136
Take it up unto thy master's use.—Villain, not for thy life: take up my mistress' gown for thy master's use! iv 3 159
Take no unkindness of his hasty words: . . . commend me to thy master iv 3 170
You saw my master wink and laugh upon you? iv 4 75
My master hath appointed me to go to Saint Luke's, to bid the priest iv 4 102
I'll see the church o' your back; and then come back to my master's v 1 6
But who is here? mine old master Vincentio! now we are undone v 1 44
You notorious villain, didst thou never see thy master's father? v 1 55
What, my old worshipful old master? yes, marry, sir v 1 56
O, he hath murdered his master! Lay hold on him, I charge you v 1 91
Like his greyhound, Which runs himself and catches for his master v 2 53
There shall your master have a thousand loves *All's Well* i 1 180
My master, my dear lord he is; and I His servant live i 3 164
Your lord and master did well to make his recantation ii 3 194
To what is count's man: count's master is of another style ii 3 204
Your lord and master's married; there's news for you ii 3 257
He is my good lord: whom I serve above is my master.—Who? God?—Ay, sir.—The devil it is that's thy master ii 3 261
For many a man's tongue shakes out his master's undoing ii 4 24
That from the bloody course of war My dearest master, your dear son, may hie iii 4 9
Where's your master?—He met the duke in the street, sir iv 3 88
I give thee not this to suggest thee from thy master thou talkest of iv 5 47
The master I speak of ever keeps a good fire iv 5 50
I moved the king my master to speak in the behalf of my daughter iv 5 75
Tell me true, I charge you, Not fearing the displeasure of your master v 3 235
My master hath been an honourable gentleman: tricks he hath had in him v 3 238
My lord and master loves you *T. Night* i 5 271
If I did love you in my master's flame, With such a suffering i 5 283
Keep your purse: My master, not myself, lacks recompense i 5 304
Let your fervour, like my master's, be Placed in contempt! i 5 306
Unless the master were the man i 5 313
My master loves her dearly; And I, poor monster, fond as much on him ii 2 34
As I am man, My state is desperate for my master's love ii 2 38
My masters, are you mad? or what are you? Have you no wit? ii 3 93
But the fool should be as oft with your master as with my mistress iii 1 46
Never more Will I my master's tears to you deplore iii 1 174
With the same 'haviour that your passion bears Goes on my master's grief iii 4 227
Nothing but this; your true love for my master iii 4 233
Where he sits crowned in his master's spite v 1 131
I am most apt to embrace your offer. Your master quits you v 1 329
And since you call'd me master for so long, Here is my hand: you shall from this time be Your master's mistress v 1 332
My dagger muzzled, Lest it should bite its master *W Tale* i 2 157
And my ground to do't Is the obedience to a master i 2 354
Two of my best sheep, which I fear the wolf will sooner find than the master iii 3 68

Master. My master hath sent for me; to whose feeling sorrows I might be some allay *W. Tale* iv 2 7
O master, if you did but hear the pedlar at the door iv 4 181
My master, whom I so much thirst to see iv 4 523
I know not what impediment this complaint may be to the flight of my master iv 4 730
A double occasion, gold and a means to do the prince my master good iv 4 866
Wrecked the same instant of their master's death v 2 76
That rare Italian master, Julio Romano v 2 105
Give me your good report to the prince my master v 2 163
Follow us: we'll be thy good masters v 2 188
And like a dog that is compell'd to fight, Snatch at his master *K. John* iv 1 117
Impatience hath his privilege.—'Tis true, to hurt his master, no man else iv 3 33
My master, God omnipotent, Is mustering in his clouds *Richard II.* iii 3 85
Have gotten leave To look upon my sometimes royal master's face v 5 75
No more opposed Against acquaintance . . . : The edge of war, like an ill-sheathed knife, No more shall cut his master *1 Hen. IV.* i 1 18
Now, my masters, happy man be his dole, say I: every man to his business ii 2 80
Set on four and bound them, and were masters of their wealth ii 4 280
Well, here I am set.—And here I stand: judge, my masters ii 4 483
Now, my masters, for a true face and good conscience ii 4 550
And send you back again to your master, for a jewel *2 Hen. IV.* i 2 21
Boy, tell him I am deaf.—You must speak louder; my master is deaf i 2 78
What foolish master taught you these manners? ii 1 202
And how doth the martlemas, your master?—In bodily health, sir ii 2 110
Is your master here in London?—Yea, my lord.—Where sups he? ii 2 156
A proper gentlewoman, sir, and a kinswoman of my master's ii 2 170
No word to your master that I am yet come to town: there's for your silence ii 2 177
I am the worse, when one says swagger: feel, masters, how I shake ii 4 113
Away, you mouldy rogue, away! I am meat for your master ii 4 135
Whether the fiery Trigon, his man, be not lisping to his master's old tables ii 4 289
He is not his craft's master; he doth not do it right iii 2 297
I would humour his men with the imputation of being near their master v 1 81
I'll to the king my master that is dead, And tell him who hath sent me v 2 40
Our master Says that you savour too much of your youth *Hen. V.* i 2 249
Pistol, you must come to my master, and you, hostess: he is very sick ii 1 86
Your own reasons turn into your bosoms, As dogs upon their masters ii 2 83
Between the promise of his greener days And these he masters now ii 4 137
He is enforced to retire, and the Duke of Exeter is master of the pridge iii 6 100
What shall I know of thee?—My master's mind.—Unfold it iii 6 123
So far my king and master; so much my office iii 6 144
Tell thy master here I am; My ransom is this frail and worthless trunk iii 6 162
Go, bid thy master well advise himself: If we may pass, we will iii 6 168
If a servant, under his master's command transporting a sum of money, be assailed by robbers and die in many irreconciled iniquities, you may call the business of the master the author of the servant's damnation iv 1 158
The king is not bound to answer the particular endings of his soldiers, the father of his son, nor the master of his servant iv 1 165
And with wild rage Yerk out their armed heels at their dead masters iv 7 83
Master of the cross-bows, Lord Rambures; Great Master of France iv 8 99
Farewell, my masters; to my task will I. *1 Hen. VI.* i 1 152
Away, my masters! trouble us no more; But join in friendship iii 1 144
The leaves Did represent my master's blushing cheeks iv 1 93
That the paleness of this flower Bewray'd the faintness of my master's heart iv 1 107
My masters, let's stand close: my lord protector will come *2 Hen. VI.* i 3 1
Did the Duke of York say he was rightful heir to the crown?—That my master was? no, forsooth: my master said that he was i 3 33
Take this fellow in, and send for his master with a pursuivant presently i 3 37
Though in this place most master wear no breeches i 3 149
This is the man That doth accuse his master of high treason i 3 185
My masters; the duchess, I tell you, expects performance of your promises i 4 1
They know their master loves to be aloft ii 1 11
Good master, my wife desired some damsons, And made me climb ii 1 102
My masters of Saint Alban's, have you not beadles in your town? ii 1 135
Be merry, Peter, and fear not thy master: fight for credit of the 'prentices ii 3 71
I am never able to deal with my master, he hath learnt so much fence ii 3 78
Peter! what more?—Thump.—Thump! then see thou thump thy master well ii 3 85
Fellow, thank God, and the good wine in thy master's way ii 3 99
What is my ransom, master? let me know.—A thousand crowns iv 1 15
Wear it as a herald's coat, To emblaze the honour that thy master got. iv 10 76
Came on the part of York, press'd by his master *3 Hen. VI.* ii 5 66
Come on, my masters, each man take his stand iv 3 1
Courage, my masters! honour now or never! But follow me iv 3 24
So Judas kiss'd his master, And cried 'all hail!' v 7 33
Cannot thy master sleep these tedious nights? *Richard III.* iii 2 6
Go, bid thy master rise and come to me iii 2 31
To bar my master's heirs in true descent, God knows I will not do it iii 2 54
They who brought me in my master's hate, I live to look upon their tragedy iii 2 58
He will lose his head ere give consent His master's son, as worshipful he terms it, Shall lose the royalty of England's throne iii 4 41
Thus doth he force the swords of wicked men To turn their own points on their masters' bosoms v 1 24
Be not too bold, For Dickon thy master is bought and sold v 3 305
Each following day Became the next day's master *Hen. VIII.* i 1 17
Suggests the king our master To this last costly treaty i 1 164
And point by point the treasons of his master He shall again relate i 2 7
The king our master—Whose honour heaven shield from soil!—even he escapes not Language unmannerly i 2 25
His master would be served before a subject, if not before the king ii 2 8
Guilty, To give up willingly that noble title Your master wed me to iii 1 141
The king, Mine and your master, with his own hand gave me iii 2 247
In the way of loyalty and truth Toward the king, my ever royal master iii 2 273
I am a poor fall'n man, unworthy now To be thy lord and master iii 2 414
Must I needs forgo So good, so noble and so true a master? iii 2 423
Found thee a way, out of his wreck, to rise in; A sure and safe one, though thy master miss'd it iii 2 438
The king has made him master O' the jewel house iv 1 110
Beside that of the jewel house, is made master O' the rolls v 1 34
Ween you of better luck, I mean, in perjured witness, than your master, Whose minister you are? v 1 136
And give it To a most noble judge, the king my master v 3 101
Each Trojan that is master of his heart, Let him to field *Troi. and Cres.* i 1 4
Great Hector's sword had lack'd a master, But for these instances i 3 76
I love you now; but not, till now, so much But I might master it iii 2 129

Master. Thy master now lies thinking in his bed Of thee and me, and sighs *Troi. and Cres.* v 2 78
I'll frush it and unlock the rivets all, But I'll be master of it v 6 30
Stand, ho! yet are we masters of the field: Never go home v 10 1
Why, masters, my good friends, mine honest neighbours, Will you undo yourselves? *Coriolanus* i 1 63
Masters o' the people, We do request your kindest ears ii 2 55
Masters of the people, Your multiplying spawn how can he flatter? ii 2 81
How now, my masters! have you chose this man?—He has our voices, sir ii 3 163
Masters, lay down your weapons.—Go not home.—Meet on the market-place iii 1 331
Hear me, my masters, and my common friends,— He's sentenced iii 3 108
I cannot get him out o' the house: prithee, call my master to him iv 5 23
Tell my master what a strange guest he has here.—And I shall iv 5 38
I serve not thy master.—How, sir! do you meddle with my master? iv 5 49
But a greater soldier than he, you wot one.—Who, my master? iv 5 172
Go, masters, get you home; be not dismay'd iv 6 150
My noble masters, hear me speak v 6 133
Tread not upon him. Masters all, be quiet; Put up your swords v 6 135
He should not choose But give them to his master for a present *T. Andron.* iv 3 75
Like stinging bees in hottest summer's day Led by their master v 1 15
The quarrel is between our masters and us their men *Rom. and Jul.* i 1 23
Say 'better:' here comes one of my master's kinsmen i 1 66
Whither should they come?—Up.—Whither?—To supper; to our house. —Whose house?—My master's i 2 80
Now I'll tell you without asking: my master is the great rich Capulet i 2 84
Am I the master here, or you? go to. You'll not endure him! i 5 80
He will answer the letter's master, how he dares, being dared ii 4 11
There's my master, One that you love.—Who is it?—Romeo v 3 128
I dare not, sir: My master knows not but I am gone hence v 3 132
I dreamt my master and another fought, And that my master slew him v 3 138
I brought my master news of Juliet's death; And then in post he came v 3 272
What made your master in this place?—He came with flowers v 3 280
And by and by my master drew on him; And then I ran away v 3 284
But you well know, Things of like value differing in the owners Are prized by their masters *T. of Athens* i 1 171
Be not ceased With slight denial, nor then silenced when—'Commend me to your master'—and the cap Plays in the right hand, thus ii 1 18
My master is awaked by great occasion To call upon his own ii 2 21
If you did know, my lord, my master's wants ii 2 29
When men come to borrow of your masters, they approach sadly ii 2 105
Thy very bountiful good lord and master iii 1 11
Now I see thou art a fool, and fit for thy master iii 1 53
O you gods, I feel my master's passion! iii 1 59
Doors, that were ne'er acquainted with their wards Many a bounteous year, must be employ'd Now to guard sure their master iii 3 40
It should seem by the sum, Your master's confidence was above mine iii 4 31
Why then preferr'd you not your sums and bills, When your false masters eat of my lord's meat? iii 4 50
I perceive our masters may throw their caps at their money iii 4 101
Large-handed robbers your grave masters are, And pill by law iv 1 11
Maid, to thy master's bed; Thy mistress is o' the brothel! iv 1 12
Hear you, master steward, where's our master? Are we undone? cast off? iv 2 1
Such a house broke! So noble a master fall'n! All gone! iv 2 6
Let's shake our heads, and say, As 'twere a knell unto our master's fortunes, 'We have seen better days' iv 2 26
My dearest master!—Away! what art thou?—Have you forgot me, sir? iv 3 478
For many so arrive at second masters, Upon their first lord's neck iv 3 512
Worthy master; in whose breast Doubt and suspect, alas, are placed too late iv 3 518
O, let me stay, And comfort you, my master.—If thou hatest curses, Stay not iv 3 541
Hail, worthy Timon!—Our late noble master! v 1 58
Men at some time are masters of their fates *J. Cæsar* i 2 139
Let our hearts, as subtle masters do, Stir up their servants to an act of rage, And after seem to chide 'em ii 1 175
Thus, Brutus, did my master bid me kneel iii 1 123
So says my master Antony.—Thy master is a wise and valiant Roman iii 1 137
Is thy master coming?—He lies to-night within seven leagues of Rome iii 1 285
Cæsar has had great wrong.—Has he, masters? iii 2 115
O masters, if I were disposed to stir Your hearts and minds to mutiny iii 2 126
Pindarus is come To do you salutation from his master iv 2 5
My noble master will appear Such as he is, full of regard and honour iv 2 11
What man is that?—My master's man. Strato, where is thy master? v 5 53
How died my master, Strato?—I held the sword, and he did run on it v 5 64
Take him to follow thee, That did the latest service to my master v 5 67
Her husband's to Aleppo gone, master o' the Tiger *Macbeth* i 3 7
We are sent To give thee from our royal master thanks i 3 101
Thou 'rt mad to say it: Is not thy master with him? i 5 33
Is thy master stirring? Our knocking has awaked him; here he comes ii 3 47
Our royal master's murder'd!—Woe, alas! What, in our house? ii 3 92
Let every man be master of his time Till seven at night iii 1 41
Say, if thou'dst rather hear it from our mouths, Or from our masters? iv 1 63
You are welcome, masters; welcome, all *Hamlet* ii 2 440
It is the false steward, that stole his master's daughter iv 5 173
Till by some elder masters, of known honour, I have a voice and precedent v 2 259
Loved as my father, as my master follow'd *Lear* i 1 143
Thy master, whom thou lovest, Shall find thee full of labours i 4 6
You have that in your countenance which I would fain call master i 4 30
You, sir, more knave than fool, after your master i 4 337
The noble duke my master, My worthy arch and patron, comes to-night ii 1 60
Come, I'll flesh ye; come on, young master.—Weapons! arms! ii 2 49
And turn their halcyon beaks With every gale and vary of their masters ii 2 85
It pleased the king his master very late To strike at me ii 2 123
You shall do small respect, show too bold malice Against the grace and person of my master, Stocking his messenger ii 2 138
His fault is much, and the good king his master Will check him for't ii 2 148
Hail to thee, noble master!—Ha! Makest thou this shame thy pastime? ii 4 4
Though I die for it, . . . the king my old master must be relieved iii 3 19
Come hither, friend: where is the king my master?—Here, sir iii 6 93
Take up thy master: If thou shouldst dally half an hour iii 6 99
Where's your master?—Madam, within; but never man so changed iv 2 2
A servant that he bred, thrill'd with remorse, Opposed against the act, bending his sword To his great master iv 2 75
The safer sense will ne'er accommodate His master thus iv 6 82
I am a king, My masters, know you that iv 6 204
Witness the world, that I create thee here My lord and master v 3 78
I am come To bid my king and master aye good night v 3 235
O my good master!—Prithee, away.—'Tis noble Kent, your friend v 3 267

Master. I have a journey, sir, shortly to go; My master calls me, I must not say no *Lear* v 3 322
We cannot all be masters, nor all masters Cannot be truly follow'd *Othello* i 1 43
Wears out his time, much like his master's ass i 1 47
Reverend signiors, My very noble and approved good masters i 3 77
Bring thou the master to the citadel; He is a good one ii 1 211
Hard at hand comes the master and main exercise, the incorporate conclusion ii 1 268
Help, ho!—Lieutenant,—sir,—Montano,—sir;—Help, masters! ii 3 160
What is the matter, masters? Honest Iago, that look'st dead with grieving, Speak ii 3 176
Masters, play here; I will content your pains; Something that's brief iii 1 1
Masters, have your instruments been in Naples, that they speak i' the nose? iii 1 3
Nay, stare not, masters: it is true, indeed v 2 188
By sea He is an absolute master.—So is the fame *Ant. and Cleo.* ii 2 166
He that can endure To follow with allegiance a fall'n lord Does conquer him that did his master conquer iii 13 45
If Cæsar please, our master Will leap to be his friend iii 13 50
Perchance to-morrow You'll serve another master iv 2 28
I turn you not away; but, like a master Married to your good service, stay till death iv 2 30
How now, masters!—How now! How now! do you hear this? iv 3 19
Say that I wish he never find more cause To change a master iv 5 16
To incline himself to Cæsar, And leave his master Antony iv 6 15
Wouldst thou be window'd in great Rome and see Thy master thus? iv 14 73
My dear master, My captain, and my emperor, let me say, Before I strike this bloody stroke, farewell iv 14 89
And, Eros, Thy master dies thy scholar: to do thus I learn'd of thee iv 14 102
He was my master; and I wore my life To spend upon his haters v 1 8
If your master Would have a queen his beggar, you must tell him v 2 15
Do not abuse my master's bounty by The undoing of yourself v 2 43
Know, sir, that I Will not wait pinion'd at your master's court v 2 53
Sir, the gods Will have it thus; my master and my lord I must obey v 2 116
My master, and my lord!—Not so v 2 190
Your son drew on my master.—Ha! No harm, I trust, is done? *Cymbeline* i 1 160
My master rather play'd than fought And had no help of anger i 1 162
Why came you from your master?—On his command i 1 169
I am the master of my speeches, and would undergo what's spoken i 4 152
Upon him Will I first work: he's for his master, And enemy to my son i 5 28
I'll tell thee on the instant thou art then As great as is thy master i 5 51
The agent for his master And the remembrancer of her to hold The hand-fast to her lord i 5 76
Search for a jewel that too casually Hath left mine arm: it was thy master's ii 3 147
The famed Cassibelan, who was once at point—O giglot fortune!—to master Cæsar's sword iii 1 31
I know your master's pleasure and he mine iii 1 86
O master! what a strange infection Is fall'n into thy ear! iii 2 3
O my master! Thy mind to her is now as low as were Thy fortunes iii 2 9
Come, fellow, be thou honest: Do thou thy master's bidding iii 4 67
Thy master is not there, who was indeed The riches of it iii 4 72
And if I do not [die] by thy hand, thou art No servant of thy master's iii 4 78
Thou art too slow to do thy master's bidding, When I desire it too iii 4 100
It cannot be But that my master is abused iii 4 123
Am right sorry that I must report ye My master's enemy iii 5 4
Hast any of thy late master's garments in thy possession? iii 5 125
You, Polydore, have proved best woodman and Are master of the feast iii 6 29
Good masters, harm me not: Before I enter'd here, I call'd iii 6 46
This was my master, A very valiant Briton and a good iv 2 368
There is no more such masters: I may wander From east to occident, cry out for service, Try many, all good, serve truly, never Find such another master iv 2 374
Thou movest no less with thy complaining than Thy master in bleeding iv 2 376
I'll hide my master from the flies, as deep As these poor pickaxes can dig iv 2 388
And rather father thee than master thee iv 2 395
I heard no letter from my master since I wrote him Imogen was slain iv 3 36
Never master had A page so kind, so duteous, diligent, So tender v 5 85
I know not why, wherefore, To say 'live, boy:' ne'er thank thy master; live v 5 96
Your life, good master, Must shuffle for itself.—The boy disdains me v 5 104
Thou 'rt my good youth, my page; I'll be thy master: walk with me v 5 119
I had a feigned letter of my master's Then in my pocket v 5 279
In my master's garments, Which he enforced from me, away he posts v 5 282
Throws her eye On him, her brothers, me, her master v 5 395
My good master, I will yet do you service.—Happy be you! v 5 403
We have no reason to desire it, Commended to our master, not to us *Per.* i 3 38
Sir, you are music's master.—The worst of all her scholars, my good lord ii 5 30
You must be her master, And she will be your scholar ii 5 38
Your master will be dead ere you return iii 2 7
The boatswain whistles, and The master calls, and trebles their confusion iv 1 65
Well, follow me, my masters, you shall have your money presently iv 2 57
What canst thou wish thine enemy to be?—Why, I could wish him to be my master, or rather, my mistress iv 6 170
If that thy master would gain by me, Proclaim that I can sing, weave iv 6 193
But since my master and mistress have bought you, there's no going but by their consent iv 6 207
Master constable *Meas. for Meas.* ii 1; *Much Ado* iii 3; iv 2
Master doctor *Mer. Wives* ii 3; iii 1; iii 2; iii 4; iv 5; v 3; v 5
Master parson *Mer. Wives* i 4; iii 1; *L. L. Lost* iv 2; *T. Night* iv 2
Master-cord. I would 'twere something that would fret the string, The master-cord on's heart *Hen. VIII.* iii 2 106
Master gentleman. Write down, master gentleman Conrade *Much Ado* iv 2 17
Master guest. Moreover, bully,—but first, master guest *Mer. Wives* ii 3 76
Master-gunner. Chief master-gunner am I of this town 1 *Hen. VI.* i 4 6
Master-leaver. A master-leaver and a fugitive *Ant. and Cleo.* iv 9 22
Master mayor, why stand you in a doubt? 3 *Hen. VI.* iv 7 27
Master reasons. Her quirks, her reasons, her master reasons *Pericles* iv 6 8
Master schoolmaster, he that is likest to a hogshead *L. L. Lost* iv 2 87
Master spirits. The choice and master spirits of this age *J. Cæsar* iii 1 163
Master steward, where's our master? Are we undone? *T. of Athens* iv 2 1
Master tapster. What's your name, Master tapster? *Meas. for Meas.* ii 1 223
Master young gentleman, I pray you *Mer. of Venice* ii 2 40
Master young man, you, I pray you, which is the way? ii 2 34
Masterdom. Which shall to all our nights and days to come Give solely sovereign sway and masterdom *Macbeth* i 5 71
Mastered. Not by might master'd but by special grace *L. L. Lost* i 1 153
As if he master'd there a double spirit Of teaching and of learning 1 *Hen. IV.* v 2 64
I will not say Thou shalt be so well master'd *Cymbeline* iv 2 383

Masterless. What mean these masterless and gory swords? *Rom. and Jul.* v 3 142
Gains or loses Your sword or mine, or masterless leaves both *Cymbeline* ii 4 60
Masterly. Thou dost speak masterly . . *T. Night* ii 4 23
Masterly done: The very life seems warm upon her lip . *W. Tale* v 3 65
And gave you such a masterly report For art and exercise *Hamlet* iv 7 97
Unless the bookish theoric, Wherein the toged consuls can propose As masterly as he: mere prattle, without practice . . *Othello* i 1 26
Masterpiece. Confusion now hath made his masterpiece! . *Macbeth* ii 3 71
Mastership. What news with your mastership?—With my master's ship? why, it is at sea . . *T. G. of Ver.* iii 1 280
An't please your mastership . *Mer. of Venice* ii 2 61
When the sea was calm all boats alike Show'd mastership in floating *Coriolanus* iv 1 7
Mastic. When rank Thersites opes his mastic jaws, We shall hear music, wit and oracle . . *Troi. and Cres.* i 3 73
Mastiff. England breeds very valiant creatures; their mastiffs are of unmatchable courage . . *Hen. V.* iii 7 151
The men do sympathize with the mastiffs in robustious and rough coming on . . iii 7 159
Pride alone Must tarre the mastiffs on, as 'twere their bone *Troi. and Cres.* i 3 392
Mastiff, greyhound, mongrel grim, Hound or spaniel, brach or lym *Lear* iii 6 71
Match. Done. The wager?—A laughter.—A match! . . *Tempest* ii 1 34
But tell me true, will't be a match?—Ask my dog . *T. G. of Ver.* ii 5 35
I have sought To match my friend Sir Thurio to my daughter . iii 1 62
And, sure, the match Were rich and honourable . iii 1 63
If it be a match, as nothing is impossible,— What then? . iii 1 379
Thou know'st how willingly I would effect The match . iii 2 23
To keep me from a most unholy match . iv 3 30
The hour is fixed; the match is made . *Mer. Wives* ii 2 304
We have lingered about a match between Anne Page and my cousin Slender . . iii 2 58
Come not to my child.—She is no match for you . iii 4 77
Her mother, ever strong against that match And firm for Doctor Caius iv 6 27
This is the body That took away the match from Isabel *Meas. for Meas.* v 1 211
I have but lean luck in the match . *Com. of Errors* iii 2 94
I hold it a sin to match in my kindred . *Much Ado* ii 1 68
God match me with a good dancer! . ii 1 111
His grace hath made the match, and all grace say Amen to it ii 1 315
I would fain have it a match, and I doubt not but to fashion it ii 1 384
You perhaps may think, Because she is something lower than myself, That I can match her . *M. N. Dream* iii 2 305
There I have another bad match . *Mer. of Venice* iii 1 46
Why, if two gods should play some heavenly match And on the wager lay two earthly women, And Portia one, there must be something else Pawn'd with the other . iii 5 84
I could match this beginning with an old tale . *As Y. Like It* i 2 127
Out of all reasonable match . iii 2 87
Every one fault seeming monstrous till his fellow-fault came to match it iii 2 374
Was ever match clapp'd up so suddenly? . *T. of Shrew* ii 1 327
The gain I seek is, quiet in the match . ii 1 332
Of all mad matches never was the like . iii 2 244
Pass my daughter a sufficient dower, The match is made . iv 4 46
A match! 'tis done.—Who shall begin?—That will I . v 2 74
If thou proceed As high as word, my deed shall match thy meed *All's W.* ii 1 213
Half won is match well made; match, and well make it . iv 3 254
Then shall we have a match. I have letters sent me That set him high in fame . . v 3 30
She'll not match above her degree . *T. Night* i 3 116
No settled senses of the world can match The pleasure of that madness *W. Tale* v 3 72
This is a match, And made between's by vows . v 3 137
If love ambitious sought a match of birth . *K. John* ii 1 430
At this match, With swifter spleen than powder can enforce, The mouth of passage shall we fling wide ope, And give you entrance: but without this match, The sea enraged is not half so deaf . ii 1 447
Son, list to this conjunction, make this match . ii 1 468
For this match made up Her presence would have interrupted much . ii 1 541
Whoever wins, on that side shall I lose; Assured loss before the match be play'd . iii 1 336
Have I not here the best cards for the game, To win this easy match? . v 2 106
And make some pretty match with shedding tears . *Richard II.* iii 3 165
Now shall we know if Gadshill have set a match . *1 Hen. IV.* i 2 119
What cunning match have you made with this jest of the drawer? . ii 4 101
Tell him he hath made a match with such a wrangler *Hen. V.* i 2 264
Yet is he poor, And our nobility will scorn the match . *1 Hen. VI.* v 3 96
Whom should we match with Henry, being a king, But Margaret, that is daughter to a king? . v 5 66
Gives away his own, To match with her that brings no vantages *2 Hen. VI.* i 1 131
And such a piece of service will you do, If you oppose yourselves to match Lord Warwick . v 1 156
Match to match I have encounter'd him . v 2 10
The match is made; she seals it with a curtsy . *3 Hen. VI.* iii 2 57
I wis your grandam had a worser match . *Richard III.* i 3 102
Whose humble means match not his haughty mind . iv 2 37
Both they Match not the high perfection of my loss . iv 4 66
To match us in comparisons with dirt . *Troi. and Cres.* i 3 194
Affronted with the match and weight Of such a winnow'd purity in love iii 2 173
I'll make my match to live, The kiss you take is better than you give . iv 5 37
It were no match, your nail against his horn . iv 5 46
I would my arms could match thee in contention . iv 5 205
But I'll endeavour deeds to match these words . iv 5 259
Thy hand upon that match . iv 5 270
Art thou for Hector's match? Art thou of blood and honour? . v 4 28
You shall ha't, worthy sir.—A match, sir . *Coriolanus* ii 3 86
In this match I hold me highly honour'd of your grace . *T. Andron.* i 1 244
The all-seeing sun Ne'er saw her match . *Rom. and Jul.* i 2 98
Switch and spurs, switch and spurs; or I'll cry a match . ii 4 74
How to lose a winning match, Play'd for a pair of stainless maidenhoods iii 2 12
I think you are happy in this second match, For it excels your first . iii 5 224
What strange, Which manifold record not matches? . *T. of Athens* i 1 5
'Twould be a sight indeed, If one could match you . *Hamlet* iv 7 101
For you, great king, I would not from your love make such a stray, To match you where I hate . *Lear* i 1 213
How shall I live and work, To match thy goodness? . iv 7 2
Not to affect many proposed matches Of her own clime . *Othello* iii 3 229
May fall to match you with her country forms And happily repent . iii 3 237
To lose't or give't away were such perdition As nothing else could match iii 4 68
Forsook so many noble matches, Her father and her country and her friends . . iv 2 125
Thy match was mortal to him, and pure grief Shore his old thread in twain v 2 205
Match. Gracious madam, I that do bring the news made not the match *Ant. and Cleo.* ii 5 67
So is the queen, That most desired the match . *Cymbeline* i 1 12
I dare you to this match: here's my ring.—I will have it no lay . i 4 158
I must go up and down like a cock that nobody can match . ii 1 24
Cadwal and I Will play the cook and servant; 'tis our match . iii 6 30
Matched. A sharp wit match'd with too blunt a will . *L. L. Lost* ii 1 49
But match'd in mouth like bells, Each under each . *M. N. Dream* iv 1 128
Here comes another of the tribe: a third cannot be matched *Mer. of Ven.* iii 1 81
I am content, in a good father's care, To have him match'd *T. of Shrew* iv 4 32
Strength match'd with strength, and power confronted power *K. John* ii 1 330
This match'd with other did, my gracious lord . *1 Hen. IV.* i 1 49
Such barren pleasures, rude society, As thou art match'd withal . iii 2 15
When we have match'd our rackets to these balls . *Hen. V.* i 2 261
His few bad words are matched with as few good deeds . iii 2 41
And had he match'd according to his state, He might have kept that glory to this day . *3 Hen. VI.* ii 2 152
The harder match'd, the greater victory . v 1 70
His daughter meanly have I match'd in marriage . *Richard III.* iv 3 37
That fair for which love groan'd for and would die, With tender Juliet match'd, is now not fair . *Rom. and Jul.* ii Prol. 4
Alone, in company, still my care hath been To have her match'd . iii 5 180
Unequal match'd, Pyrrhus at Priam drives; in rage strikes wide *Hamlet* ii 2 493
Matching. As matching to his youth and vanity . *Hen. V.* ii 4 130
Matching more for wanton lust than honour . *3 Hen. VI.* iii 3 210
When I shall turn the business of my soul To such exsufflicate and blown surmises, Matching thy inference . *Othello* iii 3 183
Matchless. Sole inheritor Of all perfections that a man may owe, Matchless Navarre . *L. L. Lost* ii 1 7
Not yet mature, yet matchless, firm of word . *Troi. and Cres.* iv 5 97
Mate. The gunner and his mate Loved Mall, Meg and Marian *Tempest* ii 2 49
Bestow thy fawning smiles on equal mates . *T. G. of Ver.* iii 1 158
These are my mates, that make their wills their law . v 4 14
Thou, that hast no unkind mate to grieve thee . *Com. of Errors* ii 1 38
Our masquing mates by this time for us stay . *Mer. of Venice* ii 6 59
Is it your will To make a stale of me amongst these mates?—Mates, maid! how mean you that? no mates for you . *T. of Shrew* i 1 58
As if He had been aboard, carousing to his mates After a storm . iii 2 173
I, an old turtle, Will wing me to some wither'd bough and there My mate, that's never to be found again, Lament till I am lost *W. Tale* v 3 134
You poor, base, rascally, cheating, lack-linen mate! . *2 Hen. IV.* ii 4 134
Thou shalt be fortunate, If thou receive me for thy warlike mate *1 Hen. VI.* i 2 92
To be disgraced by an inkhorn mate . iii 1 99
That is good deceit Which mates him first that first intends deceit *2 Hen. VI.* iii 1 265
And thou that art his mate, make boot of this . iv 1 13
We'll forward towards Warwick and his mates . *3 Hen. VI.* iv 7 82
How now, my hardy, stout resolved mates! . *Richard III.* i 3 340
Dare mate a sounder man than Surrey can be . *Hen. VIII.* iii 2 274
As true as steel, . . . As sun to day, as turtle to her mate *Troi. and Cres.* iii 2 185
Leak'd is our bark, And we, poor mates, stand on the dying deck, Hearing the surges threat . *T. of Athens* iv 2 20
The mind much sufferance doth o'erskip, When grief hath mates *Lear* iii 6 114
One self mate and mate could not beget Such different issues . iv 3 36
My competitor In top of all design, my mate in empire . *Ant. and Cleo.* v 1 43
A prize! a prize!—Half-part, mates, half-part . *Pericles* iv 1 95
Mated. Not mad, but mated; how, I do not know . *Com. of Errors* iii 2 54
I think you are all mated or stark mad . v 1 281
That, being mad herself, she's madly mated . *T. of Shrew* iii 2 246
The hind that would be mated by the lion Must die for love . *All's Well* i 1 102
How shall she be endow'd, If she be mated with an equal husband?—Three talents on the present . *T. of Athens* i 1 140
My mind she has mated, and amazed my sight . *Macbeth* v 1 86
Material. A material fool! . *As Y. Like It* iii 3 32
Made His business more material . *W. Tale* i 2 216
Whose absence is no less material to me Than is his father's . *Macbeth* iii 1 136
She that herself will sliver and disbranch From her material sap, perforce must wither And come to deadly use . *Lear* iv 2 35
Outstood my time; which is material To the tender of our present *Cymb.* i 6 207
Mathematics. The mathematics and the metaphysics, Fall to them as you find your stomach serves you . *T. of Shrew* i 1 37
Cunning in music and the mathematics . ii 1 56
As cunning in . . . languages as the other in music and mathematics ii 1 82
Matin. The glow-worm shows the matin to be near . *Hamlet* i 5 89
Matron. Please it this matron and this gentle maid To eat with us to-night, the charge and thanking Shall be for me . *All's Well* iii 5 100
Matrons flung gloves, Ladies and maids their scarfs and handkerchers *Coriolanus* ii 1 279
Come, civil night, Thou sober-suited matron, all in black *Rom. and Jul.* iii 2 11
Matrons, turn incontinent! Obedience fail in children! *T. of Athens* iv 1 3
Strike me the counterfeit matron; It is her habit only that is honest . iv 3 112
Your wives, your daughters, Your matrons and your maids, could not fill up The cistern of my lust . *Macbeth* iv 3 62
Rebellious hell, If thou canst mutine in a matron's bones *Hamlet* iii 4 83
Maids, matrons, . . . This viperous slander enters . *Cymbeline* iii 4 40
Matter. What impossible matter will he make easy next? *Tempest* ii 1 88
The setting of thine eye and cheek proclaim A matter from thee . ii 1 230
And most poor matters Point to rich ends . iii 1 3
They vanish'd strangely.—No matter, since They have left their viands behind . iii 3 40
No matter, since I feel The best is past . iii 3 50
Come, come, open the matter in brief: what said she? *T. G. of Ver.* i 1 135
Open your purse, that the money and the matter may be both at once delivered . i 1 138
It is no matter if the tied were lost . ii 3 41
How stands the matter with them? . ii 5 21
No matter who's displeased when you are gone . ii 7 66
Nay then, no matter; stay with me awhile . iii 1 58
There's some great matter she'ld employ me in . iv 3 3
I will make a Star-chamber matter of it . *Mer. Wives* i 1 2
If matters grow to your likings . i 1 79
What matter have you against me?—Marry, sir, I have matter in my head . i 1 127
There is three umpires in this matter, as I understand . i 1 139
You hear all these matters denied, gentlemen; you hear it . i 1 193
I will description the matter to you, if you be capacity of it . i 1 222
Let them say 'tis grossly done; so it be fairly done, no matter . ii 2 149
The mirth whereof so larded with my matter, That neither singly can be manifested, Without the show of both . iv 6 14
The matter will be known to-night, or never . v 1 11

Matter. But 'tis no matter; better a little chiding than a great deal of heart-break . . . . *Mer. Wives* v 3 10
Have I laid my brain in the sun and dried it, that it wants matter to prevent so gross o'erreaching as this? . . . . v 5 144
And leaves unquestion'd Matters of needful value . . *Meas. for Meas.* i 1 56
Go to: no matter for the dish, sir.—No, indeed, sir, not of a pin . ii 1 98
Few of any wit in such matters . . . . ii 1 282
Well; the matter?—I have a brother is condemn'd to die . . ii 2 33
As the matter now stands, he will avoid your accusation . . iii 1 201
What sayest thou to this tune, matter and method? . . . iii 2 50
Swerve not from the smallest article of it, neither in time, matter . iv 2 108
The matter being afoot, keep your instruction . . . . iv 5 3
Pardon it; The phrase is to the matter.—Mended again. The matter . v 1 90
Whom it concerns to hear this matter forth . . . . . v 1 255
I will debate this matter at more leisure . . . *Com. of Errors* iv 1 100
What is the matter?—I do not know the matter: he is 'rested on the case . . . . iv 2 41
I can see yet without spectacles and I see no such matter . *Much Ado* i 1 192
I have almost matter enough in me for such an embassage . . . i 1 281
I was born to speak all mirth and no matter . . . . . ii 1 344
In the meantime I will so fashion the matter . . . . . ii 2 47
The sport will be, when they hold one an opinion of another's dotage, and no such matter . . . . ii 3 225
Of this matter Is little Cupid's crafty arrow made . . . . iii 1 21
Her wit Values itself so highly that to her All matter else seems weak . iii 1 54
An there be any matter of weight chances, call up me . . . iii 3 91
Speaks a little off the matter . . . . iii 5 11
By this time our sexton hath reformed Signior Leonato of the matter . v 1 263
Why, what's the matter, That you have such a February face? . . v 4 40
They swore that you were well-nigh dead for me.—'Tis no such matter . v 4 82
How low soever the matter, I hope in God for high words . *L. L. Lost* i 1 194
The matter is to me, sir, as concerning Jaquenetta . . . . i 1 203
We will talk no more of this matter.—Till there be more matter in the shin . . . . iii 1 119
O vain petitioner! beg a greater matter . . . . . . v 2 207
That is the very defect of the matter, sir . . . *Mer. of Venice* ii 2 152
As the matter falls . . . . iii 2 204
I was always plain with you, and so now I speak my agitation of the matter . . . . iii 5 4
That for a tricksy word Defy the matter . . . . . . iii 5 75
And yet no matter: why should we go in? . . . . . v 1 50
A quarrel, ho, already! what's the matter? . . . . . v 1 146
I came to acquaint you with a matter . . . . *As Y. Like It* i 1 129
I love to cope him in these sullen fits, For then he's full of matter . ii 1 68
No matter whither, so you come not here . . . . . . ii 3 30
I think of as many matters as he, but I give heaven thanks and make no boast . . . . ii 5 37
It is a hard matter for friends to meet . . . . . . iii 2 194
I'll write it straight; The matter's in my head and in my heart . . iii 5 137
When you were gravelled for lack of matter, you might take occasion to kiss . . . . iv 1 74
For lovers lacking—God warn us!—matter, the cleanliest shift is to kiss.—How if the kiss be denied?—Then she puts you to entreaty, and there begins new matter . . . . iv 1 77
Sing it: 'tis no matter how it be in tune, so it make noise enough . iv 2 9
There was no great matter in the ditty, yet the note was very untuneable . . . . v 3 36
I have promised to make all this matter even. Keep you your word . v 4 18
Out of these convertites There is much matter to be heard . . v 4 191
A good matter, surely: comes there any more of it? . . *T. of Shrew* i 1 255
Nay, 'tis no matter, sir, what he 'leges in Latin . . . . i 2 28
A swearing Jack, That thinks with oaths to face the matter out . . ii 1 291
Then go with me to make the matter good . . . . . iv 2 114
Her matter was, she loved your son . . . . . . *All's Well* i 3 114
What's the matter, That this distemper'd messenger of wet, The many-colour'd Iris, rounds thine eye? . . . . i 3 156
Trust him not in matter of heavy consequence . . . . . ii 5 49
Though you understand it not yourselves, no matter . . . . iv 1 4
Has sat i' the stocks all night, poor gallant knave.—No matter . . iv 3 118
There is no fitter matter . . . . iv 5 81
Howe'er the matter fall, Shall tax my fears of little vanity . . v 3 121
We'll sift this matter further . . . . v 3 124
Sure, you have some hideous matter to deliver, when the courtesy of it is so fearful . . . . *T. Night* i 5 221
I hold the olive in my hand; my words are as full of peace as matter i 5 227
On a forgotten matter we can hardly make distinction of our hands . ii 3 174
Art thou a churchman?—No such matter, sir . . . . . iii 1 5
The matter, I hope, is not great, sir, begging but a beggar . . iii 1 61
My matter hath no voice, lady, but to your own . . . vouchsafed ear . iii 1 99
It is no matter how witty, so it be eloquent and full of invention . iii 2 46
Though thou write with a goose-pen, no matter: about it . . . iii 2 54
How dost thou, man? what is the matter with thee? . . . . iii 4 27
More matter for a May morning . . . . iii 4 156
That is not the matter I challenge thee for . . . . . iii 4 172
Do you know of this matter?—I know the knight is incensed . . iii 4 284
Let him let the matter slip, and I'll give him my horse, grey Capilet . iii 4 314
There is not in the world either malice or matter to alter it . *W. Tale* i 1 37
He's all my exercise, my mirth, my matter . . . . . . i 2 166
The matter, The loss, the gain, the ordering on't, is all Properly ours . ii 1 168
Nor night nor day no rest: it is but weakness To bear the matter thus . ii 3 2
The whole matter And copy of the father, eye, nose, lip . . . ii 3 98
Heavy matters! heavy matters! . . . . iii 3 115
A million of beating may come to a great matter . . . . iv 3 63
I love a ballad but even too well, if it be doleful matter merrily set down . . . . iv 4 189
Would, as it were, mean mischief and break a foul gap into the matter iv 4 198
Here is more matter for a hot brain . . . . iv 4 699
There may be matter in it . . . . iv 4 874
Like an old tale still, which will have matter to rehearse . . . v 2 67
I thought she had some great matter there in hand . . . . v 2 113
And pick strong matter of revolt and wrath . . . . *K. John* iii 4 167
And, O, what better matter breeds for you Than I have named! . . iii 4 170
And quench his fiery indignation Even in the matter of mine innocence iv 1 64
And brought in matter that should feed this fire . . . . v 2 85
Where is the duke my father with his power?—No matter where *Richard II.* iii 2 144
Let me see the writing.—My lord, 'tis nothing.—No matter, then, who see it . . . . v 2 58
A matter of small consequence, Which for some reasons I would not have seen . . . . v 2 61

Matter. I'll read you matter deep and dangerous . . . 1 *Hen. IV.* i 3 190
If matters should be looked into, for their own credit sake . . ii 1 79
Instinct is a great matter . . . . ii 4 301
Both in word and matter . . . . ii 4 479
A trifle, some eight-penny matter . . . . iii 3 119
The big year, swoln with some other grief, Is thought with child by the stern tyrant war, And no such matter . . . 2 *Hen. IV.* Ind. 15
There were matters against you for your life . . . . . i 2 151
'Tis no matter if I do halt; I have the wars for my colour . . i 2 275
How now! whose mare's dead? what's the matter? . . . . ii 1 47
I will devise matter enough out of this Shallow to keep Prince Harry in continual laughter the wearing out of six fashions . . . v 1 87
But though we think it so, it is no matter . . . . *Hen. V.* ii 4 42
You shall be soon dispatch'd . . . : A night is but small breath and little pause To answer matters of this consequence . . . . ii 4 146
You take the matter otherwise than is meant . . . . . iii 2 136
If these men do not die well, it will be a black matter for the king . iv 1 151
'Tis no matter for his swellings nor his turkey-cocks . . . v 1 17
Having any occasion to write for matter of grant . . . . v 2 365
I will work To bring this matter to the wished end . 1 *Hen. VI.* iii 3 28
The Dauphin and his train Approacheth, to confer about some matter . v 4 101
Now the matter grows to compromise, Stand'st thou aloof upon comparison? . . . . v 4 149
Marriage is a matter of more worth Than to be dealt in by attorneyship v 5 55
We'll hear more of your matter before the king . . 2 *Hen. VI.* i 3 38
These are no women's matters . . . . i 3 120
But, to the matter that we have in hand . . . . . . i 3 162
I never said nor thought any such matter . . . . . . i 3 191
Make up no factious numbers for the matter; In thine own person answer . . . . ii 1 40
Sleeping or waking, 'tis no matter how, So he be dead . . . iii 1 263
Go with me; I have great matters to impart to thee . . . iii 2 299
Thou hast appointed justices of peace, to call poor men before them about matters they were not able to answer . . . . . . iv 7 46
Matter of marriage was the charge he gave me . . 3 *Hen. VI.* iii 3 258
My thoughts aim at a further matter . . . . . . iv 1 125
I'll hence to London on a serious matter . . . . . . v 5 47
Brother of Gloucester, you mistake the matter . . . *Richard III.* i 3 62
Is it not an easy matter To make William Lord Hastings of our mind? . iii 1 161
In deep designs and matters of great moment . . . . . iii 7 67
I read in's looks Matter against me; and his eye reviled Me *Hen. VIII.* i 1 126
A choice hour To hear from him a matter of some moment . . . i 2 163
The king hath found Matter against him that for ever mars The honey of his language . . . . iii 2 21
If they shall chance, In charging you with matters, to commit you . v 1 146
For my part, I'll meddle nor make no more i' the matter *Troi. and Cres.* i 1 86
Nor, princes, is it matter new to us That we come short of our suppose i 3 10
And what hath mass or matter, by itself Lies rich in virtue and unmingled . . . . i 3 29
Speak, Prince of Ithaca; and be't of less expect That matter needless, of importless burden, Divide thy lips . . . . i 3 71
Then would come some matter from him; I see none now . . . ii 1 9
Then will Ajax lack matter, if he have lost his argument . . . ii 3 103
And never suffers matter of the world Enter his thoughts . . . ii 3 196
No, no, no such matter; you are wide . . . . . . iii 1 97
I scarce have leisure to salute you, My matter is so rash . . . iv 2 62
I beseech you, on my knees I beseech you, what's the matter? . . iv 2 94
Words, words, mere words, no matter from the heart . . . v 3 108
Where go you With bats and clubs? The matter? speak . *Coriolanus* i 1 57
Will you not be angry?—Well, well, sir, well.—Why, 'tis no great matter . . . . ii 1 31
I can't say your worships have delivered the matter well . . . ii 1 63
When you are hearing a matter between party and party, if you chance to be pinched with the colic, you make faces like mummers . . ii 1 81
The matter?—Hath he not pass'd the noble and the common? . . iii 1 28
Not by your own instruction, Nor by the matter which your heart prompts you . . . . iii 2 54
What is the matter That being pass'd for consul with full voice, I am so dishonour'd that the very hour You take it off again? . . iii 3 58
We need not put new matter to his charge . . . . . iii 3 76
To the tribunal plebs, to take up a matter of brawl . *T. Andron.* iv 3 93
Many a matter hath he told to thee, Meet and agreeing with thine infancy . . . . v 3 164
What is your will?—This is the matter:—Nurse, give leave *Rom. and Jul.* i 3 7
Conceit, more rich in matter than in words, Brags of his substance . ii 6 30
Was ever book containing such vile matter So fairly bound? . . iii 2 83
Never trouble Peter for the matter . . . . iv 4 18
Intending other serious matters, . . . They froze me into silence *T. of A.* ii 2 219
What does his cashiered worship mutter?—No matter what; he's poor iii 4 62
Some that were hang'd, No matter:—wear them, betray with them . iv 3 146
I meddle with no tradesman's matters, nor women's matters . *J. Cæsar* i 1 25
Casca will tell us what the matter is . . . . . . i 2 189
When it serves For the base matter to illuminate So vile a thing as Cæsar! . . . . i 3 110
When I ask'd you what the matter was, You stared upon me with ungentle looks . . . . ii 1 241
If thou consider rightly of the matter, Cæsar has had great wrong . iii 2 114
That matter is answered directly . . . . iii 3 25
How covert matters may be best disclosed, And open perils surest answered . . . . iv 1 46
Your face, my thane, is as a book where men May read strange matters. To beguile the time, Look like the time . . . . *Macbeth* i 5 64
Thy commandment all alone shall live Within the book and volume of my brain, Unmix'd with baser matter . . . . . *Hamlet* i 5 104
More matter, with less art.—Madam, I swear I use no art at all . ii 2 95
What is the matter, my lord?—Between who?—I mean, the matter that you read . . . . ii 2 195
We'll wait upon you.—No such matter: I will not sort you with the rest . . . . ii 2 274
Whose judgements in such matters cried in the top of mine . . ii 2 459
There were no sallets in the lines to make the matter savoury, nor no matter in the phrase . . . . ii 2 463
And like a neutral to his will and matter, Did nothing . . . ii 2 503
He beseech'd me to entreat your majesties To hear and see the matter . iii 1 23
Variable objects shall expel This something-settled matter in his heart iii 1 181
Do you think I meant country matters?—I think nothing, my lord . iii 2 123
Therefore no more, but to the matter . . . . iii 2 336
And I the matter will re-word; which madness Would gambol from . iii 4 143
Or paddling in your neck with his damn'd fingers, Make you to ravel all this matter out . . . . iii 4 186

Matter. There's matter in these sighs, these profound heaves *Hamlet* iv 1 1
Wherein necessity, of matter beggar'd, Will nothing stick our person to arraign In ear and ear iv 5 92
This nothing's more than matter iv 5 174
Yet are they much too light for the bore of the matter iv 6 27
He shall recover his wits there; or, if he do not, it's no great matter there v 1 167
I loved you ever: but it is no matter v 1 313
We'll put the matter to the present push v 1 318
Sir, this is the matter,— I beseech you, remember v 2 106
The phrase would be more german to the matter v 2 166
Sir, I love you more than words can wield the matter *Lear* i 1 56
You know the character to be your brother's?—If the matter were good, my lord, I durst swear it were his i 2 68
What grows of it, no matter; advise your fellows so i 3 23
He would not!—My lord, I know not what the matter is i 4 61
When priests are more in word than matter iii 2 81
There's a division betwixt the dukes; and a worse matter than that iii 3 9
If the matter of this paper be certain, you have mighty business in hand iii 5 16
He is posted hence on serious matter iv 5 8
Thou speak'st In better phrase and matter than thou didst iv 6 8
O, matter and impertinency mix'd! Reason in madness! iv 6 178
Come; no matter vor your foins iv 6 251
If ever I did dream of such a matter, Abhor me *Othello* i 1 5
What is the reason of this terrible summons? What is the matter there? i 1 83
Why, what's the matter?—My daughter! O, my daughter!—Dead? i 3 58
Good Brabantio, Take up this mangled matter at the best i 3 173
I have but an hour Of love, of worldly matters and direction, To spend i 3 300
More of this matter cannot I report: But men are men ii 3 240
Iago, Thy honesty and love doth mince this matter, Making it light ii 3 247
There's matter in't indeed, if he be angry iii 4 139
Good madam, what's the matter with my lord?—With who? iv 2 98
What's the matter with thee now? v 2 105
Hear me this prayer, though thou deny me a matter of more weight *Ant. and Cleo.* i 2 71
I could have given less matter A better ear ii 1 31
Every time Serves for the matter that is then born in't ii 2 10
But small to greater matters must give way.—Not if the small come first ii 2 11
I earnestly beseech, Touch you the sourest points with sweetest terms, Nor curstness grow to the matter ii 2 25
If you'll patch a quarrel, As matter whole you have not to make it with ii 2 53
I do not much dislike the matter, but The manner of his speech ii 2 113
We have cause to be glad that matters are so well digested ii 2 178
We had much more monstrous matter of feast, which worthily deserved noting ii 2 187
Pour out the pack of matter to mine ear, The good and bad together ii 5 54
I think thou'rt mad. The matter? ii 7 63
Assuredly you know me.—No matter, sir, what I have heard or known v 2 73
This matter of marrying his king's daughter, wherein he must be weighed rather by her value than his own, words him, I doubt not, a great deal from the matter *Cymbeline* i 4 14
The matter? Triumphs for nothing and lamenting toys Is jollity for apes iv 2 192
I am amazed with matter iv 3 28
I stand on fire: Come to the matter.—All too soon I shall v 5 169
New matter still? v 5 243
Now this matter must be look'd to, For her relapse is mortal *Pericles* iii 2 109
It is no matter *T. G. of Ver.* iii 1; *Much Ado* v 1; *As Y. Like It* iii 3; *1 Hen. IV.* v 1; *2 Hen. IV.* v 5; *Troi. and Cres.* ii 1; ii 3; v 2; *Coriolanus* ii 3; iv 6; *J. Cæsar* i 1; ii 1; iii 3; *Hamlet* v 2; *Ant. and Cleo.* ii 5; iii 3
It is no matter for that *T. G. of Ver.* iii 1; *Mer. Wives* i 4; *T. Night* iv 1; *Coriolanus* iv 5
That's no matter *Much Ado* v 1; *As Y. Like It* iii 2; iv 3; *Coriolanus* ii 3
What's the matter? *Tempest* ii 1; ii 2; *T. G. of Ver.* ii 3; v 4; *Mer. Wives* ii 1; iii 3; iv 5; *Meas. for Meas.* ii 1; ii 2; *Com. of Errors* iv 2; *Much Ado* iii 2; *As Y. Like It* ii 3; *T. of Shrew* i 2; v 1; *All's Well* ii 3; iii 2; *T. Night* v 1; *Richard II.* ii 1; v 2; v 3; *1 Hen. IV.* ii 4; *2 Hen. IV.* ii 1; ii 4; *Hen. V.* iv 8; *2 Hen. VI.* iii 2; *Richard III.* i 1; *Hen. VIII.* v 1; *Troi. and Cres.* ii 1; iv 2; *Coriolanus* ii 1; v 2; *Rom. and Jul.* iv 5; *J. Cæsar* iv 3; *Macbeth* ii 3; *Hamlet* ii 1; iii 4; iv 5; *Lear* i 4; ii 2; *Othello* i 2; ii 3; iv 1; iv 2; v 1; v 2; *Ant. and Cleo.* i 3; *Cymbeline* i 1; i 6; iii 4; iii 6; *Pericles* iv 6
Matthew. Thither I will send you Matthew Goffe *2 Hen. VI.* iv 5 11
Mattock. 'Tis you must dig with mattock and with spade *T. Andron.* iv 3 11
Give me that mattock and the wrenching iron *Rom. and Jul.* v 3 22
We took this mattock and this spade from him, As he was coming v 3 185
Mattress. A certain queen to Cæsar in a mattress *Ant. and Cleo.* ii 6 71
Mature. Since their more mature dignities and royal necessities made separation of their society *W. Tale* i 1 27
A true knight, Not yet mature, yet matchless *Troi. and Cres.* iv 5 97
This lies glowing, I can tell you, and is almost mature *Coriolanus* iv 3 26
In the mature time With this ungracious paper strike the sight *Lear* iv 6 282
'Tis to be chid As we rate boys, who, being mature in knowledge, Pawn their experience to their present pleasure *Ant. and Cleo.* i 4 31
Most praised, most loved, A sample to the youngest, to the more mature A glass that feated them *Cymbeline* i 1 48
When once he was mature for man, In Britain where was he That could stand up his parallel? v 4 52
Maturity. The seeded pride That hath to this maturity blown up In rank Achilles *Troi. and Cres.* i 3 317
Maud, Bridget, Marian, Cicely, Gillian, Ginn! *Com. of Errors* iii 1 31
Maudlin. Send forth your amorous token for fair Maudlin *All's Well* v 3 68
Maugre. I love thee so, that, maugre all thy pride, Nor wit nor reason can my passion hide *T. Night* iii 1 163
This maugre all the world will I keep safe *T. Andron.* iv 2 110
I protest, Maugre thy strength, youth, place, and eminence *Lear* v 3 131
Maul. I'll so maul you and your toasting-iron *K. John* iv 3 99
'Tis sport to maul a runner *Ant. and Cleo.* iv 7 14
Mauri. 'Integer vitæ, scelerisque purus, Non eget Mauri jaculis, nec arcu.'—O, 'tis a verse in Horace *T. Andron.* iv 2 21
Mauritania. He goes into Mauritania and takes away with him the fair Desdemona *Othello* iv 2 229
Mauvais. Ce sont mots de son mauvais, corruptible, gros *Hen. V.* iii 4 56
Maw. Do thou but think What 'tis to cram a maw *Meas. for Meas.* iii 2 23
Your maw, like mine, should be your clock And strike you home *C. of Er.* i 2 66
Maw. Bid the winter come To thrust his icy fingers in my maw *K. John* v 7 37
In thy throat, And in thy hateful lungs, yea, in thy maw, perdy *Hen. V.* ii 1 52
Thou detestable maw, thou womb of death! *Rom. and Jul.* v 3 45
Then they could smile and fawn upon his debts And take down the interest into their gluttonous maws *T. of Athens* iii 4 52
If charnel-houses and our graves must send Those that we bury back, our monuments Shall be the maws of kites *Macbeth* iii 4 73
Witches' mummy, maw and gulf Of the ravin'd salt-sea shark iv 1 23
Maxim. This maxim out of love I teach: Achievement is command; ungain'd, beseech *Troi. and Cres.* i 2 318
May it please you *T. G. of Ver.* i 3 39
And, may I say to thee, this pride . . . hath drawn my love from her iii 1 72
If any man may, you may as soon as any *Mer. Wives* ii 2 245
He speaks holiday, he smells April and May iii 2 70
You may, I may not; you are yet unsworn *Meas. for Meas.* i 4 9
Which princes, would they, may not disannul *Com. of Errors* i 1 145
Come again when you may iii 1 41
And may it be that you have quite forgot A husband's office? iii 2 1
Her cousin, an she were not possessed with a fury, exceeds her as much in beauty as the first of May doth the last of December *Much Ado* i 1 194
May this be so?—I will not think it iii 2 120
Despite his nice fence and his active practice, His May of youth v 1 76
Why should I joy in any abortive birth? At Christmas I no more desire a rose Than wish a snow in May's new-fangled mirth *L. L. Lost* i 1 106
Love, whose month is ever May, Spied a blossom passing fair iv 3 102
To do observance to a morn of May *M. N. Dream* i 1 167
Shine comforts from the east, That I may back to Athens by daylight iii 2 433
No doubt they rose up early to observe The rite of May iv 1 138
I never may believe These antique fables v 1 2
May you stead me? will you pleasure me? *Mer. of Venice* i 3 7
Here do I choose, and thrive I as I may! ii 7 60
Maids are May when they are maids, but the sky changes *As Y. Like It* iv 1 148
Haply to wive and thrive as best I may *T. of Shrew* i 2 56
It may not be.—Let me entreat you.—It cannot be iii 2 200
Thank both heaven and me! You may so in the end *All's Well* iv 2 68
But, come what may, I do adore thee so *T. Night* ii 1 48
More matter for a May morning iii 4 156
What would my lord, but that he may not have? v 1 104
If you may please to think I love the king *W. Tale* iv 4 532
I may not go without you to the kings.—Thou mayst, thou shalt *K. John* iii 1 66
May this be possible? may this be true? v 4 21
To find out right with wrong, it may not be *Richard II.* ii 3 145
Worst in this royal presence may I speak iv 1 115
She came adorned hither like sweet May, Sent back like Hallowmas v 1 79
The moon shines fair; you may away by night *1 Hen. IV.* iii 1 142
As full of spirit as the month of May, And gorgeous as the sun iv 1 101
I am coming on, To venge me as I may *Hen. V.* i 2 292
When time shall serve, there shall be smiles; but that shall be as it may ii 1 7
I will live so long as I may, that's the certain of it; and when I cannot live any longer, I will do as I may ii 1 15
Things must be as they may: men may sleep, and they may have their throats about them at that time ii 1 23
It must be as it may: though patience be a tired mare, yet she will plod ii 1 25
Whoe'er he be, you may not be let in *1 Hen. VI.* i 3 7
Upon the which, that every one may read, Shall be engraved ii 2 14
And crown her Queen of England ere the thirtieth of May *2 Hen. VI.* i 1 49
But be it as it may: I here entail The crown to thee *3 Hen. VI.* i 1 194
With all the heed I may *Richard III.* iii 1 187
Hark, what good sport is out of town to-day!—Better at home, if 'would I might' were 'may' *Troi. and Cres.* i 1 117
I'll spring up in his tears, an 'twere a nettle against May i 2 191
Whom may you else oppose, That can from Hector bring his honour off? i 3 333
Sweet lord, thou hast a fine forehead.—Ay, you may, you may iii 1 118
You are never without your tricks: you may, you may *Coriolanus* ii 3 39
You may not pass, you must return v 2 5
And chance it as it may *T. of Athens* i 1 129
Come what come may *Macbeth* i 3 146
Who may I rather challenge for unkindness Than pity for mischance! iii 4 42
For your desire to know what is between us, O'ermaster't as you may *Ham.* i 5 140
With all his crimes broad blown, as flush as May iii 3 81
O rose of May! Dear maid, kind sister, sweet Ophelia! iv 5 157
May you suspect Who they should be that have thus mangled you? *Oth.* v 1 78
May be. As little by such toys as may be possible *T. G. of Ver.* i 2 82
May be the knave bragged of that he could not compass *Mer. Wives* iii 3 211
May be he tells you true iv 2 11
I'll know His pleasure; may be he will relent *Meas. for Meas.* ii 2 3
May be I will call upon you anon iv 1 23
But be it as it may be, I will marry thee *As Y. Like It* iii 3 42
May be the amorous count solicits her *All's Well* iii 5 72
May be he will not touch young Arthur's life *K. John* iii 4 160
And may be so we shall *1 Hen. IV.* iv 3 113
Happily met, my lady and my wife!—That may be, sir, when I may be a wife.—That may be must be *Rom. and Jul.* iv 1 19
It may be I shall raise you by and by *J. Cæsar* iv 3 247
It may be I shall otherwise bethink me iv 3 251
May be she pluck'd it off To send it me *Cymbeline* ii 4 104
That, may be, hath endured a grief Might equal yours *Pericles* v 1 88
May-day. As fit as . . . a morris for May-day *All's Well* ii 2 25
As 'tis to make 'em sleep On May-day morning *Hen. VIII.* v 4 15
May-morn. In the very May-morn of his youth, Ripe for exploits *Hen. V.* i 2 120
Mayor. How London doth pour out her citizens! The mayor and all his brethren in best sort v Prol. 25
Peace, mayor! thou know'st little of my wrongs *1 Hen. VI.* i 3 59
Mayor, farewell: thou dost but what thou mayst i 3 86
To London, where we will have the mayor's sword borne before us *2 Hen. VI.* iv 3 16
The lord mayor craves aid of your honour from the Tower iv 5 4
But, master mayor, if Henry be your king, Yet Edward at the least is Duke of York.—True, my good lord *3 Hen. VI.* iv 7 20
Why, master mayor, why stand you in a doubt? Open the gates iv 7 27
My lord, the mayor of London comes to greet you *Richard III.* iii 1 17
Is Catesby gone?—He is; and, see, he brings the mayor along iii 5 13
Lord mayor,— Look to the drawbridge there! iii 5 14
The mayor towards Guildhall hies him in all post iii 5 73
I reprehended them; And ask'd the mayor what meant this wilful silence iii 7 28
Will not the mayor then and his brethren come?—The mayor is here at hand iii 7 44
The lord mayor knocks. Welcome, my lord: I dance attendance here iii 7 55
Tell him, myself, the mayor and citizens, In deep designs . . . Are come to have some conference with his grace iii 7 66

Mayor. When last I was at Exeter, The mayor in courtesy show'd me the castle . . . *Richard III.* iv 2 107
He sent command to the lord mayor straight To stop the rumour *Hen. VIII.* ii 1 151
To you, my good lord mayor, And your good brethren, I am much beholding . . . v 5 70
Maypole. How low am I, thou painted maypole? speak *M. N. Dream* iii 2 296
Mayst. Thou mayst perceive how well I like it *T. G. of Ver.* i 3 35
Thou dost but what thou mayst . . . *1 Hen. VI.* i 3 86
Long mayst thou live to wail thy children's loss! . *Richard III.* i 3 204
Remain in't as thou mayst . . . *Ant. and Cleo.* ii 6 29
Maze. Here's a maze trod indeed Through forth-rights and meanders! *Tempest* iii 3 2
This is as strange a maze as e'er men trod . . . v 1 242
The nine men's morris is fill'd up with mud, And the quaint mazes in the wanton green For lack of tread are undistinguishable *M. N. D.* ii 1 99
I have thrust myself into this maze, Haply to wive and thrive *T. of S.* i 2 55
Mazed. Change Their wonted liveries, and the mazed world, By their increase, now knows not which is which . *M. N. Dream* ii 1 113
A little herd of England's timorous deer, Mazed with a yelping kennel of French curs! . . . *1 Hen. VI.* iv 2 47
That many mazed considerings did throng And press'd in *Hen. VIII.* ii 4 185
Mazzard. Knocked about the mazzard with a sexton's spade . *Hamlet* v 1 97
Let me go, sir, Or I'll knock you o'er the mazzard . *Othello* ii 3 155
Me, poor man, my library Was dukedom large enough *Tempest* i 2 109
And thence retire me to my Milan . . . v 1 310
I am the dog—Oh! the dog is me, and I am myself *T. G. of Ver.* ii 3 25
He thrusts me himself into the company of three or four gentlemanlike dogs . . . iv 4 18
O me unhappy!—Look to the boy . . . v 4 84
The humour rises; it is good: humour me the angels . *Mer. Wives* i 3 64
Come me to what was done to her . . *Meas. for Meas.* ii 1 121
I do repent me, as it is an evil . . . ii 3 35
Let me excuse me, and believe me so . . . iv 1 12
I cannot, nor I will not, hold me still . *Com. of Errors* iv 2 17
She leans me out at her mistress' chamber-window. *Much Ado* iii 3 155
Get you from our court.—Me, uncle?—You, cousin *As Y. Like It* i 3 44
I hear no harm.—No, say'st me so, friend? . *T. of Shrew* i 2 190
A foolish knight,— That's me, I warrant you . *T. Night* ii 5 87
Build me thy fortunes upon the basis of valour . . iii 2 35
Will either of you bear me a challenge to him? . . iii 2 43
Scout me for him at the corner of the orchard like a bum-baily . iii 4 193
But hear me this: Since you to non-regardance cast my faith . v 1 123
Or both yourself and me Cry lost, and so good night! *W. Tale* i 2 410
Imagine me, Gentle spectators, that I now may be In fair Bohemia . iv 1 19
O me! it is my mother. How now, good lady! . *K. John* i 1 220
Me rather had my heart might feel your love . *Richard II.* iii 3 192
To quit their griefs, Tell thou the lamentable tale of me . . v 1 44
I followed me close, came in foot and hand . . *1 Hen. IV.* ii 4 241
See how this river comes me cranking in . . . iii 1 98
It [sherris] ascends me into the brain; dries me there all the foolish and dull and crudy vapours . . *2 Hen. IV.* iv 3 105
And think me honoured To feast so great a warrior . *1 Hen. VI.* ii 3 81
It [my shame] will . . . show itself, attire me how I can . *2 Hen. VI.* ii 4 109
Me seemeth then it is no policy, Respecting what a rancorous mind he bears . . . iii 1 23
Here on this molehill will I sit me down . . *3 Hen. VI.* ii 5 14
Peace, tawny slave, half me and half thy dam! . *T. Andron.* v 1 27
Rests me his minim rest, one, two, and the third in your bosom *R. and J.* ii 4 22
Where I have learn'd me to repent the sin Of disobedient opposition . iv 2 17
O me, O me! My child, my only life, Revive, look up! . iv 5 19
He plucked me ope his doublet and offered them his throat . *J. Cæsar* i 2 267
A man no mightier than thyself or me In personal action . i 3 76
O, yet I do repent me of my fury, That I did kill them . *Macbeth* ii 3 112
The cloudy messenger turns me his back, And hums . . iii 6 41
O, woe is me, To have seen what I have seen, see what I see! *Hamlet* iii 1 168
Wind me into him, I pray you . . . *Lear* i 2 106
Whip me such honest knaves . . . *Othello* i 1 49
Is she as tall as me?—She is not, madam . *Ant. and Cleo.* iii 3 14
And make a conquest of unhappy me . . *Pericles* i 4 69
The word, 'Me pompæ provexit apex' . . . ii 2 30
Come you between, And save poor me, the weaker . . iv 1 91
Meacock. A meacock wretch can make the curstest shrew *T. of Shrew* ii 1 315
Mead. And flat meads thatch'd with stover . . *Tempest* iv 1 63
In dale, forest or mead, By paved fountain or by rushy brook *M. N. D.* ii 1 83
It blots thy beauty as frosts do bite the meads . *T. of Shrew* v 2 139
The even mead, that erst brought sweetly forth The freckled cowslip *Hen. V.* v 2 48
And as our vineyards, fallows, meads and hedges, Defective in their natures, grow to wildness . . . v 2 54
One hour's storm will drown the fragrant meads; What will whole months of tears thy father's eyes? . . *T. Andron.* ii 4 54
With plenteous rivers and wide-skirted meads . *Lear* i 1 66
Meadow. Do paint the meadows with delight . *L. L. Lost* v 2 907
As meadows, yet not dry, With miry slime left on them *T. Andron.* iii 1 125
Meadow-fairies, look you sing . . *Mer. Wives* v 5 69
Meagre. Thou meagre lead, Which rather threatenest . *Mer. of Venice* iii 2 104
Turning . . . The meagre cloddy earth to glittering gold . *K. John* iii 1 80
As hollow as a ghost, As dim and meagre as an ague's fit . iii 4 85
Of ashy semblance, meagre, pale and bloodless . *2 Hen. VI.* iii 2 162
Meagre were his looks, Sharp misery had worn him to the bones *R. and J.* v 1 40
Meal. What strange fish Hath made his meal on thee? . *Tempest* ii 1 113
One fruitful meal would set me to't . . *Meas. for Meas.* iv 3 161
Unquiet meals make ill digestions . . *Com. of Errors* v 1 74
And but one meal on every day beside . . *L. L. Lost* i 1 40
Give them great meals of beef and iron and steel . *Hen. V.* iii 7 161
Give me but the ten meals I have lost, and I'ld defy them all *2 Hen. VI.* iv 10 66
Why hast thou not served thyself in to my table so many meals? *T. and C.* ii 3 45
Meal and bran together He throws without distinction . *Coriolanus* iii 1 322
Whose hours, whose bed, whose meal, and exercise, Are still together . iv 4 14
If I were a huge man, I should fear to drink at meals . *T. of Athens* i 2 51
To keep with you at meals, comfort your bed . . *J. Cæsar* ii 1 284
Ere we will eat our meal in fear and sleep In the affliction of these terrible dreams That shake us nightly . . *Macbeth* iii 2 17
Let's to-night Be bounteous at our meal . . *Ant. and Cleo.* iv 2 10
Here's money for my meat: I would have left it on the board so soon As I had made my meal . . . *Cymbeline* iii 6 52
Nature hath meal and bran, contempt and grace . . iv 2 27
Mealed. Were he meal'd with that Which he corrects, then were he tyrannous; But this being so, he's just . . *Meas. for Meas.* iv 2 86

Mealy. Men, like butterflies, Show not their mealy wings but to the summer, And not a man, for being simply man, Hath any honour *Troi. and Cres.* iii 3 79
Mean. But for the miracle, I mean our preservation . *Tempest* ii 1 7
Here is every thing advantageous to life.—True; save means to live . ii 1 50
I mean, in a sort.—That sort was well fished for . . ii 1 103
Since they did plot The means that dusky Dis my daughter got . iv 1 89
What do you mean To dote thus on such luggage? . . iv 1 230
Supportable To make the dear loss, have I means much weaker Than you v 1 146
You mistake; I mean the pound,—a pinfold . . *T. G. of Ver.* i 1 113
What means this passion at his name?—Pardon, dear madam . i 2 16
There wanteth but a mean to fill your song.—The mean is drown'd . i 2 95
Hast thou observed that? even she, I mean.—Why, sir, I know her not ii 1 49
I mean that her beauty is exquisite, but her favour infinite . ii 1 59
What means your ladyship? do you not like it?—Yes, yes . ii 1 127
Tut, man, I mean thou'lt lose the flood . . . ii 3 46
Here he means to spend his time awhile: I think 'tis no unwelcome news to you . . . ii 4 80
Too mean a servant To have a look of such a worthy mistress . ii 4 107
And all the means Plotted and 'greed on for my happiness . ii 4 182
Tell me some good mean How, with my honour, I may undertake A journey . . . ii 7 5
They have devised a mean How he her chamber-window will ascend . iii 1 38
For 'get you gone,' she doth not mean 'away!' . . iii 1 101
But she I mean is promised by her friends Unto a youthful gentleman iii 1 106
'Friend,' quoth I, 'you mean to whip the dog?' 'Ay, marry, do I,' quoth he . . . iv 4 27
Be my mean To bring me where to speak with Madam Silvia . iv 4 113
The more degenerate and base art thou, To make such means for her as thou hast done And leave her on such slight conditions . v 4 137
What mean you by that saying?—Please you, I'll tell you . v 4 167
Briefly, I do mean to make love to Ford's wife . *Mer. Wives* i 3 47
I had never so good means, as desire, to make myself acquainted with you ii 2 189
Whatsoever I have merited, either in my mind or in my means . ii 2 211
Do not marry me to yond fool.—I mean it not; I seek you a better husband . . . iii 4 88
Her father means she shall be all in white . . iv 6 35
Which means she to deceive, father or mother?—Both . iv 6 46
No man means evil but the devil, and we shall know him by his horns v 2 15
By the woman's means?—Ay, sir, by Mistress Overdone's means *M. for M.* ii 1 84
Your honour cannot come to that yet.—No, sir, nor I mean it not . ii 1 124
Does your worship mean to geld and splay all the youth of the city? . ii 1 242
Let her have needful, but not lavish, means . . ii 2 24
'Tis all as easy Falsely to take away a life true made As to put metal in restrained means To make a false one . . ii 4 48
There were No earthly mean to save him . . . ii 4 95
It oft falls out, To have what we would have, we speak not what we mean . . . ii 4 118
The evil that thou causest to be done, That is thy means to live . iii 2 22
For other means was none . . . *Com. of Errors* i 1 76
Many a man would take you at your word, And go indeed, having so good a mean . . . i 2 18
I mean not cuckold-mad; But, sure, he is stark mad . . ii 1 58
I am glad to see you in this merry vein: What means this jest? . ii 2 21
Thou drunkard, thou, what didst thou mean by this? . . iii 1 10
Though my cates be mean, take them in good part . . iii 1 28
A crow without feather? Master, mean you so? . . iii 1 81
I will depart in quiet, And, in despite of mirth, mean to be merry . iii 1 108
This woman that I mean, My wife—but, I protest, without desert—Hath oftentimes upbraided me withal . . . iii 1 111
He gains by death that hath such means to die . . iii 2 51
A wondrous fat marriage.—How dost thou mean a fat marriage? . iii 2 95
What Adam dost thou mean?—Not that Adam that kept the Paradise . iv 3 15
I hope you do not mean to cheat me so . . . iv 3 79
I will not let him stir Till I have used the approved means I have v 1 103
When mean you to go to church? . . . *Much Ado* ii 1 370
Means your lordship to be married to-morrow? . . iii 2 91
The fashion of a doublet, or a hat, or a cloak, is nothing to a man.—Yes, it is apparel.—I mean, the fashion . . iii 3 128
What means the fool, trow?—Nothing I . . . iii 4 59
What do you mean, my lord?—Not to be married . . iv 1 44
Nor age so eat up my invention, Nor fortune made such havoc of my means . . . iv 1 197
Policy of mind, Ability in means and choice of friends . iv 1 201
Claudio did mean, upon his words, to disgrace Hero . iv 2 56
And knows me, How pitiful I deserve,—I mean in singing . v 2 30
Things hid and barr'd, you mean, from common sense? . *L. L. Lost* i 1 57
Now for the ground which; which, I mean, I walked upon . i 1 242
Pretty and apt.—How mean you, sir? I pretty, and my saying apt? . i 2 20
My beauty, though but mean, Needs not the painted flourish of your praise . . . ii 1 13
He rather means to lodge you in the field . . . ii 1 85
I mean setting thee at liberty, enfreedoming thy person . . iii 1 124
As I for praise alone now seek to spill The poor deer's blood, that my heart means no ill . . . iv 1 35
He can sing A mean most meanly; and in ushering Mend him who can v 2 328
If you my favour mean to get, A twelvemonth shall you spend . v 2 830
Herein mean I to enrich my pain . . *M. N. Dream* i 1 250
I mean, that my heart unto yours is knit So that but one heart we can make of it . . . ii 2 47
I understand not what you mean by this . . . iii 2 236
Heavens shield Lysander, if they mean a fray! . . iii 2 447
And thus she means, videlicet:—Asleep, my love? What, dead? . v 1 330
By something showing a more swelling port Than my faint means would grant continuance . . . *Mer. of Venice* i 1 125
My extremest means Lie all unlock'd to your occasions . . i 1 138
O my Antonio, had I but the means To hold a rival place with one of them! . . . i 1 173
It is no mean happiness, therefore, to be seated in the mean . i 2 8
Yet his means are in supposition . . . i 3 17
Land-rats and water-rats, water-thieves and land-thieves, I mean pirates i 3 24
To yield myself His wife who wins me by that means I told you . ii 1 19
But stop my house's ears, I mean my casements . . ii 5 34
Subject to the same diseases, healed by the same means . . iii 1 65
When your honours mean to solemnize The bargain of your faith . iii 2 194
And do you, Gratiano, mean good faith?—Yes, faith, my lord . iii 2 212
Engaged my friend to his mere enemy, To feed my means . iii 2 266
If on earth he do not mean it, then In reason he should never come to heaven . . . iii 5 82
No lawful means can carry me Out of his envy's reach . . iv 1 9

Mean. I do beseech you, Make no more offers, use no farther means *Mer. of Venice* iv 1 81
You take my life When you do take the means whereby I live iv 1 377
The clerk that never means to do it, Unless he live until he be a man v 1 282
Have by underhand means laboured to dissuade him *As Y. Like It* i 1 146
Never leave thee till he hath ta'en thy life by some indirect means or other i 1 159
An you mean to mock me after, you should not have mocked me before i 2 220
That could give more, but that her hand lacks means i 2 259
This night he means To burn the lodging where you use to lie ii 3 22
If he fail of that, He will have other means to cut you off ii 3 25
With unbashful forehead woo The means of weakness and debility ii 3 51
Flow as hugely as the sea, Till that the weary very means do ebb ii 7 73
Who can come in and say that I mean her, When such a one as she such is her neighbour? Or what is he of basest function That says his bravery is not on my cost, Thinking that I mean him? ii 7 77
He that wants money, means and content is without three good friends iii 2 26
'Od's my little life, I think she means to tangle my eyes too! iii 5 44
Here comes the man you mean v 1 10
That means, Travelling some journey, to repose him here *T. of Shrew* Ind. 1 75
Mates, maid! how mean you that? no mates for you i 1 59
If I can by any means light on a fit man i 1 112
He that has the two fair daughters: is't he you mean?—Even he i 2 223
You mean not her to— Perhaps, him and her, sir: what have you to do? i 2 225
I see you do not mean to part with her ii 1 64
Women are made to bear, and so are you.—No such jade as you, if me you mean.—Alas! good Kate ii 1 202
Then show it me.—Had I a glass, I would.—What, you mean my face? ii 1 236
Keep you warm.—Marry, so I mean, sweet Katharine, in thy bed ii 1 269
Who woo'd in haste and means to wed at leisure iii 2 11
Yet never means to wed where he hath woo'd iii 2 17
Petruchio means but well, Whatever fortune stays him from his word iii 2 22
That by degrees we mean to look into, And watch our vantage iii 2 145
My haste doth call me hence, And therefore here I mean to take my leave iii 2 190
She says your worship means to make a puppet of her iv 3 105
Lay hands on the villain: I believe a' means to cozen somebody v 1 40
You miss my sense: I mean, Hortensio is afeard of you v 2 19
Mistress, how mean you that?—Thus I conceive by him v 2 21
A very mean meaning.—Right, I mean you.—And I am mean indeed, respecting you v 2 31
Am I your bird? I mean to shift my bush; And then pursue me v 2 46
For our gentlemen that mean to see The Tuscan service *All's Well* i 2 13
You might be my daughter-in-law: God shield you mean it not! i 3 174
Thou shalt have my leave and love, Means and attendants i 3 258
Let me see what he writes, and when he means to come iii 2 12
She is too mean To have her name repeated iii 5 63
I mean, the business is not ended, as fearing to hear of it hereafter iv 3 110
There's place and means for every man alive iv 3 375
Though time seem so adverse and means unfit v 1 26
With what good speed Our means will make us means v 1 35
What a plague means my niece, to take the death of her brother thus? I am sure care's an enemy to life *T. Night* i 3 1
What means this lady? Fortune forbid my outside have not charm'd her! ii 2 18
If you prized my lady's favour at any thing more than contempt, you would not give means for this uncivil rule ii 3 132
I am bound to your niece, sir; I mean, she is the list of my voyage iii 1 85
My legs do better understand me, sir, than I understand what you mean by bidding me taste my legs.—I mean, to go, sir, to enter iii 1 90
There is no Christian, that means to be saved by believing rightly, can ever believe such impossible passages of grossness iii 2 75
If you mean well, Now go with me and with this holy man iv 3 22
What means Sicilia?—He something seems unsettled *W. Tale* i 2 146
Mark my counsel, Which must be even as swiftly follow'd as I mean to utter it i 2 410
The queen is spotless I' the eyes of heaven and to you; I mean, In this ii 1 132
Very good ones; but they are most of them means and bases iv 3 46
Nature is made better by no mean But nature makes that mean iv 4 90
Your hand, my Perdita: so turtles pair, That never mean to part iv 4 155
Would, as it were, mean mischief and break a foul gap into the matter iv 4 197
I cannot speak So well, nothing so well; no, nor mean better iv 4 392
That thou no more shalt see this knack, as never I mean thou shalt iv 4 440
When he shall miss me,—as, in faith, I mean not To see him any more iv 4 505
What course I mean to hold Shall nothing benefit your knowledge iv 4 513
By which means I saw whose purse was best in picture iv 4 614
My letters, by this means being there So soon as you arrive iv 4 632
I am courted now with a double occasion, gold and a means to do the prince my master good iv 4 865
But few, And those but mean v 1 93
By any means prove a tall fellow v 2 183
Yet, to avoid deceit, I mean to learn *K. John* i 1 215
What means this scorn, thou most untoward knave? i 1 243
By whose help I mean to chastise it ii 1 117
What dost thou mean by shaking of thy head? Why dost thou look so sadly on my son? What means that hand upon that breast of thine? iii 1 19
A soul counts thee her creditor And with advantage means to pay thy love iii 3 22
No, no; when Fortune means to men most good, She looks upon them with a threatening eye iii 4 119
For even the breath of what I mean to speak Shall blow each dust, each straw, each little rub, Out of the path iii 4 127
How oft the sight of means to do ill deeds Make deeds ill done! iv 2 219
He means to recompense the pains you take By cutting off your heads v 4 15
Ere further leisure yield them further means *Richard II.* i 4 40
Light vanity, insatiate cormorant, Consuming means, soon preys upon itself ii 1 39
The pleasure that some fathers feed upon, Is my strict fast; I mean, my children's looks ii 1 80
And shortly mean to touch our northern shore ii 1 288
The means that heaven yields must be embraced, And not neglected iii 2 29
Heaven's offer we refuse, The proffer'd means of succour and redress.—He means, my lord, that we are too remiss iii 2 32
Which for some reasons I would not have seen.—Which for some reasons, sir, I mean to see v 2 63
What means our cousin, that he stares and looks So wildly? v 3 24
How now! what means death in this rude assault? v 5 106
Send me your prisoners with the speediest means *1 Hen. IV.* i 3 120

Mean. Being the agents, or base second means, The cords, the ladder *1 Hen. IV.* i 3 165
And make the Douglas' son your only mean For powers in Scotland i 3 261
Carrier, what time do you mean to come to London? ii 1 46
What a plague mean ye to colt me thus?—Thou liest; thou art not colted ii 2 39
Smooth-tongue, Spanish-pouch,— O Lord, sir, who do you mean? ii 4 81
I would your grace would take me with you: whom means your grace? ii 4 507
He means to visit us, For he hath heard of our confederacy iv 4 37
Opposed by such means As you yourself have forged against yourself v 1 67
Who never promiseth but he means to pay v 4 43
But what mean I To speak so true at first? *2 Hen. IV.* Ind. 27
Your means are very slender, and your waste is great.—I would it were otherwise; I would my means were greater, and my waist slenderer i 2 159
I take but two shirts out with me, and I mean not to sweat extra-ordinarily i 2 235
Thus have you heard our cause and known our means i 3 1
Would be better satisfied How in our means we should advance ourselves i 3 7
When we mean to build, We first survey the plot, then draw the model i 3 41
'I will imitate the honourable Romans in brevity:' he sure means brevity in breath, short-winded ii 2 135
With all appliances and means to boot iii 1 29
When means and lavish manners meet together iv 4 64
Do you mean to stop any of William's wages, about the sack he lost? v 1 24
For competence of life I will allow you, That lack of means enforce you not to evil v 5 71
We must needs admit the means How things are perfected *Hen. V.* i 1 68
They know your grace hath cause and means and might i 2 125
We do not mean the coursing snatchers only, But fear the main intend-ment i 2 143
With men of courage and with means defendant ii 4 8
None of you so mean and base, That hath not noble lustre in your eyes iii 1 29
He is white-livered and red-faced; by the means whereof a' faces it out iii 2 34
That mean and gentle all Behold, as may unworthiness define iv Prol. 45
Be stern: By this means shall we sound what skill she hath *1 Hen. VI.* i 2 63
Shall we disturb him, since he keeps no mean?—He may mean more than we poor men do know i 2 121
Beware your beard; I mean to tug it and to cuff you soundly i 3 48
By what means got'st thou to be released? i 4 25
Since there's no remedy, I mean to prove this lady's courtesy ii 2 58
You perceive my mind?—I do, my lord, and mean accordingly ii 2 60
What means he now? Go ask him whither he goes ii 3 28
Gentlemen, what means this silence? Dare no man answer in a case of truth? ii 4 1
Except you mean with obstinate repulse To slay your sovereign iii 1 113
Our sacks shall be a mean to sack the city iii 2 10
Let's get us from the walls; For Talbot means no goodness by his looks iii 2 72
What means his grace, that he hath changed his style? iv 1 50
Mean and right poor iv 6 23
Submission, Dauphin! . . . We English warriors wot not what it means iv 7 55
As the only means To stop effusion of our Christian blood v 1 8
Is now conjoin'd in one, And means to give you battle presently v 2 13
Hast thou by secret means Used intercession to obtain a league? v 4 147
To be at your command; Command, I mean, of virtuous chaste intents v 5 20
What means this passionate discourse? *2 Hen. VI.* i 1 104
Unto Saint Alban's, Where as the king and queen do mean to hawk i 2 58
What means this noise? Fellow, what miracle dost thou proclaim? ii 1 59
If you mean to save yourself from whipping, leap me over this stool ii 1 143
By this means Your lady is forthcoming yet at London ii 1 178
By wicked means to frame our sovereign's fall iii 1 52
By means whereof the towns each day revolted iii 1 63
Who cannot steal a shape that means deceit? iii 1 79
Stay'd the soldiers' pay; By means whereof his highness hath lost France iii 1 106
Murder'd By Suffolk and the Cardinal Beaufort's means iii 2 124
My thoughts do hourly prophesy Mischance unto my state by Suffolk's means iii 2 284
Jack Cade the clothier means to dress the commonwealth iv 2 6
The first thing we do, let's kill all the lawyers.—Nay, that I mean to do iv 2 85
If we mean to thrive and do good, break open the gaols iv 3 17
We'll devise a mean To reconcile you all unto the king iv 8 71
Be resolute; I mean to take possession of my right *3 Hen. VI.* i 1 44
Belike he means, . . . To aspire unto the crown and reign as king i 1 51
Words and threats Shall be the war that Henry means to use i 1 73
The army of the queen mean to besiege us.—She shall not need i 2 64
I am too mean a subject for thy wrath i 3 19
What befel me on a day In this self-place where now we mean to stand iii 1 11
I think he means to beg a child of her iii 2 27
Ay, but thou canst do what I mean to ask.—Why, then I will iii 2 48
'Tis the fruits of love I mean.—The fruits of love I mean, my loving liege iii 2 58
I did not mean such love.—Why, then you mean not as I thought you did iii 2 64
I know I am too mean to be your queen, And yet too good to be your concubine.—You cavil, widow: I did mean, my queen iii 2 97
And so I chide the means that keeps me from it iii 2 141
With patience calm the storm, While we bethink a means to break it off iii 3 39
I have advertised him by secret means iv 5 9
And supply his place; I mean, in bearing weight of government iv 6 51
By fair or foul means we must enter in iv 7 14
But when the fox hath once got in his nose, He'll soon find means to make the body follow iv 7 26
We'll debate By what safe means the crown may be recover'd iv 7 52
Know you what this means? Look here, I throw my infamy at thee v 1 81
I mean, my lords, those powers that the queen Hath raised in Gallia have arrived our coast v 3 7
Doth she swoon? use means for her recovery v 5 45
What means this armed guard That waits upon your grace? *Richard III.* i 1 42
Our brother is imprison'd by your means, Myself disgraced i 3 78
Every man that means to live well endeavours to trust to himself and to live without it [conscience] i 4 147
What means this scene of rude impatience? ii 2 38
Your grace knows how to bear with him.—You mean, to bear me iii 1 128
And make pursuit where he did mean no chase iii 2 30
Till Richard wear the garland of the realm.—How! wear the garland! dost thou mean the crown? iii 2 41
Pronounced your part,—I mean, your voice,—for crowning of the king iii 4 29
His apparent open guilt omitted, I mean, his conversation with Shore's wife iii 5 31

Mean. He fears you mean no good to him . *Richard III.* iii 7 87
The king! why, who's that?—I cry you mercy: I mean the lord protector . iv 1 19
A discontented gentleman, Whose humble means match not his haughty mind . iv 2 37
Two deep enemies, Foes to my rest . . . , I mean those bastards . iv 2 76
Let me have open means to come to them, And soon I'll rid you from the fear of them . iv 2 77
I mean, that with my soul I love thy daughter, And mean to make her queen . iv 4 262
Who dost thou mean shall be her king?—Even he that makes her queen iv 4 264
I'll play the eaves-dropper, To see if any mean to shrink from me . v 3 222
One that made means to come by what he hath, And slaughter'd those that were the means to help him . v 3 248
For want of means, poor rats, had hang'd themselves . v 3 331
Who did guide, I mean, who set the body and the limbs Of this great sport together, as you guess? *Hen. VIII.* i 1 46
Compell'd by hunger And lack of other means, in desperate manner . i 2 35
Never found again But where they mean to sink ye . ii 1 131
All the clerks, I mean the learned ones, in Christian kingdoms . ii 2 93
He, I mean the bishop, did require a respite . ii 4 177
What should this mean? What sudden anger's this? how have I reap'd it? . iii 2 203
Till I find more than will or words to do it, I mean your malice . iii 2 237
By what means got, I leave to your own conscience . iii 2 327
If heaven had pleased to have given me longer life And able means, we had not parted thus . iv 2 153
Ween you of better luck, I mean, in perjured witness, than your master? . v 1 136
Some of ye, I see, More out of malice than integrity, Would try him to the utmost, had ye mean . v 3 146
What Troy means fairly shall be spoke aloud . *Troi. and Cres.* i 3 259
And may that soldier a mere recreant prove, That means not, hath not, or is not in love! If then one is, or hath, or means to be, That one meets Hector . i 3 288
You depend upon him, I mean?—Sir, I do depend upon the lord . iii 1 4
Command, I mean, friend.—Who shall I command, sir? . iii 1 27
What mean these fellows? Know they not Achilles? . iii 3 70
No man alive can love in such a sort The thing he means to kill . iv 1 24
Then we shall ha' means to vent Our musty superfluity . *Coriolanus* i 1 229
We'll put you, Like one that means his proper harm, in manacles . i 9 57
I thank you. I mean to stride your steed . i 9 71
You are censured here in the city, I mean of us o' the right-hand file . ii 1 25
Envied against the people, seeking means To pluck away their power . iii 3 95
I cannot help it now, Unless, by using means, I lame the foot Of our design . iv 7 7
Yet I wish, sir,—I mean for your particular,—you had not Join'd . iv 7 13
Who, as I hear, mean to solicit him For mercy to his country . v 1 72
Interrupter of the good That noble-minded Titus means to thee! *T. An.* i 1 209
I know not what it means; away with her!—O, let me teach thee! . ii 3 157
But, lovely niece, that mean is cut from thee . ii 4 40
Look by and by to have thy sons with thee. Their heads, I mean . iii 1 203
Alas, sweet aunt, I know not what you mean . iv 1 4
What means my niece Lavinia by these signs? . iv 1 8
Somewhat doth she mean: See, Lucius, see how much she makes of thee iv 1 9
I think she means that there was more than one Confederate in the fact iv 1 38
She is deliver'd.—To whom?—I mean, she is brought a-bed . iv 2 62
Have by my means been butcher'd wrongfully . iv 4 55
The eagle suffers little birds to sing, And is not careful what they mean iv 4 84
For what I mean to do See here in bloody lines I have set down . v 2 13
Hark, wretches! how I mean to martyr you . v 2 181
You know your mother means to feast with me, And calls herself Revenge . v 2 185
I fear the emperor means no good to us . v 3 10
I mean, an we be in choler, we'll draw . *Rom. and Jul.* i 1 4
Have you importuned him by any means? . i 1 151
Nay, that's not so.—I mean, sir, in delay We waste our lights in vain . i 4 44
We mean well in going to this mask; But 'tis no wit to go . i 4 48
And she as much in love, her means much less To meet her new-beloved any where: But passion lends them power, time means, to meet ii Prol. 11
'Tis in vain To seek him here that means not to be found . ii 1 42
Bid her devise Some means to come to shrift this afternoon . ii 4 192
Hadst thou no poison mix'd, no sharp-ground knife, No sudden mean of death, though ne'er so mean? . iii 3 45
Find thou the means, and I'll find such a man . iii 5 104
Let's see for means: O mischief, thou are swift To enter in the thoughts of desperate men! . v 1 35
What mean these masterless and gory swords To lie discolour'd? . v 3 142
Bid me devise some mean To rid her from this second marriage . v 3 240
That heaven finds means to kill your joys with love . v 3 293
His means most short, his creditors most strait . *T. of Athens* i 1 96
Shouldst have kept one [farewell] to thyself, for I mean to give thee none . i 1 276
What means that trump? . i 2 120
That I might so have rated my expense, As I had leave of means . ii 2 136
What heart, head, sword, force, means, but is Lord Timon's? . ii 2 176
When the means are gone that buy this praise, The breath is gone whereof this praise is made . ii 2 178
Uncover, dogs, and lap.—What does his lordship mean? . iii 6 96
What man didst thou ever know unthrift that was beloved after his means? . iv 3 312
Who, without those means thou talkest of, didst thou ever know beloved? . iv 3 313
I understand thee; thou hadst some means to keep a dog . iv 3 317
Our hope in him is dead: let us return, And strain what other means is left unto us . v 1 230
By humble message and by promised means . v 4 20
By means whereof this breast of mine hath buried Thoughts . *J. Cæsar* i 2 49
What means this shouting? I do fear, the people Choose Cæsar for their king . i 2 79
We have the falling sickness.—I know not what you mean by that . i 2 259
'Tis Cæsar that you mean; is it not, Cassius?—Let it be who it is . i 3 79
They say the senators to-morrow Mean to establish Cæsar as a king . i 3 86
Half their faces buried in their cloaks, That by no means I may discover them By any mark of favour . ii 1 75
His means, If he improve them, may well stretch so far As to annoy us all . ii 1 158
Portia, what mean you? wherefore rise you now? It is not for your health . ii 1 234
Were he not in health, He would embrace the means to come by it . ii 1 259
Mean. That which melteth fools; I mean, sweet words, Low-crooked court'sies . *J. Cæsar* iii 1 42
No place will please me so, no mean of death, As here by Cæsar . iii 1 161
But what compact mean you to have with us? . iii 1 215
Hear this testament—Which, pardon me, I do not mean to read . iii 2 136
Let our alliance be combined, Our best friends made, our means stretch'd . iv 1 44
They mean this night in Sardis to be quarter'd . iv 2 28
I can raise no money by vile means . iv 3 71
So shall he waste his means, weary his soldiers, Doing himself offence . iv 3 200
They mean to warn us at Philippi here, Answering before we do demand v 1 5
What is't you say? the life?—Mean you his majesty? . *Macbeth* ii 3 75
Thriftless ambition, that wilt ravin up Thine own life's means! . ii 4 29
Now I am bent to know, By the worst means, the worst . iii 4 135
How will you live?—As birds do, mother.—What, with worms and flies?—With what I get, I mean . iv 2 33
It is myself I mean: in whom I know All the particulars of vice . iv 3 50
What's the disease he means?—'Tis call'd the evil . iv 3 146
Good God, betimes remove The means that makes us strangers! . iv 3 163
Remove from her the means of all annoyance, And still keep eyes upon her . v 1 84
What does this mean, my lord?—The king doth wake to-night *Hamlet* i 4 7
What may this mean, That thou, dead corse, again in complete steel Revisit'st thus the glimpses of the moon? . i 4 51
What means, and where they keep, What company, at what expense . ii 1 8
But, if't be he I mean, he's very wild; Addicted so and so . ii 1 18
And more above, hath his solicitings, As they fell out by time, by means, and place, All given to mine ear . ii 2 127
What is the matter, my lord?—Between who?—I mean, the matter that you read . ii 2 197
And suddenly contrive the means of meeting between him and my daughter . ii 2 216
I think their inhibition comes by the means of the late innovation . ii 2 347
As it is most like, if their means are no better . ii 2 366
Are you honest?—My lord?—Are you fair?—What means your lordship? iii 1 106
Lady, shall I lie in your lap?—No, my lord.—I mean, my head upon your lap? . iii 2 121
What means this, my lord?—Marry, this is miching mallecho; it means mischief . iii 2 148
Be not you ashamed to show, he'll not shame to tell you what it means iii 2 156
And let them know, both what we mean to do, And what's untimely done . iv 1 39
What dost thou mean by this?—Nothing but to show you . iv 3 31
Sith I have cause and will and strength and means To do't . iv 4 45
Let's have no words of this; but when they ask you what it means, say you this . iv 5 47
For my means, I'll husband them so well, They shall go far with little iv 5 138
His means of death, his obscure funeral, No trophy, sword . iv 5 213
Give these fellows some means to the king . iv 6 13
What should this mean? Are all the rest come back? Or is it some abuse? iv 7 50
If he be now return'd, As checking at his voyage, and that he means No more to undertake it, I will work him To an exploit . iv 7 63
Weigh what convenience both of time and means May fit us to our shape iv 7 150
I mean, my lord, the opposition of your person in trial . v 2 178
Convey the business as I shall find means, and acquaint you withal *Lear* i 2 110
You have heard of the news abroad; I mean the whispered ones? . ii 1 8
I'll work the means To make thee capable . ii 1 86
Out, varlet, from my sight!—What means your grace? . ii 4 190
What mean your graces? Good my friends, consider You are my guests iii 7 30
Our means secure us, and our mere defects Prove our commodities . iv 1 22
There is means, madam: Our foster-nurse of nature is repose . iv 4 11
Lest his ungovern'd rage dissolve the life That wants the means to lead it iv 4 20
Either say thou'lt do't, Or thrive by other means . v 3 34
Mean you to enjoy him?—The let-alone lies not in your good will . v 3 78
What means that bloody knife?—'Tis hot, it smokes . v 3 223
I pant for life: some good I mean to do, Despite of mine own nature . v 3 243
Found good means To draw from her a prayer of earnest heart *Othello* i 3 151
So shall you have a shorter journey to your desires by the means I shall then have to prefer them . ii 1 285
I'll devise a mean to draw the Moor Out of the way . iii 1 39
A man that languishes in your displeasure.—Who is't you mean? . iii 3 44
When I have a suit Wherein I mean to touch your love indeed . iii 3 81
Thou dost mean something: I heard thee say even now, thou likedst not that . iii 3 108
Hold him off awhile, You shall by that perceive him and his means . iii 3 249
To furnish me with some swift means of death For the fair devil . iii 3 477
I do beseech you That by your virtuous means I may again Exist . iii 4 111
Naked in bed, Iago, and not mean harm! It is hypocrisy against the devil: They that mean virtuously, and yet do so, The devil their virtue tempts, and they tempt heaven . iv 1 5
What do you mean by this haunting of me?—Let the devil and his dam haunt you! What did you mean by that same handkerchief you gave me? . iv 1 152
Those that do teach young babes Do it with gentle means and easy tasks iv 2 112
I have wasted myself out of my means . iv 2 188
If thou hast that in thee indeed, which I have greater reason to believe now than ever, I mean purpose, courage and valour . iv 2 218
How do you mean, removing of him?—Why, by making him uncapable iv 2 234
Alas, my lord, what do you mean by that?—Well, do it, and be brief . v 2 29
You shall be yet far fairer than you are.—He means in flesh *Ant. and Cleo.* i 2 17
They know, By the height, the lowness, or the mean, if dearth Or foison follow: the higher Nilus swells, The more it promises . ii 7 22
For better might we Have loved without this mean, if on both parts This be not cherish'd . iii 2 32
Know, that to-morrow the last of many battles We mean to fight . iv 1 12
What does he mean?—To make his followers weep . iv 2 23
It signs well, does it not?—No.—Peace, I say! What should this mean? iv 3 16
Like the spirit of a youth That means to be of note, begins betimes . iv 4 27
This blows my heart: If swift thought break it not, a swifter mean Shall outstrike thought . iv 6 35
Know you what Cæsar means to do with me?—I am loath to tell you v 2 106
He that hath her—I mean, that married her, alack, good man! *Cymbeline* i 1 18
Take it; It is an earnest of a further good That I mean to thee . i 5 66
Blest be those, How mean so'er, that have their honest wills . i 6 8
Though it be allow'd in meaner parties—Yet who than he more mean? ii 3 122
What means do you make to him? . ii 4 3
O, for such means! Though peril to my modesty, not death on't, I would adventure.—Well, then, here's the point . iii 4 154
Your means abroad, You have me, rich; and I will never fail . iii 4 180
Thou shouldst neither want my means for thy relief nor my voice . iii 5 115

Mean. Foundations fly the wretched ; such, I mean, Where they should be relieved . . . . . *Cymbeline* iii 6 7
I mean, the lines of my body are as well drawn as his . . . iv 1 9
'Those runagates!' Means he not us? I partly know him . . iv 2 64
Being scarce made up, I mean, to man, he had not apprehension . iv 2 110
What does he mean? since death of my dear'st mother It did not speak before . . . . iv 2 190
Though mean and mighty, rotting Together, have one dust . . iv 2 246
Some falls are means the happier to arise . . . . iv 2 403
But end it by some means for Imogen . . . . . v 3 83
If this be so, the gods do mean to strike me To death with mortal joy . v 5 234
You holp us, sir, As you did mean indeed to be our brother . . v 5 423
He hath found the meaning, for which we mean To have his head *Pericles* i 1 143
Who makes the fairest show means most deceit . . . i 4 75
He had need mean better than his outward show Can any way speak . ii 2 48
What means the nun? she dies! help, gentlemen! . . . iii 3 15
By all means *Mer. Wives* iv 2 230; *T. Night* iii 2 62
By no means *Meas. for Meas.* iii 1; *Much Ado* ii 1; *M. N. Dream* i 1; *As Y. Like It* iii 2; *T. of Athens* i 2; *J. Cæsar* ii 1; *Hamlet* i 3; i 4; iii 1; *Lear* ii 1; ii 4; iv 3; *Pericles* ii 5
What do you [dost thou] mean? *T. Night* i 3; *J. Cæsar* iii 3; *Macbeth* ii 2; *Lear* iii 7; *Othello* iii 3
What means this? *As Y. Like It* iii 5; *Hen. V.* iv 7; 1 *Hen. VI.* i 3; *Hen. VIII.* v 2; *T. Andron.* iv 1; *Hamlet* iii 2; *Ant. and Cleo.* iv 2
What mean you? *Com. of Errors* i 2; *L. L. Lost* v 2; *Hen. VIII.* v 1; *J. Cæsar* ii 2; *Ant. and Cleo.* ii 5; iv 2; *Pericles* ii 1; iv 1
Mean affairs. If one of mean affairs May plod it in a week, why may not I Glide thither in a day? . . . . *Cymbeline* iii 2 52
Mean-apparelled. Oftentimes he goes but mean-apparell'd *T. of Shrew* iii 2 75
Mean array. Neither art thou the worse For this poor furniture and mean array . . . . iv 3 182
Mean attempts. Such bare, such lewd, such mean attempts 1 *Hen IV.* iii 2 13
Mean attire. I'll put myself in poor and mean attire *As Y. Like It* i 3 113
Mean-born. Let pale-faced fear keep with the mean-born man 2 *Hen. VI.* iii 1 335
Inquire me out some mean-born gentleman, Whom I will marry straight to Clarence' daughter . . . . *Richard III.* iv 2 54
Mean condition. If one so rude and of so mean condition May pass into the presence of a king . . . . . 2 *Hen. VI.* v 1 64
Mean dependance. 'Tis a cause that hath no mean dependance Upon our joint and several dignities . . . *Troi. and Cres.* ii 2 192
Mean eyes. Yet you do well To show Lord Timon that mean eyes have seen The foot above the head . . *T. of Athens* i 1 93
Mean habiliments. We will unto your father's Even in these honest mean habiliments . . . . . *T. of Shrew* iv 3 172
Mean happiness. It is no mean happiness therefore, to be seated in the mean . . . . *Mer. of Venice* i 2 7
Mean meaning. A very mean meaning . . *T. of Shrew* v 2 31
Mean men. That which in mean men we intitle patience Is pale cold cowardice in noble breasts . . . *Richard II.* i 2 33
Mean obsequies. All in vain are these mean obsequies . 2 *Hen. VI.* iii 2 146
Mean task. This my mean task Would be as heavy to me as odious *Tempest* iii 1 4
Meander. Here's a maze trod indeed Through forth-rights and meanders! iii 3 3
Meaner. My meaner ministers Their several kinds have done . . iii 3 87
Thou and thy meaner fellows your last service Did worthily perform . iv 1 35
That very hour and in the self-same inn A meaner woman was delivered Of such a burden, male twins . . . *Com. of Errors* i 1 55
Some Florentine, Some Neapolitan, or meaner man of Pisa . *T. of Shrew* i 2 210
Whom I from meaner form Have bench'd and rear'd to worship *W. Tale* i 2 313
Choked with ambition of the meaner sort . . 1 *Hen. VI.* ii 5 123
And meaner than myself have had like fortune . . 3 *Hen. VI.* iv 1 71
Kings it [hope] makes gods, and meaner creatures kings *Richard III.* v 2 24
We live not to be grip'd by meaner persons . . *Hen. VIII.* ii 2 136
I know the sound of Marcius' tongue From every meaner man *Coriolanus* i 6 27
Youngling, learn thou to make some meaner choice *T. Andron.* ii 1 73
These hands do lack nobility, that they strike A meaner than myself; since I myself Have given myself the cause . . *Ant. and Cleo.* ii 5 83
Some natural notes about her body, Above ten thousand meaner moveables Would testify . . . . . *Cymbeline* ii 2 29
And though it be allow'd in meaner parties—Yet who than he more mean? ii 3 121
Meanest. What, thou meanest an officer?—Ay, sir . *Com. of Errors* iv 3 29
Will you win your love with a French brawl?—How meanest thou? *L. L. Lost* iii 1 10
So honour peereth in the meanest habit . . *T. of Shrew* iv 3 176
Vanquish'd as I am, I yield to thee, Or to the meanest groom 2 *Hen. VI.* ii 1 185
And make the meanest of you earls and dukes . . . iv 8 39
If thou meanest well, I greet thee well . . . . v 1 14
What mean'st thou, that thou help'st me not? . . *Richard III.* i 4 281
There's not the meanest spirit on our party Without a heart to dare or sword to draw When Helen is defended . . *Troi. and Cres.* ii 2 156
What meanest thou to curse thus?—Do I curse thee? . . . v 1 30
How now, young man! mean'st thou to fight to-day? . . . v 3 29
As far as doth the Capitol exceed The meanest house in Rome *Coriolanus* iv 2 40
Then prosecute the meanest or the best For these contempts *T. Andron.* iv 4 33
But if thou mean'st not well, I do beseech thee— Madam! *Rom. and Jul.* ii 2 150
What mean'st by this?—To go out of my dialect, which you discommend *Lear* ii 2 114
A sight most pitiful in the meanest wretch, Past speaking of in a king! iv 6 208
E'en a woman, and commanded By such poor passion as the maid that milks And does the meanest chares . . . *Ant. and Cleo.* iv 15 75
Bids thee study on what fair demands Thou mean'st to have him grant thee v 2 11
His meanest garment, That ever hath but clipp'd his body, is dearer In my respect than all the hairs above thee . . . *Cymbeline* ii 3 138
You have abused me: 'His meanest garment!'—Ay, I said so, sir . ii 3 155
Though they did change me to the meanest bird That flies . *Pericles* iv 6 108
What meanest thou? *L. L. Lost* v 2; *T. Night* iii 4; 2 *Hen. VI.* i 3; *T. Andron.* iv 2; *J. Cæsar* i 1
Meaneth. He meaneth with a corded ladder To climb celestial Silvia's chamber-window . . . . *T. G. of Ver.* ii 6 33
Meaning. When thou didst not, savage, Know thine own meaning *Tempest* i 2 356
Thou dost snore distinctly; There's meaning in thy snores . . ii 1 218
Yet I thank you, Meaning henceforth to trouble you no more *T. G. of V.* ii 1 125
The fall is in the ort 'dissolutely: the ort is, according to our meaning, 'resolutely: his meaning is good . . . . *Mer. Wives* i 1 263
Spake he so doubtfully, thou couldst not feel his meaning? *Com. of Errors* ii 1 51
The folded meaning of your words' deceit . . . . iii 2 36
There's a double meaning in that . . . *Much Ado* ii 3 267
By my troth, I have no moral meaning; I meant, plain holy-thistle . iii 4 80
There's one meaning well suited . . . . . . v 1 230
As swift as lead, sir.—The meaning, pretty ingenious? . *L. L. Lost* iii 1 59
Meaning. What's your dark meaning, mouse, of this light word? *L. L. Lost* v 2 19
We need more light to find your meaning out . . . . v 2 21
Love takes the meaning in love's conference . . *M. N. Dream* ii 2 46
Whereof who chooses his meaning chooses you . *Mer. of Venice* i 2 34
My meaning in saying he is a good man is to have you understand me that he is sufficient . . . . i 3 15
I pray thee, understand a plain man in his plain meaning . . iii 5 63
Meaning me a beast . . . . . *As Y. Like It* iv 3 49
Meaning thereby that grapes were made to eat and lips to open . v 1 38
Speakest thou in sober meanings?—By my life, I do . . . v 2 76
He hath some meaning in his mad attire . . *T. of Shrew* iii 2 126
Left me here behind, to expound the meaning or moral of his signs . iv 4 79
Now you know my meaning.—A very mean meaning . . . v 2 30
Which, if it speed, Is wicked meaning in a lawful deed . *All's Well* iii 7 45
My meaning in't, I protest, was very honest . . . . iv 3 246
And now behold the meaning . . . . v 3 305
By my troth, I would not undertake her in this company. Is that the meaning of 'accost'? . . . . . . *T. Night* i 3 62
His false cunning, Not meaning to partake with me in danger . . v 1 90
To know the meaning Of dangerous majesty . . *K. John* iv 2 212
'Tis not my meaning To raze one title of your honour out *Richard II.* ii 3 74
As who should say, 'I would thou wert the man That would divorce this terror from my heart;' Meaning the king . . . . v 4 10
Have too lavishly Wrested his meaning and authority . 2 *Hen. IV.* iv 2 58
Or shall we sparingly show you far off The Dauphin's meaning? *Hen. V.* i 2 240
I do partly understand your meaning.—Why then, rejoice therefore . iii 6 53
Teach your cousin to consent winking.—I will wink on her to consent, my lord, if you will teach her to know my meaning . . . v 2 334
Her meaning is, No way to that, for weakness, which she enter'd 1 *Hen. VI.* iii 2 24
Is as innocent From meaning treason to our royal person As is the sucking lamb or harmless dove . . . 2 *Hen. VI.* iii 1 70
Well guess'd, believe me; for that was my meaning . 3 *Hen. VI.* iv 5 22
Till then, 'tis wisdom to conceal our meaning . . . . iv 7 60
Come, come, we know your meaning . . . *Richard III.* i 3 74
I will not reason what is meant hereby, Because I will be guiltless of the meaning. Here are the keys . . . . . . i 4 95
Thus, like the formal vice, Iniquity, I moralize two meanings in one word iii 1 83
Our friends, Somewhat against our meaning, have prevented . . iii 5 55
Saying he would make his son Heir to the crown; meaning indeed his house . . . . iii 5 78
Be not so hasty to confound my meaning . . . . iv 4 261
Ever double Both in his words and meaning . . *Hen. VIII.* iv 2 39
Otherwise He knew his man.—O, meaning you *Troi. and Cres.* iii 1 142
Thou know'st our meaning . . . . *T. Andron.* ii 3 271
Write down thy mind, bewray thy meaning so . . . iv 1 3
And by still practice learn to know thy meaning . . . iii 2 45
Take our good meaning, for our judgement sits Five times in that ere once in our five wits . . . . . *Rom. and Jul.* i 4 46
Constrains a man to bow in the hams.—Meaning, to court'sy . . ii 4 58
Meaning to keep her closely at my cell, Till I conveniently could send v 3 255
To atone your fears With my more noble meaning . *T. of Athens* v 4 59
That's not my meaning . . . . . . *Hamlet* ii 1 31
I am no honest man if there be any good meaning towards you . *Lear* i 2 190
We are not the first Who, with best meaning, have incurr'd the worst . v 3 4
To be naked with her friend in bed An hour or more, not meaning any harm?—Naked in bed, Iago, and not mean harm! . . *Othello* iv 1 4
You have heard much.—I have fair meanings, sir . *Ant. and Cleo.* ii 6 67
Read, and declare the meaning . . . . . *Cymbeline* v 5 434
He has found the meaning: But I will gloze with him . *Pericles* i 1 109
He hath found the meaning, for which we mean To have his head . i 1 143
Meanly. My wife, not meanly proud of two such boys *Com. of Errors* i 1 59
He can sing A mean most meanly . . . . *L. L. Lost* v 2 328
His daughter meanly have I match'd in marriage . *Richard III.* iv 3 37
Though train'd up thus meanly . . . . *Cymbeline* iii 3 82
Meant. You have taken it wiselier than I meant you should . *Tempest* ii 1 21
Why, fool, I meant not thee; I meant thy master . *T. G. of Ver.* ii 5 51
I think my cousin meant well . . . . . *Mer. Wives* i 1 265
I will go further than I meant, to pluck all fears out of you *Meas. for Meas.* iv 2 206
He denied you had in him no right.—He meant he did me none *C. of Er.* iv 2 8
He loved my niece your daughter and meant to acknowledge it *Much Ado* i 2 13
He meant to take the present time by the top and instantly break with you of it . . . . i 2 15
I have no moral meaning; I meant, plain holy-thistle . . . iii 4 80
In faith, my hand meant nothing to my sword . . . . v 1 57
I meant not so.—What, what? first praise me and again say no? *L. L. L.* iv 1 13
To show my skill, That more for praise than purpose meant to kill . iv 1 29
Lysander riddles very prettily: Now much beshrew my manners and my pride, If Hermia meant to say Lysander lied . *M. N. Dream* ii 2 55
That 'many' may be meant By the fool multitude . *Mer. of Venice* ii 9 25
He stamp'd and swore, As if the vicar meant to cozen him *T. of Shrew* iii 2 170
I pray you, tell me what you meant by that . . . . v 2 27
In his proper stream o'erflows himself.—Is it not meant damnable in us, to be trumpeters of our unlawful intents? . . . *All's Well* iv 3 31
What, sovereign sir, I did not well I meant well . . *W. Tale* v 3 3
You take the matter otherwise than is meant . . *Hen. V.* iii 2 137
Main chance, father, you meant; but I meant Maine . 2 *Hen. VI.* i 1 212
I will take my death, I never meant him any ill . . . ii 3 91
I can give the loser leave to chide.—Far truer spoke than meant . iii 1 183
Things are often spoke and seldom meant . . . . iii 1 268
To say the truth, so Judas kiss'd his master, And cried 'all hail!' when as he meant all harm . . . . 3 *Hen. VI.* v 7 34
I will not reason what is meant hereby . . . *Richard III.* i 4 94
I reprehended them; And ask'd the mayor what meant this wilful silence iii 7 28
All the gentry; for the most part such To whom as great a charge as little honour He meant to lay upon . . . . *Hen. VIII.* i 1 78
I would have play'd The part my father meant to act upon . . i 2 195
Yet I am richer than my base accusers, That never knew what truth meant ii 1 105
A gracious king that pardons all offences Malice ne'er meant . . ii 2 69
That's to say, I meant to rectify my conscience . . . ii 4 203
I am sorry my integrity should breed, And service to his majesty and you, So deep suspicion, where all faith was meant . . . iii 1 53
He was never, But where he meant to ruin, pitiful . . . iv 2 40
Rather, If there be faith in men, meant for his trial, And fair purgation to the world, than malice . . . . v 3 151
You smile and mock me, as if I meant naughtily . *Troi. and Cres.* iv 2 38
And meant, indeed, to occupy the argument no longer . *Rom. and Jul.* ii 4 105
But thankful even for hate, that is meant love . . . . iii 5 149

Meant. Except they meant to bathe in reeking wounds, Or memorize another Golgotha, I cannot tell . . . . . . *Macbeth* i 2 39
I fear'd he did but trifle, And meant to wreck thee . *Hamlet* ii 1 113
Do you think I meant country matters?—I think nothing, my lord iii 2 123
Will he tell us what this show meant?—Ay, or any show that you'll show him . . . . iii 2 153
That praised my lord such-a-one's horse, when he meant to beg it v 1 94
This, it seems, Roderigo meant to have sent this damned villain *Othello* v 2 316
With which I meant To scourge the ingratitude that despiteful Rome Cast on my noble father . . . *Ant. and Cleo.* ii 6 21
Now the witch take me, if I meant it thus! . . . iv 2 37
But when he meant to quail and shake the orb, He was as rattling thunder . . . . v 2 85
When nature framed this piece, she meant thee a good turn . *Pericles* iv 2 151
The gods for murder seemed so content To punish them; although not done, but meant . . . . v 3 Gower 99
Meantest. Make thee beg pardon for thy passed speech And say it was thy mother that thou meant'st . . . . 2 *Hen. VI.* iii 2 222
Meantime. In the meantime let me be that I am . *Much Ado* i 3 38
In the meantime I will so fashion the matter that Hero shall be absent ii 2 47
Meantime let wonder seem familiar . . . . . . v 4 70
Meantime receive such welcome at my hand . . *L. L. Lost* ii 1 169
In the meantime I will draw a bill of properties . *M. N. Dream* i 2 107
Nerissa and myself meantime Will live as maids and widows *Mer. of Ven.* iii 2 311
Meantime the court shall hear Bellario's letter . . . iv 1 149
Meantime, forget this new-fall'n dignity . . *As Y. Like It* v 4 182
In the mean time, what hear you of these wars? . . . *All's Well* iv 3 44
Meantime, sweet sister, We will not part from hence . *T. Night* v 1 393
And in the mean time sojourn'd at my father's . . *K. John* i 1 103
Meantime but ask What you would have reform'd that is not well . iv 2 43
Mean time let this defend my loyalty . . . . *Richard II.* i 1 67
I will desire you to live in the mean time, and eat your victuals *Hen. V.* v 1 35
Meantime look gracious on thy prostrate thrall . 1 *Hen. VI.* i 2 117
Meantime your cheeks do counterfeit our roses; For pale they look ii 4 62
Meantime, in signal of my love to thee, . . . Will I . . . wear this rose ii 4 121
Meantime, this deep disgrace in brotherhood Touches me *Richard III.* i 1 111
I will deliver you, or else lie for you: Meantime, have patience . i 1 116
Meantime, God grants that we have need of you . . . i 3 77
Meantime, but think how I may do thee good . . . iv 3 33
In the mean time, against thou shalt awake, Shall Romeo by my letters know our drift . . . . . . *Rom. and Jul.* iv 1 113
Meantime forbear, And let mischance be slave to patience . . v 3 220
Meantime I writ to Romeo, That he should hither come . . v 3 246
His lordship is but merry with me; He cannot want fifty five hundred talents.—But in the mean time he wants less . . *T. of Athens* iii 2 44
Meantime we thank you for your well-took labour . *Hamlet* ii 2 83
To laugh too; though, in the mean time, some necessary question of the play be then to be considered . . . . . iii 2 47
Meantime we shall express our darker purpose . . *Lear* i 1 37
In the mean time, Let me be thought too busy in my fears . *Othello* iii 3 252
Farewell, my lord: what you shall know meantime Of stirs abroad, I shall beseech you, sir, To let me be partaker . *Ant. and Cleo.* i 4 81
The mean time, lady, I'll raise the preparation of a war . . iii 4 25
I have many other ways to die; meantime Laugh at his challenge . iv 1 5
Meanwhile must be an earnest motion Made to the queen . *Hen. VIII.* ii 4 233
Meanwhile I am possess'd of that is mine . . . . *T. Andron.* i 1 408
Meanwhile, sir, with the little skill I have, Full well shalt thou perceive how much I dare . . . . ii 1 43
Meanwhile here's money for thy charges . . . . iv 3 105
Measles. So shall my lungs Coin words till their decay against those measles, Which we disdain should tetter us . *Coriolanus* iii 1 78
Measurable. Congruent and measurable for the afternoon *L. L. Lost* v 1 97
Measure. How shall that Claribel Measure us back to Naples? *Tempest* ii 1 259
A true-devoted pilgrim is not weary To measure kingdoms with his feeble steps; Much less shall she . . . *T. G. of Ver.* ii 7 10
Come not within the measure of my wrath . . . . v 4 127
I have appointed mine host of de Jarteer to measure our weapon *M. W.* i 4 124
And twenty glow-worms shall our lanterns be, To guide our measure . v 5 83
He professes to have received no sinister measure from his judge *Meas. for Meas.* iii 2 257
Like doth quit like, and MEASURE still FOR MEASURE . . v 1 416
An ell and three quarters will not measure her from hip to hip *C. of Er.* iii 2 113
And therewithal took measure of my body . . . . iv 3 9
Did he break out into tears?—In great measure . *Much Ado* i 1 25
Why are you thus out of measure sad?—There is no measure in the occasion that breeds . . . . i 3 2
Tell him there is measure in every thing and so dance out the answer . ii 1 74
As a Scotch jig, a measure, and a cinque pace . . . ii 1 77
Mannerly-modest, as a measure, full of state and ancientry . . ii 1 80
'I measure him,' says she, 'by my own spirit' . . . ii 3 149
Measure his woe the length and breadth of mine . . . v 1 11
And justice always whirls in equal measure . . *L. L. Lost* iv 3 384
They have measured many a mile To tread a measure with you on this grass . . . . v 2 187
If they have measured many, The measure then of one is easily told . v 2 190
Tell How many inches doth fill up one mile.—Tell her, we measure them by weary steps . . . . v 2 194
Then, in our measure do but vouchsafe one change . . v 2 209
And so the measure ends.—More measure of this measure . . v 2 221
I will move storms, I will condole in some measure . *M. N. Dream* i 2 30
In some slight measure it will pay, If for his tender here I make some stay . . . . iii 2 86
Faintness constraineth me To measure out my length on this cold bed . iii 2 429
Where is the horse that doth untread again His tedious measures with the unbated fire That he did pace them first? . *Mer. of Venice* ii 6 11
Allay thy ecstasy; In measure rein thy joy; scant this excess . . iii 2 113
Therefore haste away, For we must measure twenty miles to-day . iii 4 84
Here lie I down, and measure out my grave . *As Y. Like It* ii 6 2
May in some little measure draw a belief from you, to do yourself good v 2 63
I have trod a measure; I have flattered a lady; I have been politic . v 4 45
According to the measure of their states . . . . v 4 181
Brides and bridegrooms all, With measure heap'd in joy, to the measures fall . . . . v 4 185
So, to your pleasures: I am for other than for dancing measures . v 4 199
Curst And shrewd and froward, so beyond all measure . *T. of Shrew* i 2 90
Go to the feast, revel and domineer, Carouse full measure . . iii 2 227
Your husband, being troubled with a shrew, Measures my husband's sorrow by his woe . . . . v 2 29
Though the devil lead the measure, such are to be followed . *All's Well* ii 1 58
This is hard and undeserved measure . . . . . ii 3 273

Measure. That he might take a measure of his own judgements *All's Well* iv 3 38
The triplex, sir, is a good tripping measure . . . . *T. Night* v 1 41
Then he's a rogue, and a passy measures panyn . . . . v 1 206
As your charities Shall best instruct you, measure me . *W. Tale* ii 1 114
Hath not my gait in it the measure of the court? . . . . iv 4 757
I trust we shall, If not fill up the measure of her will, Yet in some measure satisfy her so That we shall stop her exclamation *K. John* ii 1 556
Shall braying trumpets and loud churlish drums, Clamours of hell, be measures to our pomp? . . . . iii 1 304
With his shears and measure in his hand, Standing on slippers . iv 2 196
When English measure backward their own ground In faint retire . v 5 3
Thou dost consent In some large measure to thy father's death *Rich. II.* i 2 26
Thy steps no more Than a delightful measure or a dance . . i 3 291
They have let the dangerous enemy Measure our confines with such peaceful steps . . . . iii 2 125
My legs can keep no measure in delight, When my poor heart no measure keeps in grief: Therefore, no dancing . . . iii 4 7
These news, Having been well, that would have made me sick, Being sick, have in some measure made me well . . 2 *Hen. IV.* i 1 139
You do measure the heat of our livers with the bitterness of your galls i 2 198
Their memory Shall as a pattern or a measure live . . . iv 4 76
For the one, I have neither words nor measure, and for the other, I have no strength in measure, yet a reasonable measure in strength *Hen. V.* v 2 141
To add more measure to your woes, I come to tell you things 3 *Hen. VI.* ii 1 105
Or fortune given me measure of revenge . . . . . ii 3 32
Measure for measure must be answered . . . . . ii 6 55
All dissembling set aside, Tell me for truth the measure of his love iii 3 120
Our dreadful marches to delightful measures . . *Richard III.* i 1 8
I have half a dozen healths To drink to these fair ladies, and a measure To lead 'em once again . . . . . *Hen. VIII.* i 4 106
Know by measure Of their observant toil the enemies' weight *Troi. and Cres.* i 3 202
Fair desires, in all fair measure, fairly guide them! . . . iii 1 47
He cannot but with measure fit the honours Which we devise him *Cor.* ii 2 127
Yet your good will Must have that thanks from Rome, after the measure As you intended well . . . . v 1 46
Loved me above the measure of a father; Nay, godded me, indeed . v 3 10
But let them measure us by what they will; We'll measure them a measure, and be gone . . . . . *Rom. and Jul.* i 4 9
The measure done, I'll watch her place of stand . . . i 5 52
If the measure of thy joy Be heap'd like mine and that thy skill be more . . . . ii 6 24
There is no end, no limit, measure, bound, In that word's death . iii 2 125
Fall upon the ground, as I do now, Taking the measure of an unmade grave . . . . iii 3 70
And fill'd the time With all licentious measure . *T. of Athens* v 4 4
O mighty Cæsar! dost thou lie so low? Are all thy conquests, glories, triumphs, spoils, Shrunk to this little measure? . *J. Cæsar* iii 1 150
Be large in mirth; anon we'll drink a measure The table round *Macbeth* iii 4 11
By the grace of Grace, We will perform in measure, time and place . v 8 73
If you will measure your lubber's length again, tarry . . *Lear* i 4 100
My life will be too short, And every measure fail me . . iv 7 3
A measure to the health of black Othello . . . *Othello* ii 3 32
Nor for measures of lawn, nor for gowns, petticoats, nor caps . iv 3 73
But this dotage of our general's O'erflows the measure *Ant. and Cleo.* i 1 2
I must Rid all the sea of pirates; then, to send Measures of wheat to Rome . . . . ii 6 37
Cold and sickly He vented them; most narrow measure lent me . iii 4 8
That he should dream, Knowing all measures, the full Cæsar will Answer his emptiness! . . . . iii 13 35
Crush him together rather than unfold His measure duly *Cymbeline* i 1 27
O, above measure false! . . . . ii 4 113
Nor measure our good minds By this rude place we live in . iii 6 65
I have heard, you knights of Tyre Are excellent in making ladies trip; And that their measures are as excellent . . . *Pericles* ii 3 104
Measured. Whose honour cannot Be measured or confined *Tempest* v 1 122
We have measured many miles To tread a measure with her . *L. L. Lost* v 2 184
If they have measured many, The measure then of one is easily told v 2 189
If to come hither you have measured miles, And many miles . v 2 191
And so we measured swords and parted . . . *As Y. Like It* v 4 91
He had himself The lands and waters 'twixt your throne and his Measured to look upon you; whom he loves . . . *W. Tale* v 1 145
You are, I think, assured I love you not.—I am assured, if I be measured rightly, Your majesty hath no just cause to hate me 2 *Hen. IV* v 2 65
Who hath measured the ground? . . . . . . *Hen. V.* iii 7 137
Your cause of sorrow Must not be measured by his worth . *Macbeth* v 8 45
Till you had measured how long a fool you were upon the ground *Cymb.* i 2 25
Measureless liar . . . . *Coriolanus* v 6 103
Shut up In measureless content . . . . . . *Macbeth* ii 1 17
Measuring. My merry host hath had the measuring of their weapons *Mer. Wives* ii 1 215
How he comes o'er us with our wilder days, Not measuring what use we made of them . . . . *Hen. V.* i 2 268
Measuring his affections by my own . . . . *Rom. and Jul.* i 1 133
Meat. Is't near dinner-time?—I would it were, That you might kill your stomach on your meat . . . . . *T. G. of Ver.* i 2 68
I am one that am nourished by my victuals and would fain have meat . ii 1 181
By my troth, I cannot abide the smell of hot meat since . *Mer. Wives* i 1 297
That's meat and drink to me, now . . . . . . i 1 306
I wash, wring, brew, bake, scour, dress meat and drink . . . i 4 102
In the thanksgiving before meat . . . . *Meas. for Meas.* i 2 16
She is so hot because the meat is cold; The meat is cold because you come not home; You come not home because you have no stomach *Com. of Errors* i 2 47
'Your meat doth burn,' quoth I; 'My gold!' quoth he . . . ii 1 63
I think the meat wants that I have.—In good time, sir; what's that?—Basting . . . . ii 2 57
That never meat sweet-savour'd in thy taste, Unless I spake, or look'd, or touch'd or carved to thee . . . . ii 2 119
Good meat, sir, is common; that every churl affords . . . iii 1 24
Thou say'st his meat was sauced with thy upbraidings . . . v 1 74
'Twas the boy that stole your meat, and you'll beat the post *Much Ado* ii 1 206
A man loves the meat in his youth that he cannot endure in his age . ii 3 247
In despite of his heart, he eats his meat without grudging . . iii 4 90
Cover the table, serve in the meat, and we will come in . *Mer. of Venice* iii 5 64
For the meat, sir, it shall be covered . . . . . . iii 5 67
Were to put good meat into an unclean dish . . . *As Y. Like It* iii 3 36
It is meat and drink to me to see a clown . . . . . v 1 11
'Tis burnt; and so is all the meat . . . . . *T. of Shrew* iv 1 164

Meat. Be not so disquiet: The meat was well, if you were so contented *T. of Shrew* iv 1 172
She eat no meat to-day, nor none shall eat . . . . . . iv 1 200
As with the meat, some undeserved fault I'll find about the making of the bed . . . . iv 1 202
Am starved for meat, giddy for lack of sleep . . . . . iv 3 9
It is too choleric a meat. How say you to a fat tripe finely broil'd? . iv 3 19
Thou false deluding slave, That feed'st me with the very name of meat iv 3 32
Thou see'st how diligent I am To dress thy meat myself and bring it thee . . . . iv 3 40
The poorest service is repaid with thanks; And so shall mine, before you touch the meat . . . . iv 3 46
I think, sir, you can eat none of this homely meat . . . *All's Well* ii 2 49
And who abstains from meat that is not gaunt? . . . *Richard II.* ii 1 76
Away, you mouldy rogue, away! I am meat for your master *2 Hen. IV.* ii 4 135
What you want in meat, we'll have in drink: but you must bear . . v 3 30
If you be not too much cloyed with fat meat . . . . . Epil. 28
I have eat no meat these five days . . . . . *2 Hen. VI.* iv 10 41
Chaff and bran! porridge after meat! . . . *Troi. and Cres.* i 2 263
That dogs must eat, That meat was made for mouths . . *Coriolanus* i 1 211
Anger's my meat; I sup upon myself, And so shall starve with feeding iv 2 50
Your soldiers use him as the grace 'fore meat, Their talk at table . iv 7 3
And an old hare hoar Is very good meat in Lent . . *Rom. and Jul.* ii 4 143
Thy head is as full of quarrels as an egg is full of meat . . . iii 1 25
A plague o' both your houses! They have made worms' meat of me . iii 1 112
Look to the baked meats, good Angelica: Spare not for cost . . . iv 4 5
To see meat fill knaves and wine heat fools . . . *T. of Athens* i 1 271
Let my meat make thee silent.—I scorn thy meat; 'twould choke me . i 2 36
It grieves me to see so many dip their meat in one man's blood . . i 2 41
Invite them without knives; Good for their meat, and safer for their lives . . . . i 2 46
There's no meat like 'em: I could wish my best friend at such a feast . i 2 81
This slave, Unto his honour, has my lord's meat in him: Why should it thrive? . . . . iii 1 60
Why then preferr'd you not your sums and bills, When your false masters eat of my lord's meat? . . . . iii 4 50
To let the meat cool ere we can agree upon the first place . . . iii 6 76
Make the meat be beloved more than the man that gives it . . . iii 6 85
Where feed'st thou o' days, Apemantus?—Where my stomach finds meat iv 3 294
Your greatest want is, you want much of meat. Why should you want? iv 3 419
All I kept were knaves, to serve in meat to villains . . . . iv 3 485
In the names of all the gods at once, Upon what meat doth this our Cæsar feed, That he is grown so great? . . . . *J. Cæsar* i 2 149
The sauce to meat is ceremony; Meeting were bare without it *Macbeth* iii 4 36
We may again Give to our tables meat, sleep to our nights . . . iii 6 34
The funeral baked meats Did coldly furnish forth the marriage tables *Hamlet* i 2 180
Cut the egg i' the middle, and eat up the meat . . . . *Lear* i 4 174
A knave; a rascal; an eater of broken meats . . . . . ii 2 16
The green-eyed monster which doth mock The meat it feeds on *Othello* iii 3 167
The messengers of Venice stay the meat: Go in, and weep not . . iv 2 170
Sir, I will eat no meat, I'll not drink, sir . . . *Ant. and Cleo.* v 2 49
There is cold meat i' the cave; we'll browse on that, Whilst what we have kill'd be cook'd . . . . *Cymbeline* iii 6 38
Here's money for my meat: I would have left it on the board . . iii 6 50
You come in faint for want of meat, depart reeling with too much drink v 4 163
All viands that I eat do seem unsavoury, Wishing him my meat *Pericles* ii 3 32
Get fire and meat for these poor men: 'T has been a turbulent and stormy night . . . . iii 2 3
Mecænas. I do not know, Mecænas; ask Agrippa . . *Ant. and Cleo.* ii 2 17
The present need Speaks to atone you.—Worthily spoken, Mecænas . ii 2 102
Welcome from Egypt, sir.—Half the heart of Cæsar, worthy Mecænas! ii 2 175
Mechanic. The poor mechanic porters . . . . . *Hen. V.* i 2 200
Do not bid me Dismiss my soldiers, or capitulate Again with Rome's mechanics: tell me not Wherein I seem unnatural . . *Coriolanus* v 3 83
To stand On more mechanic compliment . . . . *Ant. and Cleo.* iv 4 32
Mechanic slaves With greasy aprons, rules, and hammers . . . v 2 209
Mechanical salt-butter rogue! . . . . . . *Mer. Wives* ii 2 290
A crew of patches, rude mechanicals, That work for bread *M. N. Dream* iii 2 9
Haled thither By most mechanical and dirty hand . . *2 Hen. IV.* v 5 38
Base dunghill villain and mechanical, I'll have thy head for this *2 Hen. VI.* i 3 196
Being mechanical, you ought not walk Upon a labouring day *J. Cæsar* i 1 3
Méchante. O méchante fortune! Do not run away . . . *Hen. V.* iv 5 5
Medal. He that wears her like her medal, hanging About his neck *W. Tale* i 2 307
Meddle. More to know Did never meddle with my thoughts . *Tempest* i 2 22
I will teach a scurvy jack-a-nape priest to meddle or make . *M. Wives* i 4 116
You were best meddle with buck-washing . . . . . . iii 3 165
They are to meddle with none but the prince's subjects . . *M. Ado* iii 3 34
The less you meddle or make with them, why, the more is for your honesty . . . . iii 3 55
Do not you meddle; let me deal in this . . . . v 1 101
Go ply thy needle; meddle not with her . . . . *T. of Shrew* ii 1 25
We will not meddle with him till he come . . . . *All's Well* iv 3 41
Meddle you must, that's certain, or forswear to wear iron . *T. Night* iii 4 275
Pox on't, I'll not meddle with him.—Ay, but he will not now be pacified iii 4 308
I'll not meddle with it [conscience]: it is a dangerous thing *Richard III.* i 4 137
For my part, I'll not meddle nor make no further . . *Troi. and Cres.* i 1 14
I'll not meddle in't. Let her be as she is: if she be fair, 'tis the better i 1 66
For my part, I'll meddle nor make no more i' the matter . . . i 1 85
There is a mystery—with whom relation Durst never meddle . . . iii 3 202
Do you meddle with my master?—Ay; 'tis an honester service than to meddle with thy mistress . . . . *Coriolanus* iv 5 50
Your good tongue, More than the instant army we can make, Might stop our countryman.—No, I'll not meddle . . . . v 1 38
It is written, that the shoemaker should meddle with his yard *R. and J.* i 2 40
I meddle with no tradesman's matters, nor women's matters . *J. Cæsar* i 1 25
Meddler. Not scurvy, nor a temporary meddler . . *Meas. for Meas.* v 1 145
An thou hadst hated meddlers sooner, thou shouldst have loved thyself better now . . . . *T. of Athens* iv 3 309
Meddling. 'Tis a meddling friar; I do not like the man . *Meas. for Meas.* v 1 127
On meddling monkey, or on busy ape . . . . *M. N. Dream* ii 1 181
Led so grossly by this meddling priest . . . . . *K. John* iii 1 163
O, beat away the busy meddling fiend That lays strong siege unto this wretch's soul And from his bosom purge this black despair! *2 Hen. VI.* iii 3 21
Mede. The kings of Mede and Lycaonia . . . *Ant. and Cleo.* iii 6 75
Medea. In such a night Medea gather'd the enchanted herbs . *M. of Ven.* v 1 13
Meet I an infant of the house of York, Into as many gobbets will I cut it As wild Medea young Absyrtus did . . . . *2 Hen. VI.* v 2 59
Media. Spur through Media, Mesopotamia . . . *Ant. and Cleo.* iii 1 7
Great Media, Parthia, and Armenia, He gave to Alexander . . . iii 6 14
Mediation. Noble offices thou mayst effect Of mediation *2 Hen. IV.* iv 4 25
Some nobler token I have kept apart For Livia and Octavia, to induce Their mediation . . . . *Ant. and Cleo.* v 2 170
Mediator. And, in conclusion, Nonsuits my mediators . . *Othello* i 1 16
Medice, teipsum—Protector, see to't well, protect yourself . *2 Hen. VI.* ii 1 53
Medicinable. Any impediment will be medicinable to me . . *M. Ado* ii 2 5
Whose medicinable eye Corrects the ill aspects of planets evil *Troi. and Cres.* i 3 91
I have derision medicinable, To use between your strangeness and his pride . . . . iii 3 44
Let that grieve him: Some griefs are med'cinable . . . *Cymbeline* iii 2 33
Medicinal. I Do come with words as medicinal as true . . *W. Tale* ii 3 37
Drop tears as fast as the Arabian trees Their medicinal gum . *Othello* v 2 351
Medicine. His dissolute disease will scarce obey this medicine *M. Wives* iii 3 204
A kind of medicine in itself, That skins the vice o' the top . *M. for M.* ii 2 135
The miserable have no other medicine But only hope . . . . iii 1 2
Goest about to apply a moral medicine to a mortifying mischief *M. Ado* i 3 13
But, tasting it, Their counsel turns to passion, which before Would give perceptial medicine to rage . . . . v 1 24
Out, loathed medicine! hated potion, hence! . . . *M. N. Dream* iii 2 264
If they will patiently receive my medicine . . . . *As Y. Like It* ii 7 61
Your son made me to think of this; Else Paris and the medicine and the king Had from the conversation of my thoughts Haply been absent . . . . *All's Well* i 3 239
I have seen a medicine That's able to breathe life into a stone . . ii 1 75
Plutus himself, That knows the tinct and multiplying medicine . . v 3 102
Preserver of my father, now of me, The medicine of our house *W. Tale* iv 4 598
The present time's so sick, That present medicine must be minister'd, Or overthrow incurable ensues . . . . *K. John* v 1 15
If the rascal have not given me medicines to make me love him, I'll be hanged; it could not be else; I have drunk medicines . *1 Hen. IV.* ii 2 19
May be restored With good advice and little medicine . *2 Hen. IV.* iii 1 43
More precious, Preserving life in medicine potable . . . . . iv 5 163
A goodly medicine for my aching bones! . . . *Troi. and Cres.* v 10 35
Within the infant rind of this small flower Poison hath residence and medicine power . . . . *Rom. and Jul.* ii 3 24
Let's make us medicines of our great revenge . . . *Macbeth* iv 3 214
Meet we the medicine of the sickly weal, And with him pour we in our country's purge Each drop of us . . . . v 2 27
No medicine in the world can do thee good . . . . *Hamlet* v 2 325
Restoration hang Thy medicine on my lips! . . . . . *Lear* iv 7 27
Sick, O, sick!—If not, I'll ne'er trust medicine . . . . . v 3 96
Corrupted By spells and medicines bought of mountebanks . *Othello* i 3 61
Shall ever medicine thee to that sweet sleep Which thou owedst yesterday iii 3 332
Work on, My medicine, work! Thus credulous fools are caught . iv 1 46
That great medicine hath With his tinct gilded thee . *Ant. and Cleo.* i 5 36
Great griefs, I see, medicine the less . . . . *Cymbeline* iv 2 243
By medicine life may be prolong'd, yet death Will seize the doctor too v 5 29
Meditate. I will meditate the while upon some horrid message *T. Night* iii 4 219
Grow like savages,—as soldiers will That nothing do but meditate on blood,—To swearing and stern looks . . . . . . *Hen. V.* v 2 60
Look, he meditates.—Now is that noble vessel full of grief . *J. Cæsar* v 5 12
Meditating. Are you meditating on virginity? . . . . *All's Well* i 1 121
Meditating that Shall dye your white rose in a bloody red . *1 Hen. VI.* ii 4 60
Meditating with two deep divines . . . . . *Richard III.* iii 7 75
Whilst I sit meditating On that celestial harmony I go to *Hen. VIII.* iv 2 79
We must die, Messala: With meditating that she must die once, I have the patience to endure it now . . . . *J. Cæsar* iv 3 191
Meditation. In maiden meditation, fancy-free . . *M. N. Dream* ii 1 164
Draw the curtain close; And let us all to meditation . *2 Hen. VI.* iii 3 33
With two right reverend fathers, Divinely bent to meditation *Richard III.* iii 7 62
He is not lolling on a lewd day-bed, But on his knees at meditation . iii 7 73
Like a Jack, thou keep'st the stroke Betwixt thy begging and my meditation . . . . iv 2 118
How dare you thrust yourselves Into my private meditations? *Hen. VIII.* ii 2 66
We'll leave you to your meditations How to live better . . . iii 2 345
Full of repentance, Continual meditations, tears, and sorrows . . iv 2 28
With wings as swift As meditation or the thoughts of love . *Hamlet* i 5 30
Who has a breast so pure, But some uncleanly apprehensions Keep leets and law-days and in session sit With meditations lawful? *Othello* iii 3 141
Mediterranean. And are upon the Mediterranean flote . . *Tempest* i 2 234
Mediterraneum. By the salt wave of the Mediterraneum . *L. L. Lost* v 1 61
Medlar. They would else have married me to the rotten medlar *M. for M.* iv 3 184
I'll graff it with you, and then I shall graff it with a medlar: . . for you'll be rotten ere you be half ripe, and that's the right virtue of the medlar . . . . *As Y. Like It* iii 2 125
Now will he sit under a medlar tree, And wish his mistress were that kind of fruit As maids call medlars, when they laugh alone *R. and J.* ii 1 34
There's a medlar for thee, eat it.—On what I hate I feed not.—Dost hate a medlar?—Ay, though it look like thee . *T. of Athens* iv 3 305
Medler. Come to the pedlar; Money's a medler . . . *W. Tale* iv 4 329
Meed. Duty never yet did want his meed . . . *T. G. of Ver.* ii 4 112
Vouchsafe me, for my meed, but one fair look . . . . . . v 4 23
Meed, I am sure, I have received none; unless experience *Mer. Wives* ii 2 211
To receive the meed of punishment . . . . . *L. L. Lost* i 1 270
The antique world, When service sweat for duty, not for meed *A. Y. L It* ii 3 58
Proceed As high as word, my deed shall match thy meed . *All's Well* ii 1 213
Each one already blazing by our meeds . . . . *3 Hen. VI.* ii 1 36
My meed hath got me fame: I have not stopp'd mine ears to their demands . . . . iv 8 38
And for his meed, poor lord, he is mew'd up . . . *Richard III.* i 3 139
If you be hired for meed, go back again . . . . i 4 234
And when I have my meed, I must away; For this will out . . . i 4 289
And for his meed Was brow-bound with the oak . . *Coriolanus* ii 2 101
Thanks to men Of noble minds is honourable meed . . *T. Andron.* i 1 216
There's meed for meed, death for a deadly deed! . . . . . v 3 66
No meed, but he repays Sevenfold above itself . . . *T. of Athens* i 1 288
In his meed he's unfellowed . . . . *Hamlet* v 2 149
This fool's speed Be cross'd with slowness; labour be his meed! *Cymbeline* iii 5 168
Meek. Thay can be meek that have no other cause . *Com. of Errors* ii 1 33
Hadst thou been meek, our title still had slept . . *3 Hen. VI.* ii 2 160
You're meek and humble-mouth'd . . . . . . *Hen. VIII.* ii 4 107
Courteous destroyers, affable wolves, meek bears! . . *T. of Athens* iii 6 105
O, pardon me, thou bleeding piece of earth, That I am meek and gentle with these butchers! . . . . *J. Cæsar* iii 1 255
This Duncan Hath borne his faculties so meek . . . . *Macbeth* i 7 17
Doing the honour of thy lordliness To one so meek . *Ant. and Cleo.* v 2 162
Meekly. To hear meekly, sir, and to laugh moderately . . *L. L. Lost* i 1 199

Meekness. God bless thee; and put meekness in thy mind! *Richard III.* ii 2 107
You sign your place and calling, in full seeming, With meekness and humility; but your heart Is cramm'd with arrogancy *Hen. VIII.* ii 4 109
Thy meekness saint-like, wife-like government, Obeying in commanding ii 4 138
Love and meekness, lord, Become a churchman better than ambition v 3 62
Meered. At such a point, When half to half the world opposed, he being The meered question *Ant. and Cleo.* iii 13 10
Meet. On the topmast, The yards and bowsprit, would I flame distinctly, Then meet and join *Tempest* i 2 201
We must prepare to meet with Caliban iv 1 166
Wish me partaker . . . When thou dost meet good hap *T. G. of Ver.* i 1 15
For any or for all these exercises He said that Proteus your son was meet i 3 12
He is as worthy for an empress' love As meet to be an emperor's counsellor ii 4 77
Let me have What thou thinkest meet and is most mannerly ii 7 58
If thou seest my boy, Bid him make haste and meet me at the North-gate iii 1 258
Where meet we!—At Saint Gregory's well iv 2 84
This evening coming.—Where shall I meet you?—At Friar Patrick's cell iv 3 43
The very hour That Silvia, at Friar Patrick's cell, should meet me v 1 3
Meet with me Upon the rising of the mountain-foot v 2 43
It is not meet the council hear a riot *Mer. Wives* i 1 36
Followed her with a doting observance; engrossed opportunities to meet her ii 2 204
Vherefore vill you not meet-a me?—Pray you, use your patience iii 1 82
I would my husband would meet him in this shape iv 2 86
I'll appoint my men to carry the basket again, to meet him at the door with it iv 2 97
The duke himself will be to-morrow at court, and they are going to meet him iv 3 3
Send him word they'll meet him in the park at midnight iv 4 18
Marry, this is our device; That Falstaff at that oak shall meet with us iv 4 42
They are gone but to meet the duke, villain: do not say they be fled iv 5 72
We have had ill luck; we could never meet v 5 121
He promised to meet me two hours since *Meas. for Meas.* i 2 76
From whom we thought it meet to hide our love i 2 156
A vice that most I do abhor, And most desire should meet the blow of justice ii 2 30
I do confess it, and repent it, father.—'Tis meet so, daughter ii 3 30
Much upon this time have I promised here to meet iv 1 18
If you think it meet, compound with him by the year iv 2 25
Him I'll desire To meet me at the consecrated fount iv 3 102
Who do prepare to meet him at the gates, There to give up their power iv 3 136
And why meet him at the gates, and redeliver our authorities there? iv 4 6
Give notice to such men of sort and suit as are to meet him iv 4 20
Where we'll show What's yet behind, that's meet you all should know v 1 545
Ere the ships could meet by twice five leagues *Com. of Errors* i 1 101
I'll meet with you upon the mart And afterward consort you till bed-time i 2 27
I'll meet you at that place some hour hence iii 1 122
I see a man here needs not live by shifts, When in the streets he meets such golden gifts iii 2 188
If any hour meet a sergeant, a' turns back for very fear iv 2 56
There's not a man I meet but doth salute me iv 3 1
Straight after did I meet him with a chain.—It may be so iv 4 143
We still did meet each other's man, And I was ta'en for him, and he for me v 1 386
But he'll be meet with you, I doubt it not *Much Ado* i 1 47
They never meet but there's a skirmish of wit between them i 1 63
You are come to meet your trouble i 1 97
And there will the devil meet me, like an old cuckold ii 1 46
Then the two bears will not bite one another when they meet iii 2 81
If you meet a thief, you may suspect him, by virtue of your office iii 3 53
If you meet the prince in the night, you may stay him iii 3 80
Swore he would meet her, as he was appointed, next morning at the temple iii 3 171
Set down our excommunication and meet me at the gaol iii 5 60
Sir, I shall meet your wit in the career, an you charge it against me v 1 135
Well, I will meet you, so I may have good cheer v 1 152
He and I shall meet: and, till then, peace be with him v 1 196
Or study where to meet some mistress fine *L. L. Lost* i 1 63
He and his competitors in oath Were all address'd to meet you, gentle lady ii 1 83
Of all complexions the cull'd sovereignty Do meet, as at a fair, in her fair cheek iv 3 235
And so be mock'd withal Upon the next occasion that we meet v 2 143
Let it not be sweet.—Thou grievest my gall.—Gall! bitter.—Therefore meet v 2 237
Where I did meet thee once with Helena *M. N. Dream* i 1 166
In that same place thou hast appointed me, To-morrow truly will I meet i 1 178
Meet me in the palace wood, a mile without the town, by moonlight i 2 103
If we meet in the city, we shall be dogged with company i 2 105
I pray you, fail me not.—We will meet i 2 110
At the duke's oak we meet.—Enough; hold or cut bow-strings i 2 113
And now they never meet in grove or green, . . . But they do square ii 1 28
Here am I, and wode within this wood, Because I cannot meet my Hermia ii 1 193
And look thou meet me ere the first cock crow.—Fear not, my lord ii 1 267
I am as ugly as a bear; For beasts that meet me run away for fear ii 2 95
For, you know, Pyramus and Thisby meet by moonlight iii 1 51
Meet presently at the palace; every man look o'er his part iv 2 37
By moonshine did these lovers think no scorn To meet at Ninus' tomb v 1 139
Wilt thou at Ninny's tomb meet me straightway?—'Tide life, 'tide death v 1 204
Trip away; make no stay; Meet me all by break of day v 1 429
At dinner-time, I pray you, have in mind where we must meet *M. of Ven.* i 1 71
I will seal unto this bond.—Then meet me forthwith at the notary's i 3 173
Meet me at our synagogue; go, good Tubal; at our synagogue iii 1 134
And so farewell, till we shall meet again iii 4 40
It is very meet The Lord Bassanio live an upright life iii 5 78
I must away this night toward Padua, And it is meet I presently set forth iv 1 404
I pray you, know me when we meet again: I wish you well iv 1 419
It is a hard matter for friends to meet; but mountains may be removed with earthquakes and so encounter *As Y. Like It* iii 2 195
Let's meet as little as we can.—I do desire we may be better strangers iii 2 273
If I could meet that fancy-monger, I would give him some good counsel iii 2 382
Who hath promised to meet me in this place of the forest and to couple us iii 3 44
If ever,—as that ever may be near,—You meet in some fresh cheek the power of fancy iii 5 29
I would love you, if I could. To-morrow meet me all together v 2 121
As you love Rosalind, meet: as you love Phebe, meet: and as I love no woman, I'll meet v 2 129
So your doctors hold it very meet *T. of Shrew Ind.* 2 133
Both our inventions meet and jump in one i 1 195
And where two raging fires meet together They do consume the thing that feeds their fury ii 1 133
Do you hear, ho? you must meet my master to countenance my mistress iv 1 100

Meet. Did I not bid thee meet me in the park? *T. of Shrew* iv 1 133
Upon entreaty have a pleasant alms; If not, elsewhere they meet with charity iv 3 6
And in no sense is meet or amiable v 2 141
I'll beat him, . . . if I can meet him with any convenience *All's Well* ii 3 253
I'll beat him, an if I could but meet him again ii 3 256
Remain with me till they meet together iv 5 92
O dear heaven, bless! Or, ere they meet, in me, O nature, cesse! v 3 72
If it end so meet, The bitter past, more welcome is the sweet v 3 333
Direct thy feet Where thou and I henceforth may never meet *T. Night* v 1 172
There is no lady living So meet for this great errand *W. Tale* ii 2 46
Should I now meet my father, He would not call me son iv 4 671
Meets he on the way The father of this seeming lady v 1 190
When I shall meet him in the court of heaven I shall not know him *K. John* iii 4 87
Lords, I will meet him at Saint Edmundsbury: It is our safety iv 3 11
'Twill be Two long days' journey, lords, or ere we meet iv 3 20
Now powers from home and discontents at home Meet in one line iv 3 152
Now keep your holy word: go meet the French v 1 5
Forage, and run To meet displeasure farther from the doors v 1 60
Yet, I know, Our party may well meet a prouder foe v 1 79
And other lords, If you think meet, this afternoon will post v 7 94
Which to maintain I would allow him odds, And meet him *Richard II.* i 1 63
Nor never by advised purpose meet To plot, contrive i 3 188
Go, muster up your men, And meet me presently at Berkeley ii 2 119
If heart's presages be not vain, We three here part that ne'er shall meet again ii 2 143
Well, we may meet again.—I fear me, never ii 2 149
Methinks King Richard and myself should meet With no less terror than the elements Of fire and water iii 3 54
Come, ladies, go, To meet at London London's king in woe iii 4 97
I dare meet Surrey in a wilderness iv 1 74
No word like 'pardon' for kings' mouths so meet v 3 118
Did lately meet in the intestine shock *1 Hen. IV.* i 1 12
Therefore we meet not now i 1 30
Lies that this same fat rogue will tell us when we meet at supper i 2 211
Provide us all things necessary and meet me to-morrow night in Eastcheap i 2 216
Shall happily meet, To bear our fortunes in our own strong arms i 3 297
If they meet not with St. Nicholas' clerks, I'll give thee this neck ii 1 67
They dare not meet each other; Each takes his fellow for an officer ii 2 113
Have I not all their letters to meet me in arms by the ninth? ii 3 29
Set forth To meet your father and the Scottish power, As is appointed us iii 1 85
And that shall be the day . . . This gallant Hotspur, this all-praised knight, And your unthought-of Harry chance to meet iii 2 141
Meet me to-morrow in the temple hall at two o'clock in the afternoon iii 3 223
Nor did he think it meet To lay so dangerous and dear a trust On any soul iv 1 33
Shall, hot horse to horse, Meet and ne'er part till one drop down a corse iv 1 123
The king with mighty and quick-raised power Meets with Lord Harry iv 4 13
'Tis not well That you and I should meet upon such terms As now we meet v 1 10
And posted day and night To meet you on the way, and kiss your hand v 1 36
A sword, whose temper I intend to stain With the best blood that I can meet v 2 95
I'll murder all his wardrobe, piece by piece, Until I meet the king v 3 28
Bend you with your dearest speed, To meet Northumberland v 5 37
Will you have Doll Tearsheet meet you at supper? *2 Hen. IV.* ii 1 176
It is not meet that I should be sad, now my father is sick ii 2 42
I must go and meet with danger there, Or it will seek me in another place ii 3 48
Fain would I go to meet the archbishop, But many thousand reasons hold me ii 3 65
This is the old fashion; you two never meet but you fall to some discord ii 4 61
Are these things then necessities? Then let us meet them like necessities iii 1 93
Please you, lords, In sight of both our battles we may meet iv 1 179
Pleaseth your lordship To meet his grace just distance 'tween our armies iv 1 226
But for you, rebels, look to taste the due Meet for rebellion iv 2 117
When means and lavish manners meet together iv 4 64
We meet like men that had forgot to speak.—We do remember v 2 22
As many ways meet in one town; As many fresh streams meet in one salt sea; As many lines close in the dial's centre *Hen. V.* i 2 208
It is most meet we arm us 'gainst the foe ii 4 15
I say 'tis meet we all go forth To view the sick and feeble parts ii 4 21
Is it meet, think you, that we should also, look you, be an ass and a fool? iv 1 79
He hath not told his thought to the king?—No; nor it is not meet he should iv 1 104
If we no more meet till we meet in heaven, . . . warriors all, adieu! iv 3 7
But we shall meet, and break our minds at large.—Gloucester, we will meet; to thy cost, be sure *1 Hen. VI.* i 3 81
Be choked with thy ambition! And so farewell until I meet thee next ii 4 113
Dare ye come forth and meet us in the field? iii 2 61
Thou shalt see I'll meet thee to thy cost.—Well, miscreant, I'll be there as soon as you; And, after, meet you sooner than you would iii 4 43
I vow'd, base knight, when I did meet thee next, To tear the garter from thy craven's leg iv 1 14
And pale destruction meets thee in the face iv 2 27
And now they meet where both their lives are done iv 3 38
But meet him now, and, be it in the morn, When every one will give the time of day, He knits his brow *2 Hen. VI.* iii 1 13
'Tis meet he be condemn'd by course of law iii 1 237
'Tis meet that lucky ruler be employ'd iii 1 291
Lording it in London streets, Crying 'Villiago!' unto all they meet iv 8 48
Go and meet him, And ask him what's the reason of these arms iv 9 36
Meet me to-morrow in Saint George's field, You shall have pay v 1 46
Meet I an infant of the house of York, Into as many gobbets will I cut it v 2 57
We'll meet her in the field.—What, with five thousand men? *3 Hen. VI.* i 2 65
Take leave until we meet again, Where'er it be, in heaven or in earth ii 3 42
And lose no hour, Till we meet Warwick with his foreign power iv 7 149
Yet, as we may, we'll meet both thee and Warwick iv 7 86
You left poor Henry at the Bishop's palace, And, ten to one, you'll meet him in the Tower v 1 46
I here proclaim myself thy mortal foe, With resolution, wheresoe'er I meet thee—As I will meet thee v 1 95
For Warwick bids you all farewell, to meet in heaven.—Away, away, to meet the queen's great power! v 2 50
Is't meet that he Should leave the helm? v 4 6
So part we sadly in this troublous world, To meet with joy in sweet Jerusalem v 5 8

Meet. It is meet so few should fetch the prince *Richard III.* ii 2 139
The tender prince Would fain have come with me to meet your grace iii 1 29
Entreat of her To meet you at the Tower and welcome you iii 1 139
'Tis better with me now Than when I met thee last where now we meet iii 2 101
Let us all embrace: And take our leave, until we meet in heaven iii 3 25
Who meets us here? my niece Plantagenet Led in the hand of her kind aunt? iv 1 1
Let me but meet you, ladies, one hour hence iv 1 29
You shall have letters from me to my son To meet you on the way iv 1 51
Bid him levy straight The greatest strength and power he can make, And meet me presently at Salisbury iv 4 450
I'll muster up my friends, and meet your grace iv 4 489
Then in a moment, see How soon this mightiness meets misery *Hen. VIII.* Prol. 30
Heard by fame Of this so noble and so fair assembly This night to meet here i 4 68
There ye shall meet about this weighty business ii 2 140
I am joyful To meet the least occasion that may give me Remembrance of my father-in-law iii 2 7
Each thing meets In mere oppugnancy *Troi. and Cres.* i 3 110
If then one is, or hath, or means to be [in love], That one meets Hector i 3 290
Yes, 'tis most meet: whom may you else oppose? i 3 333
It is supposed He that meets Hector issues from our choice i 3 347
Therefore 'tis meet Achilles meet not Hector i 3 358
Do not consent That ever Hector and Achilles meet i 3 363
It was thought meet Paris should do some vengeance on the Greeks ii 2 72
But when I meet you arm'd as black defiance As heart can think iv 1 12
When contention and occasion meet, By Jove, I'll play the hunter for thy life iv 1 16
His purpose meets you iv 1 36
How my achievements mock me! I will go meet them iv 2 72
Great Agamemnon comes to meet us here iv 5 159
To-morrow do I meet thee, fell as death; To-night all friends iv 5 269
I will not meet with you to-morrow night: I prithee, Diomed, visit me no more v 2 73
Would I could meet that rogue Diomed! I would croak like a raven v 2 190
Distraction, frenzy and amazement, Like witless antics, one another meet v 3 86
I would fain see them meet v 4 6
Thou boy-queller, show thy face; Know what it is to meet Achilles angry v 5 46
If we and Caius Marcius chance to meet, 'Tis sworn between us we shall ever strike Till one can do no more *Coriolanus* i 2 34
If e'er again I meet him beard to beard, He's mine, or I am his i 10 11
Remains That, in the official marks invested, you Anon do meet the senate ii 3 149
Summon'd To meet anon, upon your approbation ii 3 152
In a rebellion, When what's not meet, but what must be, was law iii 1 168
In a better hour, Let what is meet be said it must be meet iii 1 170
Go not home.—Meet on the market-place. We'll attend you there iii 1 332
Let's not meet her.—Why?—They say she's mad iv 2 8
Could I meet 'em But once a-day, it would unclog my heart Of what lies heavy iv 2 46
I will go meet the ladies v 4 55
We will meet them, And help the joy v 4 64
An if we miss to meet him handsomely *T. Andron.* ii 3 268
Such wither'd herbs as these Are meet for plucking up, and therefore mine iii 1 179
Many a matter hath he told to thee, Meet and agreeing with thine infancy v 3 165
Her means much less To meet her new-beloved any where: But passion lends them power, time means, to meet *Rom. and Jul.* ii Prol. 12
This bud of love, by summer's ripening breath, May prove a beauteous flower when next we meet ii 2 122
In half an hour she promised to return. Perchance she cannot meet him ii 5 3
And, if we meet, we shall not scape a brawl iii 1 3
Since birth, and heaven, and earth, all three do meet In thee at once iii 3 120
O, think'st thou we shall ever meet again?—I doubt it not iii 5 51
Farewell! God knows when we shall meet again iv 3 14
What, do we meet together?—Ay, and I think One business *T. of Athens* iii 4 3
Wherever we shall meet, for Timon's sake, Let's yet be fellows iv 2 24
Cut throats: All that you meet are thieves iv 3 449
How rarely does it meet with this time's guise, When man was wish'd to love his enemies! iv 3 472
We sin against our own estate, When we may profit meet, and come too late v 1 45
I'll meet you at the turn v 1 50
Fit I meet them v 1 57
Find a time Both meet to hear and answer such high things *J. Cæsar* i 2 170
Therefore it is meet That noble minds keep ever with their likes i 2 314
When these prodigies Do so conjointly meet, let not men say 'These are their reasons; they are natural' i 3 29
It is not meet, Mark Antony, so well beloved of Cæsar, Should outlive Cæsar ii 1 155
Break up the senate till another time, When Cæsar's wife shall meet with better dreams ii 2 99
It is not meet you know how Cæsar loved you iii 2 146
This is a slight unmeritable man, Meet to be sent on errands iv 1 13
Hark! he is arrived. March gently on to meet him iv 2 31
It is not meet That every nice offence should bear his comment iv 3 7
There is some grudge between 'em, 'tis not meet They be alone iv 3 125
With your will, go on; We'll along ourselves, and meet them at Philippi iv 3 225
I am fresh of spirit and resolved To meet all perils very constantly v 1 92
Whether we shall meet again I know not. Therefore our everlasting farewell take: For ever, and for ever, farewell, Cassius! If we do meet again, why, we shall smile v 1 115
If we do meet again, we'll smile indeed; If not, 'tis true this parting was well made v 1 121
I go to meet The noble Brutus v ? 73
Did I not meet thy friends? and did not they Put on my brows this wreath? v 3 81
When shall we three meet again In thunder, lightning, or in rain? *Macb.* i 1 1
Where the place?—Upon the heath.—There to meet with Macbeth i 1 7
Let us meet, And question this most bloody piece of work ii 3 133
Meet i' the hall together ii 3 140
At the pit of Acheron Meet me i' the morning iii 5 16
I will not report after her.—You may to me: and 'tis most meet you should v 1 18
Near Birnam wood Shall we well meet them; that way are they coming v 2 6
Meet. Meet we the medicine of the sickly weal *Macbeth* v 2 27
If you do meet Horatio and Marcellus, . . . bid them make haste *Hamlet* i 1 1?
My tables,—meet it is I set it down i 5 107
As I perchance hereafter shall think meet To put an antic disposition on i 5 171
Each opposite that blanks the face of joy Meet what I would have well! iii 2 231
'Tis meet that some more audience than a mother, Since nature makes them partial, should o'erhear The speech, of vantage iii 3 31
O, 'tis most sweet, When in one line two crafts directly meet iii 4 210
O, methought, there was nothing meet v 1 72
O, a pit of clay for to be made For such a guest is meet v 1 105
All with me's meet that I can fashion fit *Lear* i 2 200
We'll no more meet, no more see one another: But yet thou art my flesh, my blood, my daughter ii 4 223
Thou'ldst shun a bear; But if thy flight lay toward the raging sea, Thou'ldst meet the bear i' the mouth iii 4 11
Where thou shalt meet Both welcome and protection iii 6 98
If she live long, And in the end meet the old course of death, Women will all turn monsters iii 7 101
Would I could meet him, madam! I should show What party I do follow iv 5 39
Till time and I think meet iv 7 11
It seems not meet, nor wholesome to my place, To be produced *Othello* i 1 146
At nine i' the morning here we'll meet again i 3 280
Where shall we meet i' the morning?—At my lodging.—I'll be with thee betimes i 3 381
Let's meet him and receive him.—Lo, where he comes! ii 1 182
Do thou meet me presently at the harbour. Come hither ii 1 215
Meet me by and by at the citadel: I must fetch his necessaries ashore ii 1 291
I shall not dine at home; I meet the captains at the citadel iii 3 59
You'll never meet a more sufficient man iii 4 91
Something of moment then: I will go meet him iii 4 138
Many worthy and chaste dames even thus, All guiltless, meet reproach iv 1 48
The bawdy wind that kisses all it meets iv 2 78
'Tis meet I should be used so, very meet iv 2 107
When we shall meet at compt, This look of thine will hurl my soul from heaven, And fiends will snatch at it v 2 273
Most meet That first we come to words *Ant. and Cleo.* ii 6 2
Fetch My best attires: I am again for Cydnus, To meet Mark Antony v 2 229
If she first meet the curled Antony, He'll make demand of her, and spend that kiss Which is my heaven to have v 2 304
You do not meet a man but frowns *Cymbeline* i 1 1
Is't not meet That I did amplify my judgement in Other conclusions? i 5 16
He never can meet more mischance than come To be but named of thee ii 3 137
I'll meet you in the valleys iii 3 78
I am near to the place where they should meet iv 1 2
I would revenges, That possible strength might meet, would seek us iv 2 160
Let's withdraw; And meet the time as it seeks us iv 3 33
And long of her it was That we meet here so strangely v 5 272
Did you e'er meet?—Ay, my good lord.—And at first meeting loved v 5 378
For she must overboard straight.—As you think meet *Pericles* iii 1 55
Meet food. Such meet food to feed it *Much Ado* i 1 122
Meet hour. Find me a meet hour ii 2 33
Meeter. Sends you, meeter for your spirit, This tun of treasure *Hen. V.* i 2 254
But I will tell you at some meeter season *Ant. and Cleo.* v 1 49
Meetest. I am a tainted wether of the flock, Meetest for death *M. of Ven.* iv 1 115
Then keep thy vow, sirrah, when thou meetest the fellow *Hen. V.* iv 7 152
York is meetest man To be your regent in the realm of France *2 Hen. VI.* i 3 163
There, at your meet'st advantage of the time *Richard III.* iii 5 74
Meeting. Nor Befitting this first meeting *Tempest* v 1 165
Let's appoint him a meeting; give him a show of comfort *Mer. Wives* ii 1 97
Missing your meetings and appointments iii 1 92
I have received from her another embassy of meeting iii 5 132
Appoint a meeting with this old fat fellow iv 4 15
At the very instant of Falstaff's and our meeting v 3 16
If a merry meeting may be wished, God prohibit it! *Much Ado* v 1 335
At wakes and wassails, meetings, markets, fairs *L. L. Lost* v 2 318
Meeting her of late behind the wood, Seeking sweet favours *M. N. Dream* iv 1 53
Meeting with Salerio by the way, He did intreat me, past all saying nay, To come with him along *Mer. of Venice* iii 2 231
I would fain see this meeting *As Y. Like It* iii 3 46
Where meeting with an old religious man v 4 166
Journeys end in lovers meeting, Every wise man's son doth know *T. N.* ii 3 44
Is whispering nothing? Is leaning cheek to cheek? is meeting noses? *W. Tale* i 2 285
This your sheep-shearing Is as a meeting of the petty gods iv 4 4
Retired, As if you were a feasted one and not The hostess of the meeting iv 4 64
Did you see the meeting of the two kings?—No.—Then have you lost a sight v 2 43
Let belief and life encounter so As doth the fury of two desperate men Which in the very meeting fall and die *K. John* iii 1 33
Plays fondly with her tears and smiles in meeting *Richard II.* iii 2 9
With no less terror than the elements Of fire and water, when their thundering shock At meeting tears the cloudy cheeks of heaven iii 3 57
Appoint them a place of meeting, wherein it is at our pleasure to fail, and then will they adventure *1 Hen. IV.* i 2 190
On Thursday we ourselves will march: our meeting Is Bridgenorth iii 2 174
Shall lose his sway, Meeting the check of such another day v 5 42
And concludes in hearty prayers That your attempts may overlive the hazard And fearful meeting of their opposite *2 Hen. IV.* iv 1 16
Peace to this meeting, wherefore we are met! *Hen. V.* v 2 1
So happy be the issue . . . Of this good day and of this gracious meeting v 2 13
The wound that bred this meeting here Cannot be cured by words *3 Hen. VI.* ii 2 121
Our stern alarums changed to merry meetings *Richard III.* i 1 7
As knots, by the conflux of meeting sap, Infect the sound pine *T. and C.* i 3 7
And meeting him will tell him that my lady Was fairer than his grandam i 3 298
Meeting two such wealsmen as you are *Coriolanus* ii 1 59
And appoint the meeting Even at his father's house *T. Andron.* iv 4 102
Patience perforce with wilful choler meeting Makes my flesh tremble in their different greeting *Rom. and Jul.* i 5 91
And went further, which is now Our point of second meeting *Macbeth* iii 1 86
The sauce to meat is ceremony; Meeting were bare without it iii 4 37
You have displaced the mirth, broke the good meeting iii 4 109
So much for him. Now for ourself and for this time of meeting *Hamlet* i 2 26
And suddenly contrive the means of meeting between him and my daughter ii 2 216
At first meeting loved; Continued so, until we thought he died *Cymbeline* v 5 379

Meeting-place. This is the very description of their meeting-place *Cymb.* iv 1 26
Meetly. You can do better yet; but this is meetly . . *Ant. and Cleo.* i 3 81
Meg. The gunner and his mate Loved Mall, Meg and Marian . *Tempest* ii 2 50
How now, Meg!—Whither go you, George? Hark you . *Mer. Wives* ii 1 152
No, pray thee, good Meg, I'll wear this . . . . *Much Ado* iii 4 8
Help to dress me, good coz, good Meg, good Ursula . . . iii 4 98
I thank thee, Meg; these words content me much . 2 *Hen. VI.* iii 2 26
Mehercle, if their sons be ingenuous, they shall want no instruction; if their daughters be capable, I will put it to them . *L. L. Lost* iv 2 80
Meilleur. Le François que vous parlez, il est meilleur que l'Anglois lequel je parle . . . . *Hen. V.* v 2 200
Meiny. They summon'd up their meiny, straight took horse . *Lear* ii 4 35
Meisen. Is at this day in Germany call'd Meisen . *Hen. V.* i 2 53
Melancholies. How melancholies I am! . . . *Mer. Wives* iii 1 13
Melancholy. She is lumpish, heavy, melancholy . *T. G. of Ver.* iii 2 62
You should have heard him so loud and so melancholy . *Mer. Wives* i 4 96
Why art thou melancholy?—I melancholy! I am not melancholy . ii 1 156
Very oft, When I am dull with care and melancholy, Lightens my humour with his merry jests . . . . *Com. of Errors* i 2 20
Sweet recreation barr'd, what doth ensue But moody and dull melancholy? . . . . v 1 79
The duke himself in person Comes this way to the melancholy vale . v 1 120
He is of a very melancholy disposition . . *Much Ado* ii 1 6
Half Count John's melancholy in Signior Benedick's face . . . ii 1 14
Not marked or not laughed at, strikes him into melancholy . . ii 1 154
I found him here as melancholy as a lodge in a warren . . . ii 1 221
A pleasant-spirited lady.—There's little of the melancholy element in her . . . . ii 1 357
The sweet youth's in love.—The greatest note of it is his melancholy . iii 2 54
We are high-proof melancholy and would fain have it beaten away . v 1 123
Besieged with sable-coloured melancholy . . . *L. L. Lost* i 1 234
What sign is it when a man of great spirit grows melancholy? . . i 2 2
How canst thou part sadness and melancholy, my tender juvenal? . i 2 7
Most rude melancholy, valour gives thee place . . . iii 1 69
I do love: and it hath taught me to rhyme and to be melancholy; and here is part of my rhyme, and here my melancholy . . . . iv 3 13
He made her melancholy, sad, and heavy; And so she died . . v 2 14
Turn melancholy forth to funerals . . . *M. N. Dream* i 1 15
Fish not, with this melancholy bait, For this fool gudgeon *Mer. of Venice* i 1 101
Indeed, my lord, The melancholy Jaques grieves at that *As Y. Like It* ii 1 26
The hairy fool, Much marked of the melancholy Jaques . . . ii 1 41
More, more, I prithee, more.—It will make you melancholy . . ii 5 10
I can suck melancholy out of a song, as a weasel sucks eggs . . ii 5 13
Under the shade of melancholy boughs . . . . . ii 7 111
I am glad of your departure: adieu, good Monsieur Melancholy . . iii 2 312
You are a melancholy fellow.—I am so; I do love it better than laughing iv 1 3
I have neither the scholar's melancholy, which is emulation . . iv 1 10
It is a melancholy of mine own, compounded of many simples . . iv 1 15
And melancholy is the nurse of frenzy . . *T. of Shrew* Ind. 2 135
'Let me not live,'—This his good melancholy oft began . . *All's Well* i 2 56
I take my young lord to be a very melancholy man . . . iii 2 4
I know a man that had this trick of melancholy sold a goodly manor for a song . . . . iii 2 9
Why is he melancholy?—Perchance he's hurt . . . . . iii 5 89
Now, the melancholy god protect thee . . . *T. Night* ii 4 75
With a green and yellow melancholy She sat like patience on a monument, Smiling at grief . . . . ii 4 116
If I lose a scruple of this sport, let me be boiled to death with melancholy . . . . ii 5 3
Unsuitable to her disposition, being addicted to a melancholy as she is ii 5 223
He is gone aboard a new ship to purge melancholy . . *W. Tale* iv 4 790
If that surly spirit, melancholy, Had baked thy blood . *K. John* iii 3 42
With clog of conscience and sour melancholy . . *Richard II.* v 6 20
I am as melancholy as a gib cat or a lugged bear . 1 *Hen. IV.* i 2 83
What sayest thou to a hare, or the melancholy of Moor-ditch? . i 2 88
To thick-eyed musing and cursed melancholy . . . . ii 3 49
Arouse the jades that drag the tragic melancholy night . 2 *Hen. VI.* iv 1 4
My mind was troubled with deep melancholy . . . . v 1 34
The king is sickly, weak and melancholy . . . *Richard III.* i 1 136
The melancholy flood, With that grim ferryman which poets write of . i 4 45
The weary way hath made you melancholy . . . . iii 1 3
O, that thou wouldst as well afford a grave As thou canst yield a melancholy seat! Then would I hide my bones . . . . . iv 4 32
Saw'st thou the melancholy Lord Northumberland? . . . v 3 68
He is melancholy without cause, and merry against the hair *Tr. and Cr.* i 2 27
Sick of proud heart: you may call it melancholy, if you will favour the man . . . . ii 3 94
If you do, our melancholy upon your head! . . . . iii 1 76
What signifies my deadly-standing eye, My silence and my cloudy melancholy, My fleece of woolly hair that now uncurls? *T. Andron.* ii 3 33
Our instruments [turn] to melancholy bells . . *Rom. and Jul.* iv 5 86
A poor unmanly melancholy sprung From change of fortune *T. of Athens* iv 3 203
The falling-from of his friends drove him into this melancholy . iv 3 402
O hateful error, melancholy's child . . . . *J. Cæsar* v 3 67
Out of my weakness and my melancholy, As he is very potent with such spirits, Abuses me to damn me . . . . . . *Hamlet* ii 2 630
There's something in his soul, O'er which his melancholy sits on brood iii 1 173
My cue is villanous melancholy, with a sigh like Tom o' Bedlam . *Lear* i 2 147
O sovereign mistress of true melancholy, The poisonous damp of night disponge upon me . . . . *Ant. and Cleo.* iv 9 12
O melancholy! Who ever yet could sound thy bottom? . *Cymbeline* iv 2 203
Thou diedst, a most rare boy, of melancholy . . . . iv 2 208
The sad companion, dull-eyed melancholy . . . *Pericles* i 2 2
Yet pause awhile: Yon knight doth sit too melancholy . . . ii 3 54
I pity his misfortune, And will awake him from his melancholy . . ii 3 91
Who, hearing of your melancholy state, Did come to see you . . v 1 222
Melford. What's here! 'Against the Duke of Suffolk, for enclosing the commons of Melford.' . . . . 2 *Hen. VI.* i 3 25
Melius. Et bonum quo antiquius, eo melius . . . *Pericles* i Gower 10
Mell. Men are to mell with, boys are not to kiss . . *All's Well* iv 3 257
Mellifluous. A mellifluous voice, as I am true knight . *T. Night* ii 3 54
Mellow. Till I had made mine own occasion mellow . . . i 2 43
So, now prosperity begins to mellow And drop into the rotten mouth of death . . . . *Richard III.* iv 4 1
As Hercules Did shake down mellow fruit . . *Coriolanus* iv 6 100
But fall, unshaken, when they mellow be . . . *Hamlet* iii 2 201
Shook down my mellow hangings, nay, my leaves . . *Cymbeline* iii 3 63
Mellowed. Even in the downfall of his mellow'd years . 3 *Hen. VI.* iii 3 104
Mellow'd by the stealing hours of time . . . *Richard III.* iii 7 168
Mellowing. Delivered upon the mellowing of occasion . . *L. L. Lost* iv 2 72

Melodious. And melodious were it, would you sing it . . *T. G. of Ver.* i 2 86
Shallow rivers, to whose falls Melodious birds sings madrigals *Mer. Wives* iii 1 18
Hounds and horns and sweet melodious birds . . *T. Andron.* ii 3 27
Like a sweet melodious bird, it sung Sweet varied notes . . . iii 1 85
Till that her garments, heavy with their drink, Pull'd the poor wretch from her melodious lay To muddy death . . . . *Hamlet* iv 7 183
Melody. My tongue should catch your tongue's sweet melody *M. N. Dream* i 1 189
Philomel, with melody Sing in our sweet lullaby . . . ii 2 13
Lull'd with sound of sweetest melody . . . 2 *Hen. IV.* iii 1 14
You shall not bob us out of our melody . . . *Troi. and Cres.* iii 1 75
The birds chant melody on every bush . . . *T. Andron.* ii 3 12
Poor harmless fly, That, with his pretty buzzing melody, Came here to make us merry! . . . . iii 2 64
With the shadow of his wings He can at pleasure stint their melody . iv 4 86
Melt. Candied be they And melt ere they molest! . . *Tempest* ii 1 280
Shall never melt Mine honour into lust . . . . . . iv 1 27
A little time will melt her frozen thoughts . . *T. G. of Ver.* iii 2 9
They would melt me out of my fat drop by drop and liquor fishermen's boots with me . . . . *Mer. Wives* iv 5 99
Is the opinion that fire cannot melt out of me . . . *Much Ado* i 1 234
So he dissolved, and showers of oaths did melt . . *M. N. Dream* i 1 245
To melt myself away in water-drops! . . . *Richard II.* iv 1 262
Nay, if you melt, then will she run mad . . . 1 *Hen. IV.* iii 1 212
When tempest of commotion, like the south Borne with black vapour, doth begin to melt And drop . . . . 2 *Hen. IV.* ii 4 393
And the continent, Weary of solid firmness, melt itself Into the sea! . iii 1 48
For I should melt at an offender's tears . . . 2 *Hen. VI.* iii 1 126
Cold snow melts with the sun's hot beams . . . . . iii 1 223
I, that did never weep, now melt with woe . . . 3 *Hen. VI.* ii 3 46
And, now I fall, thy tough commixture melts . . . . . ii 6 6
As red as fire! nay, then her wax must melt . . . . . iii 2 51
Hearts of most hard temper Melt and lament for her . *Hen. VIII.* ii 3 12
You have holp . . . To melt the city leads upon your pates *Coriolanus* iv 6 82
I melt, and am not Of stronger earth than others . . . . v 3 28
In winter with warm tears I'll melt the snow . . . *T. Andron.* iii 1 20
Thou art made of tears, And tears will quickly melt thy life away . iii 2 51
Come hither, boy; come, come, and learn of us To melt in showers . v 3 161
O, that this too too solid flesh would melt! . . . . *Hamlet* i 2 129
To flaming youth let virtue be as wax, And melt in her own fire . . iii 4 85
If it hath ruffian'd so upon the sea, What ribs of oak, when mountains melt on them, Can hold the mortise? . . . . . *Othello* ii 1 8
Let Rome in Tiber melt! . . . . *Ant. and Cleo.* i 1 33
The gold I give thee will I melt and pour Down thy ill-uttering throat ii 5 34
Melt Egypt into Nile! and kindly creatures Turn all to serpents! . ii 5 78
Now, gods and devils! Authority melts from me . . . . iii 13 90
Do discandy, melt their sweets On blossoming Cæsar . . . iv 12 22
O, see, my women, The crown o' the earth doth melt . . . iv 15 63
Nor let pity, which Even women have cast off, melt thee . *Pericles* iv 1 7
That on the touching of her lips I may Melt and no more be seen . . v 3 43
Melted. Were all spirits and Are melted into air, into thin air *Tempest* iv 1 150
Till the wicked fire of lust have melted him in his own grease *Mer. Wives* ii 1 69
But manhood is melted into courtesies . . . . *Much Ado* iv 1 321
My love to Hermia, Melted as the snow . . . . *M. N. Dream* iv 1 171
To what metal this counterfeit lump of ore will be melted . *All's Well* iii 6 40
And so, with shrieks, She melted into air . . . . *W. Tale* iii 3 37
Melted by the windy breath Of soft petitions . . . . *K. John* ii 1 477
My heart hath melted at a lady's tears, Being an ordinary inundation . v 2 47
Had not God, for some strong purpose, steel'd The hearts of men, they must perforce have melted . . . . *Richard II.* v 2 35
Didst thou never see Titan kiss a dish of butter? pitiful-hearted Titan, that melted at the sweet tale of the sun's! . . . . 1 *Hen. IV.* ii 4 134
Rush on his host, as doth the melted snow Upon the valleys . *Hen. V.* iii 5 50
Being three parts melted away with rotten dews . . *Coriolanus* ii 3 35
Melted down thy youth In different beds of lust . *T. of Athens* iv 3 256
And what seem'd corporal melted As breath into the wind . *Macbeth* i 3 81
Follow'd him, till he had melted from The smallness of a gnat to air *Cymb.* i 3 20
Melteth. Against whose charms faith melteth into blood . *Much Ado* ii 1 187
Thaw'd from the true quality With that which melteth fools . *J. Cæsar* iii 1 42
Melting. As the morning steals upon the night, Melting the darkness *Tempest* v 1 66
A sea of melting pearl, which some call tears . . *T. G. of Ver.* iii 1 224
A tear for pity and a hand Open as day for melting charity 2 *Hen. IV.* iv 4 32
And that will quickly dry thy melting tears . . . 3 *Hen. VI.* i 4 174
Steel thy melting heart . . . . ii 2 41
Melting with tenderness and kind compassion . . . *Richard III.* iv 3 7
And stain the sun with fog, as sometime clouds When they do hug him in their melting bosoms . . . . *T. Andron.* iii 1 214
And to steel with valour The melting spirits of women . . *J. Cæsar* ii 1 122
Whose subdued eyes, Albeit unused to the melting mood, Drop tears *Oth.* v 2 349
Melun. The Count Melun, a noble lord of France . . . *K. John* iv 3 15
My Lord Melun, let this be copied out, And keep it safe . . . v 2 1
It is the Count Melun.—Wounded to death.—Fly, noble English . . v 4 9
What news?—The Count Melun is slain; the English lords By his persuasion are again fall'n off . . . . v 5 10
Member. Being members of my occupation, using painting . *M. for M.* iv 2 39
Instruments of some more mightier member That sets them on . . v 1 237
Here comes a member of the commonwealth . . . . *L. L. Lost* iv 1 41
You are a good member of the commonwealth . . . . . iv 2 78
And he says, you are no good member of the commonwealth *M. of Ven.* iii 5 37
All members of our cause, both here and hence . . 2 *Hen. IV.* iv 1 171
The slave, a member of the country's peace, Enjoys it . . *Hen. V.* iv 1 298
As a branch and member of this royalty . . . . . . v 2 5
As fester'd members rot but by degree . . . 1 *Hen. VI.* iii 1 192
I'll lop a member off and give it you In earnest of a further benefit . v 3 15
Count wisdom as no member of the war . . . *Troi. and Cres.* i 3 198
Thou shouldst not bear from me a Greekish member Wherein my sword had not impressure made Of our rank feud . . . . . . iv 5 130
All the body's members Rebell'd against the belly . . *Coriolanus* i 1 99
It tauntingly replied To the discontented members . . . . i 1 115
The senators of Rome are this good belly, And you the mutinous members . . . . i 1 153
We being members, should bring ourselves to be monstrous members . ii 3 13
That . . . I may again Exist, and be a member of his love . *Othello* iii 4 112
Let our finger ache, and it indues Our other healthful members even to that sense Of pain . . . . iii 4 147
When old robes are worn out, there are members to make new *A. and C.* i 2 171
Memento mori. I make as good use of it as many a man doth of a Death's-head or a memento mori . . . . 1 *Hen. IV.* iii 3 35
Memorable. Witness our too much memorable shame . . *Hen. V.* ii 4 53
He sends you this most memorable line . . . . . . ii 4 88

Memorable. I wear it for a memorable honour *Hen. V.* iv 7 109
Worn as a memorable trophy of predeceased valour v 1 76
Memorandum. If there were any thing in thy pocket but tavern-reckonings, memorandums of bawdy-houses 1 *Hen. IV.* iii 3 179
Memorial. Let us satisfy our eyes With the memorials *T. Night* iii 3 23
The primitive statue, and oblique memorial of cuckolds *Troi. and Cres.* v 1 61
Takes my glove, And gives memorial dainty kisses to it, As I kiss thee v 2 80
Memorize. Or memorize another Golgotha *Macbeth* i 2 40
Memorized. I persuade me, from her Will fall some blessing to this land, which shall In it be memorized *Hen. VIII.* iii 2 52
Memory. Made such a sinner of his memory, To credit his own lie *Tempest* i 2 101
Who shall be of as little memory When he is earth'd ii 1 233
The building fall And leave no memory of what it was *T. G. of Ver.* v 4 10
He is a good sprag memory *Mer. Wives* iv 1 84
Yet hath my night of life some memory *Com. of Errors* v 1 314
Else your memory is bad *L. L. Lost* iv 1 99
Begot in the ventricle of memory, nourished in the womb of pia mater iv 2 71
Why, that contempt will kill the speaker's heart, And quite divorce his memory from his part v 2 150
Now have toil'd their unbreathed memories *M. N. Dream* v 1 74
By the near guess of my memory *Mer. of Venice* i 3 55
The fool hath planted in his memory An army of good words iii 5 71
O my sweet master! O you memory Of old Sir Rowland! *As Y. Like It* ii 3 3
Many things of worthy memory, which now shall die in oblivion *T. of S.* iv 1 84
Good Paulina, Who hast the memory of Hermione, I know, in honour *W. Tale* v 1 50
Whose memory is written on the earth With yet appearing blood 2 *Hen. IV.* iv 1 81
And keep no tell-tale to his memory That may repeat and history his loss iv 1 202
Their memory Shall as a pattern or a measure live iv 4 75
That action, hence borne out, May waste the memory of the former days iv 5 216
Your grandfather of famous memory *Hen. V.* iv 7 95
In memory of her when she is dead 1 *Hen. VI.* i 6 23
I'll note you in my book of memory, To scourge you for this apprehension ii 4 101
That ever living man of memory iv 3 51
Cancelling your fame, Blotting your names from books of memory 2 *Hen. VI.* i 1 100
I thank my memory, I yet remember Some of these articles *Hen. VIII.* iii 2 303
Some little memory of me will stir him—I know his noble nature iii 2 417
Can dearly witness, Yet freshly pitied in our memories v 3 31
When time is old . . . , yet let memory, From false to false, among false maids in love, Upbraid my falsehood! *Troi. and Cres.* iii 2 196
I am weary; yea, my memory is tired *Coriolanus* i 9 91
A good memory, And witness of the malice and displeasure Which thou shouldst bear me iv 5 77
To make coals cheap,—a noble memory! v 1 17
Yet he shall have a noble memory v 6 155
I would forget it fain; But, O, it presses to my memory, Like damned guilty deeds to sinners' minds *Rom. and Jul.* iii 2 110
Of whose memory Hereafter more *T. of Athens* v 4 80
Yea, beg a hair of him for memory *J. Cæsar* iii 2 139
That memory, the warder of the brain, Shall be a fume *Macbeth* i 7 65
Minister to a mind diseased, Pluck from the memory a rooted sorrow v 3 41
Though yet of Hamlet our dear brother s death The memory be green *Hamlet* i 2 2
And these few precepts in thy memory See thou character i 3 58
'Tis in my memory lock'd, And you yourself shall keep the key of it i 3 85
While memory holds a seat In this distracted globe i 5 96
From the table of my memory I'll wipe away all trivial fond records i 5 98
If it live in your memory, begin at this line ii 2 470
Then there's hope a great man's memory may outlive his life half a year iii 2 140
Purpose is but the slave to memory, Of violent birth, but poor validity iii 2 198
To divide him inventorially would dizzy the arithmetic of memory v 2 119
I embrace my fortune: I have some rights of memory in this kingdom v 2 400
These weeds are memories of those worser hours *Lear* iv 7 7
It comes o'er my memory, As doth the raven o'er the infected house *Oth.* iv 1 20
Till by degrees the memory of my womb . . . Lie graveless *A. and C.* iii 13 163
Be witness to me, O thou blessed moon, When men revolted shall upon record Bear hateful memory, poor Enobarbus did Before thy face repent! iv 9 9
Why should I write this down, that's riveted, Screw'd to my memory? *Cymbeline* ii 2 44
When thou shalt be disedged by her That now thou tirest on, how thy memory Will then be pang'd by me iii 4 97
But our great court Made me to blame in memory iii 5 51
Memphis. A statelier pyramis to her I'll rear Than Rhodope's or Memphis' ever was 1 *Hen. VI.* i 6 22
Men. Where's the master? Play the men *Tempest* i 1 11
To the most of men this is a Caliban And they to him are angels i 2 480
Milan and Naples have Moe widows in them of this business' making Than we bring men to comfort them ii 1 134
No occupation; all men idle, all; And women too, but innocent and pure ii 1 154
Ebbing men, indeed, Most often do so near the bottom run ii 1 226
My brother's servants Were then my fellows; now they are my men ii 1 274
Do you put tricks upon's with savages and men of Ind? ii 2 61
Nor have I seen More that I may call men than you, good friend, And my dear father: how features are abroad, I am skilless of iii 1 51
There were such men Whose heads stood in their breasts iii 3 46
You are three men of sin iii 3 53
Where man doth not inhabit; you 'mongst men Being most unfit to live iii 3 57
With such-like valour men hang and drown Their proper selves iii 3 59
This is as strange a maze as e'er men trod v 1 242
Mark but the badges of these men, my lords, Then say if they be true v 1 267
O, they love least that let men know their love *T. G. of Ver.* i 2 32
Other men, of slender reputation, Put forth their sons to seek preferment i 3 6
The loose encounters of lascivious men ii 7 41
All these are servants to deceitful men.—Base men, that use them to so base effect! ii 7 72
Kept severely from resort of men, That no man hath access by day to her iii 1 108
Such as the fury of ungovern'd youth Thrust from the company of awful men iv 1 46
Madam Julia's gown, Which served me as fit, by all men's judgements iv 4 167
The old saying is, Black men are pearls in beauteous ladies' eyes v 2 12
In love Who respects friend?—All men but Proteus v 4 54
It is the lesser blot, modesty finds, Women to change their shapes than men their minds.—Than men their minds! 'tis true. v 4 109
These banish'd men . . . Are men endued with worthy qualities v 4 153
You have beaten my men, killed my deer, and broke open my lodge *M. W.* i 1 114
Men. I keep but three men and a boy yet, till my mother be dead *Mer. Wives* i 1 284
I'll exhibit a bill in the parliament for the putting down of men ii 1 30
I shall think the worse of fat men, as long as I have an eye to make difference of men's liking ii 1 56
These that accuse him . . . are a yoke of his discarded men ii 1 182
Were they his men?—Marry, were they.—I like it never the better for that ii 1 184
Let us not be laughing-stocks to other men's humours iii 1 88
Give your men the charge; we must be brief iii 3 7
These lisping hawthorn-buds, that come like women in men's apparel iii 3 78
Or—it is whiting-time—send him by your two men to Datchet-mead iii 3 141
Good heart, that was not her fault: she does so take on with her men iii 5 41
I'll appoint my men to carry the basket again, to meet him at the door iv 2 97
I'll first direct my men what they shall do with the basket iv 2 101
We are simple men; we do not know what's brought to pass under the profession of fortune-telling iv 2 183
Do not say they be fled; Germans are honest men iv 5 74
When gods have hot backs what shall poor men do? v 5 13
I have great hope in that; for in her youth There is a prone and speechless dialect, Such as move men *Meas. for Meas.* i 2 189
You must not speak with men But in the presence of the prioress i 4 10
Let him learn to know, when maidens sue, Men give like gods i 4 81
Are there not men in your ward sufficient to serve it? ii 1 281
Could great men thunder As Jove himself does, Jove would ne'er be quiet ii 2 110
Great men may jest with saints; 'tis wit in them ii 2 127
Ever till now, When men were fond, I smiled and wonder'd how ii 2 187
Women! Help Heaven! men their creation mar In profiting by them ii 4 127
But that you will needs buy and sell men and women like beasts iii 2 2
A gentle provost: seldom when The steeled gaoler is the friend of men iv 2 90
Give notice to such men of sort and suit as are to meet him iv 4 19
They say, best men are moulded out of faults v 1 444
A small spare mast, Such as seafaring men provide for storms *Com. of Er.* i 1 81
Loath to leave unsought Or that or any place that harbours men i 1 137
Men, more divine, the masters of all these, Lords of the wide world ii 1 20
What he hath scanted men in hair he hath given them in wit ii 2 81
Thou didst conclude hairy men plain dealers without wit ii 2 87
Have you not heard men say, That Time comes stealing on by night and day? iv 2 59
He, sir, that takes pity on decayed men and gives them suits of durance iv 3 26
It is written, they appear to men like angels of light iv 3 56
'Tis pity that thou livest To walk where any honest men resort v 1 28
Unlawful love? A sin prevailing much in youthful men v 1 52
One of these men is Genius to the other; And so of these v 1 332
By men of Epidamnum he and I And the twin Dromio all were taken up v 1 349
Not till God make men of some other metal than earth *Much Ado* ii 1 62
He both pleases men and angers them ii 1 146
Is it not strange that sheeps' guts should hale souls out of men's bodies? ii 3 62
Men were deceivers ever, One foot in sea and one on shore ii 3 65
The fraud of men was ever so, Since summer first was leavy ii 3 74
Are you good men and true?—Yea, or else it were pity iii 3 1
You shall comprehend all vagrom men iii 3 26
You may say they are not the men you took them for iii 3 50
Such kind of men, the less you meddle or make with them, why, the more is for your honesty iii 3 55
We are like to prove a goodly commodity, being taken up of these men's bills iii 3 191
God's a good man; an two men ride of a horse, one must ride behind iii 5 40
All men are not alike; alas, good neighbour! iii 5 43
We are now to examination these men.—And we must do it wisely iii 5 64
O, what men dare do! what men may do! what men daily do, not knowing what they do! iv 1 19
And men are only turned into tongue, and trim ones too iv 1 322
Masters, I charge you, in the prince's name, accuse these men iv 2 40
Master constable, let these men be bound, and brought to Leonato's iv 2 67
Men Can counsel and speak comfort to that grief Which they themselves not feel; but, tasting it, Their counsel turns to passion v 1 20
'Tis all men's office to speak patience To those that wring under the load of sorrow v 1 27
Give me no counsel: My griefs cry louder than advertisement.—Therein do men from children nothing differ v 1 33
He shall kill two of us, and men indeed v 1 80
Like to have had our two noses snapped off with two old men without teeth v 1 116
How now? two of my brother s men bound! v 1 215
Officers, what offence have these men done?—Marry, sir, they have committed false report v 1 218
Here stand a pair of honourable men v 1 276
That now men grow hard-hearted and will lend nothing for God's sake v 1 320
No words!—Of other men's secrets, I beseech you *L. L. Lost* i 1 232
And men sit down to that nourishment which is called supper i 1 239
What great men have been in love?—Hercules, master i 2 68
Let them be men of good repute and carriage i 2 72
His disgrace is to be called boy; but his glory is to subdue men i 2 187
And make them men of note—do you note me? iii 1 25
Some men must love my lady and some Joan iii 1 207
I am betray'd, by keeping company With men like men of inconstancy iv 3 180
For wisdom's sake, a word that all men love, Or for love's sake, a word that loves all men, Or for men's sake, the authors of these women, Or women's sake, by whom we men are men iv 3 358
Light wenches may prove plagues to men forsworn iv 3 385
Men of peace, well encountered v 1 37
Where will you find men worthy enough? v 1 131
Nor God, nor I, delights in perjured men v 2 346
Vice you should have spoke; For virtue's office never breaks men's troth v 2 350
Will you hear the dialogue that the two learned men have compiled? v 2 895
The cuckoo then, on every tree, Mocks married men v 2 909
Either to die the death or to abjure For ever the society of men *M. N. Dream* i 1 66
By all the vows that ever men have broke, In number more than ever women spoke i 1 175
The nine men's morris is fill'd up with mud ii 1 98
We cannot fight for love, as men may do; We should be woo'd ii 1 241
As the heresies that men do leave Are hated most of those they did deceive ii 2 139
I am no such thing; I am a man as other men are iii 1 45
Henceforth be never number'd among men! iii 2 67
If you were men, as men you are in show, You would not use a gentle lady so iii 2 151

Men. And will you rent our ancient love asunder, To join with men in scorning your poor friend? It is not friendly . . *M. N. Dream* iii 2 216
If our sport had gone forward, we had all been made men . . iv 2 18
Hard-handed men that work in Athens here, Which never labour'd in their minds till now . . . . . . v 1 72
They may pass for excellent men . . . . . v 1 220
Men whose visages Do cream and mantle like a standing pond *Mer. of Ven.* i 1 88
I must be one of these same dumb wise men . . . i 1 106
Chapels had been churches and poor men's cottages princes' palaces . i 2 15
Holy men at their death have good inspirations . . . i 2 31
He, of all the men that ever my foolish eyes looked upon, was the best deserving a fair lady . . . . . . i 2 129
Ships are but boards, sailors but men : there be land-rats and water-rats i 3 23
And thrift is blessing, if men steal it not . . . . i 3 91
Good fortune then ! To make me blest or cursed'st among men . ii 1 46
Men that hazard all Do it in hope of fair advantages . . ii 7 18
Who chooseth me shall gain what many men desire ii 7 37 ; ii 9 24
Other men have ill luck too . . . . . . iii 1 102
I fear you speak upon the rack, Where men enforced do speak any thing iii 2 33
A golden mesh to entrap the hearts of men Faster than gnats in cobwebs iii 2 122
It is the most impenetrable cur That ever kept with men . . iii 3 19
When we are both accoutred like young men, I'll prove the prettier fellow . . . . iii 4 63
That men shall swear I have discontinued school Above a twelvemonth iii 4 75
Why, shall we turn to men?—Fie, what a question's that ! . iii 4 78
Some men there are love not a gaping pig . . . iv 1 47
Do all men kill the things they do not love?—Hates any man the thing he would not kill? . . . . . . iv 1 66
That souls of animals infuse themselves Into the trunks of men . iv 1 133
That 'scuse serves many men to save their gifts . . . iv 1 444
We shall have old swearing That they did give the rings away to men . v 2 16
And a many merry men with him . . . *As Y. Like It* i 1 121
The more pity, that fools may not speak wisely what wise men do foolishly . . . . i 2 93
The little foolery that wise men have makes a great show . . i 2 96
Three proper young men, of excellent growth and presence . i 2 129
Be it known unto all men by these presents . . . i 2 132
Thus men may grow wiser every day . . . . . i 2 145
To some kind of men Their graces serve them but as enemies . ii 3 10
With holy bell been knoll'd to church And sat at good men's feasts . ii 7 122
All the world's a stage, And all the men and women merely players . ii 7 140
Owe no man hate, envy no man's happiness, glad of other men's good . iii 2 79
Horns? Even so. Poor men alone? No, no ; the noblest deer hath them . . . . iii 3 57
I fear you have sold your own lands to see other men's . . iv 1 23
Men have died from time to time and worms have eaten them, but not for love . . . . iv 1 107
Men are April when they woo, December when they wed . . iv 1 147
And he did render him the most unnatural That lived amongst men . iv 3 124
Every day Men of great worth resorted to this forest . . v 4 161
I charge you, O women, for the love you bear to men, . . . and I charge you, O men, for the love you bear to women . . . . Epil. 13
And how my men will stay themselves from laughter . *T. of Shrew* Ind. 1 134
You know no house nor no such maid, Nor no such men . . Ind. 2 94
Such names and men as these Which never were nor no man ever saw Ind. 2 97
Are you my wife and will not call me husband? My men should call me 'lord' . . . . Ind. 2 107
Prefer them hither ; for to cunning men I will be very kind . . i 1 97
Such wind as scatters young men through the world To seek their fortunes . . . . i 2 50
Of all the men alive I never yet beheld that special face Which I could fancy more than any other . . . . . . ii 1 10
'Tis a world to see, How tame, when men and women are alone . . ii 1 314
He is old, I young.—And may not young men die, as well as old? . . ii 1 393
Face not me : thou hast braved many men ; brave not me . . iv 3 126
Go, call my men, and let us straight to him ; And bring our horses . iv 3 186
Is there no military policy, how virgins might blow up men? *All's Well* i 1 133
If men could be contented to be what they are, there were no fear in marriage . . . . i 3 54
For I the ballad will repeat, Which men full true shall find . . i 3 65
It is presumption in us when The help of heaven we count the act of men ii 1 155
But for me, I have an answer will serve all men . . . ii 2 14
I think thou wast created for men to breathe themselves upon thee . ii 3 271
That's the loss of men, though it be the getting of children . iii 2 44
My integrity ne'er knew the crafts That you do charge men with . iv 2 34
I see that men make ropes in such a scarre That we'll forsake ourselves iv 2 38
My mother told me just how he would woo, As if she sat in's heart ; she says all men Have the like oaths . . . . . . iv 2 70
Men are to mell with, boys are not to kiss . . . iv 3 257
Made such pestiferous reports of men very nobly held . . iv 3 340
But, O strange men ! That can such sweet use make of what they hate iv 4 21
She whom all men praised and whom myself, Since I have lost, have loved . . . . v 3 53
She hath abjured the company And sight of men . . . *T. Night* i 2 41
I take these wise men, that crow so at these set kind of fools, no better than the fools' zanies . . . . i 5 95
And 'Three merry men be we' . . . . . . ii 3 82
Thy mind is a very opal. I would have men of such constancy put to sea ii 4 78
What dost thou know?—Too well what love women to men may owe . ii 4 108
We men may say more, swear more : but indeed Our shows are more than will . . . . ii 4 119
But wise men, folly-fall'n, quite taint their wit . . . iii 1 75
I have heard of some kind of men that put quarrels purposely on others iii 4 266
These wise men that give fools money get themselves a good report . iv 1 23
'Gainst knaves and thieves men shut their gate . . . v 1 404
There's comfort in't Whiles other men have gates and those gates open'd, As mine, against their will . . . . *W. Tale* i 2 197
Never Saw I men scour so on their way . . . . . ii 1 35
The men are not yet cold under water . . . . . iii 3 107
These are flowers Of middle summer, and I think they are given To men of middle age . . . . iv 4 108
He utters them as he had eaten ballads and all men's ears grew to his tunes . . . . iv 4 186
There are cozeners abroad ; therefore it behoves men to be wary . iv 4 257
Come to the pedlar ; Money's a medler, That doth utter all men's ware-a iv 4 330
Swine-herds, that have made themselves all men of hair . . iv 4 333
Since these good men are pleased, let them come in ; but quickly now . iv 4 350
And he, and more Than he, and men, the earth, the heavens, and all . iv 4 382
How blessed are we that are not simple men ! . . . . iv 4 772
Tell me, for you seem to be honest plain men, what you have to the king iv 4 824

Men. Women will love her, that she is a woman More worth than any man ; men, that she is The rarest of all women . . *W. Tale* v 1 111
Who now Has these poor men in question. Never saw I Wretches so quake . . . . v 1 198
Shall I produce the men?—Let them approach . . . *K. John* i 1 46
Of that I doubt, as all men's children may . . . . i 1 63
Lest men should say 'Look, where three-farthings goes !' . . i 1 143
And have is have, however men do catch . . . . i 1 173
Call for our chiefest men of discipline . . . . ii 1 39
Some trumpet summon hither to the walls These men of Angiers . . ii 1 199
You men of Angiers, and my loving subjects,— You loving men of Angiers . . . . ii 1 204
You men of Angiers, open wide your gates . . . . ii 1 300
He feasts, mousing the flesh of men, In undetermined differences of kings . . . . ii 1 354
He that wins of all, Of kings, of beggars, old men, young men, maids . ii 1 570
Let belief and life encounter so As doth the fury of two desperate men iii 1 32
What, shall our feast be kept with slaughter'd men? . . . iii 1 302
Making that idiot, laughter, keep men's eyes And strain their cheeks . iii 3 45
No, no ; when Fortune means to men most good, She looks upon them with a threatening eye . . . . iii 4 119
Save me ! my eyes are out Even with the fierce looks of these bloody men iv 1 74
Drive these men away, And I will sit as quiet as a lamb . . iv 1 79
Thrust but these men away, and I'll forgive you, Whatever torment you do put me to . . . . iv 1 83
The faiths of men ne'er stained with revolt . . . . iv 2 6
Men's mouths are full of it . . . . . . iv 2 161
Old men and beldams in the streets Do prophesy upon it dangerously . iv 2 185
What penny hath Rome borne, What men provided, what munition sent? v 2 98
How God and good men hate so foul a liar . . . . *Richard II.* i 1 114
That [reputation] away, Men are but gilded loam or painted clay . i 1 179
That which in mean men we intitle patience Is pale cold cowardice in noble breasts . . . . i 2 33
Like two men That vow a long and weary pilgrimage . . . i 3 48
What is six winters? they are quickly gone.—To men in joy . . i 3 261
When they shall know what men are rich, They shall subscribe them . i 4 49
They say the tongues of dying men Enforce attention like deep harmony ii 1 5
More are men's ends mark'd than their lives before . . . ii 1 11
This happy breed of men, this little world, This precious stone . . ii 1 45
Can sick men play so nicely with their names? . . . ii 1 84
Should dying men flatter with those that live?—No, no, men living flatter those that die . . . . ii 1 88
With eight tall ships, three thousand men of war, Are making hither . ii 1 286
Gentlemen, go, muster up your men, And meet me presently at Berkeley ii 2 118
And what stir Keeps good old York there with his men of war? . ii 3 52
There stands the castle, by yon tuft of trees, Mann'd with three hundred men . . . . ii 3 54
Rescued the Black Prince, that young Mars of men . . . ii 3 101
Base men by his endowments are made great . . . . ii 3 139
Rich men look sad and ruffians dance and leap . . . ii 4 12
Bring forth these men. Bushy and Green, I will not vex your souls . iii 1 1
Yet, to wash your blood From off my hands, here in the view of men I will unfold some causes of your deaths . . . . . iii 1 6
Leaving me no sign, Save men's opinions and my living blood . . iii 1 26
The breath of worldly men cannot depose The deputy elected by the Lord iii 2 56
Then, if angels fight, Weak men must fall, for heaven still guards the right iii 2 62
O, call back yesterday, bid time return, And thou shalt have twelve thousand fighting men ! . . . . iii 2 70
But now the blood of twenty thousand men Did triumph in my face . iii 2 76
Wise men ne'er sit and wail their woes . . . . iii 2 178
Men judge by the complexion of the sky The state and inclination of the day . . . . iii 2 194
Had he done so to great and growing men, They might have lived to bear iii 4 61
Thou, Aumerle, didst send two of thy men To execute the noble duke at Calais . . . . iv 1 81
And this land be call'd The field of Golgotha and dead men's skulls . iv 1 144
Yet I well remember The favours of these men : were they not mine? . iv 1 168
By confessing them, the souls of men May deem that you are worthily deposed . . . . iv 1 226
That every day under his household roof Did keep ten thousand men . iv 1 283
A king of beasts, indeed ; if aught but beasts, I had been still a happy king of men . . . . v 1 36
The love of wicked men converts to fear ; That fear to hate . . v 1 66
Bad men, you violate A twofold marriage, 'twixt my crown and me . v 1 71
As in a theatre, the eyes of men, After a well-graced actor leaves the stage, Are idly bent on him that enters next . . . . v 2 23
Even so, or with much more contempt, men's eyes Did scowl on gentle Richard . . . . v 2 27
Had not God, for some strong purpose, steel'd The hearts of men. . v 2 35
So is it in the music of men's lives . . . . . v 5 44
Though it [music] have holp madmen to their wits, In me it seems it will make wise men mad . . . . v 5 63
Let men say we be men of good government . . . *1 Hen. IV.* i 2 30
The fortune of us that are the moon's men doth ebb and flow like the sea i 2 36
If men were to be saved by merit, what hole in hell were hot enough for him? . . . . i 2 119
Falstaff, Bardolph, Peto and Gadshill shall rob those men . . i 2 182
By how much better than my word I am, By so much shall I falsify men's hopes . . . . i 2 235
Redeeming time when men think least I will . . . . i 2 241
That men of your nobility and power Did gage them both in an unjust behalf . . . . i 3 172
Go to ; 'homo' is a common name to all men . . . . ii 1 105
On, bacons, on ! What, ye knaves ! young men must live . . ii 2 96
The thieves have bound the true men. Now could thou and I rob the thieves . . . . ii 2 98
And in thy face strange motions have appear'd, Such as we see when men restrain their breath . . . . ii 3 64
There live not three good men unhanged in England . . . ii 4 144
As we were sharing, some six or seven fresh men set upon us . . ii 4 200
O monstrous ! eleven buckram men grown out of two ! . . . ii 4 243
How couldst thou know these men in Kendal green, when it was so dark? . . . . ii 4 257
Then to beslubber our garments with it and swear it was the blood of true men . . . . ii 4 343
A hue and cry Hath follow'd certain men unto this house.—What men? ii 4 557
It may be so : if he have robb'd these men, He shall be answerable . ii 4 570
Of many men I do not bear these crossings . . . . iii 1 35
All the courses of my life do show I am not in the roll of common men iii 1 43
Loseth men's hearts and leaves behind a stain . . . . iii 1 187

Men. So common-hackney'd in the eyes of men, So stale and cheap 1 *Hen. IV.* iii 2 40
That men would tell their children 'This is he;' Others would say 'Where, which is Bolingbroke?' iii 2 48
Dress'd myself in such humility That I did pluck allegiance from men's hearts iii 2 52
That, being daily swallow'd by men's eyes, They surfeited with honey iii 2 70
Render'd such aspect As cloudy men use to their adversaries iii 2 83
Let's away; Advantage feeds him fat, while men delay iii 2 180
For men must think, If we without his help can make a head To push against a kingdom, with his help We shall o'erturn it topsy-turvy down iv 1 79
They'll fill a pit as well as better: tush, man, mortal men, mortal men iv 2 73
Being men of such great leading as you are iv 3 17
Wherein the fortune of ten thousand men Must bide the touch iv 4 9
Dear men Of estimation and command in arms iv 4 31
And all his men Upon the foot of fear, fled with the rest v 5 19
Stuffing the ears of men with false reports 2 *Hen. IV.* Ind. 8
So did our men, heavy in Hotspur's loss i 1 121
Your son had only but the corpse, But shadows and the shows of men, to fight i 1 193
And they did fight with queasiness, constrain'd, As men drink potions i 1 197
Men of all sorts take a pride to gird at me i 2 7
I am not only witty in myself, but the cause that wit is in other men i 2 12
Five and twenty thousand men of choice i 3 11
We fortify in paper and in figures, Using the names of men instead of men i 3 57
O thoughts of men accursed! Past and to come seems best i 3 107
O miracle of men! him did you leave, Second to none, unseconded by you ii 3 33
Die men like dogs! give crowns like pins! Have we not Hiren here? ii 4 188
You see, my good wenches, how men of merit are sought after ii 4 405
There is a history in all men's lives, Figuring the nature of the times deceased iii 1 80
Here come two of Sir John Falstaff's men, as I think iii 2 60
Have you provided me here half a dozen sufficient men? iii 2 103
You need not to have pricked me; there are other men fitter to go out than I iii 2 126
Come, sir, which men shall I have?—Four of which you please iii 2 258
They are your likeliest men, and I would have you served with the best iii 2 273
O, give me the spare men, and spare me the great ones iii 2 288
Lord, Lord, how subject we old men are to this vice of lying! iii 2 326
He burst his head for crowding among the marshal's men iii 2 348
Nor do I as an enemy to peace Troop in the throngs of military men iv 1 62
We are denied access unto his person Even by those men that most have done us wrong iv 1 79
Our men more perfect in the use of arms, Our armour all as strong iv 1 155
Against ill chances men are ever merry; But heaviness foreruns the good event iv 2 81
Let our trains March by us, that we may peruse the men iv 2 94
Use his men well, Davy; for they are arrant knaves, and will backbite v 1 35
It is a wonderful thing to see the semblable coherence of his men's spirits and his v 1 73
If I had a suit to Master Shallow, I would humour his men with the imputation of being near their master: if to his men, I would curry with Master Shallow v 1 80
Wise bearing or ignorant carriage is caught, as men take diseases, one of another: therefore let men take heed of their company v 1 85
We meet like men that had forgot to speak v 2 22
Thou art now one of the greatest men in this realm v 3 92
Know the grave doth gape For thee thrice wider than for other men v 5 58
Lands which men devout By testament have given to the church *Hen. V.* i 1 9
And the mute wonder lurketh in men's ears i 1 49
'Tis ever common That men are merriest when they are from home i 2 272
Men may sleep, and they may have their throats about them at that time ii 1 23
It is most lamentable to behold. Sweet men, come to him ii 1 125
Show men dutiful? Why, so didst thou: seem they grave and learned? ii 2 127
Oaths are straws, men's faiths are wafer-cakes, And hold-fast is the only dog ii 3 53
To line and new repair our towns of war With men of courage ii 4 8
The orphans' cries, The dead men's blood, the pining maidens' groans ii 4 107
Be copy now to men of grosser blood, And teach them how to war iii 1 24
Be merciful, great duke, to men of mould iii 2 23
He hath heard that men of few words are the best men iii 2 38
I knew by that piece of service the men would carry coals iii 2 49
They would have me as familiar with men's pockets as their gloves iii 2 51
Or like to men proud of destruction Defy us to our worst iii 3 4
You men of Harfleur, Take pity of your town and of your people iii 3 27
What men have you lost, Fluellen? iii 6 102
The men do sympathize with the mastiffs in robustious and rough coming on iii 7 158
There is some soul of goodness in things evil, Would men observingly distil it out iv 1 5
'Tis good for men to love their present pains Upon example iv 1 18
Even as men wrecked upon a sand, that look to be washed off the next tide iv 1 100
And a many poor men's lives saved iv 1 128
Howsoever you speak this to feel other men's minds iv 1 131
If these men do not die well, it will be a black matter for the king that led them to it iv 1 151
If these men have defeated the law and outrun native punishment, though they can outstrip men, they have no wings to fly from God iv 1 177
So that here men are punished for before-breach of the king's laws iv 1 179
What infinite heart's-ease Must kings neglect, that private men enjoy! iv 1 254
Art thou [ceremony] aught else but place, degree and form, Creating awe and fear in other men? iv 1 264
Leaving them but the shales and husks of men iv 2 18
Of fighting men they have full three score thousand iv 3 3
O that we now had here But one ten thousand of those men in England That do no work to-day! iv 3 17
And if to live, The fewer men, the greater share of honour iv 3 22
It yearns me not if men my garments wear iv 3 26
Old men forget; yet all shall be forgot iv 3 49
Why, now thou hast unwish'd five thousand men iv 3 76
Dying like men, though buried in your dunghills, They shall be famed iv 3 99
The French have reinforced their scatter'd men iv 6 36
I'll tell you there is good men porn at Monmouth iv 7 56
To sort our nobles from our common men iv 7 77
Knights and squires, Full fifteen hundred, besides common men iv 8 84
None else of name; and of all other men But five and twenty iv 8 110

Men. And to England then; Where ne'er from France arrived more happy men *Hen. V.* iv 8 131
Behold, the English beach Pales in the flood with men v Prol. 10
What says she, fair one? that the tongues of men are full of deceits? v 2 121
Hath pursued the story, In little room confining mighty men Epil. 3
His brandish'd sword did blind men with his beams 1 *Hen. VI.* i 1 10
What treachery was used?—No treachery; but want of men and money i 1 69
No leisure had he to enrank his men i 1 115
Salisbury craveth supply, And hardly keeps his men from mutiny i 1 160
And he may well in fretting spend his gall, Nor men nor money hath he to make war i 2 17
Who ever saw the like? what men have I! Dogs! cowards! dastards! i 2 22
He may mean more than we poor men do know i 2 122
Draw, men, for all this privileged place; Blue coats to tawny coats i 3 46
All manner of men assembled here in arms this day against God's peace i 3 74
How farest thou, mirror of all martial men? i 4 74
Cheer up thy hungry-starved men; Help Salisbury to make his testament i 5 16
All France will be replete with mirth and joy, When they shall hear how we have play'd the men i 6 16
They did amongst the troops of armed men Leap o'er the walls for refuge ii 2 24
For when a world of men Could not prevail with all their oratory, Yet hath a woman's kindness over-ruled ii 2 48
And that I'll prove on better men than Somerset ii 4 98
The arbitrator of despairs, Just death, kind umpire of men's miseries ii 5 29
An uproar, I dare warrant, Begun through malice of the bishop's men iii 1 76
Gloucester's men . . . Have fill'd their pockets full of pebble stones iii 1 78
My forces and my power of men are yours iii 3 83
In which assault we lost twelve hundred men iv 1 24
Good Lord, what madness rules in brainsick men! iv 1 111
Small curs are not regarded when they grin; But great men tremble when the lion roars 2 *Hen. VI.* iii 1 19
Men's flesh preserved so whole do seldom win iii 1 301
To Ireland will you lead a band of men, Collected choicely? iii 1 312
'Tis politicly done, To send me packing with an host of men iii 1 342
'Twas men I lack'd and you will give them me: I take it kindly iii 1 345
I wear no knife to slaughter sleeping men iii 2 197
Pernicious blood-sucker of sleeping men! iii 2 226
The traitorous Warwick with the men of Bury Set all upon me iii 2 240
Blaspheming God and cursing men on earth iii 2 372
Can I make men live, whether they will or no? iii 3 10
Who, with their drowsy, slow and flagging wings, Clip dead men's graves iv 1 6
Small things make base men proud iv 1 106
Great men oft die by vile bezonians iv 1 134
Which is as much to say as, let the magistrates be labouring men iv 2 19
Follow me. Now show yourselves men; 'tis for liberty iv 2 193
Spare none but such as go in clouted shoon; For they are thrifty honest men iv 2 196
O graceless men! they know not what they do iv 4 38
Thou hast men about thee that usually talk of a noun and a verb iv 7 42
Thou hast appointed justices of peace, to call poor men before them iv 7 46
Thou oughtest not to let thy horse wear a cloak, when honester men than thou go in their hose and doublets iv 7 55
You men of Kent,— What say you of Kent? iv 7 59
Great men have reaching hands: oft have I struck Those that I never saw iv 7 86
Long sitting to determine poor men's causes Hath made me full of sickness iv 7 93
Men shall hold of me in capite iv 7 131
Now is Cade driven back, his men dispersed iv 9 34
I have eat no meat these five days; yet, come thou and thy five men iv 10 42
And dead men's cries do fill the empty air v 2 4
York not our old men spares; No more will I their babes v 2 51
He slily stole away and left his men 3 *Hen. VI.* i 1 3
Or I will fill the house with armed men i 1 167
She is hard by with twenty thousand men i 2 51
We'll meet her in the field.—What, with five thousand men? i 2 67
Let's set our men in order, And issue forth and bid them battle straight i 2 70
Five men to twenty! though the odds be great, I doubt not, uncle, of our victory i 2 72
I am too mean a subject for thy wrath: Be thou revenged on men i 3 20
They have demean'd themselves Like men born to renown by life or death i 4 8
So true men yield, with robbers so o'ermatch'd i 4 64
For with a band of thirty thousand men Comes Warwick ii 2 68
A thousand men have broke their fasts to-day, That ne'er shall dine unless thou yield the crown ii 2 127
Sad-hearted men, much overgone with care, Here sits a king more woful than you are ii 5 123
Let me embrace thee, sour adversity, For wise men say it is the wisest course iii 1 25
A man at least, for less I should not be; And men may talk of kings iii 1 58
Ah, simple men, you know not what you swear! iii 1 83
Commanded always by the greater gust; Such is the lightness of you common men iii 1 89
Thou and Oxford, with five thousand men, Shall cross the seas iii 3 234
You in our behalf Go levy men, and make prepare for war iv 1 131
To-morrow then belike shall be the day, If Warwick be so near as men report iv 3 8
What fates impose, that men must needs abide iv 3 58
He shall here find his friends with horse and men To set him free iv 5 12
For few men rightly temper with the stars iv 6 29
For many men that stumble at the threshold Are well foretold that danger lurks within iv 7 11
Let's levy men, and beat him back again iv 8 6
Shalt find Men well inclined to hear what thou command'st iv 8 16
Great lords, wise men ne'er sit and wail their loss But cheerly seek how to redress their harms v 4 1
I'll plague ye for that word.—Ay, thou wast born to be a plague to men v 5 28
Men ne'er spend their fury on a child v 5 57
Men for their sons, wives for their husbands, And orphans for their parents' timeless death—Shall rue the hour that ever thou wast born v 6 41
And this word 'love,' which greybeards call divine, Be resident in men like one another And not in me v 6 82
Two braver men Ne'er spurr'd their coursers at the trumpet's sound v 7 8
Why, this it is, when men are ruled by women *Richard III.* i 1 62
It is our way, If we will keep in favour with the king, To be her men and wear her livery i 1 80
But shall I live in hope?—All men, I hope, live so i 2 201

Men. Because I cannot flatter and speak fair, Smile in men's faces *Richard III.* i 3 48
A thousand fearful wrecks; Ten thousand men that fishes gnaw'd upon i 4 25
Some lay in dead men's skulls i 4 29
Are you call'd forth from out a world of men To slay the innocent? i 4 186
I hate it, and desire all good men's love ii 1 61
When clouds appear, wise men put on their cloaks ii 3 32
Untimely storms make men expect a dearth ii 3 35
Truly, the souls of men are full of dread ii 3 38
By a divine instinct men's minds mistrust Ensuing dangers ii 3 42
Oft have I heard of sanctuary men; But sanctuary children ne'er till now iii 1 55
'Tis a vile thing to die, my gracious lord, When men are unprepared iii 2 65
So 'twill do With some men else, who think themselves as safe As thou and I iii 2 68
When I met this holy man, Those men you talk of came into my mind iii 2 118
O momentary grace of mortal men, Which we more hunt for than the grace of God! iii 4 98
When holy and devout religious men Are at their beads, 'tis hard to draw them thence, So sweet is zealous contemplation iii 7 92
Even that, I hope, which pleaseth God above, And all good men iii 7 110
Cousin of Buckingham, and you sage, grave men iii 7 227
And die, ere men can say, God save the queen! iv 1 63
Come, muster men: my counsel is my shield; We must be brief iv 3 56
Men shall deal unadvisedly sometimes, Which after hours give leisure to repent iv 4 292
Go muster men; but, hear you, leave behind Your son, George Stanley iv 4 496
What men of name resort to him? iv 5 8
Thus doth he force the swords of wicked men To turn their own points on their masters' bosoms v 1 23
Call for some men of sound direction: Let's want no discipline v 3 16
If we be conquer'd, let men conquer us, And not these bastard Bretons v 3 332
What men of name are slain on either side? v 5 12
Those suns of glory, those two lights of men *Hen. VIII.* i 1 6
Men might say, Till this time pomp was single, but now married i 1 14
Men fear'd the French would prove perfidious, To the king's danger i 2 156
Is't possible the spells of France should juggle Men into such strange mysteries? i 3 2
Abusing better men than they can be, Out of a foreign wisdom i 3 28
And understand again like honest men; Or pack to their old playfellows i 3 32
Men of his way should be most liberal; They are set here for examples i 3 61
Nor build their evils on the graves of great men ii 1 67
Both Fell by our servants, by those men we loved most ii 1 122
Loves him with that excellence That angels love good men with ii 2 35
All men's honours Lie like one lump before him ii 2 48
These reverend fathers; men Of singular integrity and learning ii 4 58
Now I think on't, They should be good men iii 1 22
To deliver, Like free and honest men, our just opinions iii 1 60
Ye speak like honest men; pray God, ye prove so! iii 1 69
With my weak wit, And to such men of gravity and learning iii 1 73
Full little, God knows, looking Either for such men or such business iii 1 76
Holy men I thought ye, Upon my soul, two reverend cardinal virtues iii 1 102
Now, all my joy Trace the conjunction!—My amen to't!—All men's! iii 2 45
Follow your envious courses, men of malice; You have Christian warrant for 'em iii 2 243
By the main assent Of all these learned men she was divorced iv 1 32
Those men are happy; and so are all are near her iv 1 50
Men's evil manners live in brass; their virtues We write in water iv 2 45
But to those men that sought him sweet as summer iv 2 54
Those men are happy that shall have 'em iv 2 147
My men; they are the poorest, But poverty could never draw 'em from me iv 2 148
But we all are men, In our own natures frail, and capable Of our flesh v 3 10
Men that make Envy and crooked malice nourishment Dare bite the best v 3 43
Your painted gloss discovers, To men that understand you, words and weakness v 3 72
Men so noble, However faulty, yet should find respect For what they have been v 3 74
Men's prayers then would seek you, not their fears v 3 83
I take my cause Out of the gripes of cruel men v 3 100
I had thought I had had men of some understanding And wisdom v 3 135
Was rather, If there be faith in men, meant for his trial v 3 151
We are but men; and what so many may do, Not being torn a-pieces, we have done v 4 79
All the best men are ours; for 'tis ill hap, If they hold when their ladies bid 'em clap Epil. 13
Stands alone.—So do all men, unless they are drunk *Troi. and Cres.* i 2 17
Men prize the thing ungain'd more than it is i 2 315
The protractive trials of great Jove To find persistive constancy in men i 3 21
In the reproof of chance Lies the true proof of men i 3 34
This Trojan scorns us; or the men of Troy Are ceremonious courtiers i 3 233
If he fail, Yet go we under our opinion still That we have better men i 3 384
Young men, whom Aristotle thought Unfit to hear moral philosophy ii 2 166
An all men were o' my mind,— Wit would be out of fashion ii 3 225
At whose request do these men play?—That's to't indeed iii 1 31
I wish'd myself a man, Or that we women had men's privileges Of speaking first iii 2 136
Let all constant men be Troiluses, all false women Cressids iii 2 210
Greatness, once fall'n out with fortune, Must fall out with men too iii 3 76
Men, like butterflies, Show not their mealy wings but to the summer iii 3 78
I do enjoy At ample point all that I did possess, Save these men's looks iii 3 90
O heavens, what some men do, While some men leave to do! iii 3 132
How some men creep in skittish fortune's hall, Whiles others play the idiots! iii 3 134
Those wounds heal ill that men do give themselves iii 3 229
Prithee, tarry: You men will never tarry iv 2 16
Dare all imminence that gods and men Address their dangers in v 10 13
Though soft-conscienced men can be content to say it was for his country *Coriolanus* i 1 38
That the gods sent not Corn for the rich men only i 1 212
You souls of geese, That bear the shapes of men i 4 35
Know you on which side They have placed their men of trust? i 6 52
And four shall quickly draw out my command, Which men are best inclined i 6 85
You two are old men: tell me one thing that I shall ask you ii 1 15
I must be content to bear with those that say you are reverend grave men ii 1 66
Death, that dark spirit, in 's nervy arm doth lie; Which, being advanced, declines, and then men die ii 1 178
Yet, by the faith of men, We have some old crab-trees at home ii 1 204

Men. I have seen the dumb men throng to see him and The blind to hear him *Coriolanus* ii 1 278
There have been many great men that have flattered the people ii 2 9
As weeds before A vessel under sail, so men obey'd ii 2 110
He did Run reeking o'er the lives of men, as if 'Twere a perpetual spoil ii 2 123
Have you not known The worthiest men have done't? ii 3 55
Keep Rome in safety, and the chairs of justice Supplied with worthy men! iii 3 35
Whose loves I prize As the dead carcasses of unburied men iii 3 122
That common chances common men could bear iv 1 5
If I had fear'd death, of all the men i' the world I would have 'voided thee iv 5 87
Peace is a very apoplexy, lethargy; mulled, deaf, sleepy, insensible; a getter of more bastard children than war's a destroyer of men iv 5 241
And it [peace] makes men hate one another iv 5 245
Tullus Aufidius, The second name of men, obeys his points iv 6 125
You guard like men; 'tis well: but, by your leave, I am an officer of state v 2 2
The book of his good acts, whence men have read His fame unparallel'd v 2 15
Let him choose Out of my files, his projects to accomplish, My best and freshest men v 6 35
Pages blush'd at him and men of heart Look'd wondering each at other v 6 99
Cut me to pieces, Volsces; men and lads, Stain all your edges on me v 6 112
Thanks to men Of noble minds is honourable meed *T. Andron.* i 1 215
I do remit these young men's heinous faults i 1 484
O reverend tribunes! O gentle, aged men! Unbind my sons, reverse the doom of death iii 1 23
And tribunes with their tongues doom men to death iii 1 47
If that be call'd deceit, I will be honest, And never, whilst I live, deceive men so iii 1 190
Let fools do good, and fair men call for grace iii 1 205
I have heard my grandsire say full oft, Extremity of griefs would make men mad iv 1 19
No big-boned men framed of the Cyclops' size; But metal, Marcus iv 3 46
A matter of brawl betwixt my uncle and one of the emperial's men iv 3 94
A power Of high-resolved men, bent to the spoil iv 4 64
He can at pleasure stint their melody: Even so mayst thou the giddy men of Rome iv 4 87
Make poor men's cattle break their necks v 1 132
Oft have I digg'd up dead men from their graves, And set them upright v 1 135
Rapine and Murder; therefore called so, Cause they take vengeance of such kind of men v 2 63
We worldly men Have miserable, mad, mistaking eyes v 2 65
You sad-faced men, people and sons of Rome, By uproar sever'd v 3 67
O, pardon me; For when no friends are by, men praise themselves v 3 118
Therefore I will push Montague's men from the wall, and thrust his maids to the wall *Rom. and Jul.* i 1 21
The quarrel is between our masters and us their men i 1 24
When I have fought with the men, I will be cruel with the maids i 1 26
Draw, if you be men. Gregory, remember thy swashing blow i 1 69
Put up thy sword, Or manage it to part these men with me i 1 76
What, ho! you men, you beasts, That quench the fire of your pernicious rage i 1 90
Once more, on pain of death, all men depart i 1 110
'Tis not hard, I think, For men so old as we to keep the peace i 2 3
Such comfort as do lusty young men feel When well-apparell'd April on the heel Of limping winter treads i 2 26
No less! nay, bigger; women grow by men i 3 95
Drawn with a team of little atomies Athwart men's noses i 4 58
When good manners shall lie all in one or two men's hands and they unwashed too, 'tis a foul thing i 5 5
Young men's love then lies Not truly in their hearts, but in their eyes ii 3 67
Pronounce this sentence then, Women may fall, when there's no strength in men ii 3 80
Though his face be better than any man's, yet his leg excels all men's ii 5 41
We talk here in the public haunt of men iii 1 53
Men's eyes were made to look, and let them gaze; I will not budge iii 1 57
There's no trust, No faith, no honesty in men; all perjured iii 2 86
Flies may do this, but I from this must fly: They are free men, but I am banished iii 3 42
Madmen have no ears.—How should they, when that wise men have no eyes? iii 3 62
O fortune, fortune! all men call thee fickle iii 5 60
O'er-cover'd quite with dead men's rattling bones, With reeky shanks iv 1 82
Answer me like men iv 5 127
O mischief, thou art swift To enter in the thoughts of desperate men! v 1 36
If you had the strength Of twenty men, it would dispatch you straight v 1 79
There is thy gold, worse poison to men's souls v 1 80
How oft when men are at the point of death Have they been merry! v 3 88
With instruments upon them, fit to open These dead men's tombs v 3 201
This gentleman of mine hath served me long: To build his fortune I will strain a little, For 'tis a bond in men *T. of Athens* i 1 144
He speaks the common tongue, Which all men speak with him i 1 175
O you gods, what a number of men eat Timon, and he sees 'em not! i 2 40
I wonder men dare trust themselves with men i 2 44
Great men should drink with harness on their throats i 2 53
Rich men sin, and I eat root. Much good dich thy good heart, Apemantus! i 2 72
Spend our flatteries, to drink those men Upon whose age we void it up again i 2 142
Men shut their doors against a setting sun i 2 150
Where be our men?—Here, my lord, in readiness.—Our horses! i 2 171
O, that men's ears should be To counsel deaf, but not to flattery! i 2 256
Poor rogues, and usurers' men! bawds between gold and want! ii 2 61
Are you three usurers' men?—Ay, fool ii 2 101
When men come to borrow of your masters, they approach sadly, and go away merry ii 2 105
Men and men's fortunes could I frankly use As I can bid thee speak ii 2 188
One of Lord Timon's men? a gift, I warrant iii 1 4
One of his men was with the Lord Lucullus to borrow so many talents iii 2 12
Timon's money Has paid his men their wages iii 2 77
He does deny him, in respect of his, What charitable men afford to beggars iii 2 82
Men must learn now with pity to dispense; For policy sits above conscience iii 2 93
Why do fond men expose themselves to battle, And not endure all threats? iii 5 42
Nor more willingly leaves winter; such summer-birds are men iii 6 34
Were your godheads to borrow of men, men would forsake the gods iii 6 84
Plagues, incident to men, Your potent and infectious fevers heap On Athens! iv 1 21

Men. For bounty, that makes gods, does still mar men *T. of Athens* iv 2 41
Therefore, be abhorr'd All feasts, societies, and throngs of men! iv 3 21
This [gold] Will . . Pluck stout men's pillows from below their heads iv 3 32
Those milk-paps, That through the window-bars bore at men's eyes, Are not within the leaf of pity writ iv 3 116
Consumptions sow In hollow bones of man; strike their sharp shins, And mar men's spurring iv 3 153
I never did thee harm.—Yes, thou spokest well of me.—Call'st thou that harm?—Men daily find it iv 3 174
Men report Thou dost affect my manners, and dost use them iv 3 198
Myself, Who had the world as my confectionary, The mouths, the tongues, the eyes and hearts of men At duty iv 3 261
Why shouldst thou hate men? They never flatter'd thee iv 3 269
If thou hadst not been born the worst of men, Thou hadst been a knave iv 3 275
What things in the world canst thou nearest compare to thy flatterers?—Women nearest; but men, men are the things themselves iv 3 320
What wouldst thou do with the world, Apemantus, if it lay in thy power?—Give it the beasts, to be rid of the men iv 3 324
Wouldst thou have thyself fall in the confusion of men, and remain a beast? iv 3 326
Moe things like men! Eat, Timon, and abhor them iv 3 398
We are not thieves, but men that much do want iv 3 418
Nor on the beasts themselves, the birds, and fishes; You must eat men iv 3 428
I have forgot all men; Then, if thou grant'st thou'rt a man, I have forgot thee iv 3 480
As rich men deal gifts, Expecting in return twenty for one iv 3 516
Thou shalt build from men; Hate all, curse all, show charity to none iv 3 533
Give to dogs What thou deny'st to men; let prisons swallow 'em iv 3 537
Be men like blasted woods, And may diseases lick up their false bloods! iv 3 538
Wilt thou whip thine own faults in other men? v 1 41
Have I once lived to see two honest men? v 1 59
Let it go naked, men may see't the better v 1 70
We are hither come to offer you our service.—Most honest men! v 1 76
Ye're honest men: ye've heard that I have gold; I am sure you have v 1 79
At all times alike Men are not still the same v 1 125
Sack fair Athens, And take our goodly aged men by the beards v 1 175
Graves only be men's works and death their gain! Sun, hide thy beams! v 1 225
Here lie I, Timon; who, alive, all living men did hate v 4 72
As proper men as ever trod upon neat's leather *J. Cæsar* i 1 28
Why dost thou lead these men about the streets? i 1 32
O you hard hearts, you cruel men of Rome, Knew you not Pompey? i 1 41
For this fault, Assemble all the poor men of your sort i 1 62
Make him fly an ordinary pitch, Who else would soar above the view of men i 1 79
With himself at war, Forgets the shows of love to other men i 2 47
If you know That I do fawn on men and hug them hard i 2 75
I cannot tell what you and other men Think of this life i 2 93
We petty men Walk under his huge legs and peep about i 2 136
Men at some time are masters of their fates i 2 139
Let me have men about me that are fat; Sleek-headed men and such as sleep o' nights i 2 192
He thinks too much: such men are dangerous i 2 195
He is a great observer and he looks Quite through the deeds of men i 2 203
Such men as he be never at heart's ease Whiles they behold a greater than themselves, And therefore are they very dangerous i 2 208
Which gives men stomach to digest his words With better appetite i 2 305
Who swore they saw Men all in fire walk up and down the streets i 3 25
Let not men say 'These are their reasons; they are natural' i 3 29
Men may construe things after their fashion, Clean from the purpose of the things themselves i 3 34
What night is this!—A very pleasing night to honest men i 3 43
It is the part of men to fear and tremble, When the most mighty gods by tokens send Such dreadful heralds i 3 54
Why old men fool and children calculate i 3 65
Know I these men that come along with you?—Yes, every man of them ii 1 89
If not the face of men, The sufferance of our souls, the time's abuse ii 1 114
Swear priests and cowards and men cautelous, Old feeble carrions ii 1 129
Unto bad causes swear Such creatures as men doubt ii 1 132
His silver hairs Will purchase us a good opinion And buy men's voices ii 1 146
He will never follow any thing That other men begin ii 1 152
We all stand up against the spirit of Cæsar; And in the spirit of men there is no blood ii 1 168
Unicorns may be betray'd with trees, And bears with glasses, elephants with holes, Lions with toils, and men with flatterers ii 1 206
Boy! Lucius! Fast asleep? . . . Thou hast no figures, nor no fantasies, Which busy care draws in the brains of men ii 1 232
Unfold to me . . . what men to-night Have had resort to you ii 1 275
A piece of work that will make sick men whole ii 1 327
Dying men did groan, And ghosts did shriek and squeal about the streets ii 2 23
Of all the wonders that I yet have heard, It seems to me most strange that men should fear ii 2 35
Great men shall press For tinctures, stains, relics and cognizance ii 2 88
There is but one mind in all these men ii 3 6
These lowly courtesies Might fire the blood of ordinary men iii 1 37
So in the world; 'tis furnish'd well with men, And men are flesh and blood, and apprehensive iii 1 67
Men, wives and children stare, cry out and run As it were doomsday iii 1 97
'Tis but the time And drawing days out, that men stand upon iii 1 100
So often shall the knot of us be call'd The men that gave their country liberty iii 1 118
A curse shall light upon the limbs of men iii 1 262
This foul deed shall smell above the earth With carrion men, groaning for burial iii 1 275
Try, In my oration, how the people take The cruel issue of these bloody men iii 1 294
Had you rather Cæsar were living and die all slaves, than that Cæsar were dead, to live all free men? iii 2 26
The evil that men do lives after them; The good is oft interred with their bones iii 2 80
Brutus is an honourable man; So are they all, all honourable men iii 2 88
O judgement! thou art fled to brutish beasts, And men have lost their reason iii 2 110
You are not wood, you are not stones, but men; And, being men, hearing the will of Cæsar, It will inflame you, it will make you mad iii 2 147
Action, nor utterance, nor the power of speech, To stir men's blood iii 2 227
Which, out of use and staled by other men, Begin his fashion iv 1 38
But hollow men, like horses hot at hand, Make gallant show iv 2 23
For mine own part, I shall be glad to learn of noble men iv 3 54

Men. Love, and be friends, as two such men should be *J. Cæsar* iv 3 131
Even so great men great losses should endure iv 3 193
There is a tide in the affairs of men, Which, taken at the flood, leads on to fortune; Omitted, all the voyage of their life Is bound in shallows iv 3 218
Call . . my men; I'll have them sleep on cushions in my tent iv 3 242
Since the affairs of men rest still incertain, Let's reason with the worst v 1 96
Why dost thou show to the apt thoughts of men The things that are not? v 3 68
I had rather have Such men my friends than enemies v 4 29
With furbish'd arms and new supplies of men Began a fresh assault *Macb.* i 2 32
Nor would we deign him burial of his men i 2 60
Your face, my thane, is as a book where men May read strange matters i 5 63
Where we are, There's daggers in men's smiles ii 3 146
Sirrah, a word with you: attend those men Our pleasure? iii 1 45
We are men, my liege.—Ay, in the catalogue ye go for men iii 1 92
As hounds and greyhounds, mongrels, spaniels, curs, . . . are clept All by the name of dogs . . : and so of men iii 1 101
He does usually, So all men do, from hence to the palace gate Make it their walk iii 3 13
Men must not walk too late iii 6 7
'Twould have anger'd any heart alive To hear the men deny't iii 6 16
Who must hang them?—Why, the honest men iv 2 55
There are liars and swearers enow to beat the honest men and hang up them iv 2 58
And like good men Bestride our down-fall'n birthdom iv 3 3
Old Siward, with ten thousand warlike men, Already at a point iv 3 134
Good men's lives Expire before the flowers in their caps iv 3 171
Turn, hell-hound, turn!—Of all men else I have avoided thee v 8 4
Sit still, my soul: foul deeds will rise, Though all the earth o'erwhelm them, to men's eyes *Hamlet* i 2 258
Oft it chances in particular men, That for some vicious mole of nature in them, . . . that these men . . . Shall in the general censure take corruption From that particular fault i 4 23
Sure I am two men there are not living To whom he more adheres ii 2 20
The satirical rogue says here that old men have grey beards ii 2 199
For the law of writ and the liberty, these are the only men ii 2 421
Wise men know well enough what monsters you make of them iii 1 143
That I have thought some of nature's journeymen had made men and not made them well, they imitated humanity so abominably iii 2 38
Since my dear soul was mistress of her choice And could of men distinguish iii 2 69
To my shame, I see The imminent death of twenty thousand men iv 4 60
Young men will do't, if they come to't; By cock, they are to blame iv 5 61
But our cold maids do dead men's fingers call them iv 7 172
'Twill not be seen in him there; there the men are as mad as he v 1 170
Let this same be presently perform'd, Even while men's minds are wild v 2 405
That which ordinary men are fit for, I am qualified in *Lear* i 4 36
This is not altogether fool, my lord.—No, faith, lords and great men will not let me i 4 166
Wise men are grown foppish, They know not how their wits to wear i 4 182
Men so disorder'd, so debosh'd and bold i 4 263
Such men as may besort your age, And know themselves and you i 4 272
Men of choice and rarest parts, That all particulars of duty know i 4 285
Horses are tied by the heads, dogs and bears by the neck, monkeys by the loins, and men by the legs ii 4 9
All that follow their noses are led by their eyes but blind men ii 4 71
O heavens, If you do love old men, if your sweet sway Allow obedience ii 4 193
Return to her, and fifty men dismiss'd? No, rather I abjure all roofs ii 4 210
O, sir, to wilful men, The injuries that they themselves procure Must be their schoolmasters ii 4 305
All the plagues that in the pendulous air Hang fated o'er men's faults iii 4 70
Our power Shall do a courtesy to our wrath, which men May blame iii 7 26
Think that the clearest gods, who make them honours Of men's impossibilities, have preserved thee iv 6 74
Go to, they are not men o' their words: they told me I was every thing iv 6 106
Men must endure Their going hence, even as their coming hither v 2 9
Know thou this, that men Are as the time is v 3 30
Howl, howl, howl, howl! O, you are men of stones v 3 257
Though in the trade of war I have slain men, Yet do I hold it very stuff o' the conscience To do no contrived murder *Othello* i 2 1
I fetch my life and being From men of royal siege i 2 22
The Anthropophagi and men whose heads Do grow beneath their shoulders i 3 144
Men do their broken weapons rather use Than their bare hands i 3 174
Of a free and open nature, That thinks men honest that but seem to be so i 3 406
Ye men of Cyprus, let her have your knees. Hail to thee, lady! ii 1 84
Base men being in love have then a nobility in their natures ii 1 217
As if some planet had unwitted men ii 3 182
But men are men; the best sometimes forget ii 3 241
As men in rage strike those that wish them best ii 3 243
That men should put an enemy in their mouths to steal away their brains! ii 3 291
Men should be what they seem; Or those that be not, would they might seem none!—Certain, men should be what they seem iii 3 126
There are a kind of men so loose of soul, That in their sleeps will mutter their affairs iii 3 416
In such cases Men's natures wrangle with inferior things iii 4 144
Nay, we must think men are not gods, Nor of them look for such observances As fit the bridal iii 4 148
If I court moe women, you'll couch with moe men iv 3 57
O, these men, these men! iv 3 60
And have not we affections, Desires for sport, and frailty, as men have? iv 3 102
Kill men i' the dark!—Where be these bloody thieves?—How silent is this town! v 1 63
Yet she must die, else she'll betray more men v 2 6
It is the very error of the moon; She comes more nearer earth than she was wont, And makes men mad v 2 111
You have done well, That men must lay their murders on your neck v 2 170
Let heaven and men and devils, let them all, All, all, cry shame against me, yet I'll speak v 2 221
A man who is the abstract of all faults That all men follow *Ant. and Cleo.* i 4 10
Men's reports Give him much wrong'd i 4 39
The demi-Atlas of this earth, the arm And burgonet of men i 5 24
If thou with Cæsar paragon again My man of men i 5 72
If the great gods be just, they shall assist The deeds of justest men ii 1 2
Would we had all such wives, that the men might go to wars with the women! ii 2 66
Whose beauty claims No worse a husband than the best of men ii 2 131

Men. All men's faces are true, whatsome'er their hands are . *A. and C.* ii 6 102
Why, this it is to have a name in great men's fellowship . . . ii 7 13
Cæsar? Why, he's the Jupiter of men.—What's Antony? The god of Jupiter . . . iii 2 9
Wars 'twixt you twain would be As if the world should cleave, and that slain men Should solder up the rift . . . iii 4 31
The trees by the way Should have borne men . . . iii 6 47
A good rebuke, Which might have well becomed the best of men . iii 7 27
So our leader's led, And we are women's men . . . . . iii 7 71
I see men's judgements are A parcel of their fortunes . . . iii 13 31
When mine hours Were nice and lucky, men did ransom lives Of me for jests . . . . iii 13 180
He thinks, being twenty times of better fortune, He is twenty men to one . . . . iv 2 4
I wish I could be made so many men, And all of you clapp'd up together in An Antony . . . . iv 2 16
O, my fortunes have Corrupted honest men! . . . . . iv 5 17
Make a jolly march; Bear our hack'd targets like the men that owe them . . . . iv 8 31
When men revolted shall upon record Bear hateful memory . . iv 9 8
Noblest of men, woo't die? Hast thou no care of me? . . iv 15 59
Young boys and girls Are level now with men; the odds is gone . iv 15 66
But you, gods, will give us Some faults to make us men . . v 1 33
Rememberest thou any that have died on't?—Very many, men and women too . . . . v 2 250
Which the gods give men To excuse their after wrath . . . v 2 289
What, are men mad? Hath nature given them eyes? . . *Cymbeline* i 6 32
But, heavens know, Some men are much to blame . . . . i 6 77
He enchants societies into him; Half all men's hearts are his . . i 6 168
He sits 'mongst men like a descended god: He hath a kind of honour . i 6 169
They are in a trunk, Attended by my men . . . . . . i 6 197
His meanest garment, That ever hath but clipp'd his body, is dearer In my respect than all the hairs above thee, Were they all made such men . . . . ii 3 141
Our countrymen Are men more order'd than when Julius Cæsar Smiled at their lack of skill . . . . . . ii 4 21
Is there no way for men to be but women Must be half-workers? . ii 5 1
Julius Cæsar, whose remembrance yet Lives in men's eyes . . iii 1 3
Lovers And men in dangerous bonds pray not alike . . . iii 2 37
O, Men's vows are women's traitors! . . . . . . iii 4 56
True honest men being heard, like false Æneas, Were in his time thought false . . . . iii 4 60
So thou, Posthumus, Wilt lay the leaven on all proper men . . iii 4 64
Great men, That had a court no bigger than this cave . . . iii 6 82
Since the common men are now in action . . . . . . iii 7 2
Let me make men know More valour in me than my habits show . v 1 29
The odds Is that we scarce are men and you are gods . . . v 2 10
The strait pass was damm'd With dead men hurt behind . . v 3 12
Cried to those that fled, 'Our Britain's harts die flying, not our men' v 3 24
You are more clement than vile men, Who of their broken debtors take a third, A sixth, a tenth . . . . v 4 18
Whose father then, as men report Thou orphans' father art . . v 4 39
Open'd, in despite Of heaven and men, her purposes . . . v 5 59
He was too good to be Where ill men were . . . . . v 5 159
The purchase is to make men glorious . . . . *Pericles* i Gower 9
Which to prevent he made a law, To keep her still, and men in awe i Gower 36
Her thoughts the king Of every virtue gives renown to men! . . i 1 14
As sick men do Who know the world, see heaven, but, feeling woe, Gripe not at earthly joys as erst they did . . . . . i 1 47
So I bequeath a happy peace to you And all good men . . . i 1 51
O you powers That give heaven countless eyes to view men's acts, Why cloud they not their sights perpetually? . . . . . . i 1 73
Those men Blush not in actions blacker than the night . . . i 1 134
Our men be vanquish'd ere they do resist . . . . . i 2 27
Whereas reproof, obedient and in order, Fits kings, as they are men i 2 43
Whose men and dames so jetted and adorn'd, Like one another's glass . i 4 26
Let not our ships and number of our men Be like a beacon fired . i 4 86
And harbourage for ourself, our ships, and men . . . . i 4 100
The curse of heaven and men succeed their evils! . . . . i 4 104
Be quiet then as men should be, Till he hath pass'd necessity ii Gower 5
He, doing so, put forth to seas, Where when men been, there's seldom ease . . . . ii Gower 28
I am thinking of the poor men that were cast away before us even now ii 1 19
I marvel how the fishes live in the sea.—Why, as men do a-land . ii 1 31
How from the finny subject of the sea These fishers tell the infirmities of men; And from their watery empire recollect All that may men approve or men detect! . . . . ii 1 53
Whom nature gat For men to see, and seeing wonder at . . . ii 2 7
Time's the king of men, He's both their parent, and he is their grave ii 3 45
Since men take women's gifts for impudence . . . . . ii 3 69
Was by the rough seas reft of ships and men . . . . . ii 3 84
Since they [ladies] love men in arms as well as beds . . . ii 3 98
Get fire and meat for these poor men: 'T has been a turbulent and stormy night . . . . iii 2 3
Such a maidenhead were no cheap thing, if men were as they have been iv 2 65
If it please the gods to defend you by men, then men must comfort you, men must feed you, men must stir you up . . . . iv 2 97
Menace. Your eyes do menace me: why look you pale? . *Richard III.* i 4 175
And fearfully did menace me with death, If I did stay *Rom. and Jul.* v 3 133
Who ever knew the heavens menace so? . . . . *J. Cæsar* i 3 44
Divisions in state, menaces and maledictions against king and nobles *Lear* i 2 159
Menaced. From this league Peep'd harms that menaced him *Hen. VIII.* i 1 183
To whom by oath he menaced Revenge upon the cardinal . . i 2 137
Menaphon. That most famous warrior, Duke Menaphon *Com. of Errors* v 1 368
Menas. Menecrates and Menas, famous pirates . . *Ant. and Cleo.* i 4 48
I know not, Menas, How lesser enmities may give way to greater . ii 1 42
Give me your hand, Menas: if our eyes had authority, here they might take two thieves kissing . . . . ii 6 99
Here's to thee, Menas! . . . . ii 7 92
And Lepidus, Since Pompey's feast, as Menas says, is troubled With the green sickness . . . . iii 2 5
Men at arms. Have at you, then, affection's men at arms . *L. L. Lost* iv 3 290
Men-children. Bring forth men-children only; For thy undaunted mettle should compose Nothing but males . . . *Macbeth* i 7 72
Mend. Canst thou believe thy living is a life, So stinkingly depending? Go mend, go mend . . . . . . *Meas. for Meas.* iii 2 28
Thus I mend it . . . . *Com. of Errors* ii 2 107
That's a fault that water will mend.—No, sir, 'tis in grain . iii 2 107
We'll mend our dinner here? . . . . iv 3 60
Serve God, love me, and mend . . . . . . *Much Ado* v 2 95

Mend. Where fair is not, praise cannot mend the brow . *L. L. Lost* iv 1 17
In ushering Mend him who can: the ladies call him sweet . . v 2 329
If you pardon, we will mend . . . . . . *M. N. Dream* v 1 437
We will mend thy wages . . . . *As Y. Like It* ii 4 94
Mend the instance . . . . iii 2 70
And so God mend me, and by all pretty oaths . . . . iv 1 193
God mend your voices! . . . . v 3 42
I'll mend it with a largess . . . . . . *T. of Shrew* i 2 151
You pluck my foot awry: Take that, and mend the plucking off the other iv 1 151
'Twould mend the lottery well . . . . . . *All's Well* i 3 92
He will look upon his boot and sing; mend the ruff and sing . iii 2 7
Bid the dishonest man mend himself; if he mend, he is no longer dishonest; if he cannot, let the botcher mend him . . *T. Night* i 5 50
Doth he not mend?—Yes, and shall do till the pangs of death shake him i 5 80
This is an art Which does mend nature, change it rather . *W. Tale* iv 4 96
Garlic, To mend her kissing with! . . . . iv 4 163
I cannot mend it, I must needs confess, Because my power is weak and all ill left . . . . *Richard II.* ii 3 153
Revolt our subjects? that we cannot mend . . . . . iii 2 100
Ere I lead this life long, I'll sew nether stocks and mend them *1 Hen. IV.* ii 4 130
'As true as I live,' and 'as God shall mend me' . . . . iii 1 255
His highness is fallen into this same whoreson apoplexy.—Well, God mend him! . . . . *2 Hen. IV.* i 2 124
I would thou wert a man's tailor, that thou mightst mend him and make him fit to go . . . . iii 2 176
It will serve you to mend your shoes . . . . . *Hen. V.* iv 8 74
God mend all! . . . . *Hen. VIII.* i 2 201
You have now a broken banquet; but we'll mend it . . . i 4 61
Cardinal sins and hollow hearts I fear ye: Mend 'em, for shame, my lords iii 1 105
Let her be as she is: if she be fair, 'tis the better for her; an she be not, she has the mends in her own hands . . *Troi. and Cres.* i 1 68
Mend and charge home, Or, by the fires of heaven, I'll leave the foe And make my wars on you . . . . . . *Coriolanus* i 4 38
Something too rough; You must return and mend it . . . iii 2 26
What here shall miss, our toil shall strive to mend *Rom. and Jul.* Prol. 14
God shall mend my soul! You'll make a mutiny among my guests! . i 5 81
You mend the jewel by the wearing it . . . *T. of Athens* i 1 172
I will mend thy feast.—First mend my company, take away thyself.—So I shall mend mine own, by the lack of thine.—'Tis not well mended so, it is but botch'd . . . . iv 3 284
'Tis not monstrous in you, neither wish I You take much pains to mend v 1 92
My long sickness Of health and living now begins to mend . . v 1 190
What is amiss plague and infection mend! . . . . . v 1 224
Be not out with me: yet, if you be out, sir, I can mend you . *J. Cæsar* i 1 18
I would set my life on any chance, To mend it, or be rid on't *Macbeth* iii 1 114
Your dull ass will not mend his pace with beating . . . *Hamlet* v 1 64
Mend your speech a little, Lest it may mar your fortunes . . *Lear* i 1 96
Mend when thou canst; be better at thy leisure: I can be patient . ii 4 232
Since it is as it is, mend it for your own good . . . *Othello* ii 3 304
Heaven me such uses send, Not to pick bad from bad, but by bad mend! iv 3 106
Our worser thoughts heavens mend! . . . . . *Ant. and Cleo.* i 2 64
Still he mends; But this is not the best . . . . . . i 3 82
To mend the petty present, I will piece Her opulent throne with kingdoms . . . . i 5 45
Your crown's awry; I'll mend it . . . . v 2 322
They are people such That mend upon the world . . . *Cymbeline* ii 4 26
Heaven mend all! . . . . v 5 68
Mended. Well, that fault may be mended with a breakfast *T. G. of Ver.* iii 1 328
Mended again. The matter; proceed . . . *Meas. for Meas.* v 1 91
Think but this, and all is mended . . . . . *M. N. Dream* v 1 431
Be patient; to-morrow 't shall be mended . . . *T. of Shrew* iv 1 179
Very well mended. Kiss him for that . . . . . . v 2 25
Would that have mended my hair? . . . . . *T. Night* i 3 102
Any thing that's mended is but patched . . . . . . i 5 52
Show now your mended faiths . . . . *K. John* v 7 75
Which he mended thus, By now forswearing that he is forsworn *1 Hen. IV.* v 2 38
Will this gear ne'er be mended? . . . . . *Troi. and Cres.* i 1 6
'Tis not well mended so, it is but botch'd; If not, I would it were *T. of A.* iv 3 285
Upon my mended judgement—if I offend not to say it is mended *Cymb.* i 4 49
Mender. A mender of bad soles . . . . *J. Cæsar* i 1 15
Mending. Happy are they that hear their detractions and can put them to mending . . . . *Much Ado* ii 3 239
Why, this is like the mending of highways In summer . *Mer. of Venice* v 1 263
When he speaks, 'Tis like a chime a-mending . . *Troi. and Cres.* i 3 159
Menecrates and Menas, famous pirates . . . *Ant. and Cleo.* i 4 48
Menelaus. Helen of Greece was fairer far than thou, Although thy husband may be Menelaus . . . . *3 Hen. VI.* ii 2 147
Within whose strong immures The ravish'd Helen, Menelaus' queen, With wanton Paris sleeps . . . . . . *Troi. and Cres.* Prol. 9
Let Paris bleed: 'tis but a scar to scorn; Paris is gored with Menelaus' horn . . . . i 1 115
Who, in your thoughts, merits fair Helen best, Myself or Menelaus? . iv 1 54
The first was Menelaus' kiss; this, mine: Patroclus kisses you . . iv 5 32
Who must we answer?—The noble Menelaus . . . . . iv 5 176
In what place of the field doth Calchas keep?—At Menelaus' tent . iv 5 279
But to be Menelaus! I would conspire against destiny . . . v 1 69
I care not to be the louse of a lazar, so I were not Menelaus . . v 1 72
Sweet Lord Menelaus.—Sweet draught: 'sweet' quoth 'a! sweet sink . v 1 81
Menenius Agrippa; one that hath always loved the people *Coriolanus* i 1 52
Menenius, you are known well enough too . . . . . ii 1 49
Honourable Menenius, my boy Marcius approaches; for the love of Juno, let's go.—Ha! Marcius coming home!—Ay, worthy Menenius ii 1 110
Ever right.—Menenius ever, ever . . . . ii 1 209
Noble Menenius, Be you then as the people's officer . . . iii 1 329
With old Menenius, and those senators That always favour'd him . iii 3 7
Thou old and true Menenius, Thy tears are salter than a younger man's iv 1 21
Is this Menenius?—'Tis he, 'tis he: O, he is grown most kind of late . iv 6 10
It is lots to blanks, My name hath touch'd your ears: it is Menenius v 2 11
Remember my name is Menenius, always factionary on the party of your general . . . . v 2 30
And love thee no worse than thy old father Menenius does! . . v 2 76
Another word, Menenius, I will not hear thee speak . . . v 2 97
Now, sir, is your name Menenius?—'Tis a spell, you see, of much power v 2 101
Menon. The fierce Polydamas Hath beat down Menon . *Troi. and Cres.* v 5 7
Mental. The still and mental parts, That do contrive how many hands shall strike, When fitness calls them on . . . . . . i 3 200
'Twixt his mental and his active parts Kingdom'd Achilles in commotion rages And batters down himself . . . . ii 3 184
What a mental power This eye shoots forth! . . . *T. of Athens* i 1 31

Menteith. The Earl of Athol, Of Murray, Angus, and Menteith 1 *Hen. IV.* i 1 73
Mention. And sleep in dull cold marble, where no mention Of me more must be heard of *Hen. VIII.* iii 2 433
And, dying, mention it within their wills *J. Cæsar* iii 2 140
Mentioned. And remember well, I mentioned a son o' the king's *W. Tale* iv 1 22
And hid the gold within the letter mention'd *T. Andron.* v 1 107
Mentis. Tanta est erga te mentis integritas, regina serenissima *Hen. VIII.* iii 1 40
Menton. De sin. Le col, de nick; le menton, de sin *Hen. V.* iii 4 38
Mephostophilus. How now, Mephostophilus! *Mer. Wives* i 1 132
Mercade. Welcome, Mercade; But that thou interrupt'st our merriment.—I am sorry, madam *L. L. Lost* v 2 724
Mercatante. A mercatante, or a pedant, I know not what *T. of Shrew* iv 2 63
Mercatio. What think'st thou of the rich Mercatio?—Well of his wealth; but of himself, so so *T. G. of Ver.* i 2 12
Mercenary. My mind was never yet more mercenary *Mer. of Venice* iv 1 418
Lie drown'd and soak'd in mercenary blood *Hen. V.* iv 7 79
Sixteen hundred mercenaries iv 8 93
He waged me with his countenance, as if I had been mercenary *Coriol.* v 6 41
Mercer. Master Three-pile the mercer *Meas. for Meas.* iv 3 11
Merchandise. As from a voyage, rich with merchandise *M. N. Dream* ii 1 134
I know, Antonio Is sad to think upon his merchandise *Mer. of Venice* i 1 40
My merchandise makes me not sad.—Why, then you are in love i 1 45
Were he out of Venice, I can make what merchandise I will iii 1 134
So, if a son that is by his father sent about merchandise do sinfully miscarry upon the sea *Hen. V.* iv 1 155
Wert thou as far As that vast shore wash'd with the farthest sea, I would adventure for such merchandise *Rom. and Jul.* ii 2 84
The merchandise which thou hast brought from Rome Are all too dear for me: lie they upon thy hand *Ant. and Cleo.* ii 5 104
Merchant. Every day some sailor's wife, The masters of some merchant and the merchant Have just our theme of woe *Tempest* ii 1 5
Merchant of Syracusa, plead no more *Com. of Errors* i 1 3
Sprung from the rancorous outrage of your duke To merchants i 1 7
Therefore, merchant, I'll limit thee this day To seek thy life i 1 151
A Syracusian merchant Is apprehended for arrival here i 2 3
I am invited, sir, to certain merchants, Of whom I hope to make much benefit i 2 24
Perhaps some merchant hath invited him ii 1 4
A reverend Syracusian merchant, Who put unluckily into this bay v 1 124
Even there where merchants most do congregate *Mer. of Venice* i 3 50
What news among the merchants? iii 1 26
How doth that royal merchant, good Antonio? iii 2 242
Twenty merchants, The duke himself, and the magnificoes Of greatest port, have all persuaded with him iii 2 281
The penalty, Which is a pound of this poor merchant's flesh iv 1 23
Losses Enow to press a royal merchant down iv 1 29
I acquainted him with the cause in controversy between the Jew and Antonio the merchant iv 1 156
Which is the merchant here, and which the Jew? iv 1 174
This strict court of Venice Must needs give sentence 'gainst the merchant there iv 1 205
And lawfully by this the Jew may claim A pound of flesh, to be by him cut off Nearest the merchant's heart iv 1 233
You, merchant, have you any thing to say? iv 1 263
A pound of that same merchant's flesh is thine: The court awards it iv 1 299
A merchant of great traffic through the world *T. of Shrew* i 1 12
Now I play a merchant's part, And venture madly on a desperate mart ii 1 328
I have heard of him; A merchant of incomparable wealth iv 2 98
There's a whole merchant's venture of Bourdeaux stuff in him 2 *Hen. IV.* ii 4 68
Where some, like magistrates, correct at home, Others, like merchants, venture trade abroad *Hen. V.* i 2 192
This is a riddling merchant for the nonce 1 *Hen. VI.* ii 3 57
For France hath flaw'd the league, and hath attach'd Our merchants' goods at Bourdeaux *Hen. VIII.* i 1 96
Let it be call'd the wild and wandering flood, Ourself the merchant *Troi. and Cres.* i 1 106
Let us, like merchants, show our foulest wares, And think, perchance, they'll sell i 3 359
We turn not back the silks upon the merchant, When we have soil'd them ii 2 69
And turn'd crown'd kings to merchants ii 2 83
What saucy merchant was this, that was so full of his ropery? *R. and J.* ii 4 153
I know the merchant *T. of Athens* i 1 7
Art not thou a merchant?—Ay, Apemantus.—Traffic confound thee! i 1 242
And believe, Cæsar's no merchant, to make prize with you Of things that merchants sold *Ant. and Cleo.* v 2 183
Merchant-like. Therefore, when merchant-like I sell revenge, Broke be my sword! 2 *Hen. VI.* iv 1 41
Merchant-marring. And not one vessel 'scape the dreadful touch Of merchant-marring rocks? *Mer. of Venice* iii 2 274
Merciful. Though the seas threaten, they are merciful *Tempest* v 1 178
Merciful Heaven, Thou rather with thy sharp and sulphurous bolt Split'st the unwedgeable and gnarled oak Than the soft myrtle *Meas. for Meas.* ii 2 114
Be good to me; your honour is accounted a merciful man iii 2 203
You have been always called a merciful man *Much Ado* iii 3 64
Then must the Jew be merciful.—On what compulsion must I? *M. of V.* iv 1 182
Be merciful: Take thrice thy money; bid me tear the bond iv 1 233
You are a merciful general *All's Well* iv 3 144
Though a present death Had been more merciful *W. Tale* ii 3 185
O, let us yet be merciful.—So may your highness, and yet punish too *Hen. V.* ii 2 47
Be merciful, great duke, to men of mould iii 2 23
Forsake this groom: The king is merciful, if you revolt 2 *Hen. VI.* iv 2 133
I shall both find your lordship judge and juror, You are so merciful *Hen. VIII.* v 3 61
Only in The merciful construction of good women Epil. 10
Wilt thou draw near the nature of the gods? Draw near them then in being merciful: Sweet mercy is nobility's true badge *T. Andron.* i 1 118
Be merciful, say 'death;' For exile hath more terror in his look *R. and J.* iii 3 12
If thou be merciful, Open the tomb, lay me with Juliet v 3 72
Merciful powers, Restrain in me the cursed thoughts that nature Gives way to in repose! *Macbeth* ii 1 7
Merciful heaven! What, man! ne'er pull your hat upon your brows iv 3 207
Not yet quite dead? I that am cruel am yet merciful; I would not have thee linger in thy pain *Othello* v 2 86
Mercifully. Mock me mercifully *Hen. V.* v 2 214
Merciless. O, had the gods done so, I had not now Worthily term'd them merciless to us! *Com. of Errors* i 1 100
All preparation for a bloody siege And merciless proceeding *K. John* ii 1 214
Merciless. A ragged multitude Of hinds and peasants, rude and merciless 2 *Hen. VI.* iv 4 33
The foe is merciless, and will not pity 3 *Hen. VI.* ii 6 25
O, 'twas the foulest deed to slay that babe, And the most merciless! *Richard III.* i 3 184
The merciless Macdonwald—Worthy to be a rebel *Macbeth* i 2 9
Mercurial. This is his hand; His foot Mercurial *Cymbeline* iv 2 310
Mercury. The words of Mercury are harsh after the songs of Apollo *L. L. Lost* v 2 940
Now Mercury endue thee with leasing, for thou speakest well of fools! *T. Night* i 5 105
Who being, as I am, littered under Mercury *W. Tale* iv 3 25
Be Mercury, set feathers to thy heels, And fly like thought *K. John* iv 2 174
Gallantly arm'd, Rise from the ground like feather'd Mercury 1 *Hen. IV.* iv 1 106
Following the mirror of all Christian kings, With winged heels, as English Mercuries *Hen. V.* ii Prol. 7
By your first order died, And that a winged Mercury did bear *Rich. III.* ii 1 88
Then fiery expedition be my wing, Jove's Mercury, and herald for a king! iv 3 55
Fly like chidden Mercury from Jove, Or like a star disorb'd *T. and C.* ii 2 45
And, Mercury, lose all the serpentine craft of thy caduceus! ii 3 13
Apollo, Pallas, Jove, or Mercury, Inspire me! *T. Andron.* iv 1 66
Here, boy, to Pallas: here, to Mercury: To Saturn, Caius iv 3 55
See, here's to Jove, and this to Mercury; This to Apollo iv 4 14
A station like the herald Mercury New-lighted on a heaven-kissing hill *Hamlet* iii 4 58
Had I great Juno's power, The strong-wing'd Mercury should fetch thee up, And set thee by Jove's side *Ant. and Cleo.* iv 15 35
Mercutio and his brother Valentine *Rom. and Jul.* i 2 70
Peace, peace, Mercutio, peace! Thou talk'st of nothing i 4 95
Call, good Mercutio.—Nay, I'll conjure too. Romeo! humours! madman! ii 1 6
Pardon, good Mercutio, my business was great ii 4 53
Good Mercutio, let's retire: The day is hot, the Capulets abroad iii 1 1
Mercutio, thou consort'st with Romeo,— Consort! what, dost thou make us minstrels? iii 1 48
I am for you.—Gentle Mercutio, put thy rapier up.—Come, sir iii 1 87
Tybalt, Mercutio, the prince expressly hath Forbidden bandying in Verona streets: Hold, Tybalt! good Mercutio! iii 1 91
Brave Mercutio's dead! That gallant spirit hath aspired the clouds iii 1 121
Alive, in triumph! and Mercutio slain! Away to heaven, respective lenity, And fire-eyed fury be my conduct now! iii 1 127
Mercutio's soul Is but a little way above our heads, Staying for thine iii 1 131
Which way ran he that kill'd Mercutio? Tybalt, that murderer, which way ran he? iii 1 142
There lies the man, slain by young Romeo, That slew thy kinsman, brave Mercutio.—Tybalt, my cousin! iii 1 150
But that he tilts With piercing steel at bold Mercutio's breast iii 1 164
An envious thrust from Tybalt hit the life Of stout Mercutio iii 1 174
Romeo slew him, he slew Mercutio; Who now the price of his dear blood doth owe?—Not Romeo, prince, he was Mercutio's friend iii 1 187
Let me peruse this face. Mercutio's kinsman, noble County Paris! v 3 75
Mercy. The king my father wreck'd.—Alack, for mercy! *Tempest* i 2 436
Mercy, mercy! This is a devil, and no monster ii 2 101
I'll turn my mercy out o' doors and make a stock-fish of thee iii 2 78
At this hour Lie at my mercy all mine enemies iv 1 264
Unless I be relieved by prayer, Which pierces so that it assaults Mercy itself Epil. 18
Mortality and mercy in Vienna Live in thy tongue and heart *M. for M.* i 1 45
Mercy is not itself, that oft looks so; Pardon is still the nurse of second woe ii 1 297
I do think that you might pardon him, And neither heaven nor man grieve at the mercy ii 2 50
Not . . . the deputed sword, The marshal's truncheon, nor the judge's robe, Become them with one half so good a grace As mercy does ii 2 63
Mercy then will breathe within your lips, Like man new made ii 2 78
Lawful mercy Is nothing kin to foul redemption ii 4 112
There is a devilish mercy in the judge, If you'll implore it iii 1 65
Mercy to thee would prove itself a bawd iii 1 150
He knew the service, and that instructed him to mercy iii 2 128
This would make mercy swear and play the tyrant iii 2 207
When vice makes mercy, mercy's so extended, That for the fault's love is the offender friended iv 2 115
The very mercy of the law cries out Most audible v 1 412
Should she kneel down in mercy of this fact, Her brother's ghost his paved bed would break v 1 439
I crave death more willingly than mercy; 'Tis my deserving v 1 481
Take this mercy to provide For better times to come v 1 489
God, for thy mercy! they are loose again *Com. of Errors* iv 4 147
If I know more of any man alive Than that which maiden modesty doth warrant, Let all my sins lack mercy! *Much Ado* iv 1 182
Now mercy goes to kill, And shooting well is then accounted ill *L. L. L.* iv 1 24
Write, 'Lord have mercy on us' on those three; They are infected v 2 419
That lie within the mercy of your wit v 2 856
And leave thee to the mercy of wild beasts *M. N. Dream* ii 1 228
I cry your worships mercy, heartily: I beseech your worship's name iii 1 182
Gaoler, look to him: tell not me of mercy *Mer. of Venice* iii 3 1
He tells me flatly, there is no mercy for me in heaven iii 5 35
Uncapable of pity, void and empty From any dram of mercy iv 1 6
Then 'tis thought Thou'lt show thy mercy and remorse more strange Than is thy strange apparent cruelty iv 1 20
How shalt thou hope for mercy, rendering none? iv 1 88
The quality of mercy is not strain'd, It droppeth as the gentle rain iv 1 184
But mercy is above this sceptred sway; It is enthroned in the hearts of kings, It is an attribute to God himself iv 1 193
Earthly power doth then show likest God's When mercy seasons justice iv 1 197
We do pray for mercy; And that same prayer doth teach us all to render The deeds of mercy iv 1 202
The offender's life lies in the mercy Of the duke iv 1 355
Beg mercy of the duke.—Beg that thou mayst have leave to hang thyself iv 1 363
What mercy can you render him, Antonio?—A halter gratis; nothing else iv 1 378
Cupid have mercy! not a word? *As Y. Like It* i 3 2
Were I not the better part made mercy, I should not seek an absent argument iii 1 2
Cry the man mercy; love him; take his offer iii 5 61
O mercy, God! what masquing stuff is here? What's this *T. of Shrew* iv 3 87
God's mercy, maiden! does it curd thy blood To say I am thy mother? *All's Well* i 3 155
I would you had kneel'd, my lord, to ask me mercy.—I would I had; so I had broke thy pate, And ask'd thee mercy for't ii 1 66
Lord have mercy on thee for a hen! ii 3 224

Mercy. For our pleasure and his penance, till our very pastime, tired out of breath, prompt us to have mercy on him *T. Night* iii 4 152
Fare thee well; and God have mercy upon one of our souls! He may have mercy upon mine; but my hope is better iii 4 184
What foolish boldness brought thee to their mercies? v 1 73
These petty brands That calumny doth use—O, I am out—That mercy does, for calumny will sear Virtue itself *W. Tale* ii 1 73
And that there thou leave it, Without more mercy, to it own protection ii 3 178
Whom I proclaim a man of truth, of mercy iii 2 158
Name of mercy, when was this, boy? iii 3 105
If I talk to him, with his innocent prate He will awake my mercy *K. John* iv 1 26
You do lack That mercy which fierce fire and iron extends iv 1 120
Beyond the infinite and boundless reach Of mercy iv 3 118
God for his mercy! what a tide of woes! *Richard II.* ii 2 98
And make you stoop Unto the sovereign mercy of the king iii 3 157
Let them have That mercy which true prayer ought to have v 3 110
Let my soul Want mercy, if I do not join with him *1 Hen. IV.* i 3 132
And roared for mercy and still run and roared, as ever I heard bull-calf ii 4 286
There is no seeming mercy in the king.—Did you beg any? God forbid! v 2 35
Here I commit my body to your mercies *2 Hen. IV.* Epil. 15
This offer comes from mercy, not from fear iv 1 150
Rouse up fear and trembling, and do observance to my mercy iv 3 17
That's mercy, but too much security: Let him be punish'd *Hen. V.* ii 2 44
Sir, You show great mercy, if you give him life ii 2 50
I do confess my fault; And do submit me to your highness' mercy ii 2 77
The mercy that was quick in us but late, By your own counsel is suppress'd and kill'd: You must not dare, for shame, to talk of mercy ii 2 79
God quit you in his mercy! Hear your sentence ii 2 166
God of his mercy give You patience to endure, and true repentance! ii 2 179
Take mercy On the poor souls for whom this hungry war Opens his vasty jaws ii 4 103
Therefore to our best mercy give yourselves iii 3 3
The gates of mercy shall be all shut up iii 3 10
We yield our town and lives to thy soft mercy iii 3 48
Fortify it strongly 'gainst the French: Use mercy to them all iii 3 54
Besides, in mercy, The constable desires thee thou wilt mind Thy followers of repentance iv 3 83
As I suck blood, I will some mercy show iv 4 68
And not a man of them that we shall take Shall taste our mercy iv 7 68
O Lord, have mercy on us, wretched sinners! *1 Hen. VI.* i 4 70
O Lord, have mercy on me, woful man! i 4 71
Heaven, be thou gracious to none alive, If Salisbury wants mercy at thy hands! i 4 86
Then God take mercy on brave Talbot's soul! iv 3 34
And left thee to the mercy of the law *2 Hen. VI.* i 3 137
But God in mercy so deal with my soul, As I in duty love my king! i 3 160
The spite of man prevaileth against me. O Lord, have mercy upon me! i 3 219
Will ye relent, And yield to mercy whilst 'tis offer'd you? iv 8 12
Better ten thousand base-born Cades miscarry Than you should stoop unto a Frenchman's mercy iv 8 50
And kneel for grace and mercy at my feet; I am thy sovereign *3 Hen. VI.* i 1 75
Yield to our mercy, proud Plantagenet.—Ay, to such mercy as his ruthless arm, With downright payment, show'd unto my father i 4 30
Open Thy gate of mercy, gracious God! My soul flies through these wounds i 4 177
Let him be gently used.—Revoke that doom of mercy ii 6 46
Clifford, ask mercy and obtain no grace ii 6 69
My mercy dried their water-flowing tears iv 8 43
Bend thy knee, Call Edward king and at his hands beg mercy v 1 23
There's no hoped-for mercy with the brothers More than with ruthless waves v 4 35
God take King Edward to his mercy, And leave the world for me! *Richard III.* i 1 151
Have mercy, Jesu!—Soft! I did but dream v 3 178
Cry mercy, lords and watchful gentlemen, That you have ta'en a tardy sluggard here.—How have you slept? v 3 224
Call him to present trial: if he may Find mercy in the law, 'tis his; if none, Let him not seek 't of us *Hen. VIII.* i 2 212
For further life in this world I ne'er hope, Nor will I sue, although the king have mercies More than I dare make faults ii 1 70
Far from his succour, from the king, from all That might have mercy on the fault iii 2 262
And now has left me, Weary and old with service, to the mercy Of a rude stream, that must for ever hide me iii 2 363
Is there no other way of mercy, But I must needs to the Tower? v 3 92
Juno have mercy! how came it cloven? *Troi. and Cres.* i 2 133
If e'er thou stand at mercy of my sword, Name Cressid iv 4 116
You have a vice of mercy in you, Which better fits a lion than a man v 3 37
At once let your brief plagues be mercy, And linger not our sure destructions on! v 10 8
What good condition can a treaty find I' the part that is at mercy? *Cor.* i 10 7
I would not buy Their mercy at the price of one fair word iii 3 91
We are all undone, unless The noble man have mercy iv 6 108
A mile before his tent fall down, and knee The way into his mercy v 1 6
Mean to solicit him For mercy to his country v 1 73
While the Volsces May say 'This mercy we have show'd;' the Romans, 'This we received' v 3 137
I am glad thou hast set thy mercy and thy honour At difference in thee v 3 200
He wants nothing of a god but eternity and a heaven to throne in.—Yes, mercy, if you report him truly v 4 27
Mark what mercy his mother shall bring from him v 4 29
There is no more mercy in him than there is milk in a male tiger v 4 30
Sweet mercy is nobility's true badge *T. Andron.* i 1 119
And at thy mercy shall they stoop and kneel v 2 118
Mercy but murders, pardoning those that kill *Rom. and Jul.* iii 1 202
This is dear mercy, and thou seest it not.—'Tis torture, and not mercy iii 3 28
Live, and hereafter say, A madman's mercy bade thee run away v 3 67
Nothing emboldens sin so much as mercy *T. of Athens* iii 5 3
To kill, I grant, is sin's extremest gust; But, in defence, by mercy, 'tis most just iii 5 55
Spare not the babe, Whose dimpled smiles from fools exhaust their mercy iv 3 119
But shift away: there's warrant in that theft Which steals itself, when there's no mercy left *Macbeth* ii 3 152
The king-becoming graces, As justice, verity, temperance, stableness, Bounty, perseverance, mercy, lowliness iv 3 93
Here, as before, never, so help you mercy *Hamlet* i 5 169
So grace and mercy at your most need help you i 5 180
Whereto serves mercy But to confront the visage of offence? iii 3 46
God ha' mercy on his soul! And of all Christian souls, I pray God iv 5 199
They have dealt with me like thieves of mercy iv 6 21

Mercy. He may enguard his dotage with their powers, And hold our lives in mercy *Lear* i 4 350
Is it the fashion, that discarded fathers Should have thus little mercy on their flesh? iii 4 75
As for the mercy Which he intends to Lear and to Cordelia, The battle done, and they within our power, Shall never see his pardon v 1 65
Then heaven Have mercy on me!—Amen, with all my heart! *Othello* v 2 34
Then Lord have mercy on me!—I say, amen.—And have you mercy too! v 2 57
Whip him, fellows, Till, like a boy, you see him cringe his face, And whine aloud for mercy *Ant. and Cleo.* iii 13 101
Wert thou a man, Thou wouldst have mercy on me v 2 175
And question'dst every sail: if he should write, And I not have it, 'twere a paper lost, As offer'd mercy is *Cymbeline* i 3 4
So children temporal fathers do appease; Gods are more full of mercy v 4 13
This mercy shows we'll joy in such a son *Pericles* i 1 118
Cry you mercy *T. G. of Ver.* v 4 94; *Lear* iii 6 54
I cry you (thee) mercy *Mer. Wives* iii 5; *Meas. for Meas.* iv 1; *Much Ado* i 2; ii 1; *1 Hen. IV.* i 3; iv 2; *1 Hen. VI.* v 3; *2 Hen. VI.* i 3; *Richard III.* i 3; ii 2; iv 4; *Hen. VIII.* v 3; *Rom. and Jul.* iv 5; *Othello* iv 2; v 1
Mercy-lacking.—Creatures of note for mercy-lacking uses *K. John* iv 1 121
Mercy on me! I have a great dispositions to cry *Mer. Wives* iii 1 22
Mercy on me! Methinks no body should be sad but I *K. John* iv 1 12
Mercy o' me, what a multitude are here! They grow still too *Hen. VIII.* v 4 71
Mercy on us!—We split, we split! *Tempest* i 1 63
Mercy on 's, a barne; a very pretty barne! *W. Tale* iii 3 70
Mercy sake. 'Pless you from his mercy sake, all of you! *Mer. Wives* iii 1 42
Mercy upon us!—Art thou afeard?—No, monster, not I *Tempest* iii 2 141
Mere. Out, alas, sir! cozenage, mere cozenage! *Mer. Wives* iv 5 64
The mere effusion of thy proper loins *Meas. for Meas.* iii 1 30
Upon his mere request, Being come to knowledge that there was complaint v 1 152
A mere anatomy, a mountebank *Com. of Errors* v 1 238
She must lie here on mere necessity *L. L. Lost* i 1 149
If I break faith, this word shall speak for me; I am forsworn on 'mere necessity' i 1 155
He speaks the mere contrary i 2 35
Engaged my friend to his mere enemy, To feed my means *Mer. of Venice* iii 2 265
Is but a quintain, a mere lifeless block *As Y. Like It* i 2 263
Swearing that we Are mere usurpers, tyrants ii 1 61
Second childishness and mere oblivion ii 7 165
Most friendship is feigning, most loving mere folly ii 7 181
Whose judgements are Mere fathers of their garments *All's Well* i 2 62
The mere word's a slave Debosh'd on every tomb ii 3 144
Think you it is so?—Ay, surely, mere the truth iii 5 58
My determinate voyage is mere extravagancy *T. Night* ii 1 12
It is but weakness To bear the matter thus; mere weakness *W. Tale* ii 3 2
This is mere falsehood iii 2 142
The prince your son, with mere conceit and fear Of the queen's speed, is gone iii 2 145
Mere dislike Of our proceedings kept the earl from hence *1 Hen. IV.* iv 1 64
Honour is a mere scutcheon v 1 143
But this is mere digression from my purpose *2 Hen. IV.* iv 1 140
And learning a mere hoard of gold kept by a devil iv 3 124
Submission, Dauphin! 'tis a mere French word *1 Hen. VI.* iv 7 54
In regard King Henry gives consent, Of mere compassion and of lenity v 4 125
Mere instinct of love and loyalty . . . Makes them thus forward *2 Hen. VI.* iii 2 250
Your mere enforcement shall acquittance me *Richard III.* iii 7 233
Madam, this is a mere distraction *Hen. VIII.* iii 1 112
Out of mere ambition iii 2 324
To the mere undoing Of all the kingdom iii 2 329
I am stifled With the mere rankness of their joy iv 1 59
What discord follows! each thing meets In mere oppugnancy *Tr. and Cr.* i 3 111
And may that soldier a mere recreant prove, That means not, hath not, or is not in love! i 3 287
I with great truth catch mere simplicity iv 4 106
Words, words, mere words, no matter from the heart v 3 108
But in mere spite *Coriolanus* iv 5 88
A mere satiety of commendations *T. of Athens* i 1 166
Whose bare unhoused trunks, To the conflicting elements exposed, Answer mere nature iv 3 231
I am sick of this false world, and will love nought But even the mere necessities upon't iv 3 377
The mere want of gold, and the falling-from of his friends iv 3 401
When thy first griefs were but a mere conceit v 4 14
It was mere foolery; I did not mark it *J. Cæsar* i 2 236
The wine of life is drawn, and the mere lees Is left *Macbeth* ii 3 100
Foisons to fill up your will, Of your mere own iv 3 89
Pitiful to the eye, The mere despair of surgery, he cures iv 3 152
But mere implorators of unholy suits *Hamlet* i 3 129
Fair judgement, Without the which we are pictures, or mere beasts iv 5 86
This is mere madness: And thus awhile the fit will work on him v 1 307
They are weary? They have travell'd all the night? Mere fetches *Lear* ii 4 90
Full oft 'tis seen, Our means secure us, and our mere defects Prove our commodities iv 1 22
Mere prattle, without practice, Is all his soldiership *Othello* i 1 26
But I, for mere suspicion in that kind, Will do as if for surety i 3 395
Putting on the mere form of civil and humane seeming ii 1 243
Tidings now arrived, importing the mere perdition of the Turkish fleet ii 2 3
The loyalty well held to fools does make Our faith mere folly *Ant. and Cleo.* iii 13 43
To thy further fear, Nay, to thy mere confusion, thou shalt know *Cymb.* iv 2 92
Your pleasure was my mere offence, my punishment Itself v 5 334
Seldom but that pity begets you a good opinion, and that opinion a mere profit *Pericles* iv 2 132
Merely. We are merely cheated of our lives by drunkards *Tempest* i 1 59
Merely, thou art death's fool *Meas. for Meas.* iii 1 11
Thoughts are no subjects; Intents but merely thoughts.—Merely, my lord v 1 459
That's the scene that I would see, which will be merely a dumb-show *Much Ado* ii 3 226
He shall have merely justice and his bond *Mer. of Venice* iv 1 339
All the world's a stage, And all the men and women merely players: They have their exits and their entrances *As Y. Like It* ii 7 140
Love is merely a madness iii 2 420
To forswear the full stream of the world and to live in a nook merely monastic iii 2 441
What things are we!—Merely our own traitors *All's Well* iv 3 25
What they will inform, Merely in hate, 'gainst any of us all *Richard II.* ii 1 243
These external manners of laments Are merely shadows to the unseen grief iv 1 297

Merely. As far as I see, all the good our English Have got by the late voyage is but merely A fit or two o' the face . . . *Hen. VIII.* i 3 6
Merely to revenge him on the emperor . . . . . ii 1 162
I propose not merely to myself The pleasures . *Troi. and Cres.* ii 2 146
This is clean kam.—Merely awry . . . . *Coriolanus* iii 1 305
That their society, as their friendship, may Be merely poison ! *T. of A.* iv 1 32
That which I show, heaven knows, is merely love . . . iv 3 522
I turn the trouble of my countenance Merely upon myself . *J. Cæsar* i 2 39
Things rank and gross in nature Possess it merely . . *Hamlet* i 2 137
The very substance of the ambitious is merely the shadow of a dream . ii 2 264
It is merely a lust of the blood and a permission of the will . *Othello* i 3 339
The horse were merely lost . . . . . *Ant. and Cleo.* iii 7 9
Give up yourself merely to chance and hazard, From firm security . iii 7 48
Mine honour was not yielded, But conquer'd merely . . . iii 13 62
Some falling Merely through fear . . . . *Cymbeline* v 3 11
Merest. He cried upon it at the merest loss . . . *T. of Shrew* Ind. 1 23
Meridian. From that full meridian of my glory, I haste now to my setting : I shall fall Like a bright exhalation . . *Hen. VIII.* iii 2 224
Merit. Plead a new state in thy unrival'd merit . . *T. G. of Ver.* v 4 144
Let her consider his frailty, and then judge of my merit *Mer. Wives* iii 5 52
What a merit were it in death to take this poor maid ! *Meas. for Meas.* iii 1 240
Let it be thy part To praise him more than ever man did merit *M. Ado* iii 1 19
Never gives to truth and virtue that Which simpleness and merit purchaseth . . . . iii 1 70
See, see, my beauty will be saved by merit ! . . . *L. L. Lost* iv 1 21
Our sport shall be to take what they mistake : And what poor duty cannot do, noble respect Takes it in might, not merit *M. N. Dream* v 1 92
Who shall go about To cozen fortune and be honourable Without the stamp of merit ? . . . . . *Mer. of Venice* ii 9 39
That clear honour Were purchased by the merit of the wearer ! . ii 9 43
This kindness merits thanks . . . . *T. of Shrew* iv 3 41
Who ever strove To show her merit, that did miss her love ? *All's Well* i 1 242
Inspired merit so by breath is barr'd . . . . ii 1 151
France is a dog-hole, and it no more merits The tread of a man's foot ii 3 291
The merit of service is seldom attributed to the true and exact performer iii 6 63
And your father's blest, As he from heaven merits it . *W. Tale* v 1 175
Nothing do I see in you . . . That I can find should merit any hate *K. John* ii 1 520
By the merit of vile gold, dross, dust, Purchase corrupted pardon of a man iii 1 165
A dearer merit, not so deep a maim As to be cast forth in the common air, Have I deserved at your highness' hands . *Richard II.* i 3 156
Right noble is thy merit, well I wot . . . . . v 6 18
If men were to be saved by merit, what hole in hell were hot enough for him ? This is the most omnipotent villain *1 Hen. IV.* i 2 120
You see, my good wenches, how men of merit are sought after *2 Hen. IV.* ii 4 405
And shall forget the office of our hand, Sooner than quittance of desert and merit . . . . *Hen. V.* ii 2 34
A fellow, look you now, of no merits . . . . . v 1 8
May Iden live to merit such a bounty ! . . *2 Hen. VI.* v 1 81
The force of his own merit makes his way . . *Hen. VIII.* i 1 64
And choice . . . Makes merit her election . *Troi. and Cres.* i 3 349
What merit's in that reason which denies The yielding of her up ? . ii 2 24
The will dotes that is attributive To what infectiously itself affects, Without some image of the affected merit . . . ii 2 60
Nor, by my will, assubjugate his merit . . . . . ii 3 202
Our head shall go bare till merit crown it . . . . iii 2 99
As place, riches, favour, Prizes of accident as oft as merit . iii 3 83
Who, in your thoughts, merits fair Helen best, Myself or Menelaus ? . iv 1 53
He merits well to have her, that doth seek her, Not making any scruple of her soilure . . . . iv 1 55
Both merits poised, each weighs nor less nor more . . . iv 1 65
I do not call your faith in question So mainly as my merit . . iv 4 87
And all his faults To Marcius shall be honours, though indeed In aught he merit not . . . . *Coriolanus* i 1 280
He should have show'd us His marks of merit . . . . ii 3 172
This so dishonour'd rub, laid falsely I' the plain way of his merit . iii 1 61
But he has a merit, To choke it in the utterance . . . iv 7 48
Wisely too fair, To merit bliss by making me despair . *Rom. and Jul.* i 1 228
Hear all, all see, And like her most whose merit most shall be . i 2 31
You bate too much of your own merits . . . *T. of Athens* i 2 212
The less they deserve, the more merit is in your bounty . *Hamlet* ii 2 558
The insolence of office and the spurns That patient merit of the unworthy takes . . . . iii 1 74
Our largest bounty may extend Where nature doth with merit challenge *Lear* i 1 54
A provoking merit, set a-work by a reproveable badness in himself . iii 5 8
So to use them As we shall find their merits and our safety May equally determine . . . . v 3 44
One that, in the authority of her merit, did justly put on the vouch of very malice itself . . . . *Othello* ii 1 147
Reputation is . . . oft got without merit, and lost without deserving . ii 3 270
Nor from mine own weak merits will I draw The smallest fear or doubt of her revolt ; For she had eyes, and chose me . . . iii 3 187
Nor my service past, nor present sorrows, Nor purposed merit in futurity iii 4 117
If for the sake of merit thou wilt hear me, Rise . *Ant. and Cleo.* ii 7 61
When we fall, We answer others' merits in our name . . v 2 178
If there were wealth enough for the purchase, or merit for the gift *Cymb.* i 4 91
I chiefly, That set thee on to this desert, am bound To load thy merit richly i 5 74
Why hast thou thus adjourn'd The graces for his merits due ? . v 4 79
It pleaseth you, my royal father, to express My commendations great, whose merit's less . . . . *Pericles* ii 2 9
'Tis more by fortune, lady, than by merit.—Call it by what you will ii 3 12
Merited. Whatsoever I have merited, either in my mind or in my means, meed, I am sure, I have received none . . *Mer. Wives* ii 2 210
Do a poor wronged lady a merited benefit . *Meas. for Meas.* iii 1 206
How I was in your grace, How merited to be so . . *W. Tale* i 2 49
And I have merited some love at his hands . . *Hen. V.* ii 6 25
More hath it merited ; that let it have . . . *T. Andron.* iii 1 197
More of thee merited than a band of Clotens Had ever scar for *Cymbeline* v 5 304
Meritorious. It hath done meritorious service . . *Mer. Wives* iv 2 217
And meritorious shall that hand be call'd . . . *K. John* iii 1 176
Seeing the deed is meritorious . . . . *2 Hen. VI.* iii 1 270
Merlin. Of the dreamer Merlin and his prophecies . *1 Hen. IV.* iii 1 150
This prophecy Merlin shall make . . . . . *Lear* iii 2 95
Mermaid. O, train me not, sweet mermaid, with thy note *Com. of Errors* iii 2 45
I'll stop mine ears against the mermaid's song . . . . iii 2 169
And heard a mermaid on a dolphin's back . . *M. N. Dream* ii 1 150
I'll drown more sailors than the mermaid shall . . *3 Hen. VI.* iii 2 186
Her gentlewomen, like the Nereides, So many mermaids *Ant. and Cleo.* ii 2 212
At the helm A seeming mermaid steers . . . . . ii 2 214

Mermaid-like, awhile they bore her up . . . . *Hamlet* iv 7 177
Merops' son,—Wilt thou aspire to guide the heavenly car? *T. G. of Ver.* iii 1 153
Merrier. These jests are out of season ; Reserve them till a merrier hour than this . . . . . . *Com. of Errors* i 2 69
But a merrier man, Within the limit of becoming mirth, I never spent an hour's talk withal . . . . . . *L. L. Lost* ii 1 66
And neeze and swear A merrier hour was never wasted there *M. N. Dream* ii 1 57
And would you yet I were merrier? . . . . *As Y. Like It* i 2 4
You are sad.—Indeed, I have been merrier . . . *K. John* iv 1 12
A merrier day did never yet greet Rome . . . . *Coriolanus* v 4 45
I am merrier to die than thou art to live . . . *Cymbeline* v 4 175
Merriest. 'Twas never merry world since, of two usuries, the merriest was put down . . . . *Meas. for Meas.* iii 2 7
'Tis ever common That men are merriest when they are from home *Hen. V.* i 2 272
Between two girls, which hath the merriest eye . . *1 Hen. VI.* ii 4 15
Merrily. On the bat's back I do fly After summer merrily . *Tempest* v 1 92
Merrily, merrily shall I live now Under the blossom that hangs on the bough . . . . v 1 93
There is either liquor in his pate or money in his purse when he looks so merrily . . . . *Mer. Wives* ii 1 198
Look'd he or red or pale, or sad or merrily ? . . *Com. of Errors* iv 2 4
Holding a trencher, jesting merrily . . . . . *L. L. Lost* v 2 477
Full merrily Hath this brave manage, this career, been run . . v 2 481
What, you look merrily ! . . . . . . *As Y. Like It* ii 7 11
And the other lives merrily because he feels no pain . . . iii 2 340
I play the noble housewife with the time, To entertain't so merrily with a fool . . . . *All's Well* ii 2 63
Jog on, jog on, the foot-path way, And merrily hent the stile-a *W. Tale* iv 3 133
I love a ballad but even too well, if it be doleful matter merrily set down iv 4 189
Now could thou and I rob the thieves and go merrily to London *1 Hen. IV.* ii 2 100
Now merrily to horse : The thieves are all scatter'd and possess'd with fear ii 2 111
Doomsday is near ; die all, die merrily . . . . . iv 1 134
Look how we can, or sad or merrily, Interpretation will misquote our looks . . . . v 2 12
Roam here and there So merrily, And ever among so merrily *2 Hen. IV.* v 3 22
Full merrily the humble-bee doth sing . . . *Troi. and Cres.* v 10 42
I will merrily accompany you home . . . . *Coriolanus* iv 3 41
Though news be sad, yet tell them merrily . . *Rom. and Jul.* ii 5 22
They enter my mistress' house merrily, and go away sadly *T. of Athens* ii 2 107
Look fresh and merrily ; Let not our looks put on our purposes *J. Cæsar* ii 1 224
Merriman. Brach Merriman, the poor cur is emboss'd *T. of Shrew* Ind. 1 17
Merriment. Rather . . . A merriment than a vice . *Meas. for Meas.* ii 4 116
They do it but in mocking merriment . . . . *L. L. Lost* v 2 139
Here was a consent, Knowing aforehand of our merriment, To dash it . v 2 461
Welcome, Mercade ; But that thou interrupt'st our merriment . v 2 725
And therefore met your loves In their own fashion, like a merriment . v 2 794
Stir up the Athenian youth to merriments . . . *M. N. Dream* i 1 13
I see you all are bent To set against me for your merriment . . iii 2 146
We have friends That purpose merriment . . . *Mer. of Venice* ii 2 212
Mirth and merriment, Which bars a thousand harms . *T. of Shrew* Ind. 2 137
See the truth hereof ; For our first merriment hath made thee jealous . iv 5 76
And strain their cheeks to idle merriment . . . . *K. John* iii 3 46
He will drive you out of your revenge and turn all to a merriment *2 Hen. IV.* ii 4 324
Yet nature's tears are reason's merriment . . . *Rom. and Jul.* iv 5 83
Flashes of merriment, that were wont to set the table on a roar *Hamlet* v 1 210
Merriness. Well, sir, be it as the style shall give us cause to climb in the merriness . . . . *L. L. Lost* i 1 202
Merry. Be merry ; you have cause, So have we all, of joy *Tempest* ii 1 1
Thou makest me merry ; I am full of pleasure . . . . iii 2 125
Come hither from the furrow and be merry . . . . iv 1 135
I cannot be merry.—Come, we'll have you merry . *T. G. of Ver.* iv 2 29
You are merry, so am I ; ha, ha ! then there's more sympathy *Mer. Wives* ii 1 8
Wives may be merry, and yet honest too . . . . . iv 2 107
Rather rejoicing to see another merry, than merry at any thing *M. for M.* iii 2 249
And, in despite of mirth, mean to be merry . . *Com. of Errors* iii 1 108
Your man and you are marvellous merry, sir . . . . iv 3 59
Laugh when I am merry and claw no man in his humour . *Much Ado* i 3 18
And there live we as merry as the day is long . . . . ii 1 52
It may be I go under that title because I am merry . . . ii 1 213
The count is neither sad, nor sick, nor merry, nor well . . ii 1 304
Your silence most offends me, and to be merry best becomes you . . ii 1 346
Some merry mocking lord, belike ; is't so?—They say so . *L. L. Lost* ii 1 52
Such a merry, nimble, stirring spirit, She might ha' been a grandam ere she died . . . . v 2 16
Though my mocks come home by me, I will now be merry . . v 2 638
A very good piece of work, I assure you, and a merry . *M. N. Dream* i 2 15
Merry and tragical ! tedious and brief ! That is, hot ice and wondrous strange snow . . . . v 1 58
You are sad, Because you are not merry : and 'twere as easy For you to laugh and leap and say you are merry, Because you are not sad *M. of V.* i 1 48
I would have stay'd till I had made you merry, If worthier friends had not prevented me . . . . i 1 60
Be merry, and employ your chiefest thoughts To courtship . . ii 8 43
I am never merry when I hear sweet music . . . . . v 1 69
I pray thee, Rosalind, sweet my coz, be merry . *As Y. Like It* i 2 2
Therefore, my sweet Rose, my dear Rose, be merry.—From henceforth I will . . . . i 2 25
Here was he merry, hearing of a song . . . . . ii 7 4
I had rather have a fool to make me merry than experience to make me sad iv 1 28
I will do that when you are disposed to be merry . . . iv 1 156
God rest you merry, sir . . . . v 1 65
Though he be merry, yet withal he's honest . . *T. of Shrew* iii 2 25
Be mad and merry, or go hang yourselves . . . . . iii 2 228
Nay, good sweet Kate, be merry. Off with my boots, you rogues ! . iv 1 146
What if a man bring him a hundred pound or two, to make merry withal? v 1 23
She has her health : she's very merry ; but yet she is not well *All's Well* ii 4 3
Tell's a tale.—Merry or sad shall't be?—As merry as you will *W. Tale* ii 1 23
Be merry, gentle ; Strangle such thoughts as these . . . iv 4 46
I could be merry now. Hubert, I love thee . . . *K. John* iii 3 67
So I were out of prison and kept sheep, I should be as merry as the day is long ; And so I would be here . . . . iv 1 18
Be merry, for our time of stay is short . . . *Richard II.* ii 1 223
Shall we be merry?—As merry as crickets, my lad . . *1 Hen. IV.* ii 4 99
Shall we be merry? shall we have a play extempore? . . . ii 4 308
If to be old and merry be a sin, then many an old host that I know is damned . . . . ii 4 518
Come sing me a bawdy song ; make me merry . . . . iii 3 16
Against ill chances men are ever merry . . . . *2 Hen. IV.* iv 2 81
Therefore be merry, coz ; since sudden sorrow Serves to say thus, 'some good thing comes to-morrow' . . . . iv 2 83

Merry. Be merry, Master Bardolph; and, my little soldier there, be merry . . . *2 Hen. IV.* v 3 33
Be merry, be merry, my wife has all . . . v 3 35
'Tis merry in hall when beards wag all, And welcome merry Shrove-tide v 3 38
Who, I? I have been merry twice and once ere now v 3 42
And make you merry with fair Katharine of France . . . . Epil. 30
Make merry, man, With thy confederates in this weighty cause *2 Hen. VI.* i 2 85
Hume must make merry with the duchess' gold i 2 87
Be merry, Peter, and fear not thy master: fight for credit of the 'prentices ii 3 70
I prithee, grieve, to make me merry, York . *3 Hen. VI.* i 4 86
See How soon this mightiness meets misery: And, if you can be merry then, I'll say A man may weep upon his wedding-day *Hen. VIII.* Prol. 31
He would have all as merry As, first, good company, good wine, good welcome, Can make good people . . . . i 4 5
That noble lady, Or gentleman, that is not freely merry, Is not my friend i 4 36
Ladies, you are not merry: gentlemen, Whose fault is this? . . . i 4 42
Sweet partner, I must not yet forsake you: let's be merry . . . i 4 104
He is melancholy without cause, and merry against the hair *Troi. and Cres.* i 2 27
As merry as when our nuptial day was done . . . *Coriolanus* i 6 31
Make my aunt merry with some pleasing tale . . *T. Andron.* iii 2 47
Poor harmless fly, That, with his pretty buzzing melody, Came here to make us merry! . . . . iii 2 65
I pray, come and crush a cup of wine. Rest you merry! *Rom. and Jul.* i 2 86
Hold, then; go home, be merry, give consent To marry Paris . . iv 1 89
How oft when men are at the point of death Have they been merry! . v 3 89
They approach sadly, and go away merry . *T. of Athens* ii 2 106
I know his lordship is but merry with me . . . . iii 2 42
Commend me to my lord; Say I am merry . . *J. Cæsar* ii 4 45
Fortune is merry, And in this mood will give us any thing . . iii 2 271
You are merry, my lord.—Who, I?—Ay, my lord.—O God, your only jig-maker. What should a man do but be merry? . *Hamlet* iii 2 129
I prithee, be merry; thy wit shall ne'er go slip-shod . . *Lear* i 5 11
I am not merry; but I do beguile The thing I am . . *Othello* ii 1 123
Therefore be merry, Cassio; For thy solicitor shall rather die Than give thy cause away . . . . iii 3 26
I slept the next night well, was free and merry . . . iii 3 340
Was he sad or merry?—Like to the time o' the year between the extremes Of hot and cold, he was nor sad nor merry . *Ant. and Cleo.* i 5 50
He was not merry, Which seem'd to tell them his remembrance lay In Egypt with his joy . . . . i 5 56
Be'st thou sad or merry, The violence of either thee becomes, So does it no man else . . . . i 5 59
'Twas merry when You wager'd on your angling . . . ii 5 15
None a stranger there So merry and so gamesome . *Cymbeline* i 6 60
She hath despised me rejoicingly, and I'll be merry in my revenge . iii 5 150
Are you merry, knights?—Who can be other in this royal presence? *Per.* ii 3 48
Merry ballad. This is a merry ballad, but a very pretty one . *W. Tale* iv 4 291
Merry bells. And bid the merry bells ring to thine ear That thou art crowned . . . . *2 Hen. IV.* iv 5 112
Merry bond. Give him direction for this merry bond *Mer. of Venice* i 3 174
Merry cheer. Bid your friends welcome, show a merry cheer . iii 2 314
Ne'er let my heart know merry cheer indeed, Till all the Andronici be made away . . . . . . *T. Andron.* ii 3 188
Merry cheerer. Her vine, the merry cheerer of the heart . *Hen. V.* v 2 41
Merry day. Heaven give you many, many merry days! . *Mer. Wives* v 5 254
If ever I do see the merry days of desolation that I have seen *L. L. Lost* i 2 164
I'll lay A plot shall show us all a merry day . . *Richard II.* iv 1 334
Merry devil. Our house is hell, and thou, a merry devil, Didst rob it of some taste of tediousness . . . . *Mer. of Venice* ii 3 2
Merry dump. Play me some merry dump, to comfort me *Rom. and Jul.* iv 5 108
Merry feast. Small cheer and great welcome makes a merry feast *C. of Er.* iii 1 26
Merry fellow. A merry fellow and carest for nothing . *T. Night* iii 1 30
Merry fooling. In this kind of merry fooling . . *Tempest* ii 1 177
Merry Greek. Then she's a merry Greek indeed . *Troi. and Cres.* i 2 118
A woful Cressid 'mongst the merry Greeks! . . . . iv 4 58
Merry heart. In faith, lady, you have a merry heart . *Much Ado* ii 1 324
A merry heart goes all the day, Your sad tires in a mile-a . *W. Tale* iv 3 134
So merrily, And ever among so merrily.—There's a merry heart! *2 Hen. IV.* v 3 24
And drink unto the leman mine; And a merry heart lives long-a . v 3 50
Merry host. My merry host . . . . . *Mer. Wives* ii 1 215
Merry hour. Out of question, you were born in a merry hour *Much Ado* ii 1 347
Revels, dances, masks and merry hours Forerun fair Love . *L. L. Lost* iv 3 379
Merry humour. Is your merry humour alter'd? . *Com. of Errors* ii 2 7
Saving your merry humour, here's the note . . . . iv 1 27
Merry inclination. This merry inclination Accords not with the sadness of my suit . . . . . . *3 Hen. VI.* iii 2 76
Merry jest. Lightens my humour with his merry jests . *Com. of Errors* i 2 21
My hand cut off and made a merry jest . . *T. Andron.* v 2 175
Merry larks. And merry larks are ploughmen's clocks . *L. L. Lost* v 2 914
Merry look. Whilst I at home starve for a merry look . *Com. of Errors* ii 1 88
See where she comes from shrift with merry look . *Rom. and Jul.* iv 2 15
Merry mad-cap. Biron, the merry mad-cap lord . . *L. L. Lost* ii 1 215
Merry madness. I am as mad as he, If sad and merry madness equal be *T. Night* iii 4 16
Merry man. You are a merry man, sir . . . . *Com. of Errors* iii 2 183
And a many merry men with him . . . *As Y. Like It* i 1 121
And, to be noted for a merry man, He'll woo a thousand *T. of Shrew* iii 2 14
And 'Three merry men be we' . . . . . *T. Night* ii 3 82
My husband—God be with his soul! A' was a merry man *Rom. and Jul.* i 3 40
Merry march. Which pillage they with merry march bring home *Hen. V.* i 2 195
Merry meeting. I humbly give you leave to depart; and if a merry meeting may be wished, God prohibit it! . . . . *Much Ado* v 1 335
Our stern alarums changed to merry meetings . . *Richard III.* i 1 7
Merry message. This was a merry message . . . *Hen. V.* i 2 298
Merry mistress. Fair sir, and you my merry mistress . *T. of Shrew* iv 5 53
Merry night. No more of that.—Ha! 'twas a merry night *2 Hen. IV.* iii 2 210
Merry note. Tu-whit; Tu-who, a merry note . . *L. L. Lost* v 2 938
And turn his merry note Unto the sweet bird's throat . *As Y. Like It* ii 5 3
Merry passion. Lest . . . You break into some merry passion *T. of S.* Ind. 1 97
Merry sconce. I shall break that merry sconce of yours . *Com. of Errors* i 2 79
Merry Shrove-tide. Welcome merry Shrove-tide . . *2 Hen. IV.* v 3 38
Merry song. A merry song, come: it grows late; we'll to bed . . ii 4 299
And sing The merry songs of peace to all his neighbours . *Hen. VIII.* v 5 36
Merry sport. And, in a merry sport, If you repay me not on such a day, . . . let the forfeit Be nominated for an equal pound Of your fair flesh . . . . *Mer. of Venice* i 3 146
Merry tales. He hears merry tales and smiles not . . . i 2 52
That I had my good wit out of the 'Hundred Merry Tales' . *Much Ado* ii 1 135
Merry tears. Made mine eyes water; but more merry tears The passion of loud laughter never shed . . . . *M. N. Dream* v 1 69
Merry vein. I am glad to see you in this merry vein . *Com. of Errors* ii 2 20
Merry wanderer. I am that merry wanderer of the night *M. N. Dream* ii 1 43
Merry war. There is a kind of merry war . . . *Much Ado* i 1 62
Merry whoreson. Well said; a merry whoreson, ha! . *Rom. and Jul.* iv 4 19
Merry wind. The merry wind Blows fair from land . *Com. of Errors* iv 1 90
Merry words. Cheer his grace with quick and merry words *Richard III.* i 3 5
Merry world. 'Twas never merry world since, of two usuries, the merriest was put down . . . . . *Meas. for Meas.* iii 2 6
'Twas never merry world Since lowly feigning was call'd compliment *T. Night* iii 1 109
It was never merry world in England since gentlemen came up *2 Hen. VI.* iv 2 9
Merry year. Do nothing but eat, and make good cheer, And praise God for the merry year . . . . . . *2 Hen. IV.* v 3 19
Mervailous. In thy most mervailous face . . . *Hen. V.* ii 1 50
Mesh. Such a hare is madness the youth, to skip o'er the meshes of good counsel the cripple . . . . . *Mer. of Venice* i 2 22
A golden mesh to entrap the hearts of men Faster than gnats in cobwebs . . . . iii 2 122
Meshed. She says she drinks no other drink but tears, Brew'd with her sorrow, mesh'd upon her cheeks . . . *T. Andron.* iii 2 38
Mesopotamia. Spur through Media, Mesopotamia *Ant. and Cleo.* iii 1 8
Mess. I had as lief you would tell me of a mess of porridge *Mer. Wives* iii 1 63
You three fools lack'd me fool to make up the mess *L. L. Lost* iv 3 207
A mess of Russians left us but of late . . . . v 2 361
Welcome! one mess is like to be your cheer . *T. of Shrew* iv 4 70
Lower messes Perchance are to this business purblind . *W. Tale* i 2 227
Our feasts In every mess have folly and the feeders Digest it with a custom . . . . iv 4 11
He and his toothpick at my worship's mess . . *K. John* i 1 190
Coming in to borrow a mess of vinegar . . *2 Hen. IV.* ii 1 103
By the mess, ere theise eyes of mine take themselves to slomber *Hen. V.* iii 2 122
Where are your mess of sons to back you now? . *3 Hen. VI.* i 4 73
Nature on each bush Lays her full mess before you . *T. of Athens* iv 3 424
And his crib shall stand at the king's mess . . *Hamlet* v 2 89
He that makes his generation messes To gorge his appetite . . *Lear* i 1 119
I will chop her into messes . . . . . *Othello* iv 1 211
Message. Your message done, hie home unto my chamber *T. G. of Ver.* iv 4 93
How many women would do such a message? . . . . iv 4 95
I do entreat your patience To hear me speak the message I am sent on . iv 4 117
It was by private message.—For which I do discharge you *Meas. for Meas.* v 1 465
You take pleasure then in the message? . . . *Much Ado* ii 3 262
A message well sympathized . . . . . *L. L. Lost* iii 1 52
Sometimes from her eyes I did receive fair speechless messages *M. of V.* i 1 164
And then show you the heart of my message . . *T. Night* i 5 203
I will meditate the while upon some horrid message for a challenge . iii 4 220
I speak amazedly; and it becomes My marvel and my message *W. Tale* v 1 188
My Lord of Hereford, my message is to you . . *Richard II.* iii 3 69
A merry message.—We hope to make the sender blush at it *Hen. V.* i 2 298
This is his claim, his threatening and my message . . . ii 4 110
According as your ladyship desired, By message craved . . *1 Hen. VI.* ii 3 13
On what submissive message art thou sent?—Submission! . . iv 7 53
'Tis like the commons, rude unpolish'd hinds, Could send such message to their sovereign . . . . . . *2 Hen. VI.* iii 2 272
Go tell this heavy message to the king. Ay me! what is this world! . iii 2 379
I go of message from the queen to France . . . . iv 1 113
By her woman I sent your message . . . . *Hen. VIII.* v 1 64
Now, by thy looks I guess thy message . . . . . v 1 162
May one, that is a herald and a prince, Do a fair message? *Troi. and Cres.* i 3 219
Let me be privileged by my place and message, To be a speaker free . iv 4 132
Thou'lt do thy message, wilt thou not?—Ay, with my dagger *T. Andron.* iv 1 117
Here's the son of Lucius; He hath some message to deliver us . . iv 2 2
Æmilius, do this message honourably . . . . . iv 4 104
Henceforward do your messages yourself . . *Rom. and Jul.* ii 5 66
By humble message and by promised means . . *T. of Athens* v 4 20
Who, almost dead for breath, had scarcely more Than would make up his message.—Give him tending . . . . . *Macbeth* i 5 38
Some holy angel Fly to the court of England and unfold His message! . iii 6 47
He hath not fail'd to pester us with message . . . *Hamlet* i 2 22
Mar a curious tale in telling it, and deliver a plain message bluntly *Lear* i 4 36
Give to a gracious message An host of tongues; but let ill tidings tell Themselves when they be felt . . . . *Ant. and Cleo.* ii 5 86
I come With message unto princely Pericles . . . *Pericles* i 3 33
My message must return from whence it came . . . i 3 36
Messala. Bring Messala with you Immediately to us . *J. Cæsar* iv 3 141
Had you your letters from your wife, my lord?—No, Messala . iv 3 182
Why, farewell, Portia. We must die, Messala . . . iv 3 190
Messala!—What says my general?—Messala, This is my birth-day; as this very day Was Cassius born. Give me thy hand, Messala . v 1 70
Ride, ride, Messala, ride, and give these bills Unto the legions on the other side . . . . v 2 1
Hie you, Messala, And I will seek for Pindarus the while . . v 3 78
Where, where, Messala, doth his body lie?—Lo, yonder, and Titinius mourning it . . . . v 3 91
Where is thy master?—Free from the bondage you are in, Messala . v 5 54
Wilt thou bestow thy time with me?—Ay, if Messala will prefer me . v 5 62
Messaline. My father was that Sebastian of Messaline . *T. Night* ii 1 18
What countryman? what name? what parentage?—Of Messaline . v 1 239
Messenger. Whose watery arch and messenger am I . . *Tempest* iv 1 71
Hail, many-colour'd messenger, that ne'er Dost disobey the wife of Jupiter . . . . iv 1 76
I must go send some better messenger . . . *T. G. of Ver.* i 1 159
Or fearing else some messenger that might her mind discover, Herself hath taught her love himself to write unto her lover . . . ii 1 173
I will be thankful To any happy messenger from thence . . . ii 4 53
His tears pure messengers sent from his heart . . . . ii 7 77
There is a messenger That stays to bear my letters to my friends . . iii 1 52
Now am I, unhappy messenger, To plead for that which I would not obtain . . . . iv 4 104
She shall be our messenger to this paltry knight . *Mer. Wives* ii 1 163
I have another messenger to your worship . . . . ii 2 98
One Lucio As then the messenger,— That's I . *Meas. for Meas.* v 1 74
Methinks your maw, like mine, should be your clock And strike you home without a messenger . . . . . *Com. of Errors* i 2 67
For God's sake, send some other messenger . . . . ii 1 77
My wife is in a wayward mood to-day, And will not lightly trust the messenger . . . . iv 4 5
Messengers Of strong prevailment in unharden'd youth . *M. N. Dream* i 1 34
Here comes my messenger.—How now, mad spirit! . . . iii 2 4
Here stays without A messenger with letters . . *Mer. of Venice* iv 1 108
But there is come a messenger before, To signify their coming . . v 1 117

Messenger. Were you made the messenger? . . . *As Y. Like It* i 2 62
Pardon me; I am but as a guiltless messenger . . . iv 3 12
This distemper'd messenger of wet, The many-colour'd Iris . *All's Well* i 3 157
O you leaden messengers, That ride upon the violent speed of fire . iii 2 111
Dispatch the most convenient messenger . . . iii 4 34
Provide this messenger: My heart is heavy and mine age is weak . iii 4 40
Tell me your mind: I am a messenger . . . *T. Night* i 5 219
Run after that same peevish messenger . . . i 5 319
The cunning of her passion Invites me in this churlish messenger . ii 2 24
Lo, upon thy wish, Our messenger Chatillon is arrived! *K. John* ii 1 51
'Tis not the roundure of your old-faced walls Can hide you from our messengers of war . . . ii 1 260
Some speedy messenger bid her repair To our solemnity . . ii 1 554
For he perhaps shall need Some messenger betwixt me and the peers . iv 2 179
Call in the messengers sent from the Dauphin . *Hen. V.* i 2 221
Thou baleful messenger, out of my sight! . . *2 Hen. VI.* iii 2 48
Art thou a messenger, or come of pleasure?—A messenger . v 1 16
Such a messenger As shall revenge his death before I stir *3 Hen. VI.* i 1 99
You shall be the messenger.—And I, I hope, shall reconcile them all . i 1 272
Then, England's messenger, return in post . . . iii 3 222
Now, messenger, what letters or what news From France? . iv 1 84
He shent our messengers . . . *Troi. and Cres.* ii 3 86
Lest you shall chance to whip your information And beat the messenger who bids beware Of what is to be dreaded . *Coriolanus* iv 6 54
There is a messenger from Rome Desires to be admitted. *T. Andron.* v 1 152
Thou art As glorious to this night, being o'er my head, As is a winged messenger of heaven . . . *Rom. and Jul.* ii 2 28
I could not send it,—here it is again,—Nor get a messenger to bring it thee . . . v 2 15
I hope it remains not unkindly with your lordship that I returned you an empty messenger.—O, sir, let it not trouble you . *T. of Athens* iii 6 41
Yon gray lines That fret the clouds are messengers of day *J. Cæsar* ii 1 104
With an absolute 'Sir, not I,' The cloudy messenger turns me his back *Macbeth* iii 6 41
That she should lock herself from his resort, Admit no messengers *Ham.* ii 2 144
If your messenger find him not there, seek him i' the other place yourself . . . iv 3 36
The several messengers From hence attend dispatch . *Lear* ii 1 126
What is the matter?—The messengers from our sister and the king . ii 2 54
You shall do small respect, show too bold malice Against the grace and person of my master, Stocking his messenger . . ii 2 139
The king must take it ill, That he's so slightly valued in his messenger ii 2 153
'Tis strange that they should so depart from home, And not send back my messenger . . . ii 4 2
Meeting here the other messenger, Whose welcome, I perceived, had poison'd mine . . . ii 4 38
The galleys Have sent a dozen sequent messengers . *Othello* i 2 41
Whose messengers are here about my side, Upon some present business i 2 89
What, ho! what, ho!—A messenger from the galleys . i 3 13
The messengers of Venice stay the meat: Go in, and weep not iv 2 170
Call in the messengers. As I am Egypt's queen, Thou blushest *A. and C.* i 1 29
The messengers!—Let Rome in Tiber melt! . . . i 1 32
No messenger, but thine . . . i 1 52
Met'st thou my posts?—Ay, madam, twenty several messengers . i 5 62
Sir, this should be answer'd.—'Tis done already, and the messenger gone . . . iii 6 31
Which had superfluous kings for messengers Not many moons gone by iii 12 5
A messenger from Cæsar.—What, no more ceremony! See, my women! iii 13 37
Most kind messenger, Say to great Cæsar this . . iii 13 73
My messenger He hath whipp'd with rods; dares me to personal combat . . . iv 1 2
The messenger Came on my guard; and at thy tent is now Unloading of his mules . . . iv 6 22
Cæsar hath sent— Too slow a messenger. O, come apace, dispatch! . v 2 324

Messina. Don Peter of Arragon comes this night to Messina *Much Ado* i 1 2
He hath an uncle here in Messina will be very much glad of it . i 1 18
He set up his bills here in Messina and challenged Cupid at the flight . i 1 39
She would not have his head on her shoulders for all Messina . i 1 116
A couple of as arrant knaves as any in Messina . . iii 5 35
As pretty a piece of flesh as any is in Messina . . iv 2 85
Your brother the bastard is fled from Messina . . v 1 193
Possess the people in Messina here How innocent she died . v 1 290
Your brother John is ta'en in flight, And brought with armed men back to Messina . . . v 4 128

Met. They all have met again And are upon the Mediterranean flote *Temp.* i 2 233
And breasted The surge most swoln that met him . . ii 1 117
I met her deity Cutting the clouds towards Paphos . iv 1 92
Give us particulars of thy preservation; How thou hast met us here . v 1 136
You are very well met: by your leave, good mistress . *Mer. Wives* i 1 200
They took me on their shoulders; met the jealous knave their master in the door . . . iii 5 102
As Falstaff, she and I, are newly met . . . iv 4 52
Very well met, and well come. What is the news?. *Meas. for Meas.* iv 1 26
My very worthy cousin, fairly met! . . . v 1 1
I remember you, sir, by the sound of your voice: I met you at the prison . . . v 1 331
Here's a villain that would face me down He met me on the mart *Com. of Errors* iii 1 7
And in the instant that I met with you He had of me a chain . iv 1 9
With drawn swords Met us again and madly bent on us Chased us away v 1 152
In the street I met him And in his company that gentleman . v 1 225
By the way we met My wife, her sister, and a rabble more . v 1 235
These are the parents to these children, Which accidentally are met together . . . v 1 361
Exceedingly well met . . . *L. L. Lost* ii 1 145
Therefore met your loves In their own fashion, like a merriment . v 2 793
Ill met by moonlight, proud Titania . . *M. N. Dream* ii 1 60
Never, since the middle summer's spring, Met we on hill, in dale, forest or mead . . . ii 1 83
Are we all met?—Pat, pat . . . iii 1 1
A crew of patches, rude mechanicals, That work for bread upon Athenian stalls, Were met together to rehearse a play . . . iii 2 11
Fair lovers, you are fortunately met . . . iv 1 182
I met a fool i' the forest, A motley fool; a miserable world! As I do live by food, I met a fool . . . *As Y. Like It* ii 7 12
You are very well met: God 'ild you for your last company . iii 3 75
I met the duke yesterday and had much question with him . iii 4 38
Know'st thou the youth that spoke to me erewhile?—Not very well, but I have met him oft . . . iii 5 106
Till you met your wife's wit going to your neighbour's bed . iv 1 170
Met. No sooner met but they looked, no sooner looked but they loved *As Y. Like It* v 2 36
This is the motley-minded gentleman that I have so often met in the forest . . . v 4 42
We met, and found the quarrel was upon the seventh cause . v 4 51
But when the parties were met themselves, one of them thought but of an If . . . v 4 105
That reason wonder may diminish, How thus we met . . v 4 146
I have met a gentleman Hath promised me to help me . *T. of Shrew* i 2 172
Here is a gentleman whom by chance I met, Upon agreement from us to his liking, Will undertake to woo curst Katharine . . i 2 182
You are happily met . . . iv 4 19
Happily met; the happier for thy son . . iv 5 59
We met him thitherward; for thence we came . *All's Well* iii 2 55
Better 'twere I met the ravin lion when he roar'd . . iii 2 120
Now, sir, have I met you again? there's for you . *T. Night* iv 1 26
Even now I met him With customary compliment . *W. Tale* i 2 370
Behind the tuft of pines I met them; never Saw I men scour so on their way . . . ii 1 34
I met Lord Bigot . . . , With eyes as red as new-enkindled fire *K. John* iv 2 162
Nor met with fortune other than at feasts, Full of warm blood, of mirth v 2 58
Hath now himself met with the fall of leaf . *Richard II.* iii 4 49
At Holmedon met, Where they did spend a sad and bloody hour *1 Hen. IV.* i 1 55
I tell thee, He durst as well have met the devil alone . i 3 116
His father loves him not And would be glad he met with some mischance i 3 232
Douglas and the English rebels met The eleventh of this month . iii 2 165
A mad fellow met me on the way and told me I had unloaded all the gibbets . . . iv 2 39
Met him in boroughs, cities, villages, Attended him on bridges . iv 3 69
So many of his shadows thou hast met And not the very king . v 4 30
Said he . . . that rebellion Had met ill luck? . . *2 Hen. IV.* i 1 51
As I came along, I met and overtook a dozen captains, Bare-headed . ii 4 387
God knows, my son, By what by-paths and indirect crook'd ways I met this crown . . . iv 5 186
I met this man with my glove in his cap . . *Hen. V.* iv 8 32
Peace to this meeting, wherefore we are met! . . . v 2 1
Fairly met: So are you, princes English, every one . . v 2 10
Your eyes, which hitherto have borne in them Against the French, that met them in their bent, The fatal balls of murdering basilisks . v 2 16
I muse we met not with the Dauphin's grace, His new-come champion *1 Hen. VI.* ii 2 19
Before we met or that a stroke was given, Like to a trusty squire did run away . . . iv 1 22
Young John, who two hours since I met in travel toward his warlike father . . . iv 3 36
But still, where danger was, still there I met him . . *2 Hen. VI.* v 3 11
We at Saint Alban's met, Our battles join'd . . *3 Hen. VI.* ii 1 120
When you and I met at Saint Alban's last, Your legs did better service than your hands . . . ii 2 103
I thought my mother . . . Would long ere this have met us *Richard III.* iii 1 21
'Tis better with me now Than when I met thee last where now we meet iii 2 101
When I met this holy man, Those men you talk of came into my mind . iii 2 117
The cause why we are met Is, to determine of the coronation . iii 4 1
Those two lights of men Met in the vale of Andren . . *Hen. VIII.* i 1 7
If he speak of Buckingham, pray, tell him You met him half in heaven ii 1 88
Have I with all my full affections Still met the king? . . iii 1 130
Speak to the business, master secretary: Why are we met in council? . v 3 2
We met by chance; you did not find me here . *Troi. and Cres.* iv 2 73
Yonder comes news. A wager they have met.—My horse to yours, no *Coriolanus* i 4 1
Has our general met the enemy?—They lie in view; but have not spoke as yet . . . i 4 3
Whom We met here both to thank and to remember With honours . ii 2 51
Tarquin's self he met, And struck him on his knee . . ii 2 98
How often he had met you, sword to sword . . . iii 1 13
Heartily well met, and most glad of your company. . . iv 3 53
A craftier Tereus, cousin, hast thou met . . *T. Andron.* ii 4 41
How now, my masters! What, have you met with her? . iv 3 36
Where and how We met, we woo'd, and made exchange of vow *R. and J.* ii 3 62
O honey nurse, what news? Has thou met with him? . . ii 5 19
Happily met, my lady and my wife!—That may be, sir, when I may be a wife . . . iv 1 18
I met the youthful lord at Laurence' cell; And gave him what becomed love I might . . . iv 2 25
You are kindly met, sir.—Fare thee well . . *T. of Athens* iii 2 30
Thou shalt be met with thanks, Allow'd with absolute power . v 1 164
I met a courier, one mine ancient friend . . . v 2 6
I met a lion, Who glared upon me, and went surly by *J. Cæsar* i 3 20
They met me in the day of success . . . *Macbeth* i 5 1
We might have met them dareful, beard to beard, And beat them backward home . . . v 5 6
We have met with foes That strike beside us . . . v 7 28
Would I had met my dearest foe in heaven Or ever I had seen that day! *Hamlet* i 2 182
He met the night-mare, and her nine-fold . . *Lear* iii 4 126
His knights, Hot questrists after him, met him at gate . . iii 7 17
I marvel our mild husband Not met us on the way . . iv 2 2
He is not here.—No, my good lord; I met him back again . iv 2 91
Why, he was met even now As mad as the vex'd sea . . iv 4 1
In this habit Met I my father with his bleeding rings . . v 3 189
Many of the consuls, raised and met, Are at the duke's already . *Othello* i 2 43
Come, Desdemona, Once more, well met at Cyprus . . ii 1 214
They met so near with their lips that their breaths embraced together ii 1 265
When she first met Mark Antony, she pursed up his heart, upon the river of Cydnus . . . *Ant. and Cleo.* ii 2 191
Let me have your hand: I did not think, sir, to have met you here . ii 6 50
We should have met you By sea and land; supplying every stage With an augmented greeting . . . iii 6 53
The story Proud Cleopatra, when she met her Roman . *Cymbeline* ii 4 70
Have we thus met? O, never say hereafter But I am truest speaker . v 5 375
How parted with your brothers? how first met them? . . v 5 386
There, when my maiden priests are met together, Before the people all *Pericles* v 1 243
Well met *Mer. Wives* iii 2; *Com. of Errors* iv 3; *As Y. Like It* v 3; *K. John* ii 1; iv 3; *Richard II.* ii 2; *Hen. V.* ii 1; *Richard III.* iii 2; iv 1; *Hen. VIII.* i 1; ii 2; *T. of Athens* iii 4; *Ant. and Cleo.* ii 6
You are well met *As Y. Like It* iii 3; *T. of Shrew* i 2; *W. Tale* v 2; *Hen. VIII.* iv 1; *Coriolanus* iv 2

Metal. No use of metal, corn, or wine, or oil . . . *Tempest* ii 1 153
Let there be some more test made of my metal . . *Meas. for Meas.* i 1 49

Metal. As easy Falsely to take away a life true made As to put metal in restrained means To make a false one . . . *Meas. for Meas.* ii 4 48
As dear As all the metal in your shop will answer . *Com. of Errors* iv 1 82
Not till God make men of some other metal than earth . . *Much Ado* ii 1 63
Is not lead a metal heavy, dull, and slow? . . *L. L. Lost* iii 1 60
When did friendship take A breed for barren metal of his friend? *M. of V.* i 3 135
Thou makest thy knife keen ; but no metal can, No, not the hangman's axe, bear half the keenness Of thy sharp envy . . . iv 1 124
That you were made of is metal to make virgins . *All's Well* i 1 141
Good sparks and lustrous, a word, good metals . . . . ii 1 42
And to what metal this counterfeit lump of ore will be melted . . iii 6 39
How now, my metal of India! . . . . . *T. Night* ii 5 17
O, it grieves my soul, That I must draw this metal from my side To be a widow-maker! . . . . . . *K. John* v 2 16
That metal, that self mould, that fashion'd thee Made him a man *Rich. II.* i 2 23
Like bright metal on a sullen ground . . *1 Hen. IV.* i 2 236
For from his metal was his party steel'd . . . . *2 Hen. IV.* i 1 116
I would to God that the inclusive verge Of golden metal that must round my brow Were red-hot steel! . . . . . *Richard III.* iv 1 60
The imperial metal, circling now thy brow, Had graced the tender temples of my child . . . . . . iv 4 382
Now I feel Of what coarse metal ye are moulded, envy . *Hen. VIII.* iii 2 239
The fineness of which metal is not found In fortune's love *Troi. and Cres.* i 3 22
No big-boned men framed of the Cyclops' size ; But metal, Marcus, steel to the very back . . . . . . *T. Andron.* iv 3 47
They have all been touch'd and found base metal . *T. of Athens* iii 3 6
See, whether their basest metal be not moved . . *J. Cæsar* i 1 66
Thy honourable metal may be wrought From that it is disposed . . i 2 313
Here's metal more attractive . . . . . *Hamlet* iii 2 116
Like some ore Among a mineral of metals base, Shows itself pure . iv 1 26
I am made Of the self-same metal that my sister is . . . *Lear* i 1 71
The blest infusions That dwell in vegetives, in metals, stones *Pericles* iii 2 36
Metamorphosed. Julia, thou hast metamorphosed me . *T. G. of Ver.* i 1 66
Now you are metamorphosed with a mistress . . . . ii 1 32
Metamorphoses. 'Tis Ovid's Metamorphoses ; My mother gave it me *T. Andron.* iv 1 42
Metaphor. You need not to stop your nose, sir ; I spake but by a metaphor.—Indeed, sir, if your metaphor stink, I will stop my nose ; or against any man's metaphor . . . . *All's Well* v 2 12
What's your metaphor?—It's dry, sir . . . . *T. Night* i 3 76
Metaphysical. Which fate and metaphysical aid doth seem To have thee crown'd withal . . . . *Macbeth* i 5 30
Metaphysics. The mathematics and the metaphysics, Fall to them as you find your stomach serves you . . . . *T. of Shrew* i 1 37
Mete. Let the mark have a prick in't, to mete at, if it may be *L. L. Lost* iv 1 134
By which his grace must mete the lives of others . *2 Hen. IV.* iv 4 77
Metellus. This, Cinna ; and this, Metellus Cimber . *J. Cæsar* ii 1 96
Now, good Metellus, go along by him : He loves me well . . ii 1 218
Now, Metellus : what, Trebonius! I have an hour's talk in store for you . ii 2 120
Trust not Trebonius ; mark well Metellus Cimber . . . ii 3 3
Metellus Cimber throws before thy seat An humble heart . . iii 1 34
Now, Decius Brutus, yours ; now yours, Metellus ; Yours, Cinna . iii 1 187
Meteor. I will awe him with my cudgel : it shall hang like a meteor o'er the cuckold's horns . . . . . *Mer. Wives* ii 2 292
What observation madest thou in this case Of his heart's meteors tilting in his face? . . . . . . *Com. of Errors* iv 2 6
Call them meteors, prodigies and signs, Abortives, presages . *K. John* iii 4 157
The vaulty top of heaven Figured quite o'er with burning meteors . v 2 53
Meteors fright the fixed stars of heaven . . *Richard II.* ii 4 9
Like the meteors of a troubled heaven, All of one nature . *1 Hen. IV.* i 1 10
My lord, do you see these meteors? do you behold these exhalations? . ii 4 351
Be no more an exhaled meteor, A prodigy of fear . . . v 1 19
I missed the meteor once, and hit that woman . . *Hen. VIII.* v 4 52
It is some meteor that the sun exhales . . . *Rom. and Jul.* iii 5 13
Mete-yard. Take thou the bill, give me thy mete-yard . *T. of Shrew* iv 3 153
Metheglin. Given to . . . sack and wine and metheglins . *Mer. Wives* v 5 167
Metheglin, wort, and malmsey . . . . *L. L. Lost* v 2 233
Methinks he hath no drowning mark upon him . . . *Tempest* i 1 31
Methinks our garments are now as fresh as when we put them on . ii 1 68
And yet methinks I see it in thy face, What thou shouldst be . . ii 1 206
Do you understand me?—Methinks I do . . . . . ii 1 269
Methinks, should not be chronicled for wise . . *T. G. of Ver.* i 1 41
And yet methinks I do not like this tune . . . . . i 2 90
Methinks my zeal to Valentine is cold, And that I love him not as I was wont . . . . ii 4 203
Now, my young guest, methinks you 're allycholly . . . iv 2 26
Methinks that she loved you as well As you do love your lady . iv 4 84
Methinks you prescribe to yourself very preposterously . *Mer. Wives* ii 2 249
Methinks there would be no period to the jest . . . . iv 2 236
Methinks there should be terrors in him that he should not come . iv 4 23
Methinks his flesh is punished, he shall have no desires . . iv 4 24
Methinks strangely, for he hath not used it before . *Meas. for Meas.* iv 2 120
Angelo perceives he's safe ; Methinks I see a quickening in his eye . v 1 500
Methinks your maw, like mine, should be your clock . *Com. of Errors* i 2 66
They speak us fair, give us gold : methinks they are such a gentle nation iv 4 157
Methinks you are my glass, and not my brother . . . v 1 417
Methinks she's too low for a high praise, too brown for a fair praise *Much Ado* i 1 173
I am not as I have been.—So say I : methinks you are sadder . . iii 2 16
Do you speak in the sick tune?—I am out of all other tune, methinks . iii 4 43
I know not, but methinks you look with your eyes as other women do . iii 4 91
I think scorn to sigh : methinks I should outswear Cupid . *L. L. Lost* i 2 67
But to have a love of that colour, methinks Samson had small reason for it . . . . i 2 91
A time, methinks, too short To make a world-without-end bargain in . v 2 798
But, O, methinks, how slow This old moon wanes! . . *M. N. Dream* i 1 3
I love thee.—Methinks, mistress, you should have little reason for that iii 1 145
The moon methinks looks with a watery eye . . . . iii 1 203
Methinks I am marvellous hairy about the face . . . . iv 1 26
Methinks I have a great desire to a bottle of hay . . . . iv 1 36
Methinks I see these things with parted eye, When every thing seems double.—So methinks . . . . iv 1 194
The wall, methinks, being sensible, should curse again . . . v 1 183
Methinks she should not use a long one [passion] for such a Pyramus . v 1 322
Having made one [eye], Methinks it should have power to steal both his *Mer. of Venice* iii 2 125
And now methinks I have a mind to it . . . . . iv 1 433
And now methinks You teach me how a beggar should be answer'd . iv 1 439
In such a night Troilus methinks mounted the Troyan walls . . v 1 4
Methinks it sounds much sweeter than by day . . . . v 1 100

Methinks. This night methinks is but the daylight sick . *Mer. of Venice* v 1 124
When a man thanks me heartily, methinks I have given him a penny *As Y. Like It* ii 5 28
But, gentle sir, methinks you walk like a stranger . *T. of Shrew* i 2 87
Methinks he looks as though he were in love . . . . iii 1 88
Methinks you frown : And wherefore gaze this goodly company? . . iii 2 95
'Twere good, methinks, to steal our marriage . . . . iii 2 142
He would always say—Methinks I hear him now . *All's Well* i 2 53
Methinks in thee some blessed spirit doth speak His powerful sound within an organ weak . . . . ii 1 178
Methinks, thou art a general offence, and every man should beat thee . ii 3 269
Methinks sometimes I have no more wit than a Christian . *T. Night* i 3 88
Methinks I feel this youth's perfections . . . . i 5 315
Very oft we pity enemies.—Why, then, methinks 'tis time to smile again iii 1 137
Methinks his words do from such passion fly, That he believes himself iii 4 407
This is strange : methinks My favour here begins to warp . *W. Tale* i 2 364
The celestial habits, Methinks I so should term them . . . iii 1 5
Methinks I play as I have seen them do In Whitsun pastorals . . iv 4 133
Methinks a father Is at the nuptial of his son a guest That best becomes the table . . . . iv 4 405
Methinks I see Leontes opening his free arms and weeping His welcomes forth . . . . iv 4 558
Would I were dead, but that, methinks, already—What was he that did make it? . . . . v 3 62
Still, methinks, There is an air comes from her . . . . v 3 77
Methinks I see this hurly all on foot . . . . *K. John* iii 4 169
Mercy on me! Methinks no body should be sad but I . . . iv 1 13
I am amazed, methinks, and lose my way Among the thorns and dangers iv 3 140
Even there, methinks, an angel spake . . . . . . v 2 64
Methinks I am a prophet new inspired . . . *Richard II.* ii 1 31
Methinks, Some unborn sorrow, ripe in fortune's womb, Is coming towards me . . . . ii 2 9
You are my father, for methinks in you I see old Gaunt alive . ii 3 117
Methinks King Richard and myself should meet With no less terror than the elements Of fire and water . . . . . . iii 3 54
Tell Bolingbroke—for yond methinks he stands . . . . iii 3 91
Methinks it were an easy leap . . . . . *1 Hen. IV.* i 3 201
Methinks my moiety . . . In quantity equals not one of yours . . iii 1 96
Methinks they are exceeding poor and bare, too beggarly . . iv 2 74
Methinks now you are in an excellent good temperality . *2 Hen. IV.* ii 4 24
This revolt of thine, methinks, is like Another fall of man *Hen. V.* ii 2 141
Methinks I could not die any where so contented as in the king's company . . . . iv 1 131
I would not lose so great an honour As one man more, methinks, would share from me . . . . iv 3 32
Methinks your looks are sad, your cheer appall'd . . *1 Hen. VI.* i 2 48
My lord, methinks, is very long in talk . . . . . i 2 118
Methinks, my father's execution Was nothing less than bloody tyranny ii 5 99
Methinks my lord should be religious And know the office that belongs to such . . . . iii 1 54
Methinks his lordship should be humbler ; It fitteth not a prelate so to plead . . . . iii 1 56
Methinks I should revive the soldiers' hearts . . . . iii 2 97
Methinks you do not well To bear with their perverse objections . iv 1 128
He smiles, methinks, as who should say, Had death been French, then death had died to-day . . . . iv 7 27
And yet, methinks, I could be well content To be mine own attorney . v 3 165
Methinks the realms of England, France and Ireland Bear that proportion to my flesh and blood . . . . . *2 Hen. VI.* i 1 232
Methinks, you watch'd her well: A pretty plot, well chosen to build upon! . . . . i 4 58
Methinks I should not thus be led along, Mail'd up in shame . . ii 4 30
Methinks he should stand in fear of fire, being burnt i' the hand for stealing of sheep . . . . iv 2 66
Methinks already in this civil broil I see them lording it in London streets . . . . iv 8 46
You are old enough now, and yet, methinks, you lose *3 Hen. VI.* i 1 113
Had he 'scaped, methinks we should have heard The happy tidings . ii 1 6
Methinks, 'tis prize enough to be his son . . . . . ii 1 20
Ay, now methinks I hear great Warwick speak . . . . ii 1 186
Methinks it were a happy life, To be no better than a homely swain . ii 5 21
The other his pale cheeks, methinks, presenteth . . . . ii 5 100
Methinks these peers of France should smile at that . . . iii 3 91
And yet methinks your grace hath not done well . . . . iv 1 51
What thinks your lordship? Methinks the power that Edward hath in field Should not be able to encounter mine . . . . . . iv 8 35
Methinks a woman of this valiant spirit Should . . . Infuse his breast v 4 39
And since, methinks, I would not grow so fast . *Richard III.* ii 4 14
Methinks the truth should live from age to age . . . . iii 1 76
How much, methinks, I could despise this man! . *Hen. VIII.* iii 2 297
I am able now, methinks, Out of a fortitude of soul I feel, To endure . iii 2 387
Reach a chair : So ; now, methinks, I feel a little ease . . iv 2 4
Methinks I could Cry the amen . . . . v 1 23
For that, methinks, is the curse dependant on those . *Troi. and Cres.* ii 3 21
Who do, methinks, find out Something not worth in me such rich beholding . . . . iii 3 90
Methinks I hear hither your husband's drum . . *Coriolanus* i 3 32
Methinks I see him stamp thus, and call thus : 'Come on, you cowards!' i 3 35
Though thou speak'st truth, Methinks thou speak'st not well . . i 6 14
He has it now, and by his looks methinks 'Tis warm at's heart . ii 3 159
Methinks I do digress too much, Citing my worthless praise *T. Andron.* v 3 116
O God, I have an ill-divining soul! Methinks I see thee, now thou art below, As one dead in the bottom of a tomb . *Rom. and Jul.* iii 5 55
And yet, methinks, it should not, For he hath still been tried a holy man . . . . iv 3 28
O, look! methinks I see my cousin's ghost Seeking out Romeo . iv 3 55
Methinks they should invite them without knives . *T. of Athens* i 2 45
Mine eyes cannot hold out water, methinks . . . . . i 2 111
Methinks, I could deal kingdoms to my friends, And ne'er be weary . i 2 226
Methinks, false hearts should never have sound legs . . . i 2 240
Methinks he should the sooner pay his debts, And make a clear way to the gods . . . . iii 4 76
Methinks thou art more honest now than wise . . . . iv 3 509
Methinks there is much reason in his sayings . . *J. Cæsar* iii 2 113
To fright you thus, methinks, I am too savage . *Macbeth* iv 2 70
Methinks I see my father.—Where, my lord?—In my mind's eye *Hamlet* i 2 184
But, soft! methinks I scent the morning air ; Brief let me be . i 5 58
The lady doth protest too much, methinks.—O, but she'll keep her word . . . . iii 2 240
Methinks it is like a weasel.—It is backed like a weasel . . . iii 2 396

Methinks. But yet methinks it is very sultry and hot for my complexion *Hamlet* v 2 101
Methinks you are too much of late i' the frown *Lear* i 4 208
Methinks the ground is even.—Horrible steep. Hark, do you hear the sea? iv 6 3
Methinks thy voice is alter'd; and thou speak'st In better phrase and matter than thou didst iv 6 7
In nothing am I changed But in my garments.—Methinks you're better spoken iv 6 10
Methinks he seems no bigger than his head iv 6 16
Far off, methinks, I hear the beaten drum iv 6 292
Methinks I should know you, and know this man; Yet I am doubtful . iv 7 64
Methinks our pleasure might have been demanded, Ere you had spoke so far v 3 62
Methinks the wind hath spoke aloud at land *Othello* ii 1 5
What an eye she has! methinks it sounds a parley of provocation ii 3 22
An inviting eye; and yet methinks right modest ii 3 24
Methinks it should be now a huge eclipse Of sun and moon v 2 99
Methinks, if you did love him dearly, You do not hold the method to enforce The like from him *Ant. and Cleo.* i 3 6
Why, methinks, by him, This creature's no such thing iii 3 43
Methinks I hear Antony call; I see him rouse himself To praise my noble act v 2 286
Now methinks Thy favour's good enough *Cymbeline* iii 4 50
Whereupon—Methinks, I see him now— Ay, so thou dost, Italian fiend! v 5 209
Method. What sayest thou to this tune, matter and method? *M. for M.* iii 2 51
I will beat this method in your sconce *Com. of Errors* ii 2 34
To answer by the method, in the first of his heart *T. Night* i 5 244
Or am not able Verbatim to rehearse the method of my pen 1 *Hen. VI.* iii 1 13
And fall somewhat into a slower method *Richard III.* i 2 116
Though this be madness, yet there is method in't *Hamlet* ii 2 208
But called it an honest method, as wholesome as sweet ii 2 465
If you did love him dearly You do not hold the method to enforce The like from him *Ant. and Cleo.* i 3 7
Methought. The clouds methought would open and show riches *Tempest* iii 2 150
Methought the billows spoke and told me of it iii 3 96
He beat him most unpitifully, methought *Mer. Wives* iv 2 215
Methought all his senses were lock'd in his eye *L. L. Lost* ii 1 242
Methought a serpent eat my heart away, And you sat smiling *M. N. D.* ii 2 149
Methought I was enamour'd of an ass iv 1 82
Methought I was—there is no man can tell what. Methought I was,—and methought I had,—but man is but a patched fool, if he will offer to say what methought I had iv 1 213
Methought you said you neither lend nor borrow Upon advantage *Mer. of Venice* i 3 70
Methought he was a brother to your daughter *As Y. Like It* v 4 29
When I said 'a mother,' Methought you saw a serpent *All's Well* i 3 147
Methought you said You saw one here in court could witness it v 3 199
Methought she purged the air of pestilence! *T. Night* i 1 20
Methought her eyes had lost her tongue, For she did speak in starts ii 2 21
Methought it did relieve my passion much, More than light airs ii 4 4
To his image, which methought did promise Most venerable worth, did I devotion iii 4 396
Methoughts I did recoil Twenty-three years *W. Tale* i 2 154
How like, methought, I then was to this kernel, This squash, this gentleman i 2 159
Methought I heard the shepherd say, he found the child v 2 7
The sun of heaven methought was loath to set *K. John* v 5 1
Methought he had made two holes in the ale-wife's new petticoat 2 *Hen. IV.* ii 2 88
Methought a' made a shrewd thrust at your belly ii 4 227
Methought yesterday your mistress shrewdly shook your back *Hen. V.* iii 7 51
The king Prettily, methought, did play the orator 1 *Hen. VI.* iv 1 175
Methought this staff, mine office-badge in court, Was broke in twain 2 *Hen. VI.* i 2 25
Methought I sat in seat of majesty In the cathedral church i 2 36
Methought he bore him in the thickest troop As doth a lion 3 *Hen. VI.* ii 1 13
Methought that Gloucester stumbled *Richard III.* i 4 18
Lord, Lord! methought, what pain it was to drown! i 4 21
Methought I saw a thousand fearful wrecks i 4 24
Had you such leisure in the time of death To gaze upon the secrets of the deep?—Methought I had i 4 36
Who pass'd, methought, the melancholy flood, With that grim ferryman i 4 45
Methoughts, a legion of foul fiends Environ'd me about i 4 58
Methought the souls of all that I had murder'd Came to my tent; and every one did threat To-morrow's vengeance on the head of Richard v 3 204
Methought their souls, whose bodies Richard murder'd, Came to my tent, and cried on victory v 3 230
First, methought I stood not in the smile of heaven *Hen. VIII.* ii 4 186
He had, sir, a kind of face, methought,—I cannot tell how to term it *Coriolanus* iv 5 164
Methought I heard a voice cry 'Sleep no more!' *Macbeth* ii 2 35
I look'd toward Birnam, and anon, methought, The wood began to move v 5 34
Methought It lifted up it head and did address Itself to motion *Hamlet* i 2 215
In youth, when I did love, did love, Methought it was very sweet v 1 70
For, ah, my behove, O, methought, there was nothing meet v 1 72
Methought I lay Worse than the mutines in the bilboes v 2 5
As I stood here below, methought his eyes Were two full moons *Lear* iv 6 69
Methought thy very gait did prophesy A royal nobleness v 3 175
Methought Great Jupiter, upon his eagle back'd, Appear'd to me *Cymb.* v 5 426
Metre. I think thou never wast where grace was said.—No? a dozen times at least.—What, in metre? *Meas. for Meas.* i 2 22
Praises, of whose taste the wise are fond, Lascivious metres *Richard II.* ii 1 19
One of these same metre ballad-mongers 1 *Hen. IV.* iii 1 130
Metropolis. The great metropolis and see of Rome *K. John* v 2 72
Mette le au mon pocket: depeche, quickly *Mer. Wives* i 4 56
Mettest. Thou mettest with things dying, I with things new-born *W. T.* iii 3 117
Met'st thou my posts?—Ay, madam, twenty several messengers *Ant. and Cleo.* i 5 61
Mettle. You are gentlemen of brave mettle; you would lift the moon out of her sphere *Tempest* ii 1 182
If you take it not patiently, why, your mettle is the more *Meas. for Meas.* iii 2 80
Thou hast mettle enough in thee to kill care *Much Ado* v 1 133
Therein suits His folly to the mettle of my speech *As Y. Like It* ii 7 82
I care not who knows so much of my mettle *T. Night* iii 4 300
For your service done him, So much against the mettle of your sex v 1 330
An if thou hast the mettle of a king *K. John* ii 1 401
A Corinthian, a lad of mettle, a good boy 1 *Hen. IV.* ii 4 13
That rascal hath good mettle in him; he will not run ii 4 383
Mettle. Now their pride and mettle is asleep, Their courage with hard labour tame 1 *Hen. IV.* iv 3 22
O, this boy Lends mettle to us all! v 4 24
I did not think Master Silence had been a man of this mettle 2 *Hen. IV.* v 3 41
Show us here The mettle of your pasture *Hen. V.* iii 1 27
Where have they this mettle? Is not their climate foggy, raw and dull? iii 5 15
Our madams mock at us, and plainly say Our mettle is bred out iii 5 29
By this day and this light, the fellow has mettle enough in his belly iv 8 67
They are as children but one step below, Even of your mettle *Rich. III.* iv 4 302
And every Greek of mettle, let him know, What Troy means fairly shall be spoke aloud *Troi. and Cres.* i 3 258
Whose self-same mettle, Whereof thy proud child, arrogant man, is puff'd, Engenders the black toad and adder blue *T. of Athens* iv 3 179
He was quick mettle when he went to school *J. Cæsar* i 2 300
Nor the insuppressive mettle of our spirits ii 1 134
But hollow men, like horses hot at hand, Make gallant show and promise of their mettle iv 2 24
Thy undaunted mettle should compose Nothing but males *Macbeth* i 7 73
Of unimproved mettle hot and full *Hamlet* i 1 96
Why, now I see there's mettle in thee *Othello* iv 2 207
I do think there is mettle in death, which commits some loving act upon her, she hath such a celerity in dying *Ant. and Cleo.* i 2 147
Mew. Why will you mew her up, Signior Baptista, for this fiend? *T. of S.* i 1 87
To mew up Your tender kinsman and to choke his days *K. John* iv 2 57
I had rather be a kitten and cry mew 1 *Hen. IV.* iii 1 129
The cat will mew and dog will have his day *Hamlet* v 1 315
Mewed. For aye to be in shady cloister mew'd *M. N. Dream* i 1 71
And therefore has he closely mew'd her up, Because she will not be annoy'd with suitors *T. of Shrew* i 1 188
This day should Clarence closely be mew'd up, About a prophecy *Richard III.* i 1 38
More pity that the eagle should be mew'd, While kites and buzzards prey at liberty i 1 132
And for his meed, poor lord, he is mew'd up i 3 139
To-night she is mew'd up to her heaviness *Rom. and Jul.* iii 4 11
Thrice the brinded cat hath mew'd *Macbeth* iv 1 1
Mewling. At first the infant, Mewling and puking in the nurse's arms. And then the whining school-boy *As Y. Like It* ii 7 144
Mexico. He hath a third at Mexico, a fourth for England *Mer. of Venice* i 3 20
From Tripolis, from Mexico and England, From Lisbon, Barbary and India iii 2 271
Mi. Ut, re, sol, la, mi, fa. Under pardon, sir *L. L. Lost* iv 2 102
'B mi,' Bianca, take him for thy lord, 'C fa ut,' that loves with all affection: . . . 'E la mi,' show pity, or I die *T. of Shrew* iii 1 75
O, these eclipses do portend these divisions! fa, sol, la, mi *Lear* i 2 149
Mice. Long run by the hideous law, As mice by lions *Meas. for Meas.* i 4 64
Or piteous they will look, like drowned mice 1 *Hen. VI.* i 2 12
But mice and rats, and such small deer, Have been Tom's food for seven long year *Lear* iii 4 144
The fishermen, that walk upon the beach, Appear like mice iv 6 18
Michael. Hie, good Sir Michael; bear this sealed brief 1 *Hen. IV.* iv 4 1
Knight of the noble order of Saint George, Worthy Saint Michael 1 *Hen. VI.* iv 7 69
One Michael Cassio, a Florentine *Othello* i 1 20
Michael Cassio, Lieutenant to the warlike Moor Othello ii 1 26
I'll have our Michael Cassio on the hip, Abuse him to the Moor ii 1 314
Good Michael, look you to the guard to-night ii 3 1
Iago is most honest. Michael, good night ii 3 7
How comes it, Michael, you are thus forgot? ii 3 188
I had rather have this tongue cut from my mouth Than it should do offence to Michael Cassio ii 3 222
Whatever shall become of Michael Cassio, He's never any thing but your true servant iii 3 8
What! Michael Cassio, That came a-wooing with you! iii 3 70
Did Michael Cassio, when you woo'd my lady, Know of your love? iii 3 94
For Michael Cassio, I dare be sworn I think that he is honest iii 3 124
Michaelmas. A fortnight afore Michaelmas *Mer. Wives* i 1 212
Let me see—about Michaelmas next 1 *Hen. IV.* ii 4 60
Micher. Shall the blessed sun of heaven prove a micher and eat blackberries? a question not to be asked ii 4 450
Miching. Marry, this is miching mallecho; it means mischief *Hamlet* iii 2 147
Mickle. The one ne'er got me credit, the other mickle blame *C. of Er.* iii 1 45
An oath of mickle might; and fury shall abate *Hen. V.* ii 1 70
If I to-day die not with Frenchmen's rage, To-morrow I shall die with mickle age: By me they nothing gain 1 *Hen. VI.* iv 6 35
Bend thy knee to me That bows unto the grave with mickle age 2 *Hen. VI.* v 1 174
O, mickle is the powerful grace that lies In herbs, plants *Rom. and Jul.* ii 3 15
Microcosm. If you see this in the map of my microcosm *Coriolanus* ii 1 68
Mid. What is the time o' the day?—Past the mid season *Tempest* i 2 239
About the mid of night come to my tent And help to arm me *Rich. III.* v 3 77
Mid-age. Virgins and boys, mid-age and wrinkled eld *Troi. and Cres.* ii 2 104
Midas. Gaudy gold, Hard food for Midas, I will none of thee *M. of Ven.* iii 2 102
Mid-day. More dazzled and drove back his enemies Than mid-day sun fierce bent against their faces 1 *Hen. VI.* i 1 14
These eyes . . . Have been as piercing as the mid-day sun 3 *Hen. VI.* v 2 17
Middest. Have through the very middest of you! 2 *Hen. VI.* iv 8 64
Middle. Upon the heavy middle of the night *Meas. for Meas.* iv 1 35
Never, since the middle summer's spring *M. N. Dream* ii 1 82
We are for you: sit i' the middle *As Y. Like It* v 3 10
Now here, At upper end o' the table, now i' the middle *W. Tale* iv 4 59
Flowers Of middle summer, and I think they are given To men of middle age iv 4 107
In the market-place, The middle centre of this cursed town 1 *Hen. VI.* ii 2 6
Change thy colour, Murder thy breath in middle of a word *Richard III.* iii 5 2
Beginning in the middle, starting thence away *Troi. and Cres.* Prol. 28
Our general is cut i' the middle and but one half of what he was *Coriol.* iv 5 210
The middle of humanity thou never knewest *T. of Athens* iv 3 300
In the dead vast and middle of the night *Hamlet* i 2 198
Then you live about her [fortune's] waist, or in the middle of her favours? ii 2 237
What two crowns shall they be?—Why, after I have cut the egg i' the middle, and eat up the meat, the two crowns of the egg. When thou clovest thy crown i' the middle, and gavest away both parts, thou borest thy ass on thy back o'er the dirt *Lear* i 4 174
Thou hast pared thy wit o' both sides, and left nothing i' the middle i 4 205
Thou canst tell why one's nose stands i' the middle on's face? i 5 20
But even the very middle of my heart Is warm'd by the rest *Cymbeline* i 6 27
Middle-earth. But, stay; I smell a man of middle-earth *Mer. Wives* v 5 84

Midnight. One midnight Fated to the purpose . . . . *Tempest* i 2 128
Thou call'dst me up at midnight to fetch dew From the still-vex'd Bermoothes . . . . i 2 228
All's hush'd as midnight yet . . . . iv 1 207
You whose pastime Is to make midnight mushrooms . . . v 1 39
Meet him in the park at midnight? Fie, fie! he'll never come *M. W.* iv 4 19
Doth all the winter-time, at still midnight, Walk round about an oak . iv 4 30
Be you in the Park about midnight, at Herne's oak . . . v 1 12
'Tis now dead midnight . . . . *Meas. for Meas.* iv 2 67
For women are light at midnight . . . . . . v 1 281
Bear it coldly but till midnight, and let the issue show itself *Much Ado* iii 2 132
Midnight, assist our moan; Help us to sigh and groan, Heavily, heavily v 3 16
We must starve our sight From lovers' food till morrow deep midnight *M. N. Dream* i 1 223
And will to-morrow midnight solemnly Dance . . . . iv 1 93
The iron tongue of midnight hath told twelve: Lovers, to bed . v 1 370
As true a lover As ever sigh'd upon a midnight pillow . *As Y. Like It* ii 4 27
By midnight look to hear further from me . . . *All's Well* iii 6 82
When midnight comes, knock at my chamber-window . . . iv 2 54
We shall not then have his company to-night?—Not till after midnight iv 3 34
Not to be a-bed after midnight is to be up betimes . . *T. Night* ii 3 2
To be up after midnight and to go to bed then, is early: so that to go to bed after midnight is to go to bed betimes . . . . . ii 3 7
Wishing clocks more swift? Hours, minutes? noon, midnight? *W. Tale* i 2 290
The midnight bell Did, with his iron tongue and brazen mouth, Sound on into the drowsy race of night . . . . . *K. John* iii 3 37
And with my hand at midnight held your head . . . . iv 1 45
The pupil age of this present twelve o'clock at midnight . 1 *Hen. IV.* ii 4 107
What doth gravity out of his bed at midnight? . . . . ii 4 325
We have heard the chimes at midnight . . . *2 Hen. IV.* iii 2 228
And leave your England, as dead midnight still . *Hen. V.* iii Prol. 19
'Tis midnight; I'll go arm myself.—The Dauphin longs for morning . iii 7 97
The lights burn blue. It is now dead midnight. Cold fearful drops stand on my trembling flesh . . . . . *Richard III.* v 3 180
Affairs that walk, As they say spirits do, at midnight, have In them a wilder nature than the business That seeks dispatch by day *Hen. VIII.* v 1 14
'Tis midnight, Charles; Prithee, to bed . . . . v 1 72
Were I as patient as the midnight sleep, By Jove, 'twould be my mind! *Coriolanus* iii 1 85
It is after midnight; and ere day We will awake him . *J. Cæsar* i 3 163
You secret, black, and midnight hags! What is't you do? . *Macbeth* iv 1 48
Thou mixture rank, of midnight weeds collected . . *Hamlet* iii 2 268
Let me be his undertaker: you shall hear more by midnight . *Othello* iv 1 225
Fill our bowls once more; Let's mock the midnight bell *Ant. and Cleo.* iii 13 185
Or have charged him, At the sixth hour of morn, at noon, at midnight, To encounter me with orisons! . . . . *Cymbeline* i 3 31
What hour is it?—Almost midnight, madam.—I have read three hours then . . . . ii 2 2
Here's a few flowers; but 'bout midnight, more . . . iv 2 283
Midriff. There's no room for faith, truth, nor honesty in this bosom of thine; it is all filled up with guts and midriff . 1 *Hen. IV.* iii 3 175
Midst. Our helpful ship was splitted in the midst . *Com. of Errors* i 1 104
Shiver and look pale, Make periods in the midst of sentences *M. N. Dream* v 1 96
First kiss me, Kate, and we will.—What, in the midst of the street? *T. of Shrew* v 1 149
I would ne'er have fled, But that they left me 'midst my enemies 1 *Hen. VI.* i 2 24
But, in the midst of this bright-shining day, I spy a black, suspicious, threatening cloud . . . . . . 3 *Hen. VI.* v 3 3
Unless, by not so doing, our good city Cleave in the midst *Coriolanus* iii 2 28
Here I'll sit i' the midst: Be large in mirth . . *Macbeth* iii 4 10
I' the midst o' the fight, When vantage like a pair of twins appear'd, Both as the same . . . . . *Ant. and Cleo.* iii 10 11
Then in the midst a tearing groan did break The name of Antony . . iv 14 31
Midsummer. Leander, he would have lived many a fair year, though Hero had turned nun, if it had not been for a hot midsummer night *As Y. Like It* iv 1 102
Why, this is very midsummer madness . . . *T. Night* iii 4 61
And gorgeous as the sun at midsummer . . 1 *Hen. IV.* iv 1 102
Midway. He were an excellent man that were made just in the midway between him and Benedick . . . . . . *Much Ado* ii 1 8
Midway between your tents and walls of Troy . *Troi. and Cres.* i 3 278
Choughs that wing the midway air Show scarce so gross as beetles *Lear* iv 6 13
No midway 'Twixt these extremes at all . . *Ant. and Cleo.* iii 4 19
A battery through his deafen'd parts, Which now are midway stopp'd *Pericles* v 1 48
Midwife. Does it work upon him?—Like aqua-vitæ with a midwife *T. Night* ii 5 216
Officious With Lady Margery, your midwife there . . *W. Tale* ii 3 160
Here's the midwife's name to't, one Mistress Tale-porter . . iv 4 272
So, Green, thou art the midwife to my woe . . *Richard II.* ii 2 62
But the midwives say the children are not in the fault; whereupon the world increases . . . . 2 *Hen. IV.* ii 2 28
My mother a Plantagenet,— I knew her well: she was a midwife 2 *Hen. VI.* iv 2 46
The midwife wonder'd and the women cried . 3 *Hen. VI.* v 6 74
How many saw the child?—Cornelia the midwife and myself . . . —The empress, the midwife, and yourself: Two may keep counsel when the third's away . . . . *T. Andron.* iv 2 141
Send the midwife presently to me. The midwife and the nurse well made away, Then let the ladies tattle what they please . . iv 2 167
She is the fairies' midwife . . . . . *Rom. and Jul.* i 4 54
Divinest patroness, and midwife gentle To those that cry by night *Per.* iii 1 11
Might. Then tell me If this might be a brother . . *Tempest* i 2 118
Would I might But ever see that man! . . . . . i 2 168
That I might sing it, madam, to a tune . . *T. G. of Ver.* i 2 80
With all his might For thee to fight . . . *Mer. Wives* ii 1 18
But might you do't, and do the world no wrong? . *Meas. for Meas.* ii 2 53
No might nor greatness in mortality Can censure 'scape . . . iii 2 196
Every man with his affects is born, Not by might master'd *L. L. Lost* i 1 153
Of his almighty dreadful little might . . . . . iii 1 205
By east, west, north, and south, I spread my conquering might . v 2 566
But I might see young Cupid's fiery shaft Quench'd *M. N. Dream* ii 1 161
All my powers, address your love and might To honour Helen! . . ii 2 143
Whose liquor hath this virtuous property, To take from thence all error with his might . . . . iii 2 368
What poor duty cannot do, noble respect Takes it in might, not merit . v 1 92
Lord worshipped might he be! . . . . *Mer. of Venice* ii 2 98
Who might be your mother, That you insult, exult? . *As Y. Like It* iii 5 35
Might. Now I find thy saw of might, 'Who ever loved that loved not at first sight?' . . . . *As Y. Like It* iii 5 82
Love no god, that would not extend his might, only where qualities were level; Dian no queen of virgins . . . . *All's Well* i 3 118
Might you not know she would do as she has done? . . . iii 4 2
England shall give him office, honour, might . . 2 *Hen. IV.* iv 5 130
Give entertainment to the might of it . . . . . iv 5 174
O God, that right should thus overcome might! . . . . iv 4 28
They know your grace hath cause and means and might . *Hen. V.* i 2 125
An oath of mickle might; and fury shall abate . . . . ii 1 70
Hark, what good sport is out of town to-day!—Better at home, if 'would I might' were 'may' . . . . *Troi. and Cres.* i 1 117
To be wise and love Exceeds man's might; that dwells with gods above iii 2 164
What we did was mildly as we might . . . . *T. Andron.* i 1 475
I have a man's mind, but a woman's might . . *J. Cæsar* ii 4 8
I should not urge thy duty past thy might . . . . iv 3 261
Before my God, I might not this believe Without the sensible and true avouch Of mine own eyes . . . . *Hamlet* i 1 56
Put upon you what restraint and grievance The law, with all his might to enforce it on, Will give him cable . . . . *Othello* i 2 16
Which till to-night I ne'er might say before . . . . ii 3 236
In wholesome wisdom He might not but refuse you . . . iii 1 50
I may not breathe my censure What he might be: if what he might he is not, I would to heaven he were! . . . . . . iv 1 282
Cleopatra does confess thy greatness; Submits her to thy might *Ant. and Cleo.* iii 12 17
Think you there was, or might be, such a man As this I dream'd of? . v 2 93
Would I might never O'ertake pursued success, but I do feel, By the rebound of yours, a grief that smites My very heart at root . v 2 102
Mightful. My lords, you know, as know the mightful gods *T. Andron.* iv 4 5
Mightier. Instruments of some more mightier member . *Meas. for Meas.* v 1 237
Turn your forces from this paltry siege And stir them up against a mightier task . . . . *K. John* ii 1 55
By your espials were discovered Two mightier troops . 1 *Hen. VI.* iv 3 7
But mightier crimes are laid unto your charge . 2 *Hen. VI.* iii 1 134
A man no mightier than thyself or me In personal action . *J. Cæsar* i 3 76
Mad as the sea and wind, when both contend Which is the mightier *Hamlet* iv 1 8
Mightiest. 'Tis [mercy] mightiest in the mightiest . *Mer. of Venice* iv 1 188
The mightiest space in fortune nature brings To join like likes and kiss like native things . . . . *All's Well* i 1 237
Herein all breathless lies The mightiest of thy greatest enemies *Rich. II.* v 6 32
But kings and mightiest potentates must die . . 1 *Hen. VI.* iii 2 136
As rigour of tempestuous gusts Provokes the mightiest hulk against the tide . . . . v 5 6
In the most high and palmy state of Rome, A little ere the mightiest Julius fell, The graves stood tenantless . . . . *Hamlet* i 1 114
Mightily. Whose estimation do you mightily hold up . . *Much Ado* ii 2 25
Hero hath been falsely accused, the prince and Claudio mightily abused v 2 100
If he do not mightily grace himself on thee . . . *As Y. Like It* i 1 155
Her [Fortune's] benefits are mightily misplaced . . . . i 2 38
I warrant your grace, you shall not entreat him to a second, that have so mightily persuaded him from a first . . . . i 2 218
Strive mightily, but eat and drink as friends . . . *T. of Shrew* i 2 279
How mightily sometimes we make us comforts of our losses!—And how mightily some other times we drown our gains in tears! *All's Well* iv 3 76
And kindreds are mightily strengthened . . . . 2 *Hen. IV.* ii 2 30
Therein thou wrong'st thy children mightily . . . 3 *Hen. VI.* iii 2 74
His physicians fear him mightily . . . . *Richard III.* i 1 137
Good king, to be so mightily abused! . . . . *T. Andron.* ii 3 87
There's never a one of you but trusts a knave, That mightily deceives you.—Do we, my lord? . . . . *T. of Athens* v 1 97
Where am I? Fair daylight? I am mightily abused . . . *Lear* iv 7 53
O, never was there queen So mightily betray'd . . *Ant. and Cleo.* i 3 25
Mightiness. Will't please your mightiness to wash your hands? *T. of S.* Ind. 2 78
Let us fear The native mightiness and fate of him . . *Hen. V.* ii 4 64
Your mightiness on both parts best can witness . . . . v 2 28
In a moment, see How soon this mightiness meets misery *Hen. VIII.* Prol. 30
And with that painted hope braves your mightiness . *T. Andron.* ii 3 126
Mighty. The most mighty Neptune Seem to besiege . . *Tempest* i 2 204
Love's a mighty lord And hath so humbled me . . *T. G. of Ver.* ii 4 136
Your hearts are mighty, your skins are whole . . *Mer. Wives* ii 1 111
You do yourself mighty wrong, Master Ford . . . . . iii 3 221
We were encounter'd by a mighty rock . . . *Com. of Errors* i 1 102
Most mighty duke, vouchsafe me speak a word . . . . v 1 282
I may example my digression by some mighty precedent . *L. L. Lost* i 2 122
Address'd a mighty power; which were on foot . *As Y. Like It* v 4 162
Say that he dreams, For he is nothing but a mighty lord *T. of Shrew* Ind. 1 65
O, that a mighty man of such descent, Of such possessions and so high esteem, Should be infused with so foul a spirit! . . . . Ind. 2 15
A mighty man of Pisa; by report I know him well . . . . ii 1 105
Pour'd all together, Would quite confound distinction, yet stand off In differences so mighty . . . . *All's Well* ii 3 128
Did to his majesty, his mother and his lady Offence of mighty note . v 3 14
As his person's mighty, Must it [his jealousy] be violent . *W. Tale* i 2 453
In himself too mighty, And in his parties, his alliance . . . ii 3 20
More than the stripes I have received, which are mighty ones and millions . . . . iv 3 61
Colbrand the giant, that same mighty man . . . . *K. John* i 1 225
How like you this wild counsel, mighty states? . . . . ii 1 395
Persever not, but hear me, mighty kings.—Speak on with favour . . ii 1 421
That yon green boy shall have no sun to ripe The bloom that promiseth a mighty fruit . . . . ii 1 473
I had a mighty cause To wish him dead . . . . . . iv 2 205
Withhold thine indignation, mighty heaven! . . . . . v 6 37
Most mighty liege, and my companion peers, Take from my mouth the wish of happy years . . . . *Richard II.* i 3 93
King Richard, he is in the mighty hold Of Bolingbroke . . . iii 4 83
I will from henceforth rather be myself, Mighty and to be fear'd, than my condition . . . . 1 *Hen. IV.* i 3 6
A mighty and a fearful head they are, If promises be kept . . . iii 2 167
Hitherwards intended speedily, With strong and mighty preparation . iv 1 93
The king with mighty and quick-raised power Meets with Lord Harry . iv 4 12
Suppose within the girdle of these walls Are now confined two mighty monarchies . . . . *Hen. V.* Prol. 20
Look back into your mighty ancestors . . . . . . i 2 102
Whiles his most mighty father on a hill Stood smiling to behold his lion's whelp . . . . i 2 108
In the very May-morn of his youth, Ripe for exploits and mighty enterprises . . . . i 2 121

Mighty. Such a mighty sum As never did the clergy at one time Bring in *Hen. V.* i 2 133
Model to thy inward greatness, Like little body with a mighty heart ii Prol. 17
'Tis best to weigh The enemy more mighty than he seems . . . ii 4 44
Any thing that may not misbecome The mighty sender, doth he prize you at . . . ii 4 119
He'll make your Paris Louvre shake for it, Were it the mistress-court of mighty Europe . . . ii 4 133
The mighty, or the huge, or the magnanimous, are all one reckonings . iv 7 17
Which like a mighty whiffler 'fore the king Seems to prepare his way v Prol. 12
Our bending author hath pursued the story, In little room confining mighty men . Epil. 3
Welcome, high prince, the mighty Duke of York! *1 Hen. VI.* iii 1 177
Are not the speedy scouts return'd again, That dogg'd the mighty army? iv 3 2
Cannot do him good, So mighty are his vowed enemies *2 Hen. VI.* iii 1 220
Whiles I in Ireland nourish a mighty band, I will stir up in England some black storm . . . iii 1 348
For daring to affy a mighty lord Unto the daughter of a worthless king iv 1 80
A mighty power Of gallowglasses and stout kerns Is marching hitherward in proud array . . . iv 9 25
Play'd the orator, Inferring arguments of mighty force . *3 Hen. VI.* ii 2 44
Now sways it this way, like a mighty sea . . . ii 5 5
Smooths the wrong, Inferreth arguments of mighty strength . iii 1 49
Mighty lord, this merry inclination Accords not with the sadness of my suit . . . iii 2 76
Are mighty gossips in this monarchy *Richard III.* i 1 83
How the poor soul did forsake The mighty Warwick, and did fight for me . . . ii 1 110
Who hath committed them?—The mighty dukes Gloucester and Buckingham . . . ii 4 44
Be not you spoke with, but by mighty suit . . . iii 7 46
So much is my poverty of spirit, So mighty and so many my defects iii 7 160
Being a bark to brook no mighty sea . . . iii 7 162
Refuse not, mighty lord, this proffer'd love . . . iii 7 202
Say, she shall be a high and mighty queen.—To wail the title iv 4 347
White-liver'd runagate, what doth he there?—I know not, mighty sovereign . . . iv 4 466
Most mighty sovereign, You have no cause to hold my friendship doubtful . . . iv 4 492
The Earl of Richmond Is with a mighty power landed at Milford . iv 4 535
His regiment lies half a mile at least South from the mighty power of the king . . . v 3 38
Bearing a state of mighty moment in't . *Hen. VIII.* ii 4 213
His promises were, as he then was, mighty; But his performance, as he is now, nothing . . . iv 2 41
To the high and mighty princess of England, Elizabeth! . v 5 3
All princely graces, That mould up such a mighty piece as this is . v 5 27
Most mighty for thy place and sway. *Troi. and Cres.* i 3 60
And mighty states characterless are grated To dusty nothing iii 2 195
And cry you all amain, 'Achilles hath the mighty Hector slain' . v 8 14
A reason mighty, strong, and effectual *T. Andron.* v 3 43
She whom mighty kingdoms court'sy to . . . v 3 74
'Tis said he gave unto his steward a mighty sum *T. of Athens* v 1 8
It is the part of men to fear and tremble, When the most mighty gods by tokens send Such dreadful heralds to astonish us *J. Cæsar* i 3 55
Those that with haste will make a mighty fire Begin it with weak straws i 3 107
What can be avoided Whose end is purposed by the mighty gods? ii 2 27
Most mighty Cæsar, let me know some cause, Lest I be laugh'd at ii 2 69
The senate have concluded To give this day a crown to mighty Cæsar ii 2 94
The mighty gods defend thee! . . . ii 3 9
Most high, most mighty, and most puissant Cæsar . . . iii 1 33
Cæsar was mighty, bold, royal, and loving . . . iii 1 127
O mighty Cæsar! dost thou lie so low? . . . iii 1 148
Then burst his mighty heart . . . iii 2 190
And sell the mighty space of our large honours For so much trash? iv 3 25
Young Octavius and Mark Antony Come down upon us with a mighty power . . . iv 3 169
On our former ensign Two mighty eagles fell, and there they perch'd v 1 81
O Julius Cæsar, thou art mighty yet! Thy spirit walks abroad v 3 94
High and mighty, You shall know I am set naked on your kingdom *Hamlet* iv 7 43
'Tis dangerous when the baser nature comes Between the pass and fell incensed points Of mighty opposites . . . v 2 62
If the matter of this paper be certain, you have mighty business in hand *Lear* iii 5 17
O you mighty gods! This world I do renounce . . . iv 6 34
What charms, What conjuration and what mighty magic . *Othello* i 3 92
The Turk with a most mighty preparation makes for Cyprus . . . i 3 221
Cæsar and Lepidus Are in the field: a mighty strength they carry *Ant. and Cleo.* ii 1 17
Be not angry, Most mighty princess, that I have adventured *Cymbeline* i 6 172
Though mean and mighty, rotting Together, have one dust iv 2 246
Mighty sir, These two young gentlemen . . . are none of mine v 5 327
Here have you seen a mighty king His child, I wis, to incest bring *Pericles* ii Gower 1
My derivation was from ancestors Who stood equivalent with mighty kings . . . v 1 92

Milan. Twelve year since, Thy father was the Duke of Milan . *Tempest* i 2 54
She said thou wast my daughter; and thy father Was Duke of Milan . i 2 58
He needs will be Absolute Milan . . . i 2 109
And bend The dukedom yet unbow'd—alas, poor Milan! . i 2 115
And confer fair Milan With all the honours on my brother . i 2 126
One midnight Fated to the purpose did Antonio open The gates of Milan i 2 130
The Duke of Milan And his brave son being twain.—The Duke of Milan And his more braver daughter could control thee . i 2 437
O thou mine heir Of Naples and of Milan, what strange fish Hath made his meal on thee? . ii 1 112
Milan and Naples have Moe widows in them of this business' making Than we bring men to comfort them . ii 1 132
Twenty consciences, That stand 'twixt me and Milan, candied be they! ii 1 279
As thou got'st Milan, I'll come by Naples . ii 1 291
Remember . . . that you three From Milan did supplant good Prospero iii 3 70
I will discase me, and myself present As I was sometime Milan . v 1 86
Behold, sir king, The wronged Duke of Milan, Prospero . v 1 107
That very duke Which was thrust forth of Milan . v 1 160
Daughter to this famous Duke of Milan, Of whom so often I have heard v 1 192
Was Milan thrust from Milan, that his issue Should become kings of Naples? . v 1 205
Retire me to my Milan, where Every third thought shall be my grave . v 1 310
To Milan let me hear from thee by letters Of thy success *T. G. of Ver.* i 1 57
Milan. All happiness bechance to thee in Milan!—As much to you at home! *T. G. of Ver.* i 1 61
But now he parted hence, to embark for Milan . i 1 71
Welcome to Milan!—Forswear not thyself, sweet youth, for I am not welcome . ii 5 2
Whence came you?—From Milan.—Have you long sojourned there? . iv 1 19
I saw the Duchess of Milan's gown that they praise so . *Much Ado* iii 4 16
I Pandulph, of fair Milan cardinal . *K. John* iii 1 138
My holy lord of Milan, from the king I come, to learn how you have dealt . v 2 120

Milch. Would have made milch the burning eyes of heaven . *Hamlet* ii 2 540

Milch-kine. And makes milch-kine yield blood . *Mer. Wives* iv 4 33
I have a hundred milch-kine to the pail . *T. of Shrew* ii 1 359

Mild. A virtuous gentlewoman, mild and beautiful! . *T. G. of Ver.* iv 4 185
Mild, or come not near me; noble, or not I for an angel . *Much Ado* ii 3 34
Ravish savage ears And plant in tyrants mild humility . *L. L. Lost* iv 3 349
A foolish mild man; an honest man, look you, and soon dashed . v 2 584
The mild hind Makes speed to catch the tiger . *M. N. Dream* ii 1 232
She in mild terms begg'd my patience . iv 1 63
In me what strange effect Would they work in mild aspect! *As Y. Like It* iv 3 53
Maid's mild behaviour and sobriety . *T. of Shrew* i 1 71
Her wondrous qualities and mild behaviour . ii 1 50
To smooth his fault I should have been more mild . *Richard II.* i 3 240
In peace was never gentle lamb more mild . ii 1 174
But be thou mild and blush not at my shame . *2 Hen. VI.* ii 4 48
We know the time since he was mild and affable . iii 1 9
The duke is virtuous, mild and too well given To dream on evil . iii 1 72
And that my sovereign's presence makes me mild, I would, false murderous coward, on thy knee Make thee beg pardon . iii 2 219
Breathe my soul into the air, As mild and gentle as the cradle-babe iii 2 392
Women are soft, mild, pitiful and flexible; Thou stern, obdurate *3 Hen. VI.* i 4 141
The tiger will be mild whiles she doth mourn . iii 1 39
For of that sin My mild entreaty shall not make you guilty . iii 1 91
These were her words, utter'd with mild disdain . iv 1 98
O, he was gentle, mild, and virtuous!—The fitter for the King of heaven, that hath him . *Richard III.* i 2 104
But if she be obdurate To mild entreaties . iii 1 40
I will be mild and gentle in my speech.—And brief, good mother . iv 4 160
More mild, but yet more harmful, kind in hatred . iv 4 172
Be more mild and tractable . *T. Andron.* i 1 470
It almost turns my dangerous nature mild . *T. of Athens* iv 3 499
I marvel our mild husband Not met us on the way . *Lear* iv 2 1
And testy wrath Could never be her mild companion . *Pericles* i 1 18
He's father, son, and husband mild; I mother, wife, and yet his child i 1 68
Now, mild may be thy life! For a more blustrous birth had never babe iii 1 27

Milder. I find her milder than she was . *T. G. of Ver.* v 2 2
If the gentle spirit of moving words Can no way change you to a milder form . v 4 56
No mates for you, Unless you were of gentler, milder mould *T. of Shrew* i 1 60
Why did you wish me milder? would you have me False to my nature? *Coriolanus* iii 2 14

Mildest. Ah, what sharp stings are in her mildest words! . *All's Well* iii 4 18
To stir a mutiny in the mildest thoughts . *T. Andron.* iv 1 85

Mildews the white wheat, and hurts the poor creature of earth . *Lear* iii 4 123

Mildewed. Like a mildew'd ear, Blasting his wholesome brother *Hamlet* iii 4 64

Mildly. She never reprehended him but mildly . *Com. of Errors* v 1 87
Deal mildly with his youth . *Richard II.* ii 1 69
Take thy correction mildly, kiss the rod . v 1 32
Arm yourself To answer mildly . *Coriolanus* iii 2 139
The word is 'mildly.' Pray you, let us go . iii 2 142
I will answer in mine honour.—Ay, but mildly.—Well, mildly be it then. Mildly! . iii 2 144
That what we did was mildly as we might . *T. Andron.* i 1 475

Mildness. Hearing thy mildness praised in every town . *T. of Shrew* ii 1 192
Thou with mildness entertain'st thy wooers, With gentle conference ii 1 252
He is famed for mildness, peace, and prayer . *3 Hen. VI.* ii 1 156
Makes me bridle passion And bear with mildness my misfortune's cross iv 4 20
My mildness hath allay'd their swelling griefs . iv 8 42
In the mildness of your sleepy thoughts . *Richard III.* iii 7 123
Yet, under pardon, You are much more attask'd for want of wisdom Than praised for harmful mildness . *Lear* i 4 367

Mile. This boy will carry a letter twenty mile, as easy as a cannon will shoot point-blank twelve score . *Mer. Wives* iii 2 33
He were as good go a mile on his errand . *Meas. for Meas.* iii 2 38
He would have walked ten mile a-foot to see a good armour . *Much Ado* ii 3 17
That no woman shall come within a mile of my court . *L. L. Lost* i 1 120
The letter is too long by half a mile . v 2 54
We have measured many miles To tread a measure with her on this grass . v 2 184
Ask them how many inches Is in one mile . v 2 189
If to come hither you have measured miles, And many miles, the princess bids you tell How many inches doth fill up one mile . v 2 191
How many weary steps, Of many weary miles you have o'ergone, Are number'd in the travel of one mile? . v 2 196
Meet me in the palace wood, a mile without the town . *M. N. Dream* i 2 104
There is a monastery two miles off: And there will we abide *M. of Ven.* iii 4 31
Therefore haste away, For we must measure twenty miles to-day . iii 4 84
Within these ten days if that thou be'st found So near our public court as twenty miles, Thou diest for it . *As Y. Like It* i 3 46
I have a kinsman not past three quarters of a mile hence . *W. Tale* iv 3 86
Married a tinker's wife within a mile where my land and living lies iv 3 104
These high wild hills and rough uneven ways Draws out our miles *Richard II.* ii 3 5
Why have they dared to march So many miles upon her peaceful bosom! . ii 3 93
Eight yards of uneven ground is threescore and ten miles afoot with me; and the stony-hearted villains know it . *1 Hen. IV.* ii 2 27
Thou and I have thirty miles to ride yet ere dinner time . iii 3 222
Pamper'd jades of Asia, Which cannot go but thirty mile a-day *2 Hen. IV.* ii 4 179
I must a dozen mile to-night . iii 2 310
Fill the cup, and let it come; I'll pledge you a mile to the bottom . v 3 57
Not to come near our person by ten mile . v 5 69
Will it never be day? I will trot to-morrow a mile, and my way shall be paved with English faces . *Hen. V.* iii 7 87
Some six miles off the duke is with the soldiers . *3 Hen. VI.* ii 1 144
Why dost thou run so many mile about, When thou mayst tell thy tale a nearer way? Once more, what news? . *Richard III.* iv 4 461
His regiment lies half a mile at least South from the mighty power . v 3 37
At Dunstable, six miles off From Ampthill . *Hen. VIII.* iv 1 27

Mile. How far off lie these armies?—Within this mile and half *Coriolanus* i 4 8
Boils and plagues Plaster you o'er, that you may be abhorr'd Further than seen and one infect another Against the wind a mile! . . . i 4 34
'Tis not a mile; briefly we heard their drums . . . i 6 16
How couldst thou in a mile confound an hour, And bring thy news so late? i 6 17
I was forced to wheel Three or four miles about . . . i 6 20
A mile before his tent fall down, and knee The way into his mercy . v 1 5
My lord, I aim a mile beyond the moon . . . *T. Andron.* iv 3 65
Villain and he be many miles asunder . . . . *Rom. and Jul.* iii 5 82
Within this mile break forth a hundred springs . . *T. of Athens* iv 3 421
His horses go about.—Almost a mile . . . *Macbeth* iii 3 12
Within this three mile may you see it coming; I say, a moving grove . v 5 37
For many miles about There's scarce a bush . . . *Lear* ii 4 304
Thou wilt o'ertake us, hence a mile or twain . . . iv 1 44
How many score of miles may we well ride 'Twixt hour and hour? *Cymb.* iii 2 69
Why hast thou abused So many miles with a pretence? . . . iii 4 106
Pray, how far thither? 'Ods pittikins! can it be six mile yet? . iv 2 293
Mile-a. A merry heart goes all the day, Your sad tires in a mile-a *W. Tale* iv 3 135
Mile-end. The officer at a place there called Mile-end . *All's Well* iv 3 302
I remember at Mile-end Green, when I lay at Clement's Inn 2 *Hen. IV.* iii 2 298
Milford. Richmond Is with a mighty power landed at Milford *Rich. III.* iv 4 535
How far it is To this same blessed Milford . . . *Cymbeline* iii 2 61
There's no more to say; Accessible is none but Milford way . . . iii 2 84
My revenge is now at Milford: would I had wings to follow it! . . iii 5 161
To Milford go, And find not her whom thou pursuest . . . iii 5 165
Milford, When from the mountain-top Pisanio show'd thee, Thou wast within a ken: O Jove! I think Foundations fly the wretched . . iii 6 4
I have a kinsman who Is bound for Italy; he embark'd at Milford . iii 6 62
Which directed him To seek her on the mountains near to Milford . v 5 281
Milford-Haven. I am in Cambria, at Milford-Haven: what your own love will out of this advise you, follow . . . *Cymbeline* iii 2 44
He is at Milford-Haven: read, and tell me How far 'tis thither . iii 2 51
Take away her life: I shall give thee opportunity at Milford-Haven . iii 4 29
Lucius the Roman, comes to Milford-Haven To-morrow . . . iii 4 145
I desire of you A conduct over-land to Milford-Haven . . . iii 5 8
Meet thee at Milford-Haven!—I forgot to ask him one thing . . iii 5 133
How long is't since she went to Milford-Haven?—She can scarce be there yet . . . . iii 5 153
Whither bound?—To Milford-Haven.—What's your name?—Fidele, sir iii 6 59
Attending You here at Milford-Haven with your ships . . . iv 2 335
Militarist. The gallant militarist,—that was his own phrase *All's Well* iv 3 161
Military. Speak from thy lungs military . . *Mer. Wives* iv 5 18
Most military sir, salutation . . . . *L. L. Lost* v 1 38
Is there no military policy, how virgins might blow up men? *All's Well* i 1 132
Holds from all soldiers chief majority And military title capital 1 *Hen. IV.* iii 2 110
In military rules, humours of blood, He was the mark and glass, copy and book, That fashion'd others . . . . . 2 *Hen. IV.* ii 3 30
Nor do I as an enemy to peace Troop in the throngs of military men . iv 1 62
He will maintain his argument as well as any military man in the world *Hen. V.* iii 2 86
As touching the direction of the military discipline; that is the point . iii 2 107
Milk. They'll take suggestion as a cat laps milk . . . *Tempest* ii 1 288
She can milk; look you, a sweet virtue in a maid with clean hands *T. G. of Ver.* iii 1 277
'Imprimis: She can milk.'—Ay, that she can.—'Item: She brews good ale' . . . . iii 1 302
One sweet word with thee.—Honey, and milk, and sugar . *L. L. Lost* v 2 231
Tom bears logs into the hall And milk comes frozen home in pail . v 2 925
Skim milk, and sometimes labour in the quern . *M. N. Dream* ii 1 36
Come, come to me, With hands as pale as milk . . . v 1 345
Who, inward search'd, have livers white as milk . *Mer. of Venice* iii 2 86
He weeps like a wench that had shed her milk . . *All's Well* iv 3 124
One would think his mother's milk were scarce out of him . *T. Night* i 5 171
The innocent milk in it most innocent mouth, Haled out to murder *W. T.* iii 2 101
I'll queen it no inch farther, But milk my ewes and weep . . iv 4 461
For moving such a dish of skim milk with so honourable an action 1 *Hen. IV.* ii 3 36
I would the milk Thy mother gave thee when thou suck'dst her breast Had been a little ratsbane for thy sake! . . . 1 *Hen. VI.* v 4 27
There is no more mercy in him than there is milk in a male tiger *Coriol.* v 4 30
The milk thou suck'dst from her did turn to marble . *T. Andron.* ii 3 144
Adversity's sweet milk, philosophy . . . . *Rom. and Jul.* iii 3 55
I fear thy nature; It is too full o' the milk of human kindness *Macbeth* i 5 18
Come to my woman's breasts, And take my milk for gall! . . . i 5 49
I have given suck, and know How tender 'tis to love the babe that milks me . . . . i 7 55
Had I power, I should Pour the sweet milk of concord into hell . . iv 3 98
It doth posset And curd, like eager droppings into milk . *Hamlet* i 5 69
The vines of France and milk of Burgundy Strive to be interess'd *Lear* i 1 86
Commanded By such poor passion as the maid that milks *Ant. and Cleo.* iv 15 74
With fingers long, small, white as milk . . . *Pericles* iv Gower 22
Milked. I remember the kissing of her batlet and the cow's dugs that her pretty chopt hands had milked . . . . *As Y. Like It* ii 4 51
Milking-time. Is there not milking-time, when you are going to bed, or kiln-hole, to whistle off these secrets? . . . *W. Tale* iv 4 246
Milk-liver'd man! That bear'st a cheek for blows . . . *Lear* iv 2 50
Milkmaid. Yet 'tis a milkmaid; yet 'tis not a maid. . *T. G. of Ver.* iii 1 268
And thy head stands so tickle on thy shoulders that a milkmaid, if she be in love, may sigh it off . . . . . *Meas. for Meas.* i 2 177
Milk-pap. Those milk-paps, That through the window-bars bore at men's eyes, Are not within the leaf of pity writ . *T. of Athens* iv 3 115
Milksop. Boys, apes, braggarts, Jacks, milksops! . . . *Much Ado* v 1 91
A paltry fellow, . . . A milk-sop, one that never in his life Felt so much cold as over shoes in snow . . . *Richard III.* v 3 325
Milk-white. Even in the milk-white bosom of thy love . *T. G. of Ver.* iii 1 250
A little western flower, Before milk-white, now purple . *M. N. Dream* ii 1 167
Then will I raise aloft the milk-white rose . . 2 *Hen. VI.* i 1 254
But where the bull and cow are both milk-white, They never do beget a coal-black calf . . . . . . *T. Andron.* v 1 31
Four milk-white horses, trapp'd in silver . . . *T. of Athens* i 2 189
Milky. Has friendship such a faint and milky heart, It turns in less than two nights? O you gods! . . . . iii 1 57
His sword, Which was declining on the milky head Of reverend Priam *Hamlet* ii 2 500
This milky gentleness and course of yours Though I condemn not *Lear* i 4 364
Mill. More sacks to the mill! O heavens, I have my wish! . *L. L. Lost* iv 3 81
Or thou goest to the grange or mill.—If to either, thou dost ill *W. Tale* iv 4 309
At the cypress grove: I pray you—'Tis south the city mills . *Coriolanus* i 10 31
More water glideth by the mill Than wots the miller of . *T. Andron.* ii 1 85
Poor pelting villages, sheep-cotes, and mills . . . . *Lear* ii 3 18
Mille. Sur mes genoux je vous donne mille remercimens . . *Hen. V.* iv 4 57
Miller. Two Edward shovel-boards, that cost me two shilling and two pence a-piece of Yead Miller . . . . . *Mer. Wives* i 1 160
More water glideth by the mill Than wots the miller of . *T. Andron.* ii 1 86
Milliner. No milliner can so fit his customers with gloves *W. Tale* iv 4 192
He was perfumed like a milliner . . . . . 1 *Hen. IV.* i 3 36
Million. Few in millions Can speak like us . . . *Tempest* ii 1 7
O, give ye good even! here's a million of manners . *T. G. of Ver.* ii 1 105
Millions of false eyes Are stuck upon thee . . . *Meas. for Meas.* iv 1 60
Fate o'er-rules, that, one man holding troth, A million fail *M. N. Dream* iii 2 93
He hath disgraced me, and hindered me half a million *Mer. of Venice* iii 1 57
I'll buckler thee against a million . . . . *T. of Shrew* iii 2 241
Stripes I have received, which are mighty ones and millions . *W. Tale* iv 3 61
A million of beating may come to a great matter . . . iv 3 62
A thousand pound, Hal! a million: thy love is worth a million 1 *Hen. IV.* iii 3 155
Since a crooked figure may Attest in little place a million . *Hen. V.* Prol. 16
Within thine eyes sat twenty thousand deaths, In thy hands clutch'd as many millions, in Thy lying tongue both numbers *Coriolanus* iii 3 71
I would not for a million of gold The cause were known . *T. Andron.* ii 1 49
Some that smile have in their hearts, I fear, Millions of mischiefs *J. C.* iv 1 51
The play, I remember, pleased not the million . . . *Hamlet* ii 2 457
If thou prate of mountains, let them throw Millions of acres on us! . v 1 304
There's millions now alive That nightly lie in those unproper beds Which they dare swear peculiar . . . . . *Othello* iv 1 68
How many boys and wenches must I have?—If every of your wishes had a womb, And fertile every wish, a million . *Ant. and Cleo.* i 2 39
Whose heart I thought I had, for she had mine; Which whilst it was mine had annex'd unto't A million more, now lost . . . iv 14 18
If you buy ladies' flesh at a million a dram, you cannot preserve it from tainting . . . . *Cymbeline* i 4 147
Spare your arithmetic: never count the turns; Once, and a million! . ii 4 143
Mill-sixpence. Seven groats in mill-sixpences . . . *Mer. Wives* i 1 158
Millstone. Your eyes drop millstones . . . *Richard III.* i 3 354
He will weep.—Ay, millstones; as he lesson'd us to weep . . i 4 246
Hecuba laughed that her eyes ran o'er.—With mill-stones *Troi. and Cres.* i 2 158
Mill-wheel. Didst vent thy groans As fast as mill-wheels strike *Tempest* i 2 281
Milo. Bull-bearing Milo his addition yield To sinewy Ajax *Troi. and Cres.* ii 3 258
Mimic. And forth my mimic comes . . . *M. N. Dream* iii 2 19
Mince. Hold up your head, and mince . . . . *Mer. Wives* v 1 9
I know no ways to mince it in love, but directly to say 'I love you' *Hen. V.* v 2 130
Thy throat shall cut, And mince it sans remorse . . *T. of Athens* iv 3 122
Minces virtue, and does shake the head To hear of pleasure's name *Lear* iv 6 122
Thy honesty and love doth mince this matter, Making it light *Othello* ii 3 247
Speak to me home, mince not the general tongue . *Ant. and Cleo.* i 2 109
Minced. A minced man: and then to be baked with no date in the pie, for then the man's date's out . . . *Troi. and Cres.* i 2 279
Mincing. And turn two mincing steps Into a manly stride *Mer. of Venice* iii 4 67
Set my teeth nothing on edge, Nothing so much as mincing poetry 1 *Hen. IV.* iii 1 134
Which gifts, Saving your mincing, the capacity Of your soft cheveril conscience would receive . . . . . . *Hen. VIII.* ii 3 31
When she saw Pyrrhus make malicious sport In mincing with his sword her husband's limbs . . . . *Hamlet* ii 2 537
Mind. Shall we give o'er and drown? Have you a mind to sink? *Tempest* i 1 42
But how is it That this lives in thy mind? . . . . i 2 49
All dedicated To closeness and the bettering of my mind . . . i 2 90
For still 'tis beating in my mind, your reason For raising this sea-storm i 2 176
O, that you bore The mind that I do! . . . . . ii 1 267
I'll fall flat; Perchance he will not mind me . . . . ii 2 17
A turn or two I'll walk, To still my beating mind . . . iv 1 163
As with age his body uglier grows, So his mind cankers . . . iv 1 192
Since I saw thee, The affliction of my mind amends . . . v 1 115
Do not infest your mind with beating on The strangeness of this business . . . . v 1 246
Being so hard to me that brought your mind, I fear she'll prove as hard to you in telling your mind . . . . . *T. G. of Ver.* i 1 148
I'll show my mind According to my shallow simple skill . . i 2 7
O, they love least that let men know their love.—I would I knew his mind . . . . i 2 33
I see you have a month's mind to them . . . . . i 2 137
Or fearing else some messenger that might her mind discover . . ii 1 173
That hath more mind to feed on your blood than live in your air . ii 4 27
He is complete in feature and in mind With all good grace . . ii 4 73
But when I call to mind your gracious favours Done to me . . iii 1 6
Dumb jewels often in their silent kind More than quick words do move a woman's mind . . . . iii 1 91
You are already Love's firm votary. And cannot soon revolt and change your mind . . . . iii 2 59
Entreated me to call and know her mind . . . . . iv 3 2
He bears an honourable mind, And will not use a woman lawlessly . v 3 13
It is the lesser blot, modesty finds, Women to change their shapes than men their minds.—Than men their minds! 'tis true . . . v 4 109
So Got udge me, that is a virtuous mind . . . *Mer. Wives* i 1 192
Notwithstanding that, I know Anne's mind,—that's neither here nor there . . . . i 4 112
Never a woman in Windsor knows more of Anne's mind than I do . i 4 137
I have to show to the contrary.—Faith, but you do, in my mind . ii 1 39
Have a nay-word, that you may know one another's mind . . ii 2 132
Whatsoever I have merited, either in my mind or in my means . . ii 2 211
How full of chollors I am, and trempling of mind! . . . iii 1 12
Keep in that mind; I'll deserve it.—Nay, I must tell you, so you do; or else I could not be in that mind . . . . . . iii 3 89
Knowing my mind, you wrong me, Master Fenton . . . . iii 4 80
Send quickly to Sir John, to know his mind . . . . . iv 4 83
Talk not to me; my mind is heavy . . . . . . iv 6 2
Shuffle her away, While other sports are tasking of their minds . iv 6 30
The guiltiness of my mind, the sudden surprise of my powers . . v 5 130
Rebate and blunt his natural edge With profits of the mind *Meas. for Meas.* i 4 61
Fasting maids whose minds are dedicate To nothing temporal . . ii 2 154
Yet hath he in him such a mind of honour . . . . ii 4 179
Fit his mind to death, for his soul's rest . . . . . ii 4 187
My mind promises with my habit no loss shall touch her by my company . . . . iii 1 181
Time out of mind . . . . . . iv 2 17; *Rom. and Jul.* i 4 69
To transport him in the mind he is Were damnable . *Meas. for Meas.* iv 3 72
Did but convey unto our fearful minds A doubtful warrant *Com. of Errors* i 1 68
Jugglers that deceive the eye, Dark-working sorcerers that change the mind . . . . i 2 99
Know'st thou his mind?—Ay, ay, he told his mind upon mine ear . ii 1 48

Mind. I am transformed, master, am I not?—I think thou art in mind, and so am I.—Nay, master, both in mind and in my shape *Com. of Errors* ii 2 198
For servants must their masters' minds fulfil iv 1 113
Foolish, blunt, unkind, Stigmatical in making, worse in mind iv 2 22
God keep your ladyship still in that mind! *Much Ado* i 1 135
Would the cook were of my mind! i 3 75
A time too brief, too, to have all things answer my mind ii 1 376
Before God! and, in my mind, very wise ii 3 192
It would better fit your honour to change your mind iii 2 119
Both strength of limb and policy of mind, Ability in means iv 1 200
In some reclusive and religious life, Out of all eyes, tongues, minds iv 1 245
Fare you well, boy: you know my mind v 1 188
I'll hold my mind, were she an Ethiope v 4 38
The mind shall banquet, though the body pine *L. L. Lost* i 1 25
Whoe'er a' was, a' show'd a mounting mind iv 1 4
But omne bene, say I; being of an old father's mind iv 2 33
What would these strangers? know their minds, Boyet v 2 174
Henceforth my wooing mind shall be express'd In russet yeas v 2 412
I wish you the peace of mind, most royal couplement! v 2 534
There are Worthies a-coming will speak their mind in some other sort v 2 589
Being over-full of self-affairs, My mind did lose it *M. N. Dream* i 1 114
Helen, to you our minds we will unfold i 1 208
Love looks not with the eyes, but with the mind i 1 234
Nor hath Love's mind of any judgement taste i 1 236
I had no judgement when to her I swore.—Nor none, in my mind, now you give her o'er iii 2 135
As if our hands, our sides, voices and minds, Had been incorporate iii 2 207
Their minds transfigured so together, More witnesseth than fancy's images v 1 24
Hard-handed men that work in Athens here, Which never labour'd in their minds till now v 1 73
Your mind is tossing on the ocean *Mer. of Venice* i 1 8
At dinner-time, I pray you, have in mind where we must meet i 1 71
I have a mind presages me such thrift i 1 175
He grows kind.—I like not fair terms and a villain's mind i 3 181
'Rouse up a brave mind,' says the fiend, 'and run' ii 2 13
And better in my mind not undertook ii 4 7
By Jacob's staff, I swear, I have no mind of feasting forth to-night ii 5 37
Fast bind, fast find; A proverb never stale in thrifty mind ii 5 55
A golden mind stoops not to shows of dross ii 7 20
Let it not enter in your mind of love ii 8 42
Not sick, my lord, unless it be in mind; Nor well, unless in mind iii 2 237
My people do already know my mind iii 4 37
I have within my mind A thousand raw tricks of these bragging Jacks iii 4 76
Gratify this gentleman, For, in my mind, you are much bound to him iv 1 407
My mind was never yet more mercenary iv 1 418
Nothing else but only this; And now methinks I have a mind to it iv 1 433
And all the world was of my father's mind *As Y. Like It* i 2 248
Invest me in my motley; give me leave To speak my mind ii 7 59
Let no fair be kept in mind But the fair of Rosalind iii 2 99
I am not in the mind but I were better to be married of him than of another iii 3 91
I would not have my right Rosalind of this mind iv 1 110
And by him seal up thy mind iv 3 58
He sent me word, if I said his beard was not cut well, he was in the mind it was v 4 75
And frame your mind to mirth and merriment *T. of Shrew* Ind. 2 137
Tell me thy mind; for I have Pisa left And am to Padua come i 1 21
My lord, you nod; you do not mind the play.—Yes, by Saint Anne, do I i 1 254
Nay, look you, sir, he tells you flatly what his mind is i 2 78
This gentleman is happily arrived, My mind presumes, for his own good and ours i 2 214
Was it [music] not to refresh the mind of man After his studies? iii 1 11
I am no child, no babe: Your betters have endured me say my mind iv 3 75
Our purses shall be proud, our garments poor; For 'tis the mind that makes the body rich iv 3 174
And the moon changes even as your mind iv 5 20
My mind hath been as big as one of yours, My heart as great v 2 170
For where an unclean mind carries virtuous qualities, there commendations go with pity *All's Well* i 1 48
He and his physicians Are of a mind i 3 244
An thy mind stand to't, boy, steal away bravely ii 1 29
This is his majesty; say your mind to him ii 1 98
I have no mind to Isbel since I was at court iii 2 13
If the quick fire of youth light not your mind, You are no maiden iv 2 5
A mind that suits With this thy fair and outward character *T. Night* i 2 50
I am a fellow o' the strangest mind i' the world i 3 120
Tell me your mind: I am a messenger i 5 219
Your lord does know my mind; I cannot love him i 5 276
And fear to find Mine eye too great a flatterer for my mind i 5 328
She bore a mind that envy could not but call fair ii 1 30
Make thy doublet of changeable taffeta, for thy mind is a very opal ii 4 77
Not black in my mind, though yellow in my legs iii 4 28
Wonder not, nor admire not in thy mind iii 4 166
In nature there's no blemish but the mind; None can be call'd deform'd but the unkind iii 4 401
The bells of Saint Bennet, sir, may put you in mind; one, two, three v 1 42
Yet shall the oracle Give rest to the minds of others *W. Tale* ii 1 191
If thou hast The ordering of the mind too, 'mongst all colours No yellow in't! ii 3 106
But that the good mind of Camillo tardied My swift command iii 2 163
They themselves are o' the mind, if it be not too rough for some that know little but bowling, it will please plentifully iv 4 337
Your heart is full of something that does take Your mind from feasting iv 4 358
I think affliction may subdue the cheek, But not take in the mind iv 4 588
If I had a mind to be honest, I see Fortune would not suffer me iv 4 862
I'll not seek far—For him, I partly know his mind v 3 142
Your mind is all as youthful as your blood *K. John* iii 4 125
This murder had not come into my mind iv 2 223
Which, howsoever rude exteriorly, Is yet the cover of a fairer mind iv 2 258
His [death's] siege is now Against the mind, the which he pricks and wounds v 7 17
Now put it, God, in the physician's mind To help him to his grave! *Richard II.* i 4 59
Nay, speak thy mind; and let him ne'er speak more That speaks thy words again to do thee harm! ii 1 230
Richard, with the eyes of heavy mind I see thy glory like a shooting star Fall ii 4 18
The which, how far off from the mind of Bolingbroke It is iii 3 45

Mind. Now, Bagot, freely speak thy mind; What thou dost know *Richard II.* iv 1 2
Before I freely speak my mind herein, You shall not only take the sacrament iv 1 327
What, is my Richard both in shape and mind Transform'd and weaken'd? v 1 26
The mind of Bolingbroke is changed; You must to Pomfret v 1 51
But now I know thy mind; thou dost suspect That I have been disloyal v 2 104
Sweet York, sweet husband, be not of that mind v 2 107
I am not yet of Percy's mind, the Hotspur of the north *1 Hen. IV.* ii 4 114
I say the earth was not of my mind, If you suppose as fearing you it shook iii 1 22
Under whose government come they along?—His letters bear his mind, not I iv 1 20
Holy in his thoughts, He's follow'd both with body and with mind *2 Hen. IV.* i 1 203
To speak truth, This present grief had wiped it from my mind i 1 211
'Tis with my mind As with the tide swell'd up unto his height ii 3 62
An captains were of my mind, they would truncheon you out ii 4 153
Other gambol faculties a' has, that show a weak mind and an able body ii 4 273
I'll ne'er bear a base mind: an't be my destiny, so; an't be not, so iii 2 252
Thou'rt a good fellow.—Faith, I'll bear no base mind iii 2 257
To diet rank minds sick of happiness iv 1 64
The incessant care and labour of his mind Hath wrought the mure that should confine it in So thin that life looks through iv 4 118
O my son, God put it in thy mind to take it hence! iv 5 179
Be it thy course to busy giddy minds With foreign quarrels iv 5 214
With uncurbed plainness Tell us the Dauphin's mind *Hen. V.* i 2 245
To-morrow shall you know our mind at full.—Dispatch us with all speed ii 4 140
Grapple your minds to sternage of this navy iii Prol. 18
Still be kind, And eke out our performance with your mind iii Prol. 35
Partly for the satisfaction, look you, of my mind iii 2 106
If I find a hole in his coat, I will tell him my mind iii 6 89
What shall I know of thee?—My master's mind.—Unfold it iii 6 123
And when the mind is quicken'd, out of doubt, The organs, though defunct and dead before, Break up their drowsy grave and newly move iv 1 20
Howsoever you speak this to feel other men's minds iv 1 131
Who with a body fill'd and vacant mind Gets him to rest iv 1 286
Fight valiantly to-day: And yet I do thee wrong to mind thee of it iv 3 13
All things are ready, if our minds be so iv 3 71
Perish the man whose mind is backward now! iv 3 72
The constable desires thee thou wilt mind Thy followers of repentance iv 3 84
Therefore, queen of all, Katharine, break thy mind to me in broken English v 2 265
In your fair minds let this acceptance take Epil. 14
Cease, cease these jars and rest your minds in peace *1 Hen. VI.* i 1 44
But we shall meet, and break our minds at large i 3 81
You perceive my mind?—I do, my lord, and mean accordingly ii 2 59
Be not dismay'd, fair lady; nor misconstrue The mind of Talbot ii 3 74
Call we to mind, and mark but this for proof iii 3 68
I dare not speak: I'll call for pen and ink, and write my mind v 3 66
With as humble lowliness of mind She is content to be at your command v 5 18
The mutual conference that my mind hath had, By day, by night *2 Hen. VI.* i 1 25
I know your mind; 'Tis not my speeches that you do mislike i 1 139
I cannot go before, While Gloucester bears this base and humble mind i 2 62
All his mind is bent to holiness, To number Ave-Maries on his beads i 3 58
'Tis but a base ignoble mind That mounts no higher than a bird can soar ii 1 13
My lord, break we off; we know your mind at full ii 2 77
Ill can thy noble mind abrook The abject people gazing on thy face ii 4 10
Me seemeth then it is no policy, Respecting what a rancorous mind he bears iii 1 24
Had I first been put to speak my mind, I think I should have told iii 1 43
But, in my mind, that were no policy iii 1 238
By this I shall perceive the commons' mind iii 1 374
Sirs, stand apart; the king shall know your mind iii 2 242
There's no better sign of a brave mind than a hard hand iv 2 22
Oft have I heard that grief softens the mind And makes it fearful iv 4 1
Continue still in this so good a mind iv 9 17
My mind was troubled with deep melancholy v 1 34
Thou talk'st as if thou wert a king.—Why, so I am, in mind *3 Hen. VI.* iii 1 60
We will consider of your suit; And come some other time to know our mind iii 2 17
You partly may perceive my mind.—My mind will never grant what I perceive iii 2 67
Let thy dauntless mind Still ride in triumph over all mischance iii 3 17
I mind to tell him plainly what I think iv 1 8
And to that end I shortly mind to leave you.—Leave me, or tarry iv 1 64
Belike she minds to play the Amazon iv 1 106
But if you mind to hold your true obedience, Give me assurance iv 1 140
Though fortune's malice overthrow my state, My mind exceeds the compass of her wheel iv 3 47
Fearless minds climb soonest unto crowns iv 7 62
My mind presageth happy gain and conquest v 1 71
Suspicion always haunts the guilty mind v 6 11
Since the heavens have shaped my body so, Let hell make crook'd my mind v 6 79
Thou wast provoked by thy bloody mind *Richard III.* i 2 99
Let me put in your minds, if you forget, What you have been ere now i 3 131
Take the devil in thy mind, and believe him not i 4 151
And not a man of you Had so much grace to put it in my mind ii 1 120
God bless thee; and put meekness in thy mind, Love, charity ii 2 107
By a divine instinct men's minds mistrust Ensuing dangers ii 3 42
My lord, you shall o'er-rule my mind for once. Come on iii 1 57
Is it not an easy matter To make William Lord Hastings of our mind? iii 1 162
God keep your lordship in that gracious mind! iii 2 56
Those men you talk of came into my mind iii 2 118
Who knows the lord protector's mind herein? Who is most inward with the noble duke?—Your grace, we think, should soonest know his mind iii 4 7
The right idea of your father, Both in your form and nobleness of mind iii 7 14
A discontented gentleman, Whose humble means match not his haughty mind iv 2 37
I have consider'd in my mind The late demand that you did sound me in iv 2 86
I am thus bold to put your grace in mind Of what you promised me iv 2 113
'Which once,' quoth Forrest, 'almost changed my mind; But O! the devil' iv 3 15
Write to me very shortly, And you shall understand from me her mind iv 4 429
My mind is changed, sir, my mind is changed iv 4 456

Mind. These letters will resolve him of my mind *Richard III.* iv 5 19
I have not that alacrity of spirit, Nor cheer of mind, that I was wont to have v 3 74
His mind and place Infecting one another, yea, reciprocally *Hen. VIII.* i 1 161
The mind growing once corrupt, They turn to vicious forms i 2 116
A bounteous mind indeed, A hand as fruitful as the land that feeds us i 3 55
You bear a gentle mind, and heavenly blessings Follow such creatures ii 3 57
Sir, call to mind That I have been your wife, in this obedience ii 4 34
She is a gallant creature, and complete In mind and feature iii 2 50
He did it with a serious mind; a heed Was in his countenance iii 2 80
It may well be; There is a mutiny in's mind iii 2 120
And bear the inventory Of your best graces in your mind iii 2 138
The citizens, I am sure, have shown at full their royal minds iv 1 8
There are that dare; and I myself have ventured To speak my mind of him v 1 41
I will play no more to-night; My mind's not on't; you are too hard for me v 1 57
At what ease Might corrupt minds procure knaves as corrupt To swear? v 1 132
My mind gave me, In seeking tales and informations Against this man . . . Ye blew the fire that burns ye v 3 109
In whom the tempers and the minds of all Should be shut up *Troi. and Cres.* i 3 57
Nor once deject the courage of our minds, Because Cassandra's mad ii 2 121
Great minds, of partial indulgence To their benumbed wills ii 2 177
Your mind is the clearer, Ajax, and your virtues the fairer ii 3 163
An all men were o' my mind,— Wit would be out of fashion ii 3 225
With a mind That doth renew swifter than blood decays iii 2 169
Appear it to your mind That, through the sight I bear in things to love, I have abandon'd Troy iii 3 3
You know my mind, I'll fight no more 'gainst Troy iii 3 56
My mind is troubled, like a fountain stirr'd; And I myself see not the bottom of it.—Would the fountain of your mind were clear again, that I might water an ass at it! iii 3 311
That's my mind too iv 1 6
Nay, but do, then; And let your mind be coupled with your words v 2 15
This fault in us I find, The error of our eye directs our mind v 2 110
Minds sway'd by eyes are full of turpitude v 2 112
She could not publish more, Unless she said 'My mind is now turn'd whore' v 2 114
Bastard in mind, bastard in valour, in every thing illegitimate v 7 18
Trust ye? With every minute you do change a mind *Coriolanus* i 1 186
Call thither all the officers o' the town, Where they shall know our mind i 5 29
Your minds, Pre-occupied with what you rather must do Than what you should ii 3 239
Were I as patient as the midnight sleep, By Jove, 'twould be my mind! —It is a mind That shall remain a poison where it is, Not poison any further iii 1 86
By my body's action teach my mind A most inherent baseness iii 2 122
And yet my mind gave me his clothes made a false report of him iv 5 157
Why, noble lords, Will you be put in mind of his blind fortune? v 6 118
Thanks to men Of noble minds is honourable meed *T. Andron.* i 1 216
Write down thy mind, bewray thy meaning so ii 4 3
That I might rail at him, to ease my mind! ii 4 35
She but lost her tongue, And in a tedious sampler sew'd her mind ii 4 39
And arm the minds of infants to exclaims iv 1 86
Tell on thy mind; I say thy child shall live v 1 69
That bloody mind, I think, they learn'd of me v 1 101
I am Revenge: sent from the infernal kingdom, To ease the gnawing vulture of thy mind v 2 31
Since it is my father's mind That I repair to Rome, I am content v 3 1
A troubled mind drave me to walk abroad *Rom. and Jul.* i 1 127
Being black put us in mind they hide the fair i 1 237
My mind misgives Some consequence yet hanging in the stars i 4 106
It presses to my memory, Like damned guilty deeds to sinners' minds iii 2 111
Commend me to your daughter.—I will, and know her mind early to-morrow iii 4 10
You say you do not know the lady's mind: Uneven is the course iv 1 4
And doleful dumps the mind oppress iv 5 129
What says Romeo? Or, if his mind be writ, give me his letter v 2 3
You see how all conditions, how all minds, As well of glib and slippery creatures as Of grave and austere quality, tender down Their services *T. of Athens* i 1 52
The noblest mind he carries That ever govern'd man i 1 291
'Tis pity bounty had not eyes behind, That man might ne'er be wretched for his mind i 2 170
Never mind Was to be so unwise, to be so kind ii 2 5
His right noble mind, illustrious virtue, And honourable carriage iii 2 87
I'ld rather than the worth of thrice the sum, Had sent to me first, but for my mind's sake iii 3 23
Lust and liberty Creep in the minds and marrows of our youth iv 1 26
I'll ever serve his mind with my best will iv 2 49
With liquorish draughts And morsels unctuous, greases his pure mind iv 3 195
Would poison were obedient and knew my mind!—Where wouldst thou send it? iv 3 297
What viler thing upon the earth than friends Who can bring noblest minds to basest ends! iv 3 471
Heaven knows, is merely love, Duty and zeal to your unmatched mind iv 3 523
If I be alive and your mind hold and your dinner worth the eating *J. C.* i 2 205
It is meet That noble minds keep ever with their likes i 2 315
Our fathers' minds are dead, And we are govern'd With our mothers' spirits i 3 82
You have some sick offence within your mind ii 1 268
If you shall send them word you will not come, Their minds may change ii 2 96
There is but one mind in all these men, and it is bent against Cæsar ii 3 6
I have a man's mind, but a woman's might ii 4 8
Yet have I a mind That fears him much iii 1 144
If I were disposed to stir Your hearts and minds to mutiny and rage iii 2 127
Have mind upon your health, tempt me no farther iv 3 36
Now I change my mind, And partly credit things that do presage v 1 78
Think not, thou noble Roman, That ever Brutus will go bound to Rome; He bears too great a mind v 1 113
There's no art To find the mind's construction in the face *Macbeth* i 4 12
Or art thou but A dagger of the mind, a false creation? ii 1 38
Balm of hurt minds, great nature's second course ii 2 39
To that dauntless temper of his mind, He hath a wisdom iii 1 52
For Banquo's issue have I filed my mind iii 1 65
Than on the torture of the mind to lie In restless ecstasy iii 2 21
O, full of scorpions is my mind, dear wife! iii 2 36
No mind that's honest But in it shares some woe iv 3 197
Infected minds To their deaf pillows will discharge their secrets v 1 80

Mind. My mind she has mated, and amazed my sight. I think, but dare not speak *Macbeth* v 1 86
The mind I sway by and the heart I bear Shall never sag with doubt v 3 9
Cure her of that. Canst thou not minister to a mind diseased? v 3 40
Compass'd with thy kingdom's pearl, That speak my salutation in their minds v 8 57
A mote it is to trouble the mind's eye *Hamlet* i 1 112
A will most incorrect to heaven, A heart unfortified, a mind impatient i 2 96
Methinks I see my father.—Where, my lord?—In my mind's eye, Horatio i 2 185
As this temple waxes, The inward service of the mind and soul Grows wide i 3 13
But to my mind, though I am native here And to the manner born i 4 14
Taint not thy mind, nor let thy soul contrive Against thy mother aught i 5 85
The flash and outbreak of a fiery mind, A savageness in unreclaimed blood ii 1 33
To me it is a prison.—Why then, your ambition makes it one; 'tis too narrow for your mind ii 2 259
The lady shall say her mind freely, or the blank verse shall halt for't ii 2 338
Whether 'tis nobler in the mind to suffer The slings and arrows of outrageous fortune, Or to take arms iii 1 57
To the noble mind Rich gifts wax poor when givers prove unkind iii 1 100
O, what a noble mind is here o'erthrown! The courtier's, soldier's iii 1 158
The single and peculiar life is bound, With all the strength and armour of the mind, To keep itself from noyance iii 3 12
She may strew Dangerous conjectures in ill-breeding minds iv 5 15
If your mind dislike any thing, obey it v 2 227
Let this same be presently perform'd, Even while men's minds are wild v 2 405
My dimensions are as well compact, My mind as generous *Lear* i 2 8
Whose mind and mine, I know, in that are one, Not to be over-ruled i 3 15
He cannot flatter, he, An honest mind and plain, he must speak truth! ii 2 105
When nature, being oppress'd, commands the mind To suffer with the body ii 4 109
When the mind's free, The body's delicate iii 4 11
The tempest in my mind Doth from my senses take all feeling else iii 4 12
A serving-man, proud in heart and mind; that curled my hair iii 4 87
Who alone suffers suffers most i' the mind iii 6 111
The mind much sufferance doth o'erskip, When grief hath mates iii 6 113
My son Came then into my mind; and yet my mind Was then scarce friends with him iv 1 36
These things sting His mind so venomously iv 3 48
To know our enemies' minds, we'ld rip their hearts iv 6 265
To deal plainly, I fear I am not in my perfect mind iv 7 63
Trust not your daughters' minds By what you see them act *Othello* i 1 171
I saw Othello's visage in his mind i 3 253
But to be free and bounteous to her mind i 3 265
She that could think and ne'er disclose her mind ii 1 157
Hath all those requisites in him that folly and green minds look after ii 1 251
It were well The general were put in mind of it. Perhaps he sees it not ii 3 137
Farewell the tranquil mind! farewell content! Farewell the plumed troop! iii 3 348
Patience, I say; your mind perhaps may change.—Never iii 3 452
Is true of mind and made of no such baseness As jealous creatures are iii 4 27
Fetch me the handkerchief: my mind misgives iii 4 89
Heaven keep that monster [jealousy] from Othello's mind! iii 4 163
I'll not expostulate with her, lest her body and beauty unprovide my mind again iv 1 218
How foolish are our minds! If I do die before thee, prithee, shroud me In one of those same sheets iv 3 23
That song to-night Will not go from my mind iv 3 31
We bring forth weeds, When our quick minds lie still *Ant. and Cleo.* i 2 114
I have a mind to strike thee ere thou speak'st ii 5 42
Bear'st thou her face in mind? is't long or round?—Round even to faultiness iii 3 32
Choose your own company, and command what cost Your heart has mind to iii 4 38
'Tis one of those odd tricks which sorrow shoots Out of the mind iv 2 15
Less noble mind Than she which by her death our Cæsar tells 'I am conqueror of myself' iv 14 60
As the fits and stirs of's mind Could best express *Cymbeline* i 3 12
She holds her virtue still and I my mind i 4 69
If she be furnish'd with a mind so rare, She is alone the Arabian bird i 6 16
And to expound His beastly mind to us i 6 153
Keep unshaked That temple, thy fair mind! ii 1 69
Thy mind to her is now as low as were Thy fortunes iii 2 10
What is in thy mind That makes thee stare thus? iii 4 4
If you could wear a mind Dark as your fortune is iii 4 146
Nor measure our good minds By this rude place we live in iii 6 65
I had no mind To hunt this day iv 2 147
I would we were all of one mind, and one mind good v 4 212
He began His mistress' picture; which by his tongue being made, And then a mind put in 't, either our brags Were crack'd of kitchen-trulls, or his description Proved us unspeaking sots v 5 176
Our mind partakes Her private actions to your secrecy *Pericles* i 1 152
The passions of the mind, That have their first conception by mis-dread, Have after-nourishment and life by care i 2 11
Keep your mind, till you return to us, Peaceful and comfortable! i 2 34
Drew sleep out of mine eyes, blood from my cheeks, Musings into my mind i 2 97
Now to Marina bend your mind iv Gower 5
Bear you it in mind, Old Helicanus goes along behind iv 4 15
Had I brought hither a corrupted mind, Thy speech had alter'd it iv 6 111

Minded. Were I so minded, I here could pluck his highness' frown upon you And justify you traitors *Tempest* v 1 126
Let me be punish'd, that have minded you Of what you should forget *W. Tale* iii 2 226
But to know How you stand minded in the weighty difference *Hen. VIII.* iii 1 58
So many so minded, Wave thus, to express his disposition *Coriolanus* i 6 73
I minded him how royal 'twas to pardon When it was less expected v 1 18
To stop the inundation of her tears; Which, too much minded by herself alone, May be put from her by society *Rom. and Jul.* iv 1 13
One minded like the weather, most unquietly *Lear* iii 1 2

Minding. We do not come as minding to content you *M. N. Dream* v 1 113
Yet sit and see, Minding true things by what their mockeries be *Hen. V.* iv Prol. 53
The most high gods not minding longer To withhold the vengeance *Per.* ii 4 3
How absolute she's in't, Not minding whether I dislike or no! ii 5 20

Mindless. A mindless slave, Or else a hovering temporizer *W. Tale* i 2 301
Mindless of thy worth, Forgetting thy great deeds *T. of Athens* iv 3 93

Mine. Should presently extirpate me and mine *Tempest* i 2 125
And his and mine loved darling iii 3 93

Mine. You, brother mine, that entertain'd ambition . *Tempest* v 1 75
She was mine, and not mine, twice or thrice in that last article
T. G. of Ver. iii 1 365
For the revolt of mine is dangerous . . . *Mer. Wives* i 3 111
Go to; let that be mine: Do you your office . . . *Meas. for Meas.* ii 2 12
I'll make it my morn prayer To have it added to the faults of mine . ii 4 72
What's mine is yours and what is yours is mine . . . v 1 543
But mine and mine I loved and mine I praised And mine that I was proud on, mine so much That I myself was to myself not mine, Valuing of her . . . *Much Ado* iv 1 138
The lady is dead upon mine and my master's false accusation . v 1 249
He's a good friend of mine . . . . *L. L. Lost* iv 1 54
Mine own, and not mine own . . . . . *M. N. Dream* iv 1 197
As much as in him lies, mines my gentility with my education
As Y. Like It i 1 21
I would not wed her for a mine of gold . . *T. of Shrew* i 2 92
This is hers, If whilst I live she will be only mine.—That 'only' came well in . . . . ii 1 364
If you like me, she shall have me and mine . . . ii 1 385
One that fixes No bourn 'twixt his and mine . . *W. Tale* i 2 134
Wondrous affable and as bountiful As mines of India . 1 *Hen. IV.* iii 1 169
And yet, for mine own part, sir, I do not care; but rather, because I am unwilling, and, for mine own part, have a desire to stay with my friends; else, sir, I did not care, for mine own part, so much
2 *Hen. IV.* iii 2 239
Captain Fluellen, you must come presently to the mines . *Hen. V.* iii 2 59
To the mines! tell you the duke, it is not so good to come to the mines iii 2 61
The mines is not according to the disciplines of the war . . iii 2 63
Have you quit the mines? have the pioners given o'er? . . . iii 2 92
This title honours me and mine . . . . 3 *Hen. VI.* iv 1 72
So thrive I and mine! . . . . . . *Richard III.* ii 1 24
O God, I fear thy justice will take hold On me, and you, and mine, and yours for this! . . . . ii 1 132
Every man that stood Show'd like a mine . . . *Hen. VIII.* i 1 22
Close our hands with holy words, Then love-devouring death do what he dare; It is enough I may but call her mine . *Rom. and Jul.* ii 6 8
Nor what is mine shall never do thee good: Trust to't, bethink you . iii 5 196
A heart Dearer than Plutus' mine, richer than gold . *J. Cæsar* iv 3 102
Thrice to thine and thrice to mine And thrice again, to make up nine
Macbeth i 3 35
I will delve one yard below their mines, And blow them at the moon
Hamlet iii 4 208
Mine and my father's death come not upon thee, Nor thine on me! . v 2 341
'Twas mine, 'tis his, and has been slave to thousands . *Othello* iii 3 158
But with a little act upon the blood, Burn like the mines of sulphur . iii 3 329
The bawdy wind that kisses all it meets Is hush'd within the hollow mine of earth, And will not hear it . . . . . . iv 2 79
O Antony, Thou mine of bounty! . . . . *Ant. and Cleo.* iv 6 32
O, behold, How pomp is follow'd! mine will now be yours; And, should we shift estates, yours would be mine . . . . . . v 2 152
O, gentlemen, help! Mine and your mistress! . . . *Cymbeline* v 5 230
When all, for mine, if I may call offence, Must feel war's blow *Pericles* i 2 92
Mineral. Like some ore Among a mineral of metals base . *Hamlet* iv 1 26
Abused her delicate youth with drugs or minerals That weaken motion
Othello i 2 74
The thought whereof Doth, like a poisonous mineral, gnaw my inwards ii 1 306
She did confess she had For you a mortal mineral . . . *Cymbeline* v 5 50
Minerva. Hark, Tranio! thou may'st hear Minerva speak . *T. of Shrew* i 1 84
For feature, laming The shrine of Venus, or straight-pight Minerva
Cymbeline v 5 164
Mingle. To mingle friendship far is mingling bloods . . *W.Tale* i 2 109
That knew'st this was the prince, and wouldst adventure To mingle faith with him! . . . . iv 4 471
Back to the sea, Where it shall mingle with the state of floods 2 *Hen. IV.* v 2 132
I'll report it Where senators shall mingle tears with smiles *Coriolanus* i 9 3
Ourself will mingle with society, And play the humble host *Macbeth* iii 4 3
Then fly, false thanes, And mingle with the English epicures . . v 3 8
Those that mingle reason with your passion Must be content to think you old, and so—But she knows what she does . . *Lear* ii 4 237
O heavenly mingle! Be'st thou sad or merry, The violence of either thee becomes, So does it no man else . . . *Ant. and Cleo.* i 5 59
To flatter Cæsar, would you mingle eyes With one that ties his points? iii 13 156
Though grey Do something mingle with our younger brown, yet ha' we A brain . . . . iv 8 20
Blast you the city's ear; Make mingle with our rattling tabourines . iv 8 37
Grief and patience, rooted in him both, Mingle their spurs together
Cymbeline iv 2 58
We'll mingle our bloods together in the earth . . . . *Pericles* i 2 113
Mingled. My blood is mingled with the crime of lust *Com. of Errors* ii 2 143
Then confess What treason there is mingled with your love *Mer. of Ven.* iii 2 27
Just the difference Betwixt the constant red and mingled damask
As Y. Like It iii 5 123
The web of our life is of a mingled yarn, good and ill together *All's Well* iv 3 83
And part your mingled colours once again . . . *K. John* ii 1 389
Carded his state, Mingled his royalty with capering fools 1 *Hen. IV.* iii 2 63
Their blood, Mingled with venom of suggestion . 2 *Hen. IV.* iv 4 45
And make a quagmire of your mingled brains . . . 1 *Hen. VI.* i 4 109
Beauty and honour in her are so mingled . . . *Hen. VIII.* ii 3 76
Love's not love When it is mingled with regards that stand Aloof from the entire point . . . . *Lear* i 1 242
Loved thee, and her fortunes mingled With thine entirely . *A. and C.* iv 14 24
Have mingled sums To buy a present . . . . *Cymbeline* i 6 186
Their discipline, Now mingled with their courages, will make known . ii 4 24
Mingling. To mingle friendship far is mingling bloods . . *W. Tale* i 2 109
We nourish 'gainst our senate The cockle of rebellion . . . By mingling them with us, the honour'd number . . . *Coriolanus* iii 1 72
Minikin. Thy sheep be in the corn; And for one blast of thy minikin mouth, Thy sheep shall take no harm . . . . *Lear* iii 6 45
Minim. Rests me his minim rest, one, two . . *Rom. and Jul.* ii 4 22
Minimè, honest master; or rather, master, no . . *L. L. Lost.* iii 1 61
Minimo. Redime te captum quam queas minimo . . *T. of Shrew* i 1 167
Minimus. You minimus, of hindering knot-grass made *M. N. Dream* iii 2 329
Mining. Whiles rank corruption, mining all within, Infects unseen *Ham.* iii 4 148
Minion. Mars's hot minion is return'd again . . . *Tempest* iv 1 98
How now, minion!—Keep tune there still, so you will sing *T. G. of Ver.* i 2 88
It is too sharp.—You, minion, are too saucy . . . . . i 2 92
His company must do his minion's grace . . . *Com. of Errors* ii 1 87
Do you hear, you minion? you'll let us in, I hope? . . . . iii 1 54
You'll cry for this, minion, if I beat the door down . . . . iii 1 59
You minion, you, are these your customers? . . . . . iv 4 63
Minion, thou liest. Is't not Hortensio? . . . . . *T. of Shrew* ii 1 13
But this your minion, whom I know you love . . . . *T. Night* v 1 128
Fortune shall cull forth Out of one side her happy minion . *K. John* ii 1 392
Who is sweet Fortune's minion and her pride . . . . 1 *Hen. IV.* i 1 83
Let us be Diana's foresters, gentlemen of the shade, minions of the moon . . . . i 2 30
She vaunted 'mongst her minions t'other day . . . . 2 *Hen. VI.* i 3 87
Give me my fan: what, minion! can ye not? . . . . . . i 3 141
Go, rate thy minions, proud insulting boy! . . . . 3 *Hen. VI.* ii 2 84
This minion stood upon her chastity, Upon her nuptial vow *T. Andron.* ii 3 124
Mistress minion, you, Thank me no thankings . . *Rom. and Jul.* iii 5 152
The Athenian minion, whom the world Voiced so regardfully *T. of Athens* iv 3 80
Like valour's minion carved out his passage . . . . *Macbeth* i 2 19
Beauteous and swift, the minions of their race, Turn'd wild in nature . ii 4 15
Minion, your dear lies dead, And your unblest fate hies . . . *Othello* v 1 33
The exile of her minion is too new; She hath not yet forgot him *Cymb.* ii 3 46
Minister. The ministers for the purpose hurried thence . . *Tempest* i 2 131
She did confine thee, By help of her more potent ministers . . . i 2 275
To minister occasion to these gentlemen, who are of such sensible and nimble lungs . . . . ii 1 173
I and my fellows Are ministers of Fate . . . . iii 3 61
My meaner ministers Their several kinds have done . . . . iii 3 87
You gave me bitter pills, And I must minister the like to you *T. G. of V.* ii 4 150
We two will still be the ministers . . . . . . *Mer. Wives* iv 2 234
Even for our kitchens We kill the fowl of season: shall we serve heaven With less respect than we do minister To our gross selves?
Meas. for Meas. ii 2 86
Make me know The nature of their crimes, that I may minister To them ii 3 7
Sometimes you do blench from this to that, As cause doth minister . iv 5 6
O you blessed ministers above, Keep me in patience! . . . . v 1 115
How sweetly you do minister to love! . . . . . *Much Ado* i 1 314
Minister such assistance as I shall give you direction . . . . i 1 385
He that of greatest works is finisher Oft does them by the weakest minister: So holy writ in babes hath judgement shown . *All's Well* ii 1 140
Thy physic I will try, That ministers thine own death if I die . . ii 1 189
In a most weak—and debile minister, great power, great transcendence ii 3 40
Unless you laugh and minister occasion to him, he is gagged . *T. Night* i 5 93
They have here propertied me; keep me in darkness, send ministers to me . . . . iv 2 100
Advise you what you say; the minister is here . . . . . iv 2 102
Durst not tempt a minister of honour, Lest she should be denied *W. Tale* ii 2 50
I chose Camillo for the minister to poison My friend Polixenes . . iii 2 161
For I may never lift An angry arm against His minister. . *Richard II.* i 2 41
O, then how quickly should this arm of mine, Now prisoner to the palsy, chastise thee And minister correction to thy fault! . . . . . ii 3 105
Your lordship may minister the potion of imprisonment to me 2 *Hen. IV.* i 2 145
Master Dumbe, our minister, was by then . . . . ii 4 95
Consume to ashes, Thou foul accursed minister of hell! . 1 *Hen. VI.* v 4 93
Such as my wit affords And over-joy of heart doth minister . 2 *Hen. VI.* i 1 31
For a minister of my intent, I have seduced a headstrong Kentishman . iii 1 355
O war, thou son of hell, Whom angry heavens do make their minister! . v 2 34
Avaunt, thou dreadful minister of hell! . . . . . *Richard III.* i 2 46
Sin, death, and hell have set their marks on him, And all their ministers attend on him . . . . i 3 294
Who made thee, then, a bloody minister? . . . . i 4 226
Make us thy ministers of chastisement, That we may praise thee! . . v 3 113
But minister communication of A most poor issue . . . *Hen. VIII.* i 1 86
What his high hatred would effect wants not A minister in his power . ii 1 108
Ween you of better luck, I mean, in perjured witness, than your master, Whose minister you are? . . . . v 1 137
Ships, Fraught with the ministers and instruments Of cruel war
Troi. and Cres. Prol. 4
Minister Unto the appetite and affection common Of the whole body *Cor.* i 1 106
And that not in the presence Of dreaded justice, but on the ministers That do distribute it . . . . iii 3 98
These are my ministers, and come with me . . . . *T. Andron.* v 2 60
Are these thy ministers? what are they call'd?—Rapine and Murder . v 2 61
Now will I hence about thy business, And take my ministers along with me . . . . v 2 133
That unaptness made your minister, Thus to excuse yourself *T. of Athens* ii 2 140
Slaves and fools, Pluck the grave wrinkled senate from the bench, And minister in their steads! . . . . iv 1 6
You murdering ministers, Wherever in your sightless substances You wait on nature's mischief! . . . . *Macbeth* i 5 49
Canst thou not minister to a mind diseased? . . . . . . v 3 40
Therein the patient Must minister to himself.—Throw physic to the dogs v 3 46
The cruel ministers Of this dead butcher and his fiend-like queen . v 8 68
Angels and ministers of grace defend us! . . . . . *Hamlet* i 4 39
Heaven hath pleased it so, To punish me with this and this with me, That I must be their scourge and minister . . . . . . iii 4 175
Servile ministers, That have with two pernicious daughters join'd *Lear* iii 2 21
Which the time shall more favourably minister . . . . *Othello* ii 1 277
If I quench thee, thou flaming minister, I can again thy former light restore . . . . v 2 8
The high gods, To do you justice, make them ministers Of us
Ant. and Cleo. iii 6 88
Whose ministers would prevail Under the service of a child as soon . iii 13 23
He is dead, Cæsar; Not by a public minister of justice . . . . v 1 20
'Tis paltry to be Cæsar; Not being Fortune, he's but Fortune's knave, A minister of her will . . . . v 2 4
He that strikes The venison first shall be the lord o' the feast; To him the other two shall minister . . . . *Cymbeline* iii 3 76
Or hath more ministers than we That draw his knives i' the war . . v 3 72
Ministered. With full and holy rite be minister'd . . *Tempest* iv 1 17
And take upon command what help we have That to your wanting may be minister'd . . . . *As Y. Like It* ii 7 126
The present time's so sick, That present medicine must be minister'd, Or overthrow incurable ensues . . . . *K. John* v 1 15
What if it be a poison, which the friar Subtly hath minister'd?
Rom. and Jul. iv 3 25
Which he took, As we do air, fast as 'twas minister'd . . *Cymbeline* i 1 45
Nothing can be minister'd to nature That can recover him . *Pericles* iii 2 8
Minister'st a potion unto me That thou wouldst tremble to receive thyself . . . . i 2 68
Ministering. A ministering angel shall my sister be . . *Hamlet* v 1 264
Ministration. My course, Which holds not colour with the time, nor does The ministration and required office . . . . *All's Well* ii 5 65
Minnow. That base minnow of thy mirth . . . . *L. L. Lost* i 1 251
Hear you this Triton of the minnows? mark you His absolute 'shall'?
Coriolanus iii 1 89

Minola. Her father is Baptista Minola, An affable and courteous gentleman: Her name is Katharina Minola . . . *T. of Shrew* i 2 97
Which is the readiest way To the house of Signior Baptista Minola? . i 2 221
We'll over-reach the greybeard, Gremio, The narrow prying father, Minola . . . . iii 2 148
Give assurance to Baptista Minola, As if he were the right Vincentio . iv 2 69
Minority. He shall present Hercules in minority . . *L. L. Lost* v 1 141
Quoniam he seemeth in minority, Ergo I come with this apology . v 2 596
Which, in the minority of them both, his majesty, out of a self-gracious remembrance, did first propose . . . *All's Well* iv 5 77
His minority Is put unto the trust of Richard Gloucester *Richard III.* i 3 11
Minos. I, Dædalus; my poor boy, Icarus; Thy father, Minos, that denied our course . . . . 3 *Hen. VI.* v 6 22
Minotaur. Thou mayst not wander in that labyrinth; There Minotaurs and ugly treasons lurk . . . . 1 *Hen. VI.* v 3 189
Minstrel. I will bid thee draw, as we do the minstrels . . *Much Ado* v 1 129
Tush, none but minstrels like of sonneting! . . *L. L. Lost* iv 3 158
Hark, hark! I hear the minstrels play . . *T. of Shrew* iii 2 185
Consort! what, dost thou make us minstrels? an thou make minstrels of us, look to hear nothing but discords . . . *Rom. and Jul.* iii 1 50
No money, on my faith, but the gleek; I will give you the minstrel iv 5 116
Minstrelsy. I will use him for my minstrelsy . . *L. L. Lost* i 1 177
Every room Hath blazed with lights and bray'd with minstrelsy *T. of A.* ii 2 170
What minstrelsy, and pretty din, The regent made. . *Pericles* v 2 272
Mint. That hath a mint of phrases in his brain . *L. L. Lost* i 1 166
I am that flower,— That mint.—That columbine . . . v 2 661
With some excellent jests, fire-new from the mint . . *T. Night* iii 2 24
Hot lavender, mints, savory, marjoram . . *W. Tale* iv 4 104
Whose gall coins slanders like a mint . . . *Troi. and Cres.* i 3 193
Minute. The very minute bids thee ope thine ear; Obey . . *Tempest* i 2 37
The minute of their plot Is almost come . . . . iv 1 141
The good humour is to steal at a minute's rest. . . *Mer. Wives* i 3 31
Better three hours too soon than a minute too late . . . ii 2 328
The Windsor bell hath struck twelve; the minute draws on . . v 5 2
Or groan for love? or spend a minute's time In pruning me? . *L. L. Lost* iv 3 182
At the latest minute of the hour . . . . . . v 2 797
I'll put a girdle round about the earth In forty minutes *M. N. Dream* ii 1 176
Then, for the third part of a minute, hence . . . . ii 2 2
I do repent The tedious minutes I with her have spent . . . iii 2 112
Sighing every minute and groaning every hour . *As Y. Like It* iii 2 321
He that will divide a minute into a thousand parts and break but a part of the thousandth part of a minute in the affairs of love . . iv 1 45
If you break one jot of your promise or come one minute behind your hour . . . . iv 1 195
Knew the true minute when Exception bid him speak . *All's Well* i 2 39
Or four and twenty times the pilot's glass Hath told the thievish minutes . . . . ii 1 169
But falls into abatement and low price, Even in a minute . *T. Night* i 1 14
No interim, not a minute's vacancy, Both day and night . . v 1 98
Wishing clocks more swift? Hours, minutes? noon, midnight? *W. Tale* i 2 290
Entertain an hour, One minute, nay, one quiet breath of rest *K. John* iii 4 134
And like the watchful minutes to the hour, Still and anon cheer'd up the heavy time . . . . iv 1 46
Why, uncle, thou hast many years to live.—But not a minute, king, that thou canst give . . . . *Richard II.* i 3 226
My thoughts are minutes; and with sighs they jar, Their watches on unto mine eyes, the outward watch . . . . . . v 5 51
So sighs and tears and groans Show minutes, times, and hours . v 5 58
Unless hours were cups of sack and minutes capons . 1 *Hen. IV.* i 2 8
Every minute now Should be the father of some stratagem 2 *Hen. IV.* i 1 7
The examples Of every minute's instance, present now . . iv 1 83
A guard . . . That walked about me every minute while . 1 *Hen. VI.* i 4 54
And think it but a minute spent in sport. . 2 *Hen. VI.* iii 2 338
To see the minutes how they run, How many make the hour 3 *Hen. VI.* ii 5 25
So minutes, hours, days, months, and years, Pass'd over to the end they were created, Would bring white hairs unto a quiet grave . . ii 5 38
Could not find His hour of speech a minute . . *Hen. VIII.* ii 2 121
Who fed him every minute With words of sovereignty . . . . i 2 149
Trust ye? With every minute you do change a mind . . *Coriolanus* i 1 186
Will speak more in a minute than he will stand to in a month *R. and J.* ii 4 156
The exchange of joy That one short minute gives me in her sight . ii 6 5
Husband, friend! I must hear from thee every day in the hour, For in a minute there are many days . . . . . . iii 5 45
When I came, some minute ere the time Of her awaking . . v 3 257
Every minute of his being thrusts Against my near'st of life . *Macbeth* iii 1 117
Each minute teems a new one . . . . iv 3 176
Entreated him along With us to watch the minutes of this night *Hamlet* i 1 27
Sweet, not lasting, The perfume and suppliance of a minute . . i 3 9
For every minute is expectancy Of more arrivance . . *Othello* ii 1 41
What damned minutes tells he o'er Who dotes, yet doubts . . iii 3 169
There's not a minute of our lives should stretch Without some pleasure now. What sport to-night? . . . . *Ant. and Cleo.* i 1 46
For quick accumulation of renown, Which he achieved by the minute . iii 1 20
With news the time's with labour, and throes forth, Each minute, some iii 7 82
One vice, but of a minute old, for one Not half so old as that *Cymbeline* ii 5 31
Should by the minute feed on life and lingering By inches waste you . v 5 51
The shipman's toil, With whom each minute threatens life or death *Per.* i 3 25
I leap into the seas, Where's hourly trouble for a minute's ease . ii 4 44
My mother was the daughter of a king; Who died the minute I was born v 1 160
Thaisa was my mother, who did end The minute I began . . v 1 214
Minute-jack. You fools of fortune, trencher-friends, time's flies, Cap and knee slaves, vapours, and minute-jacks! . . . *T. of Athens* iii 6 107
Minutely. Now minutely revolts upbraid his faith-breach . *Macbeth* v 2 18
Minx. Get him to pray.—My prayers, minx! . . . *T. Night* iii 4 133
Let her live.—Damn her, lewd minx! O, damn her! . . *Othello* iii 3 475
This is some minx's token, and I must take out the work? . iv 1 159
Mirable. Not Neoptolemus so mirable . . . *Troi. and Cres.* iv 5 142
Miracle. But for the miracle, I mean our preservation . . *Tempest* ii 1 6
One dear son Shall I twice lose.—A most high miracle! . . v 1 177
It was a miracle to 'scape suffocation . . . . *Mer. Wives* iii 5 119
From whence, I think, you are come by miracle . *Com. of Errors* v 1 264
A miracle! here's our own hands against our hearts . . *Much Ado* v 4 91
Which therein works a miracle in nature . . *Mer. of Venice* iii 2 90
Love wrought these miracles . . . . . *T. of Shrew* v 1 127
Seas have dried When miracles have by the greatest been denied *All's W.* ii 1 144
They say miracles are past. . . . . ii 3 1
'Tis that miracle and queen of gems That nature pranks her in *T. Night* ii 4 88
How, Camillo, May this, almost a miracle, be done? . . *W. Tale* iv 4 545
In her eye I find A wonder, or a wondrous miracle . . *K. John* ii 1 497
I have 'scaped by miracle. I am eight times thrust through . 1 *Hen. IV.* ii 4 184

Miracle. And him, O wondrous him! O miracle of men! . . 2 *Hen. IV.* ii 3 33
It must be so; for miracles are ceased . . . . *Hen. V.* i 1 67
Be not offended, nature's miracle . . . . . . 1 *Hen. VI.* v 3 54
Chosen from above, By inspiration of celestial grace, To work exceeding miracles on earth . . . . v 4 41
The holy maid with child!—The greatest miracle that e'er ye wrought v 4 66
What means this noise? Fellow, what miracle dost thou proclaim? 2 *Hen. VI.* ii 1 60
A miracle! a miracle!—Come to the king and tell him what miracle . ii 1 61
My lords, Saint Alban here hath done a miracle . . . . ii 1 131
Duke Humphrey has done a miracle to-day . . . . . ii 1 161
But you have done more miracles than I; You made in a day, my lord, whole towns to fly . . . . ii 1 163
I think they have swallowed one another: I would laugh at that miracle: yet, in a sort, lechery eats itself. . . . . *Troi. and Cres.* v 4 37
A faith that reason without miracle Could never plant in me . *Lear* i 1 225
Nothing almost sees miracles But misery . . . . . ii 2 172
Thy life's a miracle. Speak yet again . . . . . iv 6 55
Yet who this should be Doth miracle itself, loved before me . *Cymbeline* iv 2 29
And who to thank, Besides the gods, for this great miracle . *Pericles* v 3 58
Miraculous. His word is more than the miraculous harp *Tempest* ii 1 86
'Tis call'd the evil: A most miraculous work in this good king *Macbeth* iv 3 147
They have proclaim'd their malefactions; For murder, though it have no tongue, will speak With most miraculous organ . . *Hamlet* ii 2 623
Miranda. Had I not Four or five women once that tended me?—Thou hadst, and more, Miranda . . . . *Tempest* i 2 48
Miranda, twelve year since, Thy father was the Duke of Milan . i 2 53
What is your name?—Miranda.—O my father, I have broke your hest to say so!—Admired Miranda! Indeed the top of admiration! . . iii 1 36
I am in my condition A prince, Miranda; I do think, a king . . iii 1 60
Mire. Fright me with urchin-shows, pitch me i' the mire . . ii 2 5
They threw me off from behind one of them, in a slough of mire *M. W.* iv 5 69
They threw on him Great pails of puddled mire . *Com. of Errors* v 1 173
Your wit's too hot, it speeds too fast, 'twill tire.—Not till it leave the rider in the mire . . . . *L. L. Lost* ii 1 121
We'll draw thee from the mire Of this sir-reverence love *Rom. and Jul.* i 4 41
Honest water, which ne'er left man i' the mire . *T. of Athens* i 2 60
Paint till a horse may mire upon your face . . . . iv 3 147
Where may we set our horses?—I' the mire . . . *Lear* ii 2 5
Spit, and throw stones, cast mire upon me . . . *Cymbeline* v 5 222
Mired. Who smirched thus and mired with infamy . . *Much Ado* iv 1 135
Mirror. Your changed complexions are to me a mirror . . *W. Tale* i 2 381
An if my word be sterling yet in England, Let it command a mirror hither straight, That it may show me what a face I have, Since it is bankrupt of his majesty . . . . . . *Richard II.* iv 1 265
Following the mirror of all Christian kings, With winged heels *Hen. V.* ii Prol. 6
How farest thou, mirror of all martial men? . . 1 *Hen. VI.* i 4 74
Henry the Fourth, Whose wisdom was a mirror to the wisest 3 *Hen. VI.* iii 3 84
But now two mirrors of his princely semblance Are crack'd in pieces by malignant death, And I for comfort have but one false glass *Richard III.* ii 2 51
Bounteous Buckingham, The mirror of all courtesy . . *Hen. VIII.* ii 1 53
It is very much lamented, Brutus, That you have no such mirrors as will turn Your hidden worthiness into your eye . . *J. Cæsar* i 2 56
To hold, as 'twere, the mirror up to nature . . . . *Hamlet* iii 2 24
To make true diction of him, his semblable is his mirror . . v 2 124
Cæsar is touch'd.—When such a spacious mirror's set before him, He needs must see himself . . . . . . *Ant. and Cleo.* v 1 34
For death remember'd should be like a mirror . . . *Pericles* i 1 45
Mirth. One fading moment's mirth [bought] With twenty watchful, weary, tedious nights . . . . *T. G. of Ver.* i 1 30
We will include all jars With triumphs, mirth and rare solemnity . . v 4 161
I was then frugal of my mirth: Heaven forgive me! . *Mer. Wives* iii 1 28
She enlargeth her mirth so far that there is shrewd construction made of her . . . . ii 2 231
The mirth whereof so larded with my matter, That neither singly can be manifested, Without the show of both . . . . . . iv 6 14
My mirth it much displeased, but pleased my woe *Meas. for Meas.* iv 1 13
And, in despite of mirth, mean to be merry . . *Com. of Errors* iv 1 108
I was born to speak all mirth and no matter . . . *Much Ado* ii 1 343
From the crown of his head to the sole of his foot, he is all mirth . iii 2 10
Than wish a snow in May's new-fangled mirth . . *L. L. Lost* i 1 106
That low-spirited swain, that base minnow of thy mirth . . i 1 251
But a merrier man, Within the limit of becoming mirth . . . ii 1 67
Good at such eruptions and sudden breaking out of mirth . . . v 1 121
And mirth is in his face.—O, I am stabb'd with laughter! . . v 2 79
Makes most form in mirth, When great things labouring perish in their birth . . . . v 2 520
It is impossible: Mirth cannot move a soul in agony . . . v 2 867
Awake the pert and nimble spirit of mirth . . . *M. N. Dream* i 1 14
The whole quire hold their hips and laugh, And waxen in their mirth . ii 1 56
Here come the lovers, full of joy and mirth . . . . . v 1 28
Where is our usual manager of mirth? What revels are in hand? . . v 1 35
'Very tragical mirth.' Merry and tragical! tedious and brief! . . v 1 57
With mirth and laughter let old wrinkles come . *Mer. of Venice* i 1 80
I would entreat you rather to put on Your boldest suit of mirth . ii 2 211
I show more mirth than I am mistress of. . . . *As Y. Like It* i 2 3
Then is there mirth in heaven, When earthly things made even Atone . v 4 114
Mirth and merriment, Which bars a thousand harms . *T. of Shrew* Ind. 2 137
'Tis not hereafter; Present mirth hath present laughter . *T. Night* ii 3 49
He's all my exercise, my mirth, my matter . . . *W. Tale* i 2 166
With these forced thoughts, I prithee, darken not The mirth o' the feast iv 4 42
Entertain them sprightly, And let's be red with mirth . . . iv 4 54
Full of warm blood, of mirth, of gossiping . . . *K. John* v 2 59
Chide him for faults, and do it reverently, When you perceive his blood inclined to mirth . . . . 2 *Hen. IV.* iv 4 38
Spare in diet, Free from gross passion or of mirth or anger . *Hen. V.* ii 2 132
Pardon the frankness of my mirth . . . . v 2 318
All France will be replete with mirth and joy . . . 1 *Hen. VI.* i 6 15
Laughest thou, wretch? thy mirth shall turn to moan . . . ii 3 44
Make yourself mirth with your particular fancy . . *Hen. VIII.* ii 3 101
Like that mirth fate turns to sudden sadness . . *Troi. and Cres.* i 1 40
Then, forsooth, the faint defects of age Must be the scene of mirth . i 3 173
As she is now, she will but disease our better mirth . *Coriolanus* i 3 117
Indeed, I must not. I wish you much mirth.—Well, then, farewell . i 3 123
From this day forth, I'll use you for my mirth . . *J. Cæsar* iv 3 49
Hath Cassius lived To be but mirth and laughter to his Brutus? . iv 3 114
Be large in mirth; anon we'll drink a measure The table round *Macbeth* iii 4 11
You have displaced the mirth, broke the good meeting . . . iii 4 109
With mirth in funeral and with dirge in marriage . . . *Hamlet* i 2 12

Mirth. I have of late—but wherefore I know not—lost all my mirth *Ham.* ii 2 307
He was disposed to mirth; but on the sudden A Roman thought hath struck him *Ant. and Cleo.* i 2 86
If you find him sad, Say I am dancing; if in mirth, report That I am sudden sick: quick, and return i 3 4
To give a kingdom for a mirth i 4 18
Is he disposed to mirth? I hope he is.—Exceeding pleasant. *Cymbeline* i 6 58
Which are often the sadness of parting, as the procuring of mirth v 4 163
How well this honest mirth becomes their labour! *Pericles* ii 1 99
Prepare for mirth, for mirth becomes a feast ii 3 7
Mirthful. With stately triumphs, mirthful comic shows 3 *Hen. VI.* v 7 43
Mirth-moving. Turns to a mirth-moving jest *L. L. Lost* ii 1 71
Miry. Thou shouldst have heard in how miry a place *T. of Shrew* iv 1 77
As meadows, yet not dry, With miry slime left on them *T. Andron.* iii 1 126
Misadventure. Have patience: Your looks are pale and wild, and do import Some misadventure *Rom. and Jul.* v 1 29
What misadventure is so early up, That calls our person v 3 188
Misadventured. Whose misadventured piteous overthrows Do with their death bury their parents' strife Prol. 7
Misanthropos. I am Misanthropos, and hate mankind *T. of Athens* iv 3 53
Misapplied. Virtue itself turns vice, being misapplied *Rom. and Jul.* ii 3 21
Misbecame. What I have done that misbecame my place 2 *Hen. IV.* v 2 100
Misbecome. Any thing that may not misbecome The mighty sender, doth he prize you at *Hen. V.* ii 4 118
Misbecomed. Have misbecomed our oaths and gravities *L. L. Lost* v 2 778
Misbegot. Which indeed Is valour misbegot *T. of Athens* iii 5 29
Misbegotten. That misbegotten devil, Faulconbridge *K. John* v 4 4
And free from other misbegotten hate *Richard II.* i 1 33
Three misbegotten knaves in Kendal green came at my back 1 *Hen. IV.* ii 4 246
Contaminated, base And misbegotten blood I spill of thine 1 *Hen. VI.* iv 6 22
Misbehaved. Like a misbehaved and sullen wench *Rom. and Jul.* iii 3 143
Misbeliever. You call me misbeliever, cut-throat dog *Mer. of Venice* i 3 112
Misbelieving. And hither hale that misbelieving Moor *T. Andron.* v 3 143
Miscall. My heart will sigh when I miscall it so *Richard II.* i 3 263
Thou dost miscall retire: I do not fly *Troi. and Cres.* v 4 21
Miscarried. The great soldier who miscarried at sea *Meas. for Meas.* iii 1 217
Accidentally, or by the way of progression, hath miscarried *L. L. Lost* iv 2 144
There miscarried A vessel of our country richly fraught *Mer. of Venice* ii 8 29
My ships have all miscarried, my creditors grow cruel iii 2 318
I once did lend my body for his wealth; Which, but for him that had your husband's ring, Had quite miscarried v 1 251
Then threw he down himself and all their lives That by indictment and by dint of sword Have since miscarried 2 *Hen. IV.* iv 1 129
All that have miscarried By underhand corrupted foul injustice *Rich. III.* v 1 5
The cardinal's letters to the pope miscarried *Hen. VIII.* iii 2 30
If aught in this Miscarried by my fault *Rom. and Jul.* v 3 267
Our sister's man is certainly miscarried *Lear* v 1 5
Miscarry. If they miscarry, we miscarry too *K. John* v 4 3
If thou marry, Hang me by the neck, if horns that year miscarry *L. L. L.* iv 1 114
I would not have him miscarry for the half of my dowry *T. Night* iii 4 70
Though we here fall down, We have supplies to second our attempt: If they miscarry, theirs shall second them 2 *Hen. IV.* iv 2 46
An the child I now go with do miscarry, thou wert better thou hadst struck thy mother v 4 10
But I pray God the fruit of her womb miscarry! v 4 15
So, if a son that is by his father sent about merchandise do sinfully miscarry upon the sea, the imputation of his wickedness, by your rule, should be imposed upon his father *Hen. V.* iv 1 155
If he miscarry, farewell wars in France 1 *Hen. VI.* iv 3 16
Better ten thousand base-born Cades miscarry Than you should stoop unto a Frenchman's mercy 2 *Hen. VI.* iv 8 49
Not concluded yet: But so it must be, if the king miscarry *Richard III.* i 3 16
What miscarries Shall be the general's fault *Coriolanus* i 1 270
If you miscarry, Your business of the world hath so an end *Lear* v 1 44
Be near at hand; I may miscarry in 't.—Here, at thy hand: be bold *Oth.* v 1 6
Miscarrying. Who miscarrying, What heart receives from hence the conquering part, To steel a strong opinion to themselves? *Troi. and Cres.* i 3 351
Mischance. Make yourself ready in your cabin for the mischance of the hour, if it so hap *Tempest* i 1 28
Be patient, for the prize I'll bring thee to Shall hoodwink this mischance iv 1 206
Some foul mischance Torment me for my love's forgetfulness! *T. G. of Ver.* ii 2 11
A thousand more mischances than this one Have learn'd me how to brook this patiently v 3 3
Nimble mischance, that art so light of foot *Richard II.* iii 4 92
But that I think his father loves him not And would be glad he met with some mischance, I would have him poison'd 1 *Hen. IV.* i 3 232
The devil and mischance look big Upon the maidenhead of our affairs iv 1 58
Lords, view these letters full of bad mischance 1 *Hen. VI.* i 1 89
To be shame's scorn and subject of mischance! iv 6 49
My thoughts do hourly prophesy Mischance 2 *Hen. VI.* iii 2 284
Mischance and sorrow go along with you! iii 2 300
But now mischance hath trod my title down 3 *Hen. VI.* iii 3 8
Let thy dauntless mind Still ride in triumph over all mischance iii 3 18
I long till Edward fall by war's mischance, For mocking marriage iii 3 254
In despite of all mischance, Of thee thyself and all thy complices iv 3 43
Farewell, York's wife, and queen of sad mischance *Richard III.* iv 4 114
Forbear, And let mischance be slave to patience *Rom. and Jul.* v 3 221
I rather challenge for unkindness Than pity for mischance! *Macbeth* iii 4 43
And never come mischance between us twain! *Hamlet* iii 2 238
Lest more mischance, On plots and errors, happen v 2 405
'Tis some mischance; the cry is very direful *Othello* v 1 38
He never can meet more mischance than come To be but named of thee *Cymbeline* ii 3 137
Mischief. For mischiefs manifold, . . . Thou know'st, was banish'd *Temp.* i 2 264
If hollowly, invert What best is boded me to mischief! iii 1 71
Do that good mischief which may make this island Thine own for ever iv 1 217
Devise something: any extremity rather than a mischief *Mer. Wives* iv 2 76
Goest about to apply a moral medicine to a mortifying mischief *Much Ado* i 3 13
Will it serve for any model to build mischief on? i 3 49
I pray God his bad voice bode no mischief ii 3 83
O day untowardly turned!—O mischief strangely thwarting! iii 2 135
Do not believe But I shall do thee mischief in the wood.—Ay, in the temple, in the town, the field, You do me mischief *M. N. Dream* ii 1 237
Come, boy, with me; my thoughts are ripe in mischief *T. Night* v 1 132
Where some stretch-mouthed rascal would, as it were, mean mischief *W. Tale* iv 4 197
Some airy devil hovers in the sky And pours down mischief *K. John* iii 2 3
A portent Of broached mischief to the unborn times 1 *Hen. IV.* v 1 21
In good faith, he cares not what mischief he does 2 *Hen. IV.* ii 1 16
Mischief. Alack, what mischiefs might he set abroach In shadow of such greatness! 2 *Hen. IV.* iv 2 14
And so success of mischief shall be born iv 2 47
Break out into a second course of mischief *Hen. V.* iv 3 106
Some sudden mischief may arise of it iv 7 186
This sudden mischief never could have fall'n 1 *Hen. VI.* ii 1 59
You see what mischief and what murder too Hath been enacted through your enmity iii 1 115
That damned sorceress Hath wrought this hellish mischief unawares iii 2 39
A plaguing mischief light on Charles and thee! v 3 39
Till mischief and despair Drive you to break your necks or hang yourselves v 4 90
O God, what mischiefs work the wicked ones! 2 *Hen. VI.* ii 1 186
The name of Henry the Fifth hales them to an hundred mischiefs iv 8 59
But that my heart's on future mischief set, I would speak blasphemy v 2 84
I do the wrong, and first begin to brawl. The secret mischiefs that I set abroach I lay unto the grievous charge of others *Richard III.* i 3 325
He is subtle, and as prone to mischief As able to perform 't *Hen. VIII.* i 1 160
Ha! what, so rank? Ah ha! There's mischief in this man i 2 187
With that devil-monk, Hopkins, that made this mischief ii 1 22
I heartily forgive 'em: Yet let 'em look they glory not in mischief ii 1 66
Foreseeing those fell mischiefs Our reasons laid before him v 1 49
Hath done To thee particularly . . . Great hurt and mischief *Coriolanus* iv 5 73
I shall never come to bliss Till all these mischiefs be return'd *T. Andron.* iii 1 274
Complots of mischief, treason, villanies Ruthful to hear v 1 65
And what not done, that thou hast cause to rue, Wherein I had no stroke of mischief in it? v 1 110
Let's see for means: O mischief, thou art swift To enter in the thoughts of desperate men! *Rom. and Jul.* v 1 35
Grant I may ever love, and rather woo Those that would mischief me than those that do! *T. of Athens* iv 3 475
Leave us, Publius; lest that the people, Rushing on us, should do your age some mischief *J. Cæsar* iii 1 93
Mischief, thou art afoot, Take thou what course thou wilt! iii 2 265
And some that smile have in their hearts, I fear, Millions of mischiefs iv 1 51
You murdering ministers, Wherever in your sightless substances You wait on nature's mischief! *Macbeth* i 5 51
This is miching mallecho; it means mischief *Hamlet* iii 2 148
That with the mischief of your person it would scarcely allay *Lear* i 2 178
You have one eye left To see some mischief on him iii 7 82
That not know'st Fools do those villains pity who are punish'd Ere they have done their mischief iv 2 55
To mourn a mischief that is past and gone Is the next way to draw new mischief on *Othello* i 3 204
Here they're but felt, and seen with mischief's eyes *Pericles* i 4 8
Mischievous. Most mischievous foul sin, in chiding sin *As Y. Like It* ii 7 64
Think him as a serpent's egg Which, hatch'd, would, as his kind, grow mischievous, And kill him in the shell *J. Cæsar* ii 1 33
Misconceived. No, misconceived! Joan of Arc hath been A virgin from her tender infancy 1 *Hen. VI.* v 4 49
Misconstruction. It pleased the king his master very late To strike at me, upon his misconstruction *Lear* ii 2 124
Misconstrue. He misconstrues all that you have done *As Y. Like It* i 2 277
Be not dismay'd, fair lady; nor misconstrue The mind of Talbot 1 *Hen. VI.* ii 3 73
Who haply may Misconstrue us in him and wail his death *Richard III.* iii 5 61
Misconstrued. Lest through thy wild behaviour I be misconstrued *Mer. of Venice* ii 2 197
So much misconstrued in his wantonness 1 *Hen. IV.* v 2 69
Alas, thou hast misconstrued every thing! *J. Cæsar* v 3 84
Miscreant. Thou art a traitor and a miscreant, Too good to be so and too bad to live *Richard II.* i 1 39
Well, miscreant, I'll be there as soon as you 1 *Hen. VI.* iii 4 44
Curse, miscreant, when thou comest to the stake v 3 44
O, vassal! miscreant!—Dear sir, forbear *Lear* i 1 163
Miscreate. Or nicely charge your understanding soul With opening titles miscreate *Hen. V.* i 2 16
Misdeed. I am clear from this misdeed of Edward's 3 *Hen. VI.* iii 3 183
O God! if my deep prayers cannot appease thee, But thou wilt be avenged on my misdeeds, Yet execute thy wrath in me alone *Rich. III.* i 4 70
Misdemeaned. You, that best should teach us, Have misdemean'd yourself, and not a little *Hen. VIII.* v 3 14
Misdemeanour. If you can separate yourself and your misdemeanours, you are welcome *T. Night* ii 3 106
Misdoubt. I do not misdoubt my wife *Mer. Wives* ii 1 192
Let this letter be read: Our parson misdoubts it *L. L. Lost* iv 3 194
That I could neither believe nor misdoubt *All's Well* i 3 130
If you misdoubt me that I am not she, I know not how I shall assure you iii 7 1
For full well he knows He cannot so precisely weed this land As his misdoubts present occasion 2 *Hen. IV.* iv 1 206
Steel thy fearful thoughts, And change misdoubt to resolution 2 *Hen. VI.* iii 1 332
This sudden stab of rancour I misdoubt *Richard III.* iii 2 89
Do you misdoubt This sword and these my wounds? *Ant. and Cleo.* iii 7 63
Misdoubteth. The bird that hath been limed in a bush, With trembling wings misdoubteth every bush 3 *Hen. VI.* v 6 14
Mis-dread. The passions of the mind, That have their first conception by mis-dread, Have after-nourishment and life by care *Pericles* i 2 12
Misenum. Where lies he?—About the mount Misenum *Ant. and Cleo.* ii 2 163
Miser. Rich honesty dwells like a miser, sir, in a poor house *As Y. Like It* v 4 63
Doth, like a miser, spoil his coat with scanting A little cloth *Hen. V.* ii 4 47
Decrepit miser! base ignoble wretch! 1 *Hen. VI.* v 4 7
As misers do by beggars, neither gave to me Good word nor look *T. and C.* iii 3 143
I can compare our rich misers to nothing so fitly as to a whale *Pericles* ii 1 33
Miserable. If he be not born to be hanged, our case is miserable *Tempest* i 1 36
Have you the tongues?—My youthful travel therein made me happy, Or else I often had been miserable *T. G. of Ver.* iv 1 35
O miserable, unhappy that I am!—Unhappy were you, madam v 4 28
The miserable have no other medicine But only hope *Meas. for Meas.* iii 1 2
So fortunate, But miserable most, to love unloved *M. N. Dream* iii 2 234
I met a fool i' the forest, A motley fool; a miserable world! *As Y. Like It* ii 7 13
In which hurtling From miserable slumber I awaked iv 3 133
O miserable lady! But, for me, What case stand I in? *W. Tale* i 2 351
Get you therefore hence, Poor miserable wretches *Hen. V.* ii 2 178
For what's more miserable than discontent? 2 *Hen. VI.* iii 1 201
O miserable age! virtue is not regarded in handicrafts-men iv 2 11
O gross and miserable ignorance! iv 2 178
But that I hate thee deadly, I should lament thy miserable state 3 *Hen. VI.* i 4 85
O, pity, God, this miserable age! ii 5 88
Witch sweet ladies with my words and looks. O miserable thought! and more unlikely Than to accomplish twenty golden crowns! iii 2 151

Miserable. If ever he have wife, let her be made As miserable by the death of him As I am made by my poor lord! . . *Richard III.* i 2 27
Judge what 'twere to lose it, and be miserable! . . . . i 3 258
O, I have pass'd a miserable night, So full of ugly sights . . i 4 2
Miserable England! I prophesy the fearfull'st time to thee . . iii 4 105
And be thy wife—if any be so mad—As miserable by the life of thee! . iv 1 76
They told me they would bind me here Unto the body of a dismal yew, And leave me to this miserable death . *T. Andron.* ii 3 108
Bid Æneas tell the tale twice o'er, How Troy was burnt and he made miserable . . . . . . iii 2 28
I made thee miserable What time I threw the people's suffrages On him iv 3 18
We worldly men Have miserable, mad, mistaking eyes . . . . v 2 66
Take heed, take heed, for such die miserable . *Rom. and Jul.* iii 3 145
Wretched, hateful day! Most miserable hour that e'er time saw! . . iv 5 44
Thou shouldst desire to die, being miserable.—Not by his breath that is more miserable . . . . *T. of Athens* iv 3 248
There is no time so miserable but a man may be true . . iv 3 462
O nation miserable, With an untitled tyrant bloody-scepter'd! *Macbeth* iv 3 103
Send the old and miserable king To some retention . . *Lear* v 3 46
What miserable praise hast thou for her that's foul and foolish? *Othello* ii 1 140
The miserable change now at my end Lament nor sorrow at *Ant. and Cleo.* iv 15 51
But most miserable Is the desire that's glorious . . *Cymbeline* i 6 6
Miserably. Lest in revenge thereof, sith God is just, He be as miserably slain as I . . . . . *3 Hen. VI.* i 3 42
Miséricorde. O, prenez miséricorde! ayez pitié de moi! . *Hen. V.* iv 4 12
Misery acquaints a man with strange bed-fellows . . *Tempest* ii 2 41
Perhaps, my son, Thou shamest to acknowledge me in misery *Com. of Errors* v 1 322
You would be, sweet madam, if your miseries were in the same abundance as your good fortunes are . . *Mer. of Venice* i 2 4
How little is the cost I have bestow'd In purchasing the semblance of my soul From out the state of hellish misery! . . . iii 4 21
From which lingering penance Of such misery doth she cut me off . iv 1 272
Thus misery doth part The flux of company . *As Y. Like It* ii 1 51
We two will rail against our mistress the world and all our misery . iii 2 296
Sorrow on thee and all the pack of you, That triumph thus upon my misery! Go, get thee gone, I say . . *T. of Shrew* iv 3 34
Better 'twere I met the ravin lion . . . ; better 'twere That all the miseries which nature owes Were mine at once . *All's Well* iii 2 122
Many a maid hath been seduced by them; and the misery is, example, that so terrible shows in the wreck of maidenhood . . iii 5 23
Do not tempt my misery . . . . . *T. Night* iii 4 383
That he did but see The flatness of my misery! . *W. Tale* iii 2 123
A wild dedication of yourselves To unpath'd waters, undream'd shores, most certain To miseries enough . . . . iv 4 579
Whose miseries are to be smiled at, their offences being so capital . iv 4 822
Though bearing misery, I desire my life Once more to look on him . v 1 137
Misery's love, O, come to me! . . . . *K. John* iii 4 35
Misery makes sport to mock itself . . . *Richard II.* ii 1 85
Away with these disgraceful wailing robes! Wounds will I lend the French instead of eyes, To weep their intermissive miseries *1 Hen. VI.* i 1 88
The arbitrator of despairs, Just death, kind umpire of men's miseries . ii 5 29
A gentler heart did never sway in court; But kings and mightiest potentates must die, For that's the end of human misery . . iii 2 137
I'll prepare My tear-stain'd eyes to see her miseries . *2 Hen. VI.* ii 4 16
Engirt with misery, For what's more miserable than discontent? . iii 1 200
Not that I pity Henry's misery, But seek revenge . . *3 Hen. VI.* iii 3 264
O ill-dispersing wind of misery! . . . . *Richard III.* iv 1 53
So many miseries have crazed my voice . . . . iv 4 17
Airy succeeders of intestate joys, Poor breathing orators of miseries! . iv 4 129
In a moment, see How soon this mightiness meets misery *Hen. VIII.* Prol. 30
I will not wish ye half my miseries; I have more charity . . iii 1 108
I am able now, methinks, Out of a fortitude of soul I feel, To endure more miseries and greater far . . . . . iii 2 389
I did not think to shed a tear In all my miseries . . . iii 2 429
The leanness that afflicts us, the object of our misery . *Coriolanus* i 1 21
He covets less Than misery itself would give . . . ii 2 131
Speed thee straight, And make my misery serve thy turn . . iv 5 94
For you, be that you are, long; and your misery increase with your age! v 2 113
We will mourn with thee: O, could our mourning ease thy misery! *T. Andron.* ii 4 57
Let us, that have our tongues, Plot some device of further misery . iii 1 134
Let reason govern thy lament.—If there were reason for these miseries, Then into limits could I bind my woes . . . . iii 1 220
These miseries are more than may be borne . . . . iii 1 244
When my heart, all mad with misery, Beats in this hollow prison of my flesh . . . . iii 2 9
Can you read?—Ay, mine own fortune in my misery *Rom. and Jul.* i 2 60
Meagre were his looks, Sharp misery had worn him to the bones . v 1 41
Who would not wish to be from wealth exempt, Since riches point to misery and contempt? . . . . . *T. of Athens* iv 2 32
I have heard in some sort of thy miseries.—Thou saw'st them, when I had prosperity.—I see them now . . . . . iv 3 76
Thou flatter'st misery.—I flatter not; but say thou art a caitiff . iv 3 234
Willing misery Outlives incertain pomp, is crown'd before . . iv 3 242
Live, and love thy misery.—Long live so, and so die . . . iv 3 396
Here, take: the gods out of my misery Have sent thee treasure . iv 3 531
Their life Is bound in shallows and in miseries . *J. Cæsar* iv 3 221
Nothing almost sees miracles But misery . . . . *Lear* ii 2 173
When we our betters see bearing our woes, We scarcely think our miseries our foes . . . . iii 6 110
I'll repair the misery thou dost bear With something rich about me iv 1 79
Is gone, In pity of his misery, to dispatch His nighted life . . iv 5 12
'Twas yet some comfort, When misery could beguile the tyrant's rage . iv 6 63
How have you known the miseries of your father?—By nursing them . v 3 180
When we in our viciousness grow hard—O misery on't! *Ant. and Cleo.* iii 13 112
To shift his being Is to exchange one misery with another . *Cymbeline* i 5 55
O noble misery, To be i' the field, and ask 'what news?' of me! . v 3 64
Since, Jupiter, our son is good, Take off his miseries . . . v 4 86
Then shall Posthumus end his miseries, Britain be fortunate . v 4 144; v 5 441
Hear these tears! The misery of Tarsus may be theirs . . *Pericles* i 4 55
Some neighbouring nation, Taking advantage of our misery . . i 4 66
We have heard your miseries as far as Tyre . . . . i 4 88
Your present kindness Makes my past miseries sports . . . ii 3 41
Misfortune. By misfortunes was my life prolong'd . *Com. of Errors* i 1 120
Make misfortune drunk With candle-wasters . . . *Much Ado* v 1 17
Every object that might make me fear Misfortune to my ventures, out of doubt Would make me sad . . . *Mer. of Venice* i 1 21
Never dare misfortune cross her foot, Unless she do it under this excuse ii 4 36
Or, if misfortune miss the first career . . . *Richard II.* i 2 49
Misfortune. In this thought they find a kind of ease, Bearing their own misfortunes on the back Of such as have before endured the like *Richard II.* v 5 29
Are you yet to learn What late misfortune is befall'n? . *3 Hen. VI.* iv 4 3
Makes me bridle passion And bear with mildness my misfortune's cross iv 4 20
What, amazed At my misfortunes? can thy spirit wonder? *Hen. VIII.* iii 2 374
And bakes the elf-locks in foul sluttish hairs, Which once untangled much misfortune bodes . . . . *Rom. and Jul.* i 4 91
O, give me thy hand, One writ with me in sour misfortune's book! . v 3 82
Only by misfortune of the seas Bereft of ships and men . . *Pericles* ii 3 88
I pity his misfortune, And will awake him from his melancholy . . ii 3 90
Misgive. My heart misgives me . . . . . *Mer. Wives* v 5 226
So doth my heart misgive me, in these conflicts What may befall him *3 Hen. VI.* iv 6 94
My mind misgives Some consequence yet hanging in the stars *R. and J.* i 4 106
Fetch me the handkerchief: my mind misgives . . . *Othello* iii 4 89
Misgiving. My misgiving still Falls shrewdly to the purpose *J. Cæsar* iii 1 145
Misgoverned. Rude misgovern'd hands . . . *Richard II.* v 2 5
Misgovernment. I am sorry for thy much misgovernment . *Much Ado* iv 1 100
Misgraffed. Or else misgraffed in respect of years . *M. N. Dream* i 1 137
Misguide. Fortune Fall deep in love with thee; and her great charms Misguide thy opposers' swords! . . . . *Coriolanus* i 5 23
Mishap. To tell sad stories of my own mishaps . *Com. of Errors* i 1 121
Whom the fates have mark'd To bear the extremity of dire mishap! . i 1 142
What! shall we curse the planets of mishap? . . *1 Hen. VI.* i 1 23
Secure from worldly chances and mishaps . . . *T. Andron.* i 1 152
Misheard. Thou hast misspoke, misheard; Be well advised . *K. John* iii 1 4
Misinterpret. You did make him misinterpret me . *Richard II.* iii 1 18
Misinterpreting. Your exposition misinterpreting . . . *Pericles* i 1 112
Mislead. Lights that do mislead the morn . . *Meas. for Meas.* iv 1 4
Mislead night-wanderers, laughing at their harm . *M. N. Dream* ii 1 39
Misleader. That villanous abominable misleader of youth . *1 Hen. IV.* ii 4 508
I banish thee, on pain of death, As I have done the rest of my misleaders, Not to come near our person . . . *2 Hen. IV.* v 5 68
Thou mad misleader of thy brain-sick son! . . *2 Hen. VI.* v 1 163
Misleading. To plague thee for thy foul misleading me . *3 Hen. VI.* v 1 97
Misled. If their wisdoms be misled in this . . . *Much Ado* iv 1 189
Your son was misled with a snipt-taffeta fellow . . *All's Well* iv 5 1
You have misled a prince, a royal king . . . *Richard II.* iii 1 8
Herein misled by your suggestion . . . . *1 Hen. IV.* iv 3 51
We love our people well; even those we love That are misled . . v 1 105
You have misled the youthful prince.—The young prince hath misled me: I am the fellow with the great belly, and he my dog *2 Hen. IV.* i 2 163
Ambassadors from the king Unto the commons whom thou hast misled *2 Hen. VI.* iv 9 8
Our people and our peers are both misled . . *3 Hen. VI.* iii 3 35
Mislike me not for my complexion . . . *Mer. of Venice* ii 1 1
'Tis not my speeches that you do mislike, But 'tis my presence *2 Hen. VI.* i 1 140
Setting your scorns and your mislike aside, Tell me some reason *3 Hen. VI.* iv 1 24
If he mislike My speech and what is done, tell him . *Ant. and Cleo.* iii 13 147
Misordered. The time misorder'd doth, in common sense, Crowd us and crush us to this monstrous form . . . *2 Hen. IV.* iv 2 33
Misplace. Do you hear how he misplaces? . . . *Meas. for Meas.* ii 1 90
Misplaced. Her [Fortune's] benefits are mightily misplaced *As Y. Like It* i 2 38
The misplaced John . . . . *K. John* iii 4 133
I'll have this crown of mine cut from my shoulders Ere I will see the crown so foul misplaced . . . . . *Richard III.* iii 2 44
Misprised. You spend your passion on a misprised mood *M. N. Dream* iii 2 74
I am altogether misprised: but it shall not be so long . *As Y. Like It* i 1 177
Your reputation shall not therefore be misprised . . . . i 2 192
Misprising. Disdain and scorn ride sparkling in her eyes, Misprising what they look on . . . . . . *Much Ado* iii 1 52
By the misprising of a maid too virtuous . . . *All's Well* iii 2 33
A little proudly, and great deal misprizing The knight opposed *T. and C.* iv 5 74
Misprision. There is some strange misprision in the princes . *Much Ado* iv 1 187
Incision Would let her out in saucers: sweet misprision! . *L. L. Lost* iv 3 98
Of thy misprision must perforce ensue Some true love turn'd *M. N. D.* iii 2 90
That dost in vile misprision shackle up My love . . *All's Well* ii 3 159
Misprision in the highest degree! . . . . . *T. Night* i 5 61
Either envy, therefore, or misprision Is guilty of this fault *1 Hen. IV.* i 3 27
Misproud. Impairing Henry, strengthening misproud York *3 Hen. VI.* ii 6 7
Misquote. Look how we can, or sad or merrily, Interpretation will misquote our looks . . . . *1 Hen. IV.* v 2 13
Misreport. A man that never yet Did, as he vouches, misreport your grace . . . . *Meas. for Meas.* v 1 148
Miss. But, as 'tis, We cannot miss him . . . . *Tempest* i 2 311
He could not miss't . . . . ii 1 40
He misses not much.—No; he doth but mistake the truth totally . ii 1 56
I shall miss thee; But yet thou shalt have freedom . . . v 1 95
That will not miss you morning nor evening prayer . *Mer. Wives* ii 2 102
I will not miss her . . . . iii 5 56
You find not the apostraphas, and so miss the accent . *L. L. Lost* iv 2 124
Miss that which one unworthier may attain . *Mer. of Venice* ii 1 37
So may you miss me; But if you do, you'll make me wish a sin . iii 2 12
You are very sensible, and yet you miss my sense . *T. of Shrew* v 2 18
Who ever strove To show her merit, that did miss her love? *All's Well* i 1 242
Be sure of this, What I can help thee to thou shalt not miss . . i 3 262
Your free undertaking cannot miss A thriving issue . . *W. Tale* ii 2 44
When he shall miss me,—as, in faith, I mean not To see him any more iv 4 505
Or, if misfortune miss the first career . . . *Richard II.* i 2 49
O, I should have a heavy miss of thee, If I were much in love with vanity! Death hath not struck so fat a deer to-day . *1 Hen. IV.* v 4 105
Hit or miss, Our project's life this shape of sense assumes *Troi. and Cres.* i 3 384
He would miss it rather Than carry it but by the suit of the gentry *Cor.* ii 1 253
An if we miss to meet him handsomely . . . *T. Andron.* ii 3 268
What here shall miss, our toil shall strive to mend . *Rom. and Jul.* Prol. 14
Well, in that hit you miss . . . . i 1 214
I laid their daggers ready; He could not miss 'em . . *Macbeth* ii 2 13
To our dear friend Banquo, whom we miss . . . . iii 4 90
I would the friends we miss were safe arrived . . . . v 8 35
May miss our name, And hit the woundless air . . . *Hamlet* iv 1 43
Two beggars told me I could not miss my way . . . *Cymbeline* iii 6 9
Missed. A health to all that shot and miss'd . . . *T. of Shrew* v 2 51
Oft have shot at them, Howe'er unfortunate I miss'd my aim *1 Hen. VI.* i 4 4
A sure and safe one, though thy master miss'd it . *Hen. VIII.* iii 2 438
I missed the meteor once, and hit that woman . . . . v 4 52
Your Coriolanus Is not much miss'd, but with his friends *Coriolanus* iv 6 13
He that hath miss'd the princess is a thing Too bad . . *Cymbeline* i 1 16
You shall be miss'd at court, And that will well confirm it . . iii 4 129
Lest, being miss'd, I be suspected of Your carriage from the court . iii 4 189

Missed. How can she be with him? When was she miss'd? He is in Rome . . . . *Cymbeline* iii 5 90
Mis-shaped. Until my mis-shaped trunk that bears this head Be round impaled with a glorious crown . . . 3 *Hen. VI.* iii 2 170
Mis-shapen. This mis-shapen knave, His mother was a witch *Tempest* v 1 268
A foul mis-shapen stigmatic, Mark'd by the destinies . . 3 *Hen. VI.* ii 2 136
Thou perjured George, And thou mis-shapen Dick . . . v 5 35
Serious vanity! Mis-shapen chaos of well-seeming forms! *Rom. and Jul.* i 1 185
Thy wit, that ornament to shape and love, Mis-shapen in the conduct of them both, Like powder in a skilless soldier's flask, Is set a-fire . iii 3 131
Mis-sheathed. This dagger hath mista'en,—for, lo, his house Is empty on the back of Montague,—And it mis-sheathed in my daughter's bosom! . . . . v 3 205
Missing. There are yet missing of your company Some few . *Tempest* v 1 254
For missing your meetings and appointments . . *Mer. Wives* iii 1 92
The roynish clown . . . is also missing . . . *As Y. Like It* ii 2 9
If in her marriage my consent be missing . . *T. of Athens* i 1 138
Macduff is missing, and your noble son . . . . *Macbeth* v 8 38
The day that she was missing he was here . . *Cymbeline* iv 3 17
Cloten, Upon my lady's missing, came to me With his sword drawn . v 5 275
Missingly. I have missingly noted, he is of late much retired . *W. Tale* iv 2 35
Mission. Made emulous missions 'mongst the gods themselves *Tr. and Cr.* iii 3 189
Missive. Whiles I stood rapt in the wonder of it, came missives from the king . . . . *Macbeth* i 5 7
And with taunts Did gibe my missive out of audience . *Ant. and Cleo.* ii 2 74
Misspoke. It is not so; thou hast misspoke, misheard . *K. John* iii 1 4
Mist. I'll say as they say and persever so And in this mist at all adventures go . . . . *Com. of Errors* ii 2 218
Breaking through the foul and ugly mists Of vapours . 1 *Hen. IV.* i 2 226
She's dead as earth. Lend me a looking-glass; If that her breath will mist or stain the stone, Why, then she lives . . . *Lear* v 3 262
Mistake. He doth but mistake the truth totally . . *Tempest* ii 1 57
You mistake; I mean the pound,—a pinfold . . *T. G. of Ver.* i 1 113
Well, your old vice still; mistake the word . . . . iii 1 283
The music likes you not.—You mistake; the musician likes me not . iv 2 57
You must not, sir, mistake my niece . . . *Much Ado* i 1 61
I mistake your shape and making quite . . *M. N. Dream* ii 1 32
Our sport shall be to take what they mistake . . . . v 1 90
Her benefits are mightily misplaced, and the bountiful blind woman doth most mistake in her gifts to women . . *As Y. Like It* i 2 39
Mistake me not so much To think my poverty is treacherous . . i 3 66
Mistake me not; I speak but as I find . . *T. of Shrew* ii 1 66
Mistake no more: I am not Licio, Nor a musician, as I seem to be . iv 2 16
You mistake, sir. Pray, what do you think is his name? . . v 1 82
Mary Accost,— You mistake, knight: 'accost' is front her . *T. Night* i 3 59
You do mistake me, sir.—No, sir, no jot; I know your favour well . iii 4 362
What was my first? it has an elder sister, Or I mistake you . *W. Tale* i 2 99
You, my lord, Do but mistake.—You have mistook, my lady . . ii 1 81
You scarce can right me throughly then to say You did mistake—No; if I mistake In those foundations which I build upon, The centre is not big enough to bear A school-boy's top . . . ii 1 100
Therefore proceed. But yet hear this; mistake me not; no life . ii 2 110
The better act of purposes mistook Is to mistake again . *K. John* iii 1 274
Mistake me not, my lord; 'tis not my meaning . *Richard II.* ii 3 74
Your grace mistakes; only to be brief, Left I his title out . iii 3 9
Mistake not, uncle, further than you should.—Take not, good cousin, further than you should, Lest you mistake the heavens are o'er our heads . . . . iii 3 14
If I mistake not, thou art Harry Monmouth . . . 1 *Hen. IV.* v 4 59
You mistake me, sir.—Why, sir, did I say you were an honest man? 2 *Hen. IV.* i 2 91
Gentlemen both, you will mistake each other . . . *Hen. V.* iii 2 146
As you did mistake The outward composition of his body . 1 *Hen. VI.* ii 3 74
I do not mistake; But thou mistakest me much to think I do 2 *Hen. VI.* v 1 129
I do mistake my person all this while . . . *Richard III.* i 2 253
Brother of Gloucester, you mistake the matter . . . . ii 3 62
My pretty cousins, you mistake me much . . . . ii 2 8
Your rage mistakes us.—The more shame for ye . *Hen. VIII.* iii 1 101
Not out of hope—Mistake me not—to save my life . *Coriolanus* v 5 86
You mistake my love: I gave it freely ever . . *T. of Athens* i 2 9
You Mistake my fortunes; I am wealthy in my friends . . ii 2 193
I do proclaim One honest man—mistake me not—but one . . iv 3 504
You do mistake your business; my brother never Did urge me *A. and C.* ii 2 45
You did mistake him, sure.—I cannot tell: long is it since I saw him *Cymbeline* iv 2 102
Mistaken. Thou hast mistaken his letter . . . *L. L. Lost* iv 1 108
What hast thou done? thou hast mistaken quite . *M. N. Dream* iii 2 88
It may be you have mistaken him, my lord.—And shall do so ever, though I took him at's prayers . . . . . *All's Well* ii 5 43
And she, mistaken, seems to dote on me. What will become of this? *T. Night* ii 2 36
You are too much mistaken in this king . . . . *Hen. V.* ii 4 30
Unless I have mista'en his colours much . . *Richard III.* v 3 35
I am sorry To hear this of him; and could wish he were Something mistaken in't.—No, not a syllable . . . *Hen. VIII.* i 1 195
And unproperly Show duty, as mistaken all this while . *Coriolanus* v 3 55
Look how our daughter bleeds! This dagger hath mista'en *Rom. and Jul.* v 3 203
I beseech you, pardon me, my lord, if I be mistaken . . *Lear* i 4 70
Either your unparagoned mistress is dead, or she's outprized by a trifle.—You are mistaken . . . . . . *Cymbeline* i 4 89
Mistakest. Thou mistakest me.—Why, fool, I meant not thee *T. G. of V.* ii 5 49
Thou mistakest, Or else committ'st thy knaveries wilfully *M. N. Dream* iii 2 345
I do not mistake; But thou mistakest me much to think I do 2 *Hen. VI.* v 1 130
Mistaketh. Sometime for three-foot stool mistaketh me *M. N. Dream* ii 1 52
Mistaking. Told thee no lies, made thee no mistakings . . *Tempest* i 2 248
I have lost my edifice by mistaking the place where I erected it *M. Wives* ii 2 225
Either this is envy in you, folly, or mistaking . *Meas. for Meas.* iii 2 150
Yet sinn'd I not But in mistaking . . . . *Much Ado* v 1 285
Pardon, old father, my mistaking eyes . . . *T. of Shrew* iv 5 45
Pardon, I pray thee, for my mad mistaking . . . . iv 5 49
Kneel again; For thy mistaking so, we pardon thee . . 2 *Hen. VI.* v 1 128
We worldly men Have miserable, mad, mistaking eyes . . *T. Andron.* v 2 66
Back, foolish tears, . . . Your tributary drops belong to woe, Which you, mistaking, offer up to joy . . . *Rom. and Jul.* iii 2 104
If you violently proceed against him, mistaking his purpose . . *Lear* i 2 90
Mistempered. This inundation of mistemper'd humour . *K. John* v 1 12
Throw your mistemper'd weapons to the ground . *Rom. and Jul.* i 1 94
Mis-termed. Then banished, Is death mis-term'd . . . . iii 3 21
Mistership. Wouldst thou speak with us?—Yea, forsooth, an your mistership be emperial . . . . . *T. Andron.* iv 4 40
Mistful. I must perforce compound With mistful eyes . . *Hen. V.* iv 6 34
Misthink. How will the country for these woful chances Misthink the king and not be satisfied! . . . . . 3 *Hen. VI.* ii 5 108
Misthought. Be it known, that we, the greatest, are misthought For things that others do . . . . . . *Ant. and Cleo.* v 2 176
Mistletoe. O'ercome with moss and baleful mistletoe *T. Andron.* ii 3 95
Mist-like. Unless the breath of heart-sick groans, Mist-like, infold me from the search of eyes . . . . *Rom. and Jul.* iii 3 73
Mistook. You mistook, sir; I say, she did nod . . *T. G. of Ver.* i 1 120
Who bade you call her?—Your worship, sir; or else I mistook . ii 1 10
O, cry you mercy, sir, I have mistook: This is the ring you sent to Silvia v 4 94
Out upon you! how am I mistook in you! . . *Mer. Wives* iii 3 111
They mistook their erection.—So did I mine, to build upon a foolish woman's promise . . . . iii 5 41
This letter is mistook, it importeth none here . . *L. L. Lost* iv 1 57
Their several counsels they unbosom shall To loves mistook . . v 2 142
And the youth, mistook by me, Pleading for a lover's fee *M. N. Dream* iii 2 112
I mistook. Did not you tell me I should know the man By the Athenian garments he had on? . . . . iii 2 347
I did but tell her she mistook her frets . . . *T. of Shrew* ii 1 150
So comes it, lady, you have been mistook . . . *T. Night* v 1 266
You, my lord, Do but mistake.—You have mistook, my lady . *W. Tale* ii 1 81
The better act of purposes mistook Is to mistake again . . *K. John* iii 1 274
You have but mistook me all this while . . . *Richard II.* iii 2 174
By the honour of my blood, My father's purposes have been mistook 2 *Hen. IV.* iv 2 56
Or else you may be marvellously mistook . . . *Hen. V.* iii 6 85
Had he mistook him and sent to me, I should ne'er have denied *T. of A.* iii 2 25
Then, Brutus, I have much mistook your passion . . *J. Cæsar* i 2 48
Purposes mistook Fall'n on the inventors' heads . . . *Hamlet* v 2 395
What's he that hath so much thy place mistook To set thee here? *Lear* ii 4 12
Mistreading. The rod of heaven To punish my mistreadings 1 *Hen. IV.* iii 2 11
Mistress. My mistress show'd me thee and thy dog and thy bush *Tempest* ii 2 144
The mistress which I serve quickens what's dead . . . . iii 1 6
My sweet mistress Weeps when she sees me work . . . . iii 1 11
O most dear mistress, The sun will set before I shall discharge What I must strive to do . . . . iii 1 21
Noble mistress; 'tis fresh morning with me When you are by at night . iii 1 33
I'll be your servant, Whether you will or no.—My mistress, dearest . iii 1 86
Mistress line, is not this my jerkin? . . . . . . iv 1 235
Now you are metamorphosed with a mistress . . . *T. G. of Ver.* ii 1 32
Madam and mistress, a thousand good-morrows . . . . ii 1 102
O, be not like your mistress; be moved, be moved . . . ii 3 181
Servant!—Mistress?—Master, Sir Thurio frowns on you . . ii 4 2
His mistress Did hold his eyes lock'd in her crystal looks . . ii 4 88
Too low a mistress for so high a servant.—Not so, sweet lady: but too mean a servant To have a look of such a worthy mistress . . ii 4 106
You are welcome to a worthless mistress.—I'll die on him that says so ii 4 113
Sovereign to all the creatures on the earth.—Except my mistress . ii 4 154
That my poor mistress, moved therewithal, Wept bitterly . . iv 4 175
I give thee this For thy sweet mistress' sake, because thou lovest her . iv 4 182
I hope my master's suit will be but cold, Since she respects my mistress' love so much . . . . iv 4 187
I'll use thee kindly for thy mistress' sake, That used me so . . iv 4 207
I must of another errand to Sir John Falstaff from my two mistresses *M. W.* iii 4 115
A couple of Ford's knaves, his hinds, were called forth by their mistress iii 5 100
I suspect without cause, mistress, do I? . . . . . . iv 2 138
A respected fellow; and his mistress is a respected woman *M. for M.* ii 1 171
How doth my dear morsel, thy mistress? Procures she still, ha? . iii 2 56
The clock hath strucken twelve upon the bell; My mistress made it one upon my cheek . . . . *Com. of Errors* i 2 46
To pay the saddler for my mistress' crupper . . . . i 2 56
I from my mistress come to you in post; If I return, I shall be post indeed i 2 63
Sir, to dinner: My mistress and her sister stays for you . . i 2 76
Some of my mistress' marks upon my shoulders . . .—Thy mistress' marks? what mistress, slave, hast thou? . . . . . . i 2 83
Why, mistress, sure my master is horn-mad.—Horn-mad, thou villain! ii 1 57
'My mistress, sir,' quoth I; 'Hang up thy mistress! I know not thy mistress; out on thy mistress!'—Quoth who?—Quoth my master . ii 1 67
'I know,' quoth he, 'no house, no wife, no mistress' . . . ii 1 71
You received no gold? Your mistress sent to have me home to dinner? ii 2 10
Thou didst deny the gold's receipt And told'st me of a mistress and a dinner . . . . ii 2 18
Some other mistress hath thy sweet aspects . . . . . ii 2 113
Sweet mistress,—what your name is else, I know not . . . iii 2 29
Master, is this Mistress Satan?—It is the devil . . . . iv 3 49
O mistress, mistress, shift and save yourself! . . . . . v 1 168
She leans me out at her mistress' chamber-window . . *Much Ado* iii 3 156
Or study where to meet some mistress fine, When mistresses from common sense are hid . . . . *L. L. Lost* i 1 63
An your waist, mistress, were as slender as my wit, One o' these maids' girdles for your waist should be fit . . . . iv 1 49
My love, her mistress, is a gracious moon, She an attending star . iv 3 230
Your mistresses dare never come in rain, For fear their colours should be wash'd away . . . . iv 3 270
Then homeward every man attach the hand Of his fair mistress . . iv 3 376
And every one his love-feat will advance Unto his several mistress . v 2 124
White-handed mistress, one sweet word with thee . . . . v 2 230
Madam, and pretty mistresses, give ear . . . . . v 2 286
The bouncing Amazon, Your buskin'd mistress . . . *M. N. Dream* ii 1 71
My mistress with a monster is in love . . . . . . iii 2 6
You, mistress, all this coil is 'long of you . . . . . iii 2 339
Mistress, look out at window, for all this . . . *Mer. of Venice* ii 5 40
You saw the mistress, I beheld the maid; You loved, I loved for intermission . . . . iii 2 200
I got a promise of this fair one here To have her love, provided that your fortune Achieved her mistress . . . . iii 2 210
For affection, Mistress of passion, sways it to the mood Of what it likes or loathes . . . . iv 1 51
My mistress will before the break of day Be here at Belmont . . v 1 29
Ceremoniously let us prepare Some welcome for the mistress of the house v 1 38
Signify, I pray you. Within the house, your mistress is at hand . v 1 52
With sweetest touches pierce your mistress' ear . . . . v 1 67
I show more mirth than I am mistress of . . . *As Y. Like It* i 2 4
As you have exceeded all promise, Your mistress shall be happy . . i 2 257
In the morning early they found the bed untreasured of their mistress . ii 2 7
Wearying thy hearer in thy mistress' praise . . . . . ii 4 38
Sighing like furnace, with a woeful ballad Made to his mistress' eyebrow ii 7 149
And we two will rail against our mistress the world . . . iii 2 295
He was to imagine me his love, his mistress . . . . . iii 2 428

Mistress. Mistress and master, you have oft inquired After the shepherd *As Y. Like It* iii 4 50
Praising the proud disdainful shepherdess That was his mistress . . iii 4 54
To tangle my eyes too! No, faith, proud mistress, hope not after it . iii 5 45
But, mistress, know yourself: down on your knees, And thank heaven, fasting, for a good man's love . . . . . iii 5 57
Who could be out, being before his beloved mistress? . . . iv 1 83
Our master and mistress seeks you; come, away, away! . . . v 1 66
That we may yet again have access to our fair mistress . *T. of Shrew* i 1 119
A fine musician to instruct our mistress . . . . i 2 174
Contrive this afternoon, And quaff carouses to our mistress' health i 2 277
I must be gone.—Faith, mistress, then I have no cause to stay . iii 1 86
We are beset with thieves; Rescue thy mistress, if thou be a man iii 2 239
Mistress, what's your opinion of your sister? . . . . iii 2 245
Winter tames man, woman and beast; for it hath tamed my old master and my new mistress and myself . . . . iv 1 26
But wilt thou make a fire, or shall I complain on thee to our mistress? iv 1 32
My master and mistress are almost frozen to death.—There's fire ready . iv 1 39
First, know, my horse is tired; my master and mistress fallen out iv 1 57
We came down a foul hill, my master riding behind my mistress iv 1 70
You must meet my master to countenance my mistress . . . iv 1 101
Now, mistress, profit you in what you read? . . . . iv 2 6
While you, sweet dear, prove mistress of my heart! . . . iv 2 10
You jest: but have you both forsworn me?—Mistress, we have . iv 2 49
Mistress, what cheer?—Faith, as cold as can be . . . iv 3 37
The gown is not for me.—You are i' the right, sir: 'tis for my mistress iv 3 158
Villain, not for thy life: take up my mistress' gown for thy master's use! iv 3 161
Good morrow, gentle mistress: where away? . . . . iv 5 27
You my merry mistress, That with your strange encounter much amazed me . . . . iv 5 53
Ay, mistress bride, hath that awaken'd you? . . . . . v 2 42
My mistress sends you word That she is busy and she cannot come v 2 80
Go to your mistress; Say, I command her come to me.—I know her answer . . . . v 2 95
Be comfortable to my mother, your mistress . . *All's Well* i 1 86
A mother and a mistress and a friend, A phœnix, captain and an enemy i 1 181
I am a mother to you.—Mine honourable mistress.—Nay, a mother i 3 145
To each of you one fair and virtuous mistress Fall, when Love please! marry, to each, but one! . . . . ii 3 63
Your lord and master's married; there's news for you: you have a new mistress . . . . ii 3 258
She deserves a lord That twenty such rude boys might tend upon And call her hourly mistress . . . . iii 2 85
And fortune play upon thy prosperous helm, As thy auspicious mistress! iii 3 8
Whose dear perfection hearts that scorn'd to serve Humbly call'd mistress . . . . v 3 19
O mistress mine, where are you roaming? O, stay and hear . *T. Night* ii 3 40
But the fool should be as oft with your master as with my mistress . iii 1 46
And that no woman has; nor never none Shall mistress be of it . iii 1 172
Here is my hand: you shall from this time be Your master's mistress v 1 334
Orsino's mistress and his fancy's queen . . . . . v 1 397
To satisfy . . . the entreaties Of our most gracious mistress.—Satisfy! The entreaties of your mistress! satisfy! Let that suffice *W. Tale* i 2 233
I would not be a stander-by to hear My sovereign mistress clouded so . i 2 280
I cannot Believe this crack to be in my dread mistress . . . i 2 322
When you shall know your mistress Has deserved prison, then abound in tears . . . . ii 1 119
You will not own it.—More than mistress of Which comes to me in name of fault, I must not At all acknowledge . . . iii 2 60
My father hath made her mistress of the feast, and she lays it on . iv 3 42
Present yourself That which you are, mistress o' the feast . . iv 4 68
Mopsa must be your mistress: marry, garlic, To mend her kissing with! iv 4 162
Where you may Enjoy your mistress . . . . . . iv 4 539
She seems a mistress To most that teach . . . . . iv 4 593
Fortunate mistress,—let my prophecy Come home to ye! . . . iv 4 662
I'ld beg your precious mistress, Which he counts but a trifle . v 1 223
Governed, as the sea is, by our noble and chaste mistress the moon *1 Hen. IV.* i 2 32
The art and practic part of life Must be the mistress to this theoric *Hen. V.* i 1 52
'Wonder of nature,'—I have heard a sonnet begin so to one's mistress . iii 7 45
My horse is my mistress.—Your mistress bears well.—Me well; which is the prescript praise and perfection of a good and particular mistress . . . . iii 7 47
Methought yesterday your mistress shrewdly shook your back . iii 7 52
I had rather have my horse to my mistress.—I had as lief have my mistress a jade . . . . iii 7 62
My mistress wears his own hair.—I could make as true a boast as that, if I had a sow to my mistress . . . . . . iii 7 64
Thou makest use of any thing.—Yet do I not use my horse for my mistress iii 7 71
Let his . . . body lie, Until the queen his mistress bury it *2 Hen. VI.* iv 1 143
I like it well that our fair queen and mistress Smiles at her news *3 Hen. VI.* iii 3 167
Our mistress' sorrows we were pitying . . . . *Hen. VIII.* ii 3 53
Some will thank you, If you speak truth, for their poor mistress' sake . iii 1 47
Like the lily, That once was mistress of the field and flourish'd . iii 1 152
A knight's daughter, To be her mistress' mistress! the queen's queen! . iii 2 95
And my good mistress will Remember in my prayers . . . v 1 77
That loves his mistress more than in confession . *Troi. and Cres.* i 3 269
So, so; rub on, and kiss the mistress . . . . . iii 2 52
Thinking it harder for our mistress to devise imposition enough than for us to undergo any difficulty imposed . . . . . . iii 2 85
And to Diomed You shall be mistress, and command him wholly . iv 4 122
Do you meddle with my master?—Ay; 'tis an honester service than to meddle with thy mistress . . . . . *Coriolanus* iv 5 53
More dances my rapt heart Than when I first my wedded mistress saw Bestride my threshold . . . . iv 5 123
Our general himself makes a mistress of him . . . . . iv 5 207
Rome's royal mistress, mistress of my heart . . *T. Andron.* i 1 241
And fit thy thoughts To mount aloft with thy imperial mistress . ii 1 13
I am as able and as fit as thou To serve, and to deserve my mistress' grace . . . . ii 1 34
Wilt thou betray thy noble mistress thus?—My mistress is my mistress; this myself, The vigour and the picture of my youth . . . iv 2 106
Show me a mistress that is passing fair . . *Rom. and Jul.* i 1 240
Ah ha, my mistresses! which of you all Will now deny to dance? . i 5 20
'Twould anger him To raise a spirit in his mistress' circle . . ii 1 24
And in his mistress' name I conjure only but to raise up him . ii 1 28
And wish his mistress were that kind of fruit As maids call medlars ii 1 35
Commend me to thy mistress.—Now God in heaven bless thee! . . ii 4 205
Well, sir; my mistress is the sweetest lady . . . . . ii 4 211

Mistress. O, he is even in my mistress' case, Just in her case! O woful sympathy! . . . . *Rom. and Jul.* iii 3 84
Mistress minion, you, Thank me no thankings, nor proud me no prouds iii 5 152
Mistress! what, mistress! Juliet! fast, I warrant her, she . . iv 5 1
How does your mistress!—She's e'en setting on water to scald such chickens as you are . . . . . . *T. of Athens* ii 2 70
Look you, here comes my mistress' page . . . . . . ii 2 75
I think no usurer but has a fool to his servant: my mistress is one . ii 2 104
They enter my mistress' house merrily, and go away sadly: the reason? ii 2 107
Each man to his stool, with that spur as he would to the lip of his mistress . . . . iii 6 74
Maid, to thy master's bed; Thy mistress is o' the brothel! . . iv 1 13
Bid thy mistress, when my drink is ready, She strike upon the bell *Macb.* ii 1 31
I, the mistress of your charms, The close contriver of all harms . iii 5 6
I went round to work, And my young mistress thus I did bespeak *Hamlet* ii 2 140
What, my young lady and mistress! . . . . ii 2 444
Since my dear soul was mistress of her choice And could of men distinguish . . . . iii 2 68
Conjuring the moon To stand auspicious mistress . . . *Lear* ii 1 42
Half breathless, panting forth From Goneril his mistress salutations ii 4 32
Served the lust of my mistress' heart, and did the act of darkness with her . . . . iii 4 89
Come hither, mistress. Is your name Goneril?—She cannot deny it . iii 6 51
Get horses for your mistress.—Farewell, sweet lord, and sister . . iii 7 20
If you dare venture in your own behalf, A mistress's command . . iv 2 21
And when your mistress hears thus much from you, I pray, desire her call her wisdom to her . . . . iv 5 34
As duteous to the vices of thy mistress As badness would desire . . iv 6 258
Come hither, gentle mistress: Do you perceive in all this noble company Where most you owe obedience? . . . . . *Othello* i 3 178
Opinion, a sovereign mistress of effects, throws a more safer voice on you i 3 225
He'll be as full of quarrel and offence As my young mistress' dog . ii 3 53
My wife must move for Cassio to her mistress; I'll set her on . ii 3 389
You are jealous now That this is from some mistress, some remembrance iii 4 186
By their own importunate suit, Or voluntary dotage of some mistress . iv 1 27
You, mistress, That have the office opposite to Saint Peter! . . iv 2 90
For you, mistress, Save you your labour . . . . . v 1 100
Look you pale, mistress? Do you perceive the gastness of her eye? . v 1 105
Come, mistress, you must tell's another tale . . . . v 1 125
Sweet Desdemona! O sweet mistress, speak!—A guiltless death I die . v 2 121
O mistress, villany hath made mocks with love! . . . . v 2 151
Help! help, ho! help! The Moor hath kill'd my mistress! . . v 2 167
My mistress here lies murder'd in her bed,— O heavens forfend! . v 2 185
Ay, ay: O, lay me by my mistress' side . . . . . v 2 237
And companion me with my mistress . . . *Ant. and Cleo.* i 2 30
All the east, Say thou, shall call her mistress . . . . i 5 47
Antonius dead!—If thou say so, villain, Thou kill'st thy mistress . ii 5 27
O sovereign mistress of true melancholy, The poisonous damp of night disponge upon me . . . . iv 9 12
My mistress loved thee, and her fortunes mingled With thine entirely iv 14 24
The queen my mistress, Confined in all she has, her monument . v 1 52
I found her trimming up the diadem On her dead mistress . . v 2 346
To his mistress, For whom he now is banish'd, her own price Proclaims how she esteem'd him . . . . *Cymbeline* i 1 50
My queen! my mistress! O lady, weep no more . . . . i 1 92
Where each of us fell in praise of our country mistresses . . i 4 62
Either your unparagoned mistress is dead, or she's outprized by a trifle i 4 87
Your Italy contains none so accomplished a courtier to convince the honour of my mistress . . . . i 4 105
I should get ground of your fair mistress, make her go back . . i 4 114
My mistress exceeds in goodness the hugeness of your unworthy thinking i 4 156
If I bring you no sufficient testimony that I have enjoyed the dearest bodily part of your mistress, my ten thousand ducats are yours . i 4 162
Tell thy mistress how The case stands with her; do't as from thyself . i 5 66
But think Thou hast thy mistress still, to boot, my son . . i 5 69
And you his mistress, only For the most worthiest fit! . . . i 6 161
When you have given good morning to your mistress, Attend the queen ii 3 66
Had I not brought The knowledge of your mistress home, I grant We were to question further . . . . ii 4 51
All-worthy villain! Discover where thy mistress is at once . . iii 5 95
The same suit he wore when he took leave of my lady and mistress . iii 5 129
How fit his garments serve me! Why should his mistress, who was made by him that made the tailor, not be fit too? . . . . iv 1 3
Thy mistress enforced; thy garments cut to pieces before thy face . iv 1 18
But, for my mistress, I nothing know where she remains, why gone . iv 3 13
Nor hear I from my mistress, who did promise To yield me often tidings iv 3 38
Britain, I have kill'd thy mistress, peace! I'll give no wound to thee v 1 20
It is my mistress: Since she is living, let the time run on To good or bad v 5 127
Not dispraising whom we praised, . . . he began His mistress' picture v 5 175
O, gentlemen, help! Mine and your mistress! . . . . v 5 230
Does the world go round?—How come these staggers on me?—Wake, my mistress! . . . . v 5 233
How fares my mistress?—O, get thee from my sight; Thou gavest me poison . . . . v 5 235
'If Pisanio Have,' said she, 'given his mistress that confection Which I gave him for cordial, she is served As I would serve a rat' . . v 5 246
As you do love, fill to your mistress' lips . . . . *Pericles* ii 3 51
'Tis well, mistress; your choice agrees with mine . . . . ii 5 18
Yea, mistress, are you so peremptory? . . . . . . ii 5 73
Look to your little mistress, on whose grace You may depend hereafter iii 3 40
She would with rich and constant pen Vail to her mistress Dian iv Gower 29
Here she comes weeping for her only mistress' death . . . iv 1 11
I could wish him [mine enemy] to be my master, or rather, my mistress iv 6 170
But since my master and mistress have bought you, there's no going but by their consent . . . . iv 6 207

Mistress-court. He'll make your Paris Louvre shake for it, Were it the mistress-court of mighty Europe . . . . . *Hen. V.* ii 4 133

Mistrust. I will never mistrust my wife again . . . *Mer. Wives* v 5 141
Because I will not do them the wrong to mistrust any, I will do myself the right to trust none . . . . . . *Much Ado* i 1 246
That ugly treason of mistrust, Which makes me fear . *Mer. of Venice* iii 2 28
Yet your mistrust cannot make me a traitor . . *As Y. Like It* i 3 58
In time I may believe, yet I mistrust.—Mistrust it not . *T. of Shrew* ii 1 51
And yet we have but trivial argument, More than mistrust *2 Hen. VI.* iii 1 242
In a curious bed, When care, mistrust, and treason waits on him *3 Hen. VI.* ii 5 54
Many a thousand, Which now mistrust no parcel of my fear . . v 6 38
By a divine instinct men's minds mistrust Ensuing dangers *Richard III.* ii 3 42
No cause to mistrust; But yet, you see, how soon the day o'ercast . iii 2 87
Thou wilt revolt, and fly to him, I fear.—No, mighty liege; therefore mistrust me not . . . . iv 4 479

Mistrust. Mistrust of my success hath done this deed.—Mistrust of good success hath done this deed *J. Cæsar* v 3 65
He needs not our mistrust, since he delivers Our offices *Macbeth* iii 3 2
Mistrusted. All's true that is mistrusted *W. Tale* ii 1 48
This is an accident of hourly proof, Which I mistrusted not *Much Ado* ii 1 189
It had been vicious To have mistrusted her *Cymbeline* v 5 66
Mistrustful. I hold it cowardice To rest mistrustful where a noble heart Hath pawn'd an open hand in sign of love 3 *Hen. VI.* iv 2 8
Mistrusting them, Hoised sail and made away for Brittany *Richard III.* iv 4 528
Misty. From their misty jaws Breathe foul contagious darkness 2 *Hen. VI.* iv 1 6
Devouring receptacle, As hateful as Cocytus' misty mouth *T. Andron.* ii 3 236
Not a hollow cave or lurking-place, No vast obscurity or misty vale v 2 36
And jocund day Stands tiptoe on the misty mountain tops *Rom. and Jul.* iii 5 10
Misuse. We cannot misuse him enough *Mer. Wives* iv 2 105
Proof enough to misuse the prince, to vex Claudio, to undo Hero *M. Ado* ii 2 28
Such vile terms, As had she studied to misuse me so *T. of Shrew* ii 1 160
Upon whose dead corpse there was such misuse 1 *Hen. IV.* i 1 43
Wouldst thou turn our offers contrary? Misuse the tenour of thy kinsman's trust? v 5 5
He misuses thy favours so much 2 *Hen. IV.* ii 2 138
O, who shall believe But you misuse the reverence of your place? iv 2 23
How have I been behaved, that he might stick The small'st opinion on my least misuse? *Othello* iv 2 109
Misused. O, she misused me past the endurance of a block! *Much Ado* ii 1 246
You have simply misused our sex in your love-prate *As Y. Like It* iv 1 205
I have misused the king's press damnably 1 *Hen. IV.* iv 2 13
Swear not by time to come; for that thou hast Misused ere used, by time misused o'erpast *Richard III.* iv 4 396
Misusest. Then, by myself— Thyself thyself misusest iv 4 376
Mite. Virginity breeds mites, much like a cheese *All's Well* i 1 154
Losing a mite, a mountain gain *Pericles* ii Gower 8
Mithridates, king Of Comagene *Ant. and Cleo.* iii 6 73
Mitigate. Pray, uncle Gloucester, mitigate this strife 1 *Hen. VI.* iii 1 88
I have spoke thus much To mitigate the justice of thy plea *Mer. of Ven.* iv 1 203
To mitigate the scorn he gives his uncle, He prettily and aptly taunts himself: So cunning and so young is wonderful *Richard III.* iii 1 133
Mitigation. Behold, behold, where Madam Mitigation comes! *M. for M.* i 2 45
Without any mitigation or remorse of voice *T. Night* ii 3 98
How now for mitigation of this bill? *Hen. V.* i 1 70
Mix. Brothers, you mix your sadness with some fear 2 *Hen. IV.* v 2 46
Mixed. More lusty red Than that mix'd in his cheek *As Y. Like It* iii 5 122
By fair persuasions mix'd with sugar'd words 1 *Hen. VI.* iii 3 18
This goodly summer with your winter mix'd *T. Andron.* v 2 172
Hadst thou no poison mix'd, no sharp-ground knife? *Rom. and Jul.* iii 3 44
His life was gentle, and the elements So mix'd in him that Nature might stand up And say to all the world 'This was a man!' *J. Cæsar* v 5 74
O, matter and impertinency mix'd! Reason in madness! *Lear* iv 6 178
Mixture. But when the planets In evil mixture to disorder wander, What plagues and what portents! *Troi. and Cres.* i 3 95
Come, vial. What if this mixture do not work at all? *Rom. and Jul.* iv 3 21
Thou mixture rank, of midnight weeds collected *Hamlet* iii 2 268
With some mixtures powerful o'er the blood, Or with some dram conjured to this effect, He wrought upon her *Othello* i 3 104
M, O, A, I, doth sway my life *T. Night* ii 5 118
Moan. Now come I to my sister; mark the moan she makes *T. G. of Ver.* ii 3 33
Midnight, assist our moan; Help us to sigh and groan *Much Ado* v 3 16
O wall, full often hast thou heard my moans! *M. N. Dream* v 1 190
These yellow cowslip cheeks Are gone, are gone: Lovers, make moan v 1 341
Nor do I now make moan to be abridged From such a noble rate *M. of V.* i 1 126
I oft deliver'd from his forfeitures Many that have at times made moan to me iii 3 23
So longest way shall have the longest moans *Richard II.* v 1 90
Laughest thou, wretch? thy mirth shall turn to moan 1 *Hen. VI.* ii 3 44
Whiles, in his moan, the ship splits on the rock, Which industry and courage might have saved 3 *Hen. VI.* v 4 10
To hear the piteous moan that Rutland made *Richard III.* i 2 158
Alas, I am the mother of these moans! ii 2 80
Heart-sorrowing peers, That bear this mutual heavy load of moan ii 2 113
And makes her pew-fellow with others' moan iv 4 58
Let us pay betimes A moiety of that mass of moan to come *Tr. and Cr.* ii 2 107
With tears distill'd by moans *Rom. and Jul.* v 3 15
He is gone, he is gone, And we cast away moan *Hamlet* iv 5 198
The fresh streams ran by her, and murmur'd her moans *Othello* iv 3 45
Fear not slander, censure rash;—Thou hast finish'd joy and moan *Cymb.* iv 2 273
And made the night-bird mute, That still records with moan *Pericles* iv Gower 27
Moat. Or as a moat defensive to a house *Richard II.* ii 1 48
Moated. There, at the moated grange, resides . . . Mariana *M. for M.* iii 1 277
Mobled. 'But who, O, who had seen the mobled queen—' 'The mobled queen?'—That's good; 'mobled queen' is good *Hamlet* ii 2 525
Mock. How you the purpose cherish Whiles thus you mock it! *Tempest* ii 1 225
Lo, how he mocks me! wilt thou let him, my lord? iii 2 34
The sea mocks Our frustrate search on land iii 3 9
Let's go in, gentlemen; but, trust me, we'll mock him *Mer. Wives* iii 3 243
Dis-horn the spirit, And mock him home to Windsor iv 4 64
Like the forfeits in a barber's shop, As much in mock as mark *M. for M.* v 1 324
I hope you will not mock me with a husband.—It is your husband mock'd you with a husband v 1 422
Nay, mock not, mock not *Much Ado* i 1 287
She mocks all her wooers out of suit ii 1 364
If I should speak, She would mock me into air iii 1 75
A better death than die with mocks, Which is as bad as die with tickling iii 1 79
We are wise girls to mock our lovers so.—They are worse fools *L. L. Lost* v 2 58
They do it but in mocking merriment; And mock for mock is only my intent v 2 140
Look, how you butt yourself in these sharp mocks! v 2 251
Let's mock them still, as well known as disguised v 2 301
We are descried; they'll mock us now downright v 2 389
Though my mocks come home by me, I will now be merry v 2 637
The world's large tongue Proclaims you for a man replete with mocks v 2 853
The cuckoo then, on every tree, Mocks married men v 2 909
Can you not hate me, as I know you do, But you must join in souls to mock me too? *M. N. Dream* iii 2 150
Both are rivals, and love Hermia; And now both rivals, to mock Helena iii 2 156
I pray you, though you mock me, gentlemen, Let her not hurt me iii 2 299
Yea, mock the lion when he roars for prey *Mer. of Venice* ii 1 30
Let us sit and mock the good housewife Fortune from her wheel *As Y. L. It* i 2 34
An you mean to mock me after, you should not have mocked me before i 2 220
Afflict me with thy mocks, pity me not iii 5 33
When you have our roses, You barely leave our thorns to prick ourselves And mock us with our bareness *All's Well* iv 2 20
Mock. Such a headstrong potent fault it is, That it but mocks reproof *T. Night* iii 4 225
What colour are your eyebrows?—Blue, my lord.—Nay, that's a mock *W. Tale* ii 1 14
Let no man mock me, For I will kiss her v 3 79
And mock the deep-mouth'd thunder *K. John* v 2 173
Gnarling sorrow hath less power to bite The man that mocks at it *Rich. II.* i 3 293
Misery makes sport to mock itself ii 1 85
I mock my name, great king, to flatter thee ii 1 87
Mock not my senseless conjuration, lords iii 2 23
Cover your heads and mock not flesh and blood With solemn reverence iii 2 171
And the spirits of the wise sit in the clouds and mock us 2 *Hen. IV.* ii 2 156
How chances mock, and changes fill the cup of alteration With divers liquors! iii 1 51
For now a time is come to mock at form iv 5 119
To spurn at your most royal image And mock your workings in a second body v 2 90
Sadly I survive, To mock the expectation of the world v 2 126
This mock of his Hath turn'd his balls to gun-stones *Hen. V.* i 2 281
Many a thousand widows Shall this his mock mock out of their dear husbands; Mock mothers from their sons, mock castles down i 2 285
Sweeten the bitter mock you sent his majesty ii 4 122
Womby vaultages of France Shall chide your trespass and return your mock ii 4 125
Our madams mock at us, and plainly say Our mettle is bred out iii 5 28
Good God! why should they mock poor fellows thus? iv 3 92
He was full of jests, and gipes, and knaveries, and mocks iv 7 52
Fall to: if you can mock a leek, you can eat a leek v 1 39
When you take occasions to see leeks hereafter, I pray you, mock at 'em v 1 58
Will you mock at an ancient tradition, begun upon an honourable respect? v 1 74
Your majesty shall mock at me; I cannot speak your England v 2 102
But, good Kate, mock me mercifully v 2 214
Thou shouldst be mad; And I, to make thee mad, do mock thee thus 3 *Hen. VI.* i 4 90
They mock thee, Clifford: swear as thou wast wont ii 6 76
An envious mountain on my back, Where sits deformity to mock my body iii 2 158
Uncle, my brother mocks both you and me *Richard III.* iii 1 129
Come, come, you mock me; this is not the way To win your daughter iv 4 284
Even for revenge mock my destruction! v 1 9
Let it alone; my state now will but mock me *Hen. VIII.* ii 1 101
You smile and mock me, as if I meant naughtily *Troi. and Cres.* iv 2 38
How my achievements mock me! iv 2 71
By Mars his gauntlet, thanks! Mock not, that I affect the untraded oath iv 5 178
To such as boasting show their scars A mock is due iv 5 291
Why, then, farewell; Thou never shalt mock Diomed again v 2 99
The gods begin to mock me *Coriolanus* i 9 79
'Tis his kind of speech: he did not mock us ii 3 169
Now again Of him that did not ask, but mock, bestow Your sued-for tongues ii 3 215
I mock at death With as big heart as thou iii 2 127
I'll trust, by leisure, him that mocks me once *T. Andron.* i 1 301
The babbling echo mocks the hounds, Replying shrilly ii 3 17
For this proud mock I'll be thy slaughter-man iv 4 58
It were a mock Apt to be render'd *J. Cæsar* ii 2 96
Away, and mock the time with fairest show *Macbeth* i 7 81
And the surfeited grooms Do mock their charge with snores ii 2 6
I came to see your father's funeral.—I pray thee, do not mock me *Hamlet* i 2 177
Follow that lord; and look you mock him not ii 2 571
Not one now, to mock your own grinning? quite chap-fallen? v 1 211
You mock me, sir.—No, by this hand v 2 268
One side will mock another; the other too *Lear* iii 7 71
Pray, do not mock me: I am a very foolish fond old man iv 7 59
Would ever have, to incur a general mock, Run from her guardage *Othello* i 2 69
It is the green-eyed monster which doth mock The meat it feeds on iii 3 166
If she be false, O, then heaven mocks itself! I'll not believe't iii 3 278
Have you not hurt your head?—Dost thou mock me?—I mock you! no iv 1 61
O mistress, villany hath made mocks with love! v 2 151
The good gods will mock me presently, When I shall pray *Ant. and Cleo.* iii 4 15
Fill our bowls once more; Let's mock the midnight bell iii 13 185
Mock not, Enobarbus.—I tell you true iv 6 25
Blue promontory With trees upon't, that nod unto the world, And mock our eyes with air iv 14 7
Being so frustrate, tell him he mocks The pauses that he makes v 1 2
I hear Antony call; I see him rouse himself To praise my noble act; I hear him mock The luck of Cæsar v 2 288
It is a recreation to be by And hear him mock the Frenchman *Cymbeline* i 6 76
What an infinite mock is this, that a man should have the best use of eyes to see the way of blindness! v 4 195
The rarest dream that e'er dull sleep Did mock sad fools withal *Pericles* v 1 164
Mockable. As ridiculous in the country as the behaviour of the country is most mockable at the court *As Y. Like It* iii 2 49
Mocked. I shall be rather praised for this than mocked *Mer. Wives* iii 2 49
If he be not amazed, he will be mocked; if he be amazed, he will every way be mocked v 3 20
In time the rod Becomes more mock'd than fear'd *Meas. for Meas.* i 3 27
It is your husband mock'd you with a husband v 1 423
Their several counsels they unbosom shall To loves mistook, and so be mock'd withal *L. L. Lost* v 2 142
And they, well mock'd, depart away with shame v 2 156
Laughed at my losses, mocked at my gains, scorned my nation *M. of Ven.* iii 1 58
An you mean to mock me after, you should not have mock'd me before: but come your ways *As Y. Like It* i 2 221
How the poor souls roared, and the sea mocked them; and how the poor gentleman roared and the bear mocked him *W. Tale* iii 3 101
Prepare To see the life as lively mock'd as ever Still sleep mock'd death v 3 19
The fixure of her eye has motion in't, As we are mock'd with art v 3 68
And like the owl by day, If he arise, be mock'd and wonder'd at 3 *Hen. VI.* v 4 57
Reflecting gems, Which woo'd the slimy bottom of the deep, And mock'd the dead bones that lay scatter'd by *Richard III.* i 4 33
A mother only mock'd with two sweet babes iv 4 87
If we shall stand still, In fear our motion will be mock'd or carp'd at, We should take root here where we sit *Hen. VIII.* i 2 86
He mock'd us when he begg'd our voices *Coriolanus* ii 3 167
Call't not a plot: The people cry you mock'd them iii 1 42
And who resist Are mock'd for valiant ignorance iv 6 104
Thy griefs their sports, thy resolution mock'd *T. Andron.* iii 1 239
Well mock'd.—No, my good lord; he speaks the common tongue *T. of A.* i 1 173
Who would be so mock'd with glory? or to live But in a dream of friendship? iv 2 33

Mocked. When thou wast in thy gilt and thy perfume, they mocked thee *T. of Athens* iv 3 303
And smiles in such a sort As if he mock'd himself . . *J. Cæsar* i 2 206
I cannot find those runagates; that villain Hath mock'd me . *Cymbeline* iv 2 63
With marriage wherefore was he mock'd, To be exiled? . . v 4 58
O, I am mock'd, And thou by some incensed god sent hither To make the world to laugh at me . . . . *Pericles* v 1 143
Mocker. Well said, old mocker . . . . . *L. L. Lost* v 2 552
Never did mockers waste more idle breath . *M. N. Dream* iii 2 168
In truth, I know it is a sin to be a mocker . *Mer. of Venice* i 2 62
If thou diest before I come, thou art a mocker of my labour *As Y. Like It* ii 6 13
Our very priests must become mockers . . *Coriolanus* ii 1 93
Both with an R.—Ah, mocker! that's the dog's name *Rom. and Jul.* ii 4 223
Mockery. A lousy knave, to have his gibes and his mockeries! *M. Wives* iii 3 260
On old Hiems' thin and icy crown An odorous chaplet of sweet summer buds Is, as in mockery, set . . *M. N. Dream* ii 1 111
Wherefore was I to this keen mockery born? . . . . iii 2 123
What mockery will it be, To want the bridegroom! *T. of Shrew* iii 2 4
Observe him, for the love of mockery . . *T. Night* ii 5 22
The truth thou art unsure To swear, swears only not to be forsworn; Else what a mockery should it be to swear! . . *K. John* iii 1 285
O that I were a mockery king of snow! . *Richard II.* iv 1 260
Yet sit and see, Minding true things by what their mockeries be *Hen. V.* iv Prol. 53
I'll be chief to bring him down again: Not that I pity Henry's misery, But seek revenge on Edward's mockery . 3 *Hen. VI.* iii 3 265
I wonder he is so fond To trust the mockery of unquiet slumbers *Richard III.* iii 2 27
Quite out of fashion, like a rusty mail In monumental mockery *T. and C.* iii 3 153
Was not this mockery? . . . . . *Coriolanus* ii 3 181
Hence, horrible shadow! Unreal mockery, hence! . *Macbeth* iii 4 107
And our vain blows malicious mockery . . . *Hamlet* i 1 146
What cannot be preserved when fortune takes Patience her injury a mockery makes . . . . . *Othello* i 3 207
Will you rhyme upon't, And vent it for a mockery? . . *Cymbeline* v 3 56
Mockest. Thou mock'st me. Thou shalt buy this dear . *M. N. Dream* iii 2 426
Mocking. You do blaspheme the good in mocking me . *Meas. for Meas.* i 4 38
Some merry mocking lord, belike; is't so?—They say so . *L. L. Lost* ii 1 52
We are wise girls to mock our lovers so.—They are worse fools to purchase mocking so . . . . v 2 59
They do it but in mocking merriment . . . . v 2 139
So shall we stay, mocking intended game, And they, well mock'd, depart away . . . . v 2 156
The tongues of mocking wenches are as keen As is the razor's edge invisible . . . . v 2 256
Nay, but the devil take mocking . . *As Y. Like It* iii 2 226
Come, come, you're mocking: we will have no telling *T. of Shrew* iv 2 132
Mocking the air with colours idly spread, And find no check . *K. John* v 1 72
Reproach and everlasting shame Sits mocking in our plumes . *Hen. V.* iv 5 5
I long till Edward fall by war's mischance, For mocking marriage with a dame of France . . . . . 3 *Hen. VI.* iii 3 255
King Lewis Becomes your enemy, for mocking him About the marriage iv 1 30
In his tent Lies mocking our designs . . *Troi. and Cres.* i 3 146
A pestilence on him! now will he be mocking: I shall have such a life! iv 2 21
Go hang yourself, you naughty mocking uncle! . . . iv 2 26
It is a pretty mocking of the life . . . *T. of Athens* i 1 35
The smile mocking the sigh, that it would fly From so divine a temple, to commix With winds that sailors rail at . . *Cymbeline* iv 2 54
Mock-water. A word, Mounseur Mockwater.—Mock-vater! vat is dat? —Mock-water, in our English tongue, is valour, bully.—By gar, den, I have as mush mock-vater as de Englishman *Mer. Wives* ii 3 60
Mode. And now my death Changes the mode . . 2 *Hen. IV.* iv 5 200
Model. Will it serve for any model to build mischief on? . *Much Ado* i 3 48
Who was the model of thy father's life . . *Richard II.* i 2 28
Nothing can we call our own but death And that small model of the barren earth Which serves as paste and cover to our bones . . iii 2 153
Showing, as in a model, our firm estate . . . . iii 4 42
Ah, thou, the model where old Troy did stand, Thou map of honour . v 1 11
We first survey the plot, then draw the model . 2 *Hen. IV.* i 3 42
What do we then but draw anew the model In fewer offices? . . i 3 46
Survey The plot of situation and the model, Consent upon a sure foundation . . . . i 3 51
Like one that draws the model of a house Beyond his power to build it i 3 58
O England! model to thy inward greatness, Like little body with a mighty heart, What mightst thou do! . . *Hen. V.* ii Prol. 16
I'll draw the form and model of our battle . *Richard III.* v 3 24
The model of our chaste loves, his young daughter . *Hen. VIII.* iv 2 132
I had my father's signet in my purse, Which was the model of that Danish seal . . . . *Hamlet* v 2 50
Princes are A model, which heaven makes like to itself . *Pericles* ii 2 11
Modena. When thou once Wast beaten from Modena, where thou slew'st Hirtius and Pansa . . . . . . *Ant. and Cleo.* i 4 57
Moderate. O love, Be moderate; allay thy ecstasy . *Mer. of Venice* iii 2 112
Moderate lamentation is the right of the dead . *All's Well* i 1 64
On a moderate pace I have since arrived but hither . *T. Night* ii 2 3
Be moderate, be moderate.—Why tell you me of moderation? *T. and C.* iv 4 1
The grief is fine, full, perfect, that I taste, . . . as strong As that which causeth it: how can I moderate it? . . . . . iv 4 5
There is not so much left, to furnish out A moderate table . *T. of Athens* iii 4 117
Stay'd it long?—While one with moderate haste might tell a hundred *Ham.* i 2 238
Moderately. To hear meekly, sir, and to laugh moderately . *L. L. Lost* i 1 200
Therefore love moderately; long love doth so . . *Rom. and Jul.* ii 6 14
Moderation. Why tell you me of moderation? The grief is fine, full, perfect, that I taste . . . . . *Troi. and Cres.* iv 4 2
Modern. Full of wise saws and modern instances . *As Y. Like It* ii 7 156
And betray themselves to every modern censure worse than drunkards iv 1 7
To make modern and familiar, things supernatural and causeless *All's W.* ii 3 2
Her infinite cunning, with her modern grace, Subdued me to her rate: she got the ring . . . . v 3 216
Which scorns a modern invocation . . . *K. John* iii 4 42
Which modern lamentation might have moved . . *Rom. and Jul.* iii 2 120
Where violent sorrow seems A modern ecstasy . . *Macbeth* iv 3 170
These thin habits and poor likelihoods Of modern seeming . *Othello* i 3 109
Things of such dignity As we greet modern friends withal *Ant. and Cleo.* v 2 167
Modest. A civil modest wife . . . . . *Mer. Wives* ii 2 101
Mistress Ford, the honest woman, the modest wife . . . iv 2 136
Joy could not show itself modest enough without a badge of bitterness *Much Ado* i 1 22
Is she not a modest young lady? . . . . . . i 1 166
I will do any modest office, my lord, to help my cousin to a good husband . . . . ii 1 390
Modest. Comes not that blood as modest evidence To witness simple virtue? . . . . *Much Ado* iv 1 38
Their savage eyes turn'd to a modest gaze . *Mer. of Venice* v 1 78
His will hath in it a more modest working . *As Y. Like It* i 2 215
He cut it to please himself: this is called the Quip Modest . . v 4 79
I perish, Tranio, If I achieve not this young modest girl . *T. of Shrew* i 1 161
She's not froward, but modest as the dove; She is not hot . . ii 1 295
Humbly entreating from your royal thoughts A modest one . *All's Well* ii 1 131
You must confine yourself within the modest limits of order . *T. Night* i 3 9
Give me modest assurance if you be the lady of the house . . i 5 192
Fie, thou dishonest Satan! I call thee by the most modest terms . iv 2 36
Banish'd till their conversations Appear more wise and modest 2 *Hen. IV.* v 5 107
Garnish'd and deck'd in modest complement . . *Hen. V.* ii 2 134
How modest in exception, and withal How terrible in constant resolution . . . . ii 4 34
In peace there's nothing so becomes a man As modest stillness and humility . . . . iii 1 4
Bids them good morrow with a modest smile . . . . iv Prol. 33
Or modest Dian circled with her nymphs . . 3 *Hen. VI.* iv 8 21
Her grace rose, and with modest paces Came to the altar . *Hen. VIII.* iv 1 82
She is young, and of a noble modest nature, I hope she will deserve well iv 2 135
I could say more, But reverence to your calling makes me modest . v 3 69
Modest as morning when she coldly eyes The youthful Phœbus *T. and C.* i 3 229
Modest doubt is call'd The beacon of the wise . . . . ii 2 15
He will not spare to gird the gods.—Be-mock the modest moon *Coriol.* i 1 261
Which, to the spire and top of praises vouch'd, Would seem but modest i 9 25
Too modest are you; More cruel to your good report than grateful To us i 9 53
Do not cry havoc, where you should but hunt With modest warrant . iii 1 276
Modest wisdom plucks me From over-credulous haste . *Macbeth* iv 3 119
Resolve me, with all modest haste . . . . *Lear* ii 4 25
All my reports go with the modest truth; Nor more nor clipp'd, but so iv 7 5
An inviting eye; and yet methinks right modest . . *Othello* ii 3 25
Octavia, with her modest eyes And still conclusion . *Ant. and Cleo.* iv 15 27
Further to boast were neither true nor modest . . *Cymbeline* v 5 18
O, sir, I can be modest . . . . *Pericles* iv 6 41
Falseness cannot come from thee; for thou look'st Modest as Justice . v 1 122
Modestly. I could wish he would modestly examine himself . *Much Ado* ii 3 216
I never in my life Did hear a challenge urged more modestly . 1 *Hen. IV.* v 2 53
Words sweetly placed and modestly directed . . 1 *Hen. VI.* v 3 179
There they stand yet, and modestly I think, The fall of every Phrygian stone will cost A drop of Grecian blood . . *Troi. and Cres.* iv 5 222
I, your glass, Will modestly discover to yourself That of yourself which you yet know not of . . . . *J. Cæsar* i 2 69
Modesty. By my modesty, The jewel in my dower . . *Tempest* iii 1 53
Now, by my modesty, a goodly broker! . . . *T. G. of Ver.* i 2 41
Since maids, in modesty, say 'no' to that Which they would have the profferer construe 'ay' . . . . i 2 55
She, in modesty, Or else for want of idle time, could not again reply . ii 1 171
It is the lesser blot, modesty finds, Women to change their shapes than men their minds . . . . v 4 108
And yet he would not swear; praised women's modesty . *Mer. Wives* ii 1 58
Pluck the borrowed veil of modesty from the so seeming Mistress Page iii 2 42
Can it be That modesty may more betray our sense Than woman's lightness? . . . O, fie, fie, fie . . . . . *Meas. for Meas.* ii 2 169
I have laboured for the poor gentleman to the extremest shore of my modesty . . . . iii 2 266
Her sober virtue, years and modesty, Plead on her part . *Com. of Errors* iii 1 90
Ay, but not rough enough.—As roughly as my modesty would let me . v 1 60
Her blush is guiltiness, not modesty . . . . . *Much Ado* iv 1 43
Than that which maiden modesty doth warrant . . . . iv 1 181
I know not by what power I am made bold, Nor how it may concern my modesty, In such a presence here to plead my thoughts *M. N. D.* i 1 60
You do impeach your modesty too much . . . . . . ii 1 214
Lie further off; in human modesty . . . . ii 2 57
Have you no modesty, no maiden shame, No touch of bashfulness? . iii 2 285
In the modesty of fearful duty I read as much as from the rattling tongue . . . . v 1 101
Allay with some cold drops of modesty Thy skipping spirit *Mer. of Ven.* ii 2 195
Wanted the modesty To urge the thing held as a ceremony . . v 1 205
Atalanta's better part, Sad Lucretia's modesty . . *As Y. Like It* iii 2 156
Pastime passing excellent, If it be husbanded with modesty *T. of Shrew* Ind. 1 68
But I am doubtful of your modesties . . . . . Ind. 1 94
One as famous for a scolding tongue As is the other for beauteous modesty . . . . i 2 255
Her beauty and her wit, Her affability and bashful modesty . . ii 1 49
Then we wound our modesty and make foul the clearness of our deservings, when of ourselves we publish them . . *All's Well* i 3 6
Though there were no further danger known but the modesty which is so lost . . . . iii 5 30
I perceive in you so excellent a touch of modesty . . . *T. Night* ii 1 13
Tell me, in the modesty of honour . . . . . . v 1 343
The forms of it, and the sobriety of it, and the modesty of it . *Hen. V.* iv 1 75
A maid yet rosed over with the virgin crimson of modesty . . v 2 324
With modesty admiring thy renown . . . . 1 *Hen. VI.* ii 2 39
Her looks do argue her replete with modesty . . 3 *Hen. VI.* iii 2 84
Deliver this with modesty to the queen . . . *Hen. VIII.* ii 2 137
Whom I most hated living, thou hast made me, With thy religious truth and modesty, Now in his ashes honour . . . . . iv 2 74
Win straying souls with modesty again, Cast none away . . v 3 64
Hood my unmann'd blood . . . With thy black mantle; till strange love, grown bold, Think true love acted simple modesty *Rom. and Jul.* iii 2 16
Who, even in pure and vestal modesty, Still blush, as thinking their own kisses sin . . . . iii 3 38
Gave him what becomed love I might, Not stepping o'er the bounds of modesty . . . . iv 2 27
I have told more of you to myself than you can with modesty speak in your own behalf . . . . *T. of Athens* i 2 97
Then, in a friend, it is cold modesty . . . . . *J. Cæsar* iii 1 213
There is a kind of confession in your looks which your modesties have not craft enough to colour . . . . *Hamlet* ii 2 289
Set down with as much modesty as cunning . . . . ii 2 461
With this special observance, that you o'erstep not the modesty of nature . . . . iii 2 21
Such an act That blurs the grace and blush of modesty . . . iii 4 41
But to follow him thither with modesty enough, and likelihood to lead it . . . . v 1 230
I should make very forges of my cheeks, That would to cinders burn up modesty, Did I but speak thy deeds . . . . *Othello* iv 2 75
If beauty, wisdom, modesty, can settle The heart of Antony, Octavia is A blessed lottery to him . . . . . *Ant. and Cleo.* ii 2 246

Modesty. And I will boot thee with what gift beside Thy modesty can beg . . . . *Ant. and Cleo.* ii 5 72
Though peril to my modesty, not death on't, I would adventure *Cymb.* iii 4 155
Modicum. What modicums of wit he utters! . . . *Troi. and Cres.* ii 1 74
Modo. The prince of darkness is a gentleman: Modo he's called . *Lear* iii 4 149
Mahu, of stealing; Modo, of murder. . . . . . iv 1 63
Module. Bring forth this counterfeit module . . . . *All's Well* iv 3 114
All this thou seest is but a clod And module of confounded royalty *K. John* v 7 58
Moe. Milan and Naples have Moe widows in them of this business' making Than we bring men to comfort them . . . *Tempest* ii 1 133
Shrieking, howling, jingling chains, And moe diversity of sounds . . v 1 234
Moe reasons for this action At our more leisure shall I render *M. for M.* i 3 48
Yet in this life Lie hid moe thousand deaths: yet death we fear . . iii 1 40
Sing no more ditties, sing no moe, Of dumps so dull and heavy *Much Ado* ii 3 72
Well, keep me company but two years moe *Mer. of Venice* i 1 108
Mar no moe of my verses with reading them ill-favouredly *As Y. Like It* iii 2 278
I multiply With one 'We thank you' many thousands moe *W. Tale* i 2 8
Let's first see moe ballads; we'll buy the other things anon . iv 4 278
I am past moe children, but thy sons and daughters will be all gentle-men born . . . . . v 2 137
Thus hath he sworn And I with him, and many moe with me *K. John* v 4 17
And many moe Of noble blood in this declining land *Richard II.* ii 1 239
And many moe corrivals and dear men Of estimation . 1 *Hen. IV.* iv 4 31
And of their feather many moe proud birds . . 3 *Hen. VI.* ii 1 170
I have no moe sons of the royal blood For thee to murder *Richard III.* iv 4 199
With many moe confederates, are in arms . . . . iv 4 504
And many moe of noble fame and worth . . . . iv 5 13
By my life, That promises moe thousands . . *Hen. VIII.* ii 3 97
I cannot promise But that you shall sustain moe new disgraces . iii 2 5
Further, sir, Stands in the gap and trade of moe preferments . v 1 36
Here come moe voices . . . . . . *Coriolanus* ii 3 132
Like a philosopher, with two stones moe than's artificial one *T. of A.* ii 2 117
Moe things like men! Eat, Timon, and abhor them . . iv 3 398
His antidotes are poison, and he slays Moe than you rob . iv 3 436
Is he alone!—No, sir, there are moe with him. . . *J. Cæsar* ii 1 72
Send out moe horses; skirr the country round . *Macbeth* v 3 35
If I court moe women, you'll couch with moe men . . *Othello* iv 3 57
As I said, there is no moe such Cæsars . . . *Cymbeline* iii 1 36
Moiety. Forgive a moiety of the principal . . *Mer. of Venice* iv 1 26
Lady, have a better cheer; If thou engrossest all the griefs are thine, Thou robb'st me of a moiety . . . . *All's Well* iii 2 69
A moiety of my rest Might come to me again . . . *W. Tale* ii 3 8
A fellow of the royal bed, which owe A moiety of the throne . . iii 2 40
Well, give me the moiety. Are you a party in this business? . iv 4 842
Methinks my moiety, north from Burton here, In quantity equals not one of yours . . . . . 1 *Hen. IV.* iii 1 96
And for my English moiety take the word of a king and a bachelor *Hen. V.* v 2 229
On me, whose all not equals Edward's moiety? . . *Richard III.* i 2 250
O, what cause have I, Thine being but a moiety of my grief, To overgo thy plaints! . . . . . . ii 2 60
You have half our power: The other moiety, ere you ask, is given *Hen. VIII.* i 2 12
Let us pay betimes A moiety of that mass of moan to come *Troi. and Cres.* ii 2 107
Against the which, a moiety competent Was gaged by our king *Hamlet* i 1 90
That curiosity in neither can make choice of either's moiety . *Lear* i 1 7
In the name lay A moiety of the world . . *Ant. and Cleo.* v 1 19
I dare thereupon pawn the moiety of my estate to your ring *Cymbeline* i 4 118
Moist Hesperus hath quench'd his sleepy lamp . . *All's Well* ii 1 167
Write till your ink be dry, and with your tears Moist it again *T. G. of V.* iii 2 76
Have you not a moist eye? a dry hand? a yellow cheek? . 2 *Hen. IV.* i 2 203
My tears, The moist impediments unto my speech? . . iv 5 140
When at their mothers' moist eyes babes shall suck . . 1 *Hen. VI.* i 1 49
Bounding between the two moist elements, Like Perseus' horse *T. and C.* i 3 41
The moist star Upon whose influence Neptune's empire stands *Hamlet* i 1 118
This hand is moist, my lady.—It yet hath felt no age . *Othello* iii 4 36
Hot, hot, and moist: this hand of yours requires A sequester from liberty . . . . iii 4 39
Now no more The juice of Egypt's grape shall moist this lip *Ant. and Cleo.* v 2 285
Moistened. There she shook The holy water from her heavenly eyes, And clamour moisten'd . . . . . *Lear* iv 3 33
Moisture. I cannot weep; for all my body's moisture Scarce serves to quench my furnace-burning heart . . 3 *Hen. VI.* ii 1 79
Moldwarp. He angers me With telling me of the moldwarp 1 *Hen. IV.* iii 1 149
Mole. Tread softly, that the blind mole may not Hear a foot fall *Tempest* iv 1 194
The mole in my neck, the great wart on my left arm *Com. of Errors* iii 2 147
Never mole, hare lip, nor scar, Nor mark prodigious, such as are Despised in nativity, Shall upon their children be . *M. N. Dream* v 1 418
My father had a mole upon his brow. . . . *T. Night* v 1 249
I will bring these two moles, these blind ones, aboard him . *W. Tale* iv 4 868
Patch'd with foul moles and eye-offending marks . *K. John* iii 1 47
That for some vicious mole of nature in them, As, in their birth *Hamlet* i 4 24
Well said, old mole! canst work i' the earth so fast? . . i 5 162
On her left breast A mole cinque-spotted, like the crimson drops I' the bottom of a cowslip . . . . . *Cymbeline* ii 2 38
Under her breast—Worthy the pressing—lies a mole, right proud Of that most delicate lodging . . . . . . ii 4 135
Upon his neck a mole, a sanguine star; It was a mark of wonder . v 5 364
The blind mole casts Copp'd hills towards heaven . . *Pericles* i 1 100
Molehill. Make him stand upon this molehill here, That raught at mountains with outstretched arms . . . 3 *Hen. VI.* i 4 67
Here on this molehill will I sit me down . . . . ii 5 14
As if Olympus to a molehill should In supplication nod . *Coriolanus* v 3 30
Molest. Candied be they And melt ere they molest! . . *Tempest* ii 1 280
Who doth molest my contemplation? . . . *T. Andron.* v 2 9
Molestation. Do but stand upon the foaming shore . . .: I never did like molestation view On the enchafed flood . . *Othello* ii 1 16
Mollification. Some mollification for your giant . . *T. Night* i 5 218
Mollis. Which we call 'mollis aer;' and 'mollis aer' We term it 'mulier' *Cymbeline* v 5 447
Molten. I am as hot as molten lead, and as heavy too . 1 *Hen. IV.* v 3 34
Let molten coin be thy damnation, Thou disease of a friend! *T. of Athens* iii 1 55
Mine own tears Do scald like molten lead . . . . *Lear* iv 7 48
Mome, malt-horse, capon, coxcomb, idiot, patch! . . *Com. of Errors* iii 1 32
Moment. One fading moment's mirth [bought] With twenty watchful, weary, tedious nights . . . . . *T. G. of Ver.* i 1 30
If I would but go to hell for an eternal moment or so *Mer. Wives* ii 1 50
When in that moment, so it came to pass, Titania waked *M. N. Dream* iii 2 33
In a moment threw him and broke three of his ribs *As Y. Like It* i 2 135
Moment. Lean but upon a rush, The cicatrice and capable impressure Thy palm some moment keeps . . *As Y. Like It* iii 5 24
His incensement at this moment is so implacable . *T. Night* iii 4 260
Then, in a moment, Fortune shall cull forth Out of one side her happy minion, To whom in favour she shall give the day . *K. John* ii 1 391
At that very moment Consideration, like an angel, came . *Hen. V.* i 1 27
In a moment look to see The blind and bloody soldier . . iii 3 33
What towns of any moment but we have? . . 1 *Hen. VI.* i 2 5
Subverts your towns And in a moment makes them desolate . . ii 3 66
Who in a moment even with the earth Shall lay your stately . . . towers iv 2 12
An oath is of no moment, being not took Before a true and lawful magistrate, That hath authority over him that swears 3 *Hen. VI.* i 2 22
In deep designs and matters of great moment . *Richard III.* iii 7 67
Then in a moment, see How soon this mightiness meets misery *Hen. VIII.* Prol. 29
A choice hour To hear from him a matter of some moment . . i 2 163
The question did at first so stagger me, Bearing a state of mighty moment in't . . . . ii 4 213
Because we have business of more moment, We will be short with you v 3 51
In this extant moment . . . . *Troi. and Cres.* iv 5 168
On the moment Follows his strides, his lobbies fill . . *T. of Athens* i 1 79
Who can be wise, amazed, temperate and furious, Loyal and neutral, in a moment? No man . . . . . *Macbeth* ii 3 115
Acquaint you with the perfect spy o' the time, The moment on't . iii 1 131
From this moment The very firstlings of my heart shall be The first-lings of my hand . . . . . . iv 1 146
I would not . . . Have you so slander any moment leisure . *Hamlet* i 3 133
Enterprises of great pitch and moment . . . . iii 1 86
If, on the tenth day following, Thy banish'd trunk be found in our dominions, The moment is thy death . . . . *Lear* i 1 181
I ran it through, even from my boyish days, To the very moment that he bade me tell it . . . . . *Othello* i 3 133
And can he be angry? Something of moment then . . iii 4 138
I have seen her die twenty times upon far poorer moment *Ant. and Cleo.* i 2 147
A small request, And yet of moment too . . . *Cymbeline* i 6 182
Momentany as a sound, Swift as a shadow . . *M. N. Dream* i 1 143
Momentary. Jove's lightnings, the precursors O' the dreadful thunder-claps, more momentary And sight-outrunning were not . *Tempest* i 2 202
Why would he for the momentary trick Be perdurably fined? *M. for M.* iii 1 114
O momentary grace of mortal men! . . *Richard III.* iii 4 98
The fit is momentary; upon a thought He will again be well *Macbeth* iii 4 55
Momentary-swift. More momentary-swift than thought *Troi. and Cres.* iv 2 14
Monachum. Cucullus non facit monachum *M. for M.* v 1 263; *T. N.* i 5 62
Monarch. That is all one, my fair, sweet, honey monarch . *L. L. Lost* v 2 531
And what is music then? Then music is Even as the flourish when true subjects bow To a new-crowned monarch . *Mer. of Venice* iii 2 50
It [mercy] becomes The throned monarch better than his crown . iv 1 189
Save you, fair queen!—And you, monarch! . . . *All's Well* i 1 118
Were I crown'd the most imperial monarch, Thereof most worthy *W. T.* iv 4 383
Know the gallant monarch is in arms . . . . *K. John* v 2 148
That man that sits within a monarch's heart . . 2 *Hen. IV.* iv 2 11
A kingdom for a stage, princes to act And monarchs to behold *Hen. V.* Prol. 4
Your brother kings and monarchs of the earth Do all expect that you should rouse yourself . . . . i 2 122
Never was monarch better fear'd and loved Than is your majesty . . ii 2 25
His neigh is like the bidding of a monarch . . . . iii 7 30
That's a perilous shot out of an elder-gun, that a poor and a private dis-pleasure can do against a monarch! . . . . . iv 1 211
Your lips . . . should sooner persuade Harry of England than a general petition of monarchs . . . . v 2 306
You speedy helpers, that are substitutes Under the lordly monarch of the north, Appear and aid me in this enterprise . . 1 *Hen. VI.* v 3 6
Hath that poor monarch taught thee to insult? . . 3 *Hen. VI.* i 4 124
Such it seems As may beseem a monarch like himself . . iii 3 122
The greatest monarch now alive may glory In such an honour *Hen. VIII.* v 3 164
Where honour may be crown'd Sole monarch of the universal earth *Rom. and Jul.* iii 2 94
With a monarch's voice Cry 'Havoc,' and let slip the dogs of war *J. C.* iii 1 272
Our monarchs and outstretched heroes the beggars' shadows . *Hamlet* ii 2 270
Who would not make her husband a cuckold to make him a monarch? *Othello* iv 3 77
A morsel for a monarch . . . . *Ant. and Cleo.* i 5 31
Come, thou monarch of the vine, Plumpy Bacchus with pink eyne! . ii 7 120
The gates of monarchs Are arch'd so high that giants may jet through And keep their impious turbans on . . . *Cymbeline* iii 3 4
Who has a book of all that monarchs do, He's more secure to keep it shut than shown . . . . . . *Pericles* i 1 94
Monarchize. Allowing him a breath, a little scene, To monarchize, be fear'd, and kill with looks . . . . *Richard II.* iii 2 165
Monarcho. A phantasime, a Monarcho, and one that makes sport *L. L. Lost* iv 1 101
Monarchy. Let higher Italy,—Those bated that inherit but the fall Of the last monarchy . . . . . *All's Well* ii 1 14
Suppose within the girdle of these walls Are now confined two mighty monarchies . . . . . . *Hen. V.* Prol. 20
Let them know Of what a monarchy you are the head . . ii 4 73
This small inheritance my father left me Contenteth me, and worth a monarchy. I seek not to wax great by others' waning 2 *Hen. VI.* iv 10 21
Are mighty gossips in this monarchy . . *Richard III.* i 1 83
What scourge for perjury Can this dark monarchy afford false Clarence? i 4 51
Monastery. Perchance entering into some monastery . *Meas. for Meas.* iv 2 217
There is a monastery two miles off; And there will we abide *Mer. of Ven.* iii 4 31
I have solemnly interr'd At Chertsey monastery this noble king *Richard III.* i 2 215
From our troops I stray'd To gaze upon a ruinous monastery *T. Andron.* v 1 21
Monastic. And to live in a nook merely monastic . . *As Y. Like It* iii 2 441
Monday. Not till Monday, my dear son . . . . *Much Ado* ii 1 374
He swore a thing to me on Monday night, which he forswore on Tuesday morning . . . . v 1 169
A purse of gold most resolutely snatched on Monday night and most dissolutely spent on Tuesday morning . . . 1 *Hen. IV.* i 2 39
Monday! ha! ha! Well, Wednesday is too soon, O' Thursday let it be *Rom. and Jul.* iii 4 18
You say right, sir: o' Monday morning; 'twas so indeed *Hamlet* ii 2 406
Monde. Je ne voudrais prononcer ces mots devant les seigneurs de France pour tout le monde . . . . . . *Hen. V.* iii 4 59
How answer you, la plus belle Katharine du monde? . . . v 2 231
Money. Will money buy 'em?—Very like . . . *Tempest* v 1 265
That the money and the matter may be both at once delivered *T. G. of V.* i 1 137
When you looked sadly, it was for want of money . . . ii 1 31

Money. Seven hundred pounds of moneys, and gold and silver *Mer Wives* i 1 52
Hold, there's money for thee; let me have thy voice in my behalf i 4 167
Either liquor in his pate or money in his purse when he looks so merrily ii 1 198
Wilt thou, after the expense of so much money, be now a gainer? ii 2 147
They say, if money go before, all ways do lie open . . . ii 2 175
Money is a good soldier, sir, and will on . . . . ii 2 176
I have a bag of money here troubles me . . . . ii 2 177
There is money; spend it, spend it; spend more; spend all I have ii 2 241
I will first make bold with your money; next, give me your hand. . ii 2 263
Want no money, Sir John; you shall want none . . . ii 2 268
They say the jealous wittolly knave hath masses of money . . ii 2 284
I would not break with her for more money than I'll speak of . iii 2 57
He sent me word to stay within: I like his money well . . iii 5 59
Has cozened all the hosts of Readins . of horses and money . iv 5 81
He hath enjoyed nothing of Ford's but his buck-basket, his cudgel, and twenty pounds of money . . . . v 5 118
To Windsor, to one Master Brook, that you have cozened of money v 5 176
I think to repay that money will be a biting affliction . . . v 5 178
Money buys lands, and wives are sold by fate . . . . v 5 246
I do it for some piece of money, and go through with all *Meas. for Meas.* ii 1 284
Of which he made five marks, ready money . . . . iv 3 8
There is your money that I had to keep . . *Com. of Errors* i 2 8
Tell me this, I pray: Where have you left the money that I gave you? i 2 54
Tell me, and dally not, where is the money? . . . . i 2 59
Answer me In what safe place you have bestow'd my money . . i 2 78
By some device or other The villain is o'er-raught of all my money . i 2 96
I greatly fear my money is not safe . . . . . i 2 105
To save the money that he spends in tiring . . . . ii 1 98
At supper-time I'll visit you And then receive my money for the chain iii 2 180
Receive the money now, For fear you ne'er see chain nor money more . iii 2 181
At five o'clock I shall receive the money for the same . . iv 1 11
I am not furnish'd with the present money . . . . iv 1 34
I hope you have; Or else you may return without your money . iv 1 44
The chain!—Why, give it to my wife and fetch your money . . iv 1 54
What should I answer you?—The money that you owe me for the chain iv 1 63
Will you send him, mistress, redemption, the money in his desk? iv 2 46
There's the money, bear it straight, And bring thy master home immediately . . . . iv 2 63
Some tender money to me; some invite me; Some other give me thanks iv 3 4
I'll give thee, ere I leave thee, so much money, To warrant thee . iv 4 2
I think he brings the money. How now, sir! have you that I sent you for? . . . . iv 4 8
But where's the money?—Why, sir, I gave the money for the rope . iv 4 11
Alas, I sent you money to redeem you, By Dromio here, who came in haste for it.—Money by me! heart and good-will you might; But surely, master, not a rag of money . . . . . . iv 4 86
I sent you money, sir, to be your bail, By Dromio; but I think he brought it not . . . . v 1 382
With a good leg and a good foot, uncle, and money enough *Much Ado* ii 1 16
Well, a horn for my money, when all's done . . . . ii 3 63
If he be sad, he wants money . . . . iii 2 20
Borrows money in God's name, the which he hath used so long and never paid . . . . v 1 319
Although not valued to the money's worth . . . *L. L. Lost* ii 1 137
We much rather had depart withal And have the money by our father lent . . . . ii 1 148
To you, Antonio, I owe the most, in money and in love . *Mer. of Venice* i 1 131
Neither have I money nor commodity To raise a present sum . . i 1 178
Go, presently inquire, and so will I, Where money is . . . i 1 184
He lends out money gratis And brings down The rate of usance . . i 3 45
You have rated me About my moneys and my usances . . . i 3 109
You come to me, and you say 'Shylock, we would have moneys' . i 3 117
Moneys is your suit. What should I say to you? Should I not say 'Hath a dog money?' . . . . i 3 122
You call'd me dog; and for these courtesies I'll lend you thus much moneys? . . . . i 3 130
If thou wilt lend this money, lend it not As to thy friends . . . i 3 133
Supply your present wants and take no doit Of usance for my moneys . i 3 142
He was wont to lend money for a Christian courtesy . . . iii 1 51
If he had The present money to discharge the Jew, He would not take it . . . . iii 2 276
Tell not me of mercy; This is the fool that lent out money gratis . . iii 3 2
We shall not shortly have a rasher on the coals for money . . . iii 5 28
Is he not able to discharge the money?—Yes, here I tender it for him . iv 1 208
Shylock, there's thrice thy money offer'd thee. . . . . iv 1 227
Be merciful: Take thrice thy money; bid me tear the bond . . iv 1 234
Here is the money.—Soft! The Jew shall have all justice; soft! no haste iv 1 319
I think you have no money in your purse . . . *As Y. Like It* ii 4 13
He that wants money, means and content is without three good friends iii 2 26
Would take her with all faults, and money enough . *T. of Shrew* i 1 134
Why, nothing comes amiss, so money comes withal . . . . i 2 82
I have bills for money by exchange From Florence and must here deliver them . . . . iv 2 89
So that you had her wrinkles and I her money . . *All's Well* ii 4 21
I begin to love, as an old man loves money, with no stomach . . iii 2 17
Let's to bed, knight. Thou hadst need send for more money *T. Night* ii 3 199
Send for money, knight: if thou hast her not i' the end, call me cut . ii 3 202
I must entreat of you some of that money.—What money, sir? . . iii 4 374
Let's see the event.—I dare lay any money 'twill be nothing yet . . iii 4 432
There's money for thee: if you tarry longer, I shall give worse payment iv 1 20
These wise men that give fools money get themselves a good report . iv 1 23
You can fool no more money out of me at this throw . . . v 1 44
Mine honest friend, Will you take eggs for money? . . *W. Tale* i 2 161
I am robbed, sir, and beaten; my money and apparel ta'en from me . iv 3 64
Dost lack any money? I have a little money for thee . . . iv 3 82
I shall there have money, or any thing I want: offer me no money, I pray you; that kills my heart . . . . iv 3 87
He sings several tunes faster than you'll tell money . . . iv 4 185
If I were not in love with Mopsa, thou shouldst take no money of me . iv 4 234
Have I not told thee how I was cozened by the way and lost all my money? . . . . iv 4 255
Come to the pedlar; Money's a medler, That doth utter all men's ware-a . . . . iv 4 329
Dreading the curse that money may buy out . . . *K. John* iii 1 164
We seize into our hands His plate, his goods, his money. *Richard II.* ii 1 210
He hath not money for these Irish wars . . . . . ii 1 259
How shall we do for money for these wars? . . . . . ii 2 104
There's money of the king's coming down the hill . . *1 Hen. IV.* ii 2 56
Your money!—Villains!—Got with much ease. . . . . ii 2 109
But, by the Lord, lads, I am glad you have the money . . . ii 4 305

Money. The money shall be paid back again with advantage . *1 Hen. IV.* ii 4 599
Paid money that I borrowed, three or four times; lived well . . . iii 3 20
If I did not think thou hadst been an ignis fatuus or a ball of wildfire, there's no purchase in money . . . . iii 3 46
You owe me money, Sir John; and now you pick a quarrel to beguile me of it . . . . iii 3 76
You owe money here besides, Sir John, for your diet and by-drinkings, and money lent you, four and twenty pound . . . . . iii 3 83
The money is paid back again.—O, I do not like that paying back. . iii 3 200
There shalt thou know thy charge; and there receive Money and order iii 3 226
Will you give me money, captain?—Lay out, lay out . . . iv 2 4
He that will caper with me for a thousand marks, let him lend me the money, and have at him! . . . . . . *2 Hen. IV.* i 2 217
What money is in my purse?—Seven groats and two pence . . . i 2 262
What is the gross sum that I owe thee?—Marry, if thou wert an honest man, thyself and the money too . . . . ii 1 93
The one you may do with sterling money, and the other with current repentance . . . . ii 1 131
What stuff wilt have a kirtle of? I shall receive money o' Thursday . ii 4 298
I owe her money; and whether she be damned for that, I know not . ii 4 367
John a Gaunt loved him well, and betted much money on his head . iii 2 50
If a servant, under his master's command transporting a sum of money, be assailed by robbers . . . . *Hen. V.* iv 1 159
I will none of your money.—It is with a good will; I can tell you. . iv 8 72
What treachery was used?—No treachery; but want of men and money *1 Hen. VI.* i 1 69
Nor men nor money hath he to make war . . . . . i 2 17
Talk like . . . market men That come to gather money for their corn . iii 2 5
You shall first receive The sum of money which I promised . . v 1 52
Keep me here, Without discharge, money, or furniture . *2 Hen. VI.* i 3 172
Will, thou shalt have my hammer: and here, Tom, take all the money that I have . . . . ii 3 76
And did he not, in his protectorship, Levy great sums of money? . iii 1 61
There shall be no money; all shall eat and drink on my score . . iv 2 79
Henry hath money, you are strong and manly; God on our side, doubt not . . . . iv 8 53
Such as give Their money out of hope they may believe . *Hen. VIII.* Prol. 8
The wars for my money . . . . *Coriolanus* iv 5 248
Meanwhile here's money for thy charges . . . *T. Andron.* iv 3 105
How much money must I have?—Come, sirrah, you must be hanged . iv 4 46
What will you give us?—No money, on my faith, but the gleek *R. and J.* iv 5 115
Importune him for my moneys; be not ceased With slight denial *T. of Athens* ii 1 16
What, You come for money?—Is't not your business too?—It is . ii 2 10
Say, that my occasions have found time to use 'em toward a supply of money . . . . ii 2 201
This is no time to lend money, especially upon bare friendship . . iii 1 45
Fie, no, do not believe it; he cannot want for money . . . iii 2 10
I have received some small kindnesses from him, as money, plate, jewels and such-like trifles . . . . iii 2 23
Timon's money Has paid his men their wages . . . . . iii 2 76
I think One business does command us all; for mine Is money . . iii 4 5
Your lord sends now for money.—Most true, he does . . . iii 4 18
He wears jewels now of Timon's gift, For which I wait for money . . iii 4 20
E'en as if your lord should wear rich jewels, And send for money for 'em . . . . iii 4 24
What do ye ask of me, my friend?—We wait for certain money here, sir.—Ay, If money were as certain as your waiting, 'Twere sure enough . . . . iii 4 46
I perceive our masters may throw their caps at their money . . iii 4 102
While they have told their money and let out Their coin upon large interest, I myself Rich only in large hurts . . . . . iii 5 107
Royal cheer, I warrant you.—Doubt not that, if money and the season can yield it . . . . iii 6 57
Take thy physic first—thou too—and thou;—Stay, I will lend thee money . . . . iii 6 111
More counsel with more money, bounteous Timon . . . . iv 3 167
I can raise no money by vile means . . . . *J. Cæsar* iv 3 71
Give him this money and these notes, Reynaldo . . . *Hamlet* ii 1 1
There was, for a while, no money bid for argument . . . . ii 2 372
There's money for thee.—O, let me kiss that hand! . . . *Lear* iv 6 134
No eyes in your head, nor no money in your purse? . . . iv 6 149
I say, put money in thy purse. (Repeated) . . . . *Othello* i 3 347
Make all the money thou canst . . . . i 3 361
My money is almost spent; I have been to-night exceedingly well cudgelled . . . . ii 3 371
And so, with no money at all and a little more wit, return again . . ii 3 374
But, masters, here's money for you: and the general so likes your music iii 1 11
We have done our course; there's money for your pains: I pray you, turn the key . . . . iv 2 93
Cæsar gets money where He loses hearts . . . *Ant. and Cleo.* ii 1 13
This is the brief of money, plate, and jewels, I am possess'd of: 'tis exactly valued . . . . v 2 138
Here's money for my meat: I would have left it on the board *Cymbeline* iii 6 50
Money, youth?—All gold and silver rather turn to dirt! . . . iii 6 53
This Cloten was a fool, an empty purse; There was no money in't . iv 2 114
We lost too much money this mart by being too wenchless . *Pericles* iv 2 4
Well, follow me, my masters, you shall have your money presently . iv 2 58
Where a man may serve seven years for the loss of a leg, and have not money enough in the end to buy him a wooden one . . . . iv 6 183

Money-bag. There is some ill a-brewing towards my rest, For I did dream of money-bags to-night . . . . . . *Mer. of Venice* ii 5 18
A usurer's wife was brought to bed of twenty money-bags *W. Tale* iv 4 267

Moneyed. The doctor is well money'd, and his friends Potent *Mer. Wives* iv 4 88

Mongrel. Thou mongrel beef-witted lord! . . . *Troi. and Cres.* ii 1 14
They set me up, in policy, that mongrel cur, Ajax, against that dog of as bad a kind, Achilles . . . . v 4 14
As hounds and greyhounds, mongrels, spaniels, curs . *Macbeth* iii 1 93
I think the world's asleep. How now! where's that mongrel? . *Lear* i 4 53
Beggar, coward, pandar, and the son and heir of a mongrel bitch . ii 2 24
Mastiff, greyhound, mongrel grim, Hound or spaniel, brach or lym . iii 6 71

Monk. The king, I fear, is poison'd by a monk . . . *K. John* v 6 23
A monk, I tell you; a resolved villain, Whose bowels suddenly burst out . . . . v 6 29
A monk o' the Chartreux.—O, Nicholas Hopkins? . . . *Hen. VIII.* i 1 221
He doubted 'Twould prove the verity of certain words Spoke by a holy monk . . . . i 2 160
I told my lord the duke, by the devil's illusions The monk might be deceived . . . . i 2 179
But all hoods make not monks . . . . iii 1 23

Monkey. Thou liest, thou jesting monkey, thou *Tempest* iii 2 52
On meddling monkey, or on busy ape *M. N. Dream* ii 1 181
Showed me a ring that he had of your daughter for a monkey *M. of Ven.* iii 1 124
I would not have given it for a wilderness of monkeys iii 1 128
More giddy in my desires than a monkey *As Y. Like It* iv 1 154
Yet lecherous as a monkey *2 Hen. IV.* iii 2 338
The strain of man's bred out Into baboon and monkey *T. of Athens* i 1 260
God help thee, poor monkey! But how wilt thou do for a father? *Macb.* iv 2 59
Horses are tied by the heads, dogs and bears by the neck, monkeys by the loins, and men by the legs *Lear* ii 4 9
Were they as prime as goats, as hot as monkeys *Othello* iii 3 403
This is the monkey's own giving out iv 1 131
Goats and monkeys! iv 1 274
Apes and monkeys 'Twixt two such shes would chatter this way and Contemn with mows the other *Cymbeline* i 6 39

Monmouth. And that no man might draw short breath to-day But I and Harry Monmouth *1 Hen. IV.* v 2 50
If I mistake not, thou art Harry Monmouth v 4 59
That Harry Monmouth fell Under the wrath of noble Hotspur's sword *2 Hen. IV.* Ind. 29
Harry Monmouth's brawn, the hulk Sir John, Is prisoner to your son i 1 19
Rendering faint quittance, wearied and out-breathed, To Harry Monmouth i 1 109
Against the Welsh, himself and Harry Monmouth i 3 83
To-day might I, hanging on Hotspur's neck, Have talk'd of Monmouth's grave ii 3 45
Ay, he was porn at Monmouth, Captain Gower *Hen. V.* iv 7 12
You sall find, in the comparisons between Macedon and Monmouth, that the situations, look you, is both alike iv 7 26
There is a river in Macedon; and there is also moreover a river at Monmouth: it is called Wye at Monmouth iv 7 29
If you mark Alexander's life well, Harry of Monmouth's life is come after it iv 7 34
As Alexander killed his friend Cleitus, being in his ales and his cups; so also Harry Monmouth, being in his right wits iv 7 49
I'll tell you there is good men porn at Monmouth iv 7 56
Wearing leeks in their Monmouth caps iv 7 104
Since Henry Monmouth first began to reign, Before whose glory I was great in arms, This loathsome sequestration have I had *1 Hen. VI.* ii 5 23
That Henry born at Monmouth should win all And Henry born at Windsor lose all iii 1 198

Monopoly. If I had a monoply out, they would have part on't *Lear* i 4 167

Mons. On the top of the mountain?—Or mons, the hill *L. L. Lost* v 1 89

Monsieur. We'll not run, Monsieur Monster *Tempest* iii 2 21
Ha! the prince and Monsieur Love! *Much Ado* ii 3 38
Monsieur, are you not lettered?—Yes, yes; he teaches boys *L. L. Lost* v 1 47
This is the ape of form, monsieur the nice v 2 325
The French lord, Monsieur Le Bon *Mer. of Venice* i 2 58
Bon jour, Monsieur Le Beau: what's the news? *As Y. Like It* i 2 104
What is the sport, monsieur, that the ladies have lost? i 2 142
Monsieur the challenger, the princesses call for you i 2 175
Monsieur! what a life is this, That your poor friends must woo your company? ii 7 9
Do you hear, monsieur? a word with you *All's Well* ii 3 191
Is there any unkindness between my lord and you, monsieur? ii 5 36
How now, monsieur! this drum sticks sorely in your disposition iii 6 46
For Monsieur Malvolio, let me alone with him *T. Night* ii 3 144
Dieu vous garde, monsieur.—Et vous aussi; votre serviteur iii 1 78
Good morrow, sweet Hal. What says Monsieur Remorse? *1 Hen. IV.* i 2 125
I The crowns will take.—Petit monsieur, que dit-il? *Hen. V.* iv 4 52
Now I would pray our monsieurs To think an English courtier may be wise, And never see the Louvre *Hen. VIII.* i 3 21
There is a Frenchman his companion, one An eminent monsieur *Cymbeline* i 6 65

Monster. O, 'twas a din to fright a monster's ear! *Tempest* ii 1 314
There would this monster make a man; any strange beast there makes a man ii 2 31
This is some monster of the isle with four legs ii 2 67
Four legs and two voices: a most delicate monster! ii 2 94
This is a devil, and no monster: I will leave him ii 2 102
This is a very shallow monster! I afeard of him! A very weak monster! ii 2 148
A most poor credulous monster! Well drawn, monster, in good sooth! ii 2 150
A most perfidious and drunken monster! ii 2 155
I shall laugh myself to death at this puppy-headed monster. A most scurvy monster! I could find in my heart to beat him ii 2 159
But that the poor monster's in drink: an abominable monster! ii 2 162
A most ridiculous monster, to make a wonder of a poor drunkard! ii 2 169
Farewell, master; farewell, farewell!—A howling monster; a drunken monster! ii 2 183
Freedom, hey-day, freedom!—O brave monster! Lead the way ii 2 192
He were a brave monster indeed, if they [his eyes] were set in his tail iii 2 12
By this light, thou shalt be my lieutenant, monster, or my standard iii 2 18
We'll not run, Monsieur Monster.—Nor go neither iii 2 21
Thou liest, most ignorant monster: I am in case to justle a constable iii 2 28
Wilt thou tell a monstrous lie, being but half a fish and half a monster? iii 2 33
That a monster should be such a natural! iii 2 36
The poor monster's my subject and he shall not suffer indignity iii 2 42
Interrupt the monster one word further, and, by this hand, I'll turn my mercy out o' doors iii 2 77
A murrain on your monster, and the devil take your fingers! iii 2 88
Monster, I will kill this man: his daughter and I will be king and queen iii 2 114
At thy request, monster, I will do reason, any reason iii 2 128
Do you hear, monster? If I should take a displeasure against you, look you,— Thou wert but a lost monster iv 1 201
O, ho, monster! we know what belongs to a frippery iv 1 224
Monster, come, put some lime upon your fingers, and away with the rest iv 1 246
Monster, lay-to your fingers: help to bear this away iv 1 251
You shall have sport; I will show you a monster *Mer. Wives* iii 2 82
Will you go, gentles?—Have with you to see this monster iii 2 93
O thou monster Ignorance, how deformed dost thou look! *L. L. Lost* iv 2 24
No marvel though Demetrius Do, as a monster, fly my presence *M. N. D.* ii 2 97
My mistress with a monster is in love iii 2 6
And then I will her charmed eye release From monster's view iii 2 377
And when I break that oath, let me turn monster *As Y. Like It* i 2 23
A very monster in apparel, and not like a Christian footboy *T. of Shrew* iii 2 71
I wonder, sir, sith wives are monsters to you, And that you fly them as you swear them lordship, Yet you desire to marry *All's Well* v 3 155
My master loves her dearly; And I, poor monster, fond as much on him *T. Night* ii 2 35

Monster. Will break the back of man, the heart of monster *W. Tale* iv 4 798
I would set an ox-head to your lion's hide, And make a monster of you *K. John* ii 1 293
And be a carrion monster like thyself iii 4 33
The blunt monster with uncounted heads, The still-discordant wavering multitude, Can play upon it *2 Hen. IV.* Ind. 18
These English monsters! *Hen V.* ii 2 85
It is a pity Would move a monster *Hen. VIII.* ii 3 11
In all Cupid's pageant there is presented no monster *Troi. and Cres.* iii 2 81
They that have the voice of lions and the act of hares, are they not monsters? iii 2 96
A great-sized monster of ingratitudes iii 3 147
He's grown a very land-fish, languageless, a monster iii 3 265
Ingratitude is monstrous, and for the multitude to be ingrateful, were to make a monster of the multitude *Coriolanus* ii 3 11
His peremptory 'shall,' being but The horn and noise o' the monster's iii 1 95
O, had the monster seen those lily hands! *T. Andron.* ii 4 44
The lean abhorred monster [death] keeps Thee here in dark *Rom. and Jul.* v 3 104
Hang thee, monster!—Pardon him, sweet Timandra *T. of Athens* iv 3 87
Teem with new monsters, whom thy upward face Hath to the marbled mansion all above Never presented! iv 3 190
We'll have thee, as our rarer monsters are, Painted upon a pole *Macbeth* v 8 25
Wise men know well enough what monsters you make of them *Hamlet* iii 1 144
That monster, custom, who all sense doth eat, Of habits devil iii 4 161
Her offence Must be of such unnatural degree, That monsters it *Lear* i 1 223
He cannot be such a monster— Nor is not, sure i 2 102
Monster ingratitude! i 5 43
If she live long, And in the end meet the old course of death, Women will all turn monsters iii 7 102
Humanity must perforce prey on itself, Like monsters of the deep iv 2 50
He echoes me, As if there were some monster in his thought *Othello* iii 3 107
O, beware, my lord, of jealousy; It is the green-eyed monster iii 3 166
'Tis [jealousy] a monster Begot upon itself, born on itself.—Heaven keep that monster from Othello's mind! iii 4 161
A horned man's a monster and a beast.—There's many a beast then in a populous city, And many a civil monster iv 1 63
Adultery! Wherefore write you not What monster's her accuser? *Cymb.* iii 2 2
The imperious seas breed monsters, for the dish Poor tributary rivers as sweet fish iv 2 35
Being an ugly monster, 'Tis strange he [death] hides him in fresh cups v 3 70
That monster envy, oft the wrack Of earned praise *Pericles* iv Gower 12

Monstered. Than idly sit To hear my nothings monster'd *Coriolanus* ii 2 81

Monster-like, be shown For poor'st diminutives, for doits *Ant. and Cleo.* iv 12 36

Monstrous. Wilt thou tell a monstrous lie? *Tempest* iii 2 32
Though they are of monstrous shape, yet, note, Their manners are more gentle-kind than of Our human generation iii 3 31
O, it is monstrous, monstrous! iii 3 95
And more faults than hairs,— That's monstrous *T. G. of Ver.* iii 1 374
I'll speak in a monstrous little voice *M. N. Dream* i 2 54
O monstrous! O strange! we are haunted iii 1 107
Ladies, you, whose gentle hearts do fear The smallest monstrous mouse v 1 223
Every one fault seeming monstrous till his fellow-fault came *As Y. L. It* iii 2 373
O monstrous beast! how like a swine he lies! *T. of Shrew* Ind. 1 34
O monstrous arrogance! iv 3 107
Thus strangers may be haled and abused: O monstrous villain! v 1 112
Needs must intimate Skill infinite or monstrous desperate *All's Well* ii 1 187
It must be an answer of most monstrous size that must fit all demands ii 2 34
Poor trespasses, More monstrous standing by *W. Tale* iii 2 191
Is all as monstrous to our human reason v 1 41
Thou monstrous slanderer of heaven and earth!—Thou monstrous injurer of heaven and earth! Call not me slanderer *K. John* ii 1 173
O monstrous! eleven buckram men grown out of two! *1 Hen. IV.* ii 4 243
I blushed to hear his monstrous devices ii 4 344
The sheriff with a most monstrous watch is at the door ii 4 530
O monstrous! but one half-pennyworth of bread to this intolerable deal of sack! ii 4 591
A huge half-moon, a monstrous cantle out iii 1 100
In the visitation of the winds, Who take the ruffian billows by the top, Curling their monstrous heads *2 Hen. IV.* iii 1 23
The time misorder'd doth, in common sense, Crowd us and crush us to this monstrous form, To hold our safety up iv 2 34
O monstrous treachery! can this be so? *1 Hen. VI.* iv 1 61
So bad a death argues a monstrous life *2 Hen. VI.* iii 3 30
He can write and read and cast accompt.—O monstrous! iv 2 94
O monstrous coward! what, to come behind folks? iv 7 88
Is't Cade that I have slain, that monstrous traitor? iv 10 71
And fight against that monstrous rebel Cade v 1 62
O monstrous traitor! I arrest thee, York, Of capital treason v 1 106
O monstrous fault, to harbour such a thought! *3 Hen. VI.* iii 2 164
O monstrous, monstrous! and so falls it out *Richard III.* iii 2 66
And this is Edward's wife, that monstrous witch iii 4 72
Hath into monstrous habits put the graces That once were his *Hen. VIII.* i 2 122
In all Cupid's pageant there is presented no monster.—Nor nothing monstrous neither?—Nothing, but our undertakings *Troi. and Cres.* iii 2 82
Ingratitude is monstrous, and for the multitude to be ingrateful, were to make a monster of the multitude; of the which we being members, should bring ourselves to be monstrous members *Coriol.* ii 3 10
O monstrous! what reproachful words are these? *T. Andron.* i 1 308
Shall I endure this monstrous villany? iv 4 51
Alas, kind lord! He's flung in rage from this ingrateful seat Of monstrous friends *T. of Athens* iv 2 46
I am rapt and cannot cover The monstrous bulk of this ingratitude With any size of words v 1 68
'Tis not monstrous in you, neither wish I You take much pains to mend v 1 91
Why all these things change from their ordinance Their natures and preformed faculties To monstrous quality *J. Cæsar* i 3 68
To make them instruments of fear and warning Unto some monstrous state i 3 71
Where wilt thou find a cavern dark enough To mask thy monstrous visage? ii 1 81
It is the weakness of mine eyes That shapes this monstrous apparition iv 3 277
Who cannot want the thought how monstrous It was? *Macbeth* iii 6 8
Is it not monstrous that this player here, But in a fiction, in a dream of passion, Could force his soul so to his own conceit? *Hamlet* ii 2 577
Should in this trice of time Commit a thing so monstrous *Lear* i 1 220
What a monstrous fellow art thou, thus to rail on one that is neither known of thee nor knows thee! ii 2 27
Most monstrous! oh! Know'st thou this paper?—Ask me not what I know v 3 159
Hell and night Must bring this monstrous birth to the world's light *Oth.* i 3 410

Monstrous. The wind-shaked surge, with high and monstrous mane *Oth.* ii 1 13
'Tis monstrous. Iago, who began't? ii 3 217
O monstrous world! Take note, take note, O world, To be direct and honest is not safe iii 3 377
O monstrous! monstrous!—Nay, this was but his dream iii 3 427
'Tis a strange truth.—O monstrous act!—Villany, villany, villany! v 2 190
We had much more monstrous matter of feast *Ant. and Cleo.* ii 2 187
'But yet' is as a gaoler to bring forth Some monstrous malefactor ii 5 53
It's monstrous labour, when I wash my brain, And it grows fouler ii 7 105
Of monstrous lust the due and just reward *Pericles* v 3 Gower 86

Monstrously. That self chain about his neck Which he forswore most monstrously to have *Com. of Errors* v 1 11

Monstrousness. O, see the monstrousness of man When he looks out in an ungrateful shape! *T. of Athens* iii 2 79

Monstruosity. This is the monstruosity in love, lady, that the will is infinite and the execution confined *Troi. and Cres.* iii 2 87

Montacute. A warrant from The king to attach Lord Montacute *Hen. VIII.* i 1 217

Montague. My brother Montague shall post to London 3 *Hen. VI.* i 2 55
Warwick came to seek you out; And therefore comes my brother Montague ii 1 167
Valiant Richard, Montague, Stay we no longer, dreaming of renown ii 1 198
These letters are for you, Sent from your brother, Marquess Montague iii 3 164
And you too, Somerset and Montague, Speak freely what you think iv 1 27
Knows not Montague that of itself England is safe, if true within itself? iv 1 39
But, ere I go, Hastings and Montague, Resolve my doubt iv 1 134
So God help Montague as he proves true! iv 1 143
Thou, brother Montague, in Buckingham, Northampton and in Leicestershire iv 8 14
My loving Montague, And all at once, once more a happy farewell iv 8 30
How far off is our brother Montague? Where is the post that came from Montague?—By this at Daintry v 1 4
Montague, Montague, for Lancaster! v 1 67
Now, Montague, sit fast; I seek for thee, That Warwick's bones may keep thine company v 2 3
Ah, Montague, If thou be there, sweet brother, take my hand, And with thy lips keep in my soul awhile! v 2 33
Come quickly, Montague, or I am dead.—Ah, Warwick! Montague hath breathed his last; And to the latest gasp cried out for Warwick v 2 39
Say Warwick was our anchor; what of that? And Montague our topmast; what of him? v 4 14
With them, the two brave bears, Warwick and Montague v 7 10
A dog of the house of Montague moves me *Rom. and Jul.* i 1 9
I will take the wall of any man or maid of Montague's i 1 16
I will push Montague's men from the wall, and thrust his maids to the wall i 1 21
Draw thy tool; here comes two of the house of the Montagues i 1 38
Peace! I hate the word, As I hate hell, all Montagues, and thee i 1 78
Beat them down! Down with the Capulets! down with the Montagues! i 1 81
Old Montague is come, And flourishes his blade in spite of me i 1 84
Capulet and Montague Have thrice disturb'd the quiet of our streets i 1 97
Montague, come you this afternoon, To know our further pleasure in this case i 1 107
But Montague is bound as well as I, In penalty alike i 2 1
If you be not of the house of Montagues, I pray, come and crush a cup of wine i 2 85
This, by his voice, should be a Montague. Fetch me my rapier, boy i 5 56
This is a Montague, our foe, A villain that is hither come in spite i 5 63
His name is Romeo, and a Montague; The only son of your great enemy i 5 138
'Tis but thy name that is my enemy; Thou art thyself, though not a Montague ii 2 39
What's Montague? it is nor hand, nor foot, Nor arm ii 2 40
Art thou not Romeo and a Montague?—Neither, fair saint, if either thee dislike ii 2 60
In truth, fair Montague, I am too fond ii 2 98
Sweet Montague, be true. Stay but a little, I will come again ii 2 137
Prince, as thou art true, For blood of ours, shed blood of Montague iii 1 154
He is a kinsman to the Montague; Affection makes him false iii 1 181
This is that banish'd haughty Montague, That murder'd my love's cousin v 3 49
Stop thy unhallow'd toil, vile Montague! Can vengeance be pursued further than death? v 3 54
Run to the Capulets: Raise up the Montagues: some others search v 3 178
This dagger hath mista'en,—for, lo, his house Is empty on the back of Montague,—And it mis-sheathed in my daughter's bosom! v 3 204
Come, Montague; for thou art early up, To see thy son and heir more early down.—Alas, my liege, my wife is dead to-night v 3 208
Capulet! Montague! See, what a scourge is laid upon your hate v 3 291
O brother Montague, give me thy hand: This is my daughter's jointure, for no more Can I demand v 3 296

Montano, Your trusty and most valiant servitor *Othello* i 3 39
Help, ho!—Lieutenant,—sir,—Montano,—sir;—Help, masters! ii 3 159
Montano,—gentlemen,—Have you forgot all sense of place and duty? ii 3 166
Worthy Montano, you were wont be civil ii 3 190
Montano and myself being in speech, There comes a fellow crying out for help ii 3 225

Montant. To see thee pass thy punto, thy stock, thy reverse, thy distance, thy montant *Mer. Wives* ii 3 27

Montez à cheval! My horse! varlet! laquais! ha! *Hen. V.* iv 2 2

Montferrat. In company of the Marquis of Montferrat *Mer. of Venice* i 2 126

Montgomery. This is Sir John Montgomery, Our trusty friend, unless I be deceived 3 *Hen. VI.* iv 7 40
Thanks, good Montgomery; but we now forget Our title to the crown iv 7 45
Long live Edward the Fourth!—Thanks, brave Montgomery iv 7 77

Month. I must Once in a month recount what thou hast been *Tempest* i 2 262
I see you have a month's mind to them *T. G. of Ver.* i 2 137
Whereon this month I have been hammering i 3 18
Have you long sojourned there?—Some sixteen months iv 1 21
From whom my absence was not six months old *Com. of Errors* i 1 45
He hath every month a new sworn brother *Much Ado* i 1 72
I tell him we shall stay here at the least a month i 1 150
I had rather pray a month with mutton and porridge *L. L. Lost* i 1 304
What was a month old at Cain's birth, that's not five weeks old as yet? iv 2 36
The moon was a month old when Adam was no more iv 2 39
The moon is never but a month old iv 2 47
Love, whose month is ever May, Spied a blossom passing fair iv 3 102
She is gone; she is two months on her way v 2 679
Three thousand ducats; well.—Ay, sir, for three months.—For three months; well *Mer. of Venice* i 3 2
Three thousand ducats for three months and Antonio bound i 3 9
But soft! how many months Do you desire? i 3 59
And for three months.—I had forgot; three months; you told me so i 3 67
Three thousand ducats; 'tis a good round sum. Three months from twelve *Mer. of Venice* i 3 105
Within these two months, that's a month before This bond expires, I do expect return Of thrice three times the value of this bond i 3 159
There can be no dismay; My ships come home a month before the day i 3 183
I would detain you here some month or two Before you venture for me iii 2 9
Thy loving voyage Is but for two months victuall'd *As Y. Like It* v 4 198
He was much famed.—Some six months since *All's Well* i 2 71
His wife some two months since fled from his house iv 3 56
I have to-night dispatched sixteen businesses, a month's length a-piece iv 3 99
A month ago I went from hence, And then 'twas fresh in murmur *T. N.* i 2 31
I'll stay a month longer. I am a fellow o' the strangest mind i' the world i 3 119
Having been three months married to her, sitting in my state ii 5 49
And for three months before, No interim, not a minute's vacancy v 1 97
Three months this youth hath tended upon me; But more of that anon v 1 102
I'll give him my commission To let him there a month *W. Tale* i 2 41
Three crabbed months had sour'd themselves to death i 2 102
Is it true, think you?—Very true, and but a month old iv 4 270
'Tis in three parts.—We had the tune on't a month ago iv 4 300
There was not full a month Between their births v 1 117
Not a month 'Fore your queen died, she was more worth such gazes v 1 225
Our doctors say this is no month to bleed *Richard II.* i 1 157
'Tis full three months since I did see him last v 3 2
But this our purpose now is twelve month old 1 *Hen. IV.* i 1 28
Argument for a week, laughter for a month, and a good jest for ever ii 2 101
All their letters to meet me in arms by the ninth of the next month ii 3 30
Thou naughty varlet, tell me, where hast thou been this month? ii 4 475
The English rebels met The eleventh of this month at Shrewsbury iii 2 166
As full of spirit as the month of May, And gorgeous as the sun at midsummer iv 1 101
The seasons change their manners, as the year Had found some months asleep and leap'd them over 2 *Hen. IV.* iv 4 124
Like pale ghosts, Faintly besiege us one hour in a month 1 *Hen. VI.* i 2 8
For eighteen months concluded by consent 2 *Hen. VI.* i 1 42
The day of combat shall be the last of the next month i 3 225
To his majesty's parliament, Holden at Bury the first of this next month ii 4 71
But I was made a king at nine months old iv 9 4
When I was crown'd I was but nine months old 3 *Hen. VI.* i 1 112
So minutes, hours, days, months, and years, Pass'd over to the end they were created, Would bring white hairs unto a quiet grave ii 5 38
I was anointed king at nine months old iii 1 76
Edward, her lord, whom I, some three months since, Stabb'd *Rich. III.* i 2 241
Henry the Sixth Was crown'd in Paris but at nine months old ii 3 17
I'll find A Marshalsea shall hold ye play these two months *Hen. VIII.* v 4 90
I have loved you night and day For many weary months *Troi. and Cres.* iii 2 123
Some two months hence my will shall here be made v 10 53
I'll follow thee a month, devise with thee Where thou shalt rest *Coriol.* iv 1 38
One hour's storm will drown the fragrant meads; What will whole months of tears thy father's eyes? *T. Andron.* ii 4 55
Will speak more in a minute than he will stand to in a month *R. and J.* ii 4 157
Cast me not away! Delay this marriage for a month, a week iii 5 201
He hath put me off To the succession of new days this month *T. of A.* ii 2 20
Yet may your pains, six months, Be quite contrary iv 3 143
The sun arises . . . Some two months hence up higher toward the north He first presents his fire *J. Cæsar* ii 1 109
But two months dead: nay, not so much, not two *Hamlet* i 2 138
Within a month—Let me not think on't—Frailty, thy name is woman! i 2 145
A little month, or ere those shoes were old i 2 147
And my father died within these two hours.—Nay, 'tis twice two months iii 2 136
O heavens! die two months ago, and not forgotten yet? iii 2 139
If you find him not within this month, you shall nose him as you go up the stairs into the lobby iv 3 38
Two months since, Here was a gentleman of Normandy iv 7 82
Our father will hence to-night.—That's most certain, and with you; next month with us *Lear* i 1 290
If, till the expiration of your month, You will return and sojourn with my sister, Dismissing half your train ii 4 205
I must needs be gone; My twelve months are expired *Pericles* iii 3 2
A man who for this three months hath not spoken To any one v 1 24

Monthly. O, swear not by the moon, the inconstant moon, That monthly changes in her circled orb *Rom. and Jul.* ii 2 110
Ourself, by monthly course, With reservation of an hundred knights, By you to be sustain'd, shall our abode Make with you by due turns *Lear* i 1 134

Montjoy. Where is Montjoy the herald? speed him hence: Let him greet England with our sharp defiance *Hen. V.* iii 5 36
Therefore, lord constable, haste on Montjoy iii 5 61
What is thy name? I know thy quality.—Montjoy iii 6 147
There's for thy labour, Montjoy. Go, bid thy master well advise himself iii 6 167
We shall your tawny ground with your red blood Discolour: and so, Montjoy, fare you well iii 6 171

Monument. For ever be confixed here, A marble monument *Meas. for Meas.* v 1 233
On your family's old monument Hang mournful epitaphs *Much Ado* iv 1 208
He shall live no longer in monument than the bell rings and the widow weeps v 2 81
Is this the monument of Leonato?—It is v 3 1
And wherefore gaze this goodly company, As if they saw some wondrous monument, Some comet? *T. of Shrew* iii 2 97
In your fine frame hath love no quality? If the quick fire of youth light not your mind, You are no maiden, but a monument *All's Well* iv 2 6
She sat like patience on a monument, Smiling at grief *T. Night* ii 4 117
Burgundy Enshrines thee in his heart and there erects Thy noble deeds as valour's monuments 1 *Hen. VI.* iii 2 120
Defacing monuments of conquer'd France 2 *Hen. VI.* i 1 102
Nor let the rain of heaven wet this place, To wash away my woful monuments iii 2 342
This monument of the victory will I bear iv 3 12
Our bruised arms hung up for monuments *Richard. III.* i 1 6
Goodness and he fill up one monument! *Hen. VIII.* ii 1 94
This monument five hundred years hath stood *T. Andron.* i 1 350
Which, like a taper in some monument, Doth shine upon the dead man's earthy cheeks ii 3 228
Lavinia shall forthwith Be closed in our household's monument v 3 194
Make the bridal bed In that dim monument where Tybalt lies *R. and J.* iii 5 203
Her body sleeps in Capel's monument, And her immortal part with angels lives v 1 18
Now must I to the monument alone; Within this three hours will fair Juliet wake v 2 23
As I discern, It burneth in the Capels' monument v 3 127

Monument. And all run, With open outcry, toward our monument *Rom. and Jul.* v 3 193
In post he came from Mantua To this same place, to this same monument v 3 274
O monument And wonder of good deeds evilly bestow'd! *T. of Athens* iv 3 466
If charnel-houses and our graves must send Those that we bury back, our monuments Shall be the maws of kites *Macbeth* iii 4 72
This grave shall have a living monument . . *Hamlet* v 1 320
To the monument! There lock yourself, and send him word you are dead . . *Ant. and Cleo.* iv 13 3
To the monument! Mardian, go tell him I have slain myself . iv 13 6
Hence, Mardian, And bring me how he takes my death. To the monument! . . iv 13 10
Where is she?—Lock'd in her monument . . iv 14 120
Look out o' the other side your monument; His guard have brought him iv 15 8
The queen my mistress, Confined in all she has, her monument, Of thy intents desires instruction . . v 1 53
Take up her bed; And bear her women from the monument . v 2 360
O sleep, thou ape of death, lie dull upon her! And be her sense but as a monument, Thus in a chapel lying! . *Cymbeline* ii 2 32
Those rich-left heirs that let their fathers lie Without a monument! iv 2 227
For a monument upon thy bones, And e'er-remaining lamps, the belching whale And humming water must o'erwhelm thy corpse *Pericles* iii 1 62
We wept after her hearse, And yet we mourn: her monument Is almost finish'd . . iv 3 42

Monumental. He hath given her his monumental ring . *All's Well* iv 3 20
Out of fashion, like a rusty mail In monumental mockery *Tr. and Cr.* iii 3 153
And smooth as monumental alabaster . . *Othello* v 2 5

Mood. A gentleman, Who, in my mood, I stabb'd . *T. G. of Ver.* iv 1 51
Abetting him to thwart me in my mood . *Com. of Errors* ii 2 172
My wife is in a wayward mood to-day . . iv 4 4
You spend your passion on a misprised mood . *M. N. Dream* iii 2 74
For affection, Mistress of passion, sways it to the mood Of what it likes or loathes . *Mer. of Venice* iv 1 51
I am now, sir, muddied in fortune's mood . *All's Well* v 2 5
He must observe their mood on whom he jests . *T. Night* iii 1 69
Does show the mood of a much troubled breast *K. John* iv 2 73
Why, what a wasp-stung and impatient fool Art thou to break into this woman's mood! . 1 *Hen. IV.* i 3 237
His moods, and his displeasures, and his indignations . *Hen. V.* iv 7 38
Whom I, some three months since, Stabb'd in my angry mood *Rich. III.* i 2 242
One on's father's moods.—Indeed, la, 'tis a noble child . *Coriolanus* i 3 72
Thou art as hot a Jack in thy mood as any in Italy . *Rom. and Jul.* iii 1 13
When Fortune in her shift and change of mood Spurns down her late beloved, all his dependants . . . let him slip down *T. of Athens* i 1 84
Fortune is merry, And in this mood will give us any thing *J. Cæsar* iii 2 272
With all forms, moods, shapes of grief, That can denote me truly *Hamlet* i 2 82
She is importunate, indeed distract: Her mood will needs be pitied . iv 5 3
Bring oil to fire, snow to their colder moods . *Lear* ii 2 83
O the blest gods! so will you wish on me, When the rash mood is on ii 4 172
You are but now cast in his mood, a punishment more in policy *Othello* ii 3 274
Of one whose subdued eyes, Albeit unused to the melting mood, Drop tears as fast as the Arabian trees Their medicinal gum . v 2 349
In that mood The dove will peck the estridge . *Ant. and Cleo.* iii 13 196
Half the flood Hath their keel cut: but fortune's mood Varies again *Pericles* iii Gower 46

Moody. How now? moody? What is't thou canst demand? *Tempest* i 2 244
What doth ensue But moody and dull melancholy? *Com. of Errors* v 1 79
Majesty might never yet endure The moody frontier of a servant brow. You have good leave to leave us . . 1 *Hen. IV.* i 3 19
Nor moody beggars, starving for a time Of pellmell havoc and confusion v 1 81
Being moody, give him line and scope . 2 *Hen. IV.* iv 4 39
The duke Hath banish'd moody discontented fury . 1 *Hen. VI.* iii 1 123
After many moody thoughts . 3 *Hen. VI.* iv 6 13
If that your moody discontented souls Do through the clouds behold this present hour, Even for revenge mock my destruction! *Rich. III.* v 1 7
Observe, observe, he's moody . *Hen. VIII.* iii 2 75
As soon moved to be moody, and as soon moody to be moved . *R. and J.* iii 1 14
Music, moody food Of us that trade in love . *Ant. and Cleo.* ii 5 1

Moody-mad and desperate stags . 1 *Hen. VI.* iv 2 50

Moon. You would lift the moon out of her sphere . *Tempest* ii 1 183
Unless the sun were past—The man i' the moon's too slow . ii 1 249
Hast thou not dropp'd from heaven?—Out o' the moon, I do assure thee. ii 2 141
I was the man i' the moon when time was . ii 2 142
His mother was a witch, and one so strong That could control the moon v 1 270
Thy complexion shifts to strange effects, After the moon *Meas. for Meas.* iii 1 25
What is Dictynna?—A title to Phœbe, to Luna, to the moon . *L. L. Lost* iv 2 39
The moon was a month old when Adam was no more . iv 2 40
The moon is never but a month old . . iv 2 47
Nor shines the silver moon one half so bright . iv 3 30
My love, her mistress, is a gracious moon; She an attending star . iv 3 230
My face is but a moon, and clouded too.—Blessed are clouds, to do as such clouds do! Vouchsafe, bright moon, and these thy stars, to shine . v 2 203
Thus change I like the moon . . v 2 212
You took the moon at full, but now she's changed.—Yet still she is the moon . . v 2 214
Four happy days bring in Another moon: but, O, methinks, how slow This old moon wanes! . *M. N. Dream* i 1 3
The moon, like to a silver bow New-bent in heaven . . i 1 10
Chanting faint hymns to the cold fruitless moon . i 1 73
By the next new moon—The sealing-day betwixt my love and me . i 1 83
I do wander every where, Swifter than the moon's sphere . ii 1 7
The moon, the governess of floods, Pale in her anger, washes all the air ii 1 103
Flying between the cold moon and the earth, Cupid all arm'd . ii 1 156
Cupid's fiery shaft Quench'd in the chaste beams of the watery moon . ii 1 162
Doth the moon shine that night we play our play? . iii 1 52
The moon may shine in at the casement . iii 1 59
The moon methinks looks with a watery eye . iii 1 203
I'll believe as soon This whole earth may be bored and that the moon May through the centre creep . iii 2 53
We the globe can compass soon, Swifter than the wandering moon . iv 1 103
Leave it to his discretion, and let us listen to the moon . v 1 242
This lanthorn doth the horned moon present; Myself the man i' the moon do seem to be . . v 1 249
The man should be put into the lanthorn. How is it else the man i' the moon? . . v 1 252
I am aweary of this moon: would he would change! . v 1 255
All that I have to say, is, to tell you that the lanthorn is the moon; I, the man in the moon . . v 1 262
Why, all these should be in the lanthorn; for all these are in the moon v 1 266

Moon. Well shone, Moon. Truly, the moon shines with a good grace *M. N. Dream* v 1 272
Sweet Moon, I thank thee for thy sunny beams; I thank thee, Moon, for shining now so bright . . v 1 277
My soul is in the sky: Tongue, lose thy light; Moon, take thy flight . v 1 310
Now the hungry lion roars, And the wolf behowls the moon . v 1 379
The moon shines bright: in such a night as this, When the sweet wind did gently kiss the trees . *Mer. of Venice* v 1 1
When the moon shone, we did not see the candle . v 1 92
Peace, ho! the moon sleeps with Endymion And would not be awaked . . v 1 109
By yonder moon I swear you do me wrong . v 1 142
'Tis like the howling of Irish wolves against the moon *As Y. Like It* v 2 119
Good Lord, how bright and goodly shines the moon!—The moon! the sun: it is not moonlight now . *T. of Shrew* iv 5 2
I say it is the moon that shines so bright.—I know it is the sun . iv 5 4
It shall be moon, or star, or what I list, Or ere I journey to your father's house . . iv 5 7
Be it moon, or sun, or what you please: An if you please to call it a rush-candle, Henceforth I vow it shall be so for me . iv 5 13
I say it is the moon.—I know it is the moon.—Nay, then you lie: it is the blessed sun . iv 5 16
And the moon changes even as your mind . iv 5 20
If you have reason, be brief: 'tis not that time of moon with me to make one in so skipping a dialogue . *T. Night* i 5 213
You may as well Forbid the sea for to obey the moon . *W. Tale* i 2 427
Now the ship boring the moon with her main-mast . iii 3 93
The pale moon shines by night . . iv 3 16
Never gazed the moon Upon the water as he'll stand . iv 4 172
They say five moons were seen to-night; Four fixed, and the fifth did whirl about The other four . *K. John* iv 2 182
Ere the six years that he hath to spend Can change their moons *Rich. II.* i 3 220
The pale-faced moon looks bloody on the earth . ii 4 10
We that take purses go by the moon and the seven stars 1 *Hen. IV.* i 2 15
Let us be Diana's foresters, gentlemen of the shade, minions of the moon . . i 2 30
Being governed, as the sea is, by our noble and chaste mistress the moon i 2 32
The fortune of us that are the moon's men doth ebb and flow like the sea i 2 35
It were an easy leap, To pluck bright honour from the pale-faced moon i 3 202
The moon shines fair; you may away by night . iii 1 142
I in the clear sky of fame o'ershine you as much as the full moon doth the cinders of the element . 2 *Hen. IV.* iv 3 57
Presenteth them unto the gazing moon So many horrid ghosts *Hen. V.* iv Prol. 27
A good heart, Kate, is the sun and the moon; or rather the sun and not the moon; for it shines bright and never changes . v 2 171
And dogged York, that reaches at the moon 2 *Hen. VI.* iii 1 158
That I, being govern'd by the watery moon, May send forth plenteous tears to drown the world! . *Richard III.* ii 2 69
And anon he casts His eye against the moon . *Hen. VIII.* iii 2 118
His thinkings are below the moon, not worth His serious considering . iii 2 134
As true as steel, as plantage to the moon, As sun to day *Troi. and Cres.* iii 2 184
The sun borrows of the moon, when Diomed keeps his word . v 1 102
Threw their caps As they would hang them on the horns o' the moon *Coriolanus* i 1 217
Being moved, he will not spare to gird the gods.—Be-mock the modest moon . . i 1 261
My as fair as noble ladies,—and the moon, were she earthly, no nobler ii 1 108
Where against My grained ash an hundred times hath broke, And scarr'd the moon with splinters . iv 5 115
You are smelt Above the moon: we must be burnt for you . v 1 32
The noble sister of Publicola, The moon of Rome . . v 3 65
So pale did shine the moon on Pyramus . *T. Andron.* ii 3 231
My lord, I aim a mile beyond the moon; Your letter is with Jupiter by this . . iv 3 65
Arise, fair sun, and kill the envious moon . *Rom. and Jul.* ii 2 4
By yonder blessed moon I swear That tips with silver all these fruit-tree tops— O, swear not by the moon, the inconstant moon . ii 2 107
How came the noble Timon to this change?—As the moon does, by wanting light to give: But then renew I could not, like the moon; There were no suns to borrow of . *T. of Athens* iii 3 68
The moon's an arrant thief, And her pale fire she snatches from the sun iv 3 440
The sea's a thief, whose liquid surge resolves The moon into salt tears . iv 3 443
I had rather be a dog, and bay the moon, Than such a Roman *J. Cæsar* iv 3 27
How goes the night, boy?—The moon is down; I have not heard the clock.—And she goes down at twelve . *Macbeth* ii 1 2
Upon the corner of the moon There hangs a vaporous drop profound . iii 5 23
Gall of goat, and slips of yew Sliver'd in the moon's eclipse . iv 1 28
The chariest maid is prodigal enough, If she unmask her beauty to the moon: Virtue itself 'scapes not calumnious strokes . *Hamlet* i 3 37
What may this mean, That thou, dead corse, again in complete steel Revisit'st thus the glimpses of the moon . . i 4 53
And thirty dozen moons with borrow'd sheen About the world have times twelve thirties been . . iii 2 167
So many journeys may the sun and moon Make us again count o'er! . iii 2 171
I will delve one yard below their mines, And blow them at the moon . iii 4 209
Collected from all simples that have virtue Under the moon . iv 7 146
These late eclipses in the sun and moon portend no good to us . *Lear* i 2 112
We make guilty of our disasters the sun, the moon, and the stars . i 2 131
Mumbling of wicked charms, conjuring the moon To stand auspicious mistress . . ii 1 41
Though it be night, yet the moon shines . . ii 2 34
For all beneath the moon Would I not leap upright . iv 6 26
Methought his eyes Were two full moons; he had a thousand noses . iv 6 70
Packs and sects of great ones, That ebb and flow by the moon . v 3 19
Till now some nine moons wasted . *Othello* i 3 84
To follow still the changes of the moon With fresh suspicions . iii 3 178
Heaven stops the nose at it and the moon winks . . iv 2 77
Methinks it should be now a huge eclipse Of sun and moon . v 2 100
It is the very error of the moon; She comes more nearer earth than she was wont, And makes men mad . . v 2 109
Had superfluous kings for messengers Not many moons gone by *Ant. and Cleo.* iii 12 6
Moon and stars! Whip him . . . Whip him, fellows . iii 13 95
Alack, our terrene moon Is now eclipsed! . . iii 13 153
Be witness to me, O thou blessed moon, When men revolted shall upon record Bear hateful memory, poor Enobarbus did Before thy face repent! . . iv 9 7
Let me lodge Lichas on the horns o' the moon . . iv 12 45
There is nothing left remarkable Beneath the visiting moon . iv 15 68
His face was as the heavens; and therein stuck A sun and moon . v 2 80

Moon. I am marble-constant; now the fleeting moon No planet is of mine *Ant. and Cleo.* v 2 240
If Cæsar can hide the sun from us with a blanket, or put the moon in his pocket, we will pay him tribute for light . . *Cymbeline* iii 1 44
One twelve moons more she'll wear Diana's livery . . . *Pericles* ii 5 10
If King Pericles Come not home in twice six moons . . iii Gower 31
But sea-room, an the brine and cloudy billow kiss the moon, I care not iii 1 46
Such a piece of slaughter The sun and moon ne'er look'd upon! . iv 3 3
Moonbeam. To fan the moonbeams from his sleeping eyes *M. N. Dream* iii 1 176
Moon-calf. How camest thou to be the siege of this moon-calf? *Tempest* ii 2 111
I hid me under the dead moon-calf's gaberdine for fear of the storm . ii 2 115
How now, moon-calf! how does thine ague? . . . . ii 2 139
Moon-calf, speak once in thy life, if thou beest a good moon-calf . iii 2 25
Moonish. Being but a moonish youth . . . *As Y. Like It* iii 2 430
Moonlight. Thou hast by moonlight at her window sung *M. N. Dream* i 1 30
Meet me in the palace wood, a mile without the town, by moonlight . i 2 104
Ill met by moonlight, proud Titania . . . . . . ii 1 60
If you will patiently dance in our round And see our moonlight revels . ii 1 141
There is two hard things; that is, to bring the moonlight into a chamber iii 1 49
For, you know, Pyramus and Thisby meet by moonlight . . iii 1 51
How sweet the moonlight sleeps upon this bank! . . *Mer. of Venice* v 1 54
Shines the moon!—The moon! the sun: it is not moonlight now *T. of S.* iv 5 3
Moonshine. By moonshine do the green sour ringlets make *Tempest* v 1 37
You moonshine revellers, and shades of night . . *Mer. Wives* v 5 42
And turn him about, Till candles and starlight and moonshine be out . v 5 106
Thou now request'st but moonshine in the water . . *L. L. Lost* v 2 208
Look in the almanac; find out moonshine, find out moonshine *M. N. D.* iii 1 55
Say he comes to disfigure, or to present, the person of Moonshine . . iii 1 62
This man, with lanthorn, dog, and bush of thorn, Presenteth Moonshine v 1 137
By moonshine did these lovers think no scorn To meet at Ninus' tomb v 1 138
Let Lion, Moonshine, Wall, and lovers twain at large discourse . v 1 151
How chance Moonshine is gone before Thisbe comes back and finds her lover? . . . . v 1 318
Moonshine and Lion are left to bury the dead . . . . v 1 355
The collars of the moonshine's watery beams . . *Rom. and Jul.* i 4 62
I am some twelve or fourteen moonshines Lag of a brother . . *Lear* i 2 5
I'll make a sop o' the moonshine of you . . . . . ii 2 35
Moor. The Moor is with child by you, Launcelot.—It is much that the Moor should be more than reason . . . *Mer. of Venice* iii 5 42
Ah, my sweet Moor, sweeter to me than life! . . *T. Andron.* ii 3 51
Your Moor and you Are singled forth to try experiments . . ii 3 68
Why are you sequester'd from all your train, . . . Accompanied but with a barbarous Moor? . . . . ii 3 78
Now will I hence to seek my lovely Moor . . . . . ii 3 190
It was a black ill-favour'd fly, Like to the empress' Moor . . iii 2 67
As if it were the Moor Come hither purposely to poison me . . iii 2 72
We are not brought so low, But that between us we can kill a fly That comes in likeness of a coal-black Moor . . . . . iii 2 78
O, tell me, did you see Aaron the Moor? . . . . . iv 2 52
But if you brave the Moor, The chafed boar, the mountain lioness, The ocean swells not so as Aaron storms . . . . . iv 2 137
She laugh'd, and told the Moor he should not choose But give them . iv 3 74
Well are you fitted, had you but a Moor . . . . . v 1 85
The empress never wags But in her company there is a Moor . . v 2 88
In the emperor's court There is a queen, attended by a Moor . . v 2 105
Take you in this barbarous Moor, This ravenous tiger . . . v 3 4
An irreligious Moor, Chief architect and plotter of these woes . . v 3 121
Hither hale that misbelieving Moor . . . . . . v 3 143
See justice done on Aaron, that damn'd Moor . . . . v 3 201
Could you on this fair mountain leave to feed, And batten on this moor? Ha! have you eyes? . . . . *Hamlet* iii 4 67
Whether I in any just term am affined To love the Moor . *Othello* i 1 40
It is as sure as you are Roderigo, Were I the Moor, I would not be Iago i 1 57
Your daughter and the Moor are now making the beast with two backs i 1 117
To the gross clasps of a lascivious Moor . . . . . i 1 127
It seems not meet, nor wholesome to my place, To be produced—as, if I stay, I shall—Against the Moor . . . . i 1 148
Where didst thou see her? O unhappy girl! With the Moor, say'st thou? . . . . i 1 165
Do you know Where we may apprehend her and the Moor? . . i 1 178
Holla! stand there!—Signior, it is the Moor.—Down with him, thief! . i 2 57
Here comes Brabantio and the valiant Moor . . . . . i 3 47
Here is the man, this Moor, whom now, it seems, Your special mandate for the state-affairs Hath hither brought . . . . . . i 3 71
So much I challenge that I may profess Due to the Moor my lord . . i 3 189
Come hither, Moor: I here do give thee that with all my heart Which, but thou hast already, with all my heart I would keep from thee . i 3 192
That I did love the Moor to live with him, My downright violence and storm of fortunes May trumpet to the world . . . . i 3 249
Adieu, brave Moor; use Desdemona well.—Look to her, Moor . . i 3 292
It cannot be that Desdemona should long continue her love to the Moor i 3 349
These Moors are changeable in their wills . . . . . i 3 352
I hate the Moor: my cause is hearted; thine hath no less reason . i 3 373
I hate the Moor; And it is thought abroad, that 'twixt my sheets He has done my office . . . . i 3 392
The Moor is of a free and open nature, That thinks men honest . i 3 405
Cassio, Lieutenant to the warlike Moor Othello, Is come on shore: the Moor himself at sea . . . . ii 1 27
Yet he looks sadly, And prays the Moor be safe . . . . ii 1 33
Thanks, you the valiant of this warlike isle, That so approve the Moor! ii 1 44
The Moor! I know his trumpet.—'Tis truly so.—Let's meet him . . ii 1 179
Mark me with what violence she first loved the Moor, but for bragging ii 1 225
Sympathy in years, manners and beauties; all which the Moor is defective in . . . . ii 1 233
Begin to heave the gorge, disrelish and abhor the Moor . . . ii 1 237
If she had been blessed, she would never have loved the Moor. Blessed pudding! . . . . ii 1 258
The Moor, howbeit that I endure him not, Is of a . . . noble nature . ii 1 297
For that I do suspect the lusty Moor Hath leap'd into my seat . . ii 1 304
Yet that I put the Moor At least into a jealousy . . . . ii 1 309
I'll have our Michael Cassio on the hip, Abuse him to the Moor . . ii 1 315
Make the Moor thank me, love me and reward me, For making him egregiously an ass . . . . ii 1 317
'Tis great pity that the noble Moor Should hazard such a place as his own second With one of an ingraft infirmity . . . . . ii 3 143
It were an honest action to say So to the Moor.—Not I, for this fair island . . . . ii 3 147
Probal to thinking and indeed the course To win the Moor again . . ii 3 345
And then for her To win the Moor—were't to renounce his baptism . ii 3 349
And she for him pleads strongly to the Moor . . . . . ii 3 361

Moor. And by how much she strives to do him good, She shall undo her credit with the Moor . . . . *Othello* ii 3 365
I'll set her on; Myself the while to draw the Moor apart . . . ii 3 391
I'll devise a mean to draw the Moor Out of the way . . . . iii 1 39
The Moor replies, That he you hurt is of great fame in Cyprus . . iii 1 47
This was her first remembrance from the Moor . . . . . iii 3 291
What handkerchief! Why, that the Moor first gave to Desdemona . iii 3 308
The Moor already changes with my poison . . . . . . iii 3 325
And then Cried 'Cursed fate that gave thee to the Moor!' . . . iii 3 426
But my noble Moor Is true of mind and made of no such baseness . iii 4 26
Is this the noble Moor whom our full senate Call all in all sufficient? . iv 1 275
The Moor's abused by some most villanous knave, Some base notorious knave . . . . iv 2 139
Some such squire he was That turn'd your wit the seamy side without, And made you to suspect me with the Moor . . . . . iv 2 147
The Moor May unfold me to him; there stand I in much peril . . v 1 20
Help! help, ho! help! The Moor hath kill'd my mistress! Murder! . v 2 167
O thou dull Moor! that handkerchief thou speak'st of I found by fortune v 2 225
Take you this weapon, Which I have here recover'd from the Moor . v 2 240
Moor, she was chaste; she loved thee, cruel Moor . . . . v 2 249
And seize upon the fortunes of the Moor, For they succeed on you . v 2 366
Moor-ditch. What sayest thou to a hare, or the melancholy of Moor-ditch?—Thou hast the most unsavoury similes . . 1 *Hen. IV.* i 2 88
Moorfields. Is this Moorfields to muster in? . . . . *Hen. VIII.* v 4 33
Moorship. And I—God bless the mark!—his Moorship's ancient . *Othello* i 1 33
Mop. Each one, tripping on his toe, Will be here with mop and mow *Temp.* iv 1 47
Mope. To mope with his fat-brained followers . . . . *Hen. V.* iii 7 143
Or but a sickly part of one true sense Could not so mope . . *Hamlet* iii 4 81
Moping. And were brought moping hither . . . . . *Tempest* v 1 240
Mopping. Flibbertigibbet, of mopping and mowing . . . . *Lear* iv 1 64
Mopsa must be your mistress: marry, garlic, To mend her kissing! *W. Tale* iv 4 162
If I were not in love with Mopsa, thou shouldst take no money of me iv 4 233
Moral. To apply a moral medicine to a mortifying mischief . *Much Ado* i 3 13
Benedictus! why Benedictus? you have some moral in this Benedictus.—Moral! no, by my troth, I have no moral meaning . . . . iii 4 78
But no man's virtue nor sufficiency To be so moral when he shall endure The like himself . . . . v 1 30
There's the moral. Now the l'envoy.—I will add the l'envoy. Say the moral again.—The fox, the ape, the humble-bee . . *L. L. Lost* iii 1 87
Now will I begin your moral, and do you follow with my l'envoy . . iii 1 94
A good moral, my lord: it is not enough to speak, but to speak true *M. N. Dream* v 1 120
When I did hear The motley fool thus moral on the time *As Y. Like It* ii 7 29
We do admire This virtue and this moral discipline . . *T. of Shrew* i 1 30
Has left me here behind, to expound the meaning or moral of his signs iv 4 79
Thy father's moral parts Mayst thou inherit too! . . . *All's Well* i 2 21
Mark, silent king, the moral of this sport . . . . *Richard II.* iv 1 290
She [Fortune] is painted also with a wheel, to signify to you, which is the moral of it, that she is turning . . . . *Hen. V.* iii 6 36
Fortune is an excellent moral . . . . iii 6 40
Thus may we gather honey from the weed, And make a moral of the devil himself . . . . iv 1 12
This moral ties me over to time and a hot summer . . . . v 2 339
Whom Aristotle thought Unfit to hear moral philosophy *Troi. and Cres.* ii 2 167
These moral laws Of nature and of nations speak aloud . . . . ii 2 184
The moral of my wit Is 'plain and true;' there's all the reach of it . iv 4 109
A thousand moral paintings I can show . . . . *T. of Athens* i 1 90
Whiles thou, a moral fool, sit'st still, and criest 'Alack' . . *Lear* iv 2 58
A pretty moral . . . . *Pericles* ii 1 39
Moraler. Come, you are too severe a moraler . . . . *Othello* ii 3 301
Morality. I had as lief have the foppery of freedom as the morality of imprisonment . . . . *Meas. for Meas.* i 2 138
Moralize. What said Jacques? Did he not moralize? . *As Y. Like It* ii 1 44
I pray thee, moralize them . . . . *T. of Shrew* iv 4 81
I moralize two meanings in one word . . . . *Richard III.* iii 1 83
Mordake. Of prisoners, Hotspur took Mordake the Earl of Fife 1 *Hen. IV.* i 1 71
And sends me word, I shall have none but Mordake Earl of Fife . . i 1 95
He is there too, and one Mordake, and a thousand blue-caps more . ii 4 391
But there is Mordake, Vernon, Lord Harry Percy . . . . . iv 4 24
More. None that I more love than myself . . . . . . *Tempest* i 1 22
We will not hand a rope more . . . . i 1 25
More to know Did never meddle with my thoughts . . . . . i 2 21
Made thee more profit Than other princesses can that have more time . i 2 172
Thou think'st there is no more such shapes as he . . . . i 2 478
I am more serious than my custom: you Must be so too . . . ii 1 219
Lead the way without any more talking . . . . ii 2 178
O, she is Ten times more gentle than her father's crabbed . . . iii 1 8
Nor have I seen More that I may call men than you . . . . iii 1 51
All the more it seeks to hide itself, The bigger bulk it shows . . iii 1 80
But my rejoicing At nothing can be more . . . . iii 1 94
Their manners are more gentle-kind than of Our human generation . iii 3 32
Be more abstemious, Or else, good night your vow! . . . . iv 1 53
That's more to me than my wetting . . . . iv 1 211
Look, sir! here is more of us . . . . v 1 216
No more of stay! to-morrow thou must go . . . . *T. G. of Ver.* i 3 75
I would have had them writ more movingly . . . . . . ii 1 134
You are not young, no more am I . . . . . . *Mer. Wives* ii 1 7
And what he gets more of her than sharp words, let it lie on my head . ii 1 190
Moe reasons for this action At our more leisure shall I render *M. for M.* i 3 49
I speak not as desiring more; But rather wishing a more strict restraint i 4 3
If you should need a pin, You could not with more tame a tongue desire it . . . . ii 2 46
A young man More fit to do another such offence Than die for this . ii 3 14
Go to; no more words . . . . iii 2 218
A man that apprehends death no more dreadfully but as a drunken sleep iv 2 149
If he be less, he's nothing; but he's more, Had I more name for badness v 1 59
Charges she more than me?—Not that I know . . . . . . v 1 200
And, for the most, become much more the better For being a little bad v 1 445
O, let me say no more! Gather the sequel by that went before *C. of Er.* i 1 95
Why should their [men's] liberty than ours be more? . . . . ii 1 10
Men, more divine, the masters of all these, Lords of the wide world . ii 1 20
Wrong not that wrong with a more contempt . . . . . . ii 2 174
More authority, dear boy, name more . . . . . *L. L. Lost* i 2 70
I am all these three.—And three times as much more, and yet nothing at all . . . . iii 1 48
The moon was a month old when Adam was no more . . . . iv 2 40
There is two or three lords and ladies more married . *M. N. Dream* iv 2 17
And to trouble you with no more suit . . . . *Mer. of Venice* i 2 112
She is indeed more than I took her for . . . . iii 5 46
Two things provided more . . . . iv 1 386

More. Giving thy sum of more To that which had too much *As Y. Like It* ii 1 48
I never loved my brother in my life.—More villain thou . . . iii 1 15
So much is a horn more precious than to want . . . iii 3 63
By so much the more shall I to-morrow be at the height of heart-heaviness v 2 49
I have no more; And she can have no more than all I have *T. of Shrew* ii 1 383
A horse and a man Is more than one, And yet not many . . . iii 2 87
The more my wrong, the more his spite appears . . . iv 3 2
There is more owing her than is paid; and more shall be paid *All's Well* i 3 108
I was very late more near her than I think she wished me . . i 3 110
I care no more for than I do for heaven . . . . i 3 170
More should I question thee, and more I must, Though more to know could not be more to trust . . . . ii 1 208
Go to, you're a dry fool; I'll no more of you . . *T. Night* i 5 45
A murderous guilt shows not itself more soon Than love that would seem hid . . . . iii 1 159
More matter for a May morning . . . . . . iii 4 156
More than I love these eyes, more than my life, More, by all mores v 1 138
Inform yourselves We need no more of your advice . . *W. Tale* ii 1 168
Be prosperous In more than this deed does require! . . . ii 3 190
And he, and more Than he, and men, the earth, the heavens, and all iv 4 381
Here is that gold I have: I'll make it as much more . . . iv 4 838
So much the more our carver's excellence . . . . . v 3 30
I conjure thee but slowly; run more fast . . . *K. John* iv 2 269
He that no more must say is listen'd more . . . *Richard II.* ii 1 9
More are men's ends mark'd than their lives before . . . ii 1 11
This and much more, much more than twice all this . . . iii 1 28
More is to be said and to be done Than out of anger can be uttered 1 *Hen. IV.* i 1 106
No more of that, Hal, an thou lovest me! . . . . ii 4 312
Whereof a little More than a little is by much too much . . . iii 2 73
It lends a lustre and more great opinion, A larger dare . . . iv 1 77
Make less thy body hence, and more thy grace . 2 *Hen. IV.* v 5 56
And on his more advice we pardon him . . . . . *Hen. V.* ii 2 43
Once more unto the breach, dear friends, once more . . . iii 1 1
More will I do; Though all that I can do is nothing worth . . iv 1 319
I find thou art no less than fame hath bruited And more than may be gather'd by thy shape . . . . . 1 *Hen. VI.* ii 3 69
More than I seem, and less than I was born to . 3 *Hen. VI.* iii 1 56
The more we stay, the stronger grows our foe.—The more I stay, the more I'll succour thee . . . . iii 3 40
Add water to the sea And give more strength to that which hath too much . . . . v 4 9
But for our hearts, he knows no more of mine, Than I of yours; Nor I no more of his, than you of mine . . . *Richard III.* iii 4 11
There is no more but so: say it is done, And I will love thee . iv 2 81
More than I have said, loving countrymen, The leisure and enforcement of the time Forbids to dwell upon . . . . . . v 3 237
I do not know What kind of my obedience I should tender; More than my all is nothing . . . . . *Hen. VIII.* ii 3 67
Sir Thomas More is chosen Lord Chancellor in your place . . iii 2 393
I'll ha' more. An ordinary groom is for such payment. I will have more v 1 173
Said I for this, the girl was like to him? I will have more, or else unsay't. . . . . v 1 175
What is he more than another?—No more than what he thinks he is.—Is he so much? . . . . *Troi. and Cres.* ii 3 151
I would have been much more a fresher man, Had I expected thee v 6 20
For your voices have Done many things, some less, some more *Coriolanus* ii 3 137
To beg of thee, it is my more dishonour Than thou of them . . iii 2 124
But I thought there was more in him than I could think . . iv 5 167
Some death more long in spectatorship, and crueller in suffering . v 2 71
One more, most welcome, makes my number more . *Rom. and Jul.* i 2 23
But no more deep will I endart mine eye Than your consent . . i 3 98
Pale with grief, That thou her maid art far more fair than she . ii 2 6
Shall I hear more, or shall I speak at this? . . . . ii 2 37
The more I give to thee, The more I have . . . . . ii 2 134
Conceit, more rich in matter than in words, Brags of his substance . ii 6 30
More honourable state, more courtship lives In carrion-flies than Romeo iii 3 34
More light and light it grows.—More light and light; more dark and dark our woes! . . . . iii 5 35
And more than that I know thee, I not desire to know . *T. of Athens* iv 3 57
More counsel with more money, bounteous Timon . . . iv 3 167
When crouching marrow in the bearer strong Cries of itself 'No more' v 4 10
For Mark Antony, think not of him; For he can do no more than Cæsar's arm When Cæsar's head is off . . . *J. Cæsar* ii 1 182
Ingratitude, more strong than traitors' arms . . . . iii 2 189
And, at more time, The interim having weigh'd it, let us speak *Macbeth* i 3 153
Only I have left to say, More is thy due than more than all can pay i 4 21
They have more in them than mortal knowledge . . . . i 5 3
Then you were a man; And, to be more than what you were, you would Be so much more the man . . . . i 7 50
My poor country Shall have more vices than it had before, More suffer and more sundry ways than ever . . . . . . iv 3 47
No more.—No more but so?—Think it no more . . . *Hamlet* i 3 9
And more above, hath his solicitings . . . All given to mine ear . ii 2 126
The less they deserve, the more merit is in your bounty . . ii 2 557
Did these bones cost no more the breeding, but to play at loggats with 'em? v 1 100
Thy mother's poison'd: I can no more: the king, the king's to blame v 2 331
In this plainness Harbour more craft and more corrupter ends . *Lear* ii 2 108
Have you no more to say?—Few words, but, to effect, more than all yet iii 1 51
What you have charged me with, that have I done; And more, much more v 3 163
I am no less in blood than thou art, Edmund; If more, the more thou hast wrong'd me . . . . v 3 168
You look as you had something more to say . . . . v 3 201
To amplify too much, would make much more, And top extremity . v 3 206
Let's have no more of this; let's to our affairs.—Forgive us our sins! *Oth.* ii 3 115
More of this matter cannot I report: But men are men . . . ii 3 240
She holds it a vice in her goodness not to do more than she is requested ii 3 327
Nay, yet there's more in this: I prithee, speak to me as to thy thinkings . . . . iii 3 130
If more thou dost perceive, let me know more; Set on thy wife to observe iii 3 239
Why did I marry? This honest creature doubtless Sees and knows more, much more, than he unfolds . . . . iii 3 243
One more, one more. Be thus when thou art dead, and I will kill thee, And love thee after . . . . v 2 17
One more, and this the last: So sweet was ne'er so fatal . . v 2 19
O Spartan dog, More fell than anguish, hunger, or the sea! . . v 2 362
Add more, From thine invention, offers . . *Ant. and Cleo.* iii 12 28
There cannot be a pinch in death More sharp than this is . *Cymbeline* i 1 131
I am not vexed more at any thing in the earth: a pox on't! . . ii 1 19
No less young, more strong, more strong, not beneath him in fortunes . . iv 1 11

More. To shame the guise o' the world, I will begin The fashion, less without and more within . . . . . . *Cymbeline* v 1 33
Is there more?—More, sir, and worse . . . . . . v 5 48
Which doth give me A more content in course of true delight *Pericles* iii 2 39
More and less. Of that and all the progress, more and less, Resolvedly more leisure shall express . . . . . . *All's Well* v 3 332
The more and less came in with cap and knee . . 1 *Hen. IV.* iv 3 68
And more and less do flock to follow him . . . 2 *Hen. IV.* i 1 209
Both more and less have given him the revolt . . . *Macbeth* v 4 12
So tell him, with the occurrents, more and less . . *Hamlet* v 2 368
More and more. You do advance your cunning more and more *M. N. Dream* iii 2 128
Came more and more and fought on part and part . *Rom. and Jul.* i 1 121
I love thee more and more: think more and more What's best to ask *Cymbeline* v 5 109
More better. Nor that I am more better Than Prospero . . *Tempest* i 2 19
For the more better assurance, tell them . . *M. N. Dream* iii 1 21
More braver. The Duke of Milan And his more braver daughter could control thee, If now 'twere fit to do't . . . . . *Tempest* i 2 439
More corrupter. In this plainness Harbour more craft and more corrupter ends . . . . *Lear* ii 2 108
More elder. How much more elder art thou than thy looks! *Mer. of Ven.* iv 1 251
More fairer than fair, beautiful than beauteous . . *L. L. Lost* iv 1 62
What in me was purchased, Falls upon thee in a more fairer sort 2 *Hen. IV.* iv 5 201
More fitter. Dispose of her To some more fitter place *Meas. for Meas.* ii 2 17
More harder. This hard house—More harder than the stones whereof 'tis raised . . . . *Lear* iii 2 64
More-having. And my more-having would be as a sauce To make me hunger more . . . . *Macbeth* iv 3 81
More headier. And am fall'n out with my more headier will . *Lear* ii 4 111
More hotter. His fisnomy is more hotter in France . *All's Well* iv 5 42
More kinder. Where he shall find The unkindest beast more kinder than mankind . . . . *T. of Athens* iv 1 36
More larger. With a more larger list of sceptres . *Ant. and Cleo.* iii 6 76
More mightier. Instruments of some more mightier member *Meas. for Meas.* v 1 237
More, more. And more, more strong, then lesser is my fear, I shall indue you with . . . . *K. John* iv 2 42
And more, More fearful, is deliver'd.—What more fearful? *Coriolanus* iv 6 62
If there be more, more woeful, hold it in . . . . *Lear* v 3 202
More nearer. Come you more nearer . . . . . *Hamlet* ii 1 11
She comes more nearer earth than she was wont . . *Othello* v 2 110
More or less. If they speak more or less than truth, they are villains and the sons of darkness . . . . 1 *Hen. IV.* ii 4 190
Well, more or less, or ne'er a whit at all . . *T. Andron.* iv 2 53
Without debatement further, more or less . . . *Hamlet* v 2 45
More proudlier. He bears himself more proudlier, Even to my person, than I thought he would . . . . . . *Coriolanus* iv 7 8
More rawer. Why do we wrap the gentleman in our more rawer breath? *Hamlet* v 2 129
More richer. Your wisdom should show itself more richer . . iii 2 316
I am sure, my love's More richer than my tongue . . . *Lear* i 1 80
More safer. Throws a more safer voice on you . . . *Othello* i 3 226
More sharper than your swords . . . . . . *Hen. V.* iii 5 39
More softer. There is no lady of more softer bowels *Troi. and Cres.* ii 2 11
More sounder. A more sounder instance, come *As Y. Like It* iii 2 62
More stronger. There is no English soul More stronger to direct you than yourself . . . . *Hen. VIII.* i 1 147
More wider. Divides more wider than the sky and earth *Troi. and Cres.* v 2 149
This is no proof, Without more wider and more overt test . *Othello* i 3 107
More worse. My sister may receive it much more worse . . *Lear* ii 2 155
More worthier. Avert your liking a more worthier way . . . i 1 214
As a walled town is more worthier than a village . *As Y. Like It* iii 3 60
I'll give my reasons, More worthier than their voices . *Coriolanus* iii 1 120
Moreover, God saw him when he was hid in the garden . *Much Ado* v 1 181
They have committed false report; moreover, they have spoken untruths v 1 220
Yes, madam, and moreover Some thousand verses . *L. L. Lost* v 2 49
Adding thereto moreover That he would wed me, or else die my lover . v 2 446
Tell me, moreover, hast thou sounded him? . . *Richard II.* i 1 8
And there is also moreover a river at Monmouth . . *Hen. V.* iv 7 28
And am moreover suitor that I may Produce his body . *J. Cæsar* iii 1 227
Moreover that we much did long to see you . . . *Hamlet* ii 2 2
Fish for fasting-days, and moreo'er puddings and flap-jacks *Pericles* ii 1 86
Morgan. He hath confessed himself to Morgan, whom he supposes to be a friar . . . . *All's Well* iv 3 125
Myself, Belarius, that am Morgan call'd, They take for natural father *Cymbeline* iii 3 106
I, old Morgan, Am that Belarius whom you sometime banish'd . v 5 332
Morisco. I have seen Him caper upright like a wild Morisco 2 *Hen. VI.* iii 1 365
Morn. And in the morn I'll bring you to your ship . . . *Tempest* v 1 306
And so, good rest.—As wretches have o'ernight That wait for execution in the morn . . . . *T. G. of Ver.* iv 2 134
I'll make it my morn prayer . . . . . *Meas. for Meas.* ii 4 71
Those eyes, the break of day, Lights that do mislead the morn . iv 1 4
I beseech you, let it be proclaimed betimes i' the morn . . . iv 4 18
But the next morn betimes, His purpose surfeiting, he sends a warrant For my poor brother's head . . . . v 1 101
That certain he would fight: yea From morn till night . *L. L. Lost* v 2 660
To do observance to a morn of May . . . . *M. N. Dream* i 1 167
I fear we shall out-sleep the coming morn . . . . . v 1 372
She is not hot, but temperate as the morn . . *T. of Shrew* ii 1 296
Have in these parts from morn till even fought . . *Hen. V.* iii 1 20
I gave a noble to the priest The morn that I was wedded . 1 *Hen. VI.* v 4 24
Be it in the morn, When every one will give the time of day 2 *Hen. VI.* iii 1 13
That right for right Hath dimm'd your infant morn to aged night *Richard III.* iv 4 16
The early village-cock Hath twice done salutation to the morn . v 3 210
Dear, trouble not yourself: the morn is cold . . *Troi. and Cres.* iv 2 1
As when the golden sun salutes the morn . . . *T. Andron.* ii 1 5
The morn is bright and grey, The fields are fragrant, and the woods are green . . . . ii 2 1
The grey-eyed morn smiles on the frowning night . *Rom. and Jul.* ii 3 1
It was the lark, the herald of the morn, No nightingale . . . iii 5 6
What day is that?—Marry, my child, early next Thursday morn . . iii 5 113
Each new morn New widows howl, new orphans cry . . *Macbeth* iv 3 4
The cock, that is the trumpet to the morn . . . . *Hamlet* i 1 150
But, look, the morn, in russet mantle clad, Walks o'er the dew of yon high eastward hill . . . . i 1 166
In the morn and liquid dew of youth Contagious blastments are most imminent . . . . i 3 41

Morn. Why, then, to-morrow night; or Tuesday morn; On Tuesday noon, or night; on Wednesday morn: I prithee, name the time *Othello* iii 3 60
That night I laugh'd him into patience: and next morn, Ere the ninth hour, I drunk him to his bed . . . *Ant. and Cleo.* ii 5 20
The morn is fair. Good morrow, general . . . iv 4 24
The night Is shiny; and they say we shall embattle By the second hour i' the morn . . . . iv 9 4
Or have charged him, At the sixth hour of morn, at noon, at midnight, To encounter me with orisons . . . *Cymbeline* i 3 31
The night to the owl and morn to the lark less welcome . iii 6 94
'Tis the ninth hour o' the morn.—Brother, farewell.—I wish ye sport . iv 2 30
Early in blustering morn this lady was Thrown upon this shore *Pericles* v 3 22
Morn-dew. I was of late as petty to his ends As is the morn-dew on the myrtle-leaf To his grand sea . . . . . *Ant. and Cleo.* iii 12 9
Morning. 'Tis fresh morning with me When you are by at night *Tempest* iii 1 33
As the morning steals upon the night, Melting the darkness . . v 1 65
Last morning you could not see to wipe my shoes . *T. G. of Ver.* ii 1 86
I had myself twenty angels given me this morning . *Mer. Wives* ii 2 74
And one, I tell you, that will not miss you morning nor evening prayer ii 2 102
And hath sent your worship a morning's draught of sack . . ii 2 153
I do invite you to-morrow morning to my house to breakfast . iii 3 246
Her husband goes this morning a-birding; she desires you once more to come to her . . . . iii 5 46
See that Claudio Be executed by nine to-morrow morning *Meas. for Meas.* ii 1 34
To-morrow morning are to die Claudio and Barnardine . . iv 2 7
You shall hear more ere morning.—Happily You something know . iv 2 98
He that drinks all night, and is hanged betimes in the morning, may sleep the sounder all the next day . . . iv 3 49
There died this morning of a cruel fever One Ragozine . . iv 3 74
Good morning to you, fair and gracious daughter.—The better, given me by so holy a man . . . . . . iv 3 116
I am at him upon my knees every morning and evening . *Much Ado* ii 1 31
A' brushes his hat o' mornings; what should that bode? . . iii 2 42
Swore he would meet her, as he was appointed, next morning at the temple . . . . iii 3 172
We would have them this morning examined before your worship . iii 5 51
He swore a thing to me on Monday night, which he forswore on Tuesday morning . . . . v 1 170
To-morrow morning come you to my house . . . . v 1 295
Until to-morrow morning, lords, farewell . . . . v 1 337
I will come to your worship to-morrow morning . *L. L. Lost* iii 1 162
I with the morning's love have oft made sport . *M. N. Dream* iii 2 389
For the morning now is something worn . . . . iv 1 187
Very vilely in the morning, when he is sober . *Mer. of Venice* i 2 92
On Black-Monday last at six o'clock i' the morning . . ii 5 26
He plies the duke at morning and at night . . . iii 2 279
In the morning early will we both Fly toward Belmont . . iv 1 456
Good news: my master will be here ere morning . . . v 1 48
It is almost morning, And yet I am sure you are not satisfied Of these events . . . . v 1 295
Saw her a-bed, and in the morning early They found the bed untreasured of their mistress . . . . . *As Y. Like It* ii 2 6
But why did he swear he would come this morning, and comes not? . iii 4 21
To be whipped at the high cross every morning . . *T. of Shrew* i 1 137
The morning wears, 'tis time we were at church . . iii 2 113
His lordship will next morning for France . . . *All's Well* iv 3 91
If the business be of any difficulty, and this morning your departure hence, it requires haste of your lordship . . . iv 3 108
It shall be done to-morrow morning, if I live . . *T. Night* iii 4 116
More matter for a May morning . . . . . iii 4 156
His eyes were set at eight i' the morning . . . . v 1 205
I should have given't you to-day morning . . . . v 1 294
To-morrow morning let us meet him then . . . *K. John* iv 3 18
A purse of gold most resolutely snatched on Monday night and most dissolutely spent on Tuesday morning . . . 1 *Hen. IV.* i 2 40
My lads, to-morrow morning, by four o'clock, early at Gadshill! . i 2 139
There be four of us here have ta'en a thousand pound this day morning ii 4 176
There let him sleep till day. I'll to the court in the morning . ii 4 595
Be with me betimes in the morning; and so, good morrow . . ii 4 600
And in the morning early shall my uncle Bring him our purposes . iv 3 110
Will it never be morning? . . . . . *Hen. V.* iii 7 6
I would it were morning; for I would fain be about the ears of the English . . . . iii 7 90
The Dauphin longs for morning.—He longs to eat the English . iii 7 98
The clocks do toll, And the third hour of drowsy morning name . iv Prol. 16
Sit patiently and inly ruminate The morning's danger . . iv Prol. 25
Is not that the morning which breaks yonder?—I think it be . iv 1 88
I'll requite it With sweet rehearsal of my morning's dream . 2 *Hen. VI.* i 2 24
See how the morning opes her golden gates, And takes her farewell of the glorious sun! . . . . . . 3 *Hen. VI.* ii 1 21
Like to the morning's war, When dying clouds contend with growing light . . . . ii 5 1
Sorrow breaks seasons and reposing hours, Makes the night morning, and the noon-tide night . . . . *Richard III.* i 4 77
By the second hour in the morning Desire the earl to see me . . v 3 31
Prepare thy battle early in the morning . . . . v 3 88
How far into the morning is it, lords?—Upon the stroke of four . v 3 234
This found I on my tent this morning . . . . v 3 303
You he bade Attend him here this morning . . . *Hen. VIII.* iii 2 82
This morning Papers of state he sent me to peruse, As I required . iii 2 120
Hath commanded To-morrow morning to the council-board He be convented . . . . v 1 51
Have moved us and our council, that you shall This morning come before us . . . . v 1 101
Keep comfort to you; and this morning see You do appear before them v 1 144
'Tis as much impossible . . . as 'tis to make 'em sleep On May-day morning . . . . v 4 15
When were you at Ilium?—This morning . . *Troi. and Cres.* i 2 47
Modest as morning when she coldly eyes The youthful Phœbus . i 3 229
To-morrow morning call some knight to arms That hath a stomach . ii 1 136
Whose youth and freshness Wrinkles Apollo's, and makes stale the morning . . . . ii 2 79
Leave! an you take leave till to-morrow morning,— Pray you, content you . . . . iii 2 150
It is great morning . . . . . iv 3 1; *Cymbeline* iv 2 61
How have we spent this morning! The prince must think me tardy and remiss . . . . *Troi. and Cres.* iv 4 142
And I do stand engaged to many Greeks, Even in the faith of valour, to appear This morning to them . . . . v 3 70

Morning. One that converses more with the buttock of the night than with the forehead of the morning . . . *Coriolanus* ii 1 57
The veins unfill'd, our blood is cold, and then We pout upon the morning v 1 52
You have pray'd well to-day: This morning for ten thousand of your throats I'ld not have given a doit . . . . . v 4 59
Many a morning hath he there been seen, With tears augmenting the fresh morning's dew . . . . . *Rom. and Jul.* i 1 137
'Tis almost morning; I would have thee gone . . . ii 2 177
Yon grey is not the morning's eye, 'Tis but the pale reflex of Cynthia's brow . . . . iii 5 19
When the bridegroom in the morning comes To rouse thee from thy bed, there art thou dead . . . . iv 1 107
I'll have this knot knit up to-morrow morning . . . . iv 2 24
Shall I be married then to-morrow morning? No, no: this shall forbid it . . . . iv 3 22
Have I thought long to see this morning's face, And doth it give me such a sight as this? . . . . iv 5 41
Take this letter; early in the morning See thou deliver it . . v 3 23
What misadventure is so early up, That calls our person from our morning's rest?—What should it be? . . . . . v 3 189
A glooming peace this morning with it brings . . . . v 3 305
Honest friend, I prithee, but repair to me next morning *T. of Athens* ii 2 25
The morning comes upon's: we'll leave you, Brutus . *J. Cæsar* ii 1 221
Wherefore rise you now? It is not for your health thus to commit Your weak condition to the raw cold morning . . . ii 1 236
Is Brutus sick? and is it physical To walk unbraced and suck up the humours Of the dank morning? . . . . . . ii 1 263
This morning are they fled away and gone . . . . v 1 84
What is the night?—Almost at odds with morning, which is which *Macb.* iii 4 127
Get you gone, And at the pit of Acheron Meet me i' the morning . . iii 5 16
I this morning know Where we shall find him most conveniently *Hamlet* i 1 174
You say right, sir: o' Monday morning; 'twas so indeed . . ii 2 407
To-morrow is Saint Valentine's day, All in the morning betime . iv 5 49
We'll go to supper i' the morning. So, so, so.—And I'll go to bed at noon . . . . *Lear* iii 6 91
At nine i' the morning here we'll meet again . . . *Othello* i 3 280
Where shall we meet i' the morning?—At my lodging . . i 3 381
In the morning I will beseech the virtuous Desdemona to undertake for me . . . . ii 3 336
By the mass, 'tis morning; Pleasure and action make the hours seem short . . . . ii 3 384
And did want Of what I was i' the morning . . *Ant. and Cleo.* ii 2 77
This morning, like the spirit of a youth That means to be of note, begins betimes . . . . iv 4 26
The soldier That has this morning left thee would have still Follow'd thy heels.—Who's gone this morning? . . . . . iv 5 5
It's almost morning, is't not?—Day, my lord . . *Cymbeline* ii 3 10
I am advised to give her music o' mornings; they say it will penetrate ii 3 13
When you have given good morning to your mistress, Attend the queen ii 3 66
I do think I saw't this morning . . . . . . ii 3 150
This gate Instructs you how to adore the heavens and bows you To a morning's holy office . . . . iii 3 4
Morning air. Methinks I scent the morning air . . . *Hamlet* i 5 58
Morning cock. But even then the morning cock crew loud, And at the sound it shrunk in haste away, And vanish'd from our sight . . i 2 218
Morning dew. Their heads are hung With ears that sweep away the morning dew . . . . *M. N. Dream* iv 1 126
As fresh as morning dew distill'd on flowers . . *T. Andron.* ii 3 201
Morning drops. So sweet a kiss the golden sun gives not To those fresh morning drops upon the rose . . . *L. L. Lost* iv 3 27
Morning face. The whining school-boy, with his satchel And shining morning face . . . . *As Y. Like It* ii 7 146
Morning field. Yon island carrions, desperate of their bones, Ill-favouredly become the morning field . . . *Hen. V.* iv 2 40
Morning lark. I do hear the morning lark . . *M. N. Dream* iv 1 99
Thou hast hawks will soar Above the morning lark . *T. of Shrew* Ind. 2 46
Morning roses. As clear As morning roses newly wash'd with dew . ii 1 174
Morning story. Here begins his morning story right . *Com. of Errors* v 1 356
Morning sun. When the morning sun shall raise his car . 3 *Hen. VI.* iv 7 80
Morning taste. Will the cold brook, Candied with ice, caudle thy morning taste, To cure thy o'er-night's surfeit? . . *T. of Athens* iv 3 226
Morocco. And there is a forerunner come from a fifth, the Prince of Morocco . . . . *Mer. of Venice* i 2 137
Pause there, Morocco, And weigh thy value with an even hand . ii 7 24
Morris. The nine men's morris is fill'd up with mud . *M. N. Dream* ii 1 98
As a pancake for Shrove Tuesday, a morris for May-day . . *All's Well* ii 2 25
Morris-dance. Busied with a Whitsun morris-dance . . *Hen. V.* ii 4 25
Morris-pike. He that sets up his rest to do more exploits with his mace than a morris-pike . . . . . . *Com. of Errors* iv 3 28
Morrow. A thousand times good morrow . . . *T. G. of Ver.* iv 3 6
Give your worship good morrow . . . . . *Mer. Wives* ii 2 34
We must starve our sight From lovers' food till morrow deep midnight *M. N. Dream* i 1 223
But what a fool am I to chat with you, When I should bid good morrow to my bride! . . . . *T. of Shrew* iii 2 124
Shorten my days thou canst with sullen sorrow, And pluck nights from me, but not lend a morrow . . . . . *Richard II.* i 3 228
Be with me betimes in the morning; and so, good morrow . 1 *Hen. IV.* ii 4 601
Many good morrows to your majesty!—Is it good morrow? 2 *Hen. IV.* iii 1 32
Bids them good morrow with a modest smile . . *Hen. V.* iv Prol. 33
Do my good morrow to them, and anon Desire them all to my pavilion iv 1 26
There's some conceit or other likes him well, When he doth bid good morrow with such a spirit . . . . . *Richard III.* iii 4 52
Good morrow.—Ay, and good next day too . . *Troi. and Cres.* iii 3 68
I would not buy Their mercy . . . ; Nor check my courage for what they can give, To have't with saying 'Good morrow' *Coriolanus* iii 3 93
Good morrow, cousin.—Is the day so young?—But new struck nine *Rom. and Jul.* i 1 166
Parting is such sweet sorrow, That I shall say good night till it be morrow . . . . ii 2 186
It argues a distemper'd head So soon to bid good morrow to thy bed ii 3 34
God ye good morrow, gentlemen.—God ye good den, fair gentlewoman ii 4 115
Good morrow to thee, gentle Apemantus!—Till I be gentle, stay thou for thy good morrow . . . . *T. of Athens* i 1 178
Vouchsafe good morrow from a feeble tongue . . *J. Cæsar* ii 1 313
And when goes hence?—To-morrow, as he purposes.—O, never Shall sun that morrow see! . . . . *Macbeth* i 5 62
Morsel. To the perpetual wink for aye might put This ancient morsel *Tempest* ii 1 286
How doth my dear morsel, thy mistress? . . . *Meas. for Meas.* iii 2 56

Morsel. From forth this morsel of dead royalty . . . . *K. John* iv 3 143
Now comes in the sweetest morsel of the night . . . 2 *Hen. IV.* ii 4 396
Camest thou to a morsel of this feast, Having fully dined before *Coriol.* i 9 10
Thou womb of death, Gorged with the dearest morsel of the earth *Rom. and Jul.* v 3 46
With liquorish draughts And morsels unctuous, greases his pure mind, That from it all consideration slips ! . . . . *T. of Athens* iv 3 195
I was A morsel for a monarch . . . . . *Ant. and Cleo.* i 5 31
I found you as a morsel cold upon Dead Cæsar's trencher . . iii 13 116
Thou mayst cut a morsel off the spit . . . . *Pericles* iv 2 142
Mort du vinaigre ! is not this Helen ? . . . . *All's Well* ii 3 50
And then to sigh, as 'twere The mort o' the deer . . *W. Tale* i 2 118
Mort de ma vie ! . . . . . . *Hen. V.* iii 5 11 ; iv 5 3
And are the cities, that I got with wounds, Deliver'd up again with peaceful words ? Mort Dieu ! . . . . 2 *Hen. VI.* i 1 123
Mortal. She is mortal ; But by immortal Providence she's mine *Tempest* v 1 188
Who, with our spleens, Would all themselves laugh mortal *M. for M.* ii 2 123
Insensible of mortality, and desperately mortal . . . . iv 2 152
Mortal and intestine jars 'Twixt thy seditious countrymen *Com. of Errors* i 1 11
A stuffed man : but for the stuffing,—well, we are all mortal *Much Ado* i 1 60
Than whom no mortal so magnificent ! . . . *L. L. Lost* iii 1 180
How far dost thou excel, No thought can think, nor tongue of mortal tell . . . . iv 3 42
And deny himself for Jove, Turning mortal for thy love . . . iv 3 120
The human mortals want their winter here . . *M. N. Dream* ii 1 101
But she, being mortal, of that boy did die . . . . . ii 1 135
I pray thee, gentle mortal, sing again . . . . . . iii 1 140
Nod to him, elves, and do him courtesies.—Hail, mortal !—Hail ! . . iii 1 178
Lord, what fools these mortals be ! . . . . . . iii 2 115
That I sleeping here was found With these mortals on the ground . iv 1 107
We that are true lovers run into strange capers ; but as all is mortal in nature, so is all nature in love mortal in folly . . *As Y. Like It* ii 4 56
Excessive grief the enemy to the living.—If the living be enemy to the grief, the excess makes it soon mortal . . . . *All's Well* i 1 67
This news is mortal to the queen . . . . . *W. Tale* iii 2 149
Are you all afraid ? Alas, I blame you not ; for you are mortal *Rich. III.* i 2 44
When I was mortal, my anointed body By thee was punched full of deadly holes . . . . v 3 124
I, her frail son, amongst my brethren mortal . . *Hen. VIII.* iii 2 148
How may A stranger to those most imperial looks Know them from eyes of other mortals ? . . . . . . *Troi. and Cres.* i 3 225
Mortal, to cut it off ; to cure it, easy . . . . *Coriolanus* iii 1 297
Most dangerously you have with him prevail'd, If not most mortal to him . . . . v 3 189
As is a winged messenger of heaven Unto the white-upturned wondering eyes Of mortals . . . . . . *Rom. and Jul.* ii 2 30
That living mortals, hearing them, run mad . . . . . iv 3 48
You all know, security Is mortals' chiefest enemy . *Macbeth* iii 5 33
Unless things mortal move them not at all, Would have made milch the burning eyes of heaven . . . . *Hamlet* ii 2 539
Exposing what is mortal and unsure To all that fortune, death and danger dare, Even for an egg-shell . . . . iv 4 51
Is't possible, a young maid's wits Should be as mortal as an old man's life ? . . . . iv 5 160
So mortal that, but dip a knife in it, Where it draws blood no cataplasm so rare, Collected from all simples . . . . . . iv 7 143
I am glad thy father's dead : Thy match was mortal to him . *Othello* v 2 205
We see how mortal an unkindness is to them [women] *Ant. and Cleo.* i 2 138
It had been pity you should have been put together with so mortal a purpose as then each bore . . . . *Cymbeline* i 4 44
Speak, man : thy tongue May take off some extremity, which to read Would be even mortal to me . . . . iii 4 18
This matter must be look'd to, For her relapse is mortal *Pericles* iii 2 110
Mortal accidents. Be not with mortal accidents opprest *Cymbeline* v 4 99
Mortal act. He finished indeed his mortal act That day . *T. Night* v 1 254
Mortal arbitrement. The knight is incensed against you, even to a mortal arbitrement . . . . iii 4 286
Mortal body. Thou hadst but power over his mortal body *Richard III.* i 2 47
As any mortal body hearing it Should straight fall mad . *T. Andron.* iii 3 103
Mortal breathing. This mortal-breathing saint . . *Mer. of Venice* ii 7 40
To the extremest point Of mortal breathing . . . *Richard II.* iv 1 48
Mortal bugs. Those that would die or ere resist are grown The mortal bugs o' the field . . . . *Cymbeline* v 3 51
Mortal business. This is no mortal business . . . *Tempest* i 2 406
Mortal coil. When we have shuffled off this mortal coil . *Hamlet* iii 1 67
Mortal consequences. The spirits that know All mortal consequences have pronounced me thus . . . . *Macbeth* v 3 5
Mortal custom. Pay his breath To time and mortal custom . . iv 1 100
Mortal drugs. Such mortal drugs I have . . . . *Rom. and Jul.* v 1 66
Mortal ears might hardly endure the din . . . . *T. of Shrew* i 1 178
Mortal engines. O you mortal engines, whose rude throats The immortal Jove's dread clamours counterfeit, Farewell ! . . *Othello* iii 3 355
Mortal eye. By heaven, the wonder in a mortal eye ! . . *L. L. Lost* iv 3 85
You are mortal, And mortal eyes cannot endure the devil *Richard III.* i 2 44
Damn them then, If ever mortal eyes do see them bolster ! . . *Othello* iii 3 399
Mortal flies. No more, thou thunder-master, show Thy spite on mortal flies . . . . *Cymbeline* v 4 31
Mortal foe. I return his sworn and mortal foe . . . . 3 *Hen. VI.* iii 3 257
I here proclaim myself thy mortal foe . . . . v 1 94
Mortal fortune. Or bide the mortal fortune of the field . . . ii 2 83
Mortal fury. Not Death himself In mortal fury half so peremptory, As we to keep this city . . . . *K. John* ii 1 454
Mortal gate. Alone he enter'd The mortal gate of the city . *Coriolanus* ii 2 115
Mortal griefs. What kind of god art thou, that suffer'st more Of mortal griefs than do thy worshippers ? . . . . . . *Hen. V.* iv 1 259
Mortal grossness. And I will purge thy mortal grossness so That thou shalt like an airy spirit go . . . . . . *M. N. Dream* iii 1 163
Mortal hand. Without the assistance of a mortal hand . . *K. John* iii 1 158
Mortal house. This mortal house I'll ruin . . . *Ant. and Cleo.* v 2 51
Mortal hurt. Got his mortal hurt In my behalf . . *Rom. and Jul.* iii 1 115
Mortal instruments. The Genius and the mortal instruments Are then in council . . . . *J. Cæsar* ii 1 66
Mortal joy. If this be so, the gods do mean to strike me To death with mortal joy . . . . *Cymbeline* v 5 235
Mortal kind. If my offence be of such mortal kind . . . . *Othello* iii 4 115
Mortal knowledge. More in them than mortal knowledge . . *Macbeth* i 5 3
Mortal living. Dead life, poor mortal living ghost . . *Richard III.* iv 4 26
Mortal man. Tush, man, mortal men, mortal men . . . 1 *Hen. IV.* iv 2 73
How many years a mortal man may live . . . . 3 *Hen. VI.* ii 5 29
O momentary grace of mortal men ! . . . . . . *Richard III.* iii 4 98
Mortal mineral. She had For you a mortal mineral . . . *Cymbeline* v 5 50
Mortal motion. He gives me the stuck in with such a mortal motion, that it is inevitable . . . . *T. Night* iii 4 304
Mortal murders. Twenty mortal murders on their crowns . *Macbeth* iii 4 81
Mortal natures. As having sense of beauty, do omit Their mortal natures, letting go safely by The divine Desdemona . . . *Othello* ii 1 72
Mortal night. This was a goodly person, Till the disaster that, one mortal night, Drove him to this . . . . *Pericles* v 1 37
Mortal officer. The gods can have no mortal officer More like a god than you . . . . v 3 62
Mortal paradise. When thou didst bower the spirit of a fiend In mortal paradise of such sweet flesh . . . . *Rom. and Jul.* iii 2 82
Mortal paw. A chafed lion by the mortal paw . . . . *K. John* iii 1 259
Mortal poison. Would it were mortal poison, for thy sake ! *Richard III.* i 2 146
Mortal preparation. Encourage myself in my certainty, put myself into my mortal preparation . . . . *All's Well* iii 6 81
Mortal revenge upon these traitorous Goths . . . *T. Andron.* iv 1 93
Mortal seeming. He hath a kind of honour sets him off, More than a mortal seeming . . . . *Cymbeline* i 6 171
Mortal-staring. And put thy fortune to the arbitrement Of bloody strokes and mortal-staring war . . . . *Richard III.* v 3 90
Mortal state. To wear our mortal state to come with her *Hen. VIII.* ii 4 228
Mortal sting. Who 'scapes the lurking serpent's mortal sting ? 3 *Hen. VI.* ii 2 15
Mortal stroke. Lest, in her greatness, by some mortal stroke She do defeat us . . . . *Ant. and Cleo.* v 1 64
Mortal sword. Should by my mortal sword Be drain'd *Troi. and Cres.* iv 5 134
Let us rather Hold fast the mortal sword . . . . *Macbeth* iv 3 3
Mortal temples. Within the hollow crown That rounds the mortal temples of a king . . . . *Richard II.* iii 2 161
Mortal thing. She excels each mortal thing . . . . *T. G. of Ver.* iv 2 51
Mortal thoughts. Come, you spirits That tend on mortal thoughts, unsex me here ! . . . . *Macbeth* i 5 42
Mortal times. The purest treasure mortal times afford Is spotless reputation . . . . *Richard II.* i 1 177
Mortal touch. Whose double tongue may with a mortal touch Throw death . . . . iii 2 21
Mortal Venus. The mortal Venus, the heart-blood of beauty, love's invisible soul . . . . *Troi. and Cres.* iii 1 34
Mortal vessel. A tempest, which his mortal vessel tears . *Pericles* iv 4 30
Mortal views. A holy parcel of the fairest dames, That ever turn'd their —backs—to mortal views ! . . . . . . *L. L. Lost* v 2 161
Mortal woe. Though death be poor, it ends a mortal woe *Richard II.* ii 1 152
Mortal world. Be my last breathing in this mortal world ! 2 *Hen. VI.* i 2 21
Mortal worm. The mortal worm might make the sleep eternal . . iii 2 263
Mortal wretch. Come, thou mortal wretch, With thy sharp teeth this knot intrinsicate Of life at once untie . . . *Ant. and Cleo.* v 2 306
Mortality and mercy in Vienna Live in thy tongue and heart *M. for M.* i 1 45
No might nor greatness in mortality Can censure 'scape . . . iii 2 196
Fearless of what's past, present, or to come ; insensible of mortality . iv 2 152
He was skilful enough to have lived still, if knowledge could be set up against mortality . . . . *All's Well* i 1 35
We cannot hold mortality's strong hand . . . . *K. John* iv 2 82
Doth by the idle comments that it makes Foretell the ending of mortality v 7 5
The swords That make such waste in brief mortality . . *Hen. V.* i 2 28
Break out into a second course of mischief, Killing in relapse of mortality . . . . iv 3 107
I beg mortality, Rather than life preserved with infamy . 1 *Hen. VI.* iv 5 32
Winged through the lither sky, In thy despite shall 'scape mortality . iv 7 22
From this instant, There's nothing serious in mortality . *Macbeth* ii 3 98
Let me kiss that hand !—Let me wipe it first ; it smells of mortality *Lear* iv 6 136
What mortality is ! . . . . *Cymbeline* iv 1 16
I thank thee, who hath taught My frail mortality to know itself *Pericles* i 1 42
Lest this great sea of joys rushing upon me O'erbear the shores of my mortality, And drown me with their sweetness . . . . . v 1 195
Mortally. Struck down Some mortally, some slightly touch'd *Cymbeline* v 3 10
Your shafts of fortune, though they hurt you mortally, Yet glance full wanderingly on us . . . . *Pericles* iii 3 6
Yet I was mortally brought forth, and am No other than I appear . v 1 105
Mortar. I will tread this unbolted villain into mortar . . *Lear* ii 2 71
Mortar-piece. He stands there, like a mortar-piece, to blow us *Hen. VIII.* v 4 48
Mortified. My loving lord, Dumain is mortified . . . *L. L. Lost* i 1 28
His wildness, mortified in him, Seem'd to die too . . . *Hen. V.* i 1 26
Thou, like an exorcist, hast conjured up My mortified spirit *J. Cæsar* ii 1 324
For their dear causes Would to the bleeding and the grim alarm Excite the mortified man . . . . *Macbeth* v 2 5
Strike in their numb'd and mortified bare arms Pins, wooden pricks *Lear* ii 3 15
Mortifying. To apply a moral medicine to a mortifying mischief *M. Ado* i 3 13
And let my liver rather heat with wine Than my heart cool with mortifying groans . . . . *Mer. of Venice* i 1 82
Mortimer, Leading the men of Herefordshire to fight . . 1 *Hen. IV.* i 1 38
That we at our own charge shall ransom straight His brother-in-law, the foolish Mortimer . . . . i 3 80
I shall never hold that man my friend Whose tongue shall ask me for one penny cost To ransom home revolted Mortimer.—Revolted Mortimer ! . . . . i 3 92
Such deadly wounds ; Nor never could the noble Mortimer Receive so many, and all willingly . . . . i 3 110
But, sirrah, henceforth Let me not hear you speak of Mortimer . . i 3 119
Speak of Mortimer ! 'Zounds, I will speak of him . . . . . i 3 130
But I will lift the down-trod Mortimer As high in the air as this unthankful king . . . . i 3 135
Trembling even at the name of Mortimer.—I cannot blame him . . i 3 144
Did King Richard then Proclaim my brother Edmund Mortimer Heir ? . i 3 156
He said he would not ransom Mortimer ; Forbad my tongue to speak of Mortimer ; But I will find him when he lies asleep, And in his ear I'll holla 'Mortimer !' . . . . i 3 219
I'll have a starling shall be taught to speak Nothing but 'Mortimer' . i 3 225
And then the power of Scotland and of York, To join with Mortimer, ha ? i 3 281
I'll steal to Glendower and Lord Mortimer . . . . i 3 295
Lord Edmund Mortimer, my lord of York and Owen Glendower . . ii 3 26
I fear my brother Mortimer doth stir About his title . . . . ii 3 84
I'll play Percy, and that damned brawn shall play Dame Mortimer his wife ii 4 124
O, Glendower.—Owen, Owen, the same ; and his son-in-law Mortimer . ii 4 376
Lord Mortimer, and cousin Glendower, Will you sit down ? . . . iii 1 3
I am afraid my daughter will run mad, So much she doteth on her Mortimer . . . . iii 1 146
Come, come, Lord Mortimer ; you are as slow As hot Lord Percy is on fire to go . . . . iii 1 268
Douglas, Mortimer, Capitulate against us and are up . . . . iii 2 119
Lord Mortimer of Scotland hath sent word . . . . iii 2 164

Mortimer. There is Douglas and Lord Mortimer.—No, Mortimer is not there — *1 Hen. IV.* iv 4 22
Let dying Mortimer here rest himself — *1 Hen. VI.* ii 5 2
These grey locks . . . Argue the end of Edmund Mortimer — ii 5 7
Thus the Mortimers, In whom the title rested, were suppress'd — ii 5 91
Here dies the dusky torch of Mortimer, Choked with ambition — ii 5 122
Philippe, a daughter, Who married Edmund Mortimer — *2 Hen. VI.* ii 2 36
Roger Earl of March, who was the son Of Edmund Mortimer — ii 2 49
John Cade of Ashford, . . . Under the title of John Mortimer — iii 1 359
For that John Mortimer, which now is dead, . . . he doth resemble — iii 1 372
My father was a Mortimer,— He was an honest man, and a good bricklayer iv 2 41
I will make myself a knight presently. Rise up Sir John Mortimer — iv 2 129
Edmund Mortimer, Earl of March, Married the Duke of Clarence' daughter — iv 2 144
Jack Cade proclaims himself Lord Mortimer — iv 4 28
Now is Mortimer lord of this city — iv 6 1
Henceforward it shall be treason for any that calls me other than Lord Mortimer — iv 6 7
Be it known unto thee by these presence, even the presence of Lord Mortimer — iv 7 33
Thy grandfather, Roger Mortimer, Earl of March — *3 Hen. VI.* i 1 106
Sir John and Sir Hugh Mortimer, mine uncles, You are come to Sandal in a happy hour — i 2 62
Mortise. If it hath ruffian'd so upon the sea, What ribs of oak, when mountains melt on them, Can hold the mortise? — *Othello* ii 1 9
Mortised. To whose huge spokes ten thousand lesser things Are mortised and adjoin'd — *Hamlet* iii 3 20
Morton. Say, Morton, didst thou come from Shrewsbury? *2 Hen. IV.* i 1 64
Yet speak, Morton; Tell thou an earl his divination lies — i 1 87
Mose. And like to mose in the chine — *T. of Shrew* iii 2 51
Moss. It is dross, Usurping ivy, brier, or idle moss — *Com. of Errors* ii 2 180
O'ercome with moss and baleful mistletoe — *T. Andron.* ii 3 95
Yea, and furr'd moss besides, when flowers are none — *Cymbeline* iv 2 228
Mossed. Under an oak, whose boughs were moss'd with age *As Y. L. It* iv 3 105
These moss'd trees, That have outlived the eagle — *T. of Athens* iv 3 223
Moss-grown. Topples down Steeples and moss-grown towers *1 Hen. IV.* iii 1 33
Most. To the most of men this is a Caliban — *Tempest* i 2 480
Ebbing men, indeed, Most often do so near the bottom run — ii 1 227
It struck mine ear most terribly.—I heard nothing — ii 1 313
Most poor matters Point to rich ends — iii 1 3
Most busy lest, when I do it — iii 1 15
Fair encounter Of two most rare affections! — iii 1 75
But this thing dare not,— That's most certain — iii 2 64
A most high miracle! — v 1 177
The most forward bud Is eaten by the canker ere it blow — *T. G. of Ver.* i 1 45
Let me have What thou thinkest meet and is most mannerly — ii 7 58
Is at most odds with his own gravity and patience. *Mer. Wives* iii 1 54
The stealth of our most mutual entertainment — *Meas. for Meas.* i 2 158
There is a vice that most I do abhor — ii 2 29
The sense of death is most in apprehension — iii 1 78
And, for the most, become much more the better For being a little bad v 1 445
Why, all delights are vain; but that most vain, Which with pain purchased doth inherit pain — *L. L. Lost* i 1 72
And when it hath the thing it hunteth most, 'Tis won as towns with fire i 1 146
As the heresies that men do leave Are hated most of those they did deceive, So thou . . . Of all be hated, but the most of me! *M. N. D.* ii 2 142
But miserable most, to love unloved — ii 2 234
To try whose right, Of thine or mine, is most in Helena — iii 2 337
Love, therefore, and tongue-tied simplicity In least speak most — v 1 105
To you, Antonio, I owe the most, in money and in love. *Mer. of Venice* i 1 131
Works a miracle in nature, Making them lightest that wear most of it. iii 2 91
Boys and women are for the most part cattle of this colour *As Y. Like It* iii 2 435
That seeming to be most which we indeed least are — *T. of Shrew* v 2 175
This she delivered in the most bitter touch of sorrow — *All's Well* i 3 122
Oft expectation fails and most oft there Where most it promises, and oft it hits Where hope is coldest and despair most fits — ii 1 145
I have for the most part been aired abroad — *W. Tale* iv 2 5
And when I wander here and there, I then do most go right — iv 3 18
He has his health and ampler strength indeed Than most have of his age iv 4 415
She seems a mistress To most that teach — iv 4 594
Discover how with most advantage They may vex us — *1 Hen. VI.* i 4 12
Most part of all this night — ii 1 67
But always resolute in most extremes — iv 1 38
Have we not lost most part of all the towns? — v 4 108
Since he affects her most, It most of all these reasons bindeth us — v 5 60
For the most part such To whom as great a charge as little honour He meant to lay upon — *Hen. VIII.* i 1 76
You speak of two The most remark'd i' the kingdom — v 1 33
This is the most despiteful gentle greeting — *Troi. and Cres.* iv 1 32
I have the most cause to be glad — *Coriolanus* iv 3 56
That most are busied when they're most alone — *Rom. and Jul.* i 1 134
Hear all, all see, And like her most whose merit most shall be — i 2 31
The most you sought was her promotion — iv 5 71
'Tis honour with most lands to be at odds — *T. of Athens* iii 5 116
I had most need of blessing, and 'Amen' Stuck in my throat *Macbeth* ii 2 32
Within this hour at most I will advise you — iii 1 128
So grace and mercy at your most need help you — *Hamlet* i 5 180
Who for the most part are capable of nothing but inexplicable dumb-shows — iii 2 12
Most choice, forsaken; and most loved, despised! — *Lear* i 1 254
Most sure and vulgar: every one hears that, Which can distinguish sound iv 6 214
He compeers the best.—That were the most, if he should husband you v 3 70
At every house I'll call; I may command at most — *Othello* i 1 182
Most potent, grave, and reverend signiors — i 3 76
A grievous wreck and sufferance On most part of their fleet — ii 1 24
For the most part, too, they are foolish that are so *Ant. and Cleo.* i 3 34
Fortune knows We scorn her most when most she offers blows — iii 11 74
I am alone the villain of the earth, And feel I am so most — iv 6 31
Most best. But that I love thee best, O most best, believe it. *Hamlet* ii 2 122
Balm of your age, Most best, most dearest — *Lear* i 1 219
Most boldest. The most boldest and best hearts of Rome *J. Cæsar* iii 1 121
Most bravest. From this most bravest vessel of the world Struck the main-top! — *Cymbeline* iv 2 319
Most coldest. The most patient man in loss, the most coldest — ii 3 2
Most dearest. Sweet villain! Most dear'st! my collop! — *W. Tale* i 2 137
Balm of your age, Most best, most dearest — *Lear* i 1 219
Most gladness. Dispatch we The business we have talk'd of.—With most gladness — *Ant. and Cleo.* ii 2 169
Most heaviest. It hath been the longest night That e'er I watch'd and the most heaviest — *T. G. of Ver.* iv 2 141
Most master. In this place most master wear no breeches *2 Hen. VI.* i 3 149
Most of all. Fire that's closest kept burns most of all — *T. G. of Ver.* i 2 30
But, most of all, agreeing with the proclamation — *Meas. for Meas.* i 2 80
Yet show some pity.—I show it most of all when I show justice — ii 2 100
Evils that take leave, On their departure most of all show evil *K. John* iii 4 115
And he of these that can do most of all Cannot do more *2 Hen. VI.* i 3 75
God's wrong is most of all — *Richard III.* iv 4 377
Most poorest. The basest and most poorest shape — *Lear* ii 3 7
Most quiet. And are enforced from our most quiet there *2 Hen. IV.* iv 1 71
Most stay. My most stay Can be but brief — *Meas. for Meas.* iv 1 44
Most stillest. In the calmest and most stillest night *2 Hen. IV.* iii 1 28
Most unkindest. This was the most unkindest cut of all *J. Cæsar* iii 2 187
Most worst. Whose every word deserves To taste of thy most worst *W. Tale* iii 2 180
Most worthiest. The worthiest sir that ever Country call'd his! and you his mistress, only For the most worthiest fit! — *Cymbeline* i 6 162
Mot. J'ai gagné deux mots d'Anglois vîtement — *Hen. V.* iii 4 14
Je m'en fais la répétition de tous les mots que vous m'avez appris — iii 4 26
Vous prononcez les mots aussi droit que les natifs d'Angleterre — iii 4 41
Ce sont mots de son mauvais, corruptible, gros, et impudique — iii 4 56
Je ne voudrais prononcer ces mots devant les seigneurs de France — iii 4 58
Mote. You found his mote; the king your mote did see; But I a beam do find in each of three — *L. L. Lost* iv 3 161
A mote will turn the balance — *M. N. Dream* v 1 324
To lose your eyes.—O heaven, that there were but a mote in yours! *K. John* iv 1 92
Therefore should every soldier in the wars do as every sick man in his bed, wash every mote out of his conscience — *Hen. V.* iv 1 189
A mote it is to trouble the mind's eye — *Hamlet* i 1 112
Like motes and shadows see them move awhile — *Pericles* iv 4 21
Moth. Who was Samson's love, my dear Moth?—A woman, master *L. L. L.* i 2 80
What shall some see?—Nay, nothing, Master Moth, but what they look upon — i 2 167
Moth, follow.—Like the sequel, I — iii 1 134
Peaseblossom! Cobweb! Moth! and Mustardseed! *M. N. Dream* iii 1 165
Thus hath the candle singed the moth. O, these deliberate fools! *M. of V.* ii 9 79
You would be another Penelope: yet, they say, all the yarn she spun in Ulysses' absence did but fill Ithaca full of moths — *Coriolanus* i 3 94
If I be left behind, A moth of peace — *Othello* i 3 257
Mother. Thy mother was a piece of virtue, and She said thou wast my daughter — *Tempest* i 2 56
As wicked dew as e'er my mother brush'd With raven's feather — i 2 321
This island's mine, by Sycorax my mother, Which thou takest from me i 2 331
His mother was a witch, and one so strong That could control the moon v 1 269
My mother weeping, my father wailing, my sister crying *T. G. of Ver.* ii 3 7
This left shoe is my father: no, no, this left shoe is my mother — ii 3 17
This shoe, with the hole in it, is my mother, and this my father — ii 3 20
Now come I to my mother: O, that she could speak now like a wood woman! — ii 3 30
Well, I kiss her; why, there 'tis; here's my mother's breath up and down — ii 3 32
I keep but three men and a boy yet, till my mother be dead *Mer. Wives* i 1 285
I'll be sworn, As my mother was, the first hour I was born — ii 2 39
Good mother, do not marry me to yond fool.—I mean it not — iii 4 87
Her mother, ever strong against that match And firm for Doctor Caius iv 6 27
To this her mother's plot She seemingly obedient — iv 6 32
Her father means she shall be all in white, . . . her mother hath intended . . . That quaint in green she shall be loose enrobed — iv 6 38
Which means she to deceive, father or mother?—Both, my good host iv 6 46
Pardon, good father! good my mother, pardon! — v 5 229
No longer staying but to give the mother Notice of my affair *M. for M.* i 4 86
Heaven shield my mother play'd my father fair! — iii 1 141
She became A joyful mother of two goodly sons *Com. of Errors* i 1 51
So I, to find a mother and a brother, In quest of them, unhappy, lose myself — i 2 39
This is your daughter.—Her mother hath many times told me so *M. Ado* i 1 105
Lest I should prove the mother of fools — ii 1 295
You were born in a merry hour.—No, sure, my lord, my mother cried ii 1 348
My father's wit and my mother's tongue, assist me! *L. L. Lost* i 2 100
Pray you, sir, whose daughter?—Her mother's, I have heard — ii 1 202
Then was Venus like her mother, for her father is but grim — v 2 255
Robin Starveling, you must play Thisby's mother — *M. N. Dream* i 2 63
His mother was a votaress of my order — ii 1 123
Peaseblossom.—I pray you, commend me to Mistress Squash, your mother — iii 1 191
I am much afeard my lady his mother played false with a smith *M. of V.* i 2 48
This Jacob from our holy Abram was, As his wise mother wrought in his behalf, The third possessor — i 3 74
Launcelot, the Jew's man, and I am sure Margery your wife is my mother ii 2 95
So the sins of my mother should be visited upon me — iii 5 15
Truly then I fear you are damned both by father and mother — iii 5 18
Thus when I shun Scylla, your father, I fall into Charybdis, your mother iii 5 20
And why, I pray you? Who might be your mother, That you insult, exult, and all at once, Over the wretched? — *As Y. Like It* iii 5 35
From my mother-wit.—A witty mother! witless else her son *T. of Shrew* ii 1 266
Art thou his father?—Ay, sir; so his mother says, if I may believe her v 1 34
Be comfortable to my mother, your mistress — *All's Well* i 1 86
To speak on the part of virginity, is to accuse your mothers — i 1 149
A mother and a mistress and a friend — i 1 181
You know, Helen, I am a mother to you.—Mine honourable mistress — i 3 144
Nay, a mother? Why not a mother? When I said 'a mother,' Methought you saw a serpent: what's in 'mother,' That you start at it? I say, I am your mother — i 3 145
You ne'er oppress'd me with a mother's groan, Yet I express to you a mother's care — i 3 153
God's mercy, maiden! does it curd thy blood To say I am thy mother? i 3 156
I am your mother.—Pardon, madam; The Count Rousillon cannot be my brother — i 3 160
You are my mother, madam; would you were,—So that my lord your son were not my brother,—Indeed my mother! or were you both our mothers, I care no more for than I do for heaven, So I were not his sister — i 3 169
Daughter and mother So strive upon your pulse. What, pale again? — i 3 174
There's letters from my mother: what the import is, I know not yet — ii 3 293
Acquaint my mother with my hate to her, And wherefore I am fled — ii 3 304
My mother greets me kindly: is she well?—She is not well — ii 4 1
And now you should be as your mother was When your sweet self was got iv 2 9
My mother did but duty; such, my lord, As you owe to your wife — iv 2 12
Knock at my chamber-window: I'll order take my mother shall not hear — iv 2 55

Mother. My mother told me just how he would woo, As if she sat in's heart *All's Well* iv 2 69
You have not given him his mother's letter?—I have delivered it iv 3 2
Buried a wife, mourned for her; writ to my lady mother I am returning iv 3 102
If she had partaken of my flesh, and cost me the dearest groans of a mother, I could not have owed her a more rooted love iv 5 12
Did to his majesty, his mother and his lady Offence of mighty note v 3 13
I am her mother, sir, whose age and honour Both suffer under this complaint we bring, And both shall cease, without your remedy v 3 162
She does abuse our ears: to prison with her.—Good mother, fetch my bail v 3 296
O my dear mother, do I see you living?—Mine eyes smell onions v 3 320
One would think his mother's milk were scarce out of him *T. Night* i 5 170
I am yet so near the manners of my mother, that upon the least occasion more mine eyes will tell tales of me ii 1 42
Go, play, boy, play: thy mother plays, and I Play too *W. Tale* i 2 187
The queen your mother rounds apace ii 1 16
Conceiving the dishonour of his mother, He straight declined, droop'd ii 3 13
A great king's daughter, The mother to a hopeful prince iii 2 41
If such thing be, thy mother Appear'd to me last night iii 3 17
Poor wretch, That for thy mother's fault art thus exposed To loss! iii 3 50
Your mother was most true to wedlock, prince v 1 124
The majesty of the creature in resemblance of the mother v 2 40
Cries 'O, thy mother, thy mother!' then asks Bohemia forgiveness v 2 56
The princess hearing of her mother's statue v 2 103
That which my daughter came to look upon, The statue of her mother v 3 14
Fair madam: kneel And pray your mother's blessing v 3 120
Silence, good mother; hear the embassy *K. John* i 1 6
You came not of one mother then, it seems.—Most certain of one mother i 1 58
As I think, one father: But for the certain knowledge of that truth I put you o'er to heaven and to my mother i 1 62
Thou dost shame thy mother And wound her honour with this diffidence i 1 64
Heaven guard my mother's honour and my land! i 1 70
Whether I be as true begot or no, That still I lay upon my mother's head i 1 76
Your tale must be how he employ'd my mother i 1 98
Large lengths of seas and shores Between my father and my mother lay i 1 106
Brother by the mother's side, give me your hand i 1 163
O me! it is my mother. How now, good lady! What brings you here? i 1 220
Therefore, good mother, To whom am I beholding for these limbs? i 1 238
Thou most untoward knave.—Knight, knight, good mother, Basilisco-like i 1 244
But, mother, I am not Sir Robert's son i 1 246
Then, good my mother, let me know my father; Some proper man, I hope: who was it, mother? i 1 249
Ay, my mother, With all my heart I thank thee for my father! i 1 269
O, take his mother's thanks, a widow's thanks! ii 1 32
I think His father never was so true begot: It cannot be, an if thou wert his mother ii 1 131
There's a good mother, boy, that blots thy father ii 1 132
Good my mother, peace! I would that I were low laid in my grave ii 1 163
His mother shames him so, poor boy, he weeps ii 1 166
His grandam's wrongs, and not his mother's shames, Draws those heaven-moving pearls from his poor eyes ii 1 168
This day hath made Much work for tears in many an English mother ii 1 303
Ugly and slanderous to thy mother's womb, Full of unpleasing blots iii 1 44
Why thou against the church, our holy mother, So wilfully dost spurn iii 1 141
Be champion of our church, Or let the church, our mother, breathe her curse, A mother's curse, on her revolting son iii 1 256
My mother is assailed in our tent, And ta'en, I fear iii 2 6
O, this will make my mother die with grief! iii 3 5
Where is my mother's care, That such an army could be drawn in France? iv 2 117
Her ear Is stopp'd with dust; the first of April died Your noble mother iv 2 121
What! mother dead! How wildly then walks my estate in France! iv 2 127
My mother dead! iv 2 181
You bloody Neroes, ripping up the womb Of your dear mother England v 2 153
Then, England's ground, farewell; sweet soil, adieu; My mother, and my nurse, that bears me yet! *Richard II.* i 3 307
And I, a gasping new-deliver'd mother, Have woe to woe ii 2 65
As a long-parted mother with her child Plays fondly with her tears and smiles iii 2 8
Good mother, be content; it is no more Than my poor life must answer v 2 82
And wilt thou pluck my fair son from mine age, And rob me of a happy mother's name? v 2 93
Let your mother in, I know she is come to pray for your foul sin v 3 81
Unto my mother's prayers I bend my knee v 3 97
Your mother well hath pray'd, and prove you true.—Come, my old son v 3 145
Whose arms were moulded in their mothers' womb To chase these pagans in those holy fields *1 Hen. IV.* i 1 23
Give him as much as will make him a royal man, and send him back again to my mother ii 4 322
I have partly thy mother's word, partly my own opinion ii 4 444
So it would have done at the same season, if your mother's cat had but kittened iii 1 19
Thou wert better thou hadst struck thy mother *2 Hen. IV.* v 4 11
Mock mothers from their sons, mock castles down *Hen. V.* i 2 286
Dishonour not your mothers iii 1 22
Whiles the mad mothers with their howls confused Do break the clouds iii 3 39
All my mother came into mine eyes And gave me up to tears iv 6 31
When at their mothers' moist eyes babes shall suck *1 Hen. VI.* i 1 49
God's mother deigned to appear to me i 2 78
Christ's mother helps me, else I were too weak i 2 106
Helen, the mother of great Constantine i 2 142
So much fear'd abroad That with his name the mothers still their babes ii 3 17
By my mother I derived am From Lionel Duke of Clarence ii 5 74
Langley, Duke of York, Marrying my sister that thy mother was ii 5 86
As looks the mother on her lowly babe When death doth close his tender dying eyes, See, see the pining malady of France iii 3 47
O, if you love my mother, Dishonour not her honourable name! iv 5 13
Shall all thy mother's hopes lie in one tomb?—Ay, rather than I'll shame my mother's womb iv 5 34
In thee thy mother dies, our household's name, My death's revenge iv 6 38
I did beget her, all the parish knows: Her mother liveth yet, can testify v 4 12
I gave a noble to the priest The morn that I was wedded to her mother v 4 24
I would the milk Thy mother gave thee when thou suck'dst her breast Had been a little ratsbane for thy sake! v 4 28
Now, by God's mother, priest, I'll shave your crown for this *2 Hen. VI.* i 1 51
Hadst thou been his mother, thou couldst have better told ii 1 81
His eldest sister, Anne, My mother, being heir unto the crown ii 2 44

Mother. Thy mother took into her blameful bed Some stern untutor'd churl *2 Hen. VI.* iii 2 212
It was thy mother that thou meant'st, That thou thyself wast born in bastardy iii 2 222
Gentle as the cradle-babe Dying with mother's dug between its lips iii 2 393
Like ambitious Sylla, overgorged With gobbets of thy mother's bleeding heart iv 1 85
My mother a Plantagenet,— I knew her well; she was a midwife iv 2 44
Whoever got thee, there thy mother stands; For, well I wot, thou hast thy mother's tongue *3 Hen. VI.* ii 2 133
How will my mother for a father's death Take on with me! ii 5 103
'Twill grieve your grace my sons should call you father.—No more than when my daughters call thee mother iii 2 101
And, by God's mother, I, being but a bachelor, Have other some iii 2 103
Why, love forswore me in my mother's womb iii 2 153
Sweet Ned! speak to thy mother, boy! Canst thou not speak? v 5 51
Thy mother felt more than a mother's pain, And yet brought forth less than a mother's hope v 6 49
I have often heard my mother say I came into the world with my legs forward v 6 70
Whose ugly and unnatural aspect May fright the hopeful mother *Richard III.* i 2 24
Die neither mother, wife, nor England's queen! i 3 209
Thou slander of thy mother's heavy womb! i 3 231
By God's holy mother, She hath had too much wrong i 3 306
Yet thou art a mother, And hast the comfort of thy children left thee ii 2 55
Was never mother had so dear a loss! Alas, I am the mother of these moans! ii 2 79
Comfort, dear mother: God is much displeased That you take with unthankfulness his doing ii 2 89
Madam, bethink you, like a careful mother, Of the young prince ii 2 96
Madam, my mother, I do cry you mercy; I did not see your grace ii 2 104
Make me die a good old man! That is the butt-end of a mother's blessing ii 2 110
Madam, and you, my mother, will you go To give your censures? ii 2 143
Both by the father and mother.—Better it were they all came by the father ii 3 22
Ay, mother; but I would not have it so ii 4 8
He should be gracious.—Why, madam, so, no doubt, he is.—I hope he is; but yet let mothers doubt ii 4 22
I thought my mother, and my brother York, Would long ere this have met us iii 1 20
What, will our mother come?—On what occasion, God he knows, not I, The queen your mother, and your brother York, Have taken sanctuary iii 1 25
The tender prince Would fain have come with me to meet your grace, But by his mother was perforce withheld iii 1 30
If my weak oratory Can from his mother win the Duke of York iii 1 38
Myself and my good cousin Buckingham Will to your mother iii 1 138
Incensed by his subtle mother To taunt and scorn you? iii 1 152
Ingenious, forward, capable: He is all the mother's, from the top to toe iii 1 156
When that my mother went with child Of that unsatiate Edward iii 5 86
But touch this sparingly, as 'twere far off; Because you know, my lord, my mother lives iii 5 94
Now, by the holy mother of our Lord, The citizens are mum iii 7 2
He was contract to Lady Lucy—Your mother lives a witness to that vow iii 7 180
A poor petitioner, A care-crazed mother of a many children iii 7 184
I am their mother; who should keep me from them? iv 1 22
I am their father's mother; I will see them iv 1 23
Their aunt I am in law, in love their mother: Then bring me to their sights iv 1 24
As mother, And reverend looker on, of two fair queens iv 1 30
Be of good cheer: mother, how fares your grace?—O Dorset, speak not! iv 1 38
Thy mother's name is ominous to children iv 1 41
And make me die . . . Nor mother, wife, nor England's counted queen iv 1 47
Hover about me with your airy wings And hear your mother's lamentation! iv 4 14
I thank thee, that this carnal cur Preys on the issue of his mother's body iv 4 57
A mother only mock'd with two sweet babes iv 4 87
A most distressed widow; For joyful mother, one that wails the name iv 4 99
I will be mild and gentle in my speech.—And brief, good mother iv 4 161
From my soul I love thy daughter.—My daughter's mother thinks it iv 4 256
A grandam's name is little less in love Than is the doting title of a mother iv 4 300
Again shall you be mother to a king iv 4 317
Go, then, my mother, to thy daughter go: Make bold her bashful years with your experience iv 4 325
She shall be a high and mighty queen.—To wail the title, as her mother doth iv 4 348
Good mother,—I must call you so—Be the attorney of my love to her iv 4 412
Shall I go win my daughter to thy will?—And be a happy mother iv 4 427
How fares our loving mother?—I, by attorney, bless thee from thy mother v 3 82
A paltry fellow, Long kept in Bretagne at our mother's cost v 3 324
And a little To love her for her mother's sake *Hen. VIII.* iv 2 137
God's blest mother! I swear he is true-hearted v 1 153
Like unbridled children, grown Too headstrong for their mother *Troi. and Cres.* iii 2 131
My mother's blood Runs on the dexter cheek iv 5 127
But the just gods gainsay That any drop thou borrow'dst from thy mother, My sacred aunt, should by my mortal sword Be drain'd! iv 5 133
Let it not be believed for womanhood! Think, we had mothers v 2 130
What hath she done, prince, that can soil our mothers? v 2 134
Let's leave the hermit pity with our mothers v 3 45
Thy wife hath dream'd; thy mother hath had visions v 3 63
He did it to please his mother, and to be partly proud *Coriolanus* i 1 39
When for a day of kings' entreaties a mother should not sell him an hour from her beholding i 3 9
Pray now, no more: my mother, Who has a charter to extol her blood, When she does praise me grieves me i 9 13
Look, sir, your mother!—O, You have, I know, petition'd all the gods For my prosperity! ii 1 186
Such eyes the widows in Corioli wear, And mothers that lack sons ii 1 196
Know, good mother, I had rather be their servant in my way ii 1 218
I muse my mother Does not approve me further iii 2 7
Let Thy mother rather feel thy pride than fear Thy dangerous stoutness iii 2 126
Be content: Mother, I am going to the market-place; Chide me no more iii 2 131
Is this the promise that you made your mother? iii 3 86
Nay, mother, Where is your ancient courage? iv 1 2

Mother. Nay, mother, Resume that spirit, when you were wont to say, If you had been the wife of Hercules, Six of his labours you'ld have done *Coriolanus* iv 1 15
Farewell, my wife, my mother: I'll do well yet iv 1 20
My mother, you wot well My hazards still have been your solace iv 1 27
Come, my sweet wife, my dearest mother, and My friends of noble touch iv 1 48
Here comes his mother.—Let's not meet her.—Why?—They say she's mad iv 2 8
Nay, I hear nothing: his mother and his wife Hear nothing from him iv 6 18
For one poor grain or two! I am one of those, his mother, wife, his child v 1 29
So that all hope is vain, Unless his noble mother, and his wife; Who, as I hear, mean to solicit him For mercy to his country v 1 71
Wife, mother, child, I know not. My affairs Are servanted to others v 2 88
My mother bows; As if Olympus to a molehill should In supplication nod v 3 29
I prate, And the most noble mother of the world Leave unsaluted v 3 49
Making the mother, wife, and child to see The son, the husband and the father tearing His country's bowels v 3 101
Thou shalt no sooner March to assault thy country than to tread—Trust to't, thou shalt not—on thy mother's womb v 3 124
There's no man in the world More bound to's mother v 3 159
Thou hast never in thy life Show'd thy dear mother any courtesy v 3 161
Thou restrain'st from me the duty which To a mother's part belongs v 3 168
O mother, mother! What have you done? v 3 182
O my mother, mother! O! You have won a happy victory to Rome v 3 185
Were you in my stead, would you have heard A mother less? or granted less? v 3 193
Some hope the ladies of Rome, especially his mother, may prevail with him v 4 6
He loved his mother dearly.—So did he me v 4 15
He no more remembers his mother now than an eight-year-old horse v 4 17
Mark what mercy his mother shall bring from him v 4 29
Repeal him with the welcome of his mother v 5 5
And given up, For certain drops of salt, your city Rome, I say 'your city, to his wife and mother v 6 94
Rue the tears I shed, A mother's tears in passion for her son *T. Andron.* i 1 106
She will a handmaid be to his desires, A loving nurse, a mother to his youth i 1 332
Although our mother, unadvised, Gave you a dancing-rapier by your side ii 1 38
Nor would your noble mother for much more Be so dishonour'd ii 1 51
Our gracious mother! Why doth your highness look so pale and wan? ii 3 89
Revenge it, as you love your mother's life ii 3 114
You shall know, my boys, Your mother's hand shall right your mother's wrong ii 3 121
At thy teat thou hadst thy tyranny. Yet every mother breeds not sons alike ii 3 146
For our father's sake and mother's care, Now let me show a brother's love iii 1 182
I have but kill'd a fly.—But how, if that fly had a father and mother? iii 2 60
I know my noble aunt Loves me as dear as e'er my mother did iv 1 23
'Tis Ovid's Metamorphoses; My mother gave it me iv 1 43
If I were a man, Their mother's bed-chamber should not be safe iv 1 108
Here lacks but your mother for to say amen iv 2 44
Let us go; and pray to all the gods For our beloved mother in her pains iv 2 47
Thou hast undone our mother.—Villain, I have done thy mother iv 2 75
It shall not live.—It shall not die.—Aaron, it must; the mother wills it so iv 2 82
By this our mother is for ever shamed.—Rome will despise her iv 2 112
Go pack with him, and give the mother gold, And tell them both iv 2 155
Had nature lent thee but thy mother's look, Villain, thou mightst have been an emperor v 1 29
Will hold thee dearly for thy mother's sake v 1 36
That codding spirit had they from their mother v 1 99
You know your mother means to feast with me, And calls herself Revenge v 2 185
I'll play the cook, And see them ready 'gainst their mother comes v 2 206
They are both baked in that pie; Whereof their mother daintily hath fed v 3 61
Younger than she are happy mothers made *Rom. and Jul.* i 2 12
Younger than you, . . . ladies of esteem, Are made already mothers i 3 71
I was your mother much upon these years That you are now a maid i 3 72
Madam, your mother craves a word with you.—What is her mother?—Marry, bachelor, Her mother is the lady of the house, And a good lady i 5 113
The earth that's nature's mother is her tomb ii 3 9
Where is your mother?—Where is my mother! why, she is within ii 5 59
How oddly thou repliest! 'Your love says, like an honest gentleman, Where is your mother?' ii 5 63
Why follow'd not, when she said 'Tybalt's dead,' Thy father, or thy mother? iii 2 119
'Romeo is banished,' to speak that word, Is father, mother, Tybalt, Romeo, Juliet, All slain, all dead iii 2 123
Where is my father, and my mother, nurse?—Weeping and wailing iii 2 127
Your lady mother is coming to your chamber: The day is broke iii 5 39
Who is't that calls? is it my lady mother? Is she not down so late? iii 5 66
O, sweet my mother, cast me not away! Delay this marriage for a month iii 5 200
Thy mother's of my generation: what's she, if I be a dog? *T. of Athens* i 1 204
Whose proof, nor yells of mothers, maids, nor babes, Nor sight of priests in holy vestments bleeding, Shall pierce a jot iv 3 124
Common mother, thou, Whose womb unmeasurable, and infinite breast, Teems, and feeds all iv 3 177
If Cæsar had stabbed their mothers, they would have done no less! *J. C.* i 2 278
Our fathers' minds are dead, And we are govern'd with our mothers' spirits i 3 83
That mothers shall but smile when they behold Their infants quarter'd iii 1 267
That rash humour which my mother gave me Makes me forgetful iv 3 120
When you are over-earnest with your Brutus, He'll think your mother chides iv 3 123
O error, soon conceived, Thou never comest unto a happy birth, But kill'st the mother that engender'd thee! v 3 71
How will you live?—As birds do, mother *Macbeth* iv 2 32
Why should I, mother? Poor birds they are not set for iv 2 36
Was my father a traitor, mother?—Ay, that he was iv 2 44
Young fry of treachery!—He has kill'd me, mother: Run away, I pray you! iv 2 84
Alas, poor country! . . . It cannot Be call'd our mother, but our grave iv 3 166
Macduff was from his mother's womb Untimely ripp'd v 8 15
'Tis not alone my inky cloak, good mother *Hamlet* i 2 77

Mother. Let not thy mother lose her prayers, Hamlet: I pray thee, stay with us *Hamlet* i 2 118
So loving to my mother That he might not beteem the winds of heaven Visit her face too roughly i 2 140
Do not mock me, fellow-student; I think it was to see my mother's wedding i 2 178
Taint not thy mind, nor let thy soul contrive Against thy mother aught i 5 86
Horridly trick'd With blood of fathers, mothers, daughters, sons ii 2 480
That it were better my mother had not borne me iii 1 125
Let his queen mother all alone entreat him To show his grief iii 1 190
Dear Hamlet, sit by me.—No, good mother, here's metal more attractive iii 2 116
How cheerfully my mother looks, and my father died within these two hours iii 2 134
Your mother, in most great affliction of spirit, hath sent me to you iii 2 323
Make me a wholesome answer, I will do your mother's commandment iii 2 328
My mother, you say,— Then thus she says; your behaviour hath struck her into amazement and admiration iii 2 336
O wonderful son, that can so astonish a mother! But is there no sequel at the heels of this mother's admiration? iii 2 341
We shall obey, were she ten times our mother iii 2 346
I will come to my mother by and by. They fool me to the top of my bent iii 2 400
Soft! now to my mother. O heart, lose not thy nature! iii 2 410
He's going to his mother's closet: Behind the arras I'll convey myself iii 3 27
'Tis meet that some more audience than a mother, Since nature makes them partial, should o'erhear The speech, of vantage iii 3 31
My mother stays: This physic but prolongs thy sickly days iii 3 95
Mother, mother, mother!—I'll warrant you, Fear me not: withdraw iii 4 6
Now, mother, what's the matter?—Hamlet, thou hast thy father much offended.—Mother, you have my father much offended iii 4 8
You are the queen, your husband's brother's wife; And—would it were not so!—you are my mother iii 4 16
Almost as bad, good mother, As kill a king, and marry with his brother iii 4 28
Amazement on thy mother sits: O, step between her and her fighting soul iii 4 112
Hamlet in madness hath Polonius slain, And from his mother's closet hath he dragg'd him iv 1 35
Farewell, dear mother.—Thy loving father, Hamlet.—My mother: father and mother is man and wife; man and wife is one flesh; and so, my mother iv 3 51
How stand I then, That have a father kill'd, a mother stain'd? iv 4 57
Brands the harlot Even here, between the chaste unsmirched brow Of my true mother iv 5 120
The queen his mother Lives almost by his looks iv 7 11
Even his mother shall uncharge the practice And call it accident iv 7 68
He that hath kill'd my king and whored my mother v 2 64
Thy mother's poison'd: I can no more: the king, the king's to blame v 2 330
Drink off this potion. Is thy union here? Follow my mother v 2 338
I cannot conceive you.—Sir, this young fellow's mother could *Lear* i 1 13
Though this knave came something saucily into the world before he was sent for, yet was his mother fair i 1 23
My father compounded with my mother under the dragon's tail i 2 140
I have used it, nuncle, ever since thou madest thy daughters thy mother i 4 188
Turn all her mother's pains and benefits To laughter and contempt i 4 308
O, how this mother swells up toward my heart! ii 4 56
If thou shouldst not be glad, I would divorce me from thy mother's tomb ii 4 133
So much duty as my mother show'd To you, preferring you before her father, So much I challenge that I may profess Due to the Moor my lord *Othello* i 3 186
That handkerchief Did an Egyptian to my mother give iii 4 56
My mother had a maid call'd Barbara: She was in love iv 3 26
It was a handkerchief, an antique token My father gave my mother v 2 217
Thou hast a sister by the mother's side, Admired Octavia *Ant. and Cleo.* ii 2 120
When Cæsar and your brother were at blows, Your mother came to Sicily ii 6 46
Look here, love; This diamond was my mother's: take it, heart *Cymbeline* i 1 112
They dare not fight with me, because of the queen my mother ii 1 22
That such a crafty devil as is his mother Should yield the world this ass! ii 1 57
A father by thy step-dame govern'd, A mother hourly coining plots ii 1 64
Good morrow to your majesty and to my gracious mother ii 3 41
I will inform your father.—Your mother too: She's my good lady ii 3 157
My mother seem'd The Dian of that time: so doth my wife The nonpareil of this ii 5 8
Son, let your mother end iii 1 39
Euriphile, Thou wast their nurse; they took thee for their mother iii 3 104
Ne'er long'd my mother so To see me first, as I have now iii 4 2
Some jay of Italy, Whose mother was her painting, hath betray'd him iii 4 52
Plenty and peace breeds cowards: hardness ever Of hardiness is mother iii 6 22
But my mother . . . shall turn all into my commendations iv 1 22
I have sent Cloten's clotpoll down the stream, In embassy to his mother iv 2 185
What does he mean? since death of my dear'st mother It did not speak before iv 2 190
Where shall's lay him?—By good Euriphile, our mother iv 2 234
Sing him to the ground, As once our mother iv 2 237
Sleep, thou hast been a grandsire, and begot A father to me; and thou hast created A mother and two brothers v 4 125
Imogen, Thy mother's dead.—I am sorry for't, my lord.—O, she was naught v 5 270
Lapp'd In a most curious mantle, wrought by the hand Of his queen mother v 5 362
Am I A mother to the birth of three? Ne'er mother Rejoiced deliverance more v 5 369
I am no viper, yet I feed On mother's flesh which did me breed *Pericles* i 1 65
He's father, son, and husband mild; I mother, wife, and yet his child i 1 69
She an eater of her mother's flesh, By the defiling of her parent's bed i 1 130
Those mothers who, to nousle up their babes, Thought nought too curious i 4 42
Ay me! poor maid, Born in a tempest, when my mother died iv 1 19
That these pirates, Not enough barbarous, had not o'erboard thrown me For to seek my mother! iv 2 71
I was born at sea.—At sea! what mother?—My mother was the daughter of a king v 1 158
What was thy mother's name? tell me but that v 1 202
Is it no more to be your daughter than To say my mother's name was Thaisa? Thaisa was my mother v 1 212
My heart Leaps to be gone into my mother's bosom v 3 45

Mother earth. Where is this young gallant that is so desirous to lie with his mother earth? *As Y. Like It* i 2 213

Mother Prat; come, give me your hand.—I'll prat her *Mer. Wives* iv 2 191

Mother-queen. With him along is come the mother-queen *K. John* ii 1 62

Mother's son. That would hang us, every mother's son . *M. N. Dream* i 2 80
Come, sit down, every mother's son, and rehearse your parts . iii 1 75
Now, by my mother's son, and that's myself . *T. of Shrew* iv 5 6
My mother's son did get your father's heir . *K. John* i 1 128
Ten thousand bloody crowns of mothers' sons . *Richard II.* iii 3 96
Whose son art thou?—My mother's son, sir.—Thy mother's son! like enough, and thy father's shadow . 2 *Hen. IV.* iii 2 138
Mother-wit. It is extempore, from my mother-wit . *T. of Shrew* ii 1 265
Mothy. His horse hipped with an old mothy saddle . iii 2 49
Motion. Incite them to quick motion . *Tempest* iv 1 39
Here she comes.—O excellent motion! O exceeding puppet! *T. G. of V.* ii 1 100
It were a goot motion if we leave our pribbles and prabbles . *Mer. Wives* i 1 55
Give ear to his motions, Master Slender . i 1 221
Shall I lose my doctor? no; he gives me the potions and the motions . iii 1 105
He gives her folly motion and advantage . iii 2 35
The firm fixture of thy foot would give an excellent motion to thy gait in a semi-circled farthingale . iii 3 68
Your father and my uncle hath made motions: if it be my luck, so . iii 4 67
Never feels The wanton stings and motions of the sense *Meas. for Meas.* i 4 59
This sensible warm motion to become A kneaded clod . iii 1 120
He is a motion generative; that's infallible . iii 2 119
I have a motion much imports your good . v 1 541
Made daily motions for our home return . *Com. of Errors* i 1 60
We in your motion turn and you may move us . iii 2 24
Full of forms, figures, shapes, objects, . . . motions . *L. L. Lost* iv 2 69
Motion and long-during action tires The sinewy vigour of the traveller iv 3 307
With the motion of all elements, Courses as swift as thought in every power . iv 3 329
The music plays; vouchsafe some motion to it.—Our ears vouchsafe it v 2 216
Never will I trust to speeches penn'd, Nor to the motion of a schoolboy's tongue, Nor never come in vizard to my friend . v 2 403
With what art You sway the motion of Demetrius' heart *M. N. Dream* i 2 193
What demi-god Hath come so near creation? Move these eyes? Or whether, riding on the balls of mine, Seem they in motion? *M. of V.* iii 2 118
There's not the smallest orb which thou behold'st But in his motion like an angel sings . v 1 61
The motions of his spirit are dull as night And his affections dark . v 1 86
O excellent motion! Fellows, let's be gone.—The motion's good indeed and be it so . *T. of Shrew* i 2 280
And make you dance canary With spritely fire and motion . *All's Well* ii 1 78
In what motion age will give me leave . ii 3 247
The great figure of a council frames By self-unable motion . iii 1 13
And of other motions, as promising her marriage . v 3 264
All true lovers are Unstaid and skittish in all motions else *T. Night* ii 4 18
Their love may be call'd appetite, No motion of the liver, but the palate ii 4 101
Taste your legs, sir; put them to motion . iii 1 87
He gives me the stuck in with such a mortal motion . iii 4 304
I'll make the motion: stand here, make a good show on't . iii 4 316
Then he compassed a motion of the Prodigal Son *W. Tale* iv 3 103
The fixure of her eye has motion in't, As we are mock'd with art . v 3 67
From the inward motion to deliver Sweet, sweet, sweet poison *K. John* i 1 212
Lions more confident, mountains and rocks More free from motion . ii 1 453
This vile-drawing bias, This sway of motion, this Commodity . ii 1 578
Five moons were seen to-night; Four fixed, and the fifth did whirl about The other four in wondrous motion . iv 2 184
Within this bosom never enter'd yet The dreadful motion of a murderous thought . iv 2 255
Let not the world see fear and sad distrust Govern the motion of a kingly eye: Be stirring as the time . v 1 47
O, I am scalded with my violent motion, And spleen of speed! . v 7 49
Give it him, To keep his anger still in motion . 1 *Hen. IV.* i 3 226
In thy face strange motions have appear'd . ii 3 63
Two stars keep not their motion in one sphere . v 4 65
To be scoured to nothing with perpetual motion . 2 *Hen. IV.* i 2 247
A' shall charge you and discharge you with the motion of a pewterer's hammer . iii 2 281
Have I, in my poor and old motion, the expedition of thought? . iv 3 37
In divers functions, Setting endeavour in continual motion . *Hen. V.* i 2 185
In motion of no less celerity Than that of thought . iii Prol. 2
A foe to citizens, One that still motions war and never peace 1 *Hen. VI.* i 3 63
How doth your grace affect their motion? . v 1 7
Yes, I agree, and thank you for your motion . 3 *Hen. VI.* iii 3 244
From sincere motions, by intelligence, And proofs . *Hen. VIII.* i 1 153
If we shall stand still, In fear our motion will be mock'd or carp'd at . i 2 86
Meanwhile must be an earnest motion Made to the queen . ii 4 233
Things in motion sooner catch the eye Than what not stirs *Tr. and Cr.* iii 3 183
Hasty and tinder-like upon too trivial motion . *Coriolanus* ii 1 56
We do request your kindest ears, and after, Your loving motion toward the common body, To yield what passes here . ii 2 57
He was a thing of blood, whose every motion Was timed with dying cries ii 2 113
A beggar's tongue Make motion through my lips! . iii 2 118
Tell me, Andronicus, doth this motion please thee? . *T. Andron.* i 1 243
Had she affections and warm youthful blood, She would be as swift in motion as a ball . *Rom. and Jul.* ii 5 13
Vile earth, to earth resign; end motion here! . iii 2 59
Still in motion Of raging waste? It cannot hold; it will not *T. of Athens* ii 1 3
What, all in motion? Henceforth be no feast, Whereat a villain's not a welcome guest . iii 6 112
Between the acting of a dreadful thing And the first motion . *J. Cæsar* ii 1 64
Unassailable holds on his rank, Unshaked of motion . iii 1 70
His corporal motion govern'd by my spirit . iv 1 33
Nor our strong sorrow Upon the foot of motion . *Macbeth* ii 3 131
It lifted up it head and did address Itself to motion . *Hamlet* i 2 217
Sense, sure, you have, Else could you not have motion? . iii 4 72
The scrimers of their nation, He swore, had neither motion, guard, nor eye iv 7 102
When in your motion you are hot and dry . iv 7 158
In fell motion, With his prepared sword, he charges home . *Lear* ii 1 52
Abused her delicate youth with drugs or minerals That weaken motion *Othello* i 2 75
Of spirit so still and quiet, that her motion Blush'd at herself . i 3 95
We have reason to cool our raging motions, our carnal stings . i 3 335
He that stirs next to carve for his own rage Holds his soul light; he dies upon his motion . ii 3 174
Lackeying the varying tide, To rot itself with motion . *Ant. and Cleo.* i 4 47
Your reason?—I see it in My motion, have it not in my tongue . ii 3 14
She creeps: Her motion and her station are as one . iii 3 22
This object, which Takes prisoner the wild motion of mine eye *Cymbeline* i 6 103
The cutter Was as another nature, dumb; outwent her, Motion and breath left out . ii 4 85
No motion That tends to vice in man, but I affirm It is the woman's part ii 5 20

Motion. My ingenious instrument! Hark, Polydore, it sounds! But what occasion Hath Cadwal now to give it motion? . *Cymbeline* iv 2 188
The want is but to put those powers in motion That long to move . iv 3 31
Have you a working pulse? and are no fairy? Motion! Well; speak on *Pericles* v 1 156
Motionless. In their pale dull mouths the gimmal bit Lies foul with chew'd grass, still and motionless . *Hen. V.* iv 2 50
Motive. Thy father's wealth Was the first motive that I woo'd thee *Mer. Wives* iii 4 14
This was your motive For Paris, was it? . *All's Well* i 3 236
As it hath fated her to be my motive And helper to a husband . iv 4 20
As all impediments in fancy's course Are motives of more fancy . v 3 215
What motive may Be stronger with thee than the name of wife? *K. John* iii 1 313
The slavish motive of recanting fear . *Richard II.* i 1 193
For me, the gold of France did not seduce; Although I did admit it as a motive The sooner to effect what I intended . *Hen. V.* ii 2 156
Her wanton spirits look out At every joint and motive of her body *Troi. and Cres.* iv 5 57
Could never be the motive Of our so frank donation . *Coriolanus* iii 1 129
Nor are they living Who were the motives . *T. of Athens* v 4 27
If these be motives weak, break off betimes . *J. Cæsar* ii 1 116
Wife and child, Those precious motives, those strong knots of love *Macb.* iv 3 27
This, I take it, Is the main motive of our preparations . *Hamlet* i 1 105
The very place puts toys of desperation, Without more motive, into every brain . i 4 76
What would he do, Had he the motive and the cue for passion That I have? ii 2 587
The other motive, Why to a public count I might not go . iv 7 16
I am satisfied in nature, Whose motive, in this case, should stir me most v 2 256
Nor fear to lose it, Thy safety being the motive . *Lear* i 1 159
Alas the heavy day! Why do you weep? Am I the motive of these tears? . *Othello* iv 2 43
For which myself, the ignorant motive, do So far ask pardon *A. and C.* ii 2 96
Though you did love this youth, I blame ye not; You had a motive *Cymb.* v 5 268
These, And your three motives to the battle . v 5 388
Motley. I met a fool i' the forest, A motley fool! . *As Y. Like It* ii 7 13
And rail'd on Lady Fortune in good terms, In good set terms and yet a motley fool . ii 7 17
When I did hear The motley fool thus moral on the time . ii 7 29
O noble fool! A worthy fool! Motley's the only wear . ii 7 34
O that I were a fool! I am ambitious for a motley coat . ii 7 43
Invest me in my motley; give me leave To speak my mind . ii 7 58
Will you be married motley? . iii 3 79
That's as much to say as I wear not motley in my brain *T. Night* i 5 63
To see a fellow In a long motley coat guarded with yellow *Hen. VIII.* Prol. 16
The sweet and bitter fool Will presently appear; The one in motley here, The other found out there . *Lear* i 4 160
Motley-minded. This is the motley-minded gentleman . *As Y. Like It* v 4 41
Motto. The motto thus, in Spanish, 'Piu por dulzura que por fuerza' *Per.* ii 2 27
The motto, 'In hac spe vivo' . ii 2 44
Mought. Which sounded like a clamour in a vault, That mought not be distinguished . 3 *Hen. VI.* v 2 45
Mould. Unless you were of gentler, milder mould . *T. of Shrew* i 1 60
The very mould and frame of hand, nail, finger . *W. Tale* ii 3 103
That self mould that fashion'd thee Made him a man . *Richard II.* i 2 23
Be merciful, great duke, to men of mould . *Hen. V.* iii 2 23
All princely graces, That mould up such a mighty piece as this is *Hen. VIII.* v 5 27
Were there but this single plot to lose, This mould of Marcius, they to dust should grind it . *Coriolanus* iii 2 103
The honour'd mould Wherein this trunk was framed . v 3 22
New honours come upon him, Like our strange garments, cleave not to their mould But with the aid of use . *Macbeth* i 3 145
The glass of fashion and the mould of form . *Hamlet* iii 1 161
Crack nature's moulds, all germens spill at once . *Lear* iii 2 8
Moulded. They say, best men are moulded out of faults . *Meas. for Meas.* v 1 444
Two lovely berries moulded on one stem . *M. N. Dream* iii 3 211
Why, this was moulded on a porringer; A velvet dish . *T. of Shrew* iv 3 64
These eyes, these brows, were moulded out of his . *K. John* ii 1 100
Whose arms were moulded in their mothers' womb To chase these pagans 1 *Hen. IV.* i 1 23
Now I feel Of what coarse metal ye are moulded, envy . *Hen. VIII.* iii 2 239
All with one consent praise new-born gawds, Though they are made and moulded of things past . *Troi. and Cres.* iii 3 177
Great nature, like his ancestry, Moulded the stuff so fair . *Cymbeline* v 4 49
Where, by the loss of maidenhead, A babe is moulded . *Pericles* iii Gower 11
Mouldeth. I'll haunt thee like a wicked conscience still, That mouldeth goblins swift as frenzy's thoughts . *Troi. and Cres.* v 10 29
Mouldy. Away, you mouldy rogue, away! . 2 *Hen. IV.* ii 4 134
I'll thrust my knife in your mouldy chaps . ii 4 139
He lives upon mouldy stewed prunes and dried cakes . ii 4 158
So, so, so, so, so, so, so: yea, marry, sir: Ralph Mouldy! . iii 2 109
Is thy name Mouldy?—Yea, an't please you.—'Tis the more time thou wert used . iii 2 115
Things that are mouldy lack use . iii 2 119
Go to: peace, Mouldy; you shall go. Mouldy, it is time you were spent iii 2 127
Sir, a word with you: I have three pound to free Mouldy and Bullcalf iii 2 261
Mouldy, stay at home till you are past service . iii 2 268
Whose wit was mouldy ere your grandsires had nails . *Troi. and Cres.* ii 1 115
Moult. And your secrecy to the king and queen moult no feather *Hamlet* ii 2 306
Moulten. A clip-wing'd griffin and a moulten raven . 1 *Hen. IV.* iii 1 152
Mounsieur Cobweb, good mounsieur . *M. N. Dream* iv 1 10
Do not fret yourself too much in the action, mounsieur . iv 1 15
Give me your neaf, Mounsieur Mustardseed . iv 1 20
Pray you, leave your courtesy, good mounsieur.—What's your will? . iv 1 21
Mount. And mount Their pricks at my footfall . *Tempest* ii 2 11
But mount you presently and meet with me . *T. G. of Ver.* v 2 45
But all's brave that youth mounts and folly guides . *As Y. Like It* iii 4 49
There will we mount, and thither walk on foot . *T. of Shrew* iv 3 188
What power is it which mounts my love so high? . *All's Well* i 1 235
Amen, amen! Mount, chevaliers! to arms! . *K. John* ii 1 287
Let France and England mount Their battering cannon . ii 1 381
O then, tread down my need, and faith mounts up; Keep my need up, and faith is trodden down! . v 1 215
And when I mount, alive may I not light, If I be traitor! . *Richard II.* i 1 82
Full of tears am I, Drinking my griefs, whilst you mount up on high . iv 1 189
Mount thee upon his horse; Spur post, and get before him to the king v 2 111
Mount, mount, my soul! thy seat is up on high . v 5 112
And let desert mount.—Thine's too heavy to mount . 2 *Hen. IV.* iv 3 61
But only in patient stillness while his rider mounts him . *Hen. V.* iii 7 25
How our steeds for present service neigh!—Mount them . iv 2 9
Let the trumpets sound The tucket sonance and the note to mount . iv 2 35

Mount. And here will Talbot mount, or make his grave . . 1 *Hen. VI.* ii 1 34
Mount on my swiftest horse; And I'll direct thee how thou shalt escape iv 5 9
She will light to listen to the lays, And never mount . 2 *Hen. VI.* i 3 94
'Tis but a base ignoble mind That mounts no higher than a bird can soar ii 1 14
He is near you in descent, And should you fall, he is the next will mount iii 1 22
Mount you, my lord; towards Berwick post amain . . 3 *Hen. VI.* ii 5 128
When I should mount with wings of victory . . . *Richard III.* v 3 106
Know you not, The fire that mounts the liquor till't run o'er, In seeming to augment it wastes it? . . . . *Hen. VIII.* i 1 144
Arm thy heart, and fit thy thoughts, To mount aloft with thy imperial mistress, And mount her pitch . . . . . . *T. Andron.* ii 1 13
The base o' the mount Is rank'd with all deserts . . *T. of Athens* i 1 64
Bowing his head against the steepy mount To climb his happiness . . i 1 75
Mount thou my horse, and hide thy spurs in him . . . *J. Cæsar* v 3 15
It is a massy wheel, Fix'd on the summit of the highest mount *Hamlet* iii 3 18
Stood challenger on mount of all the age For her perfections . . iv 7 28
So he nodded, And soberly did mount an arm-gaunt steed *Ant. and Cleo.* i 5 48
We shall, As I conceive the journey, be at the Mount Before you . . ii 4 6
As common as the stairs That mount the Capitol . . *Cymbeline* i 6 106
Mount, eagle, to my palace crystalline . . . . . v 4 113
Unto thy value I will mount myself Upon a courser, whose delightful steps Shall make the gazer joy to see him tread . . . *Pericles* ii 1 163
Mountain. Thou shalt be as free As mountain winds . . *Tempest* i 2 499
Turfy mountains, where live nibbling sheep . . . . . . iv 1 62
Hey, Mountain, hey!—Silver! there it goes, Silver!—Fury, Fury! . iv 1 256
More pinch-spotted make them Than pard or cat o' mountain . . iv 1 262
I should have been a mountain of mummy . . . *Mer. Wives* iii 5 18
But for the mountain of mad flesh that claims marriage of me *Com. of Er.* iv 4 158
Into a mountain of affection the one with the other . *Much Ado* ii 1 382
Do you not educate youth at the charge-house on the top of the mountain? —Or mons, the hill.—At your sweet pleasure, for the mountain *L. L. Lost* v 1 88
We will, fair queen, up to the mountain's top . . . *M. N. Dream* iv 1 114
Small and undistinguishable, Like far-off mountains turned into clouds iv 1 193
As well forbid the mountain pines To wag their high tops *Mer. of Venice* iv 1 75
But mountains may be removed with earthquakes . . *As Y. Like It* iii 2 195
Ay, to the proof; as mountains are for winds, That shake not, though they blow perpetually . . . . *T. of Shrew* ii 1 141
Ungracious wretch, Fit for the mountains and the barbarous caves! *T. N.* iv 1 52
A thousand knees Ten thousand years together, naked, fasting, Upon a barren mountain, and still winter In storm perpetual, could not move the gods To look that way thou wert . . . *W. Tale* iii 2 213
Mountains and rocks More free from motion . . . . *K. John* ii 1 452
Here's a large mouth, indeed, That spits forth death and mountains! . ii 1 458
As a little snow, tumbled about, Anon becomes a mountain . . . iii 4 177
On the barren mountains let him starve . . . . 1 *Hen. IV.* i 3 89
That wish'd him on the barren mountains starve . . . . . i 3 159
Gross as a mountain, open, palpable . . . . ii 4 250
The goats ran from the mountains, and the herds Were strangely clamorous to the frighted fields . . . . iii 1 39
See the revolution of the times Make mountains level . 2 *Hen. IV.* iii 1 47
Our peace shall stand as firm as rocky mountains . . . . iv 1 188
His mountain sire, on mountain standing, Up in the air . *Hen. V.* ii 4 57
Though we upon this mountain's basis by Took stand . . . . iv 2 30
Thou damned and luxurious mountain goat, Offer'st me brass? . iv 4 20
Strong-fixed is the house of Lancaster And like a mountain . 1 *Hen. VI.* ii 5 103
Make him stand upon this molehill here, That raught at mountains with outstretched arms . . . . 3 *Hen. VI.* i 4 68
To make an envious mountain on my back, Where sits deformity . . iii 2 157
Like a mountain cedar, reach his branches To all the plains about him *Hen. VIII.* v 5 54
The strong-ribb'd bark through liquid mountains cut . *Troi. and Cres.* i 3 40
The mountain lioness, The ocean swells not so as Aaron storms *T. An.* iv 2 138
His dependants Which labour'd after him to the mountain's top *T. Athens* i 1 86
Set a huge mountain 'tween my heart and tongue! . *J. Cæsar* ii 4 7
Could you on this fair mountain leave to feed? . . . *Hamlet* iii 4 66
The sun no sooner shall the mountains touch . . . . . iv 1 29
White his shroud as the mountain snow . . . . . . iv 5 35
Till of this flat a mountain you have made, To o'ertop old Pelion . . v 1 275
If thou prate of mountains, let them throw Millions of acres on us! . v 1 303
If it hath ruffian'd so upon the sea, What ribs of oak, when mountains melt on them, Can hold the mortise? . . . . . . *Othello* ii 1 8
A forked mountain, or blue promontory, With trees upon't *Ant. and Cleo.* iv 14 5
Now for our mountain sport: up to yond hill . . . *Cymbeline* iii 3 10
But up to the mountains! This is not hunters' language . . . iii 3 73
As the rudest wind, That by the top doth take the mountain pine . iv 2 175
We'll higher to the mountains; there secure us . . . . iv 4 8
Which directed him To seek her on the mountains near to Milford . v 5 281
For who digs hills because they do aspire Throws down one mountain to cast up a higher . . . . *Pericles* i 4 6
I'll show you those in troubles reign, Losing a mite, a mountain gain ii Gower. 8
Mountaineer. Who would believe that there were mountaineers Dewlapp'd like bulls? . . . . *Tempest* iii 3 44
What are you That fly me thus? some villain mountaineers? *Cymbeline* iv 2 71
Yield, rustic mountaineer . . . . iv 2 100
Who call'd me traitor, mountaineer . . . . iv 2 120
A very valiant Briton and a good, That here by mountaineers lies slain iv 2 370
Mountain-foot. Upon the rising of the mountain-foot . *T. G. of Ver.* v 2 46
Mountain-foreigner. Ha, thou mountain-foreigner! . . *Mer. Wives* i 1 164
Mountainous error be too highly heapt For truth to o'er-peer . *Coriolanus* ii 3 127
Mountain-squire. You called me yesterday mountain-squire . *Hen. V.* v 1 37
Mountain top. Well could I curse away a winter's night, Though standing naked on a mountain top . . . . . . 2 *Hen. VI.* iii 2 336
As on a mountain-top the cedar shows That keeps his leaves . . . v 1 205
Orpheus with his lute made trees, And the mountain tops that freeze, Bow themselves when he did sing . . . . *Hen. VIII.* iii 1 4
Jocund day Stands tiptoe on the misty mountain tops . *Rom. and Jul.* iii 5 10
Milford, When from the mountain-top Pisanio show'd thee, Thou wast within a ken . . . . *Cymbeline* iii 6 5
Mountant. Hold up, you sluts, Your aprons mountant . *T. of Athens* iv 3 135
Mountanto. I pray you, is Signior Mountanto returned from the wars or no? . . . . *Much Ado* i 1 30
Mountebank. Disguised cheaters, prating mountebanks . *Com. of Errors* i 2 101
A mere anatomy, a mountebank, A threadbare juggler . . . . v 1 238
I'll mountebank their loves, Cog their hearts from them *Coriolanus* iii 2 132
I bought an unction of a mountebank . . . . . *Hamlet* iv 7 142
Corrupted By spells and medicines bought of mountebanks . . *Othello* i 3 61
Mounted. Encounters mounted are Against your peace . . *L. L. Lost* v 2 82
In such a night Troilus methinks mounted the Troyan walls *Mer. of Venice* v 1 4
Mounted. No jewel is like Rosalind. Her worth, being mounted on the wind, Through all the world bears Rosalind . . . *As Y. Like It* iii 2 95
The cannons have their bowels full of wrath, And ready mounted *K. John* ii 1 211
Myself, well mounted, hardly have escaped . . . . v 6 42
Mounted upon a hot and fiery steed . . . . . *Richard II.* v 2 8
Bolingbroke and he, Being mounted and both roused in their seats 2 *Hen. IV.* iv 1 118
His affections are higher mounted than ours . . . . *Hen. V.* iv 1 111
Let him shun castles; Safer shall he be upon the sandy plains Than where castles mounted stand . . . . 2 *Hen. VI.* i 4 72
That beggars mounted run their horse to death . . . 3 *Hen. VI.* i 4 127
What, will the aspiring blood of Lancaster Sink in the ground? I thought it would have mounted . . . . v 6 62
And now are mounted Where powers are your retainers . *Hen. VIII.* iv 4 112
Like a full-acorn'd boar, a German one, Cried 'O!' and mounted *Cymb.* ii 5 17
Mounteth. For courage mounteth with occasion . . . *K. John* ii 1 82
Mounting. The sea, mounting to the welkin's cheek . . . *Tempest* i 2 4
Whoe'er a' was, a' show'd a mounting mind . . . *L. L. Lost* iv 1 4
This is worshipful society And fits the mounting spirit like myself *K. John* i 1 206
Down, king! For night-owls shriek where mounting larks should sing *Richard II.* iii 3 183
Thou ladder wherewithal The mounting Bolingbroke ascends my throne v 1 56
Instead of mounting barbed steeds . . . . . *Richard III.* i 1 10
Mounting his eyes, He did discharge a horrible oath . . *Hen. VIII.* i 2 205
Mourn. Then shall he mourn, If ever love had interest in his liver *M. Ado* iv 1 232
To-night I'll mourn with Hero . . . . v 1 339
If in black my lady's brows be deck'd, It mourns that painting and usurping hair Should ravish doters with a false aspect . *L. L. Lost* iv 3 259
And that his lady mourns at his disease . . . *T. of Shrew* Ind. 1 62
O, this it is that makes your lady mourn! . . . . . . Ind. 2 28
His soul is in heaven, fool.—The more fool, madonna, to mourn for your brother's soul being in heaven . . . . *T. Night* i 5 76
I am out of service: But shall I go mourn for that, my dear? *W. Tale* iv 3 15
Some will mourn in ashes, some coal-black . . . *Richard II.* v 1 49
Come, mourn with me for that I do lament, And put on sullen black . v 6 47
For this I shall have time enough to mourn . . . 2 *Hen. IV.* i 1 136
We mourn in black: why mourn we not in blood? . . 1 *Hen. VI.* i 1 17
Mourn not, except thou sorrow for my good . . . . . . ii 5 111
He dies, we lose; I break my warlike word; We mourn, France smiles iv 3 32
Why only, Suffolk, mourn I not for thee? . . . . 2 *Hen. VI.* iii 2 383
No, my love, I should not mourn, but die for thee . . . . iv 4 25
The hope thereof makes Clifford mourn in steel . . 3 *Hen. VI.* i 1 58
The tiger will be mild whiles she doth mourn . . . . . iii 1 39
No more than from my soul I mourn for yours . . *Richard III.* iv 1 89
O, who hath any cause to mourn but I? . . . . iv 4 34
And all the world shall mourn her . . . . . *Hen. VIII.* iv 5 63
Bear from hence his body; And mourn you for him . . *Coriolanus* v 6 144
We will mourn with thee: O, could our mourning ease thy misery! *T. An.* ii 4 56
You all did love him once, not without cause: What cause withholds you then, to mourn for him? . . . . *J. Cæsar* iii 2 108
Into the madness wherein now he raves, And all we mourn for *Hamlet* ii 2 151
To mourn a mischief that is past and gone Is the next way to draw new mischief on . . . . *Othello* i 3 204
Be resolved he lives to govern us, Or dead, give's cause to mourn *Pericles* ii 4 32
We wept after her hearse, And yet we mourn . . . . . iv 3 42
To mourn thy crosses, with thy daughter's, call And give them repetition v 1 246
Mourned. The pretty babes, That mourn'd for fashion . *Com. of Errors* i 1 74
Buried a wife, mourned for her . . . . . . *All's Well* iv 3 102
Thou wouldest not have mourn'd so much for me . . 2 *Hen. VI.* iv 4 24
Here comes his body, mourned by Mark Antony . . . *J. Cæsar* iii 2 45
A beast, that wants discourse of reason, Would have mourn'd longer *Ham.* i 2 151
Mourner. Please thee leave these sad designs To him that hath more cause to be a mourner . . . . *Richard III.* i 2 212
I am no mourner for that news . . . . iii 2 51
Tarry for the mourners, and stay dinner . . . *Rom. and Jul.* iv 5 150
Mournest. Good madonna, why mournest thou?—Good fool, for my brother's death . . . . *T. Night* i 5 72
Mournful. On your family's old monument Hang mournful epitaphs *M. Ado* iv 1 209
The treacherous manner of his mournful death . . 1 *Hen. VI.* ii 2 16
As the mournful crocodile With sorrow snares relenting passengers 2 *Hen. VI.* iii 1 226
Give me thy hand, That I may dew it with my mournful tears . . iii 2 340
No mournful bell shall ring her burial . . . . *T. Andron.* v 3 197
Mournfully. Beat thou the drum, that it speak mournfully . *Coriolanus* v 6 151
Mourning. All three distracted And the remainder mourning . *Tempest* v 1 13
Maintain a mourning ostentation . . . . . . *Much Ado* iv 1 207
Though the mourning brow of progeny Forbid the smiling courtesy of love . . . . *L. L. Lost* v 2 754
And till that instant shut My woeful self up in a mourning house . v 2 818
The thrice three Muses mourning for the death Of Learning *M. N. Dream* v 1 52
Grace my mournings here; In weeping after this untimely bier *Richard II.* v 6 51
And she a mourning widow of her nobles . . . . . *Hen. V.* i 2 158
How now, madam! Still lamenting and mourning for Suffolk's death? 2 *Hen. VI.* iv 4 22
Shall we go throw away our coats of steel, And wrap our bodies in black mourning gowns? . . . . 3 *Hen. VI.* ii 1 161
I and ten thousand in this luckless realm Had left no mourning widows ii 6 19
Tell him, my mourning weeds are laid aside . . . iii 3 229; iv 1 104
Hail, Rome, victorious in thy mourning weeds! . . . . *T. Andron.* i 1 70
We will mourn with thee: O, could our mourning ease thy misery! . ii 4 57
No funeral rite, nor man in mourning weeds, No mournful bell shall ring v 3 196
Here is a mourning Rome, a dangerous Rome, No Rome of safety *J. Cæsar* iii 1 288
Where, Messala, doth his body lie?—Lo, yonder, and Titinius mourning it v 3 92
'Tis sweet and commendable in your nature, Hamlet, To give these mourning duties to your father . . . . *Hamlet* i 2 88
My mourning and important tears hath pitied . . . . . *Lear* iv 4 26
Mourningly. Spoke of him admiringly and mourningly . . *All's Well* i 1 34
Mouse. What's your dark meaning, mouse, of this light word? *L. L. Lost* v 2 19
Ladies, you, whose gentle hearts do fear The smallest monstrous mouse that creeps on floor . . . . *M. N. Dream* v 1 223
Not a mouse Shall disturb this hallow'd house . . . . . . v 1 394
Good my mouse of virtue, answer me . . . . . *T. Night* i 5 69
As valiant as the wrathful dove or most magnanimous mouse 2 *Hen. IV.* iii 2 171
Playing the mouse in absence of the cat . . . . . *Hen. V.* i 2 172
The mouse ne'er shunn'd the cat as they did budge . . *Coriolanus* i 6 44
Dun's the mouse, the constable's own word . . . *Rom. and Jul.* i 4 40
'Zounds, a dog, a rat, a mouse, a cat, to scratch a man to death! . . iii 1 104
And every cat and dog And little mouse, every unworthy thing . . iii 3 31
Have you had quiet guard?—Not a mouse stirring . . . . *Hamlet* i 1 10
Pinch wanton on your cheek; call you his mouse . . . . . iii 4 183

Mouse. Look, look, a mouse! Peace, peace; this piece of toasted cheese will do't . . . . *Lear* iv 6 89
The cat, with eyne of burning coal, Now couches fore the mouse's hole; And crickets sing . . . . *Pericles* iii Gower 6
Believe me, la, I never kill'd a mouse, nor hurt a fly . . . iv 1 78
Moused. Well moused, Lion.—And so the lion vanished . *M. N. Dream* v 1 274
Mouse-eaten. That stale old mouse-eaten dry cheese, Nestor *Troi. and Cres.* v 4 11
Mouse-hunt. Ay, you have been a mouse-hunt in your time *Rom. and Jul.* iv 4 11
Mouse-trap. What do you call the play?—The Mouse-trap . *Hamlet* iii 2 247
Mousing. Now he feasts, mousing the flesh of men . . *K. John* ii 1 354
Was by a mousing owl hawk'd at and kill'd . . . *Macbeth* ii 4 13
Mouth. What, must our mouths be cold? . . . . . *Tempest* i 1 56
Open your mouth; here is that which will give language to you . . ii 2 85
Open your mouth; this will shake your shaking . . . ii 2 87
I will pour some in thy other mouth.—Stephano!—Doth thy other mouth call me? Mercy, mercy! This is a devil . . . ii 2 99
Than to suffer The flesh-fly blow my mouth . . . iii 1 63
See'st thou here, This is the mouth o' the cell: no noise, and enter . iv 1 216
Whom to call brother Would even infect my mouth . . . v 1 131
Now, blasphemy, That swear'st grace o'erboard, not an oath on shore? Hast thou no mouth by land? . . . . v 1 220
Why dost thou stop my mouth?—For fear thou shouldst lose thy tongue.—Where should I lose my tongue? . . *T. G. of Ver.* ii 3 51
She hath a sweet mouth.—That makes amends for her sour breath . iii 1 330
Let us command to know that of your mouth or of your lips . *Mer. Wives* i 1 235
Divers philosophers hold that the lips is parcel of the mouth . . i 1 237
Heaven in my mouth, As if I did but only chew his name *Meas. for Meas.* ii 4 4
O perilous mouths, That bear in them one and the self-same tongue, Either of condemnation or approof! . . . . ii 4 172
He would mouth with a beggar, though she smelt brown bread and garlic . . . . iii 2 194
Came I hither, To speak, as from his mouth, what he doth know Is true v 1 155
And put your trial in the villain's mouth Which here you come to accuse . . . . v 1 304
In foul mouth And in the witness of his proper ear, To call him villain v 1 309
If I had my mouth, I would bite . . . . . . *Much Ado* i 3 36
Half Signior Benedick's tongue in Count John's mouth . . . ii 1 13
Stop his mouth with a kiss, and let not him speak neither . . ii 1 322
Thy wit is as quick as the greyhound's mouth; it catches . . v 2 12
I was told you were in a consumption.—Peace! I will stop your mouth v 4 98
I only have made a mouth of his eye, By adding a tongue . *L. L. Lost* ii 1 251
Make mouths upon me when I turn my back . . *M. N. Dream* iii 2 238
Slow in pursuit, but match'd in mouth like bells, Each under each . iv 1 128
Her mantle she did fall, Which Lion vile with bloody mouth did stain . v 1 144
I had rather be married to a death's-head with a bone in his mouth *Mer. of Venice* i 2 56
Your worship was the last man in our mouths . . . . i 3 61
With his mouth full of news . . . . . *As Y. Like It* i 2 98
Seeking the bubble reputation Even in the cannon's mouth . . ii 7 153
Till thou canst quit thee by thy brother's mouth Of what we think . iii 1 11
I would thou couldst stammer, that thou mightst pour this concealed man out of thy mouth . . . . iii 2 210
Take the cork out of thy mouth that I may drink thy tidings . . iii 2 213
You must borrow me Gargantua's mouth first: 'tis a word too great for any mouth of this age's size . . . . iii 2 239
Who with her head nimble in threats approach'd The opening of his mouth . . . . iv 3 111
When he had a desire to eat a grape, would open his lips when he put it into his mouth . . . . v 1 38
And not a jot of Tranio in your mouth . . . *T. of Shrew* i 1 241
My very lips might freeze to my teeth, my tongue to the roof of my mouth . . . . iv 1 8
As the nun's lip to the friar's mouth . . . . *All's Well* ii 2 28
I'ld give bay Curtal and his furniture, My mouth no more were broken than these boys' . . . . ii 3 66
Tongue, I must put you into a butter-woman's mouth . . . iv 1 45
Yes, by Saint Anne, and ginger shall be hot i' the mouth too . *T. Night* ii 3 127
I'll deliver thy indignation to him by word of mouth . . . ii 3 141
I will deliver his challenge by word of mouth . . . . iii 4 209
From the rude sea's enraged and foamy mouth . . . . v 1 81
Nor shall you be safer Than one condemn'd by the king's own mouth *W. Tale* i 2 445
The innocent milk in it most innocent mouth, Haled out to murder . iii 2 101
She [Fortune] drops booties in my mouth . . . . . iv 4 864
Then take my king's defiance from my mouth . . *K. John* i 1 21
Their battering cannon charged to the mouths . . . . ii 1 382
Turn thou the mouth of thy artillery, As we will ours . . . ii 1 403
From north to south: Austria and France shoot in each other's mouth . ii 1 414
The mouth of passage shall we fling wide ope, And give you entrance ii 1 449
Here's a large mouth, indeed, That spits forth death and mountains! ii 1 457
And from the mouth of England Add thus much more . . iii 1 152
Will't not be? Will not a calf's-skin stop that mouth of thine? . iii 1 299
O husband, hear me! ay, alack, how new Is husband in my mouth! iii 1 306
The midnight bell Did, with his iron tongue and brazen mouth, Sound on iii 3 38
O, that my tongue were in the thunder's mouth! . . . iii 4 38
Men's mouths are full of it . . . . iv 2 161
Young Arthur's death is common in their mouths . . . iv 2 187
With open mouth swallowing a tailor's news . . . . iv 2 195
Take from my mouth the wish of happy years . . . *Richard II.* i 3 94
A heavy sentence, . . . And all unlook'd for from your highness' mouth i 3 155
Within my mouth you have engaol'd my tongue . . . i 3 166
That word 'grace' In an ungracious mouth is but profane . . ii 3 89
One kiss shall stop our mouths, and dumbly part . . . v 1 95
My knees grow to the earth, My tongue cleave to my roof within my mouth . . . . v 3 31
His words come from his mouth, ours from our breast . . . v 3 102
No word like 'pardon' for kings' mouths so meet . . . v 3 118
From your own mouth, my lord, did I this deed . . . v 6 37
We in the world's wide mouth Live scandalized . . *1 Hen. IV.* i 3 153
That I did pluck allegiance from men's hearts, Loud shouts and salutations from their mouths . . . . iii 2 53
Made a friend of him, To fill the mouth of deep defiance up . . iii 2 116
I had as lief they would put ratsbane in my mouth as offer to stop it with security . . . . *2 Hen. IV.* i 2 48
Our thighs pack'd with wax, our mouths with honey . . . iv 5 77
Our history shall with full mouth Speak freely of our acts, or else our grave, Like Turkish mute, shall have a tongueless mouth *Hen. V.* i 2 230
Yea, in thy maw, perdy, And, which is worse, within thy nasty mouth! ii 1 53
Touch her soft mouth, and march.—Farewell, hostess . . . ii 3 61
Mouth. Coward dogs Most spend their mouths when what they seem to threaten Runs far before them . . . . . . *Hen. V.* ii 4 70
Behold the ordnance on their carriages, With fatal mouths gaping iii Prol. 27
Foolish curs, that run winking into the mouth of a Russian bear! . iii 7 154
In their pale dull mouths the gimmal bit Lies foul with chew'd grass . iv 2 49
Our names, Familiar in his mouth as household words . . . iv 3 52
It is not well done, mark you now, to take the tales out of my mouth . iv 7 45
The liberty that follows our places stops the mouth of all find-faults . v 2 298
And have their provender tied to their mouths . . *1 Hen. VI.* i 2 11
Between two dogs, which hath the deeper mouth . . . ii 4 12
Was in the mouth of every sucking babe . . . . . iii 1 197
To take occasion from their mouths To raise a mutiny . . . iv 1 130
To have thee with thy lips to stop my mouth . . *2 Hen. VI.* iii 2 396
Now will I dam up this thy yawning mouth For swallowing the treasure iv 1 73
Only that the laws of England may come out of your mouth . . iv 7 8
He was thrust in the mouth with a spear, and 'tis not whole yet . . iv 7 10
My mouth shall be the parliament of England . . . . iv 7 17
Suppose that I am now my father's mouth . . . *3 Hen. VI.* v 5 18
See, see! dead Henry's wounds Open their congeal'd mouths! *Rich. III.* i 2 56
With curses in her mouth, tears in her eyes . . . . i 2 233
Now prosperity begins to mellow And drop into the rotten mouth of death . . . . iv 4 2
I'll to the king; And from a mouth of honour quite cry down This Ipswich fellow's insolence . . . . *Hen. VIII.* i 1 137
This makes bold mouths: Tongues spit their duties out . . . i 2 60
No doubt he's noble; He had a black mouth that said other of him . i 3 58
His master would be served before a subject, if not before the king; which stopped our mouths . . . . ii 2 9
And you, O fate! . . . have your mouth fill'd up Before you open it . ii 3 87
Who dare cross 'em, Bearing the king's will from his mouth expressly? iii 2 235
Which, since they are of you, and odious, I will not taint my mouth with . . . . iii 2 332
Stop their mouths with stubborn bits, and spur 'em, Till they obey the manage . . . . v 3 23
Stop my mouth.—And shall, albeit sweet music issues thence *T. and C.* iii 2 141
He will spend his mouth, and promise, like Brabbler the hound . v 1 98
Ajax hath lost a friend And foams at mouth, and he is arm'd and at it . v 5 36
That dogs must eat, That meat was made for mouths . . *Coriolanus* i 1 211
These are the tribunes of the people, The tongues o' the common mouth iii 1 22
You being their mouths, why rule you not their teeth? . . . iii 1 36
His heart's his mouth: What his breast forges, that his tongue must vent . . . . iii 1 257
He shall well know The noble tribunes are the people's mouths . . iii 1 271
It is spoke freely out of many mouths—How probable I do not know . iv 6 64
Confusion fall— Nay, then I'll stop your mouth . . *T. Andron.* ii 3 185
What subtle hole is this, Whose mouth is cover'd with rude-growing briers? . . . . ii 3 199
This fell devouring receptacle, As hateful as Cocytus' misty mouth . ii 3 236
At the elder-tree Which overshades the mouth of that same pit . . ii 3 273
Sirs, stop his mouth, and let him speak no more . . . v 1 151
Stop close their mouths, let them not speak a word. Is he sure bound? v 2 165
Stop their mouths, let them not speak to me; But let them hear what fearful words I utter . . . . v 2 168
My tears will choke me, if I ope my mouth . . . . v 3 175
To whose foul mouth no healthsome air breathes in . *Rom. and Jul.* iv 3 34
Seal up the mouth of outrage for a while . . . . . v 3 216
Would I had a rod in my mouth, that I might answer thee *T. of Athens* ii 2 79
What remains will hardly stop the mouth Of present dues . . ii 2 156
Who had the world as my confectionary, The mouths, the tongues, the eyes, and hearts of men At duty . . . . iv 3 261
Yours is as fair a name; Sound them, it doth become the mouth as well; Weigh them, it is as heavy . . . . . *J. Cæsar* i 2 145
Foamed at mouth, and was speechless . . . . . . i 2 255
Thy wounds . . . , Which, like dumb mouths, do ope their ruby lips . iii 1 260
And bid me say to you by word of mouth . . . . . iii 1 280
Show you sweet Cæsar's wounds, poor poor dumb mouths, And bid them speak for me . . . . iii 2 229
Say, if thou'dst rather hear it from our mouths, Or from our masters?—Call 'em; let me see 'em . . . . . . *Macbeth* iv 1 62
The head is not more native to the heart, The hand more instrumental to the mouth . . . . *Hamlet* i 2 48
But if you mouth it, as many of your players do, I had as lief the town-crier spoke my lines . . . . iii 2 3
Give it breath with your mouth, and it will discourse most eloquent music . . . . iii 2 374
With divine ambition puff'd Makes mouths at the invisible event . . iv 4 50
Nay, an thou'lt mouth, I'll rant as well as thou . . . v 1 306
Where should we have our thanks?—Not from his mouth . . v 2 383
Of that I shall have also cause to speak, And from his mouth whose voice will draw on more . . . . v 2 403
Unhappy that I am, I cannot heave My heart into my mouth . . *Lear* i 1 94
For there was never yet fair woman but she made mouths in a glass . iii 2 36
Thou'ldst shun a bear; But if thy flight lay toward the raging sea, Thou'ldst meet the bear i' the mouth . . . . iii 4 11
Is it not as this mouth should tear this hand For lifting food to't? . iii 4 15
And for one blast of thy minikin mouth, Thy sheep shall take no harm iii 6 45
Be thy mouth or black or white, Tooth that poisons if it bite . . iii 6 69
Shut your mouth, dame, Or with this paper shall I stop it . . v 3 154
Your name is great In mouths of wisest censure . . . *Othello* ii 3 193
I had rather have this tongue cut from my mouth Than it should do offence . . . . ii 3 221
O God, that men should put an enemy in their mouths to steal away their brains! . . . . ii 3 292
Had I as many mouths as Hydra, such an answer would stop them all . ii 3 308
The lethargy must have his quiet course: If not, he foams at mouth . iv 1 55
He will not say so.—No, his mouth is stopp'd . . . . v 2 71
For I wear not My dagger in my mouth . . . . *Cymbeline* iv 2 79
Came to me With his sword drawn; foam'd at the mouth, and swore . v 5 276
These mouths, who but of late, earth, sea, and air, Were all too little to content and please, . . . They are now starved . . *Pericles* i 4 34
And crickets sing at the oven's mouth, E'er the blither for their drouth . . . . iii Gower 7
A Spaniard's mouth so watered, that he went to bed to her very description . . . . iv 2 108
Mouthed. Those mouthed wounds, which valiantly he took . *1 Hen. IV.* i 3 97
First mouthed, to be last swallowed . . . . . . *Hamlet* iv 2 20
Mouth-filling. A good mouth-filling oath . . . . *1 Hen. IV.* iii 1 259
Mouth-friend. You knot of mouth-friends! . . . . *T. of Athens* iii 6 99
Mouthful. Driving the poor fry before him, and at last devours them all at a mouthful . . . . *Pericles* ii 1 35

Mouth-honour. Curses, not loud but deep, mouth-honour . *Macbeth* v 3 27
Mouth-made vows, Which break themselves in swearing! *Ant. and Cleo.* i 3 30
Move. Most lying slave, Whom stripes may move, not kindness! *Tempest* i 2 345
Pity move my father To be inclined my way! . i 2 446
Dumb jewels often in their silent kind More than quick words do move a woman's mind . *T. G. of Ver.* iii 1 91
I have great hope in that; for in her youth There is a prone and speechless dialect, Such as move men . *Meas. for Meas.* i 2 189
To me she speaks; she moves me for her theme *Com. of Errors* ii 2 183
We in your motion turn and you may move us . iii 2 24
With words that in an honest suit might move . iv 2 14
Let me but move one question to your daughter *Much Ado* iv 1 74
I fear these stubborn lines lack power to move . *L. L. Lost* iv 3 55
It did move him to passion, and therefore let's hear it . iv 3 202
No, to the death, we will not move a foot . v 2 146
To move wild laughter in the throat of death? It cannot be; it is impossible: Mirth cannot move a soul in agony . v 2 865
O that my prayers could such affection move! . *M. N. Dream* i 1 197
Let the audience look to their eyes; I will move storms . i 2 29
And thy fair virtue's force perforce doth move me On the first view to say, to swear, I love thee . iii 1 143
Thy paleness moves me more than eloquence . *Mer of Venice* iii 2 106
Move these eyes? Or whether, riding on the balls of mine, Seem they in motion? . iii 2 116
Speak to him, ladies; see if you can move him *As Y. Like It* i 2 172
Your gentleness shall force More than your force move us to gentleness ii 7 103
And then they perceive not how Time moves . iii 2 351
Whiles you chid me, I did love; How then might your prayers move! iv 3 55
Which seem to move and wanton with her breath . *T. of Shrew* Ind. 2 54
I saw her coral lips to move And with her breath she did perfume the air . i 1 179
She moves me not, or not removes, at least, Affection's edge in me . i 2 72
The Florentine will move us For speedy aid . *All's Well* i 2 6
Eat, speak, and move under the influence of the most received star . ii 1 56
Move the still-peering air, That sings with piercing . iii 2 113
What the devil should move me to undertake the recovery of this drum? iv 1 37
Lips, do not move; No man must know . *T. Night* ii 5 109
Thou perhaps mayst move That heart, which now abhors, to like his love . iii 1 175
This is not the way: do you not see you move him? . iii 4 121
If this letter move him not, his legs cannot . iii 4 188
There is no tongue that moves, none, none i' the world, So soon as yours could win me . *W. Tale* i 2 20
A thousand knees Ten thousand years together . . . could not move the gods To look that way thou wert. . iii 2 214
Move still, still so, And own no other function . iv 4 142
No, the bagpipe could not move you . iv 4 184
No longer shall you gaze on't, lest your fancy May think anon it moves v 3 61
I'll make the statue move indeed, descend And take you by the hand . v 3 88
'Tis as easy To make her speak as move . v 3 94
What doth move you to claim your brother's land? *K. John* i 1 91
If he see aught in you that makes him like, That any thing he sees, which moves his liking . ii 1 512
Whose restraint Doth move the murmuring lips of discontent . iv 2 53
Why then your fears, which, as they say, attend The steps of wrong, should move you to mew up Your tender kinsman? . iv 2 57
You stars that move in your right spheres, Where be your powers? . v 7 74
Ere I move, What my tongue speaks my right drawn sword may prove *Richard II.* i 1 45
Pity may move thee 'pardon' to rehearse . v 3 128
What thou speakest may move and what he hears may be believed *1 Hen. IV.* i 2 172
Move in that obedient orb again Where you did give a fair and natural light . v 1 17
The immortal part needs a physician; but that moves not him *2 Hen. IV.* ii 2 113
By his light Did all the chivalry of England move To do brave acts . ii 3 20
Did he suspire, that light and weightless down Perforce must move . iv 5 34
And newly move, With casted slough and fresh legerity . *Hen. V.* iv 1 22
I shall never move thee in French, unless it be to laugh at me . v 2 197
Thy words move rage and not remorse in me . *2 Hen. VI.* iv 1 112
Beshrew me, but his passion moves me so . *3 Hen. VI.* i 4 150
This is he that moves both wind and tide . iii 3 48
End thy frantic curse, Lest to thy harm thou move our patience *Richard III.* i 3 248
Is well-spoken, and perhaps May move your hearts to pity, if you mark him . i 3 349
In this just suit come I to move your grace . iii 7 140
It is a pity Would move a monster . *Hen. VIII.* ii 3 11
This royal infant—heaven still move about her! . v 5 18
We dare not move the question of our place . *Troi. and Cres.* ii 3 89
What moves Ajax thus to bay at him? . ii 3 98
He is much sorry, If any thing more than your sport and pleasure Did move your greatness . ii 3 118
How novelty may move, and parts with person . iv 4 81
Scratches with briers, Scars to move laughter only *Coriolanus* iii 3 52
Being assured none but myself could move thee . v 2 80
He moves like an engine, and the ground shrinks before his treading v 4 19
Ere he express himself, or move the people With what he would say v 6 55
And, sith there's no justice in earth nor hell, We will solicit heaven and move the gods . *T. Andron.* iv 3 50
Even in the time When it should move you to attend me most . v 3 92
A dog of the house of Montague moves me . *Rom. and Jul.* i 1 10
To move is to stir; and to be valiant is to stand . i 1 11
A dog of that house shall move me to stand . i 1 14
I'll look to like, if looking liking move . i 3 97
I have a soul of lead So stakes me to the ground I cannot move . i 4 16
Saints do not move, though grant for prayer's sake.—Then move not, while my prayer's effect I take . i 5 107
That we have had no time to move our daughter . iii 4 2
I have need of many orisons To move the heavens to smile upon my state . iv 3 4
The heavens do lour upon you for some ill; Move them no more . iv 5 95
How big imagination Moves in this lip! . *T. of Athens* i 1 33
My free drift Halts not particularly, but moves itself In a wide sea of wax . i 1 46
Yet, more to move you, Take my deserts to his, and join 'em both . iii 5 78
If I could pray to move, prayers would move me . *J. Cæsar* iii 1 59
And put a tongue In every wound of Cæsar that should move The stones of Rome to rise and mutiny . iii 2 233
Let us not wrangle: bid them move away . iv 2 45
Move. Towards his design Moves like a ghost . *Macbeth* ii 1 56
What is't that moves your highness?—Which of you have done this? . iii 4 48
They say, blood will have blood: Stones have been known to move and trees to speak . iii 4 123
But float upon a wild and violent sea Each way and move . iv 2 22
Those he commands move only in command, Nothing in love . v 2 19
I look'd toward Birnam, and anon, methought, The wood began to move . v 5 35
Might move More grief to hide than hate to utter love . *Hamlet* ii 1 118
Doubt thou the stars are fire; Doubt that the sun doth move . ii 2 117
The instant burst of clamour that she made, Unless things mortal move them not at all, Would have made milch the burning eyes of heaven ii 2 539
The instances that second marriage move Are base respects of thrift . iii 2 192
Her speech is nothing, Yet the unshaped use of it doth move The hearers iv 5 8
Hadst thou thy wits, and didst persuade revenge, It could not move thus . iv 5 169
As the star moves not but in his sphere, I could not but by her . iv 7 15
Where he arrives he moves All hearts against us . *Lear* iv 5 10
My wife must move for Cassio to her mistress; I'll set her on *Othello* ii 3 389
If I have any grace or power to move you, His present reconciliation take . iii 3 46
If I do find him fit, I'll move your suit And seek to effect it . iii 4 166
If Cæsar move him, Let Antony look over Cæsar's head. *Ant. and Cleo.* ii 2 4
To be called into a huge sphere, and not to be seen to move in't . ii 7 17
It is just so high as it is, and moves with it own organs . ii 7 49
For our faults Can never be so equal, that your love Can equally move with them . iii 4 36
And what thou think'st his very action speaks In every power that moves iii 12 36
Yet I'll move him To walk this way . *Cymbeline* i 1 103
I'll move the king To any shape of thy preferment such As thou'lt desire i 5 70
Yet Report should render him hourly to your ear As truly as he moves iii 4 154
From whence he moves His war for Britain.—'Tis not sleepy business . iii 5 25
Were it Toad, or Adder, Spider, 'Twould move me sooner . iv 2 91
The want is but to put those powers in motion That long to move . iv 3 32
How durst thy tongue move anger to our face? . *Pericles* i 2 54
Do as I bid you, or you'll move me else . ii 3 71
Like motes and shadows see them move awhile . iv 4 21
Moveable. I knew you at the first You were a moveable.—Why, what's a moveable?—A join'd-stool . *T. of Shrew* ii 1 198
We do seize to us The plate, coin, revenues, and moveables *Richard II.* ii 1 161
Look to my chattels and my movables: Let senses rule . *Hen. V.* ii 3 50
And the moveables Whereof the king my brother stood possess'd *Richard III.* iii 1 195
The earldom of Hereford and the moveables The which you promised . iv 2 93
Ah, but some natural notes about her body, Above ten thousand meaner moveables Would testify . *Cymbeline* ii 2 29
Moved. You do look, my son, in a moved sort . *Tempest* iv 1 146
Be kindlier moved than thou art . v 1 24
Why he, of all the rest, hath never moved me . *T. G. of Ver.* i 2 27
O, be not like your mistress; be moved, be moved . ii 1 181
My poor mistress, moved there withal, Wept bitterly . iv 4 175
If he had been throughly moved, you should have heard him *Mer. Wives* i 4 95
It hath not moved him at all . *Meas. for Meas.* iv 2 161
If speaking, why, a vane blown with all winds; If silent, why, a block moved with none. *Much Ado* iii 1 67
Hector trembles.—Pompey is moved. More Ates, more Ates! stir them on! . *L. L. Lost* v 2 694
Nor is not moved with concord of sweet sounds . *Mer. of Venice* v 1 84
Myself am moved to woo thee for my wife.—Moved! in good time: let him that moved you hither Remove you hence . *T. of Shrew* ii 1 195
A woman moved is like a fountain troubled, Muddy, ill-seeming, thick v 2 142
I moved the king my master to speak in the behalf of my daughter *All's W.* iv 5 75
Are you moved, my lord?—No, in good earnest . *W. Tale* i 2 150
The king is moved, and answers not to this . *K. John* iii 1 217
I would he were the best In all this presence that hath moved me *Richard II.* iv 1 32
An the fire of grace be not quite out of thee, now shalt thou be moved. Give me a cup of sack . *1 Hen. IV.* ii 4 422
My father, in kind heart and pity moved, Swore him assistance . iv 3 64
The reason moved these warlike lords to this . *1 Hen. VI.* i 5 70
Moved with compassion of my country's wreck . iv 1 56
Moved with remorse of these outrageous broils . v 4 97
I know no pain they can inflict upon him Will make him say I moved him to those arms . *2 Hen. VI.* iii 1 378
Prayers and tears have moved me, gifts could never . iv 7 73
Such like toys as these Have moved his highness to commit me *Rich. III.* i 1 61
End thy frantic curse, Lest to thy harm thou move our patience.—Foul shame upon you! you have all moved mine . i 3 249
In no worldly suit would he be moved, To draw him from his holy exercise . iii 7 63
Now, what moved me to't . *Hen. VIII.* ii 4 167
Remember How under my oppression I did reek, When I first moved you ii 4 209
I then moved you, My Lord of Canterbury; and got your leave . ii 4 217
A pestilence That does infest the land: with which they moved Have broken with the king . v 1 46
Grievous complaints of you! which, being consider'd, Have moved us v 1 100
Hector, whose patience Is, as a virtue, fix'd, to-day was moved *Tr. and Cr.* i 2 5
To this effect, Achilles, have I moved you . iii 3 216
O, be not moved, Prince Troilus: Let me be privileged by my place iv 4 131
You are moved, prince; let us depart, I pray you . v 2 36
Being moved, he will not spare to gird the gods . *Coriolanus* i 1 260
I was hardly moved to come to thee . v 2 78
And highly moved to wrath To be controll'd . *T. Andron.* i 1 419
The lion moved with pity did endure To have his princely paws pared all away . ii 3 151
Then must my sea be moved with her sighs . iii 1 228
The tender boy, in passion moved, Doth weep to see his grandsire's heaviness . iii 2 48
I strike quickly, being moved.—But thou art not quickly moved to strike.—A dog of the house of Montague moves me . *Rom. and Jul.* i 1 7
To be valiant is to stand: therefore, if thou art moved, thou runn'st away . i 1 12
And hear the sentence of your moved prince . i 1 95
As soon moved to be moody, and as soon moody to be moved . iii 1 13
Which modern lamentation might have moved . iii 2 120
I promise you, my lord, you moved me much . *T. of Athens* i 2 118
Your city, In part for his sake moved . v 2 13
See, whether their basest metal be not moved . *J. Cæsar* i 1 66
I would not, so with love I might entreat you, Be any further moved . i 2 167
And scorn'd his spirit That could be moved to smile at any thing . i 2 207

Moved. Are not you moved, when all the sway of earth Shakes like a thing unfirm? *J. Cæsar* i 3 3
I have moved already Some certain of the noblest-minded Romans i 3 121
I could be well moved, if I were as you iii 1 58
Know you how much the people may be moved By that which he will utter? iii 1 234
Belike they had some notice of the people, How I had moved them iii 2 276
When Cæsar lived, he durst not thus have moved me iv 3 58
Virtue, as it never will be moved, Though lewdness court it *Hamlet* i 5 53
I am guiltless, as I am ignorant Of what hath moved you *Lear* i 4 296
O, then it moved her.—Not to a rage iv 3 17
Though that the queen on special cause is here, Her army is moved on iv 6 220
This speech of yours hath moved me, And shall perchance do good v 3 199
But I do see you're moved: I am to pray you not to strain my speech To grosser issues nor to larger reach *Othello* iii 3 217
My lord, I see you're moved.—No, not much moved iii 3 224
Tell him I have moved my lord on his behalf, and hope all will be well iii 4 19
Is he angry?—May be the letter moved him iv 1 246
Warr'd upon him; although, I think, Not moved by Antony *Ant. and Cleo.* ii 1 42
What was't That moved pale Cassius to conspire? ii 6 15
On our terrible seas, Like egg-shells moved upon their surges *Cymbeline* iii 1 28
I moved her to't, Having received the punishment before v 5 342
Thou Hast moved us: what seest thou in our looks?—An angry brow *Per.* i 1 51
Mover. O thou eternal Mover of the heavens! 2 *Hen. VI.* iii 3 19
These movers that do prize their hours At a crack'd drachma! *Coriolanus* i 5 5
Poisonous compounds, Which are the movers of a languishing death *Cymb.* i 5 9
Movest. Do bravely, horse! for wot'st thou whom thou movest? *Ant. and Cleo.* i 5 22
O sun, Burn the great sphere thou movest in! iv 15 10
Thou movest no less with thy complaining than Thy master in bleeding *Cymbeline* iv 2 375
Moveth. He stirreth not, he moveth not; The ape is dead *Rom. and Jul.* ii 1 15
Moving. Standing, speaking, moving, And yet so fast asleep *Tempest* ii 1 214
If the gentle spirit of moving words Can no way change you *T. G. of Ver.* v 4 55
Heaven give thee moving graces! *Meas. for Meas.* ii 2 36
Dost think I am so muddy, so unsettled, To . . . Give scandal to the blood o' the prince my son . . . , Without ripe moving to't? *W. Tale* i 2 332
Will sympathize The heavy accent of thy moving tongue *Richard II.* v 1 47
O, I could divide myself and go to buffets, for moving such a dish of skim milk with so honourable an action! 1 *Hen. IV.* ii 3 35
Mars his true moving, even as in the heavens So in the earth, to this day is not known 1 *Hen. VI.* i 2 1
Soon won with moving words 3 *Hen. VI.* iii 1 34
Not moving From the casque to the cushion *Coriolanus* iv 7 42
Within this three mile may you see it coming; I say, a moving grove *Macbeth* v 5 38
In form and moving how express and admirable! *Hamlet* ii 2 317
Of moving accidents by flood and field, Of hair-breadth scapes *Othello* i 3 135
Ha! no more moving? Still as the grave v 2 93
The blow thou hadst Shall make thy peace for moving me to rage *Ant. and Cleo.* ii 5 70
Moving-delicate. More moving-delicate and full of life *Much Ado* iv 1 230
Movingly. I would have had them writ more movingly *T. G. of Ver.* ii 1 134
Mow. Sometime like apes that mow and chatter at me *Tempest* ii 2 9
Each one, tripping on his toe, Will be here with mop and mow iv 1 47
To mow down thorns that would annoy our foot, Is worthy praise 2 *Hen. VI.* iii 1 67
I am not Samson, nor Sir Guy, nor Colbrand, To mow 'em down before me *Hen. VIII.* v 4 23
Like to a harvest-man that's task'd to mow Or all or lose his hire *Coriol.* i 3 39
He will mow all down before him, and leave his passage polled iv 5 214
Those that would make mows at him while my father lived *Hamlet* ii 2 381
Apes and monkeys 'Twixt two such shes would chatter this way and Contemn with mows the other *Cymbeline* i 6 41
Mowbray. What dost thou object Against the Duke of Norfolk, Thomas Mowbray? *Richard II.* i 1 29
Now, Thomas Mowbray, do I turn to thee, And mark my greeting well i 1 35
What doth our cousin lay to Mowbray's charge? It must be great i 1 84
That Mowbray hath received eight thousand nobles In name of lendings for your highness' soldiers i 1 88
All the treasons for these eighteen years Complotted and contrived in this land Fetch from false Mowbray their first head and spring i 1 97
He is our subject, Mowbray; so art thou: Free speech and fearless I to thee allow.—Then, Bolingbroke, . . . thou liest i 1 122
Where shame doth harbour, even in Mowbray's face i 1 195
Thou goest to Coventry, there to behold Our cousin Hereford and fell Mowbray fight: O, sit my husband's wrongs on Hereford's spear, That it may enter butcher Mowbray's breast! i 2 46
Be Mowbray's sins so heavy in his bosom, That they may break his foaming courser's back! i 2 50
My name is Thomas Mowbray, Duke of Norfolk i 3 16
Mowbray and myself are like two men That vow a long and weary pilgrimage i 3 48
O, let no noble eye profane a tear For me, if I be gored with Mowbray's spear: As confident as is the falcon's flight Against a bird, do I with Mowbray fight i 3 60
Steel my lance's point, That it may enter Mowbray's waxen coat i 3 75
To prove the Duke of Norfolk, Thomas Mowbray, A traitor to his God i 3 107
Then was Jack Falstaff, now Sir John, a boy, and page to Thomas Mowbray, Duke of Norfolk 2 *Hen. IV.* iii 2 29
O, my good Lord Mowbray, Construe the times to their necessities iv 1 103
You speak, Lord Mowbray, now you know not what iv 1 130
Mowbray, you overween to take it so; This offer comes from mercy iv 1 149
You are well encounter'd here, my cousin Mowbray iv 2 1
Health to my lord and gentle cousin, Mowbray.—You wish me health in very happy season iv 2 78
Lord archbishop, and you, Lord Mowbray, Of capital treason I attach you both iv 2 108
Mowbray, the Bishop Scroop, Hastings and all Are brought to the correction of your law iv 4 84
Mowed. What valiant foemen, like to autumn's corn, Have we mow'd down in tops of all their pride! 3 *Hen. VI.* v 7 4
Mower. And there the strawy Greeks, ripe for his edge, Fall down before him, like the mower's swath *Troi. and Cres.* v 5 25
Mowing like grass Your fresh-fair virgins and your flowering infants *Hen. V.* iii 3 13
Flibbertigibbet, of mopping and mowing *Lear* iv 1 64
Moy. Ayez pitié de moi!—Moy shall not serve; I will have forty moys *Hen. V.* iv 4 14
O pardonnez moi!—Say'st thou me so? is that a ton of moys? iv 4 23

Moyses. He hath outrun us, But Moyses and Valerius follow him *T. G. of Ver.* v 3 8
Much. And think'st it much to tread the ooze Of the salt deep *Tempest* i 2 252
When thou camest first, Thou strokedst me and madest much of me i 2 333
And a birth indeed Which throes thee much to yield ii 1 231
If I can recover him and keep him tame, I will not take too much for him ii 2 80
O, but I love his lady too too much *T. G. of Ver.* ii 4 205
Much upon this riddle runs the wisdom of the world *Meas. for Meas.* iii 2 242
Much upon this time have I promised here to meet iv 1 17
My inwardness and love Is very much unto the prince *Much Ado* iv 1 248
I must confess that I have heard so much *M. N. Dream* i 1 111
O brave touch! Could not a worm, an adder, do so much? iii 2 71
'Twere good you do so much for charity *Mer. of Venice* iv 1 261
Giving thy sum of more To that which had too much *As Y. Like It* ii 1 49
Either too much at once, or none at all iii 2 212
My friends told me as much, and I thought no less iv 1 188
By so much the more shall I to-morrow be at the height of heart-heaviness, by how much I shall think my brother happy v 2 49
Be comfortable to my mother, your mistress, and make much of her *All's Well* i 1 87
The fellow has a deal of that too much, Which holds him much to have iii 2 92
I told him you were sick; he takes on him to understand so much *T. N.* i 5 149
Hermione was not so much wrinkled, nothing So aged as this seems.—O, not by much.—So much the more our carver's excellence *W. Tale* v 3 28
How much unlook'd for is this expedition!—By how much unexpected, by so much We must awake endeavour for defence *K. John* ii 1 80
By how much better than my word I am, By so much shall I falsify men's hopes 1 *Hen. IV.* i 2 235
Whereof a little More than a little is by much too much iii 2 73
With two points on your shoulder? much! 2 *Hen. IV.* ii 4 143
So much the worse, if your own rule be true iv 2 86
Witness our too much memorable shame *Hen. V.* ii 4 53
Must needs be granted to be much at one v 2 204
Or been reguerdon'd with so much as thanks 1 *Hen. VI.* iii 4 23
'Tis much when sceptres are in children's hands iv 1 192
I thought as much; he would be above the clouds 2 *Hen. VI.* ii 1 15
It serves you well, my lord, to say so much.—I say no more than truth iii 1 119
'Tis resolutely spoke.—Not resolute, except so much were done iii 1 267
What, think you much to pay two thousand crowns, And bear the name and port of gentlemen? iv 1 18
You said so much before, and yet you fled 3 *Hen. VI.* ii 2 106
Much is your sorrow; mine ten times so much ii 5 112
I told your majesty as much before iii 3 179
Make much of him, my lords, for this is he Must help you iv 6 75
And give more strength to that which hath too much v 4 9
So much the more dangerous, By how much the estate is green *Rich. III.* ii 2 127
Wear it, enjoy it, and make much of it v 5 7
Whereof We cannot feel too little, hear too much *Hen. VIII.* i 2 128
So much the more Must pity drop upon her ii 3 17
I will say thus much for him, if a prince May be beholding to a subject v 3 156
Much attribute he hath, and much the reason Why we ascribe it to him *Troi. and Cres.* ii 3 125
See how much she makes of thee *T. Andron.* iv 1 10
I was your mother much upon these years That you are now a maid *Rom. and Jul.* i 3 72
Good heart, and, i' faith, I will tell her as much ii 4 185
Courage, man; the hurt cannot be much iii 1 98
By this count I shall be much in years Ere I again behold my Romeo! iii 5 46
This only child; But now I see this one is one too much iii 5 167
My lord, you moved me much.—Much! *T. of Athens* i 2 118
Is't possible the world should so much differ, And we alive that lived? iii 1 49
We attend his lordship; pray, signify so much iii 4 38
Thus much of this [gold] will make black white, foul fair, Wrong right iv 3 28
He is given To sports, to wildness and much company *J. Cæsar* ii 1 189
To be more than what you were, you would Be so much more the man *Macbeth* i 7 51
If thy speech be sooth, I care not if thou dost for me as much v 5 41
So much for him. Now for ourself and for this time of meeting: Thus much the business is *Hamlet* i 2 27
Something too much of this iii 2 79
But so much was our love, We would not understand what was most fit iv 1 19
There might be thought, Though nothing sure, yet much unhappily iv 5 13
A love that makes breath poor, and speech unable; Beyond all manner of so much I love you *Lear* i 1 62
So much as I have perused, I find it not fit for your o'er-looking i 2 39
His fault is much ii 2 148
We that are young Shall never see so much, nor live so long v 3 326
By how much she strives to do him good, She shall undo her credit *Oth.* ii 3 364
I shall have so much experience for my pains ii 3 373
To have so much to do To bring him in! Trust me, I could do much iii 3 73
'Tis better to be much abused Than but to know't a little iii 3 336
'Tis very much: Make her amends; she weeps iv 1 254
That thy cheek So much as lank'd not *Ant. and Cleo.* i 4 71
Make as much of me As when mine empire was your fellow too iv 2 21
In himself, 'tis much *Cymbeline* i 6 79
The bird is dead That we have made so much on iv 2 198
I thought as much *Pericles* i 4 62
As much as to say *T. G. of Ver.* iii 1; *Com. of Errors* iv 3; *Much Ado* iii 3; *T. Night* i 5; 2 *Hen. IV.* ii 2: *Rom. and Jul.* ii 4
Much example. There's much example for't *T. of Athens* i 2 47
Much fool. And much fool may you find in you *All's Well* ii 4 36
Much goodness. Thanks, good friend Escalus, for thy much goodness: There's more behind *Meas. for Meas.* v 1 534
Much ill. Come near me; now I am much ill 2 *Hen. IV.* iv 4 111
Much misgovernment. I am sorry for thy much misgovernment *M. Ado* iv 1 100
Much Orlando. Past two o'clock? and here much Orlando! *As Y. Like It* iv 3 2
Much sorry. I am much sorry, sir *Cymbeline* ii 3 109
Much unkindly. I take it much unkindly *Othello* i 1 1
Much unwelcome. I fear We shall be much unwelcome *Troi. and Cres.* iv 1 45
Muck. And look'd upon things precious as They were The common muck of the world *Coriolanus* ii 2 130
Mud. The nine men's morris is fill'd up with mud *M. N. Dream* ii 1 98
The purest spring is not so free from mud As I am clear 2 *Hen. VI.* iii 1 101
There was a lady once, 'tis an old story, That would not be a queen, that would she not, For all the mud in Egypt *Hen. VIII.* ii 3 92
Here stands the spring whom you have stain'd with mud *T. Andron.* v 2 171
Your serpent of Egypt is bred now of your mud by the operation of your sun: so is your crocodile *Ant. and Cleo.* ii 7 31
Rather on Nilus' mud Lay me stark naked v 2 58

Mudded. I'll seek him deeper than e'er plummet sounded And with him there lie mudded *Tempest* iii 3 102
I wish Myself were mudded in that oozy bed Where my son lies v 1 151
Muddied. I am now, sir, muddied in fortune's mood *All's Well* v 2 4
Has fallen into the unclean fishpond of her displeasure, and, as he says, is muddied withal v 2 23
The people muddied Thick and unwholesome in their thoughts *Hamlet* iv 5 81
Muddy. The reasonable shore That now lies foul and muddy *Tempest* v 1 82
Empty it in the muddy ditch close by the Thames side *Mer. Wives* iii 3 15
To what, my love, shall I compare thine eyne? Crystal is muddy *M. N. Dream* iii 2 139
Whilst this muddy vesture of decay Doth grossly close it in *M. of Ven.* v 1 64
A woman moved is like a fountain troubled, Muddy, ill-seeming *T. of Shrew* v 2 143
Dost think I am so muddy, so unsettled? *W. Tale* i 2 325
This stream through muddy passages Hath held his current *Richard II.* v 3 62
Farewell, you muddy knave 1 *Hen. IV.* ii 1 106
You muddy rascal, is that all the comfort you give me? 2 *Hen. IV.* ii 4 43
Hang yourself, you muddy conger, hang yourself! ii 4 58
Till that her garments, heavy with their drink, Pull'd the poor wretch from her melodious lay To muddy death *Hamlet* iv 7 184
Muddy-mettled. A dull and muddy-mettled rascal ii 2 594
Muffle your false love with some show of blindness *Com. of Errors* iii 2 8
Muffle your face, Dismantle you *W. Tale* iv 4 665
What, with a torch! muffle me, night, awhile *Rom. and Jul.* v 3 21
Muffled. What muffled fellow's that? *Meas. for Meas.* v 1 491
We have caught the woodcock, and will keep him muffled *All's Well* iv 1 100
A plague upon him! muffled! he can say nothing of me: hush, hush! iv 3 134
The Duke of Suffolk muffled up in rags! 2 *Hen. VI.* iv 1 46
Alas, that love, whose view is muffled still, Should, without eyes, see pathways to his will! *Rom. and Jul.* i 1 177
Is not that his steward muffled so? He goes away in a cloud *T. of A.* iii 4 41
Muffler. He might put on a hat, a muffler and a kerchief *Mer. Wives* iv 2 73
There's her thrummed hat and her muffler too iv 2 81
I spy a great peard under his muffler iv 2 205
Fortune is painted blind, with a muffler afore her eyes *Hen. V.* iii 6 33
Muffling. In his mantle muffling up his face *J. Cæsar* iii 2 191
Mugs. Come, neighbour Mugs, we'll call up the gentlemen 1 *Hen. IV.* ii 1 49
Mulberry. Purple grapes, green figs, and mulberries *M. N. Dream* iii 1 170
Thisby, tarrying in mulberry shade, His dagger drew, and died v 1 149
Humble as the ripest mulberry That will not hold the handling *Coriol.* iii 2 79
Mule. Which, like your asses and your dogs and mules, You use in abject and in slavish parts *Mer. of Venice* iv 1 91
Tongue, I must put you into a butter-woman's mouth and buy myself another of Bajazet's mule *All's Well* iv 1 46
They must be dieted like mules And have their provender tied to their mouths 1 *Hen. VI.* i 2 10
Bare-headed plodded by my foot-cloth mule 2 *Hen. VI.* iv 1 54
And grew so ill He could not sit his mule *Hen. VIII.* iv 2 16
To be a dog, a mule, a cat, a fitchew, a toad, a lizard *Troi. and Cres.* v 1 67
That to's power he would Have made them mules *Coriolanus* ii 1 263
And at thy tent is now Unloading of his mules *Ant. and Cleo.* iv 6 24
Muleter. Base muleters of France! 1 *Hen. VI.* iii 2 68
Your ships are not well mann'd; Your mariners are muleters *A. and C.* iii 7 36
Muli. Not far, one Muli lives, my countryman; His wife but yesternight was brought to bed *T. Andron.* iv 2 152
Mulier. In terram Salicam mulieres nee succedant *Hen. V.* i 2 38
And 'mollis aer' We term it 'mulier:' which 'mulier' I divine Is this most constant wife *Cymbeline* v 5 448
Mulled. Peace is a very apoplexy, lethargy; mulled, deaf *Coriolanus* iv 5 239
Mulmutius. Say, then, to Cæsar, Our ancestor was that Mulmutius which Ordain'd our laws *Cymbeline* iii 1 55
Mulmutius made our laws, Who was the first of Britain which did put His brows within a golden crown iii 1 59
Multiplied. Your grace's title shall be multiplied 2 *Hen. VI.* i 2 73
Although by his sight his sin be multiplied ii 1 71
Multiply. I multiply With one 'We thank you' many thousands moe That go before it *W. Tale* i 2 7
Multiplying. Plutus himself, That knows the tinct and multiplying medicine *All's Well* v 3 102
Your multiplying spawn how can he flatter? *Coriolanus* ii 2 82
Take thou that too, with multiplying bans! *T. of Athens* iv 1 34
The multiplying villanies of nature Do swarm upon him *Macbeth* i 2 11
Multipotent. By Jove multipotent *Troi. and Cres.* iv 5 129
Multitude. Which the rude multitude call the afternoon *L. L. Lost* v 1 95
The fool multitude, that choose by show *Mer. of Venice* ii 9 26
I will not choose what many men desire, Because I will not jump with common spirits And rank me with the barbarous multitudes ii 9 33
Among the buzzing pleased multitude iii 2 182
O, what love I note In the fair multitude of those her hairs! *K. John* iii 4 62
For every honour sitting on his helm, Would they were multitudes! 1 *Hen. IV.* iii 2 143
As pages follow'd him Even at the heels in golden multitudes iv 3 73
The still-discordant wavering multitude 2 *Hen. IV.* Ind. 19
Since they, so few, watch such a multitude 1 *Hen. VI.* i 1 161
See how the giddy multitude do point, And nod their heads! 2 *Hen. VI.* ii 4 21
Stay, Salisbury, With the rude multitude till I return iii 2 135
His army is a ragged multitude Of hinds and peasants iv 4 32
Was ever feather so lightly blown to and fro as this multitude iv 8 58
Not fit to govern and rule multitudes, Which darest not, no, nor canst not rule a traitor v 1 94
Why come you not? what! multitudes, and fear? 3 *Hen. VI.* i 4 39
Why with some little train . . . ?—Marry, my lord, lest, by a multitude, The new-heal'd wound of malice should break out *Richard III.* ii 2 124
Mercy o' me, what a multitude are here! They grow still too *Hen. VIII.* v 4 71
Advantageous care Withdrew me from the odds of multitude *T. and C.* v 4 23
Ingratitude is monstrous, and for the multitude to be ingrateful, were to make a monster of the multitude *Coriolanus* ii 3 11
He himself stuck not to call us the many-headed multitude ii 3 18
How shall this bisson multitude digest The senate's courtesy? iii 1 131
Only be patient till we have appeased The multitude *J. Cæsar* iii 1 180
He's loved of the distracted multitude, Who like not in their judgement, but their eyes *Hamlet* iv 3 4
Laying by That nothing-gift of differing multitudes *Cymbeline* iii 6 86
Multitudinous. Pluck out The multitudinous tongue *Coriolanus* iii 1 156
This my hand will rather The multitudinous seas incarnadine *Macbeth* ii 2 62
Mum. I said nothing.—Mum, then, and no more *Tempest* iii 2 59
I come to her in white, and cry 'mum;' she cries 'budget' *Mer. Wives* v 2 6
But what needs either your 'mum' or her 'budget?' the white will decipher her v 2 10

Mum. I went to her in white, and cried 'mum,' and she cried 'budget' *Mer. Wives* v 5 209
Speak not you to him till we call upon you.—Mum *Meas. for Meas.* v 1 283
Go to, mum, you are he: graces will appear, and there's an end *M. Ado* ii 1 128
Well said, master; mum! and gaze your fill *T. of Shrew* i 1 73
Seal up your lips, and give no words but mum 2 *Hen. VI.* i 2 89
The citizens are mum and speak not a word *Richard III.* iii 7 3
So your face bids me, though you say nothing. Mum, mum *Lear* i 4 215
Mumble-news. Some mumble-news, some trencher-knight *L. L. Lost* v 2 464
Mumbling. Peace, you mumbling fool! *Rom. and Jul.* iii 5 174
Mumbling of wicked charms, conjuring the moon *Lear* ii 1 41
Mummer. If you chance to be pinched with the colic, you make faces like mummers *Coriolanus* ii 1 83
Mummy. I should have been a mountain of mummy *Mer. Wives* iii 5 18
Scale of dragon, tooth of wolf, Witches' mummy *Macbeth* iv 1 23
Dyed in mummy which the skilful Conserved of maidens' hearts *Othello* iii 4 74
Mun. Blows the cold wind: Says suum, mun, ha, no nonny *Lear* iii 4 103
Munch. I could munch your good dry oats *M. N. Dream* iv 1 36
Munched. A sailor's wife had chestnuts in her lap, And munch'd, and munch'd, and munch'd *Macbeth* i 3 5
Mundane. Lost This queen, worth all our mundane cost *Pericles* iii 2 71
Muniment. With other muniments and petty helps *Coriolanus* i 1 122
Munition. What penny hath Rome borne, What men provided, what munition sent? *K. John* v 2 98
I'll to the Tower . . . , To view the artillery and munition 1 *Hen. VI.* i 1 168
Mural. Now is the mural down between the two neighbours *M. N. Dream* v 1 208
Murder. Let's alone And do the murder first *Tempest* iv 1 232
Away with him, away with him! better shame than murder *Mer. Wives* iv 2 46
What, is't murder?—No.—Lechery?—Call it so *Meas. for Meas.* i 2 141
What, will you murder me? Thou gaoler, thou, I am thy prisoner *Com. of Errors* iv 4 112
He murder cries and help from Athens calls *M. N. Dream* iii 2 26
Truth will come to light; murder cannot be hid long *Mer. of Venice* ii 2 83
Thou tell'st me there is murder in mine eye: 'Tis pretty, sure! *As Y. L. It* iii 5 10
Help, help! here's a madman will murder me.—Help, son! *T. of Shrew* v 1 61
He that hangs himself is a virgin: virginity murders itself *All's Well* i 1 151
If you will not murder me for my love, let me be your servant *T. Night* ii 1 36
I am appointed him to murder you.—By whom, Camillo? *W. Tale* i 2 412
The innocent milk in it most innocent mouth, Haled out to murder iii 2 102
And would incense me To murder her I married v 1 62
Hadst not thou been by, . . . This murder had not come into my mind *K. John* iv 2 223
Murder, as hating what himself hath done, Doth lay it open iv 3 37
The height, the crest, or crest unto the crest, Of murder's arms iv 3 47
All murders past do stand excused in this iv 3 51
By envy's hand and murder's bloody axe *Richard II.* i 2 21
Thou showest the naked pathway to thy life, Teaching stern murder how to butcher thee i 2 32
Then thieves and robbers range abroad unseen In murders and in outrage iii 2 40
Then murders, treasons and detested sins, The cloak of night being pluck'd from off their backs, Stand bare and naked, trembling at themselves iii 2 44
I'll murder all his wardrobe, piece by piece, Until I meet the king 1 *Hen. IV.* v 3 27
Murder, murder! Ah, thou honey-suckle villain! 2 *Hen. IV.* ii 1 55
God let me not live, but I will murder your ruff for this ii 4 144
So; murder, I warrant now. Alas, alas! put up your naked weapons ii 4 221
Rob, murder, and commit The oldest sins the newest kind of ways iv 5 126
We shall see wilful adultery and murder committed *Hen. V.* ii 1 40
Treason and murder ever kept together, As two yoke-devils ii 2 105
Didst bring in Wonder to wait on treason and on murder ii 2 110
Whiles yet the cool and temperate wind of grace O'erblows the filthy and contagious clouds Of heady murder iii 3 32
Some peradventure have on them the guilt of premeditated and contrived murder iv 1 171
Thou that contrivedst to murder our dead lord 1 *Hen. VI.* i 3 34
See what mischief and what murder too Hath been enacted through your enmity iii 1 115
Murder not then the fruit within my womb v 4 63
Murder indeed, that bloody sin, I tortured Above the felon 2 *Hen. VI.* iii 1 131
That slanders me with murder's crimson badge iii 2 200
But that the guilt of murder bucklers thee And I should rob the deathsman of his fee iii 2 216
Thrust from the crown By shameful murder of a guiltless king iv 1 95
Unless you be possess'd with devilish spirits, You cannot but forbear to murder me v 7 81
Ah, Clifford, murder not this innocent child! 3 *Hen. VI.* i 3 8
Why, I can smile, and murder whiles I smile iii 2 182
Murder is thy alms-deed; Petitioners for blood thou ne'er put'st back v 5 79
If not by war, by surfeit die your king, As ours by murder! *Richard III.* i 3 198
Who sent you hither? Wherefore do you come?—To, to, to— To murder me? i 4 178
The great King of kings Hath in the tables of his law commanded That thou shalt do no murder i 4 202
Vengeance doth he hurl on thee, For false forswearing and for murder too i 4 207
He sends ye not to murder me for this; For in this sin he is as deep as I i 4 219
Like Pilate, would I wash my hands Of this most grievous guilty murder i 4 280
Quake, and change thy colour, Murder thy breath in middle of a word iii 5 2
This day had plotted, in the council-house To murder me iii 5 39
Murder her brothers, and then marry her! Uncertain way of gain! iv 2 63
Murder, stern murder, in the direst degree v 3 197
O wondrous thing! How easily murder is discovered! *T. Andron.* ii 3 287
Such a place there is . . . , By nature made for murders and for rapes iv 1 58
His traitorous sons, That died by law for murder of our brother iv 4 54
For I must talk of murders, rapes and massacres, Acts of black night v 1 63
Confer with me of murder and of death: There's not a hollow cave or lurking-place, No vast obscurity or misty vale, Where bloody murder or detested rape Can couch for fear, but I will find them out v 2 34
Lo, by thy side where Rape and Murder stands v 2 45
I'll do this heavy task, So thou destroy Rapine and Murder there v 2 59
Are these thy ministers? what are they call'd?—Rapine and Murder v 2 62
Rapine and Murder, you are welcome too v 2 83
And when thou find'st a man that's like thyself, Good Murder, stab him v 2 100
Nay, nay, let Rape and Murder stay with me v 2 134
The one is Murder, Rape is the other's name; And therefore bind them v 2 157
If they do see thee, they will murder thee *Rom. and Jul.* ii 2 70
Mercy but murders, pardoning those that kill iii 1 202
Thou cutt'st my head off with a golden axe, And smilest upon the stroke that murders me iii 3 23
As if that name, Shot from the deadly level of a gun, Did murder her iii 3 104

Murder. Uncomfortable time, why camest thou now To murder, murder our solemnity? *Rom. and Jul.* iv 5 61
There is thy gold, worse poison to men's souls, Doing more murders in this loathsome world, Than these poor compounds that thou mayst not sell v 1 81
Search, seek, and know how this foul murder comes v 3 198
I am the greatest, able to do least, Yet most suspected, as the time and place Doth make against me, of this direful murder v 3 225
My thought, whose murder yet is but fantastical, Shakes so my single state of man that function Is smother'd in surmise *Macbeth* i 3 139
Wither'd murder, Alarum'd by his sentinel, the wolf ii 1 52
There's one did laugh in's sleep, and one cried 'Murder!' ii 2 23
Macbeth does murder sleep, the innocent sleep ii 2 36
Most sacrilegious murder hath broke ope The Lord's anointed temple! ii 3 72
Ring the alarum-bell. Murder and treason! Banquo and Donalbain! ii 3 79
The repetition, in a woman's ear, Would murder as it fell ii 3 91
Murders have been perform'd Too terrible for the ear iii 4 77
But now they rise again, With twenty mortal murders on their crowns iii 4 81
This is more strange Than such a murder is iii 4 83
Now does he feel His secret murders sticking on his hands v 2 17
Revenge his foul and most unnatural murder.—Murder!—Murder most foul, as in the best it is; But this most foul, strange and unnatural *Hamlet* i 5 26
That lend a tyrannous and damned light To their lord's murder ii 2 483
Dost thou hear me, old friend; can you play the Murder of Gonzago? ii 2 563
Murder, though it have no tongue, will speak With most miraculous organ ii 2 622
I'll have these players Play something like the murder of my father ii 2 624
This play is the image of a murder done in Vienna iii 2 248
It hath the primal eldest curse upon't, A brother's murder iii 3 38
But, O, what form of prayer Can serve my turn? 'Forgive me my foul murder?' That cannot be; since I am still possess'd Of those effects for which I did the murder iii 3 52
What wilt thou do? thou wilt not murder me? Help, help, ho! iii 4 21
No place, indeed, should murder sanctuarize iv 7 128
As if it were Cain's jaw-bone, that did the first murder! v 1 86
It is no vicious blot, murder, or foulness, No unchaste action *Lear* i 1 230
By no means what?—Persuade me to the murder of your lordship ii 1 46
'Tis worse than murder, To do upon respect such violent outrage ii 4 23
Mahu, of stealing; Modo, of murder iv 1 63
Though in the trade of war I have slain men, Yet do I hold it very stuff o' the conscience To do no contrived murder *Othello* i 2 3
How shall I murder him, Iago?—Did you perceive how he laughed at his vice? iv 1 178
I am maim'd for ever. Help, ho! murder! murder! v 1 27
What, ho! no watch? no passage? murder! murder! v 1 37
Who's there? whose noise is this that cries on murder?—We do not know v 1 48
How silent is this town!—Ho! murder! murder!—What may you be? v 1 64
Makest me call what I intend to do A murder, which I thought a sacrifice v 2 65
O, my good lord, yonder's foul murders done!—What, now? v 2 106
Then murder's out of tune, And sweet revenge grows harsh v 2 115
Help, ho! help! The Moor hath kill'd my mistress! Murder! murder! v 2 167
You have done well, That men must lay their murders on your neck v 2 170
And your reports have set the murder on v 2 187
What's amiss, May it be gently heard: when we debate Our trivial difference loud, we do commit Murder in healing wounds *A. and C.* ii 2 22
How! that I should murder her? Upon the love and truth and vows which I Have made to thy command? I, her? *Cymbeline* iii 2 11
But his Jovial face—Murder in heaven?—How!—'Tis gone iv 2 312
How many Must murder wives much better than themselves! v 1 4
Murder's as near to lust as flame to smoke *Pericles* i 1 138
How Thaliard came full bent with sin And had intent to murder him ii Gower 24
Till cruel Cleon, with his wicked wife, Did seek to murder me v 1 174
Was nursed with Cleon; who at fourteen years He sought to murder v 3 9
The gods for murder seemed so content To punish them; although not done, but meant v 3 Gower 98
Murdered. It cannot be but thou hast murder'd him; So should a murderer look, so dead, so grim.—So should the murder'd look, and so should I, Pierced through the heart with your stern cruelty *M. N. Dream* iii 2 56
O, he hath murdered his master! Lay hold on him *T. of Shrew* v 1 90
Why seek'st thou to possess me with these fears? Why urgest thou so oft young Arthur's death? Thy hand hath murder'd him *K. John* iv 2 205
Some poison'd by their wives; some sleeping kill'd; All murder'd *Richard II.* iii 2 160
Though I did wish him dead, I hate the murderer, love him murdered v 6 40
Did return To be deposed and shortly murdered *1 Hen. IV.* i 3 152
Pray God you have not murdered some of them ii 4 209
And, like the bees, Are murdered for our pains *2 Hen. IV.* iv 5 79
As with an enemy That had before my face murder'd my father iv 5 168
As all you know, Harmless Richard was murder'd traitorously *2 Hen. VI.* ii 2 27
And God in justice hath reveal'd to us The truth and innocence of this poor fellow, Which he had thought to have murder'd wrongfully ii 3 107
That good Duke Humphrey traitorously is murder'd iii 2 123
He was murder'd here; The least of all these signs were probable iii 2 177
A Roman sworder and banditto slave Murder'd sweet Tully iv 1 136
Thou wilt stay with me?—Ay, to be murder'd by his enemies *3 Hen. VI.* i 1 260
Let them fight that will, For I have murdered where I should not kill ii 5 122
My grandam told me he was murder'd there *Richard III.* iii 1 145
Methought the souls of all that I had murder'd Came to my tent v 3 204
Methought their souls, whose bodies Richard murder'd Came to my tent v 3 230
Poor Bassianus here lies murdered *T. Andron.* ii 3 263
Find the huntsman out That should have murder'd Bassianus here ii 3 279
Some bring the murder'd body, some the murderers: Let them not speak ii 3 300
'Twas her two sons that murder'd Bassianus; They cut thy sister's tongue v 1 91
Chiron and Demetrius Were they that murdered our emperor's brother v 3 98
Some word there was, worser than Tybalt's death, That murder'd me: I would forget it fain *Rom. and Jul.* iii 2 109
An hour but married, Tybalt murdered, Doting like me iii 3 66
Did murder her; as that name's cursed hand Murder'd her kinsman iii 3 104
This is that banish'd haughty Montague, That murder'd my love's cousin v 3 50
Glamis hath murder'd sleep *Macbeth* ii 2 42
O Banquo, Banquo, Our royal master's murder'd! ii 3 92
Your royal father's murder'd.—O, by whom?—Those of his chamber ii 3 105
For them the gracious Duncan have I murder'd; Put rancours in the vessel of my peace Only for them iii 1 66
Were, on the quarry of these murder'd deer, To add the death of you iv 3 206
I, the son of a dear father murder'd, Prompted to my revenge *Hamlet* ii 2 612
O, falsely, falsely murder'd!—Alas, what cry is that? *Othello* v 2 117
Why, how should she be murder'd?—Alas, who knows? v 2 126
Murdered. My mistress here lies murder'd in her bed,— O heavens forfend! *Othello* v 2 185
Threats the throat of that his officer That murder'd Pompey *A. and C.* iii 5 20
Murderer. The one has my pity; not a jot the other, Being a murderer, though he were my brother *Meas. for Meas.* iv 2 65
That Angelo's a murderer; is't not strange? v 1 39
Where is the bush That we must stand and play the murderer in? *L. L. L.* iv 1 8
So should a murderer look, so dead, so grim *M. N. Dream* iii 2 57
Yet you, the murderer, look as bright, as clear, As yonder Venus iii 2 60
That eyes . . . Should be call'd tyrants, butchers, murderers! *As Y. L. It* iii 5 14
O, for shame, for shame, Lie not, to say mine eyes are murderers! iii 5 19
I have dogged him, like his murderer *T. Night* iii 2 82
Put it up again.—Not till I sheathe it in a murderer's skin *K. John* iv 3 80
Thou art a murderer.—Do not prove me so; Yet I am none iv 3 90
What wilt thou do, renowned Faulconbridge? Second a villain and a murderer? iv 3 102
Though I did wish him dead, I hate the murderer *Richard II.* v 6 40
Unless it were a bloody murderer, Or foul felonious thief *2 Hen. VI.* iii 1 128
Being accused a crafty murderer, His guilt should be but idly posted over iii 1 254
Æolus would not be a murderer, But left that hateful office unto thee iii 2 92
And we, I hope, sir, are no murderers iii 2 181
O Ned, sweet Ned! speak to thy mother, boy! Canst thou not speak? O traitors! murderers! *3 Hen. VI.* v 5 52
What's worse than murderer, that I may name it? v 5 58
Which says that G Of Edward's heirs the murderer shall be *Richard III.* i 1 40
Either heaven with lightning strike the murderer dead, Or earth, gape open wide and eat him quick! i 2 64
Which of you, . . If two such murderers as yourselves came to you, Would not entreat for life? i 4 268
Is there a murderer here? No. Yes, I am: Then fly. What, from myself? v 3 184
He's dead; and at the murderer's horse's tail, In beastly sort, dragg'd through the shameful field *Troi. and Cres.* v 10 4
Do this, and be a charitable murderer *T. Andron.* ii 3 178
Some bring the murder'd body, some the murderers: Let them not speak ii 3 300
Out on thee, murderer! thou kill'st my heart iii 2 54
And find out murderers in their guilty caves v 2 52
Show me a murderer, I'll deal with him v 2 93
And when thou find'st a man that's like thyself, Good Murder, stab him; he's a murderer v 2 100
Tybalt, that murderer, which way ran he? *Rom. and Jul.* iii 1 143
Doth she not think me an old murderer? iii 3 94
He doth grieve my heart.—That is, because the traitor murderer lives iii 5 85
We shall be call'd purgers, not murderers *J. Cæsar* ii 1 180
They were villains, murderers: the will! read the will iii 2 160
As his host, Who should against his murderer shut the door *Macbeth* i 7 15
There, the murderers, Steep'd in the colours of their trade ii 3 120
Grease that's sweaten From the murderer's gibbet throw Into the flame iv 1 66
Begin, murderer; pox, leave thy damnable faces, and begin *Hamlet* iii 2 263
You shall see anon how the murderer gets the love of Gonzago's wife iii 2 275
A murderer and a villain; A slave that is not twentieth part the tithe Of your precedent lord iii 4 96
A plague upon you, murderers, traitors all! I might have saved her *Lear* v 3 269
An honourable murderer, if you will; For nought I did in hate *Othello* v 2 294
Ay me, most credulous fool, Egregious murderer, thief, any thing! *Cymb.* v 5 211
Cleon's wife, with envy rare, A present murderer does prepare *Per.* iv Gower 38
Dionyza does appear, With Leonine, a murderer iv Gower 52
Murdering. The fatal balls of murdering basilisks *Hen. V.* v 2 17
Their chiefest prospect murdering basilisks! *2 Hen. VI.* iii 2 324
But set his murdering knife unto the root *3 Hen. VI.* ii 6 49
If murdering innocents be executing, Why, then thou art an executioner v 6 32
And art thou yet to thy own soul so blind, That thou wilt war with God by murdering me? *Richard III.* i 4 260
Murdering impossibility, to make What cannot be, slight work *Coriolanus* v 3 61
And take my milk for gall, you murdering ministers! *Macbeth* i 5 49
Murdering-piece. This, Like to a murdering-piece, in many places Gives me superfluous death *Hamlet* iv 5 95
Murderous. A murderous guilt shows not itself more soon Than love that would seem hid *T. Night* iii 1 159
Never enter'd yet The dreadful motion of a murderous thought *K. John* iv 2 255
And for his sake wear the detested blot Of murderous subornation *1 Hen. IV.* i 3 163
Upon thy eye-balls murderous tyranny Sits in grim majesty *2 Hen. VI.* iii 2 49
I would, false murderous coward, on thy knee Make thee beg pardon iii 2 220
Who can be bound by any solemn vow To do a murderous deed, to rob a man? v 1 185
And set the murderous Machiavel to school *3 Hen. VI.* iii 2 193
Queen Margaret saw Thy murderous falchion smoking in his blood *Richard III.* i 2 94
Withal, what I have been, and what I am.—A murderous villain i 3 134
A cockatrice hast thou hatch'd . . . , Whose unavoided eye is murderous iv 1 56
No doubt the murderous knife was dull and blunt Till it was whetted on thy stone-hard heart iv 4 226
And wonder greatly that man's face can fold In pleasing smiles such murderous tyranny *T. Andron.* ii 3 267
Stay, murderous villains! will you kill your brother? ii 3 267
O murderous slumber, Lay'st thou thy leaden mace upon my boy? *J. C.* iv 3 267
This murderous shaft that's shot Hath not yet lighted *Macbeth* ii 3 147
Thou incestuous, murderous, damned Dane, Drink off this potion *Hamlet* v 2 336
Deserve our thanks, Bringing the murderous coward to the stake *Lear* ii 1 64
The post unsanctified Of murderous lechers iv 6 282
O murderous slave! O villain!—O damn'd Iago! O inhuman dog! *Othello* v 1 61
O murderous coxcomb! what should such a fool Do with so good a woman? v 2 233
Have I not found it Murderous to the senses? *Cymbeline* iv 2 328
Mure. The incessant care and labour of his mind Hath wrought the mure that should confine it in So thin that life looks through *2 Hen. IV.* iv 4 119
Murk. Ere twice in murk and occidental damp Moist Hesperus hath quench'd his sleepy lamp *All's Well* ii 1 166
Murkiest. The murkiest den, The most opportune place *Tempest* iv 1 25
Murky. Hell is murky!—Fie, my lord, fie! a soldier, and afeard? *Macbeth* v 1 41
Murmur. The current that with gentle murmur glides *T. G. of Ver.* ii 7 25
A month ago I went from hence, And then 'twas fresh in murmur *T. Night* i 2 32
And heard thee murmur tales of iron wars *1 Hen. IV.* ii 3 51
A time When creeping murmur and the poring dark Fills the wide vessel of the universe *Hen. V.* iv Prol. 2
Murmured. The fresh streams ran by her, and murmur'd her moans *Oth.* iv 3 45
Murmurer. For living murmurers There's places of rebuke *Hen. VIII.* ii 2 131
Murmurest. If thou more murmur'st, I will rend an oak And peg thee in his knotty entrails *Tempest* i 2 294
Murmuring. The rank of osiers by the murmuring stream *As Y. Like It* iv 3 80
Whose restraint Doth move the murmuring lips of discontent *K. John* iv 2 53

Murmuring. The murmuring surge, That on the unnumber'd idle pebbles chafes . . . . *Lear* iv 6 20
He's speaking now, Or murmuring . . . *Ant. and Cleo.* i 5 25
Murrain. A murrain on your monster! . . . *Tempest* iii 2 88
Thou canst strike, canst thou? a red murrain o' thy jade's tricks! *T. and C.* ii 1 20
A murrain on't! I took this for silver . . . *Coriolanus* i 5 3
Murray. The Earl of Athol, Of Murray, Angus, and Menteith 1 *Hen. IV.* i 1 73
Murrion. And crows are fatted with the murrion flock . *M. N. Dream* ii 1 97
Muscadel. Quaff'd off the muscadel And threw the sops all in the sexton's face . . . *T. of Shrew* iii 2 174
Muscle. Thy food shall be The fresh-brook muscles . . *Tempest* i 2 463
Muscovit. Twenty adieus, my frozen Muscovits . . *L. L. Lost* v 2 265
Muscovite. Apparell'd thus, Like Muscovites or Russians, as I guess . v 2 121
Let us complain to them what fools were here, Disguised like Muscovites v 2 303
Muscovy. Why look you pale? Sea-sick, I think, coming from Muscovy v 2 393
Muse. I cannot too much muse Such shapes, such gesture . *Tempest* iii 3 36
Muse not that I thus suddenly proceed . . . *T. G. of Ver.* i 3 64
Why muse you, sir? 'tis dinner-time . . . . . ii 1 176
Well, I will muse no further . . . . *Mer. Wives* v 5 253
The thrice three Muses mourning for the death Of Learning *M. N. Dream* v 1 52
Rather muse than ask why I entreat you . . . *All's Well* ii 5 70
I muse your majesty doth seem so cold . . . *K. John* iii 1 317
I muse you make so slight a question . . . 2 *Hen. IV.* iv 1 167
O for a Muse of fire! . . . . . . *Hen. V.* Prol. 1
I muse we met not with the Dauphin's grace . . 1 *Hen. VI.* ii 2 19
I muse my Lord of Gloucester is not come! . . 2 *Hen. VI.* iii 1 1
You muse what chat we two have had . . . 3 *Hen. VI.* iii 2 109
I muse why she's at liberty.—I cannot blame her . *Richard III.* i 3 305
I muse my mother Does not approve me further . *Coriolanus* iii 2 7
Do not muse at me, my most worthy friends; I have a strange infirmity, which is nothing To those that know me . . . *Macbeth* iii 4 85
It plucks out brains and all: but my Muse labours . *Othello* ii 1 128
Mused. Cæsar's father oft, When he hath mused of taking kingdoms in, Bestow'd his lips on that unworthy place . . *Ant. and Cleo.* iii 13 83
Mushroom. Whose pastime Is to make midnight mushrooms . *Tempest* v 1 39
Music. Where should this music be? i' the air or the earth? . i 2 387
This music crept by me upon the waters, Allaying both their fury and my passion With its sweet air . . . . . . i 2 391
A brave kingdom to me, where I shall have my music for nothing . iii 2 154
What harmony is this? My good friends, hark!—Marvellous sweet music! . . . . iii 3 19
Advanced their eyelids, lifted up their noses As they smelt music . iv 1 178
When I have required Some heavenly music, which even now I do . v 1 52
Makes sweet music with the enamell'd stones . . *T. G. of Ver.* ii 7 28
Except I be by Silvia in the night, There is no music in the nightingale iii 1 179
Let us into the city presently To sort some gentlemen well skill'd in music . . . . iii 2 92
Now must we to her window, And give some evening music to her ear . iv 2 17
We'll have you merry: I'll bring you where you shall hear music . iv 2 31
But shall I hear him speak?—Ay, that you shall.—That will be music . iv 2 35
The music likes you not.—You mistake; the musician likes me not . iv 2 55
I perceive you delight not in music.—Not a whit, when it jars so . iv 2 66
Hark, what fine change is in the music!—Ay, that change is the spite . iv 2 68
I thank you for your music, gentlemen. Who is that that spake? . iv 2 86
Music oft hath such a charm To make bad good . *Meas. for Meas.* iv 1 14
Never words were music to thine ear, . . . Unless I spake *Com. of Errors* ii 2 116
Where is my cousin, your son? hath he provided this music? *Much Ado* i 2 2
The fault will be in the music, cousin, if you be not wooed in good time ii 1 72
There was no music with him but the drum and the fife . . ii 3 14
Shall we hear this music?—Yea, my good lord. How still the evening is! ii 3 39
The music ended, We'll fit the kid-fox with a pennyworth . . ii 3 44
Tax not so bad a voice To slander music any more than once . . ii 3 47
I pray thee, get us some excellent music . . . . . ii 3 87
Now, music, sound, and sing your solemn hymn . . . . v 3 11
We'll have dancing afterward.—First, of my word; therefore play, music v 4 123
One whom the music of his own vain tongue Doth ravish *L. L. Lost* i 1 167
Thy voice his dreadful thunder, Which, not to anger bent, is music . iv 2 120
Play, music, then! Nay, you must do it soon. Not yet! no dance! . v 2 211
The music plays; vouchsafe some motion to it.—Our ears vouchsafe it v 2 216
The rude sea grew civil at her song And certain stars shot madly from their spheres, To hear the sea-maid's music . *M. N. Dream* ii 1 154
What, wilt thou hear some music, my sweet love? . . . iv 1 29
I have a reasonable good ear in music. Let's have the tongs and the bones . . . . iv 1 31
Music call; and strike more dead Than common sleep of all these five the sense . . . . iv 1 86
Music, ho! music, such as charmeth sleep! . . . . . iv 1 88
Sound, music! Come, my queen, take hands with me, And rock the ground whereon these sleepers be . . . . . . iv 1 90
My love shall hear the music of my hounds . . . . . iv 1 111
What masque? what music? How shall we beguile The lazy time? . v 1 40
Let music sound while he doth make his choice *Mer. of Venice* iii 2 43
If he lose, he makes a swan-like end, Fading in music . . . iii 2 45
He may win; And what is music then? Then music is Even as the flourish when true subjects bow To a new-crowned monarch . . iii 2 48
Your mistress is at hand; And bring your music forth into the air . v 1 53
Here will we sit and let the sounds of music Creep in our ears . v 1 55
Pierce your mistress' ear And draw her home with music . . . v 1 68
I am never merry when I hear sweet music . . . . . v 1 69
If they but hear perchance a trumpet sound, Or any air of music touch their ears, You shall perceive them make a mutual stand, Their savage eyes turn'd to a modest gaze By the sweet power of music . v 1 76
Since nought so stockish, hard and full of rage, But music for the time doth change his nature . . . . v 1 82
The man that hath no music in himself, Nor is not moved with concord of sweet sounds, Is fit for treasons . . . . . . v 1 83
Music! hark!—It is your music, madam, of the house . . . v 1 97
Is there any else longs to see this broken music in his sides? *As Y. Like It* i 2 150
Give us some music; and, good cousin, sing . . . . ii 7 173
And fall into our rustic revelry. Play, music . . . . v 4 184
Procure me music ready when he wakes . . . *T. of Shrew* Ind. 1 50
Wilt thou have music? hark! Apollo plays And twenty caged nightingales do sing: Or wilt thou sleep? . . . . . . Ind. 2 37
Music and poesy use to quicken you . . . . . . i 1 36
She taketh most delight In music, instruments and poetry . . . i 1 93
A schoolmaster Well seen in music . . . . . . i 2 134
Cunning in music and the mathematics . . . . . ii 1 56
As cunning in Greek, Latin, and other languages, as the other in music ii 1 82
And when in music we have spent an hour, Your lecture shall have leisure iii 1 7
That never read so far To know the cause why music was ordain'd! . iii 1 10
Music. My lessons make no music in three parts . . *T. of Shrew* iii 1 60
Every night he comes With musics of all sorts . . . *All's Well* iii 7 40
If music be the food of love, play on; Give me excess of it . *T. Night* i 1 1
I can sing And speak to him in many sorts of music . . . i 2 58
Give me some music. Now, good morrow, friends . . . . ii 4 1
Save thee, friend, and thy music: dost thou live by thy tabor? . iii 1 1
I had rather hear you to solicit that Than music from the spheres . iii 1 121
It is as fat and fulsome to mine ear As howling after music . . v 1 113
It is my father's music To speak your deeds . . . *W. Tale* iv 4 529
Music, awake her; strike! 'Tis time; descend; be stone no more . v 3 98
The setting sun, and music at the close . . . *Richard II.* ii 1 12
How sour sweet music is, When time is broke and no proportion kept! So is it in the music of men's lives . . . . . . v 5 42
This music mads me; let it sound no more . . . . . v 5 61
Now, Esperance! Percy! and set on. Sound all the lofty instruments of war, And by that music let us all embrace . . . 1 *Hen. IV.* v 2 99
Mistress Tearsheet would fain hear some music. Dispatch 2 *Hen. IV.* ii 4 14
The music is come, sir.—Let them play. Play, sirs . . . ii 4 245
Unless some dull and favourable hand Will whisper music to my weary spirit.—Call for the music in the other room . . . . iv 5 3
I heard a bird so sing, Whose music, to my thinking, pleased the king v 5 114
You shall hear A fearful battle render'd you in music . . *Hen. V.* i 1 44
Congreeing in a full and natural close, Like music . . . . i 2 183
Come, your answer in broken music; for thy voice is music . . v 2 263
A warning bell, Sings heavy music to thy timorous soul 1 *Hen. VI.* iv 2 40
How irksome is this music to my heart! . . 2 *Hen. VI.* ii 1 56
Their music frightful as the serpent's hiss! . . . . iii 2 326
Thou sing'st sweet music . . . . . . *Richard III.* iv 2 79
And, by'r lady, Held current music too . . . *Hen. VIII.* i 3 47
Let the music knock it . . . . i 4 108
To his music plants and flowers Ever sprung . . . . iii 1 6
In sweet music is such art, Killing care and grief of heart . . iii 1 12
With all the choicest music of the kingdom, Together sung 'Te Deum' iv 1 91
Bid the music leave, They are harsh and heavy to me . . . iv 2 94
We shall hear music, wit and oracle . . . *Troi. and Cres.* i 3 74
What music is this?—I do but partly know, sir: it is music in parts . iii 1 17
Who play they to?—To the hearers, sir.—At whose pleasure, friend?—At mine, sir, and theirs that love music . . . . . iii 1 26
Fair prince, here is good broken music.—You have broke it, cousin . iii 1 52
Stop my mouth.—And shall, albeit sweet music issues thence . . iii 2 142
What music will be in him when Hector has knocked out his brains, I know not . . . . iii 3 303
Young lords, beware! an should the empress know This discord's ground, the music would not please . . . . *T. Andron.* ii 1 70
How silver-sweet sound lovers' tongues by night, Like softest music to attending ears! . . . . *Rom. and Jul.* ii 2 167
Thou shamest the music of sweet news By playing it to me with so sour a face . . . . ii 5 23
Let rich music's tongue Unfold the imagined happiness . . . ii 6 27
The county will be here with music straight, For so he said he would . iv 4 21
'Then music with her silver sound'—why 'silver sound?' . . iv 5 130
It is 'music with her silver sound,' because musicians have no gold . iv 5 142
Music with her silver sound With speedy help doth lend redress . iv 5 145
Let 'em have kind admittance: Music, make their welcome! *T. of Athens* i 2 135
Farewell; and come with better music . . . . . i 2 252
Feast your ears with the music awhile, if they will fare so harshly . iii 6 36
I hear a tongue, shriller than all the music . . . *J. Cæsar* i 2 16
He hears no music; Seldom he smiles . . . . . . i 2 204
This is a sleepy tune. O murderous slumber, Lay'st thou thy leaden mace upon my boy, That plays thee music? . . . . . iv 3 269
And let him ply his music.—Well, my lord . . . *Hamlet* ii 1 73
That suck'd the honey of his music vows . . . . . iii 1 164
Come, some music! come, the recorders! . . . . . iii 2 302
Give it breath with your mouth, and it will discourse most eloquent music . . . . iii 2 375
There is much music, excellent voice, in this little organ . . iii 2 384
My pulse, as yours, doth temperately keep time, And makes as healthful music: it is not madness . . . . iii 4 141
For his passage, The soldiers' music and the rites of war Speak loudly . v 2 410
Please you, draw near. Louder the music there! . . . *Lear* iv 7 25
I'll set down the pegs that make this music, As honest as I am *Othello* ii 1 203
The general so likes your music, that he desires you, for love's sake, to make no more noise with it . . . . iii 1 12
If you have any music that may not be heard, to't again . . . iii 1 16
But, as they say, to hear music the general does not greatly care . iii 1 17
Hark, canst thou hear me? I will play the swan, And die in music . v 2 248
Give me some music; music, moody food Of us that trade in love *A. and C.* ii 5 1
My music playing far off, I will betray Tawny-finn'd fishes . . ii 5 11
Make battery to our ears with the loud music . . . . ii 7 115
Hark!—Music i' the air.—Under the earth.—It signs well, does it not? iv 3 14
I would this music would come: I am advised to give her music o' mornings; they say it will penetrate . . . . . *Cymbeline* ii 3 12
If this penetrate, I will consider your music the better . . . ii 3 32
I have assailed her with music, but she vouchsafes no notice . . ii 3 44
Which you'll make him know, If that his head have ear in music . iii 4 178
Who, finger'd to make man his lawful music, Would draw heaven down *Pericles* i 1 82
Loud music is too harsh for ladies' heads . . . . . ii 3 97
I am beholding to you For your sweet music this last night . . ii 5 26
Sir, you are music's master.—The worst of all her scholars, my good lord ii 5 30
The rough and woeful music that we have, Cause it to sound, beseech you iii 2 88
The viol once more: how thou stirr'st, thou block! The music there! iii 2 91
Train'd In music, letters; who hath gain'd Of education all the grace iv Gower 8
Mark'd he your music?—No, nor look'd on us . . . . . v 1 81
But, what music?—My lord, I hear none.—None! The music of the spheres! . . . . v 1 228
Most heavenly music! It nips me unto listening . . . . . v 1 234
Musical. And well could wish You had not found me here so musical *Meas. for Meas.* iv 1 11
As sweet and musical As bright Apollo's lute . . . *L. L. Lost* iv 3 342
Mark the musical confusion Of hounds and echo in conjunction *M. N. D.* iv 1 115
I never heard So musical a discord, such sweet thunder . . . iv 1 123
Here was he merry, hearing of a song.—If he, compact of jars, grow musical, We shall have shortly discord in the spheres *As Y. Like It* ii 7 5
Then should you be nothing but musical, for you are altogether governed by humours . . . . 1 *Hen. IV.* iii 1 237
The basest horn of his hoof is more musical than the pipe of Hermes *Hen. V.* iii 7 18
Musician. You mistake; the musician likes me not . . *T. G. of Ver.* iv 2 57
Of good discourse, an excellent musician . . . . *Much Ado* ii 3 36

Musician. Would be thought No better a musician than the wren *Mer. of Venice* v 1 106
I have neither the scholar's melancholy, which is emulation, nor the musician's, which is fantastical . *As Y. Like It* iv 1 11
A fine musician to instruct our mistress . *T. of Shrew* i 2 174
Will my daughter prove a good musician?—I think she'll sooner prove a soldier . . . . ii 1 145
Our fine musician groweth amorous . . . . . iii 1 63
The narrow-prying father, Minola, The quaint musician, amorous Licio iii 2 149
Mistake no more: I am not Licio, Nor a musician, as I seem to be . iv 2 17
Suppose the singing birds musicians . . *Richard II.* i 3 288
And those musicians that shall play to you Hang in the air a thousand leagues from hence . . . . *1 Hen. IV.* iii 1 226
By'r lady, he is a good musician . . . . . . iii 1 235
Pay the musicians, sirrah. Farewell, hostess; farewell, Doll *2 Hen. IV.* ii 4 403
Cause the musicians play me that sad note I named my knell *Hen. VIII.* iv 2 78
Know you the musicians?—Wholly, sir.—Who play they to? *Troi. and Cres.* iii 1 21
Musicians, play. A hall, a hall! give room! and foot it, girls *Rom. and Jul.* i 5 27
Musicians, O, musicians, 'Heart's ease, Heart's ease' . . iv 5 102
I say 'silver sound,' because musicians sound for silver . . iv 5 136
It is 'music with her silver sound,' because musicians have no gold iv 5 143
Admirable musician: O! she will sing the savageness out of a bear *Oth.* iv 1 199
Musing. Made wit with musing weak, heart sick with thought *T. G. of V.* i 1 69
She is given too much to allicholy and musing *Mer. Wives* i 4 164
To thick-eyed musing and cursed melancholy . . *1 Hen. IV.* ii 3 49
He should still Dwell in his musings . . *Hen. VIII.* iii 2 133
Musing and sighing, with your arms across . . *J. Cæsar* ii 1 240
Drew sleep out of mine eyes, blood from my cheeks, Musings into my mind, with thousand doubts . . . *Pericles* i 2 97
Musk. Smelling so sweetly, all musk, and so rushling *Mer. Wives* ii 2 68
Musk-cat. Fortune's cat,—but not a musk-cat . . . *All's Well* v 2 21
Musket. To be the mark Of smoky muskets . . . . iii 2 111
Muskos. I know you are the Muskos' regiment: And I shall lose my life for want of language . . . . iv 1 76
Musk-rose. With sweet musk-roses and with eglantine *M. N. Dream* ii 1 252
Some to kill cankers in the musk-rose buds, Some war with rere-mice . ii 2 3
And stick musk-roses in thy sleek smooth head . . iv 1 3
Muss. Of late, when I cried 'Ho!' Like boys unto a muss, kings would start forth, And cry 'Your will?' *Ant. and Cleo.* iii 13 91
Mussel-shell. Ay, marry, was it, mussel-shell *Mer. Wives* iv 5 29
Must. What, must our mouths be cold? . . . *Tempest* i 1 56
Whither I must, I must; and, to conclude, This evening must I leave you . . . . *1 Hen. IV.* ii 3 109
We must away all night . . . . iv 2 63
He must, and will. Prithee now, say you will, and go about it *Coriolanus* iii 2 97
That may be, sir, when I may be a wife.—That may be must be *R. and J.* iv 1 20
What must be shall be.—That's a certain text . . . iv 1 21
I hear thou must, and nothing may prorogue it . . . iv 1 48
Must it be so? it must not be . . . *T. of Athens* iii 5 89
And I must be from thence! My wife kill'd too? . . *Macbeth* iv 3 212
I must not think there are Evils enow to darken all his goodness *Ant. and Cleo.* i 4 10
To prepare This body, like to them, to what I must . . *Pericles* i 1 44
Mustachio. Dally with my excrement, with my mustachio *L. L. Lost* v 1 110
None of these mad mustachio purple-hued malt-worms *1 Hen. IV.* ii 1 83
Mustard. Swore by his honour the mustard was naught: now I'll stand to it, the pancakes were naught and the mustard was good *As Y. L. It* i 2 68
He had sworn it away before ever he saw those pancakes or that mustard i 2 85
What say you to a piece of beef and mustard? . . *T. of Shrew* iv 3 23
The mustard is too hot a little.—Why then, the beef, and let the mustard rest. . . . . iv 3 25
Nay then, I will not: you shall have the mustard, Or else you get no beef iv 3 27
Then both, or one, or any thing thou wilt.—Why then, the mustard iv 3 30
His wit's as thick as Tewksbury mustard . . *2 Hen. IV.* ii 4 262
Mustardseed. Peaseblossom! Cobweb! Moth! and Mustardseed! *M. N. Dream* iii 1 165
Good Master Mustardseed, I know your patience well . . iii 1 196
Give me your neaf, Mounsieur Mustardseed . . . iv 1 20
Muster. Why does my blood thus muster to my heart? *Meas. for Meas.* ii 4 20
You'll be surprised: Muster your wits; stand in your own defence *L. L. Lost* v 2 85
There do muster true gait, eat, speak, and move . *All's Well* ii 1 55
Gentlemen, will you go muster men? . . . *Richard II.* ii 2 108
Go, muster up your men, And meet me presently at Berkeley . ii 2 118
Come, let us take a muster speedily: Doomsday is near . *1 Hen. IV.* iv 1 133
Who but Rumour, who but only I, Make fearful musters? *2 Hen. IV.* Ind. 12
Our present musters grow upon the file To five and twenty thousand men i 3 10
The vital commoners and inland petty spirits muster me all to their captain . . . . iv 3 120
Defences, musters, preparations, Should be maintain'd . . *Hen. V.* ii 4 18
For the effusion of our blood, the muster of his kingdom too faint a number . . . . iii 6 139
I have true-hearted friends, Not mutinous in peace, yet bold in war; Those will I muster up . . . . . *3 Hen. VI.* iv 8 11
Oxford, wondrous well beloved, In Oxfordshire shalt muster up thy friends . . . . iv 8 18
Come, muster men: my counsel is my shield; We must be brief *Rich. III.* iv 3 56
I'll muster up my friends, and meet your grace . . . iv 4 489
Well, Go muster men; but, hear you, leave behind Your son . iv 4 496
We would muster all From twelve to seventy . . *Coriolanus* iv 5 134
Hasten his musters and conduct his powers . . . *Lear* iv 2 16
Those his goodly eyes, That o'er the files and musters of the war Have glow'd like plated Mars . . . . . *Ant. and Cleo.* i 1 3
Muster-book. We have a number of shadows to fill up the muster-book *2 Hen. IV.* iii 2 146
Mustered. An army have I muster'd in my thoughts . *1 Hen. VI.* i 1 101
I, then in London, keeper of the king, Muster'd my soldiers *3 Hen. VI.* ii 1 112
Command our present numbers Be muster'd . . *Cymbeline* iv 2 344
We being not known, not muster'd Among the bands . . iv 4 10
Muster-file. The muster-file, rotten and sound, upon my life, amounts not to fifteen thousand poll . . . . . . *All's Well* iv 3 189
Mustering. God omnipotent Is mustering in his clouds *Richard II.* iii 3 86
Musty. You had musty victual, and he hath holp to eat it . *Much Ado* i 1 50
Being entertained for a perfumer, as I was smoking a musty room . i 3 61
Then we shall ha' means to vent Our musty superfluity . . *Coriolanus* i 1 230
He could not stay to pick them in a pile Of noisome musty chaff . . v 1 26
You are the musty chaff; and you are smelt Above the moon . . v 1 31
Musty. Green earthen pots, bladders and musty seeds . *Rom. and Jul.* v 1 46
'While the grass grows,'—the proverb is something musty . *Hamlet* iii 2 359
And wast thou fain, poor father, To hovel thee with swine, and rogues forlorn, In short and musty straw? . . . . . *Lear* iv 7 40
Mutability. That she [Fortune] is turning, and inconstant, and mutability, and variation . . . . *Hen. V.* iii 6 36
Nice longing, slanders, mutability, All faults that may be named, nay, that hell knows, Why, hers [woman's], in part or all . *Cymbeline* ii 5 26
Mutable. The mutable, rank-scented many . . *Coriolanus* iii 1 66
Mutation. O world! But that thy strange mutations make us hate thee, Life would not yield to age . . . . . . *Lear* iv 1 11
Though his humour Was nothing but mutation . . . *Cymbeline* iv 2 133
Mute. Hush, and be mute, Or else our spell is marr'd . *Tempest* iv 1 126
No point, quoth I; my servant straight was mute . . *L. L. Lost* v 2 277
Say she be mute and will not speak a word; Then I'll commend her volubility, And say she uttereth piercing eloquence *T. of Shrew* ii 1 175
Thanks, sir; all the rest is mute . . . . *All's Well* ii 3 83
Be you his eunuch, and your mute I'll be . . . *T. Night* i 2 62
To a vision so apparent rumour Cannot be mute . . *W. Tale* i 2 271
And the mute wonder lurketh in men's ears . . . *Hen. V.* i 1 49
Our grave, Like Turkish mute, shall have a tongueless mouth . i 2 232
My woe-wearied tongue is mute and dumb . . *Richard III.* iv 4 18
O, why should wrath be mute, and fury dumb? . *T. Andron.* v 3 184
Or given my heart a winking, mute and dumb . . . *Hamlet* ii 2 137
That are but mutes or audience to this act . . . . v 2 346
That thou wilt be a voluntary mute to my design . . *Cymbeline* iii 5 158
When to the lute She sung, and made the night-bird mute *Pericles* iv Gower 26
Mutest. 'Tis your graces That from my mutest conscience to my tongue Charms this report out . . . . *Cymbeline* i 6 116
Mutine. Do like the mutines of Jerusalem, Be friends awhile . *K. John* ii 1 378
Rebellious hell, If thou canst mutine in a matron's bones . *Hamlet* iii 4 83
Methought I lay Worse than the mutines in the bilboes . . . v 2 6
Mutineer. If you prove a mutineer,—the next tree! . *Tempest* iii 2 41
Mutiner. Worshipful mutiners, Your valour puts well forth . *Coriolanus* i 1 254
Mutinous. Call'd forth the mutinous winds . . . *Tempest* v 1 42
How fell, how butcherly, Erroneous, mutinous, and unnatural! *3 Hen. VI.* ii 5 90
I have true-hearted friends, Not mutinous in peace, yet bold in war iv 8 10
The discontented members, the mutinous parts . . *Coriolanus* i 1 115
The senators of Rome are this good belly, And you the mutinous members i 1 153
The dearth is great; The people mutinous . . . . i 2 11
Then let the mutinous winds Strike the proud cedars 'gainst the fiery sun v 3 59
Mutiny. Whom right and wrong Have chose as umpire of their mutiny *L. L. Lost* i 1 170
The spirit of my father, which I think is within me, begins to mutiny against this servitude . . . . *As Y. Like It* i 1 24
Where will doth mutiny with wit's regard . . . *Richard II.* ii 1 28
Disorder, horror, fear and mutiny Shall here inhabit . . . iv 1 142
And hardly keeps his men from mutiny . . . *1 Hen. VI.* i 1 160
To take occasion from their mouths To raise a mutiny betwixt yourselves iv 1 131
I'll either make thee stoop and bend thy knee, Or sack this country with a mutiny . . . . v 1 62
Myself have calm'd their spleenful mutiny . . *2 Hen. VI.* iii 2 128
Was wont to cheer his dad in mutinies . . . *3 Hen. VI.* i 4 77
'Tis [conscience] a blushing shamefast spirit that mutinies in a man's bosom; it fills one full of obstacles . . . . *Richard III.* i 4 142
It may well be; There is a mutiny in's mind . . *Hen. VIII.* iii 2 120
What mutiny! What raging of the sea! shaking of earth! *Troi. and Cres.* i 3 96
Their mutinies and revolts, wherein they show'd Most valour *Coriolanus* iii 1 126
Let them go on; This mutiny were better put in hazard, Than stay, past doubt, for greater. . . . . ii 3 264
To stir a mutiny in the mildest thoughts . . . *T. Andron.* iv 1 85
From ancient grudge break to new mutiny . . *Rom and Jul.* Prol. 3
You'll make a mutiny among my guests! You will set cock-a-hoop! i 5 82
Where's Publius?—Here, quite confounded with this mutiny *J. Cæsar* iii 1 86
If I were disposed to stir Your hearts and minds to mutiny and rage . iii 2 127
Sweet friends, let me not stir you up To such a sudden flood of mutiny iii 2 215
That should move The stones of Rome to rise and mutiny . . iii 2 234
We'll mutiny.—We'll burn the house of Brutus . . . iii 2 235
In cities, mutinies; in countries, discord; in palaces, treason . *Lear* i 2 116
Even out of that will I cause these of Cyprus to mutiny . *Othello* ii 1 282
Away, I say; go out, and cry a mutiny . . . . ii 3 157
My very hairs do mutiny; for the white Reprove the brown *A. and C.* iii 11 13
The mutiny he there hastes t' oppress . . . *Pericles* iii Gower 29
Mutius. Give Mutius burial with our brethren . . . *T. Andron.* i 1 348
Mutius' deeds do plead for him; He must be buried with his brethren . i 1 356
Entreat of thee To pardon Mutius and to bury him . . . i 1 363
He is not with himself; let us withdraw.—Not I, till Mutius' bones be buried . . . . i 1 369
Let not young Mutius, then, that was thy joy, Be barr'd his entrance here i 1 382
There lie thy bones, sweet Mutius, with thy friends . . . i 1 387
No man shed tears for noble Mutius; He lives in fame . . . i 1 389
Mutter. How now, wool-sack! what mutter you? . . *1 Hen. IV.* ii 4 148
What mutter you, or what conspire you, lords? . . *3 Hen. VI.* i 1 165
What does his cashiered worship mutter?—No matter what *T. of Athens* iii 4 61
There are a kind of men so loose of soul, That in their sleeps will mutter their affairs . . . . *Othello* iii 3 417
Muttered. Amongst the soldiers this is muttered . . *1 Hen. VI.* i 1 70
Mutton. I, a lost mutton, gave your letter to her, a laced mutton, and she, a laced mutton, gave me, a lost mutton, nothing for my labour *T. G. of Ver.* i 1 103
Here's too small a pasture for such store of muttons . . . i 1 106
The duke, I say to thee again, would eat mutton on Fridays *Meas. for Meas.* iii 2 192
I had rather pray a month with mutton and porridge . *L. L. Lost* i 1 304
Is not so estimable, profitable neither, As flesh of muttons *Mer. of Venice* i 3 168
Do not your courtier's hands sweat? and is not the grease of a mutton as wholesome as the sweat of a man? . . . . . *As Y. L. It* iii 2 57
Give thanks, sweet Kate; or else shall I? What's this? mutton? *T. of Shrew* iv 1 163
I can cut a caper.—And I can cut the mutton to't . . *T. Night* i 3 130
What's a joint of mutton or two in a whole Lent? . . *2 Hen. IV.* ii 4 376
A joint of mutton, and any pretty little tiny kickshaws . . . v 1 28
Mutual. One feast, one house, one mutual happiness . *T. G. of Ver.* v 4 173
The stealth of our most mutual entertainment . . *Meas. for Meas.* i 2 158
Every region near Seem'd all one mutual cry . . *M. N. Dream* iv 1 122
You shall perceive them make a mutual stand . . *Mer. of Venice* v 1 77
Confirm'd by mutual joinder of your hands . . . *T. Night* v 1 160
In mutual well-beseeming ranks, March all one way . . *1 Hen. IV.* i 1 14
The mutual conference that my mind hath had, By day, by night *2 Hen. VI.* i 1 25
Heart-sorrowing peers, That bear this mutual heavy load of moan *Rich. III.* ii 2 113

Mutual. Choice, being mutual act of all our souls . *Troi. and Cres.* i 3 348
To knit again This scatter'd corn into one mutual sheaf . *T. Andron.* v 3 71
Beat forth our brains, And make a mutual closure of our house . v 3 134
There is division, Although as yet the face of it be cover'd With mutual cunning, 'twixt Albany and Cornwall . *Lear* iii 1 21
When such a mutual pair And such a twain can do't . *Ant. and Cleo.* i 1 37
Mutualities. When these mutualities so marshal the way . *Othello* ii 1 267
Mutually. Who mutually hath answer'd my affection . *Mer. Wives* iv 6 10
Pinch him, fairies, mutually; Pinch him for his villany . v 5 103
Your most offenceful act Was mutually committed?—Mutually *M. for M.* ii 3 27
Devise, instruct, walk, feel, And, mutually participate . *Coriolanus* i 1 106
Muzzle. I am trusted with a muzzle and enfranchised with a clog *Much Ado* i 3 34
From curb'd license plucks The muzzle of restraint 2 *Hen. IV.* iv 5 132
This butcher's cur is venom-mouth'd, and I Have not the power to muzzle him; therefore best Not wake him in his slumber *Hen. VIII.* i 1 121
Muzzled. My dagger muzzled, Lest it should bite its master . *W. Tale* i 2 156
Like to a muzzled bear, Save in aspect . *K. John* ii 1 249
Myrmidon. The Myrmidons are no bottle-ale houses *T. Night* ii 3 29
That will physic the great Myrmidon *Troi. and Cres.* i 3 378
Patroclus' wounds have roused his drowsy blood, Together with his mangled Myrmidons . v 5 33
Come here about me, you my Myrmidons; Mark what I say . v 7 1
On, Myrmidons, and cry you all amain, 'Achilles hath the mighty Hector slain' . v 8 13
Myrtle. Thou rather with thy sharp and sulphurous bolt Split'st the unwedgeable and gnarled oak Than the soft myrtle . *Meas. for Meas.* ii 2 117
Myrtle-leaf. I was of late as petty to his ends As is the morn-dew on the myrtle-leaf To his grand sea . *Ant. and Cleo.* iii 12 9
Myself. None that I more love than myself . *Tempest* i 1 22
I leave myself, my friends and all, for love . *T. G. of Ver.* i 1 65
I am the dog—Oh! the dog is me, and I am myself . ii 3 25
You know him well?—I know him as myself . ii 4 62
If I keep them, I needs must lose myself; If I lose them, thus find I by their loss For Valentine myself, for Julia Silvia. I to myself am dearer than a friend . ii 6 20
To die is to be banish'd from myself; And Silvia is myself . iii 1 171
I would have daffed all other respects and made her half myself *M. Ado* ii 3 177
So much for praising myself, who, I myself will bear witness, is praiseworthy . v 2 89
I had as lief have been myself alone.—And so had I *As Y. Like It* iii 2 269
Then, by myself— Thyself thyself misusest *Richard III.* iv 4 376
Myself myself confound! Heaven and fortune bar me happy hours! . iv 4 399
Shall I forget myself to be myself?—Ay, if yourself's remembrance wrong yourself . iv 4 420

Myself. What do I fear? myself? there's none else by: Richard loves Richard; that is, I am I. Is there a murderer here? No. Yes, I am: Then fly. What, from myself? Great reason why: Lest I revenge. What, myself upon myself? Alack, I love myself. Wherefore? for any good That I myself have done unto myself? O, no! alas, I rather hate myself For hateful deeds committed by myself! *Richard III.* v 3 182
No soul shall pity me: Nay, wherefore should they, since that I myself Find in myself no pity to myself? . v 3 202
Myself hath often over-heard them say *T. Andron.* iv 4 74
Mystery. To thy great comfort in this mystery of ill opinions *Mer. Wives* ii 1 73
He will discredit our mystery . *Meas. for Meas.* iv 2 30
Do you call, sir, your occupation a mystery?—Ay, sir; a mystery . iv 2 36
Painting, sir, I have heard say, is a mystery; and your whores, sir, being members of my occupation, using painting, do prove my occupation a mystery . iv 2 39
But what mystery there should be in hanging, if I should be hanged, I cannot imagine.—Sir, it is a mystery . iv 2 41
Now I see The mystery of your loneliness *All's Well* i 3 177
If you think your mystery in stratagem can bring this instrument of honour again into his native quarter iii 6 68
Plutus himself . Hath not in nature's mystery more science . v 3 103
This mystery remained undiscovered *W. Tale* v 2 130
Is't possible the spells of France should juggle Men into such strange mysteries? *Hen. VIII.* i 3 2
There is a mystery—with whom relation Durst never meddle—in the soul of state; Which hath an operation more divine. *Troi. and Cres.* iii 3 201
Those mysteries which heaven Will not have earth to know *Coriolanus* iv 2 35
Manners, mysteries, and trades, Degrees, observances . *T. of Athens* iv 1 18
He thus advises us; not to have us thrive in our mystery . iv 3 458
You would pluck out the heart of my mystery *Hamlet* iii 2 382
By the sacred radiance of the sun, The mysteries of Hecate . *Lear* i 1 112
Take upon's the mystery of things, As if we were God's spies v 3 16
Your mystery, your mystery: nay, dispatch *Othello* iv 2 30
Mytilene is full of gallants *Pericles* iv 2 3
Patience, then, And think you now are all in Mytilene . iv 4 51
But there never came her like in Mytilene . iv 6 31
There's a barge put off from Mytilene, And in it is Lysimachus the governor . v 1 3
We have a maid in Mytilene, I durst wager, Would win some words of him v 1 43
A crew of pirates came and rescued me; Brought me to Mytilene. v 1 177
But Here is the regent, sir, of Mytilene Speaks nobly of her . v 1 188
What minstrelsy, and pretty din, The regent made in Mytilene v 2 273
But her better stars Brought her to Mytilene . v 3 10

N

Nag. 'Tis like the forced gait of a shuffling nag . 1 *Hen. IV.* iii 1 135
Know we not Galloway nags? 2 *Hen. IV.* ii 4 205
Yon ribaudred nag of Egypt,—Whom leprosy o'ertake! *Ant. and Cleo.* iii 10 10
Naiad. You nymphs, call'd Naiads, of the windring brooks *Tempest* iv 1 128
Nail. And I with my long nails will dig thee pig-nuts ii 2 172
I'll yield him thee asleep, Where thou mayst knock a nail into his head iii 2 69
As one nail by strength drives out another *T. G. of Ver.* ii 4 193
Some devils ask but the parings of one's nail, A rush, a hair *Com. of Er.* iv 3 72
With these nails I'll pluck out these false eyes . iv 4 107
Icicles hang by the wall And Dick the shepherd blows his nail *L. L. Lost* v 2 923
I am not yet so low But that my nails can reach unto thine eyes *M. N. Dream* iii 2 298
Let not him that plays the lion pare his nails . iv 2 41
We may blow our nails together, and fast it fairly out . *T. of Shrew* i 1 109
Thou yard, three-quarters, half-yard, quarter, nail! . iv 3 109
As the nail to his hole, the cuckold to his horn *All's Well* ii 2 26
What would you have me to do? 'Tis too late to pare her nails now . v 2 31
Like a mad lad, Pare thy nails, dad *T. Night* iv 2 140
The very mould and frame of hand, nail, finger *W. Tale* ii 3 103
These vain weak nails May tear a passage through the flinty ribs Of this hard world, my ragged prison walls . *Richard II.* v 5 19
What, is the old king dead?—As nail in door 2 *Hen. IV.* v 3 127
Les ongles? nous les appelons de nails . *Hen. V.* iii 4 16
Écoutez; dites-moi, si je parle bien: de hand, de fingres, et de nails . iii 4 18
Every one may pare his nails with a wooden dagger . iv 4 76
With my nails digg'd stones out of the ground, To hurl at the beholders of my shame . 1 *Hen. VI.* i 4 45
The very parings of our nails Shall pitch a field when we are dead iii 1 102
Could I come near your beauty with my nails . 2 *Hen. VI.* i 3 144
What time the shepherd, blowing of his nails, Can neither call it perfect day nor night . 3 *Hen. VI.* ii 5 3
These nails should rend that beauty from my cheeks *Richard III.* i 2 126
Till that my nails were anchor'd in thine eyes . iv 4 231
Whose wit was mouldy ere your grandsires had nails on their toes *Troi. and Cres.* ii 1 115
It were no match, your nail against his horn . iv 5 46
One fire drives out one fire; one nail, one nail *Coriolanus* iv 7 54
With her nails She'll flay thy wolvish visage *Lear* i 4 329
Strike in their numb'd and mortified bare arms Pins, wooden pricks, nails . ii 3 16
Because I would not see thy cruel nails Pluck out his poor old eyes iii 7 56
Be shown For poor'st diminutives, for doits; and let Patient Octavia plough thy visage up With her prepared nails . *Ant. and Cleo.* iv 12 39
I'll never see't; for, I am sure, my nails Are stronger than mine eyes . v 2 223
Nail'd For our advantage on the bitter cross 1 *Hen. IV.* i 1 26
Naked. Dine, sup, and sleep, Upon the very naked name of love *T. G. of Ver.* ii 4 142
You consenting to't, Would bark your honour from that trunk you bear, And leave you naked . *Meas. for Meas.* iii 1 73
And come with naked swords . *Com. of Errors* iv 4 148
The naked truth of it is, I have no shirt *L. L. Lost* v 2 716
But go with speed To some forlorn and naked hermitage . v 2 805
Therefore, on, or strip your sword stark naked . *T. Night* iii 4 275

Naked. Naked, fasting, Upon a barren mountain *W. Tale* iii 2 212
Till unfenced desolation Leave them as naked as the vulgar air *K. John* ii 1 387
Thou showest the naked pathway to thy life *Richard II.* i 2 31
Wallow naked in December snow By thinking on fantastic summer's heat . i 3 298
Stand bare and naked, trembling at themselves . iii 2 46
Upon the naked shore at Ravenspurgh . 1 *Hen. IV.* iv 3 77
Leaves his part-created cost A naked subject to the weeping clouds 2 *Hen. IV.* i 3 61
Put up your naked weapons, put up your naked weapons ii 4 222
When a' was naked, he was, for all the world, like a forked radish iii 2 333
Your naked infants spitted upon pikes . *Hen. V.* iii 3 38
There is not work enough for all our hands; Scarce blood enough in all their sickly veins To give each naked curtle-axe a stain . iv 2 21
The naked, poor and mangled Peace . v 2 34
If conjure up love in her in his true likeness, he must appear naked and blind . v 2 321
If she deny the appearance of a naked blind boy in her naked seeing self v 2 324
The truth appears so naked on my side That any purblind eye may find it out.—And on my side it is so well apparell'd 1 *Hen. VI.* ii 4 20
And he but naked, though lock'd up in steel, Whose conscience with injustice is corrupted 2 *Hen. VI.* iii 2 234
Curse away a winter's night, Though standing naked on a mountain top iii 2 336
And make him, naked, foil a man at arms 3 *Hen. VI.* v 4 42
I lay it naked to the deadly stroke, And humbly beg the death *Richard. III.* i 2 178
Thus I clothe my naked villany With old odd ends stolen out of holy writ . i 3 336
Gave himself, All thin and naked, to the numb cold night . ii 1 117
He would not in mine age Have left me naked to mine enemies *Hen. VIII.* iii 2 457
Nor sleep nor sanctuary, Being naked, sick, nor fane nor Capitol *Coriolanus* i 10 20
I cannot Put on the gown, stand naked and entreat them . ii 2 141
My naked weapon is out: quarrel, I will back thee *Rom. and Jul.* i 1 39
Timon will be left a naked gull, Which flashes now a phœnix *T. of Athens* ii 1 31
Creatures Whose naked natures live in all the spite Of wreakful heaven iv 3 228
Let it [ingratitude] go naked, men may see't the better . v 1 70
There is my dagger, And here my naked breast *J. Cæsar* iv 3 101
Pity, like a naked new-born babe, Striding the blast *Macbeth* i 7 21
When we have our naked frailties hid, That suffer in exposure ii 3 132
You shall know I am set naked on your kingdom . *Hamlet* iv 7 44
'Naked!' And in a postscript here, he says 'alone' iv 7 52
Poor naked wretches, wheresoe'er you are *Lear* iii 4 28
Bless thee, master!—Is that the naked fellow?—Ay, my lord iv 1 42
Bring some covering for this naked soul . iv 1 46
Sirrah, naked fellow,— Poor Tom's a-cold. I cannot daub it further iv 1 53
Or to be naked with her friend in bed An hour or more, not meaning any harm?—Naked in bed, Iago, and not mean harm! . *Othello* iv 1 3
Put in every honest hand a whip To lash the rascals naked through the world . iv 2 143
Speak with me, Or, naked as I am, I will assault thee . v 2 258
Rather on Nilus' mud Lay me stark naked! *Ant. and Cleo.* v 2 59
Whose naked breast Stepp'd before targes of proof . *Cymbeline* v 5 4

Nakedness. Why seek'st thou then to cover with excuse That which appears in proper nakedness? *Much Ado* iv 1 177
His ceremonies laid by, in his nakedness he appears but a man *Hen. V.* iv 1 109
Nothing I'll bear from thee, But nakedness, thou detestable town! *T. of Athens* iv 1 33
And with presented nakedness out-face The winds *Lear* ii 3 11
Name. What cares these roarers for the name of king? *Tempest* i 1 18
And teach me how To name the bigger light, and how the less i 2 335
Thou dost here usurp The name thou owest not i 2 454
No kind of traffic Would I admit; no name of magistrate ii 1 149
What is your name?—Miranda.—O my father, I have broke your hest to say so! iii 1 36
I' the name of something holy, sir, why stand you In this strange stare? iii 3 94
The thunder, That deep and dreadful organ-pipe, pronounced The name iii 3 99
Which is worthiest love?—Please you repeat their names *T. G. of Ver.* i 2 7
How now! what means this passion at his name? i 2 16
But I, being in the way, Did in your name receive it i 2 40
I throw thy name against the bruising stones i 2 111
Poor wounded name! my bosom as a bed Shall lodge thee i 2 114
Till I have found each letter in the letter, Except mine own name i 2 120
Lo, here in one line is his name twice writ i 2 123
Sith so prettily He couples it to his complaining names i 2 127
I guess the sequel; And yet I will not name it ii 1 123
Dine, sup and sleep, Upon the very naked name of love ii 4 142
Thou art an Hebrew, a Jew, and not worth the name of a Christian ii 5 58
That, indeed, know not their fathers and therefore have no names iii 1 323
Do not name Silvia thine; if once again, Verona shall not hold thee v 4 128
Peter Simple, you say your name is?—Ay, for fault of a better *Mer. Wives* i 4 16
Picked—with the devil's name!—out of my conversation ii 1 24
Letter for letter, but that the name of Page and Ford differs! ii 1 72
He hath a thousand of these letters, writ with blank space for different names ii 1 77
O, odious is the name!—What name, sir!—The horn, I say ii 1 123
My name is Corporal Nym; I speak and I avouch; 'tis true: my name is Nym ii 1 137
Tell him my name is Brook; only for a jest ii 1 224
Brook is his name?—Ay, sir.—Call him in. Such Brooks are welcome ii 2 154
There is a gentlewoman in this town; her husband's name is Ford ii 2 199
Terms! names! Amaimon sounds well; Lucifer, well; Barbason, well; yet they are devils' additions, the names of fiends: but Cuckold! Wittol!—Cuckold! the devil himself hath not such a name ii 2 310
Master Slender's serving-man, and friend Simple by your name iii 1 3
I cannot tell what the dickens his name is iii 2 20
What do you call your knight's name, sirrah?—Sir John Falstaff iii 2 21
He, he; I can never hit on's name iii 2 25
To carry me in the name of foul clothes to Datchet-lane iii 5 101
Fie on her! never name her, child, if she be a whore iv 1 65
I'll to him again in name of Brook: He'll tell me all his purpose iv 4 76
In the lawful name of marrying, To give our hearts united ceremony iv 6 50
Crier Hobgoblin, make the fairy oyes.—Elves, list your names v 5 46
And this deceit loses the name of craft, Of disobedience v 5 239
And, for a name, Now puts the drowsy and neglected act Freshly on me: 'tis surely for a name *Meas. for Meas.* i 2 173
Who may, in the ambush of my name, strike home i 3 41
As school-maids change their names By vain though apt affection i 4 47
How now, sir! What's your name? and what's the matter? ii 1 45
My name is Elbow: I do lean upon justice, sir ii 1 48
A poor widow's tapster.—Your mistress' name?—Mistress Overdone ii 1 208
Bring me in the names of some six or seven, the most sufficient of your parish ii 1 286
Heaven in my mouth, As if I did but only chew his name ii 4 5
My unsoil'd name, the austereness of my life, My vouch against you ii 4 155
What's yet in this That bears the name of life? iii 1 39
This night's the time That I should do what I abhor to name iii 1 102
I have heard of the lady, and good words went with her name iii 1 220
I am bound to call upon you; and, I pray you, your name? iii 2 168
If he be less, he's nothing; but he's more, Had I more name for badness v 1 59
One so like the other As could not be distinguish'd but by names *Com. of Errors* i 1 53
His case was like, Reft of his brother, but retain'd his name i 1 129
No man that hath a name, By falsehood and corruption doth it shame ii 1 112
Nay, not sure, in a thing falsing.—Certain ones then.—Name them ii 2 97
And hurl the name of husband in my face ii 2 137
How can she thus then call us by our names? Unless it be by inspiration ii 2 168
O villain! thou hast stolen both mine office and my name iii 1 44
If thou hadst been Dromio to-day in my place, Thou wouldst have changed thy face for a name or thy name for an ass iii 1 47
Sweet mistress,—what your name is else, I know not, Nor by what wonder you do hit of mine iii 2 29
What's her name?—Nell, sir; but her name and three quarters, that's an ell and three quarters, will not measure her from hip to hip iii 2 110
And every one doth call me by my name iv 3 3
Is not your name, sir, call'd Antipholus? And is not that your bondman? v 1 286
But few of any sort, and none of name *Much Ado* i 1 7
I know none of that name, lady: there was none such in the army i 1 32
But keep your way, i' God's name; I have done i 1 144
But had a rougher task in hand Than to drive liking to the name of love i 1 302
Thus answer I in name of Benedick ii 1 179
I have wooed in thy name, and fair Hero is won ii 1 310
Name the day of marriage, and God give thee joy! ii 1 311
When I do name him, let it be thy part To praise him iii 1 18
Indeed, he hath an excellent good name iii 1 98
Come hither, neighbour Seacole. God hath blessed you with a good name iii 3 14
You are to bid any man stand, in the prince's name iii 3 27
Goes up and down like a gentleman: I remember his name iii 3 136
We charge you, in the prince's name, stand! iii 3 177
What kind of catechising call you this?—To make you answer truly to your name iv 1 80
Who can blot that name With any just reproach? iv 1 81
I am a gentleman, sir, and my name is Conrade.—Write down, master gentleman Conrade iv 2 15
I charge you, in the prince's name, accuse these men iv 2 40
Borrows money in God's name, the which he hath used so long and never paid v 1 319
Whose names yet run smoothly in the even road of a blank verse v 2 33
Name. Which is Beatrice?—I answer to that name. What is your will? *Much Ado* v 4 73
Your oaths are pass'd; and now subscribe your names *L. L. Lost* i 1 19
Earthly godfathers of heaven's lights That give a name to every fixed star i 1 89
And every godfather can give a name i 1 93
Let me read the same; And to the strict'st decrees I'll write my name i 1 117
So to the laws at large I write my name i 1 156
An appertinent title to your old time, which we may name tough i 2 18
More authority, dear boy, name more i 2 71
And wrong the reputation of your name, In so unseeming to confess receipt ii 1 155
I desire her name.—She hath but one for herself; to desire that were a shame ii 1 199
What's her name in the cap?—Rosaline, by good hap ii 1 209
Remuneration! why, it is a fairer name than French crown iii 1 142
When tongues speak sweetly, then they name her name iii 1 167
Sweet fellowship in shame!—One drunkard loves another of the name iv 3 50
It is Biron's writing, and here is his name iv 3 203
That he was fain to seal on Cupid's name v 2 9
Will you vouchsafe with me to change a word?—Name it v 2 239
Sweet Jude! nay, why dost thou stay?—For the latter end of his name.—For the ass to the Jude; give it him:—Jud-as, away! v 2 630
Here is the scroll of every man's name, which is thought fit *M. N. Dream* i 2 4
Read the names of the actors, and so grow to a point i 2 9
Name what part I am for, and proceed i 2 20
Now name the rest of the players i 2 41
O, how fit a word Is that vile name to perish on my sword! ii 2 107
Another prologue must tell he is not a lion.—Nay, you must name his name iii 1 37
Let him name his name, and tell them plainly he is Snug the joiner iii 1 46
I beseech your worship's name.—Cobweb iii 1 183
Gives to airy nothing A local habitation and a name v 1 17
This grisly beast, which Lion hight by name v 1 140
It doth befall That I, one Snout by name, present a wall v 1 157
O that I had a title good enough to keep his name company! *M. of Ven.* iii 1 16
Both stand forth.—Is your name Shylock?—Shylock is my name iv 1 176
A friend! what friend? your name, I pray you, friend?—Stephano is my name v 1 27
Thou art a fool: she robs thee of thy name *As Y. Like It* i 3 82
I'll have no worse a name than Jove's own page i 3 126
I care not for their names; they owe me nothing ii 5 21
What woman in the city do I name, When that I say the city-woman? ii 7 74
Survey With thy chaste eye, from thy pale sphere above, Thy huntress' name iii 2 4
But didst thou hear without wondering how thy name should be hanged and carved upon these trees? iii 2 182
Rosalind is your love's name?—Yes, just.—I do not like her name.—There was no thought of pleasing you when she was christened iii 2 280
Hangs odes upon hawthorns and elegies on brambles, all, forsooth, deifying the name of Rosalind iii 2 381
Is thy name William?—William, sir.—A fair name v 1 22
As you have books for good manners: I will name you the degrees v 4 96
I have forgot your name; but, sure, that part Was aptly fitted *T. of S.* Ind. 1 86
Twenty more such names and men as these Which never were Ind. 2 97
Tell me her father's name and 'tis enough; For I will board her i 2 94
But if you have a stomach, to't i' God's name i 2 195
Whence are you, sir? what may I call your name?—Petruchio is my name ii 1 67
Good morrow, Kate; for that's your name, I hear.—Well have you heard ii 1 183
Which hath two letters for her name fairly set down in studs iii 2 62
You are like to Sir Vincentio. His name and credit shall you undertake iv 2 106
He does it under name of perfect love iv 3 12
Thou false deluding slave, That feed'st me with the very name of meat iv 3 32
Why, what, i' devil's name, tailor, call'st thou this? iv 3 92
Come on, i' God's name; once more toward our father's iv 5 1
My name is call'd Vincentio; my dwelling Pisa; And bound I am to Padua iv 5 55
Why, this is flat knavery, to take upon you another man's name v 1 38
What do you think is his name?—His name! as if I knew not his name v 1 83
His name is Tranio.—Away, away, mad ass! his name is Lucentio v 1 86
I am from humble, he from honour'd name *All's Well* i 3 162
My maiden's name Sear'd otherwise ii 1 175
For all that life can rate Worth name of life in thee hath estimate ii 1 183
My low and humble name to propagate ii 1 200
Thou dislikest Of virtue for the name: but do not so ii 3 131
Good alone Is good without a name. Vileness is so ii 3 136
Both my revenge and hate Loosing upon thee, in the name of justice ii 3 172
He was my son; But I do wash his name out of my blood iii 2 70
Whilst I from far His name with zealous fervour sanctify iii 4 11
The honour of a maid is her name; and no legacy is so rich as honesty iii 5 13
She is too mean To have her name repeated iii 5 64
They told me that your name was Fontibell.—No, my good lord, Diana iv 2 1
A' has an English name; but his fisnomy is more hotter in France than there iv 5 41
Come on, my son, in whom my house's name Must be digested v 3 73
Wrapp'd in a paper, which contain'd the name Of her that threw it v 3 94
'Tis but the shadow of a wife you see, The name and not the thing v 3 309
Who governs here?—A noble duke, in nature as in name *T. Night* i 2 25
I have heard my father name him: He was a bachelor then i 2 28
Halloo your name to the reverberate hills i 5 291
Close, in the name of jesting! ii 5 23
M,—why, that begins my name.—Did not I say he would work it out? ii 5 138
For every one of these letters are in my name ii 5 154
I would, therefore, my sister had had no name, sir.—Why, man?—Why, sir, her name's a word iii 1 20
What is your name?—Cesario is your servant's name, fair princess iii 1 107
Which way is he, in the name of sanctity? iii 4 93
Noble sir, Be pleased that I shake off these names you give me v 1 76
What kin are you to me? What countryman? what name? what parentage? v 1 238
O, would her name were Grace! *W. Tale* i 2 99
My wife's a hobby-horse, deserves a name As rank as any flax-wench i 2 276
A sickness Which puts some of us in distemper, but I cannot name the disease i 2 386
Which no less adorns Our gentry than our parents' noble names i 2 393
And my name Be yoked with his that did betray the Best! i 2 418
More than mistress of Which comes to me in name of fault iii 2 61
Therefore bring forth, And in Apollo's name, his oracle iii 2 119

Name. Name of mercy, when was this? *W. Tale* iii 3 105
Now take upon me, in the name of Time, To use my wings iv 1 3
I mentioned a son o' the king's, which Florizel I now name to you iv 1 23
I' the name of me— O, help me, help me! iv 3 54
Let me be unrolled and my name put in the book of virtue! iv 3 131
Here's the midwife's name to't, one Mistress Tale-porter iv 4 272
The place of your dwelling, your names, your ages, of what having iv 4 740
You pity not the state, nor the remembrance Of his most sovereign name v 1 26
What is thy name?—Philip, my liege, so is my name begun *K. John* i 1 157
And if his name be George, I'll call him Peter; For new-made honour doth forget men's names i 1 186
Legitimation, name and all is gone i 1 248
In the name of God How comes it then that thou art call'd a king? ii 1 106
With slaughter coupled to the name of kings ii 1 349
She again wants nothing, to name want, If want it be not that she is not he ii 1 435
Do in his name religiously demand Why thou against the church iii 1 140
What earthy name to interrogatories Can task the free breath of a sacred king? iii 1 147
Thou canst not, cardinal, devise a name So slight, unworthy and ridiculous, To charge me to an answer, as the pope iii 1 149
How new, Is husband in my mouth! even for that name, Which till this time my tongue did ne'er pronounce iii 1 306
What motive may Be stronger with thee than the name of wife? iii 1 314
I am not mad: this hair I tear is mine; My name is Constance iii 4 46
The deed, which both our tongues held vile to name iv 2 241
Honourable rescue and defence Cries out upon the name of Salisbury v 2 19
And on our actions set the name of right With holy breath v 2 67
When we were happy we had other names v 4 8
With a foul traitor's name stuff I thy throat *Richard II.* i 1 44
Hath received eight thousand nobles In name of lendings i 1 89
My fair name, Despite of death that lives upon my grave, To dark dishonour's use thou shalt not have i 1 167
Ask him his name and orderly proceed To swear him i 3 9
In God's name and the king's, say who thou art And why thou comest i 3 11
What is thy name? and wherefore comest thou hither? i 3 31
Furbish new the name of John a Gaunt, Even in the lusty haviour of his son i 3 76
If ever I were traitor, My name be blotted from the book of life! i 3 202
How is't with aged Gaunt?—O, how that name befits my composition! ii 1 73
Can sick men play so nicely with their names? ii 1 84
Since thou dost seek to kill my name in me, I mock my name, great king, to flatter thee ii 1 86
But what, o' God's name, doth become of this? ii 1 251
That is not yet known; what I cannot name; 'tis nameless woe, I wot ii 2 40
None else of name and noble estimate ii 3 56
My answer is—to Lancaster; And I am come to seek that name in England ii 3 71
Is not the king's name twenty thousand names? Arm, arm, my name! a puny subject strikes At thy great glory iii 2 85
O that I were as great As is my grief, or lesser than my name! iii 3 137
Must he lose The name of king? o' God's name, let it go iii 3 146
And long live Henry, fourth of that name!—In God's name, I'll ascend the regal throne iv 1 112
I have no name, no title, No, not that name was given me at the font iv 1 255
Alack the heavy day, That I have worn so many winters out, And know not now what name to call myself! iv 1 259
Shall I obtain it?—Name it, fair cousin iv 1 304
And wilt thou pluck my fair son from mine age, And rob me of a happy mother's name? v 2 93
Read not my name there; My heart is not confederate with my hand v 3 52
Would to God thou and I knew where a commodity of good names were to be bought *1 Hen. IV.* i 2 94
Those prisoners in your highness' name demanded i 3 23
Trembling even at the name of Mortimer.—I cannot blame him i 3 144
Go to; 'homo' is a common name to all men ii 1 104
Can call them all by their christen names, as Tom, Dick, and Francis ii 4 8
To sweeten which name of Ned, I give thee this pennyworth of sugar ii 4 24
It is known to many in our land by the name of pitch ii 4 455
There is a virtuous man whom I have often noted in thy company, but I know not his name ii 4 461
Now I remember him, his name is Falstaff ii 4 468
Good cousin Hotspur, For by that name as oft as Lancaster Doth speak of you, his cheek looks pale iii 1 8
How 'scapes he agues, in the devil's name? iii 1 69
He held me last night at least nine hours In reckoning up the several devils' names That were his lackeys iii 1 157
Had his great name profaned with their scorns, And gave his countenance, against his name, To laugh at gibing boys iii 2 64
Whose . . . great name in arms Holds from all soldiers chief majority iii 2 108
This, in the name of God, I promise here iii 2 153
Some Envy your great deservings and good name iv 3 35
Name your griefs; and with all speed You shall have your desires iv 3 48
I am content that he shall take the odds Of his great name and estimation v 1 98
An adopted name of privilege, A hare-brain'd Hotspur v 2 18
He calls us rebels, traitors; and will scourge With haughty arms this hateful name in us v 2 41
What is thy name, that in the battle thus Thou crossest me? v 3 1
A gallant knight he was, his name was Blunt v 3 20
Thou speak'st as if I would deny my name v 4 60
My name is Harry Percy.—Why, then I see A very valiant rebel of the name v 4 61
Would to God Thy name in arms were now as great as mine! v 4 70
A gentleman well bred and of good name *2 Hen. IV.* i 1 26
Were it worse than the name of rebellion can tell how to make it i 2 90
Do you set down your name in the scroll of youth, that are written down old with all the characters of age? i 2 201
I would to God my name were not so terrible to the enemy as it is i 2 244
We fortify in paper and in figures, Using the names of men instead of men i 3 57
What a disgrace is it to me to remember thy name! ii 2 16
Every man must know that, as oft as he has occasion to name himself ii 2 120
Where nothing but the sound of Hotspur's name Did seem defensible ii 3 37
I am in good name and fame with the very best ii 4 81
You are in an ill name ii 4 98
For taking their names upon you before you have earned them ii 4 154
I saw it, and told John a Gaunt he beat his own name iii 2 349
To establish here a peace indeed, Concurring both in name and quality iv 1 87
Our battle is more full of names than yours, Our men more perfect iv 1 154
That is intended in the general's name iv 1 166

Name. Your grace of York, in God's name, then, set forward *2 Hen. IV.* iv 1 227
Employ the countenance and grace of heaven, As a false favourite doth his prince's name, In deeds dishonourable iv 2 25
What's your name, sir? of what condition are you, and of what place, I pray? iv 3 1
I am a knight, sir; and my name is Colevile of the dale iv 3 3
Doth any name particular belong Unto the lodging where I first did swoon? iv 5 233
We charge you, in the name of God, take heed *Hen. V.* i 2 23
Let us be worried and our nation lose The name of hardiness and policy i 2 220
In whose name [God's] Tell you the Dauphin I am coming on i 2 290
Fetch forth the lazar kite of Cressid's kind, Doll Tearsheet she by name ii 1 81
Gave thee no instance why thou shouldst do treason, Unless to dub thee with the name of traitor ii 2 120
Captivated by the hand Of that black name, Edward, Black Prince ii 4 56
He wills you, in the name of God Almighty, That you divest yourself ii 4 77
I am a soldier, A name that in my thoughts becomes me best iii 3 6
And such fellows are perfect in the great commanders' names iii 6 74
What is thy name? I know thy quality.—Montjoy iii 6 146
He never did harm, that I heard of.—Nor will do none to-morrow: he will keep that good name still iii 7 111
The clocks do toll, And the third hour of drowsy morning name iv Prol. 16
We shall much disgrace With four or five most vile and ragged foils, Right ill-disposed in brawl ridiculous, The name of Agincourt iv Prol. 52
What is thy name?—Harry le Roy.—Le Roy! a Cornish name iv 1 48
My name is Pistol call'd.—It sorts well with your fierceness iv 1 62
So! in the name of Jesu Christ, speak lower iv 1 65
And rouse him at the name of Crispian iv 3 43
Our names, Familiar in his mouth as household words iv 3 51
Art thou a gentleman? what is thy name? discuss iv 4 5
Come hither, boy: ask me this slave in French What is his name iv 4 25
What call you the town's name where Alexander the Pig was born? iv 7 13
It is out of my prains what is the name of the other river iv 7 31
He was full of jests, and gipes, and knaveries, and mocks; I have forgot his name iv 7 53
I charge you in his majesty's name, apprehend him iv 8 18
None else of name; and of all other men But five and twenty iv 8 110
Name not religion, for thou lovest the flesh *1 Hen. VI.* i 1 41
Then come, o' God's name; I fear no woman i 2 102
Excellent Pucelle, if thy name be so i 2 110
We charge and command you, in his highness' name i 3 77
So great fear of my name 'mongst them was spread That they supposed I could rend bars of steel i 4 50
Wretched shall France be only in my name i 4 97
God is our fortress, in whose conquering name Let us resolve to scale their flinty bulwarks ii 1 26
Using no other weapon but his name ii 1 81
So much fear'd abroad That with his name the mothers still their babes ii 3 17
God save King Henry, of that name the sixth! iv 1 2
Doth but usurp the sacred name of knight iv 1 40
That, Talbot dead, great York might bear the name iv 4 9
That Talbot's name might be in thee revived iv 5 3
Is my name Talbot? and am I your son? And shall I fly? iv 5 12
O, if you love my mother, Dishonour not her honourable name! iv 5 14
Thou never hadst renown, nor canst not lose it.—Yes, your renowned name iv 5 41
In thee thy mother dies, our household's name, My death's revenge iv 6 38
Who art thou? say, that I may honour thee.—Margaret my name v 3 51
Say, Earl of Suffolk—if thy name be so—What ransom must I pay? v 3 72
In Henry's royal name, As deputy unto that gracious king v 3 160
Blotting your names from books of memory *2 Hen. VI.* i 1 100
And so, I pray you, go, in God's name, and leave us i 4 12
By the eternal God, whose name and power Thou tremblest at, answer i 4 28
Tell me, sirrah, what's my name?—Alas, master, I know not.—What's his name?—I know not.— . . . What's thine own name? ii 1 117
Thou mightst as well have known all our names as thus to name the several colours we do wear ii 1 128
And give her as a prey to law and shame, That hath dishonour'd Gloucester s honest name ii 1 199
O' God's name, see the lists and all things fit: Here let them end it ii 3 54
My joy is death; Death, at whose name I oft have been afear'd ii 4 89
I do arrest you in his highness' name iii 1 136
So shall my name with slander's tongue be wounded iii 2 68
What, think you much to pay two thousand crowns, And bear the name and port of gentlemen? iv 1 19
Thy name affrights me, in whose sound is death iv 1 33
Thy name is Gaultier, being rightly sounded.—Gaultier or Walter iv 1 37
Never yet did base dishonour blur our name, But with our sword we wiped away the blot iv 1 39
Dost thou use to write thy name? or hast thou a mark to thyself? iv 2 110
I thank God, I have been so well brought up that I can write my name iv 2 113
He has a familiar under his tongue; he speaks not o' God's name iv 7 115
The name of Henry the Fifth hales them to an hundred mischiefs iv 8 58
Hath not essentially but by circumstance The name of valour v 2 40
Richard, I bear thy name; I'll venge thy death *3 Hen. VI.* ii 1 87
His name that valiant duke hath left with thee ii 1 89
We charge you, in God's name, and the king's, To go with us unto the officers.—In God's name, lead; your king's name be obey'd iii 1 97
You that will follow me to this attempt, Applaud the name of Henry iv 2 27
Two of thy name, both Dukes of Somerset, Have sold their lives v 1 72
What's worse than murderer, that I may name it? v 5 58
Upon what cause?—Because my name is George *Richard III.* i 1 46
For my name of George begins with G, It follows in his thought that I am he i 1 58
Fairer than tongue can name thee i 2 81
And thou unfit for any place but hell.—Yes, one place else, if you will hear me name it.—Some dungeon i 2 110
He lives that loves thee better than he could.—Name him i 2 142
Why, that was he.—The selfsame name, but one of better nature i 2 143
I had thought That thou hadst call'd me all these bitter names i 3 236
So that, betwixt their titles and low names, There's nothing differs but the outward fame i 4 82
In God's name, what art thou?—A man, as you are i 4 169
And, like a traitor to the name of God, Didst break that vow i 4 210
In God's name, speak: when is the royal day? iii 4 3
But you, my noble lords, may name the time iii 4 19
Thy mother's name is ominous to children iv 1 41
Rougemont: at which name I started, Because a bard of Ireland told me once, I should not live long after I saw Richmond iv 2 108
For joyful mother, one that wails the name iv 4 99

Name. What comfortable hour canst thou name, That ever graced me in thy company? *Richard III.* iv 4 173
My tongue should to thy ears not name my boys Till that my nails were anchor'd in thine eyes . iv 4 230
A grandam's name is little less in love Than is the doting title of a mother . iv 4 299
What men of name resort to him? . iv 5 8
In God's name, cheerly on, courageous friends . v 2 14
Besides, the king's name is a tower of strength . v 3 12
What men of name are slain on either side? . v 5 12
This top-proud fellow, Whom from the flow of gall I name not *Hen. VIII.* i 1 152
Half your suit Never name to us; you have half our power . i 2 11
I have this day received a traitor's judgement, And by that name must die . ii 1 59
Restored me to my honours, and, out of ruins, Made my name once more noble . ii 1 115
Life, honour, name and all That made me happy at one stroke has taken For ever from the world . ii 1 116
If not, i' the name of God, Your pleasure be fulfill'd! . ii 4 56
How, i' the name of thrift, Does he rake this together! . iii 2 109
'Tis so lately alter'd, that the old name Is fresh about me . iv 1 98
When I shall dwell with worms, and my poor name Banish'd the kingdom iv 2 126
Thank you, good lord archbishop: What is her name?—Elizabeth . v 5 10
His honour and the greatness of his name Shall be, and make new nations v 5 52
I'll tell you them all by their names as they pass by *Troi. and Cres.* i 2 199
Or rather, right and wrong, Between whose endless jar justice resides, Should lose their names . i 3 118
Call you yourself Æneas?—Ay, Greek, that is my name . i 3 246
However it is spread in general name, Relates in purpose to Achilles . i 3 322
Had it our name, the value of one ten, What merit's in that reason which denies The yielding of her up? . ii 2 23
We will not name desert before his birth . iii 2 101
Let all pitiful goers-between be called to the world's end after my name iii 2 209
I have abandon'd Troy, left my possession, Incurr'd a traitor's name . iii 3 6
O you gods divine! Make Cressid's name the very crown of falsehood, If ever she leave Troilus! . iv 2 106
If e'er thou stand at mercy of my sword, Name Cressid . iv 4 117
If not Achilles, sir, What is your name?—If not Achilles, nothing . iv 5 76
The worthiest of them tell me name by name . iv 5 160
Name her not now, sir; she's a deadly theme . iv 5 181
That I may give the local wound a name And make distinct the very breach whereout Hector's great spirit flew . iv 5 244
Let all untruths stand by thy stained name, And they'll seem glorious . v 2 179
Ignomy and shame Pursue thy life, and live aye with thy name! . v 10 34
Holding Corioli in the name of Rome . *Coriolanus* i 6 37
His name?—By Jupiter! forgot. I am weary; yea, my memory is tired . i 9 90
He gives my son the whole name of the war . ii 1 149
Where he hath won, With fame, a name to Caius Marcius . ii 1 181
Call the people: in whose name myself Attach thee as a traitorous innovator . iii 1 174
And, being angry, does forget that ever He heard the name of death . iii 1 260
As I do know the consul's worthiness, So can I name his faults . iii 1 279
In the name o' the people And in the power of us the tribunes . iii 3 99
I know you well, sir, and you know me: your name, I think, is Adrian iv 3 2
What wouldst thou? thy name? Why speak'st not? speak, man: what's thy name? . iv 5 58
Necessity Commands me name myself . iv 5 63
A name unmusical to the Volscians' ears; And harsh in sound to thine . iv 5 64
Say, what's thy name? Thou hast a grim appearance . iv 5 65
Though thy tackle's torn, Thou show'st a noble vessel: what's thy name? . iv 5 68
Prepare thy brow to frown; know'st thou me yet?—I know thee not: thy name?—My name is Caius Marcius . iv 5 70
Only that name remains; The cruelty and envy of the people, Permitted by our dastard nobles, who Have all forsook me, hath devour'd the rest. . iv 5 79
Aufidius, The second name of men, obeys his points . iv 6 125
Yet one time he did call me by my name: I urged our old acquaintance v 1 9
Forbad all names; He was a kind of nothing, titleless, Till he had forged himself a name o' the fire Of burning Rome . v 1 14
It is lots to blanks, My name hath touch'd your ears . v 2 11
The virtue of your name Is not here passable . v 2 12
Go back.—Prithee, fellow, remember my name is Menenius . v 2 29
Now, sir, is your name Menenius?—'Tis a spell, you see, of much power v 2 101
That brought you forth this boy, to keep your name Living to time . v 3 126
The benefit Which thou shalt thereby reap is such a name, Whose repetition will be dogg'd with curses . v 3 143
His name remains To the ensuing age abhorr'd . v 3 147
Dost thou think I'll grace thee with that robbery thy stol'n name Coriolanus in Corioli? . v 6 89
Hear'st thou, Mars?—Name not the god, thou boy of tears! . v 6 101
Let us entreat, by honour of his name . *T. Andron.* i 1 39
And name thee in election for the empire . i 1 183
To advance Thy name and honourable family, Lavinia will I make my empress. . i 1 239
Brother, for in that name doth nature plead,— Father, and in that name doth nature speak,— Speak thou no more . i 1 370
Barbarous Tamora, For no name fits thy nature but thy own! . ii 3 119
Ah, beastly creature! The blot and enemy to our general name! . ii 3 183
When I did name her brothers, then fresh tears Stood on her cheeks . iii 1 111
That ever death should let life bear his name! . iii 1 249
Ah, wherefore dost thou urge the name of hands? . iii 2 26
As if we should forget we had no hands, If Marcus did not name the word of hands! . iii 2 33
When I have writ my name Without the help of any hand at all . iv 1 70
King, be thy thoughts imperious, like thy name . iv 4 81
Whose name was once our terror, now our comfort . v 1 10
And in their ears tell them my dreadful name, Revenge . v 2 39
Thou art too much deceived; The one is Murder, Rape is the other's name v 2 157
Find those persons out Whose names are written there *Rom. and Jul.* i 2 36
I am sent to find those persons whose names are here writ, and can never find what names the writing person hath here writ . i 2 43
Ask his name: if he be married, My grave is like to be my wedding bed i 5 136
His name is Romeo, and a Montague; The only son of your great enemy i 5 138
In his mistress' name I conjure only but to raise up him . ii 1 28
Deny thy father and refuse thy name; Or, if thou wilt not, be but sworn my love, And I'll no longer be a Capulet . ii 2 34
'Tis but thy name that is my enemy; Thou art thyself . ii 2 38
O, be some other name! What's in a name? . ii 2 42
That which we call a rose By any other name would smell as sweet . ii 2 44

Name. Doff thy name, And for that name which is no part of thee Take all myself . *Rom. and Jul.* ii 2 47
By a name I know not how to tell thee who I am . ii 2 53
My name, dear saint, is hateful to myself, Because it is an enemy to thee ii 2 55
Tear the cave where Echo lies, And make her airy tongue more hoarse than mine, With repetition of my Romeo's name . ii 2 164
It is my soul that calls upon my name . ii 2 165
I have forgot that name, and that name's woe . ii 3 46
I am the youngest of that name, for fault of a worse . ii 4 129
Both with an R.—Ah, mocker! that's the dog's name . ii 4 223
Good Capulet,—which name I tender As dearly as my own,—be satisfied iii 1 74
Up, sir, go with me; I charge thee in the prince's name, obey . iii 1 145
Every tongue that speaks But Romeo's name speaks heavenly eloquence iii 2 33
Ah, poor my lord, what tongue shall smooth thy name, When I, thy three-hours wife, have mangled it? . iii 2 98
As if that name, Shot from the deadly level of a gun, Did murder her; as that name's cursed hand Murder'd her kinsman . iii 3 102
In what vile part of this anatomy Doth my name lodge? . iii 3 107
While Verona by that name is known . v 3 300
You know me, Apemantus?—Thou know'st I do: I call'd thee by thy name.—Thou art proud Apemantus . *T. of Athens* i 1 187
I have been bold—For that I knew it the most general way—To them to use your signet and your name . ii 2 210
What is thy name? Is man so hateful to thee, That art thyself a man? iv 3 51
There is no leprosy but what thou speak'st.—If I name thee . iv 3 368
Allow'd with absolute power and thy good name Live with authority v 1 165
Here lies a wretched corse, of wretched soul bereft: Seek not my name v 4 71
I love The name of honour more than I fear death . *J. Cæsar* i 2 89
'Cæsar'? Why should that name be sounded more than yours? Write them together, yours is as fair a name; Sound them, it doth become the mouth as well; Weigh them, it is as heavy . i 2 143
Now, in the names of all the gods at once . i 2 148
If my name were liable to fear, I do not know the man I should avoid So soon . i 2 199
Writings all tending to the great opinion That Rome holds of his name . i 2 323
Now could I, Casca, name to thee a man Most like this dreadful night . i 3 72
O, name him not: let us not break with him . ii 1 150
I am not sick, if Brutus have in hand Any exploit worthy the name of honour . ii 1 317
What is your name?—Whither are you going?—Where do you dwell? iii 3 5
I dwell by the Capitol.—Your name, sir, truly.—Truly, my name is Cinna iii 3 28
Pluck but his name out of his heart, and turn him going . iii 3 38
These many, then, shall die; their names are prick'd . iv 1 1
The name of Cassius honours this corruption . iv 3 15
I will proclaim my name about the field: I am the son of Marcus Cato, ho! . v 4 3
For brave Macbeth—well he deserves that name . *Macbeth* i 2 16
I' the name of truth, Are ye fantastical? . i 3 52
Malcolm, whom we name hereafter The Prince of Cumberland . i 4 38
This diamond he greets your wife withal, By the name of most kind hostess . ii 1 16
Who's there, i' the name of Beelzebub? . ii 3 4
Knock, knock! Who's there, in the other devil's name? . ii 3 9
O horror, horror, horror! Tongue nor heart Cannot conceive nor name thee! . ii 3 70
He chid the sisters When first they put the name of king upon me . iii 1 58
Shoughs, water-rugs and demi-wolves are clept All by the name of dogs iii 1 95
What is't you do?—A deed without a name . iv 1 49
This tyrant, whose sole name blisters our tongues . iv 3 12
Sudden, malicious, smacking of every sin That has a name . iv 3 60
What is thy name?—Thou'lt be afraid to hear it.—No; though thou call'st thyself a hotter name Than any is in hell.—My name's Macbeth . v 7 5
Let me not think on't—Frailty, thy name is woman! . *Hamlet* i 2 146
Your poor servant ever.—Sir, my good friend; I'll change that name with you . i 2 163
I have been so affrighted!—With what, i' the name of God? . ii 1 76
With this regard their currents turn awry, And lose the name of action iii 1 88
Gonzago is the duke's name; his wife, Baptista . iii 2 249
His poison'd shot may miss our name, And hit the woundless air . iv 1 43
To gain a little patch of ground That hath in it no profit but the name . iv 4 19
If your name be Horatio, as I am let to know it is . iv 6 11
Daisies, and long purples That liberal shepherds give a grosser name . iv 7 171
I have a voice and precedent of peace, To keep my name ungored . v 2 261
What a wounded name, Things standing thus unknown, shall live behind me! . v 2 355
She names my very deed of love; Only she comes too short . *Lear* i 1 73
Only we still retain The name, and all the additions to a king . i 1 138
Your name, fair gentlewoman?—This admiration, sir, is much o' the savour Of other your new pranks . i 4 257
And in the most exact regard support The worships of their name . i 4 288
Come hither, mistress. Is your name Goneril?—She cannot deny it . iii 6 51
Once or twice she heaved the name of 'father' Pantingly forth . iv 3 27
That minces virtue, and does shake the head To hear of pleasure's name iv 6 123
I know thee well enough; thy name is Gloucester: Thou must be patient iv 6 181
Thy soldiers, All levied in my name, have in my name Took their discharge v 3 104
What are you? Your name, your quality? . v 3 120
My name is lost; By treason's tooth bare-gnawn and canker-bit . v 3 121
In wisdom I should ask thy name . v 3 141
Thou worse than any name, read thine own evil . v 3 156
Your name is great In mouths of wisest censure . *Othello* ii 3 192
And spend your rich opinion for the name Of a night-brawler . ii 3 195
O thou invisible spirit of wine, if thou hast no name to be known by, let us call thee devil! . ii 3 284
I prithee, name the time, but let it not Exceed three days . iii 3 62
Good name in man and woman, dear my lord, Is the immediate jewel of their souls: Who steals my purse steals trash; ... But he that filches from me my good name Robs me of that which not enriches him . iii 3 155
Her name, that was as fresh As Dian's visage, is now begrimed and black iii 3 386
Am I that name, Iago?—What name, fair lady?—Such as she says. . iv 2 118
It is the cause, my soul,—Let me not name it to you, you chaste stars! v 2 2
Belike my children shall have no names . *Ant. and Cleo.* i 2 36
Name Cleopatra as she is call'd in Rome; Rail thou in Fulvia's phrase . i 2 110
Who, high in name and power, Higher than both in blood and life. . i 2 196
Pompey's name strikes more Than could his war resisted . i 4 54
More laugh'd at, that I should Once name you derogately, when to sound your name It not concern'd me . ii 2 34
Why, this it is to have a name in great men's fellowship . ii 7 12
Signify what in his name, That magical word of war, we have effected . iii 1 30

Name. Promise, And in our name, what she requires . *Ant. and Cleo.* iii 12 28
What's her name, Since she was Cleopatra? . . . . . iii 13 98
Then in the midst a tearing groan did break The name of Antony . . iv 14 32
She render'd life, Thy name so buried in her . . . iv 14 34
The death of Antony Is not a single doom; in the name lay A moiety of the world.—He is dead, Cæsar . . . . . v 1 18
And, when we fall, We answer others' merits in our name . . v 2 178
Husband, I come: Now to that name my courage prove my title! . v 2 291
What's his name and birth?—I cannot delve him to the root . *Cymbeline* i 1 27
Expected to prove so worthy as since he hath been allowed the name of . i 4 3
His fortunes all lie speechless and his name Is at last gasp . . i 5 52
Sell me your good report.—How! my good name? . . . ii 3 89
She hath bought the name of whore thus dearly. There, take thy hire . ii 4 128
War and confusion In Cæsar's name pronounce I 'gainst thee . . iii 1 67
A pain that only seems to seek out danger I' the name of fame and honour . . . . . . iii 3 51
When a soldier was the theme, my name Was not far off . . iii 3 59
The event Is yet to name the winner . . . . . iii 3 15
What's your name?—Fidele, sir. I have a kinsman who Is bound for Italy iii 6 60
Hear but my name, and tremble.—What's thy name?—Cloten, thou villain.—Cloten, thou double villain, be thy name, I cannot tremble at it . . . . . . iv 2 87
Thy name?—Fidele, sir.—Thou dost approve thyself the very same: Thy name well fits thy faith, thy faith thy name, . . iv 2 379
The fit and apt construction of thy name, Being Leo-natus . v 5 444
And pride so great, The name of help grew odious to repeat *Pericles* i 4 31
He gains from his subjects the name of good by his government . ii 1 110
We desire to know of him, Of whence he is, his name and parentage . ii 3 74
My name, Pericles; My education been in arts and arms . . ii 3 81
What trade, sir?—Why, I cannot name't but I shall offend.—I cannot be offended with my trade. Please you to name it . . iv 6 75
For what thou professest, a baboon, could he speak, Would own a name too dear . . . . . . iv 6 190
Sure, all's effectless; yet nothing we'll omit That bears recovery's name v 1 54
Thy name, my most kind virgin? Recount, I do beseech thee . v 1 141
The name Was given me by one that had some power, My father, and a king . . . . v 1 149
What was thy mother's name? tell me but that . . . v 1 202
Is it no more to be your daughter than To say my mother's name was Thaisa? . . . . v 1 212
Did you not name a tempest, A birth, and death? . . . v 3 33

Named. They are not to be named, my lord, Not to be spoke of *M. Ado* iv 1 96
What you will have it named, even that it is . *T. of Shrew* iv 5 21
And, O, what better matter breeds for you Than I have named! *K. John* iii 4 171
The friends you have named uncertain; the time itself unsorted *1 Hen. IV.* ii 3 12
He that outlives this day, and comes safe home, Will stand a tip-toe when this day is named . . . *Hen. V.* iv 3 42
And the pretence for this Is named, your wars in France *Hen. VIII.* i 2 60
Cause the musicians play me that sad note I named my knell . iv 2 79
By deed-achieving honour newly named . . *Coriolanus* ii 1 190
[Censorinus,] nobly named so . . . . . . ii 3 251
Marcius, Whom late you have named for consul . . . iii 1 196
O, how my heart abhors To hear him named, and cannot come to him, To wreak the love I bore my cousin! . *Rom. and Jul.* iii 5 101
He is already named, and gone to Scone to be invested . *Macbeth* ii 4 31
Henceforth be earls, the first that ever Scotland In such an honour named . . . . v 8 64
Like a sister am most loath to call Your faults as they are named *Lear* i 1 274
Did my father's godson seek your life? He whom my father named? . ii 1 94
The south-fog rot him!—He never can meet more mischance than come To be but named of thee . . . *Cymbeline* ii 3 138
All faults that may be named, nay, that hell knows, Why, hers [woman's] ii 5 27
Marina, whom, For she was born at sea, I have named so . *Pericles* iii 3 13
Can you remember what I call'd the man? I have named him oft . v 3 53

Nameless. The secret nameless friend of yours . *T. G. of Ver.* ii 1 111
She hath many nameless virtues . . . . . . iii 1 319
What I cannot name; 'tis nameless woe, I wot . *Richard II.* ii 2 40

Namely, no time to recover hair lost by nature . *Com. of Errors* ii 2 103
Namely, some love that drew him oft from home . . . v 1 56
To him that owes it, namely this young prince . *K. John* ii 1 248
Namely, to appeal each other of high treason . *Richard II.* i 1 27
The borrow'd glories that by gift of heaven, By law of nature and of nations, 'long To him and to his heirs; namely, the crown *Hen. V.* ii 4 81
I do beweep to many simple gulls; Namely, to Hastings, Derby, Buckingham. . . . . . *Richard III.* i 3 329

Namest. As thou namest them, I will describe them . *Mer. of Venice* i 2 40

Naming. Receive The confirmation of my promised gift, Which but attends thy naming . . . . . *All's Well* ii 3 57
Whose very naming punishes me with the remembrance *W. Tale* iv 2 24
Why, 'tis this naming of him does him harm . *Troi. and Cres.* ii 3 239
My fortunes against any lay worth naming . . *Othello* ii 3 330

Nan. This hat is Nan, our maid . . . *T. G. of Ver.* ii 3 23
Good faith, it is such another Nan . . . *Mer. Wives* i 4 160
I cannot get thy father's love; Therefore no more turn me to him, sweet Nan . . . . iii 4 2
Farewell, gentle mistress: farewell, Nan . . . iii 4 98
I pray thee, once to-night Give my sweet Nan this ring . . iii 4 104
Nan Page my daughter and my little son And three or four more . iv 4 47
My Nan shall be the queen of all the fairies, Finely attired in a robe of white . . . . iv 4 71
In that time Shall Master Slender steal my Nan away And marry her at Eton . . . . iv 4 74
He hath my good will, And none but he, to marry with Nan Page iv 4 85
'Twixt twelve and one, Must my sweet Nan present the Fairy Queen iv 6 20
Where is Nan now and her troop of fairies, and the Welsh devil Hugh? v 3 12

Nap. By my fay, a goodly nap . . . *T. of Shrew* Ind. 2 83
Let your bounty take a nap, I will awake it anon . *T. Night* v 1 52
To dress the commonwealth, and turn it, and set a new nap upon it *2 Hen. VI.* iv 2 7
I'll strive, with troubled thoughts, to take a nap *Richard III.* v 3 104

Nape. O that you could turn your eyes toward the napes of your necks, and make but an interior survey of your good selves! *Coriolanus* ii 1 43

Napkin. Rammed me in with foul shirts and smocks, socks, foul stockings, greasy napkins . . . . *Mer. Wives* iii 5 92
To that youth he calls his Rosalind He sends this bloody napkin *As Y. Like It* iv 3 94
Give this napkin Dyed in his blood unto the shepherd youth . iv 3 155
An onion will do well for such a shift, Which in a napkin being close convey'd Shall in despite enforce a watery eye . *T. of Shrew* Ind. 1 127
The half shirt is two napkins tacked together . *1 Hen. IV.* iv 2 47

Napkin. I stain'd this napkin with the blood That valiant Clifford, with his rapier's point, Made issue from the bosom of the boy *3 Hen. VI.* i 4 79
Keep thou the napkin, and go boast of this . . . i 4 159
The ruthless queen gave him to dry his cheeks A napkin steeped in the harmless blood Of sweet young Rutland . . . ii 1 62
Well I wot Thy napkin cannot drink a tear of mine . *T. Andron.* iii 1 140
His napkin, with his true tears all bewet, Can do no service on her sorrowful cheeks . . . . . . iii 1 146
Kiss dead Cæsar's wounds And dip their napkins in his sacred blood *J. Cæsar* iii 2 138
Come in time; have napkins enow about you; here you'll sweat for't *Macbeth* ii 3 6
Here, Hamlet, take my napkin, rub thy brows . *Hamlet* v 2 299
Let me but bind it hard, within this hour It will be well.—Your napkin is too little: Let it alone . . . *Othello* iii 3 287
I am glad I have found this napkin: This was her first remembrance from the Moor . . . . . . iii 3 290
I will in Cassio's lodging lose this napkin, And let him find it . iii 3 321

Naples. Confederates—So dry he was for sway—wi' the King of Naples To give him annual tribute . . . *Tempest* i 2 112
This King of Naples, being an enemy To me inveterate . . i 2 121
And are upon the Mediterranean flote, Bound sadly home for Naples i 2 235
What wert thou, if the King of Naples heard thee?—A single thing, as I am now, that wonders To hear thee speak of Naples . i 2 431
Myself am Naples, Who with mine eyes, never since at ebb, beheld The king my father wreck'd . . . . . i 2 434
I'll make you The queen of Naples.—Soft, sir! one word more . i 2 449
O thou mine heir Of Naples and of Milan, what strange fish Hath made his meal on thee? . . . . . . ii 1 112
Milan and Naples have Moe widows in them of this business' making Than we bring men to comfort them . . . ii 1 132
Who's the next heir of Naples?—Claribel.—She that is queen of Tunis. ii 1 245
She that from Naples Can have no note, unless the sun were post . ii 1 247
'Tis true, my brother's daughter's queen of Tunis; So is she heir of Naples . . . . ii 1 256
How shall that Claribel Measure us back to Naples? . . ii 1 259
There be that can rule Naples As well as he that sleeps . . ii 1 262
As thou got'st Milan, I'll come by Naples . . . ii 1 292
If I can recover him and keep him tame and get to Naples with him, he's a present for any emperor . . . . . ii 2 72
If in Naples I should report this now, would they believe me? . iii 3 27
O heavens, that they were living both in Naples, The king and queen there! . . . . v 1 149
Was Milan thrust from Milan, that his issue Should become kings of Naples? . . . . v 1 206
In the morn I'll bring you to your ship and so to Naples . . v 1 307
'Tis true, I must be here confined by you, Or sent to Naples . Epil. 5
Margaret my name, and daughter to a king, The King of Naples *1 Hen. VI.* v 3 52
Though her father be the King of Naples, Duke of Anjou and Maine, yet is he poor . . . . v 3 94
'Twas neither Charles nor yet the duke I named, But Reignier, king of Naples . . . . v 4 78
Her father is a king, The King of Naples and Jerusalem . . v 5 40
O blood-bespotted Neapolitan, Outcast of Naples! . . *2 Hen. VI.* v 1 118
King of Naples, Of both the Sicils and Jerusalem . . *3 Hen. VI.* i 4 121
Iron of Naples hid with English gilt . . . . . ii 2 139
Have your instruments been in Naples, that they speak i' the nose thus? . . . . *Othello* iii 1 4

Napless. The napless vesture of humility . . *Coriolanus* ii 1 250

Napping. I should blush, I know, To be o'erheard and taken napping so . . . . *L. L. Lost* iv 3 130
Nay, I have ta'en you napping, gentle love . *T. of Shrew* iv 2 46

Naps. Stephen Sly and old John Naps of Greece . . Ind. 2 95

Narbon. Was this gentlewoman the daughter of Gerard de Narbon? *All's Well* i 1 43
Gerard de Narbon was my father; In what he did profess, well found . ii 1 104

Narcissus. Hadst thou Narcissus in thy face, to me Thou wouldst appear most ugly . . . . . *Ant. and Cleo.* ii 5 96

Narine. Le cheval volant, the Pegasus, chez les narines de feu! *Hen. V.* iii 7 15

Narrow. A shoulder-clapper, one that countermands The passages of alleys, creeks and narrow lands . . *Com. of Errors.* iv 2 38
In the narrow seas that part The French and English *Mer. of Venice* ii 8 28
Antonio hath a ship of rich lading wrecked on the narrow seas . iii 1 4
I am for the house with the narrow gate . . *All's Well* iv 5 53
Loose companions, Even such, they say, as stand in narrow lanes *Richard II.* v 3 8
Sirs, you four shall front them in the narrow lane . *1 Hen. IV.* ii 2 63
Whose high upreared and abutting fronts The perilous narrow ocean parts asunder . . . . *Hen. V.* Prol. 22
Poor mechanic porters crowding in Their heavy burdens at his narrow gate . . . . i 2 201
Charming the narrow seas To give you gentle pass . . ii Prol. 38
Stern Falconbridge commands the narrow seas . . *3 Hen. VI.* i 1 239
Hath pass'd in safety through the narrow seas . . . iv 8 3
Honour travels in a strait so narrow, Where one but goes abreast *Troi. and Cres.* iii 3 154
O, here's a wit of cheveril, that stretches from an inch narrow to an ell broad!—I stretch it out for that word 'broad' *Rom. and Jul.* ii 4 88
Why, man, he doth bestride the narrow world Like a Colossus *J. Cæsar* i 2 135
Here the street is narrow: . . . I'll get me to a place more void . ii 4 33
To me it is a prison.—Why then, your ambition makes it one; 'tis too narrow for your mind . . . . . . *Hamlet* ii 2 259
Cold and sickly He vented them; most narrow measure lent me *Ant. and Cleo.* iii 4 8
This was strange chance: A narrow lane, an old man, and two boys *Cymbeline* v 3 52

Narrowly. If my cousin do not look exceeding narrowly to thee *M. Ado.* v 4 118
My fellow-schoolmaster Doth watch Bianca's steps so narrowly *T. of S.* iii 2 141
Search the market narrowly . . . . . *Pericles* iv 2 3

Narrow-mouthed. As wine comes out of a narrow-mouthed bottle *As Y. Like It* iii 2 211

Narrow-prying. The narrow-prying father, Minola . . *T. of Shrew* ii 2 148

Naso. Ovidius Naso was the man: and why, indeed, Naso, but for smelling out the odoriferous flowers of fancy? . *L. L. Lost* iv 2 127

Nasty. In thy hateful lungs, yea, in thy maw, perdy, And, which is worse, within thy nasty mouth! . . . . . *Hen. V.* ii 1 53
Honeying and making love Over the nasty sty . . *Hamlet* iii 4 94

Nathaniel. Sir Nathaniel, will you hear an extemporal epitaph on the death of the deer? . . . . . . *L. L. Lost* iv 2 50
Did they please you, Sir Nathaniel?—Marvellous well for the pen . iv 2 157

Nathaniel. Call forth Nathaniel, Joseph, Nicholas, Philip, Walter, Sugarsop *T. of Shrew* iv 1 91
Where is Nathaniel, Gregory, Philip?—Here, here, sir; here, sir iv 1 125
Nathaniel's coat, sir, was not fully made iv 1 135

Natifs d'Angleterre. Vous prononcez les mots aussi droit que les natifs d'Angleterre *Hen. V.* iii 4 41

Nation. Methinks they are such a gentle nation *Com. of Errors* iv 4 158
He hates our sacred nation, and he rails *Mer. of Venice* i 3 49
Mocked at my gains, scorned my nation, thwarted my bargains iii 1 59
The curse never fell upon our nation till now; I never felt it till now iii 1 89
Since that the trade and profit of the city Consisteth of all nations iii 3 31
The courtesy of nations allows you my better *As Y. Like It* i 1 49
If you could find out a country where but women were that had received so much shame, you might begin an impudent nation *All's Well* iv 3 363
Whose villanous saffron would have made all the unbaked and doughy youth of a nation in his colour iv 5 4
O nation, that thou couldst remove! *K. John* v 2 33
To thrill and shake Even at the crying of your nation's crow v 2 144
Our tardy apish nation Limps after in base imitation *Richard II.* ii 1 22
It was alway yet the trick of our English nation, if they have a good thing, to make it too common 2 *Hen. IV.* i 2 241
Our state may go In equal rank with the best govern'd nation v 2 137
And our nation lose The name of hardiness and policy *Hen. V.* i 2 219
By gift of heaven, By law of nature and of nations ii 4 80
There is not many of your nation— Of my nation! What ish my nation? Ish a villain, and a bastard, and a knave, and a rascal—What ish my nation? Who talks of my nation? iii 2 131
Nor should that nation boast it so with us, But be extirped 1 *Hen. VI.* iii 3 23
A lordly nation That will not trust thee but for profit's sake iii 3 62
Remember where we are; In France, amongst a fickle wavering nation iv 1 138
Our nation's terror and their bloody scourge! iv 2 16
The states of Christendom . . . Have earnestly implored a general peace Betwixt our nation and the aspiring French v 4 99
Wherever the bright sun of heaven shall shine, His honour and the greatness of his name Shall be, and make new nations *Hen. VIII.* v 5 53
There is a law in each well-order'd nation To curb those raging appetites that are Most disobedient *Troi. and Cres.* ii 2 180
These moral laws Of nature and of nations speak aloud ii 2 185
Abated captives to some nation That won you without blows! *Coriolanus* iii 3 132
I would not be a Roman, of all nations; I had as lieve be a condemned man iv 5 186
Hath yoked a nation strong, train'd up in arms *T. Andron.* i 1 30
Come, damned earth, Thou common whore of mankind, that put'st odds Among the rout of nations *T. of Athens* iv 3 43
O nation miserable, With an untitled tyrant bloody-scepter'd! *Macbeth* iv 3 103
Makes us traduced and tax'd of other nations *Hamlet* i 4 18
The nation holds it no sin to tarre them to controversy ii 2 370
He is the brooch indeed And gem of all the nation iv 7 95
The scrimers of their nation, He swore, had neither motion, guard, nor eye iv 7 101
Wherefore should I Stand in the plague of custom, and permit The curiosity of nations to deprive me? *Lear* i 2 4
She shunn'd The wealthy curled darlings of our nation *Othello* i 2 68
Some neighbouring nation, Taking advantage of our misery *Pericles* i 4 65
If we had of every nation a traveller, we should lodge them with this sign iv 2 123

Native. Say in brief the cause Why thou departed'st from thy native home *Com. of Errors* i 1 30
For still her cheeks possess the same Which native she doth owe *L. L. L.* i 2 111
For native blood is counted painting now iv 3 263
The scarfed bark puts from her native bay *Mer. of Venice* ii 6 15
The poor dappled fools, Being native burghers of this desert city *As Y. Like It* ii 1 23
And what's worse, To fright the animals and to kill them up In their assign'd and native dwelling-place ii 1 63
Are you native of this place?—As the cony that you see dwell where she is kindled iii 2 356
To join like likes and kiss like native things *All's Well* i 1 238
And choice breeds A native slip to us from foreign seeds i 3 152
Can bring this instrument of honour again into his native quarter iii 6 70
Have sold their fortunes at their native homes *K. John* ii 1 69
Whose passage, vex'd with thy impediment, Shall leave his native channel ii 1 337
And chase the native beauty from his cheek iii 4 83
My native English now I must forego *Richard II.* i 3 160
Which robs my tongue from breathing native breath i 3 173
Chasing the royal blood With fury from his native residence ii 1 119
And fright our native peace with self-born arms ii 3 80
This earth shall have a feeling and these stones Prove armed soldiers, ere her native king Shall falter iii 2 25
In his true, native and most proper shape 2 *Hen. IV.* iv 1 37
We bear our civil swords and native fire As far as France v 5 112
Whose right Suits not in native colours with the truth *Hen. V.* i 2 17
And let us fear The native mightiness and fate of him ii 4 64
He bids you then resign Your crown and kingdom, indirectly held From him the native and true challenger ii 4 95
Poor we may call them in their native lords iii 5 26
If these men have defeated the law and outrun native punishment iv 1 176
A many of our bodies shall no doubt Find native graves iv 3 96
He could not speak English in the native garb v 1 80
From England's bank Drove back again unto my native clime 2 *Hen. VI.* iii 2 84
Spare England, for it is your native coast iv 8 52
Did I put Henry from his native right? 3 *Hen. VI.* iii 3 190
That in their country did them that disgrace, We fear to warrant in our native place! *Troi. and Cres.* ii 2 96
Your native town you enter'd like a post *Coriolanus* v 6 50
Back, foolish tears, back to your native spring *Rom. and Jul.* iii 2 102
For no pulse Shall keep his native progress, but surcease iv 1 97
The senator shall bear contempt hereditary, The beggar native honour *T. of Athens* iv 3 11
If thou path, thy native semblance on, Not Erebus itself were dim enough To hide thee from prevention *J. Cæsar* ii 1 83
The head is not more native to the heart *Hamlet* i 2 47
Though I am native here And to the manner born i 4 14
Thus the native hue of resolution Is sicklied o'er with the pale cast of thought iii 1 84
Or like a creature native and indued Unto that element iv 7 180
The native act and figure of my heart In compliment extern *Othello* i 1 62
Base men being in love have then a nobility in their natures more than is native to them ii 1 218

Nativity. They say there is divinity in odd numbers, either in nativity, chance, or death *Mer. Wives* v 1 4
I have served him from the hour of my nativity to this instant *C. of Er.* iv 4 32
My children both, And you the calendars of their nativity v 1 404
Vows so born, In their nativity all truth appears *M. N. Dream* iii 2 125
Nor mark prodigious, such as are Despised in nativity v 1 420
Lisp and wear strange suits, disable all the benefits of your own country, be out of love with your nativity *As Y. Like It* iv 1 36
At my nativity The front of heaven was full of fiery shapes 1 *Hen. IV.* iii 1 13
The earth shook to see the heavens on fire, And not in fear of your nativity iii 1 26
Now cursed be the time Of thy nativity! 1 *Hen. VI.* v 4 27
To whom the heavens in thy nativity Adjudged an olive branch 3 *Hen. VI.* iv 6 33
Seal'd in thy nativity The slave of nature and the son of hell! *Rich. III.* i 3 229
My nativity was under Ursa major *Lear* i 2 140
Thou hast as chiding a nativity As fire, air, water, earth, and heaven can make, To herald thee from the womb *Pericles* iii 1 32

Natural. A thing divine, for nothing natural I ever saw so noble *Tempest* i 2 418
That a monster should be such a natural! iii 2 37
Scarce think Their eyes do offices of truth, their words Are natural breath v 1 157
These are not natural events; they strengthen From strange to stranger v 1 227
Rebate and blunt his natural edge With profits of the mind *Meas. for Meas.* i 4 60
Go to your bosom; . . . if it confess A natural guiltiness such as is his ii 2 139
In his love toward her ever most kind and natural iii 1 229
Which is the natural man, And which the spirit? *Com. of Errors* v 1 333
But, as in health, come to my natural taste, Now I do wish it *M. N. D.* iv 1 179
Villanous contriver against me his natural brother *As Y. Like It* i 1 151
When Fortune makes Nature's natural the cutter-off of Nature's wit i 2 52
This is not Fortune's work neither, but Nature's; who perceiveth our natural wits too dull to reason of such goddesses and hath sent this natural for our whetstone i 2 55
Whose loves Are dearer than the natural bond of sisters i 2 288
Such a one is a natural philosopher iii 2 33
Natural rebellion, done i' the blaze of youth *All's Well* v 3 6
Hath all the good gifts of nature.—He hath indeed, almost natural: for besides that he's a fool, he's a great quarreller *T. Night* i 3 30
He does it with a better grace, but I do it more natural ii 3 89
A natural perspective, that is and is not! v 1 224
Our natural goodness Imparts this *W. Tale* ii 1 164
Comes it not something near?—Her natural posture! v 3 23
No natural exhalation in the sky, No scope of nature *K. John* iii 4 153
They will pluck away his natural cause And call them meteors, prodigies iii 4 156
A natural coward, without instinct 1 *Hen. IV.* ii 4 542
Curbs himself even of his natural scope When you come 'cross his humour iii 1 171
In that obedient orb again Where you did give a fair and natural light v 1 18
Congreeing in a full and natural close, Like music *Hen. V.* i 2 182
What mightst thou do, that honour would thee do, Were all thy children kind and natural! ii Prol. 19
Working so grossly in a natural cause ii 2 107
Will you have them weep our horses' blood? How shall we, then, behold their natural tears? iv 2 13
Natural graces that extinguish art 1 *Hen. VI.* v 3 192
Whom should he follow but his natural king? 3 *Hen. VI.* i 1 82
He hath made a solemn vow Never to lie and take his natural rest iv 3 5
God, I pray him, That none of you may live your natural age! *Rich. III.* i 3 213
From me receive that natural competency Whereby they live *Coriolanus* i 1 143
And from her womb children of divers kind We sucking on her natural bosom find *Rom. and Jul.* ii 3 12
This drivelling love is like a great natural, that runs lolling up and down ii 4 96
The painting is almost the natural man *T. of Athens* i 1 157
Sweet king-killer [gold], and dear divorce 'Twixt natural son and sire! iv 3 383
Thou art even natural in thine art v 1 88
When these prodigies Do so conjointly meet, let not men say 'These are their reasons; they are natural' *J. Cæsar* i 3 30
And keep the natural ruby of your cheeks, When mine is blanch'd *Macb.* iii 4 115
He loves us not; He wants the natural touch iv 2 9
Upon a wretch whose natural gifts were poor To those of mine! *Hamlet* i 5 51
It courses through The natural gates and alleys of the body i 5 67
There is something in this more than natural, if philosophy could find it out ii 2 385
The heart-ache and the thousand natural shocks That flesh is heir to iii 1 62
Thy natural magic and dire property, On wholesome life usurp immediately iii 2 270
Loyal and natural boy, I'll work the means To make thee capable *Lear* ii 1 86
I am even The natural fool of fortune iv 6 195
I do agnize A natural and prompt alacrity I find in hardness *Othello* i 3 233
It is not Cæsar's natural voice to hate Our great competitor *Ant. and Cleo.* i 4 2
And, of that natural luck, He beats thee 'gainst the odds ii 3 26
Some natural notes about her body, Above ten thousand meaner moveables Would testify *Cymbeline* ii 2 28
The natural bravery of your isle, which stands As Neptune's park iii 1 18
Myself, Belarius, that am Morgan call'd, They take for natural father iii 3 107
That she held the very garment of Posthumus in more respect than my noble and natural person iii 5 140
This is he; Who hath upon him still that natural stamp v 5 366
Her art sisters the natural roses *Pericles* v Gower 7

Naturalize. My instruction shall serve to naturalize thee *All's Well* i 1 223

Naturally. Aptly fitted and naturally perform'd *T. of Shrew* Ind. 1 87
Though I am not naturally honest, I am so sometimes by chance *W. Tale* iv 4 732
Subject to fears, A woman, naturally born to fears *K. John* iii 1 15
The cold blood he did naturally inherit of his father 2 *Hen. IV.* iv 3 128

Nature. In my false brother Awaked an evil nature *Tempest* i 2 93
Had that in't which good natures Could not abide to be with i 2 359
My father's of a better nature, sir, Than he appears by speech i 2 496
All things in common nature should produce Without sweat or endeavour ii 1 159
Nature should bring forth, Of it own kind, all foison, all abundance ii 1 162
A devil, a born devil, on whose nature Nurture can never stick iv 1 188
You, brother mine, that entertain'd ambition, Expell'd remorse and nature v 1 76
There is in this business more than nature Was ever conduct of v 1 243
And love you 'gainst the nature of love,—force ye *T. G. of Ver.* v 4 58
I see what thou wert, if Fortune thy foe were not, Nature thy friend. Come, thou canst not hide it *Mer. Wives* iii 3 70
The nature of our people, Our city's institutions *Meas. for Meas.* i 1 10
Nature never lends The smallest scruple of her excellence i 1 37

Nature. A power I have, but of what strength and nature I am not yet instructed . . . . *Meas. for Meas.* i 1 80
Our natures do pursue, Like rats that ravin down their proper bane . i 2 132
And yet my nature never in the fight To do in slander . . . i 3 42
The strumpet, With all her double vigour, art and nature . . ii 2 184
Make me know The nature of their crimes, that I may minister To them accordingly . . . . ii 3 7
As good To pardon him that hath from nature stolen A man already made . . . . ii 4 43
The weariest and most loathed worldly life That age, ache, penury and imprisonment Can lay on nature is a paradise To what we fear of death . . . . iii 1 131
Nature dispenses with the deed so far That it becomes a virtue . iii 1 135
To practise his judgement with the disposition of natures . . iii 1 165
My end Was wrought by nature, not by vile offence . *Com. of Errors* i 1 35
There's no time for a man to recover his hair that grows bald by nature ii 2 74
No time to recover hair lost by nature . . . . ii 2 104
Nature never framed a woman's heart Of prouder stuff . *Much Ado* iii 1 49
Nature, drawing of an antique, Made a foul blot . . . iii 1 63
To be a well-favoured man is the gift of fortune ; but to write and read comes by nature . . . . iii 3 16
Grieved I, I had but one? Chid I for that at frugal nature's frame? . iv 1 130
As prodigal of all dear grace As Nature was in making graces dear *L. L. Lost* ii 1 10
Of that nature that to your huge store Wise things seem foolish . v 2 377
Nature shows art, That through thy bosom makes me see thy heart *M. N. Dream* ii 2 104
O wherefore, Nature, didst thou lions frame? . . . . . v 1 296
And the blots of Nature's hand Shall not in their issue stand . v 1 416
Nature hath framed strange fellows in her time . *Mer. of Venice* i 1 51
To offend, and judge, are distinct offices And of opposed natures . ii 9 62
Works a miracle in nature, Making them lightest that wear most of it . iii 2 90
Of a strange nature is the suit you follow . . . . iv 1 177
Since nought so stockish, hard and full of rage, But music for the time doth change his nature . . . . v 1 82
The something that nature gave me his countenance seems to take from me : he lets me feed with his hinds . . . *As Y. Like It* i 1 18
Nay, now thou goest from Fortune's office to Nature's . . . i 2 44
Fortune reigns in gifts of the world, not in the lineaments of Nature . i 2 45
When Nature hath made a fair creature, may she not by Fortune fall into the fire? . . . . i 2 46
Though Nature hath given us wit to flout at Fortune . . . i 2 48
There is Fortune too hard for Nature, when Fortune makes Nature's natural the cutter-off of Nature's wit . . . . i 2 52
Peradventure this is not Fortune's work neither, but Nature's . . i 2 55
But as all is mortal in nature, so is all nature in love mortal in folly . ii 4 56
Let my officers of such a nature Make an extent upon his house and lands . . . . iii 1 16
He that hath learned no wit by nature nor art may complain of good breeding . . . . iii 2 31
Therefore Heaven Nature charged That one body should be fill'd With all graces wide-enlarged . . . . iii 2 149
Nature presently distill'd Helen's cheek, but not her heart . . iii 2 152
I see no more in you than in the ordinary Of nature's sale-work . . iii 5 43
Nature, stronger than his just occasion, Made him give battle . . iv 3 130
Though the nature of our quarrel yet never brooked parle *T. of Shrew* i 1 116
Had it stretched so far, would have made nature immortal *All's Well* i 1 22
It is not politic in the commonwealth of nature to preserve virginity . i 1 138
There's little can be said in't ; 'tis against the rule of nature . . i 1 148
A desperate offendress against nature . . . . . . i 1 153
The mightiest space in fortune nature brings To join like likes . i 1 237
Frank nature, rather curious than in haste, Hath well composed thee . i 2 20
Nature and sickness Debate it at their leisure . . . . i 2 74
So it was with me when I was young : If ever we are nature's, these are ours . . . . i 3 135
It is the show and seal of nature's truth, Where love's strong passion is impress'd in youth . . . . i 3 138
'Tis often seen Adoption strives with nature . . . . i 3 151
Labouring art can never ransom nature From her inaidible estate . . ii 1 121
She is young, wise, fair ; In these to nature she's immediate heir . ii 3 139
I have kept of them tame, and know their natures . . . . ii 5 50
The younger of our nature, That surfeit on their ease . . . iii 1 17
My son corrupts a well-derived nature With his inducement . . iii 2 90
Better 'twere That all the miseries which nature owes Were mine at once . . . . iii 2 122
There is something in't that stings his nature . . . . iv 3 4
The tenderness of her nature became as a prey to her grief . . iv 3 61
I con him no thanks for't, in the nature he delivers it . . . iv 3 175
My offences being many, I would repent out the remainder of nature . iv 3 272
The most virtuous gentlewoman that ever nature had praise for creating iv 5 10
Jades' tricks ; which are their own right by the law of nature . . iv 5 65
Let him not ask our pardon ; The nature of his great offence is dead . v 3 23
Or, ere they meet, in me, O nature, cesse ! . . . . . v 3 72
Hath not in nature's mystery more science Than I have in this ring . v 3 103
Whose nature sickens but to speak a truth . . . . . v 3 207
A noble duke, in nature as in name . . . . . *T. Night* i 2 25
Though that nature with a beauteous wall Doth oft close in pollution . i 2 48
And hath all the good gifts of nature . . . . . . i 3 29
For thou seest it will not curl by nature . . . . . . i 3 105
Whose red and white Nature's own sweet and cunning hand laid on . i 5 258
In dimension and the shape of nature A gracious person . . . i 5 280
'Tis that miracle and queen of gems That nature pranks her in attracts my soul . . . . ii 4 89
The offence is not of such a bloody nature . . . . . iii 3 30
Of what nature the wrongs are thou hast done him, I know not . . iii 4 241
In nature there's no blemish but the mind ; None can be call'd deformed but the unkind . . . . iii 4 401
Nor can there be that deity in my nature, Of here and every where . v 1 234
Lady, you have been mistook : But nature to her bias drew in that . v 1 267
How sometimes nature will betray its folly, Its tenderness *W. Tale* i 2 151
Not noted, is't, But of the finer natures? . . . . . . i 2 226
And is By law and process of great nature thence Freed and enfranchised ii 2 60
Thou, good goddess Nature, which hast made it So like to him that got it . . . . ii 3 104
So long as nature Will bear up with this exercise, so long I daily vow to use it . . . . iii 2 241
Carnations and streak'd gillyvors, Which some call nature's bastards . iv 4 83
There is an art which in their piedness shares With great creating nature . . . . iv 4 88
Yet nature is made better by no mean But nature makes that mean . iv 4 89

Nature. Over that art Which you say adds to nature, is an art That nature makes . . . . *W. Tale* iv 4 91
This is an art Which does mend nature, change it rather, but The art itself is nature.—So it is . . . . iv 4 96
Let nature crush the sides o' the earth together And mar the seeds within ! . . . . iv 4 489
Yet nature might have made me as these are, Therefore I will not disdain . . . . iv 4 773
The affection of nobleness which nature shows above her breeding . v 2 40
Would beguile Nature of her custom, so perfectly he is her ape . v 2 108
Which heaven shall take in nature of a fee . . . *K. John* ii 1 170
At thy birth, dear boy, Nature and Fortune join'd to make thee great . iii 1 52
Of Nature's gifts thou mayst with lilies boast . . . . iii 1 53
No scope of nature, no distemper'd day, No common wind . . iii 4 154
By the hand of nature mark'd, Quoted and sign'd to do a deed of shame iv 2 221
And you have slander'd nature in my form . . . . . iv 2 256
Some of those seven are dried by nature's course, Some of those branches by the Destinies cut . . . . . *Richard II.* i 2 14
This fortress built by Nature for herself Against infection . . ii 1 43
Like the meteors of a troubled heaven, All of one nature 1 *Hen. IV.* i 1 11
Diseased nature oftentimes breaks forth In strange eruptions . . iii 1 27
The king hath sent to know The nature of your griefs . . . iv 3 42
Like to a title-leaf, Foretells the nature of a tragic volume 2 *Hen. IV.* i 1 61
Now let not Nature's hand Keep the wild flood confined ! let order die ! i 1 153
Speaking thick, which nature made his blemish . . . . ii 3 24
O gentle sleep, Nature's soft nurse, how have I frighted thee? . iii 1 6
There is a history in all men's lives, Figuring the nature of the times deceased . . . . iii 1 81
I see no reason in the law of nature but I may snap at him . . iii 2 357
A peace is of the nature of a conquest . . . . . iv 2 89
They do observe Unfather'd heirs and loathly births of nature . iv 4 122
Nature, love, and filial tenderness, Shall, O dear father, pay thee plenteously . . . . iv 5 39
How quickly nature falls into revolt When gold becomes her object ! . iv 5 66
He's walk'd the way of nature ; And to our purposes he lives no more . v 2 4
The honey-bees, Creatures that by a rule in nature teach *Hen. V.* i 2 188
Saw his heroical seed, and smiled to see him, Mangle the work of nature ii 4 60
By gift of heaven, By law of nature and of nations, 'long To him . ii 4 80
Summon up the blood, Disguise fair nature with hard-favour'd rage . iii 1 8
I once writ a sonnet in his praise and began thus : 'Wonder of nature' iii 7 43
Defective in their natures, grow to wildness . . . . . v 2 55
And then in sequel all, According to their firm proposed natures . v 2 362
A most pernicious usurer, Froward by nature, enemy to peace 1 *Hen. VI.* iii 1 18
She hath bewitch'd me with her words, Or nature makes me suddenly relent . . . . iii 3 59
Be not offended, nature's miracle, Thou art allotted to be ta'en by me . v 3 54
He is a fox, By nature proved an enemy to the flock 2 *Hen. VI.* iii 1 258
Being opposites of such repairing nature . . . . . v 3 22
She did corrupt frail nature with some bribe 3 *Hen. VI.* iii 2 155
When nature brought him to the door of death . . . . v 3 105
His head by nature framed to wear a crown, His hand to wield a sceptre iv 6 72
Zeal to right prevails More than the nature of a brother's love . v 1 79
Cheated of feature by dissembling nature, Deform'd *Richard III.* i 1 19
Why, that was he.—The selfsame name, but one of better nature . i 2 143
Framed in the prodigality of nature, Young, valiant, wise . . i 2 244
Seal'd in thy nativity The slave of nature and the son of hell ! . i 3 230
The most replenished sweet work of nature, That from the prime creation e'er she framed . . . . iv 3 18
So long as heaven and nature lengthens it . . . . . iv 4 353
You know his nature, That he's revengeful . . *Hen. VIII.* i 1 108
Still exaction ! The nature of it? in what kind, let's know, Is this exaction? . . . . i 2 53
Learned, and a most rare speaker ; To nature none more bound . i 2 112
Methought I stood not in the smile of heaven ; who had Commanded nature . . . . ii 4 188
Out of his noble nature, Zeal and obedience he still bore your grace . iii 1 62
Nature does require Her times of preservation . . . . iii 2 146
I know his noble nature—not to let Thy hopeful service perish too . iii 2 418
She is young, and of a noble modest nature, I hope she will deserve well . . . . iv 2 135
Times to repair our nature With comforting repose, and not for us To waste . . . . v 1 3
A wilder nature than the business That seeks dispatch by day . v 1 15
We all are men, In our own natures frail, and capable Of our flesh . v 3 11
I'm sure Thou hast a cruel nature and a bloody . . . . v 3 129
A man into whom nature hath so crowded humours *Troi. and Cres.* i 2 22
The nature of the sickness found, Ulysses, What is the remedy? . i 3 140
Abilities, gifts, natures, shapes, Severals and generals of grace exact . i 3 179
Nature craves All dues be render'd to their owners . . . ii 2 173
If this law Of nature be corrupted through affection . . . ii 2 177
These moral laws Of nature and of nations speak aloud . . . ii 2 185
And thy parts of nature Thrice famed, beyond all erudition . . ii 3 253
All That time, acquaintance, custom and condition Made tame and most familiar to my nature . . . . iii 3 10
Nature, what things there are Most abject in regard and dear in use ! . iii 3 127
One touch of nature makes the whole world kin . . . . iii 3 175
The secrets of nature Have not more gift in taciturnity . . . iv 2 74
They're loving, well composed with gifts of nature . . . . iv 4 79
Thou core of envy ! Thou crusty batch of nature, what's the news? . v 1 5
How the poor world is pestered with such waterflies, diminutives of nature ! . . . . v 1 39
Within my soul there doth conduce a fight Of this strange nature . v 2 148
What he cannot help in his nature, you account a vice in him *Coriolanus* i 1 42
Such a nature, Tickled with good success, disdains the shadow Which he treads on at noon . . . . i 1 263
Nature teaches beasts to know their friends . . . . . ii 1 6
So his gracious nature Would think upon you for your voices . . ii 3 195
It would have gall'd his surly nature, Which easily endures not article ii 3 203
If, as his nature is, he fall in rage With their refusal . . . ii 3 266
Thus we debase The nature of our seats . . . . . iii 1 136
This man hath marr'd his fortune.—His nature is too noble for the world iii 1 255
Pluck him thence ; Lest his infection, being of catching nature, Spread iii 1 310
Why did you wish me milder? would you have me False to my nature? iii 2 15
I would dissemble with my nature where My fortunes and my friends at stake required I should do so in honour . . . . . . iii 2 62
He leads them like a thing Made by some other deity than nature . iv 6 91
Yet his nature In that's no changeling . . . . . . iv 7 10
As is the osprey to the fish, who takes it By sovereignty of nature . iv 7 35
Or whether nature, Not to be other than one thing . . . . iv 7 41
But, out, affection ! All bond and privilege of nature, break ! . v 3 25

Nature. An aspect of intercession, which Great nature cries 'Deny not' *Coriolanus* v 3 33
To this end, He bow'd his nature, never known before But to be rough v 6 25
Wilt thou draw near the nature of the gods? . . . *T. Andron.* i 1 117
Brother, for in that name doth nature plead,— Father, and in that name doth nature speak,— Speak thou no more . . . . . i 1 370
Barbarous Tamora, For no name fits thy nature but thy own! . . ii 3 119
By nature made for murders and for rapes.—O, why should nature build so foul a den, Unless the gods delight in tragedies? . . . . iv 1 58
Had nature lent thee but thy mother's look . . . . . v 1 29
Gentle people, give me aim awhile, For nature puts me to a heavy task v 3 150
Like a loving child, Shed yet some small drops from thy tender spring, Because kind nature doth require it so . . . . . . v 3 168
Raise a spirit in his mistress' circle Of some strange nature *Rom. and Jul.* ii 1 25
The earth that's nature's mother is her tomb . . . . ii 3 9
Now art thou what thou art, by art as well as by nature . . . ii 4 95
O nature, what hadst thou to do in hell, When thou didst bower the spirit of a fiend In mortal paradise of such sweet flesh? . . . iii 2 80
Fond nature bids us all lament, Yet nature's tears are reason's merriment iv 5 83
I will say of it, It tutors nature . . . . *T. of Athens* i 1 37
His large fortune Upon his good and gracious nature hanging . . i 1 56
The base o' the mount Is rank'd with all deserts, all kind of natures . i 1 65
For since dishonour traffics with man's nature, He is but outside . . i 1 158
A noble nature May catch a wrench—would all were well—tis pity . ii 2 217
And nature, as it grows again toward earth, Is fashion'd for the journey, dull and heavy . . . . ii 2 227
Let not that part of nature Which my lord paid for, be of any power To expel sickness, but prolong his hour! . . . . . . iii 1 64
Of such a nature is his politic love . . . . . . iii 3 35
Not nature, To whom all sores lay siege, can bear great fortune, But by contempt of nature . . . . iv 3 6
There's nothing level in our cursed natures, But direct villany . . iv 3 19
I will make thee Do thy right nature . . . . . . iv 3 44
That nature, being sick of man's unkindness, Should yet be hungry! . iv 3 176
This is in thee a nature but infected; A poor unmanly melancholy . iv 3 202
Creatures Whose naked natures live in all the spite Of wreakful heaven iv 3 228
Whose bare unhoused trunks, To the conflicting elements exposed, Answer mere nature . . . . iv 3 231
Thy nature did commence in sufferance, time Hath made thee hard in't iv 3 268
The bounteous housewife, nature, on each bush Lays her full mess . iv 3 423
It almost turns my dangerous nature mild . . . . . iv 3 499
Your friends fall'n off, Whose thankless natures—O abhored spirits! . v 1 63
With other incident throes That nature's fragile vessel doth sustain . v 1 204
His discontents are unremoveably Coupled to nature . . . . v 1 228
A tithed death—If thy revenges hunger for that food Which nature loathes . . . . v 4 33
And those our droplets which From niggard nature fall . . . v 4 77
Why all these things change from their ordinance Their natures *J. Cæsar* i 3 67
How that might change his nature, there's the question . . . ii 1 13
Like to a little kingdom, suffers then The nature of an insurrection . ii 1 69
I have as much of this in art as you, But yet my nature could not bear it so . . . . iv 3 195
The deep of night is crept upon our talk, And nature must obey necessity . . . . iv 3 227
That Nature might stand up And say to all the world 'This was a man!' v 5 74
The multiplying villanies of nature Do swarm upon him *Macbeth* i 2 11
And make my seated heart knock at my ribs, Against the use of nature i 3 137
Yet do I fear thy nature; It is too full o' the milk of human kindness . i 5 17
That no compunctious visitings of nature Shake my fell purpose . . i 5 46
Wherever in your sightless substances You wait on nature's mischief! . i 5 51
When in swinish sleep Their drenched natures lie as in a death . i 7 68
Restrain in me the cursed thoughts that nature Gives way to in repose! ii 1 8
Now o'er the one half-world Nature seems dead . . . . ii 1 50
That death and nature do contend about them, Whether they live or die ii 2 7
Balm of hurt minds, great nature's second course . . . . ii 2 39
His gash'd stabs look'd like a breach in nature For ruin's wasteful entrance . . . . ii 3 119
Turn'd wild in nature, broke their stalls, flung out . . . . ii 4 16
'Gainst nature still! Thriftless ambition, that wilt ravin up Thine own life's means! . . . . ii 4 27
In his royalty of nature Reigns that which would be fear'd . . iii 1 50
Do you find Your patience so predominant in your nature? . . . iii 1 87
Every one According to the gift which bounteous nature Hath in him closed . . . . iii 1 98
In them nature's copy's not eterne.—There's comfort yet . . . iii 2 38
With twenty trenched gashes on his head; The least a death to nature iii 4 28
The worm that's fled Hath nature that in time will venom breed . iii 4 30
You lack the season of all natures, sleep . . . . . . iii 4 141
Though the treasure Of nature's germens tumble all together . . iv 1 59
Shall live the lease of nature, pay his breath To time and mortal custom iv 1 99
A good and virtuous nature may recoil In an imperial charge . . iv 3 19
Boundless intemperance In nature is a tyranny . . . . . iv 3 67
Abjure The taints and blames I laid upon myself, For strangers to my nature . . . . iv 3 125
A great perturbation in nature, to receive at once the benefit of sleep, and do the effects of watching! . . . . v 1 10
Yet so far hath discretion fought with nature . . . . *Hamlet* i 2 5
All that lives must die, Passing through nature to eternity . . . i 2 73
'Tis sweet and commendable in your nature . . . . . . i 2 87
'Tis a fault to heaven, A fault against the dead, a fault to nature . i 2 102
Things rank and gross in nature Possess it merely . . . . i 2 136
A violet in the youth of primy nature, Forward, not permanent . . i 3 7
For nature, crescent, does not grow alone In thews and bulk . . i 3 11
For some vicious mole of nature in them, As, in their birth—wherein they are not guilty, Since nature cannot choose his origin . . . i 4 24
Being nature's livery, or fortune's star . . . . . . i 4 32
And we fools of nature So horridly to shake our disposition With thoughts beyond the reaches of our souls . . . . . . i 4 54
Till the foul crimes done in my days of nature Are burnt and purged away i 5 12
O, horrible! most horrible! If thou hast nature in thee, bear it not . i 5 81
As oft as any passion under heaven That does afflict our natures . . ii 1 106
With this special observance, that you o'erstep not the modesty of nature iii 2 22
Any thing so overdone is from the purpose of playing, whose end, both at the first and now, was and is, to hold, as 'twere, the mirror up to nature . . . . iii 2 25
That I have thought some of nature's journeymen had made men . . iii 2 37
O heart, lose not thy nature; let not ever The soul of Nero enter this firm bosom . . . . iii 2 411
'Tis meet that some more audience than a mother, Since nature makes them partial, should o'erhear The speech, of vantage . . . iii 3 32

Nature. But 'tis not so above; There is no shuffling, there the action lies In his true nature . . . . *Hamlet* iii 3 62
For use almost can change the stamp of nature . . . . . iii 4 168
To my sick soul, as sin's true nature is, Each toy seems prologue to some great amiss . . . . iv 5 17
Nature is fine in love, and where 'tis fine, It sends some precious instance of itself After the thing it loves . . . . . . iv 5 161
These feats, So crimeful and so capital in nature . . . . . iv 7 7
Nature her custom holds, Let shame say what it will . . . . iv 7 188
'Tis dangerous when the baser nature comes Between the pass and fell incensed points Of mighty opposites . . . . v 2 60
To let this canker of our nature come In further evil . . . . v 2 69
To this effect, sir; after what flourish your nature will . . . . v 2 188
That might your nature, honour and exception Roughly awake . . v 2 242
I am satisfied in nature, Whose motive, in this case, should stir me most v 2 255
Which of you shall we say doth love us most? That we our largest bounty may extend Where nature doth with merit challenge . *Lear* i 1 54
Which nor our nature nor our place can bear . . . . . . i 1 174
A wretch whom nature is ashamed Almost to acknowledge hers . . i 1 215
Is it but this,—a tardiness in nature? . . . . i 1 238
Thou, nature, art my goddess; to thy law My services are bound . . i 2 1
Who, in the lusty stealth of nature, take More composition . . . i 2 11
Though the wisdom of nature can reason it thus and thus, yet nature finds itself scourged by the sequent effects . . . . . . i 2 113
The king falls from bias of nature; there's father against child . . i 2 121
Whose nature is so far from doing harms, That he suspects none . . i 2 196
Like an engine, wrench'd my frame of nature From the fix'd place . i 4 290
Hear, nature, hear; dear goddess, hear! Suspend thy purpose! . . i 4 297
I will forget my nature. So kind a father! Be my horses ready? . . i 5 35
Natures of such deep trust we shall much need . . . . . ii 1 117
You cowardly rascal, nature disclaims in thee: a tailor made thee . ii 2 59
Smooth every passion That in the natures of their lords rebel . . ii 2 82
And constrains the garb Quite from his nature . . . . . ii 2 104
We are not ourselves When nature, being oppress'd, commands the mind To suffer with the body . . . . ii 4 109
You are old; Nature in you stands on the very verge Of her confine . ii 4 149
Thy tender-hefted nature shall not give Thee o'er to harshness . . ii 4 174
Thou better know'st The offices of nature, bond of childhood . . ii 4 181
Allow not nature more than nature needs, Man's life's as cheap as beast's ii 4 269
Nature needs not what thou gorgeous wear'st, Which scarcely keeps thee warm . . . . ii 4 272
Crack nature's moulds, all germens spill at once, That make ingrateful man! . . . . iii 2 8
Man's nature cannot carry The affliction nor the fear . . . . iii 2 48
The tyranny of the open night's too rough For nature to endure . . iii 4 3
Nothing could have subdued nature To such a lowness but his unkind daughters . . . . iii 4 72
That nature thus gives way to loyalty, something fears me to think of . iii 5 4
Is there any cause in nature that makes these hard hearts? . . . iii 6 82
Oppressed nature sleeps: This rest might yet have balm'd thy broken sinews . . . . iii 6 104
Enkindle all the sparks of nature, To quit this horrid act . . . iii 7 86
That nature, which contemns it origin, Cannot be border'd certain in itself . . . . iv 2 32
Our foster-nurse of nature is repose, The which he lacks . . . iv 4 12
My snuff and loathed part of nature should Burn itself out . . . iv 6 39
Nature's above art in that respect . . . . iv 6 86
O ruin'd piece of nature! This great world Shall so wear out to nought iv 6 137
Thou hast one daughter, Who redeems nature from the general curse Which twain have brought her to . . . . iv 6 210
O you kind gods, Cure this great breach in his abused nature! . . iv 7 15
Some good I mean to do, Despite of mine own nature . . . . v 3 244
My particular grief Is of so flood-gate and o'erbearing nature . *Othello* i 3 56
For nature so preposterously to err, Being not deficient, blind . . i 3 62
In spite of nature, Of years, of country, credit, every thing . . i 3 96
That will confess perfection so could err Against all rules of nature . i 3 101
The blood and baseness of our natures would conduct us to most preposterous conclusions . . . . i 3 332
Of a free and open nature, That thinks men honest that but seem to be so i 3 405
As having sense of beauty, do omit Their mortal natures . . . ii 1 72
Base men being in love have then a nobility in their natures . . ii 1 218
Very nature will instruct her in it and compel her to some second choice ii 1 237
Howbeit that I endure him not, Is of a constant, loving, noble nature . ii 1 298
Perhaps he sees it not; or his good nature Prizes the virtue that appears in Cassio, And looks not on his evils . . . . ii 3 138
I confess it is my nature's plague To spy into abuses . . . . iii 3 146
I would not have your free and noble nature, Out of self-bounty, be abused . . . . iii 3 199
And yet, how nature erring from itself,— Ay, there's the point . . iii 3 227
Matches Of her own clime, complexion, and degree, Whereto we see in all things nature tends . . . . iii 3 231
Dangerous conceits are, in their natures, poisons . . . . . iii 3 326
In such cases Men's natures wrangle with inferior things . . . iii 4 144
I tremble at it. Nature would not invest herself in such shadowing passion without some instruction . . . . iv 1 40
Is this the nature Whom passion could not shake? . . . . . iv 1 276
Thou cunning'st pattern of excelling nature . . . . . . v 2 11
You shall close prisoner rest, Till that the nature of your fault be known v 2 336
In nature's infinite book of secrecy A little I can read *Ant. and Cleo.* i 2 9
The nature of bad news infects the teller . . . . . . i 2 99
It cannot be thus long, the sides of nature Will not sustain it . . i 3 16
O'er-picturing that Venus where we see The fancy outwork nature . ii 2 206
The air; which, but for vacancy, Had gone to gaze on Cleopatra too And made a gap in nature . . . . ii 2 223
Strange it is, That nature must compel us to lament Our most persisted deeds . . . . v 1 29
Nature wants stuff To vie strange forms with fancy . . . . . v 2 97
To imagine An Antony, were nature's piece 'gainst fancy . . . v 2 99
If thou and nature can so gently part, The stroke of death is as a lover's pinch, Which hurts, and is desired . . . . v 2 297
Upon importance of so slight and trivial a nature . . *Cymbeline* i 4 45
And will not trust one of her malice with A drug of such damn'd nature i 5 36
Hath nature given them eyes To see this vaulted arch? . . . . i 6 32
That play with all infirmities for gold Which rottenness can lend nature! i 6 125
The cutter Was as another nature, dumb; outwent her, Motion and breath left out . . . . ii 4 84
How hard it is to hide the sparks of nature! . . . . . . iii 3 79
Nature prompts them In simple and low things to prince it . . . iii 3 84
If sleep charge nature, To break it with a fearful dream of him . . iii 4 44
Yet famine, Ere clean it o'erthrow nature, makes it valiant . . . iii 6 20

Nature. O noble strain! O worthiness of nature! breed of greatness! *Cymbeline* iv 2 25
Nature hath meal and bran, contempt and grace . iv 2 27
Thou divine Nature, how thyself thou blazon'st In these two princely boys! . . . . iv 2 170
Nature doth abhor to make his bed With the defunct . . iv 2 357
Who was he That, otherwise than noble nature did, Hath alter'd that good picture? . . . . iv 2 364
Or could this carl, A very drudge of nature's, have subdued me? . . v 2 5
Whilst in the womb he stay'd Attending nature's law . . v 4 38
Great nature, like his ancestry, Moulded the stuff so fair . . v 4 48
I had rather thou shouldst live while nature will Than die ere I hear more v 5 151
Postures beyond brief nature . . . . v 5 165
All offices of nature should again Do their due functions . . v 5 257
It was wise nature's end in the donation, To be his evidence now . . v 5 367
At whose conception, till Lucina reign'd, Nature this dowry gave *Pericles* i 1 9
And I, as fits my nature, do obey you . . . . ii 1 4
Like beauty's child, whom nature gat For men to see, and seeing wonder at . . . . ii 2 6
There's nothing can be minister'd to nature That can recover him . iii 2 8
'Tis most strange, Nature should be so conversant with pain . . . iii 2 25
I can speak of the disturbances That nature works, and of her cures . iii 2 38
Death may usurp on nature many hours, And yet the fire of life kindle again . . . . iii 2 82
Nature awakes; a warmth Breathes out of her . . . iii 2 93
If to that my nature need a spur, The gods revenge it upon me and mine! iii 3 23
When nature framed this piece, she meant thee a good turn . . iv 2 150
With her neeld composes Nature's own shape, of bud, bird, branch v Gower 6

Naught. If I do not carve most curiously, say my knife's naught *M. Ado* v 1 157
Say 'paragon:' a paramour is, God bless us, a thing of naught *M. N. D.* iv 2 14
Be better employed, and be naught awhile *As Y. Like It* i 1 39
The mustard was naught: now I'll stand to it, the pancakes were naught i 2 68
A good life; but in respect that it is a shepherd's life, it is naught . iii 2 15
Though, in pure truth, it was corrupt and naught *Hen. V.* i 2 73
Naught to do with Mistress Shore! I tell thee, fellow, He that doth naught with her, excepting one, Were best he do it secretly, alone *Richard III.* i 1 98
All perjured, All forsworn, all naught, all dissemblers . *Rom. and Jul.* iii 2 87
Naught that I am, Not for their own demerits, but for mine . *Macbeth* iv 3 225
You are naught, you are naught: I'll mark the play *Hamlet* iii 2 157
Beloved Regan, Thy sister's naught . . . . . . *Lear* ii 4 136
Naught, naught, all naught! I can behold no longer . *Ant. and Cleo.* iii 10 1
All's but naught; Patience is sottish . . . . . . iv 15 78
Thy mother's dead.—I am sorry for't, my lord.—O, she was naught *Cymb.* v 5 271

Naughtily. You smile and mock me, as if I meant naughtily *Tr. and Cr.* iv 2 38

Naughty. It is a naughty house.—How dost thou know that? *M. for M.* ii 1 77
Thou naughty varlet!—Away! you are an ass, you are an ass *Much Ado* iv 2 74
This naughty man Shall face to face be brought to Margaret . . v 1 306
O, these naughty times Put bars between the owners and their rights! And so, though yours, not yours . . . *Mer. of Venice* iii 2 18
I do wonder, Thou naughty gaoler, that thou art so fond To come abroad with him at his request . . . . iii 3 9
How far that little candle throws his beams! So shines a good deed in a naughty world . . . . v 1 91
He's a good drum, my lord, but a naughty orator . *All's Well* v 3 254
Thou naughty varlet, tell me, where hast thou been this month? 1 *Hen. IV.* ii 4 474
A sort of naughty persons, lewdly bent . . . 2 *Hen. VI.* ii 1 167
Whiles here he lived Upon this naughty earth . . *Hen. VIII.* ii 1 138
Go hang yourself, you naughty mocking uncle! . *Troi. and Cres.* iv 2 26
Hast not slept to-night? would he not, a naughty man, let it sleep? . iv 2 34
What trade, thou knave? thou naughty knave, what trade? . *J. Cæsar* i 1 16
'Tis a naughty night to swim in . . . . . . *Lear* iii 4 116
Naughty lady, These hairs, which thou dost ravish from my chin, Will quicken, and accuse thee . . . . iii 7 37

Navarre shall be the wonder of the world . . . *L. L. Lost* i 1 12
The welkin's vicegerent and sole dominator of Navarre . . . i 1 222
The sole inheritor Of all perfections that a man may owe, Matchless Navarre . . . . ii 1 7
All-telling fame Doth noise abroad, Navarre hath made a vow . ii 1 22
Navarre had notice of your fair approach; And he and his competitors in oath Were all address'd to meet you . . . . . ii 1 81
Here comes Navarre.—Fair princess, welcome to the court of Navarre . ii 1 89
This civil war of wits were much better used On Navarre and his book-men . . . . ii 1 227
Navarre is infected.—With what?—With that which we lovers entitle affected . . . . ii 1 230

Nave. Would not this nave of a wheel have his ears cut off? . 2 *Hen. IV.* ii 4 278
He unseam'd him from the nave to the chaps . . . *Macbeth* i 2 22
Bowl the round nave down the hill of heaven . . . *Hamlet* ii 2 518

Navel. Even when the navel of the state was touch'd . *Coriolanus* iii 1 123

Navigation. Though the yesty waves Confound and swallow navigation up; Though bladed corn be lodged . . . . . *Macbeth* iv 1 54

Navy. Our navy is address'd, our power collected . . 2 *Hen. IV.* iv 4 5
Grapple your minds to sternage of this navy . . *Hen. V.* iii Prol. 18
On the western coast Rideth a puissant navy . . . *Richard III.* iv 4 434
The Breton navy is dispersed by tempest. . . . . . iv 4 523
Out of pity, taken A load would sink a navy . . . *Hen. VIII.* iii 2 383
And that is it Hath made me rig my navy; at whose burthen The anger'd ocean foams . . . . *Ant. and Cleo.* ii 6 20
Our great navy's rigg'd.—For Italy and Cæsar . . . . iii 5 20
'Twas a shame no less Than was his loss, to course your flying flags, And leave his navy gazing . . . . iii 13 12
Our force by land Hath nobly held; our sever'd navy too Have knit again . . . . iii 13 170
If to-morrow Our navy thrive, I have an absolute hope Our landmen will stand up . . . . iv 3 10

Nay. You shall find Many, nay, almost any . . . *Tempest* iii 3 34
Nay, now you are too flat . . . . *T. G. of Ver.* i 2 93
But she loves you?—Ay, and we are bethroth'd: nay, more . . ii 4 179
Nay then, no matter; stay with me awhile . . . . iii 1 58
'Tis not so.—Nay, but I know 'tis so: I saw him . *Meas. for Meas.* i 2 67
Are not you my husband?—No; I say nay to that . *Com. of Errors* v 1 371
By yea and nay, sir, then I swore in jest . . . *L. L. Lost* i 1 54
A critic, nay, a night-watch constable . . . . . iii 1 178
Full many a man doth mark, And dares not answer nay *M. N. Dream* iii 1 136
He did intreat me, past all saying nay, To come with him *Mer. of Venice* iii 2 232
My maiden's name Sear'd otherwise; nay, worse—if worse—extended With vilest torture let my life be ended . . . *All's Well* ii 1 176
If thou hadst said him nay, it had been sin . . . *K. John* i 1 275
In weightier things you'll say a beggar nay . . . *Richard III.* iii 1 119
Nay. Play the maid's part, still answer nay, and take it . *Richard III.* iii 7 51
If you plead as well for them As I can say nay to thee for myself . . iii 7 53
I'll frown and be perverse and say thee nay, So thou wilt woo *R. and J.* ii 2 96

Nayward. I'll be sworn you would believe my saying, Howe'er you lean to the nayward . . . . *W. Tale* ii 1 64

Nay-word. And in any case have a nay-word, that you may know one another's mind . . . . *Mer. Wives* ii 2 131
I have spoke with her and we have a nay-word how to know one another v 2 5
If I do not gull him into a nayword . . . . *T. Night* ii 3 146

Nazarite. To eat of the habitation which your prophet the Nazarite conjured the devil into . . . . *Mer. of Venice* i 3 35

Ne. Neighbour voctur nebour; neigh abbreviated ne . *L. L. Lost* v 1 26
All perishen of man, of pelf, Ne aught escapen but himself *Pericles* ii Gower 36

Neaf. Give me your neaf . . . . *M. N. Dream* iv 1 20
Pistol, I would be quiet.—Sweet knight, I kiss thy neif . . 2 *Hen. IV.* ii 4 200

Néanmoins, je reciterai une autre fois ma leçon ensemble . . *Hen. V.* iii 4 60
Néanmoins, pour les écus que vous l'avez promis, il est content de vous donner la liberté, le franchisement . . . . iv 4 54

Neapolitan. Some food we had and some fresh water that A noble Neapolitan, Gonzalo, . . . did give us . . . . *Tempest* i 2 161
O Stephano, two Neapolitans 'scaped!—Prithee, do not turn me about. ii 2 118
There is the Neapolitan prince.—Ay, that's a colt indeed *Mer. of Venice* i 2 43
But, he! why, he hath a horse better than the Neapolitan's . . . i 2 63
I will some other be, some Florentine, Some Neapolitan. . *T. of Shrew* i 1 210
O blood-bespotted Neapolitan, Outcast of Naples! . . . 2 *Hen. VI.* v 1 117

Near. Ebbing men, indeed, Most often do so near the bottom run *Tempest* ii 1 227
It will go near to remove his fit. . . . . ii 2 78
Is't near dinner-time?—I would it were . . . *T. G. of Ver.* i 2 67
I am to break with thee of some affairs That touch me near . . iii 1 60
Come near the house, I pray you . . . . . *Mer. Wives* i 4 140
It draws something near to the speech we had to such a purpose *M. for M.* i 2 79
She's very near her hour . . . . ii 2 16
Whose contents Shall witness to him I am near at home . . iv 3 99
And very near upon The duke is entering . . . . iv 6 14
Good sir, draw near to me, I'll speak to him . *Com. of Errors* v 1 12
You are very near my brother in his love . . . *Much Ado* ii 1 169
Beetles black, approach not near . . . . *M. N. Dream* ii 2 22
The burnish'd sun, To whom I am a neighbour and near bred *Mer. of Ven.* ii 1 3
This comes too near the praising of myself . . . . iii 4 22
Let not that doctor e'er come near my house . . . . v 1 223
Within these ten days if that thou be'st found So near our public court as twenty miles, Thou diest for it . . . *As Y. Like It* i 3 46
If ever,—as that ever may be near,—You meet in some fresh cheek the power of fancy . . . . iii 5 28
But till that time Come not thou near me . . . . . iii 5 32
Would have gone near To fall in love with him . . . . iii 5 125
If you do love Rosalind so near the heart as your gesture cries it out . v 2 68
Signior Baptista may remember me, Near twenty years ago *T. of Shrew* iv 4 4
I was very late more near her than I think she wished me . *All's Well* i 3 110
And I have heard herself come thus near . . . . *T. Night* ii 5 29
O, ho! do you come near me now? . . . . iii 4 71
He so near to Hermione hath done Hermione . . . *W. Tale* v 2 109
Comes it not something near?—Her natural posture! . . . v 3 23
Near or far off, well won is still well shot . . . *K. John* i 1 174
As near as I could sift him on that argument . . . *Richard II.* i 1 12
A prince by fortune of my birth, Near to the king in blood, and near in love . . . . iii 1 17
How far off lies your power?—Nor near nor farther off, my gracious lord, Than this weak arm . . . . iii 2 64
Better far off than near, be ne'er the near . . . . . v 1 88
I would humour his men with the imputation of being near their master 2 *Hen. IV.* v 1 81
When his holy state is touch'd so near . . . 1 *Hen. VI.* iii 1 58
I sought every country far and near . . . . . . v 4 3
You shall go near To call them both a pair of crafty knaves . 2 *Hen. VI.* i 2 102
Proud Frenchwoman: Could I come near your beauty with my nails . i 3 144
He is near you in descent, And should you fall, he is the next will mount . . . . iii 1 21
Tell me their words as near as thou canst guess them . 3 *Hen. VI.* iv 1 90
Emulation now, who shall be nearest, Will touch us all too near *Rich. III.* ii 3 26
You and he are near in love . . . . iii 4 14
Ely with Richmond troubles me more near Than Buckingham . . iv 3 49
It is not yet near day . . . . v 3 220
I will have none so near else . . . . . *Hen. VIII.* ii 2 135
In such a point of weight, so near mine honour,—More near my life . iii 1 71
A man of his place, and so near our favour . . . . . v 2 30
I aim'd so near, when I supposed you loved . . *Rom. and Jul.* i 1 211
She that makes dainty, She, I'll swear, hath corns; am I come near ye now? . . . . i 5 22
Vouchsafe me a word; it does concern you near.—Near! why then, another time I'll hear thee . . . . . . *T. of Athens* i 2 183
Pray you, walk near: I'll speak with you anon . . . . ii 2 132
I cannot, by the progress of the stars, Give guess how near to day *J. C.* ii 1 3
Be near me, that I may remember you.—Cæsar, I will: and so near will I be, That your best friends shall wish I had been further . . ii 2 124
Where we are, There's daggers in men's smiles: the near in blood, The nearer bloody . . . . *Macbeth* ii 3 146
Now near enough: your leavy screens throw down . . . . v 6 1
The terms of our estate may not endure Hazard so near us *Hamlet* iii 3 6
They are not near my conscience . . . . v 2 58
They met so near with their lips that their breaths embraced *Othello* ii 1 265
Touch me not so near . . . . ii 3 220
If it touch not you, it comes near nobody . . . . . iv 1 210
Be near at hand; I may miscarry in't.—Here, at thy hand: be bold . v 1 6
'Twould braid yourself too near for me to tell it . . . *Pericles* i 1 93
Murder's as near to lust as flame to smoke . . . . . i 1 138

Near guess. By the near guess of my memory . . *Mer. of Venice* i 3 55

Near-legged before and with a half-checked bit . . *T. of Shrew* iii 2 57

Near occasions. Which many my near occasions did urge me to put off *T. of Athens* ii 6 11

Nearer. Come a little nearer this ways . . . . *Mer. Wives* ii 2 46
A' must shoot nearer, or he'll ne'er hit the clout . . *L. L. Lost* iv 1 136
I confess your coming before me is nearer to his reverence *As Y. Like It* i 1 54
Thy conceit is nearer death than thy powers . . . . ii 6 8
Nearer in bloody thoughts, but not in blood . . . *Richard III.* i 1 92
I could have given my uncle's grace a flout, To touch his growth nearer than he touch'd mine . . . . ii 4 25
Why dost thou run so many mile about, When thou mayst tell thy tale a nearer way? . . . . iv 4 462
What nearer debt in all humanity Than wife is to the husband? *T. and C.* ii 2 175

Nearer. Often wished myself poorer, that I might come nearer to you *T. of Athens* i 2 105
The near in blood, The nearer bloody *Macbeth* ii 3 147
Your ladyship is nearer to heaven than when I saw you last . *Hamlet* ii 2 445
Who, being born your vassal, Am something nearer . . *Cymbeline* v 5 114
Nearest. To be by him cut off Nearest the merchant's heart *Mer. of Ven.* iv 1 233
'Nearest his heart:' those are the very words . . . . iv 1 254
I have congied with the duke, done my adieu with his nearest *All's Well* iv 3 101
I have trusted thee, Camillo, With all the nearest things to my heart, as well My chamber-councils *W. Tale* i 2 236
And my near'st of kin Cry fie upon my grave! . . . . iii 2 54
I love the king And through him what is nearest to him . . iv 4 533
My near'st and dearest enemy . . . . . . 1 *Hen. IV.* iii 2 123
The son of the king, nearest his father, Harry Prince of Wales 2 *Hen. IV.* ii 2 130
It is but eight years since This Percy was the man nearest my soul . iii 1 61
Emulation now, who shall be nearest, Will touch us all too near *Rich. III.* ii 3 25
What things in the world canst thou nearest compare to thy flatterers? —Women nearest; but men, men are the things themselves *T. of A.* iv 3 319
Sons, kinsmen, thanes, And you whose places are the nearest *Macbeth* i 4 36
Yet do I fear thy nature; It is too full o' the milk of human kindness To catch the nearest way . . . . i 5 19
Every minute of his being thrusts Against my near'st of life . . iii 1 118
Nearly. I would have some confidence with you that decerns you nearly *Much Ado* iii 5 4
And confer with you Of something nearly that concerns yourselves *M. N. Dream* i 1 126
I doubt some danger does approach you nearly . . . *Macbeth* iv 2 67
Not a little I have to say of what most nearly appertains to us both *Lear* i 1 287
As nearly as I may, I'll play the penitent to you . *Ant. and Cleo.* ii 2 91
Nearness. Such neighbour nearness to our sacred blood Should nothing privilege him . . . . *Richard II.* i 1 119
Our nearness to the king in love Is near the hate of those love not the king . . . . ii 2 127
Neat. A knight well-spoken, neat and fine . . . *T. G. of Ver.* i 2 10
Is all ready, and all things neat? . . . . *T. of Shrew* iv 1 117
We must be neat; not neat, but cleanly . . . *W. Tale* i 2 123
And yet the steer, the heifer and the calf Are all call'd neat . . i 2 125
Neat, and trimly dress'd, Fresh as a bridegroom . . 1 *Hen. IV.* i 3 33
Wherein neat and cleanly, but to carve a capon and eat it? . . ii 4 502
Bore him in the thickest troop As doth a lion in a herd of neat 3 *Hen. VI.* ii 1 14
Stand, rogue, stand; you neat slave, strike . . . . *Lear* ii 2 45
Sluttery to such neat excellence opposed Should make desire vomit emptiness, Not so allured to feed . . . . . *Cymbeline* i 6 44
How angel-like he sings!—But his neat cookery! . . . . iv 2 48
Neat-herd. Three carters, three shepherds, three neat-herds *W. Tale* iv 4 332
Would I were A neat-herd's daughter, and my Leonatus Our neighbour shepherd's son!—Thou foolish thing! . . . . *Cymbeline* i 1 149
Neatly. Nor believe he can have every thing in him by wearing his apparel neatly . . . . *All's Well* iv 3 168
Neat's foot. What say you to a neat's foot?—'Tis passing good *T. of Shrew* iv 3 17
Neat's-leather. He's a present for any emperor that ever trod on neat's-leather . . . . *Tempest* ii 2 73
When they are in great danger, I recover them. As proper men as ever trod upon neat's leather have gone upon my handiwork . *J. Cæsar* i 1 29
Neat's tongue. Silence is only commendable In a neat's tongue dried and a maid not vendible . . . . . . *Mer. of Venice* i 1 112
You starveling, you elf-skin, you dried neat's tongue! . 1 *Hen. IV.* ii 4 271
Neb. How she holds up the neb, the bill to him! . . *W. Tale* i 2 183
Nebuchadnezzar. I am no great Nebuchadnezzar, sir; I have not much skill in grass . . . . *All's Well* iv 5 21
Nec. Non eget Mauri jaculis, nec arcu . . . *T. Andron.* iv 2 21
Necessaries. Rich garments, linens, stuffs and necessaries . *Tempest* i 2 164
I must unto the road, to disembark Some necessaries . *T. G. of Ver.* ii 4 188
Since we have locks to safeguard necessaries . . . *Hen. V.* i 2 176
Such necessaries As are behoveful for our state . . *Rom. and Jul.* iv 3 7
My necessaries are embark'd: farewell . . . . *Hamlet* i 3 1
I must fetch his necessaries ashore . . . . . *Othello* ii 1 292
Necessarily. If he do fear God, a' must necessarily keep peace *Much Ado* ii 3 201
Necessary. Dispossessing all my other parts Of necessary fitness *Meas. for Meas.* ii 4 23
A harmless necessary cat . . . . . . *Mer. of Venice* iv 1 55
As horns are odious, they are necessary . . . *As Y. Like It* iii 3 52
A quick eye, and a nimble hand, is necessary for a cut-purse . *W. Tale* iv 4 686
Which though it be great pity, yet it is necessary . . . . iv 4 804
Provide us all things necessary and meet me to-morrow night 1 *Hen. IV.* i 2 216
Such things become the hatch and brood of time; And by the necessary form of this King Richard might create a perfect guess 2 *Hen. IV.* iii 1 87
It is necessary, look your grace, that he keep his vow . *Hen. V.* iv 7 146
It were but necessary you were waked . . . 2 *Hen. VI.* iii 2 261
We must not stint Our necessary actions, in the fear To cope malicious censurers; which ever, As ravenous fishes, do a vessel follow *Hen. VIII.* i 2 77
Omission to do what is necessary Seals a commission to a blank of danger; And danger, like an ague, subtly taints . *Troi. and Cres.* iii 3 230
You are well understood to be a perfecter giber for the table than a necessary bencher in the Capitol . . . . . *Coriolanus* ii 1 91
The fault's Bloody; 'tis necessary he should die . . *T. of Athens* iii 5 2
This shall make Our purpose necessary and not envious . *J. Cæsar* ii 1 178
Seeing that death, a necessary end, Will come when it will come . . ii 2 36
Some necessary question of the play be then to be considered *Hamlet* iii 2 47
Most necessary 'tis that we forget To pay ourselves what to ourselves is debt . . . . iii 2 202
His personal return was most required and necessary . . *Lear* iv 3 7
Sir, I will eat no meat, I'll not drink, sir; If idle talk will once be necessary, I'll not sleep neither . . . . *Ant. and Cleo.* v 2 50
Necessitied. I bade her, if her fortunes ever stood Necessitied to help, that by this token I would relieve her . . . . *All's Well* v 3 85
Necessity. To make a virtue of necessity . . . *T. G. of Ver.* iv 1 62
I have a sword and it shall bite upon my necessity . . *Mer. Wives* ii 1 136
Hiding mine honour in my necessity . . . . . . ii 2 25
What need the bridge much broader than the flood? The fairest grant is the necessity. Look, what will serve is fit . . . *Much Ado* i 1 319
She must lie here on mere necessity . . . . *L. L. Lost* i 1 149
Necessity will make us all forsworn Three thousand times . . i 1 150
This word shall speak for me; I am forsworn on 'mere necessity' . i 1 155
I'll rather dwell in my necessity . . . . *Mer. of Venice* i 3 157
The which my love and some necessity Now lays upon you . . . iii 4 34
Let me go with you; I'll do the service of a younger man In all your business and necessities . . . . *As Y. Like It* ii 3 55
I have eat none yet.—Nor shalt not, till necessity be served . . ii 7 89
Necessity. Must of necessity hold his virtue to you . . *All's Well* i 1 9
My necessity Makes me to ask you for my purse . . . *T. Night* iii 4 368
His dishonesty appears in leaving his friend here in necessity . . iii 4 422
Since their more mature dignities and royal necessities made separation of their society . . . . *W. Tale* i 1 28
So it should now, Were there necessity in your request . . . i 2 22
One of these two must be necessities, Which then will speak . . iv 4 38
Thou must think there's a necessity in't . . . . . iv 4 649
Teach thy necessity to reason thus; There is no virtue like necessity. Think not the king did banish thee . . . . *Richard II.* i 3 277
I am sworn brother, sweet, To grim Necessity . . . . v 1 21
I had no such intent, But that necessity so bow'd the state 2 *Hen. IV.* iii 1 73
Are these things then necessities? Then let us meet them like necessities: And that same word even now cries out on us . . . . . iii 1 92
Construe the times to their necessities . . . . . iv 1 104
Yet that is but a crush'd necessity . . . . . *Hen. V.* i 2 175
God comfort him in this necessity! . . . . 1 *Hen. VI.* iv 3 15
From deceit bred by necessity . . . . . . 3 *Hen. VI.* iii 3 68
Urge the necessity and state of times, And be not peevish-fond *Rich. III.* iv 4 416
These should be hours for necessities, Not for delights . . *Hen. VIII.* v 1 2
His legs are legs for necessity, not for flexure . . *Troi. and Cres.* ii 3 114
It must omit Real necessities, and give way the while To unstable slightness . . . . *Coriolanus* iii 1 147
Necessity Commands me name myself . . . . . . iv 5 62
Bid him suppose some good necessity Touches his friend *T. of Athens* ii 2 236
Showed what necessity belonged to't, and yet was denied . . . iii 2 14
Had his necessity made use of me, I would have put my wealth into donation . . . . iii 2 89
I am sick of this false world, and will love nought But even the mere necessities upon't . . . . iv 3 377
Welcome, good Messala. Now sit we close about this taper here, And call in question our necessities . . . . . . *J. Cæsar* iv 3 165
And nature must obey necessity . . . . iv 3 227
Wherein necessity, of matter beggar'd, Will nothing stick our person to arraign In ear and ear . . . . *Hamlet* iv 5 92
As if we were villains by necessity; fools by heavenly compulsion *Lear* i 2 132
That then necessity Will call discreet proceeding . . . . i 4 232
To be a comrade with the wolf and owl,—Necessity's sharp pinch! . ii 4 214
Where is this straw, my fellow? The art of our necessities is strange, That can make vile things precious . . . . iii 2 70
Yet, for necessity of present life, I must show out a flag and sign of love, Which is indeed but sign . . . . *Othello* i 1 156
I will show you such a necessity in his death that you shall think yourself bound to put it on him . . . . iv 2 247
The strong necessity of time commands Our services awhile *Ant. and Cleo.* i 3 42
You could not lack, I am certain on't, Very necessity of this thought . ii 2 58
Be you not troubled with the time, which drives O'er your content these strong necessities . . . . iii 6 83
Be quiet then as men should be, Till he hath pass'd necessity *Pericles* ii Gower 6
In like necessity—The which the gods protect thee from!—may defend thee . . . . ii 1 134
There's no further necessity of qualities can make her be refused . . iv 2 53
Neck. I'll manacle thy neck and feet together . . . *Tempest* i 2 461
His neck will come to your waist,—a cord, sir . *Meas. for Meas.* iii 2 42
The mole in my neck, the great wart on my left arm *Com. of Errors* iii 2 148
'Tis so; and that self chain about his neck . . . . . v 1 10
When he ran in here, These people saw the chain about his neck . v 1 258
An thou wilt needs thrust thy neck into a yoke . . . *Much Ado* i 1 203
About your neck, like an usurer's chain . . . . . ii 1 196
Break the neck of the wax, and every one give ear . . *L. L. Lost* iv 1 59
But, if thou marry, Hang me by the neck, if horns that year miscarry . iv 1 114
And half his face must be seen through the lion's neck . *M. N. Dream* iii 1 38
My conscience, hanging about the neck of my heart *Mer. of Venice* ii 2 14
I had as lief thou didst break his neck as his finger . *As Y. Like It* i 1 153
With bills on their necks, 'Be it known unto all men by these presents' i 2 131
And a chain, that you once wore, about his neck . . . . iii 2 192
Falls not the axe upon the humbled neck But first begs pardon . . iii 5 5
About his neck A green and gilded snake had wreathed itself . . iv 3 108
She hung about my neck; and kiss on kiss She vied so fast *T. of Shrew* ii 1 310
He took the bride about the neck And kiss'd her lips . . . iii 2 179
Thou mayst slide from my shoulder to my heel with no greater a run but my head and my neck . . . . iv 1 16
Item, two grey eyes, with lids to them; item, one neck, one chin *T. Night* i 5 267
Wilt thou set thy foot o' my neck?—Or o' mine either? . . . ii 5 206
He that wears her like her medal, hanging About his neck . . *W. Tale* i 2 308
The mantle of Queen Hermione's, her jewel about the neck of it . . v 2 37
She hangs about his neck: If she pertain to life let her speak too . v 3 112
With signs of war about his aged neck . . . . *Richard II.* ii 2 74
Have stoop'd my neck under your injuries . . . . . iii 1 19
Bareheaded, lower than his proud steed's neck, Bespake them thus . v 2 19
And break the neck Of that proud man that did usurp his back . . v 5 88
I'll give thee this neck.—No, I'll none of it: I pray thee, keep that for the hangman . . . . 1 *Hen. IV.* ii 1 68
And in the neck of that, task'd the whole state . . . . iv 3 92
Had my sweet Harry had but half their numbers, To-day might I, hanging on Hotspur's neck, Have talk'd of Monmouth's grave 2 *Hen. IV.* ii 3 44
Comment appelez-vous le col?—De neck, madame.—De nick . *Hen. V.* iii 4 35
As cold a night as 'tis, he could wish himself in Thames up to the neck iv 1 120
And over Suffolk's neck He threw his wounded arm and kiss'd his lips iv 6 24
Let his neck answer for it, if there is any martial law in the world . iv 8 45
Will hang upon my tongue like a new-married wife about her husband's neck . . . . v 2 190
These are his substance, sinews, arms and strength, With which he yoketh your rebellious necks . . . . 1 *Hen. VI.* ii 3 64
Direct mine arms I may embrace his neck . . . . . . ii 5 37
Till mischief and despair Drive you to break your necks or hang yourselves v 4 91
And smooth my way upon their headless necks . . . 2 *Hen. VI.* i 2 65
I took a costly jewel from my neck, A heart it was, bound in with diamonds . . . . iii 2 106
Hang him with his pen and ink-horn about his neck . . . iv 2 117
Will you needs be hanged with your pardons about your necks? . . iv 8 23
And humbly thus, with halters on their necks, Expect your highness' doom . . . . iv 9 11
Yield not thy neck To fortune's yoke . . . . 3 *Hen. VI.* iii 3 16
Now thy proud neck bears half my burthen'd yoke; From which even here I slip my weary neck, And leave the burthen of it all on thee *Richard III.* iv 4 111
Like a jewel, has hung twenty years About his neck . . *Hen. VIII.* ii 2 33
Rouse yourself; and the weak wanton Cupid Shall from your neck unloose his amorous fold . . . . *Troi. and Cres.* iii 3 223

Neck. If Hector break not his neck i' the combat, he'll break 't himself in vain-glory . . . . *Troi. and Cres.* iii 3 259
A plague upon Antenor! I would they had broke 's neck! . . . iv 2 79
But a plague break thy neck for frighting me! . . . . v 4 34
He'll beat Aufidius' head below his knee And tread upon his neck *Coriol.* i 3 50
O that you could turn your eyes toward the napes of your necks! . . ii 1 43
Seven hurts i' the body.—One i' the neck, and two i' the thigh . ii 1 167
The kitchen malkin pins Her richest lockram 'bout her reechy neck . ii 1 225
And that is there which looks With us to break his neck . . iii 3 30
He hath left undone That which shall break his neck or hazard mine . iv 7 25
When we banished him, we respected not them [the gods]; and, he returning to break our necks, they respect not us . . . . v 4 37
You must be hanged.—Hanged! by'r lady, then I have brought up a neck to a fair end . . . . *T. Andron.* iv 4 49
Make poor men's cattle break their necks . . . . . v 1 132
Ay, while you live, draw your neck out o' the collar . *Rom. and Jul.* i 1 5
Sometime she driveth o'er a soldier's neck, And then dreams he of cutting foreign throats . . . . i 4 82
Many so arrive at second masters, Upon their first lord's neck *T. of Athens* iv 3 513
Damned Casca, like a cur, behind Struck Cæsar on the neck *J. Cæsar* v 1 44
He cures, Hanging a golden stamp about their necks *Macbeth* iv 3 153
Paddling in your neck with his damn'd fingers *Hamlet* iii 4 185
To try conclusions, in the basket creep, And break your own neck down iii 4 196
Horses are tied by the heads, dogs and bears by the neck *Lear* ii 4 8
Let go thy hold when a great wheel runs down a hill, lest it break thy neck with following it . . . . ii 4 74
With his strong arms He fasten'd on my neck, and bellow'd out . v 3 212
And, by this hand, she falls me thus about my neck *Othello* iv 1 140
You have done well, That men must lay their murders on your neck . v 2 170
To proclaim it civilly, were like A halter'd neck which does the hangman thank For being yare about him . . *Ant. and Cleo.* iii 13 130
The first stone Drop in my neck: as it determines, so Dissolve my life! iii 13 161
O thou day o' the world, Chain mine arm'd neck! . . . iv 8 14
Bending down His corrigible neck, his face subdued To penetrative shame iv 14 74
Thus mine enemy fell, And thus I set my foot on's neck *Cymbeline* iii 3 92
Your neck, sir, is pen, book and counters; so the acquittance follows v 4 173
Upon his neck a mole, a sanguine star; It was a mark of wonder . v 5 364

Necklace. Bugle bracelet, necklace amber . . *W. Tale* iv 4 224

Nectar. If all their sand were pearl, The water nectar *T. G. of Ver.* ii 4 171
What will it be, When that the watery palate tastes indeed Love's thrice repured nectar? . . . . . *Troi. and Cres.* iii 2 23

Ned Poins and I will walk lower . . . . . 1 *Hen. IV.* ii 2 63
Ned, where are our disguises?—Here, hard by . . . ii 2 78
Ned, prithee, come out of that fat room, and lend me thy hand to laugh a little . . . . ii 4 1
I tell thee, Ned, thou hast lost much honour, that thou wert not with me ii 4 22
But, sweet Ned,—to sweeten which name of Ned, I give thee this pennyworth of sugar . . . . ii 4 23
But do you use me thus, Ned? must I marry your sister? . 2 *Hen. IV.* ii 2 150
Shall we steal upon them, Ned, at supper?—I am your shadow, my lord ii 2 173
No abuse, Ned, i' the world; honest Ned, none . . . ii 4 345
Why not Ned and I For once allow'd the skilful pilot's charge? 3 *Hen. VI.* v 4 19
O Ned, sweet Ned! speak to thy mother, boy! . . . v 5 51
Young Ned, for thee, thine uncles and myself Have in our armours watch'd the winter's night . . . . v 7 16
Where is thy brother Clarence? And little Ned Plantagenet? *Rich. III.* iv 4 146

Nedar. Made love to Nedar's daughter, Helena . *M. N. Dream* i 1 107
This, Lysander; this Demetrius is; This Helena, old Nedar's Helena . iv 1 135

Need. He needs will be Absolute Milan . . . *Tempest* i 2 108
It must needs be of subtle, tender and delicate temperance . . ii 1 41
Knife, gun, or need of any engine, Would I not have . . ii 1 161
His spirits hear me And yet I needs must curse . . . ii 2 4
By your patience, I needs must rest me . . . . iii 3 4
Please you taste of what is here?—Not I.—Faith, sir, you need not fear iii 3 43
She hath not writ to me?—What need she, when she hath made you write to yourself? . . . . . . *T. G. of Ver.* ii 1 158
For Valentine, I need not cite him to it: I will send him hither to you ii 4 85
To disembark Some necessaries that I needs must use . . ii 4 188
If I keep them, I needs must lose myself . . . . ii 6 20
You must needs have them with a codpiece . . . . ii 7 53
To take a note of what I stand in need of . . . . ii 7 84
What need a man care for a stock with a wench, when she can knit him a stock? . . . . iii 1 311
She can wash and scour.—A special virtue; for then she need not be washed and scoured . . . . iii 1 314
I have entertained thee, Partly that I have need of such a youth . iv 4 69
My valour?—O, sir, she makes no doubt of that.—She needs not . v 2 21
I'll ne'er put my finger in the fire, and need not . *Mer. Wives* i 4 91
And the boy never need to understand any thing . . . ii 2 132
And would needs speak with you presently . . . . iii 3 94
I am half afraid he will have need of washing . . . iii 3 193
Farewell, sir: she must needs go in; Her father will be angry . iii 4 96
But what needs either your 'mum' or her 'budget?' . . v 2 9
You took the wrong.—What need you tell me that? . . . v 5 202
Nor need you, on mine honour, have to do With any scruple *M. for M.* i 1 64
Though you change your place, you need not change your trade . i 2 111
Take order for the drabs and the knaves, you need not to fear the bawds ii 1 247
If you should need a pin, You could not with more tame a tongue desire it . . . . ii 2 45
Must he needs die?—Maiden, no remedy . . . . . ii 2 48
Where their untaught love Must needs appear offence . . ii 4 30
You will needs buy and sell men and women like beasts . . iii 2 2
The business he hath helmed must upon a warranted need give him a better proclamation . . . . iii 2 152
This needs must be a practice . . . . v 1 123
What needs all that, and a pair of stocks in the town? *Com. of Errors* iii 1 60
What need she be acquainted? What simple thief brags of his own attaint? . . . . iii 2 15
I see a man here needs not live by shifts . . . . iii 2 187
These ducats pawn I for my father here.—It shall not need . . v 1 390
An thou wilt needs thrust thy neck into a yoke *Much Ado* i 1 202
What need the bridge much broader than the flood? . . . i 1 318
Let that appear when there is no need of such vanity . . iii 3 22
For when rich villains have need of poor ones, poor ones may make what price they will . . . . iii 3 121
Good Lord Boyet, my beauty, though but mean, Needs not the painted flourish of your praise . . . . . . *L. L. Lost* ii 1 14
Dost thou tear it?—A toy, my liege, a toy: your grace needs not fear it iv 3 201
Fie, painted rhetoric! O, she needs it not . . . . iv 3 239
Dark needs no candle now, for dark is light . . . . iv 3 269

Need. We need more light to find your meaning out . . *L. L. Lost* v 2 21
Well said, old mocker: I must needs be friends with thee . . v 2 552
You must needs play Pyramus.—Well, I will undertake it *M. N. Dream* i 2 90
Then will two at once woo one; That must needs be sport alone . iii 2 119
No epilogue, I pray you; for your play needs no excuse . . v 1 363
When the players are all dead, there need none to be blamed . v 1 364
You need not fear, lady, the having any of these lords . *Mer. of Venice* i 2 109
Well then, it now appears you need my help . . . . i 3 115
I must needs tell thee all . . . . ii 4 30
Whose souls do bear an equal yoke of love, There must be needs a like proportion Of lineaments, of manners and of spirit . . . iii 4 14
Antonio, Being the bosom lover of my lord, Must needs be like my lord . . . . iii 4 18
Nay, you need not fear us, Lorenzo: Launcelot and I are out . iii 5 33
This strict court of Venice Must needs give sentence 'gainst the merchant iv 1 205
If it be true that good wine needs no bush, 'tis true that a good play needs no epilogue . . . . . . *As Y. Like It* Epil. 4
I' faith, sir, you shall never need to fear . . . *T. of Shrew* i 1 61
But they may chance to need thee at home . . . . . v 1 4
Keep your hundred pounds to yourself: he shall need none, so long as I live . . . . v 1 25
Entreat her! Nay, then she must needs come . . . . v 2 88
Why under Mars?—The wars have so kept you under that you must needs be born under Mars . . . . . . *All's Well* i 1 210
Wilt thou needs be a beggar?—I do beg your good will in this case . i 3 22
I am driven on by the flesh; and he must needs go that the devil drives i 3 31
Thou this to hazard needs must intimate Skill infinite . . ii 1 186
Thy casement I need not open, for I look through thee . . ii 3 225
Strengthen'd with what apology you think May make it probable need ii 4 52
My appointments have in them a need Greater than shows itself . ii 5 72
I hope I need not to advise you further . . . . . iii 5 27
You shall not need to fear me.—I hope so . . . . iii 5 31
Between these main parcels of dispatch effected many nicer needs . iv 3 105
I need not to ask you if gold will corrupt him to revolt . . iv 3 309
You need but plead your honourable privilege . . . . iv 5 95
Nay, you need not to stop your nose, sir; I spake but by a metaphor v 2 11
He that is well hanged in this world needs to fear no colours *T. Night* i 5 6
Farewell, dear heart, since I must needs be gone . . . ii 3 110
Thou hadst need send for more money . . . . . ii 3 199
And he is yours, and his must needs be yours . . . . iii 1 112
Dear venom, give thy reason.—You must needs yield your reason, Sir . iii 2 4
I'll be with you again, In a trice, Like to the old Vice, Your need to sustain . . . . iv 2 135
If it be so, We need no grave to bury honesty . . *W. Tale* ii 1 155
What need we Commune with you of this? . . . . . ii 1 161
Inform yourselves We need no more of your advice . . . ii 1 168
I am satisfied and need no more Than what I know . . . ii 1 189
I know not what I shall incur to pass it, Having no warrant.—You need not fear it . . . . ii 2 58
Jove send her A better guiding spirit! What needs these hands? . ii 3 127
The need I have of thee thine own goodness hath made . . iv 2 13
Alack, poor soul! thou hast need of more rags to lay on thee . . iv 3 57
He shall not need to grieve At knowing of thy choice . . iv 4 426
I needs must think it honesty . . . . iv 4 498
Most opportune to our need I have A vessel rides fast by . . iv 4 511
I would your spirit were easier for advice, Or stronger for your need . iv 4 517
'Tis not a visitation framed, but forced By need and accident . v 1 92
In the extremity of the one, it must needs be . . . . v 2 21
Needs must you lay your heart at his dispose . . *K. John* i 1 263
Speaks not from her faith, But from her need.—O, if thou grant my need, Which only lives but by the death of faith, That need must needs infer this principle, That faith would live again by death of need . . . . iii 1 211
O then, tread down my need, and faith mounts up; Keep my need up, and faith is trodden down! . . . . iii 1 216
I will denounce a curse upon his head.—Thou shalt not need . . iii 1 320
That John may stand, then Arthur needs must fall . . . iii 4 139
What need you be so boisterous-rough? I will not struggle . . iv 1 76
Your vile intent must needs seem horrible . . . . . iv 1 96
A brace of tongues Must needs want pleading for a pair of eyes . iv 1 99
His passion is so ripe, it needs must break . . . . iv 2 79
He perhaps shall need Some messenger betwixt me and the peers . iv 2 178
Whom he hath used rather for sport than need . . . . v 2 175
I shall not need transport my words by you . . *Richard II.* ii 3 81
I cannot mend it, I must needs confess, Because my power is weak . ii 3 153
Needs must I like it well: I weep for joy . . . . iii 2 4
I live with bread like you, feel want, Taste grief, need friends . iii 2 176
What I have I need not to repeat; And what I want it boots not to complain . . . . iii 4 17
Being so great, I have no need to beg.—Yet ask.—And shall I have? . iv 1 309
They love not poison that do poison need, Nor do I thee . . v 6 38
When we need Your use and counsel, we shall send for you 1 *Hen. IV.* i 3 20
To prove that true Needs no more but one tongue . . . i 3 96
Not ready yet, Nor shall we need his help these fourteen days . iii 1 88
You must needs learn, lord, to amend this fault . . . iii 1 180
Be near at hand, For we shall presently have need of you . . iii 2 3
Many tales devised, Which oft the ear of greatness needs must hear . iii 2 24
I was as virtuously given as a gentleman need to be . . . iii 3 17
You are so fat, Sir John, that you must needs be out of all compass . iii 3 25
My good lord, you need not fear; There is Douglas and Lord Mortimer iv 4 21
What need I be so forward with him that calls not on me? . . v 1 129
I need no more weight than mine own bowels . . . . . v 3 35
Lead me, my lord? I do not need your help . . . . . v 4 10
But what need I thus My well-known body to anatomize? 2 *Hen. IV.* Ind. 20
Make friends with speed: Never so few, and never yet more need . i 1 215
Doth not the king lack subjects? do not the rebels need soldiers? . i 2 87
If ye will needs say I am an old man, you should give me rest . i 2 242
That he should draw his several strengths together And come against us in full puissance, Need not be dreaded . . . . . . i 3 78
Marry, the immortal part needs a physician . . . . . ii 2 112
Therefore captains had need look to't . . . . . . ii 4 163
You need not to have pricked me; there are other men fitter to go out than I . . . . iii 2 125
There is no need of any such redress; Or if there were, it not belongs to you . . . . iv 1 97
What thing, in honour, had my father lost, That need to be revived and breathed in me? . . . . iv 1 114
That thou wilt needs invest thee with my honours Before thy hour be ripe . . . . iv 5 96
Now, sir, a new link to the bucket must needs be had . . . v 1 24

Need. Therefore we must needs admit the means How things are perfected . . . *Hen. V.* i 1 68
I hoped there was no need to trouble himself with any such thoughts yet ii 3 22
He cared not who knew it.—He needs not; it is no hidden virtue in him iii 7 118
Certainly thou art so near the gulf, Thou needs must be englutted iv 3 83
I need not to be ashamed of your majesty, praised be God iv 7 118
And, captain, you must needs be friends with him iv 8 65
But thy speaking of my tongue, and I thine, most truly-falsely, must needs be granted to be much at one v 2 204
And thou must therefore needs prove a good soldier-breeder . v 2 219
Now he is gone, my lord, you need not fear . 1 *Hen. VI.* v 2 17
I shall be rescued by the French; And then I need not crave his courtesy v 3 105
They say 'A crafty knave does need no broker' . 2 *Hen. VI.* i 2 100
If he be old enough, what needs your grace To be protector? . i 3 121
Her fume needs no spurs, She'll gallop far enough to her destruction . i 3 153
Alas, sir, we did it for pure need ii 1 157
They have been up these two days.—They have the more need to sleep now iv 2 3
Turn it, and set a new nap upon it.—So he had need, for 'tis threadbare iv 2 8
Valiant I am.—A' must needs; for beggary is valiant iv 2 58
He need not fear the sword; for his coat is of proof iv 2 64
Will you needs be hanged with your pardons about your necks? . iv 8 22
A subtle traitor needs no sophister v 1 191
The army of the queen mean to besiege us.—She shall not need 3 *Hen. VI.* i 2 65
What, with five thousand men?—Ay, with five hundred, father, for a need i 2 67
It needs not, nor it boots thee not, proud queen i 4 125
In thy need such comfort come to thee As now I reap at thy too cruel hand! i 4 165
And spite of spite needs must I rest awhile ii 3 5
Art thou here too? Nay, then I see that Edward needs must down iv 3 42
What fates impose, that men must needs abide iv 3 58
Lest in our need he might infect another And make him of like spirit v 4 46
If any such be here—as God forbid!—Let him depart before we need his help v 4 49
I need not add more fuel to your fire v 4 70
God grant we never may have need of you!—Meantime, God grants that we have need of you *Richard III.* i 3 76
He needs no indirect nor lawless course To cut off those that have offended i 4 224
When I have most need to employ a friend ii 1 36
My lord protector needs will have it so iii 1 141
I fear no uncles dead.—Nor none that live, I hope.—An if they live, I hope I need not fear iii 1 148
They do need the priest; Your honour hath no shriving work in hand iii 2 115
Nay, for a need, thus far come near my person iii 5 85
There needs no such apology iii 7 104
There's no need of me, And much I need to help you, if need were iii 7 165
He hath no friends but who are friends for fear, Which in his greatest need will shrink from him v 2 21
I had my trial, And, must needs say, a noble one *Hen. VIII.* ii 1 119
We had need pray, And heartily, for our deliverance ii 2 45
Your grace must needs deserve all strangers' loves, You are so noble ii 2 102
He was a fool; For he would needs be virtuous ii 2 133
What's the need? It hath already publicly been read ii 4 2
You are call'd back.—What need you note it? pray you, keep your way ii 4 128
Must I needs forgo So good, so noble and so true a master? iii 2 422
Is there no other way of mercy, But I must needs to the Tower? v 3 93
All that stand about him are under the line, they need no other penance v 4 45
He that will have a cake out of the wheat must needs tarry the grinding.—Have I not tarried? *Troi. and Cres.* i 1 16
Helen must needs be fair, When with your blood you daily paint her thus i 1 93
Hector shall not have his wit this year.—He shall not need it i 2 93
She has a marvellous white hand, I must needs confess,— Without the rack i 2 151
If you'll avouch 'twas wisdom Paris went—As you must needs, for you all cried 'Go, go,'—If you'll confess he brought home noble prize —As you must needs, for you all clapp'd your hands ii 2 85
You depend upon a noble gentleman; I must needs praise him iii 1 7
Come, come, what need you blush? shame's a baby iii 2 42
Let us cast away nothing, for we may live to have need of such a verse iv 4 23
What need these tricks?—Prithee, be silent, boy v 1 14
I need not be barren of accusations; he hath faults *Coriolanus* i 1 45
Keep your great pretences veil'd till when They needs must show themselves i 2 21
He did solicit you in free contempt When he did need your loves ii 3 209
Peace! We need not put new matter to his charge iii 3 76
Ay, and it [peace] makes men hate one another.—Reason; because they then less need one another iv 5 248
We hear not of him, neither need we fear him; His remedies are tame iv 6 1
The emperor needs her not, Nor her, nor thee *T. Andron.* i 1 299
That, whenever you have need, You may be armed and appointed well iv 2 15
I have given her physic, And you must needs bestow her funeral iv 2 163
So that perforce you must needs stay a time iv 3 41
'Twas no need, I trow, To bid me trudge *Rom. and Jul.* i 3 33
Claps me his sword upon the table and says 'God send me no need of thee!' and by the operation of the second cup draws it on the drawer, when indeed there is no need iii 1 10
Utter your gravity o'er a gossip's bowl; For here we need it not iii 5 176
Or, if he do, it needs must be by stealth iii 5 217
I have need of many orisons To move the heavens to smile upon my state iv 3 3
What, are you busy, ho? need you my help?—No, madam iv 3 6
Get thee to bed, and rest; for thou hast need iv 3 13
My dismal scene I needs must act alone iv 3 19
Marry, and amen, how sound is she asleep! I must needs wake her iv 5 9
An if a man did need a poison now, Whose sale is present death in Mantua, Here lives a caitiff wretch would sell it him v 1 50
O, this same thought did but forerun my need v 1 53
Famine is in thy cheeks, Need and oppression starveth in thine eyes v 1 70
I am not of that feather to shake off My friend when he must need me. I do know him A gentleman that well deserves a help *T. of Athens* i 1 101
Give me your hand; We must needs dine together i 1 164
You must needs dine with me: go not you hence Till I have thank'd you i 1 253
But where there is true friendship, there needs none [ceremony] i 2 18
To trust . . . a keeper with my freedom; Or my friends, if I should need 'em i 2 70
What need we have any friends, if we should ne'er have need of 'em? i 2 99
What need these feasts, pomps and vain-glories? i 2 248
Immediate are my needs, and my relief Must not be toss'd and turn'd to me in words, But find supply immediate ii 1 25
I must needs confess, I have received some small kindnesses from him. iii 2 21
Must he needs trouble me in't,—hum!—'bove all others? iii 3 1
I need not tell him that; he knows you are too diligent iii 4 39

Need. He hath conjured me beyond them, and I must needs appear *T. of Athens* iii 6 13
Lend to each man enough, that one need not lend to another iii 6 83
Must thou needs stand for a villain in thine own work? v 1 39
My honest-natured friends, I must needs say you have a little fault v 1 90
The plague That needs must light on this ingratitude *J. Cæsar* i 1 60
His worth and our great need of him You have right well conceited i 3 161
What need we any spur but our own cause, To prick us to redress? ii 1 123
To think that or our cause or our performance Did need an oath ii 1 136
Kneel not, gentle Portia.—I should not need, if you were gentle Brutus ii 1 279
I have the same dagger for myself, when it shall please my country to need my death iii 2 51
I had most need of blessing, and 'Amen' Stuck in my throat *Macbeth* ii 2 32
He needs not our mistrust, since he delivers Our offices iii 3 2
What need I fear of thee? But yet I'll make assurance double sure iv 1 82
What need we fear who knows it, when none can call our power to account? v 1 42
More needs she the divine than the physician v 1 82
Pour we in our country's purge Each drop of us.—Or so much as it needs v 2 29
There needs no ghost, my lord, come from the grave To tell us this *Ham.* i 5 125
So grace and mercy at your most need help you i 5 180
Moreover that we much did long to see you, The need we have to use you did provoke Our hasty sending ii 2 3
You could, for a need, study a speech of some dozen or sixteen lines? ii 2 566
If thou wilt needs marry, marry a fool iii 1 143
How now, Ophelia! You need not tell us what Lord Hamlet said; We heard it all iii 1 187
Such love must needs be treason in my breast iii 2 188
Doth love on fortune tend; For who not needs shall never lack a friend iii 2 217
When he needs what you have gleaned, it is but squeezing you iv 2 21
Her mood will needs be pitied iv 5 3
And you must needs have heard, how I am punish'd With sore distraction v 2 240
The quality of nothing hath not such need to hide itself *Lear* i 2 34
If thou follow him, thou must needs wear my coxcomb i 4 116
Thou wast a pretty fellow when thou hadst no need to care for her frowning i 4 211
Natures of such deep trust we shall much need ii 1 117
But yet thou art my flesh, my blood, my daughter; Or rather a disease that's in my flesh, Which I must needs call mine ii 4 226
What, fifty followers? Is it not well? What should you need of more? ii 4 241
What need you five and twenty, ten, or five . . . ?—What need one? ii 4 264
O, reason not the need: our basest beggars Are in the poorest thing superfluous: Allow not nature more than nature needs, Man's life's as cheap as beast's ii 4 267
Nature needs not what thou gorgeous wear'st, Which scarcely keeps thee warm ii 4 272
But, for true need,—You heavens, give me that patience, patience I need! ii 4 273
Hath put himself from rest, And must needs taste his folly ii 4 294
From that place I shall no leading need iv 1 81
I must needs after him, madam, with my letter iv 5 15
Thou must needs be sure My spirit and my place have in them power *Othello* i 1 102
If thou wilt needs damn thyself, do it a more delicate way than drowning i 3 359
He protests he loves you And needs no other suitor but his likings iii 1 51
I cannot give it vital growth again, It must needs wither v 2 15
She said so: I must needs report the truth v 2 128
What needs this iteration, woman? v 2 150
Then must thou needs find out new heaven, new earth *Ant. and Cleo.* i 1 17
Remember that the present need Speaks to atone you ii 2 101
What needs more words? Good night ii 7 132
Your presence needs must puzzle Antony iii 7 11
I have myself resolved upon a course Which has no need of you; be gone iii 11 10
So, haply, are they friends to Antony.—He needs as many, sir, as Cæsar has; Or needs not us iii 13 49
When such a spacious mirror's set before him, He needs must see himself v 1 35
Who is so full of grace, that it flows over On all that need v 2 25
We shall have need To employ you towards this Roman *Cymbeline* ii 3 67
You'll give me leave to spare, when you shall find You need it not ii 4 66
What shall I need to draw my sword? the paper Hath cut her throat already iii 4 34
To show less sovereignty than they, must needs Appear unkinglike iii 5 6
To lapse in fulness Is sorer than to lie for need iii 6 13
Who needs must know of her departure and Dost seem so ignorant iv 3 10
Our cowards, Like fragments in hard voyages, became The life o' the need v 3 45
You shall not need, my fellow peers of Tyre, Further to question me *Per.* i 3 11
But bring they what they will and what they can, What need we fear? i 4 77
But tidings to the contrary Are brought your eyes; what need speak I? ii Gower 16
He had need mean better than his outward show Can any way speak ii 2 48
I must needs be gone; My twelve months are expired iii 3 1
But if to that my nature need a spur, The gods revenge it upon me and mine! iii 3 23
And give you gold for such provision As our intents will need v 1 259
So had you need *As Y. Like It* ii 7; *T. of Shrew* i 1; 1 *Hen. VI.* i 1
'Tis more than need *L. L. Lost* iv 3 289; *K. John* i 1 179.

Needed. I, who never knew how to entreat, Nor never needed that I should entreat *T. of Shrew* iv 3 8
Give me my armour.—'Tis not needed yet *Macbeth* v 3 33
What needed, then, that terrible dispatch of it into your pocket? *Lear* i 2 32

Needer. And lose advantage, which doth ever cool I' the absence of the needer *Coriolanus* iv 1 44

Needest. Nor need'st thou much importune me to that *T. G. of Ver.* i 3 17
When thou needest him, there thou shalt find him 1 *Hen. IV.* ii 2 74
Therefore stay yet; thou need'st not to be gone *Rom. and Jul.* iii 5 16
If't be summer news, Smile to't before; if winterly, thou need'st But keep that countenance still *Cymbeline* iii 4 13

Needful. Leaves unquestion'd Matters of needful value *Meas. for Meas.* i 1 56
Most biting laws, The needful bits and curbs to headstrong weeds i 3 20
Lord Angelo is severe.—It is but needful ii 1 296
Let her have needful, but not lavish, means ii 2 24
I would do more than that, if more were needful ii 3 9
It is needful that you frame the season for your own harvest *Much Ado* i 3 26
Therefore to's seemeth it a needful course *L. L. Lost* i 1 25
They shall be no more than needful there *All's Well* iv 3 93
'Fore whose throne 'tis needful, Ere I can perfect mine intents, to kneel iv 4 3
So it should now, Were there necessity in your request, although 'Twere needful I denied it *W. Tale* i 2 23
No noise, my lord; but needful conference About some gossips ii 3 40
O, let us pay the time but needful woe *K. John* v 7 110

Needful. I hope no less, yet needful 'tis to fear . . . 1 *Hen. IV.* iv 4 34
'Tis needful that the most immodest word Be look'd upon 2 *Hen. IV.* iv 4 70
Thou princely leader of our English strength, Never so needful 1 *Hen. VI.* iv 3 18
He was lately sent From your kind aunt, Duchess of Burgundy, With aid of soldiers to this needful war . . . 3 *Hen. VI.* ii 1 147
And haste is needful in this desperate case . . . iv 1 129
It is more than needful Forthwith that Edward be pronounced a traitor iv 6 53
And give him from me this most needful scroll . . *Richard III.* v 3 41
'Tis a needful fitness That we adjourn this court . . *Hen. VIII.* ii 4 231
As we walk, To our own selves bend we our needful talk *Troi. and Cres.* iv 4 141
Sort such needful ornaments As you think fit to furnish me *R. and J.* iv 2 34
This, and what needful else That calls upon us, by the grace of Grace, We will perform . . . *Macbeth* v 8 71
We shall acquaint him with it, As needful in our loves *Hamlet* i 1 173
A very riband in the cap of youth, Yet needful too . . . iv 7 79
Bestow Your needful counsel to our business . . *Lear* ii 1 129
I am now from home, and out of that provision Which shall be needful for your entertainment . . . ii 4 209
With what else needful your good grace shall think . . *Othello* i 3 287
Her son gone, So needful for this present . . *Cymbeline* iv 3 8
No needful thing omitted . . . *Pericles* v 3 68
Needle. Have with our needles created both one flower *M. N. Dream* iii 2 204
Go ply thy needle; meddle not with her . . *T. of Shrew* ii 1 25
How did you desire it should be made?—Marry, sir, with needle and thread . . . iv 3 121
Their thimbles into armed gauntlets change, Their needles to lances *K. John* v 2 157
It is as hard to come as for a camel To thread the postern of a small needle's eye . . . *Richard II.* v 5 17
Gentlewomen that live honestly by the prick of their needles *Hen. V.* ii 1 37
Has not so much wit . . . As will stop the eye of Helen's needle *T. and C.* ii 1 87
So delicate with her needle: an admirable musician . *Othello* iv 1 199
I would they were in Afric both together; Myself by with a needle, that I might prick The goer-back . . . *Cymbeline* i 1 168
Till the diminution Of space had pointed him sharp as my needle . i 3 19
Or when she would with sharp needle wound The cambric, which she made more sound By hurting it . . . . *Pericles* iv Gower 23
Needless. In brief, to set the needless process by . *Meas. for Meas.* v 1 92
How needless was it then to ask the question! . *L. L. Lost* ii 1 117
Weeping into the needless stream . . *As Y. Like It* ii 1 46
And do sigh At each his needless heavings . . *W. Tale* ii 3 35
O, bravely came we off, When with a volley of our needless shot, After such bloody toil, we bid good night! . . *K. John* v 5 5
Pray God, I say, I prove a needless coward! . *Richard III.* iii 2 90
Matter needless, of importless burden . . *Troi. and Cres.* i 3 71
To beg of Hob and Dick, that do appear, Their needless vouchers *Coriol.* ii 3 124
They [friends] were the most needless creatures living, should we ne'er have use for 'em . . . *T. of Athens* i 2 100
Needless diffidences, banishment of friends, dissipation of cohorts *Lear* i 2 161
To taint his nobler heart and brain With needless jealousy . *Cymbeline* v 4 66
Needlework. Valance of Venice gold in needlework . *T. of Shrew* ii 1 356
Needly. If sour woe delights in fellowship And needly will be rank'd with other griefs . . . *Rom. and Jul.* iii 2 117
Needy. A needy, hollow-eyed, sharp-looking wretch . *Com. of Errors* v 1 240
Because I would not tax the needy commons . 2 *Hen. VI.* iii 1 116
And joy comes well in such a needy time . *Rom. and Jul.* iii 5 106
And in his needy shop a tortoise hung, An alligator stuff'd . . v 1 42
And this same needy man must sell it me . . . v 1 54
Our ships . . . Are stored with corn to make your needy bread *Pericles* i 4 95
Neeld. With her neeld composes Nature's own shape, of bud, bird, branch, or berry . . . . v Gower 5
Neeze and swear A merrier hour was never wasted there *M. N. Dream* ii 1 56
Nefas. Sit fas aut nefas, till I find the stream To cool this heat, a charm to calm these fits . . *T. Andron.* ii 1 133
Negation. Why, my negation hath no taste of madness *Troi. and Cres.* v 2 127
Negative. If your four negatives make your two affirmatives . *T. Night* v 1 24
If thou wilt confess, Or else be impudently negative . *W. Tale* i 2 274
Neglect. Made me neglect my studies, lose my time . *T. G. of Ver.* i 1 67
She did neglect her looking-glass And threw her sun-expelling mask away iv 4 157
Which, out of my neglect, was never done . . . v 4 90
I conjure thee . . . That thou neglect me not, with that opinion That I am touch'd with madness! . . *Meas. for Meas.* v 1 50
It is a plague That Cupid will impose for my neglect Of his almighty dreadful little might . . . *L. L. Lost* iii 1 204
Use me but as your spaniel, spurn me, strike me . *M. N. Dream* ii 1 206
Lose and neglect the creeping hours of time . *As Y. Like It* ii 7 112
Hath put on a religious life And thrown into neglect the pompous court v 4 188
Wherefore, gentle maiden, Do you neglect them? . . *W. Tale* iv 4 86
Awhile we must neglect Our holy purpose to Jerusalem . 1 *Hen. IV.* i 1 101
He loves thee, and thou dost neglect him . . 2 *Hen. IV.* iv 4 21
What infinite heart's-ease Must kings neglect, that private men enjoy! *Hen. V.* iv 1 254
If we haply 'scape, As well we may, if not through your neglect 2 *Hen. VI.* v 2 80
I hope, My absence doth neglect no great designs . *Richard III.* iii 4 25
Earnest in the service of my God, Neglect the visitation of my friends iii 7 107
Good Cromwell, Neglect him not; make use now, and provide For thine own future safety . . . *Hen. VIII.* iii 2 420
And on your heads Clap round fines for neglect . . . v 4 84
Nor construe any further my neglect . . *J. Cæsar* i 2 45
I stand in pause where I shall first begin, And both neglect . *Hamlet* iii 3 43
'Tis strange that from their cold'st neglect My love should kindle to inflamed respect . . . *Lear* i 1 257
I have perceived a most faint neglect of late . . . i 4 73
Infirmity doth still neglect all office Whereto our health is bound . ii 4 107
Neglected. Puts the drowsy and neglected act Freshly on me *M. for M.* i 2 174
For your fair sakes have we neglected time . *L. L. Lost* v 2 765
A beard neglected, which you have not . . *As Y. Like It* iii 2 395
But to my own disgrace Neglected my sworn duty in that case *Rich. II.* i 1 134
The means that heaven yields must be embraced, And not neglected . iii 2 30
Left by the fatal and neglected English Upon our fields . *Hen. V.* ii 4 13
If once it be neglected, ten to one We shall not find like opportunity.—To say the truth, it is your policy . . 1 *Hen. VI.* v 4 157
Which of the peers Have uncontemn'd gone by him, or at least Strangely neglected? . . . *Hen. VIII.* iii 2 11
The specialty of rule hath been neglected . *Troi. and Cres.* i 3 78
With speed to England, For the demand of our neglected tribute *Hamlet* iii 1 178
The origin and commencement of his grief Sprung from neglected love . iii 1 186
These bloody accidents must excuse my manners, That so neglected you *Othello* v 1 95
The which you both denied.—Neglected, rather . . *Ant. and Cleo.* ii 2 89
Neglected. As jewels lose their glory if neglected, So princes their renowns if not respected . . . . *Pericles* ii 2 12
Neglectest. If thou neglect'st or dost unwillingly What I command, I'll rack thee with old cramps . . . . *Tempest* i 2 368
Neglecting. Neglecting worldly ends, all dedicated To closeness . i 2 89
The neglecting it May do much danger . . *Rom. and Jul.* v 2 19
Neglecting an attempt of ease and gain . . . *Othello* i 3 29
Neglectingly. Answer'd neglectingly I know not what . 1 *Hen. IV.* i 3 52
Neglection. Sleeping neglection doth betray to loss The conquest of our scarce cold conqueror . . . 1 *Hen. VI.* iv 3 49
And this neglection of degree it is That by a pace goes backward, with a purpose It hath to climb . . *Troi. and Cres.* i 3 127
If neglection Should therein make me vile . . *Pericles* iii 3 20
Negligence. This is thy negligence . . *N. N. Dream* iii 2 345
You either fear his humour or my negligence . *T. Night* i 4 5
It is something of my negligence, nothing of my purpose . . iii 4 280
In every one of these no man is free, But that his negligence, his folly, fear, Among the infinite doings of the world, Sometime puts forth *W. Tale* i 2 252
If industriously I play'd the fool, it was my negligence . . . i 2 257
O negligence! Fit for a fool to fall by . . *Hen. VIII.* iii 2 213
My rest and negligence befriends thee now . *Troi. and Cres.* v 6 17
Both the worlds I give to negligence, Let come what comes . *Hamlet* iv 5 134
Put on what weary negligence you please, You and your fellows *Lear* i 3 12
Wise in our negligence, have secret feet In some of our best ports . iii 1 32
When, by night and negligence, the fire Is spied in populous cities *Othello* i 1 76
She let it drop by negligence, And, to the advantage, I being here, took't up . . . . . . iii 3 311
Howsoe'er 'tis strange, Or that the negligence may well be laugh'd at, Yet is it true, sir . . . . . *Cymbeline* i 1 66
Negligent student! learn her by heart . . *L. L. Lost* iii 1 36
A servant grafted in my serious trust And therein negligent . *W. Tale* i 2 247
I may be negligent, foolish and fearful; In every one of these no man is free . . . . . . i 2 250
O, negligent and heedless discipline! . . 1 *Hen. VI.* iv 2 44
Lay negligent and loose regard upon him . *Troi. and Cres.* iii 3 41
How you were wrong led, And we in negligent danger *Ant. and Cleo.* iii 6 81
Celerity is never more admired Than by the negligent . . iii 7 26
Negotiate. Let every eye negotiate for itself And trust no agent *Much Ado* ii 1 185
Have you any commission from your lord to negotiate with my face? *T. Night* i 5 250
Negotiation. Is such a wrest in their affairs That their negotiations all must slack, Wanting his manage . . *Troi. and Cres.* iii 3 24
Negro. I shall answer that better to the commonwealth than you can the getting up of the negro's belly . . *Mer. of Venice* iii 5 42
Neif. *See* Neaf
Neigh. Neighbour vocatur nebour; neigh abbreviated ne . *L. L. Lost* v 1 26
And neigh, and bark, and grunt, and roar, and burn . *M. N. Dream* iii 1 113
His neigh is like the bidding of a monarch . . *Hen. V.* iii 7 29
Steed threatens steed, in high and boastful neighs . . iv Prol. 10
Hark, how our steeds for present service neigh! . . . iv 2 8
Horses did neigh, and dying men did groan . . *J. Cæsar* ii 2 23
You'll have your nephews neigh to you . . . *Othello* i 1 112
And The neighs of horse to tell of her approach . *Ant. and Cleo.* iii 6 45
It is not likely That when they hear the Roman horses neigh, That they will waste their time upon our note, To know from whence we are . . . . . . *Cymbeline* iv 4 17
Neighbour. To these violent proceedings all my neighbours shall cry aim *M. Wives* iii 2 45
One word more, honest neighbours . . . *Much Ado* iii 3 97
What would you with me, honest neighbour? . . . . iii 5 2
Neighbours, you are tedious . . . . . . iii 5 20
All men are not alike; alas, good neighbour! . . . iii 5 44
An old instance, Beatrice, that lived in the time of good neighbours . v 2 79
Neighbour vocatur nebour; neigh abbreviated ne . *L. L. Lost* v 1 25
Warily I stole into a neighbour thicket by . . . v 2 94
He is a marvellous good neighbour, faith, and a very good bowler . v 2 586
Pity that some honest neighbours will not make them friends *M. N. D.* iii 1 149
Now is the mural down between the two neighbours . . v 1 209
What think you of the Scottish lord, his neighbour? *Mer. of Venice* i 2 84
The burnish'd sun, To whom I am a neighbour and near bred . ii 1 3
Made her neighbours believe she wept for the death of a third husband iii 1 10
Who can come in and say that I mean her, When such a one as she such is her neighbour? . . . *As Y. Like It* ii 7 78
Till you met your wife's wit going to your neighbour's bed . iv 1 170
West of this place, down in the neighbour bottom . . . iv 3 79
Neighbour, this is a gift very grateful, I am sure of it . *T. of Shrew* ii 1 76
I am your neighbour, and was suitor first . . . ii 1 336
Neighbours and friends, though bride and bridegroom wants For to supply the places at the table, You know there wants no junkets at the feast . . . . . iii 2 248
I have told my neighbour how you have been solicited . *All's Well* iii 5 15
His pond fish'd by his next neighbour, by Sir Smile, his neighbour *W. T.* i 2 195
Be pilot to me and thy places shall Still neighbour mine . . i 2 449
From very nothing, and beyond the imagination of his neighbours . iv 2 45
Be witness to't.—And this my neighbour too?—And he, and more Than he . . . . iv 4 381
I make a vow, Such neighbour nearness to our sacred blood Should nothing privilege him . . . . . *Richard II.* i 1 119
The dire aspect Of civil wounds plough'd up with neighbours' sword . i 3 128
Come, neighbour: the boy shall lead our horses down the hill 1 *Hen. IV.* ii 2 82
I must live among my neighbours; I'll no swaggerers . 2 *Hen. IV.* ii 4 80
Now, neighbour confines, purge you of your scum . . iv 5 124
Who hath been still a giddy neighbour to us . . *Hen. V.* i 2 145
Though France himself and such another neighbour Stand in our way iii 6 165
Our bad neighbour makes us early stirrers . . . iv 1 6
Will yearly on the vigil feast his neighbours . . . iv 3 45
Canst thou love me?—I cannot tell.—Can any of your neighbours tell? v 2 208
Fear not, neighbour, you shall do well enough . . 2 *Hen. VI.* ii 3 60
And here, neighbour, here's a cup of charneco . . . ii 3 62
Here's a pot of good double beer, neighbour: drink, and fear not your man ii 3 65
He cannot lie with his neighbour's wife, but it [conscience] detects him: 'tis a blushing shamefast spirit . . . *Richard III.* i 4 141
Neighbour, well met: whither away so fast?—I promise you, I scarcely know . . . . ii 3 1
Buckingham No more shall be the neighbour to my counsel . . iv 2 43
Cheer your neighbours. Ladies, you are not merry: gentlemen, Whose fault is this? . . . . . *Hen. VIII.* i 4 41
As, of late days, our neighbours, The upper Germany, can dearly witness v 3 29
And sing The merry songs of peace to all his neighbours . . v 5 36

Neighbour. My good friends, mine honest neighbours, Will you undo yourselves? . . . . *Coriolanus* i 1 63
God-den, our neighbours.—God-den to you all, god-den to you all . iv 6 20
Farewell, kind neighbours: we wish'd Coriolanus Had loved you as we did iv 6 24
We will home to Rome, And die among our neighbours . . . v 3 173
Sweeten with thy breath This neigbour air . . . *Rom. and Jul.* ii 6 27
Forgetting thy great deeds, when neighbour states, But for thy sword and fortune, trod upon them . . . . *T. of Athens* iv 3 94
And at every putting-by mine honest neighbours shouted . *J. Cæsar* i 2 231
I'll lug the guts into the neighbour room . . . *Hamlet* iii 4 212
Would I were A neat-herd's daughter, and my Leonatus Our neighbour shepherd's son!—Thou foolish thing! . . . *Cymbeline* i 1 150
Would I had put my estate and my neighbour's on the approbation of what I have spoke! . . . . i 4 134
Hush, my gentle neighbours! Lend me your hands . *Pericles* iii 2 107
Neighboured. Wholesome berries thrive and ripen best Neighbour'd by fruit of baser quality . . . . . *Hen. V.* i 1 62
Being of so young days brought up with him, And sith so neighbour'd to his youth and haviour . . . . . *Hamlet* ii 2 12
Shall to my bosom Be as well neighbour'd, pitied, and relieved . *Lear* i 1 121
Neighbourhood. Shook and trembled at the ill neighbourhood *Hen. V.* i 2 154
Plant neighbourhood and Christian-like accord In their sweet bosoms . v 2 381
Domestic awe, night-rest, and neighbourhood . . . *T. of Athens* iv 1 17
Neighbouring. He hath a smack of all neighbouring languages *All's Well* iv 1 18
Your tenants, friends and neighbouring gentlemen . . 1 *Hen. IV.* iii 1 90
But, you know, strange fowl light upon neighbouring ponds *Cymbeline* i 4 97
We have descried, upon our neighbouring shore, A portly sail of ships *Pericles* i 4 60
Some neighbouring nation, Taking advantage of our misery . . . i 4 65
Neighbourly. He hath a neighbourly charity in him . *Mer. of Venice* i 2 85
Thou hast my love: is not that neighbourly? . . *As Y. Like It* iii 5 90
Neighbour-stained. Rebellious subjects, enemies to peace, Profaners of this neighbour-stained steel . . . *Rom. and Jul.* i 1 89
Neighed. An arm-gaunt steed, Who neigh'd so high, that what I would have spoke Was beastly dumb'd by him . . *Ant. and Cleo.* i 5 49
Neighing in likeness of a filly foal . . . *M. N. Dream* ii 1 46
Colts, Fetching mad bounds, bellowing and neighing loud *Mer. of Venice* v 1 73
Have I not in a pitched battle heard Loud 'larums, neighing steeds, and trumpets' clang? . . . . *T. of Shrew* i 2 207
Their neighing coursers daring of the spur . . 2 *Hen. IV.* iv 1 119
Farewell the neighing steed, and the shrill trump! . . *Othello* iii 3 351
Neither. We'll not run, Monsieur Monster.—Nor go neither . *Tempest* iii 2 22
Nay, that cannot be so neither . . . . . *T. G. of Ver.* ii 3 18
That's neither here nor there . . . *Mer. Wives* i 4 112; *Othello* iv 3 59
That neither singly can be manifested, Without the show of both *M. W.* iv 6 15
In debating which was best, we shall part with neither *Com. of Errors* iii 1 67
Then let your servants bring my husband forth.—Neither . . v 1 94
This was no damsel neither, sir; she was a virgin . . *L. L. Lost* i 1 294
But say that he or we, as neither have, Received that sum . . ii 1 133
Neither savouring of poetry, wit, nor invention . . . iv 2 165
Will you have me, or your pearl again?—Neither of either . . v 2 459
Thou art as wise as thou art beautiful.—Not so, neither *M. N. Dream* iii 1 152
Neither have I money nor commodity To raise a present sum *M. of Ven.* i 1 178
Is not so estimable, profitable neither, As flesh of muttons . . i 3 167
Nay, I'll fit you, And not be all day neither . . . *All's Well* ii 1 94
I have felt so many quirks of joy and grief, That the first face of neither, on the start, Can woman me unto 't . . . . . . iii 2 52
But be it; let it live. It shall not neither . . . *W. Tale* ii 3 158
Neither.—What, neither?—Neither . . . . . . iv 4 311
Of sorrow or of joy?—Of either, madam.—Of neither, girl *Richard II.* iii 4 12
Neither in birth or for authority, The bishop will be overborne 1 *Hen. VI.* v 1 59
I know it pleaseth neither of us well . . . *Richard III.* i 1 113
You know neither me, yourselves, nor any thing . . *Coriolanus* ii 1 75
Say you so? come on.—Nothing, neither way . . . *Hamlet* v 2 312
Curiosity in neither can make choice of either's moiety . . *Lear* i 1 6
I am not valiant neither, But every puny whipster gets my sword *Othello* v 2 243
Thersites' body is as good as Ajax,' When neither are alive *Cymbeline* iv 2 253
Many dream not to find, neither deserve, And yet are steep'd in favours v 4 130
Nell. What's her name?—Nell, sir; but her name and three quarters, that's an ell and three quarters, will not measure her *Com. of Errors* iii 2 111
He swears thou art to marry his sister Nell . . 2 *Hen. IV.* ii 2 140
It is certain, corporal, that he is married to Nell Quickly . *Hen. V.* ii 1 20
Nor shall my Nell keep lodgers.—No, by my troth, not long . . ii 1 33
News have I, that my Nell is dead i' the spital Of malady of France . v 1 86
O Nell, sweet Nell, if thou dost love thy lord, Banish the canker of ambitious thoughts . . . . . . 2 *Hen. VI.* i 2 17
Come, Nell, thou wilt ride with us?—Yes, my good lord, I'll follow presently . . . . i 2 59
Sweet Nell, ill can thy noble mind abrook The abject people gazing on thy face, With envious looks . . . . ii 4 10
Be patient, gentle Nell; forget this grief.—Ah, Gloucester, teach me to forget myself! . . . . ii 4 26
Ah, Nell, forbear! thou aimest all awry; I must offend before I be attainted . . . . ii 4 58
Thy greatest help is quiet, gentle Nell . . . . . . ii 4 67
My Nell, I take my leave: and, master sheriff, Let nor her penance exceed the king's commission . . . . ii 4 74
Nell, he is full of harmony . . . . . *Troi. and Cres.* iii 1 56
I would fain have armed to-day, but my Nell would not have it so . iii 1 150
Let the porter let in Susan Grindstone and Nell . . *Rom. and Jul.* i 5 11
Nemean. Thus dost thou hear the Nemean lion roar . *L. L. Lost* iv 1 90
My fate cries out, And makes each petty artery in this body As hardy as the Nemean lion's nerve . . . . . . *Hamlet* i 4 83
Nemesis. Your kingdom's terror and black Nemesis . 1 *Hen. VI.* iv 7 78
Neoptolemus. Not Neoptolemus so mirable . . . *Troi. and Cres.* iv 5 142
Nephew Of his nephew Proteus, your son.—Why, what of him? *T. G. of V.* i 3 3
Since you could not be my son-in-law, Be yet my nephew *Much Ado* v 1 297
How like you the young German, the Duke of Saxony's nephew? *M. of V.* i 2 91
When your young nephew Titus lost his leg . . . *T. Night* v 1 66
Thy nephew and right royal sovereign . . . . *K. John* i 1 15
Brother, the king hath made your nephew mad . . 1 *Hen. IV.* i 3 138
Tell your nephew, The Prince of Wales doth join with all the world In praise of Henry Percy . . . . v 1 85
My nephew must not know, Sir Richard, The liberal and kind offer . v 2 1
My nephew's trespass may be well forgot . . . . . v 2 16
The Prince of Wales stepp'd forth before the king, And, nephew, challenged you to single fight . . . . v 2 47
Charles Duke of Orleans, nephew to the king . . . *Hen. V.* iv 8 81
But tell me, keeper, will my nephew come? . . . 1 *Hen. VI.* ii 5 17
My lord, your loving nephew now is come . . . . . ii 5 33
Nephew. Thus ignobly used, Your nephew, late despised Richard, comes 1 *Hen. VI.* ii 5 36
Henry the Fourth, grandfather to this king, Deposed his nephew Richard . . . . ii 5 64
With silence, nephew, be thou politic . . . . . . ii 5 101
Nephew, what means this passionate discourse . . 2 *Hen. VI.* i 1 104
When I imagine ill Against my king and nephew, virtuous Henry . i 2 20
Clarence and Gloucester, love my lovely queen; And kiss your princely nephew, brothers both . . . . . . 3 *Hen. VI.* v 7 27
Thy nephews' souls bid thee despair and die! . . . *Richard III.* v 3 154
Now he has crack'd the league Between us and the emperor, the queen's great nephew, He dives into the king's soul . . *Hen. VIII.* ii 2 26
You should be lord ambassador from the emperor, My royal nephew . iv 2 110
Among the Greeks A lord of Trojan blood, nephew to Hector *Tr. and Cr.* i 2 13
Welcome, nephews, from successful wars, You that survive, and you that sleep in fame! . . . . *T. Andron.* i 1 172
My nephew Mutius' deeds do plead for him; He must be buried . . i 1 356
Suffer thy brother Marcus to inter His noble nephew here in virtue's nest . . . . i 1 376
The tribune and his nephews kneel for grace; I will not be denied . i 1 480
My hand hath been but idle; let it serve To ransom my two nephews . iii 1 173
Rome's emperor, and nephew, break the parle . . . . . v 3 19
Who set this ancient quarrel new abroach? Speak, nephew, were you by when it began? . . . . *Rom. and Jul.* i 1 112
Impotent and bed-rid, scarcely hears Of this his nephew's purpose *Ham.* i 2 30
He sent out to suppress His nephew's levies . . . . . ii 2 62
This is one Lucianus, nephew to the king.—You are as good as a chorus iii 2 254
Who commands them, sir?—The nephew to old Norway, Fortinbras . iv 4 14
You'll have your nephews neigh to you . . . . . *Othello* i 1 112
Neptune. The fire and cracks Of sulphurous roaring the most mighty Neptune Seem to besiege . . . . *Tempest* i 2 204
Ye that on the sands with printless foot Do chase the ebbing Neptune v 1 35
And sat with me on Neptune's yellow sands . . *M. N. Dream* ii 1 126
The eastern gate, all fiery-red, Opening on Neptune with fair blessed beams . . . . iii 2 392
Jupiter Became a bull, and bellow'd; the green Neptune A ram *W. Tale* iv 4 28
To the fearful usage, At least ungentle, of the dreadful Neptune . v 1 154
That Neptune's arms, who clippeth thee about, Would bear thee from the knowledge of thyself! . . . . *K. John* v 2 34
Whose rocky shore beats back the envious siege Of watery Neptune *Richard II.* ii 1 63
The beachy girdle of the ocean Too wide for Neptune's hips 2 *Hen. IV.* iii 1 51
Either to harbour fled, Or made a toast for Neptune . *Troi. and Cres.* i 3 45
Shall dizzy with more clamour Neptune's ear . . . . v 2 174
He would not flatter Neptune for his trident . . . *Coriolanus* iii 1 256
Yet rich conceit Taught thee to make vast Neptune weep for aye On thy low grave, on faults forgiven . . . . . *T. of Athens* v 4 78
Will all great Neptune's ocean wash this blood Clean from my hand? *Macb.* ii 2 60
The moist star Upon whose influence Neptune's empire stands *Hamlet* i 1 119
Full thirty times hath Phœbus' cart gone round Neptune's salt wash . iii 2 166
Let Neptune hear we bid a loud farewell To these great fellows *A. and C.* ii 7 139
And o'er green Neptune's back With ships made cities . . . iv 14 58
The natural bravery of your isle, which stands As Neptune's park *Cymb.* iii 1 19
Their vessel shakes On Neptune's billow . . . . *Pericles* iii Gower 45
Give you up to the mask'd Neptune and The gentlest winds of heaven . iii 3 36
The city strived God Neptune's annual feast to keep . . . v Gower 17
Being on shore, honouring of Neptune's triumphs . . . . v 1 17
Nereides. Her gentlewomen, like the Nereides, So many mermaids, tended her i' the eyes . . . . *Ant. and Cleo.* ii 2 211
Nerissa, my little body is aweary of this great world *Mer. of Venice* i 2 1
Is it not hard, Nerissa, that I cannot choose one nor refuse none? . i 2 28
I will do any thing, Nerissa, ere I'll be married to a sponge . . i 2 107
Nerissa and the rest, stand all aloof. Let music sound . . . iii 2 42
Is this true, Nerissa?—Madam, it is, so you stand pleased withal . iii 2 210
Nerissa, cheer yon stranger; bid her welcome . . . . iii 2 240
My maid Nerissa and myself meantime Will live as maids and widows . iii 2 311
Only attended by Nerissa here, Until her husband and my lord's return iii 4 29
Come on, Nerissa; I have work in hand That you yet know not of . iii 4 57
Shall they see us?—They shall, Nerissa; but in such a habit, That they shall think we are accomplished With that we lack . . . . iii 4 60
Nerrissa teaches me what to believe: I'll die for't but some woman had the ring . . . . v 1 207
There you shall find that Portia was the doctor, Nerissa there her clerk v 1 270
The first inter'gatory That my Nerissa shall be sworn on is, Whether till the next night she had rather stay, Or go to bed now . . . v 1 301
While I live I'll fear no other thing So sore as keeping safe Nerissa's ring . . . . v 1 307
Nero. You bloody Neroes, ripping up the womb Of your dear mother England, blush for shame . . . . *K. John* v 2 152
Like thee, Nero, Play on the lute, beholding the towns burn 1 *Hen. VI.* i 4 95
Nero will be tainted with remorse, To hear and see her plaints 3 *Hen. VI.* iii 1 40
Let not ever The soul of Nero enter this firm bosom . . *Hamlet* iii 2 412
Nero is an angler in the lake of darkness . . . . . . *Lear* iii 6 7
Nerve. Thy nerves are in their infancy again . . . *Tempest* i 2 484
We do learn By those that know the very nerves of state *Meas. for Meas.* i 4 53
Nerve and bone of Greece, Heart of our numbers . . *Troi. and Cres.* i 3 55
The strongest nerves and small inferior veins From me receive that natural competency Whereby they live . . . . *Coriolanus* i 1 142
Take any shape but that, and my firm nerves Shall never tremble *Macb.* iii 4 102
As hardy as the Nemean lion's nerve . . . . . *Hamlet* i 4 83
Yet ha' we A brain that nourishes our nerves . . *Ant. and Cleo.* iv 8 21
He sweats, Strains his young nerves and puts himself in posture That acts my words . . . . *Cymbeline* iii 3 94
Nervii. 'Twas on a summer's evening, in his tent, That day he overcame the Nervii . . . . *J. Cæsar* iii 2 177
Nervy. Death, that dark spirit, in's nervy arm doth lie . . *Coriolanus* ii 1 177
Nessus. For rapes and ravishments he parallels Nessus . . *All's Well* iv 3 281
The shirt of Nessus is upon me . . . . . . *Ant. and Cleo.* iv 12 43
Nest. Will dig thee pig-nuts; Show thee a jay's nest . . *Tempest* ii 2 173
Far from her nest the lapwing cries away . . . *Com. of Errors* iv 2 27
A school-boy, who, being overjoyed with finding a birds' nest *Much Ado* ii 1 230
On you, who, as I take it, have stolen his birds' nest . . . ii 1 238
Show the world what the bird hath done to her own nest *As Y. Like It* iv 1 208
What's he?—E'en a crow o' the same nest . . . . *All's Well* iv 3 319
A nest of traitors! . . . . *W. Tale* ii 3 81
'Nointed over with honey, set on the head of a wasp's nest . . . iv 4 814
The gallant monarch is in arms And like an eagle o'er his aery towers, To souse annoyance that comes near his nest . . . . *K. John* v 2 150
Used us so As that ungentle gull, the cuckoo's bird, Useth the sparrow; did oppress our nest . . . . 1 *Hen. IV.* v 1 61

Nest. For once the eagle England being in prey, To her unguarded nest the weasel Scot Comes sneaking . . . . . Hen. V. i 2 170
France hath in thee found out A nest of hollow bosoms . . . ii Prol. 21
See here the tainture of thy nest, And look thyself be faultless 2 Hen. VI. ii 1 188
Seek not a scorpion's nest, Nor set no footing on this unkind shore . iii 2 86
Who finds the partridge in the puttock's nest, But may imagine how the bird was dead? . . . . . . iii 2 191
Make war with him that climb'd unto their nest . 3 Hen. VI. ii 1 31
Your aery buildeth in our aery's nest . . . Richard III. i 3 270
In that nest of spicery they shall breed Selves of themselves . iv 4 424
To inter His noble nephew here in virtue's nest . T. Andron. i 1 376
Some say that ravens foster forlorn children, The whilst their own birds famish in their nests . . . . . ii 3 154
To fetch a ladder, by the which your love Must climb a bird's nest soon when it is dark . . . . . Rom. and Jul. ii 5 76
Lady, come from that nest Of death, contagion, and unnatural sleep . v 3 151
The poor wren, The most diminutive of birds, will fight, Her young ones in her nest, against the owl . . . Macbeth iv 2 11
Swallows have built In Cleopatra's sails their nests . Ant. and Cleo. iv 12 4
We, poor unfledged, Have never wing'd from view o' the nest Cymbeline iii 3 28
I' the world's volume Our Britain seems as of it, but not in't; In a great pool a swan's nest . . . . . iii 4 142
Nestor play at push-pin with the boys . . L. L. Lost iv 3 169
Though Nestor swear the jest be laughable . . . Mer. of Venice i 1 56
I'll play the orator as well as Nestor . . 3 Hen. VI. iii 2 188
Great Agamemnon, Nestor shall apply Thy latest words Troi. and Cres. i 3 32
And such again As venerable Nestor, hatch'd in silver, Should with a bond of air, strong as the axletree On which heaven rides, knit all the Greekish ears To his experienced tongue . . . i 3 65
Now play me Nestor; hem, and stroke thy beard, As he being drest to some oration . . . . . . i 3 165
God Achilles still cries 'Excellent! 'Tis Nestor right. Now play him me, Patroclus, Arming to answer in a night alarm' . . i 3 170
Tell him of Nestor, one that was a man When Hector's grandsire suck'd i 3 291
Old Nestor, whose wit was mouldy ere your grandsires had nails on their toes . . . . ii 1 114
After so many hours, lives, speeches spent, Thus once again says Nestor ii 2 2
Here's Nestor; Instructed by the antiquary times, He must, he is, he cannot but be wise . . . . . . ii 3 261
Pardon, father Nestor, were your days As green as Ajax' and your brain so temper'd, You should not have the eminence of him, But be as Ajax ii 3 264
'Twere better she were kiss'd in general.—And very courtly counsel: I'll begin. So much for Nestor . . . . iv 5 23
'Tis the old Nestor.—Let me embrace thee, good old chronicle, That hast so long walk'd hand in hand with time: Most reverend Nestor, I am glad to clasp thee . . . . . . iv 5 201
Old Nestor tarries; and you too, Diomed, Keep Hector company . v 1 87
That stale old mouse-eaten dry cheese, Nestor . . . v 4 12
Bid Nestor bring me spices, ink and paper, My casket . Pericles iii 1 66
Nestor-like aged in an age of care . . . 1 Hen. VI. ii 5 6
Net. Let there be the same net spread for her . . Much Ado ii 3 221
Rather choose to hide them in a net Than amply to imbar their crooked titles Usurp'd from you . . . . Hen. V. i 2 93
So doth the cony struggle in the net . 3 Hen. VI. i 4 62
The net has fall'n upon me! I shall perish Under device . Hen. VIII i 1 203
Cast your nets; Happily you may catch her in the sea . T. Andron. iv 3 7
The fisher with his pencil, and the painter with his nets Rom. and Jul. i 2 42
Poor bird! thou'ldst never fear the net nor lime . Macbeth iv 2 34
Out of her own goodness make the net That shall enmesh them all Othello ii 3 367
With dead cheeks advise thee to desist For going on death's net Pericles i 1 40
What, ho, Pilch!—Ha, come and bring away the nets!—What, Patch-breech, I say! . . . . ii 1 13
I'll go draw up the net . . . . . . ii 1 98
Here's a fish hangs in the net, like a poor man's right in the law . ii 1 123
Nether. A foolish hanging of thy nether lip . 1 Hen. IV. ii 4 447
This shows you are above, You justicers, that these our nether crimes So speedily can venge! . . . . . Lear iv 2 79
I know a lady in Venice would have walked barefoot to Palestine for a touch of his nether lip . . . . . Othello iv 3 40
Alas, why gnaw you so your nether lip? . . . . v 2 43
Netherlands. Where stood Belgia, the Netherlands? . Com. of Errors iii 2 142
Nether-stocks. Ere I lead this life long, I'll sew nether stocks and mend them and foot them too . . . 1 Hen. IV. ii 4 130
When a man's over-lusty at legs, then he wears wooden nether-stocks Lear ii 4 11
Nettle. Which being spotted Is goads, thorns, nettles . W. Tale i 2 329
Yield stinging nettles to mine enemies . Richard II. iii 2 18
Out of this nettle, danger, we pluck this flower, safety . 1 Hen. IV. ii 3 10
The strawberry grows underneath the nettle . . Hen. V. i 1 60
I'll spring up in his tears, an 'twere a nettle against May Troi. and Cres. i 2 191
We call a nettle but a nettle and The faults of fools but folly Coriolanus ii 1 207
Look for thy reward Among the nettles at the elder-tree T. Andron. ii 3 272
With fantastic garlands did she come Of crow-flowers, nettles, daisies Hamlet iv 7 170
Hemlock, nettles, cuckoo-flowers, Darnel, and all the idle weeds . Lear iv 4 4
So that if we will plant nettles, or sow lettuce, set hyssop . . Othello i 3 325
Nettled. Scourged with rods, Nettled and stung with pismires 1 Hen. IV. i 3 240
Stamps, as he were nettled: I hope all's for the best . 3 Hen. VI. iii 3 169
Nettle-seed. Had I plantation of this isle, my lord,— He'ld sow't with nettle-seed.—Or docks . . . . Tempest ii 1 144
Neuter. Be it known to you I do remain as neuter . . Richard II. ii 3 159
Neutral. Who can be wise, amazed, temperate and furious, Loyal and neutral, in a moment? No man . . . Macbeth ii 3 115
And like a neutral to his will and matter, Did nothing . Hamlet ii 2 503
Came from one that's of a neutral heart, And not from one opposed Lear iii 7 48
Never a woman in Windsor knows more of Anne's mind . . Mer. Wives i 4 135
I like it never the better for that . . . . . iii 1 186
He would never else cross me thus . . . . . v 5 40
Good sister, let us dine and never fret . . Com. of Errors ii 1 6
Swear me to this, and I will ne'er say no . . L. L. Lost i 1 69
Is't not enough, young man, That I did never, no, nor never can? M. N. D. ii 2 126
As true as truest horse that yet would never tire . . . iii 1 98
Your cue is past; it is, 'never tire' . . . . iii 1 103
Never talk to me; I will weep . . . As Y. L. It iii 4 1
You understand me?—I, sir! ne'er a whit . . T. of Shrew i 1 240
An old trot with ne'er a tooth in her head . . . i 2 80
Better once than never, for never too late . . . v 1 155
Thou never spokest To better purpose.—Never?—Never, but once W. Tale i 2 89
The hopeless word of 'never to return' Breathe I against thee Richard II. i 3 152
Better far off than near, be ne'er the near . . . v 1 88
I'll be damned for never a king's son in Christendom . 1 Hen. IV. i 2 109
Never. Hast thou never an eye in thy head? . . . . 1 Hen. IV. ii 1 31
We must away all night.—Tut, never fear me . . . . iv 2 64
Never a man's thought in the world keeps the road-way better 2 Hen. IV. ii 2 62
He may be ransomed, and we ne'er the wiser . . . Hen. V. iv 1 206
Now, York, or never, steel thy fearful thoughts . 2 Hen. VI. iii 1 331
Ne'er look, ne'er look; the eagles are gone . Troi. and Cres. i 2 264
I am your debtor, claim it when 'tis due.—Never's my day . . iv 5 52
A soldier good; But, by great Mars, the captain of us all, Never like thee iv 5 199
Never go home; here starve we out the night . . . v 10 2
There's never a one of you but trusts a knave . . T. of Athens v 1 96
Thou'lt come no more, Never, never, never, never, never! . Lear v 3 308
I love thee; But never more be officer of mine . . Othello ii 3 249
The ebb'd man, ne'er loved till ne'er worth love . Ant. and Cleo. i 4 43
Never-daunted. Whose swift wrath beat down The never-daunted Percy to the earth . . . . . . 2 Hen. IV. i 1 110
Never-dying. What never-dying honour hath he got! . 1 Hen. IV. iii 2 106
Never-heard-of. There let them bide until we have devised Some never-heard-of torturing pain for them . . T. Andron. ii 3 285
Ne'er-lust-wearied Antony . . . . . Ant. and Cleo. ii 1 38
Never-needed. If you refuse your aid In this so never-needed help, yet do not Upbraid's with our distress . . . . Coriolanus v 1 34
Never-quenching. That hand shall burn in never-quenching fire That staggers thus my person . . . . Richard II. v 5 109
Never so. Who would give a bird the lie, though he cry 'cuckoo' never so? M. N. Dream iii 1 139
If thou dost intend Never so little show of love to her, Thou shalt aby it iii 2 334
Never so weary, never so in woe . . . . . iii 2 442
If it be ne'er so false, a true gentleman may swear it . W. Tale v 2 175
Creep time ne'er so slow, Yet it shall come for me to do thee good K. John iii 3 31
Wilt know again, Being ne'er so little urged, another way Richard II. v 1 64
Who, ne'er so tame, so cherish'd and lock'd up, Will have a wild trick of his ancestors . . . . . . 1 Hen. IV. v 2 10
Make friends with speed: Never so few, and never yet more need 2 Hen. IV. i 1 215
Be his cause never so spotless . . . . Hen. V. iv 1 167
Be he ne'er so vile, This day shall gentle his condition . . iv 3 62
Though ne'er so cunningly you smother it . 1 Hen. VI. iv 1 110
It shall be so, disdain they ne'er so much . . . . v 3 98
New customs, Though they be never so ridiculous, Nay, let 'em be unmanly, yet are follow'd . . . . . Hen. VIII. i 3 3
Tell me true—For I must ever doubt, though ne'er so sure T. of Athens iv 3 514
Never-surfeited. The never-surfeited sea . . . Tempest iii 3 55
Nevertheless. I will love thee ne'er the less, my girl . T. of Shrew i 1 77
Yet ne'ertheless, My spritely brethren, I propend to you Troi. and Cres. ii 2 189
Never-touched. Want will perjure The ne'er-touch'd vestal Ant. and Cleo. iii 12 31
Never-withering. Poor shadows of Elysium, hence, and rest Upon your never-withering banks of flowers . . . . Cymbeline v 4 98
Never-yet-beaten. The ne'er-yet-beaten horse of Parthia We have jaded out o' the field . . . . . Ant. and Cleo. iii 1 33
Nevil. Which of you was by—You, cousin Nevil? . . 2 Hen. IV. iii 1 66
I will take the Nevils' parts And make a show of love . 2 Hen. VI. i 1 240
And he of these that can do most of all Cannot do more in England than the Nevils: Salisbury and Warwick are no simple peers . i 3 76
If thy claim be good, The Nevils are thy subjects to command . ii 2 8
Whose fruit thou art And never of the Nevils' noble race . iii 2 215
And the Nevils all, Whose dreadful swords were never drawn in vain . iv 1 91
Old Nevil's crest, The rampant bear chain'd to the ragged staff v 1 202
New. Kiss the book: I will furnish it anon with new contents Tempest ii 2 146
'Ban, 'Ban, Cacaliban Has a new master: get a new man . . ii 2 189
O brave new world, That has such people in't!—'Tis new to thee . v 1 184
Once more, new servant, welcome . . . . T. G. of Ver. ii 4 118
Repeal thee home again Plead a new state in thy unrival'd merit . v 4 144
An old cloak makes a new jerkin . . . Mer. Wives i 3 18
This secrecy of thine shall be a tailor to thee and shall make thee a new doublet and hose . . . . iii 3 35
'Tis painted about with the story of the Prodigal, fresh and new . iv 5 9
This new governor Awakes me all the enrolled penalties Meas. for Meas. i 2 169
Are you a god? would you create me new? . . Com. of Errors iii 2 39
He hath every month a new sworn brother . . . Much Ado i 1 73
Now will he lie ten nights awake, carving the fashion of a new doublet ii 3 19
That would be as great a soil in the new gloss of your marriage as to show a child his new coat and forbid him to wear it . . . iii 2 6
I like the new tire within excellently . . . . iii 4 13
A man in all the world's new fashion planted . . L. L. Lost i 1 165
By the next new moon—The sealing-day betwixt my love and me M. N. D. i 1 83
To seek new friends and stranger companies . . . . i 1 219
That shall seek The squirrel's hoard, and fetch thee new nuts . iv 1 40
Now thou and I are new in amity . . . . . iv 1 92
Good strings to your beards, new ribbons to your pumps . . iv 2 37
A fortnight hold we this solemnity, In nightly revels and new jollity . v 1 377
Who, indeed, gives rare new liveries . . . Mer. of Venice ii 2 117
Soon at supper shalt thou see Lorenzo, who is thy new master's guest . ii 3 6
To bid my old master the Jew to sup to-night with my new master . ii 4 18
Since this fortune falls to you, Be content and seek no new . . iii 2 135
If that the youth of my new interest here Have power to bid you welcome iii 2 224
What's the new news at the new court? . . . As Y. Like It i 1 101
The old duke is banished by his younger brother the new duke . . i 1 105
Then she puts you to entreaty, and there begins new matter . . iv 1 81
News, old news, and such news as you never heard of!—Is it new and old too? how may that be? . . . . . T. of Shrew iii 2 32
Petruchio is coming in a new hat and an old jerkin . . . . iii 2 43
It [winter] hath tamed my old master and my new mistress . . . iv 1 26
The serving-men in their new fustian, their white stockings . . iv 1 49
Whose apprehensive senses All but new things disdain . All's Well i 2 61
Your lord and master's married; there's news for you: you have a new mistress . . . . ii 3 258
He does smile his face into more lines than is in the new map T. Night iii 2 85
We shall Present our services to a fine new prince One of these days W. T. ii 1 17
He is gone aboard a new ship to purge melancholy and air himself . iv 4 790
Every wink of an eye some new grace will be born . . . v 2 120
Bearing their birthrights proudly on their backs, To make a hazard of new fortunes here . . . . . . K. John ii 1 71
The devil tempts thee here In likeness of a new untrimmed bride . iii 1 209
Alack, how new Is husband in my mouth! . . . . iii 1 305
For putting on so new a fashion'd robe . . . . iv 2 27
New flight; And happy newness, that intends old right . . v 4 60
And furbish new the name of John a Gaunt, Even in the lusty haviour of his son . . . . Richard II. i 3 76
Where doth the world thrust forth a vanity—So it be new, there's no respect how vile—That is not quickly buzz'd into his ears? . ii 1 25
And daily new exactions are devised, As blanks, benevolences . . ii 1 249

New. As I intend to thrive in this new world . . . *Richard II.* iv 1 78
Your care is gain of care, by new care won . . . iv 1 197
Our holy lives must win a new world's crown . . . v 1 24
Bear you well in this new spring of time, Lest you be cropp'd . v 2 50
Come, my old son : I pray God make thee new . . . v 3 146
And breathe short-winded accents of new broils . *1 Hen. IV.* i 1 3
Charles' wain is over the new chimney . . . ii 1 3
Trent shall run In a new channel, fair and evenly . . iii 1 103
Thus did I keep my person fresh and new . . . iii 2 55
With a new wound in your thigh, come you along with me . v 4 131
The young lion repents ; marry, not in ashes and sackcloth, but in new silk and old sack . . . *2 Hen. IV.* i 2 222
Methought he had made two holes in the ale-wife's new petticoat . ii 2 89
And keep no tell-tale to his memory That may repeat and history his loss To new remembrance . . . iv 1 204
Health to my sovereign, and new happiness Added to that that I am to deliver ! . . . iv 4 81
Now, sir, a new link to the bucket must needs be had . v 1 23
This new and gorgeous garment, majesty, Sits not so easy on me as you think . . . v 2 44
If I had had time to have made new liveries . . . v 5 11
I Richard's body have interred new . . . *Hen. V.* iv 1 312
They will pluck The gay new coats o'er the French soldiers' heads iv 3 118
But, hark ! what new alarum is this same? . . . iv 6 35
And lay new platforms to endamage them . . *1 Hen. VI.* ii 1 77
Thy friendship makes us fresh.—And doth beget new courage in our breasts . . . iii 3 87
To my determined time thou gavest new date . . . iv 6 9
Surfeiting in joys of love, With his new bride . *2 Hen. VI.* i 1 252
Means to dress the commonwealth, and turn it, and set a new nap upon it . . . iv 2 7
Come, thou new ruin of old Clifford's house . . . v 2 61
Caused him, by new act of parliament, To blot out me . *3 Hen. VI.* ii 2 91
Lewis of France is sending over masquers To revel it with him and his new bride . . . iii 3 225 ; iv 1 95
What think you Of this new marriage? . . . iv 1 2
Doing what you gave in charge, Is now dishonoured by this new marriage . . . iv 1 33
Have bestow'd the heir Of the Lord Bonville on your new wife's son . iv 1 57
Follow him To his new kingdom of perpetual rest . *Richard III.* ii 2 46
The devil is a niggard, Or has given all before, and he begins A new hell in himself . . . *Hen. VIII.* i 1 72
New customs, Though they be never so ridiculous, Nay, let 'em be unmanly, yet are follow'd . . . i 3 2
They have all new legs, and lame ones . . . i 3 11
I hear of none, but the new proclamation That's clapp'd upon the court-gate . . . i 3 17
My new secretary : I find him a fit fellow . . . ii 2 116
I cannot promise But that you shall sustain moe new disgraces . iii 2 5
Is there no way to cure this? No new device to beat this from his brains? . . . iii 2 217
With new opinions, Divers and dangerous . . . v 3 17
Do not I know you for a favourer Of this new sect? . . v 3 81
Her ashes new create another heir, As great in admiration as herself . v 5 42
His honour and the greatness of his name Shall be, and make new nations . . . v 5 53
Nor, princes, is it matter new to us . . *Troi. and Cres.* i 3 10
And here, to do you service, am become As new into the world . iii 3 12
They Upon their ancient malice will forget With the least cause these his new honours . . . *Coriolanus* ii 1 245
Tullus Aufidius then had made new head? . . . iii 1 1
Peace ! We need not put new matter to his charge . . iii 3 76
He water'd his new plants with dews of flattery . . v 6 23
And set abroad new business for you all . . *T. Andron.* i 1 192
These words, these looks, infuse new life in me . . i 1 461
But dawning day new comfort hath inspired . . . ii 2 10
From ancient grudge break to new mutiny . . *Rom. and Jul.* Prol. 3
Take thou some new infection to thy eye, And the rank poison of the old will die . . . i 2 50
Such antic, lisping, affecting fantasticoes ; these new tuners of accents ! ii 4 30
These perdona-mi's, who stand so much on the new form, that they cannot sit at ease on the old bench . . . ii 4 36
Did'st thou not fall out with a tailor for wearing his new doublet before Easter? with another, for tying his new shoes with old riband? . iii 1 30
Whiter than new snow on a raven's back . . . iii 2 19
As is the night before some festival To an impatient child that hath new robes And may not wear them . . . iii 2 30
He hath put me off To the succession of new days this month *T. of Athens* ii 2 20
It should not be, by the persuasion of his new feasting . . iii 6 9
Teem with new monsters, whom thy upward face Hath to the marbled mansion all above Never presented ! . . . iv 3 190
To stale with ordinary oaths my love To every new protester *J. Cæsar* i 2 74
These applauses are For some new honours that are heap'd on Cæsar . i 2 134
Your voice shall be as strong as any man's In the disposing of new dignities . . . iii 1 178
With furbish'd arms and new supplies of men . . *Macbeth* i 2 32
New honours come upon him, Like our strange garments, cleave not to their mould But with the aid of use . . . i 3 144
Approach the chamber, and destroy your sight With a new Gorgon . ii 3 77
Well, may you see things well done there : adieu ! Lest our old robes sit easier than our new ! . . . ii 4 38
It were a good sign that I should quickly have a new father . iv 2 63
Each new morn New widows howl, new orphans cry, new sorrows Strike heaven . . . iv 3 5
That of an hour's age doth hiss the speaker : Each minute teems a new one iv 3 176
I sat me down, Devised a new commission, wrote it fair . *Hamlet* v 2 32
He'll shape his old course in a country new . . *Lear* i 1 190
This admiration, sir, is much o' the savour Of other your new pranks . i 4 259
Therefore be content to slubber the gloss of your new fortunes . *Othello* i 3 228
The hearts of old gave hands ; But our new heraldry is hands, not hearts iii 4 47
But if she lost it Or made a gift of it, my father's eye Should hold her loathed and his spirits should hunt After new fancies . . . iii 4 63
Then must thou needs find out new heaven, new earth . *Ant. and Cleo.* i 1 17
That when old robes are worn out, there are members to make new . i 2 172
Your old smock brings forth a new petticoat . . . i 2 175
He hath waged New wars 'gainst Pompey ; made his will . . iii 4 4
The exile of her minion is too new ; She hath not yet forgot him *Cymb.* ii 3 46
I had it from the queen.—New matter still?—It poison'd me . . v 5 243
So, on your patience evermore attending, New joy wait on you ! *Pericles* v 3 Gower 101

New abroach. Who set this ancient quarrel new abroach? *Rom. and Jul.* i 1 111
New-added. Refresh d, new-added, and encouraged . *J. Cæsar* iv 3 209
New-adopted. Unfriended, new-adopted to our hate . . *Lear* i 1 206
New-apparelled. The picture of old Adam new-apparelled *Com. of Errors* iv 3 14
New-appearing. My unblown flowers, new-appearing sweets ! *Richard III.* iv 4 10
New a-work. Aroused vengeance sets him new a-work . *Hamlet* ii 2 510
New baptized. Call me but love, and I'll be new baptized *Rom. and Jul.* ii 2 50
New beaten. Go back again, and be new beaten home? . *Com. of Errors* ii 1 76
New before. And even before this truce, but new before . *K. John* iii 1 233
New-begot. Let not sloth dim your honours new-begot . *1 Hen. VI.* i 1 79
New-beloved. To meet her new-beloved any where . *Rom. and Jul.* ii Prol. 12
New-bent. The moon, like to a silver bow New-bent in heaven *M. N. Dream* i 1 11
New-born. Till new-born chins Be rough and razorable . *Tempest* ii 1 249
Beauty doth varnish age, as if new-born . . . *L. L. Lost* iv 3 244
Thou mettest with things dying, I with things new-born . *W. Tale* iii 3 117
That all with one consent praise new-born gawds . *Troi. and Cres.* iii 3 176
Pity, like a naked new-born babe, Striding the blast . *Macbeth* i 7 21
Heart with strings of steel, Be soft as sinews of the new-born babe ! *Hamlet* iii 3 71
New-built. Her new-built virtue and obedience . . *T. of Shrew* v 2 118
To be depender on a thing that leans, Who cannot be new built *Cymbeline* i 5 59
New-burned. Falsehood falsehood cures, as fire cools fire Within the scorched veins of one new-burn'd . . . *K. John* iii 1 278
New-christened. Belike his majesty hath some intent That you shall be new-christen'd in the Tower . . *Richard III.* i 1 50
New come. Here stays without A messenger with letters from the doctor, New come from Padua . . *Mer. of Venice* iv 1 109
Welcome, my son : who are the violets now That strew the green lap of the new come spring? . . . *Richard II.* v 2 47
His new-come champion, virtuous Joan of Arc . *1 Hen. IV.* ii 2 20
New committed to the Bishop of York . . *3 Hen. VI.* iv 4 11
New-conceived. That shows what future evils, Either new, or by remissness new-conceived . . . *Meas. for Meas.* ii 2 96
New-create. Is it his use? Or did the letters work upon his blood, And new-create this fault? . . . *Othello* iv 1 287
New created The creatures that were mine . . *Tempest* i 2 81
New-crowned. Even as the flourish when true subjects bow To a new-crowned monarch . . . *Mer. of Venice* iii 2 50
To this effect, before you were new crown'd, We breathed our counsel *K. John* iv 2 35
New cut off. Whiles thy head is warm and new cut off . *3 Hen. VI.* v 1 55
New-dated. I have received New-dated letters . . *2 Hen. IV.* iv 1 8
New-delivered. And I, a gasping new-deliver'd mother . *Richard II.* ii 2 65
But who comes here? the new-deliver'd Hastings? . . *Richard III.* i 1 121
New-devised. A new-devised courtesy . . . *L. L. Lost* ii 2 66
New-dyed. Rather new-dyed than stained with salt water . *Tempest* ii 1 63
New-enkindled. With eyes as red as new-enkindled fire . *K. John* iv 2 163
New-fallen. Meantime, forget this new-fall'n dignity . *As Y. Like It* v 4 182
Nor claim no further than your new-fall'n right . . *1 Hen. IV.* v 1 44
New-fangled. Than wish a snow in May's new-fangled mirth . *L. L. Lost* i 1 106
More new-fangled than an ape . . . *As Y. Like It* iv 1 152
New-fired. Set on your foot, And with a heart new-fired I follow you, To do I know not what . . . *J. Cæsar* ii 1 332
New formed. Changed 'em, Or else new form'd 'em . . *Tempest* i 2 83
New-found. And full of new-found oaths . . *T. G. of Ver.* iv 4 135
New haled. Even like a man new haled from the rack . *1 Hen. VI.* ii 5 3
New hatched. Confused events New hatch'd to the woeful time *Macbeth* ii 3 64
But do not dull thy palm with entertainment Of each new-hatch'd, unfledged comrade . . . *Hamlet* i 3 65
New-healed. I am loath to gall a new-healed wound . *2 Hen. IV.* i 2 167
Lest . . . The new-heal'd wound of malice should break out *Richard III.* ii 2 125
New inspired. Methinks I am a prophet new inspired . *Richard II.* ii 1 31
New killed. And Juliet, dead before, Warm and new kill'd *Rom. and Jul.* v 3 197
New lamenting With new lamenting ancient oversights . *2 Hen. IV.* ii 3 47
New lighted. Sir Walter Blunt, new lighted from his horse . *1 Hen. IV.* i 1 63
Like the herald Mercury New-lighted on a heaven-kissing hill *Hamlet* iii 4 59
New lost. With his bleeding rings, Their precious stones new lost *Lear* v 3 190
New-made. Like man new made . . . *Meas. for Meas.* ii 2 79
To seal love's bonds new-made . . . *Mer. of Venice* ii 6 6
For new-made honour doth forget men's names . . *K. John* i 1 187
Pledge for his truth And lasting fealty to the new made king *Richard II.* v 2 45
Suffolk, the new-made duke that rules the roast . *2 Hen. VI.* i 1 109
The great and new-made Duke of Suffolk . . . i 2 95
'Tis not his new-made bride shall succour him . . *3 Hen. VI.* iii 3 207
To wait upon this new-made empress . . *T. Andron.* i 1 20
Bid me go into a new-made grave And hide me with a dead man in his shroud . . . *Rom. and Jul.* iv 1 84
Whose untimely death Banish'd the new-made bridegroom from this city v 3 235
New-married. This new-married man approaching here *Meas. for Meas.* v 1 405
Like a new-married wife about her husband's neck . . *Hen. V.* v 2 190
Somewhat too early for new-married ladies . . *T. Andron.* ii 2 15
New news. What's the new news at the new court?—There's no news at the court, sir, but the old news . . . *As Y. Like It* i 1 101
New opened. I feel my heart new open'd . . *Hen. VIII.* iii 2 366
New over. And shall make your lord, That which he is, new o'er *Cymb.* i 6 165
New-planted. His private arbours and new-planted orchards *J. Cæsar* iii 2 253
New reaped. His chin new reap'd Show'd like a stubble-land at harvest-home . . . *1 Hen. IV.* i 3 34
New repair. To line and new repair our towns of war . *Hen. V.* ii 4 7
New-risen. And sits as one new-risen from a dream . . *T. of Shrew* iv 1 189
A holy prophetess new risen up . . . *1 Hen. VI.* i 4 102
New-sad. And entreat, Out of a new-sad soul . . *L. L. Lost* v 2 741
New-shed. Upon whose leaves are drops of new-shed blood *T. Andron.* ii 3 200
New-store. To new-store France with bastard warriors . *Hen. V.* iii 5 31
New struck. Is the day so young?—But new struck nine *Rom. and Jul.* i 1 167
New-taken. It is the prettiest villain : she fetches her breath as short as a new-ta'en sparrow . . . *Troi. and Cres.* iii 2 36
New told. This act is as an ancient tale new told . *K. John* iv 2 18
New-transformed. And the hounds Should drive upon thy new-transformed limbs . . . *T. Andron.* ii 3 64
New-trimmed. Which ever, As ravenous fishes, do a vessel follow That is new-trimm'd . . . *Hen. VIII.* i 2 80
New-trothed. So says the prince and my new-trothed lord . *Much Ado* iii 1 38
New-tuned. Which they trick up with new-tuned oaths . *Hen. V.* iii 6 80
New-varnished. And how much honour Pick'd from the chaff and ruin of the times To be new-varnish'd ! . . . *Mer. of Venice* ii 9 49
New woo. I'll reconcile me to Polixenes, New woo my queen *W. Tale* iii 2 157
New-year's gift. I'll have my brains ta'en out and buttered, and give them to a dog for a new-year's gift . . . *Mer. Wives* iii 5 8

Newer. The remembrance of my former love Is by a newer object quite forgotten . . . . *T. G. of Ver.* ii 4 195
What old or newer torture Must I receive? . . . . *W. Tale* iii 2 178
Here comes newer comfort . . . . . *Macbeth* v 8 53
O Cassio, whence came this? This is some token from a newer friend *Othello* iii 4 181
Newest. A kind of not of the newest Poor-John . . *Tempest* ii 2 28
Toys for your head Of the new'st and finest, finest wear-a *W. Tale* iv 4 327
Rob murder, and commit The oldest sins the newest kind of ways *2 Hen. IV.* iv 5 127
What bloody man is that? He can report, As seemeth by his plight, of the revolt The newest state . . . *Macbeth* i 2 3
Which would be worn now in their newest gloss, Not cast aside so soon i 7 34
What's the newest grief?—That of an hour's age doth hiss the speaker . iv 3 174
Newgate. Must we all march?—Yea, two and two, Newgate fashion *1 Hen. IV.* iii 3 104
Newly. Upon a sudden, As Falstaff, she and I, are newly met *M. Wives* iv 4 52
Who, newly in the seat, that it may know He can command, lets it straight feel the spur . . . *Meas. for Meas.* i 2 165
Is there none of Pygmalion's images, newly made woman, to be had now? . . . . iii 2 47
He hath ta'en you newly into his grace . . . *Much Ado* i 3 23
I will have that subject newly writ o'er . . . *L. L. Lost* i 2 120
To wail friends lost Is not by much so wholesome-profitable As to rejoice at friends but newly found . . . . v 2 761
She looks as clear As morning roses newly wash'd with dew *T. of Shrew* ii 1 174
But that you are but newly come, You might have heard it else proclaim'd . . . . . . iv 2 86
What thou dost know Hath newly pass'd between this youth and me *T. Night* v 1 158
A piece many years in doing and now newly performed . . *W. Tale* v 2 105
The statue is but newly fix'd, the colour's Not dry . . . v 3 47
This royal hand and mine are newly knit . . . *K. John* iii 1 226
And shall these hands, so lately purged of blood, So newly join'd in love, so strong in both, Unyoke this seizure? . . . iii 1 240
The dangers of the days but newly gone . . . *2 Hen. IV.* iv 1 80
Have but their stings and teeth newly ta'en out . . . iv 5 206
And newly move, With casted slough and fresh legerity . *Hen. V.* iv 1 22
The Duke of York is newly come from Ireland . . *2 Hen. VI.* iv 9 24
Newly preferr'd from the king's secretary . . *Hen. VIII.* iv 1 102
By deed-achieving honour newly named . . . *Coriolanus* ii 1 190
You are but newly planted in your throne . . *T. Andron.* i 1 444
Comes back to Romeo, Who had but newly entertain'd revenge *Rom. and Jul.* iii 1 176
And Juliet bleeding, warm, and newly dead . . . v 3 175
There are certain nobles of the senate Newly alighted . *T. of Athens* i 2 181
And came into the world When sects and factions were newly born . iii 5 30
What's more to do, Which would be planted newly with the time *Macb.* v 8 65
Here is newly come to court Laertes . . . *Hamlet* v 2 110
Whose breath, indeed, these hands have newly stopp'd . *Othello* v 2 202
The hated, grown to strength, Are newly grown to love . *Ant. and Cleo.* i 3 49
Three kings I had newly feasted, and did want Of what I was i' the morning . . . . ii 2 76
Newness. Whether it be the fault and glimpse of newness *Meas. for Meas.* i 2 162
New flight; And happy newness, that intends old right . . *K. John* v 4 61
Newness Of Cloten's death—we being not known, not muster'd Among the bands—may drive us to a render Where we have lived *Cymbeline* iv 4 9
News. The best news is, that we have safely found Our king . *Tempest* v 1 221
Let me hear from thee by letters Of thy success in love and what news else Betideth here . . . . . *T. G. of Ver.* i 1 58
Lend me the letter; let me see what news.—There is no news, my lord i 3 55
What say you to a letter from your friends Of much good news? . ii 4 52
Here he means to spend his time awhile: I think 'tis no unwelcome news to you . . . . ii 4 81
My ears are stopt and cannot hear good news . . . iii 1 205
What news with your mastership?—With my master's ship? . . iii 1 279
What news, then, in your paper?—The blackest news that ever thou heardest . . . . iii 1 284
This news distracts me!—This punk is one of Cupid's carriers *M. Wives* ii 2 140
This news is old enough, yet it is every day's news . . *Meas. for Meas.* iii 2 243
Very well met, and well come. What is the news from this good deputy? . . . . iv 1 27
I can tell you strange news that you yet dreamt not of . *Much Ado* i 2 4
Thus answer I in name of Benedick, But hear these ill news with the ears of Claudio . . . . . . ii 1 180
Will you come presently?—Will you go hear this news? . . v 2 103
He is Cupid's grandfather and learns news of him . *L. L. Lost* ii 1 254
The news I bring Is heavy in my tongue . . . . v 2 726
What news on the Rialto? . . . *Mer. of Venice* i 3 39; iii 1 1
Well, old man, I will tell you news of your son: give me your blessing ii 2 82
How now, Shylock! what news among the merchants? . . . iii 1 25
How now, Tubal! what news from Genoa? hast thou found my daughter? iii 1 83
No news of them? Why, so: and I know not what's spent in the search iii 1 94
Good news, good news! ha, ha! where? in Genoa? . . . iii 1 111
What's the news from Venice? How doth that royal merchant, good Antonio? . . . . iii 2 241
There's a post come from my master, with his horn full of good news . v 1 47
I have better news in store for you Than you expect . . . v 1 274
What's the new news at the new court?—There's no news at the court, sir, but the old news . . . *As Y. Like It* i 1 102
With his mouth full of news . . . . . . i 2 98
I'll tell you news indifferent good for either . . . *T. of Shrew* i 2 181
News, old news, and such news as you never heard of! . . iii 2 30
Why, is it not news, to hear of Petruchio's coming?—Is he come? . iii 2 33
But say, what to thine old news?—Why, Petruchio is coming in a new hat and an old jerkin . . . . . . iii 2 42
Grumio, the news.—Why, 'Jack, boy! ho! boy!' and as much news as will thaw . . . . iv 1 42
Every thing in order?—All ready; and therefore, I pray thee, news . iv 1 55
Your lord and master's married; there's news for you . *All's Well* ii 3 258
Yonder is heavy news within between two soldiers and my young lady . iii 2 35
Nay, there is some comfort in the news, some comfort . . iii 2 38
What news from her?—So please my lord, I might not be admitted *T. N.* i 1 23
What is the news i' the court?—None rare, my lord . . *W. Tale* i 2 367
This news is mortal to the queen: look down And see what death is doing . . . . iii 2 149
But let Time's news Be known when 'tis brought forth . . iv 1 26
This news which is called true is so like an old tale . . v 2 30
This news hath made thee a most ugly man . . *K. John* iii 1 37
If that young Arthur be not gone already Even at that news he dies . iii 4 164
News. Do not seek to stuff My head with more ill news, for it is full *K. John* iv 2 134
O my gentle cousin, Hear'st thou the news abroad, who are arrived? . iv 2 160
With open mouth swallowing a tailor's news . . . . iv 2 195
This news was brought to Richard but even now . . . v 3 12
This tyrant fever burns me up, And will not let me welcome this good news . . . . v 3 15
Ah, foul shrewd news! beshrew thy very heart! I did not think to be so sad to-night As this hath made me . . . . v 5 14
News fitting to the night, Black, fearful, comfortless and horrible . v 6 19
Show me the very wound of this ill news: I am no woman, I'll not swoon at it . . . . v 6 21
My heart hath one poor string to stay it by, Which holds but till thy news be uttered . . . . v 7 56
You breathe these dead news in as dead an ear . . . v 7 65
The wind sits fair for news to go to Ireland, But none returns *Richard II.* ii 2 123
The news is very fair and good, my lord . . . . . iii 3 5
How dares thy harsh rude tongue sound this unpleasing news? . . iii 4 74
Little joy have I To breathe this news; yet what I say is true . iii 4 82
Gardener, for telling me these news of woe, Pray God the plants thou graft'st may never grow . . . . . . iii 4 100
What news from Oxford? hold those justs and triumphs? . . v 2 52
The latest news we hear Is that the rebels have consumed with fire Our town . . . . v 6 1
All athwart there came A post from Wales loaden with heavy news *1 Hen. IV.* i 1 37
More uneven and unwelcome news Came from the north . . i 1 50
As by discharge of their artillery . . the news was told . i 1 58
There's villanous news abroad: here was Sir John Bracy from your father . . . . ii 4 367
Thy father's beard is turned white with the news . . . ii 4 394
But wherefore do I tell these news to thee? . . . . iii 2 121
Now, Hal, to the news at court: for the robbery, lad, how is that answered? . . . . iii 3 197
Welcome, by my soul.—Pray God my news be worth a welcome . iv 1 87
Which gape and rub the elbow at the news Of hurlyburly innovation v 1 77
Not a man of them brings other news Than they have learn'd of me: from Rumour's tongues . . . . *2 Hen. IV.* Ind. 38
I bring you certain news from Shrewsbury.—Good, an God will! . i 1 12
A gentleman well bred and of good name, That freely render'd me these news for true . . . . i 1 27
Here comes my servant Travers, whom I sent On Tuesday last to listen after news . . . . i 1 29
Look, here comes more news.—Yea, this man's brow, like to a title-leaf, Foretells the nature of a tragic volume . . . . i 1 59
The first bringer of unwelcome news Hath but a losing office . i 1 100
This is the news at full.—For this I shall have time enough to mourn . i 1 135
These news, Having been well, that would have made me sick, Being sick, have in some measure made me well . . . . i 1 137
I have heard better news . . . . ii 1 179
Go, captain, and deliver to the army This news of peace . . iv 2 70
Our news shall go before us to his majesty, Which, cousin, you shall bear to comfort him . . . . iv 3 84
Look, here's more news.—From enemies heaven keep your majesty! . iv 4 93
And wherefore should these good news make me sick? . . . iv 4 102
I should rejoice now at this happy news; And now my sight fails . iv 4 109
Heard he the good news yet? Tell it him.—He alter'd much upon the hearing it . . . . iv 5 11
There's one Pistol come from the court with news.—From the court! . v 3 85
Tidings do I bring and lucky joys And golden times and happy news of price . . . . v 3 100
And shall good news be baffled? Then, Pistol, lay thy head in Furies' lap . . . . v 3 109
If, sir, you come with news from the court, I take it there's but two ways, either to utter them, or to conceal them . . . v 3 115
News have I, that my Nell is dead i' the spital Of malady of France *Hen. V.* v 1 86
If Henry were recall'd to life again, These news would cause him once more yield the ghost . . . . . *1 Hen. VI.* i 1 67
Where's the Prince Dauphin? I have news for him . . . i 2 46
These news, my lords, may cheer our drooping spirits . . v 2 1
I'll over then to England with this news . . . . v 3 167
Cold news for me, for I had hope of France . *2 Hen. VI.* i 1 237; iii 1 87
Thither go these news, as fast as horse can carry them: A sorry breakfast . . . . i 4 78
This news, I think, hath turn'd your weapon's edge . . ii 1 180
What news from France?—That all your interest in those territories Is utterly bereft you . . . . iii 1 83
Cold news, Lord Somerset: but God's will be done!—Cold news for me iii 1 86
Ay me! what is this world! what news are these! . . . iii 2 380
Come, cousin, let us tell the queen these news . . *3 Hen. VI.* i 1 182
Had he been ta'en, we should have heard the news; Had he been slain, we should have heard the news . . . . . . ii 1 4
If we should recount Our baleful news, and at each word's deliverance Stab poniards in our flesh till all were told, The words would add more anguish than the wounds . . . . ii 1 97
Ten days ago I drown'd these news in tears . . . . ii 1 104
If this news be true, Poor queen and son, your labour is but lost . iii 1 31
I like it well that our fair queen and mistress Smiles at her news . iii 3 168
Now, messenger, what letters or what news From France? . . iv 1 84
These news I must confess are full of grief . . . . iv 4 13
Unsavoury news! but how made he escape? . . . . iv 6 80
Where slept our scouts, or how are they seduced, That we could hear no news? . . . . v 1 20
Even now we heard the news: ah, couldst thou fly! . . . v 2 32
Ere ye come there, be sure to hear some news . . . . v 5 48
What news abroad?—No news so bad abroad as this at home *Richard III.* i 1 134
Now, by Saint Paul, this news is bad indeed . . . . i 1 138
Hear you the news abroad?—Ay, that the king is dead.—Bad news, by'r lady; seldom comes the better . . . . . ii 3 3
Doth this news hold of good King Edward's death?—Ay, sir, it is too true . . . . ii 3 7
What news?—Such news, my lord, as grieves me to unfold . . ii 4 38
For joy of this good news, Give Mistress Shore one gentle kiss the more iii 1 184
What news, what news, in this our tottering state?—It is a reeling world iii 2 37
And thereupon he sends you this good news . . . . iii 2 48
I am no mourner for that news, Because they have been still mine enemies iii 2 51
Towards three or four o'clock Look for the news that the Guildhall affords iii 5 102
Or else I swoon With this dead-killing news . . . . iv 1 36
Despiteful tidings! O unpleasing news! . . . . . iv 1 37
Dorset is fled to Richmond?—I hear that news, my lord . . . iv 2 89

News. Am I happy in thy news? *Richard III.* iv 3 24
Good news or bad, that thou comest in so bluntly?—Bad news, my lord iv 3 45
What news with you?—None good, my lord, to please you with the hearing; Nor none so bad, but it may well be told iv 4 457
Nothing but songs of death? Take that, until thou bring me better news iv 4 510
My liege, the Duke of Buckingham is taken; That is the best news iv 4 534
These news are every where; every tongue speaks 'em *Hen. VIII.* ii 2 39
I should be glad to hear such news as this Once every hour iii 2 24
That's news indeed iii 2 402
From the queen what is the news? v 1 61
You and I must walk a turn together; I have news to tell you v 1 94
What news, Æneas, from the field to-day? *Troi. and Cres.* i 1 111
By my troth, I knew you not: what news with you so early? iv 2 48
What's the matter?—The news is, sir, the Volsces are in arms *Coriolanus* i 1 228
Go with me; and I'll tell you excellent news of your husband i 3 101
I do not jest with you; there came news from him last night i 3 104
Yonder comes news. A wager they have met.—My horse to yours, no. i 4 1
How couldst thou in a mile confound an hour, And bring thy news so late? i 6 18
The augurer tells me we shall have news to-night.—Good or bad? ii 1 2
What's the news in Rome? iv 3 10
O slaves, I can tell you news,—news, you rascals!—What, what? iv 5 181
The bottom of the news is, our general is cut i' the middle iv 5 210
Some news is come That turns their countenances iv 6 58
We hear fearful news iv 6 139
I do not like this news.—Nor I.—Let's to the Capitol iv 6 158
Good news, good news; the ladies have prevail'd v 4 43
That you are both decipher'd, that's the news *T. Andron.* iv 2 8
News, news from heaven! Marcus, the post is come iv 3 77
Though news be sad, yet tell them merrily *Rom. and Jul.* ii 5 22
Thou shamest the music of sweet news By playing it to me with so sour a face ii 5 23
I would thou hadst my bones, and I thy news. Nay, come, I pray thee, speak ii 5 27
Is thy news good, or bad? answer to that; Say either, and I'll stay the circumstance: Let me be satisfied, is't good or bad? ii 5 35
Now comes the wanton blood up in your cheeks, They'll be in scarlet straight at any news ii 5 73
O, here comes my nurse, And she brings news iii 2 32
Ay me! what news? why dost thou wring thy hands? iii 2 36
These are news indeed!—Here comes your father; tell him so yourself iii 5 124
My dreams presage some joyful news at hand v 1 2
News from Verona!—How now, Balthasar! Dost thou not bring me letters? v 1 12
Pardon me for bringing these ill news, Since you did leave it for my office v 1 22
I brought my master news of Juliet's death; And then in post he came v 3 272
Tell Antony, Brutus is ta'en.—I'll tell the news *J. Cæsar* v 4 17
The king hath happily received, Macbeth, The news of thy success *Macb.* i 3 90
Give him tending; He brings great news i 5 39
What news more?—All is confirm'd, my lord, which was reported v 3 30
Laertes, what's the news with you? You told us of some suit *Hamlet* i 2 42
Thou still hast been the father of good news ii 2 42
My news shall be the fruit to that great feast ii 2 52
What's the news?—None, my lord, but that the world's grown honest ii 2 240
But your news is not true. Let me question more in particular ii 2 243
My lord, I have news to tell you.—My lord, I have news to tell you ii 2 408
I cannot live to hear the news from England v 2 365
I know no news, my lord.—What paper were you reading?—Nothing *Lear* i 2 29
You have heard of the news abroad; I mean the whispered ones? ii 1 8
I have heard strange news.—If it be true, all vengeance comes too short ii 1 89
Another way, The news is not so tart iv 2 88
Laugh At gilded butterflies, and hear poor rogues Talk of court news v 3 14
There is no composition in these news That gives them credit *Othello* i 3 1
News, lads! our wars are done ii 1 20
This likewise is a friend.—See for the news ii 1 96
Besides these beneficial news, it is the celebration of his nuptial ii 2 7
The nature of bad news infects the teller *Ant. and Cleo.* i 2 99
This is stiff news i 2 104
What's the matter?—I know, by that same eye, there's some good news i 3 19
This is the news: he fishes, drinks, and wastes The lamps of night in revel i 4 4
Gracious madam, I that do bring the news made not the match ii 5 67
Though it be honest, it is never good To bring bad news ii 5 86
There's strange news come, sir.—What, man?—Cæsar and Lepidus have made wars upon Pompey iii 5 2
My news I might have told hereafter.—'Twill be naught: But let it be iii 5 22
The news is true, my lord; he is descried; Cæsar has taken Toryne iii 7 55
With news the time's with labour, and throes forth, Each minute, some iii 7 81
You clasp young Cupid's tables. Good news, gods! *Cymbeline* iii 2 39
If't be summer news, Smile to't before; if winterly, thou need'st But keep that countenance still iii 4 12
O noble misery, To be i' the field, and ask 'what news?' of me! v 3 65
Thou bring'st good news; I am called to be made free v 4 201
What are thy news? *3 Hen. VI.* iii 3 171
What's the news? *Tempest* v 1; *Mer. of Venice* ii 4; *As Y. Like It* i 2; *T. of Shrew* i 1; *K. John* v 6; *Richard II.* v 6; *2 Hen. IV.* ii 1; *Troi. and Cres.* v 1; *Coriolanus* v 4; *T. Andron.* iv 2; *T. of Athens* iii 6; *Othello* i 2; iv 1
What's the news with you? *Meas. for Meas.* i 2; iv 3; *M. N. Dream* i 1; *Othello* iii 4
What is thy (your) news? *T. G. of Ver.* iii i; *2 Hen. IV.* v 3; *Richard III.* ii 4
What news? *Mer. Wives* i 4; *Meas. for Meas.* iii 2; iv 2; *Much Ado* i 3; v 1; *M. N. Dream* iii 2; *Mer. of Venice* i 2; *T. of Shrew* v 2; *K. John* v 5; *Richard II.* i 4; *1 Hen. IV.* ii 2; v 2; *2 Hen. IV.* i 1; ii 1; ii 4; iv 1; *2 Hen. VI.* iii 2; iv 3; *3 Hen. VI.* i 2; iv 6; *Richard III.* ii 4; iv 4; *Hen. VIII.* i 3; *Coriolanus* iv 6; *Rom. and Jul.* ii 5; iii 2; iii 3; *T. of Athens* i 2; *J. Cæsar* v 3; *Macbeth* i 7; *Hamlet* i 5; iv 7; *Lear* i 2; iv 2; *Ant. and Cleo.* iv 3; *Cymbeline* i 1
What news abroad? *Meas. for Meas.* iii 2; *K. John* v 6; *3 Hen. VI.* ii 1; *Richard III.* i 1; *Hen. VIII.* iii 2
What news with you? *Mer. Wives* iii 3; *T of Shrew* iv 3; *K. John* iv 2; *2 Hen. VI.* v 1; *Richard III.* iv 2; iv 4; *T. Andron.* iv 4
News-crammed. Then shall we be news-crammed *As Y. Like It* i 2 101
Newsmonger. Smiling pick-thanks and base newsmongers *1 Hen. IV.* iii 2 25
Newts and blind-worms, do no wrong *M. N. Dream* ii 2 11
Engenders the black toad and adder blue, The gilded newt *T. of Athens* iv 3 182
Eye of newt and toe of frog, Wool of bat and tongue of dog *Macbeth* iv 1 14
Next. He whom next thyself Of all the world I loved *Tempest* i 2 68
The next ensuing hour some foul mischance Torment me! *T. G. of Ver.* ii 2 11

Next. What dangerous action, stood it next to death, Would I not undergo for one calm look! *T. G. of Ver.* v 4 41
I will first make bold with your money; next, give me your hand *M. W.* ii 2 263
If they lead to any ill, I will leave them at the next turning *Much Ado* ii 1 160
Turn up on your right hand at the next turning, but, at the next turning of all, on your left; marry, at the very next turning, turn of no hand *Mer. of Venice* ii 2 43
And I speak the truth the next way *All's Well* i 3 63
Before you, and next unto high heaven, I love your son i 3 199
Come, good boy, the next way home *W. Tale* iii 3 131
Go you the next way with your findings iii 3 132
The eyes of men, After a well-graced actor leaves the stage, Are idly bent on him that enters next *Richard II.* v 2 25
'Tis the next way to turn tailor *1 Hen. IV.* iii 1 264
Thy promises are like Adonis' gardens, That one day bloom'd and fruitful were the next *1 Hen. VI.* i 6 7
Consider, lords, he is the next of blood *2 Hen. VI.* i 1 151
Next time I'll keep my dreams unto myself i 2 53
He is near you in descent, And should you fall, he is the next will mount iii 1 22
Humphrey being dead, as he shall be, And Henry put apart, the next for me iii 1 383
Each following day Became the next day's master *Hen. VIII.* i 1 17
Loved him next heaven iii 1 130
Since I had my office, I have kept you next my heart iii 2 157
Good morrow.—Ay, and good next day too *Troi. and Cres.* iii 3 69
Well, bury him, and bury me the next *T. Andron.* i 1 386
Come when you are next prepared for *Othello* iv 1 167
Give me but this [wife] I have, And sear up my embracements from a next With bonds of death! *Cymbeline* i 1 116
Nibbling. Turfy mountains, where live nibbling sheep *Tempest* iv 1 62
And as pigeons bill, so wedlock would be nibbling *As Y. Like It* iii 3 83
Nicander. Bid Nicander Bring me the satin coffer *Pericles* iii 1 67
Nicanor. Know you me yet?—Nicanor? no.—The same, sir *Coriolanus* iv 3 6
You will be welcome with this intelligence, Nicanor iv 3 31
Nice. Whom I affect; but she is nice and coy *T. G. of Ver.* iii 1 82
Despite his nice fence and his active practice *Much Ado* v 1 75
These are humours; these betray nice wenches *L. L. Lost* iii 1 24
We'll not be nice: take hands v 2 219
Be not nice.—We can afford no more at such a price v 2 222
This is the ape of form, monsieur the nice v 2 325
I am not solely led By nice direction of a maiden's eyes *Mer. of Venice* ii 1 14
Nor the lawyer's, which is politic, nor the lady's, which is nice *As Y. L. It* iv 1 14
I am not so nice, To change true rules for old inventions *T. of Shrew* iii 1 80
Goaded with most sharp occasions, Which lay nice manners by *All's Well* v 1 15
He that stands upon a slippery place Makes nice of no vile hold *K. John* iii 4 138
To set so rich a main On the nice hazard of one doubtful hour *1 Hen. IV.* iv 1 48
Hence, therefore, thou nice crutch! *2 Hen. IV.* i 1 145
Never, O never, do his ghost the wrong To hold your honour more precise and nice With others than with him! ii 3 40
Every idle, nice and wanton reason Shall to the king taste of this action iv 1 191
O Kate, nice customs curtsy to great kings *Hen. V.* v 2 293
For upholding the nice fashion of your country in denying me a kiss v 2 299
But in these nice sharp quillets of the law, Good faith, I am no wiser than a daw *1 Hen. VI.* ii 4 17
Why, brother, wherefore stand you on nice points? *3 Hen. VI.* iv 7 58
The respects thereof are nice and trivial *Richard III.* iii 7 175
To prenominate in nice conjecture Where thou wilt hit me dead *T. and C.* iv 5 250
Bade him bethink How nice the quarrel was *Rom. and Jul.* iii 1 159
The letter was not nice but full of charge Of dear import v 2 18
It is not meet That every nice offence should bear his comment *J. Cæsar* iv 3 8
O, relation Too nice, and yet too true! *Macbeth* iv 3 174
Or feed upon such nice and waterish diet *Othello* iii 3 15
When mine hours Were nice and lucky *Ant. and Cleo.* iii 13 180
Change of prides, disdain, Nice longing, slanders, mutability *Cymbeline* ii 5 26
Nicely. They that dally nicely with words may quickly make them wanton *T. Night* iii 1 17
Can sick men play so nicely with their names? *Richard II.* ii 1 84
Nicely charge your understanding soul With opening titles miscreate *Hen. V.* i 2 15
Haply a woman's voice may do some good, When articles too nicely urged he stood on v 2 94
Twenty silly ducking observants That stretch their duties nicely *Lear* ii 2 110
What safe and nicely I might well delay By rule of knighthood, I disdain v 3 144
Two winking Cupids Of silver, each on one foot standing, nicely Depending on their brands *Cymbeline* ii 4 90
Let not conscience, Which is but cold, inflaming love i' thy bosom, Inflame too nicely *Pericles* iv 1 6
Nicely-gawded. Their nicely-gawded cheeks *Coriolanus* ii 1 233
Niceness. Fear and niceness—The handmaids of all women *Cymbeline* iii 4 158
Nice-preserved. Now perforce we will enjoy That nice-preserved honesty of yours *T. Andron.* ii 3 135
Nicer. And between these main parcels of dispatch effected many nicer needs *All's Well* iv 3 105
Nicety. Lay by all nicety and prolixious blushes *Meas. for Meas.* ii 4 162
Nicholas. There; and Saint Nicholas be thy speed! *T. G. of Ver.* iii 1 300
Joseph, Nicholas, Philip, Walter, Sugarsop and the rest *T. of Shrew* iv 1 92
If they meet not with Saint Nicholas' clerks, I'll give thee this neck.—No, I'll none of it *1 Hen. IV.* ii 1 68
I know thou worshippest Saint Nicholas as truly as a man of falsehood may ii 1 71
A monk o' the Chartreux.—O, Nicholas Hopkins?—He *Hen. VIII.* i 1 221
He was brought to this By a vain prophecy of Nicholas Hopkins i 2 147
Give my charge up to Sir Nicholas Vaux, Who undertakes you to your end ii 1 96
Nick. He loved her out of all nick *T. G. of Ver.* iv 2 76
His man with scissors nicks him like a fool *Com. of Errors* v 1 175
Nick Bottom, the weaver.—Ready *M. N. Dream* i 2 18
Nicked. The itch of his affection should not then Have nick'd his captainship *Ant. and Cleo.* iii 13 8
Nickname. You nickname virtue; vice you should have spoke *L. L. Lost* v 2 349
Speak to my gossip Venus one fair word, One nick-name for her purblind son and heir, Young Adam Cupid *Rom. and Jul.* ii 1 12
You jig, you amble, and you lisp, and nick-name God's creatures *Hamlet* iii 1 151
Niece. What is he that you ask for, niece?—My cousin means Signior Benedick of Padua *Much Ado* i 1 34
Faith, niece, you tax Signior Benedick too much; but he'll be meet with you i 1 46
You must not, sir, mistake my niece i 1 61
You will never run mad, niece.—No, not till a hot January i 1 93
He loved my niece your daughter and meant to acknowledge it i 2 12
By my troth, niece, thou wilt never get thee a husband ii 1 19
Well, niece, I trust you will be ruled by your father ii 1 53
Well, niece, I hope to see you one day fitted with a husband ii 1 60

Niece. Niece, will you look to those things I told you of?—I cry you mercy, uncle . . . . *Much Ado* ii 1 351
What was it you told me of to-day, that your niece Beatrice was in love? ii 3 93
I am sorry for your niece. Shall we go seek Benedick, and tell him? . ii 3 207
God knows I loved my niece; And she is dead, slander'd to death . v 1 87
Your niece regards me with an eye of favour . . . . . . v 4 22
This duke Hath ta'en displeasure 'gainst his gentle niece *As Y. Like It* i 2 290
You, niece, provide yourself: If you outstay the time, upon mine honour, And in the greatness of my word, you die . . . . i 3 89
O my dear niece, welcome thou art to me! . . . . . v 4 153
What a plague means my niece, to take the death of her brother thus? I am sure care's an enemy to life . . . . *T. Night* i 3 1
He's drunk nightly in your company.—With drinking healths to my niece . . . . i 3 40
He's a coward and a coystrill that will not drink to my niece . . i 3 43
Your niece will not be seen; or if she be, it's four to one she'll none of me i 3 112
I can write very like my lady your niece . . . . . . ii 3 174
He shall think, by the letters that thou wilt drop, that they come from my niece, and that she's in love with him . . . . . ii 3 179
If I cannot recover your niece, I am a foul way out . . . . ii 3 200
My fortunes having cast me on your niece give me this prerogative . ii 5 78
Will you encounter the house? my niece is desirous you should enter . iii 1 83
I am bound to your niece, sir; I mean, she is the list of my voyage . iii 1 85
I saw your niece do more favours to the count's serving-man than ever she bestowed upon me . . . . iii 2 6
My niece is already in the belief that he's mad . . . . iii 4 149
Of good capacity and breeding; his employment between his lord and my niece confirms no less . . . . iii 4 205
Here he comes with your niece: give them way till he take leave . iii 4 216
As the old hermit of Prague, that never saw pen and ink, very wittily said to a niece of King Gorboduc, 'That that is is' . . . . iv 2 16
I am now so far in offence with my niece that I cannot pursue with any safety this sport to the upshot . . . . iv 2 75
Make this match; Give with our niece a dowry large enough . *K. John* ii 1 469
What say these young ones? What say you, my niece? . . . ii 1 521
Did I let pass the abuse done to my niece? . . . . *3 Hen. VI.* iii 3 188
You have no judgement, niece . . . . . . *Troi. and Cres.* i 2 99
Good niece, do, sweet niece . . . . i 2 194
My niece is horribly in love with a thing you have, sweet queen . iii 1 106
Commend me to your niece.—I will, sweet queen . . . . iii 1 159
Who is this? my niece, that flies away so fast! . . . *T. Andron.* ii 4 11
Gentle niece, what stern ungentle hands Have lopp'd and hew'd and made thy body bare Of her two branches? . . . . . . ii 4 16
But, lovely niece, that mean is cut from thee . . . . . ii 4 40
See how my wretched sister sobs and weeps.—Patience, dear niece . iii 1 138
Thy niece and I, poor creatures, want our hands . . . . iii 2 5
Sit down, sweet niece: brother, sit down by me . . . . . iv 1 65
Write thou, good niece; and here display, at last, What God will have discover'd for revenge . . . . iv 1 73
Signior Placentio and his lovely nieces . . . . *Rom. and Jul.* i 2 70
I scarce did know you, uncle: there lies your niece, Whose breath, indeed, these hands have newly stopp'd . . . . . *Othello* v 2 201
Moreover, if you please, a niece of mine Shall there attend you *Pericles* iii 4 15

Niggard. Why is Time such a niggard of hair? . . . *Com. of Errors* ii 2 78
The devil is a niggard, Or has given all before . . . *Hen. VIII.* i 1 70
And those our droplets which From niggard nature fall . *T. of Athens* v 4 77
The deep of night is crept upon our talk, And nature must obey necessity; Which we will niggard with a little rest . . *J. Cæsar* iv 3 228
Be not a niggard of your speech: how goes't? . . . . *Macbeth* iv 3 180
Niggard of question; but, of our demands, Most free in his reply *Hamlet* iii 1 13

Niggardly. Fee'd every slight occasion that could but niggardly give me sight of her . . . . *Mer. Wives* ii 2 205
To a niggardly host and more sparing guest . . *Com. of Errors* iii 1 27
The niggardly rascally sheep-biter . . . . . . *T. Night* ii 5 6
Of a weak and niggardly projection . . . . . *Hen. V.* ii 4 46

Nigh. But was not this nigh shore? . . . . . . *Tempest* i 2 216
Here comes your man; now is your husband nigh . *Com. of Errors* ii 1 43
Never harm, Nor spell, nor charm, Come our lovely lady nigh *M. N. D.* ii 2 18
Then I well perceive you are not nigh . . . . ii 2 155
Freeze, freeze, thou bitter sky, That dost not bite so nigh As benefits forgot . . . . *As Y. Like It* ii 7 185
Most noble sir, That which I shall report will bear no credit, Were not the proof so nigh . . . . *W. Tale* v 1 180
And grapple with him ere he come so nigh . . . *K. John* v 1 61
I am on fire To hear this rich reprisal is so nigh And yet not ours. Come, let me taste my horse . . . . *1 Hen. IV.* iv 1 118
Was I for this nigh wreck'd upon the sea? . . . *2 Hen. VI.* iii 2 82
My lord, cheer up your spirits: our foes are nigh . . *3 Hen. VI.* ii 2 56
How nigh is Clarence now?—At Southam I did leave him with his forces v 1 8
Ah, who is nigh? come to me, friend or foe, And tell me who is victor? v 2 5
Please you, therefore, draw nigh, and take your places . *T. Andron.* v 3 24
To do worse to you were fell cruelty, Which is too nigh your person *Macb.* iv 2 72
Being anger'd, her revenge being nigh, Bade her wrong stay . *Othello* iii 3 153
So nigh at least That though his actions were not visible, yet Report should render him hourly to your ear As truly as he moves *Cymbeline* iii 4 151

Night. Urchins Shall, for that vast of night that they may work, All exercise on thee . . . . *Tempest* i 2 327
And teach me how To name the bigger light, and how the less, That burn by day and night . . . . i 2 336
'Tis fresh morning with me When you are by at night . . . iii 1 34
When I shall think, or Phœbus' steeds are founder'd, Or Night kept chain'd below . . . . iv 1 31
Be more abstemious, Or else, good night your vow! . . . . iv 1 54
As the morning steals upon the night, Melting the darkness . . . v 1 65
To my poor cell, where you shall take your rest For this one night . v 1 302
One fading moment's mirth [bought] With twenty watchful, weary, tedious nights . . . . *T. G. of Ver.* i 1 31
Last night she enjoined me to write some lines to one she loves . . ii 1 93
This night he meaneth with a corded ladder To climb celestial Silvia's chamber-window . . . . ii 6 33
My friend This night intends to steal away your daughter . . . iii 1 11
No man hath access by day to her.—Why, then, I would resort to her by night.—Ay, but the doors be lock'd and keys kept safe, That no man hath recourse to her by night . . . . iii 1 110
When would you use it? pray, sir, tell me that.—This very night . iii 1 124
What's here? 'Silvia, this night I will enfranchise thee' . . . iii 1 151
Except I be by Silvia in the night, There is no music in the nightingale iii 1 178
Visit by night your lady's chamber-window With some sweet concert . iii 2 83
The night's dead silence Will well become such sweet-complaining grievance . . . . iii 2 85

Night. And thy advice this night I'll put in practice . . *T. G. of Ver.* iii 2 89
By this pale queen of night . . . . iv 2 100
It hath been the longest night That e'er I watch'd and the most heaviest iv 2 140
We'll have a posset for't soon at night, in faith . . . *Mer. Wives* i 4 9
Thine own true knight, By day or night, Or any kind of light . . ii 1 16
Take heed, have open eye, for thieves do foot by night . . . ii 1 126
Come you to me at night; you shall know how I speed . . . ii 2 277
There want not many that do fear In deep of night to walk by this Herne's oak . . . . iv 4 40
The night is dark; light and spirits will become it well . . . v 2 13
Which, at the very instant of Falstaff's and our meeting, they will at once display to the night . . . . v 3 17
You moonshine revellers, and shades of night . . . . . v 5 42
Soon at night I'll send him certain word of my success *Meas. for Meas.* i 4 88
This will last out a night in Russia, When nights are longest there . ii 1 139
This night's the time That I should do what I abhor to name . . iii 1 101
If for this night he entreat you to his bed, give him promise of satisfaction iii 1 274
I made my promise Upon the heavy middle of the night To call upon him iv 1 35
But make haste; The vaporous night approaches . . . . . iv 1 58
The best and wholesomest spirits of the night Envelope you! . . iv 2 76
He that drinks all night, and is hanged betimes in the morning, may sleep the sounder all the next day . . . . iv 3 49
I have been drinking hard all night . . . . iv 3 57
But Tuesday night last gone in's garden-house He knew me as a wife . v 1 229
Good night to your redress! . . . . v 1 301
As good to wink, sweet love, as look on night . . . *Com. of Errors* iii 2 58
Time comes stealing on by night and day . . . . . . iv 2 60
Faith, stay here this night; they will surely do us no harm . . iv 4 155
Ne'er may I look on day, nor sleep on night, But she tells to your highness simple truth! . . . . v 1 210
Yet hath my night of life some memory, My wasting lamps some fading glimmer left . . . . v 1 314
Don Peter of Arragon comes this night to Messina . . . . *Much Ado* i 1 2
He loved my niece your daughter and meant to acknowledge it this night i 2 14
There's a partridge wing saved, for the fool will eat no supper that night ii 1 156
I am for you, though it cost me ten nights' watchings . . . ii 1 388
At any unseasonable instant of the night . . . . ii 2 17
And bring them to see this the very night before the intended wedding ii 2 46
Now will he lie ten nights awake, carving the fashion of a new doublet ii 3 18
Get us some excellent music; for to-morrow night we would have it . ii 3 88
She'll be up twenty times a night, and there will she sit in her smock . ii 3 137
See her chamber-window entered, even the night before her wedding-day iii 2 117
If you hear a child cry in the night, you must call to the nurse . . iii 3 69
If you meet the prince in the night, you may stay him . . . iii 3 80
Bids me a thousand times good night . . . . iii 3 157
Partly by the dark night, which did deceive them . . . . iii 3 167
Shame her with what he saw o'er night and send her home again . . iii 3 174
Did see her, hear her, at that hour last night Talk with a ruffian . iv 1 91
Were you her bedfellow last night?—No, truly not; although, until last night, I have this twelvemonth been her bedfellow . . . . . iv 1 149
He swore a thing to me on Monday night, which he forswore on Tuesday morning . . . . v 1 169
Who in the night overheard me confessing to this man . . . . v 1 241
Pardon, goddess of the night, Those that slew thy virgin knight . . v 3 12
Now, unto thy bones good night! Yearly will I do this rite . . . v 3 22
And then, to sleep but three hours in the night, And not be seen to wink of all the day—When I was wont to think no harm all night And make a dark night too of half the day . . . . . . *L. L. Lost* i 1 42
Have no more profit of their shining nights Than those that walk and wot not what they [the stars] are . . . . i 1 90
As thy eye-beams, when their fresh rays have smote The night of dew that on my cheeks down flows . . . . iv 3 29
O, but for my love, day would turn to night! . . . . . . iv 3 233
Black is the badge of hell, The hue of dungeons and the suit of night . iv 3 255
Certain he would fight; yea From morn till night, out of his pavilion . v 2 660
Four days will quickly steep themselves in night; Four nights will quickly dream away the time; And then the moon, like to a silver bow New-bent in heaven, shall behold the night Of our solemnities *M. N. Dream* i 1 11
Brief as the lightning in the collied night . . . . i 1 145
If thou lovest me then, Steal forth thy father's house to-morrow night . i 1 164
To-morrow night, when Phœbe doth behold Her silver visage in the watery glass . . . . i 1 209
In our interlude before the duke and the duchess, on his wedding-day at night . . . . i 2 7
Request you and desire you to con them by to-morrow night . . . i 2 103
Thou speak'st aright; I am that merry wanderer of the night . . ii 1 43
Didst thou not lead him through the glimmering night? . . . . ii 1 77
No night is now with hymn or carol blest . . . . ii 1 102
In the spiced Indian air, by night, Full often hath she gossip'd by my side . . . . ii 1 124
To trust the opportunity of night And the ill counsel of a desert place . ii 1 217
For that It is not night when I do see your face, Therefore I think I am not in the night . . . . ii 1 221
There sleeps Titania sometime of the night, Lull'd in these flowers . ii 1 253
So, good night, with lullaby . . . . ii 2 19
Good night, sweet friend: Thy love ne'er alter till thy sweet life end! . ii 2 60
Night and silence.—Who is here? Weeds of Athens he doth wear . ii 2 70
Doth the moon shine that night we play our play? . . . . . iii 1 52
Dark night, that from the eye his function takes, The ear more quick of apprehension makes . . . . iii 2 177
Who more engilds the night Than all yon fiery oes and eyes of light . iii 2 187
Since night you loved me; yet since night you left me . . . . iii 2 275
What, have you come by night And stolen my love's heart from him? . iii 2 283
Overcast the night; The starry welkin cover thou anon With drooping fog iii 2 355
Night's swift dragons cut the clouds full fast . . . . . . iii 2 379
And must for aye consort with black-brow'd night . . . . . iii 2 387
O weary night, O long and tedious night, Abate thy hours! . . . iii 2 431
Think no more of this night's accidents But as the fierce vexation of a dream . . . . iv 1 73
Then, my queen, in silence sad, Trip we after night's shade . . . iv 1 101
Tell me how it came this night That I sleeping here was found . . iv 1 105
In the night, imagining some fear, How easy is a bush supposed a bear! v 1 21
All the story of the night told over . . . . v 1 23
This grisly beast, which Lion hight by name, The trusty Thisby, coming first by night, Did scare away . . . . v 1 141
O grim-look'd night! O night with hue so black! O night, which ever art when day is not! O night, O night! alack, alack, alack! . . v 1 171
I fear we shall out-sleep the coming morn As much as we this night have overwatch'd . . . . v 1 373

Night. This palpable-gross play hath well beguiled The heavy gait of night *M. N. Dream* v 1 375
Now it is the time of night That the graves all gaping wide, Every one lets forth his sprite v 1 386
I am glad 'tis night, you do not look on me, For I am much ashamed *Mer. of Venice* ii 6 34
Come at once; For the close night doth play the runaway ii 6 47
Your daughter spent in Genoa, as I heard, in one night fourscore ducats iii 1 114
He plies the duke at morning and at night iii 2 279
I must away this night toward Padua iv 1 403
In such a night as this, When the sweet wind did gently kiss the trees v 1 1
In such a night Troilus methinks mounted the Troyan walls v 1 3
In such a night Did Thisbe fearfully o'ertrip the dew v 1 6
In such a night Stood Dido with a willow in her hand v 1 9
In such a night Medea gather'd the enchanted herbs v 1 12
In such a night Did Jessica steal from the wealthy Jew v 1 14
In such a night Did young Lorenzo swear he loved her well v 1 17
In such a night Did pretty Jessica, like a little shrew, Slander her love v 1 20
I hear the footing of a man.—Who comes so fast in silence of the night? v 1 25
Soft stillness and the night Become the touches of sweet harmony v 1 56
The motions of his spirit are dull as night v 1 86
This night methinks is but the daylight sick; It looks a little paler v 1 124
By these blessed candles of the night v 1 220
Lie not a night from home; watch me like Argus v 1 230
The doctor's clerk In lieu of this last night did lie with me v 1 262
Whether till the next night she had rather stay, Or go to bed now v 1 302
This night he means To burn the lodging where you use to lie *As Y. L. It* ii 3 22
Thou, thrice-crowned queen of night, survey With thy chaste eye iii 2 2
That a great cause of the night is lack of the sun iii 2 29
Leander, he would have lived many a fair year, though Hero had turned nun, if it had not been for a hot midsummer night iv 1 103
This happy number That have endured shrewd days and nights with us v 4 179
Let me entreat of you To pardon me yet for a night or two *T. of Shrew* Ind. 2 121
Is this your speeding? nay, then, good night our part! ii 1 303
You will away to-night?—I must away to-day, before night come iii 2 192
To-morrow't shall be mended, And, for this night, we'll fast for company iv 1 180
Last night she slept not, nor to-night she shall not iv 1 201
She shall watch all night: And if she chance to nod I'll rail and brawl iv 1 208
And there, this night, We'll pass the business privately and well iv 4 56
To watch the night in storms, the day in cold, Whilst thou liest warm at home v 2 150
God give you good night!—Now, go thy ways v 2 187
I will be gone . . . Come, night; end, day! For with the dark, poor thief, I'll steal away *All's Well* iii 2 131
Tell me what a sprat you shall find him; which you shall see this very night iii 6 114
Every night he comes With musics of all sorts and songs iii 7 39
And on your finger in the night I'll put Another ring iv 2 61
And this night he fleshes his will in the spoil of her honour iv 3 19
Has sat i' the stocks all night, poor gallant knave iv 3 117
When saucy trusting of the cozen'd thoughts Defiles the pitchy night iv 4 24
But this exceeding posting day and night Must wear your spirits low v 1 1
Since you have made the days and nights as one, To wear your gentle limbs in my affairs v 1 3
He hence removed last night and with more haste Than is his use v 1 23
I had talk of you last night v 2 57
You must come in earlier o' nights *T. Night* i 3 5
A foolish knight that you brought in one night here to be her wooer i 3 16
And sing them loud even in the dead of night i 5 290
Thou wast in very gracious fooling last night ii 3 23
Have you no wit, manners, nor honesty, but to gabble like tinkers at this time of night? ii 3 95
For this night, to bed, and dream on the event ii 3 191
That old and antique song we heard last night ii 4 3
Love's night is noon iii 1 160
Go see your lodging.—I am not weary, and 'tis long to night iii 3 21
Not a minute's vacancy, Both day and night did we keep company v 1 99
And all those swearings keep as true in soul As doth that orbed continent the fire That severs day from night v 1 279
Or both yourself and me Cry lost, and so good night! *W. Tale* i 2 411
Nor night nor day no rest: it is but weakness To bear the matter thus ii 3 1
Didst counsel and aid them, for their better safety, to fly away by night ii 2 22
If such thing be, thy mother Appear'd to me last night iii 3 18
The pale moon shines by night iv 3 16
Now blessed be the hour, by night or day, When I was got! *K. John* i 1 165
The midnight bell Did, with his iron tongue and brazen mouth, Sound on into the drowsy race of night iii 3 39
O amiable lovely death! . . . Arise forth from the couch of lasting night, Thou hate and terror to prosperity iii 4 27
Young gentlemen would be as sad as night, Only for wantonness iv 1 15
In sooth, I would you were a little sick, That I might sit all night and watch with you iv 1 30
Are wreck'd three nights ago on Goodwin Sands v 3 11
This night, whose black contagious breath Already smokes about the burning crest Of the old, feeble and day-wearied sun, Even this ill night, your breathing shall expire v 4 33
An hour or two before The stumbling night did part our weary powers v 5 18
Unkind remembrance! thou and eyeless night Have done me shame v 6 12
Here walk I in the black brow of night, To find you out v 6 17
News fitting to the night, Black, fearful, comfortless and horrible v 6 19
Half my power this night, Passing these flats, are taken by the tide v 6 39
For in a night the best part of my power, As I upon advantage did remove, Were in the Washes all unwarily Devoured by the unexpected flood v 7 61
To dwell in solemn shades of endless night *Richard II.* i 3 177
My oil-dried lamp and time-bewasted light Shall be extinct with age and endless night i 3 222
Pluck nights from me, but not lend a morrow i 3 228
Please to enter in the castle And there repose you for this night ii 3 161
The cloak of night being pluck'd from off their backs, Stand bare iii 2 45
Who all this while hath revell'd in the night Whilst we were wandering with the antipodes iii 2 48
Let them hence away, From Richard's night to Bolingbroke's fair day iii 2 218
In winter's tedious nights sit by the fire With good old folks v 1 40
With Cain go wander thorough shades of night v 6 43
Let not us that are squires of the night's body be called thieves of the day's beauty *1 Hen. IV.* i 2 27
A purse of gold most resolutely snatched on Monday night and most dissolutely spent on Tuesday morning i 2 39

Night. Who studies day and night To answer all the debt he owes to you *1 Hen. IV.* i 3 184
If he fall in, good night! or sink or swim i 3 194
I heard him tell it to one of his company last night at supper ii 1 62
I think you are more beholding to the night than to fern-seed for your walking invisible ii 1 98
A business that this night may execute iii 1 82
The moon shines fair; you may away by night iii 1 142
He held me last night at least nine hours In reckoning up iii 1 156
Making such difference 'twixt wake and sleep As is the difference betwixt day and night iii 1 220
When thou rannest up Gadshill in the night to catch my horse iii 3 43
Thou hast saved me a thousand marks in links and torches, walking with thee in the night iii 3 49
The other night I fell asleep here behind the arras and had my pocket picked iii 3 112
The king, I can tell you, looks for us all: we must away all night iv 2 63
And posted day and night To meet you on the way v 1 35
Yet once ere night I will embrace him with a soldier's arm v 2 73
Drew Priam's curtain in the dead of night *2 Hen. IV.* i 1 72
Your day's service at Shrewsbury hath a little gilded over your night's exploit on Gad's-hill i 2 169
I will ride thee o' nights like the mare ii 1 83
Where lay the king last night?—At Basingstoke, my lord ii 1 181
When wilt thou leave fighting o' days and foining o' nights? ii 4 252
Now comes in the sweetest morsel of the night ii 4 397
Canst thou, O partial sleep, give thy repose To the wet sea-boy in an hour so rude, And in the calmest and most stillest night, With all appliances and means to boot, Deny it to a king? iii 1 28
Do you remember since we lay all night in the windmill in Saint George's field? iii 2 207
No more of that.—Ha! 'twas a merry night. And is Jane Nightwork alive? iii 2 210
That keep'st the ports of slumber open wide To many a watchful night! iv 5 25
He whose brow with homely biggen bound Snores out the watch of night iv 5 28
Have you a ruffian that will swear, drink, dance, Revel the night? iv 5 126
Doth the man of war stay all night, sir? v 1 31
An we shall be merry, now comes in the sweet o' the night v 3 53
I am fortune's steward—get on thy boots: we'll ride all night v 3 138
As it were, to ride day and night v 5 21
I shall be sent for soon at night v 5 96
Grew like the summer grass, fastest by night *Hen. V.* i 1 65
You shall be soon dispatch'd with fair conditions: A night is but small breath and little pause To answer matters of this consequence ii 4 145
It now draws toward night: Beyond the river we'll encamp ourselves iii 6 179
What a long night is this! I will not change my horse with any that treads iii 7 11
Through the foul womb of night The hum of either army stilly sounds iv Prol. 4
In high and boastful neighs Piercing the night's dull ear iv Prol. 11
And chide the cripple tardy-gaited night iv Prol. 20
Nor doth he dedicate one jot of colour Unto the weary and all-watched night iv Prol. 38
Behold, as may unworthiness define, A little touch of Harry in the night iv Prol. 47
Why, the enemy is loud; you hear him all night iv 1 77
As cold a night as 'tis, he could wish himself in Thames up to the neck iv 1 119
Horrid night, the child of hell iv 1 288
Like a lackey, from the rise to set Sweats in the eye of Phœbus and all night Sleeps in Elysium iv 1 290
Winding up days with toil and nights with sleep iv 1 296
And my poor soldiers tell me, yet ere night They'll be in fresher robes iv 3 116
Please your majesty, a rascal that swaggered with me last night iv 7 131
Witness the night, your garments, your lowliness iv 8 55
At night, when you come into your closet, you'll question this gentlewoman about me v 2 210
Hung be the heavens with black, yield day to night! *1 Hen. VI.* i 1 1
This night the siege assuredly I'll raise i 2 130
This happy night the Frenchmen are secure, Having all day caroused ii 1 11
Most part of all this night, Within her quarter and mine own precinct I was employ'd in passing to and fro ii 1 67
Night is fled, Whose pitchy mantle over-veil'd the earth ii 2 1
As far as I could well discern For smoke and dusky vapours of the night ii 2 27
A pair of loving turtle-doves That could not live asunder day or night ii 2 31
This brawl to-day . . . Shall send between the red rose and the white A thousand souls to death and deadly night ii 4 127
By day, by night, waking and in my dreams *2 Hen. VI.* i 1 26
My troublous dream this night doth make me sad i 2 22
My lords, he did speak them to me in the garret one night i 3 194
Deep night, dark night, the silent of the night, The time of night when Troy was set on fire i 4 19
Invite my Lords of Salisbury and Warwick To sup with me to-morrow night i 4 84
Let never day nor night unhallow'd pass ii 1 85
For this night we will repose us here: To-morrow toward London ii 1 200
Dark shall be my light and night my day ii 4 40
I have watch'd the night, Ay, night by night, in studying good iii 1 111
Well could I curse away a winter's night iii 2 335
Loud-howling wolves arouse the jades That drag the tragic melancholy night iv 1 4
Soldiers, defer the spoil of the city until night iv 7 143
Soldiers, stay and lodge by me this night *3 Hen. VI.* i 1 32
The shepherd, blowing of his nails, Can neither call it perfect day nor night ii 5 4
May yet ere night yield both my life and them To some man else ii 5 59
But, in night's coverture, Thy brother being carelessly encamp'd, . . . We may surprise and take him at our pleasure iv 2 13
Well cover'd with the night's black mantle iv 2 22
These gates must not be shut But in the night or in the time of war iv 7 36
Now, for this night, let's harbour here in York iv 7 79
The thorny wood, Which . . . Must by the roots be hewn up yet ere night v 4 69
Let Æsop fable in a winter's night v 5 25
Thine uncles and myself Have in our armours watch'd the winter's night v 7 17
Black night o'ershade thy day, and death thy life! *Richard III.* i 2 131
O, I have pass'd a miserable night, So full of ugly sights! i 4 2
I would not spend another such a night, Though 'twere to buy a world of happy days, So full of dismal terror was the time! i 4 5

Night. Unto the kingdom of perpetual night *Richard III.* i 4 47
Sorrow breaks seasons and reposing hours, Makes the night morning, and the noon-tide night i 4 77
Gave himself, All thin and naked, to the numb cold night ii 1 117
When the sun sets, who doth not look for night? ii 3 34
Last night, I hear, they lay at Northampton; At Stony-Stratford will they be to-night ii 4 1
One night, as we did sit at supper, My uncle Rivers talk'd how I did grow ii 4 10
Cannot thy master sleep these tedious nights?—So it should seem iii 2 6
And Anne my wife hath bid the world good night iv 3 39
Say, that right for right Hath dimm'd your infant morn to aged night iv 4 16
Forbear to sleep the nights, and fast the days iv 4 118
Of all one pain, save for a night of groans Endured of her iv 4 303
Day, yield me not thy light; nor, night, thy rest! iv 4 401
Into the blind cave of eternal night v 3 62
About the mid of night come to my tent And help to arm me v 3 77
All comfort that the dark night can afford Be to thy person! v 3 80
Now this masque Was cried incomparable; and the ensuing night Made it a fool and beggar *Hen. VIII.* i 1 27
By day and night, He's traitor to the height i 2 213
This night he makes a supper, and a great one, To many lords and ladies i 3 52
I was spoke to, with Sir Henry Guildford This night to be comptrollers i 3 67
This night he dedicates To fair content and you i 4 2
Of this so noble and so fair assembly This night to meet here i 4 68
Three nights after this, About the hour of eight iv 2 25
Good hour of night, Sir Thomas! v 1 5
Many good nights, my lord: I rest your servant v 1 55
I wish your highness A quiet night v 1 77
Less valiant than the virgin in the night *Troi. and Cres.* i 1 11
Now play him me, Patroclus, Arming to answer in a night alarm i 3 171
I have loved you night and day For many weary months iii 2 122
Dreaming night will hide our joys no longer, I would not from thee.—Night hath been too brief iv 2 10
Help to trim my tent: This night in banqueting must all be spent v 1 51
Good night and welcome, both at once, to those That go or tarry v 1 84
I will not meet with you to-morrow night v 2 73
This whole night Hath nothing been but shapes and forms of slaughter v 3 11
We'll forth and fight, Do deeds worth praise and tell you them at night v 3 93
How the sun begins to set; How ugly night comes breathing at his heels v 8 6
The dragon wing of night o'erspreads the earth v 8 17
Never go home; here starve we out the night v 10 2
I do not jest with you; there came news from him last night *Coriolanus* i 3 104
One that converses more with the buttock of the night than with the forehead of the morning ii 1 57
And feasts the nobles of the state At his house this night iv 4 10
Let me have war, say I; it exceeds peace as far as day does night iv 5 237
I have been troubled in my sleep this night, But dawning day new comfort hath inspired *T. Andron.* ii 2 9
Here, at dead time of the night, A thousand fiends, a thousand hissing snakes ii 3 99
So pale did shine the moon on Pyramus When he by night lay bathed in maiden blood ii 3 232
For all the frosty nights that I have watch'd iii 1 5
Acts of black night, abominable deeds, Complots of mischief v 1 64
Set fire on barns and hay-stacks in the night v 1 133
He did discourse To love-sick Dido's sad attending ear The story of that baleful burning night v 3 83
Locks fair daylight out And makes himself an artificial night *R. and J.* i 1 146
This night I hold an old accustom'd feast i 2 20
At my poor house look to behold this night Earth-treading stars i 2 24
Such delight Among fresh female buds shall you this night Inherit i 2 29
Of all days in the year, Come Lammas-eve at night shall she be fourteen i 3 17
Can you love the gentleman? This night you shall behold him at our feast i 3 80
Go, girl, seek happy nights to happy days i 3 106
In this state she gallops night by night Through lovers' brains i 4 70
This is that very Mab That plats the manes of horses in the night i 4 89
Some consequence yet hanging in the stars Shall bitterly begin his fearful date With this night's revels i 4 109
She hangs upon the cheek of night Like a rich jewel in an Ethiope's ear i 5 47
For I ne'er saw true beauty till this night i 5 55
A villain that is hither come in spite, To scorn at our solemnity this night i 5 65
Hid himself among these trees, To be consorted with the humorous night ii 1 31
Her eyes in heaven Would through the airy region stream so bright That birds would sing and think it were not night ii 2 22
Thou art As glorious to this night, being o'er my head, As is a winged messenger of heaven ii 2 27
What man art thou that thus bescreen'd in night So stumblest on my counsel? ii 2 52
I have night's cloak to hide me from their sight ii 2 75
This mask of night is on my face, Else would a maiden blush bepaint my cheek ii 2 85
Pardon me, And not impute this yielding to light love, Which the dark night hath so discovered ii 2 106
Good night, good night! as sweet repose and rest Come to thy heart as that within my breast! ii 2 123
Blessed night! I am afeard, Being in night, all this is but a dream ii 2 139
A thousand times good night!—A thousand times the worse, to want thy light ii 2 155
How silver-sweet sound lovers' tongues by night! ii 2 166
Good night, good night! parting is such sweet sorrow, That I shall say good night till it be morrow ii 2 185
The grey-eyed morn smiles on the frowning night, Chequering the eastern clouds with streaks of light ii 3 1
Now, ere the sun advance his burning eye, The day to cheer and night's dank dew to dry ii 3 6
You gave us the counterfeit fairly last night ii 4 48
To the high top-gallant of my joy Must be my convoy in the secret night ii 4 203
I am the drudge and toil in your delight, But you shall bear the burden soon at night ii 5 78
Phaëthon would whip you to the west, And bring in cloudy night immediately iii 2 4
Spread thy close curtain, love-performing night iii 2 5
Night. If love be blind, It best agrees with night. Come, civil night, Thou sober-suited matron, all in black *Rom. and Jul.* iii 2 10
Come, night; come, Romeo; come, thou day in night iii 2 17
Lie upon the wings of night Whiter than new snow on a raven's back iii 2 18
Come, gentle night, come, loving, black-brow'd night, Give me my Romeo iii 2 20
Cut him out in little stars, And he will make the face of heaven so fine That all the world will be in love with night iii 2 24
So tedious is this day As is the night before some festival To an impatient child that hath new robes iii 2 29
Your Romeo will be here at night: I'll to him; he is hid at Laurence' cell iii 2 140
O Lord, I could have stay'd here all the night To hear good counsel iii 3 159
Night's candles are burnt out, and jocund day Stands tiptoe on the misty mountain tops iii 5 9
Some meteor that the sun exhales, To be to thee this night a torch-bearer iii 5 14
God's bread! it makes me mad: Day, night, hour, tide, time, work, play, Alone, in company, still my care hath been To have her match'd iii 5 178
To-morrow night look that thou lie alone; Let not thy nurse lie with thee iv 1 91
And that very night Shall Romeo bear thee hence to Mantua iv 1 116
We shall be short in our provision: 'Tis now near night iv 2 39
Let me now be left alone, And let the nurse this night sit up with you iv 3 10
The horrible conceit of death and night, Together with the terror of the place iv 3 37
Where, as they say, At some hours in the night spirits resort iv 3 44
Faith, you'll be sick to-morrow For this night's watching iv 4 8
I have watch'd ere now All night for lesser cause, and ne'er been sick iv 4 10
For the next night, I warrant, The County Paris hath set up his rest, That you shall rest but little iv 5 5
O son! the night before thy wedding-day Hath Death lain with thy wife iv 5 35
What, with a torch! muffle me, night, awhile v 3 21
And never from this palace of dim night Depart again v 3 107
I writ to Romeo, That he should hither come as this dire night v 3 247
Lord Timon, this thy creature By night frequents my house *T. of Athens* i 1 117
How many prodigal bits have slaves and peasants This night englutted! ii 2 175
Has friendship such a faint and milky heart, It turns in less than two nights? O you gods! iii 1 58
Where liest o' nights, Timon?—Under that's above me iv 3 292
When the day serves, before black-corner'd night v 1 47
Sleek-headed men and such as sleep o' nights *J. Cæsar* i 2 193
I will this night, In several hands, in at his windows throw, As if they came from several citizens, Writings i 2 319
The bird of night did sit Even at noon-day upon the market-place i 3 26
What night is this!—A very pleasing night to honest men i 3 42
I have walk'd about the streets, Submitting me unto the perilous night i 3 47
Now could I, Casca, name to thee a man Most like this dreadful night i 3 73
This fearful night, There is no stir or walking in the streets i 3 126
What a fearful night is this! There's two or three of us have seen strange sights i 3 137
O conspiracy, Shamest thou to show thy dangerous brow by night, When evils are most free? ii 1 78
I have been up this hour, awake all night ii 1 88
What watchful cares do interpose themselves Betwixt your eyes and night? ii 1 99
These apparent prodigies, The unaccustom'd terror of this night ii 1 199
To dare the vile contagion of the night And tempt the rheumy and unpurged air To add unto his sickness ii 1 265
Antony, that revels long o' nights, Is notwithstanding up ii 2 116
They mean this night in Sardis to be quarter'd iv 2 28
The deep of night is crept upon our talk, And nature must obey necessity iv 3 226
This was an ill beginning of the night iv 3 234
O setting sun, As in thy red rays thou dost sink to night v 3 61
And, Romans, yet ere night We shall try fortune in a second fight v 3 109
The ghost of Cæsar hath appear'd to me Two several times by night; at Sardis once, And, this last night, here in Philippi fields v 5 18
Night hangs upon mine eyes; my bones would rest v 5 41
Sleep shall neither night nor day Hang upon his pent-house lid *Macbeth* i 3 19
Come, thick night, And pall thee in the dunnest smoke of hell i 5 51
Put This night's great business into my dispatch; Which shall to all our nights and days to come Give solely sovereign sway i 5 69
How goes the night, boy?—The moon is down; I have not heard the clock ii 1 1
I dreamt last night of the three weird sisters ii 1 20
I believe drink gave thee the lie last night ii 3 42
The night has been unruly: where we lay, Our chimneys were blown down ii 3 59
The obscure bird Clamour'd the livelong night ii 3 65
'Twas a rough night.—My young remembrance cannot parallel A fellow to it ii 3 66
But this sore night Hath trifled former knowings ii 4 3
By the clock, 'tis day, And yet dark night strangles the travelling lamp ii 4 7
Is't night's predominance, or the day's shame, That darkness does the face of earth entomb, When living light should kiss it? ii 4 8
I must become a borrower of the night For a dark hour or twain iii 1 27
Adieu, Till you return at night iii 1 36
Let every man be master of his time Till seven at night iii 1 42
The shard-borne beetle with his drowsy hums Hath rung night's yawning peal iii 2 43
Come, seeling night, Scarf up the tender eye of pitiful day iii 2 46
Good things of day begin to droop and drowse; Whiles night's black agents to their preys do rouse iii 2 53
Good night: Stand not upon the order of your going, But go at once iii 4 118
Good night; and better health Attend his majesty!—A kind good night to all! iii 4 120
What is the night?—Almost at odds with morning, which is which iii 4 126
This night I'll spend Unto a dismal and a fatal end iii 5 20
We may again Give to our tables meat, sleep to our nights iii 6 34
Toad, that under cold stone Days and nights has thirty one iv 1 7
Receive what cheer you may: The night is long that never finds the day iv 3 240
I have two nights watched with you, but can perceive no truth in your report v 1 1
Entreated him along With us to watch the minutes of this night *Hamlet* i 1 27
That are so fortified against our story What we have two nights seen i 1 33
Last night of all, When yond same star that's westward from the pole Had made his course i 1 35
What art thou that usurp'st this time of night? i 1 46

Night. This sweaty haste Doth make the night joint-labourer with the day *Hamlet* i 1 78
The bird of dawning singeth all night long i 1 160
The nights are wholesome; then no planets strike, No fairy takes i 1 162
Two nights together had these gentlemen, Marcellus and Bernardo, on their watch, In the dead vast and middle of the night, Been thus encounter'd i 2 196
And I with them the third night kept the watch i 2 208
Would the night were come! Till then sit still, my soul i 2 256
To thine own self be true, And it must follow, as the night the day, Thou canst not then be false to any man i 3 79
Making night hideous i 4 54
I am thy father's spirit, Doom'd for a certain term to walk the night i 5 10
O day and night, but this is wondrous strange! i 5 164
Go to your rest; at night we'll feast together: Most welcome home! ii 2 84
To expostulate . . . Why day is day, night night, and time is time, Were nothing but to waste night, day and time ii 2 89
He whose sable arms, Black as his purpose, did the night resemble ii 2 475
Can you play the Murder of Gonzago?—Ay, my lord.—We'll ha't to-morrow night ii 2 565
My good friends, I'll leave you till night: you are welcome to Elsinore ii 2 572
As I think, they have already order This night to play before him iii 1 21
Sport and repose lock from me day and night! iii 2 227
'Tis now the very witching time of night, When churchyards yawn iii 2 406
Strengthen your patience in our last night's speech v 1 317
Your skill shall, like a star i' the darkest night, Stick fiery off indeed v 2 267
The mysteries of Hecate, and the night *Lear* i 1 112
When saw you my father last?—Why, the night gone by i 2 168
By day and night he wrongs me i 3 3
You have now the good advantage of the night ii 1 24
He's coming hither; now, i' the night, i' the haste ii 1 26
Thus out of season, threading dark-eyed night ii 1 121
Draw, you rogue: for, though it be night, yet the moon shines ii 2 34
There shall he sit till noon.—Till noon! till night, my lord; and all night too ii 2 142
The night before there was no purpose in them Of this remove ii 4 3
They are weary? They have travell'd all the night? Mere fetches ii 4 90
Alack, the night comes on, and the bleak winds Do sorely ruffle ii 4 303
Shut up your doors, my lord; 'tis a wild night: My Regan counsels well ii 4 311
This night, wherein the cub-drawn bear would couch iii 1 12
Here's a night pities neither wise man nor fool iii 2 13
Things that love night Love not such nights as these iii 2 42
Bring us to this hovel.—This is a brave night to cool a courtezan iii 2 79
I have received a letter this night; 'tis dangerous to be spoken iii 3 10
The tyranny of the open night's too rough For nature to endure iii 4 2
In such a night To shut me out! Pour on; I will endure. In such a night as this! O Regan, Goneril! iii 4 17
This cold night will turn us all to fools and madmen iii 4 80
'Tis a naughty night to swim in iii 4 116
Though their injunction be to bar my doors, And let this tyrannous night take hold upon you iii 4 156
The grief hath crazed my wits. What a night's this! iii 4 175
The sea, with such a storm as his bare head In hell-black night endured, would have buoy'd up, And quench'd the stelled fires iii 7 60
I' the last night's storm I such a fellow saw iv 1 34
What, i' the storm? i' the night? Let pity not be believed! iv 3 30
Mine enemy's dog, Though he had bit me, should have stood that night Against my fire iv 7 37
Nor I know not Where I did lodge last night iv 7 68
When, by night and negligence, the fire Is spied in populous cities *Othello* i 1 76
At this odd-even and dull watch o' the night i 1 124
Get weapons, ho! And raise some special officers of night i 1 183
The goodness of the night upon you, friends! What is the news? i 2 35
The galleys Have sent a dozen sequent messengers This very night i 2 42
How! the duke in council! In this time of the night! i 2 94
Hell and night Must bring this monstrous birth to the world's light i 3 409
He hath not yet made wanton the night with her ii 3 17
What, man! 'tis a night of revels: the gallants desire it ii 3 45
Nor know I aught By me that's said or done amiss this night ii 3 201
In night, and on the court and guard of safety! 'Tis monstrous ii 3 216
Why, then, to-morrow night; or Tuesday morn; On Tuesday noon, or night iii 3 60
I saw't not, thought it not, it harm'd not me: I slept the next night well iii 3 340
What, keep a week away? seven days and nights? Eight score eight hours? iii 4 173
Bring me on the way a little, And say if I shall see you soon at night iii 4 198
Get me some poison, Iago; this night: I'll not expostulate with her iv 1 216
If thou hast that in thee indeed, which I have greater reason to believe now than ever, I mean purpose, courage and valour, this night show it: if thou the next night following enjoy not Desdemona, take me from this world by treachery iv 2 219
It is now high supper-time, and the night grows to waste iv 2 249
Two or three groan: it is a heavy night: These may be counterfeits v 1 42
This is the night That either makes me or fordoes me quite v 1 128
Come, my queen; Last night you did desire it *Ant. and Cleo.* i 1 55
He fishes, drinks, and wastes The lamps of night in revel i 4 5
His faults in him seem as the spots of heaven, More fiery by night's blackness i 4 13
We did sleep day out of countenance, and made the night light with drinking ii 2 182
I laugh'd him out of patience; and that night I laugh'd him into patience ii 5 19
Ay, are you thereabouts? Why, then, good night indeed iii 10 30
Come, Let's have one other gaudy night iii 13 183
Did desire you To burn this night with torches iv 2 41
The night Is shiny; and they say we shall embattle By the second hour iv 9 2
O, bear me witness, night,— What man is this?—Stand close, and list iv 9 5
The poisonous damp of night disponge upon me iv 9 13
It was much like an argument that fell out last night *Cymbeline* i 4 61
I will make bold To send them to you, only for this night i 6 198
From fairies and the tempters of the night Guard me, beseech ye ii 2 9
Swift, swift, you dragons of the night, that dawning May bare the raven's eye! ii 2 48
I do think I saw't this morning: confident I am Last night 'twas on mine arm ii 3 151
I'll make a journey twice as far, to enjoy A second night of such sweet shortness which Was mine ii 4 44
But in one night, A storm or robbery, call it what you will, Shook down my mellow hangings, nay, my leaves iii 3 61

Night. Hath Britain all the sun that shines? Day, night, Are they not but in Britain? *Cymbeline* iii 4 139
May This night forestall him of the coming day! iii 5 69
For two nights together Have made the ground my bed iii 6 2
'Tis almost night: you shall have better cheer Ere you depart iii 6 67
The night to the owl and morn to the lark less welcome iii 6 94
Herbs that have on them cold dew o' the night Are strewings fitt'st for graves iv 2 284
'Ods pittikins! can it be six mile yet?—I have gone all night iv 2 294
Last night the very gods show'd me a vision iv 2 346
Those men Blush not in actions blacker than the night *Pericles* i 1 135
Peaceful night, The tomb where grief should sleep i 2 4
Under the covering of a careful night, Who seem'd my good protector i 2 81
His son's like a glow-worm in the night, The which hath fire in darkness ii 3 43
I am beholding to you For your sweet music this last night ii 5 26
Divinest patroness, and midwife gentle To those that cry by night iii 1 12
'T has been a turbulent and stormy night.—I have been in many; but such a night as this, Till now, I ne'er endured iii 2 4
She died at night; I'll say so. Who can cross it? iv 3 16
A goodly person, Till the disaster that, one mortal night, Drove him to this v 1 37
Night-bird. She sung, and made the night-bird mute iv Gower 26
Night-brawler. You unlace your reputation thus And spend your rich opinion for the name Of a night-brawler *Othello* ii 3 196
Night-cap. Threw up their sweaty night-caps *J. Cæsar* i 2 247
For I fear Cassio with my night-cap too *Othello* ii 1 316
Night-crow. The night-crow cried, aboding luckless time *3 Hen. VI.* v 6 45
Night-dog. When night-dogs run, all sorts of deer are chased *Mer. Wives* v 5 252
Nighted. Cast thy nighted colour off *Hamlet* i 2 68
Gone, In pity of his misery, to dispatch His nighted life *Lear* iv 5 13
Night-flies. Hush'd with buzzing night-flies to thy slumber *2 Hen. IV.* iii 1 11
Night-foe. Wherefore else guard we his royal tent, But to defend his person from night-foes? *3 Hen. VI.* iv 3 22
Night-gown. But a night-gown in respect of yours *Much Ado* iii 4 18
Hark! more knocking. Get on your nightgown, lest occasion call us, And show us to be watchers *Macbeth* ii 2 70
I have seen her rise from her bed, throw her nightgown upon her v 1 5
Wash your hands, put on your nightgown; look not so pale v 1 69
Shall I go fetch your night-gown?—No, unpin me here *Othello* iv 3 34
Nightingale. Except I be by Silvia in the night, There is no music in the nightingale *T. G. of Ver.* iii 1 179
To the nightingale's complaining notes Tune my distresses v 4 5
I will roar you an 'twere any nightingale *M. N. Dream* i 2 86
The nightingale, if she should sing by day, When every goose is cackling, would be thought No better a musician than the wren *Mer. of Venice* v 1 104
Apollo plays And twenty caged nightingales do sing *T. of Shrew* Ind. 2 38
Why then I'll tell her plain She sings as sweetly as a nightingale ii 1 172
Nightingales answer daws *T. Night* iii 4 38
It was the nightingale, and not the lark *Rom. and Jul.* iii 5 2
It was the lark, the herald of the morn, No nightingale iii 5 7
The foul fiend haunts poor Tom in the voice of a nightingale *Lear* iii 6 32
My nightingale, We have beat them to their beds *Ant. and Cleo.* iv 8 18
Nightly. With nightly tears and daily heart-sore sighs *T. G. of Ver.* ii 4 132
I nightly lodge her in an upper tower iii 1 35
My thoughts do harbour with my Silvia nightly iii 1 140
And nightly, meadow-fairies, look you sing *Mer. Wives* v 5 69
Then nightly sings the staring owl, Tu-whit; Tu-who *L. L. Lost* v 2 927
The clamorous owl that nightly hoots *M. N. Dream* ii 2 6
A fortnight hold we this solemnity, In nightly revels and new jollity v 1 377
He's drunk nightly in your company *T. Night* i 3 39
When shall I see you?—I will corrupt the Grecian sentinels, To give thee nightly visitation *Troi. and Cres.* iv 4 75
I have nightly since Dreamt of encounters 'twixt thyself and me *Coriol.* iv 5 128
Here nothing breeds, Unless the nightly owl or fatal raven *T. Andron.* ii 3 97
Nightly she sings on yon pomegranate tree *Rom. and Jul.* iii 5 4
Chain me with roaring bears; Or shut me nightly in a charnel-house iv 1 81
Thy canopy is dust and stones;—Which with sweet water nightly I will dew v 3 14
The obsequies that I for thee will keep Nightly shall be to strew thy grave v 3 17
In the affliction of these terrible dreams That shake us nightly *Macbeth* iii 2 19
Why this same strict and most observant watch So nightly toils *Hamlet* i 1 72
There's millions now alive That nightly lie in those unproper beds *Othello* iv 1 69
Give me my nightly wearing, and adieu: We must not now displease him iv 3 16
Night-mare. He met the night-mare, and her nine-fold *Lear* iii 4 126
Night-oblation. I will offer night-oblations to thee *Pericles* v 3 70
Night-owl. Shall we rouse the night-owl in a catch? *T. Night* ii 3 60
For night-owls shriek where mounting larks should sing *Richard II.* iii 3 183
Like the night-owl's lazy flight, Or like an idle thresher *3 Hen. VI.* ii 1 130
Night-raven. I had as lief have heard the night-raven *Much Ado* ii 3 84
Night-rest. Domestic awe, night-rest, and neighbourhood *T. of Athens* iv 1 17
Night-rule. What night-rule now about this haunted grove? *M. N. Dream* iii 2 5
Night-shriek. The time has been, my senses would have cool'd To hear a night-shriek *Macbeth* v 5 11
Night-taper. The honey-bags steal from the humble-bees, And for night-tapers crop their waxen thighs *M. N. Dream* iii 1 172
Night-tripping. O that it could be proved That some night-tripping fairy had exchanged In cradle-clothes our children! *1 Hen. IV.* i 1 87
Night-walking heralds That trudge betwixt the king and Mistress Shore *Richard III.* i 1 72
Night-wanderer. Mislead night-wanderers, laughing at their harm? Those that Hobgoblin call you *M. N. Dream* ii 1 39
Night-watch. A critic, nay, a night-watch constable *L. L. Lost* iii 1 178
Nightwork. And is Jane Nightwork alive? *2 Hen. IV.* iii 2 211
She's old; and had Robin Nightwork by old Nightwork before I came iii 2 222
Nihil. 'Tis 'semper idem,' for 'obsque hoc nihil est' v 5 31
Nile. 'Where's my serpent of old Nile?' For so he calls me *Ant. and Cleo.* i 5 25
Melt Egypt into Nile! and kindly creatures Turn all to serpents! ii 5 78
They take the flow o' the Nile By certain scales i' the pyramid ii 7 20
Lie graveless, till the flies and gnats of Nile Have buried them for prey! iii 13 166
Have slime upon them, such as the aspic leaves Upon the caves of Nile v 2 356
'Tis slander, . . . whose tongue Outvenoms all the worms of Nile *Cymb.* iii 4 37
Nill. And, will you, nill you, I will marry you *T. of Shrew* ii 1 273
It is, will he, nill he, he goes,—mark you that *Hamlet* v 1 19
I nill relate, action may Conveniently the rest convey *Pericles* iii Gower 55
Nilus. And now, like Nilus, it disdaineth bounds *T. Andron.* iii 1 71
E'en as the o'erflowing Nilus presageth famine *Ant. and Cleo* i 2 49
By the fire That quickens Nilus' slime, I go from hence Thy soldier i 3 69
The higher Nilus swells, The more it promises ii 7 23
Rather on Nilus' mud Lay me stark naked! v 2 58
Hast thou the pretty worm of Nilus there, That kills and pains not? v 2 243

Nimble. Of such sensible and nimble lungs that they always use to laugh at nothing . . . . *Tempest* ii 1 174
I find not Myself disposed to sleep.—Nor I ; my spirits are nimble . ii 1 202
And instruct thee how To snare the nimble marmoset . . . ii 2 174
Nimble jugglers that deceive the eye, Dark-working sorcerers *Com. of Er.* i 2 98
Universal plodding poisons up The nimble spirits in the arteries *L. L. L.* iv 3 306
Had she been light, like you, Of such a merry, nimble, stirring spirit . v 2 16
A heavy heart bears not a nimble tongue . . . . . . v 2 747
Awake the pert and nimble spirit of mirth *M. N. Dream* i 1 14
You have a nimble wit : I think 'twas made of Atalanta's heels *As Y. L. It* iii 2 293
About his neck A green and gilded snake had wreathed itself, Who with her head nimble in threats approach'd The opening of his mouth . iv 3 110
A nimble hand is necessary for a cut-purse . . . *W. Tale* iv 4 685
His shears and measure in his hand, Standing on slippers, which his nimble haste Had falsely thrust upon contrary feet . . *K. John* iv 2 197
Nimble mischance, that art so light of foot *Richard II.* iii 4 92
With nimble wing We were enforced, for safety sake, to fly . 1 *Hen. IV.* v 1 64
Quick, forgetive, full of nimble fiery and delectable shapes 2 *Hen. IV.* iv 3 108
There's nought in France That can be with a nimble galliard won *Hen. V.* i 2 252
The nimble gunner With linstock now the devilish cannon touches iii Prol. 32
You have dancing shoes With nimble soles : I have a soul of lead *R. and J.* i 4 15
Nimble lightnings, dart your blinding flames Into her scornful eyes ! *Lear* ii 4 167
In the most terrible and nimble stroke Of quick, cross lightning . iv 7 34
Winds of all the corners kiss'd your sails, To make your vessel nimble *Cymbeline* ii 4 29
Gently quench Thy nimble, sulphurous flashes ! *Pericles* iii 1 6
Nimble-footed. Being nimble-footed, he hath outrun us . *T. G. of Ver.* v 3 7
The nimble-footed madcap Prince of Wales . . 1 *Hen. IV.* iv 1 95
Nimbleness. Doing himself offence ; whilst we, lying still, Are full of rest, defence, and nimbleness . . . *J. Cæsar* iv 3 202
Nimble-pinioned. Therefore do nimble-pinion'd doves draw love, And therefore hath the wind-swift Cupid wings *Rom. and Jul.* ii 5 7
Nimbler. I have heard of riding wagers, Where horses have been nimbler than the sands That run i' the clock's behalf . . *Cymbeline* iii 2 74
Nimbly. That rise thus nimbly by a true king's fall *Richard II.* iv 1 318
You carried your guts away as nimbly, with as quick dexterity 1 *Hen. IV.* ii 4 285
He capers nimbly in a lady's chamber *Richard III.* i 1 12
The air Nimbly and sweetly recommends itself *Macbeth* i 6 2
Nine. Come to her between eight and nine *Mer. Wives* iii 5 47
Between nine and ten, sayest thou?—Eight and nine, sir . . iii 5 54
See that Claudio Be executed by nine to-morrow morning *Meas. for Meas.* ii 1 34
Hath she had any more than one husband?—Nine, sir ; Overdone by the last . . . . ii 1 212
One that is a prisoner nine years old . . . . . iv 2 135
I have studied eight or nine wise words to speak to you *Much Ado* iii 2 74
And three times thrice is nine.—Not so, sir ; under correction, sir *L. L. L.* v 2 488
I hope, sir, three times thrice, sir,— Is not nine . . . v 2 492
By Jove, I always took three threes for nine . . . . v 2 496
Eleven widows and nine maids is a simple coming-in for one man *M. of V.* ii 2 171
'Tis nine o'clock : our friends all stay for you . . . . ii 6 63
'Tis but an hour ago since it was nine *As Y. Like It* ii 7 24
I was seven of the nine days out of the wonder before you came . iii 2 184
Among nine bad if one be good, There's yet one good in ten *All's Well* i 3 82
Look, where the youngest wren of nine comes *T. Night* iii 2 71
Nine changes of the watery star hath been The shepherd's note *W. Tale* i 2 1
The eldest is eleven ; The second and the third, nine, and some five . ii 1 145
Fancies too weak for boys, too green and idle For girls of nine . iii 2 183
These nine in buckram that I told thee of . . 1 *Hen. IV.* ii 4 236
He held me last night at least nine hours In reckoning up the several devils' names . . . . iii 1 156
Deep prophecy she hath, Exceeding the nine sibyls of old Rome 1 *Hen. VI.* i 2 56
No sooner was I crept out of my cradle But I was made a king, at nine months old . . . . . . 2 *Hen. VI.* iv 9 4
When I was crown'd I was but nine months old 3 *Hen. VI.* i 1 112
I was anointed king at nine months old . . . iii 1 76
Henry the Sixth Was crown'd in Paris but at nine months old *Rich. III.* ii 3 17
It's supper-time, my lord : It's nine o'clock . . . v 3 48
Sixty and nine, that wore Their crownets regal . *Troi. and Cres.* Prol 5
I will buy nine sparrows for a penny . . . . . ii 1 77
Good morrow, cousin.—Is the day so young?—But new struck nine *Rom. and Jul.* i 1 167
At what o'clock to-morrow Shall I send to thee?—At the hour of nine . ii 2 169
The clock struck nine when I did send the nurse . . . ii 5 1
And from nine till twelve Is three long hours . . . . ii 5 10
Good king of cats, nothing but one of your nine lives . . iii 1 81
What do you think the hour?—Labouring for nine . *T. of Athens* iii 4 8
Weary se'nnights nine times nine Shall he dwindle, peak *Macbeth* i 3 22
Thrice to thine and thrice to mine And thrice again, to make up nine . i 3 36
Pour in sow's blood, that hath eaten Her nine farrow . . iv 1 65
He will last you some eight year or nine year : a tanner will last you nine year.—Why he more than another? . . . . *Hamlet* v 1 183
He hath laid on twelve for nine . . . . . . v 2 175
He hath been out nine years, and away he shall again . *Lear* i 1 33
Nine or ten times I had thought to have yerk'd him here under the ribs *Othello* i 2 4
Till now some nine moons wasted . . . . . . i 3 84
At nine i' the morning here we'll meet again . . . . i 3 280
I would have him nine years a-killing . . . . . iv 1 188
I heard of an Egyptian That had nine hours lien dead, Who was by good appliance recovered . . . . *Pericles* iii 2 85
Nine-fold. He met the night-mare, and her nine-fold . *Lear* iii 4 126
Nine men's morris. The nine men's morris is fill'd up with mud *M. N. Dream* ii 1 98
Nine-score and seventeen pounds . . . *Meas. for Meas.* iv 3 6
I have foundered nine score and odd posts . . 2 *Hen. IV.* iv 3 39
Nineteen. So long that nineteen zodiacs have gone round *Meas. for Meas.* i 2 172
These boiled brains of nineteen and two-and-twenty . *W. Tale* iii 3 65
Canidius, Our nineteen legions thou shalt hold by land . *Ant. and Cleo.* iii 7 59
Nine Worthies. None so fit as to present the Nine Worthies . *L. L. Lost* v 1 130
Ten times better than the Nine Worthies . . 2 *Hen. IV.* ii 4 238
Ninny. What a pied ninny's this! . . . . *Tempest* iii 2 71
I'll meet thee, Pyramus, at Ninny's tomb *M. N. Dream* iii 1 99
This is old Ninny's tomb. Where is my love? . . . v 1 268
Ninth. Ajax : he will be the ninth Worthy . . *L. L. Lost* v 2 581
To meet me in arms by the ninth of the next month . 1 *Hen. IV.* ii 3 29
But in the way of bargain, mark ye me, I'll cavil on the ninth part of a hair iii 1 140
His pia mater is not worth the ninth part of a sparrow . *Troi. and Cres.* ii 1 78
What is't o'clock?—About the ninth hour . . . *J. Cæsar* ii 4 23
Next morn, Ere the ninth hour, I drunk him to his bed . *Ant. and Cleo.* ii 5 21
'Tis the ninth hour o' the morn . . . . . *Cymbeline* iv 2 30

'**Ninus'** tomb,' man : why, you must not speak that yet . *M. N. Dream* iii 1 100
By moonshine did these lovers think no scorn To meet at Ninus' tomb v 1 139
Niobe. Make wells and Niobes of the maids and wives . *Troi. and Cres.* v 10 19
She follow'd my poor father's body, Like Niobe, all tears *Hamlet* i 2 149
Nips youth i' the head and follies doth emmew . . *Meas. for Meas.* iii 1 91
If frosts and fasts, hard lodging and thin weeds, Nip not the gaudy blossoms of your love . . . . *L. L. Lost* v 2 812
Here's snip and nip and cut and slish and slash . *T. of Shrew* iv 3 90
Nips his root, And then he falls, as I do . . *Hen. VIII.* iii 2 357
These tidings nip me, and I hang the head As flowers with frost *T. An.* iv 4 70
Most heavenly music ! It nips me unto listening . . *Pericles* v 1 235
Nipped. When blood is nipp'd and ways be foul . . *L. L. Lost* v 2 926
Nipping. Barren winter, with his wrathful nipping cold . 2 *Hen. VI.* ii 4 3
It is very cold.—It is a nipping and an eager air *Hamlet* i 4 2
Nipple. When it did taste the wormwood on the nipple Of my dug and felt it bitter . . . . *Rom. and Jul.* i 3 30
I would, while it was smiling in my face, Have pluck'd my nipple from his boneless gums, And dash'd the brains out *Macbeth* i 7 57
Nit. Ah, heavens, it is a most pathetical nit ! . . *L. L. Lost* iv 1 150
Thou flea, thou nit, thou winter-cricket thou ! . . *T. of Shrew* iv 3 110
No. Though the ship were no stronger than a nutshell . *Tempest* i 1 50
No more amazement : tell your piteous heart There's no harm done . i 2 14
Master of a full poor cell, And thy no greater father . . i 2 21
O you wonder ! If you be maid or no?—No wonder, sir ; But certainly a maid . . . . i 2 427
Thou think'st there is no more such shapes as he . . . i 2 478
Prithee, no more : thou dost talk nothing to me . . . ii 1 170
Say, this were death . . ; why, they were no worse Than now they are ii 1 261
Here lies your brother, No better than the earth he lies upon . ii 1 281
I do now let loose my opinion ; hold it no longer . . . ii 2 37
I shall no more to sea, to sea, Here shall I die ashore . . ii 2 44
I'll bear him no more sticks, but follow thee, Thou wondrous man . ii 2 167
No more dams I'll make for fish ; Nor fetch in firing At requiring . ii 2 184
But I'll be your servant, Whether you will or no . . . iii 1 86
I said nothing.—Mum, then, and no more . . . . iii 2 59
I can go no further, sir ; My old bones ache . . . . iii 3 1
Even here I will put off my hope and keep it No longer for my flatterer iii 3 8
Whether thou be'st he or no, Or some enchanted trifle . . v 1 111
No more yet of this ; For 'tis a chronicle of day by day . . v 1 162
See it be return'd ; Or else return no more into my sight *T. G. of Ver.* i 2 47
Since maids, in modesty, say 'no' to that Which they would have the profferer construe 'ay' . . . . i 2 55
What thou want'st shall be sent after thee : No more of stay ! . i 3 75
No, believe me.—No believing you, indeed, sir . . . ii 1 161
I would it were no worse.—I'll warrant you, 'tis as well . . ii 1 169
And has no more pity in him than a dog . . . . . ii 3 11
No more, gentlemen, no more : here comes my father . . ii 4 47
'She can fetch and carry.' Why, a horse can do no more . . iii 1 275
For 'tis no trusting to yond foolish lout . . . . iv 4 71
Sir, I thank you ; by yea and no, I do . . . *Mer. Wives* i 1 88
And the very yea and the no is, the French doctor, my master . i 4 99
You are not young, no more am I . . . . . . ii 1 7
By yea and no, I think the 'oman is a witch indeed . . iv 2 202
Whether one Nym, sir, that beguiled him of a chain, had the chain or no iv 5 34
In nothing good, But graciously to know I am no better *Meas. for Meas.* ii 4 77
We are made to be no stronger Than faults may shake our frames . ii 4 132
Thou'rt by no means valiant . . . . iii 1 15
Thou art deceived in me, friar. But no more of this . . . iii 2 179
Away with her to prison ! Go to ; no more words . . . iii 2 218
Nay, but it is not so.—It is no other . . . . . iv 3 122
How might she tongue me ! Yet reason dares her no . . . iv 4 28
If she be mad,—as I believe no other . . . . . v 1 60
Dare no more stretch this finger of mine than he Dare rack his own . v 1 316
Rely upon it till my tale be heard, And hold no longer out . . v 1 371
A stubborn soul, That apprehends no further than this world . . v 1 486
O, let me say no more ! Gather the sequel by that went before *C. of Er.* i 1 95
Make up the sum, And live ; if no, then thou art doom'd to die . i 1 155
No longer will I be a fool, To put the finger in the eye and weep . ii 2 205
He denied you had in him no right.—He meant he did me none . iv 2 7
Is not your husband mad?—His incivility confirms no less . . iv 4 49
Being no other but as she is, I do not like her . . . *Much Ado* i 1 177
She cannot endure to hear tell of a husband.—O, by no means . . ii 1 364
At Christmas I no more desire a rose . . . . *L. L. Lost* i 1 105
Is she wedded or no?—To her will, sir, or so . . . . ii 1 211
The moon was a month old when Adam was no more . . . iv 2 40
Henceforth my wooing mind shall be express'd In russet yeas and honest kersey noes . . . . v 2 413
Which by no means we may extenuate . . . *M. N. Dream* i 1 120
Thou shalt remain here, whether thou wilt or no . . . iii 1 156
See me no more, whether he be dead or no . . . . iii 2 81
Can you tell me whether one Launcelot, that dwells with him, dwell with him or no? . . . . *Mer. of Venice* ii 2 49
Is that my prize? are my deserts no better? . . . . ii 9 60
I'll take no more ; And you in love shall not deny me this . . iv 1 428
No better a musician than the wren . . . . . . v 1 106
Love no man in good earnest ; nor no further in sport neither *As Y. L. It* i 2 30
I'll have no worse a name than Jove's own page . . . i 3 126
You have said ; but whether wisely or no, let the forest judge . . iii 2 130
Had not that been as proper?—By no means, sir . . . iii 2 326
The oath of a lover is no stronger than the word of a tapster . . iii 4 34
My friends told me as much, and I thought no less . . . iv 1 188
I have no more ; And she can have no more than all I have *T. of Shrew* ii 1 384
With no greater a run but my head and my neck . . . iv 1 15
No note upon my parents, his all noble . . . *All's Well* i 3 163
I care no more for than I do for heaven, So I were not his sister . i 3 170
Can't no other, But, I your daughter, he must be my brother? . i 3 171
Till I have no wife, I have nothing in France . . . . iii 2 77
Though there were no further danger known . . . . iii 5 29
Suppose no other but that he is carried into the leaguer of the adversaries . . . . iii 6 27
I love not many words.—No more than a fish loves water . . iii 6 92
The duke knows him for no other but a poor officer of mine . . iv 3 225
Go to, you're a dry fool ; I'll no more of you . . . *T. Night* i 5 45
He'll speak with you, will you or no . . . . . . i 5 163
No less adorns Our gentry than our parents' noble names *W. Tale* i 2 393
Inform yourselves We need no more of your advice. . . . ii 1 168
To this I am most constant, Though destiny say no . . . iv 4 46
He that no more must say is listen'd more . . . *Richard II.* ii 1 9
I know you wise, but yet no farther wise Than Harry Percy's wife 1 *Hen. IV.* ii 3 110

No. No more of that, Hal, an thou lovest me! . . . *1 Hen. IV.* ii 4 312
With hearts in their bellies no bigger than pins' heads . . iv 2 23
Whether I shall ever see thee again or no, there is nobody cares *2 Hen. IV.* ii 4 73
There is no need of any such redress . . . . iv 1 97
We hope no other from your majesty . . . . v 2 62
And those few I have Almost no better than so many French *Hen. V.* iii 6 156
I am no wiser than a daw . . . . *1 Hen. VI.* ii 4 18
No more can I be serv'd from your side, Than can yourself yourself in twain divide . . . . . iv 5 48
Brave death by speaking, whether he will or no . . . iv 7 25
They will guard you, whether you will or no . . *2 Hen. VI.* iii 2 265
Tell us whether they will come or no . . . *Richard III.* iii 1 23
But for our hearts, he knows no more of mine, Than I of yours; Nor I no more of his, than you of mine . . . iii 4 13
He fears you mean no good to him . . . . iii 7 87
Lend thine ear: There is no more but so . . . iv 2 81
He hopes it is no other But for your health . *Troi. and Cres.* ii 3 119
What is he more than another?—No more than what he thinks he is ii 3 152
I wish no better Than have him hold that purpose . . *Coriolanus* ii 1 255
If they love they know not why, they hate upon no better a ground ii 2 12
Now you have left your voices, I have no further with you . ii 3 181
Know, I pray you,— I'll know no further . . . iii 3 87
Here's no sound jest! . . . . . . *T. Andron.* iv 2 26
No more deep will I endart mine eye Than your consent *Rom. and Jul.* i 3 98
This is no time to lend money . . . *T. of Athens* iii 1 44
When crouching marrow in the bearer strong Cries of itself 'No more' v 4 10
That by no means I may discover them . . . *J. Cæsar* ii 1 75
He can do no more than Cæsar's arm When Cæsar's head is off ii 1 182
A thing of custom: 'tis no other . . . *Macbeth* iii 4 97
We learn no other but the confident tyrant Keeps still in Dunsinane v 4 8
I think it be no other but e'en so . . . . *Hamlet* i 1 108
No more.—No more but so?—Think it no more . . . i 3 10
Be thou familiar, but by no means vulgar . . . . i 3 61
But from what cause he will by no means speak . . . iii 1 6
And must the inheritor himself have no more, ha?—Not a jot more v 1 121
Must there no more be done?—No more be done . . . v 1 258
Have you no more to say?—Few words, but, to effect, more than all yet *Lear* iii 1 51
Through the hawthorn blows the cold wind: Says suum, mun, ha, no, nonny . . . . iii 4 103
And by no means Will yield to see his daughter . . . iv 3 42
Methinks he seems no bigger than his head . . . iv 6 16
To say 'ay' and 'no' to every thing that I said!—'Ay' and 'no' too was no good divinity . . . . . . iv 6 100
I know my price, I am worth no worse a place . . . *Othello* i 1 11
Let's have no more of this; let's to our affairs . . . ii 3 115
If 'twere no other,— 'Tis but so, I warrant . . . iv 2 168
Whose beauty claims No worse a husband than the best of men *A. and C.* ii 2 131
There is no moe such Cæsars . . . . *Cymbeline* iii 1 36
No more ado With that harsh, noble, simple nothing . . iii 4 134
Thou movest no less with thy complaining than Thy master in bleeding iv 2 375
Which yet from her by no means can I get . . . *Pericles* ii 5 6
I can no more 2 *Hen. VI.* iii 2; *Hen. VIII.* iv 2; *Hamlet* v 2; *Ant. and Cleo.* iv 15

No had. I had a mighty cause To wish him dead, but thou hadst none to kill him.—No had, my lord! . . . . *K. John* iv 2 207

No one. The owner of no one good quality . . . *All's Well* iii 6 12
He's poor in no one fault, but stored with all . . *Coriolanus* ii 1 20

No otherwise. We do no otherwise than we are will'd . *1 Hen. VI.* i 3 10

Noah. 'Tis in grain; Noah's flood could not do it . *Com. of Errors* iii 2 108
They have been grand-jurymen since before Noah was a sailor *T. Night* iii 2 18

Nob. Hob, nob, is his word; give't or take't . . . iii 4 263
I would not be sir Nob in any case . . . . *K. John* i 1 147

Nobility. In this action contrives against his own nobility . *All's Well* iv 3 29
Let his nobility remain in's court . . . . . v 5 52
Forget Your worth, your greatness and nobility . . *K. John* iv 3 86
Great affections wrestling in thy bosom Doth make an earthquake of nobility . . . . v 2 42
Betwixt the wind and his nobility . . . . *1 Hen. IV.* i 3 45
That men of your nobility and power Did gage them both in an unjust behalf . . . . i 3 172
With nobility and tranquillity . . . . . . ii 1 84
Here is my speech. Stand aside, nobility . . . . ii 4 429
From such a field as this, Where stain'd nobility lies trodden on . iv 4 13
Smiling to behold his lion's whelp Forage in blood of French nobility *Hen. V.* i 2 110
Awake, English nobility! Let not sloth dim your honours new-begot *1 Hen. VI.* i 1 78
King Henry's peers and chief nobility Destroy'd themselves . . . iv 1 146
This jarring discord of nobility, This shouldering of each other . iv 1 188
Yet is he poor, And our nobility will scorn the match . . v 3 96
And conversed with such As, like to pitch, defile nobility . *2 Hen. VI.* ii 1 196
And such high vaunts of his nobility . . . . . iii 1 50
True nobility is exempt from fear . . . . . iv 1 129
The nobility think scorn to go in leather aprons . . . iv 2 13
All recreants and dastards, and delight to live in slavery to the nobility iv 8 29
Myself disgraced, and the nobility Held in contempt . *Richard III.* i 3 79
O, that your young nobility could judge What 'twere to lose it [honour], and be miserable! . . . . i 3 257
Like her true nobility, she has Carried herself towards me . *Hen. VIII.* ii 4 142
If we live thus tamely, To be thus jaded by a piece of scarlet, Farewell nobility . . . . iii 2 281
As you respect the common good, the state Of our despised nobility . iii 2 291
Would the nobility lay aside their ruth, And let me use my sword *Coriol.* i 1 201
I sin in envying his nobility . . . . . . i 1 234
It is a purposed thing, and grows by plot, To curb the will of the nobility . . . . iii 1 39
The nobility are vex'd, whom we see have sided In his behalf . iv 2 2
The nobility of Rome are his: The senators and patricians love him too iv 7 29
To virtue consecrate, To justice, continence and nobility . *T. Andron.* i 1 15
O sacred receptacle of my joys, Sweet cell of virtue and nobility! . i 1 93
Sweet mercy is nobility's true badge . . . . . i 1 119
True nobility Warrants these words in princely courtesy . . i 1 271
With no less nobility of love Than that which dearest father bears his son, Do I impart toward you . . . . *Hamlet* i 2 110
Base men being in love have then a nobility in their natures . *Othello* ii 1 218
These hands do lack nobility, that they strike A meaner *Ant. and Cleo.* ii 5 82

Noble. Nothing natural I ever saw so noble . . . *Tempest* i 2 419
Let there be some more test made of my metal, Before so noble and so great a figure Be stamp'd upon it . . . *Meas. for Meas.* i 1 50

Noble. Thou art not noble; For all the accommodations that thou bear'st Are nursed by baseness . . . *Meas. for Meas.* iii 1 13
Thou art too noble to conserve a life In base appliances . . iii 1 88
There she lost a noble and renowned brother . . . iii 1 228
My noble and well-warranted cousin, Whom it concerns . . v 1 254
Mild, or come not near me; noble, or not I for an angel *Much Ado* ii 3 35
How wise, how noble, young, how rarely featured . . . iii 1 60
You have a noble and a true conceit Of god-like amity *Mer. of Venice* iii 4 2
No note upon my parents, his all noble . . . *All's Well* i 3 163
Noble she was, and thought I stood engaged . . . . v 3 95
Yet I suppose him virtuous, know him noble . . . *T. Night* i 5 277
My love, more noble than the world, Prizes not quantity of dirty lands ii 4 84
Be not amazed; right noble is his blood . . . . . v 1 271
How would he look, to see his work so noble Vilely bound up? *W. Tale* iv 4 21
Nothing she does or seems But smacks of something greater than herself, Too noble for this place . . . . iv 4 159
He seems to be the more noble in being fantastical: a great man, I'll warrant . . . . iv 4 778
Where the warlike Smalus, That noble honour'd lord, is fear'd and loved v 1 158
My nobles leave me; and my state is braved, Even at my gates *K. John* iv 2 243
Your nobles will not hear you, but are gone To offer service to your enemy . . . . v 1 33
So, nobles, shall you all, That knit your sinews to the strength of mine v 2 62
Received eight thousand nobles In name of lendings . . *Richard II.* i 1 88
The nobles hath he fined For ancient quarrels, and quite lost their hearts ii 1 247
The nobles they are fled, the commons they are cold . . ii 2 88
Would God that any in this noble presence Were enough noble to be upright judge Of noble Richard! . . . . iv 1 117
Thy pains, Fitzwater, shall not be forgot; Right noble is thy merit v 6 18
Our noble and chaste mistress the moon . . . *1 Hen. IV.* i 2 32
Let it be but twenty nobles . . . . . . *2 Hen. IV.* ii 1 167
Fly to Scotland, Till that the nobles and the armed commons Have of their puissance made a little taste . . . . . . ii 3 51
Your noble and right well remember'd father's . . . . iv 1 112
Believe not the word of the noble: therefore let me have right . iv 3 59
How many nobles then should hold their places, That must strike sail to spirits of vile sort! . . . . v 2 17
Never king of England Had nobles richer and more loyal subjects *Hen. V.* i 2 127
And she a mourning widow of her nobles . . . . i 2 158
A noble shalt thou have, and present pay . . . . ii 1 112
I shall have my noble?—In cash most justly paid . . . ii 1 119
Your nobles, jealous of your absence, Seek through your camp to find you . . . . iv 1 302
To sort our nobles from our common men . . . . iv 7 77
Of princes, in this number, And nobles bearing banners, there lie dead One hundred twenty six . . . . iv 8 87
Good God, these nobles should such stomachs bear! . *1 Hen. VI.* i 3 90
Depart to Paris to the king, For there young Henry with his nobles lie iii 2 129
I gave a noble to the priest The morn that I was wedded to her mother v 4 23
Nor be rebellious to the crown of England, Thou, nor thy nobles . v 4 172
And all the peers and nobles of the realm Have been as bondmen *2 Hen. VI.* i 3 129
Noble she is, but if she have forgot Honour and virtue . . ii 1 194
Well, nobles, well, 'tis politicly done, To send me packing with an host of men . . . . iii 1 341
But, noble as he is, look where he comes . . . . . v 3 14
That scarce, some two days since, were worth a noble *Richard III.* i 3 82
Less noble and less loyal, Nearer in bloody thoughts, but not in blood ii 1 91
Why or for what these nobles were committed Is all unknown to me . ii 4 47
A beggar's book Outworths a noble's blood . . . *Hen. VIII.* i 1 123
No doubt he's noble; He had a black mouth that said other of him i 3 57
Your grace is noble: Let me have such a bowl may hold my thanks . i 4 38
Having heard by fame Of this so noble and so fair assembly . . i 4 67
Stay there, sir, And see the noble ruin'd man you speak of . . ii 1 54
Restored me to my honours, and, out of ruins, Made my name once more noble . . . . ii 1 115
Your grace must needs deserve all stranger's loves, You are so noble ii 2 103
As you are truly noble, As you respect the common good . . iii 2 289
Must I needs forgo So good, so noble and so true a master? . . iii 2 423
She is young, and of a noble modest nature, I hope she will deserve well iv 2 135
Will deserve . . . A right good husband, let him be a noble . iv 2 146
Men so noble, However faulty, yet should find respect For what they have been . . . . v 3 74
Nor none so noble Whose life were ill bestow'd or death unfamed *Troi. and Cres.* ii 2 158
I have a roisting challenge sent amongst The dull and factious nobles . ii 2 209
No less noble, much more gentle, and altogether more tractable . ii 3 159
And call him noble that was now your hate . . . *Coriolanus* i 1 187
He would miss it rather Than carry it but by the suit of the gentry to him And the desire of the nobles . . . . . . ii 1 255
The nobles bended, As to Jove's statue . . . . . ii 1 281
He's right noble: Let him be call'd for . . . . ii 2 133
Hath he not pass'd the noble and the common? . . . . ii 3 29
You must inquire your way, Which you are out of, with a gentler spirit, Or never be so noble as a consul . . . . . . iii 1 56
Help Marcius, help, You that be noble; help him, young and old! . iii 1 228
This man has marr'd his fortune.—His nature is too noble for the world iii 1 255
You are too absolute; Though therein you can never be too noble . iii 2 40
I am in this, Your wife, your son, these senators, the nobles . . iii 2 65
The people against the senators, patricians, and nobles . . iv 3 15
The nobles receive so to heart the banishment of that worthy Coriolanus iv 3 22
And feasts the nobles of the state At his house this night . . iv 4 9
The cruelty and envy of the people, Permitted by our dastard nobles . iv 5 81
The nobles in great earnestness are going All to the senate-house . iv 6 57
We loved him; but, like beasts And cowardly nobles, gave way . . iv 6 122
The man was noble, But with his last attempt he wiped it out . . v 3 145
The man is noble and his fame folds-in This orb o' the earth . . v 6 126
Lose not so noble a friend on vain suppose, Nor with sour looks afflict his gentle heart . . . . *T. Andron.* i 1 440
There are certain nobles of the senate Newly alighted . . *T. of Athens* i 2 180
So noble a master fall'n! . . . . iv 2 6
Thus much of this [gold] will make black white, foul fair, Wrong right, base noble, old young, coward valiant . . . . iv 3 29
Noble and young, When thy first griefs were but a mere conceit . v 4 13
Thou art noble; yet, I see, Thy honourable metal may be wrought From that it is disposed . . . . *J. Cæsar* i 2 312
Brutus is noble, wise, valiant, and honest; Cæsar was mighty, bold, royal . . . . iii 1 126
Shaking the bloody fingers of thy foes, Most noble! . . . . iii 1 199
He is noble, wise, judicious, and best knows The fits o' the season *Macb.* iv 2 16
Were I king, I should cut off the nobles for their lands . . . iv 3 79

Noble. What a piece of work is a man! how noble in reason! . *Hamlet* ii 2 316
Now see that noble and most sovereign reason, Like sweet bells jangled iii 1 165
And the noble and true-hearted Kent banished! his offence, honesty! *Lear* i 2 126
Menaces and maledictions against king and nobles . . . i 2 160
A credulous father! and a brother noble, Whose nature is so far from doing harms, That he suspects none! . . . . i 2 195
When nobles are their tailors' tutors . . . . . iii 2 83
Yet am I noble as the adversary I come to cope . . . . v 3 123
But what art thou That hast this fortune on me! If thou 'rt noble, I do forgive thee . . . . v 3 165
My very noble and approved good masters . . . . *Othello* i 3 77
It is Othello's pleasure, our noble and valiant general . . . ii 2 1
Three lads of Cyprus, noble swelling spirits . . . . ii 3 57
Thy demon, that's thy spirit which keeps thee, is noble *Ant. and Cleo.* ii 3 20
Thy spirit Is all afraid to govern thee near him: But, he away, 'tis noble ii 3 30
Then, what's brave, what's noble, Let's do it after the high Roman fashion . . . . iv 15 86
He words me, girls, he words me, that I should not Be noble to myself v 2 192
More noble than that runagate to your bed . . *Cymbeline* i 6 137
I had rather not be so noble as I am; they dare not fight with me . ii 1 20
No more ado With that harsh, noble, simple nothing, That Cloten . iii 4 135
She held the very garment of Posthumus in more respect than my noble and natural person . . . . iii 5 139
Go search like nobles, like noble subjects . . . *Pericles* ii 4 50
My actions are as noble as my thoughts . . . . . ii 5 59
Thou art a piece of virtue, and I doubt not but thy training hath been noble . . . . iv 6 119
You shall prevail, Were it to woo my daughter; for it seems You have been noble towards her . . . . v 1 264
Noble act. If this inducement force her not to love, Send her a story of thy noble acts . . . . *Richard III.* iv 4 280
I see him rouse himself To praise my noble act . . *Ant. and Cleo.* v 2 288
Noble ancestors. Basely yielded upon compromise That which his noble ancestors achieved with blows . . . . . *Richard II.* ii 1 254
Noble ancestry. To draw forth your noble ancestry From the corruption of abusing times . . . . . . *Richard III.* iii 7 198
Noble anger. Touch me with noble anger . . . . *Lear* ii 4 279
Noble Antony, go up.—For Brutus' sake, I am beholding to you *J. Cæsar* iii 2 69
Room for Antony, most noble Antony . . . . . iii 2 170
Noble auditory, be it known to you . . . *T. Andron.* v 3 96
Noble aunt. My noble aunt Loves me as dear as e'er my mother did . iv 1 22
Noble bachelors. This youthful parcel Of noble bachelors stand at my bestowing . . . . *All's Well* ii 3 59
Noble beast. As once Europa did at lusty Jove, When he would play the noble beast in love . . . . . . *Much Ado* v 4 47
Here come two noble beasts in, a man and a lion . *M. N. Dream* v 1 220
Noble benefits. When these so noble benefits shall prove Not well disposed . . . . *Hen. VIII.* i 2 115
Noble bevy. None here, he hopes, In all this noble bevy, has brought with her One care abroad . . . . i 4 4
Noble birth. Knights of the garter were of noble birth . 1 *Hen. VI.* iv 1 34
You have suborn'd this man, Of purpose to obscure my noble birth . v 4 22
Noble blood. And many moe Of noble blood . . *Richard II.* ii 1 240
Rome, thou hast lost the breed of noble bloods! . . *J. Cæsar* i 2 151
Your swords, made rich With the most noble blood of all this world . iii 1 156
Behold it stain'd With his most noble blood . . *Ant. and Cleo.* v 1 26
Noble blows. More noble blows than ever thou wise words *Coriolanus* iv 2 21
Noble born. The queen of earthly queens: she's noble born *Hen. VIII.* ii 4 141
Noble bottom. With the most noble bottom of our fleet . . *T. Night* v 1 60
Noble boy. A noble boy! Who would not do thee right? *K. John* ii 1 18
Noble breasts. That which in mean men we intitle patience Is pale cold cowardice in noble breasts . . . . . . *Richard II.* i 2 34
Noble brother, you have done me wrong . . . *J. Cæsar* iv 2 37
Noble Brutus. Have wish'd that noble Brutus had his eyes . . . i 2 62
O Cassius, if you could But win the noble Brutus to our party . i 3 141
But will follow The fortunes and affairs of noble Brutus . . iii 1 135
The noble Brutus is ascended: silence!—Be patient till the last . iii 2 11
Seek him, Titinius, whilst I go to meet The noble Brutus . . v 3 74
I dare assure thee that no enemy Shall ever take alive the noble Brutus v 4 22
Noble Cæsar. Good morrow, Antony.—So to most noble Cæsar . ii 2 118
When the noble Cæsar saw him stab, Ingratitude, more strong than traitors' arms, Quite vanquish'd him . . . . iii 2 188
Noble captains. Call all his noble captains to my lord . *Ant. and Cleo.* iii 13 189
Noble carelessness. Out of his noble carelessness lets them plainly see't . . . . *Coriolanus* ii 2 16
Noble carriage. A pleasing eye and a most noble carriage . 1 *Hen. IV.* ii 4 466
Noble Cassius. Noble, noble Cassius, Good night . . *J. Cæsar* iv 3 232
Fly, therefore, noble Cassius, fly far off . . . . . v 3 11
Noble Cato. O young and noble Cato, art thou down? . . . v 4 9
Noble change. And never live to show the incredulous world The noble change that I have purposed! . . . 2 *Hen. IV.* iv 5 155
Noble chevalier. And cannot help the noble chevalier . 1 *Hen. VI.* iv 3 14
Noble child. 'Tis a noble child.—A crack, madam . *Coriolanus* i 3 73
Noble combat. But O, the noble combat that 'twixt joy and sorrow was fought in Paulina! . . . . *W. Tale* v 2 79
O, what a noble combat hast thou fought Between compulsion and a brave respect! . . . . *K. John* v 2 43
Noble company. Your noble company.—Of much less value is my company Than your good words . . . . . *Richard II.* ii 3 18
Welcome all. A noble company! what are their pleasures? *Hen. VIII.* i 4 64
Come hither, gentle mistress: Do you perceive in all this noble company Where most you owe obedience? . . . . . *Othello* i 3 180
Noble consul. To our noble consul Wish we all joy *Coriolanus* ii 2 156
Noble corse. Let him be regarded As the most noble corse that ever herald Did follow to his urn . . . . v 6 145
Noble counsel. Choose such limbs of noble counsel . 2 *Hen. IV.* v 2 135
Noble counsellor. Well supplied with noble counsellors . *Hen. V.* ii 4 33
Thou art a grave and noble counsellor, Most wise in general . *Pericles* v 1 184
Noble count. I was preserved to serve this noble count . . *T. Night* v 1 263
Noble countenance. Turn from me, then, that noble countenance, Wherein the worship of the whole world lies . *Ant. and Cleo.* iv 14 85
Noble country. Slain manfully in arms, In right and service of their noble country . . . . *T. Andron.* i 1 197
Noble cousin. His noble cousin is right welcome hither . *Richard II.* iii 3 122
Noble creature. A brave vessel, Who had, no doubt, some noble creature in her, Dash'd all to pieces . . . . *Tempest* i 2 7
Noble cunning. Fortune's blows, When most struck home, being gentle wounded, craves A noble cunning . . . . *Coriolanus* iv 1 9
Noble deed. To grace this latter age with noble deeds . 1 *Hen. IV.* v 1 92
And there erects Thy noble deeds as valour's monuments 1 *Hen. VI.* iii 2 120
Noble deed. If he tell us his noble deeds, we must also tell him our noble acceptance of them . . . . *Coriolanus* ii 3 8
What poor an instrument May do a noble deed! . . . *Ant. and Cleo.* v 3 237
Noble device. Learned, full of noble device . . . *As Y. Like It* i 1 173
Noble duke. A noble duke, in nature as in name . . *T. Night* i 2 25
The noble duke hath sworn his coming is But for his own *Richard II.* ii 3 148
Thou, Aumerle, didst send two of thy men To execute the noble duke . iv 1 82
Have patience, noble duke; I may not open . . 1 *Hen. VI.* i 3 18
And all to have the noble duke alive . . . . 2 *Hen. VI.* iii 2 64
Forbear your conference with the noble duke . . *Richard III.* i 1 104
For the instalment of this noble duke In the seat royal . . . iii 1 163
Who is most inward with the noble duke? . . . . . iii 4 8
Being nothing like the noble duke my father . . . . iii 5 92
Noble dust. Why may not imagination trace the noble dust of Alexander, till he find it stopping a bung-hole? . . . . . *Hamlet* v 1 225
Noble earl. Three knights . . . slain to-day, A noble earl . 1 *Hen. IV.* v 5 7
Noble earl, I bring you certain news from Shrewsbury . 2 *Hen. IV.* i 1 11
But, as the rest, so fell that noble earl And was beheaded . 1 *Hen. VI.* ii 5 90
Your wondrous rare description, noble earl, Of beauteous Margaret . . v 5 1
O' Thursday, tell her, She shall be married to this noble earl *R. and J.* iii 4 21
Noble eminence. In noble eminence enthroned and sphered *Tr. and Cr.* i 3 90
Noble emperor. Lords, accompany Your noble emperor . . *T. Andron.* i 1 334
O noble emperor, do not fight by sea . . . *Ant. and Cleo.* iii 7 62
Noble empress, you have heard of me?—I cannot tell . . . . v 2 71
Noble-ending. A testament of noble-ending love . . . *Hen. V.* iv 6 27
Noble English. Fly, noble English . . . . . . *K. John* v 4 10
O noble English, that could entertain With half their forces the full pride of France And let another half stand laughing by! *Hen. V.* i 2 111
Noble enterprise. So is he now in execution Of any bold or noble enterprise . . . . *J. Cæsar* i 2 302
Noble estimate. None else of name and noble estimate . *Richard II.* ii 3 56
Noble eye. O, let no noble eye profane a tear For me . . . . i 3 59
Noble family. Come they of noble family? Why, so didst thou *Hen. V.* ii 2 129
Noble father. This gentleman, Whom I would save, had a most noble father . . . . *Meas. for Meas.* ii 1 7
Not one of those but had a noble father . . . *All's Well* ii 3 68
Will you not, sons?—Ay, noble father, if our words will serve 2 *Hen. VI.* v 1 139
My noble father, Three times to-day I holp him to his horse . . . v 3 7
The curse my noble father laid on thee, When thou didst crown his warlike brows with paper . . . . *Richard III.* i 3 174
Call us wretches, orphans, castaways, If that our noble father be alive? ii 2 7
My noble father, Henry of Buckingham . . . *Hen. VIII.* ii 1 107
O noble father, you lament in vain: The tribunes hear you not *T. An.* iii 1 27
Farewell, Andronicus, my noble father, The wofull'st man that ever lived . . . . iii 1 289
Do not for ever with thy vailed lids Seek for thy noble father in the dust: Thou know'st 'tis common . . . . *Hamlet* i 2 71
If it assume my noble father's person, I'll speak to it . . . i 2 244
He which hath your noble father slain Pursued my life . . . iv 7 4
So have I a noble father lost; A sister driven into desperate terms . iv 7 25
My noble father, I do perceive here a divided duty . *Othello* i 3 180
With which I meant To scourge the ingratitude that despiteful Rome Cast on my noble father . . . . *Ant. and Cleo.* ii 6 23
Noble father-in-law! Tell me, how fares our loving mother? *Richard III.* v 3 81
Noble feast. Here's a noble feast toward . . . . *T. of Athens* iii 6 68
Noble feat. And got a calf in that same noble feat . . *Much Ado* v 4 50
Noble fellow. Those Italian fields, Where noble fellows strike *All's Well* ii 3 308
These lords, my noble fellows, if they please, Can clear me in 't *W. Tale* ii 3 142
O noble fellow! Who sensibly outdares his senseless sword *Coriolanus* i 4 52
A noble fellow, I warrant him.—The worthy fellow is our general . v 2 115
Noble foe. And find the welcome of a noble foe . . *Troi. and Cres.* i 3 309
Noble fool. O noble fool! A worthy fool! . . . *As Y. Like It* ii 7 33
Noble fortunes. If thou dost As this instructs thee, thou dost make thy way To noble fortunes . . . . *Lear* v 3 30
Noble friend, Let me embrace thine age . . . . *Tempest* v 1 120
My most noble friends, I pray you all, Speak plainly . 2 *Hen. IV.* iii 3 2
His noble friends and fellows, whom to leave Is only bitter to him *Hen. VIII.* ii 1 73
I prithee, noble friend, home to thy house . . *Coriolanus* iii 1 234
Till then, my noble friend, chew upon this . . . *J. Cæsar* i 2 171
My worthy lord, Your noble friends do lack you . . *Macbeth* iii 4 84
You lords and noble friends, know our intent . . . *Lear* v 3 296
Noble friends, That which combined us was most great . *Ant. and Cleo.* ii 2 17
Whom I commend to you as a noble friend of mine . *Cymbeline* i 4 32
Myself and other noble friends Are partners in the business . . i 6 183
Noble fury. With a noble fury and fair spirit . . . *T. of Athens* iii 5 18
I never saw Such noble fury in so poor a thing . . *Cymbeline* v 5 8
Noble general. You feed too much on this dislike.—Our noble general, do not do so . . . . *Troi. and Cres.* ii 3 237
Heaven bless the isle of Cyprus and our noble general Othello! *Othello* ii 2 12
Noble gentleman. The king is a noble gentleman . . . *L. L. Lost* v 1 100
Belike, some noble gentleman that means, Travelling some journey, to repose him here . . . . *T. of Shrew* Ind. 1 75
Baptista is a noble gentleman, To whom my father is not all unknown i 2 240
So qualified as may beseem The spouse of any noble gentleman . . iv 5 67
Spoke like a sprightful noble gentleman . . . . *K. John* iv 2 177
And a head Of gallant warriors, noble gentlemen . . 1 *Hen. IV.* iv 4 26
While he, renowned noble gentleman, Yields up his life . 1 *Hen. VI.* iv 4 24
Humphrey Duke of Gloucester Did bear him like a noble gentleman 2 *Hen. VI.* i 1 184
The noble gentleman gave up the ghost . . . 3 *Hen. VI.* ii 3 22
You depend upon a noble gentleman . . . . *Troi. and Cres.* iii 1 6
This noble gentleman . . . Is in opinion and in honour wrong'd *T. An.* i 1 415
The gallant, young and noble gentleman, The County Paris *R. and J.* iii 5 114
A noble gentleman 'tis, if he would not keep so good a house *T. of Athens* iii 1 23
Do you know this noble gentleman, Edmund?—No, my lord . . *Lear* i 1 25
A noble gentleman of Rome, Comes from my lord with letters *Cymbeline* i 6 10
Noble goose. Breaks his staff like a noble goose . . *As Y. Like It* iii 4 48
Noble gossips, ye have been too prodigal . . . . *Hen. VIII.* v 5 13
Noble grace. My next poor petition Is, that his noble grace would have some pity Upon my wretched women . . . . iv 2 139
Rather to show a noble grace to both parts . . . *Coriolanus* v 3 121
Noble grapes. Will you eat no grapes, my royal fox? Yes, but you will my noble grapes . . . . *All's Well* ii 1 74
Noble gull-catcher. Here comes my noble gull-catcher . *T. Night* ii 5 205
Noble Hamlet. Exchange forgiveness with me, noble Hamlet *Hamlet* v 2 340
Noble hand. His noble hand Did win what he did spend *Richard II.* ii 1 179
Stay, father! for that noble hand of thine, That hath thrown down so many enemies, Shall not be sent . . . . . *T. Andron.* iii 1 163
Noble Harry. The Lord in heaven bless thee, noble Harry! *Hen. V.* iv 1 33

Noble having. You greet with present grace and great prediction Of noble having and of royal hope . . . *Macbeth* i 3 56
Noble heart. He is touch'd To the noble heart . *W. Tale* iii 2 223
I hold it cowardice To rest mistrustful where a noble heart Hath pawn'd an open hand in sign of love . . . 3 *Hen. VI.* iv 2 8
Must I with base tongue give my noble heart A lie? *Coriolanus* iii 2 100
Prepare thy aged eyes to weep; Or, if not so, thy noble heart to break: I bring consuming sorrow to thine age . *T. Andron.* iii 1 60
Now cracks a noble heart. Good night, sweet prince . . *Hamlet* v 2 370
If my speech offend a noble heart, Thy arm may do thee justice *Lear* v 3 127
Iago,— What say'st thou, noble heart?—What will I do? . *Othello* i 3 303
Noble heroes, my sword and yours are kin . . *All's Well* ii 1 40
Noble horsemanship. To turn and wind a fiery Pegasus And witch the world with noble horsemanship . . 1 *Hen. IV.* iv 1 110
Noble hostess. Fair and noble hostess, We are your guest . *Macbeth* i 6 24
Noble house. Now fair befal thee and thy noble house! *Richard III.* i 3 282
He springs of The noble house o' the Marcians . *Coriolanus* ii 3 246
Noble housewife. I play the noble housewife with the time, To entertain't so merrily with a fool . . *All's Well* ii 2 62
Noble husband. For recordation to my noble husband . 2 *Hen. IV.* ii 3 61
Ah, so much interest have I in thy sorrow As I had title in thy noble husband! I have bewept a worthy husband's death *Richard III.* ii 2 48
Noble image. He, the noble image of my youth 2 *Hen. IV.* iv 4 55
Noble isle. This noble isle doth want her proper limbs *Richard III.* iii 7 125
Noble judge. O noble judge! O excellent young man! *Mer. of Venice* iv 1 246
So says the bond: doth it not, noble judge? . iv 1 253
I take my cause Out of the gripes of cruel men, and give it To a most noble judge, the king my master *Hen. VIII.* v 3 101
Noble jury. His noble jury and foul cause can witness . iii 2 269
Noble king. After I have solemnly interr'd At Chertsey monastery this noble king . . . . . . *Richard III.* i 2 215
Noble kinsman. His noble kinsman: most degenerate king! *Richard II.* ii 1 262
Noble knight. Doubtless he would have made a noble knight 1 *Hen. VI.* iv 7 44
Noble knot. I would he had continued to his country As he began, and not unknit himself The noble knot he made *Coriolanus* iv 2 32
Noble lady. Such as he hath observed in noble ladies Unto their lords *T. of Shrew* Ind. 1 111
You're welcome, my fair guests: that noble lady, Or gentleman, that is not freely merry, Is not my friend *Hen. VIII.* i 4 35
Noble lady, I am sorry my integrity should breed . . . So deep suspicion iii 1 50
She that carries up the train Is that old noble lady, Duchess of Norfolk iv 1 52
What is your pleasure with me?—Noble lady, First, mine own service . iv 2 114
How now, my as fair as noble ladies,—and the moon, were she earthly, no nobler . . . . . . *Coriolanus* ii 1 107
Noble lady! Come, go with us; speak fair: you may salve so . iii 2 69
Noble life. That prefer A noble life before a long . iii 1 153
Noble liver. I will inflame thy noble liver 2 *Hen. IV.* v 5 33
Noble lord. God give thee joy of him! the noble lord Most honourably doth uphold his word . . . *L. L. Lost* v 2 448
As being overjoy'd To see her noble lord restored to health *T. of Shrew* Ind. 1 121
O noble lord, bethink thee of thy birth . . . . Ind. 2 32
How fares my noble lord?—Marry, I fare well . Ind. 2 102
Use a more spacious ceremony to the noble lords *All's Well* ii 1 52
One day too late, I fear me, noble lord, Hath clouded all thy happy days on earth: O, call back yesterday! *Richard II.* iii 2 67
Princes and noble lords, What answer shall I make to this base man? iv 1 19
My royal father, cheer these noble lords . 3 *Hen. VI.* ii 2 78
But you, my noble lords, may name the time . *Richard III.* iii 4 19
My noble lords and cousins all, good morrow. I have been long a sleeper iii 4 23
My noble lord and father, live in fame! . *T. Andron.* i 1 158
Great reason that my noble lord be rated For sauciness . . ii 3 81
I hope my noble lord esteems me honest . *Othello* iv 2 65
Most like a noble lord in love and one That had a royal lover *Cymbeline* v 5 171
Most noble lord . *Richard II.* ii 3 63; 2 *Hen. IV.* iv 1 59
My noble lord. *Tempest* iii 2; *M. N. Dream* i 1; v 1; *T. Night* i 4; *Richard II.* i 1; 1 *Hen. IV.* ii 4; 2 *Hen. IV.* i 1; ii 1; iv 2; iv 5; *Hen. V.* iv 3; 1 *Hen. VI.* iii 4; v 5; 2 *Hen. VI.* iii 2; v 2; *Richard III.* i 3; iii 2; *Hen. VIII.* v 3; *T. of Athens* iii 6; v 1; *Hamlet* i 5; *Lear* i 1; *Othello* iii 3; *Cymbeline* iii 5
Noble lord *T. G. of Ver.* iii 1; *Meas. for Meas.* v 1; *T. of Shrew* Ind. 2; *Richard II.* ii 3; iii 3; 2 *Hen. VI.* i 3; *Richard III.* i 1; i 2; iii 1; *Coriolanus* v 6; *T. of Athens* i 1; v 4; *Ant. and Cleo.* iv 14
Noble lordship. He commends him to your noble lordship *Richard III.* iii 2 8
Noble lustre. There is none of you so mean and base, That hath not noble lustre in your eyes . . *Hen. V.* iii 1 30
Noble Macbeth. What he hath lost noble Macbeth hath won *Macbeth* i 2 67
Noble madam. May it please you, noble madam, to withdraw *Hen. VIII.* iii 1 27
Noble madam, Men's evil manners live in brass . iv 2 44
Noble man. If there be not in our Grecian host One noble man that hath one spark of fire . . *Troi. and Cres.* i 3 294
We are all undone, unless The noble man have mercy *Coriolanus* iv 6 108
Think'st thou it honourable for a noble man Still to remember wrongs? v 3 154
For mine own part, I shall be glad to learn of noble men *J. Cæsar* iv 3 54
Noble master. That's my noble master! . . . *Tempest* i 2 299
Hold, hold!—My noble masters, hear me speak *Coriolanus* v 6 133
Hail, worthy Timon!—Our late noble master! *T. of Athens* v 1 58
My noble master will appear Such as he is . *J. Cæsar* iv 2 11
Hail to thee, noble master!—Ha! Makest thou this shame thy pastime? *Lear* ii 4 4
Noble matches. Hath she forsook so many noble matches? . *Othello* iv 2 125
Noble meaning. To atone your fears With my more noble meaning, not a man Shall pass his quarter . *T. of Athens* v 4 59
Noble memory. A pair of tribunes that have rack'd for Rome, To make coals cheap,—a noble memory! . *Coriolanus* v 1 17
Yet he shall have a noble memory . v 6 155
Noble mind. Ill can thy noble mind abrook The abject people gazing on thy face . . . 2 *Hen. VI.* ii 4 10
And thanks to men Of noble minds is honourable meed . *T. Andron.* i 1 216
His right noble mind, illustrious virtue *T. of Athens* iii 2 87
It is meet That noble minds keep ever with their likes *J. Cæsar* i 2 315
To the noble mind Rich gifts wax poor when givers prove unkind *Ham.* iii 1 100
O, what a noble mind is here o'erthrown! . . iii 1 158
Less noble mind Than she which by her death our Cæsar tells 'I am conqueror of myself' . . . *Ant. and Cleo.* iv 14 60
Noble-minded. The fraud of England, not the force of France, Hath now entrapp'd the noble-minded Talbot 1 *Hen. VI.* iv 4 37
Interrupter of the good That noble-minded Titus means to thee! *T. Andron.* i 1 209
Noble misery. O noble misery, To be i' the field, and ask 'what news?' of me! . . . . *Cymbeline* v 3 64
Noble mistress; 'tis fresh morning with me When you are by *Tempest* iii 1 33
Do you love my son?—Your pardon, noble mistress! *All's Well* i 3 192
Wilt thou betray thy noble mistress thus? *T. Andron.* iv 2 106
My noble mistress, Here is a box; I had it from the queen *Cymbeline* iii 4 190
Noble Moor. 'Tis great pity that the noble Moor Should hazard such a place as his own second With one of an ingraft infirmity . *Othello* ii 3 143
Is this the noble Moor whom our full senate Call all in all sufficient? iv 1 275
Noble mother. The first of April died Your noble mother . *K. John* iv 2 121
His noble mother, and his wife; Who, as I hear, mean to solicit him *Coriolanus* v 1 71
You gods! I prate, And the most noble mother of the world Leave unsaluted . . . v 3 49
Nor would your noble mother for much more Be so dishonour'd *T. An.* ii 1 51
Noble names. Which no less adorns Our gentry than our parents' noble names . . . *W. Tale* i 2 393
Noble nature. Out of his noble nature, Zeal and obedience *Hen. VIII.* iii 1 62
Some little memory of me will stir him—I know his noble nature . iii 2 418
A noble nature May catch a wrench . . *T. of Athens* ii 2 217
Is of a constant, loving, noble nature *Othello* ii 1 298
I would not have your free and noble nature, Out of self-bounty, be abused . . . . iii 3 199
Or who was he That, otherwise than noble nature did, Hath alter'd that good picture? . . . . . . *Cymbeline* iv 2 364
Noble nephew. Suffer thy brother Marcus to inter His noble nephew here in virtue's nest . . *T. Andron.* i 1 376
Noble offer. I'll presently Acquaint the queen of your most noble offer *W. Tale* ii 2 48
Noble offices thou mayst effect Of mediation 2 *Hen. IV.* iv 4 24
Noble one. I had my trial, And, must needs say, a noble one *Hen. VIII.* ii 1 119
Noble parentage. Of noble parentage, Of fair demesnes *Rom. and Jul.* iii 5 181
Noble partner. You shall have two noble partners . *Hen. VIII.* v 3 168
My noble partners, and myself, thus pray . v 5 6
My noble partner You greet with present grace and great prediction *Macbeth* i 3 54
Then, noble partners, The rather, for I earnestly beseech *Ant. and Cleo.* ii 2 22
Noble parts. And humbly prays you That with your other noble parts you'll suit In giving him his right . . *T. of Athens* ii 2 23
Noble passion. This noble passion, Child of integrity, hath from my soul Wiped the black scruples . . *Macbeth* iv 3 114
Noble patience. And sweetly In all the rest show'd a most noble patience . . . *Hen. VIII.* ii 1 36
Noble patricians, patrons of my right *T. Andron.* i 1 1
Noble peer. Hail, royal prince!—Thanks, noble peer *Richard II.* v 5 67
See you, my princes and my noble peers, These English monsters! *Hen. V.* ii 2 84
O, what a scandal is it to our crown, That two such noble peers as ye should jar! . . . . . 1 *Hen. VI.* iii 1 70
Thou bloody prison, Fatal and ominous to noble peers! . *Richard III.* iii 3 10
Noble Percy. Till then in blood by noble Percy lie . 1 *Hen. IV.* v 4 110
Noble person. Take good heed You charge not in your spleen a noble person And spoil your nobler soul . . *Hen. VIII.* i 2 174
Noble philosopher, your company . . . *Lear* iii 4 177
Noble pleasure. At your noble pleasure *Ant. and Cleo.* i 2 116
Noble pledge. My heart is thirsty for that noble pledge *J. Cæsar* iv 3 160
Noble plot. Why, it cannot choose but be a noble plot . 1 *Hen. IV.* i 3 279
Noble prelate. Into the bosom creep Of that same noble prelate . i 3 267
Noble presence. Would God that any in this noble presence Were enough noble to be upright judge! . *Richard II.* iv 1 117
The tender love I bear your grace, my lord, Makes me most forward in this noble presence To doom the offenders *Richard III.* iii 4 66
Noble prince. Go draw aside the curtains and discover The several caskets to this noble prince *Mer. of Venice* ii 7 2
Behold, there stand the caskets, noble prince . ii 9 4
You, my noble prince, With other princes that may best be spared *K. John* v 7 96
And doubt you not, right noble princes both . *Richard III.* iii 5 64
But Edward lives.—True, noble prince.—O bitter consequence! . iv 2 15
O noble prince, I can discover all The unlucky manage *Rom. and Jul.* iii 1 147
Noble prisoner. Kill Brutus, and be honour'd in his death.—We must not. A noble prisoner! . . *J. Cæsar* v 4 15
Noble prize. If you'll confess he brought home noble prize—As you must needs . . . *Troi. and Cres.* ii 2 86
Noble purpose. To be a soldier?—Such is his noble purpose *All's Well* iii 2 73
Noble queen. My noble queen, let former grudges pass 3 *Hen. VI.* iii 3 195
His noble queen Well struck in years, fair, and not jealous *Richard III.* i 1 91
Noble race. And never of the Nevils' noble race 2 *Hen. VI.* iii 2 215
Pupils lacks she none of noble race *Pericles* v Gower 9
Noble rate. Nor do I now make moan to be abridged From such a noble rate . . *Mer. of Venice* i 1 127
Noble respect. And what poor duty cannot do, noble respect Takes it in might, not merit . *M. N. Dream* v 1 91
Noble rite. No noble rite nor formal ostentation *Hamlet* iv 5 215
Noble Roman. He is a noble Roman and well given *J. Cæsar* i 2 197
Every one doth wish You had but that opinion of yourself Which every noble Roman bears of you . . ii 1 93
Think not, thou noble Roman, That ever Brutus will go bound to Rome v 1 111
Noble ruin. The noble ruin of her magic, Antony *Ant. and Cleo.* iii 10 19
Noble scar. A scar nobly got, or a noble scar, is a good livery of honour; so belike is that . . . *All's Well* iv 5 105
Noble scenes. Such noble scenes as draw the eye to flow *Hen. VIII.* Prol. 4
Noble Scots. Those same noble Scots That are your prisoners,— I'll keep them all . . . . . 1 *Hen. IV.* i 3 212
Noble self. Rome, the nurse of judgement, Invited by your noble self, hath sent One general tongue unto us *Hen. VIII.* ii 2 95
The duke's in council, and your noble self, I am sure, is sent for *Othello* i 2 92
Noble senate. What's the matter, That in these several places of the city You cry against the noble senate? . *Coriolanus* i 1 190
Noble sense. O brave Iago, honest and just, That hast such noble sense of thy friend's wrong! . . . *Othello* v 1 32
Noble servant. He was A noble servant to them . *Coriolanus* iv 7 36
Noble service. To gratify his noble service that Hath thus stood for his country . . . ii 2 44
Most willing spirits, That promise noble service *Cymbeline* iv 2 339
Noble shape. Thy noble shape is but a form of wax, Digressing from the valour of a man . . *Rom. and Jul.* iii 3 126
Noble ship. A noble ship of Venice Hath seen a grievous wreck *Othello* ii 1 22
Noble sinews. Now are we well resolved; and, by God's help, And yours, the noble sinews of our power . *Hen. V.* i 2 223
Noble sir. *Much Ado* v 1; *T. Night* v 1; *W. Tale* v 1; *Coriolanus* v 6; *Macbeth* ii 3; *Ant. and Cleo.* iii 11; *Pericles* v 3
Noble sister. The noble sister of Publicola, The moon of Rome, chaste as the icicle . . . . *Coriolanus* v 3 64

Noble sister. Farewell, Lavinia, my noble sister; O, would thou wert as thou tofore hast been! . . . *T. Andron.* iii 1 293
Noble soldier. Let us go see your son, I pray you: I long to talk with the young noble soldier . . . *All's Well* iv 5 109
Noble son. Here are the heads of thy two noble sons; And here's thy hand, in scorn to thee sent back . . . *T. Andron.* iii 1 237
These sorrowful drops upon thy blood-stain'd face, The last true duties of thy noble son! . . . v 3 155
Macduff is missing, and your noble son.—Your son, my lord, has paid a soldier's debt . . . *Macbeth* v 8 38
I will be brief: your noble son is mad: Mad call I it . . . *Hamlet* ii 2 92
Noble sort. None of noble sort Would so offend a virgin and extort A poor soul's patience . . . *M. N. Dream* iii 2 159
Noble spirit. Challenged The noble spirits to arms . . . *Hen. VIII.* i 1 35
A noble spirit, As yours was put into you, ever casts Such doubts, as false coin, from it . . . iii 1 169
If our betters play at that game, we must not dare To imitate them; faults that are rich are fair.—A noble spirit! . . . *T. of Athens* i 2 14
Noble spoken. Do So far ask pardon as befits mine honour To stoop in such a case.—'Tis noble spoken . . . *Ant. and Cleo.* ii 2 98
Noble state. He is much sorry, If any thing more than your sport and pleasure Did move your greatness and this noble state To call upon him . . . *Troi. and Cres.* ii 3 118
Noble steed. My noble steed, known to the camp, I give him *Coriolanus* i 9 61
Noble stock Was graft with crab-tree slip . . . 2 *Hen. VI.* iii 2 213
She's such a one, that, were I well assured Came of a gentle kind and noble stock, I'ld wish no better choice . . . *Pericles* v 1 68
Noble story. Think ye see The very persons of our noble story As they were living . . . *Hen. VIII.* Prol. 26
Noble strain. He is of a noble strain, of approved valour . *Much Ado* ii 1 394
O noble strain! O worthiness of nature! breed of greatness! *Cymbeline* iv 2 24
To think of what a noble strain you are, And of how coward a spirit *Per.* iv 3 24
Noble strength. You do unbend your noble strength, to think So brain-sickly of things . . . *Macbeth* ii 2 45
Noble subjects. Go search like nobles, like noble subjects . *Pericles* ii 4 50
Noble substance. The dram o. eale Doth all the noble substance of a doubt To his own scandal . . . *Hamlet* i 4 37
Noble sufferance. They do prank them in authority, Against all noble sufferance . . . *Coriolanus* iii 1 24
Noble temper. A noble temper dost thou show in this . *K. John* v 2 40
You have a gentle, noble temper A soul as even as a calm *Hen. VIII.* iii 1 165
But not every man patient after the noble temper of your lordship *Cymb.* ii 3 6
Noble thanes. The noble thanes do bravely in the war . *Macbeth* v 7 26
Noble thankfulness. You learn me noble thankfulness . *Much Ado* iv 1 31
Noble thing. But that I see thee here, Thou noble thing! more dances my rapt heart Than when I first my wedded mistress saw *Coriol.* iv 5 122
Noble thought. Lay a more noble thought upon mine honour Than for to think that I would sink it here . . . *All's Well* v 3 180
Thy Doll, and Helen of thy noble thoughts, Is in base durance 2 *Hen. IV.* v 5 35
Noble title. I dare not make myself so guilty, To give up willingly that noble title . . . *Hen. VIII.* iii 1 140
Noble touch. Come, my sweet wife, my dearest mother, and My friends of noble touch . . . *Coriolanus* iv 1 49
Noble tribunes. The noble tribunes are the people's mouths . . . iii 1 271
The gods preserve our noble tribunes! . . . iii 3 143
Hear me, grave fathers! noble tribunes, stay! For pity of mine age *T. Andron.* iii 1 1
Noble troop. What is't?—A noble troop of strangers . *Hen. VIII.* i 4 53
Or gild again the noble troops that waited Upon my smiles . iii 2 411
Noble uncle. How fares our noble uncle, Lancaster? *Richard II.* ii 1 71
Noble uncle, . . . Look on my wrongs with an indifferent eye . ii 3 115
Noble uncle, thus ignobly used, Your nephew, late despised Richard, comes.—Direct mine arms I may embrace his neck . 1 *Hen. VI.* ii 5 35
Is not this a heavy case, To see thy noble uncle thus distract? *T. An.* iv 3 26
My noble uncle, do you know the cause? . *Rom. and Jul.* i 1 149
Noble vessel. Though thy tackle's torn, Thou show'st a noble vessel: what's thy name? . . . *Coriolanus* iv 5 68
Now is that noble vessel full of grief, That it runs over . *J. Cæsar* v 5 13
Noble weakness. On the sudden dropp'd.—O noble weakness! *A. and C.* v 2 347
Noble wife. You, that have turn'd off a first so noble wife, May justly diet me . . . *All's Well* v 3 220
O ye gods, Render me worthy of this noble wife! . *J. Cæsar* ii 1 303
Noble wish. Throng our large temples with the shows of peace, And not our streets with war!—Amen, amen.—A noble wish *Coriolanus* iii 3 38
Noble woman. But yet a brain that leads my use of anger To better vantage.—Well said, noble woman! . . . iii 2 31
Noble youth. He was indeed the glass Wherein the noble youth did dress themselves . . . 2 *Hen. IV.* ii 3 22
But know, thou noble youth, The serpent that did sting thy father's life Now wears his crown . . . *Hamlet* i 5 38
That is Laertes, A very noble youth: mark . . . v 1 247
Nobleman. To justify this worthy nobleman, So vulgarly and personally accused . . . *Meas. for Meas.* v 1 159
A paper from fortune's close-stool to give to a nobleman! . *All's Well* v 2 18
He cried to me for help and said his name was Antigonus, a nobleman *W. Tale* iii 3 99
Out, dunghill! darest thou brave a nobleman? . . *K. John* iv 3 87
There is a nobleman of the court at door would speak with you 1 *Hen. IV.* ii 4 317
The least of which haunting a nobleman Loseth men's hearts . iii 1 186
Many a nobleman lies stark and stiff Under the hoofs of vaunting enemies v 3 42
I'll purge, and leave sack, and live cleanly as a nobleman should do v 4 169
Here comes the nobleman that committed the prince for striking him 2 *Hen. IV.* i 2 62
God forbid any malice should prevail, That faultless may condemn a nobleman! Pray God he may acquit him! . 2 *Hen. VI.* iii 2 24
What nobleman is that That with the king here resteth in his tent? 3 *Hen. VI.* iv 3 9
If I blush, It is to see a nobleman want manners . *Hen. VIII.* iii 2 308
There is a nobleman in town, one Paris, that would fain lay knife aboard; but she, good soul, had as lief see a toad . *Rom. and Jul.* ii 4 213
The nobleman would have dealt with her like a nobleman . *Pericles* iv 6 147
Noblemen. Hear sweet discourse, converse with noblemen *T. G. of Ver.* i 3 31
Then you, belike, suspect these noblemen As guilty . 2 *Hen. VI.* iii 2 186
Nobleness. Worthy his youth and nobleness of birth . *T. G. of Ver.* i 3 33
To see his nobleness! Conceiving the dishonour of his mother, He straight declined, droop'd, took it deeply . *W. Tale* ii 3 12
Any thing, my lord, That my ability may undergo And nobleness impose ii 3 165
The affection of nobleness which nature shows above her breeding v 2 40
I did infer your lineaments, Being the right idea of your father, Both in your form and nobleness of mind . . . *Richard III.* iii 7 14

Nobleness. When did he regard The stamp of nobleness in any person Out of himself?—My lords, you speak your pleasures *Hen. VIII.* iii 2 12
Call'd them Time-pleasers, flatterers, foes to nobleness *Coriolanus* iii 1 45
The god of soldiers, With the consent of supreme Jove, inform Thy thoughts with nobleness! . . . v 3 72
What! to you, Whose star-like nobleness gave life and influence To their whole being! . . . *T. of Athens* v 1 66
But signs of nobleness, like stars, shall shine On all deservers *Macbeth* i 4 41
Methought thy very gait did prophesy A royal nobleness . *Lear* v 3 176
The nobleness of life Is to do thus; when such a mutual pair And such a twain can do't . . . *Ant. and Cleo.* i 1 36
My queen and Eros Have by their brave instruction got upon me A nobleness in record . . . iv 14 99
Let the world see His nobleness well acted . . . v 2 45
More charming With their own nobleness, which could have turn'd A distaff to a lance, gilded pale looks . . . *Cymbeline* v 3 33
I hold it ever, Virtue and cunning were endowments greater Than nobleness and riches . . . *Pericles* iii 2 28
Nobler. Yet with my nobler reason 'gainst my fury Do I take part *Temp.* v 1 26
But kindness, nobler ever than revenge . . *As Y. Like It* iv 3 129
I find that she, which late Was in my nobler thoughts most base, is now The praised of the king . . . *All's Well* ii 3 178
And make conceive a bark of baser kind By bud of nobler race *W. Tale* iv 4 95
Better conquest never canst thou make Than arm thy constant and thy nobler parts Against these giddy loose suggestions . *K. John* iii 1 291
Take good heed You charge not in your spleen a noble person And spoil your nobler soul . . . *Hen. VIII.* i 2 175
Making their way With those of nobler bulk . . *Troi. and Cres.* i 3 37
How now, my as fair as noble ladies,—and the moon, were she earthly, no nobler . . . *Coriolanus* ii 1 108
My nobler friends, I crave their pardons . . . iii 1 64
Yet will I still Be thus to them.—You do the nobler . . iii 2 6
A nobler man, a braver warrior, Lives not this day . *T. Andron.* i 1 25
There's not a nobler man in Rome than Antony . *J. Cæsar* iii 2 121
Whether 'tis nobler in the mind to suffer The slings and arrows of outrageous fortune, Or to take arms against a sea of troubles *Hamlet* iii 1 57
O Antony, Nobler than my revolt is infamous, Forgive me *A. and C.* iv 9 19
Some nobler token I have kept apart For Livia and Octavia . v 2 168
This life Is nobler than attending for a check . *Cymbeline* iii 3 22
To taint his nobler heart and brain With needless jealousy . v 4 65
Be not, as is our fangled world, a garment Nobler than that it covers . v 4 135
A nobler sir ne'er lived 'Twixt sky and ground . . v 5 145
Noblesse. Then true noblesse would Learn him forbearance from so foul a wrong . . . *Richard II.* iv 1 119
Noblest. Some defect in her Did quarrel with the noblest grace she owed And put it to the foil . . . *Tempest* iii 1 45
The noblest deer hath them [horns] as huge as the rascal *As Y. Like It* iii 3 57
Will you go hunt, my lord?—What, Curio?—The hart.—Why, so I do, the noblest that I have . . . *T. Night* i 1 18
On, you noblest English, Whose blood is fet from fathers of war-proof! *Hen. V.* iii 1 17
The noblest hateful love that e'er I heard of . *Troi. and Cres.* iv 1 33
The noblest that survives, The eldest son of this distressed queen *T. An.* i 1 102
The noblest mind he carries That ever govern'd man . *T. of Athens* i 1 291
What viler thing upon the earth than friends Who can bring noblest minds to basest ends! . . . iv 3 471
Thou art the ruins of the noblest man That ever lived . *J. Cæsar* iii 1 256
If thou wert the noblest of thy strain, Young man, thou couldst not die more honourable . . . v 1 59
This was the noblest Roman of them all . . . v 5 68
Let us haste to hear it, And call the noblest to the audience . *Hamlet* v 2 398
'Tis your noblest course . . . *Ant. and Cleo.* iii 13 78
The greatest prince o' the world, The noblest . . iv 15 55
Noblest of men, woo't die? Hast thou no care of me? . . . iv 15 59
He is one of the noblest note . . . *Cymbeline* i 6 22
I'll give it; Yea, though thou do demand a prisoner, The noblest ta'en v 5 100
Noblest-minded. I have moved already Some certain of the noblest-minded Romans To undergo with me an enterprise . *J. Cæsar* i 3 122
Nobly. I should sin To think but nobly of my grandmother *Tempest* i 2 119
Some kinds of baseness Are nobly undergone . . . iii 1 3
Know you such a one?—But by the ear, that hears most nobly of him *All's Well* iii 5 53
And made such pestiferous reports of men very nobly held . iv 3 341
A scar nobly got, or a noble scar, is a good livery of honour . iv 5 105
I think nobly of the soul, and no way approve his opinion *T. Night* iv 2 59
A savage jealousy That sometime savours nobly . . v 1 123
Very nobly Have you deserved . . . *W. Tale* iv 4 528
Come, bring your luggage nobly on your back . 1 *Hen. IV.* v 4 160
Then both parties nobly are subdued, And neither party loser 2 *Hen. IV.* iv 2 90
You are more nobly born, Despoiled of your honour in your life 2 *Hen. VI.* ii 3 9
Then, nobly, York; 'tis for a crown thou fight'st . v 2 16
Receive 'em nobly, and conduct 'em Into our presence *Hen. VIII.* i 4 58
'Tis nobly spoken: Take notice, lords, he has a loyal breast iii 2 99
The rod, and bird of peace, and all such emblems Laid nobly on her iv 1 90
Must not so stale his palm, nobly acquired . *Troi. and Cres.* ii 3 201
I had rather had eleven die nobly for their country than one voluptuously surfeit out of action . . . *Coriolanus* i 3 27
Bear The addition nobly ever! . . . i 9 66
Never shame to hear What you have nobly done . . . ii 2 72
You have deserved nobly of your country, and you have not deserved nobly . . . ii 3 94
He has done nobly, and cannot go without any honest man's voice ii 3 139
[Censorinus,] nobly named so, Twice being [by the people chosen] censor ii 3 251
And do contest As hotly and as nobly with thy love As ever in ambitious strength I did Contend against thy valour . . iv 5 117
To him that, for your honour and your state, Will use you nobly *T. An.* i 1 260
And will nobly him remunerate . . . i 1 398
Nobly train'd, Stuff'd, as they say, with honourable parts *Rom. and Jul.* iii 5 182
'Tis most nobly spoken . . . *T. of Athens* v 4 63
When every drop of blood That every Roman bears, and nobly bears, Is guilty of a several bastardy . . . *J. Cæsar* ii 1 137
Was not that nobly done? Ay, and wisely too . *Macbeth* iii 6 14
Sir, you speak nobly.—Why is this reason'd? . . *Lear* v 1 28
Our force by land Hath nobly held . . . *Ant. and Cleo.* iii 13 170
Bruised pieces, go; You have been nobly borne . . iv 14 43
Nobly he yokes A smiling with a sigh . . . *Cymbeline* iv 2 51
The forlorn soldier, that so nobly fought . . . v 5 405
Live, And deal with others better.—Nobly doom'd! . . v 5 420
Nobody. This is the tune of our catch, played by the picture of Nobody *Tempest* iii 2 136

Nobody. Nobody but has his fault; but let that pass *Mer. Wives* i 4 14
I warrant thee, nobody hears i 2 51
Truly, I am so glad you have nobody here iv 2 19
Nobody marks you.—What, my dear Lady Disdain! are you yet living? *Much Ado* i 1 118
An bad thinking do not wrest true speaking, I'll offend nobody iii 4 34
Said I, 'a good wit:' 'Just,' said she, 'it hurts nobody' v 1 165
I would out-night you, did no body come *Mer. of Venice* v 1 23
I am a poor fellow, sir.—Why, be so still; here's nobody will steal that from thee *W. Tale* iv 4 645
Methinks no body should be sad but I *K. John* iv 1 13
Nothing confutes me but eyes, and nobody sees me 1 *Hen. IV.* v 4 129
Whether I shall ever see thee again or no, there is nobody cares 2 *Hen. IV.* ii 4 73
She has nobody to do any thing about her when I am gone iii 2 246
Trust nobody, for fear you be betray'd 2 *Hen. VI.* iv 4 58
Ill blows the wind that profits nobody 3 *Hen. VI.* ii 5 55
I'll speak with nobody *Troi. and Cres.* ii 3 75
He'll answer nobody; he professes not answering iii 3 269
If it touch not you, it comes near nobody *Othello* iv 1 210
Let nobody blame him; his scorn I approve,—Nay, that's not next iv 3 52
Nobody come? then shall I bleed to death v 1 45
O, who hath done this deed?—Nobody; I myself. Farewell v 2 124
And I must go up and down like a cock that nobody can match *Cymbeline* ii 1 24
Honest! good fellow, what's that? If it be a day fits you, search out of the calendar, and nobody look after it *Pericles* ii 1 59

Noces. Les dames et demoiselles pour être baisées devant leur noces, il n'est pas la coutume de France *Hen. V.* v 2 280

Nod. What said she?—Ay.—Nod—Ay—why, that's noddy *T. G. of Ver.* i 1 119
I say, she did nod; and you ask me if she did nod; and I say, 'Ay' i 1 120
Nod to him, elves, and do him courtesies *M. N. Dream* iii 1 177
My lord, you nod; you do not mind the play *T. of Shrew* i 1 254
And if she chance to nod I'll rail and brawl iv 1 209
Courteous feathers, which bow the head and nod at every man *All's W.* iv 5 112
With wrinkled brows, with nods, with rolling eyes *K. John* iv 2 192
See how the giddy multitude do point, And nod their heads! 2 *Hen. VI.* ii 4 22
Nay, he nods at us, as who should say, I'll be even with you iv 7 99
Deceive and cog, Duck with French nods and apish courtesy *Richard III.* i 3 49
Like a drunken sailor on a mast, Ready, with every nod, to tumble down iii 4 102
You shall see him nod at me.—Will he give you the nod? *Troi. and Cres.* i 2 211
I will practise the insinuating nod *Coriolanus* ii 3 107
As if Olympus to a molehill should In supplication nod v 3 31
Nor wink, nor nod, nor kneel, nor make a sign *T. Andron.* iii 2 43
And returns in peace Most rich in Timon's nod *T. of Athens* i 1 62
With certain half-caps and cold-moving nods They froze me into silence ii 2 221
And Cassius is A wretched creature and must bend his body, If Cæsar carelessly but nod on him *J. Cæsar* i 2 118
If thou dost nod, thou break'st thy instrument; I'll take it from thee iv 3 271
How say you? Why, what care I? If thou canst nod, speak too *Macb.* iii 4 70
As her winks, and nods, and gestures yield them *Hamlet* iv 5 11
Blue promontory With trees upon't, that nod unto the world *A. and C.* iv 14 6

Nodded. So he nodded, And soberly did mount an arm-gaunt steed i 5 47
No, my most wronged sister; Cleopatra Hath nodded him to her iii 6 66

Nodding. Where oxlips and the nodding violet grows *M. N. Dream* ii 1 250
Your enemies, with nodding of their plumes, Fan you into despair! *Cor.* iii 3 126

Noddle. I will smite his noddles *Mer. Wives* iii 1 125
To comb your noddle with a three-legg'd stool *T. of Shrew* i 1 64

Noddy. What said she?—Ay.—Nod—Ay—why, that's noddy *T. G. of Ver.* i 1 119
You ask me if she did nod; and I say, 'Ay.'—And that set together is noddy i 1 122
Having nothing but the word 'noddy' for my pains i 1 131

'Nointed. I have 'nointed an Athenian's eyes *M. N. Dream* iii 2 351
Who shall be flayed alive; then 'nointed over with honey *W. Tale* iv 4 813

Noise. There was a noise, That's verily *Tempest* ii 1 320
Be not afeard: the isle is full of noises, Sounds and sweet airs iii 2 144
This is the mouth o' the cell: no noise, and enter iv 1 216
With strange and several noises Of roaring, shrieking, howling v 1 232
Alas, what noise?—Heaven forgive our sins! *Mer. Wives* v 5 34
But, hark, what noise? Heaven give your spirits comfort! *M. for M.* iv 2 72
How now! what noise? That spirit's possess'd with haste iv 2 91
Who makes that noise there? What are you? iv 3 27
Who is that at the door that keeps all this noise? *Com. of Errors* iii 1 61
You shall also make no noise in the streets *Much Ado* iii 3 36
All-telling fame Doth noise abroad, Navarre hath made a vow *L. L. Lost* ii 1 22
You must understand he goes but to see a noise that he heard *M. N. D.* iii 1 93
Stand aside: the noise they make Will cause Demetrius to awake iii 2 116
You may as well forbid the mountain pines To wag their high tops and to make no noise *Mer. of Venice* iv 1 76
When the sweet wind did gently kiss the trees And they did make no noise v 1 3
'Tis no matter how it be in tune, so it make noise enough *As Y. Like It* iv 2 10
These balls bound; there's noise in it *All's Well* ii 3 314
What noise there, ho?—No noise, my lord *W. Tale* ii 3 39
Bear me hence From forth the noise and rumour of the field *K. John* v 4 45
Let's march without the noise of threatening drum *Richard II.* iii 3 51
My office is To noise abroad that Harry Monmouth fell 2 *Hen. IV.* Ind. 29
See if thou canst find out Sneak's noise ii 4 13
Let there be no noise made, my gentle friends iv 5 1
Less noise, less noise! iv 5 7
Not so much noise, my lords: sweet prince, speak low iv 5 16
What noise is this? what traitors have we here? 1 *Hen. VI.* i 3 15
What tumult's in the heavens? Whence cometh this alarum and the noise? i 4 99
Be vigilant: If any noise or soldier you perceive ii 1 2
What means this noise? Fellow, what miracle dost thou proclaim? 2 *Hen. VI.* ii 1 59
What noise is this?—Why, how now lords! your wrathful weapons drawn! iii 2 236
What noise is this I hear? Dare any be so bold to sound retreat? iv 8 3
The noise of thy cross-bow Will scare the herd 3 *Hen. VI.* iii 1 6
Methought, what pain it was to drown! What dreadful noise of waters in mine ears! What ugly sights of death within mine eyes! *Rich. III.* i 4 22
Such hideous cries, that with the very noise I trembling waked i 4 60
Hark! what noise is this!—Oh, who shall hinder me to wail and weep? ii 2 33
They That come to hear a merry bawdy play, A noise of targets *Hen. VIII.* Prol. 15
Such a noise arose As the shrouds make at sea in a stiff tempest iv 1 71
You'll leave your noise anon, ye rascals: do you take the court for Paris-garden? v 4 1
What was his cause of anger?—The noise goes, this *Troi. and Cres.* i 2 12
What noise? what shriek is this?—'Tis our mad sister ii 2 97
O, they are at it!—Their noise be our instruction *Coriolanus* i 4 22
And hark, what noise the general makes! To him! i 5 10
Before him he carries noise, and behind him he leaves tears ii 1 175
Certain of your brethren roar'd and ran From the noise of our own drums ii 3 60
His peremptory 'shall,' being but The horn and noise o' the monster's iii 1 95
Unshout the noise that banish'd Marcius v 5 4
And had no welcomes home: but he returns, Splitting the air with noise v 6 52
Here are no storms, No noise, but silence and eternal sleep *T. Andron.* i 1 155
Ring a hunter's peal, That all the court may echo with the noise ii 2 6
Let us sit down and mark their yelping noise ii 3 20
I heard a child cry underneath a wall. I made unto the noise v 1 25
What noise is this? Give me my long sword, ho! *Rom. and Jul.* i 1 82
I hear some noise within; dear love, adieu! ii 2 136
My lord! my lady!—What noise is here?—O lamentable day! iv 5 17
I hear some noise. Lady, come from that nest Of death v 3 151
Lead, boy: which way?—Yea, noise? then I'll be brief v 3 169
But then a noise did scare me from the tomb v 3 262
Bid every noise be still: peace yet again! *J. Cæsar* i 2 14
What was the second noise for?—Why, for that too i 2 224
The noise of battle hurtled in the air, Horses did neigh ii 2 22
Hark, boy! what noise is that?—I hear none, madam ii 4 16
I have done the deed. Didst thou not hear a noise? *Macbeth* ii 2 15
How is't with me, when every noise appals me? ii 2 58
Why sinks that cauldron? and what noise is this? iv 1 106
What is that noise?—It is the cry of women, my good lord v 5 7
That way the noise is. Tyrant, show thy face! v 7 14
Capable of nothing but inexplicable dumb-shows and noise *Hamlet* iii 2 14
What have I done, that thou darest wag thy tongue In noise so rude against me? iii 4 40
But soft, what noise? who calls on Hamlet? O, here they come iv 2 3
Alack, what noise is this?—Where are my Switzers? iv 5 96
What warlike noise is this? v 2 360
Or whether gasted by the noise I made, Full suddenly he fled *Lear* ii 1 57
Lie here and rest awhile.—Make no noise, make no noise; draw the curtains iii 6 89
Tom, away! Mark the high noises iii 6 118
But, hark! what noise?—'Help! help!' *Othello* ii 3 149
The general so likes your music, that he desires you, for love's sake, to make no more noise with it iii 1 13
Who's there? whose noise is this that cries on murder? v 1 48
What noise is this? Not dead? not yet quite dead? v 2 85
The noise was here. Ha! no more moving? Still as the grave v 2 93
Cleopatra, catching but the least noise of this, dies instantly *A. and C.* i 2 145
And gives his potent regiment to a trull, That noises it against us iii 6 96
Peace! what noise?—List, list!—Hark!—Music i' the air iv 3 13
Follow the noise so far as we have quarter; Let's see how it will give off iv 3 22
Bring our crown and all. Wherefore's this noise? v 2 233
There's no answer That will be given to the loudest noise we make *Cymbeline* iii 5 44
The noise is round about us.—Let us from it iv 4 1

Noised. Let it be noised That through our intercession this revokement And pardon comes *Hen. VIII.* i 2 105
It is noised he hath a mass of treasure *T. of Athens* iv 3 404

Noiseless. The inaudible and noiseless foot of Time *All's Well* v 3 41
France spreads his banners in our noiseless land *Lear* iv 2 56

Noisemaker. You whoreson, insolent noisemaker! *Tempest* i 1 47

Noisome. Foul breath is noisome; therefore I will depart unkissed *Much Ado* v 2 53
I will go root away The noisome weeds *Richard II.* iii 4 38
So bees with smoke and doves with noisome stench Are from their hives and houses driven away 1 *Hen. VI.* i 5 23
He could not stay to pick them in a pile Of noisome musty chaff *Coriol.* v 1 26
The seeing these effects will be Both noisome and infectious *Cymbeline* i 5 26

Nole. An ass's nole I fixed on his head *M. N. Dream* iii 2 17

Nominate. Thy young days, which we may nominate tender *L. L. Lost* i 2 16
Can you nominate in order now the degrees of the lie? *As Y. Like It* v 4 92
Sight may distinguish of colours, but suddenly to nominate them all, it is impossible 2 *Hen. VI.* ii 1 130

Nominated. Who is intituled, nominated, or called *L. L. Lost* v 1 8
The forfeit Be nominated for an equal pound Of your fair flesh *M. of Ven.* i 3 150
Is it so nominated in the bond?—It is not so express'd: but what of that? iv 1 259

Nomination. I will look again on the intellect of the letter, for the nomination of the party writing to the person written unto *L. L. Lost* iv 2 138
Are all things fitting for that royal time?—It is, and wants but nomination.—To-morrow, then *Richard III.* iii 4 5
What imports the nomination of this gentleman? *Hamlet* v 2 133

Nominativo. Singulariter, nominativo, hic hæc, hoc *Mer. Wives* iv 1 42
Nominativo, hig, hag, hog; pray you, mark: genitivo, hujus iv 1 44

Nonage. In his nonage council under him *Richard III.* ii 3 13

Nonce. I have cases of buckram for the nonce 1 *Hen. IV.* i 2 201
This is a riddling merchant for the nonce 1 *Hen VI.* ii 3 57
And that he calls for drink, I'll have prepared him A chalice for the nonce *Hamlet* iv 7 161

Noncome. Here's that shall drive some of them to a noncome *Much Ado* iii 5 67

None that I more love than myself *Tempest* i 1 22
Save means to live.—Of that there's none, or little ii 1 51
Away with the rest.—I will have none on't iv 1 248
You writ them, sir, at my request; But I will none of them *T. G. of Ver.* ii 1 133
Did you perceive her earnest?—She gave me none, except an angry word ii 1 164
Lest it should ravel and be good to none iii 2 52
And that's far worse than none; better have none Than plural faith v 4 51
Who's at home besides yourself?—Why, none but mine own people *Mer. Wives* iv 2 14
None better knows than you *Meas. for Meas.* i 3 7
If I do lose thee, I do lose a thing That none but fools would keep iii 1 8
And this it was, for other means was none *Com. of Errors* i 1 76
He is the bridle of your will.—There's none but asses will be bridled so ii 1 14
He denied you had in him no right.—He meant he did me none iv 2 8
Whose will still wills It should none spare *L. L. Lost* ii 1 51
None offend where all alike do dote iv 3 126
Tush, none but minstrels like of sonneting! iv 3 158
Else none at all in aught proves excellent iv 3 354
Thou hast spoken no word all this while.—Nor understood none neither v 1 158
None are so surely caught, when they are catch'd, As wit turn'd fool v 2 69
We'll none of that: that have I told my love *M. N. Dream* iv 1 46
My father hath no child but I, nor none is like to have *As Y. Like It* i 2 19

None. Forbear, and eat no more.—Why, I have eat none yet *As Y. L. It* ii 7 88
That is the dowry of his wife; 'tis none of his own getting . iii 3 56
I'll none of it: hence! make your best of it . . *T. of Shrew* iv 3 100
You can eat none of this homely meat . . . *All's Well* ii 2 48
It's four to one she'll none of me . . . *T. Night* i 3 113
He left this ring behind him, Would I or not: tell him I'll none of it i 5 321
You should put your lord into a desperate assurance she will none of him . . . ii 2 9
To force that on you, in a shameful cunning, Which you knew none of yours . . . iii 1 128
Nor never none Shall mistress be of it, save I alone . . iii 1 171
Satisfaction can be none but by pangs of death and sepulchre . iii 4 262
Say 'tis not your seal, not your invention: You can say none of this v 1 342
No, by my life, Privy to none of this . . *W. Tale* ii 1 96
She's a changeling and none of your flesh and blood . . iv 4 705
He must know 'tis none of your daughter nor my sister . . iv 4 850
That none so small advantage shall step forth . . *K. John* iii 4 151
Nor I greatly care not: God knows I had as lief be none as one *Rich. II.* v 2 49
He shall be none; We'll keep him here . . . v 2 99
Detraction will not suffer it. Therefore I'll none of it . 1 *Hen. IV.* v 1 142
Grow till you come unto it: I will none of you . 2 *Hen. IV.* iii 2 271
Take it, God, For it is none but thine! . . *Hen. V.* iv 8 117
Alack, my lord, that fault is none of yours . *Richard III.* i 1 47
But none can cure their harms by wailing them . . ii 2 103
For one commanding all, obey'd of none . . . iv 4 104
What news with you?—None good, my lord, to please you with the hearing; nor none so bad, but it may well be told . . iv 4 458
And the late marriage made of none effect . *Hen. VIII.* iv 1 33
He is true-hearted; and a soul None better in my kingdom . v 1 155
If he overhold his price so much, We'll none of him . *Troi. and Cres.* ii 3 143
He! no, she'll none of him . . . . . . iii 1 110
Abound'st in all, And usest none in that true use indeed *Rom. and Jul.* iii 3 124
None that I know will be, much that I fear may chance . *J. Cæsar* ii 4 32
Now lies he there, And none so poor to do him reverence . iii 2 125
I dare do all that may become a man; Who dares do more is none *Macb.* i 7 47
There is none but he Whose being I do fear . . . iii 1 54
Throw physic to the dogs; I'll none of it . . . . v 3 47
Our thoughts are ours, their ends none of our own . . *Hamlet* iii 2 223
For no man, sir.—What woman, then?—For none, neither . v 1 144
None does offend, none, I say, none; I'll able 'em . . *Lear* iv 6 172
None our parts so poor, But was a race of heaven . *Ant. and Cleo.* i 3 36
Your Italy contains none so accomplished a courtier . *Cymbeline* i 4 103
None a stranger there So merry and so gamesome . . . i 6 59
If you can penetrate her with your fingering, so; we'll try with tongue too: if none will do, let her remain . . . ii 3 17
Other of them may have crook'd noses, but to owe such straight arms, none . . . . iii 1 38

None-sparing. To the event Of the none-sparing war *All's Well* iii 2 108

Nonino. It was a lover and his lass, With a hey, and a ho, and a hey nonino *As Y. Like It* v 3 18

Non nobis. Let there be sung 'Non nobis' and 'Te Deum' *Hen. V.* iv 8 128

Nonny. Converting all your sounds of woe Into Hey nonny, nonny *Much Ado* ii 3 71
Hey non nonny, nonny, hey nonny . . . *Hamlet* iv 5 165
Blows the cold wind: Says suum, mun, ha, no, nonny . *Lear* iii 4 103

Nonpareil. And that most deeply to consider is The beauty of his daughter; he himself Calls her a nonpareil . . *Tempest* iii 2 108
Though you were crown'd The nonpareil of beauty . . *T. Night* i 5 273
If thou didst it, Thou art the nonpareil . . *Macbeth* iii 4 19
Spake you of Cæsar? How! the nonpareil! . *Ant. and Cleo.* iii 2 11
My mother seem'd The Dian of that time: so doth my wife The nonpareil of this. O, vengeance, vengeance! . . *Cymbeline* ii 5 8

Non-performance. Whereof the execution did cry out Against the non-performance . . . . . . *W. Tale* i 1 261

Non-regardance. Since you to non-regardance cast my faith . *T. Night* v 1 124

Nonsuit. And, in conclusion, Nonsuits my mediators . *Othello* i 1 16

Nook. In the deep nook, where once Thou call'dst me up at midnight *Tempest* i 2 227
So by many winding nooks he strays With willing sport *T. G. of Ver.* ii 7 31
To live in a nook merely monastic . . *As Y. Like It* iii 2 441

Nook-shotten. In that nook-shotten isle of Albion . *Hen. V.* iii 5 14

Noon. At any time 'fore noon . . . . *Meas. for Meas.* ii 2 160
Love's night is noon . . . . . *T. Night* iii 1 160
Wishing clocks more swift? Hours, minutes? noon, midnight? *W. Tale* i 2 290
That, ere the next Ascension-day at noon, Your highness should deliver up your crown . . . . . *K. John* iv 2 151
And on that day at noon, whereon he says I shall yield up my crown, let him be hang'd . . . . iv 2 156
Unbuttoning thee after supper and sleeping upon benches after noon 1 *Hen. IV.* i 2 4
Such a nature, Tickled with good success, disdains the shadow Which he treads on at noon . . . . . *Coriolanus* i 1 265
The bawdy hand of the dial is now upon the prick of noon *Rom. and Jul.* ii 4 119
Great business must be wrought ere noon . . *Macbeth* iii 5 22
As I have life and honour, There shall he sit till noon . *Lear* ii 2 141
We'll go to supper i' the morning. So, so, so.—And I'll go to bed at noon iii 6 92
Why, then, to-morrow night; or Tuesday morn; On Tuesday noon, or night . . . . *Othello* iii 3 61
To reel the streets at noon . . . . *Ant. and Cleo.* i 4 20
Or have charged him, At the sixth hour of morn, at noon, at midnight, To encounter me with orisons . . . *Cymbeline* i 3 31

Noon-day. Yesterday the bird of night did sit Even at noon-day upon the market-place, Hooting and shrieking . . *J. Cæsar* i 3 27

Noontide. I have bedimm'd The noontide sun . . *Tempest* v 1 42
And that the moon May through the centre creep and so displease Her brother's noontide with the Antipodes . . *M. N. Dream* iii 2 55
Now Phaëthon hath tumbled from his car, And made an evening at the noontide prick . . . . . . 3 *Hen. VI.* i 4 34
Makes the night morning, and the noon-tide night . *Richard III.* i 4 77

Nor. This is no mortal business, nor no sound That the earth owes *Temp.* i 2 406
Thou hast spoken no word all this while.—Nor understood none neither *L. L. Lost* v 1 158
I neither lend nor borrow By taking nor by giving of excess *Mer. of Venice* i 3 63
Nor no further in sport neither . . . *As Y. Like It* i 2 30
Nor never none Shall mistress be of it, save I alone . *T. Night* iii 1 171
Nor this is not my nose neither . . . . . iv 1 8
I know not, nor I greatly care not . . . *Richard II.* v 2 48
It is nor hand, nor foot, Nor arm, nor face, nor any other part Belonging to a man . . . . . . *Rom. and Jul.* ii 2 40
Pitied nor hated, to the face of peril Myself I'll dedicate . *Cymbeline* v 1 20

Norbery. Sir John Norbery, Sir Robert Waterton . . *Richard II.* ii 1 284

Norfolk. What dost thou object Against the Duke of Norfolk? . . i 1 29
Thomas of Norfolk, what say'st thou to this? . . . . i 1 110
We'll calm the Duke of Norfolk, you your son . . . . i 1 159
Throw down, my son, the Duke of Norfolk's gage.—And, Norfolk, throw down his . . . . i 1 161
The Duke of Norfolk, sprightfully and bold, Stays but the summons of the appellant's trumpet . . . . . . i 3 3
Norfolk, for thee remains a heavier doom . . . . i 3 148
Norfolk, so far as to mine enemy . . . . . . i 3 193
Besides, I heard the banish'd Norfolk say . . . . iv 1 80
Some honest Christian trust me with a gage, That Norfolk lies . iv 1 84
These differences shall all rest under gage Till Norfolk be repeal'd . . iv 1 87
Many a time hath banish'd Norfolk fought For Jesu Christ in glorious Christian field . . . . iv 1 92
Why, bishop, is Norfolk dead?—As surely as I live, my lord . . iv 1 101
Page to Thomas Mowbray, Duke of Norfolk . . 2 *Hen. IV.* iii 2 29
Were you not restored To all the Duke of Norfolk's signories? . iv 1 111
We'll all assist you; he that flies shall die.—Thanks, gentle Norfolk 3 *Hen. VI.* i 1 31
'Tis not thy southern power, Of Essex, Norfolk, Suffolk, nor of Kent . i 1 156
I'll keep London with my soldiers.—And I to Norfolk with my followers i 1 208
Thou, Richard, shalt to the Duke of Norfolk, And tell him privily of our intent . . . . i 2 38
Norfolk and myself, In haste, post-haste, are come to join with you . ii 1 138
Where is the Duke of Norfolk, gentle Warwick? And when came George? . . . . ii 1 142
Norfolk sends you word by me, The queen is coming with a puissant host . . . . ii 1 206
And thou, son Clarence, Shalt stir up in Suffolk, Norfolk and in Kent iv 8 12
A riotous gentleman Lately attendant on the Duke of Norfolk *Rich. III.* ii 1 101
Some light-foot friend post to the Duke of Norfolk . . . iv 4 440
Norfolk, we must have knocks; ha! must we not?—We must both give and take . . . . v 3 5
Good Norfolk, hie thee to thy charge; Use careful watch . . v 3 53
Stir with the lark to-morrow, gentle Norfolk.—I warrant you, my lord . v 3 56
John Duke of Norfolk, Thomas Earl of Surrey, Shall have the leading of this foot and horse . . . . v 3 296
What think'st thou, Norfolk?—A good direction, warlike sovereign . v 3 301
Jockey of Norfolk, be not too bold, For Dickon thy master is bought and sold . . . . v 3 304
Rescue, my Lord of Norfolk, rescue, rescue! . . . . v 4 1
What men of name are slain on either side?—John Duke of Norfolk . v 5 13
My Lord of Norfolk, as you are truly noble, . . . Produce the grand sum of his sins . . . . . . *Hen. VIII.* iii 2 289
Next, the Duke of Norfolk, He to be earl marshal . . . iv 1 18
She that carries up the train Is that old noble lady, Duchess of Norfolk iv 1 52
You shall have two noble partners with you; the old Duchess of Norfolk, and Lady Marquess Dorset . . . . . . v 3 169

Normandy. In Normandy, saw I this Longaville . *L. L. Lost* ii 1 43
Victorious Warwick Received deep scars in France and Normandy 2 *Hen. VI.* i 1 87
These counties were the keys of Normandy . . . . i 1 114
The state of Normandy Stands on a tickle point . . . i 1 215
What canst thou answer to my majesty for giving up of Normandy? . iv 7 30
I sold not Maine, I lost not Normandy, Yet, to recover them, would lose my life . . . . iv 7 70
Two months since, Here was a gentleman of Normandy . *Hamlet* iv 7 83

Normans, but bastard Normans, Norman bastards! . . *Hen. V.* iii 5 10
The false revolting Normans thorough thee Disdain to call us lord 2 *Hen. VI.* iv 1 87
A Norman was't?—A Norman . . . . . *Hamlet* iv 7 91

North. To run upon the sharp wind of the north . . *Tempest* i 2 254
By east, west, north, and south, I spread my conquering might *L. L. Lost* v 2 566
You are now sailed into the north of my lady's opinion . *T. Night* iii 2 28
'Tis powerful, think it, From east, west, north and south . *W. Tale* i 2 203
We from the west will send destruction Into this city's bosom.—I from the north.—Our thunder from the south . . . *K. John* ii 1 411
From north to south: Austria and France shoot in each other's mouth ii 1 413
Nor entreat the north To make his bleak winds kiss my parched lips . v 7 39
I towards the north, Where shivering cold and sickness pines the clime; My wife to France . . . . *Richard II.* v 1 76
More uneven and unwelcome news Came from the north . 1 *Hen. IV.* i 1 51
Send danger from the east unto the west, So honour cross it from the north to south, And let them grapple . . . . . i 3 196
I am not yet of Percy's mind, the Hotspur of the north . . ii 4 115
That same mad fellow of the north, Percy . . . . ii 4 369
Methinks my moiety, north from Burton here, In quantity equals not one of yours . . . . iii 1 96
A little charge will trench him here And on this north side win this cape of land . . . . iii 1 113
There are twenty weak and wearied posts Come from the north 2 *Hen. IV.* ii 4 386
Like youthful steers unyoked, they take their courses East, west, north, south . . . . iv 2 104
The Percies of the north . . . . . 1 *Hen. VI.* ii 5 67
Under the lordly monarch of the north . . . . . v 3 6
Where wert thou born?—At Berwick in the north . 2 *Hen. VI.* ii 1 84
While we pursued the horsemen of the north, He slily stole away 3 *Hen. VI.* i 1 2
With all speed post with him toward the north . *Richard III.* iii 2 17
My friends are in the north.—Cold friends to Richard: what do they in the north, When they should serve their sovereign in the west? iv 4 484
They were young and handsome, and of the best breed in the north *Hen. VIII.* ii 2 4
They would fly east, west, north, south . . . *Coriolanus* ii 3 24
At the lodge Upon the north side of this pleasant chase . *T. Andron.* ii 3 255
The wind, who wooes Even now the frozen bosom of the north *R. and J.* i 4 101
The sun arises . . . Some two months hence up higher toward the north He first presents his fire . . . . . *J. Cæsar* ii 1 109
I peace! No, I will speak as liberal as the north . . *Othello* v 2 220
Comes in my father And like the tyrannous breathing of the north Shakes all our buds from growing . . . . *Cymbeline* i 3 36
The grisled north Disgorges such a tempest forth . . *Pericles* iii Gower 47
When I was born, the wind was north . . . . . iv 1 52

Northampton. Montague, in Buckingham, Northampton and in Leicestershire, shalt find Men well inclined . . . 3 *Hen. VI.* iv 8 15
Last night, I hear, they lay at Northampton . *Richard III.* ii 4 1
Northampton, I Arrest thee of high treason . . . *Hen. VIII.* i 1 200

Northamptonshire. I, a gentleman Born in Northamptonshire *K. John* i 1 51

North-east. The north-east wind, Which then blew bitterly against our faces, Awaked the sleeping rheum . . . *Richard II.* i 4 6

Northerly. 'Tis very cold ; the wind is northerly.—It is indifferent cold, my lord, indeed . . . . *Hamlet* v 2 99
Northern. I will not fight with a pole, like a northern man *L. L. Lost* v 2 701
Or the fann'd snow that 's bolted By the northern blasts twice o'er *W. Tale* iv 4 376
And shortly mean to touch our northern shore . *Richard II.* ii 1 288
And all your northern castles yielded up . . . . . . iii 2 201
The time will come, That I shall make this northern youth exchange His glorious deeds for my indignities . . . . 1 *Hen. IV.* iii 2 145
Proud northern lord, Clifford of Cumberland . . 2 *Hen. VI.* v 2 6
The northern lords that have forsworn thy colours Will follow mine 3 *Hen. VI.* i 1 251
The queen with all the northern earls and lords Intend here to besiege you i 2 49
The angry northern wind Will blow these sands . *T. Andron.* iv 1 104
I am constant as the northern star . . . . *J. Cæsar* iii 1 60
North-gate. Bid him make haste and meet me at the North-gate *T. G. of V.* iii 1 258
Express opinions Where is best place to make our battery next.—I think, at the north gate . . . . 1 *Hen. VI.* i 4 66
North-north-east. It standeth north-north-east and by east . *L. L. Lost* i 1 248
North-north-west. I am but mad north-north-west . *Hamlet* ii 2 396
North pole. By the north pole, I do challenge thee . . *L. L. Lost* v 2 699
North star. There were no living near her ; she would infect to the north star . . . . *Much Ado* ii 1 258
Northumberland. Be confident to speak, Northumberland : We three are but thyself . . . . *Richard II.* ii 1 274
Why have you not proclaim'd Northumberland And all the rest revolted faction traitors ?—We have . . . . . . ii 2 56
It would beseem the Lord Northumberland To say 'King Richard' iii 3 7
Northumberland, say thus the king returns : His noble cousin is right welcome . . . . iii 3 121
Shall we call back Northumberland, and send Defiance to the traitor ? . iii 3 129
Most mighty prince, my Lord Northumberland, What says King Bolingbroke ? . . . . iii 3 172
Gentle Northumberland, If thy offences were upon record, Would it not shame thee in so fair a troop To read a lecture of them ? . iv 1 229
Northumberland, thou ladder wherewithal The mounting Bolingbroke ascends my throne . . . . . v 1 55 ; 2 *Hen. IV.* iii 1 70
Part us, Northumberland ; I towards the north, Where shivering cold and sickness pines the clime ; My wife to France . *Richard II.* v 1 76
And makest me sin In envy that my Lord Northumberland Should be the father to so blest a son . . . . . 1 *Hen. IV.* i 1 79
My Lord Northumberland, We license your departure with your son i 3 122
Old Northumberland, and that sprightly Scot of Scots, Douglas . ii 4 376
When the lords . . Perceived Northumberland did lean to him . iv 3 67
I fear, Sir Michael, What with the sickness of Northumberland . iv 4 14
Westmoreland Towards York shall bend you with your dearest speed, To meet Northumberland . . . . v 5 37
Where Hotspur's father, old Northumberland, Lies crafty-sick 2 *Hen. IV.* Ind. 36
And approach The ragged'st hour that time and spite dare bring To frown upon the enraged Northumberland ! . . . . i 1 152
Our supplies live largely in the hope Of great Northumberland . i 3 13
Whether our present five and twenty thousand May hold up head without Northumberland ?—With him, we may . . . . i 3 17
My Lord Northumberland will soon be cool'd . . . . . iii 1 44
'Tis not ten years gone Since Richard and Northumberland, great friends, Did feast together . . . . iii 1 58
When Richard, with his eye brimful of tears, Then check'd and rated by Northumberland, Did speak these words . . . . iii 1 68
King Richard might create a perfect guess That great Northumberland, then false to him, Would of that seed grow to a greater falseness iii 1 89
They say the bishop and Northumberland Are fifty thousand strong iii 1 95
I have received New-dated letters from Northumberland . . iv 1 8
The great Lord of Northumberland, Whose warlike ears could never brook retreat, Cheer'd up the drooping army 3 *Hen. VI.* i 1 4
Earl of Northumberland, he slew thy father, And thine, Lord Clifford i 1 54
Come, bloody Clifford, rough Northumberland, I dare your quenchless fury to more rage . . . . i 4 27
What, weeping-ripe, my Lord Northumberland ? . . . i 4 172
I wonder how our princely father 'scaped, Or whether he be 'scaped away or no From Clifford's and Northumberland's pursuit . ii 1 3
The proud insulting queen, With Clifford and the haught Northumberland ii 1 169
Northumberland, I hold thee reverently . . . . . ii 2 109
Two Cliffords, as the father and the son, And two Northumberlands v 7 8
Northumberland, then present, wept to see it . . *Richard III.* i 3 187
Saw'st thou the melancholy Lord Northumberland ? . . . v 3 68
What said Northumberland as touching Richmond ? . . . v 3 271
The stout Earl Northumberland Arrested him at York, and brought him forward, As a man sorely tainted . . . *Hen. VIII.* iv 2 12
Macduff Is gone to pray the holy king, upon his aid To wake Northumberland and warlike Siward . . . . *Macbeth* iii 6 31
Northward. Bring me the fairest creature northward born *Mer. of Venice* ii 1 4
To you The remnant northward, lying off from Trent . 1 *Hen. IV.* iii 1 79
When my heart's dear Harry Threw many a northward look to see his father Bring up his powers . . . . . . 2 *Hen. IV.* ii 3 13
Norway himself, With terrible numbers . . . . . *Macbeth* i 2 50
Sweno, the Norways' king, craves composition . . . . i 2 59
Whether he was combined With those of Norway, or did line the rebel With hidden help and vantage . . . . i 3 112
The very armour he had on When he the ambitious Norway combated *Hamlet* i 1 61
By Fortinbras of Norway, Thereto prick'd on by a most emulate pride i 1 82
Hath in the skirts of Norway here and there Shark'd up a list of lawless resolutes . . . . i 1 97
We have here writ To Norway, uncle of young Fortinbras . . i 2 28
We here dispatch You, good Cornelius, and you, Voltimand, For bearers of this greeting to old Norway . . . . i 2 35
The ambassadors from Norway, my good lord, Are joyfully return'd . ii 2 40
What from our brother Norway ?—Most fair return of greetings and desires . . . . ii 2 59
Old Norway, overcome with joy, Gives him three thousand crowns in annual fee . . . . ii 2 72
Whose powers are these ?—They are of Norway, sir.—How purposed ? . iv 4 10
Who commands them, sir ?—The nephew to old Norway, Fortinbras iv 4 14
Nor will it yield to Norway or the Pole A ranker rate, should it be sold in fee . . . . iv 4 21
Norweyan. The Norweyan lord surveying vantage, With furbish'd arms and new supplies of men Began a fresh assault . . *Macbeth* i 2 31
Where the Norweyan banners flout the sky And fan our people cold . i 2 49
In viewing o'er the rest o' the selfsame day, He finds thee in the stout Norweyan ranks . . . . i 3 95

Nose. Lifted up their noses As they smelt music . . . *Tempest* iv 1 177
At which my nose is in great indignation . . . . . . iv 1 200
Inscrutable, invisible, As a nose on a man's face . . *T. G. of Ver.* ii 1 142
Liberty plucks justice by the nose ; The baby beats the nurse *M. for M.* i 3 29
Has he affections in him, That thus can make him bite the law by the nose ? iii 2 109
Did not I pluck thee by the nose for thy speeches ? . . . . v 1 343
Where America, the Indies ?—Oh, sir, upon her nose *Com. of Errors* iii 2 137
Sent whole armadoes of caracks to be ballast at her nose . . . iii 2 141
We had like to have had our two noses snapped off . *Much Ado* v 1 115
Through the nose, as if you snuffed up love by smelling love . *L. L. Lost* iii 1 16
I am Alisander,— Your nose says, no, you are not ; for it stands too right v 2 568
Your nose smells 'no' in this, most tender-smelling knight . v 2 569
And birds sit brooding in the snow And Marian's nose looks red and raw v 2 934
These lily lips, This cherry nose . . . . *M. N. Dream* v 1 338
Then it was not for nothing that my nose fell a-bleeding on Black-Monday . . . . *Mer. of Venice* ii 5 24
When the bagpipe sings i' the nose . . . . iv 1 49
The big round tears Coursed one another down his innocent nose *As Y. L. It* ii 1 39
With spectacles on nose and pouch on side . . . . . ii 7 159
I'll slit the villain's nose, that would have sent me to the gaol *T. of Shrew* v 1 134
Thou wert best set thy lower part where thy nose stands . *All's Well* ii 3 267
Nay, you need not to stop your nose, sir ; I spake but by a metaphor.—Indeed, sir, if your metaphor stink, I will stop my nose . . v 2 11
For Malvolio's nose is no whipstock . . . . . *T. Night* ii 3 28
To hear by the nose, it is dulcet in contagion . . . . ii 3 58
I smell a device.—I have't in my nose too . . . . . ii 3 177
Nor this is not my nose neither. Nothing that is so is so . . iv 1 8
Is whispering nothing ? Is leaning cheek to cheek ? is meeting noses ? Kissing with inside lip ? . . . . *W. Tale* i 2 285
I have seen a lady's nose That has been blue, but not her eyebrows . ii 1 14
You smell this business with a sense as cold As is a dead man's nose . ii 1 152
The whole matter And copy of the father, eye, nose, lip . . . ii 3 99
Gloves as sweet as damask roses ; Masks for faces and for noses . iv 4 223
A good nose is requisite also, to smell out work for the other senses . iv 4 686
Receives not thy nose court-odour from me ? . . . . . iv 4 757
He is oft led by the nose with gold . . . . iv 4 832
A pouncet-box, which ever and anon He gave his nose . . 1 *Hen. IV.* i 3 39
We must have bloody noses and crack'd crowns, And pass them current ii 3 96
Yea, and to tickle our noses with spear-grass to make them bleed . . ii 4 340
Thou bearest the lantern in the poop, but 'tis in the nose of thee . iii 3 29
Let them coin his nose, let them coin his cheeks . . . . iii 3 90
Honest Bardolph, whose zeal burns in his nose . . 2 *Hen. IV.* ii 4 357
His nose was as sharp as a pen, and a' babbled of green fields *Hen. V.* ii 3 17
Do you not remember, a' saw a flea stick upon Bardolph's nose ? . ii 3 43
His lips blows at his nose, and it is like a coal of fire, sometimes plue and sometimes red ; but his nose is executed, and his fire's out . iii 6 109
The king is dead.—Rear up his body ; wring him by the nose 2 *Hen. VI.* iii 2 34
But when the fox hath once got in his nose, He'll soon find means to make the body follow . . . . 3 *Hen. VI.* iv 7 25
You would swear directly Their very noses had been counsellors To Pepin or Clotharius, they keep state so . . . . *Hen. VIII.* i 3 9
There be moe wasps that buzz about his nose Will make this sting the sooner . . . . iii 2 55
Twenty of the dog-days now reign in 's nose . . . . . v 4 44
Three times was his nose discharged against me . . . . v 4 47
Too flaming a praise for a good complexion. I had as lief Helen's golden tongue had commended Troilus for a copper nose . *Troi. and Cres.* i 2 115
In love, i' faith, to the very tip of the nose . . . . . iii 1 139
For that I have not wash'd My nose that bled . . . . *Coriolanus* i 9 48
To see your wives dishonour'd to your noses . . . . . iv 6 83
For one poor grain or two, to leave unburnt, And still to nose the offence v 1 28
What, hast not thou full often struck a doe, And borne her cleanly by the keeper's nose ? . . . . *T. Andron.* ii 1 94
Drawn with a team of little atomies Athwart men's noses *Rom. and Jul.* i 4 58
Sometime she gallops o'er a courtier's nose, And then dreams he of smelling out a suit . . . . i 4 77
With a tithe-pig's tail Tickling a parson's nose as a' lies asleep, Then dreams he of another benefice . . . . i 4 80
Down with the nose, Down with it flat ; take the bridge quite away *T. of A.* iv 3 157
Sliver'd in the moon's eclipse, Nose of Turk and Tartar's lips *Macbeth* iv 1 29
Plucks off my beard, and blows it in my face ? Tweaks me by the nose ? *Hamlet* ii 2 601
You shall nose him as you go up the stairs into the lobby . . iv 3 38
Thou canst tell why one's nose stands i' the middle on's face ?—No.—Why, to keep one's eyes of either side's nose . . . . *Lear* i 5 19
All that follow their noses are led by their eyes but blind men . ii 4 70
There's not a nose among twenty but can smell him that's stinking ii 4 71
He had a thousand noses, Horns whelk'd and waved like the enridged sea iv 6 70
Will as tenderly be led by the nose As asses are . . . *Othello* i 3 407
Have your instruments been in Naples, that they speak i' the nose thus ? iii 1 4
Pish ! Noses, ears, and lips.—Is't possible ?—Confess—handkerchief !—O devil ! . . . . iv 1 42
I see that nose of yours, but not that dog I shall throw it to . . iv 1 146
Heaven stops the nose at it and the moon winks . . . . iv 2 77
Where would you choose it ?—Not in my husband's nose *Ant. and Cleo.* i 2 63
Against the blown rose may they stop their nose That kneel'd unto the buds . . . . iii 13 39
We will nothing pay For wearing our own noses . . . *Cymbeline* iii 1 14
There is no moe such Cæsars : other of them may have crook'd noses, but to owe such straight arms, none . . . . iii 1 37
Nosegay. Rings, gawds, conceits, Knacks, trifles, nosegays *M. N. Dream* i 1 34
She hath made me four and twenty nosegays for the shearers *W. Tale* iv 3 44
Nose-herb. They are not herbs, you knave ; they are nose-herbs *All's Well* iv 5 20
Noseless, handless, hack'd and chipp'd . . . *Troi. and Cres.* v 5 34
Nose-painting. What three things does drink especially provoke ?—Marry, sir, nose-painting, sleep, and urine . . . *Macbeth* ii 3 31
Nostril. While Stephano breathes at nostrils . . . *Tempest* ii 2 65
The rankest compound of villanous smell that ever offended nostril *M. W.* iii 5 94
A savour that may strike the dullest nostril . . . . *W. Tale* i 2 421
Set the teeth and stretch the nostril wide, Hold hard the breath *Hen. V.* iii 1 15
His hair uprear'd, his nostrils stretch'd with struggling 2 *Hen. VI.* iii 2 171
Let our crooked smokes climb to their nostrils From our blest altars *Cymbeline* v 5 477
A delicate odour.—As ever hit my nostril . . . . *Pericles* iii 2 62
Not. I not doubt He came alive to land.—No, no, he's gone . *Tempest* ii 1 121
I find not Myself disposed to sleep . . . . ii 1 201
Green sour ringlets make, Whereof the ewe not bites . . . . v 1 38
Whether thou be'st he or no, Or some enchanted trifle to abuse me, As late I have been, I not know . . . . v 1 113
With such discourse as, I not doubt, shall make it Go quick away . v 1 303

Not. Give me not the boots.—No, I will not, for it boots thee not *T. G. of Ver.* i 1 27
I not deny, The jury, passing on the prisoner's life, May in the sworn twelve have a thief or two Guiltier than him they try *Meas. for Meas.* ii 1 18
Did not I tell thee yea? hadst thou not order? . . . ii 2 8
Went'st not thou to her for a purse of ducats? . . . *Com. of Errors* iv 4 90
Such carping is not commendable.—No, not to be so odd . *Much Ado* iii 1 72
Sweet prince, why speak not you?—What should I speak? . . iv 1 64
She will not add to her damnation A sin of perjury; she not denies it . iv 1 175
Did not I dance with you in Brabant once? . . . *L. L. Lost* ii 1 114
The fairest is confession. Were not you here but even now disguised? v 2 433
Might not you Forestall our sport, to make us thus untrue? . . . v 2 472
Are not you he That frights the maidens of the villagery? *M. N. Dream* ii 1 34
Do not you think The duke was here, and bid us follow him? . . iv 1 199
Thou hast my love: is not that neighbourly? . . . *As Y. Like It* iii 5 90
Wedded her, not bedded her; and sworn to make the 'not' eternal *All's Well* iii 2 23
'Tis not fit you know, I not acquaint My father of this business *W. Tale* iv 4 423
Come not before him.—I not purpose it . . . . . iv 4 483
No need of any such redress; Or if there were, it not belongs to you.— Why not to him in part? . . . . . 2 *Hen. IV.* iv 1 98
It not appears to me Either from the king or in the present time . iv 1 107
Had not you come upon your cue, my lord . . . *Richard III.* iii 4 27
She was often cited by them, but appear'd not . . . *Hen. VIII.* iv 1 29
Things in motion sooner catch the eye Than what not stirs *Troi. and Cres.* iii 3 184
He'll answer nobody; he professes not answering . . . iii 3 270
And more than that I know thee, I not desire to know . *T. of Athens* iv 3 58
If it be now, 'tis not to come; if it be not to come, it will be now; if it be not now, yet it will come: the readiness is all . . *Hamlet* v 2 232
If they not thought the profits of my death Were very pregnant and potential spurs To make thee seek it . . . . . *Lear* ii 1 77
I marvel our mild husband Not met us on the way . . . . iv 2 2
That what they do delay, they not deny . . . *Ant. and Cleo.* ii 1 3
When to sound your name It not concern'd me . . . . ii 2 35
Many years, Though Cloten then but young, you see, not wore him From my remembrance . . . . *Cymbeline* iv 4 25
Not a jot *Meas. for Meas.* iv 2; *T. of Shrew* i 1; *Hamlet* v 1; *Othello* iii 3
Not a whit *T. G. of Ver.* iv 2; *Mer. Wives* i 1; *M. N. Dream* iii 1; *As Y. Like It* iii 2; *T. of Shrew* ii 1; 1 *Hen. IV.* ii 4; iv 3; *Richard III.* iii 4; *Troi. and Cres.* v 1; *Rom. and Jul.* iv 4; *Hamlet* v 2; *Cymbeline* ii 4
Not for the world *Tempest* v 1; *L. L. Lost* ii 1; *Rom. and Jul.* ii 2
Not any, but abide the change of time . . . . *Cymbeline* ii 4 4
Not appearance. For not appearance and The king's late scruple, by the main assent Of all these learned men she was divorced *Hen. VIII.* iv 1 30
Not-fearing. In our not-fearing Britain . . . . *Cymbeline* iv 4 19
Not in it. Which the wenches say is a gallimaufry of gambols because they are not in't . . . . *W. Tale* iv 4 336
I' the world's volume Our Britain seems as of it, but not in 't *Cymbeline* iii 4 141
Not so. Nay, but it is not so.—It is no other . . *Meas. for Meas.* iv 3 121
It is not so, nor 'twas not so, but, indeed, God forbid it should be so *Much Ado* i 1 219
A most intelligencing bawd!—Not so . . . . . *W. Tale* ii 3 68
Well, 'tis not so, my lord high constable; But though we think it so, it is no matter . . . . *Hen. V.* ii 4 41
Not that I loved Cæsar less, but that I loved Rome more . . *J. Cæsar* iii 2 22
Not that I know. Charges she more than me?—Not that I know *M. for M.* v 1 200
Hath there been such a time . . . That I have positively said 'Tis so,' When it proved otherwise?—Not that I know . . . *Hamlet* ii 2 155
Notable. How sayest thou, that my master is become a notable lover?— I never knew him otherwise.—Than how?—A notable lubber *T. G. of V.* ii 5 44
We shall find this friar a notable fellow . . . *Meas. for Meas.* v 1 268
Thou wilt prove a notable argument . . . . . *Much Ado* i 1 258
A most notable coward, an infinite and endless liar . . *All's Well* iii 6 10
On that vice in him will my revenge find notable cause to work *T. Night* ii 3 166
Wouldst thou not be glad to have the niggardly rascally sheep-biter come by some notable shame? . . . . ii 5 6
It cannot but turn him into a notable contempt . . . . ii 5 224
Set upon Aguecheek a notable report of valour . . . . iii 4 210
Notable pirate! thou salt-water thief! . . . . . . v 1 72
A notable passion of wonder appeared in them . . . *W. Tale* v 2 17
Mark the fleers, the gibes, and notable scorns, That dwell in every region of his face . . . . *Othello* iv 1 83
O notable strumpet! . . . . v 1 78
Notably. And very notably discharged . . . . *M. N. Dream* v 1 368
Notary. This kindness will I show. Go with me to a notary, seal me there Your single bond . . . . . *Mer. of Venice* i 3 145
I will seal unto this bond.—Then meet me forthwith at the notary's . i 3 173
Notched. He scotched him and notched him like a carbonado *Coriolanus* iv 5 199
Note. From Naples Can have no note, unless the sun were post *Tempest* ii 1 248
Yet, note, Their manners are more gentle-kind . . . . iii 3 31
Give me a note: your ladyship can set . . . . *T. G. of Ver.* i 2 81
Take a note of what I stand in need of . . . . . ii 7 84
And to the nightingale's complaining notes Tune my distresses . . v 4 5
That is the very note of it . . . . . . *Mer. Wives* i 1 172
Neither press, coffer, chest, trunk, well, vault, but he hath an abstract for the remembrance of such places, and goes to them by his note . iv 2 64
Now 'tis awake, Takes note of what is done . . . *Meas. for Meas.* ii 2 94
I have ta'en a due and wary note upon't . . . . . iv 1 38
My lord hath sent you this note; and by me this further charge . . iv 2 106
Nor wish'd to hold my peace.—I wish you now, then; Pray you, take note of it . . . . v 1 80
O, train me not, sweet mermaid, with thy note . . *Com. of Errors* iii 2 45
Here's the note How much your chain weighs to the utmost carat . iv 1 27
Benedick, didst thou note the daughter of Signior Leonato? *Much Ado* i 1 163
If thou wilt hold longer argument, Do it in notes.—Note this before my notes; There's not a note of mine that's worth the noting . . ii 3 56
These are very crotchets that he speaks; Note, notes, forsooth, and nothing . . . . ii 3 59
The sweet youth's in love.—The greatest note of it is his melancholy . iii 2 54
How if a' will not stand?—Why, then, take no note of him, but let him go . . . . iii 3 29
Which is the villain? let me see his eyes, That, when I note another man like him, I may avoid him . . . . . . v 1 270
Sigh a note and sing a note, sometime through the throat . *L. L. Lost* iii 1 14
And make them men of note—do you note me? . . . . iii 1 25
Ill, to example ill, Would from my forehead wipe a perjured note. . iv 3 125
Folly in fools bears not so strong a note As foolery in the wise . . v 2 75
Tu-who, a merry note, While greasy Joan doth keel the pot . . . v 2 929
The throstle with his note so true . . . . *M. N. Dream* iii 1 130

Note. Whose note full many a man doth mark, And dares not answer nay *M. N. Dream* iii 1 135
Sing again: Mine ear is much enamour'd of thy note . . . iii 1 141
First, rehearse your song by rote, To each word a warbling note . . v 1 405
But note me, signior . . . . *Mer. of Venice* i 3 98
Fair lady, by your leave; I come by note, to give and to receive . . iii 2 141
And, look, what notes and garments he doth give thee . . . iii 4 51
Do but note a wild and wanton herd, Or race of youthful and unhandled colts . . . . v 1 71
Give order to my servants that they take No note at all of our being absent . . . . v 1 120
And turn his merry note Unto the sweet bird's throat . *As Y. Like It* ii 5 3
I'll give you a verse to this note that I made yesterday . . . ii 5 48
'Tis he: slink by, and note him . . . . iii 2 267
There was no great matter in the ditty, yet the note was very untuneable v 3 36
'D sol re,' one clef, two notes have I . . . *T. of Shrew* iii 1 77
Here is the note of the fashion to testify . . . . . iv 3 130
The note lies in's throat, if he say I said so . . . . iv 3 133
At last, though long, our jarring notes agree . . . . v 2 1
No note upon my parents, his all noble . . . . *All's Well* i 3 163
My love hath in't a bond, Whereof the world takes note . . . i 3 195
As notes whose faculties inclusive were More than they were in note . i 3 233
I will bestow some precepts of this virgin Worthy the note . . iii 5 104
Answer to what I shall ask you out of a note . . . . iv 3 146
Did to his majesty, his mother and his lady Offence of mighty note . v 3 14
Hurt him in eleven places: my niece shall take note of it . *T. Night* iii 2 38
I did some service; of such note indeed, That were I ta'en here it would scarce be answer'd . . . . iii 3 27
In the habit of some sir of note . . . . iii 4 82
A good note; that keeps you from the blow of the law . . . iii 4 168
He shall conceal it Whiles you are willing it shall come to note . . iv 3 29
And heavens so shine, That they may fairly note this act of mine! . iv 3 35
A gentleman of the greatest promise that ever came into my note *W. Tale* i 1 40
Nine changes of the watery star hath been The shepherd's note . . i 2 2
A note infallible Of breaking honesty—horsing foot on foot . . i 2 287
I have heard, sir, of such a man, who hath a daughter of most rare note iv 2 48
That's out of my note . . . . iv 3 49
For which the heavens, taking angry note, Have left me issueless . . v 1 173
The changes I perceived in the king and Camillo were very notes of admiration . . . . v 2 12
O, what love I note In the fair multitude of those her hairs! *K. John* iii 4 61
Creatures of note for mercy-lacking uses . . . . . iv 1 121
Taking note of thy abhorr'd aspect, Finding thee fit for bloody villany iv 2 224
Perusing o'er these notes, May know wherefore we took the sacrament . v 2 5
Once more, the more to aggravate the note, With a foul traitor's name stuff I thy throat . . . . *Richard II.* i 1 43
Or to take note how many pair of silk stockings thou hast . 2 *Hen. IV.* ii 2 17
Note this; the king is weary Of dainty and such picking grievances . iv 1 197
Here is now the smith's note for shoeing and plough-irons.—Let it be cast and paid . . . . v 1 19
We will hear, note, and believe in heart . . . . *Hen. V.* i 2 30
The king hath note of all that they intend . . . . . ii 2 6
With busy hammers closing rivets up, Give dreadful note of preparation iv Prol. 14
Upon his royal face there is no note How dread an army hath enrounded him . . . . iv Prol. 35
Let the trumpets sound The tucket sonance and the note to mount . iv 2 35
This note doth tell me of ten thousand French That in the field lie slain iv 8 85
I'll note you in my book of memory . . . . . 1 *Hen. VI.* ii 4 101
First note that he is near you in descent . . . 2 *Hen. VI.* iii 1 21
A raven's note, Whose dismal tune bereft my vital powers . . . iii 2 40
After many moody thoughts At last by notes of household harmony They quite forget their loss of liberty . . . . 3 *Hen. VI.* iv 6 14
But, spider-like, Out of his self-drawing web, he gives us note, The force of his own merit makes his way . . . . . *Hen. VIII.* i 1 63
These exactions, Whereof my sovereign would have note, they are Most pestilent to the hearing . . . . i 2 48
Note This dangerous conception in this point . . . . . i 2 138
I speak sincerely, and high note's Ta'en of your many virtues . . ii 3 59
You are call'd back.—What need you note it? pray you, keep your way iii 4 128
Cause the musicians play me that sad note I named my knell . . iv 2 78
Do you note How much her grace is alter'd on the sudden? . . iv 2 95
Mark him; note him. O brave Troilus! . . . *Troi. and Cres.* i 2 251
In self-assumption greater Than in the note of judgement . . . ii 3 134
Rouse him and give him note of our approach . . . . . iv 1 43
Give with thy trumpet a loud note to Troy, Thou dreadful Ajax . . iv 5 3
Bid my trumpet sound!—No notes of sally, for the heavens, sweet brother . . . . v 3 14
Being once subdued in armed tail, Sweet honey and sweet notes together fail . . . . v 10 45
Note me this, good friend . . . . *Coriolanus* i 1 131
Which, without note, here's many else have done . . . . i 9 49
They have ta'en note of us: keep on your way . . . . . iv 2 10
Note but this fool . . . . iv 2 17
I have a note from the Volscian state, to find you out there . . iv 3 11
Ingrate forgetfulness shall poison, rather Than pity note how much . v 2 93
The king my brother shall have note of this . . . *T. Andron.* ii 3 85
Sweet varied notes, enchanting every ear! . . . . . iii 1 86
Note how she quotes the leaves . . . . iv 1 50
What doth her beauty serve, but as a note Where I may read who pass'd that passing fair? . . . . *Rom. and Jul.* i 1 241
Therefore be patient, take no note of him . . . . . i 5 73
That is not the lark, whose notes do beat The vaulty heaven . . iii 5 21
I will carry no crotchets: I'll re you, I'll fa you; do you note me?— An you re us and fa us, you note us . . . . iv 5 121
If I were a huge man, I should fear to drink at meals; Lest they should spy my windpipe's dangerous notes . . . . *T. of Athens* i 2 52
What is your will?—My lord, here is a note of certain dues.—Dues! . ii 2 16
As I took note of the place, it cannot be far where he abides . . v 1 1
Pluck Casca by the sleeve; And he will, after his sour fashion, tell you What hath proceeded worthy note to-day . . . . *J. Cæsar* i 2 181
Take good note What Cæsar doth, what suitors press to him . . ii 4 14
Ever note, Lucilius, When love begins to sicken and decay, It useth an enforced ceremony . . . . iv 2 19
You must note beside, That we have tried the utmost of our friends . iv 3 213
Where never Roman shall take note of him . . . . . v 3 50
There shall be done A deed of dreadful note . . . . *Macbeth* iii 2 44
The rest That are within the note of expectation Already are i' the court iii 3 10
If much you note him, You shall offend him and extend his passion . iii 4 56
By this great clatter, one of greatest note Seems bruited . . . v 7 21

Note. Let the world take note, You are the most immediate to our throne . . . . *Hamlet* i 2 108
Or such ambiguous giving out, to note That you know aught of me . i 5 178
Give him this money and these notes . . . . . ii 1 1
Give him heedful note ; For I mine eyes will rivet to his face . iii 2 89
I did very well note him . . . . iii 2 301
You would sound me from my lowest note to the top of my compass . iii 2 383
By the Lord, Horatio, these three years I have taken note of it . v 1 151
Besides, his picture I will send far and near, that all the kingdom May have due note of him . . . . . . *Lear* ii 1 85
Sir, I do know you ; And dare, upon the warrant of my note, Commend a dear thing to you . . . . iii 1 18
Therefore I do advise you, take this note : My lord is dead . . iv 5 29
Take thou this note ; go follow them to prison . . . v 3 27
Note, if your lady strain his entertainment . . *Othello* iii 3 250
Take note, take note, O world, To be direct and honest is not safe . iii 3 377
Take but good note, and you shall see in him The triple pillar of the world transform'd Into a strumpet's fool . . *Ant. and Cleo.* i 1 11
To-night we'll wander through the streets and note The qualities of people . . . . i 1 53
Note him, Note him, good Charmian, 'tis the man ; but note him . . i 5 53
A lower place, note well, May make too great an act . . iii 1 12
Three in Egypt Cannot make better note . . . . . iii 3 26
From which the world should note Something particular . . . iii 13 21
Like the spirit of a youth That means to be of note, begins betimes . iv 4 27
Let us bear him To the court of guard ; he is of note . . iv 9 32
Left these notes Of what commands I should be subject to . *Cymbeline* i 1 171
He was then of a crescent note, expected to prove so worthy . . i 4 2
Who has the note of them? . . . . i 5 2
He is one of the noblest note, to whose kindnesses I am most infinitely tied . . . . i 6 22
But my design, To note the chamber : I will write all down . . ii 2 24
Ah, but some natural notes about her body, Above ten thousand meaner moveables Would testify . . . . ii 2 28
You are curb'd from that enlargement by The consequence o' the crown, and must not soil The precious note of it . . . . . ii 3 127
There's no motion That tends to vice in man, but I affirm It is the woman's part : be it lying, note it, The woman's . . . ii 5 22
My report was once First with the best of note . . . iii 3 58
I do note That grief and patience, rooted in him both, Mingle their spurs . . . . iv 2 56
Sing him to the ground, As once our mother ; use like note and words iv 2 237
For notes of sorrow out of tune are worse Than priests and fanes that lie iv 2 241
Shall find I love my country, Even to the note o' the king . . iv 3 44
That they will waste their time upon our note, To know from whence we are . . . . iv 4 20
He brags his service As if he were of note . . . . v 3 94
Averring notes Of chamber-hanging, pictures, this her bracelet . v 5 203
Note it not you, Thaisa ?—What is it To me, my father? *Pericles* ii 3 57
I would have you note, this is an honourable man.—I desire to find him so, that I may worthily note him . . . . . iv 6 54

Note-book. I will make a prief of it in my note-book . *Mer. Wives* i 1 147
His note-book, his counsel-keeper . . . . *2 Hen. IV.* ii 4 290
All his faults observed, Set in a note-book, learn'd . *J. Cæsar* iv 3 98

Noted. I noted her not ; but I looked on her . . *Much Ado* i 1 165
An amber-colour'd raven was well noted . . . *L. L. Lost* iv 3 88
Saw sighs reek from you, noted well your passion . . . iv 3 140
To be noted for a merry man, He'll woo a thousand . *T. of Shrew* iii 2 14
Not noted, is't, But of the finer natures? . . . *W. Tale* i 2 225
But I have missingly noted, he is of late much retired . . iv 2 35
Whose worth and honesty Is richly noted . . . . . v 3 145
The antique and well noted face Of plain old form . . *K. John* iv 2 21
And, sirrah, I have cases of buckram for the nonce, to immask our noted outward garments . . . . . . *1 Hen. IV.* i 2 202
There is a virtuous man whom I have often noted in thy company . ii 4 460
And never noted in him any study, Any retirement . . *Hen. V.* i 1 57
Effeminate remorse, Which we have noted in you to your kin *Rich. III.* iii 7 212
This is noted, And generally . . . . . *Hen. VIII.* ii 1 46
Any man may sing her, if he can take her cliff ; she's noted *Troi. and Cres.* v 2 11
These slips have made him noted long . . . *T. Andron.* ii 3 86
Which late I noted In tatter'd weeds . . . *Rom. and Jul.* v 1 38
I have noted thee always wise . . . . *T. of Athens* iii 1 33
You have condemn'd and noted Lucius Pella . . *J. Cæsar* iv 3 2
Such wanton wild, and usual slips As are companions noted and most known To youth and liberty . . . . . *Hamlet* ii 1 23
No more of that ; I have noted it well . . . . *Lear* i 4 81
The gravity and stillness of your youth The world hath noted *Othello* ii 3 192
A thing more made of malice than of duty : We have noted it *Cymbeline* iii 5 34

Notedly. Do you remember what you said of the duke?—Most notedly, sir.—Do you so, sir? . . . . . . *Meas. for Meas.* v 1 335

Notest. Tell me what thou notest about the field . *J. Cæsar* v 3 22

Note-worthy. When thou haply seest Some rare note-worthy object in thy travel . . . . *T. G. of Ver.* i 1 13

Nothing. I have done nothing but in care of thee . . *Tempest* i 2 16
Nothing of him that doth fade But doth suffer a sea-change . . i 2 399
I might call him A thing divine, for nothing natural I ever saw so noble i 2 418
There's nothing ill can dwell in such a temple . . . i 2 457
Prithee, no more : thou dost talk nothing to me . . . ii 1 170
Of such sensible and nimble lungs that they always use to laugh at nothing . . . . ii 1 175
'Twas you we laughed at.—Who in this kind of merry fooling am nothing to you : so you may continue and laugh at nothing still . . ii 1 178
I heard nothing.—O, 'twas a din to fright a monster's ear! . . ii 1 313
But my rejoicing At nothing can be more . . . . iii 1 94
But you'll lie like dogs and yet say nothing neither . . . iii 2 23
Why, I said nothing.—Mum, then, and no more. Proceed . . iii 2 58
Why, what did I? I did nothing. I'll go farther off . . . iii 2 80
Where I shall have my music for nothing . . . . . iii 2 154
Is nothing but heart-sorrow And a clear life ensuing . . . iii 3 81
Of my instruction hast thou nothing bated In what thou hadst to say . iii 3 85
She, a laced mutton, gave me . . . nothing for my labour *T. G. of Ver.* i 1 103
Having nothing but the word 'noddy' for my pains . . . i 1 131
What said she? nothing?—No, not so much as 'Take this for thy pains' . . . . i 1 150
What is't that you took up so gingerly?—Nothing.—Why didst thou stoop, then? . . . . i 2 71
Is that paper nothing.—Nothing concerning me . . . i 2 74
All I can is nothing To her whose worth makes other worthies nothing ii 4 165
Ask my dog : if he say ay, it will ; if he say, no, it will ; if he shake his tail and say nothing, it will . . . . ii 5 38
Nothing. What then?—Nothing.—Can nothing speak? Master, shall I strike?—Who wouldst thou strike?—Nothing.—Villain, forbear.—Why, sir, I'll strike nothing . . . . *T. G. of Ver.* iii 1 198
I'll have her : and if it be a match, as nothing is impossible,—What then?—Why, then will I tell thee . . . . . iii 1 379
This, or else nothing, will inherit her . . . . . iii 2 87
Have you any thing to take to?—Nothing but my fortune . . iv 1 43
I' faith, I'll eat nothing ; I thank you as much as though I did *M. Wives* i 1 290
I'll eat nothing, I thank you, sir . . . . . . i 1 315
I would have nothing lie on my head : I cannot be thus satisfied . iii 1 194
Truly, for mine own part, I would little or nothing with you . . iii 4 66
And such daubery as this is, beyond our element : we know nothing . iv 2 187
Why, sir, they were nothing but about Mistress Anne Page . . iv 5 47
And I paid nothing for it neither, but was paid for my learning . . iv 5 62
He hath enjoyed nothing of Ford's but his buck-basket, his cudgel . v 5 116
She and I, long since contracted, Are now so sure that nothing can dissolve us . . . . v 5 237
When I, that censure him, do so offend, Let mine own judgement pattern out my death, And nothing come in partial . . *Meas. for Meas.* ii 1 31
That do nothing but use their abuses in common houses . . . ii 1 42
What was done to Elbow's wife, once more?—Once, sir? there was nothing done to her once . . . . ii 1 146
For every pelting, petty officer Would use his heaven for thunder ; Nothing but thunder! . . . . ii 2 114
Fasting maids whose minds are dedicate To nothing temporal . . ii 2 155
Have it added to the faults of mine, And nothing of your answer . ii 4 73
In nothing good, But graciously to know I am no better . . . ii 4 76
Lawful mercy Is nothing kin to foul redemption . . . . ii 4 113
But, by chance, nothing of what is writ . . . . . iv 2 218
When once our grace we have forgot, Nothing goes right . . iv 4 37
If he be less, he's nothing ; but he's more, Had I more name for badness v 1 58
Are you a maid?—No, my lord.—A widow, then?—Neither, my lord.—Why, you are nothing then . . . . v 1 177
Honest in nothing but in his clothes . . . . . . v 1 264
Do yet but kneel by me ; Hold up your hands, say nothing ; I'll speak all v 1 443
There's nothing situate under heaven's eye But hath his bound, in earth, in sea, in sky . . . . *Com. of Errors* ii 1 16
Dost thou not know?—Nothing, sir, but that I am beaten . . ii 2 42
For this something that you gave me for nothing.—I'll make you amends next, to give you nothing for something . . . . . ii 2 53
Good meat, sir, is common ; that every churl affords.—And welcome more common ; for that's nothing but words . . . . . iii 1 25
That chain will I bestow—Be it for nothing but to spite my wife . iii 1 118
Thou art sensible in nothing but blows, and so is an ass . . iv 4 28
And have nothing at his hands for my service but blows . . iv 4 33
Bear me witness That I was sent for nothing but a rope! . . iv 4 94
Will you be bound for nothing? be mad, good master : cry 'The devil!' iv 4 130
Come, stand by me ; fear nothing. Guard with halberds! . . v 1 185
There's a skirmish of wit between them.—Alas! he gets nothing by that *Much Ado* i 1 65
Is too like an image and says nothing . . . . . ii 1 10
So you walk softly and look sweetly and say nothing, I am yours for the walk . . . . ii 1 92
These are very crotchets that he speaks ; Note, notes, forsooth, and nothing . . . . ii 3 59
That her ear lose nothing Of the false sweet bait that we lay for it . iii 1 32
The fashion of a doublet, or a hat, or a cloak, is nothing to a man . iii 3 126
What means the fool, trow?—Nothing I . . . . . iii 4 60
What have I to give you back . . . ?—Nothing, unless you render her again iv 1 30
I do love nothing in the world so well as you : is not that strange? . iv 1 269
It were as possible for me to say I loved nothing so well as you . iv 1 272
Believe me not ; and yet I lie not ; I confess nothing, nor I deny nothing iv 1 274
Therein do men from children nothing differ . . . . v 1 33
In faith, my hand meant nothing to my sword.—Tush, tush, man . v 1 57
She was charged with nothing But what was true and very full of proof v 1 104
And, briefly, I desire nothing but the reward of a villain . . v 1 250
That now men grow hard-hearted and will lend nothing for God's sake v 1 321
Another Hero!—Nothing certainer : One Hero died defiled, but I do live v 4 62
If a man will be beaten with brains, a' shall wear nothing handsome . v 4 105
Since I do purpose to marry, I will think nothing to any purpose that the world can say against it . . . . v 4 106
In reason nothing.—Something then in rhyme . . . *L. L. Lost* i 1 99
What shall some see?—Nay, nothing, Master Moth, but what they look upon . . . . i 2 167
I will say nothing : I thank God I have as little patience as another man ; and therefore I can be quiet . . . . . . i 2 170
Nothing becomes him ill that he would well . . . . ii 1 46
Nothing but fair is that which you inherit . . . . iv 1 20
Imitari is nothing : so doth the hound his master, the ape his keeper . iv 2 130
What makes treason here?—Nay, it makes nothing, sir.—If it mar nothing neither, The treason and you go in peace away together . iv 3 191
Where nothing wants that want itself doth seek . . . iv 3 237
But what of this? are we not all in love?—Nothing so sure . . iv 3 283
He hath drawn my picture in his letter!—Any thing like?—Much in the letters ; nothing in the praise . . . . v 2 40
What would you with the princess?—Nothing but peace and gentle visitation . . . . v 2 179
We number nothing that we spend for you : Our duty is so rich, so infinite v 2 198
You may do it extempore, for it is nothing but roaring . *M. N. Dream* i 2 71
Weigh oath with oath, and you will nothing weigh . . . iii 2 131
Be certain, nothing truer ; 'tis no jest That I do hate thee . . iii 2 280
'Little' again! nothing but 'low' and 'little'! . . . iii 2 326
Your will?—Nothing, good mounsieur, but to help Cavalery Cobweb to scratch . . . . iv 1 24
He would have deserved it : sixpence a day in Pyramus, or nothing . iv 2 24
Gives to airy nothing A local habitation and a name . . . v 1 16
I have heard it over, And it is nothing, nothing in the world . . v 1 78
He says they can do nothing in this kind.—The kinder we, to give them thanks for nothing . . . . v 1 88
His speech was like a tangled chain ; nothing impaired, but all disordered v 1 126
He is but one.—Less than an ace, man ; for he is dead ; he is nothing . v 1 315
But even now worth this, And now worth nothing . . *Mer. of Venice* i 1 36
I do know of these That therefore only are reputed wise For saying nothing . . . . i 1 97
Gratiano speaks an infinite deal of nothing, more than any man in all Venice . . . . i 1 113
Her name is Portia, nothing undervalued To Cato's daughter . . i 1 165
They are as sick that surfeit with too much as they that starve with nothing . . . . i 2 7
Ay, that's a colt indeed, for he doth nothing but talk of his horse . i 2 45

Nothing. He doth nothing but frown, as who should say 'If you will not have me, choose' *Mer. of Venice* i 2 50
I say nothing to him, for he understands not me, nor I him i 2 73
Alas, fifteen wives is nothing! ii 2 170
Was wont to tell me that I could do nothing without bidding ii 5 9
It was not for nothing that my nose fell a-bleeding on Black-Monday ii 5 24
Every something, being blent together, Turns to a wild of nothing, save of joy iii 2 184
Rating myself at nothing, you shall see How much I was a braggart iii 2 260
When I told you My state was nothing, I should then have told you That I was worse than nothing iii 2 262
Soft! no haste: He shall have nothing but the penalty iv 1 322
Thou shalt have nothing but the forfeiture, To be so taken at thy peril, Jew iv 1 343
Nothing is good, I see, without respect v 1 99
But I, his brother, gain nothing under him but growth *As Y. Like It* i 1 15
Besides this nothing that he so plentifully gives me, the something that nature gave me his countenance seems to take from me i 1 17
What make you here?—Nothing: I am not taught to make any thing i 1 32
For my soul, yet I know not why, hates nothing more than he i 1 172
Nothing remains but that I kindle the boy thither i 1 178
I shall do . . . the world no injury, for in it I have nothing i 2 203
By reason of his absence, there is nothing That you will feed on ii 4 85
Nay, I care not for their names; they owe me nothing. Will you sing? ii 5 22
Go find him out, And we will nothing waste till you return ii 7 134
'Tis good to be sad and say nothing.—Why then, 'tis good to be a post iv 1 8
To have seen much and to have nothing, is to have rich eyes and poor hands iv 1 24
I will weep for nothing, like Diana in the fountain iv 1 154
'Tis The royal disposition of that beast To prey on nothing that doth seem as dead iv 3 119
Say that he dreams, For he is nothing but a mighty lord *T. of Shrew* Ind. 1 65
Let them want nothing that my house affords Ind. 1 104
Thou art a lord and nothing but a lord Ind. 2 63
Why, nothing comes amiss, so money comes withal i 2 82
Why, that's nothing; an he begin once, he'll rail in his rope-tricks i 2 111
I call them forth to credit her.—Why, she comes to borrow nothing of them iv 1 107
Evermore cross'd and cross'd; nothing but cross'd! iv 5 10
Now we are undone and brought to nothing v 1 45
We sit to chat as well as eat.—Nothing but sit and sit, and eat and eat! v 2 12
Padua affords nothing but what is kind v 2 14
Thus he his special nothing ever prologues *All's Well* ii 1 95
He that cannot make a leg, put off's cap, kiss his hand and say nothing, has neither leg, hands, lip, nor cap ii 2 11
Yet art thou good for nothing but taking up; and that thou'rt scarce worth ii 3 218
I say nothing.—Marry, you are the wiser man ii 4 22
To say nothing, to do nothing, to know nothing, and to have nothing, is to be a great part of your title; which is within a very little of nothing ii 4 25
Lies three thirds and uses a known truth to pass a thousand nothings with ii 5 33
Sir, I can nothing say, But that I am your most obedient servant ii 5 76
What would you have?—Something; and scarce so much: nothing, indeed ii 5 88
Till I have no wife, I have nothing in France.—'Tis bitter iii 2 77
Nothing in France, until he have no wife! There's nothing here that is too good for him But only she iii 2 82
I was well born, Nothing acquainted with these businesses iii 7 5
It nothing steads us To chide him from our eaves; for he persists iii 7 41
And what think you he hath confessed?—Nothing of me, has a'? iv 3 129
He can say nothing of me iv 3 135
What shall be done to him?—Nothing, but let him have thanks iv 3 195
He has every thing that an honest man should not have; what an honest man should have, he has nothing iv 3 292
Be bold you do so grow in my requital As nothing can unroot you v 1 6
And she is dead; which nothing, but to close Her eyes myself, could win me to believe, More than to see this ring v 3 118
There is no slander in an allowed fool, though he do nothing but rail; nor no railing in a known discreet man, though he do nothing but reprove *T. Night* i 5 103
Fetch him off, I pray you; he speaks nothing but madman: fie on him! i 5 114
Though she harbours you as her kinsman, she's nothing allied to your disorders ii 3 104
That's it that always makes a good voyage of nothing ii 4 81
I warrant thou art a merry fellow and carest for nothing iii 1 31
If that be to care for nothing, sir, I would it would make you invisible iii 1 34
You'll nothing, madam, to my lord by me? iii 1 148
What's the matter? does he rave?—No, madam, he does nothing but smile iii 4 11
Nothing that can be can come between me and the full prospect of my hopes iii 4 89
It is something of my negligence, nothing of my purpose iii 4 280
I know the knight is incensed . . . ; but nothing of the circumstance more iii 4 286
Let's see the event.—I dare lay any money 'twill be nothing yet iii 4 432
Nothing that is so is so.—I prithee, vent thy folly somewhere else iv 1 9
How vexest thou this man! talkest thou nothing but of ladies? iv 2 30
You broke my head for nothing; and that that I did, I was set on to do't v 1 188
I think you set nothing by a bloody coxcomb v 1 194
If nothing lets to make us happy both But this v 1 256
With what's unreal thou coactive art, And fellow'st nothing *W. Tale* i 2 142
Is whispering nothing? Is leaning cheek to cheek? is meeting noses? i 2 284
Is this nothing? Why, then the world and all that's in't is nothing; The covering sky is nothing; Bohemia nothing; My wife is nothing; nor nothing have these nothings, If this be nothing i 2 292
Part of his theme, but nothing Of his ill-ta'en suspicion i 2 459
So surprised my sense, That I was nothing iii 1 11
That thou betray'dst Polixenes, 'twas nothing; That did but show thee, of a fool, inconstant And damnable ingrateful iii 2 186
Therefore betake thee To nothing but despair iii 2 211
Take your patience to you, And I'll say nothing iii 2 233
There is nothing in the between [sixteen and three-and-twenty] but getting wenches with child iii 3 61
We are lucky, boy; and to be so still requires nothing but secrecy iii 3 130
That from very nothing, and beyond the imagination of his neighbours, is grown into an unspeakable estate iv 2 44
Apprehend Nothing but jollity iv 4 25
When you do dance, I wish you A wave o' the sea, that you might ever do Nothing but that iv 4 142
Nothing she does or seems But smacks of something greater than herself iv 4 157

Nothing. Fear not thou, man, thou shalt lose nothing here.—I hope so, sir *W. Tale* iv 4 258
You have let him go And nothing marted with him iv 4 363
I cannot speak So well, nothing so well; no, nor mean better iv 4 392
Lies he not bed-rid? and again does nothing But what he did being childish? iv 4 412
I am but sorry, not afeard; delay'd, But nothing alter'd iv 4 475
What course I mean to hold Shall nothing benefit your knowledge iv 4 514
Nothing so certain as your anchors, who Do their best office iv 4 581
'Twas nothing to geld a codpiece of a purse iv 4 623
No hearing, no feeling, but my sir's song, and admiring the nothing of it iv 4 626
We'll make an instrument of this, omit Nothing may give us aid iv 4 638
The complaint they have to the king concerns him nothing iv 4 870
The news, Rogero?—Nothing but bonfires: the oracle is fulfilled v 2 24
Hermione was not so much wrinkled, nothing So aged as this seems v 3 28
Thy eld'st son's son, Infortunate in nothing but in thee *K. John* ii 1 178
And she again wants nothing, to name want, If want it be not that she is not he ii 1 435
Nothing do I see in you, Though churlish thoughts themselves should be your judge, That I can find should merit any hate ii 1 518
Hang no more in doubt.—Hang nothing but a calf's skin, most sweet lout iii 1 220
A rage whose heat hath this condition, That nothing can allay, nothing but blood iii 1 342
Thou'rt damn'd as black—nay, nothing is so black iv 3 121
All Kent hath yielded; nothing there holds out But Dover castle v 1 30
I make a vow, Such neighbour nearness to our sacred blood Should nothing privilege him *Richard II.* i 1 120
And stay For nothing but his majesty's approach i 3 6
What says he?—Nay, nothing; all is said: His tongue is now a stringless instrument ii 1 148
My inward soul With nothing trembles: at some thing it grieves ii 2 12
Like perspectives, which rightly gazed upon Show nothing but confusion ii 2 19
Though on thinking on no thought I think, Makes me with heavy nothing faint and shrink ii 2 32
'Tis nothing but conceit, my gracious lady.—'Tis nothing less ii 2 33
For nothing hath begot my something grief; Or something hath the nothing that I grieve ii 2 36
We are on the earth, Where nothing lives but crosses, cares and grief ii 2 79
Discomfort guides my tongue And bids me speak of nothing but despair iii 2 66
Nothing can we call our own but death And that small model of the barren earth Which serves as paste and cover to our bones iii 2 152
In your lord's scale is nothing but himself, And some few vanities iii 4 85
Ay, no; no, ay; for I must nothing be; Therefore no no, for I resign to thee iv 1 201
Make me, that nothing have, with nothing grieved iv 1 216
Let me see the writing.—My lord, 'tis nothing.—No matter, then, who see it v 2 58
'Tis nothing but some bond, that he is enter'd into For gay apparel v 2 65
By and by Think that I am unking'd by Bolingbroke, And straight am nothing v 5 38
Nor I nor any man that but man is With nothing shall be pleased v 5 40
Before I knew thee, Hal, I knew nothing *1 Hen. IV.* i 2 105
But when they seldom come, they wish'd for come, And nothing pleaseth but rare accidents i 2 231
I'll have a starling shall be taught to speak Nothing but 'Mortimer' i 3 225
Never leave calling 'Francis,' that his tale to me may be nothing but 'Anon' ii 4 35
There is nothing but roguery to be found in villanous man ii 4 138
Wherein villanous, but in all things? wherein worthy, but in nothing? ii 4 505
What hast thou found?—Nothing but papers, my lord ii 4 583
That would set my teeth nothing on edge, Nothing so much as mincing poetry iii 1 133
Then should you be nothing but musical iii 1 236
Let him pay.—He? alas, is poor; he hath nothing iii 3 88
With the losers let it sympathise, For nothing can seem foul to those that win v 1 8
You were in place and in account Nothing so strong and fortunate as I v 1 38
And you did swear . . . That you did nothing purpose 'gainst the state v 1 43
Nothing but a colossus can do thee that friendship v 1 123
Nothing confutes me but eyes, and nobody sees me v 4 129
Wear nothing but high shoes, and bunches of keys at their girdles *2 Hen. IV.* i 2 44
Better to be eaten to death with a rust than to be scoured to nothing with perpetual motion i 2 246
If a man will make courtesy and say nothing, he is virtuous ii 1 136
My honour is at pawn; And, but my going, nothing can redeem it ii 3 8
Where nothing but the sound of Hotspur's name Did seem defensible ii 3 37
Come we to full points here; and are etceteras nothing? ii 4 198
An a' do nothing but speak nothing, a' shall be nothing here ii 4 207
His face is Lucifer's privy-kitchen, where he doth nothing but roast malt-worms ii 4 361
Hath done nothing but prate to me of the wildness of his youth iii 2 327
Then, then, when there was nothing could have stay'd My father iv 1 123
So that skill in the weapon is nothing without sack, for that sets it a-work iv 3 123
What would my lord and father?—Nothing but well to thee iv 4 19
We shall Do nothing but eat, and make good cheer v 3 18
Lack nothing: be merry v 3 73
Good lieutenant! good corporal! offer nothing here *Hen. V.* ii 1 42
I desire Nothing but odds with England ii 4 129
In peace there's nothing so becomes a man As modest stillness iii 1 3
And we talk, and, be Chrish, do nothing: 'tis shame for us all iii 2 117
That in our marches through the country, there be nothing compelled from the villages, nothing taken but paid for iii 6 115
More will I do; Though all that I can do is nothing worth iv 1 320
Shame and eternal shame, nothing but shame! Let us die in honour iv 5 10
You shall be a woodmonger, and buy nothing of me but cudgels v 1 70
And nothing teems But hateful docks, rough thistles, kecksies, burs v 2 51
Grow like savages,—as soldiers will That nothing do but meditate on blood v 2 60
I am left out; for me nothing remains *1 Hen. VI.* i 1 174
Be not amazed, there's nothing hid from me i 2 68
By me they nothing gain an if I stay iv 6 36
Will nothing turn your unrelenting hearts? v 4 59
Tut, this was nothing but an argument *2 Hen. VI.* i 2 32
Nor stir at nothing till the axe of death Hang over thee ii 4 49
The pissing-conduit run nothing but claret wine this first year of our reign iv 6 4
Nothing so heavy as these woes of mine v 2 65
Bring forth that fatal screech-owl to our house, That nothing sung but death to us and ours *3 Hen. VI.* ii 6 57
Where having nothing, nothing can he lose iii 3 152

Nothing. Subjects may challenge nothing of their sovereigns 3 *Hen. VI.* iv 6 6
I challenge nothing but my dukedom, As being well content with that alone iv 7 23
And of all my lands Is nothing left me but my body's length v 2 26
And I nothing to back my suit at all, But the plain devil and dissembling looks, And yet to win her, all the world to nothing! *Richard III.* i 2 236
What doth she say, my Lord of Buckingham?—Nothing that I respect. i 3 296
So that, betwixt their titles and low names, There's nothing differs but the outward fame i 4 83
Nothing can proceed that toucheth us Whereof I shall not have intelligence iii 2 23
Left nothing fitting for the purpose Untouch'd, or slightly handled iii 7 18
But nothing spake in warrant from himself iii 7 33
I swear— By nothing; for this is no oath iv 4 368
Out on you, owls! nothing but songs of death? iv 4 509
It will help me nothing To plead mine innocence *Hen. VIII.* i 1 207
More than my all is nothing: nor my prayers Are not words duly hallow'd ii 3 67
There's nothing I have done yet, o' my conscience, Deserves a corner iii 1 30
Ye turn me into nothing: woe upon ye And all such false professors! iii 1 114
Nothing but death Shall e'er divorce my dignities iii 1 141
Poor undeserver, I Can nothing render but allegiant thanks iii 2 176
So looks the chafed lion Upon the daring huntsman that has gall'd him; Then makes him nothing iii 2 208
His promises were, as he then was, mighty; But his performance, as he is now, nothing iv 2 42
I fear nothing What can be said against me v 1 125
You did nothing, sir.—I am not Samson, nor Sir Guy, nor Colbrand v 4 21
Then though my heart's content firm love doth bear, Nothing of that shall from mine eyes appear *Troi. and Cres.* i 2 321
Strong joints, true swords; and, Jove's accord, Nothing so full of heart i 3 239
Soft infancy, that nothing canst but cry ii 2 105
Things small as nothing, for request's sake only, He makes important ii 3 179
Love, love, nothing but love, still more! iii 1 125
He eats nothing but doves, love, and that breeds hot blood iii 1 140
Nor nothing monstrous neither?—Nothing, but our undertakings iii 2 82
And mighty states characterless are grated To dusty nothing iii 2 196
That he raves in saying nothing iii 3 249
Nothing but heavenly business Should rob my bed-mate of my company iv 1 4
Let us cast away nothing, for we may live to have need iv 4 23
I'll nothing do on charge: to her own worth She shall be prized iv 4 135
If not Achilles, sir, What is your name?—If not Achilles, nothing iv 5 76
The one almost as infinite as all, The other blank as nothing iv 5 81
To an ass, were nothing; he is both ass and ox: to an ox, were nothing v 1 65
Nothing but lechery! all incontinent varlets! v 1 105
And this whole night Hath nothing been but shapes and forms of slaughter v 3 12
They nothing doubt prevailing and to make it brief wars *Coriolanus* i 3 111
Leave nothing out for length ii 2 53
Than idly sit To hear my nothings monster'd ii 2 81
Purpose so barr'd, it follows, Nothing is done to purpose iii 1 149
And waked half dead with nothing iv 5 132
This peace is nothing, but to rust iron, increase tailors iv 5 234
I hear nothing: his mother and his wife Hear nothing from him iv 6 18
Nothing but his report.—Yes, worthy sir, The slave's report is seconded iv 6 61
He was a kind of nothing, titleless, Till he had forged himself a name v 1 13
He wants nothing of a god but eternity and a heaven to throne in v 4 24
Foul-spoken coward, that thunder'st with thy tongue, And with thy weapon nothing darest perform! *T. Andron.* ii 1 59
Here nothing breeds, Unless the nightly owl or fatal raven ii 3 96
O, be to me, though thy hard heart say no, Nothing so kind, but something pitiful!—I know not what it means ii 3 156
Nothing grieves me heartily indeed But that I cannot do ten thousand more v 1 143
And cut the winds, Who nothing hurt withal hiss'd him in scorn *R. and J.* i 1 119
O brawling love! O loving hate! O any thing, of nothing first create! i 1 183
Peace, peace, Mercutio, peace! Thou talk'st of nothing.—True, I talk of dreams, Which are the children of an idle brain, Begot of nothing but vain fantasy i 4 96
She speaks, yet she says nothing: what of that? Her eye discourses ii 2 12
An thou make minstrels of us, look to hear nothing but discords iii 1 51
Good king of cats, nothing but one of your nine lives iii 1 80
A plague o' both your houses! I am sped. Is he gone, and hath nothing? iii 1 95
O, she says nothing, sir, but weeps and weeps iii 3 99
And all the world to nothing, That he dares ne'er come back to challenge you iii 5 215
And I am nothing slow to slack his haste iv 1 3
I hear thou must, and nothing may prorogue it, On Thursday next be married iv 1 48
How fares my Juliet? that I ask again; For nothing can be ill, if she be well v 1 16
Thou art proud, Apemantus.—Of nothing so much as that I am not like Timon.—Whither art going? *T. of Athens* i 1 189
That's a deed thou'lt die for.—Right, if doing nothing be death by the law i 1 195
Hang thyself!—No, I will do nothing at thy bidding i 1 278
No, I'll nothing: for if I should be bribed too, there would be none left to rail upon thee i 2 244
Give my horse to Timon, Ask nothing, give it him, it foals me, straight, And able horses ii 1 9
'Faith, nothing but an empty box, sir iii 1 16
Nothing doubting your present assistance therein.—La, la, la, la! 'nothing doubting,' says he? iii 1 20
Money, plate, jewels, and such-like trifles, nothing comparing to his iii 2 24
Nothing emboldens sin so much as mercy iii 5 3
For these my present friends, as they are to me nothing, so in nothing bless them, and to nothing are they welcome iii 6 93
Nothing I'll bear from thee, But nakedness, thou detestable town! iv 1 32
Where's our master? Are we undone? cast off? nothing remaining? iv 2 2
There's nothing level in our cursed natures, But direct villany iv 3 19
When there is nothing living but thee, thou shalt be welcome iv 3 360
Break open shops; nothing can you steal, But thieves do lose it iv 3 450
Let prisons swallow 'em, Debts wither 'em to nothing iv 3 538
What have you now to present unto him?—Nothing at this time v 1 20
Nothing but himself which looks like man Is friendly with him v 1 121
My long sickness Of health and living now begins to mend, And nothing brings me all things v 1 191
No talk of Timon, nothing of him expect v 2 14
That you do love me, I am nothing jealous *J. Cæsar* i 2 162

Nothing. Before the eyes of both our armies here, Which should perceive nothing but love from us, Let us not wrangle *J. Cæsar* iv 2 44
You shall not come to them.—Nothing but death shall stay me iv 3 128
Nor nothing in your letters writ of her?—Nothing iv 3 183
Didst thou see anything?—Nothing, my lord.—Sleep again, Lucius iv 3 299
Nothing afeard of what thyself didst make, Strange images of death *Macb.* i 3 96
Function Is smother'd in surmise, and nothing is But what is not i 3 141
Nothing in his life Became him like the leaving it i 4 7
Thy undaunted mettle should compose Nothing but males i 7 74
From this instant, There's nothing serious in mortality: All is but toys ii 3 98
To be thus is nothing; But to be safely thus iii 1 48
Malice domestic, foreign levy, nothing, Can touch him further iii 2 25
I have a strange infirmity, which is nothing To those that know me iii 4 86
The malevolence of fortune nothing Takes from his high respect iii 6 28
All is the fear and nothing is the love; As little is the wisdom iv 2 12
Where nothing, But who knows nothing, is once seen to smile iv 3 166
Our power is ready; Our lack is nothing but our leave iv 3 237
Those he commands move only in command, Nothing in love v 2 20
We doubt it nothing v 4 2; *Hamlet* i 2 41
It is a tale Told by an idiot, full of sound and fury, Signifying nothing *Macbeth* v 5 28
Has this thing appear'd again to-night?—I have seen nothing *Hamlet* i 1 22
Were nothing but to waste night, day and time ii 2 89
There is nothing either good or bad, but thinking makes it so ii 2 256
Pyrrhus stood, And like a neutral to his will and matter, Did nothing ii 2 504
His whole function suiting With forms to his conceit? and all for nothing! ii 2 583
Peak, Like John-a-dreams, unpregnant of my cause, And can say nothing ii 2 596
Capable of nothing but inexplicable dumb-shows and noise iii 2 13
For thou hast been As one, in suffering all, that suffers nothing iii 2 71
I have nothing with this answer, Hamlet; these words are not mine iii 2 101
Do you think I meant country matters?—I think nothing, my lord iii 2 124
Yet, though I distrust, Discomfort you, my lord, it nothing must iii 2 176
Do you see nothing there?—Nothing at all; yet all that is I see.—Nor did you nothing hear?—No, nothing but ourselves iii 4 131
The king is a thing— A thing, my lord!—Of nothing: bring me to him iv 2 32
What dost thou mean by this?—Nothing but to show you how a king may go a progress through the guts of a beggar iv 3 32
O, from this time forth, My thoughts be bloody, or be nothing worth! iv 4 66
Her speech is nothing, Yet the unshaped use of it doth move The hearers iv 5 7
Indeed would make one think there might be thought, Though nothing sure, yet much unhappily iv 5 13
Will nothing stick our person to arraign In ear and ear iv 5 93
This nothing's more than matter iv 5 174
He could nothing do but wish and beg Your sudden coming o'er iv 7 105
And nothing is at a like goodness still iv 7 117
O, the time, for, ah, my behove, O, methought, there was nothing v 1 72
If not, I will gain nothing but my shame and the odd hits v 2 184
Say you so? come on.—Nothing, neither way.—Have at you now! v 2 312
What can you say to draw A third more opulent than your sisters? Speak.—Nothing, my lord.—Nothing!—Nothing.—Nothing will come of nothing: speak again *Lear* i 1 89
Give but that portion which yourself proposed . . .—Nothing: I have sworn; I am firm i 1 248
I know no news, my lord.—What paper were you reading?—Nothing, my lord i 2 31
The quality of nothing hath not such need to hide itself. Let's see: come, if it be nothing, I shall not need spectacles i 2 34
Find out this villain, Edmund; it shall lose thee nothing; do it carefully i 2 125
This is nothing, fool.—Then 'tis like the breath of an unfee'd lawyer; you gave me nothing for't i 4 141
Can you make no use of nothing, nuncle?—Why, no, boy; nothing can be made out of nothing i 4 144
Thou hast pared thy wit o' both sides, and left nothing i' the middle i 4 205
Thou art an O without a figure: I am better than thou art now; I am a fool, thou art nothing i 4 213
I will hold my tongue; so your face bids me, though you say nothing i 4 215
Have you nothing said Upon his party 'gainst the Duke of Albany? ii 1 27
And art nothing but the composition of a knave, beggar, coward ii 2 22
Away! I have nothing to do with thee.—Draw, you rascal ii 2 37
Nothing almost sees miracles But misery ii 2 172
Poor Tom! That's something yet: Edgar I nothing am ii 3 21
Tears his white hair, Which the impetuous blasts, with eyeless rage, Catch in their fury, and make nothing of iii 1 9
I will be the pattern of all patience; I will say nothing iii 2 38
Most savage and unnatural!—Go to; say you nothing iii 3 8
What, have his daughters brought him to this pass? Couldst thou save nothing? iii 4 66
Nothing could have subdued nature To such a lowness but his unkind daughters iii 4 72
The wretch that thou hast blown unto the worst Owes nothing to thy blasts iv 1 9
You're much deceived: in nothing am I changed But in my garments iv 6 9
There is nothing done, if he return the conqueror: then am I the prisoner iv 6 270
Thou art in nothing less Than I have here proclaim'd thee v 3 94
What . . . can you say to this?—Nothing, but this is so *Othello* i 3 75
He bears the sentence well that nothing bears But the free comfort i 3 212
Do not put me to't; For I am nothing, if not critical ii 1 120
Nothing can or shall content my soul Till I am even'd with him ii 1 307
Your Dane, your German, and your swag-bellied Hollander—Drink, ho!—are nothing to your English ii 3 81
Yet, I persuade myself, to speak the truth Shall nothing wrong him ii 3 224
I remember a mass of things, but nothing distinctly; a quarrel, but nothing wherefore ii 3 289
What dost thou say?—Nothing, my lord: or if—I know not what. iii 3 36
Prithee, no more: let him come when he will; I will deny thee nothing iii 3 76
I will deny thee nothing: Whereon, I do beseech thee, grant me this, To leave me but a little to myself iii 3 83
Who steals my purse steals trash; 'tis something, nothing iii 3 157
And give't Iago: what he will do with it Heaven knows, not I; I nothing but to please his fantasy iii 3 299
I had been happy, if the general camp, Pioneers and all, had tasted her sweet body, So I had nothing known iii 3 347
For nothing canst thou to damnation add Greater than that iii 3 372
Nay, but be wise: yet we see nothing done; She may be honest yet iii 3 432
So they do nothing, 'tis a venial slip: But if I give my wife a handkerchief iv 1 9

Nothing. Patience; Or I shall say you are all in all in spleen, And nothing of a man . . . . *Othello* iv 1 90
You have seen nothing then?—Nor ever heard, nor ever did suspect . iv 2 1
To fetch her fan, her gloves, her mask, nor nothing?—Never, my lord . iv 2 9
And said nothing but what I protest intendment of doing . . iv 2 205
Fear nothing; I'll be at thy elbow: It makes us, or it mars us . v 1 3
Demand me nothing: what you know, you know . . . v 2 303
Speak of me as I am; nothing extenuate, Nor set down aught in malice v 2 342
Under a compelling occasion, let women die: it were pity to cast them away for nothing; though, between them and a great cause, they should be esteemed nothing . . . . . *Ant. and Cleo.* i 2 142
Her passions are made of nothing but the finest part of pure love . . i 2 152
In each thing give him way, cross him in nothing . . . i 3 9
I can do nothing But what indeed is honest to be done . . . i 5 15
I must be laugh'd at, If, or for nothing or a little, I Should say myself offended, and with you Chiefly . . . . . ii 2 31
Let this fellow Be nothing of our strife . . . . ii 2 80
All great fears, which now import their dangers, Would then be nothing ii 2 136
Enjoy thy plainness, It nothing ill becomes thee . . . ii 6 81
There's nothing in her yet: The fellow has good judgement . . iii 3 27
Methinks, by him, This creature's no such thing.—Nothing, madam . iii 3 44
Welcome to Rome; Nothing more dear to me . . . . iii 6 86
Heard you of nothing strange about the streets?—Nothing. What news? iv 3 3
And there is nothing left remarkable Beneath the visiting moon . iv 15 67
Be of good cheer; You're fall'n into a princely hand, fear nothing . v 2 22
This is my treasurer: let him speak, my lord, Upon his peril, that I have reserved To myself nothing . . . . . . v 2 144
My resolution's placed, and I have nothing Of woman in me . . v 2 238
Give it nothing, I pray you, for it is not worth the feeding . . v 2 270
I something fear my father's wrath; but nothing—Always reserved my holy duty—what His rage can do on me . . . *Cymbeline* i 1 86
I would abate her nothing, though I profess myself her adorer . i 4 73
I do nothing doubt you have store of thieves . . . . i 4 106
The description Of what is in her chamber nothing saves The wager . ii 4 94
The vows of women Of no more bondage be, to where they are made, Than they are to their virtues; which is nothing . . . ii 4 112
You lie; And I will kill thee, if thou dost deny Thou'st made me cuckold.—I'll deny nothing . . . . ii 4 146
We will nothing pay For wearing our own noses . . . iii 1 13
O, this life Is nobler than attending for a check, Richer than doing nothing for a bauble . . . . iii 3 23
We have seen nothing; We are beastly . . . . . iii 3 39
My fault being nothing—as I have told you oft . . . . iii 3 65
No more ado With that harsh, noble, simple nothing, That Cloten . iii 4 135
Time hath nothing blurr'd those lines of favour Which then he wore . iv 2 104
Though his humour Was nothing but mutation . . . . iv 2 133
Triumphs for nothing and lamenting toys Is jollity for apes . . iv 2 193
Nothing ill come near thee! . . . . iv 2 279
A bolt of nothing, shot at nothing, Which the brain makes of fumes . iv 2 300
What art thou?—I am nothing: or if not, Nothing to be were better . iv 2 367
I nothing know where she remains, why gone, Nor when she purposes return . . . . iv 3 14
A doubt In such a time nothing becoming you, Nor satisfying us . . iv 4 15
The lane is guarded: nothing routs us but The villany of our fears . v 2 12
For three performers are the file when all The rest do nothing . . v 3 31
And so I am awake. Poor wretches that depend On greatness' favour dream as I have done, Wake and find nothing . . . . v 4 129
'Tis still a dream, or else such stuff as madmen Tongue and brain not; either both or nothing . . . . v 4 147
But since the gods Will have it thus, that nothing but our lives May be call'd ransom, let it come . . . . v 5 79
The wrongs he did me Were nothing prince-like . . . . v 5 293
Her face the book of praises, where is read Nothing but curious pleasures, as from thence Sorrow were ever razed . . . *Pericles* i 1 16
Like an hypocrite, The which is good in nothing but in sight . . i 1 123
And left me breath Nothing to think on but ensuing death . . ii 1 7
I can compare our rich misers to nothing so fitly as to a whale . ii 1 33
Here's nothing to be got now-a-days, unless thou canst fish for't . ii 1 73
There's nothing can be minister'd to nature Than can recover him . iii 2 8
Report what a sojourner we have; you'll lose nothing by custom . iv 2 150
Sure, all's effectless; yet nothing we'll omit That bears recovery's name v 1 53
Nothing at all. I could perceive nothing at all from her; no, not so much as a ducat . . . . *T. G. of Ver.* i 1 144
Three times as much more, and yet nothing at all . . *L. L. Lost* iii 1 49
What hath she done, prince, that can soil our mothers?—Nothing at all, unless that this were she . . . . *Troi. and Cres.* v 2 135
Do you see nothing there?—Nothing at all . . . *Hamlet* iii 4 132
What from the cape can you discern at sea?—Nothing at all . *Othello* ii 1 2
Nothing but this. Impose on thee nothing but this . . *L. L. Lost* iii 1 131
Came nothing else along with that?—Nothing but this! yes . . v 2 6
What shall you ask of me that I'll deny, That honour saved may upon asking give?—Nothing but this; your true love for my master *T. N.* iii 4 233
What say you of Kent?—Nothing but this; 'tis 'bona terra, mala gens' *2 Hen. VI.* iv 7 61
Nothing else. My duty will I boast of; nothing else . *T. G. of Ver.* ii 4 111
A plain kerchief, Sir John: my brows become nothing else *Mer. Wives* iii 3 63
Why, will shall break it; will and nothing else . . *L. L. Lost* ii 1 100
Came nothing else along with that?—Nothing but this! yes . . v 2 5
What says that fool of Hagar's offspring, ha?—His words were, 'Farewell mistress;' nothing else . . . . *Mer. of Venice* ii 5 45
If it will feed nothing else, it will feed my revenge . . . iii 1 55
What mercy can you render him, Antonio?—A halter gratis; nothing else iv 1 379
I will have nothing else but only this; And now methinks I have a mind to it . . . . iv 1 432
What must I call her?—Madam.—Al'ce madam, or Joan madam?—'Madam,' and nothing else . . . . *T. of Shrew* Ind. 2 113
The father, all whose joy is nothing else But fair posterity . *W. Tale* iv 4 419
Boast of nothing else But that I was a journeyman to grief? . *Richard II.* i 3 273
Be sure I count myself in nothing else so happy As in a soul remembering my good friends . . . . ii 3 46
The lion dying thrusteth forth his paw, And wounds the earth, if nothing else, with rage To be o'erpower'd . . . . . v 1 30
Thinking of nothing else, putting all affairs else in oblivion . *2 Hen. IV.* v 5 26
As if there were nothing else to be done but to see him . . . v 5 28
Talking of hawking; nothing else, my lord . . . *2 Hen. VI.* ii 1 50
And take his thanks that yet hath nothing else . . *3 Hen. VI.* v 4 59
Wars and lechery; nothing else holds fashion . . *Troi. and Cres.* v 2 196
I would the gods had nothing else to do But to confirm my curses! *Coriolanus* iv 2 45
For we have nothing else to ask, but that Which you deny already . v 3 88

Nothing else. Art not thou the carrier?—Ay, of my pigeons, sir; nothing else . . . . *T. Andron.* iv 3 87
This breaking of his has been but a try for his friends.—Nothing else: you shall see him a palm in Athens again . . *T. of Athens* v 1 12
What should I do? Run to the Capitol, and nothing else? And so return to you, and nothing else? . . . . . *J. Cæsar* ii 4 11
To define true madness, What is't but to be nothing else but mad? *Ham.* ii 2 94
To lose't or give't away were such perdition As nothing else could match.—Is't possible? . . . . *Othello* iii 4 68
There's a palm presages chastity, if nothing else . . *Ant. and Cleo.* i 2 47
You shall have time to wrangle in when you have nothing else to do . ii 2 106
Nothing-gift. Laying by That nothing-gift of differing multitudes *Cymb.* iii 6 86
Nothing in the world. My husband says my son profits nothing in the world at his book . . . . *Mer. Wives* iv 1 15
I do love nothing in the world so well as you . . *Much Ado* iv 1 269
I do nothing in the world but lie, and lie in my throat . *L. L. Lost* iv 3 12
I have heard it over, And it is nothing, nothing in the world *M. N. D.* v 1 78
Some dear friend dead; else nothing in the world Could turn so much the constitution Of any constant man . . . *Mer. of Venice* iii 2 248
She's very well and wants nothing i' the world . . *All's Well* ii 4 5
Nothing in this world can make me joy . . . *K. John* iii 4 107
Nothing less. My father's execution Was nothing less than bloody tyranny . . . . *1 Hen. VI.* ii 5 100
Nothing like. What complexion is she of?—Swart, like my shoe, but her face nothing like so clean kept . . . *Com. of Errors* iii 2 105
Our old ling and our Isbels o' the country are nothing like your old ling and your Isbels o' the court . . . . . *All's Well* iii 2 15
Being nothing like the noble duke my father . . *Richard III.* iii 5 92
I have told you what I have seen and heard; but faintly, nothing like the image and horror of it . . . . *Lear* i 2 191
Nothing more. Law is strict, and war is nothing more . *T. of Athens* iii 5 85
And who else would trace him, his umbrage, nothing more . *Hamlet* v 2 125
If aught within that little seeming substance, Or all of it, with our displeasure pieced, And nothing more, may fitly like your grace, She's there, and she is yours . . . . *Lear* i 1 203
Notice. I'll give her father notice Of their disguising . *T. G. of Ver.* ii 6 36
No longer staying but to give the mother Notice of my affair *M. for M.* i 4 87
Give notice to such men of sort and suit as are to meet him . . iv 4 19
And shall, at the least of thy sweet notice, bring her to trial *L. L. Lost* i 1 279
Navarre had notice of your fair approach . . . . . ii 1 81
I had myself notice of my brother's purpose herein . *As Y. Like It* i 1 145
I have no certain notice . . . . *2 Hen. IV.* i 3 85
Bring me just notice of the numbers dead On both our parts *Hen. V.* iv 7 122
I'll by a sign give notice to our friends . . . *1 Hen. VI.* iii 2 8
Myself had notice of your conventicles . . . *2 Hen. VI.* iii 1 166
And undiscover'd come to me again And given me notice of their villanies . . . . iii 1 370
Break off your talk, And give us notice of his inclination *Richard III.* iii 1 178
Give notice, that no manner of person At any time have recourse unto the princes . . . . iii 5 108
The state takes notice of the private difference Betwixt you . *Hen. VIII.* i 1 101
Nay, gave notice He was from thence discharged? . . . . ii 4 33
Take notice, lords, he has a loyal breast, For you have seen him open't iii 2 200
To my poor unworthy notice, He mock'd us . . . *Coriolanus* ii 3 166
She will beshrew me much that Romeo Hath had no notice . *R. and J.* v 2 26
Belike they had some notice of the people, How I had moved them *J. C.* iii 2 275
To no more Will I give place or notice . . . . . *Lear* ii 4 252
Take no notice, nor build yourself a trouble . . . *Othello* iii 3 150
Let our officers Have notice what we purpose . . *Ant. and Cleo.* i 2 184
Who shall take notice of thee: I'll move the king . . *Cymbeline* i 5 70
I have assailed her with music, but she vouchsafes no notice . . ii 3 45
And towards himself, his goodness forespent on us, We must extend our notice . . . . ii 3 65
Take notice that I am in Cambria, at Milford-Haven . . . . iii 2 44
I'll give but notice you are dead and send him Some bloody sign of it iii 4 127
Notify. She gives you to notify that her husband will be absence *M. W.* ii 2 85
If she will stir hither, I shall seem to notify unto her . . *Othello* iii 1 31
Noting. Note this before my notes; There's not a note of mine that's worth the noting . . . . *Much Ado* ii 3 57
By noting of the lady I have mark'd A thousand blushing apparitions To start into her face . . . . iv 1 160
Noting this penury, to myself I said, 'An if a man did need a poison now, . . . Here lives a caitiff wretch would sell it him' *R. and J.* v 1 49
Which worthily deserved noting . . . . . *Ant. and Cleo.* ii 2 188
Notion. His own notion . . . shall join To thrust the lie unto him *Cor.* v 6 107
And all things else that might To half a soul and to a notion crazed Say, 'Thus did Banquo' . . . . *Macbeth* iii 1 83
His notion weakens, his discernings Are lethargied . . . *Lear* i 4 248
Notorious. Two notorious benefactors.—Benefactors? Well; what benefactors are they? are they not malefactors? . . *Meas. for Meas.* ii 1 50
You have been a notorious bawd.—Sir, I have been an unlawful bawd . iv 2 14
One Ragozine, a most notorious pirate . . . . . . iv 3 75
I shall have law in Ephesus, To your notorious shame . *Com. of Errors* iv 1 84
You notorious villain, didst thou never see thy master's father? *T. of S.* v 1 54
I would it were not notorious . . . . . . *All's Well* i 1 41
I love him for his sake; And yet I know him a notorious liar . . i 1 111
Madam, you have done me wrong, Notorious wrong.—Have I? *T. Night* v 1 337
And made the most notorious geck and gull That e'er invention play'd on v 1 351
Alençon! that notorious Machiavel! . . . . . *1 Hen. VI.* v 4 74
Your goodness, Since you provoke me, shall be most notorious *Hen. VIII.* iii 2 288
Wherein I did not some notorious ill . . . . . *T. Andron.* v 1 127
Some most villanous knave, Some base notorious knave . . *Othello* iv 2 140
He's gone, but his wife's kill'd.—'Tis a notorious villain . . . v 2 239
Notoriously. There was never man so notoriously abused . *T. Night* iv 2 94
He hath been most notoriously abused . . . . . . v 1 388
Not-pated, agate-ring, puke-stocking, caddis-garter . . . *1 Hen. IV.* ii 4 78
Notwithstanding. But notwithstanding, man, I'll do you your master what good I can . . . . *Mer. Wives* i 4 97
But notwithstanding,—to tell you in your ear . . . . i 4 108
But notwithstanding that, I know Anne's mind . . . . i 4 111
But, notwithstanding, haste; make no delay . . . *M. N. Dream* iii 2 394
The man is, notwithstanding, sufficient . . . *Mer. of Venice* i 3 26
Notwithstanding, use your pleasure . . . . . . iii 2 322
You are welcome notwithstanding . . . . v 1 239
Antony, that revels long o' nights, Is notwithstanding up . . *J. Cæsar* ii 2 117
But, notwithstanding, with my personal eye Will I look to't . *Othello* ii 3 5
Nought knowing Of whence I am, nor that I am more better . *Tempest* i 2 18
When that's gone He shall drink nought but brine . . . iii 2 74
War with good counsel, set the world at nought . . *T. G. of Ver.* i 1 68
But she is nice and coy And nought esteems my aged eloquence . . iii 1 83

Nought but mine eye Could have persuaded me . . . *T. G. of Ver.* v 4 64
They stay for nought at all But for their owner . . *Com. of Errors* iv 1 91
Too much to know is to know nought but fame . . *L. L. Lost* i 1 92
Jack shall have Jill; Nought shall go ill . . *M. N. Dream* iii 2 462
Since nought so stockish, hard and full of rage, But music for the time doth change his nature . . *Mer. of Venice* v 1 81
How unwillingly I left the ring, When nought would be accepted but the ring . . . . v 1 197
If love have touch'd you, nought remains but so, 'Redime te captum quam queas minimo' . . . *T. of Shrew* i 1 166
His important blood will nought deny That she'll demand . *All's Well* iii 7 21
Nought enters there, Of what validity and pitch soe'er, But falls into abatement and low price . . . . *T. Night* i 1 11
That lack'd sight only, nought for approbation But only seeing *W. Tale* ii 1 177
And bitter shame hath spoil'd the sweet world's taste, That it yields nought but shame and bitterness . . *K. John* iii 4 111
Nought shall make us rue, If England to itself do rest but true . v 7 117
The blood is hot that must be cool'd for this: Yet can I not of such tame patience boast As to be hush'd and nought at all to say *Rich. II.* i 1 53
Gaunt as a grave, Whose hollow womb inherits nought but bones . ii 1 83
Which, look'd on as it is, is nought but shadows Of what it is not . ii 2 23
To have a son set your decrees at nought . . . 2 *Hen. IV.* v 2 85
For Doll is in. Pistol speaks nought but truth . . . v 5 40
There's nought in France That can be with a nimble galliard won *Hen. V.* i 2 251
Glory is like a circle in the water, Which never ceaseth to enlarge itself Till by broad spreading it disperse to nought . . 1 *Hen. VI.* i 2 135
Nought rests for me in this tumultuous strife But to make open proclamation . . . . i 3 70
And can do nought but wail her darling's loss . . 2 *Hen. VI.* iii 1 216
What, worse than nought? nay, then, a shame take all! . . iii 1 307
Live thou to joy thy life; Myself no joy in nought but that thou livest iii 2 366
This hand was made to handle nought but gold . . . . v 1 7
Can you deny all this?—With this, my lord, myself have nought to do. —Naught to do with Mistress Shore! . . . *Richard III.* i 1 97
Bad is the world; and all will come to nought . . . . iii 6 13
To the disposing of it nought rebell'd . . . . *Hen. VIII.* i 1 43
Who shall report he has A better wife, let him in nought be trusted . ii 4 135
That she beloved knows nought that knows not this . *Troi. and Cres.* i 2 314
Which are indeed nought else But the protractive trials of great Jove . i 3 19
'Tis for Agamemnon's ears.—He hears nought privately . . . i 3 249
Law shall scorn him further trial Than the severity of the public power Which he so sets at nought . . . . *Coriolanus* iii 1 270
Mark; for we'll Hear nought from Rome in private. Your request? v 3 93
Remaineth nought, but to inter our brethren . . . *T. Andron.* i 1 146
There nought hath pass'd, But even with law . . . . iv 4 7
Nourish and bring him up; Or else I will discover nought to thee . v 1 85
The continuance of their parents' rage, Which, but their children's end, nought could remove . . . . *Rom. and Jul.* Prol. 11
For nought so vile that on the earth doth live But to the earth some special good doth give . . . . ii 3 17
He's but a mad lord, and nought but humour sways him *T. of Athens* iii 6 121
I am sick of this false world, and will love nought But even the mere necessities upon't . . . . iv 3 376
Nought's had, all's spent, Where our desire is got without content *Macb.* iii 2 4
He knows thy thought: Hear his speech, but say thou nought . iv 1 70
Knowing nought, like dogs, but following . . . *Lear* ii 2 86
This great world Shall so wear out to nought . . . iv 6 138
Wears out his time, much like his master's ass, For nought but provender, and when he's old, cashier'd . . . . *Othello* i 1 48
And what's to come of my despised time Is nought but bitterness . i 1 163
You charge me most unjustly.—With nought but truth . . . iv 2 187
For nought I did in hate, but all in honour . . . . v 2 295
If we draw lots, he speeds; His cocks do win the battle still of mine, When it is all to nought . . . . *Ant. and Cleo.* ii 3 37
Good troth, I have stol'n nought, nor would not, though I had found Gold strew'd i' the floor . . . . *Cymbeline* iii 6 49
Such precious deeds in one that promised nought But beggary and poor looks . . . . v 5 9
Mothers who, to nousle up their babes, Thought nought too curious *Per.* i 4 43

Noun. How many numbers is in nouns?—Two.—Truly, I thought there had been one number more, because they say, ''Od's nouns' *M. Wives* iv 1 22
Usually talk of a noun and a verb, and such abominable words 2 *Hen. VI.* iv 7 43

Nourish. They are the books, the arts, the academes, That show, contain and nourish all the world . . . *L. L. Lost* iv 3 353
Such as you Nourish the cause of his awaking . . *W. Tale* ii 3 36
Worse than the sun in March, This praise doth nourish agues 1 *Hen. IV.* iv 1 112
When at their mothers' moist eyes babes shall suck, Our isle be made a nourish of salt tears . . . . 1 *Hen. VI.* i 1 50
Whiles I in Ireland nourish a mighty band, I will stir up in England some black storm . . . . . 2 *Hen. VI.* iii 1 348
In soothing them, we nourish 'gainst our senate The cockle of rebellion *Coriolanus* iii 1 69
Thou shalt vow . . . To save my boy, to nourish and bring him up *T. An.* v 1 84
Yet ha' we A brain that nourishes our nerves . *Ant. and Cleo.* iv 8 21

Nourished. I am one that am nourished by my victuals . *T. G. of Ver.* ii 1 180
Begot in the ventricle of memory, nourished in the womb of pia mater *L. L. Lost* iv 2 71
Tell me where is fancy bred, Or in the heart or in the head? How begot, how nourished? Reply, reply . . *Mer. of Venice* iii 2 65
Or nourish'd him as I did with my blood . . 3 *Hen. VI.* i 1 222
They nourish'd disobedience, fed The ruin of the state . *Coriolanus* iii 1 117
Thy child shall live, and I will see it nourish'd . . *T. Andron.* v 1 60
Being vex'd [love is], a sea nourish'd with lovers' tears . *Rom. and Jul.* i 1 198
Our poesy is as a gum, which oozes From whence 'tis nourish'd *T. of A.* i 1 22

Nourisher. Balm of hurt minds, great nature's second course, Chief nourisher in life's feast . . . . *Macbeth* ii 2 40

Nourisheth. 'Tis age that nourisheth . . . *T. of Shrew* ii 1 341
It lives by that which nourisheth it . . . *Ant. and Cleo.* ii 7 50

Nourishing. 'Tis as I should entreat you wear your gloves, Or feed on nourishing dishes, or keep you warm . . . *Othello* iii 3 78

Nourishment. When beasts most graze, birds best peck, and men sit down to that nourishment which is called supper . *L. L. Lost* i 1 239
Men that make Envy and crooked malice nourishment . *Hen. VIII.* v 3 44
How durst thy tongue move anger to our face?—How dare the plants look up to heaven, from whence They have their nourishment? *Per.* i 2 56

Nousle. Those mothers who, to nousle up their babes, Thought nought too curious . . . . i 4 42

Novelty is only in request . . . . *Meas. for Meas.* iii 2 237
I may truly say, it is a novelty to the world . . . *All's Well* ii 3 22
How novelty may move, and parts with person . *Troi. and Cres.* iv 4 81

No-verbs. He gives me the proverbs and the no-verbs *Mer. Wives* iii 1 107

Novi hominem tanquam te . . . . . . *L. L. Lost* v 1 10

Novice. A novice of this place . . . . . *Meas. for Meas.* i 4 19
O, you are novices! . . . . *T. of Shrew* ii 1 313
Mars dote on you for his novices! . . . . . *All's Well* ii 1 48
Gallant-springing brave Plantagenet, That princely novice *Richard III.* i 4 228
'Tis thou Hast sold me to this novice . . . *Ant. and Cleo.* iv 12 14

Novum. Abate throw at novum . . . . . *L. L. Lost* v 2 547

Now. I pray now, keep below . . . . . . *Tempest* i 1 12
Now would I give a thousand furlongs of sea for an acre of barren ground i 1 69
Now on the beak, Now in the waist, the deck, in every cabin, I flamed . i 2 196
Lo, now, lo! Here comes a spirit of his, and to torment me . . ii 2 14
Alas, now, pray you, Work not so hard . . . . . iii 1 15
How now shall this be compassed? Canst thou bring me to the party? iii 2 66
Now, trust me, 'tis an office of great worth . . . *T. G. of Ver.* i 2 44
Now trust me, madam, it came hardly off . . . . . ii 1 115
Here! go; the desk, the purse! sweet, now, make haste *Com. of Errors* iv 2 29
Good now, hold thy tongue.—Nay, rather persuade him to hold his hands iv 4 22
Now, for your answer . . . . . . *Mer. of Venice* iv 1 52
Would now like him, now loathe him; then entertain him *As Y. Like It* iii 2 436
Her eye is sick on't: I observe her now . . . *All's Well* i 3 142
Will you be mine, now you are doubly won? . . . . v 3 315
Now here, At upper end o' the table, now i' the middle . *W. Tale* iv 4 58
Let them come in; but quickly now . . . . . iv 4 351
Lo, now! now see the issue of your peace . . . *K. John* iii 4 21
Now that their souls are topfull of offence . . . . iii 4 180
And come ye now to tell me John hath made His peace with Rome? v 2 91
So, now I have mine own again, be gone . . . *Richard II.* v 1 99
Soldiers, adieu! I have what I would have, Now my old arms are young John Talbot's grave . . . . . . 1 *Hen. VI.* iv 7 32
Now, York, or never, steel thy fearful thoughts . 2 *Hen. VI.* iii 1 331
Now one the better, then another best; both tugging to be victors 3 *Hen. VI.* ii 5 10
And, now I fall, thy tough commixture melts . . . . ii 6 6
Now is the winter of our discontent Made glorious summer *Richard III.* i 1 1
But, now thy beauty is proposed my fee, My proud heart sues . . i 2 170
The two kings, Equal in lustre, were now best, now worst *Hen. VIII.* i 1 29
Now good or bad, 'tis but the chance of war . *Troi. and Cres.* Prol. 31
Ay, good now, love, love, nothing but love . . . . iii 1 122
But, now you have it, take it.—Whose was it? . . . . v 2 90
This is strange now: do you two know how you are censured here? *Cor.* ii 1 24
Now you have left your voices, I have no further with you . . ii 3 180
Though you hear now, too late—yet now's a time . *T. of Athens* ii 2 152
Now I am alone. O, what a rogue and peasant slave am I! . *Hamlet* ii 2 575
Why, how now, Hamlet!—What's the matter now? . . . iii 4 13
Now or whensoever, provided I be so able as now . . . . v 2 210
If it be now, 'tis not to come; if it be not to come, it will be now; if it be not now, yet it will come: the readiness is all . . . v 2 232
If it were now to die, 'Twere now to be most happy . *Othello* ii 1 191
Your serpent of Egypt is bred now of your mud *Ant. and Cleo.* ii 7 29
Leave me, I pray, a little: pray you now: Nay, do so . . iii 11 22
No more tribute, pray you now . . . . . *Cymbeline* iii 1 46
How now! *Tempest* i 2: ii 1; v 1; *T. G. of Ver.* i 2; i 3; ii 1; iii 1; *Mer. Wives* i 1; i 4; *Meas. for Meas.* i 2; *Com. of Errors* ii 2; *Much Ado* i 2; *L. L. Lost* iv 3; *M. N. Dream* i 1; *Mer. of Venice* i 2; *T. of Shrew* iv 1; *T. Night* iii 4; *W. Tale* ii 2; 1 *Hen. VI.* iv 4; 2 *Hen. VI.* i 1; *Rom. and Jul.* iii 5; *Hamlet* iii 4
What now? . . . . . *Com. of Errors* i 2 42; *Troi. and Cres.* v 3 98

Now-a-days. To say the truth, reason and love keep little company together now-a-days . . . . . . *M. N. Dream* iii 1 148
We have many pocky corses now-a-days . . . . *Hamlet* v 1 181
Here's nothing to be got now-a-days, unless thou canst fish for't *Pericles* ii 1 73

Now and then. And swear but now and then . . *Mer. of Venice* ii 2 200
Loose now and then A scatter'd smile, and that I'll live upon *As Y. L. It* iii 5 103
A rogue, that now and then goes to the wars . . . *Hen. V.* iii 6 71
Now and then an ample tear trill'd down Her delicate cheek . *Lear* iv 3 14

Now-born. Whose ceremony Shall seem expedient on the now-born brief, And be perform'd to-night . . . . . *All's Well* ii 3 186

Nowhere. No, nor nowhere else but in your brain . *Mer. Wives* iv 2 166
I can no where find him like a man . . . . *As Y. Like It* ii 7 2

Noyance. The single and peculiar life is bound, With all the strength and armour of the mind, To keep itself from noyance . *Hamlet* iii 3 13

Nubibus. Under the which is writ, 'Invitis nubibus' 2 *Hen. VI.* iv 1 99

Numa. Ancus Marcius, Numa's daughter's son, Who, after great Hostilius, here was king . . . . . . *Coriolanus* ii 3 247

Numb. Yet are these feet, whose strengthless stay is numb, Unable to support this lump of clay . . . . 1 *Hen. VI.* ii 5 13
Gave himself, All thin and naked, to the numb cold night? *Richard III.* ii 1 117
Thy brother, I, Even like a stony image, cold and numb *T. Andron.* iii 1 259

Numbed. Strike in their numb'd and mortified bare arms Pins, wooden pricks, nails . . . . *Lear* ii 3 15

Number. How many numbers is in nouns?—Two.—Truly, I thought there had been one number more . . . . *Mer. Wives* iv 1 21
Hast thou no understandings for thy cases and the numbers of the genders? . . . . iv 1 72
This is the third time; I hope good luck lies in odd numbers . v 1 3
There is divinity in odd numbers, either in nativity, chance, or death . v 1 4
Our compell'd sins Stand more for number than for accompt *M. for M.* ii 4 58
A victory is twice itself when the achiever brings home full numbers *Much Ado* i 1 9
Here are only numbers ratified . . . . . *L. L. Lost* iv 2 125
These numbers will I tear, and write in prose . . . . iv 3 57
Now the number is even.—True, true; we are four . . . iv 3 211
In leaden contemplation have found out Such fiery numbers as the prompting eyes Of beauty's tutors have enrich'd you with . . iv 3 322
Nay, I have verses too, I thank Biron: The numbers true . . v 2 35
We number nothing that we spend for you . . . . . v 2 198
By all the vows that ever men have broke, In number more than ever women spoke . . . . *M. N. Dream* i 1 176
Every of this happy number That have endured shrewd days and nights with us Shall share the good . . . . *As Y. Like It* v 4 178
After our ship did split, When you and those poor number saved with you Hung on our driving boat . . . . *T. Night* i 2 10
'No man must know.' What follows? the numbers altered! . . ii 5 111
Belike you slew great number of his people . . . . iii 3 29
Or add a royal number to the dead . . . . . *K. John* ii 1 347
Amazement hurries up and down The little number of your doubtful friends . . . . v 1 36
From the number of his banish'd years Pluck'd four away . *Richard II.* i 3 210
Even so look'd he, Accomplish'd with the number of thy hours . . ii 1 177

Number. And all the number of his fair demands Shall be accomplish'd — Richard II. iii 3 123
The number of the king exceedeth ours: For God's sake, cousin, stay till all come in — 1 Hen. IV. iv 3 28
Shall we go draw our numbers and set on? — 2 Hen. IV. i 3 109
Had my sweet Harry had but half their numbers, To-day might I, hanging on Hotspur's neck, Have talk'd of Monmouth's grave — ii 3 43
Rumour doth double, like the voice and echo, The numbers of the fear'd — iii 1 98
Prick him, for we have a number of shadows to fill up the muster-book — iii 2 145
Here is two more called than your number; you must have but four here — iii 2 201
Send discoverers forth To know the numbers of our enemies — iv 1 4
I judge their number Upon or near the rate of thirty thousand — iv 1 21
That shall convert those tears By number into hours of happiness — v 2 61
Sorry am I his numbers are so few — Hen. V. iii 5 56
For the effusion of our blood, the muster of his kingdom too faint a number — iii 6 139
My people are with sickness much enfeebled, My numbers lessened — iii 6 155
Proud of their numbers and secure in soul — iv Prol. 17
Take from them now The sense of reckoning, if the opposed numbers Pluck their hearts from them — iv 1 308
Bring me just notice of the numbers dead On both our parts — iv 7 122
Are the dead number'd?—Here is the number of the slaughter'd French — iv 8 78
Of princes, in this number, And nobles bearing banners, there lie dead One hundred twenty six — iv 8 86
A royal fellowship of death! Where is the number of our English dead? — iv 8 107
I humbly pray them to admit the excuse Of time, of numbers — v Prol. 4
His mind is bent to holiness, To number Ave-Maries on his beads — 2 Hen. VI. i 3 59
Make up no factious numbers for the matter; In thine own person answer thy abuse — ii 1 40
A shame take all!—And, in the number, thee that wishest shame! — iii 1 308
The common people by numbers swarm to us — 3 Hen. VI. iv 2 2
Go, hie thee, hie thee from this slaughter-house, Lest thou increase the number of the dead — Richard III. iv 1 45
Who hath descried the number of the foe? — v 3 9
And condemn'd upon't.—I am sorry for't.—So are a number more — Hen. VIII. ii 1 9
So much I am happy Above a number — iii 1 34
Heart of our numbers, soul and only spirit — Troi. and Cres. i 3 56
'As true as Troilus' shall crown up the verse, And sanctify the numbers — iii 2 190
The dreadful Sagittary Appals our numbers: haste we — v 5 15
Take Convenient numbers to make good the city — Coriolanus i 5 13
A certain number, Though thanks to all, must I select from all — i 6 80
Presently, when you have drawn your number, Repair to the Capitol — ii 3 261
By mingling them with us, the honour'd number — iii 1 72
Within thine eyes sat twenty thousand deaths, In thy hands clutch'd as many millions, in Thy lying tongue both numbers — iii 3 72
Behold Dissentious numbers pestering streets — iv 6 7
Of five and twenty valiant sons, Half of the number that King Priam had, Behold the poor remains — T. Andron. i 1 80
I have invited many a guest, Such as I love; and you, among the store, One more, most welcome, makes my number more — Rom. and Jul. i 2 23
May stand in number, though in reckoning none — i 2 33
Now is he for the numbers that Petrarch flowed in — ii 4 41
What a number of men eat Timon, and he sees 'em not! — T. of Athens i 2 40
May these add to the number that may scald thee! — iii 1 54
But let not therefore my good friends be grieved—Among which number, Cassius, be you one — J. Cæsar i 2 44
Yet in the number I do know but one That unassailable holds on his rank — iii 1 68
Will you be prick'd in number of our friends? — iii 1 216
Cassius, go you into the other street, And part the numbers — iii 2 4
The enemy, marching along by them, By them shall make a fuller number up — iv 3 208
Norway himself, With terrible numbers — Macbeth i 2 51
Thereby shall we shadow The numbers of our host and make discovery Err in report of us — v 4 6
I am ill at these numbers; I have not art to reckon my groans — Hamlet ii 2 120
Fight for a plot Whereon the numbers cannot try the cause — iv 4 63
Sith that both charge and danger Speak 'gainst so great a number? — Lear ii 4 243
But kept a reservation to be follow'd With such a number — ii 4 256
Creeps apace Into the hearts of such as have not thrived Upon the present state, whose numbers threaten — Ant. and Cleo. i 3 52
Scribes, bards, poets, cannot Think, speak, cast, write, sing, number — iii 2 17
Let all the number of the stars give light To thy fair way! — iii 2 65
From which place We may the number of the ships behold — iii 9 3
The words of your commission Will tie you to the numbers and the time Of their dispatch.—We will discharge our duty — Cymbeline iii 7 15
Command our present numbers Be muster'd — iv 2 343
Let not our ships and number of our men Be like a beacon fired to amaze your eyes — Pericles i 4 86
I have cried her almost to the number of her hairs — iv 2 100
It gives a good report to a number to be chaste — iv 6 43

Numbered. How many weary steps, Of many weary miles you have o'ergone, Are number'd in the travel of one mile? — L. L. Lost v 2 197
Henceforth be never number'd among men! — M. N. Dream iii 2 67
Of as able body as when he numbered thirty — All's Well iv 5 86
When Viola from her birth Had number'd thirteen years — T. Night v 1 252
Are the dead number'd?—Here is the number of the slaughter'd French — Hen. V. iv 8 79
The sands are number'd that make up my life — 3 Hen. VI. i 4 25
A sibyl, that had number'd in the world The sun to course two hundred compasses, In her prophetic fury sew'd the work — Othello iii 4 70
The twinn'd stones Upon the number'd beach? — Cymbeline i 6 36

Numbering. The numbers true; and, were the numbering too, I were the fairest goddess on the ground — L. L. Lost v 2 35
The task he undertakes Is numbering sands and drinking oceans dry — Richard II. ii 2 146
Now hath time made me his numbering clock: My thoughts are minutes — v 5 50
Numbering our Ave-Maries with our beads? — 3 Hen. VI. ii 1 162

Numberless. There cannot be those numberless offences 'Gainst me, that I cannot take peace with — Hen. VIII. ii 1 84
That numberless upon me stuck as leaves Do on the oak — T. of Athens iv 3 263

Numbers. In the book of Numbers is it writ, When the man dies, let the inheritance Descend unto the daughter — Hen. V. i 2 98

Numbness. Bequeath to death your numbness — W. Tale v 3 102

Nun. And have you nuns no farther privileges? — Meas. for Meas. i 4 1
Endure the livery of a nun, For aye to be in shady cloister mew'd, To live a barren sister all your life — M. N. Dream i 1 70
A nun of winter's sisterhood kisses not more religiously — As Y. Like It iii 4 17
Leander, he would have lived many a fair year, though Hero had turned nun, if it had not been for a hot midsummer night — iv 1 102

Nun. As the nun's lip to the friar's mouth — All's Well ii 2 28
They shall be praying nuns, not weeping queens — Richard III. iv 4 201
Come, I'll dispose of thee Among a sisterhood of holy nuns — Rom. and Jul. v 3 157

Nuncio. She will attend it better in thy youth Than in a nuncio's of more grave aspect — T. Night i 4 28

Nuncle. How now, nuncle! Would I had two coxcombs and two daughters! — Lear i 4 117
Sirrah, I'll teach thee a speech.—Do.—Mark it, nuncle — i 4 130
Can you make no use of nothing, nuncle?—Why, no, boy — i 4 144
Give me an egg, nuncle, and I'll give thee two crowns — i 4 170
I have used it, nuncle, ever since thou madest thy daughters thy mother — i 4 187
Prithee, nuncle, keep a schoolmaster that can teach thy fool to lie — i 4 195
I had rather be any kind o' thing than a fool: and yet I would not be thee, nuncle — i 4 204
For, you know, nuncle, The hedge-sparrow fed the cuckoo so long — i 4 234
Nuncle Lear, nuncle Lear, tarry and take the fool with thee — i 4 338
If thou wert my fool, nuncle, I'ld have thee beaten for being old before thy time — i 5 45
Cry to it, nuncle, as the cockney did to the eels — ii 4 123
O nuncle, court holy-water in a dry house is better than this rain-water out o' door — iii 2 10
Good nuncle, in, and ask thy daughters' blessing — iii 2 12
Come not in here, nuncle, here's a spirit. Help me, help me! — iii 4 39
Prithee, nuncle, tell me whether a madman be a gentleman or a yeoman? — iii 6 10

Nunnery. Get thee to a nunnery: why wouldst thou be a breeder of sinners? I am myself indifferent honest — Hamlet iii 1 122
We are arrant knaves, all; believe none of us. Go thy ways to a nunnery — iii 1 132
Get thee to a nunnery, go: farewell. Or, if thou wilt needs marry, marry a fool — iii 1 142
To a nunnery, go, and quickly too. Farewell — iii 1 145

Nuptial. I have hope to see the nuptial Of these our dear-beloved solemnized — Tempest v 1 308
Affianced to her by oath, and the nuptial appointed — Meas. for Meas. iii 1 222
The nuptial finish'd, Let him be whipt and hang'd — v 1 518
This looks not like a nuptial — Much Ado iv 1 69
The catastrophe is a nuptial — L. L. Lost iv 1 78
Our nuptial hour Draws on apace — M. N. Dream i 1 1
I must employ you in some business Against our nuptial — i 1 125
Not sorting with a nuptial ceremony — v 1 55
Toil'd their unbreathed memories With this same play, against your nuptial — v 1 75
Straight shall our nuptial rites be solemnized — Mer. of Venice ii 9 6
Clubs cannot part them.—They shall be married to-morrow, and I will bid the duke to the nuptial — As Y. Like It v 2 47
Celebration of that nuptial which We two have sworn shall come — W. Tale iv 4 50
A father Is at the nuptial of his son a guest That best becomes the table — iv 4 406
Whom his grace affects, Must be companion of his nuptial bed — 1 Hen. VI. v 5 58
And lastly, to confirm that amity With nuptial knot — 3 Hen. VI. iii 3 55
This minion stood upon her chastity, Upon her nuptial vow — T. Andron. ii 3 125
'Tis since the nuptial of Lucentio, Come pentecost as quickly as it will, Some five and twenty years — Rom. and Jul. i 5 37
Banishment of friends, dissipation of cohorts, nuptial breaches — Lear i 2 162
Besides these beneficial news, it is the celebration of his nuptial — Othello ii 2 8
Yet there, my queen, We'll celebrate their nuptials — Pericles v 3 80

Nuptial-day. A play Intended for great Theseus' nuptial-day — M. N. D. iii 2 12
As merry as when our nuptial day was done — Coriolanus i 6 31

Nurse. That, like a testy babe, will scratch the nurse And presently all humbled kiss the rod! — T. G. of Ver. i 2 58
Time is the nurse and breeder of all good — iii 1 243
Which is in the manner of his nurse, or his dry nurse — Mer. Wives i 2 4
The baby beats the nurse, and quite athwart Goes all decorum — M. for M. i 3 30
Pardon is still the nurse of second woe — ii 1 298
I will attend my husband, be his nurse, Diet his sickness — Com. of Errors v 1 98
If you hear a child cry in the night, you must call to the nurse and bid her still it.—How if the nurse be asleep? — Much Ado iii 3 70
At first the infant, Mewling and puking in the nurse's arms — As Y. Like It ii 7 144
Let her never nurse her child herself, for she will breed it like a fool! — iv 1 178
Melancholy is the nurse of frenzy — T. of Shrew Ind. 2 135
I am glad you did not nurse him — W. Tale i 1 56
Commend it strangely to some place Where chance may nurse or end it — ii 3 183
Come on, poor babe: Some powerful spirit instruct the kites and ravens To be thy nurses! — ii 3 187
I am too old to fawn upon a nurse — Richard II. i 3 170
Sweet soil, adieu; My mother, and my nurse, that bears me yet! — i 3 307
This England, This nurse, this teeming womb of royal kings — ii 1 51
An if I were thy nurse, thy tongue to teach, 'Pardon' should be the first word of thy speech — v 3 113
O gentle sleep, Nature's soft nurse, how have I frighted thee? — 2 Hen. IV. iii 1 6
Mangled Peace, Dear nurse of arts, plenties and joyful births — Hen. V. v 2 35
Being put to nurse, Was by a beggar-woman stolen away — 2 Hen. VI. iv 2 150
I am your sorrow's nurse, And I will pamper it with lamentations — Richard III. ii 2 87
Who told thee this?—Grandam, his nurse.—His nurse! why, she was dead ere thou wert born — ii 4 32
Rough cradle for such little pretty ones! Rude ragged nurse! — iv 1 102
Rome, the nurse of judgement — Hen. VIII. ii 2 94
Truth shall nurse her, Holy and heavenly thoughts still counsel her — v 5 29
The bleared sights Are spectacled to see him: your prattling nurse Into a rapture lets her baby cry While she chats him — Coriolanus ii 1 222
Alack, or we must lose The country, our dear nurse, or else thy person, Our comfort in the country — v 3 110
But at his nurse's tears He whined and roar'd away your victory — v 6 97
She will a handmaid be to his desires, A loving nurse — T. Andron. i 1 332
Be unto us as is a nurse's song Of lullaby to bring her babe asleep — ii 3 28
It shall not die.—Aaron, it must; the mother wills it so.—What, must it, nurse? — iv 2 83
The midwife and the nurse well made away, Then let the ladies tattle — iv 2 167
Nurse, where's my daughter? call her forth to me — Rom. and Jul. i 3 1
Nurse, give leave awhile, We must talk in secret:—nurse, come back again — i 3 7
It stinted and said 'Ay.'—And stint thou too, I pray thee, nurse, say I — i 3 58
Were not I thine only nurse, I would say thou hadst suck'd wisdom from thy teat — i 3 67
The nurse cursed in the pantry, and every thing in extremity — i 3 102
I hear some noise within; dear love, adieu! Anon, good nurse! — ii 2 137
A gentleman, nurse, that loves to hear himself talk — ii 4 155
What wilt thou tell her, nurse? thou dost not mark me — ii 4 187

Nurse. And stay, good nurse, behind the abbey wall: Within this hour my man shall be with thee, And bring thee cords . *Rom. and Jul.* ii 4 199
What say'st thou, my dear nurse?—Is your man secret? . . . ii 4 207
The clock struck nine when I did send the nurse; In half an hour she promised to return . . . . ii 5 1
O honey nurse, what news? Hast thou met with him? . . . . ii 5 18
Now, good sweet nurse,—O Lord, why look'st thou sad? . . . . ii 5 21
Sweet, sweet, sweet nurse, tell me, what says my love? . . . . ii 5 55
Hie you to the cell.—Hie to high fortune! Honest nurse, farewell . ii 5 80
O, here comes my nurse, And she brings news . . . . . . iii 2 31
Now, nurse, what news? What hast thou there? the cords? . . . iii 2 34
Where is my father, and my mother, nurse?—Weeping and wailing over Tybalt's corse . . . . iii 2 127
Come, nurse; I'll to my wedding-bed; And death, not Romeo, take my maidenhead! . . . . iii 2 136
Nurse!—Ah sir! ah sir! Well, death's the end of all . . . . iii 3 91
Go before, nurse: commend me to thy lady . . . . . . iii 3 155
O God!—O nurse, how shall this be prevented? . . . . . iii 5 206
What say'st thou? hast thou not a word of joy? Some comfort, nurse iii 5 214
To-morrow night look that thou lie alone; Let not thy nurse lie with thee in thy chamber . . . . iv 1 92
But, gentle nurse, I pray thee, leave me to myself to-night . . iv 3 1
Let me now be left alone, And let the nurse this night sit up with you iv 3 10
I'll call them back again to comfort me: Nurse! What should she do here? . . . . iv 3 18
Fetch more spices, nurse.—They call for dates and quinces in the pastry iv 4 1
Nurse! Wife! What, ho! What, nurse, I say! Go waken Juliet . iv 4 23
And to the marriage Her nurse is privy . . . . . . v 3 266
Never palates more the dug, The beggar's nurse and Cæsar's *A. and C.* v 2 8
Dost thou not see my baby at my breast, That sucks the nurse asleep? v 2 313
Thou wast their nurse; they took thee for their mother . *Cymbeline* iii 3 104
Their nurse, Euriphile, Whom for the theft I wedded, stole these children . . . . v 5 340
You have A nurse of me . . . . *Pericles* iv 1 25
My father, as nurse said, did never fear, But cried, 'Good seamen!' . iv 1 53
She is dead. Nurses are not the fates To foster it, nor ever to preserve iv 3 14
As my good nurse Lychorida hath oft Deliver'd weeping . . . v 1 161
Nursed. Thou art not noble; For all the accommodations that thou bear'st Are nursed by baseness . . . . . . *Meas. for Meas.* iii 1 15
A Bohemian born, but here nursed up and bred . . . . . iv 2 134
And they have nursed this woe, in feeding life . . *T. Andron.* iii 1 74
Thou wast the prettiest babe that e'er I nursed . *Rom. and Jul.* i 3 60
A good lady, and a wise and virtuous: I nursed her daughter . . i 5 117
She at Tarsus Was nursed with Cleon . . . . . *Pericles* v 3 8
Nurse-like. So duteous, diligent, So tender over his occasions, true, So feat, so nurse-like . . . . *Cymbeline* v 5 88
Nurser. See, where he lies inhearsed in the arms Of the most bloody nurser of his harms! . . . . *1 Hen. VI.* iv 7 46
Nursery. Fair Padua, nursery of arts . . . . *T. of Shrew* i 1 2
A nursery to our gentry, who are sick For breathing and exploit *All's W.* i 2 16
Breed a nursery of like evil, To overbulk us all . . *Troi. and Cres.* i 3 319
I loved her most, and thought to set my rest On her kind nursery *Lear* i 1 126
From their nursery Were stol'n, and to this hour no guess in knowledge Which way they went . . . . *Cymbeline* i 1 59
Nursh-a. De maid is love-a me: my nursh-a Quickly tell me so mush *Mer. Wives* iii 2 66
Nursing. Ere he would have hanged a man for the getting a hundred bastards, he would have paid for the nursing a thousand *M. for M.* iii 2 126
Nursing. How have you known the miseries of your father?—By nursing them . . . . *Lear* v 3 181
First pay me for the nursing of thy sons; And let it be confiscate all, so soon As I have received it.—Nursing of my sons! . *Cymbeline* v 5 322
There I'll leave it At careful nursing . . . . . *Pericles* iii 1 81
Nurture. A born devil, on whose nature Nurture can never stick *Tempest* iv 1 189
Yet am I inland bred And know some nurture . . . *As Y. Like It* ii 7 97
Nut. A hair, a drop of blood, a pin, A nut, a cherry-stone *Com. of Errors* iv 3 74
I have a venturous fairy that shall seek The squirrel's hoard, and fetch thee new nuts . . . . *M. N. Dream* iv 1 40
Sweetest nut hath sourest rind, Such a nut is Rosalind . *As Y. Like It* iii 2 116
I do think him as concave as a covered goblet or a worm-eaten nut . iii 4 27
There can be no kernel in this light nut . . . *All's Well* ii 5 48
Were as good crack a fusty nut with no kernel . *Troi. and Cres.* ii 1 111
Thou wilt quarrel with a man for cracking nuts . *Rom. and Jul.* iii 1 21
Nuthook. I will say 'marry trap' with you, if you run the nuthook's humour on me; that is the very note of it . . . *Mer. Wives* i 1 171
Nut-hook, nut-hook, you lie. Come on; I'll tell thee what . *2 Hen. IV.* v 4 8
Nutmeg. Gave Hector a gift,— A gilt nutmeg.—A lemon . *L. L. Lost* v 2 652
Mace; dates?—none, that's out of my note; nutmegs, seven *W. Tale* iv 3 50
He's of the colour of the nutmeg.—And of the heat of the ginger *Hen. V.* iii 7 20
Nutriment. Has my lord's meat in him: Why should it thrive and turn to nutriment, When he is turn'd to poison? . . . *T. of Athens* iii 1 61
Nutshell. Though the ship were no stronger than a nutshell *Tempest* i 1 50
I could be bounded in a nutshell and count myself a king of infinite space, were it not that I have bad dreams . . . . *Hamlet* ii 2 260
Nym. Your cony-catching rascals, Bardolph, Nym, and Pistol *Mer. Wives* i 1 129
My name is Corporal Nym; I speak and I avouch; 'tis true: my name is Nym . . . . ii 1 138
I have grated upon my good friends for three reprieves for you and your coach-fellow Nym . . . . ii 2 7
One Nym, sir, that beguiled him of a chain . . . . . iv 5 33
Good Corporal Nym, show thy valour, and put up your sword *Hen. V.* ii 1 45
Corporal Nym, an thou wilt be friends, be friends . . . . ii 1 107
I'll live by Nym, and Nym shall live by me; Is not this just? . . ii 1 115
Nym, thou hast spoke the right; His heart is fracted and corroborate . ii 1 129
Nym, rouse thy vaunting veins: Boy, bristle thy courage up . . ii 3 4
For Nym, he hath heard that men of few words are the best men . . iii 2 38
Nym and Bardolph are sworn brothers in filching . . . . iii 2 47
Nymph. Go make thyself like a nymph o' the sea . . . *Tempest* i 2 301
Which spongy April at thy hest betrims, To make cold nymphs chaste crowns . . . . iv 1 66
You nymphs, call'd Naiads, of the windring brooks . . . . iv 1 128
Come, temperate nymphs, and help to celebrate A contract of true love iv 1 132
And these fresh nymphs encounter every one In country footing . iv 1 137
Thou gentle nymph, cherish thy forlorn swain! . . *T. G. of Ver.* v 4 12
Fare thee well, nymph; ere he do leave this grove, Thou shalt fly him and he shall seek thy love . . . . . . *M. N. Dream* ii 1 245
O Helen, goddess, nymph, perfect, divine! . . . . . iii 2 137
Who even but now did spurn me with his foot, To call me goddess, nymph . . . . iii 2 226
But, soft! what nymphs are these?—My lord, this is my daughter . iv 1 132
Or modest Dian circled with her nymphs . . . *3 Hen. VI.* iv 8 21
And want love's majesty To strut before a wanton ambling nymph *Richard III.* i 1 17
Like the stately Phœbe 'mongst her nymphs . . *T. Andron.* i 1 316
To wanton with this queen, This goddess, this Semiramis, this nymph . ii 1 22
Nymph, in thy orisons Be all my sins remember'd . . . *Hamlet* iii 1 89

O

O. O that your face were not so full of O's! . . . . . *L. L. Lost* v 2 45
More engilds the night Than all yon fiery oes and eyes of light *M. N. D.* iii 2 188
Or may we cram Within this wooden O the very casques That did affright the air at Agincourt? . . . . *Hen. V.* Prol. 13
Rise and stand; Why should you fall into so deep an O? *Rom. and Jul.* iii 3 90
Now thou art an O without a figure: I am better than thou art *Lear* i 4 212
His face was as the heavens; and therein stuck A sun and moon, which kept their course, and lighted The little O, the earth *Ant. and Cleo.* v 2 81
Like a full-acorn'd boar, a German one, Cried 'O!' and mounted *Cymb.* ii 5 17
Oak. I will rend an oak And peg thee in his knotty entrails . *Tempest* i 2 294
And rifted Jove's stout oak With his own bolt . . . . . v 1 45
At still midnight, Walk round about an oak . . *Mer. Wives* iv 4 31
There want not many that do fear In deep of night to walk by this Herne's oak . . . . iv 4 40
This is our device; That Falstaff at that oak shall meet with us . iv 4 42
To-night at Herne's oak, just 'twixt twelve and one . . . iv 6 19
Be you in the Park about midnight, at Herne's oak . . . . v 1 12
They are all couched in a pit hard by Herne's oak . . . . v 3 15
Our dance of custom round about the oak Of Herne the hunter . . v 5 79
Thou rather with thy sharp and sulphurous bolt Split'st the unwedgeable and gnarled oak Than the soft myrtle . . *Meas. for Meas.* ii 2 116
An oak but with one green leaf on it would have answered her *M. Ado* ii 1 247
Those thoughts to me were oaks, to thee like osiers bow'd *L. L. Lost* iv 2 112
At the duke's oak we meet . . . . . . *M. N. Dream* i 2 113
Under an oak whose antique root peeps out Upon the brook *As Y. Like It* ii 1 31
Under an oak, whose boughs were moss'd with age . . . . iv 3 105
His opinion, which is rotten As ever oak or stone was sound . *W. Tale* ii 3 90
And many strokes, though with a little axe, Hew down and fell the hardest-timber'd oak . . . . *3 Hen. VI.* ii 1 55
The splitting wind Makes flexible the knees of knotted oaks *T. and C.* i 3 50
Swims with fins of lead And hews down oaks with rushes . *Coriolanus* i 1 185
To a cruel war I sent him; from whence he returned, his brows bound with oak . . . . i 3 16
He proved best man i' the field, and for his meed Was brow-bound with the oak . . . . ii 2 102
He's the rock, the oak not to be wind-shaken . . . . . v 2 117
Yet to charge thy sulphur with a bolt That should but rive an oak . v 3 153
That numberless upon me stuck as leaves Do on the oak *T. of Athens* iv 3 264
Oak. The oaks bear mast, the briers scarlet hips . *T. of Athens* iv 3 422
Tempests, when the scolding winds Have rived the knotty oaks *J. Cæsar* i 3 6
What ribs of oak, when mountains melt on them, Can hold the mortise? *Othello* ii 1 8
To seel her father's eyes up close as oak . . . . . iii 3 210
Care no more to clothe and eat; To thee the reed is as the oak *Cymbeline* iv 2 267
Oak-cleaving. Vaunt-couriers to oak-cleaving thunderbolts . *Lear* iii 2 5
Oaken. He comes the third time home with the oaken garland *Coriolanus* ii 1 138
Oar. Thou art to post after with oars . . . *T. G. of Ver.* i 3 37
The pleasant'st angling is to see the fish Cut with her golden oars the silver stream . . . . *Much Ado* iii 1 27
The oars were silver, Which to the tune of flutes kept stroke *A. and C.* ii 2 199
Oar'd Himself with his good arms in lusty stroke To the shore *Tempest* ii 1 118
Oaten. When shepherds pipe on oaten straws . . *L. L. Lost* v 2 913
Oath. The strongest oaths are straw To the fire i' the blood *Tempest* iv 1 52
Now, blasphemy, That swear'st grace o'erboard, not an oath on shore? v 1 219
Here is her oath for love, her honour's pawn . *T. G. of Ver.* i 3 47
And even that power which gave me first my oath Provokes me to this threefold perjury . . . . ii 6 4
With twenty thousand soul-confirming oaths . . . . . ii 6 16
A thousand oaths, an ocean of his tears . . . . . . ii 7 69
His words are bonds, his oaths are oracles, His love sincere . . ii 7 75
Stuff'd with protestations And full of new-found oaths . . . iv 4 135
For whose dear sake thou didst then rend thy faith Into a thousand oaths; and all those oaths Descended into perjury . . . . v 4 48
Behold her that gave aim to all thy oaths, And entertain'd 'em deeply . v 4 101
Your red-lattice phrases, and your bold-beating oaths *Mer. Wives* ii 2 29
Affianced to her by oath, and the nuptial appointed *Meas. for Meas.* iii 1 222
Pardon me, good father; it is against my oath . . . . iv 2 195
What he with his oath And all probation will make up full clear . v 1 156
Think'st thou thy oaths, Though they would swear down each particular saint, Were testimonies against his worth and credit? . v 1 242
Against our laws, Against my crown, my oath, my dignity *Com. of Errors* i 1 144
With circumstance and oaths so to deny This chain . . . . v 1 16
It is a branch and parcel of mine oath, A charitable duty of my order . v 1 106
I'll take my oath on it, till he have made an oyster of me . *Much Ado* ii 3 26
Partly by his oaths, which first possessed them . . . . iii 3 166
Your oaths are pass'd; and now subscribe your names . *L. L. Lost* i 1 19

Oath. If you are arm'd to do as sworn to do, Subscribe to your deep oaths *L. L. Lost* i 1 23
Your oath is pass'd to pass away from these i 1 49
Or, having sworn too hard a keeping oath, Study to break it i 1 65
Although I seem so loath, I am the last that will last keep his oath i 1 161
These oaths and laws will prove an idle scorn i 1 311
He and his competitors in oath Were all address'd to meet you ii 1 82
Than seek a dispensation for his oath, To let you enter ii 1 87
Hear me, dear lady; I have sworn an oath ii 1 97
'Tis deadly sin to keep that oath, my lord, And sin to break it ii 1 105
What fool is not so wise To lose an oath to win a paradise? iv 3 73
And Jove, for your love, would infringe an oath iv 3 144
O, who can give an oath? where is a book? That I may swear iv 3 250
Let us once lose our oaths to find ourselves, Or else we lose ourselves to keep our oaths iv 3 362
The virtue of your eye must break my oath v 2 348
I hate a breaking cause to be Of heavenly oaths, vow'd with integrity v 2 356
Your oath once broke, you force not to forswear.—Despise me, when I break this oath of mine v 2 440
By my life, my troth, I never swore this lady such an oath v 2 451
For your fair sakes have we neglected time, Play'd foul play with our oaths v 2 766
In your heavenly eyes, Have misbecomed our oaths and gravities v 2 778
This shall you do for me: Your oath I will not trust v 2 804
He hail'd down oaths that he was only mine *M. N. Dream* i 1 243
So he dissolved, and showers of oaths did melt i 1 245
Two bosoms interchained with an oath ii 2 49
One man holding troth, A million fail, confounding oath on oath iii 2 93
Weigh oath with oath, and you will nothing weigh iii 2 131
Hath ta'en his oath, And comes to his election presently *Mer. of Venice* ii 9 2
I am enjoin'd by oath to observe three things ii 9 9
I'll keep my oath, Patiently to bear my wroth ii 9 77
Swearing till my very roof was dry With oaths of love iii 2 207
I have sworn an oath that I will have my bond iii 3 5
An oath, an oath, I have an oath in heaven: Shall I lay perjury upon my soul? iv 1 228
Though not for me, yet for your vehement oaths, You should have been respective and have kept it v 1 155
A thing stuck on with oaths upon your finger v 1 168
Swear by your double self, And there's an oath of credit v 1 246
By my soul I swear I never more will break an oath with thee v 1 248
When I break that oath, let me turn monster *As Y. Like It* i 2 23
By mine honour, but I was bid to come for you.—Where learned you that oath? i 2 65
Then a soldier, Full of strange oaths and bearded like the pard ii 7 150
The oath of a lover is no stronger than the word of a tapster iii 4 33
Speaks brave words, swears brave oaths and breaks them bravely iii 4 44
And so God mend me, and by all pretty oaths that are not dangerous iv 1 193
That thinks with oaths to face the matter out *T. of Shrew* ii 1 291
Protesting oath on oath, That in a twink she won me to her love ii 1 311
And here I take the like unfeigned oath, Never to marry with her iv 2 32
That I may surely keep mine oath, I will be married to a wealthy widow iv 2 36
With oaths kept waking and with brawling fed iv 3 10
Oaths, tokens, and all these engines of lust *All's Well* iii 5 20
With the divine forfeit of his soul upon oath iii 6 34
Three great oaths would scarce make that be believed iv 1 64
'Tis not the many oaths that makes the truth, But the plain single vow that is vow'd true iv 2 21
If I should swear by God's great attributes, I loved you dearly, would you believe my oaths, When I did love you ill? iv 2 26
Therefore your oaths Are words and poor conditions, but unseal'd iv 2 29
She says all men Have the like oaths iv 2 71
When he swears oaths, bid him drop gold, and take it iv 3 252
He professes not keeping of oaths; in breaking 'em he is stronger than Hercules iv 3 282
Ask him upon his oath, if he does think He had not my virginity v 3 185
Legitimate, sir, upon the oaths of judgement and reason *T. Night* iii 2 16
A terrible oath, with a swaggering accent sharply twanged off iii 4 197
There's no remedy, sir; he will fight with you for's oath sake iii 4 326
Pray God, he keep his oath!—I do assure you, 'tis against my will iii 4 341
I had thought, sir, to have held my peace until You had drawn oaths from him not to stay *W. Tale* i 2 29
Though you would seek to unsphere the stars with oaths i 2 48
As or by oath remove or counsel shake The fabric of his folly i 2 428
She's dead; I'll swear't. If word nor oath Prevail not, go and see iii 2 204
The thrower-out Of my poor babe, according to thine oath iii 3 30
And most accursed am I To be by oath enjoin'd to this iii 3 53
It becomes thy oath full well, Thou to me thy secrets tell iv 4 306
Not . . . for all the sun sees or The close earth wombs or the profound seas hides In unknown fathoms, will I break my oath iv 4 502
Good my lords, bear witness to his oath.—You tempt him over-much v 1 72
I do not believe thee, man; I have a king's oath to the contrary *K. John* iii 1 10
Like a civil war set'st oath to oath, Thy tongue against thy tongue iii 1 264
And makest an oath the surety for thy truth Against an oath iii 1 282
Thy voluntary oath Lives in this bosom, dearly cherished iii 3 23
Remember well, Upon your oath of service to the pope v 1 23
Hast thou, according to thy oath and band, Brought hither? *Richard II.* i 1 2
Speak truly, on thy knighthood and thy oath i 3 14
Engaged by my oath—Which God defend a knight should violate! i 3 17
Take an oath with thee. Lay on our royal sword your banish'd hands i 3 178
Keep the oath that we administer: You never shall, so help you truth and God! i 3 182
The one is my sovereign, whom both my oath And duty bids defend ii 2 112
Let him ne'er see joy that breaks that oath! ii 3 151
God pardon all oaths that are broke to me! iv 1 214
Cracking the strong warrant of an oath, Mark'd with a blot iv 1 235
Let me unkiss the oath 'twixt thee and me; And yet not so, for with a kiss 'twas made v 1 74
And givest such sarcenet surety for thy oaths *1 Hen. IV.* iii 1 256
Swear me, Kate, like a lady as thou art, A good mouth-filling oath iii 1 259
I would swear by thy face; my oath should be, 'By this fire' iii 3 39
Laid gifts before him, proffer'd him their oaths iv 3 71
Broke oath on oath, committed wrong on wrong iv 3 101
You swore to us, And you did swear that oath at Doncaster v 1 42
O, it is much that a lie with a slight oath and a jest with a sad brow will do with a fellow! *2 Hen. IV.* v 1 92
As I am a soldier.—An oath of mickle might *Hen. V.* ii 1 70
By this sword, I will.—Sword is an oath, and oaths must have their course ii 1 106
For oaths are straws, men's faiths are wafer-cakes ii 3 53
Oath. Which they trick up with new-tuned oaths *Hen. V.* iii 6 80
By the white hand of my lady, he's a gallant prince.—Swear by her foot, that she may tread out the oath iii 7 104
Is it fit this soldier keep his oath?—He is a craven and a villain else iv 7 138
It is necessary, look your grace, that he keep his vow and his oath iv 7 147
Downright oaths, which I never use till urged, nor never break for urging v 2 151
We'll take your oath, And all the peers', for surety of our leagues v 2 399
And may our oaths well kept and prosperous be! v 2 402
Remember, lords, your oaths to Henry sworn *1 Hen. VI.* i 1 162
Take your oath, That you elect no other king but him iv 1 3
Can this be so, That in alliance, amity and oaths, There should be found such false dissembling guile? iv 1 62
Deface your honour with reproach?—As doth a ruler with unlawful oaths v 5 30
A dreadful oath, sworn with a solemn tongue! *2 Hen. VI.* iii 2 158
Against thy oath and true allegiance sworn v 1 20
Canst thou dispense with heaven for such an oath? v 1 181
It is great sin to swear unto a sin, But greater sin to keep a sinful oath v 1 183
No other reason for this wrong But that he was bound by a solemn oath? v 1 190
Take an oath To cease this civil war *3 Hen. VI.* i 1 196
This oath I willingly take and will perform i 1 201
I took an oath that he should quietly reign i 2 15
For a kingdom any oath may be broken: I would break a thousand oaths to reign one year i 2 16
An oath is of no moment, being not took Before a true and lawful magistrate i 2 22
Your oath, my lord, is vain and frivolous. Therefore, to arms! i 2 27
And trust not simple Henry nor his oaths i 2 59
But how is it that great Plantagenet Is crown'd so soon, and broke his solemn oath? i 4 100
Rob his temples of the diadem, Now in his life, against your holy oath? i 4 105
Here's for my oath, here's for my father's death i 4 175
To dash our late decree in parliament Touching King Henry's oath ii 1 119
He swore consent to your succession, His oath enrolled in the parliament ii 1 173
All the crew are gone, To frustrate both his oath and what beside ii 1 175
I was adopted heir by his consent: Since when, his oath is broke ii 2 89
What, not an oath? nay, then the world goes hard When Clifford cannot spare his friends an oath ii 6 77
Did you never swear, and break an oath?—No, never such an oath iii 1 72
And tell me, then, have you not broke your oaths?—No iii 1 79
But do not break your oaths; for of that sin My mild entreaty shall not make you guilty iii 1 90
Perhaps thou wilt object my holy oath: To keep that oath were more impiety Than Jephthah's v 1 89
I am bound by oath, and therefore pardon me *Richard III.* iv 1 28
I swear— By nothing; for this is no oath iv 4 368
If thou hadst fear'd to break an oath by Him, The unity the king thy brother made Had not been broken iv 4 378
If thou hadst fear'd to break an oath by Him, The imperial metal, circling now thy brow, Had graced the tender temples of my child iv 4 381
To whom by oath he menaced Revenge *Hen. VIII.* i 2 137
Mounting his eyes, He did discharge a horrible oath i 2 206
Swear the oaths now to her that you have sworn to me *Troi. and Cres.* iii 2 44
When their rhymes, Full of protest, of oath and big compare, Want similes iii 2 182
By Mars his gauntlet, thanks! Mock not, that I affect the untraded oath iv 5 178
Both taxing me and gaging me to keep An oath that I have sworn v 1 47
Do not hold me to mine oath; Bid me do any thing but that v 2 26
What he would do, He sent in writing after me; what he would not, Bound with an oath to yield to his conditions *Coriolanus* v 1 69
Breaking his oath and resolution like A twist of rotten silk v 6 95
Who should I swear by? thou believest no god: That granted, how canst thou believe an oath? *T. Andron.* v 1 72
Yet, for I know thou art religious, . . . Therefore I urge thy oath v 1 78
I know An idiot holds his bauble for a god And keeps the oath which by that god he swears v 1 80
Grant I may never prove so fond, To trust man on his oath *T. of Athens* i 2 66
Spare your oaths, I'll trust to your conditions iv 3 138
To stale with ordinary oaths my love To every new protester *J. Cæsar* i 2 73
Let us swear our resolution.—No, not an oath ii 1 114
What other oath Than honesty to honesty engaged, That this shall be? ii 1 126
To think that or our cause or our performance Did need an oath ii 1 136
Come now, keep thine oath; Now be a freeman v 3 40
Propose the oath, my lord.—Never to speak of this *Hamlet* i 5 152
Makes marriage-vows As false as dicers' oaths iii 4 45
Indeed, la, without an oath, I'll make an end on't iv 5 57
Dower'd with our curse, and stranger'd with our oath *Lear* i 1 207
Swore as many oaths as I spake words, and broke them iii 4 90
He's mad that trusts in the tameness of a wolf, a horse's health, a boy's love, or a whore's oath iii 6 21
I here take my oath before this honourable assembly, she kicked the poor king her father iii 6 49
It is the privilege of mine honours, My oath, and my profession v 3 130
I heard the clink and fall of swords, And Cassio high in oath *Othello* ii 3 235
To deny each article with oath Cannot remove nor choke the strong conception That I do groan withal v 2 54
You have broken The article of your oath *Ant. and Cleo.* ii 2 82
But, on, Cæsar; The article of my oath ii 2 87
This hand, whose touch, whose every touch, would force the feeler's soul To the oath of loyalty *Cymbeline* i 6 102
Must take me up for swearing; as if I borrowed mine oaths of him and might not spend them at my pleasure ii 1 5
When a gentleman is disposed to swear, it is not for any standers-by to curtail his oaths ii 1 12
Whose strength I will confirm with oath ii 4 64
Two villains, whose false oaths prevail'd Before my perfect honour iii 3 66
I'll take thy word for faith, not ask thine oath: Who shuns not to break one will sure crack both *Pericles* i 2 120
If a king bid a man be a villain, he's bound by the indenture of his oath to be one i 3 9
Thy oath remember; thou hast sworn to do't: 'Tis but a blow iv 1 1
Oathable. You are not oathable *T. of Athens* iv 3 135
Oath-breaking. I told him gently of our grievances, Of his oath-breaking *1 Hen. IV.* v 2 38
Oats. Rich leas Of wheat, rye, barley, vetches, oats and pease *Tempest* iv 1 61
A peck of provender: I could munch your good dry oats *M. N. Dream* iv 1 36
The oats have eaten the horses *T. of Shrew* iii 2 207
Poor fellow, never joyed since the price of oats rose *1 Hen. IV.* ii 1 14
I cannot draw a cart, nor eat dried oats; If it be man's work, I'll do't *Lear* v 3 38

Ob. Item, Bread, ob.—O monstrous! but one half-pennyworth of bread to this intolerable deal of sack! . 1 *Hen. IV.* ii 4 590
Obduracy. Thou thinkest me as far in the devil's book as thou and Falstaff for obduracy and persistency . 2 *Hen. IV.* ii 2 50
Obdurate. If your heart be so obdurate, Vouchsafe me yet your picture for my love . *T. G. of Ver.* iv 2 120
Since he stands obdurate And that no lawful means can carry me Out of his envy's reach . *Mer. of Venice* iv 1 8
If when you make your prayers, God should be so obdurate as yourselves, How would it fare with your departed souls? 2 *Hen. VI.* iv 7 122
Stern, obdurate, flinty, rough, remorseless . 3 *Hen. VI.* i 4 142
Be sudden in the execution, Withal obdurate, do not hear him plead *Richard III.* i 3 347
But if she be obdurate To mild entreaties . iii 1 39
Be not obdurate, open thy deaf ears . *T. Andron.* ii 3 160
Obedience. Weigh'd between loathness and obedience . *Tempest* ii 1 130
Answer his requiring with a plausible obedience *Meas. for Meas.* iii 1 254
Turn'd her obedience, which is due to me, To stubborn harshness *M. N. Dream* i 1 37
My lord and husband; I am your wife in all obedience *T. of Shrew* Ind. 2 109
Show more sign of her obedience, Her new-built virtue and obedience . v 2 117
Craves no other tribute at thy hands But love, fair looks and true obedience . v 2 153
My ground to do't Is the obedience to a master *W. Tale* i 2 354
Commend my best obedience to the queen . ii 2 36
And make them tame to their obedience . *K. John* iv 2 262
The purpose of the king: From whose obedience I forbid my soul . iv 3 64
Our discontented counties do revolt; Our people quarrel with obedience v 1 9
And calmly run on in obedience . v 4 56
When, Harry, when? Obedience bids I should not bid again *Richard II.* i 1 163
And true obedience, of this madness cured, Stoop tamely 2 *Hen. IV.* iv 2 41
Let me no more from this obedience rise . iv 5 147
To which is fixed, as an aim or butt, Obedience . *Hen. V.* i 2 187
Our obedience to the king wipes the crime of it out of us . iv 1 138
Bring him in obedience to your yoke . 1 *Hen. VI.* v 1 164
Vows obedience And humble service till the point of death . v 1 167
This arm, that hath reclaim'd To your obedience fifty fortresses . iii 4 6
If you mind to hold your true obedience, Give me assurance 3 *Hen. VI.* iv 1 140
Put meekness in thy mind, Love, charity, obedience! *Richard III.* ii 2 108
This tractable obedience is a slave To each incensed will . *Hen. VIII.* i 2 64
I do not know What kind of my obedience I should tender; More than my all is nothing . ii 3 66
Speak my thanks and my obedience, As from a blushing handmaid . ii 3 71
I have been your wife, in this obedience, Upward of twenty years . ii 4 35
Out of his noble nature, Zeal and obedience he still bore your grace . iii 1 63
All the fellowship I hold now with him Is only my obedience . iii 1 122
The hearts of princes kiss obedience, So much they love it . iii 1 162
One that, in all obedience, makes the church The chief aim of his honour v 3 117
Who should withhold me? Not fate, obedience . *Troi. and Cres.* v 3 52
Their obedience fails To the greater bench . *Coriolanus* iii 1 166
Have we not had a taste of his obedience? . iii 1 318
Matrons, turn incontinent! Obedience fail in children! *T. of Athens* iv 1 4
Broke their stalls, flung out, Contending 'gainst obedience . *Macbeth* ii 4 17
March we on, To give obedience where 'tis truly owed . v 2 26
That which should accompany old age, As honour, love, obedience . v 3 25
Who, in her duty and obedience, mark, Hath given me this . *Hamlet* ii 2 107
This, in obedience, hath my daughter shown me . ii 2 125
You have obedience scanted, And well are worth the want . *Lear* i 1 281
It would make a great gap in your own honour, and shake in pieces the heart of his obedience . i 2 92
Liars, and adulterers, by an enforced obedience of planetary influence . i 2 135
Whose virtue and obedience doth this instant So much commend itself ii 1 115
O heavens, If you do love old men, if your sweet sway Allow obedience ii 4 194
Come hither, gentle mistress: Do you perceive in all this noble company Where most you owe obedience? . *Othello* i 3 180
I hourly learn A doctrine of obedience . *Ant. and Cleo.* v 2 31
Past grace? obedience?—Past hope, and in despair . *Cymbeline* i 1 136
You sin against Obedience, which you owe your father . iii 3 117
When thou see'st him, A little witness my obedience . iii 4 68
You must forget to be a woman; change Command into obedience . iii 4 158
Obedient. Whom I, with this obedient steel, three inches of it, Can lay to bed for ever . *Tempest* ii 1 283
She seemingly obedient likewise hath Made promise to the doctor *M. W.* iv 6 33
Always obedient to your grace's will . *Meas. for Meas.* i 1 26
Floating straight, obedient to the stream . *Com. of Errors* i 1 87
Kisses the base ground with obedient breast? . *L. L. Lost* iv 3 225
Sith it your pleasure is, And I am tied to be obedient . *T. of Shrew* i 1 217
These kites That bate and beat and will not be obedient . iv 1 199
And he whose wife is most obedient To come at first when he doth send for her, Shall win the wager . v 2 67
Froward, peevish, sullen, sour, And not obedient to his honest will . v 2 158
Do thine own fortunes that obedient right . *All's Well* ii 3 167
I can nothing say, But that I am your most obedient servant . ii 5 77
Seven of my people, with an obedient start, make out for him *T. Night* ii 5 64
Acting this in an obedient hope . v 1 348
Your most obedient counsellor . *W. Tale* ii 3 55
If my reason Will thereto be obedient, I have reason . iv 4 494
And move in that obedient orb again . 1 *Hen. IV.* v 1 17
Call my sovereign yours, And do him homage as obedient subjects 1 *Hen. VI.* iv 2 7
Like obedient subjects, follow him To his new kingdom *Richard III.* ii 2 45
And your most obedient subject.—Art thou, indeed? . iv 2 68
A loyal and obedient subject is Therein illustrated . *Hen. VIII.* iii 2 180
Would poison were obedient and knew my mind! *T. of Athens* iv 3 296
I had daughters.—Which they will make an obedient father . *Lear* i 4 255
Whate'er you be, I am obedient . *Othello* iii 3 89
Out of my sight!—I will not stay to offend you.- Truly, an obedient lady iv 1 259
And she can weep, sir, weep; And she's obedient, as you say, obedient, Very obedient . iv 1 266
Soft, soft! we'll no defence; Obedient as the scabbard . *Cymbeline* iii 4 82
Whereas reproof, obedient and in order, Fits kings, as they are men *Per.* i 2 42
He, obedient to their dooms, Will take the crown . iii Gower 32
Obeisance. Call him 'madam,' do him obeisance . *T. of Shrew* Ind. 1 108
Oberon is passing fell and wrath . *M. N. Dream* ii 1 20
And jealous Oberon would have the child Knight of his train . ii 1 24
I jest to Oberon and make him smile . ii 1 44
But, room, fairy! here comes Oberon.—And here my mistress . ii 1 58
Why should Titania cross her Oberon? . ii 1 119
So awake when I am gone; For I must now to Oberon . ii 2 83
My Oberon! what visions have I seen! . iv 1 81
Obey. Ope thine ear; Obey and be attentive . *Tempest* i 2 38
I must obey: his art is of such power . i 2 372
Come on; obey: Thy nerves are in their infancy again . i 2 483
My charms crack not; my spirits obey; and time Goes upright . v 1 2
His dissolute disease will scarce obey this medicine *Mer. Wives* iii 3 204
If he bid you set it down, obey him: quickly, dispatch . iv 2 112
Let's obey his humour a little further . iv 2 210
Ere I learn love, I'll practise to obey . *Com. of Errors* ii 1 29
If we obey them not, this will ensue . ii 2 193
Arrest him at my suit.—I do; and charge you in the duke's name to obey me . iv 1 70
I do obey thee till I give thee bail . iv 1 80
I did obey, and sent my peasant home For certain ducats . v 1 231
Never speak: we charge you let us obey you to go with us *Much Ado* iii 3 189
Young blood doth not obey an old decree . *L. L. Lost* iv 3 217
I shall obey you in all fair commands . *Mer. of Venice* iii 4 36
Obey the bride, you that attend on her . *T. of Shrew* iii 2 225
When they are bound to serve, love and obey . v 2 164
Obey our will, which travails in thy good . *All's Well* ii 3 165
He desires Some private speech with you.—I shall obey his will . ii 5 62
He does obey every point of the letter that I dropped . *T. Night* iii 2 82
Take him away: he knows I know him well.—I must obey . iii 4 366
Put your grace in your pocket, sir, for this once, and let your flesh and blood obey it . v 1 36
You may as well Forbid the sea for to obey the moon . *W. Tale* i 2 427
I willingly obey your command . iv 2 60
Till you do live to see a son of mine Offend you and obey you 2 *Hen. IV.* v 2 106
Let them obey that know not how to rule . 2 *Hen. VI.* v 1 6
Obey, audacious traitor; kneel for grace.—Wouldst have me kneel? . v 1 108
He is arrested, but will not obey . v 1 136
And be you kings, command, and I'll obey . 3 *Hen. VI.* iii 1 93
Whom they must obey? Nay, whom they shall obey, and love thee too iv 1 78
We are the queen's abjects, and must obey . *Richard III.* i 1 105
The will of heaven Be done in this and all things! I obey *Hen. VIII.* i 1 210
And spur 'em, Till they obey the manage . v 3 24
Shall more obey than to the edge of steel . *Troi. and Cres.* iii 1 165
He cares not; he'll obey conditions . iv 5 72
My major vow lies here, this I'll obey . v 1 49
I will obey you in every thing hereafter . *Coriolanus* i 3 115
Obey, I charge thee, And follow to thine answer . iii 1 176
Obeys his points As if he were his officer . iv 6 125
I'll never Be such a gosling to obey instinct . v 3 35
Yet should both ear and heart obey my tongue . *T. Andron.* iv 4 99
I do apprehend thee: Obey, and go with me . *Rom. and Jul.* v 3 57
Thy saints for aye Be crown'd with plagues that thee alone obey! *T. of A.* v 1 56
And nature must obey necessity . *J. Cæsar* iv 3 227
I shall in all my best obey you, madam . *Hamlet* i 2 120
Look to't, I charge you: come your ways.—I shall obey, my lord . i 3 136
Let's follow; 'tis not fit thus to obey him . i 4 88
But we both obey, And here give up ourselves . ii 2 29
We shall obey, were she ten times our mother . iii 2 345
If your mind dislike any thing, obey it . v 2 227
Obey you, love you, and most honour you . *Lear* i 1 100
Obey thy parents, keep thy word justly; swear not . iii 4 82
My duty cannot suffer To obey in all your daughters' hard commands . iii 4 154
You are a royal one, and we obey you . iv 6 205
The weight of this sad time we must obey . v 3 323
What if I do obey? How may the duke be therewith satisfied? *Othello* i 2 87
We must obey the time . i 3 301
Let him command, And to obey shall be in me remorse, What bloody business ever . iii 3 468
Sir, I obey the mandate, And will return to Venice . iv 1 270
Let me have leave to speak: 'Tis proper I obey him, but not now . v 2 196
The very dice obey him . *Ant. and Cleo.* ii 3 33
Her tongue will not obey her heart, nor can Her heart inform her tongue iii 2 47
My sword, made weak by my affection, would Obey it on all cause . iii 11 68
My master and my lord I must obey . v 2 117
By your command, Which my love makes religion to obey . v 2 199
Our bloods No more obey the heavens than our courtiers Still seem as does the king . *Cymbeline* i 1 2
Obey her, Save when command to your dismission tends . ii 3 56
Do your best wills, And make me blest to obey! . v 1 9
And I, as fits my nature, do obey you . *Pericles* ii 1 4
We cannot but obey The powers above us . iii 3 9
Obeyed. At this time His tongue obey'd his hand . *All's Well* i 2 41
In God's name, lead; your king's name be obey'd . 3 *Hen. VI.* iii 1 99
For one commanding all, obey'd of none . *Richard III.* iv 4 104
The will of heaven be done, and the king's pleasure By me obey'd! *Hen. VIII.* i 1 216
Loved him next heaven? obey'd him? . iii 1 130
Bear the business in some other fight, As cause will be obey'd *Coriolanus* i 6 83
As weeds before A vessel under sail, so men obey'd . ii 2 110
A dog's obeyed in office . *Lear* iv 6 163
One that but performs The bidding of the fullest man, and worthiest To have command obey'd . *Ant. and Cleo.* iii 13 88
Obeyedest. Thy liege, Whom thou obeyed'st thirty and six years 3 *Hen. VI.* iii 3 96
Obeying with my wind when I do blow, And yielding to another when it blows . iii 1 86
Wife-like government, Obeying in commanding . *Hen. VIII.* ii 4 139
Dexterity so obeying appetite That what he will he does *Troi. and Cres.* v 5 27
Obidicut. Of lust, as Obidicut . *Lear* iv 1 62
Object. Think on thy Proteus, when thou haply seest Some rare noteworthy object in thy travel . *T. G. of Ver.* i 1 13
Upon a homely object Love can wink . ii 4 98
My former love Is by a newer object quite forgotten . ii 4 195
He doth object I am too great of birth . *Mer. Wives* iii 4 4
Dishonour not your eye By throwing it on any other object *M. for M.* v 1 23
That never words were music to thine ear, That never object pleasing in thine eye, . . . Unless I spake, or look'd . *Com. of Errors* ii 2 117
His eye begets occasion for his wit; For every object that the one doth catch The other turns to a mirth-moving jest . *L. L. Lost* ii 1 70
A foolish extravagant spirit, full of forms, figures, shapes, objects, ideas iv 2 69
Varying in subjects as the eye doth roll To every varied object . v 2 775
The object and the pleasure of mine eye, Is only Helena *M. N. Dream* iv 1 175
Every object that might make me fear Misfortune to my ventures, out of doubt Would make me sad . *Mer. of Venice* i 1 20
Compounded of many simples, extracted from many objects *As Y. L. It* iv 1 17
He threw his eye aside, And mark what object did present itself . iv 3 104
Extended or contracted all proportions To a most hideous object *All s W.* v 3 52

Object. Could thought, without this object, Form such another? *K. John* iv 3 44
What dost thou object Against the Duke of Norfolk? . *Richard II.* i 1 28
For sorrow's eye, glazed with blinding tears, Divides one thing entire to many objects . . . ii 2 17
How quickly nature falls into revolt When gold becomes her object! *2 Hen. IV.* iv 5 67
On this unworthy scaffold to bring forth So great an object . *Hen. V.* Prol. 11
This blot that they object against your house . . *1 Hen. VI.* ii 4 116
I with sudden and extemporal speech Purpose to answer what thou canst object . . . iii 1 7
Doth not the object cheer your heart, my lord? . . . *3 Hen. VI.* ii 2 4
Perhaps thou wilt object my holy oath . . . v 1 89
Have now the fatal object in my eye Where my poor young was limed . v 6 16
The saying did not hold In him that did object the same to thee *Richard III.* ii 4 17
And his eye reviled Me, as his abject object . . *Hen. VIII.* i 1 127
His contemplation were above the earth, And fix'd on spiritual object . iii 2 132
And reason flies the object of all harm . . *Troi. and Cres.* ii 2 41
The present eye praises the present object . . . iii 3 180
For Hector in his blaze of wrath subscribes To tender objects . . iv 5 106
The leanness that afflicts us, the object of our misery . . *Coriolanus* i 1 21
O brother, with the dismall'st object hurt That ever eye with sight made heart lament! . . *T. Andron.* ii 3 204
Ay me, this object kills me! . . . . iii 1 64
Swear against objects; Put armour on thine ears . *T. of Athens* iv 3 122
And dreadful objects so familiar . . . *J. Cæsar* iii 1 266
And of the truth herein This present object made probation . *Hamlet* i 1 156
Variable objects shall expel This something-settled matter in his heart . iii 1 180
She, that even but now was your best object . . . *Lear* i 1 217
And with this horrible object . . . Enforce their charity . . . ii 3 17
Where's the king? and where's Cordelia? See'st thou this object, Kent? . . v 3 238
In such cases Men's natures wrangle with inferior things, Though great ones are their object . . . *Othello* iii 4 145
The object poisons sight; Let it be hid . . . v 2 364
This object, which Takes prisoner the wild motion of mine eye *Cymbeline* i 6 102
Or fruitful object be In eye of Imogen, that best Could deem his dignity v 4 55
Hitting Each object with a joy . . . . . v 5 396
Hath taught My frail mortality to know itself, And by those fearful objects to prepare This body, like to them, to what I must *Pericles* i 1 43
Objected. It is well objected . . . *1 Hen. VI.* ii 4 43
Objection. You do not well To bear with their perverse objections iv 1 129
As for your spiteful false objections, Prove them . *2 Hen. VI.* i 3 158
Speak on, sir; I dare your worst objections . *Hen. VIII.* iii 2 307
Obligation. Who writes himself 'Armigero,' in any bill, warrant, quittance, or obligation . . . *Mer. Wives* i 1 11
He can make obligations, and write court-hand . *2 Hen. VI.* iv 2 100
A thousand pounds a year for pure respect! No other obligation! *Hen. VIII.* ii 3 96
The obligation of our blood forbids A gory emulation 'twixt us *T. and C.* iv 5 122
Bound In filial obligation for some term To do obsequious sorrow *Hamlet* i 2 91
By the obligation of our ever-preserved love . . . ii 2 295
I cannot think my sister in the least Would fail her obligation . *Lear* ii 4 144
Obliged. To keep obliged faith unforfeited . *Mer. of Venice* ii 6 7
Oblique memorial of cuckolds . . *Troi. and Cres.* v 1 60
All is oblique; There's nothing level in our cursed natures *T. of Athens* iv 3 18
Oblivion. It deserves, with characters of brass, A forted residence 'gainst the tooth of time And razure of oblivion *Meas. for Meas.* v 1 13
Second childishness and mere oblivion, Sans teeth, sans eyes *As Y. L. It* ii 7 165
Things of worthy memory, which now shall die in oblivion *T. of Shrew* iv 1 85
Where dust and damn'd oblivion is the tomb Of honour'd bones *All's Well* ii 3 147
And deeper than oblivion we do bury The incensing relics of it . v 3 24
Thinking of nothing else, putting all affairs else in oblivion . *2 Hen. IV.* v 5 27
From the dust of old oblivion raked . . . *Hen. V.* ii 4 87
In the swallowing gulf Of blind forgetfulness and dark oblivion *Richard III.* iii 7 129
And blind oblivion swallow'd cities up . *Troi. and Cres.* iii 2 194
Time hath, my lord, a wallet at his back, Wherein he puts alms for oblivion . . . iii 3 146
And what's to come is strew'd with husks And formless ruin of oblivion iv 5 167
Now nor Lucius nor Lavinia lives But in oblivion . *T. Andron.* iii 1 296
Whether it be Bestial oblivion, or some craven scruple *Hamlet* iv 4 40
O, my oblivion is a very Antony, And I am all forgotten *Ant. and Cleo.* i 3 90
Oblivious. With some sweet oblivious antidote . *Macbeth* v 3 43
Obloquy. Which were the greatest obloquy i' the world *All's Well* iv 2 44
Which obloquy set bars before my tongue . . *1 Hen. VI.* ii 5 49
Obscene. I did encounter that obscene and most preposterous event *L. L. Lost* i 1 244
O, forfend it, God, That in a Christian climate souls refined Should show so heinous, black, obscene a deed! . *Richard II.* iv 1 131
Thou whoreson, obscene, greasy tallow-catch . *1 Hen. IV.* ii 4 252
Obscenely. It comes so smoothly off, so obscenely . *L. L. Lost* iv 1 145
There we may rehearse most obscenely and courageously *M. N. Dream* i 2 111
Obscure. To make plain Some obscure precedence . *L. L. Lost* iii 1 83
O base and obscure vulgar! . . . . . iv 1 69
It were too gross To rib her cerecloth in the obscure grave *Mer. of Venice* ii 7 51
Being season'd with a gracious voice, Obscures the show of evil? . . iii 2 77
I will drop in his way some obscure epistles of love *T. Night* ii 3 168
A little grave, A little little grave, an obscure grave . *Richard II.* iii 3 154
You have suborn'd this man, Of purpose to obscure my noble birth *1 Hen. VI.* v 4 22
Obscure and lowly swain . . . . . *2 Hen. VI.* iv 1 50
And wander'd hither to an obscure plot . . *T. Andron.* ii 3 77
The obscure bird Clamour'd the livelong night . *Macbeth* ii 3 64
His obscure funeral—No trophy, sword, nor hatchment o'er his bones *Hamlet* iv 5 213
An index and obscure prologue to the history of lust . *Othello* ii 1 264
Obscured. All couched in a pit, . . . with obscured lights *Mer. Wives* v 3 15
You may marvel why I obscured myself . *Meas. for Meas.* v 1 395
What obscured light the heavens did grant . *Com. of Errors* i 1 67
'Tis an office of discovery, love; And I should be obscured *Mer. of Ven.* ii 6 44
A great magician, Obscured in the circle of this forest . *As Y. Like It* v 4 34
Your high self . . . you have obscured With a swain's wearing *W. Tale* iv 4 8
The prince obscured his contemplation Under the veil of wildness *Hen. V.* i 1 63
Even since then hath Richard been obscured, Deprived of honour *1 Hen. VI.* ii 5 26
And what obscured in this fair volume lies Find written in the margent of his eyes . . . *Rom. and Jul.* i 3 85
Who hath most fortunately been inform'd Of my obscured course . *Lear* ii 2 175
Obscurely Cæsar's ambition shall be glanced at . . *J. Cæsar* i 2 323
Obscuring and hiding from me all gentleman-like qualities *As Y. Like It* i 1 72
Obscurity. There's not a hollow cave or lurking-place, No vast obscurity or misty vale, Where bloody murder or detested rape Can couch for fear, but I will find them out . . *T. Andron.* v 2 36
Obsequies. But all in vain are these mean obsequies *2 Hen. VI.* iii 2 146
These tears are my sweet Rutland's obsequies . . . *3 Hen. VI.* i 4 147
My tributary tears I render, for my brethren's obsequies *T. Andron.* i 1 160
The obsequies that I for thee will keep Nightly shall be to strew thy grave and weep . . *Rom. and Jul.* v 3 16
What cursed foot wanders this way to-night, To cross my obsequies? . v 3 20
Her obsequies have been as far enlarged As we have warranty *Hamlet* v 1 249
We have done our obsequies: come, lay him down . *Cymbeline* iv 2 282
Obsequious. I see you are obsequious in your love . *Mer. Wives* iv 2 2
In obsequious fondness Crowd to his presence . *Meas. for Meas.* ii 4 28
And so obsequious will thy father be, Even for the loss of thee, having no more, As Priam was for all his valiant sons . . *3 Hen. VI.* ii 5 118
Draw you near, To shed obsequious tears upon this trunk *T. Andron.* v 3 152
Bound In filial obligation for some term To do obsequious sorrow *Hamlet* i 2 92
Doting on his own obsequious bondage, Wears out his time . *Othello* i 1 46
Obsequiously. Whilst I awhile obsequiously lament . *Richard III.* i 2 3
Observance. Followed her with a doting observance . *Mer. Wives* ii 2 203
No other tokens Between you 'greed concerning her observance? *Meas. for Meas.* iv 1 42
But there are other strict observances . . *L. L. Lost* i 1 36
To do observance to a morn of May . . *M. N. Dream* i 1 167
Use all the observance of civility, Like one well studied *Mer. of Venice* ii 2 204
And relish it with good observance . . *As Y. Like It* iii 2 247
All adoration, duty, and observance, All humbleness, all patience and impatience, All purity, all trial, all observance . . . v 2 102
And ever shall With true observance seek to eke out that Wherein toward me my homely stars have fail'd . . *All's Well* ii 5 79
I take my young lord to be a very melancholy man.—By what observance? . . . . iii 2 5
Do observance to my mercy . . . *2 Hen. IV.* iv 3 16
With due observance of thy godlike seat, Great Agamemnon *Tr. and Cr.* i 3 31
Carries on the stream of his dispose Without observance or respect of any . . . . . ii 3 175
Degrees, observances, customs, and laws . . *T. of Athens* iv 1 19
It is a custom More honour'd in the breach than the observance *Hamlet* i 4 16
With this special observance, that you o'erstep not the modesty of nature . . . . . iii 2 21
Take no notice, nor build yourself a trouble Out of his scattering and unsure observance . . . *Othello* iii 3 151
Men are not gods, Nor of them look for such observances As fit the bridal . . . . . iii 4 149
Is this certain?—Or I have no observance . . *Ant. and Cleo.* iii 3 25
Observant. And know by measure Of their observant toil the enemies' weight . . . *Troi. and Cres.* i 3 203
Why this same strict and most observant watch So nightly toils *Hamlet* i 1 71
And more corrupter ends Than twenty silly ducking observants . *Lear* ii 2 109
Observation. With good life And observation strange . *Tempest* iii 3 87
What observation madest thou in this case Of his heart's meteors tilting in his face . . . *Com. of Errors* iv 2 5
Trust not my reading nor my observations . . *Much Ado* iv 1 167
If my observation, which very seldom lies, By the heart's still rhetoric disclosed with eyes, Deceive me not now . . . *L. L. Lost* ii 1 228
How hast thou purchased this experience?—By my penny of observation . . . . iii 1 28
Now our observation is perform'd . . . *M. N. Dream* iv 1 109
He hath strange places cramm'd With observation . *As Y. Like It* ii 7 41
He is but a bastard to the time That doth not smack of observation *K. John* i 1 208
That's a foolish observation . . . *3 Hen. VI.* ii 6 108
All pressures past, That youth and observation copied there . *Hamlet* i 5 101
The observation we have made of it hath not been little . . *Lear* i 1 292
Observe. And wait the season and observe the times . *L. L. Lost* v 2 63
No doubt they rose up early to observe The rite of May . *M. N. Dream* iv 1 137
I am enjoin'd by oath to observe three things . *Mer. of Venice* ii 9 9
He had the wit which I can well observe To-day in our young lords *All's Well* i 2 32
Her eye is sick on't: I observe her now . . . . i 3 142
Say to him, I live; and observe his reports for me . . . . iii 1 46
Observe his construction of it . . . . *T. Night* ii 3 190
Observe him, for the love of mockery . . . . . ii 5 21
He must observe their mood on whom he jests . . . . iii 1 69
I shall observe him with all care and love . *2 Hen. IV.* iv 4 49
The people fear me; for they do observe Unfather'd heirs . . iv 4 121
Will ye not observe The strangeness of his alter'd countenance? *2 Hen. VI.* iii 1 4
Observe, observe, he's moody . . . . *Hen. VIII.* iii 2 75
The planets and this centre Observe degree, priority *Troi. and Cres.* i 3 86
Both observe and answer The vantage of his anger . *Coriolanus* ii 3 267
Ceremonies, Which I have seen thee careful to observe . *T. Andron.* v 1 77
I come to observe; I give thee warning on't . *T. of Athens* i 2 33
I'll show you how to observe a strange event . . . . iii 4 17
Let his very breath, whom thou 'lt observe, Blow off thy cap . iv 3 212
I do observe you now of late . . . *J. Cæsar* i 2 32
Must I observe you? must I stand and crouch Under your testy humour? iv 3 45
Observe her; stand close . . . . *Macbeth* v 1 23
Observe his inclination in yourself.—I shall, my lord . . *Hamlet* ii 1 71
I'll observe his looks; I'll tent him to the quick . . . ii 2 625
Even with the very comment of thy soul Observe mine uncle . iii 2 85
Look to your wife; observe her well with Cassio . . *Othello* iii 3 197
If more thou dost perceive, let me know more; Set on thy wife to observe . . . . iii 3 240
You shall observe him, And his own courses will denote him . . iv 1 289
Observe how Antony becomes his flaw . . *Ant. and Cleo.* iii 12 34
Observed. Hast thou observed that? even she, I mean . *T. G. of Ver.* ii 1 48
I heard your guilty rhymes, observed your fashion . . *L. L. Lost* iv 3 139
Such as he hath observed in noble ladies Unto their lords *T. of Shrew* Ind. i 111
Here is my hand; the premises observed, Thy will by my performance shall be served . . . . *All's Well* ii 1 204
Ourself and Bushy . . . Observed his courtship to the common people *Richard II.* i 4 24
The which observed, a man may prophesy, With a near aim *2 Hen. IV.* iii 1 82
He is gracious, if he be observed . . . . . iv 4 30
His temper, therefore, must be well observed . . . . iv 4 36
As young as I am, I have observed these three swashers . *Hen. V.* iii 2 29
I have observed thee always for a towardly prompt spirit *T. of Athens* iii 1 36
All his faults observed, Set in a note-book, learn'd . . *J. Cæsar* iv 3 97

Observed. Where they most breed and haunt, I have observed, The air is delicate . . . . Macbeth i 6 9
The observed of all observers . . . Hamlet iii 1 162
Pardon us, sir; with us at sea it hath been still observed . Pericles iii 1 52
Observer. There is a kind of character in thy life, That to the observer doth thy history Fully unfold . . . Meas. for Meas. i 1 29
A great observer and he looks Quite through the deeds of men J. Cæsar i 2 202
The observed of all observers . . . . . Hamlet iii 1 162
Observing of him, do bear themselves like foolish justices . 2 Hen. IV. v 1 74
We have Stood here observing him . . . Hen. VIII. iii 2 112
Underwrite in an observing kind His humorous predominance T. and C. ii 3 137
Which I observing, Took once a pliant hour . . . Othello i 3 150
Observingly. There is some soul of goodness in things evil, Would men observingly distil it out . . . . . Hen. V. iv 1 5
Obstacle. No scruple of a scruple, no obstacle . . . . T. Night iii 4 88
Fie, Joan, that thou wilt be so obstacle! . . . . 1 Hen. VI. v 4 17
It [conscience] fills one full of obstacles . . . Richard III. i 4 143
If all obstacles were cut away, And that my path were even to the crown iii 7 156
Obstinacy. Only sin And hellish obstinacy tie thy tongue . All's Well i 3 186
You do not well in obstinacy To cavil . . . 1 Hen. VI. v 4 155
Obstinate. An obstinate heretic in the despite of beauty . Much Ado i 1 236
Except you mean with obstinate repulse To slay your sovereign 1 Hen. VI. iii 1 113
The queen is obstinate, Stubborn to justice . . . Hen. VIII. ii 4 121
Let it be virtuous to be obstinate . . . . . . Coriolanus v 3 26
To persever In obstinate condolement is a course Of impious stubbornness; 'tis unmanly grief . . . . Hamlet i 2 93
Obstinately. An esperance so obstinately strong, That doth invert the attest of eyes and ears . . . . . Troi. and Cres. v 2 121
Obstruct. I begg'd His pardon for return.—Which soon he granted, Being an obstruct 'tween his lust and him . Ant. and Cleo. iii 6 61
Obstruction. To lie in cold obstruction and to rot . Meas. for Meas. iii 1 119
There is no obstruction in this . . . . . T. Night ii 5 129
This does make some obstruction in the blood, this cross-gartering . iii 4 22
And yet complainest thou of obstruction? . . . . . iv 2 43
Purge the obstructions which begin to stop Our very veins of life 2 Hen. IV. iv 1 65
Obtain. Now am I, unhappy messenger, To plead for that which I would not obtain . . . . . . T. G. of Ver. iv 4 105
As I wooed for thee to obtain her, I will join with thee to disgrace M. Ado iii 2 129
I'll beg one boon, And then be gone and trouble you no more. Shall I obtain it?—Name it . . . . . . Richard II. iv 1 304
Hast thou by secret means Used intercession to obtain a league? 1 Hen. VI. v 4 148
Titus, thou shalt obtain and ask the empery . . T. Andron. i 1 201
Yet let me obtain my wish . . . . . . Pericles v 1 35
Obtained. I have broke with her father, and his good will obtained M. Ado ii 1 311
Coming too short of thanks For my great suit so easily obtain'd L. L. L. v 2 749
Unless I be obtained by the manner of my father's will . Mer. of Venice i 2 117
Thou hast obtain'd thy suit . . . . ii 2 153
I have a suit to you.—You have obtain'd it . . . . ii 2 186
When the special thing is well obtain'd, That is, her love T. of Shrew ii 1 129
Having this obtain'd, you presently Attend his further pleasure All's Well ii 4 53
When she has obtain'd your eye, Will have your tongue too . W. Tale v 1 105
By guileful fair words peace may be obtain'd . . 1 Hen. VI. i 1 77
To know who hath obtain'd the glory of the day . . . iv 7 52
Obtaining. I am desperate of obtaining her . . T. G. of Ver. iii 2 5
For obtaining of suits, whereof the hangman hath no lean wardrobe 1 Hen. IV. i 2 80
Occasion. To minister occasion to these gentlemen . . . Tempest ii 1 173
I see it in thy face, What thou shouldst be: the occasion speaks thee . ii 1 207
When we are married and have more occasion to know one another Mer. Wives i 1 256
Fee'd every slight occasion that could but niggardly give me sight of her ii 2 204
I have pursued her as love hath pursued me; which hath been on the wing of all occasions . . . . ii 2 210
I hope, if you have occasion to use me for your own turn, you shall find me yare . . . . Meas. for Meas. iv 2 60
He heartily prays some occasion may detain us longer . Much Ado i 1 151
Why are you thus out of measure sad?—There is no measure in the occasion that breeds . . . . i 3 3
His eye begets occasion for his wit . . . . L. L. Lost ii 1 69
And delivered upon the mellowing of occasion . . . iv 2 72
And so be mock'd withal Upon the next occasion that we meet . v 2 143
Nay, I can gleek upon occasion . . . . M. N. Dream iii 1 150
And you embrace the occasion to depart . . . Mer. of Venice i 1 64
My extremest means Lie all unlock'd to your occasions . . . i 1 139
Yet more quarrelling with occasion! . . . . . iii 5 60
Speak first, and when you were gravelled for lack of matter, you might take occasion to kiss . . . . . As Y. Like It iv 1 75
O, that woman that cannot make her fault her husband's occasion! . iv 1 178
And nature, stronger than his just occasion, Made him give battle iv 3 130
I will go sit and weep Till I can find occasion of revenge T. of Shrew ii 1 36
What occasion of import Hath all so long detain'd you from your wife? iii 2 104
Goaded with most sharp occasions, Which lay nice manners by All's Well v 1 14
Till I had made mine own occasion mellow . . T. Night i 2 43
Unless you laugh and minister occasion to him, he is gagged . . i 5 94
Upon the least occasion more mine eyes will tell tales of me . . ii 1 42
Smilest thou? I sent for thee upon a sad occasion . . . . iii 4 20
You may have very fit occasion for't . . . . . . iii 4 190
To keep in darkness what occasion now Reveals before 'tis ripe . v 1 156
On the like occasion whereon my services are now on foot . W. Tale i 1 2
I am courted now with a double occasion . . . . iv 4 864
For courage mounteth with occasion . . . . K. John ii 1 82
That the time's enemies may not have this To grace occasions . ii 2 62
Withhold thy speed, dreadful occasion! . . . . . iv 2 125
I do love the favour and the form Of this most fair occasion . v 4 51
To behold the face Of that occasion that shall bring it on 1 Hen. IV. i 3 276
When he had occasion to be seen, He was but as the cuckoo is in June iii 2 74
You took occasion to be quickly woo'd To gripe the general sway . v 1 56
I well allow the occasion of our arms . . . 2 Hen. IV. i 3 5
Let us on, And publish the occasion of our arms . . . . i 3 86
Every man must know that, as oft as he has occasion to name himself . ii 2 119
Enforced from our most quiet there By the rough torrent of occasion . iv 1 72
He cannot so precisely weed this land As his misdoubts present occasion iv 1 206
As I may pick occasion . . . . . . Hen. V. iii 2 111
There is occasions and causes why and wherefore in all things . v 1 3
When you take occasions to see leeks hereafter, I pray you, mock at 'em v 1 58
Having any occasion to write for matter of grant, shall name your highness . . . . v 2 365
Especially for those occasions At Eltham Place I told your majesty.—And those occasions, uncle, were of force . 1 Hen. VI. iii 1 155
Much less to take occasion from their mouths To raise a mutiny . . iv 1 130
Occasion. 'Tis not his wont to be the hindmost man, Whate'er occasion keeps him from us now . . . 2 Hen. VI. iii 1 3
And, like a gallant in the brow of youth, Repairs him with occasion . v 3 5
What resteth more, But that I seek occasion how to rise? . 3 Hen. VI. i 2 45
And when I give occasion of offence, Then let me die . . . i 3 44
Wet my cheeks with artificial tears, And frame my face to all occasions iii 2 185
As occasion serves . . . . iii 3 236
I'll sort occasion, As index to the story we late talk'd of Richard III. ii 2 148
On what occasion, God he knows, not I . . . . . iii 1 26
I am joyful To meet the least occasion that may give me Remembrance of my father-in-law . . . . . . Hen. VIII. iii 2 7
Am right glad to catch this good occasion Most throughly to be winnow'd v 1 109
And with what vehemency The occasion shall instruct you . . . v 1 149
Had I so good occasion to lie long As you . . . Troi. and Cres. iv 1 3
When contention and occasion meet, By Jove, I'll play the hunter for thy life . . . . iv 1 16
A very little thief of occasion will rob you of a great deal of patience: give your dispositions the reins . . . . . Coriolanus ii 1 32
I dare draw as soon as another man, if I see occasion . Rom. and Jul. ii 4 168
You shall find me apt enough to that, sir, an you will give me occasion.—Could you not take some occasion without giving? . . . iii 1 45
Awaked by great occasion To call upon his own . . T. of Athens ii 2 21
My occasions have found time to use 'em toward a supply of money . ii 2 200
Having great and instant occasion to use fifty talents . . . . iii 1 19
I should ne'er have denied his occasion so many talents . . . iii 2 26
What has he sent now?—Has only sent his present occasion now . . iii 2 39
If his occasion were not virtuous, I should not urge it half so faithfully iii 2 45
I see no sense for't, But his occasions might have woo'd me first . iii 3 15
An earnest inviting, which many my near occasions did urge me to put off iii 6 12
Get on your nightgown, lest occasion call us . . . . Macbeth ii 2 70
Occasion smiles upon a second leave . . . . . Hamlet i 3 54
To gather, So much as from occasion you may glean . . . ii 2 16
What make you at Elsinore?—To visit you, my lord; no other occasion ii 2 279
How all occasions do inform against me, And spur my dull revenge! . iv 4 32
Recount the occasion of my sudden and more strange return . iv 7 47
I would breed from hence occasions, and I shall, That I may speak Lear i 3 24
Occasions, noble Gloucester, of some poise, Wherein we must have use of your advice . . . . ii 1 122
A slipper and subtle knave, a finder of occasions . . . Othello ii 1 246
Do you find some occasion to anger Cassio . . . . . ii 1 274
To take the safest occasion by the front To bring you in again . . iii 1 52
When he is gone, I would on great occasion speak with you . . iv 1 59
Under a compelling occasion, let women die . . . Ant. and Cleo. i 2 141
Will use his affection where it is: he married but his occasion here . ii 6 140
But what occasion Hath Cadwal now to give it motion? . Cymbeline iv 2 187
He comes, And brings the dire occasion in his arms Of what we blame him for . . . . iv 2 196
So kind, so duteous, diligent, So tender over his occasions . . . v 5 87
Occident. To dim his glory and to stain the track Of his bright passage to the occident . . . . Richard II. iii 3 67
I may wander From east to occident, cry out for service . Cymbeline iv 2 372
Occidental. Ere twice in murk and occidental damp Moist Hesperus hath quench'd his sleepy lamp . . . . . . All's Well ii 1 166
Occulted. Observe mine uncle: if his occulted guilt Do not itself unkennel in one speech . . . . Hamlet iii 2 85
Occupat. Gelidus timor occupat artus, it is thee I fear . 2 Hen. VI. iv 1 117
Occupation. No occupation; all men idle, all; And women too Tempest ii 1 154
Do you call, sir, your occupation a mystery?—Ay, sir Meas. for Meas. iv 2 35
Members of my occupation, using painting, do prove my occupation a mystery . . . . iv 2 40
I can bear my part; you must know 'tis my occupation . W. Tale iv 4 302
Red pestilence strike all trades in Rome, And occupations perish! Cor. iv 1 14
You that stood so much Upon the voice of occupation . . . . iv 6 97
An I had been a man of any occupation . . . . . J. Cæsar i 2 269
'Tis my occupation to be plain: I have seen better faces . Lear ii 2 98
Farewell! Othello's occupation's gone! . . . . . Othello iii 3 357
That thou couldst see my wars to-day, and knew'st The royal occupation! thou shouldst see A workman in't . . . . Ant. and Cleo. iv 4 17
Occupy. A captain! God's light, these villains will make the word as odious as the word 'occupy' . . . . . . 2 Hen. IV. ii 4 161
And meant, indeed, to occupy the argument no longer . Rom. and Jul. ii 4 105
Occurrence. All the occurrence of my fortune since Hath been between this lady and this lord . . . . T. Night v 1 264
Omit All the occurrences, whatever chanced . . . . Hen. V. v Prol. 40
Occurrent. So tell him, with the occurrents, more and less . Hamlet v 2 368
Ocean. Strays With willing sport to the wild ocean . . T. G. of Ver. ii 7 32
A thousand oaths, an ocean of his tears, And instances of infinite of love ii 7 69
She is my prize, or ocean whelm them all! . . . Mer. Wives ii 2 143
Like a drop of water That in the ocean seeks another drop Com. of Errors i 2 36
Your mind is tossing on the ocean . . . . . Mer. of Venice i 1 8
Whose foot spurns back the ocean's roaring tides . . . K. John ii 1 24
Unless thou let his silver water keep A peaceful progress to the ocean . ii 1 340
Put but a little water in a spoon, And it shall be as all the ocean, Enough to stifle such a villain up . . . . . . iv 3 132
Run on in obedience Even to our ocean, to our great King John . v 4 57
The task he undertakes Is numbering sands and drinking oceans dry Richard II. ii 2 146
The beachy girdle of the ocean Too wide for Neptune's hips 2 Hen. IV. iii 1 50
Whose high upreared and abutting fronts The perilous narrow ocean parts asunder . . . . Hen. V. Prol. 22
Swill'd with the wild and wasteful ocean . . . . . . iii 1 14
To drain Upon his face an ocean of salt tears . . . 2 Hen. VI. iii 2 143
Like to his island girt in with the ocean . . . 3 Hen. VI. iv 8 20
In the deep bosom of the ocean buried . . . . Richard III. i 1 4
And, having gilt the ocean with his beams, Gallops the zodiac T. Andron. ii 1 6
All the water in the ocean Can never turn the swan's black legs to white iv 2 101
The ocean swells not so as Aaron storms . . . . . . iv 2 139
Go sound the ocean, and cast your nets; Happily you may catch her . iv 3 7
I have seen The ambitious ocean swell and rage and foam . J. Cæsar i 3 7
Will all great Neptune's ocean wash this blood Clean from my hand? Macb. ii 2 60
Save yourself, my lord: The ocean, overpeering of his list, Eats not the flats with more impetuous haste . . . . . . Hamlet iv 5 99
That is it Hath made me rig my navy; at whose burthen The anger'd ocean foams . . . . Ant. and Cleo. ii 6 21
Whate'er the ocean pales, or sky inclips, Is thine, if thou wilt ha't . ii 7 74
His legs bestrid the ocean: his rear'd arm Crested the world . . v 2 82
Gave you some ground.—As many inches as you have oceans Cymbeline i 2 22
O'clock. By seven o'clock I'll get you such a ladder . T. G. of Ver. iii 1 126
Eleven o'clock the hour. I will prevent this, detect my wife Mer. Wives ii 2 324
Let him be sent for to-morrow, eight o'clock, to have amends . . iii 3 210

O'clock. It hath struck ten o'clock.—The night is dark . . *Mer. Wives* v 2 12
Away; disperse: but till 'tis one o'clock . . . . v 5 78
Provide your block and your axe to-morrow four o'clock *Meas. for Meas.* iv 2 56
He had of me a chain: at five o'clock I shall receive the money *C. of Er.* iv 1 10
'Tis almost five o'clock, cousin; 'tis time you were ready . *Much Ado* iii 4 52
'Tis now but four o'clock: we have two hours To furnish us . *Mer. of Ven.* ii 4 8
My nose fell a-bleeding on Black-Monday last at six o'clock i' the morning ii 5 25
Where are all the rest? 'Tis nine o'clock: our friends all stay for you . ii 6 63
'It is ten o'clock: Thus we may see,' quoth he, 'how the world wags' *As Y. Like It* ii 7 22
What is't o' clock?—You should ask me what time o' day . . iii 2 317
By two o'clock I will be with thee again.—Ay, go your ways . . iv 1 185
Is it not past two o'clock? and here much Orlando! . . . iv 3 2
Some seven o'clock, And well we may come there by dinner-time *T. of Shrew* iv 3 189
I will not go to-day; and ere I do, It shall be what o'clock I say it is . iv 3 197
Ten o'clock: within these three hours 'twill be time enough . *All's Well* iv 1 27
To the pupil age of this present twelve o'clock at midnight 1 *Hen. IV.* ii 4 107
Meet me to-morrow in the temple hall at two o'clock in the afternoon . iii 3 224
Is it good morrow, lords?—'Tis one o'clock, and past . 2 *Hen IV.* iii 1 34
'Twill be two o'clock ere they come from the coronation . . v 5 3
Is it four o'clock?—It is.—Then go we in . . . *Hen. V.* i 1 93
Two o'clock: but, let me see, by ten We shall have each a hundred Englishmen . . . . iii 7 168
I go; and towards three or four o'clock Look for the news *Richard III.* iii 5 101
If to-morrow be a fair day, by eleven o'clock it will go one way *T. and C.* iii 3 297
At what o'clock to-morrow Shall I send to thee? . *Rom. and Jul.* ii 2 168
The second cock hath crow'd, The curfew-bell hath rung, 'tis three o'clock . . . . iv 4 4
'Tis three o'clock; and, Romans, yet ere night We shall try fortune in a second fight . . . . *J. Cæsar* v 3 109
What's o'clock? *Meas. for Meas.* ii 1; 1 *Hen. IV.* ii i; ii 4; 2 *Hen. VI.* ii 4; *Richard III.* iv 2
What is't o'clock! *Richard III.* iii 2; v 3: *J. Cæsar* ii 2; ii 4

Octavia. A sister by the mother's side, Admired Octavia *Ant. and Cleo.* ii 2 121
To knit your hearts With an unslipping knot, take Antony Octavia to his wife . . . . ii 2 130
If beauty, wisdom, modesty, can settle The heart of Antony, Octavia is A blessed lottery to him . . . . ii 2 247
My Octavia, Read not my blemishes in the world's report . . ii 3 4
Sir, Mark Antony Will e'en but kiss Octavia, and we'll follow . ii 4 3
Free, madam! no; I made no such report: He's bound unto Octavia . ii 5 58
Madam, he's married to Octavia.—The most infectious pestilence upon thee! . . . . ii 5 60
Bid him Report the feature of Octavia, her years, Her inclination . ii 5 112
Cæsar's sister is called Octavia.—True, sir; she was the wife of Caius Marcellus.—But she is now the wife of Marcus Antonius . . ii 6 116
Octavia is of a holy, cold, and still conversation . . . ii 6 130
Then shall the sighs of Octavia blow the fire up in Cæsar . . ii 6 135
Octavia weeps To part from Rome; Cæsar is sad . . . iii 2 3
And— What, Octavia?—I'll tell you in your ear . . . iii 2 46
No, sweet Octavia, You shall hear from me still . . . iii 2 59
Didst thou behold Octavia?—Ay, dread queen.—Where?—Madam, in Rome . . . . iii 3 8
Nay, nay, Octavia, not only that,—That were excusable . . iii 4 1
Gentle Octavia, Let your best love draw to that point, which seeks Best to preserve it . . . . iii 4 20
Let patient Octavia plough thy visage up With her prepared nails . iv 12 38
Octavia, with her modest eyes And still conclusion, shall acquire no honour Demuring upon me . . . . iv 15 27
Nor once be chastised with the sober eye Of dull Octavia . . v 2 55
Some nobler token I have kept apart For Livia and Octavia . . v 2 169

Octavius. You serve Octavius Cæsar, do you not? . . *J. Cæsar* iii 1 276
No Rome of safety for Octavius yet; Hie hence, and tell him so . iii 1 289
Thou shalt discourse To young Octavius of the state of things . iii 1 296
How now, fellow!—Sir, Octavius is already come to Rome . . iii 2 267
Octavius, I have seen more days than you . . . . iv 1 18
He's a tried and valiant soldier.—So is my horse, Octavius . . iv 1 29
Octavius, Listen great things:—Brutus and Cassius Are levying powers iv 1 40
Antony, and young Octavius, come, Revenge yourselves alone on Cassius iv 3 93
Grief that young Octavius with Mark Antony Have made themselves so strong . . . . iv 3 153
Octavius and Mark Antony Come down upon us with a mighty power . iv 3 168
Octavius, lead your battle softly on, Upon the left hand . . v 1 16
Good words are better than bad strokes, Octavius . . . v 1 29
Set on at once; for I perceive But cold demeanour in Octavius' wing . v 2 4
Who, having some advantage on Octavius, Took it too eagerly . v 3 6
Octavius Is overthrown by noble Brutus' power . . . v 3 51
Bring us word unto Octavius' tent How every thing is chanced . v 4 31
I shall have glory by this losing day More than Octavius . . v 5 37
Octavius, then take him to follow thee, That did the latest service to my master . . . . v 5 66
Find me to marry me with Octavius Cæsar . . *Ant. and Cleo.* i 2 29
Marcus Octavius, Marcus Justeius, Publicola, and Cælius, are for sea . iii 7 73

Ocular. Be sure of it; give me the ocular proof . . *Othello* iii 3 360
'Od's heartlings, that's a pretty jest indeed! . . *Mer. Wives* iii 4 59
'Od's lifelings, here he is! . . . . . *T. Night* v 1 187
Od's me. By my trot, I tarry too long. Od's me! . . *Mer. Wives* i 4 64
'Od's my little life, I think she means to tangle my eyes too! No, faith, proud mistress . . . . . . *As Y. Like It* iii 5 43
'Od's my will! Her love is not the hare that I do hunt . . iv 3 17
'Od's nouns. Because they say, ''Od's nouns' . . *Mer. Wives* iv 1 25
'Od's pittikins! can it be six mile yet? . . . *Cymbeline* iv 2 293
'Od's plessed will! I will not be absence at the grace . *Mer. Wives* i 1 273

Odd. Three odd ducats more Than I stand debted . *Com. of Errors* iv 1 30
Not to be so odd and from all fashions . . . *Much Ado* iii 1 72
He is too picked, too spruce, too affected, too odd, as it were *L. L. Lost* v 1 15
I have foundered nine score and odd posts . . 2 *Hen. IV.* iv 3 40
Eighty odd years of sorrow have I seen . . *Richard III.* iv 1 96
Every man is odd.—No, Paris is not; for you know 'tis true, That you are odd, and he is even with you . . *Troi. and Cres.* iv 5 42
The general state, I fear, Can scarce entreat you to be odd with him . iv 5 265
But this is something odd . . . . *Coriolanus* ii 3 88
Your voices bear Of wounds two dozen odd . . . . ii 3 135
Even or odd, of all days in the year, Come Lammas-eve . *Rom. and Jul.* i 3 16
How strange or odd soe'er I bear myself, As I perchance hereafter shall think meet To put an antic disposition on . . . *Hamlet* i 5 170

Odd angle. In an odd angle of the isle . . . *Tempest* i 2 223
Odd behaviour. Lest over-eyeing of his odd behaviour . *T. of Shrew* Ind. i 95
Odd-conceited. Twenty odd-conceited true-love knots . *T. G. of Ver.* ii 7 46
Odd days. How long is it now To Lammas-tide?—A fortnight and odd days . . . . *Rom. and Jul.* i 3 15
Odd ends. With old odd ends stolen out of holy writ *Richard III.* i 3 337
Odd-even. At this odd-even and dull watch o' the night . *Othello* i 1 124
Odd gimmors. By some odd gimmors or device . 1 *Hen. VI.* i 2 41
Odd hits. I will win for him an I can; if not, I will gain nothing but my shame and the odd hits . . . . . *Hamlet* v 2 185
Odd humour. 'Tis some odd humour . . . *T. of Shrew* iii 2 74
Odd lads. Yet missing of your company Some few odd lads . *Tempest* v 1 255
Odd man. You're an odd man; give even, or give none.—An odd man, lady! every man is odd . . . . *Troi. and Cres.* iv 5 41
Odd numbers. This is the third time; I hope good luck lies in odd numbers . . . . *Mer. Wives* v 1 3
There is divinity in odd numbers, either in nativity, chance, or death . v 1 4
Odd quirks. I may chance have some odd quirks and remnants of wit broken on me . . . . *Much Ado* ii 3 244
Odd sayings. According to Fates and Destinies and such odd sayings *Mer. of Venice* ii 2 66
Odd shilling. Every tod yields pound and odd shilling . *W. Tale* iv 3 34
Odd time. I fear the trust Othello puts him in, On some odd time of his infirmity, Will shake this island . . . . *Othello* ii 3 132
Odd tricks. One of those odd tricks which sorrow shoots Out of the mind *Ant. and Cleo.* iv 2 14
Odd worm. But this is most fallible, the worm's an odd worm . . v 2 259

Oddest. Her madness hath the oddest frame of sense . *Meas. for Meas.* v 1 61

Oddly. But, O, how oddly will it sound that I Must ask my child forgiveness! . . . . *Tempest* v 1 197
How oddly he is suited! . . . . . . *Mer. of Venice* i 2 79
Our imputation shall be oddly poised In this wild action *Troi. and Cres.* i 3 339
How oddly thou repliest! . . . . . . *Rom. and Jul.* ii 5 61

Odds. Is at most odds with his own gravity and patience *Mer. Wives* iii 1 54
Yet death we fear, That makes these odds all even . *Meas. for Meas.* iii 1 41
Too much odds for a Spaniard's rapier . . . *L. L. Lost* i 2 183
The fox, the ape, and the humble-bee, Were still at odds, being but three.—Until the goose came out of door, Staying the odds by adding four . . . . iii 1 97
There is such odds in the man . . . . *As Y. Like It* i 2 169
Then he shall have no odds . . . . . *T. of Shrew* iv 3 155
The odds for high and low's alike . . . . . *W. Tale* v 1 207
Which to maintain I would allow him odds . . . *Richard II.* i 1 62
And with that odds he weighs King Richard down . . . iii 4 89
I am content that he shall take the odds Of his great name . 1 *Hen. IV.* v 1 97
I will lay odds . . . . 2 *Hen. IV.* v 5 111
I desire Nothing but odds with England . . . . *Hen. V.* ii 4 129
God's arm strike with us! 'tis a fearful odds . . . . iv 3 5
Yields up his life unto a world of odds . . . 1 *Hen. VI.* iv 4 25
Forsaketh yet the lists By reason of his adversary's odds . . v 5 33
A poor earl's daughter is unequal odds, And therefore may be broke . v 5 34
Took odds to combat a poor famish'd man . . 2 *Hen. VI.* iv 10 47
Five men to twenty! though the odds be great, I doubt not . 3 *Hen. VI.* i 2 72
But Hercules himself must yield to odds . . . . ii 1 53
'Twas odds, belike, when valiant Warwick fled . . . . ii 1 148
I do not know that Englishman alive With whom my soul is any jot at odds More than the infant that is born to-night *Richard III.* ii 1 70
Advantageous care Withdrew me from the odds of multitude *Troi. and Cres.* v 4 23
But now 'tis odds beyond arithmetic . . . . *Coriolanus* iii 1 245
Thou hast the odds of me; therefore no more . . *T. Andron.* v 2 19
And pity 'tis you lived at odds so long . . . *Rom. and Jul.* i 2 5
This and my food are equals; there's no odds . . . *T. of Athens* i 2 61
'Tis honour with most lands to be at odds . . . . . iii 5 116
Come, damned earth, Thou common whore of mankind, that put'st odds Among the rout of nations . . . . iv 3 42
Set them into confounding odds, that beasts May have the world in empire! . . . . iv 3 392
What is the night?—Almost at odds with morning . . *Macbeth* iii 4 127
I have been in continual practice; I shall win at the odds . *Hamlet* v 2 222
Your grace hath laid the odds o' the weaker side . . . v 2 272
But since he is better'd, we have therefore odds . . . v 2 274
He flashes into one gross crime or other, That sets us all at odds . *Lear* i 3 5
I cannot speak Any beginning to this peevish odds . . *Othello* ii 3 185
And, of that natural luck, He beats thee 'gainst the odds *Ant. and Cleo.* ii 3 27
And his quails ever Beat mine, inhoop'd, at odds . . . ii 3 38
Young boys and girls Are level now with men; the odds is gone . . iv 15 66
The odds Is that we scarce are men and you are gods . *Cymbeline* v 2 9

Ode. Once more I'll read the ode that I have writ . *L. L. Lost* iv 3 99
Hangs odes upon hawthorns and elegies on brambles . *As Y. Like It* iii 2 379

Odious. As heavy to me as odious . . . . *Tempest* iii 1 5
O, odious is the name! . . . . . . *Mer. Wives* iii 1 123
The flowers of odious savours sweet,— Odours, odours *M. N. Dream* iii 1 84
As horns are odious, they are necessary . . *As Y. Like It* iii 3 52
A divulged shame Traduced by odious ballads . . *All's Well* ii 1 175
These villains will make the word as odious as the word 'occupy' 2 *Hen. IV.* ii 4 160
The sight of me is odious in their eyes . . . 2 *Hen. VI.* iv 4 46
Many more there are; Which, since they are of you, and odious, I will not taint my mouth with . . . . . *Hen. VIII.* iii 2 331
You told a lie; an odious, damned lie; Upon my soul, a lie . *Othello* v 2 180
And pride so great, The name of help grew odious to repeat . *Pericles* i 4 31

Odoriferous. Smelling out the odoriferous flowers of fancy . *L. L. Lost* iv 2 128
O amiable lovely death! Thou odoriferous stench! . . *K. John* iii 4 26

Odorous. Comparisons are odorous: palabras, neighbour Verges *M. Ado* iii 5 18
An odorous chaplet of sweet summer buds . . *M. N. Dream* ii 1 110

Odour. Thisby, the flowers of odious savours sweet,— Odours, odours. ——odours savours sweet . . . . iii 1 85
Breathes upon a bank of violets, Stealing and giving odour! . *T. Night* i 1 7
The heavens rain odours on you!—That youth's a rare courtier: 'Rain odours' . . . . iii 1 96
'Odours' 'pregnant' and 'vouchsafed:' I'll get 'em all three all ready iii 1 101
A delicate odour.—As ever hit my nostril . . . *Pericles* iii 2 61

Œillade. Examined my parts with most judicious œillades . *Mer. Wives* i 3 68
She gave strange œillades and most speaking looks . . *Lear* iv 5 25

Œuvre. La fin couronne les œuvres . . . . 2 *Hen. VI.* v 2 28

Of. Whom I left cooling of the air with sighs . . . *Tempest* i 2 222
Which, of he or Adrian, for a good wager, first begins to crow? . ii 1 28
I am a fool To weep at what I am glad of . . . . iii 1 74
With a heart as willing As bondage e'er of freedom . . . iii 1 89
We were dead of sleep . . . . v 1 230
One that I brought up of a puppy . . . *T. G. of Ver.* iv 4 3
He came of an errand to me . . . . . *Mer. Wives* i 4 80
What he gets more of her than sharp words, let it lie on my head . . ii 1 190

Of. Spend all I have; only give me so much of your time in exchange of it . . . *Mer. Wives* ii 2 242
Are you of fourscore pounds a year?—Yes, an't please you, sir.—So. What trade are you of, sir? . . . . . *Meas. for Meas.* ii 1 204
'Tis pity of him . . . . ii 3 42
Of whence are you?—Not of this country . . . . iii 2 229
Here comes the rascal I spoke of . . . . . v 1 285
A coward, One all of luxury, an ass, a madman . . . v 1 506
Sweet mistress,—what your name is else, I know not, Nor by what wonder you do hit of mine . . . *Com. of Errors* iii 2 30
I am not of many words, but I thank you . . . *Much Ado* i 1 158
I hear as good exclamation on your worship as of any man in the city iii 5 29
They are not to be named, my lord, Not to be spoke of . . iv 1 97
And not be seen to wink of all the day . . . . *L. L. Lost* i 1 43
Bold of your worthiness, we single you . . . . ii 1 28
It was well done of you to take him at his word . . . ii 1 217
O, that a lady, of one man refused, Should of another therefore be abused! . . . . . *M. N. Dream* ii 2 134
And strike more dead Than common sleep of all these five the sense . iv 1 87
I wonder of their being here together . . . . iv 1 136
I no question make To have it of my trust or for my sake *Mer. of Venice* i 1 185
At the very next turning, turn of no hand, but turn down indirectly . ii 2 45
I am sure he had more hair of his tail than I have of my face . ii 2 104
I am provided of a torch-bearer . . . . . . ii 4 24
I have no mind of feasting forth to-night . . . . ii 5 37
If my gossip Report be an honest woman of her word . . . iii 1 8
I am sure you are not satisfied Of these events at full . . . v 1 297
Thou shalt have to pay for it of us . . . . *As Y. Like It* ii 4 93
I have been told so of many . . . . . . iii 2 361
I am not in the mind but I were better to be married of him than of another . . . . iii 3 92
God 'ild you, sir; I desire you of the like . . . . v 4 56
But did I never speak of all that time? . . . *T. of Shrew* Ind. 2 84
Thy mildness praised in every town, Thy virtues spoke of . . ii 1 193
He is mine only son, and heir to the lands of me . . . iv 1 89
I'll venture so much of my hawk or hound, But twenty times so much upon my wife . . . . v 2 72
Of six preceding ancestors, that gem, Conferr'd by testament to the sequent issue, Hath it been owed and worn . . . *All's Well* v 3 196
That did but show thee, of a fool, inconstant And damnable ingrateful *W. Tale* iii 2 187
At least if you make a care Of happy holding her . . . iv 4 367
As holding of the pope Your sovereign greatness and authority *K. John* v 1 3
It was the death of him . . . . . . *1 Hen. IV.* ii 1 14
Which men shall I have?—Four of which you please *2 Hen. IV.* iii 2 259
They say he cried out of sack.—Ay, that a' did.—And of women *Hen. V.* ii 3 29
A lad of life, an imp of fame; Of parents good, of fist most valiant . iv 1 45
So weak of courage and in judgement That they'll take no offence *3 Hen. VI.* iv 1 12
I do not like the Tower, of any place . . . *Richard III.* iii 1 68
Of all one pain, save for a night of groans Endured of her . . iv 4 303
Of his own body he was ill, and gave The clergy ill example *Hen. VIII.* iv 2 43
We lay by Our appertainments, visiting of him . . *Troi. and Cres.* ii 3 87
You should not have the eminence of him . . . . ii 3 266
What wouldst thou of us, Trojan? make demand . . . iii 3 17
Give us a prince of blood, a son of Priam, In change of him . . iii 3 27
No man is the lord of any thing, Though in and of him there be much consisting, Till he communicate his parts to others . . . iii 3 116
Who is of Rome worse hated than of you . . . *Coriolanus* i 2 13
Most likely 'tis for you: Consider of it . . . . i 2 17
'Tis thought of every one Coriolanus will carry it . . . ii 2 3
That I would have spoke of . . . . . . v 6 29
For, take't of my soul, my lord leans wondrously to discontent *T. of A.* iii 4 70
Why, I was writing of my epitaph . . . . . v 1 188
All those his lands Which he stood seized of . . . *Hamlet* i 1 89
What it should be, More than his father's death, . . . I cannot dream of ii 2 10
Being of so young days brought up with him . . . . ii 2 11
By the sovereign power you have of us . . . . ii 2 27
Nay, then, I have an eye of you.—If you love me, hold not off . ii 2 301
God ha' mercy on his soul! And of all Christian souls, I pray God iv 5 200
Heaven make thee free of it! . . . . . . v 2 343
And did want Of what I was i' the morning . . *Ant. and Cleo.* ii 2 77
Thou dost o'er-count me of my father's house . . . . ii 6 27
I' the world's volume Our Britain seems as of it, but not in't *Cymbeline* iii 4 141
You have A nurse of me . . . . . . *Pericles* iv 1 25
She was of Tyrus the king's daughter . . . . . iv 4 36
Of age. He being of age to govern of himself . . *2 Hen. VI.* i 1 166
Of himself. Nor doth he of himself know them for aught Till he behold them form'd in the applause Where they're extended *Troi. and Cres.* iii 3 118
Of itself. With eggs, sir?—Simple of itself . . . *Mer. Wives* iii 5 32
The world, who of itself is peised well . . . . *K. John* ii 1 575
Of itself England is safe, if true within itself . . *3 Hen. VI.* iv 1 39
It holds his estimate and dignity As well wherein 'tis precious of itself As in the prizer . . . . . *Troi. and Cres.* ii 2 55
Of late days . . . . *Hen. VIII.* ii 1 147; v 3 29
Of old. Sad stories chanced in the times of old . . *T. Andron.* iii 2 83
The hearts of old gave hands . . . . . *Othello* iii 4 46
Of ourselves. Since, of ourselves, ourselves are choleric . *T. of Shrew* iv 1 177
We wound our modesty and make foul the clearness of our deservings, when of ourselves we publish them . . . . *All's Well* i 3 7
Of pleasure. Art thou a messenger, or come of pleasure? . *2 Hen. VI.* v 1 16
Of purpose to obscure my noble birth . . . . *1 Hen. VI.* v 4 22
This is of purpose laid by some that hate me . . . *Hen. VIII.* v 2 14
Come again to supper to him, of purpose to have him spend less *T. of A.* iii 1 26
Of themselves. Which they'll do fast enough of themselves *Mer. Wives* iv 1 69
They [the gates] 'll open of themselves . . . *Coriolanus* i 4 19
Of yourself. Had borne the action of yourself . . . . iv 7 15
Off. Set her two courses off to sea again; lay her off . . *Tempest* i 1 53
Lead off this ground; and let's make further search . . . ii 1 323
Do not smile at me that I boast her off . . . . . iv 1 9
Now trust me, madam, it came hardly off . . . *T. G. of Ver.* ii 1 115
Inconstancy falls off ere it begins . . . . . v 4 113
Goodman Verges, sir, speaks a little off the matter . . *Much Ado* iii 5 10
When it comes so smoothly off, so obscenely, as it were, so fit *L. L. Lost* iv 1 145
Hang off, thou cat, thou burr! vile thing, let loose! *M. N. Dream* iii 2 260
Off with't while 'tis vendible . . . . . *All's Well* i 1 168
Strange is it that our bloods . . . stand off In differences so mighty . ii 3 127
Stand no more off, But give thyself unto my sick desires . . v 2 34
On mine own accord I'll off . . . . . *W. Tale* ii 3 63
Indeed, brother-in-law was the farthest off you could have been to him iv 4 723
Off. She did print your royal father off, Conceiving you . . *W. Tale* v 1 125
That before Ascension-day at noon My crown I should give off *K. John* v 1 27
Off goes his bonnet to an oyster-wench . . . . *Richard II.* i 4 31
West of this forest, scarcely off a mile . . . *2 Hen. IV.* iv 1 19
Your French hose off, and in your strait strossers . . *Hen. V.* iii 7 57
Sit like a jack-an-apes, never off . . . . . . v 2 148
Off with his head, and set it on York gates . . *3 Hen. VI.* i 4 179
He's settled, Not to come off, in his displeasure . . *Hen. VIII.* iii 2 23
That's off, that's off; I would you rather had been silent . *Coriolanus* ii 2 64
I will practise the insinuating nod and be off to them most counterfeitly ii 3 107
To my thinking, he was very loath to lay his fingers off it . *J. Cæsar* i 2 243
Some must go off . . . . *Macbeth* v 8 36
If you love me, hold not off . . . . . *Hamlet* ii 2 302
Your skill shall, like a star i' the darkest night, Stick fiery off . v 2 268
Off, off, you lendings! come, unbutton here . . . *Lear* iii 4 113
In strangeness stand no further off Than in a politic distance *Othello* iii 3 12
If you please to hold him off awhile . . . . . iii 3 248
Let me request you off . . . . . *Ant. and Cleo.* ii 7 127
And put My clouted brogues from off my feet . . *Cymbeline* iv 2 214
Off and on. Five and thirty leagues off and on . . . *Tempest* iii 2 17
An easy glove, my lord; she goes off and on at pleasure . . *All's Well* v 3 279
Come off and on swifter than he that gibbets . . *2 Hen. IV.* iii 2 281
Off-capped. Three great ones of the city, In personal suit to make me his lieutenant, Off-capp'd to him . . . . . *Othello* i 1 10
Off of. How camest thou so?—A fall off of a tree . . *2 Hen. VI.* ii 1 96
Offal. Like a barrow of butcher's offal . . . *Mer. Wives* iii 5 5
What trash is Rome, What rubbish and what offal, when it serves For the base matter to illuminate So vile a thing as Cæsar! . *J. Cæsar* i 3 109
I should have fatted all the region kites With this slave's offal *Hamlet* ii 2 608
Offence. For what offence?—For that which now torments me to rehearse: I kill'd a man . . . . . . *T. G. of Ver.* iv 1 25
If hearty sorrow Be a sufficient ransom for offence, I tender't here . v 4 75
Be not as extreme in submission As in offence . . . *Mer. Wives* iv 4 12
The offence is holy that she hath committed . . . . v 5 238
What's his offence?—Groping for trouts in a peculiar river *Meas. for Meas.* i 2 90
Make us pay down for our offence by weight The words of heaven . i 2 125
What's thy offence, Claudio?—What but to speak of would offend again i 2 139
You may not so extenuate his offence For I have had such faults . . ii 1 27
Because he hath some offences in him that thou wouldst discover if thou couldst, let him continue in his courses till thou knowest what they are . . . . ii 1 195
Who is it that hath died for this offence? There's many have committed it . . . . ii 2 88
I pity those I do not know, Which a dismiss'd offence would after gall . ii 2 102
A young man More fit to do another such offence Than die for this . ii 3 14
Where their untaught love Must needs appear offence . . . ii 4 30
And his offence is so, as it appears, Accountant to the law . . ii 4 85
He would give't thee, from this rank offence, So to offend him still . iii 1 100
What offence hath this man made you, sir? . . . . iii 2 15
Hence hath offence his quick celerity, When it is borne in high authority . . . . iv 2 113
You will think you have made no offence . . . . . iv 2 200
The offence pardons itself . . . . v 1 540
My end Was wrought by nature, not by vile offence . *Com. of Errors* i 1 35
To see a reverend Syracusian merchant, Who put unluckily into this bay . . . Beheaded publicly for his offence . . . . v 1 127
And it is an offence to stay a man against his will . . . *Much Ado* iii 3 88
There is not chastity enough in language Without offence to utter them iv 1 99
Why, then, God forgive me!—What offence, sweet Beatrice? . . iv 1 284
Hearken after their offence . . . . . . v 1 216
Officers, what offence have these men done? . . . . v 1 217
Villain, thou shalt fast for thy offences ere thou be pardoned *L. L. Lost* i 2 151
That is the way to make an offence gracious . . . . v 1 147
Worm nor snail, do no offence . . . . . *M. N. Dream* ii 2 23
Every offence is not a hate at first . . . *Mer. of Venice* iv 1 68
I am not a woman, to be touched with so many giddy offences *As Y. L. It* iii 2 367
And faster than his tongue Did make offence his eye did heal it up . iii 5 117
Is it any offence?—No; if without more words you will get you hence *T. of Shrew* i 3 231
Thou art a general offence, and every man should beat thee . *All's Well* ii 3 270
My offences being many, I would repent out the remainder of nature . iv 3 271
Offence of mighty note; but to himself The greatest wrong of all . v 3 14
Let him not ask our pardon; The nature of his great offence is dead . v 3 23
Love that comes too late, Like a remorseful pardon slowly carried, To the great sender turns a sour offence . . . . . . v 3 59
The offence is not of such a bloody nature . . . *T. Night* iii 3 30
My remembrance is very free and clear from any image of offence . iii 4 249
What my offence to him is: it is something of my negligence . . iii 4 279
If this young gentleman Have done offence, I take the fault on me . iii 4 344
I am now so far in offence with my niece . . . . . iv 2 75
The offences we have made you do we'll answer . . . *W. Tale* i 2 83
Whose miseries are to be smiled at, their offences being so capital . iv 4 822
Thou art the issue of my dear offence, Which was so strongly urged *K. John* i 1 257
To do offence and scath in Christendom . . . . . ii 1 75
Like to a muzzled bear, Save in aspect, hath all offence seal'd up . . ii 1 250
Now that their souls are topful of offence . . . . . iii 4 180
Hell make war Upon their spotted souls for this offence! *Richard II.* iii 2 134
If thy offences were upon record, Would it not shame thee? . . iv 1 230
I'll so offend, to make offence a skill . . . . *1 Hen. IV.* i 2 240
For what offence have I this fortnight been A banish'd woman? . . ii 3 41
I would I could Quit all offences with as clear excuse . . . iii 2 19
And find a time To punish this offence in other faults . . . v 2 7
All his offences live upon my head And on his father's . . . v 2 20
And find our griefs heavier than our offences . . *2 Hen. IV.* iv 1 69
We shall admit no parley.—That argues but the shame of your offence. iv 1 160
Stolen that which after some few hours Were thine without offence . iv 5 103
God of his mercy give You patience to endure, and true repentance Of all your dear offences! . . . . *Hen. V.* ii 2 181
All offences, my lord, come from the heart . . . . . iv 8 49
Had you been as I took you for, I made no offence . . . . iv 8 59
Hath the late overthrow wrought this offence? . . . *1 Hen. VI.* i 2 49
Let him perceive how ill we brook his treason And what offence it is to flout his friends . . . . iv 1 75
A poor earl's daughter is unequal odds, And therefore may be broke without offence . . . . v 5 35
And you, good uncle, banish all offence . . . . . . v 5 96
Did he not . . . Devise strange deaths for small offences done? *2 Hen. VI.* iii 1 59
And when I give occasion of offence, Then let me die . . *3 Hen. VI.* i 3 44
Which are so weak of courage and in judgement That they'll take no offence at our abuse . . . . iv 1 13

Offence. What is my offence? Where are the evidence that do accuse me? *Richard III.* i 4 187
For what offence?—The sum of all I can, I have disclosed ii 4 45
I have done some offence That seems disgracious in the city's eyes iii 7 111
There cannot be those numberless offences 'Gainst me, that I cannot take peace with *Hen. VIII.* ii 1 84
A gracious king that pardons all offences Malice ne'er meant ii 2 68
If there be No great offence belongs to't, give your friend Some touch of your late business v 1 12
They are too thin and bare to hide offences v 3 125
To make a sweet lady sad is a sour offence *Troi. and Cres.* iii 1 80
There is between my will and all offences A guard of patience v 2 53
Your virtue is To make him worthy whose offence subdues him *Coriolanus* i 1 179
For one poor grain or two, to leave unburnt, And still to nose the offence v 1 28
His last offences to us Shall have judicious hearing v 6 127
If any one relieves or pities him, For the offence he dies *T. Andron.* v 3 182
For that offence Immediately we do exile him hence *Rom. and Jul.* iii 1 191
A recompense more fruitful Than their offence can weigh *T. of Athens* v 1 154
That which would appear offence in us, His countenance, like richest alchemy, Will change to virtue *J. Cæsar* i 3 158
You have some sick offence within your mind ii 1 268
His glory not extenuated, wherein he was worthy, nor his offences enforced, for which he suffered death iii 2 43
It is not meet That every nice offence should bear his comment iv 3 8
So shall he waste his means, weary his soldiers, Doing himself offence iv 3 201
There's no offence, my lord.—Yes, by Saint Patrick, but there is, Horatio, And much offence too *Hamlet* i 5 137
With more offences at my beck than I have thoughts to put them in iii 1 127
Have you heard the argument? Is there no offence in't? iii 2 243
They do but jest, poison in jest; no offence i' the world iii 2 245
O, my offence is rank, it smells to heaven iii 3 36
Whereto serves mercy But to confront the visage of offence? iii 3 47
May one be pardon'd and retain the offence? iii 3 56
In the corrupted currents of this world Offence's gilded hand may shove by justice iii 3 58
The offender's scourge is weigh'd, But never the offence iv 3 7
And where the offence is let the great axe fall iv 5 218
Her offence Must be of such unnatural degree, That monsters it *Lear* i 1 221
The noble and true-hearted Kent banished! his offence, honesty! 'Tis strange i 2 127
Might in their working do you that offence, Which else were shame i 4 231
What's his offence?—His countenance likes me not ii 2 95
What was the offence you gave him?—I never gave him any ii 2 121
Made you no more offence but what you speak of?—None ii 4 61
All's not offence that indiscretion finds And dotage terms so ii 4 199
If that the heavens do not their visible spirits Send quickly down to tame these vile offences, It will come iv 2 47
He'll be as full of quarrel and offence As my young mistress' dog *Othello* ii 3 52
No offence to the general, nor any man of quality ii 3 109
He that is approved in this offence, Though he had twinn'd with me, both at a birth, Shall lose me ii 3 211
I had rather have this tongue cut from my mouth Than it should do offence ii 3 222
From hence I'll love no friend, sith love breeds such offence iii 3 380
If my offence be of such mortal kind iii 4 115
The business of the state does him offence, And he does chide with you iv 2 166
Take no offence that I would not offend you *Ant. and Cleo.* ii 5 99
But 'twould offend him; and in his offence Should my performance perish iii 1 26
That the false housewife Fortune break her wheel, Provoked by my offence iv 15 45
I never do him wrong, But he does buy my injuries, to be friends; Pays dear for my offences *Cymbeline* i 1 106
To bar your offence herein too, I durst attempt it against any lady i 4 122
I beseech your grace, without offence,—My conscience bids me ask i 5 6
It is not fit your lordship should undertake every companion that you give offence to.—No, I know that: but it is fit I should commit offence to my inferiors ii 1 29
Almost spent with hunger, I am fall'n in this offence iii 6 64
Your pleasure was my mere offence, my punishment Itself v 5 334
And subjects punish'd that ne'er thought offence *Pericles* i 2 28
When all, for mine, if I may call offence, Must feel war's blow i 2 92
He may my proffer take for an offence, Since men take women's gifts for impudence ii 3 68
Due to this heinous capital offence ii 4 5
Never did thought of mine levy offence ii 5 52
Say if you had, Who takes offence at that would make me glad? ii 5 72

Offenceful. So then it seems your most offenceful act Was mutually committed?—Mutually *Meas. for Meas.* ii 3 26

Offenceless. Even so as one would beat his offenceless dog to affright an imperious lion *Othello* ii 3 275

Offend. What but to speak of would offend again *Meas. for Meas.* i 2 140
When I, that censure him, do so offend, Let mine own judgement pattern out my death ii 1 29
If you head and hang all that offend that way ii 1 251
He would give't thee, from this rank offence, So to offend him still iii 1 101
If bawdy talk offend you, we'll have very little of it iv 3 188
Your silence most offends me, and to be merry best becomes you *M. Ado* ii 1 345
I cannot see how sleeping should offend iii 3 43
For, indeed, the watch ought to offend no man iii 3 87
An bad thinking do not wrest true speaking, I'll offend nobody iii 4 34
Make those that do offend you suffer too v 1 40
For none offend where all alike do dote *L. L. Lost* iv 3 126
None of noble sort Would so offend a virgin *M. N. Dream* iii 2 160
If we offend, it is with our good will. That you should think, we come not to offend, But with good will v 1 109
To offend, and judge, are distinct offices And of opposed natures *Mer. of Venice* ii 9 61
Must yield to such inevitable shame As to offend, himself being offended iv 1 58
I will no further offend you than becomes me for my good *As Y. Like It* i 1 83
Never so much as in a thought unborn Did I offend your highness i 3 54
You break into some merry passion And so offend him *T. of Shrew* Ind. 1 98
Was in mine eye The dust that did offend it *All's Well* v 3 55
If you offend him, I for him defy you *T. Night* iii 4 345
The loathsomeness of them [his rags] offends me more than the stripes *W. Tale* iv 3 59
I'll keep him so, That he shall not offend your majesty *K. John* iii 3 65
Hubert, for the wealth of all the world, Will not offend thee iv 1 132
I'll so offend, to make offence a skill *1 Hen. IV.* i 2 240

Offend. God be thanked for these rebels, they offend none but the virtuous *1 Hen. IV.* iii 3 214
The tongue offends not that reports his death *2 Hen. IV.* i 1 97
She is pistol-proof, sir; you shall hardly offend her ii 4 126
Till you do live to see a son of mine Offend you and obey you v 2 106
We'll not offend one stomach with our play *Hen. V.* ii Prol. 40
They do offend our sight iv 7 62
All offences, my lord, come from the heart: never came any from mine that might offend your majesty iv 8 51
No, my good lords, it is not that offends *1 Hen. VI.* iii 1 35
Yet, if this servile usage once offend, Go and be free again v 3 58
Thou aimest all awry; I must offend before I be attainted *2 Hen. VI.* ii 4 59
Yet look to have them buzz to offend thine ears *3 Hen. VI.* ii 6 95
Did not offend, nor were not worthy blame, If this foul deed were by v 5 54
If I be so disgracious in your sight, Let me march on, and not offend your grace *Richard III.* iv 4 178
Such things as might offend the weakest spleen *Troi. and Cres.* ii 2 128
Alas the day, how loath you are to offend daylight! iii 2 51
What offends you, lady?—Sir, mine own company iii 2 151
Name her not now, sir; she's a deadly theme.—O, pardon; I offend iv 5 182
You train me to offend you v 3 4
No more of this; it does offend my heart *Coriolanus* i 1 185
Would it offend you, then, That both should speed? *T. Andron.* ii 1 100
Or offend the stream Of regular justice in your city's bounds *T. of Athens* v 4 60
If much you note him, You shall offend him and extend his passion *Macbeth* iii 4 57
These are but wild and whirling words, my lord.—I'm sorry they offend you, heartily; Yes, 'faith, heartily *Hamlet* i 5 134
O, it offends me to the soul to hear a robustious periwig-pated fellow iii 2 9
This last surrender of his will but offend us *Lear* i 1 310
Give me the letter, sir.—I shall offend, either to detain or give it i 2 42
None does offend, none, I say, none; I'll able 'em iv 6 172
That, if my speech offend a noble heart, Thy arm may do thee justice v 3 127
Put our Cassio in some action That may offend the isle *Othello* ii 3 63
While I spare speech, which something now offends me ii 3 199
I have a salt and sorry rheum offends me; Lend me thy handkerchief iii 4 51
If you are so fond over her iniquity, give her patent to offend iv 1 209
Out of my sight!—I will not stay to offend you iv 1 258
And have you mercy too! I never did Offend you in my life v 2 59
Take no offence that I would not offend you *Ant. and Cleo.* ii 5 99
But 'twould offend him; and in his offence Should my performance perish iii 1 26
Upon my mended judgement—if I offend not to say it is mended *Cymb.* i 4 50
No more, you petty spirits of region low, Offend our hearing v 4 94
Other sorts offend as well as we.—As well as we! ay, and better *Pericles* iv 2 40
What trade, sir?—Why, I cannot name't but I shall offend iv 6 75

Offended. There was the rankest compound of villanous smell that ever offended nostril *Mer. Wives* iii 5 94
He hath but as offended in a dream *Meas. for Meas.* ii 2 4
He hath offended the law: and, sir, we take him to be a thief too iii 2 16
If he had so offended, He would have weigh'd thy brother by himself v 1 110
At length the sun ... Dispersed those vapours that offended us *Com. of Errors* i 1 90
Who have you offended, masters, that you are thus bound? *Much Ado* v 1 232
If we shadows have offended, Think but this, and all is mended *M. N. D.* v 1 430
But of force Must yield to such inevitable shame As to offend, himself being offended *Mer. of Venice* iv 1 58
Be not offended; for it hurts not him That he is loved of me *All's Well* i 3 202
Ambitious love hath so in me offended iii 4 5
Out of my sight! Be not offended *T. Night* iv 1 54
You throw a strange regard upon me, and by that I do perceive it hath offended you: Pardon me, sweet one v 1 220
Your flesh and blood has not offended the king *W. Tale* iv 4 711
What you have done hath not offended me *1 Hen. VI.* ii 3 76
Be not offended, nature's miracle, Thou art allotted to be ta'en by me v 3 54
Wherein have I offended most? Have I affected wealth or honour? *2 Hen. VI.* iv 7 103
Wherein, my friends, have I offended you?—Offended us you have not, but the king *Richard III.* i 4 182
He needs no indirect nor lawless course To cut off those that have offended him i 4 225
With no man here he is offended; For, were he, he had shown it in his looks iii 4 58
Alas, sir, In what have I offended you? *Hen. VIII.* ii 4 19
I am offended with you: Upon the love you bear me, get you in *T. and C.* v 3 77
Open thy deaf ears.—Hadst thou in person ne'er offended me, Even for his sake am I pitiless *T. Andron.* ii 3 161
All have not offended; For those that were, it is not square to take On those that are, revenges *T. of Athens* v 4 35
Spare thy Athenian cradle and those kin Which in the bluster of thy wrath must fall With those that have offended v 4 42
If any, speak; for him have I offended. I pause for a reply.—None, Brutus, none.—Then none have I offended *J. Cæsar* iii 2 36
This tongue had not offended so to-day, If Cassius might have ruled v 1 46
Be not offended: I speak not as in absolute fear of you *Macbeth* iv 3 37
It is offended.—See, it stalks away! *Hamlet* i 1 50
Hamlet, thou hast thy father much offended.—Mother, you have my father much offended iii 4 9
Bethink yourself wherein you may have offended him *Lear* i 2 175
Why not by the hand, sir? How have I offended? ii 4 198
Saints in your injuries, devils being offended *Othello* ii 1 112
I must be laugh'd at, If, or for nothing or a little, I Should say myself offended, and with you Chiefly *Ant. and Cleo.* ii 2 32
Make me not offended In your distrust iii 2 33
I have offended reputation, A most unnoble swerving iii 11 49
Soon as I can win the offended king, I will be known your advocate *Cymbeline* i 1 75
How have I offended, Wherein my death might yield her any profit? *Per.* iv 1 80
I cannot be offended with my trade. Please you to name it iv 6 76

Offendendo. It must be 'se offendendo;' it cannot be else *Hamlet* v 1 9

Offender. Yourself know how easy it is to be such an offender *M. Wives* ii 2 196
When vice makes mercy, mercy's so extended, That for the fault's love is the offender friended *Meas. for Meas.* iv 2 116
But which are the offenders that are to be examined? *Much Ado* iv 2 7
This plaintiff here, the offender, did call me ass v 1 314
The offender's life lies in the mercy Of the duke only *Mer. of Venice* iv 1 355
Time is the old justice that examines all such offenders *As Y. Like It* iv 1 204
Let him approach, A stranger, no offender *All's Well* v 3 26
On this stage, Where we're offenders now *W. Tale* v 1 59
Will rain hot vengeance on offenders heads *Richard II.* i 2 8

Offender. Other offenders we will pause upon . . . . 1 *Hen. IV.* v 5 15
The king hath wasted all his rods On late offenders . . 2 *Hen. IV.* iv 1 216
Whereon, as an offender to your father, I gave bold way to my authority v 2 81
We would have all such offenders so cut off . . . . *Hen. V.* iii 6 113
And will not you maintain the thing you teach, But prove a chief offender in the same? . . . . 1 *Hen. VI.* iii 1 130
Thy cruelty in execution Upon offenders hath exceeded law . 2 *Hen. VI.* i 3 136
Call these foul offenders to their answers . . . . . ii 1 203
You did devise Strange tortures for offenders never heard of . . iii 1 122
For I should melt at an offender's tears . . . . . iii 1 126
And the offender granted scope of speech . . . . . iii 1 176
Makes me most forward . . . To doom the offenders . *Richard III.* iii 4 67
His royal self in judgement comes to hear The cause betwixt her and this great offender . . . . . . *Hen. VIII.* v 3 121
Revenge, which makes the foul offender quake . . *T. Andron.* v 2 40
The offender's scourge is weigh'd, But never the offence . *Hamlet* iv 3 6
All vengeance comes too short Which can pursue the offender . *Lear* ii 1 91
Bind the offender, And take him from our presence . *Cymbeline* v 5 300
Offendest. Thou but offend'st thy lungs to speak so loud *Mer. of Venice* iv 1 140
Offendeth. A stone is silent, and offendeth not . *T. Andron.* iii 1 46
Offending. You chide at him, offending twice as much . . *L. L. Lost* iv 3 132
To be your prisoner should import offending . . . *W. Tale* i 2 57
Ransacking the church, Offending charity . . . . *K. John* iii 4 173
And whipp'd the offending Adam out of him . . . *Hen. V.* i 1 29
If it be a sin to covet honour, I am the most offending soul alive . . iv 3 29
The very head and front of my offending, Hath this extent, no more *Oth.* i 3 80
Offendress. As a desperate offendress against nature . . *All's Well* i 1 153
Offensive. Like an offensive wife That hath enraged him 2 *Hen. IV.* iv 1 210
What most he should dislike seems pleasant to him; What like, offensive *Lear* iv 2 11
Offer. Do not omit the heavy offer of it [sleep] . . . *Tempest* ii 1 194
That dare not offer What I desire to give, and much less take What I shall die to want . . . . iii 1 77
I take your offer and will live with you . . . . *T. G. of Ver.* iv 1 70
What, didst thou offer her this from me? . . . . . . iv 4 58
I do not think the knight would offer it . . . . *Mer. Wives* ii 1 180
If by strong hand you offer to break in Now . . *Com. of Errors* iii 1 98
Some offer me commodities to buy . . . . iv 3 6
They will scarcely believe this without trial: offer them instances *M. Ado* ii 2 41
I do embrace your offer . . . . v 1 303
If this austere insociable life Change not your offer . . *L. L. Lost* v 2 810
Methought I had,—but man is but a patched fool, if he will offer to say what methought I had . . . . . . *M. N. Dream* iv 1 216
If he should offer to choose, and choose the right casket *Mer. of Venice* i 2 99
This is kind I offer.—This were kindness . . . . . . i 3 143
A kind of hard conscience, to offer to counsel me to stay with the Jew ii 2 30
If any man in Italy have a fairer table which doth offer to swear . . ii 2 167
Make no more offers, use no farther means . . . . . iv 1 81
Your wife would give you little thanks for that, If she were by, to hear you make the offer . . . . iv 1 289
'Tis well you offer it behind her back . . . . . . iv 1 293
I take this offer, then; pay the bond thrice And let the Christian go . iv 1 318
I see, sir, you are liberal in offers: You taught me first to beg . . iv 1 438
To offer to get your living by the copulation of cattle . *As Y. Like It* iii 2 84
Cry the man mercy; love him; take his offer . . . . . iii 5 61
Will the faithful offer take Of me and all that I can make . . . iv 3 60
For my kind offer, when I make curtsy, bid me farewell . . . Epil. 23
Players That offer service to your lordship . . *T. of Shrew* Ind. 1 78
And offer me disguised in sober robes . . . . . . i 2 132
I must confess your offer is the best . . . . . . ii 1 388
What are you that offer to beat my servant? . . . . . v 1 65
That women are so simple To offer war where they should kneel for peace v 2 162
We'll take your offer kindly . . . . *All's Well* iii 5 104
If he do not . . . offer to betray you and deliver all the intelligence . iii 6 31
Madam, I am most apt to embrace your offer . . . *T. Night* v 1 328
I'll presently Acquaint the queen of your most noble offer . *W. Tale* ii 2 48
Offer me no money, I pray you; that kills my heart . . . iv 3 87
You offer him, if this be so, a wrong Something unfilial . . . iv 4 416
A ram-tender, to offer to have his daughter come into grace! . . iv 4 805
If you fondly pass our proffer'd offer . . . . *K. John* ii 1 258
Foul play; and 'tis shame That greatness should so grossly offer it . iv 2 94
We must embrace This gentle offer of the perilous time . . . iv 3 13
Your nobles will not hear you, but are gone To offer service to your enemy . . . . v 1 34
Such offers of our peace As we with honour and respect may take . v 7 84
Gone to Ravenspurgh, To offer service to the Duke of Hereford *Richard II.* ii 3 32
An offer, uncle, that we will accept . . . . ii 3 162
If heaven would, And we will not, heaven's offer we refuse . . . iii 2 31
You had rather refuse The offer of an hundred thousand crowns . . iv 1 16
To do that office of thine own good will Which tired majesty did make thee offer, The resignation of thy state . . . . . . iv 1 178
And to the fire-eyed maid of smoky war All hot and bleeding will we offer them . . . . 1 *Hen. IV.* iv 1 115
I come with gracious offers from the king . . . . . . iv 3 30
Will they take the offer of our grace, Both he and they and you, yea, every man Shall be my friend again . . . . v 1 106
We offer fair; take it advisedly . . . . v 1 114
My nephew must not know, Sir Richard, The liberal and kind offer . v 2 2
And wouldst thou turn our offers contrary? . . . . . . v 5 4
As lief they would put ratsbane in my mouth as offer to stop it 2 *Hen. IV.* i 2 48
He hath forced us to compel this offer . . . . . . iv 1 147
This offer comes from mercy, not from fear . . . . . iv 1 150
Like an offensive wife That hath enraged him on to offer strokes . . iv 1 211
His power, like to a fangless lion, May offer, but not hold . . . iv 1 219
I have made an offer to his majesty . . . . . *Hen. V.* i 1 75
How did this offer seem received, my lord? . . . . . . i 1 82
Good corporal! offer nothing here . . . . ii 1 41
The offer likes not . . . . iii Prol. 32
And for achievement offer us his ransom . . . . . . iii 5 60
'Tis as arrant a piece of knavery, mark you now, as can be offer't . iv 7 4
Here, Winchester, I offer thee my hand . . . . 1 *Hen. VI.* iii 1 126
Even with the earth Shall lay your stately and air-braving towers, If you forsake the offer of their love . . . . iv 2 14
Come, offer at my shrine, and I will help thee . . . 2 *Hen. VI.* ii 1 92
Offer him no violence, Unless he seek to thrust you out perforce 3 *Hen. VI.* iii 1 33
Offers, as I do, in a sign of peace, His service . . *Hen. VIII.* iii 1 66
You turn the good we offer into envy . . . . . . iii 1 113
If you omit The offer of this time, I cannot promise But that you shall sustain moe new disgraces . . . . iii 2 4
Offer. I am able now . . . To endure more miseries and greater far Than my weak-hearted enemies dare offer . . . *Hen. VIII.* iii 2 390
Love's full sacrifice He offers in another's enterprise . *Troi. and Cres.* i 2 309
Agamemnon is a fool to offer to command Achilles . . . . . ii 3 67
Which, as I take it, is a gentlemanlike offer . . . *Rom. and Jul.* ii 4 190
We are hither come to offer you our service . . . *T. of Athens* v 1 75
I saw Mark Antony offer him a crown . . . . . *J. Cæsar* i 2 237
Here from gracious England have I offer Of goodly thousands *Macbeth* iv 3 43
We do it wrong, being so majestical, To offer it the show of violence *Ham.* i 1 144
What wouldst thou beg, Laertes, That shall not be my offer? . . . i 2 46
And hither are they coming, to offer you service . . . . . ii 2 331
And, from some knowledge and assurance, offer This office to you *Lear* iii 1 41
Good my lord, take his offer; go into the house . . . . . iii 4 161
All that offer to defend him Stand in assured loss . . . . . iii 6 101
Tell us . . . how you take The offers we have sent you . *Ant. and Cleo.* ii 6 31
You have made me offer Of Sicily, Sardinia . . . . . . ii 6 34
I came before you here a man prepared To take this offer . . . ii 6 42
These offers, Which serve not for his vantage, he shakes off . . iii 7 33
Fortune knows We scorn her most when most she offers blows . . iii 11 74
Add more, From thine invention, offers . . . . . . iii 12 29
I will embrace Your offer. Come, dearest madam . . . *Pericles* iii 3 38
I Will offer night-oblations to thee . . . . v 3 70
Offer up. Let us on heaps go offer up our lives . . . *Hen. V.* iv 5 18
Instead of gold, we'll offer up our arms; Since arms avail not now 1 *Hen. VI.* i 1 46
Your tributary drops belong to woe, Which you, mistaking, offer up to joy *Rom. and Jul.* iii 2 104
Offer up a weak poor innocent lamb To appease an angry god *Macbeth* iv 3 16
Offered. When every grief is entertain'd that's offer'd, Comes to the entertainer— A dollar . . . . *Tempest* ii 1 16
She hath offer'd to the doom . . . A sea of melting pearl *T. G. of Ver.* iii 1 222
Thou shalt not live to brag what we have offer'd . . . . iv 1 69
Then I offered her mine own, who is a dog as big as ten of yours . iv 4 61
Until I know . . . I'll entertain the offer'd fallacy . *Com. of Errors* ii 2 188
No man is so vain That would refuse so fair an offer'd chain . . iii 2 186
I offered him my company to a willow-tree . . . . *Much Ado* ii 1 224
True wit!—Offered by a child to an old man; which is wit-old *L. L. Lost* v 1 65
Shylock, there's thrice thy money offer'd thee . . *Mer. of Venice* iv 1 227
Nay, I have offer'd all, I have no more . . . . *T. of Shrew* ii 1 383
The duke hath offered him letters of commendations . . *All's Well* iv 3 92
Fairly offer'd.—This shows a sound affection . . . *W. Tale* iv 4 389
Deny his offer'd homage, You pluck a thousand dangers on your head *Richard II.* ii 1 204
A fearful head they are . . . As ever offer'd foul play in a state 1 *Hen. IV.* iii 2 169
We offer'd to the king, And might by no suit gain our audience 2 *Hen. IV.* iv 1 75
Those bitter injuries, Which Somerset hath offer'd to my house 1 *Hen. VI.* ii 5 125
Will ye relent, And yield to mercy whilst 'tis offer'd you? 2 *Hen. VI.* iv 8 12
Have I offer'd love for this, To be so flouted? . . . *Richard III.* ii 1 77
But that time offer'd sorrow; This, general joy . . *Hen. VIII.* iii 1 6
I offer'd to awaken his regard For's private friends . . *Coriolanus* v 1 23
Once more offer'd The first conditions . . . . v 3 13
An ill thing to be offered to any gentlewoman . . . *Rom. and Jul.* ii 4 180
When the day serves, before black-corner'd night, Find what thou want'st by free and offer'd light . . . . . . *T. of Athens* v 1 48
There was a crown offered him: and being offered him, he put it by with the back of his hand, thus . . . . *J. Cæsar* i 2 220
Was the crown offered him thrice?—Ay, marry, was't . . . . i 2 228
Then he offered it to him again; then he put it by again . . . i 2 241
Then he offered it the third time; he put it the third time by . . i 2 243
He plucked me ope his doublet and offered them his throat to cut . i 2 268
I do receive your offer'd love like love, And will not wrong it *Hamlet* v 2 262
I crave no more than what your highness offer'd . . . . *Lear* i 1 197
If your will want not, time and place will be fruitfully offered . . iv 6 270
Who seeks, and will not take when once 'tis offer'd, Shall never find it more . . . . *Ant. and Cleo.* ii 7 89
If he should write, And I not have it, 'twere a paper lost, As offer'd mercy is . . . . *Cymbeline* i 3 4
He offered to cut a caper at the proclamation . . . . *Pericles* iv 2 116
Offerest. Thou offer'st fairly to thy brothers' wedding . *As Y. Like It* v 4 173
And twice as much, whate'er thou offer'st next . . *T. of Shrew* ii 1 382
Thou damned and luxurious mountain goat, Offer'st me brass? *Hen. V.* iv 4 21
Offering. My soul the faithfull'st offerings hath breathed . *T. Night* v 1 117
How ceremonious, solemn and unearthly It was i' the offering! *W. Tale* iii 1 8
There are pilgrims going to Canterbury with rich offerings . 1 *Hen. IV.* i 2 141
We of the offering side Must keep aloof from strict arbitrement . . iv 1 69
Offering their own lives in their young's defence . . . 3 *Hen. VI.* ii 2 32
A priest there offering to it his own heart . . . *Troi. and Cres.* iv 3 9
They are polluted offerings, more abhorr'd Than spotted livers . . v 3 17
Time, with his fairer hand, Offering the fortunes of his former days, The former man may make him . . . . *T. of Athens* v 1 127
Plucking the entrails of an offering forth, They could not find a heart within the beast . . . . *J. Cæsar* ii 2 39
Witchcraft celebrates Pale Hecate's offerings . . . . *Macbeth* ii 1 52
Office. They are louder than the weather or our office . . *Tempest* i 1 40
Having both the key Of officer and office, set all hearts i' the state To what tune pleased his ear . . . . i 2 84
Make our fire, Fetch in our wood and serves in offices That profit us . i 2 312
Their eyes do offices of truth, their words Are natural breath . . v 1 156
'Tis an office of great worth . . . . *T. G. of Ver.* i 2 45
'Tis an ill office for a gentleman, Especially against his very friend . iii 2 40
The office is indifferent, Being entreated to it by your friend . . . iii 2 44
I would I could do a good office between you . . . *Mer. Wives* i 1 102
We are come to you to do a good office, master parson . . . . iii 1 49
Not only, Mistress Ford, in the simple office of love, but in all the accoutrement, complement and ceremony of it . . . . . . iv 2 5
You orphan heirs of fixed destiny, Attend your office and your quality v 5 44
I have on Angelo imposed the office . . . . . *Meas. for Meas.* i 3 40
I thought, by your readiness in the office, you had continued in it some time . . . . ii 1 276
Do you your office, or give up your place . . . . . . ii 2 13
Who in his office lacks a helper: if you will take it on you . . iv 2 10
Belike thinking me remiss in mine office . . . . iv 2 119
Thus fail not to do your office, as you will answer it at your peril . iv 2 129
Hast thou or word, or wit, or impudence, That yet can do thee office? . v 1 369
Go take her hence, and marry her instantly. Do you the office, friar . v 1 383
For which I do discharge you of your office: Give up your keys . . v 1 466
O villain! thou hast stolen both mine office and my name *Com. of Errors* iii 1 44
And may it be that you have quite forgot A husband's office? . . . iii 2 2
I will attend my husband, be his nurse, Diet his sickness, for it is my office . . . . v 1 99

Office. Friendship is constant in all other things Save in the office and affairs of love: Therefore all hearts in love use their own tongues *Much Ado* ii 1 183
I will do any modest office, my lord, to help my cousin to a good husband ii 1 390
This is thy office; Bear thee well in it and leave us alone . iii 1 12
If you meet a thief, you may suspect him, by virtue of your office . iii 3 54
Shall we not lay hands on him?—Truly, by your office, you may . . iii 3 59
May a man do it?—It is a man's office, but not yours . . iv 1 268
'Tis all men's office to speak patience To those that wring under the load of sorrow . . . . v 1 27
You know your office, brother . . . . v 4 14
A double power, Above their functions and their offices *L. L. Lost* iv 3 332
For virtue's office never breaks men's troth . . . . . v 2 350
Sing me now asleep; Then to your offices and let me rest *M. N. Dream* ii 2 8
'Tis an office of discovery, love . . . . *Mer. of Venice* ii 6 43
O, that estates, degrees and offices Were not derived corruptly! . . ii 9 41
To offend, and judge, are distinct offices And of opposed natures . . ii 9 61
Stubborn Turks and Tartars, never train'd To offices of tender courtesy iv 1 33
Now thou goest from Fortune's office to Nature's . . *As Y. Like It* i 2 44
To bed with him; And each one to his office when he wakes *T. of S.* Ind. 1 73
Thy servants do attend on thee, Each in his office ready at thy beck Ind. 2 36
Thou shalt soon feel, to thy cold comfort, for being slow in thy hot office . . . . iv 1 34
A cold world, Curtis, in every office but thine . . . . . iv 1 37
That's my office.—Spoke like an officer . . . . . . v 2 36
I will no more enforce mine office on you . . . *All's Well* ii 1 129
Nor does The ministration and required office On my particular . . ii 5 65
Her death itself, which could not be her office to say is come . . iv 3 68
Time was, I did him a desired office, Dear almost as his life . . iv 4 5
Dost thou put upon me at once both the office of God and the devil? . v 2 52
Is there no exorcist Beguiles the truer office of mine eyes? . . . v 3 306
Speak your office.—It alone concerns your ear . . . . *T. Night* i 5 223
Do me this courteous office, as to know of the knight . . . iii 4 278
This is the man; do thy office.—Antonio, I arrest thee . . . iii 4 359
The office Becomes a woman best; I'll take 't upon me . . *W. Tale* ii 2 31
Wolves and bears, they say, Casting their savageness aside have done Like offices of pity . . . . ii 3 189
You ha' done me a charitable office . . . . iv 3 81
Nothing so certain as your anchors, who Do their best office . . iv 4 582
Give me the office To choose you a queen . . . . . . v 1 77
These thy offices, So rarely kind . . . . v 1 149
All things that you should use to do me wrong Deny their office *K. John* iv 1 119
Bare-ribb'd death, whose office is this day To feast upon whole thousands of the French . . . . v 2 177
I do but stay behind To do the office for thee of revenge . . . v 7 71
Unfurnish'd walls, Unpeopled offices, untrodden stones . *Richard II.* i 2 69
When the tongue's office should be prodigal To breathe the abundant dolour of the heart . . . . i 3 256
Set in the silver sea, Which serves it in the office of a wall . . . ii 1 47
Little office The hateful commons will perform for us . . . ii 2 137
He hath forsook the court, Broken his staff of office . . . ii 3 27
Who perform'd The bloody office of his timeless end . . . iv 1 5
To do that office of thine own good will . . . . . . iv 1 177
For you my staff of office did I break In Richard's time . 1 *Hen. IV.* v 1 34
Rebuke and dread correction wait on us And they shall do their office v 1 112
My office is To noise abroad that Harry Monmouth fell . 2 *Hen. IV.* Ind. 28
The first bringer of unwelcome news Hath but a losing office . . . i 1 101
What do we then but draw anew the model In fewer offices? . . . i 3 47
Master Fang and Master Snare, do me, do me, do me your offices . ii 1 45
Noble offices thou mayst effect Of mediation, after I am dead . . iv 4 24
England shall give him office, honour, might . . . . iv 5 130
A foutre for thine office! Sir John, thy tender lambkin now is king . v 3 121
Choose what office thou wilt in the land, 'tis thine . . . . v 3 129
Put thy face between his sheets, and do the office of a warming pan *Hen. V.* ii 1 88
Shall forget the office of our hand, Sooner than quittance of desert . ii 2 33
So far my king and master; so much my office . . . . iii 6 145
Thou dost thy office fairly. Turn thee back, And tell thy king . iii 6 148
My office hath so far prevail'd . . . . v 2 29
That never may ill office, or fell jealousy, . . . Thrust in between the paction of these kingdoms . . . . v 2 391
But long I will not be Jack out of office . . . 1 *Hen. VI.* i 1 175
My lord should be religious And know the office that belongs to such . iii 1 55
Thy sale of offices and towns in France, If they were known, as the suspect is great, Would make thee quickly hop without thy head 2 *Hen. VI.* i 3 138
It is my office; and, madam, pardon me . . . . . . ii 4 102
Æolus would not be a murderer, But left that hateful office unto thee . iii 2 93
Take time to do him dead.—That is my office . . . 3 *Hen. VI.* i 4 109
A peevish fool was that of Crete, That taught his son the office of a fowl! . . . . v 6 19
Both are ready in their offices, At any time . . . *Richard III.* iii 5 10
The throne majestical, The scepter'd office of your ancestors . . . iii 7 119
I'll bear thy blame And take thy office from thee, on my peril . . iv 1 26
The office did Distinctly his full function . . . . *Hen. VIII.* i 1 44
Your office, sergeant; execute it . . . . i 1 198
Not unconsider'd leave your honour, nor The dignity of your office . i 2 16
And lost your office On the complaint o' the tenants . . . . i 2 172
Your words, Domestics to you, serve your will as't please Yourself pronounce their office . . . . ii 4 115
Should Do no more offices of life to't than The grave does to the dead . ii 4 190
Sir, For holy offices I have a time . . . . iii 2 144
Since I had my office, I have kept you next my heart . . . iii 2 156
'Tis the list Of those that claim their offices this day . . . iv 1 15
In all the progress Both of my life and office, I have labour'd . . v 3 33
Season, form, Office and custom, in all line of order . *Troi. and Cres.* i 3 88
Which is that god in office, guiding men? . . . . . . i 3 231
Were I the general, thou shouldst have my office Ere that correction . v 6 4
Through the cranks and offices of man . . . . . *Coriolanus* i 1 141
I warrant him consul.—Then our office may, During his power, go sleep . . . . ii 1 238
Rather than fool it so, Let the high office and the honour go . . . ii 3 129
What are your offices? You being their mouths, why rule you not their teeth? . . . . iii 1 35
You have contrived to take From Rome all season'd office . . . iii 3 64
You shall perceive that a Jack guardant cannot office me from my son . v 2 68
All things that we ordained festival, Turn from their office to black funeral; Our instruments to melancholy bells . . *Rom. and Jul.* iv 5 85
Pardon me for bringing these ill news, Since you did leave it for my office . . . . v 1 23

Office. Which bears that office, to signify their pleasures . *T. of Athens* i 2 125
Would I were gently put out of office Before I were forced out! . . i 2 207
When all our offices have been oppress'd With riotous feeders . . ii 2 167
To vex thee.—Always a villain's office or a fool's . . . . . iv 3 237
To sell and mart your offices for gold To undeservers . *J. Cæsar* iv 3 11
That's not an office for a friend, my lord . . . . . . v 5 29
So clear in his great office, that his virtues Will plead like angels *Macb.* i 7 18
And Sent forth great largess to your offices . . . . . . ii 1 14
To show an unfelt sorrow is an office Which the false man does easy . ii 3 142
He delivers Our offices and what we have to do To the direction just . iii 3 3
Come, high or low; Thyself and office deftly show! . . . . iv 1 68
The law's delay, The insolence of office . . . . *Hamlet* iii 1 73
I hear that you have shown your father A child-like office . . *Lear* ii 1 108
Infirmity doth still neglect all office Whereto our health is bound . . ii 4 107
Thou better know'st The offices of nature, bond of childhood . . . ii 4 181
And, from some knowledge and assurance, offer This office to you . iii 1 42
A dog's obeyed in office . . . . iv 6 163
Who hath the office? send Thy token of reprieve . . . . v 3 248
The trust, the office I do hold of you, Not only take away, but let your sentence Even fall upon my life . . . . *Othello* i 3 118
It is thought abroad, that 'twixt my sheets He has done my office . . i 3 394
All offices are open, and there is full liberty of feasting . . . . ii 2 9
If partially affined, or leagued in office, Thou dost deliver more or less than truth, Thou art no soldier . . . . ii 3 218
Are you a man? have you a soul or sense? God be wi' you; take mine office . . . . iii 3 375
Give me a living reason she's disloyal.—I do not like the office . . iii 3 410
Whom I with all the office of my heart Entirely honour . . . iii 4 113
That have the office opposite to Saint Peter, And keep the gate of hell! iv 2 91
Some cogging, cozening slave, to get some office . . . . . iv 2 132
Now turn The office and devotion of their view Upon a tawny front *Ant. and Cleo.* i 1 5
Those flower-soft hands, That yarely frame the office . . . . ii 2 216
The world and my great office will sometimes Divide me from your bosom . . . . ii 3 1
Declare thine office . . . . iii 12 10
I must attend mine office, Or would have done't myself . . . . iv 6 27
It is an office of the gods to venge it, Not mine to speak on't *Cymbeline* i 6 92
This gate Instructs you how to adore the heavens and bows you To a morning's holy office . . . . iii 3 4
You are appointed for that office; The due of honour in no point omit . iii 5 10
In short time All offices of nature should again Do their due functions . v 5 257
I would wish no better office than to be beadle . . . *Pericles* ii 1 97
A stranger and distressed gentleman That never aim'd so high to love your daughter, But bent all offices to honour her . . . . . ii 5 48

Office-badge. Methought this staff, mine office-badge in court, Was broke in twain . . . . 2 *Hen. VI.* i 2 25

Officed. No, although The air of paradise did fan the house And angels officed all . . . . *All's Well* iii 2 129
So stands this squire Officed with me . . . . . . *W. Tale* i 2 172
Seel with wanton dullness My speculative and officed instruments *Othello* i 3 271

Officer. Having both the key Of officer and office . . . . *Tempest* i 2 84
An office of great worth And you an officer fit for the place *T. G. of Ver.* i 2 44
Your husband's coming hither, woman, with all the officers *Mer. Wives* iii 3 114
This comes off well; here's a wise officer . . . *Meas. for Meas.* ii 1 58
Let not your worship think me the poor duke's officer . . . . ii 1 186
Every pelting, petty officer Would use his heaven for thunder . . ii 2 112
There he must stay until the officer Arise to let him in . . . iv 2 93
Make present satisfaction, Or I'll attach you by this officer *Com. of Er.* iv 1 6
Say whether you'll answer me or no: If not, I'll leave him to the officer iv 1 61
Well, officer, arrest him at my suit . . . . iv 1 69
Arrest him, officer. I would not spare my brother in this case . . iv 1 76
What, thou meanest an officer?—Ay, sir, the sergeant of the band . iv 3 29
What wilt thou do, thou peevish officer? . . . . . . iv 4 117
For the which He did arrest me with an officer . . . . . v 1 230
Then fairly I bespoke the officer To go in person with me to my house . v 1 233
But we are the poor duke's officers . . . . . *Much Ado* iii 5 22
Let him write down the prince's officer coxcomb . . . . . iv 2 73
I am a wise fellow, and, which is more, an officer . . . . iv 2 83
Officers, what offence have these men done? . . . . . . v 1 217
Thy sweet grace's officer, Anthony Dull; a man of good repute *L. L. Lost* i 1 271
You can produce acquittances For such a sum from special officers . ii 1 162
Go, Tubal, fee me an officer . . . . . *Mer. of Venice* iii 1 131
Let my officers of such a nature Make an extent upon his house and lands: Do this expediently . . . . . . *As Y. Like It* iii 1 16
Every officer his wedding-garment on . . . . *T. of Shrew* iv 1 50
That's my office.—Spoke like an officer . . . . v 2 37
A filthy officer he is in those suggestions . . . . *All's Well* iii 5 18
The duke knows him for no other but a poor officer of mine . . iv 3 226
He had the honour to be the officer at a place there called Mile-end . iv 3 301
Calling my officers about me, in my branched velvet gown . *T. Night* ii 5 53
Command our officers at arms Be ready . . . . *Richard II.* i 1 204
Except the marshal and such officers Appointed to direct these fair designs . . . . i 3 44
Each takes his fellow for an officer . . . . . 1 *Hen. IV.* ii 2 114
Wilt thou kill God's officers and the king's? . . . 2 *Hen. IV.* ii 1 56
For these foolish officers, I beseech you I may have redress against them ii 1 117
I do desire deliverance from these officers, being upon hasty employment ii 1 139
Pluck down my officers, break my decrees . . . . . . iv 5 118
They have a king and officers of sorts . . . . . *Hen. V.* i 2 190
Art thou officer? Or art thou base, common and popular? . . . iv 1 37
Come, officer; as loud as e'er thou canst: Cry . . . 1 *Hen. VI.* i 3 72
Then broke I from the officers that led me . . . . . . i 4 44
Take some order in the town, Placing therein some expert officers . iii 2 127
So desperate thieves, all hopeless of their lives, Breathe out invectives 'gainst the officers . . . . 3 *Hen. VI.* i 4 43
We charge you, in God's name, and the king's, To go with us unto the officers . . . . iii 1 98
The thief doth fear each bush an officer . . . . v 6 12
Call thither all the officers o' the town . . . . . *Coriolanus* i 5 28
Have you thus Given Hydra here to choose an officer? . . . . iii 1 93
Be you then as the people's officer . . . . iii 1 330
I do demand, If you submit you to the people's voices, Allow their officers? iii 3 45
Beating your officers, cursing yourselves, Opposing laws with strokes . iii 3 78
Caius Marcius was A worthy officer i' the war; but insolent . . . iv 6 30
Obeys his points As if he were his officer . . . . iv 6 126
By your leave, I am an officer of state . . . . v 2 3
In his own change, or by ill officers, Hath given me some worthy cause to wish Things done, undone . . . . *J. Cæsar* iv 2 7
What not put upon His spongy officers, who shall bear the guilt? *Macbeth* i 7 71

Officer. But such officers do the king best service in the end . *Hamlet* iv 2 18
Young Laertes, in a riotous head, O'erbears your officers . iv 5 102
For, 'Certes,' says he, 'I have already chose my officer' . *Othello* i 1 17
Get weapons, ho! And raise some special officers of night . . . i 1 183
Leave some officer behind, And he shall our commission bring to you . ii 3 281
I love thee; But never more be officer of mine . . . ii 3 249
Than to deceive so good a commander with so slight, so drunken, and so indiscreet an officer . . . ii 3 280
O, 'tis foul in her.—With mine officer!—That's fouler . . . iv 1 214
Let our officers Have notice what we purpose . . *Ant. and Cleo.* i 2 183
Cæsar and Antony have ever won More in their officer than person . iii 1 17
And threats the throat of that his officer That murder'd Pompey . iii 5 19
That hath more kings his servants than Thyself domestic officers *Cymb.* iii 1 65
But a man that were to sleep your sleep, and a hangman to help him to bed, I think he would change places with his officer . . v 4 180
The gods can have no mortal officer More like a god than you *Pericles* v 3 62
Official. In the official marks invested . . . *Coriolanus* ii 3 148
Officious. You are too officious In her behalf . . *M. N. Dream* iii 2 330
Come you hither; You that have been so tenderly officious . *W. Tale* ii 3 159
Let him call me rogue for being so far officious . . . iv 4 871
Know, officious lords, I dare and must deny it . . *Hen. VIII.* iii 2 237
Officious, and not valiant, you have shamed me . . *Coriolanus* i 8 14
Come, come, be every one officious To make this banquet *T. Andron.* v 2 202
Offspring. What says that fool of Hagar's offspring? . *Mer. of Venice* ii 5 44
God shall forgive you Cœur-de-lion's death The rather that you give his offspring life . . . . . . *K. John* ii 1 13
And I the rather wean me from despair For love of Edward's offspring in my womb . . . . . . 3 *Hen. VI.* iv 4 18
Thou offspring of the house of Lancaster, The wronged heirs of York do pray for thee . . . . . *Richard III.* v 3 136
I am yours, You valiant offspring of great Priamus . *Troi. and Cres.* ii 2 207
Accursed the offspring of so foul a fiend! . . . *T. Andron.* iv 2 79
Oft. If this be he you oft have wish'd to hear from . . *T. G. of Ver.* ii 4 103
To call her bad, Whose sovereignty so oft thou hast preferr'd . ii 6 15
How oft hast thou with perjury cleft the root! . . . . v 4 103
Lose the good we oft might win By fearing to attempt . *Meas. for Meas.* i 4 78
They do you wrong to put you so oft upon't . . . . ii 1 280
Mercy is not itself, that oft looks so . . . . . . ii 1 297
It oft falls out, To have what we would have, we speak not what we mean ii 4 117
Thy best of rest is sleep, And that thou oft provokest . . . iii 1 18
Music oft hath such a charm To make bad good . . . iv 1 14
We have very oft awaked him, as if to carry him to execution . iv 2 159
Very oft, When I am dull with care and melancholy, Lightens my humour with his merry jests . . . *Com. of Errors* i 2 19
Some love that drew him oft from home . . . . . v 1 56
Oft in field, with targe and shield, did make my foe to sweat *L. L. Lost* v 2 556
I with the morning's love have oft made sport . . *M. N. Dream* iii 2 389
And by adventuring both I oft found both . . *Mer. of Venice* i 1 144
Many a time and oft In the Rialto you have rated me . . . i 3 107
I oft deliver'd from his forfeitures Many that have at times made moan iii 3 22
You have oft inquired After the shepherd . . *As Y. Like It* iii 4 50
Not very well, but I have met him oft . . . . iii 5 106
Was't you that did so oft contrive to kill him? . . . . iv 3 135
How oft did you say his beard was not well cut? . . . . v 4 87
Full oft we see Cold wisdom waiting on superfluous folly *All's Well* i 1 115
He that of greatest works is finisher Oft does them by the weakest minister . . . . ii 1 140
For youth is bought more oft than begg'd or borrow'd . *T. Night* iii 4 3
Why urgest thou so oft young Arthur's death? . . *K. John* iv 2 204
Oft have shot at them, Howe'er unfortunate I miss'd my aim 1 *Hen. VI.* i 4 3
Death, at whose name I oft have been afear'd . 2 *Hen. VI.* ii 4 89
Oft have I seen a timely-parted ghost . . . . . iii 2 161
Great men oft die by vile bezonians . . . . . . iv 1 134
Oft have I heard that grief softens the mind . . . . iv 4 1
To fear the worst oft cures the worse . . . *Troi. and Cres.* iii 2 78
Oft have you—often have you thanks therefore . . . . iii 3 20
Oft when men are at the point of death Have they been merry! *R. and J.* v 3 88
So oft as that shall be, So often shall the knot of us be call'd The men that gave their country liberty . . . . *J. Cæsar* iii 1 116
And oft before gave audience, As 'tis reported, so . . *Ant. and Cleo.* iii 6 18
Often. You have often Begun to tell me what I am, but stopp'd *Tempest* i 2 33
Ebbing men, indeed, Most often do so near the bottom run . . ii 1 227
Of whom so often I have heard renown . . . . . . v 1 193
Indeed, a sheep doth very often stray . . . *T. G. of Ver.* i 1 74
For often have you writ to her . . . . ii 1 171
Dumb jewels often in their silent kind More than quick words do move a woman's mind . . . . iii 1 90
Or else I often had been miserable . . . . . . iv 1 35
We do not act that often jest and laugh . . . *Mer. Wives* iv 2 108
Like a good thing, being often read, Grown fear'd and tedious *M. for M.* ii 4 8
How often dost thou with thy case, thy habit, Wrench awe from fools! ii 4 13
And often touching will Wear gold . . . *Com. of Errors* ii 1 111
In company I often glanced it . . . . v 1 66
By night, Full often hath she gossip'd by my side . *M. N. Dream* ii 1 125
O wall, full often hast thou heard my moans! . . . . v 1 190
All that glisters is not gold; Often have you heard that told *Mer. of Ven.* ii 7 66
My often rumination wraps me in a most humorous sadness *As Y. L. It* iv 1 19
Forswear themselves as often as they speak . . . *W. Tale* v 1 200
Unbidden guests Are often welcomest when they are gone . 1 *Hen. VI.* ii 2 56
Did he so often lodge in open field, In winter's cold? . . 2 *Hen. VI.* i 1 80
For things are often spoke and seldom meant . . . . iii 1 268
Full often, like a shag-hair'd crafty kern, Hath he conversed with the enemy . . . . iii 1 367
How often hast thou waited at my cup? . . . . . iv 1 56
Their colours, often borne in France, And now in England 3 *Hen. VI.* i 1 127
Myself have often heard him say and swear . . . . iii 3 123
Oft have you—often have you thanks therefore . *Troi. and Cres.* iii 3 20
Many a time and often I ha' dined with him . . *T. of Athens* iii 1 25
So oft as that shall be, So often shall the knot of us be call'd The men that gave their country liberty . . . . *J. Cæsar* iii 1 117
Oftener. He doth oftener ask forgiveness . . . *Meas. for Meas.* iv 2 54
My eyes are oftener wash'd than hers . . . . *M. N. Dream* ii 2 93
A hundred times and oftener . . . . . . 2 *Hen. VI.* ii 1 90
Oftener upon her knees than on her feet, Died every day she lived *Macb.* iv 3 110
Oftentimes have purposed to forbid Sir Valentine her company *T. G. of V.* iii 1 26
Without desert—Hath oftentimes upbraided me withal *Com. of Errors* iii 1 113
Yet oftentimes he goes but mean-apparell'd . . . *T. of Shrew* iii 2 75
Oftentimes excusing of a fault Doth make the fault the worse *K. John* iv 2 30
Diseased nature oftentimes breaks forth In strange eruptions 1 *Hen. IV.* iii 1 27
Oftentimes it doth present harsh rage, Defect of manners . . . iii 1 183
Oftentimes, to win us to our harm, The instruments of darkness tell us truths, Win us with honest trifles . . . . . *Macbeth* i 3 123
Oft-subdued. As you fly from your oft-subdued slaves . . 1 *Hen. VI.* i 5 32
Oft-times. When he was here, He did incline to sadness, and oft-times Not knowing why . . . . *Cymbeline* i 6 62
Oh. These lovers cry Oh! oh! they die! Yet that which seems the wound to kill, Doth turn oh! oh! to ha! ha! he! *Troi. and Cres.* iii 1 131
Oh! oh! a while, but ha! ha! ha! Oh! oh! groans out for ha! ha! ha! iii 1 135
Oh, oh, oh!—What a sigh is there! The heart is sorely charged *Macbeth* v 1 58
Oil. No use of metal, corn, or wine, or oil . . . . *Tempest* ii 1 153
This whale, with so many tuns of oil in his belly . . *Mer. Wives* ii 1 65
I think the devil will not have me damned, lest the oil that's in me should set hell on fire . . . . v 5 39
I have bought The oil, the balsamum and aqua-vitæ . *Com. of Errors* iv 1 89
'Let me not live,' quoth he, 'After my flame lacks oil' . . *All's Well* i 2 59
Oil and fire, too strong for reason's force, O'erbears it and burns on . v 3 7
What flaying? boiling? In leads or oils? . . . . *W. Tale* iii 2 178
My condition; Which hath been smooth as oil . . . 1 *Hen. IV.* i 3 7
These eyes, like lamps whose wasting oil is spent, Wax dim . 1 *Hen. VI.* ii 5 8
And beauty that the tyrant oft reclaims Shall to my flaming wrath be oil and flax . . . . 2 *Hen. VI.* v 2 55
She had all the royal makings of a queen; As holy oil *Hen. VIII.* iv 1 88
Instead of oil and balm, Thou lay'st in every gash that love hath given me The knife that made it . . . . *Troi. and Cres.* i 1 61
Like madness is the glory of this life, As this pomp shows to a little oil and root . . . . *T. of Athens* i 2 140
Bring oil to fire, snow to their colder moods; Renege, affirm . *Lear* ii 2 83
Oil-dried lamp. My oil-dried lamp and time-bewasted light Shall be extinct with age . . . . *Richard II.* i 3 221
Oily. Her lip is wet; You'll mar it if you kiss it, stain your own With oily painting . . . . *W. Tale* v 3 83
This oily rascal is known as well as Paul's . . . 1 *Hen. IV.* ii 4 575
I want that glib and oily art, To speak and purpose not . . . *Lear* i 1 227
If an oily palm be not a fruitful prognostication . . *Ant. and Cleo.* i 2 53
Old. Then thou wast not Out three years old . . . . *Tempest* i 2 41
His years but young, but his experience old . . . *T. G. of Ver.* ii 4 69
When she is able to overtake seventeen years old . . *Mer. Wives* i 1 55
He wooes both high and low, both rich and poor, Both young and old . ii 1 118
Though I now be old and of the peace, if I see a sword out, my finger itches to make one . . . . ii 3 47
'Tis old, but true, Still swine eats all the draff . . . . iv 2 109
A witch, a quean, an old cozening quean! . . . . . iv 2 180
Old, cold, withered, and of intolerable entrails . . . . v 5 161
When thou art old and rich, Thou hast neither heat, affection, limb, nor beauty, To make thy riches pleasant . . *Meas. for Meas.* iii 1 36
His child is a year and a quarter old, come Philip and Jacob . . iii 2 214
One that is a prisoner nine years old . . . . . . iv 2 135
If the old fantastical duke of dark corners had been at home . . iv 3 163
Fairly met! Our old and faithful friend, we are glad to see you . v 1 2
From whom my absence was not six months old . *Com. of Errors* i 1 45
In Ephesus I am but two hours old . . . . . . ii 2 150
He is deformed, crooked, old and sere, Ill-faced, worse bodied . iv 2 19
You always end with a jade's trick: I know you of old . *Much Ado* i 1 146
To brag What I have done being young, or what would do Were I not old v 1 62
Can you tell me by your wit What was a month old at Cain's birth, that's not five weeks old as yet? . . . . . *L. L. Lost* iv 2 36
The moon was a month old when Adam was no more . . . iv 2 40
O spite! too old to be engaged to young . . . *M. N. Dream* i 1 138
I fear he will prove the weeping philosopher when he grows old *M. of V.* i 2 54
If I live to be as old as Sibylla, I will die as chaste as Diana . . i 2 116
Had you been as wise as bold, Young in limbs, in judgement old . ii 7 71
Happy in this, she is not yet so old But she may learn . . . iii 2 162
So young a body with so old a head . . . . . . iv 1 164
Though I look old, yet I am strong and lusty . . *As Y. Like It* ii 3 47
Look you, who comes here; a young man and an old in solemn talk . ii 4 21
I have loved ere now.—No, Corin, being old, thou canst not guess . ii 4 25
The poor world is almost six thousand years old . . . . iv 1 95
How old are you, friend?—Five and twenty, sir . . . . v 1 20
I have, since I was three year old, conversed with a magician . . v 2 66
As old as Sibyl and as curst and shrewd As Socrates' Xanthippe *T. of Shrew* i 2 70
He is old, I young.—And may not young men die, as well as old? . ii 1 392
An old rusty sword ta'en out of the town-armoury . . . . iii 2 46
His horse hipped with an old mothy saddle . . . . . iii 2 49
The rest were ragged, old, and beggarly . . . . . . iv 1 140
This is a man, old, wrinkled, faded, wither'd, And not a maiden . iv 5 43
I have brought him up ever since he was three years old . . . v 1 86
You are too old, sir; let it satisfy you, you are too old . . *All's Well* ii 3 206
Scurvy, old, filthy, scurvy lord! . . . . ii 3 250
Let's take the instant by the forward top; For we are old . . . v 3 40
You see, sir, how your fooling grows old, and people dislike it *T. Night* i 5 119
That old and antique song we heard last night . . . . ii 4 3
Too old, by heaven: let still the woman take An elder than herself . ii 4 30
Mark it, Cesario, it is old and plain . . . . . . ii 4 44
What old or newer torture Must I receive? . . . . *W. Tale* iii 2 178
Is it true, think you?—Very true, and but a month old . . . iv 4 270
An old sheep-whistling rogue, a ram-tender . . . . . iv 4 804
The old, feeble, and day-wearied sun . . . . . *K. John* v 4 35
I am too old to fawn upon a nurse, Too far in years to be a pupil *Rich. II.* i 3 170
Both young and old rebel, And all goes worse than I have power to tell iii 2 119
Young and old Through casements darted their desiring eyes . . v 2 13
Though I be old, I doubt not but to ride as fast as York . . . v 2 114
But this our purpose now is twelve month old . . . 1 *Hen. IV.* i 1 28
One of them is fat and grows old: God help the while! . . . ii 4 145
Falstaff, that old white-bearded Satan . . . . . . ii 4 509
That he is old, the more the pity, his white hairs do witness it . ii 4 514
If to be old and merry be a sin, then many an old host that I know is damned . . . . ii 4 518
This advertisement is five days old . . . . iii 2 172
You that are old consider not the capacities of us that are young 2 *Hen. IV.* i 2 196
Are written down old with all the characters of age . . . . i 2 202
The truth is, I am only old in judgement and understanding . . . i 2 215
I am old.—I love thee better than I love e'er a scurvy young boy . ii 4 294
Doth she hold her own well?—Old, old, Master Shallow.—Nay, she must be old; she cannot choose but be old; certain she's old . iii 2 219
O, give me always a little, lean, old, chapt, bald shot . . . iii 2 294
Such a kind of man, So surfeit-swell'd, so old and so profane . . v 5 54
But there's a saying very old and true . . . . . *Hen. V.* i 2 166
Mine was not bridled.—O then belike she was old and gentle . . iii 7 55
Old I do wax; and from my weary limbs Honour is cudgelled . . v 1 89
Of old I know them . . . . 1 *Hen. VI.* i 2 39

Old. When I was young, as yet I am not old 1 *Hen. VI.* iii 4 17
I was made a king, at nine months old 2 *Hen. VI.* iv 9 4
Why art thou old, and want'st experience? Or wherefore dost abuse it? v 1 171
Like rich hangings in a homely house, So was his will in his old feeble body v 3 13
When I was crown'd I was but nine months old 3 *Hen. VI.* i 1 112
I was anointed king at nine months old iii 1 76
Henry the Sixth Was crown'd in Paris but at nine months old *Rich. III.* ii 3 17
My uncle grew so fast That he could gnaw a crust at two hours old ii 4 28
For making me, so young, so old a widow! iv 1 73
Rude ragged nurse, old sullen playfellow! iv 1 102
The parents live, whose children thou hast butcher'd, Old wither'd plants iv 4 394
A three-pence bow'd would hire me, Old as I am, to queen it *Hen. VIII.* ii 3 37
I am old, my lords, And all the fellowship I hold now with him Is only my obedience iii 1 120
Left me, Weary and old with service, to the mercy Of a rude stream iii 2 363
Either young or old, He or she, cuckold or cuckold-maker v 4 24
So young a man and so old a lifter *Troi. and Cres.* i 2 128
Nestor, one that was a man When Hector's grandsire suck'd: he is old now i 3 292
When time is old and hath forgot itself, When waterdrops have worn the stones of Troy iii 2 192
And that old common arbitrator, Time, Will one day end it iv 5 225
That stale old mouse-eaten dry cheese, Nestor v 4 11
Help, You that be noble; help him, young and old! *Coriolanus* iii 1 228
Go read with thee Sad stories chanced in the times of old *T. Andron.* iii 2 83
To wield old partisans, in hands as old *Rom. and Jul.* i 1 101
'Tis not hard, I think, For men so old as we to keep the peace i 2 3
Take thou some new infection to thy eye, And the rank poison of the old will die i 2 51
At twelve year old, I bade her come i 3 2
These griefs, these woes, these sorrows make me old iii 2 89
Son of sixteen, Pluck the lined crutch from thy old limping sire! *T. of A.* iv 1 14
Thus much of this [gold] will make black white, foul fair, Wrong right, base noble, old young iv 3 29
Such free and friendly conference, As he hath used of old *J. Cæsar* iv 2 18
Even for that our love of old, I prithee, Hold thou my sword-hilts v 5 27
For those of old, And the late dignities heap'd up to them *Macbeth* i 6 18
A little month, or ere those shoes were old *Hamlet* i 2 147
And you, my sinews, grow not instant old, But bear me stiffly up i 5 94
Yourself, sir, should be as old as I am, if like a crab you could go backward ii 2 206
Ere we were two days old at sea iv 6 15
How old art thou?—Not so young, sir, to love a woman for singing, nor so old to dote on her for any thing *Lear* i 4 39
As you are old and reverend, you should be wise i 4 261
I'ld have thee beaten for being old before thy time i 5 46
Thou shouldst not have been old till thou hadst been wise i 5 48
We'll teach you.—Sir, I am too old to learn: Call not your stocks for me ii 2 134
O, sir, you are old; Nature in you stands on the very verge Of her confine ii 4 148
Dear daughter, I confess that I am old; Age is unnecessary ii 4 156
If you do love old men, . . . if yourselves are old, Make it your cause ii 4 193
Those that mingle reason with your passion Must be content to think you old ii 4 238
The hard rein which both of them have borne Against the old kind king iii 1 28
'Gainst a head So old and white as this. O! O! 'tis foul! iii 2 24
The younger rises when the old doth fall iii 3 26
Your old kind father, whose frank heart gave all iii 4 20
S. Withold footed thrice the old iii 4 125
He that will think to live till he be old, Give me some help! iii 7 69
Thou old unhappy traitor, Briefly thyself remember iv 6 232
Bear with me: Pray you now, forget and forgive: I am old and foolish iv 7 84
I thought it fit To send the old and miserable king To some retention v 3 46
I am old now, And these same crosses spoil me v 3 277
Wears out his time, much like his master's ass, For nought but provender, and when he's old, cashier'd *Othello* i 1 48
The hearts of old gave hands; But our new heraldry is hands, not hearts iii 4 46
You shall paint when you are old.—Wrinkles forbid! *Ant. and Cleo.* i 2 18
Their father, Then old and fond of issue, took such sorrow *Cymbeline* i 1 37
Are changing still One vice, but of a minute old, for one Not half so old ii 5 31
What should we speak of When we are old as you? iii 3 36
At three and two years old, I stole these babes iii 3 101
To sing a song that old was sung *Pericles* i Gower 1
That excellent complexion, which did steal The eyes of young and old iv 1 42
Is it a shame to get when we are old? iv 2 32
Old abusing. Here will be an old abusing of God's patience and the king's English *Mer. Wives* i 4 5
Old accustomed. I hold an old accustom'd feast *Rom. and Jul.* i 2 20
Old acquaintance. What, old acquaintance! 1 *Hen. IV.* v 4 102
To see how many of my old acquaintance are dead! 2 *Hen. IV.* iii 2 38
Visit our house; let our old acquaintance be renewed iii 2 314
I urged our old acquaintance *Coriolanus* v 1 10
How does my old acquaintance of this isle? *Othello* ii 1 205
Old Adam. The picture of old Adam new-apparelled *Com. of Errors* iv 3 13
Thou, old Adam's likeness, set to dress this garden *Richard II.* iii 4 73
Old age. Dallies with the innocence of love, Like the old age *T. Night* ii 4 49
He that shall live this day, and see old age *Hen. V.* iv 3 44
Old age, that ill layer up of beauty, can do no more spoil upon my face v 2 248
As a bell, That warns my old age to a sepulchre *Rom. and Jul.* iv 3 207
That which should accompany old age, As honour, love, obedience *Macb.* v 3 24
Old apple-john. Withered like an old apple-john 1 *Hen. IV.* iii 3 4
Old arms. Now my old arms are young John Talbot's grave 1 *Hen. VI.* iv 7 32
If I could shake off but one seven years From these old arms *Coriolanus* iv 1 56
Old Assyrian slings. As swift as stones Enforced from the old Assyrian slings *Hen. V.* iv 7 65
Old aunt. And for an old aunt whom the Greeks held captive, He brought a Grecian queen *Troi. and Cres.* ii 2 77
Old beard. By my old beard, And every hair that's on't *All's Well* v 3 76
Old beldam. Shakes the old beldam earth 1 *Hen. IV.* iii 1 32
Old bench. Who stand so much on the new form, that they cannot sit at ease on the old bench *Rom. and Jul.* ii 4 37
Old bethrothed. With Angelo to-night shall lie His old betrothed but despised *Meas. for Meas.* iii 2 293
Old black ram. An old black ram Is tupping your white ewe *Othello* i 1 88
Old blood. Hath love in thy old blood no living fire? *Richard II.* i 2 10
Old boar. Doth the old boar feed in the old frank? 2 *Hen. IV.* ii 2 159
Old body. I'll make more of thy old body than I have done *Mer. Wives* ii 2 145
Begin to patch up thine old body for heaven 2 *Hen. IV.* ii 4 253
Old bones. I can go no further, sir; My old bones ache *Tempest* iii 3 2
Old boy. Did she see thee the while, old boy? *T. Night* ii 2 9
Old brain. Bear with my weakness; my old brain is troubled *Tempest* iv 1 159
Old breeches. A pair of old breeches thrice turned *T. of Shrew* iii 2 44
Old cakes of roses *Rom. and Jul.* v 1 47
Old care. My care is loss of care, by old care done *Richard II.* iv 1 196
Old carlot. That the old carlot once was master of *As Y. Like It* iii 5 108
Old carrion. Out upon it, old carrion! *Mer. of Venice* iii 1 38
Old chronicle. Good old chronicle, That hast so long walk'd hand in hand with time *Troi. and Cres.* iv 5 202
Old church. Ephesians, my lord, of the old church 2 *Hen. IV.* ii 2 164
Old church-window. Like god Bel's priests in the old church-window *Much Ado* iii 3 144
Old cloak. An old cloak makes a new jerkin *Mer. Wives* i 3 18
Old coat. It is an old coat.—The dozen white louses do become an old coat well i 1 18
Old cock. The old cock.—The cockerel *Tempest* ii 1 30
Old coil. Yonder's old coil at home *Much Ado* v 2 98
Old comedy. Pat he comes like the catastrophe of the old comedy *Lear* i 2 146
Old commander. A good old commander *Hen. V.* iv 1 97
Old contracting. And perform an old contracting *Meas. for Meas.* iii 2 296
Old course. He'll shape his old course in a country new *Lear* i 1 190
If she live long, And in the end meet the old course of death iii 7 101
Old courtier. Virginity, like an old courtier, wears her cap out of fashion *All's Well* i 1 169
Old crab-trees. We have some old crab-trees here at home that will not Be grafted to your relish *Coriolanus* ii 1 205
Old cramps. I'll rack thee with old cramps *Tempest* i 2 369
Old cuckold. Like an old cuckold, with horns on his head *Much Ado* ii 1 46
Old custom. Hath not old custom made this life more sweet Than that of painted pomp? *As Y. Like It* ii 1 2
Old customers. Here be many of her old customers *Meas. for Meas.* iv 3 4
Old dam. Is a kind of puppy To the old dam, treason *Hen. VIII.* i 1 176
Old dame. My old dame will be undone now 2 *Hen. IV.* ii 2 123
Old days. Since the old days of goodman Adam 1 *Hen. IV.* ii 4 105
Old Death. Here's a stay That shakes the rotten carcass of old Death Out of his rags! *K. John* ii 1 456
Old decree. Young blood doth not obey an old decree *L. L. Lost* iv 3 217
Old desire. Now old desire doth in his death-bed lie *Rom. and Jul.* ii Prol. 1
Old device. That is an old device *M. N. Dream* v 1 50
Old dog. Get you with him, you old dog.—Is 'old dog' my reward? *As Y. Like It* i 1 85
Old dugs. Shall thy old dugs once more a traitor rear? *Richard II.* v 3 90
Old duke. The old duke is banished *As Y. Like It* i 1 104
Old ears. His heart Almost impregnable, his old ears deaf *T. Andron* iv 4 98
Old ends. Ere you flout old ends any further *Much Ado* i 1 290
Old enemy. Marcius your old enemy *Coriolanus* i 2 12
Old enough. This news is old enough *Meas. for Meas.* iii 2 243
Not yet old enough for a man, nor young enough for a boy *T. Night* i 5 165
Cousin, I am too young to be your father, Though you are old enough to be my heir *Richard II.* iii 3 205
The king is old enough himself To give his censure 2 *Hen. VI.* i 3 119
If he be old enough, what needs your grace To be protector? i 3 121
You are old enough now, and yet, methinks, you lose 3 *Hen. VI.* i 1 113
The gods keep you old enough; that you may live Only in bone! *T. of A.* iii 5 104
Old experience. Of his old experience the only darling *All's Well* i 1 110
Old eyes. I see them not with my old eyes *Troi. and Cres.* i 3 366
I would not see thy cruel nails Pluck out his poor old eyes *Lear* iii 7 57
Old-faced. 'Tis not the roundure of your old-faced walls Can hide you *K. John* ii 1 259
More dishonourable ragged than an old faced ancient 1 *Hen. IV.* iv 2 34
Old familiar. I think her old familiar is asleep 1 *Hen. VI.* iii 2 122
Old fashions please me best *T. of Shrew* iii 1 81
The old fashion; you two never meet but you fall to some discord 2 *Hen. IV.* ii 4 60
Old fat fellow. A meeting with this old fat fellow *Mer. Wives* iv 4 15
Old fat man. There is a devil haunts thee in the likeness of an old fat man 1 *Hen. IV.* ii 4 493
Old fat woman. There was, mine host, an old fat woman even now with me; but she's gone *Mer. Wives* iv 5 25
Old father. Being of an old father's mind *L. L. Lost* iv 2 33
Pardon, old father, my mistaking eyes *T. of Shrew* iv 5 45
And love thee no worse than thy old father Menenius does! *Coriolanus* v 2 76
I will prefer my sons; Then spare not the old father *Cymbeline* v 5 327
Old father antic the law 1 *Hen. IV.* i 2 69
Old faults. I forgive and quite forget old faults 3 *Hen. VI.* iii 3 200
Old feet. Oft to-night Have my old feet stumbled at graves! *Rom. and Jul.* v 3 122
Old fellow. These old fellows Have their ingratitude in them hereditary: Their blood is caked, 'tis cold *T. of Athens* ii 2 223
What, art thou mad, old fellow? *Lear* ii 2 91
Old folks, you know, have discretion, as they say, and know the world *Mer. Wives* ii 2 134
See, to beguile the old folks, how the young folks lay their heads together! *T. of Shrew* i 2 139
In winter's tedious nights sit by the fire With good old folks *Richard II.* v 1 41
And the old folk, time's doting chronicles 2 *Hen. IV.* iv 4 126
But old folks, many feign as they were dead; Unwieldy, slow *R. and J.* ii 5 16
Old fond eyes, Beweep this cause again, I'll pluck ye out *Lear* i 4 323
Old fond paradoxes to make fools laugh *Othello* ii 1 139
Old fools. These tedious old fools! *Hamlet* ii 2 223
Old fools are babes again; and must be used With checks as flatteries *Lear* i 3 19
Old form. In this the antique and well noted face Of plain old form is much disfigured *K. John* iv 2 22
Old frank. Doth the old boar feed in the old frank? 2 *Hen. IV.* ii 2 160
Old friend! thy face is valanced since I saw thee last *Hamlet* ii 2 442
Our good old friend, Lay comforts to your bosom *Lear* ii 1 127
Old gentleman. The priest was good enough, for all the old gentleman's saying *As Y. Like It* v 1 4
Old ginger. A commodity of brown paper and old ginger *Meas. for Meas.* iv 3 6
Old gloves. I verily did think That her old gloves were on, but 'twas her hands *As Y. Like It* iv 3 26
Old goat. Follow to thine answer.—Hence, old goat! *Coriolanus* iii 1 177
Old gradation. Preferment goes by letter and affection, And not by old gradation *Othello* i 1 37
Old grandsire. Pardon, I pray thee, for my mad mistaking.—Do, good old grandsire *T. of Shrew* iv 5 50
The hellish Pyrrhus Old grandsire Priam seeks *Hamlet* ii 2 486
Old groans. Thy old groans ring yet in my ancient ears *Rom. and Jul.* ii 3 74
Old grub. An empty hazel nut Made by the joiner squirrel or old grub i 4 68
Old hare. And an old hare hoar Is very good meat in lent ii 4 142
Old hat. An old hat and 'the humour of forty fancies' prick'd in't for a feather *T. of Shrew* iii 2 69
Old hate. Enforce his pride, And his old hate unto you *Coriolanus* ii 3 228
Old heart. Makes old hearts fresh *W. Tale* i 1 43
God-a-mercy, old heart! thou speak'st cheerfully *Hen. V.* iv 1 34

Old heart. O, madam, my old heart is crack'd, is crack'd . . . *Lear* ii 1 92
Yet, poor old heart, he holp the heavens to rain . . . iii 7 62
Old hermit of Prague, that never saw pen and ink . . . *T. Night* iv 2 14
Old Hiems. On old Hiems' thin and icy crown . . . *M. N. Dream* ii 1 109
Old host. Then many an old host that I know is damned . 1 *Hen. IV.* iv 4 518
Old infant play. All hid ; an old infant play . . . *L. L. Lost* iv 3 78
Old inhabitants. Thou wilt be a wilderness again, Peopled with wolves, thy old inhabitants ! . . . 2 *Hen. IV.* iv 5 138
Old instance. An old, an old instance, Beatrice . . . *Much Ado* v 2 78
Old invention. I am not so nice, To change true rules for old inventions *T. of Shrew* iii 1 81
Old iron. Out of a great deal of old iron I chose forth . . 1 *Hen. VI.* i 2 101
Old Italian fox. An old Italian fox is not so kind . . *T. of Shrew* ii 1 405
Old Jack. Sayest thou so, old Jack? go thy ways . . *Mer. Wives* ii 2 144
Go thy ways, old Jack ; die when thou wilt . . . 1 *Hen. IV.* ii 4 141
Old jerkin. An old jerkin, a pair of old breeches . . *T. of Shrew* iii 2 44
Old John of Gaunt, time-honour'd Lancaster . . . *Richard II.* i 1 1
Old John of Gaunt is grievous sick, my lord . . . i 4 54
Old justice. Time is the old justice that examines all such offenders, and let Time try . . . *As Y. Like. It* iv 1 203
Old king. Is the old king dead?—As nail in door . . 2 *Hen. IV.* v 3 126
Old lad. How now, old lad?—Welcome, you . . *T. of Shrew* iv 1 113
Well, go thy ways, old lad ; for thou shalt ha't . . . v 2 181
My old lad of the castle . . . . . 1 *Hen. IV.* i 2 47
As who should say 'Old lad, I am thine own' . . *T. Andron.* iv 2 121
Old lady. How does my old lady?—So that you had her wrinkles and I her money, I would she did as you say . . . *All's Well* ii 4 19
My skin hangs about me like an old lady's loose gown . 1 *Hen. IV.* iii 3 4
Old lecher. A little fire in a wild field were like an old lecher's heart *Lear* iii 4 117
Old life. Let my old life Be sacrificed . . . *Rom. and Jul.* v 3 267
Old limbs. When service should in my old limbs lie lame *As Y. Like It* ii 3 41
To crush our old limbs in ungentle steel . . 1 *Hen. IV.* v 1 13
Old ling. Our old ling and our Isbels o' the country are nothing like your old ling and your Isbels o' the court . . *All's Well* iii 2 14
Old lion. I am as melancholy as a gib cat or a lugged bear.—Or an old lion . . . . . . 1 *Hen. IV.* i 2 84
Old lord. I needs must rest me.—Old lord, I cannot blame thee *Tempest* iii 3 4
Him that you term'd, sir, 'The good old lord, Gonzalo' . . . v 1 15
An old lord of the council rated me the other day . . 1 *Hen. IV.* i 2 94
Old love. For whose old love I have, Though I show'd sourly to him, once more offer'd The first conditions . . *Coriolanus* v 3 12
Yet our old love made a particular force . . . *T. of Athens* v 2 8
Old love-monger. Thou art an old love-monger . . *L. L. Lost* ii 1 253
Old lunes. Your husband is in his old lunes again . *Mer. Wives* iv 2 22
Old majesty. We will resign, During the life of this old majesty *Lear* v 3 299
Old man. I went to her, Master Brook, as you see, like a poor old man : but I came from her, Master Brook, like a poor old woman *Mer. Wives* v 1 17
Nay, forward, old man ; do not break off so . . *Com. of Errors* i 1 97
An old man, sir, and his wits are not so blunt as, God help, I would desire they were . . . . *Much Ado* iii 5 11
I am as honest as any man living that is an old man and no honester . iii 5 16
Nay, do not quarrel with us, good old man . . . . v 1 50
You say not right, old man.—My lord, my lord, I'll prove it . . v 1 73
Like to have had our two noses snapped off with two old men without teeth . . . . v 1 116
The old man's daughter told us all.—All, all . . . . v 1 179
To satisfy this good old man, I would bend under any heavy weight . v 1 286
True wit!—Offered by a child to an old man ; which is wit-old *L. L. Lost* v 1 65
But I pray you, ergo, old man, ergo, I beseech you . *Mer. of Venice* ii 2 59
Well, old man, I will tell you news of your son . . . ii 2 81
My father, being, I hope, an old man, shall frutify unto you . . ii 2 142
And, though I say it, though old man, yet poor man, my father . ii 2 148
There comes an old man and his three sons . . *As Y. Like It* i 2 125
O good old man, how well in thee appears The constant service of the antique world ! . . . . ii 3 56
Poor old man, thou prunest a rotten tree . . . . . ii 3 63
An old poor man, Who after me hath many a weary step Limp'd . . ii 7 129
Good old man, Thou art right welcome as thy master is . . . ii 7 197
I begin to love, as an old man loves money, with no stomach *All's Well* iii 2 17
By my life ; I am either maid, or else this old man's wife . . v 3 294
And yet I will not compare with an old man . . *T. Night* i 3 126
Would I had been by, to have helped the old man ! . . *W. Tale* iii 3 111
You're a made old man : if the sins of your youth are forgiven you . iii 3 124
Had not the old man come in with a whoo-bub against his daughter . iv 4 628
Has the old man e'er a son, sir, do you hear, an't like you, sir? . iv 4 810
I will give you as much as this old man does when the business is performed . . . . iv 4 852
He that wins of all, Of kings, of beggars, old men, young men *K. John* ii 1 570
Old men and beldams in the streets Do prophesy upon it dangerously . iv 2 185
What manner of man is he?—An old man . . . 1 *Hen. IV.* ii 4 324
If ye will needs say I am an old man, you should give me rest 2 *Hen. IV.* i 2 243
How subject we old men are to this vice of lying ! . . . iii 2 326
Is't so? Why then, say an old man can do somewhat . . . v 3 82
I know thee not, old man : fall to thy prayers . . . . v 5 51
Old men forget ; yet all shall be forgot . . . *Hen. V.* iv 3 49
York not our old men spares ; No more will I their babes . 2 *Hen. VI.* v 2 51
The good old man would fain that all were well . . 3 *Hen. VI.* iv 7 31
And many an old man's sigh and many a widow's, And many an orphan's water-standing eye . . . . . . v 6 39
Amen ; and make me die a good old man ! That is the butt-end of a mother's blessing . . . . *Richard III.* ii 2 109
An old man, broken with the storms of state . . *Hen. VIII.* iv 2 21
Let an old man embrace thee . . . . *Troi. and Cres.* iv 5 199
You two are old men : tell me one thing that I shall ask you *Coriolanus* ii 1 35
This last old man, Whom with a crack'd heart I have sent to Rome . v 3 8
Take up this good old man, and cheer the heart . . *T. Andron.* i 1 457
Here's no sound jest ! the old man hath found their guilt . . iv 2 26
Tell us, old man, how shall we be employ'd? . . . . v 2 149
Care keeps his watch in every old man's eye . . *Rom. and Jul.* ii 3 35
Here's a noble feast toward.—This is the old man still . *T. of Athens* i 6 69
Why old men fool and children calculate . . . *J. Cæsar* i 3 65
Who would have thought the old man to have had so much blood? *Macb.* v 1 44
The satirical rogue says here that old men have grey beards . *Hamlet* ii 2 199
For they say an old man is twice a child . . . . ii 2 403
Is't possible, a young maid's wits Should be as mortal as an old man's life? . . . . iv 5 160
What wilt thou do, old man? . . . Reverse thy doom . . *Lear* i 1 148
Idle old man, That still would manage those authorities That he hath given away ! . . . . i 3 16

Old Man. 'Tis they have put him on the old man's death, To have the expense and waste of his revenues . . . . *Lear* ii 1 101
O heavens, If you do love old men, if your sweet sway Allow obedience, if yourselves are old . . . . ii 4 193
A poor old man, As full of grief as age ; wretched in both ! . . ii 4 275
This house is little : the old man and his people Cannot be well bestow'd . . . . ii 4 291
Here I stand, your slave, A poor, infirm, weak, and despised old man . iii 2 20
Nay, come not near th' old man ; keep out, che vor ye . . . iv 6 245
I am a very foolish fond old man, Fourscore and upward . . . iv 7 60
Away, old man ; give me thy hand ; away ! King Lear hath lost . v 2 5
That I have ta'en away this old man's daughter, It is most true *Othello* i 3 78
This was strange chance : A narrow lane, an old man, and two boys *Cymbeline* v 3 52
Two boys, an old man twice a boy, a lane, Preserved the Britons . . v 3 57
'Tis thought the old man and his sons were angels . . . . v 3 85
And that to hear an old man sing May to your wishes pleasure bring . *Pericles* i Gower 13
Old Mantuan. Ah, good old Mantuan ! . . . *L. L. Lost* iv 2 97
Old Mantuan, old Mantuan ! who understandeth thee not, loves thee not iv 2 101
Old master. O, my old master ! who hath bound him here? *Com. of Er.* v 1 338
Take leave of thy old master and inquire My lodging out *Mer. of Venice* ii 2 162
To bid my old master the Jew to sup to-night with my new master . ii 4 17
God be with my old master ! he would not have spoke such a word *As Y. Like It* i 1 88
Winter tames man, woman and beast ; for it hath tamed my old master and my new mistress . . . . *T. of Shrew* iv 1 25
Though I die for it, . . . the king my old master must be relieved *Lear* iii 3 19
Old mocker. Well said, old mocker . . . . . *L. L. Lost* v 2 552
Old mole! canst work i' the earth so fast? . . . . *Hamlet* i 5 162
Old monument. On your family's old monument . . *Much Ado* iv 1 208
Old moon. O, methinks, how slow This old moon wanes ! *M. N. Dream* i 1 4
Old motion. Have I, in my poor and old motion, the expedition of thought? I have speeded hither . . . . 2 *Hen. IV.* iv 3 37
Old murderer. Doth she not think me an old murderer? *Rom. and Jul.* iii 3 94
Old name. The old name Is fresh about me . . . *Hen. VIII.* iv 1 98
Old news. There's no news at the court, sir, but the old news *As Y. L. It* i 1 104
News, old news, and such news as you never heard of !—Is it new and old too? . . . . *T. of Shrew* iii 2 30
But say, what to thine old news? . . . . . . iii 2 42
Old Nile. Where's my serpent of old Nile? . . . *Ant. and Cleo.* i 5 25
Old Norway. The nephew to old Norway, Fortinbras . . *Hamlet* iv 4 14
Old oblivion. From the dust of old oblivion raked . . *Hen. V.* ii 4 87
Old odd ends stolen out of holy writ . . . . *Richard III.* i 3 337
Old one. 'Tis better playing with a lion's whelp Than with an old one dying . . . . *Ant. and Cleo.* iii 13 95
Old ornament. The old ornament of his cheek hath already stuffed tennis-balls . . . . *Much Ado* iii 2 46
Old painting. Like a man after the old painting . . *L. L. Lost* iii 1 21
Old pantaloon. That we might beguile the old pantaloon *T. of Shrew* iii 1 37
Old partisans, in hands as old . . . . *Rom. and Jul.* i 1 101
Old Pelion. To o'ertop old Pelion . . . . . *Hamlet* v 1 276
Old pike. If the young dace be a bait for the old pike . 2 *Hen. IV.* iii 2 356
Old place. Doth the old boar feed in the old frank?—At the old place, my lord . . . . ii 2 161
Old play. Our wooing doth not end like an old play . *L. L. Lost* v 2 884
Ten times more valour than this roaring devil i' the old play . *Hen. V.* iv 4 76
Old playfellows. Or pack to their old playfellows . . *Hen. VIII.* i 3 33
Old prerogative. Insisting on the old prerogative . . *Coriolanus* iii 3 17
Old proverb. The old proverb is very well parted . *Mer. of Venice* ii 2 158
Might we lay the old proverb to your charge . . . *W. Tale* ii 3 96
Old rage. Yet I have a trick Of the old rage . . . *L. L. Lost* v 2 417
Old rat. Swallows the old rat and the ditch-dog . . . *Lear* iii 4 138
Old receptacles. Empty Old receptacles . . . . *Pericles* iv 6 186
Old religious man. Meeting with an old religious man . *As Y. Like It* v 4 166
Old religious uncle. An old religious uncle of mine taught me to speak iii 2 362
Old riband. Tying his new shoes with old riband . . *Rom. and Jul.* iii 1 31
Old right. And happy newness, that intends old right . . *K. John* v 4 61
Old robes. Lest our old robes sit easier than our new ! . *Macbeth* ii 4 38
When old robes are worn out, there are members to make new *A. and C.* i 2 171
Old Roman coin. The face of an old Roman coin . . *L. L. Lost* v 2 617
Old Rome. Exceeding the nine sibyls of old Rome . . 1 *Hen. VI.* i 2 56
Old ruffian. Let the old ruffian know I have many other ways to die *Ant. and Cleo.* iv 1 4
Old sack. Fat-witted, with drinking of old sack . . 1 *Hen. IV.* i 2 3
Old saying. The old saying is, Black men are pearls . *T. G. of Ver.* v 2 11
Shall I come upon thee with an old saying? . . . —So I may answer thee with one as old . . . . *L. L. Lost* iv 1 121
And the old saying is, the third pays for all . . . *T. Night* v 1 40
Old servant. Her old servant I have not seen . . . *Cymbeline* iii 5 54
Old shepherd. I was by at the opening of the fardel, heard the old shepherd deliver the manner how he found it . . . . . *W. Tale* v 2 4
The old shepherd, which stands by like a weather-bitten conduit . . v 2 59
Old shoes. I am, indeed, sir, a surgeon to old shoes . . . *J. Cæsar* i 1 27
Old signs. There is no believing old signs. . . . . *Much Ado* iii 2 41
Old sir, I know She prizes not such trifles as these are . . *W. Tale* iv 4 367
Old smell. Thou losest thy old smell. . . . . . *As Y. Like It* i 2 114
Old smock. Your old smock brings forth a new petticoat *Ant. and Cleo.* i 2 175
Old soldier, Wilt thou undo the worth thou art unpaid for? . *Cymbeline* v 5 306
Old son. Come, my old son : I pray God make thee new . *Richard II.* v 3 146
Old stock. For virtue cannot so inoculate our old stock but we shall relish of it . . . . *Hamlet* iii 1 119
Revive, be jointed to the old stock, and freshly grow *Cymbeline* v 4 143 ; v 5 440
Old story. There was a lady once, 'tis an old story . . *Hen. VIII.* ii 3 90
Old swearing. We shall have old swearing . . . *Mer. of Venice* iv 2 15
Old tables. Lisping to his master's old tables . . . 2 *Hen. IV.* ii 4 289
Old tale. There is an old tale goes . . . . . *Mer. Wives* iv 4 28
Like the old tale, my lord : 'it is not so, nor 'twas not so' . *Much Ado* i 1 218
I could match this beginning with an old tale . . . *As Y. Like It* i 2 127
This news which is called true is so like an old tale . . *W. Tale* v 2 30
Like an old tale still, which will have matter to rehearse . . . v 2 66
Were it but told you, should be hooted at Like an old tale . . . v 3 117
So we'll live, And pray, and sing, and tell old tales . . . . *Lear* v 3 12
Old tear. Upon thy cheek the stain doth sit Of an old tear *Rom. and Jul.* ii 3 76
Old thing. An old thing 'twas, but it express'd her fortune . *Othello* iv 3 29
Old thread. Pure grief Shore his old thread in twain . . . v 2 206
Old time. An appertinent title to your old time . . . *L. L. Lost* i 2 18
Old Time the clock-setter, that bald sexton Time . . . *K. John* iii 1 324
And when old time shall lead him to his end . . . *Hen. VIII.* ii 1 93
Like rams In the old time of war . . . . iv 1 78

Old traitor. Thou old traitor, I am sorry that by hanging thee I can But shorten thy life one week *W. Tale* iv 4 431
Old trot. An old trot with ne'er a tooth in her head *T. of Shrew* i 2 80
Old Troy. Ah, thou, the model where old Troy did stand *Richard II.* v 1 11
Old tune. If it be aught to the old tune, my lord, It is as fat and fulsome to mine ear As howling after music *T. Night* v 1 111
Which time she chanted snatches of old tunes *Hamlet* iv 7 178
Old turning. If a man were porter of hell-gate, he should have old turning the key *Macbeth* ii 3 2
Old turtle. I, an old turtle, Will wing me to some wither'd bough and there My mate . . . Lament *W. Tale* v 3 132
Old Utis. Here will be old Utis 2 *Hen. IV.* ii 4 21
Old Verona. Blows you to Padua here from old Verona *T. of Shrew* i 2 49
Old vice. Well, your old vice still; mistake the word *T. G. of Ver.* iii 1 283
I'll be with you again, In a trice, Like to the old Vice *T. Night* iv 2 134
Old virginity. Your old virginity is like one of our French withered pears, it looks ill, it eats drily *All's Well* i 1 174
Old ward. Thou knowest my old ward 1 *Hen. IV.* ii 4 215
Old wife. When my old wife lived *W. Tale* iv 4 55
Old Windsor way, and every way, but the town way *Mer. Wives* iii 1 6
Old wit. I'll try whether my old wit be in request With those that have but little *Coriolanus* iii 1 251
Old witnesses. All these old witnesses—I cannot err *Com. of Errors* v 317
Old woe. This borrow'd passion stands for true old woe *Pericles* iv 4 24
Old woman. He cannot abide the old woman of Brentford *Mer. Wives* iv 2 87
And has been grievously peaten as an old 'oman iv 4 22
There's an old woman, a fat woman, gone up into his chamber iv 5 12
I spake with the old woman about it.—And what says she? iv 5 35
I went to her, Master Brook, as you see, like a poor old man: but I came from her, Master Brook, like a poor old woman v 1 18
Ginger was not much in request, for the old women were all dead *Meas. for Meas.* iv 3 9
Guarded with grandsires, babies and old women *Hen. V.* iii Prol. 20
Think to front his revenges with the easy groans of old women *Coriol.* v 2 45
Old world. How green you are and fresh in this old world *K. John* iii 4 145
Old wranglers. The seas and winds, old wranglers, took a truce *T. and C.* ii 2 75
Old wrinkles. Let me play the fool: With mirth and laughter let old wrinkles come *Mer. of Venice* i 1 80
Oldcastle died a martyr, and this is not the man 2 *Hen. IV.* Epil. 33
Olden. Blood hath been shed e're now, i' the olden time *Macbeth* iii 4 75
Older. Young Romeo will be older when you have found him than he was when you sought him *Rom. and Jul.* ii 4 127
I am a soldier, I, Older in practice, abler than yourself *J. Cæsar* iv 3 31
An older and a better soldier none That Christendom gives out *Macbeth* iv 3 191
Oldest. Commit The oldest sins the newest kind of ways 2 *Hen. IV.* iv 5 127
Vows revenge as spacious as between The young'st and oldest thing *Cor.* iv 6 68
The oldest hath borne most: we that are young Shall never see so much, nor live so long *Lear* v 3 325
Oldness. Keeps our fortunes from us till our oldness cannot relish them i 2 50
Olive. 'Tis at the tuft of olives here hard by *As Y. Like It* iii 5 75
A sheep-cote fenced about with olive trees iv 3 78
I hold the olive in my hand; my words are as full of peace *T. Night* i 5 226
Peace puts forth her olive every where 2 *Hen. IV.* iv 4 87
To whom the heavens in thy nativity Adjudged an olive branch and laurel crown, As likely to be blest in peace and war 3 *Hen. VI.* iv 6 34
I will use the olive with my sword, Make war breed peace *T. of Athens* v 4 82
The three-nook'd world Shall bear the olive freely *Ant. and Cleo.* iv 6 7
Oliver. O sweet Oliver, O brave Oliver, Leave me not *As Y. Like It* iii 3 101
A most wicked Sir Oliver, Audrey, a most vile Martext v 1 5
Records, England all Olivers and Rowlands bred 1 *Hen. VI.* i 2 30
Olivia. O, when mine eyes did see Olivia first, Methought she purged the air of pestilence! *T. Night* i 1 19
He did seek the love of fair Olivia.—What's she?—A virtuous maid i 2 34
And make the babbling gossip of the air Cry out 'Olivia!' i 5 293
Were not you even now with the Countess Olivia?—Even now, sir ii 2 2
What thriftless sighs shall poor Olivia breathe! ii 2 40
Say that some lady, as perhaps there is, Hath for your love as great a pang of heart As you have for Olivia ii 4 94
Make no compare Between that love a woman can bear me And that I owe Olivia ii 4 106
Having come from a day-bed, where I have left Olivia sleeping ii 5 55
The Lady Olivia's fool?—No, indeed, sir; the Lady Olivia has no folly iii 1 36
Thou comest to the lady Olivia, and in my sight she uses thee kindly iii 4 171
Belong you to the Lady Olivia, friends?—Ay, sir v 1 9
What would my lord, but that he may not have, Wherein Olivia may seem serviceable? . . . —Gracious Olivia v 1 105
Olympian. Such rewards As victors wear at the Olympian games 3 *Hen. VI.* ii 3 53
Like an Olympian wrestling *Troi. and Cres.* iv 5 194
Olympus. O thou great thunder-darter of Olympus! ii 3 11
As if Olympus to a molehill should In supplication nod *Coriolanus* v 3 30
Now climbeth Tamora Olympus' top, Safe out of fortune's shot *T. An.* ii 1 1
O Cæsar,— Hence! wilt thou lift up Olympus? *J. Cæsar* iii 1 74
Though they do appear As huge as high Olympus iv 3 92
To o'ertop old Pelion, or the skyish head Of blue Olympus *Hamlet* v 1 277
Olympus-high. Climb hills of seas Olympus-high *Othello* ii 1 190
Omen. Fierce events, As harbingers preceding still the fates And prologue to the omen coming on *Hamlet* i 1 123
Ominous. Very ominous endings *Much Ado* v 2 39
Furnished like a hunter.—O, ominous! he comes to kill my heart *As Y. Like It* iii 2 260
Thou ominous and fearful owl of death! 1 *Hen. VI.* iv 2 15
Gloucester's dukedom is too ominous 3 *Hen. VI.* ii 6 107
Bloody prison, Fatal and ominous to noble peers! *Richard III.* iii 3 10
Thy mother's name is ominous to children iv 1 41
My dreams will, sure, prove ominous to the day *Troi. and Cres.* v 3 6
Take heed, the quarrel's most ominous to us v 7 21
When he lay couched in the ominous horse *Hamlet* ii 2 476
Omission to do what is necessary Seals a commission to a blank of danger; And danger, like an ague, subtly taints *Troi. and Cres.* iii 3 230
Omit. A most auspicious star, whose influence If now I court not but omit, my fortunes Will ever after droop *Tempest* i 2 183
Do not omit the heavy offer of it [sleep] ii 1 194
What if we do omit This reprobate till he were well inclined? *M. for M.* iv 3 77
Omit Nothing may give us aid *W. Tale* iv 4 637
Omit him not; blunt not his love 2 *Hen. IV.* iv 4 27
Omit no happy hour That may give furtherance to our expedition *Hen. V.* i 2 300
And omit All the occurrences, whatever chanced v Prol. 39
If you omit the offer of this time, I cannot promise *Hen. VIII.* iii 2 3
It must omit Real necessities, and give way the while *Coriolanus* iv 1 146
I will omit no opportunity That may convey my greetings *Rom. and Jul.* iii 5 49
Omit. As having sense of beauty, do omit Their mortal natures *Othello* ii 1 71
The due of honour in no point omit *Cymbeline* iii 5 11
Omit we all their dole and woe *Pericles* iii Gower 42
Sure, all's effectless; yet nothing we'll omit That bears recovery's name v 1 53
Omittance. But that's all one; omittance is no quittance *As Y. Like It* iii 5 133
Omitted. No time shall be omitted *L. L. Lost* iv 3 381
His apparent open guilt omitted *Richard III.* iii 5 30
Omitted, all the voyage of their life Is bound in shallows *J. Cæsar* iv 3 220
No needful thing omitted *Pericles* v 3 68
Omittest. That time serves still.—The more accursed thou, that still omitt'st it *T. of Athens* i 1 268
Omitting the sweet benefit of time *T. G. of Ver.* ii 4 65
Wherefore grieve I at an hour's poor loss, Omitting Suffolk's exile? 2 *Hen. VI.* iii 2 382
Omne. But omne bene, say I *L. L. Lost* iv 2 33
Fauste, precor gelida quando pecus omne sub umbra Ruminat iv 2 95
Omnipotent. O omnipotent Love! *Mer. Wives* v 5 8
God omnipotent, Is mustering in his clouds on our behalf *Richard II.* iii 3 85
The most omnipotent villain that ever cried 'Stand' 1 *Hen. IV.* i 2 121
On. And suck'd my verdure out on't *Tempest* i 2 87
I swam, ere I could recover the shore, five and thirty leagues off and on iii 2 17
Juno sings her blessings on you iv 1 109
We are such stuff As dreams are made on iv 1 157
How's the day?—On the sixth hour v 1 4
On a trice, so please you, Even in a dream v 1 238
Not mine; my gloves are on *T. G. of Ver.* ii 1 1
I'll die on him that says so but yourself ii 4 114
Money is a good soldier, sir, and will on *Mer. Wives* ii 2 176
On went he for a search, and away went I for foul clothes iii 5 107
He arrests him on it *Meas. for Meas.* i 4 66
Who can do good on him? v 2 71
Let him walk from whence he came, lest he catch cold on's feet *C. of Er.* iii 1 37
Was he arrested on a band?—Not on a band, but on a stronger thing iv 2 49
Ne'er may I look on day, nor sleep on night! v 1 210
I hope, when I do it, I shall do it on a full stomach *L. L. Lost* i 2 154
That he may prove More fond on her than she upon her love *M. N. Dream* ii 1 266
But wonder on, till truth make all things plain v 1 129
I verily did think That her old gloves were on, but 'twas her hands *As Y. Like It* iv 3 26
This woman's an easy glove, my lord; she goes off and on at pleasure *All's Well* v 3 279
My master loves her dearly; And I, poor monster, fond as much on him *T. Night* ii 2 35
I have tremor cordis on me: my heart dances *W. Tale* i 2 110
Many thousand on's Have the disease, and feel't not i 2 206
The king hath on him such a countenance i 2 368
On her frights and griefs, . . . She is something before her time deliver'd ii 2 23
Sound on into the drowsy race of night *K. John* iii 3 39
Though on thinking on no thought I think *Richard II.* ii 2 31
Intended or committed was this fault? If on the first, how heinous e'er it be, To win thy after-love I pardon thee v 3 34
An 'twere not as good deed as drink, to break the pate on thee 1 *Hen. IV.* ii 1 33
A thing to thank God on.—I am no thing to thank God on iii 3 134
We should on, To see how fortune is disposed to us iv 1 37
I am well spoke on; I can hear it with mine own ears 2 *Hen. IV.* ii 2 69
You are an honest woman, and well thought on ii 4 100
Come off and on swifter than he that gibbets on the brewer's bucket iii 2 281
That hath enraged him on to offer strokes iv 1 211
And on to-morrow bid them march away *Hen. V.* iii 6 181
On us thou canst not enter but by death 1 *Hen. VI.* iv 2 18
Comes thought on thought, And not a thought but thinks on dignity 2 *Hen. VI.* iii 1 337
You, that have so fair parts of woman on you *Hen. VIII.* ii 3 27
Make yourself mirth with your particular fancy, And leave me out on't ii 3 102
I would 'twere something that would fret the string, The master-cord on's heart! iii 2 106
I will play no more to-night; My mind's not on't v 1 57
How much more is his life in value with him? Would I were fairly out on't! v 3 109
With a palsy-fumbling on his gorget *Troi. and Cres.* i 3 174
Unless the fiddler Apollo get his sinews to make catlings on iii 3 306
A curse begin at very root on's heart, That is not glad to see thee! *Coriolanus* ii 1 202
Why force you this?—Because that now it lies you on to speak iii 2 52
And that the spoil got on the Antiates Was ne'er distributed iii 3 4
Worth six on him.—Nay, not so neither iv 5 174
He is so made on here within, as if he were son and heir to Mars iv 5 203
Nay, sir, but hear me on *T. of Athens* i 1 77
On the moment Follow his strides i 1 79
Three talents on the present; in future, all i 1 141
Is not my lord seen yet?—Not yet.—I wonder on't iii 4 10
Be not jealous on me, gentle Brutus *J. Cæsar* i 2 71
Or shall we on, and not depend on you? iii 1 217
Enclosed round about With horsemen, that make to him on the spur; Yet he spurs on. Now they are almost on him v 3 30
Or have we eaten on the insane root That takes the reason prisoner? *Macb.* i 3 84
Get on your nightgown, lest occasion call us ii 2 70
That it did, sir, i' the very throat on me ii 3 43
I tell you yet again, Banquo's buried; he cannot come out on's grave v 1 71
Let me not think on't—Frailty, thy name is woman! *Hamlet* i 2 146
Flashes of merriment, that were wont to set the table on a roar v 1 211
And from his mouth whose voice will draw on more v 2 403
We shall further think on't.—We must do something *Lear* i 1 311
How now, daughter! what makes that frontlet on? i 4 208
So will you wish on me, When the rash mood is on ii 4 171
Here's three on's are sophisticated! iii 4 110
But what art thou That hast this fortune on me? v 3 165
Requires your haste-post-haste appearance, Even on the instant *Othello* i 2 38
'Tis a monster Begot upon itself, born on itself iii 4 162
These are portents; but yet I hope, I hope, They do not point on me v 2 46
The borders maritime Lack blood to think on't *Ant. and Cleo.* i 4 52
Ah, this thou shouldst have done, And not have spoke on't! ii 7 80
To come thus was I not constrain'd, but did On my free will iii 6 57
My sword, made weak by my affection, would Obey it on all cause iii 11 68
Ere I could tell him How I would think on him *Cymbeline* i 3 27
Think what a chance thou changest on i 5 68
The bird is dead That we have made so much on iv 2 198
The power that I have on you is to spare you v 5 418
But what I am, want teaches me to think on *Pericles* i 1 76
On business. I shall raise you by and by On business *J. Cæsar* iv 3 248

On fire. Lest the oil that's in me should set hell on fire . *Mer. Wives* v 5 39
When the rich blood of kings is set on fire . . . . *K. John* ii 1 351
The heavens were all on fire, the earth did tremble . . 1 *Hen. IV.* iii 1 24
You are as slow As hot Lord Percy is on fire to go . . . iii 1 269
I am on fire To hear this rich reprisal is so nigh . . . . iv 1 117
Now all the youth of England are on fire . . . *Hen. V.* ii Prol. 1
But first, go and set London bridge on fire . . 2 *Hen. VI.* iv 6 16
Under hot ardent zeal would set whole realms on fire . *T. of Athens* iii 3 34
I stand on fire : Come to the matter . . . . . *Cymbeline* v 5 168
On procession. Here comes the townsmen on procession . 2 *Hen. VI.* ii 1 68
On purpose shut the doors against his way . . *Com. of Errors* iv 3 92
How still the evening is, As hush'd on purpose to grace harmony ! *M. Ado* ii 3 41
The lustful bed On purpose trimm'd up for Semiramis . *T. of Shrew* Ind. 2 41
She sends him on purpose, that I may appear stubborn to him *T. Night* iii 4 74
And spoke it on purpose to try my patience . . . 2 *Hen. IV.* ii 4 334
'Twas he inform'd against him ; And quit the house on purpose . *Lear* iv 2 94
I cross'd the seas on purpose and on promise To see your grace *Cymbeline* i 6 202
On sale. His flocks . . . Are now on sale . . . . *As Y. Like It* ii 4 84
Once. Might I but through my prison once a day Behold this maid *Tempest* i 2 490
Were I in England now, as once I was . . . . . . ii 2 29
Speak once in thy life, if thou beest a good moon-calf . . . iii 2 24
I pray thee, once to-night Give my sweet Nan this ring . *Mer. Wives* iii 4 103
Why, all the souls that were were forfeit once . . *Meas. for Meas.* ii 2 73
Better it were a brother died at once, Than that a sister, by redeeming him, Should die for ever . . . . ii 4 106
The time was once when thou unurged wouldst vow . *Com. of Errors* ii 2 115
Once this,—your long experience of her wisdom, Her sober virtue, years and modesty, Plead on her part . . . . iii 1 89
Not once, nor twice, but twenty times you have . . . . iii 2 177
'Tis once, thou lovest. . . . . *Much Ado* i 1 320
Tax not so bad a voice To slander music any more than once . . ii 3 47
An you be a cursing hypocrite once, you must be looked to . . v 1 212
Let us once lose our oaths to find ourselves . . . *L. L. Lost* iv 3 361
And so, adieu ; Twice to your visor, and half once to you . . v 2 227
Thou rememberest Since once I sat upon a promontory . *M. N. Dream* ii 1 149
O, once tell true, tell true, even for my sake ! . . . . iii 2 68
Then will two at once woo one ; That must needs be sport alone . . iii 2 118
I beseech you, Wrest once the law to your authority . *Mer. of Venice* iv 1 215
Either too much at once, or none at all . . . . *As Y. Like It* iii 2 212
Better once than never, for never too late . . . *T. of Shrew* v 1 155
Fare ye well at once : my bosom is full of kindness . . *T. Night* ii 1 40
Put your grace in your pocket, sir, for this once . . . . v 1 36
And will not . . . once remove The root of his opinion . . *W. Tale* ii 3 88
Once a day I'll visit The chapel where they lie . . . . . iii 2 239
For this once, yea, superstitiously, I will be squared by this . . iii 3 40
Is this the daughter of a king?—She is, When once she is my wife . v 1 209
That 'once,' I see by your good father's speed, Will come on very slowly v 1 210
Farewell at once, for once, for all, and ever . . . *Richard II.* ii 2 148
I hope to see London once ere I die . . . . 2 *Hen. IV.* v 3 64
Then say at once if I maintain'd the truth . . . 1 *Hen. VI.* ii 4 5
Can you . . . behold My sighs and tears and will not once relent? . iii 1 108
For this once my will shall stand for law . . . 3 *Hen. VI.* iii 1 50
Why not Ned and I For once allow'd the skilful pilot's charge? . . v 4 20
By sick interpreters, once weak ones, is Not ours . . *Hen. VIII.* i 2 82
I should be glad to hear such news as this Once every hour . . . iii 2 25
Nor once deject the courage of our minds . . . *Troi. and Cres.* ii 2 121
Once, if he do require our voices, we ought not to deny him *Coriolanus* ii 3 1
For once we stood up about the corn, he himself stuck not to call us the many-headed multitude . . . . ii 3 16
I'll play the housewife for this once . . . . *Rom. and Jul.* iv 2 43
Have I once lived to see two honest men? . . . . *T. of Athens* iv 3 ...
Who once a day . . . The turbulent surge shall cover . . . . v 1 220
Would heart of man once think it? . . . . *Hamlet* i 5 121
I heard thee speak me a speech once, but it was never acted ; or, if it was, not above once . . . . ii 2 456
To be once in doubt Is once to be resolved . . . . *Othello* iii 3 180
There is no more but this,—Away at once with love or jealousy ! . . iii 3 192
I will reward thee Once for thy spritely comfort, and ten-fold For thy good valour . . . . *Ant. and Cleo.* iv 7 15
Then let it do at once The thing why thou hast drawn it . . . iv 14 88
If idle talk will once be necessary, I'll not sleep neither . . . v 2 50
Never count the turns ; Once, and a million ! . . . *Cymbeline* ii 4 143
Once again. Hearken once again to the suit I made to thee . *Tempest* iii 2 44
And once again I do receive thee honest . . . *T. G. of Ver.* v 4 78
Yet once again proclaim it publicly . . . . *Com. of Errors* v 1 130
Here once again we sit, once again crown'd . . . *K. John* iv 2 1
This 'once again,' but that your highness pleased, Was once superfluous iv 2 3
Once before he won it of me with false dice . . . *Much Ado* ii 1 289
Once-commended. I charm you, by my once-commended beauty *J. Cæsar* ii 1 271
Once more unto the breach, dear friends, once more . . *Hen. V.* iii 1 1
Once or twice. Who asked them once or twice what they had in their basket . . . . *Mer. Wives* iii 5 103
One. I have done nothing but in care of thee, Of thee, my dear one *Temp.* i 2 17
Like one Who having into truth, by telling of it, Made such a sinner of his memory, To credit his own lie . . . . i 2 99
As if it had lungs and rotten ones . . . . ii 1 47
If but one of his pockets could speak, would it not say he lies? . . . ii 1 65
I heard a humming, And that a strange one too . . . . . ii 1 318
Yond same black cloud, yond huge one . . . . ii 2 21
Each putter-out of five for one will bring us Good warrant of . . . iii 3 48
Each one, tripping on his toe, Will be here with mop and mow . . . iv 1 46
And these fresh nymphs encounter every one In country footing . . iv 1 137
One of their kind, that relish all as sharply, Passion as they . . . v 1 23
Not one of them That yet looks on me, or would know me . . . . v 1 82
I could not ask my father For his advice, nor thought I had one . . v 1 191
One of them Is a plain fish, and, no doubt, marketable . . . . v 1 265
His mother was a witch, and one so strong That could control the moon v 1 269
This demi-devil—For he's a bastard one—had plotted with them . . v 1 273
I should have been a sore one then . . . . v 1 288
Twenty to one then he is shipp'd already . . . . *T. G. of Ver.* i 1 72
Thus will I fold them one upon another . . . . i 2 128
As one relying on your lordship's will . . . . i 3 61
My gloves are on.—Why, then, this may be yours, for this is but one . ii 1 2
To walk alone, like one that had the pestilence . . . . . . ii 1 22
To fast, like one that takes diet ; to watch, like one that fears robbing ; to speak puling, like a beggar at Hallowmas . . . . ii 1 25
When you walked, to walk like one of the lions . . . . . ii 1 29
She enjoined me to write some lines to one she loves . . . . . ii 1 94
I am one that am nourished by my victuals . . . . ii 1 179
Why, stand-under and under-stand is all one . . . . . . ii 5 34
One. When the flight is made to one so dear, Of such divine perfection *T. G. of Ver.* ii 7 12
Myself am one made privy to the plot . . . . iii 1 12
What lets but one may enter at her window? . . . . iii 1 113
And built so shelving that one cannot climb it . . . . . . iii 1 115
Let me see thy cloak : I'll get me one of such another length . . iii 1 133
It must with circumstance be spoken By one whom she esteemeth as his friend . . . . iii 2 37
Be one of them ; it's an honourable kind of thievery . . . . iv 1 39
One, lady, if you knew his pure heart's truth, You would quickly learn to know him by his voice . . . . iv 2 88
Your servant and your friend ; One that attends your ladyship's command . . . . iv 3 5
One that I brought up of a puppy ; one that I saved from drowning . iv 4 2
I have taught him, even as one would say precisely, 'thus I would teach a dog' . . . . iv 4 6
I would have, as one should say, one that takes upon him to be a dog . iv 4 12
'Out with the dog!' says one : 'What cur is that?' says another . . iv 4 22
What says she to my face?—She says it is a fair one . . . . v 2 9
A thousand more mischances than this one Have learn'd me how to brook this patiently . . . . v 3 3
Better have none Than plural faith which is too much by one . . . v 4 52
I do despise a liar as I do despise one that is false, or as I despise one that is not true . . . . *Mer. Wives* i 1 70
I hope, sir, I will do as it shall become one that would do reason . . i 1 242
And one that is your friend, I can tell you that by the way . . . i 4 149
One that is well-nigh worn to pieces with age to show himself a young gallant ! . . . . ii 1 21
I'll entertain myself like one that I am not acquainted withal . . ii 1 89
He wooes both high and low, both rich and poor, Both young and old, one with another . . . . ii 1 118
And one, I tell you, that will not miss you morning nor evening prayer ii 2 101
If there be a kind woman in Windsor, she is one . . . . . . ii 2 126
Vat be all you, one, two, tree, four, come for?—To see thee fight . . ii 3 22
If I see a sword out, my finger itches to make one . . . . . ii 3 48
Coming, with half Windsor at his heels, to search for such a one . . iii 3 122
If there is one, I shall make two in the company . . . . . iii 3 250
If I have horns to make one mad, let the proverb go with me . . iii 5 154
There was one conveyed out of my house yesterday in this basket . iv 2 152
'Tis one of the best discretions of a 'oman as ever I did look upon . iv 4 1
One that hath taught me more wit than ever I learned before . . iv 5 60
They threw me off from behind one of them, in a slough of mire . . iv 5 69
Have not they suffered? Yes, I warrant ; speciously one of them . iv 5 114
Sure, one of you does not serve heaven well, that you are so crossed . iv 5 129
'Twixt twelve and one, Must my sweet Nan present the Fairy Queen . iv 6 19
Procure the vicar To stay for me at church 'twixt twelve and one . iv 6 49
Have I lived to stand at the taunt of one that makes fritters of English? v 5 151
And one that is as slanderous as Satan?—And as poor as Job? . . v 5 163
Every one go home, And laugh this sport o'er by a country fire . . v 5 255
I do bend my speech To one that can my part in him advertise *M. for M.* i 1 42
Went to sea with the Ten Commandments, but scraped one out of the table . . . . i 2 9
Not as one would say, healthy ; but so sound as things that are hollow i 2 55
There's one yonder arrested and carried to prison . . . . . i 2 60
One who never feels The wanton stings and motions of the sense . . i 4 58
That such a one and such a one were past cure of the thing you wot of ii 1 114
No ceremony that to great ones 'longs, Not the king's crown . . ii 2 59
Repent you, fair one, of the sin you carry? . . . . ii 3 19
So play the foolish throngs with one that swoons ; Come all to help him ii 4 24
'Tis all as easy Falsely to take away a life true made As to put metal in restrained means To make a false one . . . . ii 4 49
If you be one [a woman], as you are well express'd By all external warrants, show it now . . . . ii 4 136
I have no tongue but one : . . . speak the former language . . . ii 4 139
In such a one as, you consenting to't, Would bark your honour . . iii 1 71
Left her in her tears, and dried not one of them with his comfort . . iii 1 234
One that, above all other strifes, contended especially to know himself iii 2 246
The one has my pity ; not a jot the other . . . . iv 2 64
One that is a prisoner nine years old . . . . iv 2 135
One would think it were Mistress Overdone's own house . . . . iv 3 2
One of our covent, and his confessor, Gives me this instance . . . iv 3 133
Not impossible But one, the wicked'st caitiff on the ground, May seem as shy . . . . v 1 53
Some one hath set you on : Confess the truth . . . . . . v 1 112
Who knew of your intent . . .?—One that I would were here . . . v 1 125
I am sorry, one so learned and so wise As you . . . Should slip so grossly v 1 475
And yet here's one in place I cannot pardon . . . . v 1 504
You, sirrah, that knew me for a fool, a coward, One all of luxury, an ass v 1 506
I have heard him swear himself there's one Whom he begot with child v 1 516
One so like the other As could not be distinguish'd . . *Com. of Errors* i 1 52
To him one of the other twins was bound, Whilst I had been like heedful of the other . . . . i 1 82
The clock hath strucken twelve upon the bell ; My mistress made it one upon my cheek . . . . i 2 46
For what reason?—For two ; and sound ones too.—Nay, not sound, I pray you.—Sure ones then . . . . ii 2 92
For if we two be one and thou play false, I do digest the poison . . ii 2 144
When one is one too many . . . . iii 1 35
Mine office and my name. The one ne'er got me credit, the other mickle blame . . . . iii 1 45
One that claims me, one that haunts me, one that will have me . . iii 2 82
Such a one as a man may not speak of without he say 'Sir-reverence' . iii 2 92
If every one knows us and we know none, 'Tis time, I think, to trudge iii 2 157
Who would be jealous then of such a one? . . . . iv 2 23
One whose hard heart is button'd up with steel ; A fiend, a fury . . iv 2 34
One that countermands The passages of alleys, creeks . . . . iv 2 37
It was two ere I left him, and now the clock strikes one . . . . iv 2 54
And every one doth call me by my name . . . . iv 3 3
One that thinks a man always going to bed . . . . iv 3 32
These two so like, And these two Dromios, one in semblance . . . v 1 358
And now let's go hand in hand, not one before another . . . . v 1 425
In our last conflict four of his five wits went halting off, and now is the whole man governed with one . . . . *Much Ado* i 1 67
The one is too like an image and says nothing, and the other too like my lady's eldest son, evermore tattling . . . . ii 1 9
I have many ill qualities.—Which is one?—I say my prayers aloud . . ii 1 107
I gave him use for it, a double heart for his single one . . . . ii 1 289
Thus goes every one to the world but I, and I am sunburnt . . . ii 1 331
Heigh-ho for a husband !—Lady Beatrice, I will get you one.—I would rather have one of your father's getting . . . . ii 1 334

One. I will in the interim undertake one of Hercules' labours *Much Ado* ii 1 380
Into a mountain of affection the one with the other ii 1 383
So immodest to write to one that she knew would flout her ii 3 148
We have ten proofs to one that blood hath the victory ii 3 172
The sport will be, when they hold one an opinion of another's dotage ii 3 224
One doth not know How much an ill word may empoison liking iii 1 85
Well, every one can master a grief but he that has it iii 2 28
I know who loves him.— . . . I warrant, one that knows him not iii 2 67
Five shillings to one on 't, with any man that knows the statues iii 3 84
For when rich villains have need of poor ones, poor ones may make what price they will iii 3 121
And one Deformed is one of them: I know him; a' wears a lock iii 3 182
But God send every one their heart's desire! iii 4 60
God's a good man; an two men ride of a horse, one must ride behind iii 5 40
He talk'd with you yesternight Out at your window betwixt twelve and one iv 1 85
Grieved I, I had but one? Chid I for that at frugal nature's frame? O, one too much by thee! Why had I one? iv 1 129
And men are only turned into tongue, and trim ones too iv 1 323
And one that knows the law, go to; and a rich fellow enough iv 2 86
One that hath two gowns and everything handsome about him iv 2 88
Nor let no comforter delight mine ear But such a one whose wrongs do suit with mine v 1 7
If such a one will smile and stroke his beard, Bid sorrow wag v 1 15
He shall kill two of us, and men indeed: But that's no matter; let him kill one first v 1 81
I said, thou hadst a fine wit: 'True,' said she, 'a fine little one' v 1 162
'No,' said I, 'a great wit:' 'Right,' says she, 'a great gross one' v 1 164
There will I leave you too, for here comes one in haste v 2 96
To do what, signior?—To bind me, or undo me; one of them v 4 20
There is no staff more reverend than one tipped with horn v 4 125
One whom the music of his own vain tongue Doth ravish *L. L. Lost* i 1 167
How many is one thrice told?—I am ill at reckoning i 2 41
It doth amount to one more than two.—Which the base vulgar do call three i 2 50
Of the sea-water green, sir.—Is that one of the four complexions? i 2 87
Every object that the one doth catch The other turns to a mirth-moving jest ii 1 70
Every one her own hath garnished With such bedecking ornaments of praise ii 1 78
To lodge you in the field, Like one that comes here to besiege his court ii 1 86
I desire her name.—She hath but one for herself ii 1 200
One that will do the deed Though Argus were her eunuch and her guard iii 1 200
One o' these maids' girdles for your waist should be fit iv 1 50
He came, saw, and overcame: he came, one; saw, two; overcame, three iv 1 71
A nuptial: on whose side? the king's: no, on both in one, or one in both iv 1 79
One that makes sport To the prince and his bookmates iv 1 101
So I may answer thee with one as old iv 1 124
An if one should be pierced, which is the one? iv 2 86
She hath one o' my sonnets already: the clown bore it iv 3 15
Ay me! says one; O Jove! the other cries; One, her hairs were gold iv 3 142
I'll make one in a dance, or so v 1 160
One rubb'd his elbow thus, and fleer'd and swore v 2 109
The gallants shall be task'd; For, ladies, we will every one be mask'd v 2 127
This is the flower that smiles on every one, To show his teeth v 2 331
But three?—No, sir; but it is vara fine, For every one pursents three v 2 488
The whole world again Cannot pick out five such, take each one in his vein v 2 548
The one maintained by the owl, the other by the cuckoo v 2 902
One that composed your beauties, yea, and one To whom you are but as a form in wax *M. N. Dream* i 1 48
A proper man, as one shall see in a summer's day i 2 89
The one I'll slay, the other slayeth me ii 1 190
And commit yourself Into the hands of one that loves you not ii 1 216
Hence, away! now all is well: One aloof stand sentinel ii 2 26
One must come in with a bush of thorns and a lanthorn iii 1 60
And so every one according to his cue iii 1 78
Away his fellows fly; And, at our stamp, here o'er and o'er one falls iii 2 25
Then will two at once woo one; That must needs be sport alone iii 2 118
Lo, she is one of this confederacy! iii 2 192
Like coats in heraldry, Due but to one and crowned with one crest iii 2 214
Lead these testy rivals so astray As one come not within another's way iii 2 359
Go, one of you, find out the forester iv 1 108
One sees more devils than vast hell can hold, That is, the madman v 1 9
An ace for him; for he is but one.—Less than an ace, man; for he is dead v 1 313
Her passion ends the play.—Methinks she should not use a long one v 1 322
Every one lets forth his sprite, In the church-way paths to glide v 1 388
A stage where every man must play a part, And mine a sad one *M. of Ven.* i 1 79
I must be one of these same dumb wise men i 1 106
Had I but the means To hold a rival place with one of them i 1 174
I can easier teach twenty what were good to be done, than be one of the twenty to follow mine own teaching i 2 18
Is it not hard, Nerissa, that I cannot choose one nor refuse none? i 2 28
Will, no doubt, never be chosen by any rightly but one who shall rightly love i 2 36
There is not one among them but I dote on his very absence i 2 120
He hath a great infection, sir, as one would say, to serve ii 2 133
One speak for both. What would you? ii 2 150
Like one well studied in a sad ostent To please his grandam ii 2 205
To one that I would have him help to waste His borrow'd purse ii 5 50
Never to unfold to any one Which casket 'twas I chose ii 9 10
To these injunctions every one doth swear ii 9 17
One that comes before To signify the approaching of his lord ii 9 87
I am lock'd in one of them: If you do love me, you will find me out iii 2 40
Having made one [eye], Methinks it should have power to steal both his iii 2 124
To give and to receive. Like one of two contending in a prize iii 2 142
So thou canst get a wife.—I thank your lordship, you have got me one iii 2 198
I got a promise of this fair one here To have her love iii 2 208
One in whom The ancient Roman honour more appears iii 2 296
Christians enow before; e'en as many as could well live, one by another iii 5 25
Stealing her soul with many vows of faith And ne'er a true one v 1 20
There is not one so young and so villanous this day living *As Y. Like It* i 1 160
If I be foiled, there is but one shamed that was never gracious; if killed, but one dead that is willing to be so i 2 200
Wear this for me, one out of suits with fortune, That could give more i 2 258
Cupid have mercy! not a word?—Not one to throw at a dog i 3 3
The one should be lamed with reasons and the other mad without any i 3 8
Rosalind lacks then the love Which teacheth thee that thou and I am one i 3 99
One of you question yond man If he for gold will give us any food ii 4 64
One that hath been a courtier ii 7 36
I am ambitious for a motley coat.—Thou shalt have one ii 7 44

One. Who can come in and say that I mean her, When such a one as she such is her neighbour? *As Y. Like It* ii 7 78
I know the more one sickens the worse at ease he is iii 2 24
One sleeps easily because he cannot study and the other lives merrily iii 2 338
The one lacking the burden of lean and wasteful learning iii 2 340
One that knew courtship too well, for there he fell in love iii 2 363
One of the points in the which women still give the lie to their consciences iii 2 409
Did you ever cure any so?—Yes, one, and in this manner iii 2 427
One of you will prove a shrunk panel and, like green timber, warp iii 3 89
As good cause as one would desire iii 4 5
And he [Troilus] is one of the patterns of love iv 1 99
Why then, can one desire too much of a good thing? iv 1 123
That flattering tongue of yours won me: 'tis but one cast away iv 1 189
That drink, being poured out of a cup into a glass, by filling the one doth empty the other v 1 47
I have had four quarrels, and like to have fought one v 4 49
To one his lands withheld, and to the other A land itself at large v 4 174
Let one attend him with a silver basin Full of rose-water *T. of Shrew* Ind. 1 55
Some one be ready with a costly suit Ind. 1 59
To bed with him; And each one to his office when he wakes Ind. 1 73
Take them to the buttery, And give them friendly welcome every one Ind. 1 103
Both our inventions meet and jump in one i 1 195
If thou know One rich enough to be Petruchio's wife i 2 67
Well read in poetry And other books, good ones, I warrant ye i 2 171
She may more suitors have and me for one i 2 243
Lucentio shall make one, Though Paris came in hope to speed alone i 2 246
One as famous for a scolding tongue As is the other for beauteous modesty i 2 254
Well aim'd of such a young one ii 1 236
A tender fatherly regard, To wish me wed to one half lunatic ii 1 289
A pair of boots that have been candle-cases, one buckled, another laced iii 2 46
A horse and a man Is more than one, And yet not many iii 2 87
Nay, let them go, a couple of quiet ones iii 2 242
And sits as one new-risen from a dream iv 1 189
One that scorn to live in this disguise, For such a one as leaves a gentleman, And makes a god of such a cullion iv 2 18
But do forswear her, As one unworthy all the former favours iv 2 30
Doth resemble you.—As much as an apple doth an oyster, and all one iv 2 101
Both, or one, or any thing thou wilt.—Why then, the mustard without the beef iv 3 29
When you are gentle, you shall have one too, And not till then iv 3 71
Therefore for assurance Let's each one send unto his wife v 2 66
Is that an answer?—Ay, and a kind one too v 2 83
Thy head, thy sovereign; one that cares for thee v 2 147
My mind hath been as big as one of yours v 2 170
'Twere all one That I should love a bright particular star *All's Well* i 1 96
Who comes here? One that goes with him: I love him for his sake i 1 110
How might one do, sir, to lose it to her own liking? i 1 163
And he is one— What one, i' faith?—That I wish well i 1 191
Howsome'er their hearts are severed in religion, their heads are both one i 3 58
Among nine bad if one be good, There's yet one good in ten i 3 81
One good in ten? you corrupt the song, sirrah.—One good woman in ten i 3 84
An we might have a good woman born but one every blazing star i 3 91
A man may draw his heart out, ere a' pluck one i 3 93
'Tis so; for, look, thy cheeks Confess it, th' one to th' other i 3 183
And no sword worn But one to dance with! ii 1 33
There's one arrived, If you will see her ii 1 82
One that, in her sex, her years, profession, Wisdom, . . . hath amazed me ii 1 86
Now, fair one, does your business follow us? ii 1 102
On's bed of death Many receipts he gave me; chiefly one ii 1 108
Humbly entreating from your royal thoughts A modest one, to bear me back again ii 1 131
Such thanks I give As one near death to those that wish him live ii 1 134
Such a one, thy vassal, whom I know Is free for me to ask, thee to bestow ii 1 202
To each of you one fair and virtuous mistress Fall, when Love please! marry, to each, but one! ii 3 63
Peruse them well: Not one of those but had a noble father ii 3 68
Is it not a language I speak?—A most harsh one ii 3 198
One, that she's not in heaven, whither God send her quickly! the other, that she's in earth ii 4 11
One that lies three thirds ii 5 31
Know you such a one?—But by the ear ii 5 52
Some one among us whom we must produce for an interpreter iv 1 6
We must every one be a man of his own fancy, not to know what we speak one to another iv 1 19
I must give myself some hurts, and say I got them in exploit: yet slight ones will not carry it; . . . and great ones I dare not give iv 1 41
When you are dead, you should be such a one As you are now iv 2 7
He excels his brother for a coward, yet his brother is reputed one of the best iv 3 322
One of the greatest in the Christian world Shall be my surety iv 4 2
You have made the days and nights as one, To wear your gentle limbs v 1 3
One brings thee in grace and the other brings thee out v 2 53
He gave it to a commoner o' the camp, If I be one v 3 195
Dead though she be, she feels her young one kick: So there's my riddle: one that's dead is quick v 3 303
Let thy courtesies alone, they are scurvy ones v 3 324
As, you know, What great ones do the less will prattle of *T. Night* i 2 33
Or if she be, it's four to one she'll none of me i 3 113
I am resolved on two points.—That if one break, the other will hold i 5 26
Here he comes,—one of thy kin has a most weak pia mater i 5 122
There's one at the gate.—Ay, marry, what is he? i 5 134
One would think his mother's milk were scarce out of him i 5 170
'Tis not that time of moon with me to make one in so skipping a dialogue i 5 213
Look you, sir, such a one I was this present: is't not well done? i 5 252
Even so quickly may one catch the plague? i 5 314
'Tis not the first time I have constrained one to call me knave ii 3 72
She's a beagle, true-bred, and one that adores me: what o' that? ii 3 195
My part of death, no one so true Did share it ii 4 58
That, should she fancy, it should be one of my complexion ii 5 30
Every one of these letters are in my name ii 5 153
I'll make one too ii 5 228
I am almost sick for one; though I would not have it grow on my chin iii 1 53
To one of your receiving Enough is shown iii 1 131
If one should be a prey, how much the better To fall before the lion! iii 1 139
So much As might have drawn one to a longer voyage iii 3 7
If it please the eye of one, it is with me as the very true sonnet is, 'Please one, and please all' iii 4 24
Fare thee well; and God have mercy upon one of our souls! iii 4 184
I am one that had rather go with sir priest than sir knight iii 4 298
One, sir, that for his love dares yet do more Than you have heard him brag iii 4 347

One. I am one of those gentle ones that will use the devil himself with courtesy *T. Night* iv 2 37
Though it please you to be one of my friends.—Thou shalt not be the worse v 1 29
The bells of Saint Bennet, sir, may put you in mind; one, two, three v 1 43
And grew a twenty years removed thing While one would wink v 1 93
Pardon me, sweet one, even for the vows We made each other but so late ago v 1 221
I was one, sir, in this interlude v 1 380
One that indeed physics the subject, makes old hearts fresh *W. Tale* i 1 42
If the king had no son, they would desire to live on crutches till he had one i 1 50
As twinn'd lambs that did frisk i' the sun, And bleat the one at the other i 2 68
I have spoke to the purpose twice: The one for ever earn'd a royal husband i 2 107
False As dice are to be wish'd by one that fixes No bourn 'twixt his and mine i 2 133
Inch-thick, knee-deep, o'er head and ears a fork'd one! i 2 186
I may be negligent, foolish and fearful; In every one of these no man is free i 2 251
One Who in rebellion with himself will have All that are his so too i 2 354
Nor brass nor stone nor parchment bears not one [example] i 2 360
Nor shall you be safer Than one condemn'd by the king's own mouth i 2 445
A sad tale's best for winter: I have one Of sprites and goblins ii 1 25
There may be in the cup A spider steep'd, and one may drink, depart ii 1 40
But if one present The abhorr'd ingredient to his eye ii 1 42
One that knows What she should shame to know herself ii 1 90
In the which three great ones suffer ii 1 128
A worthy lady And one whom much I honour ii 2 6
As well as one so great and so forlorn May hold together ii 2 22
Nor I, nor any But one that's here, and that's himself ii 3 83
She durst not call me so, If she did know me one [a tyrant] ii 3 124
Will never do him good, not one of you ii 3 129
The daughter of a king, our wife, and one Of us too much beloved iii 2 3
Whose honourable thoughts, Thoughts high for one so tender iii 2 197
A boy or a child, I wonder? A pretty one; a very pretty one iii 3 72
Three-man-song-men all, and very good ones iv 3 45
The loathsomeness of them offends me more than the stripes I have received, which are mighty ones iv 3 61
One of these two must be necessities, Which then will speak iv 4 38
She would to each one sip. You are retired, As if you were a feasted one iv 4 63
Shepherdess,—A fair one are you iv 4 78
For she would not exchange flesh with one that loved her iv 4 285
This is a merry ballad, but a very pretty one.—Let's have some merry ones iv 4 292
One being dead, I shall have more than you can dream of yet iv 4 398
The one He chides to hell and bids the other grow Faster than thought iv 4 563
No hope to help you, But as you shake off one to take another iv 4 580
They do not give us the lie.—Your worship had like to have given us one iv 4 751
One that will either push on or pluck back thy business there iv 4 762
Though my case be a pitiful one, I hope I shall not be flayed out of it iv 4 845
I will bring these two moles, these blind ones, aboard him iv 4 868
You are one of those Would have him wed again v 1 23
No wife: one worse, And better used, would make her sainted spirit Again possess her corpse v 1 56
The one I have almost forgot,—your pardon v 1 104
They looked as they had heard of a world ransomed, or one destroyed v 2 17
Could not say if the importance were joy or sorrow; but in the extremity of the one, it must needs be v 2 21
One of the prettiest touches of all and that which angled for mine eyes v 2 89
You precious winners all; your exultation Partake to every one v 3 132
Where we may leisurely Each one demand and answer to his part v 3 153
One that will play the devil, sir, with you *K. John* ii 1 135
Both are alike; and both alike we like. One must prove greatest ii 1 332
And two such shores to two such streams made one ii 1 443
What say these young ones? ii 1 521
One that am the tongue of these To sound the purposes of all their hearts iv 2 47
We thank you both: yet one but flatters us *Richard II.* i 1 25
My life thou shalt command, but not my shame: The one my duty owes i 1 167
Mine honour is my life; both grow in one i 1 182
Edward's seven sons, whereof thyself art one i 2 11
Had the king permitted us, One of our souls had wander'd in the air i 3 195
Both are my kinsmen: The one is my sovereign ii 2 112
Where one on his side fights, thousands will fly ii 2 147
The one in fear to lose what they enjoy, The other to enjoy by rage and war iii 4 13
Three Judases, each one thrice worse than Judas! iii 2 132
Currents that spring from one most gracious head iii 3 108
They'll talk of state; for every one doth so Against a change iii 4 27
I speak no more than every one doth know iii 4 91
Excepting one, I would he were the best In all this presence. iv 1 31
[Christ], in twelve, Found truth in all but one; I, in twelve thousand, none iv 1 171
And hate turns one or both To worthy danger and deserved death v 1 67
I greatly care not: God knows I had as lief be none as one v 2 49
Come, little ones v 5 15
Little better than one of the wicked *1 Hen. IV.* i 2 106
I'll make one; an I do not, call me villain i 2 113
Wilt thou make one?—Who, I rob? I a thief? not I, by my faith i 2 152
I heard him tell it to one of his company last night at supper ii 1 62
A plague upon it when thieves cannot be true one to another! ii 2 30
One that never spake other English in his life ii 4 26
Not three good men unhanged in England; and one of them is fat ii 4 145
O Jesu, he doth it as like one of these harlotry players as ever I see! ii 4 436
One of them is well known, my gracious lord, A gross fat man ii 4 559
My moiety, north from Burton here, In quantity equals not one of yours iii 1 97
I had rather be a kitten and cry mew Than one of these same metre ballad-mongers iii 1 130
One that no persuasion can do good upon iii 1 199
Where shall I find one that can steal well? O for a fine thief! iii 3 211
Meet and ne'er part till one drop down a corse iv 1 123
The hour is come To end the one of us v 4 69
Like a sow that hath overwhelmed all her litter but one *2 Hen. IV.* i 2 14
I will sooner have a beard grow in the palm of my hand than he shall get one on his cheek i 2 25

One. Though it be a shame to be on any side but one *2 Hen. IV.* i 2 88
Like one that draws the model of a house Beyond his power to build it i 3 58
A hundred mark is a long one for a poor lone woman to bear. ii 1 35
One you may do with sterling money, and the other with current repentance ii 1 131
I had thought weariness durst not have attached one of so high blood ii 2 3
How many pair of silk stockings thou hast, viz. these, and those that were thy peach-coloured ones! ii 2 19
The inventory of thy shirts, as, one for superfluity, and another for use! ii 2 20
As to one it pleases me, for fault of a better, to call my friend ii 2 44
It perfumes the blood ere one can say 'What's this?' ii 4 31
You cannot one bear with another's confirmities ii 4 63
What the good-year! one must bear, and that must be you ii 4 64
I am the worse, when one says swagger: feel, masters, how I shake ii 4 113
For the women?—For one of them, she is in hell already ii 4 365
O God! that one might read the book of fate! iii 1 45
My old dame will be undone now for one to do her husbandry iii 2 124
O, give me the spare men, and spare me the great ones iii 2 289
Ignorant carriage is caught, as men take diseases, one of another v 1 85
Sweet knight, thou art now one of the greatest men in this realm. v 3 91
Whose guiltless drops Are every one a woe *Hen. V.* i 2 26
I will wink and hold out mine iron: it is a simple one ii 1 9
Not one behind that doth not wish Success and conquest to attend on us ii 2 23
Who are the late commissioners?—I one, my lord ii 2 62
A' parted even just between twelve and one, even at the turning o' the tide ii 3 13
Whose chin is but enrich'd With one appearing hair iii Prol.
One that is like to be executed for robbing a church iii 6 105
I was told that by one that knows him better than you iii 7 113
A largess universal like the sun His liberal eye doth give to every one iv Prol. 44
The French may lay twenty French crowns to one, they will beat us iv 1 243
There's five to one; besides, they all are fresh iv 3 4
Now thou hast unwish'd five thousand men; Which likes me better than to wish us one iv 3 77
That every one may pare his nails with a wooden dagger iv 4 76
'Tis the gage of one that I should fight withal, if he be alive iv 7 128
Brother England; fairly met: So are you, princes English, every one v 2 11
What says she, fair one? v 2 120
For the one, I have neither words nor measure v 2 139
If thou would have such a one, take me; and take me, take a soldier v 2 174
Must needs be granted to be much at one v 2 204
God, the best maker of all marriages, Combine your hearts in one, your realms in one! v 2 388
As man and wife, being two, are one in love v 2 389
One would have lingering wars with little cost *1 Hen. VI.* i 1 74
Four of their lords I'll change for one of ours i 1 151
He fighteth as one weary of his life i 2 26
A foe to citizens, One that still motions war and never peace i 3 63
Here, through this grate, I count each one i 4 60
One of thy eyes and thy cheek's side struck off! i 4 75
That, if it chance the one of us do fail, The other yet may rise ii 1 31
Upon the which, that every one may read, Shall be engraved ii 2 14
As that slaughterer doth Which giveth many wounds when one will kill ii 5 110
No one should sway but he; No one but he should be about the king iii 1 37
For what are you, I pray, But one imperious in another's throne? iii 1 44
No reason, if I wear this rose, That any one should therefore be suspicious iv 1 153
You fled for vantage, every one will swear iv 5 28
The help of one stands me in little stead iv 6 31
And, as you please, So let them have their answers every one v 1 25
The English army, that divided was Into two parties, is now conjoin'd in one v 2 12
Or one that, at a triumph having vow'd To try his strength, forsaketh yet the lists By reason of his adversary's odds v 5 31
O God, what mischiefs work the wicked ones! *2 Hen. VI.* ii 1 186
In the morn, When every one will give the time of day iii 1 14
As the dam runs lowing up and down, Looking the way her harmless young one went iii 1 215
Were't not all one, an empty eagle were set To guard the chicken? iii 1 248
As one that surfeits thinking on a want iii 2 348
For these whose ransom we have set, It is our pleasure one of them depart iv 1 140
And thou shalt have a license to kill for a hundred lacking one iv 3 9
For me, I will make shift for one iv 8 33
If one so rude and of so mean condition May pass into the presence of a king v 1 64
Of one or both of us the time is come v 2 13
Till I root out their accursed line And leave not one alive *3 Hen. VI.* i 3 33
But buckle with thee blows, twice two for one i 4 50
What valour were it, when a cur doth grin, For one to thrust his hand between his teeth? i 4 57
Three glorious suns, each one a perfect sun ii 1 26
Each one already blazing by our meeds ii 1 36
One that was a woful looker-on ii 1 45
In protection of their tender ones ii 2 28
Now one the better, then another best; Both tugging to be victors ii 5 10
Like one that stands upon a promontory, And spies a far-off shore iii 2 135
Like one lost in a thorny wood, That rends the thorns and is rent iii 2 174
My quarrel and this English queen's are one iii 3 216
To let you understand, If case some one of you would fly from us v 4 34
In deadly hate the one against the other *Richard III.* i 1 35
He that doth naught with her, excepting one, Were best he do it secretly, alone.—What one, my lord? i 1 99
Why, that was he.—The selfsame name, but one of better nature i 2 143
Nor thou within the compass of my curse.—Nor no one here i 3 285
'Twas wont to hold me but while one would tell twenty i 4 122
It [conscience] fills one full of obstacles i 4 143
You have been factious one against the other ii 1 20
And no one in this presence But his red colour hath forsook his cheeks ii 1 84
It were lost sorrow to wail one that's lost ii 2 11
There are two councils held; And that may be determined at the one Which may make you and him to rue at the other iii 2 13
His honour and myself are at the one, And at the other is my servant iii 2 21
Rough cradle for such little pretty ones! iv 1 101
One heaved a-high, to be hurl'd down below iv 4 86
For joyful mother, one that wails the name iv 4 99
For one being sued to, one that humbly sues; For one that scorn'd at me, now scorn'd of me; For one being fear'd of all, now fearing one; For one commanding all, obey'd of none iv 4 101

One. That would I learn of you, As one that are best acquainted with her humour . *Richard III.* iv 4 269
Some one take order Buckingham be brought To Salisbury . . iv 4 539
And every one did threat To-morrow's vengeance on the head of Richard . . . . v 3 205
One raised in blood, and one in blood establish'd . . v 3 247
One that made means to come by what he hath . . . v 3 248
One that hath ever been God's enemy . . . . v 3 252
You having lands, and blest with beauteous wives, They would restrain the one, distain the other . . . . . v 3 322
One that never in his life Felt so much cold as over shoes in snow . v 3 325
What four throned ones could have weigh'd Such a compounded one? *Hen. VIII.* i 1 11
Till this time pomp was single, but now married To one above itself . i 1 16
And, being present both, 'Twas said they saw but one . . i 1 32
One, certes, that promises no element In such a business . . i 1 48
What we oft do best, By sick interpreters, once weak ones, is Not ours i 2 82
But they are shrewd ones . . . . i 3 7
They have all new legs, and lame ones: one would take it, That never saw 'em pace before, the spavin Or springhalt reign'd among 'em i 3 11
This night he makes a supper, and a great one, To many lords and ladies . . . . i 3 52
Set here for examples.—True, they are so; But few now give so great ones . . . . i 3 63
By my life, They are a sweet society of fair ones . . . i 4 14
You are one will keep 'em waking; Pray, sit between these ladies . i 4 23
There should be one amongst 'em, by his person, More worthy this place . . . . i 4 78
What say they?—Such a one, they all confess, There is indeed . i 4 82
One of her highness' women.—By heaven, she is a dainty one . i 4 94
Lead in your ladies, every one: sweet partner, I must not yet forsake you . . . . i 4 103
That trick of state Was a deep envious one . . . ii 1 45
I had my trial, And, must needs say, a noble one . . ii 1 119
A little happier than my wretched father: Yet thus far we are one in fortunes . . . . ii 1 121
All the clerks, I mean the learned ones, in Christian kingdoms . ii 2 93
Was reckon'd one The wisest prince that there had reign'd by many A year . . . . ii 4 48
Spake one the least word that might Be to the prejudice . . ii 4 153
Have I lived thus long—let me speak myself, . . . —a wife, a true one? iii 1 126
One that ne'er dream'd a joy beyond his pleasure . . . iii 1 135
An arch one, Cranmer; one Hath crawl'd into the favour of the king . iii 2 102
Gleaning all the land's wealth into one, Into your own hands, cardinal iii 2 284
Those articles, my lord, are in the king's hand: But, thus much, they are foul ones . . . . iii 2 300
Found thee a way, out of his wreck, to rise in; A sure and safe one . iii 2 438
These are stars indeed; And sometimes falling ones . . iv 1 55
Master O' the jewel house, And one, already, of the privy council . iv 1 112
One that, by suggestion, Tied all the kingdom: simony was fair-play . iv 2 35
He was a scholar, and a ripe and good one; Exceeding wise, fair-spoken iv 2 51
One of which fell with him, Unwilling to outlive the good that did it . iv 2 59
Of which there is not one, I dare avow, And now I should not lie . . iv 2 142
Is this the honour they do one another? 'Tis well there's one above 'em yet . . . . v 2 26
One that, in all obedience, makes the church The chief aim of his honour . . . . v 3 117
Wait like a lousy footboy At chamber-door? and one as great as you are? . . . . v 3 140
We trifle time away; I long To have this young one made a Christian . v 3 180
As I have made ye one, lords, one remain; So I grow stronger . . v 3 181
Fetch me a dozen crab-tree staves, and strong ones . . . v 4 8
So shall she leave her blessedness to one, When heaven shall call her . v 5 44
This little one shall make it holiday . . . . . v 5 77
On one and other side, Trojan and Greek, Sets all on hazard *Tr. and Cr.* Prol. 21
Here's but two and fifty hairs on your chin, and one of them is white . i 2 172
Is not that a brave man? he's one of the flowers of Troy . . i 2 203
He's a man good enough: he's one o' the soundest judgements . i 2 208
You are such a woman! one knows not at what ward you lie . . i 2 282
At all these wards I lie, at a thousand watches.—Say one of your watches . . . . i 2 290
I'll watch you for that; and that's one of the chiefest of them too . i 2 292
May one, that is a herald and a prince, Do a fair message? . . i 3 218
If there be one among the fair'st of Greece That holds his honour higher i 3 265
If then one is, or hath, or means to be [in love], That one meets Hector i 3 289
One that was a man When Hector's grandsire suck'd . . . i 3 291
And such a one that dare Maintain—I know not what . . . ii 1 137
You speak Like one besotted on your sweet delights . . . ii 2 143
Vowing more than the perfection of ten and discharging less than the tenth part of one . . . . iii 2 95
If ever you prove false one to another, since I have taken such pains . iii 2 206
Do one pluck down another and together Die in the fall . . iii 3 86
For honour travels in a strait so narrow, Where one but goes abreast . iii 3 155
We two, that with so many thousand sighs Did buy each other, must poorly sell ourselves With the rude brevity and discharge of one . iv 4 43
Therefore no kiss.—I'll give you boot, I'll give you three for one . iv 5 40
The one almost as infinite as all, The other blank as nothing . . iv 5 80
One that knows the youth Even to his inches . . . . iv 5 110
As welcome as to one That would be rid of such an enemy . . iv 5 163
An honest fellow enough, and one that loves quails . . . v 1 57
Tell me whose it was.—'Twas one's that loved me better than you will . v 2 89
One cannot speak a word, But it straight starts you . . . v 2 100
One that hath always loved the people.—He's one honest enough *Coriol.* i 1 52
Being one o' the lowest, basest, poorest, Of this most wise rebellion . i 1 161
Like nor peace nor war? the one affrights you, The other makes you proud . . . . i 1 173
A petition granted them, a strange one—To break the heart of generosity . . . . i 1 214
'Tis sworn between us we shall ever strike Till one can do no more . i 2 36
I had rather had eleven die nobly for their country than one voluptuously surfeit out of action . . . . i 3 27
How he mammocked it!—One on's father's moods . . . i 3 72
And one infect another Against the wind a mile! . . . i 4 33
We'll put you, Like one that means his proper harm, in manacles . i 9 57
One that loves a cup of hot wine with not a drop of allaying Tiber in't ii 1 52
One that converses more with the buttock of the night than with the forehead of the morning . . . . ii 1 56
You are a pair of strange ones . . . . . . ii 1 89
Here's a letter from him . . . and, I think, there's one at home for you ii 1 120
Seven hurts i' the body.—One i' the neck, and two i' the thigh . ii 1 167

One. But 'tis thought of every one Coriolanus will carry it . *Coriolanus* ii 2 4
Pray now, sit down.—I had rather have one scratch my head i' the sun ii 2 79
That's thousand to one good one . . . . ii 2 83
He had rather venture all his limbs for honour Than one on's ears to hear it . . . . ii 2 85
Come by him where he stands, by ones, by twos, and by threes . . ii 3 47
Every one of us has a single honour, in giving him our own voices . ii 3 48
Let the high office and the honour go To one that would do thus . . ii 3 130
Not one amongst us, save yourself, but says He used us scornfully . ii 3 170
One thus descended, That hath beside well in his person wrought . ii 3 253
Such a one as he, who puts his 'shall,' His popular 'shall,' against a graver bench Than ever frown'd . . . . iii 1 105
How soon confusion May enter 'twixt the gap of both and take The one by the other . . . . iii 1 112
Why, shall the people give One that speaks thus their voice? . . iii 1 119
Be still and wonder, When one but of my ordinance stood up To speak iii 2 12
Too full Of the wars' surfeits, to go rove with one That's yet unbruised iv 1 46
Why stay we to be baited With one that wants her wits? . . . iv 2 44
Have you an army ready, say you?—A most royal one . . . iv 3 47
Whose plots have broke their sleep To take the one the other . . iv 4 20
What fellow's this?—A strange one as ever I looked on . . . iv 5 21
What are you?—A gentleman.—A marvellous poor one . . . iv 5 30
He turned me about with his finger and his thumb, as one would set up a top . . . . iv 5 160
But a greater soldier than he, you wot one.—Who, my master? . . iv 5 171
One cannot tell how to say that . . . . iv 5 177
But one of these—As he hath spices of them all, not all . . . iv 7 45
It was a bare petition of a state To one whom they had punish'd . . v 1 21
I am one that, telling true under him, must say, you cannot pass . . v 2 33
Rather to show a noble grace to both parts Than seek the end of one . v 3 122
Yet here he lets me prate Like one i' the stocks . . . . v 3 160
Take him up. Help, three o' the chiefest soldiers; I'll be one . . v 6 150
In this city he Hath widow'd and unchilded many a one . . . v 6 153
One fit to bandy with thy lawless sons . . . *T. Andron.* i 1 312
My foes I do repute you every one; So, trouble me no more . . i 1 366
Would it offend you, then, That both should speed?—Faith, not me.—Nor me, so I were one . . . . ii 1 102
When did the tiger's young ones teach the dam? . . . . ii 3 142
All the service I require of them Is that the one will help to cut the other iii 1 78
I stand as one upon a rock Environ'd with a wilderness of sea . . iii 1 93
You heavy people, circle me about, That I may turn me to each one . iii 1 278
I think she means that there was more than one Confederate in the fact iv 1 38
The one is wounded with the bait, The other rotted with delicious feed iv 4 92
I have done a thousand dreadful things As willingly as one would kill a fly v 1 142
Come, be every one officious To make this banquet . . . . v 2 202
If any one relieves or pities him, For the offence he dies. . . . v 3 181
Make his will: Ah, word ill urged to one that is so ill! . *Rom. and Jul.* i 1 209
Of many mine being one May stand in number, though in reckoning none i 2 32
One fairer than my love! the all-seeing sun Ne'er saw her match . . i 2 97
But 'tis no wit to go.—Why, may one ask? . . . . . i 4 49
What's this?—A rhyme I learn'd even now Of one I danced withal . i 5 145
Like the lightning, which doth cease to be Ere one can say, 'It lightens' ii 2 120
Feasting with mine enemy, Where on a sudden one hath wounded me . ii 3 50
Bad'st me bury love.—Not in a grave, To lay one in, another out to have ii 3 84
Rests me his minim rest, one, two, and the third in your bosom . ii 4 23
Thou hast more of the wild-goose in one of thy wits than, I am sure, I have in my whole five . . . . ii 4 77
One, gentlewoman, that God hath made for himself to mar . . . ii 4 121
Did you ne'er hear say, Two may keep counsel, putting one away? . ii 4 209
You shall not stay alone Till holy church incorporate two in one . . ii 6 37
Nay, an there were two such, we should have none shortly, for one would kill the other . . . . iii 1 17
A word with one of you.—And but one word with one of us? . . . iii 1 41
Good king of cats, nothing but one of your nine lives . . . iii 1 80
Arise; one knocks; good Romeo, hide thyself.—Not I . . . iii 3 71
One who, to put thee from thy heaviness, Hath sorted out a sudden day of joy . . . . iii 5 109
This only child; But now I see this one is one too much . . . iii 5 167
May not one speak?—Peace, you mumbling fool! . . . . iii 5 174
But one, poor one, one poor and loving child, But one thing to rejoice and solace in, And cruel death hath catch'd it! . . . . iv 5 46
Every one prepare To follow this fair corse unto her grave . . iv 5 92
Going to find a bare-foot brother out, One of our order . . . v 2 6
O, give me thy hand, One writ with me in sour misfortune's book! . v 3 82
Who's there?—Here's one, a friend, and one that knows you well. . v 3 123
There's my master, One that you love.—Who is it?—Romeo . . v 3 129
Anon comes one with light to ope the tomb . . . . v 3 283
To the dumbness of the gesture One might interpret . *T. of Athens* i 1 34
One do I personate of Lord Timon's frame . . . . i 1 69
Let him slip down, Not one accompanying his declining foot . . i 1 88
My estate deserves an heir more raised Than one which holds a trencher i 1 120
How now, philosopher!—Thou liest.—Art not one?—Yes . . i 1 223
Shouldst have kept one [farewell] to thyself, for I mean to give thee none i 1 275
No porter at his gate, But rather one that smiles and still invites All . ii 1 11
No usurer but has a fool to his servant: my mistress is one . . . ii 2 104
The reason of this?—I could render one.—Do it then . . . ii 2 109
Sometime like a philosopher, with two stones moe than's artificial one. ii 2 118
One of Lord Timon's men? a gift, I warrant. Why, this hits right . iii 1 4
And one that knows what belongs to reason . . . . . iii 1 38
Tell him this from me, I count it one of my greatest afflictions . . iii 2 62
That is, one may reach deep enough, and yet Find little. . . . iii 4 15
These debts may well be called desperate ones, for a madman owes 'em. iii 4 103
Lend to each man enough, that one need not lend to another. . . iii 6 83
Who dares . . . say 'This man's a flatterer?' if one be, So are they all . iv 3 15
Let not thy sword skip one: Pity not honour'd age for his white beard iv 3 110
The one is filling still, never complete; The other, at high wish . iv 3 244
I, that I was No prodigal.—I, that I am one now . . . . iv 3 278
As rich men deal gifts, Expecting in return twenty for one . . . iv 3 517
There's never a one of you but trusts a knave, That mightily deceives you v 1 96
I love my country, and am not One that rejoices in the common wreck v 1 195
I met a courier, one mine ancient friend . . . . . v 2 6
'Twas not a crown neither, 'twas one of these coronets . . *J. Cæsar* i 2 238
Stand close awhile, for here comes one in haste . . . . i 3 131
It is Casca; one incorporate To our attempts . . . . i 3 135
Every one doth wish You had but that opinion of yourself . . ii 1 91
That great vow Which did incorporate and make us one . . . ii 1 273
There is one within, . . . Recounts most horrid sights . . . ii 2 14
Every one [star] doth shine, But there's but one in all doth hold his place iii 1 65
I do know but one That unassailable holds on his rank, Unshaked of motion . . . . iii 1 68

One. One of two bad ways you must conceit me, Either a coward or a flatterer *J. Cæsar* iii 1 192
The three-fold world divided, he should stand One of the three to share it iv 1 15
A barren-spirited fellow; one that feeds On abjects, orts and imitations iv 1 36
One of us, That struck the foremost man of all this world iv 3 21
Hated by one he loves; braved by his brother iv 3 96
He only, in a general honest thought And common good to all, made one v 5 72
Every one did bear Thy praises in his kingdom's great defence *Macbeth* i 3 98
But I have spoke With one that saw him die i 4 4
He died As one that had been studied in his death i 4 9
Our thane is coming: One of my fellows had the speed of him i 5 36
There's one did laugh in's sleep, and one cried 'Murder!' ii 2 23
One cried 'God bless us!' and 'Amen' the other ii 2 27
I know this is a joyful trouble to you; But yet 'tis one ii 3 54
Every one According to the gift which bounteous nature Hath in him closed iii 1 97
I am one, my liege, Whom the vile blows and buffets of the world Have so incensed that I am reckless what I do to spite the world iii 1 108
There's but one down; the son is fled.—We have lost Best half iii 3 20
And a bold one, that dare look on that Which might appal the devil iii 4 59
There's not a one of them but in his house I keep a servant fee'd iii 4 131
Well done! I commend your pains; And every one shall share i' the gains iv 1 40
The poor wren, The most diminutive of birds, will fight, Her young ones in her nest, against the owl iv 2 11
What is a traitor?—Why, one that swears and lies iv 2 47
Every one that does so is a traitor, and must be hanged iv 2 49
Be not found here; hence, with your little ones iv 2 69
Better Macbeth Than such an one to reign iv 3 66
If such a one be fit to govern, speak: I am as I have spoken iv 3 101
That of an hour's age doth hiss the speaker: Each minute teems a new one iv 3 176
All my pretty ones? Did you say all? O hell-kite! All? iv 3 216
Neither to you nor any one; having no witness to confirm my speech v 1 20
Out, damned spot! out, I say!—One: two: why, then 'tis time to do't v 1 40
What's he That was not born of woman? Such a one Am I to fear, or none v 7 3
By this great clatter, one of greatest note Seems bruited v 7 21
I bear a charmed life, which must not yield To one of woman born v 8 13
So, thanks to all at once and to each one v 8 74
The bell then beating one,— Peace, break thee off; look! *Hamlet* i 1 39
Stay'd it long?—While one with moderate haste might tell a hundred i 2 238
Meet it is I set it down, That one may smile, and smile, and be a villain i 5 108
Denmark's a prison.—Then is the world one.—A goodly one; in which there are many confines, . . . Denmark being one o' the worst ii 2 250
To me it is a prison.—Why then, your ambition makes it one ii 2 258
One said there were no sallets in the lines to make the matter savoury ii 2 462
No more marriages: those that are married already, all but one, shall live iii 1 155
Madness in great ones must not unwatch'd go iii 1 196
The censure of the which one must in your allowance o'erweigh a whole theatre of others iii 2 30
Thou hast been As one, in suffering all, that suffers nothing iii 2 71
And haply one as kind For husband shalt thou— O, confound the rest! iii 2 186
Get me a fellowship in a cry of players, sir?—Half a share.—A whole one, I iii 2 291
O, the recorders! let me see one iii 2 360
May one be pardon'd and retain the offence? iii 3 56
Try what repentance can: what can it not? Yet what can it when one can not repent? iii 3 66
Indeed would make one think there might be thought, Though nothing sure iv 5 12
How should I your true love know From another one? iv 5 24
Your sum of parts Did not together pluck such envy from him As did that one iv 7 76
He cried out, 'twould be a sight indeed, If one could match you iv 7 101
She chanted snatches of old tunes; As one incapable of her own distress iv 7 179
One that would circumvent God, might it not? v 1 87
Will his vouchers vouch him no more of his purchases, and double ones too? v 1 118
One that was a woman, sir; but, rest her soul, she's dead v 1 146
Not one now, to mock your own grinning? quite chap-fallen? v 1 211
And a man's life's no more than to say 'One' v 2 74
Give us the foils. Come on.—Come, one for me.—I'll be your foil v 2 265
Come, my lord.—One.—No.—Judgement.—A hit, a very palpable hit v 2 291
Let him to our sister, Whose mind and mine, I know, in that are one *Lear* i 3 15
The sweet and bitter fool Will presently appear; The one in motley here i 4 160
Little wit in thy bald crown, when thou gavest thy golden one away i 4 179
Here comes one o' the parings.—How now, daughter! i 4 206
You have heard of the news abroad; I mean the whispered ones? ii 1 8
One that wouldst be a bawd, in way of good service ii 2 20
One whom I will beat into clamorous whining ii 2 24
Thus to rail on one that is neither known of thee nor knows thee! ii 2 28
The great one that goes up the hill, let him draw thee after ii 4 75
What need one?—O, reason not the need ii 4 266
Who's there, besides foul weather?—One minded like the weather iii 1 2
One that slept in the contriving of lust, and waked to do it iii 4 92
You, sir, I entertain for one of my hundred iii 6 83
Half way down Hangs one that gathers samphire, dreadful trade! iv 6 15
And told me I had white hairs in my beard ere the black ones were there iv 6 99
Were all the letters suns, I could not see one iv 6 143
I am a king, My masters, know you that.—You are a royal one iv 6 205
Every one hears that, Which can distinguish sound iv 6 214
Which of them shall I take? Both? one? or neither? v 1 58
Packs and sects of great ones, That ebb and flow by the moon v 3 18
The one the other poison'd for my sake, And after slew herself v 3 240
I know when one is dead, and when one lives; She's dead as earth v 3 260
If fortune brag of two she loved and hated, One of them we behold v 3 281
Three great ones of the city, In personal suit *Othello* i 1 8
These fellows have some soul; And such a one do I profess myself i 1 55
You are one of those that will not serve God, if the devil bid you i 1 108
One that excels the quirks of blazoning pens ii 1 63
Come on, assay. There's one gone to the harbour? ii 1 121
Fairness and wit, The one's for use, the other useth it ii 1 131
But does foul pranks which fair and wise ones do ii 1 143
One that, in the authority of her merit, did justly put on the vouch of very malice itself ii 1 146
He is a good one, and his worthiness Does challenge much respect ii 1 212

One. Good faith, a little one; not past a pint, as I am a soldier *Othello* ii 3 68
'Tis to his virtue a just equinox, The one as long as the other ii 3 130
Swords out, and tilting one at other's breast, In opposition bloody ii 3 183
As one would beat his offenceless dog to affright an imperious lion ii 3 275
If he be not one that truly loves you, That errs in ignorance iii 3 48
Your wisdom yet, From one that so imperfectly conceits, Would take no notice iii 3 149
One may smell in such a will most rank, Foul disproportion iii 3 232
'Tis the plague of great ones: Prerogatived are they less than the base iii 3 273
I gave her such a one; 'twas my first gift iii 3 436
O, that the slave had forty thousand lives! One is too poor, too weak for my revenge iii 3 443
'Tis a good hand, A frank one.—You may, indeed, say so iii 4 44
In such cases Men's natures wrangle with inferior things, Though great ones are their object iii 4 145
My lord is fall'n into an epilepsy: This is his second fit; he had one yesterday iv 1 52
To beguile many and be beguiled by one iv 1 98
'Tis such another fitchew! marry, a perfumed one iv 1 151
Is there division 'twixt my lord and Cassio?—A most unhappy one iv 1 243
Being like one of heaven, the devils themselves Should fear to seize thee iv 2 36
To be call'd whore? would it not make one weep? iv 2 127
Which I will fashion to fall out between twelve and one iv 2 243
If I do die before thee, prithee, shroud me In one of those same sheets iv 3 25
Here's one comes in his shirt, with light and weapons v 1 47
What villains have done this?—I think that one of them is hereabout v 1 57
Such another world Of one entire and perfect chrysolite v 2 145
Of one that loved not wisely but too well; Of one not easily jealous v 2 344
Of one whose hand, Like the base Indian, threw a pearl away v 2 346
Of one whose subdued eyes, Albeit unused to the melting mood, Drop tears v 2 348
Good sir, give me good fortune.—I make not, but forsee.—Pray, then, forsee me one *Ant. and Cleo.* i 2 15
The man from Sicyon,—is there such an one?—He stays upon your will i 2 118
I'll think them every one an Antony, And say 'Ah, ha! you're caught' ii 5 14
I had rather fast from all four days Than drink so much in one ii 7 109
'Tis a noble Lepidus.—A very fine one iii 2 7
She creeps: Her motion and her station are as one iii 3 22
Throw between them all the food thou hast, They'll grind the one the other iii 5 16
Fall not a tear, I say; one of them rates All that is won and lost iii 11 69
One that but performs The bidding of the fullest man iii 13 86
'Tis better playing with a lion's whelp Than with an old one dying iii 13 95
To be abused By one that looks on feeders? iii 13 109
To flatter Cæsar, would you mingle eyes With one that ties his points? iii 13 157
When one so great begins to rage, he's hunted Even to falling iv 1 7
He thinks, being twenty times of better fortune, He is twenty men to one iv 2 4
'Tis one of those odd tricks which sorrow shoots Out of the mind iv 2 14
I look on you As one that takes his leave iv 2 29
Who's gone this morning?—Who! One ever near thee iv 5 7
Run one before, And let the queen know of our gests iv 8 1
This last day was A shrewd one to's iv 9 5
Doing the honour of thy lordliness To one so meek v 2 162
Must I be unfolded With one that I have bred? v 2 171
I heard of one of them no longer than yesterday v 2 251
The one may be sold, or given, if there were wealth enough *Cymbeline* i 4 89
The one is but frail and the other casual i 4 99
I will have it no lay.—By the gods, it is one i 4 160
I do know her spirit, And will not trust one of her malice i 5 35
One of the noblest note, to whose kindnesses I am most infinitely tied i 6 22
There is a Frenchman his companion, one An eminent monsieur i 6 64
What do you pity, sir?—Two creatures heartily.—Am I one, sir? i 6 83
And he is one The truest manner'd i 6 165
One, two, three: time, time! ii 2 51
I know her women are about her: what If I do line one of their hands? ii 3 72
I will make One of her women lawyer to me ii 3 79
One of your great knowing Should learn, being taught, forbearance ii 3 102
One bred of alms and foster'd with cold dishes ii 3 119
Your lady Is one of the fairest that I have look'd upon ii 4 32
Who knows if one of her women, being corrupted, Hath stol'n it? ii 4 116
This is not strong enough to be believed Of one persuaded well of ii 4 132
Like a full-acorn'd boar, a German one, Cried 'O!' and mounted ii 5 16
One vice, but of a minute old, for one Not half so old as that ii 5 31
Some griefs are med'cinable; that is one of them iii 2 33
If one of mean affairs May plod it in a week, why may not I? iii 2 52
Why, one that rode to's execution, man, Could never go so slow iii 2 72
One, but painted thus, Would be interpreted a thing perplex'd iii 4 6
And am almost A man already.—First, make yourself but like one iii 4 170
From every one The best she hath, and she, of all compounded, Outsells them all iii 5 72
I see a man's life is a tedious one: I have tired myself iii 6 1
Will poor folks lie, That have afflictions on them, knowing 'tis A punishment or trial? Yes; no wonder, When rich ones scarce tell true iii 6 12
Thou art one o' the false ones. Now I think on thee, My hunger's gone iii 6 15
Society is no comfort To one not sociable iv 2 13
Young one, Inform us of thy fortunes iv 2 360
Never bestrid a horse, save one that had A rider like myself iv 4 38
No reason I, since of your lives you set So slight a valuation, should reserve My crack'd one to more care iv 4 50
You married ones, If each of you should take this course! v 1 2
Every good servant does not all commands: No bond but to do just ones v 1 7
Which gave advantage to an ancient soldier, An honest one, I warrant v 3 16
Ten, chased by one, Are now each one the slaughter-man of twenty v 3 48
Yet am I better Than one that's sick o' the gout v 4 5
And cast From her his dearest one, Sweet Imogen v 4 61
What fairies haunt this ground? A book? O rare one! v 4 133
I think you'll never return to tell one v 4 191
I never saw one so prone v 4 208
Some of them too that die against their wills; so should I, if I were one v 4 211
Such precious deeds in one that promised nought But beggary v 5 9
That The Britons have razed out, though with the loss Of many a bold one v 5 71
Best of all Amongst the rarest of good ones v 5 160
Most like a noble lord in love and one That had a royal lover v 5 171
He was a prince.—A most incivil one v 5 292
Which love to all, of which thyself art one *Pericles* i 2 94
I'll take thy word for faith, not ask thine oath: Who shuns not to break one will sure crack both i 2 121
For if a king bid a man be a villain, he's bound by the indenture of his oath to be one i 3 10

One. I marvel how the fishes live in the sea.—Why, as men do a-land; the great ones eat up the little ones . . . . *Pericles* ii 1 32
Were my fortunes equal to my desires, I could wish to make one there ii 1 118
Like gods above, Who freely give to every one that comes To honour them . . . . ii 3 60
Each one betake him to his rest; To-morrow all for speeding do their best ii 3 115
And every one with claps can sound, 'Our heir-apparent is a king!' iii Gower 36
Make me blessed in your care In bringing up my child.—I have one myself . . . . iii 3 32
Therefore let's have fresh ones, whate'er we pay for them . . . iv 2 10
Why lament you, pretty one?—That I am pretty . . . . iv 2 72
Come, young one, I like the manner of your garments well . iv 2 145
Like one that superstitiously Doth swear to the gods that winter kills the flies . . . . iv 3 49
Now, pretty one, how long have you been at this trade? . . iv 6 72
Where a man may serve seven years for the loss of a leg, and have not money enough in the end to buy him a wooden one . . . . iv 6 184
A man who for this three months hath not spoken To any one . . v 1 25
Here is The lady that I sent for. Welcome, fair one! . . . v 1 65
She's such a one, that, were I well assured Came of a gentle kind . v 1 67
And such a one My daughter might have been . . . . v 1 108
Thou look'st Like one I loved indeed. What were thy friends? . v 1 126
The name Was given me by one that had some power, My father, and a king . . . . v 1 150
All is one *Mer. Wives* ii 2; *Much Ado* v 1; *All's Well* iv 3; *2 Hen. VI.* i 3; *Othello* iv 3
All's one for that . . . . . *1 Hen. IV.* ii 4 172; *Richard III.* v 3 8
It's ('tis) all one *T. Night* i 5; *W. Tale* v 2; *Hen. V.* iv 7; *Troi. and Cres.* i 1; i 2; *Rom. and Jul.* i 1
Ten to one *T. of Shrew* v 2; *2 Hen. IV.* i 1; *1 Hen. VI.* iv 1; v 4; *2 Hen. VI.* ii 1; *3 Hen. VI.* i 2; i 4; v 1; *Hen. VIII.* Epil.
That is all one *T. G. of Ver.* iii 1; *Mer. Wives* i 1; *L. L. Lost* v 2; *M. N. Dream* i 2; *As Y. Like It* iii 5; *T. of Shrew* iii 2; *T. Night* v 1; *1 Hen. IV.* iv 2
One and other. Both one and other he denies me now *Com. of Errors* iv 3 86
The one and other Diomed embraces . . . *Troi. and Cres.* iv 1 14
One and the selfsame. O perilous mouths, That bear in them one and the self-same tongue! . . . . . *Meas. for Meas.* ii 4 173
Why, sadness is one and the self-same thing, dear imp *L. L. Lost* i 2 4
One and twenty. Buried one and twenty valiant sons . . *T. Andron.* i 1 195
One another. When we are married and have more occasion to know one another . . . . *Mer. Wives* i 1 257
Have a nay-word, that you may know one another's mind . . ii 2 132
We have a nay-word how to know one another . . . . v 2 5
Then the two bears will not bite one another when they meet *Much Ado* iii 2 80
Big round tears Coursed one another down his innocent nose *As Y. L. It* ii 1 39
They were all like one another as half-pence are . . . iii 2 372
No sooner sighed but they asked one another the reason . . v 2 39
At my house; thither they send one another . . . *All's Well* iii 5 34
They will kill one another by the look, like cockatrices . *T. Night* iii 4 214
With staring on one another, to tear the cases of their eyes *W. Tale* v 2 13
They shake their heads And whisper one another . . *K. John* iv 2 189
That owes two buckets, filling one another . . . *Richard II.* iv 1 185
Why the devil should we keep knives to cut one another's throats? *Hen. V.* ii 1 96
Do pelt so fast at one another's pate . . . . *1 Hen. VI.* iii 1 82
Let them kiss one another, for they loved well . . *2 Hen. VI.* iv 7 139
And this word 'love,' which greybeards call divine, Be resident in men like one another And not in me . . . . . *3 Hen. VI.* v 6 82
Girdling one another Within their innocent alabaster arms *Richard III.* iv 3 10
His mind and place Infecting one another, yea, reciprocally *Hen. VIII.* i 1 162
Is this the honour they do one another? 'Tis well there's one above 'em yet . . . . v 2 26
Friend, we understand not one another . . . *Troi. and Cres.* iii 1 29
Distraction, frenzy and amazement, Like witless antics, one another meet v 3 86
Now they are clapper-clawing one another; I'll go look on . . v 4 1
I think they have swallowed one another: I would laugh at that miracle v 4 36
Keep you in awe, which else Would feed on one another . *Coriolanus* i 1 192
It [peace] makes men hate one another.—Reason; because they then less need one another . . . . iv 5 245
Can you love the gentleman? . . . Examine every married lineament And see how one another lends content . . . *Rom. and Jul.* i 3 84
What a precious comfort 'tis, to have so many, like brothers, commanding one another's fortunes! . . . . . . *T. of Athens* i 2 109
Love not yourselves: away, Rob one another. There's more gold . iv 3 448
Those that understood him smiled at one another . . *J. Cæsar* i 2 286
When your vile daggers Hack'd one another in the sides of Cæsar . v 1 40
We'll no more meet, no more see one another . . . . *Lear* ii 4 223
A dozen sequent messengers This very night at one another's heels *Othello* i 2 42
If you borrow one another's love for the instant . *Ant. and Cleo.* ii 2 103
As they pinch one another by the disposition, he cries out 'No more' ii 7 7
Like one another's glass to trim them by . . . . *Pericles* i 4 27
One arm. If one arm's embracement will content thee . *T. Andron.* v 2 68
One article. Let that one article rank with the rest . . *Hen. V.* v 2 374
One bad thing. From one bad thing to worse . . . *Cymbeline* iv 2 134
One battle. Set Upon one battle all our liberties . . . *J. Cæsar* v 1 76
One bear will not bite another . . . . . *Troi. and Cres.* v 7 19
One bed. One heart, one bed, two bosoms and one troth *M. N. Dream* ii 2 42
One birth. By her he had two children at one birth . *2 Hen. VI.* iv 2 147
One blast. And for one blast of thy minikin mouth, Thy sheep shall take no harm . . . . *Lear* iii 6 45
One bloody trial. To reap the harvest of perpetual peace By this one bloody trial of sharp war . . . . . . *Richard III.* v 2 16
One blow. Tut, when struck'st thou one blow in the field? *2 Hen. VI.* iv 7 84
One body. 'Tis a great charge to come under one body's hand *Mer. Wives* i 4 105
That one body should be fill'd With all graces wide-enlarged *As Y. L. It* iii 2 150
How to knit again This scatter'd corn into one mutual sheaf, These broken limbs again into one body . . . . . *T. Andron.* v 3 72
One boon. I'll beg one boon, And then be gone . . . *Richard II.* iv 1 302
One bosom. I have one heart, one bosom and one truth . *T. Night* iii 1 170
One bottom. My ventures are not in one bottom trusted *Mer. of Venice* i 1 42
One bout. The gentleman will, for his honour's sake, have one bout with you . . . . *T. Night* iii 4 337
One breast. I have a thousand spirits in one breast . . *Richard II.* iv 1 58
One breath. She will die, if he woo her, rather than she will bate one breath of her accustomed crossness . . . . . . *Much Ado* ii 3 184
One brow. Our whole kingdom To be contracted in one brow of woe *Ham.* i 2 4
One business does command us all; for mine Is money *T. of Athens* iii 4 4
One by one. If, one by one, you wedded all the world . *W. Tale* v 1 13
So, one by one, we'll weed them all at last . . . . *2 Hen. VI.* i 3 102
One by One. Emulation hath a thousand sons That one by one pursue *Troi. and Cres.* iii 3 157
Give me your hands all over, one by one . . . . *J. Cæsar* ii 1 112
One calm look. What dangerous action, stood it next to death, Would I not undergo for one calm look! . . . . . *T. G. of Ver.* v 4 42
One care. None here, he hopes, In all this noble bevy, has brought with her One care abroad . . . . *Hen. VIII.* i 4 5
One cast. Were it good To set the exact wealth of all our states All at one cast? . . . . *1 Hen. IV.* iv 1 47
One change. In our measure do but vouchsafe one change *L. L. Lost* v 2 209
One chaste man. I will find you twenty lascivious turtles ere one chaste man . . . . *Mer. Wives* ii 1 83
One chin. Item, one neck, one chin . . . . . *T. Night* i 5 267
One christening. On my Christian conscience, this one christening will beget a thousand . . . . *Hen. VIII.* v 4 37
One clef. 'D sol re,' one clef, two notes have I . *T. of Shrew* iii 1 77
One cloud of winter showers, These flies are couch'd . *T. of Athens* ii 2 180
One coal. If he could burn us all into one coal, We have deserved it *Cor.* iv 6 137
One comma. No levell'd malice Infects one comma in the course I hold *T. of Athens* i 1 48
One consent. Me shall you find ready and willing With one consent to have her so bestow'd . . . . *T. of Shrew* iv 4 35
Doth keep in one consent, Congreeing in a full and natural close *Hen. V.* i 2 181
Many things, having full reference To one consent, may work contrariously . . . . i 2 206
That all with one consent praise new-born gawds . *Troi. and Cres.* iii 3 176
The senators with one consent of love Entreat thee back *T. of Athens* v 1 143
One crest. Due but to one and crowned with one crest *M. N. Dream* iii 2 214
One crutch. I'll lean upon one crutch and fight with t'other, Ere stay behind this business . . . . *Coriolanus* i 1 246
One cup. But one cup: I'll drink for you.—I have drunk but one cup to-night . . . . *Othello* ii 3 38
One cushion. Sitting on one cushion . . . . *M. N. Dream* iii 2 205
One dainty dish. A table full of welcome makes scarce one dainty dish *Com. of Errors* iii 1 23
One danger. To eject him hence Were but one danger *Coriolanus* iii 1 288
One daughter. Thou hast one daughter, Who redeems nature from the general curse Which twain have brought her to . . . . *Lear* iv 6 209
One day. You shall one day find it . . . . . *Mer. Wives* iii 3 88
Well, you'll answer this one day. Fare ye well *Meas. for Meas.* iv 3 172
Well, I will marry one day, but to try . . *Com. of Errors* ii 1 42
And all that are assembled in this place, That by this sympathized one day's error Have suffer'd wrong . . . . v 1 397
Well, niece, I hope to see you one day fitted with a husband *Much Ado* ii 1 60
And one day in a week to touch no food . . . . *L. L. Lost* i 1 39
Affliction may one day smile again; and till then, sit thee down, sorrow! . . . . i 1 316
One day shall crown the alliance on't, so please you . *T. Night* v 1 326
One day too late, I fear me, noble lord, Hath clouded all thy happy days on earth . . . . *Richard II.* iii 2 67
No prince nor peer shall have just cause to say, God shorten Harry's happy life one day! . . . . *2 Hen. IV.* v 2 145
Adonis' gardens That one day bloom'd and fruitful were the next *1 Hen. VI.* i 6 7
'Tis but the shortening of my life one day . . . . . iv 6 37
From Tamworth thither is but one day's march . . *Richard III.* v 2 13
And with that blood will make 'em one day groan for 't . *Hen. VIII.* i 1 106
The king will know him one day.—Pray God he do! . . . . ii 2 22
Heaven will one day open The king's eyes, that so long have slept . ii 2 42
That old common arbitrator, Time, Will one day end it *Troi. and Cres.* iv 5 226
I should fear those that dance before me now Would one day stamp upon me: 't has been done . . . . *T. of Athens* i 2 149
One day he gives us diamonds, next day stones . . . . . iii 6 131
We are two lions litter'd in one day, And I the elder . . *J. Cæsar* ii 2 46
One dead. If killed, but one dead that is willing to be so *As Y. Like It* i 2 201
What's here? one dead, or drunk? . . . . . *T. of Shrew* Ind 1 31
Methinks I see thee . . . As one dead in the bottom of a tomb *R. and J.* iii 5 56
One dear son Shall I twice lose . . . . . . *Tempest* v 1 176
One defect. Carrying, I say, the stamp of one defect . . *Hamlet* i 4 31
One desperate grief cures with another's languish . *Rom. and Jul.* i 2 49
One dignity. In her fair cheek, Where several worthies make one dignity . . . . *L. L. Lost* iv 3 236
One direct way. And their consent of one direct way should be at once to all the points o' the compass . . . . . *Coriolanus* ii 3 24
One distract. Mine hair be fix'd on end, as one distract *2 Hen. VI.* iii 2 318
One doubt. To end one doubt by death Revives two greater *2 Hen. IV.* iv 1 199
Answer me one doubt, What pledge have we of thy firm loyalty? *3 Hen. VI.* iii 3 238
One doubtful hour. To set so rich a main On the nice hazard of one doubtful hour . . . . *1 Hen. IV.* iv 1 48
One dowle. May as well Wound the loud winds . . . as diminish One dowle that's in my plume . . . . *Tempest* iii 3 65
One draught above heat makes him a fool . . . . *T. Night* i 5 140
One drop. Ere thou shalt lose for me one drop of blood . *Mer. of Venice* iv 1 113
In the cutting it, if thou dost shed one drop of Christian blood . iv 1 310
None so dry or thirsty Will deign to sip or touch one drop of it *T. of Shrew* v 2 145
England, thou hast not saved one drop of blood, In this hot trial, more than we of France . . . . *K. John* ii 1 341
One drop of blood drawn from thy country's bosom Should grieve thee more than streams of foreign gore . . . . *1 Hen. VI.* iii 3 54
One drunkard loves another of the name . . . . *L. L. Lost* iv 3 50
One dust. Mean and mighty, rotting Together, have one dust *Cymbeline* iv 2 247
One England. Nor can one England brook a double reign . *1 Hen. IV.* v 4 66
One error. That one error Fills him with faults . . *T. G. of Ver.* v 4 111
One eye. As you have one eye upon my follies, as you hear them unfolded, turn another into the register of your own *Mer. Wives* ii 2 192
One eye declined for the loss of her husband, another elevated *W. Tale* v 2 81
One eye thou hast, to look to heaven for grace: The sun with one eye vieweth all the world . . . . *1 Hen. VI.* i 4 83
Farewell! one eye yet looks on thee . . . . *Troi. and Cres.* v 2 107
Set honour in one eye and death i' the other . . . *J. Cæsar* i 2 86
You have one eye left To see some mischief on him . . . *Lear* iii 7 81
One face, one voice, one habit, and two persons . . . *T. Night* v 1 223
God has given you one face, and you make yourselves another *Hamlet* iii 1 149
One fading moment's mirth With twenty watchful, weary, tedious nights . . . . *T. G. of Ver.* i 1 30
One fainting kiss. O, tell me when my lips do touch his cheeks, That I may kindly give one fainting kiss . . . . . *1 Hen. VI.* ii 5 40
One fair daughter, and no more . . . . . . *Hamlet* ii 2 426
One fair look. Vouchsafe me, for my meed, but one fair look *T. G. of Ver.* v 4 23

One fair word. I would not buy Their mercy at the price of one fair word *Coriolanus* iii 3 91
Speak to my gossip Venus one fair word *Rom. and Jul.* ii 1 11
One faith. That such immanity and bloody strife Should reign among professors of one faith 1 *Hen. VI.* v 1 14
One false glass. I for comfort have but one false glass *Richard III.* ii 2 53
One father. Most certain of one mother, mighty king; That is well known; and, as I think, one father *K. John* i 1 60
One fault. Every one fault seeming monstrous till his fellow-fault came to match it *As Y. Like It* iii 2 372
He's poor in no one fault, but stored with all *Coriolanus* ii 1 20
One favour. If thy poor devoted suppliant may But beg one favour at thy gracious hand *Richard III.* i 2 208
One feast, one house, one mutual happiness *T. G. of Ver.* v 4 173
One fell swoop. What, all my pretty chickens and their dam At one fell swoop? *Macbeth* iv 3 219
One fiend at a time, I'll fight their legions o'er *Tempest* iii 3 102
One fire drives out one fire; one nail, one nail *Coriolanus* iv 7 54
One fire burns out another's burning, One pain is lessen'd by another's anguish *Rom. and Jul.* i 2 46
One flesh. Man and wife is one flesh *Hamlet* iv 3 54
One flower. With our needles created both one flower *M. N. Dream* iii 2 204
One follower. I'll receive him gladly, But not one follower *Lear* ii 4 296
One fool's head. With one fool's head I came to woo, But I go away with two *Mer. of Venice* ii 9 75
One foot in sea and one on shore, To one thing constant never *Much Ado* ii 3 66
Him I forgive my death that killeth me When he sees me go back one foot or fly 1 *Hen. VI.* i 2 21
Nor have we won one foot, If Salisbury be lost 2 *Hen. VI.* v 3 6
Two winking Cupids Of silver, each on one foot standing *Cymbeline* ii 4 90
One foul wrong. And do him right that, answering one foul wrong, Lives not to act another *Meas. for Meas.* ii 2 103
One friend. Now I dare not say I have one friend alive *T. G. of Ver.* v 4 66
All gone! and not One friend to take his fortune by the arm! *T. of Athens* iv 2 7
One fruitful meal would set me to't *Meas. for Meas.* iv 3 161
One gender. Supply it with one gender of herbs, or distract it with many *Othello* i 3 326
One general tongue. Rome . . . hath sent One general tongue unto us, this good man *Hen. VIII.* ii 2 96
One gentleman. We will not leave one lord, one gentleman 2 *Hen. VI.* iv 2 194
One giant arm. Put the world's whole strength Into one giant arm, it shall not force This lineal honour from me 2 *Hen. IV.* iv 5 45
One girth six times pieced *T. of Shrew* iii 2 60
One glance. And never more abase our sight so low As to vouchsafe one glance unto the ground 2 *Hen. VI.* i 2 16
One glass. She would not live The running of one glass *W. Tale* i 2 306
One goat. There is one goat for you *Hen. V.* v 1 30
One good deed dying tongueless Slaughters a thousand *W. Tale* i 2 92
If one good deed in all my life I did, I do repent it *T. Andron.* v 3 189
One good quality. The owner of no one good quality *All's Well* iii 6 12
One good woman in ten, madam i 3 86
One grape. There's one grape yet; I am sure thy father drunk wine ii 3 105
One grave shall be for both *W. Tale* iii 2 237
One green leaf. An oak but with one green leaf on it would have answered her *Much Ado* ii 1 247
One habit. One face, one voice, one habit, and two persons *T. Night* v 1 223
One half. No ceremony that to great ones 'longs . . . Become them with one half so good a grace As mercy does *Meas. for Meas.* ii 2 62
Being but the one half of an entire sum Disbursed *L. L. Lost* ii 1 131
Nor shines the silver moon one half so bright iv 3 30
One half of me is yours, the other half yours *Mer. of Venice* iii 2 16
The party 'gainst the which he doth contrive Shall seize one half his goods iv 1 353
To quit the fine for one half of his goods, I am content iv 1 381
After my death the one half of my lands *T. of Shrew* ii 1 122
This youth . . . I snatch'd one half out of the jaws of death *T. Night* iii 4 394
Do't and thou hast the one half of my heart *W. Tale* i 2 348
I am out of fear Of death or death's hand for this one-half year 1 *Hen. IV.* iv 1 136
Of England's coat one half is cut away 1 *Hen. VI.* i 1 81
Take the one half of my commission *Coriolanus* iv 5 144
Our general is cut i' the middle and but one half of what he was yesterday iv 5 211
My brother wears thee not the one half so well As when thou grew'st *Cymbeline* iv 2 202
One half-pennyworth of bread to this intolerable deal of sack! 1 *Hen. IV.* ii 4 591
One half-world. Now o'er the one half-world Nature seems dead, and wicked dreams abuse The curtain'd sleep *Macbeth* ii 1 49
One-half year. I am out of fear Of death or death's hand for this one-half year 1 *Hen. IV.* iv 1 136
One hand. With one hand on his dagger *Hen. VIII.* i 2 204
O, here I lift this one hand up to heaven *T. Andron.* iii 1 207
This one hand yet is left to cut your throats v 2 182
With one hand beats cold death aside *Rom. and Jul.* iii 1 166
One have-at-him. I'll venture one have-at-him.—I another *Hen. VIII.* ii 2 85
One heart, one bed, two bosoms, and one troth *M. N. Dream* ii 2 42
My heart unto yours is knit So that but one heart we can make of it ii 2 48
With two seeming bodies, but one heart iii 2 212
I have one heart, one bosom and one truth, And that no woman has *T. Night* iii 1 170
Friends now fast sworn, Whose double bosoms seem to wear one heart *Coriolanus* iv 4 13
One heat. Even as one heat another heat expels *T. G. of Ver.* ii 4 192
One heavy bier. Thou and Romeo press one heavy bier! *Rom. and Jul.* iii 2 60
One heinous article, Containing the deposing of a king *Richard II.* iv 1 233
One hit. Have all his ventures fail'd? What, not one hit? *Mer. of Venice* iii 2 270
One honest man. I do proclaim One honest man—mistake me not—but one; No more, I pray *T. of Athens* iv 3 504
One hope. There is but one hope in it *Mer. of Venice* iii 5 7
One horse. My master riding behind my mistress,— Both of one horse?—What's that to thee? *T. of Shrew* iv 1 71
One horse, my lord, he brought even now.—What horse? a roan? 1 *Hen. IV.* ii 3 71
One hour. And after one hour more 'twill be eleven *As Y. Like It* ii 7 25
But grief makes one hour ten *Richard II.* i 3 261
Like pale ghosts, Faintly besiege us one hour in a month 1 *Hen. VI.* i 2 8
So I might live one hour in your sweet bosom *Richard III.* i 2 124
Let me but meet you, ladies, one hour hence iv 1 29
Never yet one hour in his bed Have I enjoy'd the golden dew of sleep iv 1 83
One hour's storm will drown the fragrant meads *T. Andron.* ii 4 54
One house. One feast, one house, one mutual happiness *T. G. of Ver.* v 4 173
How, in one house, Should many people, under two commands, Hold amity? 'Tis hard; almost impossible *Lear* ii 4 243
One husband. Hath she had any more than one husband?—Nine, sir; Overdone by the last *Meas. for Meas.* ii 1 210
One immortal. She sings like one immortal *Pericles* v Gower 3
One inch of delay more is a South-sea of discovery *As Y. Like It* iii 2 206
One infectious. From his presence I am barr'd, like one infectious *W. T.* iii 2 99
One jot. If you break one jot of your promise *As Y. Like It* iv 1 194
If one jot beyond The bound of honour, or in act or will That way *W. T.* iii 2 51
Nor doth he dedicate one jot of colour Unto the weary and all-watched night, But freshly looks *Hen. V.* iv Prol. 37
Neither will they bate One jot of ceremony *Coriolanus* ii 2 145
One joy. There might you have beheld one joy crown another *W. Tale* v 2 48
One key. Both warbling of one song, both in one key *M. N. Dream* iii 2 206
One kiss shall stop our mouths, and dumbly part *Richard II.* v 1 95
Farewell, farewell! one kiss, and I'll descend *Rom. and Jul.* iii 5 42
But kiss; one kiss! Rubies unparagon'd, How dearly they do't *Cymbeline* ii 2 17
One knave. My master is a kind of a knave: but that's all one, if he be but one knave *T. G. of Ver.* iii 1 263
One lamp. Now are they but one lamp, one light, one sun 3 *Hen. VI.* ii 1 31
One language. To use one language in each several clime *Pericles* iv 4 6
One leg. With a linen stock on one leg *T. of Shrew* iii 2 68
One life. And all those twenty could but kill one life *Rom. and Jul.* iii 1 184
One light. Now are they but one lamp, one light, one sun 3 *Hen. VI.* ii 1 31
One line. Here in one line is his name twice writ *T. G. of Ver.* i 2 123
Now powers from home and discontents at home Meet in one line *K. John* iv 3 152
O, 'tis most sweet, When in one line two crafts directly meet *Hamlet* iii 4 210
One lion may [speak], when many asses do *M. N. Dream* v 1 154
One little body. In one little body Thou counterfeit'st a bark, a sea, a wind *Rom. and Jul.* iii 5 131
One little hair. All the shrouds wherewith my life should sail Are turned to one thread, one little hair *K. John* v 7 54
One little word. How long a time lies in one little word! *Richard II.* i 3 213
One livery. And I will apparel them all in one livery 2 *Hen. VI.* iv 2 80
One lord. We will not leave one lord, one gentleman iv 2 194
One loving kiss. Give him for my sake but one loving kiss *L. L. Lost* ii 1 248
One lump. All men's honours Lie like one lump before him *Hen. VIII.* ii 2 49
One man. Hath not the world one man but he will wear his cap with suspicion? *Much Ado* i 1 200
I do much wonder that one man, seeing how much another man is a fool when he dedicates his behaviours to love ii 3 8
I am, as they say, but to parfect one man in one poor man *L. L. Lost* v 2 503
I thought you lord of more true gentleness. O, that a lady, of one man refused, Should of another therefore be abused! *M. N. Dream* ii 2 133
Then fate o'er-rules, that, one man holding troth, A million fail iii 2 92
Alas, fifteen wives is nothing! eleven widows and nine maids is a simple coming-in for one man *Mer. of Venice* ii 2 172
One man in his time plays many parts *As Y. Like It* ii 7 142
Into a thousand parts divide one man *Hen. V.* Prol. 24
God's will! I pray thee, wish not one man more iv 3 23
I would not lose so great an honour As one man more, methinks, would share iv 3 32
If we suffer, Out of our easiness and childish pity To one man's honour, this contagious sickness, Farewell all physic *Hen. VIII.* v 3 26
What propugnation is in one man's valour? *Troi. and Cres.* ii 2 136
How one man eats into another's pride, While pride is fasting! iii 3 136
With one man beckon'd from the rest below *T. of Athens* i 1 74
It grieves me to see so many dip their meat in one man's blood i 2 42
When went there by an age, since the great flood, But it was famed with more than with one man? *J. Cæsar* i 2 153
When could they say till now, that talk'd of Rome, That her wide walls encompass'd but one man? i 2 155
Shall Rome stand under one man's awe? What, Rome? ii 1 52
But that they would Have one man but a man *Ant. and Cleo.* ii 6 19
One mark. Many arrows, loosed several ways, Come to one mark *Hen. V.* i 2 208
One meal. And but one meal on every day beside *L. L. Lost* i 1 40
One meaning. There's one meaning well suited *Much Ado* v 1 230
One midnight Fated to the purpose *Tempest* i 2 128
One mile. Ask them how many inches Is in one mile: if they have measured many, The measure then of one is easily told *L. L. Lost* v 2 189
One mind. There is but one mind in all these men *J. Cæsar* ii 3 6
I would we were all of one mind, and one mind good *Cymbeline* v 4 212
One minute. Or come one minute behind your hour *As Y. Like It* iv 1 195
An hour, One minute, nay, one quiet breath of rest *K. John* iii 4 134
One misery. Is to exchange one misery with another *Cymbeline* i 5 55
One monument. Goodness and he fill up one monument! *Hen. VIII.* ii 1 94
One more. Yet but three? Come one more *M. N. Dream* iii 2 437
And you, among the store, One more, most welcome *Rom. and Jul.* i 2 23
One more [kiss], one more. Be thus when thou art dead *Othello* v 2 17
One more, and this the last: So sweet was ne'er so fatal v 2 19
One more fool. Now, in thy likeness, one more fool appear! *L. L. Lost* iv 3 46
One mortal night. This was a goodly person, Till the disaster that, one mortal night, Drove him to this *Pericles* v 1 37
One mother. You came not of one mother then, it seems.—Most certain of one mother *K. John* i 1 58
One mountain. Who digs hills because they do aspire Throws down one mountain to cast up a higher *Pericles* i 4 6
One mutual cry. Every region near Seem'd all one mutual cry *M. N. D.* iv 1 122
One mutual happiness. One house, one mutual happiness *T. G. of Ver.* v 4 173
One mutual sheaf. How to knit again This scatter'd corn into one mutual sheaf *T. Andron.* v 3 71
One nail. Or as one nail by strength drives out another *T. G. of Ver.* ii 4 193
One fire drives out one fire; one nail, one nail *Coriolanus* iv 7 54
One nature. All of one nature, of one substance bred 1 *Hen. IV.* i 1 11
One neck. Item, one neck, one chin, and so forth *T. Night* i 5 267
One new-burned. As fire cools fire Within the scorched veins of one new-burn'd *K. John* iii 1 278
One night. Where you shall take your rest For this one night *Tempest* v 1 302
Spent in Genoa, as I heard, in one night fourscore ducats *Mer. of Venice* iii 1 114
A foolish knight that you brought in one night here *T. Night* i 3 16
One night, as we did sit at supper *Richard III.* ii 4 10
In one night, A storm or robbery, call it what you will, Shook down my mellow hangings, nay, my leaves *Cymbeline* iii 3 61
One noble man that hath one spark of fire *Troi. and Cres.* i 3 294
One number. Two.—Truly, I thought there had been one number more, because they say, ''Od's nouns' *Mer. Wives* iv 1 24
One o'clock. Away; disperse: but till 'tis one o'clock v 5 78
'Tis one o'clock, and past.—Why, then, good morrow to you all 2 *Hen. IV.* iii 1 34
It's one o'clock, boy, is't not?—It hath struck *Hen. VIII.* v 1 1
One of my rank. Would he had been one of my rank! *Cymbeline* ii 1 17
One of my sex. I do not know One of my sex *Tempest* iii 1 49

One of these days. You'll be whipped for taxation one of these days . *As Y. Like It* i 2 91
We shall Present our services to a fine new prince One of these days *W. T.* ii 1 18
He'll yield the crow a pudding one of these days . *Hen. V.* ii 1 92
I shall leave you one o' these days . *Troi. and Cres.* v 3 104
One of this kind is Cassio . *Othello* iii 3 418
One only daughter have I, no kin else . *T. of Athens* i 1 121
Rome indeed and room enough, When there is in it but one only man *J. C.* i 2 157
One opposed. Which came from one that's of a neutral heart, And not from one opposed . *Lear* iii 7 49
One or the other. A pox of this gout! or, a gout of this pox! for the one or the other plays the rogue with my great toe . 2 *Hen. IV.* i 2 273
One or two. If dere be one or two, I shall make-a the turd *Mer. Wives* iii 3 252
That your lordship were but now confessor To one or two of these! *Hen. VIII.* i 4 16
When good manners shall lie all in one or two men's hands *Rom. and Jul.* i 5 5
One other. Let's have one other gaudy night . *Ant. and Cleo.* iii 13 183
One pain. Of all one pain, save for a night of groans . *Richard III.* iv 4 303
One pain is lessen'd by another's anguish . *Rom. and Jul.* i 2 47
One pair. I thought upon one pair of English legs Did march three Frenchmen . *Hen. V.* iii 6 158
One pardon. Twice saying 'pardon' doth not pardon twain, But makes one pardon strong . *Richard II.* v 3 135
One part of Aquitaine is bound to us . *L. L. Lost* ii 1 136
Then let confusion of one part confirm The other's peace *K. John* ii 1 359
Was ever known so great and little loss On one part and on the other? *Hen. V.* iv 8 116
The general is gone, with one part of our Roman power . *Coriolanus* i 3 109
I am half through; The one part suffer'd, the other will I do . ii 3 131
Where one part does disdain with cause, the other Insult . iii 1 143
Hath but one part wisdom And ever three parts coward *Hamlet* iv 4 42
I have one part in my heart That's sorry yet for thee *Lear* iii 2 72
One party. The devil take one party and his dam the other! *Mer. Wives* iv 5 108
One penny. I shall never hold that man my friend Whose tongue shall ask me for one penny cost . 1 *Hen. IV.* i 3 91
Nor ever had one penny bribe from France . 2 *Hen. VI.* iii 1 109
One person. Thus play I in one person many people . *Richard II.* v 5 31
Death of one person can be paid but once . *Ant. and Cleo.* iv 14 27
One phœnix At this hour reigning there . *Tempest* iii 3 23
One piece. No man living Could say, 'This is my wife' there; all were woven So strangely in one piece . *Hen. VIII.* iv 1 81
I beseech your honour, one piece for me.—Avaunt! . *Pericles* iv 6 124
One place. I thank my fortune for it, My ventures are not in one bottom trusted, Nor to one place . *Mer. of Venice* i 1 43
Shedding tears? As thus, to drop them still upon one place, Till they have fretted us a pair of graves . *Richard II.* iii 3 166
And thou unfit for any place but hell.—Yes, one place else *Richard III.* i 2 110
One player. There is not one word apt, one player fitted *M. N. Dream* v 1 65
One poor heart. He started one poor heart of mine in thee . *T. Night* iv 1 63
One poor pennyworth of sugar-candy to make thee long-winded 1 *Hen. IV.* iii 3 180
One poor request. Give me one poor request . *Hamlet* i 5 142
One poor root. Yield him, who all thy human sons doth hate, From forth thy plenteous bosom, one poor root! *T. of Athens* iv 3 186
One poor scruple. Twentieth part Of one poor scruple . *Mer. of Venice* iv 1 330
One poor string. My heart hath one poor string to stay it by *K. John* v 7 55
One power against the French, And one against Glendower . 2 *Hen. IV.* i 3 71
One prayer. But while I say one prayer!—It is too late . *Othello* v 2 83
One puritan. But one puritan amongst them . *W. Tale* iv 3 46
One purpose. So may a thousand actions, once afoot, End in one purpose *Hen. V.* i 2 212
One quarter. A proficient in one quarter of an hour . 1 *Hen. IV.* ii 4 19
Whereof take you one quarter into France . *Hen. V.* i 2 215
One question. Let me but move one question to your daughter *M. Ado* iv 1 74
One quiet breath. Nay, one quiet breath of rest . *K. John* iii 4 134
One reckonings. The mighty, or the huge, or the magnanimous, are all one reckonings . *Hen. V.* iv 7 18
One red. Making the green one red . *Macbeth* ii 2 63
One repulse. Do not, for one repulse, forego the purpose . *Tempest* iii 3 12
One respect. In one respect I'll thy assistant be . *Rom. and Jul.* ii 3 90
One rhyme. Speak but one rhyme, and I am satisfied . ii 1 9
One root. Seven fair branches springing from one root . *Richard II.* i 2 13
One rose. Wither one rose, and let the other flourish . 3 *Hen. VI.* i 5 101
One salt sea. As many fresh streams meet in one salt sea . *Hen. V.* i 2 209
One sampler. Created both one flower, Both on one sampler *M. N. Dream* iii 2 205
One sand another Not more resembles that sweet rosy lad . *Cymbeline* v 5 120
One scar. Show me one scar character'd on thy skin . 2 *Hen. VI.* iii 1 300
One scene of it comes near the circumstance Which I have told thee *Ham.* iii 2 81
Good now, play one scene Of excellent dissembling . *Ant. and Cleo.* i 3 78
One score [of miles] 'twixt sun and sun, Madam, 's enough for you *Cymb.* iii 2 70
One self-born hour. And in one self-born hour To plant and o'erwhelm custom . *W. Tale* iv 1 8
One self king. And fill'd Her sweet perfections with one self king! *T. N.* i 1 39
One seven years. If I could shake off but one seven years From these old arms and legs . *Coriolanus* iv 1 55
One shaft. When I had lost one shaft, I shot his fellow . *Mer. of Venice* i 1 140
One shape. And let it keep one shape, till custom make it Their perch and not their terror . *Meas. for Meas.* ii 1 3
One short minute. It cannot countervail the exchange of joy That one short minute gives me in her sight . *Rom. and Jul.* ii 6 5
One shot. Where, for one shot of five pence, thou shalt have five thousand welcomes . *T. G. of Ver.* ii 5 9
One show. Some policy To have one show worse than the king's *L. L. Lost* v 2 514
One side. Armado o' th' one side,—O, a most dainty man! . iv 1 146
Thou art damned like an ill-roasted egg, all on one side *As Y. Like It* iii 2 39
As a puisny tilter, that spurs his horse but on one side . iii 4 47
Comes a creature, Sometimes her head on one side, some another *W. T.* iii 3 20
Fortune shall cull forth Out of one side her happy minion *K. John* ii 1 392
Whilst he, from the one side to the other turning, Bareheaded *Richard II.* v 2 18
Make you ready your stiff bats and clubs: Rome and her rats are at the point of battle; The one side must have bale *Coriolanus* i 1 167
One side will mock another; the other too . *Lear* iii 7 71
I have much to do, But to go hang my head all at one side . *Othello* iv 3 32
One sign. From one sign of dolour to another . *W. Tale* v 2 95
One sin, I know, another doth provoke . *Pericles* i 1 137
One single word. Hear me one single word . *All's Well* v 2 37
One skull. If all our wits were to issue out of one skull, they would fly east, west, north, south . *Coriolanus* ii 3 23
One slip. I'll not put The dibble in earth to set one slip . *W. Tale* iv 4 100
One small boat. To hazard all our lives in one small boat! 1 *Hen. VI.* iv 6 33
One soft kiss. You may ride's With one soft kiss a thousand furlongs ere With spur we heat an acre . *W. Tale* i 2 95
One sole throne. Affecting one sole throne . *Coriolanus* iv 6 32
One son. Thou hast one son; for his sake pity me . 3 *Hen. VI.* i 1 40
One song. Both warbling of one song, both in one key *M. N. Dream* iii 2 206
One sore. Of one sore I an hundred make . *L. L. Lost* iv 2 63
One sorrow never comes but brings an heir . *Pericles* i 4 63
One sound cudgel. As much as one sound cudgel of four foot—You see the poor remainder—could distribute, I made no spare *Hen. VIII.* v 4 19
One spark. Could out of thee extract one spark of evil . *Hen. V.* ii 2 101
One noble man that hath one spark of fire *Troi. and Cres.* ii 3 294
One speech. For this one speech Lord Hastings well deserves To have the heir of the Lord Hungerford . 3 *Hen. VI.* iv 1 47
One speech in it I chiefly loved: 'twas Æneas' tale to Dido . *Hamlet* ii 2 467
If his occulted guilt Do not itself unkennel in one speech . iii 2 86
One sphere. Two stars keep not their motion in one sphere 1 *Hen. IV.* v 4 65
One spirit. Nor hath not One spirit to command . *Tempest* iii 2 102
Let one spirit of the first-born Cain Reign in all bosoms! . 2 *Hen. IV.* i 1 157
One spot. That there shall not be one spot of love in't *As Y. Like It* iii 2 443
One spurn. Who dies, that bears not one spurn to their graves Of their friends' gift? *T. of Athens* i 2 146
One stem. Two lovely berries moulded on one stem . *M. N. Dream* iii 2 211
One step. Twice for one step I'll groan, the way being short *Richard II.* v 1 91
They are as children but one step below, Even of your mettle *Richard III.* iv 4 301
The general's disdain'd By him one step below, he by the next *T. and C.* i 3 130
One step I have advanced thee . *Lear* v 3 28
One stomach. We'll not offend one stomach with our play *Hen. V.* ii Prol. 40
One stroke Shall free thee from the tribute which thou payest *Tempest* i 2 292
Cowardly fled, not having struck one stroke . 1 *Hen. VI.* i 1 134
Honour, name and all That made me happy at one stroke has taken For ever from the world . *Hen. VIII.* ii 1 117
One subject. Hang all the husbands That cannot do that feat, you'll leave yourself Hardly one subject . *W. Tale* ii 3 112
One substance. All of one nature, of one substance bred 1 *Hen. IV.* i 1 11
One such. But, if there be, or ever were, one such, It's past the size of dreaming . *Ant. and Cleo.* v 2 96
One sudden foil shall never breed distrust . 1 *Hen. VI.* iii 3 11
One sun. Now are they but one lamp, one light, one sun . 3 *Hen. VI.* ii 1 31
One sweet word with thee.—Honey, and milk, and sugar . *L. L. Lost* v 2 230
One syllable. Who dare speak One syllable against him? . *Hen. VIII.* v 1 39
One table. Two dishes, but to one table . *Hamlet* iv 3 26
One tear. Yet did not this cruel-hearted cur shed one tear *T. G. of Ver.* ii 3 10
One ten. Had it our name, the value of one ten, What merit's in that reason? . *Troi. and Cres.* ii 2 23
One ten thousand. O that we now had here But one ten thousand of those men in England That do no work to-day! . *Hen. V.* iv 3 17
One thing. For one thing she did They would not take her life *Tempest* i 2 266
Took pains to make thee speak, taught thee each hour One thing or other i 2 355
You would have them always play but one thing?—I would always have one play but one thing . *T. G. of Ver.* iv 2 71
'Tis one thing to be tempted, Escalus, Another thing to fall *M. for M.* ii 1 17
One foot in sea and one on shore, To one thing constant never *Much Ado* ii 3 67
Do one thing for me that I shall entreat.—When? . *L. L. Lost* iii 1 154
Though to have her and death were both one thing . *As Y. Like It* v 4 17
To labour and effect one thing specially . *T. of Shrew* i 1 120
One thing more rests, that thyself execute, to make one among these wooers . i 1 250
And one thing more, that you be never so hardy to come again *T. Night* ii 2 9
For sorrow's eye, glazed with blinding tears, Divides one thing entire to many objects . *Richard II.* ii 2 17
Shall I tell thee one thing, Poins?—Yes, faith; and let it be an excellent good thing.—It shall serve . 2 *Hen. IV.* ii 2 35
Go to; I stand the push of your one thing that you will tell . ii 2 40
Yet in this one thing let me blame your grace, For choosing me 3 *Hen. VI.* iv 6 30
Yet one thing more, good Blunt, before thou go'st . *Richard III.* v 3 33
What one thing, what another, that I shall leave you . *Troi. and Cres.* v 3 103
Tell me one thing that I shall ask you.—Well, sir . *Coriolanus* ii 1 15
There's one thing wanting, which I doubt not but Our Rome will cast upon thee . ii 1 217
Not to be other than one thing, not moving From the casque to the cushion iv 7 42
And one thing more That womanhood denies my tongue to tell *T. Andron.* ii 3 173
One poor and loving child, But one thing to rejoice and solace in *R. and J.* iv 5 47
But I can tell you one thing, my lord, and which I hear *T. of Athens* iii 2 5
Yet my heart Throbs to know one thing . *Macbeth* iv 1 101
Prithee, Horatio, tell me one thing.—What's that, my lord? *Hamlet* v 1 216
I have one thing, of a queasy question, Which I must act . *Lear* ii 1 19
I have one thing more to ask him yet . *Ant. and Cleo.* iii 3 48
I forgot to ask him one thing; I'll remember't anon . *Cymbeline* iii 5 134
I left out one thing which the queen confess'd . v 5 244
Let me ask you one thing: What do you think of my daughter? *Pericles* ii 5 32
Prithee, tell me one thing first.—Come now, your one thing . iv 6 166
One thought. So perish they That grudge one thought! 1 *Hen. VI.* iii 1 176
One thread. All the shrouds wherewith my life should sail Are turned to one thread, one little hair . *K. John* v 7 54
One three of them, by their own report, sir, hath danced *W. Tale* iv 4 345
One time. Help to search my house this one time . *Mer. Wives* iv 2 167
And pleasure will be paid, one time or another . *T. Night* ii 4 72
Will, on my life, One time or other break some gallows' back 2 *Hen. IV.* iv 3 32
To give a greater sum Than ever at one time the clergy yet Did *Hen. V.* i 1 80
Such a mighty sum As never did the clergy at one time Bring in . i 2 134
I will cut thy throat, one time or other, in fair terms . ii 1 73
Put not your worthy rage into your tongue; One time will owe another *Coriolanus* iii 1 242
Yet one time he did call me by my name: I urged our old acquaintance v 1 9
All the plagues of hell should at one time Encounter such revolt *Cymb.* i 6 111
One title. 'Tis not my meaning To raze one title of your honour out *Richard II.* ii 3 75
One to ten! Lean raw-boned rascals! . 1 *Hen. VI.* i 2 34
One tomb. Shall all thy mother's hopes lie in one tomb? . iv 5 34
One tongue. To prove that true Needs no more but one tongue 1 *Hen. IV.* i 3 96
One too much. O, one too much by thee! Why had I one? *Much Ado* iv 1 131
Now I see this one is one too much . *Rom. and Jul.* iii 5 167
One touch of nature makes the whole world kin . *Troi. and Cres.* iii 3 175
One town. As many ways meet in one town . *Hen. V.* i 2 208
One tree. In Arabia There is one tree, the phœnix' throne . *Tempest* iii 3 23
One trifling respect. If it were not for one trifling respect, I could come to such honour! . *Mer. Wives* ii 1 44
One troth. One heart, one bed, two bosoms and one troth *M. N. Dream* ii 2 42
One true sense. Or but a sickly part of one true sense Could not so mope . *Hamlet* iii 4 80

One trunk-inheriting slave . . . . *Lear* ii 2 20
One truth. I have one heart, one bosom and one truth . . *T. Night* iii 1 170
One turf shall serve as pillow for us both . . *M. N. Dream* ii 2 41
One twelve moons more she'll wear Diana's livery . *Pericles* ii 5 10
One ungot. Who is as free from touch or soil with her As she from one ungot . . . . *Meas. for Meas.* v 1 142
One unperfectness shows me another . . . *Othello* ii 3 298
One unworthier. Which one unworthier may attain *Mer. of Venice* ii 1 37
One vessel. Not one vessel 'scape the dreadful touch? . . . iii 2 273
One vial full of Edward's sacred blood . . . Is crack'd . *Richard II.* i 2 17
One vice. Changing still One vice, but of a minute old, for one Not half so old as that . . . . . *Cymbeline* ii 5 31
One villain. If thou wouldst not reside But where one villain is, then him abandon . . . . . *T. of Athens* v 1 114
One visor. But one visor remains.—And that is Claudio . *Much Ado* ii 1 164
One voice. One face, one voice, one habit, and two persons . *T. Night* v 1 223
Which with one voice Call Agamemnon head and general *Troi. and Cres.* i 3 221
One voyage. In one voyage Did Claribel her husband find . . *Tempest* v 1 208
One way. I will one way or other make you amends . *Mer. Wives* iii 1 89
About your neck . . . ? or under your arm . . . ? You must wear it one way . . . . *Much Ado* ii 1 198
I come one way of the Plantagenets . . . . . *K. John* v 6 11
In mutual well-beseeming ranks, March all one way . . *1 Hen. IV.* i 1 15
After I saw him fumble with the sheets and play with flowers and smile upon his fingers' ends, I knew there was but one way *Hen. V.* ii 3 16
One way or other, she is for a king . . . *3 Hen. VI.* iii 2 87
That my teaching And the strong course of my authority Might go one way, and safely . . . . . . *Hen. VIII.* v 3 36
By eleven o'clock it will go one way or other . . *Troi. and Cres.* iii 3 297
O, would you had had her! Some one way, some another . *Othello* i 1 177
Though he be painted one way like a Gorgon, The other way's a Mars *Ant. and Cleo.* ii 5 116
To-morrow is the day.—It will determine one way . . . iv 3 2
One weaver. That will draw three souls out of one weaver . *T. Night* ii 3 61
One week. I am sorry that by hanging thee I can But shorten thy life one week . . . . *W. Tale* iv 4 433
One 'We thank you.' I multiply With one 'We thank you' many thousands moe . . . . i 2 8
One wife. Nor how to be contented with one wife . . *3 Hen. VI.* iv 3 37
One wink. I have not slept one wink . . . . *Cymbeline* iv 3 103
One winter. With one winter's brush Fell from their boughs *T. of Athens* iv 3 264
One wise man. There's not one wise man among twenty that will praise himself . . . . *Much Ado* v 2 76
One wiser. Albeit my wrongs might make one wiser mad *Com. of Errors* v 1 217
One wish. I'ld exchange For this one wish . . . *T. of Athens* v 3 528
One woe. So two, together weeping, make one woe . . *Richard II.* v 1 86
One woe doth tread upon another's heel, So fast they follow . *Hamlet* iv 7 164
One woman is fair, yet I am well; another is wise . . *Much Ado* ii 3 28
Till all graces be in one woman, one woman shall not come in my grace ii 3 30
All my glories In that one woman I have lost for ever . *Hen. VIII.* iii 2 409
One womb. Twinn'd brothers of one womb . . . *T. of Athens* iv 3 3
One wooer. Whiles we shut the gates upon one wooer, another knocks at the door . . . . *Mer. of Venice* i 2 147
One word further, and, by this hand, I'll turn my mercy out o' doors *Tempest* iii 2 77
Vouchsafe a word, young sister, but one word . . *Meas. for Meas.* iii 1 152
Want wit in all one word to understand . . . *Com. of Errors* iii 2 153
One word in secret.—Let it not be sweet . . . *L. L. Lost* v 2 236
In all the play There is not one word apt . . . *M. N. Dream* v 1 65
Answer me in one word.—You must borrow me Gargantua's mouth first: 'tis a word too great . . . . . . *As Y. Like It* iii 2 237
Then speak again; not all thy former tale, But this one word, whether thy tale be true . . . . *K. John* iii 1 26
Hear me but one word: Let me for this my life-time reign as king *3 Hen. VI.* i 1 170
I moralize two meanings in one word . . . *Richard III.* iii 1 83
Hark, one word in your ear.—O plague and madness! *Troi. and Cres.* v 2 34
Hear me one word; Beseech you, tribunes, hear me but a word *Coriol.* iii 1 215
A word with one of you.—And but one word with one of us? *R. and J.* iii 1 42
That one word 'banished,' Hath slain ten thousand Tybalts . iii 2 113
O my friends, I have one word to say to you . . *T. of Athens* i 2 174
Let me ask you one word in private.—Importune him once more . *Lear* iii 4 165
If e'er your grace had speech with man so poor, Hear me one word . v 1 39
One word. *Tempest* ii 1; *Meas. for Meas.* i 2; *Much Ado* iii 5; *W. Tale* iv 4; *Richard II.* iii 2; *Coriolanus* i 1; *Ant. and Cleo.* i 3; iv 15
One word more Shall make me chide thee, if not hate thee . *Tempest* i 2 475
Not one word more of the consumed time . . . *All's Well* v 3 38
Not one word more: Thus part we rich in sorrow . *T. of Athens* iv 2 28
One word more. *Tempest* i 2; *Much Ado* iii 3; *Richard II.* i 2; *2 Hen. IV.* Epil.; *Macbeth* iv 1; *Hamlet* iii 4
One wound. And heal the inveterate canker of one wound By making many . . . . *K. John* v 2 14
One wrinkle. Or bend one wrinkle on my sovereign's face *Richard II.* ii 1 170
One yard. I will delve one yard below their mines . . . *Hamlet* iii 4 208
One's eyes. That blind rascally boy that abuses every one's eyes because his own are out . . . . *As Y. Like It* iv 1 219
Why, to keep one's eyes of either side's nose . . . *Lear* i 5 22
How fearful And dizzy 'tis, to cast one's eyes so low! . . . iv 6 12
One's mistress. 'Wonder of nature,'— I have heard a sonnet begin so to one's mistress . . . . *Hen. V.* iii 7 44
One's nail. Some devils ask but the parings of one's nail *Com. of Errors* iv 3 72
One's nose. Thou canst tell why one's nose stands i' the middle on's face?—No.—Why, to keep one's eyes of either side's nose *Lear* i 5 19
One's own. Who should be trusted, when one's own right hand Is perjured to the bosom? . . . . . . *T. G. of Ver.* v 4 67
Swagger? swear? and discourse fustian with one's own shadow? *Othello* ii 3 282
One's part. For taking one's part that's out of favour . . *Lear* i 4 111
One's thought. Proportion'd as one's thought would wish a man *R. and J.* iii 5 184
Oneyers, such as can hold in, such as will strike sooner than speak, and speak sooner than drink . . . . . *1 Hen. IV.* ii 1 85
Ongle. Comment appelez-vous les ongles?—Les ongles? nous les appelons de nails . . . . *Hen. V.* iii 4 15
Onion. Eat no onions nor garlic, for we are to utter sweet breath *M. N. D.* iv 2 43
An onion will do well for such a shift . . . *T. of Shrew* Ind. 1 126
Mine eyes smell onions; I shall weep anon . . *All's Well* v 3 321
The tears live in an onion that should water this sorrow *Ant. and Cleo.* i 2 176
Onion-eyed. Look, they weep, And I, an ass, am onion-eyed . . iv 2 35
Only. Not only with what my revenue yielded, But what my power might else exact . . . . *Tempest* i 2 98
He's a spirit of persuasion, only Professes to persuade . . . . ii 1 235
Only. There is not only disgrace and dishonour in that, monster, but an infinite loss . . . . *Tempest* iv 1 209
That her father likes Only for his possessions are so huge *T. G. of Ver.* ii 4 175
Only deserve my love by loving him . . . . . . ii 7 82
Only, in lieu thereof, dispatch me hence . . . . . ii 7 88
A horse cannot fetch, but only carry . . . . . iii 1 276
Tell him my name is Brook; only for a jest . . *Mer. Wives* ii 1 224
Not only bought many presents to give her, but have given largely to many . . . . ii 2 206
Spend all I have; only give me so much of your time in exchange of it ii 2 242
I shall not only receive this villanous wrong . . . . ii 2 307
My state being gall'd with my expense, I seek to heal it only by his wealth . . . . iii 4 6
Not only, Mistress Ford, in the simple office of love, but in all the accoutrement . . . . iv 2 4
This we came not to, Only for propagation of a dower . *Meas. for Meas.* i 2 154
Having bound up the threatening twigs of birch, Only to stick it in their children's sight For terror, not to use . . . . i 3 25
Moe reasons for this action At our more leisure shall I render you; Only, this one . . . . i 3 50
As if I did but only chew his name . . . . . . ii 4 5
The miserable have no other medicine But only hope . . . iii 1 3
Only he hath made an assay of her virtue to practise his judgement . iii 1 163
He made trial of you only . . . . iii 1 202
Novelty is only in request . . . . iii 2 237
No, none, but only a repair i' the dark . . . . . iv 1 43
I am loved of all ladies, only you excepted . . . *Much Ado* i 1 126
I make all use of it, for I use it only . . . . . . i 3 41
That only wounds by hearsay . . . . iii 1 23
Men are only turned into tongue, and trim ones too . . . iv 1 323
I only swore to study with your grace . . . . *L. L. Lost* i 1 51
He hail'd down oaths that he was only mine . . *M. N. Dream* i 1 243
Only give me leave, Unworthy as I am, to follow you . . . ii 1 206
That therefore only are reputed wise For saying nothing *Mer. of Venice* i 1 96
I think he only loves the world for him . . . . . . ii 8 50
To live in prayer and contemplation, Only attended by Nerissa . . iii 4 29
And discourse grow commendable in none only but parrots . . iii 5 51
The offender's life lies in the mercy Of the duke only . . . iv 1 356
Only in the world I fill up a place . . . . *As Y. Like It* i 2 204
In the spring time, the only pretty ring time . . . . . v 3 20
If whilst I live she will be only mine.—That 'only' came well in *T. of S.* ii 1 365
Would not extend his might, only where qualities were level . *All's Well* i 3 118
Had only but the corpse, But shadows and the shows of men, to fight *2 Hen. IV.* i 1 192
Only compound me with forgotten dust . . . . . . iv 5 116
Wretched shall France be only in my name . . . *1 Hen. VI.* i 4 97
Come, 'tis only I that must disgrace thee . . . . . i 5 8
Forgive me, God, For judgement only doth belong to thee *2 Hen. VI.* iii 2 140
Why only, Suffolk, mourn I not for thee? . . . . . iii 2 383
I intend but only to surprise him . . . . *3 Hen. VI.* iv 2 25
Yield, or thou diest.—Only I yield to die . . . *J. Cæsar* v 4 12
Only, I say, Things have been strangely borne . . *Macbeth* iii 6 2
He only lived but till he was a man . . . . v 8 40
Only child. We scarce thought us blest That God had lent us but this only child . . . . *Rom. and Jul.* iii 5 166
Only choice. Before the common distribution, At your only choice *Coriol.* i 9 36
Only colour. Your chestnut was ever the only colour . *As Y. Like It* iii 4 13
Only darling. Of his old experience the only darling . *All's Well* ii 1 110
Only dog. Hold-fast is the only dog, my duck . . . *Hen. V.* ii 3 54
Only drink. Your brown bastard is your only drink . . *1 Hen. IV.* ii 4 83
Only emperor. Your worm is your only emperor for diet . *Hamlet* iv 3 22
Only hate. My only love sprung from my only hate! *Rom. and Jul.* i 5 140
Only heir. Duke of Milan; and thou his only heir . . . *Tempest* i 2 58
Only Helena. The pleasure of mine eye Is only Helena . *M. N. Dream* iv 1 176
Only jig-maker. O God, your only jig-maker . . . *Hamlet* iii 2 132
Only love. My only love sprung from my only hate! . *Rom. and Jul.* i 5 140
Only love-gods. For we are the only love-gods . . *Much Ado* ii 1 402
Only man. He is the only man of Italy . . . . iii 1 92
Now is it Rome indeed and room enough, When there is in it but one only man . . . . *J. Cæsar* i 2 157
For the law of writ and the liberty, these are the only men . *Hamlet* ii 2 421
Only means. And make the Douglas' son your only mean For powers in Scotland . . . . *1 Hen. IV.* i 3 261
The only means To stop effusion of our Christian blood . *1 Hen. VI.* v 1 8
Only peace-maker. Your If is the only peace-maker . *As Y. Like It* v 4 108
Only prologue. The only prologues to a bad voice . . . . v 3 13
Only scourge. Is Talbot slain, the Frenchmen's only scourge? *1 Hen. VI.* iv 7 77
Only son. My only son Knows not my feeble key of untuned cares *C. of E.* v 1 309
She respects me as her only son . . . . . *M. N. Dream* i 1 160
The Black Prince . . . left behind him Richard, his only son *2 Hen. VI.* ii 2 19
And disinherited thine only son . . . . . *3 Hen. VI.* i 1 225
Romeo, and a Montague; The only son of your great enemy *Rom. and Jul.* i 5 139
Only suit. It is my only suit . . . . . . *As Y. Like It* ii 7 44
Only Sycorax. I never saw a woman, But only Sycorax my dam *Tempest* iii 2 109
Only thing. It is the only thing for a qualm . . . *Much Ado* iii 4 75
Only virtue. To be slow in words is a woman's only virtue *T. G. of Ver.* iii 1 339
Only wear. Motley's the only wear . . . . . *As Y. Like It* ii 7 34
Onset. To give the onset to thy good advice . . . *T. G. of Ver.* iii 2 94
The onset and retire Of both your armies . . . . . *K. John* ii 1 326
And, for an onset, Titus, to advance Thy name and honourable family, Lavinia will I make my empress . . . . . . *T. Andron.* i 1 238
Onward. When you went onward on this ended action . *Much Ado* i 1 299
Shall seem, as partly 'tis, their own, Which we have goaded onward *Cor.* ii 3 271
Ooze. And think'st it much to tread the ooze Of the salt deep *Tempest* i 2 252
Therefore my son i' the ooze is bedded . . . . . . iii 3 100
As is the ooze and bottom of the sea With sunken wreck *Hen. V.* i 2 164
Our poesy is as a gum, which oozes From whence 'tis nourish'd *T. of Athens* i 1 21
As it [the Nile] ebbs, the seedsman Upon the slime and ooze scatters his grain, And shortly comes to harvest . . . . *Ant. and Cleo.* ii 7 25
Find The ooze, to show what coast thy sluggish crare Might easiliest harbour in . . . . *Cymbeline* iv 2 205
Straight Must cast thee, scarcely coffin'd, in the ooze . *Pericles* iii 1 61
Oozy. I wish Myself were mudded in that oozy bed Where my son lies *Tempest* v 1 151
Opal For thy mind is a very opal . . . . . *T. Night* ii 4 77
Ope. The very minute bids thee ope thine ear . . . *Tempest* i 2 37
Go fetch me something: I'll break ope the gate . *Com. of Errors* iii 1 73
Do not live, Hero; do not ope thine eyes . . . *Much Ado* iv 1 125
I am Sir Oracle, And when I ope my lips let no dog bark! *Mer. of Venice* i 1 94
Ere I ope his letter, I pray you, tell me how my good friend doth . iii 2 235

Ope. The mouth of passage shall we fling wide ope, And give you entrance *K. John* ii 1 449
Ope your gates, Let in that amity which you have made . . . ii 1 536
O Henry, ope thine eyes!—He doth revive again: madam, be patient *2 Hen. VI.* iii 2 35
Then, heaven, set ope thy everlasting gates . . . iv 9 13
See how the morning opes her golden gates . . . *3 Hen. VI.* ii 1 21
Yet that thy brazen gates of heaven may ope . . . ii 3 40
Wilt thou ope the city gates, Speak gentle words and humbly bend thy knee? . . . v 1 21
When rank Thersites opes his mastic jaws, We shall hear music *T. and C.* i 3 73
So, now the gates are ope: now prove good seconds *Coriolanus* i 4 43
Which will in time Break ope the locks o' the senate . . . iii 1 138
Behold, the heavens do ope, The gods look down . . . v 3 183
Is it your trick to make me ope the door? . . . *T. Andron.* v 2 10
My tears will choke me, if I ope my mouth . . . v 3 175
Nor ope her lap to saint-seducing gold . . . *Rom. and Jul.* i 1 220
Anon comes one with light to ope the tomb . . . v 3 283
Set but thy foot Against our rampired gates, and they shall ope *T. of A.* v 4 47
He plucked me ope his doublet and offered them his throat *J. Cæsar* i 2 267
Over thy wounds now do I prophesy,—Which, like dumb mouths, do ope their ruby lips . . . iii 1 260
Most sacrilegious murder hath broke ope The Lord's anointed temple! *Macbeth* ii 3 72
To his good friends thus wide I'll ope my arms . *Hamlet* iv 5 145
Before you fight the battle, ope this letter . . . *Lear* v 1 40
Torments will ope your lips . . . *Othello* v 2 305
And winking Mary-buds begin To ope their golden eyes . *Cymbeline* ii 3 27
Thy crystal window ope; look out . . . v 4 81
To keep his bed of blackness unlaid ope *Pericles* i 2 89
Oped. Graves at my command Have waked their sleepers, oped, and let 'em forth . . . *Tempest* v 1 49
And oped their arms to embrace me as a friend *T. Andron.* v 3 108
The sepulchre . . . Hath oped his ponderous and marble jaws *Hamlet* i 4 50
I oped the coffin, Found there rich jewels; recover'd her *Pericles* v 3 23
Open. One midnight . . . did Antonio open The gates of Milan *Tempest* i 2 129
This is a strange repose, to be asleep With eyes wide open . ii 1 214
Open your mouth; here is that which will give language to you . ii 2 85
Open your mouth; this will shake your shaking . ii 2 87
Open your chaps again . ii 2 89
The clouds methought would open and show riches Ready to drop upon me iii 2 150
Come, open the matter in brief . *T. G. of Ver.* i 1 135
Open your purse, that the money and the matter may be both at once delivered . i 1 137
Beaten my men, killed my deer, and broke open my lodge *Mer. Wives* i 1 115
His thefts were too open . i 3 28
Why, then the world's mine oyster, Which I with sword will open ii 2 3
If money go before, all ways do lie open . ii 2 175
Wherein I must very much lay open mine own imperfection . ii 2 191
If I cry out thus upon no trail, never trust me when I open again iv 2 209
What's open made to justice, That justice seizes *Meas. for Meas.* ii 1 21
I will open my lips in vain, or discover his government . iii 1 198
Who talks within there? ho, open the door! *Com. of Errors* iii 1 38
Speak; Lay open to my earthy-gross conceit . iii 2 34
Leave a casement of the great chamber window, where we play, open *M. N. Dream* iii 1 58
Then open not thy lips: Firm and irrevocable is my doom *As Y. Like It* i 3 84
When he had a desire to eat a grape, would open his lips when he put it into his mouth; meaning thereby that grapes were made to eat and lips to open . v 1 37
The door is open, sir; there lies your way *T. of Shrew* iii 2 212
Thy casement I need not open, for I look through thee . *All's Well* ii 3 226
Tell me where thou hast been, or I will not open my lips so wide as a bristle may enter in way of thy excuse *T. Night* i 5 2
Thy Fates open their hands; let thy blood and spirit embrace them ii 5 159
Daylight and champain discovers not more: this is open ii 5 175
Do not then walk too open.—It doth not fit me iii 3 37
Open't, and read it.—Look then to be well edified v 1 297
Ere I could make thee open thy white hand And clap thyself my love *W. T.* i 2 103
How came the posterns So easily open? . ii 1 53
The pretence whereof being by circumstances partly laid open iii 2 19
Look thee here; take up, take up, boy; open't. So, let's see iii 3 120
This is some changeling: open't. What's within, boy? iii 3 122
These rural latches to his entrance open iv 4 449
Whereupon I command thee to open thy affair iv 4 764
Though credit be asleep and not an ear open v 2 68
You men of Angiers, open wide your gates *K. John* ii 1 300
Open your gates and give the victors way ii 1 324
Murder, as hating what himself hath done, Doth lay it open to urge on revenge . iv 3 38
Like a cunning instrument cased up, Or, being open, put into his hands That knows no touch to tune the harmony . *Richard II.* i 3 164
Mine ear is open and my heart prepared: The worst is worldly loss iii 2 93
He is come to open The purple testament of bleeding war iii 3 93
Open the door, secure, fool-hardy king: Shall I for love speak treason to thy face? Open the door, or I will break it open v 3 43
Pity me, open the door: A beggar begs that never begg'd before v 3 77
And lay open all our proceedings *1 Hen. IV.* ii 3 34
Let them alone awhile, and then open the door ii 4 96
Gross as a mountain, open, palpable . ii 4 250
To hide thee from this open and apparent shame ii 4 292
Open your ears; for which of you will stop The vent of hearing when loud Rumour speaks? *2 Hen. IV.* Ind. 1 1
He hath a tear for pity and a hand Open as day for melting charity iv 4 32
That keep'st the ports of slumber open wide To many a watchful night! iv 5 24
This door is open; he is gone this way iv 5 56
The service that I truly did his life Hath left me open to all injuries v 2 8
Their faults are open: Arrest them to the answer of the law *Hen. V.* ii 2 142
The poor souls for whom this hungry war Opens his vasty jaws ii 4 105
Open your gates. Come, uncle Exeter, Go you and enter Harfleur iii 3 51
Open the gates unto the lord protector, Or we'll burst them open *1 Hen. VI.* i 3 27
Open your city gates; Be humble to us iv 2 5
Prove them, and I lie open to the law *2 Hen. VI.* i 3 159
Let me see thine eyes: wink now: now open them ii 1 105
If we mean to thrive and do good, break open the gaols iv 3 18
Or is it fear That makes him close his eyes? I'll open them. *3 Hen VI.* i 3 11
My father's blood Hath stopp'd the passage where thy words should enter.—Then let my father's blood open it again i 3 23
Open Thy gate of mercy, gracious God! My soul flies through these wounds . i 4 177
Open. Why, master mayor, why stand you in a doubt? Open the gates *3 Hen. VI.* iv 7 28
The gates are open, let us enter too . v 1 60
Dead Henry's wounds Open their congeal'd mouths and bleed afresh! *Richard III.* i 2 56
Or earth, gape open wide and eat him quick! i 2 65
When he opens his purse to give us our reward, thy conscience flies out i 4 132
Laid open all your victories in Scotland, Your discipline in war iii 7 15
We are too open here to argue this; Let's think in private more *Hen. VIII.* ii 1 168
Heaven will one day open The king's eyes ii 2 42
A very fresh-fish here—fie, fie, fie upon This compell'd fortune!—have your mouth fill'd up Before you open it ii 3 88
Take notice, lords, he has a loyal breast, For you have seen him open't iii 2 201
Press not a falling man too far! 'tis virtue: His faults lie open to the laws iii 2 334
This day was view'd in open as his queen . iii 2 404
What, 's all the doors open here? *Troi. and Cres.* iv 2 19
His heart and hand both open and both free; For what he has he gives iv 5 100
A juggling trick,—to be secretly open v 2 24
Our gates, Which yet seem shut, we have but pinn'd with rushes; They'll open of themselves . *Coriolanus* i 4 19
Open the gates, and let me in.—Tribunes, and me *T. Andron.* i 1 62
Be not obdurate, open thy deaf ears . ii 3 160
Which [book] is it, girl, of these? Open them, boy iv 1 32
Thus I enforce thy rotten jaws to open *Rom. and Jul.* v 3 47
O, I am slain! If thou be merciful, Open the tomb, lay me with Juliet v 3 73
With instruments upon them, fit to open These dead men's tombs v 3 200
Left me open, bare For every storm that blows *T. of Athens* iv 3 265
To Athens go, Break open shops iv 3 450
Promising is the very air o' the time: it opens the eyes of expectation. v 1 25
There's my glove; Descend, and open your uncharged ports v 4 55
When the cross blue lightning seem'd to open The breast of heaven *J. C.* i 3 50
This dreadful night, That thunders, lightens, opens graves, and roars i 3 74
He is about it: The doors are open *Macbeth* ii 2 5
Open, locks, Whoever knocks! iv 1 46
Her eyes are open.—Ay, but their sense is shut v 1 28
Or your chaste treasure open To his unmaster'd importunity. *Hamlet* i 3 31
You must not put another scandal on him, That he is open to incontinency ii 1 30
Open this purse, and take What it contains *Lear* iii 1 45
All offices are open, and there is full liberty of feasting *Othello* ii 2 9
He'ld lay the future open . *Cymbeline* iii 2 29
That I should open to the listening air *Pericles* i 2 87
But even Your purse, still open ii 2 47
Whate'er it be, 'Tis wondrous heavy.—Wrench it open straight ii 2 53
The petty wrens of Tarsus will fly hence, And open this to Pericles iv 3 23
Open air. Hurried Here to this place, i' the open air *W. Tale* ii 2 106
And holds belief That, being brought into the open air, It would allay the burning quality Of that fell poison which assaileth him *K. John* v 7 7
Straying from the way; Not knowing how to find the open air, But toiling desperately to find it out . *3 Hen. VI.* iii 2 177
Well are you welcome to the open air *Richard III.* i 1 124
Here is better than the open air; take it thankfully *Lear* iii 6 1
Open banner. Are at point To show their open banner iii 1 34
Open bounty. Having often of your open bounty tasted. *T. of Athens* v 1 61
Open court. He hath refused it in the open court *Mer. of Venice* iv 1 338
Open dealing. Out with it boldly: truth loves open dealing *Hen. VIII.* iii 1 39
Open ear. To have an open ear, a quick eye, and a nimble hand, is necessary for a cut-purse . *W. Tale* iv 4 685
To whose venom sound The open ear of youth doth always listen *Rich. II.* ii 1 20
Open et cætera. That she were An open et cætera! *Rom. and Jul.* ii 1 38
Open eye. Have open eye, for thieves do foot by night *Mer. Wives* ii 1 126
Open-eyed conspiracy His time doth take *Tempest* ii 1 301
Open field. Did he so often lodge in open field? *2 Hen. VI.* iii 1 80
Open guilt. His apparent open guilt omitted *Richard III.* iii 5 30
Open hand. By my troth, thou hast an open hand *T. Night* iv 1 22
Where a noble heart Hath pawn'd an open hand in sign of love *3 Hen. VI.* iv 2 9
Open haunts. From open haunts and popularity *Hen. V.* i 1 59
Open market-place. In open market-place produced they me *1 Hen. VI.* i 4 40
Open means. Let me have open means to come to them. *Richard III.* iv 2 77
Open mouth. With open mouth swallowing a tailor's news *K. John* iv 2 195
Open nature. Of a free and open nature *Othello* i 3 405
Open night. Good my lord, enter: The tyranny of the open night's too rough For nature to endure *Lear* iii 4 2
Open outcry. Run, With open outcry, toward our monument *R. and J.* v 3 193
Open penance. After three days' open penance *2 Hen. VI.* ii 3 11
Open perils. How covert matters may be best disclosed, And open perils surest answered *J. Cæsar* iv 1 47
Open proclamation. Nought rests for me in this tumultuous strife But to make open proclamation . *1 Hen. VI.* i 3 71
Open room. It is an open room and good for winter *Meas. for Meas.* ii 1 135
Open shame. Free from these slanders and this open shame *Com. of Er.* iv 4 70
Come you, my lord, to see my open shame? *2 Hen. VI.* ii 4 19
Open streets. And feast and banquet in the open streets *1 Hen. VI.* i 6 13
Open trial. As she hath Been publicly accused, so shall she have A just and open trial *W. Tale* ii 3 205
Open ulcer. Pour'st in the open ulcer of my heart Her eyes, her hair, her cheek, her gait, her voice *Troi. and Cres.* i 1 53
Open war. If I claim by open war *3 Hen. VI.* i 2 19
Opened. As mine eyes open'd, I saw their weapons drawn *Tempest* ii 1 319
If he were opened, and you find so much blood in his liver as will clog the foot of a flea, I'll eat the rest of the anatomy *T. Night* iii 2 65
There's comfort in 't Whiles other men have gates and those gates open'd, As mine, against their will *W. Tale* i 2 197
Which I have open'd to his grace at large *Hen. V.* i 1 78
Friends.—Ay, say you so? the gates shall then be open'd *3 Hen. VI.* iv 7 26
As my hand has open'd bounty to you, My heart dropp'd love *Hen. VIII.* iii 2 184
I feel my heart new open'd iii 2 366
When they shall be open'd, black Macbeth Will seem as pure as snow *Macbeth* iv 3 52
Whether aught, to us unknown, afflicts him thus, That, open'd, lies within our remedy *Hamlet* ii 2 18
Open'd, in despite Of heaven and men, her purposes *Cymbeline* v 5 58
Thou thought'st thy griefs might equal mine, If both were open'd *Per.* v 1 133
Opener. The very opener and intelligencer Between the grace, the sanctities of heaven And our dull workings *2 Hen. IV.* iv 2 20
Opening. A planched gate, That makes his opening with this bigger key *Meas. for Meas.* iv 1 31
At the first opening of the gorgeous east *L. L. Lost* iv 3 223
Even till the eastern gate, all fiery-red, Opening on Neptune with fair blessed beams *M. N. Dream* iii 2 392
Nimble in threats approach'd The opening of his mouth. *As Y. Like It* iv 3 111

Opening. Opening his free arms and weeping His welcomes forth *W. Tale* iv 4 559
I was by at the opening of the fardel . . . v 2 3
With opening titles miscreate . . . *Hen. V.* i 2 16
We saw him at the opening of his tent . *Troi. and Cres.* ii 3 91
For mine own part, I durst not laugh, for fear of opening my lips and receiving the bad air . . . *J. Cæsar* i 2 251
But she spoke it dying, I would not Believe her lips in opening it *Cymb.* v 5 42
Openly. This chain which now you wear so openly . *Com. of Errors* v 1 17
Publish'd and proclaim'd it openly . . . *T. of Shrew* iv 2 85
Let us be clear'd Of being tyrannous, since we so openly Proceed *W. T.* iii 2 5
And my case so openly known to the world . *2 Hen. IV.* ii 1 33
My love to ye Shall show itself more openly hereafter . . iv 2 76
And calls your grace usurper openly . . . *2 Hen. VI.* iv 4 30
Be dishonour'd openly, And basely put it up without revenge? *T. Andron.* i 1 432
Dare you draw, And maintain such a quarrel openly? . . ii 1 47
Openness. Deliver with more openness your answers To my demands *Cymbeline* i 6 88
Operant. Who seeks for better of thee, sauce his palate With thy most operant poison! . . . *T. of Athens* iv 3 25
My operant powers their functions leave to do. . *Hamlet* iii 2 184
Operate. The effect doth operate another way . . *Troi. and Cres.* v 3 109
Mine Italian brain 'Gan in your duller Britain operate Most vilely *Cymb.* v 5 197
Operation. I have operations which be humours of revenge . *Mer. Wives* i 3 98
A good sherris-sack hath a two-fold operation in it . . *2 Hen. IV.* iv 3 104
An operation more divine Than breath or pen can give expressure to *Troi. and Cres.* iii 3 203
And by the operation of the second cup draws it on the drawer *R. and J.* iii 1 8
By all the operation of the orbs From whom we do exist . *Lear* i 1 113
Your serpent of Egypt is bred now of your mud by the operation of your sun: so is your crocodile . . . *Ant. and Cleo.* ii 7 30
If knife, drugs, serpents, have Edge, sting, or operation, I am safe . iv 15 26
Operative. Many simples operative, whose power Will close the eye of anguish . . . . . *Lear* iv 4 14
Ophelia. Fear it, Ophelia, fear it, my dear sister . . *Hamlet* i 3 33
Farewell, Ophelia; and remember well What I have said to you . i 3 84
What is't, Ophelia, he hath said to you?—So please you, something touching the Lord Hamlet . . . . i 3 88
In few, Ophelia, Do not believe his vows; for they are brokers . i 3 126
Ophelia! what's the matter?—O, my lord, my lord, I have been so affrighted! . . . . . ii 1 74
To the celestial and my soul's idol, the most beautified Ophelia . ii 2 110
O dear Ophelia, I am ill at these numbers; I have not art to reckon my groans . . . . . ii 2 120
That he, as 'twere by accident, may here Affront Ophelia . . iii 1 31
Ophelia, I do wish That your good beauties be the happy cause Of Hamlet's wildness . . . . . iii 1 38
Ophelia, walk you here. Gracious, so please you, We will bestow ourselves . . . . . iii 1 44
The fair Ophelia! Nymph, in thy orisons Be all my sins remember'd . iii 1 89
How now, Ophelia! You need not tell us what Lord Hamlet said; We heard it all . . . . . iii 1 186
Pretty Ophelia!—Indeed, la, without an oath, I'll make an end on't . iv 5 56
Poor Ophelia Divided from herself and her fair judgement . . iv 5 84
O rose of May! Dear maid, kind sister, sweet Ophelia! . . iv 5 158
Too much of water hast thou, poor Ophelia, And therefore I forbid my tears . . . . . iv 7 186
What, the fair Ophelia!—Sweets to the sweet: farewell! . . v 1 265
I loved Ophelia: forty thousand brothers Could not, with all their quantity of love, Make up my sum . . . v 1 292
Opinion. I do now let loose my opinion; hold it no longer . *Tempest* ii 2 36
In thy opinion which is worthiest love? . . *T. G. of Ver.* i 2 6
Do him not that wrong To bear a hard opinion of his truth . ii 7 81
To thy great comfort in this mystery of ill opinions . *Mer. Wives* ii 1 73
Yet I cannot put off my opinion so easily . . . ii 1 243
In my poor opinion, they will to't then . *Meas. for Meas.* ii 1 245
Neglect me not, with that opinion That I am touch'd with madness! . v 1 50
Is the opinion that fire cannot melt out of me . . *Much Ado* i 1 234
The sport will be, when they hold one an opinion of another's dotage . ii 3 224
Learned without opinion, and strange without heresy . *L. L. Lost* v 1 6
To be dress'd in an opinion Of wisdom, gravity *Mer. of Venice* i 1 91
Fish not, with this melancholy bait, For this fool gudgeon, this opinion i 1 102
And now, good sweet, say thy opinion . . . iii 5 76
Nay, but ask my opinion too of that . . . . iii 5 90
Thou almost makest me waver in my faith To hold opinion with Pythagoras . . . . . . iv 1 131
We turned o'er many books together: he is furnished with my opinion iv 1 157
Weed your better judgements Of all opinion that grows rank *As Y. L. It* ii 7 46
I speak not this that you should bear a good opinion of my knowledge v 2 60
What's your opinion of your sister? . . *T. of Shrew* ii 2 245
At least in my opinion . . . . *All's Well* iv 2 31
You are now sailed into the north of my lady's opinion . *T. Night* iii 2 28
Into a most hideous opinion of his rage, skill, fury and impetuosity . iii 4 212
What is the opinion of Pythagoras concerning wild fowl? . . iv 2 54
What thinkest thou of his opinion?—I think nobly of the soul, and no way approve his opinion . . . . . iv 2 60
Thou shalt hold the opinion of Pythagoras ere I will allow of thy wits . iv 2 62
Be cured Of this diseased opinion, and betimes . . *W. Tale* i 2 297
How blest am I In my just censure, in my true opinion! . . ii 1 37
Remove The root of his opinion, which is rotten As ever oak or stone was sound . . . . ii 3 89
Makes sound opinion sick and truth suspected . . *K. John* iv 2 26
Leaving me no sign, Save men's opinions and my living blood *Richard II.* iii 1 26
I have partly thy mother's word, partly my own opinion *1 Hen. IV.* ii 4 445
Want of government, Pride, haughtiness, opinion and disdain . iii 1 185
Opinion, that did help me to the crown, Had still kept loyal to possession . . . . iii 2 42
It lends a lustre and more great opinion, A larger dare . . iv 1 77
Stay, and breathe awhile: Thou hast redeem'd thy lost opinion . v 4 48
I pray you all, Speak plainly your opinions of our hopes *2 Hen. IV.* i 3 3
It shall descend with better quiet, Better opinion, better confirmation . iv 5 189
To frustrate prophecies and to raze out Rotten opinion . . v 2 128
Falstaff shall die of a sweat, unless already a' be killed with your hard opinions . . . . Epil. 33
Partly to satisfy my opinion, and partly for the satisfaction, look you, of my mind . . . . . *Hen. V.* iii 2 105
Let me have your express opinions . . . *1 Hen. VI.* i 4 64
Shall yield the other in the right opinion . . . . ii 4 42
If I, my lord, for my opinion bleed, Opinion shall be surgeon to my hurt ii 4 53
In our opinions she should be preferr'd . . . . v 5 61
In my opinion yet thou see'st not well . . . *2 Hen. VI.* ii 1 107
Opinion. Give me leave In this close walk to satisfy myself, In craving your opinion . . . . . *2 Hen. VI.* ii 2 4
Speak freely what you think.—Then this is mine opinion *3 Hen. VI.* iv 1 29
As well the fear of harm, as harm apparent, In my opinion, ought to be prevented . . . . . *Richard III.* ii 3 131
This prince hath neither claim'd it nor deserved it; And therefore, in mine opinion, cannot have it . . . . iii 1 52
To-morrow, in mine opinion, is too sudden . . . iii 4 45
Beside forfeiting Our own brains, and the opinion that we bring *Hen. VIII.* Prol. 20
Believe me, there's an ill opinion spread then Even of yourself . ii 2 125
The king's majesty Commends his good opinion of you . . ii 3 61
Every eye saw 'em, Envy and base opinion set against 'em . . iii 1 36
To deliver, Like free and honest men, our just opinions And comforts . iii 1 60
When returns Cranmer?—He is return'd in his opinions . . iii 2 64
His own opinion was his law: i' the presence He would say untruths . iv 2 37
With new opinions, Divers and dangerous . . . v 3 17
Whom opinion crowns The sinew and the forehand of our host *T. and C.* i 3 142
These twain—Who, as Ulysses says, opinion crowns With an imperial voice . . . . i 3 186
Though't be a sportful combat, Yet in the trial much opinion dwells . i 3 336
To steel a strong opinion to themselves . . . . i 3 353
We did our main opinion crush In taint of our best man . . i 3 373
Yet go we under our opinion still That we have better men . . i 3 383
Hector's opinion Is this in way of truth . . . . ii 2 188
A plague of opinion! a man may wear it on both sides, like a leather jerkin . . . . iii 3 265
Whiles others fish with craft for great opinion, I with great truth catch mere simplicity . . . . . . iv 4 105
And policy grows into an ill opinion . . . . v 4 19
Rubbing the poor itch of your opinion, Make yourselves scabs *Coriol.* i 1 169
Opinion that so sticks on Marcius shall Of his demerits rob Cominius . i 1 275
So, your opinion is, Aufidius, That they of Rome are enter'd in our counsels . . . . i 2 1
Lord Titus here Is in opinion and in honour wrong'd . *T. Andron.* i 1 416
What friendship may I do thee?—None, but to Maintain my opinion.—What is it? . . . . *T. of Athens* iv 3 71
All tending to the great opinion That Rome holds of his name *J. Cæsar* i 2 322
Every one doth wish You had but that opinion of yourself Which every noble Roman bears of you . . . . ii 1 92
O, let us have him, for his silver hairs Will purchase us a good opinion ii 1 145
He is superstitious grown of late, Quite from the main opinion he held once . . . . ii 1 196
Bid the priests do present sacrifice And bring me their opinions of success . . . . ii 2 6
I held Epicurus strong And his opinion: now I change my mind . v 1 78
I have bought Golden opinions from all sorts of people . *Macbeth* i 7 33
In the gross and scope of my opinion . . . *Hamlet* i 1 68
It is as proper to our age To cast beyond ourselves in our opinions . ii 1 115
Carries them through and through the most fond and winnowed opinions v 2 201
His very opinion in the letter! . . . . *Lear* i 2 80
Some blood drawn on me would beget opinion Of my more fierce endeavour . . . . ii 1 35
When false opinion, whose wrong thought defiles thee, In thy just proof, repeals and reconciles thee . . . . . iii 6 119
Opinion, a sovereign mistress of effects . . . *Othello* i 3 225
And spend your rich opinion for the name Of a night-brawler . ii 3 195
How have I been behaved, that he might stick The small'st opinion on my least misuse? . . . . . . iv 2 109
Even from this instant do build on thee a better opinion than ever before . . . . iv 2 209
But let us rear The higher our opinion . . *Ant. and Cleo.* ii 1 36
Or this gentleman's opinion by this worn out . . *Cymbeline* i 4 68
Which, in my opinion, o'ervalues it something . . . i 4 119
For your ill opinion and the assault you have made to her chastity you shall answer me with your sword . . . . i 4 175
The foul opinion You had of her pure honour gains or loses Your sword or mine, or masterless leaves both . . . . ii 4 58
Opinion's but a fool, that makes us scan The outward habit by the inward man. But stay, the knights are coming . *Pericles* ii 2 56
Seldom but that pity begets you a good opinion, and that opinion a mere profit.—I understand you not . . . . . iv 2 131
Opinioned. Come, let them be opinioned . . . *Much Ado* iv 2 69
Opportune. The murkiest den, The most opportune place . *Tempest* iv 1 26
Most opportune to our need I have A vessel rides fast by . *W. Tale* iv 4 511
Opportunity. Engrossed opportunities to meet her . . *Mer. Wives* ii 2 203
When I have good opportunities for the ork . . . . iii 1 15
If opportunity and humblest suit Cannot attain it . . . iii 4 20
To trust the opportunity of night And the ill counsel . *M. N. Dream* ii 1 217
The double gilt of this opportunity you let time wash off . *T. Night* iii 2 27
When there is more better opportunity to be required . . *Hen. V.* iii 2 151
Embrace we then this opportunity As fitting best . . *1 Hen. VI.* ii 1 13
Ten to one We shall not find like opportunity . . . v 4 158
For sluttish spoils of opportunity And daughters of the game *T. and C.* iv 5 62
The self-same gods that arm'd the Queen of Troy With opportunity of sharp revenge Upon the Thracian tyrant . . *T. Andron.* i 1 137
I will omit no opportunity That may convey my greetings *Rom. and Jul.* iii 5 49
You have many opportunities to cut him off . . . *Lear* iv 6 268
I will do this, if I can bring it to any opportunity . . *Othello* ii 1 290
Had I admittance and opportunity to friend . . . *Cymbeline* i 4 116
With no more advantage than the opportunity of a second conference . i 4 142
That opportunity Which then they had to take from's, to resume We have again . . . . iii 1 14
By her own command Shall give thee opportunity . . . iii 2 19
Take away her life: I shall give thee opportunity at Milford-Haven . iii 4 29
Oppose. How she opposes her against my will . . *T. G. of Ver.* iii 2 26
I do oppose My patience to his fury . . . *Mer. of Venice* iv 1 10
'Tis your counsel My lord should to the heavens be contrary, Oppose against their wills . . . . . . *W. Tale* v 1 46
Yet I alone, alone do me oppose Against the pope . . *K. John* iii 1 170
I know it, uncle, and oppose not myself Against their will *Richard II.* iii 3 18
Seen this stubborn Cade Oppose himself against a troop of kerns *2 Hen. VI.* iii 1 361
Oppose thy steadfast-gazing eyes to mine . . . . iv 10 4[illegible]
A bedlam and ambitious humour Makes him oppose himself against his king . . . . v 1 133
And such a piece of service will you do, If you oppose yourselves . . v 1 156
I am a simple woman, much too weak To oppose your cunning *Hen. VIII.* ii 4 107
Whom may you else oppose? . . . . *Troi. and Cres.* i 3 333
I wish I had a cause to seek him there, To oppose his hatred fully *Coriol.* iii 1 [illegible]

Oppose. Oppose not Scythia to ambitious Rome . *T. Andron.* i 1 132
With a noble fury and fair spirit, Seeing his reputation touch'd to death, He did oppose his foe . . . *T. of Athens* iii 5 20
All continent impediments would o'erbear That did oppose my will *Macb.* iv 3 65
And in conclusion to oppose the bolt Against my coming in . . *Lear* ii 4 179
Whom, I fear, Most just and heavy causes make oppose . . . v 1 27
Cæsar sits down in Alexandria; where I will oppose his fate *A. and C.* iii 13 169
Found no opposition But what he look'd for should oppose . *Cymbeline* ii 5 18
Opposed. Even to the opposed end of our intents . . *L. L. Lost* v 2 768
To offend, and judge, are distinct offices And of opposed natures *M. of V.* ii 9 62
Forced To give my hand opposed against my heart . *T. of Shrew* iii 2 9
And embraced, as it were, from the ends of opposed winds . *W. Tale* i 1 34
Your resolution cannot hold, when 'tis Opposed, as it must be . iv 4 37
Those opposed eyes, Which, like the meteors of a troubled heaven, All of one nature, of one substance bred . . . 1 *Hen. IV.* i 1 9
March all one way and be no more opposed Against acquaintance . i 1 15
Gelding the opposed continent as much As on the other side it takes from you . . . . iii 1 110
Doubt not, my lord, they shall be well opposed . . . iv 4 33
We stand opposed by such means As you yourself have forged . v 1 67
Towards fronting peril and opposed decay . . 2 *Hen. IV.* iv 4 66
Take from them now The sense of reckoning, if the opposed numbers Pluck their hearts from them . . . . *Hen. V.* iv 1 308
You are potently opposed; and with a malice Of as great size *Hen. VIII.* v 1 134
Eye to eye opposed Salutes each other with each other's form *T. and C.* iii 3 107
A little proudly, and great deal misprizing The knight opposed . iv 5 75
They are opposed already . . . . iv 5 94
Nor you, my brother, with your true sword drawn, Opposed to hinder me, should stop my way . . . . . . v 3 57
Two such opposed kings encamp them still In man as well as herbs, grace and rude will . . . . *Rom. and Jul.* ii 3 27
What, are my doors opposed against my passage? . *T. of Athens* iii 4 80
In general part we were opposed, Yet our old love made a particular force . . . . v 2 7
Though Birnam wood be come to Dunsinane, And thou opposed *Macbeth* v 8 31
Beware Of entrance to a quarrel, but being in, Bear't that the opposed may beware of thee . . . . . *Hamlet* i 3 67
The scrimers of their nation, He swore, had neither motion, guard, nor eye, If you opposed them . . . . . iv 7 103
Came from one that's of a neutral heart, And not from one opposed *Lear* iii 7 49
A servant that he bred, thrill'd with remorse, Opposed against the act iv 2 74
Was this a face To be opposed against the warring winds? . iv 7 32
Half to half the world opposed, he being The meered question *A. and C.* iii 13 9
Sluttery to such neat excellence opposed . . . *Cymbeline* i 6 44
Opposeless. If I could bear it longer, and not fall To quarrel with your great opposeless wills . . . . . . *Lear* iv 6 38
Opposer. Holy seems the quarrel Upon your grace's part; black and fearful On the opposer . . . . . *All's Well* iii 1 6
Now the fair goddess, Fortune, Fall deep in love with thee; and her great charms Misguide thy opposers' swords! . *Coriolanus* i 5 23
Bestrid An o'er-press'd Roman and i' the consul's view Slew three opposers . . . . ii 2 98
Tullus Aufidius will appear well in these wars, his great opposer, Coriolanus, being now in no request of his country . . iv 3 36
Opposing freely The beauty of her person to the people *Hen. VIII.* iv 1 67
Opposing laws with strokes . . . . *Coriolanus* iii 3 79
Or to take arms against a sea of troubles, And by opposing end them *Hamlet* iii 1 60
The four opposing coigns Which the world together joins *Pericles* iii Gower 17
Opposite. You imagine me too unhurtful an opposite *Meas. for Meas.* iii 2 175
Be opposite with a kinsman, surly with servants . *T. Night* ii 5 162; iii 4 76
His opposite, the youth, bears in his visage no great presage of cruelty iii 2 68
Your opposite hath in him what youth, strength, skill and wrath can furnish man withal . . . . iii 4 253
He is, indeed, sir, the most skilful, bloody and fatal opposite . iii 4 293
All form is formless, order orderless, Save what is opposite to England's love. Therefore to arms! . . . . . . *K. John* iii 1 254
How able such a work to undergo, To weigh against his opposite 2 *Hen. IV.* i 3 55
May overlive the hazard And fearful meeting of their opposite . iv 1 16
Free from a stubborn opposite intent . . 2 *Hen. VI.* iii 2 251
'Tis not enough our foes are this time fled, Being opposites of such repairing nature . . . . v 3 22
Thou art as opposite to every good As the Antipodes are unto us 3 *Hen. VI.* i 4 134
Much more to be thus opposite with heaven, For it requires the royal debt it lent you . . . . . . *Richard III.* ii 2 94
Lo, at their births good stars were opposite . . . . iv 4 215
Be opposite all planets of good luck To my proceedings! . . iv 4 402
Enacts more wonders than a man, Daring an opposite to every danger . v 4 3
Leaves nothing undone that may fully discover him their opposite *Cor.* ii 2 23
Just opposite to what thou justly seem'st, A damned saint! *R. and J.* iii 2 78
He's opposite to humanity . . . . *T. of Athens* i 1 284
Each opposite that blanks the face of joy Meet what I would have well and it destroy! . . . . *Hamlet* iii 2 230
Between the pass and fell incensed points Of mighty opposites . v 2 62
Seeing how loathly opposite I stood To his unnatural purpose . *Lear* ii 1 51
You have the captives That were the opposites of this day's strife . v 3 42
By the law of arms thou wast not bound to answer An unknown opposite . . . . v 3 153
So opposite to marriage that she shunn'd The wealthy curled darlings *Othello* i 2 67
That have the office opposite to Saint Peter, And keep the gate of hell! iv 2 91
Present pleasure, By revolution lowering, does become The opposite of itself: she's good, being gone . . . *Ant. and Cleo.* i 2 130
Opposition. Vouchsafe In your rich wisdom to excuse or hide The liberal opposition of our spirits . . . . . . *L. L. Lost* v 2 743
In single opposition, hand to hand . . . 1 *Hen. IV.* i 3 99
Your whole plot too light for the counterpoise of so great an opposition ii 3 15
I have learn'd me to repent the sin Of disobedient opposition *R. and J.* iv 2 18
Why should we in our peevish opposition Take it to heart? . *Hamlet* i 2 100
I mean, my lord, the opposition of your person in trial . . v 2 178
And tilting one at other's breast, In opposition bloody . *Othello* ii 3 184
Found no opposition But what he look'd for should oppose . *Cymbeline* ii 5 17
And more remarkable in single oppositions . . . . iv 1 14
Oppress. Did oppress our nest; Grew by our feeding . 1 *Hen. IV.* v 1 61
Why dost thou so oppress me with thine eye? . *Trio. and Cres.* iv 5 241
And doleful dumps the mind oppress . . *Rom. and Jul.* iv 5 129
This accident is not unlike my dream: Belief of it oppresses me already *Othello* i 1 144
The mutiny he there hastes t' oppress . . . . *Pericles* iii Gower 29

Oppressed. They are oppress'd with travel . . *Tempest* iii 3 15
Here's a young maid with travel much oppress'd . *As Y. Like It* ii 4 74
Oppress'd with two weak evils, age and hunger . . . ii 7 132
You ne'er oppress'd me with a mother's groan . . *All's Well* i 3 153
Usurp The dominations, royalties and rights Of this oppressed boy *K. John* ii 1 177
Being no further enemy to you Than the constraint of hospitable zeal In the relief of this oppressed child . . . . . ii 1 245
I am sick and capable of fears, Oppress'd with wrongs . . . iii 1 13
Nor much oppress'd them with great subsidies . 3 *Hen. VI.* iv 8 45
When all our offices have been oppress'd With riotous feeders *T. of A.* ii 2 167
Thrice he walk'd By their oppress'd and fear-surprised eyes . *Hamlet* i 2 203
Nature, being oppress'd, commands the mind To suffer with the body *Lear* ii 4 109
Oppressed nature sleeps: This rest might yet have balm'd thy broken sinews . . . . iii 6 104
For thee, oppressed king, am I cast down . . . . . v 3 5
Oppresseth. Since fear oppresseth strength . *Richard II.* iii 2 180
Oppressing. For, by oppressing and betraying me, Thou might'st have sooner got another service . . . . *T. of Athens* iv 3 510
Oppression. This day of shame, oppression, perjury . *K. John* iii 1 88
Our oppression hath made up this league . . . . iii 1 106
That taught me craft To counterfeit oppression of such grief *Richard II.* i 4 14
Make their sire Stoop with oppression of their prodigal weight . iii 4 31
His peers to servitude, His subjects to oppression and contempt *Hen. V.* ii 2 172
The pitiful complaints Of such as your oppression feeds upon 1 *Hen. VI.* iv 1 58
Free from oppression or the stroke of war . . . . v 3 155
You remember How under my oppression I did reek . *Hen. VIII.* ii 4 208
Thy good heart's oppression.—Why, such is love's transgression *R. and J.* i 1 190
Too great oppression for a tender thing.—Is love a tender thing? . i 4 24
Famine is in thy cheeks, Need and oppression starveth in thine eyes v 1 70
I am pigeon-liver'd and lack gall To make oppression bitter . *Hamlet* ii 2 606
I begin to find an idle and fond bondage in the oppression of aged tyranny . . . . *Lear* i 2 52
Our oppression Exceeds what we expected . . *Ant. and Cleo.* iv 7 2
The earth is throng'd By man's oppression . . . *Pericles* i 1 102
Oppressor. The oppressor's wrong, the proud man's contumely *Hamlet* iii 1 71
Opprest. Be not with mortal accidents opprest . . *Cymbeline* v 4 99
Opprobriously. To taunt and scorn you thus opprobriously . *Rich. III.* iii 1 153
Oppugnancy. Each thing meets In mere oppugnancy . *Troi. and Cres.* i 3 111
Opulency. Flatteries that follow youth and opulency . *T. of Athens* v 1 38
Opulent. What can you say to draw A third more opulent than your sisters? Speak.—Nothing, my lord . . . . . *Lear* i 1 88
I will piece Her opulent throne with kingdoms . *Ant. and Cleo.* i 5 46
Or. Served Without or grudge or grumblings . . . *Tempest* i 2 249
I shall think, or Phœbus' steeds are founder'd, Or Night kept chain'd below . . . . iv 1 30
Loath to leave unsought Or that or any place that harbours men *C. of Er.* i 1 137
Look'd he or red or pale, or sad or merrily? . . . . iv 2 4
Will make or man or woman madly dote . . *M. N. Dream* ii 1 171
Or to find both Or bring your latter hazard back again . *Mer. of Venice* i 1 150
Tell me where is fancy bred, Or in the heart or in the head? . . iii 2 64
Move these eyes? Or whether, riding on the balls of mine, Seem they in motion? . . . . iii 2 117
Or Charles or something weaker masters thee . . . *As Y. Like It* i 2 272
Am I or that or this for what he'll utter? . . . *All's Well* v 3 208
As or by oath remove or counsel shake The fabric of his folly *W. Tale* i 2 428
Or stupified Or seeming so in skill . . . . . . ii 1 165
Or I'll be thine, my fair, Or not my father's . . . . iv 4 42
I say and will in battle prove, Or here or elsewhere . . *Richard II.* i 1 93
If he fall in, good night! or sink or swim . . . 1 *Hen. IV.* i 3 194
Look how we can, or sad or merrily, Interpretation will misquote our looks . . . . v 2 12
Why the law Salique . . . Or should, or should not, bar us . *Hen. V.* i 2 12
Or there we'll sit . . . Or lay these bones in an unworthy urn . i 2 225
Or Somerset or York, all's one to me . . . 2 *Hen. VI.* i 3 105
Or you must fight, or else be hang'd . . . . . . i 3 222
Must or now be cropp'd, Or, shedding, breed . *Troi. and Cres.* i 3 318
How dearly ever parted, How much in having, or without or in . . iii 3 97
Or whether his fall enraged him, or how 'twas . *Coriolanus* i 3 69
Or let us stand to our authority, Or let us lose it . . . iii 1 208
Your son Will or exceed the common or be caught With cautelous baits iv 1 32
To think that or our cause or our performance Did need an oath *J. Cæsar* ii 1 135
Shall I find you here?—Or here, or at the Capitol . . . . iii 1 11
When you do find him, or alive or dead, He will be found like Brutus . v 4 24
He came not back: he is or ta'en or slain . . . . . v 3 3
Be thy mouth or black or white, Tooth that poisons if it bite . *Lear* iii 6 69
Or well or ill, as this day's battle's fought . . . . iv 7 98
Or I will live, Or bathe my dying honour in the blood *Ant. and Cleo.* iv 2 5
And I think He'll grant the tribute, send the arrearages, Or look upon our Romans . . . . *Cymbeline* ii 4 14
Cydnus swell'd above the banks, or for The press of boats or pride . ii 4 71
How! a page! Or dead, or sleeping on him? But dead rather . iv 2 356
Or perform my bidding, or thou livest in woe . . . *Pericles* v 1 248
Or ere. I would Have sunk the sea within the earth or ere It should the good ship so have swallow'd . . . . . . *Tempest* i 2 11
I drink the air before me, and return Or ere your pulse twice beat . v 1 103
It shall be moon, or star, or what I list, Or ere I journey *T. of Shrew* iv 5 7
'Twill be Two long days' journey, lords, or ere we meet . *K. John* iv 3 20
I doubt he will be dead or ere I come . . . . . . v 6 44
Expire before the flowers in their caps, Dying or ere they sicken *Macbeth* iv 3 173
A little month, or ere those shoes were old . . . *Hamlet* i 2 147
This heart Shall break into a hundred thousand flaws, Or ere I'll weep *Lear* ii 4 289
Those that would die or ere resist . . . . *Cymbeline* v 3 50
Or ever. Would I had met my dearest foe in heaven Or ever I had seen that day! . . . . *Hamlet* i 2 183
Why should excuse be born or e'er begot? . . . *Cymbeline* iii 2 67
Oracle. I do believe it Against an oracle . . . . *Tempest* iv 1 12
Some oracle Must rectify our knowledge . . . . . v 1 244
His words are bonds, his oaths are oracles, His love sincere *T. G. of Ver.* ii 7 75
Hear this letter with attention?—As we would hear an oracle *L. L. Lost* i 1 218
I am Sir Oracle, And when I ope my lips let no dog bark! *Mer. of Venice* i 1 94
Now from the oracle They will bring all . . . *W. Tale* ii 1 185
Yet shall the oracle Give rest to the minds of others . . . ii 1 190
Posts From those you sent to the oracle are come . . . . ii 3 194
The burst And the ear-deafening voice o' the oracle . . . iii 1 9
When the oracle, Thus by Apollo's great divine seal'd up, Shall the contents discover, something rare . . . . iii 1 18
Your honours all, I do refer me to the oracle . . . . . iii 2 116

Oracle. Therefore bring forth, And in Apollo's name, his oracle *W. Tale* iii 2 119
This seal'd-up oracle, by the hand deliver'd Of great Apollo's priest iii 2 128
There is no truth at all i' the oracle iii 2 141
Apollo, pardon My great profaneness 'gainst thine oracle! iii 2 155
Has not the divine Apollo said, Is't not the tenour of his oracle? v 1 38
Nothing but bonfires: the oracle is fulfilled v 2 24
She had one eye declined for the loss of her husband, another elevated that the oracle was fulfilled v 2 82
The oracle Gave hope thou wast in being v 3 126
These oracles are hardly attain'd, And hardly understood *2 Hen. VI.* i 4 74
My other self, my counsel's consistory, My oracle, my prophet! *Rich. III.* ii 2 152
One Hath crawl'd into the favour of the king, And is his oracle *Hen. VIII.* iii 2 104
This oracle of comfort has so pleased me v 5 67
We shall hear music, wit and oracle *Troi. and Cres.* i 3 74
Rails on our state of war, Bold as an oracle i 3 192
Wert thou an oracle to tell me so, I'ld not believe thee iv 5 252
Whom the oracle Hath doubtfully pronounced thy throat shall cut *T. of Athens* iv 3 120
Thither come, And let my grave-stone be your oracle v 1 222
Why, by the verities on thee made good, May they not be my oracles as well, And set me up in hope? *Macbeth* iii 1 9
Answering the letter of the oracle *Cymbeline* v 5 450
Orange. But civil count, civil as an orange, and something of that jealous complexion *Much Ado* ii 1 305
Give not this rotten orange to your friend iv 1 33
Orange-tawny beard, your purple-in-grain beard *M. N. Dream* i 2 96
The ousel cock so black of hue, With orange-tawny bill iii 1 129
Orange-wife. You wear out a good wholesome forenoon in hearing a cause between an orange-wife and a fosset-seller *Coriolanus* ii 1 78
Oration. There is such confusion in my powers, As, after some oration fairly spoke By a beloved prince *Mer. of Venice* iii 2 180
Hem, and stroke thy beard, As he being drest to some oration *T. and C.* i 3 166
Thy horse will sooner con an oration than thou learn a prayer without book ii 1 19
Why, sir, that is as fit as can be to serve for your oration *T. Andron.* iv 3 96
Tell me, can you deliver an oration to the emperor with a grace? iv 3 98
Fold it in the oration; For thou hast made it like an humble suppliant iv 3 116
There shall I try, In my oration, how the people take The cruel issue of these bloody men *J. Cæsar* iii 1 293
Orator. Be not thy tongue thy own shame's orator *Com. of Errors* iii 2 10
Very good orators, when they are out, they will spit *As Y. Like It* iv 1 75
He's a good drum, my lord, but a naughty orator *All's Well* v 3 254
The king Prettily, methought, did play the orator *1 Hen. VI.* iv 1 175
But you, my lord, were glad to be employ'd, To show how quaint an orator you are *2 Hen. VI.* iii 2 274
I can better play the orator.—But I have reasons strong *3 Hen. VI.* i 2 2
Full well hath Clifford play'd the orator ii 2 43
Warwick is a subtle orator, And Lewis a prince soon won with moving words iii 1 33
I'll play the orator as well as Nestor, Deceive more slily than Ulysses iii 2 188
Fear not, my lord, I'll play the orator As if the golden fee for which I plead Were for myself *Richard III.* iii 5 95
Gold were as good as twenty orators, And will, no doubt, tempt him iv 2 38
Airy succeeders of intestate joys, Poor breathing orators of miseries! iv 4 129
Reverse the doom of death; And let me say, that never wept before, My tears are now prevailing orators *T. Andron.* iii 1 26
She hath read to thee Sweet poetry and Tully's Orator iv 1 14
I am no orator, as Brutus is; But, as you know me all, a plain blunt man, That love my friend *J. Cæsar* iii 2 221
Oratory. For when a world of men Could not prevail with all their oratory, Yet hath a woman's kindness over-ruled *1 Hen. VI.* ii 2 49
If my weak oratory Can from his mother win the Duke of York *Rich. III.* iii 1 37
And when mine oratory grew to an end, I bid them that did love their country's good Cry 'God save Richard!' iii 7 20
Floods of tears will drown my oratory *T. Andron.* v 3 90
Orb. You seem to me as Dian in her orb *Much Ado* iv 1 58
I serve the fairy queen, To dew her orbs upon the green *M. N. Dream* ii 1 9
There's not the smallest orb which thou behold'st But in his motion like an angel sings *Mer. of Venice* v 1 60
Foolery, sir, does walk about the orb like the sun *T. Night* iii 1 43
Move in that obedient orb again Where you did give a fair and natural light, And be no more an exhaled meteor *1 Hen. IV.* v 1 17
The man is noble and his fame folds-in This orb o' the earth *Coriolanus* v 6 127
The inconstant moon, That monthly changes in her circled orb *R. and J.* ii 2 110
Below thy sister's orb Infect the air! *T. of Athens* iv 3 2
The bold winds speechless and the orb below As hush as death *Hamlet* ii 2 507
The orbs From whom we do exist, and cease to be *Lear* i 1 113
My good stars, that were my former guides, Have empty left their orbs, and shot their fires Into the abysm of hell *Ant. and Cleo.* iii 13 146
When he meant to quail and shake the orb, He was as rattling thunder v 2 85
Which can distinguish 'twixt The fiery orbs above and the twinn'd stones Upon the number'd beach *Cymbeline* i 6 35
That, after this strange starting from your orbs, You may reign in them now! v 5 371
In our orbs we'll live so round and safe *Pericles* i 2 122
Orbed. All those swearings keep as true in soul As doth that orbed continent the fire That severs day from night *T. Night* v 1 278
Full thirty times hath Phœbus' cart gone round Neptune's salt wash and Tellus' orbed ground *Hamlet* iii 2 166
Orchard. Walking in a thick-pleached alley in mine orchard *Much Ado* i 2 10
In my chamber-window lies a book: bring it hither to me in the orchard ii 3 4
Whisper her ear and tell her, I and Ursula Walk in the orchard iii 1 5
My master Don John saw afar off in the orchard this amiable encounter iii 3 161
How you were brought into the orchard and saw me court Margaret v 1 244
Know you where you are, sir?—O, sir, very well: here in your orchard. —Know you before whom, sir? *As Y. Like It* i 1 44
We will go walk a little in the orchard, And then to dinner *T. of Shrew* ii 1 112
I saw't i' the orchard.—Did she see thee the while, old boy? *T. Night* iii 2 8
Scout me for him at the corner of the orchard like a bum-baily iii 4 194
Let him be brought into the orchard here. Doth he still rage? *K. John* v 7 10
His lordship is walk'd forth into the orchard *2 Hen. IV.* i 1 4
You shall see my orchard, where, in an arbour, we will eat a last year's pippin of my own graffing v 3 1
Walk here i' the orchard, I'll bring her straight *Troi. and Cres.* iii 2 17
He ran this way, and leap'd this orchard wall *Rom. and Jul.* ii 1 5
The orchard walls are high and hard to climb, And the place death ii 2 63
He hath left you all his walks, His private arbours and new-planted orchards, On this side Tiber *J. Cæsar* iii 2 253
'Tis given out that, sleeping in my orchard, A serpent stung me *Hamlet* i 5 35
Sleeping within my orchard, My custom always of the afternoon i 5 59

Orchard-end. Thy intercepter . . . attends thee at the orchard-end *T. N.* iii 4 244
Ordain. Devise, ordain, impose Some gentle order *K. John* iii 1 250
Ordained. Preposterous ass, that never read so far To know the cause why music was ordain'd! *T. of Shrew* iii 1 10
Being ordain'd his special governor *1 Hen. VI.* i 1 171
A holy maid . . . Ordained is to raise this tedious siege i 2 53
When first this order was ordain'd, my lords, Knights of the garter were of noble birth iv 1 33
Wast thou ordain'd, dear father, To lose thy youth in peace? *2 Hen. VI.* v 2 45
For this, amongst the rest, was I ordain'd *3 Hen. VI.* v 6 58
This shoulder was ordain'd so thick to heave; And heave it shall v 7 23
The feast is ready, which the careful Titus Hath ordain'd to an honourable end, For peace, for love *T. Andron.* v 3 22
All things that we ordained festival, Turn from their office *Rom. and Jul.* iv 5 84
That Mulmutius which Ordain'd our laws *Cymbeline* iii 1 56
Ordaining. But fate, ordaining he should be a cuckold, held his hand *Mer. Wives* iii 5 106
Order. The several chairs of order look you scour v 5 65
Lock hand in hand; yourselves in order set v 5 81
We do the denunciation lack Of outward order *Meas. for Meas.* i 2 153
I will, as 'twere a brother of your order, Visit both prince and people i 3 44
Take order for the drabs and the knaves, you need not to fear the bawds ii 1 246
There are pretty orders beginning, I can tell you ii 1 249
Hadst thou not order? Why dost thou ask again? ii 2 8
Let her have needful, but not lavish, means; There shall be order for't ii 2 25
Bound by my charity and my blest order, I come to visit the afflicted spirits ii 3 3
Allowed by order of law a furred gown to keep him warm iii 2 8
I am a brother Of gracious order, late come from the See iii 2 232
By the vow of mine order I warrant you iv 2 180
Trust not my holy order, If I pervert your course iv 3 152
One in the prison, That should by private order else have died v 1 471
A branch and parcel of mine oath, A charitable duty of my order *C. of Er.* v 1 107
Sent him home, Whilst to take order for the wrongs I went That here and there his fury had committed v 1 146
His mother was a votaress of my order *M. N. Dream* ii 1 123
Give order to my servants that they take No note at all *Mer. of Venice* v 1 119
Can you nominate in order now the degrees of the lie? *As Y. Like It* v 4 92
This order hath Baptista ta'en, That none shall have access *T. of Shrew* i 2 126
To learn the order of my fingering, I must begin with rudiments of art iii 1 65
The carpets laid, and every thing in order iv 1 53
It was the friar of orders grey, As he forth walked on his way iv 1 148
Grumio gave order how it should be done.—I gave him no order; I gave him the stuff iv 3 119
I have . . . casketed my treasure, Given order for our horses *All's Well* ii 5 27
I'll order take my mother shall not hear iv 2 55
You must confine yourself within the modest limits of order *T. Night* i 3 9
The same I am, ere ancient'st order was Or what is now received *W. Tale* iv 1 10
Out of your grace, devise, ordain, impose Some gentle order *K. John* iii 1 251
All form is formless, order orderless iii 1 253
Such temperate order in so fierce a cause Doth want example iii 4 12
Send fair-play orders and make compromise v 1 67
Having our fair order written down v 2 4
Order the trial, marshal, and begin *Richard II.* i 3 99
If I know how or which way to order these affairs Thus thrust disorderly into my hands, Never believe me ii 2 109
There is order ta'en for you; With all swift speed you must away v 1 53
Help to order several powers To Oxford v 3 140
Shall we divide our right According to our threefold order ta'en? *1 Hen. IV.* iii 1 71
And now I live out of all order, out of all compass iii 3 22
There receive Money and order for their furniture iii 3 226
Let heaven kiss earth! now let not Nature's hand Keep the wild flood confined! let order die! *2 Hen. IV.* i 1 154
I will take such order that thy friends shall ring for thee iii 2 198
The manner and true order of the fight This packet, please it you, contains iv 4 100
Creatures that by a rule in nature teach The act of order *Hen. V.* i 2 189
Hear the shrill whistle which doth order give To sounds confused iii Prol. 9
To whom the order of the siege is given iii 2 70
If any order might be thought upon.—The devil take order now! iv 5 21
The emperor's coming in behalf of France, To order peace between them v Prol. 39
After that things are set in order here, We'll follow them *1 Hen. VI.* ii 2 32
Only give order for my funeral: And so farewell ii 5 112
Now will we take some order in the town iii 2 126
When first this order was ordain'd, my lords, Knights of the garter were of noble birth iv 1 33
Usurp the sacred name of knight, Profaning this most honourable order iv 1 41
Knight of the noble order of Saint George iv 7 68
Ere you can take due orders for a priest *2 Hen. VI.* iii 1 274
Provide me soldiers, lords, Whiles I take order for mine own affairs iii 1 320
Have calm'd their spleenful mutiny, Until they hear the order of his death iii 2 129
They are all in order and march toward us iv 2 198
But then are we in order when we are most out of order iv 2 199
Let's set our men in order, And issue forth and bid them battle straight *3 Hen. VI.* i 2 70
Until the duke take order for his burial *Richard III.* i 4 288
The order was reversed.—But he, poor soul, by your first order died ii 1 86
Now will I in, to take some privy order iii 5 106
My wife is sick and like to die: I will take order for her keeping close iv 2 53
Some one take order Buckingham be brought To Salisbury iv 4 539
Order gave each thing view *Hen. VIII.* i 1 44
There's order given for her coronation iii 2 46
Accompanied with other Learned and reverend fathers of his order iv 1 26
Season, form, Office and custom, in all line of order *Troi. and Cres.* i 3 88
Achievements, plots, orders, preventions, Excitements to the field i 3 181
Will you the knights . . . Pursue each other, or shall be divided By any voice or order of the field? iv 5 70
As you and Lord Æneas Consent upon the order of their fight, So be it iv 5 90
To order well the state, That like events may ne'er it ruinate *T. Andron.* v 3 203
By my holy order, I thought thy disposition better temper'd *R. and J.* iii 3 114
One of our order, to associate me, Here in this city visiting the sick v 2 6
Will you go see the order of the course? *J. Cæsar* i 2 25
And in the pulpit, as becomes a friend, Speak in the order of his funeral iii 1 230
Cicero is dead, And by that order of proscription iv 3 180
Stand not upon the order of your going, But go at once *Macbeth* iii 4 119
We Shall take upon's what else remains to do, According to our order v 6 6
They have already order This night to play before him *Hamlet* iii 1 20
But that great command o'ersways the order v 1 251
Give order that these bodies High on a stage be placed to the view v 2 388

Order. I have, sir, a son by order of law, some year elder than this *Lear* i 1 19
No, his mouth is stopp'd; Honest Iago hath ta'en order for't *Othello* v 2 72
Order for sea is given . *Ant. and Cleo.* iv 10 6
Dolabella, see High order in this great solemnity . . v 2 369
Reproof, obedient and in order, Fits kings, as they are men . *Pericles* i 2 42
Yours, sir, We have given order to be next our own . . ii 3 111
Ordered. I have with such provision in mine art So safely ordered *Temp.* i 2 29
'Tis vile, unless it may be quaintly order'd . . . *Mer. of Venice* ii 4 6
And thus my battle shall be ordered . *Richard III.* v 3 292
Order'd by the good discretion Of the right reverend Cardinal *Hen. VIII.* i 1 50
Within my tent his bones to-night shall lie, Most like a soldier, order'd honourably . *J. Cæsar* v 5 79
Our countrymen Are men more order'd than when Julius Cæsar Smiled at their lack of skill . *Cymbeline* ii 4 21
And bear his courses to be ordered By Lady Fortune *Pericles* iv 4 47
Ordering. The ordering on't is all Properly ours . *W. Tale* ii 1 169
If thou [Nature] hast The ordering of the mind too . . . . ii 3 106
And, for the ordering your affairs, To sing them too . iv 4 139
Have thou the ordering of this present time . *K. John* v 1 77
Orderless. All form is formless, order orderless . . iii 1 253
Orderly. Why, sir, how do you bear with me?—Marry, sir, the letter, very orderly . *T. G. of Ver.* ii 1 130
Gave such orderly and well-behaved reproof to all uncomeliness *M. Wives* ii 1 59
These things being bought and orderly bestow'd, Return in haste *M. of V.* ii 2 179
You are too blunt: go to it orderly . *T. of Shrew* ii 1 45
Make it orderly and well, According to the fashion and the time iv 3 94
Ask him his name and orderly proceed To swear him . *Richard II.* i 3 9
But, orderly to end where I begun . *Hamlet* iii 2 220
Frame yourself To orderly soliciting . *Cymbeline* ii 3 52
Ordinance. By the compulsion of their ordinance . *K. John* ii 1 218
Honours that pertain By custom and the ordinance of times . *Hen. V.* ii 4 83
Either thou wilt die, by God's just ordinance *Richard III.* iv 4 183
By God's fair ordinance conjoin together! . . v 5 31
When one but of my ordinance stood up To speak of peace or war *Cor.* iii 2 12
Why all these things change from their ordinance Their natures *J. Cæsar* i 3 66
The superfluous and lust-dieted man, That slaves your ordinance *Lear* iv 1 71
Let ordinance Come as the gods foresay it . . . . *Cymbeline* iv 2 145
Ordinant. Why, even in that was heaven ordinant . *Hamlet* v 2 48
Ordinaries. I did think thee, for two ordinaries, to be a pretty wise fellow . *All's Well* ii 3 211
Ordinary. The lunacy is so ordinary . *As Y. Like It* iii 2 423
I see no more in you than in the ordinary Of nature's sale-work . iii 5 42
I have no more wit than a Christian or an ordinary man has *T. Night* i 3 90
I saw him put down the other day with an ordinary fool . i 5 91
Hath melted at a lady's tears, Being an ordinary inundation *K. John* v 2 48
These fits Are with his highness very ordinary . *2 Hen. IV.* iv 4 115
An ordinary groom is for such payment . *Hen. VIII.* iv 2 172
Will make him fly an ordinary pitch, Who else would soar *J. Cæsar* i 1 78
Were I a common laugher, or did use To stale with ordinary oaths my love . i 2 73
These lowly courtesies Might fire the blood of ordinary men . iii 1 37
That which ordinary men are fit for, I am qualified in . *Lear* i 4 36
And for his ordinary pays his heart For what his eyes eat only *A. and C.* ii 2 230
Ordnance. Have I not heard great ordnance in the field? *T. of Shrew* i 2 204
And return your mock In second accent of his ordnance *Hen. V.* ii 4 126
Behold the ordnance on their carriages, With fatal mouths gaping iii Prol. 26
A piece of ordnance 'gainst it I have placed . *1 Hen. VI.* i 4 15
Let all the battlements their ordnance fire . *Hamlet* v 2 281
Ordure. As gardeners do with ordure hide those roots That shall first spring and be most delicate . *Hen. V.* ii 4 39
Ore. To what metal this counterfeit lump of ore will be melted *All's Well* iii 6 40
Like some ore Among a mineral of metals base, Shows itself pure *Hamlet* iv 1 25
Organ. Raise up the organs of her fantasy . *Mer. Wives* v 5 55
Given his deputation all the organs Of our own power . *Meas. for Meas.* i 1 21
Every lovely organ of her life Shall come apparell'd in more precious habit, More moving-delicate . *Much Ado* iv 1 228
Hath not a Jew hands, organs, dimensions, senses, affections? *M. of V.* iii 1 62
Methinks in thee some blessed spirit doth speak His powerful sound within an organ weak . *All's Well* ii 1 179
Thy small pipe Is as the maiden's organ, shrill and sound . *T. Night* i 4 33
When the mind is quicken'd, out of doubt, The organs, though defunct and dead before, Break up their drowsy grave and newly move *Hen. V.* iv 1 21
Doth invert the attest of eyes and ears, As if those organs had deceptious functions, Created only to calumniate *Troi. and Cres.* v 2 123
For murder, though it have no tongue, will speak With most miraculous organ . *Hamlet* ii 2 623
And there is much music, excellent voice, in this little organ . iii 2 385
If you could devise it so That I might be the organ . iv 7 71
Dry up in her the organs of increase! . *Lear* i 4 301
It is just so high as it is, and moves with it own organs . *Ant. and Cleo.* ii 7 49
Organ-pipe. The thunder, That deep and dreadful organ-pipe . *Tempest* iii 3 98
Chants a doleful hymn to his own death, And from the organ-pipe of frailty sings His soul and body to their lasting rest . *K. John* v 7 23
Orgulous. The princes orgulous, their high blood chafed *Troi. and Cres.* Prol. 2
Orient. Like round and orient pearls . *M. N. Dream* iv 1 59
From the orient to the drooping west . . . . *2 Hen. IV.* Ind. 3
The liquid drops of tears that you have shed Shall come again, transform'd to orient pearl *Richard III.* iv 4 322
He kiss'd,—the last of many doubled kisses,—This orient pearl *A. and C.* i 5 41
Orifex. Admits no orifex for a point as subtle As Ariachne's broken woof to enter . *Troi. and Cres.* v 2 151
Origin. In their birth—wherein they are not guilty, Since nature cannot choose his origin . *Hamlet* i 4 26
The origin and commencement of his grief Sprung from neglected love . iii 1 185
I fear your disposition: That nature, which contemns it origin, Cannot be border'd certain in itself . *Lear* iv 2 32
Original. We are their parents and original . *M. N. Dream* ii 1 117
It hath it original from much grief, from study *2 Hen. IV.* i 2 131
Orison. Alas, your too much love and care of me Are heavy orisons 'gainst this poor wretch! . *Hen. V.* ii 2 53
Nay, stay; let's hear the orisons he makes . *3 Hen. VI.* i 4 110
I have need of many orisons To move the heavens to smile *Rom. and Jul.* iv 3 3
Nymph, in thy orisons Be all my sins remember'd . *Hamlet* iii 1 89
Or have charged him, At the sixth hour of morn, at noon, at midnight, To encounter me with orisons . *Cymbeline* i 3 32
Orlando. Your younger brother Orlando hath a disposition to come in disguised against me to try a fall . *As Y. Like It* i 1 131
What is thy name, young man?—Orlando, my liege . i 2 234
O poor Orlando, thou art overthrown! Or Charles or something weaker masters thee . i 2 271
Orlando. Yet I hate not Orlando.—No, faith, hate him not, for my sake *As Y. Like It* i 3 35
Run, run, Orlando; carve on every tree . iii 2 9
Young Orlando, that tripped up the wrestler's heels and your heart . iii 2 224
But what talk we of fathers, when there is such a man as Orlando? iii 4 42
Why, how now, Orlando! where have you been all this while? You a lover! . iv 1 39
Sister, you shall be the priest and marry us. Give me your hand, Orlando . iv 1 125
You must begin, 'Will you, Orlando—' Go to. Will you, Orlando, have to wife this Rosalind? . iv 1 129
I do take thee, Orlando, for my husband: there's a girl goes before the priest . iv 1 139
No, no, Orlando; men are April when they woo, December when they wed iv 1 147
I cannot be out of the sight of Orlando: I'll go find a shadow and sigh iv 1 222
How say you now? Is it not past two o'clock? and here much Orlando! iv 3 2
Orlando doth commend him to you both . iv 3 92
When last the young Orlando parted from you He left a promise to return . iv 3 99
Seeing Orlando, it unlink'd itself, And with indented glides did slip away iv 3 112
Orlando did approach the man And found it was his brother . iv 3 120
But, to Orlando: did he leave him there, Food to the . . lioness? iv 3 126
Dost thou believe, Orlando, that the boy Can do all this? . v 4 1
You say, if I bring in your Rosalind, You will bestow her on Orlando here? . v 4 7
Keep you your word, O duke, to give your daughter; You yours, Orlando, to receive his daughter . v 4 20
Orleans. Therefore the Dukes of Berri and of Bretagne, Of Brabant and of Orleans, shall make forth . *Hen. V.* ii 4 5
My Lord of Orleans, and my lord high constable, you talk of horse and armour? . iii 7 7
Rien puis? l'air et le feu.—Ciel, cousin Orleans . iv 2 6
Rheims, Orleans, Paris, Guysors, Poictiers, are all quite lost *1 Hen. VI.* i 1 60
Charles is crowned king in Rheims; The Bastard of Orleans with him is join'd . i 1 93
Retiring from the siege of Orleans, Having full scarce six thousand i 1 111
Orleans is besieged; The English army is grown weak and faint . i 1 157
At pleasure here we lie near Orleans . i 2 6
What devise you on? Shall we give over Orleans, or no? . i 2 125
Save our honours; Drive them from Orleans and be immortalized . i 2 148
How Orleans is besieged, And how the English have the suburbs won . i 4 1
Now it is supper-time in Orleans . i 4 59
I must go victual Orleans forthwith . i 5 14
Pucelle is enter'd into Orleans, In spite of us . i 5 36
Advance our waving colours on the walls; Rescued is Orleans . i 6 2
Recover'd is the town of Orleans . i 6 9
Upon the which, that every one may read, Shall be engraved the sack of Orleans . ii 2 15
Mark but this for proof, Was not the Duke of Orleans thy foe? . iii 3 69
Orleans the Bastard, Charles, Burgundy, . . . compass him about . iv 4 26
Then leaden age . . . Beat down Alençon, Orleans, Burgundy . iv 6 14
The ireful bastard Orleans, that drew blood From thee, my boy . iv 6 16
The sword of Orleans hath not made me smart . iv 6 42
A marriage 'twixt the Duke of Orleans and Our daughter Mary *Hen. VIII.* ii 4 174
Sir, we have known together in Orleans . *Cymbeline* i 4 36
Ornament. Sweet ornament that decks a thing divine! . *T. G. of Ver.* ii 1 4
The old ornament of his cheek hath already stuffed tennis-balls *M. Ado* iii 2 46
Garnished With such bedecking ornaments of praise . *L. L. Lost* ii 1 79
The world is still deceived with ornament . *Mer. of Venice* iii 2 74
And approve it with a text, Hiding the grossness with fair ornament . iii 2 80
Thus ornament is but the guiled shore To a most dangerous sea . iii 2 97
Come, tailor, let us see these ornaments . *T. of Shrew* iv 3 61
He went Still in this fashion, colour, ornament . *T. Night* iii 4 417
So prove, As ornaments oft do, too dangerous . *W. Tale* i 2 158
And gave the tongue a helpful ornament . *1 Hen. IV.* iii 1 125
This ornament of knighthood . *1 Hen. VI.* iv 1 29
Clothing me in these grave ornaments . v 1 54
And deck my body in gay ornaments, And witch sweet ladies *3 Hen. VI.* iii 2 149
A book of prayer in his hand, True ornaments to know a holy man *Richard III.* iii 7 99
Rich stuffs, and ornaments of household . *Hen. VIII.* iii 2 126
Gracious Lavinia, Rome's rich ornament . *T. Andron.* i 1 52
Those sweet ornaments, Whose circling shadows kings have sought to sleep in . ii 4 18
Ancient citizens Cast by their grave beseeming ornaments *Rom. and Jul.* i 1 100
Conceit, more rich in matter than in words, Brags of his substance, not of ornament . ii 6 31
Thy wit, that ornament to shape and love . iii 3 130
Help me sort such needful ornaments As you think fit to furnish me . iv 2 34
Wouldst thou have that Which thou esteem'st the ornament of life? *Macb.* i 7 42
This ornament Makes me look dismal will I clip to form *Pericles* v 3 73
Orodes. Thy Pacorus, Orodes, Pays this for Marcus Crassus *Ant. and Cleo.* iii 1 4
Orphan. You orphan heirs of fixed destiny *Mer. Wives* v 5 43
On your head Turning the widows' tears, the orphans' cries . *Hen. V.* ii 4 106
To reave the orphan of his patrimony, To wring the widow . *2 Hen. VI.* v 1 187
Many a widow's, And many an orphan's water-standing eye . *3 Hen. VI.* v 6 40
Wives for their husbands, And orphans for their parents' timeless death—Shall rue the hour that ever thou wast born . v 6 42
Why do you look on us, and shake your head, And call us wretches, orphans, castaways, If that our noble father be alive? *Richard III.* ii 2 6
Were never orphans had so dear a loss! . ii 2 78
That his bones, When he has run his course and sleeps in blessings, May have a tomb of orphans' tears wept on 'em! *Hen. VIII.* iii 2 399
Each new morn New widows howl, new orphans cry *Macbeth* iv 3 5
Whose father then, as men report Thou orphans' father art . *Cymbeline* v 4 40
Orpheus' lute was strung with poets' sinews . *T. G. of Ver.* iii 2 78
Therefore the poet Did feign that Orpheus drew trees, stones *Mer. of Ven.* v 1 80
Orpheus with his lute made trees, And the mountain tops that freeze, Bow themselves when he did sing *Hen. VIII.* iii 1 3
Orsino! I have heard my father name him: He was a bachelor then *T. N.* i 2 28
A young gentleman much desires to speak with you.—From the Count Orsino? . i 5 109
We'll once more hear Orsino's embassy . i 5 176
Where lies your text? In Orsino's bosom.—In his bosom! . i 5 241
I am bound to the Count Orsino's court: farewell . ii 1 44
I have many enemies in Orsino's court, Else would I very shortly see thee there . ii 1 46
You're servant to the Count Orsino, youth.—And he is yours . iii 1 111
The young gentleman of the Count Orsino's is returned . iii 4 63
I arrest thee at the suit of Count Orsino.—You do mistake me, sir . iii 4 361

Orsino. Orsino, noble sir, Be pleased that I shake off these names you give me . . . . *T. Night* v 1 75
Antonio never yet was thief or pirate, Though I confess, on base and ground enough, Orsino's enemy . . . . . v 1 79
When in other habits you are seen, Orsino's mistress and his fancy's queen . . . . v 1 397
Ort. It is a fery discretion answer ; save the fall is in the ort 'dissolutely': the ort is, according to our meaning, 'resolutely' . . *Mer. Wives* i 1 262
The fractions of her faith, orts of her love . . *Troi. and Cres.* v 2 158
It is some poor fragment, some slender ort of his remainder *T. of Athens* iv 3 400
One that feeds On abjects, orts, and imitations . . *J. Cæsar* iv 1 37
Orthography. And now is he turned orthography . *Much Ado* ii 3 21
Such rackers of orthography . . . . . *L. L. Lost* v 1 22
Oscorbidulchos volivorco . . . . *All's Well* iv 1 88
Osier. Those thoughts to me were oaks, to thee like osiers bow'd *L. L. L.* iv 2 112
The rank of osiers by the murmuring stream . . *As Y. Like It* iv 3 80
I must up-fill this osier cage of ours With baleful weeds . *Rom. and Jul.* ii 3 7
Osprey. I think he'll be to Rome As is the osprey to the fish, who takes it By sovereignty of nature . . . . *Coriolanus* iv 7 34
Osric. His majesty commended him to you by young Osric *Hamlet* v 2 204
Give them the foils, young Osric. Cousin Hamlet, You know the wager? v 2 270
How is't, Laertes?—Why, as a woodcock to mine own springe, Osric ? v 2 317
Ossa. Till our ground Singeing his pate against the burning zone, Make Ossa like a wart! . . . . v 1 306
Ostent. Use all the observance of civility, Like one well studied in a sad ostent To please his grandam . . *Mer. of Venice* ii 2 205
Employ your chiefest thoughts To courtship and such fair ostents of love ii 8 44
Giving full trophy, signal and ostent Quite from himself to God *Hen. V.* v Prol. 21
And with the ostent of war will look so huge . . *Pericles* i 2 25
Ostentare. Facere, as it were, replication, or rather, ostentare, to show *L. L. Lost* iv 2 16
Ostentation. Maintain a mourning ostentation . . *Much Ado* iv 1 207
With some delightful ostentation, or show, or pageant *L. L. Lost* v 1 118
These summer-flies Have blown me full of maggot ostentation . . v 2 409
March So many miles upon her peaceful bosom, Frighting her pale-faced villages with war And ostentation of despised arms *Richard II.* ii 3 95
Keeping such vile company as thou art hath in reason taken from me all ostentation of sorrow . . . . . . *2 Hen. IV.* ii 2 54
Make good this ostentation, and you shall Divide in all with us *Coriol.* i 6 86
His obscure funeral . . . No noble rite nor formal ostentation *Hamlet* iv 5 215
And have prevented The ostentation of our love, which, left unshown, Is often left unloved . . . . . . *Ant. and Cleo.* iii 6 52
Ostler. Our horse not packed. What, ostler!—Anon, anon . *1 Hen. IV.* ii 1 4
This house is turned upside down since Robin Ostler died . . ii 1 12
Bid the ostler bring my gelding out of the stable . . . ii 1 105
Out, ye rogue! shall I be your ostler? . . . . . ii 2 45
Revolted tapsters and ostlers trade-fallen . . . . . iv 2 31
Calmly, I do beseech you.—Ay, as an ostler, that for the poorest piece Will bear the knave by the volume . . . *Coriolanus* iii 3 32
Ostrich. Make thee eat iron like an ostrich . . *2 Hen. VI.* iv 10 31
Oswald! What, have you writ that letter to my sister? . . *Lear* i 4 356
Otecake. Hugh Otecake, sir, or George Seacole ; for they can write and read . . . . *Much Ado* iii 3 11
Othello. Valiant Othello, we must straight employ you . . . *Othello* i 3 48
But, Othello, speak : Did you by indirect and forced courses Subdue and poison this young maid's affections? . . . . . . i 3 110
Say it, Othello.—Her father loved me ; oft invited me . . . i 3 127
Othello, the fortitude of the place is best known to you . . . i 3 222
I saw Othello's visage in his mind . . . . . . i 3 253
Othello, leave some officer behind, And he shall our commission bring . i 3 281
After some time, to abuse Othello's ear That he is too familiar with his wife . . . . i 3 401
Michael Cassio, Lieutenant to the warlike Moor Othello . . . ii 1 27
To throw out our eyes for brave Othello . . . . . ii 1 38
Great Jove, Othello guard, And swell his sail with thine own powerful breath! . . . . ii 1 77
O my fair warrior!—My dear Othello! . . . . . ii 1 184
It is Othello's pleasure, our noble and valiant general . . . ii 2 1
Heaven bless the isle of Cyprus and our noble general Othello! . . ii 2 13
Cyprus gallants that would fain have a measure to the health of black Othello . . . . ii 3 33
I fear the trust Othello puts him in . . . . . . ii 3 131
Worthy Othello, I am hurt to danger : Your officer, Iago, can inform you ii 3 197
Tell me, Othello : I wonder in my soul, What you would ask me, that I should deny . . . . iii 3 68
My dear Othello! Your dinner, and the generous islanders By you invited, do attend your presence . . . . . . iii 3 279
Farewell! Othello's occupation's gone! . . . . . . iii 3 357
Witness that here Iago doth give up The execution of his wit, hands, heart, To wrong'd Othello's service! . . . . . . iii 3 467
Heaven keep that monster from Othello's mind! . . . . iii 4 163
My lord, I say! Othello! How now, Cassio!—What's the matter? . iv 1 49
Here he comes : As he shall smile, Othello shall go mad . . . iv 1 101
Why, sweet Othello,— Devil!—I have not deserved this . . . iv 1 250
I took you for that cunning whore of Venice That married with Othello iv 2 90
Especial commission come from Venice to depute Cassio in Othello's place . . . . iv 2 225
Is that true? why, then Othello and Desdemona return again to Venice iv 2 227
Removing of him?—Why, by making him uncapable of Othello's place . iv 2 236
This is Othello's ancient, as I take it.—The same indeed ; a very valiant fellow . . . . v 1 51
Who's there? Othello?—Ay Desdemona.—Will you come to bed, my lord? v 2 23
Do you go back dismay'd? 'tis a lost fear ; Man but a rush against Othello's breast, And he retires. Where should Othello go? . . v 2 270
Where is this rash and most unfortunate man?—That's he that was Othello v 2 284
O thou Othello, that wert once so good, Fall'n in the practice of a damned slave, What shall be said to thee? . . . . . v 2 291
Other. Taught thee each hour One thing or other . . . *Tempest* i 2 355
Her reputation, her marriage-vow, and a thousand other her defences *Mer. Wives* ii 2 259
Nay, but it is not so.—It is no other . . . *Meas. for Meas.* iv 3 122
Every letter he hath writ hath disvouched other . . . . iv 4 2
There's other of our friends Will greet us here anon . . . iv 5 12
If she be mad,—as I believe no other . . . . . . v 1 60
The one so like the other As could not be distinguish'd but by names *Com. of Errors* i 1 52
By some device or other The villain is o'er-raught of all my money . i 2 95
The gold bides still, That others touch, and often touching will Wear gold ii 1 111
Some invite me ; Some other give me thanks for kindnesses . . iv 3 5
Both one and other he denies me now . . . . . . iv 3 86
Other. One of these men is Genius to the other . . . *Com. of Errors* v 1 332
Some gentleman or other shall 'scape a predestinate scratched face *M. Ado* i 1 135
Were she other than she is, she were unhandsome ; and being no other but as she is, I do not like her . . . . i 3 176
It were good that Benedick knew of it by some other . . . . ii 3 161
Suggestions are to other as to me . . . . . *L. L. Lost* i 1 159
To put in practice that Which each to other hath so strongly sworn . ii 1 309
Do the wise think them other? . . . . iii 1 81
Some man or other must present Wall . . . *M. N. Dream* iii 1 69
Wink each at other ; hold the sweet jest up . . . . . iii 2 239
That, he awaking when the other do, May all to Athens back again repair . . . . iv 1 71
And other of such vinegar aspect . . . . *Mer. of Venice* i 1 54
And quicken his embraced heaviness With some delight or other . . ii 8 53
Till he hath ta'en thy life by some indirect means or other *As Y. Like It* i 1 159
I am for other than for dancing measures . . . . . v 4 199
I will some other be, some Florentine . . . *T. of Shrew* i 1 209
Can't no other, But, I your daughter, he must be my brother? *All's Well* i 3 171
Hoodwink him so, that he shall suppose no other but that he is carried into the leaguer of the adversaries . . . . . . iii 6 27
The duke knows him for no other but a poor officer of mine . . iv 3 226
I met Lord Bigot and Lord Salisbury, With eyes as red as new-enkindled fire, And others more . . . . . . *K. John* iv 2 164
Nor met with fortune other than at feasts . . . . . v 2 58
Each day still better other's happiness! . . . . *Richard II.* i 1 22
And free from other misbegotten hate . . . . . . i 1 33
This match'd with other did, my gracious lord . . *1 Hen. IV.* i 1 49
And unbound the rest, and then come in the other . . . . ii 4 202
You lie . . . if you say I am any other than an honest man *2 Hen. IV.* i 2 98
Will, on my life, One time or other break some gallows' back . iv 3 32
And how accompanied? canst thou tell that?—With Poins, and other his continual followers . . . . iv 4 53
Art worst of gold : Other, less fine in carat, is more precious . . iv 5 162
We hope no other from your majesty . . . . . . v 2 62
Demanding of King Henry's life and death, And other of your highness' privy-council . . . . *2 Hen. VI.* ii 1 176
It shall be treason for any that calls me other than Lord Mortimer . iv 6 6
Gazed each on other, and look'd deadly pale . . . *Richard III.* iii 7 26
He's noble ; He had a black mouth that said other of him . *Hen. VIII.* i 3 58
And therefore is the glorious planet Sol In noble eminence enthroned and sphered Amidst the other . . . . . *Troi. and Cres.* i 3 91
We may not think the justness of each act Such and no other than event doth form it . . . . ii 2 120
He hopes it is no other But for your health and your digestion sake . ii 3 119
What the declined is He shall as soon read in the eyes of others As feel in his own fall . . . . iii 3 77
I'll lean upon one crutch and fight with t'other, Ere stay behind *Coriol.* i 1 246
Ransoming him, or pitying, threatening the other . . . . . i 6 36
Whose plots have broke their sleep To take the one the other . . iv 4 20
And you'll look pale Before you find it other . . . . . iv 6 102
Or whether nature, Not to be other than one thing . . . . iv 7 42
And men of heart Look'd wondering each at other . . . . v 6 100
Each wreathed in the other's arms . . . . . *T. Andron.* ii 3 25
Make each Prescribe to other as each other's leech . . *T. of Athens* v 4 84
He put it by thrice, every time gentler than other . . . *J. Cæsar* i 2 230
Call Claudius and some other of my men . . . . . . iv 3 242
I'll give thee a wind.—Thou 'rt kind.—And I another.—I myself have all the other . . . . *Macbeth* i 3 14
Who dares receive it other? . . . . i 7 77
Think of this, good peers, But as a thing of custom : 'tis no other . iii 4 97
Thy hair, Thou other gold-bound brow, is like the first . . . iv 1 114
We learn no other but the confident tyrant Keeps still in Dunsinane . v 4 8
I think it be no other but e'en so . . . . . . *Hamlet* i 1 108
So much for this, sir : now shall you see the other . . . . v 2 1
Every hour He flashes into one gross crime or other . . . *Lear* i 3 4
But other of your insolent retinue Do hourly carp and quarrel . . i 4 221
This admiration, sir, is much o' the savour Of other your new pranks . i 4 259
One side will mock another ; the other too . . . . . . ii 7 71
Swords out, and tilting one at other's breast . . . . *Othello* ii 3 183
If you think other, Remove your thought . . . . . . iv 2 13
To preserve this vessel for my lord From any other foul unlawful touch iv 2 84
If 'twere no other,— 'Tis but so, I warrant . . . . . iv 2 168
What is it that they do When they change us for others? Is it sport?. iv 3 98
By this marriage, . . . her love to both Would, each to other and all loves to both, Draw after her . . . . . . *Ant. and Cleo.* ii 2 138
Throw between them all the food thou hast, They'll grind the one the other . . . . iii 5 16
In his Armenia, And other of his conquer'd kingdoms, I Demand the like iii 6 36
Come, Let's have one other gaudy night . . . . . . iii 13 183
Be it known, that we, the greatest, are misthought For things that others do ; and, when we fall, We answer others' merits in our name v 2 178
There is no moe such Cæsars : other of them may have crook'd noses, but to owe such straight arms, none . . . . . . *Cymbeline* iii 1 37
Civility not seen from other, valour That wildly grows in them . . iv 2 179
Are you merry, knights?—Who can be other in this royal presence? *Per.* ii 3 49
Other business. There's other business for thee : Come, thou tortoise! *Tempest* i 2 315
Fetch us in fuel ; and be quick, thou'rt best, To answer other business i 2 367
Other cause. They can be meek that have no other cause *Com. of Errors* ii 1 33
Other day. I bruised my shin th' other day . . . . *Mer. Wives* i 1 294
I'll tell thee how Beatrice praised thy wit the other day . . *Much Ado* v 1 161
And writ to me this other day to turn him out o' the band . *All's Well* iv 3 226
I saw him put down the other day with an ordinary fool . . *T. Night* i 5 91
You denied to fight with me this other day . . . . *W. Tale* v 2 140
An old lord of the council rated me the other day in the street *1 Hen. IV.* i 2 95
And said this other day you ought him a thousand pound . . . iii 3 152
I was before Master Tisick, the debuty, t'other day . . *2 Hen. IV.* ii 4 92
She vaunted 'mongst her minions t'other day . . . *2 Hen. VI.* i 3 87
When I did correct him for his fault the other day . . . . i 3 202
Helen herself swore th' other day . . . . . *Troi. and Cres.* i 2 100
You gave Good words the other day of a bay courser I rode on *T. of Athens* i 2 217
This honourable lord did but try us this other day . . . . iii 6 3
When your lordship this other day sent to me, I was so unfortunate . iii 6 47
I saw him yesterday, or t'other day, Or then, or then . . . *Hamlet* ii 1 56
I am thinking, brother, of a prediction I read this other day . . . *Lear* i 2 153
I was the other day talking on the sea-bank with certain Venetians *Othello* iv 1 137
Other gambol faculties a' has, that show a weak mind . . *2 Hen. IV.* ii 4 272
Other graces. These are portable, With other graces weigh'd. . *Macbeth* iv 3 90
Other house. By what? by any other house or person? . . . *Tempest* i 2 42

Other means. Compell'd by hunger And lack of other means . *Hen. VIII.* i 2 35
Let us return, And strain what other means is left unto us *T. of Athens* v 1 230
Say thou'lt do't, Or thrive by other means . . *Lear* v 3 34
Other men, of slender reputation, Put forth their sons . *T. G. of Ver.* i 3 6
Other more. And her withholds from me and other more . *T. of Shrew* i 2 121
Other mouth. I will pour some in thy other mouth.—Stephano !—Doth thy other mouth call me? . . . . *Tempest* ii 2 98
Other night. The other night I fell asleep here . . 1 *Hen. IV.* iii 3 112
Other part. The other part reserved I by consent . *Richard II.* i 1 128
Other princesses. More profit Than other princesses . *Tempest* i 2 173
Other self. My other self, my counsel's consistory ! *Richard III.* ii 2 151
Other shelter. There is no other shelter hereabout . . *Tempest* ii 2 40
Other side. As much As on the other side it takes from you 1 *Hen. IV.* iii 1 111
On one and other side, Trojan and Greek . . *Troi. and Cres.* Prol. 21
Other some. Some say he is with the Emperor of Russia ; other some, he is in Rome . . . . *Meas. for Meas.* iii 2 94
How happy some o'er other some can be ! . *M. N. Dream* i 1 226
Other two. If th' other two be brained like us, the state totters *Tempest* iii 2 7
Othergates. If he had not been in drink, he would have tickled you othergates than he did . . . *T. Night.* v 1 198
Otherwhere. How if your husband start some other where? *Com. of Errors* ii 1 30
I know his eye doth homage otherwhere . . . ii 1 104
The king has sent me otherwhere . . . *Hen. VIII.* ii 2 60
This is not Romeo, he's some other where . *Rom. and Jul.* i 1 204
Otherwhiles the famish'd English, like pale ghosts, Faintly besiege us one hour in a month . . . 1 *Hen. VI.* i 2 7
Otherwise. You were kneel'd to and importuned otherwise . *Tempest* ii 1 128
I never knew him otherwise.—Than how?—A notable lubber *T. G. of Ver.* ii 5 45
I have sat in the stocks for puddings he hath stolen, otherwise he had been executed . . . . . . iv 4 34
I have stood on the pillory for geese he hath killed, otherwise he had suffered for't . . . . . . iv 4 36
If I find her honest, I lose not my labour ; if she be otherwise, 'tis labour well bestowed . . . . *Mer. Wives* ii 1 247
Three of Master Ford's brothers watch the door with pistols, that none shall issue out ; otherwise you might slip away . . iv 2 54
There is no woman's gown big enough for him ; otherwise he might put on a hat, a muffler and a kerchief, and so escape . . iv 2 72
God forbid it should be otherwise . . . *Much Ado* ii 1 222
An it be the right husband and the right wife ; otherwise 'tis light . iii 4 37
Seem'd I ever otherwise to you? . . . . iv 1 56
My presence May well abate the over-merry spleen Which otherwise would grow into extremes . . . . *T. of Shrew* Ind. 1 138
My maiden's name Sear'd otherwise . . . *All's Well* ii 1 176
Otherwise a seducer flourishes, and a poor maid is undone . v 3 146
You'll find it otherwise, I assure you . . *T. Night* iii 4 251
Prove She's otherwise, I'll keep my stables where I lodge my wife *W. Tale* ii 1 134
But yet my inward soul Persuades me it is otherwise . *Richard II.* ii 2 29
Thou art a beast to say otherwise . . 1 *Hen. IV.* iii 3 140
I would it were otherwise ; I would my means were greater . 2 *Hen. IV.* i 2 161
You stand in coldest expectation : I am the sorrier ; would 'twere otherwise . . . . v 2 32
Look you, if you take the matter otherwise than is meant . *Hen. V.* iii 2 136
You shall find the ceremonies of the wars, . . . the sobriety of it, and the modesty of it, to be otherwise . . . . iv 1 75
You find it otherwise ; and henceforth let a Welsh correction teach you v 1 82
Otherwise I renounce all confidence . . . 1 *Hen. VI.* i 2 97
We do no otherwise than we are will'd . . . . i 3 10
And otherwise will Henry ne'er presume . . . . v 5 22
Otherwise He knew his man . . . *Troi. and Cres.* ii 1 140
Would it were otherwise ; that I could beat him, whilst he railed at me ii 3 4
To report otherwise, were a malice . . *Coriolanus* ii 2 36
It may be I shall otherwise bethink me . . *J. Cæsar* iv 3 251
Hath there been such a time—I'd fain know that—That I have positively said ''Tis so,' When it proved otherwise? . *Hamlet* ii 2 155
Take this from this, if this be otherwise . . . ii 2 156
If it be so, Laertes—As how should it be so? how otherwise? . iv 7 59
I do beguile The thing I am, by seeming otherwise . *Othello* ii 1 124
You not making it appear otherwise . . . *Cymbeline* i 4 174
Or who was he That, otherwise than noble nature did, Hath alter'd that good picture? . . . . . . iv 2 364
Yet hope . . . doth tune us otherwise . . *Pericles* i 1 115
He that otherwise accounts of me, This sword shall prove he's honour's enemy . . . . ii 5 63
Otter. What beast ! why, an otter.—An otter, Sir John ! why an otter ?—Why, she's neither fish nor flesh . . 1 *Hen. IV.* iii 3 142
Ottoman. Valiant Othello, we must straight employ you Against the general enemy Ottoman . . . . *Othello* i 3 49
Ottomites. The Ottomites, reverend and gracious, Steering with due course towards the isle of Rhodes . . . . i 3 33
And do undertake These present wars against the Ottomites . i 3 235
To ourselves do that Which heaven hath forbid the Ottomites . ii 3 171
Oublie. Od's me ! Qu'ai-j'oublie ! dere is some simples in my closet *Mer. Wives* i 4 65
Ma foi, j'oublie les doigts ; mais je me souviendrai . *Hen. V* iii 4 9
O Seigneur Dieu, je m'en oublie ! de elbow . . . iii 4 33
N'avez vous pas déjà oublié ce que je vous ai enseigné? . . iii 4 45
Ouches. Your brooches, pearls, and ouches . . 2 *Hen. IV.* ii 4 53
Ought. It is spoke as a Christians ought to speak . *Mer. Wives* i 1 103
That I am sure of ; and void of all profanation in the world that good Christians ought to have . . *Meas. for Meas.* ii 1 56
He ought to enter into a quarrel with fear and trembling . *Much Ado* ii 3 202
For, indeed, the watch ought to offend no man . . . iii 3 87
You ought to consider with yourselves . . *M. N. Dream* iii 1 30
We ought to look to't . . . . . . iii 1 34
Doublet and hose ought to show itself courageous to petticoat *As Y. L. It* ii 4 7
An your ladyship will have it as it ought to be . *T. Night* v 1 303
Let them have That mercy which true prayer ought to have *Richard II.* v 3 110
And said this other day you ought him a thousand pound 1 *Hen. IV.* iii 3 152
You do not use me with that affability as in discretion you ought *Hen. V.* iii 2 139
Put him to execution ; for discipline ought to be used . . iii 6 58
Or whether that such cowards ought to wear This ornament 1 *Hen. VI.* iv 1 28
As every loyal subject ought to do . . . 3 *Hen. VI.* iv 7 44
As well the fear of harm, as harm apparent, In my opinion, ought to be prevented . . . . . *Richard III.* ii 2 131
We ought not to deny him . . . . *Coriolanus* ii 3 2
Say, then : 'tis true, I ought so . . . . ii 3 62
Being mechanical, you ought not walk Upon a labouring day *J. Cæsar* i 1 3
Which, by the right and virtue of my place, I ought to know of . i 3 270
Speak what we feel, not what we ought to say . . *Lear* v 3 324
Oughtest. Thou oughtest not to let thy horse wear a cloak 2 *Hen. VI.* iv 7 54
Ounce. My sweet ounce of man's flesh ! my incony Jew ! . . *L. L. Lost* iii 1 136
Be it ounce, or cat, or bear, Pard, or boar with bristled hair *M. N. Dream* ii 2 30
I must have an ounce or two of this malapert blood from you *T. Night* iv 1 47
Your blood had been the dearer by I know how much an ounce *W. Tale* iv 4 725
Weigh you the worth and honour of a king So great as our dread father in a scale Of common ounces? . . *Troi. and Cres.* ii 2 28
The blood he hath lost—Which, I dare vouch, is more than that he hath, By many an ounce . . . . *Coriolanus* iii 1 301
Give me an ounce of civet, good apothecary, to sweeten my imagination *Lear* iv 6 132
Ouphe. Like urchins, ouphes and fairies . . *Mer. Wives* iv 4 49
Strew good luck, ouphes, on every sacred room . . v 5 61
Our. Moe reasons . . . At our more leisure shall I render *Meas. for Meas.* i 3 49
Our old and faithful friend, we are glad to see you . . v 1 2
Why should their liberty than ours be more . *Com. of Errors* ii 1 10
Tongue-tied our queen? speak you . . . *W. Tale* i 2 27
This toil of ours should be a work of thine . . *K. John* ii 1 93
The better part of ours [horses] are full of rest.—The number of the king exceedeth ours . . . . 1 *Hen. IV.* iv 3 27
Ah, poor our sex ! this fault in us I find . . *Troi. and Cres.* v 2 109
So much strength in us As will revenge these bitter woes of ours *T. An.* iii 2 3
Queen of us, of ours, and our fair France . . *Lear* i 1 260
Our own selves. As we walk, To our own selves bend we our needful talk *Troi. and Cres.* iv 4 141
Ourself. In our remove be thou at full ourself *Meas. for Meas.* i 1 44
We cannot weigh our brother with ourself . . . ii 2 126
Learning is but an adjunct to ourself . . *L. L. Lost* iv 3 314
We charge you, on allegiance to ourself . . 1 *Hen. VI.* iii 1 86
Ourself, my lord protector, and the rest After some respite will return . iv 1 169
Do or undo, as if ourself were here . . . . 2 *Hen. VI.* iii 1 196
As ourself, Shall do and undo as him pleaseth best . 3 *Hen. VI.* ii 6 104
What touches us ourself shall be last served . . *J. Cæsar* iii 1 8
We will keep ourself Till supper-time alone . . *Macbeth* iii 1 43
Be as ourself in Denmark . . . . . *Hamlet* i 2 122
Ourselves. Fall to't, yarely, or we run ourselves aground *Tempest* i 1 4
And all of us [found] ourselves When no man was his own . v 1 212
Which, with ourselves, all rest at thy dispose . *T. G. of Ver.* iv 1 76
The truth being known, We'll all present ourselves . *Mer. Wives* iv 4 63
Which sorrow is always toward ourselves, not heaven . *Meas. for Meas.* ii 3 32
Were we burden'd with like weight of pain, As much or more we should ourselves complain . . . . *Com. of Errors* ii 1 37
Then when ourselves we see in ladies' eyes, Do we not likewise see our learning there? . . . . . *L. L. Lost* iv 3 316
And better 'twere that both of us did fast, Since, of ourselves, ourselves are choleric . . . . . *T. of Shrew* iv 1 177
Ourselves we do not owe ; What is decreed must be . *T. Night* i 5 329
We'll have this song out anon by ourselves . . *W. Tale* iv 4 315
Defy each other, and pell-mell Make work upon ourselves . *K. John* ii 1 407
Ourselves will hear The accuser and the accused freely speak. *Richard II.* i 1 16
We do debase ourselves, cousin, do we not, To look so poorly? . iii 3 127
In them and in ourselves our safety lies . . 3 *Hen. VI.* iv 1 46
We two, that with so many thousand sighs Did buy each other, must poorly sell ourselves . . . . *Troi. and Cres.* iv 4 42
To-morrow We'll hear, ourselves, again . . . *Macbeth* iii 4 32
We fat all creatures else to fat us, and we fat ourselves for maggots *Ham.* iv 3 24
We are not ourselves When nature, being oppress'd, commands the mind To suffer with the body . . . . *Lear* ii 4 108
Virtue ! a fig ! 'tis in ourselves that we are thus or thus . . *Othello* i 3 322
There is left us Ourselves to end ourselves . . *Ant. and Cleo.* iv 14 22
Leave us to ourselves ; and make yourself some comfort. . *Cymbeline* i 1 155
Ousel. The ousel cock so black of hue, With orange-tawny bill *M. N. D.* iii 1 128
Alas, a black ousel, cousin Shallow ! . . 2 *Hen. IV.* iii 2 9
Out. Then thou wast not Out three years old . . *Tempest* i 2 41
My liberty.—Before the time be out? no more ! . . . i 2 246
It is a sleepy language and thou speak'st Out of thy sleep . . ii 1 212
When the butt is out, we will drink water . . . . iii 2 1
And be a boy right out . . . . iv 1 101
Will never out of my bones . . . . . . v 1 283
Keep tune there still, so you will sing it out . . *T. G. of Ver.* i 2 89
Put forth their sons to seek preferment out . . . . i 3 7
That's monstrous : O, that that were out ! . . . . iii 1 375
They are out by lease . . . . v 2 29
Out, alas ! here comes my master . . . *Mer. Wives* i 4 37
About, about ; Search Windsor Castle, elves, within and out . . v 5 60
Till candles and starlight and moonshine be out . . . v 5 106
This will last out a night in Russia . . *Meas. for Meas.* ii 1 139
But how out of this can she avail? . . . . . iii 1 243
So turns she every man the wrong side out . . *Much Ado* iii 1 68
She would laugh me Out of myself . . . . . iii 1 76
When the age is in, the wit is out . . . . . iii 5 37
Well, sit you out : go home, Biron . . . *L. L. Lost* i 1 110
I hear your grace hath sworn out house-keeping . . . ii 1 104
I will never buy and sell out of this word . . . . iii 1 143
I' faith, your hand is out . . . . iv 1 135
An if my hand be out, then belike your hand is in . . . iv 1 137
I make no doubt The rest will ne'er come in, if he be out . . v 2 152
Out— True, out indeed.—Out of your favours . . . . v 2 164
They do not mark me, and that brings me out . . . . v 2 172
Out, dog ! out, cur ! . . . . . *M. N. Dream* iii 2 65
Out, tawny Tartar, out ! Out, loathed medicine ! hated potion, hence !. iii 2 263
At the length truth will out . . . . *Mer. of Venice* ii 2 85
You need not fear us, Lorenzo : Launcelot and I are out . . . iii 5 40
I cannot live out of her company . . . *As Y. Like It* i 3 88
Out of all reasonable match . . . . . . iii 2 87
Very good orators, when they are out, they will spit . . . iv 1 76
Who could be out, being before his beloved mistress? . . . iv 1 82
Make the doors upon a woman's wit and it will out at the casement . iv 1 163
Abuses every one's eyes because his own are out . . . iv 1 219
I cannot be out of the sight of Orlando . . . . . iv 1 221
That thinks with oaths to face the matter out . . *T. of Shrew* iv 1 291
Out, you rogue ! you pluck my foot awry . . . . . iv 1 150
On the catastrophe and heel of pastime, When it was out *All's Well* i 2 58
Made himself much sport out of him. . . . . . iv 5 68
That question's out of my part . . . . *T. Night* i 5 191
If I cannot recover your niece, I am a foul way out . . . ii 3 201
Hast smutch'd thy nose? They say it is a copy out of mine . *W. Tale* i 2 122
These petty brands That calumny doth use—O, I am out—That mercy does . . . . ii 1 72
Mace ; dates?—none, that's out of my note . . . . iv 3 49

Out. I fear, sir, my shoulder-blade is out . . . *W. Tale* iv 3 77
We 'll have this song out anon by ourselves . . . iv 4 315
Out of my dear love I 'll give thee more . . . *K. John* ii 1 157
Dreading the curse that money may buy out . . . iii 1 164
Out of your grace, devise, ordain, impose Some gentle order . . iii 1 250
Lest resolution drop Out at mine eyes in tender womanish tears . iv 1 36
My eyes are out Even with the fierce looks of these bloody men . iv 1 73
Out of my sight, and never see me more ! . . . iv 2 242
Now my soul hath elbow-room ; It would not out at windows nor at doors . . . v 7 29
The pride of kingly sway from out my heart . . *Richard II.* iv 1 206
Out of my grief and my impatience, Answer'd neglectingly . 1 *Hen. IV.* i 3 51
Play out the play . . . ii 4 531
Their date is out . . . ii 4 553
You are as a candle, the better part burnt out . . 2 *Hen. IV.* i 2 178
A' will not out ; he is true bred . . . v 3 71
And plainly say Our mettle is bred out . . *Hen. V.* iii 5 29
His nose is executed, and his fire 's out . . . iii 6 112
We 'll fight it out . . . 1 *Hen. VI.* i 2 128
Out, tawny coats ! out, scarlet hypocrite ! . . . i 3 56
Why ring not out the bells aloud throughout the town ? . . i 6 11
I would see his heart out, ere the priest Should ever get that privilege . iii 1 120
Your private grudge, my Lord of York, will out . . . iv 1 109
A warning bell, Sings heavy music to thy timorous soul ; And mine shall ring thy dire departure out . . . iv 2 41
Out, some light horsemen, and peruse their wings . . . iv 2 43
Rancour will out : proud prelate, in thy face I see thy fury . 2 *Hen. VI.* i 1 142
His eye-balls further out than when he lived . . . iii 2 169
With this, we charged again : but, out, alas ! We bodged again 3 *Hen. VI.* i 4 18
Out of my sight ! thou dost infect my eyes . . *Richard III.* i 2 149
Are you call'd forth from out a world of men To slay the innocent ? . i 4 186
I must away ; For this will out, and here I must not stay . . i 4 290
The limit of your lives is out . . . iii 3 8
And his own letter, The honourable board of council out, Must fetch him in he papers . . . *Hen. VIII.* i 1 79
And never seek for aid out of himself . . . i 2 114
If thy rare qualities . . . could speak thee out, The queen of earthly queens . . . ii 4 140
When did he regard The stamp of nobleness in any person Out of himself ? iii 2 13
O, fear him not ; His spell in that is out . . . iii 2 20
This candle burns not clear : 'tis I must snuff it ; Then out it goes . iii 2 97
I yet remember Some of these articles ; and out they shall . . iii 2 304
Would I were fairly out on't ! . . . v 3 109
There were wit in this head, an 'twould out . . *Troi. and Cres.* iii 3 256
Your eyes, half out, weep out at Pandar's fall . . . v 10 49
Your wit will not so soon out as another man's will . *Coriolanus* ii 3 30
Go, see him out at gates, and follow him . . . iii 3 138
Thou hast beat me out Twelve several times . . . iv 5 127
It is spoke freely out of many mouths . . . iv 6 64
You have pushed out your gates the very defender of them . . v 2 41
But, out, affection ! All bond and privilege of nature, break ! . . v 3 24
Like a dull actor now, I have forgot my part, and I am out . . v 3 41
Not in a grave, To lay one in, another out to have . . *Rom. and Jul.* ii 3 84
I am sorry, when he sent to borrow of me, that my provision was out *T. of Athens* iii 6 18
The gods confound . . . The Athenians both within and out that wall ! iv 1 38
Nay, stay thou out for earnest . . . iv 3 47
Be not out with me : yet, if you be out, sir, I can mend you *J. Cæsar* i 1 18
'Tis but the time And drawing days out, that men stand upon . . iii 1 100
We must out and talk . . . v 1 22
Their candles are all out . . . *Macbeth* ii 1 5
The time has been, That, when the brains were out, the man would die iii 4 79
There ran a rumour Of many worthy fellows that were out . . iv 3 183
Out, damned spot ! out, I say !—One : two : why, then 'tis time to do't v 1 39
Out, out, brief candle ! Life's but a walking shadow, a poor player . v 5 23
And now a wood Comes toward Dunsinane. Arm, arm, and out ! . . v 5 46
Out of the shot and danger of desire . . . *Hamlet* i 3 35
Lord Hamlet is a prince, out of thy star . . . ii 2 141
Let in the maid, that out a maid Never departed more . . iv 5 54
When these are gone, The woman will be out . . . iv 7 190
She should have been buried out o' Christian burial . . . v 1 28
And do but blow them to their trial, the bubbles are out . . v 2 202
He hath been out nine years, and away he shall again . . *Lear* i 1 33
So, out went the candle, and we were left darkling . . . i 4 237
I am now from home, and out of that provision Which shall be needful ii 4 208
It was great ignorance, Gloucester's eyes being out, To let him live . iv 5 9
My snuff and loathed part of nature should Burn itself out . . iv 6 40
Who loses and who wins ; who 's in, who 's out . . . v 3 15
Come hither, herald,—Let the trumpet sound,—And read out this . v 3 108
Whom love hath turn'd almost the wrong side out . . *Othello* ii 3 54
Now he denies it faintly, and laughs it out . . . iv 1 113
She gives it out that you shall marry her . . . iv 1 118
Out of my sight !—I will not stay to offend you . . . iv 1 258
I have wasted myself out of my means . . . iv 2 188
Out, and alas ! that was my lady's voice . . . v 2 119
'Twill out : I peace ! No, I will speak as liberal as the north . v 2 219
I am not so well as I should be, but I 'll ne'er out . . *Ant. and Cleo.* ii 7 36
Our hour Is fully out . . . iv 9 33
Our lamp is spent, it 's out ! . . . iv 15 85
What your own love will out of this advise you, follow . . *Cymbeline* iii 2 45
Out of your proof you speak . . . iii 3 27
I speak not out of weak surmises . . . iii 4 23
Out, sword, and to a sore purpose ! . . . iv 1 24
A tempest, which his mortal vessel tears, And yet he rides it out . *Per.* iv 4 31
Out at elbow. He 's out at elbow . . . *Meas. for Meas.* ii 1 61
Out at heels. I am almost out at heels . . *Mer. Wives* i 3 34
A good man's fortune may grow out at heels . . . *Lear* ii 2 164
Out of all cess. Wrung in the withers out of all cess . 1 *Hen. IV.* ii 1 8
Out of all count. One is painted and the other out of all count.—How painted ? and how out of count ? . . . *T. G. of Ver.* ii 1 62
Out of all nick. He loved her out of all nick . . . iv 2 76
Out of all suspicion, she is virtuous . . . *Much Ado* ii 3 166
Out of anger. More is to be said and to be done Than out of anger can be uttered . . . 1 *Hen. IV.* i 1 107
Out of anger He sent command to the lord mayor straight *Hen. VIII.* ii 1 150
Out of beef. These English are shrewdly out of beef . . *Hen. V.* iii 7 163
Out of breath. Now you run this humour out of breath . *Com. of Errors* iv 1 57
O, I am out of breath in this fond chase ! . . . *M. N. Dream* ii 2 88
Our very pastime, tired out of breath . . . *T. Night* ii 4 152
I am out of breath ; Confusion's near . . . *Coriolanus* iii 1 189

Out of breath. Do you not see that I am out of breath ?—How art thou out of breath, when thou hast breath To say to me that thou art out of breath ? . . . *Rom. and Jul.* ii 5 31
Our fortune on the sea is out of breath, And sinks . *Ant. and Cleo.* iii 10 25
Out of circumstance. His approach, So out of circumstance and sudden . . . *W. Tale* v 1 90
Or breed itself so out of circumstance . . . *Othello* iii 3 16
Out of doors. I 'll turn my mercy out o' doors . . *Tempest* iii 2 78
Why should their [men's] liberty than ours be more ?—Because their business still lies out o' door . . . *Com. of Errors* ii 1 11
Driven out of doors with it when I go from home ; welcomed home with it iv 4 37
Until the goose came out of door, Staying the odds . . *L. L. Lost* iii 1 98
Well, push him out of doors . . . *As Y. Like It* iii 1 15
Yet would you say ye were beaten out of door . . *T. of Shrew* Ind. 2 87
And bid him turn you out of doors . . . *T. Night* ii 3 78
Hence with her, out o' door . . . *W. Tale* ii 3 67
How now, foolish rheum ! Turning dispiteous torture out of door ! *K. John* iv 1 34
Have you turned him out o' doors ?—Yea, sir. The rascal's drunk 2 *Hen. IV.* ii 4 229
I will not out of doors.—Not out of doors !—She shall, she shall *Coriol.* i 3 78
Turn thy solemness out o' door, and go along with us . . i 3 120
What 's he that now is going out of door ? . . *Rom. and Jul.* i 5 132
I come to have thee thrust me out of doors . . *T. of Athens* i 2 25
Mark how the blood of Cæsar follow'd it, As rushing out of doors, to be resolved If Brutus so unkindly knock'd, or no *J. Cæsar* iii 2 183
He seem'd to find his way without his eyes ; For out o' doors he went without their helps . . . *Hamlet* ii 1 99
Holy-water in a dry house is better than this rain-water out o' door *Lear* iii 2 11
You are pictures out of doors, Bells in your parlours . . *Othello* ii 1 110
All of her that is out of door most rich ! . . . *Cymbeline* i 6 15
Out of doubt. He will print them, out of doubt . . *Mer. Wives* ii 1 79
Out of doubt Antipholus is mad . . . *Com. of Errors* iv 3 82
He cannot be heard of. Out of doubt he is transported *M. N. Dream* iv 2 3
Misfortune to my ventures, out of doubt Would make me sad *Mer. of Ven.* i 1 21
Out of doubt you do me now more wrong In making question . . i 1 155
When the mind is quicken'd, out of doubt, The organs, though defunct and dead before, Break up their drowsy grave . . *Hen. V.* iv 1 20
His fears, out of doubt, be of the same relish as ours are . . iv 1 114
Yes, certainly, and out of doubt and out of question too, and ambiguities v 1 47
Out of fashion. Wears her cap out of fashion . . . *All's Well* i 1 170
To have done is to hang Quite out of fashion . . *Troi. and Cres.* iii 3 152
I prattle out of fashion, and I dote In mine own comforts . . *Othello* ii 1 208
Poor I am stale, a garment out of fashion . . . *Cymbeline* iii 4 53
Out of fear. This will put them out of fear . . *M. N. Dream* iii 1 23
Talk not of dying : I am out of fear Of death . . 1 *Hen. IV.* iv 1 135
You speak it out of fear and cold heart . . . iv 3 7
Out of friends. I am out o' friends . . . *All's Well* i 3 42
Out of hand. Were these inward wars once out of hand . 2 *Hen. IV.* iii 1 107
Gather we our forces out of hand And set upon our boasting enemy 1 *Hen. VI.* iii 2 102
We will proclaim you out of hand ; The bruit thereof will bring you many friends . . . 3 *Hen. VI.* iv 7 63
I 'll find some cunning practice out of hand . . . *T. Andron.* v 2 77
Out of health. He 's much out of health, and keeps his chamber.—Many do keep their chambers are not sick . . *T. of Athens* iii 4 72
Out of hearing. What, out of hearing ? gone ? . . . *M. N. Dream* ii 2 152
Out of heart you love her, being out of heart that you cannot enjoy her *L. L. Lost* iii 1 45
I 'll repent, and that suddenly . . . ; I shall be out of heart shortly, and then I shall have no strength to repent . . 1 *Hen. IV.* iii 3 6
Out of his (my) (their) (your) **wits.** Out o' your wits and hearing too ? *Tempest* iii 2 86
Here 's a fellow frights English out of his wits . . *Mer. Wives* ii 1 143
I will stare him out of his wits ; I will awe him with my cudgel . ii 2 291
Fright the ladies out of their wits . . . *M. N. Dream* i 2 82
And do all they can to face me out of my wits . . . *T. Night* iv 2 101
Out of hope. I am right glad that he 's so out of hope . . *Tempest* iii 3 11
Therefore be out of hope, of question, of doubt ; Be certain *M. N. Dream* iii 2 279
Such as give Their money out of hope they may believe . *Hen. VIII.* Prol. 8
Not out of hope—Mistake me not—to save my life . . *Coriolanus* iv 5 85
Out of love. To make my master out of love with thee . *T. G. of Ver.* iv 4 210
I am so out of love with life that I will sue to be rid of it *Meas. for Meas.* iii 1 174
Out of malice To the good queen . . . *Hen. VIII.* ii 1 157
More out of malice than integrity, Would try him to the utmost . . v 3 145
Out of mind. Time out of mind *Meas. for Meas.* iv 2 17 ; *Rom. and Jul.* i 4 69
Out of nothing. Nothing can be made out of nothing . . *Lear* i 4 146
Out of office. But long I will not be Jack out of office . 1 *Hen. VI.* i 1 175
Would I were gently put out of office Before I were forced out ! *T. of A.* i 2 207
Out of patience. I 'm out of patience . . . *Tempest* i 1 58
I 'll watch him tame and talk him out of patience . . *Othello* iii 3 23
That time,—O times !—I laugh'd him out of patience ; and that night I laugh'd him into patience . . . *Ant. and Cleo.* ii 5 19
Out of pity, taken A load would sink a navy . . . *Hen. VIII.* iii 2 382
Out of question, you were born in a merry hour . . *Much Ado* ii 1 346
A double-dealer ; which, out of question, thou wilt be . . . v 4 117
Out of question so it is sometimes . . . *L. L. Lost* iv 1 30
Therefore be out of hope, of question, of doubt ; Be certain *M. N. Dream* iii 2 279
Out of question 'tis Maria's hand . . . *T. Night* v 1 355
Yes, certainly, and out of doubt and out of question too . . *Hen. V.* v 1 47
Out of season. These jests are out of season . . *Com. of Errors* ii 2 68
Was there ever any man thus beaten out of season ? . . . ii 2 48
Thus out of season, threading dark-eyed night . . . *Lear* ii 1 121
Out of service. Very rogues, now they be out of service . *Mer. Wives* ii 1 182
Turning these jests out of service, let us talk in good earnest *As Y. L. It* i 3 26
In my time wore three-pile ; but now I am out of service . . *W. Tale* iv 3 14
They will pluck The gay new coats o'er the French soldiers' heads And turn them out of service . . . *Hen. V.* iv 3 119
Out of thinking. Indeed I cannot think, if I would think my heart out of thinking . . . *Much Ado* iii 4 85
Out of town. What good sport is out of town to-day ! . *Troi. and Cres.* i 1 116
Out of tune on the strings . . . *T. G. of Ver.* iv 2 60
Out o' tune, sir : ye lie. Art any more than a steward ? . *T. Night* ii 3 122
It is the lark that sings so out of tune . . . *Rom. and Jul.* iii 5 27
Now see that noble and most sovereign reason, Like sweet bells jangled, out of tune and harsh . . . *Hamlet* iii 1 166
And scald rhymers Ballad us out o' tune . . . *Ant. and Cleo.* v 2 216
I cannot sing : I 'll weep, and word it with thee ; For notes of sorrow out of tune are worse Than priests and fanes that lie . *Cymbeline* iv 2 241
Out of use. The deed of saying is quite out of use . . *T. of Athens* v 1 28

Out of warrant. Arts inhibited and out of warrant . . *Othello* i 2 79
Out on. I know not thy mistress; out on thy mistress! *Com. of Errors* ii 1 68
Out on thee, villain! wherefore dost thou mad me? . . iv 4 129
And seem'd I ever otherwise to you?—Out on thee! Seeming! *M. Ado* iv 1 57
Out on thee, rude man! thou dost shame thy mother . *K. John* i 1 64
Out on you, owls! nothing but songs of death? . . *Richard III.* iv 4 509
Out on thee, murderer! thou kill'st my heart . . *T. Andron.* iii 2 54
We have a curse in having her: Out on her, hilding! *Rom. and Jul.* iii 5 169
Out upon. Out upon't! what have I forgot? . . *Mer. Wives* i 4 179
Out upon you! how am I mistook in you! . . . iii 3 110
Out upon thee, hind!—Here's too much 'out upon thee!' *Com. of Errors* iii 1 77
Out upon it, old carrion! rebels it at these years? . *Mer. of Venice* iii 1 38
You did bring me out.—Out upon thee, knave! . *All's Well* v 2 51
Out upon this half-faced fellowship! . . . 1 *Hen. IV.* i 3 208
Out upon ye! Heaven is above all yet . . *Hen. VIII.* iii 1 99
Out upon you! what a man are you! . . . *Rom. and Jul.* ii 4 120
Out with. Out with't, and place it for her chief virtue *T. G. of Ver.* iii 1 339
'Out with the dog!' says one: 'What cur is that?' says another iv 4 22
Keep it not; you cannot choose but lose by't: out with't *All's Well* i 1 159
If it be so, out with it boldly . . . . . *Richard II.* ii 1 233
Out with it boldly: truth loves open dealing . *Hen. VIII.* iii 1 39
Out with your knives, And cut your trusters' throats! . *T. of Athens* iv 1 9
Outbid. There is a good angel about him; but the devil outbids him too
2 *Hen. IV.* ii 4 363
Outbrave the heart most daring on the earth . . *Mer. of Venice* ii 1 28
Outbreak. The flash and outbreak of a fiery mind . *Hamlet* ii 1 33
Outbreathed. Wearied and outbreathed . . . 2 *Hen. IV.* i 1 108
Outcast. As Ovid be an outcast quite abjured . . *T. of Shrew* i 1 33
O blood-bespotted Neapolitan, Outcast of Naples! . . 2 *Hen. VI.* v 1 118
Out-craftied. That drug-damn'd Italy hath out-craftied him *Cymbeline* iii 4 15
Outcry. The villain Jew with outcries raised the duke *Mer. of Venice* ii 8 4
And all run, With open outcry . . . . *Rom. and Jul.* v 3 193
Outdare. And boldly did outdare The dangers of the time 1 *Hen. IV.* v 1 40
O noble fellow! Who sensibly outdares his senseless sword. *Coriolanus* i 4 53
Out-dared. With pale beggar-fear impeach my height Before this out-dared dastard . . . . *Richard II.* i 1 190
Outdone. He hath in this action outdone his former deeds doubly *Coriol.* ii 1 150
Out-dwell. It is marvel he out-dwells his hour . *Mer. of Venice* ii 6 3
Outface. We'll outface them, and outswear them too . . iv 2 17
That do outface it with their semblances . . *As Y. Like It* i 3 124
Threaten the threatener and outface the brow Of bragging horror *K. John* v 1 49
See if thou canst outface me with thy looks . 2 *Hen. VI.* iv 10 49
Dost thou come here to whine? To outface me with leaping in her grave? . . . . *Hamlet* v 1 301
And with presented nakedness out-face The winds . . *Lear* ii 3 11
Out-faced. We have given thee faces.—But you have out-faced them all
L. L. Lost v 2 626
Cut off the sequence of posterity, Out-faced infant state *K. John* ii 1 97
Was this the face that faced so many follies, And was at last out-faced by Bolingbroke? . . . . *Richard II.* iv 1 286
And, with a word, out-faced you from your prize . 1 *Hen. IV.* ii 4 283
Outfacing. And with no face, as 'twere, outfacing me . *Com. of Errors* v 1 244
Scambling, out-facing, fashion-monging boys . . *Much Ado* v 1 94
Outfly. His evasion, wing'd thus swift with scorn, Cannot outfly our apprehensions . . . . . . *Troi. and Cres.* ii 3 124
Out-frown. Myself could else out-frown false fortune's frown *Lear* v 3 6
Outgo. He would outgo His father by as much as a performance Does an irresolute purpose . . . . . *Hen. VIII.* i 2 207
He outgoes The very heart of kindness . . . *T. of Athens* i 1 285
The time shall not Out-go my thinking on you *Ant. and Cleo.* iii 2 61
Outgrown. My brother hath outgrown me far . *Richard III.* iii 1 104
Out-herod. It out-herods Herod: pray you, avoid it . *Hamlet* iii 2 15
Out-jest. Who labours to out-jest His heart-struck injuries . *Lear* iii 1 16
Outlaw. A poor unminded outlaw sneaking home . 1 *Hen. IV.* iv 3 58
As an outlaw in a castle keeps . . . 1 *Hen. VI.* iii 1 47
We are held as outlaws . . . . . *Cymbeline* iv 2 67
That such as we Cave here, hunt here, are outlaws . . iv 2 138
Outlawed. I had a son, Now outlaw'd from my blood . *Lear* iii 4 172
Outlawry. By proscription and bills of outlawry . *J. Cæsar* iv 3 173
Outlive. To let the wretched man outlive his wealth *Mer. of Venice* iv 1 269
If he outlive the envy of this day . . 1 *Hen. IV.* v 2 67
Strange that desire should so many years outlive performance 2 *Hen. IV.* ii 4 284
He let him outlive that day to see His greatness *Hen. V.* iv 1 194
He that outlives this day, and comes safe home, Will stand a tip-toe . iv 3 41
The duke yet lives that Henry shall depose; But him outlive 2 *Hen. VI.* i 4 34
Outlive thy glory, like my wretched self! . . *Richard III.* i 3 203
Fell with him, Unwilling to outlive the good that did it *Hen. VIII.* ii 2 60
Outlive thy father's days, And fame's eternal date! *T. Andron.* i 1 167
When ye have the honey ye desire, Let not this wasp outlive, us both to sting . . . . ii 3 132
Willing misery Outlives incertain pomp, is crown'd before *T. of Athens* iv 3 243
I think it is not meet, Mark Antony, so well beloved of Cæsar, Should outlive Cæsar . . . . *J. Cæsar* ii 1 157
There's hope a great man's memory may outlive his life half a year *Ham.* iii 2 141
The gallows-maker; for that frame outlives a thousand tenants . v 1 50
But why should honour outlive honesty? Let it go all . *Othello* v 2 245
The gods preserve you!—And you, sir, to outlive the age I am *Pericles* v 1 15
Outlived. These moss'd trees, That have outlived the eagle *T. of Athens* iv 3 224
Outliving beauty's outward, with a mind That doth renew *Troi. and Cres.* iii 2 169
Outlook. To outlook conquest and to win renown . *K. John* v 2 115
Outlustre. As that diamond of yours outlustres many I have beheld *Cymb.* i 4 79
Out-night. I would out-night you, did no body come *Mer. of Venice* v 1 23
Out-paramoured. In woman out-paramoured the Turk . *Lear* iii 4 94
Out-peer. Could not out-peer these twain . . *Cymbeline* iii 6 87
Out-pray. Our prayers do out-pray his . . *Richard II.* v 3 109
Outprized. Either your unparagoned mistress is dead, or she's outprized by a trifle . . . . *Cymbeline* i 4 88
Outrage. Provided that you do no outrages On silly women *T. G. of Ver.* iv 1 71
I have much to do To keep them from uncivil outrages . . v 4 17
Sprung from the rancorous outrage of your duke To merchants *C. of Er.* i 1 6
Hast thou delight to see a wretched man Do outrage and displeasure to himself?—He is my prisoner . . . . iv 4 119
My daughter is sometime afeard she will do a desperate outrage to herself . . . . *Much Ado* ii 3 159
I fear some outrage, and I'll follow her . . *K. John* iii 4 106
Thieves and robbers range abroad unseen In murders and in outrage
Richard II. iii 2 40
Are you not ashamed With this immodest clamorous outrage To trouble and disturb the king and us? . . . . 1 *Hen. VI.* iv 1 126
And he shall pardon thee these outrages . . . 3 *Hen. VI.* v 1 24
Outrage. My charity is outrage, life my shame . *Richard III.* i 3 277
O, preposterous And frantic outrage, end thy damned spleen! . ii 4 64
Peace, ho! no outrage: peace! . . . . *Coriolanus* v 6 125
His feigned ecstasies Shall be no shelter to these outrages *T. Andron.* iv 4 22
And have a thousand times more cause than he To do this outrage . v 3 52
Gentlemen, for shame, forbear this outrage! *Rom. and Jul.* iii 1 90
Seal up the mouth of outrage for a while, Till we can clear these ambiguities . . . . v 3 216
In that beastly fury He has been known to commit outrages *T. of Athens* iii 5 72
'Tis worse than murder, To do upon respect such violent outrage *Lear* ii 4 24
Outrageous. A most outrageous fit of madness took him *Com. of Errors* v 1 139
I never heard a passion so confused, So strange, outrageous *M. of Venice* ii 8 13
In writing I preferr'd The manner of thy vile outrageous crimes 1 *Hen. VI.* iii 1 11
Moved with remorse of these outrageous broils . . . v 4 97
When thy poor heart beats with outrageous beating . *T. Andron.* iii 2 13
Whether 'tis nobler in the mind to suffer The slings and arrows of outrageous fortune . . . . *Hamlet* iii 1 58
Outran. He, swift of foot, Outran my purpose . . *Othello* ii 3 233
Outright. 'Tis ten to one it maim'd you two outright . *T. of Shrew* v 2 62
Prince Harry slain outright; and both the Blunts Kill'd 2 *Hen. IV.* i 1 16
This kills thy father's heart outright! . . 1 *Hen. VI.* iv 4 2
Then must I chide outright . . . . 2 *Hen. VI.* i 2 41
Outroar. O, that I were Upon the hill of Basan, to outroar The horned herd! for I have savage cause . . . *Ant. and Cleo.* iii 13 127
Out-rode. Being better horsed, Out-rode me . . 2 *Hen. IV.* i 1 36
Outrun. Being nimble-footed, he hath outrun us . *T. G. of Ver.* v 3 7
I heard say he was outrun on Cotsall . . . *Mer. Wives* i 1 92
In a retreat he outruns any lackey . . . *All's Well* iv 3 323
Have defeated the law and outrun native punishment *Hen. V.* iv 1 176
You are slow: for shame, away!—Can we outrun the heavens? 2 *Hen. VI.* v 2 73
It will outrun you, father, in the end . . 3 *Hen. VI.* i 2 14
We may outrun, By violent swiftness, that which we run at *Hen. VIII.* i 1 141
The expedition of my violent love Outrun the pauser, reason *Macbeth* ii 3 117
Outrunnest. E'en so thou outrunnest grace . . *T. of Athens* ii 2 93
Outscold. We grant thou canst outscold us . . . *K. John* v 2 160
Out-scorn. Strives in his little world of man to out-scorn The to-and-fro-conflicting wind and rain . . . . *Lear* iii 1 10
Outsell. Her pretty action did outsell her gift . . . *Cymbeline* ii 4 102
And she, of all compounded, Outsells them all . . . iii 5 74
Out-shining. Whose bright out-shining beams thy cloudy wrath Hath in eternal darkness folded up . . . . . *Richard III.* i 3 268
Outside. O, what a goodly outside falsehood hath! . *Mer. of Venice* i 3 103
Many a man his life hath sold But my outside to behold . ii 7 68
We'll have a swashing and a martial outside, As many other mannish cowards have That do outface it . . . . *As Y. Like It* i 3 122
Fortune forbid my outside have not charm'd her! . *T. Night* ii 2 19
Yet for the outside of thy poverty we must make an exchange *W. Tale* iv 4 646
Show the inside of your purse to the outside of his hand, and no more ado iv 4 834
You look but on the outside of this work.—Outside or inside, I will not return Till my attempt so much be glorified . . . *K. John* v 2 110
His vanities forespent Were but the outside of the Roman Brutus *Hen. V.* ii 4 37
Therefore was I created with a stubborn outside, with an aspect of iron v 2 244
Since dishonour traffics with man's nature, He is but outside *T. of Athens* i 1 159
And make his wrongs His outsides, to wear them like his raiment, carelessly . . . . iii 5 33
Since thy outside looks so fair and warlike . . *Lear* v 3 142
For by his rusty outside he appears To have practised more the whip-stock than the lance . . . . *Pericles* ii 2 50
Out-sleep. I fear we shall out-sleep the coming morn *M. N. Dream* v 1 372
Out-speak. That it out-speaks Possession of a subject *Hen. VIII.* iii 2 127
Outsport. Let's teach ourselves that honourable stop, Not to outsport discretion . . . . *Othello* ii 3 3
Outstare. I would outstare the sternest eyes that look *Mer. of Venice* ii 1 27
I'll follow and outstare him . . . . *Hen. VIII.* i 1 129
Now he'll outstare the lightning . . . *Ant. and Cleo.* iii 13 195
Outstay. If you outstay the time . . . *As Y. Like It* i 3 90
Outstood. I have outstood my time . . . *Cymbeline* i 6 207
Outstretched. With an outstretch'd throat I'll tell the world aloud What man thou art . . . . . . *Meas. for Meas.* ii 4 153
That raught at mountains with outstretched arms . 3 *Hen. VI.* i 4 68
With his arms outstretch'd, as he would fly, Grasps in the comer *T. and C.* iii 3 167
Timon is dead, who hath outstretch'd his span . *T. of Athens* v 3 3
Our monarchs and outstretched heroes . . . *Hamlet* ii 2 270
Outstrike. This blows my heart: If swift thought break it not, a swifter mean Shall outstrike thought . . . *Ant. and Cleo.* iv 6 36
Outstrip. She will outstrip all praise And make it halt behind *Tempest* iv 1 10
Though they can outstrip men, they have no wings to fly from God *Hen. V.* iv 1 177
If thou wilt outstrip death, go cross the seas . *Richard III.* iv 1 42
Outswear. Methinks I should outswear Cupid . . *L. L. Lost* i 2 67
We'll outface them, and outswear them too . *Mer. of Venice* iv 2 17
Out-sweetened. The leaf of eglantine, whom not to slander, Out-sweeten'd not thy breath . . . . *Cymbeline* iv 2 224
Outswell. Blow, villain, till thy sphered bias cheek Outswell the colic of puff'd Aquilon . . . . *Troi. and Cres.* iv 5 9
Out-talk. What! this gentleman will out-talk us all . *T. of Shrew* i 2 248
Out-tongue. My services which I have done the signiory Shall out-tongue his complaints . . . . *Othello* i 2 19
Outvenom. Slander, Whose edge is sharper than the sword, whose tongue Outvenoms all the worms of Nile . . . . *Cymbeline* iii 4 37
Out-vied. Gremio is out-vied . . . . . *T. of Shrew* ii 1 387
Out-villained. He hath out-villained villany so far, that the rarity redeems him . . . . *All's Well* iv 3 305
Out-voice. Whose shouts and claps out-voice the deep-mouth'd sea
Hen. V. v Prol. 11
Out-wall. For confirmation that I am much more Than my out-wall *Lear* iii 1 45
Outward. Executing the outward face of royalty . . *Tempest* i 2 104
Save that we do the denunciation lack Of outward order *Meas. for Meas.* i 2 153
O, what may man within him hide, Though angel on the outward side! . . . . iii 2 286
Outward courtesies would fain proclaim Favours that keep within . v 1 15
They have a good cover; they show well outward . . *Much Ado* i 2 8
Whom she hath in all outward behaviours seemed ever to abhor . ii 3 100
He is a very proper man.—He hath indeed a good outward happiness . ii 3 190
What a Hero hadst thou been, If half thy outward graces had been placed About thy thoughts and counsels of thy heart! . . . iv 1 102
Go anticly, show outward hideousness . . . . v 1 96
When, for fame's sake, for praise, an outward part, We bend to that the working of the heart . . . . *L. L. Lost* iv 1 32
Like the martlet, Builds in the weather on the outward wall *Mer. of Ven.* ii 9 29
So may the outward shows be least themselves . . . iii 2 73

Outward. No vice so simple but assumes Some mark of virtue on his outward parts . . . . *Mer. of Venice* iii 2 82
Like a common and an outward man . . . . . . *All's Well* iii 1 11
Thou hast a mind that suits With this thy fair and outward character *T. N.* i 2 51
How quickly the wrong side may be turned outward! . . . . iii 1 14
Not alone in habit and device, Exterior form, outward accoutrement, But from the inward motion . . . . . *K. John* i 1 211
This all-changing word, Clapp'd on the outward eye of fickle France ii 1 583
Death, having prey'd upon the outward parts, Leaves them invisible . v 7 15
Some of you with Pilate wash your hands, Showing an outward pity *Richard II.* iv 1 240
My thoughts are minutes; and with sighs they jar Their watches on unto mine eyes, the outward watch . . . . v 5 52
To immask our noted outward garments . . . *1 Hen. IV.* i 2 202
They are our outward consciences, And preachers to us all . *Hen. V.* iv 1 8
He may show what outward courage he will . . . . . . iv 1 118
It yearns me not if men my garments wear; Such outward things dwell not in my desires . . . . iv 3 27
As you did mistake The outward composition of his body . *1 Hen. VI.* ii 3 75
Your interior hatred, Which in your outward actions shows itself *Richard III.* i 3 66
Princes have but their titles for their glories, An outward honour for an inward toil . . . . i 4 79
So that betwixt their titles and low names, There's nothing differs but the outward fame . . . . i 4 83
Nor more can you distinguish of a man Than of his outward show . iii 1 10
Outliving beauty's outward, with a mind That doth renew *Troi. and Cres.* iii 2 169
If these shows be not outward, which of you But is four Volsces? *Coriol.* i 6 77
As for my country I have shed my blood, Not fearing outward force . iii 1 77
I know that virtue to be in you, Brutus, As well as I do know your outward favour . . . . *J. Cæsar* i 2 91
Hang out our banners on the outward walls . . . . *Macbeth* v 5 1
Since brevity is the soul of wit, And tediousness the limbs and outward flourishes, I will be brief . . . . *Hamlet* ii 2 91
My extent to the players, which, I tell you, must show fairly outward ii 2 392
Only got the tune of the time and outward habit of encounter . v 2 198
He that helps him take all my outward worth . . . . *Lear* iv 4 10
My outward action doth demonstrate The native act and figure of my heart In compliment extern . . . . *Othello* i 1 61
Things outward Do draw the inward quality after them *Ant. and Cleo.* iii 13 32
All Is outward sorrow; though I think the king Be touch'd . *Cymbeline* i 1 9
I do not think So fair an outward and such stuff within Endows a man but he . . . . i 1 23
He had need mean better than his outward show Can any way speak *Per.* ii 2 48
Opinion's but a fool, that makes us scan The outward habit by the inward man . . . . ii 2 57
Neither in our hearts nor outward eyes Envy the great nor do the low despise . . . . ii 3 25
Outwardly. If you can bring . . . Heat outwardly or breath within *W. T.* iii 2 207
I will be patient; outwardly I will . . . . *Troi. and Cres.* v 2 68
Are ye fantastical, or that indeed Which outwardly ye show? *Macbeth* i 3 54
This will witness outwardly, As strongly as the conscience does within *Cymbeline* ii 2 35
Outward-sainted. This outward-sainted deputy . *Meas. for Meas.* iii 1 89
Outwear. Till painful study shall outwear three years . *L. L. Lost* i 1 23
Come, come, away! The sun is high, and we outwear the day *Hen. V.* iv 2 63
Outweigh. Which if we find outweighs ability, What do we then but draw anew the model In fewer offices? . . . *2 Hen. IV.* i 3 45
If any think brave death outweighs bad life . . . *Coriolanus* i 6 71
Outwent her, Motion and breath left out . . . . *Cymbeline* ii 4 84
Outwork. Where we see The fancy outwork nature . . *Ant. and Cleo.* ii 2 206
Outworth. A beggar's book Outworths a noble's blood . . *Hen. VIII.* i 1 123
Oven. The making of the cake, the heating of the oven . *Troi. and Cres.* i 1 24
Sorrow concealed, like an oven stopp'd, Doth burn the heart to cinders where it is . . . . *T. Andron.* ii 4 36
Crickets sing at the oven's mouth, E'er the blither for their drouth *Pericles* iii Gower 7
Over. Which to do Trebles thee o'er . . . . . *Tempest* ii 1 221
But one fiend at a time, I'll fight their legions o'er . . . . iii 3 103
When, after execution, judgement hath Repented o'er his doom *Meas. for Meas.* ii 2 12
So high a style, Margaret, that no man living shall come over it *M. Ado* v 2 7
To have no man come over me! why, shall I always keep below stairs? v 2 9
When they strive to be Lords o'er their lords . . . *L. L. Lost* iv 1 38
I came o'er his heart . . . . v 2 278
How happy some o'er other some can be! . . . . *M. N. Dream* i 1 226
I have heard it over, And it is nothing, nothing in the world . . . v 1 77
You shall have gold To pay the petty debt twenty times over *M. of Ven.* iii 2 309
If that will not suffice, I will be bound to pay it ten times o'er . iv 1 211
Swear his thought over By each particular star in heaven *W. Tale* i 2 424
That you may—For I do fear eyes over—to shipboard Get undescried . iv 4 668
I put you o'er to heaven and to my mother . . . *K. John* i 1 62
And dost thou now fall over to my foes? . . . . . . iii 1 127
I do at this hour joy o'er myself . . . . . *Hen. V.* ii 2 163
You have shot over.—'Tis not the first time you were overshot . iii 7 133
Something over to remember me by . . . . *Hen. VIII.* iv 2 151
How if he had boils? full, all over, generally? . . . *Troi. and Cres.* ii 1 3
I'll not over the threshold . . . . *Coriolanus* i 3 82
Give me your hands all over, one by one . . . . *J. Cæsar* ii 1 112
Being barber'd ten times o'er . . . . . . *Ant. and Cleo.* ii 2 229
And shall make your lord, That which he is, new o'er . . *Cymbeline* i 6 165
Over and above that you have suffered . . . . *Mer. Wives* v 5 177
Stand indebted, over and above, In love and service to you *Mer. of Ven.* iv 1 413
Over and beside Signior Baptista's liberality, I'll mend it . *T. of Shrew* i 2 149
Over and over. Fold it over and over . . . . *T. G. of Ver.* i 1 115
I ha' told them over and over; they lack no direction . *Mer. Wives* iii 3 18
They were never so truly turned over and over as my poor self in love *Much Ado* v 2 35
And, at our stamp, here o'er and o'er one falls . . *M. N. Dream* iii 2 25
And my sweet friend, To strew him o'er and o'er . . *W. Tale* iv 4 129
O'er and o'er divides him 'Twixt his unkindness and his kindness . . iv 4 562
I'll kill thee every where, yea, o'er and o'er . . *Troi. and Cres.* iv 5 256
Over and over he comes, and up again; catched it again . *Coriolanus* i 3 68
Over-awe. None do you like but an effeminate prince, Whom, like a school-boy, you may over-awe . . . . *1 Hen. VI.* i 1 36
Overbear. I will overbear your will . . . . . *M. N. Dream* iv 1 184
When oil and fire, too strong for reason's force, O'erbears it . *All's Well* v 3 8
It pleased your highness To overbear it . . . . . *K. John* iv 2 37
Freshly looks and over-bears attaint With cheerful semblance *Hen. V.* iv Prol. 39
To o'erbear such As are of better person than myself . *3 Hen. VI.* iii 2 166
Overbear. Whose rage doth rend Like interrupted waters and o'erbear What they are used to bear . . . . *Coriolanus* iii 1 249
Pouring war Into the bowels of ungrateful Rome, Like a bold flood o'er-bear . . . . iv 5 137
My desire All continent impediments would o'erbear . *Macbeth* iv 3 64
Young Laertes, in a riotous head, O'erbears your officers . *Hamlet* iv 5 102
Lest this great sea of joys rushing upon me O'erbear the shores of my mortality, And drown me with their sweetness . . . *Pericles* v 1 195
O'erbearing interruption, spite of France . . . . *K. John* iii 4 9
My particular grief Is of so flood-gate and o'erbearing nature . . *Othello* i 3 56
Overblow. Whiles yet the cool and temperate wind of grace O'erblows the filthy and contagious clouds . . . . . . *Hen. V.* iii 3 31
Overblown. Is the storm overblown? . . . . . . *Tempest* ii 2 114
To smile at scapes and perils overblown . . . . *T. of Shrew* v 2 3
This ague fit of fear is over-blown . . . . . *Richard II.* iii 2 190
My choler being over-blown With walking once about the quadrangle *2 Hen. VI.* i 3 155
Domestic broils Clean over-blown . . . . . . *Richard III.* ii 4 61
Overboard. A butt of sack which the sailors heaved o'erboard *Tempest* ii 2 127
Now, blasphemy, That swear'st grace o'erboard, not an oath on shore? v 1 219
What though the mast be now blown overboard? . . . *3 Hen. VI.* v 4 3
Overboard, Into the tumbling billows of the main . *Richard III.* i 4 19
Your queen must overboard: the sea works high, the wind is loud *Per.* iii 1 47
That these pirates, Not enough barbarous, had not o'erboard thrown me! . . . . iv 2 70
I threw her overboard with these very arms . . . . . . v 3 19
Overbold. Beldams as you are, Saucy and overbold . . . *Macbeth* iii 5 3
Over-boldly. If over-boldly we have borne ourselves . . *L. L. Lost* v 2 744
Over boots. You are over boots in love . . . . *T. G. of Ver.* i 1 25
Overborne. The ecstasy hath so much overborne her . . *Much Ado* ii 3 157
Which falling in the land Have every pelting river made so proud That they have overborne their continents . . . . *M. N. Dream* ii 1 92
Weak shoulders, overborne with burthening grief . . *1 Hen. VI.* ii 5 10
See the bishop be not overborne . . . . iii 1 53
Neither in birth or for authority, The bishop will be overborne by thee v 1 60
Have already O'erborne their way, consumed with fire . *Coriolanus* iv 6 78
Was ever seen An emperor in Rome thus overborne, Troubled? *T. Andron.* iv 4 2
Some dying; some their friends O'er-borne i' the former wave *Cymbeline* v 3 48
Overbulk. Breed a nursery of like evil, To overbulk us all *Troi. and Cres.* i 3 320
Overbuys me Almost the sum he pays . . . . . . *Cymbeline* i 1 146
Overcame. He came, saw, and overcame: he came, one; saw, two; overcame, three . . . : what saw he? the beggar: who overcame he? the beggar . . . . *L. L. Lost* iv 1 70
Cæsar's thrasonical brag of 'I came, saw, and overcame' *As Y. Like It* v 2 35
That I may justly say, with the hook-nosed fellow of Rome, 'I came, saw, and overcame' . . . . *2 Hen. IV.* iv 3 46
What! wherein Talbot overcame? is't so? . . . . *1 Hen. VI.* i 1 107
In thirteen battles Salisbury o'ercame . . . . i 4 78
That day he overcame the Nervii . . . . . . *J. Cæsar* iii 2 177
Brutus only overcame himself, And no man else hath honour by his death . . . . v 5 56
That day that our last king Hamlet overcame Fortinbras . *Hamlet* v 1 156
A kind of conquest Cæsar made here; but made not here his brag Of 'Came' and 'saw' and 'overcame' . . . . . *Cymbeline* iii 1 24
Over-canopied with luscious woodbine . . . . *M. N. Dream* ii 1 251
Over-careful. For this the foolish over-careful fathers Have broke their sleep with thoughts . . . . *2 Hen. IV.* iv 5 68
Overcast. Hie therefore, Robin, overcast the night . *M. N. Dream* iii 2 355
The sun's o'ercast with blood . . . . *K. John* iii 1 326
But yet, you see, how soon the day o'ercast . . *Richard III.* iii 2 88
Overcharged. If the ground be overcharged, you were best stick her.—Nay: in that you are astray . . . . *T. G. of Ver.* i 1 107
I love not to see wretchedness o'ercharged . . . *M. N. Dream* v 1 85
Her heart is but o'ercharged; she will recover . . . *W. Tale* iii 2 151
Like an overcharged gun, recoil . . . . . . *2 Hen. VI.* iii 2 331
Whispers to his pillow as to him The secrets of his overcharged soul . iii 2 376
Be blind with tears, and break o'ercharged with grief . *3 Hen. VI.* ii 5 78
They were As cannons overcharged with double cracks . *Macbeth* i 2 37
If the sea's stomach be o'ercharged with gold . . . *Pericles* iii 2 54
O'ercharging your free purses with large fines . . *1 Hen. VI.* i 3 64
Over-cloyed. Base lackey peasants, Whom their o'er-cloyed country vomits forth To desperate ventures . . . . . *Richard III.* v 3 318
Overcome. Who came? the king: why did he come? to see: why did he see? to overcome . . . . *L. L. Lost* iv 1 73
Why would you be so fond to overcome The bonny priser? *As Y. Like It* ii 3 7
O God, that right should thus overcome might! . . . *2 Hen. IV.* iv 4 27
O God, have I overcome mine enemy in this presence? . . *2 Hen. VI.* ii 3 100
In dreadful war mayst thou be overcome! . . . . *3 Hen. VI.* i 1 187
Insolent, O'ercome with pride, ambitious past all thinking *Coriolanus* iv 6 31
O'ercome with moss and baleful mistletoe . . . *T. Andron.* ii 3 95
If there were no foes, that were enough To overcome him *T. of Athens* iii 5 71
Can such things be, And overcome us like a summer's cloud, Without our special wonder? . . . . *Macbeth* iii 4 111
Old Norway, overcome with joy, Gives him three thousand crowns *Ham.* ii 2 72
She purposed . . . to O'ercome you with her show . . . *Cymbeline* v 5 54
Make a conquest of unhappy me, Whereas no glory's got to overcome *Per.* i 4 70
Over-cool. For thin drink doth so over-cool their blood . *2 Hen. IV.* iv 3 98
Over-count. At land, thou know'st How much we do o'er-count thee.—At land, indeed, Thou dost o'er-count me of my father's house *Ant. and Cleo.* ii 6 26
O'er-cover'd quite with dead men's rattling bones . . *Rom. and Jul.* iv 1 82
Over-credulous. Sought to win me Into his power, and modest wisdom plucks me From over-credulous haste . . . . . *Macbeth* iv 3 120
Over-crow. The potent poison quite o'er-crows my spirit . *Hamlet* v 2 364
Over-daring Talbot Hath sullied all his gloss of former honour *1 Hen. VI.* iv 4 5
Overdoing. I would have such a fellow whipped for o'erdoing Termagant; it out-herods Herod . . . . *Hamlet* iii 2 15
Overdone. By Mistress Overdone's means . . . . *Meas. for Meas.* ii 1 85
Mistress Overdone.—Hath she had any more than one husband?—Nine, sir; Overdone by the last . . . . ii 1 209
One would think it were Mistress Overdone's own house . . . iv 3 3
Any thing so overdone is from the purpose of playing . . *Hamlet* iii 2 22
Now this overdone, or come tardy off, though it make the unskilful laugh, cannot but make the judicious grieve . . . . . . iii 2 28
Over-dusted. And give to dust that is a little gilt More laud than gilt o'er-dusted . . . . *Troi. and Cres.* iii 3 179
Over-dyed. Were they false As o'er-dyed blacks . . . *W. Tale* i 2 132
Over-earnest. Henceforth, When you are over-earnest with your Brutus, He'll think your mother chides . . . . *J. Cæsar* iv 3 122
Over ears. Though I be o'er ears for my labour . . . . *Tempest* iv 1 214

Over-eaten. Greasy relics Of her o'er-eaten faith *Troi. and Cres.* v 2 160
Over-eye. Here sit I in the sky, And wretched fools' secrets heedfully o'er-eye *L. L. Lost* iv 3 80
Over-eyeing. Lest over-eyeing of his odd behaviour *T. of Shrew* Ind. 1 95
Overfar. Though I could not with such estimable wonder overfar believe that, yet thus far I will boldly publish her *T. Night* ii 1 29
Over-fed. Snores, . . . Made louder by the o'er-fed breast *Pericles* iii Gower 3
Overflourished. The beauteous evil Are empty trunks o'erflourish'd by the devil *T. Night* iii 4 404
Overflow. A kind overflow of kindness *Much Ado* i 1 26
Such Brooks are welcome to me, that o'erflow such liquor *Mer. Wives* ii 2 157
Make the coming hour o'erflow with joy *All's Well* ii 4 47
He that in this action contrives against his own nobility, in his proper stream o'erflows himself iv 3 30
Thy overflow of good converts to bad *Richard II.* v 3 64
When heaven doth weep, doth not the earth o'erflow? *T. Andron.* iii 1 222
Nay, but this dotage of our general's O'erflows the measure *Ant. and Cleo.* i 1 2
Our griefs are risen to the top, And now at length they overflow *Pericles* ii 4 24
Overflowed. Then must my earth with her continual tears Become a deluge, overflow'd and drown'd *T. Andron.* iii 1 230
Therefore the earth, fearing to be o'erflow'd, Hath Thetis' birth-child on the heavens bestow'd *Pericles* iv 4 40
Overflowing. As the o'erflowing Nilus presageth famine *Ant. and Cleo.* i 2 49
Overflown. Loath to have you overflown with a honey-bag *M. N. Dream* iv 1 17
Over-fond of the shepherd's daughter *W. Tale* v 2 126
Over-fraught. The grief that does not speak Whispers the o'er-fraught heart and bids it break *Macbeth* iv 3 210
Over-full. Being over-full of self-affairs, My mind did lose it *M. N. Dream* i 1 113
Overgalled. Their eyes o'ergalled with recourse of tears *Troi. and Cres.* v 3 55
Overglance. I will overglance the superscript *L. L. Lost* iv 2 135
Overglanced. But with a cursorary eye O'erglanced the articles *Hen. V.* v 2 78
Overgo. What cause have I, Thine being but a moiety of my grief, To overgo thy plaints and drown thy cries! *Richard III.* ii 2 61
Overgone. Many weary miles you have o'ergone *L. L. Lost* v 2 196
Sad-hearted men, much overgone with care *3 Hen. VI.* ii 5 123
Overgorged With gobbets of thy mother's bleeding heart *2 Hen. VI.* iv 1 84
Over-great. The o'er-great cardinal Hath show'd him gold *Hen. VIII.* i 1 222
Over-greedy. Their over-greedy love hath surfeited *2 Hen. IV.* i 3 88
Overgrow. They'll o'ergrow the garden And choke the herbs *2 Hen. VI.* iii 1 32
Overgrown. Even like an o'ergrown lion in a cave *Meas. for Meas.* i 3 22
A wretched ragged man, o'ergrown with hair *As Y. Like It* iv 3 107
Like prisoners wildly overgrown with hair *Hen. V.* v 2 43
Yourself So out of thought, and thereto so o'ergrown *Cymbeline* iv 4 33
Overgrowth. By the o'ergrowth of some complexion *Hamlet* i 4 27
Overhang. As fearfully as doth a galled rock O'erhang and jutty his confounded base *Hen. V.* iii 1 13
Overhanging. This brave o'erhanging firmament *Hamlet* ii 2 312
Over-happy. Happy, in that we are not over-happy ii 2 232
Overhasty. His father's death, and our o'erhasty marriage ii 2 57
Overhead. The street should see as she walk'd overhead *L. L. Lost* iv 3 281
Over head and ears. Knee-deep, o'er head and ears *W. Tale* i 2 186
Overhear. And overheard what you shall overhear *L. L. Lost* v 2 95
I will overhear their conference *M. N. Dream* ii 1 187
Some more audience than a mother, Since nature makes them partial, should o'erhear The speech, of vantage *Hamlet* iii 3 32
Overheard. Son, I have overheard what hath passed *Meas. for Meas.* iii 1 161
Were thus much overheard by a man of mine *Much Ado* i 2 11
Who in the night overheard me confessing to this man v 1 241
I should blush, I know, To be o'erheard and taken napping so *L. L. Lost* iv 3 130
And overheard what you shall overhear v 2 95
She secretly o'erheard Your daughter and her cousin *As Y. Like It* ii 2 11
I overheard him and his practices ii 3 26
If they have overheard me now, why, hanging *W. Tale* iv 4 639
Myself hath often over-heard them say *T. Andron.* iv 4 74
I have o'erheard a plot of death upon him *Lear* ii 1 96
Overheardest. Say that thou overheard'st us *Much Ado* iii 1 6
Thou overheard'st, ere I was ware, My true love's passion *Rom. and Jul.* ii 2 103
Overhold. If he overhold his price so much, We'll none of him *T. and C.* ii 3 142
Over-joy. Such as my wit affords And over-joy of heart *2 Hen. VI.* i 1 31
Overjoyed with finding a bird's nest *Much Ado* ii 1 230
Bid him shed tears, as being overjoy'd *T. of Shrew* Ind. 1 120
All o'erjoy'd, Save these in bonds: let them be joyful too *Cymbeline* v 5 401
Look to the lady; O, she's but o'erjoy'd *Pericles* v 3 21
Over-kind. Sicilia cannot show himself over-kind to Bohemia *W. Tale* i 1 23
Over-kindness. Your over-kindness doth wring tears from me! *Much Ado* v 1 302
Over-laboured. The crickets sing, and man's o'er-labour'd sense Repairs itself by rest *Cymbeline* ii 2 11
Over-land. I desire of you A conduct over-land to Milford-Haven iii 5 8
Overleap. I do beseech you, Let me o'erleap that custom *Coriolanus* ii 2 140
That is a step On which I must fall down, or else o'erleap *Macbeth* i 4 49
Vaulting ambition, which o'erleaps itself And falls on the other i 7 27
Over-leather. My toes look through the over-leather *T. of Shrew* Ind. 2 12
Over-leaven. Some habit that too much o'er-leavens The form of plausive manners *Hamlet* i 4 29
Overlive. That your attempts may overlive the hazard *2 Hen. IV.* iv 1 15
Over-long. O, hold me not with silence over-long! *1 Hen. VI.* v 3 13
Overlook. Your eyes, where I o'erlook Love's stories written *M. N. Dream* ii 2 121
By this hand I swear, That sways the earth this climate overlooks *K. John* ii 1 344
Willing you overlook this pedigree *Hen. V.* ii 4 90
Spirt up so suddenly into the clouds, And overlook their grafters iii 5 9
So York may overlook the town of York *3 Hen. VI.* i 4 180
Hark! a drum.—Catesby, o'erlook the walls *Richard III.* iii 5 17
Overlooks the highest-peering hills *T. Andron.* ii 1 8
I will o'erlook thy paper *Lear* v 1 50
O'erlook What shipping and what lading's in our haven *Pericles* i 2 48
Overlooked. Yet I would I had o'erlooked the letter *T. G. of Ver.* i 2 50
Vile worm, thou wast o'erlook'd even in thy birth *Mer. Wives* v 5 87
Beshrew your eyes, They have o'erlook'd me and divided me *Mer. of Venice* iii 2 15
Stoop low within those bounds we have o'erlook'd *K. John* v 4 55
When thou shalt have overlooked this, give these fellows some means to the king: they have letters for him *Hamlet* iv 6 13
Overlooking. Bequeathed to my overlooking *All's Well* i 1 45
So much as I have perused, I find it not fit for your o'er-looking *Lear* i 2 40
Over-lusty. The confident and over-lusty French *Hen. V.* iv Prol 18
When a man's over-lusty at legs, then he wears wooden nether-stocks *Lear* ii 4 10
Overmaster. For your desire to know what is between us, O'ermaster't as you may *Hamlet* i 5 140
Overmastered. Would it not grieve a woman to be overmastered with a piece of valiant dust? *Much Ado* ii 1 64
Overmasterest. Which owe the crown that thou o'ermasterest *K. John* ii 1 109
Overmatched. Who with me Set from our o'ermatch'd forces forth for aid *1 Hen. VI.* iv 4 11
So true men yield, with robbers so o'ermatch'd *3 Hen. VI.* i 4 64
Over-matching And spend her strength with over-matching waves i 4 21
Over-measure. Come, enough.—Enough, with over-measure *Coriolanus* iii 1 140
Over-merry. I'll in to counsel them; haply my presence May well abate the over-merry spleen *T. of Shrew* Ind. 1 137
Overmount. With your theme, I could O'ermount the lark *Hen. VIII.* ii 3 94
Over-mounting. Did drench His over-mounting spirit *1 Hen. VI.* iv 7 15
Over-much. You tempt him over-much *W. Tale* v 1 73
Kept an evil diet long, And overmuch consumed his royal person *Rich. III.* i 1 140
Over-name them; and as thou namest them, I will describe them *Mer. of Venice* i 2 39
Over-night. And so, good rest.—As wretches have o'ernight That wait for execution in the morn *T. G. of Ver.* iv 2 133
Shame her with what he saw o'er night *Much Ado* iii 3 174
Pardon me, madam: If I had given you this at over-night, she might have been o'erta'en *All's Well* iii 4 23
Will the cold brook, Candied with ice, caudle thy morning taste, To cure thy o'er-night's surfeit? *T. of Athens* iv 3 227
Overpaid. To be acknowledged, madam, is o'erpaid *Lear* iv 7 4
Overparted. Alas, you see how 'tis,—a little o'erparted *L. L. Lost* v 2 588
Overpassed And like a hermit overpass'd thy days *1 Hen. VI.* ii 5 117
Overpast. That thou hast wronged in the time o'erpast *Richard III.* iv 4 388
That thou hast Misused ere used, by time misused o'erpast iv 4 396
Over-pay. Which I will over-pay and pay again *All's Well* iii 7 16
Your very goodness and your company O'erpays all I can do *Cymbeline* ii 4 10
Overpeer. Do overpeer the petty traffickers *Mer. of Venice* i 1 12
In yonder tower to overpeer the city *1 Hen. VI.* i 4 11
And mountainous error be too highly heapt For truth to o'erpeer *Coriol.* ii 3 128
Overpeered. Whose top-branch overpeer'd Jove's spreading tree *3 Hen. VI.* v 2 14
Overpeering. The ocean, overpeering of his list, Eats not the flats with more impetuous haste *Hamlet* iv 5 99
Over-perch. With love's light wings did I o'er-perch these walls; For stony limits cannot hold love out *Rom. and Jul.* ii 2 66
O'er-picturing that Venus *Ant. and Cleo.* ii 2 205
Overplus. Our overplus of shipping will we burn iii 7 51
Antony Hath after thee sent all thy treasure, with His bounty overplus iv 6 22
Over-posting. You may thank the unquiet time for your quiet o'er-posting that action *2 Hen. IV.* i 2 171
Overpowered. The lion dying thrusteth forth his paw, And wounds the earth, if nothing else, with rage To be o'erpower'd *Richard II.* v 1 31
Near him, thy angel Becomes a fear, as being o'erpower'd *Ant. and Cleo.* ii 3 22
Overpressed. He bestrid An o'er-press'd Roman *Coriolanus* ii 2 97
And yet the fire of life kindle again The o'erpress'd spirits *Pericles* iii 2 84
O'erprized all popular rate *Tempest* i 2 92
Over-proud. Lest, being over-proud in sap and blood, With too much riches it confound itself *Richard II.* iii 4 59
Say we think him over-proud And under-honest *Troi. and Cres.* ii 3 132
Over-rate. You o'er-rate my poor kindness *Cymbeline* i 4 41
Over-raught. The villain is o'er-raught of all my money *Com. of Errors* i 2 96
Certain players We o'er-raught on the way *Hamlet* iii 1 17
Over-reach. We'll over-reach the greybeard *T. of Shrew* iii 2 147
And will o'erreach them in their own devices *T. Andron.* v 2 143
It might be the pate of a politician, which this ass now o'er-reaches *Ham.* v 1 87
Overreaching. To prevent so gross o'erreaching as this *Mer. Wives* v 5 145
Over-read. You shall anon over-read it at your pleasure *Meas. for Meas.* iv 2 212
Bid them o'er-read these letters, And well consider of them *2 Hen. IV.* iii 1 2
O'er-read, At your best leisure, this his humble suit *J. Cæsar* iii 1 4
It is a letter from my brother, that I have not all o'er-read *Lear* i 2 38
Over-red. Go prick thy face, and over-red thy fear *Macbeth* v 3 14
Over-ripened. Why droops my lord, like over-ripen'd corn? *2 Hen. VI.* i 2 1
Over-roasted. Feed it with such over-roasted flesh *T. of Shrew* iv 1 178
Are you ready for death?—Over-roasted rather; ready long ago *Cymbeline* v 4 154
Over-rode. I over-rode him on the way *2 Hen. IV.* i 1 30
Over-rule. Let me o'errule you now *L. L. Lost.* v 2 516
Fate o'er-rules, that, one man holding troth, A million fail *M. N. Dream* iii 2 92
You shall o'er-rule my mind for once *Richard III.* iii 1 57
Ay, my lord; So you will not o'errule me to a peace *Hamlet* iv 7 61
Over-ruled. And comes not in, o'er-ruled by prophecies *1 Hen. IV.* iv 4 18
Yet hath a woman's kindness over-ruled *1 Hen. VI.* ii 2 50
Whose mind and mine, I know, in that are one, Not to be over-ruled *Lear* i 3 16
Over-run. Where I have seen corruption boil and bubble Till it o'er-run the stew *Meas. for Meas.* v 1 321
I will o'er-run thee with policy *As Y. Like It* v 1 61
Like envious floods o'er-run her lovely face *T. of Shrew* Ind. 2 67
Why doubt'st thou of my forwardness? An army have I muster'd in my thoughts, Wherewith already France is overrun *1 Hen. VI.* i 1 102
And in thy thought o'er-run my former time *3 Hen. VI.* i 4 45
For pavement to the abject rear, O'er-run and trampled on *Troi. and Cres.* iii 3 163
A chilling sweat o'er-runs my trembling joints *T. Andron.* ii 3 212
Over-running. We may outrun, By violent swiftness, that which we run at, And lose by over-running *Hen. VIII.* i 1 141
Over-scutched. And sung those tunes to the over-scutched huswives that he heard the carmen whistle *2 Hen. IV.* iii 2 340
Overset. And since we are o'erset, venture again i 1 185
Without a sudden calm, will overset Thy tempest-tossed body *R. and J.* iii 5 137
Overshade. Fear o'ershades me *W. Tale* i 2 457
Dark cloudy death o'ershades his beams of life *3 Hen. VI.* ii 6 62
Black night o'ershade thy day, and death thy life! *Richard III.* i 2 131
The elder-tree Which overshades the mouth of that same pit *T. Andron.* ii 3 273
Overshine. I in the clear sky of fame o'ershine you as much as the full moon doth the cinders of the element *2 Hen. IV.* iv 3 57
And over-shine the earth as this the world *3 Hen. VI.* ii 1 38
Yea, overshines ourself *Troi. and Cres.* iii 1 171
Dost overshine the gallant'st dames of Rome *T. Andron.* i 1 317
Over shoes. He was more than over shoes in love *T. G. of Ver.* i 1 24
A man may go over shoes in the grime of it *Com. of Errors* iii 2 106
Being o'er shoes in blood, plunge in the deep *M. N. Dream* iii 2 48
Overshot. So study evermore is overshot *L. L. Lost* i 1 143
But are you not ashamed? nay, are you not, All three of you, to be thus much o'ershot? iv 3 160
You have shot over.—'Tis not the first time you were overshot *Hen. VI.* iii 7 134
I have o'ershot myself to tell you of it *J. Cæsar* iii 2 155
Overshowered. In sorrow all devour'd, With sighs shot through, and biggest tears o'ershower'd *Pericles* iv 4 26
Oversights. With new lamenting ancient oversights *2 Hen. IV.* ii 3 47
O'er-sized with coagulate gore, With eyes like carbuncles *Hamlet* ii 2 484
Overskip. The mind much sufferance doth o'erskip, When grief hath mates, and bearing fellowship *Lear* iii 6 113

Overslip. When that hour o'erslips me in the day Wherein I sigh not, Julia, for thy sake . . . . *T. G. of Ver.* ii 2 9
Overspread. With hostile forces he'll o'erspread the land *Pericles* i 2 24
The noble image of my youth Is overspread with them [weeds] 2 *Hen. IV.* iv 4 56
The dragon wing of night o'erspreads the earth . . *Troi. and Cres.* v 8 17
Overstain'd With slaughter's pencil . . . . . *K. John* iii 1 236
O'erstep not the modesty of nature . . . . *Hamlet* iii 2 21
Overstunk. The foul lake O'erstunk their feet . . . *Tempest* iv 1 184
Oversway. So perttaunt-like would I o'ersway his state . . *L. L. Lost* v 2 67
Never fear that: if he be so resolved, I can o'ersway him . *J. Cæsar* ii 1 203
And, but that great command o'ersways the order . . *Hamlet* v 1 251
Over-swear. All those sayings will I over-swear . . *T. Night* v 1 276
O'erswell With course disturb'd even thy confining shores . . *K. John* ii 1 337
Let floods o'erswell, and fiends for food howl on! . . *Hen. V.* ii 1 97
Fill, Lucius, till the wine o'erswell the cup . . *J. Cæsar* iv 3 161
Overt. To vouch this, is no proof, Without more wider and more overt test Than these thin habits . . . . . *Othello* i 3 107
Overtake. A quick wit.—And yet it cannot overtake your slow purse *T. G. of Ver.* i 1 133
When she is able to overtake seventeen years old . . *Mer. Wives* i 1 55
His act did not o'ertake his bad intent . . *Meas. for Meas.* v 1 456
Run and overtake him; Give him the ring . . *Mer. of Venice* iv 1 452
To break a jest Upon the company you overtake . . *T. of Shrew* iv 5 73
O'ertake me, if thou canst; I scorn thy strength . 1 *Hen. VI.* i 5 15
If the trial of the law o'ertake ye, You'll part away disgraced *Hen. VIII.* iii 1 96
That swiftest wing of recompense is slow To overtake thee . *Macbeth* i 4 18
I shall see The winged vengeance overtake such children . *Lear* iii 7 66
O'ertake us, hence a mile or twain, I' the way toward Dover . . iv 1 44
Hear me one word.—I'll overtake you . . . . . v 1 39
Yon ribaudred nag of Egypt,—Whom leprosy o'ertake! . *Ant. and Cleo.* iii 10 11
I will o'ertake thee, Cleopatra, and Weep for my pardon . . iv 14 44
Would I might never O'ertake pursued success . . . . v 2 103
Overtaken. Fair sir, you are well o'erta'en . . *Mer. of Venice* iv 2 5
Pardon me, madam: If I had given you this at over-night, She might have been o'erta'en . . . . . . *All's Well* iii 4 24
My son of York Hath almost overta'en him in his growth *Richard III.* ii 4 7
He that has but effected his good will Hath overta'en mine act *Coriol.* i 9 19
Overtaketh. Giving a gentle kiss to every sedge He overtaketh in his pilgrimage . . . . *T. G. of Ver.* ii 7 30
Over-tedious. Speak on; but be not over-tedious . . 1 *Hen. VI.* iii 3 43
Over-teemed. About her lank and all o'er-teemed loins . *Hamlet* ii 2 531
Overthrow. Hath all the glory of my overthrow . . . *Much Ado* i 3 69
That thine own trip shall be thine overthrow . . . *T. Night* v 1 170
It is in my power To o'erthrow law . . . . . *W. Tale* iv 1 8
Present medicine must be minister'd, Or overthrow incurable ensues *K. John* v 1 16
To-day, to-day, unhappy day, too late, O'erthrows thy joys, friends, fortune and thy state . . . . . *Richard II.* iii 2 72
Traitors That sought at Oxford thy dire overthrow . . . . v 6 16
Before thy most assured overthrow . . . . *Hen V.* iv 3 81
What! shall we curse the planets of mishap That plotted thus our glory's overthrow? . . . . . . 1 *Hen. VI.* i 1 24
Hath the late overthrow wrought this offence? Be not dismay'd . . i 2 49
That seeks to overthrow religion . . . . . . i 3 65
We are like to have the overthrow again . . . . . iii 2 106
Depart when heaven please, For I have seen our enemies' overthrow . iii 2 111
False allegations to o'erthrow his state . . 2 *Hen. VI.* iii 1 181
I fear thy overthrow More than my body's parting with my soul! 3 *Hen. VI.* ii 6 3
Though fortune's malice overthrow my state, My mind exceeds . iv 3 46
His overthrow heap'd happiness upon him . . *Hen. VIII.* iv 2 64
Misadventured piteous overthrows . . . *Rom. and Jul.* Prol. 7
Sudden push gives them the overthrow . . . *J. Cæsar* v 2 5
He sweats not to overthrow your Almain . . . *Othello* ii 3 85
Yet famine, Ere clean it o'erthrow nature, makes it valiant . *Cymbeline* iii 6 20
You happily may think Are like the Trojan horse was stuff'd within With bloody veins, expecting overthrow . . . *Pericles* i 4 94
Overthrown. Now my charms are all o'erthrown . . *Tempest* Epil. 1
You're shamed, you're overthrown, you're undone for ever! *Mer. Wives* iii 3 102
And all the preparation overthrown . . . . *Much Ado* ii 2 51
There's no such sport as sport by sport o'erthrown . *L. L. Lost* v 2 153
You have overthrown Alisander the conqueror! . . . . v 2 577
You have wrestled well and overthrown More than your enemies *As Y. L. It* i 2 266
O poor Orlando, thou art overthrown! . . . . . i 2 271
Your honour not o'erthrown by your desires . . *W. Tale* v 1 230
Are by the sheriff of Yorkshire overthrown . . 2 *Hen. IV.* iv 4 99
Lord Talbot was o'erthrown: The circumstance I'll tell you 1 *Hen. VI.* i 1 108
So many peers, So many captains, gentlemen and soldiers, That in this quarrel have been overthrown . . . . . . v 4 105
Most detestable death, by thee beguiled, By cruel cruel thee quite overthrown! O love! O life! . . . . *Rom. and Jul.* iv 5 57
Octavius Is overthrown by noble Brutus' power, As Cassius' legions are by Antony . . . . *J. Cæsar* v 3 52
Treasons capital, confess'd and proved, Have overthrown him *Macbeth* i 3 116
O, what a noble mind is here o'erthrown! . . *Hamlet* iii 1 158
Our wills and fates do so contrary run That our devices still are overthrown . . . . iii 2 222
Not Cæsar's valour hath o'erthrown Antony, But Antony's hath triumph'd on itself.—So it should be . . *Ant. and Cleo.* iv 15 14
Overtook. I met and overtook a dozen captains, Bare-headed . 2 *Hen. IV.* ii 4 387
The flighty purpose never is o'ertook Unless the deed go with it *Macbeth* iv 1 145
There was a' gaming; there o'ertook in's rouse . . *Hamlet* ii 1 58
Overtop. Though less than yours in past, must o'ertop yours *T. and C.* iii 3 164
Till of this flat a mountain you have made, To o'ertop old Pelion *Hamlet* v 1 276
Overtopped. This pine is bark'd, That overtopp'd them all *Ant. and Cleo.* iv 12 24
Over-topping. Who to advance and who To trash for over-topping *Tempest* i 2 81
Of wisdom O'ertopping woman's power . . . *Hen. VIII.* ii 4 88
Overtrip. In such a night Did Thisbe fearfully o'ertrip the dew *M. of Ven.* v 1 7
Overture. I hear there is an overture of peace . . . *All's Well* iv 3 46
I could not answer in that course of honour As she had made the overture v 3 99
I bring no overture of war, no taxation of homage . . *T. Night* i 5 225
I wish, my liege, You had only in your silent judgment tried it, Without more overture.—How could that be? . . . *W. Tale* ii 1 172
It was he That made the overture of thy treasons to us . . *Lear* iii 7 89
Overturn. We shall o'erturn it topsy-turvy down . . 1 *Hen. IV.* iv 1 82
But blow on them, The vapour of our valour will o'erturn them *Hen. V.* iv 2 24
Overturned. O God, I fear all will be overturn'd! . . 2 *Hen. IV.* v 2 19
Overvalue. Which, in my opinion, o'ervalues it something . *Cymbeline* i 4 120
Over-veiled. Whose pitchy mantle over-veil'd the earth . . 1 *Hen. VI.* ii 2 2
Over-view. Are we betray'd thus to thy over-view? . . *L. L. Lost* iv 3 175
Over-walk. As to o'er-walk a current roaring loud On the unsteadfast footing of a spear . . . . 1 *Hen. IV.* i 3 192

Overwatched. I fear we shall out-sleep the coming morn As much as we this night have overwatch'd . . . . . *M. N. Dream* v 1 373
Poor knave, I blame thee not; thou art o'erwatch'd . *J. Cæsar* iv 3 241
All weary and o'erwatch'd, Take vantage, heavy eyes . . *Lear* ii 2 177
Over-weathered. With over-weather'd ribs and ragged sails, Lean, rent, and beggar'd . . . . *Mer. of Venice* ii 6 18
Overween. I might be some allay, or I o'erween to think so . *W. Tale* iv 2 9
You overween to take it so . . . . . 2 *Hen. IV.* iv 1 149
My eye's too quick, my heart o'erweens too much . . 3 *Hen. VI.* iii 2 144
Thou dost over-ween in all; And so in this, to bear me down *T. Andron.* ii 1 29
Overweening. Go, base intruder! overweening slave! *T. G. of Ver.* iii 1 157
Here's an overweening rogue! . . . . . *T. Night* ii 5 34
Hurl down my gaze Upon this overweening traitor's foot . *Richard II.* i 1 147
Whose overweening arm I have pluck'd back . . 2 *Hen. VI.* iii 1 159
Oft have I seen a hot o'erweening cur Run back and bite . . . v 1 151
Lash hence these overweening rags of France . . *Richard III.* v 3 328
Overweigh. My place i' the state Will so your accusation overweigh *Meas. for Meas.* ii 4 157
Say what you can, my false o'erweighs your true . . . . ii 4 170
The censure of the which one must in your allowance o'erweigh a whole theatre of others . . . . *Hamlet* iii 2 31
Overwhelm. In one self-born hour To plant and o'erwhelm custom *W. T.* iv 1 9
Let the brow o'erwhelm it As fearfully as doth a galled rock . *Hen. V.* iii 1 11
Thou wretch, despite o'erwhelm thee! . . . *Coriolanus* iii 1 164
Foul deeds will rise, Though all the earth o'erwhelm them, to men's eyes *Hamlet* i 2 258
With the hell-hated lie o'erwhelm thy heart . . . . . *Lear* v 3 147
And humming water must o'erwhelm thy corpse . . . *Pericles* iii 1 64
Avaunt, thou damned door-keeper! Your house, but for this virgin that doth prop it, Would sink and overwhelm you . . . . . iv 6 128
Overwhelmed. Whose joy of her is overwhelm'd like mine . *Much Ado* v 1 9
Like a sow that hath overwhelmed all her litter but one . 2 *Hen. IV.* i 2 13
And wrath o'erwhelm'd my pity . . . . . *Coriolanus* i 9 86
What an if His sorrows have so overwhelm'd his wits? . *T. Andron.* iv 4 10
Whilst you were here o'erwhelmed with your grief . . *Othello* iv 1 77
Overwhelming. In tatter'd weeds, with overwhelming brows . *R. and J.* v 1 39
Over-worn. But the word is over-worn . . . . *T. Night* iii 1 66
The jealous o'erworn widow . . . . . . *Richard III.* i 1 81
Over-wrested. Such to-be-pitied and o'er-wrested seeming *Troi. and Cres.* i 3 157
Ovid. The most capricious poet, honest Ovid . . *As Y. Like It* iii 3 8
So devote to Aristotle's checks As Ovid be an outcast . . *T. of Shrew* i 1 33
'Tis Ovid's Metamorphoses; My mother gave it me . . *T. Andron.* iv 1 42
Ovidius Naso was the man: and why, indeed, Naso, but for smelling out the odoriferous flowers of fancy? . . . . . *L. L. Lost* iv 2 127
Owe. This is no mortal business, nor no sound That the earth owes *Temp.* i 2 407
Wherefore?—That such an ass should owe them . . *T. G. of Ver.* v 2 28
When they weep and kneel, All their petitions are as freely theirs As they themselves would owe them . . . . *Meas. for Meas.* i 4 83
If not a feodary, but only he Owe and succeed thy weakness . . ii 4 123
For your kindness I owe you a good turn . . . . . iv 2 62
What art thou that keepest me out from the house I owe? *Com. of Errors* iii 1 42
No wife of mine, Nor to her bed no homage do I owe . . . iii 2 43
Even just the sum that I do owe to you Is growing to me by Antipholus iv 1 7
What should I answer you?—The money that you owe me for the chain. —I owe you none till I receive the chain . . . . . iv 1 63
Time is a very bankrupt and owes more than he's worth to season . iv 2 58
If I let him go, The debt he owes will be required of me . . . iv 4 121
What is the sum he owes?—Two hundred ducats.—Say, how grows it due? . . . . iv 4 136
Being reconciled to the prince your brother, I owe you all duty *Much Ado* i 1 157
I will owe thee an answer for that . . . . . . iii 3 108
You have just his bleat.—For this I owe you: here comes other reckonings . . . . v 4 52
For still her cheeks possess the same Which native she doth owe *L. L. L.* i 2 111
The sole inheritor Of all perfections that a man may owe . . . ii 1 6
Upon thy eyes I throw All the power this charm doth owe *M. N. Dream* ii 2 79
So sorrow's heaviness doth heavier grow For debt that bankrupt sleep doth sorrow owe . . . . iii 2 85
To you, Antonio, I owe the most, in money and in love . *Mer. of Venice* i 1 131
From your love I have a warranty To unburden all my plots and purposes How to get clear of all the debts I owe . . . . . i 1 134
I owe you much, and, like a wilful youth, That which I owe is lost . i 1 147
He would rather have Antonio's flesh Than twenty times the value of the sum That he did owe him . . . . iii 2 290
What sum owes he the Jew?—For me three thousand ducats . . iii 2 299
I care not for their names; they owe me nothing . *As Y. Like It* ii 5 22
I earn that I eat, get that I wear, owe no man hate . . . iii 2 78
Tell these headstrong women What duty they do owe their lords *T. of S.* v 2 131
Such duty as the subject owes the prince Even such a woman oweth to her husband . . . . v 2 155
And yet my heart Will not confess he owes the malady . *All's Well* ii 1 9
That obedient right Which both thy duty owes and our power claims . ii 3 168
I am not worthy of the wealth I owe, Nor dare I say 'tis mine, and yet it is . . . . ii 5 84
Better 'twere That all the miseries which nature owes Were mine at once iii 2 122
My mother did but duty; such, my lord, As you owe to your wife . iv 2 13
The count's a fool, I know it, Who pays before, but not when he does owe it . . . . iv 3 259
The jeweller that owes the ring is sent for, And he shall surety me . v 3 297
Ourselves we do not owe; What is decreed must be . . *T. Night* i 5 329
Make no compare Between that love a woman can bear me And that I owe Olivia . . . . ii 4 106
What dost thou know?—Too well what love women to men may owe . ii 4 108
The visitation which he justly owes him . . . . *W. Tale* i 1 8
Behold me A fellow of the royal bed, which owe A moiety of the throne iii 2 39
Which owe the crown that thou o'ermasterest . . . *K. John* ii 1 109
Be pleased then To pay that duty which you truly owe To him that owes it . . . . ii 1 247
We owe thee much! within this wall of flesh There is a soul counts thee her creditor And with advantage means to pay thy love . . iii 3 20
I will not touch thine eye For all the treasure that thine uncle owes . iv 1 123
My life thou shalt command, but not my shame: The one my duty owes; but my fair name . . . thou shalt not have . *Richard II.* i 1 167
Swear by the duty that you owe to God . . . . . i 3 180
Like a deep well That owes two buckets, filling one another . . iv 1 185
Who studies day and night To answer all the debt he owes to you 1 *Hen. IV.* i 3 185
You owe me money, Sir John; and now you pick a quarrel to beguile me of it . . . . iii 3 75
Do I owe you a thousand pound?—A thousand pound, Hal! a million . iii 3 153

Owe. If he outlive the envy of this day, England did never owe so sweet a hope *1 Hen. IV.* v 2 68
What is the gross sum that I owe thee? *2 Hen. IV.* ii 1 91
Pay her the debt you owe her, and unpay the villany you have done her ii 1 130
I owe her money; and whether she be damned for that, I know not ii 4 366
A man can die but once: we owe God a death iii 2 251
Master Shallow, I owe you a thousand pound.—Yea, marry, Sir John v 5 77
Owe yourselves, your lives and services To this imperial throne *Hen. V.* i 2 34
If I owe you any thing, I will pay you in cudgels v 1 68
I owe him little duty, and less love *1 Hen. VI.* iv 4 34
For now we owe allegiance unto Henry *3 Hen. VI.* iv 7 19
The duty that I owe unto your majesty I seal upon the lips of this sweet babe v 7 28
Nor feels nor what he owes, but by reflection *Troi. and Cres.* iii 3 99
I do owe them still My life and services *Coriolanus* ii 2 137
Put not your worthy rage into your tongue; One time will owe another iii 1 242
Thy valiantness was mine, thou suck'dst it from me, But owe thy pride thyself iii 2 130
Though I owe My revenge properly, my remission lies In Volscian breasts v 2 89
The great danger Which this man's life did owe you v 6 139
Receive them then, the tribute that I owe *T. Andron.* i 1 251
By all the duties that I owe to Rome i 1 414
So Romeo would, were he not Romeo call'd, Retain that dear perfection which he owes Without that title *Rom. and Jul.* ii 2 46
Who now the price of his dear blood doth owe? iii 1 188
He owes For every word *T. of Athens* i 2 204
All these Owe their estates unto him iii 3 5
Mark, how strange it shows, Timon in this should pay more than he owes iii 4 22
These debts may well be called desperate ones, for a madman owes 'em iii 4 103
If by this crime he owes the law his life, Why, let the war receive't iii 5 83
I owe more tears To this dead man than you shall see me pay *J. Cæsar* v 3 101
Say from whence You owe this strange intelligence? *Macbeth* i 3 76
The service and the loyalty I owe, In doing it, pays itself i 4 22
You make me strange Even to the disposition that I owe iii 4 113
The time approaches That will with due decision make us know What we shall say we have and what we owe v 4 18
Will you, with those infirmities she owes, . . . Take her, or leave her? *Lear* i 1 205
You owe me no subscription: then let fall Your horrible pleasure iii 2 18
The wretch that thou hast blown unto the worst Owes nothing to thy blasts iv 1 9
What a full fortune does the thick-lips owe! *Othello* i 1 66
Do you perceive in all this noble company Where most you owe obedience? i 3 180
And am well studied for a liberal thanks Which I do owe you *A. and C.* ii 6 49
Make a jolly march; Bear our hack'd targets like the men that owe them iv 8 31
You sin against Obedience, which you owe your father *Cymbeline* iii 3 117
Other of them may have crook'd noses, but to owe such straight arms, none iii 1 38
Take that life, beseech you, Which I so often owe v 5 415
How achieved you these endowments, which You make more rich to owe? *Pericles* v 1 118
Owed. Some defect in her Did quarrel with the noblest grace she owed And put it to the foil *Tempest* iii 1 45
I could not have owed her a more rooted love *All's Well* iv 5 12
Of six preceding ancestors, that gem, . . . Hath it been owed and worn v 3 198
Remember since you owed no more to time Than I do now *W. Tale* v 1 219
That blood which owed the breadth of all this isle, Three foot of it doth hold: bad world the while! *K. John* iv 2 99
But, for the party that owed it, he might have more diseases *2 Hen. IV.* i 2 5
Where should be graven, if that right were right, The slaughter of the prince that owed that crown *Richard III.* iv 4 142
Humbly I thank your lordship: never may That state or fortune fall into my keeping, Which is not owed to you! *T. of Athens* i 1 151
To throw away the dearest thing he owed, As 'twere a careless trifle *Macb.* i 4 10
Well, march we on, To give obedience where 'tis truly owed v 2 26
Owedst. That sweet sleep Which thou owedst yesterday *Othello* iii 3 333
Owest. Thou dost here usurp The name thou owest not *Tempest* i 2 454
Thy love is worth a million: thou owest me thy love *1 Hen. IV.* iii 3 156
Thou owest God a death.—'Tis not due yet v 1 127
A husband and a son thou owest to me *Richard III.* i 3 170
And pay thy life thou owest me for my horse! *Troi. and Cres.* v 6 7
Lend less than thou owest *Lear* i 4 133
Thou owest the worm no silk, the beast no hide, the sheep no wool iii 4 108
Oweth. Such duty as the subject owes the prince, Even such a woman oweth to her husband *T. of Shrew* v 2 156
Owing. There is more owing her than is paid; and more shall be paid her than she'll demand *All's Well* i 3 108
Owl. In a cowslip's bell I lie; There I couch when owls do cry *Tempest* v 1 90
O spite of spites! We talk with goblins, owls and sprites *Com. of Errors* ii 2 192
Good night, my good owl *L. L. Lost* iv 1 141
In praise of the owl and the cuckoo v 2 896
The one maintained by the owl, the other by the cuckoo v 2 902
Then nightly sings the staring owl, Tu-whit; Tu-who v 2 936
The clamorous owl that nightly hoots *M. N. Dream* ii 2 6
Thou ominous and fearful owl of death, Our nation's terror! *1 Hen. VI.* iv 2 15
Like the owl by day, If he arise, be mock'd and wonder'd at *3 Hen. VI.* v 4 56
The owl shriek'd at thy birth,—an evil sign; The night-crow cried v 6 44
Out on you, owls! nothing but songs of death? *Richard III.* iv 4 509
I bade the vile owl go learn me the tenour of the proclamation *T. and C.* ii 1 99
An owl, a puttock, or a herring without a roe v 1 68
Here nothing breeds, Unless the nightly owl or fatal raven *T. Andron.* ii 3 97
It was the owl that shriek'd, the fatal bellman *Macbeth* ii 2 3
Didst thou not hear a noise?—I heard the owl scream and the crickets cry ii 2 16
On Tuesday last, A falcon, towering in her pride of place, Was by a mousing owl hawk'd at and kill'd ii 4 13
The poor wren, The most diminutive of birds, will fight, Her young ones in her nest, against the owl iv 2 11
They say the owl was a baker's daughter *Hamlet* iv 5 41
To be a comrade with the wolf and owl,—Necessity's sharp pinch! *Lear* ii 4 213
The night to the owl and morn to the lark less welcome *Cymbeline* iii 6 94
Own. Stand fast, good Fate, to his hanging: make the rope of his destiny our cable, for our own doth little advantage *Tempest* i 1 34
Made such a sinner of his memory, To credit his own lie i 2 102
He furnish'd me From mine own library with volumes i 2 167
I am all the subjects that you have, Which first was mine own king i 2 342
When thou didst not, savage, Know thine own meaning i 2 356
The fault's your own.—So is the dear'st o' the loss ii 1 135
Nature should bring forth, Of it own kind, all foison, all abundance ii 1 163
And how does your content Tender your own good fortune? ii 1 270
No woman's face remember, Save, from my glass, mine own iii 1 50
Own. As my gift and thine own acquisition Worthily purchased *Tempest* iv 1 13
Fairly spoke. Sit then and talk with her; she is thine own iv 1 32
Do that good mischief which may make this island Thine own for ever iv 1 218
And all of us [found] ourselves When no man was his own v 1 213
Two of these fellows you Must know and own v 1 275
What strength I have's mine own, Which is most faint Epil. 2
Till I have found each letter in the letter, Except mine own name *T. G. of Ver.* i 2 120
With the vantage of mine own excuse Hath he excepted most against my love i 3 82
Have I not reason to prefer mine own? ii 4 156
You shall have An fool's-head of your own *Mer. Wives* i 4 135
Thine own true knight, By day or night, Or any kind of light ii 1 15
Thyself and thy belongings Are not thine own so proper as to waste Thyself upon thy virtues, they on thee *Meas. for Meas.* i 1 31
One would think it were Mistress Overdone's own house iv 3 3
Give us the swords; we have bucklers of our own *Much Ado* v 2 19
What do you see? you see an ass-head of your own, do you? *M. N. Dream* iii 1 120
And the country proverb known, That every man should take his own iii 2 459
Mine own, and not mine own iv 1 197
And all for use of that which is mine own *Mer. of Venice* i 3 114
It is a melancholy of mine own *As Y. Like It* iv 1 16
An ill-favoured thing, sir, but mine own v 4 61
Pardon me, sir, the boldness is mine own *T. of Shrew* ii 1 89
She hath a face of her own.—Who knows not that? iv 1 102
Hold your own, in any case iv 4 6
Your own proper wisdom Brings in the champion Honour on my part *All's Well* iv 2 49
Frenzy of mine own From my remembrance clearly banish'd his *T. Night* v 1 288
'Tis a saying, sir, not due to me.—You will not own it *W. Tale* iii 2 60
I'll not remember you of my own lord, Who is lost too iii 2 231
I cannot be Mine own, nor any thing to any, if I be not thine iv 4 44
Move still, still so, And own no other function iv 4 143
Tell me, mine own, Where hast thou been preserved? v 3 123
In peace permit Our just and lineal entrance to our own *K. John* ii 1 85
His coming is But for his own *Richard II.* ii 3 149
An easy task it is to win our own iii 2 191
I come but for mine own.—Your own is yours, and I am yours, and all iii 3 196
Let us not leave till all our own be won *1 Hen. IV.* v 5 44
When your own Percy, when my heart's dear Harry, Threw many a northward look to see his father *2 Hen. IV.* ii 3 12
Doth she hold her own well?—Old, old iii 2 218
I trust ere long to choke thee with thine own *1 Hen. VI.* iii 2 46
Of the King of England's own proper cost and charges *2 Hen. VI.* i 1 61
Ready to starve and dare not touch his own i 1 229
A day will come when York shall claim his own i 1 239
Many a pound of mine own proper store iii 1 115
And let his manly face . . . steel thy melting heart To hold thine own and leave thine own with him *3 Hen. VI.* ii 2 42
Some followers of mine own, At the lower end of the hall *Richard III.* ii 7 34
She shall be loved and fear'd: her own shall bless her *Hen. VIII.* v 5 31
Now, Ajax, hold thine own! *Troi. and Cres.* iv 5 114
Not Afric owns a serpent I abhor More than thy fame and envy *Coriolanus* i 8 3
Rome must know The value of her own i 9 21
Like an unnatural dam Should now eat up her own! iii 1 294
You are darken'd in this action, sir, Even by your own iv 7 6
This prince in justice seizeth but his own *T. Andron.* i 1 281
Rape, call you it, my lord, to seize my own, My true-betrothed love? i 1 405
Griefs of mine own lie heavy in my breast *Rom. and Jul.* i 1 192
My master is awaked by great occasion To call upon his own *T. of Athens* ii 2 22
The villains fly! Myself have to mine own turn'd enemy *J. Cæsar* v 3 2
Thy spirit walks abroad, and turns our swords In our own proper entrails v 3 96
Scotland hath foisons to fill up your will, Of your mere own *Macbeth* iv 3 89
Our thoughts are ours, their ends none of our own *Hamlet* iii 2 223
Ah, mine own lord, what have I seen to-night!—What, Gertrude? iv 1 5
Add such reasons of your own As may compact it more *Lear* i 4 361
I am your own for ever *Othello* iii 3 479
He gives me so much of mine own *Ant. and Cleo.* v 2 20
To entice his own To evil should be done by none *Pericles* i Gower 27
For what thou professest, a baboon, could he speak, Would own a name too dear iv 6 190
Owner. Worthy the owner, and the owner it *Mer. Wives* v 5 64
A bark of Epidamnum That stays but till her owner comes aboard *Com. of Errors* iv 1 86
I will but teach them to sing, and restore them to the owner *Much Ado* ii 1 240
And the owner of it blest Ever shall in safety rest *M. N. Dream* v 1 426
O, these naughty times Put bars between the owners and their rights! And so, though yours, not yours *Mer. of Venice* iii 2 19
Are not you The owner of the house I did enquire for? *As Y. Like It* iv 3 90
An hourly promise-breaker, the owner of no one good quality *All's Well* iii 6 12
Grief is proud and makes his owner stoop *K. John* iii 1 69
Who is, if every owner were well placed, Indeed his king *1 Hen. IV.* iv 3 94
While as the silly owner of the goods Weeps over them *2 Hen. VI.* i 1 225
Climbing my walls in spite of me the owner iv 10 37
Nature craves All dues be render'd to their owners *Troi. and Cres.* ii 2 174
Set fire on barns and hay-stacks in the night, And bid the owners quench them with their tears *T. Andron.* v 1 134
You well know, Things of like value differing in the owners Are prized by their masters *T. of Athens* i 1 170
But, like the owner of a foul disease, To keep it from divulging, let it feed Even on the pith of life *Hamlet* iv 1 21
Owning. Cast out, like to itself, No father owning it *W. Tale* iii 2 89
Own self. This above all: to thine own self be true *Hamlet* i 3 78
Own selves. To our own selves bend we our needful talk *Troi. and Cres.* iv 4 141
Ox. I am made an ass.—Ay, and an ox too *Mer. Wives* v 5 126
It may prove an ox *L. L. Lost* v 2 250
The ox hath therefore stretch'd his yoke in vain *M. N. Dream* ii 1 93
Call you that keeping for a gentleman of my birth, that differs not from the stalling of an ox? *As Y. Like It* i 1 11
The ox hath his bow, sir, the horse his curb and the falcon her bells iii 3 80
She is . . . My horse, my ox, my ass, my any thing *T. of Shrew* iii 2 234
Roasted Manningtree ox with the pudding in his belly *1 Hen. IV.* ii 4 498
Then is sin struck down like an ox *2 Hen. VI.* iv 2 28
He is both ass and ox: to an ox, were nothing *Troi. and Cres.* v 1 65
Ox-beef. That same cowardly, giant-like ox-beef hath devoured many a gentleman of your house *M. N. Dream* iii 1 197
Oxen. Sixscore fat oxen standing in my stalls *T. of Shrew* ii 1 360
Oxen and wainropes cannot hale them together *T. Night* iii 2 64
We shall feed like oxen at a stall *1 Hen. IV.* v 2 14

Oxen. Sheep run not half so treacherous from the wolf, Or horse or oxen from the leopard, As you fly . . . . . . 1 *Hen. VI.* i 5 31
So worthless peasants bargain for their wives, As market-men for oxen v 5 54
They fell before thee like sheep and oxen 2 *Hen. VI.* iv 3 5
And now, like Ajax Telamonius, On sheep or oxen could I spend my fury v 1 27
Oxford. What news from Oxford? hold those justs and triumphs? *Rich. II.* v 2 52
And interchangeably set down their hands, To kill the king at Oxford . v 2 99
I saw the prince, And told him of those triumphs held at Oxford . v 3 14
Help to order several powers To Oxford, or where'er these traitors are. v 3 141
I have to London sent The heads of Oxford, Salisbury, Blunt, and Kent v 6 8
I have from Oxford sent to London The heads of Brocas and Sir Bennet Seely, Two of the dangerous consorted traitors That sought at Oxford thy dire overthrow . . . . v 6 13
William is become a good scholar: he is at Oxford still, is he not? 2 *Hen. IV.* iii 2 12
Oxford, how haps it, in this smooth discourse, You told not? 3 *Hen. VI.* iii 3 88
Can Oxford, that did ever fence the right, Now buckler falsehood with a pedigree? For shame! . . . . . . iii 3 98
Oxford, Vouchsafe, at our request, to stand aside . . . iii 3 109
Warwick, Thou and Oxford, with five thousand men, Shall cross the seas iii 3 234
Oxford, to prevent the worst, Forthwith we'll send him hence to Brittany iv 6 96
And thou, brave Oxford, wondrous well beloved, In Oxfordshire shalt muster up thy friends . . . . iv 8 17
Sweet Oxford, and my loving Montague . . . . . iv 8 30
Where is the post that came from valiant Oxford? . . . . v 1 1
O cheerful colours! see where Oxford comes!—Oxford, Oxford, for Lancaster! . . . . v 1 58
O, welcome, Oxford! for we want thy help . . . . . v 1 66
Oxford. And Somerset, with Oxford, fled to her . . . 3 *Hen. VI.* v 3 15
Is not Oxford here another anchor? And Somerset another goodly mast? v 4 16
Sweet Oxford, thanks.—And take his thanks that yet hath nothing else v 4 58
Away with Oxford to Hames Castle straight . . . . v 5 2
When Oxford had me down, he rescued me . . . . *Richard III.* ii 1 112
Oxford, redoubted Pembroke, Sir James Blunt, And Rice ap Thomas . iv 5 11
My Lord of Oxford,—And you, Sir Walter Herbert, stay with me . v 3 27
Ever witness for him Those twins of learning that he raised in you, Ipswich and Oxford! . . . . *Hen. VIII.* iv 2 59
Oxfordshire. And thou, brave Oxford, wondrous well beloved, In Oxfordshire shalt muster up thy friends . . . . 3 *Hen. VI.* iv 8 18
Ox-head. I would set an ox-head to your lion's hide . . *K. John* ii 1 292
Oxlip.—Where oxlips and the nodding violet grows . . *M. N. Dream* ii 1 250
Bold oxlips and The crown imperial . . . . . *W. Tale* iv 4 125
Oyes. Crier Hobgoblin, make the fairy oyes . . . . *Mer. Wives* v 5 45
Not Neoptolemus so mirable, On whose bright crest Fame with her loud'st Oyes Cries 'This is he' . . . . . . *Troi. and Cres.* iv 5 143
Oyster. The world's mine oyster, Which I with sword will open *Mer. Wives* ii 2 2
Love may transform me to an oyster; but I'll take my oath on it, till he have made an oyster of me, he shall never make me such a fool *Much Ado* ii 3 25
Rich honesty dwells like a miser, sir, in a poor house; as your pearl in your foul oyster . . . . *As Y. Like It* v 4 64
As much as an apple doth [resemble] an oyster, and all one *T. of Shrew* iv 2 101
Canst tell how an oyster makes his shell?—No.—Nor I neither . *Lear* i 5 26
The firm Roman to great Egypt sends This treasure of an oyster *Ant. and Cleo.* i 5 44
Oyster-wench. Off goes his bonnet to an oyster-wench . *Richard II.* i 4 31

P

P. And thus makes she her great P's . . . . . *T. Night* ii 5 97
Pabylon. Melodious birds sing madrigals—When as I sat in Pabylon *Mer. Wives* iii 1 24
Pace. If you can, pace your wisdom In that good path that I would wish it go . . . . *Meas. for Meas.* iv 3 137
What pace is this that thy tongue keeps?—Not a false gallop *Much Ado* iii 4 93
My legs can keep no pace with my desires . . *M. N. Dream* iii 2 445
Where is the horse that doth untread again His tedious measures with the unbated fire That he did pace them first? . . *Mer. of Venice* ii 6 12
Time travels in divers paces with divers persons . *As Y. Like It* iii 2 327
Time's pace is so hard that it seems the length of seven year . iii 2 334
Indeed, he has no pace, but runs where he will . . *All's Well* iv 5 70
On a moderate pace I have since arrived but hither . . *T. Night* ii 2 3
And with speed so pace To speak of Perdita . . . *W. Tale* iv 1 23
I will even take my leave of you, and pace softly towards my kinsman's iv 3 121
With slow but stately pace kept on his course . . *Richard II.* v 2 10
With the armed hoofs Of hostile paces . . . . 1 *Hen. IV.* i 1 9
And hold me pace in deep experiments . . . . . iii 1 48
But now two paces of the vilest earth Is room enough . . v 4 91
The English lie within fifteen hundred paces of your tents . *Hen. V.* iii 7 136
So swift a pace hath thought . . . . v Prol. 15
To climb steep hills Requires slow pace at first . . *Hen. VIII.* i 1 132
Was not one Doctor Pace In this man's place before him? . . ii 2 122
At length her grace rose, and with modest paces Came to the altar . iv 1 82
Those that tame wild horses Pace 'em not in their hands to make 'em gentle . . . . v 3 22
This neglection of degree it is That by a pace goes backward *Troi. and Cres.* i 3 128
So every step, Exampled by the first pace that is sick Of his superior . i 3 132
Bring me word thither How the world goes, that to the pace of it I may spur on my journey . . . . *Coriolanus* i 10 32
Plague upon't! I cannot bring My tongue to such a pace . . iii 3 57
With his stealthy pace, With Tarquin's ravishing strides, towards his design Moves like a ghost . . . . . . *Macbeth* ii 1 54
To-morrow, and to-morrow, and to-morrow, Creeps in this petty pace from day to day . v 5 20
Do they grow rusty?—Nay, their endeavour keeps in the wonted pace *Ham.* ii 2 354
For your dull ass will not mend his pace with beating . . v 1 64
My bloody thoughts, with violent pace, Shall ne'er look back *Othello* iii 3 457
Which with a snaffle You may pace easy . . *Ant. and Cleo.* ii 2 64
I saw her once Hop forty paces through the public street . . ii 2 234
Her eyes as jewel-like And cased as richly; in pace another Juno *Pericles* v 1 112
Paced. As we paced along Upon the giddy footing of the hatches *Rich. III.* i 4 16
And with the same full state paced back again . *Hen. VIII.* iv 1 93
She's not paced yet . . . . *Pericles* iv 6 68
Pacified. But he will not now be pacified . . . *T. Night* iii 4 309
Thou seest I am pacified still . . . . 1 *Hen. IV.* iii 3 195
Pacify yourself, Sir John: there comes no swaggerers here 2 *Hen. IV.* ii 4 87
Pacing through the forest, Chewing the food of sweet and bitter fancy, Lo, what befel! . . . . *As Y. Like It* iv 3 101
Pack. A pack of sorrows which would press you down . *T. G. of Ver.* iii 1 20
Go; Trudge, plod away o' the hoof; seek shelter, pack! *Mer. Wives* i 3 91
There's a knot, a ging, a pack, a conspiracy against me . . iv 2 123
'Tis time, I think, to trudge, pack and be gone . *Com. of Errors* iii 2 158
Thou art false in all And art confederate with a damned pack . iv 4 105
The most courageous fiend bids me pack . . . *Mer. of Venice* ii 2 11
If she do bid me pack, I'll give her thanks, As though she bid me stay by her a week . . . . *T. of Shrew* ii 1 178
Sorrow on thee and all the pack of you, That triumph thus upon my misery! . . . . iv 3 33
I'll be revenged on the whole pack of you . . . *T. Night* v 1 386
And witnesses more than my pack will hold . . . *W. Tale* iv 4 289
Come, bring away thy pack after me. Wenches, I'll buy for you both iv 4 318
Not a ribbon, . . . bracelet, horn-ring, to keep my pack from fasting iv 4 611
Now of late, not able to travel with her furred pack . 2 *Hen. VI.* iv 2 51
God keep the prince from all the pack of you! . *Richard III.* i 3 5
Or pack to their old playfellows . . . . . *Hen. VIII.* i 3 33
Ere yet the fight be done, pack up . . . . *Coriolanus* i 5 9
Go pack with him, and give the mother gold . . *T. Andron.* iv 2 155
A pack of blessings lights upon thy back; Happiness courts thee *Rom. and Jul.* iii 3 141
Pack. Hence, pack! there's gold; you came for gold, ye slaves *T. of Athens* v 1 115
Will pack when it begins to rain, And leave thee in the storm . *Lear* ii 4 81
Packs and sects of great ones, That ebb and flow by the moon . v 3 18
Pour out the pack of matter to mine ear, The good and bad *Ant. and Cleo.* ii 5 54
Packed. That goldsmith there, were he not pack'd with her, Could witness it, for he was with me . . . . *Com. of Errors* v 1 219
Who I believe was pack'd in all this wrong . . . *Much Ado* v 1 308
The gifts she looks from me are pack'd and lock'd Up in my heart *W. Tale* iv 4 369
Charles' wain is over the new chimney, and yet our horse not packed 1 *Hen. IV.* ii 1 3
Our thighs pack'd with wax, our mouths with honey . 2 *Hen. IV.* iv 5 77
Pack'd with post-horse up to heaven . . . *Richard III.* i 1 146
The bones Of all my buried ancestors are pack'd . *Rom. and Jul.* iv 3 41
She, Eros, has Pack'd cards with Cæsar, and false-play'd my glory Unto an enemy's triumph . . . . *Ant. and Cleo.* iv 14 19
Packet. So please your grace, the packet is not come . *L. L. Lost* ii 1 164
This small packet of Greek and Latin books: If you accept them, then their worth is great . . . . . . *T. of Shrew* ii 1 101
Is Gilliams with the packet gone?—He is, my lord, an hour ago 1 *Hen. IV.* ii 3 68
The manner and true order of the fight This packet, please it you, contains at large . . . . 2 *Hen. IV.* iv 4 101
The packet, Cromwell, Gave't you the king? . . *Hen. VIII.* iii 2 76
Some spirit put this paper in the packet, To bless your eye withal . iii 2 129
What cross devil Made me put this main secret in the packet? . . iii 2 215
Your intercepted packets You writ to the pope against the king . . iii 2 286
And at the door too, like a post with packets . . . v 2 32
Finger'd their packet, and in fine withdrew To mine own room again *Ham.* v 2 15
Pack-horse. Shall pack-horses And hollow pamper'd jades of Asia, Which cannot go but thirty mile a-day, Compare with Cæsars? . 2 *Hen. IV.* ii 4 177
I was a pack-horse in his great affairs . . *Richard III.* i 3 122
Packing. Here's packing, with a witness, to deceive us all! *T. of Shrew* v 1 121
'Faith, and I'll send him packing . . . . 1 *Hen. IV.* ii 4 328
Be packing, therefore, thou that wast a knight . . 1 *Hen. VI.* iv 1 46
'Tis politicly done, To send me packing with an host of men 2 *Hen. VI.* iii 1 342
And bid mine eyes be packing with my heart . . . . iii 2 111
Ere a fortnight make me elder, I'll send some packing *Richard III.* iii 2 63
This man shall set me packing . . . . . . *Hamlet* iii 4 211
What hath been seen, Either in snuffs and packings of the dukes . *Lear* iii 1 26
Who is here? What, are you packing, sirrah? . . *Cymbeline* iii 5 80
Pack-saddle. Your beards deserve not so honourable a grave as to stuff a botcher's cushion, or to be entombed in an ass's pack-saddle *Cor.* ii 1 99
Packthread. And here and there pieced with packthread *T. of Shrew* iii 2 64
Musty seeds, Remnants of packthread and old cakes of roses *Rom. and Jul.* v 1 47
Pacoras. Thy Pacorus, Orodes, Pays this for Marcus Crassus *A. and C.* iii 1 4
Paction. Thrust in between the paction of these kingdoms . *Hen. V.* v 2 393
Pad. I suffer for it.—You suffer for a pad conscience . *Mer. Wives* iii 3 235
Paddle. Didst thou not see her paddle with the palm of his hand? *Othello* ii 1 259
Paddling. But to be paddling palms and pinching fingers . *W. Tale* i 2 115
Paddling in your neck with his damn'd fingers . . *Hamlet* iii 4 185
Paddock. I come, Graymalkin!—Paddock calls.—Anon . . *Macbeth* i 1 9
Who, that's but a queen, fair, sober, wise, Would from a paddock, from a bat, a gib, Such dear concernings hide? . . . . *Hamlet* iii 4 190
Padua. Signior Benedick of Padua.—O, he's returned; and as pleasant as ever he was . . . . *Much Ado* i 1 36
And use thou all the endeavour of a man In speed to Padua *Mer. of Venice* iii 4 49
A messenger with letters from the doctor, New come from Padua . iv 1 109
Came you from Padua, from Bellario?—From both, my lord . . iv 1 119
I must away this night toward Padua, And it is meet I presently set forth . . . . iv 1 403
Here is a letter; read it at your leisure; It comes from Padua . . v 1 268
The great desire I had To see fair Padua, nursery of arts . *T. of Shrew* i 1 2
Tell me thy mind; for I have Pisa left And am to Padua come . . i 1 22
Take a lodging fit to entertain Such friends as time in Padua shall beget i 1 45
Would I had given him the best horse in Padua to begin his wooing! . i 1 148
For who shall bear your part, And be in Padua here Vincentio's son? . i 1 200
Verona, for a while I take my leave, To see my friends in Padua . . i 2 2
What happy gale Blows you to Padua here from old Verona? . . i 2 49

Padua. I come to wive it wealthily in Padua; If wealthily, then happily in Padua *T. of Shrew* i 2 75
Katharina Minola, Renown'd in Padua for her scolding tongue i 2 100
I'll leave her houses three or four as good, Within rich Pisa walls, as any one Old Signior Gremio has in Padua ii 1 370
And make assurance here in Padua Of greater sums than I have promised iii 2 136
I'll bring mine action on the proudest he That stops my way in Padua iii 2 237
Of Mantua, sir? marry, God forbid! And come to Padua, careless of your life? iv 2 79
'Tis death for any one in Mantua To come to Padua iv 2 82
I told him that your father was at Venice, And that you look'd for him this day in Padua iv 4 16
Sir, by your leave: having come to Padua To gather in some debts iv 4 24
If you will, tell what hath happened, Lucentio's father is arrived in Padua iv 4 65
My name is call'd Vincentio; my dwelling Pisa; And bound I am to Padua iv 5 56
I told you your son was well-beloved in Padua. Do you hear, sir? v 1 27
His father is come from Padua and here looking out at the window v 1 31
Padua affords this kindness, son Petruchio.—Padua affords nothing but what is kind v 2 13
Pagan. Most beautiful pagan, most sweet Jew! *Mer. of Venice* ii 3 11
Would bear thee from the knowledge of thyself, And grapple thee unto a pagan shore *K. John* v 2 36
Streaming the ensign of the Christian cross Against black pagans *Rich. II.* iv 1 95
To chase these pagans in those holy fields *1 Hen. IV.* i 1 24
What a pagan rascal is this! an infidel! ii 3 31
What pagan may that be?—A proper gentlewoman, sir *2 Hen. IV.* ii 2 168
Their clothes are after such a pagan cut too, That, sure, they've worn out Christendom *Hen. VIII.* i 3 14
Nor the gait of Christian, pagan, nor man *Hamlet* iii 2 36
For if such actions may have passage free, Bond-slaves and pagans shall our statesmen be *Othello* i 2 99
Page. *See* **Anne Page**
Say, who gave it thee?—Sir Valentine's page *T. G. of Ver.* i 2 38
Fit me with such weeds As may beseem some well-reputed page ii 7 43
What think you of this page, my lord?—I think the boy hath grace in him v 4 164
Well, let us see honest Master Page. Is Falstaff there? *Mer. Wives* i 1 67
I will peat the door for Master Page. What, hoa! Got pless your house here! i 1 73
Master Page, I am glad to see you: much good do it your good heart! i 1 82
How doth good Mistress Page?—and I thank you always with my heart, la! i 1 85
Master Page, fidelicet Master Page; and there is myself, fidelicit myself i 1 140
I have writ me here a letter to her: and here another to Page's wife i 3 66
Go bear thou this letter to Mistress Page; and thou this to Mistress Ford i 3 80
French thrift, you rogues; myself and skirted page i 3 93
I will discuss the humour of this love to Page i 3 104
I will incense Page to deal with poison i 3 110
Let it suffice thee, Mistress Page,—at the least, if the love of soldier can suffice,—that I love thee ii 1 11
Mistress Page! trust me, I was going to your house ii 1 33
O Mistress Page, give me some counsel!—What's the matter, woman? ii 1 42
Letter for letter, but that the name of Page and Ford differs! ii 1 72
Will you go, Mistress Page?—Have with you. You'll come to dinner, George ii 1 160
Good even and twenty, good Master Page! Master Page, will you go with us? ii 1 203
'Tis the heart, Master Page; 'tis here, 'tis here ii 1 235
Though Page be a secure fool, and stands so firmly on his wife's frailty ii 1 241
She was in his company at Page's house ii 1 244
Mistress Page hath her hearty commendations to you too ii 2 98
Has Ford's wife and Page's wife acquainted each other how they love me? ii 2 114
But mistress Page would desire you to send her your little page ii 2 118
Her husband has a marvellous infection to the little page; and truly Master Page is an honest man ii 2 120
Ah, ha! Mistress Ford and Mistress Page, have I encompassed you? ii 2 159
Page is an ass, a secure ass: he will trust his wife; he will not be jealous ii 2 314
I will . . . detect my wife, be revenged on Falstaff, and laugh at Page ii 2 326
Master Page, we have some salt of our youth in us; we are the sons of women, Master Page ii 3 50
Master guest, and Master Page, and eke Cavaleiro Slender ii 3 77
Well met, Mistress Page. Whither go you?—Truly, sir, to see your wife iii 2 9
Has Page any brains? hath he any eyes? hath he any thinking? iii 2 30
Pluck the borrowed veil of modesty from the so seeming Mistress Page, divulge Page himself for a secure and wilful Actæon iii 2 43
I hope I have your good will, father Page.—You have, Master Slender iii 2 61
Well, fare you well: we shall have the freer wooing at Master Page's iii 2 86
Mistress Page, remember you your cue.—I warrant thee iii 3 38
I fear you love Mistress Page.—Thou mightst as well say I love to walk by the Counter-gate iii 3 83
Here's Mistress Page at the door, sweating and blowing and looking wildly iii 3 93
'Tis my fault, Master Page: I suffer for it.—You suffer for a pad conscience iii 3 233
Come, wife; come, Mistress Page. I pray you, pardon me; pray heartily, pardon me iii 3 242
I told you, sir, my daughter is disposed of.—Nay, Master Page, be not impatient iii 4 75
Good Mistress Page, for that I love your daughter In such a righteous fashion as I do, . . . I must advance the colours of my love iii 4 82
As good luck would have it, comes in one Mistress Page iii 5 85
How near is he, Mistress Page?—Hard by; at street end; he will be here anon iv 2 39
Go, go, sweet Sir John: Mistress Page and I will look some linen for your head iv 2 83
But if it prove true, Master Page, have you any way then to unfool me again? iv 2 119
Master Page, as I am a man, there was one conveyed out of my house yesterday in this basket iv 2 151
What, ho, Mistress Page! come you and the old woman down iv 2 174
Nan Page my daughter and my little son And three or four more iv 4 47
The doctor: he hath my good will, And none but he, to marry with Nan Page iv 4 85
Mistress Page is come with me, sweetheart.—Divide me like a bribe buck v 5 25
Page. Whoa, ho! ho, father Page!—Son, how now! how now, son! *Mer. Wives* v 5 187
Vere is Mistress Page? By gar, I am cozened: I ha' married un garçon v 5 217
And his page o' t' other side, that handful of wit! *L. L. Lost* iv 1 149
The page, Hercules,— Pardon, sir; error: he is not quantity enough for that Worthy's thumb v 1 136
Their herald is a pretty knavish page v 2 97
A blister on his sweet tongue, with my heart, That put Armado's page out of his part! v 2 336
I'll make her render up her page to me *M. N. Dream* ii 1 185
So is Alcides beaten by his page *Mer. of Venice* ii 1 35
What page's suit she hath in readiness ii 4 33
I'll have no worse a name than Jove's own page *As Y. Like It* i 3 126
Here come two of the banish'd duke's pages.—Well met, honest gentleman v 3 6
Sirrah, go you to Barthol'mew my page, And see him dress'd in all suits like a lady *T. of Shrew* Ind. 1 105
Come, sir page, Look on me with your welkin eye *W. Tale* i 2 135
Pages follow'd him Even at the heels in golden multitudes *1 Hen. IV.* iv 3 72
Then was Jack Falstaff, now Sir John, a boy, and page to Thomas Mowbray, Duke of Norfolk *2 Hen. IV.* iii 2 28
Master page, good master page, sit. Proface! v 3 29
Their dwarfish pages were As cherubins, all gilt *Hen. VIII.* i 1 22
This imperious man will work us all From princes into pages ii 2 48
Who holds his state at door, 'mongst pursuivants, Pages, and footboys v 2 25
Bold gentleman, Prosperity by thy page! *Coriolanus* i 5 24
Pages blush'd at him and men of heart Look'd wondering each at other v 6 99
Where is my page? Go, villain, fetch a surgeon *Rom. and Jul.* iii 1 97
Where is the county's page, that raised the watch? v 3 279
Here comes my mistress' page.—Why, how now, captain! *T. of Athens* ii 2 75
Will these moss'd trees, That have outlived the eagle, page thy heels? iv 3 224
Who told you of this stranger?—One of your lordship's pages *Cymbeline* ii 1 45
How! a page! Or dead, or sleeping on him? But dead rather iv 2 355
Never master had A page so kind, so duteous, diligent, So tender v 5 86
Thou'rt my good youth, my page; I'll be thy master: walk with me v 5 118
Shall's have a play of this? Thou scornful page, There lie thy part v 5 228
Pages and lights, to conduct These knights unto their several lodgings! *Pericles* ii 3 109
Pageant. Like this insubstantial pageant faded *Tempest* iv 1 155
When all our pageants of delight were play'd *T. G. of Ver.* iv 4 164
Some delightful ostentation, or show, or pageant *L. L. Lost* v 1 118
Shall we their fond pageant see? *M. N. Dream* iii 2 114
Or, as it were, the pageants of the sea *Mer. of Venice* i 1 11
This wide and universal theatre Presents more woeful pageants *A. Y. L. It* ii 7 138
If you will see a pageant truly play'd iii 4 55
A woeful pageant have we here beheld *Richard II.* iv 1 321
I will not be slack To play my part in Fortune's pageant *2 Hen. VI.* i 2 67
The flattering index of a direful pageant *Richard III.* iv 4 85
In celebration of this day with shows, Pageants *Hen. VIII.* iv 1 11
With ridiculous and awkward action, Which, slanderer, he imitation calls, He pageants us *Troi. and Cres.* i 3 151
In all Cupid's pageant there is presented no monster iii 2 81
You shall see the pageant of Ajax iii 3 273
'Tis a pageant, To keep us in false gaze *Othello* i 3 18
Thou hast seen these signs; They are black vesper's pageants *A. and C.* iv 14 8
Pageantry. What pageantry, what feats, what shows *Pericles* v 2 271
Pah. And smelt so? pah! *Hamlet* v 1 221
Pah, pah! Give me an ounce of civet, good apothecary *Lear* iv 6 132
Paid. Ha, ha, ha! So, you're paid *Tempest* ii 1 36
No bed-right shall be paid Till Hymen's torch be lighted iv 1 96
Nor never welcome to a place till some certain shot be paid *T. G. of Ver.* ii 5 7
Then I am paid; And once again I do receive thee honest v 4 77
I paid nothing for it neither, but was paid for my learning *Mer. Wives* iv 5 62
And twenty pounds of money, which must be paid to Master Brook v 5 118
Ere he would have hanged a man for the getting a hundred bastards, he would have paid for the nursing a thousand *Meas. for Meas.* iii 2 126
You have paid the heavens your function iii 2 263
Yea, and paid me richly for the practice of it *Much Ado* v 1 255
Borrows money in God's name, the which he hath used so long and never paid v 1 320
And wrong the reputation of your name, In so unseeming to confess receipt Of that which hath so faithfully been paid *L. L. Lost* ii 1 157
The virgin tribute paid by howling Troy To the sea-monster *Mer. of Venice* iii 2 56
When it is paid, bring your true friend along iii 2 310
Bid me tear the bond.—When it is paid according to the tenour iv 1 235
He is well paid that is well satisfied iv 1 415
Am satisfied And therein do account myself well paid iv 1 417
Say thou wilt see the tailor paid *T. of Shrew* iv 3 166
There is more owing her than is paid; and more shall be paid her than she'll demand *All's Well* i 3 108
Thy pains not used must by thyself be paid ii 1 149
His vows are forfeited to me, and my honour's paid to him v 3 143
Pleasure will be paid, one time or another *T. Night* ii 4 72
I will not give my part of this sport for a pension of thousands to be paid from the Sophy ii 5 197
He hath paid you all he promised you: may be, he has paid you more *W. Tale* iv 4 241
Indeed, paid down More penitence than done trespass v 1 3
All my services You have paid home v 3 4
No; I'll give thee thy due, thou hast paid all there *1 Hen. IV.* i 2 60
Two I am sure I have paid, two rogues in buckram suits ii 4 213
And with a thought seven of the eleven I paid ii 4 242
The money shall be paid back again with advantage ii 4 599
Paid money that I borrowed, three or four times; lived well iii 3 20
The money is paid back again.—O, I do not like that paying back iii 3 200
I have paid Percy, I have made him sure v 3 48
'Twas time to counterfeit, or that hot termagant Scot had paid me scot and lot too v 4 115
And every third word a lie, duer paid to the hearer than the Turk's tribute *2 Hen. IV.* iii 2 330
The smith's note for shoeing and plough-irons.—Let it be cast and paid v 1 21
The sum is paid; the traitors are agreed *Hen. V.* ii Prol. 33
I shall have my noble?—In cash most justly paid ii 1 120
Nothing compelled from the villages, nothing taken but paid for iii 6 117
Now have I paid my vow unto his soul *1 Hen. VI.* ii 2 7
They set him free without his ransom paid, In spite of Burgundy iii 3 72
Rate me at what thou wilt, thou shalt be paid *2 Hen. VI.* iv 1 30
I am sure the emperor Paid ere he promised *Hen. VIII.* i 1 186
That they may have their wages duly paid 'em, And something over iv 2 150
I may make his lordship understand Wherefore you are not paid *T. of A.* ii 2 44

Paid. Let not that part of nature Which my lord paid for, be of any power To expel sickness, but prolong his hour! *T. of Athens* iii 1 65
Timon's money Has paid his men their wages iii 2 77
Fly not; stand still: ambition's debt is paid *J. Cæsar* iii 1 83
Has paid a soldier's debt: He only lived but till he was a man *Macbeth* v 8 39
They say he parted well, and paid his score: And so, God be with him! v 8 52
By heaven, thy madness shall be paid with weight *Hamlet* iv 5 156
I am paid for't now *Ant. and Cleo.* ii 5 108
Thou mine of bounty, how wouldst thou have paid My better service! iv 6 32
Death of one person can be paid but once, And that she has discharged iv 14 27
You shall hear The legions now in Gallia sooner landed In our not-fearing Britain than have tidings Of any penny tribute paid *Cymbeline* ii 4 20
Come, there's no more tribute to be paid iii 1 35
Paid More pious debts to heaven than in all The fore-end of my time iii 3 71
And though he came our enemy, remember He was paid for that iv 2 246
Sorry that you have paid too much, and sorry that you are paid too much v 4 165
Marina gets All praises, which are paid as debts, And not as given *Pericles* iv Gower 34
Pail. They threw on him Great pails of puddled mire *Com. of Errors* v 1 173
And milk comes frozen home in pail *L. L. Lost* v 2 925
At my farm I have a hundred milch-kine to the pail *T. of Shrew* ii 1 359
Pailful. Yond same cloud cannot choose but fall by pailfuls *Tempest* ii 2 24
Pain. Since thou dost give me pains, Let me remember thee what thou hast promised i 2 242
I pitied thee, Took pains to make thee speak i 2 359
On whom my pains, Humanely taken, all, all lost, quite lost iv 1 189
Now you have taken the pains to set it together, take it for your pains.—No, no; you shall have it *T. G. of Ver.* i 1 123
Having nothing but the word 'noddy' for my pains i 1 131
Well, sir, here is for your pains. What said she? i 1 139
What said she? nothing?—No, not so much as 'Take this for thy pains' i 1 152
Perchance you think too much of so much pains?—No, madam; so it stead you ii 1 118
Give my sweet Nan this ring; there's for thy pains *Mer. Wives* iii 4 104
If he be chaste, the flame will back descend And turn him to no pain v 5 90
Alas, it hath been great pains to you *Meas. for Meas.* ii 1 279
His offence is so, as it appears, Accountant to the law upon that pain ii 4 86
Lend him your kind pains To find out this abuse v 1 246
Were we burden'd with like weight of pain, As much or more we should ourselves complain *Com. of Errors* ii 1 36
If you went in pain, master, this 'knave' would go sore iii 1 65
Vouchsafe to take the pains To go with us v 1 393
I thank you for your pains.—I took no more pains for those thanks than you take pains to thank me *Much Ado* ii 3 258
Any pains that I take for you is as easy as thanks ii 3 270
I thank thee for thy care and honest pains v 1 323
There's for thy pains.—God save the foundation! v 1 326
I must entreat your pains, I think v 4 18
All delights are vain; but that most vain, Which with pain purchased doth inherit pain *L. L. Lost* i 1 73
On pain of losing her tongue i 1 124
Something else more plain, That shall express my true love's fasting pain iv 3 122
Longaville, where lies thy pain? And where my liege's? all about the breast iv 3 172
But herein mean I to enrich my pain *M. N. Dream* i 1 250
There we may rehearse most obscenely and courageously. Take pains i 2 112
Extremely stretch'd and conn'd with cruel pain v 1 80
Pray thee, take pain To allay with some cold drops of modesty Thy skipping spirit *Mer. of Venice* ii 2 194
It is worth the pains ii 6 33
Your grace hath ta'en great pains to qualify His rigorous course iv 1 7
We freely cope your courteous pains withal iv 1 412
His clerk, That took some pains in writing v 1 182
Cannot so much as a blossom yield In lieu of all thy pains *As Y. Like It* ii 3 65
Lives merrily because he feels no pain iii 2 340
To refresh the mind of man After his studies or his usual pain *T. of Shrew* iii 1 12
Gentlemen and friends, I thank you for your pains iii 2 186
Then thou lovest it not; And all my pains is sorted to no proof iv 3 43
Impossible be strange attempts to those That weigh their pains in sense and do suppose What hath been cannot be *All's Well* i 1 240
My duty then shall pay me for my pains ii 1 128
Thy pains not used must by thyself be paid ii 1 149
Brought you this letter, gentlemen?—Ay, madam; And for the contents' sake are sorry for our pains iii 2 66
Lord, how we lose our pains! v 1 24
Shall render you no blame But rather make you thank your pains for it v 1 33
Present me as an eunuch to him: It may be worth thy pains *T. Night* i 2 57
I have taken great pains to con it i 5 186
I took great pains to study it, and 'tis poetical i 5 206
I thank you for your pains: spend this for me i 5 302
You might have saved me my pains, to have taken it away yourself ii 2 6
There's for thy pains.—No pains, sir; I take pleasure in singing, sir ii 4 68
Since you make your pleasure of your pains, I will no further chide you iii 3 2
To greet a man not worth her pains *W. Tale* v 1 155
Fair fall the bones that took the pains for me! *K. John* i 1 78
My brother, Who, as you say, took pains to get this son i 1 121
Hath she no husband That will take pains to blow a horn before her? i 1 219
Very little pains Will bring this labour to an happy end iii 2 9
Let hell want pains enough to torture me iv 3 138
He means to recompense the pains you take By cutting off your heads v 4 15
On pain of death, no person be so bold Or daring-hardy *Richard II.* i 3 42
On pain to be found false and recreant i 3 106
The hopeless word of 'never to return' Breathe I against thee, upon pain of life i 3 153
They breathe truth that breathe their words in pain ii 1 8
Heaven will take our souls And plague injustice with the pains of hell iii 1 34
For your pains, Of capital treason we arrest you here iv 1 150
We thank thee, gentle Percy, for thy pains v 6 11
Thy pains, Fitzwater, shall not be forgot; Right noble is thy merit v 6 17
If you knew what pains I have bestow'd to breed this present peace *2 Hen. IV.* iv 2 73
We bring it to the hive, and, like the bees, Are murdered for our pains iv 5 79
With more than with a common pain iv 5 224
Till then, I banish thee, on pain of death v 5 67
His present and your pains we thank you for *Hen. V.* i 2 260
'Tis good for men to love their present pains Upon example iv 1 18
If you would take the pains but to examine the wars of Pompey the Great iv 1 69
I have labour'd, With all my wits, my pains and strong endeavours v 2 25

Pain. Henceforward, upon pain of death *1 Hen. VI.* i 3 79
Henceforth we banish thee, on pain of death iv 1 47
Whom I with pain have woo'd and won thereto v 3 138
Are deeply indebted for this piece of pains *2 Hen. VI.* i 4 47
No pain they can inflict upon him Will make him say I moved him iii 1 377
In pain of your dislike or pain of death iii 2 257
He shall not breathe infection in this air But three days longer, on the pain of death iii 2 288
So thou wilt let me live, and feel no pain iii 3 4
Hadst thou but loved him half so well as I, Or felt that pain which I did for him once *3 Hen. VI.* i 1 221
Exempt from envy, but not from disdain, Unless the Lady Bona quit his pain iii 3 128
Thy mother felt more than a mother's pain, And yet brought forth less than a mother's hope v 6 49
'Tis time to speak; my pains are quite forgot.—Out, devil! I remember them too well *Richard III.* i 3 117
Wert thou not banished on pain of death?—I was; but I do find more pain in banishment i 3 167
He is frank'd up to fatting for his pains i 3 314
Lord, Lord! methought, what pain it was to drown! i 4 21
Of all one pain, save for a night of groans Endured of her iv 4 303
Your country's fat shall pay your pains the hire v 3 258
A worthy fellow, and hath ta'en much pain In the king's business *Hen. VIII.* iii 2 72
I think your grace, Out of the pain you suffer'd, gave no ear to't iv 2 8
I should have ta'en some pains to bring together Yourself and your accusers v 1 119
Since I have taken such pains to bring you together *Troi. and Cres.* iii 2 207
Shall quite strike off all service I have done, In most accepted pain iii 3 30
With such a hell of pain and world of charge iv 1 57
There let them bide until we have devised Some never-heard-of torturing pain for them *T. Andron.* ii 3 285
Pray to all the gods For our beloved mother in her pains iv 2 47
On pain of torture *Rom. and Jul.* i 1 93
Once more, on pain of death, all men depart i 1 110
One pain is lessen'd by another's anguish i 2 47
Here is for thy pains.—No, truly, sir; not a penny ii 4 194
Farewell; be trusty, and I'll quit thy pains: Farewell ii 4 204
Your words have took such pains as if they labour'd *T. of Athens* iii 5 26
Let the unscarr'd braggarts of the war Derive some pain from you iv 3 162
'Tis not monstrous in you, neither wish I You take much pains to mend v 1 92
I thank you for your pains and courtesy *J. Cæsar* ii 2 115
Thane of Cawdor! The greatest is behind. Thanks for your pains *Macbeth* i 3 117
Your pains Are register'd where every day I turn The leaf to read them i 3 150
Herein I teach you How you shall bid God 'ild us for your pains i 6 13
The labour we delight in physics pain ii 3 55
O, well done! I commend your pains; And every one shall share i' the gains iv 1 39
And in this harsh world draw thy breath in pain, To tell my story *Hamlet* v 2 359
Turn all her mother's pains and benefits To laughter and contempt *Lear* i 4 308
When we have found the king,—in which your pain That way, I'll this iii 1 53
Charged me, on pain of their perpetual displeasure, neither to speak of him, entreat for him, nor any way sustain him iii 3 4
How light and portable my pain seems now! iii 6 115
That we the pain of death would hourly die Rather than die at once! v 3 185
I'll deserve your pains *Othello* i 1 184
My story being done, She gave me for my pains a world of sighs i 3 159
The issue will be, I shall have so much experience for my pains ii 3 374
Masters, play here; I will content your pains; Something that's brief iii 1 1
I have a pain upon my forehead here.—'Faith, that's with watching iii 3 284
Let our finger ache, and it indues Our other healthful members even to that sense Of pain iii 4 148
We have done our course; there's money for your pains iv 2 93
I that am cruel am yet merciful; I would not have thee linger in thy pain v 2 87
In which I bind, On pain of punishment, the world to weet *Ant. and Cleo.* i 1 39
Make thine own edict for thy pains, which we Will answer as a law iii 12 32
For this pains Cæsar hath hang'd him iv 6 15
Hast thou the pretty worm of Nilus there, That kills and pains not? v 2 244
How she died of the biting of it, what pain she felt v 2 255
I thank you for your pains: But not away to-morrow! *Cymbeline* i 6 203
You lay out too much pains For purchasing but trouble ii 3 92
A pain that only seems to seek out danger I' the name of fame and honour iii 3 50
Would I could free't!—Or I, whate'er it be, What pain it cost, what danger iii 6 81
Their pleasures here are past, so is their pain iv 2 290
'Tis most strange, Nature should be so conversant with pain, Being thereto not compell'd *Pericles* iii 2 25
And not your knowledge, your personal pain, but even Your purse, still open iii 2 46
You must take some pains to work her to your manage iv 6 69
Strike me, honour'd sir; Give me a gash, put me to present pain v 1 193
Pained. Pardon, That I, your vassal, have employ'd and pain'd Your unknown sovereignty! *Meas. for Meas.* v 1 391
Enforce the pained impotent to smile *L. L. Lost* v 2 864
Painedest. Thou hold'st a place, for which the pained'st fiend Of hell would not in reputation change *Pericles* iv 6 173
Painful. There be some sports are painful, and their labour Delight in them sets off *Tempest* iii 1 1
With most painful feeling of thy speech *Meas. for Meas.* i 2 38
If it had been painful, I would not have come *Much Ado* ii 3 261
Till painful study shall outwear three years *L. L. Lost* i 1 23
And for thy maintenance commits his body To painful labour *T. of Shrew* v 2 149
All besmirch'd With rainy marching in the painful field *Hen. V.* iv 3 111
The painful service, The extreme dangers *Coriolanus* iv 5 74
By many a dern and painful perch Of Pericles the careful search *Pericles* iii Gower 15
Painfully. Imprison'd thou didst painfully remain A dozen years *Tempest* i 2 278
As, painfully to pore upon a book To seek the light of truth *L. L. Lost* i 1 74
Painfully with much expedient march *K. John* ii 1 223
Thou hast painfully discover'd *T. of Athens* v 2 1
Paint. Does Bridget paint still? *Meas. for Meas.* iii 2 83
When was he wont to wash his face?—Yea, or to paint himself? *M. Ado* iii 2 58
Disloyal?—The word is too good to paint out her wickedness iii 2 112
Never paint me now: Where fair is not, praise cannot mend the brow *L. L. Lost* iv 1 16
Red, that would avoid dispraise, Paints itself black, to imitate her brow iv 3 265
And cuckoo-buds of yellow hue Do paint the meadows with delight v 2 907
And paint your face and use you like a fool *T. of Shrew* i 1 65

Paint. Where revenge did paint The fearful difference of incensed kings *K. John* iii 1 237
To gild refined gold, to paint the lily, To throw a perfume on the violet iv 2 11
Lest bleeding you do paint the white rose red . 1 *Hen. VI.* ii 4 50
Fools on both sides! Helen must needs be fair, When with your blood you daily paint her thus *Troi. and Cres.* i 1 94
I paint him in the character *Coriolanus* v 4 28
With man's blood paint the ground, gules, gules *T. of Athens* iv 3 59
Paint till a horse may mire upon your face iv 3 147
Excellent workman! thou canst not paint a man so bad as is thyself v 1 33
Let her paint an inch thick, to this favour she must come *Hamlet* v 1 213
You shall paint when you are old.—Wrinkles forbid! *Ant. and Cleo.* i 2 18
Painted. With colours fairer painted their foul ends *Tempest* i 2 143
Were I in England now, as once I was, and had but this fish painted ii 2 30
One is painted and the other out of all count *T. G. of Ver.* ii 1 61
So painted, to make her fair, that no man counts of her beauty ii 1 64
'Tis painted about with the story of the Prodigal, fresh and new *M. W.* iv 5 8
Let me be vilely painted, and in such great letters *Much Ado* i 1 267
My beauty, though but mean, Needs not the painted flourish of your praise: Beauty is bought by judgement of the eye *L. L. Lost* ii 1 14
Lend me the flourish of all gentle tongues,—Fie, painted rhetoric! iv 3 239
You will be scraped out of the painted cloth for this v 2 579
And therefore is wing'd Cupid painted blind *M. N. Dream* i 1 235
Pluck the wings from painted butterflies To fan the moonbeams iii 1 175
How low am I, thou painted maypole? speak; How low am I? iii 2 296
Brothers in exile, Hath not old custom made this life more sweet Than that of painted pomp? *As Y. Like It* ii 1 3
I answer you right painted cloth, from whence you have studied your questions iii 2 290
We will fetch thee straight Adonis painted by a running brook *T. of S.* Ind. 2 52
As lively painted as the deed was done Ind. 2 58
Is the adder better than the eel, Because his painted skin contents the eye? iv 3 180
No more than were I painted I would wish This youth should say 'twere well and only therefore Desire to breed by me *W. Tale* iv 4 101
Rough frown of war Is cold in amity and painted peace *K. John* iii 1 105
An innocent hand, Not painted with the crimson spots of blood iv 2 253
Men are but gilded loam or painted clay *Richard II.* i 1 179
All the walls With painted imagery v 2 16
As ragged as Lazarus in the painted cloth 1 *Hen. IV.* iv 2 28
With pennons painted in the blood of Harfleur *Hen. V.* iii 5 49
Fortune is painted blind, with a muffler afore her eyes iii 6 33
And she [Fortune] is painted also with a wheel iii 6 35
With purple falchion, painted to the hilt In blood 3 *Hen. VI.* i 4 12
Poor painted queen, vain flourish of my fortune! *Richard III.* i 3 241
I call'd thee then poor shadow, painted queen iv 4 83
That's the plain truth: your painted gloss discovers, To men that understand you, words and weakness *Hen. VIII.* v 3 71
From Cupid's shoulder pluck his painted wings *Troi. and Cres.* iii 2 15
Good traders in the flesh, set this in your painted cloths v 10 46
Alone he enter'd The mortal gate of the city, which he painted With shunless destiny *Coriolanus* ii 2 115
And with that painted hope braves your mightiness *T. Andron.* ii 3 126
Ye white-limed walls! ye alehouse painted signs! iv 2 98
We'll have no Cupid hoodwink'd with a scarf, Bearing a Tartar's painted bow of lath *Rom. and Jul.* i 4 5
Wrought he not well that painted it?—He wrought better that made the painter *T. of Athens* i 1 200
But only painted, like his varnish'd friends iv 2 36
The skies are painted with unnumber'd sparks, They are all fire *J. Cæsar* iii 1 63
'Tis the eye of childhood That fears a painted devil *Macbeth* ii 2 55
We'll have thee, as our rarer monsters are, Painted upon a pole v 8 26
So, as a painted tyrant, Pyrrhus stood *Hamlet* ii 2 502
The harlot's cheek, beautied with plastering art, Is not more ugly to the thing that helps it Than is my deed to my most painted word iii 1 53
Though he be painted one way like a Gorgon, The other way's a Mars *Ant. and Cleo.* ii 5 116
One, but painted thus, Would be interpreted a thing perplex'd *Cymbeline* iii 4 6
Painter. Yet the painter flatter'd her a little *T. G. of Ver.* iv 4 192
He's a god or a painter; for he makes faces *L. L. Lost* v 2 648
Here in her hairs The painter plays the spider *Mer. of Venice* iii 2 121
The fisher with his pencil, and the painter with his nets *Rom. and Jul.* i 2 41
He wrought better that made the painter *T. of Athens* i 1 202
Yonder comes a poet and a painter: the plague of company light upon thee! iv 3 356
A stone-cutter or a painter could not have made him so ill, though he had been but two hours at the trade *Lear* ii 2 64
Painting, sir, I have heard say, is a mystery *Meas. for Meas.* iv 2 38
Your whores, sir, being members of my occupation, using painting, do prove my occupation a mystery iv 2 40
Fashioning them like Pharaoh's soldiers in the reechy painting *M. Ado* iii 3 143
Your hands in your pocket like a man after the old painting *L. L. Lost* iii 1 21
That painting and usurping hair Should ravish doters with a false aspect iv 3 259
For native blood is counted painting now iv 3 263
You'll mar it if you kiss it, stain your own With oily painting *W. Tale* v 3 83
That their very labour Was to them as a painting *Hen. VIII.* i 1 26
If any such be here—As it were sin to doubt—that love this painting Wherein you see me smear'd *Coriolanus* i 6 68
A thousand moral paintings I can show That shall demonstrate these quick blows of Fortune's *T. of Athens* i 1 90
A piece of painting, which I do beseech Your lordship to accept i 1 155
Painting is welcome. The painting is almost the natural man i 1 156
O proper stuff! This is the very painting of your fear *Macbeth* iii 4 61
I have heard of your paintings too, well enough *Hamlet* iii 1 148
Are you like the painting of a sorrow, A face without a heart? iv 7 109
Some jay of Italy, Whose mother was her painting, hath betray'd him *Cymbeline* iii 4 52
Pair. Love hath twenty pair of eyes *T. G. of Ver.* ii 4 95
To cast up, with a pair of anchoring hooks iii 1 118
I'll do what I can to get you a pair of horns *Mer. Wives* v 1 7
There went but a pair of shears between us *Meas. for Meas.* i 2 28
What needs all that, and a pair of stocks in the town? *Com. of Errors* iii 1 60
Here stand a pair of honourable men *Much Ado* v 1 276
There shall the pairs of faithful lovers be Wedded *M. N. Dream* iv 1 96
He hath bought a pair of cast lips of Diana *As Y. Like It* iii 4 16
They made a pair of stairs to marriage v 2 41
A pair of very strange beasts, which in all tongues are called fools v 4 37
A pair of stocks, you rogue! *T. of Shrew* Ind. 1 2
A pair of old breeches thrice turned, a pair of boots that have been candle-cases, one buckled, another laced iii 2 44

Pair. Would not a pair of these have bred, sir? *T. Night* iii 1 55
So turtles pair, That never mean to part *W. Tale* iv 4 154
You promised me a tawdry-lace and a pair of sweet gloves iv 4 253
And here justified By us, a pair of kings v 3 146
A brace of tongues Must needs want pleading for a pair of eyes *K. John* iv 1 99
A pair of carved saints *Richard II.* iii 3 152
Till they have fretted us a pair of graves iii 3 167
If I hang, I'll make a fat pair of gallows 1 *Hen. IV.* ii 1 74
Show it a fair pair of heels and run from it ii 4 53
Or to take note how many pair of silk stockings thou hast 2 *Hen. IV.* ii 2 17
An thou dost, I'll canvass thee between a pair of sheets ii 4 243
I thought upon one pair of English legs Did march three Frenchmen *Hen. V.* iii 6 158
Like to a pair of loving turtle-doves That could not live asunder 1 *Hen. VI.* ii 2 30
You shall go near To call them both a pair of crafty knaves 2 *Hen. VI.* i 2 103
A pair of bleeding hearts *Richard III.* iv 4 272
What a pair of spectacles is here! Let me embrace too *Troi. and Cres.* iv 4 14
You are a pair of strange ones *Coriolanus* ii 1 89
A pair of tribunes that have rack'd for Rome, To make coals cheap v 1 16
A pair of cursed hell-hounds and their dam! *T. Andron.* v 2 144
A pair of star-cross'd lovers *Rom. and Jul.* Prol. 6
A winning match, Play'd for a pair of stainless maidenhoods iii 2 13
And let him, for a pair of reechy kisses *Hamlet* iii 4 184
The length and breadth of a pair of indentures v 1 119
When such a mutual pair And such a twain can do't *Ant. and Cleo.* i 1 37
Then, world, thou hast a pair of chaps, no more iii 5 14
I' the midst o' the fight, When vantage like a pair of twins appear'd iii 10 12
No grave upon the earth shall clip in it A pair so famous v 2 363
I know not how to wish A pair of worthier sons *Cymbeline* v 5 356
I yet am unprovided Of a pair of bases *Pericles* ii 1 167
Thou shalt have my best gown to make thee a pair ii 1 169
Paired. Had our prince, Jewel of children, seen this hour, he had pair'd Well with this lord *W. Tale* v 1 116
Pajock. And now reigns here A very, very—pajock *Hamlet* iii 2 295
Palabras, neighbour Verges.—Neighbours, you are tedious *Much Ado* iii 5 18
Palace. The cloud-clapp'd towers, the gorgeous palaces *Tempest* iv 1 152
Bring us to our palace; where we'll show What's yet behind *M. for M.* v 1 544
Meet presently at the palace; every man look o'er his part *M. N. Dream* iv 2 38
And each several chamber bless, Through this palace, with sweet peace v 1 425
If to do were as easy as to know what were good to do, chapels had been churches and poor men's cottages princes' palaces *Mer. of Venice* i 2 15
Pray heartily he be at palace *W. Tale* iv 4 731
How now, rustics! whither are you bound?—To the palace iv 4 737
The king is not at the palace; he is gone aboard a new ship iv 4 789
My jewels for a set of beads, My gorgeous palace for a hermitage *Rich. II.* iii 3 148
Peace be amongst them, if they turn to us; Else, ruin combat with their palaces! 1 *Hen. VI.* v 2 7
Set this diamond safe In golden palaces, as it becomes v 3 170
Because thy flinty heart, more hard than they, Might in thy palace perish Margaret 2 *Hen. VI.* iii 2 100
They will by violence tear him from your palace And torture him iii 2 246
Reproach and beggary Is crept into the palace of our king iv 1 102
This is the palace of the fearful king, And this the regal seat 3 *Hen. VI.* i 1 25
Now my soul's palace is become a prison: Ah, would she break from hence! ii 1 74
Here at the palace will I rest awhile iv 8 33
You left poor Henry at the Bishop's palace, And, ten to one, you'll meet him in the Tower v 1 45
I will not re-salute the streets of Rome, Or climb my palace, till from forth this place I lead espoused my bride along with me *T. Andron.* i 1 327
So near the emperor's palace dare you draw, And maintain such a quarrel? ii 1 46
The palace full of tongues, of eyes, and ears: The woods are ruthless ii 1 127
O, that deceit should dwell In such a gorgeous palace! *Rom. and Jul.* iii 2 85
I still will stay with thee; And never from this palace of dim night Depart v 3 107
For't must be done to-night, And something from the palace *Macbeth* iii 1 132
Though palaces and pyramids do slope Their heads to their foundations iv 1 57
In cities, mutinies; in countries, discord; in palaces, treason *Lear* i 2 117
Make it more like a tavern or a brothel Than a graced palace i 4 267
Where's that palace whereinto foul things Sometimes intrude not? *Oth.* iii 3 137
Had our great palace the capacity To camp this host, we all would sup together, And drink carouses *Ant. and Cleo.* iv 8 32
Though train'd up thus meanly I' the cave wherein they bow, their thoughts do hit The roofs of palaces *Cymbeline* iii 3 84
Mount, eagle, to my palace crystalline v 4 113
Thou seem'st a palace For the crown'd Truth to dwell in *Pericles* v 1 122
To rage the city turn, That him and his they in his palace burn v 3 Gower 97
Palace gate. March'd through the city to the palace gates 3 *Hen. VI.* i 1 92
Henry your foe is taken, And brought your prisoner to your palace gate iii 2 119
It did me good, before the palace gate To brave the tribune *T. Andron.* ii 2 35
They are, my lord, without the palace gate.—Bring them before us *Macb.* iii 1 47
So all men do, from hence to the palace gate Make it their walk iii 3 13
Palace wood. Meet me in the palace wood, a mile without the town *M. N. D.* i 2 104
Palamedes. Patroclus ta'en or slain, and Palamedes Sore hurt and bruised *Troi. and Cres.* v 5 13
Palate. Let their beds Be made as soft as yours and let their palates Be season'd with such viands *Mer. of Venice* iv 1 96
Their love may be call'd appetite, No motion of the liver, but the palate, That suffer surfeit, cloyment *T. Night* ii 4 101
The Trojans taste our dear'st repute With their finest palate *Tr. and Cr.* i 3 338
When that the watery palate tastes indeed Love's thrice repured nectar iii 2 22
If I could temporise with my affection, Or brew it to a weak and colder palate, The like allayment could I give my grief iv 4 7
If the drink you give me touch my palate adversely, I make a crooked face at it *Coriolanus* ii 1 61
Both your voices blended, the great'st taste, Most palates theirs iii 1 104
Sauce his palate With thy most operant poison! *T. of Athens* iv 3 24
I therefore beg it not, To please the palate of my appetite *Othello* i 3 263
They see and smell And have their palates both for sweet and sour iv 3 96
Thy palate then did deign The roughest berry *Ant. and Cleo.* i 4 63
Sleeps, and never palates more the dug, The beggar's nurse and Cæsar's v 2 7
Those palates who, not yet two summers younger, Must have inventions to delight the taste *Pericles* i 4 39
Palatine. Then there is the County Palatine.—He doth nothing but frown *Mer. of Venice* i 2 49
A better bad habit of frowning than the Count Palatine i 2 64
Palating. Not palating the taste of her dishonour *Troi. and Cres.* iv 1 59
Pale. They waxed pale for woe *T. G. of Ver.* iii 1 228
I am pale at mine heart to see thine eyes so red *Meas. for Meas.* iv 3 157

Pale. Too unruly deer, he breaks the pale And feeds from home *Com. of Errors* ii 1 100
Look'd he or red or pale, or sad or merrily? . . iv 2 4
Both man and master is possess'd; I know it by their pale and deadly looks . . . . iv 4 96
The fiend is strong within him.—Ay me, poor man, how pale and wan he looks! . . . . iv 4 111
I shall see thee, ere I die, look pale with love . . . *Much Ado* i 1 250
As I am an honest man, he looks pale. Art thou sick, or angry? . . v 1 131
You may look pale, but I should blush, I know, To be o'erheard *L. L. L.* iv 3 129
Why look you pale? Sea-sick, I think . . . . v 2 392
Why is your cheek so pale? How chance the roses there do fade so fast? *M. N. Dream* i 1 128
Over park, over pale, Thorough flood, thorough fire, I do wander . ii 1 4
The moon, the governess of floods, Pale in her anger, washes all the air ii 1 104
And pale of cheer, With sighs of love, that costs the fresh blood dear . iii 2 96
Shiver and look pale, Make periods in the midst of sentences . v 1 95
O Sisters Three, Come, come to me, With hands as pale as milk . v 1 345
Thou [silver] pale and common drudge 'Tween man and man *Mer. of Ven.* iii 2 103
I must blush and weep and thou must look pale and wonder *As Y. Like It* i 1 164
By this heaven, now at our sorrows pale, Say what thou canst . i 3 106
Why dost thou look so pale?—For fear, I promise you, if I look pale *T. of Shrew* ii 1 143
Look not pale, Bianca; thy father will not frown.—My cake is dough v 1 143
What, pale again? My fear hath catch'd your fondness . *All's Well* i 3 175
Pants and looks pale, as if a bear were at his heels . . *T. Night* iii 4 323
For the red blood reigns in the winter's pale . . *W. Tale* iv 3 4
Together with that pale, that white-faced shore, Whose foot spurns back the ocean's roaring tides . . . *K. John* ii 1 23
Look'st thou pale, France? do not let go thy hand.—Look to that, devil iii 1 195
Are you sick, Hubert? you look pale to-day: In sooth, I would you were iv 1 28
I am the cygnet to this pale faint swan, Who chants a doleful hymn . v 7 21
Pale trembling coward, there I throw my gage . *Richard II.* i 1 69
That which in mean men we intitle patience Is pale cold cowardice in noble breasts . . . . i 2 34
Darest with thy frozen admonition Make pale our cheek . . ii 1 118
Comfort, my liege: why looks your grace so pale? . . iii 2 75
Till so much blood thither come again, Have I not reason to look pale? iii 2 79
Why should we in the compass of a pale Keep law and form? . iii 4 40
What seal is that, that hangs without thy bosom? Yea, look'st thou pale? v 2 57
His cheek look'd pale, And on my face he turn'd an eye of death 1 *Hen. IV.* i 3 142
His cheek looks pale and with A rising sigh he wisheth you in heaven . iii 1 9
The day looks pale At his distemperature . . . . v 1 2
Left the liver white and pale, which is the badge of pusillanimity 2 *Hen. IV.* iv 3 113
Delivering o'er to executors pale The lazy yawning drone . *Hen. V.* i 2 203
On whom, as in despite, the sun looks pale, Killing their fruit with frowns iii 5 17
Every wretch, pining and pale before, Beholding him, plucks comfort iv Prol. 41
Behold, the English beach Pales in the flood with men . . v Prol. 10
Of France and England, whose very shores look pale With envy . v 2 378
I pluck this pale and maiden blossom here . . . . 1 *Hen. VI.* ii 4 47
Your cheeks do counterfeit our roses; For pale they look with fear . ii 4 63
This pale and angry rose . . Will I for ever and my faction wear . ii 4 107
These eyes, that see thee now well coloured, Shall see thee wither'd, bloody, pale and dead . . . . iv 2 38
Bounded in a pale, A little herd of England's timorous deer . . iv 2 45
How now! why look'st thou pale? why tremblest thou? 2 *Hen. VI.* iii 2 27
Sick with groans, Look pale as primrose with blood-drinking sighs . iii 2 63
Oft have I seen a timely-parted ghost, Of ashy semblance, meagre, pale and bloodless . . . . iii 2 162
These cheeks are pale for watching for your good . . . iv 7 90
And will you pale your head in Henry's glory, And rob his temples? 3 *Hen. VI.* i 4 103
But sever'd in a pale clear-shining sky . . . . ii 1 28
Your eyes do menace me: why look you pale? Who sent you? *Rich. III.* i 4 175
Look I so pale, Lord Dorset, as the rest?—Ay, my good lord . ii 1 83
Mark'd you not How that the guilty kindred of the queen Look'd pale? ii 1 136
But, like dumb statuas or breathing stones, Gazed each on other, and look'd deadly pale . . . . iii 7 26
How pale she looks, And of an earthy cold . . . *Hen. VIII.* iv 2 97
You i' the camlet, get up o' the rail; I'll peck you o'er the pales else . v 4 94
Grows to an envious fever Of pale and bloodless emulation *Troi. and Cres.* i 3 134
Reason and respect Make livers pale and lustihood deject . . ii 2 50
Like a bourn, a pale, a shore, confines Thy spacious and dilated parts . ii 3 260
Look, how thy eye turns pale! Look, how thy wounds do bleed at many vents! . . . . v 3 81
To break the heart of generosity, And make bold power look pale *Coriol.* i 1 216
All hurt behind; backs red, and faces pale With flight and agued fear! i 4 37
But is this true, sir?—Ay; and you'll look pale Before you find it other iv 6 101
Why doth your highness look so pale and wan?—Have I not reason, think you, to look pale? . . . . *T. Andron.* ii 3 90
So pale did shine the moon on Pyramus . . . . ii 3 231
Thy other banish'd son, with this dear sight Struck pale and bloodless iii 1 258
O, take this warm kiss on thy pale cold lips! . . . . v 3 153
Arise, fair sun, and kill the envious moon, Who is already sick and pale with grief . . . . *Rom. and Jul.* ii 2 5
That same pale hard-hearted wench, that Rosaline, Torments him so . ii 4 4
I'll warrant you, when I say so, she looks as pale as any clout . ii 4 218
Unwieldy, slow, heavy and pale as lead . . . . ii 5 17
A piteous corse, a bloody piteous corse; Pale, pale as ashes . . iii 2 55
Either my eyesight fails, or thou look'st pale.—And trust me, love, in my eye so do you. . . . . iii 5 57
I do beseech you, sir, have patience: Your looks are pale and wild . v 1 28
Romeo! O, pale! Who else? what, Paris too? And steep'd in blood? v 3 144
All the rest look like a chidden train: Calpurnia's cheek is pale *J. Cæsar* i 2 185
You look pale and gaze And put on fear and cast yourself in wonder . i 3 59
And wakes it now, to look so green and pale At what it did so freely? *Macbeth* i 7 37
Cancel and tear to pieces that great bond Which keeps me pale! . iii 2 50
Wash your hands, put on your nightgown; look not so pale . . v 1 69
You tremble and look pale: Is not this something more than fantasy? *Hamlet* i 1 53
Pale or red?—Nay, very pale.—And fix'd his eyes upon you?—Most constantly . . . . i 2 233
Oft breaking down the pales and forts of reason . . . i 4 28
The glow-worm shows the matin to be near, And 'gins to pale his uneffectual fire: Adieu, adieu! . . . . i 5 90
Pale as his shirt; his knees knocking each other . . . ii 1 81
Whereon do you look?—On him, on him! Look you, how pale he glares! iii 4 125
You that look pale and tremble at this chance . . . . v 2 345

Pale. What, look you pale? O, bear him out o' the air . . *Othello* v 1 104
Look you pale, mistress? Do you perceive the gastness of her eye? . v 1 105
Now, how dost thou look now? O ill-starr'd wench! Pale as thy smock! v 2 273
I am pale, Charmian.—Madam, he's married to Octavia *Ant. and Cleo.* ii 5 59
Whate'er the ocean pales, or sky inclips, Is thine, if thou wilt ha't . ii 7 74
Then, if you can, Be pale: I beg but leave to air this jewel . *Cymbeline* ii 4 96
Tell thee, with speechless tongues and semblance pale . . *Pericles* i 1 36
If this be true, which makes me pale to read it . . . . i 1 75
Pale ashes of the house of Lancaster! Thou bloodless remnant! *Rich. III.* i 2 6
Pale beggar-fear. Or with pale beggar-fear impeach my height *Rich. II.* i 1 189
Pale Cassius. What was't That moved pale Cassius to conspire? *A. and C.* ii 6 15
Pale cast. Thus the native hue of resolution Is sicklied o'er with the pale cast of thought . . . . *Hamlet* iii 1 85
Pale cheek. The other his pale cheeks, methinks, presenteth 3 *Hen. VI.* ii 5 100
Give colour to my pale cheek with thy blood . . . *Cymbeline* iv 2 330
Pale companion. The pale companion is not for our pomp *M. N. Dream* i 1 15
Pale complexion. Between the pale complexion of true love And the red glow of scorn . . . . *As Y. Like It* iii 4 56
Pale-dead. The gum down-roping from their pale-dead eyes . *Hen. V.* iv 2 48
Pale destruction. And pale destruction meets thee in the face 1 *Hen. VI.* iv 2 27
Pale distemperatures. At her heels a huge infectious troop Of pale distemperatures . . . . *Com. of Errors* v 1 82
Pale dull. In their pale dull mouths the gimmal bit . . *Hen. V.* iv 2 49
Pale envy. Advanced above pale envy's threatening reach *T. Andron.* ii 1 4
Pale-faced. Frighting her pale-faced villages with war . *Richard II.* ii 3 94
The pale-faced moon looks bloody on the earth . . . . ii 4 10
An easy leap, To pluck bright honour from the pale-faced moon 1 *Hen. IV.* i 3 202
Let pale-faced fear keep with the mean-born man . . 2 *Hen. VI.* iii 1 335
Pale fire. The moon's an arrant thief, And her pale fire she snatches from the sun . . . . *T. of Athens* iv 3 441
Pale flag. And death's pale flag is not advanced there . *Rom. and Jul.* v 3 96
Pale ghosts. The famish'd English, like pale ghosts, Faintly besiege us one hour in a month . . . . 1 *Hen. VI.* i 2 7
Pale-hearted. That I may tell pale-hearted fear it lies . *Macbeth* iv 1 85
Pale looks. Gilded pale looks, Part shame, part spirit renew'd *Cymbeline* iv 3 34
Pale moon. The pale moon shines by night . . . *W. Tale* iv 3 16
Pale policy. The French . . . Shake in their fear and with pale policy Seek to divert the English purposes . . . . *Hen. V.* ii Prol. 14
Pale primroses, That die unmarried . . . . . . *W. Tale* iv 4 122
Thou shalt not lack The flower that's like thy face, pale primrose *Cymbeline* iv 2 221
Pale queen. By this pale queen of night I swear . . *T. G. of Ver.* iv 2 100
Pale reflex. 'Tis but the pale reflex of Cynthia's brow *Rom. and Jul.* iii 5 20
Pale sphere. Thrice-crowned queen of night, survey With thy chaste eye, from thy pale sphere above . . . . . *As Y. Like It* iii 2 3
Pale-visaged. For your own ladies and pale-visaged maids Like Amazons come tripping after drums . . . . *K. John* v 2 154
Pale white. Blushing cheeks by faults are bred And fears by pale white shown . . . . *L. L. Lost* i 2 107
Paled in With rocks unscaleable and roaring waters . . *Cymbeline* iii 1 19
Paleness. Thy paleness moves me more than eloquence . *Mer. of Venice* iii 2 106
Pronouncing that the paleness of this flower Bewray'd the faintness of my master's heart . . . . 1 *Hen. VI.* iv 1 106
Paler. This night methinks is but the daylight sick; It looks a little paler . . . . *Mer. of Venice* v 1 125
You look paler and paler: pray you, draw homewards . *As Y. Like It* iv 3 178
Palestine. Richard, that robb'd the lion of his heart And fought the holy wars in Palestine . . . . *K. John* ii 1 4
I know a lady in Venice would have walked barefoot to Palestine for a touch of his nether lip . . . . *Othello* iv 3 39
Palfrey It is the prince of palfreys . . . . . *Hen. V.* iii 7 29
Vary deserved praise on my palfrey: it is a theme as fluent as the sea . iii 7 35
In Cheapside shall my palfry go to grass . . 2 *Hen. VI.* iv 2 75
Provide thee two proper palfreys, black as jet. . . *T. Andron.* v 2 50
Palisadoes. Of palisadoes, frontiers, parapets, Of basilisks . 1 *Hen. IV.* ii 3 55
Pall. Come, thick night, And pall thee in the dunnest smoke of hell *Macb.* i 5 52
Our indiscretion sometimes serves us well, When our deep plots do pall *Hamlet* v 2 9
Pallas. Apollo, Pallas, Jove, or Mercury, Inspire me! *T. Andron.* iv 1 66
Here, boy, to Pallas: here, to Mercury: To Saturn, Caius, not to Saturnine iv 3 55
Good boy, in Virgo's lap; give it Pallas . . . . . iv 3 64
Palled. For this, I'll never follow thy pall'd fortunes more *Ant. and Cleo.* ii 7 88
Pallet. Upon uneasy pallets stretching thee . . . 2 *Hen. IV.* iii 1 10
Palliament. This palliament of white and spotless hue . *T. Andron.* i 1 182
Palm. Hard in the palm of the hand . . . *Com. of Errors* iii 2 124
By this virgin palm now kissing thine, I will be thine . *L. L. Lost* v 2 816
Lean but upon a rush, The cicatrice and capable impressure Thy palm some moment keeps . . . . *As Y. Like It* iii 5 24
But to be paddling palms and pinching fingers . . . *W. Tale* i 2 115
Still virginalling Upon his palm!—How now, you wanton calf! . . i 2 126
When his fair angels would salute my palm . . . *K. John* ii 1 590
As now again to snatch our palm from palm, Unswear faith sworn . iii 1 244
I will sooner have a beard grow in the palm of my hand than he shall get one on his cheek . . . . 2 *Hen. IV.* i 2 24
And spirit of sense Hard as the palm of ploughman . *Troi. and Cres.* i 1 59
Must not so stale his palm, nobly acquired . . . . ii 3 201
What he shall receive of us in duty Gives us more palm in beauty . iii 1 170
Limekilns i' the palm, incurable bone-ache . . . . v 1 25
The virginal palms of your daughters . . . . *Coriolanus* v 2 46
And bear the palm for having bravely shed Thy wife and children's blood v 3 117
And palm to palm is holy palmers' kiss . . . *Rom. and Jul.* i 5 102
You shall see him a palm in Athens again . . . *T. of Athens* v 1 12
So get the start of the majestic world And bear the palm alone *J. Cæsar* i 2 131
You yourself Are much condemn'd to have an itching palm . . iv 3 10
I an itching palm! You know that you are Brutus that speak this . iv 3 12
But do not dull thy palm with entertainment Of each new-hatch'd, unfledged comrade . . . . *Hamlet* i 3 64
As love between them like the palm might flourish . . . v 2 40
He takes her by the palm: ay, well said, whisper . . . *Othello* ii 1 168
Didst thou not see her paddle with the palm of his hand? . . ii 1 259
There's a palm presages chastity, if nothing else . *Ant. and Cleo.* i 2 47
If an oily palm be not a fruitful prognostication, I cannot scratch mine ear i 2 53
Palmer. Where do the palmers lodge? . . . . . *All's Well* iii 5 38
My sceptre for a palmer's walking-staff . . . . *Richard II.* iii 3 151
Thy hand is made to grasp a palmer's staff . . . 2 *Hen. VI.* v 1 97
And palm to palm is holy palmers' kiss . . . . *Rom. and Jul.* i 5 102
Have not saints lips, and holy palmers too?—Ay, pilgrim, lips that they must use in prayer . . . . i 5 103
Palm-tree. Look here what I found on a palm-tree . . *As Y. Like It* iii 2 186
Palmy. In the most high and palmy state of Rome . . . *Hamlet* i 1 113

Palpable. Gross as a mountain, open, palpable . . . 1 *Hen. IV.* ii 4 250
Why, who's so gross, That seeth not this palpable device? *Richard III.* iii 6 11
I see thee yet, in form as palpable As this which now I draw *Macbeth* ii 1 40
A hit, a very palpable hit . . . . *Hamlet* v 2 292
'Tis probable and palpable to thinking . . . *Othello* i 2 76
Palpable-gross. This palpable-gross play hath well beguiled The heavy gait of night . . . . *M. N. Dream* v 1 374
Palsied. And doth beg the alms Of palsied eld . *Meas. for Meas.* iii 1 36
The palsied intercession of such a decayed dotant as you . *Coriolanus* v 2 46
Palsies. Cold palsies, raw eyes, dirt-rotten livers *Troi. and Cres.* v 1 23
Palsy. O, then how quickly should this arm of mine, Now prisoner to the palsy, chastise thee! *Richard II.* ii 3 104
Why dost thou quiver, man?—The palsy, and not fear, provokes me 2 *Hen. VI.* iv 7 98
Palsy-fumbling. With a palsy-fumbling on his gorget *Troi. and Cres.* i 3 174
Palter. A whoreson dog, that shall palter thus with us! . . ii 3 244
You palter.—In faith, I do not: come hither once again . . v 2 48
Have spoke the word, And will not palter . . . *J. Cæsar* ii 1 126
And be these juggling fiends no more believed, That palter with us in a double sense . . . . *Macbeth* v 8 20
Send humble treaties, dodge And palter in the shifts of lowness *A. and C.* iii 11 63
Paltering. This paltering Becomes not Rome . . *Coriolanus* iii 1 58
Paltry. She shall be our messenger to this paltry knight *Mer. Wives* ii 1 164
What's the matter?—About a hoop of gold, a paltry ring *Mer. of Venice* v 1 147
It is a paltry cap, A custard-coffin, a bauble . . *T. of Shrew* iv 3 81
A very dishonest paltry boy . . . . . *T. Night* iii 4 420
Then turn your forces from this paltry siege . . . *K. John* ii 1 54
To save a paltry life and slay bright fame . 1 *Hen. VI.* iv 6 45
O that I were a god, to shoot forth thunder Upon these paltry, servile, abject drudges! . . . . . . 2 *Hen. VI.* iv 1 105
Underneath an alehouse' paltry sign . . . . . v 2 67
A paltry fellow, Long kept in Bretagne at our mother's cost *Richard III.* v 3 323
A paltry, insolent fellow!—How he describes himself! *Troi. and Cres.* ii 3 218
'Tis paltry to be Cæsar; Not being Fortune, he's but Fortune's knave, A minister of her will . . . . . *Ant. and Cleo.* v 2 2
Paly. And through their paly flames Each battle sees the other's umber'd face . . . . *Hen. V.* iv Prol. 8
Fain would I go to chafe his paly lips With twenty thousand kisses 2 *Hen. VI.* iii 2 141
The roses in thy lips and cheeks shall fade To paly ashes *Rom. and Jul.* iv 1 100
Pamper. Pour all your tears! I am your sorrow's nurse, And I will pamper it with lamentations . . . . *Richard III.* ii 2 88
Pampered. Those pamper'd animals That rage in savage sensuality *M. Ado* iv 1 61
Hollow pamper'd jades of Asia . . . . 2 *Hen. IV.* ii 4 178
Pamphlet. With written pamphlets studiously devised . 1 *Hen. VI.* iii 1 2
Pancake. Swore by his honour they were good pancakes *As Y. Like It* i 2 67
The pancakes were naught and the mustard was good . . i 2 69
He had sworn it away before ever he saw those pancakes . . i 2 85
As a pancake for Shrove Tuesday, a morris for May-day . *All's Well* ii 2 25
Pandar. To whom you should have been a pandar . . *Mer. Wives* v 5 176
Troilus the first employer of pandars . . . *Much Ado* v 2 31
Camillo was his help in this, his pandar . . . *W. Tale* ii 1 46
Like a base pandar, hold the chamber-door . . . *Hen. V.* iv 5 14
I cannot come to Cressid but by Pandar . . *Troi. and Cres.* i 1 98
Tell me, Apollo, for thy Daphne's love, What Cressid is, what Pandar? i 1 102
Ourself the merchant, and this sailing Pandar Our doubtful hope, our convoy . . . . i 1 106
But more in Troilus thousand fold I see Than in the glass of Pandar's praise i 2 311
Call them all Pandars; let all constant men be Troiluses, all false women Cressids, and all brokers-between Pandars! . . . . . iii 2 210
Cupid grant all tongue-tied maidens here Bed, chamber, Pandar to provide this gear! . . . . iii 2 220
As many as be here of pandar's hall, Your eyes, half out, weep out at Pandar's fall . . . . v 10 48
Since frost itself as actively doth burn And reason pandars will *Hamlet* iii 4 88
Art nothing but the composition of a knave, beggar, coward, pandar *Lear* ii 2 23
If thou fear to strike and to make me certain it is done, thou art the pandar to her dishonour . . . . *Cymbeline* iii 4 32
What, are you packing, sirrah? Come hither: ah, you precious pandar! iii 5 81
Pandarly. O you pandarly rascals! . . . . *Mer. Wives* iv 2 122
Pandarus. Shall I Sir Pandarus of Troy become? . . . i 3 83
I would play Lord Pandarus of Phrygia . . . *T. Night* iii 1 58
O Pandarus! I tell thee, Pandarus,—When I do tell thee, there my hopes lie drown'd . . . . *Troi. and Cres.* i 1 48
What, art thou angry, Pandarus? what, with me?—Because she's kin to me . . . . i 1 74
Pandarus,— Not I.—Sweet Pandarus,— Pray you, speak no more to me i 1 87
But Pandarus,—O gods, how do you plague me! I cannot come to Cressid but by Pandar. . . . . i 1 97
Friend, know me better; I am the Lord Pandarus . . . iii 1 12
My Lord Pandarus; honey-sweet lord,— Go to, sweet queen, go to . iii 1 71
He hangs the lip at something: you know all, Lord Pandarus . iii 1 153
O gentle Pandarus, From Cupid's shoulder pluck his painted wings! . iii 2 14
Pandulph. I Pandulph, of fair Milan cardinal . . . *K. John* iii 1 138
The Cardinal Pandulph is within at rest, Who half an hour since came v 7 82
Panel. Then one of you will prove a shrunk panel and, like green timber, warp, warp . . . . *As Y. Like It* iii 3 89
Pang. I suffered the pangs of three several deaths . *Mer. Wives* iii 5 109
In corporal sufferance finds a pang as great As when a giant dies *Meas. for Meas.* iii 1 80
And shall do till the pangs of death shake him . . *T. Night* i 5 81
If ever thou shalt love, In the sweet pangs of it remember me . ii 4 16
Hath for your love as great a pang of heart As you have for Olivia . ii 4 93
Satisfaction can be none but by pangs of death and sepulchre . iii 4 262
I do see the cruel pangs of death Right in thine eye . *K. John* v 4 59
He cannot long hold out these pangs . . . 2 *Hen. IV.* iv 4 117
See, how the pangs of death do make him grin! . 2 *Hen. VI.* iii 3 24
In the very pangs of death he cried, Like to a dismal clangor 3 *Hen. VI.* ii 3 17
Here's the pang that pinches . . . . . *Hen. VIII.* ii 3 1
More pangs and fears than wars or women have . . . iii 2 370
Her sufferance made Almost each pang a death . . . v 1 69
To ease them of their griefs, . . . Their pangs of love *T. of Athens* v 1 203
The pangs of despised love, the law's delay, The insolence of office *Hamlet* iii 1 72
Pitying The pangs of barr'd affections . . . *Cymbeline* i 1 82
A touch more rare Subdues all pangs, all fears . . . v 5 136
Make swift the pangs Of my queen's travails! . . . *Pericles* iii 1 13
Panged. How thy memory Will then be pang'd by me! . *Cymbeline* iii 4 98
Panging. A sufferance panging As soul and body's severing *Hen. VIII.* ii 3 15
Pannier. The turkeys in my pannier are quite starved . 1 *Hen. IV.* ii 1 30
Pannonian. I am perfect That the Pannonians and Dalmatians for Their liberties are now in arms . . . . . . *Cymbeline* iii 1 74
The common men are now in action 'Gainst the Pannonians and Dalmatians . . . . iii 7 3
Pansa. Where thou slew'st Hirtius and Pansa, consuls . *Ant. and Cleo.* i 4 58
Pansies. There is pansies, that's for thoughts . . *Hamlet* iv 5 176
Pants and looks pale, as if a bear were at his heels . . *T. Night* iii 4 323
Find we a time for frighted peace to pant . . 1 *Hen. IV.* i 1 2
Now breathless wrong Shall sit and pant in your great chairs of ease *T. of Athens* v 4 11
I pant for life: some good I mean to do, Despite of mine own nature *Lear* v 3 243
Make love's quick pants in Desdemona's arms . . . *Othello* ii 1 80
Leap thou, attire and all, Through proof of harness to my heart, and there Ride on the pants triumphing! . . . *Ant. and Cleo.* iv 8 16
Pantaloon. The sixth age shifts Into the lean and slipper'd pantaloon, With spectacles on nose . . . . . . *As Y. Like It* ii 7 158
That we might beguile the old pantaloon . . . *T. of Shrew* iii 1 37
Panted. And having lost her breath, she spoke, and panted, That she did make defect perfection . . . . . *Ant. and Cleo.* ii 2 235
Pantheon. And in the sacred Pantheon her espouse . *T. Andron.* i 1 242
Ascend, fair queen, Pantheon. Lords, accompany Your noble emperor i 1 333
Panther. Please your majesty To hunt the panther and the hart with me i 1 493
I have dogs, my lord, Will rouse the proudest panther in the chase . ii 2 21
The loathsome pit Where I espied the panther fast asleep . . ii 3 194
Panthino, what sad talk was that Wherewith my brother held you? *T. G. of Ver.* i 3 1
Come on, Panthino: you shall be employ'd To hasten on his expedition i 3 76
Panting. Against the panting sides of his poor jade . 2 *Hen. IV.* i 1 45
Smother'd it within my panting bulk . . . *Richard III.* i 4 40
He never stood To ease his breast with panting . . *Coriolanus* ii 2 126
Stew'd in his haste, half breathless, panting forth . . *Lear* ii 4 31
Pantingly. She heaved the name of 'father' Pantingly forth . . iv 3 28
Pantler. She was both pantler, butler, cook . . . *W. Tale* iv 4 56
Would have made a good pantler, a' would ha' chipped bread well 2 *Hen. IV.* ii 4 258
And call me pantler and bread-chipper and I know not what . . ii 4 342
A hilding for a livery, a squire's cloth, A pantler, not so eminent *Cymb.* ii 3 129
Pantry. The nurse cursed in the pantry, and every thing in extremity. I must hence to wait . . . . *Rom. and Jul.* i 3 102
Panyn. He's a rogue, and a passy measures panyn . . . *T. Night* v 1 207
Pap. Thumped him with thy bird-bolt under the left pap . *L. L. Lost* iv 3 24
Out, sword, and wound The pap of Pyramus; Ay, that left pap *M. N. D.* v 1 302
Paper. I would I knew his mind.—Peruse this paper, madam *T. G. of Ver.* i 2 34
There, take the paper: see it be return'd; Or else return no more . i 2 46
Nothing.—Why didst thou stoop, then?—To take a paper up that I let fall.—And is that paper nothing? . . . . i 2 73
Let the papers lie: You would be fingering them, to anger me . . i 2 100
I'll kiss each several paper for amends. Look, here is writ 'kind Julia' i 2 108
Shall these papers lie like tell-tales here? . . . . . i 2 133
What news, then, in your paper?—The blackest news that ever thou heardest . . . . iii 1 284
Come, fool, come; try me in thy paper . . . . . iii 1 299
I have unadvised Deliver'd you a paper that I should not . . iv 4 128
Full of new-found oaths; which he will break As easily as I do tear his paper . . . . iv 4 136
Sir Hugh send-a you? Rugby, baille me some paper . *Mer. Wives* i 4 93
He's in for a commodity of brown paper and old ginger *Meas. for Meas.* iv 3 6
There will she sit in her smock till she have writ a sheet of paper *M. Ado* ii 3 138
Now you talk of a sheet of paper, I remember a pretty jest . . ii 3 140
Here's a paper written in his hand, A halting sonnet . . . v 4 86
Give me the paper; let me read the same . . . *L. L. Lost* i 1 116
He hath not eat paper, as it were; he hath not drunk ink . . iv 2 26
Deliver this paper into the royal hand of the king: it may concern much iv 2 145
Here comes one with a paper: God give him grace to groan! . . iv 3 19
How shall she know my griefs? I'll drop the paper: Sweet leaves, shade folly . . . . iv 3 43
He comes in like a perjure, wearing papers . . . . iv 3 48
As much love in rhyme As would be cramm'd up in a sheet of paper . v 2 7
Whiter than the paper it writ on Is the fair hand that writ *Mer. of Venice* ii 4 13
There are some shrewd contents in yon same paper . . . iii 2 246
I must freely have the half of anything That this same paper brings you iii 2 253
Here are a few of the unpleasant'st words That ever blotted paper! . iii 2 255
Here is a letter, lady; The paper as the body of my friend, And every word in it a gaping wound . . . . iii 2 267
Take your paper too, And let me have them very well perfumed *T. of Shrew* i 2 151
Here 'tis; here's a paper: shall I read it to you? . . *All's Well* iv 3 233
Commend the paper to his gracious hand . . . . . v 1 31
Deliver me this paper.—Foh! prithee, stand away: a paper from fortune's close-stool to give to a nobleman! . . . . . v 2 16
In Florence was it from a casement thrown me, Wrapp'd in a paper . v 3 94
And as many lies as will lie in thy sheet of paper . . *T. Night* iii 2 50
Help me to a candle, and pen, ink and paper . . . . iv 2 88
Good fool, help me to some light and some paper . . . iv 2 114
Some ink, paper and light; and convey what I will set down to my lady iv 2 118
From where you do remain let paper show . . . *Richard II.* i 3 250
Make dust our paper and with rainy eyes Write sorrow on the bosom of the earth . . . . iii 2 146
Read o'er this paper while the glass doth come . . . . iv 1 269
The manner of their taking may appear At large discoursed in this paper v 6 10
What hast thou found?—Nothing but papers . . . 1 *Hen. IV.* ii 4 583
We fortify in paper and in figures, Using the names of men . 2 *Hen. IV.* i 3 56
The rest the paper tells . . . . iii 1 147
What see you in those papers that you lose So much complexion? *Hen. V.* ii 2 72
Look ye, how they change! Their cheeks are paper . . . ii 2 74
Mail'd up in shame, with papers on my back . . . 2 *Hen. VI.* ii 4 31
Sends me a paper to persuade me patience . . . 3 *Hen. VI.* iii 3 176
When thou didst crown his warlike brows with paper . *Richard III.* i 3 175
Some ink and paper in my tent: I'll draw the form and model of our battle v 3 23
I will not sup to-night. Give me some ink and paper . . . v 3 49
Set it down. Is ink and paper ready?—It is, my lord . . . v 3 75
And his own letter, The honourable board of council out, Must fetch him in the papers . . . . *Hen. VIII.* i 1 80
Look'd he o' the inside of the paper?—Presently He did unseal them . iii 2 78
This morning Papers of state he sent me to peruse . . . iii 2 121
Some spirit put this paper in the packet, To bless your eye withal . iii 2 129
I must read this paper; I fear, the story of his anger. 'Tis so; This paper has undone me . . . . iii 2 208
May I be bold to ask what that contains, That paper in your hand? . iv 1 14
Had I not known those customs, I should have been beholding to your paper . . . . iv 1 21

Paper. Go tell the lords o' the city I am here: Deliver them this paper *Coriolanus* v 6 2
Get me ink and paper, And hire post-horses *Rom. and Jul.* v 1 25
I fear me thou wilt give away thyself in paper shortly *T. of Athens* i 2 248
Take this paper, And look you lay it in the prætor's chair *J. Cæsar* i 3 142
I will hie, And so bestow these papers as you bade me i 3 151
Searching the window for a flint, I found This paper, thus seal'd up ii 1 37
I have seen her, . . . unlock her closet, take forth paper, fold it, write upon 't, read it, afterwards seal it, and again return to bed *Macbeth* v 1 7
What paper were you reading?—Nothing, my lord *Lear* i 2 30
If the matter of this paper be certain, you have mighty business in hand iii 5 16
To know our enemies' minds, we'ld rip their hearts; Their papers, is more lawful iv 6 266
With this ungracious paper strike the sight Of the death-practised duke iv 6 283
Why, fare thee well: I will o'erlook thy paper v 1 50
Shut your mouth, dame, Or with this paper shall I stop it v 3 155
Know'st thou this paper?—Ask me not what I know v 3 160
He did not call; he's busy in the paper *Othello* iv 1 241
Was this fair paper, this most goodly book, Made to write 'whore' upon? iv 2 71
Here's another discontented paper, Found in his pocket too v 2 314
Ink and paper, Charmian. Welcome, my good Alexas *Ant. and Cleo.* i 5 65
Get me ink and paper: He shall have every day a several greeting i 5 76
If he should write, And I not have it, 'twere a paper lost *Cymbeline* i 3 3
O damn'd paper! Black as the ink that's on thee! iii 2 19
Why tender'st thou that paper to me, with A look untender? iii 4 11
What shall I need to draw my sword? the paper Hath cut her throat already iii 4 34
This paper is the history of my knowledge Touching her flight iii 5 99
Bid Nestor bring me spices, ink and paper, My casket and my jewels *Pericles* iii 1 66

Paper bullets. Shall quips and sentences and these paper bullets of the brain awe a man? *Much Ado* ii 3 249

Paper-faced. Thou paper-faced villain 2 *Hen. IV.* v 4 12

Paper-mill. Contrary to the king, his crown and dignity, thou hast built a paper-mill 2 *Hen. VI.* iv 7 41

Paphlagonia. Philadelphos, king Of Paphlagonia *Ant. and Cleo.* iii 6 71

Paphos. I met her deity Cutting the clouds towards Paphos and her son Dove-drawn with her *Tempest* iv 1 93
So With the dove of Paphos might the crow Vie feathers white iv Gower *Per.* 32

Papist. Old Poysam the papist *All's Well* i 3 56

Parable. Thou shalt never get such a secret from me but by a parable.—'Tis well that I get it so *T. G. of Ver.* ii 5 41

Paracelsus. Both of Galen and Paracelsus *All's Well* ii 3 12

Paradise. Let me live here ever; So rare a wonder'd father and a wife Makes this place Paradise *Tempest* iv 1 124
Is a paradise To what we fear of death *Meas. for Meas.* iii 1 131
Not that Adam that kept the Paradise *Com. of Errors* iv 3 16
What fool is not so wise To lose an oath to win a paradise? *L. L. Lost* iv 3 73
You would for paradise break faith and troth iv 3 143
Before the time I did Lysander see, Seem'd Athens as a paradise to me *M. N. Dream* i 1 205
The air of paradise did fan the house And angels officed all *All's Well* iii 2 128
His body as a paradise, To envelop and contain celestial spirits *Hen. V.* i 1 30
If ye should lead her into a fool's paradise, as they say *Rom. and Jul.* ii 4 176
Didst bower the spirit of a fiend In mortal paradise of such sweet flesh iii 2 82

Paradox. O paradox! Black is the badge of hell *L. L. Lost* iv 3 254
What is or is not, serves As stuff for these two to make paradoxes *Troi. and Cres.* i 3 184
You undergo too strict a paradox, Striving to make an ugly deed look fair *T. of Athens* iii 5 24
This was sometime a paradox, but now the time gives it proof *Hamlet* iii 1 115
These are old fond paradoxes to make fools laugh i' the alehouse *Othello* ii 1 139

Paragon. Tunis was never graced before with such a paragon to their queen *Tempest* ii 1 75
Is she not a heavenly saint?—No; but she is an earthly paragon *T. G. of V.* ii 4 146
A very paramour for a sweet voice.—You must say 'paragon:' *M. N. D.* iv 2 13
And hath he too Exposed this paragon? *W. Tale* v 1 153
The beauty of the world! the paragon of animals! *Hamlet* ii 2 320
A maid That paragons description and wild fame *Othello* ii 1 62
By Isis, I will give thee bloody teeth, If thou with Cæsar paragon again My man of men *Ant. and Cleo.* i 5 71
By Jupiter, an angel! or, if not, An earthly paragon! *Cymbeline* iii 6 44
That paragon, thy daughter,—For whom my heart drops blood v 5 147
He shall come and find Our paragon to all reports thus blasted *Pericles* iv 1 36
Therefore say what a paragon she is, and thou hast the harvest iv 2 152

Paragoned. The primest creature That's paragon'd o' the world *Hen. VIII.* ii 4 230

Parallel. For the liberal arts Without a parallel *Tempest* i 2 74
For rapes and ravishments he parallels Nessus *All's Well* iv 3 281
Whose high respect and rich validity Did lack a parallel v 3 193
As near as the extremest ends Of parallels *Troi. and Cres.* i 3 168
Whom, we know well, The world's large spaces cannot parallel ii 2 162
'Twas a rough night.—My young remembrance cannot parallel A fellow to it.—O horror, horror, horror! *Macbeth* ii 3 67
How am I then a villain To counsel Cassio to this parallel course? *Othello* ii 3 355
In Britain where was he That could stand up his parallel? *Cymbeline* v 4 54

Paralleled. His life is parallel'd Even with the stroke and line of his great justice *Meas. for Meas.* iv 2 82

Paramour. He is a very paramour for a sweet voice.—You must say 'paragon:' a paramour is, God bless us, a thing of naught *M. N. D.* iv 2 12
Encompass'd with thy lustful paramours 1 *Hen. VI.* iii 2 53
Fitter is my study and my books Than wanton dalliance with a paramour v 1 23
Remember that thou hast a wife; Then how can Margaret be thy paramour? v 3 81
Shall I believe That unsubstantial death is amorous, And that the lean abhorred monster keeps Thee here in dark to be his paramour? *Rom. and Jul.* v 3 105

Parapet. Of palisadoes, frontiers, parapets 1 *Hen. IV.* ii 3 55

Paraquito. You paraquito, answer me Directly unto this question ii 3 88

Parasite. My parasite, my soldier, statesman, all *W. Tale* i 2 168
He is a flatterer, A parasite, a keeper back of death *Richard II.* ii 2 70
When steel grows soft as the parasite's silk *Coriolanus* i 9 45
Detested parasites, Courteous destroyers, affable wolves, meek bears! *T. of Athens* iii 6 104

Parca. Ha! art thou bedlam? dost thou thirst, base Trojan, To have me fold up Parca's fatal web? *Hen. V.* v 1 21

Parcel. For divers philosophers hold that the lips is parcel of the mouth *Mer. Wives* i 1 237
It is a branch and parcel of mine oath, A charitable duty *Com. of Errors* v 1 106
A holy parcel of the fairest dames *L. L. Lost* v 2 160
I am glad this parcel of wooers are so reasonable *Mer. of Venice* i 2 119

Parcel. Had they mark'd him In parcels as I did *As Y. Like It* iii 5 125
This youthful parcel Of noble bachelors stand at my bestowing *All's Well* ii 3 58
Between these main parcels of dispatch effected many nicer v 3 104
I have about me many parcels of charge.—What hast here? ballads? *W. Tale* iv 4 261
His eloquence the parcel of a reckoning 1 *Hen. IV.* ii 4 113
That swollen parcel of dropsies, that huge bombard of sack ii 4 496
I will die a hundred thousand deaths Ere break the smallest parcel of this vow iii 2 159
I sent your grace The parcels and particulars of our grief 2 *Hen. IV.* iv 2 36
Many a thousand, Which now mistrust no parcel of my fear 3 *Hen. VI.* v 6 38
The several parcels of his plate, his treasure, Rich stuffs *Hen. VIII.* iii 2 125
Some parcels of their power are forth already, And only hitherward *Coriol.* i 2 32
'Tis, as it were, a parcel of their feast iv 5 231
Here comes a parcel of our hopeful booty *T. Andron.* ii 3 49
Whereof by parcels she had something heard, But not intentively *Othello* i 3 154
I see men's judgements are A parcel of their fortunes *Ant. and Cleo.* iii 13 32
That mine own servant should Parcel the sum of my disgraces by Addition of his envy! v 2 163

Parcel-bawd. He, sir! a tapster, sir; parcel-bawd *Meas. for Meas.* ii 1 63

Parcel-gilt. Thou didst swear to me upon a parcel-gilt goblet 2 *Hen. IV.* ii 1 94

Parcelled. Their woes are parcell'd, mine are general *Richard III.* ii 2 81

Parch. We were better parch in Afric sun Than in the pride and salt scorn of his eyes *Troi. and Cres.* i 3 370

Parched. Entreat the north To make his bleak winds kiss my parched lips And comfort me with cold *K. John* v 7 40
Hath thy fiery heart so parch'd thine entrails That not a tear can fall? 3 *Hen. VI.* i 4 87

Parching. And to sun's parching heat display'd my cheeks 1 *Hen. VI.* i 2 77
In open field, In winter's cold and summer's parching heat 2 *Hen. VI.* i 1 81
Baked and impasted with the parching streets *Hamlet* ii 2 481

Parchment. If the skin were parchment and the blows you gave were ink, Your own handwriting would tell you *Com. of Errors* iii 1 13
Nor brass nor stone nor parchment bears not one [example] *W. Tale* i 2 360
I am a scribbled form, drawn with a pen Upon a parchment *K. John* v 7 33
Bound in with shame, With inky blots and rotten parchment bonds *Richard II.* ii 1 64
That of the skin of an innocent lamb should be made parchment? that parchment, being scribbled o'er, should undo a man? 2 *Hen. VI.* iv 2 87
Here's a parchment with the seal of Cæsar; I found it in his closet *J. C.* iii 2 133
Is not parchment made of sheep-skins?—Ay, my lord, and of calf-skins *Hamlet* v 1 123

Pard. More pinch-spotted make them Than pard or cat o' mountain *Temp.* iv 1 262
Be it ounce, or cat, or bear, Pard, or boar with bristled hair *M. N. Dream* ii 2 31
Then a soldier, Full of strange oaths and bearded like the pard *As Y. L. It* ii 7 150
False As . . . Pard to the hind, or stepdame to her son *Troi. and Cres.* iii 2 201

Pardon, master; I will be correspondent to command *Tempest* i 2 296
I resign and do entreat Thou pardon me my wrongs v 1 119
As you look To have my pardon, trim it handsomely v 1 293
What means this passion at his name?—Pardon, dear madam *T. G. of Ver.* i 2 17
Did in your name receive it: pardon the fault, I pray i 2 40
Even now about it! I will pardon you iii 2 98
I pardon them and thee: Dispose of them as thou know'st their deserts v 4 158
I pray you, pardon me; pray heartily, pardon me *Mer. Wives* iii 3 243
Pardon, good father! good my mother, pardon! v 5 229
Pardon is still the nurse of second woe *Meas. for Meas.* ii 1 298
I crave your honour's pardon. What shall be done, sir? ii 2 14
You might pardon him, And neither heaven nor man grieve at the mercy ii 2 49
As good To pardon him that hath from nature stolen A man already made ii 4 43
Ignomy in ransom and free pardon Are of two houses ii 4 111
Sign me a present pardon for my brother ii 4 152
So then you hope of pardon from Lord Angelo? iii 1 1
Let me ask my sister pardon iii 1 173
What, I prithee, might be the cause?—No, pardon; 'tis a secret iii 2 142
I hope it is some pardon or reprieve For the most gentle Claudio iv 2 74
Here comes Claudio's pardon.—My lord hath sent you this note iv 2 104
This is his pardon, purchased by such sin For which the pardoner himself is in iv 2 111
She's come to know If yet her brother's pardon be come hither iv 3 112
Hath yet the deputy sent my brother's pardon? iv 3 118
To try her gracious fortune with Lord Angelo For her poor brother's pardon v 1 77
That's somewhat madly spoken.—Pardon it; The phrase is to the matter v 1 89
Pardon, my lord; I will not show my face Until my husband bid me v 1 169
What you have spoke I pardon: sit you down: We'll borrow place of him v 1 366
O, give me pardon, That I, your vassal, have employ'd and pain'd Your unknown sovereignty! v 1 390
This new-married man . . . you must pardon For Mariana's sake v 1 407
And yet here's one in place I cannot pardon v 1 504
The offence pardons itself v 1 540
For we may pity, though not pardon thee *Com. of Errors* i 1 98
I crave your pardon. Soon at five o'clock, Please you, I'll meet with you i 2 26
All women shall pardon me. Because I will not do them the wrong to mistrust any *Much Ado* i 1 244
Will you not tell me who told you so?—No, you shall pardon me ii 1 131
I cry you mercy, uncle. By your grace's pardon ii 1 354
Pardon, goddess of the night, Those that slew thy virgin knight v 3 12
O, pardon me, my stars! *L. L. Lost* iii 1 78
Under pardon, sir, what are the contents? iv 2 103
O, pardon love this wrong iv 2 121
The page, Hercules,— Pardon, sir; error v 1 137
I do entreat your grace to pardon me *M. N. Dream* i 1 58
Gentles, do not reprehend: If you pardon, we will mend v 1 437
I pardon thee thy life before thou ask it *Mer. of Venice* iv 1 369
Nay, take my life and all; pardon not that iv 1 374
He shall do this, or else I do recant The pardon that I late pronounced iv 1 392
I entreat you home with me to dinner.—I humbly do desire your grace of pardon: I must away this night iv 1 402
Grant me two things, I pray you, Not to deny me, and to pardon me iv 1 424
Only for this, I pray you, pardon me iv 1 437
Pardon this fault, and by my soul I swear I never more will break an oath v 1 247
A beard neglected, which you have not; but I pardon you for that *As Y. Like It* iii 2 395
The common executioner . . . Falls not the axe upon the humbled neck But first begs pardon iii 5 6
Let me entreat of you To pardon me yet for a night or two *T. of Shrew* Ind. 2 121
Sir, pardon me in what I have to say iv 4 38
Pardon, old father, my mistaking eyes, That have been so bedazzled iv 5 45

Pardon. Thou art a reverend father; Pardon, I pray thee, for my mad mistaking . . . *T. of Shrew* iv 5 49
I say, I am your mother.—Pardon, madam . . . *All's Well* i 3 160
Do you love my son?—Your pardon, noble mistress!—Love you my son? . . . i 3 192
Pardon, my lord, for me and for my tidings . . . ii 1 63
Then here's a man stands, that has brought his pardon . . . ii 1 65
Speak; thine answer.—Pardon, my gracious lord; for I submit . . . ii 3 174
Pray, sir, your pardon.—Well, what would you say? . . . ii 5 83
This I must say, But first I beg my pardon . . . v 3 12
Let him not ask our pardon; The nature of his great offence is dead . . v 3 22
My high-repented blames, Dear sovereign, pardon to me . . . v 3 37
Love that comes too late, Like a remorseful pardon slowly carried, To the great sender turns a sour offence . . . v 3 58
'Tis but the shadow of a wife you see, The name and not the thing.—Both, both. O, pardon! . . . v 3 309
Pardon me, sir, your bad entertainment . . . *T. Night* ii 1 34
Would you'ld pardon me . . . iii 3 24
Pardon me, sweet one, even for the vows We made each other but so late ago . . . v 1 221
Thy lewd-tongued wife, Whom for this time we pardon . . . *W. Tale* ii 3 173
Apollo, pardon My great profaneness 'gainst thine oracle! . . . iii 2 154
To chide at your extremes it not becomes me: O, pardon, that I name them! . . . iv 4 7
Your pardon, sir; for this I'll blush you thanks . . . iv 4 594
Pardon, madam: The one I have almost forgot,—your pardon . . . v 1 103
Pardon me all the faults I have committed to your worship . . . v 2 160
Both your pardons, That e'er I put between your holy looks My ill suspicion . . . v 3 147
By the merit of vile gold, dross, dust, Purchase corrupted pardon of a man, Who in that sale sells pardon from himself . . . *K. John* iii 1 166
Your grace shall pardon me, I will not back . . . v 2 78
Exactly begg'd Your grace's pardon, and I hope I had it . . . *Richard II.* i 1 141
Pardon me, if you please; if not, I, pleased Not to be pardon'd, am content . . . ii 1 187
God pardon all oaths that are broke to me! . . . iv 1 214
I do beseech your grace to pardon me: It is a matter of small consequence . . . v 2 60
Get before him to the king, And beg thy pardon ere he do accuse thee . v 2 113
May my knees grow to the earth, My tongue cleave to my roof within my mouth, Unless a pardon ere I rise or speak . . . v 3 32
How heinous e'er it be, To win thy after-love I pardon thee . . . v 3 35
If thou do pardon, whosoever pray, More sins for this forgiveness prosper may . . . v 3 83
Do not say, 'stand up'; Say 'pardon' first, and afterwards 'stand up' v 3 112
If I were thy nurse, thy tongue to teach, 'Pardon' should be the first word of thy speech . . . v 3 114
I never long'd to hear a word till now; Say 'pardon,' king . . . v 3 116
The word is short, but not so short as sweet; No word like 'pardon' for kings' mouths so meet . . . v 3 118
Say, 'pardonne moi.'—Dost thou teach pardon pardon to destroy? . . v 3 120
Speak 'pardon' as 'tis current in our land; The chopping French we do not understand . . . v 3 123
Pity may move thee 'pardon' to rehearse . . . v 3 128
Stand up.—I do not sue to stand; Pardon is all the suit I have in hand v 3 130
I pardon him, as God shall pardon me . . . v 3 131
Twice saying 'pardon' doth not pardon twain, But makes one pardon strong . . . v 3 134
With all my heart I pardon him.—A god on earth thou art . . . v 3 136
The unhappy king,—Whose wrongs in us God pardon! . . . *1 Hen. IV.* i 3 149
O, pardon me that I descend so low! . . . i 3 167
In an unjust behalf, As both of you—God pardon it!—have done . . . i 3 174
I may . . . Find pardon on my true submission.—God pardon thee! . iii 2 28
You shall have your desires with interest And pardon absolute . . . iv 3 50
Did not we send grace, Pardon and terms of love to all of you? . . . v 5 3
Sir, pardon; a soldier is better accommodated than with a wife *2 Hen. IV.* iii 2 72
Give me pardon, sir: if, sir, you come with news from the court . . . v 3 114
My courtesy, my duty; and my speech, to beg your pardons . . . Epil. 4
But pardon, gentles all, The flat unraised spirits . . . *Hen. V.* Prol. 8
It was excess of wine that set him on; And on his more advice we pardon him . . . ii 2 43
I in sufferance heartily will rejoice, Beseeching God and you to pardon me ii 2 160
My fault, but not my body, pardon, sovereign . . . ii 2 165
Twice a-day their wither'd hands hold up Toward heaven, to pardon blood iv 1 317
All that I can do is nothing worth, Since that my penitence comes after all, Imploring pardon . . . iv 1 322
I made no offence; therefore, I beseech your highness, pardon me . iv 8 60
Pardon the frankness of my mirth, if I answer you for that . . . v 2 318
Pardon my abuse: I find thou art no less than fame hath bruited *1 Hen. VI.* ii 3 67
It is my office; and, madam, pardon me . . . *2 Hen. VI.* ii 4 102
Pardon, my liege, that I have stay'd so long . . . iii 1 94
I would, false murderous coward, on thy knee Make thee beg pardon . iii 2 221
And here pronounce free pardon to them all That will forsake thee . iv 8 9
Who loves the king and will embrace his pardon, Fling up his cap . iv 8 14
Will you needs be hanged with your pardons about your necks? . . . iv 8 23
And so, with thanks and pardon to you all, I do dismiss you . . . iv 9 20
Clifford, kneel again; For thy mistaking so, we pardon thee . . . v 1 128
Art thou against us, Duke of Exeter?—His is the right, and therefore pardon me . . . *3 Hen. VI.* i 1 148
Pardon me, God, I knew not what I did! And pardon, father! . . . ii 5 69
Few words, But such as I, without your special pardon, Dare not relate iv 1 87
We pardon thee: therefore, in brief, Tell me their words . . . iv 1 89
But if an humble prayer may prevail, I then crave pardon of your majesty . . . iv 6 8
He shall pardon thee these outrages . . . v 1 24
Here sheathe thy sword, I'll pardon thee my death . . . v 5 70
O, God forgive my sins, and pardon thee! . . . v 6 60
I beseech your graces both to pardon me . . . *Richard III.* i 1 84
Yea, and forswore himself,—which Jesu pardon!—Which God revenge! i 3 136
God pardon them that are the cause of it! . . . i 3 315
Have I a tongue to doom my brother's death, And shall the same give pardon to a slave? . . . ii 1 103
You straight are on your knees for pardon, pardon; And I, unjustly too, must grant it you . . . ii 1 124
Pardon us the interruption Of thy devotion and right Christian zeal iii 7 102
There needs no such apology: I rather do beseech you pardon me . iii 7 105
I am bound by oath, and therefore pardon me . . . iv 1 28
Proclaim a pardon to the soldiers fled That in submission will return v 5 16
Bolden'd Under your promised pardon . . . *Hen. VIII.* i 2 56

Pardon. Send our letters, with Free pardon to each man . . . *Hen. VIII.* i 2 100
Let there be letters writ to every shire, Of the king's grace and pardon i 2 104
Through our intercession this revokement And pardon comes . . . i 2 107
A gracious king that pardons all offences Malice ne'er meant . . . ii 2 68
I humbly do entreat your highness' pardon; My haste made me unmannerly . . . iv 2 104
That comfort comes too late; 'Tis like a pardon after execution . . . iv 2 121
Give pardon to my speech . . . *Troi. and Cres.* i 3 357
Name her not now, sir; she's a deadly theme.—O, pardon; I offend . iv 5 182
Pardon me this brag; His insolence draws folly from my lips . . . iv 5 257
O my sweet lady, pardon . . . *Coriolanus* ii 1 197
My nobler friends, I crave their pardons . . . iii 1 65
For they have pardons, being ask'd, as free As words to little purpose . iii 2 88
I minded him how royal 'twas to pardon When it was less expected . v 1 18
Our general has sworn you out of reprieve and pardon . . . v 2 54
And conjure thee to pardon Rome, and thy petitionary countrymen . v 2 82
But entreat of thee To pardon Mutius and to bury him . . . *T. Andron.* i 1 363
And at my suit, sweet, pardon what is past . . . i 1 431
All humbled on your knees, You shall ask pardon of his majesty . . . i 1 473
Agree whose hand shall go along, For fear they die before their pardon come . . . iii 1 176
Then pardon me for reprehending thee . . . iii 2 69
God pardon sin! wast thou with Rosaline? . . . *Rom. and Jul.* ii 3 44
To blaze your marriage, reconcile your friends, Beg pardon of the prince iii 3 152
God pardon him! I do, with all my heart . . . iii 5 83
'I cannot love, I am too young; I pray you, pardon me.' But, an you will not wed, I'll pardon you . . . iii 5 188
To fall prostrate here, And beg your pardon: pardon, I beseech you! . iv 2 21
Pardon me for bringing these ill news, Since you did leave it for my office . . . v 1 22
Under favour, pardon me, If I speak like a captain . . . *T. of Athens* iii 5 40
Pardon him, sweet Timandra; for his wits Are drown'd and lost . . . iv 3 88
Doth not the day break here?—No.—O, pardon, sir, it doth . . . *J. Cæsar* ii 1 103
Pardon, Cæsar; Cæsar, pardon: As low as to thy foot doth Cassius fall iii 1 55
By your pardon; I will myself into the pulpit first . . . iii 1 235
O, pardon me, thou bleeding piece of earth, That I am meek and gentle! iii 1 254
Under your pardon . . . iv 3 213
Very frankly he confess'd his treasons, Implored your highness' pardon *Macbeth* i 4 6
But I shall crave your pardon; That which you are my thoughts cannot transpose . . . iv 3 20
Bow them to your gracious leave and pardon . . . *Hamlet* i 2 56
Your pardon and my return shall be the end of my business . . . ii 2 329
In the fatness of these pursy times Virtue itself of vice must pardon beg iii 4 154
I shall, first asking your pardon thereunto, recount the occasion . . . iv 7 46
Give me your pardon, sir: I've done you wrong; But pardon't, as you are a gentleman . . . v 2 237
Yet, under pardon, You are much more attask'd for want of wisdom *Lear* i 4 365
When I do stare, see how the subject quakes. I pardon that man's life iv 6 111
The battle done, and they within our power, Shall never see his pardon v 1 68
I humbly do beseech you of your pardon For too much loving you *Othello* iii 3 212
Heaven pardon him!—A halter pardon him! and hell gnaw his bones! iv 2 135
I cry you gentle pardon . . . v 1 93
I never gave you cause.—I do believe it, and I ask you pardon . . . v 2 300
By your most gracious pardon, I sing but after you . . . *Ant. and Cleo.* i 5 72
I told him of myself; which was as much As to have ask'd him pardon ii 2 79
Do So far ask pardon as befits mine honour To stoop in such a case . ii 2 97
Pardon what I have spoke; For 'tis a studied, not a present thought . ii 2 139
When good will is show'd, though't come too short, The actor may plead pardon . . . ii 5 9
He is married?—I crave your highness' pardon.—He is married? . . . ii 5 98
I begg'd His pardon for return.—Which soon he granted, Being an obstruct . . . iii 6 60
Thy beck might from the bidding of the gods Command me.—O, my pardon! . . . iii 11 61
Pardon, pardon!—Fall not a tear, I say . . . iii 11 68
Cried he? and begg'd a' pardon?—He did ask favour . . . iii 13 132
I will o'ertake thee, Cleopatra, and Weep for my pardon . . . iv 14 45
I dare not, dear,—Dear my lord, pardon,—I dare not, Lest I be taken . iv 15 22
By your pardon, sir, I was then a young traveller . . . *Cymbeline* i 4 46
Give me your pardon. I have spoke this, to know if your affiance Were deeply rooted . . . i 6 162
Pray, your pardon.—All's well, sir: take my power i' the court for yours i 6 178
If I do lie and do No harm by it, though the gods hear, I hope They'll pardon it . . . iv 2 379
We'll learn our freeness of a son-in-law; Pardon's the word to all . v 5 422
Pardon me, or strike me, if you please; I cannot be much lower *Pericles* i 2 46
What shall be next, Pardon old Gower,—this longs the text . . . ii Gower 40
That's your superstition.—Pardon us, sir . . . iii 1 51
Pardon me *T. G. of Ver.* ii 4; iv 4; *Mer. Wives* i 1; iv 4; *Meas. for Meas.* ii 4; iv 2; *Much Ado* ii 1; *L. L. Lost* ii 1; iv 1; iv 3; v 2; *Mer. of Venice* v 1; *As Y. Like It* ii 7; iv 1; iv 3; *T. of Shrew* ii 1; *All's Well* i 3; iii 4; *K. John* iii 1; v 6; *Richard II.* ii 2; iii 4; *1 Hen. IV.* ii 4; *2 Hen. IV.* iii 2; iv 5; *1 Hen. VI.* iv 1; *2 Hen. VI.* i 1; i 3; v 1; *3 Hen. VI.* i 1; v 1; *Troi. and Cres.* i 3; iii 2; *Coriolanus* i 3; v 6; *T. Andron.* i 1; iii 2; iv 1; v 3; *Rom. and Jul.* ii 2; *T. of Athens* i 2; *J. Cæsar* ii 2; iii 1; iii 2; *Hamlet* v 2; *Lear* i 1; i 2; i 4; ii 1; iv 7; *Othello* i 3: ii 3; iii 3; iii 4; iv 3; *Ant. and Cleo.* iv 14; *Cymbeline* iii 6

Pardoned. I have my dukedom got And pardon'd the deceiver *Tempest* Epil. 7
As you from crimes would pardon'd be, Let your indulgence set me free Epil. 19
You are pardon'd, Isabel: And now, dear maid, be you as free to us *Meas. for Meas* v 1 392
If he be like your brother, for his sake Is he pardon'd . . . v 1 496
Villain, thou shalt fast for thy offences ere thou be pardoned *L. L. Lost* i 2 152
The king hath pardon'd them, And they are all about his majesty *K. John* v 6 35
Pardon me, if you please; if not, I, pleased Not to be pardon'd *Richard II.* ii 1 188
Never will I rise up from the ground Till Bolingbroke have pardon'd thee . . . v 2 117
Some shall be pardon'd, and some punished . . . *Rom. and Jul.* v 3 308
To be forestalled ere we come to fall, Or pardon'd being down *Hamlet* iii 3 50
May one be pardon'd and retain the offence? . . . iii 3 56
By you being pardon'd, we commit no crime To use one language *Pericles* iv 4 5

Pardoner. This is his pardon, purchased by such sin For which the pardoner himself is in . . . *Meas. for Meas.* iv 2 112

Pardoning. Until thou bid me joy, By pardoning Rutland, my transgressing boy . . . *Richard II.* v 3 96
Mercy but murders, pardoning those that kill . . . *Rom. and Jul.* iii 1 202

Pardonne moi. Speak it in French, king; say, 'pardonne moi' *Richard II.* v 3 119

Pardonner. O, je vous supplie, pour l'amour de Dieu, me pardonner! *Hen. V.* iv 4 43
Encore qu'il est contre son jurement de pardonner aucun prisonnier . iv 4 54
Pardonnez-moi!—Say'st thou me so? is that a ton of moys? . . . iv 4 22
Pardonnez-moi, I cannot tell vat is 'like me' . . . . v 2 108
Pare. Let not him that plays the lion pare his nails . *M. N. Dream* iv 2 41
'Tis too late to pare her nails now . . . . . *All's Well* v 2 31
Like a mad lad, Pare thy nails, dad . . . . *T. Night* iv 2 140
That every one may pare his nails with a wooden dagger . *Hen. V.* iv 4 76
Pared my present havings, to bestow My bounties upon you *Hen. VIII.* iii 2 159
Yet have I heard,—O, could I find it now!—The lion moved with pity did endure To have his princely paws pared all away *T. Andron.* ii 3 152
Thou hast pared thy wit o' both sides, and left nothing i' the middle *Lear* i 4 204
'Parel. I'll bring him the best 'parel that I have, Come on't what will . iv 1 51
Parent. My trust, Like a good parent, did beget of him A falsehood in its contrary as great As my trust was *Tempest* i 2 94
Those, for their parents were exceeding poor, I bought . *Com. of Errors* v 1 57
These are the parents to these children, Which accidentally are met . v 1 360
On my privilege I have with the parents of the foresaid child *L. L. Lost* iv 2 162
We are their parents and original . . . . *M. N. Dream* ii 1 117
Happy the parents of so fair a child! . . . . *T. of Shrew* iv 5 39
No note upon my parents, his all noble . . . . *All's Well* i 3 163
Clerk-like experienced, which no less adorns Our gentry than our parents' noble names . . . . . . *W. Tale* i 2 393
By the honour of my parents, I have utter'd truth . . . i 2 442
Of parents good, of fist most valiant. . . . . *Hen. V.* iv 1 46
Orphans for their parents' timeless death—Shall rue the hour that ever thou wast born . . . . . . *3 Hen. VI.* v 6 42
The children live, whose parents thou hast slaughter'd, Ungovern'd youth, to wail it in their age; The parents live, whose children thou hast butcher'd, Old wither'd plants, to wail it with their age *Richard III.* iv 4 391
All comfort, joy, in this most gracious lady, Heaven ever laid up to make parents happy . . . . . *Hen. VIII.* v 5 8
And unproperly Show duty, as mistaken all this while Between the child and parent . . . . . *Coriolanus* v 3 56
Do with their death bury their parents' strife . . *Rom. and Jul.* Prol. 8
Their parents' rage, Which, but their children's end, nought could remove . . . . Prol. 10
To general filths Convert o' the instant, green virginity, Do't in your parents' eyes! . . . . . . *T. of Athens* iv 1 8
Unnaturalness between the child and the parent . . . *Lear* i 2 158
Obey thy parents; keep thy word justly; swear not . . . iii 4 83
For this from stiller seats we came, Our parents and us twain *Cymbeline* v 4 70
And she an eater of her mother's flesh, By the defiling of her parent's bed . . . . *Pericles* i 1 131
Time's the king of men, He's both their parent, and he is their grave . ii 3 46
Parentage. He asked me of what parentage I was; I told him, of as good as he . . . . *As Y. Like It* iii 4 39
That, upon knowledge of my parentage, I may have welcome *T. of Shrew* ii 1 96
What is your parentage?—Above my fortunes, yet my state is well *T. N.* i 5 296
What kin are you to me? What countryman? what name? what parentage? . . . . v 1 238
I was the next by birth and parentage . . . *1 Hen. VI.* ii 5 73
Graceless! wilt thou deny thy parentage? . . . . v 4 14
And, ignorant of his birth and parentage, Became a bricklayer *2 Hen. VI.* iv 2 152
A gentleman of noble parentage, Of fair demesnes, youthful *Rom. and Jul.* iii 5 181
Know of him, Of whence he is, his name and parentage . *Pericles* ii 3 74
Time hath rooted out my parentage . . . . . v 1 93
My fortunes—parentage—good parentage—To equal mine!—was it not thus? . . . . v 1 98
My lord, if you did know my parentage, You would not do me violence v 1 100
Report thy parentage. I think thou said'st Thou hadst been toss'd from wrong to injury . . . . . . v 1 130
She would never tell Her parentage; being demanded that, She would sit still and weep . . . . v 1 190
Parfect. But to parfect one man in one poor man . . *L. L. Lost* v 2 503
Paring. Some devils ask but the parings of one's nail . *Com. of Errors* iv 3 72
Like a cheese; consumes itself to the very paring . . *All's Well* i 1 155
The very parings of our nails Shall pitch a field when we are dead *1 Hen. VI.* iii 1 102
Thou hast pared thy wit o' both sides, and left nothing i' the middle: here comes one o' the parings . . . . . . *Lear* i 4 206
Paring-knife. A great round beard, like a glover's paring-knife *Mer. Wives* i 4 21
Paris. Though Paris came in hope to speed alone . . *T. of Shrew* i 2 247
Welcome to Paris.—My thanks and duty are your majesty's . *All's Well* i 2 22
Had you not lately an intent,—speak truly,—To go to Paris? . . . i 3 225
This was your motive For Paris, was it? speak . . . . i 3 237
Else Paris and the medicine and the king Had from the conversation of my thoughts Haply been absent then . . . . . i 3 239
Is Paris lost? is Rouen yielded up? . . . . *1 Hen. VI.* i 1 65
Depart to Paris to the king, For there young Henry with his nobles lie. iii 2 128
Now, governor of Paris, take your oath, That you elect no other king but him. . . . . iv 1 3
And now to Paris, in this conquering vein: All will be ours . . . iv 7 95
Then march to Paris, royal Charles of France, And keep not back your powers . . . . v 2 4
And thus he goes, As did the youthful Paris once to Greece . . v 5 104
In his infancy Crowned in Paris in despite of foes . . *2 Hen. VI.* i 1 94
Paris is lost: the state of Normandy Stands on a tickle point . i 1 215
I danced attendance on his will Till Paris was besieged, famish'd, and lost . . . . i 3 175
Henry the Sixth Was crown'd in Paris but at nine months old *Rich. III.* ii 3 17
Within whose strong immures The ravish'd Helen, Menelaus' queen, With wanton Paris sleeps . . . . . *Troi. and Cres.* Prol. 10
What news, Æneas . . . ?—That Paris is returned home and hurt i 1 112
Let Paris bleed: 'tis but a scar to scorn; Paris is gored with Menelaus' horn . . . . i 1 114
She praised his complexion above Paris.—Why, Paris hath colour enough . . . . i 2 107
I swear to you, I think Helen loves him better than Paris . . . i 2 117
Which of these hairs is Paris my husband? 'The forked one,' quoth he i 2 178
Helen so blushed, and Paris so chafed, and all the rest so laughed . i 2 181
Yonder comes Paris. Look ye yonder, niece; is't not a gallant man? i 2 230
Paris is dirt to him; and, I warrant, Helen, to change, would give an eye to boot . . . . i 2 259
It was thought meet Paris should do some vengeance on the Greeks ii 2 73
If you'll avouch 'twas wisdom Paris went—As you must needs . . ii 2 84
Our firebrand brother, Paris, burns us all. Cry, Trojans, cry! . ii 2 110
Paris should ne'er retract what he hath done, Nor faint in the pursuit ii 2 141
Paris. Paris, you speak Like one besotted on your sweet delights *T. and C.* ii 2 142
Paris and Troilus, you have both said well . . . . ii 2 163
Pray you, a word: do not you follow the young Lord Paris? . . . iii 1 2
I come to speak with Paris from the Prince Troilus . . . iii 1 41
She shall have it, my lord, if it be not my lord Paris.—He! no . iii 1 109
Had I so good occasion to lie long As you, Prince Paris, nothing but heavenly business Should rob my bed-mate of my company . . iv 1 4
Hear me, Paris: For every false drop in her bawdy veins A Grecian's life hath sunk . . . . iv 1 68
There is at hand Paris your brother, and Deiphobus . . . . iv 2 63
Thus popp'd Paris in his hardiment . . . . . . iv 5 28
Patroclus kisses you.—O, this is trim!—Paris and I kiss evermore for him . . . . iv 5 34
Every man is odd.—No, Paris is not; for you know 'tis true, That you are odd, and he is even with you . . . . . . iv 5 43
'Loo, Paris, 'loo! now my double-henned sparrow! 'loo, Paris, 'loo! . v 7 10
But woo her, gentle Paris, get her heart . . . *Rom. and Jul.* i 2 16
Thus then in brief: The valiant Paris seeks you for his love . . i 3 74
Read o'er the volume of young Paris' face And find delight writ there . i 3 81
Speak briefly, can you like of Paris' love?—I'll look to like . . i 3 96
There is a nobleman in town, one Paris, that would fain lay knife aboard ii 4 214
I anger her sometimes and tell her that Paris is the properer man. . ii 4 217
Sir Paris, I will make a desperate tender Of my child's love . . iii 4 12
Wife, go you to her ere you go to bed; Acquaint her here of my son Paris' love . . . . iii 4 16
The County Paris, at Saint Peter's Church, Shall happily make thee there a joyful bride . . . . iii 5 115
I will not marry yet; and, when I do, I swear, It shall be Romeo, whom you know I hate, Rather than Paris . . . . . iii 5 124
Go with Paris to Saint Peter's Church, Or I will drag thee on a hurdle . iii 5 155
An eagle, madam, Hath not so green, so quick, so fair an eye As Paris hath . . . . iii 5 223
If, rather than to marry County Paris, Thou hast the strength of will to slay thyself . . . . iv 1 71
O, bid me leap, rather than marry Paris, From off the battlements of yonder tower; Or walk in thievish ways . . . . . iv 1 77
Hold, then; go home, be merry, give consent To marry Paris . . iv 1 90
I will walk myself To County Paris, to prepare him up Against to-morrow iv 2 45
Go waken Juliet, go and trim her up; I'll go and chat with Paris . iv 4 25
The County Paris hath set up his rest, That you shall rest but little . iv 5 6
Go, Sir Paris; every one prepare To follow this fair corse unto her grave iv 5 92
Let me peruse this face. Mercutio's kinsman, noble County Paris! . v 3 75
I think He told me Paris should have married Juliet . . . v 3 78
Romeo! O, pale! Who else? what, Paris too? And steep'd in blood? . v 3 144
Thy husband in thy bosom there lies dead; And Paris too . . . v 3 156
The people in the street cry Romeo, Some Juliet, and some Paris . . v 3 192
Here lies the County Paris slain; And Romeo dead; and Juliet, dead before . . . . v 3 195
Betroth'd and would have married her perforce To County Paris . . v 3 239
Here untimely lay The noble Paris and true Romeo dead . . . v 3 259
Look you, sir, Inquire me first what Danskers are in Paris . *Hamlet* ii 1 7
Paris balls. As matching to his youth and vanity, I did present him with the Paris balls . . . . *Hen. V.* ii 4 131
Paris-garden. Do you take the court for Paris-garden? . . *Hen. VIII.* v 4 2
Paris Louvre. He'll make your Paris Louvre shake for it, Were it the mistress-court of mighty Europe . . . . . *Hen. V.* ii 4 132
Paris-ward. Their powers are marching unto Paris-ward . *1 Hen. VI.* iii 3 30
Parish. Bring me in the names of some six or seven, the most sufficient of your parish . . . . *Meas. for Meas.* ii 1 287
The parish curate, Alexander . . . . . *L. L. Lost* v 2 538
The 'why' is plain as way to parish church . . . *As Y. Like It* ii 7 52
Even such kin as the parish heifers are to the town bull . *2 Hen. IV.* ii 2 171
I did beget her, all the parish knows. . . . . *1 Hen. VI.* v 4 11
At the Rose, within the parish Saint Lawrence Poultney . *Hen. VIII.* i 2 152
To gain his colour I'ld let a parish of such Clotens blood . *Cymbeline* iv 2 168
Never leave gaping till they've swallowed the whole parish, church, steeple, bells, and all . . . . *Pericles* ii 1 38
He should never have left, till he cast bells, steeple, church, and parish, up again . . . . ii 1 47
Parishioner. I praise the Lord for you: and so may my parishioners; for their sons are well tutored by you . . . *L. L. Lost* iv 2 76
O most gentle pulpiter! what tedious homily of love have you wearied your parishioners withal! . . . . . *As Y. Like It* iii 2 164
Parish-top. Till his brains turn o' the toe like a parish-top . *T. Night* i 3 44
Parisian. 'Tis said the stout Parisians do revolt . . *1 Hen. VI.* v 2 2
'Paritor. Sole imperator and great general Of trotting 'paritors *L. L. Lost* iii 1 188
Park. I will cut his troat in de park . . . . . *Mer. Wives* i 4 115
Come, walk in the Park . . . . iii 3 240
Send him word they'll meet him in the park at midnight . . . iv 4 19
Be you in the Park about midnight, at Herne's oak. . . . v 1 12
Go before into the Park: we two must go together . . . . v 3 4
And taken following her into the park . . . . . *L. L. Lost* i 1 210
It is ycleped thy park. . . . . i 1 242
I do love that country girl that I took in the park . . . . i 2 130
For this damsel, I must keep her at the park . . . . i 2 136
The princess comes to hunt here in the park . . . . iii 1 165
First, from the park let us conduct them thither; Then homeward . iv 3 374
Over park, over pale, Thorough flood, thorough fire . . *M. N. Dream* ii 1 4
Did I not bid thee meet me in the park? . . . . *T. of Shrew* iv 1 133
Dispark'd my parks and fell'd my forest woods . . . *Richard II.* iii 1 23
O esperance! Bid Butler lead him forth into the park . . *1 Hen. IV.* ii 3 75
Why I drew you hither, Into this chiefest thicket of the park *3 Hen. VI.* iv 5 3
My parks, my walks, my manors that I had, Even now forsake me . v 2 24
Thus I found her, straying in the park, Seeking to hide herself *T. An.* iii 1 88
As Neptune's park, ribbed and paled in With rocks unscaleable *Cymb.* iii 1 19
Park-corner. Your horse stands ready at the park-corner . *3 Hen. VI.* iv 5 19
Parked. How are we park'd and bounded in a pale, A little herd of England's timorous deer! . . . . . . *1 Hen. VI.* iv 2 45
Park gate. I'll tell thee all my whole device When I am in my coach, which stays for us At the park gate . . . *Mer. of Venice* iii 4 83
Park-ward. The pittie-ward, the park-ward, every way . *Mer. Wives* iii 1 5
Parle. Of all the fair resort of gentlemen That every day with parle encounter me, In thy opinion which is worthiest love? *T. G. of Ver.* i 2 5
Their purpose is to parle, to court and dance . . . *L. L. Lost* v 2 122
The nature of our quarrel yet never brooked parle . . . *T. of Shrew* i 1 117
Our trumpet call'd you to this gentle parle . . . . *K. John* ii 1 205
Behold, the French amazed vouchsafe a parle . . . . . ii 1 226
Ere my tongue Shall wound my honour with such feeble wrong, Or sound so base a parle . . . . *Richard II.* i 1 192
This is the latest parle we will admit . . . . . *Hen. V.* iii 3 2

Parle. Alice, tu as été en Angleterre, et tu parles bien le langage *Hen. V.* iii 4 2
Écoutez ; dites-moi, si je parle bien : de hand, de fingres, et de nails . iii 4 18
Le François que vous parlez, il est meilleur que l'Anglois lequel je parle v 2 201
Go, trumpet, to the walls, and sound a parle . . . . *3 Hen. VI.* v 1 16
Break the parle ; These quarrels must be quietly debated *T. Andron.* v 3 19
When, in an angry parle, He smote the sledded Polacks on the ice *Hamlet* i 1 62
Parler. Je te prie, m'enseignez ; il faut que j'apprenne à parler *Hen. V.* iii 4 5
Parley. Because you are a banish'd man, Therefore, above the rest, we parley to you . . . . *T. G. of Ver.* iv 1 60
To parley with the sole inheritor Of all perfections . . . *L. L. Lost* ii 1 5
They are at hand, To parley or to fight . . . . *K. John* ii 1 78
Thou didst understand me by my signs And didst in signs again parley with sin . . . . iv 2 238
Send fair-play orders and make compromise, Insinuation, parley . . v 1 68
Through brazen trumpet send the breath of parley Into his ruin'd ears *Richard II.* iii 3 33
And, but for shame, In such a parley should I answer thee *1 Hen. IV.* iii 1 204
Well, by my will we shall admit no parley . . *2 Hen. IV.* iii 1 159
The town sounds a parley . . . . *Hen. V.* iii 2 149
Summon a parley ; we will talk with him . . . *1 Hen. VI.* iii 3 35
A parley with the Duke of Burgundy !—Who craves a parley with the Burgundy? . . . . iii 3 36
At your father's castle walls We'll crave a parley, to confer with him . v 3 130
And I myself, Rather than bloody war shall cut them short, Will parley with Jack Cade . . . . *2 Hen. VI.* iv 4 13
Dare any be so bold to sound retreat or parley, when I command them kill? iv 8 5
Break off the parley . . . . *3 Hen. VI.* ii 2 110
Say that the emperor requests a parley . . . *T. Andron.* iv 4 101
He craves a parley at your father's house . . . . . . v 1 159
They stand, and would have parley . . . . . *J. Cæsar* v 1 21
What's the business, That such a hideous trumpet calls to parley The sleepers of the house? . . . . *Macbeth* ii 3 87
See your entreatments at a higher rate Than a command to parley *Hamlet* i 3 123
What an eye she has ! methinks it sounds a parley of provocation *Othello* ii 3 23
Parleyed. This tongue hath parley'd unto foreign kings For your behoof *2 Hen. VI.* iv 7 82
Parlez. Le François que vous parlez, il est meilleur que l'Anglois lequel je parle . . . . *Hen. V.* v 2 200
Parliament. Why, I'll exhibit a bill in the parliament for the putting down of men . . . . *Mer. Wives* ii 1 29
I am in parliament pledge for his truth . . . *Richard II.* v 2 44
You were . . . To us the speaker in his [God's] parliament *2 Hen. IV.* iv 2 18
Now call we our high court of parliament . . . . . . v 2 134
The king hath call'd his parliament . . . . . . v 5 109
This blot . . . Shall be wiped out in the next parliament . *1 Hen. VI.* ii 4 117
And therefore haste I to the parliament . . . . . . ii 5 127
God speed the parliament ! who shall be the speaker? . . . iii 2 60
His majesty's parliament, Holden at Bury the first of this next month *2 Hen. VI.* ii 4 70
What, will your highness leave the parliament? . . . . iii 1 197
Burn all the records of the realm : my mouth shall be the parliament . iv 7 17
The king is fled to London, To call a present court of parliament . v 3 25
The queen this day here holds her parliament, But little thinks we shall be of her council . . . . *3 Hen. VI.* i 1 35
The bloody parliament shall this be call'd . . . . . . i 1 39
Here in the parliament Let us assail the family of York . . . i 1 64
Until that act of parliament be repeal'd Whereby my son is disinherited i 1 249
Was't you that revell'd in our parliament? . . . . . i 4 71
With a full intent To dash our late decree in parliament . . . ii 1 118
He swore consent to your succession, His oath enrolled in the parliament ii 1 173
Have caused him, by new act of parliament, To blot out me . . ii 2 91
Parliament-house. To make a shambles of the parliament-house ! . . i 1 71
Parlour. Good Margaret, run thee to the parlour . . *Much Ado* iii 1 1
They sit conferring by the parlour fire . . . *T. of Shrew* v 2 102
You are pictures out of doors, Bells in your parlours . . *Othello* ii 1 111
Parlous. By'r lakin, a parlous fear . . . *M. N. Dream* iii 1 14
Thou art in a parlous state, shepherd . . . *As Y. Like It* iii 2 45
A parlous boy ; go to, you are too shrewd . . *Richard III.* ii 4 35
O, 'tis a parlous boy ; Bold, quick, ingenious, forward, capable . iii 1 154
A bump as big as a young cockerel's stone ; A parlous knock *R. and J.* i 3 54
Parmaceti. Telling me the sovereign'st thing on earth Was parmaceti for an inward bruise . . . . *1 Hen. IV.* i 3 58
Parolles. Monsieur Parolles, my lord calls for you . *All's Well* i 1 201
Monsieur Parolles, you were born under a charitable star . . . i 1 204
Sweet Monsieur Parolles ! . . . . ii 1 39
O my Parolles, they have married me ! I'll to the Tuscan wars . ii 3 289
Parolles, was it not?—Ay, my good lady, he.—A very tainted fellow iii 2 87
Reports but coarsely of her.—What's his name?—Monsieur Parolles iii 5 61
This is Monsieur Parolles, the gallant militarist . . . . iv 3 161
Thine, as he vowed to thee in thine ear, Parolles . . . . iv 3 261
Rust, sword ! cool, blushes ! and, Parolles, live Safest in shame ! . iv 3 373
His name's Parolles.—I saw the man to-day, if man he be . . v 3 202
Parricide. Not confessing Their cruel parricide . . . *Macbeth* iii 1 32
The revenging gods 'Gainst parricides did all their thunders bend . *Lear* ii 1 48
Parrot. The prophecy like the parrot, 'beware the rope's-end' *Com. of Er.* iv 4 46
Evermore peep through their eyes And laugh like parrots *Mer. of Venice* i 1 53
And discourse grow commendable in none only but parrots . . iii 5 51
More clamorous than a parrot against rain . . *As Y. Like It* iv 1 152
That ever this fellow should have fewer words than a parrot ! *1 Hen. IV.* ii 4 111
Look, whether the withered elder hath not his poll clawed like a parrot *2 Hen. IV.* ii 4 282
The parrot will not do more for an almond . . *Troi. and Cres.* v 2 193
Drunk? and speak parrot? and squabble? swagger? swear? . *Othello* ii 3 281
Parrot-teacher. Well, you are a rare parrot-teacher . *Much Ado* i 1 139
Parsley. She went to the garden for parsley to stuff a rabbit *T. of Shrew* iv 4 101
Parson. A gentleman born, master parson . . . *Mer. Wives* i 1 9
I hear the parson is no jester . . . . ii 1 218
I will rather trust . . . Parson Hugh the Welshman with my cheese ii 2 317
What, the sword and the word ! do you study them both, master parson? iii 1 45
We are come to you to do a good office, master parson . . . iii 1 50
Nay, good master parson, keep in your weapon . . . . iii 1 75
Shall I lose my parson, my priest, my Sir Hugh? no . . . iii 1 106
Master Parson, quasi pers-on . . . . . *L. L. Lost* iv 2 84
Let this letter be read : Our parson misdoubts it . . . . iv 3 194
Coughing drowns the parson's saw And birds sit brooding in the snow . v 2 932
We'ld find no fault with the tithe-woman, if I were the parson *All's Well* i 3 89
Jove bless thee, master Parson.—Bonos dies, Sir Toby . *T. Night* iv 2 13
'That that is is ;' so I, being Master Parson, am master Parson . iv 2 17
Talkest thou nothing but of ladies?—Well said, master Parson . iv 2 31
With a tithe-pig's tail Tickling a parson's nose as a' lies asleep *R. and J.* i 4 80

Part. To have no screen between this part he play'd And him he play'd it for, he needs will be Absolute Milan . . . . . *Tempest* i 2 107
Yet with my nobler reason 'gainst my fury Do I take part . . v 1 27
Take your rest For this one night ; which, part of it, I'll waste . v 1 302
But, sirrah, how did thy master part with Madam Julia? *T. G. of Ver.* ii 5 11
Ere I part with thee, confer at large Of all that may concern thy love-affairs . . . . iii 1 253
Peace ! stand aside : the company parts . . . . . . iv 2 81
Our youth got me to play the woman's part . . . . . iv 4 165
I made her weep agood, For I did play a lamentable part . . . iv 4 171
Examined my parts with most judicious œillades . . *Mer. Wives* i 3 67
Setting the attraction of my good parts aside I have no other charms . ii 2 110
Trib, fairies ; come ; and remember your parts : be pold, I pray you . v 4 2
I do bend my speech To one that can my part in him advertise *M. for M.* i 1 42
Dispossessing all my other parts Of necessary fitness . . . ii 4 22
Even so The general, subject to a well-wish'd king, Quit their own part ii 4 28
But to accuse him so, That is your part . . . . . iv 6 3
Sweet Isabel, take my part ; Lend me your knees . . . . v 1 435
Her part, poor soul ! seeming as burdened With lesser weight but not with lesser woe, Was carried with more speed . . *Com. of Errors* i 1 108
Undividable, incorporate, Am better than thy dear self's better part . ii 2 125
But though my cates be mean, take them in good part . . . iii 1 28
In debating which was best, we shall part with neither . . . iii 1 67
Her sober virtue, years and modesty, Plead on her part . . . iii 1 91
It is thyself, mine own self's better part, Mine eye's clear eye . iii 2 61
In what part of her body stands Ireland? . . . . . . iii 2 118
Much deserved on his part . . . . *Much Ado* i 1 12
He is in love. With who? now that is your grace's part . . . i 1 215
And never could maintain his part but in the force of his will . . i 1 238
I will assume thy part in some disguise . . . . . . i 1 323
You may do the part of an honest man in it . . . . . ii 1 172
Troth, my lord, I have played the part of Lady Fame . . . ii 1 220
When I do name him, let it be thy part To praise him . . . iii 1 18
Fear you not my part of the dialogue . . . . . . iii 1 31
Hero and Margaret have by this played their parts with Beatrice . . iii 2 79
No part of it is mine ; This shame derives itself from unknown loins . iv 1 136
You are almost come to part almost a fray . . . . . v 1 114
Tell me for which of my bad parts didst thou first fall in love with me? v 2 60
They will not admit any good part to intermingle with them . . . v 2 64
For which of my good parts did you first suffer love for me? . . v 2 65
How canst thou part sadness and melancholy? . . . *L. L. Lost* i 2 7
A man of sovereign parts he is esteem'd ; Well fitted in arts . . ii 1 44
In surety of the which, One part of Aquitaine is bound to us . . ii 1 136
For praise, an outward part, We bend to that the working of the heart iv 1 32
My lips on thy foot, my eyes on thy picture, and my heart on thy every part . . . . iv 1 87
He is only an animal, only sensible in the duller parts . . . iv 2 28
Those parts that do fructify in us more than he . . . . iv 2 30
Which is to me some praise that I thy parts admire . . . iv 2 118
And here is part of my rhyme, and here my melancholy . . . iv 3 15
Ay, or I would these hands might never part . . . . . iv 3 57
Why, that contempt will kill the speaker's heart, And quite divorce his memory from his part . . . . v 2 150
Why take we hands, then?—Only to part friends . . . . v 2 220
Let's part the word . . . . v 2 249
A blister on his sweet tongue, with my heart, That put Armado's page out of his part ! . . . . v 2 336
The extreme parts of time extremely forms All causes to the purpose . v 2 750
If this thou do deny, let our hands part . . . . . . v 2 821
Name what part I am for, and proceed . . . *M. N. Dream* i 2 20
I could play Ercles rarely, or a part to tear a cat in, to make all split . i 2 32
Snug, the joiner ; you, the lion's part : and, I hope, here is a play fitted i 2 66
Have you the lion's part written? pray you, if it be, give it me . . i 2 68
You can play no part but Pyramus ; for Pyramus is a sweet-faced man . i 2 87
Here are your parts : and I am to entreat you, request you and desire you, to con them by to-morrow night . . . . i 2 101
For her sake do I rear up her boy, And for her sake I will not part with him . . . . ii 1 137
For the third part of a minute . . . . ii 2 2
Sit down, every mother's son, and rehearse your parts . . . iii 1 76
You speak all your part at once, cues and all . . . . . iii 1 102
And from thy hated presence part I so . . . . . . iii 2 80
To vow, and swear, and superpraise my parts, When I am sure you hate me . . . . iii 2 153
With all my heart, In Hermia's love I yield you up my part . . iii 2 165
She shall not harm thee, Helena.—No, sir, she shall not, though you take her part . . . . iii 2 322
Let her alone : speak not of Helena ; Take not her part . . . iii 2 333
Every man look o'er his part . . . . iv 2 38
Thus have I, Wall, my part discharged so . . . . . v 1 206
The better part of my affections would Be with my hopes abroad *M. of V.* i 1 16
A stage where every man must play a part, And mine a sad one . . i 1 78
He makes it a great appropriation to his own good parts . . . i 2 46
To be cut off and taken In what part of your body pleaseth me . . i 3 152
Parts that become thee happily enough . . . . . . ii 2 191
Therefore I part with him, and part with him To one that I would have him help to waste His borrow'd purse . . . . . . ii 5 49
I have too grieved a heart To take a tedious leave : thus losers part . ii 7 77
In the narrow seas that part The French and English . . . ii 8 28
I saw Bassanio and Antonio part . . . . ii 8 36
And Shylock, for his own part, knew the bird was fledged . . iii 1 31
No vice so simple but assumes Some mark of virtue on his outward parts iii 2 82
I give them with this ring ; Which when you part from, lose, or give away, Let it presage the ruin of your love . . . . . iii 2 174
When this ring Parts from this finger, then parts life from hence . iii 2 186
If every ducat in six thousand ducats Were in six parts and every part a ducat, I would not draw them . . . . iv 1 86
You use in abject and in slavish parts, Because you bought them . . iv 1 92
Or the division of the twentieth part Of one poor scruple . . . iv 1 329
You were to blame, . . . To part so slightly with your wife's first gift . v 1 167
I gave my love a ring and made him swear Never to part with it . . v 1 171
You shall have some part of your will . . . *As Y. Like It* i 1 81
Full of ambition, an envious emulator of every man's good parts . i 1 150
That all the beholders take his part with weeping . . . . i 2 140
My better parts Are all thrown down . . . . i 2 261
Wrestle with thy affections.—O, they take the part of a better wrestler ! i 3 22
Shall we be sunder'd? shall we part, sweet girl? . . . . i 3 100
Thus misery doth part The flux of company . . . . . ii 1 51
Much commend The parts and graces of the wrestler . . . . ii 2 13
And one man in his time plays many parts, His acts being seven ages . ii 7 142

Part. And so he plays his part *As Y. Like It* ii 7 157
Were I not the better part made mercy iii 1 2
Cleopatra's majesty, Atalanta's better part iii 2 155
Thus Rosalind of many parts By heavenly synod was devised iii 2 157
As boys and women are for the most part cattle of this colour iii 2 435
He that will divide a minute into a thousand parts and break but a part of the thousandth part of a minute iv 1 45
Clubs cannot part them v 2 45
You and you no cross shall part: You and you are heart in heart v 4 137
My lord, I warrant you we will play our part *T. of Shrew* Ind. 1 69
Sure, that part Was aptly fitted and naturally perform'd Ind. 1 86
Virtue and that part of philosophy Will I apply that treats of happiness i 1 18
May it be done?—Not possible; for who shall bear your part? i 1 199
Come you to part the fray? 'Con tutto il cuore, ben trovato' i 2 23
I see you do not mean to part with her ii 1 64
Is this your speeding? nay, then, good night our part! ii 1 303
Now I play a merchant's part, And venture madly on a desperate mart. ii 1 328
My lessons make no music in three parts iii 1 60
I am come to keep my word, Though in some part enforced to digress iii 2 109
And such assurance ta'en As shall with either part's agreement stand iv 4 50
Our soft conditions and our hearts Should well agree with our external parts v 2 168
To speak on the part of virginity, is to accuse your mothers *All's Well* i 1 148
Freely have they leave To stand on either part. i 2 15
Thy father's moral parts Mayst thou inherit too! i 2 21
But what at full I know, thou know'st no part ii 1 135
What is infirm from your sound parts shall fly. ii 1 170
Thou wert best set thy lower part where thy nose stands ii 3 267
To know nothing, and to have nothing, is to be a great part of your title ii 4 26
Holy seems the quarrel Upon your grace's part iii 1 5
Thus your own proper wisdom Brings in the champion Honour on my part iv 2 50
How is this justified?—The stronger part of it by her own letters iv 3 65
Ours be your patience then, and yours our parts Epil. 339
An thou let part so, Sir Andrew, would thou mightst never draw sword again.—An you part so, mistress, I would I might never *T. Night* i 3 65
And all is semblative a woman's part i 4 34
That question's out of my part i 5 191
My part of death, no one so true Did share it ii 4 58
The parts that fortune hath bestow'd upon her, Tell her, I hold as giddily as fortune ii 4 86
I will not give my part of this sport for a pension of thousands ii 5 196
Being skilless in these parts iii 3 9
That you could possibly have found in any part of Illyria iii 4 294
And, part, being prompted by your present trouble iii 4 377
Upon some stubborn and uncourteous parts We had conceived against him v 1 369
Meantime, sweet sister, We will not part from hence v 1 394
Stay your thanks a while; And pay them when you part *W. Tale* i 2 10
We'll part the time between's then i 2 18
Thy mother plays, and I Play too, but so disgraced a part i 2 188
By all the parts of man Which honour does acknowledge i 2 400
The gracious queen, part of his theme, but nothing Of his ill-ta'en suspicion! i 2 459
If The cause were not in being,—part o' the cause, She the adulteress ii 3 3
And The testimony on my part no other But what comes from myself iii 2 25
Though I have for the most part been aired abroad iv 2 5
That's likewise part of my intelligence iv 2 51
These your unusual weeds to each part of you Do give a life iv 4 1
So turtles pair, That never mean to part iv 4 155
We can both sing it: if thou'lt bear a part, thou shalt hear; 'tis in three parts iv 4 299
I can bear my part; you must know 'tis my occupation; have at it with you iv 4 301
Is it not too far gone? 'Tis time to part them. iv 4 354
I see the play so lies That I must bear a part.—No remedy iv 4 670
Mark Her eye, and tell me for what dull part in't You chose her v 1 64
Where we may leisurely Each one demand and answer to his part v 3 153
Mine eye hath well examined his parts And finds them perfect *K. John* i 1 89
Sir Robert might have eat his part in me Upon Good-Friday and ne'er broke his fast i 1 234
Then let confusion of one part confirm The other's peace ii 1 359
Dissever your united strengths, And part your mingled colours once again ii 1 389
He is the half part of a blessed man, Left to be finished by such as she ii 1 437
John, to stop Arthur's title in the whole, Hath willingly departed with a part ii 1 563
Arm thy constant and thy nobler parts Against these giddy loose suggestions iii 1 291
Upon which better part our prayers come in, If thou vouchsafe them iii 1 293
My reasonable part produces reason How I may be deliver'd of these woes iii 4 54
Remembers me of all his gracious parts, Stuffs out his vacant garments iii 4 96
Since all and every part of what we would Doth make a stand at what your highness will iv 2 38
England now is left To tug and scamble and to part by the teeth iv 3 146
And part this body and my soul With contemplation and devout desires v 4 47
The stumbling night did part our weary powers v 5 18
What art thou?—Of the part of England.—Whither dost thou go? v 6 2
Death, having prey'd upon the outward parts, Leaves them invisible v 7 15
The best part of my power, As I upon advantage did remove, Were in the Washes all unwarily Devoured v 7 61
Three parts of that receipt I had for Calais Disbursed I duly to his highness' soldiers; The other part reserved I by consent *Richard II.* i 1 126
Alas, the part I had in Woodstock's blood Doth more solicit me i 2 1
Our part therein we banish with yourselves i 3 181
To-morrow must we part; Be merry, for our time of stay is short ii 1 222
Farewell: if heart's presages be not vain, We three here part that ne'er shall meet again ii 2 143
I will not vex your souls—Since presently your souls must part your bodies iii 1 3
Part of your cares you give me with your crown iv 1 194
Take leave and part; for you must part forthwith.—Doubly divorced! v 1 70
Part us, Northumberland; I towards the north v 1 76
One kiss shall stop our mouths, and dumbly part; Thus give I mine v 1 95
'Twere no good part To take on me to keep and kill thy heart v 1 97
Did I ever call for thee to pay thy part? *1 Hen. IV.* i 2 58
How shall we part with them in setting forth? i 2 187
Hand to hand, He did confound the best part of an hour i 3 100
Yea, on his part I'll empty all these veins, And shed my dear blood i 3 133
From Trent and Severn hitherto, By south and east is to my part assign'd iii 1 75

Part. In the way of bargain, mark ye me, I'll cavil on the ninth part of a hair *1 Hen. IV.* iii 1 140
Leaves behind a stain Upon the beauty of all parts besides iii 1 188
My daughter weeps: she will not part with you iii 1 194
He had his part of it; let him pay iii 3 87
Shall, hot horse to horse, Meet and ne'er part till one drop down a corse iv 1 123
The better part of ours [horses] are full of rest iv 3 27
Even those we love That are misled upon your cousin's part v 1 105
Would to God Thy name in arms were now as great as mine!—I'll make it greater ere I part from thee v 4 71
The better part of valour is discretion; in the which better part I have saved my life v 4 121
What! you are as a candle, the better part burnt out *2 Hen. IV.* i 2 178
Every part about you blasted with antiquity i 2 207
A man can no more separate age and covetousness than a' can part young limbs and lechery i 2 257
This is the right fencing grace, my lord; tap for tap, and so part fair ii 1 207
I could discern no part of his face from the window ii 2 86
Marry, the immortal part needs a physician ii 2 112
I have done the part of a careful friend ii 4 348
Why not to him in part, and to us all? iv 1 99
Let them have pay, and part: I know it will well please them iv 2 70
And makes it course from the inwards to the parts extreme iv 3 116
This part of his conjoins with my disease, And helps to end me iv 5 64
Imagine me taking your part And in your power soft silencing your son v 2 96
'Tis 'semper idem,' for 'obsque hoc nihil est:' 'tis all in every part v 5 31
Two mighty monarchies, Whose high upreared and abutting fronts The perilous narrow ocean parts asunder *Hen. V.* Prol. 22
Into a thousand parts divide one man, And make imaginary puissance. Prol. 24
The art and practic part of life Must be the mistress to this theoric i 1 51
He seems indifferent, Or rather swaying more upon our part i 1 73
To give a greater sum Than ever at one time the clergy yet Did to his predecessors part withal i 1 81
Though high and low and lower, Put into parts, doth keep in one consent i 2 181
'Tis meet we all go forth To view the sick and feeble parts of France ii 4 22
Like so many Alexanders, Have in these parts from morn till even fought iii 1 20
Leaving their earthly parts to choke your clime iv 3 102
Bring me just notice of the numbers dead On both our parts. iv 7 123
Was ever known so great and little loss On one part and on the other? iv 8 116
I will make him eat some part of my leek, or I will peat his pate four days v 1 42
Your mightiness on both parts best can witness v 2 28
I love France so well that I will not part with a village of it v 2 183
I know, Kate, you will to her dispraise those parts in me that you love v 2 213
Promise, Kate, you will endeavour for your French part of such a boy v 2 228
Reignier, Duke of Anjou, doth take his part *1 Hen. VI.* i 1 94
Most part of all this night ii 1 67
What you see is but the smallest part And least proportion of humanity ii 3 52
And scorn both him and thee.—I'll turn my part thereof into thy throat ii 4 79
Would some part of my young years Might but redeem the passage of your age! ii 5 107
Banding themselves in contrary parts Do pelt so fast iii 1 81
Pucelle hath bravely play'd her part in this iii 3 88
We institute your grace To be our regent in these parts of France iv 1 163
Part of thy father may be saved in thee.—No part of him but will be shame in me iv 5 38
We here discharge your grace from being regent I' the parts of France *2 Hen. VI.* i 1 67
Therefore I will take the Nevils' parts And make a show of love i 1 240
I will not be slack To play my part in Fortune's pageant i 2 67
And take ten thousand leaves, Loather a hundred times to part than die iii 2 355
But these rags are no part of the duke iv 1 47
Honest men and such As would, but that they dare not, take our parts iv 2 197
Now part them again, lest they consult iv 7 140
And swallow my sword like a great pin, ere thou and I part iv 10 32
That is too much presumption on thy part v 1 38
Throw in the frozen bosoms of our part Hot coals of vengeance v 2 35
Uncurable discomfit Reigns in the hearts of all our present parts v 2 87
My father, being the Earl of Warwick's man, Came on the part of York *3 Hen. VI.* ii 5 66
To shape my legs of an unequal size; To disproportion me in every part iii 2 160
Great John of Gaunt, Which did subdue the greatest part of Spain iii 3 82
Ay, therein Clarence shall not want his part iv 6 57
So part we sadly in this troublous world, To meet with joy in sweet Jerusalem v 5 7
I repent My part thereof that I have done to her *Richard III.* i 3 308
And now in peace my soul shall part to heaven ii 1 5
This interchange of love, I here protest, Upon my part shall be unviolable ii 1 27
I'll sort occasion ... To part the queen's proud kindred from the king ii 2 150
O, then, I see, you will part but with light gifts iii 1 118
I'll give my voice, Which, I presume, he'll take in gentle part iii 4 21
Lord Hastings had pronounced your part,—I mean, your voice iii 4 28
Play the maid's part, still answer nay, and take it iii 7 51
Fled To Richmond, in those parts beyond the sea Where he abides iv 2 47
And part in just proportion our small strength v 3 26
If I thrive, the gain of my attempt The least of you shall share his part v 3 268
I can see his pride Peep through each part of him *Hen. VIII.* i 1 69
For the most part such To whom as great a charge as little honour He meant to lay upon i 1 76
That dye is on me Which makes my whitest part black i 1 209
I know but of a single part, in aught Pertains to the state i 2 41
Which compel from each The sixth part of his substance i 2 58
Sixth part of each? A trembling contribution! i 2 94
We take From every tree lop, bark, and part o' the timber i 2 96
I would have play'd The part my father meant to act upon The usurper i 2 195
You, that have so fair parts of woman on you, Have too a woman's heart ii 3 27
And thy parts Sovereign and pious else, could speak thee out, The queen of earthly queens ii 4 139
Your graces find me here part of a housewife iii 1 24
If the trial of the law o'ertake ye, You'll part away disgraced iii 1 97
A time To think upon the part of business which I bear i' the state iii 2 145
With thee and all thy best parts bound together, Weigh'd not a hair of his iii 2 258
He gave his honours to the world again, His blessed part to heaven iv 2 30
From all parts they are coming, As if we kept a fair here! v 4 72
The still and mental parts, That do contrive how many hands shall strike, When fitness calls them on *Troi. and Cres.* i 3 200
What heart receives from hence the conquering part? i 3 352
His pia mater is not worth the ninth part of a sparrow ii 1 78
For my private part, I am no more touch'd than all Priam's sons ii 2 125
Yet all his virtues, Not virtuously on his own part beheld, Do in our eyes begin to lose their gloss ii 3 127

Part. 'Twixt his mental and his active parts Kingdom'd Achilles in commotion rages . . . . *Troi. and Cres.* ii 3 184
Famed be thy tutor, and thy parts of nature Thrice famed . . . ii 3 253
Like a bourn, a pale, a shore, confines Thy spacious and dilated parts . ii 3 261
What music is this?—I do but partly know, sir: it is music in parts . iii 1 20
You shall fight your hearts out ere I part you . . . . . . ii 2 55
Vowing more than the perfection of ten and discharging less than the tenth part of one . . . . iii 2 95
No man is the lord of any thing, Though in and of him there be much consisting, Till he communicate his parts to others . . . . . iii 3 117
How novelty may move, and parts with person . . . . . iv 4 81
Come, kiss; and let us part . . . . iv 4 100
Signify this loving interview To the expecters of our Trojan part . iv 5 156
Tell me, you heavens, in which part of his body Shall I destroy him? . iv 5 242
After we part from Agamemnon's tent, To bring me thither . . . iv 5 285
Nay, but you part in anger.—Doth that grieve thee? O wither'd truth! v 2 45
Hark! a retire upon our Grecian part.—The Trojan trumpets sound the like . . . . v 8 15
The discontented members, the mutinous parts . . . *Coriolanus* i 1 115
The general is gone, with one part of our Roman power . . . . i 3 109
And stand upon my common part with those That have beheld the doing i 9 39
What good condition can a treaty find I' the part that is at mercy? . i 10 7
I find the ass in compound with the major part of your syllables . . ii 1 64
It is a part That I shall blush in acting . . . . ii 2 148
Being three parts melted away with rotten dews . . . . . ii 3 35
But that's no matter, the greater part carries it . . . . . ii 3 41
I am half through; The one part suffer'd, the other will I do . . ii 3 131
Where one part does disdain with cause, the other Insult without all reason . . . . iii 1 143
Love the fundamental part of state More than you doubt the change on't iii 1 151
We do here pronounce, Upon the part o' the people . . . . iii 1 210
You have put me now to such a part which never I shall discharge to the life . . . . iii 2 105
To have my praise for this, perform a part Thou hast not done before . iii 2 109
And most glad of your company.—You take my part from me, sir; I have the most cause to be glad of yours . . . . iv 3 55
Or rudely visit them in parts remote . . . . iv 5 148
Like a dull actor now, I have forgot my part, and I am out . . . v 3 41
Rather to show a noble grace to both parts Than seek the end of one . v 3 121
Thou restrain'st from me the duty which To a mother's part belongs . v 3 168
Do more than counterpoise a full third part The charges of the action . v 6 78
His own impatience Takes from Aufidius a great part of blame . . v 6 147
I give thee thanks in part of thy deserts . . . . . *T. Andron.* i 1 236
Lest, then, the people, . . . Upon a just survey, take Titus' part . . i 1 446
I swore I would not part a bachelor from the priest . . . . . i 1 488
If you love me, as I think you do, Let's kiss and part . . . . iii 1 288
Part, fools! Put up your swords; you know not what you do *R. and J.* i 1 71
Put up thy sword, Or manage it to part these men with me . . . i 1 76
Wield old partisans, in hands as old, . . . to part your canker'd hate . i 1 102
I drew to part them: in the instant came The fiery Tybalt . . . i 1 115
Came more and more and fought on part and part, Till the prince came, who parted either part . . . . i 1 121
Woo her, gentle Paris, get her heart, My will to her consent is but a part i 2 17
Nor arm, nor face, nor any other part Belonging to a man . . . ii 2 41
Doff thy name, And for that name which is no part of thee Take all myself ii 2 48
For this, being smelt, with that part cheers each part . . . . ii 3 25
Now, afore God, I am so vexed, that every part about me quivers . . ii 4 171
Romeo he cries aloud, 'Hold, friends! friends, part!' . . . . iii 1 170
Ere I Could draw to part them, was stout Tybalt slain . . . . iii 1 178
Affliction is enamour'd of thy parts, And thou art wedded to calamity . iii 3 2
But the kind prince, Taking thy part, hath rush'd aside the law . . iii 3 26
Tell me, In what vile part of this anatomy Doth my name lodge? . . iii 3 106
But that a joy past joy calls out on me, It were a grief, so brief to part iii 3 174
Youthful, and nobly train'd, Stuff'd, as they say, with honourable parts iii 5 183
Each part, deprived of supple government, Shall, stiff and stark and cold, appear like death . . . . iv 1 102
Heaven and yourself Had part in this fair maid; now heaven hath all . iv 5 67
Your part in her you could not keep from death, But heaven keeps his part in eternal life . . . . iv 5 70
Her body sleeps in Capel's monument, And her immortal part with angels lives . . . . v 1 19
The fellow that sits next him now, parts bread with him *T. of Athens* i 2 48
Once use our hearts, whereby we might express some part of our zeals i 2 88
That with your other noble parts you'll suit In giving him his right . ii 2 23
Canst use the time well, if the time use thee well: good parts in thee . iii 1 40
Let not that part of nature Which my lord paid for, be of any power To expel sickness, but prolong his hour! . . . . iii 1 64
How unluckily it happened, that I should purchase the day before for a little part, and undo a great deal of honour! . . . . . . iii 2 53
If not for any parts in him—Though his right arm might purchase his own time And be in debt to none . . . . iii 5 76
We must all part Into this sea of air . . . . iv 2 21
Not one word more: Thus part we rich in sorrow, parting poor . . iv 2 29
It is our part and promise . . . . v 1 123
In general part we were opposed, Yet our old love made a particular force v 2 7
In part for his sake moved . . . . v 2 13
I am not gamesome: I do lack some part Of that quick spirit *J. Cæsar* i 2 28
It is the part of men to fear and tremble, When the most mighty gods by tokens send Such dreadful heralds . . . . i 3 54
That part of tyranny that I do bear I can shake off at pleasure . . i 3 99
Three parts of him Is ours already, and the man entire Upon the next encounter yields him ours . . . . i 3 154
The clock hath stricken three.—'Tis time to part . . . . . ii 1 193
Domestic fury and fierce civil strife Shall cumber all the parts of Italy iii 1 264
Go you into the other street, And part the numbers . . . . . iii 2 4
Let him be Cæsar.—Cæsar's better parts Shall be crown'd in Brutus . iii 2 56
The greater part, the horse in general, Are come with Cassius . . iv 2 29
By your leave, gods:—this is a Roman's part . . . . . . v 3 89
And let's away, To part the glories of this happy day . . . . v 5 81
Your highness' part Is to receive our duties . . . . *Macbeth* i 4 23
Was never call'd to bear my part, Or show the glory of our art . . iii 5 8
No mind that's honest But in it shares some woe; though the main part Pertains to you alone . . . . iv 3 198
Did heaven look on, And would not take their part? . . . . . iv 3 224
For it hath cow'd my better part of man . . . . v 8 18
When yond same star that's westward from the pole Had made his course to illume that part of heaven Where now it burns *Hamlet* i 1 37
So have I heard and do in part believe it . . . . i 1 165
Thy knotted and combined locks to part . . . . i 5 18
I hold it fit that we shake hands and part . . . . i 5 128
Part. And for mine own poor part, Look you, I'll go pray . *Hamlet* i 5 131
I know his father and his friends, And in part him . . . . . ii 1 15
You cannot, sir, take from me any thing that I will more willingly part withal . . . . ii 2 220
In the secret parts of fortune . . . . ii 2 239
The humorous man shall end his part in peace . . . . . . ii 2 336
Who for the most part are capable of nothing but inexplicable dumb-shows iii 2 13
It was a brute part of him to kill so capital a calf there . . . . iii 2 110
Go not till I set you up a glass Where you may see the inmost part of you iii 4 20
Or but a sickly part of one true sense Could not so mope . . . iii 4 80
A slave that is not twentieth part the tithe Of your precedent lord . iii 4 97
O, throw away the worser part of it, And live the purer with the other half iii 4 157
How purposed, sir, I pray you?—Against some part of Poland . . iv 4 12
A thought which, quarter'd, hath but one part wisdom And ever three parts coward . . . . iv 4 42
I do not know from what part of the world I should be greeted . . iv 6 4
Your sum of parts Did not together pluck such envy from him As did that iv 7 74
What part is that, my lord?—A very riband in the cap of youth . . iv 7 77
You shall find in him the continent of what part a gentleman would see v 2 115
Have at you now!—Part them; they are incensed.—Nay, come, again . v 2 313
This coronet part betwixt you . . . . *Lear* i 1 141
The contents, as in part I understand them, are to blame . . . i 2 43
If I like thee no worse after dinner, I will not part from thee yet . . i 4 44
For taking one's part that's out of favour . . . . i 4 111
If I had a monopoly out, they would have part on't . . . . . i 4 168
Thou clovest thy crown i' the middle, and gavest away both parts . i 4 176
My train are men of choice and rarest parts . . . . . . i 4 285
And take vanity the puppet's part against the royalty of her father . ii 2 40
Make it your cause; send down, and take my part! . . . . . ii 4 195
Poor fool and knave, I have one part in my heart That's sorry yet for thee iii 2 72
There's part of a power already footed . . . . iii 3 13
My tears begin to take his part so much, They'll mar my counterfeiting iii 6 63
My snuff and loathed part of nature should Burn itself out . . . iv 6 39
He that parts us shall bring a brand from heaven, And fire us hence . v 3 22
My parts, my title and my perfect soul Shall manifest me rightly *Othello* i 2 31
What, in your own part, can you say to this?—Nothing, but this is so . i 3 74
To his honours and his valiant parts Did I my soul and fortunes consecrate i 3 254
A grievous wreck and sufferance On most part of their fleet . . . ii 1 24
Would in action glorious I had lost Those legs that brought me to a part of it! . . . . ii 3 187
Even as again they were When you yourself did part them . . . ii 3 239
I have lost the immortal part of myself, and what remains is bestial . ii 3 264
Given up himself to the contemplation, mark, and denotement of her parts ii 3 323
That he hath left part of his grief with me, To suffer with him . . iii 3 53
Many a time, When I have spoke of you dispraisingly, Hath ta'en your part . . . . iii 3 73
And have not those soft parts of conversation That chamberers have . iii 3 264
This wretch hath part confess'd his villany . . . . v 2 296
Her passions are made of nothing but the finest part of pure love *A. and C.* i 2 152
Break The cause of our expedience to the queen, And get her leave to part i 2 186
None our parts so poor, But was a race of heaven . . . . . i 3 36
Sir, you and I must part, but that's not it: Sir, you and I have loved . i 3 87
To part with unhack'd edges, and bear back Our targes undinted . . ii 6 38
We'll feast each other ere we part; and let's Draw lots who shall begin ii 6 61
There's a strong fellow, Menas.—Why?—A' bears the third part of the world, man; see'st not?—The third part, then, is drunk . . . . ii 7 96
Gentle lords, let's part; You see we have burnt our cheeks . . . ii 7 128
Octavia weeps To part from Rome; Cæsar is sad . . . . . iii 2 4
You take from me a great part of myself; Use me well in't . . . iii 2 24
For better might we Have loved without this mean, if on both parts This be not cherish'd . . . . iii 2 32
We will here part.—Farewell, my dearest sister, fare thee well . . iii 2 38
Round even to faultiness.—For the most part, too, they are foolish that are so . . . . iii 3 34
That . . . we had not rated him His part o' the isle . . . . iii 6 26
For what I have conquer'd, I grant him part . . . . . . iii 6 35
Some ditch wherein to die; the foul'st best fits My latter part of life . iv 6 39
Fortune and Antony part here: even here Do we shake hands . . iv 12 19
If thou and nature can so gently part, The stroke of death is as a lover's pinch, Which hurts, and is desired . . . . v 2 297
Your son's my father's friend; he takes his part . . . *Cymbeline* i 1 165
My ring I hold dear as my finger; 'tis part of it . . . . . i 4 145
I have enjoyed the dearest bodily part of your mistress . . . . i 4 162
Could I find out The woman's part in me! . . . . ii 5 20
No motion That tends to vice in man, but I affirm It is the woman's part ii 5 22
All faults that may be named, nay, that hell knows, Why, hers, in part or all . . . . ii 5 28
That part thou, Pisanio, must act for me, if thy faith be not tainted . iii 4 26
She hath all courtly parts more exquisite Than lady, ladies, woman . iii 5 71
But if there be Yet left in heaven as small a drop of pity As a wren's eye, fear'd gods, a part of it! . . . . iv 2 305
The Roman eagle, wing'd From the spongy south to this part of the west iv 2 349
Imogen, The great part of my comfort, gone . . . . . . iv 3 5
He's true and shall perform All parts of his subjection loyally . . iv 3 19
So I'll fight Against the part I come with . . . . v 1 25
Gilded pale looks, Part shame, part spirit renew'd . . . . . v 3 35
No more a Briton, I have resumed again The part I came in . . . v 3 76
If of my freedom 'tis the main part, take No stricter render of me than my all . . . . v 4 16
Shall's have a play of this? Thou scornful page, There lie thy part . v 5 229
There are princes and knights come from all parts of the world *Pericles* ii 1 115
It was mine own, part of my heritage . . . . ii 1 129
Her eyelids . . . Begin to part their fringes of bright gold . . . iii 2 101
The gods have done their part in you . . . . iv 2 74
At her birth, Thetis, being proud, swallow'd some part o' the earth . iv 4 39
I hear say you are of honourable parts, and are the governor of this place iv 6 87
Make a battery through his deafen'd parts, Which now are midway stopp'd v 1 47
Tell thy story; If thine consider'd prove the thousandth part Of my endurance, thou art a man . . . . v 1 136
How came you in these parts? where were you bred? . . . . . v 1 171
For my (mine own) part *Tempest* iii 2; *Mer. Wives* i 1; iii 4; *Meas. for Meas.* ii 1; *Much Ado* iii 5; iv 1; *L. L. Lost* v 2; *Mer. of Venice* ii 2; iii 1; iii 2; iii 4; v 1; *As Y. Like It* i 1; ii 4; iii 5; *All's Well* iii 2; 1 *Hen. IV.* ii 3; v 1; v 4; 2 *Hen. IV.* iii 2; *Hen. V.* ii 1; iii 2; iii 6; 2 *Hen. VI.* i 3; 3 *Hen. VI.* v 5; *Richard III.* ii 4; *Troi. and Cres.* i 1; iv 2; *Coriolanus* iv 6; v 3; *T. of Athens* iii 2; *J. Cæsar* i 2; i 3; ii 1; iv 3; *Hamlet* v 1; *Lear* ii 2; *Othello* ii 3; *Ant. and Cleo.* ii 6; *Cymbeline* v 5
For thy (your) part *Much Ado* v 4; 2 *Hen. IV.* iii 2; iv 1; *T. of Athens* iv 3; *J. Cæsar* iii 1; *Hamlet* iii 1

Partake. Not meaning to partake with me in danger . . . *T. Night* v 1 90
One may drink, depart, And yet partake no venom . . . *W. Tale* ii 1 41
Your exultation Partake to every one . . . . v 3 132
You may partake of any thing we say . . . . *Richard III.* i 1 89
News, you rascals!—What, what, what? let's partake *Coriolanus* iv 5 184
By and by thy bosom shall partake The secrets of my heart . *J. Cæsar* ii 1 305
Would not let him partake in the glory of the action . *Ant. and Cleo.* iii 5 9
Our mind partakes Her private actions to your secrecy . . *Pericles* i 1 152
Partaken. If she had partaken of my flesh, and cost me the dearest groans of a mother, I could not have owed her a more rooted love *All's Well* iv 5 11
Partaker. Wish me partaker in thy happiness When thou dost meet good hap . . . . *T. G. of Ver.* i 1 14
At first, to flatter us withal, Make us partakers of a little gain *1 Hen. VI.* ii 1 52
For your partaker Pole and you yourself, I'll note you in my book . ii 4 100
Of stirs abroad, I shall beseech you, sir, To let me be partaker *A. and C.* i 4 83
Part-created. Gives o'er and leaves his part-created cost A naked subject to the weeping clouds . . . . . . *2 Hen. IV.* i 3 60
Parted. Saw you my master?—But now he parted hence *T. G. of Ver.* i 1 71
After they closed in earnest, they parted very fairly in jest . . . ii 5 14
This ring I gave him when he parted from me . . . . . iv 4 102
As you came in to me, her assistant or go-between parted from me *M. W.* ii 2 274
Who parted with me to go fetch a chain . . . . *Com. of Errors* v 1 221
But seven years since, in Syracusa, boy, Thou know'st we parted . . v 1 321
Like to a double cherry, seeming parted, But yet an union *M. N. Dream* iii 2 209
I see these things with parted eye, When every thing seems double . iv 1 194
The wall is down that parted their fathers . . . . . v 1 359
The old proverb is very well parted . . . . *Mer. of Venice* ii 2 158
He wrung Bassanio's hand; and so they parted . . . . . ii 8 49
Here are sever'd lips, Parted with sugar breath . . . . . iii 2 119
If you had known the virtue of the ring, . . . You would not then have parted with the ring . . . . v 1 202
How parted he with thee? and when shalt thou see him again? *A. Y. L. It* iii 2 235
When last the young Orlando parted from you He left a promise to return . . . . iv 3 99
And so we measured swords and parted . . . . . . v 4 91
When his disguise and he is parted . . . . . *All's Well* iii 6 113
What said our cousin when you parted with him?—'Farewell' *Richard II.* i 4 10
You promised, when you parted with the king, To lay aside life-harming heaviness . . . . ii 2 2
A' parted even just between twelve and one . . *Hen. V.* ii 3 12
Raught at mountains with outstretched arms, Yet parted but the shadow with his hand . . . . *3 Hen. VI.* i 4 69
When we parted, Thou call'dst me king . . . . . . iv 3 30
When I parted with him, He hugg'd me in his arms . *Richard III.* i 4 251
He parted frowning from me, as if ruin Leap'd from his eyes *Hen. VIII.* iii 2 205
So she parted, And with the same full state paced back again . iv 1 92
If heaven had pleased to have given me longer life And able means, we had not parted thus . . . . iv 2 153
I had thought They had parted so much honesty among 'em . . . v 2 28
That man, how dearly ever parted, How much in having, or without or in, Cannot make boast to have that which he hath . *Troi. and Cres.* iii 3 96
Thus popp'd Paris in his hardiment, And parted thus you and your argument . . . . iv 5 29
No more infected with my country's love Than when I parted hence *Cor.* v 6 73
Till the prince came, who parted either part . . . *Rom. and Jul.* i 1 122
They say he parted well, and paid his score . . . *Macbeth* v 8 52
Kent banish'd thus! and France in choler parted! And the king gone! *Lear* i 2 23
Parted you in good terms? Found you no displeasure in him? . i 2 171
Which parted thence, As pearls from diamonds dropp'd . . . iv 3 23
Upon the crown o' the cliff, what thing was that Which parted from you? . . . . iv 6 68
They were parted With foul and violent tempest . . . *Othello* ii 1 33
The great contention of the sea and skies Parted our fellowship . . ii 1 93
The day had broke Before we parted . . . . . . iii 1 35
Was not that Cassio parted from my wife?—Cassio, my lord! No, sure iii 3 37
What, are the brothers parted? . . . . . *Ant. and Cleo.* iii 2 1
Ay me, most wretched, That have my heart parted betwixt two friends! iii 6 77
They were parted By gentlemen at hand . . . . *Cymbeline* i 1 163
As I had made my meal, and parted With prayers for the provider . iii 6 52
How parted with your brothers? how first met them? Why fled you? v 5 386
When we with tears parted Pentapolis . . . . . *Pericles* v 3 38
Partest. Thou partest a fair fray . . . . . . *L. L. Lost* v 2 484
Parthia. In Parthia did I take thee prisoner . . . . *J. Cæsar* v 3 37
If we compose well here, to Parthia . . . . *Ant. and Cleo.* ii 2 15
Say to Ventidius I would speak with him: He shall to Parthia . ii 3 32
Now, darting Parthia, art thou struck . . . . iii 1 1
The ne'er-yet-beaten horse of Parthia We have jaded out o' the field . iii 1 33
Great Media, Parthia, and Armenia, He gave to Alexander . . iii 6 14
Parthian. Labienus—This is stiff news—hath, with his Parthian force, Extended Asia from Euphrates . . . . i 2 104
Noble Ventidius, Whiles yet with Parthian blood thy sword is warm, The fugitive Parthians follow . . . . iii 1 6
Shall I do that which all the Parthian darts, Though enemy, lost aim, and could not? . . . . iv 14 70
Or, like the Parthian, I shall flying fight; Rather, directly fly *Cymbeline* i 6 20
Partial. Let mine own judgement pattern out my death, And nothing come in partial . . . . *Meas. for Meas.* ii 1 31
Plead no more; I am not partial to infringe our laws *Com. of Errors* i 1 4
A partial slander sought I to avoid, And in the sentence my own life destroy'd . . . . *Richard II.* i 3 241
Canst thou, O partial sleep, give thy repose To the wet sea-boy? *2 Hen. IV.* iii 1 26
Of partial indulgence To their benumbed wills . . *Troi. and Cres.* ii 2 178
'Tis meet that some more audience than a mother, Since nature makes them partial, should o'erhear The speech, of vantage . *Hamlet* iii 3 32
I cannot be so partial, Goneril, To the great love I bear you . *Lear* i 4 334
Partialize. Should nothing privilege him, nor partialize The unstooping firmness of my upright soul . . . . . . *Richard II.* i 1 120
Partially. If partially affined, or leagued in office . . . *Othello* ii 3 218
Participate. A spirit I am indeed; But am in that dimension grossly clad Which from the womb I did participate . . *T. Night* v 1 245
See and hear, devise, instruct, walk, feel, And, mutually participate *Cor.* i 1 106
Participation. For thou hast lost thy princely privilege With vile participation . . . . *1 Hen. IV.* iii 2 87
So married in conjunction with the participation of society . *2 Hen. IV.* v 1 77
Particle. Every particle and utensil labelled to my will . . *T. Night* i 5 264
If he do break the smallest particle Of any promise . . *J. Cæsar* ii 1 139
Parti-coated presence of loose love . . . . . . *L. L. Lost* v 2 776

Parti-coloured. Did in eaning time Fall parti-colour'd lambs *Mer. of Ven.* i 3 89
Particular. Give us particulars of thy preservation . . . *Tempest* v 1 135
The story of my life And the particular accidents gone by . . . v 1 305
That no particular scandal once can touch . . *Meas. for Meas.* iv 4 30
Though they would swear down each particular saint . . . . v 1 243
You shall recount their particular duties afterwards . . . *Much Ado* iv 1 3
Thus did she, an hour together, trans-shape thy particular virtues . v 1 172
Answer me in one word.—You must borrow me Gargantua's mouth first . . . . *As Y. Like It* iii 2 240
'Twere all one That I should love a bright particular star . *All's Well* i 1 97
My course, Which holds not colour with the time, nor does The ministration and required office On my particular . . . . . ii 5 66
I would I knew in what particular action to try him . . . . iii 6 18
And the particular confirmations, point from point . . . . iv 3 71
Let me answer to the particular of the inter'gatories: demand them singly . . . . iv 3 207
That bare eyes To see alike mine honour as their profits, Their own particular thrifts . . . . *W. Tale* i 2 311
Swear his thought over By each particular star in heaven . . . i 2 425
Each your doing, So singular in each particular . . . . . iv 4 144
Examine me upon the particulars of my life . . . *1 Hen. IV.* ii 4 414
My brother general, the commonwealth, To brother born an household cruelty, I make my quarrel in particular . . . *2 Hen. IV.* iv 1 96
I sent your grace The parcels and particulars of our grief . . . iv 2 36
I will have it in a particular ballad else, with mine own picture on the top iv 3 52
With every course in his particular . . . . iv 4 90
Doth any name particular belong Unto the lodging where I first did swoon? . . . . iv 5 233
Upon my particular knowledge of his directions . . . *Hen. V.* iii 2 84
To lay apart their particular functions and wonder at him . . . iii 7 41
The prescript praise and perfection of a good and particular mistress . iii 7 50
The king is not bound to answer the particular endings of his soldiers . iv 1 163
Whose tenours and particular effects You have enscheduled briefly . v 2 72
Where's our general?—Here I am, thou particular fellow *2 Hen. VI.* iv 2 119
Make yourself mirth with your particular fancy, And leave me out *Hen. VIII.* ii 3 101
By particular consent proceeded Under your hands and seals . . ii 4 221
Should, notwithstanding that your bond of duty, As 'twere in love's particular, be more To me, your friend, than any . . . . iii 2 189
Hath robbed many beasts of their particular additions . *Troi. and Cres.* i 2 20
A tapster's arithmetic may soon bring his particulars therein to a total i 2 124
The success, Although particular, shall give a scantling Of good or bad unto the general . . . . i 3 341
No man lesser fears the Greeks than I As far as toucheth my particular ii 2 9
Value dwells not in particular will . . . . ii 2 53
Yet is the kindness but particular; 'Twere better she were kiss'd in general . . . . iv 5 20
He's to make his requests by particulars . . . . . *Coriolanus* ii 3 48
Revenge Thine own particular wrongs . . . . iv 5 92
Yet I wish, sir,—I mean for your particular,—you had not Join'd . iv 7 13
Who loved him In a most dear particular . . . . . . v 1 3
The glorious gods sit in hourly synod about thy particular prosperity! v 2 74
Ay, that's well known: But what particular rarity? . *T. of Athens* i 1 4
His particular to foresee, Smells from the general weal . . iv 3 159
Our old love made a particular force, And made us speak like friends . v 2 8
Whereby he does receive Particular addition, from the bill That writes them all alike . . . . *Macbeth* iii 1 100
It is myself I mean: in whom I know All the particulars of vice . iv 3 51
In what particular thought to work I know not . . . *Hamlet* i 1 67
Ay, madam, it is common.—If it be, Why seems it so particular with thee? . . . . i 2 75
As he in his particular act and place May give his saying deed . i 3 26
So, oft it chances in particular men, That for some vicious mole of nature in them, As, in their birth . . . . i 4 23
Shall in the general censure take corruption From that particular fault i 4 36
Each particular hair to stand an end, Like quills upon the fretful porpentine . . . . i 5 19
Come you more nearer Than your particular demands will touch it . ii 1 12
But your news is not true. Let me question more in particular . . ii 2 244
Men of choice and rarest parts, That all particulars of duty know *Lear* i 4 286
Inform her full of my particular fear . . . . i 4 360
For his particular, I'll receive him gladly, But not one follower . . ii 4 295
These domestic and particular broils Are not the question here . . v 1 30
Nor doth the general care Take hold on me, for my particular grief *Othello* i 3 55
Your fortunes are alike.—But how, but how? give me particulars *A. and C.* i 2 57
My more particular, And that which most with you should safe my going i 3 54
From which the world should note Something particular . . . iii 13 22
O Antony, Nobler than my revolt is infamous, Forgive me in thine own particular . . . . iv 9 20
More particulars Must justify my knowledge . . . *Cymbeline* ii 4 78
Particularities. As good a man as yourself . . . in the derivation of my birth, and in other particularities . . . . . . *Hen. V.* iii 2 142
Now let the general trumpet blow his blast, Particularities and petty sounds To cease! . . . . *2 Hen. VI.* v 2 44
Particularize. The leanness that afflicts us, the object of our misery, is as an inventory to particularize their abundance . . *Coriolanus* i 1 21
Particularly. Who hath done To thee particularly and to all the Volsces Great hurt and mischief . . . . iv 5 72
My free drift Halts not particularly . . . . . *T. of Athens* i 1 46
Parties. Whence come you?—From the two parties, forsooth *Mer. Wives* iv 5 107
The parties themselves, the actors, sir, will show . . *L. L. Lost* v 2 500
When the parties were met themselves, one of them thought but of an If, as, 'If you said so, then I said so' . . . . *As Y. Like It* v 4 104
In himself too mighty, And in his parties, his alliance . . *W. Tale* ii 3 21
These promises are fair, the parties sure . . . . *1 Hen. IV.* iii 1 1
Then both parties nobly are subdued, And neither party loser *2 Hen. IV.* iv 2 90
The English army, that divided was Into two parties, is now conjoin'd in one . . . . *1 Hen. VI.* v 2 12
Here's 'In witness whereof the parties interchangeably' *Troi. and Cres.* iii 2 61
Making parties strong And feebling such as stand not in their liking Below their cobbled shoes . . . . *Coriolanus* i 1 198
All the peace you make in their cause is, calling both the parties knaves ii 1 88
Proceed by process; Lest parties, as he is beloved, break out . . iii 1 315
If you do hold the same intent wherein You wish'd us parties . . v 6 14
Bring forth the parties of suspicion . . . . . *Rom. and Jul.* v 3 222
I think the policy of that purpose made more in the marriage than the love of the parties . . . . *Ant. and Cleo.* ii 6 127
And though it be allow'd in meaner parties . . . . *Cymbeline* v 3 121
Parting. Alas! this parting strikes poor lovers dumb . *T. G. of Ver.* ii 2 21
A Jew would have wept to have seen our parting . . . . . ii 3 13

Parting. My grandam, having no eyes, look you, wept herself blind at my parting . . . *T. G. of Ver.* ii 3 15
When we have chid the hasty-footed time For parting us *M. N. Dream* iii 2 201
Often hast thou heard my moans, For parting my fair Pyramus and me! v 1 191
For so your father charged me at our parting . . . *T. of Shrew* i 1 218
Such a clamorous smack That at the parting all the church did echo . iii 2 181
I grow to you, and our parting is a tortured body *All's Well* ii 1 36
Procured his leave For present parting . . . ii 5 61
I'll give him my commission To let him there a month behind the gest Prefix'd for's parting . . . *W. Tale* i 2 42
From him, whose daughter His tears proclaim'd his, parting with her v 1 160
And say, what store of parting tears were shed? *Richard II.* i 4 5
And so by chance Did grace our hollow parting with a tear . i 4 9
At some thing it grieves, More than with parting from my lord the king ii 2 13
For there will be a world of water shed Upon the parting of your wives and you . . . *1 Hen. IV.* iii 1 95
And peace, no war, befall thy parting soul! . . . *1 Hen. VI.* ii 5 115
Away! though parting be a fretful corrosive, It is applied to a deathful wound . . . *2 Hen. VI.* iii 2 403
I fear thy overthrow More than my body's parting with my soul! *3 Hen. VI.* ii 6 4
For time is like a fashionable host That slightly shakes his parting guest by the hand . . . *Troi. and Cres.* iii 3 166
We must use expostulation kindly, For it is parting from us . iv 4 63
Parting is such sweet sorrow . . . *Rom. and Jul.* ii 2 185
Thus part we rich in sorrow, parting poor . *T. of Athens* iv 2 29
If we do meet again, why, we shall smile; If not, why then, this parting was well made . . . *J. Cæsar* v 1 119
If we do meet again, we'll smile indeed; If not, 'tis true this parting was well made . . . v 1 122
The soul and body rive not more in parting Than greatness going off *Ant. and Cleo.* iv 13 5
Stay a little: Were you but riding forth to air yourself, Such parting were too petty . . . *Cymbeline* i 1 111
That parting kiss which I had set Betwixt two charming words . . i 3 34
Which are often the sadness of parting, as the procuring of mirth . . v 4 162
I saw you lately, When you caught hurt in parting two that fought *Per.* iv 1 88
Partisan. Clubs, bills, and partisans! strike! beat them down! *R. and J.* i 1 80
Cast by their grave beseeming ornaments, To wield old partisans . . i 1 101
Shall I strike at it with my partisan?—Do, if it will not stand *Hamlet* i 1 140
I had as lief have a reed that will do me no service as a partisan I could not heave . . . *Ant. and Cleo.* ii 7 14
Make him with our pikes and partisans A grave . *Cymbeline* iv 2 399
Partition. Like to a double cherry, seeming parted, But yet an union in partition . . . *M. N. Dream* iii 2 210
It is the wittiest partition that ever I heard discourse, my lord . . v 1 168
And good from bad find no partition . . . *2 Hen. IV.* iv 1 196
And can we not Partition make with spectacles so precious 'Twixt fair and foul? . . . *Cymbeline* i 6 37
Partlet. Thou dotard! thou art woman-tired, unroosted By thy dame Partlet here . . . *W. Tale* ii 3 75
How now, Dame Partlet the hen! . . . *1 Hen. IV.* iii 3 60
Partly, seeing you are beautified With goodly shape . *T. G. of Ver.* iv 1 55
I have entertained thee, Partly that I have need of such a youth . . iv 4 69
You are partly a bawd, Pompey, howsoever you colour it *Meas. for Meas.* ii 1 231
Partly for that her promised proportions Came short of composition . v 1 219
I partly think A due sincerity govern'd his deeds . . . v 1 450
Partly by his oaths, which first possessed them, partly by the dark night, which did deceive them . . . *Much Ado* iii 3 166
I yield upon great persuasion; and partly to save your life . . v 4 96
'Tis partly my own fault . . . *M. N. Dream* iii 2 243
You may partly hope that your father got you not . *Mer. of Venice* iii 5 11
I partly guess; for I have loved ere now . . . *As Y. Like It* ii 4 24
I partly know the instrument That screws me from my true place *T. N.* v 1 125
By circumstances partly laid open . . . *W. Tale* iii 2 19
I'll not seek far—For him, I partly know his mind . . . v 3 142
I have partly thy mother's word, partly my own opinion . *1 Hen. IV.* ii 4 444
Partly to satisfy my opinion, and partly for the satisfaction, look you, of my mind . . . *Hen. V.* iii 2 105
I do partly understand your meaning.—Why then, rejoice therefore . iii 6 52
Now you partly may perceive my mind . . *3 Hen. VI.* iii 2 66
For God he knows, and you may partly see . *Richard III.* iii 7 235
I partly know the man: go, call him hither . . . iv 2 41
What music is this?—I do but partly know, sir . *Troi. and Cres.* iii 1 19
He did it to please his mother, and to be partly proud . *Coriolanus* i 1 40
This shall seem, as partly 'tis, their own, Which we have goaded onward ii 3 270
Why I descend into this bed of death, Is partly to behold my lady's face; But chiefly to take thence . . . A precious ring . *Rom. and Jul.* v 3 29
Now I change my mind, And partly credit things that do presage *J. Cæsar* v 1 79
Believe not so.—I but believe it partly . . . v 1 90
If't be your pleasure and most wise consent, As partly I find it is *Othello* i 1 123
I stand accountant for as great a sin, But partly led to diet my revenge ii 1 303
He partly begs To be desired to give . . *Ant. and Cleo.* iii 13 66
O, come apace, dispatch! I partly feel thee . . . v 2 325
'Those runagates!' Means he not us? I partly know him . *Cymbeline* iv 2 64
Partner. Wishing me with him, partner of his fortune *T. G. of Ver.* i 3 59
Your partner, as I hear, must die to-morrow . *Meas. for Meas.* i 3 37
I would be glad to receive some instruction from my fellow partner . iv 2 19
You have been always called a merciful man, partner *Much Ado* iii 3 65
Go, good partner, go, get you to Francis Seacole . . iii 5 62
Which be the malefactors?—Marry, that am I and my partner . iv 2 4
Be my present partner in this business . . . *W. Tale* iv 2 58
She shall be habited as it becomes The partner of your bed . . iv 4 558
My vows are equal partners with thy vows . . *1 Hen. VI.* iii 2 85
And will be partner of your weal or woe . . . iii 2 92
Sweet partner, I must not yet forsake you: let's be merry . *Hen. VIII.* i 4 103
You shall have two noble partners with you . . . v 3 168
My noble partners, and myself, thus pray . . . v 5 6
My partner in this action, You must report . . *Coriolanus* v 3 2
Till, at the last, I seem'd his follower, not partner . . v 6 39
My noble partner You greet with present grace and great prediction *Macb.* i 3 54
And nothing is But what is not.—Look, how our partner's rapt . i 3 142
This have I thought good to deliver thee, my dearest partner of greatness i 5 12
Hardly gave audience, or Vouchsafed to think he had partners *A. and C.* i 4 8
Noble partners, . . . Touch you the sourest points with sweetest terms ii 2 22
I, Your partner in the cause 'gainst which he fought . . ii 2 59
Myself and other noble friends Are partners in the business *Cymbeline* i 6 184
Partnered. To be partner'd With tomboys hired . . i 6 121
Partridge. Then there's a partridge wing saved, for the fool will eat no supper that night. . . . *Much Ado* ii 1 155
Partridge. Who finds the partridge in the puttock's nest, But may imagine how the bird was dead? . . . *2 Hen. VI.* iii 2 191
Party. Canst thou bring me to the party? . . *Tempest* iii 2 67
And the three party is, lastly and finally, mine host of the Garter *M. W.* i 1 142
The devil take one party and his dam the other! . . . iv 5 108
For the nomination of the party writing to the person written unto *L. L. Lost* iv 2 138
The party is gone, fellow Hector, she is gone . . . v 2 678
If . . . He seek the life of any citizen, The party 'gainst the which he doth contrive Shall seize one half his goods . *Mer. of Venice* iv 1 352
Who cries out on pride, That can therein tax any private party? *As Y. Like It* ii 7 71
I must be A party in this alteration, finding Myself thus alter'd *W. Tale* i 2 383
This child . . . is . . . not a party to The anger of the king nor guilty ii 2 61
The party tried The daughter of a king . . . iii 2 2
Are you a party in this business?—In some sort, sir . . iv 4 843
Would not cease Till she had kindled France and all the world, Upon the right and party of her son . . . *K. John* i 1 34
Whose party do the townsmen yet admit? . . . ii 1 361
A ramping fool, to brag and stamp and swear Upon my party! . . iii 1 123
Our party may well meet a prouder foe . . . v 1 79
And all your southern gentlemen in arms Upon his party *Richard II.* iii 2 203
Which on thy royal party granted once, His glittering arms he will commend to rust . . . iii 3 115
Three knights upon our party slain to-day . . . *1 Hen. IV.* v 5 6
Where hateful death put on his ugliest mask To fright our party *2 Hen. IV.* i 1 67
For from his metal was his party steel'd . . . i 1 116
A good healthy water; but, for the party that owed it, he might have more diseases than he knew for . . . i 2 4
For then both parties nobly are subdued, And neither party loser . iv 2 91
But dare maintain the party of the truth . . *1 Hen. VI.* ii 4 32
Will I upon thy party wear this rose . . . ii 4 123
To fight on Edward's party for the crown . . *Richard III.* i 3 138
And hopes to find you forward Upon his party for the gain thereof . iii 2 47
My prayers on the adverse party fight . . . iv 4 190
They came from Buckingham Upon his party . . . iv 4 528
Besides, the king's name is a tower of strength, Which they upon the adverse party want . . . v 3 13
There's not the meanest spirit on our party Without a heart *Tr. and Cr.* ii 2 156
Were half to half the world by the ears and he Upon my party, I'ld revolt, to make Only my wars with him . . *Coriolanus* i 1 238
I saw our party to their trenches driven . . . i 6 12
When you are hearing a matter between party and party . . ii 1 82
'Tis fit You make strong party, or defend yourself By calmness or by absence . . . iii 2 94
Always factionary on the party of your general . . . v 2 30
The people of Rome, for whom we stand A special party . *T. Andron.* i 1 21
O Cassius, if you could But win the noble Brutus to our party *J. Cæsar* i 3 141
Your party in converse, him you would sound . . *Hamlet* ii 1 42
Have you nothing said Upon his party 'gainst the Duke of Albany? *Lear* ii 1 28
This is the letter he spoke of, which approves him an intelligent party iii 5 12
I should show What party I do follow . . . iv 5 40
Seek him out Upon the British party . . . iv 6 256
I do suspect this trash To be a party in this injury . . . *Othello* v 1 86
I would not be the party that should desire you to touch him *A. and C.* v 2 246
To the king's party there's no going . . . *Cymbeline* iv 4 9
Party-verdict. Whereto thy tongue a party-verdict gave . *Richard II.* i 3 234
Pash. Thou want'st a rough pash and the shoots that I have, To be full like me . . . *W. Tale* i 2 128
If I go to him, with my armed fist I'll pash him o'er the face *Tr. and Cr.* ii 3 213
Pashed. Waving his beam, Upon the pashed corses of the kings . v 5 10
Pashful. Come, wherefore should you be so pashful? . . *Hen. V.* iv 8 75
Pass. 'Steal by line and level' is an excellent pass of pate *Tempest* iv 1 244
The ways are dangerous to pass. . . . *T. G. of Ver.* iv 3 24
I'll tell you as we pass along . . . v 4 168
Be avised, sir, and pass good humours . . *Mer. Wives* i 1 169
The anchor is deep: will that humour pass? . . . i 3 57
But nobody but has his fault; but let that pass . . . i 4 15
You stand on distance, your passes, stoccadoes, and I know not what ii 1 233
That I may pass with a reproof the easier . . . ii 2 194
To see thee pass thy punto, thy stock, thy reverse, thy distance, thy montant . . . ii 3 26
Why, this passes, Master Ford; you are not to go loose any longer . iv 2 127
We are simple men; we do not know what's brought to pass under the profession of fortune-telling . . . iv 2 183
When evil deeds have their permissive pass . *Meas. for Meas.* i 3 38
What know the laws That thieves do pass on thieves? . . ii 1 23
If you live to see this come to pass, say Pompey told you so . . ii 1 256
Where you may have such vantage on the duke, He shall not pass you . iv 6 12
Your grace, like power divine, Hath look'd upon my passes . . v 1 375
Being at that pass, You would keep from my heels . . *Com. of Errors* iii 1 17
Kneel to the duke before he pass the abbey . . . v 1 129
Your oath is pass'd to pass away from these . . *L. L. Lost* i 1 49
She passes praise; then praise too short doth blot . . . iv 3 241
For what is inward between us, let it pass . . . v 1 102
And of great import indeed, too, but let that pass . . . v 1 106
It came to pass, Titania waked and straightway loved an ass *M. N. D.* iii 2 33
How came these things to pass? . . . iv 1 83
They may pass for excellent men . . . v 1 219
God made him, and therefore let him pass for a man *Mer. of Venice* i 2 61
A thing not in his power to bring to pass . . . i 3 93
So shall we pass along And never stir assailants . *As Y. Like It* i 3 115
If it do come to pass That any man turn ass . . . ii 5 52
That o'er the green corn-field did pass In the spring time . . v 3 19
Though it pass your patience and mine . . . *T. of Shrew* i 1 130
Which to bring to pass, As I before imparted to your worship . iii 2 131
I will be married to a wealthy widow, Ere three days pass . . iv 2 38
My father is here look'd for every day, To pass assurance of a dower . iv 2 117
And pass my daughter a sufficient dower, The match is made . . iv 4 45
This night, We'll pass the business privately and well . . . iv 4 57
Let me never have a cause to sigh, Till I be brought to such a silly pass! v 2 124
The pilot's glass Hath told the thievish minutes how they pass *All's Well* ii 1 169
Thou didst make tolerable vent of thy travel; it might pass . . ii 3 213
Lies three thirds and uses a known truth to pass a thousand nothings with . . . ii 5 32
I do know him well, and common speech Gives him a worthy pass . ii 5 58
You did never lack advice so much, As letting her pass so . . iii 4 20
For it will come to pass That every braggart shall be found an ass . iv 3 371
And I, that am sure I lack thee, may pass for a wise man . *T. Night* i 5 38
He will not pass his word for two pence that you are no fool . . i 5 86

Pass. Nay, an thou pass upon me, I'll no more with thee . *T. Night* iii 1 48
For it comes to pass oft that a terrible oath, with a swaggering accent sharply twanged off, gives manhood more approbation . iii 4 196
I had a pass with him, rapier, scabbard, and all . iii 4 302
Here's such ado to make no stain a stain As passes colouring *W. Tale* ii 2 20
I know not what I shall incur to pass it, Having no warrant . ii 2 57
Which is enough, I'll warrant, As this world goes, to pass for honest . ii 3 72
Let me pass The same I am . iv 1 9
I tremble To think your father, by some accident, Should pass this way iv 4 20
If you fondly pass our proffer'd offer . *K. John* ii 1 258
We must have bloody noses and crack'd crowns, And pass them current too . *1 Hen. IV.* ii 3 97
That daff'd the world aside, And bid it pass . iv 1 97
If it pass against us, We lose the better half of our possession *Hen. V.* i 1 7
Charming the narrow seas To give you gentle pass . ii Prol. 39
But it must be as it may; he passes some humours and careers . ii 1 132
If we may pass, we will . iii 6 169
We will suddenly Pass our accept and peremptory answer . v 2 82
But your request shall make me let it pass . v 2 372
O, stay! I have no power to let her pass . *1 Hen. VI.* v 3 60
What ransom must I pay before I pass? . v 3 73
Till thou speak, thou shalt not pass from hence . *2 Hen. VI.* i 4 30
Let never day nor night unhallow'd pass, But still remember what the Lord hath done . ii 1 85
No, stir not, for your lives; let her pass by . ii 4 18
Disturb him not; let him pass peaceably . iii 3 25
As for these silken-coated slaves, I pass not . iv 2 136
Who hateth him . . . , Shake he his weapon at us and pass by . iv 8 18
If one so rude and of so mean condition May pass into the presence of a king . v 1 65
Proclaim'd In every borough as we pass along . *3 Hen. VI.* ii 1 195
Did I let pass the abuse done to my niece? . iii 3 188
Let former grudges pass, And henceforth I am thy true servitor . iii 3 195
Why, I, in this weak piping time of peace, Have no delight to pass away the time . *Richard III.* i 1 25
My lord, stand back, and let the coffin pass . i 2 38
I have bought a glass, That I may see my shadow as I pass . i 2 264
For curses never pass The lips of those that breathe them in the air . i 3 285
My lord, will't please you pass along? . iii 1 136
Well, let that pass. Dorset is fled . iv 2 88
And so agree The play may pass . *Hen. VIII.* Prol. 11
It's come to pass, This tractable obedience is a slave . i 2 63
The penance lies on you, if these fair ladies Pass away frowning . i 4 33
They vex me past my patience! Pray you, pass on: I will not tarry . ii 4 130
Stand here, and behold The Lady Anne pass from her coronation . iv 1 3
If your will pass, I shall both find your lordship judge and juror . v 3 59
Room, no doubt, left for the ladies, When they pass back from the christening . v 4 78
Find a way out To let the troop pass fairly . v 4 89
A most unspotted lily shall she pass To the ground . v 5 62
Shall we stand up here, and see them as they pass? . *Troi. and Cres.* i 2 194
I'll tell you them all by their names as they pass by . i 2 199
I protest, Were I alone to pass the difficulties . ii 2 139
Please it our general to pass strangely by him, As if he were forgot . iii 3 39
And put on A form of strangeness as we pass along . iii 3 51
They pass by strangely: they were used to bend, To send their smiles . iii 3 71
We do request your kindest ears, and after, Your loving motion toward the common body, To yield what passes here . *Coriolanus* ii 2 58
Please you That I may pass this doing . ii 2 143
Pass no further.—Ha! what is that?—It will be dangerous to go on . iii 1 24
If you will pass To where you are bound, you must inquire your way . iii 1 53
You may not pass, you must return . v 2 5
If you had told as many lies in his behalf as you have uttered words in your own, you should not pass . v 2 26
I am one that, telling true under him, must say, you cannot pass . v 2 34
My lord, you pass not here.—What, villain boy! . *T. Andron.* i 1 290
In dumb shows Pass the remainder of our hateful days . iii 1 132
I'll deceive you in another sort, And that you'll say, ere half an hour pass iii 1 192
I will frown as I pass by, and let them take it as they list *Rom. and Jul.* i 1 46
I'll tell thee as we pass . ii 3 63
Stay not till the watch be set, For then thou canst not pass to Mantua iii 3 149
No porter at his gate, But rather one that smiles and still invites All that pass by. It cannot hold . *T. of Athens* ii 1 12
You do yourselves but wrong to stir me up; Let me pass quietly . iii 4 54
These words become your lips as they pass thorough them . v 1 198
Not a man Shall pass his quarter, or offend the stream Of regular justice v 4 60
Pass by and curse thy fill, but pass and stay not here thy gait . v 4 73
With patient expectation, To see great Pompey pass the streets of Rome *J. Cæsar* i 1 47
He is a dreamer; let us leave him: pass . i 2 24
Cæsar is returning.—As they pass by, pluck Casca by the sleeve . i 2 179
Here will I stand till Cæsar pass along . ii 3 11
I go to take my stand, To see him pass on to the Capitol . ii 4 26
They pass by me as the idle wind, Which I respect not . iv 3 68
Please you to give quiet pass Through your dominions . *Hamlet* ii 2 77
And then, you know, 'It came to pass, as most like it was' . ii 2 437
And in a pass of practice Requite him for your father . iv 7 139
Between the pass and fell incensed points Of mighty opposites . v 2 61
The king, sir, hath laid, that in a dozen passes between yourself and him, he shall not exceed you three hits . v 2 173
Pass with your best violence; I am afeard you make a wanton of me . v 2 309
Have his daughters brought him to this pass? Couldst thou save nothing . *Lear* iii 4 65
We may not pass upon his life Without the form of justice . iii 7 24
This trusty servant Shall pass between us . iv 2 19
Hear you, sir! speak! Thus might he pass indeed: yet he revives . iv 6 47
Give the word.—Sweet marjoram.—Pass.—I know that voice . iv 6 95
Go your gait, and let poor volk pass . iv 6 243
Vex not his ghost: O, let him pass! . v 3 313
Some strange indignity, Which patience could not pass . *Othello* ii 3 246
Let him not pass, But kill him rather . v 2 241
We shall appear before him. On, there; pass along! . *Ant. and Cleo.* iii 1 37
As my farthest band Shall pass on thy approof . iii 2 27
She had a prophesying fear Of what hath come to pass . iv 14 121
The strait pass was damm'd With dead men hurt behind . *Cymbeline* v 3 11
Has broken a staff or so; so let it pass . *Pericles* ii 3 35

Passable. Go back: the virtue of your name Is not here passable *Coriol.* v 2 13
Hurt him! his body's a passable carcass, if he be not hurt . *Cymbeline* ii 1 10

Passado. The passado he respects not, the duello he regards not *L. L. Lost* i 2 184
Ah, the immortal passado! the punto reverso! the hai! *Rom. and Jul.* ii 4 26
Come, sir, your passado.—Draw, Benvolio; beat down their weapons . *Rom. and Jul.* iii 1 88

Passage. To break in Now in the stirring passage of the day *Com. of Er.* iii 1 99
A shoulder-clapper, one that countermands The passages of alleys . iv 2 38
Through the velvet leaves the wind, All unseen, can passage find *L. L. L.* iv 3 106
This young gentlewoman had a father,—O, that 'had'! how sad a passage 'tis! . *All's Well* i 1 20
I'll drink to her as long as there is a passage in my throat . *T. Night* i 3 41
Can ever believe such impossible passages of grossness . iii 2 77
So thou Shalt feel our justice, in whose easiest passage Look for no less than death . *W. Tale* iii 2 91
Impute it not a crime To me or my swift passage . iv 1 5
Whose passage, vex'd with thy impediment, Shall leave his native channel and o'erswell . *K. John* ii 1 336
The mouth of passage shall we fling wide ope, And give you entrance . ii 1 449
Through the false passage of thy throat, thou liest . *Richard II.* i 1 125
The sullen passage of thy weary steps Esteem as foil . i 3 265
Must I not serve a long apprenticehood To foreign passages? . i 3 272
And to stain the track Of his bright passage to the occident . iii 3 67
This stream through muddy passages Hath held his current . v 3 62
May tear a passage through the flinty ribs Of this hard world . v 5 20
Thou dost in thy passages of life Make me believe . *1 Hen. IV.* iii 2 8
The severals and unhidden passages Of his true titles . *Hen. V.* i 1 86
The powers we bear with us Will cut their passage through the force of France . ii 2 16
And there is gallant and most prave passages . iii 6 97
O, uncle, would some part of my young years Might but redeem the passage of your age! . *1 Hen. VI.* ii 5 108
How will she specify Where is the best and safest passage in? . iii 2 22
Boiling choler chokes The hollow passage of my poison'd voice . v 4 121
In vain thou speak'st, poor boy; my father's blood Hath stopp'd the passage where thy words should enter . *3 Hen. VI.* i 3 22
Yet that thy brazen gates of heaven may ope, And give sweet passage to my sinful soul! . ii 3 41
Unless our halberds did shut up his passage . iv 3 20
But oft have hinder'd, oft, The passages made toward it *Hen. VIII.* ii 4 165
Watch His pettish lunes, his ebbs, his flows, as if The passage and whole carriage of this action Rode on his tide . *Troi. and Cres.* ii 3 140
He will mow all down before him, and leave his passage polled *Coriolanus* iv 5 215
With bloody passage led your wars even to The gates of Rome . v 6 76
Keep then this passage to the Capitol . *T. Andron.* i 1 12
The fearful passage of their death-mark'd love . *Rom. and Jul.* Prol. 9
What, are my doors opposed against my passage? *T. of Athens* iii 4 80
Like valour's minion carved out his passage . *Macbeth* i 2 19
Make thick my blood; Stop up the access and passage to remorse! . i 5 45
When he is fit and season'd for his passage . *Hamlet* iii 3 86
I see, in passages of proof, Time qualifies the spark and fire of it . iv 7 113
For his passage, The soldiers' music and the rites of war Speak loudly . v 2 409
For if such actions may have passage free, Bond-slaves and pagans shall our statesmen be . *Othello* i 2 98
What, ho! no watch? no passage? murder! murder! . v 1 37
It is no act of common passage, but A strain of rareness . *Cymbeline* iii 4 94
Made good the passage; cried to those that fled . v 3 23

Passant. It agrees well, passant . *Mer. Wives* i 1 20

Passed. And so conclusions passed the careires . i 1 184
The women have so cried and shrieked at it, that it passed . i 1 310
You come to know what hath passed between me and Ford's wife? . iii 5 63
I have overheard what hath passed between you and your sister *M. for M.* iii 1 161
Passed sentence may not be recall'd . *Com. of Errors* i 1 148
Knowing what hath passed between you and Claudio . *Much Ado* v 2 48
Your oaths are pass'd; and now subscribe your names . *L. L. Lost* i 1 19
Your oath is pass'd to pass away from these . i 1 49
Did point you to buy them, along as you pass'd . ii 1 245
And the imperial votaress passed on, In maiden meditation *M. N. Dream* ii 1 163
Firm and irrevocable is my doom Which I have pass'd upon her *As Y. Like It* i 3 86
Hath newly pass'd between this youth and me . *T. Night* v 1 158
This practice hath most shrewdly pass'd upon thee . v 1 360
If that the injuries be justly weigh'd That have on both sides pass'd . v 1 376
Your gallery Have we pass'd through, not without much content *W. Tale* v 3 11
And thus still doing, thus he pass'd along . *Richard II.* v 2 21
Remember, as thou read'st, thy promise pass'd . v 3 51
That self bill is urged, Which in the eleventh year of the last king's reign Was like, and had indeed against us pass'd . *Hen. V.* i 1 3
'Tis certain he hath pass'd the river Somme . iii 5 1
On thy knee Make thee beg pardon for thy passed speech . *2 Hen. VI.* iii 2 221
So minutes, hours, days, months, and years, Pass'd over to the end they were created . *3 Hen. VI.* ii 5 39
Well have we pass'd and now repass'd the seas . iv 7 5
Hath pass'd in safety through the narrow seas . iv 8 3
O, I have pass'd a miserable night, So full of ugly sights! *Richard III.* i 4 2
Who pass'd, methought, the melancholy flood, With that grim ferryman . i 4 45
And that not pass'd me but By learned approbation of the judges *Hen. VIII.* i 2 70
Pray, how pass'd it?—I'll tell you in a little . ii 1 10
As he pass'd along, How earnestly he cast his eyes upon me! . v 2 11
And all the rest so laughed, that it passed. So let it now *Troi. and Cres.* i 2 182
They pass'd by me As misers do by beggars . iii 3 142
Matrons flung gloves, Ladies and maids their scarfs and handkerchers, Upon him as he pass'd . *Coriolanus* ii 1 281
You should have ta'en the advantage of his choler And pass'd him unelected . ii 3 207
Hath he not pass'd the noble and the common? . iii 1 29
Being pass'd for consul with full voice . iii 3 59
I have pass'd My word and promise . *T. Andron.* i 1 468
Nought hath pass'd, But even with law . iv 4 7
What doth her beauty serve, but as a note Where I may read who pass'd that passing fair? . *Rom. and Jul.* i 1 242
No villanous bounty yet hath pass'd my heart . *T. of Athens* ii 2 182
Is guilty of a several bastardy, If he do break the smallest particle Of any promise that hath pass'd from him . *J. Cæsar* ii 1 140
Pass'd in probation with you, How you were borne in hand . *Macbeth* iii 1 80
The battles, sieges, fortunes, That I have pass'd . *Othello* i 3 131
She loved me for the dangers I had pass'd, And I loved her . i 3 167
Be quiet then as men should be, Till he hath pass'd necessity *Per.* ii Gower 6

Passenger. Fellows, stand fast; I see a passenger . *T. G. of Ver.* iv 1 1
Provided that you do no outrages On silly women or poor passengers . iv 1 72
My mates . . . Have some unhappy passenger in chase . v 4 15
Beat our watch, and rob our passengers . *Richard II.* v 3 9
Foul felonious thief that fleeced poor passengers . *2 Hen. VI.* iii 1 129
As the mournful crocodile With sorrow snares relenting passengers . iii 1 227

Passeth. And passeth by with stiff unbowed knee . . *2 Hen. VI.* iii 1 16
But I have that within which passeth show . . . . *Hamlet* i 2 85
Passing. 'Tis a passing shame . . . . . . *T. G. of Ver.* i 2 17
What should I see then?—Your own present folly and her passing deformity . . . . ii 1 81
Is she not passing fair?—She hath been fairer, madam, than she is . iv 4 153
The jury, passing on the prisoner's life, May in the sworn twelve have a thief or two Guiltier than him they try . . *Meas. for Meas.* ii 1 19
You apprehend passing shrewdly . . . . . *Much Ado* ii 1 84
Spied a blossom passing fair Playing in the wanton air . . *L. L. Lost* iv 3 103
Oberon is passing fell and wrath . . . . . *M. N. Dream* ii 1 20
I will be bitter with him and passing short . . *As Y. Like It* iii 5 138
It will be pastime passing excellent . . . . . *T. of Shrew* Ind. 1 67
You are passing welcome, And so I pray you all to think yourselves . ii 1 113
I find you passing gentle. 'Twas told me you were rough and coy . ii 1 244
Thou art pleasant, gamesome, passing courteous, But slow in speech . ii 1 247
Though he be blunt, I know him passing wise . . . . iii 2 24
My falcon now is sharp and passing empty . . . . iv 1 193
'Tis passing good . . . . iv 3 18
Of the Vapians passing the equinoctial of Queubus . . *T. Night* ii 3 23
Let's have some merry ones.—Why, this is a passing merry one *W. Tale* iv 4 294
Half my power this night, Passing these flats, are taken by the tide *K. John* v 6 40
Believe me, I am passing light in spirit . . . *2 Hen. IV.* iv 2 85
Our air shakes them passing scornfully . . . . *Hen. V.* iv 2 42
I was employ'd in passing to and fro . . . . . *1 Hen. VI.* ii 1 69
O passing traitor, perjured and unjust! . . . . . *3 Hen. VI.* v 1 106
A cherry lip, a bonny eye, a passing pleasing tongue *Richard III.* i 1 94
His long trouble now is passing Out of this world . . *Hen. VIII.* iv 2 162
Abundantly they lack discretion, Yet are they passing cowardly *Coriol.* i 1 207
This valley fits the purpose passing well . . . . *T. Andron.* ii 3 84
Show me a mistress that is passing fair, What doth her beauty serve, but as a note Where I may read who pass'd that passing fair? *Rom. and Jul.* i 1 240
All that lives must die, Passing through nature to eternity . *Hamlet* i 2 73
One fair daughter, and no more, The which he loved passing well . . ii 2 427
I have a daughter that I love passing well . . . . . ii 2 431
She swore, in faith, 'twas strange, 'twas passing strange . *Othello* i 3 160
Passio. Hysterica passio, down, thou climbing sorrow, Thy element's below! . . . . *Lear* ii 4 57
Passion. This music crept by me upon the waters, Allaying both their fury and my passion With its sweet air . . . . *Tempest* i 2 392
Your father's in some passion That works him strongly . . . iv 1 143
Shall not myself, One of their kind, that relish all as sharply, Passion as they, be kindlier moved than thou art? . . . . . v 1 24
What means this passion at his name? . . . . *T. G. of Ver.* i 2 16
Got's will, and his passion of my heart! . . . . *Mer. Wives* iii 1 62
Till this afternoon his passion Ne'er brake into extremity of rage *C. of Er.* v 1 47
Each one with ireful passion, with drawn swords . . . . v 1 151
If my passion change not shortly, God forbid it should be otherwise *M. Ado* i 1 221
Never counterfeit of passion came so near the life of passion . . ii 3 110
What effects of passion shows she? . . . . . . ii 3 112
I will go to Benedick And counsel him to fight against his passion . iii 1 83
But, tasting it, Their counsel turns to passion . . . . . v 1 23
With,—O, with—but with this I passion to say wherewith . *L. L. Lost* i 1 264
Saw sighs reek from you, noted well your passion . . . . iv 3 140
It did move him to passion, and therefore let's hear it . . . iv 3 202
In this spleen ridiculous appears, To check their folly, passion's solemn tears . . . . v 2 118
You spend your passion on a misprised mood . . *M. N. Dream* iii 2 74
More merry tears The passion of loud laughter never shed . . v 1 70
This passion, and the death of a dear friend, would go near to make a man look sad . . . . v 1 293
She comes; and her passion ends the play . . . . . v 1 321
I never heard a passion so confused, So strange, outrageous *M. of Venice* ii 8 12
Hath not a Jew hands, organs, dimensions, senses, affections, passions? iii 1 63
How all the other passions fleet to air, As doubtful thoughts! . . iii 2 108
For affection, Mistress of passion, sways it to the mood Of what it likes or loathes . . . . iv 1 51
What passion hangs these weights upon my tongue? . *As Y. Like It* i 2 269
If thou hast not broke from company Abruptly, as my passion now makes me, Thou hast not loved . . . . ii 4 41
This shepherd's passion Is much upon my fashion . . . . ii 4 61
For every passion something and for no passion truly any thing . iii 2 433
Too great testimony in your complexion that it was a passion of earnest iv 3 172
It [to love] is to be all made of fantasy, All made of passion . . v 2 101
You break into some merry passion And so offend him . *T. of Shrew* Ind. 1 97
'Gamut' I am, the ground of all accord, 'A re,' to plead Hortensio's passion . . . . iii 1 74
Cock's passion, silence! . . . . iv 1 121
Where love's strong passion is impress'd in youth . . *All's Well* i 3 139
Invention is ashamed, Against the proclamation of thy passion . i 3 180
For your passions Have to the full appeach'd . . . . i 3 196
Cox my passion! give me your hand . . . . . . v 2 43
O, then unfold the passion of my love . . . . *T. Night* i 4 24
The cunning of her passion Invites me in this churlish messenger . ii 2 23
Methought it did relieve my passion much, More than light airs . ii 4 4
There is no woman's sides Can bide the beating of so strong a passion . ii 4 97
Maugre all thy pride, Nor wit nor reason can my passion hide . iii 1 164
With the same 'haviour that your passion bears Goes on my master's grief . . . . iii 4 226
Methinks his words do from such passion fly, That he believes himself iii 4 407
Let thy fair wisdom, not thy passion, sway . . . . . iv 1 56
Fear you his tyrannous passion more, alas, Than the queen's life? *W. Tale* ii 3 28
Cast your good counsels Upon his passion . . . . . . iv 4 507
A notable passion of wonder appeared in them . . . . . v 2 17
Idle merriment, A passion hateful to my purposes . . . *K. John* iii 3 47
Then with a passion would I shake the world . . . . . iii 4 39
His passion is so ripe, it needs must break . . . . . iv 2 79
Forgive the comment that my passion made Upon thy feature . . iv 2 263
I must speak in passion, and I will do it in King Cambyses' vein *1 Hen. IV.* ii 4 425
Not in pleasure but in passion, not in words only, but in woes also . ii 4 458
Our grandam earth, having this distemperature, In passion shook . iii 1 35
This strained passion doth you wrong, my lord . . . *2 Hen. IV.* i 1 161
Lean on your health; the which, if you give o'er To stormy passion, must perforce decay . . . . i 1 165
Till that his passions, like a whale on ground, Confound themselves . iv 4 40
Unto whose grace our passion is as subject As are our wretches fetter'd in our prisons . . . . *Hen. V.* i 2 242
Spare in diet, Free from gross passion or of mirth or anger . . . ii 2 132
Passion. Had the passions of thy heart burst out, I fear we should have seen decipher'd there More rancorous spite . *1 Hen. VI.* iv 1 183
Of all base passions, fear is most accursed . . . . . . v 2 18
Her virtues graced with external gifts Do breed love's settled passions . v 5 4
My tender youth was never yet attaint With any passion of inflaming love . . . . v 5 82
Beshrew me, but his passion moves me so That hardly can I check my eyes from tears . . . . *3 Hen. VI.* i 4 150
And with my tongue To tell the passion of my sovereign's heart . . iii 3 62
This is it that makes me bridle passion And bear with mildness . . iv 4 19
No English soul More stronger to direct you than yourself, If with the sap of reason you would quench, Or but allay, the fire of passion *Hen. VIII.* i 1 149
Do more conduce To the hot passion of distemper'd blood *Troi. and Cres.* ii 2 169
Even such a passion doth embrace my bosom . . . . . . iii 2 37
May worthy Troilus be half attach'd With that which here his passion doth express? . . . . v 2 162
O, contain yourself; Your passion draws ears hither . . . . v 2 181
Whose passions and whose plots have broke their sleep . *Coriolanus* iv 4 19
Titus, rue the tears I shed, A mother's tears in passion for her son *T. An.* i 1 106
And that my sword upon thee shall approve, And plead my passions . ii 1 36
Is not my sorrow deep, having no bottom? Then be my passions bottomless . . . . iii 1 218
The tender boy, in passion moved, Doth weep to see his grandsire's heaviness . . . . iii 2 48
But passion lends them power, time means, to meet *Rom. and Jul.* ii Prol. 13
Nay, I'll conjure too. Romeo! humours! madman! passion! lover! . ii 1 7
Thou overheard'st, ere I was ware, My true love's passion . . . ii 2 104
Our own precedent passions do instruct us What levity's in youth *T. of A.* i 1 133
O you gods, I feel my master's passion! . . . . . . iii 1 59
And with such sober and unnoted passion He did behave his anger . iii 5 21
Vexed I am Of late with passions of some difference . . *J. Cæsar* i 2 40
Then, Brutus, I have much mistook your passion . . . . . i 2 48
Thy heart is big, get thee apart and weep. Passion, I see, is catching . iii 1 283
If much you note him, You shall offend him and extend his passion *Macb.* iii 4 57
Macduff, this noble passion, Child of integrity, hath from my soul Wiped the black scruples . . . . iv 3 114
As oft as any passion under heaven That does afflict our natures *Hamlet* ii 1 105
Would have made milch the burning eyes of heaven, And passion in the gods . . . . ii 2 541
In a fiction, in a dream of passion, Could force his soul so to his own conceit . . . . ii 2 578
What would he do, Had he the motive and the cue for passion That I have? . . . . ii 2 587
In the very torrent, tempest, and, as I may say, the whirlwind of passion iii 2 8
To hear a robustious periwig-pated fellow tear a passion to tatters iii 2 11
Give me that man That is not passion's slave . . . . . iii 2 77
What to ourselves in passion we propose, The passion ending, doth the purpose lose . . . . iii 2 205
Lapsed in time and passion, lets go by The important acting . . iii 4 107
Affliction, passion, hell itself, She turns to favour and to prettiness . iv 5 188
The bravery of his grief did put me Into a towering passion . . v 2 80
Smooth every passion That in the natures of their lords rebel . *Lear* ii 2 81
Those that mingle reason with your passion Must be content to think you old . . . . ii 4 237
She was a queen Over her passion . . . . iv 3 16
'Twixt two extremes of passion, joy and grief, Burst smilingly . v 3 198
Passion, having my best judgement collied, Assays to lead the way *Oth.* ii 3 206
Close delations, working from the heart That passion cannot rule . . iii 3 124
I see, sir, you are eaten up with passion: I do repent me . . iii 3 391
Nature would not invest herself in such shadowing passion without some instruction . . . . iv 1 41
O'erwhelmed with your grief—A passion most unsuiting such a man . iv 1 78
Proceed you in your tears. Concerning this, sir,—O well-painted passion! . . . . iv 1 268
Is this the nature Whom passion could not shake? . . . . iv 1 277
Some bloody passion shakes your very frame . . . . . v 2 44
Whom every thing becomes, to chide, to laugh, To weep; whose every passion fully strives To make itself, in thee, fair and admired! *Ant. and Cleo.* i 1 50
Her passions are made of nothing but the finest part of pure love . . i 2 151
Your speech is passion: But, pray you, stir no embers up . . ii 2 12
Gods and goddesses, All the whole synod of them!—What's thy passion? iii 10 5
E'en a woman, and commanded By such poor passion as the maid that milks . . . . iv 15 74
Give her what comforts The quality of her passion shall require . . v 1 63
The passions of the mind, That have their first conception by mis-dread, Have after-nourishment and life by care . . . . *Pericles* i 2 11
This borrow'd passion stands for true old woe . . . . . iv 4 24
Passionate. Poor forlorn Proteus, passionate Proteus . *T. G. of Ver.* i 2 124
Warble, child; make passionate my sense of hearing . *L. L. Lost* iii 1 1
I am amazed at your passionate words . . . . *M. N. Dream* iii 2 220
She is sad and passionate . . . . *K. John* ii 1 544
Nephew, what means this passionate discourse? . . . *2 Hen. VI.* i 1 104
And cannot passionate our tenfold grief With folded arms *T. Andron.* iii 2 6
Come, give us a taste of your quality; come, a passionate speech *Hamlet* ii 2 452
Passioning. 'Twas Ariadne passioning For Theseus' perjury *T. G. of Ver.* iv 4 172
Passive. The sweet degrees that this brief world affords To such as may the passive drugs of it Freely command . . . *T. of Athens* iv 3 254
Passport. Here's my passport . . . . . . *All's Well* iii 2 58
His passport shall be made And crowns for convoy put into his purse *Hen. V.* iv 3 36
A passport too! Apollo, perfect me in the characters! . *Pericles* iii 2 66
Passy. Then he's a rogue, and a passy measures panyn . . *T. Night* v 1 206
Past. Past the mid season . . . . *Tempest* i 2 239
And by that destiny to perform an act Whereof what's past is prologue ii 1 253
I will here shroud till the dregs of the storm be past . . . ii 2 43
No matter, since I feel The best is past . . . . . . iii 3 51
Irreparable is the loss, and patience Says it is past her cure . . v 1 141
And ask remission for my folly past . . . . *T. G. of Ver.* i 2 65
Vat is de clock, Jack?—'Tis past the hour . . . *Mer. Wives* i 3 4
He lays before me My riots past, my wild societies . . . . iii 4 8
He's not past it yet . . . . *Meas. for Meas.* iii 2 193
Careless, reckless, and fearless of what's past, present, or to come . iv 2 151
O, she misused me past the endurance of a block! . . . *Much Ado* ii 1 246
It is past the infinite of thought . . . . ii 3 106
I say, sing.—Forbear till this company be past . . . *L. L. Lost* i 2 131
Your cue is past; it is, 'never tire' . . . . . *M. N. Dream* iii 1 103
Thou drivest me past the bounds Of maiden's patience . . . iii 2 65
Saint Valentine is past: Begin these wood-birds but to couple now? . iv 1 144

Past. Past the wit of man to say . . . *M. N. Dream* iv 1 211
His hour is almost past . . . *Mer. of Venice* ii 6 2
He did intreat me, past all saying nay . . . iii 2 232
Past all expressing . . . iii 5 78
I am past my gamut long ago . . . *T. of Shrew* iii 1 71
They say miracles are past . . . *All's Well* ii 3 1
For doing I am past . . . ii 3 246
The troop is past. Come, pilgrim, I will bring you Where you shall host iii 5 96
To marry her, I'll add three thousand crowns To what is past already . iii 7 36
'Tis past, my liege; And I beseech your majesty to make it Natural rebellion . . . v 3 4
And if it end so meet, The bitter past, more welcome is the sweet . v 3 334
As recompense of our dear services Past and to come . *W. Tale* ii 3 151
As you were past all shame,—Those of your fact are so—so past all truth . . . iii 2 85
I have a kinsman not past three quarters of a mile hence . iv 3 85
I am past moe children, but thy sons and daughters will be all gentle-men born . . . v 2 137
Which was so strongly urged past my defence . *K. John* i 1 258
All murders past do stand excused in this . . . iv 3 51
Writ in remembrance more than things long past . *Richard II.* ii 1 14
Though not clean past your youth, hath yet some smack of age *2 Hen. IV.* i 2 110
Past and to come seems best; things present worst . i 3 108
Is it good morrow, lords?—'Tis one o'clock, and past . iii 1 34
Viewing his progress through, What perils past, what crosses to ensue iii 1 55
The heat is past; follow no further now: Call in the powers . iv 3 27
Of indigent faint souls past corporal toil . . . *Hen. V.* i 1 16
Babies and old women, Either past or not arrived to pith and puissance iii Prol. 21
And myself have play'd The interim, by remembering you 'tis past v Prol. 43
But why wear you your leek to-day? Saint Davy's day is past . v 1 2
What's past and what's to come she can descry . *1 Hen. VI.* i 2 57
Here comes a man; let's stay till he be past . *3 Hen. VI.* iii 1 12
Thou seest what's past, go fear thy king withal . iii 3 226
We'll send him hence to Brittany, Till storms be past of civil enmity . iv 6 98
Harp not on that string, madam; that is past *Richard III.* iv 4 364
Myself have many tears to wash Hereafter time, for time past wrong'd by thee . . . iv 4 390
Now, the Lord help, They vex me past my patience! *Hen. VIII.* ii 4 130
You must no more call it York-place, that's past . iv 1 95
But now I am past all comforts here, but prayers . iv 2 123
He has not past three or four hairs on his chin . *Troi. and Cres.* i 2 121
Those scraps are good deeds past . . . iii 3 148
What they do in present, Though less than yours in past, must o'ertop yours . . . iii 3 164
Praise new-born gawds, Though they are made and moulded of things past . . . iii 3 177
What's past and what's to come is strew'd with husks And formless ruin iv 5 166
Well, well, 'tis done, 'tis past: and yet it is not . v 2 97
You have found, Scaling his present bearing with his past . *Coriolanus* ii 3 257
You may salve so, Not what is dangerous present, but the loss Of what is past . . . iii 2 72
The main blaze of it is past, but a small thing would make it flame again iv 3 20
O'ercome with pride, ambitious past all thinking, Self-loving . iv 6 31
Like to a bowl upon a subtle ground, I have tumbled past the throw . v 2 21
And at my suit, sweet, pardon what is past . *T. Andron* i 1 431
For you and I are past our dancing days . *Rom. and Jul.* i 5 33
I already know thy grief; It strains me past the compass of my wits . iv 1 47
His days and times are past . . . *T. of Athens* ii 1 21
'Twas due on forfeiture, my lord, six weeks And past . ii 2 31
Lord Timon's happy hours are done and past . iii 2 7
I should not urge thy duty past thy might . *J. Cæsar* iv 3 261
It was he in the times past which held you So under fortune *Macbeth* iii 1 77
I'll wipe away . . . All saws of books, all forms, all pressures past *Hamlet* i 5 100
My fault is past. But, O, what form of prayer Can serve my turn? . iii 3 51
Confess yourself to heaven; Repent what's past; avoid what is to come iii 4 150
Had he been where he thought, By this, had thought been past . *Lear* iv 6 45
And more, much more; the time will bring it out: 'Tis past, and so am I v 3 164
Until some half-hour past . . . v 3 193
When remedies are past, the griefs are ended By seeing the worst *Othello* i 3 202
To mourn a mischief that is past and gone Is the next way to draw new mischief on . . . i 3 204
Good faith, a little one; not past a pint, as I am a soldier . ii 3 68
What, are you hurt, lieutenant?—Ay, past all surgery . ii 3 260
Nor my service past, nor present sorrows, Nor purposed merit in futurity iii 4 116
Things that are past are done with me . *Ant. and Cleo.* i 2 101
She is cunning past man's thought . . . i 2 150
Whose love is never link'd to the deserver Till his deserts are past . i 2 194
But, if there be, or ever were, one such, It's past the size of dreaming . v 2 97
Fear no more the frown o' the great; Thou art past the tyrant's stroke *Cymbeline* iv 2 265
Their pleasures here are past, so is their pain . iv 2 290
It strikes me, past The hope of comfort . . . iv 3 8
Of what's past, is, and to come, the discharge . v 4 172
Thief, any thing That's due to all the villains past, in being, To come! v 5 212
Being here, Bethought me what was past, what might succeed *Pericles* i 2 83
Past all doubt. Then 'twere past all doubt You'ld call your children yours . . . *W. Tale* ii 3 80
Past care. For 'past cure is still past care' . . . *L. L. Lost* v 2 28
Things past redress are now with me past care . *Richard II.* ii 3 171
Past compare. Our weakness past compare . *T. of Shrew* v 2 174
Though they be not to be talked on, yet they are past compare *R. and J.* ii 5 43
Past cure. That such a one and such a one were past cure of the thing you wot of . . . *Meas. for Meas.* ii 1 115
For 'past cure is still past care' . . . *L. L. Lost* v 2 28
Past cure of the fives, stark spoiled with the staggers . *T. of Shrew* iii 2 54
To prostitute our past-cure malady To empirics . *All's Well* ii 1 124
My art is not past power nor you past cure . ii 1 161
Indeed we fear'd his sickness was past cure . *K. John* iv 2 86
Come weep with me; past hope, past cure, past help! . *Rom. and Jul.* iv 1 45
Past deeds. That what in time proceeds May token to the future our past deeds . . . *All's Well* iv 2 63
Past depth. Hath stepp'd into the law, which is past depth *T. of Athens* iii 5 12
Past doubt. But that's past doubt . . . *W. Tale* i 2 268
Let them go on; This mutiny were better put in hazard, Than stay, past doubt, for greater . . . *Coriolanus* ii 3 265
Past eight. 'Tis past eight already, sir.—Is it? I will then address me to my appointment . . . *Mer. Wives* iii 5 134
Past endeavours. I wish might be found in the calendar of my past endeavours . . . *All's Well* i 3 5

Past enduring. He so troubles me, 'Tis past enduring . *W. Tale* ii 1 2
Past evils. Turning past evils to advantages . *2 Hen. IV.* iv 4 78
Past fearing. That life is better life, past fearing death, Than that which lives to fear . . . *Meas. for Meas.* v 1 402
Past grace? obedience?—Past hope, and in despair; that way, past grace *Cymbeline* i 1 136
Past grief. What's gone and what's past help Should be past grief *W. T.* iii 2 224
Past help. What's gone and what's past help Should be past grief . iii 2 223
Come weep with me; past hope, past cure, past help! . *Rom. and Jul.* iv 1 45
Past hiding. Unless it swell past hiding . . . *Troi. and Cres.* i 2 294
Past hope. A wreck past hope he was . . . *T. Night* v 1 82
Come weep with me; past hope, past cure, past help! . *Rom. and Jul.* iv 1 45
Past grace? obedience?—Past hope, and in despair . *Cymbeline* i 1 137
Past joy. But that a joy past joy calls out on me, It were a grief, so brief to part with thee . . . *Rom. and Jul.* iii 3 173
Past life. My past life Hath been as continent, as chaste, as true, As I am now unhappy . . . *W. Tale* iii 2 36
Past miseries. You gods! your present kindness Makes my past miseries sports . . . *Pericles* v 3 41
Past patience. These wrongs, unspeakable, past patience *T. Andron.* v 3 126
Past power, My art is not past power nor you past cure . *All's Well* ii 1 161
Past praying for. Nay, that's past praying for . *1 Hen. IV.* ii 4 211
Past proportion. Will you with counters sum The past proportion of his infinite? . . . *Troi. and Cres.* ii 2 29
Past question. Would that have mended my hair?—Past question *T. N.* i 3 104
Past recovery. For grief that they are past recovery . *2 Hen. VI.* i 1 116
Past redress. Things past redress are now with me past care *Richard II.* ii 3 171
Past remedy. Kinsmen, his sorrows are past remedy . *T. Andron.* iv 3 31
For certainties Either are past remedies, or, timely knowing, The remedy then born—discover to me What both you spur and stop *Cymb.* i 6 97
Past-saving. What a past-saving slave is this! . *All's Well* iv 3 158
Past sense. To esteem A senseless help when help past sense we deem . ii 1 127
Past service. Stay at home till you are past service . *2 Hen. IV.* iii 2 269
Past speaking of in a king! . . . *Lear* iv 6 209
Past thought. He's there, past thought of human reason *Com. of Errors* v 1 189
O, she deceives me Past thought! . . . *Othello* i 1 167
Past two o'clock? and here much Orlando! . *As Y. Like It* iv 3 1
Past watching. Unless it swell past hiding, and then it's past watching *Troi. and Cres.* i 2 295

Paste. That small model of the barren earth Which serves as paste and cover to our bones . . . *Richard II.* iii 2 154
I will grind your bones to dust And with your blood and it I'll make a paste, And of the paste a coffin I will rear . *T. Andron.* v 2 188
And in that paste let their vile heads be baked . v 2 201
As the cockney did to the eels when she put 'em i' the paste alive *Lear* ii 4 124
Pastern. I will not change my horse with any that treads but on four pasterns . . . *Hen. V.* iii 7 13
Pasties. And make two pasties of your shameful heads *T. Andron.* v 2 190
Pastime. Whose pastime Is to make midnight mushrooms . *Tempest* v 1 38
And make a pastime of each weary step . *T. G. of Ver.* ii 7 35
We will with some strange pastime solace them . *L. L. Lost* iv 3 377
We have had pastimes here and pleasant game . v 2 360
Stay, Jaques, stay.—To see no pastime I . *As Y. Like It* v 4 201
It will be pastime passing excellent, If it be husbanded . *T. of Shrew* Ind. 1 67
Hush, master! here's some good pastime toward . i 1 68
This his good melancholy oft began, On the catastrophe and heel of pastime, When it was out . . . *All's Well* i 2 57
Till our very pastime, tired out of breath, prompt us to have mercy *T. N.* iii 4 151
How sometimes nature will betray its folly, Its tenderness, and make itself a pastime To harder bosoms! . . . *W. Tale* i 2 152
Laugh at me, make their pastime at my sorrow . ii 3 24
Our pastimes done, possess a golden slumber . *T. Andron.* ii 3 26
Did you assay him To any pastime? . . . *Hamlet* iii 1 15
That we can let our beard be shook with danger And think it pastime . iv 7 33
Makest thou this shame thy pastime? . . . *Lear* ii 4 6
Make pastime with us a day or two, or longer . *Cymbeline* iii 1 79
Pastor. Do not, as some ungracious pastors do, Show me the steep and thorny way to heaven . . . *Hamlet* i 3 47
Pastoral. I play as I have seen them do In Whitsun pastorals *W. Tale* iv 4 134
Pastoral, pastoral-comical, historical-pastoral, tragical-historical *Hamlet* ii 2 416
Pastry They call for dates and quinces in the pastry . *Rom. and Jul.* iv 4 2
Pasture. Too small a pasture for such store of muttons . *T. G. of Ver.* i 1 105
Unless we feed on your lips.—You sheep, and I pasture . *L. L. Lost* ii 1 221
Anon a careless herd, Full of the pasture, jumps along . *As Y. Like It* ii 1 53
What is he that shall buy his flock and pasture? . ii 4 88
Good pasture makes fat sheep . . . iii 2 28
And bedew Her pastures' grass with faithful English blood *Richard II.* iii 3 100
They sell the pasture now to buy the horse . *Hen. V.* ii Prol. 5
Show us here The mettle of your pasture . iii 1 27
It is the pasture lards the rother's sides . *T. of Athens* iv 3 12
Yea, like the stag, when snow the pasture sheets, The barks of trees thou browsed'st . . . *Ant. and Cleo.* i 4 65
You have locks upon you; So graze as you find pasture . *Cymbeline* v 4 2
Pasty. We have a hot venison pasty to dinner . *Mer. Wives* i 1 202
If ye pinch me like a pasty, I can say no more . *All's Well* iv 3 140
Pat. Are we all met?—Pat, pat . . . *M. N. Dream* iii 1 2
You shall see, it will fall pat as I told you . v 1 188
Nor could Come pat betwixt too early and too late . *Hen. VIII.* ii 3 84
Now might I do it pat, now he is praying; And now I'll do't *Hamlet* iii 3 73
And pat he comes like the catastrophe of the old comedy . *Lear* i 2 146
Patay. At the battle of Patay, When but in all I was six thousand strong And that the French were almost ten to one . *1 Hen. VI.* iv 1 19
Patch. What a pied ninny's this! Thou scurvy patch! . *Tempest* iii 2 71
Mome, malt-horse, capon, coxcomb, idiot, patch! . *Com. of Errors* iii 1 32
What patch is made our porter? My master stays in the street . iii 1 36
Patch grief with proverbs . . . *Much Ado* v 1 17
So were there a patch set on learning, to see him in a school. *L. L. Lost* iv 2 32
A crew of patches, rude mechanicals, That work for bread *M. N. Dream* iii 2 9
The patch is kind enough, but a huge feeder . *Mer. of Venice* ii 5 46
With a patch of velvet on's face . . . *All's Well* iv 5 100
A goodly patch of velvet: his left cheek is a cheek of two pile and a half iv 5 102
As patches set upon a little breach Discredit more in hiding of the fault Than did the fault before it was so patch'd . *K. John* iv 2 32
Begin to patch up thine old body for heaven . *2 Hen. IV.* ii 4 252
Do botch and bungle up damnation With patches, colours . *Hen. V.* ii 2 116
And patches will I get unto these cudgell'd scars, And swear I got them in the Gallia wars . . . v 1 93
What soldiers, patch? Death of thy soul! those linen cheeks of thine Are counsellors to fear . . . *Macbeth* v 3 15
A king of shreds and patches . . . *Hamlet* iii 4 102

Patch. To gain a little patch of ground That hath in it no profit but the name . . . *Hamlet* iv 4 18
O, that that earth, which kept the world in awe, Should patch a wall! v 1 239
If you'll patch a quarrel, As matter whole you have not to make it with, It must not be with this . . . *Ant. and Cleo.* ii 2 52
Patch-breech, I say!—What say you, master? . . . *Pericles* ii 1 14
Patched. Man is but a patched fool, if he will offer to say what methought I had . . . *M. N. Dream* iv 1 215
Any thing that's mended is but patched . . . *T. Night* i 5 52
Virtue that transgresses is but patched with sin; and sin that amends is but patched with virtue . . . i 5 53
Lame, foolish, crooked, swart, prodigious, Patch'd with foul moles *K. John* iii 1 47
As patches set upon a little breach Discredit more in hiding of the fault Than did the fault before it was so patch'd . . . iv 2 34
This must be patch'd With cloth of any colour . . . *Coriolanus* iii 1 252
But You patch'd up your excuses . . . *Ant. and Cleo.* ii 2 56
Patchery. Here is such patchery, such juggling! . . . *Troi. and Cres.* ii 3 77
You hear him cog, see him dissemble, Know his gross patchery *T. of A.* v 1 99
Pate. 'Steal by line and level' is an excellent pass of pate . *Tempest* iv 1 244
There is either liquor in his pate or money in his purse . *Mer. Wives* ii 1 197
She will score your fault upon my pate . . . *Com. of Errors* i 2 65
I have some marks of yours upon my pate . . . i 2 82
Back, slave, or I will break thy pate across . . . ii 1 78
As plain as the plain bald pate of father Time himself . . . ii 2 71
Let none enter, lest I break your pate . . . ii 2 220
Break any breaking here, and I'll break your knave's pate . . . iii 1 74
Fat paunches have lean pates, and dainty bits Make rich the ribs *L. L. L.* i 1 26
Rap me well, or I'll knock your knave's pate . . . *T. of Shrew* i 2 12
She struck me on the head, And through the instrument my pate made way . . . ii 1 155
I would I had; so I had broke thy pate . . . *All's Well* ii 1 68
Was this taken By any understanding pate but thine? . . . *W. Tale* i 2 223
That sly devil, That broker, that still breaks the pate of faith *K. John* ii 1 568
An 'twere not as good deed as drink, to break the pate on thee 1 *Hen. IV.* ii 1 33
Here's no scoring but upon the pate . . . v 3 32
Tell him, I'll knock his leek about his pate . . . *Hen. V.* iv 1 54
I will make him eat some part of my leek, or I will peat his pate four days . . . v 1 43
There is a groat to heal your pate . . . v 1 62
God b' wi' you, and keep you, and heal your pate . . . v 1 71
A black beard will turn white; a curled pate will grow bald . . . v 2 169
Do pelt so fast at one another's pate That many have their giddy brains knock'd out . . . 1 *Hen. VI.* iii 1 82
Let him to the Tower, And chop away that factious pate of his 2 *Hen. VI.* v 1 135
You have holp . . . To melt the city leads upon your pates *Coriolanus* iv 6 82
Then will I lay the serving-creature's dagger on your pate *Rom. and Jul.* iv 5 120
The learned pate Ducks to the golden fool: all is oblique *T. of Athens* iv 3 17
Am I a coward? Who calls me villain? breaks my pate across? *Hamlet* ii 2 599
It might be the pate of a politician, which this ass now o'er-reaches . v 1 86
To have his fine pate full of fine dirt . . . v 1 116
Till our ground, Singeing his pate against the burning zone, Make Ossa like a wart! . . . v 1 305
My invention Comes from my pate as birdlime does from frize *Othello* ii 1 127
What got he by that? You have broke his pate with your bowl *Cymbeline* ii 1 8
Patent. Ere I will yield my virgin patent up . . . *M. N. Dream* i 1 80
Which he thinks is a patent for his sauciness . . . *All's Well* iv 5 69
Call in the letters patents that he hath . . . *Richard II.* ii 1 202
I am denied to sue my livery here, And yet my letters-patents give me leave . . . ii 3 130
And, to confirm his goodness, Tied it by letters-patents *Hen. VIII.* iii 2 250
If you are so fond over her iniquity, give her patent to offend *Othello* iv 1 209
Paternal. Here I disclaim all my paternal care . . . *Lear* i 1 115
Path. Ask him why, that hour of fairy revel, In their so sacred paths he dares to tread In shape profane . . . *Mer. Wives* iv 4 59
Pace your wisdom In that good path that I would wish it go *M. for M.* iv 3 138
Every one lets forth his sprite, In the church-way paths to glide *M. N. Dream* v 1 389
If we walk not in the trodden paths . . . *As Y. Like It* i 3 15
Shall blow each dust, each straw, each little rub, Out of the path *K. John* iii 4 129
But tread the stranger paths of banishment . . . *Richard II.* i 3 143
That haunted us in our familiar paths . . . *Hen. V.* ii 4 52
Go, tread the path that thou shalt ne'er return . . . *Richard III.* i 1 117
And that my path were even to the crown, As my ripe revenue . iii 7 157
Keep then the path . . . *Troi. and Cres.* iii 3 155
A speedier course than lingering languishment Must we pursue, and I have found the path . . . *T. Andron.* ii 1 111
Flecked darkness like a drunkard reels From forth day's path *R. and J.* ii 3 4
If thou path, thy native semblance on, Not Erebus itself were dim enough To hide thee from prevention . . . *J. Cæsar* ii 1 83
Himself the primrose path of dalliance treads . . . *Hamlet* i 3 50
But what is this? Here is a path to't: 'tis some savage hold *Cymbeline* iii 6 18
Pathetical. Sweet invocation of a child; most pretty and pathetical! *L. L. Lost* i 2 103
Ah, heavens, it is a most pathetical nit! . . . iv 1 150
The most pathetical break-promise and the most hollow lover *As Y. L. It* iv 1 196
Pathway. Thou showest the naked pathway to thy life . *Richard II.* i 2 31
Alas, that love, whose view is muffled still, Should, without eyes, see pathways to his will! . . . *Rom. and Jul.* i 1 178
Patience. I'm out of patience . . . *Tempest* i 1 58
Irreparable is the loss, and patience Says it is past her cure . . . v 1 140
Have patience, gentle Julia.—I must, where is no remedy *T. G. of Ver.* ii 2 1
My patience, more than thy desert, Is privilege for thy departure hence iii 1 159
I do entreat your patience To hear me speak the message I am sent on iv 4 116
Love, lend me patience to forbear awhile . . . v 4 27
An old abusing of God's patience and the king's English . *Mer. Wives* i 4 5
Is at most odds with his own gravity and patience that ever you saw . iii 1 55
Pray you, use your patience: in good time . . . iii 1 84
Any madness I ever yet beheld seemed but tameness, civility and patience, to this his distemper . . . iv 2 28
Show your wisdom, daughter, In your close patience *Meas. for Meas.* iv 3 123
O you blessed ministers above, Keep me in patience . . . v 1 116
Give me the scope of justice; My patience here is touch'd . . . v 1 235
Patience unmoved! no marvel though she pause . *Com. of Errors* ii 1 32
No unkind mate to grieve thee, With urging helpless patience . . . ii 1 39
This fool-begg'd patience in thee will be left . . . ii 1 41
Have patience, sir; O, let it not be so! Herein you war against your reputation . . . iii 1 85
Be ruled by me: depart in patience . . . iii 1 94
Have patience, I beseech.—I cannot, nor I will not . . . iv 2 16

Patience. My master preaches patience to him and the while His man with scissors nicks him like a fool . . . *Com. of Errors* v 1 174
Prays, curses; 'O sweet Benedick! God give me patience!' *Much Ado* ii 3 154
This wedding-day Perhaps is but prolong'd: have patience and endure iv 1 256
Bring me a father that so loved his child, Whose joy of her is overwhelm'd like mine, And bid him speak of patience . . . v 1 10
Bring him yet to me, And I of him will gather patience . . . v 1 19
'Tis all men's office to speak patience To those that wring under the load of sorrow . . . v 1 27
Gentlemen both, we will not wake your patience . . . v 1 102
I know not how to pray your patience; Yet I must speak . . . v 1 281
God grant us patience! . . . *L. L. Lost* i 1 197
I thank God I have as little patience as another man . . . i 2 170
With what strict patience have I sat, To see a king transformed to a gnat! iv 3 165
I'll stay with patience; but the time is long . . . v 2 845
Let us teach our trial patience, Because it is a customary cross *M. N. D.* i 1 152
I know your patience well . . . iii 1 197
Thou drivest me past the bounds Of maiden's patience . . . iii 2 66
Extort A poor soul's patience, all to make you sport . . . iii 2 161
She in mild terms begg'd my patience . . . iv 1 63
Sweet friends, your patience for my long abode . *Mer. of Venice* ii 6 21
I do oppose My patience to his fury, and am arm'd To suffer . . . iv 1 11
Her very silence and her patience Speak to the people . *As Y. Like It* i 3 80
And never cried 'Have patience, good people'! . . . iii 2 165
Patience herself would startle at this letter And play the swaggerer . iv 3 13
We shall find a time, Audrey; patience, gentle Audrey . . . v 1 1
All humbleness, all patience and impatience, All purity, all trial . v 2 103
Patience once more, whiles our compact is urged . . . v 4 5
Your patience and your virtue well deserves it . . . v 4 193
Though it pass your patience and mine . . . *T. of Shrew* i 1 131
Sirrah, be gone, or talk not, I advise you.—Petruchio, patience . . . i 2 45
If you be gentlemen, Do me this right; hear me with patience . i 2 239
For patience she will prove a second Grissel . . . ii 1 297
Patience, I pray you; 'twas a fault unwilling . . . iv 1 159
Do not say so.—Think upon patience . . . *All's Well* iii 2 50
You must have the patience to hear it . . . iv 3 132
Ours be your patience then, and yours our parts . . . Epil. 339
She sat like patience on a monument, Smiling at grief . . . *T. Night* ii 4 117
Nay, patience, or we break the sinews of our plot . . . ii 5 83
Make False accusation blush and tyranny Tremble at patience *W. Tale* iii 2 33
Take your patience to you, And I'll say nothing . . . iii 2 232
Your patience this allowing . . . iv 1 15
O, patience! The statue is but newly fix'd, the colour's Not dry . v 3 46
Patience, good lady! comfort, gentle Constance!—No, I defy all counsel *K. John* iii 4 22
Yet can I not of such tame patience boast As to be hush'd and nought at all to say . . . *Richard II.* i 1 52
Call it not patience, Gaunt; it is despair . . . i 2 29
That which in mean men we intitle patience Is pale cold cowardice in noble breasts . . . i 2 33
And prick my tender patience to those thoughts Which honour and allegiance cannot think . . . ii 1 207
Combating with tears and smiles, The badges of his grief and patience v 2 33
Patience is stale, and I am weary of it . . . v 5 104
For accordingly You tread upon my patience . . . 1 *Hen. IV.* i 3 4
Imagination of some great exploit Drives him beyond the bounds of patience . . . i 3 200
Have done enough To put him quite beside his patience . . . iii 1 179
And spoke it on purpose to try my patience . . . 2 *Hen. IV.* ii 4 335
Not to deliberate, not to remember, not to have patience to shift me v 5 23
I was lately here in the end of a displeasing play, to pray your patience Epil. 10
Your humble patience pray, Gently to hear, kindly to judge *Hen. V.* Prol. 33
Linger your patience on; and we'll digest The abuse of distance. ii Prol. 31
It must be as it may: though patience be a tired mare, yet she will plod ii 1 26
God of his mercy give You patience to endure, and true repentance! ii 2 180
Have patience, noble duke; I may not open . . . 1 *Hen. VI.* i 3 18
But only, with your patience, that we may Taste of your wine . ii 3 78
This place commands my patience . . . iii 1 8
Patience, good lady; wizards know their times . . . 2 *Hen. VI.* i 4 18
Sort thy heart to patience; These few days' wonder will be quickly worn ii 4 68
Patience is for poltroons, such as he . . . 3 *Hen. VI.* i 1 62
With patience calm the storm, While we bethink a means to break it off iii 3 38
To soothe your forgery and his, Sends me a paper to persuade me patience iii 3 176
But stoop with patience to my fortune . . . v 5 6
I will deliver you, or else lie for you: Meantime, have patience *Rich. III.* i 1 116
How hath your lordship brook'd imprisonment?—With patience, noble lord . . . i 1 126
Have patience, madam: there's no doubt his majesty Will soon recover i 3 1
Lest to thy harm thou move our patience . . . i 3 248
Whether I will or no, I must have patience to endure the load . iii 7 230
I am much too venturous In tempting of your patience . *Hen. VIII.* i 2 55
And sweetly In all the rest show'd a most noble patience . . . ii 1 36
Now, the Lord help, They vex me past my patience! . . . ii 4 130
And to that woman, when she has done most, Yet will I add an honour, a great patience . . . iii 1 137
Good sir, have patience.—So I have. Farewell The hopes of court! iii 2 458
Patience, be near me still; and set me lower . . . iv 2 76
Good wench, let's sit down quiet, For fear we wake her: softly, gentle Patience . . . iv 2 82
Patience, is that letter, I caused you write, yet sent away? . . . iv 2 127
Nay, Patience, You must not leave me yet: I must to bed . . . iv 2 165
You must take Your patience to you, and be well contented . . . v 1 105
Their pleasures Must be fulfill'd, and I attend with patience . . . v 2 19
I shall clear myself, Lay all the weight ye can upon my patience . v 3 66
Patience herself, what goddess e'er she be, Doth lesser blench at sufferance than I do . . . *Troi. and Cres.* i 1 27
Hector, whose patience Is, as a virtue, fix'd, to-day was moved . . . i 2 4
Bid them have patience; she shall come anon . . . iv 4 54
I pray thee, stay.—You have not patience; come.—I pray you, stay v 2 42
There is between my will and all offences A guard of patience . v 2 54
You have sworn patience.—Fear me not, sweet lord . . . v 2 62
I will not be myself, nor have cognition Of what I feel: I am all patience v 2 64
I had your heart before, this follows it.—I did swear patience . . . v 2 84
I will tell you; If you'll bestow a small—of what you have little—Patience awhile, you'll hear . . . *Coriolanus* i 1 130
A very little thief of occasion will rob you of a great deal of patience . ii 1 33
Set up the bloody flag against all patience . . . ii 1 84
I cannot speak. You, tribunes To the people! Coriolanus, patience! iii 1 191
Under your patience, gentle empress . . . *T. Andron.* ii 3 66
Why have I patience to endure all this? . . . ii 3 88

Patience. See how my wretched sister sobs and weeps.—Patience, dear niece . . . . *T. Andron.* iii 1 138
Unspeakable, past patience, Or more than any living man could bear v 3 126
Patience perforce with wilful choler meeting Makes my flesh tremble in their different greeting . . . . . . *Rom. and Jul.* i 5 91
I beseech you on my knees, Hear me with patience but to speak a word iii 5 160
I do beseech you, sir, have patience: Your looks are pale and wild v 1 27
Meantime forbear, And let mischance be slave to patience . . . v 3 221
And bear this work of heaven with patience . . . . . v 3 261
What you have to say I will with patience hear . . . *J. Cæsar* i 2 169
Can I bear that with patience, And not my husband's secrets? . ii 1 301
We will hear Cæsar's will.—Have patience, gentle friends, I must not read it . . . . iii 2 145
Hear me with patience.—Peace, ho! . . . . . . iii 2 250
Meditating that she must die once, I have the patience to endure it now iv 3 192
Arming myself with patience To stay the providence of some high powers v 1 106
Do you find Your patience so predominant in your nature That you can let this go? . . . . *Macbeth* iii 1 87
You must have patience, madam.—He had none . . . . iv 2 2
Devotion, patience, courage, fortitude, I have no relish of them . iv 3 94
Be the players ready?—Ay, my lord; they stay upon your patience *Ham.* iii 2 112
Upon the heat and flame of thy distemper Sprinkle cool patience . iii 4 124
Lend your patience to us, And we shall jointly labour with your soul iv 5 210
Strengthen your patience in our last night's speech . . . v 1 317
Till then, in patience our proceeding be . . . . . v 1 322
Thou'lt not believe With how depraved a quality—O Regan!—I pray you, sir, take patience . . . . *Lear* ii 4 140
You heavens, give me that patience, patience I need! . . . ii 4 274
I will be the pattern of all patience; I will say nothing . . iii 2 37
Where is the patience now, That you so oft have boasted to retain? iii 6 61
Patience and sorrow strove Who should express her goodliest . iv 3 18
By your gracious patience, I will a round unvarnish'd tale deliver *Othello* i 3 89
What cannot be preserved when fortune takes Patience her injury a mockery makes . . . . i 3 207
He bears both the sentence and the sorrow That, to pay grief, must of poor patience borrow . . . . i 3 215
Let it not gall your patience, good Iago, That I extend my manners . ii 1 98
Some strange indignity, Which patience could not pass . . . ii 3 246
How poor are they that have not patience! What wound did ever heal but by degrees? . . . . ii 3 376
I'll watch him tame and talk him out of patience . . . . iii 3 23
O, blood, blood, blood!—Patience, I say; your mind perhaps may change iii 3 452
Patience; Or I shall say you are all in all spleen, And nothing of a man iv 1 88
I will be found most cunning in my patience . . . . . iv 1 91
I should have found in some place of my soul A drop of patience . iv 2 53
Turn thy complexion there, Patience, thou young and rose-lipp'd cherubin . . . . iv 2 63
Patience awhile, good Cassio. Come, come; Lend me a light . . v 1 87
With patience more Than savages could suffer. . . *Ant. and Cleo.* i 4 60
That time,—O times!—I laugh'd him out of patience; and that night I laugh'd him into patience . . . . ii 5 19
The most infectious pestilence upon thee!—Good madam, patience . ii 5 62
Sister, welcome: pray you, Be ever known to patience: my dear'st sister! iii 6 98
Patience is sottish, and impatience does Become a dog that's mad . iv 15 79
'Twere good You lean'd unto his sentence with what patience Your wisdom may inform you . . . . *Cymbeline* i 1 78
Beseech your patience. Peace, Dear lady daughter, peace! . . i 1 153
Have I hurt him?—No, 'faith; not so much as his patience . . i 2 9
Have patience, sir, And take your ring again; 'tis not yet won . ii 4 113
Quite besides The government of patience! . . . . . ii 4 150
Hear me with patience.—Talk thy tongue weary; speak . . iii 4 115
I do note That grief and patience, rooted in him both, Mingle their spurs together.—Grow, patience! . . . . iv 2 57
Bear with patience Such griefs as you yourself do lay upon yourself *Pericles* i 2 65
I shall with aged patience bear your yoke . . . . . . ii 4 48
Patience, good sir; do not assist the storm . . . . . iii 1 19
Patience, good sir, Even for this charge . . . . . . iii 1 26
Patience, then, And think you now are all in Mytilene . . . iv 4 50
Like Patience gazing on kings' graves, and smiling Extremity out of act v 1 139
Patience, good sir, Or here I'll cease.—Nay, I'll be patient . . v 1 145
So, on your patience evermore attending, New joy wait on you! v 3 Gower 100
By your patience *Tempest* iii 3; *As Y. Like It* v 4; *T. Night* ii 1; *Hen. V.* iii 6; *Richard III.* iv 1; *Coriolanus* i 3; i 9; *Lear* v 3

Patient. Nay, good, be patient.—When the sea is . . . *Tempest* i 1 16
For your sake Am I this patient log-man . . . . . . iii 1 67
I'll be as patient as a gentle stream . . . . *T. G. of Ver.* ii 7 34
I will be patient; I will find out this . . . . *Mer. Wives* ii 1 130
Sir Hugh hath shown himself a wise and patient churchman . . iii 3 57
De earl, de knight, de lords, de gentlemen, my patients . . . ii 3 97
O pretty Isabella, I am pale at mine heart to see thine eyes so red: thou must be patient . . . . . *Meas. for Meas.* iv 3 159
'Tis for me to be patient; I am in adversity . . *Com. of Errors* iv 4 20
You are not Pinch's patient, are you, sir? . . . . . v 1 294
If not a present remedy, at least a patient sufferance . . *Much Ado* i 3 10
Still have I borne it with a patient shrug . . . *Mer. of Venice* i 3 110
Be patient: for your father's remembrance, be at accord *As Y. Like It* i 1 66
To this most patient, sweet and virtuous wife. . . *T. of Shrew* iii 2 197
I, Thy resolved patient, on thee still rely . . . . *All's Well* ii 1 207
Sit, my preserver, by thy patient's side . . . . . . ii 3 53
Well, I must be patient; there is no fettering of authority . . ii 3 251
I must be patient: You, that have turn'd off a first so noble wife, May justly diet me . . . . v 3 219
There's some ill planet reigns: I must be patient . . . *W. Tale* ii 1 106
He is more patient Than when you left him; even now he sung *K. John* v 7 11
Wooing poor craftsmen with the craft of smiles And patient underbearing of his fortune . . . . *Richard II.* i 4 29
And thou, too careless patient as thou art . . . . . . ii 1 97
How long shall I be patient? ah, how long? . . . . . . ii 1 163
Nor my own disgrace Have ever made me sour my patient cheek . . ii 1 169
I am as poor as Job, my lord, but not so patient . . 2 *Hen. IV.* i 2 145
But how I should be your patient to follow your prescriptions, the wise may make some dram of a scruple . . . . i 2 147
Be patient, for you shall remain with us . . . . . *Hen. V.* iii 5 66
The dull elements of earth and water never appear in him, but only in patient stillness while his rider mounts him . . . . . . iii 7 24
Be patient, lords; and give them leave to speak . . 1 *Hen. VI.* iv 1 82
Be patient, gentle Nell; forget this grief. . . . 2 *Hen. VI.* ii 4 26
Be patient, gentle queen, and I will stay.—Who can be patient in such extremes? Ah, wretched man! . . . . 3 *Hen. VI.* i 1 214
Patient. Why art thou patient, man? thou shouldst be mad . 3 *Hen. VI.* i 4 89
Let me have Some patient leisure to excuse myself . . *Richard III.* i 2 82
I can no longer hold me patient . . . . i 3 157
Either be patient, and entreat me fair, Or with the clamorous report of war Thus will I drown your exclamations. . . . . . . iv 4 151
Let me speak with him?—No, my good lord; therefore be patient . v 1 2
Be patient yet.—I will, when you are humble; nay, before *Hen. VIII.* ii 4 73
He brings his physic After his patient's death . . . . . iii 2 41
The sea being smooth, How many shallow bauble boats dare sail Upon her patient breast! . . . . *Troi. and Cres.* i 3 36
He will be the physician that should be the patient . . . . ii 3 224
Who keeps the tent now?—The surgeon's box, or the patient's wound . v 1 12
I will be patient; outwardly I will . . . . v 2 68
Choler! Were I as patient as the midnight sleep, By Jove, 'twould be my mind! . . . . *Coriolanus* iii 1 85
And patient fools, Whose children he hath slain, their base throats tear With giving him glory . . . . v 6 52
Patient yourself, madam, and pardon me. . . . . *T. Andron.* i 1 121
The which if you with patient ears attend . . . *Rom. and Jul.* Prol. 13
Therefore be patient, take no note of him . . . . . . i 5 73
Be patient, for the world is broad and wide . . . . . iii 3 16
And there have sat The live-long day, with patient expectation *J. Cæsar* i 1 46
Only be patient till we have appeased The multitude . . . . iii 1 179
The noble Brutus is ascended: silence!—Be patient till the last . iii 2 12
Will you be patient? will you stay awhile? . . . . . . iii 2 154
How does your patient, doctor?—Not so sick, my lord . . *Macbeth* v 3 37
Therein the patient Must minister to himself.—Throw physic to the dogs v 3 45
And the spurns That patient merit of the unworthy takes . . *Hamlet* iii 1 74
We must be patient: but I cannot choose but weep . . . . iv 5 69
As patient as the female dove, When that her golden couplets are disclosed v 1 309
I can be patient; I can stay with Regan, I and my hundred knights *Lear* ii 4 233
Bear free and patient thoughts . . . . iv 6 80
Thou must be patient; we came crying hither . . . . . iv 6 182
You must awhile be patient: What I can do I will . . . . *Othello* iii 4 129
Stand you awhile apart; Confine yourself but in a patient list . . iv 1 76
The most patient man in loss, the most coldest . . . *Cymbeline* ii 3 1
It would make any man cold to lose.—But not every man patient. . ii 3 5
If you'll be patient, I'll no more be mad; That cures us both . . iv 3 108
Fair one, all goodness that consists in bounty Expect even here, where is a kingly patient . . . . *Pericles* v 1 71
Nay, I'll be patient. Thou little know'st how thou dost startle me v 1 146
Be patient *Tempest* iv 1; *T. G. of Ver.* v 3; *Com. of Errors* ii 1; iv 4; v 1; *Much Ado* iv 1; *T. of Shrew* ii 1; iv 1; *T. Night* ii 3; iv 2; *Richard II.* v 3; 2 *Hen. IV.* iv 4; *Hen. V.* ii 1; 1 *Hen. VI.* iv 2; 2 *Hen. VI.* i 3; iii 2; *Richard III.* iii 5; *Hen. VIII.* v 4; *Coriolanus* v 1; *Lear* i 4; *Cymbeline* ii 4

Patiently. A thousand more mischances than this one Have learn'd me how to brook this patiently . . . . . . *T. G. of Ver.* v 3 4
Repent you, fair one, of the sin you carry?—I do; and bear the shame most patiently . . . . *Meas. for Meas.* ii 3 20
If you take it not patiently, why, your mettle is the more . . iii 2 79
Perchance you will not bear them patiently . . . *Com. of Errors* i 2 86
For there was never yet philosopher That could endure the toothache patiently . . . . *Much Ado* v 1 36
If you will patiently dance in our round . . . . *M. N. Dream* ii 1 140
I'll keep my oath, Patiently to bear my wroth . . *Mer. of Venice* ii 9 78
If they will patiently receive my medicine . . . *As Y. Like It* ii 7 61
I embrace this fortune patiently, Since not to be avoided it falls 1 *Hen. IV.* v 5 12
Sit patiently and inly ruminate The morning's danger . . *Hen. V.* iv Prol. 24
Therefore, patiently and yielding . . . . v 2 300
Then patiently hear my impatience . . . . . *Richard III.* iv 4 156
March patiently along . . . . *Troi. and Cres.* v 9 7
Here stooping to your clemency, We beg your hearing patiently *Hamlet* iii 2 161
Shake patiently my great affliction off . . . . . . *Lear* iv 6 36
Since patiently and constantly thou hast stuck to the bare fortune of that beggar Posthumus . . . . *Cymbeline* iii 5 118
Good heavens, Hear patiently my purpose . . . . . . v 1 22

Patine. Look how the floor of heaven Is thick inlaid with patines of bright gold . . . . *Mer. of Venice* v 1 59

Patrician. We are accounted poor citizens, the patricians good *Coriolanus* i 1 16
I tell you, friends, most charitable care Have the patricians of you . i 1 68
For the dearth, The gods, not the patricians, make it . . . i 1 75
Where great patricians shall attend and shrug, I' the end admire . i 9 4
I am known to be a humorous patrician . . . . ii 1 51
The good patricians must be visited . . . . ii 1 212
O good but most unwise patricians! . . . . iii 1 91
Tribunes! Patricians! Citizens! What, ho! Sicinius! Brutus! Coriolanus! . . . . iii 1 186
The people against the senators, patricians, and nobles . . . iv 3 15
The nobility of Rome are his: The senators and patricians love him too iv 7 30
Subscribed by the consuls and patricians . . . . v 6 82
Noble patricians, patrons of my right . . . . . . *T. Andron.* i 1 1
Patricians, draw your swords, and sheathe them not Till Saturninus be Rome's emperor . . . . i 1 204
With voices and applause of every sort, Patricians and plebeians, we create Lord Saturninus Rome's great emperor . . . . . . i 1 231
Lest, then, the people, and patricians too, Upon a just survey, take Titus' part, And so supplant you . . . . i 1 445

Patrick. Where shall I meet you?—At Friar Patrick's cell *T. G. of Ver.* iv 3 43
About the very hour That Silvia, at Friar Patrick's cell, should meet me v 1 3
Besides, she did intend confession At Patrick's cell this even . . v 2 42
There's no offence, my lord.—Yes, by Saint Patrick, but there is *Hamlet* i 5 136

Patrimony. Give me Bianca for my patrimony. . . . *T. of Shrew* iv 4 22
Pity him, Bereft and gelded of his patrimony . . . *Richard II.* ii 1 237
To reave the orphan of his patrimony . . . . . 2 *Hen. VI.* v 1 187
General, Take thou my soldiers, prisoners, patrimony . . . *Lear* v 3 75

Patroclus. With him Patroclus Upon a lazy bed the livelong day Breaks scurril jests . . . . *Troi. and Cres.* i 3 146
Now play him me, Patroclus, Arming to answer in a night alarm . i 3 170
Sir Valour dies; cries 'O, enough, Patroclus; Or give me ribs of steel!'. i 3 176
I will hold my peace when Achilles' brach bids me, shall I?—There's for you, Patroclus . . . . ii 1 127
Then tell me, Patroclus, what's Achilles?—Thy lord, Thersites . . ii 3 48
What's thyself?—Thy knower, Patroclus: then tell me, Patroclus, what art thou! . . . . ii 3 51
Achilles is my lord; I am Patroclus' knower, and Patroclus is a fool ii 3 57
Achilles is a fool; Thersites is a fool, and, as aforesaid, Patroclus is a fool . . . . ii 3 64
Thersites is a fool to serve such a fool; and Patroclus is a fool positive ii 3 70
Patroclus, I'll speak with nobody. Come in with me, Thersites . . ii 3 75

Patroclus. Hear comes Patroclus.—No Achilles with him *Troi. and Cres.* ii 3 111
Hear you, Patroclus : We are too well acquainted with these answers . ii 3 121
Let Patroclus make demands to me, you shall see the pageant of Ajax . iii 3 272
Patroclus kisses you.—O, this is trim !—Paris and I kiss evermore for him . iv 5 33
Patroclus, let us feast him to the height . v 1 3
My sweet Patroclus, I am thwarted quite From my great purpose . v 1 42
Patroclus will give me any thing for the intelligence of this whore . v 2 192
Patroclus ta'en or slain, and Palamedes Sore hurt and bruised . v 5 13
Go, bear Patroclus' body to Achilles ; And bid the snail-paced Ajax arm v 5 17
Patroclus' wounds have roused his drowsy blood . v 5 32
Patron. Twenty years Have I been patron to Antipholus *Com. of Errors* v 1 327
My soul's earth's god, and body's fostering patron . *L. L. Lost* i 1 223
I'll plead for you As for my patron . *T. of Shrew* i 2 156
I do ; and will repute you ever The patron of my life and liberty . iv 2 113
Confess who set thee up and pluck'd thee down, Call Warwick patron and be penitent . *3 Hen. VI.* v 1 27
Noble patricians, patrons of my right . *T. Andron.* i 1 1
The good Andronicus, Patron of virtue, Rome's best champion . i 1 65
The five best senses Acknowledge thee their patron . *T. of Athens* i 2 130
As my great patron thought on in my prayers . *Lear* i 1 144
My master, My worthy arch and patron, comes to-night . ii 1 61
Patronage. As an outlaw in a castle keeps And useth it to patronage his theft . *1 Hen. VI.* iii 1 48
As well as you dare patronage The envious barking of your saucy tongue iii 4 32
Patroness. This is The patroness of heavenly harmony . *T. of Shrew* iii 1 5
Behold our patroness, the life of Rome ! . *Coriolanus* v 5 1
O Divinest patroness, and midwife gentle To those that cry by night ! *Pericles* iii 1 11
Patrum. I have some of 'em in Limbo Patrum, and there they are like to dance these three days . *Hen. VIII.* v 4 67
Pattern. Let mine own judgement pattern out my death *Meas. for Meas.* ii 1 30
Pattern in himself to know, Grace to stand, and virtue go . iii 2 277
He [Troilus] is one of the patterns of love . *As Y. Like It* iv 1 100
Which is more Than history can pattern . *W. Tale* iii 2 37
By the pattern of mine own thoughts I cut out The purity of his . iv 4 393
So we could find some pattern of our shame . *K. John* iii 4 16
And their memory Shall as a pattern or a measure live . *2 Hen. IV.* iv 4 76
And deface The patterns that by God and by French fathers Had twenty years been made . *Hen. V.* ii 4 61
A pattern of celestial peace . *1 Hen. VI.* v 5 65
Behold this pattern of thy butcheries . *Richard III.* i 2 54
A pattern to all princes living with her . *Hen. VIII.* v 5 23
A pattern, precedent, and lively warrant, For me . *T. Andron.* v 3 44
I will be the pattern of all patience ; I will say nothing . *Lear* iii 2 37
Thou cunning'st pattern of excelling nature . *Othello* v 2 11
Pattern'd by that the poet here describes . *T. Andron.* iv 1 57
Pattle. Fought a most prave pattle here in France . *Hen. V.* iv 7 98
Pauca verba, Sir John ; goot worts . *Mer. Wives* i 1 123
Slice, I say ! pauca, pauca : slice ! that's my humour . i 1 134
Vir sapit qui pauca loquitur . *L. L. Lost* iv 2 83
Sir, I do invite you too ; you shall not say me nay : pauca verba . iv 2 171
Paucas pallabris ; let the world slide : sessa ! . *T. of Shrew* Ind. 1 5
I have, and I will hold, the quondam Quickly For the only she ; and—pauca, there's enough . *Hen. V.* ii 1 83
Paul. This oily rascal is known as well as Paul's . *1 Hen. IV.* ii 4 576
I bought him in Paul's, and he'll buy me a horse in Smithfield *2 Hen. IV.* i 2 58
Now, by Saint Paul, this news is bad indeed . *Richard III.* i 1 138
Towards Chertsey with your holy load, Taken from Paul's to be interred there . i 2 30
Set down the corse ; or, by Saint Paul, I'll make a corse of him that disobeys . i 2 36
By Saint Paul, I'll strike thee to my foot, And spurn upon thee . i 2 41
By holy Paul, they love his grace but lightly . i 3 45
Now, by Saint Paul I swear, I will not dine until I see the same . iii 4 78
Fairly is engross'd, That it may be this day read o'er in Paul's . iii 6 3
By the apostle Paul, shadows to-night Have struck more terror to the soul of Richard Than can the substance of ten thousand soldiers . v 3 216
Paulina. Thou ne'er shalt see Thy wife Paulina more . *W. Tale* iii 3 36
Good Paulina, Who hast the memory of Hermione, I know, in honour . v 1 49
Fear thou no wife ; I'll have no wife, Paulina . v 1 69
Will you swear Never to marry but by my free leave ?—Never, Paulina v 1 71
My true Paulina, We shall not marry till thou bid'st us . v 1 81
Here comes the Lady Paulina's steward : he can deliver you more . v 2 28
A handkerchief and rings of his that Paulina knows . v 2 72
But O, the noble combat that 'twixt joy and sorrow was fought in Paulina ! . v 2 80
Her mother's statue, which is in the keeping of Paulina . v 2 104
O grave and good Paulina, the great comfort That I have had of thee ! . v 3 1
O Paulina, We honour you with trouble . v 3 8
But yet, Paulina, Hermione was not so much wrinkled, nothing So aged v 3 27
O sweet Paulina, Make me to think so twenty years together ! . v 3 70
I could afflict you farther.—Do, Paulina . v 3 75
Knowing by Paulina that the oracle Gave hope thou wast in being . v 3 126
O, peace, Paulina ! Thou shouldst a husband take by my consent, As I by thine a wife . v 3 135
Good Paulina, Lead us from hence, where we may leisurely Each one demand . v 3 151
Paunch him with a stake, Or cut his wezand with thy knife . *Tempest* iii 2 98
Fat paunches have lean pates . *L. L. Lost* i 1 26
What, a coward, Sir John Paunch ? . *1 Hen. IV.* ii 2 69
Ye fat paunch, an ye call me coward, by the Lord, I'll stab thee . ii 4 159
Pause. Without any pause or staggering . *Mer. Wives* iii 3 12
Patience unmoved ! no marvel though she pause . *Com. of Errors* ii 1 32
Pause awhile, And let my counsel sway you in this case . *Much Ado* iv 1 202
Take time to pause . *M. N. Dream* i 1 83
Pause there, Morocco, And weigh thy value with an even hand *M. of Ven.* ii 7 24
Too long a pause for that which you find there . ii 9 53
I pray you, tarry : pause a day or two Before you hazard . iii 2 1
Why doth the Jew pause ? take thy forfeiture . iv 1 335
Then give me leave to read philosophy, And while I pause, serve in your harmony . *T. of Shrew* iii 1 14
Say briefly, gentle lord ; We coldly pause for thee . *K. John* ii 1 53
Peace, lady ! pause, or be more temperate . iii 1 195
Hadst thou but shook thy head or made a pause . iv 2 231
Then pause not ; for the present time's so sick, That present medicine must be minister'd . v 2 20
It may be I will go with you : but yet I'll pause . *Richard II.* ii 3 168
What, drunk with choler ? stay and pause awhile . *1 Hen. IV.* i 3 129
There did he pause : but let me tell the world . v 2 66
Pause. Other offenders we will pause upon . *1 Hen. IV.* v 5 15
And pause us, till these rebels, now afoot, Come underneath the yoke of government . *2 Hen. IV.* iv 4 9
A night is but small breath and little pause To answer matters of this consequence . *Hen. V.* ii 4 145
Pause, and take thy breath . *1 Hen. VI.* iv 6 4
What seest thou in me, York ? why dost thou pause ? . *2 Hen. VI.* v 2 19
I'll never pause again, never stand still . *3 Hen. VI.* ii 3 30
Good fortune bids us pause, And smooth the frowns of war . ii 6 31
It were dishonour to deny it her.—It were no less ; but yet I'll make a pause . iii 2 10
And twenty times made pause to sob and weep . *Richard III.* i 2 162
And humbly beg the death upon my knee. Nay, do not pause . i 2 180
Give me some breath, some little pause, my lord, Before I positively speak . iv 2 24
Puts back leave-taking, justles roughly by All time of pause *Tr. and Cr.* iv 4 37
I have seen thee pause and take thy breath . iv 5 192
Pause, if thou wilt.—I do disdain thy courtesy, proud Trojan . v 6 14
If any, speak ; for him have I offended. I pause for a reply . *J. Cæsar* iii 2 36
My heart is in the coffin there with Cæsar, And I must pause till it come back to me . iii 2 112
So, after Pyrrhus' pause, Aroused vengeance sets him new a-work *Hamlet* ii 2 509
In that sleep of death what dreams may come When we have shuffled off this mortal coil, Must give us pause . iii 1 68
I stand in pause where I shall first begin, And both neglect . iii 3 42
This sudden sending him away must seem Deliberate pause . iv 3 9
Sir, this gentleman Steps in to Cassio, and entreats his pause *Othello* ii 3 229
Being done, there is no pause . v 2 82
Being so frustrate, tell him he mocks The pauses that he makes *A. and C.* v 1 3
Yet pause awhile : Yon knight doth sit too melancholy . *Pericles* ii 3 53
Pauser. My violent love Outrun the pauser, reason . *Macbeth* ii 3 117
Pausingly. With demure confidence This pausingly ensued . *Hen. VIII.* i 2 168
Pauvre. Paysans, pauvres gens de France ; Poor market folks *1 Hen. VI.* iii 2 14
Paved. Her brother's ghost his paved bed would break . *Meas. for Meas.* v 1 440
O, if the streets were paved with thine eyes, Her feet were much too dainty for such tread ! . *L. L. Lost* iv 3 278
By paved fountain or by rushy brook . *M. N. Dream* ii 1 84
My way shall be paved with English faces . *Hen. V.* iii 7 87
When the way was made, And paved with gold . *Hen. VIII.* i 1 188
Pavement. Or, like a gallant horse fall'n in first rank, Lie there for pavement to the abject rear . *Troi. and Cres.* iii 3 162
The marble pavement closes, he is enter'd His radiant roof *Cymbeline* v 4 120
Pavilion. Come to our pavilion : Boyet is disposed . *L. L. Lost* ii 1 249
It is the king's most sweet pleasure and affection to congratulate the princess at her pavilion . v 1 94
Certain he would fight ; yea From morn till night, out of his pavilion . v 2 660
And anon Desire them all to my pavilion . *Hen. V.* iv 1 27
Now on Dardan plains The fresh and yet unbruised Greeks do pitch Their brave pavilions . *Troi. and Cres.* Prol. 15
Let me touch your hand ; To our pavilion shall I lead you, sir . i 3 305
She did lie In her pavilion—cloth-of-gold of tissue . *Ant. and Cleo.* ii 2 204
Pavilioned. Whose hearts have left their bodies here in England And lie pavilion'd in the fields of France . *Hen. V.* i 2 129
Paw. France, thou mayst hold a serpent by the tongue, A chafed lion by the mortal paw . *K. John* iii 1 259
The lion dying thrusteth forth his paw, And wounds the earth *Rich. II.* v 1 29
Who, being suffer'd with the bear's fell paw, Hath clapp'd his tail between his legs and cried . *2 Hen. VI.* v 1 153
So looks the pent-up lion o'er the wretch That trembles under his devouring paws . *3 Hen. VI.* i 3 13
Yet have I heard, . . . The lion moved with pity did endure To have his princely paws pared all away . *T. Andron.* ii 3 152
Pawn. Here is her oath for love, her honour's pawn . *T. G. of Ver.* i 3 47
Now she hath enfranchised them Upon some other pawn for fealty . ii 4 91
I have been content, sir, you should lay my countenance to pawn *M. W.* ii 2 5
Come, lay their swords to pawn. Follow me, lads of peace . iii 1 113
These ducats pawn I for my father here.—It shall not need *Com. of Errors* v 1 389
I'll pawn the little blood which I have left To save the innocent *W. Tale* ii 3 166
I'll make it as much more and leave this young man in pawn till I bring it . iv 4 839
And remain, as he says, your pawn till it be brought you . iv 4 853
To lie like pawns lock'd up in chests and trunks . *K. John* v 2 141
Take up mine honour's pawn . *Richard II.* i 1 74
Redeem from broking pawn the blemish'd crown . ii 1 293
There is my honour's pawn ; Engage it to the trial, if thou darest . iv 1 70
I must be fain to pawn both my plate and the tapestry . *2 Hen. IV.* ii 1 153
I' faith, I am loath to pawn my plate, so God save me, la ! . ii 1 167
Well, you shall have it, though I pawn my gown . ii 1 171
Alas, sweet wife, my honour is at pawn . ii 3 7
They'll pawn their swords for my enfranchisement . *2 Hen. VI.* v 1 113
Thereon I pawn my credit and mine honour . *3 Hen. VI.* iii 3 116
He would pawn his fortunes To hopeless restitution . *Coriolanus* iii 1 15
Pawn me to this your honour, she is his . *T. of Athens* i 1 147
I'll pawn my victories, all My honours to you, upon his good returns . i 5 81
My life I never held but as a pawn To wage against thy enemies . *Lear* i 1 157
I dare pawn down my life for him . i 2 92
Pawn their experience to their present pleasure . *Ant. and Cleo.* i 4 32
I dare thereupon pawn the moiety of my estate to your ring . *Cymbeline* i 4 118
And pawn mine honour for their safety . i 6 194
Pawned. Till he hath pawned his horses to mine host of the Garter *M. W.* ii 1 99
There must be something else Pawn'd with the other, for the poor rude world Hath not her fellow . *Mer. of Venice* iii 5 87
Have I not pawn'd to you my majesty ? . *K. John* iii 1 98
Will you thus break your faith ?—I pawn'd thee none . *2 Hen. IV.* iv 2 112
I hold it cowardice To rest mistrustful where a noble heart Hath pawn'd an open hand in sign of love . *3 Hen. VI.* iv 2 9
Her father to the king of France Hath pawn'd the Sicils and Jerusalem v 7 39
For which your honour and your faith is pawn'd . *Richard III.* iv 2 92
The garter, blemish'd, pawn'd his knightly virtue . iv 4 370
I raised him, and I pawn'd Mine honour for his truth . *Coriolanus* v 6 21
Pax. He hath stolen a pax, and hanged must a' be : A damned death ! *Hen. V.* iii 6 42
But Exeter hath given the doom of death For pax of little price . iii 6 47
Pay. He shall pay for him that hath him, and that soundly . *Tempest* ii 2 81
He that dies pays all debts . iii 2 140
I will pay thy graces Home both in word and deed . v 1 70
Do what she will, say what she will, take all, pay all . *Mer. Wives* ii 2 123
They shall have my horses ; but I'll make them pay . iv 3 11
Thus can the demigod Authority Make us pay down for our offence by weight The words of heaven . *Meas. for Meas.* i 2 125

Pay. So disguise shall, by the disguised, Pay with falsehood false exacting *Meas. for Meas.* iii 2 295
Haste still pays haste, and leisure answers leisure v 1 415
Sixpence, that I had o' Wednesday last To pay the saddler *Com. of Errors* i 2 56
If I should pay your worship those again, Perchance you will not bear them patiently i 2 85
To pay a fine for a periwig and recover the lost hair of another man ii 2 76
Either consent to pay this sum for me Or I attach you by this officer.—Consent to pay thee that I never had! iv 1 72
Here's that, I warrant you, will pay them all iv 4 10
Knowing how the debt grows, I will pay it iv 4 124
If any friend will pay the sum for him, He shall not die v 1 131
Haply I see a friend will save my life And pay the sum v 1 284
Pay him the due of honey-tongued Boyet *L. L. Lost* v 2 334
Which now in some slight measure it will pay *M. N. Dream* iii 2 86
Wherein it doth impair the seeing sense, It pays the hearing double recompense iii 2 180
He borrowed a box of the ear of the Englishman and swore he would pay him again when he was able *Mer. of Venice* i 2 87
Look he keep his day, Or he shall pay for this ii 8 26
Pay him six thousand, and deface the bond; Double six thousand iii 2 301
You shall have gold To pay the petty debt twenty times over iii 2 309
Pray God, Bassanio come To see me pay his debt, and then I care not! iii 3 36
If that will not suffice, I will be bound to pay it ten times o'er iv 1 211
Repent but you that you shall lose your friend, And he repents not that he pays your debt iv 1 279
If the Jew do cut but deep enough, I'll pay it presently with all my heart iv 1 281
I take this offer, then; pay the bond thrice And let the Christian go iv 1 318
Buy thou the cottage, pasture and the flock, And thou shalt have to pay for it of us *As Y. Like It* ii 4 93
You will not pay for the glasses you have burst?—No *T. of Shrew* Ind. 1 7
Tailor, I'll pay thee for thy gown to-morrow iv 3 168
My duty then shall pay me for my pains *All's Well* ii 1 128
Let me buy your friendly help thus far, Which I will over-pay and pay again iii 7 16
After he scores, he never pays the score iv 3 253
He ne'er pays after-debts, take it before iv 3 255
The count's a fool, I know it, Who pays before, but not when he does owe it iv 3 259
Choose thou thy husband, and I'll pay thy dower v 3 328
Which we will pay, With strife to please you, day exceeding day Epil. 337
She that hath a heart of that fine frame To pay this debt of love *T. Night* i 1 34
I'll pay thee bounteously, Conceal me what I am i 2 52
I take pleasure in singing, sir.—I'll pay thy pleasure then ii 4 71
Oft good turns Are shuffled off with such uncurrent pay iii 3 16
For which, if I be lapsed in this place, I shall pay dear iii 3 37
He pays you as surely as your feet hit the ground they step on iii 4 305
And the old saying is, the third pays for all v 1 40
Means to pay Bohemia the visitation which he justly owes him *W. Tale* i 1 7
You pay a great deal too dear for what's given freely i 1 18
Stay your thanks a while; And pay them when you part i 2 10
So you shall pay your fees When you depart, and save your thanks i 2 53
If this prove true, they'll pay for't ii 1 146
And you shall pay well for 'em iv 4 321
They often give us soldiers the lie: but we pay them for it with stamped coin iv 4 747
Our abbeys and our priories shall pay This expedition's charge *K. John* i 1 48
Be pleased then To pay that duty which you truly owe To him that owes it ii 1 247
A soul counts thee her creditor And with advantage means to pay thy love iii 3 22
O, let us pay the time but needful woe v 7 110
God for his Richard hath in heavenly pay A glorious angel *Richard II.* iii 2 60
If we prevail, their heads shall pay for it iii 2 126
Where fearing dying pays death servile breath iii 2 185
How dare thy joints forget To pay their awful duty to our presence? iii 3 76
Did I ever call for thee to pay thy part? *1 Hen. IV.* i 2 57
This loose behaviour I throw off And pay the debt I never promised i 2 233
Lost that title of respect Which the proud soul ne'er pays but to the proud i 3 9
Think we think ourselves unsatisfied, Till he hath found a time to pay us i 3 288
To fight against me under Percy's pay iii 2 126
He had his part of it; let him pay.—He? alas, he is poor iii 3 87
Let them coin his nose, let them coin his cheeks: I'll not pay a denier iii 3 91
Knows at what time to promise, when to pay iv 3 53
There is many a soul Shall pay full dearly for this encounter v 1 84
'Tis not due yet; I would be loath to pay him before his day v 1 129
We, as the spring of all, shall pay for all v 2 23
Who never promiseth but he means to pay v 4 43
Pay her the debt you owe her, and unpay the villany *2 Hen. IV.* ii 1 129
You'll pay me all together?—Will I live? ii 1 173
Pay the musicians, sirrah ii 4 403
Let them have pay, and part: I know it will well please them iv 2 70
Love, and filial tenderness, Shall, O dear father, pay thee plenteously iv 5 40
I meant indeed to pay you with this Epil. 12
I will pay you some and, as most debtors do, promise you infinitely Epil. 16
You'll pay me the eight shillings I won of you at betting?—Base is the slave that pays *Hen. V.* ii 1 98
A noble shalt thou have, and present pay ii 1 112
I beseech your highness to forgive, Although my body pay the price of it ii 2 154
The word is 'Pitch and Pay': Trust none; For oaths are straws ii 3 51
And ay 'll pay't as valorously as I may, that sall I suerly do iii 2 125
If I live to see it, I will never trust his word after.—You pay him then iv 1 209
Five hundred poor I have in yearly pay iv 1 315
If I owe you any thing, I will pay you in cudgels v 1 68
His ransom there is none but I shall pay *1 Hen. VI.* i 1 148
My body shall Pay recompense, if you will grant my suit v 3 19
What ransom must I pay before I pass? For I perceive I am thy prisoner v 3 73
Upon condition thou wilt swear To pay him tribute, and submit thyself v 4 130
Did he not, in his protectorship, Levy great sums of money through the realm For soldiers' pay in France, and never sent it? *2 Hen. VI.* iii 1 62
You took bribes of France, And, being protector, stay'd the soldiers' pay iii 1 105
I never robb'd the soldiers of their pay, Nor ever had one penny bribe iii 1 108
What, think you much to pay two thousand crowns, And bear the name and port of gentlemen? iv 1 18
He that made us pay one and twenty fifteens, and one shilling to the pound iv 7 24

Pay. The proudest peer in the realm shall not wear a head on his shoulders, unless he pay me tribute *2 Hen. VI.* iv 7 127
But she shall pay to me her maidenhead ere they have it iv 7 130
You shall have pay and every thing you wish v 1 47
With promise of high pay and great rewards *3 Hen. VI.* ii 1 134
They shall have wars and pay for their presumption iv 1 114
Doubt not of the day, And, that once gotten, doubt not of large pay iv 7 88
Discharge the common sort With pay and thanks v 5 88
Edward for Edward pays a dying debt *Richard III.* iv 4 21
Your country's fat shall pay your pains the hire v 3 258
For which I pay 'em A thousand thanks *Hen. VIII.* i 4 73
The honour of it Does pay the act of it iii 2 182
Let us pay betimes A moiety of that mass of moan to come *Troi. and Cres.* ii 2 106
Words pay no debts, give her deeds iii 2 58
Howsoever, he shall pay for me ere he has me iii 3 298
Turn thy false face, thou traitor, And pay thy life thou owest me for my horse! v 6 7
But that he pays himself with being proud *Coriolanus* i 1 33
But cannot make my heart consent to take A bribe to pay my sword i 9 38
As many coxcombs As you threw caps up will he tumble down, And pay you for your voices iv 6 136
O, were the sum of these that I should pay Countless and infinite, yet would I pay them! *T. Andron.* v 3 158
Your lives shall pay the forfeit of the peace *Rom. and Jul.* i 1 104
Thou canst not teach me to forget.—I'll pay that doctrine, or else die in debt i 1 244
The world will be in love with night And pay no worship to the garish sun iii 2 25
My poverty, but not my will, consents.—I pay thy poverty v 1 76
I'll pay the debt, and free him.—Your lordship ever binds him *T. of A.* i 1 103
If I should pay you for't as 'tis extoll'd, it would unclew me quite i 1 167
He is worthy of thee, and to pay thee for thy labour i 1 231
He owes For every word: he is so kind that he now Pays interest for't i 2 206
The greatest of your having lacks a half To pay your present debts ii 2 154
Mark, how strange it shows, Timon in this should pay more than he owes iii 4 22
He should the sooner pay his debts, And make a clear way to the gods iii 4 76
Five thousand crowns, my lord.—Five thousand drops pays that iii 4 97
There's gold to pay thy soldiers: Make large confusion iv 3 126
I did send To you for gold to pay my legions *J. Cæsar* iv 3 76
Friends, I owe more tears To this dead man than you shall see me pay v 3 102
Only to herald thee into his sight, Not pay thee *Macbeth* i 3 103
Only I have left to say, More is thy due than more than all can pay i 4 21
The service and the loyalty I owe, In doing it, pays itself i 4 23
Shall live the lease of nature, pay his breath To time and mortal custom iv 1 99
That this great king may kindly say, Our duties did his welcome pay iv 1 132
You have ta'en these tenders for true pay, Which are not sterling *Hamlet* i 3 106
If he steal aught the whilst this play is playing, And 'scape detecting, I will pay the theft iii 2 94
Necessary 'tis that we forget To pay ourselves what to ourselves is debt iii 2 203
And thy free awe Pays homage to us iv 3 64
To pay five ducats, five, I would not farm it iv 4 20
He bears both the sentence and the sorrow That, to pay grief, must of poor patience borrow *Othello* i 3 215
So thy cheek pays shame When shrill-tongued Fulvia scolds *Ant. and Cleo.* i 1 31
And for his ordinary pays his heart For what his eyes eat only ii 2 230
Thy Pacorus, Orodes, Pays this for Marcus Crassus iii 1 5
When perforce he could not But pay me terms of honour, cold and sickly He vented them iii 4 7
That thou depart'st hence safe, Does pay thy labour richly iv 14 37
He does buy my injuries, to be friends; Pays dear for my offences *Cymb.* i 1 106
Overbuys me Almost the sum he pays i 1 147
Debtor to you for courtesies, which I will be ever to pay and yet pay still i 4 39
And we will nothing pay For wearing our own noses iii 1 13
Why should we pay tribute? If Cæsar can hide the sun from us with a blanket, or put the moon in his pocket, we will pay him tribute for light iii 1 43
So, if I prove a good repast to the spectators, the dish pays the shot v 4 158
First pay me for the nursing of thy sons; And let it be confiscate all, so soon As I have received it v 5 322
Promising To pay our wonted tribute, from the which We were dissuaded v 5 462
Or pay you with unthankfulness in thought *Pericles* i 4 102
If that ever my low fortune's better, I'll pay your bounties ii 1 149
Let's have fresh ones, whate'er we pay for them iv 2 11
Thy sacred physic shall receive such pay As thy desires can wish v 1 74

Payest. Draw thy sword: one stroke Shall free thee from the tribute which thou payest *Tempest* ii 1 293

Paying. As I say, paying for them very honestly *Meas. for Meas.* ii 1 105
More nor less to others paying Than by self-offences weighing iii 2 279
Dumbly have broke off, Not paying me a welcome *M. N. Dream* v 1 99
My bond to the Jew is forfeit; and since in paying it, it is impossible I should live, all debts are cleared between you and I *Mer. of Venice* iii 2 320
Your breathing shall expire, Paying the fine of rated treachery *K. John* v 4 37
O, I do not like that paying back; 'tis a double labour *1 Hen. IV.* iii 3 201

Payment. Your father here doth intimate The payment of a hundred thousand crowns *L. L. Lost* ii 1 130
And not demands, On payment of a hundred thousand crowns, To have his title ii 1 145
Fair payment for foul words is more than due iv 1 19
If he come to-morrow, I'll give him his payment *As Y. Like It* i 1 166
Too little payment for so great a debt *T. of Shrew* v 2 154
If you tarry longer, I shall give worse payment *T. Night* iv 1 21
Even with the bloody payment of your deaths *1 Hen. IV.* i 3 186
That were but light payment, to dance out of your debt *2 Hen. IV.* Epil. 20
I will give treason his payment into plows *Hen. V.* iv 8 15
Such mercy as his ruthless arm, With downright payment, show'd unto my father *3 Hen. VI.* i 4 32
I'll ha' more. An ordinary groom is for such payment *Hen. VIII.* v 1 172
He humbly prays your speedy payment *T. of Athens* ii 2 28
You have work'd for me; there's payment for you v 1 116
Would thou hadst less deserved, That the proportion both of thanks and payment Might have been mine! *Macbeth* i 4 19
The comfort is, you shall be called to no more payments *Cymbeline* v 4 161

Paysan. I ha' married un garçon, a boy; un paysan, by gar *Mer. Wives* v 5 219
Paysans, pauvres gens de France; Poor market folks *1 Hen. VI.* iii 2 14

Pea. Rich leas Of wheat, rye, barley, vetches, oats, and pease *Tempest* iv 1 61
This fellow pecks up wit as pigeons pease *L. L. Lost* v 2 315
I had rather have a handful or two of dried peas *M. N. Dream* iv 1 42
Peas and beans are as dank here as a dog *1 Hen. IV.* ii 1 9

Peace. If you can command these elements to silence, and work the peace of the present *Tempest* i 1 24

Peace. Incensed the seas and shores, yea, all the creatures, Against your peace . . . . . *Tempest* iii 3 75
We wish your peace . . . . iv 1 163
How likes she my discourse?—Ill, when you talk of war.—But well, when I discourse of love and peace?—But better, indeed, when you hold your peace . . . . . *T. G. of Ver.* v 2 17
In the county of Gloucester, justice of peace and 'Coram' . *Mer. Wives* i 1 6
He's a justice of peace in his country, simple though I stand here . i 1 226
A justice of peace sometime may be beholding to his friend for a man . i 1 283
Peace, I pray you.—Peace-a your tongue. Speak-a your tale . i 4 84
You have yourself been a great fighter, though now a man of peace . ii 3 45
Though I now be old and of the peace, if I see a sword out, my finger itches . . . . ii 3 47
I am sworn of the peace . . . . . . ii 3 55
Peace, I say, Gallia and Gaul, French and Welsh! . . . iii 1 99
Follow me, lads of peace; follow, follow, follow . . . iii 1 113
Peace your tattlings! . . . . iv 1 26
Heaven grant us its peace, but not the King of Hungary's! *M. for M.* i 2 4
There's not a soldier of us all, that, in the thanksgiving before meat, do relish the petition well that prays for peace . . . i 2 17
Peace be in this place! . . . . . . ii 4 6
He calls again; I pray you, answer him.—Peace and prosperity! . i 4 15
Peace here; grace and good company! . . . . . iii 1 44
You were not bid to speak.—No, my good lord; Nor wish'd to hold my peace . . . . v 1 79
Peace, doting wizard, peace! I am not mad . . . *Com. of Errors* iv 4 61
If he do fear God, a' must necessarily keep peace: if he break the peace, he ought to enter into a quarrel with fear and trembling *Much Ado* ii 3 202
Depart in peace, and let the child wake her with crying . . iii 3 73
Pray thee, fellow, peace: I do not like thy look, I promise thee . iv 2 46
Peace! I will stop your mouth . . . . . . v 4 98
Peace!—Be to me and every man that dares not fight! . . *L. L. Lost* i 1 228
Treason and you go in peace away together . . . . iv 3 192
Men of peace, well encountered.—Most military sir, salutation . v 1 37
Peace! the peal begins . . . . v 1 46
Arm, wenches, arm! encounters mounted are Against your peace . v 2 83
What would they, say they?—Nothing but peace and gentle visitation . v 2 181
Peace! for I will not have to do with you . . . . v 2 428
I wish you the peace of mind, most royal couplement! . . . v 2 534
And all things shall be peace . . . . . *M. N. Dream* iii 2 377
And each several chamber bless, Through this palace, with sweet peace v 1 425
Peace, ho! the moon sleeps with Endymion . . *Mer. of Venice* v 1 109
Peace, ho! I bar confusion: 'Tis I must make conclusion *As Y. Like It* v 4 131
I would not wed her for a mine of gold.—Hortensio, peace! *T. of Shrew* i 2 93
I wonder what it bodes.—Marry, peace it bodes, and love and quiet life v 2 108
I am ashamed that women are so simple To offer war where they should kneel for peace . . . . v 2 162
Bless him at home in peace . . . . . . *All's Well* iii 4 10
I hear there is an overture of peace.—Nay, I assure you, a peace concluded . . . . iv 3 46
Peace, you rogue, no more o' that. Here comes my lady . *T. Night* i 5 32
My words are as full of peace as matter . . . . . i 5 227
Begin, fool: it begins 'Hold thy peace.'—I shall never begin if I hold my peace . . . . ii 3 73
For the love o' God, peace! . . . . . . ii 3 92
O, peace! Contemplation makes a rare turkey-cock of him . . ii 5 35
O, peace! now he's deeply in: look how imagination bows him . ii 5 47
Though our silence be drawn from us with cars, yet peace . . ii 5 71
O, peace! and the spirit of humours intimate reading aloud to him! ii 5 93
Go to; peace, peace; we must deal gently with him: let me alone . iii 4 105
I will make your peace with him if I can . . . . iii 4 296
Let thy fair wisdom, not thy passion, sway In this uncivil and unjust extent Against thy peace . . . . iv 1 58
What, ho, I say! peace in this prison! . . . . . iv 2 21
That my most jealous and too doubtful soul May live at peace . iv 3 28
Pursue him, and entreat him to a peace . . . . . v 1 389
I had thought, sir, to have held my peace until You had drawn oaths from him not to stay . . . . . . *W. Tale* i 2 28
Hold your peaces . . . . ii 1 139
And so depart in peace: Be thou as lightning in the eyes of France *K. John* i 1 23
The peace of heaven is theirs that lift their swords In such a just and charitable war . . . . ii 1 35
May from England bring That right in peace which here we urge in war ii 1 47
Peace be to France, if France in peace permit Our just and lineal entrance to our own; If not, bleed France, and peace ascend to heaven ii 1 84
Whiles we, God's wrathful agent, do correct Their proud contempt that beats His peace to heaven . . . . ii 1 88
Peace be to England, if that war return From France to England, there to live in peace . . . . ii 1 89
Wide havoc made For bloody power to rush upon your peace . . ii 1 221
And leave your children, wives and you in peace . . . ii 1 257
Then let confusion of one part confirm The other's peace . . ii 1 360
Vouchsafe awhile to stay, And I shall show you peace and fair-faced league . . . . ii 1 417
A most base and vile-concluded peace . . . . . ii 1 586
Gone to be married! gone to swear a peace! False blood to false blood join'd! . . . . iii 1 1
And rough frown of war Is cold in amity and painted peace . . iii 1 105
Let not the hours of this ungodly day Wear out the day in peace . iii 1 110
Lady Constance, peace!—War! war! no peace! peace is to me a war . iii 1 112
Deep-sworn faith, peace, amity, true love Between our kingdoms . iii 1 231
No longer than we well could wash our hands To clap this royal bargain up of peace . . . . iii 1 235
And on the marriage-bed Of smiling peace to march a bloody host . iii 1 246
Thou mayest hold . . . A fasting tiger safer by the tooth Than keep in peace that hand which thou dost hold . . . . . iii 1 261
The fat ribs of peace Must by the hungry now be fed upon . . iii 3 9
Lo, now! now see the issue of your peace.—Patience, good lady! . iii 4 21
O fair affliction, peace!—No, no, I will not, having breath to cry . iii 4 36
I'll make a peace between your soul and you . . . . iv 2 250
Keep the peace, I say.—Stand by, or I shall gall you . . iv 3 93
Now for the bare-pick'd bone of majesty Doth dogged war bristle his angry crest And snarleth in the gentle eyes of peace . . iv 3 150
The legate of the pope hath been with me, And I have made a happy peace with him . . . . v 1 63
Perchance the cardinal cannot make your peace . . . . v 1 74
That, like a lion foster'd up at hand, It may lie gently at the foot of peace v 2 76
And come ye now to tell me John hath made His peace with Rome? . v 2 92
Must I back Because that John hath made his peace with Rome? . v 2 96
Turn thy face in peace; We grant thou canst outscold us . . v 2 159

Peace. Where I may think the remnant of my thoughts In peace *K. John* v 4 47
Such offers of our peace As we with honour and respect may take . v 7 84
To wake our peace, which in our country's cradle Draws the sweet infant breath of gentle sleep . . . . *Richard II.* i 3 132
Might from our quiet confines fright fair peace . . . i 3 137
In war was never lion raged more fierce, In peace was never gentle lamb more mild . . . . ii 1 174
More hath he spent in peace than they in wars . . . ii 1 255
And fright our native peace with self-born arms . . . ii 3 80
I warrant they have made peace with Bolingbroke.—Peace have they made . . . . iii 2 127
Would they make peace? terrible hell make war Upon their spotted souls! iii 2 133
Their peace is made With heads, and not with hands . . iii 2 137
Ere the crown he looks for live in peace, Ten thousand bloody crowns . iii 3 95
Change the complexion of her maid-pale peace To scarlet indignation . iii 3 98
Sweet peace conduct his sweet soul to the bosom Of good old Abraham! iv 1 103
Peace shall go sleep with Turks and infidels, And in this seat of peace tumultuous wars . . . . iv 1 139
Peace, foolish woman.—I will not peace . . . . . v 2 80
So as thou livest in peace, die free from strife . . . . v 6 27
Find we a time for frighted peace to pant . . . *1 Hen. IV.* i 1 2
Therefore, I say,— Peace, cousin, say no more . . . . i 3 187
Peace, ye fat-kidneyed rascal! what a brawling dost thou keep! . ii 2 5
Peace, ye fat-guts! lie down . . . . . . ii 2 33
Peace, good pint-pot; peace, good tickle-brain . . . ii 4 438
Peace, cousin Percy; you will make him mad . . . . iii 1 51
And shake the peace and safety of our throne . . . . iii 2 117
The cankers of a calm world and a long peace . . . . iv 2 33
Whereupon You conjure from the breast of civil peace Such bold hostility iv 3 43
To sue his livery and beg his peace, With tears of innocency . . iv 3 62
You have deceived our trust, And made us doff our easy robes of peace v 1 12
Rebellion lay in his way, and he found it.—Peace, chewet, peace! . v 1 29
I speak of peace, while covert enmity Under the smile of safety wounds the world . . . . . . *2 Hen. IV.* Ind. 9
Look you pray, all you that kiss my lady Peace at home . . i 2 233
What is the matter? keep the peace here, ho! . . . . ii 1 67
Peace, good Doll! do not speak like a death's-head . . . ii 4 254
One of the king's justices of the peace . . . . . iii 2 65
Good Master Silence, it well befits you should be of the peace . . iii 2 99
Peace, fellow, peace; stand aside: know you where you are? . . iii 2 130
God send us peace! At your return visit our house . . . iii 2 313
Say on, my Lord of Westmoreland, in peace: What doth concern your coming? . . . . iv 1 29
Whose see is by a civil peace maintain'd, Whose beard the silver hand of peace hath touch'd, Whose learning and good letters peace hath tutor'd, Whose white investments figure innocence, The dove and very blessed spirit of peace . . . . iv 1 42
Wherefore do you so ill translate yourself Out of the speech of peace that bears such grace, Into the harsh and boisterous tongue of war? iv 1 48
Nor do I as an enemy to peace Troop in the throngs of military men . iv 1 61
Not to break peace or any branch of it, But to establish here a peace . iv 1 85
In sight of both our battles we may meet; And either end in peace . iv 1 180
My bosom tells me That no conditions of our peace can stand . . iv 1 184
If we can make our peace Upon such large terms and so absolute As our conditions shall consist upon, Our peace shall stand as firm as rocky mountains . . . . iv 1 185
Our peace will, like a broken limb united, Grow stronger for the breaking iv 1 222
Both against the peace of heaven and him . . . . . iv 2 29
Good my Lord of Lancaster, I am not here against your father's peace iv 2 31
Go, captain, and deliver to the army This news of peace . . iv 2 70
If you knew what pains I have bestow'd to breed this present peace . iv 2 74
The word of peace is render'd: hark, how they shout! . . . iv 2 87
A peace is of the nature of a conquest; For then both parties nobly are subdued, And neither party loser . . . . . iv 2 89
But Peace puts forth her olive every where . . . . iv 4 87
Daily grew to quarrel and to bloodshed, Wounding supposed peace . iv 5 196
How I came by the crown, O God forgive; And grant it may with thee in true peace live! . . . . iv 5 220
Health, peace, and happiness to my royal father!—Thou bring'st me happiness and peace, son John . . . . . . iv 5 227
Peace be with him that hath made us heavy!—Peace be with us! . v 2 25
That war, or peace, or both at once, may be As things acquainted and familiar to us . . . . v 2 138
So get you hence in peace; and tell the Dauphin . . *Hen. V.* i 2 294
For peace itself should not so dull a kingdom . . . . ii 4 16
In peace there's nothing so becomes a man As modest stillness . . iii 1 3
Gored the gentle bosom of peace with pillage and robbery . . iv 1 174
The slave, a member of the country's peace, Enjoys it; but in gross brain little wots What watch the king keeps to maintain the peace iv 1 298
God's peace! I would not lose so great an honour . . . iv 3 31
The emperor's coming in behalf of France, To order peace . . v Prol. 39
Peace to this meeting, wherefore we are met! . . . . v 2 1
Poor and mangled Peace, Dear nurse of arts, plenties and joyful births v 2 34
My speech entreats That I may know the let, why gentle Peace Should not expel these inconveniences . . . . . . v 2 65
If, Duke of Burgundy, you would the peace, Whose want gives growth to the imperfections Which you have cited, you must buy that peace v 2 68
Cease, cease these jars and rest your minds in peace . . *1 Hen. VI.* i 1 44
Without expense at all, By guileful fair words peace may be obtain'd . i 1 77
That you, being supreme magistrates, Thus contumeliously should break the peace!—Peace, mayor! thou know'st little of my wrongs i 3 58
A foe to citizens, One that still motions war and never peace . . i 3 63
Assembled here in arms this day against God's peace and the king's . i 3 75
Fair be all thy hopes And prosperous be thy life in peace and war! . ii 5 114
Thou art a most pernicious usurer, Froward by nature, enemy to peace iii 1 18
Who preferreth peace More than I do?—except I be provoked . . iii 1 33
Hold your slaughtering hands and keep the peace . . . . iii 1 87
Who should study to prefer a peace, If holy churchmen take delight in broils? . . . . iii 1 110
Then be at peace, except ye thirst for blood . . . . iii 1 117
York and Somerset, Quiet yourselves, I pray, and be at peace . . iv 1 115
Let this dissension first be tried by fight, And then your highness shall command a peace . . . . iv 1 117
As we hither came in peace, So let us still continue peace and love . iv 1 160
But, if you frown upon this proffer'd peace, You tempt the fury of my three attendants . . . . iv 2 9
They humbly sue unto your excellence To have a godly peace . . v 1 5
Therefore are we certainly resolved To draw conditions of a friendly peace v 1 38
Peace be amongst them, if they turn to us . . . . v 2 6
I kiss these fingers for eternal peace . . . . . v 3 48

Peace. Yet so my fancy may be satisfied, And peace established 1 *Hen. VI.* v 3 92
The states of Christendom . . . Have earnestly implored a general peace v 4 98
Shall we at last conclude effeminate peace? . . . . . v 4 107
If we conclude a peace, It shall be with such strict and severe covenants v 4 113
And suffer you to breathe in fruitful peace . . . . . v 4 127
Let your drums be still, For here we entertain a solemn peace . v 4 175
His alliance will confirm our peace . . . . . . v 5 42
Whereas the contrary bringeth bliss, And is a pattern of celestial peace v 5 65
Here are the articles of contracted peace . . . 2 *Hen. VI.* i 1 40
Peace, headstrong Warwick!—Image of pride, why should I hold my peace? . . . . i 3 179
Let me be blessed for the peace I make . . . . . ii 1 36
And go in peace, Humphrey, no less beloved Than when thou wert protector to thy king . . . . ii 3 26
When I am dead and gone, May honourable peace attend thy throne! . ii 3 38
Peace to his soul, if God's good pleasure be! . . . . . iii 3 26
Thou hast appointed justices of peace, to call poor men before them iv 7 45
Free pardon to them all That will forsake thee and go home in peace iv 8 10
A messenger from Henry . . . To know the reason of these arms in peace v 1 18
Thus war hath given thee peace, for thou art still. Peace with his soul! v 2 29
Wast thou ordain'd, dear father, To lose thy youth in peace? . . v 2 46
Sons, peace!—Peace, thou! and give King Henry leave to speak 3 *Hen. VI.* i 1 120
In dreadful war mayst thou be overcome, Or live in peace abandon'd! . i 1 188
As famous and as bold in war As he is famed for mildness, peace, and prayer . . . . ii 1 156
And thou this day hadst kept thy chair in peace . . . . . ii 6 20
Peace, impudent and shameless Warwick, peace! . . . . iii 3 156
To whom the heavens in thy nativity Adjudged an olive branch and laurel crown, As likely to be blest in peace and war . . . iv 6 35
I have true-hearted friends, Not mutinous in peace, yet bold in war . iv 8 10
Peace, wilful boy, or I will charm your tongue . . . . v 5 31
That thou mightst repossess the crown in peace . . . . v 7 19
Now am I seated as my soul delights, Having my country's peace and brothers' loves . . . . v 7 36
I, in this weak piping time of peace, Have no delight . *Richard III.* i 1 24
Say, then, my peace is made.—That shall you know hereafter . . i 2 198
Hurl down their indignation On thee, the troubler of the poor world's peace! . . . . i 3 221
Peace, master marquess, you are malapert . . . . . i 3 255
They ascend the sky, And there awake God's gentle-sleeping peace . i 3 288
Make peace with God, for you must die, my lord.—Hast thou that holy feeling in thy soul, To counsel me to make my peace with God? . i 4 256
Now in peace my soul shall part to heaven, Since I have set my friends at peace on earth . . . . ii 1 5
To make the perfect period of this peace . . . . . . ii 1 44
We have done deeds of charity; Made peace of enmity, fair love of hate ii 1 50
Reconcile me to his friendly peace: 'Tis death to me to be at enmity . ii 1 59
I entreat true peace of you, Which I will purchase with my duteous service . . . . ii 1 62
Peace, children, peace! the king doth love you well . . . ii 2 17
I hope the king made peace with all of us . . . . . ii 2 132
The peace of England and our persons' safety Enforced us to this execution . . . . iii 5 45
Your discipline in war, wisdom in peace, Your bounty, virtue . . iii 7 16
I to my grave, where peace and rest lie with me! . . . . iv 1 95
Infer fair England's peace by this alliance.—Which she shall purchase with still lasting war . . . . iv 4 343
Cheerly on, courageous friends, To reap the harvest of perpetual peace v 2 15
Sleep in peace, and wake in joy; Good angels guard thee! . . v 3 155
If you do sweat to put a tyrant down, You sleep in peace . . v 3 256
With smooth-faced peace, With smiling plenty and fair prosperous days . . . . v 5 33
Let them not live to taste this land's increase That would with treason wound this fair land's peace! . . . . v 5 39
Now civil wounds are stopp'd, peace lives again: That she may long live here, God say amen! . . . . v 5 40
The peace between the French and us not values The cost *Hen. VIII.* i 1 88
This tempest, Dashing the garment of this peace, aboded The sudden breach . . . . i 1 93
A proper title of a peace; and purchased At a superfluous rate! . . i 1 98
He would please to alter the king's course, And break the foresaid peace i 1 190
There cannot be those numberless offences 'Gainst me, that I cannot take peace with . . . . ii 1 85
Was by that wretch betray'd, And without trial fell; God's peace be with him! . . . . ii 1 111
That he ran mad and died.—Heaven's peace be with him! . . . ii 2 130
Peace to your highness!—Your graces find me here part of a housewife iii 1 23
Offers, as I do, in a sign of peace, His service and his counsel . iii 1 66
Within me A peace above all earthly dignities, A still and quiet conscience . . . . iii 2 379
Still in thy right hand carry gentle peace, To silence envious tongues . iii 2 445
The rod, and bird of peace, and all such emblems . . . . iv 1 89
He gave his honours to the world again, His blessed part to heaven, and slept in peace . . . . iv 2 30
Spirits of peace, where are ye? are ye all gone, And leave me here in wretchedness behind ye? . . . . iv 2 83
As you wish Christian peace to souls departed . . . . iv 2 156
Nor is there living, I speak it with a single heart, my lords, A man that more detests, more stirs against, Both in his private conscience and his place, Defacers of a public peace, than I do . . . . v 3 41
And sing The merry songs of peace to all his neighbours . . . v 5 36
Nor shall this peace sleep with her . . . . . . v 5 40
Peace, plenty, love, truth, terror, That were the servants to this chosen infant . . . . v 5 48
Peace, you ungracious clamours! peace, rude sounds! . *Troi. and Cres.* i 1 92
Brave Troilus! the prince of chivalry!—Peace, for shame, peace! . i 2 250
Courtiers as free, as debonair, unarm'd, As bending angels; that's their fame in peace . . . . i 3 236
But peace, Æneas, Peace, Trojan; lay thy finger on thy lips! . . i 3 239
Peace, fool!—I would have peace and quietness, but the fool will not . ii 1 89
Peace!—I will hold my peace when Achilles' brach bids me, shall I? . ii 1 124
The wound of peace is surety, Surety secure . . . . . ii 2 14
I will fill them with prophetic tears.—Peace, sister, peace! . . ii 2 103
You rascal!—Peace, fool! I have not done . . . . . ii 3 60
I have a woman's longing . . . To see great Hector in his weeds of peace iii 3 239
What would you have, you curs, That like nor peace nor war? *Coriolanus* i 1 173
All the peace you make in their cause is, calling both the parties knaves ii 1 87
Coriolanus! Citizens! Peace, peace, peace! Stay, hold, peace! . . iii 1 188
Hear me, people; peace!—Let's hear our tribune: peace! . . . iii 1 192
Where he shall answer, by a lawful form, In peace, to his utmost peril iii 1 326

Peace. To yawn, be still and wonder, When one but of my ordinance stood up To speak of peace or war . . . . *Coriolanus* iii 2 13
Tell me, In peace what each of them by the other lose . . . iii 2 44
How is it less or worse, That it shall hold companionship in peace With honour, as in war? . . . . iii 2 49
Plant love among's! Throng our large temples with the shows of peace! iii 3 36
Peace, peace; be not so loud.—If that I could for weeping, you should hear . . . . iv 2 12
This peace is nothing, but to rust iron, increase tailors . . . iv 5 234
Let me have war, say I; it exceeds peace as far as day does night . iv 5 237
Peace is a very apoplexy, lethargy; mulled, deaf, sleepy, insensible . iv 5 238
It cannot be denied but peace is a great maker of cuckolds . . iv 5 244
Ay, and it [peace] makes men hate one another . . . . iv 5 245
His remedies are tame i' the present peace And quietness of the people iv 6 2
Commanding peace Even with the same austerity and garb As he controll'd the war . . . . iv 7 43
I beseech you, peace: Or, if you 'ld ask, remember this before . . v 3 78
Be blest For making up this peace! . . . . v 3 140
Aufidius, though I cannot make true wars, I'll frame convenient peace v 3 191
What peace you'll make, advise me: for my part, I'll not to Rome . v 3 197
All the swords In Italy, and her confederate arms, Could not have made this peace . . . . v 3 209
Made peace With no less honour to the Antiates Than shame to the Romans . . . . v 6 79
Peace, both, and hear me speak.—Cut me to pieces, Volsces . . . v 6 111
Peace, ho! no outrage: peace! The man is noble . . . . v 6 125
Stand, Aufidius, And trouble not the peace . . . . . v 6 129
As suitors should, Plead your deserts in peace and humbleness *T. Andron.* i 1 45
There greet in silence, as the dead are wont, And sleep in peace! . . i 1 91
No noise, but silence and eternal sleep: In peace and honour rest you here, my sons!—In peace and honour live Lord Titus long; My noble lord and father, live in fame! . . . . i 1 156
These lovers will not keep the peace . . . . ii 1 37
Peace, tender sapling; thou art made of tears . . . . . iii 2 50
'Peace, villain, peace!'—even thus he rates the babe . . . iv 2 33
I do but keep the peace: put up thy sword . . . *Rom. and Jul.* i 1 75
What, drawn, and talk of peace! I hate the word, As I hate hell . . i 1 77
Rebellious subjects, enemies to peace . . . . i 1 88
To wield old partisans, in hands as old, Canker'd with peace . . . i 1 102
Disturb our streets again, Your lives shall pay the forfeit of the peace . i 1 104
'Tis not hard, I think, For men so old as we to keep the peace . . i 2 3
Peace, I have done. God mark thee to his grace! . . . . i 3 59
Peace, peace, Mercutio, peace! Thou talk'st of nothing . . . i 4 95
Sleep dwell upon thine eyes, peace in thy breast! Would I were sleep and peace, so sweet to rest! . . . . ii 2 188
Could not take truce with the unruly spleen Of Tybalt deaf to peace . iii 1 163
Peace, you mumbling fool! Utter your gravity o'er a gossip's bowl . iii 5 174
Peace, ho, for shame! confusion's cure lives not in these confusions . iv 5 65
What mean these masterless and gory swords To lie discolour'd by this place of peace? . . . . v 3 143
A glooming peace this morning with it brings . . . . . v 3 305
Even he drops down The knee before him and returns in peace *T. of Athens* i 1 61
It hath pleased the gods to remember my father's age, And call him to long peace. He is gone happy . . . . i 2 3
Piety, and fear, Religion to the gods, peace, justice, truth . . iv 1 16
Let us first see peace in Athens . . . . iv 3 461
Here is his cave. Peace and content be here! Lord Timon! Timon! Look out . . . . v 1 130
Who, like a boar too savage, doth root up His country's peace . . v 1 169
Make war breed peace, make peace stint war, make each Prescribe to other . . . . v 4 83
Bid every noise be still: peace yet again! . . . . *J. Cæsar* i 2 14
Peace! count the clock.—The clock hath stricken three . . . ii 1 192
Nor heaven nor earth have been at peace to-night . . . . ii 2 1
Waving our red weapons o'er our heads, Let's all cry 'Peace, freedom!' iii 1 110
To see thy Antony making his peace, Shaking the bloody fingers of thy foes . . . . iii 1 197
My countrymen,—Peace, silence! Brutus speaks.—Peace, ho! . . iii 2 59
Peace! let us hear what Antony can say . . . . . . iii 2 76
Peace, peace! you durst not so have tempted him.—I durst not!—No . iv 3 59
That we may, Lovers in peace, lead on our days to age! . . . iv 3 95
Not for all the world.—Peace then! no words . . . . . v 5 7
Peace! the charm's wound up . . . . *Macbeth* i 3 37
That no compunctious visitings of nature shake my fell purpose, nor keep peace between The effect and it! . . . . i 5 47
Prithee, peace: I dare do all that may become a man . . . . i 7 45
Put rancours in the vessel of my peace Only for them . . . . iii 1 67
Better be with the dead, Whom we, to gain our peace, have sent to peace iii 2 20
Uproar the universal peace, confound All unity on earth . . . iv 3 99
The tyrant has not batter'd at their peace!—No; they were well at peace when I did leave 'em . . . . iv 3 178
Peace, break thee off; look, where it comes again! . . . *Hamlet* i 1 40
I'll speak to it, though hell itself should gape And bid me hold my peace i 2 246
The humorous man shall end his part in peace . . . . . ii 2 336
Leave wringing of your hands: peace! sit you down, And let me wring your heart . . . . iii 4 34
This is the imposthume of much wealth and peace, That inward breaks iv 4 27
Will you be ruled by me?—Ay, my lord; So you will not o'errule me to a peace.—To thine own peace . . . . iv 7 61
As peace should still her wheaten garland wear . . . . . v 2 41
I have a voice and precedent of peace, To keep my name ungored . . v 2 260
Peace, Kent! Come not between the dragon and his wrath . . *Lear* i 1 123
So be my grave my peace, as here I give Her father's heart from her! . i 1 127
Peace be with Burgundy? Since that respects of fortune are his love, I shall not be his wife . . . . i 1 250
Whipped for lying; and sometimes I am whipped for holding my peace . i 4 202
Keep peace, upon your lives: He dies that strikes again . . . ii 2 52
Peace, sirrah! You beastly knave, know you no reverence? . . . ii 2 74
Look, look, a mouse! Peace, peace; this piece of toasted cheese will do't . . . . iv 6 89
When the thunder would not peace at my bidding . . . . iv 6 104
Rude am I in my speech, And little bless'd with the soft phrase of peace *Othello* i 3 82
If I be left behind, A moth of peace, and he go to the war . . . i 3 257
Practising upon his peace and quiet Even to madness . . . . ii 1 319
Nor am I yet persuaded to put up in peace what already I have foolishly suffered . . . . iv 2 181
Peace, and be still!—I will so. What's the matter? . . . . v 2 46
This deed of thine is no more worthy heaven Than thou wast worthy her.—Peace, you were best . . . . v 2 161

Peace. Come, hold your peace.—'Twill out, 'twill out: I peace! *Othello* v 2 219
Thy soldier, servant; making peace or war As thou affect'st *Ant. and Cleo.* i 3 70
Could not with graceful eyes attend those wars Which fronted mine own peace . . . ii 2 61
Though I make this marriage for my peace, I' the east my pleasure lies ii 3 39
The blow thou hadst Shall make thy peace for moving me to rage ii 5 70
Take that, divide it; fly, And make your peace with Cæsar.—Fly! not we iii 11 6
Peace! what noise?—List, list!—Hark!—Music i' the air . . iv 3 13
The time of universal peace is near . . . . . iv 6 5
Peace, peace! Dost thou not see my baby at my breast? . . v 2 311
Beseech your patience. Peace, Dear lady daughter, peace! . *Cymbeline* i 1 153
Plenty and peace breeds cowards: hardness ever Of hardiness is mother iii 6 21
Now peace be here, Poor house, that keep'st thyself! . . iii 6 35
Britain be fortunate and flourish in peace and plenty . . v 4 145; v 5 442
Peace, peace! see further; he eyes us not; forbear . . v 5 124
Whose issue Promises Britain peace and plenty.—Well; My peace we will begin . . . . v 5 458
The fingers of the powers above do tune the harmony of this peace . v 5 467
Publish we this peace To all our subjects . . . . v 5 478
And in the temple of great Jupiter Our peace we'll ratify . . v 5 483
Never was a war did cease, Ere bloody hands were wash'd, with such a peace . . . . v 5 485
So I bequeath a happy peace to you And all good men . . *Pericles* i 1 50
Peace, peace, and give experience tongue . . . . . i 2 37
When Signior Sooth here does proclaim a peace, He flatters you . i 2 44
I'll present myself. Peace to the lords of Tyre! . . . i 3 30
By the semblance Of their white flags display'd, they bring us peace . i 4 72
Welcome is peace, if he on peace consist; If wars, we are unable to resist i 4 83
Here to have death in peace is all he'll crave . . . ii 1 11
Peace be at your labour, honest fishermen . . . . ii 1 56
My twelve months are expired, and Tyrus stands In a litigious peace . iii 3 3
But, not to be a troubler of your peace, I will end here . . v 1 153
Hold thy peace *Mer. Wives* iv 1; *T. Night* ii 3; iii 4; *Richard II.* iii 4; *1 Hen. VI.* iii 2; *Rom. and Jul.* i 3
I prithee [pray thee], peace *Tempest* ii 1; *Much Ado* v 1; *2 Hen. IV.* ii 1; *2 Hen. VI.* ii 1; *Richard III.* ii 1; *Ant. and Cleo.* iii 13
Peace be with him! *M. for M.* v 1; *Much Ado* v 1; *Hen. VIII.* iv 2
Peace be with you! *Mer. Wives* iii 5; *Meas. for Meas.* iii 2; *Mer. of Venice* iv 1; *Rom. and Jul.* iii 1
Peace, I pray you . . . . . . *Mer. Wives* i 1 138; i 4 84

Peace with honour. Hold companionship in peace With honour *Coriol.* iii 2 49

Peaceable. The most peaceable way for you . . *Much Ado* iii 3 61
So to be called for his peaceable reign and good government . *Pericles* ii 1 108

Peaceably. Thou and I are too wise to woo peaceably . . *Much Ado* v 2 73
Disturb him not; let him pass peaceably . . *2 Hen. VI.* iii 3 25

Peaceful. Unless thou let his silver water keep A peaceful progress to the ocean . . . . *K. John* ii 1 340
Why have they dared to march So many miles upon her peaceful bosom? *Richard II.* ii 3 93
Where is Green? That they have let the dangerous enemy Measure our confines with such peaceful steps? . . . . . . iii 2 125
That their souls May make a peaceful and a sweet retire . *Hen. V.* iv 3 86
How many would the peaceful city quit, To welcome him! . . v Prol. 33
I see our wars Will turn unto a peaceful comic sport . *1 Hen. VI.* ii 2 45
It is thus agreed That peaceful truce shall be proclaim'd in France . v 4 117
And are the cities, that I got with wounds, Deliver'd up again with peaceful words? . . . . *2 Hen. VI.* i 1 122
And smooth the frowns of war with peaceful looks . . *3 Hen. VI.* ii 6 32
His looks are full of peaceful majesty . . . . . iv 6 71
Brotherhoods in cities, Peaceful commerce . . *Troi. and Cres.* i 3 105
Not an hour, In the day's glorious walk, or peaceful night . *Pericles* i 2 4
Keep your mind, till you return to us, Peaceful and comfortable! . i 2 36

Peace-maker. Your If is the only peace-maker . . *As Y. Like It* v 4 108
For blessed are the peacemakers on earth . . *2 Hen. VI.* ii 1 35
Pray, think us Those we profess, peace-makers, friends, and servants *Hen. VIII.* iii 1 167

Peace-parted. We should profane the service of the dead To sing a requiem and such rest to her As to peace-parted souls . *Hamlet* v 1 261

Peach. For some four suits of peach-coloured satin, which now peaches him a beggar . . . . . . *Meas. for Meas.* iv 3 12
If I be ta'en, I'll peach for this . . . *1 Hen. IV.* ii 2 47

Peach-coloured. Four suits of peach-coloured satin *Meas. for Meas.* iv 3 12
Those that were thy peach-coloured ones . . *2 Hen. IV.* ii 2 19

Peacock. Her peacocks fly amain . . . . *Tempest* iv 1 74
'Fly pride,' says the peacock . . . *Com. of Errors* iv 3 81
You may as well go about to turn the sun to ice with fanning in his face with a peacock's feather . . . . . *Hen. V.* iv 1 213
Triumph for a while And like a peacock sweep along his tail *1 Hen. VI.* iii 3 6
He stalks up and down like a peacock,—a stride and a stand *Tr. and Cr.* iii 3 252

Peak. He shall live a man forbid: Weary se'nnights nine times nine Shall he dwindle, peak and pine . . . . . . *Macbeth* i 3 23
A dull and muddy-mettled rascal, peak, Like John-a-dreams . *Hamlet* ii 2 594

Peaking. The peaking Cornuto her husband . . . *Mer. Wives* iii 5 71

Peal. Peace! the peal begins . . . . . *L. L. Lost* iv 1 46
Gazing in a doubt Whether those peals of praise be his or no *Mer. of Ven.* iii 2 146
And ring a hunter's peal, That all the court may echo . *T. Andron.* ii 2 5
I promised your grace a hunter's peal.—And you have rung it lustily ii 2 13
Ere to black Hecate's summons The shard-borne beetle with his drowsy hums Hath rung night's yawning peal . . . *Macbeth* iii 2 43

Pear. Till I were as crest-fallen as a dried pear . . *Mer. Wives* iv 5 103
Like one of our French withered pears, it looks ill, it eats drily *All's Well* i 1 175
'Tis a withered pear; it was formerly better . . . . i 1 176
I hope your majesty is pear me testimony and witness . *Hen. V.* iv 8 38
O, that she were An open et cætera, thou a poperin pear! *Rom. and Jul.* ii 1 38

Peard. I think the 'oman is a witch indeed: I like not when a 'oman has a great peard; I spy a great peard under his muffler *Mer. Wives* iv 2 204

Pearl. Full fathom five thy father lies; Of his bones are coral made; Those are pearls that were his eyes . . . . . *Tempest* i 2 398
She is mine own, And I as rich in having such a jewel As twenty seas, if all their sand were pearl . . . . . . *T. G. of Ver.* ii 4 170
A sea of melting pearl, which some call tears . . . iii 1 224
But pearls are fair; and the old saying is, Black men are pearls in beauteous ladies' eyes.—'Tis true; such pearls as put out ladies' eyes . . . . v 2 11
Like sapphire, pearl and rich embroidery, Buckled below fair knight-hood's bending knee . . . . *Mer. Wives* v 5 75
Laced with silver, set with pearls . . . . *Much Ado* iii 4 20
Fire enough for a flint, pearl enough for a swine . *L. L. Lost* iv 2 91
This and these pearls to me sent Longaville . . . . v 2 53
Will you have me, or your pearl again?—Neither of either . . v 2 458

Pearl. Decking with liquid pearl the bladed grass . *M. N. Dream* i 1 211
Go seek some dewdrops here And hang a pearl in every cowslip's ear . ii 1 15
That same dew, which sometime on the buds Was wont to swell like round and orient pearls . . . . iv 1 59
Rich honesty dwells like a miser, sir, in a poor house; as your pearl in your foul oyster . . . . *As Y. Like It* v 4 63
Their harness studded all with gold and pearl . . *T. of Shrew* Ind. 2 44
Fine linen, Turkey cushions boss'd with pearl, Valance of Venice gold . ii 1 355
Why, sir, what 'cerns it you if I wear pearl and gold? . . . v 1 77
This pearl she gave me, I do feel't and see't . . . *T. Night* iv 3 2
Draws those heaven-moving pearls from his poor eyes . . *K. John* ii 1 169
Our chains and our jewels.—'Your brooches, pearls, and ouches' *2 Hen. IV.* ii 4 53
The crown imperial, The intertissued robe of gold and pearl . *Hen. V.* iv 1 279
Wedges of gold, great anchors, heaps of pearl, Inestimable stones *Richard III.* i 4 26
The liquid drops of tears that you have shed Shall come again, trans-form'd to orient pearl . . . . iv 4 322
Her bed is India; there she lies, a pearl . . . *Troi. and Cres.* i 1 103
She is a pearl, Whose price hath launch'd above a thousand ships ii 2 81
I will be bright, and shine in pearl and gold . . *T. Andron.* ii 1 19
This is the pearl that pleased your empress' eye . . . v 1 42
I see thee compass'd with thy kingdom's pearl . . . *Macbeth* v 8 56
Hamlet, this pearl is thine. . . . . . . *Hamlet* v 2 293
What guests were in her eyes; which parted thence, As pearls from diamonds dropp'd . . . . *Lear* iv 3 24
Like the base Indian, threw a pearl away Richer than all his tribe *Othello* v 2 347
He kiss'd,—the last of many doubled kisses,—This orient pearl *A. and C.* i 5 41
I'll set thee in a shower of gold, and hail Rich pearls upon thee . ii 5 46

Peasant. How now, you whoreson peasant! Where have you been these two days loitering? . . . . *T. G. of Ver.* iv 4 47
She's fled unto that peasant Valentine; And Eglamour is in her company v 2 35
Thou shalt know I will predominate over the peasant . *Mer. Wives* ii 2 294
Hence, prating peasant! fetch thy master home . *Com. of Errors* ii 1 81
I did obey, and sent my peasant home For certain ducats . . iv 1 231
You have trained me like a peasant . . . *As Y. Like It* i 1 72
How my men will stay themselves from laughter When they do homage to this simple peasant . . . . . *T. of Shrew* Ind. 1 135
You peasant swain! you whoreson malt-horse drudge! . . . iv 1 132
Made glory base and sovereignty a slave, Proud majesty a subject, state a peasant . . . . *Richard II.* iv 1 252
This have I rumour'd through the peasant towns . *2 Hen. IV.* Ind. 33
Whose spirit lent a fire Even to the dullest peasant in his camp . i 1 113
Whose hours the peasant best advantages . . . *Hen. V.* iv 1 301
Our superfluous lackeys and our peasants . . . were enow To purge this field of such a hilding foe . . . . iv 2 26
Cuppele gorge, permafoy, Peasant, unless thou give me crowns . iv 4 40
So do our vulgar drench their peasant limbs In blood of princes . iv 7 80
Like peasant foot-boys do they keep the walls . . *1 Hen. VI.* iii 2 69
And like me to the peasant boys of France . . . . iv 6 48
Deny me not, I prithee, gentle Joan.—Peasant, avaunt! . . v 4 21
So worthless peasants bargain for their wives, As market-men for oxen v 5 53
His army is a ragged multitude Of hinds and peasants . *2 Hen. VI.* iv 4 33
Base peasants, do ye believe him? will you needs be hanged with your pardons about your necks? . . . . iv 8 21
Base lackey peasants, Whom their o'er-cloyed country vomits forth *Richard III.* v 3 317
The bounty of this lord! How many prodigal bits have slaves and peasants This night englutted! . . . . *T. of Athens* ii 2 174
To wring From the hard hands of peasants their vile trash *J. Cæsar* iv 3 74
O, what a rogue and peasant slave am I! . . . . *Hamlet* ii 2 576
The toe of the peasant comes so near the heel of the courtier. . v 1 152
Give me thy sword. A peasant stand up thus! . . *Lear* iii 7 80
Wherefore, bold peasant, Darest thou support a publish'd traitor? iv 6 235
And suit myself As does a Briton peasant . . . *Cymbeline* v 1 24

Peasantry. How much low peasantry would then be glean'd From the true seed of honour! . . . . . . *Mer. of Venice* ii 9 46

Peascod. Commend me to Mistress Squash, your mother, and to Master Peascod, your father . . . . *M. N. Dream* iii 1 191
I remember the wooing of a peascod instead of her . *As Y. Like It* ii 4 52
As a squash is before 'tis a peascod . . . . *T. Night* i 5 167
That's a shealed peascod . . . . *Lear* i 4 219

Peascod-time. I have known thee these twenty-nine years, come peas-cod-time . . . . *2 Hen. IV.* ii 4 413

Peaseblossom! Cobweb! Moth! and Mustardseed! . . *M. N. Dream* iii 1 165
Good Master Peaseblossom, I shall desire you of more acquaintance . iii 1 192
Where's Peaseblossom?—Ready.—Scratch my head, Peaseblossom . iv 1 5

Peat. I will peat the door for Master Page. What, hoa! . *Mer. Wives* i 1 73
A pretty peat! it is best Put finger in the eye, an she knew why *T. of S.* i 1 78
Or I will peat his pate four days . . . . . *Hen. V.* v 1 43

Peaten. And has been grievously peaten as an old 'oman *Mer. Wives* iv 4 22

Pebble. He is a stone, a very pebble stone . . . *T. G. of Ver.* ii 3 11
And what is 'a stone,' William?—A pebble . . . *Mer. Wives* iv 1 35
Have fill'd their pockets full of pebble stones . . *1 Hen. VI.* iii 1 80
When suddenly a file of boys behind 'em, loose shot, delivered such a shower of pebbles . . . . *Hen. VIII.* v 4 60
Then let the pebbles on the hungry beach Fillip the stars *Coriolanus* v 3 58
For charitable prayers, Shards, flints and pebbles should be thrown on her . . . . *Hamlet* v 1 254
The murmuring surge, That on the unnumber'd idle pebbles chafes *Lear* iv 6 21

Peck. In the circumference of a peck, hilt to point, heel to head *M. Wives* iii 5 113
About the sixth hour; when beasts most graze, birds best peck *L. L. Lost* i 1 239
This fellow pecks up wit as pigeons pease, And utters it again . v 2 315
A peck of provender: I could munch your good dry oats *M. N. Dream* iv 1 35
So doves do peck the falcon's piercing talons . . . *3 Hen. VI.* i 4 41
And doves will peck in safeguard of their brood . . . ii 2 18
One Gilbert Peck, his chancellor . . . . *Hen. VIII.* i 1 219
Sir Gilbert Peck his chancellor; and John Car, Confessor to him. . ii 1 20
You i' the camlet, get up o' the rail; I'll peck you o'er the pales else v 4 94
And bring in The crows to peck the eagles . . *Coriolanus* iii 1 139
But I will wear my heart upon my sleeve For daws to peck at . *Othello* i 1 65
In that mood The dove will peck the estridge . . *Ant. and Cleo.* iii 13 197

Pecked. A leg of Rome shall not return to tell What crows have peck'd them here . . . . *Cymbeline* v 3 93

Peculiar. Groping for trouts in a peculiar river . . *Meas. for Meas.* i 2 91
In will peculiar and in self-admission . . . *Troi. and Cres.* ii 3 176
The single and peculiar life is bound, With all the strength and armour of the mind, To keep itself from noyance . . . . *Hamlet* iii 3 11
Not I for love and duty, But seeming so, for my peculiar end *Othello* i 1 60
Or keep you warm, Or sue to you to do a peculiar profit To your own person iii 3 79

Peculiar. There's millions now alive That nightly lie in those unproper beds Which they dare swear peculiar . . . . . *Othello* iv 70
And so much For my peculiar care . . . . *Cymbeline* v 5 83
Pecus. Precor gelida quando pecus omne sub umbra Ruminat *L. L. Lost* iv 2 95
Ped. There will we make our peds of roses . . . *Mer. Wives* iii 1 19
Pedant. A domineering pedant o'er the boy . . . *L. L. Lost* iii 1 179
The pedant, the braggart, the hedge-priest, the fool, and the boy . v 2 545
But, wrangling pedant, this is The patroness of heavenly harmony *T. of Shrew* iii 1 4
How fiery and forward our pedant is! . . . . iii 1 48
But I have cause to pry into this pedant: Methinks he looks as though he were in love . . . . iii 1 87
A mercatante, or a pedant, I know not what; but formal in apparel . iv 2 63
Like a pedant that keeps a school i' the church . . . *T. Night* iii 2 80
Pedantical. Spruce affectation, Figures pedantical . . . *L. L. Lost* v 2 408
Pedascule, I'll watch you better yet . . . . *T. of Shrew* iii 1 50
Pedigree. Willing you overlook this pedigree . . . . *Hen. V.* ii 4 90
He From John of Gaunt doth bring his pedigree . . . 1 *Hen. VI.* ii 5 77
But for the rest, you tell a pedigree Of threescore and two years 3 *Hen. VI.* iii 3 92
Can Oxford, that did ever fence the right, Now buckler falsehood with a pedigree? For shame! . . . . iii 3 99
Pedlar. He is wit's pedler, and retails his wares At wakes . *L. L. Lost* v 2 317
By birth a pedlar, by education a cardmaker . . *T. of Shrew* Ind. 2 20
If you did but hear the pedlar at the door, you would never dance again after a tabor and pipe . . . . *W. Tale* iv 4 181
You have of these pedlars, that have more in them than you'ld think . iv 4 217
Pedlar, let's have the first choice . . . . iv 4 319
Come to the pedlar; Money's a medler . . . . . . iv 4 328
I would have ransack'd The pedlar's silken treasury . . . . iv 4 361
Let me pocket up my pedlar's excrement . . . . iv 4 734
She was, indeed, a pedler's daughter, and sold many laces 2 *Hen. VI.* iv 2 48
I had rather be a pedlar . . . . *Richard III.* i 3 149
Pedro. Much deserved on his part and equally remembered by Don Pedro *Much Ado* i 1 13
Don Pedro is approached . . . . i 1 95
Look; Don Pedro is returned to seek you . . . . . . i 1 204
Find me a meet hour to draw Don Pedro and the Count Claudio alone . ii 2 34
Peeled. The skilful shepherd peel'd me certain wands . *Mer. of Venice* i 3 85
Peel'd priest, dost thou command me to be shut out? . 1 *Hen. VI.* i 3 30
Peep. Now, when thou wakest, with thine own fool's eyes peep *M. N. D.* iv 1 89
Evermore peep through their eyes And laugh like parrots *Mer. of Venice* i 1 52
Under an oak whose antique root peeps out Upon the brook *As Y. Like It* ii 1 31
Which gratitude Through flinty Tartar's bosom would peep forth *All's W.* iv 4 7
Not a dangerous action can peep out his head but I am thrust upon it 2 *Hen. IV.* i 2 238
And faintly through a rusty beaver peeps . . . . *Hen. V.* iv 2 44
Where thou darest not peep . . . . 2 *Hen. VI.* ii 1 42
These five days have I hid me in these woods and durst not peep out . iv 10 4
I can see his pride Peep through each part of him . . . *Hen. VIII.* i 1 69
And durst not once peep out . . . . *Coriolanus* iv 6 46
And peep about To find ourselves dishonourable graves . . *J. Cæsar* i 2 137
Nor heaven peep through the blanket of the dark, To cry 'Hold!' *Macb.* i 5 54
Forth at your eyes your spirits wildly peep . . . . *Hamlet* iii 4 119
Such divinity doth hedge a king, That treason can but peep to what it would . . . . iv 5 124
No vessel can peep forth, but 'tis as soon Taken as seen . *Ant. and Cleo.* i 4 53
To-night I'll force The wine peep through their scars . . . iii 13 191
Peep through thy marble mansion; help; Or we poor ghosts will cry *Cymbeline* v 4 87
Peeped. Methought he had made two holes in the ale-wife's new petticoat and so peeped through . . . . 2 *Hen. IV.* ii 2 89
From this league Peep'd harms that menaced him . . *Hen. VIII.* i 1 183
Peepeth. Your youth, And the true blood which peepeth fairly through't, Do plainly give you out an unstain'd shepherd *W. Tale* iv 4 148
Peeping. All his behaviours did make their retire To the court of his eye, peeping thorough desire . . . . . . *L. L. Lost* ii 1 235
Peer. O king Stephano! O peer! O worthy Stephano! . . *Tempest* iv 1 221
So buffets himself on the forehead, crying, 'Peer out, peer out!' *M. Wives* iv 2 26
When daffodils begin to peer . . . . *W. Tale* iv 3 1
O, make a league with me, till I have pleased My discontented peers! *K. John* iv 2 127
He perhaps shall need Some messenger betwixt me and the peers . . iv 2 179
O, haste thee to the peers, Throw this report on their incensed rage! . iv 2 260
Most mighty liege, and my companion peers . . . *Richard II.* i 3 93
But in the balance of great Bolingbroke, Besides himself, are all the English peers . . . . iii 4 88
How bloodily the sun begins to peer Above yon busky hill! . 1 *Hen. IV.* v 1 1
What peer hath been suborn'd to grate on you? . 2 *Hen. IV.* iv 1 90
No prince nor peer shall have just cause to say, God shorten Harry's happy life one day! . . . . v 2 144
Then hear me, gracious sovereign, and you peers . . *Hen. V.* i 2 33
See you, my princes and my noble peers, These English monsters! . ii 2 84
Sold your king to slaughter, His princes and his peers to servitude . ii 2 171
The English are embattled, you French peers . . . . . iv 2 14
For yet a many of your horsemen peer And gallop o'er the field . . iv 7 88
And, princes French, and peers, health to you all! . . . . . v 2 8
We'll take your oath, And all the peers', for surety of our leagues . v 2 400
O, what a scandal is it to our crown, That two such noble peers as ye should jar! . . . . 1 *Hen. VI.* iii 1 70
This late dissension grown betwixt the peers Burns under feigned ashes of forged love . . . . iii 1 189
My gracious prince, and honourable peers . . . . . . iii 4 1
That for a toy, a thing of no regard, King Henry's peers and chief nobility Destroy'd themselves . . . . iv 1 146
Winchester will not submit, I trow, Or be inferior to the proudest peer v 1 57
Is all our travail turn'd to this effect? After the slaughter of so many peers? . . . . v 4 103
Upon my bended knee, In sight of England and her lordly peers 2 *Hen. VI.* i 1 11
Brave peers of England, pillars of the state . . . . . . i 1 75
O peers of England, shameful is this league! . . . . . . i 1 98
Suffolk concluded on the articles, The peers agreed . . . . i 1 218
And Humphrey with the peers be fall'n at jars . . . . . i 1 253
Salisbury and Warwick are no simple peers . . . . . . i 3 77
The peers and nobles of the realm Have been as bondmen to thy sovereignty . . . . i 3 129
Dangerous peer, That smooth'st it so with king and commonweal! . ii 1 21
No more than well becomes So good a quarrel and so bad a peer . . ii 1 28
Peace, good queen, And whet not on these furious peers . . . ii 1 34
The king and all the peers are here at hand . . . . . . iii 2 10
Peer. The proudest peer in the realm shall not wear a head on his shoulders, unless he pay me tribute . . . . 2 *Hen. VI.* iv 7 127
Back'd by the power of Warwick, that false peer . . 3 *Hen. VI.* i 1 52
Our people and our peers are both misled, Our treasure seized . . iii 3 35
Methinks these peers of France should smile at that . . . . iii 3 91
You peers, continue this united league . . . . *Richard III.* ii 1 2
Princely peers, a happy time of day! . . . . ii 1 47
Made peace of enmity, fair love of hate, Between these swelling wrong-incensed peers . . . . ii 1 51
Heart-sorrowing peers, That bear this mutual heavy load of moan . ii 2 112
O thou bloody prison, Fatal and ominous to noble peers! . . . iii 3 10
Where be the bending peers that flatter'd thee? . . . . . iv 4 95
His peers, upon this evidence, Have found him guilty of high treason *Hen. VIII.* ii 1 26
Which of the peers Have uncontemn'd gone by him? . . . . iii 2 9
First, all you peers of Greece, go to my tent . . . *Troi. and Cres.* iv 5 271
Think of this, good peers, But as a thing of custom . . *Macbeth* iii 4 96
King Stephen was a worthy peer, His breeches cost him but a crown *Oth.* ii 3 92
You shall not need, my fellow peers of Tyre, Further to question *Pericles* i 3 11
When peers thus knit, a kingdom ever stands . . . . . . ii 4 58
Peered. An hour before the worshipp'd sun Peer'd forth the golden window of the east . . . . *Rom. and Jul.* i 1 126
Peereth. So honour peereth in the meanest habit . . *T. of Shrew* iv 3 176
Peering in maps for ports and piers and roads . . *Mer. of Venice* i 1 19
No shepherdess, but Flora Peering in April's front . . . *W. Tale* iv 4 3
Like a proud river peering o'er his bounds . . . . *K. John* iii 1 23
Even through the hollow eyes of death I spy life peering *Richard II.* ii 1 271
Peerless. But you, O you, So perfect and so peerless! . . *Tempest* iii 1 47
Ay, the most peerless piece of earth, I think, That e'er the sun shone bright on . . . . *W. Tale* v 1 94
As she lived peerless, So her dead likeness, I do well believe, Excels . v 3 14
Her peerless feature, joined with her birth . . . 1 *Hen. VI.* v 5 68
It is a peerless kinsman . . . . *Macbeth* i 4 58
I bind . . . the world to weet We stand up peerless . *Ant. and Cleo.* i 1 40
That her daughter Might stand peerless . . . . *Pericles* iv Gower 40
Peesel. Good Captain Peesel, be quiet; 'tis very late, i' faith . 2 *Hen. IV.* ii 4 174
Peevish. She is peevish, sullen, froward, Proud, disobedient *T. G. of Ver.* iii 1 68
Why, this it is to be a peevish girl, That flies her fortune . . . v 2 49
He is something peevish that way: but nobody but has his fault *M. W.* i 4 14
Why, thou peevish sheep, What ship of Epidamnum stays for me? *Com. of Errors* iv 1 93
What wilt thou do, thou peevish officer? . . . . . . iv 4 117
And creep into the jaundice By being peevish . . . *Mer. of Venice* i 1 86
'Tis but a peevish boy; yet he talks well . . . *As Y. Like It* iii 5 110
When she is froward, peevish, sullen, sour . . . *T. of Shrew* v 2 157
Besides, virginity is peevish, proud, idle, made of self-love . *All's Well* i 1 156
Run after that same peevish messenger . . . . . *T. Night* i 5 319
Wrong'd as we are by this peevish town . . . . . *K. John* ii 1 402
A peevish self-will'd harlotry . . . 1 *Hen. IV.* iii 1 198; *Rom. and Jul.* iv 2 14
What a wretched and peevish fellow is this king of England *Hen. V.* iii 7 142
I scorn thee and thy fashion, peevish boy . . . 1 *Hen. VI.* ii 4 76
Leave this peevish broil And set this unaccustom'd fight aside . . iii 1 92
I will not so presume To send such peevish tokens to a king . . . v 3 186
What a peevish fool was that of Crete! . . . . 3 *Hen. VI.* v 6 18
My woful banishment, Could all but answer for that peevish brat? *Richard III.* i 3 194
Fie, what an indirect and peevish course! . . . . iii 1 31
When Richmond was a little peevish boy . . . . iv 2 100
The gods are deaf to hot and peevish vows . . . *Troi. and Cres.* v 3 16
A peevish schoolboy, worthless of such honour! . . . . *J. Cæsar* v 1 61
Why should we in our peevish opposition Take it to heart? *Hamlet* i 2 100
I cannot speak Any beginning to this peevish odds . . . *Othello* ii 3 185
Or else break out in peevish jealousies, Throwing restraint upon us . iv 3 90
Beseech you, sir, desire My man's abode where I did leave him: he Is strange and peevish . . . . *Cymbeline* i 6 54
If the peevish baggage would but give way to customers . *Pericles* iv 6 20
Your peevish chastity, which is not worth a breakfast . . . . iv 6 130
Peevish-fond. And be not peevish-fond in great designs . *Richard III.* iv 4 417
Peevishly. Come, sir, you peevishly threw it to her . . *T. Night* ii 2 14
Peg. I will rend an oak And peg thee in his knotty entrails . *Tempest* i 2 295
I'll set down the pegs that make this music, As honest as I am *Othello* ii 1 203
Peg-a-Ramsey. Malvolio's a Peg-a-Ramsey . . . . *T. Night* ii 3 81
Pegasus. In Genoa, Where we were lodgers at the Pegasus *T. of Shrew* iv 4 5
To turn and wind a fiery Pegasus And witch the world . 1 *Hen. IV.* iv 1 109
Le cheval volant, the Pegasus, chez les narines de feu! . . *Hen. V.* iii 7 15
Peise. 'Tis to peize the time, To eke it and to draw it out *Mer. of Venice* iii 2 22
To take a nap, Lest leaden slumber peise me down to-morrow *Richard III.* v 3 105
Peised. Commodity, the bias of the world, The world, who of itself is peised well . . . . *K. John* ii 1 575
Pelf. Immortal gods, I crave no pelf . . . . . *T. of Athens* i 2 63
All perishen of man, of pelf, Ne aught escapen but himself *Pericles* ii Gower 35
Pelican. That blood already, like the pelican, Hast thou tapp'd out and drunkenly caroused . . . . *Richard II.* ii 1 126
Like the kind life-rendering pelican, Repast them with my blood *Hamlet* iv 5 146
Judicious punishment! 'twas this flesh begot Those pelican daughters *Lear* iii 4 77
Pelion. I had rather be a giantess, and lie under Mount Pelion *Mer. Wives* ii 1 82
To o'ertop old Pelion, or the skyish head Of blue Olympus . . *Hamlet* v 1 276
Pella. Condemn'd and noted Lucius Pella For taking bribes . *J. Cæsar* iv 3 2
Pelleted. My brave Egyptians all, By the discandying of this pelleted storm, Lie graveless . . . . *Ant. and Cleo.* iii 13 165
Pell-mell, down with them! . . . . *L. L. Lost* iv 3 368
Defy each other, and pell-mell Make work upon ourselves . *K. John* ii 1 406
Moody beggars, starving for a time Of pell-mell havoc and confusion 1 *Hen. IV.* v 1 82
Let us to't pell-mell; if not to heaven, then hand in hand to hell *Rich. III.* v 3 312
To't, luxury, pell-mell! . . . . *Lear* iv 6 119
Peloponnesus. Toward Peloponnesus are they fled . . *Ant. and Cleo.* iii 10 31
Pelt. Do pelt so fast at one another's pate . . . . 1 *Hen. VI.* iii 1 82
The chidden billow seems to pelt the clouds . . . . . *Othello* ii 1 12
Pelting. Every pelting, petty officer . . . . . . *Meas. for Meas.* ii 2 112
Have every pelting river made so proud That they have overborne their continents . . . . *M. N. Dream* ii 1 91
Is now leased out . . . Like to a tenement or pelting farm *Richard II.* ii 1 60
We have had pelting wars . . . . *Troi. and Cres.* iv 5 267
Poor pelting villages, sheep-cotes, and mills . . . . . *Lear* ii 3 18
Wheresoe'er you are, That bide the pelting of this pitiless storm . iii 4 29
Pembroke. Honourable conduct let him have: Pembroke, look to't *K. John* i 1 30
Pembroke and Stafford, you in our behalf Go levy men . 3 *Hen. VI.* iv 1 130
When I have fought with Pembroke and his fellows, I'll follow you . iv 3 54
Where is princely Richmond now?—At Pembroke . . *Richard III.* iv 5 7

Pembroke. Oxford, redoubted Pembroke, Sir James Blunt, And Rice ap Thomas . . . . *Richard III.* iv 5 11
The Earl of Pembroke keeps his regiment . . . . v 3 29
And Does purpose honour to you no less flowing Than Marchioness of Pembroke; to which title A thousand pound a year *Hen. VIII.* ii 3 63
Marchioness of Pembroke! A thousand pounds a year for pure respect! ii 3 94
Bullen! No, we'll no Bullens. Speedily I wish To hear from Rome. The Marchioness of Pembroke! . . . . iii 2 90
Pen. Side-stitches that shall pen thy breath up . . . *Tempest* i 2 326
How my father stole two geese out of a pen . *Mer. Wives* iii 4 41
Pick out mine eyes with a ballad-maker's pen . . . . *Much Ado* i 1 255
Bid him bring his pen and inkhorn to the gaol . . . . iii 5 63
That draweth from my snow-white pen the ebon-coloured ink *L. L. Lost* i 1 245
Devise, wit; write, pen; for I am for whole volumes in folio . i 2 191
Marvellous well for the pen . . . . iv 2 158
Never durst poet touch a pen to write Until his ink were temper'd with Love's sighs . . . . iv 3 346
The poet's pen Turns them to shapes . . . *M. N. Dream* v 1 15
I'll mar the young clerk's pen . . . . . *Mer. of Venice* v 1 237
To give great Charlemain a pen in's hand And write to her . *All's Well* ii 1 80
I will presently pen down my dilemmas . . . . . . iii 6 80
The old hermit of Prague, that never saw pen and ink . . *T. Night* iv 2 15
Help me to a candle, and pen, ink and paper . . . . . iv 2 87
In a semicircle, Or a half-moon made with a pen . . *W. Tale* ii 1 11
I am a scribbled form, drawn with a pen Upon a parchment . *K. John* v 7 32
Turning your books to graves, your ink to blood, Your pens to lances *2 Hen. IV.* iv 1 51
His nose was as sharp as a pen, and a' babbled of green fields *Hen. V.* ii 3 17
With rough and all-unable pen, Our bending author hath pursued the story . . . . Epil. 1
Or am not able Verbatim to rehearse the method of my pen *1 Hen. VI.* iii 1 13
I'll call for pen and ink, and write my mind . . . . v 3 66
Hang him with his pen and ink-horn about his neck . *2 Hen. VI.* iv 2 117
Not in confidence Of author's pen or actor's voice . *Troi. and Cres.* Prol. 24
More divine Than breath or pen can give expressure to . . . iii 3 204
Heaven guide thy pen to print thy sorrows plain! . . *T. Andron.* iv 1 75
Give me pen and ink. Sirrah, can you with a grace deliver a supplication? iv 3 106
And private in his chamber pens himself . . . *Rom. and Jul.* i 1 144
Read o'er the volume of young Paris' face And find delight writ there with beauty's pen . . . . i 3 82
Keep . . . thy pen from lenders' books . . . . . *Lear* iii 4 100
One that excels the quirks of blazoning pens . . . . *Othello* ii 1 63
Away with her, And pen her up.—Beseech your patience *Cymbeline* i 1 153
Your neck, sir, is pen, book and counters; so the acquittance follows . v 4 173
She would with rich and constant pen Vail to her mistress *Pericles* iv Gower 28
Penalty. Awakes me all the enrolled penalties . . . *Meas. for Meas.* i 2 170
And an express command, under penalty . . . . . . iv 2 177
Unless a thousand marks be levied, To quit the penalty. *Com. of Errors* i 1 23
Let's see the penalty. 'On pain of losing her tongue.' Who devised this penalty? . . . . *L. L. Lost* i 1 123
And why?—To fright them hence with that dread penalty . . . i 1 128
If he break, thou mayst with better face Exact the penalty *Mer. of Venice* i 3 138
Where thou now exact'st the penalty, Which is a pound of this poor merchant's flesh . . . . iv 1 22
I crave the law, The penalty and forfeit of my bond . . . . iv 1 207
The intent and purpose of the law Hath full relation to the penalty . iv 1 248
He shall have nothing but the penalty . . . . iv 1 322
This day acquitted Of grievous penalties . . . . . . iv 1 410
Here feel we but the penalty of Adam, The seasons' difference *As Y. L. It* ii 1 5
But Montague is bound as well as I, In penalty alike *Rom. and Jul.* i 2 2
Penance. My penance is to call Lucetta back And ask remission for my folly past . . . . *T. G. of Ver.* i 2 64
I have done penance for contemning Love . . . . . ii 4 129
As he in penance wander'd through the forest . . . . . v 2 38
'Tis your penance but to hear The story of your loves discovered . v 4 170
Impose me to what penance your invention Can lay upon my sin *M. Ado* v 1 283
And bide the penance of each three years' day . . *L. L. Lost* i 1 115
You must suffer him to take no delight nor no penance . . . i 2 134
I have no shirt; I go woolward for penance . . . . . v 2 717
From which lingering penance Of such misery doth she cut me off *Mer. of Ven.* iv 1 271
Make her bear the penance of her tongue . . . *T. of Shrew* i 1 89
We may carry it thus, for our pleasure and his penance *T. Night* iii 4 151
After three days' open penance done . . . . *2 Hen. VI.* ii 3 11
Come you, my lord, to see my open shame? Now thou dost penance too ii 4 20
Master sheriff, Let not her penance exceed the king's commission . ii 4 75
Madam, your penance done, throw off this sheet . . . . ii 4 105
They should find easy penance.—Faith, how easy?—As easy as a down-bed would afford it . . . . *Hen. VIII.* i 4 17
Gentlemen, The penance lies on you, if these fair ladies Pass away frowning . . . . i 4 32
All that stand about him are under the line, they need no other penance v 4 45
Pence. Where, for one shot of five pence, thou shalt have five thousand welcomes . . . . *T. G. of Ver.* ii 5 10
That cost me two shilling and two pence a-piece . . . *Mer. Wives* i 1 160
Didst not thou share? hadst thou not fifteen pence? . . . ii 2 14
If she say I am not fourteen pence on the score for sheer ale *T. of Shrew* Ind. 2 24
He will not pass his word for two pence that you are no fool *T. Night* i 5 87
I would not be in some of your coats for two pence . . . iv 1 33
Your face hath got five hundred pound a year, Yet sell your face for five pence and 'tis dear . . . . *K. John* i 1 153
What money is in my purse?—Seven groats and two pence *2 Hen. IV.* i 2 263
Hold, there is twelve pence for you; and I pray you to serve God *Hen. V.* iv 8 68
How tastes it? is it bitter? forty pence, no . . . *Hen. VIII.* ii 3 89
Pencil. Fair as a text B in a copy-book.—'Ware pencils, ho! . *L. L. Lost* v 2 43
They were besmear'd and overstain'd With slaughter's pencil *K. John* iii 1 237
The fisher with his pencil, and the painter with his nets *Rom. and Jul.* i 2 41
Pencilled. These pencill'd figures are Even such as they give out *T. of Athens* i 1 159
Pendent. With ribands pendent, flaring 'bout her head . *Mer. Wives* iv 6 42
Blown with restless violence round about The pendent world *M. for M.* iii 1 126
This bird Hath made his pendent bed and procreant cradle . *Macbeth* i 6 8
On the pendent boughs her coronet weeds Clambering to hang *Hamlet* iv 7 173
A tower'd citadel, a pendent rock, A forked mountain . *Ant. and Cleo.* iv 14 4
Pendragon. Stout Pendragon in his litter sick Came to the field and vanquished his foes . . . . *1 Hen. VI.* iii 2 95
Pendulous. All the plagues that in the pendulous air Hang fated o'er men's faults . . . . *Lear* iii 4 69
Penelope. You would be another Penelope: yet, they say, all the yarn she spun in Ulysses' absence did but fill Ithaca full of moths *Coriolanus* i 3 92
Penetrable. I am not made of stones, But penetrable to your kind entreats. . . . . *Richard III.* iii 7 225
Sit you down, And let me wring your heart; for so I shall, If it be made of penetrable stuff . . . . *Hamlet* iii 4 36
Penetrate. Thy groans Did make wolves howl and penetrate the breasts Of ever angry bears . . . . *Tempest* i 2 288
Sad sighs, deep groans, nor silver-shedding tears, Could penetrate her uncompassionate sire . . . . *T. G. of Ver.* iii 1 231
I am advised to give her music o' mornings; they say it will penetrate *Cymbeline* ii 3 14
If you can penetrate her with your fingering, so; we'll try with tongue too ii 3 15
If this penetrate, I will consider your music the better . . . ii 3 31
Penetrative. His face subdued To penetrative shame . *Ant. and Cleo.* iv 14 75
Penitence. By penitence the Eternal's wrath's appeased *T. G. of Ver.* v 4 81
Try your penitence, if it be sound, Or hollowly put on . *Meas. for Meas.* ii 3 22
Indeed, paid down More penitence than done trespass . . *W. Tale* v 1 4
Fear, and not love, begets his penitence: Forget to pity him *Richard II.* v 3 56
All that I can do is nothing worth, Since that my penitence comes after all, Imploring pardon . . . . *Hen. V.* iv 1 321
Repent in bootless penitence . . . . *3 Hen. VI.* ii 6 70
Penitent. They being penitent, The sole drift of my purpose doth extend Not a frown further . . . . *Tempest* v 1 28
Your hangman is a more penitent trade than your bawd *Meas. for Meas.* iv 2 53
Shave the head, and tie the beard; and say it was the desire of the penitent . . . . iv 2 188
So deep sticks it in my penitent heart That I crave death more willingly v 1 480
But we that know what 'tis to fast and pray Are penitent for your default to-day . . . . *Com. of Errors* i 2 52
Of enjoin'd penitents There's four or five . . . . *All's Well* iii 5 97
I from thee departed Thy penitent reform'd . . . . *W. Tale* i 2 239
The penitent king, my master, hath sent for me . . . . iv 2 7
Whose very naming punishes me with the remembrance of that penitent iv 2 25
What have we done? Didst ever hear a man so penitent? *2 Hen. VI.* iii 2 4
Call Warwick patron and be penitent . . . . . *3 Hen. VI.* v 1 27
Much it joys me too, To see you are become so penitent. *Richard III.* i 2 221
In faith, he's penitent; And yet his trespass, in our common reason—Save that they say, the wars must make examples Out of their best—is not almost a fault To incur a private check . . *Othello* iii 3 63
As nearly as I may, I'll play the penitent to you . *Ant. and Cleo.* ii 2 92
You good gods, give me The penitent instrument to pick that bolt! *Cymb.* v 4 10
Penitential. With bitter fasts, with penitential groans *T. G. of Ver.* ii 4 131
Penitently. Hath he borne himself penitently in prison? *Meas. for Meas.* iv 2 147
Penker. Go, Lovel, with all speed to Doctor Shaw; Go thou to Friar Penker . . . . *Richard III.* iii 5 104
Penknife. He presents no mark to the enemy; the foeman may with as great aim level at the edge of a penknife . . . *2 Hen. IV.* iii 2 286
Penned. Nor to their penn'd speech render we no grace *L. L. Lost* v 2 147
And to what end Their shallow shows and prologue vilely penn'd . v 2 305
O, never will I trust to speeches penn'd! . . . . . . v 2 402
It is excellently well penned, I have taken great pains to con it *T. Night* i 5 185
As sweet as ditties highly penn'd, Sung by a fair queen . *1 Hen. IV.* iii 1 209
Penning. Read thou this challenge; mark but the penning of it . *Lear* iv 6 142
Pennon. With pennons painted in the blood of Harfleur . *Hen. V.* iii 5 49
Penny. Ay, and her father is make her a petter penny . *Mer. Wives* i 1 62
I will not lend thee a penny.—Why, then the world's mine oyster . ii 2 1
Not a penny. I have been content, sir, you should lay my countenance to pawn . . . . ii 2 4
How hast thou purchased this experience?—By my penny of observation *L. L. Lost* iii 1 28
What's the price of this inkle?—One penny . . . . . iii 1 140
An I had but one penny in the world, thou shouldst have it to buy gingerbread . . . . v 1 74
When a man thanks me heartily, methinks I have given him a penny *As Y. Like It* ii 5 29
Nay, by Saint Jamy, I hold you a penny . . . *T. of Shrew* iii 2 85
You beg a single penny more: come, you shall ha't . *All's Well* v 2 39
What penny hath Rome borne, What men provided? . *K. John* v 2 97
I shall never hold that man my friend Whose tongue shall ask me for one penny cost . . . . *1 Hen. IV.* i 3 91
Lend me a thousand pound to furnish me forth?—Not a penny *2 Hen. IV.* i 2 252
A friend i' the court is better than a penny in purse . . . v 1 34
Nor ever had one penny bribe from France . . . *2 Hen. VI.* iii 1 109
There shall be in England seven halfpenny loaves sold for a penny iv 2 71
Take an inventory of all I have, To the last penny . *Hen. VIII.* iii 2 452
I will buy nine sparrows for a penny . . . . *Troi. and Cres.* ii 1 77
Here is for thy pains.—No, truly, sir; not a penny *Rom. and Jul.* ii 4 195
You shall hear The legions now in Gallia sooner landed . . . Than have tidings Of any penny tribute paid . . . . *Cymbeline* ii 4 20
Penny cord. Let not Bardolph's vital thread be cut With edge of penny cord and vile reproach . . . . *Hen. V.* iii 6 50
O, the charity of a penny cord! it sums up thousands in a trice *Cymb.* v 4 170
Pennyworth. We'll fit the kid-fox with a pennyworth . . *Much Ado* ii 3 45
Your pennyworth is good, an your goose be fat . . *L. L. Lost* iii 1 103
And swear that I have a poor pennyworth in the English *Mer. of Venice* i 2 77
Though the pennyworth on his side be the worst, yet hold thee, there's some boot . . . . *W. Tale* iv 4 650
I give thee this pennyworth of sugar . . . . . *1 Hen. IV.* ii 4 25
The sugar thou gavest me, 'twas a pennyworth, wast't not? . . ii 4 65
One poor pennyworth of sugar-candy to make thee long-winded . iii 3 180
Pirates may make cheap pennyworths of their pillage . *2 Hen. VI.* i 1 222
You take your pennyworths now; Sleep for a week . *Rom. and Jul.* iv 5 4
Pense. Les doigts? je pense qu'ils sont appelés de fingres . *Hen. V.* iii 4 10
Je pense que je suis le bon écolier; j'ai gagné deux mots d'Anglois vitement . . . . iii 4 13
Je pense que vous êtes gentilhomme de bonne qualité . . . iv 4 2
Je pense, le plus brave, vaillant, et très distingué seigneur d'Angleterre iv 4 59
Pension. I will not give my part of this sport for a pension of thousands to be paid from the Sophy . . . . *T. Night* ii 5 197
'Tis no matter if I do halt; I have the wars for my colour, and my pension shall seem the more reasonable . . . *2 Hen. IV.* i 2 276
And, squire-like, pension beg To keep base life afoot . . *Lear* ii 4 217
Pensioner. There has been earls, nay, which is more, pensioners *M. Wives* ii 2 79
The cowslips tall her pensioners be . . . . . *M. N. Dream* ii 1 10
Pensive. How like you our choice, That you stand pensive? *3 Hen. VI.* iv 1 10
My leisure serves me, pensive daughter, now . . *Rom. and Jul.* iv 1 39
Pent. Let me not be pent up, sir: I will fast, being loose . *L. L. Lost* i 2 160
And, in thy closet pent up, rue my shame . . . . *2 Hen. VI.* ii 4 24
Being pent from liberty, as I am now . . . . . *Richard III.* i 4 267
O, cut my lace in sunder, that my pent heart May have some scope to beat! . . . . iv 1 34

Pent. The son of Clarence have I pent up close . . *Richard III.* iv 3 36
Pent to linger But with a grain a day . . . *Coriolanus* iii 3 89
Pentapolis. This is called Pentapolis, and our king the good Simonides *Per.* ii 1 104
Brought hither to Pentapolis, Y-ravished the regions round . . iii Gower 34
Who, frighted from my country, did wed At Pentapolis the fair Thaisa v 3 4
When we with tears parted Pentapolis, The king my father gave you such a ring . . . . v 3 38
The fair-betrothed of your daughter Shall marry her at Pentapolis . v 3 72
Pentecost. At Pentecost, When all our pageants of delight were play'd *T. G. of Ver.* iv 4 163
Since Pentecost the sum is due . . . *Com. of Errors* iv 1 1
'Tis since the nuptial of Lucentio, Come Pentecost as quickly as it will, Some five and twenty years . . . *Rom. and Jul.* i 5 38
Penthesilea. Good night, Penthesilea.—Before me, she's a good wench *T. Night* ii 3 193
Pent-house. Stand thee close, then, under this pent-house . *Much Ado* iii 3 110
This is the pent-house under which Lorenzo Desired us to make stand *Mer. of Venice* ii 6 1
Sleep shall neither night nor day Hang upon his pent-house lid *Macbeth* i 3 20
Penthouse-like. With your hat penthouse-like o'er the shop of your eyes; with your arms crossed . . . *L. L. Lost* iii 1 17
Pent-up. So looks the pent-up lion o'er the wretch That trembles under his devouring paws . . . . . . *3 Hen. VI.* i 3 12
Close pent-up guilts, Rive your concealing continents . . *Lear* iii 2 57
Penurious. The want whereof doth daily make revolt In my penurious band . . . . *T. of Athens* iv 3 92
Penury. The weariest and most loathed worldly life That age, ache, penury and imprisonment Can lay on nature *Meas. for Meas.* iii 1 130
Shall I keep your hogs and eat husks with them? What prodigal portion have I spent, that I should come to such penury? *As Y. L. It* i 1 42
Knowing no burden of heavy tedious penury . . . . . iii 2 343
Then crushing penury Persuades me I was better when a king *Richard II.* v 5 34
Noting this penury, to myself I said, 'An if a man did need a poison now, Whose sale is present death in Mantua, Here lives a caitiff wretch would sell it him' . . . *Rom. and Jul.* v 1 49
The basest and most poorest shape That ever penury, in contempt of man, Brought near to beast . . . . . *Lear* ii 3 8
People. So dear the love my people bore me . . . *Tempest* i 2 141
All abundance, To feed my innocent people . . . . ii 1 164
I saw such islanders—For, certes, these are people of the island . iii 3 30
How beauteous mankind is! O brave new world, That has such people in't! . . . . v 1 184
I warrant thee, nobody hears; mine own people, mine own people *M. W.* ii 2 52
Who's at home besides yourself?—Why, none but mine own people . iv 2 14
The nature of our people, Our city's institutions . *Meas. for Meas.* i 1 10
I love the people, But do not like to stage me to their eyes . . i 1 68
Sith 'twas my fault to give the people scope, 'Twould be my tyranny to strike and gall them . . . . i 3 35
I will, as 'twere a brother of your order, Visit both prince and people . i 3 45
If these be good people in a commonweal that do nothing but use their abuses in common houses, I know no law . . . . . ii 1 42
Be quiet, people. Wherefore throng you hither? . . *Com. of Errors* v 1 38
Good people, enter and lay hold on him.—No, not a creature enters . v 1 91
These people saw the chain about his neck . . . . . v 1 258
And people sin upon purpose, because they would go thither *Much Ado* ii 1 266
Possess the people in Messina here How innocent she died . . v 1 290
Or pricket sore, or else sorel; the people fall a-hooting . *L. L. Lost* iv 2 61
And never rest, But seek the weary beds of people sick . . . v 2 832
Let none of your people stir me . . . . *M. N. Dream* iv 1 43
That thinks he hath done well in people's eyes, Hearing applause *M. of V.* iii 2 143
My people do already know my mind . . . . . . iii 4 37
You drop manna in the way Of starved people . . . . . v 1 295
Upon no other argument But that the people praise her . *As Y. Like It* i 2 292
Her very silence and her patience Speak to the people . . . i 3 81
Why do people love you? And wherefore are you gentle, strong and valiant? . . . . ii 3 5
And never cried 'Have patience, good people!' . . . . . iii 2 166
'Tis Hymen peoples every town . . . . v 4 149
Who of my people hold him in delay? . . . . *T. Night* i 5 112
Now you see, sir, how your fooling grows old, and people dislike it . i 5 119
Seven of my people, with an obedient start, make out for him . . ii 5 64
Belike you slew great number of his people . . . . . iii 3 29
Let some of my people have a special care of him . . . . iii 4 69
Are all the people mad? . . . . iv 1 29
Bade me . . . to frown Upon Sir Toby and the lighter people . . v 1 347
My people did expect my hence departure Two days ago . *W. Tale* i 2 450
This act so evilly born shall cool the hearts Of all his people . *K. John* iii 4 150
I find the people strangely fantasied; Possess'd with rumours . . iv 2 144
Our discontented counties do revolt; Our people quarrel with obedience v 1 9
Observed his courtship to the common people . . . *Richard II.* i 4 24
And these same thoughts people this little world, In humours like the people of this world . . . . v 5 10
Thus play I in one person many people, And none contented . . v 5 31
A thousand of his people butchered . . . . . *1 Hen. IV.* i 1 42
We love our people well; even those we love That are misled . . v 1 104
A rescue! a rescue!—Good people, bring a rescue or two . *2 Hen. IV.* ii 1 62
Didst thou not, when she was gone downstairs, desire me to be no more so familiarity with such poor people? . . . . . . ii 1 108
The people fear me; for they do observe Unfather'd heirs . . iv 4 121
You men of Harfleur, Take pity of your town and of your people *Hen. V.* iii 3 28
Let us quit all And give our vineyards to a barbarous people . . iii 5 4
Whiles a more frosty people Sweat drops of gallant youth in our rich fields . . . . iii 5 24
My people are with sickness much enfeebled . . . . . iii 6 154
For your expenses . . . , Among the people gather up a tenth *1 Hen. VI.* v 5 93
What! did my brother Henry spend his youth, His valour, coin and people, in the wars? . . . . *2 Hen. VI.* i 1 79
Be wise and circumspect. What though the common people favour him i 1 158
Have made thee fear'd and honour'd of the people . . . . i 1 198
Ill can thy noble mind abrook The abject people gazing on thy face . ii 4 11
And when I start, the envious people laugh And bid me be advised how I tread . . . . ii 4 35
God save your majesty!—I thank you, good people . . . iv 2 78
It is to you, good people, that I speak, Over whom, in time to come, I hope to reign . . . . iv 2 137
The rascal people, thirsting after prey, Join with the traitor . . iv 4 51
Sweet is the country, because full of riches; The people liberal, valiant iv 7 68
The common people swarm like summer flies . . . *3 Hen. VI.* ii 6 8
Our people and our peers are both misled, Our treasure seized . . iii 3 35
But is he gracious in the people's eye? . . . . . . iii 3 117
People. All hitherto goes well; The common people by numbers swarm to us . . . . *3 Hen. VI.* iv 2 2
Nor how to study for the people's welfare . . . . . . iv 3 39
And that the people of this blessed land May not be punish'd with my thwarting stars . . . . iv 6 21
Doth march amain to London; And many giddy people flock to him . iv 8 5
The people were not wont To be spoke to but by the recorder *Rich. III.* iii 7 29
As merry As, first, good company, good wine, good welcome, Can make good people . . . . *Hen. VIII.* i 4 7
All good people, You that thus far have come to pity me, Hear what I say ii 1 55
Opposing freely The beauty of her person to the people . . . iv 1 68
Which when the people Had the full view of, such a noise arose . iv 1 70
Pray'd devoutly. Then rose again and bow'd her to the people . . iv 1 85
As you wish Christian peace to souls departed, Stand these poor people's friend, and urge the king . . . . iv 2 157
Hark! do you not hear the people cry 'Troilus'? *Troi. and Cres.* i 2 244
First, you know Caius Marcius is chief enemy to the people . *Coriolanus* i 1 8
Worthy Menenius Agrippa; one that hath always loved the people . i 1 53
When we were chosen tribunes for the people,—Mark'd you his lip and eyes? . . . . i 1 258
The dearth is great; The people mutinous . . . . . i 2 11
We shall have news to-night.—Good or bad?—Not according to the prayer of the people . . . . ii 1 4
There will be large cicatrices to show the people . . . . ii 1 164
Nor, showing, as the manner is, his wounds To the people . . . ii 1 252
We must suggest the people in what hatred He still hath held them . ii 1 261
At some time when his soaring insolence Shall touch the people . . ii 1 271
He's vengeance proud, and loves not the common people . . . ii 2 7
Many great men that have flattered the people, who ne'er loved them . ii 2 9
Now, to seem to affect the malice and displeasure of the people is as bad as that which he dislikes, to flatter them for their love . . . ii 2 25
Having been supple and courteous to the people . . . . . ii 2 30
Masters o' the people, We do request your kindest ears . . . . ii 2 55
We shall be blest to do, if he remember A kinder value of the people . ii 2 63
He loves your people; But tie him not to be their bedfellow . . ii 2 68
But your people, I love them as they weigh . . . . . ii 2 77
Masters of the people, Your multiplying spawn how can he flatter? . ii 2 81
It then remains That you do speak to the people . . . . ii 2 139
The people Must have their voices; neither will they bate One jot of ceremony . . . . ii 2 143
A part That I shall blush in acting, and might well Be taken from the people . . . . ii 2 150
We recommend to you, tribunes of the people, Our purpose to them . ii 2 155
You see how he intends to use the people.—May they perceive's intent! ii 2 159
If he would incline to the people, there was never a worthier man . ii 3 42
You have not indeed loved the common people . . . . . ii 3 99
I will, sir, flatter my sworn brother, the people, to earn a dearer estimation ii 3 102
The gods give him joy, and make him good friend to the people! . ii 3 143
The tribunes Endue you with the people's voice . . . . . ii 3 147
The people do admit you, and are summon'd To meet anon . . . ii 3 151
Will you along?—We stay here for the people . . . . . ii 3 158
Will you dismiss the people? . . . . ii 3 162
[Censorinus,] nobly named so, Twice being [by the people chosen] censor ii 3 252
To the Capitol, come: We will be there before the stream o' the people ii 3 269
These are the tribunes of the people, The tongues o' the common mouth iii 1 21
The people are incensed against him.—Stop, Or all will fall in broil . iii 1 32
The people cry you mock'd them, and of late, When corn was given them gratis, you repined . . . . iii 1 42
Scandal'd the suppliants for the people, call'd them Time-pleasers . iii 1 44
You show too much of that For which the people stir . . . iii 1 53
The people are abused; set on. This paltering Becomes not Rome . iii 1 58
You speak o' the people, As if you were a god to punish, not A man of their infirmity . . . . iii 1 80
'Twere well We let the people know't . . . . . . iii 1 83
Though there the people had more absolute power . . . . iii 1 116
Why, shall the people give One that speaks thus their voice? . . iii 1 118
What should the people do with these bald tribunes? . . . . iii 1 165
Call the people: in whose name myself Attach thee as a traitorous innovator . . . . iii 1 174
Hear me, people; peace!—Let's hear our tribune: peace! Speak . iii 1 192
What is the city but the people?—True, The people are the city . iii 1 199
By the consent of all, we were establish'd The people's magistrates . iii 1 202
We do here pronounce, Upon the part o' the people, in whose power We were elected theirs, Marcius is worthy Of present death . . iii 1 210
The noble tribunes are the people's mouths, And we their hands . . iii 1 271
If, by the tribunes' leave, and yours, good people, I may be heard . iii 1 282
Be you then as the people's officer. Masters, lay down your weapons . iii 1 330
Because that now it lies you on to speak To the people . . . iii 2 53
If he evade us there, Enforce him with his envy to the people . . iii 3 3
Assemble presently the people hither . . . . . . iii 3 12
Draw near, ye people.—List to your tribunes. Audience! peace, I say! iii 3 39
I do demand, If you submit you to the people's voices, Allow their officers? iii 3 44
For which you are a traitor to the people.—How! traitor! . . . iii 3 66
The fires i' the lowest hell fold-in the people! Call me their traitor! . iii 3 68
Mark you this, people!—To the rock, to the rock with him! . . iii 3 74
He has, As much as in him lies, from time to time Envied against the people . . . . iii 3 95
In the name o' the people And in the power of us the tribunes . . iii 3 99
Never more To enter our Rome gates: i' the people's name, I say it shall be so . . . . iii 3 104
He is banish'd, As enemy to the people and his country . . . iii 3 118
The people's enemy is gone, is gone!—Our enemy is banish'd! . . iii 3 136
The people against the senators, patricians, and nobles . . . iv 3 14
They are in a ripe aptness to take all power from the people . . iv 3 24
The cruelty and envy of the people, Permitted by our dastard nobles . iv 5 80
His remedies are tame i' the present peace And quietness of the people iv 6 3
Go whip him 'fore the people's eyes:—his raising; Nothing but his report iv 6 60
The people Deserve such pity of him as the wolf Does of the shepherds iv 6 109
Their people Will be as rash in the repeal, as hasty To expel him thence iv 7 31
Intends to appear before the people, hoping To purge himself with words v 6 7
We must proceed as we do find the people.—The people will remain uncertain . . . . v 6 16
Ere he express himself, or move the people With what he would say, let him feel your sword . . . . v 6 55
The people of Rome, for whom we stand A special party . *T. Andron.* i 1 20
And to my fortunes and the people's favour Commit my cause . . i 1 54
The people of Rome, Whose friend in justice thou hast ever been . . i 1 179
Would thou wert shipp'd to hell, Rather than rob me of the people's hearts! . . . . i 1 207
I will restore to thee The people's hearts, and wean them from themselves i 1 211

People. People of Rome, and people's tribunes here, I ask your voices *T. Andron.* i 1 217
The people will accept whom he admits . . . . . i 1 222
Lest, then, the people, and patricians too, Upon a just survey, take Titus' part . . . . i 1 445
You heavy people, circle me about, That I may turn me to each one of you iii 1 277
I made thee miserable What time I threw the people's suffrages On him iv 3 19
However these disturbers of our peace Buz in the people's ears . iv 4 7
'Tis he the common people love so much . . . . . iv 4 73
You sad-faced men, people and sons of Rome, By uproar sever'd . v 3 67
Gentle people, give me aim awhile, For nature puts me to a heavy task v 3 149
The people in the street cry Romeo, Some Juliet *Rom. and Jul.* v 3 191
The senators of Athens, together with the common lag of people *T. of A.* iii 6 91
But in the plainer and simpler kind of people, the deed of saying is quite out of use . . . . v 1 27
I do fear, the people Choose Cæsar for their king . *J. Cæsar* i 2 79
And then the people fell a-shouting . . . . . i 2 222
If the tag-rag people did not clap him and hiss him . . . i 2 261
O, he sits high in all the people's hearts . . . . i 3 157
People and senators, be not affrighted ; Fly not ; stand still . . iii 1 82
Lest that the people, Rushing on us, should do your age some mischief iii 1 92
Know you how much the people may be moved By that which he will utter? . . . . iii 1 234
There shall I try, In my oration, how the people take the cruel issue . iii 1 293
Belike they had some notice of the people, How I had moved them . iii 2 275
The people 'twixt Philippi and this ground Do stand but in a forced affection . . . . iv 3 204
We cut him off, If at Philippi we do face him there, These people at our back . . . . iv 3 212
The Norweyan banners flout the sky And fan our people cold *Macbeth* i 2 50
I have bought Golden opinions from all sorts of people . . i 7 33
Strangely-visited people, All swoln and ulcerous, pitiful to the eye . iv 3 150
The castle's gently render'd : The tyrant's people on both sides do fight v 7 25
The people muddied, Thick and unwholesome in their thoughts *Hamlet* iv 5 81
You strike my people . . . . . . *Lear* i 4 277
Go, go, my people.—My lord, I am guiltless, as I am ignorant . i 4 294
How, in one house, Should many people, under two commands, Hold amity? . . . . ii 4 244
This house is little : the old man and his people Cannot be well bestow'd ii 4 291
Who is conductor of his people?—As 'tis said, the bastard son of Gloucester . . . . iv 7 88
Strike on the tinder, ho! Give me a taper! call up all my people! *Oth.* i 1 142
The town is empty ; on the brow o' the sea Stand ranks of people . ii 1 54
In a town of war, Yet wild, the people's hearts brimful of fear . ii 3 214
She was a charmer, and could almost read The thoughts of people . iii 4 58
We'll wander through the streets and note The qualities of people *Ant. and Cleo.* i 1 54
Dear goddess, hear that prayer of the people . . . . i 2 74
Our slippery people, Whose love is never link'd to the deserver Till his deserts are past . . . . i 2 192
The people love me, and the sea is mine ; My powers are crescent . ii 1 9
The city cast Her people out upon her ; and Antony, Enthroned i' the market-place, did sit alone . . . . ii 2 219
The people know it ; and have now received His accusations . iii 6 22
Your mariners are muleters, reapers, people Ingross'd by swift impress iii 7 36
The worm is not to be trusted but in the keeping of wise people . v 2 267
They are people such That mend upon the world . *Cymbeline* ii 4 25
For which the people's prayers still fall upon you . *Pericles* iii 3 19
How dost thou find the inclination of the people, especially of the younger? . . . . iv 2 104
Before the people all, Reveal how thou at sea didst lose thy wife . v 1 244
Peopled. I had peopled else This isle with Calibans. *Tempest* i 2 350
This shadowy desert, unfrequented woods, I better brook than flourishing peopled towns . . . . . . *T. G. of Ver.* v 4 3
No, the world must be peopled . . . . *Much Ado* ii 3 251
Be a wilderness again, Peopled with wolves, thy old inhabitants! *2 Hen. IV.* iv 5 138
So work the honey-bees, Creatures that by a rule in nature teach The act of order to a peopled kingdom . . . . . *Hen. V.* i 2 189
Pepin. A man when King Pepin of France was a little boy . *L. L. Lost* iv 1 122
Whose simple touch Is powerful to araise King Pepin . *All's Well* ii 1 79
King Pepin, which deposed Childeric, Did . . . Make claim and title to the crown of France . . . . . . *Hen. V.* i 2 65
King Pepin's title and Hugh Capet's claim, King Lewis his satisfaction, all appear To hold in right and title of the female . . . i 2 87
Their very noses had been counsellors To Pepin or Clotharius *Hen. VIII.* i 3 10
Pepper. I warrant there's vinegar and pepper in't . *T. Night* iii 4 158
Pepper-box. 'Tis impossible he should ; he cannot creep into a halfpenny purse, nor into a pepper-box . . . . *Mer. Wives* iii 5 149
Peppercorn. An I have not forgotten what the inside of a church is made of, I am a peppercorn . . . . . *1 Hen. IV.* iii 3 9
Peppered. I have peppered two of them ; two I am sure I have paid . ii 4 212
I have led my ragamuffins where they are peppered . . . v 3 37
I am peppered, I warrant, for this world . . *Rom. and Jul.* iii 1 102
Pepper-gingerbread. And leave 'in sooth,' And such protest of pepper-gingerbread . . . . *1 Hen. IV.* iii 1 260
Peradventure. Which peradventure prings goot discretions with it *Mer. W.* i 1 44
That peradventures shall tell you another tale . . . . i 1 78
If peradventure he shall ever return to have hearing of this *M. for M.* iii 1 209
He tells me that, if peradventure He speak against me on the adverse side, I should not think it strange . . . . . . iv 6 5
The better prepared for an answer, if peradventure this be true *Much Ado* i 2 24
Which, peradventure not marked or not laughed at, strikes him into melancholy . . . . ii 1 153
Peradventure, to make it the more gracious, I shall sing it *M. N. Dream* iv 1 224
Peradventure this is not Fortune's work neither, but Nature's *As Y. L. It* i 2 54
The king Yet speaks and peradventure may recover . *K. John* v 6 31
Peradventure I will with ye to the court . . *2 Hen. IV.* iii 2 315
Peradventure I shall think you do not use me with that affability as in discretion you ought to use me . . . . *Hen. V.* iii 2 137
Some peradventure have on them the guilt of premeditated and contrived murder . . . . iv 1 170
More good toward you peradventure than is in your knowledge to dream of iv 8 4
Peradventure some of the best of 'em were hereditary hangmen *Coriol.* ii 1 102
If thou wert the fox, the lion would suspect thee, when peradventure thou wert accused by the ass . . . . *T. of Athens* iv 3 333
Though peradventure I stand accountant for as great a sin . *Othello* ii 1 301
Perceive. I perceive, these lords At this encounter do so much admire That they devour their reason . . . . . . *Tempest* v 1 153
Well, I perceive I must be fain to bear with you . . *T. G. of Ver.* i 1 127
Perceive. Why, couldst thou perceive so much from her?—Sir, I could perceive nothing at all from her ; no, not so much as a ducat *T. G. of Ver.* i 1 142
That thou mayst perceive how well I like it . . . . i 3 35
Do you not perceive the jest?—No, believe me . . . ii 1 159
But did you perceive her earnest?—She gave me none . . ii 1 163
And, that thou mayst perceive my fear of this . . . iii 1 33
I perceive you delight not in music.—Not a whit, when it jars so. . iv 2 66
Read, read ; perceive how I might be knighted *Mer. Wives* ii 1 55
Ha, do I perceive dat? have you make-a de sot of us? . . . iii 1 118
I do begin to perceive that I am made an ass . . . . v 5 124
He will relent ; He's coming ; I perceive't . . *Meas. for Meas.* ii 2 125
I do perceive These poor informal women are no more But instruments of some more mightier member . . . . v 1 235
I perceive your grace, like power divine, Hath look'd upon my passes . v 1 374
By this Lord Angelo perceives he's safe . . . . . v 1 499
Did he tempt thee so? Mightst thou perceive austerely in his eye That he did plead in earnest? . . . . . *Com. of Errors* iv 2 2
They say I will bear myself proudly, if I perceive the love come from her *Much Ado* ii 3 234
Then I well perceive you are not nigh . . *M. N. Dream* ii 2 155
Now I perceive they have conjoin'd all three To fashion this false sport iii 2 193
I perceive A weak bond holds you . . . . . iii 2 267
Now I perceive that she hath made compare Between our statures . iii 2 290
You shall perceive them make a mutual stand *Mer. of Venice* v 1 77
And then they perceive not how Time moves . . *As Y. Like It* iii 2 350
I charge you, O men, for the love you bear to women—as I perceive by your simpering, none of you hates them . . . . Epil. 16
Now I well perceive You have but jested with me all this while *T. of S.* ii 1 19
Now I perceive thou art a reverend father ; Pardon, I pray thee . iv 5 48
I perceive, by this demand, you are not altogether of his council *All's W.* iv 3 52
I perceive, sir, by the general's looks, we shall be fain to hang you . iv 3 268
That you may well perceive I have not wrong'd you, One of the greatest in the Christian world Shall be my surety . . . . . iv 4 1
But I perceive in you so excellent a touch of modesty *T. Night* ii 1 12
If 'twere so, She could not sway her house . . With such a smooth, discreet and stable bearing As I perceive she does . . . iv 3 20
By that I do perceive it hath offended you : Pardon me, sweet one . v 1 220
I am angling now, Though you perceive me not how I give line *W. Tale* i 2 181
He would not stay at your petitions ; made His business more material.—Didst perceive it? . . . . i 2 216
He shall not perceive But that you have your father's bosom there . iv 4 573
You perceive she stirs : Start not ; her actions shall be holy . . v 3 103
And well shall you perceive how willingly I will both hear and grant you your requests . . . . . . *K. John* iv 2 45
Woe doth the heavier sit, Where it perceives it is but faintly borne *Richard II.* i 3 281
When he perceives the envious clouds are bent To dim his glory . iii 3 65
Now I perceive the devil understands Welsh . *1 Hen. IV.* iii 1 233
Then you perceive the body of our kingdom How foul it is *2 Hen. IV.* iii 1 38
Chide him for faults, and do it reverently, When you perceive his blood inclined to mirth . . . . iv 4 38
For God doth know, so shall the world perceive . . . . v 5 61
I will be the man yet that shall make you great.—I cannot well perceive how . . . . v 5 86
I do perceive he is not the man that he would gladly make show to the world he is . . . . *Hen. V.* iii 6 87
If any noise or soldier you perceive . . . , Let us have knowledge *1 Hen. VI.* ii 1 2
You perceive my mind?—I do, my lord, and mean accordingly . ii 2 59
Your honours shall perceive how I will work . . . . iii 2 27
By the sound of drum you may perceive Their powers are marching . iii 3 29
Let him perceive how ill we brook his treason . . . . iv 1 74
A fickle wavering nation : If they perceive dissension in our looks . iv 1 139
I perceive that will be verified Henry the Fifth did sometime prophesy v 1 30
Thou shalt well perceive That, neither in birth or for authority, The bishop will be overborne by thee . . . . v 1 58
What ransom must I pay before I pass? For I perceive I am thy prisoner v 3 74
By his death we do perceive his guilt . . *2 Hen. VI.* iii 3 104
By this I shall perceive the commons' mind . . . . iii 1 374
But now you partly may perceive my mind . . *3 Hen. VI.* iii 2 66
My mind will never grant what I perceive Your highness aims at . iii 2 67
What shall we do, if we perceive Lord Hastings will not yield? *Rich. III.* iii 1 191
What of his heart perceive you in his face By any likelihood he show'd to-day? . . . . iii 4 56
When they once perceive The least rub in your fortunes, fall away Like water from ye . . . . *Hen. VIII.* ii 1 128
That you may, fair lady, Perceive I speak sincerely . . . ii 3 9
I may perceive These cardinals trifle with me . . . . ii 4 235
'I do,' quoth he, 'perceive My king is tangled in affection' . . iii 2 34
The king in this perceives him, how he coasts And hedges his own way iii 2 38
Lest Hector or my father should perceive me, I have . . . Buried this sigh in wrinkle of a smile . . . . . *Troi. and Cres.* i 1 36
A maiden battle, then? O, I perceive you . . . . iv 5 87
When my face is fair, you shall perceive Whether I blush or no *Coriolanus* i 9 69
You see how he intends to use the people.—May they perceive's intent! ii 2 160
Did you perceive He did solicit you in free contempt? . . . ii 3 207
You shall perceive that a Jack guardant cannot office me from my son v 2 67
Full well shalt thou perceive how much I dare . *T. Andron.* ii 1 44
Dost thou not perceive That Rome is but a wilderness of tigers? . iii 1 53
You shall perceive how you Mistake my fortunes . *T. of Athens* ii 2 192
But, I perceive, Men must learn now with pity to dispense . . iii 2 92
I perceive our masters may throw their caps at their money . . iii 4 101
I'll about, And drive away the vulgar from the streets : So do you too, where you perceive them thick . . . . . *J. Cæsar* i 1 76
O, now you weep ; and, I perceive, you feel The dint of pity . . iii 2 197
Before the eyes of both our armies here, Which should perceive nothing but love from us, Let us not wrangle . . . . . iv 2 44
I perceive But cold demeanour in Octavius' wing . . . . v 2 3
Are those my tents where I perceive the fire?—They are, my lord . v 3 13
I have two nights watched with you, but can perceive no truth in your report. When was it she last walked? . . . . *Macbeth* v 1 2
I'll take the ghost's word for a thousand pound. Didst perceive? *Hamlet* iii 2 298
I now perceive, it was not altogether your brother's evil disposition *Lear* iii 5 6
Read thine own evil : No tearing, lady ; I perceive you know it . v 3 157
Do you perceive in all this noble company Where most you owe obedience?—My noble father, I do perceive here a divided duty *Othello* i 3 179
If more thou dost perceive, let me know more : Set on thy wife to observe iii 3 239
Hold him off awhile, You shall by that perceive him and his means . iii 3 249
Did you perceive how he laughed at his vice? . . . . iv 1 180
Look you pale, mistress? Do you perceive the gastness of her eye? . v 1 106

Perceive. For, I perceive, Four feasts are toward *Ant. and Cleo.* ii 6 74
He's very knowing; I do perceive't iii 3 27
Consider, When you above perceive me like a crow, That it is place which lessens and sets off *Cymbeline* iii 3 12
I perceive he was a wise fellow, and had good discretion *Pericles* i 3 4
Perceived. Are all these things perceived in me?—They are all perceived without ye *T. G. of Ver.* ii 1 34
The changes I perceived in the king and Camillo were very notes *W. Tale* v 2 11
When the lords and barons of the realm Perceived Northumberland did lean to him *1 Hen. IV.* iv 3 67
Whom I have weekly sworn to marry since I perceived the first white hair on my chin *2 Hen. IV.* i 2 270
Save that there was not time enough to hear, As I perceived his grace would fain have done *Hen. V.* i 1 85
When he perceived me shrink and on my knee, His bloody sword he brandish'd over me *1 Hen. VI.* iv 7 5
When he perceived the common herd was glad he refused the crown *J. C.* i 2 266
I perceived it, I must tell you that, Before my daughter told me *Hamlet* ii 2 133
I have perceived a most faint neglect of late *Lear* i 4 73
Whose welcome, I perceived, had poison'd mine ii 4 39
That my charity be not of him perceived: if he ask for me, I am ill iii 3 17
We perceived, both how you were wrong led *Ant. and Cleo.* iii 6 80
When I did push thee back—Which was when I perceived thee *Pericles* v 1 128
Perceiveth our natural wits too dull to reason *As Y. Like It* i 2 55
Perch. Till custom make it Their perch and not their terror *Meas. for Meas.* ii 1 4
That wrens make prey where eagles dare not perch *Richard III.* i 3 71
By many a dern and painful perch Of Pericles the careful search *Per.* iii Gower 15
Perchance he will not mind me *Tempest* ii 2 17
Perchance you think too much of so much pains?—No, madam *T. G. of V.* ii 1 118
Letters of strange tenour; perchance of the duke's death; perchance entering into some monastery; but, by chance, nothing of what is writ *Meas. for Meas.* iv 2 216
Perchance, publicly, she'll be ashamed v 1 277
Perchance you will not bear them patiently *Com. of Errors* i 2 86
Perchance I will be there as soon as you iv 1 39
You may think perchance that I think you are in love *Much Ado* iii 4 81
An you saw her in the light.—Perchance light in the light *L. L. Lost* v 2 199
Perchance till after Theseus' wedding day *M. N. Dream* ii 1 139
Perchance you wonder at this show; But wonder on v 1 128
Ladies, you . . . May now perchance both quake and tremble here v 1 224
If they but hear perchance a trumpet sound, Or any air of music *M. of V.* v 1 75
Why is he melancholy?—Perchance he's hurt i' the battle *All's Well* iii 5 90
Perchance he is not drown'd: what think you, sailors?—It is perchance that you yourself were saved.—O my poor brother! and so perchance may he be *T. Night* i 2 5
Let him send no more; Unless, perchance, you come to me again i 5 300
I frown the while; and perchance wind up my watch ii 5 66
Lower messes Perchance are to this business purblind *W. Tale* i 2 228
The want of which vain dew Perchance shall dry your pities ii 1 110
Nay, it perchance will sparkle in your eyes *K. John* iv 1 115
To know the meaning Of dangerous majesty, when perchance it frowns iv 2 213
Perchance the cardinal cannot make your peace v 1 74
Show our foulest wares, And think, perchance, they'll sell *Troi. and Cres.* i 3 360
Lest perchance he think We dare not move the question of our place ii 3 88
Perchance, my lord, I show more craft than love iii 2 160
Perchance she weeps because they kill'd her husband; Perchance because she knows them innocent *T. Andron.* iii 1 114
Perchance she cannot meet him: that's not so *Rom. and Jul.* ii 5 3
Perchance some single vantages you took *T. of Athens* ii 2 138
What you have spoke, it may be so perchance *Macbeth* iv 3 11
I have lost my hopes.—Perchance even there where I did find my doubts iv 3 25
I will watch to-night; Perchance 'twill walk again *Hamlet* i 2 243
As I perchance hereafter shall think meet To put an antic disposition on i 5 171
Or perchance, 'I saw him enter such a house of sale' ii 1 59
To die, to sleep; To sleep: perchance to dream: ay, there's the rub iii 1 65
Then what I have to do Will want true colour; tears perchance for blood iii 4 130
His countenance likes me not.—No more, perchance, does mine *Lear* ii 2 97
If, sir, perchance She have restrain'd the riots of your followers ii 4 144
Something deeper, Whereof perchance these are but furnishings iii 1 29
This speech of yours hath moved me, And shall perchance do good v 3 200
Though I perchance am vicious in my guess *Othello* iii 3 145
'Tis proper I obey him, but not now. Perchance, Iago, I will ne'er go home v 2 197
Nay, hear them, Antony: Fulvia perchance is angry *Ant. and Cleo.* i 1 20
Perchance! nay, and most like: You must not stay here longer i 1 25
Perchance to-morrow You'll serve another master iv 2 27
Which first, perchance, she'll prove on cats and dogs *Cymbeline* i 5 38
Perchance he spoke not, but, Like a full-acorn'd boar, a German one, Cried 'O!' and mounted ii 5 15
Perched. Two mighty eagles fell, and there they perch'd *J. Cæsar* v 1 81
Percies. The Percies of the north, Finding his usurpation most unjust, Endeavour'd my advancement to the throne *1 Hen. VI.* ii 5 67
Percussion. With thy grim looks and The thunder-like percussion of thy sounds, Thou madest thine enemies shake *Coriolanus* i 4 59
Percy. The Lord Northumberland, his son young Henry Percy *Richard II.* ii 2 53
It is my son, young Harry Percy, Sent from my brother Worcester ii 3 21
I tender you my service, Such as it is . . .—I thank thee, gentle Percy ii 3 45
We thank thee, gentle Percy, for thy pains v 6 11
The gallant Hotspur there, Young Harry Percy *1 Hen. IV.* i 1 53
O that it could be proved That some night-tripping fairy had exchanged In cradle-clothes our children where they lay, And call'd mine Percy! i 1 89
What think you, coz, Of this young Percy's pride? i 1 92
Those prisoners in your highness' name demanded, Which Harry Percy here at Holmedon took i 3 24
Whate'er Lord Harry Percy then had said To such a person i 3 71
Thou dost belie him, Percy, thou dost belie him i 3 113
'Gentle Harry Percy,' and 'kind cousin'; O, the devil take such cozeners! i 3 254
I know you wise, but yet no farther wise Than Harry Percy's wife ii 3 111
I am not yet of Percy's mind, the Hotspur of the north ii 4 114
I'll play Percy, and that damned brawn shall play Dame Mortimer his wife ii 4 123
That same mad fellow of the north, Percy, and he of Wales ii 4 369
That fiend Douglas, that spirit Percy, and that devil Glendower ii 4 405
Sit, cousin Percy; sit, good cousin Hotspur, For by that name as oft as Lancaster Doth speak of you, his cheek looks pale iii 1 7
Peace, cousin Percy; you will make him mad iii 1 51
To-morrow, cousin Percy, you and I And my good Lord of Worcester will set forth To meet your father iii 1 83
Fie, cousin Percy! how you cross my father!—I cannot choose iii 1 147
She and my aunt Percy Shall follow in your conduct speedily iii 1 196
Percy. You are as slow As hot Lord Percy is on fire to go *1 Hen. IV.* iii 1 269
And even as I was then is Percy now iii 2 96
Percy, Northumberland, The Archbishop's grace of York, Douglas, Mortimer, Capitulate against us and are up iii 2 118
To fight against me under Percy's pay, To dog his heels iii 2 126
I will redeem all this on Percy's head iii 2 132
Percy is but my factor, good my lord, To engross up glorious deeds iii 2 147
Percy stands on high; And either we or they must lower lie iii 3 227
Percy is already in the field.—What, is the king encamped? iv 2 81
I fear the power of Percy is too weak To wage an instant trial with the king iv 4 19
Mortimer is not there.—But there is Mordake, Vernon, Lord Harry Percy iv 4 24
If Lord Percy thrive not, ere the king Dismiss his power, he means to visit us iv 4 36
The Prince of Wales doth join with all the world In praise of Henry Percy v 1 87
Now, Esperance! Percy! and set on. Sound all the lofty instruments of war v 2 97
I have paid Percy, I have made him sure v 3 48
If Percy be alive, thou get'st not my sword v 3 51
Well, if Percy be alive, I'll pierce him. If he do come in my way, so v 3 59
I saw him hold Lord Percy at the point With lustier maintenance v 4 21
I have two boys Seek Percy and thyself about the field v 4 32
Thou speak'st as if I would deny my name.—My name is Harry Percy v 4 61
I am the Prince of Wales; and think not, Percy, To share with me in glory any more v 4 63
Nor can one England brook a double reign, Of Harry Percy and the Prince of Wales v 4 67
No, Percy, thou art dust, And food for—For worms, brave Percy v 4 85
Till then in blood by noble Percy lie v 4 110
I am afraid of this gunpowder Percy, though he be dead v 4 124
There is Percy: if your father will do me any honour, so; if not, let him kill the next Percy himself v 4 143
Why, Percy I killed myself and saw thee dead v 4 147
The noble Percy slain, and all his men Upon the foot of fear v 5 19
He told me that rebellion had bad luck And that young Harry Percy's spur was cold *2 Hen. IV.* i 1 42
Said he young Harry Percy's spur was cold? Of Hotspur Coldspur? i 1 49
But Priam found the fire ere he his tongue, And I my Percy's death ere thou report'st it i 1 75
Yet, for all this, say not that Percy's dead i 1 93
Whose swift wrath beat down The never-daunted Percy to the earth i 1 110
Put not you on the visage of the times And be like them to Percy troublesome ii 3 4
When your own Percy, when my heart's dear Harry, Threw many a northward look to see his father ii 3 12
It is but eight years since This Percy was the man nearest my soul iii 1 61
Perdie, your doors were lock'd and you shut out *Com. of Errors* iv 4 74
Perdita. And, for the babe Is counted lost for ever, Perdita, I prithee, call't *W. Tale* iii 3 33
And with speed so pace To speak of Perdita, now grown in grace iv 1 24
Thou dearest Perdita, With these forced thoughts, I prithee, darken not The mirth o' the feast iv 4 40
Your hand, my Perdita: so turtles pair, That never mean to part iv 4 154
Hark, Perdita. I'll hear you by and by iv 4 517
My prettiest Perdita! But O, the thorns we stand upon! iv 4 595
O Perdita, what have we twain forgot! Pray you, a word iv 4 674
Turn, good lady; Our Perdita is found v 3 121
Perdition. Not so much perdition as an hair Betid to any *Tempest* i 2 30
Lingering perdition, worse than any death Can be at once iii 3 77
This shall end without the perdition of souls *T. Night* iii 4 318
Condemn them to her service Or to their own perdition *W. Tale* iv 4 389
The perdition of th' athversary hath been very great, reasonable great *Hen. V.* iii 6 103
Bi-fold authority! where reason can revolt Without perdition *T. and C.* v 2 145
His definement suffers no perdition in you *Hamlet* v 2 117
Upon certain tidings now arrived, importing the mere perdition of the Turkish fleet *Othello* ii 2 3
Perdition catch my soul, But I do love thee! iii 3 90
To lose't or give't away were such perdition As nothing else could match iii 4 67
Perdona-mi. These fashion-mongers, these perdona-mi's, who stand so much on the new form *Rom. and Jul.* ii 4 35
Perdonato. Mi perdonato, gentle master mine *T. of Shrew* i 1 25
Perdu. O seigneur! le jour est perdu, tout est perdu! *Hen. V.* iv 5 2
To watch—poor perdu!—With this thin helm? *Lear* iv 7 35
Perdurable. O perdurable shame! let's stab ourselves *Hen. V.* iv 5 7
Knit to thy deserving with cables of perdurable toughness *Othello* i 3 343
Perdurably. If it were damnable, he being so wise, Why would he for the momentary trick Be perdurably fined? *Meas. for Meas.* iii 1 115
Perdy. My lady is unkind, perdy *T. Night* iv 2 81
In thy throat, And in thy hateful lungs, yea, in thy maw, perdy *Hen. V.* ii 1 52
If the king like not the comedy, Why then, belike, he likes it not, perdy *Hamlet* iii 2 305
The knave turns fool that runs away; The fool no knave, perdy *Lear* ii 4 86
Pere. Dat is as it sall please de roi mon père *Hen. V.* v 2 267
Peregrinate. Too affected, too odd, as it were, too peregrinate *L. L. Lost* v 1 15
Peremptorily I speak it *1 Hen. IV.* ii 4 472
Peremptory. Excuse it not, for I am peremptory *T. G. of Ver.* i 3 71
What peremptory eagle-sighted eye Dares look upon the heaven of her brow, That is not blinded? *L. L. Lost* iv 3 226
His humour is lofty, his discourse peremptory, his tongue filed v 1 11
I am as peremptory as she proud-minded *T. of Shrew* ii 1 132
No, not Death himself In mortal fury half so peremptory *K. John* ii 1 454
Your presence is too bold and peremptory *1 Hen. IV.* i 3 17
We will suddenly Pass our accept and peremptory answer *Hen. V.* v 2 82
What, cardinal, is your priesthood grown peremptory? *2 Hen. VI.* ii 1 23
How insolent of late he is become, How proud, how peremptory! iii 1 8
Towards Coventry bend we our course, Where peremptory Warwick now remains *3 Hen. VI.* iv 8 59
With his peremptory 'shall' *Coriolanus* iii 1 94
We are peremptory to dispatch This viperous traitor iii 1 286
Are you so peremptory? I am glad on't with all my heart *Pericles* ii 5 73
Perfect. But you, O you, So perfect and so peerless, are created Of every creature's best! *Tempest* iii 1 47
O heaven! were man But constant, he were perfect *T. G. of Ver.* v 4 111
Her cause and yours I'll perfect him withal *Meas. for Meas.* iv 3 146
When you have A business for yourself, pray heaven you then Be perfect v 1 82
'Tis not so much worth; but I hope I was perfect *L. L. Lost* v 2 562
Take pains; be perfect *M. N. Dream* i 2 112
O Helen, goddess, nymph, perfect, divine! iii 2 137
So holy and so perfect is my love *As Y. Like It* iii 5 99

Perfect. Ere I can perfect mine intents . . . . . . *All's Well* iv 4 4
Thou art perfect then, our ship hath touch'd upon The deserts of Bohemia?—Ay, my lord . . . *W. Tale* iii 3 1
I'll show thee a precedent.—Francis!—Thou art perfect . 1 *Hen. IV.* ii 4 39
That pretty Welsh Which thou pour'st down from these swelling heavens I am too perfect in . . . . iii 1 203
Thou art perfect in lying down . . . . iii 1 229
Our men more perfect in the use of arms . . . 2 *Hen. IV.* iv 1 155
Such fellows are perfect in the great commanders' names *Hen. V.* iii 6 73
The grief is fine, full, perfect, that I taste . *Troi. and Cres.* iv 4 3
As perfect As begging hermits in their holy prayers . *T. Andron.* iii 2 40
That you would once use our hearts, whereby we might express some part of our zeals, we should think ourselves for ever perfect *T. of Athens* i 2 90
Our health but sickly in his life, Which in his death were perfect *Macb.* iii 1 108
I had else been perfect, Whole as the marble, founded as the rock . iii 4 21
I am not to you known, Though in your state of honour I am perfect . iv 2 66
I am perfect That the Pannonians and Dalmatians for Their liberties are now in arms . . . . *Cymbeline* iii 1 73
What hast thou done?—I am perfect what: cut off one Cloten's head . iv 2 118
Apollo, perfect me in the characters! . . . . . *Pericles* iii 2 67
In the rest you said Thou hast been godlike perfect . . . . v 1 208
Perfect age. Sons at perfect age, and fathers declining . . . *Lear* i 2 77
Perfect chrysolite. If heaven would make me such another world Of one entire and perfect chrysolite . . . . . *Othello* v 2 145
Perfect conscience. With such cozenage—is't not perfect conscience, To quit him with this arm? . . . . . . *Hamlet* v 2 67
Perfect courtier. I will return perfect courtier . . . *All's Well* i 1 221
Perfect day. Can neither call it perfect day nor night . . 3 *Hen. VI.* ii 5 4
Perfect gallows. His complexion is perfect gallows . . . *Tempest* i 1 32
Perfect goodness. The credit that thy lady hath of thee Deserves thy trust, and thy most perfect goodness Her assured credit *Cymbeline* i 6 158
Perfect guess. King Richard might create a perfect guess 2 *Hen. IV.* iii 1 88
Perfect honour. Let it look Like perfect honour . . *Ant. and Cleo.* i 3 80
Two villains, whose false oaths prevail'd Before my perfect honour *Cymbeline* iii 3 67
Perfect image. No counterfeit, but the true and perfect image of life indeed . . . . 1 *Hen. IV.* v 4 120
Perfect love. He does it under name of perfect love . *T. of Shrew* iv 3 12
To choose for wealth and not for perfect love . . . 1 *Hen. VI.* v 5 50
So prosper I, as I swear perfect love! . . . . *Richard III.* ii 1 16
By heaven, I come in perfect love to him . . . . . iii 7 90
Perfect man. He cannot be a perfect man, Not being tried and tutor'd in the world . . . . *T. G. of Ver.* i 3 20
Perfect mind. I fear I am not in my perfect mind . . . *Lear* iv 7 63
Perfect period. To make the perfect period of this peace *Richard III.* ii 1 44
Perfect Richard. Mine eye hath well examined his parts And finds them perfect Richard . . . . *K. John* i 1 90
Perfect self. For since the substance of your perfect self Is else devoted, I am but a shadow . . . . . . *T. G. of Ver.* iv 2 124
Perfect soul. My parts, my title and my perfect soul Shall manifest me rightly . . . . *Othello* i 2 31
Perfect spy. Acquaint you with the perfect spy o' the time *Macbeth* iii 1 130
Perfect sun. Three glorious suns, each one a perfect sun . 3 *Hen. VI.* ii 1 26
Perfect thought. Thou hast a perfect thought . . . *K. John* v 6 6
Perfect ways. From her shall read the perfect ways of honour *Hen. VIII.* v 5 38
Perfect wits. I knew he was not in his perfect wits . *Com. of Errors* v 1 42
Perfect woman. From the all that are took something good, To make a perfect woman . . . . *W. Tale* v 1 15
Perfect wrong. Since law itself is perfect wrong . . . *K. John* iii 1 189
Perfect yellow. Her hair is auburn, mine is perfect yellow *T. G. of Ver.* iv 4 194
Your French-crown-colour beard, your perfect yellow *M. N. Dream* i 2 98
Perfected how to grant suits, How to deny them . . . *Tempest* i 2 79
Experience is by industry achieved And perfected by the swift course of time . . . . *T. G. of Ver.* i 3 23
Therefore we must needs admit the means How things are perfected *Hen. V.* i 1 69
Perfecter. You are well understood to be a perfecter giber for the table than a necessary bencher in the Capitol . . *Coriolanus* ii 1 91
Perfectest. Silence is the perfectest herald of joy . . . *Much Ado* ii 1 317
I have learned by the perfectest report . . . . . *Macbeth* i 5 2
Perfection. I would with such perfection govern, sir, To excel the golden age . . . . *Tempest* ii 1 167
To clothe mine age with angel-like perfection . . *T. G. of Ver.* ii 4 66
Is it mine, or Valentine's praise, Her true perfection, or my false transgression, That makes me reasonless to reason thus? . . . . ii 4 197
When I look on her perfections, There is no reason but I shall be blind ii 4 211
To one so dear, Of such divine perfection . . . . . . ii 7 13
To think that she is by And feed upon the shadow of perfection . . iii 1 177
A man of such perfection As we do in our quality much want . . iv 1 57
I trust it will grow to a most prosperous perfection *Meas. for Meas.* iii 1 272
It is the witness still of excellency To put a strange face on his own perfection . . . . *Much Ado* ii 3 49
Sole inheritor Of all perfections that a man may owe . *L. L. Lost* ii 1 6
How many things by season season'd are To their right praise and true perfection! . . . . *Mer. of Venice* v 1 108
Whose words all ears took captive, Whose dear perfection hearts that scorn'd to serve Humbly call'd mistress . . *All's Well* v 3 18
And fill'd Her sweet perfections with one self king . . *T. Night* i 1 39
Methinks I feel this youth's perfections With an invisible and subtle stealth To creep in at mine eyes . . . . i 5 315
Alas, that they are so; To die, even when they to perfection grow! . ii 4 42
A fair divided excellence, Whose fulness of perfection lies in him *K. John* ii 1 440
Would turn their own perfection to abuse, To seem like him 2 *Hen. IV.* ii 3 27
The prescript praise and perfection of a good and particular mistress *Hen. V.* iii 7 50
The chief perfections of that lovely dame, Had I sufficient skill to utter them, Would make a volume of enticing lines . . 1 *Hen. VI.* v 5 12
All her perfections challenge sovereignty . . . . 3 *Hen. VI.* iii 2 86
Vouchsafe, divine perfection of a woman . . . . *Richard III.* i 2 75
Because both they Match not the high perfection of my loss . . iv 4 66
Vowing more than the perfection of ten and discharging less than the tenth part of one . . . . *Troi. and Cres.* iii 2 94
No perfection in reversion shall have a praise in present . . . iii 2 99
Retain that dear perfection which he owes Without that title *R. and J.* ii 2 46
Smoke and lukewarm water Is your perfection . . *T. of Athens* iii 6 100
Stood challenger on mount of all the age For her perfections *Hamlet* iv 7 29
It is a judgement maim'd and most imperfect That will confess perfection so could err Against all rules of nature . . . *Othello* i 3 100
When she speaks, is it not an alarum to love?—She is indeed perfection ii 3 28
Perfection. She spoke, and panted, That she did make defect perfection *Ant. and Cleo.* ii 2 236
To glad her presence, The senate-house of planets all did sit, To knit in her their best perfections . . . . *Pericles* i 1 11
He's no man on whom perfections wait That, knowing sin within, will touch the gate . . . . i 1 79
Perfectly. Would beguile Nature of her custom, so perfectly he is her ape . . . . *W. Tale* v 2 108
This they con perfectly in the phrase of war . . . *Hen. V.* iii 6 79
I would have her learn, my fair cousin, how perfectly I love her . . v 2 310
As perfectly is ours as yours, my lord . . . . *Troi. and Cres.* iii 3 206
Perfectness. Is this your perfectness? be gone, you rogue! *L. L. Lost* v 2 173
The prince will in the perfectness of time Cast off his followers 2 *Hen. IV.* iv 4 74
Perfidious. That a brother should Be so perfidious! . . . *Tempest* i 2 68
A most perfidious and drunken monster! . . . . . . ii 2 154
He's quoted for a most perfidious slave . . . . . *All's Well* v 3 205
Men fear'd the French would prove perfidious, To the king's danger *Hen. VIII.* i 2 156
Perfidiously He has betray'd your business . . . . *Coriolanus* v 6 91
Perforce. Which perforce, I know, Thou must restore . . *Tempest* v 1 133
Perforce, against all checks, rebukes and manners, I must advance the colours of my love . . . . *Mer. Wives* iii 4 84
He rush'd into my house and took perforce My ring away *Com. of Errors* iv 3 95
And take perforce my husband from the abbess . . . . . v 1 117
She perforce withholds the loved boy . . . . *M. N. Dream* ii 1 26
Perforce I must confess I thought you lord of more true gentleness . ii 2 131
And thy fair virtue's force perforce doth move me On the first view to say, to swear, I love thee . . . . iii 1 143
Of thy misprision must perforce ensue Some true love turn'd . . iii 2 90
For what he hath taken away from thy father perforce, I will render thee again in affection . . . . *As Y. Like It* i 2 21
He that perforce robs lions of their hearts May easily win a woman's *K. John* i 1 268
And force perforce Keep Stephen Langton, chosen archbishop Of Canterbury . . . . iii 1 142
My rights and royalties Pluck'd from my arms perforce *Richard II.* ii 3 121
They must perforce have melted And barbarism itself have pitied him . v 2 35
The which, if you give o'er To stormy passion, must perforce decay *2 Hen. IV.* i 1 165
And one against Glendower; perforce a third Must take up us . . i 3 72
These unseason'd hours perforce must add Unto your sickness . iii 1 105
As the state stood then, Was force perforce compell'd to banish him . iv 1 116
With venom of suggestion—As, force perforce, the age will pour it in . iv 4 46
I must perforce compound With mistful eyes . . . . *Hen. V.* iv 6 33
For he perforce must do thee right, because he hath not the gift to woo in other places . . . . v 2 161
How I am braved and must perforce endure it! . . . 1 *Hen. VI.* ii 4 115
And, force perforce, I'll make him yield the crown . 2 *Hen. VI.* i 1 258
Offer him no violence, Unless he seek to thrust you out perforce 3 *Hen. VI.* i 1 34
And made him to resign his crown perforce . . . . . . i 1 142
Away with her; go, bear her hence perforce.—Nay, never bear me hence . . . . v 5 68
Meantime, have patience.—I must perforce . . . . *Richard III.* i 1 116
The tender prince Would fain have come with me to meet your grace, But by his mother was perforce withheld . . . . . . iii 1 30
Go with him, And from her jealous arms pluck him perforce . . . iii 1 36
Would not know them, and yet must Perforce be their acquaintance *Hen. VIII.* i 2 47
Which perforce I, her frail son, amongst my brethren mortal, Must give my tendance to . . . . iii 2 147
An universal wolf, So doubly seconded with will and power, Must make perforce an universal prey . . . . *Troi. and Cres.* i 3 123
And so must you resolve, That what you cannot as you would achieve, You must perforce accomplish as you may . . *T. Andron.* ii 1 107
Now perforce we will enjoy That nice-preserved honesty of yours . . ii 3 134
So that perforce you must needs stay a time . . . . . iv 3 41
Patience perforce with wilful choler meeting . . . *Rom. and Jul.* i 5 91
Betroth'd and would have married her perforce . . . . . v 3 238
These hot tears, which break from me perforce . . . . *Lear* i 4 320
To take't again perforce! Monster ingratitude! . . . . . i 5 43
This weaves itself perforce into my business . . . . . . ii 1 17
She that herself will sliver and disbranch From her material sap, perforce must wither And come to deadly use . . . . . . iv 2 35
Humanity must perforce prey on itself, Like monsters of the deep . iv 2 49
It will cost thee dear: Thou hast no weapon, and perforce must suffer *Oth.* v 2 256
When perforce he could not But pay me terms of honour, cold and sickly He vented them . . . . *Ant. and Cleo.* iii 4 6
I must perforce Have shown to thee such a declining day . . . v 1 37
Of him I gather'd honour; Which he to seek of me again, perforce, Behoves me keep at utterance . . . . *Cymbeline* iii 1 72
Perform. To perform an act Whereof what's past is prologue . *Tempest* ii 1 252
For yet ere supper-time must I perform Much business appertaining . iii 1 95
Thou and thy meaner fellows your last service Did worthily perform . iv 1 36
Pay with falsehood false exacting, And perform an old contracting *Meas. for Meas.* iii 2 296
You should refuse to perform your father's will, if you should refuse to accept him . . . . *Mer. of Venice* i 2 100
And here, where you are, they are coming to perform it . *As Y. Like It* i 2 122
Here is the place appointed for the wrestling, and they are ready to perform it . . . . i 2 155
The treachery of the two fled hence Be left her to perform . *W. Tale* ii 1 196
Swear by this sword Thou wilt perform my bidding.—I will, my lord.—Mark and perform it, see'st thou! . . . . ii 3 169
Wanted Less impudence to gainsay what they did Than to perform it first . . . . iii 2 58
What good love may I perform for you? . . . . . *K. John* iv 1 49
Little office The hateful commons will perform for us . *Richard II.* ii 2 138
This, in the name of God, I promise here: The which if He be pleased I shall perform . . . . 1 *Hen. IV.* iii 2 154
Which, by mine honour, I will perform with a most Christian care *2 Hen. IV.* iv 2 115
This oath I willingly take and will perform . . . . 3 *Hen. VI.* i 1 201
And what God will, that let your king perform . . . . . iii 1 100
I will perform it to enfranchise you . . . . . *Richard III.* i 1 110
They did perform Beyond thought's compass . . . . *Hen. VIII.* i 1 35
He is subtle, and as prone to mischief As able to perform 't . . . i 1 161
And yet reserve an ability that they never perform . *Troi. and Cres.* iii 2 93
But when he performs, astronomers foretell it . . . . . . v 1 99
For what miscarries Shall be the general's fault, though he perform To the utmost of a man . . . . *Coriolanus* i 1 271

Perform. To have my praise for this, perform a part Thou hast not done before . . . *Coriolanus* iii 2 109
Foul-spoken coward, that thunder'st with thy tongue, and with thy weapon nothing darest perform! . . . *T. Andron.* ii 1 59
Precedent, and lively warrant, For me, most wretched, to perform the like . . . v 3 45
Ten thousand worse than ever yet I did Would I perform, if I might . v 3 188
Send me word to-morrow, By one that I'll procure to come to thee, Where and what time thou wilt perform the rite . *Rom. and Jul.* ii 2 146
Promise me friendship, but perform none: if thou wilt not promise, the gods plague thee, for thou art a man! if thou dost perform, confound thee, for thou art a man! . . . *T. of Athens* iv 3 72
What cannot you and I perform upon The unguarded Duncan? *Macbeth* i 7 69
We shall, my lord, Perform what you command us . . . iii 1 127
I'll charm the air to give a sound, While you perform your antic round iv 1 130
By the grace of Grace, We will perform in measure, time and place v 8 73
And an act hath three branches; it is, to act, to do, and to perform *Ham.* v 1 13
If I do vow a friendship, I'll perform it To the last article . *Othello* iii 3 21
Perform't, or else we damn thee . . . *Ant. and Cleo.* i 1 24
This if she perform, She shall not sue unheard . . . iii 12 23
One that but performs The bidding of the fullest man . . . iii 13 86
What villany soe'er I bid thee do, to perform it directly and truly *Cymb.* iii 5 113
I dare be bound he's true and shall perform All parts of his subjection loyally . . . iv 3 18
Away! and, to be blest, Let us with care perform his great behest . v 4 122
Which, to preserve mine honour, I'll perform . . *Pericles* ii 2 16
And what ensues in this fell storm Shall for itself itself perform iii Gower 54
Perform my bidding, or thou livest in woe; Do it, and happy . v 1 248
Hail, Dian! to perform thy just command, I here confess myself the king of Tyre . . . v 3 1
Performance. The premises observed, Thy will by my performance shall be served . . . *All's Well* ii 1 205
Strange that desire should so many years outlive performance 2 *Hen. IV.* ii 4 284
Still be kind, And eke out our performance with your mind *Hen. V.* iii Prol. 35
The duchess, I tell you, expects performance of your promises 2 *Hen. VI.* i 4 2
By as much as a performance Does an irresolute purpose *Hen. VIII.* i 2 208
His promises were, as he then was, mighty; But his performance, as he is now, nothing . . . iv 2 42
Were it not glory that we more affected Than the performance of our heaving spleens . . . *Troi. and Cres.* ii 2 196
You shall piece it out with a piece of your performance . . iii 1 55
They say all lovers swear more performance than they are able . iii 2 91
Why should our endeavour be so loved and the performance so loathed? v 10 39
Performance is ever the duller for his act . . *T. of Athens* v 1 26
Performance is a kind of will or testament . . . v 1 29
To think that or our cause or our performance Did need an oath *J. Cæsar* ii 1 135
It [drink] provokes the desire, but it takes away the performance *Macb.* ii 3 33
Besides her walking and other actual performances . . v 1 13
If this should fail, And that our drift look through our bad performance, 'Twere better not assay'd . . . *Hamlet* iv 7 152
Your words and performances are no kin together . . *Othello* iv 2 185
In his offence Should my performance perish . . *Ant. and Cleo.* iii 1 27
Get this done as I command you.—Performance shall follow *Pericles* iv 2 67
Performed. Hast thou, spirit, Perform'd to point the tempest? *Tempest* i 2 194
Thy charge Exactly is perform'd . . . i 2 238
Let me remember thee what thou hast promised, Which is not yet perform'd . . . i 2 244
Bravely the figure of this harpy hast thou Perform'd, my Ariel . iii 3 84
Let this be duly performed; with a thought that more depends on it *Meas. for Meas.* iv 2 127
Now our observation is perform'd . . *M. N. Dream* iv 1 109
Sure, that part Was aptly fitted and naturally perform'd *T. of Shrew* Ind. 1 87
To steal our marriage; Which once perform'd, let all the world say no iii 2 143
Whose ceremony Shall seem expedient on the now-born brief, And be perform'd to-night . . . *All's Well* ii 3 187
And so The king's will be perform'd! . . . *W. Tale* ii 1 115
I will give you as much as this old man does when the business is performed . . . iv 4 852
You have done enough, and have perform'd A saint-like sorrow . v 1 1
Speak of something wildly By us perform'd before . . . v 1 130
A piece many years in doing and now newly performed . . v 2 105
Perform'd in this wide gap of time since first We were dissever'd . v 3 154
O, let thy vow First made to heaven, first be to heaven perform'd! *K. John* iii 1 266
Is sworn against thyself And may not be performed by thyself . iii 1 269
Who perform'd The bloody office of his timeless end *Richard II.* iv 1 4
Swore him assistance and perform'd it too . . 1 *Hen. IV.* iv 3 65
Be it your charge, my lord, To see perform'd the tenour of our word 2 *Hen. IV.* v 5 75
Thus Joan la Pucelle hath perform'd her word . . 1 *Hen. VI.* i 6 3
I have perform'd my task and was espoused . . 2 *Hen. VI.* i 1 9
Let us in, and with all speed provide To see her coronation be perform'd i 1 74
That's not suddenly to be perform'd, But with advice and silent secrecy ii 2 67
A charge, Lord York, that I will see perform'd . . iii 1 321
'Tis but to love a king.—That's soon perform'd 3 *Hen. VI.* iii 2 54
I wish the bastards dead; And I would have it suddenly perform'd *Richard III.* iv 2 19
Which perform'd, the choir . . . Together sung 'Te Deum' *Hen. VIII.* iv 1 90
Report A little of that worthy work perform'd . *Coriolanus* ii 2 49
See, lord and father, how we have perform'd Our Roman rites *T. Andron.* i 1 142
Villanies Ruthful to hear, yet piteously perform'd . . v 1 66
When Cæsar says 'do this,' it is perform'd . . *J. Cæsar* i 2 10
Murders have been perform'd Too terrible for the ear . *Macbeth* iii 4 77
It takes From our achievements, though perform'd at height, The pith and marrow of our attribute . . . *Hamlet* i 4 21
Let this same be presently perform'd, Even while men's minds are wild v 2 404
Tigers, not daughters, what have you perform'd? . . *Lear* iv 2 40
I have perform'd Your pleasure and my promise . *Ant. and Cleo.* v 2 203
To see perform'd the dreaded act which thou So sought'st to hinder . v 2 334
Like hardiment Posthumus hath To Cymbeline perform'd . *Cymbeline* v 4 76
So, this was well ask'd, 'twas so well perform'd . *Pericles* ii 3 99
It greets me as an enterprise of kindness Perform'd to your sole daughter iv 3 39
Performer. The merit of service is seldom attributed to the true and exact performer . . . *All's Well* iii 6 65
Performers of this heinous, bloody deed . . *T. Andron.* iv 1 80
For three performers are the file when all The rest do nothing *Cymbeline* v 3 30
Performing. That will ask some tears in the true performing of it *M. N. D.* i 2 27
Perfume. They are an excellent perfume.—I am stuffed, cousin; I cannot smell . . . *Much Ado* iii 4 63
And with her breath she did perfume the air . . *T. of Shrew* i 1 180
Have them very well perfumed: For she is sweeter than perfume itself i 2 153
Perfume. Perfume for a lady's chamber . . . *W. Tale* iv 4 225
To paint the lily, To throw a perfume on the violet . . *K. John* iv 2 12
It perfumes the blood ere one can say 'What's this?' . 2 *Hen. IV.* iv 3 104
Whose smoke, like incense, doth perfume the sky . *T. Andron.* i 1 145
Wear silk, drink wine, lie soft; Hug their diseased perfumes *T. of Athens* iv 3 207
When thou wast in thy gilt and thy perfume, they mock'd thee . iv 3 302
All the perfumes of Arabia will not sweeten this little hand . *Macbeth* v 1 57
Sweet, not lasting, The prefume and suppliance of a minute . *Hamlet* i 3 9
Their perfume lost, Take these again . . . iii 1 99
Thou owest the worm no silk, the beast no hide, the sheep no wool, the cat no perfume . . . *Lear* iii 4 110
A strange invisible perfume hits the sense . *Ant. and Cleo.* ii 2 217
Hast thou not learn'd me how To make perfumes? distil? preserve? *Cymb.* i 5 13
'Tis her breathing that Perfumes the chamber thus . . ii 2 19
Perfumed. Or as 'twere perfumed by a fen . . *Tempest* ii 1 48
The courtier's hands are perfumed with civet . . . *As Y. Like It* iii 2 65
Take your paper too, And let me have them very well perfumed *T. of Shrew* i 2 152
He was perfumed like a milliner . . 1 *Hen. IV.* i 3 36
In the perfumed chambers of the great . . . 2 *Hen. IV.* iii 1 12
Then will I raise aloft the milk-white rose, With whose sweet smell the air shall be perfumed . . . 2 *Hen. VI.* i 1 255
'Tis such another fitchew! marry, a perfumed one . . *Othello* iv 1 150
Purple the sails, and so perfumed that The winds were love-sick *A. and C.* ii 2 198
Perfumer. Being entertained for a perfumer . . *Much Ado* i 3 60
Perge, good Master Holofernes, perge . . . *L. L. Lost* iv 2 54
Perhaps. If haply won, perhaps a hapless gain . *T. G. of Ver.* i 1 32
Perhaps some merchant hath invited him . . *Com. of Errors* ii 1 4
This wedding-day Perhaps is but prolong'd . . *Much Ado* iv 1 256
Trow you what he call'd me?—Qualm, perhaps . . *L. L. Lost* v 2 279
I'll be an auditor; An actor too perhaps, if I see cause . *M. N. Dream* iii 1 82
You perhaps may think, Because she is something lower than myself, That I can match her . . . iii 2 303
Go in: Perhaps I will return immediately . . . *Mer. of Venice* ii 5 52
Perhaps you mark'd not what's the pith of all . . *T. of Shrew* i 1 171
Being perhaps, for aught I see, two and thirty, a pip out . . i 2 32
She may perhaps call him half a score knaves or so . . . i 2 110
Yea, and perhaps with more successful words Than you . . i 2 158
The malignancy of my fate might perhaps distemper yours . *T. Night* ii 1 5
Say that some lady, as perhaps there is, Hath for your love as great a pang ii 4 92
Thou perhaps mayst move That heart, which now abhors, to like . iii 1 175
Perhaps they had ere this, but that they stay . . *Richard II.* ii 1 289
Your mistress shrewdly shook your back.—So perhaps did yours *Hen. V.* iii 7 53
I have perhaps some shallow spirit of judgement . . 1 *Hen. VI.* ii 4 16
Your grace may starve perhaps before that time . . . iii 2 48
O, would he did! and so perhaps he doth . . . 3 *Hen. VI.* ii 6 64
Perhaps thou wilt object my holy oath . . . v 1 89
A king, perhaps, perhaps . . . *Richard III.* iv 2 101
Perhaps thy childishness will move him more . . *Coriolanus* v 3 157
Made me down to throw my books, and fly,—Causeless, perhaps *T. An.* iv 1 26
Perhaps you have learned it without book . *Rom. and Jul.* i 2 61
Which give some soil perhaps to my behaviours . . *J. Cæsar* i 2 42
Perhaps he loves you now . . . *Hamlet* i 3 14
For two special reasons; Which may to you, perhaps, seem much unsinew'd . . . iv 7 10
Periapt. Now help, ye charming spells and periapts . 1 *Hen. VI.* v 3 2
Pericles. Prince Pericles,—That would be son to great Antiochus *Pericles* i 1 25
Prince Pericles, touch not, upon thy life, For that's an article within our law . . . i 1 87
My lord, prince Pericles is fled.—As thou Wilt live, fly after . . i 1 162
Ne'er return Unless thou say 'Prince Pericles is dead' . . i 1 166
Till Pericles be dead, My heart can lend no succour to my head . i 1 170
Here must I kill King Pericles; and if I do it not, I am sure to be hanged i 3 2
From him I come With message unto princely Pericles . . i 3 33
Keep it, my Pericles; it hath been a shield 'Twixt me and death . ii 1 132
A gentleman of Tyre; my name, Pericles; My education been in arts and arms . . . ii 3 81
Forbear your suffrages; If that you love Prince Pericles, forbear . ii 4 42
By many a dern and painful perch Of Pericles the careful search . iii Gower 16
If King Pericles Come not home in twice six moons, He, obedient to their dooms, Will take the crown . . . iii Gower 30
This stage the ship, upon whose deck The sea-tost Pericles appears to speak . . . iii Gower 60
I, King Pericles, have lost This queen, worth all our mundane cost . iii 2 70
If thou livest, Pericles, thou hast a heart That even cracks for woe! . iii 2 76
Behold, Her eyelids, cases to those heavenly jewels Which Pericles hath lost . . . iii 2 100
But since King Pericles, My wedded lord, I ne'er shall see again, A vestal livery will I take me to . . . iii 4 8
Imagine Pericles arrived at Tyre, Welcomed and settled . . iv Gower 1
What canst thou say When noble Pericles shall demand his child? . iv 3 13
The petty wrens of Tarsus will fly hence, And open this to Pericles . iv 3 23
And as for Pericles, What should he say? We wept after her hearse . iv 3 40
Pericles Is now again thwarting the wayward seas . . . iv 4 9
And Pericles, in sorrow all devour'd, With sighs shot through . iv 4 25
Let Pericles believe his daughter's dead . . . iv 4 46
In your supposing once more put your sight Of heavy Pericles . v Gower 22
I am the daughter to King Pericles, If good King Pericles be . v 1 180
I am Pericles of Tyre: but tell me now My drown'd queen's name . v 1 206
The heir of kingdoms and another like To Pericles thy father . v 1 210
Voice and favour! You are, you are—O royal Pericles! . . v 3 14
O, my lord, Are you not Pericles? Like him you spake. . . v 3 32
In Pericles, his queen and daughter, seen, Although assail'd with fortune fierce and keen, Virtue preserved from fell destruction's blast . . . v 3 Gower 87
When fame Had spread their cursed deed, and honour'd name Of Pericles . . . v 3 Gower 97
Perigenia. Theseus? Didst thou not lead him through the glimmering night From Perigenia, whom he ravished? . *M. N. Dream* ii 1 78
Perigort. At a marriage-feast, Between Lord Perigort and the beauteous heir Of Jaques Falconbridge . . . *L. L. Lost* ii 1 41
Peril. I fear not mine own shame so much as his peril *Mer. Wives* iii 3 130
I'll take it as a peril to my soul, It is no sin at all, but charity *M. for M.* ii 4 65
Pleased you to do't at peril of your soul, Were equal poise of sin and charity . . . ii 4 67
Fail not to do your office, as you will answer it at your peril . . iv 2 130
Stay, on thy peril: I alone will go . . . *M. N. Dream* ii 2 87
Lest, to thy peril, thou aby it dear . . . iii 2 175
Without the peril of the Athenian law . . . iv 1 158
Then there is the peril of waters, winds, and rocks . *Mer. of Venice* i 3 25
To be in peril of my life with the edge of a feather-bed . . i 2 173

Peril. Thou shalt have nothing but the forfeiture, To be so taken at thy peril . . . *Mer. of Venice* iv 1 344
His own peril on his forwardness . . . *As Y. Like It* i 2 159
Are not these woods More free from peril than the envious court? . ii 1 4
In peril to incur your former malady . . *T. of Shrew* Ind. 2 124
Time it is, when raging war is done, To smile at scapes and perils overblown . . . . . . v 2 3
Thou know'st no part, I knowing all my peril, thou no art . *All's Well* ii 1 136
Tongue, I must put you into a butter-woman's mouth and buy myself another of Bajazet's mule, if you prattle me into these perils . . iv 1 47
I saw your brother, Most provident in peril . . . *T. Night* i 2 12
On your displeasure's peril and on mine . . . *W. Tale* ii 3 45
I do in justice charge thee, On thy soul's peril and thy body's torture . ii 3 181
On peril of a curse, Let go the hand of that arch-heretic . *K. John* iii 1 191
But if not, then know The peril of our curses light on thee . . iii 1 295
As full of peril and adventurous spirit As to o'er-walk a current roaring loud On the unsteadfast footing of a spear . . 1 *Hen. IV.* i 3 191
He walk'd o'er perils, on an edge, More likely to fall in . 2 *Hen. IV.* i 1 170
The gain proposed Choked the respect of likely peril fear'd . . i 1 184
Viewing his progress through, What perils past, what crosses to ensue . iii 1 55
O, with what wings shall his affections fly Towards fronting peril! . iv 4 66
All these bold fears Thou see'st with peril I have answered . . iv 5 197
Thousands more, that yet suspect no peril . . 2 *Hen. VI.* iii 1 152
Must Edward fall, which peril heaven forfend! . 3 *Hen. VI.* ii 1 191
The extreme peril of the case . . . Enforced us to this . *Richard III.* iii 5 44
I'll bear thy blame And take thy office from thee, on my peril . . iv 1 26
If without peril it be possible . . . . v 3 39
Though perils did Abound, as thick as thought could make 'em *Hen. VIII.* iii 2 194
That seeks his praise more than he fears his peril . *Troi. and Cres.* i 3 267
He shall answer, by a lawful form, In peace, to his utmost peril *Coriol.* iii 1 326
Banish him our city, In peril of precipitation From off the rock Tarpeian . . . . iii 3 102
There lies more peril in thine eye Than twenty of their swords *R. and J.* ii 2 71
And strain what other means is left unto us In our dear peril *T. of Athens* v 1 231
Go sit in council, How covert matters may be best disclosed, And open perils surest answered . . . . . . *J. Cæsar* iv 1 47
I am fresh of spirit and resolved To meet all perils very constantly . v 1 92
Wast thou not charged at peril? . . . . . *Lear* iii 7 52
If he do resist, Subdue him at his peril . . . . *Othello* i 2 81
The Moor May unfold me to him; there stand I in much peril . . v 1 21
Drink carouses to the next day's fate, Which promises royal peril *Ant. and Cleo.* iv 8 35
Let him speak, my lord, Upon his peril, that I have reserved To myself nothing . . . . v 2 143
I had rather seal my lips, than, to my peril, Speak that which is not . v 2 146
I will from hence to-day.—You know the peril . . *Cymbeline* i 1 80
Though peril to my modesty, not death on't, I would adventure . . iii 4 155
Thus, unknown, Pitied nor hated, to the face of peril Myself I'll dedicate v 1 28
You do not know, or jump the after inquiry on your own peril . . v 4 189
Perilous. O perilous mouths, That bear in them one and the self-same tongue, Either of condemnation or approof! . *Meas. for Meas.* ii 4 172
We must embrace This gentle offer of the perilous time . *K. John* iv 3 13
A perilous gash, a very limb lopp'd off . . . . 1 *Hen. IV.* iv 1 43
In the adventure of this perilous day . . . . . . v 2 96
The perilous narrow ocean parts asunder . . . . *Hen. V.* Prol. 22
That's a perilous shot out of an elder-gun . . . . . iv 1 209
You know a sword employ'd is perilous . . . *Troi. and Cres.* ii 2 40
Walk'd about the streets, Submitting me unto the perilous night *J. Cæsar* i 3 47
And with some sweet oblivious antidote Cleanse the stuff'd bosom of that perilous stuff Which weighs upon the heart . . *Macbeth* v 3 44
You speak like a green girl, Unsifted in such perilous circumstance *Ham.* i 3 102
We do fear this body hath a tail More perilous than the head *Cymbeline* iv 2 145
Period. And yet—A pretty period! . . . . *T. G. of Ver.* ii 1 122
I have lived long enough: this is the period of my ambition *Mer. Wives* iii 3 47
There would be no period to the jest, should he not be publicly shamed iv 2 237
Make periods in the midst of sentences . . . *M. N. Dream* v 1 96
Upon thy sight My worldly business makes a period . 2 *Hen. IV.* iv 5 231
The period of thy tyranny approacheth . . . 1 *Hen. VI.* iv 2 17
And prove the period of their tyranny . . . 2 *Hen. VI.* iii 1 149
Now here a period of tumultuous broils . . . 3 *Hen. VI.* v 5 1
O, let me make the period to my curse! . . . *Richard III.* i 3 238
To make the perfect period of this peace . . . . . ii 1 44
There's his period, To sheathe his knife in us . . *Hen. VIII.* i 2 209
Which failing, Periods his comfort . . . . *T. of Athens* i 1 99
My point and period will be throughly wrought, Or well or ill . *Lear* iv 7 97
This would have seem'd a period To such as love not sorrow . . v 3 204
O bloody period!—All that's spoke is marr'd . . *Othello* v 2 357
Tend me to-night; May be it is the period of your duty *Ant. and Cleo.* iv 2 25
The star is fall'n.—And time is at his period.—Alas, and woe! . . iv 14 107
Perish. Supposing that they saw the king's ship wreck'd And his great person perish . . . . *Tempest* i 2 237
Go, go, be gone, to save your ship from wreck, Which cannot perish having thee aboard . . . . . . *T. G. of Ver.* i 1 157
Take my defiance! Die, perish! . . . . *Meas. for Meas.* iii 1 144
When great things labouring perish in their birth . . *L. L. Lost* v 2 521
O, how fit a word Is that vile name to perish on my sword! *M. N. Dream* ii 2 107
I perish, Tranio, If I achieve not this young modest girl . *T. of Shrew* i 1 160
'Twill bring you gain, or perish on the seas . . . . . . ii 1 331
We see the wind sit sore upon our sails, And yet we strike not, but securely perish . . . . *Richard II.* ii 1 266
And where they would be safe, they perish . . . *Hen. V.* iv 1 182
Perish the man whose mind is backward now! . . . . . iv 3 72
So perish they That grudge one thought against your majesty! 1 *Hen. VI.* iii 1 175
Perish, base prince, ignoble Duke of York! . . . . . . iii 1 178
I'll have a bout with you again, Or else let Talbot perish with this shame . . . . iii 2 57
Confounded be your strife! And perish ye, with your audacious prate! iv 1 124
Because thy flinty heart, more hard than they, Might in thy palace perish Margaret . . . . 2 *Hen. VI.* iii 2 100
For God forbid so many simple souls Should perish by the sword! . iv 4 11
Or I with grief and extreme age shall perish . *Richard III.* iv 4 185
I shall perish Under device and practice . . . *Hen. VIII.* i 1 203
Like the lily, That once was mistress of the field and flourish'd, I'll hang my head and perish . . . . iii 1 153
I know his noble nature—not to let Thy hopeful service perish too . iii 2 419
Haste we, Diomed, To reinforcement, or we perish all *Troi. and Cres.* v 5 16
By not so doing, our good city Cleave in the midst, and perish *Coriolanus* iii 2 28
Now the red pestilence strike all trades in Rome, And occupations perish! . . . . iv 1 14
Perish. Are mock'd for valiant ignorance, And perish constant fools *Coriolanus* iv 6 105
Let her rot, and perish, and be damned to-night . . *Othello* iv 1 191
Tie up thy discontented sword, And carry back to Sicily much tall youth That else must perish here . . . . *Ant. and Cleo.* ii 6 8
'Twould offend him; and in his offence Should my performance perish . iii 1 27
Or this, or perish . . . . *Cymbeline* iii 5 101
He 'scaped the land, to perish at the sea . . . . *Pericles* i 3 29
Perished. Poor souls, they perish'd . . . . . *Tempest* i 2 9
But are they, Ariel, safe?—Not a hair perish'd . . . . . i 2 217
Having in that perished vessel the dowry of his sister *Meas. for Meas.* iii 1 225
And must be buried but as an intent That perish'd by the way . . v 1 458
Perishen. All perishen of man, of pelf, Ne aught escapen but himself *Pericles* ii Gower 35
Perishest. Abandon the society of this female, or, clown, thou perishest; or, to thy better understanding, diest . . . *As Y. Like It* v 1 56
Perisheth. And Talbot perisheth by your default . . 1 *Hen. VI.* iv 4 28
Perishing. I love not to see wretchedness o'ercharged And duty in his service perishing . . . . *M. N. Dream* v 1 86
And let the stinking elder, grief, untwine His perishing root with the increasing vine! . . . . *Cymbeline* iv 2 60
Periwig. I'll get me such a colour'd periwig . . *T. G. of Ver.* iv 4 196
To pay a fine for a periwig . . . . . . *Com. of Errors* ii 2 76
Periwig-pated. To hear a robustious periwig-pated fellow tear a passion to tatters . . . . *Hamlet* iii 2 10
Perjure. Why, he comes in like a perjure, wearing papers *L. L. Lost* iv 3 48
Women are not In their best fortunes strong; but want will perjure The ne'er-touch'd vestal . . . . . . *Ant. and Cleo.* iii 12 30
Perjured. Thou subtle, perjured, false, disloyal man! . *T. G. of Ver.* iv 2 95
I do detest false perjured Proteus . . . . v 4 39
Who should be trusted, when one's own right hand Is perjured to the bosom! . . . . v 4 68
O perjured woman! They are both forsworn . . . *Com. of Errors* v 1 212
There did this perjured goldsmith swear me down . . . . v 1 227
For you'll prove perjured if you make me stay . . *L. L. Lost* i 1 113
Nay, to be perjured, which is worst of all . . . . . iii 1 196
Am I the first that have been perjured so?—I could put thee in comfort iv 3 51
Ill, to example ill, Would from my forehead wipe a perjured note . iv 3 125
You'll not be perjured, 'tis a hateful thing . . . . . iv 3 157
Nor God, nor I, delights in perjured men . . . . . . v 2 346
Your grace is perjured much, Full of dear guiltiness . . . . v 2 800
As waggish boys in game themselves forswear, So the boy Love is perjured every where . . . . *M. N. Dream* i 1 241
Arm, arm, you heavens, against these perjured kings! . *K. John* iii 1 107
But, ere sunset, Set armed discord 'twixt these perjured kings! . . iii 1 111
Thou art perjured too, And soothest up greatness . . . . iii 1 120
If he be perjured, see you now, his reputation is as arrant a villain and a Jacksauce, as ever his black shoe trod upon God's ground *Hen. V.* iv 7 147
Now, perjured Henry! wilt thou kneel for grace? . . 3 *Hen. VI.* ii 2 81
O passing traitor, perjured and unjust! . . . . . . v 1 106
Lascivious Edward, and thou perjured George . . . . . v 5 34
False, fleeting, perjured Clarence . . . . . *Richard III.* i 4 55
Ween you of better luck, I mean, in perjured witness, than your master, Whose minister you are . . . . *Hen. VIII.* v 1 136
There's no trust, No faith, no honesty in men; all perjured *Rom. and Jul.* iii 2 86
Thou perjured, and thou simular man of virtue That art incestuous *Lear* iii 2 54
O perjured woman! thou dost stone my heart . . . . *Othello* v 2 63
Goodly and gallant shall be false and perjured From thy great fail *Cymbeline* iii 4 65
Perjuries. At lovers' perjuries, They say, Jove laughs . *Rom. and Jul.* ii 2 92
Perjury. And even that power which gave me first my oath Provokes me to this threefold perjury . . . . . . *T. G. of Ver.* ii 6 5
'Twas Ariadne passioning For Theseus' perjury and unjust flight . . iv 4 173
And all those oaths Descended into perjury, to love me . . . v 4 49
How oft hast thou with perjury cleft the root! . . . . . v 4 103
She will not add to her damnation A sin of perjury . . *Much Ado* iv 1 175
Why, this is flat perjury, to call a prince's brother villain . . iv 2 44
Persuade my heart to this false perjury . . . . *L. L. Lost* iv 3 62
Some quillets, how to cheat the devil.—Some salve for perjury . . iv 3 289
Thus pour the stars down plagues for perjury . . . . . v 2 394
Now, to our perjury to add more terror, We are again forsworn . . v 2 470
Your sins are rack'd, You are attaint with faults and perjury . . v 2 829
I have an oath in heaven: Shall I lay perjury upon my soul? *Mer. of Venice* iv 1 229
This day of shame, oppression, perjury . . . . *K. John* iii 1 88
Beguiling virgins with the broken seals of perjury . . *Hen. V.* iv 1 172
And there's for twitting me with perjury . . . 3 *Hen. VI.* v 5 40
What scourge for perjury Can this dark monarchy afford? *Richard III.* i 4 50
Perjury, perjury, in the high'st degree; Murder, stern murder . . v 3 196
Thy dear love sworn but hollow perjury . . . . *Rom. and Jul.* iii 3 128
Take heed, Take heed of perjury; thou art on thy death-bed . *Othello* v 2 51
Perked. Than to be perk'd up in a glistering grief . . *Hen. VIII.* ii 3 21
Perkes. I beseech you, sir, to countenance William Visor of Woncot against Clement Perkes of the hill . . . . . 2 *Hen. IV.* v 1 42
Permanent. Forward, not permanent, sweet, not lasting . . *Hamlet* i 3 8
Permission. What Antony shall speak, I will protest He speaks by leave and by permission . . . . *J. Cæsar* iii 1 239
Speak all good you can devise of Cæsar, And say you do't by our permission . . . . iii 1 247
Which Mark Antony, By our permission, is allow'd to make . . iii 2 64
It [love] is merely a lust of the blood and a permission of the will. *Othello* i 3 340
Permissive. When evil deeds have their permissive pass . *Meas. for Meas.* i 3 38
Permit. Shall we thus permit A blasting and a scandalous breath to fall On him so near us? . . . . v 1 121
Peace be to France, if France in peace permit Our just and lineal entrance to our own . . . . *K. John* ii 1 84
But time will not permit . . . . *Richard II.* ii 2 121
Will you permit that I shall stand condemn'd A wandering vagabond? . ii 3 119
I imitate the sun, Who doth permit the base contagious clouds To smother up his beauty . . . . 1 *Hen. IV.* i 2 222
I will, if that my fading breath permit . . . . 1 *Hen. VI.* ii 5 61
Wishing me to permit John de la Car, my chaplain, a choice hour *Hen. VIII.* i 2 161
Aged custom, But by your voices, will not so permit me . *Coriolanus* ii 3 177
My compassionate heart Will not permit mine eyes once to behold The thing whereat it trembles by surmise . . . . . *T. Andron.* ii 3 218
And permit The curiosity of nations to deprive me . . . . *Lear* i 2 3
With what haste The weight we must convey with's will permit *Ant. and Cleo.* iii 1 36
You some permit To second ills with ills, each elder worse . *Cymbeline* v 1 13

Permitted. Had the king permitted us, One of our souls had wander'd in the air . . . *Richard II.* i 3 194
The cruelty and envy of the people, Permitted by our dastard nobles *Coriolanus* iv 5 81
Pernicious. Most pernicious purpose! Seeming, seeming! *Meas. for Meas.* ii 4 150
I went To this pernicious caitiff deputy,— That's somewhat madly spoken . . . v 1 88
Thou foolish friar, and thou pernicious woman . . . v 1 241
This pernicious slave, Forsooth, took on him as a conjurer *Com. of Errors* v 1 241
They would else have been troubled with a pernicious suitor *Much Ado* i 1 130
The pernicious and indubitate beggar Zenelophon . . *L. L. Lost* iv 1 66
On the casque Of thy adverse pernicious enemy . . *Richard II.* i 3 82
I will not vex your souls—Since presently your souls must part your bodies—With too much urging your pernicious lives . . . iii 1 4
Is there no plot To rid the realm of this pernicious blot? . . . iv 1 325
Thou art a most pernicious usurer . . . *1 Hen. VI.* iii 1 17
Forsaken your pernicious faction And join'd with Charles . . . iv 1 59
Pernicious protector, dangerous peer! . . . *2 Hen. VI.* ii 1 21
Pernicious blood-sucker of sleeping men! . . . iii 2 226
Which are heresies, And, not reform'd, may prove pernicious *Hen. VIII.* v 3 19
Quench the fire of your pernicious rage With purple fountains *R. and J.* i 1 91
Let this pernicious hour Stand aye accursed in the calendar! *Macbeth* iv 1 133
This avarice Sticks deeper, grows with more pernicious root . . iv 3 85
O most pernicious woman! O villain, villain, smiling, damned villain! *Hamlet* i 5 105
Servile ministers, That have with two pernicious daughters join'd *Lear* iii 2 22
If he say so, may his pernicious soul Rot half a grain a day! . *Othello* v 2 155
O the pernicious caitiff! . . . v 2 318
Perniciously. All the commons Hate him perniciously *Hen. VIII.* ii 1 50
Peroration. What means this passionate discourse, This peroration with such circumstance? . . . *2 Hen. VI.* i 1 105
Perpend. He loves the gallimaufry: Ford, perpend . . *Mer. Wives* ii 1 119
Learn of the wise, and perpend . . . *As Y. Like It* iii 2 69
Therefore perpend, my princess, and give ear . . . *T. Night* v 1 307
Perpend my words, O Signieur Dew, and mark . . *Hen. V.* iv 4 8
Thus it remains, and the remainder thus. Perpend *Hamlet* ii 2 105
Perpendicular. Runs o' horseback up a hill perpendicular . *1 Hen. IV.* ii 4 378
Perpendicularly. Ten masts at each make not the altitude Which thou hast perpendicularly fell . . . *Lear* iv 6 54
Perpetual. To the perpetual wink for aye might put This ancient morsel, this Sir Prudence . . . *Tempest* ii 1 285
That it may stand till the perpetual doom . . . *Mer. Wives* v 5 62
Perpetual durance?—Ay, just; perpetual durance, a restraint *M. for M.* iii 1 67
Six or seven winters more respect Than a perpetual honour . . . iii 1 77
And a perpetual succession for it perpetually . . . *All's Well* iv 3 313
Upon a barren mountain, and still winter In storm perpetual *W. Tale* iii 2 214
Upon them shall The causes of their death appear, unto Our shame perpetual . . . iii 2 239
Return with me again, To push destruction and perpetual shame Out of the weak door of our fainting land . . . *K. John* v 7 77
Thou art a perpetual triumph, an everlasting bonfire-light! *1 Hen. IV.* iii 3 46
Than to be scoured to nothing with perpetual motion . *2 Hen. IV.* i 2 246
And warriors faint! why, 'twere perpetual shame . *3 Hen. VI.* v 4 51
Unto the kingdom of perpetual night . . . *Richard III.* i 4 47
Like obedient subjects, follow him To his new kingdom of perpetual rest ii 2 46
If yet your gentle souls fly in the air And be not fix'd in doom perpetual iv 4 12
To reap the harvest of perpetual peace By this one bloody trial . v 2 15
He did Run reeking o'er the lives of men, as if 'Twere a perpetual spoil *Coriolanus* ii 2 124
To thine and Albany's issue Be this perpetual . . . *Lear* i 1 68
Charged me, on pain of their perpetual displeasure . . . iii 3 5
To hold you in perpetual amity, To make you brothers *Ant. and Cleo.* ii 2 127
Perpetually. As mountains are for winds, That shake not, though they blow perpetually . . . *T. of Shrew* ii 1 142
And a perpetual succession for it perpetually . . . *All's Well* iv 3 314
Why cloud they not their sights perpetually? . . . *Pericles* i 1 74
Perpetual-sober. Forgive my general and exceptless rashness, You perpetual-sober gods! . . . *T. of Athens* iv 3 503
Perpetuity. Yet we should, for perpetuity, Go hence in debt *W. Tale* i 2 5
Coupled in bonds of perpetuity . . . *1 Hen. VI.* iv 7 20
He had rather Groan so in perpetuity than be cured By the sure physician, death, who is the key To unbar these locks *Cymbeline* v 4 6
Perplex. What canst thou say but will perplex thee more? . *K. John* iii 1 222
Perplexed. I am perplex'd, and know not what to say . . . iii 1 221
Till you do return, I rest perplexed with a thousand cares . *1 Hen. VI.* v 5 95
Not easily jealous, but being wrought Perplex'd in the extreme *Othello* v 2 346
One, but painted thus, Would be interpreted a thing perplex'd *Cymbeline* iii 4 7
But remain Perplex'd in all . . . iv 3 41
Why stands he so perplex'd?—What wouldst thou, boy? . . v 5 108
Perplexity. And all our house in a great perplexity . . *T. G. of Ver.* ii 3 9
In perplexity and doubtful dilemma . . . *Mer. Wives* iv 5 85
Avaunt, perplexity! What shall we do? . . . *L. L. Lost* v 2 298
Per se. They say he is a very man per se, And stands alone *Troi. and Cres.* i 2 15
Persecuted. He hath persecuted time with hope . . *All's Well* i 1 16
Persecution. With presented nakedness out-face The winds and persecutions of the sky . . . *Lear* ii 3 12
Persecutor. A persecutor, I am sure, thou art . . *3 Hen. VI.* v 6 31
Perseus. It is a beast for Perseus: he is pure air and fire . *Hen. V.* iii 7 22
Bounding between the two moist elements, Like Perseus' horse *T. and C.* i 3 42
I have seen thee, As hot as Perseus, spur thy Phrygian steed . iv 5 186
Persever. Ay, and perversely she persevers so . . *T. G. of Ver.* iii 2 28
I'll say as they say and persever so . . . *Com. of Errors* ii 2 217
Ay, do, persever, counterfeit sad looks . . . *M. N. Dream* iii 2 237
And will you persever to enjoy her? . . . *As Y. Like It* v 2 4
Instruct my daughter how she shall persever . . . *All's Well* iii 7 37
Say thou art mine, and ever My love as it begins shall so persever . iv 2 37
Persever not, but hear me, mighty kings.—Speak on with favour *K. John* ii 1 421
To persever In obstinate condolement is a course Of impious stubbornness; 'tis unmanly grief . . . *Hamlet* i 2 92
I will persevere in my course of loyalty, though the conflict be sore between that and my blood . . . *Lear* iii 5 23
Persever in that clear way thou goest, And the gods strengthen thee! *Pericles* iv 6 113
Perseverance, dear my lord, Keeps honour bright . *Troi. and Cres.* iii 3 150
The king-becoming graces, As justice, verity, . . . perseverance *Macbeth* iv 3 93
Persia. I am bound To Persia and want guilders for my voyage *C. of Er.* iv 1 4
Persian. By this scimitar That slew the Sophy and a Persian prince That won three fields of Sultan Solyman . . . *Mer. of Venice* ii 1 25
I do not like the fashion of your garments: you will say they are Persian attire; but let them be changed . . . *Lear* iii 6 85

Persist. He persists As if his life lay on't . . . *All's Well* iii 7 42
To persist In doing wrong extenuates not wrong . *Troi. and Cres.* ii 2 186
Persisted. Strange it is, That nature must compel us to lament Our most persisted deeds . . . *Ant. and Cleo.* v 1 30
Persistency. Thou thinkest me as far in the devil's book as thou and Falstaff for obduracy and persistency . . . *2 Hen. IV.* ii 2 50
Persistive. Nought else But the protractive trials of great Jove To find persistive constancy in men . . . *Troi. and Cres.* i 3 21
Person. Canst thou remember A time before we came unto this cell? . . . By what? by any other house or person? . . . *Tempest* i 2 42
They saw the king's ship wreck'd And his great person perish . . i 2 237
Thou mightst call him A goodly person . . . i 2 416
We two, my lord, Will guard your person . . . ii 1 197
And yet she takes exceptions at your person . . *T. G. of Ver.* v 2 3
It is that fery person for all the orld, as just as you will desire *Mer. Wives* i 1 50
Of great admittance, authentic in your place and person . . ii 2 236
Having received wrong by some person . . . iii 1 53
How I may formally in person bear me Like a true friar *Meas. for Meas.* i 3 47
His wife is a more respected person than any of us all . . ii 1 173
Finding yourself desired of such a person . . . ii 4 91
Do no stain to your own gracious person . . . iii 1 208
And did supply thee at thy garden-house In her imagined person . v 1 213
Did not you say you knew that Friar Lodowick to be a dishonest person? . . . v 1 262
You must, sir, change persons with me, ere you make that my report . v 1 339
And never rise until my tears and prayers Have won his grace to come in person hither . . . *Com. of Errors* v 1 116
Anon, I'm sure, the duke himself in person Comes this way . . v 1 119
I bespoke the officer To go in person with me to my house . . v 1 234
That puts the world into her person, and so gives me out . *Much Ado* ii 1 216
You, constable, are to present the prince's own person . . . iii 3 79
Our watch, sir, have indeed comprehended two aspicious persons . . iii 5 50
Which is the duke's own person? . . . *L. L. Lost* i 1 182
I myself reprehend his own person, for I am his grace's tharborough: but I would see his own person in flesh and blood . . . i 1 184
I mean setting thee at liberty, enfreedoming thy person . . . iii 1 125
Master Parson, quasi pers-on . . . iv 2 85
For the nomination of the party writing to the person written unto . iv 2 139
Say he comes to disfigure, or to present, the person of Moonshine *M. N. Dream* iii 1 62
The best wit of any handicraft man in Athens.—Yea, and the best person too . . . iv 2 11
Be assured, My purse, my person, my extremest means, Lie all unlock'd to your occasions . . . *Mer. of Venice* i 1 138
Time travels in divers paces with divers persons . *As Y. Like It* iii 2 327
Well in her person I say I will not have you.—Then in mine own person I die.—No, faith, die by attorney . . . iv 1 92
There was not any man died in his own person, videlicet, in a love-cause iv 1 97
We have our philosophical persons . . . *All's Well* ii 3 2
And in dimension and the shape of nature A gracious person *T. Night* i 5 281
Is there no respect of place, persons, nor time in you? . . ii 3 99
He must observe their mood on whom he jests, The quality of persons . iii 1 70
One face, one voice, one habit, and two persons, A natural perspective! v 1 223
As his person's mighty, Must it [jealousy] be violent . *W. Tale* i 2 453
So have we thought it good From our free person she should be confined ii 1 194
It is his highness' pleasure that the queen Appear in person here in court iii 2 10
Since fate, against thy better disposition, Hath made thy person for the thrower-out Of my poor babe . . . iii 3 29
Asks thee the son forgiveness, As 'twere i' the father's person . iv 4 561
Tender your persons to his presence, whisper him in your behalfs . iv 4 826
To greet a man not worth her pains, much less The adventure of her person . . . v 1 156
Against whose person, So sacred as it is, I have done sin . . v 1 171
Her sin, All punish'd in the person of this child . . *K. John* ii 1 189
And bear possession of our person here, Lord of our presence . ii 1 366
Good reverend father, make my person yours . . . iii 1 224
On pain of death, no person be so bold Or daring-hardy . *Richard II.* i 3 42
We will ourself in person to this war . . . i 4 42
I shall not need transport my words by you; Here comes his grace in person . . . ii 3 82
And sends allegiance and true faith of heart To his most royal person . iii 3 38
These grievous crimes Committed by your person and your followers . iv 1 224
Thus play I in one person many people, And none contented . . v 5 31
That hand shall burn in never-quenching fire That staggers thus my person . . . v 5 110
Said To such a person and in such a place, At such a time . *1 Hen. IV.* i 3 72
Thus did I keep my person fresh and new . . . iii 2 55
I have learn'd, The king himself in person is set forth . . . iv 1 91
What art thou, That counterfeit'st the person of a king? . . v 4 28
And made her serve your uses both in purse and in person . *2 Hen. IV.* ii 1 127
Here doth he wish his person, with such powers As might hold sortance with his quality . . . iv 1 10
We are denied access unto his person . . . iv 1 78
I then did use the person of your father . . . v 2 73
And blunt the sword That guards the peace and safety of your person . v 2 88
Speak in your state What I have done that misbecame my place, My person . . . v 2 101
Not to come near our person by ten mile . . . v 5 69
Therefore take heed how you impawn our person . . *Hen. V.* i 2 21
Enlarge the man committed yesterday, That rail'd against our person . ii 2 41
In their dear care And tender preservation of our person . . ii 2 59
Hear your sentence. You have conspired against our royal person . ii 2 167
Touching our person seek we no revenge . . . ii 2 174
And for our disgrace, his own person, kneeling at our feet . . iii 6 140
He is a friend to Alençon, and an enemy to our person . . . iv 7 164
In thine own person answer thy abuse . . *2 Hen. VI.* ii 1 41
A sort of naughty persons, lewdly bent . . . ii 1 167
It is no policy . . . That he should come about your royal person . iii 1 26
As innocent From meaning treason to our royal person As is the sucking lamb . . . iii 1 70
Those that care to keep your royal person From treason's secret knife . iii 1 173
In care of your most royal person . . . iii 2 254
So might your grace's person be in danger . . . iv 4 45
To o'erbear such As are of better person than myself . *3 Hen. VI.* iii 2 167
In kindness and unfeigned love, First, to do greetings to thy royal person iii 3 52
Myself in person will straight follow you . . . iv 1 133
Ay, wherefore else guard we his royal tent, But to defend his person from night-foes? . . . iv 3 22
What! loss of some pitch'd battle against Warwick?—No, but the loss of his own royal person . . . iv 4 5

Person. His majesty, Tendering my person's safety . . . *Richard III.* i 1 44
He hath kept an evil diet long, And overmuch consumed his royal person i 1 140
My dukedom to a beggarly denier, I do mistake my person all this while i 2 253
Since every Jack became a gentleman, There's many a gentle person made a Jack . . . i 3 73
The peace of England and our persons' safety, Enforced us to this execution . . . iii 5 45
Nay, for a need, thus far come near my person . . . iii 5 85
That no manner of person At any time have recourse unto the princes . iii 5 108
All comfort that the dark night can afford Be to thy person ! . . v 3 81
Think ye see The very persons of our noble story . . *Hen. VIII.* Prol. 26
Is he in person ready?—Ay, please your grace . . . . i 1 117
Or proclaim There's difference in no persons . . . . i 1 139
In person I'll hear him his confessions justify . . . . i 2 5
Traduced by ignorant tongues, which neither know My faculties nor person i 2 73
To your high person His will is most malignant . . . i 2 140
Take good heed You charge not in your spleen a noble person . . i 2 174
There should be one amongst 'em, by his person, More worthy this place i 4 78
And fit it with such furniture as suits The greatness of his person . ii 1 100
We live not to be grip'd by meaner persons . . . . ii 2 136
And prove it too, against mine honour aught, My bond to wedlock, or my love and duty, Against your sacred person . . . ii 4 41
You tender more your person's honour than Your high profession spiritual . . . ii 4 116
Whether ever I . . . spake one the least word that might Be to the prejudice of her present state, Or touch of her good person? . . ii 4 155
Unsolicited I left no reverend person in this court . . . ii 4 220
For no dislike i' the world against the person of the good queen . ii 4 223
I am a woman, lacking wit To make a seemly answer to such persons . iii 1 178
When did he regard The stamp of nobleness in any person Out of himself? iii 2 12
Evermore they pointed To the good of your most sacred person . iii 2 173
Opposing freely The beauty of her person to the people . . . iv 1 68
I, with mine enemies, Will triumph o'er my person; which I weigh not, Being of those virtues vacant . . . v 1 124
Now, good angels Fly o'er thy royal head, and shade thy person ! . v 1 160
He's one o' the soundest judgements in Troy, whosoever, and a proper man of person . . . *Troi. and Cres.* i 2 209
Why will he not upon our fair request Untent his person? . . ii 3 178
At the request of Paris my lord, who's there in person . . . iii 1 33
Procure safe-conduct for his person . . . . . iii 3 277
Is the prince there in person? . . . . . iv 1 2
How novelty may move, and parts with person . . . iv 4 81
Considering how honour would become such a person . *Coriolanus* i 3 11
If any fear Lesser his person than an ill report . . . i 6 70
One thus descended, That hath beside well in his person wrought . ii 3 254
That of all things upon the earth he hated Your person most . . iii 1 15
Thyself, forsooth, hereafter theirs, so far As thou hast power and person iii 2 86
He bears himself more proudlier, Even to my person, than I thought he would . . . iv 7 9
Alack, or we must lose The country, our dear nurse, or else thy person, Our comfort in the country . . . v 3 110
Served his designments In mine own person . . . . v 6 36
And to the love and favour of my country Commit myself, my person, and the cause . . . *T. Andron.* i 1 59
Be your charge, as it is ours, To attend the emperor's person carefully ii 2 8
Hadst thou in person ne'er offended me, Even for his sake am I pitiless ii 3 161
Find those persons out Whose names are written there . *Rom. and Jul.* i 2 35
I am sent to find those persons whose names are here writ, and can never find what names the writing person hath here writ . . i 2 42
That calls our person from our morning's rest . . . v 3 189
There is no harm intended to your person, Nor to no Roman else *J. C.* iii 1 90
Here had we now our country's honour roof'd, Were the graced person of our Banquo present . . . *Macbeth* iii 4 41
How say'st thou, that Macduff denies his person At our great bidding? iii 4 128
To do worse to you were fell cruelty, Which is too nigh your person . iv 2 72
If it assume my noble father's person, I'll speak to it . . *Hamlet* i 2 244
He may not, as unvalued persons do, Carve for himself . . . i 3 19
Will nothing stick our person to arraign In ear and ear . . . iv 5 93
Do not fear our person: There's such divinity doth hedge a king . . iv 5 122
I mean, my lord, the opposition of your person in trial . . . v 2 179
With the mischief of your person it would scarcely allay . *Lear* i 2 179
Show too bold malice Against the grace and person of my master . . ii 2 138
Are my brother's powers set forth?—Ay, madam.—Himself in person there? . . . iv 5 2
He led our powers; Bore the commission of my place and person . . v 3 64
He hath a person and a smooth dispose To be suspected . *Othello* i 3 403
Or keep you warm, Or sue to you to do a peculiar profit To your own person . . . iii 3 80
Eight wild-boars roasted whole at a breakfast, and but twelve persons there; is this true? . . . *Ant. and Cleo.* ii 2 184
For her own person, It beggar'd all description . . . ii 2 202
Cæsar and Antony have ever won More in their officer than person . iii 1 17
If not denounced against us, why should not we Be there in person? . iii 7 6
Can he be there in person? 'tis impossible; Strange that his power should be . . . iii 7 57
Death of one person can be paid but once, And that she has discharged iv 14 27
What's your lordship's pleasure?—Your lady's person: is she ready? *Cymbeline* ii 3 86
She held the very garment of Posthumous in more respect than my noble and natural person . . . iii 5 140
I create you Companions to our person and will fit you With dignities . v 5 21
Married your royalty, was wife to your place; Abhorr'd your person . v 5 40
This her bracelet,—O cunning, how I got it!—nay, some marks Of secret on her person . . . v 5 206
This was a goodly person, Till the disaster that, one mortal night, Drove him to this . . . *Pericles* v 1 36
Personage. With her personage, her tall personage, Her height, forsooth, she hath prevail'd with him . . . *M. N. Dream* iii 2 292
You are more saucy with lords and honourable personages . *All's Well* ii 3 278
Of what personage and years is he? . . . *T. Night* i 5 164
Personal. Importunes personal conference with his grace . *L. L. Lost* ii 1 32
Their encounters, though not personal, have been royally attorneyed with interchange of gifts, letters . . . *W. Tale* i 1 29
Left behind him here, When he was personal in the Irish war *1 Hen. IV.* iv 3 88
Only, we want a little personal strength . . *2 Hen. IV.* iv 4 8
A man no mightier than thyself or me In personal action . *J. Cæsar* i 3 77
For my part, I know no personal cause to spurn at him, But for the general . . . ii 1 11
When he reads Thy personal venture in the rebels' fight, His wonders and his praises do contend . . . *Macbeth* i 3 91
Personal. Giving to you no further personal power To business with the king . . . *Hamlet* i 2 36
His personal return was most required and necessary . . *Lear* iv 3 6
In personal suit to make me his lieutenant, Off-capp'd to him . *Othello* i 1 9
But, notwithstanding, with my personal eye Will I look to't . . ii 3 5
Dares me to personal combat . . . *Ant. and Cleo.* iv 1 3
Not your knowledge, your personal pain, but even Your purse, still open *Pericles* iii 2 46
Personally. So vulgarly and personally accused . *Meas. for Meas.* v 1 160
Personally I lay my claim To my inheritance of free descent *Richard II.* ii 3 135
I could not personally deliver to her What you commanded me *Hen. VIII.* v 1 62
Personate. One do I personate of Lord Timon's frame . *T. of Athens* i 1 69
The lofty cedar, royal Cymbeline, Personates thee . . *Cymbeline* v 5 454
Personated. He shall find himself most feelingly personated . *T. Night* ii 3 173
Personating. It must be a personating of himself . *T. of Athens* v 1 35
Perspective. Contempt his scornful perspective did lend me . *All's Well* v 3 48
One habit and two persons, A natural perspective, that is and is not! *T. N.* v 1 224
Like perspectives, which rightly gazed upon Show nothing but confusion, eyed awry Distinguish form . . . *Richard II.* ii 2 18
Perspectively. You see them perspectively . . . *Hen. V.* v 2 347
Perspicuous. The purpose is perspicuous even as substance *Troi. and Cres.* i 3 324
Persuade. He's a spirit of persuasion, only Professes to persuade *Tempest* ii 1 236
Cease to persuade, my loving Proteus . . . *T. G. of Ver.* i 1 1
Persuade me not; I will make a Star-chamber matter of it . *Mer. Wives* i 1 1
What made me love thee? let that persuade thee there's something extraordinary in thee . . . iii 3 74
She will play with reason and discourse, And well she can persuade *Meas. for Meas.* i 2 191
Do you persuade yourself that I respect you?—Good friar, I know you do iv 1 53
Whiles I Persuade this rude wretch willingly to die . . . iv 3 85
Hold thy tongue.—Nay, rather persuade him to hold his hands *C. of Er.* iv 4 23
Did not the heavenly rhetoric of thine eye . . . Persuade my heart to this false perjury . . . *L. L. Lost* iv 3 62
If your love do not persuade you to come, let not my letter *Mer. of Ven.* iii 2 324
These are counsellors That feelingly persuade me what I am *As Y. Like It* ii 1 11
Persuade him that he hath been lunatic . . *T. of Shrew* Ind. 1 63
We will persuade him, be it possible, To put on better ere he go to church iii 2 127
I am ready to distrust mine eyes And wrangle with my reason that persuades me To any other trust . . . *T. Night* iv 3 14
The silence often of pure innocence Persuades when speaking fails *W. Tale* ii 2 42
It may be so; but yet my inward soul Persuades me it is otherwise *Richard II.* ii 2 29
Then crushing penury Persuades me I was better when a king . . v 5 35
And they should sooner persuade Harry of England than a general petition of monarchs . . . *Hen. V.* v 2 304
Let me persuade you to forbear awhile . . *1 Hen. VI.* iii 1 105
Let us now persuade you.—Not to be gone from hence . . . iii 2 93
Let me persuade you take a better course . . . iv 1 132
Your discretions better can persuade Than I am able to instruct or teach iv 1 158
Stay my thoughts, My thoughts, that labour to persuade my soul *2 Hen. VI.* iii 2 137
Sends me a paper to persuade me patience . . *3 Hen. VI.* iii 3 176
We shall soon persuade Both him and all his brothers unto reason . iv 7 33
Lord cardinal, will your grace Persuade the queen? . *Richard III.* iii 1 33
I persuade me, from her Will fall some blessing to this land *Hen. VIII.* iii 2 50
Call my father to persuade . . . *Troi. and Cres.* v 3 30
If I cannot persuade thee Rather to show a noble grace to both parts Than seek the end of one . . . *Coriolanus* v 3 120
It [drink] persuades him, and disheartens him . . . *Macbeth* ii 3 37
Hadst thou thy wits, and didst persuade revenge, It could not move thus *Hamlet* iv 5 168
What?—Persuade me to the murder of your lordship . . *Lear* ii 1 46
This act persuades me That this remotion of the duke and her Is practice ii 4 114
Persuade me rather to be slave and sumpter To this detested groom . ii 4 219
Yet, I persuade myself, to speak the truth Shall nothing wrong him *Oth.* ii 3 223
Ah, balmy breath, that dost almost persuade Justice to break her sword! v 2 16
There did persuade Great Herod to incline himself to Cæsar *Ant. and Cleo.* iv 6 13
Persuaded. Hath here almost persuaded,—For he's a spirit of persuasion, only Professes to persuade . . . *Tempest* ii 1 234
Nought but mine eye Could have persuaded me . *T. G. of Ver.* v 4 65
How I persuaded, how I pray'd, and kneel'd . *Meas. for Meas.* v 1 93
But I persuaded them, if they loved Benedick, To wish him wrestle with affection . . . *Much Ado* iii 1 41
The magnificoes Of greatest port have all persuaded with him *M. of Ven.* iii 2 283
That have so mightily persuaded him from a first . *As Y. Like It* i 2 219
The best persuaded of himself . . . *T. Night* ii 3 162
I have persuaded him the youth's a devil . . . iii 4 321
He would make you believe it was done in fight, and persuaded us to do the like . . . *1 Hen. IV.* ii 4 339
Who then persuaded you to stay at home? . . *2 Hen. IV.* ii 3 15
We are well persuaded We carry not a heart with us from hence That grows not in a fair consent with ours . . . *Hen. V.* ii 2 20
Are you now persuaded That Talbot is but shadow of himself? *1 Hen. VI.* ii 3 61
Thrice I led him off, Persuaded him from any further act . *2 Hen. VI.* v 3 10
A wise stout captain, and soon persuaded ! . . *3 Hen. VI.* iv 7 30
O, be persuaded ! do not count it holy To hurt by being just *T. and C.* v 3 19
These are almost thoroughly persuaded . . . *Coriolanus* i 1 205
By the marks of sovereignty, knowledge, and reason, I should be false persuaded I had daughters . . . *Lear* i 4 254
She is persuaded I will marry her, out of her own love and flattery *Othello* iv 1 132
I will indeed no longer endure it, nor am I yet persuaded to put up in peace what already I have foolishly suffered . . . iv 2 180
This is not strong enough to be believed Of one persuaded well of *Cymbel.* ii 4 132
Persuading. 'Zounds, it [conscience] is even now at my elbow, persuading me not to kill the duke . . . *Richard III.* i 4 150
Exceeding wise, fair-spoken, and persuading . . *Hen. VIII.* iv 2 52
Almost charmed me from my profession, by persuading me to it *T. of A.* iv 3 455
Persuasion. For he's a spirit of persuasion . . . *Tempest* ii 1 235
You may temper her by your persuasion . . *T. G. of Ver.* iii 2 64
Whose persuasion is I come about my brother . . *Meas. for Meas.* iv 1 47
Neither my coat, integrity, nor persuasion can with ease attempt you . iv 2 205
I will not die to-day for any man's persuasion . . . iv 3 63
With what persuasion did he tempt thy love? . . *Com. of Errors* iv 2 13
I yield upon great persuasion; and partly to save your life . *Much Ado* v 4 95
A good persuasion: therefore, hear me . . . *M. N. Dream* i 1 156
As prisoners to her womanly persuasion . . . *T. of Shrew* v 2 120
Is't possible that my deserts to you Can lack persuasion? . *T. Night* iii 4 383
The English lords By his persuasion are again fall'n off . . *K. John* v 5 11
God give thee the spirit of persuasion and him the ears of profiting *1 Hen. IV.* i 2 170

Persuasion. A peevish self-will'd harlotry, one that no persuasion can do good upon . . . 1 *Hen. IV.* iii 1 199
Can lift your blood up with persuasion . . . . . . v 2 79
By fair persuasions mix'd with sugar'd words . 1 *Hen. VI.* iii 3 18
The best persuasions to the contrary Fail not to use *Hen. VIII.* v 1 147
Or that persuasion could but thus convince me . *Troi. and Cres.* iii 2 171
It should not be, by the persuasion of his new feasting . *T. of Athens* iii 6 8
The persuasion of his augurers May hold him . . . *J. Cæsar* ii 1 200
You are a great deal abused in too bold a persuasion . *Cymbeline* i 4 125
Pert. This pert Biron was out of countenance quite . . *L. L. Lost* v 2 272
Awake the pert and nimble spirit of mirth . . *M. N. Dream* i 1 14
Pertain. No more pertains to me, my lord, than you . *Mer. of Venice* iii 2 202
If she pertain to life let her speak too . . *W. Tale* v 3 113
And all wide-stretched honours that pertain By custom *Hen. V.* ii 4 82
I know but of a single part, in aught Pertains to the state . *Hen. VIII.* i 2 42
No mind that's honest But in it shares some woe ; though the main part Pertains to you alone . . . . . *Macbeth* iv 3 199
Little of this great world can I speak, More than pertains to feats of broil and battle . . . . *Othello* i 3 87
Pertaining. With all their honourable points of ignorance Pertaining thereunto . . . . . *Hen. VIII.* i 3 27
Pertinent. 'Good' should be pertinent ; But, so it is, it is not *W. Tale* i 2 221
My caution was more pertinent Than the rebuke you give it . *Coriolanus* ii 2 67
Pertly. Appear, and pertly ! No tongue ! all eyes ! be silent *Tempest* iv 1 58
Yonder walls, that pertly front your town . . *Troi. and Cres.* iv 5 219
Perttaunt-like. So perttaunt-like would I o'ersway his state . *L. L. Lost* v 2 67
Perturbation. All disquiet, horror and perturbation follows her *M. Ado* ii 1 268
From much grief, from study and perturbation of the brain . 2 *Hen. IV.* i 2 132
O polish'd perturbation ! golden care ! . . . . . iv 5 23
Thy wife, That never slept a quiet hour with thee, Now fills thy sleep with perturbations . . . . . *Richard III.* v 3 161
A great perturbation in nature . . . . *Macbeth* v 1 10
Perturbed. Rest, rest, perturbed spirit ! . . . *Hamlet* i 5 183
The perturb'd court, For my being absent . . . *Cymbeline* iii 4 108
Perusal. He falls to such perusal of my face As he would draw it *Hamlet* ii 1 90
Peruse this paper, madam . . . . . . *T. G. of Ver.* i 2 34
Madam, please you peruse this letter . . . . . iv 4 126
I'll view the manners of the town, Peruse the traders . *Com. of Errors* i 2 13
Peruse this as thou goest . . . . . *Mer. of Ven.* ii 4 39
Peruse them well : Not one of those but had a noble father . *All's Well* ii 3 67
Peruse that letter. You must not now deny it is your hand . *T. Night* v 1 338
Peruse this writing here, and thou shalt know The treason *Richard II.* v 3 49
Let our trains March by us, that we may peruse the men . 2 *Hen. IV.* iv 2 94
I hear the enemy : Out, some light horsemen, and peruse their wings 1 *Hen. VI.* iv 2 43
This morning Papers of state he sent me to peruse . . *Hen. VIII.* iii 2 121
Let me peruse this face . . . . . *Rom. and Jul.* v 3 74
He, being remiss, Most generous and free from all contriving, Will not peruse the foils . . . . . *Hamlet* iv 7 137
That by thy comfortable beams I may Peruse this letter . . *Lear* ii 2 172
Though the catalogue of his endowments had been tabled by his side and I to peruse him by items . . . . . *Cymbeline* i 4 7
I am unworthy for her schoolmaster.—She thinks not so ; peruse this writing else . . . . *Pericles* ii 5 41
Perused. I have perused the note . . . . . *T. of Shrew* i 2 145
Our fair appointments may be well perused . . *Richard II.* iii 3 53
Have you perused the letters from the pope ? . . 1 *Hen. VI.* v 1 1
I have perused her well . . . . . . *Hen VIII.* ii 3 75
I have with exact view perused thee . . . *Troi. and Cres.* iv 5 232
Have you with heed perused What I have written to you ? . *Coriolanus* v 6 62
So much as I have perused, I find it not fit for your o'er-looking . *Lear* i 2 39
Perusing. Both they and we, perusing o'er these notes, May know wherefore we took the sacrament . . . . . *K. John* v 2 5
Perverse. If I were covetous, ambitious or perverse, As he will have me, how am I so poor ? . . . . . . 1 *Hen. VI.* iii 1 29
You do not well To bear with their perverse objections . . . iv 1 129
If thou think'st I am too quickly won, I'll frown and be perverse *R. and J.* ii 2 96
Perversely. Ay, and perversely she persevers so . *T. G. of Ver.* iii 2 28
Perverseness. Still so cruel ?—Still so constant, lord.—What, to perverseness ? you uncivil lady . . . . . *T. Night* v 1 115
Pervert. Trust not my holy order, If I pervert your course *Meas. for Meas.* iv 3 153
Follow him, and pervert the present wrath He hath against himself *Cymb.* ii 4 151
Perverted. He hath perverted a young gentlewoman . *All's Well* iv 3 17
Peseech. I peseech you heartily, scurvy, lousy knave . *Hen. V.* v 1 23
Pester. He hath not fail'd to pester us with message . *Hamlet* i 2 22
Pestered. To be so pester'd with a popinjay . . 1 *Hen. IV.* i 3 50
Ah, how the poor world is pestered with such waterflies ! *Troi. and Cres.* v 1 38
Who then shall blame His pester'd senses to recoil and start ? *Macbeth* v 2 23
Pestering. Behold Dissentious numbers pestering streets *Coriolanus* iv 6 7
Pestiferous. Made such pestiferous reports . . *All's Well* iv 3 340
Thy lewd, pestiferous and dissentious pranks . . . 1 *Hen. VI.* iii 1 15
Pestilence. To walk alone, like one that had the pestilence ! *T. G. of Ver.* ii 1 22
He is sooner caught than the pestilence . . . *Much Ado* i 1 87
Methought she purged the air of pestilence ! . . *T. Night* i 1 20
Or suppose Devouring pestilence hangs in our air . . *Richard II.* i 3 284
Yet know, my master, God omnipotent, Is mustering in his clouds on our behalf Armies of pestilence . . . . . . iii 3 87
A most arch heretic, a pestilence That does infect the land *Hen. VIII.* v 1 45
A pestilence on him ! now will he be mocking . . *Troi. and Cres.* iv 2 21
Now the red pestilence strike all trades in Rome ! . *Coriolanus* iv 1 13
In a house Where the infectious pestilence did reign . *Rom. and Jul.* v 2 10
A pestilence on him for a mad rogue ! . . . *Hamlet* v 1 196
I'll pour this pestilence into his ear . . . *Othello* ii 3 362
The most infectious pestilence upon thee . . . *Ant. and Cleo.* ii 5 61
How appears the fight ?—On our side like the token'd pestilence . iii 10 9
Pestilent. They are Most pestilent to the hearing . . *Hen. VIII.* i 2 49
What a pestilent knave is this same ! . . . *Rom. and Jul.* iv 5 147
A foul and pestilent congregation of vapours . . . *Hamlet* ii 2 315
And wants not buzzers to infect his ear With pestilent speeches . iv 5 91
A pestilent gall to me ! . . . . . . *Lear* i 4 127
A pestilent complete knave ; and the woman hath found him already *Oth.* ii 1 252
The next time I do fight, I'll make death love me ; for I will contend Even with his pestilent scythe . . . *Ant. and Cleo.* iii 13 194
Petar. Let it work ; For 'tis the sport to have the enginer Hoist with his own petar . . . . . . *Hamlet* iii 4 207
Peter. This letter, then, to Friar Peter give . . *Meas. for Meas.* iv 3 142
I would Friar Peter—O, peace ! the friar is come . . . iv 6 9
So deliver I up my apes, and away to Saint Peter for the heavens *M. Ado* ii 1 50
There was no link to colour Peter's hat . . . *T. of Shrew* iv 1 137
Peter, didst ever see the like ?—He kills her in her own humour . . iv 1 182

Peter. And if his name be George, I'll call him Peter . . *K. John* i 1 186
A fig for Peter !—Here, Peter, I drink to thee : and be not afraid.—Be merry, Peter, and fear not thy master . . . . 2 *Hen. VI.* ii 3 67
What 's thy name ?—Peter, forsooth.—Peter ! what more ?—Thump . ii 3 82
And therefore, Peter, have at thee with a downright blow ! . . . ii 3 92
Hold, Peter, hold ! I confess, I confess treason.—Take away his weapon ii 3 96
O Peter, thou hast prevailed in right ! . . . . . ii 3 101
Peter !—Anon !—My fan, Peter.—Good Peter, to hide her face *Rom. and Jul.* ii 4 110
Send thy man away.—Peter, stay at the gate . . . . ii 5 20
The County Paris, at Saint Peter's Church, Shall happily make thee there a joyful bride.—Now, by Saint Peter's Church and Peter too, He shall not make me there a joyful bride . . . . . iii 5 115
Sirrah, fetch drier logs : Call Peter, he will show thee where they are. —I have a head, sir, that will find out logs, And never trouble Peter iv 4 16
You, mistress, That have the office opposite to Saint Peter, And keep the gate of hell ! . . . . *Othello* iv 2 91
Peter Bullcalf. Who is next ?—Peter Bullcalf o' the green ! 2 *Hen. IV.* iii 2 183
Peter Quince, say what the play treats on . . . *M. N. Dream* i 2 8
Now, good Peter Quince, call forth your actors by the scroll . i 2 15
Francis Flute, the bellows-mender.—Here, Peter Quince . . i 2 45
Peter Quince,— What sayest thou, bully Bottom ? . . . iii 1 7
Heigh-ho ! Peter Quince ! Flute, the bellows-mender ! Snout, the tinker ! . . . . iv 1 207
I will get Peter Quince to write a ballad of this dream . . . iv 1 220
Peter Simple, you say your name is ?—Ay, for fault of a better *Mer. Wives* i 4 15
Peter Turph and Henry Pimpernell And twenty more such names and men as these Which never were nor no man ever saw *T. of Shrew* Ind. 2 96
Petit monsieur, que dit-il ? . . . . . . *Hen. V.* iv 4 52
Petition. Do relish the petition well that prays for peace *Meas. for Meas.* i 2 16
All their petitions are as freely theirs As they themselves would owe them . . . . i 4 82
That if any crave redress of injustice, they should exhibit their petitions in the street . . . . iv 4 11
Please you To give this poor petition to the king . . *All's Well* v 1 19
Here 's a petition from a Florentine . . . . . . v 3 130
He would not stay at your petitions . . . . . *W. Tale* i 2 215
Do not receive affliction At my petition . . . . . iii 2 225
But your petition Is yet unanswer'd . . . . . . iii 2 228
Melted by the windy breath Of soft petitions, pity and remorse *K. John* ii 1 478
At my desires, and my requests, and my petitions . . . *Hen. V.* v 1 25
And they should sooner persuade Harry of England than a general petition of monarchs . . . . v 2 305
And that is my petition, noble lord . . . . 1 *Hen. VI.* iv 1 101
That you would love yourself . . . is the point Of my petition *Hen. VIII.* i 2 17
My next poor petition Is, that his noble grace would have some pity Upon my wretched women . . . . iv 2 138
I look'd You would have given me your petition . . . . v 1 118
Thou dost not use me courteously, To shame the zeal of my petition to thee In praising her . . . . *Troi. and Cres.* iv 4 124
Consort with me in loud and dear petition, Pursue we him on knees . v 3 9
And a petition granted them, a strange one . . . *Coriolanus* i 1 214
It was a bare petition of a state To one whom they had punish'd . . v 1 20
Does reason our petition with more strength Than thou hast to deny't v 3 176
I pray you, deliver him this petition . . . . *T. Andron.* iv 3 14
If the redress will follow, thou receivest Thy full petition . *J. Cæsar* ii 1 58
What, urge you your petitions in the street ? Come to the Capitol . iii 1 11
Wrung from me my slow leave By laboursome petition . . *Hamlet* i 2 59
Many our contriving friends in Rome Petition us at home *Ant. and Cleo.* i 2 190
Petitionary. With most petitionary vehemence . . *As Y. Like It* iii 2 199
Pardon Rome, and thy petitionary countrymen . . *Coriolanus* v 2 82
Petitioned. You have, I know, petition'd all the gods For my prosperity ! ii 1 187
Petitioner. O vain petitioner ! beg a greater matter . . *L. L. Lost* v 2 207
Let us, that are poor petitioners, speak too . . . *T. of Shrew* ii 1 72
I am but a poor petitioner of our whole township . . 2 *Hen. VI.* i 3 26
Petitioners for blood thou ne'er put'st back . . . 3 *Hen. VI.* v 5 80
A poor petitioner, A care-crazed mother of a many children *Richard III.* iii 7 183
Peto. Falstaff, Bardolph, Peto and Gadshill shall rob those men 1 *Hen. IV.* i 2 182
Poins ! Hal ! a plague upon you both ! Bardolph ! Peto ! . . . ii 2 22
You fought fair ; so did you, Peto ; so did you, Bardolph . . . ii 4 330
Banish Peto, banish Bardolph, banish Poins : but for sweet Jack Falstaff ii 4 521
Be with me betimes in the morning ; and so, good morrow, Peto . . ii 4 601
Go, Peto, to horse, to horse ; for thou and I have thirty miles to ride . iii 3 220
Bid my lieutenant Peto meet me at town's end . . . . . iv 2 9
Peto, how now ! what news ? . . . . . . 2 *Hen. IV.* ii 4 383
Petrarch. Now is he for the numbers that Petrarch flowed in *R. and J.* ii 4 41
Petruchio. My old friend Grumio ! and my good friend Petruchio ! *T. of S.* i 2 21
Alla nostra casa ben venuto, molto honorato signor mio Petruchio . i 2 26
Petruchio, patience ; I am Grumio's pledge . . . . . i 2 45
Petruchio, shall I then come roundly to thee ? . . . . . i 2 59
If thou know One rich enough to be Petruchio's wife . . . . i 2 67
Petruchio, since we are stepp'd thus far in, I will continue that I broach'd in jest. I can, Petruchio, help thee to a wife with wealth enough . . . . i 2 83
Petruchio, I must go with thee, For in Baptista's keep my treasure is . i 2 117
Now shall my friend Petruchio do me grace . . . . . i 2 131
Peace, Grumio ! it is the rival of my love. Petruchio, stand by a while i 2 143
The motion 's good indeed and be it so, Petruchio, I shall be your ben venuto . . . . i 2 282
Petruchio is my name ; Antonio's son, A man well known throughout all Italy . . . . ii 1 68
Petruchio, I pray, Let us, that are poor petitioners, speak too . . ii 1 71
Petruchio, will you go with us, Or shall I send my daughter Kate to you ? ii 1 167
But here she comes ; and now, Petruchio, speak. Good morrow, Kate ii 1 182
Now, Signior Petruchio, how speed you with my daughter ? . . ii 1 283
Hark, Petruchio ; she says she'll see thee hang'd first . . . ii 1 302
Give me your hands ; God send you joy, Petruchio ! 'tis a match . ii 1 321
There is mad Petruchio's wife, If it would please him come and marry her ! . . . . iii 2 19
Petruchio means but well, Whatever fortune stays him from his word . iii 2 22
Is it not news, to hear of Petruchio's coming ? . . . . . iii 2 33
Petruchio is coming in a new hat and an old jerkin . . . . iii 2 43
Didst thou not say he comes ?—Who ? that Petruchio came ?—Ay, that Petruchio came . . . . iii 2 79
I warrant him, Petruchio is Kated . . . . iii 2 247
The taming-school ! what, is there such a place ?—Ay, mistress, and Petruchio is the master . . . . iv 2 56
Petruchio, fie ! you are to blame. Come, Mistress Kate, I'll bear you company . . . . iv 3 43
Petruchio, go thy ways ; the field is won . . . . . . iv 5 23
Well, Petruchio, this has put me in heart. Have to my widow ! . . iv 5 77

Petruchio. Brother Petruchio, sister Katharina, And thou, Hortensio, with thy loving widow, Feast with the best, and welcome to my house *T. of Shrew* v 2 6
Padua affords this kindness, son Petruchio v 2 13
O ho, Petruchio! Tranio hits you now v 2 57
Now, fair befal thee, good Petruchio! The wager thou hast won v 2 111
Petrucio. What's he that now is going out of door?—Marry, that, I think, be young Petrucio *Rom. and Jul.* i 5 133
Petter. It is petter that friends is the sword, and end it *Mer. Wives* i 1 42
Ay, and her father is make her a petter penny i 1 61
Nay, it is petter yet. Give her this letter i 2 7
Which you and yourself and all the world know to be no petter *Hen. V.* v 1 7
Petticoat. If we walk not in the trodden paths, our very petticoats will catch them *As Y. Like It* i 3 15
Doublet and hose ought to show itself courageous to petticoat ii 4 7
Here in the skirts of the forest, like fringe upon a petticoat iii 2 354
I'll pull them off myself, Yea, all my raiment, to my petticoat *T. of Shrew* ii 1 5
Methought he had made two holes in the ale-wife's new petticoat and so peeped through 2 *Hen. IV.* ii 2 89
Wilt thou make as many holes in an enemy's battle as thou hast done in a woman's petticoat? iii 2 166
You might still have worn the petticoat, And ne'er have stol'n the breech 3 *Hen. VI.* v 5 23
I would not do such a thing for a joint-ring, nor for measures of lawn, nor for gowns, petticoats, nor caps *Othello* iv 3 74
Your old smock brings forth a new petticoat *Ant. and Cleo.* i 2 176
Pettiness. Which in weight to re-answer, his pettiness would bow under *Hen. V.* iii 6 136
Pettish. Yea, watch his pettish lunes, his ebbs, his flows *Troi. and Cres.* ii 3 139
Pettitoes. That he would not stir his pettitoes till he had both tune and words *W. Tale* iv 4 619
Petty. And I for such like petty crimes as these *T. G. of Ver.* iv 1 52
Every pelting, petty officer *Meas. for Meas.* ii 2 112
Do overpeer the petty traffickers *Mer. of Venice* i 1 12
You shall have gold To pay the petty debt twenty times over iii 2 309
These petty brands That calumny doth use *W. Tale* ii 1 71
Your sheep-shearing Is as a meeting of the petty gods iv 4 4
The vital commoners and inland petty spirits 2 *Hen. IV.* iv 3 119
And pretty traps to catch the petty thieves *Hen. V.* i 2 177
To dowry, Some petty and unprofitable dukedoms iii Prol. 31
Except some petty towns of no import 1 *Hen. VI.* i 1 91
These are petty faults to faults unknown 2 *Hen. VI.* iii 1 64
The lives of those which we have lost in fight Be counterpoised with such a petty sum! iv 1 22
Now let the general trumpet blow his blast, Particularities and petty sounds To cease! v 2 44
The petty rebel, dull-brain'd Buckingham *Richard III.* iv 4 332
With other muniments and petty helps *Coriolanus* i 1 122
He had no power, But was a petty servant to the state ii 3 186
This petty brabble will undo us all *T. Andron.* ii 1 62
And we petty men Walk under his huge legs and peep about *J. Cæsar* i 2 136
To-morrow, and to-morrow, and to-morrow, Creeps in this petty pace from day to day *Macbeth* v 5 20
Each petty artery in this body As hardy as the Nemean lion's nerve *Ham.* i 4 82
Each small annexment, petty consequence, Attends the boisterous ruin iii 3 21
Nor for gowns, petticoats, nor caps, nor any petty exhibition *Othello* iv 3 74
To mend the petty present *Ant. and Cleo.* i 5 45
I did not think This amorous surfeiter would have donn'd his helm For such a petty war ii 1 34
May cement their divisions and bind up The petty difference ii 1 49
I was of late as petty to his ends As is the morn-dew on the myrtle-leaf iii 12 8
'Tis exactly valued; Not petty things admitted v 2 140
Nay, stay a little: Were you but riding forth to air yourself, Such parting were too petty *Cymbeline* i 1 111
No more, you petty spirits of region low, Offend our hearing v 4 93
The petty wrens of Tarsus will fly hence, And open this to Pericles *Per.* iv 3 22
Peu. Tu parles bien le langage.—Un peu, madame *Hen. V.* iii 4 3
Je ne doute point d'apprendre, par la grace de Dieu, et en peu de temps iii 4 44
Pew. Hath laid knives under his pillow, and halters in his pew *Lear* iii 4 55
Pew-fellow. And makes her pew-fellow with others' moan *Richard III.* iv 4 58
Pewter. I have . . . Pewter and brass and all things that belong To house or housekeeping *T. of Shrew* ii 1 357
Five year! by'r lady, a long lease for the clinking of pewter 1 *Hen. IV.* ii 4 51
Pewterer's hammer. A' shall charge you and discharge you with the motion of a pewterer's hammer 2 *Hen. IV.* iii 2 281
Phaëthon. Why, Phaëthon,—for thou art Merops' son,—Wilt thou aspire to guide the heavenly car? *T. G. of Ver.* iii 1 153
Like glistering Phaëthon, Wanting the manage of unruly jades *Rich. II.* iii 3 178
Now Phaëthon hath tumbled from his car, And made an evening at the noontide prick 3 *Hen. VI.* i 4 33
O Phœbus, hadst thou never given consent That Phaëthon should check thy fiery steeds, Thy burning car never had scorch'd the earth! ii 6 12
Such a waggoner As Phaëthon would whip you to the west, And bring in cloudy night immediately *Rom. and Jul.* iii 2 3
Phantasime. A phantasime, a Monarcho *L. L. Lost* iv 1 101
I abhor such fanatical phantasimes v 1 20
Phantasma. Between the acting of a dreadful thing And the first motion, all the interim is Like a phantasma, or a hideous dream *J. Cæsar* ii 1 65
Pharamond. This, which they produce from Pharamond, 'In terram Salicam mulieres ne succedant' *Hen. V.* i 2 37
Pharamond The founder of this law and female bar i 2 41
Four hundred one and twenty years After defunction of King Pharamond i 2 58
Pharaoh. Like Pharaoh's soldiers in the reechy painting *Much Ado* iii 3 142
If to be fat be to be hated, then Pharaoh's lean kine are to be loved. No, my good lord 1 *Hen. IV.* ii 4 520
Pharsalia. At Pharsalia, Where Cæsar fought with Pompey *A. and C.* iii 7 32
Pheasant. Advocate's the court-word for a pheasant *W. Tale.* iv 4 768
I have no pheasant, cock nor hen iv 4 770
Phebe. O Phebe, Phebe, Phebe!—Alas, poor shepherd! *As Y. Like It* ii 4 43
Sweet Phebe, do not scorn me; do not, Phebe iii 5 1
O dear Phebe, If ever,—as that ever may be near iii 5 27
Sweet Phebe,— Ha, what say'st thou, Silvius?—Sweet Phebe, pity me iii 5 84
Thou shalt bear it: wilt thou, Silvius?—Phebe, with all my heart iii 5 136
My errand is to you, fair youth; My gentle Phebe bid me give you this iv 3 7
I protest, I know not the contents: Phebe did write it iv 3 22
I never heard it yet; Yet heard too much of Phebe's cruelty iv 3 38
She Phebes me: mark how the tyrant writes iv 3 39
It [to love] is to be all made of sighs and tears; And so am I for Phebe v 2 91
As you love Rosalind, meet: as you love Phebe, meet v 2 129
Phebe. You say, that you'll have Phebe, if she will? *As Y. Like It* v 4 16
Keep your word, Phebe, that you'll marry me, Or else refusing me, to wed this shepherd v 4 21
Pheezar. Thou'rt an emperor, Cæsar, Keisar, and Pheezar *Mer. Wives* i 3 10
Pheeze. I'll pheeze you, in faith.—A pair of stocks, you rogue! *T. of S.* Ind. 1 1
An a' be proud with me, I'll pheeze his pride *Troi. and Cres.* ii 3 215
Phibbus. And Phibbus' car Shall shine from far *M. N. Dream* i 2 37
Philadelphos, king Of Paphlagonia *Ant. and Cleo.* iii 6 70
Philario. My residence in Rome at one Philario's, Who to my father was a friend *Cymbeline* i 1 97
Philarmonus!—Here, my good lord.—Read, and declare the meaning v 5 433
Philemon. My visor is Philemon's roof; within the house is Jove *M. Ado* ii 1 99
Philemon, ho!—Doth my lord call?—Get fire and meat *Pericles* iii 2 1
Philip. Call forth Nathaniel, Joseph, Nicholas, Philip *T. of Shrew* iv 1 92
Where is Nathaniel, Gregory, Philip? iv 1 125
Philip of France, in right and true behalf Of thy deceased brother Geffrey's son *K. John* i 1 7
What is thy name?—Philip, my liege, so is my name begun; Philip, good old sir Robert's wife's eldest son i 1 158
Kneel thou down Philip, but rise more great, Arise sir Richard i 1 161
Good leave, good Philip.—Philip! sparrow i 1 231
Philip of France, if thou be pleased withal, Command thy son and daughter to join hands ii 1 531
Philip of France, on peril of a curse, Let go the hand of that arch-heretic iii 1 191
King Philip, listen to the cardinal iii 1 198
Philip, what say'st thou to the cardinal?—What should he say? iii 1 202
Do so, King Philip; hang no more in doubt.—Hang nothing but a calf's-skin iii 1 219
Austria's head lie there, While Philip breathes iii 2 4
Philip, make up: My mother is assailed in our tent iii 2 5
His father was called Philip of Macedon *Hen. V.* iv 7 21
Helen, the mother of great Constantine, Nor yet Saint Philip's daughters, were like thee 1 *Hen. VI.* i 2 143
Philip and Jacob. A year and a quarter old, come Philip and Jacob *Meas. for Meas.* iii 2 214
Philippan. Then put my tires and mantles on him, whilst I wore his sword Philippan *Ant. and Cleo.* ii 5 23
Philippe, a daughter, Who married Edmund Mortimer, Earl of March 2 *Hen. VI.* ii 2 35
Roger Earl of March, who was the son Of Edmund Mortimer, who married Philippe, Sole daughter unto Lionel Duke of Clarence ii 2 49
Philippi. Bending their expedition toward Philippi *J. Cæsar* iv 3 170
What do you think Of marching to Philippi presently? iv 3 197
The people 'twixt Philippi and this ground Do stand but in a forced affection, For they have grudged us contribution iv 3 204
From which advantage shall we cut him off, If at Philippi we do face him iv 3 211
We'll along ourselves, and meet them at Philippi iv 3 225
Why comest thou?—To tell thee thou shalt see me at Philippi iv 3 284
Then I shall see thee again?—Ay, at Philippi.—Why, I will see thee at Philippi, then iv 3 286
They mean to warn us at Philippi here, Answering before we do demand v 1 5
Two mighty eagles fell, and there they perch'd, Gorging and feeding from our soldiers' hands; Who to Philippi here consorted us v 1 83
The ghost of Cæsar hath appear'd to me Two several times by night; at Sardis once, And, this last night, here in Philippi fields v 5 19
Since Julius Cæsar, Who at Philippi the good Brutus ghosted *A. and C.* ii 6 13
He wept When at Philippi he found Brutus slain iii 2 55
He at Philippi kept His sword e'en like a dancer iii 11 35
Phillida. In the shape of Corin sat all day, Playing on pipes of corn and versing love To amorous Phillida *M. N. Dream* ii 1 68
Philomel, with melody Sing in our sweet lullaby ii 2 13
His Philomel must lose her tongue to-day *T. Andron.* ii 3 43
Cut those pretty fingers off, That could have better sew'd than Philomel ii 4 43
This is the tragic tale of Philomel, And treats of Tereus' treason iv 1 47
For worse than Philomel you used my daughter, And worse than Progne I will be revenged v 2 195
She hath been reading late The tale of Tereus; here the leaf's turn'd down Where Philomel gave up *Cymbeline* ii 2 46
Philomela. Fair Philomela, she but lost her tongue, And in a tedious sampler sew'd her mind *T. Andron.* ii 4 38
Ravish'd and wrong'd, as Philomela was iv 1 52
Philosopher. Divers philosophers hold that the lips is parcel of the mouth *Mer. Wives* i 1 236
Never yet philosopher That could endure the toothache patiently *M. Ado* v 1 35
I fear he will prove the weeping philosopher when he grows old *M. of V.* i 2 53
Such a one is a natural philosopher *As Y. Like It* iii 2 33
The heathen philosopher, when he had a desire to eat a grape, would open his lips when he put it into his mouth v 1 36
I will make him a philosopher's two stones to me 2 *Hen. IV.* iii 2 355
How now, philosopher!—Thou liest.—Art not one?—Yes *T. of Athens* i 1 221
Sometime like a philosopher, with two stones moe than's artificial one ii 2 117
Come with me, fool, come.—I do not always follow lover, elder brother and woman; sometime the philosopher ii 2 131
First let me talk with this philosopher. What is the cause of thunder? *Lear* iii 4 159
I do beseech your grace,—O, cry you mercy, sir. Noble philosopher, your company iii 4 177
With him; I will keep still with my philosopher iii 4 181
Philosophical. We have our philosophical persons *All's Well* ii 3 2
Philosophy. I pine and die; With all these living in philosophy *L. L. Lost* i 1 32
Hast any philosophy in thee, shepherd? *As Y. Like It* iii 2 22
That part of philosophy Will I apply that treats of happiness *T. of Shrew* i 1 18
Continue your resolve To suck the sweets of sweet philosophy i 1 28
Give me leave to read philosophy, And while I pause, serve in your harmony iii 1 13
Preach some philosophy to make me mad *K. John* iii 4 51
Young men, whom Aristotle thought Unfit to hear moral philosophy *Troi. and Cres.* ii 2 167
Adversity's sweet milk, philosophy *Rom. and Jul.* iii 3 55
Hang up philosophy! Unless philosophy can make a Juliet iii 3 57
I am sick of many griefs.—Of your philosophy you make no use, If you give place to accidental evils *J. Cæsar* iv 3 145
Even by the rule of that philosophy By which I did blame Cato v 1 101
There are more things in heaven and earth, Horatio, Than are dreamt of in your philosophy *Hamlet* i 5 167
There is something in this more than natural, if philosophy could find it out ii 2 385
Philostrate, Stir up the Athenian youth to merriments *M. N. Dream* i 1 12
Is there no play, To ease the anguish of a torturing hour? Call Philostrate v 1 38

Philoten. Ripe for marriage-rite; this maid Hight Philoten *Pericles* iv Gower 18
This Philoten contends in skill With absolute Marina . . . . iv Gower 30
This so darks in Philoten all graceful marks . . . . iv Gower 36
Philotus. And Sir Philotus too!—Good day at once . . . *T. of Athens* iii 4 6
Phlegmatic. I beseech you, be not so phlegmatic . . . *Mer. Wives* i 4 79
Phœbe. What is Dictynna?—A title to Phœbe, to Luna, to the moon *L. L. Lost* iv 2 39
When Phœbe doth behold Her silver visage in the watery glass *M. N. D.* i 1 209
Like the stately Phœbe 'mongst her nymphs . . . . *T. Andron.* i 1 316
Phœbus. When I shall think, or Phœbus' steeds are founder'd, Or Night kept chain'd below . . . . *Tempest* iv 1 30
And look, the gentle day, Before the wheels of Phœbus . . *Much Ado* v 3 26
Where Phœbus' fire scarce thaws the icicles . . . *Mer. of Venice* ii 1 5
Die unmarried, ere they can behold Bright Phœbus in his strength *W. T.* iv 4 124
We that take purses go by the moon and the seven stars, and not by Phœbus, he, 'that wandering knight so fair' . . . 1 *Hen. IV.* i 2 16
His brave fleet With silken streamers the young Phœbus fanning *Hen. V.* iii Prol. 6
From the rise to set Sweats in the eye of Phœbus . . . . . iv 1 290
O Phœbus, hadst thou never given consent That Phaëthon should check thy fiery steeds, Thy burning car never had scorch'd the earth! 3 *Hen. VI.* ii 6 11
Modest as morning when she coldly eyes The youthful Phœbus *T. and C.* i 3 230
To the wanton spoil Of Phœbus' burning kisses . . . *Coriolanus* ii 1 234
Gallop apace, you fiery-footed steeds, Towards Phœbus' lodging *R. and J.* iii 2 2
Full thirty times hath Phœbus' cart gone round Neptune's salt wash *Hamlet* iii 2 165
Like the wreath of radiant fire On flickering Phœbus' front . *Lear* ii 2 114
That am with Phœbus' amorous pinches black . . *Ant. and Cleo.* i 5 28
He has deserved it, were it carbuncled Like holy Phœbus' car . . iv 8 29
And golden Phœbus never be beheld Of eyes again so royal! . . . v 2 320
Hark! the lark at heaven's gate sings, And Phœbus 'gins arise *Cymbeline* ii 3 22
Stakes this ring; And would so, had it been a carbuncle Of Phœbus' wheel . . . . v 5 190
Phœnicia. Armenia He gave to Alexander; to Ptolemy he assign'd Syria, Cilicia, and Phœnicia . . . . *Ant. and Cleo.* iii 6 16
Phœnician. Let the Egyptians And the Phœnicians go a-ducking . . iii 7 65
Phœnix. In Arabia There is one tree, the phœnix' throne, one phœnix At this hour reigning there . . . . . . *Tempest* iii 3 23
Home to your house, the Phœnix, sir, to dinner . *Com. of Errors* i 2 75
Thy mistress' marks? what mistress, slave, hast thou?—Your worship's wife, my mistress at the Phœnix . . . . . . i 2 88
To have me home to dinner? My house was at the Phœnix? Wast thou mad? . . . . ii 2 11
And that she could not love me, Were man as rare as phœnix *As Y. L. It* iv 3 17
A phœnix, captain and an enemy, A guide, a goddess . . *All's Well* i 1 182
That Antonio That took the Phœnix and her fraught from Candy *T. Night* v 1 64
From their ashes shall be rear'd A phœnix . . . . 1 *Hen. VI.* iv 7 93
My ashes, as the phœnix, may bring forth A bird . . . 3 *Hen. VI.* i 4 35
But as when The bird of wonder dies, the maiden phœnix, Her ashes new create another heir, As great in admiration as herself *Hen. VIII.* v 5 41
Timon will be left a naked gull, Which flashes now a phœnix *T. of Athens* ii 1 32
Photinus. 'Tis said in Rome That Photinus an eunuch and your maids Manage this war . . . . *Ant. and Cleo.* iii 7 15
Phrase. What phrase is this, 'He hears with ear'? . . *Mer. Wives* i 1 151
'Convey,' the wise it call. 'Steal!' foh! a fico for the phrase! . . i 3 33
I will not say, pity me; 'tis not a soldier-like phrase . . . . ii 1 13
Your cat-a-mountain looks, your red-lattice phrases . . . . ii 2 28
That's somewhat madly spoken.—Pardon it; The phrase is to the matter. —Mended again. The matter; proceed . . . *Meas. for Meas.* v 1 90
That hath a mint of phrases in his brain . . . . *L. L. Lost* i 1 166
Taffeta phrases, silken terms precise, Three-piled hyperboles . . . v 2 406
The gallant militarist,—that was his own phrase . . *All's Well* iv 3 162
'This, and my good wishes:'—her very phrases! . . . *T. Night* ii 5 102
Write from it, if you can, in hand or phrase . . . . . . v 1 340
Good phrases are surely, and ever were, very commendable 2 *Hen. IV.* iii 2 76
Accommodated! it comes of 'accommodo:' very good; a good phrase . iii 2 79
Phrase call you it? by this good day, I know not the phrase . . iii 2 81
This they con perfectly in the phrase of war . . . *Hen. V.* iii 6 79
Are all one reckonings, save the phrase is a little variations . . iv 7 19
These suns—For so they phrase 'em . . . . . *Hen. VIII.* i 1 34
Sodden business! there's a stewed phrase indeed! . . *Troi. and Cres.* iii 1 45
I am proverb'd with a grandsire phrase . . . . *Rom. and Jul.* i 4 37
Or—not to crack the wind of the poor phrase . . . . *Hamlet* i 3 108
They clepe us drunkards, and with swinish phrase Soil our addition . i 4 19
Or by pronouncing of some doubtful phrase, As 'Well, well, we know' . i 5 175
According to the phrase or the addition Of man and country . . ii 1 47
That's an ill phrase, a vile phrase; 'beautified' is a vile phrase . ii 2 111
No matter in the phrase that might indict the author of affectation . ii 2 463
Whose phrase of sorrow Conjures the wandering stars . . . . v 1 278
The phrase would be more german to the matter . . . . v 2 165
Thou speak'st In better phrase and matter than thou didst . . *Lear* iv 6 8
And little bless'd with the soft phrase of peace . . . *Othello* i 3 82
Rail thou in Fulvia's phrase; and taunt my faults . *Ant. and Cleo.* i 2 111
Phrygia. I would play Lord Pandarus of Phrygia . . . *T. Night* iii 1 58
From the Athenian bay Put forth toward Phrygia . *Troi. and Cres.* Prol. 7
His smiling becomes him better than any man in all Phrygia . . i 2 136
Phrygian. Tester I'll have in pouch when thou shalt lack, Base Phrygian Turk! . . . . *Mer. Wives* i 3 97
I have seen thee, As hot as Perseus, spur thy Phrygian steed *Tr. and Cr.* iv 5 186
The fall of every Phrygian stone will cost A drop of Grecian blood . iv 5 223
You vile abominable tents, Thus proudly pight upon our Phrygian plains v 10 24
Phrynia and Timandra had gold of him . . . . *T. of Athens* v 1 5
Physic. Master Caius, that calls himself doctor of physic *Mer. Wives* iii 1 4
'Tis a physic That's bitter to sweet end . . . *Meas. for Meas.* iv 6 7
To the most wholesome physic of thy health-giving air . . *L. L. Lost* i 1 235
Alack, let it blood.—Would that do it good?—My physic says 'ay' . ii 1 188
Begin you to grow upon me? I will physic your rankness *As Y. Like It* i 1 91
I will not cast away my physic but on those that are sick . . iii 2 376
Sweet practiser, thy physic I will try . . . . . *All's Well* ii 1 188
I am sure the younger of our nature, That surfeit on their ease, will day by day Come here for physic . . . . iii 1 19
I know my physic will work with him . . . . *T. Night* ii 3 188
It is a gallant child; one that indeed physics the subject *W. Tale* i 1 43
Physic for't there is none . . . . i 2 200
For the health and physic of our right . . . . . *K. John* v 2 21
In poison there is physic . . . . 2 *Hen. IV.* i 1 137
If he be sick with joy, he'll recover without physic . . . . iv 5 15
I will see what physic the tavern affords . . . 1 *Hen. VI.* iii 1 147
'Tis time to give 'em physic, their diseases Are grown so catching *Hen. VIII.* i 3 36
Physic. He brings his physic After his patient's death . *Hen. VIII.* iii 2 40
That gentle physic, given in time, had cured me . . . . . iv 2 122
If we suffer, Out of our easiness and childish pity To one man's honour, this contagious sickness, Farewell all physic . . . . . . v 3 27
That will physic the great Myrmidon . . . . *Troi. and Cres.* i 3 378
And wish To jump a body with a dangerous physic That's sure of death without it . . . . *Coriolanus* iii 1 154
The violent fit o' the time craves it as physic For the whole state . . ii 2 33
I have given her physic, And you must needs bestow her funeral *T. An.* iv 2 162
Both our remedies Within thy help and holy physic lies *Rom. and Jul.* ii 3 52
What, dost thou go? Soft! take thy physic first—thou too *T. of Athens* iii 6 110
The labour we delight in physics pain . . . . . *Macbeth* ii 3 55
Therein the patient Must minister to himself.—Throw physic to the dogs v 3 47
This physic but prolongs thy sickly days. . . . . *Hamlet* iii 3 96
Take physic, pomp; Expose thyself to feel what wretches feel . *Lear* iii 4 33
Let that grieve him: Some griefs are med'cinable; that is one of them, For it doth physic love . . . . *Cymbeline* iii 2 34
The sceptre, learning, physic, must All follow this, and come to dust . iv 2 268
Sharp physic is the last . . . . *Pericles* i 1 72
'Tis known, I ever Have studied physic . . . . iii 2 32
Since I came, Diseases have been sold dearer than physic . . . iv 6 105
Thy sacred physic shall receive such pay As thy desires can wish . v 1 74
Physical. The blood I drop is rather physical Than dangerous *Coriolanus* i 5 19
Is Brutus sick? and is it physical To walk unbraced and suck up the humours Of the dank morning? . . . . *J. Cæsar* ii 1 261
Physician. Not an eye that sees you but is a physician to comment on your malady . . . . *T. G. of Ver.* ii 1 42
Though Love use Reason for his physician, he admits him not for his counsellor . . . . *Mer. Wives* ii 1 5
You have showed yourself a wise physician . . . . . . ii 3 56
Master Doctor Caius, the renowned French physician . . . . iii 1 61
Will you cast away your child on a fool, and a physician? . . . iii 4 101
Your physicians have expressly charged . . . *T. of Shrew* Ind. 2 123
He hath abandoned his physicians . . . . . . *All's Well* i 1 15
How long is't, count, Since the physician at your father's died? . . i 2 70
He and his physicians Are of a mind; he, that they cannot help him . i 3 243
A poor physician's daughter my wife! . . . . ii 3 122
Hear me, who profess Myself your loyal servant, your physician *W. Tale* ii 3 54
This we prescribe, though no physician . . . . *Richard II.* i 1 154
Put it, God, in the physician's mind To help him to his grave immediately! i 4 59
To the cure Of those physicians that first wounded thee . . . ii 1 99
He was much fear'd by his physicians . . . . 1 *Hen. IV.* iv 1 24
I care not if I do become your physician . . . 2 *Hen. IV.* i 2 143
Marry, the immortal part needs a physician . . . . . . ii 2 112
I take not on me here as a physician . . . . iv 1 60
Sickly, weak, and melancholy And his physicians fear him mightily *Richard III.* i 1 137
'Tis Butts, The king's physician: as he pass'd along, How earnestly he cast his eyes upon me! . . . . *Hen. VIII.* v 2 11
He will be the physician that should be the patient . *Troi. and Cres.* ii 3 223
It gives me an estate of seven years' health; in which time I will make a lip at the physician . . . . *Coriolanus* ii 1 127
His friends, like physicians, Thrive, give him over . . *T. of Athens* iii 3 11
Trust not the physician; His antidotes are poison . . . . iv 3 434
More needs she the divine than the physician . . . . *Macbeth* v 1 82
Kill thy physician, and the fee bestow Upon thy foul disease . *Lear* i 1 166
Then have we a prescription to die when death is our physician *Othello* i 3 311
Most probable That so she died; for her physician tells me She hath pursued conclusions infinite Of easy ways to die . *Ant. and Cleo.* v 2 357
Since he had rather Groan so in perpetuity than be cured By the sure physician, death . . . . *Cymbeline* v 4 7
The queen is dead.—Who worse than a physician Would this report become? . . . . v 5 27
Thou speak'st like a physician, Helicanus, That minister'st a potion unto me That thou wouldst tremble to receive thyself . *Pericles* i 2 67
Pia mater. Nourished in the womb of pia mater . . *L. L. Lost* iv 2 71
One of thy kin has a most weak pia mater . . . . *T. Night* i 5 123
His pia mater is not worth the ninth part of a sparrow . *Troi. and Cres.* ii 1 77
Pibble pabble. I warrant you, that there is no tiddle taddle nor pibble pabble in Pompey's camp . . . . *Hen. V.* iv 1 71
Pible. He has pray his Pible well, dat he is no come . *Mer. Wives* iii 3 7
Picardy. Wallon and Picardy are friends to us . . . 1 *Hen. VI.* ii 1 10
Picardy Hath slain their governors, surprised our forts . 2 *Hen. VI.* iv 1 88
Pick. Pistol, did you pick Master Slender's purse? . . *Mer. Wives* i 1 154
Pick out mine eyes with a ballad-maker's pen . . . . *Much Ado* i 1 254
The whole world again Cannot pick out five such . . *L. L. Lost* v 2 548
Pick his teeth and sing . . . . *All's Well* iii 2 8
We may pick a thousand salads ere we light on such another herb . iv 5 15
And pick strong matter of revolt and wrath . . . *K. John* iii 4 167
Could the world pick thee out three such enemies again? . 1 *Hen. IV.* ii 4 403
Now you pick a quarrel . . . . iii 3 76
This house is turned bawdy-house; they pick pockets . . . . iii 3 114
As I may pick occasion . . . . *Hen. V.* iii 2 111
I climbed into this garden, to see if I can eat grass, or pick a sallet 2 *Hen. VI.* iv 10 9
As high As I could pick my lance . . . . . . *Coriolanus* i 1 204
He could not stay to pick them in a pile Of noisome musty chaff . . v 1 25
Chill pick your teeth, zir: come; no matter vor your foins . *Lear* iv 6 250
Heaven me such uses send, Not to pick bad from bad, but by bad mend! *Othello* iv 3 106
You good gods, give me The penitent instrument to pick that bolt! *Cymb.* v 4 10
If in our youths we could pick up some pretty estate, 'twere not amiss to keep our door hatched . . . . *Pericles* iv 2 36
Pick-axe. A pick-axe, and a spade, a spade, For and a shrouding sheet *Hamlet* v 1 102
An't please the gods, I'll hide my master from the flies, as deep As these poor pickaxes can dig . . . . *Cymbeline* iv 2 389
Pickbone. Francis Pickbone, and Will Squele . . . 2 *Hen. IV.* iii 2 23
Picked. At pick'd leisure Which shall be shortly . . . *Tempest* v 1 247
Picked—with the devil's name!—out of my conversation *Mer. Wives* ii 1 24
He . . . hath pick'd out an act, Under whose heavy sense your brother's life Falls into forfeit . . . . *Meas. for Meas.* i 4 64
He is too picked, too spruce, too affected, too odd, as it were *L. L. Lost* v 1 14
Out of this silence yet I pick'd a welcome . . . *M. N. Dream* v 1 100
Pick'd from the chaff and ruin of the times To be new-varnish'd *M. of V.* ii 9 48
And twice to-day pick'd out the dullest scent . . *T. of Shrew* Ind. 1 24
I picked and cut most of their festival purses . . . *W. Tale* iv 4 627
Then I suck my teeth and catechize My picked man of countries *K. John* i 1 193
Have you inquired yet who picked my pocket? . . 1 *Hen. IV.* iii 3 61
I'll be sworn my pocket was picked . . . . iii 3 70

Picked. Shall I not take mine ease in mine inn but I shall have my pocket picked? . . . . 1 *Hen. IV.* iii 3 94
I fell asleep here behind the arras and had my pocket picked . . iii 3 113
You confess then, you picked my pocket?—It appears so . . iii 3 190
Pick'd from the worm-holes of long-vanish'd days . . *Hen. V.* ii 4 86
Leave their false vows with him, Like empty purses pick'd *T. of Athens* iv 2 12
To be honest . . . is to be one man picked out of ten thousand *Hamlet* ii 2 179
The age is grown so picked that the toe of the peasant comes so near the heel of the courtier, he galls his kibe . . . . . . v 1 151
Besides what hotter hours, Unregister'd in vulgar fame, you have Luxuriously pick'd out . . . . . *Ant. and Cleo.* iii 13 120
This secret Will force him think I have pick'd the lock . *Cymbeline* ii 2 41
Picker. You once did love me.—So I do still, by these pickers and stealers *Hamlet* iii 2 348
Picking. You were beaten in Italy for picking a kernel out of a pomegranate *All's Well* ii 3 276
A great man, I'll warrant; I know by the picking on's teeth *W. Tale* iv 4 780
Thou variest no more from picking of purses than giving direction doth from labouring; thou layest the plot how . . . 1 *Hen. IV.* ii 1 56
Charge an honest woman with picking thy pocket! . . . iii 3 176
The king is weary Of dainty and such picking grievances 2 *Hen. IV.* iv 1 198
Pickle. How camest thou in this pickle?—I have been in such a pickle since I saw you last . . . . *Tempest* v 1 281
Stew'd in brine, Smarting in lingering pickle . *Ant. and Cleo.* ii 5 66
Pickle-herring. A plague o' these pickle-herring! . . . *T. Night* i 5 129
Picklock. We have found upon him, sir, a strange picklock *Meas. for Meas.* iii 2 18
Pick-purse. Is this true, Pistol?—No; it is false, if it is a pick-purse *Mer. Wives* i 1 163
Are pick-purses in love, and we deserve to die . . . *L. L. Lost* iv 3 209
I think he is not a pick-purse nor a horse-stealer . . *As Y. Like It* iii 4 24
Ho! chamberlain!—At hand, quoth pick-purse . . . 1 *Hen. IV.* ii 1 53
Pick-thanks. By smiling pick-thanks and base newsmongers . . . iii 2 25
Pickt-hatch. To your manor of Pickt-hatch! . . . . *Mer. Wives* ii 2 19
Picture. What is this same?—This is the tune of our catch, played by the picture of Nobody . . . . *Tempest* iii 2 136
Love her! 'Tis but her picture I have yet beheld, And that hath dazzled my reason's light . . . . *T. G. of Ver.* ii 4 209
Vouchsafe me yet your picture for my love, The picture that is hanging in your chamber . . . . iv 2 122
Tell my lady I claim the promise for her heavenly picture . . iv 4 92
From my master, Sir Proteus, madam.—O, he sends you for a picture . iv 4 120
Bring my picture there. Go give your master this: tell him from me . iv 4 122
Alas, how love can trifle with itself! Here is her picture . . iv 4 189
You may come and see the picture, she says, that you wot of *Mer. Wives* ii 2 90
What, have you got the picture of old Adam new-apparelled? *Com. of Er.* iv 3 13
If I do not love her, I am a Jew. I will go get her picture . *Much Ado* ii 3 273
I profane my lips on thy foot, my eyes on thy picture . . *L. L. Lost* iv 1 87
O, he hath drawn my picture in his letter!—Any thing like? . . v 2 38
He is a proper man's picture . . . . . . *Mer. of Venice* i 2 78
One of them contains my picture, prince: If you choose that, then I am yours . . . . ii 7 11
One of these three contains her heavenly picture . . . . ii 7 48
All the pictures fairest lined Are but black to Rosalind . *As Y. Like It* iii 2 97
And hang it round with all my wanton pictures . . *T. of Shrew* Ind. 1 47
Dost thou love pictures? . . . . Ind. 2 51
Are they like to take dust, like Mistress Mall's picture? . *T. Night* i 3 136
We will draw the curtain and show you the picture . . . . i 5 252
Did you never see the picture of 'we three?' . . . . . ii 3 17
'Tis my picture; Refuse it not; it hath no tongue to vex you . . iii 4 228
I saw whose purse was best in picture . . . . *W. Tale* iv 4 615
Going to see the queen's picture . . . . v 2 187
I will have it in a particular ballad else, with mine own picture on the top on't . . . . 2 *Hen. IV.* iv 3 53
Long time thy shadow hath been thrall to me, For in my gallery thy picture hangs . . . . 1 *Hen. VI.* ii 3 37
Were but his picture left amongst you here, It would amaze the proudest iv 7 83
Come, draw this curtain, and let's see your picture *Troi. and Cres.* iii 2 50
Thou picture of what thou seemest, and idol of idiot-worshippers . v 1 6
Had I but seen thy picture in this plight, It would have madded me *T. Andron.* iii 1 103
This myself, The vigour and the picture of my youth . . . iv 2 108
What have you there?—A picture, sir . . . . *T. of Athens* i 1 26
How likest thou this picture, Apemantus?—The best, for the innocence i 1 197
The sleeping and the dead Are but as pictures . . . *Macbeth* ii 2 54
Forty, fifty, an hundred ducats a-piece for his picture in little *Hamlet* ii 2 383
Look here, upon this picture, and on this, The counterfeit presentment of two brothers . . . . iii 4 53
Divided from herself and her fair judgement, Without the which we are pictures, or mere beasts . . . . iv 5 86
His picture I will send far and near . . . . . . *Lear* ii 1 83
You are pictures out of doors, Bells in your parlours . . *Othello* ii 1 110
I will write all down: Such and such pictures; there the window *Cymb.* ii 2 25
Who was he That, otherwise than noble nature did, Hath alter'd that good picture? . . . . iv 2 365
Therein He was as calm as virtue—he began His mistress' picture . v 5 175
Averring notes Of chamber-hanging, pictures, this her bracelet . v 5 204
Yon king's to me like to my father's picture . . . *Pericles* ii 3 37
I have drawn her picture with my voice . . . . . . iv 2 101
Pictured. Your death has eyes in's head then; I have not seen him so pictured . . . . *Cymbeline* v 4 185
Picture-like. That it was no better than picture-like to hang by the wall, if renown made it not stir . . . . . *Coriolanus* i 3 12
Pid. When I give watch-'ords, do as I pid you . . *Mer. Wives* v 4 4
Pie. By cock and pie, you shall not choose, sir! . . . . . i 1 316
It is a paltry cap, A custard-coffin, a bauble, a silken pie *T. of Shrew* iv 3 82
Your date is better in your pie and your porridge than in your cheek *All's Well* i 1 173
I must have saffron to colour the warden pies . . . *W. Tale* iv 3 49
By cock and pie, sir, you shall not away to-night . 2 *Hen. IV.* v 1 1
And chattering pies in dismal discords sung . . . 3 *Hen. VI.* v 6 48
No man's pie is freed From his ambitious finger . . *Hen. VIII.* i 1 52
A minced man: and then to be baked with no date in the pie *T. and C.* i 2 280
There they are both, baked in that pie; Whereof their mother daintily hath fed . . . . *T. Andron.* v 3 60
A lenten pie, that is something stale and hoar ere it be spent *R. and J.* ii 4 139
Piece. A brave vessel, Who had, no doubt, some noble creature in her, Dash'd all to pieces . . . . *Tempest* i 2 8
Thy mother was a piece of virtue . . . . i 2 56
Not a holiday fool there but would give a piece of silver . . ii 2 31
One that is well-nigh worn to pieces with age . . . *Mer. Wives* ii 1 22
He pieces out his wife's inclination . . . . . *Mer. Wives* iii 2 34
Defend me from that Welsh fairy, lest he transform me to a piece of cheese! . . . . v 5 86
'Tis time I were choked with a piece of toasted cheese . . . v 5 147
Thou art good velvet; thou'rt a three-piled piece . . *Meas. for Meas.* i 2 33
I do it for some piece of money . . . . ii 1 284
To be overmastered with a piece of valiant dust . . . *Much Ado* ii 1 64
The most dangerous piece of lechery that ever was known . . iii 3 180
As pretty a piece of flesh as any is in Messina . . . . . iv 2 85
Is this such a piece of study? . . . . . . *L. L. Lost* i 2 53
Cut me to pieces with thy keen conceit . . . . . . v 2 399
A very good piece of work, I assure you, and a merry . *M. N. Dream* i 2 14
Thou worms-meat, in respect of a good piece of flesh indeed! *As Y. L. It* iii 2 68
'Tis a very excellent piece of work . . . . . *T. of Shrew* i 1 258
Who is that calls so coldly?—A piece of ice . . . . . iv 1 14
What say you to a piece of beef and mustard? . . . . . iv 3 23
I bid thy master cut out the gown; but I did not bid him cut it to pieces iv 3 129
Half of the which dare not shake the snow from off their cassocks, lest they shake themselves to pieces . . . . *All's Well* iv 3 193
Thou wert as witty a piece of Eve's flesh as any in Illyria *T. Night* i 5 30
That piece of song, That old and antique song we heard last night . ii 4 2
Their transformations Were never for a piece of beauty rarer *W. Tale* iv 4 32
Thou, fresh piece Of excellent witchcraft . . . . . . iv 4 433
The prince himself is about a piece of iniquity . . . . iv 4 693
If I thought it were a piece of honesty to acquaint the king withal, I would not do't . . . . iv 4 695
The most peerless piece of earth, I think, That e'er the sun shone bright on v 1 94
He was torn to pieces with a bear . . . . v 2 68
A piece many years in doing . . . . v 2 104
Shall we thither and with our company piece the rejoicing? . . v 2 117
O royal piece! There's magic in thy majesty . . . . . v 3 38
To take off so much grief from you as he Will piece up in himself . v 3 56
Cut him to pieces.—Keep the peace, I say . . . . *K. John* iv 3 93
Except like curs to tear us all to pieces . . . . *Richard II.* ii 2 139
Twice for one step I'll groan, the way being short, And piece the way out with a heavy heart . . . . v 1 92
Never call a true piece of gold a counterfeit . . . 1 *Hen. IV.* ii 4 540
I will kill all his coats; I'll murder all his wardrobe, piece by piece . v 3 27
I would make him eat a piece of my sword . . . . . v 4 157
A little quiver fellow, and a' would manage you his piece thus 2 *Hen. IV.* iii 2 301
The hopes we have in him touch ground And dash themselves to pieces iv 1 18
Piece out our imperfections with your thoughts . . . *Hen. V.* Prol. 23
We'll bend it to our awe, Or break it all to pieces . . . . i 2 225
I knew by that piece of service the men would carry coals . . iii 2 49
There's not a piece of feather in our host . . . . . iv 3 112
'Tis as arrant a piece of knavery, mark you now, as can be offer't . iv 7 3
And then I will tell him a little piece of my desires . . . v 1 14
A piece of ordnance 'gainst it I have placed . . . . 1 *Hen. VI.* i 4 15
And spurn in pieces posts of adamant . . . . i 4 52
Hew them to pieces, hack their bones asunder . . . . . iv 7 47
Break thou in pieces and consume to ashes, Thou foul accursed minister! v 4 92
And on the pieces of the broken wand Were placed the heads 2 *Hen. VI.* i 2 28
The king and commonweal Are deeply indebted for this piece of pains . i 4 47
And such a piece of service will you do, If you oppose yourselves . v 1 155
And if they fall, they dash themselves to pieces . . *Richard III.* i 3 260
With a piece of scripture, tell them that God bids us do good for evil . i 3 334
Crack'd in pieces by malignant death . . . . ii 2 52
Whom I did suborn To do this ruthless piece of butchery . . . iv 3 5
Rush all to pieces on thy rocky bosom . . . . iv 4 234
If we live thus tamely, To be thus jaded by a piece of scarlet *Hen. VIII.* iii 2 280
No man living Could say 'This is my wife' there; all were woven So strangely in one piece . . . . iv 1 81
This is a piece of malice . . . . v 2 8
What so many may do, Not being torn a-pieces, we have done . . v 4 80
All princely graces, That mould up such a mighty piece as this is . v 5 27
You shall piece it out with a piece of your performance *Troi. and Cres.* iii 1 55
Would drink up The lees and dregs of a flat tamed piece . . iv 1 62
Twice five hundred and their friends to piece 'em . . *Coriolanus* ii 3 220
As an ostler, that for the poorest piece Will bear the knave by the volume iii 3 32
Cut me to pieces, Volsces; men and lads, Stain all your edges on me . v 6 112
Let him die for't.—Tear him to pieces. Do it presently . . v 6 121
Go, give that changing piece To him that flourish'd for her *T. Andron.* i 1 309
Which, cunningly effected, will beget A very excellent piece of villany ii 3 7
I am a pretty piece of flesh.—'Tis well thou art not fish *Rom. and Jul.* i 1 34
Good thou, save me a piece of marchpane . . . . . . i 5 9
What a head have I! It beats as it would fall in twenty pieces . ii 5 50
Let's see your piece.—'Tis a good piece.—So 'tis . . *T. of Athens* i 1 28
A piece of painting, which I do beseech Your lordship to accept . . i 1 155
He's but a filthy piece of work . . . . i 1 202
When dinner's done, Show me this piece . . . . i 1 255
And just of the same piece Is every flatterer's spirit . . . . iii 2 71
What would he have borrowed of you?—A thousand pieces . . iii 6 23
I will promise him an excellent piece . . . . v 1 21
Thus must I piece it out . . . . *J. Cæsar* ii 1 51
A piece of work that will make sick men whole . . . . . ii 1 327
O, pardon me, thou bleeding piece of earth, That I am meek and gentle! iii 1 254
Tear him to pieces; he's a conspirator . . . . iii 3 30
Be ready, gods, with all your thunderbolts; Dash him to pieces! . . iv 3 82
Let us meet, And question this most bloody piece of work . *Macbeth* ii 3 134
Cancel and tear to pieces that great bond Which keeps me pale! . . iii 2 49
Say, What, is Horatio there?—A piece of him . . . . *Hamlet* i 1 19
What a piece of work is a man! how noble in reason! how infinite in faculty! . . . . ii 2 315
Pray God, your voice, like a piece of uncurrent gold, be not cracked . ii 2 447
Will the king hear this piece of work? . . . . iii 2 51
'Tis a knavish piece of work: but what o' that? . . . . . iii 2 251
And shake in pieces the heart of his obedience . . . . *Lear* i 2 92
Caitiff, to pieces shake, That under covert and convenient seeming Hast practised on man's life . . . . iii 2 55
I will piece out the comfort with what addition I can . . . . iii 6 2
Look, look, a mouse! Peace, peace; this piece of toasted cheese will do't iv 6 90
O ruin'd piece of nature! This great world Shall so wear out to nought iv 6 137
There's a poor piece of gold for thee . . . . . . *Othello* iii 1 26
I'll tear her all to pieces.—Nay, but be wise: yet we see nothing done iii 3 431
A likely piece of work, that you should find it in your chamber! . iv 1 156
Sir, you had then left unseen a wonderful piece of work *Ant. and Cleo.* i 2 160
I will piece Her opulent throne with kingdoms . . . . . i 5 45
The piece of virtue, which is set Betwixt us as the cement of our love . iii 2 28
No more a soldier: bruised pieces, go; You have been nobly borne . iv 14 42
To imagine An Antony, were nature's piece 'gainst fancy . . . . v 2 99

Piece. A piece of work So bravely done, so rich . . . . *Cymbeline* ii 4 72
To pieces with me!—O, Men's vows are women's traitors! . . iii 4 55
Thy mistress enforced; thy garments cut to pieces before thy face . iv 1 19
Why should we be tender To let an arrogant piece of flesh threat us? . iv 2 127
'Tween man and man they weigh not every stamp; Though light, take pieces for the figure's sake . . . . v 4 25
And be embraced by a piece of tender air . . . . . v 4 140; v 5 437
Wager'd with him Pieces of gold 'gainst this . . . . v 5 183
Take in your arms this piece Of your dead queen . *Pericles* iii 1 17
The stuff we have, a strong wind will blow it to pieces . . . iv 2 20
I have gone through for this piece, you see: if you like her, so . . iv 2 48
I cannot be bated one doit of a thousand pieces . . . . iv 2 56
When nature framed this piece, she meant thee a good turn . . iv 2 151
Such a piece of slaughter The sun and moon ne'er look'd upon! . . iv 3 2
Thou art a piece of virtue, and I doubt not but thy training hath been noble . . . . iv 6 118
I beseech your honour, one piece for me.—Avaunt, thou damned door-keeper! . . . . iv 6 124
If she were a thornier piece of ground than she is, she shall be ploughed iv 6 153
Pieced. One girth six times pieced . . . . . *T. of Shrew* iii 2 61
Here and there pieced with packthread . . . . . . iii 2 63
There she stands: If aught within that little seeming substance, Or all of it, with our displeasure pieced, And nothing more, may fitly like your grace, She's there, and she is yours . . . . . *Lear* i 1 202
Pie-corner. A' comes continuantly to Pie-corner—saving your manhoods —to buy a saddle . . . . 2 *Hen. IV.* ii 1 28
Pied. What a pied ninny's this! Thou scurvy patch! . . *Tempest* iii 2 71
Daisies pied and violets blue And lady-smocks all silver-white *L. L. Lost* v 2 904
The eanlings which were streak'd and pied . . *Mer. of Venice* i 3 80
Comment appelez-vous le pied et la robe?—De foot, madame; et de coun *Hen. V.* iii 4 53
Piedness. There is an art which in their piedness shares With great creating nature . . . . *W. Tale* iv 4 87
Pier. Peering in maps for ports and piers and roads . . *Mer. of Venice* i 1 19
You have seen The well-appointed king at Hampton pier *Hen. V.* iii Prol. 4
Pierce. That even Ambition cannot pierce a wink beyond . *Tempest* ii 1 242
Relieved by prayer, Which pierces so that it assaults Mercy itself Epil. 17
Throw away that thought; Believe not that the dribbling dart of love Can pierce a complete bosom . . . . . *Meas. for Meas.* i 3 3
Honest plain words best pierce the ear of grief . . *L. L. Lost* v 2 763
And loosed his love-shaft smartly from his bow, As it should pierce a hundred thousand hearts . . . . . . *M. N. Dream* ii 1 160
Can no prayers pierce thee? . . . . . . *Mer. of Venice* iv 1 126
With sweetest touches pierce your mistress' ear . . . . v 1 67
Hearing how our plaints and prayers do pierce, Pity may move thee *Richard II.* v 3 127
Sir Pierce of Exton, who lately came from the king . . . v 5 100
If Percy be alive, I'll pierce him . . . . . 1 *Hen. IV.* v 3 59
Were thy heart as hard as steel, As thou hast shown it flinty by thy deeds, I come to pierce it . . . . 3 *Hen. VI.* i 1 203
Her tears will pierce into a marble heart; The tiger will be mild . . iii 1 38
Can curses pierce the clouds and enter heaven? . . *Richard III.* i 3 195
Thy woes will make them sharp, and pierce like mine . . . iv 4 125
Let some graver eye Pierce into that . . . . . *Hen. VIII.* i 1 68
That the appalled air May pierce the head of the great combatant *Troi. and Cres.* iv 5 5
By and by, the din of war gan pierce His ready sense . . *Coriolanus* ii 2 119
Able to pierce a corslet with his eye; talks like a knell . . . v 4 21
And pierce the inmost centre of the earth . . . *T. Andron.* iv 3 12
Nor yells of mothers, maids, nor babes, Nor sight of priests in holy vestments bleeding, Shall pierce a jot . . . *T. of Athens* iv 3 126
It shall as level to your judgement pierce As day does to your eye *Ham.* iv 5 151
A father's curse Pierce every sense about thee! . . . . *Lear* i 4 323
How far your eyes may pierce I cannot tell: Striving to better, oft we mar i 4 368
Did your letters pierce the queen? . . . . iv 3 11
Arm it [sin] in rags, a pigmy's straw does pierce it . . . . iv 6 171
Whose solid virtue The shot of accident, nor dart of chance, Could neither graze nor pierce . . . . *Othello* iv 1 279
My bended hook shall pierce Their slimy jaws . . *Ant. and Cleo.* ii 5 12
The air is quick there, And it pierces and sharpens the stomach *Pericles* iv 1 29
Pierced. The preyful princess pierced and prick'd a pretty pleasing pricket . . . . *L. L. Lost* iv 2 58
An if one should be pierced, which is the one? . . . . iv 2 86
Pierced through the heart with your stern cruelty . . *M. N. Dream* iii 2 59
Pierced to the soul with slander's venom'd spear . . *Richard II.* i 1 171
Whose loss hath pierced him deep and scarr'd his heart . *T. Andron.* iv 4 31
Not the lark, That pierced the fearful hollow of thine ear *Rom. and Jul.* iii 5 3
But words are words; I never yet did hear That the bruised heart was pierced through the ear . . . . *Othello* i 3 219
It pierced me thorough . . . . *Pericles* iv 3 35
Pierceth. Thus most invectively he pierceth through The body of the country, city, court . . . . *As Y. Like It* ii 1 58
Piercing a hogshead! a good lustre of conceit in a tuft of earth *L. L. Lost* iv 2 89
She uttereth piercing eloquence . . . . . . *T. of Shrew* ii 1 177
Move the still-peering air, That sings with piercing . . *All's Well* iii 2 114
So much to my good comfort, as it is Now piercing to my soul *W. Tale* v 3 34
In high and boastful neighs Piercing the night's dull ear *Hen. V.* iv Prol. 11
Hath not thy rose a thorn Plantagenet?—Ay, sharp and piercing 1 *Hen. VI.* ii 4 70
So doves do peck the falcon's piercing talons . . . 3 *Hen. VI.* i 4 41
These eyes . . . Have been as piercing as the mid-day sun . . v 2 17
More piercing statutes daily, to chain up and restrain the poor *Coriolanus* i 1 86
There is the man of my soul's hate, Aufidius, Piercing our Romans . i 5 12
He tilts With piercing steel at bold Mercutio's breast *Rom. and Jul.* iii 1 164
Piercing steel and darts envenomed Shall be as welcome . *J. Cæsar* v 3 76
Piety. Thou villain, thou art full of piety, as shall be proved *Much Ado* iv 2 81
How his piety Does my deeds make the blacker! . . . *W. Tale* ii 2 172
With forms being fetch'd From glistering semblances of piety *Hen. V.* ii 2 117
But must my sons be slaughter'd . . . ? O, if to fight for king and commonweal Were piety in thine, it is in these . . *T. Andron.* i 1 115
O cruel, irreligious piety!—Was ever Scythia half so barbarous? . . i 1 130
Piety, and fear, Religion to the gods, peace, justice, truth *T. of Athens* iv 1 15
Pig. The capon burns, the pig falls from the spit . *Com. of Errors* i 2 44
'The pig,' quoth I, 'is burn'd;' 'My gold!' quoth he: 'My mistress, sir,' quoth I . . . . ii 1 66
Some men there are love not a gaping pig . . . *Mer. of Venice* iv 1 47
There is no firm reason to be render'd, Why he cannot abide a gaping pig iv 1 54
Where Alexander the Pig was born!—Alexander the Great.—Why, I pray you, is not pig great? the pig, or the great, or the mighty, or the huge, or the magnanimous, are all one reckonings . *Hen. V.* iv 7 14
Weke, weke! so cries a pig prepared to the spit . . *T. Andron.* iv 2 146

Pigeon. This fellow pecks up wit as pigeons pease . . . *L. L. Lost* v 2 315
O, ten times faster Venus' pigeons fly To seal love's bonds! *Mer. of Venice* ii 6 5
With his mouth full of news.—Which he will put on us, as pigeons feed their young . . . . *As Y. Like It* i 2 99
And as pigeons bill, so wedlock would be nibbling . . . . iii 3 82
But for William cook: are there no young pigeons?—Yes, sir 2 *Hen. IV.* v 1 18
Some pigeons, Davy, a couple of short-legged hens, a joint of mutton . v 1 27
Art not thou the carrier?—Ay, of my pigeons, sir; nothing else *T. An.* iv 3 87
I am going with my pigeons to the tribunal plebs . . . . iv 3 92
Make no more ado, But give your pigeons to the emperor . . iv 3 103
I have brought you a letter and a couple of pigeons . . . . iv 4 44
Pigeon-egg. Thou pigeon-egg of discretion . . . . *L. L. Lost* v 1 77
Pigeon-livered. But I am pigeon-liver'd and lack gall . *Hamlet* ii 2 605
Pight. You vile abominable tents, Thus proudly pight upon our Phrygian plains . . . . *Troi. and Cres.* v 10 24
When I dissuaded him from his intent, And found him pight to do it *Lear* ii 1 67
Pigmies. Do you any embassage to the Pigmies . . *Much Ado* ii 1 278
Pigmy. Prepared To whip this dwarfish war, these pigmy arms *K. John* v 2 135
Arm it [sin] in rags, a pigmy's straw does pierce it . . . *Lear* iv 6 171
Pig-nut. I with my long nails will dig thee pig-nuts . *Tempest* ii 2 172
Pigrogromitus. Thou spokest of Pigrogromitus . . . *T. Night* ii 3 23
Pike. Sword, pike, knife, gun, or need of any engine . *Tempest* ii 1 161
You must put in the pikes with a vice . . . . *Much Ado* v 2 21
To come off the breach with his pike bent bravely . . 2 *Hen. IV.* ii 4 55
If the young dace be a bait for the old pike . . . . . iii 2 356
Your naked infants spitted upon pikes . . . . . *Hen. V.* iii 3 38
Trail'st thou the puissant pike?—Even so . . . . . . iv 1 40
He wanted pikes to set before his archers . . . . 1 *Hen. VI.* i 1 116
The soldiers should have toss'd me on their pikes Before I would have granted to that act . . . . 3 *Hen. VI.* i 1 244
Let us revenge this with our pikes, ere we become rakes *Coriolanus* i 1 23
Beat thou the drum, that it speak mournfully: Trail your steel pikes . v 6 152
Make him with our pikes and partisans A grave . . *Cymbeline* iv 2 399
And to grin like lions Upon the pikes o' the hunters . . . v 3 39
Pilate. Though some of you with Pilate wash your hands Showing an outward pity; yet you Pilates Have here deliver'd me to my sour cross, And water cannot wash away your sin . . *Richard II.* iv 1 239
How fain, like Pilate, would I wash my hands Of this most grievous guilty murder done! . . . . *Richard III.* i 4 279
Pilch. What, ho, Pilch!—Ha, come and bring away the nets! *Pericles* ii 1 12
Pilchard. Fools are as like husbands as pilchards are to herrings; the husband's the bigger . . . . *T. Night* iii 1 39
Pilcher. Will you pluck your sword out of his pilcher by the ears? make haste, lest mine be about your ears ere it be out *Rom. and Jul.* iii 1 84
Pile. I must remove Some thousands of these logs and pile them up *Tempest* iii 1 10
I would the lightning had Burnt up those logs that you are enjoin'd to pile! . . . . iii 1 17
I'll bear your logs the while: pray, give me that; I'll carry it to the pile iii 1 25
His left cheek is a cheek of two pile and a half . . . *All's Well* iv 5 103
What piles of wealth hath he accumulated To his own portion! *Hen. VIII.* iii 2 107
In heaps and piles of ruin . . . . *Coriolanus* iii 1 207
Or pile ten hills on the Tarpeian rock . . . . . . iii 2 3
He could not stay to pick them in a pile Of noisome musty chaff . v 1 25
And on a pile Ad manes fratrum sacrifice his flesh . . *T. Andron.* i 1 97
Upon a pile of wood, Let's hew his limbs till they be clean consumed . i 1 128
Now pile your dust upon the quick and dead . . . . *Hamlet* v 1 274
Piled. I had as lief be a list of an English kersey as be piled, as thou art piled, for a French velvet . . . . . . *Meas. for Meas.* i 2 35
Whose foundation Is piled upon his faith . . . . *W. Tale* i 2 430
And piled up The canker'd heaps of strange-achieved gold . 2 *Hen. IV.* iv 5 71
Pilfering. To defend Our inland from the pilfering borderers . *Hen. V.* i 2 142
Such as basest and contemned'st wretches For pilferings and most common trespasses Are punish'd with . . . . . . *Lear* ii 2 151
Pilgrim. A true-devoted pilgrim is not weary To measure kingdoms with his feeble steps . . . . *T. G. of Ver.* ii 7 9
I am Saint Jaques' pilgrim, thither gone . . . . *All's Well* iii 4 4
Look, here comes a pilgrim: I know she will lie at my house . . iii 5 33
God save you, pilgrim! whither are you bound? . . . . . iii 5 35
Tarry, holy pilgrim, But till the troops come by . . . . . iii 5 42
I know your hostess As ample as myself.—Is it yourself?—If you shall please so, pilgrim . . . . iii 5 47
Come, pilgrim, I will bring you Where you shall host . . . iii 5 96
There are pilgrims going to Canterbury with rich offerings . 1 *Hen. IV.* i 2 140
My lips, two blushing pilgrims, ready stand To smooth that rough touch with a tender kiss . . . . *Rom. and Jul.* i 5 97
Good pilgrim, you do wrong your hand too much . . . . . i 5 99
For saints have hands that pilgrims' hands do touch, And palm to palm is holy palmers' kiss . . . . i 5 101
Have not saints lips, and holy palmers too?—Ay, pilgrim, lips that they must use in prayer . . . . i 5 104
Pilgrimage. Giving a gentle kiss to every sedge He overtaketh in his pilgrimage . . . . *T. G. of Ver.* ii 7 30
Let him be prepared; For that's the utmost of his pilgrimage *M. for M.* ii 1 36
That master so their blood, To undergo such maiden pilgrimage *M. N. D.* i 1 75
What lady is the same To whom you swore a secret pilgrimage? *M. of V.* i 1 120
How brief the life of man Runs his erring pilgrimage . *As Y. Like It* iii 2 138
Her pretence is a pilgrimage to Saint Jaques le Grand . . *All's Well* iv 3 57
Like two men That vow a long and weary pilgrimage . . *Richard II.* i 3 49
Thou canst help time to furrow me with age, But stop no wrinkle in his pilgrimage . . . . i 3 230
Which finds it an inforced pilgrimage . . . . i 3 264
His time is spent, our pilgrimage must be . . . . . . ii 1 154
In prison hast thou spent a pilgrimage . . . . . 1 *Hen. VI.* ii 5 116
Wretched, hateful day! Most miserable hour that e'er time saw In lasting labour of his pilgrimage! . . . . . *Rom. and Jul.* iv 5 45
I ask'd his blessing, and from first to last Told him my pilgrimage *Lear* v 3 196
A prayer of earnest heart That I would all my pilgrimage dilate *Othello* i 3 153
Pill. You gave me bitter pills, And I must minister the like *T. G. of Ver.* ii 4 149
My belly's as cold as if I had swallowed snowballs for pills *Mer. Wives* iii 5 24
Large-handed robbers your grave masters are, And pill by law *T. of A.* iv 1 12
Pillage. Which pillage they with merry march bring home . *Hen. V.* i 2 195
Gored the gentle bosom of peace with pillage and robbery . . . iv 1 174
Young Talbot was not born To be the pillage of a giglot wench 1 *Hen. VI.* iv 7 41
Pirates may make cheap pennyworths of their pillage . 2 *Hen. VI.* i 1 222
Thy sons make pillage of her chastity . . . . *T. Andron.* ii 3 44
Pillar. And set it down With gold on lasting pillars . . *Tempest* v 1 208
I charge you by the law, Whereof you are a well-deserving pillar *M. of V.* iv 1 239
Brave peers of England, pillars of the state . . . 2 *Hen. VI.* i 1 75
And call them pillars that will stand to us . . . . 3 *Hen. VI.* ii 3 51

Pillar. And from these shoulders, These ruin'd pillars, out of pity, taken A load would sink a navy, too much honour . *Hen. VIII.* iii 2 382
I wonder now how yonder city stands When we have here her base and pillar by us . *Troi. and Cres.* iv 5 212
You shall see in him The triple pillar of the world . *Ant. and Cleo.* i 1 12
Pilled. The commons hath he pill'd with grievous taxes . *Richard II.* ii 1 246
Hear me, you wrangling pirates, that fall out In sharing that which you have pill'd from me! . *Richard III.* i 3 159
Pillicock sat on Pillicock-hill: Halloo, halloo, loo, loo! . *Lear* iii 4 78
Pillory. I have stood on the pillory for geese he hath killed *T. G. of Ver.* iv 4 35
And there I stood amazed for a while, As on a pillory . *T. of Shrew* ii 1 157
Pillow. One turf shall serve as pillow for us both . *M. N. Dream* ii 2 41
As true a lover As ever sigh'd upon a midnight pillow . *As Y. Like It* ii 4 27
Here I'll fling the pillow, there the bolster . *T. of Shrew* iv 1 204
Set me the crown upon my pillow here . 2 *Hen. IV.* iv 5 5
Why doth the crown lie there upon his pillow, Being so troublesome? . iv 5 21
Where is the crown? who took it from my pillow? . iv 5 58
A good soft pillow for that good white head Were better . *Hen. V.* iv 1 14
Sometime he calls the king And whispers to his pillow as to him The secrets of his overcharged soul . 2 *Hen. VI.* iii 2 375
A book of prayers on their pillow lay . *Richard III.* iv 3 14
Fair thoughts be your fair pillow! . *Troi. and Cres.* iii 1 49
And make his dead trunk pillow to our lust . *T. Andron.* ii 3 130
He danced thee on his knee, Sung thee asleep, his loving breast thy pillow . v 3 163
Pluck stout men's pillows from below their heads . *T. of Athens* iv 3 32
So were their daggers, which unwiped we found Upon their pillows *Macb.* ii 3 109
Infected minds To their deaf pillows will discharge their secrets . v 1 81
Hath laid knives under his pillow, and halters in his pew . *Lear* iii 4 55
Have I my pillow left unpress'd in Rome? . *Ant. and Cleo.* iii 13 106
Weariness Can snore upon the flint, when resty sloth Finds the down pillow hard . *Cymbeline* iii 6 35
Who is this Thou makest thy bloody pillow? . iv 2 363
Lay the babe Upon the pillow: hie thee, whiles I say A priestly farewell *Pericles* iii 1 69
Let me rest.—A pillow for his head: So, leave him all . v 1 237
Pilot. Or four and twenty times the pilot's glass Hath told the thievish minutes how they pass . *All's Well* ii 1 168
Be pilot to me and thy places shall Still neighbour mine . *W. Tale* i 2 448
Yet lives our pilot still. Is't meet that he Should leave the helm and like a fearful lad With tearful eyes add water to the sea? 3 *Hen. VI.* v 4 6
And, though unskilful, why not Ned and I For once allow'd the skilful pilot's charge? . v 4 20
Eyes and ears, Two traded pilots 'twixt the dangerous shores Of will and judgement . *Troi. and Cres.* ii 2 64
I am no pilot; yet, wert thou as far As that vast shore wash'd with the farthest sea, I would adventure for such merchandise *Rom. and Jul.* ii 2 82
Thou desperate pilot, now at once run on The dashing rocks thy sea-sick weary bark! . v 3 117
Here I have a pilot's thumb, Wreck'd as homeward he did come *Macbeth* i 3 28
His pilot Of very expert and approved allowance . *Othello* ii 1 48
These letters give, Iago, to the pilot; And by him do my duties to the senate . iii 2 1
Think his pilot thought . *Pericles* iv 4 18
Pimpernell. Henry Pimpernell And twenty more such names *T. of S.* Ind. 2 96
Pin. From a pound to a pin? . *T. G. of Ver.* i 1 115
A round hose, madam, now's not worth a pin, Unless you have a codpiece to stick pins on . ii 7 56
Tut, a pin! this shall be answered . *Mer. Wives* i 1 117
No matter for the dish, sir.—No, indeed, sir, not of a pin *Meas. for Meas.* ii 1 99
If you should need a pin, You could not with more tame a tongue desire it . ii 2 45
But my life, I'ld throw it down for your deliverance As frankly as a pin iii 1 106
A rush, a hair, a drop of blood, a pin, A nut, a cherry-stone *Com. of Er.* iv 3 73
Then will she get the upshoot by cleaving the pin . *L. L. Lost* iv 1 138
I would not care a pin, if the other three were in . iv 3 18
This gallant pins the wenches on his sleeve . v 2 321
Scratch thee but with a pin, and there remains Some scar of it *As Y. L. It* iii 5 21
And all eyes Blind with the pin and web but theirs . *W. Tale* i 2 291
Pins and poking-sticks of steel, What maids lack from head to heel . iv 4 228
And so locks her in embracing, as if she would pin her to her heart . v 2 84
And with a little pin Bores through his castle wall. . *Richard II.* iii 2 169
My wretchedness unto a row of pins, They'll talk of state . iii 4 26
With hearts in their bellies no bigger than pins' heads . 1 *Hen. IV.* iv 2 24
Die men like dogs! give crowns like pins! . 2 *Hen. IV.* ii 4 189
His apparel is built upon his back and the whole frame stands upon pins iii 2 156
Which show like pins' heads to her . iv 3 58
I'll make thee . . . swallow my sword like a great pin . 2 *Hen. VI.* iv 10 32
I'll tell you what,— Foh, foh! come, tell a pin: you are forsworn *Troi. and Cres.* v 2 22
The kitchen malkin pins Her richest lockram 'bout her reechy neck *Cor.* ii 1 224
Shot thorough the ear with a love-song; the very pin of his heart cleft with the blind bow-boy's butt-shaft . *Rom. and Jul.* ii 4 15
I do not set my life at a pin's fee . *Hamlet* i 4 65
Strike in their numb'd and mortified bare arms Pins, wooden pricks *Lear* ii 3 16
He gives the web and the pin, squints the eye, and makes the hare-lip . iii 4 122
I will not swear these are my hands: let's see; I feel this pin prick . iv 7 56
Pin-buttock. The pin-buttock, the quatch-buttock . *All's Well* ii 2 18
Pinch. Each pinch more stinging Than bees that made 'em . *Tempest* i 2 329
They'll nor pinch, Fright me with urchin-shows, pitch me i' the mire . ii 2 4
He'll fill our skins with pinches, Make us strange stuff . iv 1 233
Whose inward pinches therefore are most strong . v 1 77
Encircle him about And, fairy-like, to pinch the unclean knight *M. W.* iv 4 57
Let the supposed fairies pinch him sound And burn him with their tapers . iv 4 61
And when the doctor spies his vantage ripe, To pinch her by the hand. iv 6 44
There pinch the maids as blue as bilberry . v 5 49
Pinch them, arms, legs, backs, shoulders, sides, and shins . v 5 58
And, as you trip, still pinch him to your time . v 5 96
Pinch him, fairies, mutually; Pinch him for his villany; Pinch him, and burn him . v 5 103
They'll suck our breath or pinch us black and blue *Com. of Errors* ii 2 194
Good Doctor Pinch, you are a conjurer; Establish him in his true sense again . iv 4 50
One Pinch, a hungry lean-faced villain, A mere anatomy, a mountebank . v 1 237
You are not Pinch's patient, are you, sir? . v 1 294
If ye pinch me like a pasty, I can say no more . *All's Well* iv 3 140
All studies here I solemnly defy, Save how to gall and pinch this Bolingbroke . 1 *Hen. IV.* i 3 229
Pinch. The gout galls the one, and the pox pinches the other 2 *Hen. IV.* i 2 258
O majesty! When thou dost pinch thy bearer . iv 5 29
Not rascal-like, to fall down with a pinch, But rather, moody-mad 1 *Hen. VI.* iv 2 49
Here's the pang that pinches . *Hen. VIII.* ii 3 1
Pinch wanton on your cheek; call you his mouse . *Hamlet* iii 4 183
To be a comrade with the wolf and owl,—Necessity's sharp pinch. *Lear* ii 4 214
That am with Phœbus' amorous pinches black . *Ant. and Cleo.* i 5 28
As they pinch one another by the disposition, he cries out 'No more' . ii 7 7
The stroke of death is as a lover's pinch, Which hurts, and is desired . v 2 298
There cannot be a pinch in death More sharp than this is . *Cymbeline* i 1 130
Pinched. Thou shalt be pinch'd As thick as honeycomb . *Tempest* i 2 328
Thou art pinch'd for't now. . v 1 74
I shall be pinch'd to death . v 1 276
The air hath starved the roses in her cheeks And pinch'd the lily-tincture of her face . *T. G. of Ver.* iv 4 160
What, have I pinch d you, Signior Gremio? . *T. of Shrew* ii 1 373
He has discover'd my design, and I Remain a pinch'd thing . *W. Tale* ii 1 51
You might have pinched a placket, it was senseless . iv 4 622
Oft the teeming earth Is with a kind of colic pinch'd . 1 *Hen. IV.* iii 1 29
As a bear, encompass'd round with dogs, Who having pinch'd a few and made them cry, The rest stand all aloof . 3 *Hen. VI.* ii 1 16
If you chance to be pinched with the colic, you make faces . *Coriolanus* ii 1 82
Pinching. Paddling palms and pinching fingers . *W. Tale* i 2 115
How, In this our pinching cave, shall we discourse The freezing hours away? We have seen nothing . *Cymbeline* iii 3 38
Pinch-spotted. More pinch-spotted make them Than pard or cat o' mountain . *Tempest* iv 1 261
Pindarus. Is Cassius near?—He is at hand; and Pindarus is come To do you salutation . *J. Cæsar* iv 2 4
Your master, Pindarus, In his own change, or by ill officers, Hath given me some worthy cause to wish Things done, undone . iv 2 6
Pindarus, Bid our commanders lead their charges off A little . iv 2 47
Go, Pindarus, get higher on that hill; My sight was ever thick . v 3 20
O Cassius, Far from this country Pindarus shall run, Where never Roman shall take note of him . v 3 49
Where did you leave him?—All disconsolate, With Pindarus his bondman v 3 56
What, Pindarus! where art thou, Pindarus? . v 3 72
Hie you, Messala, And I will seek for Pindarus the while . v 3 79
Pine. She did confine thee . . . Into a cloven pine . *Tempest* i 2 277
It was mine art, When I arrived and heard thee, that made gape The pine . i 2 293
And by the spurs pluck'd up The pine and cedar . v 1 48
The mind shall banquet, though the body pine . *L. L. Lost* i 1 25
To love, to wealth, to pomp, I pine and die . i 1 31
As well forbid the mountain pines To wag their high tops *Mer. of Venice* iv 1 75
I pine, I perish, Tranio, If I achieve not this young modest girl *T. of S.* i 1 160
Behind the tuft of pines I met them . *W. Tale* ii 1 34
Fires the proud tops of the eastern pines . *Richard II.* iii 2 42
Go to Flint castle: there I'll pine away; A king, woe's slave . iii 2 209
Towards the north, Where shivering cold and sickness pines the clime . v 1 77
Within a loathsome dungeon, there to pine . 1 *Hen. VI.* ii 5 57
Thus droops this lofty pine and hangs his sprays . 2 *Hen. VI.* ii 3 45
As knots, by the conflux of meeting sap, Infect the sound pine *T. and C.* i 3 8
Weary se'nnights nine times nine Shall he dwindle, peak and pine *Macbeth* i 3 23
All which we pine for now . iii 6 37
Where yond pine does stand, I shall discover all . *Ant. and Cleo.* iv 12 1
This pine is bark'd, That overtopp'd them all. Betray'd I am . iv 12 23
As the rudest wind, That by the top doth take the mountain pine *Cymb.* iv 2 175
Makes both my body pine and soul to languish . *Pericles* i 2 31
Pined. Pity the dearth that I have pined in . *T. G. of Ver.* ii 7 16
She pined in thought, And with a green and yellow melancholy She sat like patience on a monument . *T. Night* ii 4 115
For whom, and not for Tybalt, Juliet pined . *Rom. and Jul.* v 3 236
Since my young lady's going into France, sir, the fool hath much pined away.—No more of that . *Lear* i 4 80
Pinfold. I mean the pound,—a pinfold.—From a pound to a pin? *T. G. of V.* i 1 114
If I had thee in Lipsbury pinfold, I would make thee care for me . *Lear* ii 2 9
Pining. The pining maidens' groans, For husbands, fathers and betrothed lovers . *Hen. V.* ii 4 107
Every wretch, pining and pale before, Beholding him, plucks comfort iv Prol. 41
See, see the pining malady of France; Behold the wounds 1 *Hen. VI.* iii 3 49
Pinion him like a thief, bring him before us . *Lear* iii 7 23
'Tis his schoolmaster: An argument that he is pluck'd, when hither He sends so poor a pinion of his wing . *Ant. and Cleo.* iii 12 4
Pinioned. You must be pinioned . *Mer. Wives* iv 2 129
Know, sir, that I Will not wait pinion'd at your master's court *Ant. and Cleo.* v 2 53
Pink. Nay, I am the very pink of courtesy . *Rom. and Jul.* ii 4 61
Thou monarch of the vine, Plumpy Bacchus with pink eyne! *A. and C.* ii 7 121
Pinked. A haberdasher's wife of small wit near him, that railed upon me till her pinked porringer fell off her head . *Hen. VIII.* v 4 50
Pinnace. Sail like my pinnace to these golden shores . *Mer. Wives* i 3 89
Whilst our pinnace anchors in the Downs . 2 *Hen. VI.* iv 1 9
This villain here, Being captain of a pinnace, threatens more Than Bargulus the strong Illyrian pirate . iv 1 107
Pinned. Our gates, Which yet seem shut, we have but pinn'd with rushes; They'll open of themselves . *Coriolanus* i 4 18
Pinse. Leave your desires, and fairies will not pinse you . *Mer. Wives* v 5 137
Pint. Score a pint of bastard in the Half-moon . 1 *Hen. IV.* ii 4 29
Not past a pint, as I am a soldier . *Othello* ii 3 68
Pint-pot. Peace, good pint-pot; peace, good tickle-brain . 1 *Hen. IV.* ii 4 438
Pioned. Banks with pioned and twilled brims . *Tempest* iv 1 64
Pioner. Have you quit the mines? have the pioners given o'er? *Hen. V.* iii 2 92
Well said, old mole! canst work i' the earth so fast? A worthy pioner! *Hamlet* i 5 163
I had been happy, if the general camp, Pioners and all, had tasted her sweet body, So I had nothing known . *Othello* iii 3 346
Pious. Now, pious sir, You will demand of me why I do this? *M. for M.* i 3 16
Is not this course pious? . *Hen. VIII.* ii 2 37
And thy parts Sovereign and pious else, could speak thee out, The queen ii 4 140
He whose pious breath seeks to convert you . *T. of Athens* iv 3 140
Did he not straight In pious rage the two delinquents tear? . *Macbeth* iii 6 12
Lives in the English court, and is received Of the most pious Edward . iii 6 27
Breathing like sanctified and pious bawds, The better to beguile *Hamlet* i 3 130
The first row of the pious chanson will show you more . ii 2 438
With devotion's visage And pious action we do sugar o'er The devil himself iii 1 48
Paid More pious debts to heaven than in all The fore-end of my time *Cymb.* iii 3 72
Unless you play the pious innocent . *Pericles* iv 3 17
Pip. Being perhaps, for aught I see, two and thirty, a pip out *T. of Shrew* i 2 22

Pipe. Now had he rather hear the tabor and the pipe . . *Much Ado* ii 3 15
When shepherds pipe on oaten straws . . . . . *L. L. Lost* v 2 913
Playing on pipes of corn and versing love To amorous Phillida *M. N. D.* ii 1 67
His big manly voice, Turning again toward childish treble, pipes And whistles in his sound . . . . . *As Y. Like It* ii 7 162
Thy small pipe Is as the maiden's organ, shrill and sound . *T. Night* i 4 32
You would never dance again after a tabor and pipe . *W. Tale* iv 4 183
Rumour is a pipe Blown by surmises, jealousies, conjectures 2 *Hen. IV.* Ind. 15
His hoof is more musical than the pipe of Hermes . . *Hen. V.* iii 7 18
Now crack thy lungs, and split thy brazen pipe . *Troi. and Cres.* iv 5 7
Into a pipe Small as an eunuch, or the virgin voice . *Coriolanus* iii 2 113
When we have stuff'd These pipes and these conveyances of our blood . v 1 54
Then we may go pipe for justice . . . . *T. Andron.* iv 3 24
Faith, we may put up our pipes, and be gone . . *Rom. and Jul.* iv 5 96
Your statue spouting blood in many pipes . . . *J. Cæsar* ii 2 85
Are not a pipe for fortune's finger To sound what stop she please *Hamlet* iii 2 75
Will you play upon this pipe?—My lord, I cannot.—I pray you . iii 2 366
Do you think I am easier to be played on than a pipe? . . . iii 2 387
Put up your pipes in your bag, for I'll away: go; vanish into air . *Oth.* iii 1 20
Piper. Strike up, pipers . . . . . . *Much Ado* v 4 131
Pipe-wine. I shall drink in pipe-wine first with him . *Mer. Wives* iii 2 90
Piping. The winds, piping to us in vain . . *M. N. Dream* ii 1 88
I, in this weak piping time of peace, Have no delight . *Richard III.* i 1 24
Pippin. There's pippins and cheese to come . . . *Mer. Wives* i 2 13
We will eat a last year's pippin of my own graffing . . 2 *Hen. IV.* v 3 2
Pirate. Thou concludest like the sanctimonious pirate . *Meas. for Meas.* i 2 8
Ragozine, a most notorious pirate . . . . . . iv 3 75
Water-thieves and land-thieves, I mean pirates . *Mer. of Venice* i 3 25
Notable pirate! thou salt-water thief! . . . . *T. Night* v 1 72
Antonio never yet was thief or pirate . . . . . v 1 77
Pirates may make cheap pennyworths of their pillage . 2 *Hen. VI.* i 1 222
Threatens more Than Bargulus the strong Illyrian pirate . . iv 1 108
And Suffolk dies by pirates . . . . iv 1 138
Having 'scaped a tempest, Is straightway calm'd and boarded with a pirate iv 9 33
Hear me, you wrangling pirates, that fall out In sharing that which you have pill'd from me! . . . *Richard III.* i 3 158
A pirate of very warlike appointment gave us chase . *Hamlet* iv 6 15
Menecrates and Menas, famous pirates, Make the sea serve them *A. and C.* i 4 48
I must Rid all the sea of pirates; then, to send Measures of wheat to Rome ii 6 36
These roguing thieves serve the great pirate Valdes . *Pericles* iv 1 97
That these pirates, Not enough barbarous, had not o'erboard thrown me! iv 2 69
A crew of pirates came and rescued me; Brought me to Mytilene . v 1 176
Pisa renown'd for grave citizens . . . . *T. of Shrew* i 1 10; iv 2 95
I have Pisa left And am to Padua come . . . . . i 1 21
Some Florentine, Some Neapolitan, or meaner man of Pisa . . i 1 210
A mighty man of Pisa; by report I know him well . . . ii 1 105
I'll leave her houses three or four as good, Within rich Pisa walls . ii 1 369
'Simois,' I am Lucentio, 'hic est,' son unto Vincentio of Pisa . iii 1 33
We'll fit him to our turn,—And he shall be Vincentio of Pisa . iii 2 135
Have you ever been at Pisa?—Ay, sir, in Pisa have I often been . iv 2 93
One mess is like to be your cheer: Come, sir; we will better it in Pisa iv 4 71
My name is call'd Vincentio; my dwelling Pisa; And bound I am to Padua iv 5 55
Tell Signior Lucentio that his father is come from Pisa . . v 1 29
Pisanio. But, good Pisanio, When shall we hear from him? *Cymbeline* i 3 22
He's for his master, And enemy to my son. How now, Pisanio! . i 5 29
Fare thee well, Pisanio; Think on my words . . . . i 5 84
Hear'st thou, Pisanio? He is at Milford-Haven: read, and tell me How far 'tis thither . . . . iii 2 50
True Pisanio,—Who long'st, like me, to see thy lord . . iii 2 54
Pisanio! man! Where is Posthumus? What is in thy mind, That makes thee stare thus? . . . . iii 4 3
Thy mistress, Pisanio, hath played the strumpet in my bed . iii 4 21
That part thou, Pisanio, must act for me, if thy faith be not tainted iii 4 26
That man of hers, Pisanio, her old servant, I have not seen these two days iii 5 54
Pisanio, thou that stand'st so for Posthumus! He hath a drug of mine iii 5 56
Milford, When from the mountain-top Pisanio show'd thee, Thou wast within a ken . . . . iii 6 5
Near to the place where they should meet, if Pisanio have mapped it truly iv 1 2
I am sick still; heart-sick. Pisanio, I'll now taste of thy drug iv 2 37
Pisanio, All curses madded Hecuba gave the Greeks, And mine to boot, be darted on thee! . . . . iv 2 312
Damn'd Pisanio Hath with his forged letters,—damn'd Pisanio—From this most bravest vessel of the world Struck the main-top! . iv 2 317
Pisanio might have kill'd thee at the heart, And left this head on. How should this be? Pisanio? . . . . . iv 2 322
That confirms it home: This is Pisanio's deed, and Cloten's . . iv 2 329
O Pisanio! Every good servant does not all commands . . v 1 5
'If Pisanio Have,' said she, 'given his mistress that confection . . . , she is served As I would serve a rat' . . . . . v 5 245
Pish!—Pish for thee, Iceland dog! . . . . *Hen. V.* ii 1 43
Pish! But, sir, be you ruled by me . . . . . *Othello* ii 1 270
Pish! Noses, ears, and lips.—Is't possible?—Confess—handkerchief! iv 1 42
Pismire. Scourged with rods, Nettled and stung with pismires 1 *Hen. IV.* i 3 240
Piss. Send me a cool rut-time, Jove, or who can blame me to piss my tallow? . . . . *Mer. Wives* v 5 16
Pissing. He had not been there—bless the mark!—a pissing while, but all the chamber smelt him . . . . . . *T. G. of Ver.* iv 4 21
Pissing-conduit. I charge and command that, of the city's cost, the pissing-conduit run nothing but claret wine . 2 *Hen. VI.* iv 6 3
Pistol. Your cony-catching rascals, Bardolph, Nym, and Pistol *Mer. Wives* i 1 129
Pistol!—he hears with ears . . . . i 1 149
Pistol, did you pick Master Slender's purse? . . . . . i 1 154
No quips now, Pistol! . . . . i 3 45
Three of Master Ford's brothers watch the door with pistols . . iv 2 53
Ah, rogue!—Pistol him, pistol him . . . . *T. Night* ii 5 42
Rides at high speed and with his pistol kills a sparrow flying 1 *Hen. IV.* ii 4 380
If Percy be alive, thou get'st not my sword; but take my pistol . v 3 53
Sir, Ancient Pistol's below, and would speak with you . 2 *Hen. IV.* ii 4 74
Welcome, Ancient Pistol. Here, Pistol, I charge you with a cup of sack ii 4 120
No more, Pistol; I would not have you go off here; discharge yourself of our company, Pistol.—No, good Captain Pistol; not here . ii 4 146
Pistol, I would be quiet.—Sweet knight, I kiss thy neif . . ii 4 199
There's one Pistol come from the court with news.—From the court! . v 3 85
What wind blew you hither, Pistol?—Not the ill wind which blows no man to good . . . . v 3 89
I am thy Pistol and thy friend, And helter-skelter have I rode to thee . v 3 97
And shall good news be baffled? Then, Pistol, lay thy head in Furies' lap v 3 110
When Pistol lies, do this; and fig me, like The bragging Spaniard . v 3 124
Pistol, I will double-charge thee with dignities . . . . v 3 130
O sweet Pistol! Away, Bardolph! Come, Pistol, utter more to me . v 3 138
Pistol. Go with me; for the man is dead that you and Pistol beat amongst you . . . . 2 *Hen. IV.* v 4 19
God bless thy lungs, good knight.—Come here, Pistol; stand behind me v 5 10
For Doll is in. Pistol speaks nought but truth . . . . v 5 40
Go with me to dinner: come, Lieutenant Pistol; come, Bardolph . . v 5 95
Are Ancient Pistol and you friends yet?—For my part, I care not *Hen. V.* ii 1 3
Here comes Ancient Pistol and his wife . . . . . ii 1 28
How now, mine host Pistol!—Base tike, call'st thou me host? . . ii 1 30
Pistol's cock is up, And flashing fire will follow . . . . ii 1 55
If you grow foul with me, Pistol, I will scour you with my rapier . ii 1 59
Mine host Pistol, you must come to my master, and you, hostess . ii 1 85
For Pistol, he hath a killing tongue and a quiet sword . . . iii 2 35
What do you call him?—He is called Aunchient Pistol.—I know him not iii 6 19
Aunchient Pistol, I do partly understand your meaning.—Why then, rejoice . . . . iii 6 52
My name is Pistol call'd.—It sorts well with your fierceness . . iv 1 62
The rascally, scauld, beggarly, lousy, pragging knave, Pistol . v 1 6
God pless you, Aunchient Pistol! you scurvy, lousy knave, God pless you! v 1 18
If I can get him within my pistol's length, I'll make him sure enough *Per.* i 1 168
Pistol-proof. She is pistol-proof, sir; you shall hardly offend her 2 *Hen. IV.* ii 4 125
Pit. They are all couched in a pit hard by Herne's oak . *Mer. Wives* v 3 14
Be pold, I pray you; follow me into the pit . . . . v 4 3
She, O, she is fallen Into a pit of ink! . . . . *Much Ado* iv 1 142
Long mayst thou live in Richard's seat to sit, And soon lie Richard in an earthy pit! . . . . *Richard II.* iv 1 219
Food for powder; they'll fill a pit as well as better . 1 *Hen. IV.* iv 2 72
When they show'd me this abhorred pit . . . *T. Andron.* ii 3 98
Tumble me into some loathsome pit . . . . . . ii 3 176
Straight will I bring you to the loathsome pit Where I espied the panther ii 3 193
Like to a slaughter'd lamb, In this detested, dark, blood-drinking pit ii 3 224
A precious ring, that lightens all the hole, . . . And shows the ragged entrails of the pit . . . . ii 3 230
I may be pluck'd into the swallowing womb Of this deep pit . . ii 3 240
Look for thy reward Among the nettles at the elder-tree, Which overshades the mouth of that same pit . . . . . . ii 3 273
Was ever heard the like? This is the pit, and this the elder-tree . ii 3 277
Drag them from the pit unto the prison: There let them bide . ii 3 283
Are they in this pit? O wondrous thing! How easily murder is discovered! . . . . ii 3 286
Our enemies have beat us to the pit . . . . *J. Cæsar* v 5 23
At the pit of Acheron Meet me i' the morning . . . *Macbeth* iii 5 15
Conscience and grace, to the profoundest pit! I dare damnation *Hamlet* iv 5 132
O, a pit of clay for to be made For such a guest is meet . . v 1 104
There's hell, there's darkness, there's the sulphurous pit . . *Lear* iv 6 130
Pitch. The sky, it seems, would pour down stinking pitch . *Tempest* i 2 3
They'll nor pinch, Fright me with urchin-shows, pitch me i' the mire ii 2 5
She loved not the savour of tar nor of pitch . . . . ii 2 54
Shall we desire to raze the sanctuary And pitch our evils there? *Meas. for Meas.* ii 2 172
I think they that touch pitch will be defiled . . *Much Ado* iii 3 60
I am toiling in a pitch,—pitch that defiles: defile! a foul word *L. L. Lost* iv 3 3
Nought enters there, Of what validity and pitch soe'er . *T. Night* i 1 12
How high a pitch his resolution soars! . . . *Richard II.* i 1 109
It is known to many in our land by the name of pitch: this pitch, as ancient writers do report, doth defile . . 1 *Hen. IV.* ii 4 455
The word is 'Pitch and Pay:' Trust none; For oaths are straws *Hen. V.* ii 3 51
Were the whole frame here, It is of such a spacious lofty pitch 1 *Hen. VI.* ii 3 55
Between two hawks, which flies the higher pitch . . . ii 4 11
The very parings of our nails Shall pitch a field when we are dead . iii 1 103
Place barrels of pitch upon the fatal stake . . . . v 4 57
But what a point, my lord, your falcon made, And what a pitch she flew above the rest! . . . . 2 *Hen. VI.* ii 1 6
Their master loves to be aloft And bears his thoughts above his falcon's pitch . . . . ii 1 12
And conversed with such As, like to pitch, defile nobility . . ii 1 196
Here pitch our battle; hence we will not budge . 3 *Hen. VI.* v 4 66
Seduced the pitch and height of all his thoughts . *Richard III.* iii 7 188
Here pitch our tents, even here in Bosworth field . . . v 3 1
All men's honours Lie like one lump before him, to be fashion'd Into what pitch he please . . . . *Hen. VIII.* ii 2 50
On Dardan plains The fresh and yet unbruised Greeks do pitch Their brave pavilions . . . . *Troi. and Cres.* Prol. 14
Mount aloft with thy imperial mistress, And mount her pitch *T. An.* ii 1 14
And so bound, I cannot bound a pitch above dull woe . *Rom. and Jul.* i 4 21
Will make him fly an ordinary pitch, Who else would soar . *J. Cæsar* i 1 78
Enterprises of great pitch and moment . . . . *Hamlet* iii 1 86
So will I turn her virtue into pitch . . . . *Othello* ii 3 366
Pitch-ball. With two pitch-balls stuck in her face for eyes *L. L. Lost* iii 1 199
Pitched. They have pitched a toil; I am toiling in a pitch . iv 3 2
Have I not in a pitched battle heard Loud 'larums? . *T. of Shrew* i 2 206
Sharp stakes pluck'd out of hedges They pitched in the ground 1 *Hen. VI.* i 1 118
On either hand thee there are squadrons pitch'd . . . iv 2 23
What! loss of some pitch'd battle against Warwick? . 3 *Hen. VI.* iv 4 4
And all the lands thou hast Lie in a pitch'd field . *T. of Athens* i 2 231
Pitchers have ears, and I have many servants . . *T. of Shrew* iv 4 52
Be not angry with the child.—Pitchers have ears . *Richard III.* ii 4 37
Pitchy. When saucy trusting of the cozen'd thoughts Defiles the pitchy night . . . . *All's Well* iv 4 24
Night is fled, Whose pitchy mantle over-veil'd the earth . 1 *Hen. VI.* ii 2 2
But I will sort a pitchy day for thee . . . . 3 *Hen. VI.* v 6 85
Piteous. Tell your piteous heart There's no harm done . *Tempest* i 2 14
Piteous plainings of the pretty babes, That mourn'd for fashion *C. of Er.* i 1 73
And the big round tears Coursed one another down his innocent nose In piteous chase . . . . *As Y. Like It* ii 1 40
In an act of this importance 'twere Most piteous to be wild . *W. Tale* ii 1 182
O, the most piteous cry of the poor souls! . . . . . iii 3 91
In thy piteous heart plant thou thine ear . . . *Richard. II.* v 3 126
Piteous they will look, like drowned mice . . . 1 *Hen. VI.* i 2 12
Alas, it was a piteous deed! . . . . . . 3 *Hen. VI.* i 4 163
O piteous spectacle! O bloody times! . . . . . . ii 5 73
To hear the piteous moan that Rutland made . . *Richard III.* i 2 158
The most arch act of piteous massacre That ever yet this land was guilty of iv 3 2
At hand, at hand, Ensues his piteous and unpitied end . . . iv 4 74
Whose misadventured piteous overthrows . . . *Rom. and Jul.* Prol. 7
A piteous corse, a bloody piteous corse; Pale, pale as ashes . . iii 2 54
O woful sympathy! Piteous predicament! . . . . . iii 3 86
The true ground of all these piteous woes . . . . . v 3 180
O piteous spectacle!—O noble Cæsar!—O woful day! . *J. Cæsar* iii 2 202
A look so piteous in purport As if he had been loosed out of hell *Hamlet* ii 1 82
A sigh so piteous and profound As it did seem to shatter all his bulk . ii 1 94

Piteous. Lest with this piteous action you convert My stern effects *Ham.* iii 4 128
Told the most piteous tale of Lear and him That ever ear received *Lear* v 3 214
Piteously. Villanies Ruthful to hear, yet piteously perform'd *T. Andron.* v 1 66
And word it, prithee, piteously *Ant. and Cleo.* iv 13 9
Pitfall. Poor bird! thou 'ldst never fear the net nor lime, The pitfall nor the gin *Macbeth* iv 2 35
Pith. That's my pith of business *Meas. for Meas.* i 4 70
Perhaps you mark'd not what's the pith of all *T. of Shrew* i 1 171
Guarded with grandsires, babies and old women, Either past or not arrived to pith and puissance *Hen. V.* iii Prol. 21
It takes From our achievements, though perform'd at height, The pith and marrow of our attribute *Hamlet* i 4 22
To keep it from divulging, let it feed Even on the pith of life iv 1 23
Since these arms of mine had seven years' pith, Till now *Othello* i 3 83
Pithless. And pithless arms, like to a wither'd vine 1 *Hen. VI.* ii 5 11
Pithy. In a briefer sort, More pleasant, pithy and effectual *T. of Shrew* iii 1 68
Pitié. O, prenez miséricorde! ayez pitié de moi! *Hen. V.* iv 4 12
Pitied I pitied thee, Took pains to make thee speak *Tempest* i 2 353
Lamented, pitied and excused Of every hearer *Much Ado* iv 1 218
If ever from your eyelids wiped a tear And know what 'tis to pity and be pitied *As Y. Like It* ii 7 117
You know, And therefore know how far I may be pitied *All's Well* v 3 161
Which I receive much better Than to be pitied of thee *W. Tale* iii 2 235
They must perforce have melted And barbarism itself have pitied him *Richard II.* v 2 36
She's a woman to be pitied much 3 *Hen. VI.* iii 1 36
But all Was either pitied in him or forgotten *Hen. VIII.* ii 1 29
Yet freshly pitied in our memories v 3 31
The gracious Duncan Was pitied of Macbeth: marry, he was dead *Macb.* iii 6 4
She is importunate, indeed distract: Her mood will needs be pitied *Ham.* iv 5 3
Shall to my bosom Be as well neighbour'd, pitied, and relieved *Lear* i 1 121
My mourning and important tears hath pitied iv 4 26
I know your plight is pitied Of him that caused it *Ant. and Cleo.* v 2 33
And, when we fall, We answer others' merits in our name, Are therefore to be pitied v 2 179
Pitied nor hated, to the face of peril Myself I'll dedicate *Cymbeline* v 1 28
Pitiedest. Thou pitied'st Rutland; I will pity thee 3 *Hen. VI.* ii 6 74
Pities. Considers she my possessions?—O, ay; and pities them *T. G. of V.* v 2 26
The want of which vain dew Perchance shall dry your pities *W. Tale* ii 1 110
A begging prince what beggar pities not? *Richard III.* i 4 274
If any power pities wretched tears, To that I call! *T. Andron.* iii 1 209
If any one relieves or pities him, For the offence he dies v 3 181
Here's a night pities neither wise man nor fool *Lear* iii 2 13
Pitiful. Alas, I should be a pitiful lady! *Mer. Wives* iii 3 56
And knows me, and knows me, How pitiful I deserve *Much Ado* v 2 29
Making such pitiful dole over them *As Y. Like It* i 2 139
Pitiful rumour may report my flight, To consolate thine ear *All's Well* iii 2 130
The ballad is very pitiful and as true.—Is it true too? *W. Tale* iv 4 286
Though my case be a pitiful one, I hope I shall not be flayed out of it iv 4 845
Good ground, be pitiful and hurt me not! *K. John* iv 3 2
Hadst thou groan'd for him As I have done, thou wouldst be more pitiful. But now I know thy mind *Richard II.* v 2 103
Thy precious rich crown for a pitiful bald crown! 1 *Hen. IV.* ii 4 420
I did never see such pitiful rascals iv 2 70
Who should be pitiful, if you be not? 1 *Hen. VI.* iii 1 109
The pitiful complaints Of such as your oppression feeds upon iv 1 57
Women are soft, mild, pitiful and flexible 3 *Hen. VI.* i 4 141
Be pitiful, dread lord, and grant it then iii 2 32
I would to God my heart were flint, like Edward's; Or Edward's soft and pitiful, like mine *Richard III.* i 3 141
He was never, But where he meant to ruin, pitiful *Hen. VIII.* iv 2 40
Let all pitiful goers-between be called to the world's end after my name; call them all Pandars *Troi. and Cres.* iii 2 208
O, be to me, though thy hard heart say no, Nothing so kind, but something pitiful! *T. Andron.* ii 3 156
Be pitiful to my condemned sons, Whose souls are not corrupted iii 1 8
Well you know, this is a pitiful case *Rom. and Jul.* iv 5 99
Pitiful sight! here lies the county slain v 3 174
Our hearts you see not; they are pitiful *J. Cæsar* iii 1 169
Come, seeling night, Scarf up the tender eye of pitiful day! *Macbeth* iii 2 47
All swoln and ulcerous, pitiful to the eye, The mere despair of surgery iv 3 151
And shows a most pitiful ambition in the fool that uses it *Hamlet* iii 2 49
A sight most pitiful in the meanest wretch *Lear* iv 6 208
'Twas passing strange, 'Twas pitiful, 'twas wondrous pitiful *Othello* i 3 161
'Tis pitiful; but yet Iago knows v 2 210
It grieved my heart to hear what pitiful cries they made to us *Pericles* ii 1 22
Pitiful-hearted. Didst thou never see Titan kiss a dish of butter? pitiful-hearted Titan! 1 *Hen. IV.* ii 4 134
Pitifully. Trust me, he beat him most pitifully *Mer. Wives* iv 2 212
As you are great, be pitifully good *T. of Athens* iii 5 52
Which pitifully disaster the cheeks *Ant. and Cleo.* ii 7 18
A strong wind will blow it to pieces, they are so pitifully sodden *Per.* iv 2 21
Pitiless. A fiend, a fury, pitiless and rough *Com. of Errors* iv 2 35
Must you be therefore proud and pitiless? *As Y. Like It* iii 5 40
Even for his sake am I pitiless *T. Andron.* ii 3 162
Wheresoe'er you are, That bide the pelting of this pitiless storm *Lear* iii 4 29
Pittance. You are like to have a thin and slender pittance *T. of Shrew* iv 4 61
Pittie-ward. The pittie-ward, the park-ward, every way *Mer. Wives* iii 1 5
Pittikins. 'Ods pittikins! can it be six mile yet? *Cymbeline* iv 2 293
Pity. Alack, for pity! I, not remembering how I cried out then, Will cry it o'er again *Tempest* i 2 132
To sigh To the winds whose pity, sighing back again, Did us but loving wrong i 2 150
Pity move my father To be inclined my way! i 2 446
Sir, have pity; I'll be his surety i 2 474
A very pebble stone, and has no more pity in him than a dog *T. G. of Ver.* ii 3 12
Pity the dearth that I have pined in, By longing for that food so long ii 7 16
Madam, I pity much your grievances iv 3 37
I cannot choose But pity her.—Wherefore shouldst thou pity her? iv 4 83
'Tis pity love should be so contrary iv 4 88
Why do I pity him That with his very heart despiseth me? iv 4 98
Because I love him, I must pity him iv 4 101
'Twere pity two such friends should be long foes v 4 118
I will not say, pity me; 'tis not a soldier-like phrase *Mer. Wives* ii 1 13
Courage! there will be pity taken on you *Meas. for Meas.* i 2 112
It is pity of her life, for it is a naughty house ii 1 77
Yet show some pity.—I show it most of all when I show justice; For then I pity those I do not know ii 2 99
Whose very comfort Is still a dying horror!—'Tis pity of him ii 3 42
If my brother wrought by my pity, it should not be so with him ii 2 223
The one has my pity; not a jot the other *Meas. for Meas.* iv 2 64
Excludes all pity from our threatening looks *Com. of Errors* i 1 10
Do not break off so; For we may pity, though not pardon thee i 1 98
He, sir, that takes pity on decayed men and gives them suits of durance iv 3 26
'Tis pity that thou livest To walk where any honest men resort v 1 27
They seem to pity the lady: it seems her affections have their full bent. Love me! why, it must be requited *Much Ado* ii 3 231
If I do not take pity of her, I am a villain; if I do not love her, I am a Jew ii 3 271
It were pity but they should suffer salvation, body and soul iii 3 2
I will have thee; but, by this light, I take thee for pity v 4 93
Not wounding, pity would not let me do't *L. L. Lost* iv 1 27
It were pity you should get your living by reckoning v 2 497
Ay me, for pity! what a dream was here! *M. N. Dream* ii 2 147
If you think I come hither as a lion, it were pity of my life iii 1 44
The more the pity that some honest neighbours will not make them friends iii 1 148
To love unloved? This you should pity rather than despise iii 2 235
If you have any pity, grace, or manners iii 2 241
See'st thou this sweet sight? Her dotage now I do begin to pity iv 1 52
If I should as lion come in strife Into this place, 'twere pity on my life v 1 229
Beshrew my heart, but I pity the man v 1 295
But I bar to-night: you shall not gauge me By what we do to-night.—No, that were pity *Mer. of Venice* ii 2 209
An inhuman wretch Uncapable of pity, void and empty From any dram of mercy iv 1 5
Forgive a moiety of the principal; Glancing an eye of pity on his losses iv 1 27
The more pity, that fools may not speak wisely what wise men do foolishly.—By my troth, thou sayest true *As Y. Like It* i 2 92
In pity of the challenger's youth I would fain dissuade him i 2 170
People praise her for her virtues And pity her for her good father's sake i 2 293
Her very silence and her patience Speak to the people, and they pity her i 3 81
I pity her And wish, for her sake more than for mine own, My fortunes were more able to relieve her ii 4 75
And know what 'tis to pity and be pitied ii 7 117
And wiped our eyes Of drops that sacred pity hath engender'd ii 7 123
Though it be pity to see such a sight, it well becomes the ground iii 2 255
When that time comes, Afflict me with thy mocks, pity me not; As till that time I shall not pity thee iii 5 33
Sweet Phebe, pity me.—Why, I am sorry for thee, gentle Silvius iii 5 85
Do you pity him? no, he deserves no pity. Wilt thou love such a woman? iv 3 66
'D sol re,' one clef, two notes have I: 'E la mi,' show pity, or I die *T. of Shrew* iii 1 78
There commendations go with pity *All's Well* i 1 50
'Tis pity— What's pity?—That wishing well had not a body in't i 1 193
Give pity To her, whose state is such that cannot choose i 3 219
In the name of justice, Without all terms of pity ii 3 173
I'll have no more pity of his age than I would have of— I'll beat him ii 3 254
I like him well.—'Tis pity he is not honest iii 5 85
I do pity his distress in my similes of comfort v 2 25
O, you should not rest Between the elements of air and earth, But you should pity me! *T. Night* i 5 295
An we do not, it is pity of our lives ii 5 14
I pity you.—That's a degree to love.—No, not a grize; for 'tis a vulgar proof, That very oft we pity enemies iii 1 134
'Tis pity she's not honest, honourable *W. Tale* ii 1 68
Wolves and bears, they say, Casting their savageness aside have done Like offices of pity ii 3 189
But see The flatness of my misery, yet with eyes Of pity, not revenge! iii 2 124
I'll take it up for pity: yet I'll tarry till my son come iii 3 78
I cannot say 'tis pity She lacks instructions iv 4 592
Though it be great pity, yet it is necessary iv 4 804
You pity not the state, nor the remembrance Of his most sovereign name v 1 25
Melted by the windy breath Of soft petitions, pity and remorse *K. John* ii 1 478
He doth espy Himself love's traitor: this is pity now ii 1 507
And is't not pity, O my grieved friends? v 2 24
Unless you call it good to pity him *Richard II.* ii 1 236
O, what pity is it That he had not so trimm'd and dress'd his land! iii 4 55
Though some of you with Pilate wash your hands Showing an outward pity iv 1 240
Look up, behold, That you in pity may dissolve to dew v 1 9
Forget to pity him, lest thy pity prove A serpent that will sting thee v 3 57
Pity me, open the door: A beggar begs that never begg'd before v 3 77
Say 'pardon,' king; let pity teach thee how: the word is short v 3 116
Hearing how our plaints and prayers do pierce, Pity may move thee v 3 128
And that it was great pity, so it was 1 *Hen. IV.* i 3 59
Were't not for laughing, I should pity him.—How the rogue roar'd! ii 2 117
That he is old, the more the pity, his white hairs do witness it ii 4 514
My father, in kind heart and pity moved, Swore him assistance iv 3 64
He hath a tear for pity and a hand Open as day for melting charity 2 *Hen. IV.* iv 4 31
You men of Harfleur, Take pity of your town and of your people *Hen. V.* iii 3 28
Where—O for pity!—we shall much disgrace . . . The name of Agincourt iv Prol. 49
Again in pity of my hard distress 1 *Hen. VI.* ii 5 87
Pity the city of London, pity us! iii 1 77
For God's sake, pity my case 2 *Hen. VI.* i 3 218
Pity was all the fault that was in me iii 1 125
Is cold in great affairs, Too full of foolish pity iii 1 225
Which makes me hope you are not void of pity iv 7 69
Henceforth I will not have to do with pity v 2 56
Sweet Clifford, pity me!—Such pity as my rapier's point affords 3 *Hen. VI.* i 3 36
Thou hast one son; for his sake pity me i 3 40
This too much lenity And harmful pity must be laid aside ii 2 10
Were it not pity that this goodly boy Should lose his birthright? ii 2 34
And we, in pity of the gentle king, Had slipp'd our claim until another age ii 2 161
O, pity, God, this miserable age! ii 5 88
O, pity, pity, gentle heaven, pity! ii 5 96
The foe is merciless, and will not pity; For at their hands I have deserved no pity ii 6 25
Thou pitied'st Rutland; I will pity thee ii 6 74
'Twere pity they should lose their father's lands iii 2 31
Not that I pity Henry's misery, But seek revenge on Edward's mockery iii 3 264
'Twere pity To sunder them that yoke so well together iv 1 22
My pity hath been balm to heal their wounds iv 8 41
I, that have neither pity, love, nor fear v 6 68
More pity that the eagle should be mew'd, While kites and buzzards prey at liberty *Richard III.* i 1 132
No beast so fierce but knows some touch of pity i 2 71

Pity. Is well-spoken, and perhaps May move your hearts to pity, if you mark him . . . . *Richard III.* i 3 349
My friend, I spy some pity in thy looks . . . . i 4 270
I pity thy complaining.—No more than from my soul I mourn for yours iv 1 88
Pity, you ancient stones, those tender babes Whom envy hath immured within your walls! . . . . iv 1 99
Tear-falling pity dwells not in this eye . . . . iv 2 66
There is no creature loves me; And if I die, no soul shall pity me: Nay, wherefore should they, since that I myself Find in myself no pity to myself? . . . . v 3 201
Those that can pity, here May, if they think it well, let fall a tear; The subject will deserve it . . . . . . *Hen. VIII.* Prol. 5
You that thus far have come to pity me, Hear what I say . . ii 1 56
I have done; and God forgive me!—O, this is full of pity! . . . ii 1 137
It is a pity Would move a monster . . . . ii 3 10
She's a stranger now again.—So much the more Must pity drop upon her ii 3 18
I desire you do me right and justice; And to bestow your pity on me . ii 4 14
If you have any justice, any pity; If ye be any thing but churchmen's habits . . . . iii 1 116
Where no pity, No friends, no hope; no kindred weep for me . . iii 1 149
Whilst your great goodness, out of holy pity, Absolved him with an axe iii 2 263
From these shoulders, . . . out of pity, taken A load would sink a navy iii 2 382
Have some pity Upon my wretched women . . . . . . iv 2 139
If we suffer, Out of our easiness and childish pity To one man's honour v 3 25
And would, as I shall pity, I could help! . . . . *Troi. and Cres.* iv 3 11
Let's leave the hermit pity with our mothers . . . . . v 3 45
I would your cambric were sensible as your finger, that you might leave pricking it for pity . . . . *Coriolanus* i 3 96
But then Aufidius was within my view, And wrath o'erwhelm'd my pity i 9 86
The people Deserve such pity of him as the wolf Does of the shepherds iv 6 110
For mine own part, When I said, banish him, I said, 'twas pity . . iv 6 140
And his injury The gaoler to his pity . . . . v 1 65
Ingrate forgetfulness shall poision, rather Than pity note how much . v 2 93
To his surname Coriolanus 'longs more pride Than pity to our prayers . v 3 171
'Tis pity they should take him for a stag . . . . *T. Andron.* ii 3 71
Do thou entreat her show a woman pity . . . . . . ii 3 147
Yet have I heard,—O, could I find it now!—The lion moved with pity did endure To have his princely paws pared all away . . . . ii 3 151
Stay! For pity of mine age . . . . iii 1 2
If they did hear, They would not mark me, or if they did mark, They would not pity me . . . . iii 1 35
Her life was beast-like, and devoid of pity . . . . . . v 3 199
And pity 'tis you lived at odds so long . . . . *Rom. and Jul.* i 2 5
Is there no pity sitting in the clouds? . . . . iii 5 198
'Tis pity bounty had not eyes behind . . . . . *T. of Athens* i 2 169
A noble nature May catch a wrench—would all were well—'tis pity . ii 2 218
Men must learn now with pity to dispense; For policy sits above conscience . . . . iii 2 93
Pity is the virtue of the law, And none but tyrants use it cruelly . . iii 5 8
I am thy friend, and pity thee, dear Timon.—How dost thou pity him whom thou dost trouble? I had rather be alone . . . . . iv 3 97
Pity not honour'd age for his white beard; He is an usurer . . iv 3 111
Are not within the leaf of pity writ, But set them down horrible traitors iv 3 117
Pity's sleeping: Strange times, that weep with laughing, not with weeping! . . . . iv 3 492
In pity of our aged and our youth, I cannot choose but tell him . . v 1 179
Pity to the general wrong of Rome—As fire drives out fire, so pity pity —Hath done this deed . . . . *J. Cæsar* iii 1 171
All pity choked with custom of fell deeds . . . . . . iii 1 269
O, now you weep; and, I perceive, you feel The dint of pity . . . iii 2 198
Pity, like a naked new-born babe, Striding the blast . . *Macbeth* i 7 21
Who may I rather challenge for unkindness Than pity for mischance! . iii 4 43
Alas, poor ghost!—Pity me not, but lend thy serious hearing *Hamlet* i 5 5
That he is mad, 'tis true: 'tis true 'tis pity; And pity 'tis 'tis true . ii 2 97
And the more pity that great folk should have countenance in this world to drown or hang themselves . . . . v 1 30
When I desired their leave that I might pity him, they took from me the use of mine own house . . . . *Lear* iii 3 3
O pity! Sir, where is the patience now, That you so oft have boasted? iii 6 61
Who is too good to pity thee . . . . iii 7 90
That not know'st Fools do those villains pity who are punish'd Ere they have done their mischief . . . . iv 2 54
What, i' the storm? i' the night? Let pity not be believed! . . . iv 3 31
Gone, In pity of his misery, to dispatch His nighted life . . . iv 5 12
Who, by the art of known and feeling sorrows, Am pregnant to good pity iv 6 227
Had you not been their father, these white flakes Had challenged pity . iv 7 31
I should e'en die with pity, To see another thus . . . . . iv 7 53
This judgement of the heavens, that makes us tremble, Touches us not with pity . . . . v 3 232
She loved me for the dangers I had pass'd, And I loved her that she did pity them . . . . *Othello* i 3 168
Do but see his vice; 'Tis to his virtue a just equinox, The one as long as the other: 'tis pity of him . . . . ii 3 130
'Tis great pity that the noble Moor Should hazard such a place as his own second With one of an ingraft infirmity . . . . . . ii 3 143
But yet the pity of it, Iago! O Iago, the pity of it, Iago! . . . iv 1 206
It were pity to cast them [women] away for nothing *Ant. and Cleo.* i 2 142
'Tis pity of him.—Let his shames quickly Drive him to Rome . . i 4 71
Pity me, Charmian, But do not speak to me . . . . . . ii 5 118
Welcome, dear madam. Each heart in Rome does love and pity you . iii 6 92
Therefore, he Does pity, as constrained blemishes, Not as deserved . iii 13 59
Our care and pity is so much upon you, That we remain your friend . v 2 188
Their story is No less in pity than his glory . . . . . . v 2 365
Pity you should have been put together with so mortal a purpose *Cymb.* i 4 43
Whilst I am bound to wonder, I am bound To pity too.—What do you pity, sir? . . . . i 6 82
You look on me: what wreck discern you in me Deserves your pity? . i 6 85
Your cause doth strike my heart With pity, that doth make me sick . i 6 119
And Sinon's weeping Did scandal many a holy tear, took pity From most true wretchedness . . . . iii 4 62
If there be Yet left in heaven as small a drop of pity As a wren's eye . iv 2 304
Came crying 'mongst his foes, A thing of pity! . . . . . . v 4 47
Not pity of myself, Who am no more but as the tops of trees *Pericles* i 2 28
Entreats you pity him; He asks of you, that never used to beg . . ii 1 65
I pity his misfortune, And will awake him from his melancholy . . ii 3 90
Nor let pity, which Even women have cast off, melt thee, but be A soldier iv 1 6
To weep that you live as ye do makes pity in your lovers: seldom but that pity begets you a good opinion, and that opinion a mere profit iv 2 130
Pitying My father's loss, like a most royal prince . . *Hen. VIII.* ii 1 112
Our mistress' sorrows we were pitying . . . . ii 3 53
Pitying. Condemning some to death, and some to exile; Ransoming him, or pitying, threatening the other . . . . *Coriolanus* i 6 36
Pitying The pangs of barr'd affections . . . . . *Cymbeline* i 1 81
Piu por dulzura que por fuerza . . . . *Pericles* ii 2 27
Pius. Chosen Andronicus, surnamed Pius For many good and great deserts to Rome . . . . *T. Andron.* i 1 23
Pizzle. You bull's pizzle, you stock-fish! . . . . . 1 *Hen. IV.* ii 4 271
Place. Sometime I'ld divide, And burn in many places . . *Tempest* i 2 199
Fresh springs, brine-pits, barren place and fertile . . . . . i 2 338
'Tis best we stand upon our guard, Or that we quit this place . . ii 1 322
The murkiest den, The most opportune place . . . . . . iv 1 26
Go bring the rabble, O'er whom I give thee power, here to this place . iv 1 38
Here on this grass-plot, in this very place, To come and sport . . iv 1 73
So rare a wonder'd father and a wife Makes this place Paradise . . iv 1 124
Enforce them to this place, And presently . . . . . . v 1 100
An office of great worth And you an officer fit for the place *T. G. of Ver.* i 2 45
Never welcome to a place till some certain shot be paid . . . . ii 5 6
I pray thee, out with't, and place it for her chief virtue . . . iii 1 339
They do no more adhere and keep place together . . *Mer. Wives* ii 1 63
Hath appointed them contrary places . . . . ii 1 217
I have lost my edifice by mistaking the place where I erected it . . ii 2 226
In other places she enlargeth her mirth . . . . ii 2 231
Of great admittance, authentic in your place and person . . . ii 2 236
A man of his place, gravity and learning, so wide of his own respect . iii 1 57
Have I not stay for him to kill him? have I not, at de place I did appoint? iii 1 95
Look you, this is the place appointed . . . . iii 1 97
I have deceived you both; I have directed you to wrong places . . iii 1 110
I will search impossible places . . . . iii 5 151
He hath an abstract for the remembrance of such places . . . iv 2 64
It concerns me To look into the bottom of my place . *Meas. for Meas.* i 1 79
Though you change your place, you need not change your trade . . i 2 110
Whether the tyranny be in his place, Or in his eminence that fills it up i 2 167
My absolute power and place here in Vienna . . . . . . i 3 13
Peace be in this place! . . . . i 4 6
A novice of this place . . . . i 4 19
Upon his place, And with full line of his authority . . . . i 4 55
Had time cohered with place or place with wishing . . . . ii 1 11
How long have you been in this place of constable? . . . . ii 1 273
Do you your office, or give up your place . . . . . . ii 2 13
Dispose of her To some more fitter place, and that with speed . . ii 2 17
O place, O form, How often dost thou with thy case, thy habit, Wrench awe from fools! . . . . ii 4 12
Whose credit with the judge, or own great place, Could fetch your brother ii 4 92
My place i' the state Will so your accusation overweigh . . . ii 4 156
And the place answer to convenience . . . . iii 1 258
To stead up your appointment, go in your place . . . . . iii 1 261
At that place call upon me . . . . iii 1 278
O place and greatness! millions of false eyes Are stuck upon thee . iv 1 60
I will give him a present shrift and advise him for a better place . iv 2 224
Your provost knows the place where he abides And he may fetch him . v 1 252
Know you where you are?—Respect to your great place! . . . v 1 294
We'll borrow place of him. Sir, by your leave . . . . . v 1 367
And yet here's one in place I cannot pardon . . . . . . v 1 504
We shall employ thee in a worthier place . . . . v 1 537
Loath to leave unsought Or that or any place that harbours men *C. of Er.* i 1 137
Answer me In what safe place you have bestow'd my money . . . i 2 78
If thou hadst been Dromio to-day in my place, Thou wouldst have changed thy face for a name . . . . iii 1 46
I'll meet you at that place some hour hence . . . . . . iii 1 122
He took this place for sanctuary, And it shall privilege him . . v 1 94
The melancholy vale, The place of death and sorry execution . . v 1 121
And all that are assembled in this place . . . . v 1 396
War-thoughts Have left their places vacant . . . . *Much Ado* i 1 304
Here's no place for you maids . . . . ii 1 48
Dost thou not suspect my place? dost thou not suspect my years? . iv 2 76
Do not forget to specify, when time and place shall serve, that I am an ass v 1 264
Fit in his place and time . . . . *L. L. Lost* i 1 98
Now for the ground which; . . . Then for the place where . . . i 1 243
But to the place where; it standeth north-north-east and by east from the west corner . . . . i 1 247
Thy own wish wish I thee in every place! . . . . ii 1 179
Most rude melancholy, valour gives thee place . . . . . . iii 1 69
To that place the sharp Athenian law Cannot pursue us *M. N. Dream* i 1 162
In that same place thou hast appointed me, To-morrow truly will I meet i 1 177
What worser place can I beg in your love,—And yet a place of high respect with me? . . . . ii 1 208
To trust the opportunity of night And the ill counsel of a desert place ii 1 218
Here's a marvellous convenient place for our rehearsal . . . iii 1 3
But I will not stir from this place, do what they can . . . . iii 1 125
Thou see'st these lovers seek a place to fight . . . . . . iii 2 354
Thou runn'st before me, shifting every place, And darest not stand . iii 2 423
Bring them in: and take your places, ladies . . . . . . v 1 84
If I should as lion come in strife Into this place, 'twere pity on my life v 1 229
Hand in hand, with fairy grace, Will we sing, and bless this place . v 1 407
My ventures are not in one bottom trusted, Nor to one place *Mer. of Ven.* i 1 43
O my Antonio, had I but the means To hold a rival place with one of them! . . . . i 1 174
If you repay me not on such a day, In such a place, such sum or sums i 3 148
Lest through thy wild behaviour I be misconstrued in the place I go to ii 2 197
The Goodwins, I think they call the place; a very dangerous flat . iii 1 5
Will acknowledge you and Jessica In place of Lord Bassanio and myself iii 4 39
I do know A many fools, that stand in better place . . . . iii 5 73
Some three or four of you Go give him courteous conduct to this place iv 1 148
You are welcome: take your place. Are you acquainted? . . . iv 1 170
The quality of mercy is not strain'd, It droppeth as the gentle rain from heaven Upon the place beneath . . . . iv 1 186
He lets me feed with his hinds, bars me the place of a brother *As Y. L. It* i 1 20
Here is the place appointed for the wrestling, and they are ready . i 2 154
In the world I fill up a place, which may be better supplied . . i 2 204
I do in friendship counsel you To leave this place . . . . . i 2 274
To the which place a poor sequester'd stag . . . Did come to languish . ii 1 33
Show me the place: I love to cope him in these sullen fits . . ii 1 66
This is no place; this house is but a butchery . . . . . ii 3 27
When I was at home, I was in a better place: but travellers must be content . . . . ii 4 18
If that love or gold Can in this desert place buy entertainment . . ii 4 72
I like this place, And willingly could waste my time in it . . . ii 4 94
He hath strange places cramm'd With observation . . . . . ii 7 40
Are you native of this place?—As the cony that you see dwell where she is kindled . . . . iii 2 356

Place. The vicar of the next village, who hath promised to meet me in this place *As Y. Like It* iii 3 45
West of this place, down in the neighbour bottom iv 3 79
The murmuring stream Left on your right hand brings you to the place iv 3 81
As how I came into that desert place iv 3 142
When I am alone, why, then I am Tranio; But in all places else your master Lucentio *T. of Shrew* i 1 249
Stand you so assured, As firmly as yourself were still in place i 2 157
Though bride and bridegroom wants For to supply the places at the table iii 2 249
Lucentio, you shall supply the bridegroom's place iii 2 251
Thou shouldst have heard in how miry a place, how she was bemoiled iv 1 77
The taming-school! what, is there such a place? iv 2 55
An I had thee in place where, thou shouldst know it iv 3 151
And place your hands below your husband's foot v 2 177
These fix'd evils sit so fit in him, That they take place, when virtue's steely bones Look bleak i' the cold wind *All's Well* i 1 114
Who were below him He used as creatures of another place i 2 42
You are loved, sir . . . —I fill a place, I know't i 2 69
What place make you special, when you put off that with such contempt? ii 2 5
From lowest place when virtuous things proceed, The place is dignified by the doer's deed ii 3 133
You know your places well; When better fall, for your avails they fell iii 1 21
Yond's that same knave That leads him to these places iii 5 86
That time and place with this deceit so lawful May prove coherent iii 7 38
Was faithfully confirmed by the rector of the place iv 3 69
He had the honour to be the officer at a place there called Mile-end iv 3 302
There's place and means for every man alive iv 3 375
His grace is at Marseilles; to which place We have convenient convoy iv 4 9
I was bred and born Not three hours' travel from this very place *T. Night* i 2 23
Give us the place alone i 5 235
Is there no respect of place, persons, nor time in you? ii 3 99
Let all the rest give place ii 4 82
Say, My love can give no place, bide no denay ii 4 127
I know my place as I would they should do theirs ii 5 60
Hurt him in eleven places iii 2 37
For which, if I be lapsed in this place, I shall pay dear iii 3 36
The instrument That screws me from my true place in your favour v 1 126
Do not embrace me till each circumstance Of place, time, fortune, do cohere v 1 259
Like a cipher, Yet standing in rich place *W. Tale* i 2 7
Be pilot to me and thy places shall Still neighbour mine i 2 448
O thou thing! Which I'll not call a creature of thy place ii 1 83
Bear it To some remote and desert place quite out Of our dominions ii 3 176
Commend it strangely to some place Where chance may nurse or end it ii 3 182
Hurried Here to this place, i' the open air, before I have got strength iii 2 106
This place is famous for the creatures Of prey that keep upon't iii 3 12
Places remote enough are in Bohemia iii 3 31
Thou shalt accompany us to the place iv 2 53
Nothing she does or seems But smacks of something greater than herself, Too noble for this place iv 4 159
Have you thought on A place whereto you'll go? iv 4 548
The place of your dwelling, your names, your ages, of what having iv 4 739
Let's from this place. What! look upon my brother v 3 146
Would I might never stir from off this place *K. John* i 1 145
He that stands upon a slippery place Makes nice of no vile hold iii 4 137
All places that the eye of heaven visits Are to a wise man ports *Rich. II.* i 3 275
To drop them still upon one place, Till they have fretted us a pair of graves iii 3 166
Here in this place I'll set a bank of rue, sour herb of grace iii 4 104
Fellow, give place; here is no longer stay v 5 95
Choose out some secret place, some reverend room, More than thou hast v 6 25
Appoint them a place of meeting, wherein it is at our pleasure to fail *1 Hen. IV.* i 2 190
Said To such a person and in such a place, At such a time i 3 72
What do you call the place?—A plague upon it, it is in Gloucestershire i 3 242
We must all to the wars, and thy place shall be honourable ii 4 596
I'll have the current in this place damm'd up iii 1 101
Thy place in council thou hast rudely lost iii 2 32
A braver place In my heart's love hath no man than yourself iv 1 7
You were in place and in account Nothing so strong and fortunate as I v 1 37
Doth this become your place, your time and business? *2 Hen. IV.* ii 1 72
As familiar with me as my dog; and he holds his place ii 2 116
Doth the old boar feed in the old frank?—At the old place, my lord ii 2 161
I must go and meet with danger there, Or it will seek me in another place ii 3 49
Or to the place of difference call the swords Which must decide it iv 1 181
O, who shall believe But you misuse the reverence of your place? iv 2 23
What's your name, sir? of what condition are you, and of what place? iv 3 2
A traitor your degree, and the dungeon your place, a place deep enough iv 3 8
Thou hast a better place in his affection Than all thy brothers iv 4 22
Which, as immediate from thy place and blood, Derives itself to me iv 5 42
How many nobles then should hold their places, That must strike sail to spirits of vile sort! v 2 17
Your highness pleased to forget my place v 2 77
Speak in your state What I have done that misbecame my place v 2 100
A crooked figure may Attest in little place a million *Hen. V.* Prol. 16
Shall join together at the latter day and cry all 'We died at such a place' iv 1 144
Art thou aught else but place, degree and form? iv 1 263
Will it give place to flexure and low bending? iv 1 272
You know your places: God be with you all! iv 3 78
Much more cause, Did they this Harry. Now in London place him v Prol. 35
It was in a place where I could not breed no contention with him v 1 11
For he perforce must do thee right, because he hath not the gift to woo in other places v 2 163
The liberty that follows our places stops the mouth of all find-faults v 2 297
Each hath his place and function to attend: I am left out *1 Hen. VI.* i 1 173
To try her skill, Reignier, stand thou as Dauphin in my place i 2 61
Thy scarlet robes as a child's bearing-cloth I'll use to carry thee out of this place i 3 43
Am I dared and bearded to my face? Draw, men, for all this privileged place i 3 46
Express opinions Where is best place to make our battery next i 4 65
Sirs, take your places and be vigilant ii 1 1
'Tis sure they found some place But weakly guarded ii 1 73
He bears him on the place's privilege, Or durst not, for his craven heart, say thus ii 4 86
When they are cloy'd With long continuance in a settled place ii 5 106
This place commands my patience, Or thou shouldst find iii 1 8
Especially for those occasions At Eltham Place I told your majesty iii 1 156
Take heed, be wary how you place your words iii 2 3

Place. We will bestow you in some better place, Fitter for sickness *1 Hen. VI.* iii 2 88
We'll set thy statue in some holy place, And have thee reverenced iii 3 14
If we could do that, France were no place for Henry's warriors iii 3 22
And in our coronation take your place iii 4 27
O God, that Somerset, who in proud heart Doth stop my cornets, were in Talbot's place! iv 3 25
Place barrels of pitch upon the fatal stake v 4 57
Though Humphrey's pride And greatness of his place be grief to us *2 Hen. VI.* i 1 173
If Somerset be unworthy of the place, Let York be regent i 3 108
I am protector of the realm; And, at his pleasure, will resign my place i 3 124
Though in this place most master wear no breeches i 3 149
If I be appointed for the place, My Lord of Somerset will keep me here i 3 170
Let these have a day appointed them For single combat in convenient place i 3 212
From hence to prison back again; From thence unto the place of execution ii 3 6
Were't not all one, an empty eagle were set To guard the chicken from a hungry kite, As place Duke Humphrey for the king's protector? iii 1 250
Lords, take your places; and, I pray you all, Proceed no straiter iii 2 19
Nor let the rain of heaven wet this place iii 2 341
Kent, in the Commentaries Cæsar writ, Is term'd the civil'st place of all this isle iv 7 66
Alas, he hath no home, no place to fly to iv 8 40
Give place: by heaven, thou shalt rule no more v 1 104
Henry had none, but did usurp the place *3 Hen. VI.* i 2 25
Off with the traitor's head, And rear it in the place your father's stands ii 6 86
'Tis no land of thine; Thy place is fill'd, thy sceptre wrung from thee iii 1 16
To strengthen and support King Edward's place iii 1 52
To take their rooms, ere I can place myself iii 2 132
I have heard that she was there in place iv 1 103
Let me blame your grace, For choosing me when Clarence is in place iv 6 31
Yoke together, like a double shadow To Henry's body, and supply his place iv 6 50
Let Æsop fable in a winter's night; His currish riddles sort not with this place v 5 26
He was fitter for that place than earth.—And thou unfit for any place but hell.—Yes, one place else, if you will hear me name it *Richard III.* i 2 108
Never came poison from so sweet a place i 2 147
To those whose dealings have deserved the place, And those who have the wit to claim the place iii 1 49
I do not like the Tower, of any place. Did Julius Cæsar build that place, my lord?—He did, my gracious lord, begin that place iii 1 68
At Crosby Place, there shall you find us both iii 1 190
Thou didst usurp my place, and dost thou not Usurp the just proportion of my sorrow? iv 4 109
Which buys A place next to the king *Hen. VIII.* i 1 66
His mind and place Infecting one another, yea, reciprocally i 1 161
I am a suitor.—Arise, and take place by us i 2 10
'Tis but the fate of place i 2 75
Sweet ladies, will it please you sit? Sir Harry, Place you that side i 4 20
There should be one amongst 'em, by his person, More worthy this place i 4 79
I would not be so sick though for his place: But this cannot continue ii 2 83
Not to deny her that A woman of less place might ask by law ii 2 112
Was not one Doctor Pace In this man's place before him? ii 2 123
For living murmurers There's places of rebuke. He was a fool ii 2 132
The most convenient place that I can think of For such receipt of learning is Black-Friars ii 2 138
But, conscience, conscience! O, 'tis a tender place ii 2 144
You sign your place and calling, in full seeming, With meekness and humility ii 4 108
Wrong you? alas, our places, The way of our profession is against it iii 1 156
To stay the judgement o' the divorce; for if It did take place iii 2 34
With his own hand gave me; Bade me enjoy it, with the place and honours iii 2 248
Sir Thomas More is chosen Lord chancellor in your place iii 2 394
Having brought the queen To a prepared place in the choir, fell off iv 1 64
A man of his place, and so near our favour, To dance attendance v 2 30
More stirs against, Both in his private conscience and his place v 3 40
He had better starve Than but once think this place becomes thee not v 3 133
Is this a place to roar in? Fetch me a dozen crab-tree staves v 4 7
They fell on; I made good my place v 4 57
Here's an excellent place; here we may see most bravely *Troi. and Cres.* i 2 197
Most mighty for thy place and sway i 3 60
The planets and this centre Observe degree, priority and place i 3 86
Crowns, sceptres, laurels, But by degree, stand in authentic place i 3 108
In full as proud a place As broad Achilles i 3 189
The ram that batters down the wall, For the great swing and rudeness of his poise, They place before his hand that made the engine i 3 208
We fear to warrant in our native place ii 2 96
Lest perchance he think We dare not move the question of our place ii 3 89
As place, riches, favour, Prizes of accident as oft as merit iii 3 82
Finds bottom in the uncomprehensive deeps, Keeps place with thought iii 3 199
Let me be privileged by my place and message, To be a speaker free iv 4 132
Tell me, I beseech you, In what place of the field doth Calchas keep? iv 5 278
This place is dangerous; The time right deadly v 2 38
What's the matter, That in these several places of the city You cry against the noble senate? *Coriolanus* i 1 189
Fame, at the which he aims, In whom already he's well graced, can not Better be held nor more attain'd than by A place below the first i 1 270
There will be large cicatrices to show the people, when he shall stand for his place ii 1 165
Nay, keep your place.—Sit, Coriolanus; never shame to hear ii 2 70
And now, arriving A place of potency and sway o' the state ii 3 190
That hath beside well in his person wrought To be set high in place ii 3 255
Poor gentleman, take up some other station; here's no place for you iv 5 33
All places yield to him ere he sits down iv 7 28
I will not re-salute the streets of Rome, Or climb my palace, till from forth this place I lead espoused my bride along with me *T. Andron.* i 1 327
What villain was it spake that word?—He that would vouch it in any place but here i 1 360
These two have 'ticed me hither to this place: A barren detested vale ii 3 92
Be call'd a gentle queen, And with thine own hands kill me in this place! ii 3 169
A very fatal place it seems to me. Speak, brother, hast thou hurt thee? ii 3 202
Ay, such a place there is, where we did hunt—O, had we never, never hunted there! iv 1 55
Received for the emperor's heir, And substituted in the place of mine iv 2 159
Please you, therefore, draw nigh, and take your places v 3 24

Place. From the place where you behold us now, . . . all headlong cast us down *T. Andron.* v 3 130
The measure done, I'll watch her place of stand *Rom. and Jul.* i 5 52
And the place death, considering who thou art ii 2 64
By whose direction found'st thou out this place?—By love ii 2 79
Withdraw unto some private place, And reason coldly of your grievances iii 1 54
The horrible conceit of death and night, Together with the terror of the place,—As in a vault iv 3 38
What mean these masterless and gory swords To lie discolour'd by this place of peace? v 3 143
This is the place; there, where the torch doth burn v 3 171
Most suspected, as the time and place Doth make against me v 3 224
And then in post he came from Mantua To this same place v 3 274
What made your master in this place?—He came with flowers v 3 280
I'm angry at him, That might have known my place *T. of Athens* iii 3 14
The place which I have feasted, does it now, Like all mankind, show me an iron heart? iii 4 83
Your diet shall be in all places alike. Make not a city feast of it, to let the meat cool ere we can agree upon the first place: sit, sit iii 6 75
Place thieves And give them title, knee and approbation With senators iv 3 35
Why this spade? this place? This slave-like habit? and these looks of care? iv 3 204
As I took note of the place, it cannot be far where he abides v 1 1
By all description this should be the place. Who's here? speak, ho! v 3 1
He shall wear his crown . . . In every place, save here in Italy *J. Cæsar* i 3 88
By the right and virtue of my place, I ought to know ii 1 269
I'll get me to a place more void, and there Speak to great Cæsar ii 4 37
What, is the fellow mad?—Sirrah, give place iii 1 10
Every one doth shine, But there's but one in all doth hold his place iii 1 65
Tell him, so please him come unto this place, He shall be satisfied iii 1 140
No place will please me so, no mean of death, As here by Cæsar iii 1 161
Here comes his body, mourned by Mark Antony: who, though he had no hand in his death, shall receive the benefit of his dying, a place in the commonwealth iii 2 47
I fear there will a worse come in his place iii 2 116
Look, in this place ran Cassius' dagger through iii 2 178
We'll burn his body in the holy place iii 2 259
Of your philosophy you make no use, If you give place to accidental evils iv 3 146
Good reasons must, of force, give place to better iv 3 203
I know Wherefore they do it: they could be content To visit other places v 1 9
Where the place?—Upon the heath.—There to meet with Macbeth *Macb.* i 1 6
Sons, kinsmen, thanes, And you whose places are the nearest i 4 36
Nor time nor place Did then adhere, and yet you would make both i 7 51
Why did you bring these daggers from the place? They must lie there ii 2 48
This place is too cold for hell ii 3 19
A falcon, towering in her pride of place, Was by a mousing owl hawk'd at and kill'd ii 4 12
The table's full.—Here is a place reserved, sir.—Where?—Here iii 4 46
Wisdom! to leave his wife, to leave his babes, His mansion and his titles in a place From whence himself does fly? iv 2 7
Where is your husband?—I hope, in no place so unsanctified Where such as thou mayst find him iv 2 81
By the grace of Grace, We will perform in measure, time and place v 8 73
As he in his particular act and place May give his saying deed *Hamlet* i 3 26
The very place puts toys of desperation, Without more motive, into every brain That looks so many fathoms to the sea i 4 75
And more above, hath his solicitings, As they fell out by time, by means and place, All given to mine ear ii 2 127
They are coming to the play; I must be idle: Get you a place iii 2 96
It will but skin and film the ulcerous place iii 4 147
Bestow this place on us a little while iv 1 4
If your messenger find him not there, seek him i' the other place yourself iv 3 37
Like to a murdering-piece, in many places Gives me superfluous death. iv 5 95
No place, indeed, should murder sanctuarize iv 7 128
Which nor our nature nor our place can bear *Lear* i 1 174
Stood I within his grace, I would prefer him to a better place i 1 277
I will place you where you shall hear us confer of this i 2 98
Come place him here by me, Do thou for him stand i 4 156
Like an engine, wrench'd my frame of nature From the fix'd place i 4 291
O sir, fly this place; Intelligence is given where you are hid ii 1 22
No place, That guard, and most unusual vigilance, Does not attend my taking ii 3 3
What's he that hath so much thy place mistook To set thee here? ii 4 12
Ere I was risen from the place that show'd My duty kneeling ii 4 29
Bring but five and twenty: to no more Will I give place or notice ii 4 252
Here is the place, my lord; good my lord, enter iii 4 1
Bring in the evidence. Thou robed man of justice, take thy place iii 6 38
Stop her there! Arms, arms, sword, fire! Corruption in the place! iii 6 58
From that place I shall no leading need iv 1 80
Come on, sir; here's the place: stand still iv 6 11
Change places; and, handy-dandy, which is the justice, which is the thief? iv 6 156
If your will want not, time and place will be fruitfully offered iv 6 269
His bed my gaol; from the loathed warmth whereof deliver me, and supply the place for your labour iv 6 273
I am mainly ignorant What place this is iv 7 66
Have you never found my brother's way To the forfended place? v 1 11
The question of Cordelia and her father Requires a fitter place v 3 59
He led our powers; Bore the commission of my place and person v 3 64
I protest, Maugre thy strength, youth, place, and eminence v 3 131
The dark and vicious place where thee he got Cost him his eyes v 3 172
I know my price, I am worth no worse a place *Othello* i 1 11
My spirit and my place have in them power To make this bitter to thee i 1 103
It seems not meet, nor wholesome to my place, To be produced i 1 146
Neither my place nor aught I heard of business Hath raised me from my bed i 3 53
Ancient, conduct them: you best know the place i 3 121
The fortitude of the place is best known to you i 3 223
I crave fit disposition for my wife, Due reference of place i 3 238
Cassio's a proper man: let me see now: To get his place i 3 399
I hold him to be unworthy of his place that does those things ii 3 105
'Tis great pity that the noble Moor Should hazard such a place as his own second With one of an ingraft infirmity ii 3 144
Gentlemen,—Have you forgot all sense of place and duty? ii 3 167
It hath pleased the devil drunkenness to give place to the devil wrath ii 3 298
As the time, the place, and the condition of this country stands ii 3 302
I will ask him for my place again; he shall tell me I am a drunkard! ii 3 306
Importune her help to put you in your place again ii 3 325

Place. I being absent and my place supplied, My general will forget my love *Othello* iii 3 17
I give thee warrant of thy place: assure thee, If I do vow a friendship, I'll perform it To the last article iii 3 20
Fit that Cassio have his place, For, sure, he fills it up with great ability iii 3 246
She was here even now; she haunts me in every place iv 1 137
Cassio shall have my place iv 1 272
I should have found in some place of my soul A drop of patience iv 2 52
Who keeps her company? What place? what time? what form? iv 2 138
Especial commission come from Venice to depute Cassio in Othello's place iv 2 226
By making him uncapable of Othello's place; knocking out his brains iv 2 236
To you, lord governor, Remains the censure of this hellish villain; The time, the place, the torture v 2 369
Say, our pleasure, To such whose place is under us, requires Our quick remove from hence *Ant. and Cleo.* i 2 202
The while I'll place you: then the boy shall sing ii 7 116
I have done enough; a lower place, note well, May make too great an act iii 1 12
Sossius, One of my place in Syria, his lieutenant iii 1 18
From which place We may the number of the ships behold iii 9 2
Yet he that can endure To follow with allegiance a fall'n lord Does conquer him that did his master conquer, And earns a place i' the story iii 13 46
Bestow'd his lips on that unworthy place, As it rain'd kisses iii 13 84
And we, Your scutcheons and your signs of conquest, shall Hang in what place you please v 2 136
It is a manacle of love; I'll place it Upon this fairest prisoner *Cymbeline* i 1 122
Consider, When you above perceive me like a crow, That it is place which lessens and sets off iii 3 13
We will fear no poison, which attends In place of greater state iii 3 78
Why hast thou abused So many miles with a pretence? this place? iii 4 106
I am most glad You think of other place iii 4 144
Nor measure our good minds By this rude place we live in iii 6 66
I am near to the place where they should meet iv 1 1
In this place we left them: I wish my brother make good time with him iv 2 107
Reverence, That angel of the world, doth make distinction Of place 'tween high and low iv 2 249
Accommodated by the place, more charming With their own nobleness v 3 32
I think he would change places with his officer v 4 180
Married your royalty, was wife to your place; Abhorr'd your person v 5 39
Briefly die their joys That place them on the truth of girls and boys v 5 107
To attain In suit the place of's bed v 5 185
Nor the time nor place Will serve our long inter'gatories v 5 391
He would have well becomed this place v 5 406
To place upon the volume of your deeds, As in a title-page, your worth *Pericles* ii 3 3
Here take your place: Marshal the rest, as they deserve their grace ii 3 18
Sir, yonder is your place.—Some other is more fit ii 3 23
Here is a thing too young for such a place iii 1 15
Which makes her both the heart and place Of general wonder iv Gower 10
Did you ever hear the like?—No, nor never shall do in such a place as this iv 5 3
Do you know this house to be a place of such resort, and will come into't? iv 6 85
I hear say you are of honourable parts, and are the governor of this place iv 6 88
Come, bring me to some private place: come, come iv 6 98
O, that the gods Would set me free from this unhallow'd place! iv 6 107
A place, for which the pained'st fiend Of hell would not in reputation change iv 6 173
O, that the gods Would safely deliver me from this place! iv 6 191
I will see what I can do for thee: if I can place thee, I will iv 6 204
Here we her place; And to her father turn our thoughts again v Gower 11
What is your place?—I am the governor of this place you lie before v 1 20
Where do you live?—Where I am but a stranger: from the deck You may discern the place v 1 116
Placed. I know they virtuously are placed *T. G. of Ver.* iv 3 38
Planted and placed and possessed by my master *Much Ado* iii 3 159
If half thy outward graces had been placed About thy thoughts! iv 1 102
Wise, fair and true, Shall she be placed in my constant soul *Mer. of Ven.* ii 6 57
Let your fervour, like my master's, be Placed in contempt! *T. Night* i 5 307
Who is, if every owner were well placed, Indeed his king 1 *Hen. IV.* iv 3 94
I will take up that with 'Give the devil his due.'—Well placed *Hen. V.* iii 7 128
He, being in the vaward, placed behind With purpose to relieve 1 *Hen. VI.* i 1 132
A piece of ordnance 'gainst it I have placed i 4 15
Words sweetly placed and modestly directed v 3 179
Thou shalt be placed as viceroy under him v 4 131
And on the pieces of the broken wand Were placed the heads 2 *Hen. VI.* i 2 29
Myself have limed a bush for her, And placed a quire of such enticing birds i 3 92
From off the gates of York fetch down the head, Your father's head, which Clifford placed there 3 *Hen. VI.* ii 6 53
Our archers shall be placed in the midst *Richard III.* v 3 295
Two women placed together makes cold weather *Hen. VIII.* i 4 22
Know you on which side They have placed their men of trust? *Coriol.* i 6 52
In whose breast Doubt and suspect, alas, are placed too late *T. of A.* iv 3 519
Upon my head they placed a fruitless crown *Macbeth* iii 1 61
I'll be placed, so please you, in the ear Of all their conference *Hamlet* iii 1 192
Subscribed it, gave't the impression, placed it safely v 2 52
Give order that these bodies High on a stage be placed to the view v 2 389
My resolution's placed, and I have nothing Of woman in me *A. and C.* v 2 238
Though most ungentle fortune Have placed me in this sty *Pericles* iv 6 104
Recover'd her, and placed her Here in Diana's temple v 3 24
How she came placed here in the temple; No needful thing omitted v 3 67
Placentio. Signior Placentio and his lovely nieces *Rom. and Jul.* i 2 69
Placeth. Thy friend no less Than those she placeth highest! *Coriolanus* i 5 25
Placing therein some expert officers 1 *Hen. VI.* iii 2 127
She being down, I have the placing of the British crown *Cymbeline* iii 5 65
Plack. Your great-uncle Edward the Plack Prince of Wales *Hen. V.* iv 7 97
Placket. Dread prince of plackets, king of codpieces *L. L. Lost* iii 1 186
Will they wear their plackets where they should bear their faces? *W. T.* iv 4 245
You might have pinched a placket, it was senseless iv 4 622
Or rather, the bone-ache! for that, methinks, is the curse dependant on those that war for a placket *Troi. and Cres.* ii 3 22
Keep thy foot out of brothels, thy hand out of plackets *Lear* iii 4 100
Plague. A plague upon this howling! *Tempest* i 1 39
The red plague rid you For learning me your language! i 2 364
A plague upon the tyrant that I serve! ii 2 166
I will plague them all, Even to roaring iv 1 192

Plague. To keep me from a most unholy match, Which heaven and fortune still rewards with plagues . . . *T. G. of Ver.* iv 3 31
Come what plague could have come after it . . . . . *Much Ado* ii 3 85
O mischief strangely thwarting!—O plague right well prevented! . iii 2 136
It is a plague That Cupid will impose for my neglect . *L. L. Lost* iii 1 203
Light wenches may prove plagues to men forsworn . . . . iv 3 385
Thus pour the stars down plagues for perjury . . . . . v 2 394
They have the plague, and caught it of your eyes . . . . v 2 421
I'll plague him; I'll torture him: I am glad of it . *Mer. of Venice* iii 1 121
The ambition in my love thus plagues itself . . . *All's Well* i 1 101
'Twas pretty, though a plague, To see him every hour . . . . i 1 103
A plague upon him! muffled! he can say nothing of me: hush, hush! . iv 3 134
I'll no more drumming; a plague of all drums! . . . . . iv 3 331
What a plague means my niece? . . . . . . *T. Night* i 3 1
A plague o' these pickle-herring! How now, sot! . . . . . i 5 128
How now! Even so quickly may one catch the plague? . . . . i 5 314
Plague on't, an I thought he had been valiant and so cunning iii 4 311
He is not only plagued for her sin, But God hath made her sin and her the plague On this removed issue, plagued for her And with her plague . . . . *K. John* ii 1 185
Too well, too well I feel The different plague of each calamity . iii 4 60
And plague injustice with the pains of hell . . . *Richard II.* iii 1 34
If any plague hang over us, 'tis he . . . . v 3 3
What a plague have I to do with a buff jerkin? . . . 1 *Hen. IV.* i 2 51
What do you call the place?—A plague upon it, it is in Gloucestershire i 3 243
A plague on thee! hast thou never an eye in thy head? . . . ii 1 31
Poins! Hal! a plague upon you both! Bardolph! Peto! . . . ii 2 21
A plague upon it when thieves cannot be true one to another! . . ii 2 29
What a plague mean ye to colt me thus?—Thou liest; thou art not colted ii 2 39
A plague of all cowards, I say, and a vengeance too! . . . ii 4 127
A plague upon such backing! give me them that will face me . . ii 4 166
A plague of sighing and grief! it blows a man up like a bladder . ii 4 365
What a plague call you him?—O, Glendower . . . . . . ii 4 373
If I become not a cart as well as another man, a plague on my bringing up! ii 4 546
A plague upon it! I have forgot the map . . . . . . iii 1 5
The smell whereof shall breed a plague in France . . *Hen. V.* iv 3 103
A plague upon that villain Somerset, That thus delays! 1 *Hen. VI.* iv 3 9
Or we will plague thee with incessant wars . . . . . . v 4 154
A plague upon them! wherefore should I curse them? . 2 *Hen. VI.* iii 2 309
To plague thee for thy foul misleading me . . . 3 *Hen. VI.* v 1 97
I'll plague ye for that word.—Ay, thou wast born to be a plague to men v 5 27
When have I injured thee? when done thee wrong? Or thee? or thee? or any of your faction? A plague upon you all! *Richard III.* i 3 58
If heaven have any grievous plague in store Exceeding those that I can wish upon thee, O, let them keep it till thy sins be ripe! . . . i 3 217
Plague of your policy! You sent me deputy for Ireland *Hen. VIII.* iii 2 259
O gods, how do you plague me! . . . . . *Troi. and Cres.* i 1 97
But when the planets In evil mixture to disorder wander, What plagues! i 3 96
The plague of Greece upon thee, thou mongrel beef-witted lord! . ii 1 13
A plague of opinion! a man may wear it on both sides, like a leather jerkin iii 3 265
A plague upon Antenor! I would they had broke's neck! . . iv 2 78
One word in your ear.—O plague and madness! . . . . . v 2 35
A plague break thy neck for frighting me! . . . . . . v 4 34
Let your brief plagues be mercy, And linger not our sure destructions on! v 10 8
Boils and plagues Plaster you o'er, that you may be abhorr'd! *Coriolanus* i 4 31
But for our gentlemen, The common file—a plague! tribunes for them! i 6 43
Plague upon't! I cannot bring My tongue to such a pace . . . ii 3 56
The hoarded plague o' the gods Requite your love! . . . . iv 2 11
The gods will plague thee, That thou restrain'st from me the duty which To a mother's part belongs . . . . v 3 166
Which oft the angry Mab with blisters plagues . . *Rom. and Jul.* i 4 75
A plague o' both your houses! They have made worms' meat of me iii 1 111
A plague upon him, dog! . . . . *T. of Athens* ii 2 50
Plagues, incident to men, Your potent and infectious fevers heap On Athens! . . . . iv 1 21
If thou wilt not promise, the gods plague thee, for thou art a man! . iv 3 73
Be as a planetary plague, when Jove Will o'er some high-viced city hang his poison In the sick air . . . . iv 3 108
Plague all; That your activity may defeat and quell The source of all erection. There's more gold . . . . iv 3 162
More man? plague, plague! . . . . iv 3 197
Yonder comes a poet and a painter: the plague of company light upon thee! iv 3 357
A plague on thee! thou art too bad to curse . . . . . . iv 3 365
And thy saints for aye Be crown'd with plagues that thee alone obey! . v 1 56
I thank them; and would send them back the plague, Could I but catch it . . . . v 1 140
Go, live still; Be Alcibiades your plague, you his! . . . . . v 1 192
What is amiss plague and infection mend! . . . . v 1 224
A plague consume you wicked caitiffs left! . . . . v 4 71
Pray to the gods to intermit the plague . . . . . *J. Cæsar* i 1 59
We but teach Bloody instructions, which, being taught, return To plague the inventor . . . . *Macbeth* i 7 10
If thou dost marry, I'll give thee this plague for thy dowry . *Hamlet* iii 1 140
My virtue or my plague, be it either which—She's so conjunctive to my life . . . . iv 7 13
Wherefore should I Stand in the plague of custom? . . . . *Lear* i 2 3
A plague upon your epileptic visage! Smile you my speeches? . . ii 2 87
Vengeance! plague! death! confusion! Fiery? what quality? . . ii 4 96
All the plagues that in the pendulous air Hang fated o'er men's faults . iii 4 69
'Tis the times' plague, when madmen lead the blind . . . . iv 1 48
Thou whom the heavens' plagues Have humbled to all strokes . . iv 1 67
The gods are just, and of our pleasant vices Make instruments to plague us . . . . v 3 171
A plague upon you, murderers, traitors all! I might have saved her . v 3 269
And, though he in a fertile climate dwell, Plague him with flies *Othello* i 1 71
I confess, it is my nature's plague To spy into abuses . . . . iii 3 146
'Tis the plague of great ones; Prerogatived are they less than the base . iii 3 273
Even then this forked plague is fated to us When we do quicken . . iii 3 276
'Tis the strumpet's plague To beguile many and be beguiled by one . iv 1 97
It were fit That all the plagues of hell should at one time Encounter such revolt . . . . *Cymbeline* i 6 111
The very devils cannot plague them better . . . . ii 5 35
A plague on them, they ne'er come but I look to be washed . *Pericles* ii 1 28
Plagued. He is not only plagued for her sin, But God hath made her sin and her the plague On this removed issue, plagued for her And with her plague . . . . *K. John* ii 1 184
And God, not we, hath plagued thy bloody deed . . *Richard III.* i 3 181
Ay, come:—O Jove!—do come:—I shall be plagued . *Troi. and Cres.* v 2 105
Plague-sore. Thou art a boil, A plague-sore, an embossed carbuncle, In my corrupted blood . . . . *Lear* ii 4 227

Plaguing. A plaguing mischief light on Charles and thee! . 1 *Hen. VI.* v 3 39
Plaguy. He is so plaguy proud . . . . . . *Troi. and Cres.* ii 3 187
Plain. Prompt me, plain and holy innocence! . . . . . *Tempest* iii 1 82
That my love may appear plain and free . . . . *T. G. of Ver.* v 4 82
To be received plain, I'll speak more gross . . . *Meas. for Meas.* ii 4 82
As plain as the plain bald pate of father Time . . . *Com. of Errors* ii 2 70
He was wont to speak plain and to the purpose, like an honest man *Much Ado* ii 3 19
An epilogue or discourse, to make plain Some obscure precedence *L. L. Lost* iii 1 82
Something else more plain, That shall express my true love's fasting pain iv 3 121
To tell you plain, I'll find a fairer face not wash'd to-day . . . iv 3 272
And to confirm it plain, You gave me this . . . . v 2 452
My scutcheon plain declares that I am Alisander . . . . . . v 2 567
But wonder on, till truth make all things plain . . *M. N. Dream* v 1 129
I was always plain with you . . . . *Mer. of Venice* iii 5 4
You were to blame, I must be plain with you . . . . v 1 166
The 'why' is plain as way to parish church . . . *As Y. Like It* ii 7 52
Knock at the gate! O heavens! Spake you not these words plain? *T. of Shrew* i 2 40
I'll tell her plain She sings as sweetly as a nightingale . . . . ii 1 171
'Tis not the many oaths that makes the truth, But the plain single vow that is vow'd true . . . . *All's Well* iv 2 22
If it appear not plain and prove untrue, Deadly divorce step between me and you! . . . . v 3 318
Mark it, Cesario, it is old and plain . . . . . . *T. Night* ii 4 44
As plain as I see you now . . . . iii 2 11
To be plain, I think there is not half a kiss to choose . . *W. Tale* iv 4 174
Up higher to the plain; where we'll set forth In best appointment *K. John* ii 1 295
The antique and well noted face Of plain old form is much disfigured . iv 2 22
Plain well-meaning soul . . . . *Richard II.* ii 1 128
While here we march Upon the grassy carpet of this plain . . . iii 3 50
Balk'd in their own blood . . . On Holmedon's plains . . 1 *Hen. IV.* i 1 70
Then plain and right must my possession be . . . 2 *Hen. IV.* iv 5 223
In which array, brave soldier, doth he lie, Larding the plain . *Hen. V.* iv 6 8
Take a fellow of plain and uncoined constancy . . . . . . v 2 161
Which is so plain that Exeter doth wish His days may finish ere that hapless time . . . . 1 *Hen. VI.* iii 1 200
No more but, plain and bluntly, 'To the king!' . . . . . . iv 1 51
To be plain, They, knowing Dame Eleanor's aspiring humour, Have hired me to undermine the duchess . . . . 2 *Hen. VI.* i 2 96
Safer shall he be upon the sandy plains Than where castles mounted stand . . . . i 4 71
To tell thee plain, I aim to lie with thee.—To tell you plain, I had rather lie in prison . . . . 3 *Hen. VI.* iii 2 69
Be plain, Queen Margaret, and tell thy grief; It shall be eased . . iii 3 19
Shall I be plain? I wish the bastards dead . . . *Richard III.* iv 2 18
Plain and not honest is too harsh a style . . . . iv 4 360
I will lead forth my soldiers to the plain . . . . v 3 291
Like a mountain cedar, reach his branches To all the plains about *Hen. VIII.* v 5 55
On Dardan plains The fresh and yet unbruised Greeks do pitch Their brave pavilions . . . . *Troi. and Cres.* Prol. 13
Look, how many Grecian tents do stand Hollow upon this plain . . i 3 80
The moral of my wit Is 'plain and true;' there's all the reach of it . iv 4 110
You vile abominable tents, Thus proudly pight upon our Phrygian plains v 10 24
And run like swallows o'er the plain . . . . . . *T. Andron.* ii 2 24
Let them not speak a word; the guilt is plain . . . . . . ii 3 301
This sandy plot is plain; guide, if thou canst, This after me . . . iv 1 69
Heaven guide thy pen to print thy sorrows plain! . . . . . . iv 1 75
Be plain, good son, and homely in thy drift . . . *Rom. and Jul.* ii 3 55
But, as you know me all, a plain blunt man, That love my friend *J. C.* iii 2 222
There are no tricks in plain and simple faith . . . . iv 2 22
Goose, if I had you upon Sarum plain, I'ld drive ye cackling home *Lear* ii 2 89
Sir, 'tis my occupation to be plain: I have seen better faces . . ii 2 98
An honest mind and plain, he must speak truth! An they will take it, so; if not, he's plain . . . . ii 2 105
Of how unnatural and bemadding sorrow The king hath cause to plain . iii 1 39
Chill be plain with you . . . . iv 6 248
What's dumb in show I'll plain with speech . . *Pericles* iii Gower 14
Plain a case. Have the gods envy?—Ay, ay, ay, ay; 'tis too plain a case *Troi. and Cres.* iv 4 31
Plain a stop. So easy and so plain a stop . . . . . 2 *Hen. IV.* Ind. 17
Plain accent. He that beguiled you in a plain accent was a plain knave *Lear* ii 2 117
Plain cannon fire. He speaks plain cannon fire . . . . *K. John* ii 1 462
Plain case. Why, 'tis a plain case . . . . . *Com. of Errors* iv 3 22
Plain Clarence. Go, tread the path that thou shalt ne'er return, Simple, plain Clarence! . . . . *Richard III.* i 1 118
Plain conveniency. With all brief and plain conveniency *Mer. of Venice* iv 1 82
Plain dealer. Thou didst conclude hairy men plain dealers without wit *Com. of Errors* ii 2 88
Plain-dealing. In plain dealing, Pompey, I shall have you whipt *Meas. for Meas.* ii 1 263
It must not be denied but I am a plain-dealing villain . . *Much Ado* i 3 33
Now to plain-dealing; lay these glozes by . . . . *L. L. Lost* iv 3 370
Or hast thou a mark to thyself, like an honest plain-dealing man? 2 *Hen. VI.* iv 2 111
Not so well as plain-dealing, which will not cost a man a doit *T. of Athens* i 1 216
Plain devil. The plain devil and dissembling looks . . *Richard III.* i 2 237
Plain face. Knavery's plain face is never seen till used . . *Othello* ii 1 321
Plain fellows. We are but plain fellows, sir.—A lie; you are rough and hairy . . . . *W. Tale* iv 4 743
Plain fish. One of them Is a plain fish . . . . . . *Tempest* v 1 266
Plain form. Be brief; only to the plain form of marriage . *Much Ado* iv 1 2
Plain highway. Without any slips of prolixity or crossing the plain highway of talk . . . . *Mer. of Venice* iii 1 13
Plain holy-thistle. I meant, plain holy-thistle . . . . *Much Ado* iii 4 80
Plain Judas. Judas Maccabæus clipt is plain Judas . . . *L. L. Lost* v 2 603
Plain Kate. You are call'd plain Kate, And bonny Kate . . *T. of Shrew* ii 1 186
Plain kerchief. A plain kerchief, Sir John: my brows become nothing else . . . . *Mer. Wives* iii 3 62
Plain king. Thou wouldst find me such a plain king that thou wouldst think I had sold my farm to buy my crown . . . . . *Hen. V.* v 2 128
Plain knave. He that beguiled you in a plain accent was a plain knave *Lear* ii 2 118
Plain man. Some plain man recount their purposes . . *L. L. Lost* v 2 176
I pray thee, understand a plain man in his plain meaning *Mer. of Venice* iii 5 62
You seem to be honest plain men . . . . *W. Tale* iv 4 824
Cannot a plain man live and think no harm? . . . *Richard III.* i 3 51

Plain masonry. Creaking my shoes on the plain masonry . *All's Well* ii 1 31
Plain meaning. Understand a plain man in his plain meaning *M. of V.* iii 5 63
Plain message. And deliver a plain message bluntly . . *Lear* i 4 35
Plain pocketing up. It is plain pocketing up of wrongs . . *Hen. V.* iii 2 54
Plain proceeding. What plain proceeding is more plain than this? *2 Hen. VI.* ii 2 53
Plain shock. In plain shock and even play of battle . . *Hen. V.* iv 8 114
Plain soldier. I speak to thee plain soldier . . . . v 2 156
Plain-song. The plain-song cuckoo gray . . *M. N. Dream* iii 1 134
The humour of it is too hot, that is the very plain-song of it. The plain-song is most just; for humours do abound . . . *Hen. V.* iii 2 6
May bring his plain-song And have an hour of hearing . *Hen. VIII.* i 3 45
Plain statute-caps. Better wits have worn plain statute-caps *L. L. Lost* v 2 281
Plain tale. A plain tale shall put you down . . . 1 *Hen. IV.* ii 4 281
Plain terms. Is indeed deceased, or, as you would say in plain terms, gone to heaven . . . . *Mer. of Venice* ii 2 68
Setting all this chat aside, Thus in plain terms . *T. of Shrew* ii 1 271
In plain terms tell her my loving tale . . . *Richard III.* iv 4 359
I would not, in plain terms, from this time forth, Have you so slander any moment leisure . . . . *Hamlet* i 3 132
Plain truth. You are a sectary, That's the plain truth . *Hen. VIII.* v 3 71
Plain way. Laid falsely I' the plain way of his merit . *Coriolanus* iii 1 61
Plain words. Honest plain words best pierce the ear of grief . *L. L. Lost* v 2 763
Plainer. The plainer dealer, the sooner lost . . . *Com. of Errors* ii 2 89
Follow me, then, To plainer ground . . . . *M. N. Dream* iii 2 404
But, beseech your grace, Be plainer with me . . . *W. Tale* i 2 265
But in the plainer and simpler kind of people, the deed of saying is quite out of use . . . . *T. of Athens* v 1 27
Plainest. Do I not in plainest truth Tell you, I do not, nor I cannot love you? . . . . *M. N. Dream* ii 1 200
I took him for the plainest harmless creature That breathed *Richard III.* iii 5 25
Plaining. Piteous plainings of the pretty babes . *Com. of Errors* i 1 73
After our sentence plaining comes too late . . . *Richard II.* i 3 175
Plainly conceive, I love you . . . . *Meas. for Meas.* ii 4 141
He struck so plainly, I could too well feel his blows . *Com. of Errors* ii 1 52
But I must tell thee plainly, Claudio undergoes my challenge *Much Ado* v 2 57
And tell them plainly he is Snug the joiner . . *M. N. Dream* iii 1 47
Now my foes tell me plainly I am an ass . . . *T. Night* v 1 20
Who mayst see Plainly as heaven sees earth and earth sees heaven *W. Tale* i 2 315
Do plainly give you out an unstain'd shepherd . . . iv 4 149
Once or twice I was about to speak and tell him plainly . . iv 4 454
Tongues of heaven, Plainly denouncing vengeance upon John *K. John* iii 4 159
Speak plainly your opinions of our hopes . . . 2 *Hen. IV.* i 3 3
Hear me more plainly . . . . iv 1 66
Our madams mock at us, and plainly say Our mettle is bred out *Hen. V.* iii 5 28
I mind to tell him plainly what I think . . . 3 *Hen. VI.* iv 1 8
Which plainly signified That I should snarl and bite and play the dog . v 6 76
An honest tale speeds best being plainly told . . *Richard III.* iv 4 358
And out of his noble carelessness lets them plainly see't . *Coriolanus* ii 2 16
Report to the Volscian lords, how plainly I have borne this business . v 3 3
Then plainly know my heart's dear love is set On the fair daughter of rich Capulet . . . . *Rom. and Jul.* ii 3 57
To deal plainly, I fear I am not in my perfect mind . . *Lear* iv 7 62
Plainness. And now in plainness do confess to thee . . *T. of Shrew* i 1 157
Your plainness and your shortness please me well . . . iv 4 39
Therefore with frank and with uncurbed plainness Tell us *Hen. V.* i 2 244
For the truth and plainness of the case, I pluck this pale and maiden blossom here . . . . 1 *Hen. VI.* ii 4 46
Thy plainness and thy housekeeping, Hath won the greatest favour 2 *Hen. VI.* i 1 191
Whilst some with cunning gild their copper crowns, With truth and plainness I do wear mine bare . . . . *Troi. and Cres.* iv 4 108
Let pride, which she calls plainness, marry her . . *Lear* i 1 131
To plainness honour's bound, When majesty stoops to folly . . i 1 150
In this plainness Harbour more craft and more corrupter ends . ii 2 107
In honest plainness thou hast heard me say . . . *Othello* i 1 97
Enjoy thy plainness, It nothing ill becomes thee . *Ant. and Cleo.* ii 6 80
Plaint. Hearing how our plaints and prayers do pierce . *Richard II.* v 3 127
Bootless are plaints, and cureless are my wounds . 3 *Hen. VI.* ii 6 23
And Nero will be tainted with remorse, To hear and see her plaints . iii 1 41
What cause have I, Thine being but a moiety of my grief, To overgo thy plaints and drown thy cries! . . . . . *Richard III.* ii 2 61
Plaintiff. Come, bring away the plaintiffs . . . *Much Ado* v 1 261
This plaintiff here, the offender, did call me ass . . . v 1 314
Thou shalt be both the plaintiff and the judge Of thine own cause *T. N.* v 1 362
Plaited. Time shall unfold what plaited cunning hides . . *Lear* i 1 283
Planched. And to that vineyard is a planched gate . *Meas. for Meas.* iv 1 30
Planet. I was not born under a rhyming planet . . *Much Ado* v 2 41
It is a bawdy planet, that will strike Where 'tis predominant *W. Tale* i 2 201
There's some ill planet reigns: I must be patient . . . . ii 1 105
What! shall we curse the planets of mishap? . . . 1 *Hen. VI.* i 1 23
Combat with adverse planets in the heavens! . . . . . i 1 54
Hath this lovely face Ruled, like a wandering planet, over me? 2 *Hen. VI.* iv 4 16
Be opposite all planets of good luck To my proceedings! *Richard III.* iv 4 402
The planets and this centre Observe degree, priority and place *T. and C.* i 3 85
Therefore is the glorious planet Sol In noble eminence enthroned . . i 3 89
Whose medicinable eye Corrects the ill aspects of planets evil . i 3 92
But when the planets In evil mixture to disorder wander, What plagues! i 3 94
And with a sudden re-inforcement struck Corioli like a planet *Coriolanus* ii 2 118
Some planet strike me down, That I may slumber in eternal sleep! *T. Andron.* ii 4 14
The nights are wholesome; then no planets strike . . . *Hamlet* i 1 162
As if some planet had unwitted men . . . . . *Othello* ii 3 182
Now the fleeting moon No planet is of mine . . *Ant. and Cleo.* v 2 241
To glad her presence, The senate-house of planets all did sit . *Pericles* i 1 10
Planetary. Be as a planetary plague, when Jove Will o'er some high-viced city hang his poison In the sick air . . . *T. of Athens* iv 3 108
By an enforced obedience of planetary influence . . . *Lear* i 2 135
Plank. To crouch in litter of your stable planks . . . *K. John* v 2 140
Do not fight by sea; Trust not to rotten planks . . *Ant. and Cleo.* iii 7 63
Plants with goodly burthen bowing . . . . . *Tempest* iv 1 113
Such barren plants are set before us, that we thankful should be *L. L. L.* iv 2 29
His lines would ravish savage ears And plant in tyrants mild humility iv 3 349
Abuses our young plants with carving 'Rosalind' on their barks *As Y. Like It* iii 2 378
It is in us to plant thine honour where We please . . . *All's Well* ii 3 163
I will plant you two, and let the fool make a third . . *T. Night* ii 3 188
And in one self-born hour To plant and o'erwhelm custom . *W. Tale* iv 1 9
Pray God the plants thou graft'st may never grow . *Richard II.* iii 4 101
Thou, which know'st the way To plant unrightful kings . . . v 1 63
Plant. In thy piteous heart plant thou thine ear . . *Richard II.* v 3 126
Amongst a grove, the very straightest plant . . . . 1 *Hen. IV.* i 1 82
And plant this thorn, this canker, Bolingbroke . . . . i 3 176
Plant neighbourhood and Christian-like accord In their sweet bosoms *Hen. V.* v 2 381
They laboured to plant the rightful heir . . . . . 1 *Hen. VI.* ii 5 80
I'll plant Plantagenet, root him up who dares . . . 3 *Hen. VI.* i 1 48
This may plant courage in their quailing breasts; For yet is hope . ii 3 54
His love was an eternal plant, Whereof the root was fix'd in virtue's ground . . . . iii 3 124
How sweet a plant have you untimely cropp'd! . . . . . v 5 62
And plant your joys in living Edward's throne . . *Richard III.* ii 2 100
Her royal stock graft with ignoble plants . . . . . iii 7 127
We will plant some other in the throne . . . . . iii 7 216
The parents live, whose children thou hast butcher'd, Old wither'd plants iv 4 394
To his music plants and flowers Ever sprung . . . *Hen. VIII.* iii 1 6
Every man shall eat in safety, Under his own vine, what he plants . v 5 35
Plant love among's! Throng our large temples with the shows of peace! *Coriolanus* iii 3 35
He water'd his new plants with dews of flattery . . . v 6 23
O, mickle is the powerful grace that lies In herbs, plants, stones *R. and J.* ii 3 16
Full soon the canker death eats up that plant . . . . ii 3 30
Welcome hither: I have begun to plant thee, and will labour To make thee full of growing . . . . *Macbeth* i 4 28
Within this hour at most I will advise you where to plant yourselves . iii 1 129
A faith that reason without miracle Could never plant in me . . *Lear* i 1 226
If we will plant nettles, or sow lettuce, set hyssop . . . *Othello* i 3 325
Some o' their plants are ill-rooted already . . . *Ant. and Cleo.* ii 7 2
Plant those that have revolted in the van . . . . . iv 6 9
How dare the plants look up to heaven? . . . . . *Pericles* i 2 55
Plantage. As true as steel, as plantage to the moon . *Troi. and Cres.* iii 2 184
Plantagenet. Arthur Plantagenet lays most lawful claim To this fair island . . . . *K. John* i 1 9
Bear his name whose form thou bear'st: Kneel thou down Philip, but rise more great, Arise sir Richard and Plantagenet . . . . i 1 162
The very spirit of Plantagenet! I am thy grandam, Richard . . . i 1 167
Young Plantagenet, Son to the elder brother of this man . . . ii 1 238
Befriend me so much as to think I come one way of the Plantagenets . v 6 11
That some night-tripping fairy had exchanged In cradle-clothes our children where they lay, And call'd mine Percy, his Plantagenet! 1 *Hen. IV.* i 1 89
England is thine, Ireland is thine, France is thine, and Henry Plantagenet is thine . . . . *Hen. V.* v 2 259
'Remember to avenge me on the French.' Plantagenet, I will 1 *Hen. VI.* i 4 95
I pluck this white rose with Plantagenet . . . . . ii 4 36
No, Plantagenet, 'Tis not for fear but anger that thy cheeks Blush . ii 4 64
Hath not thy rose a thorn, Plantagenet? . . . . . . ii 4 69
Where false Plantagenet dare not be seen . . . . . . ii 4 74
Turn not thy scorns this way, Plantagenet . . . . . ii 4 77
Richard Plantagenet, my lord, will come: We sent unto the Temple . ii 5 18
Richard Plantagenet, my friend, is he come?—Ay, noble uncle . . ii 5 34
In honour of a true Plantagenet And for alliance sake . . . ii 5 52
Plantagenet, I see, must hold his tongue . . . . . iii 1 61
Which in the right of Richard Plantagenet We do exhibit to your majesty iii 1 150
Rise, Richard, like a true Plantagenet . . . . . . iii 1 172
My mother a Plantagenet,— I knew her well; she was a midwife 2 *Hen. VI.* iv 2 44
Unless Plantagenet, Duke of York, be king . . . 3 *Hen. VI.* i 1 40
I'll plant Plantagenet, root him up who dares: Resolve thee, Richard . i 1 48
Plantagenet, of thee and these thy sons, Thy kinsmen and thy friends, I'll have more lives Than drops of blood were in my father's veins . i 1 95
Give King Henry leave to speak.—Plantagenet shall speak first . i 1 121
Plantagenet, for all the claim thou lay'st, Think not that Henry shall be so deposed.—Deposed he shall be . . . . i 1 152
Richard Plantagenet, Enjoy the kingdom after my decease . . . i 1 174
Long live King Henry! Plantagenet, embrace him . . . . i 1 202
Plantagenet! I come, Plantagenet! And this thy son's blood cleaving to my blade Shall rust upon my weapon, till thy blood, Congeal'd with this, do make me wipe off both . . . . i 3 49
Yield to our mercy, proud Plantagenet . . . . . . i 4 30
But how is it that great Plantagenet Is crown'd so soon? . . . i 4 99
We, the sons of brave Plantagenet, Each one already blazing by our meeds . . . . ii 1 35
That Plantagenet, Which held thee dearly as his soul's redemption . ii 1 101
Edward Plantagenet, arise a knight; And learn this lesson . . . ii 2 61
Is not the causer of the timeless deaths Of these Plantagenets, Henry and Edward, As blameful as the executioner? . . . *Richard III.* i 2 118
He lives that loves thee better than he could.—Name him.—Plantagenet i 2 142
Gallant-springing brave Plantagenet, That princely novice . . . i 4 227
Famous Plantagenet, most gracious prince, Lend favourable ears . . iii 7 100
Who meets us here? my niece Plantagenet Led in the hand of her kind aunt? . . . . iv 1 1
Edward Plantagenet, why art thou dead?—Plantagenet doth quit Plantagenet. Edward for Edward pays a dying debt . . . iv 4 19
Where is thy brother Clarence? And little Ned Plantagenet, his son? . iv 4 146
Plantain. O, sir, plantain, a plain plantain! no l'envoy, no l'envoy; no salve, sir, but a plantain! . . . . *L. L. Lost* iii 1 74
Plantain-leaf is excellent for that.—For what, I pray thee?—For your broken shin . . . . *Rom. and Jul.* i 2 52
Plantation. Had I plantation of this isle, my lord . . . *Tempest* ii 1 143
Planted and placed and possessed by my master . . . *Much Ado* iii 3 159
A man in all the world's new fashion planted . . . *L. L. Lost* i 1 165
The fool hath planted in his memory An army of good words *M. of Ven.* iii 5 71
Anointed, crowned, planted many years . . . . *Richard II.* iv 1 127
He hath so planted his honours in their eyes . . . *Coriolanus* ii 2 32
You are but newly planted in your throne . . . . *T. Andron.* i 1 444
Thy temples should be planted presently With horns, as was Actæon's . ii 3 62
What's more to do, Which would be planted newly with the time *Macbeth* v 8 65
Yet at the first I saw the treasons planted . . . *Ant. and Cleo.* i 3 26
Planteth. It engenders choler, planteth anger . . . *T. of Shrew* iv 1 175
Plash. As he that leaves A shallow plash to plunge him in the deep . i 1 23
Plashy. With all good speed at Plashy visit me . . . *Richard II.* i 2 66
Get thee to Plashy, to my sister Gloucester . . . . . ii 2 90
I should to Plashy too; But time will not permit . . . . ii 2 120
Plaster. You rub the sore, When you should bring the plaster *Tempest* ii 1 139
Let him have some plaster, or some loam . . . *M. N. Dream* iii 1 70
I am not glad that such a sore of time Should seek a plaster . *K. John* v 2 13
Boils and plagues Plaster you o'er, that you may be abhorr'd! *Coriolanus* i 4 32
Plasterer. Villain, thy father was a plasterer . . . . 2 *Hen. VI.* iv 2 140
Plastering. Beautied with plastering art . . . . . *Hamlet* iii 1 51

Plat. That very Mab That plats the manes of horses in the night *R. and J.* i 4 89
Plate. My house . . . Is richly furnished with plate and gold *T. of Shrew* ii 1 349
We do seize to us The plate, coin, revenues and moveables *Richard II.* ii 1 161
We seize into our hands His plate, his goods, his money and his lands ii 1 210
I must be fain to pawn both my plate and the tapestry . 2 *Hen. IV.* ii 1 153
The several parcels of his plate, his treasure, Rich stuffs *Hen. VIII.* iii 2 125
Remove the court-cupboard, look to the plate . *Rom. and Jul.* i 5 8
As money, plate, jewels and such-like trifles . *T. of Athens* iii 2 23
Plate sin with gold, And the strong lance of justice hurtless breaks *Lear* iv 6 169
Realms and islands were As plates dropp'd from his pocket *Ant. and Cleo.* v 2 92
This is the brief of money, plate, and jewels, I am possess'd of . v 2 138
'Tis plate of rare device, and jewels Of rich and exquisite form *Cymbeline* i 6 189
Plated. Thus plated in habiliments of war . . . *Richard II.* i 3 28
Those his goodly eyes, That o'er the files and musters of the war Have glow'd like plated Mars . . . *Ant. and Cleo.* i 1 4
Platform. And lay new platforms to endamage them . 1 *Hen. VI.* ii 1 77
But where was this?—My lord, upon the platform where we watch'd *Ham.* i 2 213
Upon the platform, 'twixt eleven and twelve, I'll visit you . i 2 252
To the platform, masters; come, let's set the watch . *Othello* ii 3 124
Plausible. Answer his requiring with a plausible obedience . *M. for M.* iii 1 253
Plausive. His plausive words He scatter'd not in ears . *All's Well* i 2 53
It must be a very plausive invention that carries it . iv 1 29
Some habit that too much o'er-leavens The form of plausive manners *Ham.* i 4 30
Plautus. Seneca cannot be too heavy, nor Plautus too light . ii 2 420
Play. Where's the master? Play the men . . *Tempest* i 1 11
What foul play had we, that we came from thence? . i 2 60
By foul play, as thou say'st, were we heaved thence . i 2 62
He will shoot no more but play with sparrows And be a boy right out . iv 1 100
Sweet lord, you play me false.—No, my dear'st love, I would not . v 1 172
For a score of kingdoms you should wrangle, And I would call it fair play . . . v 1 175
What is this maid with whom thou wast at play? . v 1 185
He plays false, father.—How? out of tune? . . *T. G. of Ver.* iv 2 59
You would have them always play but one thing?—I would always have one play but one thing . . . iv 2 70
When a man's servant shall play the cur with him, look you, it goes hard iv 4 1
Our youth got me to play the woman's part . iv 4 165
I made her weep agood, For I did play a lamentable part . iv 4 171
Master Slender is let the boys leave to play.—Blessing of his heart! *Mer. Wives* iv 1 12
Go your ways, and play; go . . . iv 1 81
She hath prosperous art When she will play with reason *Meas. for Meas.* i 2 190
I would not— . . . Tongue far from heart—play with all virgins so . i 4 33
Plays such fantastic tricks before high heaven As make the angels weep ii 2 121
So play the foolish throngs with one that swoons . ii 4 24
This would make mercy swear and play the tyrant . iii 2 207
If we two be one and thou play false, I do digest the poison *Com. of Errors* ii 2 144
Dromio, play the porter well . . . ii 2 213
Or do you play the flouting Jack? . . *Much Ado* i 1 185
And all Europa shall rejoice at thee, As once Europa did at lusty Jove, When he would play the noble beast in love . v 4 47
Therefore play, music. Prince, thou art sad; get thee a wife . v 4 123
That aged ears play truant at his tales . . *L. L. Lost* ii 1 74
Where is the bush That we must stand and play the murderer in? . iv 1 8
And he from forage will incline to play . iv 1 93
All hid, all hid; an old infant play . iv 3 78
And Nestor play at push-pin with the boys . iv 3 169
I will play three myself.—Thrice-worthy gentleman! . v 1 150
I'll make one in a dance, or so; or I will play On the tabor . v 1 160
The music plays; vouchsafe some motion to it.—Our ears vouchsafe it v 2 216
Sweet, adieu: Since you can cog, I'll play no more with you . v 2 235
When he plays at tables, chides the dice In honourable terms . v 2 326
Unless you play the honest Troyan, the poor wench is cast away . v 2 681
For your fair sakes have we neglected time, Play'd foul play with our oaths . . . v 2 766
Our wooing doth not end like an old play; Jack hath not Jill . v 2 884
A twelvemonth and a day, And then 'twill end.—That's too long for a play v 2 888
Here is the scroll of every man's name, which is thought fit, through all Athens, to play in our interlude . *M. N. Dream* i 2 5
Say what the play treats on, then read the names of the actors . i 2 9
Marry, our play is, The most lamentable comedy . i 2 11
I could play Ercles rarely, or a part to tear a cat in, to make all split . i 2 31
Let not me play a woman; I have a beard coming . i 2 49
You shall play it in a mask, and you may speak as small as you will . i 2 51
Let me play Thisby too, I'll speak in a monstrous little voice . i 2 53
No; you must play Pyramus: and, Flute, you Thisby . i 2 57
Robin Starveling, you must play Thisby's mother . i 2 62
I hope, here is a play fitted . . . i 2 67
Let me play the lion too: I will roar . i 2 72
You can play no part but Pyramus . . i 2 87
What beard were I best to play it in?—Why, what you will . i 2 93
And then you will play barefaced . . i 2 100
I will draw a bill of properties, such as our play wants . i 2 108
Doth the moon shine that night we play our play? . iii 1 53
Leave a casement of the great chamber window, where we play, open . iii 1 58
What, a play toward! I'll be an auditor; An actor too perhaps . iii 1 81
To rehearse a play Intended for great Theseus' nuptial-day . iii 2 11
I will sing it in the latter end of a play . iv 1 223
If he come not, then the play is marred: it goes not forward, doth it? iv 2 5
For the short and the long is, our play is preferred . iv 2 39
Let not him that plays the lion pare his nails . iv 2 41
Is there no play, To ease the anguish of a torturing hour? . v 1 36
A play there is, my lord, some ten words long, Which is as brief as I have known a play . . . v 1 61
For in all the play There is not one word apt, one player fitted . v 1 64
What are they that do play it?—Hard-handed men that work in Athens v 1 71
And now have toil'd their unbreathed memories With this same play . v 1 75
I will hear that play; For never anything can be amiss, When simpleness and duty tender it . . . v 1 81
Here she comes; and her passion ends the play . v 1 321
No epilogue, I pray you; for your play needs no excuse. Never excuse v 1 362
This palpable-gross play hath well beguiled The heavy gait of night . v 1 374
A stage where every man must play a part, And mine a sad one.—Let me play the fool . . *Mer. of Venice* i 1 78
If Hercules and Lichas play at dice Which is the better man . ii 1 32
If a Christian did not play the knave and get thee, I am much deceived ii 3 12
When you shall please to play the thieves for wives, I'll watch as long ii 6 23
Come at once; For the close night doth play the runaway . ii 6 47
In her hairs The painter plays the spider . . iii 2 121
We'll play with them the first boy for a thousand ducats . iii 2 216

Play. How every fool can play upon the word! . . *Mer. of Venice* iii 5 48
If two gods should play some heavenly match . iii 5 84
This wide and universal theatre Presents more woeful pageants than the scene Wherein we play in . . *As Y. Like It* ii 7 139
And one man in his time plays many parts, His acts being seven ages . ii 7 142
And so he plays his part . . . ii 7 157
And under that habit play the knave with him . iii 2 314
And you shall say I'll prove a busy actor in their play . iii 4 62
Patience herself would startle at this letter And play the swaggerer . iv 3 14
What, to make thee an instrument and play false strains upon thee! . iv 3 68
And fall into our rustic revelry. Play, music! . v 4 184
A good play needs no epilogue . . . Epil. 4
Good plays prove the better by the help of good epilogues . . Epil. 6
Nor cannot insinuate with you in the behalf of a good play . . Epil. 9
I charge you, O women, for the love you bear to men, to like as much of this play as please you . . . Epil. 14
I charge you, O men, for the love you bear to women, . . . that between you and the women the play may please . . Epil. 18
My lord, I warrant you we will play our part . *T. of Shrew* Ind. 1 69
There is a lord will hear you play to-night . Ind. 1 93
For yet his honour never heard a play . Ind. 1 96
Apollo plays And twenty caged nightingales do sing . Ind. 2 37
Even as the waving sedges play with wind . Ind. 2 55
Hearing your amendment, Are come to play a pleasant comedy . Ind. 2 132
They thought it good you hear a play And frame your mind to mirth Ind. 2 136
Let them play it. Is not a comonty a Christmas gambold? . Ind. 2 139
My lord, you nod; you do not mind the play . i 1 254
Now I play a merchant's part, And venture madly on a desperate mart ii 1 328
Take you your instrument, play you the whiles . iii 1 22
Hark, hark! I hear the minstrels play . iii 2 185
While I play the good husband at home, my son and my servant spend all at the university . . v 1 71
And death should have play for lack of work . *All's Well* i 1 23
I play the noble housewife with the time, To entertain't so merrily ii 2 62
Then go thou forth; And fortune play upon thy prosperous helm! . iii 3 7
So lust doth play With what it loathes for that which is away . iv 4 24
The king's a beggar, now the play is done . . Epil. 335
If music be the food of love, play on . . *T. Night* i 1 1
He plays o' the viol-de-gamboys, and speaks three or four languages . i 3 26
And yet, by the very fangs of malice I swear, I am not that I play . i 5 196
Seek him out, and play the tune the while . ii 4 14
And perchance wind up my watch, or play with my—some rich jewel . ii 5 66
Shall I play my freedom at tray-trip, and become thy bond-slave? . ii 5 208
I would play Lord Pandarus of Phrygia . . iii 1 58
This fellow is wise enough to play the fool . iii 1 67
What, man! 'tis not for gravity to play at cherry-pit with Satan . iii 4 129
Primo, secundo, tertio, is a good play . v 1 39
That's all one, our play is done, And we'll strive to please you every day . . . v 1 416
Go, play, boy, play: thy mother plays, and I Play too . . *W. Tale* i 2 187
I Remain a pinch'd thing; yea, a very trick For them to play at will . ii 1 52
Like a bank for love to lie and play on . iv 4 130
Methinks I play as I have seen them do In Whitsun pastorals . iv 4 133
My care To have you royally appointed as if The scene you play were mine . . . iv 4 604
I see the play so lies That I must bear a part . iv 4 669
If she did play false, the fault was hers . . *K. John* i 1 118
What the devil art thou?—One that will play the devil, sir, with you . ii 1 135
Victory, with little loss, doth play Upon the dancing banners . ii 1 307
I'ld play incessantly upon these jades . . ii 1 385
The glorious sun Stays in his course and plays the alchemist . iii 1 78
Play fast and loose with faith? so jest with heaven? . iii 1 242
Whiles warm life plays in that infant's veins . iii 4 132
It is apparent foul play; and 'tis shame . iv 2 93
According to the fair play of the world, Let me have audience . v 2 118
Can sick men play so nicely with their names? . *Richard II.* ii 1 84
As a long-parted mother with her child Plays fondly with her tears and smiles in meeting . . . iii 2 9
I play the torturer, by small and small To lengthen out the worst . iii 2 198
Shall we play the wantons with our woes? . iii 3 164
Madam, we'll play at bowls . . . iii 4 3
Thus play I in one person many people, And none contented . v 5 31
This is no world To play with mammets and to tilt with lips . 1 *Hen. IV.* ii 3 95
And bid you play it off . . . ii 4 18
Darest thou be so valiant as to play the coward with thy indenture? . ii 4 52
I'll play Percy, and that damned brawn shall play Dame Mortimer his wife . . . ii 4 122
What, shall we be merry? shall we have a play extempore? . ii 4 309
Dost thou speak like a king? Do thou stand for me, and I'll play my father . . . ii 4 477
Play out the play: I have much to say in the behalf of that Falstaff . ii 4 531
And those musicians that shall play to you Hang in the air . iii 1 226
As ever offer'd foul play in a state . . iii 2 169
The southern wind Doth play the trumpet to his purposes . v 1 4
To it, Hal! Nay, you shall find no boy's play here, I can tell you . v 4 76
Art thou alive? Or is it fantasy that plays upon our eyesight? . v 4 138
The still-discordant wavering multitude Can play upon it 2 *Hen. IV.* Ind. 20
For the one or the other plays the rogue with my great toe . i 2 274
Thus we play the fools with the time . . ii 2 154
I'll thrust my knife in your mouldy chaps, an you play the saucy cuttle ii 4 139
The music is come, sir.—Let them play. Play, sirs . ii 4 246
A' plays at quoits well, and eats conger and fennel . ii 4 266
I was lately here in the end of a displeasing play . . Epil. 10
Gently to hear, kindly to judge, our play . *Hen. V.* Prol. 34
When we have match'd our rackets to these balls, We will, in France, by God's grace, play a set Shall strike his father's crown into the hazard . . . i 2 262
And we'll digest The abuse of distance; force a play . ii Prol. 32
For, if we may, We'll not offend one stomach with our play . ii Prol. 40
I saw him fumble with the sheets and play with flowers . ii 3 15
Play with your fancies . . . iii Prol. 7
When lenity and cruelty play for a kingdom, the gentler gamester is the soonest winner . . . iii 6 119
Over-lusty French Do the low-rated English play at dice . iv Prol. 19
Had ten times more valour than this roaring devil i' the old play . iv 4 76
In plain shock and even play of battle . . iv 8 114
Doth Fortune play the huswife with me now? . . v 1 85
And like thee, Nero, Play on the lute, beholding the towns burn 1 *Hen. VI.* i 4 96
The king Prettily, methought, did play the orator . iv 1 175
As plays the sun upon the glassy streams . v 3 62

Play. I will not be slack To play my part in Fortune's pageant *2 Hen. VI.* i 2 67
But mine is made the prologue to their play . . . . . . iii 1 151
What, wilt thou on thy death-bed play the ruffian? . . . . . v 1 164
I can better play the orator.—But I have reasons . *3 Hen. VI.* i 2 2
I'll play the orator as well as Nestor, Deceive more slily than Ulysses . iii 2 188
You shall give me leave To play the broker in mine own behalf . iv 1 63
Belike she minds to play the Amazon . . . . iv 1 106
Which plainly signified That I should snarl and bite and play the dog . v 6 77
And seem a saint, when most I play the devil . . *Richard III.* i 3 338
I'll play the orator As if the golden fee for which I plead Were for myself . . . . iii 5 95
Play the maid's part, still answer nay, and take it . . . . . iii 7 51
Now do I play the touch, To try if thou be current gold indeed . iv 2 8
The beholders of this tragic play, The adulterate Hastings, Rivers, Vaughan . . . . iv 4 68
Under our tents I'll play the eaves-dropper . . . . . v 3 221
The play may pass, if they be still and willing . . *Hen. VIII.* Prol. 11
Only they That come to hear a merry bawdy play . . . Will be deceived Prol. 14
An honest country lord, as I am, beaten A long time out of play . i 3 45
You are a merry gamester, My Lord Sands.—Yes, if I make my play . i 4 46
Every thing that heard him play, Even the billows of the sea, Hung their heads, and then lay by . . . . iii 1 9
Thou hast forced me, Out of thy honest truth, to play the woman . iii 2 430
Cause the musicians play me that sad note I named my knell . iv 2 78
I will play no more to-night; My mind's not on't; you are too hard for me . . . . v 1 56
I did never win of you before.—But little, Charles; Nor shall not, when my fancy's on my play . . . . v 1 60
You play the spaniel, And think with wagging of your tongue to win me v 3 126
I'll find A Marshalsea shall hold ye play these two months . . v 4 90
'Tis ten to one this play can never please All that are here . . Epil. 1
All the expected good we're like to hear For this play at this time, is only in The merciful construction of good women . . . Epil. 9
Our play Leaps o'er the vaunt and firstlings of those broils, Beginning in the middle, starting thence away To what may be digested in a play . . . . *Troi. and Cres.* Prol. 26
Play me Nestor; hem, and stroke thy beard, As he being drest to some oration . . . . i 3 165
Now play him me, Patroclus, Arming to answer in a night alarm . i 3 170
Who play they to?—To the hearers, sir.—At whose pleasure, friend? . iii 1 23
Thou art too cunning. At whose request do these men play? . . iii 1 31
Pardon me—If I confess much, you will play the tyrant . . iii 2 127
I'll play the hunter for thy life With all my force . . . iv 1 17
Nor heel the high lavolt, nor sweeten talk, Nor play at subtle games . iv 4 89
O, 'tis fair play.—Fool's play, by heaven . . . . . v 3 43
I must have you play the idle huswife with me this afternoon *Coriolanus* i 3 76
Rather say I play The man I am . . . . iii 2 15
If thy stumps will let thee play the scribe . . *T. Andron.* ii 4 4
Bring them in, for I'll play the cook . . . . v 2 205
Come, musicians, play. A hall, a hall! give room! and foot it, girls *Rom. and Jul.* i 5 27
Day, night, hour, tide, time, work, play, Alone, in company . . iii 5 178
'Twixt my extremes and me this bloody knife Shall play the umpire . iv 1 63
Let me alone; I'll play the housewife for this once . . . . iv 2 43
And madly play with my forefathers' joints . . . . . iv 3 51
O, an you will have me live, play 'Heart's ease.'—Why 'Heart's ease'? —O, musicians, because my heart itself plays 'My heart is full of woe' . . . . iv 5 103
O, play me some merry dump, to comfort me.—Not a dump we; 'tis no time to play now . . . . iv 5 107
If our betters play at that game, we must not dare To imitate them *T. of Athens* i 2 12
And the cap Plays in the right hand, thus . . . . . . ii 1 19
The public body, which doth seldom Play the recanter . . . v 1 149
He loves no plays, As thou dost, Antony; he hears no music *J. Cæsar* i 2 203
Lay'st thou thy leaden mace upon my boy, That plays thee music? . iv 3 269
Wouldst not play false, And yet wouldst wrongly win . *Macbeth* i 5 22
Ourself will mingle with society, And play the humble host . . iii 4 4
O, I could play the woman with mine eyes And braggart with my tongue! . . . . iv 3 230
Why should I play the Roman fool, and die On mine own sword? . v 8 1
These indeed seem, For they are actions that a man might play *Hamlet* i 2 84
My father's spirit in arms! all is not well; I doubt some foul play . i 2 256
He that plays the king shall be welcome . . . . . . ii 2 332
The play, I remember, pleased not the million . . . . . ii 2 456
An excellent play, well digested in the scenes . . . . . ii 2 460
We'll hear a play to-morrow. Dost thou hear me, old friend; can you play the Murder of Gonzago? . . . . ii 2 560
I have heard That guilty creatures sitting at a play Have by the very cunning of the scene Been struck so to the soul that presently They have proclaim'd their malefactions . . . . . . ii 2 618
I'll have these players Play something like the murder of my father . ii 2 624
The play's the thing Wherein I'll catch the conscience of the king . ii 2 633
They have already order This night to play before him . . . iii 1 21
That he may play the fool no where but in's own house . . . iii 1 136
After the play Let his queen mother all alone entreat him . . iii 1 189
O, there be players that I have seen play, and heard others praise . iii 2 33
Let those that play your clowns speak no more than is set down for them . . . . iii 2 43
Though, in the mean time, some necessary question of the play be then to be considered . . . . iii 2 47
There is a play to-night before the king . . . . . . iii 2 80
If he steal aught the whilst this play is playing, And 'scape detecting, I will pay the theft . . . . iii 2 93
They are coming to the play; I must be idle: Get you a place . . iii 2 95
Belike this show imports the argument of the play . . . . iii 2 150
You are naught, you are naught: I'll mark the play . . . . iii 2 158
Madam, how like you this play?—The lady doth protest too much . iii 2 239
What do you call the play?—The Mouse-trap. Marry, how? Tropically iii 2 246
This play is the image of a murder done in Vienna . . . . iii 2 248
Give o'er the play.—Give me some light: away! . . . . . iii 2 279
Why, let the stricken deer go weep, The hart ungalled play . . iii 2 283
Will you play upon this pipe?—My lord, I cannot.—I pray you . iii 2 366
How unworthy a thing you make of me! You would play upon me . iii 2 380
Though you can fret me, yet you cannot play upon me . . . iii 2 389
He could nothing do but wish and beg Your sudden coming o'er, to play with him . . . . iv 7 106
Did these bones cost no more the breeding, but to play at loggats with 'em? . . . . v 1 100
Ere I could make a prologue to my brains, They had begun the play . v 2 31

Play. He sends to know if your pleasure hold to play with Laertes *Ham.* v 2 206
Use some gentle entertainment to Laertes before you fall to play . . v 2 217
I embrace it freely; And will this brother's wager frankly play . . v 2 264
Give him the cup.—I'll play this bout first; set it by awhile . . v 2 295
That such a king should play bo-peep . . . . . *Lear* i 4 193
You are my guests: do me no foul play, friends . . . . . iii 7 31
Bad is the trade that must play fool to sorrow, Angering itself and others iv 1 40
Do not believe That . . . I thus would play and trifle . . *Othello* i 1 133
You rise to play and go to bed to work . . . . ii 1 116
Which now again you are most apt to play the sir in . . . . ii 1 175
What's he then that says I play the villain? . . . . . . ii 3 342
Even as her appetite shall play the god With his weak function . . ii 3 353
Masters, play here; I will content your pains; Something that's brief iii 1 1
Loves company, Is free of speech, sings, plays and dances well . . iii 3 185
I will play the swan, And die in music . . . . v 2 247
Play one scene Of excellent dissembling . . . *Ant. and Cleo.* i 3 78
As nearly as I may, I'll play the penitent to you . . . . . ii 2 92
If thou dost play with him at any game, Thou art sure to lose . . ii 3 25
Let's to billiards: come, Charmian.—My arm is sore; best play with Mardian . . . . ii 5 4
Come, you'll play with me, sir?—As well as I can, madam . . . ii 5 6
When thou hast done this chare, I'll give thee leave To play till doomsday . . . . v 2 232
Your crown's awry; I'll mend it, and then play . . . . . . v 2 322
Diseased ventures That play with all infirmities for gold *Cymbeline* i 6 124
Cadwal and I Will play the cook and servant; 'tis our match . . iii 6 30
'Tis said a woman's fitness comes by fits. Therein I must play the workman . . . . iv 1 7
Why should we be tender To let an arrogant piece of flesh threat us, Play judge and executioner all himself, For we do fear the law? . iv 2 128
I prithee, to our rock; You and Fidele play the cooks . . . iv 2 164
Do not play in wench-like words with that Which is so serious . iv 2 230
Shall's have a play of this? Thou scornful page, There lie thy part . v 5 228
A whale; a' plays and tumbles, driving the poor fry before him *Pericles* ii 1 34
In that vast tennis-court, have made the ball For them to play upon . ii 1 65
Unless you play the pious innocent, And for an honest attribute cry out 'She died by foul play' . . . . iv 3 17
Our scene must play His daughter's woe . . . . iv 4 48
New joy wait on you! Here our play has ending . . . . v 3 Gower 101

Played. To have no screen between this part he play'd And him he play'd it for . . . . *Tempest* i 2 107
Felt a fever of the mad and play'd Some tricks of desperation . . i 2 209
This is the tune of our catch, play'd by the picture of Nobody . . iii 2 135
Has done little better than played the Jack with us . . . . iv 1 197
I have play'd the sheep in losing him . . . *T. G. of Ver.* i 1 73
At Pentecost, When all our pageants of delight were play'd . . iv 4 164
Since I plucked geese, played truant and whipped top . *Mer. Wives* v 1 27
Heaven shield my mother play'd my father fair! . *Meas. for Meas.* iii 1 141
My lord, I have played the part of Lady Fame . . . *Much Ado* ii 1 220
Hero and Margaret have by this played their parts with Beatrice . . iii 2 79
Well bandied both; a set of wit well play'd . . . *L. L. Lost* v 2 29
We neglected time, Play'd foul play with our oaths . . . . v 2 766
A stranger Pyramus than e'er played here . . . *M. N. Dream* iii 1 90
It was play'd When I from Thebes came last a conqueror . . . v 1 50
He hath played on his prologue like a child on a recorder . . . v 1 122
If he that writ it had played Pyramus and hanged himself in Thisbe's garter, it would have been a fine tragedy . . . . v 1 365
I am much afeard my lady his mother played false with a smith *M. of V.* i 2 48
Slept together, Rose at an instant, learn'd, play'd, eat together *As Y. L. It* i 3 76
If you will see a pageant truly play'd, . . . Go hence a little . . iii 4 55
Once he play'd a farmer's eldest son . . . *T. of Shrew* Ind. 1 84
Wherein have you played the knave with fortune? . . *All's Well* v 2 32
If this were played upon a stage now, I could condemn it as an improbable fiction . . . . *T. Night* iii 4 140
And made the most notorious geck and gull That e'er invention play'd on v 1 352
A fool That seest a game play'd home, the rich stake drawn, And takest it all for jest . . . . *W. Tale* i 2 248
If industriously I play'd the fool, it was my negligence . . . i 2 257
More Than history can pattern, though devised And play'd to take spectators . . . . iii 2 38
Whoever wins, on that side shall I lose; Assured loss before the match be play'd . . . . *K. John* iii 1 336
Have I not here the best cards for the game, To win this easy match play'd for a crown? . . . . v 2 106
The Black Prince, Who on the French ground play'd a tragedy *Hen. V.* i 2 106
Be these the wretches that we play'd at dice for? . . . . . iv 5 8
And myself have play'd The interim, by remembering you 'tis past v Prol. 42
If Sir John Fastolfe had not play'd the coward . . *1 Hen. VI.* i 1 131
All France will be replete with mirth and joy, When they shall hear how we have play'd the men . . . . i 6 16
Pucelle hath bravely play'd her part in this, And doth deserve a coronet iii 3 88
I lose, indeed; Beshrew the winners, for they play'd me false! *2 Hen. VI.* iii 1 184
Full well hath Clifford play'd the orator . . . *3 Hen. VI.* ii 2 43
Look upon, as if the tragedy Were play'd in jest by counterfeiting actors ii 3 28
I would have play'd The part my father meant to act . . *Hen. VIII.* i 2 194
You have play'd your prize: God give you joy, sir! . . *T. Andron.* i 1 399
I play'd the cheater for thy father's hand . . . . . . v 1 111
Learn me how to lose a winning match, Play'd for a pair of stainless maidenhoods . . . . *Rom. and Jul.* iii 2 13
What might you . . . think, If I had play'd the desk or table-book? *Ham.* ii 2 136
My lord, you played once i' the university, you say? . . . . iii 2 104
Do you think I am easier to be played on than a pipe? . . . . iii 2 387
Those happy smilets, That play'd on her ripe lip . . . . *Lear* iv 3 22
As many to the vantage as would store the world they played for *Othello* iv 3 86
As well a woman with an eunuch play'd As with a woman *Ant. and Cleo.* ii 5 5
With half the bulk o' the world play'd as I pleased . . . . . iii 11 64
My master rather play'd than fought And had no help of anger *Cymbeline* i 1 162
Thy mistress, Pisanio, hath played the strumpet in my bed . . . iii 4 22
But being play'd upon before your time, Hell only danceth at so harsh a chime . . . . *Pericles* i 1 84

Playedst. I fear Thou play'dst most foully for't . . *Macbeth* iii 1 3

Player. Now name the rest of the players . . . *M. N. Dream* i 2 42
For in all the play There is not one word apt, one player fitted . v 1 65
Never excuse; for when the players are all dead, there need none to be blamed . . . . v 1 364
All the world's a stage, And all the men and women merely players: They have their exits and their entrances . . *As Y. Like It* ii 7 140
Players That offer service to your lordship . . . *T. of Shrew* Ind. 1 77
Your honour's players, hearing your amendment, Are come to play Ind. 2 131
He doth it as like one of these harlotry players as ever I see! *1 Hen. IV.* ii 4 437

Player. Like a strutting player, whose conceit Lies in his hamstring *Troi. and Cres.* i 3 153
As they use to do the players in the theatre *J. Cæsar* i 2 263
A poor player That struts and frets his hour upon the stage *Macbeth* v 5 24
What lenten entertainment the players shall receive from you *Hamlet* ii 2 329
What players are they?—Even those you were wont to take delight in ii 2 339
If they should grow themselves to common players—as it is most like ii 2 365
Unless the poet and the player went to cuffs in the question ii 2 373
There are the players.—Gentlemen, you are welcome to Elsinore ii 2 386
Lest my extent to the players, which, I tell you, must show fairly outward, should more appear like entertainment than yours ii 2 391
I will prophesy he comes to tell me of the players ii 2 406
Good my lord, will you see the players well bestowed? ii 2 547
Is it not monstrous that this player here, But in a fiction, in a dream of passion, Could force his soul so to his own conceit? ii 2 577
I'll have these players Play something like the murder of my father ii 2 623
It so fell out, that certain players We o'er-raught on the way iii 1 16
If you mouth it, as many of your players do, I had as lief the town-crier spoke my lines iii 2 3
O, there be players that I have seen play, and heard others praise iii 2 32
Bid the players make haste. Will you two help to hasten them? iii 2 54
Be the players ready?—Ay, my lord; they stay upon your patience iii 2 111
The players cannot keep counsel; they'll tell all iii 2 152
Would not this . . . get me a fellowship in a cry of players, sir? iii 2 289
Nor tripped neither, you base foot-ball player *Lear* i 4 96
Bells in your parlours, . . . Players in your housewifery *Othello* ii 1 113
Playest. Proud dream, That play'st so subtly with a king's repose *Hen. V.* iv 1 275
Playeth. And lulls him whilst she playeth on her back *T. Andron.* iv 1 99
Playfellow. Farewell, sweet playfellow: pray thou for us *M. N. Dream* i 1 220
In those unfledged days was my wife a girl; Your precious self had then not cross'd the eyes Of my young play-fellow *W. Tale* i 2 80
Shall I be your playfellow?—No, I'll none of you ii 1 3
Heart's discontent and sour affliction Be playfellows to keep you company! There's two of you *2 Hen. VI.* iii 2 302
Rude ragged nurse, old sullen playfellow! *Richard III.* iv 1 102
Two tender playfellows for dust iv 4 385
Or pack to their old playfellows *Hen. VIII.* i 3 33
Familiar with My playfellow, your hand *Ant. and Cleo.* iii 13 125
It is your fault that I have loved Posthumus: You bred him as my playfellow, and he is A man worth any woman *Cymbeline* i 1 145
To seek her as a bed-fellow, In marriage-pleasures play-fellow *Pericles* i Gower 34
Playhouse. There is the playhouse now, there must you sit *Hen. V.* ii Prol. 36
Youths that thunder at a playhouse, and fight for bitten apples *Hen. VIII.* v 4 64
Playing. I bruised my shin th' other day with playing *Mer. Wives* i 1 294
Spied a blossom passing fair Playing in the wanton air *L. L. Lost* iv 3 104
Sat all day, Playing on pipes of corn and versing love *M. N. Dream* ii 1 67
An the duke had not given him sixpence a day for playing Pyramus, I'll be hanged; he would have deserved it iv 2 22
If all the year were playing holidays, To sport would be as tedious as to work; But when they seldom come, they wish'd for come *1 Hen. IV.* i 2 228
Playing the mouse in absence of the cat *Hen. V.* i 2 172
If good, thou shamest the music of sweet news By playing it to me with so sour a face *Rom. and Jul.* ii 5 24
Any thing so overdone is from the purpose of playing *Hamlet* iii 2 23
If he steal aught the whilst this play is playing, And 'scape detecting iii 2 93
My music playing far off, I will betray Tawny-finn'd fishes *Ant. and Cleo.* ii 5 11
'Tis better playing with a lion's whelp Than with an old one dying iii 13 94
Playing-day. 'Tis a playing-day, I see *Mer. Wives* iv 1 9
Plea. The plea of no less weight Than Aquitaine *L. L. Lost* ii 1 7
In law, what plea so tainted and corrupt But, being season'd with a gracious voice, Obscures the show of evil? *Mer. of Venice* iii 2 75
But none can drive him from the envious plea Of forfeiture, of justice iii 2 284
Though justice be thy plea, consider this iv 1 198
I have spoke thus much To mitigate the justice of thy plea iv 1 203
That is my brother's plea and none of mine *K. John* i 1 67
Pleached. Bid her steal into the pleached bower *Much Ado* iii 1 7
Thus with pleach'd arms, bending down His corrigible neck *A. and C.* iv 14 73
Plead. To plead for love deserves more fee than hate *T. G. of Ver.* i 2 48
I will so plead That you shall say my cunning drift excels iv 2 82
Unhappy messenger, To plead for that which I would not obtain iv 4 105
Repeal thee home again, Plead a new state in thy unrival'd merit v 4 144
For which I would not plead, but that I must; For which I must not plead, but that I am At war 'twixt will and will not *Meas. for Meas.* ii 2 31
He cannot plead his estimation with you iv 2 27
I will plead against it with my life iv 2 192
Plead no more; I am not partial to infringe our laws *Com. of Errors* i 1 3
Plead you to me, fair dame? I know you not ii 2 149
Her sober virtue, years, and modesty, Plead on her part iii 1 91
Mightst thou perceive austerely in his eye That he did plead in earnest? iv 2 3
If he were mad, he would not plead so coldly v 1 272
In such a presence here to plead my thoughts *M. N. Dream* i 1 61
I'll plead for you As for my patron *T. of Shrew* i 2 155
Here I swear I'll plead for you myself ii 1 15
'Gamut' I am, the ground of all accord, 'A re,' to plead Hortensio's passion iii 1 74
His love and wisdom . . . may plead For amplest credence *All's Well* i 2 10
You need but plead your honourable privilege iv 5 95
And let the tongue of war Plead for our interest *K. John* v 2 165
Pleads he in earnest? look upon his face *Richard II.* v 3 100
Such as will enter at a lady's ear And plead his love-suit *Hen. V.* v 2 101
It fitteth not a prelate so to plead *1 Hen. VI.* iii 1 57
O Henry, let me plead for gentle Suffolk! *2 Hen. VI.* iii 2 289
If thou dost plead for him, Thou wilt but add increase unto my wrath iii 2 291
Used to command, untaught to plead for favour iv 1 122
Our swords shall plead it in the field *3 Hen. VI.* i 1 103
Have been An earnest advocate to plead for him *Richard III.* i 3 87
Be sudden in the execution, Withal obdurate, do not hear him plead i 3 347
Yet none of you would once plead for his life ii 1 130
I'll play the orator As if the golden fee for which I plead Were for myself iii 5 96
If you plead as well for them As I can say nay to thee for myself, No doubt we'll bring it to a happy issue iii 7 52
Plead what I will be, not what I have been iv 4 414
It will help me nothing To plead mine innocence *Hen. VIII.* i 1 208
The elect o' the land, who are assembled To plead your cause ii 4 61
The lustre in your eye . . . Pleads your fair usage *Troi. and Cres.* iv 4 121
My loving followers, Plead my successive title with your swords *T. An.* i 1 4
And, as suitors should, Plead your deserts in peace and humbleness i 1 45
My nephew Mutius' deeds do plead for him i 1 356
Brother, for in that name doth nature plead i 1 370
Plead. And wise Laertes' son Did graciously plead for his funerals *T. Andron.* i 1 381
Leave to plead my deeds: 'Tis thou and those that have dishonour'd me i 1 424
And that my sword upon thee shall approve, And plead my passions ii 1 36
For thy brothers let me plead. Grave tribunes, once more I entreat of you iii 1 30
Then go successantly, and plead to him iv 4 113
Crack the lawyer's voice, That he may never more false title plead, Nor sound his quillets shrilly *T. of Athens* iv 3 154
His virtues Will plead like angels, trumpet-tongued *Macbeth* i 7 19
And she for him pleads strongly to the Moor *Othello* ii 3 361
As well as I can, madam.—And when good will is show'd, though 't come too short, The actor may plead pardon *Ant. and Cleo.* ii 5 9
Pleaded. Then pleaded I for you.—And what said he? *Com. of Errors* iv 2 11
If he suppose that I have pleaded truth *1 Hen. VI.* ii 4 29
He pleaded still not guilty and alleged Many sharp reasons *Hen. VIII.* ii 1 13
Pleader. Silenced their pleaders *Coriolanus* ii 1 263
But, sure, if you Would be your country's pleader v 1 36
Pleading for a lover's fee *M. N. Dream* iii 2 113
A brace of tongues Must needs want pleading for a pair of eyes *K. John* iv 1 99
That thou mightst win the more thy father's love, Pleading so wisely in excuse of it *2 Hen. IV.* iv 5 181
He shall die, an it be but for pleading so well for his life *2 Hen. VI.* iv 7 113
I will be deaf to pleading and excuses *Rom. and Jul.* iii 1 197
Pleasance. That we should, with joy, pleasance, revel and applause, transform ourselves into beasts! *Othello* ii 3 293
Pleasant. Thou hast neither heat, affection, limb, nor beauty, To make thy riches pleasant *Meas. for Meas.* iii 1 38
You are pleasant, sir, and speak apace iii 2 120
He's returned; and as pleasant as ever he was *Much Ado* i 1 37
By my troth, most pleasant: how both did fit it! *L. L. Lost* iv 1 131
Pleasant without scurrility, witty without affection v 1 4
We have had pastimes here and pleasant game v 2 360
In our maiden council, rated them At courtship, pleasant jest and courtesy v 2 790
Are come to play a pleasant comedy *T. of Shrew* Ind. 2 132
Fruitful Lombardy, The pleasant garden of great Italy i 1 4
Your ancient, trusty, pleasant servant Grumio i 2 47
Thou art pleasant, gamesome, passing courteous, But slow in speech ii 1 247
Take it not unkindly, pray, That I have been thus pleasant with you both iii 1 58
To teach you gamut in a briefer sort, More pleasant, pithy and effectual iii 1 68
Like pleasant travellers, to break a jest Upon the company you overtake iv 5 72
It hath been to us rare, pleasant, speedy *W. Tale* iii 1 13
A very pleasant thing indeed and sung lamentably iv 4 190
Gave His body to that pleasant country's earth *Richard II.* iv 1 98
Welcome these pleasant days! *2 Hen. IV.* v 3 148
We are glad the Dauphin is so pleasant with us *Hen. V.* i 2 259
Tell the pleasant prince this mock of his Hath turn'd his balls to gun-stones i 2 281
What were it else But like a pleasant slumber in thy lap? *2 Hen. VI.* iii 2 390
I am glad Your grace is grown so pleasant *Hen. VIII.* i 4 90
Come, you are pleasant.—With your theme, I could O'ermount the lark ii 3 93
Well, sweet queen, you are pleasant with me *Troi. and Cres.* iii 1 67
At the lodge Upon the north side of this pleasant chase *T. Andron.* ii 3 255
And then awake as from a pleasant sleep *Rom. and Jul.* iv 1 106
I have upon a high and pleasant hill Feign'd Fortune *T. of Athens* i 1 63
This castle hath a pleasant seat *Macbeth* i 6 1
Heavens make our presence and our practices Pleasant and helpful to him!—Ay, Amen! *Hamlet* ii 2 39
What most he should dislike seems pleasant to him *Lear* iv 2 10
The gods are just, and of our pleasant vices Make instruments to plague us v 3 170
Is he disposed to mirth? I hope he is.—Exceeding pleasant *Cymbeline* i 6 59
Pleasantest. The pleasant'st angling is to see the fish Cut with her golden oars the silver stream *Much Ado* iii 1 26
Pleasantly. Think'st thou to catch my life so pleasantly? *Troi. and Cres.* iv 5 249
Pleasant-spirited. By my troth, a pleasant-spirited lady *Much Ado* ii 1 355
Please. Or else my project fails, Which was to please *Tempest* Epil. 13
I will write, Please you command, a thousand times as much *T. G. of Ver.* ii 1 120
If it please you, so; if not, why, so.—If it please me, madam, what then?—Why, if it please you, take it for your labour ii 1 137
And will employ thee in some service presently.—In what you please iv 4 46
How dost thou?—The better that it pleases your good worship to ask *Mer. Wives* i 4 144
I know not which pleases me better iii 3 189
I am a woeful suitor to your honour, Please but your honour hear me *Meas. for Meas.* ii 2 28
That you might know it, would much better please me Than to demand what 'tis ii 4 32
Please you to do't, I'll take it as a peril to my soul ii 4 64
A word with you.—As many as you please iii 1 51
Do no stain to your own gracious person; and much please the absent duke iii 1 209
I had rather it would please you I might be whipt v 1 511
It seems he hath great care to please his wife *Com. of Errors* ii 1 56
Since that my beauty cannot please his eye, I'll weep what's left away ii 1 114
What is your will that I shall do with this?—What please yourself iii 2 175
Go home with it and please your wife withal iii 2 178
I will please you what you will demand iv 4 52
To make curtsy and say 'Father, as it please you' *Much Ado* ii 1 56
Or else make another curtsy and say 'Father, as it please me' ii 1 59
I may say so, when I please.—And when please you to say so? ii 1 95
He both pleases men and angers them, and then they laugh at him ii 1 146
An excellent musician, and her hair shall be of what colour it please God ii 3 37
You are tedious.—It pleases your worship to say so iii 5 21
Study me how to please the eye indeed *L. L. Lost* i 1 80
Perge; so it shall please you to abrogate scurrility iv 2 55
But to return to the verses: did they please you? iv 2 157
If, before repast, it shall please you to gratify the table with a grace iv 2 161
It will please his grace . . . sometime to lean upon my poor shoulder v 1 107
This fellow pecks up wit as pigeons pease, And utters it again when God doth please v 2 316
That sport best pleases that doth least know how v 2 517
There are things in this comedy of Pyramus and Thisby that will never please *M. N. Dream* iii 1 10
Those things do best please me That befal preposterously iii 2 120
If you please To shoot another arrow that self way *Mer. of Venice* i 1 147
Of Launcelot, an't please your mastership ii 2 61
Like one well studied in a sad ostent To please his grandam ii 2 206
When you shall please to play the thieves for wives, I'll watch as long ii 6 23
I am not bound to please thee with my answers iv 1 65

Please. So please my lord the duke and all the court To quit the fine *Mer. of Venice* iv 1 380
Let me go, I say.—I will not, till I please . . . *As Y. Like It* i 1 69
My voice is ragged: I know I cannot please you.—I do not desire you to please me; I do desire you to sing . . . ii 5 16
Will you sing?—More at your request than to please myself . . . ii 5 23
Leaving his wealth and ease, A stubborn will to please . . . ii 5 55
Withal, as large a charter as the wind, To blow on whom I please . . ii 7 49
Words do well When he that speaks them pleases those that hear . . iii 5 112
And I am your Rosalind.—It pleases him to call you so . . . iv 1 66
I will content you, if what pleases you contents you . . . v 2 127
He cut it to please himself . . . v 4 78
I charge you, O women, . . . to like as much of this play as please you Epil. 14
Between you and the women the play may please . . . Epil. 18
Will't please your mightiness to wash your hands? . *T. of Shrew* Ind. 2 78
Yea, and to marry her, if her dowry please.—So said, so done, is well . i 2 185
In sign whereof, Please ye we may contrive this afternoon . . i 2 276
I'll not be tied to hours nor 'pointed times, But learn my lessons as I please myself . . . iii 1 20
Old fashions please me best; I am not so nice, To change true rules . iii 1 80
There is mad Petruchio's wife, If it would please him come and marry her! iii 2 20
I wil not go to-day; No, nor to-morrow, not till I please myself . . iii 2 211
For me, I'll not be gone till I please myself . . . iii 2 214
I will be free Even to the uttermost, as I please, in words . . iv 3 80
This is the house: please it you that I call? . . . iv 4 1
If you please to like No worse than I . . . iv 4 32
Your plainness and your shortness please me well . . . iv 4 39
Be it moon, or sun, or what you please: An if you please to call it a rush-candle, Henceforth I vow it shall be so for me . . iv 5 13
In token of which duty, if he please, My hand is ready . . . v 2 178
To each of you one fair and virtuous mistress Fall, when Love please! marry, to each, but one! . . . *All's Well* ii 3 64
It is in us to plant thine honour where We please to have it grow . . ii 3 164
Is it yourself?—If you shall please so . . . iii 5 47
Please it this matron and this gentle maid To eat with us . . iii 5 100
Your will?—That it will please you To give this poor petition to the king v 1 18
Howe'er it pleases you to take it so, The ring was never hers . . v 3 88
Which we will pay, With strife to please you, day exceeding day . . Epil. 4
So please my lord, I might not be admitted . . *T. Night* i 1 24
An it would please you to take leave of her, she is very willing . . ii 3 107
If it please the eye of one, it is with me as the very true sonnet is, 'Please one, and please all' . . . iii 4 23
Though it please you to be one of my friends . . . v 1 28
What shall I do?—Even what it please my lord . . . v 1 119
Think of me as you please . . . v 1 318
Our play is done, And we'll strive to please you every day . . v 1 417
I dare my life lay down and will do't, sir, Please you to accept it *W. Tale* ii 1 131
If't please the queen to send the babe, I know not what I shall incur . ii 2 55
These lords, my noble fellows, if they please, Can clear me in't . . ii 3 142
To prate and talk for life and honour 'fore Who please to come and hear iii 2 43
Which may, if fortune please, both breed thee, pretty, And still rest thine iii 3 48
I, that please some, try all, both joy and terror Of good and bad . . iv 1 1
It will please plentifully . . . iv 4 338
If you may please to think I love the king . . . iv 4 532
Please you to interpose, fair madam: kneel And pray . . . v 3 119
If thou please, Thou mayst befriend me . . . *K. John* v 6 9
And wish, so please my sovereign, ere I move . . *Richard II.* i 1 45
To please the king I did; to please myself I cannot do it . . ii 2 5
Fare you well; Unless you please to enter in the castle And there repose iii 3 160
Thou shouldst please me better, wouldst thou weep . . . iii 4 20
When he please again to be himself . . . *1 Hen. IV.* i 2 224
With some fine colour that may please the eye . . . v 1 75
Please it your honour . . . *2 Hen. IV.* i 1 5
To one it pleases me, for fault of a better, to call my friend . . ii 2 44
Which men shall I have?—Four of which you please . . . iii 2 259
If this may please you, Discharge your powers . . . iv 2 60
Let them have pay, and part: I know it will well please them . . iv 2 71
If they do this,—As, if God please, they shall . . *Hen. V.* iv 3 120
God pless it and preserve it, as long as it pleases his grace . . iv 7 114
I would fain see it once, an please God of his grace that I might see . iv 7 171
Wilt thou have me?—Dat is as it sall please de roi mon père.—Nay, it will please him well, Kate; it shall please him, Kate . . v 2 267
Now, quiet soul, depart when heaven please . . *1 Hen. VI.* iii 2 110
And, as you please, So let them have their answers every one . . v 1 24
A proper man; No shape but his can please your dainty eye . . v 3 38
Madam, are ye so content?—An if my father please, I am content . v 3 127
Command in Anjou what your honour pleases.—Thanks, Reignier . v 3 147
My daughter shall be Henry's, if he please . . . v 3 156
So, now dismiss your army when ye please . . . v 4 173
Here are the articles of contracted peace . . . —They please us well *2 Hen. VI.* i 1 63
When he please to make commotion, 'Tis to be fear'd they all will follow iii 1 29
I will, my lord, so please his majesty.—Why, our authority is his consent iii 1 315
I'll cross the sea, To effect this marriage, so it please my lord *3 Hen. VI.* ii 6 98
An if what pleases him shall pleasure you . . . iii 2 22
Please you dismiss me, either with 'ay' or 'no' . . . iii 2 78
And only claim Our dukedom till God please to send the rest . . iv 7 47
Which if thou please to hide in this true bosom . . *Richard III.* i 2 176
Please thee leave these sad designs To him that hath more cause . . i 2 211
And may direct his course as please himself . . . ii 2 129
Where you please, and shall be thought most fit For your best health . iii 1 66
My lord, will't please you pass along? . . . iii 1 136
How goes the world with thee?—The better that your lordship please to ask . . . iii 2 99
To-morrow will it please you to be crown'd?—Even when you please . iii 7 242
What news with you?—None good, my lord, to please you with the hearing . . . iv 4 458
And meet your grace Where and what time your majesty shall please . iv 4 490
Thus desired, That he would please to alter the king's course *Hen. VIII.* i 1 189
Thus the cardinal Does buy and sell his honour as he pleases . . i 1 192
Some of these Should find a running banquet ere they rested, I think would better please 'em . . . i 4 13
Lie like one lump before him, to be fashion'd Into what pitch he please ii 2 50
As I am made without him, so I'll stand, If the king please . . ii 2 53
The capacity Of your soft cheveril conscience would receive, If you might please to stretch it . . . ii 3 33
Your words, Domestics to you, serve your will as't please Yourself . ii 4 114
That it shall please you to declare, in hearing Of all these ears . . ii 4 145
If you please To trust us in your business, we are ready . . iii 1 172
May it please your grace,— No, sir, it does not please me . . v 3 134

Please. The old Duchess of Norfolk, and Lady Marquess Dorset: will these please you? . . . *Hen. VIII.* v 3 170
'Tis ten to one this play can never please All that are here . . Epil. 1
Let it please both, Thou great, and wise, to hear Ulysses speak *Troi. and Cres.* i 3 68
Please it our great general To call together all his state of war . ii 3 270
Please it our general to pass strangely by him, As if he were forgot . iii 3 39
I am not warm yet; let us fight again.—As Hector pleases . . iv 5 119
But that that likes not you pleases me best . . . v 2 103
He did it to please his mother, and to be partly proud . *Coriolanus* i 1 39
Please you to march; And four shall quickly draw out my command . i 6 83
Please it your honours To call me to your senate . . . v 6 140
Doth this motion please thee?—It doth, my worthy lord . *T. Andron.* i 1 243
An should the empress know This discord's ground, the music would not please . . . ii 1 70
Then let the ladies tattle what they please . . . ii 2 168
Bid him demand what pledge will please him best . . . iv 4 106
If it please me which thou speak'st, Thy child shall live . . v 1 59
An if it please thee! why, assure thee, Lucius, 'Twill vex thy soul to hear v 1 61
Would it please thee, good Andronicus, To send for Lucius . . v 2 111
Will't please you eat? will't please your highness feed? . . v 3 54
Tell A whispering tale in a fair lady's ear, Such as would please *R. and J.* i 5 26
Please it your lordship . . . *T. of Athens* ii 2 19
It pleases time and fortune to lie heavy Upon a friend of mine . . iii 5 10
Always a villain's office or a fool's. Dost please thyself in't? . . iv 3 238
If thou couldst please me with speaking to me . . . iv 3 350
Therefore, so please thee to return with us . . . v 1 162
Whoso please To stop affliction, let him take his haste . . . v 1 212
To-morrow, if you please to speak with me, I will come home *J. Cæsar* i 2 308
If it will please Cæsar To be so good to Cæsar as to hear me . . ii 4 28
Tell him, so please him come unto this place, He shall be satisfied . iii 1 140
No place will please me so, no mean of death, As here by Cæsar . . iii 1 161
I have the same dagger for myself, when it shall please my country to need my death . . . iii 2 51
Make your vaunting true, And it shall please me well . . . iv 3 53
Had he Duncan's sons under his key—As, an't please heaven, he shall not—they should find What 'twere to kill a father . *Macbeth* iii 6 19
Put on him What forgeries you please . . . *Hamlet* ii 1 20
If it will please you To show us so much gentry and good will . . ii 2 21
That it might please you to give quiet pass Through your dominions . ii 2 77
My lord, do as you please . . . iii 1 188
They are not a pipe for fortune's finger To sound what stop she please . iii 2 76
If it shall please you to make me a wholesome answer . . . iii 2 327
God bless you, sir.—Let him bless thee too.—He shall, sir, an't please him . . . iv 6 8
If it please his majesty, 'tis the breathing time of day with me . . v 2 181
If it shall please you to suspend your indignation . . *Lear* i 2 86
Put on what weary negligence you please, You and your fellows . . i 3 12
Make your own purpose, How in my strength you please . . . ii 1 114
With you, goodman boy, an you please . . . ii 2 48
Let not my worser spirit tempt me again To die before you please! . iv 6 223
I can discover him, if you please To get good guard and go along *Othello* i 1 179
I therefore beg it not, To please the palate of my appetite . . i 3 263
Tainting his discipline; or from what other course you please . . ii 1 276
If you please to hold him off awhile, You shall by that perceive him . iii 3 248
I nothing but to please his fantasy . . . iii 3 299
Good, good: the justice of it pleases: very good . . . iv 1 222
If it might please you, to enforce no further The griefs . *Ant. and Cleo.* ii 2 99
If Cæsar please, our master Will leap to be his friend . . . iii 13 50
It much would please him, That of his fortunes you should make a staff iii 13 67
He that unbuckles this, till we do please To daff't for our repose . . iv 4 12
Their preparation is to-day by sea; We please them not by land . . iv 10 2
Good my fellows, do not please sharp fate To grace it with your sorrows iv 14 135
But please your thoughts In feeding them with those my former fortunes wherein I lived . . . iv 15 52
If thou please To take me to thee, as I was to him I'll be to Cæsar . v 1 9
If he please To give me conquer'd Egypt for my son . . . v 2 18
To Cæsar I will speak what you shall please, If you'll employ me to him v 2 69
And your signs of conquest, shall Hang in what place you please . . v 2 136
First you please To greet your lord with writing, do't to-night . *Cymbeline* i 6 205
First, an't please the gods, I'll hide my master from the flies . . iv 2 387
I'll tell you, sir, in private, if you please To give me hearing . . v 5 115
To glad your ear, and please your eyes . . . *Pericles* i Gower 4
But since he's gone, the king's seas must please . . . i 3 28
Who but of late, earth, sea, and air, Were all too little to content and please . . . i 4 35
Now, by the gods, he could not please me better . . . ii 3 72
Or tie my treasure up in silken bags, To please the fool and death . iii 2 42
Perhaps they will but please themselves upon her . . . iv 1 101
If it please the gods to defend you by men, then men must comfort you iv 2 96
Now please you wit The epitaph is for Marina writ By wicked Dionyza iv 4 31
I cannot be offended with my trade. Please you to name it . . iv 6 77
An please you . . . *1 Hen. VI.* v 4 10
An't (shall) please you *Meas. for Meas.* ii 1; *L. L. Lost* i 1; v 2; *Mer. of Venice* ii 4; *W. Tale* iv 4; *2 Hen. IV.* iii 2; *Hen. V.* iv 7; *Coriolanus* i 1; *J. Cæsar* iv 3
If it please you *Meas. for Meas.* v 1; *Much Ado* iii 2; *Mer. of Venice* i 3; *2 Hen. VI.* ii 1; *Richard III.* v 5; *Macbeth* iii 6
If you please *L. L. Lost* i 1; v 2; *As Y. Like It* v 2; *All's Well* ii 3; *T. Night* iii 4; *Richard II.* ii 1; *Troi. and Cres.* iv 1; *Othello* i 3; *Cymbeline* i 6; *Pericles* i 2; iii 4
May it please you *T. G. of Ver.* i 3; *All's Well* i 3; *Richard II.* iii 3; iv 1; *Hen. VIII.* iii 1; *T. Andron.* iv 2; *Cymbeline* i 6
Please it you *L. L. Lost* v 2; *2 Hen. IV.* iv 4; *2 Hen. VI.* v 1
Please it your grace *T. G. of Ver.* iii 1; *Much Ado* i 1; *2 Hen. IV.* iii 1; *2 Hen. VI.* iv 9; *Othello* i 3
Please it your majesty *L. L. Lost* v 2; *All's Well* ii 3; *2 Hen. VI.* i 3; ii 3: *Richard III.* iv 4
Please you *Tempest* i 2; ii 1; v 1; *T. G. of Ver.* i 2; i 3; ii 1; iv 4; v 4; *Com. of Errors* i 2; *W. Tale* ii 2; v 1; *2 Hen. IV.* iv 1; *Hen. VIII.* i 2; ii 4; *Troi. and Cres.* iv 3; *Coriolanus* ii 2; *T. Andron.* v 3; *T. of Athens* i 2; ii 2; *Lear* iv 7; *Ant. and Cleo.* iv 4; *Cymbeline* ii 2; iii 4; *Pericles* v Gower
Please your grace *Com. of Errors* v 1; *L. L. Lost* ii 1; *M. N. Dream* v 1; *Mer. of Venice* iv 1; *2 Hen. IV.* ii 1; iv 1: iv 5; *2 Hen. VI.* i 1; i 3; ii 1; ii 4; *Richard III.* iii 7; *Hen. VIII.* i 1; i 4; iii 1; v 3; *Othello* i 3
Please your highness *W. Tale* i 2; ii 3; *2 Hen. VI.* ii 3; *3 Hen. VI.* iii 2; *Hen. VIII.* ii 4; iv 2; *Macbeth* iii 1; iii 4; *Lear* iv 7; *Cymbeline* i 1; v 5

Please your honour *Meas. for Meas.* ii 1; iii 2; *T. of Shrew* Ind. 1; Ind. 2; *Hen. VIII.* v 4; *T. of Athens* i 2; iii 2
Please your ladyship *As Y. Like It* i 2 120; *W. Tale* ii 2 46
Please your lordship *T. G. of Ver.* i 3; *T. of Shrew* Ind. 1; Ind. 2; *All's Well* iii 6; *2 Hen. IV.* i 2; *T. of Athens* iii 1; *Lear* i 2
Please your majesty *All's Well* v 3; *1 Hen. IV.* iii 2; *Hen. V.* i 2; iii 6; iv 7; iv 8; *1 Hen. VI.* iii 4; *T. Andron.* i 1; *Lear* iv 7; *Cymbeline* iv 3; *Pericles* ii 5
Please your worship *Mer. Wives* i 1; ii 2; *2 Hen. IV.* v 3; *Richard III.* i 1
So please you *Tempest* v 1; *Meas. for Meas.* iii 2; *As Y. Like It* i 1; i 2; iv 3; *T. Night* v 1; *W. Tale* ii 2; ii 3; *2 Hen. IV.* iv 2; *Hen. V.* v 2; *Hen. VIII.* i 1; *Troi. and Cres.* iv 4; iv 5; *Rom. and Jul.* i 1; iv 3; *J. Cæsar* iv 3; *Macbeth* i 5; v 3; *Hamlet* i 3; iii 1; *Cymbeline* iv 2; v 5
Will it please you? *Tempest* iii 3; *T. G. of Ver.* i 2; *Meas. for Meas.* iv 1; *M. N. Dream* v 1; *W. Tale* iv 4; *Richard II.* v 5; *Hen. VIII.* i 4; *T. Andron.* v 3; *Hamlet* iv 4; *Ant. and Cleo.* ii 5

Pleased. Set all hearts i' the state To what tune pleased his ear *Tempest* i 2 85
Wilt thou be pleased to hearken once again to the suit I made to thee? iii 2 44
If you be pleased, retire into my cell And there repose iv 1 161
She would be best pleased To be so anger'd with another letter *T. G. of V.* i 2 102
I fear me, he will scarce be pleased withal ii 7 67
Who by repentance is not satisfied Is nor of heaven nor earth, for these are pleased v 4 80
In your grace To unloose this tied-up justice when you pleased *M. for M.* i 3 32
Pleased you to do't at peril of your soul, Were equal poise of sin and charity ii 4 67
My mirth it much displeased, but pleased my woe iv 1 13
O, an the heavens were so pleased that thou wert but my bastard! *L. L. L.* v 1 79
Let's hold more chat.—In private, then.—I am best pleased with that v 2 229
It pleased them to think me worthy of Pompion the Great v 2 506
If you be well pleased with this And hold your fortune *Mer. of Venice* iii 2 136
Among the buzzing pleased multitude iii 2 182
Is this true, Nerissa?—Madam, it is, so you stand pleased withal iii 2 211
I thank you for your wish, and am well pleased To wish it back on you iii 4 43
What if my house be troubled with a rat And I be pleased to give ten thousand ducats To have it baned? iv 1 45
If you had pleased to have defended it With any terms of zeal v 1 204
Thou shouldst have better pleased me with this deed, Hadst thou descended from another house *As Y. Like It* i 2 240
Seeking the food he eats And pleased with what he gets ii 5 43
I would kiss as many of you as had beards that pleased me Epil 20
If she and I be pleased, what's that to you? *T. of Shrew* ii 1 305
She will be pleased; then wherefore should I doubt? iv 4 107
This young maid might do her A shrewd turn, if she pleased *All's Well* iii 5 71
If the heavens had been pleased, would we had so ended! *T. Night* ii 1 21
Be pleased that I shake off these names you give me v 1 76
Since these good men are pleased, let them come in *W. Tale* iv 4 350
My senses, better pleased with madness, Do bid it welcome iv 4 495
Be pleased then To pay that duty which you truly owe *K. John* ii 1 246
If thou be pleased withal, Command thy son and daughter to join hands ii 1 531
If heaven be pleased that you must use me ill, Why then you must iv 1 55
I am best pleased to be from such a deed iv 1 86
This 'once again,' but that your highness pleased, Was once superfluous iv 2 3
O, make a league with me, till I have pleased My discontented peers! iv 2 126
Pardon me, if you please; if not, I, pleased Not to be pardon'd, am content withal *Richard II.* ii 1 187
And thou with all pleased, that hast all achieved! iv 1 217
Nor I nor any man that but man is With nothing shall be pleased v 5 40
I promise here: The which if He be pleased I shall perform *1 Hen. IV.* iii 2 154
It pleased your majesty to turn your looks Of favour from myself v 1 30
Your highness pleased to forget my place *2 Hen. IV.* v 2 77
I heard a bird so sing, Whose music, to my thinking, pleased the king v 5 114
Heaven and our Lady gracious hath it pleased To shine on my contemptible estate *1 Hen. VI.* i 2 74
Nay, be not angry; I am pleased again *2 Hen. VI.* i 2 55
Maintains my state And sends the poor well pleased from my gate iv 10 25
It hath pleased him that three times to-day You have defended me v 3 18
Before it pleased his majesty To raise my state *3 Hen. VI.* i 1 67
The articles o' the combination drew As Himself pleased *Hen. VIII.* i 1 170
The king Is pleased you shall to the Tower i 1 213
I have spoke long: be pleased yourself to say How far you satisfied me ii 4 210
If heaven had pleased to have given me longer life And able means iv 2 152
This oracle of comfort has so pleased me, That when I am in heaven I shall desire To see what this child does v 5 67
Out of whorish loins Are pleased to breed out your inheritors *T. and C.* iv 1 64
Pleased with this dainty bait, thus goes to bed v 8 20
Was pleased to let him seek danger where he was like to find fame *Cor.* i 3 13
Alone I fought in your Corioli walls, And made what work I pleased i 8 9
The senate, Coriolanus, are well pleased To make thee consul ii 2 136
If thou be pleased with this my sudden choice *T. Andron.* i 1 318
This is the pearl that pleased your empress' eye v 1 42
It hath pleased the gods to remember my father's age *T. of Athens* i 2 2
Th' ear, Taste, touch and smell, pleased from thy table rise i 2 132
Clap him and hiss him, according as he pleased and displeased them *J. C.* i 2 262
The play, I remember, pleased not the million *Hamlet* ii 2 456
Heaven hath pleased it so, To punish me with this and this with me iii 4 173
Better thou Hadst not been born than not to have pleased me better *Lear* i 1 237
It pleased the king his master very late To strike at me ii 2 123
It hath pleased the devil drunkenness to give place to the devil wrath *Othello* ii 3 297
Had it pleased heaven To try me with affliction iv 2 47
Be pleased to catch at mine intent By what did here befal me *A. and C.* ii 2 41
Be pleased to tell us—For this is from the present—how you take The offers we have sent you ii 6 29
Now Pleased fortune does of Marcus Crassus' death Make me revenger iii 1 2
Herod of Jewry dare not look upon you But when you are well pleased iii 3 4
With half the bulk o' the world play'd as I pleased iii 11 64
Left these notes Of what commands I should be subject to, When't pleased you to employ me *Cymbeline* i 1 173
Prunes the immortal wing and cloys his beak, As when his god is pleased v 4 119
Be pleased awhile v 5 356
God give you joy!—What, are you both pleased? *Pericles* ii 5 88
That the strict fates had pleased you had brought her hither! iii 3 8

Please-man. Some carry-tale, some please-man *L. L. Lost* v 2 463

Pleasest. And how thou pleasest, God, dispose the day! *Hen. V.* iv 3 132
If thou pleasest not, I yield thee up my life *Ant. and Cleo.* v 1 11

Pleaseth you walk with me down to his house *Com. of Errors* iv 1 12
Certain special honours it pleaseth his greatness to impart *L. L. Lost* v 1 112

Pleaseth. To be cut off and taken In what part of your body pleaseth me *Mer. of Venice* i 3 152
In respect it is in the fields, it pleaseth me well *As Y. Like It* iii 2 18
And nothing pleaseth but rare accidents *1 Hen. IV.* i 2 231
She will sing the song that pleaseth you iii 1 216
Pleaseth your lordship To meet his grace *2 Hen. IV.* iv 1 225
Pleaseth your grace to answer them directly iv 2 52
Pleaseth your grace To appoint some of your council presently *Hen. V.* v 2 78
What wills Lord Talbot pleaseth Burgundy *1 Hen. VI.* iii 2 130
Warwick, as ourself, Shall do and undo as him pleaseth best *3 Hen. VI.* ii 6 105
I know it pleaseth neither of us well *Richard III.* i 1 113
What is your grace's pleasure?—Even that, I hope, which pleaseth God above iii 7 109
When it pleaseth their deities to take the wife of a man from him, it shows to man the tailors of the earth *Ant. and Cleo.* i 2 168
Have you brought those drugs?—Pleaseth your highness, ay *Cymbeline* i 5 5
It pleaseth you, my royal father, to express My commendations great *Per.* ii 2 8
If it please your majesty.—It pleaseth me so well, that I will see you wed ii 5 92

Pleasing. The pleasing punishment that women bear *Com. of Errors* i 1 47
That never words were music to thine ear, That never object pleasing ii 2 117
The preyful princess pierced and prick'd a pretty pleasing pricket *L. L. L.* iv 2 58
There was no thought of pleasing you when she was christened *As Y. L. It* iii 2 283
It is more pleasing stuff.—What, household stuff? *T. of Shrew* Ind. 2 142
I never saw a better-fashion'd gown, More quaint, more pleasing iv 3 102
Of a cheerful look, a pleasing eye and a most noble carriage *1 Hen. IV.* ii 4 465
Charming your blood with pleasing heaviness iii 1 218
Your dislike, to whom I would be pleasing, Doth cloud my joys *3 Hen. VI.* iv 1 73
To the lascivious pleasing of a lute *Richard III.* i 1 13
A cherry lip, a bonny eye, a passing pleasing tongue i 1 94
A pleasing cordial ii 1 41
Can make seem pleasing to her tender years iv 4 342
We are convented Upon a pleasing treaty *Coriolanus* ii 2 59
And wonder greatly that man's face can fold In pleasing smiles such murderous tyranny *T. Andron.* ii 3 267
O, that delightful engine of her thoughts, That blabb'd them with such pleasing eloquence iii 1 83
Make my aunt merry with some pleasing tale iii 2 47
She swooned almost at my pleasing tale v 1 119
What night is this!—A very pleasing night to honest men *J. Cæsar* i 3 43
The devil hath power To assume a pleasing shape *Hamlet* ii 2 629
My ears were never better fed With such delightful pleasing harmony *Pericles* ii 5 28

Pleasure. I come to answer thy best pleasure *Tempest* i 2 190
But The mistress which I serve quickens what's dead And makes my labours pleasures iii 1 7
I am full of pleasure: Let us be jocund iii 2 125
Your father would speak with you.—I wait upon his pleasure *T. G. of V.* ii 4 117
To know what service It is your pleasure to command me in iv 3 10
What I do is to pleasure you *Mer. Wives* i 1 251
It is admirable pleasures and fery honest knaveries iv 4 80
I come to know your pleasure *Meas. for Meas.* i 1 27
What is't your worship's pleasure I shall do with this wicked caitiff? ii 1 192
I'll know His pleasure; may be he will relent ii 2 3
I am come to know your pleasure.—That you might know it, would much better please me Than to demand what 'tis ii 4 31
What pleasure was he given to?—Rather rejoicing to see another merry iii 2 248
You shall anon over-read it at your pleasure iv 2 213
Punish them to your height of pleasure v 1 240
And see our pleasure herein executed v 1 527
You take pleasure then in the message? *Much Ado* ii 3 262
I will bid thee draw, as we do the minstrels; draw, to pleasure us v 1 129
The duke's pleasure is, that you keep Costard safe *L. L. Lost* i 2 132
Before we enter his forbidden gates, To know his pleasure ii 1 27
Where all those pleasures live that art would comprehend iv 2 114
Or mons, the hill.—At your sweet pleasure, for the mountain v 1 90
It is the king's most sweet pleasure and affection v 1 92
Remote from all the pleasures of the world v 2 806
When I had at my pleasure taunted her *M. N. Dream* iv 1 62
The object and the pleasure of mine eye Is only Helena iv 1 175
May you stead me? will you pleasure me? *Mer. of Venice* i 3 7
Notwithstanding, use your pleasure iii 2 323
Unless you could teach me to forget a banished father, you must not learn me how to remember any extraordinary pleasure *As Y. L. It* i 2 7
I did not then entreat to have her stay; It was your pleasure i 3 72
To your pleasures: I am for other than for dancing measures v 4 198
No profit grows where is no pleasure ta'en *T. of Shrew* i 1 39
Leave shall you have to court her at your pleasure i 1 54
Sir, to your pleasure humbly I subscribe i 1 81
Sith it your pleasure is, And I am tied to be obedient i 1 216
Nor hast thou pleasure to be cross in talk ii 1 251
Or is it else your pleasure, Like pleasant travellers, to break a jest? iv 5 71
Do you hear, monsieur? a word with you.—Your pleasure, sir? *All's Well* ii 3 193
Even to the world's pleasure and the increase of laughter ii 4 37
Make the coming hour o'erflow with joy And pleasure drown the brim ii 4 48
Attend his further pleasure.—In every thing I wait upon his will ii 4 54
Be it his pleasure iii 1 16
I'll whisper with the general, and know his pleasure iv 3 330
This woman's an easy glove, my lord; she goes off and on at pleasure v 3 279
This story know, To make the even truth in pleasure flow v 3 326
There's for thy pains.—No pains, sir; I take pleasure in singing, sir.—I'll pay thy pleasure then *T. Night* ii 4 69
Pleasure will be paid, one time or another ii 4 72
Since you make your pleasure of your pains, I will no further chide you iii 3 2
He attends your ladyship's pleasure.—I'll come to him iii 4 65
We may carry it thus, for our pleasure and his penance iii 4 151
It is his highness' pleasure that the queen Appear in person here *W. Tale* iii 2 9
No settled senses of the world can match The pleasure of that madness v 3 73
We shall be blest To do your pleasure and continue friends *K. John* iii 1 252
The proud day, Attended with the pleasures of the world, Is all too wanton iii 3 35
But that your royal pleasure must be done iv 2 17
A holy vow, Never to taste the pleasures of the world iv 3 68
Call it a travel that thou takest for pleasure *Richard II.* i 3 262
The pleasure that some fathers feed upon, Is my strict fast ii 1 79
A place of meeting, wherein it is at our pleasure to fail *1 Hen. IV.* i 2 191
What is't that takes from thee Thy stomach, pleasure and thy golden sleep? ii 3 44
Not in pleasure but in passion, not in words only, but in woes also ii 4 458
Such barren pleasures, rude society, As thou art match'd withal iii 2 14
Deliver him Up to his pleasure, ransomless and free v 5 28

Pleasure. I'll drink no more than will do me good, for no man's pleasure, I . . . . *2 Hen. IV.* ii 4 129
One of the king's justices of the peace: what is your good pleasure? . iii 2 65
Now are we well prepared to know the pleasure Of our fair cousin *Hen. V.* i 2 234
I would desire the duke to use his good pleasure, and put him to execution . . . . iii 6 57
God's will and his pleasure, captain, I beseech you now, come apace iv 8 2
At pleasure here we lie near Orleans . . . . . *1 Hen. VI.* i 2 6
My loving lords, our pleasure is That Richard be restored to his blood . iii 1 158
Although you break it when your pleasure serves . . . v 4 164
Ye grow too hot: It was the pleasure of my lord the king *2 Hen. VI.* i 1 138
Hast thou not worldly pleasure at command? . . . . . i 2 45
'Tis his highness' pleasure You do prepare to ride unto Saint Alban's . i 2 56
I am protector of the realm; And, at his pleasure, will resign my place i 3 124
At your pleasure, my good lord. Who's within there, ho! . . i 4 82
Bring him near the king; His highness' pleasure is to talk with him . ii 1 73
Where thou art, there is the world itself, With every several pleasure . iii 2 363
Peace to his soul, if God's good pleasure be! . . . . iii 3 26
For these whose ransom we have set, It is our pleasure one of them depart . . . . iv 1 140
Art thou a messenger, or come of pleasure?—A messenger . . v 1 16
More care to keep Than in possession any jot of pleasure . *3 Hen. VI.* ii 2 53
Resolve me now; And what your pleasure is, shall satisfy me . iii 2 20
An if what pleases him shall pleasure you . . . . . iii 2 22
What other pleasure can the world afford? . . . . . iii 2 147
We may surprise and take him at our pleasure . . . . iv 2 17
I'll well requite thy kindness, For that it made my imprisonment a pleasure . . . . iv 6 11
Such a pleasure as incaged birds Conceive . . . . . iv 6 12
Mirthful comic shows, Such as befits the pleasure of the court . v 7 44
And hate the idle pleasures of these days . . . . *Richard III.* i 1 31
The sorrow that I have, by right is yours, And all the pleasures you usurp are mine . . . . i 3 173
He sends to know your lordship's pleasure, If presently you will take horse . . . . iii 2 15
I have not sounded him, nor he deliver'd His gracious pleasure . iii 4 18
What is your grace's pleasure?—Even that, I hope, which pleaseth God above . . . . iii 7 108
Speak suddenly; be brief.—Your grace may do your pleasure . iv 2 21
What is't your highness' pleasure I shall do At Salisbury? . . iv 4 452
'Tis his highness' pleasure You shall to the Tower . . *Hen. VIII.* i 1 206
The will of heaven be done, and the king's pleasure By me obey'd! . i 1 215
By my life, This is against our pleasure . . . . . i 2 68
A noble company! what are their pleasures? . . . . i 4 64
Pray 'em take their pleasures . . . . i 4 74
We come To know your royal pleasure.—Ye are too bold . . ii 2 71
I' the name of God, Your pleasure be fulfill'd! . . . . ii 4 57
Lord cardinal, To you I speak.—Your pleasure, madam? . . ii 4 69
What are your pleasures with me, reverend lords? . . . iii 1 26
Can you think, lords, That any Englishman dare give me counsel? Or be a known friend, 'gainst his highness' pleasure? . . . iii 1 85
One that ne'er dream'd a joy beyond his pleasure . . . . iii 1 135
My lords, you speak your pleasures . . . . . . iii 2 13
Hear the king's pleasure, cardinal . . . . . . iii 2 228
Lord cardinal, the king's further pleasure is . . . . iii 2 337
He attends your highness' pleasure.—Bring him to us . . . v 1 83
It is my duty To attend your highness' pleasure . . . . v 1 91
But their pleasures Must be fulfill'd, and I attend with patience . v 2 18
To dance attendance on their lordships' pleasures . . . v 2 31
And has done [waited] half an hour, to know your pleasures . . v 3 6
We will be short with you. 'Tis his highness' pleasure, And our consent v 3 52
There to remain till the king's further pleasure Be known unto us . v 3 90
Like or find fault; do as your pleasures are . . *Troi. and Cres.* Prol. 30
Good niece, do, sweet niece Cressida.—At your pleasure . . i 2 196
Give me ribs of steel! I shall split all In pleasure of my spleen . i 3 178
I propose not merely to myself The pleasures such a beauty brings with it . . . . ii 2 147
Pleasure and revenge Have ears more deaf than adders . . . ii 2 171
He is much sorry, If any thing more than your sport and pleasure Did move your greatness . . . . ii 3 117
At whose pleasure, friend?—At mine, sir, and theirs that love music . iii 1 25
You speak your fair pleasure, sweet queen . . . . . iii 1 51
Give your dispositions the reins, and be angry at your pleasures *Coriol.* ii 1 34
Keep there: now talk at pleasure of your safety . . *T. Andron.* iv 2 134
With the shadow of his wings He can at pleasure stint their melody . iv 4 86
Madam, depart at pleasure; leave us here.—Farewell, Andronicus . v 2 145
Come you this afternoon, To know our further pleasure . *Rom. and Jul.* i 1 108
To them say, My house and welcome on their pleasure stay . . i 2 37
And thou must stand by too, and suffer every knave to use me at his pleasure?—I saw no man use you at his pleasure . . . . ii 4 164
Let them gaze; I will not budge for no man's pleasure, I . . iii 1 58
We'll share a bounteous time In different pleasures . . *T. of Athens* i 1 264
A forerunner, my lord, which bears that office, to signify their pleasures i 2 126
You have done our pleasures much grace, fair ladies . . . i 2 151
Here's to thee.—Your lordship speaks your pleasure . . . iii 1 35
I count it one of my greatest afflictions, say, that I cannot pleasure such an honourable gentleman . . . . iii 2 63
That part of tyranny that I do bear I can shake off at pleasure *J. Cæsar* i 3 100
Dwell I but in the suburbs Of your good pleasure? . . . . ii 1 286
Fates, we will know your pleasures: That we shall die, we know . iii 1 98
Now, whilst your purpled hands do reek and smoke, Fulfil your pleasure iii 1 159
He hath left them you, And to your heirs for ever, common pleasures . iii 2 255
So please you, we will stand and watch your pleasure . . . iv 3 249
To make their audit at your highness' pleasure . . *Macbeth* i 6 27
He hath been in unusual pleasure . . . . ii 1 13
Sirrah, a word with you: attend those men Our pleasure? . . iii 1 46
A thing of custom: 'tis no other; Only it spoils the pleasure of the time iii 4 98
You may Convey your pleasures in a spacious plenty, And yet seem cold iv 3 71
Seyton!—What is your gracious pleasure?—What news more? . v 3 30
So by your companies To draw him on to pleasures . . *Hamlet* ii 2 15
Put your dread pleasures more into command Than to entreaty . ii 2 28
Or in his rage, Or in the incestuous pleasure of his bed . . iii 3 90
Where is he?—Without, my lord; guarded, to know your pleasure . iv 3 14
He sends to know if your pleasure hold to play with Laertes . . v 2 206
I am constant to my purposes; they follow the king's pleasure . v 2 209
No less in space, validity, and pleasure . . . . *Lear* i 1 83
'Tis the duke's pleasure, Whose disposition, all the world well knows, Will not be rubb'd nor stopp'd . . . . ii 2 159
'Tis not in thee To grudge my pleasures . . . . . ii 4 177
Then let fall Your horrible pleasure; here I stand, your slave . . iii 2 19

Pleasure. Do as I bid thee, or rather do thy pleasure; Above the rest, be gone . . . . *Lear* iv 1 49
That minces virtue, and does shake the head To hear of pleasure's name iv 6 123
He's full of alteration And self-reproving: bring his constant pleasure v 1 4
Good guard, Until their greater pleasures first be known . . v 3 2
Methinks our pleasure might have been demanded, Ere you had spoke so far . . . . v 3 62
I beseech you, If't be your pleasure and most wise consent . *Othello* i 1 122
If thou canst cuckold him, thou dost thyself a pleasure, me a sport . i 3 376
It is Othello's pleasure, our noble and valiant general . . . ii 2 1
So much was his pleasure should be proclaimed . . . . ii 2 8
Pleasure and action make the hours seem short . . . . ii 3 385
Senators of Venice greet you.—I kiss the instrument of their pleasures iv 1 231
You may take him at your pleasure: I will be near to second your attempt iv 2 244
Not a minute of our lives should stretch Without some pleasure *A. and C.* i 1 47
Fare thee well awhile.—At your noble pleasure . . . . i 2 116
Present pleasure, By revolution lowering, does become The opposite . i 2 128
Say, our pleasure, To such whose place is under us, requires Our quick remove from hence . . . . i 2 201
Pawn their experience to their present pleasure . . . . i 4 32
What's your highness' pleasure?—Not now to hear thee sing . . i 5 8
Though I make this marriage for my peace, I' the east my pleasure lies ii 3 40
Whom He may at pleasure whip, or hang, or torture, As he shall like . iii 13 150
Still be't yours, Bestow it at your pleasure . . . . . v 2 182
Make your best use of this: I have perform'd Your pleasure and my promise . . . . v 2 204
I dedicate myself to your sweet pleasure . . . *Cymbeline* i 6 136
As if I borrowed mine oaths of him and might not spend them at my pleasure . . . . ii 1 6
What's your lordship's pleasure?—Your lady's person: is she ready? . ii 3 85
Me of my lawful pleasure she restrain'd And pray'd me oft forbearance ii 5 9
I know your master's pleasure and he mine: All the remain is 'Welcome!' . . . . iii 1 86
Their pleasures here are past, so is their pain . . . . iv 2 290
These flowers are like the pleasures of the world . . . iv 2 296
What pleasure, sir, find we in life, to lock it From action and adventure? iv 4 2
Wherein Our pleasure his full fortune doth confine . . . . iv 4 110
Your pleasure was my mere offence, my punishment Itself . . v 5 334
To hear an old man sing May to your wishes pleasure bring *Pericles* i Gower 14
Her face the book of praises, where is read Nothing but curious pleasures i 1 16
Which pleasure fits an husband, not a father . . . . i 1 129
Here pleasures court mine eyes, and mine eyes shun them . . i 2 6
Yet neither pleasure's art can joy my spirits, Nor yet the other's distance comfort me . . . . i 2 9
I am at your grace's pleasure . . . . ii 3 112
It is your grace's pleasure to commend; Not my desert . . . ii 5 29
Ay, and you shall live in pleasure.—No.—Yes, indeed shall you . iv 2 81
Take her away; use her at thy pleasure . . . . . iv 6 151
What is thy (your) pleasure? *Tempest* iv 1; *All's Well* i 3; *Hen. VIII.* iv 2; *T. of Athens* ii 1; *Othello* iv 2; *Ant. and Cleo.* i 2

Plebeian. With the plebeians swarming at their heels . *Hen. V.* v Prol. 27
Dull tribunes, That, with the fusty plebeians, hate thine honours *Coriol.* 1 9 7
Devour him; as the hungry plebeians would the noble Marcius . ii 1 10
Being the herdsmen of the beastly plebeians . . . . ii 1 106
You are plebeians, If they be senators . . . . . . iii 1 101
The plebeians have got your fellow-tribune And hale him up and down v 4 39
With voices and applause of every sort, Patricians and plebeians *T. And.* i 1 231
Let him take thee, And hoist thee up to the shouting plebeians *Ant. and Cleo.* iv 12 34

Plebeii. If he should still malignantly remain Fast foe to the plebeii, your voices might Be curses to yourselves . . *Coriolanus* ii 3 192

Plebs. I am going with my pigeons to the tribunal plebs . *T. Andron.* iv 3 92

Pledge. I am Grumio's pledge . . . . *T. of Shrew* i 2 45
I am in parliament pledge for his truth . . . . *Richard II.* v 2 44
I pledge your grace . . . . *2 Hen. IV.* v 2 73
Fill the cup, and let it come; I'll pledge you a mile to the bottom . v 3 57
There is my pledge; accept it, Somerset . . . *1 Hen. VI.* ii 4 120
Bear her this jewel, pledge of my affection . . . . v 1 47
I'll pledge you all . . . . *2 Hen. VI.* ii 3 66
Command my eldest son, nay, all my sons, As pledges of my fealty . v 1 50
Answer me one doubt, What pledge have we of thy firm loyalty? *3 Hen. VI.* iii 3 239
And here, to pledge my vow, I give my hand . . . . iii 3 250
Here's to your ladyship: and pledge it, madam . . *Hen. VIII.* i 4 47
Now the pledge; now, now, now!—Here, Diomed . *Troi. and Cres.* v 2 65
O, all you gods! O pretty, pretty pledge! . . . . . v 2 77
He leaves his pledges dearer than his life . . . *T. Andron.* iii 1 292
Bid him demand what pledge will please him best . . . iv 4 106
Let the emperor give his pledges . . . . v 1 163
Pledges the breath of him in a divided draught . . *T. of Athens* i 2 48
My heart is thirsty for that noble pledge . . . *J. Cæsar* iv 3 160
And all to all.—Our duties, and the pledge . . . *Macbeth* iii 4 92
The kettle-drum and trumpet thus bray out The triumph of his pledge *Ham.* i 4 12
There is my pledge; I'll prove it on thy heart . . . *Lear* v 3 93
With that recognizance and pledge of love Which I first gave her *Othello* v 2 214
This health to Lepidus!—Bear him ashore. I'll pledge it for him *Ant. and Cleo.* ii 7 91
I thank both him and you, and pledge him freely . . . *Pericles* ii 3 78

Pleine. Les langues des hommes sont pleines de tromperies . *Hen. V.* v 2 119

Plenteous. Her plenteous womb Expresseth his full tilth *Meas. for Meas.* i 4 43
I shall think it a most plenteous crop To glean the broken ears *As Y. Like It* iii 5 101
Like over-ripen'd corn, Hanging the head at Ceres' plenteous load *2 Hen. VI.* i 2 2
Plenteous tears to drown the world! . . . . *Richard III.* ii 2 70
Take it from a heart that wishes towards you Honour and plenteous safety . . . . *Hen. VIII.* i 1 104
Come freely To gratulate thy plenteous bosom . . *T. of Athens* i 2 131
How full of valour did he bear himself In the last conflict, and made plenteous wounds! . . . . iii 5 66
From forth thy plenteous bosom, one poor root! . . . . iv 3 186
My plenteous joys, Wanton in fulness, seek to hide themselves In drops of sorrow . . . . *Macbeth* i 4 33
With plenteous rivers and wide-skirted meads . . . *Lear* i 1 66
Of so high and plenteous wit and invention . . . *Othello* iv 1 201

Plenteously. Shall, O dear father, pay thee plenteously . *2 Hen. IV.* iv 5 40

Plenties. Peace, Dear nurse of arts, plenties and joyful births *Hen. V.* v 2 35

Plentiful. Being, as it is, so plentiful an excrement . *Com. of Errors* ii 2 79
If reasons were as plentiful as blackberries, I would give no man a reason upon compulsion . . . . *1 Hen. IV.* ii 4 265

Plentiful. They have a plentiful lack of wit *Hamlet* ii 2 202
Having work More plentiful than tools to do't *Cymbeline* v 3 9
Plentifully. We shall be rich ere we depart, If fairings come thus plentifully in *L. L. Lost* v 2 2
Besides this nothing that he so plentifully gives me *As Y. Like It* i 1 17
It will please plentifully *W. Tale* iv 4 338
Plenty. Earth's increase, foison plenty *Tempest* iv 1 110
As there is no more plenty in it, it goes much against my stomach *As Y. Like It* iii 2 21
What's to come is still unsure: In delay there lies no plenty *T. Night* ii 3 51
With smooth-faced peace, With smiling plenty *Richard III.* v 5 34
Peace, plenty, love, truth, terror *Hen. VIII.* v 5 48
Made plenteous wounds!—He has made too much plenty with 'em *T. of Athens* iii 5 67
Here's a farmer, that hanged himself on the expectation of plenty *Macb.* ii 3 6
You may Convey your pleasures in a spacious plenty, And yet seem cold iv 3 71
Plenty and peace breeds cowards *Cymbeline* iii 6 21
Britain be fortunate and flourish in peace and plenty v 4 145; v 5 442
Whose issue Promises Britain peace and plenty v 5 458
A city on whom plenty held full hand, For riches strew'd herself even in the streets *Pericles* i 4 22
Those cities that of plenty's cup And her prosperities so largely taste i 4 52
Pless. What, hoa! Got pless your house here!—Who's there? *Mer. Wives* i 1 74
'Pless my soul, how full of chollors I am, and trempling of mind! iii 1 11
'Pless you from his mercy sake, all of you! iii 1 42
God pless your majesty!—How now, Fluellen! *Hen. V.* iii 6 92
God pless it and preserve it, as long as it pleases his grace! iv 7 113
God pless you, Aunchient Pistol! you scurvy, lousy knave, God pless you! v 1 18
Plessed. Od's plessed will! I will not be absence at the grace *Mer. Wives* i 1 273
Plessing. Here is Got's plessing, and your friend, and Justice Shallow i 1 76
Pliant. Which I observing, Took once a pliant hour *Othello* i 3 151
Plied. He plied them both with excellent praises *Ant. and Cleo.* iii 2 14
Plies. He plies the duke at morning and at night *Mer. of Venice* iii 2 279
He plies her hard; and much rain wears the marble 3 *Hen. VI.* iii 2 50
Canst thou not guess wherefore she plies thee thus? *T. Andron.* iv 1 15
This honest fool Plies Desdemona to repair his fortunes *Othello* ii 3 360
Plight. I think myself in better plight for a lender than you are *M. Wives* ii 2 172
Plight me the full assurance of your faith *T. Night* iv 3 26
You see My plight requires it *W. Tale* ii 1 118
And, as thou seest, ourselves in heavy plight 3 *Hen. VI.* iii 3 37
To keep her constancy in plight and youth *Troi. and Cres.* iii 2 168
Had I but seen thy picture in this plight, It would have madded me *T. Andron.* iii 1 103
Rather comfort his distressed plight Than prosecute the meanest or the best iv 4 32
What bloody man is that? He can report, As seemeth by his plight *Macbeth* i 2 2
That lord whose hand must take my plight shall carry Half my love *Lear* i 1 103
Bid her alight, And her troth plight iii 4 128
I know your plight is pitied Of him that caused it *Ant. and Cleo.* v 2 33
I will remain The loyal'st husband that did e'er plight troth *Cymbeline* i 1 96
Plighted. Quick Biron hath plighted faith to me *L. L. Lost* v 2 283
Give thee her hand, for sign of plighted faith 1 *Hen. VI.* v 3 162
Plighter. This kingly seal And plighter of high hearts *Ant. and Cleo.* iii 13 126
Plod. Trudge, plod away o' the hoof; seek shelter, pack! *Mer. Wives* i 3 91
Barefoot plod I the cold ground upon, With sainted vow *All's Well* iii 4 6
Though patience be a tired mare, yet she will plod *Hen. V.* ii 1 26
Tell me How far 'tis thither. If one of mean affairs May plod it in a week, why may not I Glide thither in a day? *Cymbeline* iii 2 53
Plodded. And plodded like a man for working-days *Hen. V.* i 2 277
Bare-headed plodded by my foot-cloth mule And thought thee happy 2 *Hen. VI.* iv 1 54
Plodder. Small have continual plodders ever won Save base authority from others' books *L. L. Lost* i 1 86
Plodding. Universal plodding poisons up The nimble spirits iv 3 305
Plood. All the water in Wye cannot wash your majesty's Welsh plood out of your pody *Hen. V.* iv 7 112
Ploody. It is good for your green wound and your ploody coxcomb v 1 45
Plot. Dost thou like the plot? *Tempest* iii 2 117
Since they did plot The means that dusky Dis my daughter got iv 1 88
The minute of their plot Is almost come iv 1 141
Love, lend me wings to make my purpose swift, As thou hast lent me wit to plot this drift! *T. G. of Ver.* ii 6 43
Myself am one made privy to the plot iii 1 12
Then she plots, then she ruminates, then she devises *Mer. Wives* ii 2 320
Good plots, they are laid iii 2 39
I will lay a plot to try that iii 3 202
But let our plot go forward iv 4 13
What shall be done with him? what is your plot? iv 4 45
To this her mother's plot She seemingly obedient iv 6 32
The provost knows our purpose and our plot *Meas. for Meas.* iv 5 2
This green plot shall be our stage *M. N. Dream* iii 1 3
From your love I have a warranty To unburden all my plots *Mer. of Ven.* i 1 133
To-night Let us assay our plot *All's Well* iii 7 44
Who cannot be crushed with a plot? iv 3 360
Patience, or we break the sinews of our plot *T. Night* ii 5 84
There is a plot against my life, my crown *W. Tale* ii 1 47
To cull the plots of best advantages *K. John* ii 1 40
John lays you plots; the times conspire with you iii 4 146
That he did plot the Duke of Gloucester's death *Richard II.* i 1 100
Nor never by advised purpose meet To plot, contrive, or complot any ill i 3 189
This blessed plot, this earth, this realm, this England ii 1 50
Is there no plot To rid the realm of this pernicious blot? iv 1 324
And I'll lay A plot shall show us all a merry day iv 1 334
Thoughts tending to ambition, they do plot Unlikely wonders v 5 18
It cannot choose but be a noble plot 1 *Hen. IV.* i 3 279
Thou layest the plot how ii 1 57
Your whole plot too light for the counterpoise of so great an opposition ii 3 14
Our plot is a good plot as ever was laid: our friends true and constant ii 3 18
A good plot, good friends, and full of expectation; an excellent plot ii 3 19
When we mean to build, We first survey the plot 2 *Hen. IV.* i 3 42
Survey The plot of situation and the model, Consent upon a sure foundation i 3 51
The plot is laid: if all things fall out right 1 *Hen. VI.* ii 3 4
I'll maintain my words On any plot of ground in Christendom ii 4 89
A pretty plot, well chosen to build upon 2 *Hen. VI.* i 4 59
In this private plot be we the first ii 2 60
Plots have I laid, inductions dangerous, By drunken prophecies *Rich. III.* i 1 32
Tell me what they deserve That do conspire my death with devilish plots? iii 4 62
Plot. These are the limbs o' the plot: no more, I hope *Hen. VIII.* i 1 220
Is posted, as the agent of our cardinal, To second all his plot iii 2 60
Achievements, plots, orders, preventions *Troi. and Cres.* i 3 181
It is a purposed thing, and grows by plot *Coriolanus* iii 1 38
Call't not a plot: The people cry you mock'd them iii 1 41
Were there but this single plot to lose, This mould of Marcius iii 2 102
Whose passions and whose plots have broke their sleep iv 4 19
You do but plot your deaths By this device *T. Andron.* ii 1 78
Many unfrequented plots there are Fitted by kind for rape and villany ii 1 115
And wander'd hither to an obscure plot ii 3 77
Plot some device of further misery, To make us wonder'd at in time to come iii 1 134
This sandy plot is plain; guide, if thou canst, This after me iv 1 69
Ravish a maid, or plot the way to do it v 1 129
Where, they say, he keeps, To ruminate strange plots of dire revenge v 2 6
Fight for a plot Whereon the numbers cannot try the cause *Hamlet* iv 4 62
Our indiscretion sometimes serves us well, When our deep plots do pall v 2 9
Lest more mischance, On plots and errors, happen v 2 406
I'ld turn it all To thy suggestion, plot, and damned practice *Lear* ii 1 75
I prithee, take him in thy arms; I have o'erheard a plot of death upon him iii 6 96
A plot upon her virtuous husband's life iv 6 279
The witch shall die: To the young Roman boy she hath sold me, and I fall Under this plot *Ant. and Cleo.* iv 12 49
A father by thy step-dame govern'd, A mother hourly coining plots *Cymbeline* ii 1 64
Let us Find out the prettiest daisied plot we can iv 2 398
Plot-proof. Out of the blank And level of my brain, plot-proof *W. Tale* ii 3 6
Plotted. This demi-devil . . . had plotted with them To take my life *Temp.* v 1 273
And all the means Plotted and 'greed on for my happiness *T. G. of Ver.* ii 4 183
And now 'tis plotted *T. of Shrew* i 1 193
In that dead time when Gloucester's death was plotted *Richard II.* iv 1 10
What I know Is ruminated, plotted and set down 1 *Hen. IV.* i 3 274
The planets of mishap That plotted thus our glory's overthrow 1 *Hen. VI.* i 1 24
This expedition was by York and Talbot Too rashly plotted iv 4 3
Thousands more, that yet suspect no peril, Will not conclude their plotted tragedy 2 *Hen. VI.* iii 1 153
This day had plotted, in the council-house To murder me *Richard III.* iii 5 38
Plotter. Chief architect and plotter of these woes *T. Andron.* v 3 122
Plough. I have vowed to Jaquenetta to hold the plough for her sweet love three years *L. L. Lost* v 2 893
Yoke you like draught-oxen and make you plough up the wars *T. and C.* ii 1 117
Let the Volsces Plough Rome, and harrow Italy *Coriolanus* v 3 34
Sooner this sword shall plough thy bowels up *T. Andron.* iv 2 87
Let Patient Octavia plough thy visage up With her prepared nails *Ant. and Cleo.* iv 12 38
Ploughed. Civil wounds plough'd up with neighbours' sword *Richard II.* i 3 128
Which we ourselves have plough'd for, sow'd, and scatter'd *Coriolanus* iii 1 71
He plough'd her, and she cropp'd *Ant. and Cleo.* ii 2 233
An if she were a thornier piece of ground than she is, she shall be ploughed.—Hark, hark, you gods! *Pericles* iv 6 154
Ploughest. 'Tis thou that rigg'st the bark and plough'st the foam *T. of A.* v 1 53
Plough-irons. The smith's note for shoeing and plough-irons 2 *Hen. IV.* v 1 20
Ploughman. The ox hath therefore stretch'd his yoke in vain, The ploughman lost his sweat *M. N. Dream* ii 1 94
Whilst the heavy ploughman snores, All with weary task fordone v 1 380
Hard as the palm of ploughman *Troi. and Cres.* i 1 59
Ploughmen. And merry larks are ploughmen's clocks *L. L. Lost* v 2 914
Plough-torn. O, a root,—dear thanks!—Dry up thy marrows, vines, and plough-torn leas! *T. of Athens* iv 3 193
Plow. I think a' will plow up all, if there is not better directions *Hen. V.* iii 2 68
I will give treason his payment into plows, I warrant you iv 8 15
Pluck. Lend thy hand, And pluck my magic garment from me *Tempest* i 2 24
I'll pluck thee berries; I'll fish for thee and get thee wood enough ii 2 164
Were I so minded, I here could pluck his highness' frown upon you v 1 127
A team of horse shall not pluck that from me *T. G. of Ver.* iii 1 266
Pluck the borrowed veil of modesty *Mer. Wives* iii 2 41
Pluck me out all the linen iv 2 155
And liberty plucks justice by the nose *Meas. for Meas.* i 3 29
I know your virtue hath a license in't, Which seems a little fouler than it is, To pluck on others ii 4 147
I will go further than I meant, to pluck all fears out of you iv 2 206
O, I will to him and pluck out his eyes! iv 3 124
Did not I pluck thee by the nose for thy speeches? v 1 343
If a crow help us in, sirrah, we'll pluck a crow together *Com. of Errors* iii 1 83
With these nails I'll pluck out these false eyes iv 4 107
Pluck off the bull's horns and set them in my forehead *Much Ado* i 1 265
Pluck up, my heart, and be sad v 1 207
My hand is sworn Ne'er to pluck thee from thy thorn *L. L. Lost* iv 3 112
Vow, alack, for youth unmeet, Youth so apt to pluck a sweet! iv 3 114
Do thy best To pluck this crawling serpent from my breast *M. N. Dream* ii 2 146
And pluck the wings from painted butterflies To fan the moonbeams iii 1 175
Pluck the young sucking cubs from the she-bear *Mer. of Venice* ii 1 29
And pluck commiseration of his state From brassy bosoms iv 1 30
Nor pluck it from his finger, for the wealth That the world masters v 1 173
Beware my sting.—My remedy is then, to pluck it out *T. of Shrew* ii 1 212
How she waded through the dirt to pluck him off me iv 1 80
Out, you rogue! you pluck my foot awry iv 1 150
Pluck up thy spirits; look cheerfully upon me iv 3 38
What heaven more will, That thee may furnish and my prayers pluck down, Fall on thy head! *All's Well* i 1 78
A man may draw his heart out, ere a' pluck one i 3 93
To pluck his indignation on thy head iii 2 32
May rather pluck on laughter than revenge *T. Night* v 1 374
I fear, the angle that plucks our son thither *W. Tale* iv 2 52
Pluck but off these rags; and then, death, death! iv 3 55
Take your sweetheart's hat And pluck it o'er your brows iv 4 665
One that will either push on or pluck back thy business iv 4 762
Whose valour plucks dead lions by the beard *K. John* ii 1 138
They will pluck away his natural cause And call them meteors iii 4 156
And pluck nights from me, but not lend a morrow *Richard II.* i 3 228
You pluck a thousand dangers on your head ii 1 205
Caterpillars of the commonwealth, Which I have sworn to weed and pluck away ii 3 167
When they from thy bosom pluck a flower, Guard it, I pray thee iii 2 19
Your cares set up do not pluck my cares down iv 1 195
Another way To pluck him headlong from the usurped throne v 1 65
Wilt thou pluck my fair son from mine age? v 2 92
He would unto the stews, And from the common'st creature pluck a glove v 3 17
An easy leap, To pluck bright honour from the pale-faced moon 1 *Hen. IV.* i 3 202
And pluck up drowned honour by the locks i 3 205

Pluck. Out of this nettle, danger, we pluck this flower, safety 1 *Hen. IV.* ii 3 10
I did pluck allegiance from men's hearts . . . . iii 2 52
Go, pluck him by the elbow; I must speak with him 2 *Hen. IV.* i 2 81
Which is almost to pluck a kingdom down And set another up . . i 3 49
Pluck down my officers, break my decrees . . . . iv 5 118
The fifth Harry from curb'd license plucks The muzzle of restraint . iv 5 131
To pluck down justice from your awful bench . . . . v 2 86
Beholding him, plucks comfort from his looks *Hen. V.* iv Prol. 42
If the opposed numbers Pluck their hearts from them . . . iv 1 309
They will pluck The gay new coats o'er the French soldiers' heads iv 3 117
From off this brier pluck a white rose with me . . . 1 *Hen. VI.* ii 4 30
Pluck a red rose from off this thorn with me . . . . ii 4 33
I pluck this white rose with Plantagenet . . . . . ii 4 36
I pluck this red rose with young Somerset . . . . . ii 4 37
Stay, lords and gentlemen, and pluck no more . . . . ii 4 39
I pluck this pale and maiden blossom here . . . . . ii 4 47
Prick not your finger as you pluck it off . . . . . ii 4 49
I am bound to you, That you on my behalf would pluck a flower . ii 4 129
Thus comes York to claim his right, And pluck the crown from feeble Henry's head . . . . 2 *Hen. VI.* v 1 2
Shall we suffer this? let's pluck him down . . . 3 *Hen. VI.* i 1 59
This strong right hand of mine Can pluck the diadem from faint Henry's head . . . . ii 1 153
Cannot get a crown? Tut, were it farther off, I'll pluck it down . iii 2 195
And from the cross-row plucks the letter G . . . *Richard III.* i 1 55
Go with him, And from her jealous arms pluck him perforce . . iii 1 36
But I am in So far in blood that sin will pluck on sin . . . iv 2 65
Then you are weakly made: pluck off a little . . . *Hen. VIII.* ii 3 40
'The forked one,' quoth he, 'pluck't out, and give it him' *Troi. and Cres.* i 2 179
Ajax employ'd plucks down Achilles' plumes . . . . . i 3 386
From Cupid's shoulder pluck his painted wings . . . . iii 2 15
Do one pluck down another and together Die in the fall . . . iii 3 86
See him pluck Aufidius down by the hair, As children from a bear *Coriol.* i 3 33
Would pluck reproof and rebuke from every ear that heard it . . ii 2 37
At once pluck out The multitudinous tongue . . . . . iii 1 155
Pursue him to his house, and pluck him thence . . . . iii 1 309
Seeking means To pluck away their power . . . . . iii 3 96
To pluck from them their tribunes for ever . . . . . iv 3 25
But hope to pluck a dainty doe to ground . . . *T. Andron.* ii 2 26
I have no strength to pluck thee to the brink . . . . ii 3 241
To pluck proud Lucius from the warlike Goths . . . . iv 4 110
And with a silk thread plucks it back again . . . *Rom. and Jul.* ii 2 181
Will you pluck your sword out of his pilcher by the ears? . . iii 1 83
And pluck the mangled Tybalt from his shroud . . . . iv 3 52
Pluck the grave wrinkled senate from the bench! . . *T. of Athens* iv 1 5
Son of sixteen, Pluck the lined crutch from thy old limping sire! . iv 1 14
Pluck stout men's pillows from below their heads . . . . iv 3 32
As they pass by, pluck Casca by the sleeve . . . *J. Cæsar* i 2 179
Pluck down benches.—Pluck down forms, windows, any thing . . iii 2 263
Pluck but his name out of his heart, and turn him going . . iii 3 38
What hands are here? ha! they pluck out mine eyes . . *Macbeth* ii 2 59
Modest wisdom plucks me From over-credulous haste . . . iv 3 119
Canst thou not . . . Pluck from the memory a rooted sorrow? . . v 3 41
Plucks off my beard, and blows it in my face? . . . *Hamlet* ii 2 600
You would pluck out the heart of my mystery . . . . iii 2 382
O, such a deed As from the body of contraction plucks The very soul . iii 4 46
Your sum of parts Did not together pluck such envy from him As did that one . . . . iv 7 75
Pluck them asunder . . . . v 1 287
Old fond eyes, Beweep this cause again, I'll pluck ye out . . *Lear* i 4 324
Hang him instantly.—Pluck out his eyes.—Leave him to my displeasure iii 7 5
By the kind gods, 'tis most ignobly done To pluck me by the beard . iii 7 36
I would not see thy cruel nails Pluck out his poor old eyes . . iii 7 57
May all the building in my fancy pluck Upon my hateful life . . iv 2 86
To pluck the common bosom on his side . . . . . . v 3 49
It plucks out brains and all: but my Muse labours . . *Othello* ii 1 128
The hand could pluck her back that shoved her on . . *Ant. and Cleo.* i 2 131
His speech sticks in my heart.—Mine ear must pluck it thence . . i 5 42
Can from the lap of Egypt's widow pluck The ne'er-lust-wearied Antony ii 1 37
Off, pluck off; The seven-fold shield of Ajax cannot keep The battery from my heart . . . . iv 14 37
I would not thy good deeds should from my lips Pluck a hard sentence *Cymbeline* v 5 289

Plucked. And by the spurs pluck'd up The pine and cedar . . *Tempest* v 1 47
Since I plucked geese, played truant and whipped top . *Mer. Wives* v 1 26
All houses in the suburbs of Vienna must be plucked down *Meas. for Meas.* i 2 99
Whose house, sir, was, as they say, plucked down in the suburbs . ii 1 65
We must have your doublet and hose plucked over your head *As You Like It* iv 1 207
Hath pluck'd on France To tread down fair respect of sovereignty *K. John* iii 1 57
You were crown'd before, And that high royalty was ne'er pluck'd off . iv 2 5
Hath from the number of his banish'd years Pluck'd four away *Rich. II.* i 3 211
My rights and royalties Pluck'd from my arms perforce and given away ii 3 121
The cloak of night being pluck'd from off their backs, Stand bare and naked . . . . iii 2 45
Pluck'd up root and all by Bolingbroke . . . . . . iii 4 52
I plucked this glove from his helm . . . . . *Hen. V.* iv 7 162
Sharp stakes pluck'd out of hedges They pitched in the ground 1 *Hen. VI.* i 1 117
Whose overweening arm I have pluck'd back . . 2 *Hen. VI.* iii 1 159
Confess who set thee up and pluck'd thee down . . 3 *Hen. VI.* v 1 26
All this from my remembrance brutish wrath Sinfully pluck'd *Rich. III.* ii 1 119
And pluck'd two crutches from my feeble limbs . . . . ii 2 58
This long-usurped royalty From the dead temples of this bloody wretch Have I pluck'd off . . . . v 5 6
When youth with comeliness plucked all gaze his way . . *Coriolanus* i 3 8
From him pluck'd Either his gracious promise . . . . ii 3 200
I may be pluck'd into the swallowing womb Of this deep pit *T. Andron.* ii 3 239
These growing feathers pluck'd from Cæsar's wing Will make him fly an ordinary pitch . . . . *J. Cæsar* i 1 77
He plucked me ope his doublet and offered them his throat to cut . i 2 267
Their hats are pluck'd about their ears, And half their faces buried . ii 1 73
As he pluck'd his cursed steel away, Mark how the blood of Cæsar follow'd it . . . . iii 2 181
Have pluck'd my nipple from his boneless gums . . . *Macbeth* i 7 57
Not without that harmful stroke, which since Hath pluck'd him after *Lear* iv 2 78
And then kiss me hard, As if he pluck'd up kisses by the roots *Othello* iii 3 423
Now he tells how she plucked him to my chamber . . . . iv 1 145
When I have pluck'd the rose, I cannot give it vital growth again . v 2 13
An argument that he is pluck'd, when hither He sends so poor a pinion of his wing . . . . *Ant. and Cleo.* iii 12 3

Plucked. May be she pluck'd it off To send it me.—She writes so to you? *Cymbeline* ii 4 104
Which grows to the stalk; never plucked yet, I can assure you *Pericles* iv 6 46

Plucker. Thou setter up and plucker down of kings . 3 *Hen. VI* ii 3 37

Plucking the grass, to know where sits the wind . *Mer. of Venice* i 1 18
Out, you rogue! you pluck my foot awry: Take that, and mend the plucking off the other . . . . *T. of Shrew* iv 1 151
What I was, I am; More straining on for plucking back . *W. Tale* iv 4 476
Plucking to unfix an enemy, He doth unfasten so and shake a friend 2 *Hen. IV.* iv 1 208
Such wither'd herbs as these Are meet for plucking up . *T. Andron.* iii 1 179
Plucking the entrails of an offering forth, They could not find a heart within the beast . . . . *J. Cæsar* ii 2 39

Plue. It is like a coal of fire, sometimes plue and sometimes red *Hen. V.* iii 6 110

Plum. It grandam will Give it a plum, a cherry, and a fig . *K. John* ii 1 162
Thou lovedst plums well, that wouldst venture so . 2 *Hen. VI.* ii 1 101

Plume. As diminish One dowle that's in my plume . . . *Tempest* iii 3 65
Change for an idle plume, Which the air beats for vain . *Meas. for Meas.* ii 4 11
What plume of feathers is he that indited this letter? . . *L. L. Lost* iv 1 96
Which is the Frenchman?—He; That with the plume . . *All's Well* iii 5 81
How he jets under his advanced plumes! . . . . . *T. Night* ii 5 37
Reproach and everlasting shame Sits mocking in our plumes . *Hen. V.* iv 5 5
We'll pull his plumes and take away his train . . . 1 *Hen. VI.* iii 3 7
Ajax employ'd plucks down Achilles' plumes . . . *Troi. and Cres.* i 3 386
Your enemies, with nodding of their plumes, Fan you into despair! *Cor.* iii 3 126
To get his place and to plume up my will In double knavery . . *Othello* i 3 399

Plumed. All plumed like estridges . . . . . 1 *Hen. IV.* iv 1 98
With plumed helm thy state begins to threat . . . . *Lear* iv 2 57
Farewell the plumed troop, and the big wars! . . . . *Othello* iii 3 349

Plume-plucked. I come to thee From plume-pluck'd Richard *Richard II.* iv 1 108

Plummet. I'll seek him deeper than e'er plummet sounded . *Tempest* iii 3 101
And deeper than did ever plummet sound I'll drown my book . . v 1 56
Ignorance itself is a plummet o'er me . . . . . *Mer. Wives* v 5 173

Plump. Banish plump Jack, and banish all the world . 1 *Hen. IV.* ii 4 527

Plumpy. Come, thou monarch of the vine, Plumpy Bacchus! *A. and C.* ii 7 121

Plum-tree. A fall off a tree.—A plum-tree, master . . . 2 *Hen. VI.* ii 1 97
Their eyes purging thick amber and plum-tree gum . . *Hamlet* ii 2 201

Plunge. Being o'er shoes in blood, plunge in the deep . *M. N. Dream* iii 2 48
As he that leaves A shallow plash to plunge him in the deep . *T. of Shrew* i 1 23
Do not plunge thyself too far in anger . . . . . *All's Well* ii 3 222
Which is past depth To those that, without heed, do plunge into't *T. of Athens* iii 5 13
Would perhaps plunge him into far more choler . . . *Hamlet* iii 2 318

Plunged. All but mariners Plunged in the foaming brine . . *Tempest* i 2 211
Thou wouldst have plunged thyself In general riot . *T. of Athens* iv 3 255
Accoutred as I was, I plunged in And bade him follow . . *J. Cæsar* i 2 105

Plural. Better have none Than plural faith . . . *T. G. of Ver.* v 4 52
What is your genitive case plural, William? . . . . *Mer. Wives* iv 1 59

Plurisy. Goodness, growing to a plurisy, Dies in his own too much *Ham.* iv 7 118

Pluto. To Pluto's damned lake . . . . . . 2 *Hen. IV.* ii 4 169
By the dreadful Pluto, if thou dost not, Though the great bulk Achilles be thy guard, I'll cut thy throat . . . . *Troi. and Cres.* iv 4 129
I do not like this fooling.—Nor I, by Pluto . . . . . v 2 102
Instance, O instance! strong as Pluto's gates . . . . . v 2 153
Pluto and hell! All hurt behind . . . . . . *Coriolanus* i 4 36
When you come to Pluto's region, I pray you, deliver him this *T. An.* iv 3 13
Pluto sends you word, If you will have Revenge from hell, you shall . iv 3 37

Plutus himself, That knows the tinct and multiplying medicine *All's Well* v 3 101
Knows almost every grain of Plutus' gold . . . *Troi. and Cres.* iii 3 197
Plutus, the god of gold, Is but his steward . . . *T. of Athens* i 1 287
A heart Dearer than Plutus' mine, richer than gold . . *J. Cæsar* iv 3 102

Ply. Will you go, sister? Shepherd, ply her hard . . *As Y. Like It* iii 5 76
Keep house and ply his book, welcome his friends . . *T. of Shrew* i 1 201
Go ply thy needle; meddle not with her . . . . . . ii 1 25
See, here he comes, and I must ply my theme . . . *T. Andron.* v 2 80
And let him ply his music.—Well, my lord . . . . *Hamlet* ii 1 73
Ply Desdemona well, and you are sure on't . . . . *Othello* iv 1 107

Po. Talking of the Alps and Apennines, The Pyrenean and the river Po *K. John* i 1 203

Pocket. If but one of his pockets could speak, would it not say he lies?—Ay, or very falsely pocket up his report. . . . . *Tempest* ii 1 65
I think he will carry this island home in his pocket and give it his son . ii 1 91
Mette le au mon pocket . . . . *Mer. Wives* i 4 56
For putting the hand in the pocket and extracting it clutched *M. for M.* iii 2 49
Here's another Writ in my cousin's hand, stolen from her pocket *M. Ado* v 4 89
Your hands in your pocket like a man after the old painting . *L. L. Lost* iii 1 20
Wear prayer-books in my pocket, look demurely . . *Mer. of Venice* ii 2 201
I think I have his letter in my pocket . . . . . *All's Well* iv 3 228
Put your grace in your pocket, sir, for this once . . . *T. Night* v 1 35
Let me pocket up my pedlar's excrement. . . . . . *W. Tale* iv 4 734
I must pocket up these wrongs . . . . *K. John* iii 1 200
Search his pockets. What hast thou found? . . . 1 *Hen. IV.* ii 4 580
Have you inquired yet who picked my pocket? . . . . . iii 3 61
I'll be sworn my pocket was picked . . . . iii 3 70
Shall I not take mine ease in mine inn but I shall have my pocket picked? . . . . iii 3 93
I fell asleep here behind the arras and had my pocket picked . . iii 3 113
This house is turned bawdy-house; they pick pockets . . . . iii 3 114
Charge an honest woman with picking thy pocket! . . . . . iii 3 176
If there were anything in thy pocket but tavern-reckonings, . . . if thy pocket were enriched with any other injuries but these, I am a villain . . . . iii 3 178
You will not pocket up wrong: art thou not ashamed? . . . . iii 3 183
You confess then, you picked my pocket?—It appears so by the story . iii 3 190
They would have me as familiar with men's pockets as their gloves *Hen. V.* iii 2 51
Which makes much against my manhood, if I should take from another's pocket to put into mine . . . . iii 2 54
I have another leek in my pocket, which you shall eat . . . . v 1 65
Have fill'd their pockets full of pebble stones . . . 1 *Hen. VI.* iii 1 80
Here's a villain!—Has a book in his pocket with red letters in't 2 *Hen. VI.* iv 2 97
Brings a' victory in his pocket? . . . . *Coriolanus* ii 1 135
Here's the book I sought for so; I put it in the pocket of my gown *J. C.* iv 3 253
From a shelf the precious diadem stole, And put it in his pocket *Hamlet* iii 4 101
What needed, then, that terrible dispatch of it into your pocket? *Lear* i 2 33
Let's see these pockets: the letters that he speaks of May be my friends iv 6 261
Here is a letter Found in the pocket of the slain Roderigo . . *Othello* v 2 309
Now here's another discontented paper, Found in his pocket too . . v 2 315
You Did pocket up my letters, and with taunts Did gibe *Ant. and Cleo.* ii 2 73
Realms and islands were As plates dropp'd from his pocket . . . v 2 92

Pocket. If Cæsar can hide the sun from us with a blanket, or put the moon in his pocket, we will pay him tribute for light . *Cymbeline* iii 1 44
I had a feigned letter of my master's Then in my pocket . v 5 280
Pocketing. It is plain pocketing up of wrongs . *Hen. V.* iii 2 54
Pocky. We have many pocky corses now-a-days . *Hamlet* v 1 181
Pody. If there be any pody in the house, . . . heaven forgive my sins at the day of judgement . *Mer. Wives* iii 3 224
All the water in Wye cannot wash your majesty's Welsh plood out of your pody, I can tell you that . *Hen. V.* iv 7 112
Poem. Scene individable, or poem unlimited . *Hamlet* ii 2 419
Poesy. Much is the force of heaven-bred poesy . *T. G. of Ver.* iii 2 72
For the elegancy, facility, and golden cadence of poesy, caret *L. L. Lost* iv 2 126
Music and poesy use to quicken you . *T. of Shrew* i 1 36
Our poesy is as a gum, which oozes From whence 'tis nourish'd *T. of A.* i 1 21
Poet. For Orpheus' lute was strung with poets' sinews . *T. G. of Ver.* iii 2 78
Never durst poet touch a pen to write Until his ink were temper'd with Love's sighs . *L. L. Lost* iv 3 346
The lunatic, the lover and the poet Are of imagination all compact *M. N. Dream* v 1 7
The poet's eye, in a fine frenzy rolling, Doth glance from heaven to earth, from earth to heaven . v 1 12
The poet's pen Turns them to shapes and gives to airy nothing A local habitation and a name . v 1 15
Therefore the poet Did feign that Orpheus drew trees, stones *Mer. of Ven.* v 1 79
The most capricious poet, honest Ovid, was among the Goths *As Y. L. It* iii 3 8
If thou wert a poet, I might have some hope thou didst feign . iii 3 26
In good truth, the poet makes a most excellent description of it *Hen. V.* iii 6 39
And all that poets feign of bliss and joy . *3 Hen. VI.* i 2 31
That grim ferryman which poets write of . *Richard III.* i 4 46
And fell asleep As Cerberus at the Thracian poet's feet . *T. Andron.* ii 4 51
Pattern'd by that the poet here describes . iv 1 57
How now, poet!—How now, philosopher!—Thou liest . *T. of Athens* i 1 220
Art not a poet?—Yes.—Then thou liest: look in thy last work, where thou hast feigned him a worthy fellow . i 1 226
Yonder comes a poet and a painter: the plague of company light upon thee! . iv 3 356
I am Cinna the poet.—Tear him for his bad verses . *J. Cæsar* iii 3 33
Unless the poet and the player went to cuffs in the question . *Hamlet* ii 2 372
Scribes, bards, poets, cannot Think, speak, cast, write, sing *A. and C.* iii 2 16
Poetical. Truly, I would the gods had made thee poetical *As Y. Like It* iii 3 16
I do not know what 'poetical' is: is it honest in deed and word? . iii 3 17
Do you wish then that the gods had made me poetical?—I do, truly . iii 3 24
I took great pains to study it, and 'tis poetical . *T. Night* i 5 207
Poetry. Neither savouring of poetry, wit, nor invention . *L. L. Lost* iv 2 165
For all the world like cutler's poetry Upon a knife . *Mer. of Venice* v 1 149
The truest poetry is the most feigning; and lovers are given to poetry, and what they swear in poetry may be said as lovers they do feign *As Y. Like It* iii 3 19
She taketh most delight In music, instruments, and poetry . *T. of Shrew* i 1 93
Well read in poetry And other books, good ones, I warrant ye . i 2 170
That would set my teeth nothing on edge, Nothing so much as mincing poetry . *1 Hen. IV.* iii 1 134
She hath read to thee Sweet poetry and Tully's Orator . *T. Andron.* iv 1 14
Poictiers. To Ireland, Poictiers, Anjou, Touraine, Maine. . *K. John* i 1 11
Anjou and fair Touraine, Maine, Poictiers, . . . Shall gild her bridal bed ii 1 487
Then do I give Volquessen, Touraine, Maine, Poictiers and Anjou . ii 1 528
Rheims, Orleans, Paris, Guysors, Poictiers, are all quite lost *1 Hen. VI.* i 1 61
Maine, Blois, Poictiers, and Tours, are won away, 'Long all of Somerset iv 3 45
Poins. He kept company with the wild prince and Poins. *Mer. Wives* iii 2 74
Poins! Now shall we know if Gadshill have set a match . *1 Hen. IV.* i 2 118
Poins! Poins, and be hanged! Poins!—Peace, ye fat-kidneyed rascal! . ii 2 4
Where's Poins, Hal?—He is walked up to the top of the hill . ii 2 7
Poins! Hal! a plague upon you both! Bardolph! Peto! . ii 2 21
Front them in the narrow lane; Ned Poins and I will walk lower . ii 2 63
An the Prince and Poins be not two arrant cowards . ii 2 105
There's no more valour in that Poins than in a wild-duck . ii 2 107
Are not you a coward? answer me to that: and Poins there? . ii 4 158
No, my good lord; banish Peto, banish Bardolph, banish Poins . ii 4 522
Shall I tell thee one thing, Poins?—Yes, faith . *2 Hen. IV.* ii 2 35
Be not too familiar with Poins; for he misuses thy favours so much . ii 2 138
Here will be the prince and Master Poins anon . ii 4 17
They say Poins has a good wit.—He a good wit? hang him, baboon! . ii 4 260
A bastard son of the kings? And art not thou Poins his brother? . ii 4 308
Poins, I feel me much to blame, So idly to profane the precious time . ii 4 390
Point. Hast thou, spirit, Perform'd to point the tempest? . *Tempest* i 2 194
But then exactly do All points of my command . i 2 500
Most poor matters Point to rich ends . iii 1 4
How sharp the point of this remembrance is! . v 1 138
Ay, there's the point, sir.—Marry, is it; the very point of it *Mer. Wives* i 1 229
In the circumference of a peck, hilt to point, heel to head . iii 5 113
We may soon our satisfaction have Touching that point . *Meas. for Meas.* i 1 84
O, let him marry her.—This is the point . i 4 49
Whether you had not sometime in your life Err'd in this point . ii 1 15
You are therein in the right: but to the point . ii 1 100
Let me know the point.—O, I do fear thee . iii 1 73
Agree with his demands to the point . iii 1 254
By this, I think, the dial points at five . *Com. of Errors* v 1 118
Just so much as you may take upon a knife's point . *Much Ado* ii 3 264
Hath no man's dagger here a point for me? . iv 1 110
Examine him upon that point . v 1 322
Will you prick't with your eye?—No point, with my knife . *L. L. Lost* ii 1 190
Did point you to buy them, along as you pass'd . iii 1 245
No point, quoth I; my servant straight was mute . v 2 277
Then read the names of the actors, and so grow to a point *M. N. Dream* i 2 10
Touching now the point of human skill . ii 2 119
This fellow doth not stand upon points . v 1 118
That I did suit me all points like a man . *As Y. Like It* i 3 118
The thorny point Of bare distress hath ta'en from me the show Of smooth civility . ii 7 94
That is one of the points in the which women still give the lie to their consciences . iii 2 409
Now must the world point at poor Katharine . *T. of Shrew* iii 2 18
With a broken hilt, and chapeless; with two broken points . iii 2 49
So that from point to point now have you heard . *All's Well* iii 1 1
Which makes her story true, even to the point of her death . iv 3 67
Confirmations, point from point, to the full arming of the verity . iv 3 72
Let us from point to point this story know . v 3 325
I am resolved on two points.—That if one break, the other will hold *T. Night* i 5 25
He does obey every point of the letter that I dropped to betray him . iii 2 83

Point. The fail Of any point in't shall not only be Death to thyself but to thy lewd-tongued wife . *W. Tale* ii 3 171
Betwixt the firmament and it you cannot thrust a bodkin's point . iii 3 87
But that's not to the point . iii 3 91
Points more than all the lawyers in Bohemia can learnedly handle . iv 4 206
I'll point you where you shall have such receiving As shall become . iv 4 537
The which shall point you forth at every sitting What you must say . iv 4 572
As in a theatre, whence they gape and point . *K. John* ii 1 375
Turn face to face and bloody point to point . ii 1 390
Is Harry Hereford arm'd?—Yea, at all points . *Richard II.* i 3 2
And with thy blessings steel my lance's point . i 3 74
His golden beams to you here lent Shall point on me and gild my banishment . i 3 147
And I will turn thy falsehood to thy heart . . . with my rapier's point iv 1 40
To prove it on thee to the extremest point Of mortal breathing . iv 1 47
Whereto my finger, like a dial's point, Is pointing still . v 5 53
Beat Cut's saddle, put a few flocks in the point . *1 Hen. IV.* ii 1 7
Thou knowest my old ward; here I lay, and thus I bore my point . ii 4 216
I made me no more ado but took all their seven points in my target, thus . ii 4 224
Their points being broken,— Down fell their hose . ii 4 238
Here lies the point; why, being son to me, art thou so pointed at? . ii 4 448
I came not to hear this.—Then to the point . iv 3 89
If life did ride upon a dial's point, Still ending at the arrival of an hour v 2 84
I saw him hold Lord Percy at the point . v 4 21
Upon mine honour, for a silken point I'll give my barony . *2 Hen. IV.* i 1 53
God's light, with two points on your shoulder? much! . ii 4 142
Come we to full points here; and are etceteras nothing? . ii 4 198
And hides a sword from hilts unto the point . *Hen. V.* ii Prol. 9
As touching the direction of the military discipline; that is the point . iii 2 108
Je ne doute point d'apprendre, par la grace de Dieu, et en peu de temps iii 4 43
The state of Normandy Stands on a tickle point . *2 Hen. VI.* i 1 216
But what a point, my lord, your falcon made, And what a pitch she flew! ii 1 5
See how the giddy multitude do point, And nod their heads! . ii 4 21
Ne'er shall this blood be wiped from thy point . iv 10 74
Pity me!—Such pity as my rapier's point affords . *3 Hen. VI.* i 3 37
Clifford, with his rapier's point, Made issue from the bosom of the boy i 4 80
Broach'd with the steely point of Clifford's lance . ii 3 16
Carve out dials quaintly, point by point, Thereby to see the minutes . ii 5 24
Why, brother, wherefore stand you on nice points? . iv 7 58
My breast can better brook thy dagger's point Than can my ears that tragic history . v 6 27
But that thy brothers beat aside the point . *Richard III.* i 2 96
Thus doth he force the swords of wicked men To turn their own points on their masters' bosoms . v 1 24
Point by point the treasons of his master He shall again relate *Hen. VIII.* i 2 7
That you would love yourself . . . is the point Of my petition . i 2 16
Note This dangerous conception in this point . i 2 139
To this point hast thou heard him At any time speak aught? . i 2 145
I speak my good lord cardinal to this point, And thus far clear him . ii 4 166
The sharp thorny points Of my alleged reasons drive this forward . ii 4 224
But in this point All his tricks founder . iii 2 39
I have touch'd the highest point of all my greatness . iii 2 223
I do enjoy At ample point all that I did possess . *Troi. and Cres.* iii 3 89
Admits no orifex for a point as subtle As Ariachne's broken woof to enter v 2 151
It remains, As the main point of this our after-meeting . *Coriolanus* ii 2 43
Our then dictator, Whom with all praise I point at, saw him fight . ii 2 94
One direct way should be at once to all the points o' the compass . ii 3 25
You are at point to lose your liberties . iii 1 194
In this point charge him home, that he affects Tyrannical power . iii 3 1
Aufidius, The second name of men, obeys his points As if he were his officer . iv 6 125
They are near the city?—Almost at point to enter . v 4 64
And bids thee christen it with thy dagger's point . *T. Andron.* iv 2 70
I'll broach the tadpole on my rapier's point . iv 2 85
'Tis true, 'tis true; witness my knife's sharp point . v 3 63
And from her bosom took the enemy's point . v 3 111
Who, all as hot, turns deadly point to point . *Rom. and Jul.* iii 1 165
Swifter than his tongue, His agile arm beats down their fatal points . iii 1 171
There's a fearful point! . iv 3 32
Seeking out Romeo, that did spit his body Upon a rapier's point . iv 3 57
Who would not wish to be from wealth exempt, Since riches point to misery and contempt? . *T. of Athens* iv 2 32
For any benefit that points to me, Either in hope or present, I'ld exchange For this one wish . iv 3 526
Leap in with me into this angry flood, And swim to yonder point *J. Cæsar* i 2 104
Ere we could arrive the point proposed, Cæsar cried 'Help me, Cassius!' i 2 110
I believe, they are portentous things Unto the climate that they point upon . i 3 32
Here, as I point my sword, the sun arises . ii 1 106
To you our swords have leaden points, Mark Antony . iii 1 173
Therefore I took your hands, but was, indeed, Sway'd from the point . iii 1 219
Either led or driven, as we point the way . iv 1 23
Point against point rebellious, arm 'gainst arm . *Macbeth* i 2 56
All our service In every point twice done and then done double . i 6 15
I did so, and went further, which is now Our point of second meeting . iii 1 86
The blood-bolter'd Banquo smiles upon me, And points at them for his iv 1 124
Old Siward, with ten thousand warlike men, Already at a point . iv 3 135
A figure like your father, Armed at point exactly, cap-a-pe . *Hamlet* i 2 200
Shake hands and part: You, as your business and desire shall point you i 5 129
To this point I stand, That both the worlds I give to negligence . iv 5 133
I'll touch my point With this contagion, that, if I gall him slightly, It may be death . iv 7 147
For here lies the point: if I drown myself wittingly, it argues an act . v 1 10
Between the pass and fell incensed points Of mighty opposites . v 2 61
The point envenom'd too! Then, venom, to thy work . v 2 332
Love's not love When it is mingled with regards that stand Aloof from the entire point . *Lear* i 1 243
'Tis politic and safe to let him keep At point a hundred knights . i 4 347
And are at point To show their open banner . iii 1 33
My point and period will be throughly wrought, Or well or ill . iv 7 97
But, alas, to make me A fixed figure for the time of scorn To point his slow unmoving finger at! . *Othello* iv 2 55
These are portents; but yet I hope, I hope, They do not point on me . v 2 46
Touch you the sourest points with sweetest terms . *Ant. and Cleo.* ii 2 24
Let your best love draw to that point, which seeks Best to preserve it . iii 4 21
At such a point, When half to half the world opposed . iii 13 8
To flatter Cæsar, would you mingle eyes With one that ties his points? iii 13 157
Who was once at point—O giglot fortune!—to master Cæsar's sword *Cymbeline* iii 1 30

Point. That drug-damn'd Italy hath out-craftied him, And he's at some hard point *Cymbeline* iii 4 16
Well, then, here's the point: You must forget to be a woman iii 4 156
You are appointed for that office; The due of honour in no point omit iii 5 11
In that point I will conclude to hate her, nay, indeed, To be revenged iii 5 77
But even before, I was At point to sink for food iii 6 17
In a time When fearful wars point at me iv 3 7
Thy lopp'd branches point Thy two sons forth v 5 454
Make my senses credit thy relation To points that seem impossible *Per.* v 1 125
Tell him O'er, point by point, for yet he seems to doubt v 1 227
There's the point *Mer. Wives* i 1; *2 Hen. IV.* i 3; *Othello* iii 3; *Ant. and Cleo.* ii 6
'Point. He'll woo a thousand, 'point the day of marriage *T. of Shrew* iii 2 15
Point-blank. As easy as a cannon will shoot point-blank twelve score *Mer. Wives* iii 2 34
Now art thou within point-blank of our jurisdiction regal *2 Hen. VI.* iv 7 28
Point-devise. Such insociable and point-devise companions *L. L. Lost* v 1 21
You are rather point-device in your accoutrements *As Y. Like It* iii 2 401
I will be point-devise the very man *T. Night* ii 5 177
Pointed. Why, being son to me, art thou so pointed at? *1 Hen. IV.* ii 4 449
Evermore they pointed To the good of your most sacred person *Hen. VIII.* iii 2 172
Till the diminution Of space had pointed him sharp as my needle *Cymb.* i 3 19
'It hath been a shield 'Twixt me and death;'—and pointed to this brace *Pericles* ii 1 133
'Pointed. I'll not be tied to hours nor 'pointed times *T. of Shrew* iii 1 19
This is the 'pointed day iii 2 1
Pointest. Will these moss'd trees, That have outlived the eagle, page thy heels, And skip where thou point'st out? *T. of Athens* iv 3 225
Pointing. Whereto my finger, like a dial's point, Is pointing *Richard II.* v 5 54
With celerity, find Hector's purpose Pointing on him *Troi. and Cres.* i 3 331
Pointing-stock. A wonder and a pointing-stock *2 Hen. VI.* ii 4 46
Point of battle. Rome and her rats are at the point of battle *Coriolanus* i 1 166
Point of death. Like to the Egyptian thief at point of death, Kill what I love *T. Night* v 1 121
Vows obedience And humble service till the point of death *1 Hen. VI.* iii 1 168
Cardinal Beaufort is at point of death *2 Hen. VI.* iii 2 369
Oft when men are at the point of death Have they been merry *R. and J.* v 3 88
Point of envy. Dignified enough, Even to the point of envy *Cymbeline* ii 3 133
Point of fox. O Signieur Dew, thou diest on point of fox *Hen. V.* iv 4 9
Point of friendship. 'Tis a point of friendship *1 Hen. IV.* v 1 122
Point of honour. Takes on the point of honour to support So dissolute a crew *Richard II.* v 3 11
Point of ignorance. With all their honourable points of ignorance Pertaining thereunto *Hen. VIII.* i 3 26
Point of war. To a loud trumpet and a point of war *2 Hen. IV.* iv 1 52
Point of weight. But how to make ye suddenly an answer, In such a point of weight *Hen. VIII.* iii 1 71
Point of wisdom. Do so, it is a point of wisdom *Richard III.* i 4 99
Poise. Were equal poise of sin and charity *Meas. for Meas.* ii 4 68
Poise the cause in justice' equal scales, Whose beam stands sure *2 Hen. VI.* ii 1 204
So is the equal poise of this fell war *3 Hen. VI.* ii 5 13
For the great swing and rudeness of his poise *Troi. and Cres.* i 3 207
Occasions, noble Gloucester, of some poise *Lear* ii 1 122
If the balance of our lives had not one scale of reason to poise another of sensuality *Othello* i 3 331
It shall be full of poise and difficult weight And fearful to be granted iii 3 82
Poised. Our imputation shall be oddly poised In this *Troi. and Cres.* i 3 339
Both merits poised, each weighs nor less nor more iv 1 65
You saw her fair, none else being by, Herself poised with herself *R. and J.* i 2 100
Poising. We, poising us in her defective scale, Shall weigh thee to the beam *All's Well* ii 3 161
Poison. Guilt, Like poison given to work a great time after *Tempest* iii 3 105
I will incense Page to deal with poison *Mer. Wives* i 3 110
I do digest the poison of thy flesh *Com. of Errors* ii 2 145
Clamours of a jealous woman Poisons more deadly than a mad dog's tooth v 1 70
The poison of that lies in you to temper *Much Ado* ii 2 21
I have drunk poison whiles he utter'd it v 1 253
Universal plodding poisons up The nimble spirits in the arteries *L. L. L.* iv 3 305
If you tickle us, do we not laugh? if you poison us, do we not die? *Mer. of Venice* iii 1 68
He will practise against thee by poison *As Y. Like It* i 1 157
I will deal in poison with thee, or in bastinado, or in steel v 1 60
Were I his lady, I would poison that vile rascal *All's Well* iii 5 87
What dish o' poison has she dressed him! *T. Night* ii 5 123
A lingering dram that should not work Maliciously like poison *W. Tale* i 2 321
I chose Camillo for the minister to poison My friend Polixenes iii 2 161
Sweet, sweet, sweet poison for the age's tooth *K. John* i 1 213
It would allay the burning quality Of that fell poison which assaileth him v 7 9
Within me is a hell; and there the poison Is as a fiend confined v 7 46
No balm can cure but his heart-blood Which breathed this poison *Rich. II.* i 1 173
They love not poison that do poison need v 6 38
Let a cup of sack be my poison *1 Hen. IV.* ii 2 49
In poison there is physic *2 Hen. IV.* i 1 137
Hide not thy poison with such sugar'd words *2 Hen. VI.* iii 2 45
Poison be their drink! Gall, worse than gall, the daintiest that they taste! iii 2 321
Bid the apothecary Bring the strong poison that I bought of him iii 3 18
Whose tongue more poisons than the adder's tooth! *3 Hen. VI.* i 4 112
Why dost thou spit at me?—Would it were mortal poison! *Richard III.* i 2 146
Never came poison from so sweet a place.—Never hung poison on a fouler toad i 2 147
Attended to their sugar'd words, But look'd not on the poison of their hearts iii 1 14
All goodness Is poison to thy stomach *Hen. VIII.* iii 2 283
A mind That shall remain a poison where it is, Not poison any further *Coriolanus* iii 1 87
Let them not lick The sweet which is their poison iii 1 157
Ingrate forgetfulness shall poison, rather Than pity note how much v 2 92
As if it were the Moor Come hither purposely to poison me *T. Andron.* iii 2 73
Take thou some new infection to thy eye, And the rank poison of the old will die *Rom. and Jul.* i 2 51
Within the infant rind of this small flower Poison hath residence ii 3 24
Shall poison more Than the death-darting eye of cockatrice iii 2 46
Hadst thou no poison mix'd, no sharp-ground knife, No sudden mean of death? iii 3 44
If you could find out but a man To bear a poison, I would temper it iii 5 98
What if it be a poison, which the friar Subtly hath minister'd? iv 3 24
If a man did need a poison now, Whose sale is present death in Mantua, Here lives a caitiff wretch would sell it him v 1 50
Poison. Let me have A dram of poison, such soon-speeding gear As will disperse itself through all the veins *Rom. and Jul.* v 1 60
There is thy gold, worse poison to men's souls, Doing more murders in this loathsome world, Than these poor compounds that thou mayst not sell v 1 80
I sell thee poison; thou hast sold me none v 1 83
Come, cordial and not poison, go with me To Juliet's grave v 1 85
Poison, I see, hath been his timeless end v 3 162
I will kiss thy lips; Haply some poison yet doth hang on them v 3 165
He writes that he did buy a poison Of a poor 'pothecary v 3 288
Has my lord's meat in him: Why should it thrive and turn to nutriment, When he is turn'd to poison? *T. of Athens* iii 1 62
That their society, as their friendship, may Be merely poison! iv 1 32
Who seeks for better of thee, sauce his palate With thy most operant poison! iv 3 25
When Jove Will o'er some high-viced city hang his poison In the sick air iv 3 109
Would poison were obedient and knew my mind!—Where wouldst thou send it?—To sauce thy dishes iv 3 296
Trust not the physician; His antidotes are poison iv 3 435
Nor steel, nor poison, Malice domestic, foreign levy, nothing, Can touch him further *Macbeth* iii 2 24
They do but jest, poison in jest; no offence i' the world. *Hamlet* iii 2 244
He poisons him i' the garden for's estate. His name's Gonzago iii 2 272
O, this is the poison of deep grief iv 5 76
He is justly served; It is a poison temper'd by himself v 2 339
The potent poison quite o'er-crows my spirit v 2 364
Be thy mouth or black or white, Tooth that poisons of it bite *Lear* iii 6 70
I pray, weep not: If you have poison for me, I will drink it iv 7 72
Rouse him: make after him, poison his delight *Othello* i 1 68
Did you by indirect and forced courses Subdue and poison this young maid's affections? i 3 112
Dangerous conceits are, in their natures, poisons iii 3 325
If there be cords, or knives, Poison, or fire . . . I'll not endure it iii 3 389
Get me some poison, Iago; this night: I'll not expostulate with her iv 1 216
Do it not with poison, strangle her in her bed iv 1 220
This is thy work: the object poisons sight; Let it be hid v 2 364
Hath yet but life, And not a serpent's poison *Ant. and Cleo.* i 2 201
Now I feed myself With most delicious poison i 5 27
From my cold heart let heaven engender hail, And poison it in the source iii 13 160
If they had swallow'd poison, 'twould appear By external swelling v 2 348
Away! Thou'rt poison to my blood *Cymbeline* i 1 128
She doth think she has Strange lingering poisons i 5 34
Such boil'd stuff As well might poison poison! i 6 126
We will fear no poison, which attends In place of greater state iii 3 77
Whose life, But that her flight prevented it, she had Ta'en off by poison v 5 47
O, give me cord, or knife, or poison, Some upright justicer! v 5 213
O, get thee from my sight; Thou gavest me poison v 5 237
The queen, sir, very oft importuned me To temper poisons for her v 5 250
Though they feed On sweetest flowers, yet they poison breed *Pericles* i 1 133
Poison and treason are the hands of sin, Ay, and the targets i 1 139
Behold, here's poison, and here's gold; We hate the prince of Tyre i 1 155
Poisoned. Thou wouldst have poison'd good Camillo's honour *W. Tale* iii 2 189
The king, I fear, is poison'd by a monk *K. John* v 6 23
How fares your majesty?—Poison'd,—ill fare—dead, forsook, cast off v 7 35
Some poison'd by their wives; some sleeping kill'd. *Richard II.* iii 2 159
I would have him poison'd with a pot of ale *1 Hen. IV.* i 3 233
O ceremony, . . . What drink'st thou oft, instead of homage sweet, But poison'd flattery? *Hen. V.* iv 1 268
Boiling choler chokes The hollow passage of my poison'd voice *1 Hen. VI.* v 4 121
My valour's poison'd With only suffering stain by him *Coriolanus* i 10 17
Commends the ingredients of our poison'd chalice To our own lips *Macbeth* i 7 11
Round about the cauldron go; In the poison'd entrails throw iv 1 5
As level as the cannon to his blank, Transports his poison'd shot *Hamlet* iv 1 43
It is the poison'd cup: it is too late v 2 303
Dear Hamlet,—The drink, the drink! I am poison'd v 2 321
Thy mother's poison'd: I can no more: the king, the king's to blame v 2 330
The other messenger, Whose welcome, I perceived, had poison'd mine *Lear* ii 4 39
Your lady: and her sister By her is poisoned; she hath confess'd it v 3 227
Edmund was beloved: The one the other poison'd for my sake v 3 240
When poison'd hours had bound me up From mine own knowledge *Ant. and Cleo.* ii 2 90
Who was last with them?—A simple countryman, that brought her figs: This was his basket.—Poison'd, then v 2 343
'Twas at a feast,—O, would Our viands had been poison'd! *Cymbeline* v 5 156
I had it from the queen.—New matter still?—It poison'd me v 5 243
O villain Leonine! Whom thou hast poison'd too! *Pericles* iv 3 10
Poisoner. I must be the poisoner Of good Polixenes *W. Tale* i 2 352
Poisoning. Didst perceive?—Very well, my lord.—Upon the talk of the poisoning? *Hamlet* iii 2 300
Poisonous. Thou poisonous slave, got by the devil himself! *Tempest* i 2 319
As speedy in your end As all the poisonous potions in the world *1 Hen. IV.* v 4 56
Be poisonous too and kill thy forlorn queen *2 Hen. VI.* iii 2 77
To help thee curse that poisonous bunch-back'd toad *Richard III.* i 3 246
Those cold ways, That seem like prudent helps, are very poisonous Where the disease is violent *Coriolanus* iii 1 221
You might condemn us As poisonous of your honour v 3 135
With poisonous spite and envy *T. of Athens* i 2 144
The thought whereof Doth, like a poisonous mineral, gnaw my inwards *Othello* ii 1 306
The poisonous damp of night disponge upon me *Ant. and Cleo.* iv 9 13
Poisonous compounds, Which are the movers of a languishing death *Cymbeline* i 5 8
Poisonous-tongued. As poisonous-tongued as handed iii 2 5
Poke. Then he drew a dial from his poke *As Y. Like It* ii 7 20
Poking-stick. Pins and poking-sticks of steel *W. Tale* iv 4 228
Polack. When, in an angry parle, He smote the sledded Polacks *Hamlet* i 1 63
Which to him appear'd To be a preparation 'gainst the Polack ii 2 63
To employ those soldiers, So levied as before, against the Polack ii 2 75
Why, then the Polack never will defend it iv 4 23
You from the Polack wars, and you from England v 2 387
Poland. He supposes me travell'd to Poland *Meas. for Meas.* i 3 14
Her rags and the tallow in them will burn a Poland winter *Com. of Errors* iii 2 100
How purposed, sir, I pray you?—Against some part of Poland *Hamlet* iv 4 12
Goes it against the main of Poland, sir, Or for some frontier? iv 4 15
Young Fortinbras, with conquest come from Poland v 2 361
Pold. Be pold, I pray you; follow me into the pit *Mer. Wives* v 4 2
Pole. By the north pole, I do challenge thee *L. L. Lost* v 2 699
I will not fight with a pole, like a northern man v 2 700
Turn not thy scorns this way, Plantagenet.—Proud Pole, I will *1 Hen. VI.* ii 4 78

Pole. Away, away, good William de la Pole! We grace the yeoman by conversing . . . . . . 1 *Hen. VI.* ii 4 80
Your partaker Pole and you yourself, I'll note you in my book of memory. . . . . ii 4 100
And so farewell until I meet thee next.—Have with thee, Pole . ii 4 114
In signal of my love to thee, Against proud Somerset and William Pole ii 4 122
Fie, de la Pole! disable not thyself; Hast not a tongue? . v 3 67
Agreed between the French king Charles, and William de la Pole 2 *Hen. VI.* i 1 44
And on the pieces of the broken wand Were placed the heads of Edmund Duke of Somerset, And William de la Pole . . . . . i 2 30
Pole, when in the city Tours Thou ran'st a tilt in honour of my love . i 3 53
Thy prisoner is a prince, The Duke of Suffolk, William de la Pole . iv 1 45
Yes, Pole.—Pole!—Pool! Sir Pool! lord! Ay, kennel, puddle, sink . iv 1 70
Sooner dance upon a bloody pole Than stand uncover'd to the vulgar groom . . . . iv 1 127
I'll see if his head will stand steadier on a pole, or no . . . iv 7 101
Strike off his head, and bring them both upon two poles hither . iv 7 119
We'll have thee, as our rarer monsters are, Painted upon a pole *Macbeth* v 8 26
Yond same star that's westward from the pole . . . *Hamlet* i 1 36
Nor will it yield to Norway or the Pole A ranker rate, should it be sold iv 4 21
And quench the guards of the ever-fixed pole . . . . *Othello* ii 1 15
O, wither'd is the garland of the war, The soldier's pole is fall'n *A. and C.* iv 15 65
Polecats! there are fairer things than polecats, sure . . *Mer. Wives* iv 1 29
You witch, you hag, you baggage, you polecat! . . . . iv 2 195
Pole-clipt. Thy pole-clipt vineyard; And thy sea-marge, sterile *Tempest* iv 1 68
Polemon and Amyntas, The kings of Mede and Lycaonia . *Ant. and Cleo.* iii 6 74
Poli. Magni Dominator poli, Tam lentus audis scelera? . *T. Andron.* iv 1 81
Policies. Search out thy wit for secret policies . . 1 *Hen. VI.* iii 3 12
Policy. Both strength of limb and policy of mind . . *Much Ado* iv 1 200
'Tis some policy To have one show worse than the king's . *L. L. Lost* v 2 513
I will o'er-run thee with policy . . . . . . *As Y. Like It* v 1 62
If she be curst, it is for policy, For she's not froward . *T. of Shrew* ii 1 294
Is there no military policy, how virgins might blow up men? *All's Well* i 1 132
Redeem it by some laudable attempt either of valour or policy *T. Night* iii 2 31
Policy I hate: I had as lief be a Brownist as a politician . . iii 2 33
Smacks it not something of the policy? . . . . . *K. John* ii 1 396
That were some love but little policy . . . . . *Richard II.* v 1 84
Never did base and rotten policy Colour her working with such deadly wounds . . . . 1 *Hen. IV.* i 3 108
It proceeds from policy, not love . . . . . 2 *Hen. IV.* iv 1 148
Turn him to any cause of policy, The Gordian knot of it he will unloose, Familiar as his garter . . . . *Hen. V.* i 1 45
And our nation lose The name of hardiness and policy . . . i 2 220
And with pale policy Seek to divert the English purposes . ii Prol. 14
The gates of Rouen, Through which our policy must make a breach 1 *Hen. VI.* iii 2 2
To say the truth, it is your policy To save your subjects . . v 4 159
Did my brother Bedford toil his wits, To keep by policy what Henry got? . . . . 2 *Hen. VI.* i 1 84
Me seemeth then it is no policy, Respecting what a rancorous mind he bears . . . . iii 1 23
That he should die is worthy policy . . . . . . iii 1 235
In my mind, that were no policy . . . . . . iii 1 238
With all his far-fet policy . . . . iii 1 293
By devilish policy art thou grown great . . . . . iv 1 83
With powerful policy strengthen themselves . . . . 3 *Hen. VI.* i 2 58
'Tis but his policy to counterfeit . . . . ii 6 65
It is his policy To haste thus fast . . . . iv 2 24
Plague of your policy! . . . . *Hen. VIII.* iii 2 259
They tax our policy, and call it cowardice . . . *Troi. and Cres.* i 3 197
I'll play the hunter for thy life With all my force, pursuit and policy iv 1 18
The policy of those crafty swearing rascals . . . . . v 4 10
They set me up, in policy, that mongrel cur . . . . . v 4 14
And policy grows into an ill opinion . . . . . . v 4 18
I have heard you say, Honour and policy, like unsever'd friends, I' the war do grow together . . . . *Coriolanus* iii 2 42
Which, for your best ends, You adopt your policy . . . . iii 2 48
Desperation Is all the policy, strength and defence, That Rome can make . . . . iv 6 127
'Tis policy and stratagem must do That you affect . . *T. Andron.* ii 1 104
Wherefore didst thou this?—O Lord, sir, 'tis a deed of policy . iv 2 148
For policy sits above conscience . . . . . . *T. of Athens* iii 2 94
Or else this brain of mine Hunts not the trail of policy so sure As it hath used to do . . . . *Hamlet* ii 2 47
This policy and reverence of age makes the world bitter to the best of our times; keeps our fortunes from us . . . . . *Lear* i 2 48
A punishment more in policy than in malice . . . . *Othello* ii 3 274
That policy may either last so long, Or feed upon such nice and waterish diet . . . . iii 3 14
Out of her impatience, which not wanted Shrewdness of policy too *Ant. and Cleo.* ii 2 69
The policy of that purpose made more in the marriage than the love . ii 6 126
Polished. O polish'd perturbation! golden care! . . 2 *Hen. IV.* iv 5 23
Politic. Am I politic? am I subtle? am I a Machiavel? . *Mer. Wives* iii 1 103
So politic a state of evil that they will not admit any good part *Much Ado* v 2 63
I have neither the scholar's melancholy, . . . nor the soldier's, which is ambitious, nor the lawyer's, which is politic . . *As Y. Like It* iv 1 14
I have been politic with my friend, smooth with mine enemy . . v 4 46
Not politic in the commonwealth of nature to preserve virginity *All's Well* i 1 137
As for you, interpreter, you must seem very politic . . . iv 1 24
I will be proud, I will read politic authors . . . . *T. Night* ii 5 175
With silence, nephew, be thou politic . . . . 1 *Hen. VI.* ii 5 101
Enrich'd With politic grave counsel . . . . . *Richard III.* ii 3 20
Bites his lip with a politic regard . . . . . *Troi. and Cres.* iii 3 254
The devil knew not what he did when he made man politic *T. of Athens* iii 3 29
Of such a nature is his politic love . . . . iii 3 35
A certain convocation of politic worms are e'en at him . . *Hamlet* iv 3 21
'Tis politic and safe to let him keep At point a hundred knights . *Lear* i 4 346
In strangeness stand no further off Than in a politic distance *Othello* iii 3 13
Politician. We are politicians . . . . *T. Night* ii 3 80
I had as lief be a Brownist as a politician . . . . . . iii 2 34
Stung with pismires, when I hear Of this vile politician . 1 *Hen. IV.* i 3 241
It might be the pate of a politician, which this ass now o'er-reaches *Ham.* v 1 86
Like a scurvy politician, seem To see the things thou dost not *Lear* iv 6 175
Politicly. Thus have I politicly begun my reign . *T. of Shrew* iv 1 191
'Tis politicly done, To send me packing with an host of men 2 *Hen. VI.* iii 1 341
Polixenes. I must be the poisoner Of good Polixenes . *W. Tale* i 2 353
'Tis Polixenes Has made thee swell thus . . . . . . ii 1 61
You have mistook, my lady, Polixenes for Leontes . . . . ii 1 82
Camillo and Polixenes Laugh at me, make their pastime at my sorrow . ii 3 23
Polixenes. This brat is none of mine; It is the issue of Polixenes *W. Tale* ii 3 93
Arraigned of high treason, in committing adultery with Polixenes . iii 2 15
Sir, before Polixenes Came to your court, how I was in your grace . iii 2 47
For Polixenes, With whom I am accused, I do confess I loved him as in honour he required . . . . iii 2 62
You had a bastard by Polixenes, And I but dream'd it . . . iii 2 84
Hermione is chaste; Polixenes blameless; Camillo a true subject. . iii 2 133
I'll reconcile me to Polixenes, New woo my queen, recall the good Camillo . . . . iii 2 156
I chose Camillo for the minister to poison My friend Polixenes . . iii 2 162
That thou betray'dst Polixenes, 'twas nothing; That did but show thee, of a fool, inconstant And damnable ingrateful . . . . . . iii 2 186
This being indeed the issue Of King Polixenes, it should here be laid . iii 3 44
One that gives out himself Prince Florizel, Son of Polixenes . . v 1 86
Poll. The muster-file, rotten and sound, upon my life, amounts not to fifteen thousand poll . . . . *All's Well* iv 3 190
Look, whether the withered elder hath not his poll clawed like a parrot 2 *Hen. IV.* ii 4 282
We are the greater poll, and in true fear They gave us our demands *Cor.* iii 1 134
A catalogue Of all the voices that we have procured Set down by the poll iii 3 10
His beard was as white as snow, All flaxen was his poll . . *Hamlet* iv 5 196
Poll-axe. Your lion, that holds his poll-axe sitting on a close-stool *L. L. L.* v 2 580
Polled. Mow all down before him, and leave his passage polled *Coriolanus* iv 5 215
Pollusion. I say, the pollusion holds in the exchange . . *L. L. Lost* iv 2 46
Polluted. You, that are polluted with your lusts . . . 1 *Hen. VI.* v 4 43
They are polluted offerings, more abhorr'd Than spotted livers *T. and C.* v 3 17
Pollution. Her body stoop To such abhorr'd pollution *Meas. for Meas.* ii 4 183
Nature with a beauteous wall Doth oft close in pollution . . *T. Night* i 2 49
Polonius. Have you your father's leave? What says Polonius? *Hamlet* i 2 57
Hamlet in madness hath Polonius slain . . . . iv 1 34
Now, Hamlet, where's Polonius?—At supper.—At supper! where? . iv 3 17
Where is Polonius?—In heaven; send thither to see . . . . iv 3 34
The people muddied, Thick and unwholesome in their thoughts and whispers, For good Polonius' death . . . . iv 5 83
Poltroon. Patience is for poltroons, such as he . . . 3 *Hen. VI.* i 1 62
Polydamas. The fierce Polydamas Hath beat down Menon *Troi. and Cres.* v 5 6
Polydore. This Polydore, The heir of Cymbeline and Britain . *Cymbeline* iii 3 86
You, Polydore, have proved best woodman and Are master of the feast iii 6 28
Would, Polydore, thou hadst not done't! though valour Becomes thee iv 2 155
Polydore, I love thee brotherly, but envy much Thou hast robb'd me of this deed . . . . iv 2 157
I'll stay Till hasty Polydore return, and bring him To dinner presently iv 2 165
My ingenious instrument! Hark, Polydore, it sounds! But what occasion? . . . . iv 2 187
Let us, Polydore, though now our voices Have got the mannish crack, sing him to the ground . . . . iv 2 235
This gentleman, whom I call Polydore, Most worthy prince, as yours, is true Guiderius . . . . v 5 357
Polyxena. And better would it fit Achilles much To throw down Hector than Polyxena . . . . *Troi. and Cres.* iii 3 208
Polyxenes is slain, Amphimachus and Thoas deadly hurt . . . v 5 11
Pomander. Not a ribbon, glass, pomander, brooch . . *W. Tale* iv 4 609
Pomegranate. You were beaten in Italy for picking a kernel out of a pomegranate . . . . *All's Well* ii 3 276
Pomegranate-tree. Nightly she sings on yon pomegranate-tree: Believe me, love, it was the nightingale . . . . . *Rom. and Jul.* iii 5 4
Pomewater. Ripe as the pomewater . . . . . . *L. L. Lost* iv 2 4
Pomfret. Here's a prophet, that I brought with me From forth the streets of Pomfret . . . . *K. John* iv 2 148
You must to Pomfret, not unto the Tower . . . . *Richard II.* v 1 52
'I would thou wert the man That would divorce this terror from my heart;' Meaning the king at Pomfret . . . . v 4 10
With the blood Of fair King Richard, scraped from Pomfret stones 2 *Hen. IV.* i 1 205
To Pomfret; where, as all you know, Harmless Richard was murder'd 2 *Hen. VI.* ii 2 26
Lord Rivers and Lord Grey are sent to Pomfret . . *Richard III.* ii 4 42
His ancient knot of dangerous adversaries To-morrow are let blood at Pomfret-castle . . . . iii 1 183
Your enemies, The kindred of the queen, must die at Pomfret . . iii 2 50
The lords at Pomfret, when they rode from London, Were jocund. . iii 2 85
Your friends at Pomfret, they do need the priest . . . . iii 2 115
O Pomfret, Pomfret! O thou bloody prison, Fatal and ominous to noble peers! . . . . iii 3 9
Triumphing at mine enemies, How they at Pomfret bloodily were butcher'd . . . . iii 4 92
Let me sit heavy on thy soul to-morrow, Rivers, that died at Pomfret! v 3 140
Pomgarnet. Look down into the Pomgarnet, Ralph . . 1 *Hen. IV.* ii 4 42
Pommel. The pommel of Cæsar's falchion . . . . *L. L. Lost* v 2 618
Pomp. To love, to wealth, to pomp, I pine and die . . . . i 1 31
The pale companion is not for our pomp . . . . *M. N. Dream* i 1 15
I will wed thee in another key, With pomp, with triumph . . . i 1 19
Brothers in exile, Hath not old custom made this life more sweet Than that of painted pomp? . . . . *As Y. Like It* ii 1 3
I am for the house with the narrow gate, which I take to be too little for pomp to enter. . . . . *All's Well* iv 5 54
Not for Bohemia, nor the pomp that may Be thereat glean'd . *W. Tale* iv 4 499
To this unlook'd for, unprepared pomp . . . . . *K. John* ii 1 560
Shall braying trumpets and loud churlish drums, Clamours of hell, be measures to our pomp? . . . . iii 1 304
To be possess'd with double pomp, To guard a title that was rich before iv 2 9
Adverse foreigners affright my towns With dreadful pomp of stout invasion! . . . . iv 2 173
Confusion waits, As doth a raven on a sick-fall'n beast, The imminent decay of wrested pomp . . . . iv 3 154
There the antic sits, Scoffing his state and grinning at his pomp *Rich. II.* iii 2 163
All pomp and majesty I do forswear; My manors, rents, revenues I forego iv 1 211
Whence, set forth in pomp, She came adorned hither like sweet May . v 1 78
The tide of pomp That beats upon the high shore of this world *Hen. V.* iv 1 281
I will slay myself, For living idly here in pomp and ease . 1 *Hen. VI.* i 1 142
To think upon my pomp shall be my hell . . . . 2 *Hen. VI.* ii 4 41
What is pomp, rule, reign, but earth and dust? . . . 3 *Hen. VI.* v 2 27
Till this time pomp was single, but now married . . . *Hen. VIII.* i 1 15
Only to show his pomp as well in France As here at home . . . i 1 163
Still growing in a majesty and pomp, the which To leave a thousand-fold more bitter than 'Tis sweet at first to acquire . . . . . ii 3 7
Much better She ne'er had known pomp . . . . ii 3 13
Vain pomp and glory of this world, I hate ye: I feel my heart new open'd . . . . iii 2 365
But safer triumph is this funeral pomp . . . . . *T. Andron.* i 1 176

Pomp. Like madness is the glory of this life, As this pomp shows *T. of Athens* i 2 140
What need these feasts, pomps and vain-glories? . . . i 2 249
To have his pomp and all what state compounds But only painted . iv 2 35
Willing misery Outlives incertain pomp, is crown'd before . iv 3 243
No, let the candied tongue lick absurd pomp . . . *Hamlet* iii 2 65
Take physic, pomp; Expose thyself to feel what wretches feel . *Lear* iii 4 33
And all quality, Pride, pomp and circumstance of glorious war! *Othello* iii 3 354
Behold, How pomp is follow'd! mine will now be yours; And, should we shift estates, yours would be mine . . . *Ant. and Cleo.* v 2 151
Pompæ. A wreath of chivalry; The word, 'Me pompæ provexit apex' *Pericles* ii 2 30
Pompeius. Sextus Pompeius Hath given the dare to Cæsar *Ant. and Cleo.* i 2 190
Sextus Pompeius Makes his approaches to the port of Rome . . i 3 45
Having in Sicily Sextus Pompeius spoil'd. . . . . iii 6 25
Pompey. What's your name, Master tapster?—Pompey.—What else?—Bum, sir . . . . . . *Meas. for Meas.* ii 1 225
How would you live, Pompey? by being a bawd? . . . ii 1 236
If you live to see this come to pass, say Pompey told you so . . ii 1 256
Pompey, I shall beat you to your tent, and prove a shrewd Cæsar to you ii 1 262
Noble Pompey! What, at the wheels of Cæsar? art thou led in triumph? . . . . iii 2 45
Art going to prison, Pompey?—Yes, faith, sir.—Why, 'tis not amiss, Pompey . . . . iii 2 63
Farewell, good Pompey. Commend me to the prison, Pompey: you will turn good husband now, Pompey . . . . iii 2 72
I hope, sir, your good worship will be my bail.—No, indeed, will I not, Pompey . . . . iii 2 77
I will pray, Pompey, to increase your bondage . . . Adieu, trusty Pompey . . . . iii 2 78
I Pompey am,— You lie, you are not he.—I Pompey am *L. L. Lost* v 2 550
I Pompey am, Pompey surnamed the Big,— The Great.—It is, 'Great,' sir . . . . v 2 553
If your ladyship would say, 'Thanks, Pompey,' I had done.—Great thanks, great Pompey . . . . v 2 559
My hat to a halfpenny, Pompey proves the best Worthy . . . v 2 563
Then shall Hector be . . . hanged for Pompey that is dead by him . v 2 688
Greater than great, great, great, great Pompey! Pompey the Huge! v 2 692
Hector trembles.—Pompey is moved. More Ates, more Ates! stir them on! . . . . v 2 694
Do you not see Pompey is uncasing for the combat? . . . v 2 707
You may not deny it: Pompey hath made the challenge . . . v 2 712
There is no tiddle taddle nor pibble pabble in Pompey's camp *Hen. V.* iv 1 72
You hard hearts, you cruel men of Rome, Knew you not Pompey? *J. Cæsar* i 1 42
Have sat The live-long day, with patient expectation, To see great Pompey . . . . i 1 47
Now strew flowers in his way That comes in triumph over Pompey's blood? . . . . i 1 56
They stay for me In Pompey's porch . . . . . i 3 126
All this done, Repair to Pompey's porch, where you shall find us . i 3 147
That done, repair to Pompey's theatre . . . . . i 3 152
Ligarius doth bear Cæsar hard, Who rated him for speaking well of Pompey . . . . ii 1 216
That now on Pompey's basis lies along No worthier than the dust . iii 1 115
At the base of Pompey's statua, Which all the while ran blood, great Cæsar fell . . . . iii 2 192
As Pompey was, am I compell'd to set Upon one battle all our liberties v 1 75
The condemn'd Pompey, Rich in his father's honour *Ant. and Cleo.* i 3 49
Pompey is strong at sea; And it appears he is beloved of those That only have fear'd Cæsar . . . . i 4 36
Pompey's name strikes more Than could his war resisted . . i 4 54
Assemble we immediate council: Pompey Thrives in our idleness . i 4 75
Great Pompey Would stand and make his eyes grow in my brow . i 5 31
Know, worthy Pompey, That what they do delay, they not deny . ii 1 2
If you borrow one another's love for the instant, you may, when you hear no more words of Pompey, return it again . . . ii 2 105
I did not think to draw my sword 'gainst Pompey . . . ii 2 156
Of us must Pompey presently be sought, Or else he seeks out us . ii 2 161
Thou canst not fear us, Pompey, with thy sails . . . ii 6 24
Your mother came to Sicily and did find Her welcome friendly.—I have heard it, Pompey . . . . ii 6 47
Let's Draw lots who shall begin.—That will I, Pompey . . . ii 6 62
Thy father, Pompey, would ne'er have made this treaty . . . ii 6 84
Pompey doth this day laugh away his fortune.—If he do, sure, he cannot weep't back again . . . . ii 6 109
Pompey, a word.—Say in mine ear: what is't? . . . . ii 7 42
Will this description satisfy him?—With the health that Pompey gives him . . . . ii 7 57
Hast thou drunk well?—No, Pompey, I have kept me from the cup . ii 7 72
This health to Lepidus!—Bear him ashore. I'll pledge it for him, Pompey . . . . ii 7 91
They have dispatch'd with Pompey, he is gone; The other three are sealing . . . . iii 2 2
Cæsar is sad; and Lepidus, Since Pompey's feast, as Menas says, is troubled With the green sickness . . . . . iii 2 5
He hath waged New wars 'gainst Pompey; made his will . . iii 4 4
Cæsar and Lepidus have made wars upon Pompey.—This is old . iii 5 5
Cæsar, having made use of him in the wars 'gainst Pompey, presently denied him rivality . . . . iii 5 8
Not resting here, accuses him of letters he had formerly wrote to Pompey . . . . iii 5 11
And threats the throat of that his officer That murder'd Pompey . iii 5 20
In Cæsar's fleet Are those that often have 'gainst Pompey fought . iii 7 38
I found you as a morsel cold upon Dead Cæsar's trencher; nay, you were a fragment Of Cneius Pompey's . . . . iii 13 118
Pompey the Great. In the beastliest sense you are Pompey the Great *Meas. for Meas.* ii 1 230
Because of his great limb or joint, shall pass Pompey the Great *L. L. Lost* v 1 136
Take the pains but to examine the wars of Pompey the Great *Hen. V.* iv 1 70
Savage islanders [stabbed] Pompey the Great . . *2 Hen. VI.* iv 1 138
Our slippery people . . . begin to throw Pompey the Great and all his dignities Upon his son. . . . . *Ant. and Cleo.* i 2 195
Pompion the Great. I am, as they say, but to parfect one man in one poor man, Pompion the Great . . . *L. L. Lost* v 2 503
It pleased them to think me worthy of Pompion the Great . . v 2 507
Pompous. And thrown into neglect the pompous court . *As Y. Like It* v 4 188
To undeck the pompous body of a king . . . *Richard II.* iv 1 250
The o'er-fed breast Of this most pompous marriage-feast *Pericles* iii Gower 4
Pond. Is yet a devil; His filth within being cast, he would appear A pond as deep as hell . . . . *Meas. for Meas.* iii 1 94
Pond. Men whose visages Do cream and mantle like a standing pond *Mer. of Venice* i 1 89
And his pond fish'd by his next neighbour . . . . *W. Tale* i 2 195
It had froze them up, As fish are in a pond . . *2 Hen. IV.* i 1 200
But, you know, strange fowl light upon neighbouring ponds . *Cymbeline* i 4 98
Ponder. This tempest will not give me leave to ponder On things would hurt me more . . . . *Lear* iii 4 24
Ponderous. To draw with idle spiders' strings Most ponderous and substantial things! . . . . . *Meas. for Meas.* iii 2 290
If your more ponderous and settled project May suffer alteration *W. Tale* iv 4 535
Why the sepulchre . . . Hath oped his ponderous and marble jaws *Ham.* i 4 50
Poniard. She speaks poniards, and every word stabs . *Much Ado* ii 1 255
Betake thee to thy faith, for seventeen poniards are at thy bosom *All's W.* iv 1 83
Stab poniards in our flesh till all were told, The words would add more anguish than the wounds . . . . . . *3 Hen. VI.* ii 1 98
Give me thy poniard; you shall know, my boys, Your mother's hand shall right your mother's wrong . . . . *T. Andron.* ii 3 120
Six French rapiers and poniards, with their assigns . . *Hamlet* v 2 157
Pont. King Malchus of Arabia; King of Pont . . . *Ant. and Cleo.* iii 6 72
Pontic. Like to the Pontic sea, Whose icy current and compulsive course Ne'er feels retiring ebb . . . . . *Othello* iii 3 453
Pontifical. My presence, like a robe pontifical, Ne'er seen but wonder'd at *1 Hen. IV.* iii 2 56
Ponton. A prisoner Call'd the brave Lord Ponton de Santrailles *1 Hen. VI.* i 4 28
Pooh. Affection! pooh! you speak like a green girl . . *Hamlet* i 3 101
Pool. I left them I' the filthy-mantled pool . . . *Tempest* iv 1 182
Ay, but to lose our bottles in the pool . . . . . iv 1 208
Pole!—Pool! Sir Pool! lord! Ay, kennel, puddle, sink *2 Hen. VI.* iv 1 70
Drinks the green mantle of the standing pool . . . *Lear* iii 4 139
I' the world's volume Our Britain seems as of it, but not in't; In a great pool a swan's nest . . . . . . *Cymbeline* iii 4 142
Poop. Thou art our admiral, thou bearest the lantern in the poop *1 Hen. IV.* iii 3 29
The poop was beaten gold; Purple the sails . . *Ant. and Cleo.* ii 2 197
Pooped. Ay, she quickly pooped him; she made him roast-meat for worms . . . . *Pericles* iv 2 25
Poor. A most poor credulous monster! . . . . *Tempest* ii 2 149
Here is writ 'love-wounded Proteus.' Poor wounded name! *T. G. of Ver.* i 2 114
Poor forlorn Proteus, passionate Proteus, To the sweet Julia . . i 2 124
And high and low beguiles the rich and poor . . . *Mer. Wives* i 3 95
He wooes both high and low, both rich and poor, Both young and old . ii 1 117
Poor cuckoldly knave! I know him not: yet I wrong him to call him poor . . . . ii 2 283
If . . . the poor unvirtuous fat knight should be any further afflicted . iv 2 232
Stones whose rates are either rich or poor As fancy values them *M. for M.* ii 2 150
If thou art rich, thou'rt poor . . . . iii 1 25
Most uprighteously do a poor wronged lady a merited benefit . . iii 1 206
These poor informal women are no more But instruments of some more mightier member That sets them on . . . . . v 1 236
Those, for their parents were exceeding poor, I bought . *Com. of Errors* i 1 57
I am not mad.—O, that thou wert not, poor distressed soul! . . iv 4 62
Wherefore throng you hither?—To fetch my poor distracted husband hence . . . . v 1 39
Alas, poor hurt fowl! now will he creep into sedges . . *Much Ado* ii 1 209
To your huge store Wise things seem foolish and rich things but poor *L. L. Lost* v 2 378
If it be preferment To leave a rich Jew's service, to become The follower of so poor a gentleman . . . . . *Mer. of Venice* ii 2 157
The poor rude world Hath not her fellow. . . . . . . iii 5 87
Bequeathed me by will but poor a thousand crowns . *As Y. Like It* i 1 2
A poor unworthy brother of yours . . . . i 1 36
I'll put myself in poor and mean attire . . . . . . i 3 113
The poor dappled fools, Being native burghers of this desert city . ii 1 22
To the which place a poor sequester'd stag . . . Did come to languish . ii 1 33
Wherefore do you look Upon that poor and broken bankrupt there? . ii 1 57
Esteemed him No better than a poor and loathsome beggar *T. of Shrew* Ind. 1 123
Our purses shall be proud, our garments poor . . . . iv 3 173
'Tis not so well that I am poor, though many of the rich are damned *All's Well* i 3 18
My friends were poor, but honest; so's my love . . . . i 3 201
How shall they credit A poor unlearned virgin? . . . . i 3 246
Has sat i' the stocks all night, poor gallant knave . . . iv 3 117
A truth's a truth, the rogues are marvellous poor . . . . iv 3 179
He looks like a poor, decayed, ingenious, foolish, rascally knave . v 2 24
O world, how apt the poor are to be proud! . . . *T. Night* iii 1 138
And me, poor lowly maid, Most goddess-like prank'd up . *W. Tale* iv 4 9
And the fire-robed god, Golden Apollo, a poor humble swain . . iv 4 30
Though death be poor, it ends a mortal woe . . . *Richard II.* ii 1 152
Evermore thanks, the exchequer of the poor . . . . . ii 3 65
Such poor, such bare, such lewd, such mean attempts . *1 Hen. IV.* iii 2 13
Alas, he is poor; he hath nothing.—How! poor? look upon his face . iii 3 88
They are exceeding poor and bare, too beggarly . . . . iv 2 75
A poor unminded outlaw sneaking home . . . . . . iv 3 58
While his blood was poor, Upon the naked shore at Ravenspurgh . . iv 3 76
Deny it, if thou canst.—My lord, this is a poor mad soul *2 Hen. IV.* ii 1 113
You poor, base, rascally, cheating, lack-linen mate! . . . ii 4 133
Have I, in my poor and old motion, the expedition of thought? . iv 3 37
A stomach and no food; Such are the poor, in health . . . iv 4 106
Poor mechanic porters crowding in Their heavy burdens . *Hen. V.* i 2 200
Get you therefore hence, Poor miserable wretches, to your death . . ii 2 178
Poor we may call them in their native lords . . . . . iii 5 26
For our losses, his exchequer is too poor . . . . . iii 6 138
The poor condemned English, Like sacrifices, by their watchful fires Sit patiently . . . . iv Prol. 22
Some crying for a surgeon, some upon their wives left poor behind them iv 1 146
That's a perilous shot out of an elder-gun, that a poor and a private displeasure can do against a monarch! . . . . . iv 1 210
Five hundred poor I have in yearly pay . . . . . iv 1 315
Do but behold yon poor and starved band . . . . . iv 2 16
Poor and mangled Peace, Dear nurse of arts, plenties and joyful births v 2 34
Notwithstanding the poor and untempering effect of my visage . v 2 240
If I were covetous, ambitious or perverse, As he will have me, how am I so poor? . . . . *1 Hen. VI.* iii 1 30
Base And misbegotten blood I spill of thine, Mean and right poor . iv 6 23
Yet is he poor, And our nobility will scorn the match . . . v 3 95
Disgrace not so your king, That he should be so abject, base and poor . v 5 49
Sufficeth that I have maintains my state And sends the poor well pleased from my gate . . . . *2 Hen. VI.* iv 10 25
Took odds to combat a poor famish'd man . . . . . iv 10 47
Poor harmless lambs abide their enmity . . . . *3 Hen. VI.* ii 5 75

Poor. Poor key-cold figure of a holy king! *Richard III.* i 2 5
If thy poor devoted suppliant may But beg one favour at thy gracious hand . . . . . i 2 207
Poor painted queen, vain flourish of my fortune! . i 3 241
Poor mortal living ghost, Woe's scene, world's shame, grave's due by life usurp'd . iv 4 26
Airy succeeders of intestate joys, Poor breathing orators of miseries! . iv 4 129
What can be their business With me, a poor weak woman? *Hen. VIII.* iii 1 20
How may I deserve it, That am a poor and humble subject to you? . v 3 166
Am I poor of late? 'Tis certain, greatness, once fall'n out with fortune, Must fall out with men too . . *Troi. and Cres.* iii 3 74
What things again most dear in the esteem And poor in worth! . . iii 3 130
More piercing statutes daily, to chain up and restrain the poor *Coriolanus* i 1 87
In what enormity is Marcius poor in, that you two have not in abundance? . . . . ii 1 18
He's poor in no one fault, but stored with all.—Especially in pride . ii 1 20
'Twas never my desire yet to trouble the poor with begging . ii 3 76
To my poor unworthy notice, He mock'd us when he begg'd our voices ii 3 166
Poor harmless fly! . . . . . *T. Andron.* iii 2 63
Although the cheer be poor, 'Twill fill your stomachs . v 3 28
Only poor, That when she dies with beauty dies her store *Rom. and Jul.* i 1 221
Come hither, man. I see that thou art poor: Hold, there is forty ducats v 1 58
The world affords no law to make thee rich; Then be not poor, but break it . . . . v 1 74
Poor living corse, closed in a dead man's tomb! . . v 2 30
When he was poor, Imprison'd, and in scarcity of friends *T. of Athens* ii 2 233
He's poor, and that's revenge enough . . . iii 4 62
Let me be recorded by the righteous gods, I am as poor as you . iv 2 5
Not one word more: Thus part we rich in sorrow, parting poor . iv 2 29
Poor honest lord, brought low by his own heart, Undone by goodness! iv 2 37
And thatch your poor thin roofs With burthens of the dead . . iv 3 144
A poor unmanly melancholy sprung From change of fortune . . iv 3 203
He likewise enriched poor straggling soldiers . . . v 1 7
When that the poor have cried, Cæsar hath wept . *J. Cæsar* iii 2 96
Now lies he there, And none so poor to do him reverence . iii 2 125
Show you sweet Cæsar's wounds, poor poor dumb mouths, And bid them speak for me . . . . . . iii 2 229
All our service In every point twice done and then done double Were poor and single business to contend Against those honours *Macbeth* i 6 16
To offer up a weak poor innocent lamb To appease an angry god . iv 3 16
Upon a wretch whose natural gifts were poor To those of mine! *Hamlet* i 5 51
What so poor a man as Hamlet is May do, to express his love and friending to you, God willing, shall not lack . . . . . i 5 185
Beggar that I am, I am even poor in thanks; but I thank you . ii 2 280
To the noble mind Rich gifts wax poor when givers prove unkind . iii 1 101
Why should the poor be flatter'd? . . . . iii 2 64
The poor advanced makes friends of enemies . . . iii 2 215
A love that makes breath poor, and speech unable . *Lear* i 1 61
Most rich, being poor; Most choice, forsaken; and most loved, despised! i 1 253
A very honest-hearted fellow, and as poor as the king.—If thou be as poor for a subject as he is for a king, thou art poor enough . i 4 21
Low farms, Poor pelting villages, sheep-cotes, and mills . ii 3 18
Fortune, that arrant whore, Ne'er turns the key to the poor . . ii 4 53
Here I stand, your slave, A poor, infirm, weak, and despised old man . iii 2 20
Poor naked wretches, wheresoe'er you are . . . iii 4 28
Unaccommodated man is no more but such a poor, bare, forked animal iii 4 112
Ah, that good Kent! He said it would be thus, poor banish'd man! . iii 4 169
'Tis poor mad Tom.—And worse I may be yet . . iv 1 28
The poor distressed Lear's i' the town . . . iv 3 40
What thing was that Which parted from you?—A poor unfortunate beggar iv 6 68
If e'er your grace had speech with man so poor . . v 1 38
I have very poor and unhappy brains for drinking . *Othello* ii 3 35
How poor are they that have not patience! . . . ii 3 376
He that filches from me my good name Robs me of that which not enriches him And makes me poor indeed . . . iii 3 161
Poor and content is rich and rich enough, But riches fineless is as poor as winter To him that ever fears he shall be poor . . iii 3 172
O, that the slave had forty thousand lives! One is too poor, too weak iii 3 443
None our parts so poor, But was a race of heaven . *Ant. and Cleo.* i 3 36
Mine honesty Shall not make poor my greatness . . ii 2 93
Though thou think me poor, I am the man Will give thee all the world ii 7 70
An argument that he is pluck'd, when hither He sends so poor a pinion of his wing . . . . iii 12 4
It is my birth-day: I had thought to have held it poor . . iii 13 186
What poor an instrument May do a noble deed! he brings me liberty v 2 236
Poor venomous fool, Be angry, and dispatch . . . v 2 308
Hath referr'd herself Unto a poor but worthy gentleman . *Cymbeline* i 1 7
The thanks I give Is telling you that I am poor of thanks . ii 3 94
His shipping—Poor ignorant baubles!—on our terrible seas, Like egg-shells . . . . iii 1 27
For the dish Poor tributary rivers as sweet fish . . iv 2 36
Poor sick Fidele! I'll willingly to him . . . iv 2 166
I never saw Such noble fury in so poor a thing . . v 5 8

Poor abuses. The poor abuses of the time want countenance *1 Hen. IV.* i 2 174

Poor accoutrements. Could I repair what she will wear in me, As I can change these poor accoutrements . . . *T. of Shrew* iii 2 121

Poor agent. O world! world! world! thus is the poor agent despised! *Troi. and Cres.* v 10 36

Poor allottery. Give me the poor allottery my father left me by testament . . . . *As Y. Like It* i 1 76

Poor Andromache shrills her dolours forth! . *Troi. and Cres.* v 3 84

Poor Anne. Hear the lamentations of poor Anne . *Richard III.* i 2 9

Poor Antonio. It will go hard with poor Antonio . *Mer. of Venice* iii 2 292

Poor Antony. They have earn'd the waste. Poor Antony! *Ant. and Cleo.* iv 1 16

Poor ape. Alas, poor ape, how thou sweatest! . . . *2 Hen. IV.* ii 4 233

Poor as Job. As poor as Job?—And as wicked as his wife? *Mer. Wives* v 5 164
I am as poor as Job, my lord, but not so patient . *2 Hen. IV.* i 2 144

Poor babe. Come on, poor babe: Some powerful spirit instruct the kites and ravens To be thy nurses! . . . *W. Tale* ii 3 185
Since fate . . Hath made thy person for the thrower-out Of my poor babe . . . . iii 3 30

Poor bankrupt. O, break, my heart! poor bankrupt, break at once! *Rom. and Jul.* iii 2 57

Poor Barbara. I have much to do, But to go hang my head all at one side, And sing it like poor Barbara . . . *Othello* iv 3 33

Poor bark. All these the enemies to our poor bark . *3 Hen. VI.* v 4 28
Like a poor bark, of sails and tackling reft, Rush all to pieces *Rich. III.* iv 4 233

Poor Bassianus. This deep pit, poor Bassianus' grave . *T. Andron.* ii 3 240
Poor Bassianus here lies murdered . . . . ii 3 263

Poor bastards. 'Tis not our bringing up of poor bastards . *Pericles* iv 2 15

Poor beetle. And the poor beetle, that we tread upon, In corporal sufferance finds a pang as great As when a giant dies *Meas. for Meas.* iii 1 79

Poor beggar. Like a poor beggar, raileth on the rich . *K. John* ii 1 592

Poor beseeming. I am, sir, The soldier that did company these three In poor beseeming . . . . *Cymbeline* v 5 409

Poor bird! thou'ldst never fear the net nor lime, The pitfall nor the gin.—Why should I, mother? Poor birds they are not set for *Macb.* iv 2 34

Poor body. Tell me thy reason why thou wilt marry.—My poor body, madam, requires it . . . . . . *All's Well* i 3 30
Where, wretches, their poor bodies Must lie and fester . *Hen. V.* iv 3 87

Poor Bolingbroke. Nor the prevention of poor Bolingbroke About his marriage . . . . *Richard II.* ii 1 167

Poor boy. Here's my son, sir, a poor boy,— Not a poor boy, sir, but the rich Jew's man . . . . . *Mer. of Venice* ii 2 129
His mother shames him so, poor boy, he weeps . . *K. John* ii 1 166
Strike him, Aumerle. Poor boy, thou art amazed . *Richard II.* v 2 85
Poor boy! he smiles, methinks, as who should say, Had death been French, then death had died to-day . . . *1 Hen. VI.* iv 7 27
Let me live.—In vain thou speak'st, poor boy . . *3 Hen. VI.* i 3 21
I, Dædalus; my poor boy, Icarus; Thy father, Minos . . v 6 21
Hath my poor boy done aught but well, Whose face I never saw? *Cymb.* v 4 35

Poor brother. And that's my pith of business 'Twixt you and your poor brother . . . . *Meas. for Meas.* i 4 71
To try her gracious fortune with Lord Angelo For her poor brother's pardon . . . . v 1 77

Poor Brutus, with himself at war, Forgets the shows of love . *J. Cæsar* i 2 46

Poor Buckingham. I am the shadow of poor Buckingham . *Hen. VIII.* i 1 224

Poor caitiff. Alas, poor caitiff!—Look, how he laughs already! *Othello* iv 1 109

Poor Cassio. Let's go see poor Cassio dress'd . . . . v 1 124

Poor castle. Vouchsafe To visit her poor castle . . *1 Hen. VI.* ii 2 41

Poor cat. Letting 'I dare not' wait upon 'I would,' Like the poor cat i' the adage . . . . *Macbeth* i 7 45

Poor cell. Master of a full poor cell . . . . *Tempest* i 2 20
I invite your highness and your train To my poor cell . . v 1 301

Poor cheek. Hath homely age the alluring beauty took From my poor cheek? . . . . *Com. of Errors* ii 1 90

Poor chicken. So the poor chicken should be sure of death *2 Hen. VI.* iii 1 251

Poor child. Thy sins are visited in this poor child . *K. John* ii 1 179
I envy at their liberty, And will again commit them to their bonds, Because my poor child is a prisoner . . . . . iii 4 75
I'll go with thee, And find the inheritance of this poor child . iv 2 97

Poor children. O, spare my guiltless wife and my poor children! *Rich. III.* i 4 72

Poor chin! many a wart is richer . . . *Troi. and Cres.* i 2 155

Poor citizens. We are accounted poor citizens, the patricians good *Coriol.* i 1 15

Poor city. There is no more mercy in him than there is milk in a male tiger; that shall our poor city find . . . . . v 4 31

Poor Clarence! is it for a wife That thou art malcontent? *3 Hen. VI.* iv 1 59
Poor Clarence did forsake his father, Warwick . *Richard III.* i 3 135
Who pronounced The bitter sentence of poor Clarence' death? . i 4 191
Come, Hastings, help me to my closet. Oh, poor Clarence! . ii 1 133
Poor Clarence, by thy guile betrayed to death! . . v 3 133

Poor Claudio! There is no remedy . . . . *Meas. for Meas.* ii 1 299
And dispose For henceforth of poor Claudio . . . *Much Ado* v 1 304

Poor Clifford! how I scorn his worthless threats! . *3 Hen. VI.* i 1 101

Poor company. From these that my poor company detest *M. N. Dream* iii 2 434

Poor competitor. Let me in.—Tribunes, and me, a poor competitor *T. An.* i 1 63

Poor compounds that thou mayst not sell . . *Rom. and Jul.* v 1 82

Poor conditions. Your oaths Are words and poor conditions *All's Well* iv 2 30

Poor Cordelia. Then poor Cordelia! And yet not so . . *Lear* i 1 78

Poor corpse. Not a friend greet My poor corpse . . *T. Night* ii 4 63

Poor country. Bleed, bleed, poor country! Great tyranny! *Macbeth* iv 3 31
Yet my poor country Shall have more vices than it had before . iv 3 46

Poor cousin. I am the king's poor cousin, sir . . *2 Hen. IV.* ii 2 125

Poor craftsmen. Wooing poor craftsmen with the craft of smiles And patient underbearing of his fortune . . . . *Richard II.* i 4 28

Poor creature. I do now remember the poor creature, small beer *2 Hen. IV.* ii 2 13
Thy niece and I, poor creatures, want our hands . *T. Andron.* iii 2 5
Mildews the white wheat, and hurts the poor creature of earth . *Lear* iii 4 124

Poor cur. Brach Merriman, the poor cur is emboss'd . *T. of Shrew* Ind. 1 17

Poor deer. As if for praise alone now seek to spill The poor deer's blood, that my heart means no ill . . . . . *L. L. Lost* iv 1 35
'Poor deer,' quoth he 'thou makest a testament As worldlings do' *As Y. Like It* ii 1 47

Poor descent. Falsehood, cowardice and poor descent, Three things that women highly hold in hate . . . . *T. G. of Ver.* iii 2 32

Poor Desdemona! I am glad thy father's dead . . *Othello* v 2 204

Poor discontents. That may please the eye Of fickle changelings and poor discontents . . . . *1 Hen. IV.* v 1 76

Poor disposer. Your poor disposer's sick . . *Troi. and Cres.* iii 1 101

Poor doing. I would it were hell-pains for thy sake, and my poor doing eternal . . . . *All's Well* ii 3 246

Poor drunkard. To make a wonder of a poor drunkard! . *Tempest* ii 2 170

Poor duke. I am the poor duke's constable . . *Meas. for Meas.* ii 1 47
Let not your worship think me the poor duke's officer . . ii 1 186
Alas, poor duke! the task he undertakes Is numbering sands *Rich. II.* ii 2 145

Poor duty. And what poor duty cannot do, noble respect Takes it in might, not merit . . . . *M. N. Dream* v 1 91

Poor earl. A poor earl's daughter is unequal odds, And therefore may be broke without offence . . . . . *1 Hen. VI.* v 5 34
Is not a dukedom, sir, a goodly gift?—Ay, by my faith, for a poor earl to give . . . . *3 Hen. VI.* iv 1 32

Poor Edward Bohun. I was lord high constable And Duke of Buckingham; now, poor Edward Bohun. . . . *Hen. VIII.* ii 1 103

Poor Egyptian. Whence are you?—A poor Egyptian yet *Ant. and Cleo.* v 1 52

Poor England. And make poor England weep in streams of blood! *Richard III.* v 5 37

Poor Enobarbus did Before thy face repent! . *Ant. and Cleo.* iv 9 9

Poor epitome. This is a poor epitome of yours . . *Coriolanus* v 3 68

Poor esquire. A poor esquire of this county . . *2 Hen. IV.* iii 2 63
Alexander Iden, that's my name; A poor esquire of Kent . *2 Hen. VI.* v 1 75

Poor eyes. Draws those heaven-moving pearls from his poor eyes *K. John* ii 1 169
I pour the helpless balm of my poor eyes . . . *Richard III.* i 2 13
All the tears that thy poor eyes let fall May run into that sink *T. An.* iii 2 18

Poor fallen man. I am a poor fall'n man . . . . *Hen. VIII.* iii 2 413

Poor fancy. Wishes and tears, poor fancy's followers . *M. N. Dream* i 1 155

Poor father. O my poor father! The heaven sets spies upon us *W. Tale* v 1 202
Ere those shoes were old With which she follow'd my poor father's body . . . . *Hamlet* i 2 148
And wast thou fain, poor father, To hovel thee with swine? . . *Lear* iv 7 38

Poor fellow. I am a poor fellow that would live . . . *Meas. for Meas.* ii 1 234
'Tis not unknown to you, madam, I am a poor fellow . . . *All's Well* i 3 15
I am a poor fellow, sir.—Why, be so still; here's nobody will steal that from thee . . . . *W. Tale* iv 4 644
Poor fellow, never joyed since the price of oats rose . . 1 *Hen. IV.* ii 1 13
Good God! why should they mock poor fellows thus? . . *Hen. V.* iv 3 92
And God in justice hath reveal'd to us The truth and innocence of this poor fellow . . . . 2 *Hen. VI.* ii 3 106
Poor females. Cupid is a knavish lad, Thus to make poor females mad *M. N. Dream* iii 2 441
Poor folks. Will poor folks lie, That have afflictions on them? *Cymbeline* iii 6 9
Poor fool. Alas, poor fool! why do I pity him That with his very heart despiseth me? . . . . *T. G. of Ver.* iv 4 98
I thank it, poor fool, it keeps on the windy side of care . *Much Ado* ii 1 326
Alas, poor fool, how have they baffled thee! . . . *T. Night* v 1 377
So many weeks ere the poor fools will ean . . . 3 *Hen. VI.* ii 5 36
Come, your hovel. Poor fool and knave, I have one part in my heart That's sorry yet for thee . . . . . . *Lear* iii 2 72
And my poor fool is hang'd! No, no, no life! . . . . v 3 305
Thus may poor fools Believe false teachers . . . *Cymbeline* iii 4 86
Poor four. A hundred upon poor four of us . . . 1 *Hen. IV.* ii 4 180
Poor fragment. It is some poor fragment, some slender ort of his remainder . . . . *T. of Athens* iv 3 400
Poor friend. And will you rent our ancient love asunder, To join with men in scorning your poor friend? . . *M. N. Dream* iii 2 216
What a life is this, That your poor friends must woo your company? *As Y. Like It* ii 7 10
Sir, I am a poor friend of yours, that loves you . . *All's Well* ii 2 45
Poor fry. Driving the poor fry before him . . . *Pericles* ii 1 34
Poor furniture. Neither art thou the worse For this poor furniture and mean array . . . . *T. of Shrew* iv 3 182
Poor gentleman. Yet I live like a poor gentleman born . *Mer. Wives* i 1 286
I have laboured for the poor gentleman . . . *Meas. for Meas.* iii 2 265
Now I remember me, They say, poor gentleman, he's much distract *T. N.* v 1 287
How the poor gentleman roared and the bear mocked him . *W. Tale* iii 3 102
Poor gentleman! his wrong doth equal mine . . . 1 *Hen. VI.* ii 5 22
I knew thou wouldst be his death. O, poor gentleman! *Troi. and Cres.* iv 2 91
Pray you, poor gentleman, take up some other station . *Coriolanus* iv 5 32
Burning shame Detains him from Cordelia.—Alack, poor gentleman! *Lear* iv 3 49
Poor gentlewoman! my master wrongs her much . *T. G. of Ver.* iv 4 146
But mark how heavily this befell to the poor gentlewoman *Meas. for Meas.* iii 1 227
Poor ghost. Alas, poor ghost!—Pity me not, but lend thy serious hearing To what I shall unfold . . . . . . *Hamlet* i 5 4
Remember thee! Ay, thou poor ghost, while memory holds a seat . i 5 96
Or we poor ghosts will cry To the shining synod of the rest . *Cymbeline* v 4 88
Poor girl. Bianca, stand aside. Poor girl! she weeps . *T. of Shrew* ii 1 24
Here's a letter come from yond poor girl.—Let me read. *Troi. and Cres.* v 3 99
Poor Gloucester! Lost he his other eye? . . . . *Lear* iv 2 80
Poor grain. 'Twas folly, for one poor grain or two, to leave unburnt, And still to nose the offence.—For one poor grain or two! I am one of those; his mother, wife, his child . . . *Coriolanus* v 1 27
Poor groom. I was a poor groom of thy stable, king . *Richard II.* v 5 72
Poor habiliments. My riches are these poor habiliments *T. G. of Ver.* iv 1 13
Poor Hamlet. His madness is poor Hamlet's enemy . *Hamlet* v 2 250
Poor hands. To have seen much and to have nothing, is to have rich eyes and poor hands . . . . . . *As Y. Like It* iv 1 25
Poor Harry of England! he longs not for the dawning as we do *Hen. V.* iii 7 140
Poor Hastings. Margaret, now thy heavy curse Is lighted on poor Hastings' wretched head! . . . . . *Richard III.* iii 4 95
Poor heart. In spite of your heart, I think; alas, poor heart! *Much Ado* v 2 69
He started one poor heart of mine in thee . . . *T. Night* v 1 63
My legs can keep no measure in delight, When my poor heart no measure keeps in grief . . . . *Richard II.* iii 4 8
Ah, poor heart! he is so shaked of a burning quotidian tertian *Hen. V.* ii 1 123
Even so thy breast encloseth my poor heart . . *Richard III.* i 2 205
Poor heart, adieu! I pity thy complaining . . . . iv 1 88
Alas, poor heart, that kiss is comfortless As frozen water *T. Andron.* iii 1 251
When thy poor heart beats with outrageous beating . . iii 2 13
Is my poor heart so for a kinsman vex'd . . *Rom. and Jul.* iii 5 96
Which the poor heart would fain deny, and dare not . *Macbeth* v 3 28
Let not the creaking of shoes nor the rustling of silks betray thy poor heart to woman . . . . *Lear* iii 4 98
Poor hen. She, poor hen, fond of no second brood, Has cluck'd thee to the wars . . . . *Coriolanus* v 3 162
Poor Henry. How shall poor Henry live? . . . . 3 *Hen. VI.* iii 3 214
You left poor Henry at the Bishop's palace . . . . v 1 45
Poor host. I request you To give my poor host freedom . *Coriolanus* i 9 87
Poor house. Rich honesty dwells like a miser, sir, in a poor house *A. Y. L. It* v 4 63
That you have vouchsafed . . . my poor house to visit . *W. Tale* v 3 6
They have done my poor house grace . . . *Hen. VIII.* i 4 73
At my poor house look to behold this night Earth-treading stars *R. and J.* i 2 24
Now peace be here, Poor house, that keep'st thyself! . *Cymbeline* iii 6 36
Poor humour. A poor humour of mine, sir, to take that that no man else will . . . . *As Y. Like It* v 4 61
Poor I am but his stale . . . . . *Com. of Errors* ii 1 101
Poor I was slain when Bassianus died . . . *T. Andron.* iii 3 171
Poor I am stale, a garment out of fashion . . *Cymbeline* iii 4 53
Poor ignorance. This insculpture, which With wax I brought away, whose soft impression Interprets for my poor ignorance *T. of Athens* v 4 69
Poor image. If I had thought the sight of my poor image Would thus have wrought you . . . . *W. Tale* v 3 57
Poor infant. My reasons are too deep and dead; Too deep and dead, poor infants, in their grave . . . . *Richard III.* iv 4 363
Yet, for the love Of this poor infant, this fresh-new sea-farer, I would it would be quiet . . . . . . *Pericles* iii 1 41
Poor instructions. Under my poor instructions . . *All's Well* iv 4 27
Poor isle. Prospero [found] his dukedom In a poor isle . *Tempest* v 1 212
Poor issue. Communication of A most poor issue . *Hen. VIII.* i 1 87
Poor itch. Rubbing the poor itch of your opinion . . *Coriolanus* i 1 169
Poor Jack Falstaff. And what should poor Jack Falstaff do in the days of villany? . . . . 1 *Hen. IV.* iii 3 187
Poor Jack, farewell! I could have better spared a better man . v 4 103
Poor jade, is wrung in the withers out of all cess . . . ii 1 7
And that is the next way to give poor jades the bots . . ii 1 10
Struck his armed heels Against the panting sides of his poor jade 2 *Hen. IV.* i 1 45
Their poor jades Lob down their heads, dropping the hides and hips *Hen. V.* iv 2 46
Poor-John. A kind of not of the newest Poor-John . *Tempest* ii 2 28
Thou art not fish; if thou hadst, thou hadst been poor John *Rom. and Jul.* i 1 37
Poor judgment. With what poor judgement he hath now cast her off appears too grossly . . . . *Lear* i 1 294
Poor Katharine. Now must the world point at poor Katharine *T. of S.* iii 2 18
Poor kindness. You o'er-rate my poor kindness . . *Cymbeline* i 4 41
Poor king. The poor King Reignier, whose large style Agrees not with the leanness of his purse . . . . . 2 *Hen. VI.* i 1 111
See how my sword weeps for the poor king's death! . 3 *Hen. VI.* v 6 63
She kicked the poor king her father . . . . *Lear* iii 6 50
Poor kingdom. O my poor kingdom, sick with civil blows! 2 *Hen. IV.* iv 5 134
Poor knave. You are ambitious for poor knaves' caps and legs *Coriolanus* ii 1 76
What, thou speak'st drowsily? Poor knave, I blame thee not *J. Cæsar* iv 3 241
Poor knight, What dreadful dole is here! . . . *M. N. Dream* v 1 282
Dian no queen of virgins, that would suffer her poor knight surprised, without rescue . . . . *All's Well* i 3 120
When every case in law is right; No squire in debt, nor no poor knight *Lear* iii 2 86
Poor lady. Alas, poor lady, desolate and left! . . *T. G. of Ver.* iv 4 179
He would make but a sport of it and torment the poor lady worse *M. Ado* ii 3 163
Alas, poor lady! 'Tis a hard bondage to become the wife Of a detesting lord.—I warrant, good creature . . . *All's Well* iii 5 66
If it be so, as 'tis, Poor lady, she were better love a dream . *T. Night* ii 2 27
Alas, poor lady! She's a stranger now again . . *Hen. VIII.* ii 3 16
Poor lady, she'll run mad When she shall lack it . . *Othello* iii 3 317
Poor last. Of many thousand kisses the poor last I lay upon thy lips *Ant. and Cleo.* iv 15 20
Poor life. It is no more Than my poor life must answer . *Richard II.* v 2 83
Poor likelihoods Of modern seeming . . . . *Othello* i 3 108
Poor lone woman. A hundred mark is a long one for a poor lone woman to bear . . . . 2 *Hen. IV.* ii 1 35
Poor looks. Such precious deeds in one that promised nought But beggary and poor looks . . . . . . *Cymbeline* v 5 10
Poor lord! is't I That chase thee from thy country? . *All's Well* iii 2 105
And for his meed, poor lord, he is mew'd up . *Richard III.* i 3 139
Poor loss. But wherefore grieve I at an hour's poor loss? 2 *Hen. VI.* iii 2 381
Poor lovers. Alas! this parting strikes poor lovers dumb *T. G. of Ver.* ii 2 21
Poor Maccabæus, how hath he been baited! . . *L. L. Lost* v 2 634
Poor maid. What a merit were it in death to take this poor maid from the world! . . . . *Meas. for Meas.* iii 1 241
A manly enterprise, To conjure tears up in a poor maid's eyes! *M. N. D.* iii 2 158
Otherwise a seducer flourishes, and a poor maid is undone . *All's Well* v 3 146
Having no external thing to lose But the word 'maid,' cheats the poor maid of that . . . . *K. John* ii 1 572
Ay me! poor maid, Born in a tempest, when my mother died *Pericles* iv 1 18
Poor malice. Whilst our poor malice Remains in danger . *Macbeth* iii 2 14
Poor man. Me, poor man, my library Was dukedom large enough *Temp.* i 2 109
When gods have hot backs, what shall poor men do? . *Mer. Wives* v 5 13
Ay me, poor man, how pale and wan he looks! . *Com. of Errors* iv 4 111
Though I be but a poor man, I am glad to hear it . . *Much Ado* iii 5 30
I am, as they say, but to parfect one man in one poor man . *L. L. Lost* v 2 503
Chapels had been churches and poor men's cottages princes' palaces *Mer. of Venice* i 2 15
A poor man's son: his father, though I say it, is an honest exceeding poor man . . . . ii 2 53
And, though I say it, though old man, yet poor man, my father . . ii 2 149
There is an old poor man, Who after me hath many a weary step Limp'd in pure love . . . . *As Y. Like It* ii 7 129
Poor men alone? No, no; the noblest deer hath them as huge as the rascal . . . . iii 3 57
I am a poor man, and at your majesty's command . . *All's Well* v 3 251
Alas, poor man! a million of beating may come to a great matter *W. Tale* iv 3 62
I spake with him; who now Has these poor men in question . . v 1 198
Many a poor man's son would have lien still . . . *K. John* iv 1 50
And a many poor men's lives saved . . . . . *Hen. V.* iv 1 128
He may mean more than we poor men do know . . 1 *Hen. VI.* i 2 122
Thou hast appointed justices of peace, to call poor men before them about matters they were not able to answer . . 2 *Hen. VI.* iv 7 46
Long sitting to determine poor men's causes Hath made me full of sickness . . . . iv 7 93
O, how wretched Is that poor man that hangs on princes' favours! *Hen. VIII.* iii 2 367
And grew so ill He could not sit his mule.—Alas, poor man! . iv 2 16
There's none stands under more calumnious tongues Than I myself, poor man . . . . v 1 113
I sometime lay here in Corioli At a poor man's house . . *Coriolanus* i 9 83
Thy napkin cannot drink a tear of mine, For thou, poor man, hast drown'd it with thine own . . . . . . *T. Andron.* iii 1 141
Alas, poor man! grief has so wrought on him, He takes false shadows for true substances . . . . iii 2 79
Make poor men's cattle break their necks . . . . v 1 132
And, for this fault, Assemble all the poor men of your sort . *J. Cæsar* i 1 62
Poor man! I know he would not be a wolf, But that he sees the Romans are but sheep . . . . i 3 104
Another purse; in it a jewel Well worth a poor man's taking . *Lear* iv 6 29
What are you?—A most poor man, made tame to fortune's blows . iv 6 225
I am thinking of the poor men that were cast away before us *Pericles* ii 1 19
Here's a fish hangs in the net, like a poor man's right in the law . ii 1 123
Get fire and meat for these poor men . . . . . . ii 2 3
Poor Margaret. I, poor Margaret, With this my son, Prince Edward, Henry's heir, Am come to crave thy just and lawful aid 3 *Hen. VI.* iii 3 30
And say poor Margaret was a prophetess! . . *Richard III.* i 3 301
Poor Mariana advantaged, and the corrupt deputy scaled *Meas. for Meas.* iii 1 264
Poor market folks that come to sell their corn . 1 *Hen. VI.* iii 2 15
Poor mates. Leak'd is our bark, And we, poor mates, stand on the dying deck . . . . *T. of Athens* iv 2 20
Poor matters. Most poor matters Point to rich ends . . *Tempest* iii 1 3
Poor me. Come you between, And save poor me, the weaker . *Pericles* iv 1 91
Poor merchant. A pound of this poor merchant's flesh . *Mer. of Venice* iv 1 23
Poor Milan. Bend The dukedom yet unbow'd—alas, poor Milan!—To most ignoble stooping . . . . *Tempest* i 2 115
Poor mistress. My poor mistress, moved therewithal, Wept bitterly *T. G. of Ver.* iv 4 175
Will thank you, If you speak truth, for their poor mistress' sake *Hen. VIII.* iii 1 47
Poor monarch. Hath that poor monarch taught thee to insult? 3 *Hen. VI.* i 4 124
Poor monkey. God help thee, poor monkey! But how wilt thou do for a father? . . . . *Macbeth* iv 2 59
Poor monster. The poor monster's my subject . . . *Tempest* iii 2 42
And I, poor monster, fond as much on him . . . *T. Night* ii 2 35
Poor my lord, what tongue shall smooth thy name? . *Rom. and Jul.* iii 2 98
Poor name. And my poor name Banish'd the kingdom . *Hen. VIII.* iv 2 126
Poor number. You and those poor number saved with you . *T. Night* i 2 10
Poor officer. The duke knows him for no other but a poor officer of mine *All's Well* iv 3 226

Poor old eyes. Because I would not see thy cruel nails Pluck out his poor old eyes — *Lear* iii 7 57
Poor old heart, he holp the heavens to rain — iii 7 62
Poor old Jack. If there were not two or three and fifty upon poor old Jack, then am I no two-legged creature — *1 Hen. IV.* ii 4 207
Poor old man. I went to her, Master Brook, as you see, like a poor old man: but I came from her, Master Brook, like a poor old woman — *Mer. Wives* v 1 17
The poor old man, their father, making such pitiful dole over them — *As Y. Like It* i 2 138
Poor old man, thou prunest a rotten tree — ii 3 63
You see me here, you gods, a poor old man, As full of grief as age — *Lear* ii 4 275
Poor old woman. I went to her, Master Brook, as you see, like a poor old man: but I came from her, Master Brook, like a poor old woman — *Mer. Wives* v 1 18
Poor Olivia. What thriftless sighs shall poor Olivia breathe! — *T. Night* ii 2 40
Poor one. When rich villains have need of poor ones, poor ones may make what price they will — *Much Ado* iii 3 121
What are you?—A gentleman.—A marvellous poor one — *Coriolanus* iv 5 30
But one, poor one, one poor and loving child — *Rom. and Jul.* iv 5 46
Poor Ophelia Divided from herself and her fair judgement — *Hamlet* iv 5 84
Too much of water hast thou, poor Ophelia — iv 7 186
Poor opinion. Truly, sir, in my poor opinion — *Meas. for Meas.* ii 1 245
Poor Orlando, thou art overthrown! — *As Y. Like It* i 2 271
Poor our sex. Ah, poor our sex! this fault in us I find, The error of our eye directs our mind — *Troi. and Cres.* v 2 109
Poor part. For mine own poor part, Look you, I'll go pray — *Hamlet* i 5 131
Poor passengers. Provided that you do no outrages On silly women or poor passengers — *T. G. of Ver.* iv 1 72
Or foul felonious thief that fleeced poor passengers — *2 Hen. VI.* iii 1 129
Poor passion. Such poor passion as the maid that milks And does the meanest chares — *Ant. and Cleo.* iv 15 74
Poor patience. To pay grief, must of poor patience borrow — *Othello* i 3 215
Poor pennyworth. And swear that I have a poor pennyworth in the English — *Mer. of Venice* i 2 76
One poor penny-worth of sugar-candy to make thee long-winded *1 Hen. IV.* iii 3 180
Poor people. Didst thou not, when she was gone down stairs, desire me to be no more so familiarity with such poor people? — *2 Hen. IV.* ii 1 108
As you wish Christian peace to souls departed, Stand these poor people's friend — *Hen. VIII.* iv 2 157
Poor perdu. To watch—poor perdu!—With this thin helm? — *Lear* iv 7 35
Poor petition. Give this poor petition to the king — *All's Well* v 1 19
My next poor petition Is — *Hen. VIII.* iv 2 138
Poor petitioner. I pray, Let us, that are poor petitioners, speak too *T. of S.* ii 1 72
I am but a poor petitioner of our whole township — *2 Hen. VI.* i 3 26
A poor petitioner, A care-crazed mother of a many children *Richard III.* iii 7 183
Poor phrase. Not to crack the wind of the poor phrase — *Hamlet* i 3 108
Poor physician. A poor physician's daughter my wife! — *All's Well* ii 3 122
A poor physician's daughter, thou dislikest Of virtue for the name — ii 3 130
Poor pickaxes. As deep As these poor pickaxes can dig — *Cymbeline* iv 2 389
Poor piece. There's a poor piece of gold for thee — *Othello* iii 1 26
Poor player. Life's but a walking shadow, a poor player — *Macbeth* v 5 24
Poor 'pothecary. He writes that he did buy a poison Of a poor 'pothecary — *Rom. and Jul.* v 3 289
Poor praise. In their poor praise he humbled — *All's Well* i 2 45
Poor prattler, how thou talk'st! — *Macbeth* iv 2 64
Poor price. His qualities being at this poor price — *All's Well* iv 3 308
Poor princess, Thou divine Imogen, what thou endurest! — *Cymbeline* ii 1 61
Poor prisoner. My poor prisoner, I am innocent as you — *W. Tale* ii 2 28
Like a poor prisoner in his twisted gyves — *Rom. and Jul.* ii 2 180
Poor Proteus! thou hast entertain'd A fox — *T. G. of Ver.* iv 4 96
Poor queen! so that thy state might be no worse, I would my skill were subject to thy curse — *Richard II.* iii 4 102
Deposed the rightful king, Sent his poor queen to France *2 Hen. VI.* ii 2 25
Poor queen! how love to me and to her son Hath made her break out into terms of rage! — *3 Hen. VI.* i 1 264
If this news be true, Poor queen and son, your labour is but lost — iii 1 32
In thy prayers remember The estate of my poor queen — *Hen. VIII.* v 1 74
Poor rag. If thou wilt curse, thy father, that poor rag, Must be thy subject — *T. of Athens* iv 3 271
Poor rats. For want of means, poor rats, had hang'd themselves *Rich. III.* v 3 331
Poor remainder. The poor remainder of Andronici — *T. Andron.* v 3 131
Poor remains. Behold the poor remains, alive and dead! — i 1 81
Come, poor remains of friends, rest on this rock — *J. Cæsar* v 5 1
Poor request. Give me one poor request — *Hamlet* i 5 142
Poor Richard! where rode he the whilst? — *Richard II.* v 2 22
Poor right hand. This poor right hand of mine Is left to tyrannize upon my breast — *T. Andron.* iii 2 7
Poor rogue. And the commanders very poor rogues — *All's Well* iv 3 153
Poor rogues, I pray you, say.—Well, that's set down — iv 3 176
Poor rogues, and usurers' men! bawds between gold and want! *T. of A.* ii 2 60
And compounded thee Poor rogue hereditary — iv 3 274
And hear poor rogues Talk of court news — *Lear* v 3 13
Alas, poor rogue! I think, i' faith, she loves me — *Othello* iv 1 112
Poor Romeo. Alas, poor Romeo! he is already dead — *Rom. and Jul.* ii 4 13
Poor root. Forth thy plenteous bosom, one poor root! — *T. of Athens* iv 3 186
Poor ropes, you are beguiled, Both you and I — *Rom. and Jul.* iii 2 132
Poor Rosalind, whither wilt thou go? — *As Y. Like It* i 3 92
Poor sacrifices of our enmity! — *Rom. and Jul.* v 3 304
Poor scruple. The twentieth part Of one poor scruple — *Mer. of Venice* iv 1 330
Poor seat. We never valued this poor seat of England — *Hen. V.* i 2 269
Poor self. For my poor self, I am combined by a sacred vow And shall be absent — *Meas. for Meas.* iv 3 148
They were never so truly turned over and over as my poor self in love — *Much Ado* v 2 35
And his poor self, A dedicated beggar to the air — *T. of Athens* iv 2 12
As I my poor self did exchange for you, To your so infinite loss *Cymbeline* i 1 119
Poor servant. An honest poor servant of yours — *T. of Athens* iv 3 482
Your poor servant ever.—Sir, my good friend — *Hamlet* i 2 162
Poor services. You have heard of my poor services — *W. Tale* iv 4 527
Poor servitors. Thus are poor servitors, When others sleep upon their quiet beds, Constrain'd to watch in darkness — *1 Hen. VI.* ii 1 5
Poor shadow. I call'd thee then poor shadow, painted queen *Rich. III.* iv 4 83
Poor shadows of Elysium, hence, and rest — *Cymbeline* v 4 97
Poor shepherd. Alas, poor shepherd! searching of thy wound, I have by hard adventure found mine own — *As Y. Like It* ii 4 44
Alas, poor shepherd!—Do you pity him? no, he deserves no pity — iv 3 65
Poor ship. As a duck for life that dives, So up and down the poor ship drives — *Pericles* iii Gower 50
Poor shoulder. To lean upon my poor shoulder — *L. L. Lost* v 1 108
Poor show. This poor show doth better — *2 Hen. IV.* v 5 13
Poor sire. And graced thy poor sire with his bridal-day — *3 Hen. VI.* ii 2 155
Poor soldier. And my poor soldiers tell me, yet ere night They'll be in fresher robes — *Hen. V.* iv 3 116
The poor soldier that so richly fought — cannot be found — *Cymbeline* v 5 3
Poor son. Let's make further search For my poor son — *Tempest* ii 1 324
Thou slewest my husband Henry in the Tower, And Edward, my poor son, at Tewksbury — *Richard III.* i 3 120
Poor souls, they perish'd — *Tempest* i 2 9
Poor soul, She speaks this in the infirmity of sense — *Meas. for Meas.* v 1 46
But, O, poor souls, Come you to seek the lamb here of the fox? — v 1 299
Her part, poor soul! seeming as burdened With lesser weight *Com. of Er.* i 1 108
One that before the judgement carries poor souls to hell — iv 2 40
God help, poor souls, how idly do they talk! — iv 4 132
But if thou strive, poor soul, what art thou then? Food for his rage — *L. L. Lost* iv 1 94
And extort A poor soul's patience, all to make you sport *M. N. Dream* iii 2 161
And through Wall's chink, poor souls, they are content To whisper — v 1 134
She, poor soul, Knows not which way to stand, to look, to speak — *T. of Shrew* iv 1 187
O, the most piteous cry of the poor souls! — *W. Tale* iii 3 92
How the poor souls roared, and the sea mocked them — iii 3 101
Alack, poor soul! thou hast need of more rags to lay on thee — iv 3 57
O, good sir, tenderly, O!—Alas, poor soul! — iv 3 75
She is in hell already, and burns poor souls — *2 Hen. IV.* ii 4 366
The poor souls for whom this hungry war Opens his vasty jaws *Hen. V.* ii 4 104
Poor soul, God's goodness hath been great to thee — *2 Hen. VI.* ii 1 84
And thou, poor soul, Art then forsaken, as thou went'st forlorn! — *3 Hen. VI.* iii 1 53
But he, poor soul, by your first order died — *Richard III.* ii 1 87
Who told me how the poor soul did forsake The mighty Warwick? — ii 1 109
Not a man would speak, Nor I, ungracious, speak unto myself For him, poor soul — ii 1 128
Poor soul, I envy not thy glory; To feed my humour, with thyself no harm — iv 1 64
Woful welcomer of glory!—Adieu, poor soul, that takest thy leave of it! iv 1 91
Poor soul, thy face is much abused with tears — *Rom. and Jul.* iv 1 29
Poor soul! his eyes are red as fire with weeping — *J. Cæsar* iii 2 120
The poor soul sat sighing by a sycamore tree — *Othello* iv 3 41
Poor souls, it grieved my heart to hear what pitiful cries they made to us to help them — *Pericles* ii 1 21
Poor state. And the poor state Esteem him as a lamb — *Macbeth* iv 3 53
Poor steward. Ne'er did poor steward wear a truer grief For his undone lord than mine eyes for you — *T. of Athens* iv 3 487
Poor string. My heart hath one poor string to stay it by — *K. John* v 7 55
Poor Suffolk. Thus is poor Suffolk ten times banished *2 Hen. VI.* iii 2 357
Poor suitors have strong breaths — *Coriolanus* i 1 61
Poor suppliant. Vanquish'd thereto by the fair grace and speech Of the poor suppliant — *All's Well* v 3 134
Poor thief. For with the dark, poor thief, I'll steal away — iii 2 132
Poor thing, condemn'd to loss! — *W. Tale* iii 3 192
They were warmer that got this than the poor thing is here — iii 3 77
Poor third. So the poor third is up — *Ant. and Cleo.* iii 5 12
Poor three. We have but poor three, and they can do no more than they can do — *Pericles* iv 2 7
Poor Tom! That's something yet: Edgar I nothing am — *Lear* ii 3 20
Fathom and half, fathom and half! Poor Tom! — iii 4 38
Who's there?—A spirit, a spirit: he says his name's poor Tom — iii 4 43
Who gives any thing to poor Tom? — iii 4 51
Do poor Tom some charity, whom the foul fiend vexes — iii 4 61
Poor Tom; that eats the swimming frog, the toad, the tadpole — iii 4 134
Poor Tom's a-cold.—Go in with me — iii 4 152
The foul fiend haunts poor Tom in the voice of a nightingale — iii 6 31
Poor Tom, thy horn is dry — iii 6 78
Sirrah, naked fellow,— Poor Tom's a-cold. I cannot daub it further — iv 1 54
Poor Tom hath been scared out of his good wits — iv 1 59
Five fiends have been in poor Tom at once — iv 1 61
Give me thy arm: Poor Tom shall lead thee — iv 1 82
Poor tongue. O time's extremity, Hast thou so crack'd and splitted my poor tongue? — *Com. of Errors* v 1 308
Poor Transylvanian. The poor Transylvanian is dead — *Pericles* iv 2 23
Poor trash. This poor trash of Venice — *Othello* ii 1 312
Poor trespasses, More monstrous standing by — *W. Tale* iii 2 190
Poor Troilus. He is himself.—Himself! Alas, poor Troilus! I would he were — *Troi. and Cres.* i 2 77
Poor Turlygod! poor Tom! That's something yet — *Lear* ii 3 20
Poor underserver, I Can nothing render but allegiant thanks *Hen. VIII.* iii 2 175
Poor unfledged, Have never wing'd from view o' the nest — *Cymbeline* iii 3 27
Poor unknown. I am ashamed To look upon the holy sun, to have The benefit of his blest beams, remaining So long a poor unknown — iv 4 43
Poor validity. Purpose is but the slave to memory, Of violent birth, but poor validity — *Hamlet* iii 2 199
Poor virgin. A poor virgin, sir, an ill-favoured thing, sir, but mine own — *As Y. Like It* v 4 60
Poor virginity. Bless our poor virginity from underminers and blowers up! — *All's Well* i 1 131
Poor virtue. We catch of you; grant that, my poor virtue — *2 Hen. IV.* ii 4 51
Poor volk. Go your gait, and let poor volk pass — *Lear* iv 6 243
Poor we. And to poor we Thine enmity's most capital — *Coriolanus* v 3 103
Poor wealth. Whilst this poor wealth lasts — *T. of Athens* iv 3 495
Poor wench. The poor wench is cast away — *L. L. Lost* v 2 682
Alas, poor wenches, where are now your fortunes! — *Hen. VIII.* iii 1 148
Poor whore. For tearing a poor whore's ruff — *2 Hen. IV.* ii 4 156
Poor widow. A tapster; a poor widow's tapster — *Meas. for Meas.* ii 1 207
I am a poor widow of Eastcheap, and he is arrested at my suit *2 Hen. IV.* ii 1 76
Are you not ashamed to enforce a poor widow to so rough a course? — ii 1 89
Poor woman. I think you have killed the poor woman — *Mer. Wives* iv 2 198
Alas, poor women! make us but believe, Being compact of credit, that you love us — *Com. of Errors* iii 2 21
Satisfy the poor woman — *2 Hen. IV.* ii 1 143
A most poor woman, and a stranger, Born out of your dominions — *Hen. VIII.* ii 4 15
Poor world. The troubler of the poor world's peace! — *Richard II.* i 3 221
The poor world is almost six thousand years old — *As Y. Like It* iv 1 94
How the poor world is pestered with such waterflies! — *Troi. and Cres.* v 1 37
Poor worm, thou art infected! This visitation shows it — *Tempest* iii 1 31
Thou dost fear the soft and tender fork Of a poor worm *Meas. for Meas.* iii 1 17
The blind mole casts Copp'd hills towards heaven, to tell the earth is throng'd By man's oppression; and the poor worm doth die for't — *Pericles* i 1 102

Poor wren. The poor wren, The most diminutive of birds, will fight, Her young ones in her nest, against the owl . . . . . *Macbeth* iv 2 9
Poor wretch, That for thy mother's fault art thus exposed ! *W. Tale* iii 3 49
Alas, your too much love and care of me Are heavy orisons 'gainst this poor wretch ! . . . . *Hen. V.* ii 2 53
She, poor wretch, for grief can speak no more . . 3 *Hen. VI.* iii 1 47
Alas, poor wretch ! ah, poor capocchia ! hast not slept to-night? *Troi. and Cres.* iv 2 32
But, look, where sadly the poor wretch comes reading . *Hamlet* ii 2 168
Pull'd the poor wretch from her melodious lay To muddy death . iv 7 183
Poor wretches that depend On greatness' favour dream as I have done *Cymbeline* v 4 127
Poor Yorick. Alas, poor Yorick ! I knew him, Horatio . . *Hamlet* v 1 203
Poor York. Alas, poor York ! but that I hate thee deadly, I should lament thy miserable state . . . . . 3 *Hen. VI.* i 4 84
Poor young. Where my poor young was limed, was caught . . v 6 17
Poorer. We, the poorer born, Whose baser stars do shut us up in wishes *All's Well* i 1 196
We lost a jewel of her ; and our esteem Was made much poorer by it . v 3 2
I have often wished myself poorer, that I might come nearer to you *T. of Athens* i 2 104
I have seen her die twenty times upon far poorer moment *Ant. and Cleo.* i 2 146
Poorest. The poorest service is repaid with thanks . *T. of Shrew* iv 3 45
How many thousand of my poorest subjects Are at this hour asleep ! 2 *Hen. IV.* iii 1 4
Let God for ever keep it from my head And make me as the poorest vassal is ! . . . . iv 5 176
They are the poorest, But poverty could never draw 'em from me *Hen. VIII.* iv 2 148
Being one o' the lowest, basest, poorest, Of this most wise rebellion, thou go'st foremost . . . . . *Coriolanus* i 1 161
As an ostler, that for the poorest piece Will bear the knave by the volume iii 3 32
When, Caius, Rome is thine, Thou art poor'st of all ; then shortly art thou mine . . . . iv 7 57
The basest and most poorest shape That ever penury, in contempt of man, Brought near to beast . . . . . *Lear* ii 3 7
Our basest beggars Are in the poorest thing superfluous . ii 4 268
Most monster-like, be shown For poor'st diminutives, for doits *A. and C.* iv 12 37
Poorly. To look so poorly and to speak so fair . *Richard II.* iii 3 128
Their ragged curtains poorly are let loose . . *Hen. V.* iv 2 41
Must poorly sell ourselves . . . . . *Troi. and Cres.* iv 4 42
Be not lost So poorly in your thoughts . . . *Macbeth* ii 2 72
But who comes here? My father, poorly led? . . . *Lear* iv 1 10
I'll rob none but myself ; and let me die, Stealing so poorly *Cymbeline* iv 2 16
Pope. Here comes the holy legate of the pope.—Hail, you anointed deputies of heaven ! . . . . iii 1 135
I Pandulph, of fair Milan cardinal, And from Pope Innocent the legate iii 1 139
This, in our foresaid holy father's name, Pope Innocent, I do demand . iii 1 146
Thou canst not, cardinal, devise a name So slight, unworthy and ridiculous, To charge me to an answer, as the pope . . . iii 1 151
So tell the pope, all reverence set apart To him and his usurp'd authority iii 1 159
I alone, alone do me oppose Against the pope and count his friends my foes . . . . iii 1 171
As holding of the pope Your sovereign greatness and authority . . v 1 3
My breath that blew this tempest up, Upon your stubborn usage of the pope . . . . v 1 18
On this Ascension-day, remember well, Upon your oath of service to the pope . . . . v 1 23
In spite of pope or dignities of church, Here by the cheeks I'll drag thee up and down.—Gloucester, thou wilt answer this before the pope 1 *Hen. VI.* i 3 50
Have you perused the letters from the pope, The emperor? . . . v 1 1
I would the college of the cardinals Would choose him pope and carry him to Rome, And set the triple crown upon his head . 2 *Hen. VI.* i 3 65
So I leave him To him that made him proud, the pope . *Hen. VIII.* ii 2 56
I do refuse you for my judge ; and here, Before you all, appeal unto the pope . . . . ii 4 119
The cardinal's letters to the pope miscarried . . . iii 2 30
'To the Pope !' The letter, as I live, with all the business I writ to's holiness . . . . iii 2 220
The goodness of your intercepted packets You writ to the pope . . iii 2 287
Popedom. To gain the popedom, And fee my friends in Rome. . iii 2 212
Poperin. That she were, O, that she were An open et cætera, thou a poperin pear ! . . . . *Rom. and Jul.* ii 1 38
Popilius Lena. I wish your enterprise to-day may thrive.—What enterprise, Popilius? . . . . *J. Cæsar* iii 1 14
What said Popilius Lena?—He wish'd to-day our enterprise might thrive iii 1 15
Popilius Lena speaks not of our purposes ; For, look, he smiles . iii 1 23
Popinjay. To be so pester'd with a popinjay . 1 *Hen. IV.* i 3 50
Popish. With twenty popish tricks and ceremonies . *T. Andron.* v 1 76
Popped. Thus popp'd Paris in his hardiment . *Troi. and Cres.* iv 5 28
Popp'd in between the election and my hopes . . *Hamlet* v 2 65
Poppy. Not poppy, nor mandragora, Nor all the drowsy syrups *Othello* iii 3 330
Pops. A' pops me out At least from fair five hundred pound a year *K. John* i 1 68
Popular. O'er-prized all popular rate . . . *Tempest* i 2 92
Art thou officer? Or art thou base, common and popular? . *Hen. V.* iv 1 38
Seld-shown flamens Do press among the popular throngs . *Coriolanus* ii 1 230
I will counterfeit the bewitchment of some popular man . . ii 3 109
Puts his 'shall,' His popular 'shall,' against a graver bench Than ever frown'd . . . . iii 1 106
And, in a violent popular ignorance, given your enemy your shield . v 2 43
Popularity. Enfeoff'd himself to popularity . 1 *Hen. IV.* iii 2 69
Any retirement, any sequestration From open haunts and popularity *Hen. V.* i 1 59
Populous. And for because the world is populous And here is not a creature but myself . . . . *Richard II.* v 5 3
A wilderness is populous enough, So Suffolk had thy heavenly company : For where thou art, there is the world itself . 2 *Hen. VI.* iii 2 360
By night and negligence, the fire Is spied in populous cities . *Othello* i 1 77
There's many a beast then in a populous city, And many a civil monster iv 1 64
Nay, the dust Should have ascended to the roof of heaven, Raised by your populous troops . . . . . . *Ant. and Cleo.* iii 6 50
I doubt not but this populous city will Yield many scholars . *Pericles* iv 6 197
Porch. Take-a your rapier, and come after my heel to the court.—'Tis ready, sir, here in the porch . . . . *Mer. Wives* i 4 63
Not Romans—as they are not, Though calved i' the porch o' the Capitol *Coriolanus* iii 1 240
They stay for me In Pompey's porch . . . . *J. Cæsar* i 3 126
All this done, Repair to Pompey's porch, where you shall find us . . i 3 147
And in the porches of my ears did pour The leperous distilment *Hamlet* i 5 63

Pore. Painfully to pore upon a book To seek the light of truth *L. L. Lost* i 1 74
In that each of you have forsworn his book, Can you still dream and pore and thereon look? . . . . iv 3 298
Poring. The poring dark Fills the wide vessel of the universe *Hen. V.* iv Prol. 2
Pork. To smell pork ; to eat of the habitation which your prophet the Nazarite conjured the devil into . . . *Mer. of Venice* i 3 34
In converting Jews to Christians, you raise the price of pork . . iii 5 39
Pork-eaters. If we grow all to be pork-eaters, we shall not shortly have a rasher on the coals for money . . . . iii 5 27
Porn. O, 'tis a gallant king !—Ay, he was porn at Monmouth . *Hen. V.* iv 7 12
I think it is in Macedon where Alexander is porn . . . iv 7 24
Porpentine. Bring it, I pray you, to the Porpentine . *Com. of Errors* iii 1 116
Here is the chain. I thought to have ta'en you at the Porpentine . iii 2 172
You use this dalliance to excuse Your breach of promise to the Porpentine . . . . iv 1 49
Parted with me to go fetch a chain, Promising to bring it to the Porpentine . . . . v 1 222
What say you?—Sir, he dined with her there, at the Porpentine . . v 1 275
His thighs with darts Were almost like a sharp-quill'd porpentine 2 *Hen. VI.* iii 1 363
Do not, porpentine, do not : my fingers itch . . *Troi. and Cres.* ii 1 27
And each particular hair to stand an end, Like quills upon the fretful porpentine . . . . *Hamlet* i 5 20
Porpus. When I saw the porpus how he bounced and tumbled *Pericles* ii 1 26
Porridge. He receives comfort like cold porridge . . *Tempest* ii 1 10
I had as lief you would tell me of a mess of porridge . *Mer. Wives* iii 1 64
That at dinner they should not drop in his porridge . *Com. of Errors* ii 2 100
I had rather pray a month with mutton and porridge . *L. L. Lost* i 1 305
Your date is better in your pie and your porridge than in your cheek *All's Well* i 1 173
They want their porridge and their fat bull-beeves . . 1 *Hen. VI.* i 2 9
Chaff and bran ! porridge after meat ! . . *Troi. and Cres.* i 2 263
Set ratsbane by his porridge . . . . *Lear* iii 4 56
Porringer. Why, this was moulded on a porringer . *T. of Shrew.* iv 3 64
That railed upon me till her pinked porringer fell off her head *Hen. VIII.* v 4 50
Port. Peering in maps for ports and piers and roads . *Mer. of Venice* i 1 19
Showing a more swelling port Than my faint means would grant continuance . . . . i 1 124
And the magnificoes Of greatest port have all persuaded with him . iii 2 283
In my stead, Keep house and port and servants, as I should *T. of Shrew* i 1 208
'Priami,' is my man Tranio, 'regia,' bearing my port . . . iii 1 36
At the Saint Francis here beside the port . . . . *All's Well* iii 5 39
All places that the eye of heaven visits Are to a wise man ports *Rich. II.* i 3 276
Golden care! That keep'st the ports of slumber open wide 2 *Hen. IV.* iv 5 24
The warlike Harry, like himself, Assume the port of Mars *Hen. V.* Prol. 6
And bear the name and port of gentlemen . . 2 *Hen. VI.* iv 1 19
Have to the port of Athens sent their ships . . *Troi. and Cres.* Prol. 3
He touch'd the ports desired . . . . ii 2 76
At the port, lord, I'll give her to thy hand . . . . . iv 4 113
Let the ports be guarded . . . . *Coriolanus* i 7 1
Him I accuse The city ports by this hath enter'd . . . . v 6 6
If Aaron now be wise, Then is all safe, the anchor's in the port *T. An.* iv 4 38
Descend, and open your uncharged ports . . . *T. of Athens* v 4 55
And the very ports they blow, All the quarters that they know *Macbeth* i 3 15
All ports I'll bar ; the villain shall not 'scape . . . *Lear* ii 1 82
No port is free ; no place, That guard, and most unusual vigilance, Does not attend my taking . . . . ii 3 3
Wise in our negligence, have secret feet In some of our best ports . iii 1 33
Sextus Pompeius Makes his approaches to the port of Rome *Ant. and Cleo.* i 3 46
To the ports The discontents repair . . . . . . i 4 38
Early though 't be, have on their riveted trim, And at the port expect you iv 4 23
We'll hand in hand, And with our sprightly port make the ghosts gaze iv 14 52
Port le Blanc, a bay In Brittany . . . . . *Richard II.* ii 1 277
Portable. Like an engine Not portable . . . *Troi. and Cres.* ii 3 144
All these are portable, With other graces weigh'd . . *Macbeth* iv 3 89
How light and portable my pain seems now! . . . . *Lear* iii 6 115
Portage. Let it pry through the portage of the head . *Hen. V.* iii 1 10
Even at the first Thy loss is more than can thy portage quit . *Pericles* iii 1 35
Portal. From out the fiery portal of the east . . *Richard II.* iii 3 64
Look, where he goes, even now, out at the portal ! . . *Hamlet* iii 4 136
Portance. Thinking upon his services, took from you The apprehension of his present portance . . . . . . *Coriolanus* ii 3 232
Of my redemption thence And portance in my travels' history *Othello* i 3 139
Portcullised. Within my mouth you have engaol'd my tongue, Doubly portcullis'd with my teeth and lips . . . . *Richard II.* i 3 167
Portend. What should that alphabetical position portend? . *T. Night* ii 5 130
What think you they portend?—Hot livers and cold purses . 1 *Hen. IV.* ii 4 354
These late eclipses in the sun and moon portend no good to us . *Lear* i 2 113
O, these eclipses do portend these divisions ! . . . . . i 2 149
Alack, our terrene moon Is now eclipsed ; and it portends alone The fall of Antony ! . . . . *Ant. and Cleo.* iii 13 154
Yet still it's strange What Cloten's being here to us portends *Cymbeline* iv 2 182
Which portends—Unless my sins abuse my divination—Success to the Roman host . . . . iv 2 350
Portent. O, what portents are these? . . . . . 1 *Hen. IV.* ii 3 65
A prodigy of fear and a portent Of broached mischief to the unborn times v 1 20
But when the planets In evil mixture to disorder wander, What plagues and what portents ! . . . . *Troi. and Cres.* i 3 96
These does she apply for warnings, and portents . . *J. Cæsar* ii 2 80
These are portents ; but yet I hope, I hope, They do not point on me *Oth.* v 2 45
Portentous. Black and portentous must this humour prove *Rom. and Jul.* i 1 147
They are portentous things Unto the climate that they point upon *J. C.* i 3 31
That this portentous figure Comes armed through our watch . *Hamlet* i 1 109
Porter. I know not how I may deserve to be your porter *Mer Wives* ii 2 181
Dromio, play the porter well . . . . *Com. of Errors* ii 2 213
Shall I be porter at the gate?—Ay ; and let none enter . . . ii 2 219
What patch is made our porter? My master stays in the street . iii 1 36
What art thou that keepest me out from the house I owe?—The porter for this time, sir . . . . iii 1 43
He carried the town-gates on his back like a porter . *L. L. Lost* i 2 75
Poor mechanic porters crowding in Their heavy burdens . *Hen. V.* i 2 200
Porter, remember what I gave in charge . . . 1 *Hen. VI.* ii 3 1
Good master porter, I belong to the larder . . . *Hen. VIII.* v 4 4
Where are these porters, These lazy knaves? . . . . . v 4 73
Achilles ! a drayman, a porter, a very camel . . *Troi. and Cres.* i 2 270
Has the porter his eyes in his head? . . . . *Coriolanus* iv 5 13
He'll go, he says, and sowl the porter of Rome gates by the ears . iv 5 213
As thou lovest me, let the porter let in Susan Grindstone *Rom. and Jul.* i 5 10
No porter at his gate, But rather one that smiles and still invites All that pass by . . . . *T. of Athens* ii 1 10

Porter. If a man were porter of hell-gate, he should have old turning the key . . . *Macbeth* ii 3 2
I pray you, remember the porter . . . ii 3 23
Thou shouldst have said, 'Good porter, turn the key' . . . *Lear* iii 7 64
Portia. Her name is Portia, nothing undervalued To Cato's daughter, Brutus' Portia . . . *Mer. of Venice* i 1 166
Try what my credit can in Venice do: That shall be rack'd, even to the uttermost, To furnish thee to Belmont, to fair Portia . i 1 182
The Hyrcanian deserts and the vasty wilds Of wide Arabia are as throughfares now For princes to come view fair Portia . ii 7 43
They come, As o'er a brook, to see fair Portia . . ii 7 47
Portia, adieu. I have too grieved a heart To take a tedious leave . ii 7 76
How much unlike art thou to Portia! How much unlike my hopes! . ii 9 56
What find I here? Fair Portia's counterfeit! . iii 2 115
By your leave, I bid my very friends and countrymen, Sweet Portia, welcome . iii 2 227
O sweet Portia, Here are a few of the unpleasant'st words! . iii 2 253
For never shall you lie by Portia's side With an unquiet soul . iii 2 307
If two gods should play some heavenly match And on the wager lay two earthly women, And Portia one, there must be something else Pawn'd with the other . iii 5 86
That is the voice, Or I am much deceived, of Portia . v 1 111
Sweet Portia, If you did know to whom I gave the ring . v 1 192
Portia, forgive me this enforced wrong . v 1 240
There you shall find that Portia was the doctor, Nerissa there her clerk v 1 269
Portia, what mean you? wherefore rise you now? *J. Cæsar* ii 1 234
Why, so I do. Good Portia, go to bed . ii 1 260
Kneel not, gentle Portia.—I should not need, if you were gentle Brutus ii 1 278
If it be no more, Portia is Brutus' harlot, not his wife . ii 1 287
Portia, go in awhile; And by and by thy bosom shall partake The secrets of my heart . ii 1 304
No man bears sorrow better. Portia is dead.—Ha! Portia!—She is dead iv 3 147
Portia, art thou gone?—No more, I pray you . iv 3 166
Farewell, Portia. We must die, Messala: With meditating that she must die once, I have the patience to endure it now . iv 3 190
Portion. With him, the portion and sinew of her fortune *Meas. for Meas.* iii 1 230
What prodigal portion have I spent? *As Y. Like It* i 1 41
And all things answerable to this portion . *T. of Shrew* ii 1 361
I give my daughter to him, and will make Her portion equal his *W. Tale* iv 4 397
And have no portion in the choice myself . *1 Hen. VI.* v 3 125
What piles of wealth hath he accumulated To his own portion! *Hen. VIII.* iii 2 108
Give but that portion which yourself proposed *Lear* i 1 245
Portly. Sometimes the beam of her view gilded my foot, sometimes my portly belly . *Mer. Wives* i 3 69
Your argosies with portly sail, Like signiors and rich burghers *M. of Ven.* i 1 9
Greatness too which our own hands Have holp to make so portly *1 Hen. IV.* i 3 13
A goodly portly man, i' faith, and a corpulent; of a cheerful look . ii 4 464
Shall find him by his large and portly size *Troi. and Cres.* iv 5 162
He bears him like a portly gentleman . *Rom. and Jul.* i 5 68
A portly sail of ships make hitherward . *Pericles* i 4 61
Portotartarosa. Hoodman comes! Portotartarosa . *All's Well* iv 3 136
Portrait. What's here? the portrait of a blinking idiot! . *Mer. of Venice* ii 9 54
Portraiture. For, by the image of my cause, I see The portraiture of his: I'll court his favours . *Hamlet* v 2 78
Portugal. It cannot be sounded: my affection hath an unknown bottom, like the bay of Portugal . *As Y. Like It* iv 1 213
Pose. Say you so? then I shall pose you quickly . *Meas. for Meas.* ii 4 51
Posies. Make our peds of roses, And a thousand fragrant posies *Mer. Wives* iii 1 20
Position. What should that alphabetical position portend? . *T. Night* ii 5 130
I do not strain at the position,—It is familiar . *Troi. and Cres.* iii 3 112
It is a most pregnant and unforced position . *Othello* ii 1 240
But pardon me; I do not in position Distinctly speak of her . iii 3 234
Positive. It is as positive as the earth is firm . *Mer. Wives* iii 2 49
'Tis positive 'gainst all exceptions . *Hen. V.* iv 2 25
Patroclus is a fool positive . *Troi. and Cres.* ii 3 70
Positively. Give me some breath, some little pause, my lord, Before I positively speak herein *Richard III.* iv 2 25
Hath there been such a time—I'd fain know that—That I have positively said ''Tis so,' When it proved otherwise? *Hamlet* ii 2 154
Possess. What a strange drowsiness possesses them! *Tempest* ii 1 199
Possess his books; for without them He's but a sot, as I am . iii 2 100
I will possess him with yellowness . *Mer. Wives* i 3 110
If aught possess thee from me, it is dross, Usurping ivy *Com. of Errors* ii 2 179
Possess the people in Messina here How innocent she died . *Much Ado* v 1 290
For still her cheeks possess the same Which native she doth owe *L. L. L.* i 2 110
O, I am yours, and all that I possess! . v 2 383
Possess us, possess us; tell us something of him *T. Night* ii 3 149
Would make her sainted spirit Again possess her corpse *W. Tale* v 1 58
Why seek'st thou to possess me with these fears? . *K. John* iv 2 203
'Tis in reversion that I do possess . *Richard II.* ii 2 38
Sweetened with the hope to have The present benefit which I possess . ii 3 14
Nor did the French possess the Salique land Until four hundred one and twenty years After defunction of King Pharamond . *Hen. V.* i 2 56
No man should possess him with any appearance of fear . iv 1 115
O God of battles! steel my soldiers' hearts; Possess them not with fear iv 1 307
This the regal seat: possess it, York . *3 Hen. VI.* i 1 26
Go thou to sanctuary, and good thoughts possess thee! *Richard III.* iv 1 94
The which you promised I should possess . iv 2 94
I am most joyful, madam, such good dreams Possess your fancy *Hen. VIII.* iv 2 94
I do enjoy At ample point all that I did possess *Troi. and Cres.* iii 3 89
I'll give her to thy hand; And by the way possess thee what she is . iv 4 114
Away, my disposition, and possess me Some harlot's spirit! *Coriolanus* iii 2 111
Our pastimes done, possess a golden slumber . *T. Andron.* ii 3 26
I know not, I, nor can I guess, Unless some fit or frenzy do possess her iv 1 17
So shall you share all that he doth possess, By having him *Rom. and Jul.* i 3 93
Possess them with the heaviest sound That ever yet they heard *Macbeth* iv 3 202
Things rank and gross in nature Possess it merely . *Hamlet* i 2 137
I profess Myself an enemy to all other joys, Which the most precious square of sense possesses . *Lear* i 1 76
Who since possesses chambermaids and waiting-women . iv 1 65
Be a child o' the time.—Possess it, I'll make answer . *Ant. and Cleo.* ii 7 107
To the sea-side straightway: I will possess you of that ship and treasure . iii 11 21
And let instructions enter Where folly now possesses . *Cymbeline* i 5 48
Possessed. Thy conscience Is so possess'd with guilt . *Tempest* i 2 471
My ears are stopt and cannot hear good news, So much of bad already hath possess'd them . *T. G. of Ver.* iii 1 206
I have possess'd him my most stay Can be but brief *Meas. for Meas.* iv 1 44
Possessed. What noise? That spirit's possess'd with haste *Meas. for Meas.* iv 2 91
I am possess'd with an adulterate blot . *Com. of Errors* ii 2 142
Possess'd with such a gentle sovereign grace, Of such enchanting presence . iii 2 165
Both man and master is possess'd . iv 4 95
And with no face, as 'twere, outfacing me, Cries out, I was possess'd . v 1 245
Her cousin, an she were not possessed with a fury, exceeds her *Much Ado* i 1 193
Planted and placed and possessed by my master . iii 3 159
Partly by his oaths, which first possessed them, partly by the dark night iii 3 167
As well derived as he, As well possess'd; my love is more *M. N. Dream* i 1 100
Is he yet possess'd How much ye would? . *Mer. of Venice* i 3 65
I have possess'd your grace of what I purpose . iv 1 35
That he do record a gift, Here in the court, of all he dies possess'd iv 1 389; v 1 293
Tell me how long you would have her after you have possessed her *As Y. Like It* iv 1 144
Possessed with the glanders and like to mose in the chine *T. of Shrew* iii 2 50
He is, sure, possessed, madam.—Why, what's the matter? . *T. Night* iii 4 9
If all the devils of hell be drawn in little, and Legion himself possessed him, yet I'll speak to him . iii 4 95
And thou possessed with a thousand wrongs . *K. John* iii 3 41
To be possess'd with double pomp, To guard a title that was rich before iv 2 9
Some reasons of this double coronation I have possess'd you with . iv 2 41
I find the people strangely fantasied; Possess'd with rumours . iv 2 145
Deposing thee before thou wert possess'd, Which art possess'd now to depose thyself *Richard II.* ii 1 108
We do seize to us The plate, coin, revenues and moveables, Whereof our uncle Gaunt did stand possess'd . ii 1 162
The thieves are all scatter'd and possess'd with fear . *1 Hen. IV.* ii 2 112
The king is certainly possess'd Of all our purposes . iv 1 40
And that we now possess'd The utmost man of expectation . *2 Hen. IV.* i 3 64
I am possess'd With more than half the Gallian territories . *1 Hen. VI.* v 4 138
Unless you be possess'd with devilish spirits . *2 Hen. VI.* iv 7 80
This man, whom hand to hand I slew in fight, May be possessed with some store of crowns . *3 Hen. VI.* ii 5 57
And the moveables Whereof the king my brother stood possess'd *Rich. III.* iii 1 196
Possess'd him with a scruple That will undo her . *Hen. VIII.* ii 1 158
Possess'd he is with greatness . *Troi. and Cres.* ii 3 180
Exposed myself, From certain and possess'd conveniences, To doubtful fortunes . iii 3 7
Is the senate possessed of this? . *Coriolanus* ii 1 145
Meanwhile I am possess'd of that is mine . *T. Andron.* i 1 408
I have bought the mansion of a love, But not possess'd it *Rom. and Jul.* iii 2 27
How sweet is love itself possess'd, When but love's shadows are so rich! v 1 10
I am still possess'd Of those effects for which I did the murder *Hamlet* iii 3 53
This is the brief of money, plate, and jewels, I am possess'd of *Ant. and Cleo.* v 2 139
Possesseth. Weakness possesseth me, and I am faint . *K. John* v 3 17
Possession. That her father likes Only for his possessions *T. G. of Ver.* ii 4 175
For me and my possessions she esteems not . iii 1 79
Considers she my possessions?—O, ay; and pities them . v 2 25
Here she stands: Take but possession of her with a touch . v 4 130
Upon a true contract I got possession of Julietta's bed *Meas. for Meas.* i 2 150
For his possessions, Although by confiscation they are ours, We do instate and widow you withal . v 1 427
Slander lives upon succession, For ever housed where it gets possession *Com. of Errors* iii 1 106
I charge thee, Satan, housed within this man, To yield possession to my holy prayers . iv 4 58
How long hath this possession held the man? . v 1 44
Then we find The virtue that possession would not show us . *Much Ado* iv 1 223
Of such descent, Of such possessions, and so high esteem *T. of Shrew* Ind. 2 16
One half of my lands, And in possession twenty thousand crowns . ii 1 123
To-night, When I should take possession of the bride . *All's Well* ii 5 28
Our strong possession and our right for us.—Your strong possession much more than your right . *K. John* i 1 39
Shall we give the signal to our rage And stalk in blood to our possession? ii 1 266
And bear possession of our person here, Lord of our presence . ii 1 366
His words do take possession of my bosom . iv 1 32
Broke the possession of a royal bed . *Richard II.* iii 1 13
And his high sceptre yields To the possession of thy royal hand . iv 1 110
Opinion, that did help me to the crown, Had still kept loyal to possession And left me in reputeless banishment . *1 Hen. IV.* iii 2 43
Then plain and right must my possession be . *2 Hen. IV.* iv 5 223
If it pass against us, We lose the better half of our possession *Hen. V.* i 1 8
Th' athversary was have possession of the pridge . iii 6 98
Je quand sur le possession de France, et quand vous avez le possession de moi,—let me see, what then? . v 2 192
I mean to take possession of my right . *3 Hen. VI.* i 1 44
A thousand-fold more care to keep Than in possession any jot of pleasure ii 2 53
Now to London, To see these honours in possession . ii 6 110
At such proud rate, that it out-speaks Possession of a subject *Hen. VIII.* iii 2 128
To deliver her possession up On terms of base compulsion! *Tr. and Cr.* ii 2 152
I have abandon'd Troy, left my possession, Incurr'd a traitor's name . iii 3 5
'Tis a chough; but, as I say, spacious in the possession of dirt *Hamlet* v 2 90
Whip me, ye devils, From the possession of this heavenly sight! *Othello* v 2 278
Now boast thee, death, in thy possession lies A lass unparallel'd *Ant. and Cleo.* v 2 318
Hast any of thy late master's garments in thy possession? *Cymbeline* iii 5 126
Possessor. The third possessor; ay, he was the third . *Mer. of Venice* i 3 75
Sole possessor of my love . *3 Hen. VI.* iii 3 24
Posset. We'll have a posset for't soon at night . *Mer. Wives* i 4 8
Thou shalt eat a posset to-night at my house . v 5 180
I have drugg'd their possets, That death and nature do contend *Macbeth* ii 2 6
With a sudden vigour it doth posset And curd, like eager droppings into milk, The thin and wholesome blood . *Hamlet* i 5 68
Possibilities. Seven hundred pounds and possibilities is goot gifts *M. W.* i 1 65
Speak with possibilities, And do not break into these deep extremes *T. Andron.* iii 1 215
Possibility. I know thou'rt valiant; and, to the possibility of thy soldiership, will subscribe for thee . *All's Well* iii 6 88
I have speeded hither with the very extremest inch of possibility *2 Hen. IV.* iv 3 39
Coveting for more, Be cast from possibility of all . *1 Hen. VI.* v 4 146
Possible. Give me a note: your ladyship can set.—As little by such toys as may be possible . *T. G. of Ver.* i 2 82
O, sir, you are deceived.—'Tis not possible . *Meas. for Meas.* iii 2 132
Is't possible?—Very easily possible . *Much Ado* i 1 74
Is it possible disdain should die while she hath such meet food to feed it? i 1 121
If she should make tender of her love, 'tis very possible he'll scorn it . ii 3 186

Possible. Is it possible that any villany should be so dear?—Thou shouldst rather ask if it were possible any villany should be so rich *Much Ado* iii 3 117
It were as possible for me to say I loved nothing so well as you . . iv 1 272
It goes not forward, doth it?—It is not possible . *M. N. Dream* iv 2 7
Is it possible A cur can lend three thousand ducats? *Mer. of Venice* i 3 122
Is it possible, on such a sudden, you should fall into so strong a liking with old Sir Rowland's youngest son? *As Y. Like It* i 3 27
Can it be possible that no man saw them? It cannot be . . ii 2 1
Is't possible that on so little acquaintance you should like her? . . v 2 1
Is it possible That love should of a sudden take such hold? . *T. of Shrew* i 1 151
Till I found it to be true, I never thought it possible or likely . i 1 154
May it be done?—Not possible; for who shall bear your part? . . i 1 199
We will persuade him, be it possible, To put on better ere he go to church iii 2 127
Is't possible you will away to-night?—I must away to-day . iii 2 191
Is't possible, friend Licio, that Mistress Bianca Doth fancy any other? iv 2 1
Is it possible he should know what he is, and be that he is? . *All's Well* iv 1 48
It were not possible, with well-weighing sums of gold, to corrupt him . iv 3 203
Is't possible that my deserts to you Can lack persuasion? *T. Night* iii 4 382
Thou dost make possible things not so held . . . *W. Tale* i 2 139
Any thing possible.—It shall be possible . . . ii 3 167
May this be possible? may this be true? . . . *K. John* v 4 21
It is not possible, it cannot be . . . . 1 *Hen. IV.* v 2 4
A good conscience will make any possible satisfaction . 2 *Hen. IV.* Epil. 21
May it be possible, that foreign hire Could out of thee extract one spark of evil That might annoy my finger? . . . *Hen. V.* ii 2 100
Is it possible dat I sould love de enemy of France?—No; it is not possible v 2 178
Ask me what question thou canst possible, And I will answer 1 *Hen. VI.* i 2 87
If without peril it be possible . . . . *Richard III.* v 3 39
That former fabulous story, Being now seen possible enough, got credit, That Bevis was believed . . . . *Hen. VIII.* i 1 37
Is't possible the spells of France should juggle Men into such strange mysteries? . . . . i 3 1
Tell not me: I know this cannot be.—Not possible . *Coriolanus* iv 6 56
If it be possible for you to displace it with your little finger . v 4 4
Is't possible that so short a time can alter the condition of a man? . v 4 9
Is't possible the world should so much differ? . . *T. of Athens* iii 1 49
O heavens! is't possible, a young maid's wits Should be as mortal as an old man's life? . . . . . . *Hamlet* iv 5 159
Is't not possible to understand in another tongue? . . . . v 2 131
It is possible enough to judgement . . . . . *Othello* i 3 9
Desdemona is directly in love with him.—With him! why, 'tis not possible . . . . ii 1 222
I would revenges, That possible strength might meet, would seek us *Cymbeline* iv 2 160
Is it possible? *Much Ado* i 1; ii 3; *As Y. Like It* iii 2; *T. Night* iii 4; *Troi. and Cres.* iv 2; iv 4; *J. Cæsar* iv 3; *Hamlet* ii 2; v 2; *Othello* ii 3; iii 3; iii 4; iv 1; iv 2

Possibly. When possibly I can, I will return . . *T. G. of Ver.* ii 2 3
Such public shame as the rest of the court can possibly devise *L. L. Lost* i 1 133
The most . . . fatal opposite that you could possibly have found *T. N.* iii 4 294
I long to hear how you were found; How possibly preserved *Pericles* v 3 57

Possitable. You must speak possitable, if you can carry her your desires towards her . . . . *Mer. Wives* i 1 244

Post. She that from Naples Can have no note, unless the sun were post—The man i' the moon's too slow . . . . . *Tempest* ii 1 248
I fear my Julia would not deign my lines, Receiving them from such a worthless post . . . . . . *T. G. of Ver.* i 1 161
Thy master is shipped and thou art to post after with oars . . ii 3 37
I from my mistress come to you in post; If I return, I shall be post indeed, For she will score your fault upon my pate *Com. of Errors* i 2 63
Go hie thee presently, post to the road . . . . iii 2 152
'Twas the boy that stole your meat, and you'll beat the post *Much Ado* ii 1 207
I post from love: good lover, let me go . . *L. L. Lost* iv 3 188
I long to see Quick Cupid's post that comes so mannerly *Mer. of Venice* ii 9 100
There's a post come from my master, with his horn full of good news . v 1 46
Why, 'tis good to be sad and say nothing.—Why then, 'tis good to be a post . . . . *As Y. Like It* iv 1 9
He'll stand at your door like a sheriff's post . . . *T. Night* i 5 157
I am no fee'd post, lady; keep your purse . . . . i 5 303
I have dispatch'd in post To sacred Delphos . . *W. Tale* ii 1 182
Posts From those you sent to the oracle are come An hour since . ii 3 193
Myself on every post Proclaim'd a strumpet . . . . iii 2 102
This afternoon will post To consummate this business happily *K. John* v 7 94
Curbs me From giving reins and spurs to my free speech; Which else would post until it had return'd These terms of treason *Richard II.* i 1 56
Away with me in post to Ravenspurgh . . . . ii 1 296
What, are there no posts dispatch'd for Ireland? . . . ii 2 103
Post you to London, and you will find it so . . . . iii 4 90
Spur post, and get before him to the king, And beg thy pardon . v 2 112
There came A post from Wales loaden with heavy news . 1 *Hen. IV.* i 1 37
The posts come tiring on . . . . . 2 *Hen. IV.* Ind. 37
Get posts and letters, and make friends with speed . . . i 1 214
There are twenty weak and wearied posts Come from the north . . ii 4 385
If I be not sent away post, I will see you again ere I go . . ii 4 408
I have foundered nine score and odd posts . . . . iv 3 40
A' never broke any man's head but his own, and that was against a post when he was drunk . . . . *Hen. V.* iii 2 44
Rend bars of steel And spurn in pieces posts of adamant 1 *Hen. VI.* i 4 52
Post, my lord, to France; Agree to any covenants . . . v 5 87
Give me leave, my Lord of York, To be the post . 2 *Hen. VI.* i 4 81
What news? Why comest thou in such post? . . 3 *Hen. VI.* i 2 48
You shall stay with me; My brother Montague shall post to London . i 2 55
Tidings, as swiftly as the posts could run, Were brought me . . ii 1 109
Mount you, my lord; towards Berwick post amain . . . ii 5 128
This is some post to us or thee . . . . . . iii 3 162
Then, England's messenger, return in post, And tell false Edward . iii 3 222
Where is the post that came from valiant Oxford? . . . v 1 1
Where's Richard gone?—To London, all in post . . . . v 5 84
Determine Who they shall be that straight shall post to Ludlow *Rich. III.* ii 2 142
Take horse with him, And with all speed post with him . . . iii 2 17
The mayor towards Guildhall hies him in all post . . . . iii 5 73
Some light-foot friend post to the Duke of Norfolk . . . iv 4 440
Fly to the duke: Post thou to Salisbury . . . . . iv 4 443
Your highness told me I should post before.—My mind is changed . iv 4 455
And at the door too, like a post with packets . . . *Hen. VIII.* v 2 32
Posts, like the commandment of a king, Sans check to good and bad *Troi. and Cres.* i 3 93
Your native town you enter'd like a post, And had no welcomes *Coriol.* v 6 50
And presently took post to tell it you . . . *Rom. and Jul.* v 1 21
I brought my master news of Juliet's death; And then in post he came . . . . *Rom. and Jul.* v 3 273
Post back with speed, and tell him what hath chanced *J. Cæsar* iii 1 287
As thick as hail Came post with post . . . . *Macbeth* i 3 98
Most wicked speed, to post With such dexterity to incestuous sheets! *Hamlet* i 2 156
Came there a reeking post, Stew'd in his haste, half breathless . *Lear* ii 4 30
Post speedily to my lord your husband; show him this letter . iii 7 1
Our posts shall be swift and intelligent betwixt us . . . iii 7 11
The post unsanctified Of murderous lechers . . . . . iv 6 281
Met'st thou my posts?—Ay, madam, twenty several messengers *A. and C.* i 5 61
Away to Britain Post I in this design . . . . *Cymbeline* v 5 192
Away he posts With unchaste purpose . . . . . . v 5 283
Only I carry winged time Post on the lame feet of my rhyme *Per.* iv Gower 48

Posted day and night To meet you on the way . . . 1 *Hen. IV.* v 1 35
His guilt should be but idly posted over . . . 2 *Hen. VI.* iii 1 255
Nor posted off their suits with slow delays . . 3 *Hen. VI.* iv 8 40
Is posted, as the agent of our cardinal, To second all his plot *Hen. VIII.* iii 2 59
He is posted hence on serious matter . . . . . *Lear* iv 5 8
The swiftest harts have posted you by land . . . *Cymbeline* ii 4 27

Poster. The weird sisters, hand in hand, Posters of the sea and land *Macb.* i 3 33

Posterior. In the posteriors of this day, which the rude multitude call the afternoon . . . . *L. L. Lost* v 1 94
The posterior of the day, most generous sir, is liable, congruent and measurable for the afternoon . . . . v 1 96

Posterity. All whose joy is nothing else But fair posterity . *W. Tale* iv 4 420
For amends to his posterity, At our importance hither is he come *K. John* ii 1 6
Thou hast under-wrought his lawful king, Cut off the sequence of posterity ii 1 96
Posterity, await for wretched years . . . . 1 *Hen. VI.* i 1 48
Methinks the truth should live from age to age, As 'twere retail'd to all posterity . . . . *Richard III.* iii 1 77
What then! He'ld make an end of thy posterity . . *Coriolanus* iv 2 26
Her severity Cuts beauty off from all posterity . *Rom. and Jul.* i 1 226
Yet it was said It should not stand in thy posterity . . *Macbeth* iii 1 4

Postern. Out at the postern by the abbey-wall . . *T. G. of Ver.* v 1 9
That wounds the unsisting postern with these strokes *Meas. for Meas.* iv 2 92
By twos and threes at several posterns Clear them o' the city *W. Tale* i 2 438
It is in mine authority to command The keys of all the posterns . . i 2 464
How came the posterns So easily open? . . . . . ii 1 52
As for a camel To thread the postern of a small needle's eye *Richard II.* v 5 17

Post-haste. Hath sent post haste To entreat your majesty to visit him i 4 55
In haste, post-haste, are come to join with you . 3 *Hen. VI.* ii 1 139
And the chief head Of this post-haste and romage in the land *Hamlet* i 1 107
He requires your haste-post-haste appearance, Even on the instant *Othello* i 2 37

Post-horse. Making the wind my post-horse . . . 2 *Hen. IV.* Ind. 4
Till George be pack'd with post-horse up to heaven . *Richard III.* i 1 146
Get me ink and paper, And hire post-horses . . . *Rom. and Jul.* v 1 26

Posthumus. The king he takes the babe To his protection, calls him Posthumus Leonatus . . . . *Cymbeline* i 1 41
For you, Posthumus, So soon as I can win the offended king, I will be known your advocate . . . . i 1 74
It is your fault that I have loved Posthumus: You bred him as my playfellow . . . . i 1 144
And your, increasing in love, Leonatus Posthumus . . . . iii 2 49
Where is Posthumus? What is in thy mind, That makes thee stare thus? iii 4 4
So thou, Posthumus, Wilt lay the leaven on all proper men . . iii 4 63
Posthumus, thou that didst set up My disobedience 'gainst the king . iii 4 90
Pretty and full of view; yea, haply, near The residence of Posthumus . iii 4 151
Since the exile of Posthumus, most retired Hath her life been . . iii 5 36
Pisanio, thou that stand'st so for Posthumus! . . . . iii 5 56
Wing'd with fervour of her love, she's flown To her desired Posthumus iii 5 62
Disdaining me and throwing favours on The low Posthumus . . iii 5 76
Is she with Posthumus? From whose so many weights of baseness cannot A dram of worth be drawn . . . . iii 5 87
Is this letter true?—Sir, as I think.—It is Posthumus' hand . . iii 5 108
Constantly thou hast stuck to the bare fortune of that beggar Posthumus iii 5 120
Even there, thou villain Posthumus, will I kill thee . . . iii 5 135
She held the very garment of Posthumus in more respect . . iii 5 139
Then had my prize Been less, and so more equal ballasting To thee, Posthumus . . . . iii 6 79
Posthumus, thy head, which now is growing upon thy shoulders, shall within this hour be off . . . . iv 1 16
A headless man! The garments of Posthumus! I know the shape of's leg . . . . iv 2 308
O Posthumus! alas, Where is thy head? where's that? Ay me! . iv 2 320
That from me was Posthumus ript, Came crying 'mongst his foes . v 4 45
Like hardiment Posthumus hath To Cymbeline perform'd . . . v 4 75
Then shall Posthumus end his miseries, Britain be fortunate v 4 144; v 5 441
The good Posthumus—What should I say? he was too good to be Where ill men were . . . . v 5 157
Posthumus, Most like a noble lord in love and one That had a royal lover v 5 170
I am Posthumus, That kill'd thy daughter . . . . . v 5 217
Every villain Be call'd Posthumus Leonatus; and Be villany less than 'twas! . . . . v 5 224
O, my lord Posthumus! You ne'er kill'd Imogen till now . . v 5 230
See, Posthumus anchors upon Imogen . . . . . . v 5 393

Posting. This exceeding posting day and night Must wear your spirits low; we cannot help it . . . . *All's Well* v 1 1
My time Runs posting on in Bolingbroke's proud joy . *Richard II.* v 5 59
'Tis slander, . . . whose breath Rides on the posting winds . *Cymbeline* iii 4 38

Postmaster. 'Tis a postmaster's boy . . . . . *Mer. Wives* v 5 199
And yet it was not Anne, but a postmaster's boy . . . . v 5 211

Post-post-haste. Write from us to him; post-post-haste dispatch . *Othello* i 3 46

Postscript. Jove and my stars be praised! Here is yet a postscript *T. N.* ii 5 188
'Naked!' And in a postscript here, he says 'alone' . . *Hamlet* iv 7 53

Posture. Comes it not something near?—Her natural posture! *W. Tale* v 3 23
In most strange postures We have seen him set himself . *Hen. VIII.* iii 2 118
As if that whatsoever god who leads him Were slily crept into his human powers And gave him graceful posture . . . *Coriolanus* ii 1 237
The posture of your blows are yet unknown . . . *J. Cæsar* v 1 33
And I shall see Some squeaking Cleopatra boy my greatness I' the posture of a whore . . . . *Ant. and Cleo.* v 2 221
And puts himself in posture That acts my words . . *Cymbeline* iii 3 94
Venus, or straight-pight Minerva, Postures beyond brief nature . v 5 165

Posy. Whose posy was For all the world like cutler's poetry *Mer. of Venice* v 1 148
What talk you of the posy or the value? . . . . . v 1 151
Is this a prologue, or the posy of a ring?—'Tis brief, my lord *Hamlet* iii 2 162

Pot. While greasy Joan doth keel the pot . . . . *L. L. Lost* v 2 930
For God's sake, a pot of small ale . . . . *T. of Shrew* Ind. 2 1
And once again, a pot o' the smallest ale . . . . . Ind. 2 77

Pot. Were not I a little pot and soon hot, my very lips might freeze to my teeth *T. of Shrew* iv 1 6
I would have him poison'd with a pot of ale 1 *Hen. IV.* i 3 233
I would give all my fame for a pot of ale and safety *Hen. V.* iii 2 13
Here's a pot of good double beer, neighbour 2 *Hen. VI.* ii 3 64
The three-hooped pot shall have ten hoops iv 2 72
It hath served me instead of a quart pot to drink in iv 10 16
There was more temperate fire under the pot of her eyes *Troi. and Cres.* i 2 161
They have shut him in.—To the pot, I warrant him *Coriolanus* i 4 47
Green earthen pots, bladders and musty seeds *Rom. and Jul.* v 1 46
Swelter'd venom sleeping got, Boil thou first i' the charmed pot *Macbeth* iv 1 9
Potable. Preserving life in medicine potable 2 *Hen. IV.* iv 5 163
Potations. To forswear thin potations and to addict themselves to sack iv 3 135
Hath to-night caroused Potations pottle-deep *Othello* ii 3 56
Potatoes. Let the sky rain potatoes *Mer. Wives* v 5 21
Potato-finger. How the devil Luxury, with his fat rump and potato-finger, tickles these together! *Troi. and Cres.* v 2 56
Potch. I'll potch at him some way Or wrath or craft may get him *Coriol.* i 10 15
Potency. I would to heaven I had your potency! *Meas. for Meas.* ii 2 67
Read The cardinal's malice and his potency Together *Hen. VIII.* i 1 105
Presuming on their changeful potency *Troi. and Cres.* iv 4 99
And now, arriving A place of potency and sway o' the state *Coriolanus* ii 3 190
And either . . . the devil, or throw him out With wondrous potency *Hamlet* iii 4 170
Our potency made good, take thy reward *Lear* i 1 175
Potent. She did confine thee, By help of her more potent ministers *Tempest* i 2 275
What, Ariel! my industrious servant, Ariel!—What would my potent master? iv 1 34
Graves at my command Have waked their sleepers, oped, and let 'em forth By my so potent art v 1 50
His friends Potent at court *Mer. Wives* iv 4 89
A land itself at large, a potent dukedom *As Y. Like It* v 4 175
Such a headstrong potent fault it is, That it but mocks reproof *T. Night* iii 4 224
A lady's 'Verily' 's As potent as a lord's *W. Tale* i 2 51
Back to the stained field, You equal potents, fiery kindled spirits! *K. John* ii 1 358
No man so potent breathes upon the ground But I will beard him 1 *Hen. IV.* iv 1 11
I do believe, Induced by potent circumstances *Hen. VIII.* ii 4 76
The reasons are more potent and heroical *Troi. and Cres.* iii 3 192
Your potent and infectious fevers heap On Athens! *T. of Athens* iv 1 22
Here's another, More potent than the first *Macbeth* iv 1 76
As he is very potent with such spirits, Abuses me to damn me *Hamlet* ii 2 631
O, I die, Horatio; The potent poison quite o'er-crows my spirit v 2 364
Most potent, grave, and reverend signiors *Othello* i 3 76
I learned it in England, where, indeed, they are most potent in potting ii 3 79
And gives his potent regiment to a trull *Ant. and Cleo.* iii 6 95
No longer exercise Upon a valiant race thy harsh And potent injuries *Cymbeline* v 4 84
O you most potent gods! what's here? *Pericles* iii 2 63
Potentates. With commendation from great potentates *T. G. of Ver.* ii 4 79
Dost thou infamonize me among potentates? *L. L. Lost* v 2 684
Kings and mightiest potentates must die 1 *Hen. VI.* iii 2 136
Potential. The profits of my death Were very pregnant and potential spurs To make thee seek it *Lear* ii 1 78
Is much beloved, And hath in his effect a voice potential *Othello* i 2 13
Potently. You are potently opposed; and with a malice *Hen. VIII.* v 1 134
Though I most powerfully and potently believe *Hamlet* ii 2 204
'Pothecary. He did buy a poison Of a poor 'pothecary *Rom. and Jul.* v 3 289
Give this to the 'pothecary, And tell me how it works *Pericles* iii 2 9
Pother. Such a pother As if that whatsoever god who leads him Were slily crept into his human powers *Coriolanus* ii 1 234
Let the great gods, That keep this dreadful pother o'er our heads, Find out their enemies now *Lear* iii 2 50
Potion. He gives me the potions and the motions *Mer. Wives* iii 1 105
Out, loathed medicine! hated potion, hence! *M. N. Dream* iii 2 264
With no rash potion, But with a lingering dram *W. Tale* i 2 319
As speedy in your end As all the poisonous potions in the world 1 *Hen. IV.* v 4 56
They did fight with queasiness, constrain'd, As men drink potions 2 *Hen. IV.* i 1 197
Your lordship may minister the potion of imprisonment to me i 2 145
Then gave I her, so tutor'd by my art, A sleeping potion *Rom. and Jul.* v 3 244
Being the time the potion's force should cease v 3 249
Thou incestuous, murderous, damned Dane, Drink off this potion *Hamlet* v 2 337
Minister'st a potion unto me That thou wouldst tremble to receive *Pericles* i 2 68
Potpan. Where's Potpan, that he helps not to take away? *Rom. and Jul.* i 5 1
Antony, and Potpan!—Ay, boy, ready.—You are looked for i 5 11
Pots. And wild Half-can that stabbed Pots *Meas. for Meas.* iv 3 19
Potter. My thoughts are whirled like a potter's wheel 1 *Hen. VI.* i 5 19
Potting. I learned it in England, where, indeed, they are most potent in potting *Othello* ii 3 79
Pottle. I'll give you a pottle of burnt sack to give me recourse to him *Mer. Wives* ii 1 223
Go brew me a pottle of sack finely.—With eggs, sir?—Simple of itself iii 5 30
He gives your Hollander a vomit, ere the next pottle can be filled *Othello* ii 3 87
Pottle-deep. Hath to-night caroused Potations pottle-deep ii 3 56
Pottle-pot. Is't such a matter to get a pottle-pot's maidenhead? 2 *Hen. IV.* ii 2 83
You'll crack a quart together, ha! . . . Yea, sir, in a pottle-pot v 3 68
Pouch. Tester I'll have in pouch when thou shalt lack *Mer. Wives* i 3 96
With spectacles on nose and pouch on side *As Y. Like It* ii 7 159
Poulter's hare. Hang me up by the heels for a rabbit-sucker or a poulter's hare 1 *Hen. IV.* ii 4 480
Poultice. Is this the poultice for my aching bones? *Rom. and Jul.* ii 5 65
Poultney. Within the parish Saint Lawrence Poultney *Hen. VIII.* i 2 153
Pouncet-box. And 'twixt his finger and his thumb he held A pouncet-box, which ever and anon He gave his nose 1 *Hen. IV.* i 3 38
Pound. 'Twere best pound you.—Nay, sir, less than a pound shall serve me for carrying your letter *T. G. of Ver.* i 1 110
I mean the pound,—a pinfold.—From a pound to a pin? fold it over and over i 1 113
Seven hundred pounds of moneys, and gold and silver *Mer. Wives* i 1 52
Did her grandsire leave her seven hundred pound? i 1 60
Seven hundred pounds and possibilities is goot gifts i 1 65
I sit at ten pounds a week i 3 8
I had rather than a thousand pound he were out of the house iii 3 131
O, what a world of vile ill-favour'd faults Looks handsome in three hundred pounds a-year! iii 4 33
He will make you a hundred and fifty pounds jointure iii 4 50
I'll give thee A hundred pound in gold more than your loss iv 6 5
He hath enjoyed nothing of Ford's but his buck-basket, his cudgel, and twenty pounds of money v 5 117
Pound. A man of fourscore pound a year *Meas. for Meas.* ii 1 127
Are you of fourscore pounds a year?—Yes, an't please you, sir ii 1 204
A commodity of brown paper and old ginger, nine-score and seventeen pounds iv 3 7
I buy a thousand pound a year: I buy a rope *Com. of Errors* iv 1 21
It will cost him a thousand pound ere a' be cured *Much Ado* i 1 90
All thy tediousness on me, ah?—Yea, an 'twere a thousand pound more than 'tis iii 5 27
The forfeit Be nominated for an equal pound Of your fair flesh *M. of Ven.* i 3 150
A pound of man's flesh taken from a man Is not so estimable i 3 166
I shall hardly spare a pound of flesh To-morrow to my bloody creditor iii 3 33
The penalty, Which is a pound of this poor merchant's flesh iv 1 23
The pound of flesh, which I demand of him, Is dearly bought iv 1 99
Lawfully by this the Jew may claim A pound of flesh iv 1 232
A pound of that same merchant's flesh is thine: The court awards it iv 1 299
The words expressly are 'a pound of flesh:' Take then thy bond, take thou thy pound of flesh iv 1 307
Just a pound of flesh: if thou cut'st more Or less than a just pound iv 1 326
I would not lose the dog for twenty pound *T. of Shrew* Ind 1 21
What if a man bring him a hundred pound or two, to make merry withal? v 1 22
Keep your hundred pounds to yourself: he shall need none v 1 24
I had rather than forty pound I were at home *T. Night* v 1 181
Every 'leven wether tods; every tod yields pound and odd shilling *W. T.* iv 3 34
Three pound of sugar, five pound of currants iv 3 40
Four pound of prunes, and as many of raisins o' the sun iv 3 51
Pops me out At least from fair five hundred pound a year *K. John* i 1 69
Your face hath got five hundred pound a year i 1 152
Bid her send me presently a thousand pound *Richard II.* ii 2 91
I will give thee for it a thousand pound 1 *Hen. IV.* ii 4 69
I would give a thousand pound I could run as fast as thou canst ii 4 163
There be four of us here have ta'en a thousand pound this day morning ii 4 176
And money lent you, four and twenty pound iii 3 86
Three or four bonds of forty pound a-piece iii 3 117
Said this other day you ought him a thousand pound iii 3 152
Do I owe you a thousand pound?—A thousand pound, Hal! a million iii 3 154
In exchange of a hundred and fifty soldiers, three hundred and odd pounds iv 2 15
Lend me a thousand pound to furnish me forth 2 *Hen. IV.* i 2 251
Let it be ten pound, if thou canst ii 1 160
A score of good ewes may be worth ten pounds iii 2 57
A word with you: I have three pound to free Mouldy and Bullcalf iii 2 261
I would have bestowed the thousand pound I borrowed of you v 5 12
Master Shallow, I owe you a thousand pound v 5 78
A thousand pounds by the year: thus runs the bill *Hen. V.* i 1 19
Many a pound of mine own proper store 2 *Hen. VI.* iii 1 115
Show me where he is: I'll give a thousand pound to look upon him iii 3 13
He that made us pay one and twenty fifteens, and one shilling to the pound iv 7 25
A thousand pound a year, annual support *Hen. VIII.* ii 3 64
Nor could Come pat betwixt too early and too late For any suit of pounds ii 3 85
A thousand pounds a year for pure respect! No other obligation! ii 3 95
Yet will he, within three pound, lift as much as his brother *Troi. and Cres.* i 2 126
We'll break our walls, Rather than they shall pound us up *Coriolanus* i 4 17
Will too late Tie leaden pounds to's heels iii 1 314
I'll take the ghost's word for a thousand pound *Hamlet* iii 2 298
I had a hundred pound on't *Cymbeline* ii 1 3
Granted Rome a tribute, Yearly three thousand pounds iii 1 9
Pour. The sky, it seems, would pour down stinking pitch *Tempest* i 2 3
I will pour some in thy other mouth ii 2 98
Come, let me pour in some sack to the Thames water *Mer. Wives* iii 5 22
Thus pour the stars down plagues for perjury *L. L. Lost* v 2 394
Against her lips I bob And on her wither'd dewlap pour the ale *M. N. D.* ii 1 50
Pour this concealed man out of thy mouth *As Y. Like It* iii 2 210
Or rather, bottomless, that as fast as you pour affection in, it runs out iv 1 215
In this captious and intenible sieve I still pour in the waters of my love And lack not to lose still *All's Well* i 3 209
From your sacred vials pour your graces Upon my daughter's head! *W. Tale* v 3 122
Some airy devil hovers in the sky And pours down mischief *K. John* iii 2 3
In despite of brooded watchful day, I would into thy bosom pour my thoughts iii 3 53
So foul a sky clears not without a storm: Pour down thy weather iv 2 109
As, force perforce, the age will pour it in 2 *Hen. IV.* iv 4 46
How London doth pour out her citizens! *Hen. V.* v Prol. 24
Lo, in these windows that let forth thy life, I pour the helpless balm of my poor eyes *Richard III.* i 2 13
Alas, you three, on me, threefold distress'd, Pour all your tears! ii 2 87
Force him with praises: pour in, pour in; his ambition is dry *Troi. and Cres.* ii 3 233
He outgoes The very heart of kindness.—He pours it out *T. of Athens* i 2 287
Is this the balsam that the usuring senate Pours into captains' wounds? iii 5 111
Hie thee hither, That I may pour my spirits in thine ear *Macbeth* i 5 27
Pour in sow's blood, that hath eaten Her nine farrow iv 1 64
Nay, had I power, I should Pour the sweet milk of concord into hell iv 3 98
And with him pour we in our country's purge Each drop of us v 2 28
In the porches of my ears did pour The leperous distilment *Hamlet* i 5 63
In such a night To shut me out! Pour on; I will endure *Lear* iii 4 18
I'll pour this pestilence into his ear *Othello* ii 3 362
Say that they slack their duties, And pour our treasures into foreign laps iv 3 89
Bring it to that, The gold I give thee will I melt and pour Down thy ill-uttering throat *Ant. and Cleo.* ii 5 34
Pour out the pack of matter to mine ear, The good and bad together ii 5 54
Pupils lacks she none of noble race, Who pour their bounty on her *Pericles* v Gower 10
Poured. It is a figure in rhetoric that drink, being poured out of a cup into a glass, by filling the one doth empty the other *As Y. Like It* v 1 46
Our bloods, Of colour, weight, and heat, pour'd all together, Would quite confound distinction, yet stand off In differences so mighty *All's Well* ii 3 126
I would have ransack'd The pedlar's silken treasury and have pour'd it To her acceptance *W. Tale* iv 4 361
Remember, boys, I pour'd forth tears in vain, To save your brother *T. Andron.* ii 3 163
Every one did bear Thy praises in his kingdom's great defence, And pour'd them down before him *Macbeth* i 3 100
A mad rogue! a' poured a flagon of Rhenish on my head once *Hamlet* v 1 197
Your honour has through Ephesus pour'd forth Your charity *Pericles* iii 2 43
Pourest. That pretty Welsh Which thou pour'st down 1 *Hen. IV.* iii 1 202
Pour'st in the open ulcer of my heart Her eyes, her hair, her cheek *Troi. and Cres.* i 1 53

Pouring. Came pouring, like the tide into a breach . . . *Hen. V.* i 2 149
Pouring war Into the bowels of ungrateful Rome . . *Coriolanus* iv 5 135
Pourquoi. I'll ride home to-morrow, Sir Toby.—Pourquoi, my dear knight?—What is 'pourquoi'? do or not do? . . . *T. Night* i 3 95
Pout. The veins unfill'd, our blood is cold, and then We pout upon the morning . . . . *Coriolanus* v 1 52
Poutest. Like a misbehaved and sullen wench, Thou pout'st upon thy fortune and thy love . . . *Rom. and Jul.* iii 3 144
Poverty. Letters should not be known; riches, poverty, And use of service, none . . . . . . *Tempest* ii 1 150
And what with poverty, I am custom-shrunk . . *Meas. for Meas.* i 2 85
O poverty in wit, kingly-poor flout! . . . . . *L. L. Lost* v 2 269
I am a fool, and full of poverty . . . . . . v 2 380
To view with hollow eye and wrinkled brow An age of poverty *M. of Ven.* iv 1 271
Mistake me not so much To think my poverty is treacherous *As Y. L. It* i 3 67
So holy and so perfect is my love, And I in such a poverty of grace . iii 5 100
Neither call the giddiness of it in question, the poverty of her . v 2 7
Yet for the outside of thy poverty we must make an exchange *W. Tale* iv 4 647
'Faith, for their poverty, I know not where they had that 1 *Hen. IV.* iv 2 76
Minister the potion of imprisonment to me in respect of poverty 2 *Hen. IV.* i 2 146
His coffers sound With hollow poverty and emptiness . . . i 3 75
She hath been in good case, and the truth is, poverty hath distracted her ii 1 116
In her heart she scorns our poverty . . . . 2 *Hen. VI.* i 3 84
So much is my poverty of spirit, So mighty and so many my defects *Richard III.* iii 7 159
They are the poorest, But poverty could never draw 'em from me *Hen. VIII.* iv 2 149
My poverty, but not my will, consents.—I pay thy poverty *R. and J.* v 1 75
With his disease of all-shunn'd poverty . . . *T. of Athens* iv 2 14
You houseless poverty . . . . *Lear* iii 4 26
Steep'd me in poverty to the very lips . . . . *Othello* iv 2 50
All poverty was scorn'd, and pride so great . . . *Pericles* i 4 30
Powder. With swifter spleen than powder can enforce . . *K. John* ii 1 448
Food for powder; they'll fill a pit as well as better . 1 *Hen. IV.* iv 2 72
If thou embowel me to-day, I'll give you leave to powder me and eat me too . . . . v 4 112
When that they are dead, Let me go grind their bones to powder *T. An.* v 2 199
Like fire and powder, Which as they kiss consume . *Rom. and Jul.* ii 6 10
Like powder in a skilless soldier's flask, Is set a-fire by thine own ignorance . . . . iii 3 132
Violently as hasty powder fired Doth hurry from the fatal cannon's womb v 1 64
Being dried with grief, will break to powder, And finish all *A. and C.* iv 9 17
Powdered. Ever your fresh whore and your powdered bawd *M. for M.* iii 2 61
Powdering-tub. From the powdering-tub of infamy . . *Hen. V.* ii 1 79
Power. Had I been any god of power, I would Have sunk the sea *Tempest* i 2 10
Thy father was the Duke of Milan and A prince of power . . i 2 55
Not only with what my revenue yielded, But what my power might else exact . . . . i 2 99
His art is of such power, It would control my dam's god, Setebos . . i 2 372
They are both in either's powers . . . . . . i 2 450
I will resist such entertainment till Mine enemy has more power . . i 2 466
The powers, delaying, not forgetting, have Incensed the seas and shores iii 3 73
They now are in my power . . . . iii 3 90
Go bring the rabble, O'er whom I give thee power . . . iv 1 38
Some heavenly power guide us Out of this fearful country! . . . v 1 105
One so strong That could control the moon, make flows and ebbs, And deal in her command without her power . . . . . v 1 271
Even that power which gave me first my oath Provokes me *T. G. of Ver.* ii 6 4
No more; unless the next word that thou speak'st Have some malignant power upon my life . . . . iii 1 238
The guiltiness of my mind, the sudden surprise of my powers *Mer. Wives* v 5 131
Given his deputation all the organs Of our own power . *Meas. for Meas.* i 1 22
A power I have, but of what strength and nature I am not yet instructed i 1 80
My absolute power and place here in Vienna . . . . . i 3 13
Hence shall we see, If power change purpose, what our seemers be . i 3 54
Assay the power you have.—My power? Alas, I doubt . . . i 4 76
He doth with holy abstinence subdue That in himself which he spurs on his power To qualify in others . . . . . . iv 2 85
Who do prepare to meet him at the gates, There to give up their power iv 3 137
Which shall then have no power to stand against us . . . iv 4 15
I perceive your grace, like power divine, Hath look'd upon my passes . v 1 374
Rather Make rash remonstrance of my hidden power Than let him so be lost . . . . v 1 397
Transform me then, and to your power I'll yield . *Com. of Errors* iii 2 40
Here we wander in illusions: Some blessed power deliver us from hence! iv 3 44
That advance their pride Against that power that bred it *Much Ado* iii 1 11
By that fatherly and kindly power That you have in her, bid her answer iv 1 75
Whose edge hath power to cut, whose will still wills It should none spare that come within his power . . . . *L. L. Lost* ii 1 50
Most power to do most harm, least knowing ill . . . . ii 1 58
I fear these stubborn lines lack power to move . . . . iv 3 55
Gives to every power a double power, Above their functions . . . iv 3 331
All the power thereof it doth apply To prove, by wit, worth in simplicity v 2 77
To flatter up these powers of mine with rest . . . . . v 2 824
And within his power To leave the figure or disfigure it *M. N. Dream* i 1 50
I know not by what power I am made bold . . . . . i 1 59
Ere a man hath power to say 'Behold!' The jaws of darkness do devour it . . . . i 1 147
Leave you your power to draw, And I shall have no power to follow you ii 1 197
Upon thy eyes I throw All the power this charm doth owe . . . ii 2 79
All my powers, address your love and might To honour Helen! . . . ii 2 143
Dian's bud o'er Cupid's flower Hath such force and blessed power . iv 1 79
I wot not by what power,—But by some power it is . . . iv 1 169
A thing not in his power to bring to pass . . . *Mer. of Venice* i 3 93
But her eyes,—How could he see to do them? having made one, Methinks it should have power to steal both his And leave itself unfurnish'd . . . . iii 2 125
There is such confusion in my powers, As, after some oration fairly spoke iii 2 179
If that the youth of my new interest here Have power to bid you welcome iii 2 225
If law, authority and power deny not, It will go hard with poor Antonio iii 2 291
Upon my power I may dismiss this court . . . . . . iv 1 104
His sceptre shows the force of temporal power, The attribute to awe . iv 1 190
Earthly power doth then show likest God's When mercy seasons justice iv 1 196
No power in Venice Can alter a decree established . . . . iv 1 218
There is no power in the tongue of man To alter me . . . . iv 1 241
I would she were in heaven, so she could Entreat some power to change this currish Jew . . . . iv 1 292
Their savage eyes turn'd to a modest gaze By the sweet power of music v 1 79
Thy conceit is nearer death than thy powers . . . *As. Y. Like It* ii 6 9
If ever . . . You meet in some fresh cheek the power of fancy . . iii 5 29
Power. If the scorn of your bright eyne Have power to raise such love in mine . . . . *As Y. Like It* iv 3 51
Address'd a mighty power; which were on foot, In his own conduct . v 4 162
Be able for thine enemy Rather in power than use . . . *All's Well* i 1 75
What power is it which mounts my love so high? . . . . . i 1 235
Wherein the honour Of my dear father's gift stands chief in power . ii 1 115
My art is not past power nor you past cure . . . . . ii 1 161
Give me with thy kingly hand What husband in thy power I will command . . . . ii 1 197
In a most weak—and debile minister, great power, great transcendence ii 3 40
O'er whom both sovereign power and father's voice I have to use: thy frank election make; Thou hast power to choose, and they none to forsake . . . . ii 3 60
I give Me and my service, ever whilst I live, Into your guiding power . ii 3 111
My honour's at the stake; which to defeat, I must produce my power . ii 3 157
Do thine own fortunes that obedient right Which both thy duty owes and our power claims . . . . ii 3 168
And deliver all the intelligence in his power against you . . . iii 6 33
I'll lend it thee, my dear; but have no power To give it from me . . iv 2 40
This man may help me to his majesty's ear, If he would spend his power v 1 8
And aid me with that store of power you have . . . . . v 1 20
Make their pastime at my sorrow: They should not laugh if I could reach them, nor Shall she within my power . . . . *W. Tale* ii 3 26
If powers divine Behold our human actions, as they do . . . iii 2 29
The higher powers forbid! . . . . iii 2 203
Since it is in my power To o'erthrow law . . . . . . iv 1 7
Your resolution cannot hold, when 'tis Opposed, as it must be, by the power of the king . . . . iv 4 37
Had she such power, She had just cause . . . . . . v 1 60
Though Fortune, visible an enemy, Should chase us with my father, power no jot Hath she to change our loves . . . . . v 1 217
I will prove so, sir, to my power . . . . v 2 182
Let him that was the cause of this have power To take off so much grief from you as he Will piece up in himself . . . . v 3 54
You'll think—Which I protest against—I am assisted By wicked powers v 3 91
And wide havoc made For bloody power to rush upon your peace *K. John* ii 1 221
Strength match'd with strength, and power confronted power . . ii 1 330
A greater power than we denies all this . . . . . . ii 1 368
France, shall we knit our powers And lay this Angiers even with the ground? . . . . ii 1 398
Not that I have the power to clutch my hand, When his fair angels would salute my palm . . . . ii 1 589
Then, by the lawful power that I have, Thou shalt stand cursed . . iii 1 172
For without my wrong There is no tongue hath power to curse him right iii 1 183
And raise the power of France upon his head, Unless he do submit . iii 1 193
I'll send those powers o'er to your majesty . . . . . iii 3 70
Never such a power For any foreign preparation Was levied . . . iv 2 110
Under whose conduct came those powers of France? . . . . iv 2 129
My state is braved, Even at my gates, with ranks of foreign powers . iv 2 244
Now powers from home and discontents at home Meet in one line . . iv 3 151
And from his holiness use all your power To stop their marches . . v 1 6
London hath received, Like a kind host, the Dauphin and his powers . v 1 32
And he hath promised to dismiss the powers Led by the Dauphin . . v 1 64
An hour or two before The stumbling night did part our weary powers . v 5 18
Tempt us not to bear above our power! . . . . . . v 6 38
Half my power this night, Passing these flats, are taken by the tide . v 6 39
The best part of my power . . . Devoured by the unexpected flood . v 7 61
You stars that move in your right spheres, Where be your powers? . v 7 75
Gnarling sorrow hath less power to bite The man that mocks at it *Rich. II.* i 3 292
He, our hope, might have retired his power . . . . . ii 2 46
For us to levy power Proportionable to the enemy Is all unpossible . ii 2 124
To discover What power the Duke of York had levied there . . . ii 3 34
The king is left behind, And in my loyal bosom lies his power . . ii 3 98
I cannot mend it, I must needs confess, Because my power is weak . ii 3 154
That Power that made you king Hath power to keep you king . . iii 2 27
Through our security, Grows strong and great in substance and in power iii 2 35
How far off lies your power?—Nor near nor farther off, my gracious lord, Than this weak arm . . . . iii 2 63
I know my uncle York Hath power enough to serve our turn . . iii 2 90
Both young and old rebel, And all goes worse than I have power to tell iii 2 120
Where is the duke my father with his power?—No matter where . . iii 2 143
My father hath a power; inquire of him, And learn to make a body of a limb . . . . iii 2 186
Where lies our uncle with his power? Speak sweetly, man . . . iii 2 192
That power I have, discharge; and let them go To ear the land . . iii 2 211
Hither come Even at his feet to lay my arms and power . . . iii 3 39
I'll use the advantage of my power . . . . iii 3 42
Help to order several powers To Oxford, or where'er these traitors are v 3 140
Forthwith a power of English shall we levy . . . 1 *Hen. IV.* i 1 22
That men of your nobility and power Did gage them both in an unjust behalf . . . . i 3 172
And make the Douglas' son your only mean For powers in Scotland . i 3 262
And our powers at once, As I will fashion it, shall happily meet . . i 3 296
If thou have power to raise him, bring him hither, And I'll be sworn I have power to shame him hence . . . . iii 1 60
Three times hath Henry Bolingbroke made head Against my power . . iii 1 65
Worcester will set forth To meet your father and the Scottish power . iii 1 85
Who leads his power? Under whose government come they along? . iv 1 18
He cannot draw his power this fourteen days . . . . . iv 1 126
The powers of us may serve so great a day . . . . . iv 1 132
'Tis more than time that I were there, and you too; but my powers are there already . . . . iv 2 61
The king with mighty and quick-raised power Meets with Lord Harry . iv 4 12
Whose power was in the first proportion . . . . . . iv 4 15
I fear the power of Percy is too weak To wage an instant trial . . iv 4 19
Ere the king Dismiss his power, he means to visit us . . . . iv 4 37
Then this remains, that we divide our power . . . . . v 5 34
And hath sent out A speedy power to encounter you . . 2 *Hen. IV.* i 1 133
The gentle Archbishop of York is up With well-appointed powers . . i 1 190
We should advance ourselves To look with forehead bold and big enough Upon the power and puissance of the king . . . . . i 3 9
Flattering himself in project of a power . . . . . . i 3 29
Led his powers to death And winking leap'd into destruction . . . i 3 32
Like one that draws the model of a house Beyond his power to build it i 3 59
One power against the French, And one against Glendower . . . i 3 71
You speak as having power to do wrong . . . . . . ii 1 141
Threw many a northward look to see his father Bring up his powers . ii 3 14
The powers that you already have sent forth Shall bring this prize in . iii 1 100
With such powers As might hold sortance with his quality . . . iv 1 10
And knit our powers to the arm of peace . . . . . . iv 1 177

Power. So that his power, like to a fangless lion, May offer, but not hold 2 *Hen. IV.* iv 1 218
Discharge your powers unto their several counties, As we will ours . iv 2 61
The heat is past ; follow no further now : Call in the powers . iv 3 28
Our navy is address'd, our power collected . . . . . iv 4 5
With a great power of English and of Scots, Are by the sheriff of Yorkshire overthrown . . . . iv 4 98
And by whose power I well might lodge a fear To be again displaced . iv 5 208
The image of his power lay then in me . . . . . v 2 74
Pleased to forget my place, The majesty and power of law and justice . v 2 78
Imagine me taking your part And in your power soft silencing your son v 2 97
Making defeat on the full power of France . . . *Hen. V.* i 2 107
If we, with thrice such powers left at home, Cannot defend our own doors i 2 217
By God's help, And yours, the noble sinews of our power . . i 2 223
Think you not that the powers we bear with us Will cut their passage? ii 2 15
Thus comes the English with full power upon us . . . ii 4 1
Returns us that his powers are yet not ready To raise so great a siege . iii 3 46
Go down upon him, you have power enough . . . . iii 5 53
With my soul, and my heart, and my duty, and my life, and my living, and my uttermost power . . . . iii 6 10
And take with you free power to ratify, Augment, or alter . . v 2 86
Whom with my bare fists I would execute, If I now had him brought into my power . . . . 1 *Hen. VI.* i 4 37
A holy prophetess new risen up Is come with a great power to raise the siege . . . . i 4 103
At all times will you have my power alike? Sleeping or waking? . ii 1 55
We'll follow them with all the power we have . . . . ii 2 33
You may perceive Their powers are marching unto Paris-ward . . iii 3 30
My forces and my power of men are yours . . . . . iii 3 83
On, my lords, and join our powers, And seek how we may prejudice the foe . . . . iii 3 90
Do him homage . . . ; And I'll withdraw me and my bloody power . iv 2 8
He is march'd to Bourdeaux with his power, To fight with Talbot . iv 3 4
Keep not back your powers in dalliance . . . . . v 2 5
O, stay ! I have no power to let her pass . . . . . v 3 60
By the eternal God, whose name and power Thou tremblest at 2 *Hen. VI.* i 4 28
Sorrow and grief have vanquish'd all my powers . . . . ii 1 183
Twenty times so many foes, And each of them had twenty times their power . . . . ii 4 61
A raven's note, Whose dismal tune bereft my vital powers . . . iii 2 41
Retire to Killingworth, Until a power be raised to put them down . iv 4 40
He is fled, my lord, and all his powers do yield . . . . iv 9 10
A mighty power Of gallowglasses and stout kerns Is marching hitherward iv 9 25
Then, Buckingham, I do dismiss my powers. Soldiers, I thank you all v 1 44
He means, Back'd by the power of Warwick, that false peer . 3 *Hen. VI.* i 1 52
'Tis not thy southern power, Of Essex, Norfolk, Suffolk, nor of Kent . i 1 155
Their power, I think, is thirty thousand strong . . . . ii 1 177
Hence ; and lose no hour, Till we meet Warwick with his foreign power iv 1 149
If secret powers Suggest but truth to my divining thoughts . . iv 6 68
The power that Edward hath in field Should not be able to encounter mine . . . . iv 8 35
The queen from France hath brought a puissant power . . . v 2 31
Away, away, to meet the queen's great power ! . . . . v 2 50
Those powers that the queen Hath raised in Gallia have arrived our coast . . . . v 3 7
Thou hadst but power over his mortal body . . . *Richard. III.* i 2 47
You have power in me as in a kinsman . . . . . iii 1 109
Is in the field, and still his power increaseth . . . . iv 3 48
Bid him levy straight The greatest strength and power he can make . iv 4 449
Where is thy power, then, to beat him back? Where are thy tenants? iv 4 480
The Earl of Richmond Is with a mighty power landed at Milford . iv 4 535
Six or seven thousand is their utmost power . . . . . v 3 10
Lies half a mile at least South from the mighty power of the king . v 3 38
Bid him bring his power Before sunrising, lest his son George fall . v 3 60
Bid him bring his power : I will lead forth my soldiers to the plain . v 3 290
What says Lord Stanley? will he bring his power?—My lord, he doth deny to come . . . . v 3 342
Consider further that What his high hatred would effect wants not A minister in his power . . . . . . *Hen. VIII.* i 1 108
This butcher's cur is venom-mouth'd, and I Have not the power to muzzle him . . . . i 1 121
Half your suit Never name to us ; you have half our power . . . i 2 11
By commission and main power, took 'em from me . . . . ii 2 7
Of disposition gentle, and of wisdom O'ertopping woman's power . . ii 4 88
Powers are your retainers, and your words, Domestics to you . . ii 4 113
Shook The bosom of my conscience, enter'd me, Yea, with a splitting power . . . . ii 4 183
My heart dropp'd love, my power rain'd honour, more On you than any iii 2 185
Your hand and heart, Your brain, and every function of your power . iii 2 187
By which power You maim'd the jurisdiction of all bishops . . iii 2 311
All those things you have done of late, By your power legatine . . iii 2 339
Why, how now, Cromwell !—I have no power to speak, sir . . iii 2 373
I gave ye Power as he was a counsellor to try him, Not as a groom . v 3 143
Then every thing includes itself in power, Power into will, will into appetite ; And appetite, an universal wolf, So doubly seconded with will and power, Must make perforce an universal prey *Troi. and Cres.* i 3 119
The fever whereof all our power is sick . . . . . . i 3 139
Were I alone to pass the difficulties And had as ample power as I have will ii 2 140
To-morrow We must with all our main of power stand fast . . iii 3 273
Tuned too sharp in sweetness, For the capacity of my ruder powers . iii 2 26
And all my powers do their bestowing lose . . . . . iii 2 39
We are devils to ourselves, When we will tempt the frailty of our powers iv 4 98
To break the heart of generosity, And make bold power look pale *Coriol.* i 1 216
It will in time Win upon power and throw forth greater themes . . i 1 224
They have press'd a power, but it is not known Whether for east or west i 2 9
Some parcels of their power are forth already, And only hitherward . i 2 32
Cominius the general is gone, with one part of our Roman power . . i 3 109
Both our powers, with smiling fronts encountering . . . . i 6 8
For thy revenge Wrench up thy power to the highest . . . i 8 11
To undercrest your good addition To the fairness of my power . . i 9 73
As if that whatsoever god who leads him Were slily crept into his human powers And gave him graceful posture . . . . . ii 1 236
I warrant him consul.—Then our office may, During his power, go sleep ii 1 239
That to's power he would Have made them mules . . . . ii 1 262
We may, sir, if we will.—We have power in ourselves to do it, but it is a power that we have no power to do . . . . . . ii 3 4
When he had no power, But was a petty servant to the state, He was your enemy . . . . ii 3 185
And do you think That his contempt shall not be bruising to you, When he hath power to crush? . . . . ii 3 211

Power. Lack not virtue, no, nor power, but that Which they have given to beggars . . . . *Coriolanus* iii 1 73
If he have power, Then vail your ignorance . . . . . . iii 1 97
Though there the people had more absolute power, I say, they nourish'd disobedience, fed The ruin of the state . . . . . iii 1 116
Not having the power to do the good it would, For the ill which doth control't . . . . iii 1 160
Let what is meet be said it must be meet, And throw their power i' the dust iii 1 171
Here's he that would take from you all your power . . . . iii 1 182
Upon the part o' the people, in whose power We were elected theirs . iii 1 210
He would not flatter Neptune for his trident, Or Jove for's power to thunder . . . . iii 1 257
Law shall scorn him further trial Than the severity of the public power iii 1 269
I would have had you put your power well on, Before you had worn it out iii 2 17
If You had not show'd them how ye were disposed Ere they lack'd power to cross you . . . . iii 2 23
Thyself, forsooth, hereafter theirs, so far As thou hast power and person iii 2 86
In this point charge him home, that he affects Tyrannical power . . iii 3 2
Insisting on the old prerogative And power i' the truth o' the cause . iii 3 18
You have contrived . . . to wind Yourself into a power tyrannical . iii 3 65
And here defying Those whose great power must try him . . . iii 3 80
Envied against the people, seeking means To pluck away their power . iii 3 96
In the power of us the tribunes, we, Even from this instant, banish him iii 3 100
Have the power still To banish your defenders . . . . . iii 3 127
Now we have shown our power, Let us seem humbler after it is done . iv 2 3
You shall stay too ; I would I had the power To say so to my husband iv 2 15
They are in a ripe aptness to take all power from the people . . iv 3 24
Why, thou Mars ! I tell thee, We have a power on foot . . . iv 5 125
The Volsces with two several powers Are enter'd in the Roman territories iv 6 39
Marcius, Join'd with Aufidius, leads a power 'gainst Rome . . iv 6 66
And power, unto itself most commendable, Hath not a tomb so evident as a chair To extol what it hath done . . . . iv 7 51
'Tis a spell, you see, of much power: you know the way home again . v 2 103
In the high'st degree He hath abused your powers . . . . v 6 86
If Rome have law or we have power . . . . . *T. Andron.* i 1 403
Had I the power that some say Dian had, Thy temples should be planted presently With horns, as was Actæon's . . . . . . ii 3 61
If any power pities wretched tears, To that I call ! . . . . iii 1 209
Now will I to the Goths, and raise a power, To be revenged on Rome . iii 1 300
With a power Of high-resolved men, bent to the spoil . . . iv 4 63
But passion lends them power, time means, to meet *Rom. and Jul.* ii Prol. 13
Within the infant rind of this small flower Poison hath residence and medicine power . . . . ii 3 24
If all else fail, myself have power to die . . . . . iii 5 242
Death, that hath suck'd the honey of thy breath, Hath had no power yet upon thy beauty . . . . v 3 93
A greater power than we can contradict Hath thwarted our intents . v 3 153
Magic of bounty ! all these spirits thy power Hath conjured *T. of Athens* i 1 6
What a mental power This eye shoots forth ! . . . . . i 1 31
I myself would have no power ; prithee, let my meat make thee silent . i 2 36
What a beggar his heart is, Being of no power to make his wishes good i 2 202
Be of any power To expel sickness, but prolong his hour ! . . . iii 1 65
Conceive the fairest of me, because I have no power to be kind . . iii 2 61
What wouldst thou do with the world, Apemantus, if it lay in thy power? iv 3 322
The laws, your curb and whip, in their rough power Have uncheck'd theft iv 3 446
That you had power and wealth To requite me, by making rich yourself iv 3 528
Thou shalt be met with thanks, Allow'd with absolute power . . v 1 165
Myself and such As slept within the shadow of your power . . . v 4 6
Ere thou hadst power or we had cause of fear, We sent to thee . . v 4 15
All thy powers Shall make their harbour in our town . . . . v 4 52
But life, being weary of these worldly bars, Never lacks power to dismiss itself . . . . *J. Cæsar* i 3 97
Every bondman in his own hand bears The power to cancel his captivity i 3 102
The abuse of greatness is, when it disjoins Remorse from power . . ii 1 19
Action, nor utterance, nor the power of speech, To stir men's blood . iii 2 226
Brutus and Cassius Are levying powers : we must straight make head . iv 1 42
Octavius and Mark Antony Come down upon us with a mighty power . iv 3 169
Bid him set on his powers betimes before, And we will follow . . iv 3 308
Arming myself with patience To stay the providence of some high powers v 1 107
Octavius Is overthrown by noble Brutus' power . . . . . v 3 52
Merciful powers, Restrain in me the cursed thoughts that nature Gives way to in repose ! . . . . *Macbeth* ii 1 8
Though I could With barefaced power sweep him from my sight . . iii 1 119
Tell me, thou unknown power,— He knows thy thought: hear his speech iv 1 69
Be bloody, bold, and resolute ; laugh to scorn The power of man . . iv 1 80
Nay, had I power, I should Pour the sweet milk of concord into hell . iv 3 97
By many of these trains hath sought to win me Into his power . . iv 3 119
I saw the tyrant's power a-foot: Now is the time of help . . . iv 3 185
Go we to the king ; our power is ready ; Our lack is nothing but our leave iv 3 236
Macbeth Is ripe for shaking, and the powers above Put on their instruments . . . . iv 3 238
What need we fear who knows it, when none can call our power to account? . . . . v 1 43
The English power is near, led on by Malcolm . . . . . v 2 1
No man that's born of woman Shall e'er have power upon thee . . v 3 7
But find the tyrant's power to-night, Let us be beaten, if we cannot fight v 6 7
No planets strike, No fairy takes, nor witch hath power to charm *Hamlet* i 1 163
Giving to you no further personal power To business with the king . i 2 36
O wicked wit and gifts, that have the power So to seduce ! . . . i 5 44
Both your majesties Might, by the sovereign power you have of us, Put your dread pleasures more into command Than to entreaty . . . ii 2 27
Out, out, thou strumpet, Fortune ! All you gods, In general synod, take away her power ! . . . . ii 2 516
The devil hath power To assume a pleasing shape . . . . . ii 2 628
The power of beauty will sooner transform honesty from what it is . iii 1 111
O heavenly powers, restore him ! . . . . iii 1 147
My operant powers their functions leave to do . . . . . iii 2 184
As my great power thereof may give thee sense . . . . iv 3 61
Good sir, whose powers are these?—They are of Norway, sir . . iv 4 9
I do invest you jointly with my power, Pre-eminence . . . *Lear* i 1 132
What wilt thou do, old man? Think'st thou that duty shall have dread to speak, When power to flattery bows? . . . . i 1 150
With strain'd pride To come between our sentence and our power . . i 1 173
By the power that made me, I tell you all her wealth . . . . i 1 210
And the king gone to-night! subscribed his power! Confined to exhibition ! . . . . i 2 24
Who sways, not as it hath power, but as it is suffered . . . . i 2 53
I am ashamed That thou hast power to shake my manhood thus . . i 4 319
He may enguard his dotage with their powers, And hold our lives in mercy . . . . i 4 349

Power. True it is, from France there comes a power Into this scatter'd kingdom . . . *Lear* iii 1 30
There's part of a power already footed: we must incline to the king . iii 3 14
All the power of his wits have given way to his impatience . . . iii 6 4
Our power Shall do a courtesy to our wrath, which Men may blame . iii 7 25
Let the superfluous and lust-dieted man, That slaves your ordinance, that will not see Because he doth not feel, feel your power quickly iv 1 72
Hasten his musters and conduct his powers: I must change arms at home iv 2 16
Of Albany's and Cornwall's powers you heard not? . . . iv 3 50
Are many simples operative, whose power Will close the eye of anguish iv 4 14
The British powers are marching hitherward.—'Tis known before . iv 4 21
Are my brother's powers set forth?—Ay, madam.—Himself in person there? . . . iv 5 1
Take that of me, my friend, who have the power To seal the accuser's lips iv 6 173
'Tis time to look about; the powers of the kingdom approach apace . iv 7 93
Draw up your powers. Here is the guess of their true strength and forces v 1 51
The battle done, and they within our power, Shall never see his pardon v 1 67
He led our powers; Bore the commission of my place and person . v 3 63
For us, we will resign, During the life of this old majesty, To him our absolute power . . . v 3 300
My spirit and my place have in them power To make this bitter to thee *Othello* i 1 103
The power and corrigible authority of this lies in our wills . i 3 329
Amen to that, sweet powers! I cannot speak enough of this content . ii 1 197
If I have any grace or power to move you . . . iii 3 46
Now, if this suit lay in Bianca's power, How quickly should you speed! iv 1 108
Thou hast not half that power to do me harm As I have to be hurt . v 2 162
O heaven! O heavenly powers!—Come, hold your peace . . v 2 218
Your power and your command is taken off, And Cassio rules in Cyprus v 2 331
Taunt my faults With such full license as both truth and malice Have power to utter . . . *Ant. and Cleo.* i 2 113
Who, high in name and power, Higher than both in blood and life . i 2 196
Let her not say 'tis I that keep you here: I have no power upon you . i 3 23
Equality of two domestic powers Breed scrupulous faction . . i 3 47
Beg often our own harms, which the wise powers Deny us for our good ii 1 6
My powers are crescent, and my auguring hope Says it will come to the full . . . ii 1 10
Mine honesty Shall not make poor my greatness, nor my power Work without it . . . ii 2 93
What power is in Agrippa, If I would say, 'Agrippa, be it so,' To make this good?—The power of Cæsar, and His power unto Octavia . ii 2 143
She did make defect perfection, And, breathless, power breathe forth . ii 2 237
The Jove of power make me most weak, most weak, Your reconciler! . iii 4 29
Can he be there in person? 'tis impossible; Strange that his power should be . . . iii 7 58
His whole action grows Not in the power on't: so our leader's led . iii 7 70
His power went out in such distractions as Beguiled all spies . iii 7 77
What thou think'st his very action speaks In every power that moves . iii 12 36
He calls me boy; and chides, as he had power To beat me out of Egypt iv 1 1
Had I great Juno's power, The strong-wing'd Mercury should fetch thee up . . . iv 15 34
Quicken with kissing: had my lips that power, Thus would I wear them out . . . iv 15 39
All's well, sir: take my power i' the court for yours *Cymbeline* i 6 179
Whose repair and franchise Shall, by the power we hold, be our good deed iii 1 58
The powers that he already hath in Gallia Will soon be drawn to head . iii 5 24
My mother, having power of his testiness, shall turn all into my commendations . . . iv 1 22
The want is but to put those powers in motion That long to move . iv 3 31
And so, great powers, If you will take this audit, take this life . v 4 26
A certain stuff, which, being ta'en, would cease The present power of life v 5 256
The power that I have on you is to spare you . . . v 5 418
The fingers of the powers above do tune The harmony of this peace . v 5 466
O you powers That give heaven countless eyes to view men's acts! *Per.* i 1 72
Thou know'st I have power To take thy life from thee . . i 2 56
Hath stuff'd these hollow vessels with their power, To beat us down . i 4 67
Let it suffice the greatness of your powers To have bereft a prince of all ii 1 8
Beauty hath his power and will, Which can as well inflame as it can kill ii 2 34
We cannot but obey The powers above us . . . iii 3 10
O, you have heard something of my power, and so stand aloof for more serious wooing . . . iv 6 94
The name Was given me by one that had some power, My father, and a king . . . v 1 150
This man, Through whom the gods have shown their power . v 3 60
Powerful. O powerful love! that, in some respects, makes a beast a man, in some other, a man a beast . . . *Mer. Wives* v 5 4
Whose simple touch Is powerful to araise King Pepin *All's Well* ii 1 79
Some blessed spirit doth speak His powerful sound within an organ weak ii 1 179
'Tis powerful, think it, From east, west, north and south . *W. Tale* i 2 202
Do your best To fright me with your sprites; you're powerful at it . ii 1 28
Some powerful spirit instruct the kites and ravens To be thy nurses! . ii 3 186
Gallows and knock are too powerful on the highway . . iv 3 29
With all their powerful friends, are fled to him . *Richard II.* ii 2 55
Spirits, that are cull'd Out of the powerful regions under earth *1 Hen. VI.* v 3 11
With powerful policy strengthen themselves . . . *3 Hen. VI.* i 2 58
And kept low shrubs from winter's powerful wind . . . v 2 15
Take not the quarrel from his powerful arm . . *Richard III.* i 4 223
Distinction, with a broad and powerful fan, Puffing at all *Troi. and Cres.* i 3 27
O, mickle is the powerful grace that lies In herbs, plants, stones *R. and J.* ii 3 15
For a charm of powerful trouble, Like a hell-broth boil and bubble *Macb.* iv 1 18
You fen-suck'd fogs, drawn by the powerful sun . . . *Lear* ii 4 169
With some mixtures powerful o'er the blood . . . *Othello* i 3 104
Great Jove, Othello guard, And swell his sail with thine own powerful breath! . . . ii 1 78
Who knows If the scarce-bearded Cæsar have not sent His powerful mandate to you, 'Do this, or this' . . *Ant. and Cleo.* i 1 22
Powerfully. Though I most powerfully and potently believe . *Hamlet* ii 2 203
Powerless. I give you welcome with a powerless hand . *K. John* ii 1 15
Powle. We may as well push against Powle's, as stir 'em . *Hen. VIII.* v 4 16
Pow, wow. The gods grant them true!—True! pow, wow . *Coriolanus* ii 1 157
Pox. A pox o' your throat, you bawling, blasphemous, incharitable dog! *Tempest* i 1 43
Not since widow Dido's time.—Widow! a pox o' that! How came that widow in? . . . ii 1 77
A pox o' your bottle! this can sack and drinking do . . iii 2 87
Pox of your love-letters! . . . *T. G. of Ver.* iii 1 390
A pox o' your throats! Who makes that noise there? *Meas. for Meas.* iv 3 26
Show your knave's visage, with a pox to you! . . . v 1 359
O that your face were not so full of O's!—A pox of that jest! *L. L. Lost* v 2 46
A pox on't, let it go; 'tis but a drum . . *All's Well* iii 6 48
A pox upon him for me, he's more and more a cat . . *All's Well* iv 3 295
A pox on him, he's a cat still . . . iv 3 307
Pox on't, I'll not meddle with him . . . *T. Night* iii 4 308
What a pox have I to do with my hostess of the tavern? . *1 Hen. IV.* i 2 53
The gout galls the one, and the pox pinches the other . *2 Hen. IV.* i 2 258
A pox of this gout! or, a gout of this pox! for the one or the other plays the rogue with my great toe . . . i 2 272
Have at the very eye of that proverb with 'A pox of the devil' *Hen. V.* iii 7 130
The pox of such antic, lisping, affecting fantasticoes! . *Rom. and Jul.* ii 4 29
Paint till a horse may mire upon your face. A pox of wrinkles! *T. of A.* iv 3 148
Pox, leave thy damnable faces, and begin . . . *Hamlet* iii 2 263
A pox of drowning thyself! it is clean out of the way . . *Othello* i 3 365
I am not vexed more at any thing in the earth: a pox on't . *Cymbeline* ii 1 20
Now, the pox upon her green-sickness for me!—'Faith, there's no way to be rid on't but by the way to the pox . . *Pericles* iv 6 14
Poys. Kill the poys and the luggage! 'tis expressly against the law of arms . . . *Hen. V.* iv 7 1
Poysam. Charbon the puritan and old Poysam the papist . *All's Well* i 3 56
Prabble. A goot motion if we leave our pribbles and prabbles *Mer. Wives* i 1 56
'Hang-hog' is Latin for bacon, I warrant you.—Leave your prabbles, 'oman . . . iv 1 52
Given to . . . drinkings and swearings and starings, pribbles and prabbles . . . v 5 169
I pray you to serve God, and keep you out of prawls, and prabbles *Hen. V.* iv 8 69
Practic. So that the art and practic part of life Must be the mistress to this theoric . . . i 1 51
Practice. Thy advice this night I'll put in practice . . *T. G. of Ver.* iii 2 89
We detest such vile base practices . . . iv 1 73
As pregnant in As art and practice hath enriched any . *Meas. for Meas.* i 1 13
Making practice on the times . . . iii 2 288
Thou art suborn'd against his honour In hateful practice . . v 1 107
This needs must be a practice . . . v 1 123
Let me have way, my lord, To find this practice out . . v 1 239
In practice let us put it presently . . . *Much Ado* i 1 330
Grow this to what adverse issue it can, I will put it in practice . ii 2 53
The practice of it lives in John the bastard . . . iv 1 190
Despite his nice fence and his active practice, His May of youth . v 1 75
And paid me richly for the practice of it . . . v 1 255
To put in practice that Which each to other hath so strongly sworn *L. L. L.* i 1 308
I overheard him and his practices . . . *As Y. Like It* ii 3 26
Proceed in practice with my younger daughter; She's apt to learn *T. of S.* ii 1 165
Under whose practices he hath persecuted time with hope . *All's Well* i 1 16
The dearest issue of his practice, And of his old experience the only darling . . . ii 1 109
Had the whole theoric of war in the knot of his scarf, and the practice in the chape of his dagger . . . iv 3 163
Courage and hope both teaching him the practice . . *T. Night* i 2 13
This is a practice As full of labour as a wise man's art . . iii 1 72
This practice hath most shrewdly pass'd upon thee . . . v 1 360
To my kingly guest Unclasp'd my practice . . . *W. Tale* iii 2 168
The practice and the purpose of the king . . . *K. John* iv 3 63
Conspired, And sworn unto the practices of France . . *Hen. V.* ii 2 90
God acquit them of their practices! . . . ii 2 144
None friends but such as are his friends, And none your foes but such as shall pretend Malicious practices against his state *1 Hen. VI.* iv 1 7
Upon my life, began her devilish practices . . *2 Hen. VI.* iii 1 46
From true evidence of good esteem He be approved in practice culpable iii 2 22
I shall perish Under device and practice . . . *Hen. VIII.* i 1 204
Bid him recount The fore-recited practices . . . i 2 127
How came His practices to light? . . . iii 2 29
Your enemies are many, and not small; their practices Must bear the same proportion . . . v 1 128
Be caught With cautelous baits and practice . . . *Coriolanus* iv 1 33
And by still practice learn to know thy meaning . . *T. Andron.* iii 2 45
Whilst I at a banquet hold him sure, I'll find some cunning practice . v 2 77
Older in practice, abler than yourself To make conditions . *J. Cæsar* iv 3 31
This disease is beyond my practice . . . *Macbeth* v 1 65
Heavens make our presence and our practices Pleasant and helpful! *Ham.* ii 2 38
Shall uncharge the practice And call it accident . . . iv 7 68
And in a pass of practice Requite him for your father . . iv 7 139
I have been in continual practice; I shall win at the odds . . v 2 221
The foul practice Hath turn'd itself on me; lo, here I lie, Never to rise again . . . v 2 328
On whose foolish honesty My practices ride easy . . . *Lear* i 2 198
I'ld turn it all To thy suggestion, plot, and damned practice . . ii 1 75
He did bewray his practice; and received This hurt you see . . ii 1 109
Persuades me That this remotion of the duke and her Is practice only . ii 4 116
This is practice, Gloucester: By the law of arms thou wast not bound to answer . . . v 3 151
Mere prattle, without practice, Is all his soldiership . *Othello* i 1 26
Must be driven To find out practices of cunning hell, Why this should be i 3 102
Some unhatch'd practice Made demonstrable here in Cyprus to him Hath puddled his clear spirit . . . iii 4 141
Othello, that wert once so good, Fall'n in the practice of a damned slave v 2 292
And no practice had In the brave squares of war . *Ant. and Cleo.* iii 11 39
Your highness Shall from this practice but make hard your heart *Cymb.* i 5 24
My practice so prevail'd, That I return'd with simular proof enough . v 5 199
Which secret art, By turning o'er authorities, I have, Together with my practice, made familiar . . . *Pericles* iii 2 34
These blushes of hers must be quenched with some present practice . iv 2 136
Practisants. Here enter'd Pucelle and her practisants . *1 Hen. VI.* iii 2 20
Practise. There shall he practise tilts and tournaments . *T. G. of Ver.* i 3 30
He hath made an assay of her virtue to practise his judgement *M. for M.* iii 1 164
Ere I learn love, I'll practise to obey . . *Com. of Errors* ii 1 29
And I, with your two helps, will so practise on Benedick . *Much Ado* ii 1 398
I have within my mind A thousand raw tricks of these bragging Jacks, Which I will practise . . . *Mer. of Venice* iii 4 78
He will practise against thee by poison . . . *As Y. Like It* i 1 156
I will practise on this drunken man . . *T. of Shrew* Ind. 1 36
And practise rhetoric in your common talk . . . i 1 35
My books and instruments shall be my company, On them to look and practise by myself . . . i 1 83
Shall sweet Bianca practise how to bride it? . . . iii 2 253
I will not practise to deceive, Yet, to avoid deceit, I mean to learn *K. John* i 1 214
I doubt My uncle practises more harm to me . . . iv 1 20
If thou love me, practise an answer . . . *1 Hen. IV.* ii 4 412
Let them practise and converse with spirits . . . *1 Hen. VI.* ii 1 25
That you have aught but Talbot's shadow Whereon to practise your severity . . . ii 3 47

Practise. Cry, Trojans, cry! practise your eyes with tears! *Tr. and Cr.* ii 2 108
I will practise the insinuating nod . . . . . *Coriolanus* ii 3 106
Alack, that heaven should practise stratagems Upon so soft a subject as myself! . . . . *Rom. and Jul.* iii 5 211
A friend should bear his friend's infirmities, But Brutus makes mine greater than they are.—I do not, till you practise them on me *J. C.* iv 3 88
Yet, if you there Did practise on my state, your being in Egypt Might be my question.—How intend you, practised? . *Ant. and Cleo.* ii 2 39
Practised. The children must Be practised well to this . *Mer. Wives* iv 4 65
Throttle their practised accent in their fears . . . *M. N. Dream* v 1 97
Making practised smiles, As in a looking-glass. . . . *W. Tale* i 2 116
Practised upon the easy-yielding spirit of this woman . . 2 *Hen. IV.* ii 1 125
He had no legs that practised not his gait . . . . ii 3 23
Wouldst thou have practised on me for thy use? . . *Hen. V.* ii 2 99
Have practised dangerously against your state . . 2 *Hen. VI.* ii 1 171
Caitiff, to pieces shake, That under covert and convenient seeming Hast practised on man's life. . . . . *Lear* iii 2 57
Thou hast practised on her with foul charms . . . . *Othello* i 2 73
Did practise on my state . . . —How intend you, practised? *A. and C.* ii 2 40
Canst thou catch any fishes, then?—I never practised it. . *Pericles* ii 1 71
He appears To have practised more the whipstock than the lance . . ii 2 51
Practiser. Finding barren practisers, Scarce show a harvest of their heavy toil . . . . *L. L. Lost* iv 3 325
Sweet practiser, thy physic I will try . . . . . *All's Well* ii 1 188
A practiser Of arts inhibited and out of warrant . . *Othello* i 2 78
Practising. Banished For practising to steal away a lady *T. G. of Ver.* iv 1 48
Yonder i' the sun practising behaviour to his own shadow . *T. Night* ii 5 20
Practising upon his peace and quiet Even to madness . . *Othello* ii 1 319
Præclarissimus filius noster Henricus, Rex Angliæ, et Hæres Franciæ *Hen. V.* v 2 369
Præmunire. Fall into the compass of a præmunire . . . *Hen. VIII.* iii 2 340
Prætor. And look you lay it in the prætor's chair . . *J. Cæsar* i 3 143
The throng that follows Cæsar at the heels, Of senators, of prætors . ii 4 35
Pragging. Beggarly, lousy, pragging knave . . . *Hen. V.* v 1 6
Prague. As the old hermit of Prague, that never saw pen and ink *T. Night* iv 2 15
Prain. And there is also another device in my prain . *Mer. Wives* i 1 44
Let us knog our prains together to be revenge on this same scall . . iii 1 122
I pray you, remember in your prain . . . . . . iv 1 37
It is out of my prains what is the name of the other river . *Hen. V.* iv 7 30
And also being a little intoxicates in his prains . . . . iv 7 40
Praise in departing.—They vanish'd strangely . . . . *Tempest* iii 3 39
Thou shalt find she will outstrip all praise And make it halt behind her iv 1 10
Far behind his worth Comes all the praises that I now bestow *T. G. of V.* ii 4 72
O, flatter me; for love delights in praises. . . . . . ii 4 148
Is it mine, or Valentine's praise, . . . That makes me reasonless? . . ii 4 196
Flatter and praise, commend, extol their graces . . . . iii 1 102
She will often praise her liquor.—If her liquor be good, she shall . . iii 1 350
To praise his faith which I would have dispraised . . . iv 4 107
I can tell you that by the way; I praise heaven for it . *Mer. Wives* i 4 150
I am not such a sickly creature, I give heaven praise . . iii 4 62
First he did praise my beauty, then my speech . . *Com. of Errors* iv 2 15
She's too low for a high praise, too brown for a fair praise, and too little for a great praise . . . . *Much Ado* i 1 174
Not the unhopefullest husband that I know. Thus far can I praise him ii 1 394
Let it be thy part To praise him more than ever man did merit . iii 1 19
I saw the Duchess of Milan's gown that they praise so . . . iii 4 16
Will you then write me a sonnet in praise of my beauty? . . . v 2 5
There's not one wise man among twenty that will praise himself . v 2 76
Speak you this in my praise, master?—In thy condign praise *L. L. Lost* i 2 26
I will praise an eel with the same praise . . . . . i 2 28
My beauty, though but mean, Needs not the painted flourish of your praise . . . . ii 1 14
Willing to be counted wise In spending your wit in the praise of mine . ii 1 19
Every one her own hath garnished With such bedecking ornaments of praise . . . . ii 1 79
What, what? first praise me and again say no? O short-lived-pride! iv 1 14
Where fair is not, praise cannot mend the brow . . . iv 1 17
A giving hand, though foul, shall have fair praise . . . iv 1 23
It was to show my skill, That more for praise than purpose meant to kill . . . . iv 1 29
For praise, an outward part, We bend to that the working of the heart iv 1 32
As I for praise alone now seek to spill The poor deer's blood . . iv 1 34
Do not curst wives hold that self-sovereignty Only for praise sake? . iv 1 37
Only for praise: and praise we may afford To any lady that subdues a lord . . . . iv 1 39
I praise the Lord for you: and so may my parishioners . . . . iv 2 75
Which is to me some praise that I thy parts admire . . . iv 2 118
That sings heaven's praise with such an earthly tongue . . . iv 2 122
When shall you hear that I Will praise a hand, a foot, a face, an eye? . iv 3 184
To things of sale a seller's praise belongs, She passes praise; then praise too short doth blot . . . . iv 3 240
He hath drawn my picture in his letter!—Any thing like?—Much in the letters; nothing in the praise . . . . v 2 40
Making the bold wag by their praises bolder . . . . . v 2 108
My lady, to the manner of the days, In courtesy gives undeserving praise v 2 366
The dialogue that the two learned men have compiled in praise of the owl v 2 896
Have you not set Lysander, as in scorn, To follow me and praise my eyes and face? . . . . *M. N. Dream* iii 2 223
I remember him well, and I remember him worthy of thy praise *M. of V.* i 2 133
The substance of my praise doth wrong this shadow In underprizing it iii 2 128
Still gazing in a doubt Whether those peals of praise be his or no . iii 2 146
Let me praise you while I have a stomach . . . . . iii 5 92
How many things by season season'd are To their right praise! . . v 1 108
No other argument But that the people praise her for her virtues *As Y. Like It* i 2 292
Your praise is come too swiftly home before you . . . . ii 3 9
Your brother . . . Hath heard your praises . . . . . ii 3 22
Wearying thy hearer in thy mistress' praise . . . . . ii 4 38
'Tis the best brine a maiden can season her praise in . . *All's Well* i 1 56
Making them proud of his humility, In their poor praise he humbled . i 2 45
The rather will I spare my praises towards him; Knowing him is enough ii 1 106
O, I believe with him, In argument of praise . . . . . iii 5 62
The most virtuous gentlewoman that ever nature had praise for creating iv 5 10
I will on with my speech in your praise . . . . . *T. Night* i 5 202
Come to what is important in't: I forgive you the praise . . . i 5 205
Were you sent hither to praise me? . . . . i 5 268
However we do praise ourselves, Our fancies are more giddy and unfirm ii 4 33
She did praise my leg being cross-gartered . . . . . ii 5 181
They praise me and make an ass of me . . . . . . v 1 19
May, though they cannot praise us, as little accuse us . *W. Tale* i 1 17
Praise. Cram's with praise, and make's As fat as tame things *W. Tale* i 2 91
Our praises are our wages: you may ride's With one soft kiss a thousand furlongs ere With spur we heat an acre . . . . i 2 94
Praise her but for this her without-door form . . . . . ii 1 69
Much surpassing The common praise it bears . . . . . iii 1 3
O Doricles, Your praises are too large . . . . . . iv 4 147
Well could I bear that England had this praise, So we could find some pattern of our shame . . . . *K. John* iii 4 15
Flattering sounds, As praises, of whose taste the wise are fond *Rich. II.* ii 1 18
Whilst I, by looking on the praise of him, See riot and dishonour stain the brow Of my young Harry . . . . 1 *Hen. IV.* i 1 84
Why, what a rascal art thou then, to praise him so for running! . . ii 4 386
They offend none but the virtuous: I laud them, I praise them . . iii 3 215
Worse than the sun in March, This praise doth nourish agues . . iv 1 112
The Prince of Wales doth join with all the world In praise of Henry Percy . . . . v 1 87
Trimm'd up your praises with a princely tongue . . . . . v 2 57
Making you ever better than his praise By still dispraising praise valued with you . . . . v 2 59
Adieu, and take thy praise with thee to heaven! . . . . . v 4 99
To stop my ear indeed, Thou hast a sigh to blow away this praise 2 *Hen. IV.* i 1 80
Eat, and make good cheer, And praise God for the merry year . . v 3 19
As rich with praise As is the ooze and bottom of the sea . *Hen. V.* i 2 163
The Duke of Exeter doth love thee well.—Ay, I praise God . . . iii 6 25
The man hath no wit that cannot, from the rising of the lark to the lodging of the lamb, vary deserved praise on my palfrey . . . iii 7 35
I once writ a sonnet in his praise and began thus! 'Wonder of nature' iii 7 42
Which is the prescript praise and perfection of a good and particular mistress . . . . iii 7 49
Even as your horse bears your praises; who would trot as well, were some of your brags dismounted . . . . iii 7 82
Let him cry 'Praise and glory on his head!' . . . . . iv Prol. 31
And be it death proclaimed through our host To boast of this or take that praise from God Which is his only . . . . iv 8 120
And all the priests and friars in my realm Shall in procession sing her endless praise . . . . 1 *Hen. VI.* i 6 20
This is the latest glory of thy praise That I, thy enemy, due thee withal iv 2 33
Good wishes, praise and prayers Shall Suffolk ever have of Margaret . v 3 173
Solicit Henry with her wondrous praise: Bethink thee on her virtues . v 3 190
This superficial tale Is but a preface of her worthy praise . . v 5 11
The care you have of us . . . Is worthy praise . . 2 *Hen. VI.* iii 1 68
Then, heaven, set ope thy everlasting gates, To entertain my vows of thanks and praise! . . . . iv 9 14
Nor should thy prowess want praise and esteem, But that 'tis shown ignobly . . . . v 2 22
Oft have I heard his praises in pursuit . . . . 3 *Hen. VI.* ii 1 149
In devotion spend my latter days, To sin's rebuke and my Creator's praise iv 6 44
That we may praise thee in the victory! . . . *Richard III.* v 3 114
Him in eye, Still him in praise . . . . . . *Hen. VIII.* i 1 31
When I am in heaven I shall desire To see what this child does, and praise my Maker . . . . v 5 69
She is my kinswoman; I would not, as they term it; praise her *T. and C.* i 1 45
Is too flaming a praise for a good complexion . . . . . i 2 113
More in Troilus thousand fold I see Than in the glass of Pandar's praise i 2 311
The worthiness of praise distains his worth, If that the praised himself bring the praise forth . . . . i 3 242
But what the repining enemy commends, That breath fame blows; that praise, sole pure, transcends . . . . i 3 244
That seeks his praise more than he fears his peril . . . . i 3 267
You have the honey still, but these the gall; So to be valiant is no praise at all . . . . ii 2 145
Whatever praises itself but in the deed, devours the deed in the praise . ii 3 166
Force him with praises: pour in, pour in; his ambition is dry . . ii 3 233
If he were proud,— Or covetous of praise,— Ay, or surly borne . ii 3 248
Praise him that got thee, she that gave thee suck . . . . ii 3 252
I will not praise thy wisdom . . . . ii 3 259
I must needs praise him.—The lord be praised! . . . . iii 1 7
Praise us as we are tasted, allow us as we prove . . . . iii 2 97
No perfection in reversion shall have a praise in present. . . iii 2 100
Praise new-born gawds, Though they are made and moulded of things past . . . . iii 3 176
The present eye praises the present object . . . . . iii 3 180
She is as far high-soaring o'er thy praises As thou unworthy . . iv 4 126
We'll forth and fight, Do deeds worth praise and tell you them at night v 3 93
My mother, Who has a charter to extol her blood, When she does praise me grieves me . . . . *Coriolanus* i 9 15
Which, to the spire and top of praises vouch'd, Would seem but modest i 9 24
As if I loved my little should be dieted In praises sauced with lies . i 9 53
Our then dictator, Whom with all praise I point at, saw him fight . ii 2 94
Thou hast said My praises made thee first a soldier, so, To have my praise for this, perform a part Thou hast not done before . . iii 2 108
And in his praise Have almost stamp'd the leasing . . . . v 2 21
Praise the gods, And make triumphant fires . . . . . v 5 2
Lavinia, live; outlive thy father's days, And fame's eternal date, for virtue's praise! . . . . *T. Andron.* i 1 168
But, soft! methinks I do digress too much, Citing my worthless praise v 3 117
O, pardon me; For when no friends are by, men praise themselves . v 3 118
Your jewel Hath suffer'd under praise.—What, my lord! dispraise? *T. of A.* i 1 165
I know, no man Can justly praise but what he does affect . . i 2 221
When the means are gone that buy this praise, The breath is gone whereof this praise is made. . . . . ii 2 179
Praise his most vicious stain, And call it excellent . . . . iv 3 213
Lend me your ears; I come to bury Cæsar, not to praise him *J. Cæsar* iii 2 79
His wonders and his praises do contend . . . . . *Macbeth* i 3 92
Every one did bear Thy praises in his kingdom's great defence . . i 3 99
O, there be players that I have seen play, and heard others praise *Hamlet* iii 2 32
Whose worth, if praises may go back again, Stood challenger on mount of all the age For her perfections . . . . iv 7 27
We'll put on those shall praise your excellence . . . . iv 7 132
The argument of your praise, balm of your age, Most best . *Lear* i 1 218
Got praises of the king For him attempting who was self-subdued . ii 2 128
Not being the worst Stands in some rank of praise . . . . ii 4 261
You shall not write my praise.—No, let me not . . . *Othello* ii 1 117
What wouldst thou write of me, if thou shouldst praise me? . . ii 1 118
Come, how wouldst thou praise me?—I am about it . . . . ii 1 125
What miserable praise hast thou for her that's foul and foolish? . ii 1 140
But what praise couldst thou bestow on a deserving woman indeed? . ii 1 145
Are you of good or evil?—As you shall prove us, praise us . . v 1 66
You praise yourself By laying defects of judgement to me *Ant. and Cleo.* ii 2 54
Though I lose The praise of it by telling, you must know . . ii 6 44

Praise. I will praise any man that will praise me . . . *Ant. and Cleo.* ii 6 91
Would you praise Cæsar, say 'Cæsar:' go no further . . . . iii 2 13
Indeed, he plied them both with excellent praises . . . . . iii 2 14
I hear Antony call; I see him rouse himself To praise my noble act . v 2 288
Where each of us fell in praise of our country mistresses . *Cymbeline* i 4 61
Praise Be given to your remembrance . . . . ii 4 92
Famous in Cæsar's praises, no whit less Than in his feats deserving it . iii 1 6
I'ld let a parish of such Clotens blood, And praise myself for charity . iv 2 169
Moulded the stuff so fair, That he deserved the praise o' the world . v 4 50
Sitting sadly, Hearing us praise our loves of Italy . . . . v 5 161
Whereat I, wretch, Made scruple of his praise; and wager'd with him . v 5 182
Embolden'd with the glory of her praise, Think death no hazard *Pericles* i 1 4
Her face the book of praises, where is read Nothing but curious pleasures i 1 15
That monster envy, oft the wrack Of earned praise . . . iv Gower 13
Praises, which are paid as debts, And not as given . . . . iv Gower 34
Her epitaphs In glittering golden characters express A general praise
to her . . . . iv 3 45
I praise God for you *Much Ado* v 1; *L. L. Lost* v 1; *All's Well* v 2
Praised. For good things should be praised . . . *T. G. of Ver.* iii 1 354
Yet he would not swear; praised women's modesty . *Mer. Wives* ii 1 58
God be praised for my jealousy! . . . . ii 2 324
I shall be rather praised for this than mocked . . . . . iii 2 48
Mine I loved and mine I praised And mine that I was proud on *M. Ado* iv 1 138
I'll tell thee how Beatrice praised thy wit the other day . . . v 1 160
Praised be the gods for thy foulness! . . . . *As Y. Like It* iii 3 40
Thy mildness praised in every town, Thy virtues spoke of *T. of Shrew* ii 1 192
Is now The praised of the king . . . . . . *All's Well* ii 3 179
She whom all men praised and whom myself, Since I have lost, have
loved . . . . v 3 53
Jove and my stars be praised! Here is yet a postscript . *T. Night* ii 5 188
Now blessed be the great Apollo!—Praised!—Hast thou read truth? *W. T.* iii 2 138
He is not—God be praised and blessed!—any hurt in the world *Hen. V.* iii 6 10
The day is yours.—Praised be God, and not our strength, for it! . . iv 7 90
I need not to be ashamed of your majesty, praised be God . . . iv 7 119
Here is—praised be God for it!—a most contagious treason come to
light . . . . iv 8 21
God be praised, that to believing souls Gives light in darkness! 2 *Hen. VI.* ii 1 66
God and your arms be praised, victorious friends; The day is ours
Richard III. v 5 1
She praised his complexion above Paris . . . *Troi. and Cres.* i 2 107
If she praised him above, his complexion is higher than his . . . i 2 111
The worthiness of praise distains his worth, If that the praised himself
bring the praise forth . . . . i 3 242
I must needs praise him.—The lord be praised! . . . . . iii 1 8
Tear my bright hair and scratch my praised cheeks . . . . iv 2 113
To dispraise my lord with that same tongue Which she hath praised him
with above compare So many thousand times . *Rom. and Jul.* iii 5 238
When we for recompense have praised the vile, It stains the glory in that
happy verse Which aptly sings the good . . *T. of Athens* i 1 15
For your own gifts, make yourselves praised: but reserve still to give . iii 6 81
Rashly, And praised be rashness for it, let us know, Our indiscretion
sometimes serves us well, When our deep plots do pall . *Hamlet* v 2 7
Under pardon, You are much more attask'd for want of wisdom Than
praised for harmful mildness . . . . *Lear* i 4 367
Who, having been praised for bluntness, doth affect A saucy roughness ii 2 102
Well praised! How if she be black and witty? . . . *Othello* ii 1 132
Where's the soothsayer that you praised so to the queen? *Ant. and Cleo.* i 2 3
I ha' praised ye, When you have well deserved ten times as much . . ii 6 78
Most praised, most loved, A sample to the youngest . . *Cymbeline* i 1 47
I praised her as I rated her: so do I my stone . . . . . i 4 83
Which, as I say, to vex her I will execute in the clothes that she so
praised . . . . iii 5 148
Great Jupiter be praised! Lucius is taken . . . . . . v 3 84
Not dispraising whom we praised,—therein He was as calm as virtue . v 5 173
The diamonds of a most praised water Do appear . . . *Pericles* iii 2 102
Praisest. O heavy ignorance! thou praisest the worst best . *Othello* ii 1 144
Praiseworthy. So much for praising myself, who, I myself will bear wit-
ness, is praiseworthy . . . . *Much Ado* v 2 90
Praising me as much As you in worth dispraise Sir Valentine *T. G. of Ver.* iii 2 54
So much for praising myself . . . . *Much Ado* v 2 89
Hang thou there upon the tomb, Praising her when I am dumb . . v 3 10
I am half afeard Thou wilt say anon he is some kin to thee, Thou
spend'st such high-day wit in praising him . . *Mer. of Venice* ii 9 98
This comes too near the praising of myself; Therefore no more of it . iii 4 22
On the turf, Praising the proud disdainful shepherdess . *As Y. Like It* iii 4 53
Praising what is lost Makes the remembrance dear . . . *All's Well* v 3 19
Thou dost not use me courteously, To shame the zeal of my petition to
thee In praising her . . . . *Troi. and Cres.* iv 4 125
I blame you not for praising Cæsar so; But what compact mean you to
have with us? . . . . *J. Cæsar* iii 1 214
In praising Antony, I have dispraised Cæsar.—Many times, madam
Ant. and Cleo. ii 5 107
Prancing. Trimm'd like a younker prancing to his love! . 3 *Hen. VI.* ii 1 24
Prank. And shrive you of a thousand idle pranks . . *Com. of Errors* ii 2 210
'Tis that miracle and queen of gems That nature pranks her in *T. Night* ii 4 89
Hear thou there how many fruitless pranks This ruffian hath botch'd up iv 1 59
I will tell the king all, every word, yea, and his son's pranks too *W. Tale* iv 4 718
Thy lewd, pestiferous and dissentious pranks . . 1 *Hen. VI.* iii 1 15
They do prank them in authority, Against all noble sufferance *Coriol.* iii 1 23
Tell him his pranks have been too broad to bear with . *Hamlet* iii 4 2
This admiration, sir, is much o' the savour Of other your new pranks *Lear* i 4 259
There's none so foul and foolish thereunto, But does foul pranks *Othello* ii 1 143
They do let heaven see the pranks They dare not show their husbands . iii 3 202
Pranked up. And me, poor lowly maid, Most goddess-like prank'd up
W. Tale iv 4 10
Prat. Come, Mother Prat; come, give me your hand.—I'll prat her
Mer. Wives iv 2 191
Prate. Lords that can prate As amply and unnecessarily . *Tempest* ii 1 263
All shall be well. We must give folks leave to prate . *Mer. Wives* i 4 128
I cannot cog, I cannot prate . . . . iii 3 51
Here standing To prate and talk for life and honour . *W. Tale* iii 2 42
If I talk to him, with his innocent prate He will awake my mercy *K. John* iv 1 25
Hath done nothing but prate to me of the wildness of his youth 2 *Hen. IV.* iii 2 327
Perish ye, with your audacious prate! Presumptuous vassals 1 *Hen. VI.* iv 1 124
We will not stand to prate; Talkers are no good doers . *Richard III.* i 3 351
What do you prate of service?—I talk of that, that know it *Coriolanus* iii 3 83
You gods! I prate, And the most noble mother of the world Leave
unsaluted . . . . v 3 48
Yet here he lets me prate Like one i' the stocks . . . . v 3 159
For fear Thy very stones prate of my whereabout . . . *Macbeth* ii 1 58
Prate. If thou prate of mountains, let them throw Millions of acres on us!
Hamlet v 1 303
Beat me!—Dost thou prate, rogue? . . . . . . *Othello* ii 3 153
Prated. He prated, And spoke such scurvy and provoking terms . i 2 6
Prater. A speaker is but a prater; a rhyme is but a ballad *Hen. V.* v 2 166
Pratest. Why pratest thou to thyself and answer'st not? *Com. of Errors* ii 2 195
Thou pratest, and pratest . . . . *Coriolanus* iv 5 54
Prating mountebanks, And many such-like liberties of sin *Com. of Errors* i 2 101
Hence, prating peasant! fetch thy master home . . . . ii 1 81
A prating boy, that begg'd it as a fee . . . *Mer. of Venice* v 1 164
I shall so be-mete thee with thy yard As thou shalt think on prating
whilst thou livest! . . . . *T. of Shrew* iv 3 114
Leave your prating: since these good men are pleased, let them come
W. Tale iv 4 349
An ass and a fool and a prating coxcomb . . . . *Hen. V.* iv 1 79
Think you, my lord, this little prating York Was not incensed by his
subtle mother To taunt and scorn you? . . . *Richard III.* iii 1 151
Why stay we prating here? to the Capitol! . . . *Coriolanus* i 1 49
Lord, Lord! when 'twas a little prating thing . . *Rom. and Jul.* ii 4 212
Who was in life a foolish prating knave . . . . . *Hamlet* iii 4 215
And will she love him still for prating? . . . . . *Othello* ii 1 227
Prattle. But I prattle Something too wildly . . . *Tempest* iii 1 57
I would he had some cause To prattle for himself . *Meas. for Meas.* v 1 182
If you prattle me into these perils . . . . . *All's Well* iv 1 46
As, you know, What great ones do the rest will prattle of . *T. Night* i 2 33
Thinking his prattle to be tedious . . . . . *Richard II.* v 2 26
As very infants prattle of thy pride . . . . 1 *Hen. VI.* iii 1 16
Mere prattle, without practice, Is all his soldiership . . *Othello* i 1 26
I prattle out of fashion, and I dote In mine own comforts . . . ii 1 208
Prattler. Poor prattler, how thou talk'st! . . . . *Macbeth* iv 2 64
Prattling. Prithee, no more prattling: go . . . . *Mer. Wives* v 1 1
Your prattling nurse Into a rapture lets her baby cry . *Coriolanus* ii 1 222
Prave. A' uttered as prave words at the pridge as you shall see in a
summer's day . . . . *Hen. V.* iii 6 66
And there is gallant and most prave passages . . . . . iii 6 97
I can tell your majesty, the duke is a prave man . . . . iii 6 101
As I have read in the chronicles, fought a most prave pattle here in
France . . . . iv 7 98
Prawl. Serve God, and keep you out of prawls, and prabbles . . iv 8 69
Prawns. Telling us she had a good dish of prawns . . . 2 *Hen. IV.* ii 1 104
Pray. And on a love-book pray for my success?—Upon some book I love
I'll pray for thee . . . . *T. G. of Ver.* i 1 20
A shame to call her back again And pray her to a fault for which I
chid her . . . . i 2 52
His heart as far from fraud as heaven from earth.—Pray heaven he
prove so! . . . . ii 7 79
He has pray his Pible well, dat he is no come . . . *Mer. Wives* ii 3 7
You must pray, and not follow the imaginations of your own heart . iv 2 162
There's not a soldier of us all, that, in the thanksgiving before meat, do
relish the petition well that prays for peace . . *Meas. for Meas.* i 2 16
And well she can persuade.—I pray she may . . . . . . i 2 192
I pray you home to dinner with me.—I humbly thank you . . . ii 1 292
He will relent; He's coming; I perceive't.—Pray heaven she win him! ii 2 125
When I would pray and think, I think and pray To several subjects . ii 4 1
I'll pray a thousand prayers for thy death, No word to save thee . . iii 1 146
I will pray, Pompey, to increase your bondage . . . . . iii 2 78
Farewell, good friar: I prithee, pray for me . . . . . iii 2 191
I am come to advise you, comfort you and pray with you . . . iv 3 55
Pray heaven his wisdom be not tainted! . . . . iv 4 4
We that know what 'tis to fast and pray Are penitent . *Com. of Errors* i 2 51
And prays that you will hie you home to dinner . . . . . i 2 90
Pray God our cheer May answer my good will and your good welcome . iii 1 19
My heart prays for him, though my tongue do curse . . . . iv 2 28
He heartily prays some occasion may detain us longer. I dare swear he
is no hypocrite, but prays from his heart . . . . *Much Ado* i 1 151
Weeps, sobs, beats her heart, tears her hair, prays, curses . . . ii 3 153
I know not how to pray your patience; Yet I must speak . . . v 1 281
I had rather pray a month with mutton and porridge . . *L. L. Lost* i 1 304
And I to sigh for her! to watch for her! To pray for her! Go to . . iii 1 203
I will love, write, sigh, pray, sue, and groan . . . . . iii 1 206
Farewell, sweet playfellow: pray thou for us . . . *M. N. Dream* i 1 220
I will not eat with you, drink with you, nor pray with you *Mer. of Venice* i 3 39
We do pray for mercy; And that same prayer doth teach us all to render
The deeds of mercy . . . . iv 1 200
By holy crosses, where she kneels and prays For happy wedlock hours . v 1 31
Fare you well: pray heaven I be deceived in you! . . *As Y. Like It* i 2 209
I am not fair; and therefore I pray the gods make me honest . . . iii 3 34
You are passing welcome, And so I pray you all to think yourselves
T. of Shrew ii 1 114
Mistress, your father prays you leave your books . . . . . iii 1 82
I pray the gods she may with all my heart!—Dally not with the gods . iv 4 67
I'll stay at home And pray God's blessing into thy attempt . *All's Well* i 3 260
O, pray, pray, pray! Manka revania dulche . . . . . . iv 1 86
My lady prays you to have a care of him.—Ah, ha! does she so? *T. Night* iii 4 103
Pray God, he be not bewitched! . . . . iii 4 112
Get him to say his prayers, good Sir Toby, get him to pray . . . iii 4 132
When you sing, I'ld have you buy and sell so, so give alms, Pray so
W. Tale iv 4 139
Pray heartily he be at palace . . . . iv 4 731
Kneel And pray your mother's blessing . . . . v 3 120
Let wives with child Pray that their burthens may not fall this day
K. John iii 1 90
O, upon my knee, Made hard with kneeling, I do pray to thee . . . iii 1 310
Husband, I cannot pray that thou mayst win; Uncle, I needs must pray
that thou mayst lose . . . . iii 1 331
I will pray, If ever I remember to be holy, For your fair safety . . iii 3 14
Most heartily I pray Your highness to assign our trial day . *Richard II.* i 1 150
Let's all go visit him: Pray God we may make haste, and come too
late! . . . . i 4 64
Let your mother in: I know she is come to pray for your foul sin . . v 3 82
If thou do pardon, whosoever pray, More sins for this forgiveness
prosper may . . . . v 3 83
He prays but faintly and would be denied; We pray with heart and soul v 3 103
Come, my old son: I pray God make thee new . . . . . . v 3 146
Speak sooner than drink, and drink sooner than pray . . 1 *Hen. IV.* ii 1 87
They pray continually to their saint, the commonwealth; or rather,
not pray to her, but prey on her. . . . . ii 1 88
Pray God you have not murdered some of them.—Nay, that's past
praying for . . . . ii 4 209
Hostess, clap to the doors: watch to-night, pray to-morrow . . . ii 4 306

Pray. But look you pray, all you that kiss my lady Peace at home 2 *Hen. IV.* i 2 232
I was lately here in the end of a displeasing play, to pray your patience Epil. 10
And so kneel down before you; but, indeed, to pray for the queen . Epil. 36
Your humble patience pray, Gently to hear, kindly to judge . *Hen. V.* Prol. 33
We pray you to proceed And justly and religiously unfold . . . i 2 9
He prays you to save his life: he is a gentleman of a good house . . iv 4 47
I pray you to serve God, and keep you out of prawls, and prabbles . iv 8 68
I humbly pray them to admit the excuse Of time, of numbers . . v Prol. 3
And ne'er throughout the year to church thou go'st Except it be to pray against thy foes . . . . 1 *Hen. VI.* i 1 43
I thank you all: drink, and pray for me, I pray you . . 2 *Hen. VI.* ii 3 72
Entreat her not the worse in that I pray You use her well . . ii 4 81
Heart, be wrathful still: Priests pray for enemies, but princes kill . v 2 71
O, let me pray before I take my death! To thee I pray . . 3 *Hen. VI.* i 3 36
Shield thee from Warwick's frown; And pray that I may repossess the crown . . . . v 5 29
God, I pray him, That none of you may live your natural age! *Rich. III.* i 3 212
A Christian-like conclusion, To pray for them that have done scathe to us . . . . i 3 317
Fiends roar, saints pray, To have him suddenly convey'd away . iv 4 75
Bless thee from thy mother, Who prays continually for Richmond's good . . . . v 3 84
The wronged heirs of York do pray for thee: Good angels guard thy battle! . . . . v 3 137
Thy adversary's wife doth pray for thee . . . . v 3 166
Now I would pray our monsieurs To think an English courtier may be wise, And never see the Louvre . . . . . *Hen. VIII.* i 3 21
I pay 'em A thousand thanks, an pray 'em take their pleasures . . i 4 74
All good people, Pray for me! I must now forsake ye . . . ii 1 132
We had need pray, And heartily, for our deliverance . . . . ii 2 45
There is hope All will be well.—Now, I pray God, amen! . . . ii 3 56
To his highness; Whose health and royalty I pray for . . . ii 3 73
Pray their graces To come near. What can be their business With me? iii 1 18
Ye speak like honest men; pray God, ye prove so! . . . . . iii 1 69
Seek the king; That sun, I pray, may never set! . . . . . iii 2 415
Mark her eyes!—She is going, wench: pray, pray.—Heaven comfort her! . . . . iv 2 99
I most humbly pray you to deliver This to my lord the king . . . iv 2 129
The fruit she goes with I pray for heartily, that it may find Good time v 1 21
And desired your highness Most heartily to pray for her.—What say'st thou, ha? To pray for her? what, is she crying out? . . . . v 1 66
Pray heaven, the king may never find a heart With less allegiance in it! v 3 42
My noble partners, and myself, thus pray . . . . . . v 5 6
Let one be sent To pray Achilles see us at our tent . . *Troi. and Cres.* v 9 8
We pray the gods he may deserve your loves.—Amen, sir . *Coriolanus* ii 3 165
I would say 'Thou liest' unto thee with a voice as free As I do pray the gods . . . . iii 3 74
Ourselves, our wives, and children, on our knees, Are bound to pray for you . . . . iv 6 23
Alas, how can we for our country pray, Whereto we are bound, together with thy victory, Whereto we are bound? . . . . v 3 107
And pray the Roman gods confound you both! . . . . *T. Andron.* iv 2 6
Come, let us go; and pray to all the gods For our beloved mother . iv 2 46
Pray to the devils; the gods have given us over . . . . . iv 2 48
Pray be careful all, And leave you not a man-of-war unsearch'd . . iv 3 21
They pray, grant thou, lest faith turn to despair . . *Rom. and Jul.* i 5 106
Immortal gods, I crave no pelf; I pray for no man but myself *T. of A.* i 2 64
Humbly prays you That with your other noble parts you'll suit In giving him his right . . . . ii 2 22
He humbly prays your speedy payment . . . . ii 2 28
Pray to the gods to intermit the plague . . . . . *J. Cæsar* i 1 59
If thou dost bend and pray and fawn for him, I spurn thee like a cur . iii 1 45
If I could pray to move, prayers would move me . . . . . iii 1 59
Are you so gospell'd To pray for this good man and for his issue? *Macb.* iii 1 89
Thither Macduff Is gone to pray the holy king . . . . . . iii 6 30
We pray you, throw to earth This unprevailing woe . . . *Hamlet* i 2 106
Let not thy mother lose her prayers, Hamlet: I pray thee, stay with us i 2 119
And for mine own poor part, Look you, I'll go pray . . . . i 5 132
Pray can I not, Though inclination be as sharp as will . . . iii 3 38
God ha' mercy on his soul! And of all Christian souls, I pray God . iv 5 200
Gertrude, do not drink.—I will, my lord; I pray you, pardon me . . v 2 302
Nay, get thee in. I'll pray, and then I'll sleep . . . . *Lear* iii 4 27
Pray, innocent, and beware the foul fiend . . . . . . iii 6 8
Let not my worser spirit tempt me again To die before you please!—Well pray you, father . . . . iv 6 223
Pray that the right may thrive . . . . v 2 2
So we'll live, And pray, and sing, and tell old tales, and laugh . . v 3 12
Recommends you thus, And prays you to believe him . . . *Othello* i 3 42
Yet he looks sadly, And prays the Moor be safe . . . —Pray heavens he be . . . . ii 1 33
I am to pray you not to strain my speech To grosser issues . . . iii 3 218
If thou dost slander her and torture me, Never pray more . . . iii 3 369
A closet lock and key of villanous secrets; And yet she'll kneel and pray iv 2 23
From this time forth I never will speak word.—What, not to pray? . v 2 305
She is now the wife of Marcus Antonius.—Pray ye, sir?—'Tis true *Ant. and Cleo.* ii 6 120
The good gods will mock me presently, When I shall pray, 'O, bless my lord and husband!' . . . . iii 4 16
Husband win, win brother, Prays, and destroys the prayer; no midway iii 4 19
You shall find A conqueror that will pray in aid for kindness . . v 2 27
Yet 'tis greater skill In a true hate, to pray they have their will *Cymb.* ii 5 34
Lovers And men in dangerous bonds pray not alike . . . . iii 2 37
Blest pray you be, That, after this strange starting from your orbs, You may reign in them now! . . . . v 5 370
The gods of Greece protect you! And we'll pray for you . . *Pericles* i 4 98
If you require a little space for prayer, I grant it: pray; but be not tedious . . . . iv 1 69
I pray *Tempest* i 1; *T. G. of Ver.* i 2; iii 1; *Meas. for Meas.* i 2; *Com. of Errors* i 2; ii 2; 1 *Hen. VI.* iii 1; v 5; *T. of Athens* iv 3; *Macbeth* ii 2; *Cymbeline* iii 5
I pray thee (you) *Tempest* i 2; iii 3; *T. G. of Ver.* i 3; iii 1; *Meas. for Meas.* iii 2; iv 1; *Much Ado* i 1; *T. of Shrew* iv 4; 2 *Hen. VI.* ii 3; *Richard III.* ii 4; *Troi. and Cres.* v 2; *Macbeth* iii 4; *Pericles* i 4
Pray (prefix) *Tempest* iii 1; *T. G. of Ver.* iii 1; *Hen. VIII.* iii 1; *Coriolanus* iv 5; iv 6; *Pericles* ii 1
Pray thee (you) *Tempest* i 2; ii 1; iv 1; v 1; *T. G. of Ver.* iv 2; *Mer. Wives* i 4; *Meas. for Meas.* ii 2; *Mer. of Venice* ii 2; iii 5; *Coriolanus* iv 5; *T. of Athens* ii 2; *Macbeth* iii 4; *Ant. and Cleo.* v 2
Prayed. How I persuaded, how I pray'd, and kneel'd . *Meas. for Meas.* v 1 93
How she prayed, that never prayed before . . . *T. of Shrew* iv 1 81

Prayed. Your mother well hath pray'd, and prove you true *Richard II.* v 3 145
Had not churchmen pray'd, His thread of life had not so soon decay'd 1 *Hen. VI.* i 1 33
They speak no English, thus they pray'd To tell your grace *Hen. VIII.* i 4 65
And saint-like Cast her fair eyes to heaven and pray'd devoutly . iv 1 84
Sent to me from the council, pray'd me To make great haste . . v 2 2
You have pray'd well to-day: This morning for ten thousand of your throats I'ld not have given a doit . . . . *Coriolanus* v 4 58
Yea, 'gainst the authority of manners, pray'd you . *T. of Athens* ii 2 147
Have you pray'd to-night, Desdemona?—Ay, my lord . *Othello* v 2 25
And pray'd me oft forbearance; did it with A pudency so rosy *Cymb.* ii 5 10
When last I went to visit her, She pray'd me to excuse her keeping close iii 5 46
The very gods show'd me a vision—I fast and pray'd for their intelligence . . . . iv 2 347
Prayer. All lost! to prayers, to prayers! all lost! . . . *Tempest* i 1 54
The king and prince at prayers! let's assist them, For our case is as theirs . . . . i 1 57
Vouchsafe my prayer May know if you remain upon this island . . i 2 422
Beseech you—Chiefly that I might set it in my prayers—What is your name? . . . . iii 1 35
And my ending is despair, Unless I be relieved by prayer . . . Epil. 16
Commend thy grievance to my holy prayers . . . *T. G. of Ver.* i 1 17
His worst fault is, that he is given to prayer . . . *Mer. Wives* i 4 13
And one, I tell you, that will not miss you morning nor evening prayer ii 2 102
If my wind were but long enough to say my prayers, I would repent . iv 5 105
Where you find a maid That, ere she sleep, has thrice her prayers said . v 5 54
Unless you have the grace by your fair prayer To soften Angelo *M. for M.* i 4 69
True prayers That shall be up at heaven and enter there Ere sun-rise . ii 2 151
Prayers from preserved souls, From fasting maids . . . . . ii 2 153
I am that way going to temptation, Where prayers cross . . . ii 2 159
If that be sin, I'll make it my morn prayer . . . . . . ii 4 71
I'll pray a thousand prayers for thy death, No word to save thee . . iii 1 146
If ever the duke return, as our prayers are he may . . . . . iii 2 164
But leave we him to his events, with a prayer they may prove prosperous . . . . iii 2 252
I would desire you to clap into your prayers . . . . . . iv 3 44
I charge thee, Satan, housed within this man, To yield possession to my holy prayers . . . . *Com. of Errors* iv 4 58
With wholesome syrups, drugs and holy prayers . . . . . . v 1 104
I will fall prostrate at his feet And never rise until my tears and prayers Have won his grace . . . . v 1 115
I have many ill qualities.—Which is one?—I say my prayers aloud *Much Ado* ii 1 108
O that my prayers could such affection move! . . . *M. N. Dream* i 1 197
Amen, amen, to that fair prayer, say I! . . . . ii 2 62
The more my prayer, the lesser is my grace . . . . . . ii 2 89
Thy threats have no more strength than her weak prayers . . . iii 2 250
Let me say 'amen' betimes, lest the devil cross my prayer *Mer. of Venice* iii 1 23
Let him alone: I'll follow him no more with bootless prayers . . iii 3 20
I have toward heaven breathed a secret vow To live in prayer . . iii 4 28
Can no prayers pierce thee?—No, none that thou hast wit enough to make . . . . iv 1 126
We do pray for mercy; And that same prayer doth teach us all to render The deeds of mercy . . . . iv 1 201
Whiles you chid me, I did love; How then might your prayers move! *As Y. Like It* iv 3 55
What heaven more will, That thee may furnish and my prayers pluck down, Fall on thy head! . . . . *All's Well* i 1 78
When thou hast leisure, say thy prayers . . . . i 1 228
You had my prayers to lead them on; and to keep them on, have them still . . . . ii 4 17
It may be you have mistaken him, my lord.—And shall do so ever, though I took him at's prayers . . . . ii 5 46
Shut his bosom Against our borrowing prayers . . . . . . iii 1 9
He cannot thrive, Unless her prayers, whom heaven delights to hear And loves to grant, reprieve him from the wrath Of greatest justice iii 4 27
Get him to say his prayers, good Sir Toby, get him to pray.—My prayers, minx!—No, I warrant you, he will not hear of godliness *T. Night* iii 4 131
And have in vain said many A prayer upon her grave . . *W. Tale* v 3 141
Upon which better part our prayers come in . . . . *K. John* iii 1 293
Add proof unto mine armour with thy prayers . . . *Richard II.* i 3 73
Unto my mother's prayers I bend my knee . . . . . . v 3 97
Look upon his face; His eyes do drop no tears, his prayers are in jest . v 3 101
His prayers are full of false hypocrisy; Ours of true zeal . . . v 3 107
Our prayers do out-pray his; then let them have That mercy which true prayer ought to have . . . . v 3 109
Hearing how our plaints and prayers do pierce, Pity may move thee . v 3 127
Say thy prayers, and farewell . . . . 1 *Hen. IV.* v 1 124
In hearty prayers That your attempts may overlive the hazard 2 *Hen. IV.* iv 1 14
All their prayers and love Were set on Hereford, whom they doted on . iv 1 137
I know thee not, old man: fall to thy prayers . . . . . . v 5 51
He scorns to say his prayers, lest a' should be thought a coward *Hen. V.* iii 2 40
They have said their prayers, and they stay for death . . . . iv 2 56
The church's prayers made him so prosperous.—The church! 1 *Hen. VI.* i 1 32
I would prevail, if prayers might prevail, To join your hearts in love . iii 1 67
Good wishes, praise and prayers Shall Suffolk ever have of Margaret . v 3 173
Prayers and tears have moved me, gifts could never . . 2 *Hen. VI.* iv 7 73
If when you make your prayers, God should be so obdurate as yourselves, How would it fare with your departed souls? . . . . . iv 7 121
As bold in war As he is famed for mildness, peace, and prayer 3 *Hen. VI.* ii 1 156
My love till death, my humble thanks, my prayers . . . . . iii 2 62
But if an humble prayer may prevail, I then crave pardon . . . iv 6 7
To your good prayers will scarcely say amen . . . *Richard III.* i 3 21
O God! if my deep prayers cannot appease thee . . . . . i 4 69
Whom I will importune With daily prayers all to that effect . . ii 2 15
O, remember, God, To hear her prayers for them, as now for us! . . iii 3 19
See, a book of prayer in his hand, True ornaments to know a holy man iii 7 98
A book of prayers on their pillow lay . . . . iv 3 14
My prayers on the adverse party fight . . . . iv 4 190
That high All-Seer that I dallied with Hath turn'd my feigned prayer on my head And given in earnest what I begg'd in jest . . . . v 1 21
The prayers of holy saints and wronged souls, Like high-rear'd bulwarks, stand before our faces . . . . v 3 241
Their curses now Live where their prayers did . . . *Hen. VIII.* i 2 63
Make of your prayers one sweet sacrifice, And lift my soul to heaven . ii 1 77
My vows and prayers Yet are the king's . . . . ii 1 88
My prayers Are not words duly hallow'd . . . . ii 3 67
Prayers and wishes Are all I can return . . . . ii 3 69
Almost forgot my prayers to content him? And am I thus rewarded? . iii 1 132

Prayer. He has my heart yet; and shall have my prayers While I shall have my life *Hen. VIII.* iii 1 180
I Can nothing render but allegiant thanks, My prayers to heaven for you iii 2 177
My prayers For ever and for ever shall be yours iii 2 426
But now I am past all comforts here, but prayers iv 2 123
Prithee, to bed; and in thy prayers remember The estate of my poor queen v 1 73
And my good mistress will Remember in my prayers v 1 78
Would you were half so honest! Men's prayers then would seek you v 3 83
But, I think, thy horse will sooner con an oration than thou learn a prayer without book *Troi. and Cres.* ii 1 19
I have said my prayers and devil Envy say Amen ii 3 23
What, art thou devout? wast thou in prayer?—Ay: the heavens hear me ii 3 39
I will wish her speedy strength, and visit her with my prayers *Coriolanus* i 3 88
The prayers of priests nor times of sacrifice, Embarquements all of fury, shall lift up Their rotten privilege and custom 'gainst My hate i 10 21
News to-night.—Good or bad?—Not according to the prayer of the people ii 1 4
Take my prayers with you. I would the gods had nothing else to do But to confirm my curses! iv 2 44
Thou barr'st us Our prayers to the gods, which is a comfort That all but we enjoy v 3 105
To his surname Coriolanus 'longs more pride Than pity to our prayers v 3 171
Chop off my hands too; . . . In bootless prayer have they been held up *T. Andron.* iii 1 75
For heaven shall hear our prayers; Or with our sighs we'll breathe the welkin dim, And stain the sun with fog iii 1 211
Will I be as perfect As begging hermits in their holy prayers iii 2 41
I am no baby, I, that with base prayers I should repent the evils I have done v 3 185
Thus frighted swears a prayer or two And sleeps again *Rom and Jul.* i 4 87
Have not saints lips, and holy palmers too!—Ay, pilgrim, lips that they must use in prayer i 5 104
Saints do not move, though grant for prayers' sake.—Then move not, while my prayer's effect I take i 5 107
Nor tears nor prayers shall purchase out abuses: Therefore use none iii 1 198
If I could pray to move, prayers would move me *J. Cæsar* iii 1 59
But they did say their prayers, and address'd them Again to sleep *Macb.* ii 2 25
I'll send my prayers with him iii 6 49
Hanging a golden stamp about their necks, Put on with holy prayers iv 3 154
Let not thy mother lose her prayers, Hamlet: I pray thee, stay with us *Hamlet* i 2 118
And what's in prayer but this two-fold force, To be forestalled ere we come to fall, Or pardon'd being down? iii 3 48
But, O, what form of prayer Can serve my turn? iii 3 51
For charitable prayers, Shards, flints and pebbles should be thrown on her v 1 253
As my great patron thought on in my prayers *Lear* i 1 144
Sometime with lunatic bans, sometime with prayers, Enforce their charity ii 3 19
Found good means To draw from her a prayer of earnest heart *Othello* i 3 152
This hand of yours requires A sequester from liberty, fasting and prayer iii 4 40
Being done, there is no pause.—But while I say one prayer!—It is too late v 2 83
Hear me this prayer, though thou deny me a matter of more weight *Ant. and Cleo.* i 2 70
Dear goddess, hear that prayer of the people! i 2 73
Deny us for our good; so find we profit By losing of our prayers ii 1 8
Before the gods my knee shall bow my prayers To them for you ii 3 3
When I shall pray, 'O, bless my lord and husband!' Undo that prayer, by crying out as loud, 'O, bless my brother!' iii 4 17
Husband win, win brother, Prays, and destroys the prayer; no midway iii 4 19
He sleeps.—Swoons rather; for so bad a prayer as his Was never yet for sleep iv 9 27
As I had made my meal, and parted With prayers for the provider *Cymb.* iii 6 53
I ha' strew'd his grave, And on it said a century of prayers, Such as I can iv 2 391
For which the people's prayers still fall upon you *Pericles* iii 3 19
Madam, my thanks and prayers iii 3 34
Come, say your prayers.—What mean you?—If you require a little space for prayer, I grant it: pray; but be not tedious iv 1 66
She has me her quirks, her reasons, her master reasons, her prayers, her knees iv 6 9
She sent him away as cold as a snowball; saying his prayers too iv 6 149
Prayer-book. Wear prayer-books in my pocket, look demurely *M. of Ven.* ii 2 201
Get a prayer-book in your hand, And stand betwixt two churchmen *Richard III.* iii 7 47
Prayest. The devil take thy soul!—Thou pray'st not well *Hamlet* v 1 282
Praying. We have been praying for our husbands' healths *Mer. of Venice* v 1 114
I see a good amendment of life in thee; from praying to purse-taking *1 Hen. IV.* i 2 115
Nay, that's past praying for ii 4 211
Not sleeping, to engross his idle body, But praying *Richard III.* iii 7 77
For my daughters, Richard, They shall be praying nuns, not weeping queens iv 4 201
My letters, praying on his side, . . . were slighted off *J. Cæsar* iv 3 4
Now might I do it pat, now he is praying; And now I'll do't *Hamlet* iii 3 73
A more unhappy lady, If this division chance, ne'er stood between, Praying for both parts *Ant. and Cleo.* iii 4 14
Preach. My master preaches patience to him *Com. of Errors* v 1 174
Preach some philosophy to make me mad *K. John* iii 4 51
I have heard you preach That malice was a great and grievous sin *1 Hen. VI.* iii 1 127
I will preach to thee: mark *Lear* iv 6 184
Preached. Fit for the mountains and the barbarous caves, Where manners ne'er were preach'd! *T. Night* iv 1 53
To have divinity preached there! did you ever dream of such a thing? *Pericles* iv 5 4
Preacher. Besides, they are our outward consciences, And preachers to us all *Hen. V.* iv 1 9
Preaching. His form and cause conjoin'd, preaching to stones, Would make them capable *Hamlet* iii 4 126
Preachment. And made a preachment of your high descent *3 Hen. VI.* i 4 72
Pread. He is come to me and prings me pread and salt yesterday *Hen. V.* v 1 9
Preambulate. Arts-man, preambulate, we will be singuled from the barbarous *L. L. Lost* v 1 85
Precedence. Some obscure precedence that hath tofore been sain iii 1 83
I do not like 'But yet,' it does allay The good precedence *Ant. and Cleo.* ii 5 51
Precedent. Thy case, dear friend, Shall be my precedent *Tempest* ii 1 291
That I may example my digression by some mighty precedent *L. L. Lost* i 2 122
'Twill be recorded for a precedent *Mer. of Venice* iv 1 220
Making me the precedent, Should a like language use to all degrees *W. T.* ii 1 84
Precedent. Return the precedent to these lords again *K. John* v 2 3
May be a precedent and witness good *Richard II.* ii 1 130
Step aside, and I'll show thee a precedent *1 Hen. IV.* ii 4 37
For shame, my liege, make them your precedent! *3 Hen. VI.* ii 2 33
The precedent was full as long a-doing *Richard III.* iii 6 7
Have you a precedent Of this commission? *Hen. VIII.* i 2 91
Your grace has given a precedent of wisdom Above all princes ii 2 86
A pattern, precedent, and lively warrant *T. Andron.* v 3 44
Our own precedent passions do instruct us What levity's in youth *T. of A.* i 1 133
A slave that is not twentieth part the tithe Of your precedent lord *Ham.* iii 4 98
I have a voice and precedent of peace, To keep my name ungored v 2 260
The country gives me proof and precedent Of Bedlam beggars *Lear* ii 3 13
Do it at once; Or thy precedent services are all But accidents *A. and C.* iv 14 83
A precedent Which not to read would show the Britons cold *Cymbeline* iii 1 75
Preceding. Of six preceding ancestors . . . Hath it been owed *All's Well* v 3 196
As harbingers preceding still the fates *Hamlet* i 1 122
Precept. My father's precepts I therein do forget *Tempest* iii 1 58
In action all of precept, he did show me The way twice o'er *M. for M.* iv 1 40
I will bestow some precepts of this virgin Worthy the note *All's Well* iii 5 103
Those precepts cannot be served *2 Hen. IV.* v 1 14
We may as bootless spend our vain command Upon the enraged soldiers in their spoil As send precepts to the leviathan To come ashore *Hen. V.* iii 3 26
You were used to load me With precepts that would make invincible The heart that conn'd them *Coriolanus* iv 1 10
And never learn'd The icy precepts of respect *T. of Athens* iv 3 258
These few precepts in thy memory See thou character *Hamlet* i 3 58
Preceptial. Which before Would give preceptial medicine to rage *M. Ado* v 1 24
Precinct. Within her quarter and mine own precinct *1 Hen. VI.* ii 1 68
Precious creature; I had rather crack my sinews, break my back *Tempest* iii 1 25
For love is still most precious in itself *T. G. of Ver.* ii 6 24
With juice of balm and every precious flower *Mer. Wives* v 5 66
What have I to give you back, whose worth May counterpoise this rich and precious gift? *Much Ado* iv 1 29
Every lovely organ of her life Shall come apparell'd in more precious habit iv 1 229
Held precious in the world's esteem *L. L. Lost* ii 1 4
It adds a precious seeing to the eye iv 3 333
He swore that he did hold me dear As precious eyesight v 2 445
To call me goddess, nymph, divine and rare, Precious, celestial *M. N. D.* iii 2 227
Two rich and precious stones, Stolen by my daughter! *Mer. of Venice* ii 8 20
Two thousand ducats in that; and other precious, precious jewels iii 1 91
Thy words are too precious to be cast away upon curs *As Y. Like It* i 3 4
Like the toad, ugly and venomous, Wears yet a precious jewel in his head ii 1 14
By so much is a horn more precious than to want iii 3 64
Is the jay more precious than the lark, Because his feathers are more beautiful? Or is the adder better than the eel? *T. of Shrew* iv 3 177
Your precious self had then not cross'd the eyes Of my young play-fellow *W. Tale* i 2 79
This jealousy Is for a precious creature i 2 452
His most precious queen and children are even now to be afresh lamented iv 2 27
At your request My father will grant precious things as trifles.—Would he do so, I'ld beg your precious mistress v 1 223
Go together, You precious winners all v 3 131
Turning with splendour of his precious eye The meagre cloddy earth to glittering gold *K. John* iii 1 79
A gnat, a wandering hair, Any annoyance in that precious sense iv 1 94
We hold our time too precious to be spent With such a brabbler v 2 161
Tendering the precious safety of my prince *Richard II.* i 1 32
One vial . . . Is crack'd, and all the precious liquor spilt i 2 19
As foil wherein thou art to set The precious jewel of thy home return i 3 267
This little world, This precious stone set in the silver sea ii 1 46
And threat the glory of my precious crown iii 3 90
Thy precious rich crown for a pitiful bald crown *1 Hen. IV.* ii 4 420
I feel me much to blame, So idly to profane the precious time *2 Hen. IV.* ii 4 391
Other, less fine in carat, is more precious, Preserving life iv 5 162
An urn more precious Than the rich-jewel'd coffer of Darius *1 Hen. VI.* i 6 24
Put a golden sceptre in thy hand And set a precious crown upon thy head v 3 119
And defaced The precious image of our dear Redeemer *Richard III.* ii 1 123
And never in my life, I do protest, Was it more precious to me than 'tis now iii 2 82
A base foul stone, made precious by the foil Of England's chair v 3 250
It holds his estimate and dignity As well wherein 'tis precious of itself As in the prizer *Troi. and Cres.* ii 2 55
My love admits no qualifying dross; No more my grief, in such a precious loss iv 4 10
And look'd upon things precious as they were The common muck *Coriol.* ii 2 129
As the bark . . . Returns with precious lading to the bay *T. Andron.* i 1 72
Upon his bloody finger he doth wear A precious ring ii 3 227
He that is strucken blind cannot forget The precious treasure of his eyesight lost *Rom. and Jul.* i 1 239
This precious book of love, this unbound lover i 3 87
A precious ring, a ring that I must use In dear employment v 3 31
What a precious comfort 'tis, to have so many, like brothers, commanding one another's fortunes! *T. of Athens* i 2 108
What is here? Gold? yellow, glittering, precious gold? iv 3 26
Wife and child, Those precious motives, those strong knots of love *Macb.* iv 3 27
I cannot but remember such things were, That were most precious to me iv 3 223
From a shelf the precious diadem stole, And put it in his pocket! *Hamlet* iii 4 100
It sends some precious instance of itself After the thing it loves iv 5 162
I profess Myself an enemy to all other joys, Which the most precious square of sense possesses *Lear* i 1 76
Not all the dukes of waterish Burgundy Can buy this unprized precious maid of me i 1 262
The art of our necessities is strange, That can make vile things precious iii 2 71
Met I my father with his bleeding rings, Their precious stones new lost v 3 190
Make it a darling like your precious eye *Othello* iii 4 66
Precious villain!—The woman falls; sure, he hath kill'd his wife v 2 235
I have not seen the most precious diamond that is, nor you the lady *Cymbeline* i 4 81
Can we not Partition make with spectacles so precious 'Twixt fair and foul? i 6 37
And must not soil The precious note of it with a base slave ii 3 127
Here is a box; I had it from the queen: What's in't is precious iii 4 192
I pray his absence Proceed by swallowing that, for he believes It is a thing most precious iii 5 59
Ah, you precious pandar! Villain, Where is thy lady? iii 5 81
Thou precious varlet iv 2 83
The drug he gave me, which he said was precious And cordial to me, have I not found it Murderous to the senses? iv 2 326

Precious. Such precious deeds in one that promised nought But beggary *Cymbeline* v 5 9
If That box I gave you was not thought by me A precious thing v 5 242
Precious-dear. But the brave man Holds honour far more precious-dear than life *Troi. and Cres.* v 3 28
Precious-juiced. I must up-fill this osier cage of ours With baleful weeds and precious-juiced flowers *Rom. and Jul.* ii 3 8
Preciously. The time 'twixt six and now Must by us both be spent most preciously *Tempest* i 2 241
Precious-princely. Too precious-princely for a grave *K. John* iv 3 40
Precipice. You take a precipice for no leap of danger, And woo your own destruction *Hen. VIII.* v 1 139
Precipitating. Hadst thou been aught but gossamer, feathers, air, So many fathom down precipitating, Thou'dst shiver'd like an egg *Lear* iv 6 50
Precipitation. That the precipitation might down stretch Below the beam of sight *Coriolanus* iii 2 4
Banish him our city, In peril of precipitation From off the rock Tarpeian iii 3 102
Precise. It is as much as I can do to keep the terms of my honour precise *Mer. Wives* ii 2 23
He was ever precise in promise-keeping *Meas. for Meas.* i 2 76
Lord Angelo is precise; Stands at a guard with envy i 3 50
I know not well what they are: but precise villains they are, that I am sure of ii 1 54
Taffeta phrases, silken terms precise *L. L. Lost* v 2 406
Never, O never, do his ghost the wrong To hold your honour more precise and nice With others than with him! *2 Hen. IV.* ii 3 40
Precisely. I have taught him, even as one would say precisely, 'thus I would teach a dog' *T. G. of Ver.* iv 4 6
Therefore, precisely, can you carry your good will to the maid? *Mer. Wives* i 1 237
Tell me precisely of what complexion.—Of the sea-water green *L. L. Lost* i 2 85
Such a fellow, to say precisely, were not for the court *All's Well* ii 2 12
Full well he knows He cannot so precisely weed this land *2 Hen. IV.* iv 1 205
Some craven scruple Of thinking too precisely on the event *Hamlet* iv 4 41
Preciseness. Is all your strict preciseness come to this? *1 Hen. VI.* v 4 67
Pre-contract. He is your husband on a pre-contract *Meas. for Meas.* iv 1 72
Precor. Fauste, precor gelida quando pecus omne sub umbra Ruminat,—and so forth *L. L. Lost* iv 2 95
Precurse. Even the like precurse of fierce events *Hamlet* i 1 121
Precursors. The precursors O' the dreadful thunder-claps *Tempest* i 2 201
Predeceased. A memorable trophy of predeceased valour *Hen. V.* v 1 76
Predecessor. To give a greater sum Than ever at one time the clergy yet Did to his predecessors part withal i 1 81
In the right Of your great predecessor, King Edward the Third i 2 248
Is worth all your predecessors since Deucalion *Coriolanus* ii 1 101
Take to you, as your predecessors have, Your honour with your form ii 2 147
The sacred storehouse of his predecessors *Macbeth* ii 4 34
Predestinate. Some gentleman or other shall 'scape a predestinate scratched face *Much Ado* i 1 136
Predicament. In which predicament, I say, thou stand'st *Mer. of Venice* iv 1 357
To show the line and the predicament Wherein you range *1 Hen. IV.* i 3 168
O woful sympathy! Piteous predicament! *Rom. and Jul.* iii 3 86
Prediction. For these predictions Are to the world in general as to Cæsar *J. Cæsar* ii 2 28
Great prediction Of noble having and of royal hope *Macbeth* i 3 55
This villain of mine comes under the prediction *Lear* i 2 119
I am thinking, brother, of a prediction I read this other day i 2 152
Predominance. And underwrite in an observing kind His humorous predominance *Troi. and Cres.* ii 3 138
Is't night's predominance, or the day's shame? *Macbeth* ii 4 8
Knaves, thieves, and treachers, by spherical predominance *Lear* i 2 134
Predominant. Born under Mars.—When he was predominant.—When he was retrograde, I think, rather *All's Well* i 1 211
It is a bawdy planet, that will strike Where 'tis predominant *W. Tale* i 2 202
Foul subornation is predominant And equity exiled *2 Hen. VI.* iii 1 145
And where the worser is predominant, Full soon the canker death eats up that plant *Rom. and Jul.* ii 3 29
Do you find Your patience so predominant in your nature? *Macbeth* iii 1 87
Predominate. Know I will predominate over the peasant *Mer. Wives* ii 2 294
Let your close fire predominate his smoke *T. of Athens* iv 3 142
Preeches. If you forget your 'quies,' your 'quæs,' and your 'quods,' you must be preeches *Mer. Wives* iv 1 81
Pre-eminence. Of more pre-eminence than fish and fowls *Com. of Errors* ii 1 23
I do invest you jointly with my power, Pre-eminence *Lear* i 1 133
Pre-employed. That false villain Whom I employ'd was pre-employ'd by him *W. Tale* ii 1 49
Preface. Is but a preface of her worthy praise *1 Hen. VI.* v 5 11
Prefer. Have I not reason to prefer mine own?—And I will help thee to prefer her too *T. G. of Ver.* ii 4 156
Under the colour of commending him, I have access my own love to prefer iv 2 4
Our haste from hence is of so quick condition That it prefers itself *Meas. for Meas.* i 1 55
If you . . . know any such, Prefer them hither *T. of Shrew* i 1 97
Who should be pitiful, if you be not? Or who should study to prefer a peace, If holy churchmen take delight in broils? *1 Hen. VI.* iii 1 110
Say it is done, And I will love thee, and prefer thee too *Richard III.* iv 2 82
That prefer A noble life before a long *Coriolanus* iii 1 152
This before all the world do I prefer *T. Andron.* iv 2 109
Ne'er prefer his injuries to his heart, To bring it into danger *T. of Athens* iii 5 34
Let him go, And presently prefer his suit to Cæsar *J. Cæsar* iii 1 28
Wilt thou bestow thy time with me?—Ay, if Messala will prefer me to you v 5 62
Stood I within his grace, I would prefer him to a better place *Lear* i 1 277
More overt test Than these thin habits and poor likelihoods Of modern seeming do prefer against him *Othello* i 3 109
So shall you have a shorter journey to your desires by the means I shall then have to prefer them ii 1 286
You must not so far prefer her 'fore ours of Italy *Cymbeline* i 4 70
Who lets go by no vantages that may Prefer you to his daughter ii 3 51
The Roman emperor's letters, Sent by a consul to me, should not sooner Than thine own worth prefer thee iv 2 386
Ere I arise, I will prefer my sons v 5 326
Who is the first that doth prefer himself? *Pericles* ii 2 17
Preferment. Put forth their sons to seek preferment *T. G. of Ver.* i 3 7
If it be preferment To leave a rich Jew's service, to become The follower of so poor a gentleman *Mer. of Venice* ii 2 155
In the preferment of the eldest sister *T. of Shrew* ii 1 94
Now, had I not the dash of my former life in me, would preferment drop on my head *W. Tale* v 2 123
While these do labour for their own preferment, Behoves it us to labour for the realm *2 Hen. VI.* i 1 181
She may help you to many fair preferments *Richard III.* i 3 95

Preferment. Stands in the gap and trade of moe preferments *Hen. VIII.* v 1 36
Preferment falls on him that cuts him off *Lear* iv 5 38
Preferment goes by letter and affection, And not by old gradation *Othello* i 1 36
I'll move the king To any shape of thy preferment *Cymbeline* i 5 71
Neither want my means for thy relief nor my voice for thy preferment iii 5 116
Be but duteous, and true preferment shall tender itself to thee iii 5 159
I speak against my present profit, but my wish hath a preferment in't v 4 215
Preferr'd With twenty thousand soul-confirming oaths *T. G. of Ver.* ii 6 15
The short and the long is, our play is preferred *M. N. Dream* iv 2 39
Thy master spoke with me this day, And hath preferr'd thee *Mer. of Ven.* ii 2 155
Think not, although in writing I preferr'd The manner of thy vile outrageous crimes, That therefore I have forged, or am not able Verbatim to rehearse the method of my pen *1 Hen. VI.* iii 1 10
Since he affects her most, . . . In our opinions she should be preferr'd v 5 61
Show some reason, Buckingham, Why Somerset should be preferred in this *2 Hen. VI.* i 3 117
Large gifts have I bestow'd on learned clerks, Because my book preferr'd me to the king iv 7 77
Newly preferr'd from the king's secretary *Hen. VIII.* iv 1 102
Why then preferr'd you not your sums and bills? *T. of Athens* iii 4 49
And hated For being preferr'd so well *Cymbeline* ii 3 136
He is preferr'd By thee to us iv 2 400
Preferrest. But thou preferr'st thy life before thine honour *3 Hen. VI.* i 1 246
Preferreth. Who preferreth peace More than I do? *1 Hen. VI.* iii 1 33
Preferring you before her father *Othello* i 3 187
Prefixed. The hour draws on Prefix'd by Angelo *Meas. for Meas.* iv 3 83
A month behind the gest Prefix'd for's parting *W. Tale* i 2 42
It is great morning, and the hour prefix'd Of her delivery *Troi. and Cres.* iv 3 1
At the prefixed hour of her waking, Came I to take her *Rom. and Jul.* v 3 253
Preformed. Why all these things change from their ordinance Their natures and preformed faculties *J. Cæsar* i 3 67
Pregnancy is made a tapster, and hath his quick wit wasted *2 Hen. IV.* i 2 192
Pregnant. The terms For common justice, you're as pregnant in As art and practice hath enriched any *Meas. for Meas.* i 1 12
'Tis very pregnant, The jewel that we find, we stoop and take't ii 1 23
Disguise, I see, thou art a wickedness, Wherein the pregnant enemy does much *T. Night* ii 2 29
My matter hath no voice, lady, but to your own most pregnant and vouchsafed ear.—'Odours,' 'pregnant' and 'vouchsafed:' I'll get 'em all three iii 1 100
Most true, if ever truth were pregnant by circumstance *W. Tale* v 2 34
To which the Grecians are most prompt and pregnant *Troi. and Cres.* iv 4 90
How pregnant sometimes his replies are! *Hamlet* ii 2 212
Crook the pregnant hinges of the knee Where thrift may follow fawning iii 2 66
The profits of my death Were very pregnant and potential spurs *Lear* ii 1 78
Who, by the art of known and feeling sorrows, Am pregnant to good pity iv 6 227
It is a most pregnant and unforced position *Othello* ii 1 239
'Twere pregnant they should square between themselves *Ant. and Cleo.* ii 1 45
O, 'tis pregnant, pregnant! The drug he gave me, which he said was precious And cordial to me, have I not found it Murderous to the senses? *Cymbeline* iv 2 325
The pregnant instrument of wrath Prest for this blow *Pericles* iv Gower 44
Pregnantly. That shall demonstrate these quick blows of Fortune's More pregnantly than words *T. of Athens* i 1 92
Prejudicates. Our dearest friend Prejudicates the business *All's Well* i 2 8
Prejudice. And seek how we may prejudice the foe *1 Hen. VI.* iii 3 91
Might, through their amity, Breed him some prejudice *Hen. VIII.* i 1 182
The least word that might Be to the prejudice of her present state ii 4 154
Prejudicial. Think you 'twere prejudicial to his crown? *3 Hen. VI.* i 1 144
Prelate. Into the bosom creep Of that same noble prelate *1 Hen. IV.* i 3 267
Northumberland and the prelate Scroop, Who, as we hear, are busily in arms v 5 37
With an inward wish You would desire the king were made a prelate *Hen. V.* i 1 40
Arrogant Winchester, that haughty prelate *1 Hen. VI.* i 3 23
No, prelate: such is thy audacious wickedness iii 1 14
Am I not protector, saucy priest?—And am not I a prelate of the church? iii 1 46
His lordship should be humbler; It fitteth not a prelate so to plead iii 1 57
Rancour will out: proud prelate, in thy face I see thy fury *2 Hen. VI.* i 1 142
The haughty prelate Bishop of Exeter, his brother there *Richard III.* iv 4 502
Premeditated. Great clerks have purposed To greet me with premeditated welcomes *M. N. Dream* v 1 94
Have on them the guilt of premeditated and contrived murder *Hen. V.* iv 1 170
Comest thou with deep premeditated lines? *1 Hen. VI.* iii 1 1
Premeditation. A cold premeditation for my purpose! *3 Hen. VI.* iii 2 133
Premised. O, let the vile world end, And the premised flames of the last day Knit earth and heaven together! *2 Hen. VI.* v 2 41
Premises. In lieu o' the premises Of homage *Tempest* i 2 123
Here is my hand; the premises observed, Thy will by my performance shall be served *All's Well* ii 1 204
The law I bear no malice for my death; 'T has done, upon the premises, but justice *Hen. VIII.* ii 1 63
Prenez. O, prenez miséricorde! ayez pitié de moi! *Hen. V.* iv 4 12
Prenominate. Think'st thou to catch my life so pleasantly As to prenominate in nice conjecture Where thou wilt hit me dead? *T. and C.* iv 5 250
Ever seen in the prenominate crimes The youth you breathe of guilty *Ham.* ii 1 43
'Prentice. A' was a botcher's 'prentice in Paris *All's Well* iv 3 211
From a prince to a prentice? a low transformation! *2 Hen. IV.* ii 2 194
My accuser is my 'prentice *2 Hen. VI.* i 3 201
Fear not thy master: fight for credit of the 'prentices ii 3 71
Prenzie. The prenzie Angelo! *Meas. for Meas.* iii 1 94
The damned'st body to invest and cover In prenzie guards! iii 1 97
Pre-occupied with what you rather must do Than what you should *Cor.* ii 3 240
Pre-ordinance. And turn pre-ordinance and first decree Into the law of children *J. Cæsar* iii 1 38
Preparation. To press with so little preparation upon you *Mer. Wives* ii 2 162
Allowed for your many war-like, court-like, and learned preparations ii 2 237
Furnished with divines, and have all charitable preparation *M. for M.* iii 2 222
Indeed he hath made great preparation *Much Ado* i 1 280
Jealousy shall be called assurance and all the preparation overthrown ii 2 50
We have not made good preparation *Mer. of Venice* ii 4 4
Put myself into my mortal preparation *All's Well* iii 6 82
Be yare in thy preparation, for thy assailant is quick *T. Night* iii 4 245
All preparation for a bloody siege *K. John* ii 2 111
Never such a power For any foreign preparation Was levied iv 2 111
With strong and mighty preparation *1 Hen. IV.* iv 1 93
Advised by good intelligence Of this most dreadful preparation *Hen. V.* ii Prol. 13
Defences, musters, preparations, Should be maintain'd ii 4 18
With busy hammers closing rivets up, Give dreadful note of preparation iv Prol. 14

Preparation. The time was blessedly lost wherein such preparation was gained . . . . Hen. V. iv 1 192
And here take my leave, To go about my preparation . . 1 Hen. VI. i 1 166
These three lead on this preparation Whither 'tis bent . . Coriolanus i 2 15
They are in a most warlike preparation, and hope to come upon them . iv 3 18
Who, were't so, Would have inform'd for preparation . . Macbeth i 5 34
Your royal preparation Makes us hear something . . . . v 3 57
This, I take it, Is the main motive of our preparations . . Hamlet i 1 105
Appear'd To be a preparation 'gainst the Polack . . . . ii 2 63
Advise the duke, where you are going, to a most festinate preparation Lear iii 7 10
Our preparation stands In expectation of them . . . . iv 4 22
The Turk with a most mighty preparation makes for Cyprus . Othello i 3 221
I'll raise the preparation of a war Shall stain your brother Ant. and Cleo. iii 4 26
Their preparation is to-day by sea; We please them not by land . iv 10 1
That's the way To fool their preparation . . . . . . v 2 225
Your preparation can affront no less Than what you hear of . Cymbeline iv 3 29
Prepare. Spirit, We must prepare to meet with Caliban . . Tempest iv 1 166
Therefore prepare yourself to death . . . Meas. for Meas. iii 1 169
Who can do good on him? Well, go, prepare yourself . . iv 2 72
I will have more time to prepare me . . . . . . iv 3 57
Notice to Escalus and Angelo, Who do prepare to meet him at the gates iv 3 136
Prepare, madam, prepare! Arm, wenches, arm! . . . L. L. Lost v 2 81
Go, bid them prepare.—We will turn it finely off, sir . . . v 2 510
Prepare; I will away to-night.—Madam, not so; I do beseech you, stay.—Prepare, I say . . . . v 2 737
Prepare to die For disobedience to your father's will . M. N. Dream i 1 86
Will you prepare you for this masque to-night? . Mer. of Venice ii 4 23
Bid them prepare for dinner.—That is done, sir; they have all stomachs iii 5 52
Then bid them prepare dinner.—That is done too, sir; only 'cover' is the word . . . . iii 5 56
You must prepare your bosom for his knife . . . . . iv 1 245
Most learned judge! A sentence! Come, prepare!—Tarry a little . iv 1 304
Therefore prepare thee to cut off the flesh. Shed thou no blood . iv 1 324
Let us prepare Some welcome for the mistress of the house . . v 1 37
Let your wedding be to-morrow . . . Go you and prepare Aliena As Y. L. It v 2 17
My shroud of white, stuck all with yew, O, prepare it! . . T. Night ii 4 57
Prepare you, lords; Summon a session . . . . W. Tale ii 3 201
Prepare To see the life as lively mock'd as ever Still sleep mock'd death v 3 18
They are at hand, To parley or to fight; therefore prepare. . K. John ii 1 78
Come, boy, prepare yourself.—Is there no remedy? . . . iv 1 90
When you should be told they do prepare, The tidings comes that they are all arrived . . . . iv 2 114
On Wednesday next we solemnly set down Our coronation: lords, prepare yourselves . . . . Richard II. iv 1 320
Good sometime queen, prepare thee hence for France . . . v 1 37
My lord, prepare; the king comes on apace . . . . 1 Hen. IV. v 2 90
He let him outlive that day to see His greatness and to teach others how they should prepare . . . . Hen. V. iv 1 196
Bid him prepare; for I will cut his throat . . . . . iv 4 34
The deep-mouth'd sea, Which like a mighty whiffler 'fore the king Seems to prepare his way . . . . v Prol. 13
Prepare we for our marriage . . . . v 2 398
His highness' pleasure You do prepare to ride unto Saint Alban's 2 Hen. VI. i 2 57
I'll prepare My tear-stain'd eyes to see her miseries . . . ii 4 15
Go levy men, and make prepare for war . . . . 3 Hen. VI. iv 1 131
Prepare you, lords, for Edward is at hand, Ready to fight . . v 4 60
Never, my lord; therefore prepare to die . . . Richard III. i 4 185
Prepare her ears to hear a wooer's tale . . . . . iv 4 327
Prepare thy battle early in the morning . . . . . v 3 88
Prepare there, The duke is coming: see the barge be ready Hen. VIII. ii 1 97
To furnish Rome, and to prepare the ways You have for dignities . iii 2 328
You must prepare to fight without Achilles . . Troi. and Cres. ii 3 238
What's thy name?—Prepare thy brow to frown . . Coriolanus iv 5 69
Back to Rome, and prepare for your execution: you are condemned . v 2 51
Prepare thy aged eyes to weep . . . . . T. Andron. iii 1 59
I will be revenged: And now prepare your throats . . . v 2 197
Nay, gentlemen, prepare not to be gone . . . Rom. and Jul. i 5 123
Bid my sweet prepare to chide . . . . iii 3 162
Ere you go to bed, Prepare her, wife, against this wedding-day . iii 4 32
Prepare him up Against to-morrow . . . . iv 2 45
Every one prepare To follow this fair corse unto her grave . . iv 5 92
Then, Timon, presently prepare thy grave . . . T. of Athens iv 3 378
In, and prepare: Ours is the fall, I fear; our foes the snare . . v 2 16
Bid them prepare within: I am to blame to be thus waited for J. Cæsar ii 2 118
Prepare the body then, and follow us . . . . . . iii 1 253
If you have tears, prepare to shed them now . . . . . iii 2 173
Bid the commanders Prepare to lodge their companies to-night . iv 3 140
Prepare you, generals: The enemy comes on in gallant show . v 1 12
So exasperate the king that he Prepares for some attempt of war Macb. iii 6 39
Prepare you; I your commission will forthwith dispatch . Hamlet iii 3 2
Must send thee hence With fiery quickness: therefore prepare thyself . iv 3 45
Prepare for dinner . . . . Lear i 3 26
Prepare my horses . . . . i 4 280
To prepare This body, like to them, to what I must . . Pericles i 1 43
Prepare for mirth, for mirth becomes a feast . . . . . ii 3 7
Cleon's wife, with envy rare, A present murderer does prepare . iv Gower 38
Prepared. They prepared A rotten carcass of a boat . . Tempest i 2 145
We have with a leaven'd and prepared choice Proceeded to you M. for M. i 1 52
Bring him his confessor, let him be prepared . . . . . ii 1 35
Spare him, spare him! He's not prepared for death . . . . ii 2 84
I've hope to live, and am prepared to die . . . . . iii 1 4
Let me desire to know how you find Claudio prepared . . . iii 2 254
I will acquaint my daughter withal, that she may be the better prepared for an answer . . . . Much Ado i 2 23
I am arm'd and well prepared . . . . . . Mer. of Venice iv 1 264
I'll go seek the duke: his banquet is prepared . . As Y. Like It ii 5 65
And have prepared great store of wedding cheer . . T. of Shrew iii 2 188
Prepared I was not For such a business . . . . . All's Well ii 5 66
We must away; Our waggon is prepared, and time revives us . . iv 4 34
A vessel rides fast by, but not prepared For this design . W. Tale iv 4 512
Let them be welcome then; we are prepared . . . K. John ii 1 83
He is prepared, and reason too he should . . . . . v 2 130
And is well prepared To whip this dwarfish war, these pigmy arms . v 2 134
The champions are prepared . . . . Richard II. i 3 5
Mine ear is open and my heart prepared: The worst is worldly loss . iii 2 93
Let him tell the king: we are prepared. I will set forward to-night 1 Hen. IV. ii 3 37
Who but only I Make fearful musters and prepared defence? 2 Hen. IV. Ind. 12
Now are we well prepared to know the pleasure Of our fair cousin Hen. V. i 2 234
Prepared. I am prepared: here is my keen-edged sword . . 1 Hen. VI. i 2 98
Having brought the queen To a prepared place in the choir Hen. VIII. iv 1 64
I think, you'll find They've not prepared for us . . . . Coriolanus i 2 30
They are prepared With accusations, as I hear, more strong . . iii 2 139
Who am prepared against your territories, Though not for Rome itself iv 5 140
For that I am prepared and full resolved . . . . . T. Andron. ii 1 57
Weke, weke! so cries a pig prepared to the spit . . . . . iv 2 146
Came The fiery Tybalt, with his sword prepared . Rom. and Jul. i 1 116
Therefore, good Brutus, be prepared to hear . . . . J. Cæsar i 2 66
I'll have prepared him A chalice for the nonce . . . Hamlet iv 7 160
With his prepared sword, he charges home My unprovided body . Lear ii 1 53
An you'll come to supper to-night, you may; an you will not, come when you are next prepared for . . . . Othello iv 1 168
Be prepared to know The purposes I bear . . . Ant. and Cleo. i 3 66
I came before you here a man prepared To take this offer . . . ii 6 41
Go make thee ready; Our letters are prepared . . . . . iii 3 41
Mark Antony, Hearing that you prepared for war, acquainted My grieved ear . . . . iii 6 58
No disgrace Shall fall you for refusing him at sea, Being prepared for land iii 7 41
Let Patient Octavia plough thy visage up With her prepared nails . iv 12 39
Preparedly. Desires instruction, That she preparedly may frame herself To the way she's forced to . . . . v 1 55
Preparing. The Dauphin is preparing hitherward . . . . K. John v 7 59
O my son, my son! thou art preparing fire for us . . . Coriolanus v 2 77
Preposterous. Where, I mean, I did encounter that obscene and most preposterous event . . . . L. L. Lost i 1 244
Preposterous ass, that never read so far To know the cause why music was ordain'd! . . . . T. of Shrew iii 1 9
Being in so preposterous estate as we are . . . . W. Tale v 2 159
'Good Gloucester' and 'good devil' were alike, And both preposterous 3 Hen. VI. v 6 5
O, preposterous And frantic outrage, end thy damned spleen! Rich. III. ii 4 63
Take and take again such preposterous discoveries! . Troi. and Cres. v 1 27
Our natures would conduct us to most preposterous conclusions Othello i 3 333
Preposterously. You prescribe to yourself very preposterously Mer. W. ii 2 250
And those things do best please me That befal preposterously M. N. D. iii 2 121
That wrought upon thee so preposterously . . . . Hen. V. ii 2 112
For nature so preposterously to err, Being not deficient, blind, or lame of sense, Sans witchcraft could not . . . . Othello i 3 62
Prerogatife. When the true and aunchient prerogatifes and laws of the wars is not kept . . . . Hen. V. iv 1 67
Prerogative. And executing the outward face of royalty, With all prerogative . . . . Tempest i 2 105
Then give me leave to have prerogative . . . . T. of Shrew iii 1 6
The great prerogative and rite of love . . . . . All's Well ii 4 42
Give me this prerogative of speech . . . . . . T. Night ii 5 78
Our prerogative Calls not your counsels . . . . . W. Tale ii 1 163
Shall I, . . ., Detract so much from that prerogative, As to be call'd but viceroy? . . . . 1 Hen. VI. v 4 142
The primogenitive and due of birth, Prerogative of age . Troi. and Cres. i 3 107
Insisting on the old prerogative And power i' the truth o' the cause Cor. iii 3 17
Prerogatived. 'Tis the plague of great ones; Prerogatived are they less than the base . . . . Othello iii 3 274
Presage. I have a mind presages me such thrift . . Mer. of Venice i 1 175
Let it presage the ruin of your love . . . . iii 2 175
The youth bears in his visage no great presage of cruelty . T. Night iii 2 69
The trumpet of our wrath And sullen presage of your own decay K. John i 1 28
Prodigies and signs, Abortives, presages and tongues of heaven . . iii 4 158
Farewell: if heart's presages be not vain, We three here part that ne'er shall meet again . . . . Richard II. ii 2 142
It doth presage some ill event . . . . 1 Hen. VI. iv 1 191
My dreams presage some joyful news at hand . . . Rom. and Jul. v 1 2
Now I change my mind, And partly credit things that do presage J. C. v 1 79
Yond simpering dame, Whose face between her forks presages snow Lear iv 6 121
There's a palm presages chastity, if nothing else . . Ant. and Cleo. i 2 47
Presageth. My mind presageth happy gain and conquest . 3 Hen. VI. v 1 71
E'en as the o'erflowing Nilus presageth famine . . Ant. and Cleo. i 2 49
Presaging. Henry's late presaging prophecy Did glad my heart 3 Hen. VI. iv 6 92
Prescience. By my prescience I find my zenith doth depend upon A most auspicious star . . . . Tempest i 2 180
Forestall prescience and esteem no act But that of hand Troi. and Cres. i 3 199
Vex not his prescience; be attentive . . . . Ant. and Cleo. i 2 20
Prescribe. You prescribe to yourself very preposterously . Mer. Wives ii 2 249
This we prescribe, though no physician . . . . Richard II. i 1 154
Make each Prescribe to other as each other's leech . . T. of Athens v 4 84
Prescribe not us our duties . . . . Lear i 1 279
Prescript. Which is the prescript praise and perfection of a good and particular mistress . . . . Hen. V. iii 7 49
I prescripts gave her, That she should lock herself from his resort Hamlet ii 2 142
Do not exceed The prescript of this scroll . . . Ant. and Cleo. iii 8 5
Prescription. Some prescriptions Of rare and proved effects . All's Well i 3 227
How I should be your patient to follow your prescriptions . 2 Hen. IV. i 2 147
A silly time To make prescription for a kingdom's worth . 3 Hen. VI. iii 3 94
I am thankful to you; and I'll go along By your prescription Hen. VIII. i 1 151
The most sovereign prescription in Galen is but empiricutic . Coriolanus ii 1 127
Then have we a prescription to die when death is our physician . Othello i 3 310
Presence. Repair me with thy presence . . . . . . T. G. of Ver. v 4 11
Thou makest me most unhappy.—And me, when he approacheth to your presence . . . . v 4 32
You must not speak with men But in the presence of the prioress Meas. for Meas. i 4 11
In obsequious fondness Crowd to his presence . . . . . . ii 4 29
Bear a fair presence, though your heart be tainted . . Com. of Errors iii 2 13
Of such enchanting presence and discourse . . . . . . iii 2 166
I promised your presence and the chain . . . . . . iv 1 23
Courtesy itself must convert to disdain, if you come in her presence Much Ado i 1 124
Excepting your worship's presence . . . . iii 5 34
Presence majestical would put him out . . . . . L. L. Lost v 2 102
Here is like to be a good presence of Worthies . . . . . v 2 536
Which parti-coated presence of loose love Put on by us . . . v 2 776
In such a presence here to plead my thoughts . . . M. N. Dream i 1 61
No marvel though Demetrius Do, as a monster, fly my presence thus . ii 2 97
From thy hated presence part I so: See me no more . . . . iii 2 80
From the presence of the sun, Following darkness like a dream . . v 1 392
Now he goes, With no less presence, but with much more love M. of V. iii 2 54
Although I speak it in your presence, You have a noble and a true conceit . . . . iii 4 1
Three proper young men, of excellent growth and presence As Y. Like It i 2 130
My presence May well abate the over-merry spleen . . T. of Shrew Ind. 1 136

Presence. His presence must be the whip of the other . . *All's Well* iv 3 42
Aid me with that store of power you have To come into his presence . v 1 21
Smiles become thee well; therefore in my presence still smile *T. Night* ii 5 192
Of your royal presence I'll adventure The borrow of a week . *W. Tale* i 2 38
From his presence I am barr'd, like one infectious . . . iii 2 98
Behold The sternness of his presence . . . . iv 4 24
I'll bring you where he is aboard, tender your persons to his presence . iv 4 827
She The fairest I have yet beheld, desires access To your high presence v 1 88
Lord of thy presence and no land beside . . . *K. John* i 1 137
It ill beseems this presence to cry aim To these ill-tuned repetitions . ii 1 196
Lord of our presence, Angiers, and of you . . . . . ii 1 367
Your royal presences be ruled by me . . . . . . ii 1 377
Her presence would have interrupted much . . . . . iii 1 542
The king by me requests your presence straight . . . . iv 3 22
Then call them to our presence; face to face . . . *Richard II.* i 1 15
Come I appellant to this princely presence . . . . . i 1 34
What presence must not know, From where you do remain let paper show . . . . i 3 249
The grass whereon thou tread'st the presence strew'd . . . i 3 289
Your presence makes us rich, most noble lord . . . . . ii 3 63
How dare thy joints forget To pay their awful duty to our presence? . iii 3 76
I would he were the best In all this presence that hath moved me so . iv 1 32
You were in presence then; And you can witness with me this is true . iv 1 62
Worst in this royal presence may I speak, Yet best beseeming me to speak the truth. Would God that any in this noble presence Were enough noble to be upright judge! . . . . iv 1 115
Look to thyself; Thou hast a traitor in thy presence there . . . v 3 40
Your presence is too bold and peremptory . . . . *1 Hen. IV.* i 3 17
Had I so lavish of my presence been, So common-hackney'd . . iii 2 39
Even in the presence of the crowned king . . . . . iii 2 54
My presence, like a robe pontifical, Ne'er seen but wonder'd at . iii 2 56
Being with his presence glutted, gorged and full . . . . iii 2 84
He is in presence here . . . . *2 Hen. IV.* iv 4 17
Where is my gracious Lord of Canterbury?—Not here in presence *Hen. V.* i 2 2
Unless the Dauphin be in presence here . . . . . . ii 4 111
We with our stately presence glorify . . . . . *1 Hen. VI.* i 1 21
The presence of a king engenders love Amongst his subjects . . iii 1 181
In presence of the Kings of France and Sicil . . . *2 Hen. VI.* i 1 6
'Tis not my speeches that you do mislike, But 'tis my presence . i 1 141
All in this presence are thy betters . . . . . . i 3 114
O God, have I overcome mine enemy in this presence? . . . ii 3 101
Go, call our uncle to our presence straight . . . . . iii 2 15
My sovereign's presence makes me mild . . . . . . iii 2 219
If from this presence thou darest go with me.—Away even now . . iii 2 228
How now, lords! your wrathful weapons drawn Here in our presence! iii 2 238
Be it known unto thee by these presence, even the presence of Lord Mortimer . . . . iv 7 32
If one so rude and of so mean condition May pass into the presence of a king . . . . v 1 65
What's he approacheth boldly to our presence? . . *3 Hen. VI.* iii 3 44
'Tis thy presence that exhales this blood . . . . *Richard III.* i 2 58
Sent to warn them to his royal presence . . . . . . i 3 39
To whom in all this presence speaks your grace? . . . . i 3 54
What I have said I will avouch in presence of the king . . . i 3 115
Have aught committed that is hardly borne By any in this presence . ii 1 58
Have I offer'd love for this, To be so flouted in this royal presence? . ii 1 78
No one in this presence But his red colour hath forsook his cheeks . ii 1 84
I hope, My absence doth neglect no great designs, Which by my presence might have been concluded . . . . . . iii 4 26
Makes me most forward in this noble presence To doom the offenders . iii 4 66
Were now best, now worst, As presence did present them *Hen. VIII.* i 1 30
Made suit to come in's presence . . . . i 2 197
Receive 'em nobly, and conduct 'em Into our presence . . . i 4 59
An't please your grace, the two great cardinals Wait in the presence . iii 1 17
I' the presence He would say untruths; and be ever double . . iv 2 37
I come not To hear such flattery now, and in my presence . . v 3 124
I have received much honour by your presence . . . . . v 5 72
Her presence Shall quite strike off all service I have done *Troi. and Cres.* iii 3 28
I will put on his presence . . . . iii 3 272
Given hostile strokes, and that not in the presence Of dreaded justice *Coriolanus* iii 3 97
A messenger from Rome Desires to be admitted to your presence *T. An.* v 1 153
By her presence still renew his sorrows . . . . . . v 3 42
Show a fair presence and put off these frowns . *Rom. and Jul.* i 5 75
Her beauty makes This vault a feasting presence full of light . . v 3 86
To see thy Antony making his peace, Shaking the bloody fingers of thy foes, Most noble! in the presence of thy corse . . *J. Cæsar* iii 1 199
To-night we hold a solemn supper, sir, And I'll request your presence *Macbeth* iii 1 15
From broad words and 'cause he fail'd His presence at the tyrant's feast iii 6 22
From this time Be somewhat scanter of your maiden presence *Hamlet* i 3 121
Heavens make our presence and our practices Pleasant and helpful to him! . . . . ii 2 38
This presence knows, And you must needs have heard . . . . v 2 239
At my entreaty forbear his presence till some little time hath qualified the heat of his displeasure . . . . *Lear* i 2 176
She took them, read them in my presence . . . . . . iv 3 13
The generous islanders By you invited, do attend your presence *Othello* iii 3 281
You wrong this presence; therefore speak no more. . *Ant. and Cleo.* ii 2 111
What is't you say?—Your presence needs must puzzle Antony . . iii 7 11
Here is a rural fellow That will not be denied your highness' presence . v 2 234
Bind the offender, And take him from our presence . . *Cymbeline* v 5 301
To glad her presence, The senate-house of planets all did sit . *Pericles* i 1 9
Your presence glads our days: honour we love . . . . . ii 3 21
What, are you merry, knights?—Who can be other in this royal presence? . . . . ii 3 49
Welcome, fair one! Is't not a goodly presence?—She's a gallant lady . v 1 66
Present. And work the peace of the present . . . . *Tempest* i 1 25
A present for any emperor that ever trod on neat's-leather . . ii 2 72
Some of you there present Are worse than devils . . . . iii 3 35
I will discase me, and myself present As I was sometime Milan . . v 1 85
She did scorn a present that I sent her . . . *T. G. of Ver.* iii 1 92
His dog; which to-morrow, by his master's command, he must carry for a present to his lady . . . . iv 2 80
I was sent to deliver him as a present to Mistress Silvia. . . . iv 4 7
Currish thanks is good enough for such a present . . . . iv 4 54
Not only bought many presents to give her, but have given largely to many to know what she would have given . . *Mer. Wives* ii 2 206
The folly of my soul dares not present itself . . . . . ii 2 253
The truth being known, We'll all present ourselves . . . . iv 4 63
Present. 'Twixt twelve and one, Must my sweet Nan present the Fairy Queen . . . . *Mer. Wives* iv 6 20
To the love I have in doing good a remedy presents itself *Meas. for Meas.* iii 1 204
Use him for the present and dismiss him . . . . iv 2 27
Fearless of what's past, present, or to come . . . . . . iv 2 151
For the which you are to do me both a present and a dangerous courtesy iv 2 171
You, constable, are to present the prince's own person . *Much Ado* iii 3 79
What present hast thou there?—Some certain treason . . *L. L. Lost* iv 3 189
Present the princess, sweet chuck, with some delightful ostentation . v 1 117
You shall present before her the Nine Worthies . . . . . v 1 124
Where will you find men worthy enough to present them? . . . v 1 132
He shall present Hercules in minority . . . . v 1 140
And the contents Dies in the zeal of that which it presents . . v 2 519
He presents Hector of Troy; the swain, Pompey the Great . . . v 2 537
These four will change habits, and present the other five . . v 2 542
Say he comes to disfigure, or to present, the person of Moonshine *M. N. Dream* iii 1 62
Some man or other must present Wall: and let him have some plaster . iii 1 69
This man, with lime and rough-cast, doth present Wall, that vile Wall. v 1 132
It doth befall That I, one Snout by name, present a wall . . v 1 157
This lanthorn doth the horned moon present . . . . . v 1 243
How dost thou and thy master agree? I have brought him a present *Mer. of Venice* ii 2 108
Give him a present! give him a halter: I am famish'd in his service . ii 2 112
Give me your present to one Master Bassanio . . . . . ii 2 115
Be it known unto all men by these presents . . . *As Y. Like It* i 2 132
This wide and universal theatre Presents more woeful pageants . . ii 7 138
I should not seek an absent argument Of my revenge, thou present . iii 1 4
Let's present him to the duke, like a Roman conqueror . . . . iv 2 3
He threw his eye aside, And mark what object did present itself . iv 3 104
Present her at the leet, Because she brought stone jugs *T. of Shrew* Ind. 2 89
For an entrance to my entertainment, I do present you with a man of mine . . . . ii 1 55
Be but your lordship present at his examination . . . *All's Well* iii 6 29
I'll serve this duke: Thou shalt present me as an eunuch to him *T. Night* i 2 56
Such a one I was this present . . . . i 5 253
My having is not much; I'll make division of my present with you . iii 4 380
Many a man there is, even at this present, Now while I speak this *W. T.* i 2 192
We shall Present our services to a fine new prince One of these days . ii 1 17
But if one present The abhorr'd ingredient to his eye . . . ii 1 42
I must be present at your conference.—Well, be't so, prithee . . ii 2 17
And make stale The glistering of this present . . . . . iv 1 14
Quench your blushes and present yourself That which you are . . iv 4 67
Mistress Tale-porter, and five or six honest wives that were present . iv 4 274
Make for Sicilia, And there present yourself and your fair princess . iv 4 555
To him will I present them: there may be matter in it . . . iv 4 873
Beseech you, sir, were you present at this relation? . . . . v 2 1
Nay, present your hand: When she was young you woo'd her . . v 3 107
Joy absent, grief is present for that time . . . *Richard II.* i 3 259
Be judged by subject and inferior breath, And he himself not present? iv 1 129
Great king, within this coffin I present Thy buried fear . . . v 6 30
Yet oftentimes it doth present harsh rage, Defect of manners *1 Hen. IV.* iii 1 183
Whether our present five and twenty thousand May hold up head *2 Hen. IV.* i 3 16
Past and to come seems best; things present worst . . . . i 3 108
Give me this man: he presents no mark to the enemy . . . . iii 2 284
The examples Of every minute's instance, present now . . . iv 1 83
He cannot so precisely weed this land As his misdoubts present occasion iv 1 206
His present and your pains we thank you for . . . . *Hen. V.* i 2 260
As matching to his youth and vanity, I did present him with the Paris balls . . . . ii 4 131
Je m'en fais la répétition de tous les mots que vous m'avez appris dès à présent . . . . iii 4 27
On procession, To present your highness with the man . *2 Hen. VI.* ii 1 69
In all submission and humility York doth present himself . . . v 1 59
I present your grace a traitor's head, The head of Cade . . . v 1 66
I will shortly send thy soul to heaven, If heaven will take the present *Richard III.* i 1 120
Northumberland, then present, wept to see it . . . . . . i 3 187
Present to her,—as sometime Margaret Did to thy father, steep'd in Rutland's blood,—A handkerchief . . . . iv 4 274
Such noble scenes as draw the eye to flow We now present *Hen. VIII.* Prol. 5
I was then present, saw them salute on horseback . . . . . i 1 8
Equal in lustre, were now best, now worst, As presence did present them i 1 30
And, being present both, 'Twas said they saw but one . . . i 1 31
I am sorry To see you ta'en from liberty, to look on The business present i 1 206
Cardinal Campeius; Whom once more I present unto your highness . ii 2 98
The king is present: if it be known to him That I gainsay my deed . ii 4 95
Whereupon we are Now present here together . . . . . . ii 4 202
I'm very sorry To sit here at this present, and behold That chair stand empty . . . . v 3 9
No perfection in reversion shall have a praise in present *Troi. and Cres.* iii 2 100
What they do in present, Though less than yours in past, must o'ertop yours . . . . iii 3 163
Take thou Troilus' horse; Present the fair steed to my lady Cressid . v 5 2
That you not delay the present, but . . . We prove this very hour *Coriol.* i 6 60
Present me Death on the wheel or at wild horses' heels . . . iii 2 1
You may salve so, Not what is dangerous present, but the loss Of what is past . . . . iii 2 71
Shall I be charged no further than this present? Must all determine here? . . . . iii 3 42
I also am Longer to live most weary, and present My throat to thee . iv 5 101
Presents well worthy Rome's imperial lord . . . . *T. Andron.* i 1 250
My boy, Shalt carry from me to the empress' sons Presents . . . iv 1 116
So he bade me say; And so I do, and with his gifts present Your lordships . . . . iv 2 14
He should not choose But give them to his master for a present . . iv 3 75
Three talents on the present; in future, all . . . . *T. of Athens* i 1 141
Let the presents Be worthily entertain'd . . . . i 2 190
When, for some trifling present, you have bid me Return so much . ii 2 145
I will present My honest grief unto him; and, as my lord, Still serve him . . . . iv 3 476
Any benefit that points to me, Either in hope or present, I'ld exchange iv 3 527
What have you now to present unto him?—Nothing at this time but my visitation . . . . v 1 19
For this present, I would not, so with love I might entreat you, Be any further moved . . . . *J. Cæsar* i 2 165
I did present myself Even in the aim and very flash of it . . . i 3 51
Two months hence up higher toward the north He first presents his fire ii 1 110
Thy letters have transported me beyond This ignorant present *Macbeth* i 5 58

Present. Present him eminence, both with eye and tongue *Macbeth* iii 2 31
Hath nature that in time will venom breed, No teeth for the present iii 4 31
Here had we now our country's honour roof'd, Were the graced person of our Banquo present iii 4 41
He knows not what he says : and vain it is That we present us to him *Lear* v 3 294
Justly to your grave ears I'll present How I did thrive *Othello* i 3 124
Has an eye can stamp and counterfeit advantages, though true advantage never present itself ii 1 249
At whose foot, To mend the petty present, I will piece Her opulent throne with kingdoms *Ant. and Cleo.* i 5 45
Tell us—For this is from the present—how you take The offers ii 6 30
Extemporally will stage us, and present Our Alexandrian revels v 2 217
Have mingled sums To buy a present *Cymbeline* i 6 187
I have outstood my time ; which is material To the tender of our present i 6 208
Present yourself, desire his service, tell him Wherein you're happy iii 4 176
Her son gone, So needful for this present. iv 3 8
Who with wet cheeks Were present when she finish'd v 5 36
I'll present myself. Peace to the lords of Tyre ! *Pericles* i 3 30
And stay your coming to present themselves ii 2 3
Who is the second that presents himself ?—A prince of Macedon ii 2 23
Present act. By our hands and this our present act *J. Cæsar* iii 1 166
Present action. And in what fashion, More than his singularity, he goes Upon this present action *Coriolanus* i 1 283
The man, I think, that shall set them in present action iv 3 53
Present aid. The fear of that withholds my present aid *Richard III* iv 5 5
Present alms. Beggars, that come unto my father's door, Upon entreaty have a present alms *T. of Shrew* iv 3 5
Present answer. Urge her to a present answer back *All's Well* ii 2 67
Present approach. His expedition promises Present approach *T. of Athens* v 2 4
Present assistance. Nothing doubting your present assistance iii 1 21
Present audience. We'll give them present audience *Hen V.* ii 4 67
Present bearing. Scaling his present bearing with his past *Coriolanus* ii 3 257
Present benefit. Sweetened with the hope to have The present benefit which I possess *Richard II.* ii 3 14
Present blusters. The skies look grimly And threaten present blusters *W. Tale* iii 3 4
Present breath. The endeavour of this present breath may buy That honour *L. L. Lost* i 1 5
Present business. Hear a little further And then I'll bring thee to the present business *Tempest* i 2 136
My present business calls me from you now *Com. of Errors* i 2 29
Our present business Is general woe *Lear* v 3 318
Upon some present business of the state *Othello* i 2 90
Present comfort. For present comfort and for future good *W. Tale* v 1 32
Present consul. The present consul, and last general *Coriolanus* ii 2 47
Present counsel. Out of thy long-experienced time, Give me some present counsel *Rom. and Jul.* iv 1 61
Present courage may beat down our foes *Troi. and Cres.* ii 2 201
Present court. The king is fled to London, To call a present court of parliament 2 *Hen. VI.* v 3 25
Present day. From whence this present day he is deliver'd *Richard III.* i 1 69
Present death. As who should say, if I should sleep or eat, 'Twere deadly sickness or else present death *T. of Shrew* iv 3 14
I swear to do this, though a present death Had been more merciful *W. Tale* ii 3 184
That whoso draws a sword, 'tis present death 1 *Hen. VI.* iii 4 39
Marcius is worthy Of present death *Coriolanus* iii 1 212
'Tis present death I beg ; and one thing more *T. Andron.* ii 3 173
If a man did need a poison now, Whose sale is present death *R. and J.* v 1 51
Go pronounce his present death *Macbeth* i 2 64
Which imports at full . . . The present death of Hamlet *Hamlet* iv 3 67
Present debts. The greatest of your having lacks a half To pay your present debts *T. of Athens* ii 2 154
Present deed. Each your doing, So singular in each particular, Crowns what you are doing in the present deed *W. Tale* iv 4 145
Present dower. What, in the least, Will you require in present dower with her? *Lear* i 1 195
Present dues. What remains will hardly stop the mouth Of present dues *T. of Athens* ii 2 157
Present enterprise. This present enterprise set off his head 1 *Hen. IV.* v 1 88
Present evening. I have this present evening from my sister Been well inform'd *Lear* ii 1 103
Present execution. Acquitted by a true substantial form And present execution of our wills 2 *Hen. IV.* iv 1 174
Send Colevile with his confederates To York, to present execution iv 3 80
Enforce the present execution Of what we chance to sentence *Coriolanus* iii 3 21
Present eye. The present eye praises the present object *Troi. and Cres.* iii 3 180
Present fancies. To enact My present fancies *Tempest* iv 1 122
Present fears Are less than horrible imaginings *Macbeth* i 3 137
Present folly. What should I see then?—Your own present folly and her passing deformity *T. G. of Ver.* ii 1 81
Present friends. These my present friends, as they are to me nothing, so in nothing bless them *T. of Athens* iii 6 92
Present gift. His present gift Shall furnish me *All's Well* ii 3 306
Present grace. Whose present grace to present slaves and servants Translates his rivals *T. of Athens* i 1 71
My noble partner You greet with present grace and great prediction *Macb.* i 3 55
Present grief. This present grief had wiped it from my mind 2 *Hen. IV.* i 1 211
Present havings. Pared my present havings, to bestow My bounties upon you *Hen. VIII.* iii 2 159
Present head. We were enforced, for safety sake, to fly Out of your sight and raise this present head 1 *Hen. IV.* v 1 66
Present help. Unless you send some present help *Com. of Errors* v 1 176
Present horror. And take the present horror from the time *Macbeth* ii 1 59
Present hour. And till this present hour My heavy burthen ne'er delivered *Com. of Errors* v 1 401
If I were to live this present hour, I will tell true *All's Well* iv 3 183
Let no quarrel nor no brawl to come Taint the condition of this present hour, Which I have wonder'd at *T. Night* v 1 365
If that your moody discontented souls Do through the clouds behold this present hour *Richard III.* v 1 8
There is full liberty of feasting from this present hour of five till the bell have told eleven *Othello* ii 2 10
Present hunger. It gave me present hunger To feed again *Cymbeline* ii 4 137
Present instance. Besides this present instance of his rage, Is a mad tale he told to-day *Com. of Errors* iv 3 88
Present kindness. You gods! your present kindness Makes my past miseries sports *Pericles* v 3 40
Present laughter. Present mirth hath present laughter *T. Night* ii 3 49
Present life. For necessity of present life *Othello* i 1 156
Present medicine. The present time's so sick, That present medicine must be minister'd *K. John* v 1 15
Present mirth hath present laughter *T. Night* ii 3 49
Present money. I am not furnish'd with the present money *C. of Er.* iv 1 34
Besides, it should appear, that if he had The present money to discharge the Jew, He would not take it *Mer. of Venice* iii 2 276
Present murderer. A present murderer does prepare *Pericles* iv Gower 38
Present musters. Our present musters grow upon the file To five and twenty thousand 2 *Hen. IV.* i 3 10
Present need. The present need Speaks to atone you *Ant. and Cleo.* ii 2 101
Present numbers. Command our present numbers Be muster'd *Cymbeline* iv 2 343
Present object. And of the truth herein This present object made probation *Hamlet* i 1 156
Present occasion. Has only sent his present occasion now *T. of Athens* iii 2 39
Present pain. 'Tis good for men to love their present pains *Hen. V.* iv 1 18
Strike me, honour'd sir ; Give me a gash, put me to present pain *Pericles* v 1 193
Present pardon. Sign me a present pardon for my brother *Meas. for Meas.* ii 4 152
Present parting. Procured his leave For present parting *All's Well* ii 5 61
Present partner. Be my present partner in this business *W. Tale* iv 2 57
Present parts. Uncurable discomfit Reigns in the hearts of all our present parts 2 *Hen. VI.* v 2 87
Present pay. A noble shalt thou have, and present pay *Hen. V.* ii 1 112
Present peace. If you knew what pains I have bestow'd to breed this present peace 2 *Hen. IV.* iv 2 74
His remedies are tame i' the present peace And quietness *Coriolanus* iv 6 2
Present pleasure. The present pleasure, By revolution lowering, does become The opposite of itself *Ant. and Cleo.* i 2 128
Pawn their experience to their present pleasure i 4 32
Present portance. Thinking upon his services, took from you The apprehension of his present portance *Coriolanus* ii 3 232
Present power. Would cease The present power of life *Cymbeline* v 5 256
Present practice. These blushes of hers must be quenched with some present practice *Pericles* iv 2 136
Present profession. By present profession a tinker *T. of Shrew* Ind. 2 22
Present profit. I speak against my present profit *Cymbeline* v 4 214
Present push. We'll put the matter to the present push *Hamlet* v 1 318
Present quality. If this present quality of war, Indeed the instant action : a cause on foot Lives so in hope 2 *Hen. IV.* i 3 36
Present question. Are you acquainted with the difference That holds this present question? *Mer. of Venice* iv 1 172
Present recompense. I'll make a present recompense *Mer. Wives* iv 6 55
Present reconciliation. If I have any grace or power to move you, His present reconciliation take *Othello* iii 3 47
Present remedy. If not a present remedy, at least a patient sufferance *Much Ado* i 3 9
Present sacrifice. Go bid the priests do present sacrifice *J. Cæsar* ii 2 5
Present satisfaction. Make present satisfaction, Or I'll attach you by this officer *Com. of Errors* iv 1 5
Present shame. And this shall free thee from this present shame *R. and J.* iv 1 118
Present shrift. I will give him a present shrift *Meas. for Meas.* iv 2 223
Present sickness. Join with the present sickness that I have *Richard II.* ii 1 132
Present slaves. Whose present grace to present slaves and servants Translates his rivals *T. of Athens* i 1 71
Present sorrows. Nor my service past, nor present sorrows, Nor purposed merit in futurity *Othello* iii 4 116
Present state. The least word that might Be to the prejudice of her present state *Hen. VIII.* ii 4 154
Such as have not thrived Upon the present state *Ant. and Cleo.* i 3 52
Present store. I am debating of my present store *Mer. of Venice* i 3 54
Present sum. Neither have I money nor commodity To raise a present sum i 1 179
Present summons. And got your leave To make this present summons *Hen. VIII.* ii 4 219
What are you? Your name, your quality? and why you answer This present summons? *Lear* v 3 121
Present thought. 'Tis a studied, not a present thought *Ant. and Cleo.* ii 2 140
Present time. To take the present time by the top *Much Ado* i 2 15
Therefore take the present time, With a hey, and a ho *As Y. Like It* v 3 31
Every present time doth boast itself Above a better gone *W. Tale* v 1 96
The present time's so sick, That present medicine must be minister'd *K. John* v 1 14
Have thou the ordering of this present time v 1 77
It not appears to me Either from the king or in the present time That you should have an inch of any ground 2 *Hen. IV.* iv 1 108
What by sea and land I can be able To front this present time *A. and C.* i 4 79
Present trial. Call him to present trial *Hen. VIII.* i 2 211
Present trouble. Prompted by your present trouble *T. Night* iii 4 377
Present twelve o'clock. To the pupil age of this present twelve o'clock at midnight 1 *Hen. IV.* ii 4 106
Present vengeance. I would not be a stander-by to hear My sovereign mistress clouded so, without My present vengeance taken *W. Tale* i 2 281
Present want. Supply your present wants and take no doit Of usance for my moneys *Mer. of Venice* i 3 141
His present want Seems more than we shall find it 1 *Hen. IV.* iv 1 44
Present wars. The present wars devour him *Coriolanus* i 1 262
And do undertake These present wars against the Ottomites *Othello* i 3 235
These present wars shall find I love my country *Cymbeline* iv 3 43
Present wildness. O, let me in my present wildness die! 2 *Hen. IV.* iv 5 153
Present winter. Quake in the present winter's state *Cymbeline* ii 4 5
Present wrath. Let's follow him, and pervert the present wrath He hath against himself ii 4 151
Present year. Nor is my whole estate Upon the fortune of this present year *Mer. of Venice* i 1 44
Presentation. He uses his folly like a stalking-horse and under the presentation of that he shoots his wit *As Y. Like It* v 4 112
The presentation of but what I was *Richard III.* iv 4 84
Presented. When I presented Ceres, I thought to have told thee *Tempest* iv 1 167
So ridiculous, Should be presented at our tent to us *L. L. Lost* v 2 307
Great Hercules is presented by this imp v 2 592
The shallowest thick-skin . . . , Who Pyramus presented *M. N. Dream* iii 2 14
Imaginary eyes of blood Presented thee more hideous than thou art *K. John* iv 2 266
The vilest stroke, That ever wall-eyed wrath or staring rage Presented to the tears of soft remorse iv 3 50
The image of the king whom I presented 2 *Hen. IV.* v 2 79
Which cannot in their huge and proper life Be here presented *Hen. V.* v Prol. 6
I hope ere long To be presented, by your victories, With Charles, Alençon and that traitorous rout 1 *Hen. VI.* iv 1 172
In all Cupid's pageant there is presented no monster *Troi. and Cres.* iii 2 81
He came unto my hearth ; Presented to my knife his throat *Coriolanus* v 6 31

Presented. Hath presented to you Four milk-white horses, trapp'd in silver *T. of Athens* i 2 188
Whom thy upward face Hath to the marbled mansion all above Never presented iv 3 192
I thrice presented him a kingly crown, Which he did thrice refuse *J. C.* iii 2 101
With presented nakedness outface The winds *Lear* ii 3 11
Presenteth. This man, with lanthorn, dog, and bush of thorn, Presenteth Moonshine *M. N. Dream* v 1 137
Presenteth them unto the gazing moon So many horrid ghosts *Hen. V.* iv Prol. 27
Presenting. A blinking idiot, Presenting me a schedule! *Mer. of Venice* ii 9 55
Presently extirpate me and mine Out of the dukedom *Tempest* i 2 125
Presently?—Ay, with a twink iv 1 42
Enforce them to this place, And presently, I prithee v 1 101
That, like a testy babe, will scratch the nurse And presently all humbled kiss the rod! *T. G. of Ver.* i 2 59
When you fasted, it was presently after dinner ii 1 30
I will send him hither to you presently ii 4 86
And then I'll presently attend you.—Will you make haste? ii 4 189
Come on, you madcap, I'll to the alehouse with you presently ii 5 9
Now presently I'll give her father notice Of their disguising ii 6 36
Presently go with me to my chamber, To take a note of what I stand in need of ii 7 83
Come, answer not, but to it presently! ii 7 89
And this way comes he with it presently iii 1 42
Let us into the city presently To sort some gentlemen well skill'd in music iii 2 91
My will is even this: That presently you hie you home to bed iv 2 94
I like thee well And will employ thee in some service presently iv 4 45
Go presently and take this ring with thee, Deliver it to Madam Silvia iv 4 76
Stand not to discourse, But mount you presently and meet with me v 2 45
Would needs speak with you presently.—She shall not see me *Mer. Wives* iii 3 95
Sure he is by this, or will be presently iv 1 3
He'll be here presently: let's go dress him like the witch of Brentford iv 2 99
I will presently to Saint Luke's *Meas. for Meas.* iii 1 276
'Tis an accident that heaven provides! Dispatch it presently iv 3 82
This shall be done, good father, presently iv 3 86
Go hie thee presently, post to the road *Com. of Errors* iii 2 152
See him presently discharged, For he is bound to sea and stays but for it iv 1 32
I'll prove mine honour and mine honesty Against thee presently v 1 31
He is sooner caught than the pestilence, and the taker runs presently mad *Much Ado* i 1 88
Thou wilt be like a lover presently And tire the hearer i 1 308
In practice let us put it presently i 1 330
I will presently go learn their day of marriage ii 2 57
I'll make her come, I warrant you, presently iii 1 14
Presently call the rest of the watch together and thank God iii 3 30
The smallest twine may lead me.—'Tis well consented: presently away iv 1 253
Will you come presently?—Will you go hear this news? v 2 102
Meantime let wonder seem familiar, And to the chapel let us presently v 4 71
Meet presently at the palace; every man look o'er his part *M. N. Dream* iv 2 37
Go, presently inquire, and so will I, Where money is *Mer. of Venice* i 1 183
See to my house, . . . and presently I will be with you i 3 177
The wind is come about; Bassanio presently will go aboard ii 6 65
Arragon hath ta'en his oath, And comes to his election presently ii 9 3
If the Jew do cut but deep enough, I'll pay it presently with all my heart iv 1 281
Provided more, that, for this favour, He presently become a Christian iv 1 387
It is meet I presently set forth.—I am sorry that your leisure serves you not iv 1 404
Come, you and I will thither presently iv 1 455
I will here be with thee presently *As Y. Like It* ii 6 11
Nature presently distill'd Helen's cheek, but not her heart iii 2 152
You shall go see your pupils presently *T. of Shrew* ii 1 108
My boy shall fetch the scrivener presently iv 4 59
But presently Do thine own fortunes that obedient right *All's Well* ii 3 166
Presently Attend his further pleasure.—In every thing I wait upon his will ii 4 53
This drives me to entreat you That presently you take your way for home ii 5 69
I will presently pen down my dilemmas, encourage myself in my certainty iii 6 80
Give them way till he take leave, and presently after him *T. Night* iii 4 217
For the love of God, a surgeon! Send one presently to Sir Toby v 1 176
I'll presently Acquaint the queen of your most noble offer *W. Tale* ii 2 47
Quit presently the chapel, or resolve you For more amazement v 3 86
Presently The rites of marriage shall be solemnized *K. John* ii 1 538
With purpose presently to leave this war v 7 86
To supply our wants; For we will make for Ireland presently *Richard II.* i 4 52
To my sister Gloucester; Bid her send me presently a thousand pound ii 2 91
Gentlemen, go, muster up your men, And meet me presently at Berkeley ii 2 119
I will not vex your souls—Since presently your souls must part your bodies iii 1 3
Wise men ne'er sit and wail their woes, But presently prevent the ways to wail iii 2 179
Be near at hand, For we shall presently have need of you *1 Hen. IV.* iii 2 3
He presently, as greatness knows itself, Steps me a little higher iv 3 74
What news?—The king will bid you battle presently v 2 31
You shall have letters of me presently *2 Hen. IV.* ii 1 190
You must away to court, sir, presently; A dozen captains stay at door ii 4 401
Good husband, come home presently *Hen. V.* ii 1 93
You must come presently to the mines iii 2 58
Pleaseth your grace To appoint some of your council presently To sit with us v 2 79
Presently we'll try: come, let's away about it *1 Hen. VI.* i 2 149
How can these contrarieties agree?—That will I show you presently ii 3 60
Enter, and cry 'The Dauphin!' presently, And then do execution on the watch iii 2 34
We mean Shall be transported presently to France v 1 40
And means to give you battle presently.—Somewhat too sudden, sirs, the warning is; But we will presently provide for them v 2 13
Will not brook delay; I'll to the Duke of Suffolk presently *2 Hen. VI.* i 1 171
I'll follow presently. Follow I must; I cannot go before i 2 60
Take this fellow in, and send for his master with a pursuivant presently i 3 38
Then send for one presently.—Sirrah, go fetch the beadle ii 1 139
Go, call our uncle to our presence straight . . . — I'll call him presently iii 2 18
To equal him, I will make myself a knight presently iv 2 128
Go, take him away, I say, and strike off his head presently iv 7 116
My lord, When shall we go to Cheapside . . .?—Marry, presently iv 7 136
Thou shalt to London presently, And whet on Warwick *3 Hen. VI.* i 2 36
You promised knighthood to our forward son: Unsheathe your sword, and dub him presently ii 2 59
Presently. I will away towards Barnet presently, And bid thee battle, Edward *3 Hen. VI.* v 1 110
And presently repair to Crosby Place *Richard III.* i 2 213
Send the Duke of York Unto his princely brother presently iii 1 34
He sends to know your lordship's pleasure, If presently you will take horse iii 2 16
Presently the duke Said, 'twas the fear, indeed *Hen. VIII.* i 1 157
Look'd he o' the inside of the paper?—Presently He did unseal them iii 2 78
Commands you To render up the great seal presently Into our hands iii 2 229
The king Shall understand it presently v 2 10
I shall be with you presently, good master puppy v 4 29
Tell him so.—I shall; and bring his answer presently *Troi. and Cres.* ii 3 148
Walk into her house; I'll bring her to the Grecian presently iv 3 6
Presently, when you have drawn your number, Repair to the Capitol *Cor.* ii 3 261
Assemble presently the people hither iii 3 12
But when goes this forward?—To-morrow; to-day; presently iv 5 229
Behold now presently, and swoon for what's to come upon thee v 2 72
'Tear him to pieces.' 'Do it presently' v 6 122
Thy temples should be planted presently With horns *T. Andron.* ii 3 62
See that you take no longer days, But send the midwife presently to me iv 2 166
Go, take him away, and hang him presently iv 4 45
He must not die So sweet a death as hanging presently v 1 146
Go fetch them hither to us presently.—Why, there they are both v 3 59
Do thou but call my resolution wise, And with this knife I'll help it presently *Rom. and Jul.* iv 1 54
Presently through all thy veins shall run A cold and drowsy humour iv 1 95
And presently took post to tell it you v 1 21
And, not to swell our spirit, He shall be executed presently *T. of Athens* iii 5 103
Gentlemen, our dinner . . .; we shall to't presently iii 6 38
Then, Timon, presently prepare thy grave iv 3 378
Let him go, And presently prefer his suit to Cæsar *J. Cæsar* iii 1 28
I'll fetch him presently.—I know that we shall have him well to friend iii 1 142
Let us presently go sit in council iv 1 45
What do you think Of marching to Philippi presently? iv 3 197
Such sanctity hath heaven given his hand—They presently amend *Macb.* iv 3 145
I do beseech you, both away: I'll board him presently *Hamlet* ii 2 170
I have heard That guilty creatures sitting at a play Have by the very cunning of the scene Been struck so to the soul that presently They have proclaim'd their malefactions ii 2 620
Will the king hear this piece of work?—And the queen too, and that presently iii 2 53
My lord, the queen would speak with you, and presently iii 2 392
Let this same be presently perform'd, Even while men's minds are wild v 2 404
I will seek him, sir, presently: convey the business *Lear* i 2 109
The sweet and bitter fool Will presently appear i 4 159
Deliver'd letters, spite of intermission, Which presently they read ii 4 34
Go tell the duke and 's wife I'ld speak with them, Now, presently ii 4 118
I shall attend you presently at your tent.—Sister, you'll go with us? v 1 33
Do thou meet me presently at the harbour. Come hither *Othello* ii 1 215
To be now a sensible man, by and by a fool, and presently a beast! ii 3 310
Procure me some access.—I'll send her to you presently iii 1 38
Thou art on thy death-bed.—Ay, but not yet to die.—Yes, presently v 2 52
Of us must Pompey presently be sought, Or else he seeks out us *A. and C.* ii 2 161
The good gods will mock me presently, When I shall pray iii 4 15
In the wars 'gainst Pompey, presently denied him rivality iii 5 8
My lord desires you presently: my news I might have told hereafter iii 5 22
To Dorothy my woman hie thee presently *Cymbeline* ii 3 143
Provide me presently A riding-suit iii 2 77
Bring him To dinner presently iv 2 166
Go thy ways, good mariner: I'll bring the body presently *Pericles* iii 1 82
Well, follow me, my masters, you shall have your money presently iv 2 58
Give me leave: a word, and I'll have done presently iv 6 51
Presentment. When comes your book forth?—Upon the heels of my presentment *T. of Athens* i 1 27
The counterfeit presentment of two brothers *Hamlet* iii 4 54
Preservation. But for the miracle, I mean our preservation, few in millions Can speak like us *Tempest* ii 1 7
Give us particulars of thy preservation v 1 135
In their dear care And tender preservation of our person *Hen. V.* ii 2 59
By great preservation, We live to tell it you *Richard III.* iii 5 36
Nature does require Her times of preservation *Hen. VIII.* iii 2 147
With faces fit for masks, or rather fairer Than those for preservation cased, or shame *Cymbeline* v 3 22
Preservative. And, to this preservative, of no better report than a horse-drench *Coriolanus* ii 1 129
Preserve. O, a cherubin Thou wast that did preserve me *Tempest* i 2 153
Let us both be sudden.—Now, good angels Preserve the king ii 1 307
Not politic in the commonwealth of nature to preserve virginity *All's Well* i 1 138
Which to preserve is sleep, which being spotted Is goads, thorns *W. Tale* i 2 328
That all the walls . . . had said at once, 'Jesu preserve thee!' *Richard II.* v 2 17
Well, there is sixpence to preserve thee *2 Hen. IV.* ii 2 103
O, the Lord preserve thy good grace! by my troth, welcome ii 4 315
God pless it and preserve it, as long as it pleases his grace! *Hen. V.* iv 7 113
God preserve the good Duke Humphrey! *2 Hen. VI.* i 1 162
Jesus preserve your royal majesty!—What say'st thou? majesty! i 2 70
And to preserve my sovereign from his foe, Say but the word, and I will be his priest iii 1 271
Whom God preserve better than you would wish! *Richard III.* i 3 59
The gods preserve our noble tribunes! *Coriolanus* iii 3 143
The gods preserve you both!—God-den, our neighbours iv 6 20
Eat no more Than will preserve just so much strength in us *T. Andron.* iii 2 2
The gods preserve ye!—Well fare you, gentleman *T. of Athens* i 1 162
Heaven preserve you! I dare abide no longer *Macbeth* iv 2 72
Whiles I may 'scape, I will preserve myself *Lear* ii 3 6
If to preserve this vessel for my lord From any other foul unlawful touch Be not to be a strumpet, I am none *Othello* iv 2 83
Gentle Octavia, Let your best love draw to that point, which seeks Best to preserve it *Ant. and Cleo.* iii 4 22
Cæsar cannot live To be ungentle.—So the gods preserve thee! v 1 60
If you buy ladies' flesh at a million a dram, you cannot preserve it from tainting *Cymbeline* i 4 148
Hast thou not learn'd me how To make perfumes? distil? preserve? i 5 13
Which, to preserve mine honour, I'll perform *Pericles* ii 2 16
She is dead. Nurses are not the fates To foster it, nor ever to preserve iv 3 15
The gods strengthen thee!—The good gods preserve you! iv 6 114
The gods preserve you!—And you, sir, to outlive the age I am v 1 14
Preserved. Prayers from preserved souls, From fasting maids *M. for M.* ii 2 153
By whose gentle help I was preserved *T. Night* v 1 263
Tell me, mine own, Where hast thou been preserved? *W. Tale* v 3 124
Have preserved Myself to see the issue v 3 127

Preserved. I beg mortality, Rather than life preserved with infamy 1 *Hen. VI.* iv 5 33
Men's flesh preserved so whole do seldom win . 2 *Hen. VI.* iii 1 301
Must gently be preserved, cherish'd, and kept *Richard III.* ii 2 119
That have preserved her welfare in my blood *T. Andron.* v 3 110
Think that the clearest gods, who make them honours Of men's impossibilities, have preserved thee . . . *Lear* iv 6 74
What cannot be preserved when fortune takes Patience her injury a mockery makes . . . . *Othello* i 3 206
Two boys, an old man twice a boy, a lane, Preserved the Britons *Cymb.* v 3 58
I long to hear how you were found ; How possibly preserved *Pericles* v 3 57
Virtue preserved from fell destruction's blast, Led on by heaven v 3 Gower 89
Preserver. My true preserver, and a loyal sir ! . . . . *Tempest* v 1 69
Sit, my preserver, by thy patient's side . . . . *All's Well* ii 3 53
Preserver of my father, now of me, The medicine of our house *W. Tale* iv 4 597
You whom the gods have made Preservers of my throne . *Cymbeline* v 5 2
Preserving life in medicine potable . . . 2 *Hen. IV.* iv 5 163
A madness most discreet, A choking gall and a preserving sweet *Rom. and Jul.* i 1 200
President. A charge we bear i' the war, And, as the president of my kingdom, will Appear there for a man . . *Ant. and Cleo.* iii 7 18
Press. A pack of sorrows which would press you down *T. G. of Ver.* iii 1 20
He cares not what he puts into the press, when he would put us two *Mer. Wives* ii 1 80
I make bold to press with so little preparation upon you ii 2 162
In the chambers, and in the coffers, and in the presses . iii 3 226
Neither press, coffer, chest, trunk, well, vault, but he hath an abstract for the remembrance of such places . . . . iv 2 62
She would laugh me Out of myself, press me to death with wit *Much Ado* iii 1 76
Why should he stay, whom love doth press to go? . *M. N. Dream* iii 2 184
What love could press Lysander from my side? . . . iii 2 185
Losses . . . Enow to press a royal merchant down . *Mer. of Venice* iv 1 29
You press me far, and therefore I will yield . . . iv 1 425
I press in here, sir, amongst the rest . . *As Y. Like It* v 4 57
Press me not, beseech you, so . . . . . *W. Tale* i 2 19
To purge him of that humour That presses him from sleep . ii 3 39
In their throng and press to that last hold, Confound themselves *K. John* v 7 19
I have misused the king's press damnably . . 1 *Hen. IV.* iv 2 13
I press me none but good householders, yeomen's sons . . iv 2 16
No humble suitors press to speak for right . 3 *Hen. VI.* iii 1 19
Press not a falling man too far ! 'tis virtue . *Hen. VIII.* iii 2 333
Like rams In the old time of war, would shake the press . iv 1 78
Go, break among the press, and find a way out To let the troop pass fairly . . . . v 4 88
Which bed, because it shall not speak of your pretty encounters, press it to death : away ! . . . . *Troi. and Cres.* iii 2 217
Seld-shown flamens Do press among the popular throngs . *Coriolanus* ii 1 230
God forbid I should be so bold to press to heaven in my young days *T. Andron.* iv 3 90
This is the hag, when maids lie on their backs, That presses them *R. and J.* i 4 93
End motion here ; And thou and Romeo press one heavy bier ! . iii 2 60
I would forget it fain ; But, O, it presses to my memory . . iii 2 110
What manners is in this, To press before thy father to a grave? . v 3 215
Who is it in the press that calls on me? . . *J. Cæsar* i 2 15
Great men shall press For tinctures, stains, relics and cognizance . ii 2 88
Take good note What Cæsar doth, what suitors press to him . . ii 4 15
He is address'd : press near and second him . . . iii 1 29
Press not so upon me ; stand far off.—Stand back ; room ; bear back . iii 2 171
Our Tarquin thus Did softly press the rushes, ere he waken'd The chastity he wounded . . . . . . *Cymbeline* ii 2 13
And Cydnus swell'd above the banks, or for The press of boats or pride ii 4 72
Pressed. I am press'd down with conceit . . . *Com. of Errors* iv 2 65
With half that wish the wisher's eyes be press'd ! . *M. N. Dream* ii 2 65
And sing while thou on pressed flowers dost sleep . . . iii 1 162
Every man that Bolingbroke hath press'd To lift shrewd steel *Rich. II.* iii 2 58
O, I am press'd to death through want of speaking ! . . . iii 4 72
I pressed me none but such toasts-and-butter . . 1 *Hen. IV.* iv 2 22
Unloaded all the gibbets and pressed the dead bodies . . iv 2 40
From London by the king was I press'd forth . . 3 *Hen. VI.* ii 5 64
Came on the part of York, press'd by his master . . . ii 5 66
That many mazed considerings did throng And press'd in . *Hen. VIII.* ii 4 186
The large Achilles, on his press'd bed lolling . *Troi. and Cres.* i 3 162
They have press'd a power . . . . . . *Coriolanus* i 2 9
Being press'd to the war . . . . iii 1 122
Once or twice she heaved the name of 'father' Pantingly forth, as if it press'd her heart . . . . *Lear* iv 3 28
I have this while with leaden thoughts been press'd . *Othello* iii 4 177
Pressing. Is pressing to death, whipping, and hanging . *Meas. for Meas.* v 1 528
Under her breast—Worthy the pressing—lies a mole . *Cymbeline* ii 4 135
Press-money. There's your press-money . . . . *Lear* iv 6 87
Pressure. All saws of books, all forms, all pressures past *Hamlet* i 5 100
The very age and body of the time his form and pressure . . iii 2 27
Prest. Say to me what I should do That in your knowledge may by me be done, And I am prest unto it . . *Mer. of Venice* i 1 160
Griefs of mine own lie heavy in my breast, Which thou wilt propagate, to have it prest With more of thine . . *Rom. and Jul.* i 1 193
The pregnant instrument of wrath Prest for this blow . *Pericles* iv Gower 45
Prester John. Bring you the length of Prester John's foot . *Much Ado* ii 1 276
Presume. Dare you presume to harbour wanton lines? . *T. G. of Ver.* i 2 42
Let none presume To wear an undeserved dignity . . *Mer. of Venice* ii 9 39
This gentleman is happily arrived, My mind presumes . . *T. of Shrew* i 2 214
'Regia,' presume not, 'celsa senis,' despair not . . . iii 1 44
And not presume to touch a hair of my master's horse-tail till they kiss their hands . . . . iv 1 96
I do presume, sir, that you are not fallen From the report that goes upon your goodness . . . . *All's Well* v 1 12
Which I presume shall render you no blame . . . . . v 1 32
Presume not that I am the thing I was . . . 2 *Hen. IV.* v 5 60
Durst not presume to look once in the face . . 1 *Hen. VI.* i 1 140
Like a hedge-born swain That doth presume to boast of gentle blood . iv 1 44
I dare presume, sweet prince, he thought no harm . . . iv 1 179
I will not so presume To send such peevish tokens to a king . . v 3 185
And otherwise will Henry ne'er presume . . . . . v 5 22
Dare he presume to scorn us in this manner? . 3 *Hen. VI.* iii 3 178
Hadst thou been kill'd when first thou didst presume, Thou hadst not lived to kill a son of mine . . . . v 6 35
I'll give my voice, Which, I presume, he'll take in gentle part *Rich. III.* iii 4 21
I presume That, as my hand has open'd bounty to you . *Hen. VIII.* iii 2 183
I presume, brave Hector would not lose So rich advantage *Troi. and Cres.* ii 2 203
This, I presume, will wake him . . . . ii 2 213
Presume. O that I thought it could be in a woman—As, if it can, I will presume in you . . . . . . *Troi. and Cres.* iii 2 166
Sit by the fire, and presume to know What's done i' the Capitol *Coriol.* i 1 195
Do not presume too much upon my love . . . *J. Cæsar* iv 3 63
Because thine eye Presumes to reach, all thy whole heap must die *Pericles* i 1 33
Presuming. Lean-witted fool, Presuming on an ague's privilege *Rich. II.* ii 1 116
We are devils to ourselves, When we will tempt the frailty of our powers, Presuming on their changeful potency . . *Troi. and Cres.* iv 4 99
Presumption. But most it is presumption in us when The help of heaven we count the act of men . . . . . . *All's Well* ii 1 154
Let my presumption not provoke thy wrath . . 1 *Hen. VI.* ii 3 70
Shall lose his head for his presumption . . . 2 *Hen. VI.* i 2 34
That is too much presumption on thy part . . . . . v 1 38
They shall have wars and pay for their presumption 3 *Hen. VI.* iv 1 114
Thy son I kill'd for his presumption . . . . . . v 6 34
Presumptuous. I follow him not By any token of presumptuous suit *All's Well* i 3 204
Presumptuous priest ! this place commands my patience 1 *Hen. VI.* iii 1 8
Presumptuous vassals, are you not ashamed? . . . . iv 1 125
Presumptuous dame, ill-nurtured Eleanor . . 2 *Hen. VI.* i 2 42
Which makes thee thus presumptuous and proud . 3 *Hen. VI.* i 1 157
Presupposed. In such forms which here were presupposed . *T. Night* v 1 358
Presurmise. It was your presurmise, That, in the dole of blows, your son might drop . . . . 2 *Hen. IV.* i 1 168
Pretence. For love of you, not hate unto my friend, Hath made me publisher of this pretence . . . . *T. G. of Ver.* iii 1 47
Her pretence is a pilgrimage to Saint Jaques le Grand . *All's Well* iv 3 57
The pretence whereof being by circumstances partly laid open *W. Tale* iii 2 18
Under pretence to see the queen his aunt . . *Hen. VIII.* i 1 177
The pretence for this Is named, your wars in France . . i 2 59
Nor did you think it folly To keep your great pretences veil'd *Coriolanus* i 2 20
Against the undivulged pretence I fight Of treasonous malice *Macbeth* ii 3 137
He hath wrote this to feel my affection to your honour, and to no further pretence of danger . . . . . . *Lear* i 2 95
Than as a very pretence and purpose of unkindness . . . i 4 75
Why hast thou abused So many miles with a pretence? . *Cymbeline* iii 4 106
And make pretence of wrong that I have done him . . *Pericles* i 2 91
Pretend. And none your foes but such as shall pretend Malicious practices against his state . . . . . 1 *Hen. VI.* iv 1 6
Doth this churlish superscription Pretend some alteration in good will? iv 1 54
Why shall we fight, if you pretend no title? . . 3 *Hen. VI.* iv 7 57
Whom you pretend to honour and adore . . . *T. Andron.* i 1 42
Alas, the day ! What good could they pretend? . . *Macbeth* ii 4 24
For The contract you pretend with that base wretch, . . . it is no contract, none . . . . *Cymbeline* ii 3 118
Pretended. I'll give her father notice Of their disguising and pretended flight . . . . *T. G. of Ver.* ii 6 37
Pretending in her discoveries of dishonour . *Meas. for Meas.* iii 1 236
Still pretending The satisfaction of her knowledge only . *Cymbeline* v 5 250
Pretext. My pretext to strike at him admits A good construction *Coriol.* v 6 20
Pretia. Venetia, Venetia, Chi non ti vede non ti pretia . *L. L. Lost* iv 2 100
Prettier. I'll prove the prettier fellow of the two . *Mer. of Venice* iii 4 64
Prettiest. The prettiest Kate in Christendom . . *T. of Shrew* ii 1 188
The prettiest low-born lass that ever Ran on the green-sward *W. Tale* iv 4 156
He has the prettiest love-songs for maids . . . . iv 4 193
My prettiest Perdita ! But O, the thorns we stand upon ! . . iv 4 595
One of the prettiest touches of all . . . . . . v 2 89
I'll fetch her. It is the prettiest villain . . *Troi. and Cres.* iii 2 35
Thou wast the prettiest babe that e'er I nursed . *Rom. and Jul.* i 3 60
And she hath the prettiest sententious of it, of you nd rosemary . ii 4 225
Let us Find out the prettiest daisied plot we can . . *Cymbeline* iv 2 398
Prettily. So prettily He couples it to his complaining names *T. G. of Ver.* i 2 126
Lysander riddles very prettily . . . . *M. N. Dream* ii 2 53
How prettily the young swain seems to wash The hand was fair before ! *W. Tale* iv 4 377
The king Prettily, methought, did play the orator . 1 *Hen. VI.* iv 1 175
He prettily and aptly taunts himself : So cunning and so young *Rich. III.* iii 1 134
Prettiness. Thought and affliction, passion, hell itself, She turns to favour and to prettiness . . . . . . *Hamlet* iv 5 189
Pretty. She is pretty, and honest, and gentle . . *Mer. Wives* i 4 148
A wench of excellent discourse, Pretty and witty . *Com. of Errors* iii 1 110
Pretty and apt.—How mean you, sir? I pretty, and my saying apt? or I apt, and my saying pretty?—Thou pretty, because little.—Little pretty, because little . . . . *L. L. Lost* i 2 19
Sweet invocation of a child ; most pretty and pathetical ! . . i 2 103
The preyful princess pierced and prick'd a pretty pleasing pricket iv 2 58
Fire enough for a flint, pearl enough for a swine : 'tis pretty ; it is well iv 2 91
A pretty knavish page, That well by heart hath conn'd his embassage . v 2 97
She, with pretty and with swimming gait . . *M. N. Dream* ii 1 130
And the cow's dugs that her pretty chopt hands had milked *As Y. L. It* ii 4 50
There is murder in mine eye : 'Tis pretty, sure, and very probable ! . iii 5 11
It is a pretty youth : not very pretty : But, sure, he's proud . iii 5 113
'Twas pretty, though a plague, To see him every hour . *All's Well* i 1 103
With a world Of pretty, fond, adoptious christendoms . . . i 1 188
I did think thee, for two ordinaries, to be a pretty wise fellow . ii 3 210
May, if fortune please, both breed thee, pretty, And still rest thine *W. T.* iii 3 48
I thank your pretty sweet wit for it . . . . . 2 *Hen. IV.* i 2 231
And for thy walls, a pretty slight drollery, or the story of the Prodigal ii 1 156
Any pretty little tiny kickshaws, tell William cook . . . v 1 29
The pretty and sweet manner of it forced Those waters from me *Hen. V.* iv 6 28
Stop my mouth.—And shall, albeit sweet music issues thence.—Pretty, i' faith . . . . *Troi. and Cres.* iii 2 143
O, that delightful engine of her thoughts . . . Is torn from forth that pretty hollow cage . . . . *T. Andron.* iii 1 84
Poor harmless fly, That, with his pretty buzzing melody, Came here ! . iii 2 64
Marry, sir, because silver hath a sweet sound.—Pretty ! *Rom. and Jul.* iv 5 135
I say 'silver sound,' because musicians sound for silver.—Pretty too ! . iv 5 138
With every thing that pretty is, My lady sweet, arise . *Cymbeline* ii 3 28
You should tread a course Pretty and full of view . . . iii 4 150
Pretty a piece. As pretty a piece of flesh as any is in Messina *Much Ado* iv 2 85
Pretty a proportion. Three or four thousand chequins were as pretty a proportion to live quietly . . . . *Pericles* iv 2 29
Pretty abruption. What makes this pretty abruption? . *Troi. and Cres.* iii 2 70
Pretty action. Her pretty action did outsell her gift . *Cymbeline* ii 4 102
Pretty age. My daughter's of a pretty age . . *Rom. and Jul.* i 3 10
Pretty answer. You are full of pretty answers . *As Y. Like It* iii 2 287
They laughed not so much at the hair as at his pretty answer *T. and C.* i 2 169
Pretty Arthur. Therefore never, never Must I behold my pretty Arthur more . . . . *K. John* iii 4 89
Pretty babes. Piteous plainings of the pretty babes . *Com. of Errors* i 1 73

Pretty barne. Mercy on's, a barne ; a very pretty barne! . *W. Tale* iii 3 71
Pretty boy. I'll swear, 'tis a very pretty boy . . . . *Coriolanus* i 3 63
Pretty chickens. What, all my pretty chickens and their dam At one fell swoop? . . . . *Macbeth* iv 3 218
Pretty child, sleep doubtless and secure . . . . *K. John* iv 1 130
Pretty country folks would lie, In spring time . *As Y. Like It* v 3 25
Pretty cousin. My pretty cousins, you mistake me much *Richard III.* ii 2 8
My pretty cousin, Blessing upon you! . . . . *Macbeth* iv 2 25
Pretty dimpled boys, like smiling Cupids . . *Ant. and Cleo.* ii 2 207
Pretty dimples. The pretty dimples of his chin and cheek . *W. Tale* ii 3 101
Pretty din. What minstrelsy, and pretty din, The regent made *Pericles* v 2 272
Pretty estate. If in our youths we could pick up some pretty estate, 'twere not amiss to keep our door hatched . . . . . iv 2 36
Pretty eyes. Sleep kill those pretty eyes! . . . *Troi. and Cres.* iv 2 4
Pretty fellow. Thou wast a pretty fellow when thou hadst no need to care for her frowning . . . . *Lear* i 4 210
Pretty fingers. He hath cut those pretty fingers off . *T. Andron.* ii 4 42
Pretty Flaminius. What hast thou there under thy cloak, pretty Flaminius? . . . . *T. of Athens* iii 1 15
Pretty floweret. And that same dew . . . Stood now within the pretty flowerets' eyes Like tears . . . . . . *M. N. Dream* iv 1 60
Pretty follies. Love is blind and lovers cannot see The pretty follies that themselves commit . . . . *Mer. of Venice* ii 6 37
Pretty fool, To see it tetchy and fall out with the dug! . *Rom. and Jul.* i 3 31
And, pretty fool, it stinted and said 'Ay' . . . . . i 3 48
Pretty foot. We say that Shore's wife hath a pretty foot *Richard III.* i 1 93
Pretty ingenious. As swift as lead, sir.—The meaning, pretty ingenious? Is not lead a metal heavy, dull, and slow? . . . . *L. L. Lost* iii 1 59
Pretty Isabella. O pretty Isabella, I am pale at mine heart to see thine eyes so red . . . . *Meas. for Meas.* iv 3 157
Pretty Jessica. In such a night Did pretty Jessica, like a little shrew, Slander her love . . . . *Mer. of Venice* v 1 21
Pretty jest. That's a pretty jest indeed! . . . *Mer. Wives* iii 4 59
I remember a pretty jest your daughter told us of . . *Much Ado* ii 3 141
Pretty knave. How now, my pretty knave! how dost thou? . *Lear* i 4 107
Pretty lad. This pretty lad will prove our country's bliss 3 *Hen. VI.* iv 6 70
Pretty lady, I am sorry for thy much misgovernment . *Much Ado* iv 1 99
Farewell, pretty lady : you must hold the credit of your father *All's Well* i 1 88
How do you, pretty lady?—Well, God 'ild you! . . . *Hamlet* iv 5 40
Pretty little coz. O coz, coz, coz, my pretty little coz! *As Y. Like It* iv 1 209
Pretty looks. Puts on his pretty looks, repeats his words . *K. John* iii 4 95
Pretty lordings. You were pretty lordings then? . . *W. Tale* i 2 62
Pretty match. Make some pretty match with shedding tears *Richard II.* iii 3 165
Pretty mistress. How does pretty Mistress Anne? . . *Mer. Wives* i 4 146
Madam, and pretty mistresses, give ear . . . . *L. L. Lost* v 2 286
Pretty mocking. It is a pretty mocking of the life . . *T. of Athens* i 1 35
Pretty moral. Swallowed . . . steeple, bells, and all.—A pretty moral *Pericles* ii 1 39
The motto, 'In hac spe vivo.'—A pretty moral . . . . ii 2 45
Pretty oaths. And so God mend me, and by all pretty oaths that are not dangerous . . . . *As Y. Like It* iv 1 193
Pretty one. A boy or a child, I wonder? A pretty one; a very pretty one *W. Tale* iii 3 72
This is a merry ballad, but a very pretty one . . . . . iv 4 291
Rough cradle for such little pretty ones! Rude ragged nurse! *Rich. III.* iv 1 101
All my pretty ones? Did you say all? O hell-kite! All? . *Macbeth* iv 3 216
Why lament you, pretty one?—That I am pretty . . *Pericles* iv 2 72
Now, pretty one, how long have you been at this trade? . . . iv 6 72
Pretty one, my authority shall not see thee, or else look friendly upon thee . . . . iv 6 96
Pretty Ophelia!—Indeed, la, without an oath, I'll make an end on't *Ham.* iv 5 56
Pretty orders. There are pretty orders beginning . *Meas. for Meas.* ii 1 249
Pretty peat. A pretty peat! it is best Put finger in the eye, an she knew why . . . . *T. of Shrew* i 1 78
Pretty period. A pretty period! Well, I guess the sequel; And yet I will not name it . . . . *T. G. of Ver.* ii 1 122
Pretty piece. 'Tis known I am a pretty piece of flesh . *Rom. and Jul.* i 1 34
Pretty pledge. O, all you gods! O pretty, pretty pledge! *Troi. and Cres.* v 2 77
Pretty plot. A pretty plot, well chosen to build upon! . 2 *Hen. VI.* i 4 59
Pretty reason. The reason why the seven stars are no more than seven is a pretty reason . . . . *Lear* i 5 39
Pretty redness. There was a pretty redness in his lip . *As Y. Like It* iii 5 120
Pretty ring time. In the spring time, the only pretty ring time . v 3 20
Pretty Rutland. A clout Steep'd in the faultless blood of pretty Rutland . . . . *Richard III.* i 3 178
Pretty self. Fear and niceness—The handmaids of all women, or, more truly, Woman it pretty self. . . . . *Cymbeline* iii 4 160
Pretty soul! she durst not lie Near this lack-love . . *M. N. Dream* ii 2 76
Pretty sweeting. Trip no further, pretty sweeting . . *T. Night* ii 3 43
Pretty tale. I can tell thee pretty tales of the duke *Meas. for Meas.* iv 3 175
I shall tell you A pretty tale : it may be you have heard it . *Coriolanus* i 1 93
Pretty thing. What a pretty thing man is when he goes in his doublet and hose and leaves off his wit! . . . . *Much Ado* v 1 202
I did not take my leave of him, but had Most pretty things to say *Cymb.* i 3 26
Pretty traps to catch the petty thieves . . . . *Hen. V.* i 2 177
Pretty-vaulting. The pretty-vaulting sea refused to drown me 2 *Hen. VI.* iii 2 94
Pretty virginity. There is Anne Page, which is daughter to Master Thomas Page, which is pretty virginity . . . . *Mer. Wives* i 1 46
Pretty weathercock. Where had you this pretty weathercock? . . iii 2 18
Pretty Welsh. That pretty Welsh Which thou pour'st down 1 *Hen. IV.* iii 1 201
Pretty wit. Art thou wise?—Ay, sir, I have a pretty wit *As Y. Like It* v 1 32
Pretty worm. Hast thou the pretty worm of Nilus there? *Ant. and Cleo.* v 2 243
Pretty wretch. By my holidame, The pretty wretch left crying and said 'Ay' . . . . *Rom. and Jul.* i 3 44
Pretty York. He touch'd mine.—How, my pretty York? *Richard III.* ii 4 26
I pray thee, pretty York, who told thee this?—Grandam, his nurse . ii 4 31
Pretty youth. The musician likes me not.—Why, my pretty youth?—He plays false . . . . *T. G. of Ver.* iv 2 58
Where dwell you, pretty youth?—With this shepherdess *As Y. Like It* iii 2 352
It is a pretty youth : not very pretty : But, sure, he's proud . . iii 5 113
I prithee, pretty youth, let me be better acquainted with thee . iv 1 1
Prevail. No love-broker in the world can more prevail in man's commendation with woman than report of valour . . . *T. Night* iii 2 40
If word nor oath Prevail not, go and see . . . . *W. Tale* iii 2 205
Wherein my hope is I shall so prevail To force him after . . . iv 4 678
How he did prevail I shame to speak, But truth is truth . *K. John* i 1 104
If we prevail, their heads shall pay for it . . . *Richard II.* iii 2 126
If wishes would prevail with me, My purpose should not fail with me *Hen. V.* iii 2 16
Heavens, can you suffer hell so to prevail? . . . . 1 *Hen. VI.* i 5 9
Prevail. Sleeping or waking must I still prevail? . . . 1 *Hen. VI.* ii 1 56
When a world of men Could not prevail with all their oratory, Yet hath a woman's kindness over-ruled . . . . ii 2 49
Thy grave admonishments prevail with me . . . . . . ii 5 98
I would prevail, if prayers might prevail, To join your hearts in love . iii 1 67
Whose rightful cause prevails . . . . . . 2 *Hen. VI.* ii 1 205
God forbid any malice should prevail! . . . . . . iii 2 23
Seeing gentle words will not prevail, Assail them with the army . . iv 2 184
Sometime the flood prevails, and then the wind . . . 3 *Hen. VI.* ii 5 9
But if an humble prayer may prevail, I then crave pardon . . iv 6 7
An upright zeal to right prevails More than the nature of a brother's love . . . . v 1 78
Did York's dread curse prevail so much with heaven? . . *Richard III.* i 3 191
I am strong-framed, he cannot prevail with me . . . . . i 4 155
Be of good cheer ; They shall no more prevail than we give way to *Hen. VIII.* v 1 143
The ladies of Rome, especially his mother, may prevail with him *Coriol.* v 4 6
Unless philosophy can make a Juliet, Displant a town, reverse a prince's doom, It helps not, it prevails not . . . . *Rom. and Jul.* iii 3 60
Let me, upon my knee, prevail in this . . . . *J. Cæsar* ii 2 54
Whose ministers would prevail Under the service of a child as soon As i' the command of Cæsar . . . . *Ant. and Cleo.* iii 13 23
You shall prevail, Were it to woo my daughter . . . *Pericles* v 1 262
Prevailed. You have prevail'd, my lord . . . *T. G. of Ver.* iii 2 46
Thou hast prevail'd ; I pardon them and thee . . . . . v 4 158
You have prevail'd : I will depart in quiet . *Com. of Errors* iii 1 107
With her personage, her tall personage, Her height, forsooth, she hath prevail'd with him . . . . *M. N. Dream* iii 2 293
Which often hath no less prevail'd than so On your command *W. Tale* ii 1 54
Since then my office hath so far prevail'd . . . . *Hen. V.* v 2 29
'Twas neither Charles nor yet the duke I named, But Reignier, king of Naples, that prevail'd . . . . 1 *Hen. VI.* v 4 78
Thus Suffolk hath prevail'd ; and thus he goes, As did the youthful Paris v 5 103
The Dauphin hath prevail'd beyond the seas . . . 2 *Hen. VI.* i 3 128
Thou hast prevailed in right! . . . . ii 3 101
Your enemies are his, And have prevail'd as much on him as you *Rich. III.* i 1 131
Have prevail'd Upon my body with their hellish charms . . . iii 4 63
The rabble should have first unroof'd the city, Ere so prevail'd with me *Coriolanus* i 1 223
How prevail'd you?—Will the time serve to tell? I do not think . i 6 45
Believe it, O, believe it, Most dangerously you have with him prevail'd v 3 188
Good news ; the ladies have prevail'd . . . . . . v 4 43
Rise, Titus, rise ; my empress hath prevail'd . . . *T. Andron.* i 1 459
Could it work so much upon your shape As it hath much prevail'd on your condition, I should not know you . . . . *J. Cæsar* ii 1 254
Would thou and those thy scars had once prevail'd! . *Ant. and Cleo.* iv 5 2
Give me directly to understand you have prevailed . . *Cymbeline* i 4 171
What false Italian . . . hath prevail'd On thy too ready hearing? . iii 2 5
Two villains, whose false oaths prevail'd Before my perfect honour . iii 3 66
My practice so prevail'd, That I return'd with simular proof enough . v 5 199
Prevaileth. The spite of man prevaileth against me . 2 *Hen. VI.* i 3 218
Prevailing. A sin prevailing much in youthful men *Com. of Errors* v 1 52
They nothing doubt prevailing and to make it brief wars *Coriolanus* i 3 111
My tears are now prevailing orators . . . . *T. Andron.* iii 1 26
Prevailment. Nosegays, sweetmeats, messengers Of strong prevailment in unharden'd youth . . . . *M. N. Dream* i 1 35
Prevent. Would't had been done! Thou didst prevent me . *Tempest* i 2 350
For I would prevent The loose encounters of lascivious men *T. G. of Ver.* ii 7 40
Prevent, or go thou, Like Sir Actæon he . . . . *Mer. Wives* ii 1 121
I will prevent this, detect my wife, be revenged on Falstaff . . ii 2 325
It wants matter to prevent so gross o'erreaching as this . . . v 5 144
And prevents the slander of his wife . . . . *As Y. Like It* iv 1 61
Many a good hanging prevents a bad marriage . . . *T. Night* i 5 20
My lord, wise men ne'er sit and wail their woes, But presently prevent the ways to wail . . . . *Richard II.* iii 2 179
Prevent it, resist it, let it not be so . . . . iv 1 148
You will be there, I know.—If God prevent not, I purpose so . v 2 55
And, to prevent the worst, Sir Michael, speed . . . 1 *Hen. IV.* iv 4 35
Both the degrees prevent my curses . . . . . 2 *Hen. IV.* i 2 259
To prevent the tyrant's violence, . . . I'll hence forthwith 3 *Hen. VI.* iv 4 29
To prevent the worst, Forthwith we'll send him hence to Brittany . iv 6 96
For emulation now, who shall be nearest, Will touch us all too near, if God prevent not . . . . *Richard III.* ii 3 26
Forcibly prevents Our lock'd embrasures . . . . *Troi. and Cres.* iv 4 38
Tell me not, friar, that thou hear'st of this, Unless thou tell me how I may prevent it . . . . *Rom. and Jul.* iv 1 51
A kind of hope, Which craves as desperate an execution As that is desperate which we would prevent . . . . iv 1 70
I'll teach them to prevent wild Alcibiades' wrath . *T. of Athens* v 1 206
So Cæsar may. Then, lest he may, prevent . . . . *J. Cæsar* ii 1 28
Which to prevent, Let Antony and Cæsar fall together . . . ii 1 160
Metellus Cimber throws before thy seat An humble heart,— I must prevent thee, Cimber . . . . iii 1 35
I do find it cowardly and vile, For fear of what might fall, so to prevent The time of life . . . . v 1 105
So shall my anticipation prevent your discovery . . . *Hamlet* ii 2 305
Which for to prevent, I have in quick determination Thus set it down . iii 1 175
What is your study?—How to prevent the fiend, and to kill vermin *Lear* iii 4 164
You have one eye left To see some mischief on him. O!—Lest it see more, prevent it . . . . iii 7 83
Which to prevent he made a law, To keep her still . . *Pericles* i Gower 35
Prevented. O plague right well prevented! . . . *Much Ado* iii 2 136
I would have stay'd till I had made you merry, If worthier friends had not prevented me . . . . *Mer. of Venice* i 1 61
She hath prevented me . . . . *T. of Shrew* v 2 49
Had I spoke with her, I could have well diverted her intents, Which thus she hath prevented . . . . *All's Well* iii 4 22
It was a disaster of war that Cæsar himself could not have prevented . iii 6 56
I will answer you with gait and entrance. But we are prevented *T. N.* iii 1 94
Which way to be prevented, if to be ; If not, how best to bear it *W. Tale* i 2 405
This might have been prevented and made whole . . . *K. John* i 1 35
I do at this hour joy o'er myself, Prevented from a damned enterprise *Hen. V.* ii 2 164
But that I am prevented, I should have begg'd I might have been employ'd.—Then gather strength and march . . . 1 *Hen. VI.* iv 1 71
As well the fear of harm, as harm apparent, In my opinion, ought to be prevented . . . . *Richard III.* ii 2 131
Not a whit for me ; For I, too fond, might have prevented this . . iii 4 83
Which now the loving haste of these our friends, Somewhat against our meaning, have prevented . . . . iii 5 55

Prevented. The gods have well prevented it . . . *Coriolanus* iv 6 36
O God!—O nurse, how shall this be prevented? . . . *Rom. and Jul.* iii 5 206
That future strife May be prevented now . . . . . *Lear* i 1 46
But you are come A market-maid to Rome; and have prevented The ostentation of our love . . . *Ant. and Cleo.* iii 6 51
For one death Might have prevented many . . . . iv 12 42
Whose life, But that her flight prevented it, she had Ta'en off *Cymbeline* v 5 46
Sir, I will recount it to you: But, see, I am prevented . . *Pericles* v 1 64
Prevention. Nor the prevention of poor Bolingbroke About his marriage *Richard II.* ii 1 167
But what prevention?—The king is full of grace and fair regard *Hen. V.* i 1 21
But God be thanked for prevention . . . . . ii 2 158
Nor never seek prevention of thy foes . . . *2 Hen. VI.* ii 4 57
Achievements, plots, orders, preventions . . . *Troi. and Cres.* i 3 181
Not Erebus itself were dim enough To hide thee from prevention *J. Cæsar* ii 1 85
Casca, be sudden, for we fear prevention. Brutus, what shall be done? iii 1 19
Prey. Like an o'ergrown lion in a cave, That goes not out to prey *Meas. for Meas.* i 3 23
Make a scarecrow of the law, Setting it up to fear the birds of prey . ii 1 2
And would have reft the fishers of their prey . . *Com. of Errors* i 1 116
Thus dost thou hear the Nemean lion roar 'Gainst thee, thou lamb, that standest as his prey . . . . . *L. L. Lost* iv 1 91
I do quake with fear: Methought a serpent eat my heart away, And you sat smiling at his cruel prey . . . . *M. N. Dream* ii 2 150
Yea, mock the lion when he roars for prey . . *Mer. of Venice* iii 1 30
For 'tis The royal disposition of that beast To prey on nothing that doth seem as dead . . . . . . *As Y. Like It* iv 3 119
The tenderness of her nature became as a prey to her grief *All's Well* iv 3 61
If one should be a prey, how much the better To fall before the lion than the wolf! . . . . . . *T. Night* iii 1 139
This place is famous for the creatures Of prey that keep upon't *W. Tale* iii 3 13
Light vanity, insatiate cormorant, Consuming means, soon preys upon itself . . . . . . *Richard II.* ii 1 39
Or rather, not pray to her, but prey on her . . . *1 Hen. IV.* ii 1 90
For once the eagle England being in prey . . . *Hen. V.* i 2 169
The French might have a good prey of us, if he knew of it . . iv 4 81
Like lions wanting food, Do rush upon us as their hungry prey *1 Hen. VI.* i 2 28
And give her as a prey to law and shame . . *2 Hen. VI.* ii 1 198
The rascal people, thirsting after prey . . . . iv 4 51
Made a prey for carrion kites and crows Even of the bonny beast he loved . . . . v 2 11
Be thou a prey unto the house of York, And die in bands! . *3 Hen. VI.* i 1 185
So he walks, insulting o'er his prey, And so he comes, to rend his limbs i 3 14
If with thy will it stands That to my foes this body must be prey . ii 3 39
More pity that the eagle should be mew'd, While kites and buzzards prey at liberty . . . . . . *Richard III.* i 1 133
The world is grown so bad, That wrens make prey where eagles dare not perch . . . . i 3 71
Even where his lustful eye or savage heart, Without control, listed to make his prey . . . . iii 5 84
This carnal cur Preys on the issue of his mother's body . . iv 4 57
Thus hath the course of justice wheel'd about, And left thee but a very prey to time . . . . iv 4 106
Which now, two tender playfellows for dust, Thy broken faith hath made a prey for worms . . . . . . iv 4 386
Must make perforce an universal prey, And last eat up himself *Troi. and Cres.* i 3 123
Tigers must prey, and Rome affords no prey But me and mine *T. An.* iii 1 55
Nor the god of war, Shall seize this prey out of his father's hands . iv 2 96
Throw her forth to beasts and birds of prey . . . v 3 198
Ravens, crows and kites, Fly o'er our heads and downward look on us, As we were sickly prey . . . . . *J. Cæsar* v 1 87
Whiles night's black agents to their preys do rouse . *Macbeth* iii 2 53
So lust, though to a radiant angel link'd, Will sate itself in a celestial bed, And prey on garbage . . . . . *Hamlet* i 5 57
Fox in stealth, wolf in greediness, dog in madness, lion in prey . *Lear* iii 4 97
Humanity must perforce prey on itself, Like monsters of the deep . iv 2 49
I'ld whistle her off and let her down the wind, To prey at fortune *Othello* iii 3 263
Till the flies and gnats of Nile Have buried them for prey! *Ant. and Cleo.* iii 13 167
When valour preys on reason, It eats the sword it fights with . iii 13 199
Subtle as the fox for prey, Like warlike as the wolf for what we eat *Cymbeline* iii 3 40
Preyed. Put your torches out: The wolves have prey'd . . *Much Ado* v 3 25
Death, having prey'd upon the outward parts, Leaves them invisible *K. John* v 7 15
Preyful. The preyful princess pierced and prick'd a pretty pleasing pricket . . . . *L. L. Lost* iv 2 58
Priam. Fond done, done fond, Was this King Priam's joy? . *All's Well* i 3 77
Drew Priam's curtain in the dead of night, And would have told him half his Troy was burnt; But Priam found the fire ere he his tongue *2 Hen. IV.* i 1 72
So obsequious will thy father be, Even for the loss of thee, having no more, As Priam was for all his valiant sons . . *3 Hen. VI.* ii 5 120
Priam's six-gated city . . . . . . *Troi. and Cres.* Prol. 15
At Priam's royal table do I sit . . . . . . i 1 29
We have, great Agamemnon, here in Troy A prince call'd Hector,—Priam is his father . . . . i 3 261
Yet, dread Priam, There is no lady of more softer bowels . . ii 2 10
For my private part, I am no more touch'd than all Priam's sons . ii 2 126
They're come from field: let us to Priam's hall, To greet the warriors . iii 1 161
They will almost Give us a prince of blood, a son of Priam, In change of him . . . . iii 3 26
'Tis known, Achilles, that you are in love With one of Priam's daughters iii 3 194
Is it so concluded?—By Priam and the general state of Troy . . iv 2 69
Name Cressid, and thy life shall be as safe As Priam is in Ilion . iv 4 118
The youngest son of Priam, a true knight, Not yet mature, yet matchless iv 5 96
My father's sister's son, A cousin-german to great Priam's seed . . iv 5 121
Lay hold upon him, Priam, hold him fast: He is thy crutch . . v 3 59
Royal Priam.—O Priam, yield not to him!—Do not, dear father . v 3 75
What art thou?—A bastard son of Priam's . . . . v 7 15
Hector is gone: Who shall tell Priam so, or Hecuba? . . . v 10 15
Hector's dead: There is a word will Priam turn to stone . . v 10 18
Of five and twenty valiant sons, Half of the number that King Priam had, Behold the poor remains, alive and dead! . . *T. Andron.* i 1 80
That baleful burning night When subtle Greeks surprised King Priam's Troy . . . . v 3 84
'Twas Æneas' tale to Dido; and thereabout of it especially, where he speaks of Priam's slaughter . . . . . *Hamlet* ii 2 469
With eyes like carbuncles, the hellish Pyrrhus Old grandsire Priam seeks ii 2 486
Unequal match'd, Pyrrhus at Priam drives; in rage strikes wide . ii 2 494
Priam. His sword, Which was declining on the milky head Of reverend Priam, seem'd i' the air to stick . . . . . . *Hamlet* ii 2 501
And never did the Cyclops' hammers fall On Mars's armour forged for proof eterne With less remorse than Pyrrhus' bleeding sword Now falls on Priam . . . . ii 2 514
Priami. Hic steterat Priami regia celsa senis . . *T. of Shrew* iii 1 29
'Hic steterat,' and that Lucentio that comes a-wooing, 'Priami,' is my man . . . . iii 1 35
'Hic steterat Priami,' take heed he hear us not, 'regia,' presume not . iii 1 43
Priamus. I am yours, You valiant offspring of great Priamus *Tr. and Cr.* ii 2 207
Not Priamus and Hecuba on knees . . . should stop my way . v 3 54
Priapus. She's able to freeze the god Priapus . . . *Pericles* iv 6 4
Pribble. A goot motion if we leave our pribbles and prabbles *Mer. Wives* i 1 56
Given to . . . drinkings and swearings and starings, pribbles and prabbles v 5 168
Price. And held in idle price to haunt assemblies . *Meas. for Meas.* i 3 9
When rich villains have need of poor ones, poor ones may make what price they will . . . . *Much Ado* iii 3 122
'What's the price of this inkle?'—'One penny' . . *L. L. Lost* iii 1 139
We can afford no more at such a price.—Prize you yourselves . . v 2 223
This making of Christians will raise the price of hogs *Mer. of Venice* iii 5 26
In converting Jews to Christians, you raise the price of pork . iii 5 38
His qualities being at this poor price, I need not to ask you if gold will corrupt him . . . . *All's Well* iv 3 309
Our rash faults Make trivial price of serious things we have . . v 3 61
If I were so, He might have bought me at a common price . . v 3 190
Falls into abatement and low price, Even in a minute . . *T. Night* i 1 13
If you hold your life at any price, betake you to your guard . . iii 4 252
Poor fellow, never joyed since the price of oats rose . *1 Hen. IV.* ii 1 14
Lucky joys And golden times and happy news of price . *2 Hen. IV.* v 3 100
Forgive, Although my body pay the price of it . . *Hen. V.* ii 2 154
Hath given the doom of death For pax of little price . . . iii 6 47
She is a pearl, Whose price hath launch'd above a thousand ships *Troi. and Cres.* ii 2 82
And add, That if he overhold his price so much, We'll none of him . ii 3 142
Let us kill him, and we'll have corn at our own price . . *Coriolanus* i 1 11
The price is to ask it kindly.—Kindly! Sir, I pray, let me ha't . . ii 3 81
I would not buy Their mercy at the price of one fair word . . iii 3 91
I account of them As jewels purchased at an easy price . *T. Andron.* iii 1 199
Who now the price of his dear blood doth owe? . . *Rom. and Jul.* iii 1 188
It will be of more price, Being spoke behind your back, than to your face iv 1 27
When she was dear to us, we did hold her so; But now her price is fall'n *Lear* i 1 200
I know my price, I am worth no worse a place . . . *Othello* i 1 11
It is a great price For a small vice . . . . . iv 3 69
Her own price Proclaims how she esteem'd him . . *Cymbeline* i 1 51
Her price, Boult?—I cannot be bated one doit of a thousand pieces *Per.* iv 2 54
Prick. Like hedgehogs which Lie tumbling in my barefoot way and mount Their pricks at my footfall . . . . . . *Tempest* ii 2 12
My duty pricks me on to utter that Which else no worldly good should draw from me . . . . *T. G. of Ver.* iii 1 8
As my ever-esteemed duty pricks me on . . . *L. L. Lost* iv 1 269
Will you prick't with your eye?—No point, with my knife . . ii 1 189
Let the mark have a prick in't, to mete at, if it may be . . iv 1 134
She's too hard for you at pricks, sir: challenge her to bowl . . iv 1 140
If you prick us, do we not bleed? . . . . . *Mer. of Venice* iii 1 67
He that sweetest rose will find Must find love's prick . *As Y. Like It* iii 2 118
'Tis some odd humour pricks him to this fashion . *T. of Shrew* iii 2 74
When you have our roses, You barely leave our thorns to prick ourselves And mock us with our bareness . . . . . *All's Well* iv 2 19
His siege is now Against the mind, the which he pricks and wounds With many legions of strange fantasies . . . *K. John* v 7 17
And prick my tender patience to those thoughts Which honour and allegiance cannot think . . . . . . *Richard II.* ii 1 207
What pricks you on To take advantage of the absent time? . . ii 3 78
Honour pricks me on. Yea, but how if honour prick me off? *1 Hen. IV.* v 1 131
For they never prick their finger but they say, 'There's some of the king's blood spilt' . . . . . . *2 Hen. IV.* ii 2 121
Prick him.—I was pricked well enough before . . . . iii 2 121
Shall I prick him down, Sir John?—It were superfluous . . iii 2 153
The whole frame stands upon pins: prick him no more . . iii 2 156
Prick the woman's tailor: well, Master Shallow; deep, Master Shallow iii 2 171
A likely fellow! Come, prick me Bullcalf till he roar again . iii 2 186
Gentlewomen that live honestly by the prick of their needles *Hen. V.* ii 1 36
If you would walk off, I would prick your guts a little, in good terms ii 1 61
Prick not your finger as you pluck it off . . *1 Hen. VI.* ii 4 49
Now Phaëthon hath tumbled from his car, And made an evening at the noontide prick . . . . *3 Hen. VI.* i 4 34
Do not honour him so much To prick thy finger, though to wound his heart . . . . i 4 55
What! can so young a thorn begin to prick? . . . . v 5 13
My conscience first received a tenderness, Scruple, and prick *Hen. VIII.* ii 4 171
Such indexes, although small pricks To their subsequent volumes *Troi. and Cres.* i 3 343
And it [love] pricks like thorn . . . . *Rom. and Jul.* i 4 26
Prick love for pricking, and you beat love down . . . i 4 28
The bawdy hand of the dial is now upon the prick of noon . . ii 4 119
What need we any spur but our own cause To prick us to redress? *J. C.* ii 1 124
Your brother too must die; consent you, Lepidus?—I do consent,—Prick him down . . . . iv 1 3
I have no spur To prick the sides of my intent . . *Macbeth* i 7 26
Go prick thy face, and over-red thy fear, Thou lily-liver'd boy . v 3 14
Leave her to heaven And to those thorns that in her bosom lodge, To prick and sting her . . . . *Hamlet* i 5 88
Strike in their numb'd and mortified bare arms Pins, wooden pricks *Lear* ii 3 16
I will not swear these are my hands: let's see; I feel this pin prick . iv 7 56
Myself by with a needle, that I might prick The goer-back . *Cymbeline* i 1 168
Prick-eared. Iceland dog! thou prick-ear'd cur of Iceland! . *Hen. V.* ii 1 44
Pricked. Like unback'd colts, they prick'd their ears . *Tempest* iv 1 176
The preyful princess pierced and prick'd a pretty pleasing pricket *L. L. Lost* iv 2 58
An old hat and 'the humour of forty fancies' pricked in't *T. of Shrew* iii 2 70
The fiend hath pricked down Bardolph irrecoverable . *2 Hen. IV.* ii 4 359
Prick him.—I was pricked well enough before . . . iii 2 121
You need not to have pricked me; there are other men fitter to go out iii 2 125
If he had been a man's tailor, he'ld ha' pricked you . . iii 2 164
What, dost thou roar before thou art pricked? . . . . iii 2 190
Prick'd on by public wrongs sustain'd in France . *1 Hen. VI.* iii 2 78
A round little worm Prick'd from the lazy finger of a maid *Rom. and Jul.* i 4 66
Will you be prick'd in number of our friends; Or shall we on? *J. Cæsar* iii 1 216
These many, then, shall die; their names are prick'd . . iv 1 1

Pricked. And took his voice who should be prick'd to die, In our black sentence *J. Cæsar* iv 1 16
Thereto prick'd on by a most emulate pride *Hamlet* i 1 83
Prick'd to't by foolish honesty and love *Othello* iii 3 412
Prickest. There thou prickest her with a thistle *Much Ado* iii 4 76
Pricket. 'Twas not a haud credo; 'twas a pricket *L. L. Lost* iv 2 12
To humour the ignorant, call I the deer the princess killed a pricket iv 2 53
The preyful princess pierced and prick'd a pretty pleasing pricket iv 2 58
Put L to sore, then sorel jumps from thicket; Or pricket sore, or else sorel iv 2 61
Pricking. Tooth'd briers, sharp furzes, pricking goss and thorns *Temp.* iv 1 180
I would your cambric were sensible as your finger, that you might leave pricking it for pity *Coriolanus* i 3 96
Prick love for pricking, and you beat love down *Rom. and Jul.* i 4 28
By the pricking of my thumbs, Something wicked this way comes *Macb.* iv 1 44
Prick-song. He fights as you sing prick-song *Rom. and Jul.* ii 4 21
Pride. And, may I say to thee, this pride of hers, Upon advice, hath drawn my love from her *T. G. of Ver.* iii 1 72
My gravity, Wherein—let no man hear me—I take pride *Meas. for Meas.* ii 4 10
'Fly pride,' says the peacock *Com. of Errors* iv 3 81
That advance their pride Against that power that bred it *Much Ado* iii 1 10
Can this be true? Stand I condemn'd for pride and scorn so much? iii 1 108
Contempt, farewell! and maiden pride, adieu! iii 1 109
All pride is willing pride, and yours is so *L. L. Lost* ii 1 36
Proud with his form, in his eye pride express'd ii 1 237
What, what? first praise me and again say no? O short-lived pride! iv 1 15
Now much beshrew my manners and my pride *M. N. Dream* ii 2 54
My pride fell with my fortunes *As Y. Like It* i 2 264
Why, who cries out on pride, That can therein tax any private party? ii 7 70
The greatest of my pride is to see my ewes graze and my lambs suck iii 2 81
He's proud, and yet his pride becomes him: He'll make a proper man iii 5 114
Contempt nor bitterness Were in his pride or sharpness *All's Well* i 2 37
Maugre all thy pride, Nor wit nor reason can my passion hide *T. Night* iii 1 163
The eagle-winged pride Of sky-aspiring and ambitious thoughts *Rich. II.* i 3 129
For time hath set a blot upon my pride iii 2 81
I give ... The pride of kingly sway from out my heart iv 1 206
Would he not fall down, Since pride must have a fall? v 5 88
Living, to abide Thy kingly doom and sentence of his pride v 6 23
In the very heat And pride of their contention *1 Hen. IV.* i 1 60
Who is sweet Fortune's minion and her pride i 1 83
What think you, coz, Of this young Percy's pride? i 1 92
Want of government, Pride, haughtiness, opinion and disdain iii 1 185
Their pride and mettle is asleep, Their courage with hard labour tame iv 3 22
Men of all sorts take a pride to gird at me *2 Hen. IV.* i 2 7
Infect my blood with joy, Or swell my thoughts to any strain of pride iv 5 171
O noble English, that could entertain With half their forces the full pride of France! *Hen. V.* i 2 112
Being free from vainness and self-glorious pride v Prol. 20
As very infants prattle of thy pride *1 Hen. VI.* iii 1 16
That hardly we escaped the pride of France iii 2 40
And from the pride of Gallia rescued thee iv 6 15
And, commendable proved, let's die in pride iv 6 57
And there died, My Icarus, my blossom, in his pride iv 7 16
Though Humphrey's pride And greatness of his place be grief to us *2 Hen. VI.* i 1 172
Pride went before, ambition follows him i 1 180
To bridle and suppress The pride of Suffolk and the cardinal i 1 201
I am unmeet: First, for I cannot flatter thee in pride i 3 169
Image of pride, why should I hold my peace? i 3 179
At Beaufort's pride, at Somerset's ambition ii 2 71
Thus Eleanor's pride dies in her youngest days ii 3 46
And let it make thee crest-fall'n, Ay, and allay this thy abortive pride iv 1 60
For what hath broach'd this tumult but thy pride? *3 Hen. VI.* ii 2 159
Like to autumn's corn, Have we mow'd down in tops of all their pride! v 7 4
And Richard falls in height of all his pride *Richard III.* v 3 176
The madams too, Not used to toil, did almost sweat to bear The pride upon them *Hen. VIII.* i 1 25
I can see his pride Peep through each part of him i 1 68
This priest has no pride in him?—Not to speak of ii 2 82
Your heart Is cramm'd with arrogancy, spleen, and pride ii 4 110
My high-blown pride At length broke under me iii 2 361
The seeded pride That hath to this maturity blown up *Troi. and Cres.* i 3 316
Better parch in Afric sun Than in the pride and salt scorn of his eyes i 3 371
Pride alone Must tarre the mastiffs on, as 'twere their bone i 3 391
Call it melancholy, if you will favour the man; but, by my head, 'tis pride ii 3 95
Why should a man be proud? How doth pride grow? I know not what pride is ii 3 162
He that is proud eats up himself: pride is his own glass, his own trumpet ii 3 165
Speaks not to himself but with a pride That quarrels at self-breath ii 3 181
That were to enlard his fat already pride And add more coals to Cancer ii 3 205
An a' be proud with me, I'll pheeze his pride ii 3 215
Shall pride carry it?—An 'twould, you'ld carry half ii 3 228
I have derision medicinable, To use between your strangeness and his pride iii 3 45
Pride hath no other glass To show itself but pride iii 3 47
One man eats into another's pride, While pride is fasting in his wantonness! iii 3 137
Valour and pride excel themselves in Hector iv 5 79
Weigh him well, And that which looks like pride is courtesy iv 5 82
He's poor in no one fault, but stored with all.—Especially in pride *Cor.* ii 1 22
How are we censured?—Because you talk of pride ii 1 28
You talk of pride: O that you could turn your eyes toward the napes of your necks, and make but an interior survey of your good selves! ii 1 42
Enforce his pride, And his old hate unto you ii 3 227
Let Thy mother rather feel thy pride than fear Thy dangerous stoutness iii 2 126
Thy valiantness was mine, thou suck'dst it from me, But owe thy pride thyself iii 2 130
O'ercome with pride, ambitious past all thinking, Self-loving iv 6 31
Pride, Which out of daily fortune ever taints The happy man iv 7 37
To his surname Coriolanus 'longs more pride Than pity to our prayers v 3 170
And took some pride To do myself this wrong v 6 37
Chastised with arms Our enemies' pride *T. Andron.* i 1 33
We will afflict the emperor in his pride i 3 62
Let two more summers wither in their pride *Rom. and Jul.* i 2 10
And 'tis much pride For fair without the fair within to hide i 3 89
If thou didst put this sour-cold habit on To castigate thy pride, 'twere well: but thou Dost it enforcedly *T. of Athens* iv 3 240
Pride. Wert thou the unicorn, pride and wrath would confound thee *T. of Athens* iv 3 339
A falcon, towering in her pride of place *Macbeth* ii 4 12
Thereto prick'd on by a most emulate pride, Dared to the combat *Hamlet* i 1 83
Let pride, which she calls plainness, marry her *Lear* i 1 131
With strain'd pride To come between our sentence and our power i 1 172
Infect her beauty, You fen-suck'd fogs, drawn by the powerful sun, To fall and blast her pride! ii 4 170
Whose easy-borrow'd pride Dwells in the fickle grace of her he follows ii 4 188
He, as loving his own pride and purposes, Evades them *Othello* i 1 12
'Tis pride that pulls the country down ii 3 98
Pride, pomp and circumstance of glorious war! iii 3 354
As salt as wolves in pride, and fools as gross As ignorance made drunk iii 3 404
Cydnus swell'd above the banks, or for The press of boats or pride *Cymb.* ii 4 72
Ambitions, covetings, change of prides, disdain, Nice longing, slanders ii 5 25
And pride so great, The name of help grew odious to repeat *Pericles* i 4 30
Even in the height and pride of all his glory ii 4 6
Pridge. A' uttered as prave words at the pridge *Hen. V.* iii 6 67
The king is coming, and I must speak with him from the pridge iii 6 91
The Duke of Exeter has very gallantly maintained the pridge iii 6 96
Th' athversary was have possession of the pridge; but he is enforced to retire, and the Duke of Exeter is master of the pridge iii 6 98
Prie. Je te prie, m'enseignez; il faut que j'apprenne à parler iii 4 4
Prief. I will make a prief of it in my note-book *Mer. Wives* i 1 146
Pries. Which pries not to the interior *Mer. of Venice* ii 9 28
Priest. I will teach a scurvy jack-a-nape priest to meddle or make *Mer. Wives* i 4 116
By gar, I vill kill de Jack priest i 4 123
I will not believe such a Cataian, though the priest o' the town commended him ii 1 149
There is a fray to be fought between Sir Hugh the Welsh priest and Caius the French doctor ii 1 209
He is de coward Jack priest of de vorld ii 3 32
Scurvy jack-dog priest! by gar, me vill cut his ears ii 3 65
Shall I lose my parson, my priest? iii 1 106
At the deanery, where a priest attends, Straight marry her iv 6 31
Bring you the maid, you shall not lack a priest iv 6 53
Like god Bel's priests in the old church-window *Much Ado* iii 3 144
Who ambles Time withal?—With a priest that lacks Latin *As Y. Like It* iii 2 337
Have a good priest that can tell you what marriage is iii 3 86
Come, sister, you shall be the priest and marry us iv 1 124
There's a girl goes before the priest iv 1 140
The priest was good enough, for all the old gentleman's saying v 1 3
What will be said? what mockery will it be, To want the bridegroom when the priest attends! *T. of Shrew* iii 2 5
When the priest Should ask, if Katharine should be his wife, 'Ay, by gogs-wouns,' quoth he iii 2 160
All-amazed, the priest let fall the book; And, as he stoop'd again to take it up, This mad-brain'd bridegroom took him such a cuff That down fell priest and book and book and priest iii 2 163
The old priest of Saint Luke's church is at your command at all hours iv 4 88
Take the priest, clerk, and some sufficient honest witnesses iv 4 94
Bid the priest be ready to come against you come with your appendix iv 4 103
Softly and swiftly, sir; for the priest is ready.—I fly v 1 1
Although before the solemn priest I have sworn, I will not bed her *All's Well* ii 3 286
I am one that had rather go with sir priest than sir knight *T. Night* iii 4 298
Visited by the priest, And made the most notorious geck and gull v 1 350
Seal'd-up oracle, by the hand deliver'd Of great Apollo's priest *W. Tale* iii 2 129
Put on my shroud and lay me Where no priest shovels in dust iv 4 469
No Italian priest Shall tithe or toll in our dominions *K. John* iii 1 153
Led so grossly by this meddling priest, Dreading the curse iii 1 163
Will no man say amen? Am I both priest and clerk? *Richard II.* iv 1 173
Where the sad and solemn priests Sing still for Richard's soul *Hen. V.* iv 1 318
Peel'd priest, dost thou command me to be shut out? *1 Hen. VI.* i 3 30
Priest, beware your beard; I mean to tug it and to cuff you soundly i 3 47
And all the priests and friars in my realm Shall in procession sing her endless praise i 6 19
Presumptuous priest! this place commands my patience iii 1 8
Am I not protector, saucy priest?—And am not I a prelate of the church? iii 1 45
I would see his heart out, ere the priest Should ever get that privilege of me iii 1 120
I gave a noble to the priest The morn that I was wedded to her mother v 4 23
Now, by God's mother, priest, I'll shave your crown for this *2 Hen. VI.* ii 1 51
Impious Beaufort, that false priest ii 4 53
Say but the word, and I will be his priest.—But I would have him dead, my Lord of Suffolk, Ere you can take due orders for a priest iii 1 272
Heart, be wrathful still: Priests pray for enemies, but princes kill v 2 71
Talking with a priest, lord chamberlain? Your friends at Pomfret, they do need the priest *Richard III.* iii 2 114
O, now I want the priest that spake to me iii 4 89
That blind priest, like the eldest son of fortune, Turns what he list *Hen. VIII.* ii 2 21
This priest has no pride in him?—Not to speak of ii 2 82
This good man, This just and learned priest ii 2 97
Thou art a proud traitor, priest.—Proud lord, thou liest iii 2 252
By my soul, Your long coat, priest, protects you iii 2 276
Helenus is a priest *Troi. and Cres.* i 2 245
You are for dreams and slumbers, brother priest ii 2 37
Think it an altar, and thy brother Troilus A priest there offering to it his own heart iv 3 9
The prayers of priests nor times of sacrifice, Embarquements all of fury, shall lift up Their rotten privilege and custom 'gainst My hate *Coriolanus* i 10 21
Our very priests must become mockers ii 1 93
Sith priest and holy water are so near And tapers burn so bright *T. An.* i 1 323
Sure as death I swore I would not part a bachelor from the priest i 1 488
This [gold] Will lug your priests and servants from your sides *T. of A.* iv 3 31
Nor sight of priests in holy vestments bleeding, Shall pierce a jot iv 3 125
Swear priests and cowards and men cautelous *J. Cæsar* ii 1 129
Go bid the priests do present sacrifice And bring me their opinions ii 2 5
I tell thee, churlish priest, A ministering angel shall my sister be, When thou liest howling *Hamlet* v 1 263
When priests are more in word than matter *Lear* iii 2 81
The holy priests Bless her when she is riggish *Ant. and Cleo.* ii 2 244
Should he make me Live, like Diana's priest, betwixt cold sheets? *Cymb.* i 6 133
Notes of sorrow out of tune are worse Than priests and fanes that lie iv 2 242
She'll ... make our swearers priests *Pericles* iv 6 13
There, when my maiden priests are met together v 1 243

Priesthood. Is your priesthood grown peremptory? 2 *Hen. VI.* ii 1 23
Chaplain, away! thy priesthood saves thy life 3 *Hen. VI.* i 3 3
Priest-like. Wherein, priest-like, thou Hast cleansed my bosom *W. Tale* i 2 237
We have suppler souls Than in our priest-like fasts *Coriolanus* v 1 56
Priestly. Hie thee, whiles I say A priestly farewell to her *Pericles* iii 1 70
Prig. Out upon him! prig, for my life, prig *W. Tale* iv 3 108
Primal. It hath the primal eldest curse upon 't, A brother's murder *Ham.* iii 3 37
It hath been taught us from the primal state, That he which is was wish'd until he were *Ant. and Cleo.* i 4 41
Prime. It was the first And Prospero the prime duke *Tempest* i 2 72
My prime request, Which I do last pronounce i 2 425
Losing his verdure even in the prime *T. G. of Ver.* i 1 49
For love is crowned with the prime In spring time *As Y. Like It* v 3 33
Wisdom, courage, All That happiness and prime can happy call *All's Well* ii 1 185
Lest you be cropp'd before you come to prime *Richard II.* v 2 51
How well resembles it the prime of youth! 3 *Hen. VI.* ii 1 23
That cropp'd the golden prime of this sweet prince *Richard III.* i 2 248
The most replenished sweet work of nature, That from the prime creation e'er she framed iv 3 19
Thy prime of manhood daring, bold, and venturous, Thy age confirm'd iv 4 170
Think, how thou stab'dst me in my prime of youth At Tewksbury v 3 119
Have I not made you The prime man of the state? *Hen. VIII.* iii 2 162
Were they as prime as goats, as hot as monkeys *Othello* iii 3 403
Who ever but his approbation added, Though not his prime consent, he did not flow From honourable sources *Pericles* iv 3 27
Primer. There is no primer business *Hen. VIII.* i 2 67
Primero. I never prospered since I forswore myself at primero *M. Wives* iv 5 104
Left him at primero With the Duke of Suffolk *Hen. VIII.* v 1 7
Primest. The primest creature That's paragon'd o' the world ii 4 229
Primitive. The bull,—the primitive statue, and oblique memorial of cuckolds *Troi. and Cres.* v 1 60
Primo, secundo, tertio, is a good play *T. Night* v 1 39
Primogenitive and due of birth, Prerogative of age *Troi. and Cres.* i 3 106
Primrose. Pale primroses, That die unmarried *W. Tale* iv 4 122
Look pale as primrose with blood-drinking sighs 2 *Hen. VI.* iii 2 63
That go the primrose way to the everlasting bonfire *Macbeth* ii 3 21
Himself the primrose path of dalliance treads *Hamlet* i 3 50
The violets, cowslips, and the primroses, Bear to my closet *Cymbeline* i 5 83
Thou shalt not lack The flower that's like thy face, pale primrose iv 2 221
Primrose-beds. Where often you and I Upon faint primrose-beds were wont to lie *M. N. Dream* i 1 215
Primy. A violet in the youth of primy nature *Hamlet* i 3 7
Prince. The king and prince at prayers! let's assist them *Tempest* i 1 57
Thy father was the Duke of Milan and A prince of power i 2 55
I am in my condition A prince, Miranda; I do think, a king iii 1 60
For more assurance that a living prince Does now speak to thee v 1 108
Know, worthy prince, Sir Valentine, my friend, This night intends to steal away your daughter *T. G. of Ver.* iii 1 10
He kept company with the wild prince and Poins *Mer. Wives* iii 2 74
As 'twere a brother of your order, Visit both prince and people *M. for M.* i 3 45
O worthy prince, dishonour not your eye By throwing it on any other object! v 1 22
O prince, I conjure thee, as thou believest There is another comfort! v 1 48
An arch-villain; believe it, royal prince: If he be less, he's nothing v 1 57
Then, good prince, No longer session hold upon my shame v 1 375
Come hither, Isabel. Your friar is now your prince v 1 387
Marrying a punk, my lord, is pressing to death, whipping, and hanging. —Slandering a prince deserves it v 1 530
Which princes, would they, may not disannul *Com. of Errors* i 1 145
And I to thee engaged a prince's word v 1 162
Justice, sweet prince, against that woman there! She whom thou gavest to me to be my wife! v 1 197
Being reconciled to the prince your brother, I owe you all duty *M. Ado* i 1 156
The prince and Count Claudio, walking in a thick-pleached alley i 2 9
The prince discovered to Claudio that he loved my niecė your daughter i 2 11
The prince your brother is royally entertained by Leonato i 3 45
Comes me the prince and Claudio, hand in hand, in sad conference i 3 62
If the prince do solicit you in that kind, you know your answer ii 1 70
If the prince be too important, tell him there is measure in every thing ii 1 73
What is he?—Why, he is the prince's jester: a very dull fool ii 1 142
The prince wooes for himself ii 1 181
The prince hath got your Hero.—I wish him joy of her ii 1 199
But did you think the prince would have served you thus? ii 1 203
The prince's fool! Ha? It may be I go under that title because I am merry ii 1 211
She told me, not thinking I had been myself, that I was the prince's jester ii 1 251
Go you to the prince your brother; spare not to tell him that he hath wronged his honour ii 2 22
What proof shall I make of that?—Proof enough to misuse the prince ii 2 28
Intend a kind of zeal both to the prince and Claudio ii 2 36
Ha! the prince and Monsieur Love! I will hide me in the arbour ii 3 37
There shalt thou find my cousin Beatrice Proposing with the prince iii 1 3
Like favourites, Made proud by princes iii 1 10
That Benedick loves Beatrice so entirely?—So says the prince iii 1 38
Being chosen for the prince's watch.—Well, give them their charge iii 3 6
You are to bid any man stand, in the prince's name iii 3 27
If he will not stand when he is bidden, he is none of the prince's subjects iii 3 33
They are to meddle with none but the prince's subjects iii 3 35
You, constable, are to present the prince's own person: if you meet the prince in the night, you may stay him iii 3 79
He may stay him: marry, not without the prince be willing iii 3 86
I should first tell thee how the prince, Claudio and my master . . . saw afar off in the orchard this amiable encounter iii 3 158
We charge you, in the prince's name, stand! iii 3 176
The prince, the count, Signior Benedick, Don John, and all the gallants iii 4 95
Sweet prince, you learn me noble thankfulness iv 1 31
Sweet prince, why speak not you?—What should I speak? I stand dishonour'd iv 1 64
Is this the prince? is this the prince's brother? Is this face Hero's? iv 1 71
Would the two princes lie, and Claudio lie, Who loved her so? iv 1 154
To burn the errors that these princes hold Against her maiden truth iv 1 165
There is some strange misprision in the princes iv 1 187
Your daughter here the princes left for dead iv 1 204
You know my inwardness and love Is very much unto the prince iv 1 248
Princes and counties! Surely, a princely testimony, a goodly count! iv 1 317
Masters, I charge you, in the prince's name, accuse these men iv 2 40
This man said, sir, that Don John, the prince's brother, was a villain iv 2 42
Why, this is flat perjury, to call a prince's brother villain iv 2 44

Prince. Where's the sexton? let him write down the prince's officer coxcomb *Much Ado* iv 2 73
Hero is belied; And that shall Claudio know; so shall the prince v 1 43
Sweet prince, let me go no farther to mine answer: do you hear me v 1 236
I thank you, princes, for my daughter's death: Record it with your high and worthy deeds v 1 278
Hero hath been falsely accused, the prince and Claudio mightily abused v 2 99
Did I not tell you she was innocent?—So are the prince and Claudio v 4 2
Prince, thou art sad; get thee a wife, get thee a wife v 4 124
Methought all his senses were lock'd in his eye, As jewels in crystal for some prince to buy *L. L. Lost* ii 1 243
One that makes sport To the prince and his bookmates iv 1 102
Chapels had been churches and poor men's cottages princes' palaces *Mer. of Venice* i 2 15
There is the Neapolitan prince.—Ay, that's a colt indeed i 2 43
Yourself, renowned prince, then stood as fair As any ii 1 20
By this scimitar That slew the Sophy and a Persian prince ii 1 25
Discover The several caskets to this noble prince ii 7 2
The vasty wilds Of wide Arabia are as throughfares now For princes to come view fair Portia ii 7 43
Behold, there stand the caskets, noble prince ii 9 4
As, after some oration fairly spoke By a beloved prince iii 2 181
The city-woman bears The cost of princes on unworthy shoulders *As Y. Like It* ii 7 76
Such duty as the subject owes the prince, Even such a woman oweth to her husband *T. of Shrew* v 2 155
If I cannot serve you, I can serve as great a prince as you are *All's Well* iv 5 39
What prince is that?—The black prince, sir; alias, the prince of darkness iv 5 43
But, sure, he is the prince of the world; let his nobility remain in's court iv 5 51
Are you so fond of your young prince as we Do seem to be of ours? *W. T.* i 2 164
Give scandal to the blood o' the prince my son, Who I do think is mine i 2 330
We shall Present our services to a fine new prince One of these days ii 1 17
And mannerly distinguishment leave out Betwixt the prince and beggar ii 1 87
A great king's daughter, The mother to a hopeful prince iii 2 41
The prince your son, with mere conceit and fear Of the queen's speed, is gone iii 2 145
Nor is't directly laid to thee, the death Of the young prince iii 2 196
Sir, it is three days since I saw the prince iv 2 34
I knew him once a servant of the prince iv 3 93
O cursed wretch, That knew'st this was the prince, and wouldst adventure To mingle faith with him! iv 4 470
The prince himself is about a piece of iniquity iv 4 693
I am courted now with a double occasion, gold and a means to do the prince my master good iv 4 865
Had our prince, Jewel of children, seen this hour, he had pair'd Well with this lord v 1 115
Your mother was most true to wedlock, prince v 1 124
Having both their country quitted With this young prince v 1 193
The dignity of this act was worth the audience of kings and princes v 2 87
I brought the old man and his son aboard the prince v 2 125
The prince my brother and the princess my sister called my father father v 2 153
Give me your good report to the prince my master v 2 163
I will swear to the prince thou art as honest a true fellow as any is v 2 169
The kings and the princes, our kindred, are going to see the queen's picture v 2 186
Be pleased then To pay that duty which you truly owe To him that owes it, namely this young prince *K. John* ii 1 248
Two such controlling bounds shall you be, kings, To these two princes ii 1 445
It likes us well; young princes, close your hands.—And your lips too ii 1 533
Good morrow, little prince.—As little prince, having so great a title To be more prince, as may be iv 1 10
Many a poor man's son would have lien still And ne'er have spoke a loving word to you; But you at your sick service had a prince iv 1 52
Thou, to be endeared to a king, Made it no conscience to destroy a prince iv 2 229
Who kill'd this prince?—'Tis not an hour since I left him well iv 3 103
Yet believe me, prince, I am not glad that such a sore of time Should seek a plaster by contemn'd revolt v 2 11
Where is my prince, the Dauphin?—Here: what news? v 5 9
Be of good comfort, prince; for you are born To set a form upon that indigest v 7 25
You, my noble prince, With other princes that may best be spared v 7 96
Now these her princes are come home again, Come the three corners of the world in arms, And we shall shock them v 7 115
A subject's love, Tendering the precious safety of my prince *Richard II.* i 1 32
Afore God, 'tis shame such wrongs are borne In him, a royal prince ii 1 239
When brave Gaunt, thy father, and myself Rescued the Black Prince ii 3 101
You have misled a prince, a royal king, A happy gentleman in blood iii 1 8
Myself, a prince by fortune of my birth, Near to the king in blood iii 1 16
This swears he, as he is a prince, is just iii 3 119
Mighty prince, my Lord Northumberland, What says King Bolingbroke? iii 3 172
Princes and noble lords, What answer shall I make to this base man? iv 1 19
Some two days since I saw the prince, And told him of those triumphs v 3 13
Hail, royal prince!—Thanks, noble peer; The cheapest of us is ten groats too dear v 5 67
In faith, It is a conquest for a prince to boast of 1 *Hen. IV.* i 1 77
The most comparative, rascalliest, sweet young prince i 2 91
Leave the prince and me alone: I will lay him down such reasons i 2 167
That the true prince may, for recreation sake, prove a false thief i 2 173
An the Prince and Poins be not two arrant cowards, there's no equity ii 2 105
Was it for me to kill the heir-apparent? should I turn upon the true prince? ii 4 298
The lion will not touch the true prince ii 4 300
I for a valiant lion, and thou for a true prince ii 4 304
'Sblood, my lord, they are false: nay, I'll tickle ye for a young prince ii 4 489
Almost an alien to the hearts Of all the court and princes of my blood iii 2 35
I have heard the prince tell him, I know not how oft, that that ring was copper iii 3 96
The prince is a Jack, a sneak-cup: 'sblood, an he were here, I would cudgel him like a dog iii 3 99
As thou art prince, I fear thee as I fear the roaring of the lion's whelp iii 3 166
Like a prince indeed, He made a blushing cital of himself v 2 61
Never did I hear Of any prince so wild a libertine v 2 72
If die, brave death, when princes die with us! v 2 87
Thou art a guard too wanton for the head Which princes, flesh'd with conquest, aim to hit 2 *Hen. IV.* i 1 149
If the prince put thee into my service for any other reason than to set me off, why then I have no judgement i 2 14

Prince. The juvenal, the prince your master, whose chin is not yet fledged *2 Hen. IV.* i 2 22
Here comes the nobleman that committed the prince for striking him . i 2 63
You have misled the youthful prince.—The young prince hath misled me i 2 163
For the box of the ear that the prince gave you, he gave it like a rude prince, and you took it like a sensible lord . . i 2 218
Well, God send the prince a better companion!—God send the companion a better prince! . . . . i 2 223
When the prince broke thy head for liking his father to a singing-man . ii 1 97
Small beer?—Why, a prince should not be so loosely studied as to remember so weak a composition . . . . . . ii 2 9
How many good young princes would do so, their fathers being so sick? ii 2 33
From a prince to a prentice? a low transformation! . . . ii 2 193
The prince once set a dish of apple-johns before him, and told him there were five more Sir Johns . . . . ii 4 5
Here will be the prince and Master Poins anon . . . . ii 4 16
What humour's the prince of?—A good shallow young fellow . . ii 4 256
Why does the prince love him so, then?—Because their legs are both of a bigness . . . . ii 4 264
Other gambol faculties a' has, that show a weak mind and an able body, for the which the prince admits him: for the prince himself is such another . . . . ii 4 274
No man is too good to serve's prince . . . . . . iii 2 253
The prince is here at hand: pleaseth your lordship To meet his grace . iv 1 225
Employ the countenance and grace of heaven, As a false favourite doth his prince's name, In deeds dishonourable . . . . . iv 2 25
Where is the prince your brother?—I think he's gone to hunt . . iv 4 13
How chance thou art not with the prince thy brother? . . . . iv 4 20
The prince but studies his companions Like a strange tongue . . iv 4 68
The prince will in the perfectness of time Cast off his followers . . iv 4 74
Be patient, princes; you do know, these fits Are . . . very ordinary . iv 4 114
Speak lower, princes, for the king recovers . . . . . iv 4 129
We left the prince my brother here, my liege . . . . . iv 5 52
Where is the crown? . . . The prince hath ta'en it hence: go, seek him out . . . . iv 5 60
The prince in the next room, Washing with kindly tears his gentle cheeks . . . . iv 5 83
Sweet princes, what I did, I did in honour . . . . . v 2 35
How might a prince of my great hopes forget So great indignities? . v 2 68
And, princes all, believe me, I beseech you . . . . . v 2 122
No prince nor peer shall have just cause to say, God shorten Harry's happy life one day! . . . . v 2 144
A kingdom for a stage, princes to act And monarchs to behold *Hen. V.* Prol. 3
And so the prince obscured his contemplation Under the veil of wildness i 1 63
Edward the Black Prince, Who on the French ground play'd a tragedy . i 2 105
The prince our master Says that you savour too much of your youth . i 2 249
Tell the pleasant prince this mock of his Hath turn'd his balls to gunstones . . . . i 2 281
See you, my princes and my noble peers, These English monsters! . ii 2 84
Sold your king to slaughter, His princes and his peers to servitude . ii 2 171
Think we King Harry strong; And, princes, look you strongly arm . ii 4 49
Up, princes! and, with spirit of honour edged More sharper than your swords, hie to the field . . . . iii 5 38
High dukes, great princes, barons, lords and knights . . . iii 5 46
Now forth, lord constable and princes all, And quickly bring us word . iii 5 67
You talk of horse and armour?—You are as well provided of both as any prince in the world . . . . iii 7 10
By the white hand of my lady, he's a gallant prince . . . iii 7 102
Brothers both, Commend me to the princes in our camp . . . iv 1 25
To horse, you gallant princes! straight to horse! . . . . iv 2 15
For many of our princes—woe the while!—Lie drown'd and soak'd in mercenary blood . . . . iv 7 78
So do our vulgar drench their peasant limbs In blood of princes . . iv 7 81
Of princes, in this number, And nobles bearing banners, there lie dead One hundred twenty six . . . . iv 8 86
And, princes French, and peers, health to you all! . . . . v 2 8
Fairly met: So are you, princes English, every one . . . . v 2 11
You English princes all, I do salute you . . . . . v 2 22
Will you, fair sister, Go with the princes, or stay here with us? . . v 2 91
None do you like but an effeminate prince, Whom, like a school-boy, you may over-awe . . . . *1 Hen. VI.* i 1 35
Thou art protector And lookest to command the prince and realm . . i 1 38
He is protector of the realm, And would have armour here out of the Tower, To crown himself king and suppress the prince . . . . i 3 68
The prince's espials have informed me . . . . . . i 4 8
But now thy uncle is removing hence; As princes do their courts . . ii 5 105
And ere that we will suffer such a prince, So kind a father of the commonweal, To be disgraced by an inkhorn mate, We and our wives and children all will fight . . . . iii 1 97
Sweet prince, An if your grace mark every circumstance, You have great reason to do Richard right . . . . iii 1 152
Welcome, high prince, the mighty Duke of York!—Perish, base prince, ignoble Duke of York! . . . . iii 1 178
But, ere we go, regard this dying prince, The valiant Duke of Bedford . iii 2 86
Dismay not, princes, at this accident . . . . . . iii 3 1
My gracious prince, and honourable peers, Hearing of your arrival . . iii 4 1
This is my servant: hear him, noble prince.—And this is mine . . iv 1 80
What infamy will there arise, When foreign princes shall be certified! . iv 1 144
Blame him not; I dare presume, sweet prince, he thought no harm . iv 1 179
Princes should be free.—And so shall you . . . . . v 3 114
I do embrace thee, as I would embrace The Christian prince, King Henry . . . . v 3 172
His insolence is more intolerable Than all the princes in the land *2 Hen. VI.* i 1 176
As did the fatal brand Althæa burn'd Unto the prince's heart of Calydon i 1 235
Edward the Black Prince died before his father . . . . . ii 2 18
I think I am thy married wife And thou a prince, protector of this land ii 4 29
Sometime I'll say, I am Duke Humphrey's wife, And he a prince and ruler of the land: Yet so he ruled and such a prince he was . . ii 4 43
And princes' courts be fill'd with my reproach . . . . . iii 2 69
Stay, Whitmore; for thy prisoner is a prince . . . . . iv 1 44
Inspired with the spirit of putting down kings and princes . . . iv 2 39
And show'd how well you love your prince and country . . . iv 9 16
Heart, be wrathful still: Priests pray for enemies, but princes kill . v 2 71
What wrong is this unto the prince your son! . . . *3 Hen. VI.* i 1 176
Why, that is spoken like a toward prince . . . . . . ii 2 66
All which secure and sweetly he enjoys, Is far beyond a prince's delicates ii 5 51
Warwick is a subtle orator, And Lewis a prince soon won with moving words . . . . iii 1 34
Thy father Henry did usurp; And thou no more art prince than she is queen . . . . iii 3 80

Prince. After that wise prince, Henry the Fifth . . . *3 Hen. VI.* iii 3 85
Renowned prince, how shall poor Henry live, Unless thou rescue him? iii 3 214
And, as occasion serves, this noble queen And prince shall follow . . iii 3 237
If our queen and this young prince agree, I'll join mine eldest daughter and my joy To him forthwith in holy wedlock bands . . . . iii 3 241
O brave young prince! thy famous grandfather Doth live again in thee v 4 52
But if you ever chance to have a child, Look in his youth to have him so cut off As, deathsmen, you have rid this sweet young prince! . v 5 67
So come to you and yours, as to this prince! . . . . . v 5 82
King Henry and the prince his son are gone: Clarence, thy turn is next v 6 89
Hath she forgot already that brave prince, Edward, her lord? *Rich. III.* i 2 240
That cropp'd the golden prime of this sweet prince, And made her widow i 2 248
Princes have but their titles for their glories, An outward honour for an inward toil . . . . i 4 78
Which of you, if you were a prince's son, Being pent from liberty, as I am now, If two such murderers as yourselves came to you, Would not entreat for life? . . . . i 4 266
A begging prince what beggar pities not? . . . . . . i 4 274
Bethink you, like a careful mother, Of the young prince your son . . ii 2 97
You cloudy princes and heart-sorrowing peers . . . . . ii 2 112
That, with some little train, Forthwith from Ludlow the young prince be fetch'd . . . . ii 2 121
Therefore I say . . . That it is meet so few should fetch the prince . ii 2 139
Whoever journeys to the prince, For God's sake, let not us two be behind ii 2 146
I long with all my heart to see the prince: I hope he is much grown . ii 4 4
How fares the prince?—Well, madam, and in health . . . . ii 4 40
Welcome, sweet prince, to London, to your chamber . . . . iii 1 1
Sweet prince, the untainted virtue of your years Hath not yet dived into the world's deceit . . . . iii 1 7
The tender prince Would fain have come with me to meet your grace . iii 1 28
This prince hath neither claim'd it nor deserved it . . . . . iii 1 51
You said that idle weeds are fast in growth: The prince my brother hath outgrown me far . . . . iii 1 104
He for his father's sake so loves the prince, That he will not be won . iii 1 165
The princes both make high account of you . . . . . iii 2 71
God keep the prince from all the pack of you! . . . . . iii 3 5
That no manner of person At any time have recourse unto the princes . iii 5 109
This prince is not an Edward! He is not lolling on a lewd day-bed . iii 7 71
Happy were England, would this gracious prince Take on himself the sovereignty thereof . . . . iii 7 78
Between two clergymen!—Two props of virtue for a Christian prince . iii 7 96
Famous Plantagenet, most gracious prince, Lend favourable ears . . iii 7 100
This Edward, whom our manners term the prince . . . . . iii 7 191
To the Tower, On pure heart's love to greet the tender princes . . iv 1 4
Upon the like devotion as yourselves, To gratulate the gentle princes . iv 1 10
Pray you, by your leave, How doth the prince, and my young son of York? . . . . iv 1 14
Old sullen playfellow For tender princes, use my babies well! . . iv 1 103
Ha! am I king? 'tis so: but Edward lives.—True, noble prince.—O bitter consequence, That Edward still should live! 'True, noble prince!' . . . . iv 2 15
Ah, my young princes! ah, my tender babes! My unblown flowers! . iv 4 9
Hidest thou that forehead with a golden crown, Where should be graven, if that right were right, The slaughter of the prince that owed that crown? . . . . iv 4 142
If thou hadst fear'd to break an oath by Him, The imperial metal, circling now thy brow, Had graced the tender temples of my child, And both the princes had been breathing here . . . . . iv 4 384
The wronged souls Of butcher'd princes fight in thy behalf . . v 3 122
And hither make, as great ambassadors From foreign princes *Hen. VIII.* i 4 56
Like a most royal prince, Restored me to my honours . . . . ii 1 113
This imperious man will work us all From princes into pages . . ii 2 48
Your grace has given a precedent of wisdom Above all princes . . ii 2 87
A prince most prudent, of an excellent And unmatch'd wit and judgement . . . . ii 4 46
The wisest prince that there had reign'd by many A year before . . ii 4 49
The hearts of princes kiss obedience, So much they love it . . . iii 1 162
In all you writ to Rome, or else To foreign princes, 'Ego et Rex meus' iii 2 314
O, how wretched Is that poor man that hangs on princes' favours! . iii 2 367
There is, betwixt that smile we would aspire to, That sweet aspect of princes, and their ruin, More pangs and fears . . . . . iii 2 369
He was a man Of an unbounded stomach, ever ranking Himself with princes . . . . iv 2 35
Such a prince; Not only good and wise, but most religious . . v 3 115
If a prince May be beholding to a subject, I Am, for his love and service v 3 156
A pattern to all princes living with her, And all that shall succeed . v 5 23
The princes orgulous, their high blood chafed, Have to the port of Athens sent their ships . . . . *Troi. and Cres.* Prol. 2
Princes, What grief hath set the jaundice on your cheeks? . . i 3 1
Why then, you princes, Do you with cheeks abash'd behold our works? i 3 17
May one, that is a herald and a prince, Do a fair message to his kingly ears? . . . . i 3 218
We have, great Agamemnon, here in Troy A prince call'd Hector . i 3 261
Kings, princes, lords! If there be one among the fair'st of Greece That holds his honour higher than his ease . . . . i 3 264
Fair prince, here is good broken music . . . . . . iii 1 52
Now, princes, for the service I have done you, The advantage of the time prompts me aloud To call for recompense . . . . . iii 3 1
They will almost Give us a prince of blood, a son of Priam, In change . iii 3 26
Let him be sent, great princes, And he shall buy my daughter . . iii 3 27
And, princes all, Lay negligent and loose regard upon him . . . iii 3 40
Who is that there?—It is the Lord Æneas.—Is the prince there in person? . . . . iv 1 2
So please you, save the thanks this prince expects . . . . iv 4 119
The prince must think me tardy and remiss, That swore to ride before him . . . . iv 4 143
Princes, enough, so please you.—I am not warm yet; let us fight again iv 5 117
Welcome, princes all.—So now, fair Prince of Troy, I bid good night . v 1 77
You are moved, prince; let us depart, I pray you . . . . v 2 36
What hath she done, prince, that can soil our mothers?—Nothing at all v 2 134
Have with you, prince. My courteous lord, adieu. Farewell, revolted fair! . . . . v 2 185
Courage, princes! great Achilles Is arming, weeping, cursing, vowing vengeance . . . . v 5 30
Princes, that strive by factions and by friends Ambitiously for rule *T. Andron.* i 1 18
Content thee, prince; I will restore to thee The people's hearts . . i 1 210
This prince in justice seizeth but his own . . . . . . i 1 281
Think you not how dangerous It is to jet upon a prince's right? . . ii 1 64
Wake the emperor and his lovely bride And rouse the prince . . . ii 2 5

Prince. Conflict such as was supposed The wandering prince and Dido once enjoy'd . . . . *T. Andron.* ii 3 22
You princes of the Goths, The Roman emperor greets you all by me . v 1 156
And bring with him Some of the chiefest princes of the Goths . . v 2 125
And hear the sentence of your moved prince . . *Rom. and Jul.* i 1 95
And fought on part and part, Till the prince came, who parted either part . . . . i 1 122
The prince expressly hath Forbidden bandying in Verona streets . . iii 1 91
The prince's near ally, My very friend, hath got his mortal hurt . iii 1 114
The prince will doom thee death, If thou art taken : hence, be gone ! . iii 1 139
Up, sir, go with me ; I charge thee in the prince's name, obey . iii 1 145
O noble prince, I can discover all The unlucky manage of this fatal brawl . . . . iii 1 147
O prince ! O cousin ! husband ! O, the blood is spilt Of my dear kinsman ! Prince, as thou art true, For blood of ours, shed blood of Montague . . . . iii 1 152
I beg for justice, which thou, prince, must give . . . iii 1 185
Father, what news ? what is the prince's doom ? . . . . iii 3 4
I bring thee tidings of the prince's doom.—What less than dooms-day is the prince's doom ? . . . . iii 3 8
The kind prince, Taking thy part, hath rush'd aside the law . . . iii 3 25
Unless philosophy can make a Juliet, Displant a town, reverse a prince's doom, It helps not, it prevails not . . . . . iii 3 59
Till we can find a time To blaze your marriage, reconcile your friends, Beg pardon of the prince . . . . iii 3 152
Go, tell the prince : run to the Capulets : Raise up the Montagues . v 3 177
Hold him in safety, till the prince come hither . . . . v 3 183
The heavens themselves blaze forth the death of princes . *J. Cæsar* ii 2 31
How like a deer, strucken by many princes, Dost thou here lie ! . . iii 1 209
Lord Hamlet is a prince, out of thy star ; This must not be . *Hamlet* ii 2 141
This army of such mass and charge Led by a delicate and tender prince iv 4 48
Good night, sweet prince ; And flights of angels sing thee to thy rest ! . v 2 370
That thou so many princes at a shot So bloodily hast struck . . . v 2 377
The princes, France and Burgundy, Great rivals . . . *Lear* i 1 46
Thus Kent, O princes, bids you all adieu . . . . . i 1 189
Could my good brother suffer you to do it ? A man, a prince, by him so benefited ! . . . . iv 2 45
False to thy gods, . . . Conspirant 'gainst this high-illustrious prince . v 3 135
Let sorrow split my heart, if ever I Did hate thee or thy father !—Worthy prince, I know't . . . . v 3 178
The greatest prince o' the world, The noblest . . . *Ant. and Cleo.* iv 15 54
Then revolve what tales I have told you Of courts, of princes *Cymbeline* iii 3 15
In simple and low things to prince it much Beyond the trick of others iii 3 85
This attempt I am soldier to, and will abide it with A prince's courage iii 4 187
Though you took his life, as being our foe, Yet bury him as a prince . iv 2 251
Their blood thinks scorn, Till it fly out and show them princes born iv 4 54
Dangerous fellow, hence ! Breathe not where princes are . . . v 5 238
He was a prince.—A most incivil one : the wrongs he did me Were nothing prince-like . . . . v 5 291
These gentle princes—For such and so they are—these twenty years Have I train'd up . . . . v 5 336
Whom I call Polydore, Most worthy prince, as yours, is true Guiderius v 5 358
Our brother ; Joy'd are we that you are.—Your servant, princes . . v 5 425
The beauty of this sinful dame Made many princes thither frame *Per.* i Gower 32
Yon sometimes famous princes, like thyself, Drawn by report, adventurous by desire . . . . i 1 34
I bequeath a happy peace to you And all good men, as every prince should do . . . . i 1 51
Instantly this prince must die ; For by his fall my honour must keep high . . . . i 1 148
Prince, pardon me, or strike me, if you please ; I cannot be much lower i 2 46
If there be such a dart in princes' frowns, How durst thy tongue move anger to our face ? . . . . i 2 53
Fit counsellor and servant for a prince, Who by thy wisdom makest a prince thy servant . . . . i 2 63
From whence an issue I might propagate, Are arms to princes . . i 2 74
Open to the listening air How many worthy princes' bloods were shed i 2 88
Thou show'dst a subject's shine, I a true prince . . . . i 2 124
A better prince and benign lord, That will prove awful . . ii Gower 3
To fulfil his prince' desire, Sends word of all that haps in Tyre ii Gower 21
He, good prince, having all lost, By waves from coast to coast is tost ii Gower 33
Let it suffice the greatness of your powers To have bereft a prince of all ii 1 9
There are princes and knights come from all parts of the world to just and tourney for her love . . . . ii 1 114
Princes are A model, which heaven makes like to itself : As jewels lose their glory if neglected, So princes their renowns if not respected . ii 2 10
Had princes sit, like stars, about his throne, And he the sun . . ii 3 39
Princes in this should live like gods above, Who freely give to every one that comes To honour them : And princes not doing so are like to gnats . . . . ii 3 59
Wrong not your prince you love.—Wrong not yourself, then . . . ii 4 25
Thou art the rudeliest welcome to this world That ever was prince's child iii 1 31
This prince, the fair-betrothed of your daughter, Shall marry her . . v 3 71
Prince Dauphin, you shall stay with us in Rouen . . *Hen V.* iii 5 64
Prince Florizel. When sawest thou the Prince Florizel, my son ? *W. Tale* iv 2 29
One that gives out himself Prince Florizel, Son of Polixenes . . . v 1 85
Prince-like. The wrongs he did me Were nothing prince-like *Cymbeline* v 5 293
Prince Lucifer. More deep damn'd than Prince Lucifer . . *K. John* iv 3 122
Prince of Arragon hath ta'en his oath . . . *Mer. of Venice* ii 9 2
Prince of cats. More than prince of cats, I can tell you *Rom. and Jul.* ii 4 19
Prince of chivalry. Brave Troilus ! the prince of chivalry ! . *Tr. and Cr.* i 2 249
Prince of darkness. The black prince, sir ; alias, the prince of darkness ; alias, the devil . . . . *All's Well* iv 5 44
The prince of darkness is a gentleman : Modo he's call'd, and Mahu *Lear* iii 4 148
Prince of fiends. Impious war, Array'd in flames like to the prince of fiends . . . . *Hen. V.* iii 3 16
Prince of Ithaca. Hear Ulysses speak.—Speak, Prince of Ithaca *T. and C.* i 3 70
Prince of Morocco. There is a forerunner come from a fifth, the Prince of Morocco . . . . *Mer. of Venice* i 2 137
Prince of palfreys. It is the prince of palfreys . . . *Hen. V.* iii 7 29
Prince of plackets. Dread prince of plackets, king of codpieces *L. L. Lost* iii 1 186
Prince of Wales. I am the last of noble Edward's sons, Of whom thy father, Prince of Wales, was first . . . . . *Richard II.* ii 1 172
That same sword-and-buckler Prince of Wales . . . *1 Hen. IV.* i 3 230
Though I be but Prince of Wales, yet I am the king of courtesy . . ii 4 10
You Prince of Wales !—Why, you whoreson round man, what's the matter ? . . . . ii 4 154
The Prince of Wales and I Must have some private conference . . iii 2 1
The nimble-footed madcap Prince of Wales, And his comrades . . iv 1 95
And, Prince of Wales, so dare we venture thee . . . . . v 1 101
Prince of Wales. The Prince of Wales stepp'd forth before the king *1 Hen. IV.* v 2 46
It is the Prince of Wales that threatens thee ; Who never promiseth but he means to pay . . . . v 4 42
Nor can one England brook a double reign, Of Harry Percy and the Prince of Wales . . . . v 4 67
The Prince of Wales ! Where is he ? let me see him . . *2 Hen. IV.* iv 5 54
That black name, Edward, Black Prince of Wales . . . *Hen. V.* ii 4 56
Edward the Plack Prince of Wales, as I have read in the chronicles . iv 7 97
Seven sons : The first, Edward the Black Prince, Prince of Wales *2 Hen. VI.* ii 2 11
Edward thy son, which now is Prince of Wales, For Edward my son, which was Prince of Wales . . . . *Richard III.* i 3 199
Prince Paris. Had I so good occasion to lie long As you, Prince Paris *Troi. and Cres.* iv 1 4
Princely. He was The ivy which had hid my princely trunk *Tempest* i 2 86
Princes and counties ! Surely, a princely testimony, a goodly count ! *Much Ado* iv 1 317
Submissive fall his princely feet before . . . *L. L. Lost* iv 1 92
But what warmth is there in your affection towards any of these princely suitors ? . . . . *Mer. of Venice* i 2 38
Did ever Dian so become a grove As Kate this chamber with her princely gait ? O, be thou Dian ! . . . . . *T. of Shrew* ii 1 261
Is less frequent to his princely exercises than formerly . . *W. Tale* iv 2 37
The aweless lion could not wage the fight, Nor keep his princely heart from Richard's hand . . . . *K. John* i 1 267
If . . . thy princely son Can in this book of beauty read 'I love' . ii 1 484
O death, made proud with pure and princely beauty ! . . . iv 3 35
Come I appellant to this princely presence . . . *Richard II.* i 1 34
Never gentle lamb more mild Than was that young and princely gentleman . . . . ii 1 175
You debase your princely knee To make the base earth proud with kissing it . . . . iii 3 190
But neither my good word nor princely favour . . . . v 6 42
And hold their level with thy princely heart . . *1 Hen. IV.* iii 2 17
Thou hast lost thy princely privilege With vile participation . . iii 2 86
Trimm'd up your praises with a princely tongue . . . . v 2 57
Belike then my appetite was not princely got . . . *2 Hen. IV.* ii 2 12
If I should weep ?—I would think thee a most princely hypocrite . . ii 2 58
Here come I from our princely general To know your griefs . . iv 1 141
I take your princely word for these redresses . . . . iv 2 66
The weasel Scot Comes sneaking and so sucks her princely eggs *Hen. V.* i 2 171
He is as full of valour as of kindness ; Princely in both . . . iv 3 16
Joy and good wishes To our most fair and princely cousin ! . . . v 2 4
Which of this princely train Call ye the warlike Talbot ? . *1 Hen. VI.* ii 2 34
Rise created princely Duke of York . . . . . . iii 1 173
The princely Charles of France, thy countryman . . . . iii 3 38
Pardon me, princely Henry, and the rest . . . . . iv 1 18
Thou princely leader of our English strength, Never so needful . iv 3 17
Ay, beauty's princely majesty is such, Confounds the tongue . . v 3 70
This her easy-held imprisonment Hath gain'd thy daughter princely liberty . . . . v 3 140
Upon thy princely warrant, I descend To give thee answer . . . v 3 143
To woo her little worth To be the princely bride of such a lord . . v 3 152
But hark you, Margaret ; No princely commendations to my king ? . v 3 176
This great favour done, In entertainment to my princely queen *2 Hen. VI.* i 1 72
The princely Warwick, and the Nevils all . . . . . iv 1 91
Thy hand is made to grasp a palmer's staff, And not to grace an awful princely sceptre . . . . v 1 98
Do right unto this princely Duke of York . . . *3 Hen. VI.* i 1 166
I wonder how our princely father 'scaped, Or whether he be 'scaped away ii 1 1
The noble Duke of York was slain, Your princely father . . . ii 1 47
If thou be that princely eagle's bird, Show thy descent . . . ii 1 91
I mean our princely father, Duke of York . . . . . ii 6 51
Whose arms gave shelter to the princely eagle . . . . v 2 12
Love my lovely queen ; And kiss your princely nephew . . . . v 7 27
O princely Buckingham, I'll kiss thy hand, In sign of league *Richard III.* i 3 280
Brave Plantagenet, That princely novice, was struck dead by thee . i 4 228
When that our princely father York Bless'd his three sons . . . i 4 241
Now, princely Buckingham, seal thou this league With thy embracements ii 1 29
And, princely peers, a happy time of day !—Happy, indeed . . . ii 1 47
Amongst this princely heap, if any here . . . Hold me a foe . . ii 1 53
But now two mirrors of his princely semblance Are crack'd in pieces . ii 2 51
Persuade the queen to send the Duke of York Unto his princely brother iii 1 34
Who, as thou know'st, are dear To princely Richard and to Buckingham iii 2 70
And for my sister and her princely sons, Be satisfied, dear God . . iii 3 20
Noble York My princely father then had wars in France . . . iii 5 88
If, with pure heart's love, Immaculate devotion, holy thoughts, I tender not thy beauteous princely daughter ! . . . . . . iv 4 405
Where is princely Richmond now ?—At Pembroke, or at Ha'rford-west iv 5 6
In bestowing, madam, He was most princely . . . . *Hen. VIII.* iv 2 57
And by me Sends you his princely commendations . . . . iv 2 118
Hath so far Given ear to our complaint, of his great grace And princely care . . . . v 1 49
All princely graces, That mould up such a mighty piece as this is . . v 5 26
Let me confirm my princely brother's greeting . . *Troi. and Cres.* iv 5 174
Most princely Troilus . . . . iv 5 279
I, that now Refused most princely gifts, am bound to beg . *Coriolanus* i 9 80
Princely shall be thy usage every way . . . . *T. Andron.* i 1 266
True nobility Warrants these words in princely courtesy . . . i 1 272
If ever Tamora Were gracious in those princely eyes of thine, Then hear me . . . . i 1 429
The lion moved with pity did endure To have his princely paws pared all away . . . . ii 3 152
You're fall'n into a princely hand, fear nothing . . *Ant. and Cleo.* v 2 22
The princely blood flows in his cheek . . . . . *Cymbeline* iii 3 93
And make me put into contempt the suits Of princely fellows . . . iii 4 93
Thou divine Nature, how thyself thou blazon'st In these two princely boys ! . . . . iv 2 171
Our foe was princely . . . . iv 2 249
This gentleman, my Cadwal, Arviragus, Your younger princely son . v 5 360
Which foreshow'd our princely eagle, The imperial Cæsar . . . v 5 473
I thought it princely charity to grieve them . . . . *Pericles* i 2 100
From him I come With message unto princely Pericles . . . i 3 33
Give her princely training, that she may be Manner'd as she is born . iii 3 16
Princess. And thou his only heir And princess no worse issued *Tempest* i 2 59
Here Have I, thy schoolmaster, made thee more profit Than other princesses . . . . i 2 173
Or vainly comes the admired princess hither . . . *L. L. Lost* i 1 141
Fair princess, welcome to the court of Navarre.—'Fair' I give you back ii 1 90

Princess. Dear princess, were not his requests so far From reason's yielding, your fair self should make A yielding 'gainst some reason in my breast . . . . . *L. L. Lost* ii 1 150
You may not come, fair princess, in my gates . . . ii 1 172
It is but this: The princess comes to hunt here in the park . iii 1 165
And I say beside that, 'twas a pricket that the princess killed iv 2 49
To humour the ignorant, call I the deer the princess killed a pricket . iv 2 52
The preyful princess pierced and prick'd a pretty pleasing pricket . iv 2 58
In your tears There is no certain princess that appears . iv 3 156
The king's most sweet pleasure and affection to congratulate the princess v 1 93
Present the princess, sweet chuck, with some delightful ostentation . v 1 117
What would you with the princess?—Nothing but peace and gentle visitation . . . . v 2 178
The princess bids you tell How many inches doth fill up one mile . v 2 192
Fair sir, God save you! Where's the princess?—Gone to her tent . v 2 310
My faith and this the princess I did give . . . . . v 2 454
O, let me kiss This princess of pure white, this seal of bliss! *M. N. Dream* iii 2 144
Fair princess, you have lost much good sport . . *As Y. Like It* i 2 105
The princesses call for you.—I attend them with all respect and duty . i 2 175
Young man, have you challenged Charles the wrestler?—No, fair princess i 2 180
Hisperia, the princess' gentlewoman, Confesses that she secretly o'erheard . . . . ii 2 10
Cesario is your servant's name, fair princess.—My servant, sir! *T. Night* iii 1 108
To read thus: therefore perpend, my princess, and give ear . v 1 307
For ever Unvenerable be thy hands, if thou Takest up the princess by that forced baseness! . . . . *W. Tale* ii 3 78
There present yourself and your fair princess, For so I see she must be iv 4 555
Kisses the hands Of your fresh princess . . . . . iv 4 562
Prince Florizel, Son of Polixenes, with his princess . . . v 1 86
His princess, say you, with him?—Ay, the most peerless piece of earth v 1 93
Most dearly welcome! And your fair princess,—goddess!—O, alas! . v 1 131
She lifted the princess from the earth, and so locks her in embracing . v 2 83
The princess hearing of her mother's statue . . . . v 2 102
The prince my brother and the princess my sister called my father father v 2 154
She in beauty, education, blood, Holds hand with any princess *K. John* ii 1 494
I knit my handkercher about your brows, The best I had, a princess wrought it me . . . . iv 1 43
Dat is de princess.—The princess is the better Englishwoman *Hen. V.* v 2 123
Mock me mercifully; the rather, gentle princess, because I love thee cruelly . . . . v 2 215
Teach you our princess English?—I would have her learn, my fair cousin, how perfectly I love her . . . . v 2 308
Say, gentle princess, would you not suppose Your bondage happy, to be made a queen? . . . . *1 Hen. VI.* v 3 110
Acquaint the princess With the sweet silent hours of marriage joys *Richard III.* iv 4 329
Katharine no more Shall be call'd queen, but princess dowager *Hen. VIII.* iii 2 70
I beseech you, what's become of Katharine, The princess dowager? . iv 1 23
Six miles off From Ampthill where the princess lay . . iv 1 28
Make way there for the princess.—You great fellow, Stand close up v 4 91
She shall be, to the happiness of England, An aged princess . . v 5 58
And fitting for a princess Descended of so many royal kings *A. and C.* v 2 329
He that hath miss'd the princess is a thing Too bad for bad report *Cymb.* i 1 16
We must forbear: here comes the gentleman, The queen, and princess . i 1 69
Be not angry, Most mighty princess, that I have adventured . . i 6 172
Alas, poor princess, Thou divine Imogen, what thou endurest! . . ii 1 61
The princess!—Good morrow, fairest: sister, your sweet hand . ii 3 90
I have belied a lady, The princess of this country, and the air on't Revengingly enfeebles me . . . . v 2 3
And here the bracelet of the truest princess That ever swore her faith v 5 416
A most virtuous princess.—And she is fair too, is she not? *Pericles* ii 5 34
Yet a princess To equal any single crown o' the earth . . iv 3 7
Thou shalt kneel, and justify in knowledge She is thy very princess v 1 220
Principal. Forgive a moiety of the principal . . *Mer. of Venice* iv 1 26
Give me my principal, and let me go . . . . . iv 1 336
Shall I not have barely my principal? . . . . . iv 1 342
Can you remember any of the principal evils that he laid to the charge of women?—There were none principal . . *As Y. Like It* iii 2 369
Within ten year it will make itself ten, which is a goodly increase; and the principal itself not much the worse . . . *All's Well* i 1 161
She should shame to know herself But with her most vile principal *W. T.* ii 1 92
Culling the principal of all the deer . . . *3 Hen. VI.* iii 1 4
The very principals did seem to rend, And all-to topple . *Pericles* iii 2 16
Hath your principal made known unto you who I am?—Who is my principal? . . . . iv 6 89
Principality. If not divine, Yet let her be a principality . *T. G. of Ver.* ii 4 152
To the boy Cæsar send this grizzled head, And he will fill thy wishes to the brim With principalities . . . . *Ant. and Cleo.* iii 13 19
Principle. These warlike principles Do not throw from you *All's Well* ii 1 1
That need must needs infer this principle . . . *K. John* iii 1 213
If I had a thousand sons, the first humane principle I would teach them should be, to forswear thin potations . . *2 Hen. IV.* iv 3 133
Princox. You are a princox; go: Be quiet . . . *Rom. and Jul.* i 5 88
Pring. There is also another device in my prain, which peradventure prings goot discretions with it . . . . *Mer. Wives* i 1 44
He is come to me and prings me pread and salt yesterday, look you *Hen. V.* v 1 9
Print. Abhorred slave, Which any print of goodness wilt not take! *Temp.* i 2 352
All this I speak in print, for in print I found it . . *T. G. of Ver.* ii 1 175
These are of the second edition: he will print them, out of doubt; for he cares not what he puts into the press . . . *Mer. Wives* ii 1 79
We are soft as our complexions are, And credulous to false prints *Meas. for. Meas.* ii 4 130
An thou wilt needs thrust thy neck into a yoke, wear the print of it *Much Ado* i 1 203
His heart, like an agate, with your print impress'd . *L. L. Lost* ii 1 236
I will do it, sir, in print . . . . iii 1 173
We quarrel in print, by the book . . . . *As Y. Like It* v 4 94
Although the print be little, the whole matter And copy of the father *W. Tale* ii 3 98
I love a ballad in print o' life, for then we are sure they are true . . iv 4 264
She did print your royal father off, Conceiving you . . . v 1 125
Nor attend the foot That leaves the print of blood where'er it walks *K. John* iv 3 26
Heaven guide thy pen to print thy sorrows plain! . *T. Andron.* iv 1 75
Some more time Must wear the print of his remembrance out *Cymbeline* ii 3 48
Printed. Could she here deny The story that is printed in her blood? *Much Ado* iv 1 124
O, could this kiss be printed in thy hand! . . . *2 Hen. VI.* iii 2 343
Printing their proud hoofs i' the receiving earth . . *Hen. V.* Prol. 27
Thou hast caused printing to be used . . . . *2 Hen. VI.* iv 7 39

Printless. And ye that on the sands with printless foot Do chase the ebbing Neptune . . . . *Tempest* v 1 34
Prioress. You must not speak with men But in the presence of the prioress . . . . *Meas. for Meas.* i 4 11
Priority. The planets and this centre Observe degree, priority and place *Troi. and Cres.* i 3 86
We must follow you; Right worthy you priority . . *Coriolanus* i 1 251
Priory. This is some priory. In, or we are spoil'd! . *Com. of Errors* v 1 37
Our abbeys and our priories shall pay This expedition's charge *K. John* i 1 48
Priscian! a little scratched, 'twill serve . . . *L. L. Lost* v 1 31
Priser. Why would you be so fond to overcome The bonny priser of the humorous duke? . . . . *As Y. Like It* ii 3 8
Prison. Who hadst deserved more than a prison . . . *Tempest* i 2 362
Might I but through my prison once a day Behold this maid . . i 2 490
Space enough Have I in such a prison . . . . . i 2 493
To close prison he commanded her, With many bitter threats *T. G. of Ver.* iii 1 235
There's one yonder arrested and carried to prison was worth five thousand of you all . . . . *Meas. for Meas.* i 2 61
Claudio to prison? 'tis not so.—Nay, but I know 'tis so: I saw him arrested . . . . i 2 66
Here comes Signior Claudio, led by the provost to prison . . i 2 119
Fellow, why dost thou show me thus to the world? Bear me to prison i 2 121
Your brother kindly greets you: Not to be weary with you, he's in prison . . . . i 4 25
I come to visit the afflicted spirits Here in the prison . . ii 3 5
Take him to prison, officer: Correction and instruction must both work . . . . iii 2 32
Art going to prison, Pompey?—Yes, faith, sir.—Why, 'tis not amiss . iii 2 63
Commend me to the prison, Pompey: you will turn good husband now iii 2 73
Go; away with her to prison!—Good my lord, be good to me . . iii 2 201
In our prison a common executioner, who in his office lacks a helper . iv 2 9
Hath he borne himself penitently in prison? . . . . iv 2 148
He hath evermore had the liberty of the prison; give him leave to escape hence, he would not . . . . iv 2 156
In the prison, father, There died this morning of a cruel fever One Ragozine . . . . iv 3 73
I know you'ld fain be gone. An officer! To prison with her! . v 1 121
She and that friar, I saw them at the prison: a saucy friar . v 1 135
Away with him to prison!—What can you vouch against him? . v 1 325
I met you at the prison, in the absence of the duke.—O, did you so? . v 1 331
Such a fellow is not to be talked withal. Away with him to prison! . v 1 349
One in the prison, That should by private order else have died . v 1 470
That shall bail me: . . . On, officer, to prison till it come *Com. of Errors* iv 1 108
Not that Adam that kept the Paradise, but that Adam that keeps the prison . . . . iv 3 17
Let me not be pent up, sir: I will fast, being loose.—No, sir; that were fast and loose: thou shalt to prison . . . *L. L. Lost* i 2 163
Carry me to the gaol!—Stay, officer: he shall not go to prison.—I say he shall go to prison . . . . . *T. of Shrew* v 1 98
Take her away; I do not like her now; To prison with her . *All's Well* v 3 283
What, ho, I say! peace in this prison! . . . . *T. Night* iv 2 21
Away with her! to prison! He who shall speak for her is afar off guilty But that he speaks . . . . *W. Tale* ii 1 103
When you shall know your mistress Has deserved prison, then abound in tears . . . . ii 1 120
The keeper of the prison, call to him; Let him have knowledge who I am . . . . ii 2 1
No court in Europe is too good for thee; What dost thou then in prison? ii 2 4
A grave unto a soul; Holding the eternal spirit, against her will, In the vile prison of afflicted breath . . . . . . *K. John* iii 4 19
So I were out of prison and kept sheep, I should be as merry as the day is long; And so I would be here . . . . . . iv 1 17
This is the prison. What is he lies here? . . . . iv 3 34
To seek sweet safety out In vaults and prisons . . . . v 2 143
I have been studying how I may compare This prison where I live unto the world . . . . *Richard II.* v 5 2
Indeed I had the most of them out of prison . . *1 Hen. IV.* iv 2 45
And roughly send to prison The immediate heir of England! . *2 Hen. IV.* v 2 70
Is in base durance and contagious prison . . . . . v 5 36
A Christian king; Unto whose grace our passion is as subject As are our wretches fetter'd in our prisons . . . . . *Hen. V.* i 2 243
In prison hast thou spent a pilgrimage . . . *1 Hen. VI.* ii 5 116
For prisoners ask'st thou? hell our prison is . . . . iv 7 58
Away with them to prison; and the day of combat shall be the last of the next month . . . . *2 Hen. VI.* i 3 223
To prison back again; From thence unto the place of execution . ii 3 5
Go, lead the way; I long to see my prison . . . . . ii 4 110
Thou hast put them in prison; and because they could not read, thou hast hanged them . . . . iv 7 48
I'll yield myself to prison willingly, Or unto death, to do my country good . . . . iv 9 42
Ah, let me live in prison all my days; And when I give occasion of offence, Then let me die, for now thou hast no cause . *3 Hen. VI.* i 3 43
Now my soul's palace is become a prison . . . . . ii 1 74
To tell you plain, I had rather lie in prison . . . . iii 2 70
O Pomfret, Pomfret! O thou bloody prison! . . . *Richard III.* iii 3 9
May his highness live in freedom, And this man out of prison? *Hen. VIII.* i 2 201
There is a slave, whom we have put in prison, Reports . *Coriolanus* iv 6 38
Sacrifice his flesh, Before this earthy prison of their bones . *T. Andron.* i 1 99
Sirs, drag them from the pit unto the prison . . . . ii 3 283
My heart, all mad with misery, Beats in this hollow prison of my flesh iii 2 10
Shut up in prison, kept without my food, Whipp'd and . *Rom. and Jul.* i 2 56
To prison, eyes, ne'er look on liberty! Vile earth, to earth resign! . iii 2 58
Now Ventidius is wealthy too, Whom he redeem'd from prison *T. of A.* iii 3 4
Let prisons swallow 'em, Debts wither 'em to nothing! . . . iv 3 537
What have you, my good friends, deserved at the hands of fortune, that she sends you to prison hither?—Prison, my lord! . . *Hamlet* ii 2 246
Denmark's a prison.—Then is the world one.—A goodly one; in which there are many confines, wards and dungeons . . . . ii 2 249
To me it is a prison.—Why then, your ambition makes it one . . ii 2 257
An anchor's cheer in prison be my scope! . . . . . iii 2 229
Let's away to prison: We two alone will sing like birds i' the cage *Lear* v 3 8
And we'll wear out, In a wall'd prison, packs and sects of great ones . v 3 18
Go follow them to prison: One step I have advanced thee . . v 3 27
He hath commission from thy wife and me To hang Cordelia in the prison v 3 253
To prison, till fit time Of law and course of direct session Call thee *Othello* i 2 85
Therefore be cheer'd; Make not your thoughts your prisons *Ant. and Cleo.* v 2 185
Good wax, thy leave . . . Though forfeiters you cast in prison, yet You clasp young Cupid's tables . . . . . *Cymbeline* iii 2 38
A prison for a debtor, that not dares To stride a limit . . . iii 3 34

Prison gates. Shivering shocks Shall break the locks Of prison gates *M. N. Dream* i 2 36

Prison-house. I am forbid To tell the secrets of my prison-house *Hamlet* i 5 14

Prison walls. These vain weak nails May tear a passage through the flinty ribs Of this hard world, my ragged prison walls *Richard II.* v 5 21

Prisoned. Our cage We make a quire, as doth the prison'd bird *Cymbeline* iii 3 43

Prisoner. All prisoners, sir, In the line-grove *Tempest* v 1 9

His eyes . . . , I think she holds them prisoners still *T. G. of Ver.* ii 4 92

The jury, passing on the prisoner's life, May in the sworn twelve have a thief or two Guiltier than him they try *Meas. for Meas.* ii 1 19

I would tell what 'twere to be a judge, And what a prisoner ii 2 69

You have paid the heavens your function, and the prisoner the very debt of your calling iii 2 264

I am going to visit the prisoner. Fare you well iii 2 272

One that is a prisoner nine years old iv 2 135

Now, sir, how do you find the prisoner?—A creature unprepared iv 3 70

This is another prisoner that I saved, Who should have died v 1 492

I am thy prisoner: wilt thou suffer them To make a rescue? *Com. of Errors* iv 4 113

Let him go: He is my prisoner, and you shall not have him iv 4 115

In her bosom I'll unclasp my heart And take her hearing prisoner *Much Ado* i 1 326

I discharge thee of thy prisoner, and I thank thee v 1 328

I would take Desire prisoner, and ransom him to any French courtier *L. L. Lost* i 2 65

It is not for prisoners to be too silent in their words i 2 168

In which cage of rushes I am sure you are not prisoner *As Y. Like It* iii 2 390

As prisoners to her womanly persuasion *T. of Shrew* v 2 120

Force me to keep you as a prisoner, Not like a guest *W. Tale* i 2 52

How say you? My prisoner? or my guest? i 2 55

Your guest, then, madam: To be your prisoner should import offending i 2 57

Says 'My poor prisoner, I am innocent as you' ii 2 28

This child was prisoner to the womb ii 2 59

Produce the prisoner.—It is his highness' pleasure that the queen Appear iii 2 8

Is not Angiers lost? Arthur ta'en prisoner? *K. John* iii 4 7

Again commit them to their bonds, Because my poor child is a prisoner iii 4 75

Are not you grieved that Arthur is his prisoner?—As heartily as he is glad iii 4 123

This arm of mine, Now prisoner to the palsy *Richard II.* ii 3 104

To whose flint bosom my condemned lord Is doom'd a prisoner v 1 4

Of prisoners, Hotspur took Mordake the Earl of Fife *1 Hen. IV.* i 1 70

What think you, coz, Of this young Percy's pride? the prisoners, Which he in this adventure hath surprised, To his own use he keeps i 1 92

Those prisoners in your highness' name demanded, Which Harry Percy here at Holmedon took, Were, as he says, not with such strength denied i 3 23

My liege, I did deny no prisoners i 3 29

Amongst the rest, demanded My prisoners in your majesty's behalf i 3 48

Yet he doth deny his prisoners, But with proviso and exception i 3 77

Send me your prisoners with the speediest means i 3 120

He will, forsooth, have all my prisoners i 3 140

Those same noble Scots That are your prisoners,— I'll keep them all i 3 213

Those prisoners you shall keep.—Nay, I will; that's flat i 3 218

Once more to your Scottish prisoners. Deliver them up without their ransom i 3 259

Of prisoners' ransom and of soldiers slain ii 3 57

Unless thou yield thee as my prisoner.—I was not born a yielder v 3 10

The hulk Sir John, Is prisoner to your son *2 Hen. IV.* i 1 20

Then was that noble Worcester Too soon ta'en prisoner i 1 126

To fill King Edward's fame with prisoner kings *Hen. V.* i 2 162

In a captive chariot into Rouen Bring him our prisoner iii 5 55

Who will go to hazard with me for twenty prisoners? iii 7 94

Then every soldier kill his prisoners; Give the word through iv 6 37

Most worthily, hath caused every soldier to cut his prisoner's throat iv 7 10

What prisoners of good sort are taken, uncle? iv 8 80

Like prisoners wildly overgrown with hair v 2 43

O no, he lives; but is took prisoner, And Lord Scales with him *1 Hen. VI.* i 1 145

How wert thou handled being prisoner? i 4 24

The Duke of Bedford had a prisoner Call'd the brave Lord Ponton i 4 27

If thou be he, then art thou prisoner.—Prisoner! to whom? ii 3 33

Was not the Duke of Orleans thy foe? And was he not in England prisoner? iii 3 70

Seven walled towns of strength, Beside five hundred prisoners of esteem iii 4 8

And divers gentlemen beside Were there surprised and taken prisoners iv 1 26

I come to know what prisoners thou hast ta'en And to survey the bodies of the dead.—For prisoners ask'st thou? hell our prison is iv 7 56

Be what thou wilt, thou art my prisoner. O fairest beauty, do not fear! v 3 45

So doth the swan her downy cygnets save, Keeping them prisoner underneath her wings v 3 57

What ransom must I pay before I pass? For I perceive I am thy prisoner v 3 74

See, Reignier, see, thy daughter prisoner!—To whom?—To me v 3 131

Lord cardinal, he is your prisoner.—Sirs, take away the duke *2 Hen. VI.* iii 1 187

Master, this prisoner freely give I thee iv 1 12

Thy prisoner is a prince, The Duke of Suffolk, William de la Pole iv 1 44

If we mean to thrive and do good, break open the gaols and let out the prisoners iv 3 18

Upon thine honour, is he prisoner?—Upon mine honour, he is prisoner v 1 42

Your foe is taken, And brought your prisoner to your palace gate *3 Hen. VI.* iii 2 119

Then is my sovereign slain?—Ay, almost slain, for he is taken prisoner iv 4 7

Our king, my brother, Is prisoner to the bishop here iv 5 5

Henry is my king, Warwick his subject.—But Warwick's king is Edward's prisoner v 1 39

Henry, your sovereign, Is prisoner to the foe v 4 77

How hath your lordship brook'd imprisonment?—With patience, noble lord, as prisoners must *Richard III.* i 1 126

Lord Rivers and Lord Grey are sent to Pomfret, With them Sir Thomas Vaughan, prisoners ii 4 43

Then was I going prisoner to the Tower iii 2 102

Come, bring forth the prisoners iii 3 1

An untimely ague Stay'd me a prisoner in my chamber *Hen. VIII.* i 1 5

All the whole time I was my chamber's prisoner i 1 13

All's now done, but the ceremony Of bringing back the prisoner ii 1 5

It stands agreed, I take it, by all voices, that forthwith You be convey'd to the Tower a prisoner v 3 89

You have a Trojan prisoner, call'd Antenor, Yesterday took *T. and C.* iii 3 18

Bastard Margarelon Hath Doreus prisoner v 5 8

He cried to me; I saw him prisoner; But then Aufidius was within my view, And wrath o'erwhelm'd my pity *Coriolanus* i 9 84

Give us the proudest prisoner of the Goths, That we may hew his limbs, and on a pile Ad manes fratrum sacrifice his flesh *T. Andron.* i 1 96

Prisoner. I consecrate My sword, my chariot and my prisoners; Presents well worthy *T. Andron.* i 1 249

Now, madam, are you prisoner to an emperor i 1 258

Let us go: Ransomless here we set our prisoners free i 1 274

Whom thou in triumph long Hast prisoner held, fetter'd in amorous chains ii 1 15

Like a poor prisoner in his twisted gyves *Rom. and Jul.* ii 2 180

A sin that often Drowns him, and takes his valour prisoner *T. of Athens* iii 5 69

In Parthia did I take thee prisoner; And then I swore thee *J. Cæsar* v 3 37

A noble prisoner!—Room, ho! Tell Antony, Brutus is ta'en v 4 15

The insane root That takes the reason prisoner *Macbeth* i 3 85

And with a hideous crash Takes prisoner Pyrrhus' ear *Hamlet* ii 2 499

I alone became their prisoner. They have dealt with me like thieves of mercy iv 6 20

No rescue? What, a prisoner? I am even The natural fool of fortune *Lear* iv 6 194

Then am I the prisoner, and his bed my gaol iv 6 271

Take thou my soldiers, prisoners, patrimony; Dispose of them, of me v 3 75

You shall close prisoner rest, Till that the nature of your fault be known To the Venetian state *Othello* v 2 335

You're my prisoner, but Your gaoler shall deliver you the keys *Cymbeline* i 1 72

It is a manacle of love; I'll place it Upon this fairest prisoner i 1 123

This object, which Takes prisoner the wild motion of mine eye i 6 103

Knock off his manacles; bring your prisoner to the king v 4 200

We should not, when the blood was cool, have threaten'd Our prisoners with the sword v 5 78

I'll give it; Yea, though thou do demand a prisoner, The noblest ta'en v 5 99

Prisonment. May be he will not touch young Arthur's life, But hold himself safe in his prisonment *K. John* iii 4 161

Prisonnier. Encore qu'il est contre son jurement de pardonner aucun prisonnier, néanmoins, pour les écus *Hen. V.* iv 4 54

Pristine. In the disciplines of the pristine wars of the Romans iii 2 87

Find her disease, And purge it to a sound and pristine health *Macbeth* v 3 52

Prithee. Enforce them to this place, And presently, I prithee *Tempest* v 1 101

What, I prithee, might be the cause? *Meas. for Meas.* iii 2 141

But say, I prithee, is he coming home? *Com. of Errors* ii 1 55

Marry, I prithee, do, to make sport withal *As Y. Like It* i 2 29

I prithee now with most petitionary vehemence, tell me who it is iii 2 199

I prithee *Tempest* i 2; ii 1; ii 2; iii 2; *Meas. for Meas.* i 2; i 3; *As Y. Like It* ii 4; ii 5; iii 2; iii 4; *1 Hen. VI.* v 2; v 3; *2 Hen. VI.* ii 1; *3 Hen. VI.* ii 2; *Richard III.* iv 4; *Cymbeline* iv 2

Prithee (prefix) *Tempest* ii 1; ii 2; iii 2; iv 1; *Mer. Wives* iv 1; v 1; *As Y. Like It* i 2; i 3; *W. Tale* ii 2; *Hen VIII.* i 4; *Cymb.* iv 2

Privacy. Fie! privacy? fie! *Mer. Wives* iv 5 24

Of this my privacy I have strong reasons.—But 'gainst your privacy The reasons are more potent and heroical *Troi. and Cres.* iii 3 190

Private. The private wound is deepest *T. G. of Ver.* v 4 71

No, my good lord; it was by private message *Meas. for Meas.* v 1 465

One in the prison, That should by private order else have died v 1 471

Haply, in private.—And in assemblies too *Com. of Errors* iii 1 60

I would speak with you.—In private?—If it please you *Much Ado* iii 2 86

Let's hold more chat.—In private, then *L. L. Lost* v 2 229

Please it you, As much in private, and I'll bid adieu v 2 241

One word in private with you, ere I die v 2 254

I have some private schooling for you both *M. N. Dream* i 1 116

Who cries out on pride, That can therein tax any private party? *A. Y. L. It* ii 7 71

In respect that it is private, it is a very vile life iii 2 17

And the duke, For private quarrel twixt your duke and him, Hath publish'd and proclaim'd it openly *T. of Shrew* iv 2 84

He desires Some private speech with you *All's Well* ii 5 62

Let me enjoy my private: go off *T. Night* iii 4 100

He is a devil in private brawl iii 4 259

In private brabble did we apprehend him v 1 68

Whose private with me of the Dauphin's love Is much more general than these lines import *K. John* iv 3 16

Not Gaunt's rebukes, nor England's private wrongs *Richard II.* ii 1 166

With some few private friends iii 3 4

The Prince of Wales and I Must have some private conference *1 Hen. IV.* iii 2 2

I cannot put him to a private soldier that is the leader of so many thousands: let that suffice *2 Hen. IV.* iii 2 177

Do not you grieve at this; I shall be sent for in private to him v 5 83

That a poor and a private displeasure can do against a monarch *Hen. V.* iv 1 210

What infinite heart's-ease Must kings neglect, that private men enjoy! And what have kings, that privates have not too, Save ceremony? iv 1 254

There's nothing hid from me: In private will I talk with thee apart *1 Hen. VI.* i 2 69

Your private grudge, my Lord of York, will out iv 1 109

Let not your private discord keep away The levied succours iv 4 22

In substance and authority, Retain but privilege of a private man v 4 136

In this private plot be we the first *2 Hen. VI.* ii 2 60

I myself will lead a private life *3 Hen. VI.* iv 6 42

No man shall have private conference, Of what degree soever *Richard III.* i 1 86

The state takes notice of the private difference Betwixt you *Hen. VIII.* i 1 101

We are too open here to argue this; Let's think in private more ii 1 169

I left him private, Full of sad thoughts and troubles ii 2 15

How dare you thrust yourselves Into my private meditations? ii 2 66

I would your grace would give us but an hour Of private conference— We are busy ii 2 81

First I began in private With you, my Lord of Lincoln ii 4 206

Withdraw Into your private chamber, we shall give you The full cause iii 1 28

How innocent I was From any private malice in his end iii 2 268

More stirs against, Both in his private conscience and his place v 3 40

But a private man again, You shall know many dare accuse you v 3 55

For my private part, I am no more touch'd than all Priam's sons *Troi. and Cres.* ii 2 125

One that knows the youth Even to his inches, and with private soul Did in great Ilion thus translate him to me iv 5 111

I have wounds to show you, which shall be yours in private *Coriolanus* ii 3 84

He said he had wounds, which he could show in private ii 3 174

I offer'd to awaken his regard For's private friends v 1 24

Never admitted A private whisper v 3 7

Suits, Nor from the state nor private friends, hereafter Will I lend ear to v 3 18

You Volsces, mark; for we'll Hear nought from Rome in private v 3 93

Saucy controller of our private steps! *T. Andron.* ii 3 60

Over-heard them say, When I have walked like a private man v 4 75

And private in his chamber pens himself *Rom. and Jul.* i 1 144

Withdraw unto some private place, And reason coldly of your grievances iii 1 54

Nor are they such That these great towers, trophies and schools should fall For private faults in them *T. of Athens* v 4 26

For your private satisfaction, Because I love you *J. Cæsar* ii 2 73

What private griefs they have, alas, I know not, That made them do it iii 2 217

Private. He hath left you all his walks, His private arbours *J. Cæsar* iii 2 253
He hath very oft of late Given private time to you *Hamlet* i 3 92
'Faith, her privates we.—In the secret parts of fortune? ii 2 238
Let me ask you one word in private.—Importune him once more to go *Lear* iii 4 165
What! in a town of war, Yet wild, the people's hearts brimful of fear, To manage private and domestic quarrel! *Othello* ii 3 215
Is not almost a fault To incur a private check iii 3 67
What, To kiss in private?—An unauthorized kiss iv 1 2
'Tis not a time For private stomaching.—Every time serves for the matter that is then born in't *Ant. and Cleo.* ii 2 9
To thee sues To let him breathe between the heavens and earth, A private man in Athens iii 12 15
I'll tell you, sir, in private, if you please To give me hearing *Cymbeline* v 5 115
Our mind partakes Her private actions to your secrecy *Pericles* i 1 153
Who either by public war or private treason Will take away your life i 2 104
Not a man in private conference Or council has respect with him but he ii 4 17
Come, bring me to some private place iv 6 98
Privately. I think, if you handled her privately, she would sooner confess *Meas. for Meas.* v 1 277
Tell gentle Jessica I will not fail her; speak it privately *Mer. of Venice* ii 4 21
This night, We'll pass the business privately and well *T. of Shrew* iv 4 57
She hath privately twice or thrice a day, ever since the death of Hermione, visited that removed house *W. Tale* v 2 114
He hears nought privately that comes from Troy *Troi. and Cres.* i 3 249
Be it as you shall privately determine *Othello* i 3 276
Privilege. And think my patience, more than thy desert, Is privilege for thy departure hence *T. G. of Ver.* iii 1 160
And have you nuns no farther privileges? *Meas. for Meas.* i 4 1
It shall privilege him from your hands *Com. of Errors* v 1 95
Under privilege of age to brag What I have done being young *Much Ado* v 1 60
On my privilege I have with the parents of the foresaid child *L. L. Lost* iv 2 162
I beg the ancient privilege of Athens, As she is mine *M. N. Dream* i 1 41
Your virtue is my privilege ii 1 220
What should I get therefore?—A privilege never to see me more iii 2 79
Hadst thou not the privilege of antiquity upon thee *All's Well* ii 3 220
You need but plead your honourable privilege iv 5 96
With immodest hatred The child-bed privilege denied *W. Tale* iii 2 104
Some sins do bear their privilege on earth, And so doth yours *K. John* i 1 261
Impatience hath his privilege.—'Tis true, to hurt his master, no man else iv 3 32
Nearness to our sacred blood Should nothing privilege him *Richard. II.* i 1 120
A lunatic lean-witted fool, Presuming on an ague's privilege ii 1 116
Where no venom else But only they have privilege to live ii 1 158
Thou hast lost thy princely privilege With vile participation *1 Hen. IV.* iii 2 86
And an adopted name of privilege, A hare-brain'd Hotspur v 2 18
He bears him on the place's privilege *1 Hen. VI.* ii 4 86
I would see his heart out, ere the priest Should ever get that privilege of me iii 1 121
Discover thine infirmity, That warranteth by law to be thy privilege v 4 61
Yet, in substance and authority, Retain but privilege of a private man v 4 136
But if she be obdurate To mild entreaties, God in heaven forbid We should infringe the holy privilege Of blessed sanctuary! *Richard III.* iii 1 41
You break no privilege nor charter there iii 1 54
Or that we women had men's privilege Of speaking first *Troi. and Cres.* iii 2 136
The prayers of priests nor times of sacrifice, Embarquements all of fury, shall lift up Their rotten privilege and custom 'gainst My hate *Coriolanus* i 10 23
All bond and privilege of nature, break! Let it be virtuous to be obstinate v 3 25
Why, there's the privilege your beauty bears *T. Andron.* iv 2 116
Nor age nor honour shall shape privilege iv 4 57
Know you no reverence?—Yes, sir; but anger hath a privilege *Lear* ii 2 76
It is the privilege of mine honours, My oath, and my profession v 3 129
Privileged. Draw, men, for all this privileged place *1 Hen. VI.* i 3 46
Give no limits to my tongue: I am a king, and privileged to speak *3 Hen. VI.* ii 2 120
Nay, ladies, fear not; By all the laws of war you're privileged *Hen. VIII.* i 4 52
Peace, fool! I have not done.—He is a privileged man *Troi. and Cres.* ii 3 61
Let me be privileged by my place and message, To be a speaker free iv 4 132
Privilegio. Cum privilegio ad imprimendum solum *T. of Shrew* iv 4 93
They may, 'cum privilegio,' wear away The lag end of their lewdness and be laughed at *Hen. VIII.* i 3 34
Privily. Give me your hand: I'll privily away *Meas. for Meas.* i 1 68
Tell him privily of our intent *3 Hen. VI.* i 2 39
He privily Deals with our cardinal *Hen. VIII.* i 1 183
I will seek him, and privily relieve him *Lear* iii 3 15
Privity. Without the privity o' the king *Hen. VIII.* i 1 74
Privy. Myself am one made privy to the plot *T. G. of Ver.* iii 1 12
Told me what privy marks I had about me *Com. of Errors* iii 2 146
The other half Comes to the privy coffer of the state *Mer. of Venice* iv 1 354
Ay, and privy To this their late escape.—No, by my life, Privy to none of this *W. Tale* ii 1 94
Or, if he were not privy to those faults *2 Hen. VI.* iii 1 47
And yet the king not privy to my drift *3 Hen. VI.* i 2 46
Now will I in, to take some privy order *Richard III.* iii 5 106
Is the banquet ready I' the privy chamber? *Hen. VIII.* i 4 99
And to the marriage Her nurse is privy *Rom. and Jul.* v 3 266
If thou art privy to thy country's fate *Hamlet* i 1 133
You think none but your sheets are privy to your wishes *Ant. and Cleo.* i 2 42
Privy-council. And other of your highness' privy-council *2 Hen. VI.* ii 1 176
And one, already, of the privy council *Hen. VIII.* iv 1 112
Privy-kitchen. His face is Lucifer's privy-kitchen *2 Hen. IV.* ii 4 360
Prize. Volumes that I prize above my dukedom *Tempest* i 2 168
Lest too light winning Make the prize light i 2 452
I Beyond all limit of what else i' the world Do love, prize, honour you iii 1 73
The prize I'll bring thee to Shall hoodwink this mischance iv 1 205
A prize, a prize, a prize! *T. G. of Ver.* v 4 121
She is my prize, or ocean whelm them all! *Mer. Wives* ii 2 143
What we have we prize not to the worth Whiles we enjoy it *Much Ado* iv 1 220
Prize you yourselves: what buys your company? *L. L. Lost* v 2 224
Is that my prize? are my deserts no better? *Mer. of Venice* ii 9 60
Like one of two contending in a prize, That thinks he hath done well iii 2 142
If ever he go alone again, I'll never wrestle for prize more *As Y. Like It* i 1 168
I will compound this strife: 'Tis deeds must win the prize *T. of Shrew* ii 1 344
Tell her, my love, Prizes not quantity of dirty lands *T. Night* ii 4 85
For life, I prize it As I weigh grief, which I would spare *W. Tale* iii 2 43
No life, I prize it not a straw, but for mine honour, Which I would free iii 2 111
A prize! a prize! If the springe hold, the cock's mine iv 3 31
Old sir, I know She prizes not such trifles as these are iv 4 368
More than was ever man's, I would not prize them Without her love iv 4 386
Prize. And is not this an honourable spoil? A gallant prize? *1 Hen. IV.* i 1 75
And, with a word, out-faced you from your prize ii 4 283
Shall bring this prize in very easily *2 Hen. IV.* iii 1 101
Contempt, And any thing that may not misbecome The mighty sender, doth he prize you at *Hen. V.* ii 4 119
A goodly prize, fit for the devil's grace! *1 Hen. VI.* v 3 33
Bring forth the soldiers of our prize *2 Hen. VI.* iv 1 8
I lost mine eye in laying the prize aboard iv 1 25
A prize, a prize! here's the Lord Say, which sold the towns in France iv 7 22
It is war's prize to take all vantages *3 Hen. VI.* i 4 59
Methinks, 'tis prize enough to be his son ii 1 20
Made prize and purchase of his lustful eye *Richard III.* iii 7 187
Men prize the thing ungain'd more than it is *Troi. and Cres.* i 2 315
If you'll confess he brought home noble prize—As you must needs ii 2 86
As place, riches, favour, Prizes of accident as oft as merit iii 3 83
He is my prize; I will not look upon v 6 10
These movers that do prize their hours At a crack'd drachma! *Coriolanus* i 5 5
Whose loves I prize As the dead carcasses of unburied men iii 3 121
You have play'd your prize: God give you joy, sir! *T. Andron.* i 1 399
I do prize it at my love before The reverend'st throat *T. of Athens* v 1 184
This is not Brutus, friend; but, I assure you, A prize no less *J. Cæsar* v 4 27
Oft 'tis seen the wicked prize itself Buys out the law *Hamlet* iii 3 59
Sir, I am made Of the self-same metal that my sister is, And prize me at her worth *Lear* i 1 72
A proclaim'd prize! Most happy! iv 6 230
He to-night hath boarded a land carack: If it prove lawful prize, he's made for ever *Othello* i 2 51
Prizes the virtue that appears in Cassio, And looks not on his evils ii 3 139
And to see how he prizes the foolish woman your wife! iv 1 186
And believe, Cæsar's no merchant, to make prize with you Of things that merchants sold *Ant. and Cleo.* v 2 183
Then had my prize Been less, and so more equal ballasting To thee *Cymb.* iii 6 77
A prize! a prize!—Half-part, mates, half-part *Pericles* iv 1 94
Prized. Having so ... excellent a wit As she is prized to have *M. Ado* iii 1 90
Of many faces, ... To have the touches dearest prized *As Y. Like It* iii 2 160
If you prized my lady's favour at any thing more than contempt *T. Night* ii 3 130
Which you prized Richer than sea and land *Troi. and Cres.* ii 2 91
To her own worth She shall be prized iv 4 136
A kinder value of the people than He hath hereto prized them at *Coriol.* ii 2 64
But you well know, Things of like value differing in the owners Are prized by their masters *T. of Athens* i 1 171
Is Cæsar with Antonius prized so slight? *Ant. and Cleo.* i 1 56
She gave it me, and said She prized it once *Cymbeline* ii 4 104
Prizer. But value dwells not in particular will; It holds his estimate and dignity As well wherein 'tis precious of itself As in the prizer *Troi. and Cres.* ii 2 56
Prizest. Faint-hearted Woodvile, prizest him 'fore me? *1 Hen. VI.* i 3 22
Probable. I'll resolve you, Which to you shall seem probable *Tempest* v 1 249
'Tis pretty, sure, and very probable! *As Y. Like It* iii 5 11
With what apology you think May make it probable need *All's Well* ii 4 52
And clap upon you two or three probable lies iii 6 107
The least of all these signs were probable *2 Hen. VI.* iii 2 178
It is spoke freely out of many mouths—How probable I do not know *Coriolanus* iv 6 65
I'll have't disputed on; 'Tis probable and palpable to thinking *Othello* i 2 76
Most probable That so she died *Ant. and Cleo.* v 2 356
It may be probable she lost it *Cymbeline* ii 4 115
Yet is't not probable To come alone iv 2 141
Probal. This advice is free I give and honest, Probal to thinking *Othello* ii 3 344
Probation. I, in probation of a sisterhood *Meas. for Meas.* v 1 72
And what he with his oath And all probation will make up full clear v 1 157
There is no consonancy in the sequel; that suffers under probation *T. N.* ii 5 142
Pass'd in probation with you, How you were borne in hand *Macbeth* iii 1 80
And of the truth herein This present object made probation *Hamlet* i 1 156
That the probation bear no hinge nor loop To hang a doubt on *Othello* iii 3 365
Which for more probation I can with ease produce *Cymbeline* v 5 362
Proceed. Mum, then, and no more. Proceed *Tempest* iii 2 59
Come, proceed.—Why, as I told thee, 'tis a custom with him iii 2 94
Muse not that I thus suddenly proceed *T. G. of Ver.* i 3 64
Which I was much unwilling to proceed in But for my duty ii 1 112
Well, proceed.—'Item: She hath more hair than wit iii 1 360
How easy it is to be such an offender.—Very well, sir; proceed *M. Wives* ii 2 197
Die, perish! Might but my bending down Reprieve thee from thy fate, it should proceed *Meas. for Meas.* iii 1 145
By cold gradation and well-balanced form We shall proceed with Angelo iv 3 105
But you are i' the wrong To speak before your time. Proceed v 1 87
Proceed, Solinus, to procure my fall *Com. of Errors* i 1 1
When you have seen more and heard more, proceed accordingly *M. Ado* iii 2 125
Ay me!—Shot, by heaven! Proceed, sweet Cupid *L. L. Lost* iv 3 22
O, some authority how to proceed iv 3 287
The conqueror is dismay'd. Proceed, good Alexander v 2 570
Name what part I am for, and proceed *M. N. Dream* i 2 21
Proceed, Moon.—All that I have to say, is, to tell you that the lanthorn is the moon v 1 260
The Venetian law Cannot impugn you as you do proceed *Mer. of Venice* iv 1 179
I charge you by the law, Proceed to judgement iv 1 240
Give me audience, good madam.—Proceed *As Y. Like It* iii 2 252
The marriage is not lawful.—Proceed, proceed: I'll give her iii 3 72
Proceed, proceed: we will begin these rites v 4 203
Proceed in practice with my younger daughter *T. of Shrew* ii 1 165
I said a gown.—Proceed.—'With a small compassed cape' iv 3 139
If thou proceed As high as word, my deed shall match thy meed *All's W.* ii 1 212
From lowest place when virtuous things proceed, The place is dignified ii 3 132
That what in time proceeds May token to the future our past deeds iv 2 62
Give me modest assurance if you be the lady of the house, that I may proceed in my speech *T. Night* i 5 193
Proceed in justice, which shall have due course *W. Tale* iii 2 6
Therefore proceed. But yet hear this iii 2 109
There is no truth at all i' the oracle: The sessions shall proceed iii 2 142
Proceed: No foot shall stir v 3 97
Orderly proceed To swear him in the justice of his cause *Richard II.* i 3 9
So we shall proceed Without suspicion iv 1 156
And it proceeds from policy, not love *2 Hen. IV.* iv 1 148
My learned lord, we pray you to proceed *Hen. V.* i 2 9
I'll canvass thee in thy broad cardinal's hat, If thou proceed in this thy insolence *1 Hen. VI.* i 3 37
And listen after Humphrey, how he proceeds *2 Hen. VI.* i 3 152
Proceed no straiter 'gainst our uncle Gloucester Than from true evidence iii 2 20
His brother's death Hath given them heart and courage to proceed iv 4 35
Her weakness, which, I think, proceeds From wayward sickness *Rich. III.* i 3 28

Proceed. Nothing can proceed that toucheth us Whereof I shall not have intelligence *Richard III.* iii 2 23
Against the form of law, Proceed thus rashly to the villain's death iii 5 43
That . . . is the point Of my petition.—Lady mine, proceed *Hen. VIII.* i 2 17
From this lady may proceed a gem To lighten all this isle ii 3 78
You may, then, spare that time.—Be't so. Proceed ii 4 5
That thus you should proceed to put me off ii 4 21
It's fit this royal session do proceed ii 4 66
It fits we thus proceed, or else no witness Would come against you v 1 107
Proceed, Thersites.—Agamemnon is a fool; Achilles is a fool *T. and C.* ii 3 61
Before we proceed any further, hear me speak.—Speak, speak *Coriolanus* i 1 1
Would you proceed especially against Caius Marcius?—Against him first i 1 26
No public benefit which you receive But it proceeds or comes from them i 1 157
They of Rome are enter'd in our counsels And know how we proceed i 2 3
Proceed, Cominius.—I shall lack voice ii 2 85
Temperately proceed to what you would Thus violently redress iii 1 219
Proceed by process; Lest parties, as he is beloved, break out iii 1 314
If you bring not Marcius, we'll proceed In our first way.—I'll bring him iii 1 333
Sir, I cannot tell: We must proceed as we do find the people v 6 16
I know from whence this same device proceeds *T. Andron.* iv 4 52
Proceed; directly.—Directly, I am going to Cæsar's funeral *J. Cæsar* iii 3 21
We will proceed no further in this business: He hath honour'd me *Macb.* i 7 31
So, proceed you.—'Fore God, my lord, well spoken *Hamlet* ii 2 487
But wilt thou hear me how I did proceed?—I beseech you v 2 27
If you violently proceed against him, mistaking his purpose, it would make a great gap in your own honour *Lear* i 2 89
Be govern'd by your knowledge, and proceed I' the sway of your own will iv 7 19
I humbly beseech you, proceed to the affairs of state *Othello* i 3 220
Proceed you in your tears. Concerning this, sir,—O well-painted passion! iv 1 267
I were damn'd beneath all depth in hell, But that I did proceed upon just grounds To this extremity v 2 138
The number of the ships behold, And so proceed accordingly *A. and C.* iii 9 4
Proceed.—First, her bedchamber,—Where, I confess, I slept not *Cymb.* ii 4 66
He hath a drug of mine; I pray his absence Proceed by swallowing that iii 5 58
Misinterpreting, We might proceed to cancel of your days *Pericles* i 1 113
Proceeded. We have with a leaven'd and prepared choice Proceeded to you *Meas. for Meas.* i 1 53
Proceeded well, to stop all good proceeding! *L. L. Lost* i 1 95
Proceeded further; cut me off the heads Of all the favourites *1 Hen. IV.* iv 3 85
Well proceeded, To warn false traitors from the like attempts *Rich. III.* iii 5 48
How far I have proceeded, Or how far further shall, is warranted *Hen. VIII.* ii 4 90
By particular consent proceeded Under your hands and seals ii 4 221
Proceeded The sweet degrees that this brief world affords *T. of Athens* iv 3 252
He will, after his sour fashion, tell you What hath proceeded *J. Cæsar* i 2 181
And then we will deliver you the cause, Why I, that did love Cæsar when I struck him, Have thus proceeded iii 1 183
Tell me Why you proceeded not against these feats, So crimeful *Hamlet* iv 7 6
How calm and gentle I proceeded still In all my writings *Ant. and Cleo.* v 1 75
Having thus far proceeded *Cymbeline* i 5 15
Not the wronger Of her or you, having proceeded but By both your wills ii 4 55
Proceeders. Quick proceeders, marry! *T. of Shrew* iv 2 11
Proceeding. I'll quickly cross By some sly trick blunt Thurio's dull proceeding *T. G. of Ver.* ii 6 41
And here an engine fit for my proceeding iii 1 138
And afterward determine our proceedings.—Even now about it! iii 2 97
To these violent proceedings all my neighbours shall cry aim *Mer. Wives* iii 2 44
If his own life answer the straitness of his proceeding *Meas. for Meas.* iii 2 270
Makes me unpregnant And dull to all proceedings iv 4 24
Proceeded well, to stop all good proceeding! *L. L. Lost* i 1 95
For it appears, by manifest proceeding *Mer. of Venice* iv 1 358
And make this haste as your own good proceeding *All's Well* ii 4 50
Not fearing the displeasure of your master, Which on your just proceeding I'll keep off v 3 236
Doth push on this proceeding *W. Tale* ii 1 179
Merciless proceeding by these French Confronts your city's eyes *K. John* ii 1 214
You shall have no cause To curse the fair proceedings of this day iii 1 97
You will but make it blush And glow with shame of your proceedings iv 1 114
Now, what says the world To your proceedings? iv 2 133
We swear A voluntary zeal and an unurged faith To your proceedings v 2 11
Will he to the king and lay open all our proceedings *1 Hen. IV.* ii 3 34
Mere dislike Of our proceedings kept the earl from hence iv 1 65
Is this proceeding just and honourable? *2 Hen. IV.* iv 2 110
I like this fair proceeding of the king's v 5 103
If little faults, proceeding on distemper, Shall not be wink'd at *Hen. V.* ii 2 54
The title thou usurp'st, Of benefit proceeding from our king *1 Hen. VI.* v 4 152
Such massacre And ruthless slaughters as are daily seen By our proceeding in hostility v 4 162
What plain proceeding is more plain than this? *2 Hen. VI.* ii 2 53
But a feigned friend to our proceedings *3 Hen. VI.* iv 2 11
I'll acquaint our duteous citizens With all your just proceedings *Rich. III.* iii 5 66
Be opposite all planets of good luck To my proceedings! iv 4 403
I shall anon advise you Further in the proceeding *Hen. VIII.* i 2 108
Nor no more assurance Of equal friendship and proceeding ii 4 18
In the divorce his contrary proceedings Are all unfolded iii 2 26
Follow me, sirs, and my proceedings eye *Troi. and Cres.* v 7 7
Come, we'll inform them Of our proceedings here *Coriolanus* ii 2 163
For testimony of her foul proceedings *T. Andron.* v 3 8
I have an interest in your hate's proceeding *Rom. and Jul.* iii 1 193
My dear dear love To your proceeding bids me tell you this *J. Cæsar* ii 2 103
A false creation, Proceeding from the heat-oppressed brain *Macbeth* ii 1 39
Till then, in patience our proceeding be *Hamlet* v 1 322
That then necessity Will call discreet proceeding *Lear* i 4 233
Let's then determine With the ancient of war on our proceedings v 1 32
Whoe'er he be that in this foul proceeding Hath thus beguiled your daughter of herself And you of her *Othello* i 3 65
And what mighty magic, For such proceeding I am charged withal i 3 93
To such proceeding Who ever but his approbation added *Pericles* iv 3 25
Process. In brief, to set the needless process by *Meas. for Meas.* v 1 92
And often at his very loose decides That which long process could not arbitrate *L. L. Lost* v 2 753
Tell her the process of Antonio's end *Mer. of Venice* iv 1 274
No other advantage in the process but only the losing of hope *All's Well* i 1 18
By law and process of great nature *W. Tale* ii 2 60
Much Beguiled The tediousness and process of my travel *Richard II.* ii 3 12
Ere the glass, that now begins to run, Finish the process of his sandy hour, These eyes . . . Shall see thee wither'd *1 Hen. VI.* iv 2 36
Thou shalt tell the process of their death. *Richard III.* iv 3 32
Be brief, lest that the process of thy kindness Last longer telling than thy kindness' date iv 4 253
After this process, To give her the avaunt! it is a pity *Hen. VIII.* ii 3 9
Process. If, in the course And process of this time, you can report, And prove it too, against mine honour aught *Hen. VIII.* ii 4 38
Witness the process of your speech *Troi. and Cres.* iv 1 8
Proceed by process; Lest parties, as he is beloved, break out *Coriolanus* iii 1 314
Denmark Is by a forged process of my death Rankly abused *Hamlet* i 5 37
Behind the arras I'll convey myself, To hear the process iii 3 29
Thou mayst not coldly set Our sovereign process iv 3 65
It was my hint to speak,—such was the process *Othello* i 3 142
Where's Fulvia's process? Cæsar's I would say? both? *Ant. and Cleo.* i 1 28
Procession. Come, go we in procession to the village *Hen. V.* iv 8 118
And all the priests and friars in my realm Shall in procession sing her endless praise *1 Hen. VI.* i 6 20
Here comes the townsmen on procession *2 Hen. VI.* ii 1 68
Process-server. He hath been since an ape-bearer; then a process-server, a bailiff *W. Tale* iv 3 102
Proclaim. Thine eye and cheek proclaim A matter from thee *Tempest* ii 1 229
I will proclaim myself what I am *Mer. Wives* iii 5 146
Hail, virgin, if you be, as those cheek-roses Proclaim! *Meas. for Meas.* i 4 17
These black masks Proclaim an enshield beauty ii 4 80
Seeming, seeming! I will proclaim thee, Angelo ii 4 151
And why should we proclaim it in an hour before his entering? iv 4 9
But that her tender shame Will not proclaim against her maiden loss, How might she tongue me! iv 4 27
That outward courtesies would fain proclaim Favours that keep within v 1 15
Proclaim it, provost, round about the city, Is any woman wrong'd v 1 514
Yet once again proclaim it publicly *Com. of Errors* v 1 130
The world's large tongue Proclaims you for a man replete with mocks *L. L. Lost* v 2 853
Make feasts, invite friends, and proclaim the banns *T. of Shrew* iii 2 16
I am not an impostor that proclaim Myself against the level of mine aim; But know I think and think I know. *All's Well* ii 1 158
Whom I proclaim a man of truth, of mercy *W. Tale* ii 2 158
In the hottest day prognostication proclaims iv 4 818
Other evidences proclaim her with all certainty to be the king's daughter v 2 42
To proclaim Arthur of Bretagne England's king and yours *K. John* ii 1 310
Did King Richard then Proclaim my brother Edmund Mortimer Heir to the crown? *1 Hen. IV.* i 3 156
Proclaim it, Westmoreland, through my host, That he which hath no stomach to this fight, Let him depart *Hen. V.* iv 3 34
And then I will proclaim young Henry king *1 Hen. VI.* i 1 169
In dumb significants proclaim your thoughts ii 4 26
What means this noise? Fellow, what miracle dost thou proclaim? *2 Hen. VI.* ii 1 60
Throughout every town Proclaim them traitors that are up with Cade iv 2 187
My lord! Jack Cade proclaims himself Lord Mortimer iv 4 28
And in the towns, as they do march along, Proclaims him king *3 Hen. VI.* ii 2 71
If you'll not here proclaim yourself our king, I'll leave you to your fortune iv 7 54
Brother, we will proclaim you out of hand; The bruit thereof will bring you many friends iv 7 63
Once again proclaim us king of England iv 8 54
I here proclaim myself thy mortal foe v 1 94
Proclaim a pardon to the soldiers fled *Richard III.* v 5 16
Or proclaim There's difference in no persons *Hen. VIII.* i 1 138
Whereupon the Grecians begin to proclaim barbarism *Troi. and Cres.* v 4 18
Proclaim our honours, lords, with trump and drum *T. Andron.* i 1 275
I do proclaim One honest man—mistake me not—but one *T. of Athens* iv 3 503
Run hence, proclaim, cry it about the streets *J. Cæsar* iii 1 79
I will proclaim my name about the field v 4 3
Rich, not gaudy; For the apparel oft proclaims the man *Hamlet* i 3 72
Proclaim no shame When the compulsive ardour gives the charge iii 4 85
That drop of blood that's calm proclaims me bastard iv 5 117
What I have done, That might your nature, honour and exception Roughly awake, I here proclaim was madness v 2 243
By his authority I will proclaim it *Lear* ii 1 62
Here's another, whose warp'd looks proclaim What store her heart is made on iii 6 56
Make after him, poison his delight, Proclaim him in the streets *Othello* i 1 69
Take the hint Which my despair proclaims *Ant. and Cleo.* iii 11 19
I have savage cause; And to proclaim it civilly, were like A halter'd neck which does the hangman thank For being yare about him iii 13 129
She sent you word she was dead; But, fearing since how it might work, hath sent Me to proclaim the truth iv 14 126
Her own price Proclaims how she esteem'd him *Cymbeline* i 1 52
When Signior Sooth here does proclaim a peace, He flatters you *Pericles* i 2 44
Our eyes do weep, Till tongues fetch breath that may proclaim them louder i 4 15
Why, the house you dwell in proclaims you to be a creature of sale iv 6 83
Proclaim that I can sing, weave, sew, and dance, With other virtues iv 6 194
Proclaimed. Hath this been proclaimed?—Four days ago *L. L. Lost* i 1 121
Contrary to thy established proclaimed edict i 1 262
It was proclaimed a year's imprisonment, to be taken with a wench i 1 289
It was proclaimed 'damsel.'—This was no damsel neither, sir; she was a virgin.—It is so varied too; for it was proclaimed 'virgin' i 1 293
Publish'd and proclaim'd it openly *T. of Shrew* iv 2 85
But that you are but newly come, You might have heard it else proclaim'd iv 2 87
This satisfaction The by-gone day proclaim'd *W. Tale* i 2 32
Myself on every post Proclaimed a strumpet iii 2 103
Whose daughter His tears proclaim'd his, parting with her v 1 160
Why have you not proclaim'd Northumberland And all the rest revolted faction traitors? *Richard II.* ii 2 56
What was his reason? . . . —Because your lordship was proclaimed traitor ii 3 30
Was not he proclaim'd By Richard that dead is the next of blood? *1 Hen. IV.* i 3 145
Proclaim'd at market-crosses, read in churches v 1 73
Join'd with an enemy proclaim'd *Hen. V.* ii 2 168
Be it death proclaimed through our host To boast of this or take that praise from God Which is his only iv 8 119
Agreed That peaceful truce shall be proclaim'd in France *1 Hen. VI.* v 4 117
And I proclaim'd a coward through the world! *2 Hen. VI.* i 1 43
King of England shalt thou be proclaim'd In every borough *3 Hen. VI.* i 1 194
Sound trumpet; Edward shall be here proclaim'd iv 7 69
Hath any well-advised friend proclaim'd Reward? *Richard III.* iv 4 517
The proclamation!—Thou art proclaimed a fool, I think *Troi. and Cres.* ii 1 26
This, sir, is proclaim'd through all our host ii 1 133
Have by the very cunning of the scene Been struck so to the soul that presently They have proclaim'd their malefactions *Hamlet* ii 2 621
I heard myself proclaim'd *Lear* ii 3 1

Proclaimed. A proclaim'd prize! Most happy! . . . . . *Lear* iv 6 230
Thou art in nothing else Than I have here proclaim'd thee . . . v 3 95
So much was his pleasure should be proclaimed . . . *Othello* ii 2 9
His sons he there proclaim'd the kings of kings . *Ant. and Cleo.* iii 6 13
Proclaimeth. And still proclaimeth, as he comes along . 2 *Hen. VI.* iv 9 28
Proclamation. What is your news?—Sir, there is a proclamation that you are vanished . . . . *T. G. of Ver.* iii 1 216
Is your countryman According to our proclamation gone? . . . iii 2 12
But, most of all, agreeing with the proclamation . . *Meas. for Meas.* i 2 81
The business he hath helmed must upon a warranted need give him a better proclamation . . . . iii 2 152
Did you hear the proclamation?—I do confess much of the hearing it, but little of the marking of it . . . . . *L. L. Lost* i 1 286
The dearest ring in Venice will I give you, And find it out by proclamation: Only for this, I pray you, pardon me . . *Mer. of Venice* iv 1 436
Invention is ashamed, Against the proclamation of thy passion *All's Well* i 3 180
These proclamations, So forcing faults upon Hermione . . *W. Tale* iii 1 15
Was not he proclaim'd By Richard that dead is the next of blood?—He was; I heard the proclamation . . . . . 1 *Hen. IV.* i 3 147
Nought rests for me in this tumultuous strife But to make open proclamation: Come, officer; as loud as e'er thou canst . 1 *Hen. VI.* i 3 71
Come, fellow-soldier, make thou proclamation . . 3 *Hen. VI.* iv 7 70
Is proclamation made, that who finds Edward Shall have a high reward? v 5 9
Such proclamation hath been made, my liege . . . *Richard III.* iv 4 519
The new proclamation That's clapp'd upon the court-gate *Hen. VIII.* i 3 17
Toadstool, learn me the proclamation . . . . *Troi. and Cres.* ii 1 22
The proclamation!—Thou art proclaimed a fool, I think . . . ii 1 25
I say, the proclamation!—Thou grumblest and railest every hour . . ii 1 34
I bade the vile owl go learn me the tenour of the proclamation . . ii 1 100
Be chosen with proclamations to-day, To-morrow yield up rule *T. Andron.* i 1 190
The bloody proclamation to escape, That follow'd me so near . *Lear* v 3 183
He offered to cut a caper at the proclamation . . . . *Pericles* iv 2 117
Proconsul. He creates Lucius proconsul . . . . . *Cymbeline* iii 7 8
Procrastinate. But to procrastinate his lifeless end . *Com. of Errors* i 1 159
Procreant. Leave procreants alone and shut the door . . *Othello* iv 2 28
But this bird Hath made his pendent bed and procreant cradle *Macbeth* i 6 8
Procreation. Twinn'd brothers of one womb, Whose procreation, residence, and birth, Scarce is dividant . . . . *T. of Athens* iv 3 4
Procrus. Not Shafalus to Procrus was so true.—As Shafalus to Procrus, I to you . . . . *M. N. Dream* v 1 200
Proculeius. None about Cæsar trust but Proculeius . *Ant. and Cleo.* iv 15 48
Come hither, Proculeius. Go and say, We purpose her no shame . . v 1 61
Gallus, go you along. Where's Dolabella, To second Proculeius? . . v 1 70
What's thy name?—My name is Proculeius.—Antony Did tell me of you v 2 12
Proculeius, What thou hast done thy master Cæsar knows . . . v 2 64
Procurator. As procurator to your excellence . . . . 2 *Hen. VI.* i 1 3
Procure. I shall procure-a you de good guest, de earl . *Mer. Wives* ii 3 95
You'll procure the vicar To stay for me at church 'twixt twelve and one iv 6 48
How doth my dear morsel, thy mistress? Procures she still, ha?
Meas. for Meas. iii 2 57
I am sorry that such sorrow I procure . . . . v 1 479
Procure my fall And by the doom of death end woes and all *Com. of Er.* i 1 1
Procure me music ready when he wakes . . . *T. of Shrew* Ind. 1 50
Procure your sureties for your days of answer . . . . *Richard II.* iv 1 159
I'll procure this fat rogue a charge of foot . . . . 1 *Hen. IV.* ii 4 597
He said, sir, you should procure him better assurance . . 2 *Hen. IV.* i 2 35
Something I must do to procure me grace . . . . 1 *Hen. VI.* i 4 7
Procure That Lady Margaret do vouchsafe to come . . . . . v 5 88
All these could not procure me any scathe . . . . 2 *Hen. VI.* ii 4 62
With all the friends that thou, brave Earl of March, Amongst the loving Welshmen canst procure . . . . 3 *Hen. VI.* ii 1 180
Procure knaves as corrupt To swear against you . . . *Hen. VIII.* v 1 132
Procure safe-conduct for his person . . . . . . *Troi. and Cres.* iii 3 276
Send me word to-morrow, By one that I'll procure to come *Rom. and Jul.* ii 2 145
What unaccustom'd cause procures her hither? . . . . . . iii 5 68
To wilful men, The injuries that they themselves procure Must be their schoolmasters . . . . *Lear* ii 4 306
That she will to virtuous Desdemona Procure me some access *Othello* iii 1 38
Procured. Have procured his leave For present parting . . *All's Well* ii 5 60
I have procured thee, Jack, a charge of foot . . . 1 *Hen. IV.* iii 3 208
Have you a catalogue Of all the voices that we have procured? *Coriol.* iii 3 9
Procuring. Fear no more tavern-bills; which are often the sadness of parting, as the procuring of mirth . . . . *Cymbeline* v 4 162
Prodigal. 'Tis painted about with the story of the Prodigal *Mer. Wives* iv 5 8
He that goes in the calf's skin that was killed for the Prodigal
Com. of Errors iv 3 19
As prodigal of all dear grace As Nature was in making graces dear
L. L. Lost ii 1 9
And spend his prodigal wits in bootless rhymes . . . . . v 2 64
Wherein my time something too prodigal Hath left me gaged *Mer. of Ven.* i 1 129
But yet I'll go in hate, to feed upon The prodigal Christian . . ii 5 15
Like a younker or a prodigal The scarfed bark puts from her native bay ii 6 14
How like the prodigal doth she return, With over-weather'd ribs! . ii 6 17
A bankrupt, a prodigal, who dare scarce show his head on the Rialto . iii 1 47
Shall I keep your hogs and eat husks with them? What prodigal portion have I spent, that I should come to such penury? *As Y. Like It* i 1 41
He's a very fool and a prodigal.—Fie, that you'll say so! . *T. Night* i 3 25
Then he compassed a motion of the Prodigal Son . . *W. Tale* iv 3 103
When the tongue's office should be prodigal To breathe the abundant dolour of the heart . . . . *Richard II.* i 3 256
Make their sire Stoop with oppression of their prodigal weight . . iii 4 31
You would think that I had a hundred and fifty tattered prodigals
1 *Hen. IV.* iv 2 37
For thy walls, a pretty slight drollery, or the story of the Prodigal
2 *Hen. IV.* ii 1 157
My noble gossips, ye have been too prodigal: I thank ye heartily
Hen. VIII. v 5 13
Thou tassel of a prodigal's purse, thou . . . . *Troi. and Cres.* v 1 37
The bounty of this lord! How many prodigal bits have slaves and peasants This night englutted! . . . . *T. of Athens* ii 2 174
You must consider that a prodigal course Is like the sun's . . . iii 4 12
Art thou proud yet?—Ay, that I am not thee.—I, that I was No prodigal iv 3 278
The chariest maid is prodigal enough, If she unmask her beauty to the moon: Virtue itself 'scapes not calumnious strokes . . *Hamlet* i 3 36
When the blood burns, how prodigal the soul Lends the tongue vows . i 3 116
Prodigality. Framed in the prodigality of nature, Young . *Richard III.* i 2 244
Prodigally. And prodigally gave them all to you . . . *L. L. Lost* ii 1 12
Prodigious. I have received my proportion, like the prodigious son, and am going . . . . *T. G. of Ver.* ii 3 4
Nor mark prodigious, such as are Despised in nativity . *M. N. Dream* v 1 419

Prodigious. Crooked, swart, prodigious, Patch'd with foul moles *K. John* iii 1 46
If ever he have child, abortive be it, Prodigious! . . . *Richard III.* i 2 22
It is prodigious, there will come some change . . *Troi. and Cres.* v 1 100
Prodigious birth of love it is to me . . . . . *Rom. and Jul.* i 5 142
A man no mightier than thyself or me In personal action, yet prodigious grown And fearful . . . . *J. Cæsar* i 3 77
Prodigiously. Lest that their hopes prodigiously be cross'd *K. John* iii 1 91
Prodigy. Some comet or unusual prodigy . . . . *T. of Shrew* iii 2 98
Meteors, prodigies and signs, Abortives, presages . . *K. John* iii 4 157
Now hath my soul brought forth her prodigy . . . *Richard II.* ii 2 64
An exhaled meteor, A prodigy of fear and a portent . . . 1 *Hen. IV.* v 1 20
Where's that valiant crook-back prodigy, Dicky your boy? . 3 *Hen. VI.* i 4 75
That so the shadows be not unappeased, Nor we disturb'd with prodigies on earth . . . . *T. Andron.* i 1 101
When these prodigies Do so conjointly meet, let not men say 'These are their reasons; they are natural' . . . . . . *J. Cæsar* i 3 28
These apparent prodigies, The unaccustom'd terror of this night . . ii 1 198
Proditor. Thou most usurping proditor, And not protector . 1 *Hen. VI.* i 3 31
Produce. All things in common nature should produce . . *Tempest* ii 1 159
You can produce acquittances For such a sum . . . *L. L. Lost* ii 1 161
Which to defeat, I must produce my power . . . . *All's Well* iii 3 157
Unless some one among us whom we must produce for an interpreter . iv 1 6
But loath am to produce So bad an instrument . . . . . . v 3 201
I had rather glib myself than they Should not produce fair issue *W. Tale* ii 1 150
Not able to produce more accusation Than your own weak-hinged fancy ii 3 118
Produce the prisoner.—It is his highness' pleasure that the queen Appear . . . . iii 2 8
Shall I produce the men?—Let them approach . . . *K. John* i 1 46
I can produce A will that bars the title of thy son . . . . ii 1 191
Being not mad but sensible of grief, My reasonable part produces reason iii 4 54
There is no bar To make against your highness' claim to France But this, which they produce from Pharamond . . . . . . *Hen. V.* i 2 37
Produce the grand sum of his sins . . . . . . *Hen. VIII.* iii 2 293
That I may Produce his body to the market-place . . . *J. Cæsar* iii 1 228
Ay, though thou didst produce My very character . . . . *Lear* ii 1 73
I can produce a champion that will prove What is avouched there . v 1 43
Produce their bodies, be they alive or dead . . . . . . v 3 230
Which for more probation I can with ease produce . . . *Cymbeline* v 5 363
Produced. In open market-place produced they me . . 1 *Hen. VI.* i 4 40
And that, without delay, their arguments Be now produced *Hen. VIII.* ii 4 68
It seems not meet, nor wholesome to my place, To be produced *Othello* i 1 147
Producing. An evil soul producing holy witness Is like a villain with a smiling cheek . . . . *Mer. of Venice* i 3 100
Producing forth the cruel ministers Of this dead butcher . *Macbeth* v 8 68
Proface! What you want in meat, we'll have in drink . 2 *Hen. IV.* v 3 30
Profanation. Void of all profanation in the world that good Christians ought to have . . . . *Meas. for Meas.* ii 1 55
Great men may jest with saints; 'tis wit in them, But in the less foul profanation.—Thou'rt i' the right . . . . ii 2 128
To your ears, divinity, to any other's, profanation . . . *T. Night* i 5 233
Profane. Ask him why, that hour of fairy revel, In their so sacred paths he dares to tread In shape profane . . . . . *Mer. Wives* iv 4 60
I profane my lips on thy foot, my eyes on thy picture . . *L. L. Lost* iv 1 86
O most divine Kate!—O most profane coxcomb! . . . . . iv 3 84
O, let no noble eye profane a tear For me. . . . . *Richard II.* i 3 59
My heart disdained that my tongue Should so profane the word . . i 4 13
And that word 'grace' In an ungracious mouth is but profane . . ii 3 89
Unless he do profane, steal, or usurp . . . . iii 3 81
Our holy lives must win a new world's crown, Which our profane hours here have stricken down . . . . v 1 25
I feel me much to blame, So idly to profane the precious time 2 *Hen. IV.* ii 4 391
So surfeit-swell'd, so old and so profane . . . . v 5 54
May these same instruments, which you profane, Never sound more!
Coriolanus i 9 41
If I profane with my unworthiest hand This holy shrine *Rom. and Jul.* i 5 95
We should profane the service of the dead To sing a requiem and such rest to her As to peace-parted souls . . . . *Hamlet* v 1 259
What profane wretch art thou? . . . . *Othello* i 1 115
I mine own gain'd knowledge should profane, If I would time expend with such a snipe . . . . i 3 390
Is he not a most profane and liberal counsellor?—He speaks home, madam . . . . ii 1 165
Profane fellow! Wert thou the son of Jupiter and no more But what thou art besides, thou wert too base To be his groom . *Cymbeline* ii 3 129
Profaned. Though his false finger have profaned the ring *T. G. of Ver.* iv 4 141
Had his great name profaned with their scorns . . . 1 *Hen. IV.* iii 2 64
Hear your own dignity so much profaned . . . . . 2 *Hen. IV.* v 2 93
By my George, my garter, and my crown,—Profaned, dishonour'd, and the third usurp'd . . . . *Richard III.* iv 4 367
The George, profaned, hath lost his holy honour . . . . . iv 4 369
Profanely. Not to speak it profanely . . . . *Hamlet* iii 2 34
Profaneness. Apollo, pardon My great profaneness 'gainst thine oracle!
W. Tale iii 2 155
Profaners of this neighbour-stained steel . . . . *Rom. and Jul.* i 1 89
Profaning this most honourable order . . . . . . 1 *Hen. VI.* iv 1 41
Profess. Almost persuaded,—For he's a spirit of persuasion, only Professes to persuade . . . . *Tempest* ii 1 236
And crown what I profess with kind event If I speak true! . . . iii 1 69
I profess requital to a hair's breadth . . . . . . *Mer. Wives* iv 2 3
She professes a hot-house, which, I think, is a very ill house *M. for M.* ii 1 66
He professes to have received no sinister measure from his judge . iii 2 256
By the saint whom I profess, I will plead against it with my life . iv 2 192
I profess curing it by counsel . . . . . . *As Y. Like It* iii 2 425
And since you do profess to be a suitor, You must, as we do, gratify this gentleman . . . . *T. of Shrew* i 2 272
I read that I profess, the Art to Love . . . . iv 2 8
In what he did profess, well found . . . . *All's Well* ii 1 105
He professes not keeping of oaths . . . . iv 3 282
Whether dost thou profess thyself, a knave or a fool? . . . . iv 5 23
Hear me, who profess Myself your loyal servant . . . . *W. Tale* ii 3 53
But to your protestation; let me hear What you profess . . . . iv 4 380
We profess Ourselves to be the slaves of chance and flies Of every wind iv 4 550
I profess not talking; only this—Let each man do his best . 1 *Hen. IV.* v 2 92
I do profess You speak not like yourself . . . . . *Hen. VIII.* ii 4 84
Pray, think us Those we profess, peace-makers, friends, and servants . iii 1 167
May you be happy in your wish, my lord! For, I profess, you have it . iii 2 44
I do profess That for your highness' good I ever labour'd . . . iii 2 190
He'll answer nobody; he professes not answering . *Troi. and Cres.* iii 3 270
Hear me profess sincerely . . . . *Coriolanus* i 3 24
If you know That I profess myself in banqueting . . . . *J. Cæsar* i 2 77

Profess. I conjure you, by that which you profess *Macbeth* iv 1 50
The day almost itself professes yours, And little is to do . . . v 7 27
I profess Myself an enemy to all other joys *Lear* i 1 74
What dost thou profess? what wouldst thou with us?—I do profess to be no less than I seem . . . . i 4 12
These fellows have some soul; And such a one do I profess myself *Othello* i 1 55
So much I challenge that I may profess Due to the Moor . . . i 3 188
Though I profess myself her adorer, not her friend . . *Cymbeline* i 4 73
I now Profess myself the winner of her honour . . . . . ii 4 53
I confess, I slept not, but profess Had that was well worth watching . ii 4 67
Professed. Rather rejoicing to see another merry, than merry at any thing which professed to make him rejoice . . . *Meas. for Meas.* iii 2 250
Lord Angelo hath to the public ear Profess'd the contrary . . . iv 2 103
Being a professed tyrant to their sex . . . . . *Much Ado* i 1 170
How long have you professed apprehension?—Ever since you left it . iii 4 68
Dishonour'd by a man which ever Profess'd to him . . . *W. Tale* i 2 456
A sin-absolver, and my friend profess'd . . . *Rom. and Jul.* iii 3 50
Yet thanks I must you con That you are thieves profess'd *T. of Athens* iv 3 429
Use well our father: To your professed bosoms I commit him . *Lear* i 1 275
I have professed me thy friend and I confess me knit to thy deserving with cables of perdurable toughness . . . . . . *Othello* i 3 342
Professest. For what thou professest, a baboon, could he speak, Would own a name too dear . . . . *Pericles* iv 6 189
Profession. You go against the hair of your professions . *Mer. Wives* ii 3 42
We do not know what's brought to pass under the profession of fortune-telling . . . . iv 2 184
I am as well acquainted here as I was in our house of profession *Meas. for Meas.* iv 3 2
And now by present profession a tinker . . . *T. of Shrew* Ind. 2 22
He was famous, sir, in his profession . . . . . *All's Well* i 1 29
My father's skill, which was the greatest Of his profession . . . i 3 250
In her sex, her years, profession, Wisdom and constancy, hath amazed me . . . . ii 1 86
Having flown over many knavish professions, he settled only in rogue *W. Tale* iv 3 105
Therein am I constant to my profession . . . . iv 4 698
For sport sake are content to do the profession some grace . *1 Hen. IV.* ii 1 78
I must not yield to any rites of love, For my profession's sacred *1 Hen. VI.* i 2 114
More than well beseems A man of thy profession and degree . . . iii 1 20
You tender more your person's honour than Your high profession *Hen. VIII.* ii 4 117
Wrong you? alas, our places, The way of our profession is against it . iii 1 157
There is boundless theft In limited professions . . *T. of Athens* iv 3 431
Has almost charmed me from my profession, by persuading me to it . iv 3 455
Without the sign Of your profession . . . . . *J. Cæsar* i 1 5
I had thought to have let in some of all professions . *Macbeth* ii 3 21
They hold up Adam's profession . . . . *Hamlet* v 1 35
It is the privilege of mine honours, My oath, and my profession . *Lear* v 3 130
Revengingly enfeebles me; or could this carl, A very drudge of nature's, have subdued me In my profession? . . . *Cymbeline* v 2 6
Neither is our profession any trade; it's no calling . . *Pericles* iv 2 42
When she should do for clients her fitment, and do me the kindness of our profession, she has me her quirks, her reasons . . . . iv 6 7
How long have you been of this profession?—E'er since I can remember iv 6 78
Makes our profession as it were to stink afore the face of the gods . iv 6 144
Professor. This is a creature, Would she begin a sect, might quench the zeal Of all professors else . . . . *W. Tale* v 1 108
I always thought It was both impious and unnatural That such immanity and bloody strife Should reign among professors of one faith . . . . *1 Hen. VI.* v 1 14
Woe upon ye And all such false professors! . . . *Hen. VIII.* iii 1 115
Proffers not took reap thanks for their reward . . *All's Well* ii 1 150
Why, what a candy deal of courtesy This fawning greyhound then did proffer me! . . . . *1 Hen. IV.* i 3 252
Proffers his only daughter to your grace In marriage . *1 Hen. VI.* v 1 19
For the proffer of my lord your master, I have inform'd his highness . v 1 41
This proffer is absurd and reasonless . . . . v 4 137
She should that duty leave unpaid to you, Which daily she was bound to proffer . . . . *Cymbeline* iii 5 49
He may my proffer take for an offence, Since men take women's gifts for impudence . . . . *Pericles* ii 3 68
Proffered. But if you fondly pass our proffer'd offer . . *K. John* ii 1 258
The proffer'd means of succour and redress . . . *Richard II.* iii 2 32
Laid gifts before him, proffer'd him their oaths . . *1 Hen. IV.* iv 3 71
If you frown upon this proffer'd peace, You tempt the fury *1 Hen. VI.* iv 2 9
Take to your royal self This proffer'd benefit of dignity . *Richard III.* iii 7 196
Refuse not, mighty lord, this proffer'd love . . . . . iii 7 202
Profferer. Since maids, in modesty, say 'no' to that Which they would have the profferer construe 'ay' . . . . . . *T. G. of Ver.* i 2 56
Proficient. I am so good a proficient in one quarter of an hour, that I can drink with any tinker . . . . *1 Hen. IV.* ii 4 19
Profit. Made thee more profit Than other princesses . . *Tempest* i 2 172
He does . . . Fetch in our wood and serves in offices That profit us . i 2 313
You taught me language; and my profit on't Is, I know how to curse . i 2 363
My son profits nothing in the world at his book . . *Mer. Wives* iv 1 15
Doth rebate and blunt his natural edge With profits of the mind *Meas. for Meas.* i 4 61
Correction and instruction must both work Ere this rude beast will profit . . . . iii 2 34
This nor hurts him nor profits you a jot . . . . . . iv 3 128
Have no more profit of their shining nights Than those that walk and wot not what they are . . . . *L. L. Lost* i 1 90
Their daughters profit very greatly under you . . . . . . iv 2 77
Is kind enough, but a huge feeder; Snail-slow in profit . *Mer. of Venice* ii 5 47
Since that the trade and profit of the city Consisteth of all nations . iii 3 30
Report speaks goldenly of his profit . . . . . *As Y. Like It* i 1 7
If you like upon report The soil, the profit and this kind of life . ii 4 98
If that an eye may profit by a tongue, Then should I know you . . iii 5 84
No profit grows where is no pleasure ta'en . . . *T. of Shrew* i 1 39
Profit you in what you read? . . . . iv 2 6
By my foes, sir, I profit in the knowledge of myself . . *T. Night* v 1 21
That bare eyes To see alike mine honour as their profits . . *W. Tale* i 2 310
And my profit therein the heaping friendships . . . . . iv 2 21
Noisome weeds, which without profit suck The soil's fertility *Richard II.* iii 4 38
Against the state and profit of this land . . . . . . iv 1 225
I shall sutler be Unto the camp, and profits will accrue . *Hen. V.* ii 1 117
That will not trust thee but for profit's sake . . *1 Hen. VI.* iii 3 63
Ill blows the wind that profits nobody . . . . *3 Hen. VI.* ii 5 55
In England But little for my profit . . . . . *Hen. VIII.* iii 1 83
Employ'd you where high profits might come home . . . . iii 2 158

Profit. To the good of your most sacred person and The profit of the state *Hen. VIII.* iii 2 174
Be silent, boy; I profit not by thy talk . . . *Troi. and Cres.* v 1 16
Then do we sin against our own estate, When we may profit meet, and come too late . . . . *T. of Athens* v 1 45
Profit again should hardly draw me here . . . . . *Macbeth* v 3 62
For the supply and profit of our hope . . . . . *Hamlet* ii 2 24
Their residence, both in reputation and profit, was better both ways . ii 2 344
To gain a little patch of ground That hath in it no profit but the name iv 4 19
The profits of my death Were very pregnant and potential spurs . *Lear* ii 1 77
I mine own gain'd knowledge should profane, If I would time expend with such a snipe, But for my sport and profit . . . . *Othello* i 3 392
The purchase made, the fruits are to ensue; That profit's yet to come . ii 3 10
Or keep you warm, Or sue to you to do a peculiar profit To your own person . . . . iii 3 79
I thank you for this profit; and from hence I'll love no friend . . iii 3 379
If you dare do yourself a profit and a right . . . . . iv 2 238
So find we profit By losing of our prayers . . . *Ant. and Cleo.* ii 1 7
'Tis not my profit that does lead mine honour; Mine honour, it . ii 7 82
To apprehend thus, Draws us a profit from all things we see . *Cymbeline* iii 3 18
We'll hunt no more to-day, nor seek for danger Where there's no profit iv 2 163
I speak against my present profit, but my wish hath a preferment in't v 4 214
Thou canst not do a thing in the world so soon, To yield thee so much profit. Let not conscience . . . Inflame too nicely . . *Pericles* iv 1 4
How have I offended, Wherein my death might yield her any profit? . iv 1 81
You must seem to . . . despise profit where you have most gain . . iv 2 128
But that pity begets you a good opinion, and that opinion a mere profit . . . . iv 2 132
Profitable. Flesh taken from a man Is not so estimable, profitable neither, As flesh of muttons . . . . . . *Mer. of Venice* i 3 167
The search, sir, was profitable . . . . *All's Well* ii 4 36
And follows so the ever-running year, With profitable labour *Hen. V.* iv 1 294
Profitably. Would I had a rod in my mouth, that I might answer thee profitably . . . . *T. of Athens* ii 2 80
The impediment most profitably removed . . . . . . *Othello* ii 1 286
Profited. Well read, and profited In strange concealments . *1 Hen. IV.* iii 1 166
Has not the boy profited? . . . . *2 Hen. IV.* ii 2 90
Profiting. Women! Help Heaven! men their creation mar In profiting by them . . . . *Meas. for Meas.* ii 4 128
God give thee the spirit of persuasion and him the ears of profiting *1 Hen. IV.* i 2 171
Profitless. As profitless As water in a sieve . . . *Much Ado* v 1 4
To wake and wage a danger profitless . . . . . . *Othello* i 3 30
Profound. Which of your hips has the most profound sciatica? *M. for M.* i 2 59
He is in earnest.—In most profound earnest . . . . *Much Ado* v 1 198
And profound Solomon to tune a jig . . . . . . *L. L. Lost* iv 3 168
A huge translation of hypocrisy, Vilely compiled, profound simplicity . v 2 52
With such a zealous laughter, so profound . . . . . . v 2 116
Dress'd in an opinion Of wisdom, gravity, profound conceit *Mer. of Venice* i 1 92
A magician, most profound in his art and yet not damnable *As Y. Like It* v 2 67
Are you a comedian?—No, my profound heart . . . . *T. Night* i 5 195
The profound seas hide In unknown fathoms . . . . *W. Tale* iv 4 501
I muse your majesty doth seem so cold, When such profound respects do pull you on . . . . *K. John* iii 1 318
A respect more tender, More holy and profound, than mine own life *Coriolanus* iii 3 113
Upon the corner of the moon There hangs a vaporous drop profound *Macbeth* iii 5 24
He raised a sigh so piteous and profound . . . . . *Hamlet* ii 1 94
There's matter in these sighs, these profound heaves . . . . iv 1 1
Profoundest. Conscience and grace, to the profoundest pit! . . . iv 5 132
Profoundly. Why sigh you so profoundly? . . . *Troi. and Cres.* iv 2 83
Progenitor. Usurp'd from you and your progenitors . . *Hen. V.* i 2 95
Like true subjects, sons of your progenitors, Go cheerfully together *1 Hen. VI.* iv 1 166
Have we not lost most part of all the towns, By treason, falsehood and by treachery, Our great progenitors had conquered? . . . . v 4 110
Progeny. Though the mourning brow of progeny Forbid the smiling courtesy of love . . . . *L. L. Lost* v 2 754
This same progeny of evils comes From our debate . . *M. N. Dream* ii 1 115
Doubting thy birth and lawful progeny . . . . . *1 Hen. VI.* iii 3 61
Not me begotten of a shepherd swain, But issued from the progeny of kings . . . . v 4 38
Wert thou the Hector That was the whip of your bragg'd progeny *Cor.* i 8 12
Progne. For worse than Philomel you used my daughter, And worse than Progne I will be revenged . . . . *T. Andron.* v 2 196
Prognostication. In the hottest day prognostication proclaims *W. Tale* iv 4 817
If an oily palm be not a fruitful prognostication . . *Ant. and Cleo.* i 2 54
Progress. And so in progress to be hatch'd and born . *Meas. for Meas.* ii 2 97
Of that and all the progress, more and less, Resolvedly more leisure shall express . . . . *All's Well* v 3 331
Let his silver water keep A peaceful progress to the ocean . *K. John* ii 1 340
Wipe off this honourable dew, That silverly doth progress on thy cheeks v 2 46
The hour before the heavenly-harness'd team Begins his golden progress in the east . . . . *1 Hen. IV.* iii 1 222
The happiest youth, viewing his progress through, What perils past, what crosses to ensue, Would shut the book, and sit him down and die . . . . *2 Hen. IV.* iii 1 54
The king is now in progress towards Saint Alban's . . *2 Hen. VI.* i 4 76
I' the progress of this business, Ere a determinate resolution . *Hen. VIII.* ii 4 175
In all the progress Both of my life and office, I have labour'd . . v 3 32
No pulse Shall keep his native progress, but surcease . *Rom. and Jul.* iv 1 97
I cannot, by the progress of the stars, Give guess how near to day *J. C.* ii 1 2
To show you how a king may go a progress through the guts of a beggar *Hamlet* iv 3 33
Progression. Which accidentally, or by the way of progression, hath miscarried . . . . *L. L. Lost* iv 2 144
Prohibit. If a merry meeting may be wished, God prohibit it! *Much Ado* v 1 33
Prohibition. Against self-slaughter There is a prohibition so divine That cravens my weak hand . . . . *Cymbeline* iii 4 79
Project. And sends me forth—For else his project dies . *Tempest* ii 1 299
Yet always bending Towards their project . . . . . . iv 1 175
Now does my project gather to a head: My charms crack not . . . v 1 1
Gentle breath of yours my sails Must fill, or else my project fails . Epil. 12
She cannot love, Nor take no shape nor project of affection . *Much Ado* iii 1 55
My project may deceive me, But my intents are fix'd . . *All's Well* iii 7 24
If your more ponderous and settled project May suffer alteration *W. Tale* iv 4 535
Flattering himself in project of a power . . . . *2 Hen. IV.* i 3 29
Hit or miss, Our project's life this shape of sense assumes *Troi. and Cres.* i 3 385
And cut off All fears attending on so dire a project . . . . ii 2 134

Project. Nay, let him choose Out of my files, his projects to accomplish, My best and freshest men . . . . . *Coriolanus* v 6 34
This project Should have a back or second, that might hold *Hamlet* iv 7 153
I cannot project mine own cause so well To make it clear *Ant. and Cleo.* v 2 121
Projection. Of a weak and niggardly projection . . *Hen. V.* ii 4 46
Prolixious. Lay by all nicety and prolixious blushes *Meas. for Meas.* ii 4 162
Prolixity. It is true, without any slips of prolixity . *Mer. of Venice* iii 1 13
The date is out of such prolixity *Rom. and Jul.* i 4 3
Prologue. To perform an act Whereof what's past is prologue *Tempest* ii 1 253
And, as it were, spoke the prologue of our comedy . *Mer. Wives* iii 5 75
Their shallow shows and prologue vilely penn'd *L. L. Lost* v 2 305
Write me a prologue; and let the prologue seem to say, we will do no harm with our swords . . *M. N. Dream* iii 1 18
We will have such a prologue; and it shall be written in eight and six . iii 1 24
Therefore another prologue must tell he is not a lion . . . iii 1 35
So please your grace, the Prologue is address'd . . . v 1 106
He hath rid his prologue like a rough colt . . . v 1 119
Indeed he hath played on his prologue like a child on a recorder . v 1 122
Which are the only prologues to a bad voice . *As Y. Like It* v 3 13
It is no more unhandsome than to see the lord the prologue . Epil. 3
Thus he his special nothing ever prologues . *All's Well* ii 1 95
Not so much as will serve to be prologue to an egg and butter *1 Hen. IV.* i 2 23
But mine is made the prologue to their play *2 Hen. VI.* iii 1 151
A prologue arm'd, but not in confidence Of author's pen *Troi. and Cres.* Prol. 23
No without-book prologue, faintly spoke After the prompter *R. and J.* i 4 7
Two truths are told, As happy prologues to the swelling act . *Macbeth* i 3 128
Preceding still the fates And prologue to the omen coming on *Hamlet* i 1 123
Is this a prologue, or the posy of a ring?—'Tis brief, my lord . iii 2 162
As sin's true nature is, Each toy seems prologue to some great amiss . iv 5 18
Ere I could make a prologue to my brains, They had begun the play . v 2 30
An index and obscure prologue to the history of lust *Othello* ii 1 264
Is he often thus?—'Tis evermore the prologue to his sleep . ii 3 134
Prologue-like your humble patience pray . *Hen. V.* Prol. 33
Prolong. I would prolong awhile the traitor's life . . *3 Hen. VI.* i 4 52
Be of any power To expel sickness, but prolong his hour! *T. of Athens* iii 1 66
This physic but prolongs thy sickly days . *Hamlet* iii 3 96
Prolonged. By misfortunes was my life prolong'd *Com. of Errors* i 1 120
This wedding-day Perhaps is but prolong'd: have patience . *Much Ado* iv 1 256
Not so well provided As else I would be, were the day prolong'd *Richard III.* iii 4 47
By medicine life may be prolong'd, yet death Will seize the doctor *Cymb.* v 5 29
Promethean. The books, the academes From whence doth spring the true Promethean fire . . *L. L. Lost* iv 3 304
From women's eyes this doctrine I derive: They sparkle still the right Promethean fire . . . iv 3 351
I know not where is that Promethean heat That can thy light relume *Othello* v 2 12
Prometheus. And faster bound to Aaron's charming eyes Than is Prometheus tied to Caucasus . *T. Andron.* ii 1 17
Promis. Pour les écus que vous l'avez promis, il est content de vous donner la liberté . . *Hen. V.* iv 4 55
Promise. Thou didst promise To bate me a full year . *Tempest* i 2 249
It is my promise, And they expect it from me . . iv 1 41
And promise you calm seas, auspicious gales, And sail so expeditious . v 1 314
I claim the promise for her heavenly picture *T. G. of Ver.* iv 4 92
Have you received no promise of satisfaction at her hands? . *Mer. Wives* ii 2 217
He promise to bring me where is Anne Page; by gar, he deceive me too iii 1 125
To build upon a foolish woman's promise . . . iii 5 43
She seemingly obedient likewise hath Made promise to the doctor iv 6 34
My mind promises with my habit no loss shall touch her *Meas. for Meas.* iii 1 181
Give him promise of satisfaction . . . iii 1 275
Many deceiving promises of life . . . iii 2 260
I made my promise Upon the heavy middle of the night To call upon him . . . iv 1 34
You use this dalliance to excuse Your breach of promise *Com. of Errors* iv 1 49
He hath borne himself beyond the promise of his age *Much Ado* i 1 13
Truly will I meet with thee.—Keep promise, love *M. N. Dream* i 1 179
Alack, alack, I fear my Thisby's promise is forgot! . v 1 177
If thou keep promise, I shall end this strife *Mer. of Venice* ii 3 20
Which this promise carries, 'Who chooseth me shall get as much as he deserves' . . . ii 7 6
Promise me life, and I'll confess the truth . . iii 2 34
Thou meagre lead, Which rather threatenest than dost promise aught iii 2 105
If promise last, I got a promise of this fair one here To have her love iii 2 207
I promise ye, I fear you . . . iii 5 3
If you do keep your promises in love But justly, as you have exceeded all promise, Your mistress shall be happy . *As Y. Like It* i 2 255
I come within an hour of my promise.—Break an hour's promise in love! . . . iv 1 43
If you break one jot of your promise . . iv 1 194
Therefore beware my censure and keep your promise . iv 1 200
He left a promise to return again Within an hour . . iv 3 100
To tell this story, that you might excuse His broken promise . iv 3 155
I'll promise thee she shall be rich And very rich . *T. of Shrew* i 2 62
And will not promise her to any man Until the elder sister first be wed i 2 262
Why, then the maid is mine from all the world, By your firm promise . ii 1 387
I have those hopes of her good that her education promises *All's Well* i 1 46
Oft expectation fails and most oft there Where most it promises . ii 1 146
Not helping, death's my fee; But, if I help, what do you promise me? . ii 1 193
I promise A counterpoise, if not to thy estate A balance more replete ii 3 181
Promises, enticements, oaths, tokens, and all these engines of lust iii 5 20
For the promise of his life and in the highest compulsion of base fear iii 6 30
And then to break promise with him and make a fool of him . *T. Night* ii 3 137
Nothing of that wonderful promise, to read him by his form . iii 4 290
To his image, which methought did promise Most venerable worth . iii 4 396
You do not keep promise with me . . . v 1 106
A gentleman of the greatest promise that ever came into my note *W. T.* i 1 39
Is this your promise? go to, hold your tongue . *K. John* iv 1 97
Remember, as thou read'st, thy promise pass'd *Richard II.* v 3 51
These promises are fair, the parties sure . *1 Hen. IV.* iii 1 1
This, in the name of God, I promise here: The which if He be pleased I shall perform . . . iii 2 153
A mighty and a fearful head they are, If promises be kept . iii 2 168
The king Knows at what time to promise, when to pay . iv 3 53
Eating the air on promise of supply . . . *2 Hen. IV.* i 3 28
To pray your patience for it and to promise you a better . Epil. 11
I will pay you some and, as most debtors do, promise you infinitely . Epil. 17
If hell and treason hold their promises . *Hen. V.* ii Prol. 29
Between the promise of his greener days And these he masters now . ii 4 136
No; tis hereafter to know, but now to promise . . v 2 227
Promise. Thy promises are like Adonis' gardens That one day bloom'd and fruitful were the next . . . *1 Hen. VI.* i 6 6
The duchess, I tell you, expects performance of your promises *2 Hen. VI.* i 4 2
With promise of high pay and great rewards: But all in vain. *3 Hen. VI.* ii 1 134
Promise them such rewards As victors wear at the Olympian games . ii 3 52
In conclusion wins the king from her, With promise of his sister . iii 1 51
I'll claim that promise at your grace's hands . *Richard III.* iii 1 197
I claim your gift, my due by promise . . . iv 2 91
My lord, your promise for the earldom . . . iv 2 105
And there the little souls of Edward's children Whisper the spirits of thine enemies And promise them success and victory . . iv 4 193
One, certes, that promises no element In such a business . *Hen. VIII.* i 1 48
That promises moe thousands: honour's train Is longer than his fore-skirt . . . ii 3 97
I cannot promise But that you shall sustain moe new disgraces . iii 2 4
His promises were, as he then was, mighty; But his performance, as he is now, nothing . . . iv 2 41
'Tis a girl, Promises boys hereafter . . . v 1 166
Now promises Upon this land a thousand thousand blessings . v 5 19
Give me now a little benefit, Out of those many register'd in promise, Which, you say, live to come in my behalf . *Troi. and Cres.* iii 3 15
Could promise to himself A thought of added honour torn from Hector iv 5 144
He will spend his mouth, and promise, like Brabbler the hound . v 1 98
It is your former promise.—Sir, it is; And I am constant . *Coriolanus* i 1 242
From him pluck'd Either his gracious promise, which you might, As cause had call'd you up, have held him to . . . ii 3 201
How! traitor!—Nay, temperately; your promise . . iii 3 67
Is this the promise that you made your mother? . . iii 3 86
I have pass'd My word and promise to the emperor . *T. Andron.* i 1 469
I can smooth and fill his aged ear With golden promises . iv 4 97
My hand to thee; mine honour on my promise *T. of Athens* i 1 148
His promises fly so beyond his state That what he speaks is all in debt i 2 203
Promise me friendship, but perform none: if thou wilt not promise, the gods plague thee! . . . iv 3 72
To promise is most courtly and fashionable . . v 1 29
It is our part and promise to the Athenians . . v 1 123
His expedition promises Present approach . . v 2 3
O Rome, I make thee promise; If the redress will follow *J. Cæsar* ii 1 56
If he do break the smallest particle Of any promise . ii 1 140
But hollow men, like horses hot at hand, Make gallant show and promise of their mettle . . . . iv 2 24
His absence, sir, Lays blame upon his promise *Macbeth* iii 4 44
That keep the word of promise to our ear, And break it to our hope v 8 21
Giving more light than heat, extinct in both, Even in their promise *Ham.* i 3 119
Come now, your promise.—What promise, chuck? *Othello* iii 4 48
She is persuaded I will marry her, out of her own love and flattery, not out of my promise . . . iv 1 133
The higher Nilus swells, The more it promises . *Ant. and Cleo.* ii 7 24
Quite forego The way which promises assurance . iii 7 47
Promise, And in our name, what she requires; add more . iii 12 27
And drink carouses to the next day's fate, Which promises royal peril . iv 8 35
Make your best use of this: I have perform'd Your pleasure and my promise . . . v 2 204
I cross'd the seas on purpose and on promise To see your grace *Cymbeline* i 6 202
Most willing spirits, That promise noble service . . iv 2 339
Nor hear I from my mistress, who did promise To yield me often tidings iv 3 38
So follow, to be most unlike our courtiers, As good as promise . v 4 137
Whose issue Promises Britain peace and plenty . v 5 458
I promise thee (you) *Mer. Wives* iii 2; *M. Ado* iv 2; *M. N. Dream* iii 1; *As Y. Like It* i 2; *T. of Shrew* ii 1; iii 1; *1 Hen. VI.* iv 1; *Richard III.* i 4; ii 3; v 3; *T. Andron.* ii 3; *Rom. and Jul.* iii 4; *T. of Athens* i 2; *Lear* i 2
Promise-breach. In double violation Of sacred chastity and of promise-breach . . . . *Meas. for Meas.* v 1 410
Promise-breaker. An hourly promise-breaker . *All's Well* iii 6 12
I do hate thee Worse than a promise-breaker . *Coriolanus* i 8 2
Promise-crammed. I eat the air, promise-crammed . *Hamlet* iii 2 99
Promised. Let me remember thee what thou hast promised *Tempest* i 2 243
She I mean is promised by her friends Unto a youthful gentleman of worth . . . *T. G. of Ver.* iii 1 106
'Tis past the hour, sir, that Sir Hugh promised to meet . *Mer. Wives* ii 3 5
Well, I promised you a dinner . . . iii 3 239
I have promised, and I'll be as good as my word . . iii 4 112
He promised to meet me two hours since . *Meas. for Meas.* i 2 75
He promised her marriage . . . . iii 2 212
Much upon this time have I promised here to meet . . iv 1 18
Her promised proportions Came short of composition . v 1 219
Sister, you know he promised me a chain . *Com. of Errors* ii 1 106
I promised your presence and the chain; But neither chain nor goldsmith came to me . . . iv 1 23
Is that the chain you promised me to-day? . . iv 3 47
Or, for my diamond, the chain you promised, And I'll be gone . iv 3 70
A ring he hath of mine worth forty ducats, And for the same he promised me a chain . . . iv 3 85
I promised to eat all of his killing . *Much Ado* i 1 44
The prince and Claudio promised by this hour To visit me . v 4 13
I have promised to study three years with the duke . *L. L. Lost* i 2 37
You to-day promised to tell me . *Mer. of Venice* i 1 121
Who hath promised to meet me in this place of the forest *As Y. Like It* iii 3 44
Dost thou believe, Orlando, that the boy Can do all this that he hath promised?—I sometimes do believe . . v 4 2
I have promised to make all this matter even . . v 4 18
I promised to inquire carefully About a schoolmaster . *T. of Shrew* i 2 166
I have met a gentleman Hath promised me to help me . . i 2 173
I promised we would be contributors And bear his charge of wooing . i 2 215
And make assurance here in Padua Of greater sums than I have promised iii 2 137
A second time receive The confirmation of my promised gift . *All's Well* iii 3 56
His highness hath promised me to do it . . iv 5 79
Do you know he promised me marriage?—Faith, I know more than I'll speak . . . . v 3 255
He has promised me, as he is a gentleman and a soldier . *T. Night* iii 4 338
And, for that I promised you, I'll be as good as my word . . iii 4 357
I was promised them against the feast . *W. Tale* iv 4 237
He hath promised you more than that, or there be liars . . iv 4 239
He hath paid you all he promised you: may be, he has paid you more . iv 4 241
You promised me a tawdry-lace and a pair of sweet gloves . . iv 4 252
After I have done what I promised?—Ay, sir . . iv 4 840
And he hath promised to dismiss the powers . . *K. John* v 1 64
You promised, To lay aside life-harming heaviness . *Richard II.* ii 2 2
And pay the debt I never promised . . . *1 Hen. IV.* i 2 233

Promised. I promised you redress of these same grievances *2 Hen. IV.* iv 2 113
Here I promised you I would be and here I commit my body to your mercies . . . . Epil. 14
The courses of his youth promised it not . . . *Hen. V.* i 1 24
Crowns and coronets, Promised to Harry and his followers . . ii Prol. 11
He that I gave it to in change promised to wear it in his cap : I promised to strike him, if he did . . . . iv 8 31
Her aid she promised and assured success . . *1 Hen. VI.* i 2 82
A plague upon that villain Somerset, That thus delays my promised supply ! . . . . iv 3 10
You shall first receive The sum of money which I promised . . v 1 52
Will they undertake to do me good ?—This they have promised *2 Hen. VI.* i 2 78
You promised knighthood to our forward son . *3 Hen. VI.* ii 2 58
'Tis but reason that I be released From giving aid which late I promised iii 3 148
The moveables The which you promised I should possess *Richard III.* iv 2 94
I am thus bold to put your grace in mind Of what you promised me . iv 2 114
I am sure the emperor Paid ere he promised . . *Hen. VIII.* i 1 186
I am much too venturous In tempting of your patience ; but am bolden'd Under your promised pardon . . . . i 2 56
They promised me eternal happiness . . . . . . iv 2 90
The ample proposition that hope makes In all designs begun on earth below Fails in the promised largeness . . . *Troi. and Cres.* i 3 5
Brave Hector would not lose So rich advantage of a promised glory . ii 2 204
Not to be his wife, That is another's lawful promised love . *T. Andron.* i 1 298
I promised your grace a hunter's peal.—And you have rung it lustily . ii 2 13
In half an hour she promised to return . . . *Rom. and Jul.* ii 5 2
By humble message and by promised means . . . *T. of Athens* v 4 20
Will you sup with me to-night, Casca ?—No, I am promised forth *J. C.* i 2 293
Do you not hope your children shall be kings, When those that gave the thane of Cawdor to me Promised no less to them ? . . . *Macbeth* i 3 120
That thou mightst not lose the dues of rejoicing, by being ignorant of what greatness is promised thee . . . . i 5 14
Glamis thou art, and Cawdor ; and shalt be What thou art promised . i 5 17
Thou hast it now : king, Cawdor, Glamis, all, As the weird women promised . . . . iii 1 2
Craves the conveyance of a promised march Over his kingdom *Hamlet* iv 4 3
Quoth she, before you tumbled me, You promised me to wed . . iv 5 64
Is this the promised end ?—Or image of that horror ? . . *Lear* v 3 263
Bade him anon return and here speak with me ; The which he promised *Othello* iv 1 82
Aye hopeless To have the courtesy your cradle promised . *Cymbeline* iv 4 28
Such precious deeds in one that promised nought But beggary . . v 5 9
So he thrived, That he is promised to be wived To fair Marina *Pericles* v 2 275
Promisedest. 'Twas I, indeed, thou promised'st to strike . *Hen. V.* iv 8 43
Promise-keeping. He was ever precise in promise-keeping *Meas. for Meas.* i 2 77
Promiseth. That yon green boy shall have no sun to ripe The bloom that promiseth a mighty fruit . . . . *K. John* ii 1 473
Who never promiseth but he means to pay . . . *1 Hen. IV.* v 4 43
His manly face, which promiseth Successful fortune . *3 Hen. VI.* ii 2 40
Promising to bring it to the Porpentine . . . *Com. of Errors* v 1 222
Lay our best love and credence Upon thy promising fortune . *All's Well* iii 3 3
I knew of their going to bed, and of other motions, as promising her marriage . . . . v 3 264
A course more promising Than a wild dedication of yourselves To unpath'd waters, undream'd shores. . . . . . *W. Tale* iv 4 576
Promising is the very air o' the time : it opens the eyes of expectation : performance is ever the duller for his act . . . *T. of Athens* v 1 24
We submit to Cæsar, And to the Roman empire ; promising To pay our wonted tribute, from the which We were dissuaded . *Cymbeline* v 5 461
Promontory. The strong-based promontory Have I made shake *Tempest* v 1 46
Once I sat upon a promontory, And heard a mermaid . *M. N. Dream* ii 1 149
Like one that stands upon a promontory, And spies a far-off shore *3 Hen. VI.* iii 2 135
And climb the highest promontory top . . . *T. Andron.* ii 2 22
This goodly frame, the earth, seems to me a sterile promontory *Hamlet* ii 2 311
A forked mountain, or blue promontory With trees upon't *Ant. and Cleo.* iv 14 5
Promotion. Thou art not for the fashion of these times, Where none will sweat but for promotion . . . . . . *As Y. Like It* ii 3 60
To do this deed, Promotion follows . . . . . . *W. Tale* i 2 357
And make her rich In titles, honours and promotions . . *K. John* ii 1 492
Many fair promotions Are daily given . . . . *Richard III.* i 3 80
Shall call home To high promotions and great dignity . . . iv 4 314
The high promotion of his grace of Canterbury . . *Hen. VIII.* v 2 23
The most you sought was her promotion . . . *Rom. and Jul.* iv 5 71
Prompt. It goes on, I see, As my soul prompts it . . *Tempest* i 2 420
Hence, bashful cunning ! And prompt me, plain and holy innocence ! . iii 1 82
Till our very pastime, tired out of breath, prompt us to have mercy *T. N.* iii 4 152
My voice shall sound as you do prompt mine ear . *2 Hen. IV.* v 2 119
To those that have not read the story, That I may prompt them *Hen. V.* v Prol. 2
My proud heart sues and prompts my tongue to speak . *Richard III.* i 2 171
For the service I have done you, The advantage of the time prompts me aloud To call for recompense . . . . *Troi. and Cres.* iii 3 2
Fair virtues all, To which the Grecians are most prompt and pregnant iv 4 90
Ready, when time shall prompt them, to make road Upon's again *Coriol.* iii 1 5
Not by your own instruction, Nor by the matter which your heart prompts you . . . . ii 2 54
Which never I shall discharge to the life.—Come, come, we'll prompt you iii 2 106
Some devil whisper curses in mine ear, And prompt me ! . *T. Andron.* v 3 12
By whose direction found'st thou out this place ?—By love, who first did prompt me to inquire . . . . . . *Rom. and Jul.* ii 2 80
I have observed thee always for a towardly prompt spirit *T. of Athens* iii 1 37
I do agnize A natural and prompt alacrity I find in hardness . *Othello* i 3 233
Tell him, I am prompt To lay my crown at's feet . *Ant. and Cleo.* iii 13 75
Nature prompts them In simple and low things to prince it *Cymbeline* iii 3 84
Prompted. Being prompted by your present trouble . . *T. Night* iii 4 377
Than shall my prompted sword Falling on Diomed . *Troi. and Cres.* v 2 175
I have Prompted you in the ebb of your estate . . *T. of Athens* ii 2 150
Prompted to my revenge by heaven and hell . . . *Hamlet* ii 2 613
Promptement Non, je reciterai à vous promptement . . *Hen. V.* iii 4 47
Prompter. Nor no without-book prologue, faintly spoke After the prompter, for our entrance . . . . *Rom. and Jul.* i 4 8
Were it my cue to fight, I should have known it Without a prompter *Oth.* i 2 84
Prompting. All prompting me how fair young Hero is . *Much Ado* i 1 306
As the prompting eyes Of beauty's tutors have enrich'd you with *L. L. L.* iv 3 322
Prompture. Though he hath fall'n by prompture of the blood *M. for M.* ii 4 178
Promulgate. 'Tis yet to know,—Which, when I know that boasting is an honour, I shall promulgate . . . . *Othello* i 2 21
Prone. In her youth There is a prone and speechless dialect *Meas. for Meas.* i 2 188
I am not prone to weeping, as our sex Commonly are . . *W. Tale* ii 1 108
Prone. And as prone to mischief As able to perform't . . *Hen. VIII.* i 1 160
Unless a man would marry a gallows and beget young gibbets, I never saw one so prone . . . . *Cymbeline* v 4 208
Prononcer. Je ne voudrais prononcer ces mots devant les seigneurs de France pour tout le monde . . . . *Hen. V.* iii 4 58
Prononcez. Vous prononcez les mots aussi droit que les natifs d'Angleterre . . . . iii 4 41
Pronoun. Articles are borrowed of the pronoun . . *Mer. Wives* iv 1 41
Show me now, William, some declensions of your pronouns . . iv 1 77
Pronounce. My prime request, Which I do last pronounce . *Tempest* i 2 426
And do pronounce by me Lingering perdition, worse than any death . iii 3 76
I, now the voice of the recorded law, Pronounce a sentence *M. for M.* ii 4 62
I will pronounce your sentence : you shall fast a week . *L. L. Lost* i 1 302
Det, when he should pronounce debt,—d, e, b, t, not d, e, t . . . v 1 23
She is banish'd.—Pronounce that sentence then on me . *As Y. Like It* i 3 87
I hate thee, Pronounce thee a gross lout . . . *W. Tale* i 2 301
This sessions, to our great grief we pronounce, Even pushes 'gainst our heart . . . . iii 2 1
That name, Which till this time my tongue did ne'er pronounce *K. John* iii 1 307
A heavier doom, Which I with some unwillingness pronounce *Rich. II.* i 3 149
Upon my tongues continual slanders ride, The which in every language I pronounce . . . . *2 Hen. IV.* Ind. 7
Here pronounce free pardon to them all That will forsake thee *2 Hen. VI.* iv 8 9
I do pronounce him in that very shape He shall appear in proof *Hen. VIII.* i 1 196
So good a lady that no tongue could ever Pronounce dishonour of her . ii 3 4
Your words, Domestics to you, serve your will as't please Yourself pronounce their office . . . . ii 4 115
I pray you, tell me, If what I now pronounce you have found true . iii 2 163
We do here pronounce, Upon the part o' the people *Coriolanus* iii 1 209
Let them pronounce the steep Tarpeian death . . . . . iii 3 88
Cry but 'Ay me !' pronounce but 'love' and 'dove' *Rom. and Jul.* ii 1 10
O gentle Romeo, If thou dost love, pronounce it faithfully . . ii 2 94
And art thou changed ? pronounce this sentence then, Women may fall, when there's no strength in men . . . . ii 3 79
Go pronounce his present death . . . . . . *Macbeth* i 2 64
But wherefore could not I pronounce 'Amen'? I had most need of blessing . . . . ii 2 31
We will require her welcome.—Pronounce it for me, sir, to all our friends iii 4 7
The devil himself could not pronounce a title More hateful to mine ear v 7 8
Start not so wildly from my affair.—I am tame, sir : pronounce *Hamlet* iii 2 322
Not I, Inclined to this intelligence, pronounce The beggary of his change ; but 'tis your graces . . . . . . *Cymbeline* i 6 114
Learn now, for all, That I, which know my heart, do here pronounce, By the very truth of it, I care not for you . . . . . ii 3 112
I am to pronounce Augustus Cæsar . . . thine enemy . . . iii 1 63
War and confusion In Cæsar's name pronounce I 'gainst thee . . iii 1 67
Pronounced. The thunder, That deep and dreadful organ-pipe, pronounced The name of Prosper . . . . *Tempest* iii 3 98
Good sentences and well pronounced.—They would be better, if well followed.—If to do were as easy as to know what were good to do *Mer. of Venice* i 2 11
He shall do this, or else I do recant The pardon that I late pronounced iv 1 392
He hath betrayed his followers, whose condemnation is pronounced *Hen. V.* iii 6 144
More than needful Forthwith that Edward be pronounced a traitor *3 Hen. VI.* v 6 54
Who pronounced The bitter sentence of poor Clarence' death? *Richard III.* i 4 190
William Lord Hastings had pronounced your part,—I mean, your voice iii 4 28
When he lies along, After your way his tale pronounced shall bury His reasons with his body . . . . *Coriolanus* v 6 58
The judges have pronounced My everlasting doom of banishment *T. An.* iii 1 50
Whom the oracle Hath doubtfully pronounced thy throat shall cut *T. of Athens* iv 3 121
The spirits that know All mortal consequences have pronounced me thus : 'Fear not, Macbeth' . . . . *Macbeth* v 3 5
'Gainst Fortune's state would treason have pronounced . . *Hamlet* ii 2 534
Speak the speech, I pray you, as I pronounced it to you, trippingly . iii 2 2
Pronouncing. I die pronouncing it . . . . . *Richard II.* ii 1 59
Pronouncing that the paleness of this flower Bewray'd the faintness of my master's heart . . . . *1 Hen. VI.* iv 1 106
Or by pronouncing of some doubtful phrase, As 'Well, well, we know' *Hamlet* i 5 175
Proof. Such another proof will make me cry 'baa' . . *T. G. of Ver.* i 1 97
We'll leave a proof, by that which we will do, Wives may be merry, and yet honest too . . . . *Mer. Wives* iv 2 106
I am made an ass.—Ay, and an ox too : both the proofs are extant . v 5 126
If the devil have given thee proofs for sin, Thou wilt prove his *Meas. for Meas.* iii 2 31
It is a mystery.—Proof ?—Every true man's apparel fits your thief . iv 2 45
Came not to an undoubtful proof.—It is now apparent ? . . . iv 2 143
This is an accident of hourly proof, Which I mistrusted not *Much Ado* ii 1 188
What proof shall I make of that ?—Proof enough to misuse the prince . ii 2 27
We have ten proofs to one that blood hath the victory . . . ii 3 171
If you, in your own proof, Have vanquish'd the resistance of her youth iv 1 46
She was charged with nothing But what was true and very full of proof v 1 105
I urge this childhood proof . . . . . . *Mer. of Venice* i 1 144
You have seen cruel proof of this man's strength . *As Y. Like It* i 2 184
Be thou arm'd for some unhappy words.—Ay, to the proof *T. of Shrew* ii 1 141
Thou lovest it not ; And all my pains is sorted to no proof . . iv 3 43
My fore-past proofs, howe'er the matter fall, Shall tax my fears of little vanity, Having vainly fear'd too little . . . . *All's Well* v 3 121
This is his wife ; That ring's a thousand proofs . . . . . v 3 199
Make your proof.—I must catechize you for it . . . *T. Night* i 5 67
For want of other idleness, I'll bide your proof . . . . . i 5 71
I pity you.—That's a degree to love.—No, not a grize ; for 'tis a vulgar proof, That very oft we pity enemies . . . . iii 1 135
A terrible oath, with a swaggering accent sharply twanged off, gives manhood more approbation than ever proof itself would have earned him . . . . iii 4 199
As you are like to find him in the proof of his valour . . . iii 4 292
All proofs sleeping else But what your jealousies awake *W. Tale* ii 2 113
I am proof against that title and what shame else belongs to't . . iv 4 872
That which I shall report will bear no credit, Were not the proof so nigh v 1 180
That which you hear you'll swear you see, there is such unity in the proofs . . . . v 2 36
Add proof unto mine armour with thy prayers . . *Richard II.* i 3 73
In proof whereof, there is my honour's pawn . . . . . iv 1 70
Governed, as the sea is, by the moon. As, for proof, now . *1 Hen. IV.* i 2 37
Well, we leave that to the proof . . . . ii 2 72
To gentle exercise and proof of arms . . . . v 2 55

Proof. She is pistol-proof, sir; you shall hardly offend her.—Come, I'll drink no proofs nor no bullets . . . 2 *Hen. IV.* ii 4 127
There's never none of these demure boys come to any proof . . iv 3 98
Only this proof I'll of thy valour make . . . . 1 *Hen. VI.* i 2 94
Call we to mind, and mark but this for proof . . . iii 3 68
In argument and proof of which contract, Bear her this jewel . v 1 46
This speedy and quick appearance argues proof Of your accustom'd diligence . . . . v 3 8
He need not fear the sword; for his coat is of proof . 2 *Hen. VI.* iv 2 65
As, by proof, we see The waters swell before a boisterous storm *Rich. III.* ii 3 43
Than can the substance of ten thousand soldiers Armed in proof . v 3 219
Proofs as clear as founts in July when We see each grain *Hen. VIII.* i 1 154
I do pronounce him in that very shape He shall appear in proof . i 1 197
Urged on the examinations, proofs, confessions Of divers witnesses ii 1 16
Troilus will stand to the proof, if you'll prove it so *Troi. and Cres.* i 2 142
In the reproof of chance Lies the true proof of men . . i 3 34
A proof of strength she could not publish more . . . iv 2 113
I have chastised the amorous Trojan, And am her knight by proof v 5 5
What he will he does, and does so much That proof is call'd impossibility v 5 29
And fight With hearts more proof than shields . . *Coriolanus* i 4 25
Alas, that love, so gentle in his view, Should be so tyrannous and rough in proof! . . . . *Rom. and Jul.* i 1 176
She hath Dian's wit; And, in strong proof of chastity well arm'd . i 1 216
Look thou but sweet, And I am proof against their enmity . ii 2 73
Call me before the exactest auditors And set me on the proof *T. of A.* ii 2 166
Whose proof, nor yells of mothers, maids, nor babes, Nor sight of priests in holy vestments bleeding, Shall pierce a jot . . iv 3 124
'Tis a common proof, That lowliness is young ambition's ladder *J. Cæsar* ii 1 21
I have made strong proof of my constancy . . . . ii 1 299
If arguing make us sweat, The proof of it will turn to redder drops v 1 49
Lapp'd in proof, Confronted him with self-comparisons . *Macbeth* i 2 54
Never did the Cyclops' hammers fall On Mars's armour forged for proof eterne With less remorse . . . . *Hamlet* ii 2 512
This was sometime a paradox, but now the time gives it proof . iii 1 115
What my love is, proof hath made you know . . . iii 2 179
Brass'd it so That it be proof and bulwark against sense . . iii 4 38
In passages of proof, Time qualifies the spark and fire of it [love] iv 7 113
This project Should have a back or second, that might hold, If this should blast in proof . . . . iv 7 155
The country gives me proof and precedent Of Bedlam beggars *Lear* ii 3 13
When false opinion, whose wrong thought defiles thee, In thy just proof, repeals and reconciles thee . . . . . . iii 6 120
I'll put't in proof . . . . iv 6 189
I, of whom his eyes had seen the proof . . . *Othello* i 1 28
To vouch this, is no proof, Without more wider and more overt test i 3 106
When I doubt, prove; And on the proof, there is no more but this,— Away at once with love or jealousy! . . . . . iii 3 191
I speak not yet of proof. Look to your wife; observe her well with Cassio . . . . iii 3 196
Trifles light as air Are to the jealous confirmations strong As proofs of holy writ . . . . iii 3 324
Give me the ocular proof . . . . iii 3 360
I think that thou art just and think thou art not. I'll have some proof iii 3 386
This may help to thicken other proofs That do demonstrate thinly . iii 3 430
It speaks against her with the other proofs . . . iii 3 441
My coat is better than thou know'st: I will make proof of thine . . v 1 26
Leap thou, attire and all, Through proof of harness to my heart! *Ant. and Cleo.* iv 8 15
Who knows By history, report, or his own proof, What woman is *Cymb.* i 6 70
Let proof speak . . . . iii 1 77
No life to ours.—Out of your proof you speak . . . iii 3 27
I speak not out of weak surmises, but from proof as strong as my grief iii 4 24
Whose naked breast Stepp'd before targes of proof . . . v 5 5
To be brief, my practice so prevail'd, That I return'd with simular proof v 5 200
Prop. The boy was the very staff of my age, my very prop *Mer. of Venice* ii 2 70
Do I look like a cudgel or a hovel-post, a staff or a prop? . . ii 2 72
You take my house when you do take the prop That doth sustain my house . . . . iv 1 375
Our prop to lean upon, Now thou art gone, we have no staff 3 *Hen. VI.* ii 1 68
See, where he stands between two clergymen!—Two props of virtue for a Christian prince . . . . . *Richard III.* iii 7 96
The ratifiers and props of every word . . . . *Hamlet* iv 5 105
Nor has no friends, So much as but to prop him . *Cymbeline* iv 5 60
Your house, but for this virgin that doth prop it, Would sink *Pericles* iv 6 127
Propagate. My low and humble name to propagate . . *All's Well* ii 1 200
Griefs of mine own lie heavy in my breast, Which thou wilt propagate, to have it prest With more of thine . . . *Rom. and Jul.* i 1 193
All deserts, all kind of natures, That labour on the bosom of this sphere To propagate their states . . . *T. of Athens* i 1 67
A glorious beauty, From whence an issue I might propagate . *Pericles* i 2 73
Propagation. This we came not to, Only for propagation of a dower Remaining in the coffer of her friends . . *Meas. for Meas.* i 2 154
Propend. I propend to you In resolution to keep Helen *Troi. and Cres.* ii 2 190
Propension. Your full consent Gave wings to my propension . ii 2 133
Proper. As proper a man as ever went on four legs cannot make him give ground . . . . *Tempest* ii 2 63
I have made you mad; And even with such-like valour men hang and drown Their proper selves . . . . . . iii 3 60
Thyself and thy belongings Are not thine own so proper as to waste Thyself upon thy virtues . . . . *Meas. for Meas.* i 1 31
Like rats that ravin down their proper bane, A thirsty evil . i 2 133
Which do call thee sire, The mere effusion of thy proper loins . iii 1 30
That with such vehemency he should pursue Faults proper to himself . v 1 110
In the witness of his proper ear, To call him villain . . . v 1 310
The law cries out Most audible, even from his proper tongue . v 1 413
A proper squire! And who, and who? which way looks he? *Much Ado* i 3 54
Why seek'st thou then to cover with excuse That which appears in proper nakedness? . . . . iv 1 177
Talk with a man out at a window! A proper saying! . . . iv 1 312
That the comparison May stand more proper . *Mer. of Venice* iii 2 46
Three proper young men, of excellent growth and presence *As Y. Like It* i 2 129
Why not the swift foot of Time? had not that been as proper? . iii 2 325
And out of you she sees herself more proper Than any of her lineaments can show her . . . . iii 5 55
A proper stripling and an amorous! . . . . . *T. of Shrew* i 2 144
Thus your own proper wisdom Brings in the champion Honour on my part, Against your vain assault . . . . *All's Well* iv 2 49
He that in this action contrives against his own nobility, in his proper stream o'erflows himself . . . . iv 3 29
That is an advertisement to a proper maid in Florence, one Diana . iv 3 240
Proper. Here at my house and at my proper cost . . *T. Night* v 1 327
The bastard brains with these my proper hands Shall I dash out *W. Tale* ii 3 139
With great imagination Proper to madmen . . . 2 *Hen. IV.* i 3 32
That I am a second brother and that I am a proper fellow of my hands ii 2 72
A proper gentlewoman, sir, and a kinswoman of my master's . . ii 2 169
If damn'd commotion so appear'd, In his true, native and most proper shape . . . . iv 1 37
Happy am I, that have a man so bold, That dares do justice on my proper son . . . . v 2 109
Which cannot in their huge and proper life Be here presented *Hen. V.* v Prol. 5
Of the King of England's own proper cost and charges . 2 *Hen. VI.* i 1 61
A proper jest, and never heard before! . . . . . i 1 132
Many a pound of mine own proper store . . . . . iii 1 115
This noble isle doth want her proper limbs . . *Richard III.* iii 7 125
A proper title of a peace; and purchased At a superfluous rate! *Hen. VIII.* i 1 98
Why do you now The issue of your proper wisdoms rate? *Troi. and Cres.* ii 2 89
We'll put you, Like one that means his proper harm, in manacles *Coriolanus* i 9 57
Provide thee two proper palfreys, black as jet . . *T. Andron.* v 2 50
Conceptions only proper to myself . . . . *J. Cæsar* i 2 41
Thy spirit walks abroad, and turns our swords In our own proper entrails . . . . v 3 96
O proper stuff! This is the very painting of your fear . *Macbeth* iii 4 60
It is as proper to our age To cast beyond ourselves in our opinions *Ham.* ii 1 114
Thrown out his angle for my proper life . . . . v 2 66
I cannot wish the fault undone, The issue of it being so proper . *Lear* i 1 18
Proper deformity seems not in the fiend So horrid as in woman . iv 2 60
Yea, though our proper son Stood in your action . . *Othello* i 3 69
Nor to comply with heat—the young affects In me defunct—and proper satisfaction, But to be free . . . . i 3 265
Let me have leave to speak: 'Tis proper I obey him, but not now . v 2 196
When I have slain thee with my proper hand, I'll follow those *Cymbeline* iv 2 97
Proper man. For he's a proper man . . . . *T. G. of Ver.* iv 1 10
He is a very proper man.—He hath indeed a good outward happiness *Much Ado* ii 3 189
A proper man, as one shall see in a summer's day . . *M. N. Dream* i 2 88
He is a proper man's picture . . . . *Mer. of Venice* i 2 77
Yet his pride becomes him: He'll make a proper man *As Y. Like It* iii 5 115
Your wife is like to reap a proper man . . . *T. Night* iii 1 144
Good my mother, let me know my father; Some proper man, I hope *K. John* i 1 250
A proper man; No shape but his can please your dainty eye . 1 *Hen. VI.* v 3 37
The man is a proper man, of mine honour . . 2 *Hen. VI.* iv 2 102
She finds, although I cannot, Myself to be a marvellous proper man *Richard III.* i 2 255
He's one o' the soundest judgements in Troy, whosoever, and a proper man of person . . . . *Troi. and Cres.* i 2 209
As proper men as ever trod upon neat's leather . . *J. Cæsar* i 1 28
Cassio's a proper man: let me see now: To get his place . *Othello* i 3 398
This Lodovico is a proper man.—A very handsome man . . iv 3 35
A proper man.—Indeed, he is so: I repent me much That so I harried him *Ant. and Cleo.* iii 3 41
Wilt lay the leaven on all proper men; Goodly and gallant shall be false and perjured From thy great fail . . *Cymbeline* iii 4 64
Properer. You foolish shepherd, . . . You are a thousand times a properer man Than she a woman . . . *As Y. Like It* iii 5 51
I anger her sometimes and tell her that Paris is the properer man *Rom. and Jul.* ii 4 217
We are born to do benefits: and what better or properer can we call our own than the riches of our friends? . . *T. of Athens* i 2 106
Properest. At last she concluded with a sigh, thou wast the properest man in Italy . . . . *Much Ado* v 1 174
Proper-false. How easy is it for the proper-false In women's waxen hearts to set their forms! . . . . . *T. Night* ii 2 30
Properly. He keeps me rustically at home, or, to speak more properly, stays me here at home unkept . . . *As Y. Like It* i 1 8
The loss, the gain, the ordering on't, is all Properly ours . *W. Tale* ii 1 170
To speak more properly, I will enforce it easily to my love *K. John* ii 1 514
My affairs Are servanted to others: though I owe My revenge properly, my remission lies In Volscian breasts . . . *Coriolanus* v 2 90
Propertied. They have here propertied me . . . *T. Night* iv 2 99
I am too high-born to be propertied, To be a secondary at control *K. John* v 2 79
His voice was propertied As all the tuned spheres . *Ant. and Cleo.* v 2 83
Properties. Get us properties And tricking for our fairies *Mer. Wives* iv 4 78
Of government the properties to unfold, Would seem in me to affect speech and discourse . . . . . *Meas. for Meas.* i 1 3
In the mean time I will draw a bill of properties . *M. N. Dream* i 2 108
Subdues and properties to his love and tendance All sorts *T. of Athens* i 1 57
Property. And tells me 'tis a thing impossible I should love thee but as a property . . . . *Mer. Wives* iii 4 10
Whose liquor hath this virtuous property . . *M. N. Dream* iii 2 367
That the property of rain is to wet and fire to burn . *As Y. Like It* iii 2 27
If I break time, or flinch in property Of what I spoke . *All's Well* ii 1 190
The property by what it is should go, Not by the title . . ii 3 137
Sweet love, I see, changing his property, Turns to the sourest and most deadly hate . . . . *Richard II.* iii 2 135
The second property of your excellent sherris is, the warming of the blood; which, before cold and settled . . . 2 *Hen. IV.* iv 3 111
Do not talk of him, But as a property . . . . *J. Cæsar* iv 1 40
The very ecstasy of love, Whose violent property fordoes itself *Hamlet* ii 1 103
Upon whose property and most dear life A damn'd defeat was made . ii 2 597
Thy natural magic and dire property, On wholesome life usurp immediately . . . . iii 2 270
Custom hath made it in him a property of easiness . . . v 1 75
I disclaim all my paternal care, Propinquity and property of blood *Lear* i 1 116
Is there not charms By which the property of youth and maidhood May be abused? . . . . *Othello* i 1 173
Sometimes, when he is not Antony, He comes too short of that great property Which still should go with Antony . *Ant. and Cleo.* i 1 58
Prophecy. In requital of your prophecy, hark you *Meas. for Meas.* i 1 259
The prophecy like the parrot, 'beware the rope's-end' . *Com. of Errors* iv 4 45
Let my prophecy Come home to ye! . . . . . *W. Tale* iv 4 662
The dreamer Merlin and his prophecies . . . 1 *Hen. IV.* iii 1 150
And comes not in, o'er-ruled by prophecies . . . . iv 4 18
These words, now proved a prophecy . . . 2 *Hen. IV.* iii 1 69
To frustrate prophecies and to raze out Rotten opinion . . iv 5 127
The spirit of deep prophecy she hath, Exceeding the nine sibyls 1 *Hen. VI.* i 2 55
And now I fear that fatal prophecy . . . . . . iii 1 195
Henry's late presaging prophecy Did glad my heart with hope 3 *Hen. VI.* iv 6 92
I will buz abroad such prophecies That Edward shall be fearful . . v 6 86

Prophecy. Plots have I laid, inductions dangerous, By drunken prophecies, libels and dreams . . . . *Richard III.* i 1 33
Mew'd up, About a prophecy, which says that G Of Edward's heirs the murderer shall be. . . . . i 1 39
As I can learn, He hearkens after prophecies and dreams . . . i 1 54
And, not consulting, broke Into a general prophecy *Hen VIII.* i 1 92
He was brought to this By a vain prophecy of Nicholas Hopkins . . i 2 147
That was he That fed him with his prophecies?—The same . . ii 1 23
My prophecy is but half his journey yet . . . . *Troi. and Cres.* iv 5 218
He hath a heavenly gift of prophecy . . . . . *Macbeth* iv 3 157
I'll speak a prophecy ere I go . . . . *Lear* iii 2 80
This prophecy Merlin shall make; for I live before his time . . iii 2 95
Prophesied. I prophesied, if a gallows were on land, This fellow could not drown . . . . *Tempest* v 1 217
There my life must end. It hath been prophesied to me many years, I should not die but in Jerusalem . . . . *2 Hen. IV.* iv 5 237
Say, when I am gone, I prophesied France will be lost ere long *2 Hen. VI.* i 1 146
No man but prophesied revenge for it . . . . *Richard III.* i 3 186
Harry, that prophesied thou shouldst be king, Doth comfort thee . v 3 129
Prophesier. Deceived me, like a double-meaning prophesier . *All's Well* iv 3 115
Prophesy. What of her ensues I list not prophesy . *W. Tale* iv 1 26
Old men and beldams in the streets Do prophesy upon it dangerously *K. John* iv 2 186
If you crown him, let me prophesy . . . . . *Richard II.* iv 1 136
O, I could prophesy, But that the earthy and cold hand of death Lies on my tongue: no, Percy, thou art dust . . *1 Hen. IV.* v 4 83
The which observed, a man may prophesy, With a near aim *2 Hen. IV.* iii 1 82
And here I prophesy: this brawl to-day . . . Shall send between the red rose and the white A thousand souls to death and deadly night *1 Hen. VI.* ii 4 124
I perceive that will be verified Henry the Fifth did sometime prophesy v 1 31
They in seeking that Shall find their deaths, if York can prophesy *2 Hen. VI.* ii 2 76
For, sure, my thoughts do hourly prophesy Mischance . . . iii 2 283
And thus I prophesy, that many a thousand . . . Shall rue the hour that ever thou wast born . . . . *3 Hen. VI.* v 6 37
Miserable England! I prophesy the fearfull'st time to thee *Richard III.* iii 4 106
Henry the Sixth Did prophesy that Richmond should be king . . iv 2 99
Thou didst prophesy the time would come That I should wish for thee iv 4 79
Over thy wounds now do I prophesy . . . . *J. Cæsar* iii 1 259
I will prophesy he comes to tell me of the players . . *Hamlet* ii 2 405
I do prophesy the election lights On Fortinbras: he has my dying voice v 2 366
Methought thy very gait did prophesy A royal nobleness . . *Lear* v 3 175
If I were bound to divine of this unity, I would not prophesy so *A. and C.* ii 6 125
Prophesying with accents terrible Of dire combustion . . *Macbeth* ii 3 62
She had a prophesying fear Of what hath come to pass . *Ant. and Cleo.* iv 14 120
Prophet. Like a prophet, Looks in a glass . . . *Meas. for Meas.* ii 2 94
To eat of the habitation which your prophet the Nazarite conjured the devil into . . . . *Mer. of Venice* i 3 35
A prophet I, madam; and I speak the truth the next way *All's Well* i 3 62
Here's a prophet, that I brought with me From forth the streets of Pomfret, whom I found With many hundreds treading on his heels *K. John* iv 2 147
Did not the prophet Say that before Ascension-day at noon My crown I should give off? Even so I have . . . . . . v 1 25
Methinks I am a prophet new inspired . . . . *Richard II.* ii 1 31
O, had thy grandsire with a prophet's eye Seen how his son's son should destroy his sons . . . . ii 1 104
Lean-look'd prophets whisper fearful change . . . . . ii 4 11
No prophet will I trust, if she prove false . . . *1 Hen. VI.* i 2 150
Shine it like a comet of revenge, A prophet to the fall of all our foes! . iii 2 32
His champions are the prophets and apostles . . . . *2 Hen. VI.* i 3 60
I'll hear no more: die, prophet, in thy speech . . *3 Hen. VI.* v 6 57
My other self, my counsel's consistory, My oracle, my prophet! *Richard III.* ii 2 152
How chance the prophet could not at that time Have told me? . iv 2 103
Every flower Did, as a prophet, weep what it foresaw *Troi. and Cres.* i 2 10
Prophet may you be! . . . . iii 2 190
Am like a prophet suddenly enrapt To tell thee that this day is ominous v 3 65
Jesters do oft prove prophets . . . . *Lear* v 3 71
Prophetess. Joan la Pucelle . . . , A holy prophetess . . *1 Hen. VI.* i 6 102
France, triumph in thy glorious prophetess! . . . . . i 6 8
Remember this another day, When he shall split thy very heart with sorrow, And say poor Margaret was a prophetess! *Rich. III.* i 3 301; v 1 27
Prophetic. Now hear me speak with a prophetic spirit . . *K. John* iii 4 126
Cry, Trojans, cry! lend me ten thousand eyes, And I will fill them with prophetic tears . . . . *Troi. and Cres.* ii 2 102
Or why Upon this blasted heath you stop our way With such prophetic greeting? Speak, I charge you . . . . . . *Macbeth* i 3 78
O my prophetic soul! My uncle! . . . . . . *Hamlet* i 5 40
In her prophetic fury sew'd the work; The worms were hallow'd *Othello* iii 4 72
Prophetically. And the soul of every man Prophetically doth forethink thy fall . . . . *1 Hen. IV.* iii 2 38
So prophetically proud of an heroical cudgelling . *Troi. and Cres.* iii 3 248
Prophet-like They hail'd him father to a line of kings . *Macbeth* iii 1 59
Propinquity. I disclaim all my paternal care, Propinquity . *Lear* i 1 116
Propontic. Keeps due on To the Propontic and the Hellespont *Othello* iii 3 456
Proportion. I have received my proportion, like the prodigious son, and am going . . . . *T. G. of Ver.* ii 3 3
You would have married her most shamefully, Where there was no proportion held in love . . . . . . *Mer. Wives* v 5 235
What, in metre?—In any proportion or in any language . *Meas. for Meas.* i 2 23
Her promised proportions Came short of composition . . . v 1 219
There must be needs a like proportion Of lineaments, of manners *Mer. of Venice* iii 4 14
Contracted all proportions To a most hideous object . *All's Well* v 3 51
Why should we in the compass of a pale Keep law and form and due proportion, . . . When . . . the whole land Is full of weeds? *Rich. II.* iii 4 41
How sour sweet music is, When time is broke and no proportion kept! . v 5 43
Whose power was in the first proportion . . . *1 Hen. IV.* iv 4 15
The just proportion that we gave them out . . *2 Hen. IV.* iv 1 23
We must not only arm to invade the French, But lay down our proportions to defend Against the Scot . . . . . . *Hen. V.* i 2 137
Let our proportions for these wars Be soon collected . . . i 2 304
But thou, 'gainst all proportion, didst bring in Wonder to wait on treason . . . . ii 2 109
So the proportions of defence are fill'd . . . . . . ii 4 45
Bid him therefore consider of his ransom; which must proportion the losses . . . . iii 6 134
Whom to disobey were against all proportion of subjection . . . iv 1 153
Proportion. A second Hector, for his grim aspect, And large proportion of his strong-knit limbs . . . . *1 Hen. VI.* ii 3 21
What you see is but the smallest part And least proportion of humanity ii 3 53
Bear that proportion to my flesh and blood As did the fatal brand Althæa burn'd Unto the prince's heart of Calydon *2 Hen. VI.* i 1 233
Resembled thee In courage, courtship and proportion . . . i 3 57
I, that am curtail'd of this fair proportion, Cheated of feature *Rich. III.* i 1 18
Thou didst usurp my place, and dost thou not Usurp the just proportion of my sorrow? . . . . iv 4 110
And part in just proportion our small strength . . . . . v 3 26
Your enemies are many, and not small; their practices Must bear the same proportion . . . . *Hen. VIII.* v 1 129
The planets and this centre Observe degree, priority and place, Insisture, course, proportion, season, form, Office and custom *Troi. and Cres.* i 3 87
Will you with counters sum The past proportion of his infinite? . ii 2 29
Well mayst thou know her by thy own proportion . . *T. Andron.* iv 2 106
Keeps time, distance, and proportion . . . *Rom. and Jul.* ii 4 22
Would thou hadst less deserved, That the proportion both of thanks and payment Might have been mine! . . . . . *Macbeth* i 4 19
The lists and full proportions, are all made Out of his subject *Hamlet* i 2 32
Three or four thousand chequins were as pretty a proportion to live quietly, and so give over . . . . *Pericles* iv 2 29
Proportionable. For us to levy power Proportionable to the enemy Is all unpossible . . . . *Richard II.* ii 2 125
Proportion'd as one's thought would wish a man . *Rom. and Jul.* iii 5 184
Our size of sorrow, Proportion'd to our cause, must be as great As that which makes it . . . . *Ant. and Cleo.* iv 15 5
Propose. The wager which we will propose . . . *T. of Shrew* v 2 69
So is running away, when fear proposes the safety . . *All's Well* i 1 216
His majesty, out of a self-gracious remembrance, did first propose . iv 5 78
Make the case yours; Be now the father and propose a son *2 Hen. IV.* v 2 92
Kneel thou, Whilst I propose the selfsame words to thee . *3 Hen. VI.* v 5 20
I propose not merely to myself The pleasures . . *Troi. and Cres.* ii 2 146
A thousand deaths Would I propose to achieve her whom I love *T. An.* ii 1 80
Consent to swear.—Propose the oath, my lord . . . . *Hamlet* i 5 152
What to ourselves in passion we propose, The passion ending, doth the purpose lose . . . . iii 2 204
Unless the bookish theoric, Wherein the toged consuls can propose As masterly as he . . . . *Othello* i 1 25
Proposed. Yet we ventur'd, for the gain proposed . *2 Hen. IV.* i 1 183
According to their firm proposed natures . . . . . *Hen. V.* v 2 362
But, now thy beauty is proposed my fee, My proud heart sues *Rich. III.* i 2 170
Where I may wallow in the lily-beds Proposed for the deserver *T. and C.* iii 2 14
You would not hear me, At many leisures I proposed . *T. of Athens* ii 2 137
Ere we could arrive the point proposed, Cæsar cried 'Help me!' *J. Cæsar* i 2 110
Give but that portion which yourself proposed . . . . *Lear* i 1 245
Not to affect many proposed matches Of her own clime . *Othello* iii 3 229
Proposer. By what more dear a better proposer could charge you *Hamlet* ii 2 297
Proposing. There shalt thou find my cousin Beatrice Proposing with the prince and Claudio . . . . *Much Ado* iii 1 3
It is as easy to count atomies as to resolve the propositions of a lover *As Y. Like It* iii 2 246
Proposition. The ample proposition that hope makes In all designs *T. and C.* i 3 3
Propounded. That shall make answer to such questions As by your grace shall be propounded him . . . . *2 Hen. VI.* i 2 81
Propped. Being not propp'd by ancestry . . . *Hen. VIII.* i 1 59
Propre. Le chien est retourné à son propre vomissement . *Hen. V.* iii 7 68
Propriety. Alas, it is the baseness of thy fear That makes thee strangle thy propriety . . . . *T. Night* v 1 150
Silence that dreadful bell: it frights the isle From her propriety *Othello* ii 3 176
Propugnation. What propugnation is in one man's valour? *Troi. and Cres.* ii 2 136
Prorogue. I hear thou must, and nothing may prorogue it *Rom. and Jul.* iv 1 48
Sauce his appetite; That sleep and feeding may prorogue his honour Even till a Lethe'd dulness! . . . . . . *Ant. and Cleo.* ii 1 26
Nor taken sustenance But to prorogue his grief . . . *Pericles* v 1 26
Prorogued. My life were better ended by their hate, Than death prorogued, wanting of thy love . . . . . *Rom and Jul.* ii 2 78
Proscription. In our black sentence and proscription . . *J. Cæsar* iv 1 17
By proscription and bills of outlawry . . . . . . iv 3 173
Seventy senators that died By their proscriptions . . . . iv 3 178
Cicero is dead, And by that order of proscription . . . . iv 3 180
Prose. These numbers will I tear, and write in prose . *L. L. Lost* iv 3 57
Soft! here follows prose . . . . *T. Night* ii 5 154
Prosecute. Why should not I then prosecute my right? . *M. N. Dream* i 1 105
That will the king severely prosecute . . . . *Richard II.* ii 1 244
We will prosecute by good advice Mortal revenge upon these *T. Andron.* iv 1 92
Rather comfort his distressed plight Than prosecute the meanest or the best . . . . iv 4 33
Prosecution. When I should see behind me The inevitable prosecution of Disgrace and horror. . . . . *Ant. and Cleo.* iv 14 65
Proselyte. Make proselytes Of who she but bid follow . *W. Tale* v 1 108
Proserpina, For the flowers now, that frighted thou let'st fall! . iv 4 116
And thou art as full of envy at his greatness as Cerberus is at Proserpina's beauty . . . . *Troi. and Cres.* ii 1 37
Prospect. Into the eye and prospect of his soul . . *Much Ado* iv 1 231
Between me and the full prospect of my hopes . . *T. Night* iii 4 90
Are advanced here Before the eye and prospect of your town *K. John* ii 1 208
Their chiefest prospect murdering basilisks! . . *2 Hen. VI.* iii 2 324
Stands not within the prospect of belief . . . . *Macbeth* i 3 74
It were a tedious difficulty, I think, To bring them to that prospect *Oth.* iii 3 398
Prosper. 'Twas a sweet marriage, and we prosper well . . *Tempest* ii 1 72
All the infections that the sun sucks up From bogs, fens, flats, on Prosper fall! . . . . ii 2 2
Now Prosper works upon thee . . . . ii 2 83
The winds did sing it to me, and the thunder, That deep and dreadful organ-pipe, pronounced The name of Prosper . . . . iii 3 99
Heaven prosper the right! . . . . *Mer. Wives* iii 1 30
Heaven prosper our sport! . . . . v 2 14
By that which knitteth souls and prospers loves . *M. N. Dream* i 1 172
It is now our time, That have stood by and seen our wishes prosper, To cry, good joy. . . . . *Mer. of Venice* iii 2 189
Prosper well in this, And thou shalt live as freely as thy lord *T. Night* i 4 38
Prosper you, sweet sir! . . . . *W. Tale* iv 3 126
Bid us welcome to your sheep-shearing, As your good flock shall prosper iv 4 70
More sins for this forgiveness prosper may . . *Richard II.* v 3 84
The Lord bless you! God prosper your affairs! . . *2 Hen. IV.* iii 2 313
Prosper this realm, keep it from civil broils! . . . *1 Hen. VI.* i 1 53
Prosper our colours in this dangerous fight! . . . . . iv 2 56
Hope to find the like event in love, But prosper better than the Trojan did v 5 106

Prosper. Swearing both They prosper best of all when I am thence *3 Hen. VI.* ii 5 18
So prosper I, as I swear perfect love! *Richard III.* ii 1 16
As I intend to prosper and repent, So thrive I in my dangerous attempt! iv 4 397
Neither the king nor's heirs, Tell you the duke, shall prosper *Hen. VIII.* i 2 169
Well may you prosper! *Lear* i 1 285
I grow; I prosper . . . . i 2 21
Kind gods, forgive me that, and prosper him! . . . . iii 7 92
Fairies and gods Prosper it with thee! . . . . . iv 6 30
If there be not a conscience to be used in every trade, we shall never prosper.—Thou sayest true . *Pericles* iv 2 13
Prospered. I never prospered since I forswore myself at primero *M. W.* iv 5 103
Prosperities. Those cities that of plenty's cup And her prosperities so largely taste . . . *Pericles* i 4 53
Prosperity. Peace and prosperity! . . . . *Meas. for Meas.* i 4 15
Therefore welcome the sour cup of prosperity! . . *L. L. Lost* i 1 316
A jest's prosperity lies in the ear Of him that hears it . . v 2 871
And you come To give their bed joy and prosperity *M. N. Dream* ii 1 73
And bless it to all fair prosperity . . . . . iv 1 95
You know Prosperity's the very bond of love . . *W. Tale* iv 4 584
Death, death; . . . Arise forth from the couch of lasting night, Thou hate and terror to prosperity . . . *K. John* iii 4 28
Thou shalt thrust thy hand as deep Into the purse of rich prosperity . v 2 61
O flattering glass, Like to my followers in prosperity! *Richard II.* iv 1 280
So, now prosperity begins to mellow And drop into the rotten mouth of death . . . . *Richard III.* iv 4 1
Bold gentleman, Prosperity be thy page! . . . *Coriolanus* i 5 24
You have, I know, petition'd all the gods For my prosperity! . ii 1 188
The glorious gods sit in hourly synod about thy particular prosperity! v 2 75
I have heard in some sort of thy miseries.—Thou saw'st them, when I had prosperity.—I see them now . . *T. of Athens* iv 3 77
A satire against the softness of prosperity . . . . v 1 36
Without the which there were no expectation of our prosperity *Othello* ii 1 288
Prospero. Nought knowing Of whence I am, nor that I am more better Than Prospero, master of a full poor cell . *Tempest* i 2 20
Prospero the prime duke, being so reputed In dignity, and for the liberal arts Without a parallel . . . . . i 2 72
I remember You did supplant your brother Prospero . . ii 1 271
Prospero my lord shall know what I have done: So, king, go safely on. ii 1 326
I shall have my music for nothing.—When Prospero is destroyed . iii 2 155
You three From Milan did supplant good Prospero . . . iii 3 70
Behold, sir king, The wronged Duke of Milan, Prospero . . v 1 107
But how should Prospero Be living and be here? . . . v 1 119
If thou be'st Prospero, Give us particulars of thy preservation . v 1 134
I am Prospero and that very duke Which was thrust forth of Milan . v 1 159
Prospero [found] his dukedom In a poor isle . . . . v 1 211
Prosperous. Bless this twain, that they may prosperous be . . iv 1 104
She hath prosperous art When she will play with reason *Meas. for Meas.* i 2 189
And I trust it will grow to a most prosperous perfection . . iii 1 271
But leave we him to his events, with a prayer they may prove prosperous iii 2 253
Our wealth increased By prosperous voyages . . *Com. of Errors* i 1 41
Go thou forth; And fortune play upon thy prosperous helm! *All's Well* iii 3 7
Be prosperous In more than this deed does require! . *W. Tale* ii 3 189
Thence, A prosperous south-wind friendly, we have cross'd . . v 1 161
God in thy good cause make thee prosperous! . . *Richard II.* i 3 78
The parties sure, And our induction full of prosperous hope *1 Hen. IV.* iii 1 2
And may our oaths well kept and prosperous be! . . *Hen. V.* v 2 402
The church's prayers made him so prosperous.—The church! *1 Hen. VI.* i 1 32
Fair be all thy hopes And prosperous be thy life in peace and war! . ii 5 114
With smiling plenty and fair prosperous days! . . *Richard III.* v 5 34
Heaven, from thy endless goodness, send prosperous life *Hen. VIII.* v 5 2
With most prosperous approbation . . . . . *Coriolanus* ii 1 114
Be strong and prosperous In this resolve . . . *Rom. and Jul.* iv 1 122
Live, and be prosperous: and farewell, good fellow . . v 3 42
I leave you To the protection of the prosperous gods . *T. of Athens* v 1 186
How of Cawdor? the thane of Cawdor lives, A prosperous gentleman *Macb.* i 3 73
Your good advice, Which still hath been both grave and prosperous . iii 1 22
To my unfolding lend your prosperous ear . . . *Othello* i 3 245
The time of universal peace is near: Prove this a prosperous day, the three-nook'd world Shall bear the olive freely . *Ant. and Cleo.* iv 6 6
Of all say'd yet, mayst thou prove prosperous! . . . *Pericles* i 1 59
If that thy prosperous and artificial feat Can draw him but to answer thee v 1 72
Come, let us leave her; And the gods make her prosperous! . . v 1 80
Prosperously I have attempted and With bloody passage led your wars even to The gates of Rome . . . . *Coriolanus* v 6 75
Which reason and sanity could not so prosperously be delivered of *Hamlet* ii 2 214
Prostitute. To prostitute our past-cure malady To empirics . *All's Well* ii 1 124
And prostitute me to the basest groom . . . . *Pericles* iv 6 201
Prostrate. I will fall prostrate at his feet . . . . *Com. of Errors* v 1 114
This prostrate and exterior bending . . . . *2 Hen. IV.* iv 5 149
Look gracious on thy prostrate thrall . . . . *1 Hen. VI.* i 2 117
Be you prostrate and grovel on the earth . . . . *2 Hen. VI.* i 4 13
And am enjoin'd By holy Laurence to fall prostrate here *Rom. and Jul.* iv 2 20
Being prostrate, thus he bade me say . . . . *J. Cæsar* iii 1 125
Protect. Now, the melancholy god protect thee . . . *T. Night* ii 4 75
Answer you so the lord protector?—The Lord protect him! . *1 Hen. VI.* i 3 9
Why should he, then, protect our sovereign, He being of age? *2 Hen. VI.* i 1 165
Marry, the Lord protect him, for he's a good man! Jesu bless him! i 3 5
Medice, teipsum—Protector, see to't well, protect yourself . . ii 1 54
Must you, Sir John, protect my lady here?—So am I given in charge . ii 4 79
Despite the bear-ward that protects the bear . . . . v 1 210
The king Had virtuous uncles to protect his grace . *Richard III.* ii 3 21
I mean the lord protector.—The Lord protect him from that kingly title! iv 1 20
Your long coat, priest, protects you . . . . *Hen. VIII.* iii 2 276
God and your majesty Protect mine innocence, or I fall into The trap! v 1 141
God protect thee! Into whose hand I give thy life . . . . v 5 11
That you protect this course, and put it on By your allowance *Lear* i 4 227
The gods protect you! And bless the good remainders of the court! *Cymbeline* i 1 128
The law Protects not us: then why should we be tender To let an arrogant piece of flesh threat us? . . . . . iv 2 126
The gods of Greece protect you! And we'll pray for you . *Pericles* i 4 97
In like necessity—The which the gods protect thee from!—may defend thee . . . . ii 1 135
Protected. As for you, that love to be protected . . *2 Hen. VI.* i 3 40
I see no reason why a king of years Should be to be protected like a child i 3 29
Protection. 'Therefore be well advised How you do leave me to mine own protection . . . . . . *Mer. of Venice* v 1 235
Leaving her In the protection of his son, her brother . *T. Night* i 2 38
There thou leave it, Without more mercy, to its own protection *W. Tale* ii 3 178
Protection. In this right hand, whose protection Is most divinely vow'd upon the right Of him it holds . . . . . *K. John* ii 1 236
Who should do the duke to death? Myself and Beaufort had him in protection; And we, I hope, sir, are no murderers . *2 Hen. VI.* iii 2 180
In protection of their tender ones . . . *3 Hen. VI.* ii 2 28
Put your main cause into the king's protection . . *Hen. VIII.* iii 1 93
To forfeit all your goods . . . and to be Out of the king's protection . iii 2 344
I leave you To the protection of the prosperous gods . *T. of Athens* v 1 186
Thou shalt meet Both welcome and protection . . . *Lear* iii 6 99
The king he takes the babe To his protection . . . *Cymbeline* i 1 41
May it please you To take them in protection? . . . . i 6 193
To your protection I commend me, gods. From fairies and the tempters of the night Guard me, beseech ye . . . . . . ii 2 8
Protector. Whate'er we like, thou art protector And lookest to command the prince and realm . . . . . . *1 Hen. VI.* i 1 37
Answer you so the lord protector?—The Lord protect him! so we answer him . . . . i 3 8
Whose will stands but mine? There's none protector of the realm but I i 3 12
Open the gates unto the lord protector, Or we'll burst them open . i 3 27
Thou most usurping proditor, And not protector, of the king or realm . i 3 32
That seeks to overthrow religion, Because he is protector of the realm . i 3 66
Am I not protector, saucy priest?—And am not I a prelate of the church? iii 1 45
What of that? Is not his grace protector to the king? . . . iii 1 60
Yield, my lord protector; yield, Winchester; Except you mean with obstinate repulse To slay your sovereign and destroy the realm . iii 1 112
And now, my lord protector, view the letter Sent from our uncle . iv 1 48
Ourself, my lord protector and the rest After some respite will return . iv 1 169
And so, my lord protector, see them guarded And safely brought to Dover v 1 48
My lord protector, give consent That Margaret may be England's royal queen . . . . v 5 23
Lord protector, so it please your grace, Here are the articles *2 Hen. VI.* i 1 39
There goes our protector in a rage . . . . i 1 147
For all this flattering gloss, He will be found a dangerous protector . i 1 164
If Gloucester be displaced, he'll be protector.—Or thou or I, Somerset, will be protector . . . . i 1 177
Art thou not second woman in the realm, And the protector's wife? . i 2 44
My lord protector, 'tis his highness' pleasure You do prepare to ride . i 2 56
Let's stand close: my lord protector will come this way by and by . i 3 2
Come back, fool; this is the Duke of Suffolk, and not my lord protector i 3 10
Pardon me; I took ye for my lord protector . . . . . i 3 14
'To my Lord Protector!' Are your supplications to his lordship? Let me see . . . . i 3 15
You, that love to be protected Under the wings of our protector's grace i 3 41
Beside the haughty protector, have we Beaufort The imperious churchman . . . . i 3 71
Not all these lords do vex me half so much As that proud dame, the lord protector's wife . . . . i 3 79
If he be old enough, what needs your grace To be protector of his excellence?—Madam, I am protector of the realm . . . i 3 122
My lord protector will, I doubt it not, See you well guerdon'd . . i 4 48
A sorry breakfast for my lord protector . . . . . . i 4 79
No marvel . . . My lord protector's hawks do tower so well . . ii 1 10
Pernicious protector, dangerous peer, That smooth'st it so with king! . ii 1 21
Let me be blessed for the peace I make, Against this proud protector! ii 1 37
Medice, teipsum—Protector, see to't well, protect yourself . . ii 1 54
Lady Eleanor, the protector's wife, The ringleader and head of all this rout . . . . ii 1 169
So, my lord protector, by this means Your lady is forthcoming yet at London . . . . ii 1 178
Give up thy staff: Henry will to himself Protector be . . . ii 3 24
And go in peace, Humphrey, no less beloved Than when thou wert protector . . . . ii 3 27
I think I am thy married wife And thou a prince, protector of this land ii 4 29
'Tis thought, my lord, that you took bribes of France, And, being protector, stay'd the soldiers' pay . . . . iii 1 105
Whiles I was protector, Pity was all the fault that was in me . . iii 1 124
Were't not all one, an empty eagle were set To guard the chicken from a hungry kite, As place Duke Humphrey for the king's protector? . iii 1 250
I am content he shall reign; but I'll be protector over him . . iv 2 167
Talk not of France, sith thou hast lost it all.—The lord protector lost it, and not I . . . . *3 Hen. VI.* i 1 111
The duke is made protector of the realm; And yet shalt thou be safe? . i 1 240
Warwick, Cobham, and the rest, Whom we have left protectors of the king . . . . i 2 57
And I choose Clarence only for protector . . . . . iv 6 37
I make you both protectors of this land . . . . . iv 6 41
Is it concluded he shall be protector?—It is determined *Richard III.* i 3 14
Will you go unto the Tower, my lord?—My lord protector needs will have it so . . . . iii 1 141
Who knows the lord protector's mind herein? Who is most inward? . iii 4 7
Where is my lord protector? I have sent for these strawberries . . iii 4 48
Thou protector of this damned strumpet, Tellest thou me of 'ifs'? . iii 4 76
Not as protector, steward, substitute, Or lowly factor for another's gain iii 7 133
The king! why, who's that?—I cry you mercy: I mean the lord protector iv 1 19
Under the covering of a careful night, Who seem'd my good protector *Per.* i 2 82
Protectorship. Did he not, in his protectorship, Levy great sums of money? . . . . *2 Hen. VI.* iii 1 60
In your protectorship you did devise Strange tortures for offenders . iii 1 121
Protectress. She may, I think, bestow't on any man.—She is protectress of her honour too: May she give that? . . . . *Othello* iv 1 14
Protest. When I protest true loyalty to her, She twits me with my falsehood to my friend . . . . *T. G. of Ver.* iv 2 7
To think upon her woes I do protest That I have wept . . . iv 4 149
Let thine inherit first; for, I protest, mine never shall . *Mer. Wives* ii 1 75
I have long loved her, and, I protest to you, bestowed much on her . ii 2 201
Protests to my husband he is now here . . . . . iv 2 33
I protest I love the duke as I love myself . . *Meas. for Meas.* v 1 344
This woman that I mean, My wife—but, I protest, without desert—Hath oftentimes upbraided me withal . . *Com. of Errors* iii 1 112
I protest, he had the chain of me, Though most dishonestly he doth deny it . . . . v 1 2
I protest I love thee.—Why, then, God forgive me! . . *Much Ado* iv 1 282
I was about to protest I loved you.—And do it with all thy heart.—I love you with so much of my heart that none is left to protest . iv 1 286
Do me right, or I will protest your cowardice . . . . v 1 149
I protest, I love to hear him lie . . . . . *L. L. Lost* i 1 176
I do protest I never heard of it; And if you prove it, I'll repay it ii 1 158
I protest, A world of torments though I should endure, I would not yield to be your house's guest . . . . v 2 352
I here protest, By this white glove,—how white the hand, God knows! v 2 410

Protest. I protest, the schoolmaster is exceeding fantastical . *L. L. Lost* v 2 531
On Diana's altar to protest For aye austerity . . . *M. N. Dream* i 1 89
I have a wife, whom, I protest, I love . . . . *Mer. of Venice* iv 1 290
For, I protest, her frown might kill me . . . *As Y. Like It* iv 1 110
No, I protest, I know not the contents : Phebe did write it . iv 3 21
Therein wealthiest, That I protest I simply am a maid . . *All's Well* ii 3 73
This has no holding, To swear by him whom I protest to love, That I will work against him . . . . iv 2 28
My meaning in't, I protest, was very honest in the behalf of the maid . iv 3 246
I protest, I take these wise men, that crow so at these set kind of fools, no better than the fools' zanies . . . . . *T. Night* i 5 94
He protests he will not hurt you . . . . iii 4 330
My lord, I do protest— O, do not swear! . . . . . v 1 173
But then you'll think—Which I protest against—I am assisted By wicked powers . . . . *W. Tale* v 3 90
I do protest I never loved myself Till now . . . *K. John* ii 1 501
Which, I protest, hath very much beguiled The tediousness *Richard II.* ii 3 11
I protest, my soul is full of woe, That blood should sprinkle me to make me grow . . . . v 6 45
And such protest of pepper-gingerbread . . . 1 *Hen. IV.* iii 1 260
I do protest, I have not sought the day of this dislike . . v 1 25
I protest, we are well fortified And strong enough to issue out 1 *Hen. VI.* iv 2 19
I here protest, in sight of heaven, . . . That I am clear . 3 *Hen. VI.* iii 3 181
When I know ; for I protest As yet I do not . . *Richard III.* i 1 52
This interchange of love, I here protest, Upon my part shall be unviolable . . . . ii 1 26
And never in my life, I do protest, Was it more precious to me . iii 2 81
I protest, Were I alone to pass the difficulties . *Troi. and Cres.* ii 2 138
When their rhymes, Full of protest, of oath, and big compare, Want similes . . . . iii 2 182
That, on mine honour, here I do protest . . . *T. Andron.* i 1 477
I protest unto thee—Good heart, and, i' faith, I will tell her . *R. and J.* ii 4 183
I will tell her, sir, that you do protest ; which, as I take it, is a gentlemanlike offer . . . . ii 4 189
I do protest, I never injured thee, But love thee . . . . iii 1 71
Yet, I protest, . . . Had his necessity made use of me, I would have put my wealth into donation . . . . . *T. of Athens* iii 2 86
Do villany, do, since you protest to do't, Like workmen . . iv 3 437
What Antony shall speak, I will protest He speaks by leave . *J. Cæsar* iii 1 238
If trembling I inhabit then, protest me The baby of a girl . *Macbeth* iii 4 105
Many unrough youths that even now Protest their first of manhood . v 2 11
The lady doth protest too much, methinks . . . . *Hamlet* iii 2 240
I protest, Maugre thy strength, youth, place, and eminence . *Lear* v 3 130
You advise me well.—I protest, in the sincerity of love . *Othello* ii 3 333
In wholesome wisdom He might not but refuse you, but he protests he loves you . . . . iii 1 50
Ay, and said nothing but what I protest intendment of doing . . iv 2 205
I protest, I have dealt most directly in thy affair . . . iv 2 211
I do Protest my ears were never better fed . . . . *Pericles* ii 5 27
I protest to thee, pretty one, my authority shall not see thee, or else look friendly upon thee . . . . iv 6 95
Protestation. Here is a coil with protestation ! . . . *T. G. of Ver.* i 2 99
I know they are stuff'd with protestations And full of new-found oaths iv 4 134
I can but say their protestation over . . . . *L. L. Lost* i 1 33
Upon his many protestations to marry me . . . , he won me . *All's Well* v 3 139
But to your protestation ; let me hear What you profess . *W. Tale* iv 4 379
Nor I have no cunning in protestation ; only downright oaths *Hen. V.* v 2 150
'Be thou true,' say I, to fashion in My sequent protestation *T. and C.* iv 4 68
Protested. After we had embraced, kissed, protested *Mer. Wives* iii 5 75
Protester. Were I a common laugher, or did use To stale with ordinary oaths my love To every new protester . . . . *J. Cæsar* i 2 74
Protesting oath on oath, That in a twink she won me to her love *T. of S.* ii 1 311
Proteus. Cease to persuade, my loving Proteus . . *T. G. of Ver.* i 1 1
Think on thy Proteus, when thou haply seest Some rare note-worthy object . . . . i 1 12
Thither will I bring thee, Valentine.—Sweet Proteus, no . . i 1 56
Sir Proteus, save you ! Saw you my master ?—But now he parted hence i 1 70
What think'st thou of the gentle Proteus ?—Lord, Lord ! to see what folly reigns in us ! . . . . i 2 14
Why not on Proteus, as of all the rest ?—Then thus : of many good I think him best . . . . i 2 20
Sent, I think, from Proteus. He would have given it you . . i 2 38
Indeed, I bid the base for Proteus . . . . i 2 97
And here is writ 'love-wounded Proteus.' Poor wounded name ! . i 2 113
I search it with a sovereign kiss. But twice or thrice was 'Proteus' written . . . . i 2 117
His name twice writ, 'Poor forlorn Proteus, passionate Proteus' . i 2 124
'Twas of his nephew Proteus, your son.—Why, what of him ? . i 3 3
For any or for all these exercises He said that Proteus your son was meet i 3 12
Good company ; with them shall Proteus go . . . . i 3 43
Proteus, your father calls for you : He is in haste ; therefore, I pray you, go . . . . i 3 88
Learned, like Sir Proteus, to wreathe your arms, like a malecontent ii 1 19
When you chid at Sir Proteus for going ungartered . . . ii 1 79
Proteus, you are stay'd for.—Go ; I come, I come. Alas ! this parting ii 2 19
And am going with Sir Proteus to the Imperial's court . . ii 3 5
Proteus, for that's his name, Made use and fair advantage of his days . ii 4 67
Welcome, dear Proteus ! Mistress, I beseech you, Confirm his welcome ii 4 100
You joy not in a love-discourse.—Ay, Proteus, but that life is alter'd . ii 4 128
O gentle Proteus, Love's a mighty lord And hath so humbled me . ii 4 136
Why, Valentine, what braggardism is this ?—Pardon me, Proteus . ii 4 165
Good Proteus, go with me to my chamber, In these affairs to aid me . ii 4 184
I may undertake A journey to my loving Proteus . . . ii 7 7
To one so dear, Of such divine perfection, as Sir Proteus . . ii 7 13
Better forbear till Proteus make return . . . . . ii 7 14
If Proteus like your journey when you come, No matter who's displeased ii 7 65
An ocean of his tears And instances of infinite of love Warrant me welcome to my Proteus . . . . ii 7 71
But truer stars did govern Proteus' birth ; His words are bonds . ii 7 74
Now, tell me, Proteus, what's your will with me ? . . . iii 1 3
Proteus, I thank thee for thine honest care ; Which to requite, command me . . . . iii 1 22
Sir Proteus ! Is your countryman According to our proclamation gone ? iii 2 11
Proteus, the good conceit I hold of thee—For thou hast shown some sign of good desert—Makes me the better to confer with thee . iii 2 17
And, Proteus, we dare trust you in this kind . . . . iii 2 56
Sweet Proteus, my direction-giver, Let us into the city presently . iii 2 90
How now, Sir Proteus, are you crept before us ? . . . iv 2 18
Doth this Sir Proteus that we talk on Often resort unto this gentlewoman ? . . . . iv 2 73

Proteus. Sir Proteus, as I take it.—Sir Proteus, gentle lady, and your servant . . . . *T. G. of Ver.* iv 2 90
By my halidom, I was fast asleep.—Pray you, where lies Sir Proteus ? . iv 2 137
Poor Proteus ! thou hast entertain'd A fox to be the shepherd of thy lambs . . . . iv 4 96
From my master, Sir Proteus, madam.—O, he sends you for a picture . iv 4 119
Belike she thinks that Proteus hath forsook her.—I think she doth . iv 4 151
Sir Proteus, what says Silvia to my suit ?—O, sir, I find her milder . v 2 1
Sir Proteus ! how now, Thurio ! Which of you saw Sir Eglamour of late ? v 2 31
I would have been a breakfast to the beast, Rather than have false Proteus rescue me . . . . v 4 35
As much, for more there cannot be, I do detest false perjured Proteus . v 4 39
O, 'tis the curse in love, . . . When women cannot love where they're beloved.—When Proteus cannot love where he's beloved . . . v 4 45
In love Who respects friend ?—All men but Proteus . . . v 4 54
Proteus, I am sorry I must never trust thee more . . . . v 4 68
O Proteus, let this habit make thee blush ! . . . . . v 4 104
Come, Proteus ; 'tis your penance but to hear The story of your loves . v 4 170
Add colours to the chameleon, Change shapes with Proteus 3 *Hen. VI.* iii 2 192
Protract. Else ne'er could he so long protract his speech . 1 *Hen. VI.* i 2 120
Bury him, And not protract with admiration what Is now due debt *Cymbeline* iv 2 232
Protractive. Which are indeed nought else But the protractive trials of great Jove . . . . *Troi. and Cres.* i 3 20
Proud. And, of so great a favour growing proud . . *T. G. of Ver.* ii 4 161
She is peevish, sullen, froward, Proud, disobedient, stubborn . . iii 1 69
She is proud.—Out with that too ; it was Eve's legacy, and cannot be ta'en from her . . . . iii 1 341
My wife, not meanly proud of two such boys . . . *Com. of Errors* i 1 59
I must not seem proud : happy are they that hear their detractions *M. Ado* ii 3 237
Like favourites, Made proud by princes . . . . . . iii 1 10
Mine I loved and mine I praised And mine that I was proud on . . iv 1 139
I am less proud to hear you tell my worth Than you much willing to be counted wise In spending your wit . . . . *L. L. Lost* ii 1 17
Proud of employment, willingly I go.—All pride is willing pride . ii 1 35
Proud with his form, in his eye pride express'd . . . . ii 1 237
And make him proud to make me proud that jests ! . . . v 2 66
Every pelting river made so proud . . . . . *M. N. Dream* ii 1 91
I am more proud to be Sir Rowland's son, His youngest son . *As Y. L. It* i 2 245
Proud, fantastical, apish, shallow, inconstant, full of tears . . iii 2 431
Praising the proud disdainful shepherdess That was his mistress . . iii 4 53
Must you be therefore proud and pitiless ? Why, what means this ? . iii 5 40
Shepherdess, look on him better, And be not proud . . . iii 5 79
Sure, he's proud, and yet his pride becomes him . . . iii 5 114
Nor the courtier's, which is proud, nor the soldier's, which is ambitious iv 1 12
She calls me proud, and that she could not love me . . . iv 3 16
I have loved this proud disdainful haggard . . . *T. of Shrew* iv 2 39
Our purses shall be proud, our garments poor . . . . iv 3 173
Peevish, proud, idle, made of self-love . . . . *All's Well* i 1 156
Making them proud of his humility, In their poor praise he humbled . i 2 44
Here, take her hand, Proud scornful boy, unworthy this good gift . ii 3 158
Thou shalt find what it is to be proud of thy bondage . . . ii 3 239
Our virtues would be proud, if our faults whipped them not . . iv 3 85
You are too proud ; But, if you were the devil, you are fair . *T. Night* i 5 269
I will be proud, I will read politic authors . . . . . ii 5 175
O world, how apt the poor are to be proud . . . . . iii 1 138
I will instruct my sorrows to be proud ; For grief is proud . *K. John* iii 1 68
O death, made proud with pure and princely beauty ! . . . iv 3 35
Fair cousin, you debase your princely knee To make the base earth proud with kissing it . . . . *Richard II.* iii 3 191
So proud that Bolingbroke was on his back ! . . . . . v 5 84
This hand hath made him proud with clapping him . . . . v 5 86
Which the proud soul ne'er pays but to the proud . 1 *Hen. IV.* i 3 9
Or like to men proud of destruction Defy us to our worst . *Hen. V.* iii 3 4
Proud of their numbers and secure in soul . . . . . iv Prol. 17
Thy wife is proud ; she holdeth thee in awe . . . 1 *Hen. VI.* i 1 39
Like that proud insulting ship Which Cæsar and his fortune bare at once i 2 138
With a proud majestical high scorn, He answer'd thus . . . iv 7 39
He speaks with such a proud commanding spirit . . . . iv 7 88
As stout and proud as he were lord of all . . . 2 *Hen. VI.* i 1 187
How insolent of late he is become, How proud, how peremptory ! . iii 1 8
By shameful murder of a guiltless king And lofty proud encroaching tyranny . . . . iv 1 96
Small things make base men proud . . . . iv 1 106
Farewell, and be proud of thy victory . . . . . . iv 10 77
Proud northern lord, Clifford of Cumberland . . . . v 2 6
Which makes thee thus presumptuous and proud . . . 3 *Hen. VI.* i 1 157
'Tis beauty that doth oft make women proud . . . . . i 4 128
The proud insulting queen, With Clifford and the haught Northumberland ii 1 168
Proud insulting boy ! Becomes it thee to be thus bold in terms ? . ii 2 84
While proud ambitious Edward Duke of York Usurps the regal title . iii 3 27
Speak like a subject, proud ambitious York ! . . . . . v 5 17
And the queen's sons and brothers haught and proud . *Richard III.* i 3 28
Thy age confirm'd, proud, subtle, bloody, treacherous . . . iv 4 171
So I leave him To him that made him proud, the pope . *Hen. VIII.* ii 2 56
In full as proud a place As broad Achilles . . *Troi. and Cres.* i 3 189
Were he not proud, we all should share with him . . . . i 3 368
Why should a man be proud ? How doth pride grow ? . . . ii 3 161
He that is proud eats up himself : pride is his own glass, his own trumpet ii 3 163
He is so plaguy proud that the death-tokens of it Cry 'No recovery' . ii 3 187
An a' be proud with me, I'll pheeze his pride . . . . . ii 3 215
If he were proud,—Or covetous of praise,—Ay, or surly borne . ii 3 247
Disarm great Hector.—'Twill make us proud to be his servant . iii 1 168
'Tis a burden Which I am proud to bear . . . . . . iii 3 37
So prophetically proud of an heroical cudgelling that he raves . iii 3 248
But that he pays himself with being proud . . . *Coriolanus* i 1 34
He did it to please his mother, and to be partly proud ; which he is . i 1 40
What would you have, you curs, That like nor peace nor war ? the one affrights you, The other makes you proud . . . . . . i 1 174
He is a lion That I am proud to hunt . . . . . . i 1 240
Was ever man so proud as is this Marcius ?—He has no equal . i 1 256
The present wars devour him : he is grown Too proud to be so valiant i 1 263
You blame Marcius for being proud ?—We do it not alone, sir . ii 1 36
A brace of unmeriting, proud, violent, testy magistrates, alias fools . ii 1 47
Yet you must be saying, Marcius is proud . . . . . ii 1 100
Marcius is coming home : he has more cause to be proud . . ii 1 161
Which That he will give them make I as little question As he is proud to do't . . . . ii 1 247
He's vengeance proud, and loves not the common people . . ii 2 6
Proud and ambitious tribune, canst thou tell ? . . . *T. Andron.* i 1 202

Proud. How proud I am of thee and of thy gifts Rome shall record *T. Andron.* i 1 254
Is she not proud? doth she not count her blest, Unworthy as she is, that we have wrought So worthy a gentleman to be her bridegroom? *Rom. and Jul.* iii 5 144
Not proud, you have; but thankful, that you have: Proud can I never be of what I hate . . . iii 5 148
What is this? 'Proud,' and 'I thank you,' and 'I thank you not;' And yet 'not proud' . . . iii 5 151
Thank me no thankings, nor proud me no prouds . . . iii 5 153
Thou art proud, Apemantus.—Of nothing so much as that I am not like Timon . . . *T. of Athens* i 1 188
Feasts are too proud to give thanks to the gods . . . i 2 62
I am proud, say, that my occasions have found time to use 'em . . . ii 2 199
Art thou proud yet?—Ay, that I am not thee.—I, that I was No prodigal iv 3 276
Be lion-mettled, proud; and take no care Who chafes, who frets *Macb.* iv 1 90
I am very proud, revengeful, ambitious . . . *Hamlet* iii 1 126
Base, proud, shallow, beggarly, three-suited, hundred-pound *Lear* ii 2 16
Proud of heart, to ride on a bay trotting-horse over four-inched bridges iii 4 56
A serving-man, proud in heart and mind; that curled my hair . . . iii 4 87
My demerits May speak unbonneted to as proud a fortune As this that I have reach'd . . . *Othello* i 2 23
She that was ever fair and never proud . . . ii 1 149
A province I will give thee, And make thy fortunes proud *Ant. and Cleo.* ii 5 69
Proud and disdainful, harping on what I am, Not what he knew I was iii 13 142
Let's do it after the high Roman fashion, And make death proud to take us . . . iv 15 88
Lies a mole, right proud Of that most delicate lodging . . . *Cymbeline* ii 4 135
At her birth, Thetis, being proud, swallow'd some part o' the earth *Pericles* iv 4 39
Proud adversaries. A weeder-out of his proud adversaries, A liberal rewarder of his friends . . . *Richard III.* i 3 123
Proud array. Is marching hitherward in proud array . . . *2 Hen. VI.* iv 9 27
Set not thy sweet heart on proud array . . . *Lear* iii 4 85
Proud arrogance. Be you, good lord, assured I hate not you for her proud arrogance . . . *Richard III.* i 3 24
Proud Athens. When I have laid proud Athens on a heap *T. of Athens* iv 3 101
Before proud Athens he's set down by this . . . v 3 9
Proud birds. And of their feather many moe proud birds . *3 Hen. VI.* ii 1 170
Proud Bolingbroke, I come To change blows with thee . *Richard II.* iii 2 188
My condemned lord Is doom'd a prisoner by proud Bolingbroke . . . v 1 4
Proud brag. Full well, Andronicus, Agree these deeds with that proud brag of thine . . . *T. Andron.* i 1 306
Proud cedars. Then let the mutinous winds Strike the proud cedars 'gainst the fiery sun . . . *Coriolanus* v 3 60
Proud chariot-wheels. That erst did follow thy proud chariot-wheels *2 Hen. VI.* ii 4 13
Proud child. Whose self-same mettle, Whereof thy proud child, arrogant man, is puff'd, Engenders the black toad . . . *T. of Athens* iv 3 180
Proud Cleopatra, when she met her Roman . . . *Cymbeline* ii 4 70
Proud contempt. Whiles we, God's wrathful agent, do correct Their proud contempt . . . *K. John* ii 1 88
Proud control. The proud control of fierce and bloody war . . . i 1 17
Proud dame. Not all these lords do vex me half so much As that proud dame . . . *2 Hen. VI.* i 3 79
Proud day. And the proud day, Attended with the pleasures of the world, Is all too wanton . . . *K. John* iii 3 34
Proud death, What feast is toward in thine eternal cell? . . . *Hamlet* v 2 375
Proud desire. It warm'd thy father's heart with proud desire Of bold-faced victory . . . *1 Hen. VI.* iv 6 11
Proud Diomed, believe, I come to lose my arm, or win my sleeve *T. and C.* v 3 95
Proud disdain. The red glow of scorn and proud disdain *As Y. Like It* iii 4 57
Proud dream, That play'st so subtly with a king's repose *Hen. V.* iv 1 274
Proud Duke Humphrey. And make a show of love to proud Duke Humphrey . . . *2 Hen. VI.* i 1 241
Proud earth. My unshrubb'd down, Rich scarf to my proud earth *Temp.* iv 1 82
Proud empress. I know thee well For our proud empress *T. Andron.* v 2 26
Proud foot. This England never did, nor never shall, Lie at the proud foot of a conqueror . . . *K. John* v 7 113
Proud Frenchwoman. Was it you?—Was't I! yea, I it was, proud Frenchwoman . . . *2 Hen. VI.* i 3 143
Proud heart. Swell'st thou, proud heart? I'll give thee scope to beat *Richard II.* iii 3 140
Somerset, who in proud heart Doth stop my cornets . *1 Hen. VI.* iv 3 24
My proud heart sues and prompts my tongue to speak . *Richard III.* i 2 171
Lion-sick, sick of proud heart: you may call it melancholy *Tr. and Cr.* ii 3 93
With a proud heart he wore his humble weeds . *Coriolanus* ii 3 161
All this! ay, more: fret till your proud heart break . *J. Cæsar* iv 3 42
Proud-hearted Warwick, I defy thee . . . *3 Hen. VI.* v 1 98
Proud Hereford. Hereford here, whom you call king, Is a foul traitor to proud Hereford's king . . . *Richard II.* iv 1 135
Proud hoofs. Printing their proud hoofs i' the receiving earth *Hen. V.* Prol. 27
Proud horses. Spur your proud horses hard! . . . *Richard III.* v 3 340
Proud humility. His humble ambition, proud humility . . . *All's Well* i 1 185
Proud Italy. Report of fashions in proud Italy . . . *Richard II.* ii 1 21
Proud Jack. I am no proud Jack, like Falstaff . . . *1 Hen. IV.* ii 4 12
Proud joy. My time Runs posting on in Bolingbroke's proud joy *Rich. II.* v 5 59
Proud kindred. To part the queen's proud kindred from the king *Richard III.* ii 2 150
Proud king. Revenge the jeering and disdain'd contempt Of this proud king . . . *1 Hen. IV.* i 3 184
Proud Lancaster. Nor shall proud Lancaster usurp my right *2 Hen. VI.* i 1 244
Proud London. When through proud London he came sighing on *2 Hen. IV.* i 3 104
Proud lord. Say, if thou darest, proud Lord of Warwickshire That I am faulty . . . *2 Hen. VI.* iii 2 201
Proud lord, thou liest . . . *Hen. VIII.* iii 2 252
Proud Lucius. Pluck proud Lucius from the warlike Goths *T. Andron.* iv 4 110
Proud majesty. Made glory base and sovereignty a slave, Proud majesty a subject, state a peasant . . . *Richard II.* iv 1 252
Proud man. But man, proud man, Drest in a little brief authority, Most ignorant of what he's most assured . . . *Meas. for Meas.* ii 2 117
Laid the sentence of dread banishment On yon proud man *Richard II.* iii 3 135
And break the neck Of that proud man that did usurp his back . . v 5 89
I do hate a proud man, as I hate the engendering of toads *Troi. and Cres.* ii 3 169
Supple knees Feed arrogance and are the proud man's fees . . . iii 3 49
It would discredit the blest gods, proud man, To answer such a question iv 5 247
The oppressor's wrong, the proud man's contumely . . *Hamlet* iii 1 71
Proud-minded. I am as peremptory as she proud-minded *T. of Shrew* ii 1 132
Proud mistress. I think she means to tangle my eyes too! No, faith, proud mistress, hope not after it . . . *As Y. Like It* iii 5 45
Proud mock. For this proud mock I'll be thy slaughter-man *T. Andron.* iv 4 58
Proud neck. Thy proud neck bears half my burthen'd yoke *Richard III.* iv 4 111
Proud Plantagenet. I am your butt, and I abide your shot.—Yield to our mercy, proud Plantagenet . . . *3 Hen. VI.* i 4 30
Proud Pole, I will, and scorn both him and thee . . *1 Hen. VI.* ii 4 78
Proud prelate, in thy face I see thy fury . . . *2 Hen. VI.* i 1 142
Proud protector. Let me be blessed for the peace I make Against this proud protector! . . . ii 1 37
Proud queen. I would assay, proud queen, to make thee blush, To tell thee whence thou camest . . . *3 Hen. VI.* i 4 118
Taught thee to insult? It needs not, nor it boots thee not, proud queen i 4 125
Proud rate. At such proud rate, that it out-speaks Possession of a subject . . . *Hen. VIII.* iii 2 127
Proud river. Like a proud river peering o'er his bounds *K. John* iii 1 23
Proud Rome. Farewell, proud Rome; till Lucius come again, He leaves his pledges dearer than his life . . . *T. Andron.* iii 1 291
Proud Saturnine, interrupter of the good That noble-minded Titus means to thee! . . . i 1 208
And make proud Saturnine and his empress Beg at the gates . . . iii 1 298
Proud Scot. I was not born a yielder, thou proud Scot . *1 Hen. IV.* v 3 11
Proud setter up and puller down of kings! . . *3 Hen. VI.* iii 3 157
Proud Somerset. In signal of my love to thee, Against proud Somerset *1 Hen. VI.* ii 4 122
Why I have brought this army hither Is to remove proud Somerset *2 Hen. VI.* v 1 36
Proud soul. That title of respect Which the proud soul ne'er pays but to the proud . . . *1 Hen. IV.* i 3 9
Proud steed. Bareheaded, lower than his proud steed's neck *Richard II.* v 2 19
Proud summer. Why should proud summer boast Before the birds have any cause to sing? . . . *L. L. Lost* i 1 102
Proud-swelling. The unowed interest of proud-swelling state *K. John* iv 3 147
Proud Titania. Ill met by moonlight, proud Titania . *M. N. Dream* ii 1 60
Proud titles. I better brook the loss of brittle life Than those proud titles thou hast won of me . . . *1 Hen. IV.* v 4 79
Proud tops. He fires the proud tops of the eastern pines *Richard II.* iii 2 42
Proud traitor. Thou art a proud traitor, priest.—Proud lord, thou liest *Hen. VIII.* iii 2 252
Proud Trojan. I do disdain thy courtesy, proud Trojan *Troi. and Cres.* v 6 15
Proud will. And frustrate his proud will . . . *Lear* iv 6 64
Proud words. Durst the traitor breathe out so proud words? *3 Hen. VI.* iv 1 112
Prouder. Nature never framed a woman's heart Of prouder stuff *M. Ado* iii 1 50
I know you would be prouder of the work Than customary bounty can enforce you . . . *Mer. of Venice* iii 4 8
Our party may well meet a prouder foe . . . *K. John* v 1 79
Make him fall His crest that prouder than blue Iris bends *Troi. and Cres.* i 3 380
Now is the cur Ajax prouder than the cur Achilles, and will not arm to-day . . . v 4 16
Hail, thou fair heaven! We house i' the rock, yet use thee not so hardly As prouder livers do . . . *Cymbeline* iii 3 9
Prouder than rustling in unpaid-for silk . . . iii 3 24
Proudest. They could never get her so much as sip on a cup with the proudest of them all . . . *Mer. Wives* ii 2 77
If they wrong her honour, The proudest of them shall well hear of it *Much Ado* iv 1 194
I'll bring mine action on the proudest he That stops my way *T. of Shrew* iii 2 236
And that thou and the proudest of you all shall find . . . iv 1 89
It would amaze the proudest of you all . . . *1 Hen. VI.* iv 7 84
Winchester will not submit, I trow, Or be inferior to the proudest peer v 1 57
The proudest peer in the realm shall not wear a head on his shoulders, unless he pay me tribute . . . *2 Hen. VI.* iv 7 127
Neither the king, nor he that loves him best, The proudest he that holds up Lancaster, Dares stir a wing . . . *3 Hen. VI.* i 1 46
To answer thee, Or any he the proudest of thy sort . . . ii 2 97
The proudest of you all Have been beholding to him in his life *Rich. III.* ii 1 128
Let me see the proudest He, that dares most, but wag his finger *Hen. VIII.* v 3 130
Give us the proudest prisoner of the Goths . . . *T. Andron.* i 1 96
I have dogs, my lord, Will rouse the proudest panther in the chase . ii 2 21
As she in fury shall Cut off the proud'st conspirator that lives . iv 4 26
Proudlier. He bears himself more proudlier, Even to my person, than I thought he would . . . *Coriolanus* iv 7 8
Proudly. They say I will bear myself proudly . . . *Much Ado* ii 3 234
Bearing their birthrights proudly on their backs . . *K. John* ii 1 70
So proudly as if he disdain'd the ground . . . *Richard II.* v 5 83
The tide of blood in me Hath proudly flow'd in vanity till now *2 Hen. IV.* v 2 130
Let me speak proudly . . . *Hen. V.* iv 3 108
Question her proudly; let thy looks be stern . . . *1 Hen. VI.* i 2 62
He left me proudly, as unworthy fight . . . iv 7 43
And, by that knot, looks proudly o'er the crown . *Richard III.* iv 3 42
Securely done, A little proudly . . . *Troi. and Cres.* iv 5 74
You vile abominable tents, Thus proudly pight upon our Phrygian plains v 10 24
Provand. Who have their provand Only for bearing burdens *Coriolanus* ii 1 267
Prove. If you prove a mutineer,—the next tree! . . . *Tempest* iii 2 40
This will prove a brave kingdom to me . . . iii 2 153
Now, jerkin, you are like to lose your hair and prove a bald jerkin iv 1 238
If this prove A vision of the Island, one dear son Shall I twice lose v 1 175
You call me fool.—So, by your circumstance, I fear you'll prove *T. G. of V.* i 1 37
This proves me still a sheep.—True; and thy master a shepherd . . i 1 82
It shall go hard but I'll prove it . . . i 1 86
I fear she'll prove as hard to you in telling your mind . . . i 1 147
I cannot now prove constant to myself, Without some treachery . ii 6 31
Pray heaven he prove so, when you come to him! . . . ii 7 79
This proves that thou canst not read . . . iii 1 297
More hair than wit? It may be; I'll prove it . . . iii 1 359
Longer than I prove loyal to your grace Let me not live . . . iii 2 20
Cannot be true servant to my master, Unless I prove false traitor to myself . . . iv 4 110
How Falstaff, varlet vile, His dove will prove . . . *Mer. Wives* i 3 107
But if it prove true, Master Page, have you any way then to unfool me? iv 2 119
Prove it before these varlets here, thou honourable man; prove it *M. for M.* ii 1 88
Prove this, thou wicked Hannibal, or I'll have mine action of battery . ii 1 186
I shall beat you to your tent, and prove a shrewd Cæsar to you . . ii 1 263
By the affection that now guides me most, I'll prove a tyrant to him . ii 4 169
Mercy to thee would prove itself a bawd: 'Tis best that thou diest . iii 1 150
But yet, sir, I would prove— Nay, if the devil have given thee proofs for sin, Thou wilt prove his . . . iii 2 30
Leave we him to his events, with a prayer they may prove prosperous iii 2 253
Using painting, do prove my occupation a mystery . . . iv 2 40
This may prove worse than hanging . . . iv 2 165
If it prove so, I will be gone the sooner . *Com. of Errors* i 2 103
I am an ass, indeed; you may prove it by my long ears . . . iv 4 30

Prove. I'll prove mine honour and mine honesty Against thee presently *Com. of Errors* v 1 30
Prove that ever I lose more blood with love than I will get again *M. Ado* i 1 252
If ever thou dost fall from this faith, thou wilt prove a notable argument i 1 258
Come, let us thither: this may prove food to my displeasure i 3 68
Shall we go prove what's to be done? i 3 75
Lest I should prove the mother of fools ii 1 295
If it proves so, then loving goes by haps iii 1 105
We are like to prove a goodly commodity, being taken up iii 3 190
Prove you that any man with me conversed At hours unmeet iv 1 183
I'll prove it on his body, if he dare, Despite his nice fence v 1 74
These oaths and laws will prove an idle scorn *L. L. Lost* i 1 311
A most fine figure!—To prove you a cipher i 2 59
His ignorance were wise, Where now his knowledge must prove ignorance ii 1 103
You'll prove perjured if you make me stay ii 1 113
I do protest I never heard of it; And if you prove it, I'll repay it back ii 1 159
All those three I will prove.—What wilt thou prove?—A man, if I live iii 1 40
Though to myself forsworn, to thee I'll faithful prove iv 2 111
I will prove those verses to be very unlearned iv 2 164
But I will prove, Thou being a goddess, I forswore not thee iv 3 64
I'll prove her fair, or talk till doomsday here iv 3 274
Now prove Our loving lawful, and our faith not torn iv 3 284
Love's tongue proves dainty Bacchus gross in taste iv 3 339
Else none at all in aught proves excellent iv 3 354
Then fools you were these women to forswear, Or keeping what is sworn, you will prove fools iv 3 356
Light wenches may prove plagues to men forsworn iv 3 385
To prove, by wit, worth in simplicity v 2 78
A fair lord calf.—Let's part the word.—No, I'll not be your half: Take all, and wean it; it may prove an ox v 2 250
Wise things seem foolish and rich things but poor.—This proves you wise and rich v 2 379
My hat to a halfpenny, Pompey proves the best Worthy v 2 563
We to ourselves prove false, By being once false for ever to be true v 2 782
That he may prove More fond on her than she upon her love *M. N. Dream* ii 1 265
How can these things in me seem scorn to you, Bearing the badge of faith, to prove them true? iii 2 127
I swear by that which I will lose for thee, To prove him false that says I love thee not iii 2 253
I love thee more than he can do.—If thou say so, withdraw, and prove it iii 2 255
And so far blameless proves my enterprise iii 2 350
With the help of a surgeon he might yet recover, and prove an ass v 1 317
I fear he will prove the weeping philosopher when he grows old *M. of V.* i 2 53
Let us make incision for your love, To prove whose blood is reddest ii 1 7
I would it might prove the end of his losses iii 1 20
Prove it so, Let fortune go to hell for it, not I iii 2 20
I'll prove the prettier fellow of the two iii 4 64
How prove you that, in the great heap of your knowledge? *As Y. Like It* i 2 72
One of you will prove a shrunk panel and, like green timber, warp, warp iii 3 89
You shall say I'll prove a busy actor in their play iii 4 62
Go your ways; I knew what you would prove iv 1 187
Good plays prove the better by the help of good epilogues Epil. 6
And that my deeds shall prove.—And that his bags shall prove *T. of S.* i 2 177
Give him head: I know he'll prove a jade i 2 249
Will my daughter prove a good musician?—I think she'll sooner prove a soldier ii 1 145
For patience she will prove a second Grissel ii 1 297
'Tis like you'll prove a jolly surly groom, That take it on you at the first so roundly iii 2 215
And may you prove, sir, master of your art!—While you, sweet dear, prove mistress of my heart! iv 2 9
That I'll prove upon thee, though thy little finger be armed in a thimble iv 3 148
Worthy fellows; and like to prove most sinewy sword-men *All's Well* ii 1 61
And I shall prove A lover of thy drum, hater of love iii 3 10
That time and place with this deceit so lawful May prove coherent iii 7 39
If it should prove That thou art so inhuman,—'twill not prove so v 3 115
If you shall prove This ring was ever hers, you shall as easy Prove that I husbanded her bed in Florence v 3 124
Fairer prove your honour Than in my thought it lies v 3 183
If it . . . prove untrue, Deadly divorce step between me and you! v 3 318
Those wits, that think they have thee, do very oft prove fools *T. Night* i 5 37
Good madonna, give me leave to prove you a fool.—Can you do it? i 5 64
For still we prove Much in our vows, but little in our love ii 4 120
Words are grown so false, I am loath to prove reason with them iii 1 29
I will prove it legitimate, sir, upon the oaths of judgement and reason iii 2 15
To a stranger, Unguided and unfriended, often prove Rough and unhospitable iii 3 10
But O how vile an idol proves this god! iii 4 399
Prove true, imagination, O, prove true, That I, dear brother, be now ta'en for you! iii 4 409
O, if it prove, Tempests are kind and salt waves fresh in love iii 4 418
I am afraid this great lubber, the world, will prove a cockney iv 1 15
Which if you seek to prove, I dare not stand by *W. Tale* i 2 443
Be certain what you do, sir, lest your justice Prove violence ii 1 128
If it prove She's otherwise, I'll keep my stables where I lodge my wife ii 1 133
If this prove true, they'll pay for't: by mine honour ii 1 146
If I prove honey-mouth'd, let my tongue blister ii 2 33
If the event o' the journey Prove as successful to the queen,—O be't so! iii 1 12
This is fairy gold, boy, and 'twill prove so: up with't, keep it close iii 3 128
If I make not this cheat bring out another and the shearers prove sheep iv 3 130
I will prove so, sir, to my power.—Ay, by any means prove a tall fellow v 2 182
The which if he can prove, a' pops me out At least from fair five hundred pound a year *K. John* i 1 68
He that proves the king, To him will we prove loyal ii 1 270
Doth not the crown of England prove the king? ii 1 273
Both are alike; and both alike we like. One must prove greatest ii 1 332
You think them false That give you cause to prove my saying true iii 1 28
Which, being touch'd and tried, Proves valueless iii 1 101
Prove a deadly bloodshed but a jest, Exampled by this heinous spectacle iv 3 55
Thou art a murderer.—Do not prove me so; Yet I am none iv 3 90
What my tongue speaks my right drawn sword may prove *Richard II.* i 1 46
Look, what I speak, my life shall prove it true i 1 87
I say and will in battle prove, Or here or elsewhere i 1 92
To prove myself a loyal gentleman i 1 148
To prove him, in defending of myself, A traitor to my God i 3 23

Prove. Ready here do stand in arms, To prove, by God's grace and my body's valour *Richard II.* i 3 37
To prove the Duke of Norfolk, Thomas Mowbray, A traitor to his God i 3 107
Things sweet to taste prove in digestion sour i 3 236
This earth shall have a feeling and these stones Prove armed soldiers iii 2 25
There I throw my gage, To prove it on thee to the extremest point iv 1 47
It will the woefullest division prove That ever fell upon this cursed earth iv 1 146
Forget to pity him, lest thy pity prove A serpent that will sting thee v 3 57
Your mother well hath pray'd, and prove you true v 3 145
My brain I'll prove the female to my soul, My soul the father v 5 6
The true prince may, for recreation sake, prove a false thief *1 Hen. IV.* i 2 174
To prove that true Needs no more but one tongue i 3 95
Shall the blessed sun of heaven prove a micher and eat blackberries? ii 4 450
Shall the son of England prove a thief and take purses? ii 4 452
By my faith, I am afraid he would prove the better counterfeit v 4 126
Which to prove fruit, Hope gives not so much warrant as despair *2 Hen. IV.* i 3 39
Prove that ever I dress myself handsome till thy return ii 4 302
Learn this, Thomas, And thou shalt prove a shelter to thy friends iv 4 42
And what indeed I should say will, I doubt, prove mine own marring Epil. 7
Thou must therefore needs prove a good soldier-breeder *Hen. V.* v 2 219
No prophet will I trust, if she prove false *1 Hen. VI.* i 2 150
A maid! and be so martial!—Pray God she prove not masculine ere long ii 1 22
Then, alone, since there's no remedy, I mean to prove this lady's courtesy ii 2 58
But no traitor; And that I'll prove on better men than Somerset ii 4 98
And will not you maintain the thing you teach, But prove a chief offender? iii 1 130
As for your spiteful false objections, Prove them *2 Hen. VI.* i 3 159
I am come hither . . . to prove him a knave and myself an honest man ii 3 88
And prove the period of their tyranny iii 1 149
This spark will prove a raging fire, If wind and fuel be brought to feed it iii 1 302
For death or dignity.—The first I warrant thee, if dreams prove true v 1 195
My title's good, and better far than his.—Prove it, Henry *3 Hen. VI.* i 1 131
I'll prove the contrary, if you'll hear me speak i 2 20
To prove him tyrant this reason may suffice, That Henry liveth still iii 3 71
In hope he'll prove a widower shortly, I'll wear the willow garland iii 3 227; iv 1 99
I want a kingdom, yet in marriage I may not prove inferior to yourself iv 1 122
So God help Montague as he proves true! iv 1 143
This pretty lad will prove our country's bliss iv 6 70
Since I cannot prove a lover, To entertain these fair well-spoken days, I am determined to prove a villain *Richard III.* i 1 28
In those busy days Which here you urge to prove us enemies i 3 146
I fear, I fear 'twill prove a troublous world ii 3 5
Pray God, I say, I prove a needless coward! iii 2 90
Your most obedient subject.—Art thou, indeed?—Prove me iv 2 69
Hoping the consequence Will prove as bitter, black, and tragical iv 4 7
So deal with him as I prove true to you iv 4 499
What thinkest thou, will our friends prove all true? v 3 213
When these so noble benefits shall prove Not well disposed *Hen. VIII.* i 2 115
Men fear'd the French would prove perfidious, To the king's danger i 2 156
And that he doubted 'Twould prove the verity of certain words i 2 159
If . . . you can report, And prove it too, against mine honour aught ii 4 39
Prove but our marriage lawful, by my life . . . we are contented ii 4 226
Ye speak like honest men; pray God, ye prove so! iii 1 69
Which are heresies, And, not reform'd, may prove pernicious v 3 19
But to prove to you that Helen loves Troilus,— Troilus will stand to the proof, if you'll prove it so *Troi. and Cres.* i 2 140
And may that soldier a mere recreant prove, That means not, hath not, or is not in love! i 3 287
I'll prove this truth with my three drops of blood i 3 301
Praise us as we are tasted, allow us as we prove iii 2 98
If ever you prove false one to another iii 2 206
Expressly proves That no man is the lord of any thing iii 3 114
My dreams will, sure, prove ominous to the day v 3 6
So, now the gates are ope: now prove good seconds *Coriolanus* i 4 43
Filling the air with swords advanced and darts, We prove this very hour i 6 62
When drums and trumpets shall I' the field prove flatterers, let courts and cities be Made all of false-faced soothing! i 9 43
It is the humane way: the other course Will prove too bloody iii 1 328
So use it That my revengeful services may prove As benefits to thee iv 5 95
To prove more fortunes Thou'rt tired iv 5 99
And not a hair upon a soldier's head Which will not prove a whip iv 6 134
I'll prove him, Speed how it will v 1 60
That thou mayst prove To shame unvulnerable v 3 72
What, wouldst thou have me prove myself a bastard? *T. Andron.* ii 3 148
To prove thou hast a true-divining heart, . . . look down into this den ii 3 214
Which I wish may prove More stern and bloody than the Centaurs' feast v 2 203
Black and portentous must this humour prove *Rom. and Jul.* i 1 147
I will take thy word: yet, if thou swear'st, Thou mayst prove false ii 2 92
I'll prove more true Than those that have more cunning to be strange ii 2 100
O, swear not by the moon, . . . Lest that thy love prove likewise variable ii 2 111
This bud of love, by summer's ripening breath, May prove a beauteous flower ii 2 122
For this alliance may so happy prove ii 3 91
Which added to the goose, proves thee far and wide a broad goose ii 4 90
Grant I may never prove so fond, To trust man on his oath *T. of Athens* i 2 65
So it may prove an argument of laughter iii 3 20
It could not else be, I should prove so base, To sue, and be denied iii 5 94
You said the enemy would not come down . . . : It proves not so *J. C.* v 1 4
Thou liest, abhorred tyrant; with my sword I'll prove the lie *Macbeth* v 7 11
A man faithful and honourable.—I would fain prove so *Hamlet* ii 2 131
To the noble mind Rich gifts wax poor when givers prove unkind iii 1 101
For 'tis a question left us yet to prove, Whether love lead fortune, or else fortune love iii 2 212
Full oft 'tis seen, . . . our mere defects Prove our commodities *Lear* iv 1 23
Our wishes on the way May prove effects iv 2 15
There's my gauntlet; I'll prove it on a giant iv 6 91
I can produce a champion that will prove What is avouched there v 1 43
If he should husband you.—Jesters do oft prove prophets v 3 71
Let the drum strike, and prove my title thine v 3 81
To prove upon thy heinous, manifest, and many treasons v 3 91
I'll prove it on thy heart, Ere I taste bread v 3 93
And my best spirits are bent To prove upon thy heart, whereto I speak v 3 140
If it prove lawful prize, he's made for ever *Othello* i 2 51
I dare think he'll prove to Desdemona A most dear husband ii 1 299

Prove. No, Iago; I'll see before I doubt; when I doubt, prove *Othello* iii 3 190
If I do prove her haggard, Though that her jesses were my dear heart-strings, I'ld whistle her off. . . . iii 3 260
Villain, be sure thou prove my love a whore, Be sure of it . . . iii 3 359
So prove it, That the probation bear no hinge nor loop To hang a doubt on . . . iii 3 364
If that the earth could teem with woman's tears, Each drop she falls would prove a crocodile . . . . iv 1 257
That was not so well; yet would I knew That stroke would prove the worst! . . . . iv 1 285
Are you of good or evil?—As you shall prove us, praise us . . v 1 66
That which is the strength of their amity shall prove the immediate author of their variance *Ant. and Cleo.* ii 6 137
Prove such a wife As my thoughts make thee . . . . iii 2 25
Prove this a prosperous day, the three-nook'd world Shall bear the olive iv 6 6
Husband, I come: Now to that name my courage prove my title . v 2 291
This proves me base . . . . v 2 303
Expected to prove so worthy as since he hath been allowed . *Cymbeline* i 4 2
First, perchance, she'll prove on cats and dogs, Then afterward up higher . . . . i 5 38
When to my good lord I prove untrue, I'll choke myself . . . i 5 86
I do believe, Statist though I am none, nor like to be, That this will prove a war . . . . ii 4 17
But if I were as wise as honest, then My purpose would prove well . iii 4 122
Not seen of late? Grant, heavens, that which I fear Prove false! . . iii 5 53
What he learns by this May prove his travel, not her danger . . iii 5 103
For true to thee Were to prove false, which I will never be, To him . iii 5 164
If I prove a good repast to the spectators, the dish pays the shot . v 4 157
That it was folly in me, thou mayst say, And prove it in thy feeling . v 5 68
My tears that fall Prove holy water on thee! . . . . v 5 269
But I will prove that two on's are as good As I have given out him . v 5 311
Of all say'd yet, mayst thou prove prosperous! . . . *Pericles* i 1 59
That will prove awful both in deed and word . . . . ii Gower 4
This sword shall prove he's honour's enemy . . . . . ii 5 64
Prove that I cannot, take me home again . . . . . iv 6 200
Tell thy story; If thine consider'd prove the thousandth part Of my endurance, thou art a man, and I Have suffer'd like a girl . . v 1 136
Proved the sliding of your brother A merriment *Meas. for Meas.* ii 4 115
You would all this time have proved there is no time *Com. of Errors* ii 2 101
It is proved already that you are little better than false knaves *M. Ado* iv 2 23
Thou art full of piety, as shall be proved upon thee by good witness iv 2 82
It is proved my Lady Hero hath been falsely accused . . . iv 2 98
The fool said, and so say I, and I the fool: well proved, wit! *L. L. Lost* iv 3 6
Well proved again o' my side! I will not love: if I do, hang me . iv 3 8
How art thou proved Judas?—Judas I am . . . . . v 2 604
True she is, as she hath proved herself . . . *Mer. of Venice* ii 6 55
If it be proved against an alien That by direct or indirect attempts He seek the life of any citizen, The party 'gainst the which he doth contrive Shall seize one half his goods . . . . . . iv 1 349
Prescriptions Of rare and proved effects . . . . *All's Well* i 3 228
O that it could be proved That some night-tripping fairy had exchanged In cradle-clothes our children where they lay! . . 1 *Hen. IV.* i 1 86
When Richard . . . Did speak these words, now proved a prophecy 2 *Hen. IV.* iii 1 69
And, commendable proved, let's die in pride . . 1 *Hen. VI.* iv 6 57
Is the hour to come That e'er I proved thee false . . 2 *Hen. VI.* iii 1 205
Let him die, in that he is a fox, By nature proved an enemy to the flock, . . . As Humphrey, proved by reasons, to my liege . . iii 1 258
Thy fortune, York, hadst thou been regent there, Might happily have proved far worse than his . . . . iii 1 306
It will be proved to thy face . . . . iv 7 41
Seeing thou hast proved so unnatural a father! . . . 3 *Hen. VI.* ii 1 218
And proved the subject of my own soul's curse . . . *Richard III.* iv 1 81
That same dog-fox, Ulysses, is not proved worth a blackberry *T. and C.* v 4 13
I sprang not more in joy at first hearing he was a man-child than now in first seeing he had proved himself a man . . *Coriolanus* i 3 18
When he might act the woman in the scene, He proved best man i' the field . . . . ii 2 101
To suffer lawful censure for such faults As shall be proved upon you . iii 3 47
That this fell fault of my accursed sons, Accursed, if the fault be proved in them,— If it be proved! you see it is apparent *T. Andron.* ii 3 291
Is the readiest man to kill him: 't has been proved . *T. of Athens* i 2 50
He did behave his anger, ere 'twas spent, As if he had but proved an argument . . . . iii 5 23
I thank thee, Brutus, That thou hast proved Lucilius' saying true *J. C.* v 5 59
But treasons capital, confess'd and proved, Have overthrown him *Macb.* i 3 115
Hath there been such a time—I'd fain know that—That I have positively said ''Tis so,' when it proved otherwise? . . . *Hamlet* ii 2 155
'Tis too much proved—that with devotion's visage And pious action we do sugar o'er The devil himself . . . . . . iii 1 47
He was likely, had he been put on, To have proved most royally . v 2 409
She was in love, and he she loved proved mad And did forsake her *Oth.* iv 3 27
You have seen and proved a fairer former fortune . *Ant. and Cleo.* i 2 33
You, Polydore, have proved best woodman . . . *Cymbeline* iii 6 28
His description Proved us unspeaking sots . . . . . v 5 178
Provender. Say, sweet love, what thou desirest to eat.—Truly, a peck of provender . . . . *M. N. Dream* iv 1 34
Give their fasting horses provender, And after fight with them? *Hen. V.* iv 2 58
Dieted like mules And have their provender tied to their mouths 1 *Hen. VI.* i 2 11
For that I do appoint him store of provender . . *J. Cæsar* iv 1 30
Wears out his time, much like his master's ass, For nought but provender, and when he's old, cashier'd . . . . *Othello* i 1 48
Prover. Why am I a fool?—Make that demand of the prover *Troi. and Cres.* ii 3 72
Proverb. And thereof comes the proverb . . . . *T. G. of Ver.* iii 1 305
He gives me the proverbs and the no-verbs . . *Mer. Wives* iii 1 107
If I have horns to make one mad, let the proverb go with me: I'll be horn-mad . . . . iii 5 154
Have at you with a proverb—Shall I set in my staff? *Com. of Errors* iii 1 51
Patch grief with proverbs, make misfortune drunk With candle-wasters *Much Ado* v 1 17
The country proverb known, That every man should take his own *M. N. Dream* iii 2 458
The old proverb is very well parted between . . . you *Mer. of Venice* ii 2 158
Fast bind, fast find; A proverb never stale in thrifty mind . . ii 5 55
It is yours; And, might we lay the old proverb to your charge, So like you, 'tis the worse . . . . *W. Tale* ii 3 96
You are the hare of whom the proverb goes . . . *K. John* ii 1 137
For he was never yet a breaker of proverbs . . . 1 *Hen. IV.* i 2 132
Yet do I not use my horse for my mistress, or any such proverb *Hen. V.* iii 7 72
I will cap that proverb with 'There is flattery in friendship' . . iii 7 124
Proverb. Have at the very eye of that proverb with 'A pox of the devil' *Hen. V.* iii 7 129
You are the better at proverbs, by how much 'A fool's bolt is soon shot' . . . . iii 7 131
The ancient proverb will be well effected: 'A staff is quickly found to beat a dog' . . . . 2 *Hen. VI.* iii 1 170
Sigh'd forth proverbs, That hunger broke stone walls . . *Coriolanus* i 1 209
'While the grass grows,'—the proverb is something musty . *Hamlet* iii 2 359
Proverbed. I am proverb'd with a grandsire phrase . *Rom. and Jul.* i 4 37
Proveth. This proveth Edward's love and Warwick's honesty 3 *Hen. VI.* iii 3 180
Yet hasty marriage seldom proveth well . . . . . iv 1 18
Provexit. And his device, a wreath of chivalry; The word, 'Me pompæ provexit apex' . . . . *Pericles* ii 2 30
Provide. You must provide to bottom it on me . . *T. G. of Ver.* iii 2 53
I'll provide you a chain; and I'll do what I can . *Mer. Wives* v 1 6
Provide your block and your axe to-morrow four o'clock *Meas. for Meas.* iv 2 55
O, 'tis an accident that heaven provides! . . . . . . iv 3 81
Take this mercy to provide For better times to come . . . v 1 489
A small spare mast, Such as seafaring men provide for storms *Com. of Er.* i 1 81
You, niece, provide yourself: If you outstay the time . *As Y. Like It* i 3 89
Provide the feast, father, and bid the guests . . . *T. of Shrew* ii 1 318
Provide this messenger: My heart is heavy and mine age is weak *All's Well* iii 4 40
We must to horse again. Go, go, provide . . . . . . v 1 38
Provide some carts And bring away the armour that is there *Richard II.* ii 2 106
Provide us all things necessary and meet me to-morrow night 1 *Hen. IV.* i 2 214
Somewhat too sudden, sirs, the warning is; But we will presently provide for them . . . . 1 *Hen. VI.* v 2 15
With all speed provide To see her coronation be perform'd . 2 *Hen. VI.* i 1 73
Say you consent and censure well the deed, And I'll provide his executioner . . . . iii 1 276
Provide me soldiers, lords, Whiles I take order for mine own affairs . iii 1 319
Is it for a wife That thou art malcontent? I will provide thee 3 *Hen. VI.* iv 1 60
Hence, my sovereign, to provide A salve for any sore that may betide . iv 6 87
Make use now, and provide For thine own future safety. *Hen. VIII.* iii 2 420
And Cupid grant all tongue-tied maidens here Bed, chamber, Pandar to provide this gear! . . . . *Troi. and Cres.* iii 2 220
Provide more piercing statutes daily, . . . restrain the poor *Coriolanus* i 1 86
Provide thee two proper palfreys, black as jet . . . *T. Andron.* v 2 50
What will this come to? He commands us to provide, and give great gifts, And all out of an empty coffer . . . . . *T. of Athens* i 2 198
Let in the tide Of knaves once more; my cook and I'll provide . iii 4 119
Your vessels and your spells provide, Your charms . . *Macbeth* iii 5 18
Advise him to a caution, to hold what distance His wisdom can provide iii 6 45
We will ourselves provide . . . . *Hamlet* iii 3 7
Traverse! go, provide thy money . . . . . . *Othello* i 3 378
Provide your going; Choose your own company . . *Ant. and Cleo.* iii 4 36
Provide me presently A riding-suit, no costlier . . . *Cymbeline* iii 2 77
I yet am unprovided Of a pair of bases.—We'll sure provide . *Pericles* ii 1 168
Provided. I cannot be so soon provided . . . . *T. G. of Ver.* i 3 72
Provided that you do no outrages On silly women or poor passengers iv 1 71
I have provided for you: stay awhile . . . *Meas. for Meas.* ii 3 17
Hath he provided this music?—He is very busy about it . *Much Ado* i 2 2
According to our law Immediately provided in that case *M. N. Dream* i 1 45
I am provided of a torch-bearer . . . . . *Mer. of Venice* ii 4 24
To have her love, provided that your fortune Achieved her mistress . iii 2 209
Provided more, that, for this favour, He presently become a Christian iv 1 386
Provided that you weed your better judgements Of all opinion *As Y. L. It* ii 7 45
And so we will, provided that he win her . . . *T. of Shrew* i 2 217
Provided that, when he's removed, your highness Will take again your queen as yours at first . . . . *W. Tale* i 2 335
Let's before as he bids us: he was provided to do us good . . iv 4 860
What penny hath Rome borne, What men provided? . . *K. John* v 2 98
Provided that my banishment repeal'd And lands restored again be freely granted . . . . *Richard II.* iii 3 40
I must go and meet with danger there, Or it will seek me in another place And find me worse provided . . . . . 2 *Hen. IV.* ii 3 50
Have you provided me here half a dozen sufficient men? . . . iii 2 102
His wonted followers Shall all be very well provided for . . . v 5 105
You talk of horse and armour?—You are as well provided of both as any prince in the world . . . . *Hen. V.* iii 7 9
The duchess, I tell you, expects performance of your promises.—Master Hume, we are therefore provided . . . . . 2 *Hen. VI.* i 4 3
I myself am not so well provided As else I would be . *Richard III.* iii 4 46
You shall know many dare accuse you boldly, More than, I fear, you are provided for . . . . *Hen. VIII.* v 3 57
Having now provided A gentleman of noble parentage *Rom. and Jul.* iii 5 180
The gods themselves have provided that I shall have much help *T. of A.* i 2 92
Let's be provided to show them entertainment.—I scarce know how . i 2 185
I am thinking what I shall say I have provided for him . . . v 1 35
He that's coming Must be provided for . . . . . *Macbeth* i 5 68
Now or whensoever, provided I be so able as now . . . *Hamlet* v 2 210
I look'd not for you yet, nor am provided For your fit welcome . *Lear* ii 4 235
I have spoke already, and it is provided . . . *Ant. and Cleo.* v 2 195
Provided I have your commendation for my more free entertainment *Cymbeline* i 4 166
I will use My utmost skill in his recovery, Provided That none but I and my companion maid Be suffer'd to come near him . *Pericles* v 1 77
Providence. How came we ashore?—By Providence divine . *Tempest* i 2 159
She is mortal; But by immortal Providence she's mine . . . v 1 189
The providence that's in a watchful state Knows almost every grain of Plutus' gold . . . . *Troi. and Cres.* iii 3 196
With patience To stay the providence of some high powers *J. Cæsar* v 1 107
It will be laid to us, whose providence Should have kept short, restrain'd and out of haunt, This mad young man . . . . *Hamlet* iv 1 17
There's a special providence in the fall of a sparrow . . . v 2 231
Provident. Most provident in peril . . . . . . *T. Night* i 2 12
It fits us then to be as provident As fear may teach us . *Hen. V.* ii 4 11
Providently. He that doth the ravens feed, Yea, providently caters for the sparrow . . . . *As Y. Like It* ii 3 44
Provider. Made my meal, and parted With prayers for the provider *Cymb.* iii 6 53
Province. Will unpeople the province with continency *Meas. for Meas.* iii 2 185
The king hath on him such a countenance As he had lost some province *W. Tale* i 2 369
Then do I give Volquessen, Touraine, Maine, Poictiers and Anjou, these five provinces, With her to thee . . . . . *K. John* ii 1 528
Shall Lewis have Blanch, and Blanch those provinces? . . . iii 1 3
Nor should that nation boast it so with us, But be extirped from our provinces . . . . 1 *Hen. VI.* iii 3 24
Those provinces these arms of mine did conquer . . . 2 *Hen. VI.* i 1 120

Province. I am the son of Henry the Fifth, Who made the Dauphin and the French to stoop And seized upon their towns and provinces *3 Hen. VI.* i 1 109
Say 'tis not so, a province I will give thee . . . *Ant. and Cleo.* ii 5 68
We have kiss'd away Kingdoms and provinces . . . iii 10 8
For every graff would send a caterpillar, And so afflict our province *Per.* v 1 61
Provincial. His subject am I not, Nor here provincial *Meas. for Meas.* v 1 318
With two Provincial roses on my razed shoes . . *Hamlet* iii 2 288
Provision. With such provision in mine art So safely ordered *Tempest* i 2 28
Had made provision for her following me . . *Com. of Errors* i 1 48
We shall be short in our provision : 'Tis now near night *Rom. and Jul.* iv 2 38
I am sorry, when he sent to borrow of me, that my provision was out.—I am sick of that grief too . . . . . . *T. of Athens* iii 6 18
Five days we do allot thee, for provision To shield thee from diseases of the world . . . . *Lear* i 1 176
I am now from home, and out of that provision Which shall be needful ii 4 208
Follow me, that will to some provision Give thee quick conduct . . iii 6 103
Let us beseech you That for our gold we may provision have *Pericles* v 1 56
And give you gold for such provision As our intents will need . . v 1 258
Proviso. But with proviso and exception . . . *1 Hen. IV.* i 3 78
Provocation. Let there come a tempest of provocation . *Mer. Wives* v 5 23
What an eye she has ! methinks it sounds a parley of provocation *Oth.* ii 3 23
Provoke. My tale provokes that question . . . . . *Tempest* i 2 140
And hinder them from what this ecstasy May now provoke them to . iii 3 109
And even that power which gave me first my oath Provokes me to this threefold perjury . . . . . . *T. G. of Ver.* ii 6 5
I will provoke him to 't, or let him wag . . . *Mer. Wives* ii 3 73
'Tis good ; though music oft hath such a charm To make bad good, and good provoke to harm . . . . . . *Meas. for Meas.* iv 1 15
The heaving of my lungs provokes me to ridiculous smiling *L. L. Lost* iii 1 78
Rebuke me not for that which you provoke . . . . . v 2 347
No further enemy to you Than the constraint of hospitable zeal In the relief of this oppressed child Religiously provokes . . *K. John* ii 1 246
Did you not provoke me? . . . . iv 2 207
Let my presumption not provoke thy wrath . . *1 Hen. VI.* ii 3 70
As rigour of tempestuous gusts Provokes the mightiest hulk against the tide . . . . v 5 6
Why dost thou quiver, man?—The palsy, and not fear, provokes me *2 Hen. VI.* iv 7 98
Thy deed, inhuman and unnatural, Provokes this deluge *Richard III.* i 2 61
Our duty, and thy fault, Provoke us hither now to slaughter thee . i 4 231
Your goodness, Since you provoke me, shall be most notorious *Hen. VIII.* iii 2 288
Wilt thou provoke me? then have at thee, boy ! . *Rom. and Jul.* v 3 70
Our gentle flame Provokes itself . . . . . *T. of Athens* i 1 24
What three things does drink especially provoke? . . *Macbeth* ii 3 30
Lechery, sir, it provokes, and unprovokes ; it provokes the desire, but it takes away the performance . . . . ii 3 33
The need we have to use you did provoke Our hasty sending *Hamlet* ii 2 3
Our foster-nurse of nature is repose, The which he lacks ; that to provoke in him, Are many simples operative . . . . . *Lear* iv 4 13
And haply may strike at you : provoke him, that he may *Othello* ii 1 280
Keep whole : provoke not battle, Till we have done at sea *Ant. and Cleo.* iii 8 3
He did provoke me With language that would make me spurn the sea, If it could so roar to me . . . . *Cymbeline* v 5 293
With whom the father liking took, And her to incest did provoke *Pericles* i Gower 26
One sin, I know, another doth provoke . . . . . . i 1 137
Provoked and instigated by his distemper . . *Mer. Wives* iii 5 77
Nor heady-rash, provoked with raging ire . . *Com. of Errors* v 1 216
I would to God, So my untruth had not provoked him to it *Richard II.* ii 2 101
Who preferreth peace More than I do?—except I be provoked *1 Hen. VI.* iii 1 34
Yet know, my lord, I was provoked by him . . . . iv 1 104
How will their grudging stomachs be provoked To wilful disobedience ! iv 1 141
I was provoked by her slanderous tongue . . . *Richard III.* i 2 97
Thou wast provoked by thy bloody mind . . . . . i 2 99
'Twas thy beauty that provoked me . . . . i 2 181
Of his own royal disposition, And not provoked by any suitor else . i 3 64
The king, provoked by the queen, Devised impeachments . . ii 2 21
Not soon provoked nor being provoked soon calm'd *Troi. and Cres.* iv 5 99
When you shall know—as in this rage, Provoked by him, you cannot *Coriolanus* v 6 138
Let me rail so high, That the false housewife Fortune break her wheel, Provoked by my offence . . . . . *Ant. and Cleo.* iv 15 45
Being so far provoked as I was in France, I would abate her nothing *Cymbeline* i 4 72
Provoker. Drink, sir, is a great provoker of three things . *Macbeth* ii 3 27
Provokest Thy best of rest is sleep, And that thou oft provokest ; yet grossly fear'st Thy death . . . . . *Meas. for Meas.* iii 1 18
Art so full of him, That thou provokest thyself to cast him up *2 Hen. IV.* i 3 96
Provoketh. Beauty provoketh thieves sooner than gold *As Y. Like It* i 3 112
Provoking. A provoking merit . . . . *Lear* iii 5 8
He prated, And spoke such scurvy and provoking terms . *Othello* i 2 7
Provost. Signior Claudio, led by the provost to prison *Meas. for Meas.* i 2 119
As I hear, the provost hath A warrant for his execution . . . i 4 73
Where is the provost?—Here, if it like your honour . . . ii 1 32
Hail to you, provost ! so I think you are.—I am the provost . . ii 3 1
Provost, a word with you.—As many as you please . . . iii 1 50
Provost, a word with you !—What's your will, father?—That now you are come, you will be gone . . . . iii 1 177
The best and wholesomest spirits of the night, Envelope you, good Provost ! . . . . iv 2 77
A gentle provost : seldom when The steeled gaoler is the friend of men iv 2 89
As near the dawning, provost, as it is, You shall hear more ere morning iv 2 97
There is written in your brow, provost, honesty and constancy . iv 2 163
Now will I write letters to Angelo,—The provost, he shall bear them . iv 3 98
These letters at fit time deliver me : The provost knows our purpose . iv 5 2
Your provost knows the place where he abides And he may fetch him . v 1 252
My lord, here comes the rascal I spoke of ; here with the provost . v 1 285
First, provost, let me bail these gentle three . . . . . v 1 362
Provost, how came it Claudio was beheaded At an unusual hour? . . v 1 462
Proclaim it, provost, round about the city, Is any woman wrong'd . v 1 514
Thanks, provost, for thy care and secrecy : We shall employ thee in a worthier place . . . . v 1 536
Prowess. Nor should thy prowess want praise and esteem, But that 'tis shown ignobly . . . . *2 Hen. VI.* v 2 22
Henry the Fifth, Who by his prowess conquered all France *3 Hen. VI.* iii 3 86
The which no sooner had his prowess confirm'd In the unshrinking station where he fought, But like a man he died . . *Macbeth* v 8 41

Prudence. This Sir Prudence, who Should not upbraid our course *Tempest* ii 1 286
Hold your tongue, Good prudence ; smatter with your gossips, go *Rom. and Jul.* iii 5 172
Prudent. 'Tis thought among the prudent he would quickly have the gift of a grave . . . . *T. Night* i 3 34
O prudent discipline ! . . . . *K. John* ii 1 413
Most prudent, of an excellent And unmatch'd wit . . *Hen. VIII.* ii 4 46
Those cold ways, That seem like prudent helps, are very poisonous *Coriolanus* iii 1 221
Prune. Three veneys for a dish of stewed prunes . . . *Mer. Wives* i 1 296
Longing, saving your honour's reverence, for stewed prunes *M. for M.* ii 1 93
Longing, as I said, for prunes ; and having but two in the dish, as I said ii 1 103
If you be remembered, cracking the stones of the foresaid prunes . . ii 1 111
Four pound of prunes, and as many of raisins o' the sun *W. Tale* iv 3 51
Which makes him prune himself, and bristle up The crest of youth *1 Hen. IV.* i 1 98
There's no more faith in thee than in a stewed prune . . . iii 3 128
He lives upon mouldy stewed prunes and dried cakes . *2 Hen. IV.* ii 4 159
His royal bird Prunes the immortal wing and cloys his beak *Cymbeline* v 4 118
Prunest. Poor old man, thou prunest a rotten tree . *As Y. Like It* ii 3 63
Pruning. All for want of pruning . . . . *Com. of Errors* ii 2 181
Or groan for love? or spend a minute's time In pruning me? *L. L. Lost* iv 3 183
Pry. I have cause to pry into this pedant . . . . *T. of Shrew* iii 1 87
Every loop from whence The eye of reason may pry in upon us *1 Hen. IV.* iv 1 72
To pry Into his title, the which we find Too indirect for long continuance iv 3 103
Let it pry through the portage of the head Like the brass cannon *Hen. V.* iii 1 10
Wake when others be asleep, To pry into the secrets of the state *2 Hen. VI.* i 1 250
Speak and look back, and pry on every side, Tremble and start *Rich. III.* iii 5 6
But if thou, jealous, dost return to pry In what I further shall intend to do, By heaven, I will tear thee joint by joint . *Rom. and Jul.* v 3 33
Pryed. I pry'd me through the crevice of a wall . . *T. Andron.* v 1 114
Psalm. They do no more adhere and keep place together than the Hundredth Psalm to the tune of 'Green Sleeves' . *Mer. Wives* ii 1 63
But one puritan amongst them, and he sings psalms to hornpipes *W. T.* iv 3 47
I would I were a weaver ; I could sing psalms or any thing *1 Hen. IV.* ii 4 146
Psalmist. Death, as the Psalmist saith, is certain to all . *2 Hen. IV.* iii 2 41
Psalteries and fifes, Tabors and cymbals . . . . *Coriolanus* v 4 52
Ptolemies. Nay, certainly, I have heard the Ptolemies' pyramises are very goodly things . . . . *Ant. and Cleo.* ii 7 39
Of thee craves The circle of the Ptolemies for her heirs . . . iii 12 18
Ptolemy. Nor the queen of Ptolemy More womanly than he . . . i 4 6
Let us grant, it is not Amiss to tumble on the bed of Ptolemy . . i 4 17
To Ptolemy he assign'd Syria, Cilicia, and Phœnicia . . . iii 6 15
Public. To make us public sport, Appoint a meeting . *Mer. Wives* iv 4 14
The body public be A horse whereon the governor doth ride *M. for M.* i 2 163
Lord Angelo hath to the public ear Profess'd the contrary . . iv 2 102
Our soul Cannot but yield you forth to public thanks . . . v 1 7
With public accusation, uncovered slander, unmitigated rancour *M. Ado* iv 1 307
Such public shame as the rest of the court can possibly devise *L. L. Lost* i 1 132
Nor thrust your head into the public street . . *Mer. of Ven.* ii 5 32
If that thou be'st found So near our public court as twenty miles, Thou diest for it . . . . *As Y. Like It* i 3 46
And this our life exempt from public haunt Finds tongues in trees . ii 1 15
Come, follow us ; We are to speak in public . . . *W. Tale* ii 1 197
And sit at chiefest stern of public weal . . . *1 Hen. VI.* i 1 177
In open market-place produced they me, To be a public spectacle to all i 4 41
Prick'd on by public wrongs sustain'd in France . . . . iii 2 78
Join we together, for the public good . . . *2 Hen. VI.* i 1 199
Thy wife's attire Have cost a mass of public treasury . . . i 3 134
Defacers of a public peace . . . . *Hen. VIII.* v 3 41
No public benefit which you receive But it proceeds or comes from them to you . . . . *Coriolanus* i 1 156
A traitorous innovator, A foe to the public weal . . . . iii 1 176
Law shall scorn him further trial Than the severity of the public power iii 1 269
We talk here in the public haunt of men . . . *Rom. and Jul.* iii 1 53
The public body, which doth seldom Play the recanter . *T. of Athens* v 1 148
Not a man . . . But shall be render'd to your public laws . . v 4 62
Public reasons shall be rendered Of Cæsar's death . . *J. Cæsar* iii 2 7
Let us hear Mark Antony.—Let him go up into the public chair . iii 2 68
That they know full well That gave me public leave to speak of him . iii 2 224
The other motive, Why to a public count I might not go . *Hamlet* iv 7 17
What committed ! Committed ! O thou public commoner ! *Othello* iv 2 73
I saw her once Hop forty paces through the public street *Ant. and Cleo.* ii 2 234
He hath . . . made his will, and read it To public ear . . . iii 4 5
This in the public eye?—I' the common show-place, where they exercise iii 6 11
He is dead, Cæsar ; Not by a public minister of justice, Nor by a hired knife . . . . v 1 20
'Twas a contention in public . . . . . . *Cymbeline* i 4 59
Either by public war or private treason Will take away your life *Pericles* i 2 104
Publican. How like a fawning publican he looks ! . *Mer. of Venice* i 3 42
Publication. In the publication, make no strain . *Troi. and Cres.* i 3 326
Publicly. I'll warrant they'll have him publicly shamed *Mer. Wives* iv 2 236
There would be no period to the jest, should he not be publicly shamed iv 2 237
And that, by great injunctions, I am bound To enter publicly *M. for M.* iv 3 101
If you handled her privately, she would sooner confess : perchance, publicly, she'll be ashamed . . . . v 1 278
Beheaded publicly for his offence . . . . *Com. of Errors* v 1 127
Yet once again proclaim it publicly, If any friend will pay the sum . v 1 130
For, as she hath Been publicly accused, so shall she have A just and open trial . . . . *W. Tale* ii 3 204
If God will be revenged for this deed, O, know you yet, he doth it publicly : Take not the quarrel from his powerful arm *Richard III.* i 4 222
What's the need? It hath already publicly been read . *Hen. VIII.* ii 4 3
Cleopatra and himself in chairs of gold Were publicly enthroned *A. and C.* iii 6 5
Publicola. The noble sister of Publicola, The moon of Rome *Coriolanus* v 3 64
Marcus Justeius, Publicola, and Cælius, are for sea . *Ant. and Cleo.* iii 7 74
Publish. And publish it that she is dead indeed . . . *Much Ado* iv 1 206
Whose trial shall better publish his commendation . *Mer. of Venice* iv 1 165
We wound our modesty and make foul the clearness of our deservings, when of ourselves we publish them . . . . . . *All's Well* i 3 7
Yet thus far I will boldly publish her . . . . . *T. Night* ii 1 30
Let us on, And publish the occasion of our arms . . . *2 Hen. IV.* i 3 86
A proof of strength she could not publish more . . *Troi. and Cres.* v 2 113
A constant will to publish Our daughters' several dowers . . *Lear* i 1 44
Publish we this peace To all our subjects . . . . . *Cymbeline* v 5 478
Publish'd and proclaim'd it openly . . . . *T. of Shrew* iv 2 85
How will this grieve you, When you shall come to clearer knowledge, that You thus have publish'd me ! . . . . . . *W. Tale* ii 1 98
We intend to try his grace to-day, If he be guilty, as 'tis published *2 Hen. VI.* iii 2 17

Published. Shortly, I believe, His second marriage shall be publish'd *Hen. VIII.* iii 2 68
Wherefore, bold peasant, Darest thou support a publish'd traitor? *Lear* iv 6 236
Publisher. For love of you, not hate unto my friend, Hath made me publisher of this pretence . . . *T. G. of Ver.* iii 1 47
Publishing. Shall I not lie in publishing a truth? . . *Troi. and Cres.* v 2 119
Publius. Of the same house Publius and Quintus were, That our best water brought by conduits hither . . . *Coriolanus* ii 3 249
Publius and Sempronius, you must do it; 'Tis you must dig *T. Andron.* iv 3 10
O Publius, is not this a heavy case, To see thy noble uncle thus distract? iv 3 25
Publius, how now! how now, my masters! What, have you met with her? iv 3 35
Publius, Publius, what hast thou done? See, see, thou hast shot off one of Taurus' horns . . . . iv 3 68
When Publius shot, The Bull, being gall'd, gave Aries such a knock That down fell both the Ram's horns . . . . . iv 3 70
I have work enough for you to do. Publius, come hither, Caius, and Valentine! . . . . v 2 151
Fie, Publius, fie! thou art too much deceived; The one is Murder, Rape is the other's name; And therefore bind them, gentle Publius v 2 156
I will go. And look where Publius is come to fetch me . . *J. Cæsar* ii 2 108
That Publius Cimber may Have an immediate freedom of repeal . iii 1 53
To thy foot doth Cassius fall, To beg enfranchisement for Publius Cimber iii 1 57
Where's Publius?—Here, quite confounded with this mutiny . iii 1 85
Publius, good cheer; There is no harm intended to your person, Nor to no Roman else: so tell them, Publius.—And leave us, Publius iii 1 89
Prick him down, Antony.—Upon condition Publius shall not live . iv 1 4
Pucelle. Excellent Pucelle, if thy name be so, Let me thy servant and not sovereign be . . . . *1 Hen. VI.* i 2 110
With one Joan la Pucelle join'd, A holy prophetess new risen up . i 4 101
Pucelle or puzzel, dolphin or dogfish . . . . . . i 4 107
Pucelle is enter'd into Orleans, In spite of us . . . . i 5 36
Thus Joan la Pucelle hath perform'd her word . . . . i 6 3
No longer on Saint Denis will we cry, But Joan la Pucelle . . i 6 29
But what's that Pucelle whom they term so pure?—A maid, they say . ii 1 20
Here enter'd Pucelle and her practisants . . . . . iii 2 20
Pucelle, that witch, that damned sorceress, Hath wrought this hellish mischief . . . . iii 2 38
Are ye so hot, sir? yet, Pucelle, hold thy peace . . . iii 2 58
But where is Pucelle now? I think her old familiar is asleep . . iii 2 121
Speak, Pucelle, and enchant him with thy words . . . iii 3 40
Pucelle hath bravely play'd her part in this, And doth deserve a coronet iii 3 88
Puck. Those that Hobgoblin call you and sweet Puck . *M. N. Dream* ii 1 40
My gentle Puck, come hither. Thou rememberest Since once I sat upon a promontory, And heard a mermaid . . . . . ii 1 148
Gentle Puck, take this transformed scalp From off the head of this Athenian swain . . . . iv 1 69
As I am an honest Puck . . . . v 1 438
We will make amends ere long; Else the Puck a liar call . . v 1 442
Pudding. I have sat in the stocks for puddings he hath stolen *T. G. of Ver.* iv 4 34
Revenged I will be, as sure as his guts are made of puddings *Mer. Wives* iv 1 32
Young Drop-heir that killed lusty Pudding . . *Meas. for Meas.* iv 3 17
As the pudding to his skin . . . . . . *All's Well* ii 2 29
That roasted Manningtree ox with the pudding in his belly *1 Hen. IV.* ii 4 498
He'll yield the crow a pudding one of these days . . *Hen. V.* ii 1 92
Blessed fig's-end! . . . if she had been blessed, she would never have loved the Moor. Blessed pudding! . . . . . . *Othello* ii 1 258
Fish for fasting-days, and moreo'er puddings and flap-jacks . *Pericles* ii 1 86
Puddle. Pool! Sir Pool! lord! Ay, kennel, puddle, sink *2 Hen. VI.* iv 1 71
Thou didst drink The stale of horses, and the gilded puddle *A. and C.* i 4 62
Puddled. They threw on him Great pails of puddled mire *Com. of Errors* v 1 173
Hath puddled his clear spirit . . . . . . *Othello* iii 4 143
Pudency. With A pudency so rosy the sweet view on't Might well have warm'd old Saturn . . . . *Cymbeline* ii 5 11
Pueritia. Ba, pueritia, with a horn added . . . *L. L. Lost* v 1 52
Puff. Goodman Puff of Barson.—Puff! Puff in thy teeth! . *2 Hen. IV.* v 3 94
Seld-shown flamens Do press among the popular throngs and puff To win a vulgar station . . . . *Coriolanus* ii 1 230
And, being anger'd, puffs away from thence . . *Rom. and Jul.* i 4 102
Puffed. A bag of flax?—A puffed man? . . . *Mer. Wives* v 5 160
Tapers they are, with your sweet breaths puff'd out *L. L. Lost* v 2 267
The sea puff'd up with winds Rage like an angry boar . *T. of Shrew* i 2 202
Great and puffed up with this retinue, doth any deed of courage *2 Hen. IV.* iv 3 121
Blow, villain, till thy sphered bias cheek Outswell the colic of puff'd Aquilon: Come, stretch thy chest . . . *Troi. and Cres.* iv 5 9
Whose self-same mettle, Whereof thy proud child, arrogant man, is puff'd, Engenders the black toad . . . . . *T. of Athens* iv 3 180
Like a puff'd and reckless libertine . . . . . *Hamlet* i 3 49
Whose spirit with divine ambition puff'd . . . . . iv 4 49
And, like the devil, from his very arm Puff'd his own brother *Othello* iii 4 137
Puffing. Like foggy south puffing with wind and rain *As Y. Like It* iii 5 50
Distinction, with a broad and powerful fan, Puffing at all, winnows the light away . . . . *Troi. and Cres.* i 3 28
Pugging. Doth set my pugging tooth on edge . . *W. Tale* iv 3 7
Puisny. As a puisny tilter, that spurs his horse but on one side, breaks his staff like a noble goose . . . . . *As Y. Like It* iii 4 46
Puissance. Go draw our puissance together . . . *K. John* iii 1 339
To look with forehead bold and big enough Upon the power and puissance of the king . . . . *2 Hen. IV.* i 3 9
And come against us in full puissance . . . . . . i 3 77
Till that the nobles and the armed commons Have of their puissance made a little taste . . . . ii 3 52
And make imaginary puissance . . . . . . *Hen. V.* Prol. 25
Let us deliver Our puissance into the hand of God . . . ii 2 190
Babies and old women, Either past or not arrived to pith and puissance iii Prol. 21
And fain to go with a staff, but that my puissance holds it up *2 Hen. VI.* iv 2 173
We will follow In the main battle, whose puissance on either side Shall be well winged with our chiefest horse . . . *Richard III.* v 3 299
Puissant. With your puissant arm renew their feats . *Hen. V.* i 2 116
Trail'st thou the puissant pike?—Even so . . . . . iv 1 40
A puissant and a mighty power Of gallowglasses and stout kerns *2 Hen. VI.* iv 9 25
The queen is coming with a puissant host . . *3 Hen. VI.* ii 1 207
Where is the post that came from Montague?—By this at Daintry, with a puissant troop . . . . v 1 6
The queen from France hath brought a puissant power: Even now we heard . . . . v 2 31
Gracious sovereign, on the western coast Rideth a puissant navy *Richard III.* iv 4 434
Most high, most mighty, and most puissant Cæsar . . *J. Cæsar* iii 1 33
His grief grew puissant, and the strings of life Began to crack . *Lear* v 3 216
Puke-stocking, caddis-garter, smooth-tongue . . . . *1 Hen. IV.* ii 4 78

Puking. At first the infant, Mewling and puking in the nurse's arms. And then the whining school-boy . . . . . *As Y. Like It* ii 7 144
Pulcher. What is 'fair,' William?—Pulcher.—Polecats! there are fairer things than polecats, sure . . . . . *Mer. Wives* iv 1 28
Puling. To speak puling, like a beggar at Hallowmas . *T. G. of Ver.* ii 1 26
He, like a puling cuckold, would drink up The lees and dregs of a flat tamed piece . . . . *Troi. and Cres.* iv 1 61
Leave this faint puling and lament as I do, In anger, Juno-like *Coriolanus* iv 2 52
A wretched puling fool, A whining mammet . . *Rom. and Jul.* iii 5 185
Pull. Trinculo, come forth: I'll pull thee by the lesser legs *Tempest* ii 2 108
I'll pull them off myself, Yea, all my raiment, to my petticoat *T. of Shrew* ii 1 4
Doth backward pull Our slow designs when we ourselves are dull *All's W.* i 1 233
Thou hast to pull at a smack o' the contrary . . . . ii 3 237
I muse your majesty doth seem so cold, When such profound respects do pull you on . . . . *K. John* iii 1 318
We'll pull his plumes and take away his train . . . *1 Hen. VI.* iii 3 7
Two pulls at once; His lady banish'd, and a limb lopp'd off *2 Hen. VI.* ii 3 41
Now go some and pull down the Savoy; others to the inns of court . iv 7 1
Let them pull all about mine ears . . . . . *Coriolanus* iii 2 1
And pull her out of Acheron by the heels . . . *T. Andron.* iv 3 44
What, man! ne'er pull your hat upon your brows; Give sorrow words *Macbeth* iv 3 208
Pull't off, I say . . . . v 3 54
I pull in resolution, and begin To doubt the equivocation of the fiend . v 5 42
Pull off my boots: harder, harder . . . . . . *Lear* iv 6 177
'Tis pride that pulls the country down . . . . *Othello* ii 3 98
So hangs, and lolls, and weeps upon me; so hales, and pulls me . iv 1 144
Pulled. Shall all our houses of resort in the suburbs be pulled down?—To the ground, mistress . . . . . . *Meas. for Meas.* i 2 105
And pull'd the law upon you . . . . ii 1 16
I would not take this hand from thy throat till this other had pulled out thy tongue for saying so . . . . *As Y. Like It* i 1 64
Whose bookish rule hath pull'd fair England down . *2 Hen. VI.* i 1 259
We are like to have biting statutes, unless his teeth be pulled out . iv 7 19
There was the weight that pull'd me down . . *Hen. VIII.* iii 2 407
You pull'd me by the cloak; would you speak with me? *J. Cæsar* i 2 215
Her garments, heavy with their drink, Pull'd the poor wretch from her melodious lay To muddy death . . . . . . *Hamlet* iv 7 183
Puller down. Proud setter up and puller down of kings! *3 Hen. VI.* iii 3 157
Pullet-sperm. I'll no pullet-sperm in my brewage *Mer. Wives* iii 5 32
Pulling. Marullus and Flavius, for pulling scarfs off Cæsar's images, are put to silence . . . . *J. Cæsar* i 2 289
Pulpit. Some to the common pulpits, and cry out 'Liberty, freedom!' . iii 1 80
Go to the pulpit, Brutus.—And Cassius too . . . . iii 1 84
And in the pulpit, as becomes a friend, Speak in the order of his funeral iii 1 229
By your pardon; I will myself into the pulpit first. . . . iii 1 236
You shall speak In the same pulpit whereto I am going, After my speech iii 1 250
Pulpiter. O most gentle pulpiter! . . . . *As Y. Like It* iii 2 163
Pulse. And return Or ere your pulse twice beat . . *Tempest* v 1 103
Thy pulse Beats as of flesh and blood . . . . . . v 1 113
Give me your hand and let me feel your pulse . . *Com. of Errors* iv 4 55
Gazing in mine eyes, feeling my pulse . . . . . . v 1 243
So strive upon your pulse. What, pale again? . . *All's Well* i 3 175
Have I commandment on the pulse of life? . . . *K. John* iv 2 92
My heart beats thicker than a feverous pulse . *Troi. and Cres.* iii 2 38
For no pulse Shall keep his native progress, but surcease *Rom. and Jul.* iv 1 96
My pulse, as yours, doth temperately keep time . . *Hamlet* iii 4 140
But are you flesh and blood? Have you a working pulse? *Pericles* v 1 155
Pulsidge. You are in an excellent good temperality: your pulsidge beats as extraordinarily as heart would desire . . . . *2 Hen. IV.* ii 4 25
Pump. Get your apparel together, good strings to your beards, new ribbons to your pumps . . . . *M. N. Dream* iv 2 37
Gabriel's pumps were all unpink'd i' the heel . . *T. of Shrew* iv 1 136
Then is my pump well flowered . . . . *Rom. and Jul.* ii 4 64
Follow me this jest now till thou hast worn out thy pump . . ii 4 66
Pumpion. This unwholesome humidity, this gross watery pumpion *Mer. Wives* iii 3 43
Pun. He would pun thee into shivers with his fist . *Troi. and Cres.* ii 1 42
Punched. When I was mortal, my anointed body By thee was punched full of deadly holes . . . . *Richard III.* v 3 125
Punish. That which I must speak Must either punish me, not being believed, Or wring redress from you . . . *Meas. for Meas.* v 1 31
Punish them to your height of pleasure . . . . . . v 1 240
I beseech you, punish me not with your hard thoughts *As Y. Like It* i 2 195
If I do feign, you witnesses above Punish my life! . . *T. Night* v 1 141
Which is for me less easy to commit Than you to punish . *W. Tale* i 2 59
Whose very naming punishes me with the remembrance . . . iv 2 24
Mark'd For the hot vengeance and the rod of heaven To punish my mistreadings . . . . *1 Hen. IV.* iii 2 11
And find a time To punish this offence in other faults . . . v 2 7
To punish you by the heels would amend the attention of your ears *2 Hen. IV.* i 2 141
Let us yet be merciful.—So may your highness, and yet punish too *Hen. V.* ii 2 48
God punish me With hate in those where I expect most love! *Rich. III.* ii 1 34
I will, when you are humble; nay, before, Or God will punish me *Hen. VIII.* ii 4 75
You speak o' the people, As if you were a god to punish, not A man of their infirmity . . . . *Coriolanus* iii 1 81
But reason with the fellow, Before you punish him, where he heard this iv 6 52
Heaven hath pleased it so, To punish me with this and this with me *Ham.* iii 4 174
But I will punish home: No, I will weep no more . . *Lear* iii 4 16
To punish me for what you make me do Seems much unequal *A. and C.* ii 5 100
Bid that welcome Which comes to punish us, and we punish it Seeming to bear it lightly . . . . iv 14 137
Makes both my body pine and soul to languish, And punish that before that he would punish . . . . *Pericles* i 2 32
The gods for murder seemed so content To punish them . . v 3 Gower 99
Punished. If I have too austerely punish'd you, Your compensation makes amends . . . . *Tempest* iv 1 1
Have punish'd me With bitter fasts, with penitential groans *T. G. of V.* ii 4 130
Methinks his flesh is punished, he shall have no desires . *Mer. Wives* iv 4 25
Thou shalt be heavily punished . . . . . . *L. L. Lost* i 2 155
The reason why they are not so punished and cured is, that the lunacy is so ordinary that the whippers are in love too *As Y. Like It* iii 2 423
I beseech you, rather Let me be punish'd . . . *W. Tale* iii 2 226
So your flesh and blood is not to be punished by him . . . iv 4 712
All punish'd in the person of this child, And all for her . *K. John* ii 1 189
Thou shalt be punish'd for thus frighting me . . . . . iii 1 11
Let him be punish'd, sovereign, lest example Breed, by his sufferance, more of such a kind . . . . *Hen. V.* ii 2 45

Punished. In their dear care And tender preservation of our person,
Would have him punish'd . . . . *Hen. V.* ii 2 60
Here men are punished for before-breach of the king's laws . iv 1 179
Appointed me To watch the coming of my punish'd duchess . *2 Hen. VI.* ii 4 7
And that the people of this blessed land May not be punish'd with my
thwarting stars . . . . *3 Hen. VI.* iv 6 22
It was a bare petition of a state To one whom they had punish'd *Coriol.* v 1 21
And I for winking at your discords too Have lost a brace of kinsmen:
all are punish'd . . . . *Rom. and Jul.* v 3 295
Some shall be pardon'd, and some punished . . . . . . v 3 308
And you must needs have heard, how I am punish'd . . *Hamlet* v 2 240
Such as basest and contemned'st wretches For pilferings and most
common trespasses Are punish'd with . . . . . *Lear* ii 2 152
That not know'st Fools do those villains pity who are punish'd Ere they
have done their mischief . . . . iv 2 54
Disloyal! No: She's punish'd for her truth . . . . *Cymbeline* iii 2 7
And subjects punish'd that ne'er thought offence . . . *Pericles* i 2 27
Punishment. And give him another hope, to betray him to another
punishment . . . . *Mer. Wives* iii 3 208
For we bid this be done, When evil deeds have their permissive pass
And not the punishment . . . . . . *Meas. for Meas.* i 3 39
If myself might be his judge, He should receive his punishment in
thanks . . . . i 4 28
Fainting under The pleasing punishment that women bear *Com. of Errors* i 1 47
That were a punishment too good for them . . . *Much Ado* iii 3 4
I beseech you, let it be remembered in his punishment . . . . v 1 316
I'll devise thee brave punishments for him . . . . . v 4 130
Have sent to thee, to receive the meed of punishment . *L. L. Lost* i 1 270
Vows for thee broke deserve not punishment . . . . . iv 3 63
These men have defeated the law and outrun native punishment *Hen. V.* iv 1 176
I never gave them condign punishment . . . . *2 Hen. VI.* iii 1 130
His fault was thought, And yet his punishment was cruel death *Rich. III.* ii 1 105
The honour of it Does pay the act of it; as, i' the contrary, The foulness
is the punishment . . . . *Hen. VIII.* iii 2 183
Slaughtering death, As punishment for his most wicked life . *T. Andron.* v 3 145
Judicious punishment! 'twas this flesh begot Those pelican daughters
Lear iii 4 76
Quit the house on purpose, that their punishment Might have the freer
course . . . . iv 2 94
A punishment more in policy than in malice . . . . *Othello* ii 3 274
In which I bind, On pain of punishment, the world to weet *Ant. and Cleo.* i 1 39
What's that?—A repulse: though your attempt, as you call it, deserve
more; a punishment too . . . . *Cymbeline* i 4 129
Will poor folks lie, That have afflictions on them, knowing 'tis A
punishment or trial? . . . . iii 6 11
Your pleasure was my mere offence, my punishment Itself . . . v 5 334
Having received the punishment before, For that which I did then . v 5 343
Punk. This punk is one of Cupid's carriers . . . *Mer. Wives* ii 2 141
Neither maid, widow, nor wife?—My lord, she may be a punk *M. for M.* v 1 179
Marrying a punk, my lord, is pressing to death, whipping, and hanging v 1 528
As your French crown for your taffeta punk . . . *All's Well* ii 2 24
Punto. To see thee pass thy punto, thy stock, thy reverse . *Mer. Wives* ii 3 26
Ah, the immortal passado! the punto reverso! the hai! . *Rom. and Jul.* ii 4 27
Puny. And twenty of these puny lies I'll tell . . *Mer. of Venice* iii 4 74
A puny subject strikes At thy great glory . . . . *Richard II.* iii 2 86
I question my puny drawer to what end he gave me the sugar *1 Hen. IV.* ii 4 33
Did flesh his puny sword in Frenchmen's blood . . . *1 Hen. VI.* iv 7 36
Wives with spits and boys with stones In puny battle slay me *Coriolanus* iv 4 6
I am not valiant neither, But every puny whipster gets my sword *Othello* v 2 244
Pupil. And she hath taught her suitor, He being her pupil, to become her
tutor . . . . *T. G. of Ver.* ii 1 144
I do dine to-day at the father's of a certain pupil of mine . *L. L. Lost* iv 2 160
On my privilege I have with the parents of the foresaid child or pupil . iv 2 163
You shall go see your pupils presently . . . . *T. of Shrew* iii 1 108
I am too old to fawn upon a nurse, Too far in years to be a pupil *Rich. II.* i 3 171
Where is he living . . . Which calls me pupil, or hath read to me?
1 Hen. IV. iii 1 46
What, shall King Henry be a pupil still? . . . . *2 Hen. VI.* i 3 49
Thou chid'st me oft for loving Rosaline.—For doting, not for loving,
pupil mine . . . . *Rom. and Jul.* ii 3 82
Have I not been Thy pupil long? . . . . . . *Cymbeline* i 5 12
That pupils lacks she none of noble race . . . . *Pericles* v Gower 9
Pupil age. To the pupil age of this present twelve o'clock at midnight
1 Hen. IV. ii 4 106
His pupil age Man-enter'd thus, he waxed like a sea . . *Coriolanus* ii 2 102
Pupil-like, Take thy correction mildly, kiss the rod . . *Richard II.* v 1 31
Puppet. O excellent motion! O exceeding puppet! . . . *T. G. of Ver.* ii 1 101
Fie! you counterfeit, you puppet, you!—Puppet? why so? *M. N. Dream* iii 2 288
Give him gold enough and marry him to a puppet . . . *T. of Shrew* i 2 79
Belike you mean to make a puppet of me.—Why, true; he means to make
a puppet of thee.—She says your worship means to make a puppet
of her . . . . iv 3 103
I could interpret between you and your love, if I could see the puppets
dallying.—You are keen, my lord . . . . . *Hamlet* iii 2 257
And take vanity the puppet's part . . . . . . *Lear* ii 2 39
Thou, an Egyptian puppet, shalt be shown In Rome, as well as I
Ant. and Cleo. v 2 208
Puppy. One that I brought up of a puppy . . . . *T. G. of Ver.* iv 4 3
With as little remorse as they would have drowned a blind bitch's
puppies . . . . *Mer. Wives* iii 5 11
Very wisely, puppies! . . . . *W. Tale* iv 4 726
You may stroke him as gently as a puppy greyhound . . *2 Hen. IV.* ii 4 107
Which, as I take it, is a kind of puppy To the old dam, treason *Hen. VIII.* i 1 175
I shall be with you presently, good master puppy . . . . v 4 30
Come, be a man. Drown thyself! drown cats and blind puppies *Othello* i 3 341
Puppies!—I would they had not come between us . . . *Cymbeline* i 2 22
Puppy-dog. Talks as familiarly of roaring lions As maids of thirteen do
of puppy-dogs! . . . . *K. John* ii 1 460
He has no more directions in the true disciplines of the wars, look you,
of the Roman disciplines, than is a puppy-dog . . . *Hen. V.* iii 2 78
Puppy-headed. I shall laugh myself to death at this puppy-headed
monster . . . . *Tempest* ii 2 159
Pur. *See* Purr
Purblind. This wimpled, whining, purblind, wayward boy . *L. L. Lost* iii 1 181
Lower messes Perchance are to this business purblind . . *W. Tale* i 2 228
Any purblind eye may find it out . . . . . *1 Hen. VI.* ii 4 21
Purblind Argus, all eyes and no sight . . . . *Troi. and Cres.* i 2 31
Her purblind son and heir, Young Adam Cupid . . . *Rom. and Jul.* ii 1 12
Purchase. And purchase me another dry basting . . *Com. of Errors* ii 2 63
They are worse fools to purchase mocking so . . . . *L. L. Lost* v 2 59
Purchase. Finer than you could purchase in so removed a dwelling
As Y. Like It iii 2 360
Haply your eye shall light upon some toy You have desire to purchase
T. Night iii 3 45
Get themselves a good report—after fourteen years' purchase . . iv 1 24
Your purse is not hot enough to purchase your spice . . *W. Tale* iv 3 127
Do him love and honour, Purchase the sight again of dear Sicilia . iv 4 522
By the merit of vile gold . . . Purchase corrupted pardon of a man
K. John iii 1 166
The difference Is purchase of a heavy curse from Rome . . . iii 1 205
I sent thee forth to purchase honour . . . . . *Richard II.* i 3 282
Thou shalt have a share in our purchase . . . . . *1 Hen. IV.* ii 1 101
There's no purchase in money . . . . iii 3 45
They will steal any thing, and call it purchase . . . *Hen. V.* iii 2 45
May haply purchase him a box o' th' ear . . . . . . iv 7 181
Make cheap pennyworths of their pillage And purchase friends *2 Hen. VI.* i 1 223
I'll give thee England's treasure, Enough to purchase such another
island . . . . iii 3 3
By that loss I will not purchase them . . . . *3 Hen. VI.* iii 2 73
For how can tyrants safely govern home, Unless abroad they purchase
great alliance? . . . . iii 3 70
Which I will purchase with my duteous service . . . *Richard III.* ii 1 63
Made prize and purchase of his lustful eye . . . . . iii 7 187
Infer fair England's peace by this alliance.—Which she shall purchase
with still lasting war . . . . iv 4 344
Do this, and purchase us thy lasting friends . . . *T. Andron.* ii 3 275
Nor tears nor prayers shall purchase out abuses . . *Rom. and Jul.* iii 1 198
How unluckily it happened, that I should purchase the day before!
T. of Athens iii 2 52
His right arm might purchase his own time And be in debt to none . iii 5 77
His silver hairs Will purchase us a good opinion . . . *J. Cæsar* ii 1 145
Will his vouchers vouch him no more of his purchases? . . *Hamlet* v 1 117
The purchase made, the fruits are to ensue . . . . *Othello* ii 3 9
What have I kept back?—Enough to purchase what you have made
known.—Nay, blush not . . . . . . *Ant. and Cleo.* v 2 148
If there were wealth enough for the purchase, or merit for the gift *Cymb.* i 4 91
The purchase is to make men glorious . . . . . *Pericles* i Gower 9
Against the face of death, I sought the purchase of a glorious beauty . i 2 72
Purchased. As my gift and thine own acquisition Worthily purchased,
take my daughter . . . . *Tempest* iv 1 14
Experience be a jewel that I have purchased at an infinite rate *M. Wives* ii 2 213
I have purchased as many diseases under her roof as come to— *M. for M.* i 2 46
His pardon, purchased by such sin For which the pardoner himself is in iv 2 111
All delights are vain; but that most vain, Which with pain purchased
doth inherit pain . . . . *L. L. Lost* i 1 73
How hast thou purchased this experience?—By my penny of observation iii 1 27
That clear honour Were purchased by the merit of the wearer!
Mer. of Venice ii 9 43
Look on beauty, And you shall see 'tis purchased by the weight . iii 2 89
You have among you many a purchased slave . . . . . iv 1 90
With die and drab I purchased this caparison . . . . *W. Tale* iv 3 27
What in me was purchased, Falls upon thee in a more fairer sort *2 Hen. IV.* iv 5 200
A proper title of a peace; and purchased At a superfluous rate! *Hen. VIII.* i 1 98
I account of them As jewels purchased at an easy price . *T. Andron.* iii 1 199
Hereditary, Rather than purchased . . . . . *Ant. and Cleo.* i 4 14
Purchaseth. And never gives to truth and virtue that Which simpleness
and merit purchaseth . . . . *Much Ado* iii 1 70
Purchasing. How little is the cost I have bestow'd In purchasing the
semblance of my soul! . . . . *Mer. of Venice* iii 4 20
Wondrous! ay, I warrant you, and not without his true purchasing *Cor.* ii 1 155
You lay out too much pains For purchasing but trouble . . *Cymbeline* ii 3 93
Pure. All men idle, all; And women too, but innocent and pure *Tempest* ii 1 155
Yet as pure As the unsullied lily . . . . . . *L. L. Lost* v 2 351
That pure congealed white, high Taurus' snow . . *M. N. Dream* iii 2 141
For his sake Did I expose myself, pure for his love . . . *T. Night* v 1 86
O death, made proud with pure and princely beauty! . . *K. John* iv 3 35
In my pure and immaculate valour . . . . . *2 Hen. IV.* iv 3 41
Is in your conscience wash'd As pure as sin with baptism . . *Hen. V.* i 2 32
But what's that Pucelle whom they term so pure? . . *1 Hen. VI.* ii 1 20
A pure unspotted heart, Never yet taint with love . . . . v 3 182
She hath been liberal and free.—And yet, forsooth, she is a virgin pure v 4 83
That praise, sole pure, transcends . . . . *Troi. and Cres.* i 3 244
Who, even in pure and vestal modesty, Still blush, as thinking their
own kisses sin . . . . *Rom. and Jul.* iii 3 38
All villains that do stand by thee are pure . . . *T. of Athens* iv 3 366
Black Macbeth Will seem as pure as snow . . . . *Macbeth* iv 3 53
Be they as pure as grace, As infinite as man may undergo . *Hamlet* i 4 33
Be thou as chaste as ice, as pure as snow, thou shalt not escape calumny iii 1 141
Like some ore Among a mineral of metals base, Shows itself pure . iv 1 27
Who has a breast so pure, But some uncleanly apprehensions Keep leets
and law-days? . . . . *Othello* iii 3 138
Pure air. He is pure air and fire . . . . *Hen. V.* iii 7 22
Pure blood. Contaminated, base, And misbegotten blood I spill of thine,
Mean and right poor, for that pure blood of mine . . *1 Hen. VI.* iv 6 23
Like a fountain with an hundred spouts, Did run pure blood *J. Cæsar* ii 2 78
Pure blush. No further in sport neither than with safety of a pure blush
As Y. Like It i 2 31
Pure bosom. My herald thoughts in thy pure bosom rest *T. G. of Ver.* iii 1 144
Pure brain. A halting sonnet of his own pure brain . . *Much Ado* v 4 87
His pure brain, Which some suppose the soul's frail dwelling-house *K. John* v 7 2
Pure chastity. Thou vow'dst pure chastity . . . *T. G. of Ver.* iv 3 21
Pure devotion. God knows, of pure devotion . . . . *2 Hen. VI.* ii 1 89
Pure Dian, bless thee for thy vision! . . . . . *Pericles* v 3 69
Pure election. Let desert in pure election shine . . . *T. Andron.* i 1 16
Pure fear and entire cowardice . . . . . . *2 Hen. IV.* ii 4 352
Pure gold. The water nectar and the rocks pure gold *T. G. of Ver.* ii 4 171
I will raise her statue in pure gold . . . . *Rom. and Jul.* v 3 299
Pure grief Shore his old thread in twain . . . . . *Othello* v 2 205
Pure hands. Neither bended knees, pure hands held up . *T. G. of Ver.* iii 1 229
Pure heart. If you knew his pure heart's truth . . . . . iv 2 88
On pure heart's love to greet the tender princes . . *Richard III.* iv 1 4
With pure heart's love, Immaculate devotion, holy thoughts . . . iv 4 403
Pure honour. We will not line his thin bestained cloak With our pure
honours . . . . *K. John* iv 3 25
Pure idolatry. Pure, pure idolatry. God amend us! . *L. L. Lost* iv 3 75
Pure impiety. Thou pure impiety and impious purity! . . *Much Ado* iv 1 105
Pure innocence. What follows is pure innocence . . *Mer. of Venice* i 1 145
The silence often of pure innocence Persuades when speaking fails *W. T.* ii 2 41
Pure kindness. 'Twas her brother that, in pure kindness to his horse,
buttered his hay . . . . *Lear* ii 4 127

Pure love. Many a weary step Limp'd in pure love . . *As Y. Like It* ii 7 131
With pure love and troubled brain, he hath ta'en his bow and arrows . iv 3 3
Led hither by pure love . . . . *All's Well* iii 4 38
From Scotland am I stol'n, even of pure love, To greet mine own land *3 Hen. VI.* iii 1 13
To turn your households' rancour to pure love . . *Rom. and Jul.* ii 3 92
Alack, sir, no; her passions are made of nothing but the finest part of pure love . . . . *Ant. and Cleo.* i 2 152
Pure maidens. You yourselves are cause, If your pure maidens fall into the hand Of hot and forcing violation . . . *Hen. V.* iii 3 20
Pure messenger. His thoughts immaculate, His tears pure messengers sent from his heart . . . . . *T. G. of Ver.* ii 7 77
Pure mind. Greases his pure mind . . . . . *T. of Athens* iv 3 195
Pure need. We did it for pure need . . . . *2 Hen. VI.* ii 1 157
Pure respect. A thousand pounds a year for pure respect! . *Hen. VIII.* ii 3 95
Pure scoff. All dry-beaten with pure scoff! . . . *L. L. Lost* v 2 263
Pure shame. Thy cheeks Blush for pure shame . . *1 Hen. VI.* ii 4 66
Pure soul. His pure soul unto his captain Christ . . *Richard II.* iv 1 99
Saba was never More covetous of wisdom and fair virtue Than this pure soul shall be . . . . *Hen. VIII.* v 5 26
In simple and pure soul I come to you . . . . *Othello* i 1 107
Pure spirit. Nor doth the eye itself, That most pure spirit of sense, behold itself, Not going from itself . . . *Troi. and Cres.* iii 3 106
Pure surprise and fear Made me to quit the house . . *Pericles* iii 2 17
Pure truth. Against my soul's pure truth why labour you? *Com. of Er.* iii 2 37
With some shows of truth, Though, in pure truth, it was corrupt *Hen. V.* i 2 73
Pure white. O, let me kiss This princess of pure white! . *M. N. Dream* iii 2 144
In pure white robes, Like very sanctity . . . . *W. Tale* iii 3 22
Pure wit. Welcome, pure wit! thou partest a fair fray . . *L. L. Lost* v 2 484
Purely. Strain'd purely from all hollow bias-drawing . *Troi. and Cres.* iv 5 169
Purer. If zealous love should go in search of virtue, Where should he find it purer? . . . . *K. John* ii 1 429
Throw away the worser part of it, And live the purer with the other *Ham.* iii 4 158
Change me to the meanest bird That flies i' the purer air! . *Pericles* iv 6 109
Purest. The purest treasure mortal times afford Is spotless reputation *Richard II.* i 1 177
The purest spring is not so free from mud As I am clear *2 Hen. VI.* iii 1 101
Chaste as the icicle That 's curdied by the frost from purest snow *Coriol.* v 3 66
Thou bright defiler Of Hymen's purest bed! . . . *T. of Athens* iv 3 384
If she be not honest, chaste, and true, There's no man happy; the purest of their wives Is foul as slander . . . . *Othello* iv 2 18
Purgation. Now you will be my purgation and let me loose . *L. L. Lost* iii 1 128
Thus do all traitors: If their purgation did consist in words, They are as innocent as grace itself . . . . . *As Y. Like It* i 3 55
If any man doubt that, let him put me to my purgation . . . v 4 45
We so openly Proceed in justice, which shall have due course, Even to the guilt or the purgation . . . . . *W. Tale* iii 2 7
Meant for his trial, And fair purgation to the world . . *Hen. VIII.* v 3 152
For me to put him to his purgation would perhaps plunge him into far more choler . . . . *Hamlet* iii 2 318
Purgative. What rhubarb, cyme, or what purgative drug, Would scour these English hence? . . . . *Macbeth* v 3 55
Purgatory. No world without Verona walls, But purgatory . *R. and J.* iii 3 18
I should venture purgatory for't . . . . . *Othello* iv 3 77
Purge. I will purge thy mortal grossness so That thou shalt like an airy spirit go . . . . *M. N. Dream* iii 1 163
Purge him of that humour That presses him from sleep . . *W. Tale* ii 3 38
He is gone aboard a new ship to purge melancholy and air himself . iv 4 790
The blessed gods Purge all infection from our air whilst you Do climate here! . . . . v 1 169
Let's purge this choler without letting blood . . . *Richard II.* i 1 153
I would I could Quit all offences with as clear excuse As well as I am doubtless I can purge Myself of many I am charged withal *1 Hen. IV.* iii 2 20
If I do grow great, I'll grow less; for I'll purge, and leave sack . v 4 168
Purge the obstructions which begin to stop Our very veins of life *2 Hen. IV.* iv 1 65
Now, neighbour confines, purge you of your scum . . . iv 5 124
Enow To purge this field of such a hilding foe . . . *Hen. V.* iv 2 29
But mightier crimes are laid unto your charge, Whereof you cannot easily purge yourself . . . . *2 Hen. VI.* iii 1 135
And from his bosom purge this black despair! . . . . iii 3 23
To purge his fear, I'll be thy death . . . . *3 Hen. VI.* v 6 88
Where, I know, You cannot with such freedom purge yourself *Hen. VIII.* v 1 102
Hoping To purge himself with words . . . . *Coriolanus* v 6 8
Here I stand, both to impeach and purge Myself condemned *Rom. and Jul.* v 3 226
And with him pour we in our country's purge Each drop of us *Macbeth* v 2 28
Find her disease, And purge it to a sound and pristine health . . v 3 52
Grown sick of rest, would purge By any desperate change *Ant. and Cleo.* i 3 53
We would purge the land of these drones . . . . *Pericles* ii 1 50
Purged. You must be purged too, your sins are rack'd . *L. L. Lost* v 2 828
Methought she purged the air of pestilence . . . *T. Night* i 1 20
Our fears, resolved, Be by some certain king purged and deposed *K. John* ii 1 372
These hands, so lately purged of blood, So newly join'd in love . iii 1 239
And but in purged judgement trusting neither . . . *Hen. V.* ii 2 136
My heart is purged from grudging hate . . . . *Richard III.* ii 1 9
Love is a smoke raised with the fume of sighs; Being purged, a fire sparkling in lovers' eyes . . . . . . *Rom. and Jul.* i 1 197
Thus from my lips, by yours, my sin is purged . . . . . i 5 109
I' the olden time, Ere humane statute purged the gentle weal *Macbeth* iii 4 76
Confined to fast in fires, Till the foul crimes done in my days of nature Are burnt and purged away . . . . *Hamlet* i 5 13
When she saw . . . that your rage Would not be purged, she sent you word she was dead . . . . *Ant. and Cleo.* iv 14 124
Purger. We shall be call'd purgers, not murderers . . *J. Cæsar* ii 1 180
Purging. Their eyes purging thick amber and plum-tree gum . *Hamlet* ii 2 200
Am I then revenged, To take him in the purging of his soul? . . iii 3 85
Purifies. That falsehood, in itself a sin, Thus purifies itself . *L. L. Lost* v 2 786
Purifying. Which is a purifying o' the song . . . *All's Well* i 3 87
Puritan. Young Charbon the puritan and old Poysam the papist . . i 3 56
Though honesty be no puritan, yet it will do no hurt . . . i 3 98
He is a kind of puritan.—O, if I thought that, I'ld beat him like a dog! —What, for being a puritan? . . . . . . *T. Night* ii 3 152
The devil a puritan that he is, or any thing constantly, but a time-pleaser ii 3 159
But one puritan amongst them, and he sings psalms to hornpipes *W. T.* iv 3 46
She would make a puritan of the devil . . . . *Pericles* iv 6 9
Purity. I could drive her then from the ward of her purity *Mer. Wives* ii 2 258
Thou pure impiety and impious purity! . . . . *Much Ado* iv 1 105
All patience and impatience, All purity, all trial . . *As Y. Like It* v 2 104
Sully the purity and whiteness of my sheets . . . *W. Tale* i 2 327
By the pattern of mine own thoughts I cut out The purity of his . . iv 4 394
Give a holiness, a purity, To the yet unbegotten sin of times . *K. John* iv 3 53
Purity. Of such a winnow'd purity in love . . . *Troi. and Cres.* iii 2 174
I love thee in so strain'd a purity . . . . . . iv 4 26
Who dares, In purity of manhood stand upright, And say, 'This man's a flatterer'? if one be, So are they all . . . *T. of Athens* iv 3 14
Purlieu. Where in the purlieus of this forest stands A sheep-cote fenced about with olive trees? . . . . . . *As Y. Like It* iv 3 77
Purple. Write In emerald tufts, flowers purple, blue, and white *Mer. Wives* v 5 74
Before milk-white, now purple with love's wound . *M. N. Dream* ii 1 167
Purple grapes, green figs, and mulberries . . . . . iii 1 170
Flower of this purple dye, Hit with Cupid's archery . . . iii 2 102
He is come to open The purple testament of bleeding war *Richard II.* iii 3 94
I never see thy face but I think upon hell-fire and Dives that lived in purple; for there he is in his robes, burning, burning *1 Hen. IV.* iii 3 36
With purple falchion, painted to the hilt In blood . . *3 Hen. VI.* i 4 12
The one his purple blood right well resembles . . . . ii 5 99
O, may such purple tears be alway shed From those that wish the downfall of our house! . . . . v 6 64
Did drain The purple sap from her sweet brother's body *Richard III.* iv 4 277
That quench the fire of your pernicious rage With purple fountains issuing from your veins . . . . . . *Rom. and Jul.* i 1 92
Daisies, and long purples That liberal shepherds give a grosser name *Ham.* iv 7 170
Purple the sails, and so perfumed that The winds were love-sick *A. and C.* ii 2 198
The yellows, blues, The purple violets, and marigolds . . *Pericles* iv 1 16
Purpled. With purpled hands, Dyed in the dying slaughter of their foes *K. John* ii 1 322
If you bear me hard, Now, whilst your purpled hands do reek and smoke, Fulfil your pleasure . . . . . . *J. Cæsar* iii 1 158
Purple-hued. Mad mustachio purple-hued malt-worms . *1 Hen. IV.* ii 1 83
Purple-in-grain beard, or your French-crown-colour beard *M. N. Dream* i 2 97
Purport. And with a look so piteous in purport As if he had been loosed out of hell . . . . *Hamlet* ii 1 82
Purpose. One midnight Fated to the purpose . . . *Tempest* i 2 129
The ministers for the purpose hurried thence Me and thy crying self . i 2 131
I endow'd thy purposes With words that made them known . . i 2 357
If you but knew how you the purpose cherish Whiles thus you mock it! ii 1 224
Do not, for one repulse, forego the purpose That you resolved to effect . iii 3 12
The sole drift of my purpose doth extend Not a frown further . . v 1 29
Love, lend me wings to make my purpose swift! . *T. G. of Ver.* ii 6 42
Here's the ladder for the purpose . . . . . . iii 1 152
But to the purpose . . . . iv 1 53
Have you importuned her to such a purpose? . . *Mer. Wives* ii 2 221
To what purpose have you unfolded this to me? . . . . ii 2 227
Here is the heart of my purpose . . . . ii 2 233
He'll tell me all his purpose . . . . iv 4 77
Yet hear me speak. Assist me in my purpose . . . . iv 6 3
The purpose why, is here . . . . iv 6 21
Be not angry: I knew of your purpose . . . . . v 5 214
The heavens give safety to your purposes! . . *Meas. for Meas.* i 1 74
It draws something near to the speech we had to such a purpose . i 2 79
Why I desire thee To give me secret harbour, hath a purpose . . i 3 4
Hence shall we see, If power change purpose, what our seemers be . i 3 54
Or that the resolute acting of your blood Could have attain'd the effect of your own purpose . . . . ii 1 13
You are a tedious fool: to the purpose . . . . . ii 1 120
'Tis for a good purpose . . . . ii 1 155
Believe me, on mine honour, My words express my purpose.—Ha! little honour to be much believed, And most pernicious purpose! . . ii 4 148
Angelo had never the purpose to corrupt her . . . . iii 1 163
The provost knows our purpose and our plot . . . . iv 5 2
I am advised to do it; He says, to veil full purpose . . . iv 6 4
His purpose surfeiting, he sends a warrant For my poor brother's head v 1 102
We'll touse you Joint by joint, but we will know his purpose . v 1 314
That brain'd my purpose . . . . v 1 401
I sent thee for a rope And told thee to what purpose *Com. of Errors* iv 1 97
Belike his wife, acquainted with his fits, On purpose shut the doors . iv 3 92
People sin upon purpose, because they would go thither . *Much Ado* ii 1 267
He was wont to speak plain and to the purpose, like an honest man . ii 3 20
How still the evening is, As hush'd on purpose to grace harmony! . ii 3 41
There will she hide her, To listen our purpose . . . . iii 1 12
Since I do purpose to marry, I will think nothing to any purpose that the world can say against it . . . . v 4 106
Read the purpose of my coming, And suddenly resolve me . *L. L. Lost* ii 1 109
It was to show my skill, That more for praise than purpose meant to kill iv 1 29
I will have an apology for that purpose.—An excellent device! . . v 1 143
Their purpose is to parle, to court and dance . . . . v 2 122
'Tis our will That some plain man recount their purposes . . v 2 176
We came to visit you, and purpose now To lead you to our court . v 2 343
The extreme parts of time extremely forms All causes to the purpose . v 2 751
Helen told me of their stealth, Of this their purpose hither *M. N. Dream* iv 1 166
With purpose to be dress'd in an opinion Of wisdom, gravity *Mer. of Ven.* i 1 91
From your love I have a warranty To unburden all my plots and purposes i 1 133
The devil can cite Scripture for his purpose . . . . i 3 99
We have friends That purpose merriment . . . . . ii 2 212
My purpose was not to have seen you here . . . . . iii 2 230
I have possess'd your grace of what I purpose . . . . iv 1 35
The intent and purpose of the law Hath full relation to the penalty . iv 1 247
I had myself notice of my brother's purpose herein . *As Y. Like It* i 1 145
Have you no song, forester, for this purpose? . . . . iv 2 7
Know of me then, for now I speak to some purpose . . . v 2 58
The lustful bed On purpose trimm'd up for Semiramis . *T. of Shrew* Ind. 2 41
And to be a soldier?—Such is his noble purpose . . *All's Well* iii 2 73
May be the amorous count solicits her In the unlawful purpose . . iii 5 73
Now I see The bottom of your purpose . . . . . iii 7 29
Not to know what we speak one to another; so we seem to know, is to know straight our purpose . . . . iv 1 21
Being not ignorant of the impossibility, and knowing I had no such purpose . . . . iv 1 40
All the secrets of our camp I'll show, Their force, their purposes . iv 1 94
Come, come, to the purpose: did he love this woman? . . . v 3 241
What's that to the purpose? . . . . . . *T. Night* i 3 21
My purpose is, indeed, a horse of that colour . . . . ii 3 181
She sends him on purpose, that I may appear stubborn to him . . iii 4 74
It is something of my negligence, nothing of my purpose . . . iii 4 280
Thou never spokest To better purpose . . . . . *W. Tale* i 2 89
But once before I spoke to the purpose: when? Nay, let me have't . i 2 100
Why, lo you now, I have spoke to the purpose twice . . . i 2 106
That you do change this purpose, Which being so horrible, so bloody, must Lead on to some foul issue . . . . ii 3 151
You must change this purpose, Or I my life . . . . . iv 4 39
You have As little skill to fear as I have purpose To put you to't . . iv 4 152

Purpose. He will allow no speech, which I do guess You do not purpose *W. Tale* iv 4 480
Come not before him.—I not purpose it iv 4 483
Then list to me: This follows, if you will not change your purpose iv 4 553
Besides, the gods Will have fulfill'd their secret purposes v 1 36
Still secure And confident from foreign purposes *K. John* ii 1 28
Makes it take head from all indifferency, From all direction, purpose ii 1 580
The better act of purposes mistook Is to mistake again iii 1 274
Strain their cheeks to idle merriment, A passion hateful to my purposes iii 3 47
Yet am I sworn and I did purpose, boy iv 1 124
That am the tongue of these To sound the purposes of all their hearts iv 2 48
The colour of the king doth come and go Between his purpose and his conscience iv 2 77
The shameful work of Hubert's hand; The practice and the purpose of the king iv 3 63
Let it at least be said They saw we had a purpose of defence v 1 76
With purpose presently to leave this war v 7 86
Never by advised purpose meet To plot, contrive *Richard II.* i 3 188
To what purpose dost thou hoard thy words? i 3 253
Had not God, for some strong purpose, steel'd The hearts of men v 2 34
You will be there, I know.—If God prevent not, I purpose so v 2 55
But this our purpose now is twelve month old *1 Hen. IV.* i 1 28
For this cause awhile we must neglect Our holy purpose to Jerusalem i 1 102
You start away And lend no ear unto my purposes i 3 217
The purpose you undertake is dangerous ii 3 7
The king is certainly possess'd Of all our purposes iv 1 41
In the morning early shall my uncle Bring him our purposes iv 3 111
The southern wind Doth play the trumpet to his purposes v 1 4
You swore to us . . . That you did nothing purpose 'gainst the state v 1 43
In every thing the purpose must weigh with the folly *2 Hen. IV.* ii 2 195
You knew I was at your back, and spoke it on purpose to try my patience ii 4 334
But this is mere digression from my purpose iv 1 140
And present execution of our wills To us and to our purposes confined iv 1 175
My father's purposes have been mistook iv 2 56
And had a purpose now To lead out many to the Holy Land iv 5 210
He's walk'd the way of nature; And to our purposes he lives no more v 2 5
But to the purpose, and so to the venture Epil. 7
So may a thousand actions, once afoot, End in one purpose *Hen. V.* i 2 212
The French . . . with pale policy Seek to divert the English purposes ii Prol. 15
Ever kept together, As two yoke-devils sworn to either's purpose ii 2 106
Our purposes God justly hath discover'd; And I repent my fault ii 2 151
If wishes would prevail with me, My purpose should not fail with me iii 2 17
Or any such proverb so little kin to the purpose iii 7 72
They purpose not their death, when they purpose their services iv 1 165
Placed behind With purpose to relieve and follow them *1 Hen. VI.* i 1 133
As I with sudden and extemporal speech Purpose to answer iii 1 7
Your purpose is both good and reasonable v 1 36
You have suborn'd this man, Of purpose to obscure my noble birth v 4 22
Being accused a crafty murderer, His guilt should be but idly posted over, Because his purpose is not executed *2 Hen. VI.* iii 1 256
Had I not been cited so by them, Yet did I purpose as they do entreat iii 2 282
A cold premeditation for my purpose! *3 Hen. VI.* iii 2 133
How he doth stand affected to our purpose *Richard III.* iii 1 171
But, for his purpose in the coronation, I have not sounded him iii 4 16
And timorously confess The manner and the purpose of his treason iii 5 58
Left nothing fitting for the purpose Untouch'd, or slightly handled iii 7 18
He smiled and said 'The better for our purpose' v 3 274
Were he evil used, he would outgo His father by as much as a performance Does an irresolute purpose *Hen. VIII.* i 2 209
Commends his good opinion of you, and Does purpose honour to you ii 3 62
Your royal graces, Shower'd on me daily, have been more than could My studied purposes requite iii 2 168
For certain, This is of purpose laid by some that hate me v 2 14
By a pace goes backward, with a purpose It hath to climb *Troi. and Cres.* i 3 128
He bade me take a trumpet, And to this purpose speak i 3 264
However it is spread in general name, Relates in purpose only to Achilles i 3 323
The purpose is perspicuous even as substance i 3 324
With great speed of judgement, Ay, with celerity, find Hector's purpose i 3 330
Pardon me; 'Twas not my purpose, thus to beg a kiss: I am ashamed iii 2 145
We'll execute your purpose, and put on A form of strangeness as we pass iii 3 50
I was sent for to the king; but why, I know not.—His purpose meets you iv 1 36
Tell you the lady what she is to do, And haste her to the purpose iv 3 5
Do you purpose A victor shall be known? iv 5 66
Let these threats alone, Till accident or purpose bring you to't iv 5 262
I am thwarted quite From my great purpose in to-morrow's battle v 1 43
It is the purpose that makes strong the vow; But vows to every purpose must not hold v 3 23
Since it serves my purpose, I will venture To stale 't a little more *Cor.* i 1 94
We have at disadvantage fought and did Retire to win our purpose i 6 50
When you speak best unto the purpose, it is not worth the wagging of your beards ii 1 95
I wish no better Than have him hold that purpose and to put it In execution ii 1 256
We recommend to you, tribunes of the people, Our purpose to them ii 2 156
Purpose so barr'd, it follows, Nothing is done to purpose iii 1 148
They have pardons, being ask'd, as free As words to little purpose iii 2 89
I had purpose Once more to hew thy target from thy brawn, Or lose mine arm for't iv 5 125
I purpose not to wait on fortune till These wars determine v 3 119
This valley fits the purpose passing well *T. Andron.* ii 3 84
Wouldst thou withdraw it? for what purpose, love? *Rom. and Jul.* ii 2 130
If that thy bent of love be honourable, Thy purpose marriage ii 2 144
A grey eye or so, but not to the purpose ii 4 46
Of purpose to have him spend less *T. of Athens* iii 1 26
That speak'st with every tongue, To every purpose! iv 3 390
Is very likely to load our purposes with what they travail for v 1 17
But men may construe things after their fashion, Clean from the purpose of the things themselves *J. Cæsar* i 3 35
This shall make Our purpose necessary and not envious ii 1 178
Look fresh and merrily: Let not our looks put on our purposes ii 1 225
He wish'd to-day our enterprise might thrive. I fear our purpose is discovered iii 1 17
Popilius Lena speaks not of our purposes; For, look, he smiles iii 1 23
My misgiving still Falls shrewdly to the purpose iii 1 146
That no compunctious visitings of nature Shake my fell purpose *Macbeth* i 5 47
And when goes hence?—To-morrow, as he purposes i 5 61
We coursed him at the heels, and had a purpose To be his purveyor i 6 21
Infirm of purpose! Give me the daggers ii 2 52
The flighty purpose never is o'ertook Unless the deed go with it iv 1 145

Purpose. No boasting like a fool; This deed I'll do before this purpose cool *Macbeth* iv 1 154
Impotent and bed-rid, scarcely hears Of this his nephew's purpose *Ham.* i 2 30
What should we say, my lord?—Why, any thing, but to the purpose ii 2 287
He whose sable arms, Black as his purpose, did the night resemble ii 2 475
Give him a further edge, And drive his purpose on to these delights iii 1 27
For any thing so overdone is from the purpose of playing iii 2 23
Purpose is but the slave to memory, Of violent birth, but poor validity iii 2 198
What to ourselves in passion we propose, The passion ending, doth the purpose lose iii 2 205
This visitation Is but to whet thy almost blunted purpose iii 4 111
Good.—So is it, if thou knew'st our purposes.—I see a cherub that sees them iv 3 49
For that purpose, I'll anoint my sword iv 7 141
If he by chance escape your venom'd stuck, Our purpose may hold there iv 7 163
If thou answerest me not to the purpose, confess thyself v 1 44
And the king hold his purpose, I will win for him an I can v 2 183
I am constant to my purposes v 2 208
And, in this upshot, purposes mistook Fall'n on the inventors' heads v 2 395
Meantime we shall express our darker purpose *Lear* i 1 37
I want that glib and oily art, To speak and purpose not i 1 228
If you violently proceed against him, mistaking his purpose i 2 90
Which I have rather blamed as mine own jealous curiosity than as a very pretence and purpose of unkindness i 4 75
I do beseech you To understand my purposes aright i 4 260
Suspend thy purpose, if thou didst intend To make this creature fruitful! i 4 298
Seeing how loathly opposite I stood To his unnatural purpose ii 1 52
Make your own purpose, How in my strength you please ii 1 113
The night before there was no purpose in them Of this remove ii 4 3
Good sir, to the purpose.—Who put my man i' the stocks? ii 4 184
Quit the house on purpose, that their punishment Might have the freer course iv 2 94
Might not you Transport her purposes by word? iv 5 20
Know of the duke if his last purpose hold v 1 1
Ask him his purposes, why he appears Upon this call o' the trumpet v 3 118
He, as loving his own pride and purposes, Evades them *Othello* i 1 12
Bearing with frank appearance Their purposes toward Cyprus i 3 39
He holds me well; The better shall my purpose work on him i 3 397
He, swift of foot, Outran my purpose ii 3 233
I am very ill at ease, Unfit for mine own purposes iii 3 33
If it be not for some purpose of import, Give't me again iii 3 316
If thou hast that in thee indeed, which I have greater reason to believe now than ever, I mean purpose, courage and valour, this night show it iv 2 218
There he dropp'd it for a special purpose Which wrought to his desire v 2 322
Let our officers Have notice what we purpose *Ant. and Cleo.* i 2 184
I am sorry to give breathing to my purpose i 3 14
Quarrel no more, but be prepared to know The purposes I bear i 3 67
May I never To this good purpose, that so fairly shows, Dream of impediment! ii 2 147
Your way is shorter; My purposes do draw me much about ii 4 8
And therefore have we Our written purposes before us sent ii 6 4
Thanks to you, That call'd me timelier than my purpose hither ii 6 52
The policy of that purpose made more in the marriage than the love ii 6 126
'Tis a brave army, And full of purpose iv 3 12
Go and say, We purpose her no shame v 1 62
By taking Antony's course, you shall bereave yourself Of my good purposes v 2 131
Bravest at the last, She levell'd at our purposes v 2 339
It had been pity you should have been put together with so mortal a purpose as then each bore *Cymbeline* i 4 44
This is but a custom in your tongue; you bear a graver purpose, I hope i 4 151
I cross'd the seas on purpose and on promise To see your grace i 6 202
A worthy fellow, Albeit he comes on angry purpose now ii 3 61
She hath my letter for the purpose iii 4 30
Whereunto I never Purpose return iii 4 110
But if I were as wise as honest, then My purpose would prove well iii 4 122
My horse is tied up safe: out, sword, and to a sore purpose! iv 1 25
What have you dream'd of late of this war's purpose? iv 2 345
I nothing know where she remains, why gone, Nor when she purposes return iv 3 15
Therefore, good heavens, Hear patiently my purpose v 1 22
Open'd, in despite Of heaven and men, her purposes v 5 59
Nay, nay, to the purpose v 5 178
I, dreading that her purpose Was of more danger v 5 253
Away he posts With unchaste purpose v 5 284
'Twas a fitment for The purpose I then follow'd v 5 410
And on set purpose let his armour rust Until this day *Pericles* ii 2 54
If this you purpose as ye speak ii 4 12
Nor let pity, which Even women have cast off, melt thee, but be A soldier to thy purpose iv 1 8
Untied I still my virgin knot will keep. Diana, aid my purpose! iv 2 161
Therefore I will make them acquainted with your purpose iv 6 210
My purpose was for Tarsus, there to strike The inhospitable Cleon v 1 253
Purpose-changer. That same purpose-changer *K. John* ii 1 567
Purposed. You have spoken truer than you purposed *Tempest* ii 1 20
Oftentimes have purposed to forbid Sir Valentine her company *T. G. of V.* iii 1 26
To interrupt my purposed rest *L. L. Lost* v 2 91
Let not the cloud of sorrow justle it From what it purposed v 2 759
Our purposed hunting shall be set aside *M. N. Dream* iv 1 188
Great clerks have purposed To greet me with premeditated welcomes v 1 93
Twice did he turn his back and purposed so *As Y. Like It* iv 3 128
Hadst thou but shook thy head or made a pause When I spake darkly what I purposed *K. John* iv 2 232
In my present wildness die And never live to show the incredulous world The noble change that I have purposed *2 Hen. IV.* iv 5 155
Merely to revenge him on the emperor . . . , this is purposed *Hen. VIII.* ii 1 164
What was purposed Concerning his imprisonment, was rather, If there be faith in men, meant for his trial v 3 149
It is a purposed thing, and grows by plot *Coriolanus* iii 1 38
What can be avoided Whose end is purposed by the mighty gods? *J. C.* ii 2 27
How purposed, sir, I pray you?—Against some part of Poland *Hamlet* iv 4 11
Let my disclaiming from a purposed evil Free me so far v 2 252
Your purposed low correction *Lear* ii 2 149
So am I purposed ii 4 296
Nor my service past, nor present sorrows, Nor purposed merit *Othello* iii 4 117
The heir of's kingdom, whom He purposed to his wife's sole son *Cymb.* i 1 5
She purposed, By watching, weeping, tendance, kissing, to O'ercome you v 5 52

Purposely to take His brother here and put him to the sword *As Y. Like It* v 4 163
Some kind of men that put quarrels purposely on others . *T. Night* iii 4 267
Purposely therefore Left I the court, to see this quarrel tried 2 *Hen. VI.* ii 3 52
As if it were the Moor Come hither purposely to poison me *T. Andron.* iii 2 73
Purposeth. But that, it seems, he little purposeth . *L. L. Lost* ii 1 142
Where is he now?—He purposeth to Athens . *Ant. and Cleo.* iii 1 35
Purposing the Bastard to destroy, Came in strong rescue 1 *Hen. VI.* iv 6 25
Purr. Here is a purr of fortune's, sir, or of fortune's cat . *All's Well* v 2 20
Pur! the cat is gray . . . . *Lear* iii 6 47
Purse. Beshrew me, but you have a quick wit.—And yet it cannot overtake your slow purse . . . . . *T. G. of Ver.* i 1 134
Open your purse, that the money and the matter may be both at once delivered . . . . i 1 137
She is too liberal.—Of her tongue she cannot, for that's writ down she is slow of; of her purse she shall not . . . . . iii 1 357
There is my purse; I give thee this For thy sweet mistress' sake . iv 4 181
Did you pick Master Slender's purse?—Ay, by these gloves, did he *M. W.* i 1 155
The report goes she has all the rule of her husband's purse . i 3 59
She bears the purse too; she is a region in Guiana, all gold and bounty i 3 76
There is either liquor in his pate or money in his purse when he looks so merrily . . . . ii 1 198
There's my purse; I am yet thy debtor . . . . . ii 2 138
He cannot creep into a halfpenny purse, nor into a pepper-box . iii 5 149
In the desk That's cover'd o'er with Turkish tapestry There is a purse of ducats . . . . . *Com. of Errors* iv 1 105
Here! go; the desk, the purse! sweet, now, make haste . . iv 2 29
Went'st not thou to her for a purse of ducats?—He came to me . iv 4 90
This purse of ducats I received from you . . . . . v 1 385
A good leg and a good foot, uncle, and money enough in his purse *M. Ado* ii 1 16
Thou halfpenny purse of wit, thou pigeon-egg of discretion . *L. L. Lost* v 1 77
Be assured, My purse, my person, my extremest means, Lie all unlock'd to your occasions . . . . . *Mer. of Venice* i 1 138
I will go and purse the ducats straight . . . . . i 3 175
I would have him help to waste His borrow'd purse . . . ii 5 51
I think you have no money in your purse . . . *As Y. Like It* ii 4 14
Crowns in my purse I have and goods at home . . *T. of Shrew* i 2 57
Our purses shall be proud, our garments poor. . . . . iv 3 173
Take this purse of gold, And let me buy your friendly help . *All's Well* iii 7 14
There's my purse: I give thee not this to suggest thee from thy master iv 5 46
Keep your purse: My master, not myself, lacks recompense *T. Night* i 5 303
Here's my purse. In the south suburbs, at the Elephant, Is best to lodge iii 3 38
Why I your purse?—Haply your eye shall light upon some toy . iii 3 43
My necessity Makes me to ask you for my purse . . . iii 4 369
Denied me mine own purse, Which I had recommended to his use Not half an hour before . . . . v 1 93
Your purse is not hot enough to purchase your spice . *W. Tale* iv 3 127
By which means I saw whose purse was best in picture . . . iv 4 615
'Twas nothing to geld a codpiece of a purse; I could have filed keys off iv 4 623
In this time of lethargy I picked and cut most of their festival purses . iv 4 628
I had not left a purse alive in the whole army . . . iv 4 631
Show the inside of your purse to the outside of his hand, and no more ado iv 4 833
Shalt thrust thy hand as deep Into the purse of rich prosperity *K. John* v 2 61
For their love Lies in their purses . . . . *Richard II.* ii 2 130
We that take purses go by the moon and the seven stars . 1 *Hen. IV.* i 2 15
A purse of gold most resolutely snatched on Monday night and most dissolutely spent on Tuesday morning . . . . . . i 2 38
Where shall we take a purse to-morrow, Jack? . . . . i 2 110
And traders riding to London with fat purses . . . . i 2 142
If you will go, I will stuff your purses full of crowns . . i 2 146
Thou variest no more from picking of purses than giving direction doth from labouring . . . . ii 1 56
Hot livers and cold purses . . . . ii 4 355
Shall the son of England prove a thief and take purses? . . ii 4 452
What money is in my purse?—Seven groats and two pence . 2 *Hen. IV.* i 2 262
I can get no remedy against this consumption of the purse . . i 2 265
You have, as it appears to me, practised upon the easy-yielding spirit of this woman, and made her serve your uses both in purse and in person . . . . ii 1 127
A friend i' the court is better than a penny in purse . . . v 1 34
That he should, for a foreign purse, so sell His sovereign's life *Hen. V.* ii 2 10
His passport shall be made And crowns for convoy put into his purse iv 3 37
O'ercharging your free purses with large fines . . . 1 *Hen. VI.* i 3 64
Whose large style Agrees not with the leanness of his purse . 2 *Hen. VI.* i 1 112
Where is thy conscience now?—In the Duke of Gloucester's purse *Rich. III.* i 4 131
When he opens his purse to give us our reward, thy conscience flies out i 4 132
It [conscience] made me once restore a purse of gold that I found . i 4 144
There is my purse to cure that blow of thine . . . . iv 4 516
Thou, trumpet, there's my purse. Now crack thy lungs *Troi. and Cres.* iv 5 6
Thou green sarcenet flap for a sore eye, thou tassel of a prodigal's purse v 1 37
Nor will he know his purse, or yield me this, To show him *T. of Athens* i 2 200
Timon has been this lord's father, And kept his credit with his purse . iii 2 75
I fear 'tis deepest winter in Lord Timon's purse . . . iii 4 14
Leave their false vows with him, Like empty purses pick'd . . iv 2 12
Costly thy habit as thy purse can buy, But not express'd in fancy *Ham.* i 3 70
I had my father's signet in my purse . . . . . v 2 49
His purse is empty already; all's golden words are spent . . v 2 136
For confirmation that I am much more Than my out-wall, open this purse, and take What it contains . . . . . *Lear* iii 1 45
Take this purse, thou whom the heavens' plagues Have humbled to all strokes . . . . iv 1 67
Here, friend, 's another purse; in it a jewel Well worth . . iv 6 28
No eyes in your head, nor no money in your purse? Your eyes are in a heavy case, your purse in a light . . . . . . iv 6 149
Villain, take my purse: If ever thou wilt thrive, bury my body . iv 6 252
Who hast had my purse As if the strings were thine . . *Othello* i 1 2
I say, put money in thy purse. (Repeated) . . . . i 3 347
Fill thy purse with money . . . . i 3 353
Thus do I ever make my fool my purse . . . . . i 3 389
Thou criedst 'Indeed!' And didst contract and purse thy brow together iii 3 113
Who steals my purse steals trash; 'tis something, nothing . iii 3 157
Believe me, I had rather have lost my purse Full of crusadoes . iii 4 25
He is vaulting variable ramps, In your despite, upon your purse *Cymb.* i 6 135
Wilt thou serve me?—Sir, I will.—Give me thy hand; here's my purse iii 5 124
This Cloten was a fool, an empty purse; There was no money in't . iv 2 113
Purse and brain both empty; the brain the heavier for being too light, the purse too light, being drawn of heaviness . . . . v 4 166
And not your knowledge, your personal pain, but even Your purse *Per.* iii 2 47
Purse-bearer. I'll be your purse-bearer . . . . *T. Night* iii 3 47
Pursed. When she first met Mark Antony, she pursed up his heart, upon the river of Cydnus . . . . . *Ant. and Cleo.* ii 2 192

Pursents. It is vara fine, For every one pursents three . . *L. L. Lost* v 2 488
Purse-taking. I see a good amendment of life in thee; from praying to purse-taking . . . . 1 *Hen. IV.* i 2 115
Pursue. Clap on more sails; pursue . . . . *Mer. Wives* ii 2 142
Love like a shadow flies when substance love pursues; Pursuing that that flies, and flying what pursues . . . . . . ii 2 215
May we, with the warrant of womanhood and the witness of a good conscience, pursue him with any further revenge? . . . iv 2 221
Our natures do pursue, Like rats that ravin down their proper bane, A thirsty evil . . . . *Meas. for Meas.* i 2 132
Your sense pursues not mine: either you are ignorant, Or seem so craftily ii 4 74
No reason That with such vehemency he should pursue Faults proper to himself . . . . v 1 109
To that place the sharp Athenian law Cannot pursue us *M. N. Dream* i 1 163
To the wood will he to-morrow night Pursue her . . . . i 1 248
She shall pursue it with the soul of love . . . . . ii 1 182
I love thee not, therefore pursue me not. . . . . ii 1 188
The dove pursues the griffin . . . . ii 1 232
Bootless speed, When cowardice pursues and valour flies . . ii 1 234
We trifle time: I pray thee, pursue sentence . *Mer. of Venice* iv 1 298
I mean to shift my bush; And then pursue me as you draw your bow *T. of Shrew* v 2 47
I pray you, make us friends; I will pursue the amity . *All's Well* ii 5 15
My desires, like fell and cruel hounds, E'er since pursue me . *T. Night* i 1 23
Pursue him now, lest the device take air and taint . . . iii 4 144
I cannot pursue with any safety this sport to the upshot . . iv 2 76
Pursue him, and entreat him to a peace . . . . . v 1 389
I wot your love pursues A banish'd traitor . . *Richard II.* ii 3 59
Strike up our drums, pursue the scatter'd stray . 2 *Hen. IV.* iv 2 120
Let us pursue him ere the writs go forth . . . 2 *Hen. VI.* v 3 26
Hark! the fatal followers do pursue; And I am faint and cannot fly 3 *Hen. VI.* i 4 22
Some troops pursue the bloody-minded queen, That led calm Henry . ii 6 33
To fly the boar before the boar pursues, Were to incense the boar to follow us And make pursuit where he did mean no chase *Rich. III.* iii 2 28
Emulation hath a thousand sons That one by one pursue *Troi. and Cres.* iii 3 157
Will you the knights Shall to the edge of all extremity Pursue each other? iv 5 69
Consort with me in loud and dear petition, Pursue we him on knees v 3 10
Ignomy and shame Pursue thy life, and live aye with thy name! . v 10 34
Pursue him to his house, and pluck him thence . . *Coriolanus* iii 1 309
A speedier course than lingering languishment Must we pursue *T. An.* ii 1 111
Will they pursue the quality no longer than they can sing? *Hamlet* ii 2 363
Here and hence pursue me lasting strife, If, once a widow, ever I be wife! iii 2 232
Fled this way, sir. When by no means he could— Pursue him, ho! *Lear* ii 1 45
All vengeance comes too short Which can pursue the offender . . ii 1 91
Myself the crying fellow did pursue . . . . *Othello* ii 3 230
If I knew What hoop should hold us stanch, from edge to edge O' the world I would pursue it . . . . . . *Ant. and Cleo.* ii 2 118
Fortune pursue thee! . . . . iii 12 25
I will pursue her Even to Augustus' throne . . . *Cymbeline* iii 5 100
Pursued. I have pursued her as love hath pursued me . *Mer. Wives* ii 2 208
They fled Into this abbey, whither we pursued them . *Com. of Errors* v 1 155
Had we pursued that life, And our weak spirits ne'er been higher rear'd With stronger blood . . . . *W. Tale* i 2 71
Thus far, with rough and all-unable pen, Our bending author hath pursued the story . . . . *Hen. V.* Epil. 2
While we pursued the horsemen of the north, He slily stole away 3 *Hen. VI.* i 1 2
Turn back and fly, like . . . lambs pursued by hunger-starved wolves i 4 5
So went to bed; where eagerly his sickness Pursued him still *Hen. VIII.* iv 2 25
Pursued my humour not pursuing his . . . *Rom. and Jul.* i 1 135
Can vengeance be pursued further than death? . . . . v 3 55
He which hath your noble father slain Pursued my life . . *Hamlet* iv 7 5
Is he pursued?—Ay, my good lord . . . . . *Lear* ii 1 111
Would I might never O'ertake pursued success, but I do feel, By the rebound of yours, a grief that smites My very heart at root *A. and C.* v 2 103
She hath pursued conclusions infinite Of easy ways to die . . v 2 358
Would I had done't, So the revenge alone pursued me! . . *Cymbeline* iv 2 157
Pursuer. Falling from a hill, he was so bruised That the pursuers took him . . . . 1 *Hen. IV.* v 5 22
Pursuest. Howsoever thou pursuest this act, Taint not thy mind *Hamlet* i 5 84
To Milford go, And find not her whom thou pursuest . . *Cymbeline* iii 5 166
Pursuing that that flies, and flying what pursues . . *Mer. Wives* ii 2 216
With no less confidence Than boys pursuing summer butterflies *Coriol.* iv 6 94
Pursued my humour not pursuing his . . . *Rom. and Jul.* i 1 135
Pursuit. Slow in pursuit, but match'd in mouth like bells *M. N. Dream* iv 1 128
Devise the fittest time and safest way To hide us from pursuit *As Y. L. It* ii 3 138
She writes, Pursuit would be but vain . . . . *All's Well* iii 4 25
The rather by these arguments of fear, Set forth in your pursuit *T. N.* iii 3 12
Now, have you left pursuit?—Retreat is made . . . 2 *Hen. IV.* iv 3 77
Turn head, and stop pursuit . . . . . . *Hen. V.* ii 4 69
Here sound retreat, and cease our hot pursuit . . . 1 *Hen. VI.* ii 2 3
Or whether he be 'scaped away or no From Clifford's and Northumberland's pursuit . . . . 3 *Hen. VI.* ii 1 3
Oft have I heard his praises in pursuit, But ne'er till now his scandal of retire.—Nor now my scandal . . . . ii 1 149
They follow us with wings; And weak we are and cannot shun pursuit ii 3 13
Away! for death doth hold us in pursuit . . . . . ii 5 127
To fly the boar before the boar pursues, Were to incense the boar to follow us And make pursuit where he did mean no chase *Rich. III.* iii 2 30
Ne'er retract what he hath done, Nor faint in the pursuit *Troi. and Cres.* ii 2 142
I'll play the hunter for thy life With all my force, pursuit and policy iv 1 18
Pursuivant. These grey locks, the pursuivants of death . 1 *Hen. VI.* ii 5 5
Send for his master with a pursuivant presently . . 2 *Hen. VI.* i 3 37
I now repent I told the pursuivant . . . . *Richard III.* iii 4 90
Send out a pursuivant at arms . . . . v 3 59
Who holds his state at door, 'mongst pursuivants, Pages . *Hen. VIII.* v 2 24
Pursy insolence shall break his wind With fear . . . *T. of Athens* v 4 12
Forgive me this my virtue; For in the fatness of these pursy times Virtue itself of vice must pardon beg . . . . . *Hamlet* iii 4 153
Purus. Integer vitæ, scelerisque purus, Non eget Mauri jaculis, nec arcu *T. Andron.* iv 2 20
Purveyor. We coursed him at the heels, and had a purpose To be his purveyor . . . . *Macbeth* i 6 22
Push. And made a push at chance and sufferance . . *Much Ado* v 1 38
More villain thou. Well, push him out of doors . . *As Y. Like It* iii 1 15
All other circumstances Made up to the deed, doth push on this *W. Tale* ii 1 179
Traitors! Will you not push her out? . . . . . ii 3 73
I pray you, do not push me; I'll be gone . . . . . ii 3 125
This sessions, to our great grief we pronounce, Even pushes 'gainst our heart . . . . iii 2 2

Push. One that will either push on or pluck back thy business there *W. Tale* iv 4 762
Lest they desire upon this push to trouble Your joys with like relation v 3 129
To push destruction and perpetual shame Out of the weak door of our fainting land *K. John* v 7 77
And stand the push Of every beardless vain comparative *1 Hen. IV.* iii 2 66
If we without his help can make a head To push against a kingdom iv 1 81
I stand the push of your one thing that you will tell *2 Hen. IV.* ii 2 40
The scambling and unquiet time Did push it out of farther question *Hen. V.* i 1 5
We may as well push against Powle's, as stir 'em *Hen. VIII.* v 4 16
What propugnation is in one man's valour, To stand the push and enmity of those This quarrel would excite? *Troi. and Cres.* ii 2 137
Therefore I will push Montague's men from the wall *Rom. and Jul.* i 1 21
Push! did you see my cap? *T. of Athens* iii 6 119
Sudden push gives them the overthrow *J. Cæsar* v 2 5
It is more worthy to leap in ourselves, Than tarry till they push us v 5 25
Now they rise again, With twenty mortal murders on their crowns, And push us from our stools *Macbeth* iii 4 82
This push Will cheer me ever, or disseat me now v 3 20
We'll put the matter to the present push *Hamlet* v 1 318
When I did push thee back—Which was when I perceived thee *Pericles* v 1 127
Pushed out your gates the very defender of them *Coriolanus* v 2 41
Push home. As manhood shall compound: push home *Hen. V.* ii 1 103
Push-pin. And Nestor play at push-pin with the boys! *L. L. Lost* iv 3 169
Pusillanimity. The liver white and pale, which is the badge of pusillanimity and cowardice *2 Hen. IV.* iv 3 114
Put. Dearest father, you have Put the wild waters in this roar *Tempest* i 2 2
Of all the world I loved and to him put The manage of my state i 2 69
The strangeness of your story put Heaviness in me i 2 306
And hast put thyself Upon this island as a spy, to win it From me i 2 454
Put thy sword up, traitor; Who makest a show but darest not strike i 2 469
Methinks our garments are now as fresh as when we put them on first ii 1 69
If 'twere a kibe, 'Twould put me to my slipper ii 1 277
To the perpetual wink for aye might put This ancient morsel ii 1 285
Do you put tricks upon's with savages and men of Ind? ii 2 60
Did quarrel with the noblest grace she owed And put it to the foil iii 1 46
Even here I will put off my hope and keep it No longer iii 3 7
Your rye-straw hats put on And these fresh nymphs encounter iv 1 136
Put off that gown, Trinculo; by this hand, I'll have that gown iv 1 227
Put some lime upon your fingers, and away with the rest iv 1 246
Bravely rigg'd as when We first put out to sea v 1 225
Put forth their sons to seek preferment out *T. G. of Ver.* i 3 7
And you, being in love, cannot see to put on your hose ii 1 84
Thy advice this night I'll put in practice iii 2 89
Such pearls as put out ladies' eyes v 2 13
But I'll ne'er put my finger in the fire, and need not *Mer. Wives* i 4 91
He cares not what he puts into the press, when he would put us two ii 1 80
I cannot put off my opinion so easily ii 1 243
Hath threatened to put me into everlasting liberty if I tell you of it iii 3 31
Go fetch me a quart of sack; put a toast in't iii 5 3
How should I bestow him? Shall I put him into the basket again? iv 2 48
He might put on a hat, a muffler and a kerchief, and so escape iv 2 73
Quick! we'll come dress you straight: put on the gown the while iv 2 85
I am put to know *Meas. for Meas.* i 1 5
They put forth to steal i 2 14
They had gone down too, but that a wise burgher put in for them i 2 103
Puts the drowsy and neglected act Freshly on me i 2 174
They do you wrong to put you so oft upon't ii 1 280
Why do you put these sayings upon me? ii 2 133
Try your penitence, if it be sound, Or hollowly put on ii 3 23
'Tis all as easy Falsely to take away a life true made As to put metal in restrained means To make a false one ii 4 48
'Twas never merry world since, of two usuries, the merriest was put down iii 2 7
He puts transgression to't iii 2 101
Impossible to extirp it quite, friar, till eating and drinking be put down iii 2 111
And his use was to put a ducat in her clack-dish iii 2 134
Put not yourself into amazement how these things should be iv 2 219
You must be so good, sir, to rise and be put to death iv 3 29
Put them in secret holds, both Barnardine and Claudio iv 3 91
And put your trial in the villain's mouth Which here you come to accuse v 1 304
No longer will I be a fool, To put the finger in the eye and weep *Com. of Errors* ii 2 206
I know not what use to put her to but to make a lamp of her iii 2 97
If any bark put forth, come to the mart iii 2 155
If any ship put out, then straight away iii 2 190
Is there any ship puts forth to-night? may we be gone? iv 3 35
I wonder much That you would put me to this shame and trouble v 1 14
Hoisted sail and put to sea to-day v 1 21
Who put unluckily into this bay Against the laws v 1 125
Can the world buy such a jewel?—Yea, and a case to put it into *M. Ado* i 1 184
In practice let us put it presently i 1 330
That puts the world into her person, and so gives me out ii 1 215
You have put him down, lady, you have put him down ii 1 292
Grow this to what adverse issue it can, I will put it in practice ii 2 53
The witness still of excellency To put a strange face on his own perfection ii 3 49
Happy are they that hear their detractions and can put them to mending ii 3 238
You must put in the pikes with a vice; and they are dangerous weapons v 2 21
Put your torches out: The wolves have prey'd v 3 24
Come, let us hence, and put on other weeds v 3 30
Which, put together, is in manner and form following *L. L. Lost* i 1 210
To put in practice that Which each to other hath so strongly sworn i 1 308
Easy it is to put 'years' to the word 'three,' and study three years in two words i 2 55
Here, sweet, put up this: 'twill be thine another day iv 1 109
Finely put off! iv 1 112
Finely put on, indeed! iv 1 118
Lord, Lord, how the ladies and I have put him down! iv 1 143
If their daughters be capable, I will put it to them iv 2 82
I could put thee in comfort iv 3 52
They made a doubt Presence majestical would put him out v 2 102
A blister on his sweet tongue, with my heart, That put Armado's page out of his part! v 2 336
Holding a trencher, jesting merrily? You put our page out v 2 478
But we will put it, as they say, to fortuna de la guerra v 2 533
I will not be put out of countenance.—Because thou hast no face v 2 611
Put. We have put thee in countenance.—You have put me out of countenance *L. L. Lost* v 2 623
Parti-coated presence of loose love Put on by us v 2 777
I'll put a girdle round about the earth In forty minutes *M. N. Dream* ii 1 175
This will put them out of fear iii 1 23
Your vows to her and me, put in two scales, Will even weigh iii 2 132
The man should be put into the lanthorn. How is it else the man i' the moon? v 1 251
Puts the wretch that lies in woe In remembrance of a shroud v 1 384
See these letters delivered; put the liveries to making *Mer. of Venice* ii 2 123
Put on a sober habit, Talk with respect and swear but now and then ii 2 199
I would entreat you rather to put on Your boldest suit of mirth ii 2 210
Like a younker or a prodigal The scarfed bark puts from her native bay ii 6 15
His eye being big with tears, Turning his face, he put his hand behind him ii 8 47
O, these naughty times Put bars between the owners and their rights! iii 2 19
The seeming truth which cunning times put on To entrap the wisest iii 2 100
And when she put it on, she made me vow That I should neither sell nor give nor lose it iv 1 442
Have put themselves into voluntary exile with him *As Y. Like It* i 1 106
Full of news.—Which he will put on us, as pigeons feed their young i 2 99
I'll put myself in poor and mean attire i 3 113
Therefore put I on the countenance Of stern commandment ii 7 108
So you may put a man in your belly iii 2 215
Were to put good meat into an unclean dish iii 3 36
Then she puts you to entreaty, and there begins new matter iv 1 80
When he had a desire to eat a grape, would open his lips when he put it into his mouth v 1 38
Put you in your best array; bid your friends v 2 78
If any man doubt that, let him put me to my purgation v 4 44
Take His brother here and put him to the sword v 4 164
The duke hath put on a religious life v 4 187
Wrapp'd in sweet clothes, rings put upon his fingers *T. of Shrew* Ind. 1 38
We could at once put us in readiness i 1 43
A pretty peat! it is best Put finger in the eye, an she knew why i 1 79
Puts my apparel and my countenance on, And I for my escape have put on his i 1 234
O, put me in thy books!—What is your crest? a coxcomb? ii 1 225
Go to my chamber; put on clothes of mine.—Not I, believe me iii 2 115
We will persuade him, be it possible, To put on better ere he go to church iii 2 128
This has put me in heart iv 5 77
A hundred marks, my Kate does put her down v 2 35
That had put such difference betwixt their two estates *All's Well* i 3 116
And put you in the catalogue of those That were enwombed mine i 3 149
Come on, sir; I shall now put you to the height of your breeding ii 2 1
What place make you special, when you put off that with such contempt? ii 2 6
If God have lent a man any manners, he may easily put it off at court ii 2 9
He that cannot make a leg, put off's cap, kiss his hand and say nothing ii 2 10
Nay, put me to't, I warrant you ii 2 50
He does acknowledge; But puts it off to a compell'd restraint ii 4 44
This very day, Great Mars, I put myself into thy file iii 3 9
Put him to't; let him have his way iii 6 1
Put myself into my mortal preparation iii 6 81
And would not put my reputation now In any staining act iii 7 6
Tongue, I must put you into a butter-woman's mouth iv 1 44
And on your finger in the night I'll put Another ring iv 2 61
Put it up again.—Nay, I'll read it first iv 3 243
If I put any tricks upon 'em, sir, they shall be jades' tricks iv 5 63
I put you to The use of your own virtues v 1 15
Dost thou put upon me at once both the office of God and the devil? v 2 51
She call'd the saints to surety That she would never put it from her finger v 3 109
Take her away.—I'll put in bail, my liege v 3 286
When did I see thee so put down?—Never in your life, I think; unless you see canary put me down *T. Night* i 3 86
Wit, an't be thy will, put me into good fooling! i 5 35
I saw him put down the other day with an ordinary fool i 5 90
You should put your lord into a desperate assurance she will none of him ii 2 8
I would have men of such constancy put to sea ii 4 78
Put thyself into the trick of singularity ii 5 164
Thou hast put him in such a dream ii 5 211
Being kept together and put to use iii 1 56
Taste your legs, sir; put them to motion iii 1 87
To put fire in your heart, and brimstone in your liver iii 2 21
I have heard of some kind of men that put quarrels purposely on others iii 4 266
'Tis against my will.—Put up your sword iii 4 343
My young soldier, put up your iron: you are well fleshed iv 1 42
Nay, I prithee, put on this gown and this beard iv 2 1
Well, I'll put it on, and I will dissemble myself in't iv 2 5
Put your grace in your pocket, sir, for this once v 1 35
The bells of Saint Bennet, sir, may put you in mind v 1 42
But in conclusion put strange speech upon me v 1 70
I have your own letter that induced me to the semblance I put on v 1 315
Bade me come smiling and cross-garter'd to you, To put on yellow stockings v 1 346
I speak as my understanding instructs me and as mine honesty puts it to utterance *W. Tale* i 1 21
To make us say, 'This is put forth too truly' i 2 14
We are tougher, brother, Than you can put us to't i 2 16
Verily! You put me off with limber vows i 2 47
This entertainment May a free face put on i 2 112
But that his negligence, his folly, fear, Among the infinite doings of the world, Sometime puts forth i 2 254
As rank as any flax-wench that puts to Before her troth-plight i 2 277
There is a sickness Which puts some of us in distemper i 2 385
For myself, I'll put My fortunes to your service i 2 439
So please you, madam, To put apart these your attendants ii 2 14
By that forced baseness Which he has put upon't ii 3 79
This ungentle business, Put on thee by my lord iii 3 35
You shall help to put him i' the ground iii 3 140
He, sir, he; that's the rogue that put me into this apparel iv 3 111
Let me be unrolled and my name put in the book of virtue! iv 3 131
I'll not put The dibble in earth to set one slip of them iv 4 99
You have As little skill to fear as I have purpose To put you to't iv 4 153
Puts him off, slights him, with 'Whoop, do me no harm' iv 4 200
I have put you out: But to your protestation iv 4 378
But now Some hangman must put on my shroud iv 4 468

Put. I am put to sea With her whom here I cannot hold on shore *W. Tale* iv 4 509
Who, had he himself eternity and could put breath into his work, would beguile Nature of her custom . . . . v 2 107
Your pardons, That e'er I put between your holy looks My ill suspicion v 3 148
And put the same into young Arthur's hand, Thy nephew . *K. John* i 1 14
I put you o'er to heaven and to my mother . . . . . . i 1 62
England, impatient of your just demands, Hath put himself in arms . ii 1 57
We'll put thee down, 'gainst whom these arms we bear . . . ii 1 346
I will kiss thy detestable bones And put my eyeballs in thy vaulty brows iii 4 30
Puts on his pretty looks, repeats his words . . . . . iii 4 95
Will you put out mine eyes? These eyes that never did nor never shall So much as frown on you . . . . iv 1 56
An if an angel should have come to me And told me Hubert should put out mine eyes, I would not have believed him . . . . . iv 1 69
I'll forgive you, Whatever torment you do put me to . . . . iv 1 84
Your sword is bright, sir; put it up again . . . . . iv 3 79
Put up thy sword betime; Or I'll so maul you and your toasting-iron iv 3 98
Put but a little water in a spoon, And it shall be as all the ocean . . iv 3 131
Put on The dauntless spirit of resolution . . . . . . v 1 52
Up once again; put spirit in the French: If they miscarry, we miscarry too . . . . v 4 2
Put his cause and quarrel To the disposing of the cardinal . . . v 7 91
Happily may your sweet self put on The lineal state and glory of the land! . . . . v 7 101
Put we our quarrel to the will of heaven . . . . . *Richard II.* i 2 6
Put into his hands That knows no touch to tune the harmony . . i 3 164
Now put it, God, in the physician's mind To help him to his grave! . i 4 59
The traitor lives, the true man's put to death . . . . . v 3 73
Mourn with me for that I do lament, And put on sullen black incontinent . . . . v 6 48
To put down Richard, that sweet lovely rose, And plant this thorn, this canker, Bolingbroke . . . . *1 Hen. IV.* i 3 175
Tom, beat Cut's saddle, put a few flocks in the point . . . . ii 1 7
Mark now, how a plain tale shall put you down . . . . . ii 4 281
Such a deal of skimble-skamble stuff As puts me from my faith . . iii 1 155
You . . . have done enough To put him quite beside his patience . . iii 1 179
Where hateful death put on his ugliest mask To fright our party *2 Hen. IV.* i 1 66
We will all put forth, body and goods.—'Tis more than time . . . i 1 186
If the prince put thee into my service for any other reason than to set me off, why then I have no judgement . . . . i 2 14
I had as lief they would put ratsbane in my mouth as offer to stop it . i 2 48
He hath put all my substance into that fat belly of his . . . ii 1 81
I put thee now to thy book-oath: deny it, if thou canst. . . . ii 1 111
Put on two leathern jerkins and aprons, and wait upon him . . . ii 2 189
Put not you on the visage of the times . . . . ii 3 3
They will put on two of our jerkins and aprons . . . . . ii 4 17
Put up your naked weapons, put up your naked weapons . . . . ii 4 222
I cannot put him to a private soldier that is the leader of so many thousands . . . . iii 2 177
Put me a caliver into Wart's hand, Bardolph . . . . . . iii 2 289
Hath put us in these ill-beseeming arms . . . . iv 1 84
Peace puts forth her olive every where . . . . iv 4 87
Put the world's whole strength Into one giant arm, it shall not force This lineal honour from me. . . . . iv 5 44
Thus, my most royal liege, Accusing it, I put it on my head . . . iv 5 166
O my son, God put it in thy mind to take it hence! . . . . iv 5 179
Sorrow so royally in you appears That I will deeply put the fashion on v 2 52
Put into parts, doth keep in one consent . . . . . . *Hen. V.* i 2 181
To put forth My rightful hand in a well-hallow'd cause . . . . i 2 292
Show thy valour, and put up your sword . . . . ii 1 46
Put thy face between his sheets, and do the office of a warming-pan . ii 1 87
An thou wilt not, why, then, be enemies with me too. Prithee, put up ii 1 109
I put my hand into the bed and felt them, and they were as cold as any stone . . . . ii 3 24
If I should take from another's pocket to put into mine. . . . iii 2 54
Our scions, put in wild and savage stock, Spirt up so suddenly . . iii 5 7
Put him to execution; for discipline ought to be used . . . . iii 6 58
His passport shall be made And crowns for convoy put into his purse . iv 3 37
The naked, poor and mangled Peace . . . put up her lovely visage . v 2 37
Her hedges even-pleach'd . . . Put forth disorder'd twigs . . . v 2 44
If you would put me to verses or to dance for your sake, Kate, why you undid me . . . . v 2 137
Put off your maiden blushes; avouch the thoughts of your heart . . v 2 253
To put a golden sceptre in thy hand . . . . . *1 Hen. VI.* v 3 118
Put forth thy hand, reach at the glorious gold. . . *2 Hen. VI.* i 2 11
Had not your man put up the fowl so suddenly, We had had more sport ii 1 45
Had I first been put to speak my mind, I think I should have told . iii 1 43
I come amain, To signify that rebels there are up And put the Englishmen unto the sword . . . . iii 1 284
Yet be well assured You put sharp weapons in a madman's hands . . iii 1 347
And Henry put apart, the next for me . . . . iii 1 383
Being put to nurse, Was by a beggar-woman stolen away . . . iv 2 150
Until a power be raised to put them down . . . . . . iv 4 40
Moreover, thou hast put them in prison . . . . iv 7 48
Neither by treason nor hostility To seek to put me down . *3 Hen. VI.* i 1 200
To blot out me, and put his own son in . . . . ii 2 92
Their blood upon thy head; For York in justice puts his armour on . ii 2 130
He lopp'd the branch In hewing Rutland when his leaves put forth . ii 6 48
Our soldiers put to flight, And, as thou seest, ourselves in heavy plight iii 3 36
Did I put Henry from his native right? . . . . iii 3 190
My mourning weeds are laid aside, And I am ready to put armour on . . . . iii 3 230; iv 1 105
Well, well, put up your sword . . . . . . *Richard III.* i 2 197
He is young, and his minority Is put unto the trust of Richard Gloucester . . . . i 3 12
Let me put in your minds, if you forget, What you have been ere now . i 3 131
Not a man of you Had so much grace to put it in my mind . . . ii 1 120
God bless thee; and put meekness in thy mind! . . . . . ii 2 107
It should be put To no apparent likelihood of breach . . . . ii 2 135
When clouds appear, wise men put on their cloaks . . . . . ii 3 32
Keep it to thyself—This day those enemies are put to death . . . iii 2 105
Edward put to death a citizen, Only for saying he would make his son Heir to the crown . . . . iii 5 76
These both put by, a poor petitioner . . . Made prize and purchase . iii 7 183
I am thus bold to put your grace in mind Of what you promised me . iv 2 113
There is no other way; Unless thou couldst put on some other shape . iv 4 286
Put in her tender heart the aspiring flame Of golden sovereignty . . iv 4 328
Put in their hands thy bruising irons of wrath! . . . . . . v 3 110
If you do sweat to put a tyrant down, You sleep in peace . . . v 3 255
There's in him stuff that puts him to these ends . . . *Hen. VIII.* i 1 58

Put. Whose figure even this instant cloud puts on, By darkening my clear sun . . . . *Hen. VIII.* i 1 225
Have put off The spinsters, carders, fullers, weavers . . . . i 2 32
Pray, look to't; I put it to your care . . . . i 2 102
Hath into monstrous habits put the graces That once were his . . i 2 122
Which if granted, . . . would Have put his knife into him . . . i 2 199
With some other business put the king From these sad thoughts . . ii 2 57
What cause Hath my behaviour given to your displeasure, That thus you should proceed to put me off? . . . . ii 4 21
By some of these The queen is put in anger . . . . . . ii 4 161
Put your main cause into the king's protection; He's loving . . iii 1 93
Put my sick cause into his hands that hates me? . . . . . iii 1 118
A noble spirit, As yours was put into you, ever casts Such doubts, as false coin, from it . . . . iii 1 170
Wot you what I found There,—on my conscience, put unwittingly? . iii 2 123
It's heaven's will: Some spirit put this paper in the packet . . . iii 2 129
What cross devil Made me put this main secret in the packet? . . iii 2 215
To-day he puts forth The tender leaves of hopes . . . . . iii 2 352
While it is hot, I'll put it to the issue . . . . v 1 176
I told ye all, When we first put this dangerous stone a-rolling, 'Twould fall . . . . v 3 104
She came and puts me her white hand to his cloven chin *Troi. and Cres.* i 2 131
Thy topless deputation he puts on . . . . i 3 152
And in my vantbrace put this wither'd brawn . . . . . . i 3 297
'Tis put to lottery . . . . ii 1 140
And worthier than himself Here tend the savage strangeness he puts on ii 3 135
An you draw backward, we'll put you i' the fills . . . . . iii 2 48
And put on A form of strangeness as we pass along . . . . . iii 3 50
Time hath, my lord, a wallet at his back, Wherein he puts alms for oblivion . . . . iii 3 146
I will put on his presence . . . . iii 3 272
Where injury of chance Puts back leave-taking . . . . . . iv 4 36
They have a leader, Tullus Aufidius, that will put you to't . *Coriolanus* i 1 233
Worshipful mutiners, Your valour puts well forth . . . . . i 1 255
Now put your shields before your hearts, and fight With hearts more proof than shields . . . . i 4 24
We'll put you, Like one that means his proper harm, in manacles . i 9 56
Nor on him put The napless vesture of humility . . . . . . ii 1 249
I wish no better Than have him hold that purpose and to put it In execution . . . . ii 1 256
Which time shall not want, If he be put upon't . . . . . . ii 1 272
For I cannot Put on the gown, stand naked and entreat them . . . ii 2 141
Neither will they bate One jot of ceremony.—Put them not to't . . ii 2 145
We are to put our tongues into those wounds and speak for them . . ii 3 7
This mutiny were better put in hazard, Than stay, past doubt, for greater ii 3 264
Who puts his 'shall,' His popular 'shall,' against a graver bench . iii 1 105
Shall it be put to that?—The gods forbid! . . . . . . iii 1 233
Put not your worthy rage into your tongue; One time will owe another iii 1 241
I would have had you put your power well on, Before you had worn it out . . . . iii 2 17
I would put mine armour on, Which I can scarcely bear . . . . iii 2 34
Which else would put you to your fortune and The hazard of much blood iii 2 60
You have put me now to such a part which never I shall discharge . iii 2 105
Put him to choler straight: he hath been used Ever to conquer . . iii 3 25
We need not put new matter to his charge . . . . . . iii 3 76
There is a slave, whom we have put in prison, Reports . . . . iv 6 38
Why, noble lords, Will you be put in mind of his blind fortune? . . v 6 118
Masters all, be quiet; Put up your swords . . . . . . v 6 136
Be candidatus then, and put it on . . . . . . *T. Andron.* i 1 185
Be dishonour'd openly, And basely put it up without revenge? . . i 1 433
Put up.—Not I, till I have sheathed My rapier in his bosom . . . ii 1 53
It is you that puts us to our shifts . . . . iv 2 176
Give me aim awhile, For nature puts me to a heavy task . . . v 3 150
Part, fools! Put up your swords; you know not what you do *R. and J.* i 1 72
Put up thy sword, Or manage it to part these men with me . . . i 1 75
Being black put us in mind they hide the fair . . . . . . i 1 237
Give me a case to put my visage in: A visor for a visor! . . . . i 4 29
Show a fair presence and put off these frowns . . . . . . i 5 75
Let me be ta'en, let me be put to death; I am content . . . . iii 5 17
To put thee from thy heaviness, Hath sorted out a sudden day of joy . iii 5 109
Which, too much minded by herself alone, May be put from her by society . . . . iv. 1 14
We may put up our pipes, and be gone.—Honest good fellows, ah, put up, put up . . . . iv 5 96
Pray you, put up your dagger, and put out your wit . . . . . iv 5 123
I will dry-beat you with an iron wit, and put up my iron dagger . . iv 5 126
Put this in any liquid thing you will, And drink it off . . . . v 1 77
Give me thy torch, boy: hence, and stand aloof: Yet put it out . . v 3 2
Put not another sin upon my head, By urging me to fury . . . . v 3 62
He owes For every word: . . . his land's put to their books *T. of Athens* i 2 206
Would I were gently put out of office Before I were forced out! . . i 2 207
Put on a most importunate aspect, A visage of demand . . . . ii 1 28
He hath put me off To the succession of new days this month . . . ii 2 19
Your steward puts me off, my lord . . . . ii 2 32
My indisposition put you back . . . . ii 2 139
Had his necessity made use of me, I would have put my wealth into donation . . . . iii 2 90
Who can speak broader than he that has no house to put his head in? . iii 4 64
Put in now, Titus.—My lord, here is my bill . . . . . . iii 4 85
They have e'en put my breath from me, the slaves. Creditors? devils! iii 4 104
Which many my near occasions did urge me to put off . . . . iii 6 12
Let each take some; Nay, put out all your hands . . . . . iv 2 28
Put up thy gold: go on,—here's gold,—go on; Be as a planetary plague iv 3 107
Put armour on thine ears and on thine eyes . . . . iv 3 123
The bleak air, thy boisterous chamberlain, Will put thy shirt on warm? iv 3 223
If thou didst put this sour-cold habit on To castigate thy pride, 'twere well . . . . iv 3 239
Put stuff To some she beggar and compounded thee Poor rogue hereditary iv 3 272
As common bruit doth put it . . . . v 1 196
And do you now put on your best attire? . . . . . . *J. Cæsar* i 1 53
He put it by with the back of his hand . . . . i 2 221
He put it by thrice, every time gentler than other. (Repeated) . . i 2 229
Are put to silence . . . . i 2 290
However he puts on this tardy form . . . . i 2 303
You look pale and gaze And put on fear . . . . i 3 60
We put a sting in him, That at his will he may do danger with . . ii 1 16
Look fresh and merrily; Let not our looks put on our purposes . . ii 1 225
I remember The first time ever Cæsar put it on . . . . . iii 2 175
Would ruffle up your spirits and put a tongue In every wound of Cæsar iii 2 232
Have put to death an hundred senators . . . . iv 3 175

Put. Here's the book I sought for so; I put it in the pocket of my gown *J. Cæsar* iv 3 253
They Put on my brows this wreath of victory, And bid me give it thee v 3 82
You shall put This night's great business into my dispatch *Macbeth* i 5 68
What not put upon His spongy officers? i 7 70
Let's briefly put on manly readiness, And meet i' the hall together ii 3 139
Are stol'n away and fled; which puts upon them Suspicion of the deed ii 4 26
He chid the sisters When first they put the name of king upon me iii 1 58
And put a barren sceptre in my gripe iii 1 62
Put rancours in the vessel of my peace Only for them iii 1 67
Put that business in your bosoms, Whose execution takes your enemy off iii 1 104
Now about the cauldron sing, . . . Enchanting all that you put in iv 1 43
Why then, alas, Do I put up that womanly defence? iv 2 78
Even now I put myself to thy direction iv 3 122
Hanging a golden stamp about their necks, Put on with holy prayers iv 3 154
Macbeth Is ripe for shaking, and the powers above Put on their instruments iv 3 239
Wash your hands, put on your nightgown; look not so pale v 1 68
Give me my armour.—'Tis not needed yet.—I'll put it on v 3 34
Put mine armour on; give me my staff v 3 48
Put we on Industrious soldiership v 4 15
If it be so, as so 'tis put on me, And that in way of caution *Hamlet* i 3 94
The very place puts toys of desperation . . . into every brain i 4 75
As I perchance hereafter shall think meet To put an antic disposition on i 5 172
And there put on him What forgeries you please; marry, none so rank ii 1 19
You must not put another scandal on him ii 1 29
What it should be, More than his father's death, that thus hath put him So much from the understanding of himself, I cannot dream of ii 2 8
Put your dread pleasures more into command Than to entreaty ii 2 28
Get from him why he puts on this confusion iii 1 2
With more offences at my beck than I have thoughts to put them in iii 1 128
Whereon his brains still beating puts him thus From fashion of himself iii 1 182
To put him to his purgation would perhaps plunge him into far more choler iii 2 318
Put your discourse into some frame and start not so wildly iii 2 320
We will fetters put upon this fear, Which now goes too free-footed iii 3 25
That from a shelf the precious diadem stole, And put it in his pocket! iii 4 101
He likewise gives a frock or livery, That aptly is put on iii 4 165
Yet must not we put the strong law on him iv 3 3
We put on a compelled valour iv 6 17
You must put me in your heart for friend iv 7 2
We'll put on those shall praise your excellence iv 7 132
I'll put another question to thee v 1 43
We'll put the matter to the present push v 1 318
He should the bearers put to sudden death, Not shriving-time allow'd v 2 46
The bravery of his grief did put me Into a towering passion v 2 79
Deaths put on by cunning and forced cause v 2 394
He was likely, had he been put on, To have proved most royally v 2 408
Why so earnestly seek you to put up that letter? *Lear* i 2 28
Put on what weary negligence you please i 3 12
To serve him truly that will put me in trust i 4 15
You protect this course, and put it on By your allowance i 4 227
Put away These dispositions, that of late transform you i 4 241
I can tell why a snail has a house.—Why?—Why, to put his head in i 5 32
'Tis they have put him on the old man's death ii 1 101
Rail'd, And put upon him such a deal of man, That worthied him ii 2 127
Put in his legs. Come, my good lord, away ii 2 157
As the cockney did to the eels when she put 'em i' the paste alive ii 4 124
Who put my man i' the stocks? ii 4 185
'Tis his own blame; hath put himself from rest ii 4 293
He that has a house to put's head in has a good head-piece iii 2 25
Slain by his servant, going to put out The other eye of Gloucester iv 2 71
I'll put't in proof iv 6 189
Let thy friendly hand Put strength enough to't iv 6 235
These weeds are memories of those worser hours: I prithee, put them off iv 7 8
In the heaviness of his sleep We put fresh garments on him iv 7 22
For shame, put on your gown *Othello* i 1 86
He will divorce you; Or put upon you what restraint and grievance The law, with all his might to enforce it on, Will give him cable i 2 15
I would not my unhoused free condition Put into circumscription i 2 27
I would not there reside, To put my father in impatient thoughts i 3 243
Put money in thy purse. (Repeated) i 3 345
How! is this true?—The ship is here put in ii 1 25
How now! who has put in?—'Tis one Iago, ancient to the general ii 1 65
She puts her tongue a little in her heart, And chides with thinking ii 1 107
What wouldst thou write of me, if thou shouldst praise me?—O gentle lady, do not put me to't ii 1 119
In the authority of her merit, did justly put on the vouch of very malice ii 1 147
Or failing so, yet that I put the Moor At least into a jealousy ii 1 309
Every man put himself into triumph ii 2 4
Am I to put our Cassio in some action That may offend the isle ii 3 62
I fear the trust Othello puts him in ii 3 131
It were well The general were put in mind of it ii 3 137
For Christian shame, put by this barbarous brawl ii 3 172
Importune her help to put you in your place again ii 3 324
When devils will the blackest sins put on, They do suggest at first with heavenly shows ii 3 357
Put up your pipes in your bag iii 1 20
You are eaten up with passion: I do repent me that I put it to you iii 3 392
And will upon the instant put thee to't iii 3 471
It were enough To put him to ill thinking iii 4 29
This is a trick to put me from my suit iii 4 87
If any wretch have put this in your head, Let heaven requite it! iv 2 15
Put in every honest hand a whip To lash the rascals naked iv 2 142
I will indeed no longer endure it, nor am I yet persuaded to put up in peace what already I have foolishly suffered iv 2 181
I will show you such a necessity in his death that you shall think yourself bound to put it on him iv 2 248
Wear thy good rapier bare, and put it home: Quick, quick; fear nothing v 1 2
Put out the light, and then put out the light v 2 7
But once put out thy light, Thou cunning'st pattern of excelling nature, I know not where is that Promethean heat That can thy light relume v 2 10
Ere we put ourselves in arms, dispatch we The business *Ant. and Cleo.* ii 2 168
I drunk him to his bed; Then put my tires and mantles on him ii 5 22
Mark Antony Put me to some impatience ii 6 43
Cut the cable; And, when we are put off, fall to their throats ii 7 78
Antony Shall set thee on triumphant chariots and Put garlands on thy head iii 1 11
Put yourself under his shrowd, The universal landlord iii 13 71

Put. Come, good fellow, put mine iron on *Ant. and Cleo.* iv 4 3
Go put on thy defences.—Briefly, sir iv 4 10
Order for sea is given; They have put forth the haven iv 10 7
Put colour in thy cheek iv 14 69
Not cowardly put off my helmet to My countryman iv 15 56
And put your children To that destruction which I'll guard them from v 2 131
Not what you have reserved, nor what acknowledged, Put we i' the roll of conquest: still be't yours v 2 181
Go put it to the haste v 2 196
Puts to him all the learnings that his time Could make him the receiver of; which he took, As we do air *Cymbeline* i 1 43
Pity you should have been put together with so mortal a purpose i 4 43
To be put to the arbitrement of swords i 4 52
Would I had put my estate and my neighbour's on the approbation! i 4 133
Winning will put any man into courage ii 3 8
I am much sorry, sir, You put me to forget a lady's manners ii 3 110
If Cæsar can hide the sun from us with a blanket, or put the moon in his pocket, we will pay him tribute for light iii 1 44
Against all colour here Did put the yoke upon's iii 1 52
The first of Britain which did put His brows within a golden crown iii 1 60
Strains his young nerves and puts himself in posture That acts my words iii 3 94
Put thyself Into a haviour of less fear iii 4 8
And make me put into contempt the suits Of princely fellows iii 4 92
Fortune, put them into my hand! iv 1 25
Would seek us through And put us to our answer iv 2 161
I thought he slept, and put My clouted brogues from off my feet iv 2 213
The want is but to put those powers in motion That long to move iv 3 31
Gods! if you Should have ta'en vengeance on my faults, I never Had lived to put on this v 1 9
Gods, put the strength o' the Leonati in me! v 1 31
You have put me into rhyme v 3 63
His tongue being made, And then a mind put in't v 5 176
Those arts they have as I Could put into them v 5 339
Targets, to put off the shame *Pericles* i 1 140
So puts himself unto the shipman's toil i 3 24
Put forth to seas, Where when men been, there's seldom ease ii Gower 27
I have a gown here; come, put it on; keep thee warm ii 1 83
He puts on sackcloth, and to sea iv 4 29
If put upon you, make the judgement good That thought you worthy of it iv 6 100
In your supposing once more put your sight Of heavy Pericles v Gower 21
There's a barge put off from Mytilene, And in it is Lysimachus v 1 3
Give me a gash, put me to present pain v 1 193
Putrefied. Most putrefied core, so fair without *Troi. and Cres.* v 8 1
Putrefy. They would but stink, and putrefy the air 1 *Hen. VI.* iv 7 90
Putter. Seese is not good to give putter; your belly is all putter.—'Seese' and 'putter'! *Mer. Wives* v 5 148
Putter-on. You are abused and by some putter-on *W. Tale* ii 1 141
My good lord cardinal, they vent reproaches Most bitterly on you, as putter on Of these exactions *Hen. VIII.* i 2 24
Putter-out. Which now we find Each putter-out of five for one will bring us Good warrant of *Tempest* iii 3 48
Puttest. Petitioners for blood thou ne'er put'st back 3 *Hen. VI.* v 5 80
That put'st odds Among the rout of nations *T. of Athens* iv 3 42
When thou gavest them the rod, and put'st down thine own breeches *Lear* i 4 189
Putting the hand in the pocket and extracting it clutched *Meas. for Meas.* iii 2 48
Thinking of nothing else, putting all affairs else in oblivion 2 *Hen. IV.* v 5 27
Putting it straight in expedition *Hen. V.* ii 2 191
So putting him to rage, You should have ta'en the advantage *Coriolanus* ii 3 205
If he were putting to my house the brand That should consume it, I have not the face To say 'Beseech you, cease' iv 6 115
Did you ne'er hear say, Two may keep counsel, putting one away? *Rom. and Jul.* ii 4 209
Putting-by. And at every putting-by mine honest neighbours shouted *J. C.* i 2 231
Putting down. I'll exhibit a bill in the parliament for the putting down of men *Mer. Wives* ii 1 30
Inspired with the spirit of putting down kings and princes 2 *Hen. VI.* iv 2 38
Putting off. There's a simple putting off. More, more *All's Well* ii 2 43
And, putting off his hat, said 'I will now take my leave' 2 *Hen. IV.* ii 4 7
Putting on. Show it now, By putting on the destined livery *M. for M.* ii 4 138
Awakens me with this unwonted putting-on iv 2 120
Cross-gartered, even with the swiftness of putting on *T. Night* ii 5 187
And truth suspected, For putting on so new a fashion'd robe *K. John* iv 2 27
Say, you ne'er had done't—Harp on that still—but by our putting on *Coriolanus* ii 3 260
Shame not these woods, By putting on the cunning of a carper *T. of A.* iv 3 209
Putting on the mere form of civil and humane seeming *Othello* ii 1 243
If this poor trash of Venice . . . stand the putting on ii 1 313
Puttock. Who finds the partridge in the puttock's nest, But may imagine how the bird was dead? 2 *Hen. VI.* iii 2 191
To be . . . an owl, a puttock, or a herring without a roe *Troi. and Cres.* v 1 68
I chose an eagle, And did avoid a puttock *Cymbeline* i 1 140
Puzzel. Pucelle or puzzel, dolphin or dogfish 1 *Hen. VI.* i 4 107
Puzzles the will And makes us rather bear those ills we have Than fly to others that we know not of *Hamlet* iii 1 80
Your presence needs must puzzle Antony *Ant. and Cleo.* iii 7 11
Puzzled. More puzzled than the Egyptians in their fog *T. Night* iv 2 48
Pygmalion. Is there none of Pygmalion's images, newly made woman, to be had now? *Meas. for Meas.* iii 2 47
Pyramid. Though palaces and pyramids do slope Their heads to their foundations *Macbeth* iv 1 57
They take the flow o' the Nile By certain scales i' the pyramid *A. and C.* ii 7 21
Rather make My country's high pyramides my gibbet! v 2 61
Pyramis. A statlier pyramis to her I'll rear Than Rhodope's or Memphis' ever was 1 *Hen. VI.* i 6 21
I have heard the Ptolemies' pyramises are very goodly things *Ant. and Cleo.* ii 7 40
Pyramus. Most cruel death of Pyramus and Thisby *M. N. Dream* i 2 12
You, Nick Bottom, are set down for Pyramus.—What is Pyramus? a lover, or a tyrant? i 2 23
What is Thisby? a wandering knight?—It is the lady that Pyramus must love i 2 48
Ah Pyramus, my lover dear! thy Thisby dear, and lady dear! i 2 55
No, no; you must play Pyramus; and, Flute, you Thisby i 2 57
Tom Snout, the tinker.—Here, Peter Quince.—You, Pyramus' father i 2 65
You can play no part but Pyramus; for Pyramus is a sweet-faced man i 2 87
You must needs play Pyramus.—Well, I will undertake it i 2 91
There are things in this comedy of Pyramus and Thisby that will never please iii 1 10
Pyramus must draw a sword to kill himself; which the ladies cannot abide iii 1 11

Pyramus. Let the prologue seem to say, we will do no harm with our swords and that Pyramus is not killed *M. N. Dream* iii 1 20
Tell them that I Pyramus am not Pyramus, but Bottom the weaver iii 1 22
You know, Pyramus and Thisby meet by moonlight iii 1 50
Pyramus and Thisby, says the story, did talk through the chink of a wall iii 1 64
Let him hold his fingers thus, and through that cranny shall Pyramus and Thisby whisper iii 1 73
Pyramus, you begin: when you have spoken your speech, enter into that brake iii 1 76
A stranger Pyramus than e'er played here iii 1 90
Most radiant Pyramus, most lily-white of hue, Of colour like the red rose iii 1 95
I'll meet thee, Pyramus, at Ninny's tomb.—'Ninus' tomb, man: why, you must not speak that yet; that you answer to Pyramus iii 1 99
Pyramus enter: your cue is past; it is, 'never tire' iii 1 103
The shallowest thick-skin of that barren sort, Who Pyramus presented iii 2 14
I led them on in this distracted fear, And left sweet Pyramus translated iii 2 32
When my cue comes, call me, and I will answer: my next is, 'Most fair Pyramus' iv 1 206
You have not a man in all Athens able to discharge Pyramus but he iv 2 8
An the duke had not given him sixpence a day for playing Pyramus, I'll be hanged; he would have deserved it: sixpence a day in Pyramus, or nothing iv 2 22
A tedious brief scene of young Pyramus And his love Thisbe v 1 56
And tragical, my noble lord, it is; For Pyramus therein doth kill himself v 1 67
This man is Pyramus, if you would know; This beauteous lady Thisby is v 1 130
Anon comes Pyramus, sweet youth and tall, And finds his trusty Thisby's mantle slain v 1 145
A crannied hole or chink, Through which the lovers, Pyramus and Thisby, Did whisper often very secretly v 1 160
Pyramus draws near the wall: silence!—O grim-look'd night! v 1 170
O wall, full often hast thou heard my moans, For parting my fair Pyramus and me! v 1 191

Pyramus. The lion vanished.—And then came Pyramus *M. N. Dream* v 1 276
Out, sword, and wound The pap of Pyramus; Ay, that left pap v 1 302
Her passion ends the play.—Methinks she should not use a long one for such a Pyramus v 1 323
A mote will turn the balance, which Pyramus, which Thisbe, is the better v 1 325
O Pyramus, arise! Speak, speak. Quite dumb? Dead, dead? v 1 333
If he that writ it had played Pyramus and hanged himself in Thisbe's garter, it would have been a fine tragedy v 1 365
So pale did shine the moon on Pyramus When he by night lay bathed in maiden blood *T. Andron.* ii 3 231
Pyrenean. Talking of the Alps and Apennines, The Pyrenean and the river Po *K. John* i 1 203
Pyrrhus. But it must grieve young Pyrrhus now at home, When fame shall in our islands sound her trump *Troi. and Cres.* iii 3 209
'The rugged Pyrrhus, like the Hyrcanian beast,'—it is not so:—it begins with Pyrrhus *Hamlet* ii 2 472
The rugged Pyrrhus, whose sable arms, Black as his purpose ii 2 474
With eyes like carbuncles, the hellish Pyrrhus Old grandsire Priam seeks ii 2 485
Unequal match'd, Pyrrhus at Priam drives; in rage strikes wide ii 2 494
Stoops to his base, and with a hideous crash Takes prisoner Pyrrhus' ear ii 2 499
So, as a painted tyrant, Pyrrhus stood ii 2 502
So, after Pyrrhus' pause, Aroused vengeance sets him new a-work ii 2 509
And never did the Cyclops' hammers fall . . . With less remorse than Pyrrhus' bleeding sword Now falls on Priam ii 2 513
When she saw Pyrrhus make malicious sport In mincing with his sword her husband's limbs ii 2 536
Pythagoras. Thou almost makest me waver in my faith To hold opinion with Pythagoras *Mer. of Venice* iv 1 131
I was never so berhymed since Pythagoras' time *As Y. Like It* iii 2 187
What is the opinion of Pythagoras concerning wild fowl? *T. Night* iv 2 54
Thou shalt hold the opinion of Pythagoras ere I will allow of thy wits iv 2 62

Q

Quadrangle. My choler being over-blown With walking once about the quadrangle *2 Hen. VI.* i 3 156
Quaff carouses to our mistress' health *T. of Shrew* i 2 277
Quaff'd off the muscadel And threw the sops all in the sexton's face iii 2 174
That tyranny, which never quaff'd but blood *2 Hen. IV.* iv 5 86
Quaffing. That quaffing and drinking will undo you *T. Night* i 3 14
Quagmire. And make a quagmire of your mingled brains *1 Hen. VI.* i 4 109
Through ford and whirlipool, o'er bog and quagmire *Lear* iii 4 54
Quail, crush, conclude, and quell! *M. N. Dream* v 1 292
Do this suddenly, And let not search and inquisition quail To bring again these foolish runaways *As Y. Like It* ii 2 20
An honest fellow enough, and one that loves quails *Troi. and Cres.* v 1 57
His quails ever Beat mine, inhoop'd, at odds *Ant. and Cleo.* ii 3 37
But when he meant to quail and shake the orb, He was as rattling thunder v 2 85
And my false spirits Quail to remember *Cymbeline* v 5 149
Quailing. There is no quailing now *1 Hen. IV.* iv 1 39
This may plant courage in their quailing breasts *3 Hen. VI.* ii 3 54
Quaint. My quaint Ariel, Hark in thine ear *Tempest* i 2 317
Quaint in green she shall be loose enrobed *Mer. Wives* iv 6 41
A fine, quaint, graceful and excellent fashion *Much Ado* iii 4 22
The quaint mazes in the wanton green *M. N. Dream* ii 1 99
The clamorous owl that nightly hoots and wonders At our quaint spirits ii 2 7
Tell quaint lies, How honourable ladies sought my love *Mer. of Venice* iii 4 69
The quaint musician, amorous Licio *T. of Shrew* iii 2 149
I never saw a better-fashion'd gown, More quaint, more pleasing iv 3 102
With forged quaint conceit To set a gloss upon his bold intent *1 Hen. VI.* iv 1 102
But you, my lord, were glad to be employ'd, To show how quaint an orator you are *2 Hen. VI.* iii 2 274
Quaintly. The lines are very quaintly writ *T. G. of Ver.* ii 1 128
A ladder quaintly made of cords iii 1 117
'Tis vile, unless it may be quaintly order'd *Mer. of Venice* ii 4 6
To carve out dials quaintly, point by point *3 Hen. VI.* ii 5 24
Breathe his faults so quaintly That they may seem the taints of liberty, The flash and outbreak of a fiery mind *Hamlet* ii 1 31
With your fine fancies quaintly eche *Pericles* iii Gower 13
Quake. I quake, Lest thou a feverous life shouldst entertain *M. for M.* iii 1 74
Thou wilt quake for this shortly *Much Ado* i 1 274
Look how I do quake with fear *M. N. Dream* ii 2 148
You, ladies, you . . . May now perchance both quake and tremble here v 1 224
Never saw I Wretches so quake *W. Tale* v 1 199
They will quake and tremble all this day *K. John* iii 1 18
Whose bloody deeds shall make all Europe quake *1 Hen. VI.* i 1 156
Henry the Fifth, that made all France to quake *2 Hen. VI.* iv 8 17
You quake like rebels *Richard III.* i 3 162
Come, cousin, canst thou quake, and change thy colour, Murder thy breath in middle of a word? iii 5 1
Revenge, which makes the foul offender quake *T. Andron.* v 2 40
And do such bitter business as the day Would quake to look on *Hamlet* iii 2 410
When I do stare, see how the subject quakes *Lear* iv 6 110
Quake in the present winter's state *Cymbeline* ii 4 5
Our lodgings, standing bleak upon the sea, Shook as the earth did quake; The very principals did seem to rend *Pericles* iii 2 15
Quaked. I quaked for fear *Mer. Wives* iii 5 104
Where ladies shall be frighted, And, gladly quaked, hear more *Coriolanus* i 9 6
Qualification. Whose qualification shall come into no true taste again but by the displanting of Cassio *Othello* ii 1 282
Qualified as may beseem The spouse of any noble gentleman *T. of Shrew* iv 5 66
With thoughts so qualified as your charities Shall best instruct *W. Tale* ii 1 113
This inundation of mistemper'd humour Rests by you only to be qualified: Then pause not *K. John* v 1 13
Till some little time hath qualified the heat of his displeasure *Lear* i 2 176
That which ordinary men are fit for, I am qualified in i 4 37
I have drunk but one cup to-night, and that was craftily qualified *Othello* ii 3 41

Qualify. I do not seek to quench your love's hot fire, But qualify the fire's extreme rage *T. G. of Ver.* ii 7 22
Enforce or qualify the laws As to your soul seems good *Meas. for Meas.* i 1 66
He doth with holy abstinence subdue That in himself which he spurs on his power To qualify in others iv 2 86
All this amazement can I qualify *Much Ado* v 4 67
Hath ta'en great pains to qualify His rigorous course *Mer. of Venice* iv 1 7
Your discontenting father strive to qualify *W. Tale* iv 4 543
So madly hot that no discourse of reason, Nor fear of bad success in a bad cause, Can qualify the same *Troi. and Cres.* ii 2 118
Time qualifies the spark and fire of it [love] *Hamlet* iv 7 114
Qualifying. My love admits no qualifying dross *Troi. and Cres.* iv 4 9
Qualité. Je pense que vous êtes gentilhomme de bonne qualité *Hen. V.* iv 4 3
Qualities. And show'd thee all the qualities o' the isle *Tempest* i 2 337
Qualities Beseeming such a wife as your fair daughter *T. G. of Ver.* iii 1 65
She hath more qualities than a water-spaniel iii 1 271
These banish'd men . . . Are men endued with worthy qualities v 4 153
I have many ill qualities.—Which is one?—I say my prayers aloud *Much Ado* ii 1 106
He errs, doting on Hermia's eyes, So I, admiring of his qualities *M. N. D.* i 1 231
I do in birth deserve her, and in fortunes, In graces and in qualities of breeding *Mer. of Venice* ii 7 33
Obscuring and hiding from me all gentleman-like qualities *As Y. Like It* i 1 73
Her wondrous qualities and mild behaviour *T. of Shrew* ii 1 50
Where an unclean mind carries virtuous qualities, there commendations go with pity *All's Well* i 1 49
Love no god, that would not extend his might, only where qualities were level i 3 118
His qualities being at this poor price, I need not to ask you if gold will corrupt him iv 3 308
According to your strengths and qualities, Give you advancement *2 Hen. IV.* v 5 73
And bless us with her former qualities *Hen. V.* v 2 67
She hath lived too long, To fill the world with vicious qualities *1 Hen. VI* v 4 35
Thy rare qualities, sweet gentleness, Thy meekness saint-like *Hen. VIII.* ii 4 137
Nor his qualities.—No matter.—Nor his beauty *Troi. and Cres.* i 2 94
O, mickle is the powerful grace that lies In herbs, plants, stones, and their true qualities *Rom. and Jul.* ii 3 16
I have bred her at my dearest cost In qualities of the best *T. of Athens* i 1 125
This fellow's of exceeding honesty, And knows all qualities *Othello* iii 3 259
Wander through the streets and note The qualities of people *A. and C.* i 1 54
Together with the adornment of my qualities *Cymbeline* iii 5 141
A shop of all the qualities that man Loves woman for v 5 166
Has she any qualities?—She has a good face, speaks well, and has excellent good clothes: there's no further necessity of qualities *Per.* iv 2 50
Quality. To thy strong bidding task Ariel and all his quality *Tempest* i 2 193
What a strange drowsiness possesses them!—It is the quality o' the climate ii 1 200
A man of such perfection As we do in our quality much want *T. G. of Ver.* iv 1 58
Of what quality was your love, then? *Mer. Wives* ii 2 223
You orphan heirs of fixed destiny, Attend your office and your quality v 5 44
Go to: what quality are they of? *Meas. for Meas.* ii 1 59
You know yourself, Hate counsels not in such a quality *Mer. of Venice* iii 2 6
The quality of mercy is not strain'd, It droppeth as the gentle rain iv 1 184
An hourly promise-breaker, the owner of no one good quality *All's Well* iii 6 12
But, fair soul, In your fine frame hath love no quality? iv 2 4
He must observe their mood on whom he jests, The quality of persons, and the time *T. Night* iii 1 70
The quality of the time and quarrel Might well have given us bloody argument iii 3 31
It would allay the burning quality Of that fell poison *K. John* v 7 8
The quality and hair of our attempt Brooks no division *1 Hen. IV.* iv 1 61
Envy your great deservings . . . , Because you are not of our quality iv 3 36
Yes, if this present quality of war, Indeed the instant action *2 Hen. IV.* i 3 36

Quality. With such powers As might hold sortance with his quality 2 *Hen. IV.* iv 1 11
A peace indeed, Concurring both in name and quality iv 1 87
Which swims against your stream of quality v 2 34
And wholesome berries thrive and ripen best Neighbour'd by fruit of baser quality *Hen. V.* i 1 62
What is thy name? I know thy quality iii 6 146
Knights, squires, And gentlemen of blood and quality iv 8 95
The venom of such looks, we fairly hope, Have lost their quality v 2 19
Hitting a grosser quality, is cried up For our best act *Hen. VIII.* i 2 84
Give him note of our approach, With the whole quality wherefore *Troi. and Cres.* iv 1 44
The Grecian youths are full of quality; They're loving, well composed iv 4 78
All minds, As well of glib and slippery creatures as Of grave and austere quality, tender down Their services *T. of Athens* i 1 54
Know you the quality of Lord Timon's fury? iii 6 117
Hoar the flamen, That scolds against the quality of flesh iv 3 156
Why birds and beasts from quality and kind, Why old men fool *J. Cæsar* i 3 64
Why all these things change from their ordinance Their natures and preformed faculties To monstrous quality i 3 68
Will be thaw'd from the true quality With that which melteth fools iii 1 41
Of whose true-fix'd and resting quality There is no fellow in the firmament iii 1 61
I hold ambition of so airy and light a quality *Hamlet* ii 2 268
Will they pursue the quality no longer than they can sing? ii 2 363
Come, give us a taste of your quality ii 2 452
For a quality Wherein, they say, you shine iv 7 73
In the lusty stealth of nature take More composition and fierce quality *Lear* i 2 12
The quality of nothing hath not such need to hide itself i 2 33
You know the fiery quality of the duke; How unremoveable and fix'd he is ii 4 93
Vengeance! plague! death! confusion! Fiery? what quality? ii 4 97
Thou'lt not believe With how depraved a quality—O Regan! ii 4 139
Any man of quality or degree v 3 110
What are you? Your name, your quality? v 3 120
My heart's subdued Even to the very quality of my lord *Othello* i 3 252
With such things else of quality and respect As doth import you i 3 283
No offence to the general, nor any man of quality,—I hope to be saved iii 3 110
All quality, Pride, pomp and circumstance of glorious war! iii 3 353
Whose quality, going on, The sides o' the world may danger *Ant. and Cleo.* i 2 198
Things outward Do draw the inward quality after them, To suffer all alike iii 13 33
Give her what comforts The quality of her passion shall require v 1 63
For taking a beggar without less quality *Cymbeline* i 4 24
As suits, with gentlemen of your knowing, to a stranger of his quality i 4 30
Qualm. Lay it to your heart: it is the only thing for a qualm *Much Ado* iii 4 75
And trow you what he call'd me?—Qualm, perhaps *L. L. Lost* v 2 279
Some sudden qualm hath struck me at the heart 2 *Hen. VI.* i 1 54
Qualmish. Hence! I am qualmish at the smell of leek *Hen. V.* v 1 22
Qualtitie calmie custure me! Art thou a gentleman? iv 4 4
Quando. Fauste, precor gelida quando pecus omne sub umbra Ruminat *L. L. Lost* iv 2 95
Quantity. He is not quantity enough for that Worthy's thumb *L. L. Lost* v 1 137
Things base and vile, holding no quantity, Love can transpose *M. N. D.* i 1 232
Away, thou rag, thou quantity, thou remnant! *T. of Shrew* iv 3 112
My love . . . Prizes not quantity of dirty lands *T. Night* ii 4 85
Have I not hideous death within my view, Retaining but a quantity of life, Which bleeds away? *K. John* v 4 23
My moiety . . ., In quantity equals not one of yours 1 *Hen IV.* iii 1 97
If I were sawed into quantities, I should make four dozen of such bearded hermits' staves 2 *Hen. IV.* v 1 70
Enriched poor straggling soldiers with great quantity *T. of Athens* v 1 7
To wipe out our ingratitude with loves Above their quantity v 4 18
Laugh, to set on some quantity of barren spectators to laugh too *Hamlet* iii 2 45
Women's fear and love holds quantity; In neither aught, or in extremity iii 2 177
Nor sense to ecstasy was ne'er so thrall'd But it reserved some quantity of choice, To serve in such a difference iii 4 75
Forty thousand brothers Could not, with all their quantity of love, Make up my sum v 1 293
I love thee; I have spoke it: How much the quantity, the weight as much, As I do love my father *Cymbeline* iv 2 17
Quarrel. Some defect in her Did quarrel with the noblest grace she owed And put it to the foil *Tempest* iii 1 45
I love the sport well; but I shall as soon quarrel at it as any man *M. W.* i 1 303
The Lady Beatrice hath a quarrel to you *Much Ado* ii 1 243
In the managing of quarrels you may say he is wise ii 3 197
He ought to enter into a quarrel with fear and trembling ii 3 203
Nay, do not quarrel with us, good old man v 1 50
In a false quarrel there is no true valour v 1 120
A quarrel, ho, already! what's the matter? *Mer. of Venice* v 1 146
I am the unhappy subject of these quarrels v 1 238
Jealous in honour, sudden and quick in quarrel *As Y. Like It* ii 7 151
I have had four quarrels, and like to have fought one v 4 48
We met, and found the quarrel was upon the seventh cause v 4 51
How did you find the quarrel on the seventh cause?—Upon a lie v 4 70
We quarrel in print, by the book; as you have books for good manners v 4 94
I knew when seven justices could not take up a quarrel v 4 104
Though the nature of our quarrel yet never brooked parle *T. of Shrew* i 1 116
In a quarrel since I came ashore I kill'd a man i 1 236
We will compound this quarrel i 2 27
And the duke, For private quarrel 'twixt your duke and him, Hath publish'd and proclaim'd it openly iv 2 84
Holy seems the quarrel Upon your grace's part *All's Well* iii 1 4
Albeit the quality of the time and quarrel Might well have given us bloody argument *T. Night* iii 3 31
You mistake, sir; I am sure no man hath any quarrel to me iii 4 248
I have heard of some kind of men that put quarrels purposely on others iii 4 266
I have his horse to take up the quarrel iii 4 320
He hath better bethought him of his quarrel iii 4 327
Let no quarrel nor no brawl to come Taint the condition of this present hour v 1 364
Our people quarrel with obedience *K. John* v 1 9
And put his cause and quarrel To the disposing of the cardinal v 7 91
Put we our quarrel to the will of heaven *Richard II.* i 2 6
God's is the quarrel i 2 37
Against what man thou comest, and what thy quarrel: Speak truly i 3 13
Against whom comest thou? and what's thy quarrel? Speak like a true knight i 3 33
The nobles hath he fined For ancient quarrels ii 1 248
Quarrel. I know you, Sir John: you owe me money, Sir John; and now you pick a quarrel to beguile me of it 1 *Hen. IV.* iii 3 76
O, would the quarrel lay upon our heads! v 2 48
Derives from heaven his quarrel and his cause 2 *Hen. IV.* i 1 206
I make my quarrel in particular iv 1 96
Heir from heir shall hold this quarrel up iv 2 48
The quarrel of a true inheritor iv 5 169
Which daily grew to quarrel and to bloodshed, Wounding supposed peace iv 5 195
Be it thy course to busy giddy minds With foreign quarrels iv 5 215
Though war nor no known quarrel were in question *Hen. V.* ii 4 17
His cause being just and his quarrel honourable iv 1 133
Punished for before-breach of the king's laws in now the king's quarrel iv 1 180
Let it be a quarrel between us, if you live.—I embrace it iv 1 219
If ever thou darest acknowledge it, I will make it my quarrel iv 1 225
We have French quarrels enow, if you could tell how to reckon iv 1 240
Serve God, and keep you out of prawls, and prabbles, and quarrels iv 8 69
This day Shall change all griefs and quarrels into love v 2 20
I dare say This quarrel will drink blood another day 1 *Hen. VI.* ii 4 134
The quarrel toucheth none but us alone; Betwixt ourselves let us decide it iv 1 118
I charge you, as you love our favour, Quite to forget this quarrel iv 1 136
So many peers, So many captains, gentlemen and soldiers, That in this quarrel have been overthrown v 4 105
No malice, sir; no more than well becomes So good a quarrel 2 *Hen. VI.* ii 1 28
Purposely therefore Left I the court, to see this quarrel tried ii 3 53
Thrice is he arm'd that hath his quarrel just iii 2 233
At a strife? What is your quarrel? how began it first?—No quarrel, but a slight contention 3 *Hen. VI.* i 2 5
And in that quarrel use it to the death ii 2 65
What stratagems, how fell, . . . This deadly quarrel daily doth beget! ii 5 91
In quarrel of the house of York The worthy gentleman did lose his life iii 2 6
My quarrel and this English queen's are one iii 3 216
It is a quarrel most unnatural, To be revenged on him that loveth you.—It is a quarrel just and reasonable, To be revenged on him that slew my husband *Richard III.* i 2 134
Thou didst receive the holy sacrament, To fight in quarrel of the house of Lancaster i 4 209
Take not the quarrel from his powerful arm i 4 223
Our travell'd gallants, That fill the court with quarrels, talk *Hen. VIII.* i 3 20
Though't be temporal, Yet, if that quarrel, fortune, do divorce It ii 3 14
And that's the quarrel *Troi. and Cres.* Prol. 10
Good words, Thersites.—What's the quarrel? ii 1 98
Her brain-sick raptures Cannot distaste the goodness of a quarrel ii 2 123
What propugnation is in one man's valour, To stand the push and enmity of those This quarrel would excite? ii 2 138
A good quarrel to draw emulous factions and bleed to death upon ii 3 79
And speaks not to himself but with a pride That quarrels at self-breath ii 3 182
Not for the worth that hangs upon our quarrel iii 3 217
Take heed, the quarrel's most ominous to us v 7 21
Had we no quarrel else to Rome, but that Thou art thence banish'd *Cor.* iv 5 133
In wrongful quarrel you have slain your son *T. Andron.* i 1 293
O, see what thou hast done! In a bad quarrel slain a virtuous son i 1 342
This day all quarrels die i 1 465
So near the emperor's palace dare you draw, And maintain such a quarrel? ii 1 47
Is Lavinia then become so loose, Or Bassianus so degenerate, That for her love such quarrels may be broach'd? ii 1 67
I'll go fetch thy sons To back thy quarrels ii 3 54
For all my blood in Rome's great quarrel shed iii 1 4
Break the parle; These quarrels must be quietly debated v 3 20
And basely cozen'd Of that true hand that fought Rome's quarrel out v 3 102
The quarrel is between our masters and us their men *Rom. and Jul.* i 1 23
My naked weapon is out: quarrel, I will back thee.—How! turn thy back? i 1 39
Do you quarrel, sir?—Quarrel, sir! no, sir.—If you do, sir, I am for you i 1 59
Who set this ancient quarrel new abroach? i 1 111
I dare draw as soon as another man, if I see occasion in a good quarrel, and the law on my side ii 4 168
Thou wilt quarrel with a man that hath a hair more, or a hair less iii 1 18
Thou wilt quarrel with a man for cracking nuts iii 1 20
What eye but such an eye would spy out such a quarrel? iii 1 23
Thy head is as full of quarrels as an egg is full of meat iii 1 24
An I were so apt to quarrel as thou art, any man should buy the fee-simple of my life for an hour and a quarter iii 1 34
Spoke him fair, bade him bethink How nice the quarrel was iii 1 159
Since the quarrel Will bear no colour for the thing he is *J. Cæsar* ii 1 28
Fortune, on his damned quarrel smiling *Macbeth* i 2 14
I should forge Quarrels unjust against the good and loyal iv 3 83
And the chance of goodness Be like our warranted quarrel! iv 3 137
Beware Of entrance to a quarrel, but being in, Bear't that the opposed may beware of thee *Hamlet* i 3 66
But greatly to find quarrel in a straw When honour's at the stake iv 4 55
Other of your insolent retinue Do hourly carp and quarrel *Lear* i 4 222
When he saw my best alarum'd spirits, Bold in the quarrel's right ii 1 56
Speak yet, how grew your quarrel? ii 2 66
If you did wear a beard upon your chin, I'd shake it on this quarrel iii 7 77
And not fall To quarrel with your great opposeless wills iv 6 38
Best quarrels, in the heat, are cursed By those that feel their sharpness v 3 56
He'll be as full of quarrel and offence As my young mistress' dog *Othello* ii 3 52
To manage private and domestic quarrel, In night, and on the court and guard of safety! 'Tis monstrous ii 3 215
I remember a mass of things, but nothing distinctly; a quarrel, but nothing wherefore ii 3 290
Quarrel no more, but be prepared to know The purposes *Ant. and Cleo.* ii 3 66
If you'll patch a quarrel, As matter whole you have not to make it with ii 2 52
My quarrel was not altogether slight *Cymbeline* i 4 51
Quarrelled with a man for coughing in the street *Rom. and Jul.* iii 1 26
Quarreller. Besides that he's a fool, he's a great quarreller *T. Night* i 3 31
Quarrelling. If he could right himself with quarrelling, Some of us would lie low *Much Ado* v 1 51
Yet more quarrelling with occasion! *Mer. of Venice* iii 5 60
Hath the gift of a coward to allay the gust he hath in quarrelling *T. N.* i 3 33
Thy head hath been beaten as addle as an egg for quarrelling *R. and J.* iii 1 26
And yet thou wilt tutor me from quarrelling! iii 1 32
And set quarrelling Upon the head of valour *T. of Athens* iii 5 27
Drinking, fencing, swearing, quarrelling, Drabbing *Hamlet* ii 1 25
Quarrelous. Saucy and As quarrelous as the weasel *Cymbeline* iii 4 162
Quarrelsome. This is called the Countercheck Quarrelsome *As Y. Like It* v 4 85
The fifth, the Countercheck Quarrelsome v 4 99
My master is grown quarrelsome *T. of Shrew* i 2 13

Quarries. Deserts idle, Rough quarries, rocks and hills . *Othello* i 3 141
Quarry. I'ld make a quarry With thousands of these quarter'd slaves, as high As I could pick my lance . *Coriolanus* i 1 202
To relate the manner, Were, on the quarry of these murder'd deer, To add the death of you . *Macbeth* iv 3 206
This quarry cries on havoc . . . . . . *Hamlet* v 2 375
Quart. Fetch me a quart of sack; put a toast in't . *Mer. Wives* iii 5 3
She brought stone jugs and no seal'd quarts . *T. of Shrew* Ind. 2 90
For a quart of ale is a dish for a king . . *W. Tale* iv 3 8
You'll crack a quart together, ha! will you not? . 2 *Hen. IV.* v 3 66
Quart d'écu. For a quart d'écu he will sell the fee-simple of his salvation, the inheritance of it . . . *All's Well* iv 3 311
There's a quart d'écu for you: let the justices make you and fortune friends . . . . . . v 2 35
Quart pot. When I have been dry and bravely marching, it hath served me instead of a quart pot to drink in . 2 *Hen. VI.* iv 10 16
Quarter. The salt fish is an old coat.—I may quarter, coz.—You may, by marrying.—It is marring indeed, if he quarter it . *Mer. Wives* i 1 24
If he has a quarter of your coat, there is but three skirts for yourself . i 1 28
At an instant?—Within a quarter of an hour . . . . iv 4 5
His child is a year and a quarter old, come Philip and Jacob *M. for M.* iii 2 213
So he would keep fair quarter with his bed! . *Com. of Errors* ii 1 108
What's her name?—Nell, sir; but her name and three quarters, that's an ell and three quarters, will not measure her from hip to hip iii 2 112
An hour in clamour and a quarter in rheum . *Much Ado* v 2 85
Thou thimble, Thou yard, three-quarters, half-yard, quarter, nail! *T. of S.* iv 3 109
Bring this instrument of honour again into his native quarter *All's Well* iii 6 70
I have a kinsman not past three quarters of a mile hence . *W. Tale* iv 3 85
Then stand till he be three quarters and a dram dead . iv 4 814
Keep good quarter and good care to-night . . . *K. John* v 5 20
I am so good a proficient in one quarter of an hour . 1 *Hen. IV.* ii 4 19
Not above once in a quarter—of an hour . . . . iii 3 20
If I cannot once or twice in a quarter bear out a knave against an honest man, I have but a very little credit . 2 *Hen. IV.* v 1 53
Whereof take you one quarter into France, And you withal shall make all Gallia shake . . . . . *Hen. V.* i 2 215
Had all your quarters been as safely kept As that . . 1 *Hen. VI.* ii 1 63
Within her quarter and mine own precinct I was employ'd in passing . ii 1 68
Should buy the fee-simple of my life for an hour and a quarter *R. and J.* iii 1 36
Not a man Shall pass his quarter . . . *T. of Athens* v 4 60
And the very ports they blow, All the quarters that they know *Macbeth* i 3 16
I have known her continue in this a quarter of an hour . . v 1 34
Friends all but now, even now, In quarter, and in terms like bride and groom Devesting them for bed . . . *Othello* ii 3 180
Follow the noise so far as we have quarter . *Ant. and Cleo.* iv 3 22
Quartered. Hang'd in the frowning wrinkle of her brow! And quarter'd in her heart! . . . . . *K. John* ii 1 506
This is pity now, That, hang'd and drawn and quarter'd, there should be In such a love so vile a lout as he . . . . ii 1 508
Where is Lord Stanley quarter'd, dost thou know? . *Richard III.* v 3 34
Which were the hope o' the Strand, where she was quartered *Hen. VIII.* v 4 56
I'ld make a quarry With thousands of these quarter'd slaves. *Coriolanus* i 1 203
Mothers shall but smile when they behold Their infants quarter'd with the hands of war . . . . . *J. Cæsar* iii 1 268
They mean this night in Sardis to be quarter'd . . . . iv 2 28
A thought which, quarter'd, hath but one part wisdom . *Hamlet* iv 4 42
I, that with my sword Quarter'd the world . . *Ant. and Cleo.* iv 14 58
Hear the Roman horses neigh, Behold their quarter'd fires . *Cymbeline* iv 4 18
Quartering. Lean famine, quartering steel, and climbing fire . 1 *Hen. VI.* iv 2 11
Quasi. Good morrow, master Parson.—Master Parson, quasi pers-on *L. L. Lost* iv 2 85
Quat. I have rubb'd this young quat almost to the sense. . *Othello* v 1 11
Quatch-buttock. The pin-buttock, the quatch-buttock . *All's Well* ii 2 18
Quean. A witch, a quean, an old cozening quean! . . *Mer. Wives* iv 2 180
As a scolding quean to a wrangling knave . . *All's Well* ii 2 27
Throw the quean in the channel.—Throw me in the channel! . 2 *Hen. IV.* ii 1 51
Queas. Redime te captum quam queas minimo . . *T. of Shrew* i 1 167
Queasiness. They did fight with queasiness, constrain'd . 2 *Hen. IV.* i 1 196
Queasy. In despite of his quick wit and his queasy stomach *Much Ado* ii 1 399
And I have one thing, of a queasy question, Which I must act *Lear* ii 1 19
Queasy with his insolence Already . . . *Ant. and Cleo.* iii 6 20
Queen. I'll make you The queen of Naples . . . *Tempest* i 2 449
Tunis was never graced before with such a paragon to their queen . ii 1 75
She that is queen of Tunis; she that dwells Ten leagues beyond man's life . . . . ii 1 246
His daughter and I will be king and queen,—save our graces! . iii 2 115
The queen o' the sky, Whose watery arch and messenger am I . iv 1 70
Why hath thy queen Summon'd me hither, to this short-grass'd green? iv 1 82
Tell me, heavenly bow, If Venus or her son, as thou dost know, Do now attend the queen? . . . . iv 1 88
High'st queen of state, Great Juno, comes; I know her by her gait . iv 1 101
O heavens, that they were living both in Naples, The king and queen there! . . . . v 1 150
By this pale queen of night . . . . *T. G. of Ver.* iv 2 100
My Nan shall be the queen of all the fairies . *Mer. Wives* iv 4 71
Just 'twixt twelve and one, Must my sweet Nan present the Fairy Queen . . . . iv 6 20
Our radiant queen hates sluts and sluttery . . . . v 5 50
A dowry for a queen . . . . . . *L. L. Lost* ii 1 8
One Monsieur Biron, one of the strange queen's lords . . iv 2 134
He hath framed a letter to a sequent of the stranger queen's . . iv 2 143
O queen of queens! how far dost thou excel, No thought can think . iv 3 41
By that fire which burn'd the Carthage queen . . *M. N. Dream* i 1 173
And I serve the fairy queen, To dew her orbs upon the green . . ii 1 8
I'll be gone: Our queen and all her elves come here anon . . ii 1 17
Take heed the queen come not within his sight; For Oberon is passing fell . . . . ii 1 19
Newts and blind-worms, do no wrong, Come not near our fairy queen . ii 2 12
What hempen home-spuns have we swaggering here, So near the cradle of the fairy queen? . . . . iii 1 80
I'll to my queen and beg her Indian boy . . . . iii 2 375
But first I will release the fairy queen . . . . iv 1 75
Wake you, my sweet queen . . . . . . iv 1 80
Come, my queen, take hands with me, And rock the ground . . iv 1 90
Then, my queen, in silence sad, Trip we after night's shade . . iv 1 100
We will, fair queen, up to the mountain's top . . . iv 1 114
Except to steal your thoughts, my gentle queen . *Mer. of Venice* ii 1 12
Master of my servants, Queen o'er myself . . . . iii 2 171
Thrice-crowned queen of night, survey With thy chaste eye *As Y. L. It* iii 2 2
As dear As Anna to the queen of Carthage was . *T. of Shrew* i 1 159

Queen. Save you, fair queen!—And you, monarch! . . . *All's Well* i 1 117
Dian no queen of virgins, that would suffer her poor knight surprised . i 3 119
That miracle and queen of gems That nature pranks her in . *T. Night* ii 4 88
Orsino's mistress and his fancy's queen . . . . v 1 397
Tongue-tied our queen? speak you . . . . . *W. Tale* i 2 27
We were, fair queen, Two lads that thought there was no more behind . i 2 62
Of this make no conclusion, lest you say Your queen and I are devils . i 2 82
How came't, Camillo, That he did stay?—At the good queen's entreaty. —At the queen's be't: 'good' should be pertinent . . . i 2 220
Take again your queen as yours at first, Even for your son's sake . i 2 336
Keep with Bohemia And with your queen . . . . i 2 345
He thinks . . . that you have touch'd his queen Forbiddenly . . i 2 416
Good expedition be my friend, and comfort The gracious queen! . i 2 459
The queen your mother rounds apace . . . . . ii 1 16
Beseech your highness, call the queen again.—Be certain what you do, sir . . . . ii 1 126
In the which three great ones suffer, Yourself, your queen, your son ii 1 129
That the queen is spotless I' the eyes of heaven and to you . . ii 1 131
Pray you then, Conduct me to the queen.—I may not, madam . ii 2 7
A daughter, and a goodly babe, Lusty and like to live: the queen receives Much comfort in't . . . . ii 2 27
Commend my best obedience to the queen . . . . ii 2 36
I'll presently Acquaint the queen of your most noble offer . . ii 2 48
I'll to the queen: please you, come something nearer . . ii 2 55
If't please the queen to send the babe, I know not what I shall incur to pass it, Having no warrant . . . . . . ii 2 56
This child . . . is . . . not a party to The anger of the king nor guilty of, If any be, the trespass of the queen . . . . ii 2 63
Fear you his tyrannous passion more, alas, Than the queen's life? . ii 3 29
I say, I come From your good queen.—Good queen!—Good queen, my lord, Good queen; I say good queen . . . . . ii 3 58
The good queen, For she is good, hath brought you forth a daughter . ii 3 64
For he The sacred honour of himself, his queen's, His hopeful son's, his babe's, betrays to slander . . . . ii 3 84
This most cruel usage of your queen . . . something savours Of tyranny ii 3 117
If the event o' the journey Prove as successful to the queen,—O be't so! iii 1 12
It is his highness' pleasure that the queen Appear in person here in court iii 2 9
Hermione, queen to the worthy Leontes, king of Sicilia . . . iii 2 12
Your son, with mere conceit and fear Of the queen's speed, is gone iii 2 146
This news is mortal to the queen: look down And see what death is doing . . . . iii 2 149
I'll reconcile me to Polixenes, New woo my queen, recall the good Camillo iii 2 157
The queen, the queen, The sweet'st, dear'st creature's dead . iii 2 201
Forgive a foolish woman: The love I bore your queen—lo, fool again! . iii 2 229
Bring me To the dead bodies of my queen and son: One grave shall be for both . . . . iii 2 236
His most precious queen and children are even now to be afresh lamented iv 2 27
Is as a meeting of the petty gods, And you the queen on't . . iv 4 5
All your acts are queens . . . . iv 4 146
Good sooth, she is The queen of curds and cream . . . iv 4 161
I'll queen it no inch farther, But milk my ewes and weep . . iv 4 460
What were more holy Than to rejoice the former queen is well? . v 1 30
Even now, I might have look'd upon my queen's full eyes . . v 1 53
Give me the office To choose you a queen: she shall not be so young As was your former . . . . v 1 78
Walk'd your first queen's ghost, it should take joy To see her in your arms . . . . v 1 80
We shall not marry till thou bid'st us.—That Shall be when your first queen's again in breath . . . . v 1 83
Not a month 'Fore your queen died, she was more worth such gazes . v 1 226
At the relation of the queen's death, with the manner how she came to't v 2 92
The princes, our kindred, are going to see the queen's picture . v 2 187
We honour you with trouble: but we came To see the statue of our queen v 3 10
Dear queen, that ended when I but began, Give me that hand of yours to kiss . . . . v 3 45
Thy bastard shall be king, That thou mayst be a queen! . *K. John* ii 1 123
Her dowry shall weigh equal with a queen . . . . ii 1 486
Since last I went to France to fetch his queen . . *Richard II.* i 1 131
Come on, our queen: to-morrow must we part; Be merry . . i 1 222
Then, thrice-gracious queen, More than your lord's departure weep not ii 2 24
Why, is he not with the queen?—No, my good Lord . . . ii 3 25
With your sinful hours Made a divorce betwixt his queen and him . iii 1 12
And stain'd the beauty of a fair queen's cheeks With tears . . iii 1 14
The queen is at your house; For God's sake, fairly let her be entreated iii 1 36
Poor queen! so that thy state might be no worse, I would my skill were subject to thy curse . . . . iii 4 102
Rue, even for ruth, here shortly shall be seen, In the remembrance of a weeping queen . . . . iii 4 107
If this rebellious earth Have any resting for her true king's queen . v 1 6
Good sometime queen, prepare thee hence for France . . . v 1 37
Weep not, sweet queen; for trickling tears are vain . 1 *Hen. IV.* ii 4 431
Convey my tristful queen; for tears do stop the flood-gates of her eyes ii 4 434
Sweet as ditties highly penn'd, Sung by a fair queen in a summer's bower iii 1 210
Kneel down before you; but, indeed, to pray for the queen 2 *Hen. IV.* Epil. 37
Therefore, queen of all, Katharine, break thy mind to me *Hen. V.* v 2 264
Upon that I kiss your hand, and I call you my queen . . . v 2 272
Bear me witness all, That here I kiss her as my sovereign queen . v 2 386
At high festivals Before the kings and queens of France . 1 *Hen. VI.* i 6 27
He doth intend she shall be England's queen . . . . v 1 45
Would you not suppose Your bondage happy, to be made a queen? . v 3 111
To be a queen in bondage is more vile Than is a slave in base servility . v 3 112
I'll undertake to make thee Henry's queen . . . . v 3 117
Lord protector, give consent That Margaret may be England's royal queen . . . . v 5 24
Henry is able to enrich his queen And not to seek a queen to make him rich . . . . v 5 51
Margaret shall be queen, and none but she . . . . v 5 78
Upon my bended knee, . . . Deliver up my title in the queen 2 *Hen. VI.* i 1 13
The fairest queen that ever king received . . . . . i 1 16
For this great favour done, In entertainment to my princely queen . i 1 72
With his new bride and England's dear-bought queen . . . i 1 252
In that chair where kings and queens are crown'd . . . i 2 38
Unto Saint Alban's, Where as the king and queen do mean to hawk . i 2 58
Here a' comes, methinks, and the queen with him . . . i 3 7
Am I a queen in title and in style, And must be made a subject to a duke? . . . . i 3 51
Strangers in court do take her for the queen . . . . i 3 82
I prithee, peace, good queen, And whet not on these furious peers . ii 1 33
Deposed the rightful king, Sent his poor queen to France . . ii 2 25
Why, now is Henry king, and Margaret queen . . . . ii 3 39

Queen. I never meant him any ill, nor the king, nor the queen *2 Hen. VI.* ii 3 91
And Margaret our queen Do seek subversion of thy harmless life iii 1 207
Ay me, unhappy! To be a queen, and crown'd with infamy! iii 2 71
Art thou, like the adder, waxen deaf? Be poisonous too and kill thy forlorn queen iii 2 77
Ungentle queen, to call him gentle Suffolk! No more, I say iii 2 290
Cease, gentle queen, these execrations iii 2 305
Thy lips that kiss'd the queen shall sweep the ground iv 1 75
I go of message from the queen to France; I charge thee waft me safely iv 1 113
Let his head and lifeless body lie, Until the queen his mistress bury it iv 1 143
If he revenge it not, yet will his friends; So will the queen iv 1 147
Somerset comes with the queen: Go, bid her hide him quickly from the duke v 1 83
The queen this day here holds her parliament *3 Hen. VI.* i 1 35
Come, cousin, let us tell the queen these news i 1 182
Here comes the queen, whose looks bewray her anger i 1 211
I will follow thee.—Be patient, gentle queen, and I will stay i 1 214
Poor queen! how love to me and to her son Hath made her break out into terms of rage! i 1 264
The queen with all the northern earls and lords Intend here to besiege you i 2 49
The army of the queen mean to besiege us.—She shall not need i 2 64
The army of the queen hath got the field: My uncles both are slain i 4 1
I would assay, proud queen, to make thee blush i 4 118
Taught thee to insult? It needs not, nor it boots thee not, proud queen i 4 125
See, ruthless queen, a hapless father's tears: This cloth thou dip'dst in blood of my sweet boy i 4 156
Slaughter'd by the ireful arm Of unrelenting Clifford and the queen ii 1 58
The ruthless queen gave him to dry his cheeks A napkin steeped in the harmless blood Of sweet young Rutland ii 1 61
March'd toward Saint Alban's to intercept the queen, Bearing the king ii 1 114
The coldness of the king, Who look'd full gently on his warlike queen ii 1 123
No hope to win the day; So that we fled; the king unto the queen ii 1 137
The proud insulting queen, With Clifford, . . . Have wrought the easy-melting king like wax ii 1 168
The queen is coming with a puissant host ii 1 207
The queen hath best success when you are absent ii 2 74
Margaret my queen, and Clifford too, Have chid me from the battle ii 5 16
Not that I fear to stay, but love to go Whither the queen intends ii 5 139
Some troops pursue the bloody-minded queen, That led calm Henry ii 6 33
Cut the sea to France, And ask the Lady Bona for thy queen ii 6 90
My queen and son are gone to France for aid iii 1 28
If this news be true, Poor queen and son, your labour is but lost iii 1 32
Say, what art thou that talk'st of kings and queens? iii 1 55
She shall be my love, or else my queen.—Say that King Edward take thee for his queen?—'Tis better said than done iii 2 88
I am too mean to be your queen, And yet too good to be your concubine iii 2 97
You cavil, widow: I did mean, my queen iii 2 99
Answer no more, for thou shalt be my queen iii 2 106
I was, I must confess, Great Albion's queen in former golden days iii 3 7
Why, say, fair queen, whence springs this deep despair? iii 3 12
Renowned queen, with patience calm the storm, While we bethink a means iii 3 38
And why not queen?—Because thy father Henry did usurp; And thou no more art prince than she is queen iii 3 78
Our quondam queen, You have a father able to maintain you iii 3 153
I like it well that our fair queen and mistress Smiles at her news iii 3 167
My noble queen, let former grudges pass iii 3 195
How shall Bona be revenged But by thy help to this distressed queen? iii 3 213
My quarrel and this English queen's are one iii 3 216
And, as occasion serves, this noble queen And prince shall follow iii 3 236
If our queen and this young prince agree, I'll join mine eldest daughter and my joy To him forthwith iii 3 241
Tell me some reason why the Lady Grey Should not become my wife and England's queen iv 1 26
Before it pleased his majesty To raise my state to title of a queen iv 1 68
But what said Henry's queen? For I have heard that she was there iv 1 102
Let me entreat, for I command no more, That Margaret your queen and my son Edward Be sent for, to return from France with speed iv 6 60
The queen from France hath brought a puissant power: Even now we heard the news v 1 31
Away, away, to meet the queen's great power! v 2 50
Those powers that the queen Hath raised in Gallia have arrived our coast v 3 7
The queen is valued thirty thousand strong v 3 14
Let's away to London And see our gentle queen how well she fares v 5 89
Love my lovely queen; And kiss your princely nephew, brothers both v 7 26
I think there's no man is secure But the queen's kindred *Richard III.* i 1 72
The king Is wise and virtuous, and his noble queen Well struck in years i 1 91
The queen's kindred are made gentlefolks: How say you, sir? i 1 95
We are the queen's abjects, and must obey i 1 106
I had rather be a country servant-maid Than a great queen i 3 108
Small joy have I in being England's queen i 3 110
Ere you were queen, yea, or your husband king, I was a pack-horse in his great affairs i 3 121
As little joy may you suppose in me, That I enjoy, being the queen thereof i 3 154
A little joy enjoys the queen thereof; For I am she, and altogether joyless i 3 155
Which of you trembles not that looks on me? If not, that, I being queen, you bow like subjects? i 3 161
Thyself a queen, for me that was a queen, Outlive thy glory, like my wretched self! i 3 202
And, after many lengthen'd hours of grief, Die neither mother, wife, nor England's queen! i 3 209
Poor painted queen, vain flourish of my fortune! i 3 241
Teach me to be your queen, and you my subjects: O, serve me well! i 3 252
Say it is the queen and her allies That stir the king against the duke i 3 330
Good morrow to my sovereign king and queen; And, princely peers ii 1 46
The guilty kindred of the queen Look'd pale when they did hear of Clarence' death ii 1 135
The king, provoked by the queen, Devised impeachments ii 2 21
To part the queen's proud kindred from the king ii 2 150
And the queen's sons and brothers haught and proud ii 3 28
The queen your mother, and your brother York, Have taken sanctuary iii 1 27
Persuade the queen to send the Duke of York Unto his princely brother iii 1 33
Your enemies, The kindred of the queen, must die at Pomfret iii 2 50
Going prisoner to the Tower, By the suggestion of the queen's allies iii 2 103
As mother, And reverend looker on, of two fair queens iv 1 31
Straight to Westminster, There to be crowned Richard's royal queen iv 1 33
Nor mother, wife, nor England's counted queen iv 1 47

Queen. Anointed let me be with deadly venom, And die, ere men can say, God save the queen! *Richard III.* iv 1 63
I call'd thee then poor shadow, painted queen iv 4 83
A queen in jest, only to fill the scene iv 4 91
Wherein dost thou joy? Who sues to thee and cries 'God save the queen'? iv 4 94
For queen, a very caitiff crown'd with care iv 4 100
Farewell, York's wife, and queen of sad mischance iv 4 114
For my daughters, Richard, They shall be praying nuns, not weeping queens iv 4 201
Who dost thou mean shall be her king?—Even he that makes her queen iv 4 265
The loss you have is but a son being king, And by that loss your daughter is made queen iv 4 308
Say, she shall be a high and mighty queen.—To wail the title iv 4 347
The queen hath heartily consented He shall espouse Elizabeth her daughter iv 5 17
Charles the emperor, Under pretence to see the queen his aunt *Hen. VIII.* i 1 177
Have, out of malice To the good queen, possess'd him with a scruple ii 1 158
Now he has crack'd the league Between us and the emperor, the queen's great nephew ii 2 26
The queen shall be acquainted Forthwith for what you come ii 2 108
Deliver this with modesty to the queen ii 2 137
By my troth and maidenhead, I would not be a queen ii 3 24
You would not be a queen?—No, not for all the riches under heaven ii 3 34
A three-pence bow'd would hire me, Old as I am, to queen it ii 3 37
I swear again, I would not be a queen For all the world ii 3 45
There was a lady once, 'tis an old story, That would not be a queen ii 3 91
The queen is comfortless, and we forgetful In our long absence ii 3 105
We are a queen, or long have dream'd so, certain The daughter of a king ii 4 71
The queen is obstinate, Stubborn to justice, apt to accuse it ii 4 121
The queen of earthly queens ii 4 141
By some of these The queen is put in anger ii 4 161
For no dislike i' the world against the person Of the good queen ii 4 224
Katharine our queen, before the primest creature That's paragon'd o' the world ii 4 229
The queen being absent, 'tis a needful fitness That we adjourn this court ii 4 231
Must be an earnest motion Made to the queen, to call back her appeal ii 4 234
My king is tangled in affection to A creature of the queen's iii 2 36
Katharine no more Shall be call'd queen, but princess dowager iii 2 70
The late queen's gentlewoman, a knight's daughter, To be her mistress' mistress! the queen's queen! iii 2 94
The Lady Anne, Whom the king hath in secrecy long married, This day was view'd in open as his queen, Going to chapel iii 2 404
The trumpets sound: stand close, the queen is coming iv 1 36
Having brought the queen To a prepared place in the choir, fell off iv 1 63
She had all the royal makings of a queen; As holy oil iv 1 87
What two reverend bishops Were those that went on each side of the queen? iv 1 100
The queen's in labour, They say, in great extremity v 1 18
Now, Lovell, from the queen what is the news? v 1 61
Prithee, to bed; and in thy prayers remember The estate of my poor queen v 1 74
By thy looks I guess thy message. Is the queen deliver'd? v 1 162
Sir, your queen Desires your visitation v 1 166
Give her an hundred marks. I'll to the queen v 1 170
And to your royal grace, and the good queen, . . . thus pray v 5 5
Ye must all see the queen, and she must thank ye, She will be sick else v 5 74
The ravish'd Helen, Menelaus' queen, With wanton Paris sleeps *Troi. and Cres.* Prol. 9
For an old aunt whom the Greeks held captive, He brought a Grecian queen ii 2 78
Treason were it to the ransack'd queen, Disgrace to your great worths and shame to me, Now to deliver her possession up ii 2 150
To you, fair queen! fair thoughts be your fair pillow! iii 1 48
You speak your fair pleasure, sweet queen iii 1 52
I have business to my lord, dear queen iii 1 63
Well, sweet queen, you are pleasant with me iii 1 67
Honey-sweet lord,— Go to, sweet queen, go to iii 1 73
Sweet queen, sweet queen! that's a sweet queen, i' faith iii 1 77
What says my sweet queen, my very very sweet queen? iii 1 87
Come, give me an instrument. Now, sweet queen iii 1 104
You know all, Lord Pandarus.—Not I, honey-sweet queen iii 1 154
Farewell, sweet queen.—Commend me to your niece.—I will, sweet queen iii 1 158
By the jealous queen of heaven, that kiss I carried from thee *Coriolanus* v 3 46
The eldest son of this distressed queen *T. Andron.* i 1 103
The self-same gods that arm'd the Queen of Troy i 1 136
Tamora, the Queen of Goths—When Goths were Goths and Tamora was queen i 1 140
Clear up, fair queen, that cloudy countenance i 1 263
He comforts you Can make you greater than the Queen of Goths i 1 269
Speak, Queen of Goths, dost thou applaud my choice? i 1 321
I swear, If Saturnine advance the Queen of Goths, She will a handmaid be to his desires i 1 330
How comes it that the subtle Queen of Goths Is of a sudden thus advanced? i 1 392
And make them know what 'tis to let a queen Kneel in the streets i 1 454
To wanton with this queen, This goddess, this Semiramis, this nymph ii 1 21
Believe me, queen, your swarth Cimmerian Doth make your honour of his body's hue ii 3 72
O Tamora, be call'd a gentle queen, And with thine own hands kill me! ii 3 168
Beg at the gates, like Tarquin and his queen iii 1 299
Confederate with the queen and her two sons v 1 108
In her company there is a Moor; And, would you represent our queen aright, It were convenient you had such a devil v 2 89
In the emperor's court There is a queen, attended by a Moor v 2 105
Welcome, my gracious lord; welcome, dread queen; Welcome, ye warlike Goths v 3 26
The queen that bore thee, Oftener upon her knees than on her feet, Died every day she lived *Macbeth* iv 3 109
Wherefore was that cry?—The queen, my lord, is dead v 5 16
The cruel ministers Of this dead butcher and his fiend-like queen v 8 69
Our sometime sister, now our queen *Hamlet* i 2 8
Won to his shameful lust The will of my most seeming-virtuous queen i 5 46
By a brother's hand Of life, of crown, of queen, at once dispatch'd i 5 75
What might you, Or my dear majesty your queen here, think? ii 2 135
I know the good king and queen have sent for you ii 2 291
So shall my anticipation prevent your discovery, and your secrecy to the king and queen moult no feather ii 2 306
'The mobled queen?'—That's good; 'mobled queen' is good ii 2 525
After the play Let his queen mother all alone entreat him iii 1 190

Queen. Will the king hear this piece of work?—And the queen too *Ham.* iii 2 53
The queen, your mother, in most great affliction of spirit, hath sent me iii 2 323
My lord, the queen would speak with you, and presently . . iii 2 391
I am still possess'd Of those effects for which I did the murder, My crown, mine own ambition and my queen . . . . iii 3 55
You are the queen, your husband's brother's wife . . . iii 4 15
Who, that's but a queen, fair, sober, wise, Would from a paddock, from a bat, a gib, Such dear concernings hide? . . . iii 4 189
The queen his mother Lives almost by his looks . . . iv 7 11
Letters, my lord, from Hamlet: This to your majesty; this to the queen iv 7 37
How now, sweet queen!—One woe doth tread upon another's heel iv 7 163
Here comes the king, The queen, the courtiers: who is this they follow? . . . . v 1 241
The king and queen and all are coming down . . . . v 2 212
The queen desires you to use some gentle entertainment to Laertes v 2 215
The queen carouses to thy fortune, Hamlet . . . . v 2 300
Look to the queen there, ho! . . . . v 2 314
How does the queen?—She swounds to see them bleed . . v 2 319
I am dead, Horatio. Wretched queen, adieu! . . . . v 2 344
Is queen of us, of ours, and our fair France . . . *Lear* i 1 260
Did your letters pierce the queen to any demonstration of grief? . iv 3 11
It seem'd she was a queen Over her passion . . . . iv 3 15
Though that the queen on special cause is here, Her army is moved on iv 6 219
With him I sent the queen; My reason all the same; and they are ready v 3 51
As I am Egypt's queen, Thou blushest, Antony *Ant. and Cleo.* i 1 29
Fie, wrangling queen! Whom every thing becomes, to chide, to laugh, To weep . . . . i 1 48
Come, my queen; Last night you did desire it . . . . i 1 54
Where's the soothsayer that you praised so to the queen? . . i 2 3
Hush! here comes Antony.—Not he; the queen.—Saw you my lord? . i 2 83
I must from this enchanting queen break off . . . . i 2 132
I shall break The cause of our expedience to the queen . . . i 2 185
Now, my dearest queen,— Pray you, stand farther from me . . i 3 17
O, never was there queen So mightily betray'd! . . . . i 3 24
Most sweet queen,— Nay, pray you, seek no colour for your going . i 3 31
Hear me, queen: The strong necessity of time commands Our services awhile . . . . i 3 41
Can Fulvia die?—She's dead, my queen . . . . . i 3 59
I am quickly ill, and well, So Antony loves.—My precious queen, forbear i 3 73
Not more manlike Than Cleopatra; nor the queen of Ptolemy More womanly . . . . i 4 6
Last thing he did, dear queen, He kiss'd,—the last of many doubled kisses,—This orient pearl . . . . i 5 39
Apollodorus carried— No more of that: he did so.—What, I pray you?—A certain queen to Cæsar in a mattress . . . . . ii 6 71
Most gracious majesty,— Didst thou behold Octavia?—Ay, dread queen iii 3 9
Made her Of lower Syria, Cyprus, Lydia, Absolute queen . . iii 6 11
Comfort him.—Do, most dear queen.—Do! why: what else? . . iii 11 26
The queen approaches: Her head's declined, and death will seize her . iii 11 46
Sir, the queen.—O, whither hast thou led me, Egypt? . . . iii 11 50
The queen Of audience nor desire shall fail, so she From Egypt drive her all-disgraced friend . . . . iii 12 20
The queen shall then have courtesy, so she Will yield us up . . iii 13 15
Come on, my queen; There's sap in't yet . . . . . iii 13 191
Thou fumblest, Eros; and my queen's a squire More tight at this than thou iv 4 14
We have beat him to his camp: run one before, And let the queen know iv 8 2
I made these wars for Egypt: and the queen,—Whose heart I thought I had, for she had mine . . . . iv 14 15
I come, my queen:—Eros!—Stay for me: Where souls do couch on flowers . . . . iv 14 50
My queen and Eros Have by their brave instruction got upon me A nobleness in record . . . . iv 14 97
One word, sweet queen: Of Cæsar seek your honour, with your safety iv 15 45
The queen my mistress, Confined in all she has, her monument . v 1 52
If your master Would have a queen his beggar, you must tell him, That majesty, to keep decorum, must No less beg than a kingdom . . v 2 16
Royal queen!—O Cleopatra! thou art taken, queen . . . v 2 37
Come, come, and take a queen Worth many babes and beggars! . . v 2 47
For the queen, I'll take her to my guard . . . . . v 2 66
Which is the Queen of Egypt?—It is the emperor, madam . . v 2 112
Good queen, let us entreat you.—O Cæsar, what a wounding shame is this! . . . . v 2 158
Be cheer'd; Make not your thoughts your prisons: no, dear queen . v 2 185
Where is the queen?—Behold, sir . . . . . . v 2 197
I shall remain your debtor.—I your servant. Adieu, good queen . v 2 206
Show me, my women, like a queen: go fetch My best attires . . v 2 227
So is the queen, That most desired the match . . *Cymbeline* i 1 11
We must forbear: here comes the gentleman, The queen, and princess . i 1 69
My queen! my mistress! O lady, weep no more . . . . i 1 92
Thither write, my queen, And with mine eyes I'll drink the words you send . . . . i 1 99
That mightst have had the sole son of my queen! . . . . i 1 138
What was the last That he spake to thee?—It was his queen, his queen! i 3 5
The queen, madam, Desires your highness' company . . . i 3 37
Be revenged; Or she that bore you was no queen . . . . i 6 127
They dare not fight with me, because of the queen my mother . . ii 1 22
When you have given good morning to your mistress, Attend the queen and us . . . Come, our queen . . . . . . ii 3 67
Kings, queens and states, Maids, matrons, nay, the secrets of the grave This viperous slander enters . . . . iii 4 39
Here is a box; I had it from the queen: What's in't is precious . iii 4 191
But, my gentle queen, Where is our daughter? She hath not appear'd iii 5 29
I partly know him: 'tis Cloten, the son o' the queen . . . iv 2 65
I am son to the queen.—I am sorry for't; not seeming So worthy as thy birth . . . . iv 2 93
Cut off one Cloten's head, Son to the queen, after his own report . iv 2 119
My queen Upon a desperate bed, and in a time When fearful wars point at me . . . . iv 3 5
Now for the counsel of my son and queen! I am amazed with matter iv 3 27
To sour your happiness, I must report The queen is dead . . v 5 27
O Imogen! My queen, my life, my wife! O Imogen, Imogen, Imogen! v 5 226
Thought by me A precious thing: I had it from the queen . . v 5 242
I left out one thing which the queen confess'd . . . . v 5 244
The queen, sir, very oft importuned me To temper poisons for her . v 5 249
A most curious mantle, wrought by the hand Of his queen mother . v 5 362
Our wicked queen; Whom heavens, in justice, both on her and hers, Have laid most heavy hand . . . . v 5 463
Come, queen o' the feast,—For, daughter, so you are . *Pericles* ii 3 17
By Juno, that is queen of marriage, All viands that I eat do seem unsavoury, Wishing him my meat . . . . ii 3 30

Queen. His queen with child makes her desire—Which who shall cross?—along to go . . . . *Pericles* iii Gower 40
How does my queen? Thou stormest venomously; Wilt thou spit all thyself? . . . . iii 1 7
Make swift the pangs Of my queen's travails! . . . . . iii 1 14
Take in your arms this piece Of your dead queen . . . . iii 1 18
Here's all that is left living of your queen, A little daughter . . iii 1 20
Your queen must overboard: the sea works high, the wind is loud . iii 1 47
She must overboard straight.—As you think meet. Most wretched queen! . . . . iii 1 55
I, King Pericles, have lost This queen, worth all our mundane cost . iii 2 71
This queen will live: nature awakes; a warmth Breathes out of her . iii 2 93
O your sweet queen! That the strict fates had pleased you had brought her! . . . . iii 3 7
His woeful queen we leave at Ephesus, Unto Diana there a votaress iv Gower 3
My queen's square brows; Her stature to an inch; as wand-like straight v 1 109
But tell me now My drown'd queen's name . . . . . v 1 207
Hail, madam, and my queen!—I know you not . . . . v 3 49
Will you deliver How this dead queen re-lives? . . . . v 3 64
Yet there, my queen, We'll celebrate their nuptials . . . . v 3 79
In Pericles, his queen and daughter, seen . . . Virtue preserved v 3 Gower 87
Queen Hecuba laughed that her eyes ran o'er *Troi. and Cres.* i 2 157
Here is a letter from Queen Hecuba, A token from her daughter . v 1 44
Queen Mab. I see Queen Mab hath been with you *Rom. and Jul.* i 4 53
Quell. Notwithstanding all her sudden quips, The least whereof would quell a lover's hope . . . . *T. G. of Ver.* iv 2 13
Cut thread and thrum; Quail, crush, conclude, and quell! *M. N. Dream* v 1 292
Either to quell the Dauphin utterly, Or bring him in obedience 1 *Hen. VI.* i 1 163
And so to arms, victorious father, To quell the rebels . 2 *Hen. VI.* v 1 212
Your activity may defeat and quell The source of all erection *T. of Athens* iv 3 163
His spongy officers, who shall bear the guilt Of our great quell *Macbeth* i 7 72
Quench. As soon go kindle fire with snow As seek to quench the fire of love with words . . . . *T. G. of Ver.* ii 7 20
I do not seek to quench your love's hot fire, But qualify the fire's extreme rage . . . . ii 7 21
Threw on him Great pails of puddled mire to quench the hair *Com. of Er.* v 1 173
The lady's death Will quench the wonder of her infamy . *Much Ado* iv 1 241
With satiety seeks to quench his thirst . . . *T. of Shrew* i 1 24
Her face o' fire With labour and the thing she took to quench it *W. Tale* iv 4 61
Come, quench your blushes and present yourself That which you are . iv 4 67
Would she begin a sect, might quench the zeal Of all professors else . v 1 107
Thy rage shall burn thee up, and thou shalt turn To ashes, ere our blood shall quench that fire . . . . . . *K. John* iii 1 345
And quench his fiery indignation Even in the matter of mine innocence iv 1 63
I cannot weep; for all my body's moisture Scarce serves to quench my furnace-burning heart . . . . 3 *Hen. VI.* ii 1 80
A little fire is quickly trodden out; Which, being suffer'd, rivers cannot quench . . . . iv 8 8
No English soul More stronger to direct you than yourself, If with the sap of reason you would quench, Or but allay, the fire of passion *Hen. VIII.* i 1 148
You Have blown this coal betwixt my lord and me; Which God's dew quench! . . . . ii 4 80
This is of purpose laid by some that hate me . . . To quench mine honour v 2 16
Fie, fie, fie! This is the way to kindle, not to quench . *Coriolanus* iii 1 197
Thou art preparing fire for us; look thee, here's water to quench it . v 2 78
Set fire on barns and hay-stacks in the night, And bid the owners quench them with their tears . . . . . . *T. Andron.* v 1 134
Quench the fire of your pernicious rage With purple fountains *R. and J.* i 1 91
Turn the tables up, And quench the fire, the room is grown too hot . i 5 30
And quench the guards of the ever-fixed pole . . . *Othello* ii 1 15
If I quench thee, thou flaming minister, I can again thy former light restore, Should I repent me . . . . v 2 8
Dost thou think in time She will not quench and let instructions enter Where folly now possesses? . . . . . . *Cymbeline* i 5 47
That were to blow at fire in hope to quench it . . . *Pericles* i 4 4
Gently quench Thy nimble, sulphurous flashes! . . . . iii 1 5
Quenched. That in all reason should have quenched her love *M. for M.* iii 1 250
Quench'd in the chaste beams of the watery moon . *M. N. Dream* ii 1 162
Moist Hesperus hath quench'd his sleepy lamp . . *All's Well* ii 1 167
What hath quench'd them hath given me fire . . . *Macbeth* ii 2 2
Would have buoy'd up, And quench'd the stelled fires . . *Lear* iii 7 61
Being thus quench'd Of hope, not longing . . . *Cymbeline* v 5 195
These blushes of hers must be quenched with some present practice *Per.* iv 2 135
Quenching my familiar smile with an austere regard of control *T. Night* ii 5 72
Quenching the flame of bold rebellion Even with the rebels' blood 2 *Hen. IV.* Ind. 26
Quenchless. I dare your quenchless fury to more rage . 3 *Hen. VI.* i 4 28
Quern. Skim milk, and sometimes labour in the quern . *M. N. Dream* ii 1 36
Quest. Volumes of report Run with these false and most contrarious quests Upon thy doings . . . . . . *Meas. for Meas.* iv 1 62
That his attendant . . . Might bear him company in the quest of him *Com. of Errors* i 1 130
I, to find a mother and a brother, In quest of them, unhappy, lose myself i 2 40
Many Jasons come in quest of her . . . . *Mer. of Venice* i 1 172
If lusty love should go in quest of beauty, Where should he find it fairer than in Blanch? . . . . *K. John* ii 1 426
What lawful quest have given their verdict up? . . *Richard III.* i 4 189
But is this law?—Ay, marry, is t; crowner's quest law . *Hamlet* v 1 24
What, in the least, Will you require in present dower with her, Or cease your quest of love? . . . . *Lear* i 1 196
Hath sent about three several quests To search you out . . *Othello* i 2 46
With all due diligence That horse and sail and high expense Can stead the quest . . . . *Pericles* iii Gower 21
Questant. When The bravest questant shrinks . . . *All's Well* ii 1 16
Question. My tale provokes that question . . . . *Tempest* i 2 140
Here cease more questions: Thou art inclined to sleep . . . i 2 184
That is not the question: the question is concerning your marriage *M. W.* i 1 227
Disarm them, and let them question . . . . iii 1 78
My daughter will I question how she loves you . . . . iii 4 94
Ask him some questions in his accidence . . . . . . iv 1 16
Old Escalus, Though first in question, is thy secondary *Meas. for Meas.* i 1 47
I subscribe not that, nor any other, But in the loss of question . ii 4 90
Wise! why, no question but he was . . . . iii 2 146
Give me leave to question; you shall see how I'll handle her . . v 1 272
You are my elder.—That's a question: how shall we try it? *Com. of Er.* v 1 421
Do you question me, as an honest man should do? . . . *Much Ado* i 1 167
I will send for him; and question him yourself . . . . . i 2 20
Out of question, you were born in a merry hour . . . . ii 1 346
A commodity in question, I warrant you . . . . . . iii 3 192

Question. Let me but move one question to your daughter . *Much Ado* iv 1 74
And how long is that, think you?—Question . . . v 2 84
Against her will, as it appears In the true course of all the question . v 4 6
To make thee a double-dealer; which, out of question, thou wilt be . v 4 117
How needless was it then to ask the question! . . *L. L. Lost* ii 1 117
'Tis 'long of you that spur me with such questions . . ii 1 119
Out of question so it is sometimes, Glory grows guilty of detested crimes iv 1 30
Do you not educate youth at the charge-house? . . . —I do, sans question v 1 91
Question your desires; Know of your youth . . *M. N. Dream* i 1 67
I will not stay thy questions; let me go . . . . ii 1 235
Therefore be out of hope, of question, of doubt; Be certain, nothing truer iii 2 279
You do me now more wrong In making question of my uttermost *M. of V.* i 1 156
And I no question make To have it of my trust or for my sake . . i 1 184
Shall we turn to men?—Fie, what a question's that! . . . . iii 4 79
I pray you, think you question with the Jew . . . . iv 1 70
As well use question with the wolf Why he hath made the ewe bleat . iv 1 73
Are you acquainted with the difference That holds this present question? iv 1 172
I'll stay no longer question . . . . iv 1 346
Question yond man If he for gold will give us any food . *As Y. Like It* ii 4 64
I will not trouble you As yet, to question you about your fortunes . ii 7 172
I answer you right painted cloth, from whence you have studied your questions . . . . iii 2 291
I met the duke yesterday and had much question with him . . . iii 4 39
Neither call the giddiness of it in question . . . . v 2 6
Where meeting with an old religious man, After some question with him, was converted . . . . v 4 167
Let me ask you a question . . . . . . *All's Well* i 1 123
More should I question thee, and more I must, Though more to know could not be more to trust . . . . ii 1 208
That's a bountiful answer that fits all questions . . . . ii 2 16
Will your answer serve fit to all questions? . . . . . ii 2 20
From below your duke to beneath your constable, it will fit any question . . . . ii 2 33
I will be a fool in question, hoping to be the wiser by your answer . ii 2 41
You'll run again, rather than suffer question for your residence . ii 5 42
Ask questions and sing; pick his teeth and sing . . . . iii 2 7
I'll question her. God save you, pilgrim! whither are you bound? . iii 5 35
I believe that does harm to my wit.—No question . . *T. Night* i 3 92
Would that have mended my hair?—Past question . . . . i 3 104
You call in question the continuance of his love: is he inconstant? . i 4 6
I can say little more than I have studied, and that question's out of my part . . . . i 5 191
It is, in contempt of question, her hand.—Her C's, her U's and her T's ii 5 98
I am no more mad than you are: make the trial of it in any constant question . . . . iv 2 53
Much like the character: But out of question 'tis Maria's hand . v 1 355
I'll question you Of my lord's tricks and yours when you were boys *W. T.* i 2 60
I have loved thee,— Make that thy question, and go rot! . . . i 2 324
'Tis safer to Avoid what's grown than question how 'tis born . . i 2 433
We will, not appearing what we are, have some question with the shepherd . . . . iv 2 55
I spake with him; who now Has these poor men in question . . . v 1 198
'I shall beseech you'—that is question now; And then comes answer *K. John* i 1 195
'At your service, sir:' 'No, sir,' says question, 'I, sweet sir, at yours' i 1 199
Ere answer knows what question would, Saving in dialogue of compliment i 1 200
This haste was hot in question . . . . *1 Hen. IV.* i 1 34
You paraquito, answer me Directly unto this question that I ask . . ii 3 89
I must not have you henceforth question me Whither I go . . . ii 3 106
Stand in some by-room, while I question my puny drawer . . . ii 4 33
Shall the blessed sun of heaven prove a micher and eat blackberries? a question not to be asked . . . . ii 4 451
Shall the son of England prove a thief and take purses? a question to be asked . . . . ii 4 452
And breed a kind of question in our cause . . . . . iv 1 68
He seem'd in running to devour the way, Staying no longer question *2 Hen. IV.* i 1 48
He that was in question for the robbery?—He, my lord. . . . i 2 68
The question then, Lord Hastings, standeth thus . . . . i 3 15
Consent upon a sure foundation, Question surveyors . . . . i 3 53
Wherefore do I this? so the question stands. Briefly to this end . iv 1 53
I muse you make so slight a question . . . . . . iv 1 167
Question your royal thoughts, make the case yours . . . . v 2 91
The scambling and unquiet time Did push it out of farther question *Hen. V.* i 1 5
Though war nor no known quarrel were in question . . . . ii 4 17
Question your grace the late ambassadors . . . . . ii 4 31
With all speed, lest that our king Come here himself to question our delay ii 4 142
Marry, I wad full fain hear some question 'tween you tway . . iii 2 127
And out of doubt and out of question too, and ambiguities . . v 1 48
When you come into your closet, you'll question this gentlewoman about me . . . . v 2 211
Question her proudly; let thy looks be stern . *1 Hen. VI.* i 2 62
Ask me what question thou canst possible, And I will answer unpremeditated . . . . i 2 87
Question, my lords, no further of the case, How or which way . . ii 1 72
Stubbornly he did repugn the truth About a certain question in the law iv 1 95
A spirit . . . , That shall make answer to such questions As by your grace shall be propounded him . . . . *2 Hen. VI.* i 2 80
I'll think upon the questions . . . . i 2 82
I am able to endure much.—No question of that . . . . iv 2 61
That's false.—Ay, there's the question; but I say, 'tis true . iv 2 149
Go we, brothers, to the man that took him, To question of his apprehension. . . . . *3 Hen. VI.* iii 2 122
Let your reason with your choler question What 'tis you go about *Hen. VIII.* i 1 130
Or Laid any scruple in your way, which might Induce you to the question on't . . . . ii 4 151
The question did at first so stagger me . . . . . ii 4 212
Not ever The justice and the truth o' the question carries The due o' the verdict with it . . . . v 1 130
This is her question.—That's true; make no question of that *T. and C.* i 2 173
Since the first sword was drawn about this question . . . ii 2 18
And on the cause and question now in hand Have glozed, but superficially . . . . ii 2 164
I'll decline the whole question . . . . ii 3 55
Lest perchance he think We dare not move the question of our place . ii 3 89
Do you not think he thinks himself a better man than I am?—No question . . . . ii 3 155
She'll bereave you o' the deeds too, if she call your activity in question iii 2 60

Question. 'Tis like he'll question me Why such unplausive eyes are bent on him . . . . *Troi. and Cres.* iii 3 42
Health to you, valiant sir, During all question of the gentle truce . iv 1 11
In this I do not call your faith in question So mainly as my merit iv 4 86
It would discredit the blest gods, proud man, To answer such a question iv 5 248
I as little question As he is proud to do't . . *Coriolanus* ii 1 246
No question asked him by any of the senators, but they stand bald before him . . . . iv 5 205
Now question me no more; we are espied . . *T. Andron.* ii 3 48
Examine other beauties.—'Tis the way To call hers exquisite, in question more . . . . *Rom. and Jul.* i 1 235
Stay not to question, for the watch is coming . . . . v 3 158
Where's the fool now?—He last asked the question . *T. of Athens* ii 2 60
How that might change his nature, there's the question . *J. Cæsar* ii 1 13
The question of his death is enrolled in the Capitol . . . iii 2 41
Sit we close about this taper here, And call in question our necessities iv 3 165
Live you? or are you aught That man may question? . . *Macbeth* i 3 43
I burned in desire to question them further . . . . i 5 4
Let us meet, And question this most bloody piece of work . . ii 3 134
I pray you, speak not; he grows worse and worse; Question enrages him . . . . iii 4 118
It would be spoke to.—Question it, Horatio . . . *Hamlet* i 1 45
So like the king That was and is the question of these wars . . i 1 111
Finding By this encompassment and drift of question That they do know my son . . . . ii 1 10
But your news is not true. Let me question more in particular . ii 2 244
An aery of children, little eyases, that cry out on the top of question . ii 2 356
Unless the poet and the player went to cuffs in the question . . ii 2 373
Niggard of question; but, of our demands, Most free in his reply . iii 1 13
To be, or not to be: that is the question . . . . . iii 1 56
Some necessary question of the play be then to be considered . . iii 2 47
For 'tis a question left us yet to prove, Whether love lead fortune, or else fortune love . . . . iii 2 212
Go, go, you question with a wicked tongue . . . . . iii 4 12
And twenty thousand ducats Will not debate the question of this straw iv 4 26
I must call't in question.—So you shall . . . . . iv 5 217
I'll put another question to thee . . . . . . v 1 43
When you are asked this question next, say 'a grave-maker' . . v 1 65
So jump upon this bloody question . . . . . . v 2 386
I'ld have it come to question . . . . . . *Lear* i 3 13
And I have one thing, of a queasy question, Which I must act . . ii 1 19
And thou hadst been set i' the stocks for that question, thou hadst well deserved it . . . . ii 4 66
Made she no verbal question? . . . . iv 3 26
These domestic and particular broils Are not the question here . v 1 31
Thy great employment Will not bear question . . . . v 3 33
The question of Cordelia and her father Requires a fitter place . v 3 58
So may he with more facile question bear it . . . *Othello* i 3 23
Came it by request and such fair question As soul to soul affordeth? . i 3 113
Catechize the world for him; that is, make questions, and by them answer . . . . iii 4 17
Now will I question Cassio of Bianca . . . . . iv 1 94
There be some such, no question . . . . . . iv 3 63
Your being in Egypt Might be my question . . *Ant. and Cleo.* ii 2 40
If we contend, Out of our question wipe him . . . . . ii 2 81
When half to half the world opposed, he being The meered question . iii 13 10
And had, besides this gentleman in question, Two other sons *Cymbeline* i 1 34
I wonder, doctor, Thou ask'st me such a question . . . . i 5 11
Had I not brought The knowledge of your mistress home, I grant We were to question further . . . . ii 4 52
You shall not need . . . Further to question me . . *Pericles* i 3 12
Questionable. Thou comest in such a questionable shape That I will speak to thee . . . . *Hamlet* i 4 43
Questioned. I am question'd by my fears, of what may chance *W. Tale* i 2 11
Thou hast found mine; But how, is to be question'd . . . . v 3 139
With many holiday and lady terms He question'd me . . *1 Hen. IV.* i 3 47
To every county Where this is question'd send our letters . *Hen. VIII.* i 2 99
It is not to be question'd That they had gather'd a wise council to them ii 4 50
Still question'd me the story of my life, From year to year . *Othello* i 3 129
I and my brother are not known; yourself So out of thought, and thereto so o'ergrown, Cannot be question'd . . . *Cymbeline* iv 4 34
Questionedst. I would thou grew'st unto the shores o' the haven, And question'dst every sail. . . . . i 3 2
Questioning. Feed yourselves with questioning . . *As Y. Like It* v 4 144
Questionless. That I should questionless be fortunate *Mer. of Venice* i 1 176
She questionless with her sweet harmony And other chosen attractions, would allure. . . . . *Pericles* v 1 45
Questrists. His knights, Hot questrists after him, met him at gate *Lear* iii 7 17
Queubus. Of the Vapians passing the equinoctial of Queubus . *T. Night* ii 3 25
Quick. And be quick, thou'rt best, To answer other business . *Tempest* i 2 366
Though with their high wrongs I am struck to the quick . . . v 1 25
With such discourse as, I doubt not, shall make it Go quick away . v 1 304
I had rather be set quick i' the earth And bowl'd to death with turnips! *Mer. Wives* iii 4 90
Quick, quick! we'll come dress you straight: put on the gown the while . . . . iv 2 84
Speak, breathe, discuss; brief, short, quick, snap . . . . iv 5 3
What are they? let us know.—Ay, come; quick . . . . iv 5 44
Break off thy song, and haste thee quick away. . . *Meas. for Meas.* iv 1 7
Quick, dispatch, and send the head to Angelo . . . . iv 3 96
How dearly would it touch thee to the quick! . . *Com. of Errors* ii 2 132
Thy wit is as quick as the greyhound's mouth; it catches . *Much Ado* v 2 11
And therefore apt, because quick . . . . . *L. L. Lost* i 2 25
That an eel is ingenious?—That an eel is quick . . . . i 2 30
I do say thou art quick in answers: thou heatest my blood . . i 2 31
You must not be so quick. . . . . ii 1 118
A sweet touch, a quick venue of wit! snip, snap, quick, and home! . v 1 62
She's quick; the child brags in her belly already . . . . v 2 682
Then shall Hector be whipped for Jaquenetta that is quick by him . v 2 687
So quick bright things come to confusion . . . *M. N. Dream* i 1 149
Dark night, that from the eye his function takes, The ear more quick of apprehension makes . . . . iii 2 178
If thou say so, withdraw, and prove it too.—Quick, come! . . iii 2 256
Quick, quick, I pray thee; draw the curtain straight . *Mer. of Venice* ii 9 1
Jealous in honour, sudden and quick in quarrel . . *As Y. Like It* ii 7 151
There's my riddle: one that's dead is quick . . . *All's Well* v 3 304
O spirit of love! how quick and fresh art thou . . . *T. Night* i 1 9
Be yare in thy preparation, for thy assailant is quick, skilful and deadly . . . . iii 4 245
Not to be buried, But quick and in mine arms. . . . . *W. Tale* iv 4 132

Quick. Quick is mine ear to hear of good towards him . *Richard II.* ii 1 234
Come, quick, quick, that I may lay my head in thy lap . 1 *Hen. IV.* iii 1 230
Quick, forgetive, full of nimble fiery and delectable shapes 2 *Hen. IV.* iv 3 107
The mercy that was quick in us but late, By your own counsel is suppress'd and kill'd . *Hen. V.* ii 2 79
A breach that craves a quick expedient stop! . . . 2 *Hen. VI.* iii 1 288
My eye's too quick, my heart o'erweens too much . . 3 *Hen. VI.* iii 2 144
Or earth, gape open wide and eat him quick! . . . *Richard III.* i 2 65
Entertain good comfort, And cheer his grace with quick and merry words . . . . i 3 5
O, 'tis a parlous boy; Bold, quick, ingenious, forward, capable . . iii 1 156
Your reasons are too shallow and too quick . . . . iv 4 361
Now, Mars, I prithee, make us quick in work! . . *Coriolanus* i 4 10
With lines, That wound, beyond their feeling, to the quick *T. Andron.* iv 2 28
I have touch'd thee to the quick, Thy life-blood out . . . iv 4 36
An eagle, madam, Hath not so green, so quick, so fair an eye *R. and J.* iii 5 222
O true apothecary! Thy drugs are quick . . . . v 3 120
Thou'rt quick, But yet I'll bury thee . . . *T. of Athens* iv 3 44
I'll observe his looks; I'll tent him to the quick . . *Hamlet* ii 2 626
But, to the quick o' the ulcer:—Hamlet comes back . . iv 7 124
'Tis for the dead, not for the quick . . . . . . v 1 137
Now pile your dust upon the quick and dead . . . v 1 274
Be buried quick with her, and so will I . . . . v 1 302
In the most terrible and nimble stroke Of quick, cross lightning . *Lear* iv 7 35
Put it home: Quick, quick; fear nothing . . . *Othello* v 1 3
If in mirth, report That I am sudden sick: quick, and return *A. and C.* i 3 5
Assist, good friends.—O, quick, or I am gone . . . iv 15 31
Quick, quick, good hands . . . . v 2 39
Yare, yare, good Iras; quick. Methinks I hear Antony call . v 2 286
The air is quick there, And it pierces and sharpens the stomach *Pericles* iv 1 28
Be not tedious, For the gods are quick of ear . . . iv 1 70
Quick accumulation of renown . . . *Ant. and Cleo.* iii 1 19
Quick-answer'd, saucy, and As quarrelous as the weasel . *Cymbeline* iii 4 161
Quick appearance. This speedy and quick appearance argues proof Of your accustom'd diligence . . . . 1 *Hen. VI.* v 3 8
Quick Biron hath plighted faith to me . . . *L. L. Lost* v 2 283
Quick blood. And shall our quick blood, spirited with wine, Seem frosty? *Hen. V.* iii 5 21
Quick blows. These quick blows of Fortune's . . *T. of Athens* i 1 91
Quick celerity. Hence hath offence his quick celerity, When it is borne in high authority . . . *Meas. for Meas.* iv 2 113
Quick comedians, Extemporally will stage us . *Ant. and Cleo.* v 2 216
Quick-conceiving. To your quick-conceiving discontents I'll read you matter deep and dangerous . . . . . 1 *Hen. IV.* i 3 189
Quick condition. Our haste from hence is of so quick condition That it prefers itself . . . . *Meas. for Meas.* i 1 54
Quick conduct. To some provision Give thee quick conduct . *Lear* iii 6 104
Quick consideration. Give it quick consideration, for There is no primer business . . . . . *Hen. VIII.* i 2 66
Quick conveyance. And, for her sake, Madest quick conveyance with her good aunt Anne . . . . . *Richard III.* iv 4 283
Quick Cupid. I long to see Quick Cupid's post. . . *Mer. of Venice* ii 9 100
Quick curses. Give way, dull clouds, to my quick curses! *Richard III.* i 3 196
Quick determination. Which for to prevent, I have in quick determination Thus set it down . . . . *Hamlet* iii 1 176
Quick dexterity. You carried your guts away as nimbly, with as quick dexterity . . . . . . 1 *Hen. IV.* ii 4 286
Quick dispatch. Serious business, craving quick dispatch . *L. L. Lost* ii 1 31
Quick ear. You have a quick ear.—Ay, I would I were deaf *T. G. of Ver.* iv 2 63
Quick eye. An open ear, a quick eye, and a nimble hand, is necessary for a cut-purse . . . . *W. Tale* iv 4 685
Quick fire. If the quick fire of youth light not your mind, You are no maiden . . . . . *All's Well* iv 2 5
Quick forge. In the quick forge and working-house of thought *Hen. V.* v Prol. 23
Quick freshes. I'll not show him Where the quick freshes are *Tempest* iii 2 75
Quick hand. And something lean to cutpurse of quick hand . *Hen. V.* v 1 91
Quick hunting. If this poor trash of Venice, whom I trash For his quick hunting, stand the putting on . . . *Othello* ii 1 313
Quick lie. 'Tis a quick lie, sir . . . . *Hamlet* v 1 133
Quick mettle. He was quick mettle when he went to school . *J. Cæsar* i 2 300
Quick minds. O, then we bring forth weeds, When our quick minds lie still . . . . *Ant. and Cleo.* i 2 114
Quick motion. Incite them to quick motion . . *Tempest* iv 1 39
Quick pants. Make love's quick pants in Desdemona's arms *Othello* ii 1 80
Quick proceeders, marry! . . . . *T. of Shrew* iv 2 11
Quick-raised. With mighty and quick-raised power 1 *Hen. IV.* iv 4 12
Quick recreation. Is there no quick recreation granted? *L. L. Lost* i 1 162
Quick remove. Say, our pleasure, To such whose place is under us, requires Our quick remove . . . *Ant. and Cleo.* i 2 203
Quick sail. Yet but yaw neither, in respect of his quick sail *Hamlet* v 2 120
Quick sense. A woman of quick sense . . *Troi. and Cres.* iv 5 54
Quick spirit. I am not gamesome: I do lack some part Of that quick spirit that is in Antony . . . . . . *J. Cæsar* i 2 29
Quick venue. A sweet touch, a quick venue of wit! . *L. L. Lost* v 1 62
Quick wit. You have a quick wit . . . *T. G. of Ver.* i 1 132
Despite of his quick wit and his queasy stomach, he shall fall in love *Much Ado* ii 1 399
A tapster, and hath his quick wit wasted in giving reckonings 2 *Hen. IV.* i 2 193
Quick-witted. How likes Gremio these quick-witted folks? *T. of Shrew* v 2 38
Quick words. Dumb jewels often in their silent kind More than quick words do move a woman's mind . . *T. G. of Ver.* iii 1 91
Quicken. The mistress which I serve quickens what's dead . *Tempest* iii 1 6
Go and find him out And quicken his embraced heaviness *Mer. of Venice* ii 8 52
Music and poesy use to quicken you . . *T. of Shrew* i 1 36
That's able to breathe life into a stone, Quicken a rock . *All's Well* ii 1 77
My words are dull; O, quicken them with thine! *Richard III.* iv 4 124
If I have kill'd the issue of your womb, To quicken your increase, I will beget Mine issue of your blood upon your daughter . . iv 4 297
Naughty lady, These hairs, which thou dost ravish from my chin, Will quicken, and accuse thee . . . . . *Lear* iii 7 39
Even then this forked plague is fated to us When we do quicken *Othello* iii 3 277
As summer flies are in the shambles, That quicken even with blowing iv 2 67
By the fire That quickens Nilus' slime . . *Ant. and Cleo.* i 3 69
Welcome, welcome! die where thou hast lived: Quicken with kissing . iv 15 39
Quickened. When the mind is quicken'd . . . *Hen. V.* iv 1 20
Leaden age, Quicken'd with youthful spleen and warlike rage 1 *Hen. VI.* iv 6 13
Quickening. Methinks I see a quickening in his eye *Meas. for Meas.* v 1 500
Whereon Hyperion's quickening fire doth shine . *T. of Athens* iv 3 184
Quicker. Your hands than mine are quicker for a fray *M. N. Dream* iii 2 342

Quickest. On our quick'st decrees The inaudible and noiseless foot of Time Steals ere we can effect them . . . *All's Well* v 3 40
Quicklier. Virginity being blown down, man will quicklier be blown up i 1 135
Quickly, spirit; Thou shalt ere long be free . . . *Tempest* v 1 86
A fine volley of words, gentlemen, and quickly shot off . *T. G. of Ver.* ii 4 34
I'll quickly cross By some sly trick blunt Thurio's dull proceeding . ii 6 40
You would quickly learn to know him by his voice . . . . . iv 2 89
One Mistress Quickly, which is in the manner of his nurse . *Mer. Wives* i 2 3
Mette le au mon pocket: depeche, quickly . . . . . . i 4 57
De maid is love-a me: my nursh-a Quickly tell me so mush . . . iii 2 66
Quickly, quickly! Is the buck-basket— I warrant . . . . iii 3 2
Robert! John! Go take up these clothes here quickly . . . . iii 3 155
Carry them to the laundress in Datchet-mead; quickly, come . . iii 3 157
Shall we send that foolish carrion, Mistress Quickly, to him? . . iii 3 206
Break their talk, Mistress Quickly: my kinsman shall speak for himself iii 4 22
Here's Mistress Quickly, sir, to speak with you . . . . . iii 5 20
Come to her between eight and nine: I must carry her word quickly . iii 5 48
If he bid you set it down, obey him: quickly, dispatch . . . . iv 2 112
Send quickly to Sir John, to know his mind. I'll to the doctor . . iv 4 83
Away with her to the deanery, and dispatch it quickly . . . v 3 4
Say you so? then I shall pose you quickly . . *Meas. for Meas.* ii 4 51
'Tis best that thou diest quickly . . . . . . iii 1 151
Call upon me; and dispatch with Angelo, that it may be quickly . iii 1 279
Tell him he must awake, and that quickly too . . . iv 3 33
Did I think thou wouldst not quickly die . . . *Much Ado* iv 1 126
O for your reason! quickly, sir; I long . . . . *L. L. Lost* v 2 244
Will you hear the dialogue . . . ?—Call them forth quickly; we will do so v 2 899
Four days will quickly steep themselves in night; Four nights will quickly dream away the time . . . . *M. N. Dream* i 1 8
Thou lookest cheerly, and I'll be with thee quickly . *As Y. Like It* ii 6 15
Tell me who is it quickly, and speak apace . . . . iii 2 208
Made him give battle to the lioness, Who quickly fell before him . iv 3 132
Went they not quickly, I should die with laughing . *T. of Shrew* iii 2 243
Wish too, Since I nor wax nor honey can bring home, I quickly were dissolved from my hive . . . . *All's Well* i 2 66
One, that she's not in heaven, whither God send her quickly! the other, that she's in earth, from whence God send her quickly! . . ii 4 12
Give a favour from you To sparkle in the spirits of my daughter, That she may quickly come . . . . . . v 3 76
He would quickly have the gift of a grave . . *T. Night* i 3 34
Even so quickly may one catch the plague? . . . . i 5 314
How quickly the wrong side may be turned outward! . . . iii 1 14
They that dally nicely with words may quickly make them wanton . iii 1 17
Make him believe thou art Sir Topas the curate: do it quickly . iv 2 3
Or will not else thy craft so quickly grow, That thine own trip shall be thine overthrow? . . . . v 1 169
Since these good men are pleased, let them come in; but quickly now *W. Tale* iv 4 350
Speak, ho! speak quickly, or I shoot . . . *K. John* v 6 1
Yet depart not so; Though this be all, do not so quickly go . *Richard II.* i 2 64
What is six winters? they are quickly gone.—To men in joy . i 3 260
There's no respect how vile—That is not quickly buzz'd into his ears . ii 1 26
Quickly should this arm of mine, Now prisoner to the palsy, chastise thee ii 3 103
What sayest thou, Mistress Quickly? How doth thy husband? 1 *Hen. IV.* iii 3 106
From this swarm of fair advantages You took occasion to be quickly woo'd . . . . v 1 56
Which cannot choose but bring him quickly on . . . v 2 45
Sir John, I arrest you at the suit of Mistress Quickly . 2 *Hen. IV.* ii 1 49
Canst thou deny it? Did not goodwife Keech, the butcher's wife, come in then and call me gossip Quickly? . . . . . ii 1 102
Old Mistress Quickly and Mistress Doll Tearsheet . . . ii 2 166
'I' good faith, neighbour Quickly,' says he; Master Dumbe, our minister, was by then; 'neighbour Quickly,' says he, 'receive those that are civil' . . . . ii 4 96
How quickly nature falls into revolt When gold becomes her object! . iv 5 66
Is held from falling with so weak a wind That it will quickly drop . iv 5 101
It is certain, corporal, that he is married to Nell Quickly *Hen. V.* ii 1 20
I have, and I will hold, the quondam Quickly For the only she . ii 1 82
As ever you came of women, come in quickly to Sir John . . ii 1 123
And quickly bring us word of England's fall . . . . iii 5 68
Hot as gunpowder, And quickly will return an injury . . iv 7 189
If I could win a lady at leap-frog, . . . I should quickly leap into a wife v 2 145
Or we'll burst them open, if that you come not quickly . 1 *Hen. VI.* i 3 28
And interchanging blows I quickly shed Some of his bastard blood . iv 6 19
Henry is youthful and will quickly yield . . . . . v 3 99
We'll quickly hoise Duke Humphrey from his seat . 2 *Hen. VI.* i 1 169
Would make thee quickly hop without thy head . . . i 3 140
Off with your doublet quickly.—Alas, master, what shall I do? . ii 1 151
These few days' wonder will be quickly worn . . . . ii 4 69
These faults are easy, quickly answer'd . . . . . iii 1 133
A staff is quickly found to beat a dog . . . . . iii 1 171
This Gloucester should be quickly rid the world . . . . iii 1 233
Somerset comes with the queen: Go, bid her hide him quickly from the duke . . . . v 1 84
But when the duke is slain, they'll quickly fly . . . 3 *Hen. VI.* i 1 69
Think but upon the wrong he did us all, And that will quickly dry thy melting tears . . . . i 4 174
Make prepare for war; They are already, or quickly will be landed . iv 1 132
A little fire is quickly trodden out . . . . . . iv 8 7
Belike, unlook'd-for friends.—They are at hand, and you shall quickly know . . . . v 1 15
The city being but of small defence, We'll quickly rouse the traitors . v 1 65
Come quickly, Montague, or I am dead . . . . . v 2 39
Tread on the sand; why, there you quickly sink . . . v 4 30
Dorset your son . . . This fair alliance quickly shall call home *Rich. III.* iv 4 313
Pray, speak what has happen'd.—You may guess quickly what *Hen. VIII.* ii 1 7
Quickly draw out my command, Which men are best inclined *Coriolanus* i 6 84
Thou art made of tears, And tears will quickly melt thy life away *T. An.* iii 2 51
I strike quickly, being moved.—But thou art not quickly moved to strike.—A dog of the house of Montague moves me . *Rom. and Jul.* i 1 7
Come pentecost as quickly as it will, Some five and twenty years . i 5 38
If thou think'st I am too quickly won, I'll frown and be perverse . ii 2 95
My weapon should quickly have been out, I warrant you . . ii 4 166
Were it all yours to give it in a breath, How quickly were it gone! *T. of A.* ii 2 163
If it were done when 'tis done, then 'twere well It were done quickly *Macbeth* i 7 2
It were a good sign that I should quickly have a new father . . iv 2 63
If it be mine, Keep it not from me, quickly let me have it . . iv 3 200
Thou comest to use thy tongue; thy story quickly . . . v 5 29
To a nunnery, go, and quickly too. Farewell . . . *Hamlet* iii 1 143

Quickly. Let the superfluous and lust-dieted man . . . feel your power quickly . . . . *Lear* iv 1 72
If that the heavens do not their visible spirits Send quickly down to tame these vile offences, It will come . . . . . . iv 2 47
Quickly send, Be brief in it, to the castle ; for my writ Is on the life of Lear and on Cordelia . . . . v 3 244
He 's a good fellow, I can tell you that ; He 'll strike, and quickly too . v 3 285
If this suit lay in Bianca's power, How quickly should you speed ! *Othello* iv 1 109
'Tis a wrong in your own world, and you might quickly make it right . iv 3 82
Bring in the banquet quickly ; wine enough . . *Ant. and Cleo.* i 2 11
Let it be : I am quickly ill, and well, So Antony loves . . . i 3 72
Let his shames quickly Drive him to Rome . . . . . i 4 72
Let him not leave out The colour of her hair : bring me word quickly . ii 5 114
He could so quickly cut the Ionian sea, And take in Toryne . . iii 7 23
I know he'll quickly fly my friendship too . . . . *Cymbeline* v 3 62
Come to the matter.—All too soon I shall, Unless thou wouldst grieve quickly . . . . v 5 170
She quickly pooped him, she made him roast-meat for worms *Pericles* iv 2 25
Quickness. Must send thee hence With fiery quickness . . *Hamlet* iv 3 45
Quicksand. What Clarence but a quicksand of deceit? . . 3 *Hen. VI.* v 4 26
These quick-sands, Lepidus, Keep off them, for you sink *Ant. and Cleo.* ii 7 65
Quicksilver. The rogue fled from me like quicksilver . . 2 *Hen. IV.* ii 4 248
Swift as quicksilver it courses through The natural gates . *Hamlet* i 5 66
Quid. I cry you mercy, 'tis but Quid for Quo . . 1 *Hen. VI.* v 3 109
Quiddities. Mad wag ! what, in thy quips and thy quiddities ? 1 *Hen. IV.* i 2 51
Where be his quiddities now, his quillets, his cases, his tenures ? *Hamlet* v 1 107
Quiet. Be quiet. See'st thou here, This is the mouth o' the cell *Tempest* iv 1 215
Be you quiet, monster. Mistress line, is not this my jerkin? . . iv 1 235
I am glad he is so quiet . . . . *Mer. Wives* i 4 95
Jove would ne'er be quiet . . . . *Meas. for Meas.* ii 2 111
A wretched soul, bruised with adversity, We bid be quiet *Com. of Errors* ii 1 35
I will depart in quiet, And, in despite of mirth, mean to be merry . iii 1 107
Be quiet, people. Wherefore throng you hither? . . . . v 1 38
Be quiet and depart : thou shalt not have him . . . . v 1 112
While she is here, a man may live as quiet in hell as in a sanctuary *Much Ado* ii 1 266
Therefore I can be quiet . . . . *L. L. Lost* i 2 171
Let me quiet go . . . . *M. N. Dream* iii 2 314
Happy is your grace, That can translate the stubbornness of fortune Into so quiet and so sweet a style . . . . . *As Y. Like It* ii 1 20
The gain I seek is, quiet in the match . . . *T. of Shrew* ii 1 332
I will be angry : what hast thou to do? Father, be quiet . . iii 2 219
She is much out of quiet . . . . *T. Night* iii 3 144
You have undone a man of fourscore three, That thought to fill his grave in quiet . . . . *W. Tale* iv 4 465
Drive these men away, And I will sit as quiet as a lamb . . *K. John* iv 1 80
Lie In earth as quiet as thy father's skull . . . *Richard II.* iv 1 69
Be quiet ; 'tis very late, i' faith : I beseek you now . . 2 *Hen IV.* ii 4 174
For God's sake, be quiet . . . . ii 4 192
I would be quiet.—Sweet knight, I kiss thy neif . . . . . ii 4 199
Enforced from our most quiet there By the rough torrent of occasion . iv 1 71
To thee it shall descend with better quiet . . . . . iv 5 188
Could not keep quiet in his conscience . . . . *Hen. V.* i 2 79
Quiet thy cudgel ; thou dost see I eat . . . . . . v 1 54
Quiet yourselves, I pray, and be at peace . . . 1 *Hen. VI.* iv 1 115
Sweet aunt, be quiet ; 'twas against her will.—Against her will ! 2 *Hen. VI.* i 3 146
Thy greatest help is quiet . . . . ii 4 67
Thou shalt reign in quiet while thou livest . . . 3 *Hen. VI.* i 1 173
Cannot be quiet scarce a breathing-while . . . *Richard III.* i 3 60
I shall not sleep in quiet at the Tower.—Why, what should you fear? . iii 1 142
Quiet untroubled soul, awake, awake ! Arm, fight, and conquer ! . v 3 149
O my Wolsey, The quiet of my wounded conscience . *Hen. VIII.* ii 2 75
As well For your own quiet, as to rectify What is unsettled in the king ii 4 63
Let's sit down quiet, For fear we wake her . . . . . iv 2 81
Tread not upon him. Masters all, be quiet ; Put up your swords *Coriolanus* v 6 135
Have thrice disturb'd the quiet of our streets . . *Rom. and Jul.* i 1 98
Be quiet, or—More light, more light ! For shame ! I'll make you quiet i 5 89
That Romeo should, upon receipt thereof, Soon sleep in quiet . . iii 5 100
Knock, knock ; never at quiet ! What are you? . . . *Macbeth* ii 3 18
Grating so harshly all his days of quiet . . . . *Hamlet* iii 1 3
Good my lord, be quiet.—Why, I will fight with him upon this theme . v 1 288
An hour of quiet shortly shall we see ; Till then, in patience . . v 1 321
Upon malicious bravery, dost thou come To start my quiet . . *Othello* i 1 101
Of spirit so still and quiet, that her motion Blush'd at herself . . i 3 95
Practising upon his peace and quiet Even to madness . . . . ii 1 319
It were not for your quiet nor your good, Nor for my manhood, honesty iii 3 152
Not an hour, In the day's glorious walk, or peaceful night, The tomb where grief should sleep, can breed me quiet . . . *Pericles* i 2 5
Be quiet then as men should be, Till he hath pass'd necessity . ii Gower 5
Now, mild may be thy life ! . . . Quiet and gentle thy conditions ! . iii 1 29
For the love Of this poor infant, this fresh-new sea-farer, I would it would be quiet . . . . iii 1 42
Quiet beds. Thus are poor servitors, When others sleep upon their quiet beds, Constrain'd to watch in darkness . . . 1 *Hen. VI.* ii 1 6
Quiet breast. Truth hath a quiet breast . . . . *Richard II.* i 3 96
Quiet breath. One minute, nay, one quiet breath of rest . *K. John* iii 4 134
Quiet catch. No doubt but he hath got a quiet catch . . *T. of Shrew* ii 1 333
Quiet confines. From our quiet confines fright fair peace . *Richard II.* i 3 137
Quiet conscience. A still and quiet conscience . . *Hen. VIII.* iii 2 380
Quiet consummation have ; And renowned be thy grave ! . *Cymbeline* iv 2 280
Quiet course. The lethargy must have his quiet course . . *Othello* iv 1 54
Quiet days. As I hope For quiet days, fair issue, and long life *Tempest* iv 1 24
Quiet grave. Would bring white hairs unto a quiet grave . 3 *Hen. VI.* ii 5 40
Quiet guard. Have you had quiet guard?—Not a mouse stirring *Hamlet* i 1 10
Quiet hour. I could be well content To entertain the lag-end of my life With quiet hours . . . . 1 *Hen. IV.* v 1 25
Wretched Anne thy wife, That never slept a quiet hour with thee *Rich. III.* v 3 160
Quiet life. Peace it bodes, and love and quiet life . . *T. of Shrew* v 2 108
Fie upon this quiet life ! I want work . . . . 1 *Hen. IV.* ii 4 117
Haply this life is best, If quiet life be best . . . *Cymbeline* iii 3 30
Quiet night. I wish your highness A quiet night . . . *Hen. VIII.* v 1 77
Quiet o'er-posting. You may thank the unquiet time for your quiet o'er-posting that action . . . . 2 *Hen. IV.* i 2 171
Quiet ones. Let them go, a couple of quiet ones . . *T. of Shrew* iii 2 242
Quiet pass. To give quiet pass Through your dominions . . *Hamlet* ii 2 77
Quiet rest. And so, God give you quiet rest to-night ! . *Richard III.* v 3 43
Quiet soul. Now, quiet soul, depart when heaven please 1 *Hen. VI.* iii 2 110
Thou quiet soul, sleep thou a quiet sleep ; Dream of success ! *Richard III.* v 3 164
Quiet sword. He hath a killing tongue and a quiet sword . *Hen. V.* iii 2 36
Quiet walks. Who would live turmoiled in the court, And may enjoy such quiet walks as these? . . . . . . 2 *Hen. VI.* iv 10 19
Quiet watchman. You speak like an ancient and most quiet watchman *Much Ado* iii 3 42
Quieter. The house will be the quieter . . . . *T. Night* iii 4 147
Quietly. So shall you quietly enjoy your hope . . . *T. of Shrew* iii 2 138
Upon condition I may quietly Enjoy mine own . . . 1 *Hen. VI.* v 3 153
I will undertake Your grace shall well and quietly enjoy . . . v 3 159
I took an oath that he should quietly reign . . . 3 *Hen. VI.* i 2 15
These quarrels must be quietly debated . . . . *T. Andron.* v 3 20
Let me pass quietly . . . . *T. of Athens* iii 4 54
And let the foes quietly cut their throats, Without repugnancy? . . iii 5 44
Why the sepulchre, Wherein we saw thee quietly inurn'd, Hath oped his ponderous and marble jaws, To cast thee up again . . *Hamlet* i 4 49
Were as pretty a proportion to live quietly . . . *Pericles* iv 2 29
Quietness. Am arm'd To suffer, with a quietness of spirit *Mer. of Venice* iv 1 12
To stop effusion of our Christian blood And stablish quietness 1 *Hen. VI.* v 1 10
But give me worship and quietness ; I like it better . 3 *Hen. VI.* iv 3 16
I would have peace and quietness, but the fool will not . *Troi. and Cres.* ii 1 90
His remedies are tame i' the present peace And quietness *Coriolanus* iv 6 3
And quietness, grown sick of rest, would purge . . *Ant. and Cleo.* i 3 53
O, quietness, lady !—She is dead too . . . . . . iv 15 68
Quietus. Might his quietus make With a bare bodkin . . *Hamlet* iii 1 75
Quill. The wren with little quill . . . . . *M. N. Dream* iii 1 131
We may deliver our supplications in the quill . . . 2 *Hen. VI.* i 3 4
To stand an end, Like quills upon the fretful porpentine . *Hamlet* i 5 20
Quillets. Some tricks, some quillets, how to cheat the devil . *L. L. Lost* iv 3 288
But in these nice sharp quillets of the law, Good faith, I am no wiser than a daw . . . . 1 *Hen. VI.* ii 4 17
Do not stand on quillets how to slay him . . . 2 *Hen. VI.* iii 1 261
Never more false title plead, Nor sound his quillets shrilly *T. of Athens* iv 3 155
Where be his quiddities now, his quillets, his cases, his tenures? *Hamlet* v 1 108
Prithee, keep up thy quillets. There's a poor piece of gold for thee *Oth.* iii 1 25
Quilt. How now, blown Jack ! how now, quilt !—What, Hal ! 1 *Hen. IV.* iv 2 54
Quinapalus. For what says Quinapalus? 'Better a witty fool than a foolish wit' . . . . *T. Night* i 5 39
Quince. Good Peter Quince, say what the play treats on . *M. N. Dream* i 2 8
Now, good Peter Quince, call forth your actors by the scroll . . . i 2 15
Francis Flute, the bellows-mender.—Here, Peter Quince . . . i 2 45
Peter Quince,— What sayest thou, bully Bottom? . . . . iii 1 7
Heigh-ho ! Peter Quince ! Flute, the bellows-mender ! Snout, the tinker ! iv 1 207
I will get Peter Quince to write a ballad of this dream . . . iv 1 220
They call for dates and quinces in the pastry . . *Rom. and Jul.* iv 4 2
Quintain. And that which here stands up Is but a quintain, a mere lifeless block . . . . *As Y. Like It* i 2 263
Quintessence. The quintessence of every sprite . . . . iii 2 147
And yet, to me, what is this quintessence of dust? . . . *Hamlet* ii 2 321
Quintus. Of the same house Publius and Quintus were, That our best water brought by conduits hither . . . . . *Coriolanus* ii 3 249
Quip. Notwithstanding all her sudden quips, The least whereof would quell a lover's hope . . . . *T. G. of Ver.* iv 2 12
No quips now, Pistol ! . . . . *Mer. Wives* i 3 45
Shall quips and sentences and these paper bullets of the brain awe a man from the career of his humour? . . . . . . *Much Ado* ii 3 249
This is called the Quip Modest . . . . . . *As Y. Like It* v 4 79
The first, the Retort Courteous ; the second, the Quip Modest . . v 4 97
How now, mad wag ! what, in thy quips and thy quiddities ? 1 *Hen. IV.* i 2 51
Quire. The whole quire hold their hips and laugh . *M. N. Dream* ii 1 55
Placed a quire of such enticing birds, That she will light to listen 2 *Hen. VI.* i 3 92
Our cage We make a quire, as doth the prison'd bird . *Cymbeline* iii 3 43
Quired. My throat of war be turn'd, Which quired with my drum, into a pipe Small as an eunuch ! . . . . . . *Coriolanus* iii 2 113
Quiring. Still quiring to the young-eyed cherubins . *Mer. of Venice* v 1 62
Quirk. I may chance have some odd quirks and remnants of wit broken on me, because I have railed so long against marriage . *Much Ado* ii 3 245
I have felt so many quirks of joy and grief . . . *All's Well* iii 2 51
Belike this is a man of that quirk . . . . . *T. Night* iii 4 268
One that excels the quirks of blazoning pens . . . *Othello* ii 1 63
She has me her quirks, her reasons . . . . . *Pericles* iv 6 8
Quit. The very rats Instinctively have quit it . . . . *Tempest* i 2 148
All but mariners Plunged in the foaming brine and quit the vessel . i 2 211
'Tis best we stand upon our guard, Or that we quit this place . . ii 1 322
The general, subject to a well-wish'd king, Quit their own part *M. for M.* ii 4 28
Like doth quit like, and MEASURE still FOR MEASURE . . . v 1 416
Thou'rt condemn'd : But, for those earthly faults, I quit them all . v 1 488
Your evil quits you well . . . . v 1 501
But they shall find, . . . Ability in means and choice of friends, To quit me of them throughly . . . . *Much Ado* iv 1 202
To quit the fine for one half of his goods, I am content . *Mer. of Venice* iv 1 381
Till thou canst quit thee by thy brother's mouth . . *As Y. Like It* iii 1 11
Seize thee that list : if once I find thee ranging, Hortensio will be quit with thee by changing . . . . *T. of Shrew* iii 1 92
Though yet he never harm'd me, here I quit him . . . *All's Well* v 3 300
Your master quits you . . . . *T. Night* v 1 329
Quit his fortunes here, Which you knew great . . . *W. Tale* iii 2 168
Quit presently the chapel, or resolve you For more amazement . . v 3 86
To quit their griefs, Tell thou the lamentable tale of me . *Richard II.* v 1 43
I would I could Quit all offences with as clear excuse . 1 *Hen. IV.* iii 2 19
I think thou art quit for that . . . . . 2 *Hen. IV.* ii 4 371
Let it go which way it will, he that dies this year is quit for the next . iii 2 255
God quit you in his mercy ! Hear your sentence . . *Hen. V.* ii 2 166
How now, Captain Macmorris ! have you quit the mines? . . . iii 2 92
I sall quit you with gud leve, as I may pick occasion . . . iii 2 110
Let us quit all And give our vineyards to a barbarous people . . iii 5 3
Your great seats now quit you of great shames . . . . iii 5 47
So I would he were, and I by him, at all adventures, so we were quit here iv 1 122
How many would the peaceful city quit, To welcome him ! . . v Prol. 33
Unless the Lady Bona quit his pain . . . . 3 *Hen. VI.* iii 3 128
Plantagenet doth quit Plantagenet . . . . *Richard III.* iv 4 20
Thy Edward he is dead, that stabb'd my Edward ; Thy other Edward dead, to quit my Edward . . . . iv 4 64
If you do free your children from the sword, Your children's children quit it in your age . . . . v 3 262
God safely quit her of her burthen ! . . . . *Hen. VIII.* v 1 70
In mere spite, To be full quit of those my banishers . *Coriolanus* iv 5 89
To quit the bloody wrongs upon her foes . . . . *T. Andron.* i 1 141
Be trusty, and I'll quit thy pains . . . . *Rom. and Jul.* ii 4 204
Long live so, and so die. I am quit . . . . *T. of Athens* iv 3 397
Avaunt ! and quit my sight ! let the earth hide thee ! . . *Macbeth* iii 4 93
Is't not perfect conscience, To quit him with this arm? . . *Hamlet* v 2 68

Quit. If Hamlet give the first or second hit, Or quit in answer of the third exchange . . . . *Hamlet* v 2 280
Now quit you well . . . . *Lear* ii 1 32
Enkindle all the sparks of nature, To quit this horrid act . . . iii 7 87
Quit the house on purpose, that their punishment Might have the freer course . . . . iv 2 94
We must leave thee to thy sinking, for Thy dearest quit thee *A. and C.* iii 13 65
To let a fellow that will take rewards And say 'God quit you!' be familiar! iii 13 124
He may at pleasure whip, or hang, or torture, As he shall like, to quit me iii 13 151
Took such sorrow That he quit being . . . *Cymbeline* i 1 38
Of this contradiction you shall now be quit . . . . v 4 169
Let's quit this ground, And smoke the temple with our sacrifices . . 5 397
Even at the first Thy loss is more than can thy portage quit . *Pericles* iii 1 35
Pure surprise and fear Made me to quit the house . . . iii 2 18

Quite. On whom my pains, Humanely taken, all, all lost, quite lost *Temp.* iv 1 190
My former love Is by a newer object quite forgotten . *T. G. of Ver.* ii 4 195
Quite athwart Goes all decorum . . . *Meas. for Meas.* i 3 30
This virtuous maid Subdues me quite . . . . . ii 2 186
It is impossible to extirp it quite . . . . . iii 2 110
This deed unshapes me quite . . . . . . iv 4 23
And may it be that you have quite forgot A husband's office? *C. of Er.* iii 2 1
These be the stops that hinder study quite . . *L. L. Lost* i 1 70
Why, this was quite forgot . . . . . . i 1 142
Will kill the speaker's heart, And quite divorce his memory from his part v 2 150
Either I mistake your shape and making quite . . *M. N. Dream* ii 1 32
Quite over-canopied with luscious woodbine . . . ii 1 251
What hast thou done? thou hast mistaken quite . . . iii 2 88
Which, but for him . . ., Had quite miscarried . *Mer. of Venice* v 1 251
Swears brave oaths and breaks them bravely, quite traverse *As Y. L. It* iii 4 45
Pour'd all together, Would quite confound distinction . *All's Well* ii 3 127
But wise men, folly-fall'n, quite taint their wit . . *T. Night* iii 1 75
This ship-boy's semblance hath disguised me quite . . *K. John* iv 3 4
Giving full trophy, signal and ostent Quite from himself to God *Hen. V.* v Prol. 22
France is revolted from the English quite . . . *1 Hen. VI.* i 1 90
Thy sovereign, is not quite exempt From envious malice of thy swelling heart . . . . iii 1 25
And should, if I were worthy to be judge, Be quite degraded . . iv 1 43
Till Warwick or himself be quite suppress'd . . *3 Hen. VI.* iv 3 6
The observed of all observers, quite, quite down! . . *Hamlet* iii 1 162
Were nature's piece 'gainst fancy, Condemning shadows quite *A. and C.* v 2 100

Quittance. In any bill, warrant, quittance, or obligation . *Mer. Wives* i 1 10
That's all one; omittance is no quittance . . *As Y. Like It* iii 5 133
Rendering faint quittance, wearied and out-breathed . *2 Hen. IV.* i 1 108
Shall forget the office of our hand, Sooner than quittance of desert *Hen. V.* ii 2 34
As fitting best to quittance their deceit Contrived by art . *1 Hen. VI.* ii 1 14
Breeds the giver a return exceeding All use of quittance . *T. of Athens* i 1 291

Quitted. The father of this seeming lady and Her brother, having both their country quitted . . . . . . *W. Tale* v 1 192

Quitting. I should rob the deathsman of his fee, Quitting thee thereby of ten thousand shames . . . . . *2 Hen. VI.* iii 2 218

Quiver. If Cupid have not spent all his quiver in Venice . . *Much Ado* i 1 274
Why dost thou quiver, man?—The palsy, and not fear, provokes me *2 Hen. VI.* iv 7 97
The green leaves quiver with the cooling wind . . *T. Andron.* ii 3 14
I am so vexed, that every part about me quivers . *Rom. and Jul.* ii 4 171

Quiver fellow. There was a little quiver fellow . . *2 Hen. IV.* iii 2 301

Quivering. By her fine foot, straight leg and quivering thigh And the demesnes that there adjacent lie . . . . . *Rom. and Jul.* ii 1 19

Quo. I cry you mercy, 'tis but Quid for Quo . . . *1 Hen. VI.* v 3 109

Quod me alit, me extinguit . . . . . . *Pericles* ii 2 33

Quoif. Golden quoifs and stomachers . . . . . *W. Tale* iv 4 226
Hence, thou sickly quoif! Thou art a guard too wanton for the head *2 Hen. IV.* i 1 147

Quoint. Sir Robert Waterton and Francis Quoint . . *Richard II.* ii 1 284

Quoit him down, Bardolph, like a shove-groat shilling . *2 Hen. IV.* ii 4 206
A' plays at quoits well, and eats conger and fennel . . . ii 4 266

Quondam. A whole bookful of these quondam carpet-mongers *Much Ado* v 2 32
I did converse this quondam day with a companion . . *L. L. Lost* v 1 7
I have, and I will hold, the quondam Quickly For the only she *Hen. V.* ii 1 82
Here's a deer whose skin's a keeper's fee: This is the quondam king *3 Hen. VI.* iii 1 23

Quondam. Our quondam queen, You have a father able to maintain you *3 Hen. VI.* iii 3 153
Your quondam wife swears still by Venus' glove . *Troi. and Cres.* iv 5 179

Quoniam he seemeth in minority, Ergo I come with this apology *L. L. Lost* v 2 596

Quote. How quote you my folly?—I quote it in your jerkin *T. G. of Ver.* ii 4 18
His face's own margent did quote such amazes . . . *L. L. Lost* ii 1 245
So did our looks.—We did not quote them so . . . . v 2 796
See, brother, see; note how she quotes the leaves . . *T. Andron.* iv 1 50
What care I What curious eye doth quote deformities? . *Rom. and Jul.* i 4 31

Quoted. Her amber hair for foul hath amber quoted . . *L. L. Lost* iv 3 87
He's quoted for a most perfidious slave . . . *All's Well* v 3 205
Mark'd, Quoted and sign'd to do a deed of shame . . *K. John* iv 2 222
With exact view perused thee, Hector, And quoted joint by joint *T. and C.* iv 5 233
I am sorry that with better heed and judgement I had not quoted him *Hamlet* ii 1 112

Quoth. 'Lord,' quoth he! That a monster should be such a natural! *Tempest* iii 2 36
'Friend,' quoth I, 'you mean to whip the dog?' 'Ay, marry, do I,' quoth he. 'You do him the more wrong,' quoth I *T. G. of Ver.* iv 4 28
'Tis dinner-time,' quoth I; 'My gold!' quoth he. (Repeated) *C. of Er.* ii 1 62
'My mistress, sir,' quoth I; 'Hang up thy mistress! I know not thy mistress; out on thy mistress!'—Quoth who?—Quoth my master ii 1 67
Air, quoth he, thy cheeks may blow . . . *L. L. Lost* iv 3 109
Did these rent lines show some love of thine?—Did they, quoth you? . iv 3 221
Quoth the king, 'an angel shalt thou see; Yet fear not thou' . . v 2 103
Veal, quoth the Dutchman. Is not 'veal' a calf?—A calf, fair lady! . v 2 247
Dumain was at my service, and his sword: No point, quoth I . . v 2 277
'Poor deer,' quoth he, 'thou makest a testament As worldlings do' *As Y. Like It* ii 1 47
'Ay,' quoth Jaques, 'Sweep on, you fat and greasy citizens' . . ii 1 54
'Good morrow, fool,' quoth I. 'No, sir,' quoth he, 'Call me not fool' ii 7 18
'It is ten o'clock: Thus we may see,' quoth he, 'how the world wags' ii 7 23
'Be serviceable to my son,' quoth he . . . *T. of Shrew* i 1 219
'Frets, call you these?' quoth she; 'I'll fume with them' . . ii 1 153
Ask, if Katharine should be his wife, 'Ay, by gogs-wouns,' quoth he . iii 2 162
'A health!' quoth he, as if He had been aboard, carousing to his mates iii 2 172
'Let me not live,' quoth he, 'After my flame lacks oil' . . *All's Well* i 2 58
Was this fair face the cause, quoth she, Why the Grecians sacked Troy? i 3 74
'Have I no friend?' quoth he: he spake it twice . . *Richard II.* v 4 4
Lend me thy lantern, quoth he? marry, I'll see thee hanged first *1 Hen. IV.* ii 1 44
What, ho! chamberlain!—At hand, quoth pick-purse.—That's even as fair as—at hand, quoth the chamberlain . . . . . ii 1 53
'How now, Sir John!' quoth I: 'what, man! be o' good cheer' *Hen. V.* ii 3 18
Quoth my uncle Gloucester, 'Small herbs have grace' . *Richard III.* ii 4 12
'Thanks, gentle citizens and friends,' quoth I . . . . iii 7 38
'Be thou,' quoth I, 'accursed, For making me, so young, so old a widow!' iv 1 72
'Lo, thus,' quoth Dighton, 'lay those tender babes:' 'Thus, thus,' quoth Forrest . . . . iv 3 9
'Which once,' quoth Forrest, 'almost changed my mind; But O! the devil' . . . . iv 3 15
'When he,' quoth she, 'shall split thy heart with sorrow, Remember Margaret' . . . . v 1 26
'If,' quoth he, 'I for this had been committed' . . . *Hen. VIII.* i 2 193
'I do,' quoth he, 'perceive My king is tangled in affection' . . iii 2 34
Quoth she, 'Here's but two and fifty hairs on your chin.' (Repeated) *Troi. and Cres.* i 2 171
'True is it, my incorporate friends,' quoth he . . . *Coriolanus* i 1 134
'Shake,' quoth the dove-house: 'twas no need, I trow . *Rom. and Jul.* i 3 33
Took up the child: 'Yea,' quoth he, 'dost thou fall upon thy face?' . i 3 41
'Give me,' quoth I: 'Aroint thee, witch!' the rump-fed ronyon cries *Macb.* i 3 5
Quoth she, before you tumbled me, You promised me to wed *Hamlet* iv 5 63
Quoth he, 'Say, the firm Roman to great Egypt sends This' *A. and C.* i 5 42

Quoth a'. 'The humour of it,' quoth a'! here's a fellow frights English out of his wits . . . . *Mer. Wives* ii 1 142
One good woman in ten, madam; . . . One in ten, quoth a'! *All's Well* i 3 90
Ah, sirrah! quoth-a, we shall Do nothing but eat . . . *2 Hen. IV.* v 3 17
Sweet draught: 'sweet' quoth a'! sweet sink, sweet sewer *Tr. and Cr.* v 1 82
By my troth, it is well said; 'for himself to mar,' quoth a'? *R. and J.* ii 4 124
Pray see me buried.—Die quoth-a? Now gods forbid! . . *Pericles* ii 1 82

Quotidian. He seems to have the quotidian of love upon him *As Y. L. It* iii 2 383
He is so shaked of a burning quotidian tertian . . . *Hen. V.* ii 1 124

R

R. An R.—Ah, mocker! that's the dog's name; R is for the— *R. and J.* ii 4 222

Rabato. I think your other rabato were better . . . *Much Ado* iii 4 6

Rabbit. With your arms crossed on your thin-belly doublet like a rabbit on a spit . . . . *L. L. Lost* iii 1 19
As she went to the garden for parsley to stuff a rabbit . *T. of Shrew* iv 4 101
Away, you whoreson upright rabbit, away! . . . *2 Hen. IV.* ii 2 91

Rabbit-sucker. Hang me up by the heels for a rabbit-sucker . *1 Hen. IV.* ii 4 480

Rabble. Go bring the rabble, O'er whom I give thee power . *Tempest* iv 1 37
At his heels a rabble of his companions . . . *Mer. Wives* iii 5 76
My wife, her sister, and a rabble more . . . *Com. of Errors* v 1 236
With papers on my back, And follow'd with a rabble . . *2 Hen. VI.* ii 4 32
Ye have made a fine hand, fellows: There's a trim rabble let in *Hen. VIII.* v 4 75
The rabble should have first unroof'd the city, Ere so prevail'd *Coriolanus* i 1 222
We debase The nature of our seats and make the rabble Call our cares fears iii 1 136
'Twas you incensed the rabble: Cats, that can judge as fitly of his worth iv 2 33
And to be baited with the rabble's curse . . . . *Macbeth* v 8 29
The rabble call him lord . . . . *Hamlet* iv 5 102
And your disorder'd rabble Make servants of their betters . . *Lear* i 4 277

Rabblement. The rabblement hooted and clapped . . . *J. Cæsar* i 2 245

Race. But thy vile race, Though thou didst learn, had that in't which good natures Could not abide to be with . . . . . *Tempest* i 2 358
I have begun, And now I give my sensual race the rein *Meas. for Meas.* ii 4 160
A wild and wanton herd, Or race of youthful and unhandled colts *Mer. of Venice* v 1 72
Nutmegs, seven; a race or two of ginger, but that I may beg *W. Tale* iv 3 50
Make conceive a bark of baser kind By bud of nobler race . . . iv 4 95

Race. Sound on into the drowsy race of night . . . . *K. John* iii 3 39
Whose fruit thou art And never of the Nevils' noble race . *2 Hen. VI.* iii 2 215
Forspent with toil, as runners with a race, I lay me down . *3 Hen. VI.* ii 3 1
Live, and beget a happy race of kings! . . . . *Richard III.* v 3 157
And grant, as Timon grows, his hate may grow To the whole race of mankind, high and low! . . . . *T. of Athens* iv 1 40
Beauteous and swift, the minions of their race . . . *Macbeth* ii 4 15
None our parts so poor, But was a race of heaven . . *Ant. and Cleo.* i 3 37
My pillow left unpress'd in Rome, Forborne the getting of a lawful race iii 13 107
Thy crystal window ope; look out; No longer exercise Upon a valiant race thy harsh And potent injuries . . . . . . *Cymbeline* v 4 83
That pupils lacks she none of noble race . . . . *Pericles* v Gower 9

Rack. I'll rack thee with old cramps, Fill all thy bones with aches *Tempest* i 2 369
And, like this insubstantial pageant faded, Leave not a rack behind . iv 1 156
And rack thee in their fancies . . . . . *Meas. for Meas.* iv 1 65
Take him hence; to the rack with him! . . . . . . v 1 313
The duke Dare no more stretch this finger of mine than he Dare rack his own . . . . v 1 317
But being lack'd and lost, Why, then we rack the value . . *Much Ado* iv 1 222
Let me choose; For as I am, I live upon the rack.—Upon the rack! *Mer. of Venice* iii 2 25
I fear you speak upon the rack, Where men enforced do speak any thing iii 2 32
What wheels? racks? fires? what flaying? boiling? . . . *W. Tale* iii 2 177
An I were at the strappado, or all the racks in the world, I would not tell you on compulsion . . . . *1 Hen. IV.* ii 4 262

Rack. Even like a man new haled from the rack, So fare my limbs with long imprisonment . . . . 1 *Hen. VI.* ii 5 3
I must needs confess,— Without the rack . . . *Troi. and Cres.* i 2 152
A silence in the heavens, the rack stand still . . . *Hamlet* ii 2 506
He hates him much That would upon the rack of this tough world Stretch him out longer . . . . *Lear* v 3 314
Avaunt! be gone! thou hast set me on the rack . . . *Othello* iii 3 335
Even with a thought The rack dislimns, and makes it indistinct *A. and C.* iv 14 10
Racked. You must be purged too, your sins are rack'd *L. L. Lost* v 2 828
Try what my credit can in Venice do: That shall be rack'd *Mer. of Ven* i 1 181
How have the hours rack'd and tortured me, Since I have lost thee! *T. Night* v 1 226
The commons hast thou rack'd; the clergy's bags Are lank . 2 *Hen. VI.* i 3 131
Say he be taken, rack'd and tortured . . . . . iii 1 376
A pair of tribunes that have rack'd for Rome, To make coals cheap *Cor.* v 1 16
Racker. Such rackers of orthography . . . *L. L. Lost* v 1 21
Racket. It is a low ebb of linen with thee when thou keepest not racket there . . . . 2 *Hen. IV.* ii 2 23
When we have match'd our rackets to these balls . . *Hen. V.* i 2 261
Racking. Not separated with the racking clouds . . 3 *Hen. VI.* ii 1 27
Radiance. In his bright radiance and collateral light Must I be comforted, not in his sphere . . . . . . *All's Well* i 1 99
By the sacred radiance of the sun, The mysteries of Hecate . *Lear* i 1 111
Radiant. Our radiant queen hates sluts and sluttery . *Mer. Wives* v 5 50
Most radiant Pyramus, most lily-white of hue . . *M. N. Dream* iii 1 95
Most radiant, exquisite and unmatchable beauty . . *T. Night* i 5 181
So lust, though to a radiant angel link'd, Will sate itself . *Hamlet* i 5 55
Like the wreath of radiant fire On flickering Phœbus' front . *Lear* ii 2 113
Lamentable! What, To hide me from the radiant sun and solace I' the dungeon by a snuff? . . . . . . *Cymbeline* i 6 86
The marble pavement closes, he is enter'd His radiant roof . . v 4 121
The radiant Cymbeline, Which shines here in the west . . v 5 475
Radish. I know not what you call all; but if I fought not with fifty of them, I am a bunch of radish . . . . 1 *Hen. IV.* ii 4 206
Like a forked radish, with a head fantastically carved upon it 2 *Hen. IV.* iii 2 334
Raft. Where is that son That floated with thee on the fatal raft? *Com. of Er.* v 1 348
Rag. And yet you, rogue, will ensconce your rags . *Mer. Wives* ii 2 27
Her rags and the tallow in them will burn a Poland winter *Com. of Er.* iii 2 99
Heart and good-will you might; But surely, master, not a rag of money iv 4 89
What shalt thou exchange for rags? robes . . *L. L. Lost* iv 1 84
Away, thou rag, thou quantity, thou remnant! . . *T. of Shrew* iv 3 112
Pluck but off these rags; and then, death, death! . . *W. Tale* iv 3 56
Thou hast need of more rags to lay on thee, rather than have these off iv 3 58
That shakes the rotten carcass of old Death Out of his rags! . *K. John* ii 1 457
Led on by bloody youth, guarded with rags . . 2 *Hen. IV.* iv 1 34
The Duke of Suffolk muffled up in rags!—Ay, but these rags are no part of the duke: Jove sometime went disguised . 2 *Hen. VI.* iv 1 46
Thou rag of honour! thou detested— Margaret . *Richard III.* i 3 233
Lash hence these overweening rags of France, These famish'd beggars . v 3 328
If thou wilt curse, thy father, that poor rag, Must be thy subject *T. of A.* iv 3 271
In thy rags thou knowest none, but art despised for the contrary . iv 3 303
Tear a passion to tatters, to very rags, to split the ears of the groundlings . . . . *Hamlet* iii 2 11
Fathers that wear rags Do make their children blind . . *Lear* ii 4 48
Arm it [sin] in rags, a pigmy's straw does pierce it . . . iv 6 171
Taught me to shift Into a madman's rags . . . . . v 3 187
The poor soldier that so richly fought, Whose rags shamed gilded arms *Cymbeline* v 5 4
Ragamuffin. I have led my ragamuffins where they are peppered 1 *Hen. IV.* v 3 36
Rage. In her most unmitigable rage . . . . . *Tempest* i 2 276
I do not seek to quench your love's hot fire, But qualify the fire's extreme rage . . . . *T. G. of Ver.* ii 7 22
The current that with gentle murmur glides, Thou know'st, being stopp'd, impatiently doth rage . . . . ii 7 26
Besides this present instance of his rage, Is a mad tale he told *Com. of Er.* iv 3 88
And did not I in rage depart from thence?—In verity you did . iv 4 79
My bones bear witness, That since have felt the vigour of his rage . iv 4 81
Your husband all in rage to-day Came to my house . . . iv 4 140
Till this afternoon his passion Ne'er brake into extremity of rage . . v 1 48
Bearing thence Rings, jewels, any thing his rage did like . . v 1 144
Those pamper'd animals That rage in savage sensuality . . *Much Ado* iv 1 62
Would give perceptial medicine to rage, Fetter strong madness . . v 1 24
Poor soul, what art thou then? Food for his rage . *L. L. Lost* iv 1 95
Yet I have a trick Of the old rage: bear with me, I am sick . . v 2 417
The tipsy Bacchanals, Tearing the Thracian singer in their rage *M. N. D.* v 1 49
When lion rough in wildest rage doth roar . . . . v 1 225
And am arm'd To suffer, with a quietness of spirit, The very tyranny and rage of his . . . . . . *Mer. of Venice* iv 1 13
Since nought so stockish, hard and full of rage, But music for the time doth change his nature . . . . v 1 81
Have I not heard the sea puff'd up with winds Rage like an angry boar chafed with sweat? . . . . *T. of Shrew* i 2 203
Into a most hideous opinion of his rage, skill, fury . *T. Night* iii 4 213
With dagger of lath, In his rage and his wrath, Cries, ah, ha! to the devil iv 2 137
But see how it chafes, how it rages, how it takes up the shore! *W. Tale* iii 3 90
Or shall we give the signal to our rage And stalk in blood? *K. John* ii 1 265
Each army hath a hand; And in their rage, I having hold of both, They whirl asunder and dismember me . . . . iii 1 329
A rage whose heat hath this condition, That nothing can allay, nothing but blood . . . . iii 1 341
Thy rage shall burn thee up, and thou shalt turn To ashes . . iii 1 344
O, haste thee to the peers, Throw this report on their incensed rage! . iv 2 261
Forgive the comment that my passion made Upon thy feature; for my rage was blind . . . . iv 2 264
The vilest stroke That ever wall-eyed wrath or staring rage Presented to the tears of soft remorse . . . . iv 3 49
Lest I, by marking of your rage, forget Your worth . . . iv 3 85
Doth he still rage?—He is more patient Than when you left him . v 7 11
The Dauphin rages at our very heels . . . . . . v 7 80
Full of ire, In rage deaf as the sea, hasty as fire . . *Richard II.* i 1 19
Rage must be withstood: Give me his gage: lions make leopards tame i 1 173
Deal mildly with his youth; For young hot colts being raged do rage the more . . . . ii 1 70
One in fear to lose what they enjoy, The other to enjoy by rage and war ii 4 14
So high above his limits swells the rage Of Bolingbroke . . . iii 2 109
The rage be his, whilst on the earth I rain My waters . . . iii 3 59
The lion dying thrusteth forth his paw, And wounds the earth, if nothing else, with rage To be o'erpower'd . . . . . . v 1 30
Take thy correction mildly, kiss the rod, And fawn on rage . . v 1 33
When I was dry with rage and extreme toil, Breathless and faint 1 *Hen. IV.* i 3 31
Rage. Oftentimes it doth present harsh rage, Defect of manners 1 *Hen. IV.* iii 1 183
In rage dismiss'd my father from the court; Broke oath on oath . iv 3 100
The king before the Douglas' rage Stoop'd his anointed head 2 *Hen. IV.* Ind. 31
Headstrong riot hath no curb, When rage and hot blood are his counsellors iv 4 63
I will inflame thy noble liver, And make thee rage . . . v 5 34
Summon up the blood, Disguise fair nature with hard-favour'd rage *Hen. V.* iii 1 8
Abate thy rage, abate thy manly rage, Abate thy rage, great duke! . iii 2 24
Good bawcock, bate thy rage; use lenity, sweet chuck! . . . iii 2 26
In his rages, and his furies, and his wraths, and his cholers . . iv 7 37
And with wild rage Yerk out their armed heels at their dead masters . iv 7 82
Broke his word And left us to the rage of France his sword 1 *Hen. VI.* iv 6 3
Leaden age, Quicken'd with youthful spleen and warlike rage . iv 6 13
If I to-day die not with Frenchmen's rage, To-morrow I shall die with mickle age . . . . iv 6 34
And, like a hungry lion, did commence Rough deeds of rage . . iv 7 8
Dizzy-eyed fury and great rage of heart Suddenly made him from my side to start . . . . iv 7 11
O, were mine eye-balls into bullets turn'd, That I in rage might shoot them at your faces! . . . . iv 7 80
So, there goes our protector in a rage . . . . 2 *Hen. VI.* i 1 147
From treason's secret knife and traitors' rage . . . . iii 1 174
And stop the rage betime, Before the wound do grow uncurable . iii 1 285
And this fell tempest shall not cease to rage . . . . iii 1 351
Thy words move rage and not remorse in me . . . . iv 1 112
That winter lion, who in rage forgets Aged contusions . . . v 3 2
Poor queen! how love to me and to her son Hath made her break out into terms of rage! . . . . 3 *Hen. VI.* i 1 265
I dare your quenchless fury to more rage: I am your butt . . i 4 28
Bid'st thou me rage? why, now thou hast thy wish: Wouldst have me weep? . . . . i 4 143
For raging wind blows up incessant showers, And when the rage allays, the rain begins . . . . i 4 146
Why stand we like soft-hearted women here, Wailing our losses, Whiles the foe doth rage? . . . . ii 3 26
Warwick rages like a chafed bull . . . . ii 5 126
Tush, that was in thy rage: Speak it again . . . *Richard III.* i 2 188
In that shame still live my sorrow's rage! . . . . . i 3 278
My brother's love, the devil, and my rage . . . . . i 4 229
If I unwittingly, or in my rage, Have aught committed . . . ii 1 56
Your rage mistakes us.—The more shame for ye . . *Hen. VIII.* iii 1 101
As roused with rage with rage doth sympathize . . *Troi. and Cres.* i 3 52
Kingdom'd Achilles in commotion rages And batters down himself . ii 3 185
Frown on, you heavens, effect your rage with speed! . . . v 10 6
So putting him to rage, You should have ta'en the advantage *Coriolanus* ii 3 205
If, as his nature is, he fall in rage With their refusal, both observe and answer The vantage of his anger . . . . ii 3 266
Put not your worthy rage into your tongue; One time will owe another iii 1 241
Whose rage doth rend Like interrupted waters . . . . iii 1 248
This tiger-footed rage, when it shall find The harm of unscann'd swiftness, will too late Tie leaden pounds to's heels . . . . iii 1 312
A fearful army, led by Caius Marcius . . . , rages Upon our territories iv 6 76
Desire not To allay my rages and revenges with Your colder reasons . v 3 85
When you shall know—as in this rage, Provoked by him, you cannot . v 6 137
My rage is gone; And I am struck with sorrow . . . . v 6 148
If the winds rage, doth not the sea wax mad? . . *T. Andron.* iii 1 223
The emperor, in his rage, will doom her death . . . . iv 2 114
And the continuance of their parents' rage . . . *Rom. and Jul.* Prol. 10
That quench the fire of your pernicious rage With purple fountains . i 1 91
The reason that I have to love thee Doth much excuse the appertaining rage . . . . iii 1 66
And, in this rage, with some great kinsman's bone, As with a club, dash out my desperate brains . . . . iv 3 53
Alas, kind lord! He's flung in rage from this ingrateful seat *T. of Athens* iv 2 45
To give thy rages balm, To wipe out our ingratitude with loves . v 4 16
Then, dear countryman, Bring in thy ranks, but leave without thy rage v 4 39
I have seen The ambitious ocean swell and rage and foam . *J. Cæsar* i 3 7
Stir up their servants to an act of rage, And after seem to chide 'em ii 1 176
If I were disposed to stir Your hearts and minds to mutiny and rage . iii 2 127
Did he not straight In pious rage the two delinquents tear? . *Macbeth* iii 6 12
Unequal match'd, Pyrrhus at Priam drives; in rage strikes wide *Hamlet* ii 2 494
When he is drunk asleep, or in his rage . . . . . iii 3 89
For like the hectic in my blood he rages, And thou must cure me . iv 3 68
How much I had to do to calm his rage! Now fear I this will give it start again . . . . iv 7 193
Have a continent forbearance till the speed of his rage goes slower *Lear* i 2 182
The king is in high rage.—Whither is he going? . . . . ii 4 299
Tears his white hair, Which the impetuous blasts, with eyeless rage, Catch . . . . iii 1 8
Blow, winds, and crack your cheeks! rage! blow! . . . . iii 2 1
In the fury of his heart, when the foul fiend rages, eats cow-dung for sallets . . . . iii 4 137
O, then it moved her.—Not to a rage . . . . . . iv 3 18
Lest his ungovern'd rage dissolve the life That wants the means to lead it . . . . iv 4 19
'Twas yet some comfort, When misery could beguile the tyrant's rage . iv 6 63
Be comforted, good madam: the great rage, You see, is kill'd in him . iv 7 78
He that stirs next to carve for his own rage Holds his soul light *Othello* ii 3 173
As men in rage strike those that wish them best . . . . ii 3 243
The blow thou hadst Shall make thy peace for moving me to rage *Ant. and Cleo.* ii 5 70
When one so great begins to rage, he's hunted Even to falling . iv 1 7
Teach me, Alcides, thou mine ancestor, thy rage . . . . iv 12 44
When she saw . . . that your rage Would not be purged, she sent you word she was dead . . . . iv 14 123
Marry, yet The fire of rage is in him . . . . . *Cymbeline* i 1 77
I something fear my father's wrath; but nothing—Always reserved my holy duty—what His rage can do on me . . . . . . i 1 88
He rages; none Dare come about him . . . . . . iii 5 67
Fear no more the heat o' the sun, Nor the furious winter's rages . iv 2 259
Go travel for a while, Till that his rage and anger be forgot . *Pericles* i 2 107
Till the rough seas, that spare not any man, Took it in rage . . ii 1 138
Could I rage and roar As doth the sea she lies in, yet the end Must be as 'tis . . . . iii 1 10
To rage the city turn . . . . v 3 Gower 97
Raged. For young hot colts being raged do rage the more *Richard II.* ii 1 70
In war was never lion raged more fierce . . . . . ii 1 173
Rageth. Till some little time hath qualified the heat of his displeasure; which at this instant so rageth in him . . . . *Lear* i 2 178

Ragged. Unto a ragged fearful-hanging rock . . . *T. G. of Ver.* i 2 121
Herne the hunter, . . . Doth all the winter-time, at still midnight,
Walk round about an oak, with great ragg'd horns . *Mer. Wives* iv 4 31
With over-weather'd ribs and ragged sails . . *Mer. of Venice* ii 6 18
My voice is ragged : I know I cannot please you . . *As Y. Like It* ii 5 15
A wretched ragged man, o'ergrown with hair . . . . iv 3 107
The rest were ragged, old, and beggarly . . . *T. of Shrew* iv 1 140
The flinty ribs Of this hard world, my ragged prison walls *Richard II.* v 5 21
Ragged as Lazarus in the painted cloth . . . 1 *Hen. IV.* iv 2 27
Ten times more dishonourable ragged than an old faced ancient . iv 2 33
This worm-eaten hold of ragged stone . . . 2 *Hen. IV.* Ind. 35
Thou art a very ragged wart . . . . iii 2 152
Here's Wart ; you see what a ragged appearance it is . . . iii 2 279
Never shall you see that I will beg A ragged and forestall'd remission . v 2 38
Four or five most vile and ragged foils . . . *Hen. V.* iv Prol. 50
Their ragged curtains poorly are let loose . . . . . iv 2 41
The splitting rocks cower'd in the sinking sands And would not dash
me with their ragged sides . . . . . . 2 *Hen. VI.* iii 2 98
Surprised our forts And sent the ragged soldiers wounded home . iv 1 90
His army is a ragged multitude Of hinds and peasants . . . iv 4 32
Old Nevil's crest, The rampant bear chain'd to the ragged staff . v 1 203
A ragged fatal rock . . . . 3 *Hen. VI.* v 4 27
Rude ragged nurse, old sullen playfellow For tender princes !
Richard III. iv 1 102
The ragged entrails of the pit . . . . . *T. Andron.* ii 3 230
All headlong cast us down, And on the ragged stones beat forth our
brains . . . . v 3 133
Raggedest. Now bind my brows with iron ; and approach The ragged'st
hour that time and spite dare bring ! . . . . 2 *Hen. IV.* i 1 151
Raggedness. Your loop'd and window'd raggedness . . *Lear* iii 4 31
Raging. Throw it thence into the raging sea ! . . . *T. G. of Ver.* i 2 122
Ill digestions ; Thereof the raging fire of fever bred . *Com. of Errors* v 1 75
Nor heady-rash, provoked with raging ire . . . . . v 1 216
The raging rocks And shivering shocks Shall break the locks *M. N. Dream* i 2 33
Where two raging fires meet together They do consume the thing that
feeds their fury . . . . *T. of Shrew* ii 1 133
Time it is, when raging war is done, To smile at scapes and perils
overblown . . . . v 2 2
More furious raging broils Than yet can be imagined or supposed
1 *Hen. VI.* iv 1 185
This spark will prove a raging fire, If wind and fuel be brought to feed
it with . . . . 2 *Hen. VI.* iii 1 302
Where, from thy sight, I should be raging mad . . . . iii 2 394
For raging wind blows up incessant showers . . . 3 *Hen. VI.* i 4 145
What raging of the sea ! shaking of earth ! . . *Troi. and Cres.* i 3 97
There is a law in each well-order'd nation To curb those raging appetites ii 2 181
The winds, thy sighs ; Who, raging with thy tears, and they with them,
Without a sudden calm, will overset Thy tempest-tossed body
Rom. and Jul. iii 5 136
Still in motion Of raging waste ? It cannot hold . . *T. of Athens* ii 1 4
Thou'ldst shun a bear ; But if thy flight lay toward the raging sea,
Thou'ldst meet the bear i' the mouth . . . . . *Lear* iii 4 10
We have reason to cool our raging motions, our carnal stings *Othello* i 3 334
Being troubled with a raging tooth, I could not sleep . . . iii 3 414
She'll never stint, Make raging battery upon shores of flint . *Pericles* iv 4 43
Raging-wood. How the young whelp of Talbot's, raging-wood, Did flesh
his puny sword in Frenchmen's blood ! . . . 1 *Hen. VI.* iv 7 35
Ragozine. One Ragozine, a most notorious pirate . *Meas. for Meas.* iv 3 75
Satisfy the deputy with the visage Of Ragozine, more like to Claudio . iv 3 80
That brought you home The head of Ragozine for Claudio's . . . v 1 539
'Rah, tah, tah,' would a' say ; 'bounce' would a' say . 2 *Hen. IV.* iii 2 303
Rails against all married mankind . . . . . *Mer. Wives* iv 2 23
Did not her kitchen-maid rail, taunt, and scorn me ? *Com. of Errors* iv 4 77
And sometime rail thou like Demetrius . . . . *M. N. Dream* iii 2 362
And he rails, Even there where merchants most do congregate *M. of Ven.* i 3 49
Till thou canst rail the seal from off my bond, Thou but offend'st thy
lungs . . . . iv 1 139
I'll rail against all the first-born of Egypt . . *As Y. Like It* ii 5 63
We two will rail against our mistress the world and all our misery . iii 2 295
Can a woman rail thus ?—Call you this railing ? . . . . iv 3 42
And rail upon the hostess of the house . . . . *T. of Shrew* Ind. 2 88
An he begin once, he'll rail in his rope-tricks . . . . . i 2 112
Say that she rail ; why then I'll tell her plain She sings as sweetly as
a nightingale . . . . ii 1 171
Rails, and swears, and rates, that she, poor soul, Knows not which way
to stand, to look, to speak . . . . iv 1 187
If she chance to nod I'll rail and brawl . . . . . . iv 1 209
No slander in an allowed fool, though he do nothing but rail *T. Night* i 5 102
And why rail I on this Commodity ? . . . . . *K. John* ii 1 587
Whiles I am a beggar, I will rail And say there is no sin but to be rich ii 1 593
Forgiveness, horse ! why do I rail on thee ? . . . *Richard II.* v 5 90
That I in all despite might rail at him . . . . 3 *Hen. VI.* ii 6 81
Strike alarum, drums ! Let not the heavens hear these tell-tale women
Rail on the Lord's anointed . . . . . *Richard III.* iv 4 150
You i' the camlet, get up o' the rail . . . . *Hen. VIII.* v 4 93
Rails on our state of war, Bold as an oracle . . *Troi. and Cres.* i 3 191
I shall sooner rail thee into wit and holiness . . . . . ii 1 17
I bade the vile owl go learn me the tenour of the proclamation, and he
rails upon me . . . . ii 1 100
He beats me, and I rail at him : O, worthy satisfaction ! . . . ii 3 3
Who's there ? Thersites ! Good Thersites, come in and rail . . ii 3 26
That I might rail at him, to ease my mind ! . . . *T. Andron.* ii 4 35
If I should be bribed too, there would be none left to rail upon thee,
and then thou wouldst sin the faster . . . *T. of Athens* i 2 245
An you begin to rail on society once, I am sworn not to give regard to
you . . . . i 2 250
Who can speak broader than he that has no house to put his head in ?
such may rail against great buildings . . . . . . iii 4 65
What a monstrous fellow art thou, thus to rail on one that is neither
known of thee nor knows thee ! . . . . . . *Lear* ii 2 28
See how yond justice rails upon yond simple thief . . . . iv 6 155
After her.—'Faith, I must ; she'll rail in the street else . *Othello* iv 1 170
Rail thou in Fulvia's phrase ; and taunt my faults *Ant. and Cleo.* i 2 111
Let me rail so high, That the false housewife Fortune break her wheel iv 15 43
To commix With winds that sailors rail at . . . *Cymbeline* iv 2 56
Railed. Forsworn my company and rail'd at me . . *T. G. of Ver.* iii 2 4
Railed at herself, that she should be so immodest to write . *Much Ado* ii 3 147
I have railed so long against marriage : but doth not the appetite alter ? ii 3 246
Thou hast railed on thyself . . . . . . *A. Y. Like It* i 1 65
Rail'd on Lady Fortune in good terms, In good set terms . . . ii 7 16
Railed. Enlarge the man committed yesterday, That rail'd against our
person . . . . *Hen. V.* ii 2 41
Railed upon me till her pinked porringer fell off her head *Hen. VIII.* v 4 50
He beats me, and I rail at him : O, worthy satisfaction ! would it were
otherwise ; that I could beat him, whilst he railed at me *Tr. and Cr.* ii 3 5
Insulted, rail'd, And put upon him such a deal of man . . *Lear* ii 2 126
Railer. Take that, thou likeness of this railer here . . . 3 *Hen. VI.* v 5 38
Railest. Thou grumblest and railest every hour . . *Troi. and Cres.* ii 1 35
Why rail'st thou on thy birth, the heaven, and earth ? . *Rom. and Jul.* iii 3 119
Raileth. Like a poor beggar, raileth on the rich . . . *K. John* ii 1 592
Railing. It seems his sleeps were hinder'd by thy railing *Com. of Errors* v 1 71
Call you this railing ? . . . . *As Y. Like It* iv 3 43
Did you ever hear such railing ? . . . . iv 3 46
Nor no railing in a known discreet man . . . . *T. Night* i 5 102
O, he is as tedious As a tired horse, a railing wife . . 1 *Hen. IV.* iii 1 160
I speak not to that railing Hecate, But unto thee . . 1 *Hen. VI.* iii 2 64
His railing is intolerable . . . . 2 *Hen. VI.* iii 1 172
I am a rascal ; a scurvy railing knave . . . . *Troi. and Cres.* v 4 30
Raiment. I have took upon me Such an immodest raiment *T. G. of Ver.* v 4 106
What raiment will your honour wear to-day ? . . *T. of Shrew* Ind. 2 4
Ne'er ask me what raiment I'll wear ; for I have no more doublets than
backs . . . . Ind. 2 8
I'll pull them off myself, Yea, all my raiment, to my petticoat . . ii 1 5
Our raiment And state of bodies would bewray what life We have led *Cor.* v 3 94
Make his wrongs His outsides, to wear them like his raiment *T. of Athens* iii 5 33
On my knees I beg That you'll vouchsafe me raiment, bed, and food *Lear* ii 4 158
Rain. Heavens rain grace On that which breeds between 'em ! *Tempest* iii 1 75
Let the sky rain potatoes . . . . *Mer. Wives* v 5 21
Is't not drowned i' the last rain ? . . . . . *Meas. for Meas.* iii 2 51
Stand thee close, then, under this penthouse, for it drizzles rain *M. Ado* iii 3 111
Your mistresses dare never come in rain, For fear their colours should
be wash'd away . . . . *L. L. Lost* iv 3 270
Why is your cheek so pale ? How chance the roses there do fade so
fast ?—Belike for want of rain . . . . . *M. N. Dream* i 1 130
The quality of mercy is not strain'd, It droppeth as the gentle rain from
heaven Upon the place beneath . . . . . *Mer. of Venice* iv 1 185
That the property of rain is to wet and fire to burn . *As Y. Like It* iii 2 27
Like foggy south puffing with wind and rain . . . . . iii 5 50
More clamorous than a parrot against rain, more new-fangled than an ape iv 1 152
If the boy have not a woman's gift To rain a shower of commanded tears,
An onion will do . . . . *T. of Shrew* Ind. 1 125
Most excellent accomplished lady, the heavens rain odours on you ! *T. N.* iii 1 96
That youth's a rare courtier : 'Rain odours' ; well . . . . iii 1 97
With hey, ho, the wind and the rain . . . . v 1 399 ; *Lear* iii 2 75
For the rain it raineth every day . . . . *T. Night* v 1 401 ; *Lear* iii 2 77
Being as like As rain to water, or devil to his dam . . . *K. John* ii 1 128
Our thunder from the south Shall rain their drift of bullets on this town ii 1 412
Will rain hot vengeance on offenders' heads . . . . *Richard II.* i 2 8
The rage be his, whilst on the earth I rain My waters . . . . iii 3 59
So came I a widow ; And never shall have length of life enough To rain
upon remembrance with mine eyes . . . . . 2 *Hen. IV.* ii 3 59
How now ! rain within doors, and none abroad ! . . . . . v 5 9
Constrain'd to watch in darkness, rain, and cold . . . 1 *Hen. VI.* ii 1 7
If Talbot do but thunder, rain will follow . . . . ii 2 59
Nor let the rain of heaven wet this place . . . . 2 *Hen. VI.* iii 2 341
For raging wind blows up incessant showers, And when the rage allays,
the rain begins . . . . 3 *Hen. VI.* i 4 146
He plies her hard ; and much rain wears the marble . . . . iii 2 50
The standers-by had wet their cheeks, Like trees bedash'd with rain
Richard III. i 2 164
Where are my tears ? rain, to lay this wind, or my heart will be blown
up by the root . . . . *Troi. and Cres.* iv 4 55
They will out of their burrows, like conies after rain *Coriolanus* iv 5 226
Be your heart to them As unrelenting flint to drops of rain *T. Andron.* ii 3 141
O earth, I will befriend thee more with rain, That shall distil from these
two ancient urns, Than youthful April shall . . . . . iii 1 16
But for the sunset of my brother's son It rains downright *Rom. and Jul.* iii 5 129
Rain sacrificial whisperings in his ear . . . . *T. of Athens* i 1 81
When shall we three meet again In thunder, lightning, or in rain ? *Macbeth* i 1 2
It will be rain to-night.—Let it come down . . . . . . iii 3 16
Is there not rain enough in the sweet heavens To wash it white ? *Hamlet* iii 3 45
Will pack when it begins to rain, And leave thee in the storm . *Lear* ii 4 81
Strives in his little world of man to out-scorn The to-and-fro-conflicting
wind and rain . . . . iii 1 11
Spit, fire ! spout, rain ! Nor rain, wind, thunder, fire, are my daughters iii 2 15
Such groans of roaring wind and rain I never Remember to have heard iii 2 47
Yet, poor old heart, he holp the heavens to rain . . . . . iii 7 62
You have seen Sunshine and rain at once . . . . iv 3 20
When the rain came to wet me once, and the wind to make me chatter . iv 6 102
She makes a shower of rain as well as Jove . . *Ant. and Cleo.* i 2 156
Dissolve, thick cloud, and rain ; that I may say, The gods themselves do
weep ! . . . . v 2 302
When we shall hear The rain and wind beat dark December . *Cymbeline* iii 3 37
Wind, rain, and thunder, remember, earthly man Is but a substance that
must yield to you . . . . *Pericles* ii 1 2
Rainbow. I was beaten myself into all the colours of the rainbow *M. Wives* iv 5 119
He hath ribbons of all the colours i' the rainbow . . . *W. Tale* iv 4 206
To smooth the ice, or add another hue Unto the rainbow . . *K. John* iv 2 14
Rained. Showers of blood Rain'd from the wounds of slaughter'd
Englishmen . . . . *Richard II.* iii 3 44
In short space It rain'd down fortune showering on your head 1 *Hen. IV.* v 1 47
My power rain'd honour more On you than any . . . *Hen. VIII.* iii 2 185
And in his grave rain'd many a tear . . . . . . *Hamlet* iv 5 166
Had they rain'd All kinds of sores and shames on my bare head *Othello* iv 2 48
Bestow'd his lips on that unworthy place, As it rain'd kisses *A. and C.* iii 13 85
Raineth. For the rain it raineth every day . . *T. Night* v 1 401 ; *Lear* iii 2 77
Raining the tears of lamentation . . . . . . *L. L. Lost* v 2 819
Rain-water. Court holy-water in a dry house is better than this rain-
water out o' door . . . . *Lear* iii 2 11
Rainy. Make dust our paper and with rainy eyes Write sorrow on the
bosom of the earth . . . . *Richard II.* iii 2 146
All besmirch'd With rainy marching in the painful field . . *Hen. V.* iv 3 111
Laugh'd so heartily, That both mine eyes were rainy like to his *T. An.* v 1 117
Raise up the organs of her fantasy . . . . . . *Mer. Wives* v 5 55
I'll raise all Windsor . . . . v 5 223
As this is true, Let me in safety raise me from my knees ! *Meas. for Meas.* v 1 231
Neither have I money nor commodity To raise a present sum *Mer. of Ven.* i 1 179
I cannot instantly raise up the gross Of full three thousand ducats . i 3 56
Mark me now ; now will I raise the waters . . . . . . ii 2 51
This making of Christians will raise the price of hogs . . . . iii 5 26

Raise. In converting Jews to Christians, you raise the price of pork *Mer. of Venice* iii 5 38
If the scorn of your bright eyne Have power to raise such love *As Y. L. It* iv 3 51
Her sister Began to scold and raise up such a storm . *T. of Shrew* i 1 177
This business Will raise us all.—To laughter, as I take it *W. Tale* ii 1 198
Raise the power of France upon his head, Unless he do submit *K. John* iii 1 193
O, if you raise this house against this house, It will the woefullest division prove That ever fell upon this cursed earth *Richard II.* iv 1 145
If thou have power to raise him, bring him hither 1 *Hen. IV.* iii 1 60
We were enforced, for safety sake, to . . . raise this present head v 1 66
We of the spiritualty Will raise your highness such a mighty sum *Hen. V.* i 2 133
His powers are yet not ready To raise so great a siege . iii 3 47
Take her, fair son, and from her blood raise up Issue to me . v 2 376
Let's raise the siege: why live we idly here? . . . . 1 *Hen. VI.* i 2 13
Ordained is to raise this tedious siege . . . . i 2 53
This night the siege assuredly I'll raise . . . . i 2 130
Leave off delays, and let us raise the siege . . . . i 2 146
Joan la Pucelle . . . Is come with a great power to raise the siege . i 4 103
How haps it I seek not to advance Or raise myself? . . iii 1 32
To raise a mutiny betwixt yourselves . . . . iv 1 131
Then will I raise aloft the milk-white rose . . 2 *Hen. VI.* i 1 254
Whom we raise, We will make fast within a hallow'd verge . i 4 24
Or why thou . . . Should raise so great a power without his leave . v 1 21
He, but a duke, would have his son a king, And raise his issue 3 *Hen. VI.* ii 2 22
Before it pleased his majesty To raise my state to title of a queen . iv 1 68
When the morning sun shall raise his car Above the border of this horizon . . . . iv 7 80
I'll learn to conjure and raise devils . . *Troi. and Cres.* ii 3 6
Thou must not stay: Hie to the Goths, and raise an army *T. Andron.* iii 1 286
Now will I to the Goths, and raise a power, To be revenged on Rome . iii 1 300
'Twould anger him To raise a spirit in his mistress' circle *Rom. and Jul.* ii 1 24
And in his mistress' name I conjure only but to raise up him ii 1 29
Run to the Capulets: Raise up the Montagues . . . v 3 178
I will raise her statue in pure gold . . . . v 3 299
Raise me this beggar, and deny't that lord . . *T. of Athens* iv 3 9
I can raise no money by vile means . . . . *J. Cæsar* iv 3 71
It may be I shall raise you by and by On business . . iv 3 247
Distill'd by magic sleights Shall raise such artificial sprites . *Macbeth* iii 5 27
That eyeless head of thine was first framed flesh To raise my fortunes *Lear* iv 6 232
Get more tapers; Raise all my kindred . . . . *Othello* i 1 168
Raise some special officers of night . . . . . i 1 183
It raises the greater war between him and his discretion *Ant. and Cleo.* ii 7 10
Lady, I'll raise the preparation of a war Shall stain your brother . iii 4 26
Raised. Which raised in me An undergoing stomach . *Tempest* i 2 156
He hath raised the wall and houses too . . . . ii 1 87
I did say so, When first I raised the tempest . . . v 1 6
I am waked with it when I sleep; raised with it when I sit *Com. of Errors* iv 4 36
The villain Jew with outcries raised the duke . . *Mer. of Venice* ii 8 4
Thou know'st she has raised me from my sickly bed . . *All's Well* ii 3 118
A spirit raised from depth of under-ground . . 2 *Hen. VI.* i 2 79
Retire to Killingworth, Until a power be raised to put them down . iv 4 40
I was the chief that raised him to the crown, And I'll be chief to bring him down again . . . . 3 *Hen. VI.* iii 3 262
Those powers that the queen Hath raised in Gallia have arrived our coast . . . . v 3 8
By Him that raised me to this careful height . . *Richard III.* i 3 83
One raised in blood, and one in blood establish'd . . . v 3 247
Buckingham, Who first raised head against usurping Richard *Hen. VIII.* ii 1 108
To be commanded For ever by your grace, whose hand has raised me . ii 2 120
Those twins of learning that he raised in you, Ipswich and Oxford iv 2 58
Raised only, that the weaker sort may wish Good Marcius home again *Coriolanus* iv 6 69
I raised him, and I pawn'd Mine honour for his truth . v 6 21
Love is a smoke raised with the fume of sighs . *Rom. and Jul.* i 1 196
Where is the county's page, that raised the watch? . . . v 3 279
Deserves an heir more raised Than one which holds a trencher *T. of A.* i 1 119
He raised a sigh so piteous and profound . . . *Hamlet* ii 1 94
He raised the house with loud and coward cries . . *Lear* ii 4 43
This hard house—More harder than the stones whereof 'tis raised . iii 2 64
Lead to the Sagittary the raised search . . . *Othello* i 1 159
What lights come yond?—Those are the raised father and his friends . i 2 29
Many of the consuls, raised and met, Are at the duke's already . i 2 43
Neither my place nor aught I heard of business Hath raised me from my bed . . . . i 3 54
Look, if my gentle love be not raised up! I'll make thee an example . ii 3 250
Nay, the dust Should have ascended to the roof of heaven, Raised by your populous troops . . . *Ant. and Cleo.* iii 6 50
Raising. Your reason For raising this sea-storm? . . *Tempest* i 2 177
Chased us away, till raising of more aid We came again . *Com. of Errors* v 1 153
She has raised me from my sickly bed.—But follows it, my lord, to bring me down Must answer for your raising? . . . . *All's Well* ii 3 120
To save our heads by raising of a head . . . 1 *Hen. IV.* i 3 284
Raising up wicked spirits from under ground . . 2 *Hen. VI.* ii 1 174
His raising; Nothing but his report . . . . *Coriolanus* iv 6 60
Raisins. Four pound of prunes, and as many of raisins o' the sun *W. Tale* iv 3 52
Rake. My love is buried.—Sweet lady, let me rake it from the earth *T. G. of Ver.* iv 2 116
If you hide the crown Even in your hearts, there will he rake for it *Hen. V.* ii 4 98
How, i' the name of thrift, Does he rake this together! . . *Hen. VIII.* iii 2 110
Let us revenge this with our pikes, ere we become rakes . *Coriolanus* i 1 24
Here, in the sands, Thee I'll rake up, the post unsanctified Of murderous lechers . . . . *Lear* iv 6 281
Raked. From the dust of old oblivion raked . . . *Hen. V.* ii 4 87
Raker. I am joined with no foot-land rakers . . . 1 *Hen. IV.* ii 1 81
Ralph. There were none fine but Adam, Ralph, and Gregory *T. of Shrew* iv 1 139
Francis!—Anon, anon, sir. Look down into the Pomgarnet, Ralph 1 *Hen. IV.* ii 4 42
So, so, so: yea, marry, sir: Ralph Mouldy! . . 2 *Hen. IV.* iii 2 109
Ram. The ewes, being rank, In the end of autumn turned to the rams *Mer. of Venice* i 3 82
Is your gold and silver ewes and rams?—I cannot tell; I make it breed as fast: But note me, signior . . . . i 3 96
That is another simple sin in you, to bring the ewes and the rams together . . . . *As Y. Like It* iii 2 83
A crooked-pated, old, cuckoldly ram . . . . . iii 2 87
There was never any thing so sudden but the fight of two rams . v 2 34
Jupiter Became a bull, and bellow'd; the green Neptune A ram *W. Tale* iv 4 29
Like rams In the old time of war, would shake the press *Hen. VIII.* iv 1 77
Ram. So that the ram that batters down the wall, For the great swing and rudeness of his poise, They place before his hand that made the engine . . . . *Troi. and Cres.* i 3 206
The Bull, being gall'd, gave Aries such a knock That down fell both the Ram's horns in the court . . . . . . *T. Andron.* iv 3 72
An old black ram Is tupping your white ewe . . . . *Othello* i 1 88
Ram thou thy fruitful tidings in mine ears . . *Ant. and Cleo.* ii 5 24
Let not the piece of virtue, which is set Betwixt us as the cement of our love, To keep it builded, be the ram to batter The fortress of it . iii 2 30
Rambures, Vaudemont, Beaumont, Grandpré, Roussi . *Hen. V.* iii 5 43
The master of the cross-bows, Lord Rambures . . . . iv 8 99
Rammed me in with foul shirts and smocks . . . *Mer. Wives* iii 5 90
Till that time Have we ramm'd up our gates against the world *K. John* ii 1 272
Rampallian. You rampallian! you fustilarian! . . 2 *Hen. IV.* ii 1 65
Rampant. The rampant bear chain'd to the ragged staff . 2 *Hen. VI.* v 1 203
Ramping. A ramping fool, to brag and stamp and swear! . *K. John* iii 1 122
A moulten raven, A couching lion and a ramping cat! . 1 *Hen. IV.* iii 1 153
Under whose shade the ramping lion slept . . . 3 *Hen. VI.* v 2 13
Rampired. Set but thy foot Against our rampired gates, and they shall ope *T. of Athens* v 4 47
Ramps. Whiles he is vaulting variable ramps, In your despite *Cymbeline* i 6 134
Ramston. Sir John Ramston, Sir John Norbery . . *Richard II.* ii 1 283
Ram-tender. An old sheep-whistling rogue, a ram-tender *W. Tale* iv 4 805
Ran. I guess it stood in her chin, by the salt rheum that ran *C. of Er.* iii 2 131
That I amazed ran from her as a witch . . . . . iii 2 149
She that would be your wife now ran from you . . . iv 4 152
I gain'd my freedom and immediately Ran hither . . . v 1 251
When he ran in here, These people saw the chain about his neck . v 1 257
I freely told you, all the wealth I had Ran in my veins . *Mer. of Venice* iii 2 258
In such a night Did Thisbe fearfully o'ertrip the dew And saw the lion's shadow ere himself And ran dismay'd away . . . . v 1 9
How I cried, how the horses ran away, how her bridle was burst *T. of S.* iv 1 82
The prettiest low-born lass that ever Ran on the green-sward *W. Tale* iv 4 157
Ran fearfully among the trembling reeds . . . 1 *Hen. IV.* i 3 105
You are lions too, you ran away upon instinct . . . ii 4 331
'Faith, I ran when I saw others run . . . . . ii 4 333
The goats ran from the mountains, and the herds Were strangely clamorous . . . . iii 1 39
Didst thou come from Shrewsbury?—I ran from Shrewsbury 2 *Hen. IV.* i 1 65
You knew me, as you did when you ran away by Gad's-hill . . ii 4 333
Cowardly rascals that ran from the battle ha' done this slaughter *Hen. V.* iv 7 6
Which so grieved him, That he ran mad . . . *Hen. VIII.* ii 2 130
Queen Hecuba laughed that her eyes ran o'er . *Troi. and Cres.* i 2 157
Roar'd and ran From the noise of our own drums . . *Coriolanus* ii 3 59
These fellows ran about the streets, Crying confusion . . iv 6 28
Hecuba of Troy Ran mad for sorrow . . . . *T. Andron.* iv 1 21
He ran this way, and leap'd this orchard wall . . *Rom. and Jul.* ii 1 5
Which way ran he that kill'd Mercutio? Tybalt, that murderer, which way ran he?—There lies that Tybalt . . . . . . iii 1 142
My master drew on him; And then I ran away to call the watch . v 3 285
Look, in this place ran Cassius' dagger through . . *J. Cæsar* iii 2 178
Even at the base of Pompey's statua, Which all the while ran blood, great Cæsar fell . . . . iii 2 193
With this good sword, That ran through Cæsar's bowels, search this bosom . . . . v 3 42
There ran a rumour Of many worthy fellows that were out . *Macbeth* iv 3 182
I ran it through, even from my boyish days, To the very moment *Othello* i 3 132
The fresh streams ran by her, and murmur'd her moans . . iv 3 45
Rancorous. Sprung from the rancorous outrage of your duke *Com. of Er.* i 1 6
I fear we should have seen decipher'd there More rancorous spite 1 *Hen. VI.* iv 1 185
It is no policy, Respecting what a rancorous mind he bears 2 *Hen. VI.* iii 1 24
Here's a vengeful sword, . . . That shall be scoured in his rancorous heart iii 2 199
I must be held a rancorous enemy . . . . . *Richard III.* i 3 50
Rancour. Uncovered slander, unmitigated rancour . . *Much Ado* iv 1 308
It issues from the rancour of a villain . . . *Richard II.* i 1 143
Rancour will out: proud prelate, in thy face I see thy fury . 2 *Hen. VI.* i 1 142
And charity chased hence by rancour's hand . . . . iii 1 144
The broken rancour of your high-swoln hearts . . *Richard. III.* ii 2 117
This sudden stab of rancour I misdoubt . . . . . iii 2 89
To turn your households' rancour to pure love . . *Rom. and Jul.* ii 3 92
Put rancours in the vessel of my peace Only for them . *Macbeth* iii 1 67
Random. I writ at random, very doubtfully . . *T. G. of Ver.* ii 1 117
The great care of goods at random left Drew me from kind embracements of my spouse . . . . *Com. of Errors* i 1 43
He talks at random; sure, the man is mad . . . 1 *Hen. VI.* v 3 84
Range. I am sick in displeasure to him, and whatsoever comes athwart his affection ranges evenly with mine . . . . *Much Ado* ii 2 7
I found this credit, That he did range the town to seek me out *T. Night* iv 3 7
Then thieves and robbers range abroad unseen . . *Richard II.* iii 2 39
To show the line and the predicament Wherein you range . 1 *Hen. IV.* i 3 169
In liberty of bloody hand shall range With conscience wide as hell *Hen. V.* iii 3 12
I saw him in the battle range about . . . . 3 *Hen. VI.* ii 1 11
'Tis better to be lowly born, And range with humble livers in content *Hen. VIII.* ii 3 20
Bury all, which yet distinctly ranges, In heaps and piles of ruin *Coriol.* iii 1 206
So let high-sighted tyranny range on, Till each man drop . *J. Cæsar* ii 1 118
Nor stands it safe with us To let his madness range . . *Hamlet* iii 3 2
What though you fled From that great face of war, whose several ranges Frighted each other? . . . . . . *Ant. and Cleo.* iii 13 5
Ranged. We stay'd her for your sake, Else had she with her father ranged along . . . . *As Y. Like It* i 3 70
Would lift him where most trade of danger ranged . . 2 *Hen. IV.* i 1 174
And the wide arch Of the ranged empire fall! . . . *Ant. and Cleo.* i 1 34
Rangers. 'Tis gold Which buys admittance; oft it doth; yea, and makes Diana's rangers false themselves . . . . *Cymbeline* ii 3 74
Ranging. If once I find thee ranging, Hortensio will be quit with thee by changing . . . . *T. of Shrew* iii 1 91
Cæsar's spirit, ranging for revenge, With Ate by his side . *J. Cæsar* iii 1 270
Rank. Other jests are something rank on foot . . *Mer. Wives* iv 6 22
The ewes, being rank, In the end of autumn turned to the rams *M. of V.* i 3 81
Because I will not jump with common spirits And rank me with the barbarous multitudes . . . . ii 9 33
If I keep not my rank,— Thou losest thy old smell . *As Y. Like It* i 2 113
Weed your better judgements Of all opinion that grows rank in them . ii 7 46
It is the right butter-women's rank to market . . . . iii 2 103
The rank of osiers by the murmuring stream Left on your right hand . iv 3 80
And bow'd his eminent top to their low ranks . . . *All's Well* i 2 43
Though it be as rank as a fox . . . . . . *T. Night* ii 5 136
Deserves a name As rank as any flax-wench . . . . *W. Tale* i 2 277

Rank. Braved, Even at my gates, with ranks of foreign powers *K. John* iv 2 244
And fill up Her enemies' ranks . . . v 2 29
Rescued the Black Prince, that young Mars of men, From forth the ranks of many thousand French . . . *Richard II.* ii 3 102
In mutual well-beseeming ranks, March all one way . 1 *Hen. IV.* i 1 14
Our state may go In equal rank with the best govern'd nation 2 *Hen. IV.* v 2 137
Do not run away.—Why, all our ranks are broke . *Hen. V.* iv 5 6
Burnet and green clover, Wanting the scythe, all uncorrected, rank v 2 50
Let that one article rank with the rest . . . v 2 374
Our ranks are broke, and ruin follows us . 3 *Hen. VI.* ii 3 10
To rank our chosen truth with such a show As fool and fight is *Hen. VIII.* Prol. 18
Ha! what, so rank? Ah ha! There's mischief in this man . i 2 186
How rank soever rounded in with danger . *Troi. and Cres.* i 3 196
Like a gallant horse fall'n in first rank, Lie there for pavement . iii 3 161
Labouring for destiny make cruel way Through ranks of Greekish youth iv 5 185
Bring in thy ranks, but leave without thy rage . *T. of Athens* v 4 39
Fierce fiery warriors fought upon the clouds, In ranks and squadrons and right form of war . . . *J. Cæsar* ii 2 20
I do know but one That unassailable holds on his rank, Unshaked of motion . . . iii 1 69
I know not, gentlemen, what you intend, Who else must be let blood, who else is rank . . . iii 1 152
He finds thee in the stout Norweyan ranks, Nothing afeard *Macbeth* i 3 95
If you have a station in the file, Not i' the worst rank of manhood, say't iii 1 103
Things rank and gross in nature Possess it merely . *Hamlet* i 2 136
They in France of the best rank and station Are of a most select and generous chief in that . . . i 3 73
Put on him What forgeries you please; marry, none so rank As may dishonour him; take heed of that . . . ii 1 20
Thou mixture rank, of midnight weeds collected . iii 2 268
O, my offence is rank, it smells to heaven; It hath the primal eldest curse . . . iii 3 36
Breaking forth In rank and not-to-be-endured riots . *Lear* i 4 223
Not being the worst Stands in some rank of praise . ii 4 261
Conceive, and fare thee well.—Yours in the ranks of death . iv 2 25
The town is empty; on the brow o' the sea Stand ranks of people *Othello* ii 1 54
Foh! one may smell in such a will most rank, Foul disproportion . iii 3 232
I have seen the cannon, When it hath blown his ranks into the air iii 4 135
With his banners and his well-paid ranks, The ne'er-yet-beaten horse of Parthia We have jaded out o' the field . *Ant. and Cleo.* iii 1 32
Let the world rank me in register A master-leaver and a fugitive . iv 9 21
In their thick breaths, Rank of gross diet, shall we be enclouded . v 2 212
I give him satisfaction? Would he had been one of my rank! *Cymbeline* ii 1 17
Rank Achilles. The seeded pride That hath to this maturity blown up In rank Achilles must or now be cropp'd *Troi. and Cres.* i 3 318
Rank corruption. Whiles rank corruption, mining all within, Infects unseen . . . *Hamlet* iii 4 148
Rank diseases. What rank diseases grow, And with what danger, near the heart of it . . . 2 *Hen. IV.* iii 1 39
Rank feud. Wherein my sword had not impressure made Of our rank feud . . . *Troi. and Cres.* iv 5 132
Rank fumiter. Crown'd with rank fumiter and furrow-weeds *Lear* iv 4 3
Rank fumitory. Her fallow leas The darnel, hemlock and rank fumitory Doth root upon . . . *Hen. V.* v 2 45
Rank garb. Abuse him to the Moor in the rank garb . *Othello* ii 1 315
Rank minds. To diet rank minds sick of happiness . 2 *Hen. IV.* iv 1 64
Rank offence. He would give't thee, from this rank offence, So to offend him still . . . *Meas. for Meas.* iii 1 100
Rank poison. Take thou some new infection to thy eye, And the rank poison of the old will die . *Rom. and Jul.* i 2 51
Rank-scented. The mutable, rank-scented many . *Coriolanus* iii 1 66
Rank sweat. To live In the rank sweat of an enseamed bed *Hamlet* iii 4 92
Rank Thersites. When rank Thersites opes his mastic jaws, We shall hear music . . . *Troi and Cres.* i 3 73
Rank thoughts. Lust and rank thoughts, hers, hers . *Cymbeline* ii 5 24
Rank weed. He's a rank weed, Sir Thomas . *Hen. VIII.* v 1 52
Ranked. My fortunes every way as fairly rank'd *M. N. Dream* i 1 101
Embattailed and rank'd in Kent . . . *K. John* iv 2 200
Was woe enough, if it had ended there: Or, if sour woe delights in fellowship And needly will be rank'd with other griefs *Rom. and Jul.* iii 2 117
The base o' the mount Is rank'd with all deserts . *T. of Athens* i 1 65
Ranker. I should think my honesty ranker than my wit *As Y. Like It* iv 1 85
Do not spread the compost on the weeds, To make them ranker *Hamlet* iii 4 152
Nor will it yield to Norway or the Pole A ranker rate, should it be sold iv 4 22
Rankest. I do forgive Thy rankest fault; all of them . *Tempest* v 1 132
The rankest compound of villanous smell that ever offended nostril *Mer. Wives* iii 5 93
Ranking. He was a man Of an unbounded stomach, ever ranking Himself with princes . . . *Hen. VIII.* iv 2 34
Rankle. Fell sorrow's tooth doth never rankle more Than when he bites, but lanceth not the sore . . . *Richard II.* i 3 302
And when he bites, His venom tooth will rankle to the death *Richard III.* i 3 291
Rankly. Is by a forged process of my death Rankly abused . *Hamlet* i 5 38
Rankness. I will physic your rankness . *As Y. Like It* i 1 91
Like a bated and retired flood, Leaving our rankness . *K. John* v 4 54
I am stifled With the mere rankness of their joy . *Hen. VIII.* iv 1 59
Rannest. Thou hadst fire and sword on thy side, and yet thou rannest away . . . 1 *Hen. IV.* ii 4 349
When thou rannest up Gadshill in the night to catch my horse . iii 3 43
In the city Tours Thou ran'st a tilt in honour of my love . 2 *Hen. VI.* i 3 54
Ransack. Their vow is made To ransack Troy . *Troi. and Cres.* Prol. 8
Ransacked. My coffers ransacked, my reputation gnawn at *Mer. Wives* ii 2 306
I would have ransack'd The pedlar's silken treasury and have pour'd it To her acceptance . . . *W. Tale* iv 4 360
What treason were it to the ransack'd queen! . *Troi. and Cres.* ii 2 150
Ransacking the church, Offending charity . . *K. John* iii 4 172
Ransom. If hearty sorrow Be a sufficient ransom for offence, I tender't here . . . *T. G. of Ver.* v 4 75
Ignomy in ransom and free pardon Are of two houses . *Meas. for Meas.* ii 4 111
Receiving a dishonour'd life With ransom of such shame . ii 4 35
His goods confiscate to the duke's dispose, Unless a thousand marks be levied, To quit the penalty and to ransom him . *Com. of Errors* i 1 23
I would take Desire prisoner, and ransom him to any French courtier for a new-devised courtesy . . . *L. L. Lost* i 2 65
Without rescue in the first assault or ransom afterward . *All's Well* i 3 121
Labouring art can never ransom nature From her inaidible estate . ii 1 121
O, ransom, ransom! do not hide mine eyes . iv 1 74
The world's ransom, blessed Mary's Son . *Richard II.* ii 1 56
That we at our own charge shall ransom straight His brother-in-law 1 *Hen. IV.* i 3 79
Ransom. I shall never hold that man my friend Whose tongue shall ask me for one penny cost To ransom home revolted Mortimer 1 *Hen. IV.* i 3 92
When I urged the ransom once again Of my wife's brother, then his cheek look'd pale . . . i 3 141
He would not ransom Mortimer; Forbad my tongue to speak of Mortimer i 3 219
Deliver them up without their ransom straight . i 3 260
Of prisoners' ransom and of soldiers slain . ii 3 57
There without ransom to lie forfeited . iv 3 96
And for achievement offer us his ransom . *Hen. V.* iii 5 60
Say to England that we send To know what willing ransom he will give iii 5 63
Bid him therefore consider of his ransom . iii 6 133
My ransom is this frail and worthless trunk . iii 6 163
I come to know of thee, King Harry, If for thy ransom thou wilt now compound . . . iv 3 80
If they do this,—As, if God please, they shall,—my ransom then Will soon be levied . . . iv 3 120
Come thou no more for ransom, gentle herald: They shall have none, I swear, but these my joints . . . iv 3 122
I fear thou'lt once more come again for ransom . iv 3 128
O Signieur Dew, thou diest on point of fox, Except, O signieur, thou do give to me Egregious ransom . . . iv 4 11
For his ransom he will give you two hundred crowns . iv 4 48
Is this the king we sent to for his ransom? . iv 5 9
Know'st thou not That I have fined these bones of mine for ransom? Comest thou again for ransom? . . . iv 7 72
His ransom there is none but I shall pay . 1 *Hen. VI.* i 1 148
His crown shall be the ransom of my friend . i 1 150
They set him free without his ransom paid . iii 3 72
What ransom must I pay before I pass? . v 3 73
Wilt thou accept of ransom? yea, or no . v 3 79
My daughter shall be Henry's, if he please.—That is her ransom . v 3 157
And lowly words were ransom for their fault . 2 *Hen. VI.* iii 1 127
The world shall not be ransom for thy life . iii 2 297
Here shall they make their ransom on the sand . iv 1 10
What is my ransom, master? let me know.—A thousand crowns . iv 1 15
Be not so rash; take ransom, let him live . iv 1 28
For these whose ransom we have set, It is our pleasure one of them depart . . . iv 1 139
And hither have they sent it for her ransom . 3 *Hen. VI.* v 7 40
For me, the ransom of my bold attempt Shall be this cold corpse on the earth's cold face . . . *Richard III.* v 3 265
Thy sons alive; And that shall be the ransom for their fault *T. Andron.* iii 1 156
Let it serve To ransom my two nephews from their death . iii 1 173
Commend me to him: I will send his ransom . *T. of Athens* i 1 105
He hath brought many captives home to Rome, Whose ransoms did the general coffers fill . . . *J. Cæsar* iii 2 94
Use me well; You shall have ransom . *Lear* iv 6 196
Nor purposed merit in futurity Can ransom me into his love again *Othello* iii 4 118
Men did ransom lives Of me for jests . *Ant. and Cleo.* iii 13 180
For me, my ransom's death . *Cymbeline* v 3 80
Since the gods Will have it thus, that nothing but our lives May be call'd ransom, let it come . . . v 5 80
Ransomed. They looked as they had heard of a world ransomed, or one destroyed . . . *W. Tale* v 2 16
I would he were here alone; so should he be sure to be ransomed *Hen. V.* iv 1 127
I myself heard the king say he would not be ransomed . iv 1 203
But when our throats are cut, he may be ransomed, and we ne'er the wiser . . . iv 1 206
For him was I exchanged and ransomed . 1 *Hen. VI.* i 4 29
This one thing only I will entreat; my boy, a Briton born, Let him be ransom'd: never master had A page so kind . *Cymbeline* v 5 85
Ransoming him, or pitying, threatening the other . *Coriolanus* i 6 36
Ransomless. Deliver him Up to his pleasure, ransomless and free 1 *Hen. IV.* v 5 28
Ransomless here we set our prisoners free . *T. Andron.* i 1 274
Rant. Nay, an thou'lt mouth, I'll rant as well as thou . *Hamlet* v 1 307
Ranting. Look where my ranting host of the Garter comes . *Mer Wives* ii 1 196
Rap. Knock me at this gate And rap me well . *T. of Shrew* i 2 12
He bid me knock him and rap him soundly . i 2 31
Knock me here, rap me here, knock me well, and knock me soundly i 2 41
What, dear sir, Thus raps you? Are you well?—Thanks, madam; well *Cymbeline* i 6 51
Rape. For rapes and ravishments he parallels Nessus *All's Well* iv 3 281
And done a rape Upon the maiden virtue of the crown . *K. John* ii 1 97
The soil of her fair rape Wiped off, in honourable keeping her *T. and C.* ii 2 148
Thou and thy faction shall repent this rape . *T. Andron.* i 1 404
Rape, call you it, my lord, to seize my own, My true-betrothed love? i 1 405
Many unfrequented plots there are Fitted by kind for rape and villany ii 1 116
The tragic tale of Philomel, And treats of Tereus' treason and his rape . iv 1 48
And rape, I fear, was root of thine annoy . iv 1 49
By nature made for murders and for rapes . iv 1 58
And swear with me, as . . . Lord Junius Brutus sware for Lucrece' rape iv 1 91
You are both decipher'd, that's the news, For villains mark'd with rape iv 2 9
I must talk of murders, rapes and massacres, Acts of black night . v 1 63
Or misty vale, Where bloody murder or detested rape Can couch for fear v 2 37
Lo, by thy side where Rape and Murder stands . v 2 45
Show me a villain that hath done a rape, And I am sent to be revenged on him . . . v 2 94
The one is Murder, Rape is the other's name; And therefore bind them v 2 157
Rapier. Fetch me the hat and rapier in my cell . *Tempest* v 1 84
Take your rapier, and come after my heel . *Mer. Wives* i 4 61
Rugby, my rapier!—Good master, be content.—Wherefore shall I be content-a? . . . i 4 72
The Frenchman hath good skill in his rapier . ii 1 231
Take your rapier, Jack; I vill tell you how I vill kill him . ii 3 13
Master Starve-lackey the rapier and dagger man *Meas. for Meas.* iv 3 15
Strong-jointed Samson! I do excel thee in my rapier *L. L. Lost* i 2 78
Too much odds for a Spaniard's rapier . i 2 183
Adieu, valour! rust, rapier! be still, drum! for your manager is in love i 2 187
He is knight, dubbed with unhatched rapier . *T. Night* iii 4 258
I had a pass with him, rapier, scabbard and all . iii 4 303
I will turn thy falsehood to thy heart, Where it was forged, with my rapier's point . . . *Richard II.* iv 1 40
Here's goodly stuff toward!—Give me my rapier, boy . 2 *Hen. IV.* ii 4 215
I will scour you with my rapier, as I may, in fair terms . *Hen. V.* ii 1 60
Sweet Clifford, pity me!—Such pity as my rapier's point affords 3 *Hen. VI.* i 3 37
With the blood That valiant Clifford, with his rapier's point, Made issue from the bosom of the boy . . . i 4 80
Put up.—Not I, till I have sheathed My rapier in his bosom *T. Andron.* ii 1 54
I'll broach the tadpole on my rapier's point: Nurse, give it me . iv 2 85

Rapier. This, by his voice, should be a Montague. Fetch me my rapier, boy . . . . . . *Rom. and Jul.* i 5 57
I am for you.—Gentle Mercutio, put thy rapier up . . . iii 1 87
Methinks I see my cousin's ghost Seeking out Romeo, that did spit his body Upon a rapier's point . . . . . . iv 3 57
Many wearing rapiers are afraid of goose-quills . . *Hamlet* ii 2 359
Behind the arras hearing something stir, Whips out his rapier . iv 1 10
And gave you such a masterly report For art and exercise in your defence And for your rapier most especial . . . . . . iv 7 99
What's his weapon?—Rapier and dagger.—That's two of his weapons . v 2 152
Against the which he has imponed, as I take it, six French rapiers . v 2 156
Wear thy good rapier bare, and put it home: Quick, quick . *Othello* v 1 2
Rapine. So thou destroy Rapine and Murder there . *T. Andron.* v 2 59
Are these thy ministers? what are they call'd?—Rapine and Murder . v 2 62
Rapine and Murder, you are welcome too. . . . . v 2 83
When it is thy hap To find another that is like to thee, Good Rapine, stab him . . . . v 2 103
Rapt. Being transported And rapt in secret studies . . . *Tempest* i 2 77
More dances my rapt heart Than when I first my wedded mistress saw Bestride my threshold . . . . . *Coriolanus* iv 5 122
You are rapt, sir, in some work . . . . . *T. of Athens* i 1 19
I am rapt and cannot cover The monstrous bulk of this ingratitude With any size of words . . . . v 1 67
He seems rapt withal . . . . *Macbeth* i 3 57
Look, how our partner's rapt . . . . . . i 3 142
Whiles I stood rapt in the wonder of it . . . . . i 5 6
Rapture. Her brain-sick raptures . . . . *Troi. and Cres.* ii 2 122
In this rapture I shall surely speak The thing I shall repent . . iii 2 138
Your prattling nurse Into a rapture lets her baby cry . *Coriolanus* ii 1 223
And, spite of all the rapture of the sea, This jewel holds his building on my arm . . . . *Pericles* ii 1 161
Rare. So rare a wonder'd father and a wife Makes this place Paradise *Tempest* iv 1 123
Think on thy Proteus, when thou haply seest Some rare note-worthy object in thy travel . . . . . . *T. G. of Ver.* i 1 13
As to refuse So rare a gentleman . . . . *Much Ado* iii 1 91
To call me goddess, nymph, divine and rare, Precious . *M. N. Dream* iii 2 226
Our Master Bassanio, who, indeed, gives rare new liveries *Mer. of Venice* ii 2 116
And that she could not love me, Were man as rare as phœnix *As Y. L. It* iv 3 17
My father left me some prescriptions Of rare and proved effects *All's Well* i 3 228
With such magnificence—in so rare—I know not what to say *W. Tale* i 1 14
What is the news i' the court?—None rare . . . . i 2 367
This jealousy Is for a precious creature: as she's rare, Must it be great i 2 452
As it hath been to us rare, pleasant, speedy, The time is worth the use iii 1 13
Something rare Even then will rush to knowledge . . . iii 1 20
Shall I? O rare! By the Lord, I'll be a brave judge . 1 *Hen. IV.* i 2 72
No cataplasm so rare, Collected from all simples . . *Hamlet* iv 7 144
Dearer than eye-sight, space, and liberty; Beyond what can be valued, rich or rare . . . . *Lear* i 1 58
Say this becomes him,—As his composure must be rare indeed Whom these things cannot blemish . . . . *Ant. and Cleo.* i 4 22
O, rare for Antony! . . . . ii 2 210
Lived in court—Which rare it is to do—most praised . *Cymbeline* i 1 47
I am senseless of your wrath; a touch more rare Subdues all pangs . i 1 135
If she be furnish'd with a mind so rare, She is alone the Arabian bird i 6 16
In the election of a sir so rare, Which you know cannot err . . i 6 175
Slanders so her judgement That what's else rare is choked . . iii 5 77
Make us weep to hear your fate, fair creature, Rare as you seem *Pericles* iii 2 105
What world is this?—Is not this strange?—Most rare . . iii 2 107
Cleon's wife, with envy rare, A present murderer does prepare . iv Gower 37
Rare accidents. Nothing pleaseth but rare accidents . 1 *Hen. IV.* i 2 231
Rare affections. Fair encounter Of two most rare affections! *Tempest* iii 1 75
Rare boy. Thou diedst, a most rare boy, of melancholy . *Cymbeline* iv 2 208
Rare carpenter. And Vulcan a rare carpenter . . . *Much Ado* i 1 187
Rare courtier. That youth's a rare courtier . . . *T. Night* iii 1 97
Rare description. Your wondrous rare description, noble earl, Of beauteous Margaret hath astonish'd me . . . 1 *Hen. VI.* v 5 1
Rare device. Plate of rare device, and jewels . . . *Cymbeline* i 6 189
Rare Egyptian!—Upon her landing, Antony sent to her . *Ant. and Cleo.* ii 2 223
Rare enginer. Then there's Achilles, a rare enginer! *Troi. and Cres.* ii 3 8
Rare example. By his rare example made the coward Turn terror into sport . . . . *Coriolanus* ii 2 108
Rare fashion. Your gown's a most rare fashion . . *Much Ado* iii 4 15
Rare fellow. Is not this a rare fellow, my lord? . *As Y. Like It* v 4 109
Rare fortune. O rare fortune! here comes the man . *Mer. of Venice* ii 2 118
Rare hangman. And so become a rare hangman . . 1 *Hen. IV.* i 2 76
Rare instinct. O rare instinct! . . . . . *Cymbeline* v 5 381
Rare Italian master. Performed by that rare Italian master, Julio Romano . . . . *W. Tale* v 2 105
Rare letter. We shall have a rare letter from him . . *T. Night* iii 2 60
Rare note. A daughter of most rare note . . . . *W. Tale* v 2 48
Rare one. A book? O rare one! . . . . . *Cymbeline* v 4 133
Rare parrot-teacher. You are a rare parrot-teacher . . *Much Ado* i 1 139
Rare Pompey. Most rare Pompey!—Renowned Pompey . *L. L. Lost* v 2 689
Rare qualities. Thy rare qualities, sweet gentleness . *Hen. VIII.* ii 4 137
Rare reports. Fain would mine eyes be witness with mine ears, To give their censure of these rare reports . . . 1 *Hen. VI.* ii 3 10
Rare semblance. Now thy image doth appear In the rare semblance that I loved it first . . . . *Much Ado* v 1 260
Rare solemnity. We will include all jars With triumphs, mirth, and rare solemnity . . . . *T. G. of Ver.* v 4 161
Rare speaker. Learn'd, and a most rare speaker . . *Hen. VIII.* i 2 111
Rare success. Created for his rare success in arms . 1 *Hen. VI.* iv 7 62
Rare talent. A rare talent!—If a talent be a claw . *L. L. Lost* iv 2 64
Rare turkey-cock. O, peace! Contemplation makes a rare turkey-cock of him . . . . *T. Night* ii 5 35
Rare vision. I have had a most rare vision . . *M. N. Dream* iv 1 210
Rare words! brave world! . . . . . . 1 *Hen. IV.* iii 3 229
Rarely. How wise, how noble, young, how rarely featured *Much Ado* iii 1 60
Doth not my wit become me rarely?—It is not seen enough . iii 4 70
I could play Ercles rarely . . . . . . *M. N. Dream* i 2 31
These thy offices, So rarely kind . . . . . *W. Tale* v 1 150
How rarely does it meet with this time's guise, When man was wish'd to love his enemies! . . . . . . *T. of Athens* iv 3 472
Is not this buckled well?—Rarely, rarely . . *Ant. and Cleo.* iv 4 11
Slave, soulless villain, dog! O rarely base! . . . . v 2 158
Which I wonder'd Could be so rarely and exactly wrought *Cymbeline* ii 4 75
I'ld wish no better choice, and think me rarely wed . *Pericles* v 1 69
Rareness. And won by rareness such solemnity . . 1 *Hen. IV.* iii 2 59
And his infusion of such dearth and rareness . . *Hamlet* v 2 123
Rareness. It is no act of common passage, but A strain of rareness *Cymb.* iii 4 95
Rarer. The rarer action is In virtue than in vengeance . *Tempest* v 1 27
Their transformations Were never for a piece of beauty rarer . *W. Tale* iv 4 32
We'll have thee, as our rarer monsters are, Painted upon a pole *Macbeth* v 8 25
A rarer spirit never Did steer humanity . . . *Ant. and Cleo.* v 1 31
Rarest. Who is now queen.—And the rarest that e'er came there *Tempest* ii 1 99
'Tis the rarest argument of wonder that hath shot out . *All's Well* ii 3 7
She is The rarest of all women . . . . . . *W. Tale* v 1 112
He is simply the rarest man i' the world . . . *Coriolanus* iv 5 169
My train are men of choice and rarest parts . . . . *Lear* i 4 285
And less attemptable than any the rarest of our ladies in France *Cymb.* i 4 66
You must Forget that rarest treasure of your cheek, Exposing it . iii 4 163
And was the best of all Amongst the rarest of good ones . . v 5 160
The rarest dream that e'er dull sleep Did mock sad fools withal *Pericles* v 1 163
Rarest sounds! Do ye not hear? . . . . v 1 233
Rarity. But the rarity of it is,—which is indeed almost beyond credit, —As many vouched rarities are . . . . . . *Tempest* ii 1 58
Out-villained villany so far, that the rarity redeems him *All's Well* iv 3 306
Ay, that's well known: But what particular rarity? . *T. of Athens* i 1 4
Sorrow would be a rarity most beloved, If all could so become it *Lear* iv 3 25
Rascal. This wide-chapp'd rascal . . . . . . *Tempest* i 1 60
Your cony-catching rascals, Bardolph, Nym, and Pistol . *Mer. Wives* i 1 128
What a damned Epicurean rascal is this! . . . . . ii 2 300
Dishonest rascal! I would all of the same strain were in the same distress . . . . iii 3 196
O you pandarly rascals! there's a knot, a ging, a pack . . iv 2 122
This is the rascal; this is he I spoke of . . . . *Meas. for Meas.* v 1 306
You bald-pated, lying rascal, you must be hooded, must you? . v 1 357
The noblest deer hath them [horns] as huge as the rascal *As Y. Like It* iii 3 58
I bade the rascal knock upon your gate . . . *T. of Shrew* i 2 37
Go, rascals, go, and fetch my supper in . . . . . iv 1 142
Were I his lady, I would poison that vile rascal . . *All's Well* iii 5 87
I marvel your ladyship takes delight in such a barren rascal . *T. Night* i 5 90
Indeed words are very rascals since bonds disgraced them . . iii 1 24
Why laugh you at such a barren rascal? . . . . . . v 1 383
Some stretch-mouthed rascal . . . . *W. Tale* iv 4 197
But what talk we of these traitorly rascals? . . . . . iv 4 821
Peace, ye fat-kidneyed rascal! what a brawling dost thou keep! 1 *Hen. IV.* ii 2 5
The rascal hath removed my horse, and tied him I know not where . ii 2 11
If the rascal have not given me medicines to make me love him, I'll be hanged . . . . ii 2 19
An I were now by this rascal, I could brain him with his lady's fan . ii 3 24
What a pagan rascal is this! an infidel! . . . . . ii 3 31
That rascal hath good mettle in him; he will not run.—Why, what a rascal art thou then, to praise him so for running! . . . ii 4 383
This oily rascal is known as well as Paul's . . . . ii 4 575
Thou whoreson, impudent, embossed rascal . . . . iii 3 177
I did never see such pitiful rascals.—Tut, tut; good enough to toss iv 2 70
You muddy rascal, is that all the comfort you give me? . 2 *Hen. IV.* ii 4 43
You make fat rascals, Mistress Doll.—I make them! . . . ii 4 45
Hang him, swaggering rascal! let him not come hither . . ii 4 76
Away, you cut-purse rascal! you filthy bung, away! . . . ii 4 137
Away, you bottle-ale rascal! you basket-hilt stale juggler, you! . ii 4 140
Thrust him down stairs: I cannot endure such a fustian rascal . ii 4 203
I pray thee, Jack, be quiet; the rascal's gone . . . . ii 4 224
Have you turned him out o' doors?—Yea, sir. The rascal's drunk . ii 4 230
A rascal! to brave me! . . . . ii 4 232
A rascal bragging slave! the rogue fled from me like quicksilver . ii 4 247
Come on; I'll tell thee what, thou damned tripe-visaged rascal . v 4 10
Thou atomy, thou!—Come, you thin thing; come, you rascal . v 4 34
What ish my nation? Ish a villain, and a bastard, and a knave, and a rascal—What ish my nation? . . . . *Hen. V.* iii 2 134
This is an arrant counterfeit rascal; I remember him now . . iii 6 64
The cowardly rascals that ran from the battle ha' done this slaughter iv 7 6
Please your majesty, a rascal that swaggered with me last night . iv 7 130
Lean raw-boned rascals! who would e'er suppose They had such courage and audacity? . . . . 1 *Hen. VI.* i 2 35
And reap the harvest which that rascal sow'd . . 2 *Hen. VI.* iii 1 381
A sort of vagabonds, rascals, and runaways . . . *Richard III.* v 3 316
You'll leave your noise anon, ye rascals . . . . *Hen. VIII.* v 4 1
Do you look for ale and cakes here, you rude rascals? . . . v 4 11
Patroclus is a fool.—You rascal!—Peace, fool! I have not done *T. and C.* ii 3 59
The policy of those crafty swearing rascals . . . . . v 4 11
Art thou of blood and honour?—No, no, I am a rascal; a scurvy railing knave . . . . v 4 30
Thou rascal, that art worst in blood to run . . . . *Coriolanus* i 1 163
The mouse ne'er shunn'd the cat as they did budge From rascals worse than they . . . . i 6 45
O slaves, I can tell you news,—news, you rascals! . . . iv 5 182
All, sirrah, all: I'll once more feast the rascals . . *T. of Athens* iii 4 114
'Tis most just That thou turn rascal; hadst thou wealth again, Rascals should have't . . . . iv 3 217
Yet I, A dull and muddy-mettled rascal, peak, Like John-a-dreams *Ham.* ii 2 594
Do you bandy looks with me, you rascal? . . . . . *Lear* i 4 93
A rascal; an eater of broken meats . . . . ii 2 15
Draw, you rascal: you come with letters against the king . . ii 2 38
Draw, you rascal; come your ways . . . . ii 2 42
You cowardly rascal, nature disclaims in thee . . . . ii 2 59
You rogue! you rascal!—What's the matter, lieutenant? . *Othello* ii 3 143
Put in every honest hand a whip To lash the rascals naked through the world . . . . iv 2 143
Here comes a flattering rascal; upon him Will I first work . *Cymbeline* i 5 27
Leonatus! a banished rascal; and he's another, whatsoever he be . ii 1 42
Know'st me not by my clothes?—No, nor thy tailor, rascal . . iv 2 81
Rascal beadle. Thou rascal beadle, hold thy bloody hand! . . *Lear* iv 6 164
Rascal cook. 'Tis burnt; and so is all the meat. What dogs are these! Where is the rascal cook? . . . . *T. of Shrew* iv 1 165
Rascal counters. When Marcus Brutus grows so covetous, To lock such rascal counters from his friends . . . . *J. Cæsar* iv 3 80
Rascal dogs. Out, rascal dogs! . . . . . . *T. of Athens* v 1 118
Rascal fiddler. She did call me rascal fiddler . . *T. of Shrew* ii 1 158
Rascal follower. A wonder and a pointing-stock To every idle rascal follower . . . . 2 *Hen. VI.* ii 4 47
Rascal knaves. Bring along these rascal knaves with thee *T. of Shrew* iv 1 134
Rascal-like. Not rascal-like, to fall down with a pinch, But rather, moody-mad and desperate stags . . . . . 1 *Hen. VI.* iv 2 49
Rascal people. The rascal people, thirsting after prey . 2 *Hen. VI.* iv 4 51
Rascal thieves, Here's gold. Go . . . . . *T. of Athens* iv 3 431
Rascalliest. And art indeed the most comparative, rascalliest, sweet young prince . . . . 1 *Hen. IV.* i 2 90

Rascally. The jealous rascally knave her husband will be forth *M. Wives* ii 2 276
That blind rascally boy that abuses every one's eyes *As Y. Like It* iv 1 218
He looks like a poor, decayed, ingenuous, foolish, rascally knave *All's W.* v 2 25
The niggardly rascally sheep-biter . . . . *T. Night* ii 5 6
A rascally yea-forsooth knave! . . . *2 Hen. IV.* i 2 41
Away, you rascally Althæa's dream, away! . . . ii 2 93
You poor, base, rascally, cheating, lack-linen mate! . . ii 4 133
A rascally slave! I will toss the rogue in a blanket . . ii 4 240
What an arrant, rascally, beggarly, lousy knave it is . *Hen. V.* iv 8 36
The rascally, scauld, beggarly, lousy, pragging knave . v 1 5
A whoreson rascally tisick so troubles me *Troi. and Cres.* v 3 101
Rash. Make not too rash a trial of him . . *Tempest* i 2 467
Why dost thou ask again?—Lest I might be too rash . *Meas. for Meas.* ii 2 9
Here's young Master Rash . . . . iv 3 5
This is not well, rash and unbridled boy . *All's Well* iii 2 30
Rash, inconsiderate, fiery voluntaries, With ladies' faces . *K. John* ii 1 67
His rash fierce blaze of riot cannot last . *Richard II.* ii 1 33
He ambled up and down With shallow jesters and rash bavin wits *1 Hen. IV.* iii 2 61
Be not so rash; take ransom, let him live . *2 Hen. VI.* iv 1 28
I scarce have leisure to salute you, My matter is so rash *Troi. and Cres.* iv 2 62
Deliberate, Not rash like his accusers . . *Coriolanus* i 1 133
Their people Will be as rash in the repeal, as hasty To expel him thence iv 7 32
Too rash, too unadvised, too sudden; Too like the lightning *R. and J.* ii 2 118
O, what a rash and bloody deed is this! . . *Hamlet* iii 4 27
Thou wretched, rash, intruding fool, farewell! I took thee for thy better . . . . iii 4 31
I am not splenitive and rash, Yet have I something in me dangerous v 1 284
The best and soundest of his time hath been but rash . . *Lear* i 1 299
He is rash and very sudden in choler, and haply may strike at you *Othello* ii 1 279
Why do you speak so startingly and rash? . . . iii 4 79
Thou art rash as fire, to say That she was false: O, she was heavenly true! . . . . v 2 134
Where is this rash and most unfortunate man?—That's he that was Othello . . . . v 2 283
Fear not slander, censure rash;—Thou hast finish'd joy and moan *Cymb.* iv 2 272
Rash choler. Must I give way and room to your rash choler? *J. Cæsar* iv 3 39
Rash-embraced despair, And shuddering fear . *Mer. of Venice* iii 2 109
Rash faults. Our rash faults Make trivial price of serious things we have *All's Well* v 3 60
Rash gunpowder. Strong As aconitum or rash gunpowder *2 Hen. IV.* iv 4 48
Rash haste. Then we shall repent each drop of blood That hot rash haste so indirectly shed . . . *K. John* ii 1 49
Rash humour. That rash humour which my mother gave me Makes me forgetful . . . . . . *J. Cæsar* iv 3 120
Rash-levied. Buckingham and his rash-levied army . *Richard III.* iv 3 50
Rash mood. When the rash mood is on . . . *Lear* ii 4 172
Rash potion. With no rash potion, But with a lingering dram *W. Tale* i 2 319
Rash remonstrance. And would not rather Make rash remonstrance of my hidden power . . . *Meas. for Meas.* v 1 397
Rash Virginius. Was it well done of rash Virginius To slay his daughter? *T. Andron.* v 3 36
Rash wanton. Tarry, rash wanton: am not I thy lord? . *M. N. Dream* ii 1 63
Rasher. If we grow all to be pork-eaters, we shall not shortly have a rasher on the coals for money . . *Mer. of Venice* iii 5 28
Rashly. Too rashly plotted . . . *1 Hen. VI.* iv 4 3
Against the form of law, Proceed thus rashly . . *Richard III.* iii 5 43
The father rashly slaughter'd his own son . . . v 5 25
Rashly, And praised be rashness for it . . . *Hamlet* v 2 6
Rashness. A rashness that I ever yet have shunn'd . *T. G. of Ver.* iii 1 30
Alas! I have show'd too much The rashness of a woman *W. Tale* iii 2 222
Advantage is a better soldier than rashness . . *Hen. V.* iii 6 127
This is the fruit of rashness! . . . *Richard III.* ii 1 134
Be pitifully good: Who cannot condemn rashness in cold blood? *T. of A.* iii 5 53
Forgive my general and exceptless rashness, You perpetual-sober gods! iv 3 502
Rashly, And praised be rashness for it . . *Hamlet* v 2 7
In thy best consideration, check This hideous rashness . . *Lear* i 1 153
Your reproof Were well deserved of rashness . *Ant. and Cleo.* ii 2 124
My very hairs do mutiny; for the white Reprove the brown for rashness . . . . iii 11 14
Rat. The very rats Instinctively have quit it . . *Tempest* i 2 147
I would have made you four tall fellows skip like rats . *Mer. Wives* ii 1 237
Our natures do pursue, Like rats that ravin down their proper bane, A thirsty evil; and when we drink we die . . *Meas. for Meas.* i 2 133
What if my house be troubled with a rat? . *Mer. of Venice* iv 1 44
I was never so berhymed since Pythagoras' time, that I was an Irish rat, which I can hardly remember . . *As Y. Like It* iii 2 188
For want of means, poor rats, had hang'd themselves . *Richard III.* v 3 331
Rome and her rats are at the point of battle . *Coriolanus* i 1 166
The Volsces have much corn; take these rats thither To gnaw their garners . . . . i 1 253
A dog, a rat, a mouse, a cat, to scratch a man to death! *Rom. and Jul.* iii 1 104
And, like a rat without a tail, I'll do, I'll do, and I'll do . *Macbeth* i 3 9
How now! a rat? Dead, for a ducat, dead! . . *Hamlet* iii 4 23
Hearing something stir, Whips out his rapier, cries, 'A rat, a rat!' iv 1 10
Like rats, oft bite the holy cords a-twain Which are too intrinse . *Lear* ii 2 80
Eats cow-dung for sallets; swallows the old rat and the ditch-dog . iii 4 138
Mice and rats, and such small deer, Have been Tom's food for seven long year . . . . iii 4 144
Why should a dog, a horse, a rat, have life, And thou no breath at all? v 3 306
She is served As I would serve a rat . . . *Cymbeline* v 5 248
Rat-catcher. Tybalt, you rat-catcher, will you walk? *Rom. and Jul.* iii 1 78
Ratcliff. Sir Richard Ratcliff, let me tell thee this . *Richard III.* iii 3 2
Off with his head! . . . Lovel and Ratcliff, look that it be done . iii 4 80
Be patient, they are friends, Ratcliff and Lovel . . iii 5 21
Some light-foot friend post to the Duke of Norfolk: Ratcliff, thyself . iv 4 441
'Zounds! who is there?—Ratcliff, my lord; 'tis I . . v 3 209
O Ratcliff, I have dream'd a fearful dream! . . . v 3 212
O Ratcliff, I fear, I fear,— Nay, good my lord, be not afraid of shadows v 3 214
Rate. But by being so retired, O'er-prized all popular rate *Tempest* i 2 92
My son is lost and, in my rate, she too, Who is so far from Italy removed . . . . ii 1 109
Experience be a jewel that I have purchased at an infinite rate *M. Wives* ii 2 213
Stones whose rates are either rich or poor As fancy values them *M. for M.* ii 2 150
At the highest rate, Cannot amount unto a hundred marks *Com. of Errors* i 1 24
I'll serve you, sir, five hundred at the rate . . . iv 4 14
I am a spirit of no common rate . . . *M. N. Dream* iii 1 157
Nor do I now make moan to be abridged From such a noble rate *M. of V.* i 1 127
He lends out money gratis and brings down The rate of usance here . i 3 46
Three months from twelve; then, let me see; the rate . . i 3 105
Rate. Rails, and swears, and rates, that she, poor soul, Knows not which way to stand, to look, to speak . . . *T. of Shrew* iv 1 187
All that life can rate Worth name of life in thee hath estimate *All's Well* ii 1 182
I have seen her wear it; and she reckon'd it At her life's rate . . v 3 91
Her infinite cunning, with her modern grace, Subdued me to her rate . v 3 217
When we see the figure of the house, Then must we rate the cost *2 Hen. IV.* i 3 44
I judge their number Upon or near the rate of thirty thousand . iv 1 22
What! rate, rebuke, and roughly send to prison The immediate heir of England! . . . . v 2 70
Burgundy will fast Before he'll buy again at such a rate *1 Hen. VI.* iii 2 43
Why do you rate my Lord of Suffolk thus? . . *2 Hen. VI.* iii 2 56
Rate me at what thou wilt, thou shalt be paid . . . iv 1 30
All the rest is held at such a rate As brings a thousand-fold more care to keep Than in possession any jot of pleasure . . *3 Hen. VI.* ii 2 51
Go, rate thy minions, proud insulting boy! . . . ii 2 84
A proper title of a peace; and purchased At a superfluous rate! *Hen. VIII.* i 1 99
At such proud rate, that it out-speaks Possession of a subject . . iii 2 127
Why do you now The issue of your proper wisdoms rate? *Troi. and Cres.* ii 2 89
What's their seeking?—For corn at their own rates . *Coriolanus* i 1 193
'Peace, villain, peace!'—even thus he rates the babe . *T. Andron.* v 1 33
You are to blame, my lord, to rate her so . . *Rom. and Jul.* iii 5 170
There shall no figure at such rate be set As that of true and faithful Juliet . . . . v 3 301
Set your entreatments at a higher rate Than a command to parley *Hamlet* i 3 122
Nor will it yield to Norway or the Pole A ranker rate, should it be sold iv 4 22
'Tis to be chid As we rate boys . . . *Ant. and Cleo.* i 4 31
Fall not a tear, I say; one of them rates All that is won and lost . . iii 11 69
With Juno chide, That thy adulteries Rates and revenges . *Cymbeline* v 4 34
Rated them At courtship, pleasant jest and courtesy . *L. L. Lost* v 2 789
Many a time and oft In the Rialto you have rated me *Mer. of Venice* i 3 108
If thou be'st rated by thy estimation, Thou dost deserve enough . ii 7 26
Affection is not rated from the heart . . *T. of Shrew* i 1 165
Your breathing shall expire, Paying the fine of rated treachery *K. John* v 4 37
An old lord of the council rated me the other day in the street *1 Hen. IV.* i 2 95
Rated mine uncle from the council-board . . . iv 3 99
Who with them was a rated sinew too . . . . iv 4 17
Check'd and rated by Northumberland . . *2 Hen. IV.* iii 1 68
Thus upbraided, chid and rated at . . . *2 Hen. VI.* iii 1 175
Great reason that my noble lord be rated For sauciness . *T. Andron.* i 1 81
'Tis rated As those which sell would give . . *T. of Athens* i 1 168
That I might so have rated my expense, As I had leave of means . ii 2 135
Caius Ligarius doth bear Cæsar hard, Who rated him for speaking well of Pompey . . . . *J. Cæsar* ii 1 216
That . . . we had not rated him His part o' the isle . *Ant. and Cleo.* iii 6 25
I praised her as I rated her: so do I my stone . . *Cymbeline* i 4 83
Rather like a dream than an assurance . . . *Tempest* i 2 45
I have follow'd it, Or it hath drawn me rather . . . i 2 394
Being rather new-dyed than stained with salt water . . ii 1 63
Would not bless our Europe with your daughter, But rather lose her . ii 1 125
Thou let'st thy fortune sleep—die, rather . . . ii 1 216
We heard a hollow burst of bellowing Like bulls, or rather lions . ii 1 312
I had rather crack my sinews, break my back, Than you should such dishonour undergo . . . . iii 1 26
Bring a corollary, Rather than want a spirit . . . iv 1 58
I rather think You have not sought her help . . . v 1 141
Bestow your luggage where you found it.—Or stole it, rather . v 1 300
I rather would entreat thy company . . . *T. G. of Ver.* i 1 5
'Tis not in hate of you, But rather to beget more love in you . . iii 1 97
Why not death rather than living torment? . . . iii 1 170
I had rather wink than look on them . . . . v 2 14
I had rather than forty shillings I had my Book of Songs . *Mer. Wives* i 1 205
Walk in.—I had rather walk here . . . . . i 1 293
I had rather be a giantess, and lie under Mount Pelion . . ii 1 81
Whether had you rather lead mine eyes, or eye your master's heels? . iii 2 3
I had rather than a thousand pound he were out of the house . iii 3 130
For shame! never stand 'you had rather' and 'you had rather' . iii 3 134
I had rather be set quick i' the earth And bowl'd to death with turnips! iii 4 90
Devise something: any extremity rather than a mischief . . iv 2 76
I rather will suspect the sun with cold Than thee with wantonness . iv 4 7
Not as desiring more; But rather wishing a more strict restraint *M. for M.* i 4 4
Let me ask, The rather for I now must make you know I am that Isabella i 4 22
Let us be keen, and rather cut a little, Than fall, and bruise to death . ii 1 5
But rather tell me, When I, that censure him, do so offend . . ii 1 28
Which had you rather, that the most just law Now took your brother's life; or, to redeem him, Give up your body? . . . . ii 4 52
I had rather give my body than my soul . . . . ii 4 56
I had rather my brother die by the law than my son should be unlawfully born . . . . iii 1 195
I had rather it would please you I might be whipt . . . v 1 511
Return'd so soon?—Return'd so soon! rather approach'd too late *C. of Er.* i 2 43
Hold thy tongue.—Nay, rather persuade him to hold his hands . iv 4 23
I had rather hear my dog bark at a crow than a man swear he loves me *Much Ado* i 1 132
I had rather be a canker in a hedge than a rose in his grace . . i 3 28
I had rather lie in the woollen . . . . . ii 1 33
And now had he rather hear the tabor and the pipe . . ii 3 15
She will die, if he woo her, rather than she will bate one breath of her accustomed crossness . . . . ii 3 183
Which I had rather seal with my death than repeat over to my shame . v 1 247
I had rather pray a month with mutton and porridge . *L. L. Lost* i 1 304
Facere, as it were, replication, or, rather, ostentare, to show . . iv 2 15
Untrained, or rather, unlettered, or ratherest, unconfirmed fashion . iv 2 18
I would my father look'd but with my eyes.—Rather your eyes must with his judgement look . . . . *M. N. Dream* i 1 57
Do I speak you fair? Or, rather, do I not in plainest truth Tell you, I do not, nor I cannot love you? . . . . ii 1 200
I had rather give his carcass to my hounds . . . iii 2 64
To love unloved? This you should pity rather than despise . . iii 2 235
I had rather have a handful or two of dried peas . . . iv 1 41
Did scare away, or rather did affright . . . . v 1 142
I had rather be married to a death's-head . . *Mer. of Venice* i 2 55
I had rather he should shrive me than wive me . . . i 2 144
Lend it not As to thy friends; . . . But lend it rather to thine enemy . i 3 136
Whether till the next night she had rather stay, Or go to bed now . v 1 302
For my part, I had rather bear with you than bear you . *As Y. Like It* ii 4 11
I had rather hear you chide than this man woo . . . iii 5 65
Or else my heart concealing it will break, And rather than it shall, I will be free Even to the uttermost, as I please, in words *T. of Shrew* iv 3 79
Be able for thine enemy Rather in power than use . . *All's Well* i 1 75
I knew him.—The rather will I spare my praises towards him . . ii 1 106

Rather. The rather, for I think I know your hostess As ample as myself . *All's Well* iii 5 45
And leap all civil bounds Rather than make unprofited return *T. Night* i 4 22
I had rather than forty shillings I had such a leg . . . ii 3 20
The rather by these arguments of fear, Set forth in your pursuit . iii 3 12
This is an art Which does mend nature, change it rather . *W. Tale* iv 4 96
God shall forgive you Cœur-de-lion's death The rather that you give his offspring life . . . . *K. John* ii 1 13
He will the rather do it when he sees Ourselves well sinewed to our defence . . . . v 7 87
I had rather You would have bid me argue like a father . *Richard II.* i 3 237
But be sure I will from henceforth rather be myself . . 1 *Hen. IV.* i 3 5
I had rather be a kitten and cry mew . . . . . iii 1 129
I had rather hear a brazen canstick turn'd, Or a dry wheel grate . iii 1 131
I had rather live With cheese and garlic in a windmill, far . . iii 1 161
I had rather have my horse to my mistress . . *Hen. V.* iii 7 62
I'll rather keep That which I have than, coveting for more, Be cast from possibility of all . . . . 1 *Hen. VI.* v 4 144
I rather would have lost my life betimes . . . 2 *Hen. VI.* iii 1 297
To tell you plain, I had rather lie in prison . . . 3 *Hen. VI.* iii 2 70
I had rather chop this hand off at a blow . . . . . v 1 50
I had rather be a country servant-maid Than a great queen *Richard III.* i 3 107
Kill a friend of mine?—Ay, my lord; But I had rather kill two enemies iv 2 72
He would miss it rather Than carry it but by the suit of the gentry *Cor.* ii 1 253
Rather be at a breakfast of enemies than a dinner of friends *T. of Athens* i 2 78
I'ld rather than the worth of thrice the sum . . . . iii 3 22
Had you rather Cæsar were living and die all slaves, than that Cæsar were dead, to live all free men? . . . . . . *J. Cæsar* iii 2 24
I had rather be a dog, and bay the moon, Than such a Roman . . iv 3 27
I had rather coin my heart, And drop my blood for drachmas . iv 3 72
No words.—I'll rather kill myself . . . . . . v 5 7
When Duncan is asleep—Whereto the rather shall his day's hard journey Soundly invite him . . . . *Macbeth* i 7 62
Rather than so, come fate into the list, And champion me to the utterance! . . . . iii 1 71
My lord, I will be ruled; The rather, if you could devise it so That I might be the organ . . . . *Hamlet* iv 7 70
I had rather to adopt a child than get it . . . . . *Othello* i 3 191
I had rather have this tongue cut from my mouth Than it should do offence . . . . ii 3 221
I had rather heat my liver with drinking . . . . *Ant. and Cleo.* i 2 23
The which you both denied.—Neglected, rather . . . . ii 2 89
I had rather fast from all four days Than drink so much in one . ii 7 108
I had rather seal my lips, than, to my peril, Speak that which is not . v 2 146
I had rather not be so noble as I am . . . . . *Cymbeline* ii 1 20
Which I had rather You felt than make't my boast . . . ii 3 115
Money, youth?—All gold and silver rather turn to dirt! . . . iii 6 54
I had rather Have skipp'd from sixteen years of age to sixty . . iv 2 198
Dead, or sleeping on him? But dead rather . . . . . iv 2 356
I had rather thou shouldst live while nature will Than die ere I hear more . . . . v 5 151
Ratherest. Rather, unlettered, or ratherest, unconfirmed . *L. L. Lost* iv 2 19
Rather had. Which we much rather had depart withal . . . ii 1 147
Me rather had my heart might feel your love Than my unpleased eye see your courtesy . . . . *Richard II.* iii 3 192
Who rather had, Though they themselves did suffer by't *Coriolanus* iv 6 5
Ratified. Here are only numbers ratified . . . *L. L. Lost* iv 2 125
As doubtful whether what I see be true, Until confirm'd, sign'd, ratified by you . . . . *Mer. of Venice* iii 2 149
The articles o' the combination drew As himself pleased; and they were ratified As he cried 'Thus let be' . . . . . *Hen. VIII.* i 1 170
A seal'd compact, Well ratified by law and heraldry . . *Hamlet* i 1 87
Ratifiers. The rabble . . . The ratifiers and props of every word . iv 5 105
Ratify. Here, afore Heaven, I ratify this my rich gift . . *Tempest* iv 1 8
Take with you free power to ratify, Augment, or alter . . *Hen. V.* v 2 86
By the help of these—with Him above To ratify the work . *Macbeth* iii 6 33
In the temple of great Jupiter Our peace we'll ratify . . *Cymbeline* v 5 483
Rating. And yet, dear lady, Rating myself at nothing, you shall see How much I was a braggart . . . . *Mer. of Venice* iii 2 260
Rational. The rational hind Costard . . . . . *L. L. Lost* i 2 123
Loss of virginity is rational increase . . . . . *All's Well* i 1 139
Rato-lorum. And 'Custalorum.'—Ay, and 'Rato-lorum' too *Mer. Wives* i 1 8
Ratsbane. I had as lief they would put ratsbane in my mouth 2 *Hen. IV.* i 2 48
I would the milk Thy mother gave thee when thou suck'dst her breast, Had been a little ratsbane for thy sake! . . . . . 1 *Hen. VI.* v 4 29
Laid knives under his pillow, . . set ratsbane by his porridge . *Lear* iii 4 55
Rattle. Tapers on their heads, And rattles in their hands *Mer. Wives* iv 4 51
Another shall As loud as thine rattle the welkin's ear . *K. John* v 2 172
Rattling. To the dread rattling thunder Have I given fire *Tempest* v 1 44
In the modesty of fearful duty I read as much as from the rattling tongue Of saucy and audacious eloquence . . . . *M. N. Dream* v 1 102
O'er-cover'd quite with dead men's rattling bones . *Rom. and Jul.* iv 1 82
Make mingle with our rattling tabourines . . . *Ant. and Cleo.* iv 8 37
But when he meant to quail and shake the orb, He was as rattling thunder . . . . v 2 86
Raught. And raught not to five weeks . . . . . *L. L. Lost* iv 2 41
He smiled me in the face, raught me his hand . . . *Hen. V.* iv 6 21
This staff of honour raught, there let it stand . . 2 *Hen. VI.* ii 3 43
That raught at mountains with outstretched arms . . 3 *Hen. VI.* i 4 68
The hand of death hath raught him . . . . *Ant. and Cleo.* iv 9 30
Rave. What's the matter? does he rave? . . . . *T. Night* iii 4 10
Stamp, rave, and fret, that I may sing and dance . . 3 *Hen. VI.* i 4 91
He raves in saying nothing.—How can that be? . *Troi. and Cres.* iii 3 249
There let him stand, and rave, and cry for food . . *T. Andron.* v 3 180
And, by this declension, Into the madness wherein now he raves *Hamlet* ii 2 150
Raved. Not frenzy, not Absolute madness could so far have raved *Cymb.* iv 2 135
Ravel. As you unwind her love from him, Lest it should ravel and be good to none, You must provide to bottom it on me *T. G. of Ver.* iii 2 52
Must I do so? and must I ravel out My weaved-up folly? *Richard II.* iv 1 228
Make you to ravel all this matter out . . . . . *Hamlet* iii 4 186
Ravelled. The innocent sleep, Sleep that knits up the ravell'd sleave of care . . . . *Macbeth* ii 2 37
Raven. As wicked dew as e'er my mother brush'd With raven's feather from unwholesome fen . . . . *Tempest* i 2 322
Young ravens must have food . . . . . . *Mer. Wives* i 3 38
An amber-colour'd raven was well noted . . . . *L. L. Lost* iv 2 88
Who will not change a raven for a dove? . . . *M. N. Dream* ii 2 114
He that doth the ravens feed . . . . . . *As Y. Like It* ii 3 43
To spite a raven's heart within a dove . . . . . *T. Night* v 1 134
Some powerful spirit instruct the kites and ravens To be thy nurses! *W. T.* ii 3 186

Raven. Vast confusion waits, As doth a raven on a sick-fall'n beast, The imminent decay of wrested pomp . . . . . . *K. John* iv 3 153
A clip-wing'd griffin and a moulten raven . . . . 1 *Hen. IV.* iii 1 152
Seems he a dove? his feathers are but borrow'd, For he's disposed as the hateful raven . . . . 2 *Hen. VI.* iii 1 76
A raven's note, Whose dismal tune bereft my vital powers . . . iii 2 40
The raven rook'd her on the chimney's top . . . . 3 *Hen. VI.* v 6 47
Can he not be sociable?—The raven chides blackness *Troi. and Cres.* ii 3 221
I would croak like a raven; I would bode, I would bode . . . v 2 191
Here nothing breeds, Unless the nightly owl or fatal raven *T. Andron.* ii 3 97
'Tis true; the raven doth not hatch a lark . . . . . ii 3 149
Some say that ravens foster forlorn children, The whilst their own birds famish in their nests . . . . ii 3 153
Did ever raven sing so like a lark? . . . . . . iii 1 158
Whiter than new snow on a raven's back . . . *Rom. and Jul.* iii 2 19
Beautiful tyrant! fiend angelical! Dove-feather'd raven! . . . iii 2 76
In their steads do ravens, crows and kites, Fly o'er our heads *J. Cæsar* v 1 85
The raven himself is hoarse That croaks the fatal entrance of Duncan Under my battlements . . . . *Macbeth* i 5 39
The croaking raven doth bellow for revenge . . . . *Hamlet* iii 2 264
It comes o'er my memory, As doth the raven o'er the infected house *Oth.* iv 1 21
Swift, you dragons of the night, that dawning May bare the raven's eye! . . . . *Cymbeline* ii 2 49
Raven-coloured. And let her joy her raven-colour'd love *T. Andron.* ii 3 83
Ravening first the lamb Longs after for the garbage . . *Cymbeline* i 6 49
Ravenous. Wolvish, bloody, starved and ravenous . . *Mer. of Venice* iv 1 138
Nor with thy sweets comfort his ravenous sense . . . *Richard II.* iii 2 13
I wish some ravenous wolf had eaten thee! . . . 1 *Hen. VI.* v 4 31
For he's inclined as is the ravenous wolf . . . . 2 *Hen. VI.* iii 1 78
He is equal ravenous As he is subtle . . . . . *Hen. VIII.* i 1 159
Which ever, As ravenous fishes, do a vessel follow That is new-trimm'd i 2 79
This ravenous tiger, this accursed devil . . . . *T. Andron.* v 3 5
Ravenspurgh. Away with me in post to Ravenspurgh . *Richard II.* ii 1 296
The banish'd Bolingbroke . . . is safe arrived At Ravenspurgh . . ii 2 51
A weary way From Ravenspurgh to Cotswold will be found . . ii 3 9
Is gone to Ravenspurgh, To offer service to the Duke of Hereford . ii 3 31
Then with directions to repair to Ravenspurgh . . . . ii 3 35
When you and he came back from Ravenspurgh . . . 1 *Hen. IV.* i 3 248
When I from France set foot at Ravenspurgh . . . . . iii 2 95
His vow Made to my father . . . Upon the naked shore at Ravenspurgh iv 3 77
Thus arrived From Ravenspurgh haven before the gates of York 3 *Hen. VI.* iv 7 8
Ravin. Like rats that ravin down their proper bane . *Meas. for Meas.* i 2 133
Better 'twere I met the ravin lion when he roar'd . . *All's Well* iii 2 120
Thriftless ambition, that wilt ravin up Thine own life's means! *Macbeth* ii 4 28
Ravined. Maw and gulf Of the ravin'd salt-sea shark . . . . iv 1 24
Ravish. One whom the music of his own vain tongue Doth ravish *L. L. Lost* i 1 168
That painting and usurping hair Should ravish doters with a false aspect iv 3 260
His lines would ravish savage ears And plant in tyrants mild humility iv 3 348
A volume of enticing lines, Able to ravish any dull conceit 1 *Hen. VI.* v 5 15
Her sight did ravish; but her grace in speech . . 2 *Hen. VI.* i 1 32
Ravish your wives and daughters before your faces . . . iv 8 31
Shall these enjoy our lands? . . . Ravish our daughters? *Richard III.* v 3 337
You have holp to ravish your own daughters . . *Coriolanus* iv 6 81
Some notorious ill, As . . . Ravish a maid, or plot the way to do it *T. An.* v 1 129
These hairs, which thou dost ravish from my chin, Will quicken *Lear* iii 7 38
With that suit upon my back, will I ravish her: first kill him *Cymb.* iii 5 142
I must ravish her, or she'll disfurnish us of all our cavaliers *Pericles* iv 6 11
Ravished. Now, divine air! now is his soul ravished! . . *Much Ado* ii 3 60
That aged ears play truant at his tales And younger hearings are quite ravished . . . . *L. L. Lost* ii 1 75
Didst thou not lead him through the glimmering night From Perigenia, whom he ravished? . . . . *M. N. Dream* ii 1 78
When we, Almost with ravish'd listening, could not find His hour of speech a minute . . . . *Hen. VIII.* i 2 120
The ravish'd Helen, Menelaus' queen, With wanton Paris sleeps *T. and C.* Prol. 9
So, now go tell, an if thy tongue can speak, Who 'twas that cut thy tongue and ravish'd thee . . . . *T. Andron.* ii 4 2
Wert thou thus surprised, sweet girl, Ravish'd and wrong'd? . . iv 1 52
They cut thy sister's tongue and ravish'd her And cut her hands . v 1 92
What, was she ravish'd? tell who did the deed . . . . v 3 53
'Twas Chiron and Demetrius: They ravish'd her, and cut away her tongue . . . . v 3 57
They it were that ravished our sister . . . . . . v 3 99
If she remain, Whom they have ravish'd must by me be slain *Pericles* iv 1 103
We must either get her ravished, or be rid of her . . . . iv 6 5
Ravisher. War, in some sort, may be said to be a ravisher *Coriolanus* iv 5 243
When it is thy hap To find another that is like to thee, Good Rapine, stab him; he's a ravisher . . . . *T. Andron.* v 2 103
Ravishing. Sung by a fair queen in a summer's bower, With ravishing division, to her lute . . . . 1 *Hen. IV.* iii 1 211
With his stealthy pace, With Tarquin's ravishing strides . *Macbeth* ii 1 55
Ravishment. For rapes and ravishments he parallels Nessus *All's Well* iv 3 281
Raw. In your doublet and hose this raw rheumatic day! *Mer. Wives* iii 1 47
And Marian's nose looks red and raw . . . . *L. L. Lost* v 2 934
I have within my mind A thousand raw tricks of these bragging Jacks, Which I will practice . . . . *Mer. of Venice* iii 4 77
God make incision in thee! thou art raw . . . *As Y. Like It* iii 2 76
Raw as he is, and in the hottest day prognostication proclaims, shall he be set against a brick-wall . . . . . . *W. Tale* iv 4 816
My service, Such as it is, being tender, raw and young . *Richard II.* ii 3 42
Where have they this mettle? Is not their climate foggy, raw? *Hen. V.* iii 5 16
In to our tent; the air is raw and cold . . . . *Richard III.* v 3 46
Lethargies, cold palsies, raw eyes . . . . *Troi. and Cres.* v 1 23
Once, upon a raw and gusty day, The troubled Tiber chafing *J. Cæsar* i 2 100
Wherefore rise you now? It is not for your health thus to commit Your weak condition to the raw cold morning . . . . . ii 1 236
Yet thy cicatrice looks raw and red . . . . . *Hamlet* iv 3 62
Take her in; instruct her what she has to do, that she may not be raw in her entertainment . . . . *Pericles* iv 2 60
Raw-boned. Lean raw-boned rascals! who would e'er suppose They had such courage and audacity? . . . . . . 1 *Hen. VI.* i 2 35
Rawer. Why do we wrap the gentleman in our more rawer breath? *Ham.* v 2 129
Rawly. Their children rawly left . . . . . . *Hen. V.* iv 1 147
Rawness. Why in that rawness left you wife and child? . . *Macbeth* iv 3 26
Ray. As thy eye-beams, when their fresh rays have smote The night of dew that on my cheeks down flows . . . . . *L. L. Lost* iv 3 28
With those clear rays which she infused on me That beauty am I bless'd with which you see . . . . 1 *Hen. VI.* i 2 85
With his very bulk Take up the rays o' the beneficial sun *Hen. VIII.* i 1 56
In her ray and brightness The herd hath more annoyance *Troi. and Cres.* i 3 47

Ray. Whose virtues will, I hope, Reflect on Rome as Titan's rays on earth *T. Andron.* i 1 226
O setting sun, As in thy red rays thou dost sink to-night . *J. Cæsar* v 3 61
Rayed. Sped with spavins, rayed with the yellows . *T. of Shrew* iii 2 54
Was ever man so rayed? was ever man so weary? . . iv 1 3
Raze. To raze the sanctuary And pitch our evils there *Meas. for Meas.* ii 2 171
'Tis not my meaning To raze one title of your honour out *Richard II.* ii 3 75
I have a gammon of bacon and two razes of ginger . 1 *Hen. IV.* ii 1 27
To frustrate prophecies and to raze out Rotten opinion . 2 *Hen. IV.* v 2 127
Stanley did dream the boar did raze his helm . *Richard III.* iii 4 84
I'll find a day to massacre them all And raze their faction *T. Andron.* i 1 451
Canst thou not . . . Pluck from the memory a rooted sorrow, Raze out the written troubles of the brain? . . *Macbeth* v 3 42
Razed. 'Thou shalt not steal'?—Ay, that he razed . *Meas. for Meas.* i 2 11
Razed out my imprese, leaving me no sign, Save men's opinions *Rich. II.* iii 1 25
He dreamt to-night the boar had razed his helm . *Richard III.* iii 2 11
With two Provincial roses on my razed shoes . *Hamlet* iii 2 288
My good intent May carry through itself to that full issue For which I razed my likeness . . . . . *Lear* i 4 4
Not, Caius, now for tribute; that The Britons have razed out *Cymbeline* v 5 70
As from thence Sorrow were ever razed . . *Pericles* i 1 17
Razeth your cities and subverts your towns . . 1 *Hen. VI.* ii 3 65
Razing the characters of your renown . . . . 2 *Hen. VI.* i 1 101
Razor. As keen As is the razor's edge invisible . *L. L. Lost* v 2 257
These words are razors to my wounded heart . . *T. Andron.* i 1 314
What this fourteen years no razor touch'd . . *Pericles* v 3 75
Razorable. Till new-born chins Be rough and razorable . *Tempest* ii 1 250
Razure. 'Gainst the tooth of time And razure of oblivion *Meas. for Meas.* v 1 13
Re. Ut, re, sol, la, mi, fa . . . . . *L. L. Lost* iv 2 102
'A re,' to plead Hortensio's passion; 'B mi,' Bianca, take him *T. of S.* iii 1 74
'D sol re,' one clef, two notes have I: 'E la mi,' show pity, or I die . iii 1 77
I will carry no crotchets: I'll re you, I'll fa you; do you note me?—An you re us and fa us, you note us . . *Rom. and Jul.* iv 5 121
Reach. I cannot reach so high . . . *T. G. of Ver.* i 2 87
Wilt thou reach stars, because they shine on thee? . . iii 1 156
I am not yet so low But that my nails can reach unto thine eyes *M. N. D.* iii 2 298
No lawful means can carry me Out of his envy's reach *Mer. of Venice* iv 1 10
Will you eat no grapes, my royal fox? Yes, but you will my noble grapes, an if My royal fox could reach them . *All's Well* ii 1 75
They should not laugh if I could reach them . . *W. Tale* ii 3 25
Beyond the infinite and boundless reach Of mercy . . *K. John* iv 3 117
Lift me up To reach at victory above my head . *Richard II.* i 3 72
From forth thy reach he would have laid thy shame . . ii 1 106
What may the king's whole battle reach unto? . 1 *Hen. IV.* iv 1 129
Put forth thy hand, reach at the glorious gold . 2 *Hen. VI.* i 2 11
Pleasure at command, Above the reach or compass of thy thought . i 2 46
And dogged York, that reaches at the moon . . . iii 1 158
Not all so much for love As for another secret close intent, By marrying her which I must reach unto . . *Richard III.* i 1 159
Go cross the seas, And live with Richmond, from the reach of hell iv 1 43
His sword Hath a sharp edge: it's long and . . . It reaches far *Hen. VIII.* i 1 111
Who can be angry now? what envy reach you? . . . ii 2 89
Reach a chair: So; now, methinks, I feel a little ease . iv 2 3
To me you cannot reach, you play the spaniel, And think with wagging of your tongue to win me . . . . . v 3 126
Like a mountain cedar, reach his branches To all the plains about him v 5 54
My wit Is 'plain and true;' there's all the reach of it *Troi. and Cres.* iv 4 110
Advanced above pale envy's threatening reach . *T. Andron.* ii 1 4
Reach me thy hand, that I may help thee out . . . ii 3 237
That is, because the traitor murderer lives.—Ay, madam, from the reach of these my hands . . . . *Rom. and Jul.* iii 5 86
I fear 'tis deepest winter in Lord Timon's purse; That is, one may reach deep enough, and yet Find little . . *T. of Athens* iii 4 15
With thoughts beyond the reaches of our souls . . *Hamlet* i 4 56
Thus do we of wisdom and of reach, With windlasses and with assays of bias, By indirections find directions out . . . ii 1 64
Not to strain my speech To grosser issues nor to larger reach *Othello* iii 3 219
Because thine eye Presumes to reach, all thy whole heap must die *Per.* i 1 33
Alter thy course for Tyre. When canst thou reach it?—By break of day iii 1 76
Reached. My demerits May speak unbonneted to as proud a fortune As this that I have reach'd . . . . *Othello* i 2 24
Reacheth. Is not my arm of length, That reacheth from the restful English court As far as Calais? . . . *Richard II.* iv 1 12
Reaching. Great men have reaching hands . . 2 *Hen. VI.* iv 7 86
Upon his shield Is a black Ethiope reaching at the sun . *Pericles* ii 2 20
Read. When it's writ, for my sake read it over . *T. G. of Ver.* i 1 136
Enough; I read your fortune in your eye . . . . ii 4 143
Let me read them.—Fie on thee, jolt-head! thou canst not read.—Thou liest . . . . iii 1 289
This proves that thou canst not read . . . . iii 1 298
Well, that fault may be mended with a breakfast. Read on . iii 1 329
Read over Julia's heart, thy first best love . . . v 4 46
We burn daylight: here, read, read . . . *Mer. Wives* ii 1 54
Like a good thing, being often read, Grown fear'd and tedious *M. for M.* ii 4 8
If I read it not truly, my ancient skill beguiles me . . iv 2 164
Let not my sister read it in your eye . . . *Com. of Errors* iii 2 9
'Tis double wrong, to truant with your bed And let her read it in thy looks . . . . iii 2 18
For they can write and read . . . . *Much Ado* iii 3 12
To write and read comes by nature . . . . . iii 3 16
How well he's read, to reason against reading! . *L. L. Lost* i 1 94
Let me read the same; And to the strict'st decrees I'll write my name i 1 116
Is that one of the four complexions?—As I have read, sir . i 2 88
Read the purpose of my coming, And suddenly resolve me . ii 1 109
This letter is mistook, . . . It is writ to Jaquenetta.—We will read it . iv 1 58
Be so good as read me this letter: it was given me . . iv 2 92
Once more I'll read the ode that I have writ . . . iv 3 99
Let this letter be read: Our parson misdoubts it; 'twas treason, he said.—Biron, read it over . . . . iv 3 193
For aught that I could ever read, Could ever hear . *M. N. Dream* i 1 132
Read the names of the actors, and so grow to a point . . i 2 9
In the modesty of fearful duty I read as much as from the rattling tongue v 1 102
There is a written scroll! I'll read the writing . *Mer. of Venice* ii 7 64
The portrait of a blinking idiot, Presenting me a schedule! I will read it ii 9 55
Here is a letter; read it at your leisure . . . . v 1 267
Here I read for certain that my ships Are safely come to road . v 1 287
Teaching all that read to know . . . . *As Y. Like It* iii 2 146
He fell in love. I have heard him read many lectures against it . iii 2 365
See you read no other lectures to her: You understand me *T. of Shrew* i 2 148
What will you read to her?—Whate'er I read to her, I'll plead for you . i 2 154

Read. Well read in poetry And other books, good ones . *T. of Shrew* i 2 170
That never read so far To know the cause why music was ordain'd! . iii 1 9
Then give me leave to read philosophy . . . . . iii 1 13
I am past my gamut long ago.—Yet read the gamut of Hortensio . iii 1 72
Profit you in what you read?—What, master, read you? . . . —I read that I profess, the Art to Love . . . . . . iv 2 6
Why, here is the note of the fashion to testify.—Read it . . iv 3 132
If you will have it in showing, you shall read it in . . *All's Well* ii 3 25
Might you not know she would do as she has done, By sending me a letter? Read it again . . . . iii 4 3
His confession is taken, and it shall be read to his face . iv 3 131
Here's a paper: shall I read it to you?—I do not know if it be it or no iv 3 234
Put it up again.—Nay, I'll read it first, by your favour . iv 3 244
I have read it: it is heresy . . . . . *T. Night* i 5 246
I will be proud, I will read politic authors . . . . ii 5 175
Here's the challenge, read it: I warrant there's vinegar and pepper in't iii 4 157
Is't so saucy?—Ay, is't, I warrant him: do but read . . iii 4 161
Nothing of that wonderful promise, to read him by his form . iii 4 291
Open't, and read it.—Look then to be well edified . . v 1 297
Art thou mad?—No, madam, I do but read madness . . v 1 302
Prithee, read i' thy right wits.—So I do, madonna; but to read his right wits is to read thus . . . . v 1 305
Worse than the great'st infection That e'er was heard or read! *W. Tale* i 2 424
Appear in person here in court. Silence!—Read the indictment . iii 2 11
You have not dared to break the holy seal Nor read the secrets in't iii 2 131
Break up the seals and read.—Hermione is chaste; Polixenes blameless iii 2 132
Hast thou read truth?—Ay, my lord; even so As it is here set down . iii 2 139
Though I am not bookish, yet I can read waiting-gentlewoman in the 'scape . . . . iii 3 73
He'll stand and read As 'twere my daughter's eyes . . iv 4 173
Do you not read some tokens of my son In the large composition? *K. John* i 1 87
If . . . thy princely son Can in this book of beauty read 'I love' . ii 1 485
Who hath read or heard Of any kindred action like to this? . iv 4 13
His words do take possession of my bosom. Read here, young Arthur iv 1 33
Can you not read it? is it not fair writ?—Too fairly . . iv 1 37
Have you beheld, Or have you read or heard? or could you think? iv 3 42
What more remains?—No more, but that you read These accusations *Richard II.* iv 1 222
Would it not shame thee in so fair a troop To read a lecture of them? . iv 1 232
Read o'er these articles.—Mine eyes are full of tears, I cannot see iv 1 243
Read o'er this paper while the glass doth come . . . iv 1 269
I'll read enough, When I do see the very book indeed Where all my sins are writ, and that's myself . . . . iv 1 273
Give me the glass, and therein will I read. No deeper wrinkles yet? . iv 1 276
I do repent me; read not my name there . . . . v 3 52
I will unclasp a secret book, And to your quick-conceiving discontents I'll read you matter deep and dangerous . . . 1 *Hen. IV.* i 3 190
Nothing but papers, my lord.—Let's see what they be: read them . ii 4 584
Where is he living . . . Which calls me pupil, or hath read to me? . iii 1 46
In faith, he is a worthy gentleman, Exceedingly well read . . iii 1 166
Therein should we read The very bottom and the soul of hope . iv 1 49
Proclaim'd at market-crosses, read in churches . . . v 1 73
Here are letters for you.—I cannot read them now . . . v 2 81
I have read the cause of his effects in Galen . . 2 *Hen. IV.* i 2 133
Have you read o'er the letters that I sent you?—We have, my liege . iii 1 36
That one might read the book of fate, And see the revolution of the times! iii 1 45
Here at more leisure may your highness read, With every course . iv 4 89
For you shall read that my great-grandfather Never went with his forces into France . . . . *Hen. V.* i 2 146
This same is yours: Read them; and know, I know your worthiness . ii 2 69
What read you there, That hath so cowarded and chased your blood? . ii 2 74
That you shall read In your own losses . . . . iii 6 138
As I have read in the chronicles . . . . . . iv 7 98
Vouchsafe to those that have not read the story, That I may prompt them . . . . v Prol. 1
Upon the which, that every one may read, Shall be engraved 1 *Hen. VI.* ii 2 14
For once I read That stout Pendragon in his litter sick Came to the field iii 2 94
Some sudden qualm hath struck me at the heart And dimm'd mine eyes, that I can read no further . . . . 2 *Hen. VI.* i 1 55
I never read but England's kings have had Large sums of gold and dowries with their wives . . . . i 1 128
John Southwell, read you; and let us to our work . . i 4 14
This Edmund, . . . As I have read, laid claim unto the crown . ii 2 40
He can write and read and cast accompt.—O monstrous! . iv 2 93
But stay, I'll read it over once again . . . . iv 4 14
Because they could not read, thou hast hanged them . . iv 7 49
That it may be this day read o'er in Paul's . . *Richard III.* iii 6 3
Read The cardinal's malice and his potency Together . *Hen. VIII.* i 1 104
I read in's looks Matter against me; and his eye reviled Me . i 1 125
Whilst our commission from Rome is read, Let silence be commanded . ii 4 1
What's the need? It hath already publicly been read . . ii 4 3
Wherein was read, How that the cardinal did entreat his holiness . iii 2 31
Read o'er this; And after, this: and then to breakfast with What appetite you have . . . . iii 2 201
I must read this paper; I fear, the story of his anger . . iii 2 208
You may read the rest.—I thank you, sir . . . . iv 1 19
And those about her From her shall read the perfect ways of honour . v 5 38
What the declined is He shall as soon read in the eyes of others As feel in his own fall . . . . . . *Troi. and Cres.* iii 3 77
Like a book of sport thou'lt read me o'er; But there's more in me . iv 5 239
Here's a letter come from yond poor girl.—Let me read . . v 3 100
Spare us not. Say we read lectures to you . . *Coriolanus* ii 3 243
I have been The book of his good acts, whence men have read His fame v 2 15
Deliver them this paper: having read it, Bid them repair to the market-place . . . . v 6 2
We here deliver . . . what We have compounded on.—Read it not, noble lords . . . . v 6 84
And go read with thee Sad stories chanced in the times of old *T. Andron.* iii 2 82
Thy sight is young, And thou shalt read when mine begin to dazzle . iii 2 85
Cornelia never with more care Read to her sons than she hath read to thee . . . . iv 1 13
And I have read that Hecuba of Troy Ran mad for sorrow . . iv 1 20
Thou art deeper read, and better skill'd . . . . iv 1 33
Lavinia, shall I read? This is the tragic tale of Philomel . iv 1 46
O, do ye read, my lord, what she hath writ? 'Stuprum. Chiron. Demetrius' . . . . iv 1 77
'Tis a verse in Horace; I know it well: I read it in the grammar long ago iv 2 23
As a note Where I may read who pass'd that passing fair *Rom. and Jul.* i 1 242
I pray, sir, can you read?—Ay, mine own fortune in my misery . i 2 59

Read. Can you read any thing you see?—Ay, if I know the letters and the language . . . . *Rom. and Jul.* i 2 62
Rest you merry!—Stay, fellow; I can read . . . . . i 2 66
Read o'er the volume of young Paris' face And find delight writ there . i 3 81
O, she knew well Thy love did read by rote and could not spell . ii 3 88
Read me the superscription of these letters . . . *T. of Athens* ii 2 81
Canst not read?—No.—There will little learning die then, that day thou art hanged . . . . ii 2 84
And write in thee the figures of their love, Ever to read them thine . v 1 158
What's on this tomb I cannot read; the character I'll take with wax . v 3 6
He reads much; He is a great observer . . . . *J. Cæsar* i 2 201
The exhalations whizzing in the air Give so much light that I may read ii 1 45
If thou read this, O Cæsar, thou mayst live . . . . ii 3 15
Read this schedule.—Trebonius doth desire you to o'er-read, At your best leisure, this his humble suit . . . . . . iii 1 3
O Cæsar, read mine first; for mine's a suit That touches Cæsar nearer: read it, great Cæsar . . . . iii 1 6
Delay not, Cæsar; read it instantly.—What, is the fellow mad? . iii 1 9
'Tis his will: Let but the commons hear this testament—Which, pardon me, I do not mean to read . . . . iii 2 136
We'll hear the will: read it, Mark Antony.—The will, the will! . iii 2 143
We will hear Cæsar's will.—Have patience, gentle friends, I must not read it . . . . iii 2 145
Read the will; we'll hear it, Antony; You shall read us the will . iii 2 152
You will compel me, then, to read the will? . . . . iii 2 161
When he reads Thy personal venture in the rebels' fight . . *Macbeth* i 3 90
Your pains Are register'd where every day I turn The leaf to read them i 3 152
Your face, my thane, is as a book where men May read strange matters i 5 64
I have seen her rise from her bed, throw her nightgown upon her, unlock her closet, take forth paper, fold it, write upon't, read it, afterwards seal it, and again return to bed . . . . . . v 1 7
At our more consider'd time we'll read, Answer, and think upon this business . . . . *Hamlet* ii 2 81
What do you read, my lord?—Words, words, words . . . ii 2 193
What is the matter, my lord?—Between who?—I mean, the matter that you read . . . . ii 2 197
Read on this book; That show of such an exercise may colour Your loneliness . . . . iii 1 44
Here's the commission: read it at more leisure . . . . v 2 26
I am thinking, brother, of a prediction I read this other day . . *Lear* i 2 153
Deliver'd letters, spite of intermission, Which presently they read . ii 4 34
Another way, The news is not so tart. I'll read, and answer . . iv 2 88
Did your letters pierce the queen to any demonstration of grief?—Ay, sir; she took them, read them in my presence . . . . . iv 3 13
Read thou this challenge; mark but the penning of it . . . iv 6 141
Read.—What, with the case of eyes? . . . . . . iv 6 146
Stay till I have read the letter.—I was forbid it . . . . v 1 47
Come hither, herald,—Let the trumpet sound,—And read out this . v 3 108
Thou worse than any name, read thine own evil . . . . v 3 156
Have you not read, Roderigo, Of some such thing? . . . *Othello* i 1 174
You shall yourself read in the bitter letter After your own sense . i 3 68
She was a charmer, and could almost read The thoughts of people . iii 4 57
In nature's infinite book of secrecy A little I can read . *Ant. and Cleo.* i 2 10
At thy sovereign leisure read The garboils she awaked . . . i 3 60
Read not my blemishes in the world's report: I have not kept my square ii 3 5
Made his will, and read it To public ear . . . . . iii 4 4
By her election may be truly read What kind of man he is . *Cymbeline* i 1 53
So far I read aloud . . . . i 6 26
Almost midnight, madam.—I have read three hours then . . . ii 2 3
A precedent Which not to read would show the Britons cold . . . iii 1 76
He is at Milford-Haven: read, and tell me How far 'tis thither . iii 2 51
O boys, this story The world may read in me . . . . . iii 3 56
Speak, man: thy tongue May take off some extremity, which to read Would be even mortal to me . . . . iii 4 17
Please you, read; And you shall find me, wretched man, a thing The most disdain'd of fortune . . . . iii 4 18
To write and read Be henceforth treacherous! . . . . . iv 2 316
O most delicate fiend! Who is't can read a woman? . . . . v 5 48
Read, and declare the meaning . . . . v 5 434
Lords and ladies in their lives Have read it for restoratives *Pericles* 1 Gower 8
Her face the book of praises, where is read Nothing but curious pleasures i 1 15
Scorning advice, read the conclusion, then: Which read and not expounded, 'tis decreed, As these before thee thou thyself shalt bleed . i 1 56
If this be true, which makes me pale to read it . . . . . i 1 75
Reader. And wide unclasp the tables of their thoughts To every ticklish reader! . . . . *Troi. and Cres.* iv 5 61
Readest. Remember, as thou read'st, thy promise pass'd *Richard II.* v 3 51
Readiest. Tell me, I beseech you, which is the readiest way? *T. of Shrew* iv 2 220
The readiest way to make the wench amends Is to become her husband and her father . . . . *Richard III.* i 1 155
My sons; Rome's readiest champions, repose you here . *T. Andron.* i 1 151
Parts bread with him, pledges the breath of him in a divided draught, is the readiest man to kill him . . . . . *T. of Athens* i 2 49
Readily. And where this breach now in our fortunes made May readily be stopp'd . . . . 2 *Hen. VI.* v 2 83
Readiness. To-morrow be in readiness to go . . *T. G. of Ver.* i 3 70
I thought, by your readiness in the office, you had continued in it some time. You say, seven years together? . . . *Meas. for Meas.* ii 1 275
What page's suit she hath in readiness . . . . *Mer. of Venice* ii 4 33
We could at once put us in readiness . . . . *T. of Shrew* i 1 43
Your ships already are in readiness . . . . . 1 *Hen. VI.* iii 1 186
Royal commanders, be in readiness . . . . . 3 *Hen. VI.* ii 2 67
We are in readiness.—This cheers my heart, to see your forwardness . v 4 64
All things are in readiness . . . . *Richard III.* v 3 52
I am joyful to hear of their readiness . . . . . *Coriolanus* iv 3 51
Every thing In readiness for Hymenæus stand . . . *T. Andron.* i 1 325
Where be our men?—Here, my lord, in readiness . . *T. of Athens* i 2 172
Let's briefly put on manly readiness . . . . . *Macbeth* ii 3 139
If it be not now, yet it will come: the readiness is all . . *Hamlet* v 2 234
Therefore ripely Our chariots and our horsemen be in readiness . *Cymb.* iii 5 23
Your ships: They are in readiness . . . . iv 2 336
Reading. What letter are you reading there? . . . *T. G. of Ver.* i 3 51
Now will he be swinged for reading my letter . . . . . iii 1 392
My uncle's fool, reading the challenge, subscribed for Cupid . *Much Ado* i 1 41
Reading it over, she found Benedick and Beatrice between the sheet . ii 3 142
For your writing and reading, let that appear when there is no need of such vanity . . . . iii 3 21
Call me a fool; Trust not my reading nor my observations . . iv 1 167
How well he's read, to reason against reading! . . . *L. L. Lost* i 1 94
Who is he comes here? What, Longaville! and reading! listen, ear . iv 3 45
Reading. Peace! Here comes my sister, reading: stand aside *As Y. L It* iii 2 132
I pray you, mar no moe of my verses with reading them ill-favouredly . iii 2 279
Such as his reading And manifest experience had collected . *All's Well* i 3 228
On the reading it he changed almost into another man . . . . iv 3 5
The spirit of humours intimate reading aloud to him! . . . *T. Night* ii 5 94
That you should fashion, wrest, or bow your reading . . . *Hen. V.* i 2 14
Here is Ulysses: I'll interrupt his reading. How now, Ulysses! *Troi. and Cres.* iii 3 93
What are you reading?—A strange fellow here Writes me . . . iii 3 95
Let me see; is not the leaf turn'd down Where I left reading? *J. Cæsar* iv 3 274
But, look, where sadly the poor wretch comes reading . . . *Hamlet* ii 2 168
What paper were you reading?—Nothing, my lord . . . . *Lear* i 2 30
She hath been reading late The tale of Tereus . . . . *Cymbeline* ii 2 44
Readins. Has cozened all the hosts of Readins . . . *Mer. Wives* iv 5 80
Ready. Make yourself ready in your cabin for the mischance . *Tempest* i 1 27
I am ready now. Approach, my Ariel, come . . . . . . i 2 187
The clouds methought would open and show riches Ready to drop upon me . . . . iii 2 151
Dinner is ready, and your father stays . . . . *T. G. of Ver.* i 2 131
'Tis ready, sir, here in the porch . . . . . . *Mer. Wives* i 4 63
It makes me almost ready to wrangle with mine own honesty . . . ii 1 88
My heart is ready to crack with impatience . . . . . . ii 2 301
Be ready here hard by . . . . iii 3 10
Be ready, Claudio, for your death to-morrow . . *Meas. for Meas.* iii 1 107
To-morrow you must die; go to your knees and make ready . . . iii 1 172
Who hath a story ready for your ear . . . . iv 1 56
Is the axe upon the block, sirrah?—Very ready, sir . . . . iv 3 40
Will you walk? dinner is ready . . . . *Much Ado* ii 3 216
'Tis time you were ready . . . . iii 4 53
I'll wait upon them: I am ready . . . . iii 5 61
Call her forth, brother; here's the friar ready . . . . . v 4 39
Answer as I call you. Nick Bottom, the weaver.—Ready *M. N. Dream* i 2 20
Ready.—And I.—And I.—And I.—Where shall we go? . . . . iii 1 166
Speak thou now.—Here, villain; drawn and ready . . . . iii 2 402
Where's Peaseblossom?—Ready.—Scratch my head, Peaseblossom . iv 1 6
Be ready at the farthest by five of the clock . . . *Mer. of Venice* ii 2 122
Is Antonio here?—Ready, so please your grace . . . . . iv 1 2
Call the Jew into the court.—He is ready at the door . . . . iv 1 15
Are there balance here to weigh The flesh?—I have them ready . . iv 1 256
Give me my principal, and let me go.—I have it ready for thee . . iv 1 337
Here is the place appointed for the wrestling, and they are ready to perform it . . . . *As Y. Like It* i 2 155
Where is this young gallant that is so desirous to lie with his mother earth?—Ready, sir; but his will hath in it a more modest working . i 2 214
Procure me music ready when he wakes . . . . *T. of Shrew* Ind. 1 50
If he chance to speak, be ready straight . . . . . . Ind. 1 52
Some one be ready with a costly suit And ask him what apparel he will wear . . . . Ind. 1 59
Thy servants do attend on thee, Each in his office ready at thy beck . Ind. 2 36
Grumio, my horse.—Ay, sir, they be ready: the oats have eaten the horses . . . . iii 2 207
My master and mistress are almost frozen to death.—There's fire ready iv 1 41
Where's the cook? is supper ready, the house trimmed, rushes strewed? iv 1 48
The carpets laid, and every thing in order?—All ready . . . iv 1 54
Are they all ready?—They are.—Call them forth . . . . . iv 1 97
Me shall you find ready and willing With one consent . . . . iv 4 34
Make her ready straight; And, if you will, tell what hath happened . iv 4 63
Bid the priest be ready to come against you come with your appendix . iv 4 104
Softly and swiftly, sir; for the priest is ready.—I fly . . . . v 1 2
In token of which duty, if he please, My hand is ready . . . v 2 179
Are you ready, sir?—Ay; prithee, sing . . . . . *T. Night* ii 4 50
I'll get 'em all three all ready . . . . iii 1 102
I am ready to distrust mine eyes And wrangle with my reason . . iv 3 13
My ships are ready and My people did expect my hence departure *W. Tale* i 2 449
Ready to leap out of himself for joy . . . . v 2 54
Be ready, as your lives shall answer it . . . . *Richard II.* i 1 198
Command our officers at arms Be ready to direct these home alarms . i 1 205
Who ready here do stand in arms, To prove, by God's grace . . . i 3 36
Is not ready yet, Nor shall we need his help these fourteen days 1 *Hen. IV.* iii 1 87
Go, make ready breakfast; love thy husband, look to thy servants . iii 3 192
The answer is as ready as a borrower's cap, 'I am the king's poor cousin' 2 *Hen. IV.* ii 2 124
I cannot speak; if my heart be not ready to burst . . . . . ii 4 409
We ready are to try our fortunes To the last man . . . . iv 2 43
His powers are yet not ready To raise so great a siege . . *Hen. V.* iii 3 46
All things are ready, if our minds be so . . . . . . iv 3 71
If I did but stir out of my bed, Ready they were to shoot me 1 *Hen. VI.* i 4 56
Thou shalt find us ready for thee still . . . . ii 4 104
Ready to starve and dare not touch his own . . . . 2 *Hen. VI.* i 1 229
Ready are the appellant and defendant . . . . ii 3 49
Fie on myself, that have a sword, and yet am ready to famish! . . iv 10 2
Let's away; Our army is ready; come, we'll after them . 3 *Hen. VI.* i 1 256
My mourning weeds are laid aside, And I am ready to put armour on iii 3 230; iv 1 105
The time and case requireth haste: Your horse stands ready . . . iv 5 19
Prepare you, lords, for Edward is at hand, Ready to fight . . . v 4 61
Ready to catch each other by the throat . . . . *Richard III.* i 3 189
Ready, with every nod, to tumble down . . . . iii 4 102
And both are ready in their offices, At any time, to grace my stratagems iii 5 10
Set it down. Is ink and paper ready?—It is, my lord . . . . v 3 75
Is he in person ready?—Ay, please your grace . . . . *Hen. VIII.* i 1 117
Is the banquet ready I' the privy chamber?—Yes, my lord . . . i 4 98
Prepare there, The duke is coming: see the barge be ready . . . ii 1 98
When they were ready to set out for London, . . . took 'em from me . ii 2 5
We are ready To use our utmost studies in your service . . . . iii 1 173
Is he ready To come abroad?—I think, by this he is . . . . . iii 2 82
You are strangely troublesome. Let some o' the guard be ready there . v 3 95
Bid the cheek be ready with a blush . . . . . *Troi. and Cres.* i 3 228
More ready to cry out 'Who knows what follows?' . . . . . ii 2 13
She's making her ready, she'll come straight . . . . . iii 2 31
If Hector will to-morrow Be answer'd in his challenge: Ajax is ready . iii 3 35
They are at hand and ready to effect it.—How my achievements mock me! . . . . iv 2 70
My lord, is the lady ready?—Hark! you are call'd . . . . iv 4 51
Let us make ready straight.—Yea, with a bridegroom's fresh alacrity . iv 4 146
Make you ready your stiff bats and clubs . . . . *Coriolanus* i 1 165
We never yet made doubt but Rome was ready To answer us . . . i 2 18
Ready, when time shall prompt them, to make road Upon's again . . iii 1 5
Have you a catalogue Of all the voices . . ?—I have; 'tis ready . . iii 3 10

Ready. Make them be strong and ready for this hint, When we shall hap to give't them *Coriolanus* iii 3 23
Have you an army ready, say you?—A most royal one iv 3 46
Can you think to blow out the intended fire your city is ready to flame in? v 2 49
They shall be ready at your highness' will To answer their suspicion with their lives *T. Andron.* ii 3 297
I'll play the cook, And see them ready 'gainst their mother comes v 2 206
The feast is ready, which the careful Titus Hath ordain'd v 3 21
Antony, and Potpan!—Ay, boy, ready.—You are looked for *Rom. and Jul.* i 5 12
Ready stand To smooth that rough touch with a tender kiss i 5 97
Will you be ready? do you like this haste? We'll keep no great ado iii 4 22
Come, is the bride ready to go to church?—Ready to go, but never to return iv 5 33
Lord Timon!—Ready for his friends *T. of Athens* i 2 236
Is my lord ready to come forth?—No, indeed, he is not iii 4 35
You are the first that rears your hand.—Are we all ready? *J. Cæsar* iii 1 31
Be ready, gods, with all your thunderbolts; Dash him to pieces! iv 3 81
We, at the height, are ready to decline iv 3 217
A canopy most fatal, under which Our army lies, ready to give up the ghost v 1 89
Bid thy mistress, when my drink is ready, She strike upon the bell *Macbeth* ii 1 31
I laid their daggers ready; He could not miss 'em ii 2 12
Our power is ready; Our lack is nothing but our leave iv 3 236
Go, make you ready.—How now, my lord! *Hamlet* iii 2 50
Be the players ready?—Ay, my lord; they stay upon your patience iii 2 111
The bark is ready, and the wind at help, The associates tend iv 3 46
They follow the king's pleasure: if his fitness speaks, mine is ready v 2 210
Let me not stay a jot for dinner; go get it ready *Lear* i 4 9
How now! are the horses ready?—Ready, my lord i 5 52
And bring you where both fire and food is ready iii 4 158
Seek out where thy father is, that he may be ready for our apprehension iii 5 20
There is a litter ready; lay him in't, And drive towards Dover iii 6 97
They are ready To-morrow, or at further space, to appear v 3 52
I am almost ready to dissolve, Hearing of this v 3 203
Your commission's ready; Follow me, and receive't *Ant. and Cleo.* ii 3 41
I find thee Most fit for business: go make thee ready iii 3 40
I remember now How he's employ'd: he shall in time be ready v 1 72
Your lady's person: is she ready?—Ay, To keep her chamber *Cymbeline* ii 3 86
Ready in gibes, quick-answer'd, saucy and As quarrelous as the weasel iii 4 161
Your preparation can affront no less Than what you hear of: come more, for more you're ready iv 3 30
Are you ready for death?—Over-roasted rather; ready long ago v 4 152
Hanging is the word, sir: if you be ready for that, you are well cooked v 4 156
Thus ready for the way of life or death, I wait the sharpest blow *Pericles* i 1 54
Are ready now To eat those little darlings whom they loved i 4 43
Are the knights ready to begin the triumph? ii 2 1
Stay your coming to present themselves.—Return them, we are ready ii 2 4
We have a chest beneath the hatches, caulked and bitumed ready iii 1 72
Ready braced. Even at hand a drum is ready braced *K. John* v 2 169
Ready guess. I could with a ready guess declare *Hen. V.* i 1 96
Ready hearing. Hath prevail'd On thy too ready hearing *Cymbeline* iii 2 6
Ready money. He made five marks, ready money *Meas. for Meas.* iv 3 7
Ready mounted are they to spit forth Their iron indignation *K. John* ii 1 211
Ready sense. The din of war gan pierce His ready sense *Coriolanus* ii 2 120
Ready tongue. See what a ready tongue suspicion hath *2 Hen. IV.* i 1 84
Real. Is't real that I see? *All's Well* v 3 307
It must omit Real necessities *Coriolanus* iii 1 147
Really. You will do't, sir, really *Hamlet* v 2 132
Realm. This is enough to be the decay of lust and late-walking through the realm *Mer. Wives* v 5 153
The life, the right and truth of all this realm Is fled to heaven *K. John* iv 3 144
Confess thy treasons ere thou fly the realm *Richard II.* i 3 198
We are inforced to farm our royal realm i 4 45
This blessed plot, this earth, this realm, this England ii 1 50
The Earl of Wiltshire hath the realm in farm ii 1 256
Is there no plot To rid the realm of this pernicious blot? iv 1 325
Though he divide the realm and give thee half, It is too little v 1 60
He doth fill fields with harness in the realm *1 Hen. IV.* iii 2 101
When the lords and barons of the realm Perceived Northumberland did lean to him, The more and less came in with cap and knee iv 3 66
Thou art now one of the greatest men in this realm *2 Hen. IV.* v 3 92
Salique land the French unjustly glose To be the realm of France *Hen. V.* i 2 41
The Salique law Was not devised for the realm of France i 2 55
God, the best maker of all marriages, Combine your hearts in one, your realms in one! v 2 388
Thou art protector And lookest to command the prince and realm *1 Hen. VI.* i 1 38
Prosper this realm, keep it from civil broils, Combat with adverse planets! i 1 53
There's none protector of the realm but I i 3 12
Thou most usurping proditor, And not protector, of the king or realm i 3 32
Seeks to overthrow religion, Because he is protector of the realm i 3 66
All the priests and friars in my realm Shall in procession sing i 6 19
For his acts So much applauded through the realm of France ii 2 36
Except you mean with obstinate repulse To slay your sovereign and destroy the realm iii 1 114
Hearing of your arrival in this realm, I have awhile given truce unto my wars iii 4 2
Destroy'd themselves, and lost the realm of France! iv 1 147
Marshal to Henry the Sixth Of all his wars within the realm of France iv 7 71
It were enough to fright the realm of France iv 7 82
A godly peace concluded of Between the realms of England and of France v 1 6
So my fancy may be satisfied, And peace established between these realms v 3 92
I foresee with grief The utter loss of all the realm of France v 4 112
Margaret shall now be queen, and rule the king; But I will rule both her, the king and realm v 5 108
With all the learned council of the realm *2 Hen. VI.* i 1 89
While these do labour for their own preferment, Behoves it us to labour for the realm i 1 182
The realms of England, France and Ireland Bear that proportion i 1 232
Art thou not second woman in the realm? i 2 43
Madam, I am protector of the realm; And, at his pleasure, will resign i 3 123
All the peers and nobles of the realm Have been as bondmen i 3 129
York is meetest man To be your regent in the realm of France i 3 164
Henry the Fourth Seized on the realm, deposed the rightful king ii 2 24
God and King Henry govern England's realm ii 3 30
Give up your staff, sir, and the king his realm ii 3 31
Realm. Did he not, in his protectorship, Levy great sums of money through the realm? *2 Hen. VI.* iii 1 61
I dam up this thy yawning mouth For swallowing the treasure of the realm iv 1 74
All the realm shall be in common iv 2 74
Burn all the records of the realm: my mouth shall be the parliament iv 7 16
Thou hast most traitorously corrupted the youth of the realm iv 7 36
Have I aught exacted at your hands, But to maintain the king, the realm? iv 7 75
The proudest peer in the realm shall not wear a head on his shoulders iv 7 127
No; first shall war unpeople this my realm *3 Hen. VI.* i 1 126
The duke is made protector of the realm; And yet shalt thou be safe? i 1 240
I and ten thousand in this luckless realm Had left no mourning widows ii 6 18
His state usurp'd, His realm a slaughter-house v 4 78
Never stand upright Till Richard wear the garland of the realm *Rich. III.* iii 2 40
They had gather'd a wise council to them Of every realm *Hen. VIII.* ii 4 52
I weigh'd the danger which my realms stood in By this my issue's fail. ii 4 197
Filling The whole realm, by your teaching and your chaplains v 3 16
That under hot ardent zeal would set whole realms on fire *T. of Athens* iii 3 34
This realm dismantled was Of Jove himself *Hamlet* iii 2 293
Then shall the realm of Albion Come to great confusion *Lear* iii 2 91
Friends of my soul, you twain Rule in this realm v 3 320
Realms and islands were As plates dropp'd from his pocket *Ant. and Cleo.* v 2 91
Re-answer. Which in weight to re-answer, his pettiness would bow under *Hen. V.* iii 6 136
Reap. Our corn's to reap, for yet our tithe's to sow *Meas. for Meas.* iv 1 76
They that reap must sheaf and bind *As Y. Like It* iii 2 113
To glean the broken ears after the man That the main harvest reaps iii 5 103
Proffers not took reap thanks for their reward *All's Well* ii 1 150
And yet, when wit and youth is come to harvest, Your wife is like to reap a proper man *T. Night* iii 1 144
Little vantage shall I reap thereby *Richard II.* i 3 218
And reap the harvest which that rascal sow'd *2 Hen. VI.* iii 1 381
And in thy need such comfort come to thee As now I reap at thy too cruel hand! *3 Hen. VI.* i 4 166
Of our labours thou shalt reap the gain.—I'll blast his harvest v 7 20
Though we have spent our harvest of this king, We are to reap the harvest of his son *Richard III.* ii 2 116
Cheerly on, courageous friends, To reap the harvest of perpetual peace v 2 15
The benefit Which thou shalt thereby reap is such a name, Whose repetition will be dogg'd with curses *Coriolanus* v 3 143
Holp to reap the fame Which he did end all his v 6 36
This is a thing Which you might from relation likewise reap *Cymbeline* ii 4 86
Reaped. Sow'd cockle reap'd no corn *L. L. Lost* iv 3 383
His chin new reap'd Show'd like a stubble-land at harvest-home *1 Hen. IV.* i 3 34
What sudden anger's this? how have I reap'd it? *Hen. VIII.* iii 2 204
Reapers. Your ships are not well mann'd; Your mariners are muleters, reapers, people Ingross'd by swift impress *Ant. and Cleo.* iii 7 36
Reaping. An autumn 'twas That grew the more by reaping v 2 88
Rear. Draw together; And when I rear my hand, do you the like *Tempest* ii 1 295
For her sake do I rear up her boy *M. N. Dream* ii 1 136
I'll not rear Another's issue *W. Tale* ii 3 192
She is as forward of her breeding as She is i' the rear our birth iv 4 592
Shall thy old dugs once more a traitor rear? *Richard II.* v 3 90
A statelier pyramis to her I'll rear Than Rhodope's *1 Hen. VI.* i 6 21
The king is dead.—Rear up his body; wring him by the nose *2 Hen. VI.* iii 2 34
Ay, but he's dead: off with the traitor's head, And rear it in the place your father's stands *3 Hen. VI.* ii 6 86
Or, like a gallant horse fall'n in first rank, Lie there for pavement to the abject rear *Troi. and Cres.* iii 3 162
I'll make a paste, And of the paste a coffin I will rear *T. Andron.* v 2 189
Casca, you are the first that rears your hand *J. Cæsar* iii 1 30
Keep you in the rear of your affection *Hamlet* i 3 34
Let us rear The higher our opinion *Ant. and Cleo.* ii 1 35
Reared. Had we pursued that life, And our weak spirits ne'er been higher rear'd With stronger blood *W. Tale* i 2 72
Whom I from meaner form Have bench'd and rear'd to worship i 2 314
From their ashes shall be rear'd A phœnix *1 Hen. VI.* iv 7 92
Checks and disasters Grow in the veins of actions highest rear'd *T. and C.* i 3 6
Which of your hands hath not defended Rome, And rear'd aloft the bloody battle-axe? *T. Andron.* iii 1 169
Some beast rear'd this; there does not live a man *T. of Athens* v 3 4
His legs bestrid the ocean: his rear'd arm Crested the world *A. and C.* v 2 82
Rearward. Myself would, on the rearward of reproaches, Strike at thy life *Much Ado* iv 1 128
A' came ever in the rearward of the fashion *2 Hen. IV.* iii 2 339
Now in the rearward comes the duke and his *1 Hen. VI.* iii 3 33
With a rearward following Tybalt's death, 'Romeo is banished' *R. and J.* iii 2 121
Reason. Your reason For raising this sea-storm? *Tempest* i 2 176
Who was so firm, so constant, that this coil Would not infect his reason? i 2 208
At thy request, monster, I will do reason, any reason iii 2 128
Yet with my nobler reason 'gainst my fury Do I take part v 1 26
Their rising senses Begin to chase the ignorant fumes that mantle Their clearer reason v 1 68
They devour their reason and scarce think Their eyes do offices of truth v 1 155
I think him best.—Your reason?—I have no other but a woman's reason; I think him so because I think him so *T. G. of Ver.* i 2 22
Are you reasoning with yourself?—Nay, I was rhyming: 'tis you that have the reason ii 1 150
Have I not reason to prefer mine own? ii 4 156
Or my false transgression, That makes me reasonless to reason thus ii 4 198
I love his lady too too much, And that's the reason I love him so little ii 4 206
But her picture I have yet beheld, And that hath dazzled my reason's light ii 4 210
When I look on her perfections, There is no reason but I shall be blind ii 4 212
But qualify the fire's extreme rage, Lest it should burn above the bounds of reason ii 7 23
Find me reasonable; if it be so, I shall do that that is reason *Mer. Wives* i 1 218
I will do as it shall become one that would do reason i 1 242
I will do a greater thing than that, upon your request, cousin, in any reason i 1 249
Ask me no reason why I love you; for though Love use Reason for his physician, he admits him not for his counsellor ii 1 5
Reason, you rogue, reason: think'st thou I'll endanger my soul gratis? ii 2 15
There is reasons and causes for it iii 1 48
In despite of the teeth of all rhyme and reason v 5 133
She hath prosperous art When she will play with reason *Meas. for Meas.* i 2 190
Moe reasons for this action At our more leisure shall I render you i 3 48
Reason thus with life: If I do lose thee, I do lose a thing That none but fools would keep iii 1 6

Reason. His unjust unkindness, that in all reason should have quenched her love — *Meas. for Meas.* iii 1 250
He shows his reason for that — iv 4 13
How might she tongue me! Yet reason dares her no — iv 4 28
Harp not on that, nor do not banish reason For inequality — v 1 64
Let your reason serve To make the truth appear where it seems hid — v 1 65
Many that are not mad Have, sure, more lack of reason — v 1 68
It imports no reason That with such vehemency he should pursue Faults proper to himself — v 1 108
In the why and the wherefore is neither rhyme nor reason *Com. of Errors* ii 2 49
I pray you, eat none of it.—Your reason?—Lest it make you choleric — ii 2 62
For what reason?—For two; and sound ones too — ii 2 91
Your reason was not substantial — ii 2 105
To know the reason of this strange restraint — iii 1 97
What, are you mad, that you do reason so?—Not mad, but mated — iii 2 53
How fondly dost thou reason! — iv 2 57
Hath he not reason to turn back an hour in a day? — iv 2 62
The reason that I gather he is mad, Besides this present instance — iv 3 87
And now he's there, past thought of human reason — v 1 189
Hear reason.—And when I have heard it, what blessing brings it? *M. Ado* i 3 6
I will not desire that.—You have no reason; I do it freely — iv 1 260
There thou speak'st reason — v 1 41
If justice cannot tame you, she shall ne'er weigh more reasons in her balance — v 1 211
Do not you love me?—Why, no; no more than reason — v 4 74
Do not you love me?—Troth, no; no more than reason — v 4 77
How well he's read, to reason against reading! *L. L. Lost* i 1 94
In reason nothing.—Something then in rhyme — i 1 99
Methinks Samson had small reason for it — i 2 92
A dangerous rhyme, master, against the reason of white and red — i 2 112
Were not his requests so far From reason's yielding, your fair self should make A yielding 'gainst some reason in my breast — ii 1 152
At which interview All liberal reason I will yield unto — ii 1 168
Your reason?—Why, all his behaviours did make their retire To the court of his eye — ii 1 233
Your reasons at dinner have been sharp and sententious — v 1 2
You care not for me.—Great reason; for 'past cure is still past care' — v 2 28
I know the reason, lady, why you ask.—O for your reason! — v 2 243
What reason have you for't?—The naked truth of it is, I have no shirt — v 2 715
The will of man is by his reason sway'd; And reason says you are the worthier maid *M. N. Dream* ii 2 115
Things growing are not ripe until their season: So I, being young, till now ripe not to reason — ii 2 118
Reason becomes the marshal to my will And leads me to your eyes — ii 2 120
You should have little reason for that: and yet, to say the truth, reason and love keep little company together now-a-days — iii 1 146
Fantasies, that apprehend More than cool reason ever comprehends — v 1 6
In courtesy, in all reason, we must stay the time — v 1 259
His reasons are as two grains of wheat hid in two bushels of chaff: you shall seek all day ere you find them *Mer. of Venice* i 1 115
And what's his reason? I am a Jew — iii 1 60
I did, my lord; And I have reason for it — iii 2 234
He seeks my life; his reason well I know — iii 3 21
It is much that the Moor should be more than reason — iii 5 45
There is no firm reason to be render'd, Why he cannot abide a gaping pig iv 1 53
So can I give no reason, nor I will not, More than a lodged hate — iv 1 59
I am never merry when I hear sweet music.—The reason is, your spirits are attentive — v 1 70
Our natural wits too dull to reason of such goddesses *As Y. Like It* i 2 56
Throw some of them at me; come, lame me with reasons — i 3 6
One should be lamed with reasons and the other mad without any — i 3 8
By reason of his absence, there is nothing That you will feed on — ii 4 85
An you will not be answered with reason, I must die — ii 7 100
Then thou art damned.— . . . For not being at court? Your reason — iii 2 40
Neither rhyme nor reason can express how much — iii 2 418
The reason why they are not so punished and cured is, that the lunacy is so ordinary that the whippers are in love too — iii 2 422
A traveller! By my faith, you have great reason to be sad — iv 1 22
No sooner sighed but they asked one another the reason, no sooner knew the reason but they sought the remedy — v 2 39
Feed yourselves with questioning; That reason wonder may diminish — v 4 145
I hope this reason stands for my excuse.—Ay, it stands so *T. of Shrew* Ind. 2 126
If thou ask me why, sufficeth, my reasons are both good and weighty — i 1 252
For what reason, I beseech you?—For this reason, if you'll know — i 2 235
I see no reason but supposed Lucentio Must get a father — ii 1 409
Having no other reason But that his beard grew thin and hungerly — iii 2 176
My heart as great, my reason haply more, To bandy word for word — v 2 171
Tell me thy reason why thou wilt marry *All's Well* i 3 29
Is this all your worship's reason?—Faith, madam, I have other holy reasons — i 3 33
Now have you heard The fundamental reasons of this war — iii 1 2
The reasons of our state I cannot yield — iii 1 10
My reasons are most strong; and you shall know them — iv 2 59
Oil and fire, too strong for reason's force, O'erbears it and burns on — v 3 7
If you be not mad, be gone; if you have reason, be brief *T. Night* i 5 212
If that the youth will come this way to-morrow, I'll give him reasons for't — i 5 325
Thy exquisite reason, dear knight?—I have no exquisite reason for't, but I have reason good enough — ii 3 156
Every reason excites to this, that my lady loves me — ii 5 179
Thy reason, man?—Troth, sir, I can yield you none without words; and words are grown so false, I am loath to prove reason with them — iii 1 26
Maugre all thy pride, Nor wit nor reason can my passion hide — iii 1 164
Do not extort thy reasons from this clause, For that I woo, thou therefore hast no cause; But rather reason thus with reason fetter, Love sought is good, but given unsought is better — iii 1 165
I'll not stay a jot longer.—Thy reason, dear venom, give thy reason.—You must needs yield your reason — iii 2 2
I will prove it legitimate, sir, upon the oaths of judgement and reason iii 2 16
Wonder not . . . why I do call thee so, for I will show thee no reason for't iii 4 167
I am ready to distrust mine eyes And wrangle with my reason — iv 3 14
Reason my son Should choose himself a wife, but as good reason The father . . . should hold some counsel In such a business *W. Tale* iv 4 417
For some other reasons, my grave sir, Which 'tis not fit you know — iv 4 422
If my reason Will thereto be obedient, I have reason — iv 4 493
As monstrous to our human reason As my Antigonus to break his grave — v 1 41
Thy speeches Will bring me to consider that which may Unfurnish me of reason — v 1 123
I have no reason for it; That is my brother's plea *K. John* i 1 66
My reasonable part produces reason How I may be deliver'd of these woes iii 4 54

Reason. Then, have I reason to be fond of grief? *K. John* iii 4 98
Strong reasons make strong actions — iii 4 182
Some reasons of this double coronation I have possess'd you with — iv 2 40
Our griefs, and not our manners, reason now.—But there is little reason in your grief; Therefore 'twere reason you had manners now — iv 3 29
He is prepared, and reason too he should — v 2 130
Teach thy necessity to reason thus *Richard II.* i 3 277
What was his reason? He was not so resolved when last we spake together — ii 3 28
Have I not reason to look pale and dead? — iii 2 79
It is a matter of small consequence, Which for some reasons I would not have seen.—Which for some reasons, sir, I mean to see — v 2 62
I see no reason why thou shouldst be so superfluous to demand the time of the day *1 Hen. IV.* i 2 11
I will lay him down such reasons for this adventure that he shall go — i 2 168
If he fight longer than he sees reason, I'll forswear arms — i 2 207
For divers reasons Which I shall send you written — i 3 262
And 'tis no little reason bids us speed, To save our heads — i 3 283
But hark you, Kate; I must not have you henceforth question me Whither I go, nor reason whereabout — ii 3 107
Tell us your reason: what sayest thou to this?—Come, your reason, Jack ii 4 259
Give you a reason on compulsion! if reasons were as plentiful as blackberries, I would give no man a reason upon compulsion — ii 4 264
Thou shalt find me tractable to any honest reason — iii 3 195
Every loop from whence The eye of reason may pry in upon us — iv 1 72
For any other reason than to set me off *2 Hen. IV.* i 2 15
Keeping such vile company as thou art hath in reason taken from me all ostentation of sorrow.—The reason? — ii 2 53
But many thousand reasons hold me back — ii 3 66
I see no reason in the law of nature but I may snap at him — iii 2 356
Our cause the best; Then reason will our hearts should be as good — iv 1 157
Every idle, nice and wanton reason Shall to the king taste of this action iv 1 191
Hear him but reason in divinity *Hen. V.* i 1 38
Your own reasons turn into your bosoms, As dogs upon their masters — ii 2 82
'Tis a subject for a sovereign to reason on — iii 7 38
When he sees reason of fears, as we do, his fears, out of doubt, be of the same relish as ours are — iv 1 113
In reason, no man should possess him with any appearance of fear — iv 1 115
These fellows of infinite tongue, that can rhyme themselves into ladies' favours, they do always reason themselves out again — v 2 165
We have consented to all terms of reason — v 2 358
The reason moved these warlike lords to this Was, for that . . . I was the next by birth and parentage *1 Hen. VI.* ii 5 70
You have great reason to do Richard right — iii 1 154
I see no reason, if I wear this rose, That any one should therefore be suspicious I more incline to Somerset — iv 1 152
Forsaketh yet the lists By reason of his adversary's odds — v 5 33
Since he affects her most, It most of all these reasons bindeth us — v 5 60
There's reason he should be displeased at it *2 Hen. VI.* i 1 155
Peace, son! and show some reason — i 3 116
Give me leave To show some reason, of no little force — i 3 166
I see no reason why a king of years Should be to be protected like a child — ii 3 28
Which fear if better reasons can supplant, I will subscribe — iii 1 37
'Tis York that hath more reason for his death — iii 1 245
By nature proved an enemy to the flock, Before his chaps be stain'd with crimson blood, As Humphrey, proved by reasons, to my liege iii 1 260
Furthermore, we'll have the Lord Say's head for selling the dukedom of Maine.—And good reason — iv 2 171
Go and meet him, And ask him what's the reason of these arms — iv 9 37
A messenger from Henry, our dread liege, To know the reason of these arms — v 1 18
No other reason for this wrong But that he was bound by a solemn oath? v 1 189
But I have reasons strong and forcible *3 Hen. VI.* i 2 3
And reason too: Who should succeed the father but the son? — ii 2 93
To prove him tyrant this reason may suffice, That Henry liveth still — iii 3 71
Then 'tis but reason that I be released From giving aid — iii 3 147
Setting your scorns and your mislike aside, Tell me some reason why — iv 1 25
We shall soon persuade Both him and all his brothers unto reason — iv 7 34
Had I not reason, think ye, to make haste, And seek their ruin? — v 6 72
For divers unknown reasons, I beseech you, Grant me this *Richard III.* i 2 218
I will not reason what is meant hereby, Because I will be guiltless — i 4 94
Shall I strike?—No, first let's reason with him — i 4 165
Ye cannot reason almost with a man That looks not heavily and full of fear ii 3 39
With what a sharp-provided wit he reasons! — iii 1 132
Thou know'st our reasons urged upon the way; What think'st thou? — iii 1 160
Encourage him, and show him all our reasons — iii 1 175
The reason we have sent— Look back, defend thee, here are enemies — iii 5 18
Your reasons are too shallow and too quick.—O no, my reasons are too deep and dead — iv 4 361
While we reason here, A royal battle might be won and lost — iv 4 537
Then fly. What, from myself? Great reason why: Lest I revenge — v 3 185
Let your reason with your choler question What 'tis you go about *Hen. VIII.* i 1 130
If with the sap of reason you would quench, Or but allay, the fire of passion — i 1 148
Pleaded still not guilty and alleged Many sharp reasons to defeat the law ii 1 14
With this reason: His master would be served before a subject — ii 2 7
The sharp thorny points Of my alleged reasons drive this forward — ii 4 225
Foreseeing those fell mischiefs Our reasons laid before him — v 1 50
Or those that with the fineness of their souls By reason guide *Troi. and Cres.* i 3 210
What merit's in that reason which denies The yielding of her up? — ii 2 24
With spans and inches so diminutive As fears and reasons — ii 2 32
No marvel, though you bite so sharp at reasons, You are so empty of them ii 2 33
Should not our father Bear the great sway of his affairs with reasons? — ii 2 35
You fur your gloves with reason. Here are your reasons — ii 2 38
A sword employ'd is perilous, And reason flies the object of all harm — ii 2 41
If he do set The very wings of reason to his heels — ii 2 44
If we talk of reason, Let's shut our gates and sleep — ii 2 46
Would they but fat their thoughts With this cramm'd reason: reason and respect Make livers pale and lustihood deject — ii 2 49
No discourse of reason, Nor fear of bad success in a bad cause — ii 2 116
The reasons you allege do more conduce To the hot passion of distemper'd blood Than to make up a free determination — ii 2 168
Much attribute he hath, and much the reason Why we ascribe it to him ii 3 125
Blind fear, that seeing reason leads, finds safer footing than blind reason stumbling without fear — iii 2 76
Of this my privacy I have strong reasons.—But 'gainst your privacy The reasons are more potent and heroical — iii 3 191

Reason. Bi-fold authority! where reason can revolt Without perdition, and loss assume all reason Without revolt *Troi. and Cres.* v 2 145
We'll put you, Like one that means his proper harm, in manacles, Then reason safely with you *Coriolanus* i 9 58
I'll give my reasons, More worthier than their voices iii 1 119
Where one part does disdain with cause, the other Insult without all reason iii 1 144
It [peace] makes men hate one another.—Reason; because they then less need one another iv 5 247
But reason with the fellow, Before you punish him, where he heard this iv 6 51
Desire not To allay my rages and revenges with Your colder reasons v 3 86
Perhaps thy childishness will move him more Than can our reasons v 3 158
Does reason our petition with more strength Than thou hast to deny't v 3 176
After your way his tale pronounced shall bury His reasons with his body v 6 59
And resolved withal To do myself this reason and this right *T. Andron.* i 1 279
Great reason that my noble lord be rated For sauciness ii 3 81
Have I not reason, think you, to look pale? ii 3 91
But yet let reason govern thy lament.—If there were reason for these miseries, Then into limits could I bind my woes iii 1 219
And wilt thou have a reason for this coil? iii 1 225
So great a lord Basely insinuate and send us gifts.—Had he not reason? iv 2 39
Your reason, mighty lord?—Because the girl should not survive her shame v 3 40
A reason mighty, strong, and effectual v 3 43
Thou wilt quarrel with a man for cracking nuts, having no other reason but because thou hast hazel eyes *Rom. and Jul.* iii 1 21
Withdraw unto some private place, And reason coldly of your grievances iii 1 55
The reason that I have to love thee Doth much excuse the appertaining rage iii 1 65
But love thee better than thou canst devise, Till thou shalt know the reason of my love iii 1 73
Now do you know the reason of this haste iv 1 15
Fond nature bids us all lament, Yet nature's tears are reason's merriment iv 5 83
It cannot hold; no reason Can found his state in safety *T. of Athens* ii 1 12
The reason of this?—I could render one.—Do it then ii 2 108
One that knows what belongs to reason; and canst use the time well iii 1 38
When these prodigies Do so conjointly meet, let not men say 'These are their reasons; they are natural' *J. Cæsar* i 3 30
I have not known when his affections sway'd More than his reason ii 1 21
He loves me well, and I have given him reasons; Send him but hither ii 1 219
My dear dear love To your proceeding bids me tell you this; And reason to my love is liable ii 2 104
You shall give me reasons Why and wherein Cæsar was dangerous iii 1 221
Our reasons are so full of good regard That were you, Antony, the son of Cæsar, You should be satisfied iii 1 224
I will myself into the pulpit first, And show the reason of our Cæsar's death iii 1 237
Public reasons shall be rendered Of Cæsar's death iii 2 7
I will hear Brutus speak.—I will hear Cassius; and compare their reasons iii 2 9
O judgement! thou art fled to brutish beasts, And men have lost their reason iii 2 110
Methinks there is much reason in his sayings iii 2 113
They are wise and honourable, And will, no doubt, with reasons answer you iii 2 219
I do not think it good.—Your reason?—This it is iv 3 198
Good reasons must, of force, give place to better iv 3 203
Let's reason with the worst that may befall v 1 97
Have we eaten on the insane root That takes the reason prisoner? *Macb.* i 3 85
And the receipt of reason A limbeck only i 7 66
The expedition of my violent love Outrun the pauser, reason ii 3 117
Masking the business from the common eye For sundry weighty reasons iii 1 126
You look angerly.—Have I not reason, beldams as you are? iii 5 2
As little is the wisdom, where the flight So runs against all reason iv 2 14
You cannot speak of reason to the Dane, And lose your voice *Hamlet* i 2 44
A fault against the dead, a fault to nature, To reason most absurd i 2 103
A beast, that wants discourse of reason, Would have mourn'd longer i 2 150
Oft breaking down the pales and forts of reason i 4 28
Might deprive your sovereignty of reason And draw you into madness i 4 73
If he love her not And be not from his reason fall'n thereon ii 2 165
A happiness that often madness hits on, which reason and sanity could not so prosperously be delivered of ii 2 214
By my fay, I cannot reason ii 2 272
What a piece of work is a man! how noble in reason! how infinite in faculty! ii 2 316
Now see that noble and most sovereign reason, Like sweet bells jangled iii 1 165
Since frost itself as actively doth burn And reason pandars will iii 4 88
Gave us not That capability and god-like reason To fust in us unused iv 4 38
Excitements of my reason and my blood iv 4 58
For two special reasons; Which may to you, perhaps, seem much unsinew'd iv 7 9
What is the reason that you use me thus? I loved you ever v 1 312
An exact command, Larded with many several sorts of reasons v 2 20
A faith that reason without miracle Could never plant in me *Lear* i 1 225
Though the wisdom of nature can reason it thus and thus, yet nature finds itself scourged by the sequent effects i 2 114
By the marks of sovereignty, knowledge, and reason, I should be false persuaded I had daughters i 4 253
And thereto add such reasons of your own As may compact it more i 4 361
The reason why the seven stars are no more than seven is a pretty reason i 5 38
Those that mingle reason with your passion Must be content to think you old ii 4 237
Reason not the need: our basest beggars Are in the poorest thing superfluous ii 4 267
He has some reason, else he could not beg iv 1 33
Know you the reason?—Something he left imperfect in the state iv 3 2
O, matter and impertinency mix'd! Reason in madness! iv 6 179
With him I sent the queen; My reason all the same v 3 52
Let the drum strike, and prove my title thine.—Stay yet; hear reason v 3 82
What is the reason of this terrible summons? *Othello* i 1 82
For he's embark'd With such loud reason to the Cyprus wars i 1 151
This cannot be, By no assay of reason i 3 18
If the balance of our lives had not one scale of reason to poise another of sensuality i 3 331
We have reason to cool our raging motions, our carnal stings i 3 334
My cause is hearted; thine hath no less reason i 3 374
His trespass, in our common reason—Save that, they say, the wars must make examples Out of their best—is not almost a fault iii 3 64
Now I shall have reason To show the love and duty that I bear you iii 3 193
Give me a living reason she's disloyal.—I do not like the office iii 3 409
Which I have greater reason to believe now than ever iv 2 217

Reason. Well, what is it? is it within reason and compass? *Othello* iv 2 223
I will hear further reason for this.—And you shall be satisfied iv 2 251
I have no great devotion to the deed; And yet he hath given me satisfying reasons: 'Tis but a man gone v 1 9
Your reason?—I see it in My motion, have it not in my tongue *A. and C.* ii 3 13
Though my reason Sits in the wind against me iii 10 36
That would make his will Lord of his reason iii 13 4
When valour preys on reason, It eats the sword it fights with iii 13 199
I was up so late; for that's the reason I was up so early *Cymbeline* ii 3 38
I am not very sick, Since I can reason of it iv 2 14
I have heard you say, Love's reason's without reason iv 2 22
In all safe reason He must have some attendants iv 2 131
We must lay his head to the east; My father hath a reason for't iv 2 256
No reason I, since of your lives you set So slight a valuation, should reserve My crack'd one to more care iv 4 48
It fits thee not to ask the reason why, Because we bid it *Pericles* i 1 157
Now do I see he had some reason for't i 3 8
We have no reason to desire it, Commended to our master, not to us i 3 37
Her reason to herself is only known ii 5 5
My commission Is not to reason of the deed, but do it iv 1 84
She has me her quirks, her reasons, her master reasons iv 6 8
Reasonable. The approaching tide Will shortly fill the reasonable shore That now lies foul and muddy *Tempest* v 1 81
Do you understand me?—Ay, sir, you shall find me reasonable *M. W.* i 1 217
I will marry her upon any reasonable demands i 1 233
If he be of any reasonable stature, he may creep in here iii 3 138
My jealousy is reasonable iv 2 155
All the wealth that he hath left, to be known a reasonable creature *Much Ado* i 1 71
I have a reasonable good ear in music *M. N. Dream* iv 1 31
I am glad this parcel of wooers are so reasonable *Mer. of Venice* i 2 119
Out of all reasonable match *As Y. Like It* iii 2 87
Is not your father grown incapable Of reasonable affairs? *W. Tale* iv 4 409
Who wants but something to be a reasonable man iv 4 617
Not mad but sensible of grief, My reasonable part produces reason *K. John* iii 4 54
Out of all compass, out of all reasonable compass *1 Hen. IV.* iii 3 26
'Tis no matter if I do halt; I have the wars for my colour, and my pension shall seem the more reasonable *2 Hen. IV.* i 2 276
That may with reasonable swiftness add More feathers to our wings *Hen. V.* i 2 306
The perdition of th' athversary hath been very great, reasonable great iii 6 104
I have no strength in measure, yet a reasonable measure in strength v 2 141
Your purpose is both good and reasonable *1 Hen. VI.* v 1 36
It is a quarrel just and reasonable *Richard III.* i 2 136
Reasonably. With all the rest retold, May reasonably die *1 Hen. IV.* i 3 74
Reasoned. Rightly reasoned, and in his own division *Much Ado* v 1 229
I reason'd with a Frenchman yesterday *Mer. of Venice* ii 8 27
Why is this reason'd? *Lear* v 1 28
Reasoning. What are you reasoning with yourself? *T. G. of Ver.* ii 1 147
This reasoning is not in the fashion to choose me a husband *Mer. of Ven.* i 2 23
Reasonless. That makes me reasonless to reason thus *T. G. of Ver.* ii 4 198
This proffer is absurd and reasonless *1 Hen. VI.* v 4 137
Reave. Had you that craft, to reave her Of what should stead her most?— . . . The ring was never hers *All's Well* v 3 86
To reave the orphan of his patrimony, To wring the widow *2 Hen. VI.* v 1 187
Rebate and blunt his natural edge With profits of the mind *Meas. for Meas.* i 4 60
Rebeck. What say you, Hugh Rebeck? *Rom. and Jul.* iv 5 135
Rebel. My own flesh and blood to rebel!—Out upon it, old carrion! rebels it at these years? *Mer. of Venice* iii 1 37
What is she but a foul contending rebel And graceless traitor? *T. of S.* v 2 159
Now for the rebels which stand out in Ireland *Richard II.* i 4 38
You that do abet him in this kind Cherish rebellion and are rebels all ii 3 147
Dear earth, I do salute thee with my hand, Though rebels wound thee with their horse's hoofs iii 2 7
Both young and old rebel, And all goes worse than I have power to tell iii 2 119
The rebels have consumed with fire Our town of Cicester v 6 2
A hundred thousand rebels die in this *1 Hen. IV.* iii 2 160
The English rebels met The eleventh of this month at Shrewsbury iii 2 165
God be thanked for these rebels, they offend none but the virtuous iii 3 214
He calls us rebels, traitors; and will scourge With haughty arms this hateful name in us v 2 40
Stain'd nobility lies trodden on, And rebels' arms triumph in massacres v 4 14
My name is Harry Percy.—Why, then I see A very valiant rebel of the name v 4 62
Quenching the flame of bold rebellion Even with the rebels' blood *2 Hen. IV.* Ind. 27
Is there not employment? . . . do not the rebels need soldiers? i 2 86
His grace says that which his flesh rebels against ii 4 379
An iron man, Cheering a rout of rebels with your drum iv 2 9
But for you, rebels, look to taste the due Meet for rebellion iv 2 116
A famous rebel art thou, Colevile iv 3 69
Pause us, till these rebels, now afoot, Come underneath the yoke iv 4 9
There is not now a rebel's sword unsheathed iv 4 86
If any rebel or vain spirit of mine Did with the least affection of a welcome Give entertainment to the might of it iv 5 172
If . . . we disagree, How will their grudging stomachs be provoked To wilful disobedience, and rebel! *1 Hen. VI.* iv 1 142
I come amain, To signify that rebels there are up *2 Hen. VI.* iii 1 283
What answer makes your grace to the rebels' supplication? iv 4 8
The rebels are in Southwark; fly, my lord! iv 4 27
Were the Duke of Suffolk now alive, These Kentish rebels would be soon appeased! iv 4 42
The lord mayor craves aid of your honour from the Tower to defend the city from the rebels iv 5 6
The rebels have assay'd to win the Tower iv 5 9
Will ye relent, And yield to mercy whilst 'tis offer'd you; Or let a rebel lead you to your deaths? iv 8 13
That monstrous rebel Cade, Who since I heard to be discomfited v 1 62
And so to arms, victorious father, To quell the rebels v 1 212
Look where the sturdy rebel sits, Even in the chair of state *3 Hen. VI.* i 1 50
You quake like rebels? O gentle villain, do not turn away! *Richard III.* i 3 162
The petty rebel, dull-brain'd Buckingham iv 4 332
Upon the western shore, Safe-conducting the rebels from their ships iv 4 483
If not to fight with foreign enemies, Yet to beat down these rebels here iv 4 532
O thou touch of hearts! Think, thy slave man rebels *T. of Athens* iv 3 391
Be not fond, To think that Cæsar bears such rebel blood *J. Cæsar* iii 1 40
Worthy to be a rebel, for to that The multiplying villanies of nature Do swarm upon him *Macbeth* i 2 10
Fortune, on his damned quarrel smiling, Show'd like a rebel's whore i 2 15

Rebel. When he reads Thy personal venture in the rebels' fight *Macbeth* i 3 91
Or did line the rebel With hidden help and vantage . . . i 3 112
Youth to itself rebels, though none else near *Hamlet* i 3 44
Smooth every passion That in the natures of their lords rebel *Lear* ii 2 82
Here's a young and sweating devil here, That commonly rebels *Othello* iii 4 43
And so rebel to judgement . *Ant. and Cleo.* i 4 33
That life, a very rebel to my will, May hang no longer on me . iv 9 14
I came unto your court for honour's cause, And not to be a rebel *Pericles* ii 5 62
Rebelled. To the disposing of it nought rebell'd . *Hen. VIII.* i 1 43
A time when all the body's members Rebell'd against the belly *Coriol.* i 1 100
Rebel-like. It seem'd she was a queen Over her passion; who, most rebel-like, Sought to be king o'er her . *Lear* iv 3 16
Rebelling. How dare you ghosts Accuse the thunderer, whose bolt, you know, Sky-planted batters all rebelling coasts? . *Cymbeline* v 4 96
Rebellion. What a ruthless thing is this in him, for the rebellion of a codpiece to take away the life of a man! . *Meas. for Meas.* iii 2 122
Now, God delay our rebellion! as we are ourselves, what things are we! —Merely our own traitors . *All's Well* iv 3 23
Natural rebellion, done i' the blaze of youth . v 3 6
In rebellion with himself will have All that are his so too *W. Tale* i 2 355
Thy later vows against thy first Is in thyself rebellion to thyself *K. John* iii 1 289
Rebellion, flat rebellion! . iii 1 298
Unthread the rude eye of rebellion And welcome home again discarded faith . v 4 11
Even in condition of the worst degree, In gross rebellion *Richard II.* ii 3 109
And you that do abet him in this kind Cherish rebellion and are rebels all ii 3 147
This earth shall have a feeling and these stones Prove armed soldiers, ere her native king Shall falter under foul rebellion's arms . iii 2 26
Rebellion lay in his way, and he found it . *1 Hen. IV.* v 1 28
To face the garment of rebellion With some fine colour . v 1 74
Thus ever did rebellion find rebuke . v 5 1
Rebellion in this land shall lose his sway, Meeting the check of such another day . v 5 41
Quenching the flame of bold rebellion Even with the rebels' blood *2 Hen. IV.* Ind. 26
That rebellion had bad luck And that young Harry Percy's spur was cold . i 1 41
For that same word, rebellion, did divide The action of their bodies from their souls . i 1 194
This word, rebellion, it had froze them up, As fish are in a pond . i 1 199
It is worse shame to beg than to be on the worst side, were it worse than the name of rebellion . i 2 90
If that rebellion Came like itself, in base and abject routs . iv 1 32
Seal this lawless bloody book Of forged rebellion with a seal divine . iv 1 92
But for you, rebels, look to taste the due Meet for rebellion . iv 2 117
Bringing rebellion broached on his sword. *Hen. V.* v Prol. 32
Henry the Fourth by conquest got the crown.—'Twas by rebellion *3 Hen. VI.* i 1 133
Language unmannerly, yea, such which breaks The sides of loyalty, and almost appears In loud rebellion . *Hen. VIII.* i 2 29
One o' the lowest, basest, poorest, Of this most wise rebellion *Coriolanus* i 1 162
We nourish 'gainst our senate The cockle of rebellion, insolence, sedition iii 1 70
In a rebellion, When what's not meet, but what must be, was law . iii 1 167
Rebellion's head, rise never till the wood Of Birnam rise . *Macbeth* iv 1 97
What is the cause, Laertes, That thy rebellion looks so giant-like? *Ham.* iv 5 121
Rebellious. In my youth I never did apply Hot and rebellious liquors in my blood . *As Y. Like It* ii 3 49
Here let us rest, if this rebellious earth Have any resting for her true king's queen . *Richard II.* v 1 5
With which he yoketh your rebellious necks . *1 Hen. VI.* ii 3 64
As thou art knight, never to disobey Nor be rebellious . v 4 171
Rebellious hinds, the filth and scum of Kent . *2 Hen. VI.* iv 2 130
Rebellious subjects, enemies to peace . *Rom. and Jul.* i 1 88
Point against point rebellious, arm 'gainst arm . *Macbeth* i 2 56
His antique sword, Rebellious to his arm, lies where it falls *Hamlet* ii 2 492
Rebellious hell, If thou canst mutine in a matron's bones . iii 4 82
Rebound. I do feel, By the rebound of yours, a grief that smites My very heart at root. *Ant. and Cleo.* v 2 104
Rebuke. Against all checks, rebukes and manners . *Mer. Wives* iii 4 84
Why bear you these rebukes and answer not? . *Com. of Errors* v 1 89
Rebuke me not for that which you provoke . *L. L. Lost* v 2 347
Why rebuke you him that loves you so? . *M. N. Dream* iii 2 43
Does not the stone rebuke me For being more stone than it? *W. Tale* v 3 37
To rebuke the usurpation Of thy unnatural uncle . *K. John* ii 1 9
Not Gaunt's rebukes, nor England's private wrongs *Richard II.* ii 1 166
If he will not yield, Rebuke and dread correction wait on us *1 Hen. IV.* v 1 111
Thus ever did rebellion find rebuke . v 5 1
I never knew yet but rebuke and check was the reward of valour *2 Hen. IV.* iv 3 34
I had forestall'd this dear and deep rebuke Ere you with grief had spoke iv 5 141
Rate, rebuke, and roughly send to prison The immediate heir of England! . v 2 70
In devotion spend my latter days, To sin's rebuke . *3 Hen. VI.* iv 6 44
For living murmurers There's places of rebuke . *Hen. VIII.* ii 2 132
Would pluck reproof and rebuke from every ear that heard it *Coriolanus* ii 2 38
My caution was more pertinent Than the rebuke you give it ii 2 68
Receives rebuke from Norway . *Hamlet* ii 2 69
My manners tell me We have your wrong rebuke . *Othello* i 1 131
The best of you Shall sink in my rebuke . ii 3 209
A good rebuke, Which might have well becomed the best of men *Ant. and Cleo.* iii 7 26
The gods rebuke me, but it is tidings To wash the eyes of kings . v 1 27
So tender of rebukes that words are strokes And strokes death to her *Cymbeline* iii 5 40
Thou god of this great vast, rebuke these surges! . *Pericles* iii 1 1
Rebukeable And worthy shameful check it were . *Ant. and Cleo.* iv 4 30
Rebuked. Tell him we could have rebuked him at Harfleur . *Hen. V.* iii 6 128
Under him My Genius is rebuked; as, it is said, Mark Antony's was by Cæsar . *Macbeth* iii 1 56
Rebused. Is there any man has rebused your worship? . *T. of Shrew* i 2 7
Recall the good Camillo, Whom I proclaim a man of truth *W. Tale* iii 2 157
Might liquid tears or heart-offending groans Or blood-consuming sighs recall his life, I would be blind with weeping *2 Hen. VI.* iii 2 61
Why do you make us love your goodly gifts, And snatch them straight away? We here below Recall not what we give . *Pericles* iii 1 25
Recalled. Let them be recall'd from their exile. . *T. G. of Ver.* v 4 155
And passed sentence may not be recall'd . *Com. of Errors* i 1 148
If Henry were recall'd to life again, These news would cause him once more yield the ghost . *1 Hen. VI.* i 1 66
Recant. He shall do this, or else I do recant The pardon *Mer. of Venice* iv 1 391

Recantation. Your lord and master did well to make his recantation.—Recantation! . *All's Well* ii 3 195
Recanter. The public body, which doth seldom Play the recanter, feeling in itself A lack . *T. of Athens* v 1 149
Recanting. Hollow welcomes, Recanting goodness, sorry ere 'tis shown i 2 17
My teeth shall tear The slavish motive of recanting fear. *Richard II.* i 1 193
Receipt. Thou didst deny the gold's receipt . *Com. of Errors* ii 2 17
Take the chain and bid my wife Disburse the sum on the receipt thereof iv 1 38
And wrong the reputation of your name, In so unseeming to confess receipt Of that which hath so faithfully been paid . *L. L. Lost* ii 1 156
Understand that at the receipt of your letter I am very sick *Mer. of Ven.* iv 1 151
His good receipt Shall for my legacy be sanctified . *All's Well* i 3 250
On's bed of death Many receipts he gave me; chiefly one . ii 1 108
Three parts of that receipt I had for Calais Disbursed I duly *Richard II.* i 1 126
We have the receipt of fern-seed, we walk invisible . *1 Hen. IV.* ii 1 96
The most convenient place that I can think of For such receipt of learning is Black-Friars . *Hen. VIII.* ii 2 139
The mutinous parts That envied his receipt . *Coriolanus* i 1 116
Romeo should, upon receipt thereof, Soon sleep in quiet *Rom. and Jul.* iii 5 99
And the receipt of reason A limbeck only. . *Macbeth* i 7 66
Receive. He receives comfort like cold porridge . *Tempest* ii 1 10
He would have given it you; but I, being in the way, Did in your name receive it . *T. G. of Ver.* i 2 40
What maintenance he from his friends receives, Like exhibition thou shalt have from me . i 3 68
Once again I do receive thee honest . v 4 78
I shall not only receive this villanous wrong . *Mer. Wives* ii 2 308
The cloister enter And there receive her approbation . *Meas. for Meas.* i 2 183
If myself might be his judge, He should receive his punishment in thanks . i 4 28
Made him that gracious denial which he is most glad to receive . iii 1 167
I would be glad to receive some instruction from my fellow partner . iv 2 18
He this very day receives letters of strange tenour . iv 2 215
At supper-time I'll visit you And then receive my money for the chain.—I pray you, sir, receive the money now . *Com. of Errors* iii 2 180
At five o'clock I shall receive the money for the same . iv 1 11
You owe me for the chain.—I owe you none till I receive the chain iv 1 64
Have sent to thee, to receive the meed of punishment . *L. L. Lost* i 1 269
Meantime receive such welcome at my hand As honour without breach of honour may Make tender of . ii 1 169
From her eyes I did receive fair speechless messages . *Mer. of Venice* i 1 164
I come by note, to give and to receive . iii 2 141
I rather choose to have A weight of carrion flesh than to receive Three thousand ducats . iv 1 41
If they will patiently receive my medicine . *As Y. Like It* ii 7 61
Keep you your word, O duke, to give your daughter; You yours, Orlando, to receive his daughter . v 4 20
Receive thy daughter: Hymen from heaven brought her . v 4 117
'Tis most credible; we here receive it A certainty . *All's Well* i 2 4
But think you, Helen, If you should tender your supposed aid, He would receive it? . i 3 243
Our hearts receive your warnings . ii 1 22
A second time receive The confirmation of my promised gift . ii 3 55
My wish receive, Which great Love grant! . ii 3 90
She ceased In heavy satisfaction and would never Receive the ring again v 3 101
Receive it so.—She took the ring of me: I'll none of it . *T. Night* ii 2 12
I know his youth will aptly receive it, into a most hideous opinion . iii 4 212
A goodly babe . . . : the queen receives Much comfort in't . *W. Tale* ii 2 27
What old or newer torture Must I receive? . iii 2 179
Do not receive affliction At my petition . iii 2 224
Which I receive much better Than to be pitied of thee . iii 2 234
Receives not thy nose court-odour from me? . iv 4 757
Receive thy lance; and God defend the right! . *Richard II.* i 3 101
Never could the noble Mortimer Receive so many, and all willingly *1 Hen. IV.* i 3 111
Know thy charge; and there receive Money and order for their furniture iii 3 225
'Neighbour Quickly,' says he, 'receive those that are civil' . *2 Hen. IV.* ii 4 97
'Therefore take heed what guests you receive: receive,' says he, 'no swaggering companions' . ii 4 101
What stuff wilt have a kirtle of? I shall receive money o' Thursday . ii 4 298
Almost receive The secret whispers of each other's watch *Hen. V.* iv Prol. 6
That English may as French, French Englishmen, Receive each other . v 2 396
Thou shalt be fortunate, If thou receive me for thy warlike mate *1 Hen. VI.* i 2 92
You shall first receive The sum of money which I promised . v 1 51
Sooner will receive than give . v 5 47
Receive the sentence of the law for sins . *2 Hen. VI.* ii 3 3
As willingly at thy feet I leave it As others would ambitiously receive it ii 3 36
Thou didst receive the holy sacrament, To fight in quarrel of the house of Lancaster . *Richard III.* i 4 208
Here receive we from our father Stanley Lines of fair comfort . v 2 5
Receive 'em nobly, and conduct 'em Into our presence . *Hen. VIII.* i 4 58
This from a dying man receive as certain . ii 1 125
The capacity Of your soft cheveril conscience would receive, If you might please to stretch it . ii 3 32
Receive him, And see him safe i' the Tower . v 3 96
What heart receives from hence the conquering part? . *Troi. and Cres.* i 3 352
What he shall receive of us in duty Gives us more palm in beauty . iii 1 169
Like a gate of steel Fronting the sun, receives and renders back . iii 3 122
Shall Ajax fight with Hector?—Ay, and perhaps receive much honour . iii 3 226
In kissing, do you render or receive?—Both take and give . iv 5 36
I receive the general food at first, Which you do live upon *Coriolanus* i 1 135
From me receive that natural competency Whereby they live . i 1 143
All From me do back receive the flour of all, And leave me but the bran i 1 149
No public benefit which you receive But it proceeds or comes from them i 1 156
The nobles receive so to heart the banishment of that worthy Coriolanus iv 3 22
Receive them then, the tribute that I owe . *T. Andron.* i 1 251
Receive him, then, to favour, Saturnine . i 1 421
They humbly at my feet Receive my tears and seem to weep with me . iii 1 42
Lavinia 'tween her stumps doth hold The basin that receives your guilty blood . v 2 184
Receive the blood: and when that they are dead, Let me go grind their bones to powder small . v 2 198
This accursed devil; Let him receive no sustenance, fetter him . v 3 6
Unfold the imagined happiness that both Receive in either *Rom. and Jul.* ii 6 29
There's none Can truly say he gives, if he receives . *T. of Athens* i 2 11
With more than common thanks I will receive it . i 2 214
If by this crime he owes the law his life, Why, let the war receive't . iii 5 84
Our hearts Of brothers' temper do receive you in . *J. Cæsar* iii 1 175
He did receive his letters, and is coming . iii 1 279
Though he had no hand in his death, shall receive the benefit of his dying iii 2 47

Receive. Your highness' part Is to receive our duties . . . *Macbeth* i 4 24
Who dares receive it other, As we shall make our griefs and clamour roar? . . . . i 7 77
He does receive Particular addition, from the bill That writes them all alike . . . . iii 1 99
Do faithful homage and receive free honours . . . . . iii 6 36
Receive what cheer you may: The night is long that never finds the day iv 3 239
To receive at once the benefit of sleep, and do the effects of watching! . v 1 11
Receive such thanks As fits a king's remembrance . . *Hamlet* ii 2 25
Receives rebuke from Norway, and in fine Makes vow before his uncle . ii 2 69
Admit no messengers, receive no tokens . . . . . . ii 2 144
What lenten entertainment the players shall receive from you . ii 2 330
Did he receive you well?—Most like a gentleman . . . . iii 1 10
That I have longed long to re-deliver; I pray you, now receive them . iii 1 95
I will receive it, sir, with all diligence of spirit . . . v 2 94
But till that time, I do receive your offer'd love like love . . v 2 262
Then must we look to receive from his age, not alone the imperfections of long-engraffed condition . . . . . *Lear* i 1 299
My sister may receive it much more worse . . . . ii 2 155
Why might not you, my lord, receive attendance From those? . . ii 4 246
For his particular, I'll receive him gladly, But not one follower . ii 4 295
Let's meet him and receive him.—Lo, where he comes! . . *Othello* ii 1 182
Therefore, as I am bound, Receive it from me. I speak not yet of proof iii 3 196
Your commission's ready: Follow me, and receive't *Ant. and Cleo.* ii 3 42
We must receive him According to the honour of his sender . *Cymbeline* ii 3 62
Receive it from me, then: war and confusion In Cæsar's name pronounce I iii 1 66
Your hand, my lord.—Receive it friendly . . . . . iii 5 13
For Britons slay us, or receive us For barbarous and unnatural revolts iv 4 5
Your time's expired: Either expound now, or receive your sentence *Per.* i 1 90
Minister'st a potion unto me That thou wouldst tremble to receive thyself i 2 69
What he will do graciously, I will thankfully receive . . . iv 6 66
Thy sacred physic shall receive such pay As thy desires can wish . . v 1 74

Received. Of whom I have Received a second life . . . *Tempest* v 1 195
I have received my proportion, like the prodigious son . *T. G. of Ver.* ii 3 3
But she received my dog?—No, indeed, did she not . . . iv 4 55
She hath received your letter, for the which she thanks you . *Mer. Wives* ii 2 83
Meed, I am sure, I have received none: unless experience be a jewel . ii 2 212
Have you received no promise of satisfaction at her hands? . . ii 2 217
Having received wrong by some person, is at most odds with his own gravity . . . . iii 1 53
I have received from her another embassy of meeting . . . iii 5 131
Idle-headed eld Received and did deliver to our age This tale . . iv 4 37
Drove the grossness of the foppery into a received belief . . v 5 132
So I have strew'd it in the common ear, And so it is received *M. for M.* i 3 16
To be received plain, I'll speak more gross . . . . ii 4 82
He professes to have received no sinister measure from his judge . iii 2 256
You know no Centaur? you received no gold? . . *Com. of Errors* ii 2 9
Gentle master, I received no gold . . . . . . iv 4 101
There did this perjured goldsmith swear me down That I this day of him received the chain . . . . v 1 228
No, none by me.—This purse of ducats I received from you . . v 1 385
Received a thousand ducats of Don John for accusing the Lady Hero *Much Ado* iv 2 49
Say that he or we, as neither have, Received that sum . *L. L. Lost* ii 1 134
You shall be so received As you shall deem yourself lodged in my heart ii 1 173
We have received your letters full of love . . . . . . v 2 787
What ring gave you, my lord? Not that, I hope, which you received of me.—If I could add a lie unto a fault, I would deny it *Mer. of Venice* v 1 185
The gift doth stretch itself as 'tis received . . . *All's Well* ii 1 4
Eat, speak, and move under the influence of the most received star . ii 1 57
Find out a country where but women were that had received so much shame . . . . iv 3 362
It shall scarce boot me To say, 'not guilty:' mine integrity Being counted falsehood, shall, as I express it, Be so received . *W. Tale* iii 2 29
The same I am, ere ancient'st order was Or what is now received . . iv 1 11
Offends me more than the stripes I have received . . . . iv 3 60
London hath received, Like a kind host, the Dauphin . *K. John* v 1 31
Mowbray hath received eight thousand nobles In name of lendings *Richard II.* i 1 88
But ere I last received the sacrament I did confess it . . . i 1 139
I have from Port le Blanc, a bay In Brittany, received intelligence . ii 1 278
I have received A certain instance that Glendower is dead 2 *Hen. IV.* iii 1 102
I have received New-dated letters from Northumberland . . . iv 1 7
How did this offer seem received? . . . . . *Hen. V.* i 1 82
And from his coffers Received the golden earnest of our death . . ii 2 169
The fairest queen that ever king received . . . 2 *Hen. VI.* i 1 16
York, Salisbury, and victorious Warwick, Received deep scars in France i 1 87
At Saint Alban's shrine, Within this half-hour, hath received his sight . ii 1 64
The sea received it, And so I wish'd thy body might my heart . . iii 2 108
For strokes received, and many blows repaid . . . 3 *Hen. VI.* ii 3 3
I, who at his hands received my life, Have by my hands of life bereaved him . . . . ii 5 67
I have this day received a traitor's judgement . . . *Hen. VIII.* ii 1 58
My conscience first received a tenderness, Scruple, and prick . . ii 4 170
The reverend abbot, With all his covent, honourably received him . iv 2 19
I have received much honour by your presence . . . . v 5 72
He received in the repulse of Tarquin seven hurts . . *Coriolanus* ii 1 165
I have received not only greetings, But with them change of honours . ii 1 213
Show them the unaching scars which I should hide, As if I had received them for the hire Of their breath only! . . . . . . ii 2 153
You have received many wounds for your country . . . . ii 3 113
He should have show'd us His marks of merit, wounds received for's country . . . . ii 3 172
My arm'd knees . . . bend like his That hath received an alms! . . iii 2 120
While the Volsces May say 'This mercy we have show'd; the Romans, 'This we received' . . . . v 3 138
Seeking to hide herself, as doth the deer That hath received some unrecuring wound . . . . *T. Andron.* iii 1 90
Their child shall be advanced, And be received for the emperor's heir . iv 2 158
Faithful friends, I have received letters from great Rome . . . v 1 2
Let them be received, Not without fair reward . . *T. of Athens* i 2 196
I have received some small kindnesses from him, as money, plate . . iii 2 22
I was the first man That ere received gift from him . . . iii 3 17
These walls of ours Were not erected by their hands from whom You have received your griefs . . . . v 4 24
How he received you, let me be resolved.—With courtesy . *J. Cæsar* iv 2 14
I have here received letters, That young Octavius and Mark Antony Come iv 3 167
The king hath happily received, Macbeth, The news of thy success *Macb.* i 3 89
Will it not be received, When we have mark'd with blood those sleepy two Of his own chamber . . . , That they have done't? . . . i 7 74
Received. Lives in the English court, and is received Of the most pious Edward . . . . *Macbeth* iii 6 26
But how hath she Received his love? . . . . . *Hamlet* ii 2 129
It was—as I received it, and others, whose judgements in such matters cried in the top of mine—an excellent play . . . . . ii 2 458
He received them Of him that brought them . . . . . iv 7 40
Your lord, who hath received you At fortune's alms . . . *Lear* i 1 280
He did bewray his practice; and received This hurt you see . . . ii 1 109
I have received a letter this night; 'tis dangerous to be spoken . . iii 3 10
I have received a hurt: follow me, lady . . . . . . iii 7 95
The most piteous tale of Lear and him That ever ear received . . v 3 215
Received From him that fled some strange indignity . . *Othello* ii 3 244
As I am an honest man, I thought you had received some bodily wound ii 3 267
Pray you, let Cassio be received again . . . . . iii 4 88
You have told me she hath received them and returned me expectations iv 2 191
Now I see, I see, In Fulvia's death, how mine received shall be *A. and C.* i 3 65
The people know it; and have now received His accusations . . iii 6 22
Since I received command to do this business I have not slept *Cymbeline* iii 4 102
Let it be confiscate all, so soon As I have received it . . . v 5 324
Having received the punishment before, For that which I did then . v 5 343
You have at large received The danger of the task you undertake *Pericles* i 1 1

Receiver. Puts to him all the learnings that his time Could make him the receiver of . . . . *Cymbeline* i 1 44

Receivest. If the redress will follow, thou receivest Thy full petition *J. C.* ii 1 57

Receiveth. Notwithstanding thy capacity Receiveth as the sea *T. Night* i 1 11

Receiving. I fear my Julia would not deign my lines, Receiving them from such a worthless post . . . . . . *T. G. of Ver.* i 1 161
So receiving a dishonour'd life With ransom of such shame *Meas. for Meas.* iv 4 34
To one of your receiving Enough is shown . . . *T. Night* iii 1 131
You shall have such receiving As shall become your highness *W. Tale.* iv 4 537
Printing their proud hoofs i' the receiving earth . . *Hen. V.* Prol. 27
For mine own part, I durst not laugh, for fear of opening my lips and receiving the bad air . . . . *J. Cæsar* i 2 252

Receptacle. O sacred receptacle of my joys, Sweet cell of virtue and nobility, How many sons of mine hast thou in store! . *T. Andron.* i 1 92
This fell devouring receptacle, As hateful as Cocytus' misty mouth . ii 3 235
An ancient receptacle, Where, for these many hundred years, the bones Of all my buried ancestors are pack'd . . . *Rom. and Jul.* iv 3 39
Empty Old receptacles, or common shores, of filth . . . *Pericles* iv 6 186

Recheat. I will have a recheat winded in my forehead . . *Much Ado* i 1 242

Reciprocal. Let our reciprocal vows be remembered . . . *Lear* iv 6 267

Reciprocally. His mind and place Infecting one another, yea, reciprocally *Hen. VIII.* i 1 162

Reciterai. Je reciterai à vous promptement . . . *Hen. V.* iii 4 47
Néanmoins, je reciterai une autre fois ma leçon ensemble . . . iii 4 60

Reck. And little recks to find the way to heaven By doing deeds of hospitality . . . . *As Y. Like It* ii 4 81
Fate, hear me what I say! I reck not though I end my life to-day *T. and C.* v 6 26
The primrose path of dalliance treads, And recks not his own rede *Hamlet* i 3 51
That's all I reck . . . . *Cymbeline* iv 2 154

Recking as little what betideth me As much I wish all good befortune you *T. G. of Ver.* iv 3 40

Reckless. I'll after, more to be revenged on Eglamour Than for the love of reckless Silvia . . . . v 2 52
Reckless, and fearless of what's past, present, or to come *Meas. for Meas.* iv 2 150
So flies the reckless shepherd from the wolf . . . 3 *Hen. VI.* v 6 7
You grave but reckless senators . . . . . *Coriolanus* iii 1 92
So incensed that I am reckless what I do to spite the world . *Macbeth* iii 1 110
Like a puff'd and reckless libertine . . . . . . *Hamlet* i 3 49

Reckon. I reckon this always, that a man is never undone till he be hanged, nor never welcome . . . . . . *T. G. of Ver.* ii 5 4
Whereof I reckon The casting forth to crows thy baby-daughter To be or none or little . . . . *W. Tale* iii 2 191
We have French quarrels enow, if you could tell how to reckon *Hen. V.* iv 1 241
I have no more to reckon, he to spend . . . . *T. of Athens* iii 4 56
We shall not spend a large expense of time Before we reckon . *Macbeth* v 8 61
I am ill at these numbers; I have not art to reckon my groans *Hamlet* ii 2 121
A warlike people, whom we reckon Ourselves to be . . . *Cymbeline* iii 1 53

Reckoned. You know no house nor no such maid, Nor no such men as you have reckon'd up . . . . *T. of Shrew* Ind. 2 94
She reckon'd it At her life's rate . . . . . . *All's Well* v 3 90
Was reckon'd one The wisest prince that there had reign'd *Hen. VIII.* ii 4 48
There's beggary in the love that can be reckon'd . *Ant. and Cleo.* i 1 15
All gold and silver rather turn to dirt! As 'tis no better reckon'd, but of those Who worship dirty gods . . . . . . *Cymbeline* iii 6 55

Reckoning. For truth is truth To the end of reckoning *Meas. for Meas.* v 1 46
By faith enforced To call young Claudio to a reckoning for it . *Much Ado* v 4 9
For this I owe you: here comes other reckonings . . . . v 4 52
I am ill at reckoning; it fitteth the spirit of a tapster . . *L. L. Lost* i 2 42
It were pity you should get your living by reckoning, sir . . . v 2 498
Until the twelve celestial signs Have brought about the annual reckoning v 2 808
When a man's verses cannot be understood, . . . it strikes a man more dead than a great reckoning in a little room . . *As Y. Like It* iii 3 15
A lover is no stronger than the word of a tapster; they are both the confirmer of false reckonings . . . . iii 4 35
By this reckoning he is more shrew than she . . . *T. of Shrew* iv 1 87
Thou hast called her to a reckoning many a time and oft . 1 *Hen. IV.* i 2 55
His eloquence the parcel of a reckoning . . . . . . ii 4 113
He held me last night at least nine hours In reckoning up the several devils' names That were his lackeys . . . . iii 1 157
Or I will tear the reckoning from his heart . . . . . iii 2 152
What is in that word honour? what is that honour? air. A trim reckoning! v 1 137
His quick wit wasted in giving reckonings . . . 2 *Hen. IV.* i 2 194
If the cause be not good, the king himself hath a heavy reckoning *Hen. V.* iv 1 141
Possess them not with fear; take from them now The sense of reckoning iv 1 308
The mighty, or the huge, or the magnanimous, are all one reckonings . iv 7 18
No arithmetic but her brain to set down her reckoning . *Troi. and Cres.* iii 3 254
Of honourable reckoning are you both . . . . *Rom. and Jul.* i 2 4
May stand in number, though in reckoning none . . . . i 2 33
The future comes apace: What shall defend the interim? and at length How goes our reckoning? . . . . *T. of Athens* ii 2 159
No reckoning made, but sent to my account With all my imperfections on my head: O, horrible! . . . . *Hamlet* i 5 78
And lovers' absent hours, More tedious than the dial eight score times? O weary reckoning! . . . . *Othello* iii 4 176
A heavy reckoning for you, sir . . . . *Cymbeline* v 4 159

Reclaim'd To your obedience fifty fortresses, Twelve cities 1 *Hen. VI.* iii 4 5
Prepare him up Against to-morrow: my heart is wondrous light, Since this same wayward girl is so reclaim'd . . . *Rom. and Jul.* iv 2 47

Reclaims. Beauty that the tyrant oft reclaims . . . . 2 *Hen. VI.* v 2 54

Reclusive. In some reclusive and religious life . . . . *Much Ado* iv 1 244
Recognizance. His statutes, his recognizances, his fines . *Hamlet* v 1 113
With that recognizance and pledge of love Which I first gave her *Othello* v 2 214
Recoil. Methoughts I did recoil Twenty-three years . . *W. Tale* i 2 154
The very thought of my revenges that way Recoil upon me . ii 3 20
Or like an overcharged gun, recoil . . . . . *2 Hen. VI.* iii 2 331
A good and virtuous nature may recoil In an imperial charge *Macbeth* iv 3 19
Who then shall blame His pester'd senses to recoil and start? . v 2 23
Be revenged ; Or she that bore you was no queen, and you Recoil from your great stock . . . . *Cymbeline* i 6 128
Recoiling. Her will, recoiling to her better judgement . . *Othello* iii 3 236
Recollect. And from their watery empire recollect All that may men approve or men detect! . . . . *Pericles* ii 1 54
Recollected terms Of these most brisk and giddy-paced times . *T. Night* ii 4 5
Recomforted. Ne'er through an arch so hurried the blown tide, As the recomforted through the gates . . . . *Coriolanus* v 4 51
Recomforture. In that nest of spicery they shall breed Selves of themselves, to your recomforture . . . . *Richard III.* iv 4 425
Recommend. We recommend to you, tribunes of the people . *Coriolanus* ii 2 155
The air Nimbly and sweetly recommends itself . . . *Macbeth* i 6 2
With his free duty recommends you thus . . . . . *Othello* i 3 41
Recommended. Denied me mine own purse, Which I had recommended to his use Not half an hour before . . . . *T. Night* v 1 94
Recompense. Besides, I'll make a present recompense . *Mer. Wives* iv 6 55
I may compel him to her recompense . . *Meas. for Meas.* iii 1 263
Do not recompense me in making me a cuckold . . . v 1 522
Then you do not love me?—No, truly, but in friendly recompense *M. Ado* v 4 83
That is study's god-like recompense . . . . . *L. L. Lost* i 1 58
Dark night . . . ; Wherein it doth impair the seeing sense, It pays the hearing double recompense . . . . *M. N. Dream* iii 2 180
Fortune cannot recompense me better Than to die well . *As Y. Like It* ii 3 75
Do not look for further recompense Than thine own gladness . iii 5 97
Whose thoughts more truly labour To recompense your love . *All's Well* iv 4 18
Keep your purse : My master, not myself, lacks recompense . *T. Night* i 5 304
That I may bear my evils alone : it were a bad recompense for your love, to lay any of them on you . . . . ii 1 7
This is, to give a dog, and in recompense desire my dog again . v 1 7
In recompense whereof he hath married her . . . . v 1 372
As recompense of our dear services Past and to come . *W. Tale* ii 3 150
He means to recompense the pains you take By cutting off your heads : thus hath he sworn . . . . *K. John* v 4 15
It shall be still thy true love's recompense . . . *Richard II.* ii 3 49
All my treasury Is yet but unfelt thanks, which more enrich'd Shall be your love and labour's recompense . . . . ii 3 62
When I have chased all thy foes from hence, Then will I think upon a recompense.—Meantime look gracious . . *1 Hen. VI.* i 2 116
My body shall Pay recompense, if you will grant my suit . . v 3 19
For the service I have done you, The advantage of the time prompts me aloud To call for recompense . . . . *Troi. and Cres.* iii 3 3
They know the corn Was not our recompense . . . *Coriolanus* iii 1 121
When we for recompense have praised the vile, It stains the glory in that happy verse Which aptly sings the good . . *T. of Athens* i 1 15
Gentlemen, our dinner will not recompense this long stay . . . iii 6 35
A recompense more fruitful Than their offence can weigh down by the dram . . . . v 1 153
That swiftest wing of recompense is slow To overtake thee . *Macbeth* i 4 17
If you swear still, your recompense is still That I regard it not *Cymbeline* ii 3 97
My recompense is thanks, that's all ; Yet my good will is great *Pericles* iii 4 17
Recompensed. Such love Could be but recompensed, though you were crown'd The nonpareil of beauty! . . . . . *T. Night* i 5 272
It is my father's music To speak your deeds, not little of his care To have them recompensed as thought on . . . . *W. Tale* iv 4 531
So shall his father's wrongs be recompensed . . *1 Hen. VI.* iii 1 161
Reconcile. I'll reconcile me to Polixenes . . . . *W. Tale* iii 2 156
Never write, regreet, nor reconcile This louring tempest . *Richard II.* i 3 186
We'll devise a mean To reconcile you all unto the king . *2 Hen. VI.* iv 8 72
And I, I hope, shall reconcile them all . . . *3 Hen. VI.* i 1 273
I desire To reconcile me to his friendly peace . *Richard III.* ii 1 59
Our suit Is, that you reconcile them . . . . *Coriolanus* v 3 136
Find a time To blaze your marriage, reconcile your friends *Rom. and Jul.* iii 3 151
Such welcome and unwelcome things at once 'Tis hard to reconcile *Macb.* iv 3 139
When false opinion, whose wrong thought defiles thee, In thy just proof, repeals and reconciles thee . . . . . . *Lear* iii 6 120
Reconciles them to his entreaty, and himself to the drink *Ant. and Cleo.* ii 7 8
Your ears unto your eyes I'll reconcile . . . . *Pericles* iv 4 22
Reconciled to the prince your brother, I owe you all duty . *Much Ado* i 1 156
We are reconciled, and the first view shall kill All repetition . *All's Well* v 3 21
That penitent, as thou callest him, and reconciled king . . *W. Tale* iv 2 25
King John hath reconciled Himself to Rome . . . . *K. John* v 2 69
Now York and Lancaster are reconciled . . . . *3 Hen. VI.* ii 1 204
I shall be reconciled to him again.—Never . . . *Richard III.* i 4 184
Let it be mine honour, good my lord, That I have reconciled your friends and you . . . . *T. Andron.* i 1 467
Reconciled my thoughts To thy good truth and honour . . *Macbeth* iv 3 116
Reconcilement. In my terms of honour I stand aloof ; and will no reconcilement . . . . *Hamlet* v 2 258
Reconciler. The Jove of power make me most weak, most weak, Your reconciler! . . . . *Ant. and Cleo.* iii 4 30
Reconciliation. If I have any grace or power to move you, His present reconciliation take . . . . *Othello* iii 3 47
Record. And to the nightingale's complaining notes Tune my distresses and record my woes . . . . *T. G. of Ver.* v 4 6
Mine were the very cipher of a function, To fine the faults whose fine stands in record, And let go by the actor . . *Meas. for Meas.* ii 2 40
My villany they have upon record . . . . . . *Much Ado* v 1 247
Record it with your high and worthy deeds : 'Twas bravely done . . v 1 279
Record a gift, Here in the court, of all he dies possess'd . *Mer. of Venice* iv 1 388
O, that record is lively in my soul! . . . . . . *T. Night* v 1 253
Heaven be the record to my speech! . . . . . *Richard II.* i 1 30
If thy offences were upon record, Would it not shame thee? . . iv 1 230
A countryman of ours records, England all Olivers and Rowlands *1 Hen. VI.* i 2 29
Burn all the records of the realm . . . . . *2 Hen. VI.* iv 7 16
Is it upon record, or else reported Successively from age to age? *Rich. III.* iii 1 72
Brief abstract and record of tedious days, Rest thy unrest! . . . iv 4 28
And in record, left them the heirs of shame . . . . . v 3 335
Every action that hath gone before, Whereof we have record . *Tr. and Cr.* i 3 14
Cannot be! We have record that very well it can . *Coriolanus* iv 6 49
How proud I am of thee and of thy gifts Rome shall record . *T. Andron.* i 1 255
What strange, Which manifold record not matches? . . *T. of Athens* i 1 5
From the table of my memory I'll wipe away all trivial fond records *Ham.* i 5 99
Record. Be witness to me, O thou blessed moon, When men revolted shall upon record Bear hateful memory, poor Enobarbus did Before thy face repent! . . . . *Ant. and Cleo.* iv 9 8
Have by their brave instruction got upon me A nobleness in record . iv 14 99
The record of what injuries you did us, Though written in our flesh, we shall remember As things but done by chance . . . . v 2 118
And hath as oft a slanderous epitaph As record of fair act . *Cymbeline* iii 3 53
And made the night-bird mute, That still records with moan *Pericles* iv Gower 27
Recordation. For recordation to my noble husband . . *2 Hen. IV.* ii 3 61
To make a recordation to my soul Of every syllable . *Troi. and Cres.* v 2 116
Recorded. I, now the voice of the recorded law . . *Meas. for Meas.* ii 4 61
To keep those statutes That are recorded in this schedule . *L. L. Lost* i 1 18
'Twill be recorded for a precedent . . . . *Mer. of Venice* iv 1 220
Wherein my soul recorded The history of all her secret thoughts *Rich. III.* iii 5 27
Let me be recorded by the righteous gods, I am as poor as you *T. of Athens* iv 2 4
From day to day To the last syllable of recorded time . . *Macbeth* v 5 21
I will fetch my gold and have our two wagers recorded . . *Cymbeline* i 4 181
Recorder. He hath played on his prologue like a child on a recorder ; a sound, but not in government . . . . *M. N. Dream* v 1 123
The people were not wont To be spoke to but by the recorder *Richard III.* iii 7 30
Come, some music! come, the recorders! . . . . *Hamlet* iii 2 303
O, the recorders! let me see one . . . . iii 2 360
Recount. I must Once in a month recount what thou hast been *Tempest* i 2 262
You shall recount their particular duties afterwards . . *Much Ado* iv 1 2
By the world, I recount no fable . . . . . *L. L. Lost* v 1 111
'Tis our will That some plain man recount their purposes . . . v 2 176
And by the way let us recount our dreams . . . *M. N. Dream* iv 1 204
I prithee, recount some of them . . . . . *As Y. Like It* iii 2 375
If we should recount Our baleful news . . . . *3 Hen. VI.* ii 1 96
Bid him recount The fore-recited practices . . . . *Hen. VIII.* i 2 126
No man is by ; And you recount your sorrows to a stone . *T. Andron.* iii 1 29
How I have thought of this . . . , I shall recount hereafter . *J. Cæsar* i 2 165
Recounts most horrid sights seen by the watch . . . . ii 2 16
Recount the occasion of my sudden and more strange return . *Hamlet* iv 7 46
Sit, sir, I will recount it to you : But, see, I am prevented . *Pericles* v 1 63
Thy name, my most kind virgin? Recount, I do beseech thee . . v 1 142
Recounted. When I have heard your king's desert recounted, Mine ear hath tempted judgment to desire . . . . *3 Hen. VI.* iii 3 132
Recounting. Which in recounting His grief grew puissant . . *Lear* v 3 215
Recountments. Betwixt us two Tears our recountments had most kindly bathed . . . . *As Y. Like It* iv 3 141
Recourse. That no man hath recourse to her by night . *T. G. of Ver.* iii 1 112
I'll give you a pottle of burnt sack to give me recourse to him *Mer. Wives* ii 1 223
No manner of person At any time have recourse unto the princes *Richard III.* iii 5 109
Their eyes o'ergalled with recourse of tears . . *Troi. and Cres.* v 3 55
Recover. If I can recover him and keep him tame and get to Naples *Temp.* ii 2 71
If I can recover him and keep him tame, I will not take too much for him ii 2 79
If all the wine in my bottle will recover him, I will help his ague . . ii 2 97
I swam, ere I could recover the shore, five and thirty leagues off and on iii 2 16
Fear not : the forest is not three leagues off ; If we recover that, we are sure enough . . . . *T. G. of Ver.* v 1 12
There's no time for a man to recover his hair that grows bald *Com. of Er.* ii 2 73
To pay a fine for a periwig and recover the lost hair of another man . ii 2 77
With the help of a surgeon he might yet recover . . *M. N. Dream* v 1 317
Look, he recovers.—I would I were at home . . . *As Y. Like It* iv 3 161
But give thyself unto my sick desires, Who then recover . *All's Well* iv 2 36
If I cannot recover your niece, I am a foul way out . . *T. Night* ii 3 200
Her heart is but o'ercharged ; she will recover . . . *W. Tale* iii 2 151
The king Yet speaks and peradventure may recover . . *K. John* v 6 31
Speak ; Recover breath ; tell us how near is danger . . *Richard II.* v 3 47
Speak lower, princes, for the king recovers . . . *2 Hen. IV.* iv 4 129
If he be sick with joy, he'll recover without physic . . . . iv 5 14
That so he might recover what was lost . . . . *1 Hen. VI.* ii 5 32
To recover them, would lose my life . . . . *2 Hen. VI.* iv 7 71
Wert thou as we are, We might recover all our loss again . *3 Hen. VI.* v 2 30
No doubt his majesty Will soon recover his accustom'd health *Richard III.* i 3 2
I am, indeed, sir, a surgeon to old shoes ; when they are in great danger, I recover them . . . . *J. Cæsar* i 1 28
To recover of us, by strong hand And terms compulsatory . *Hamlet* i 1 102
Why do you go about to recover the wind of me? . . . . iii 2 361
He shall recover his wits there ; or, if he do not, it's no great matter v 1 166
What, man! there are ways to recover the general again . *Othello* ii 3 273
Do you withdraw yourself a little while, He will recover straight . . iv 1 58
Come on, then ; He may recover yet . . . . *Ant. and Cleo.* iv 9 35
Those that do die of it do seldom or never recover . . . . v 2 248
Nothing can be minister'd to nature That can recover him . *Pericles* iii 2 9
Recoverable. You must consider that a prodigal course Is like the sun's ; but not, like his, recoverable . . . . . *T. of Athens* iii 4 13
Recovered. We have here recovered the most dangerous piece of lechery that ever was known . . . . *Much Ado* iii 3 179
Brief, I recover'd him, bound up his wound . . . *As Y. Like It* iv 3 151
She hath recovered the king, and undone me . . . *All's Well* ii 2 22
It is not to be recovered.—It might have been recovered.—It might ; but it is not now.—It is to be recovered . . . . . . iii 6 60
I would I had any drum of the enemy's : I would swear I recovered it . iv 1 67
Kill him whom you have recovered . . . . . *T. Night* ii 1 39
Recovered again with aqua-vitæ or some other hot infusion . *W. Tale* iv 4 815
Recover'd is the town of Orleans . . . . . *1 Hen. VI.* i 6 9
Lost, and recover'd in a day again! . . . . . . iii 2 115
Nor grieve that Rouen is so recovered : Care is no cure . . . iii 3 2
I thought ye would never have given out these arms till you had recovered your ancient freedom . . . . . *2 Hen. VI.* iv 8 27
We'll debate By what safe means the crown may be recover'd *3 Hen. VI.* iv 7 52
Why, but you are now well enough : how came you thus recovered? *Oth.* ii 3 296
Take you this weapon, Which I have here recover'd from the Moor . v 2 240
I heard of an Egyptian That had nine hours lien dead, Who was by good appliance recovered . . . . *Pericles* iii 2 86
Recover'd her, and placed her Here in Diana's temple . . . v 3 24
Look, Thaisa is Recovered.—O, let me look! . . . . . v 3 28
Recovery. If the devil have him not in fee-simple, with fine and recovery *Mer. Wives* iv 2 225
May he not do it by fine and recovery? . . . *Com. of Errors* ii 2 75
Bind him fast And bear him home for his recovery . . . . v 1 41
A further use to be made than alone the recovery of the king *All's Well* ii 3 42
What the devil should move me to undertake the recovery of this drum? iv 1 38
For grief that they are past recovery . . . . *2 Hen. VI.* i 1 116
What, doth she swoon? use means for her recovery . . *3 Hen. VI.* v 5 45
He is so plaguy proud that the death-tokens of it Cry 'No recovery' *Troi. and Cres.* ii 3 188

Recovery. His fines, his double vouchers, his recoveries: is this the fine of his fines, and the recovery of his recoveries? . . . *Hamlet* v 1 115
All's effectless; yet nothing we'll omit That bears recovery's name *Per.* v 1 54
I will use My utmost skill in his recovery . . . v 1 76
Recreant. Come, recreant; come, thou child; I'll whip thee *M. N. Dream* iii 2 409
Doff it for shame, And hang a calf's-skin on those recreant limbs *K. John* iii 1 129
A recreant and most degenerate traitor . . . *Richard II.* i 1 144
A caitiff recreant to my cousin Hereford! . . . . i 2 53
On pain to be found false and recreant . . . . i 3 106
Puff! Puff in thy teeth, most recreant coward base! . *2 Hen. IV.* v 3 96
Distrustful recreants! Fight till the last gasp . . . *1 Hen. VI.* i 2 126
You are all recreants and dastards, and delight to live in slavery *2 Hen. VI.* iv 8 28
And may that soldier a mere recreant prove, That means not, hath not, or is not in love! . . . *Troi. and Cres.* i 3 287
As a foreign recreant, be led With manacles thorough our streets *Coriolanus* v 3 114
Hear me, recreant! On thine allegiance, hear me! . . *Lear* i 1 169
Recreate. To walk abroad, and recreate yourselves . . *J. Cæsar* iii 2 256
Recreation. Sweet recreation barr'd, what doth ensue But moody and dull melancholy? . . . *Com. of Errors* v 1 78
But is there no quick recreation granted? . . *L. L. Lost* i 1 162
The gentles are at their game, and we will to our recreation . iv 2 173
Gull him into a nayword, and make him a common recreation *T. Night* ii 3 146
And tears shed there Shall be my recreation . *W. Tale* iii 2 241
The true prince may, for recreation sake, prove a false thief . *1 Hen. IV.* i 2 173
Thought most fit For your best health and recreation *Richard III.* iii 1 67
It is a recreation to be by And hear him mock . *Cymbeline* i 6 75
Rectify. Some oracle Must rectify our knowledge . . *Tempest* v 1 245
For your own quiet, as to rectify What is unsettled in the king *Hen. VIII.* ii 4 63
That's to say, I meant to rectify my conscience . . . ii 4 203
Rector. Confirmed by the rector of the place . *All's Well* iv 3 69
Rectorship. To cry Against the rectorship of judgement. *Coriolanus* ii 3 213
Recure. Which to recure, we heartily solicit Your gracious self to take on you the charge *Richard III.* iii 7 130
Red. I am pale at mine heart to see thine eyes so red *Meas. for Meas.* iv 3 158
Look'd he or red or pale, or sad or merrily? . *Com. of Errors* iv 2 4
My love is most immaculate white and red . *L. L. Lost* i 2 96
If she be made of white and red, Her faults will ne'er be known . i 2 104
Red, that would avoid dispraise, Paints itself black, to imitate her brow iv 3 264
And Marian's nose looks red and raw . . . v 2 934
There was a pretty redness in his lip, A little riper and more lusty red Than that mix'd in his cheek *As Y. Like It* iii 5 121
'Twas just the difference Betwixt the constant red and mingled damask iii 5 123
Gartered with a red and blue list . . *T. of Shrew* iii 2 69
Such war of white and red within her cheeks! . . . iv 5 30
Whose red and white Nature's own sweet and cunning hand laid on *T. N.* i 5 257
Item, two lips, indifferent red; item, two grey eyes, with lids to them i 5 266
Entertain them sprightly, And let's be red with mirth . *W. Tale* iv 4 54
With eyes as red as new-enkindled fire . . *K. John* iv 2 163
Give me a cup of sack to make my eyes look red . *1 Hen. IV.* ii 4 423
And your colour, I warrant you, is as red as any rose *2 Hen. IV.* ii 4 28
It is like a coal of fire, sometimes plue and sometimes red *Hen. V.* iii 6 111
Prick not your finger as you pluck it off, Lest bleeding you do paint the white rose red . . . . *1 Hen. VI.* ii 4 50
Meditating that Shall dye your white rose in a bloody red . ii 4 61
What colour is this cloak of?—Red, master; red as blood . *2 Hen. VI.* ii 1 110
Beaufort's red sparkling eyes blab his heart's malice . . iii 1 154
Give him a box o' the ear and that will make 'em red again . iv 7 92
As red as fire! . . . . *3 Hen. VI.* iii 2 51
We will unite the white rose and the red . *Richard III.* v 5 19
In characters as red as Mars his heart Inflamed with Venus *Troi. and Cres.* v 2 164
Backs red, and faces pale With flight and agued fear *Coriolanus* i 4 37
I tell you, he does sit in gold, his eye Red as 'twould burn Rome . v 1 64
Yet do thy cheeks look red as Titan's face . *T. Andron.* ii 4 31
Poor soul! his eyes are red as fire with weeping *J. Cæsar* iii 2 120
The multitudinous seas incarnadine, Making the green one red *Macbeth* ii 2 63
Pale or red?—Nay, very pale . . . . *Hamlet* i 2 233
Yet thy cicatrice looks raw and red . . . . iv 3 62
With red burning spits Come hissing in upon 'em . *Lear* iii 6 16
For flesh and blood, sir, white and red, you shall see a rose *Pericles* iv 6 37
Red blood. The red blood reigns in the winter's pale . *W. Tale* iv 3 4
We shall your tawny ground with your red blood Discolour *Hen. V.* iii 6 170
O setting sun, As in thy red rays thou dost sink to night, So in his red blood Cassius' day is set! . . . *J. Cæsar* v 3 61
Red-breast. I will not sing.—'Tis the next way to turn tailor, or be red-breast teacher . . . . *1 Hen. IV.* iii 1 265
Red colour. His red colour hath forsook his cheeks . *Richard III.* ii 1 85
Red dominical. My red dominical, my golden letter . *L. L. Lost* v 2 44
Red face. He in the red face had it . . . *Mer. Wives* i 1 173
Red-faced. White-livered and red-faced . . . *Hen. V.* iii 2 34
Red glow. The red glow of scorn and proud disdain *As Y. Like It* iii 4 57
Red-hipped. Kill me a red-hipped humble-bee . *M. N. Dream* iv 1 12
Red-hot. They were red-hot with drinking . . *Tempest* iv 1 171
The iron of itself, though heat red-hot, Approaching near these eyes, would drink my tears And quench his fiery indignation *K. John* iv 1 61
I would to God that the inclusive verge Of golden metal that must round my brow Were red-hot steel! . . . *Richard III.* iv 1 61
Red-lattice phrases, and your bold-beating oaths *Mer. Wives* ii 2 28
A' calls me e'en now, my lord, through a red lattice . *2 Hen. IV.* ii 2 86
Red letters. Here's a villain!—Has a book in his pocket with red letters in't . . . . . *2 Hen. VI.* iv 2 97
Red-looked. Let my tongue blister And never to my red-look'd anger be The trumpet any more. . . . *W. Tale* ii 2 34
Red murrain. A red murrain o' thy jade's tricks! . *Troi. and Cres.* ii 1 20
Red-nose. The red-nose innkeeper of Daventry *1 Hen. IV.* iv 2 51
Red pestilence. The red pestilence strike all trades in Rome! *Coriolanus* iv 1 13
Red plague. I know how to curse. The red plague rid you For learning me your language! . . . . *Tempest* i 2 364
Red rays. O setting sun, As in thy red rays thou dost sink to night, So in his red blood Cassius' day is set! . . . *J. Cæsar* v 3 61
Red rose. Of colour like the red rose on triumphant brier *M. N. Dream* iii 1 96
Pluck a red rose from off this thorn with me . *1 Hen. VI.* ii 4 33
I pluck this red rose with young Somerset . . . ii 4 37
Shall send between the red rose and the white A thousand souls to death ii 4 126
The red rose and the white are on his face . *3 Hen. VI.* ii 5 97
Their lips were four red roses on a stalk . *Richard III.* iv 3 12
Red-tailed. That red-tailed humble-bee . . *All's Well* iv 5 7
Red weapons. Waving our red weapons o'er our heads . *J. Cæsar* iii 1 109
Red wheat. Sow the headland with wheat!—With red wheat *2 Hen. IV.* v 1 17
Red wine. More [difference] between your bloods than there is between red wine and rhenish . . . *Mer. of Venice* iii 1 43
The red wine first must rise In their fair cheeks . . *Hen. VIII.* i 4 43
Redder. If arguing make us sweat, The proof of it will turn to redder drops . . . . . *J. Cæsar* v 1 49
Reddest. Let us make incision for your love, To prove whose blood is reddest, his or mine . . . *Mer. of Venice* ii 1 7
Rede. And recks not his own rede . . . *Hamlet* i 3 51
Redeem. To redeem him, Give up your body . . *Meas. for Meas.* ii 4 53
Redeem thy brother By yielding up thy body to my will . ii 4 163
Redeem your brother from the angry law. . . . iii 1 207
Take it on you to assist him, it shall redeem you from your gyves . iv 2 11
Wanting guilders to redeem their lives . . *Com. of Errors* i 1 8
Alas, I sent you money to redeem you . . . iv 4 86
With much more love Than young Alcides, when he did redeem The virgin tribute paid by howling Troy . . *Mer. of Venice* iii 2 55
Out-villained villany so far, that the rarity redeems him *All's Well* iv 3 306
Unless you do redeem it by some laudable attempt . *T. Night* iii 2 30
From the rude sea's enraged and foamy mouth Did I redeem . . v 1 82
Bequeath to death your numbness, for from him Dear life redeems you *W. Tale* v 3 103
O that these hands could so redeem my son! . *K. John* iii 4 71
Redeem from broking pawn the blemish'd crown . *Richard II.* ii 1 293
Shall our coffers, then, Be emptied to redeem a traitor home? *1 Hen. IV.* i 3 86
Yet time serves wherein you may redeem Your banish'd honours . i 3 180
He that doth redeem her thence might wear Without corrival all her dignities . . . . . . i 3 206
I will redeem all this on Percy's head . . . . iii 2 132
My honour is at pawn; And, but my going, nothing can redeem it *2 Hen. IV.* ii 3 8
Weening to redeem And have install'd me in the diadem . *1 Hen. VI.* ii 5 88
Would some part of my young years Might but redeem the passage of your age! . . . . . . ii 5 108
I every day expect an embassage From my Redeemer to redeem me hence . . . . . . *Richard III.* ii 1 4
Let me redeem my brothers both from death . . *T. Andron.* iii 1 181
How if, when I am laid into the tomb, I wake before the time that Romeo Come to redeem me? . . . *Rom. and Jul.* iv 3 32
Thou hast one daughter, Who redeems nature from the general curse Which twain have brought her to . . . *Lear* iv 6 210
It is a chance which does redeem all sorrows That ever I have felt v 3 266
Redeemed. No fault could you make, Which you have not redeem'd; indeed, paid down More . . . . *W. Tale* v 1 3
Stay, and breathe awhile: Thou hast redeem'd thy lost opinion *1 Hen. IV.* v 4 48
In fine, redeem'd I was as I desired . . . *1 Hen. VI.* i 4 34
Soldiers, this day have you redeem'd your lives . . *2 Hen. VI.* iv 9 15
Ventidius is wealthy too, Whom he redeem'd from prison *T. of Athens* iii 3 4
To renounce his baptism, All seals and symbols of redeemed sin *Othello* ii 3 350
A thing I made, which hath the king Five times redeem'd from death *Cymbeline* i 5 63
Redeemer. I every day expect an embassage From my Redeemer to redeem me hence . . . . *Richard III.* ii 1 4
And defaced The precious image of our dear Redeemer . . ii 1 123
Redeemest. Thou redeem'st thyself: but all, save thee, I fell with curses *T. of Athens* iv 3 507
Redeeming. Better it were a brother died at once, Than that a sister, by redeeming him, Should die for ever . . *Meas. for Meas.* ii 4 107
Redeeming time when men think least I will . . *1 Hen. IV.* i 2 241
Engaging and redeeming of himself With such a careless force *T. and C.* v 5 39
Redeliver. Why meet him at the gates, and redeliver our authorities there? . . . . . . *Meas. for Meas.* iv 4 6
Remembrances of yours, That I have longed long to re-deliver *Hamlet* iii 1 94
Shall I re-deliver you e'en so?—To this effect, sir . . . v 2 186
Redemption. Lawful mercy Is nothing kin to foul redemption *M. for M.* ii 4 113
You bid me seek redemption of the devil . . . . v 1 29
Send him, mistress, redemption, the money in his desk . *Com. of Errors* iv 2 46
Thou wilt be condemned into everlasting redemption for this *Much Ado* iv 2 59
O villains, vipers, damn'd without redemption! . . *Richard II.* iii 2 129
Within the year of our redemption Four hundred twenty-six *Hen. V.* i 2 60
Held thee dearly as his soul's redemption . . *3 Hen. VI.* ii 1 102
As you hope to have redemption By Christ's dear blood . *Richard III.* i 4 194
And sold to slavery, of my redemption thence And portance . . *Othello* i 3 138
Redime te captum quam queas minimo . . *T. of Shrew* i 1 167
Redness. There was a pretty redness in his lip . *As Y. Like It* iii 5 120
Redoubled. Let thy blows, doubly redoubled, Fall . . *Richard II.* i 3 80
And on my head My shames redoubled! . . *1 Hen. IV.* iii 2 144
So they Doubly redoubled strokes upon the foe . . *Macbeth* i 2 38
Redoubted. My most redoubted lord . . . . *Richard II.* iii 3 198
Assume but valour's excrement To render them redoubted *Mer. of Venice* iii 2 88
My most redoubted father, It is most meet we arm us . . *Hen. V.* ii 4 14
Lord Regent, and redoubted Burgundy . . . . *1 Hen. VI.* ii 1 8
Oxford, redoubted Pembroke, Sir James Blunt . *Richard III.* iv 5 11
Redound. As all things shall redound unto your good *2 Hen. VI.* iv 9 47
Redress. If any crave redress of injustice . . . *Meas. for Meas.* iv 4 10
That which I must speak Must either punish me, not being believed, Or wring redress from you . . . . v 1 32
Come you to seek the lamb here of the fox? Good night to your redress! . . . . v 1 301
I defy all counsel, all redress, But that which ends all counsel, true redress, Death, death . . . . *K. John* iii 4 23
Things past redress are now with me past care . *Richard II.* ii 3 171
Heaven's offer we refuse, The proffer'd means of succour and redress . iii 2 32
I beseech you I may have redress against them . *2 Hen. IV.* ii 1 118
No need of any such redress; Or if there were, it not belongs to you . iv 1 97
I take your princely word for these redresses . . . . iv 2 66
I promised you redress of these same grievances . . . iv 2 113
Those bitter injuries, which Somerset hath offer'd to my house, I doubt not but with honour to redress . . . *1 Hen. VI.* ii 5 126
And no way canst thou turn thee for redress . . . . iv 2 25
No hope to have redress? My body shall Pay recompense . . v 3 18
Not a man comes for redress of thee . . . *3 Hen. VI.* iii 1 20
Wise men ne'er sit and wail their loss, But cheerly seek how to redress their harms . . . . v 4 2
Temperately proceed to what you would Thus violently redress *Coriol.* iii 1 220
And now he writes to heaven for his redress . *T. Andron.* iv 4 13
Music with her silver sound With speedy help doth lend redress *Rom. and Jul.* iv 5 146
Use the wars as thy redress And not as our confusion . *T. of Athens* v 4 51
Be factious for redress of all these griefs . . . *J. Cæsar* i 3 118

Redress. Speak, strike, redress! Brutus, thou sleep'st: awake! *J. C.* ii 1 47
'Speak, strike, redress!' Am I entreated To speak and strike? ii 1 55
If the redress will follow, thou receivest Thy full petition ii 1 57
What need we any spur but our own cause, To prick us to redress? ii 1 124
What is now amiss That Cæsar and his senate must redress? iii 1 32
What I can redress, As I shall find the time to friend, I will *Macbeth* iv 3 9
Sir, I had thought, by making this well known unto you, To have found a safe redress *Lear* i 4 225
The fault Would not 'scape censure, nor the redresses sleep i 4 229
Redressed. If it be confessed, it is not redressed *Mer. Wives* i 1 107
Each several article herein redress'd *2 Hen. IV.* iv 1 170
These griefs shall be with speed redress'd; Upon my soul, they shall iv 2 59
Reduce. Which to reduce into our former favour You are assembled *Hen. V.* v 2 63
All springs reduce their currents to mine eyes *Richard III.* ii 2 68
Abate the edge of traitors, gracious Lord, That would reduce these bloody days again! v 5 36
Reechy. Like Pharaoh's soldiers in the reechy painting *Much Ado* iii 3 143
The kitchen malkin pins Her richest lockram 'bout her reechy neck *Cor.* ii 1 225
For a pair of reechy kisses, Or paddling in your neck *Hamlet* iii 4 184
Reed. With hair up-staring,—then like reeds, not hair *Tempest* i 2 213
His tears run down his beard, like winter's drops From eaves of reeds v 1 17
Speak between the change of man and boy With a reed voice *Mer. of Ven.* iii 4 67
Ran fearfully among the trembling reeds *1 Hen. IV.* i 3 105
I had as lief have a reed that will do me no service as a partisan I could not heave *Ant. and Cleo.* ii 7 13
Care no more to clothe and eat; To thee the reed is as the oak *Cymbeline* iv 2 267
Re-edified. Which, since, succeeding ages have re-edified *Richard III.* iii 1 71
This monument five hundred years hath stood, Which I have sumptuously re-edified *T. Andron.* i 1 351
Reek. Which is as hateful to me as the reek of a lime-kiln *Mer. Wives* iii 3 86
Saw sighs reek from you, noted well your passion *L. L. Lost* iv 3 140
You remember How under my oppression I did reek *Hen. VIII.* ii 4 208
Curs! whose breath I hate As reek o' the rotten fens *Coriolanus* iii 3 121
If you bear me hard, Now, whilst your purpled hands do reek and smoke, Fulfil your pleasure. *J. Cæsar* iii 1 158
You reek as a sacrifice: where air comes out, air comes in *Cymbeline* i 2 2
Reeking. And draw their honours reeking up to heaven *Hen. V.* iv 3 101
Where he did Run reeking o'er the lives of men *Coriolanus* ii 2 123
And sprinkles in your faces Your reeking villany *T. of Athens* iii 6 103
Except they meant to bathe in reeking wounds, Or memorize another Golgotha, I cannot tell *Macbeth* i 2 39
Came there a reeking post, Stew'd in his haste, half breathless *Lear* ii 4 30
Reeky. With dead men's rattling bones, With reeky shanks *Rom. and Jul.* iv 1 83
Reel. Would shake the press, And make 'em reel before 'em *Hen. VIII.* iv 1 79
I will make my very house reel to-night *Coriolanus* ii 1 121
Flecked darkness like a drunkard reels From forth day's path *R. and J.* ii 3 3
Keeps wassail, and the swaggering up-spring reels *Hamlet* i 4 9
To reel the streets at noon, and stand the buffet With knaves *A. and C.* i 4 20
Drink thou; increase the reels ii 7 100
Reeling. And Trinculo is reeling ripe *Tempest* v 1 279
It is a reeling world, indeed *Richard III.* iii 2 38
You come in faint for want of meat, depart reeling *Cymbeline* v 4 164
Refelled. How I pray'd, and kneel'd, How he refell'd me *Meas. for Meas.* v 1 94
Refer. Only refer yourself to this advantage iii 1 255
I do refer me to the oracle *W. Tale* iii 2 116
I'll refer me to all things of sense *Othello* i 2 64
Reference. Something that hath a reference to my state *As Y. Like It* i 3 129
All that he is hath reference to your highness *All's Well* v 3 29
I this infer, That many things, having full reference To one consent, may work contrariously *Hen. V.* i 2 205
I crave fit disposition for my wife, Due reference of place *Othello* i 3 238
Make your full reference freely to my lord *Ant. and Cleo.* v 2 23
Referred me to the coming on of time. *Macbeth* i 5 9
Hath referr'd herself Unto a poor but worthy gentleman *Cymbeline* i 1 6
Refined. Haunted With a refined traveller of Spain *L. L. Lost* i 1 164
To gild refined gold, to paint the lily *K. John* iv 2 11
That in a Christian climate souls refined Should show so heinous, black, obscene a deed! *Richard II.* iv 1 130
Reflect I not on thy baseness court-contempt? *W. Tale* iv 4 758
Whose virtues will, I hope, Reflect on Rome as Titan's rays *T. Andron.* i 1 226
Reflect upon him accordingly, as you value your trust *Cymbeline* i 6 24
Reflecting. Where eyes did once inhabit, there were crept, As 'twere in scorn of eyes, reflecting gems *Richard III.* i 4 31
Reflection. Feels not what he owes, but by reflection *Troi. and Cres.* iii 3 99
For the eye sees not itself, But by reflection *J. Cæsar* i 2 53
Since you know you cannot see yourself So well as by reflection i 2 68
As whence the sun 'gins his reflection Shipwrecking storms and direful thunders break *Macbeth* i 2 25
I have seen small reflection of her wit.—She shines not upon fools, lest the reflection should hurt her *Cymbeline* i 2 35
Reflex. May never glorious sun reflex his beams Upon the country where you make abode! *1 Hen. VI.* v 4 87
'Tis but the pale reflex of Cynthia's brow *Rom. and Jul.* iii 5 20
Reform. Forsooth, takes on him to reform Some certain edicts *1 Hen. IV.* iv 3 78
As we hear you do reform yourselves, We will *2 Hen. IV.* v 5 72
I hope we have reformed that indifferently with us, sir.—O, reform it altogether *Hamlet* iii 2 42
Reformation. Right joyful of your reformation *L. L. Lost* v 2 879
My reformation, glittering o'er my fault, Shall show more goodly *1 Hen. IV.* i 2 237
Never came reformation in a flood, With such a heady currance *Hen. V.* i 1 33
Your captain is brave, and vows reformation *2 Hen. VI.* iv 2 70
The reformation of our travell'd gallants *Hen. VIII.* i 3 19
Which reformation must be sudden too v 3 20
Reformed. They are reformed, civil, full of good *T. G. of Ver.* v 4 156
By this time our sexton hath reformed Signior Leonato of the matter *Much Ado* v 1 262
I from thee departed Thy penitent reform'd *W. Tale* i 2 239
Meantime but ask What you would have reform'd that is not well *K. John* iv 2 44
Which are heresies, And, not reform'd, may prove pernicious *Hen. VIII.* v 3 19
I hope we have reformed that indifferently with us, sir *Hamlet* iii 2 40
Refractory. To curb those raging appetites that are Most disobedient and refractory *Troi. and Cres.* ii 2 182
Refrain. Nay, ask me if I can refrain from love *K. John* ii 1 525
Scarce I can refrain The execution of my big-swoln heart *3 Hen. VI.* ii 2 110
Who could refrain, That had a heart to love? *Macbeth* ii 3 122
Refrain to-night, And that shall lend a kind of easiness To the next abstinence: the next more easy *Hamlet* iii 4 165
When he hears of her, cannot refrain From the excess of laughter *Oth.* iv 1 99
Refresh. These sweet thoughts do even refresh my labours *Tempest* iii 1 14
Was it not to refresh the mind of man After his studies? *T. of Shrew* iii 1 11
I know, sir, we weary you.—You weary those that refresh us *W. Tale* iv 4 343
And labour shall refresh itself with hope *Hen. V.* ii 2 37
Shall we refresh us, sir, upon your shore, And give you gold? *Pericles* v 1 257
Refreshed. Come on refresh'd, new-added, and encouraged *J. Cæsar* iv 3 209
Refreshing. Diffusest honey-drops, refreshing showers *Tempest* iv 1 79
Reft. And would have reft the fishers of their prey *Com. of Errors* i 1 116
Reft of his brother, but retain'd his name i 1 129
Nor my bad life reft me so much of friends *Much Ado* iv 1 198
Like a poor bark, of sails and tackling reft *Richard III.* iv 4 233
Was by the rough seas reft of ships and men *Pericles* ii 3 84
Reftest. Thinking to bar thee of succession, as Thou reft'st me of my lands *Cymbeline* iii 3 103
Refuge. I will for refuge straight to Bristol castle *Richard II.* ii 2 135
Like silly beggars Who sitting in the stocks refuge their shame v 5 26
Troops of armed men Leap o'er the walls for refuge in the field *1 Hen. VI.* ii 2 25
I did imagine what would be her refuge v 4 69
Their latest refuge Was to send him *Coriolanus* v 3 11
Must I be his last refuge? *T. of Athens* iii 3 11
Refusal. If, as his nature is, he fall in rage With their refusal, both observe and answer *Coriolanus* ii 3 267
Refuse. Mine own doors refuse to entertain me *Com. of Errors* iii 1 120
There's no man is so vain That would refuse so fair an offer'd chain iii 2 186
To refuse So rare a gentleman as Signior Benedick *Much Ado* iii 1 90
Refuse me, hate me, torture me to death! iv 1 186
That I may know The worst that may befall me in this case, If I refuse to wed Demetrius *M. N. Dream* i 1 64
I may neither choose whom I would nor refuse whom I dislike *M. of V.* i 2 25
Is it not hard, Nerissa, that I cannot choose one nor refuse none? i 2 28
You should refuse to perform your father's will, if you should refuse to accept him i 2 100
A civil doctor, Which did refuse three thousand ducats of me v 1 211
But if you do refuse to marry me, You'll give yourself to this most faithful shepherd? *As Y. Like It* v 4 13
Keep your word, Silvius, that you'll marry her, If she refuse me v 4 24
'Tis my picture; Refuse it not; it hath no tongue to vex you *T. Night* iii 4 229
If thou refuse And wilt encounter with my wrath, say so *W. Tale* ii 3 137
Then, if he were my brother's, My brother might not claim him; nor your father, Being none of his, refuse him. *K. John* i 1 127
If heaven would, And we will not, heaven's offer we refuse *Richard II.* iii 2 31
You say that you had rather refuse The offer of an hundred thousand crowns iv 1 15
Bane to those That for my surety will refuse the boys! *2 Hen. VI.* v 1 121
Refuse not, mighty lord, this proffer'd love *Richard III.* iii 7 202
If you refuse it,—as, in love and zeal, Loath to depose the child iii 7 208
I utterly abhor, yea, from my soul Refuse you for my judge *Hen. VIII.* ii 4 82
Again I do refuse you for my judge ii 4 118
I do refuse it; And stand upon my common part with those *Coriolanus* i 9 38
If you refuse your aid In this so never-needed help, yet do not Upbraid's v 1 33
Offer'd The first conditions, which they did refuse And cannot now accept v 3 14
So thou refuse to drink my dear sons' blood *T. Andron.* iii 1 22
Wherefore art thou Romeo? Deny thy father and refuse thy name *Rom. and Jul.* ii 2 34
Thrice presented him a kingly crown, Which he did thrice refuse *J. C.* iii 2 102
In wholesome wisdom He might not but refuse you *Othello* iii 1 50
And that she should love this fellow and refuse me! *Cymbeline* i 2 28
Ask your help; Which if you shall refuse, when I am dead, For that I am a man, pray see me buried *Pericles* ii 1 80
Refused. To carry that which I would have refused *T. G. of Ver.* iv 4 106
In this manner accused, in this very manner refused *Much Ado* iv 2 65
I thought you lord of more true gentleness. O, that a lady, of one man refused, Should of another therefore be abused! *M. N. Dream* ii 2 133
Here it is.—He hath refused it in the open court *Mer. of Venice* iv 1 338
But, be refused, Let the white death sit on thy cheek for ever *All's Well* ii 3 76
The pretty-vaulting sea refused to drown me *2 Hen. VI.* iii 2 94
We have had pelting wars, since you refused The Grecians' cause *Troi. and Cres.* iv 5 267
I, that now Refused most princely gifts, am bound to beg *Coriolanus* i 9 80
And still as he refused it, the rabblement hooted *J. Cæsar* i 2 245
Uttered such a deal of stinking breath because Cæsar refused the crown i 2 248
When he perceived the common herd was glad he refused the crown i 2 266
No further necessity of qualities can make her be refused *Pericles* iv 2 53
Refusing her grand hests, she did confine thee *Tempest* i 2 274
Keep your word, Phebe, that you'll marry me, Or else refusing me, to wed this shepherd *As Y. Like It* v 4 22
No disgrace Shall fall you for refusing him at sea *Ant. and Cleo.* iii 7 40
Regal. In God's name, I'll ascend the regal throne *Richard II.* iv 1 113
Why am I sent for to a king, Before I have shook off the regal thoughts Wherewith I reign'd? iv 1 163
As viceroy under him, And still enjoy thy regal dignity *1 Hen. VI.* v 4 132
Now art thou within point-blank of our jurisdiction regal *2 Hen. VI.* iv 7 29
This is the palace of the fearful king, And this the regal seat *3 Hen. VI.* i 1 26
Edward Duke of York Usurps the regal title and the seat iii 3 28
Did I impale him with the regal crown? iii 3 189
Free king Henry from imprisonment And see him seated in the regal throne iv 3 64
God and friends Have shaken Edward from the regal seat iv 6 2
And himself Likely in time to bless a regal throne iv 6 74
Once more I shall interchange My waned state for Henry's regal crown iv 7 4
Sixty and nine, that wore Their crownets regal *Troi. and Cres.* Prol. 6
Regan. What says our second daughter, Our dearest Regan? *Lear* i 1 69
Cornwall and Regan his duchess will be here with him this night ii 1 4
He's coming hither; now, i' the night, i' the haste, And Regan with him ii 1 27
If they come to sojourn at my house, I'll not be there.—Nor I, assure thee, Regan ii 1 106
I am glad to see your highness.—Regan, I think you are ii 4 131
Beloved Regan, Thy sister's naught: O Regan, she hath tied Sharp-tooth'd unkindness, like a vulture, here ii 4 135
Return you to my sister.—Never, Regan ii 4 160
No, Regan, thou shalt never have my curse ii 4 173
Who stock'd my servant? Regan, I have good hope Thou didst not know on't ii 4 191
O Regan, wilt thou take her by the hand?—Why not by the hand, sir? ii 4 197
I can be patient; I can stay with Regan, I and my hundred knights ii 4 233
What, must I come to you With five and twenty, Regan? said you so? ii 4 257
Shut up your doors, my lord; 'tis a wild night; My Regan counsels well ii 4 312
In such a night as this! O Regan, Goneril! Your old kind father, whose frank heart gave all,—O, that way madness lies iii 4 19
Then let them anatomize Regan; see what breeds about her heart iii 6 80

Regan. Regan, I bleed apace: Untimely comes this hurt: give me your arm . *Lear* iii 7 97
Regard. Full many a lady I have eyed with best regard . *Tempest* iii 1 40
A son that well deserves The honour and regard of such a father *T. G. of Ver.* ii 4 60
Regard thy danger, and along with me! . iii 1 256
Vail your regard Upon a wrong'd, I would fain have said, a maid! *Meas. for Meas.* v 1 20
Your niece regards me with an eye of favour . *Much Ado* v 4 22
The passado he respects not, the duello he regards not *L. L. Lost* i 2 185
Your worth is very dear in my regard . *Mer. of Venice* i 1 62
You have show'd a tender fatherly regard . *T. of Shrew* ii 1 288
What, no attendance? no regard? no duty? . iv 1 129
After a demure travel of regard, telling them I know my place *T. Night* ii 5 59
Quenching my familiar smile with an austere regard of control . ii 5 73
You throw a strange regard upon me . v 1 219
I have look'd on thousands, who have sped the better By my regard, but kill'd none so . *W. Tale* i 2 390
In regard of me He shortens four years of my son's exile . *Richard II.* i 3 216
Where will doth mutiny with wit's regard . ii 1 28
Wisdom cries out in the streets, and no man regards it . *1 Hen. IV.* i 2 100
Sick in the world's regard, wretched and low . iv 3 57
Virtue is of so little regard in these costermonger times . *2 Hen. IV.* i 2 191
The king is full of grace and fair regard . *Hen. V.* i 1 22
In regard of causes now in hand . i 1 77
Scorn and defiance; slight regard, contempt, And any thing . ii 4 117
Here's Beaufort, that regards nor God nor king . *1 Hen. VI.* i 3 60
Ere we go, regard this dying prince . iii 2 86
For a toy, a thing of no regard . iv 1 145
Your loss is great, so your regard should be . iv 5 22
In regard King Henry gives consent . v 4 124
Turn this way, Henry, and regard them not . *3 Hen. VI.* i 1 189
Strangely neglected? when did he regard The stamp of nobleness in any person Out of himself? . *Hen. VIII.* iii 2 11
Regard him well.—'Well!' why, I do so . *Troi. and Cres.* iii 1 67
Lay negligent and loose regard upon him . iii 3 41
Nature, what things there are Most abject in regard and dear in use! . iii 3 128
Bites his lip with a politic regard . iii 3 255
Let them Regard me as I do not flatter . *Coriolanus* iii 1 67
I offer'd to awaken his regard For's private friends . v 1 23
So let him, As he regards his aged father's life . *T. Andron.* v 2 130
I am sworn not to give regard to you . *T. of Athens* i 2 251
Our reasons are so full of good regard . *J. Cæsar* iii 1 224
Will appear Such as he is, full of regard and honour . iv 2 12
Regard Titinius, And tell me what thou notest about the field . v 3 21
Things without all remedy Should be without regard . *Macbeth* iii 2 12
If much you note him, You shall offend him and extend his passion: Feed, and regard him not . iii 4 58
On such regards of safety and allowance As therein are set down *Hamlet* ii 2 79
With this regard their currents turn awry, And lose the name of action iii 1 87
And that, in my regard, Of the unworthiest siege . iv 7 76
Love's not love When it is mingled with regards that stand Aloof from the entire point . *Lear* i 1 242
And in the most exact regard support The worships of their name . i 4 287
In which regard, Though I do hate him as I do hell-pains, Yet, for necessity of present life, I must show out a flag and sign of love *Oth.* i 1 154
Even till we make the main and the aerial blue An indistinct regard . ii 1 40
If you swear still, your recompense is still That I regard it not *Cymb.* ii 3 98
Regarded. To be regarded in her sun-bright eye . *T. G. of Ver.* iii 1 88
I regarded him not; and yet he talked wisely . *1 Hen. IV.* i 2 97
He was but as the cuckoo is in June, Heard, not regarded . iii 2 76
Small curs are not regarded when they grin . *2 Hen. VI.* iii 1 18
O miserable age! virtue is not regarded in handicrafts-men . iv 2 11
Let him be regarded As the most noble corse that ever herald Did follow to his urn . *Coriolanus* v 6 144
Brutus, come apace, And see how I regarded Caius Cassius *J. Cæsar* v 3 88
Regardfully. Whom the world Voiced so regardfully . *T. of Athens* iv 3 81
Regarding. Neither regarding that she is my child . *T. G. of Ver.* iii 1 70
Regenerate. O thou, the earthly author of my blood, Whose youthful spirit, in me regenerate . *Richard II.* i 3 70
Regent of love-rhymes, lord of folded arms . *L. L. Lost* iii 1 183
Why, cousin, wert thou regent of the world, It were a shame to let this land by lease . *Richard II.* ii 1 109
From the most gracious regent of this land, The Duke of York . ii 3 77
Regent I am of France. Give me my steeled coat. I'll fight *1 Hen. VI.* i 1 84
Lord Regent, and redoubted Burgundy . ii 1 8
York, we institute your grace To be our regent in these parts of France iv 1 163
The regent hath with Talbot broke his word And left us . iv 6 2
The regent conquers, and the Frenchmen fly . v 3 1
Lord regent, I do greet your excellence With letters of commission . v 4 94
We here discharge your grace from being regent . *2 Hen. VI.* i 1 66
Thy late exploits done in the heart of France, When thou wert regent . i 1 197
If Somerset be unworthy of the place, Let York be regent . i 3 109
York is meetest man To be your regent in the realm of France . i 3 164
If I may judge: Let Somerset be regent o'er the French . i 3 209
What counsel give you . . . ?—That Somerset be sent as regent thither iii 1 290
If York, with all his far-fet policy, Had been the regent there instead of me, He never would have stay'd in France so long . iii 1 294
Thy fortune, York, hadst thou been regent there, Might happily have proved far worse than his . iii 1 305
Here is the regent, sir, of Mytilene Speaks nobly of her . *Pericles* v 1 188
And pretty din The regent made in Mytilene To greet the king . v 2 273
Regentship. Let him be denay'd the regentship . *2 Hen. VI.* i 3 107
Regia. Hic steterat Priami regia celsa senis . *T. of Shrew* iii 1 28
'Regia,' bearing my port, 'celsa senis,' that we might beguile the old pantaloon . iii 1 36
'Regia,' presume not, 'celsa senis,' despair not . iii 1 44
Regiment. In the regiment of the Spinii one Captain Spurio . *All's Well* ii 1 42
I know you are the Muskos' regiment . iv 1 76
We'll set forth In best appointment all our regiments . *K. John* ii 1 296
The Earl of Pembroke keeps his regiment . *Richard III.* v 3 29
His regiment lies half a mile at least South from the mighty power of the king . v 3 37
Send out a pursuivant at arms To Stanley's regiment . v 3 60
Conduct him to his regiment: I'll strive . . . to take a nap . v 3 103
Turns you off; And gives his potent regiment to a trull *Ant. and Cleo.* iii 6 95
Regina. Tanta est erga te mentis integritas, regina serenissima,— O, good my lord, no Latin . *Hen. VIII.* iii 1 41
Region. Queen of Tunis; So is she heir of Naples; 'twixt which regions There is some space . *Tempest* ii 1 256
Region. She is a region in Guiana, all gold and bounty . *Mer. Wives* i 3 76
He is of too high a region; he knows too much . iii 2 75
Or to reside In thrilling region of thick-ribbed ice . *Meas. for Meas.* iii 1 123
Every region near Seem'd all one mutual cry . *M. N. Dream* iv 1 121
To other regions France is a stable . *All's Well* ii 3 300
The king hath on him such a countenance As he had lost some province and a region Loved as he loves himself . *W. Tale* i 2 369
To the English court assemble now, From every region . *2 Hen. IV.* iv 5 123
The regions of Artois, Wallon and Picardy are friends to us *1 Hen. VI.* ii 1 9
Now, ye familiar spirits, that are cull'd Out of the powerful regions under earth, Help me this once . v 3 11
And made to tremble The region of my breast . *Hen. VIII.* ii 4 184
All the regions Do smilingly revolt . *Coriolanus* iv 6 102
When you come to Pluto's region, I pray you, deliver him this *T. An.* iv 3 13
Her eyes in heaven Would through the airy region stream so bright That birds would sing . *Rom. and Jul.* ii 2 21
You said the enemy would not come down, But keep the hills and upper regions: It proves not so . *J. Cæsar* v 1 3
Anon the dreadful thunder Doth rend the region . *Hamlet* ii 2 509
Ere this I should have fatted all the region kites With this slave's offal ii 2 607
Let it fall rather, though the fork invade The region of my heart *Lear* i 1 147
Notable scorns, That dwell in every region of his face . *Othello* iv 1 84
To seek through the regions of the earth For one his like, there would be something failing In him that should compare . *Cymbeline* i 1 20
No more, you petty spirits of region low, Offend our hearing . v 4 93
Y-ravished the regions round . *Pericles* iii Gower 35
From bourn to bourn, region to region . iv 4 4
Register. As you have one eye upon my follies, as you hear them unfolded, turn another into the register of your own *Mer. Wives* ii 2 194
Let the world rank me in register A master-leaver . *Ant. and Cleo.* iv 9 21
Registered. Live register'd upon our brazen tombs . *L. L. Lost* i 1 2
But say, my lord, it were not register'd, Methinks the truth should live from age to age . *Richard III.* iii 1 75
A little benefit, Out of those many register'd in promise *Troi. and Cres.* iii 3 15
Your pains Are register'd where every day I turn The leaf . *Macbeth* i 3 151
Regreet. From whom he bringeth sensible regreets . *Mer. of Venice* ii 9 89
Unyoke this seizure and this kind regreet . *K. John* iii 1 241
As at English feasts, so I regreet The daintiest last . *Richard II.* i 3 67
Shall not regreet our fair dominions . i 3 142
Nor never write, regreet, nor reconcile This louring tempest . i 3 186
Regress. Thou shalt have egress and regress;—said I well? *Mer. Wives* ii 1 226
Reguerdon. In reguerdon of that duty done . *1 Hen. VI.* iii 1 170
Reguerdoned. Or been reguerdon'd with so much as thanks . iii 4 23
Regular. Not a man Shall pass his quarter, or offend the stream Of regular justice . *T. of Athens* v 4 61
Rehearsal. A marvellous convenient place for our rehearsal *M. N. Dream* iii 1 3
I'll requite it With sweet rehearsal of my morning's dream *2 Hen. VI.* i 2 24
Rehearse that once more . *T. G. of Ver.* iii 1 366
For what offence?—For that which now torments me to rehearse . iv 1 26
A mile without the town, by moonlight; there will we rehearse *M. N. D.* i 2 105
There we may rehearse most obscenely and courageously . i 2 110
Sit down, every mother's son, and rehearse your parts . iii 1 75
Were met together to rehearse a play . iii 2 11
First, rehearse your song by rote, To each word a warbling note . v 1 404
Like an old tale still, which will have matter to rehearse . *W. Tale* v 2 67
Pity may move thee 'pardon' to rehearse . *Richard II.* v 3 128
Or am not able Verbatim to rehearse the method of my pen *1 Hen. VI.* iii 1 13
Rehearsed. Which, when I saw rehearsed, I must confess, Made mine eyes water . *M. N. Dream* v 1 68
Thou hast incurr'd The danger formerly by me rehearsed *Mer. of Venice* iv 1 362
Those defects I have before rehearsed . *T. of Shrew* i 2 124
Reign. Lord, Lord! to see what folly reigns in us! . *T. G. of Ver.* i 2 15
A fever she Reigns in my blood and will remember'd be. *L. L. Lost* iv 3 96
Fortune reigns in gifts of the world . *As Y. Like It* i 2 44
Thus have I politicly begun my reign . *T. of Shrew* iv 1 191
Happy star reign now! . *W. Tale* i 2 363
There's some ill planet reigns: I must be patient . ii 1 105
The red blood reigns in the winter's pale . iv 3 4
Like a weather-bitten conduit of many kings' reigns . v 2 61
Where we do reign, we will alone uphold . *K. John* iii 1 157
That none so small advantage shall step forth To check his reign . iii 4 152
Civil tumult reigns Between my conscience and my cousin's death . iv 2 247
Nor can one England brook a double reign . *1 Hen. IV.* v 4 66
Let one spirit of the first-born Cain Reign in all bosoms! . *2 Hen. IV.* i 1 158
All my reign hath been but as a scene Acting that argument . iv 5 198
Which in the eleventh year of the last king's reign Was like . *Hen. V.* i 1 2
Honour's thought Reigns solely in the breast of every man . ii Prol. 4
During the time Edward the Third did reign . *1 Hen. VI.* ii 2 31
Since Henry Monmouth first began to reign . ii 5 23
When Henry the Fifth, Succeeding his father Bolingbroke, did reign . ii 5 83
It was both impious and unnatural That such immanity and bloody strife Should reign among professors of one faith . v 1 14
Edmund, in the reign of Bolingbroke, As I have read, laid claim *2 Hen. VI.* ii 2 39
Till Lionel's issue fails, his should not reign . ii 2 56
Over whom, in time to come, I hope to reign . iv 2 138
I am content he shall reign; but I'll be protector over him . iv 2 167
I charge and command that, of the city's cost, the pissing-conduit run nothing but claret wine this first year of our reign . iv 6 5
For yet may England curse my wretched reign . iv 9 49
Uncurable discomfit Reigns in the hearts of all our present parts . v 2 87
For he could not so reign his crown But that the next heir should succeed and reign . *3 Hen. VI.* i 1 146
Hear me but one word: Let me for this my life-time reign as king . i 1 171
Confirm the crown to me and to mine heirs, And thou shalt reign in quiet i 1 173
Neither by treason nor hostility To seek to put me down and reign thyself i 1 200
As thou shalt reign but by their sufferance . i 1 234
I took an oath that he should quietly reign . i 2 15
I would break a thousand oaths to reign one year . i 2 17
Why, what is pomp, rule, reign, but earth and dust? . v 2 27
Clarence still breathes; Edward still lives and reigns . *Richard III.* i 1 161
By God's good grace his son shall reign . ii 3 10
And make, no doubt, us happy by his reign . iii 7 170
Your brother's son shall never reign our king . iii 7 215
Grand tyrant of the earth, That reigns in galled eyes of weeping souls . iv 4 53
Twenty of the dog-days now reign in's nose . *Hen. VIII.* v 4 43
Where unbruised youth with unstuff'd brain Doth couch his limbs, there golden sleep doth reign . *Rom. and Jul.* ii 3 38
In a house Where the infectious pestilence did reign . v 2 10
Sun, hide thy beams! Timon hath done his reign . *T. of Athens* v 1 226
In his royalty of nature Reigns that which would be fear'd . *Macbeth* iii 1 51

Reign. Shall Banquo's issue ever Reign in this kingdom? . *Macbeth* iv 1 103
Better Macbeth Than such an one to reign . . . . . . iv 3 66
This realm dismantled was Of Jove himself; and now reigns here A very, very—pajock . . . . *Hamlet* iii 2 294
Blest pray you be, That, after this strange starting from your orbs, You may reign in them now! . . . . . . *Cymbeline* v 5 372
I'll show you those in troubles reign . . . . *Pericles* ii Gower 7
He deserves so to be called for his peaceable reign . . . . ii 1 108
Your noble self, That best know how to rule and how to reign . ii 4 38
Our son and daughter shall in Tyrus reign . . . . . v 3 82
Reigned. Why am I sent for to a king, Before I have shook off the regal thoughts Wherewith I reign'd? . . . . *Richard II.* iv 1 164
His only son, Who after Edward the Third's death reign'd as king 2 *Hen. VI.* ii 2 20
The issue of the next son should have reign'd . . . . ii 2 32
The spavin Or springhalt reign'd among 'em . . . *Hen. VIII.* i 3 13
The wisest prince that there had reign'd by many A year before . ii 4 49
Our Jovial star reign'd at his birth . . . . *Cymbline* v 4 105
Till Lucina reign'd, Nature this dowry gave . . . *Pericles* i 1 8
Reignier, Duke of Anjou, doth take his part . . . 1 *Hen. VI.* i 1 94
Reignier, stand thou as Dauphin in my place: Question her proudly i 2 61
Reignier, is't thou that thinkest to beguile me? Where is the Dauphin? i 2 65
Charles, Burgundy, Alençon, Reignier, compass him about . . iv 4 27
See, Reignier, see, thy daughter prisoner!—To whom?—To me . v 3 131
Thanks, Reignier, happy for so sweet a child . . . . v 3 148
Reignier of France, I give thee kingly thanks . . . . v 3 163
So farewell, Reignier: set this diamond safe In golden palaces, as it becomes . . . . v 3 169
'Twas neither Charles nor yet the duke I named, But Reignier . v 4 78
Reignier sooner will receive than give . . . . . v 5 47
Henry shall espouse the Lady Margaret, daughter unto Reignier 2 *Hen. VI.* i 1 47
King Reignier, whose large style Agrees not with the leanness of his purse . . . . i 1 111
Reignier, her father, to the king of France Hath pawn'd the Sicils 3 *Hen. VI.* v 7 38
Reigning. In Arabia There is one tree, the phœnix' throne, one phœnix At this hour reigning there. . . . . . *Tempest* iii 3 24
So shall I do To the freshest things now reigning . . *W. Tale* iv 1 13
Rein. Be true; do not give dalliance Too much the rein . . *Tempest* iv 1 52
Cold as if I had swallowed snowballs for pills to cool the reins *M. Wives* iii 5 24
I have begun, And now I give my sensual race the rein . *Meas. for Meas.* ii 4 160
Rein thy tongue.—I must rather give it the rein . . *L. L. Lost* v 2 662
In measure rein thy joy; scant this excess . . *Mer. of Venice* iii 2 113
He will bear you easily and reins well . . . . *T. Night* iii 4 358
When she will take the rein I let her run; But she'll not stumble *W. T.* ii 3 51
Curbs me From giving reins and spurs to my free speech . *Richard II.* i 1 55
What rein can hold licentious wickedness? . . . *Hen. V.* iii 3 22
Where every horse bears his commanding rein . . *Richard III.* ii 2 128
Ajax is grown self-will'd, and bears his head In such a rein *Tr. and Cr.* i 3 189
Spur them to ruthful work, rein them from ruth . . . v 3 48
Give your dispositions the reins, and be angry at your pleasures *Coriol.* ii 1 33
The hard rein which both of them have borne Against the old kind king *Lear* iii 1 27
Reined. Once chafed, he cannot Be rein'd again to temperance *Coriol.* iii 3 28
Re-inforce. Or betimes Let's re-inforce, or fly. . . *Cymbeline* v 2 18
Reinforced. The French have reinforced their scatter'd men . *Hen. V.* iv 6 36
Reinforcement. To reinforcement, or we perish all . *Troi. and Cres.* v 5 16
With a sudden re-inforcement struck Corioli like a planet . *Coriolanus* ii 2 117
Reiterate. Which to reiterate were sin As deep as that . *W. Tale* i 2 283
Reject. When she shall challenge this, you will reject her . *L. L. Lost* v 2 438
Rejoice. That rejoice To hear the solemn curfew . . *Tempest* v 1 39
Rejoice Beyond a common joy, and set it down With gold on lasting pillars . . . . v 1 206
I'll after, to rejoice in the boy's correction . . *T. G. of Ver.* iii 1 394
My husband will not rejoice so much at the abuse of Falstaff *Mer. Wives* v 3 8
Rather rejoicing to see another merry, than merry at any thing which professed to make him rejoice . . . . *Meas. for Meas.* iii 2 251
Embrace thy brother there; rejoice with him . . *Com. of Errors* v 1 413
All Europa shall rejoice at thee . . . . . . *Much Ado* v 4 45
To wail friends lost Is not by much so wholesome-profitable As to rejoice at friends but newly found . . . . . *L. L. Lost* v 2 761
I will forget the condition of my estate, to rejoice in yours *As Y. Like It* i 2 17
It rejoices me, that I hope I shall see him ere I die . . *All's Well* iv 5 89
What were more holy Than to rejoice the former queen is well? *W. Tale* v 1 30
Rejoice, you men of Angiers, ring your bells . . . *K. John* ii 1 312
I should rejoice now at this happy news; And now my sight fails 2 *Hen. IV.* iv 4 109
Which I in sufferance heartily will rejoice . . . *Hen. V.* ii 2 159
I do partly understand your meaning.—Why then, rejoice therefore iii 6 54
It is not a thing to rejoice at . . . . iii 6 56
Follow'd with a rabble that rejoice To see my tears . . 2 *Hen. VI.* ii 4 32
But shall we wear these honours for a day? Or shall they last, and we rejoice in them? . . . . *Richard III.* iv 2 6
I should freelier rejoice in that absence wherein he won honour than in the embracements of his bed . . . . . *Coriolanus* i 3 3
When you shall know . . ., you'll rejoice That he is thus cut off . v 6 139
But to rejoice in splendour of mine own . . . *Rom. and Jul.* i 2 106
One poor and loving child, But one thing to rejoice and solace in . iv 5 47
And am not One that rejoices in the common wreck . *T. of Athens* ii 1 195
We make holiday, to see Cæsar and to rejoice in his triumph . *J. Cæsar* i 1 35
Wherefore rejoice? What conquest brings he home? . . . i 1 37
As Cæsar loved me, I weep for him; as he was fortunate, I rejoice at it iii 2 27
Rejoiced. Ne'er mother Rejoiced deliverance more . . *Cymbeline* v 5 370
Rejoiceth. It rejoiceth my intellect . . . . . *L. L. Lost* v 1 63
Rejoicing. My rejoicing At nothing can be more . . . *Tempest* iii 1 93
Rather rejoicing to see another merry, than merry . *Meas. for Meas.* iii 2 249
Shall we thither and with our company piece the rejoicing? . *W. Tale* v 2 117
That thou mightst not lose the dues of rejoicing . . *Macbeth* i 5 13
Made Lud's town with rejoicing fires bright . . . *Cymbeline* iii 1 32
Rejoicingly. She hath despised me rejoicingly, and I'll be merry in my revenge . . . . iii 5 149
Rejoindure. Rudely beguiles our lips Of all rejoindure *Troi. and Cres.* iv 4 38
Rejourn the controversy of three pence to a second day . *Coriolanus* ii 1 79
Relapse. Killing in relapse of mortality . . . . *Hen. V.* iv 3 107
Now this matter must be look'd to, For her relapse is mortal *Pericles* iii 2 110
Relate your wrongs; in what? by whom? be brief . . *Meas. for Meas.* v 1 26
Shall relate In high-born words the worth of many a knight . *L. L. Lost* i 1 172
But such as I, without your special pardon, Dare not relate . 3 *Hen. VI.* iv 1 88
Point by point the treasons of his master He shall again relate *Hen. VIII.* i 2 8
Stand forth, and with bold spirit relate . . . . . . i 2 129
Relate. However it is spread in general name, Relates in purpose only to Achilles.—The purpose is perspicuous . . . *Troi. and Cres.* i 3 323
To relate the manner, Were, on the quarry of these murder'd deer, To add the death of you . . . . *Macbeth* iv 3 205
Thoughts speculative their unsure hopes relate . . . . v 4 19
When you shall these unlucky deeds relate, Speak of me as I am *Othello* v 2 341
And to the state This heavy act with heavy heart relate . . . v 2 371
I nill relate, action may Conveniently the rest convey . *Pericles* iii Gower 55
Relating tales of others' griefs, See if 'twill teach us to forget our own . i 4 2
Relation. No more yet of this; For 'tis a chronicle of day by day, Not a relation for a breakfast . . . . . . *Tempest* v 1 164
The intent and purpose of the law Hath full relation to the penalty, Which here appeareth due . . . . . . *Mer. of Venice* iv 1 248
Were you present at this relation?—I was . . . . *W. Tale* v 2 2
At the relation of the queen's death, with the manner how she came to't v 2 92
Lest they desire upon this push to trouble Your joys with like relation v 3 130
There is a mystery—with whom relation Durst never meddle *Tr. and Cr.* iii 3 201
Augurs and understood relations have By magot-pies and choughs and rooks brought forth The secret'st man of blood . . *Macbeth* iii 4 124
O, relation Too nice, and yet too true! . . . . . . iv 3 173
This is a thing Which you might from relation likewise reap . *Cymbeline* ii 4 86
I will believe thee, And make my senses credit thy relation . *Pericles* v 1 124
Relative. I'll have grounds More relative than this . . . *Hamlet* ii 2 633
Release. They cannot budge till your release . . . . *Tempest* v 1 11
Go release them, Ariel: My charms I'll break, their senses I'll restore v 1 30
Release me from my bands With the help of your good hands . Epil. 9
He would not, but by gift of my chaste body To his concupiscible intemperate lust, Release my brother . . . *Meas. for Meas.* v 1 99
Then I will her charmed eye release From monster's view *M. N. Dream* iii 2 376
But first I will release the fairy queen . . . . . . iv 1 75
With mine own breath release all duty's rites . . *Richard II.* iv 1 210
Released. He hath released him, Isabel, from the world . *Meas. for Meas.* iv 3 119
By what means got'st thou to be released? . . . . 1 *Hen. VI.* i 4 25
The duchies of Anjou and Maine shall be released and delivered 2 *Hen. VI.* i 1 59
'Tis but reason that I be released From giving aid . . 3 *Hen. VI.* iii 3 147
Relent. I do relent: what would thou more of man? . *Mer. Wives* ii 2 31
I'll know His pleasure; may be he will relent . . *Meas. for Meas.* ii 2 3
O, to him, to him, wench! he will relent; He's coming; I perceive't . ii 2 124
He, a marble to her tears, is washed with them, but relents not . . iii 1 239
Relent, sweet Hermia: and, Lysander, yield Thy crazed title *M. N. D.* i 1 91
I'll not be made a soft and dull-eyed fool, To shake the head, relent, and sigh, and yield To Christian intercessors . . *Mer. of Venice* iii 3 15
Behold My sighs and tears and will not once relent? . 1 *Hen. VI.* iii 1 108
Relent! What, shall a child instruct you what to do? . . . iii 1 132
She hath bewitch'd me with her words, Or nature makes me suddenly relent . . . . iii 3 59
Could it not enforce them to relent, That were unworthy? . 2 *Hen. VI.* iv 4 17
If when you make your prayers, God should be so obdurate as yourselves, How would it fare with your departed souls? And therefore yet relent . . . . iv 7 124
Will ye relent, And yield to mercy whilst 'tis offer'd you? . . iv 8 11
What shall we do?—Relent, and save your souls.—Relent! 'tis cowardly and womanish.—Not to relent is beastly, savage, devilish *Rich. III.* i 4 263
But fierce Andronicus would not relent . . . . *T. Andron.* ii 3 165
O heavens, can you hear a good man groan, And not relent? . . iv 1 124
Relenting. Beguiles him as the mournful crocodile With sorrow snares relenting passengers . . . . 2 *Hen. VI.* iii 1 227
Relenting fool, and shallow, changing woman! . . *Richard III.* iv 4 431
Reliance. His days and times are past And my reliances on his fracted dates Have smit my credit . . . . . . *T. of Athens* ii 1 22
Relic. The nature of his great offence is dead, And deeper than oblivion we do bury The incensing relics of it . . . . . *All's Well* v 3 25
The bits and greasy relics Of her o'er-eaten faith . *Troi. and Cres.* v 2 159
Great men shall press For tinctures, stains, relics . . *J. Cæsar* ii 2 89
Relief. I will give him some relief, if it be but for that . . *Tempest* ii 2 70
If you knew . . . How true a gentleman you send relief *Mer. of Venice* iii 4 6
Wherever sorrow is, relief would be . . . . *As Y. Like It* iii 5 86
In the relief of this oppressed child . . . . . *K. John* ii 1 245
To relief of lazars and weak age, Of indigent faint souls . . *Hen. V.* i 1 15
Away, for your relief! and we will live To see their day. . 2 *Hen. VI.* v 2 88
Tell thy grief; It shall be eased, if France can yield relief 3 *Hen. VI.* iii 3 20
The gates shut on me, and turn'd weeping out, To beg relief . *T. Andron.* v 3 106
My relief Must not be toss'd and turn'd to me in words . *T. of Athens* ii 1 25
For this relief much thanks: 'tis bitter cold, And I am sick at heart *Ham.* i 1 8
I am abused; and my relief Must be to loathe her . . . *Othello* iii 3 267
Thou shouldst neither want my means for thy relief nor my voice *Cymb.* iii 5 115
Relieve. Bow'd, As stooping to relieve him . . . . *Tempest* ii 1 121
When they will not give a doit to relieve a lame beggar, they will lay out ten to see a dead Indian . . . . ii 2 33
With urging helpless patience would relieve me . *Com. of Errors* ii 1 39
I pity her And wish, for her sake more than for mine own, My fortunes were more able to relieve her . . . . . . *As Y. Like It* ii 4 77
That by this token I would relieve her . . . . *All's Well* v 3 86
It did relieve my passion much . . . . . . *T. Night* ii 4 4
O that there were some virtue in my tears, That might relieve you! *K. John* v 7 45
In the vaward, placed behind With purpose to relieve . . 1 *Hen. VI.* i 1 133
What authority surfeits on would relieve us . . . *Coriolanus* i 1 17
If any one relieves or pities him, For the offence he dies. *T. Andron.* v 3 181
Show charity to none, But let the famish'd flesh slide from the bone, Ere thou relieve the beggar . . . . *T. of Athens* iv 3 536
I will seek him, and privily relieve him . . . . *Lear* iii 3 15
You are my father too, and did relieve me . . . *Cymbeline* v 5 400
And finding little comfort to relieve them, I thought it princely charity to grieve them . . . . *Pericles* i 2 99
Nor come we to add sorrow to your tears, But to relieve them . . i 4 91
This, my last boon, give me, For such kindness must relieve me . . v 2 269
Relieved. My ending is despair, Unless I be relieved by prayer *Tempest* Epil. 16
Relieved him with such sanctity of love . . . . *T. Night* iii 4 395
We might guess they relieved us humanely . . . *Coriolanus* i 1 19
O, farewell, honest soldier: Who hath relieved you? . . . *Hamlet* i 1 17
Diseases desperate grown By desperate appliance are relieved, Or not at all . . . . iv 3 10
Shall to my bosom Be as well neighbour'd, pitied, and relieved *Lear* i 1 121
Though I die for it, . . . the king my old master must be relieved . iii 3 20
If we be not relieved within this hour, We must return *Ant. and Cleo.* iv 9 1
Do not yourself such wrong, who are in this Relieved, but not betray'd v 2 41
O Jove! I think Foundations fly the wretched; such, I mean, Where they should be relieved . . . . *Cymbeline* iii 6 8
If neglection Should therein make me vile, the common body, By you relieved, would force me to my duty . . . . . *Pericles* iii 3 22

Relieving. I was employ'd in passing to and fro, About relieving of the sentinels . 1 *Hen. VI.* ii 1 70
Religion. In any religion.—Ay, why not? Grace is grace, despite of all controversy *Meas. for Meas.* i 2 24
It is religion to be thus forsworn *L. L. Lost* iv 3 363
In religion, What damned error, but some sober brow Will bless it and approve it with a text *Mer. of Venice* iii 2 77
With no less religion than if thou wert indeed my Rosalind *As Y. Like It* iv 1 201
The puritan and . . . the papist, howsome'er their hearts are severed in religion, their heads are both one *All's Well* i 3 57
It is religion that doth make vows kept *K. John* iii 1 279
But now the bishop Turns insurrection to religion 2 *Hen. IV.* i 1 201
Name not religion, for thou lovest the flesh 1 *Hen. VI.* i 1 41
That seeks to overthrow religion i 3 65
When the devout religion of mine eye Maintains such falsehood, then turn tears to fires! *Rom. and Jul.* i 2 93
Religion groans at it *T. of Athens* iii 2 83
Piety, and fear, Religion to the gods, peace, justice, truth iv 1 16
This yellow slave [gold] Will knit and break religions iv 3 34
And sweet religion makes A rhapsody of words *Hamlet* iii 4 47
By your command, Which my love makes religion to obey *Ant. and Cleo.* v 2 199
I see you have some religion in you, that you fear *Cymbeline* i 4 149
Religious. In some reclusive and religious life *Much Ado* iv 1 244
An old religious uncle of mine taught me to speak *As Y. Like It* iii 2 362
Where meeting with an old religious man, After some question with him, was converted v 4 166
If I heard you rightly, The duke hath put on a religious life? v 4 187
Religious in mine error, I adore The sun *All's Well* i 3 211
As thou lovest her, Thy love's to me religious; else, does err ii 3 190
A coward, a most devout coward, religious in it *T. Night* iii 4 424
Link'd together With all religious strength of sacred vows *K. John* iii 1 229
Hie thee to France And cloister thee in some religious house *Richard II.* v 1 23
Seem they religious? Why, so didst thou *Hen. V.* ii 2 130
She holdeth thee in awe, More than God or religious churchmen may 1 *Hen. VI.* i 1 40
My lord should be religious And know the office that belongs to such iii 1 54
When holy and devout religious men Are at their beads, 'tis hard to draw them thence *Richard III.* iii 7 92
Whom I most hated living, thou hast made me, With thy religious truth and modesty, Now in his ashes honour *Hen. VIII.* iv 2 74
You're a gentleman Of mine own way; I know you wise, religious v 1 28
Such a prince; Not only good and wise, but most religious v 3 116
Yet, for I know thou art religious And hast a thing within thee called conscience, . . . Therefore I urge thy oath *T. Andron.* v 1 74
Religious canons, civil laws are cruel; Then what should war be? *T. of Athens* iv 3 60
Holy and religious fear it is To keep those many many bodies safe *Hamlet* iii 3 8
Religiously. Sir, you have done this in the fear of God, very religiously *L. L. Lost* iv 2 153
A nun of winter's sisterhood kisses not more religiously *As Y. Like It* iii 4 18
Being no further enemy to you Than the constraint of hospitable zeal In the relief of this oppressed child Religiously provokes *K. John* ii 1 246
From Pope Innocent the legate here, Do in his name religiously demand iii 1 140
Our souls religiously confirm thy words iv 3 73
Proceed And justly and religiously unfold *Hen. V.* i 2 10
Religiously they ask a sacrifice: To this your son is mark'd *T. Andron.* i 1 124
Relinquished. To be relinquished of the artists *All's Well* ii 3 10
Reliques. My idolatrous fancy Must sanctify his reliques i 1 109
Shall we go see the reliques of this town? *T. Night* iii 3 19
Reliquit. Terras Astræa reliquit *T. Andron.* iv 3 4
Relish. One of their kind, that relish all as sharply *Tempest* v 1 23
To relish a love-song, like a robin-redbreast; to walk alone *T. G. of Ver.* ii 1 20
Though it do well, I do not relish well Their loud applause *Meas. for Meas.* i 1 70
There's not a soldier of us all, that, in the thanksgiving before meat, do relish the petition well that prays for peace i 2 16
Take a taste of my finding him, and relish it *As Y. Like It* iii 2 247
What relish is in this? how runs the stream? *T. Night* iv 1 64
Cannot or will not Relish a truth *W. Tale* ii 1 167
Some smack of age in you, some relish of the saltness of time 2 *Hen. IV.* i 2 111
His fears, out of doubt, be of the same relish as ours are *Hen. V.* iv 1 114
Now I begin to relish thy advice *Troi. and Cres.* i 3 388
The imaginary relish is so sweet That it enchants my sense iii 2 20
We have some old crab-trees here at home that will not Be grafted to your relish *Coriolanus* ii 1 206
Devotion, patience, courage, fortitude, I have no relish of them *Macbeth* iv 3 95
Virtue cannot so inoculate our old stock but we shall relish of it *Hamlet* iii 1 120
About some act That has no relish of salvation in't iii 3 92
Keeps our fortunes from us till our oldness cannot relish them *Lear* i 2 51
You may relish him more in the soldier than in the scholar *Othello* ii 1 166
Let what is here contain'd relish of love, Of my lord's health *Cymbeline* iii 2 30
Relished. It would not have relished among my other discredits *W. Tale* v 2 132
My thoughts, That never relish'd of a base descent *Pericles* ii 5 60
Re-lives. Will you deliver How this dead queen re-lives? v 3 64
Relume. But once put out thy light, . . . I know not where is that Promethean heat That can thy light relume *Othello* v 2 13
Rely upon it till my tale be heard *Meas. for Meas.* v 1 370
For I, Thy resolved patient, on thee still rely *All's Well* ii 1 207
Bade me rely on him as on my father, And he would love me *Richard III.* ii 2 25
What's his excuse?—He doth rely on none *Troi. and Cres.* ii 3 173
Which I'll guard them from, If thereon you rely *Ant. and Cleo.* v 2 133
Relying. As one relying on your lordship's will *T. G. of Ver.* i 3 61
Remain. Imprison'd thou didst painfully remain A dozen years *Tempest* i 2 278
Vouchsafe my prayer May know if you remain upon this island i 2 423
No more remains, But that to your sufficiency *Meas. for Meas.* i 1 7
Trouble being gone, comfort should remain *Much Ado* i 1 101
The ladies follow her and but one visor remains ii 1 164
Yet there remains unpaid A hundred thousand more *L. L. Lost* ii 1 134
Thou shalt remain here, whether thou wilt or no *M. N. Dream* iii 1 156
Here therefore for a while I will remain iii 2 83
Home return'd, There to remain iii 2 173
Let . . . lovers twain At large discourse, while here they do remain v 1 152
Nothing remains but that I kindle the boy thither *As Y. Like It* i 1 179
Did he ask for me? Where remains he? How parted he with thee? iii 2 235
Scratch thee but with a pin, and there remains Some scar of it iii 5 21
If love have touch'd you, nought remains but so *T. of Shrew* i 1 166
Remain there but an hour, nor speak to me *All's Well* iv 2 58
He is the prince of the world; let his nobility remain in's court iv 5 52
By his authority he remains here iv 5 69
I shall beseech your lordship to remain with me till they meet iv 5 91
Fare thee well. Remain thou still in darkness *T. Night* iv 2 61
Remain. He has discover'd my design, and I Remain a pinch'd thing *W. Tale* ii 1 51
And remain, as he says, your pawn till it be brought you iv 4 853
For thee remains a heavier doom *Richard II.* i 3 148
What presence must not know, From where you do remain let paper show i 3 250
Be it known to you I do remain as neuter ii 3 159
Send him many years of sunshine days! What more remains? iv 1 222
Where now remains a sweet reversion 1 *Hen. IV.* iv 1 53
Then this remains, that we divide our power v 5 34
Enter Harfleur; there remain, And fortify it strongly *Hen. V.* iii 3 52
Be patient, for you shall remain with us iii 5 66
I am left out; for me nothing remains 1 *Hen. VI.* i 1 174
But there remains a scruple in that too v 3 93
There it doth remain, The saddest spectacle that e'er I view'd 3 *Hen. VI.* ii 1 66
Where did you dwell . . . ?—Here in this country, where we now remain iii 1 75
What now remains, my lords, for us to do But march to London? iv 3 60
What then remains, we being thus arrived . . . , But that we enter? iv 7 7
Towards Coventry bend we our course, Where peremptory Warwick now remains iv 8 59
Thou shalt still remain the Duke of York v 1 28
She was removed to Kimbolton, Where she remains now sick *Hen. VIII.* iv 1 35
There to remain till the king's further pleasure Be known unto us v 3 90
As I have made ye one, lords, one remain; So I grow stronger v 3 181
That only like a gulf it did remain I' the midst o' the body *Coriolanus* i 1 101
Let's fetch him off, or make remain alike i 4 62
It remains, As the main point of this our after-meeting ii 2 42
It then remains That you do speak to the people ii 2 138
Remains That, in the official marks invested, you Anon do meet the senate ii 3 147
If he should still malignantly remain Fast foe to the plebeii ii 3 191
It is a mind That shall remain a poison where it is, Not poison any further.—Shall remain! Hear you this Triton of the minnows? iii 1 87
You so remain.—And so are like to do iii 1 202
I banish you; And here remain with your uncertainty! iii 3 124
While I remain above the ground, you shall Hear from me still iv 1 51
Only that name remains iv 5 79
Destroy'd his country, and his name remains To the ensuing age abhorr'd v 3 147
The people will remain uncertain whilst 'Twixt you there's difference v 6 17
Behold the poor remains, alive and dead! *T. Andron.* i 1 81
When the single sole of it is worn, the jest may remain *Rom. and Jul.* ii 4 67
Here will I remain With worms that are thy chamber-maids v 3 108
What remains will hardly stop the mouth Of present dues *T. of Athens* ii 2 156
I hope it remains not unkindly with your lordship iii 6 39
Wouldst thou have thyself fall in the confusion of men, and remain a beast with the beasts? iv 3 326
Remain assured That he's a made-up villain v 1 100
I was constant Cimber should be banish'd, And constant do remain to keep him so *J. Cæsar* iii 1 73
Come, poor remains of friends, rest on this rock v 5 1
Whilst our poor malice Remains in danger of her former tooth *Macbeth* iii 2 15
We shall take upon's what else remains to do, According to our order v 6 5
Bend you to remain Here, in the cheer and comfort of our eye *Hamlet* i 2 115
And now remains That we find out the cause of this effect ii 2 100
Thus it remains, and the remainder thus. Perpend ii 2 104
My words fly up, my thoughts remain below iii 3 97
I must be cruel, only to be kind: Thus bad begins and worse remains behind iii 4 179
To thee and thine hereditary ever Remain this ample third *Lear* i 1 82
See better, Lear; and let me still remain The true blank of thine eye i 1 160
Not in this land shall he remain uncaught; And found—dispatch ii 1 59
Neither can be enjoy'd, If both remain alive v 1 59
I have lost the immortal part of myself, and what remains is bestial *Oth.* ii 3 264
If Cassio do remain, He hath a daily beauty in his life That makes me ugly v 1 18
To you, lord governor, Remains the censure of this hellish villain v 2 368
My full heart Remains in use with you *Ant. and Cleo.* i 3 44
That thou, residing here, go'st yet with me, And I, hence fleeting, here remain with thee i 3 104
'T cannot be We shall remain in friendship, our conditions So differing ii 2 115
Since the cuckoo builds not for himself, Remain in't as thou mayst ii 6 29
Our care and pity is so much upon you, That we remain your friend v 2 189
I shall remain your debtor.—I your servant v 2 205
I will remain The loyal'st husband that did e'er plight troth *Cymbeline* i 1 95
Remain, remain thou here While sense can keep it on i 1 117
Hath been Your faithful servant: I dare lay mine honour He will remain so i 1 175
If she remain unseduced, . . . you shall answer me with your sword i 4 173
We'll try with tongue too: if none will do, let her remain ii 3 17
I am bold her honour Will remain hers ii 4 3
I know your master's pleasure and he mine: All the remain is 'Welcome!' iii 1 87
So he wishes you all happiness, that remains loyal to his vow iii 2 47
You are not well: remain here iv 2 1
I nothing know where she remains, why gone, Nor when she purposes return iv 3 14
Unscissar'd shall this hair of mine remain, Though I show ill *Pericles* iii 3 29
If she remain, Whom they have ravish'd must by me be slain iv 1 102
Remainder. And the remainder mourning over them *Tempest* v 1 13
Which is as dry as the remainder biscuit After a voyage *As Y. Like It* ii 7 39
I would repent out the remainder of nature *All's Well* iv 3 272
Cut the entail from all remainders, and a perpetual succession for it iv 3 313
Was in my debt Upon remainder of a dear account *Richard II.* i 1 130
As much as one sound cudgel of four foot—You see the poor remainder—could distribute, I made no spare *Hen. VIII.* v 4 20
The remainder viands We do not throw in unrespective sieve *T. and C.* ii 2 70
In dumb shows Pass the remainder of our hateful days *T. Andron.* iii 1 132
The poor remainder of Andronici Will, hand in hand, all headlong cast us down v 3 131
It is some poor fragment, some slender ort of his remainder *T. of Athens* iv 3 401
Thus it remains, and the remainder thus. Perpend *Hamlet* ii 2 104
And the remainder, that shall still depend, To be such men *Lear* i 4 271
The gods protect you! And bless the good remainders of the court! *Cymbeline* i 1 129
Remained. At home; Where would you had remain'd! *Com. of Errors* iv 4 69
His hand, Not sensible of fire, remain'd unscorch'd *J. Cæsar* i 3 18
Remaineth none but mad-brain'd Salisbury 1 *Hen. VI.* i 2 15
Remaineth nought, but to inter our brethren *T. Andron.* i 1 146
Remaining. A dower Remaining in the coffer of her friends *Meas. for Meas.* i 2 155
If any spark of life be yet remaining, Down, down to hell 3 *Hen. VI.* v 6 66
Are we undone? cast off? nothing remaining? *T. of Athens* iv 2 2

Remaining. Remaining now in Gallia?—With those legions . *Cymbeline* iii 7 12
I am ashamed To look upon the holy sun, to have The benefit of his blest beams, remaining So long a poor unknown . iv 4 42
Remarkable. There is nothing left remarkable Beneath the visiting moon *Ant. and Cleo.* iv 15 67
And more remarkable in single oppositions . *Cymbeline* iv 1 14
Remarked. You speak of two The most remark'd i' the kingdom *Hen. VIII.* v 1 33
Remediate. Be aidant and remediate In the good man's distress! . *Lear* iv 4 17
Remedied. Care is no cure, but rather corrosive, For things that are not to be remedied . 1 *Hen. VI.* iii 3 4
Remedy. Have patience, gentle Julia.—I must, where is no remedy *T. G. of Ver.* ii 2 2
There is no remedy; I must cony-catch . *Mer. Wives* i 3 36
You must send her your page; no remedy . ii 2 127
Stand not amazed; here is no remedy . v 5 244
Well, what remedy? . . . What cannot be eschew'd must be embraced . v 5 250
It grieves me for the death of Claudio; But there's no remedy *M. for M.* ii 1 295
But yet,—poor Claudio! There is no remedy . ii 1 299
Must he needs die?—Maiden, no remedy . ii 2 48
He that might the vantage best have took Found out the remedy . ii 2 75
Is there no remedy?—None, but such remedy as, to save a head, To cleave a heart in twain.—But is there any? . iii 1 61
To the love I have in doing good a remedy presents itself . iii 1 204
If there be no remedy for it, but that you will needs buy and sell men and women like beasts . iii 2 1
Thou lovest, And I will fit thee with the remedy . *Much Ado* i 1 321
If not a present remedy, at least a patient sufferance . i 3 9
When thou wakest, if she be by, Beg of her for remedy . *M. N. Dream* iii 2 109
'Tis partly my own fault; Which death or absence soon shall remedy . iii 2 244
I'll apply To your eye, Gentle lover, remedy . iii 2 452
No remedy, my lord, when walls are so wilful to hear without warning v 1 210
I will no longer endure it, though yet I know no wise remedy *As Y. L. It* i 1 26
I am he that is so love-shaked: I pray you, tell me your remedy . iii 2 386
No sooner knew the reason but they sought the remedy . v 2 40
I know my remedy; I must go fetch the third-borough *T. of Shrew* Ind. 1 11
Beware my sting.—My remedy is then, to pluck it out . ii 1 212
Our remedies oft in ourselves do lie . *All's Well* i 1 231
Amongst the rest There is a remedy, approved, set down . i 3 234
Can do no hurt to try, Since you set up your rest 'gainst remedy . ii 1 138
There is no remedy, sir, but you must die . iv 3 337
And both shall cease, without your remedy . v 3 164
If it will not, what remedy? . *T. Night* i 5 56
There's no remedy, sir; he will fight with you for's oath sake . iii 4 325
This comes with seeking you: But there's no remedy; I shall answer it iii 4 367
Beseech you, tenderly apply to her Some remedies for life . *W. Tale* iii 2 154
I see the play so lies That I must bear a part.—No remedy . iv 4 670
Yet, if my lord will marry,—if you will, sir, No remedy, but you will . v 1 77
Is there no remedy?—None, but to lose your eyes . *K. John* iv 1 91
Dry your eyes; Tears show their love, but want their remedies *Rich. II.* iii 3 203
I can get no remedy against this consumption of the purse . 2 *Hen. IV.* i 2 264
Well then, alone, since there's no remedy . 1 *Hen. VI.* ii 2 57
Rome shall remedy this.—Roam thither, then . iii 1 51
See, thy daughter prisoner!—To whom?—To me.—Suffolk, what remedy? v 3 132
There is remedy enough, my lord: Consent . v 3 135
I will remedy this gear ere long, Or sell my title . 2 *Hen. VI.* iii 1 91
I did steer Toward this remedy, whereupon we are Now present *Hen. VIII.* ii 4 201
If entreaties Will render you no remedy, this ring Deliver them . v 1 150
The nature of the sickness found, Ulysses, What is the remedy? *T. and C.* i 3 141
I must then to the Grecians?—No remedy . iv 4 57
You must return and mend it.—There's no remedy . *Coriolanus* iii 2 26
His remedies are tame i' the present peace And quietness . iv 6 2
Till time beget some careful remedy . *T. Andron.* iv 3 30
Kinsmen, his sorrows are past remedy . iv 3 31
Both our remedies Within thy help and holy physic lies *Rom. and Jul.* ii 3 51
I'll to the friar, to know his remedy . iii 5 241
I long to die, If what thou speak'st speak not of remedy . iv 1 67
If thou darest, I'll give thee remedy . iv 1 76
Things without all remedy Should be without regard . *Macbeth* iii 2 11
Whether aught, to us unknown, afflicts him thus, That, open'd, lies within our remedy . *Hamlet* ii 2 18
The shame itself doth speak For instant remedy . *Lear* i 4 268
Seeking to give Losses their remedies . ii 2 177
There's no remedy; 'tis the curse of service . *Othello* i 1 35
When remedies are past, the griefs are ended By seeing the worst . i 3 202
For certainties Either are past remedies, or, timely knowing, The remedy then born . *Cymbeline* i 6 98
You must Forget that rarest treasure of your cheek, Exposing it—but, O, the harder heart! Alack, no remedy! . iii 4 165
Remember whom thou hast aboard . *Tempest* i 1 20
Canst thou remember A time before we came unto this cell? . i 2 38
Let me remember thee what thou hast promised . i 2 243
Remember I have done thee worthy service; Told thee no lies . i 2 247
The ditty does remember my drown'd father . i 2 405
I remember You did supplant your brother Prospero . ii 1 270
I do not know One of my sex; no woman's face remember, Save, from my glass, mine own . iii 1 49
Remember First to possess his books; for without them He's but a sot iii 2 99
I remember the story . iii 2 156
But remember—For that's my business to you . iii 3 68
There are yet missing of your company Some few odd lads that you remember not . v 1 255
I remember the trick you served me . *T. G. of Ver.* iv 4 37
This ring I gave him when he parted from me, To bind him to remember iv 4 103
I cannot remember what I did when you made me drunk . *Mer. Wives* i 1 174
How say you? O, I should remember him . i 4 29
Remember you your cue.—I warrant thee . iii 3 38
I pray you, remember in your prain . iv 1 36
O,—vocativo, O.—Remember, William; focative is caret . iv 1 55
Remember, son Slender, my daughter . v 2 2
Come; and remember your parts: be pold, I pray you . v 4 1
Remember, Jove, thou wast a bull for thy Europa . v 5 3
As art and practice hath enriched any That we remember *Meas. for Meas.* i 1 14
Remember now my brother . iv 1 70
I remember you, sir, by the sound of your voice . v 1 330
Do you remember what you said of the duke?—Most notedly . v 1 333
I am sure you both of you remember me.—Ourselves we do remember, sir, by you . *Com. of Errors* v 1 291
Daughter, remember what I told you . *Much Ado* ii 1 69
I think I told your lordship a year since . . . —I remember . ii 2 15
Remember. I remember a pretty jest your daughter told us of *Much Ado* iii 3 141
A' goes up and down like a gentleman: I remember his name . iii 3 135
Masters, remember that I am an ass . iv 2 79
Which, as I remember, hight Costard . *L. L. Lost* i 1 258
I am much deceived but I remember the style . iv 1 98
I do beseech thee, remember thy courtesy . v 1 103
Once I sat upon a promontory . . . —I remember . *M. N. Dream* ii 1 154
Do you not remember, lady, in your father's time, a Venetian? *M. of V.* i 2 123
I remember him well, and I remember him worthy of thy praise . i 2 132
As I remember, Adam, it was upon this fashion . *As Y. Like It* i 1 1
You must not learn me how to remember any extraordinary pleasure . i 2 7
I remember, when I was in love I broke my sword upon a stone . ii 4 46
That I was an Irish rat, which I can hardly remember . iii 2 188
Can you remember any of the principal evils? . iii 2 369
I do now remember a saying, 'The fool doth think he is wise' . v 1 34
I do remember in this shepherd boy Some lively touches of my daughter's favour . v 4 26
I remember, Since once he play'd a farmer's eldest son *T. of Shrew* Ind. 1 83
And but I be deceived Signior Baptista may remember me . iv 4 3
If I can remember thee, I will think of thee at court . *All's Well* i 1 202
Say thy prayers; when thou hast none, remember thy friends . i 1 228
You remember The daughter of this lord?—Admiringly . v 3 42
If ever thou shalt love, In the sweet pangs of it remember me *T. Night* ii 4 16
Remember who commended thy yellow stockings . ii 5 166; iii 4 52
To the Elephant.—I do remember . iii 3 49
That face of his I do remember well . v 1 54
Now I remember me, They say, poor gentleman, he's much distract . v 1 286
Do you remember? 'Madam, why laugh you at such a barren rascal?' v 1 382
I'll not remember you of my own lord, Who is lost too . *W. Tale* iii 2 231
Remember well, I mentioned a son o' the king's . iv 1 21
No more ado. Remember 'stoned,' and 'flayed alive' . iv 4 834
Whilst I remember Her and her virtues, I cannot forget My blemishes in them . v 1 6
And the words that follow'd Should be 'Remember mine' . v 1 67
Remember since you owed no more to time Than I do now . v 1 219
Grandam, I will pray, If ever I remember to be holy . *K. John* iii 3 15
Well, I'll not say what I intend for thee: Remember . iii 3 69
Remembers me of all his gracious parts, Stuffs out his vacant garments iii 4 96
I remember, when I was in France, Young gentlemen would be as sad as night . iv 1 14
Remember well, Upon your oath of service to the pope . v 1 22
Do not so quickly go; I shall remember more . *Richard II.* i 2 65
Every tedious stride I make Will but remember me what a deal of world I wander from the jewels that I love . i 3 269
For that is not forgot Which ne'er I did remember . ii 3 38
Remember who you are.—I had forgot myself . iii 2 82
That I could forget what I have been, Or not remember what I must be now! . iii 3 139
Joy, being altogether wanting, It doth remember me the more of sorrow iii 4 14
I do remember well The very time Aumerle and you did talk . iv 1 60
I well remember The favours of these men: were they not mine? . iv 1 167
Remember, as thou read'st, thy promise pass'd . v 3 51
I remember, when the fight was done, When I was dry with rage 1 *Hen. IV.* i 3 30
Inclining to three score; and now I remember me, his name is Falstaff ii 4 468
I must remember you, my lord, We were the first and dearest of your friends . v 1 32
A prince should not be so loosely studied as to remember so weak a composition . 2 *Hen. IV.* ii 2 10
I do now remember the poor creature, small beer . ii 2 12
What a disgrace is it to me to remember thy name! . ii 2 16
Do not speak like a death's-head; do not bid me remember mine end . ii 4 255
Which of you was by—You, cousin Nevil, as I may remember? . iii 1 66
Do you remember since we lay all night in the windmill? . iii 2 206
I remember at Mile-end Green, when I lay at Clement's Inn . iii 2 298
I do remember him at Clement's Inn like a man made after supper . iii 2 331
We do remember; but our argument Is all too heavy to admit much talk . v 2 23
Not to deliberate, not to remember, not to have patience . v 5 22
Do you not remember, a' saw a flea stick upon Bardolph's nose? *Hen. V.* ii 3 42
An arrant counterfeit rascal; I remember him now . iii 6 65
But he'll remember with advantages What feats he did that day . iv 3 50
Remember, lords, your oaths . 1 *Hen. VI.* i 1 162
I do remember it; and here take my leave . i 1 165
When I am dead and gone, Remember to avenge me on the French . i 4 94
Porter, remember what I gave in charge . ii 3 1
When I was young, as yet I am not old, I do remember how my father said . iii 4 18
Remember where we are; In France, amongst a fickle wavering nation iv 1 137
Fond man, remember that thou hast a wife . v 3 80
Let never day nor night unhallow'd pass, But still remember what the Lord hath done . 2 *Hen. VI.* ii 1 86
Remember it and let it make thee crest-fall'n . iv 1 59
I remember it to my grief . 3 *Hen. VI.* i 1 93
My pains are quite forgot.—Out, devil! I remember them too well *Richard III.* i 3 118
Remember this another day, When he shall split thy very heart with sorrow . i 3 299
Remember our reward, when the deed is done . i 4 126
I will never more remember Our former hatred, So thrive I and mine! . ii 1 23
O, remember, God, To hear her prayers for them, as now for us! . iii 3 18
I remember, Henry the Sixth Did prophesy that Richmond should be king . iv 2 98
'When he,' quoth she, 'shall split thy heart with sorrow, Remember Margaret' . v 1 27
Yet remember this, God and our good cause fight upon our side . v 3 239
Remember whom you are to cope withal; A sort of vagabonds . v 3 315
I remember Of such a time . *Hen. VIII.* i 2 190
You remember How under my oppression I did reek . ii 4 207
I thank my memory, I yet remember Some of these articles . iii 2 303
Have their wages duly paid 'em, And something over to remember me by iv 2 151
Remember me In all humility unto his highness . iv 2 160
In thy prayers remember The estate of my poor queen . v 1 73
And my good mistress will Remember in my prayers . v 1 78
I shall remember this bold language.—Do. Remember your bold life too v 3 84
You'll remember your brother's excuse?—To a hair . *Troi. and Cres.* iii 1 155
Will you remember?—Remember! yes.—Nay, but do, then . v 2 12
What should she remember?—List . v 2 16
If you do remember, I send it through the rivers of your blood *Coriolanus* i 1 138
Whom We met here both to thank and to remember With honours . ii 2 51
We shall be blest to do, if he remember A kinder value of the people . ii 2 62

Remember. Prithee, fellow, remember my name is Menenius *Coriolanus* v 2 29
If you'ld ask, remember this before: The thing I have forsworn to grant may never Be held by you denials . v 3 79
Think'st thou it honourable for a noble man Still to remember wrongs? v 3 155
He no more remembers his mother now than an eight-year-old horse . v 4 16
Remember, boys, I pour'd forth tears in vain . *T. Andron.* ii 3 163
O, handle not the theme, to talk of hands, Lest we remember still that we have none . . . . iii 2 30
Gregory, remember thy swashing blow . *Rom. and Jul.* i 1 69
I remember it well. 'Tis since the earthquake now eleven years . i 3 22
I have forgot why I did call thee back.—Let me stand here till thou remember it.—I shall forget, to have thee still stand there . ii 2 172
I do remember an apothecary,—And hereabouts he dwells . v 1 37
As I remember, this should be the house . . . . v 1 55
I do remember well where I should be, And there I am . . v 3 149
It hath pleased the gods to remember my father's age *T. of Athens* i 2 2
I remember, my lord, you gave Good words the other day . i 2 216
I shall remember: When Cæsar says 'do this,' it is perform'd *J. Cæsar* i 2 9
There was more foolery yet, if I could remember it . . i 2 291
Disperse yourselves; but all remember What you have said . ii 1 222
Remember that you call on me to-day: Be near me, that I may remember you . . . . ii 2 122
You all do know this mantle: I remember The first time ever Cæsar put it on . . . . iii 2 174
Remember March, the ides of March remember . . iv 3 18
I pray you, remember the porter . . . *Macbeth* ii 3 23
Threescore and ten I can remember well . . . ii 4 1
I have done no harm. But I remember now I am in this earthly world iv 2 74
I cannot but remember such things were, That were most precious to me iv 3 222
Heaven and earth! Must I remember? . . . *Hamlet* i 2 143
Remember well What I have said to you.—'Tis in my memory lock'd . i 3 84
Adieu, adieu! Hamlet, remember me . . . . i 5 91
Remember thee! Ay, thou poor ghost, while memory holds a seat . i 5 95
Remember thee! Yea, from the table of my memory I'll wipe away all trivial fond records . . . . . . i 5 97
I remember, one said there were no sallets in the lines . . . ii 2 461
There's rosemary, that's for remembrance; pray, love, remember . iv 5 176
You do remember all the circumstance?—Remember it, my lord! . v 2 2
I beseech you, remember— Nay, good my lord; for mine ease, in good faith . . . . v 2 108
Remember him hereafter as my honourable friend . *Lear* i 1 27
Remember what I tell you.—Well, madam . . . i 3 21
Such groans of roaring wind and rain I never Remember to have heard . iii 2 48
Who sometime, in his better tune, remembers What we are come about iv 3 41
I do remember now: henceforth I'll bear Affliction till it do cry out itself . . . . iv 6 75
The trick of that voice I do well remember . . . iv 6 108
I remember thine eyes well enough. Dost thou squiny at me? . iv 6 139
Thou old unhappy traitor, Briefly thyself remember . . . iv 6 233
All the skill I have Remembers not these garments . . . iv 7 67
Your sisters Have, as I do remember, done me wrong . . iv 7 74
I remember a mass of things, but nothing distinctly . *Othello* ii 3 289
To-night Lay on my bed my wedding sheets: remember . . iv 2 105
Remember that the present need Speaks to atone you *Ant. and Cleo.* ii 2 101
What majesty is in her gait? Remember, If e'er thou look'dst on majesty . . . . iii 3 20
Let him alone, for I remember now How he's employ'd . . v 1 71
We shall remember As things but done by chance . . . v 2 119
You do remember This stain upon her?—Ay . *Cymbeline* ii 4 138
Remember, sir, my liege, The kings your ancestors . . . iii 1 16
I forgot to ask him one thing; I'll remember't anon . . iii 5 134
And though he came our enemy, remember He was paid for that . iv 2 245
My false spirits Quail to remember . . . . . v 5 149
Well may you, sir, Remember me at court . . . v 5 193
To remember what he does, Build his statue . *Pericles* ii Gower 13
Wind, rain, and thunder, remember, earthly man Is but a substance that must yield to you . . . . ii 1 2
I hope, sir, if you thrive, you'll remember from whence you had it . ii 1 158
I was shipp'd at sea, I well remember, Even on my eaning time . iii 4 5
Thy oath remember; thou hast sworn to do't: 'Tis but a blow . iv 1 1
Remember what I have said.—I warrant you, madam . . iv 1 47
As I can remember, by my troth, I never did her hurt in all my life . iv 1 74
How long have you been of this profession?—E'er since I can remember iv 6 79
If this but answer to my just belief, I'll well remember you . . v 1 240
Can you remember what I call'd the man? I have named him oft . v 3 52
Remembered. You being then, if you be remember'd, cracking the stones of the foresaid prunes . . . . . . *Meas. for Meas.* ii 1 110
I telling you then, if you be remembered, that such a one and such a one were past cure . . . . ii 1 114
Much deserved on his part and equally remembered by Don Pedro *M. Ado* i 1 13
Let it be remembered in his punishment . . . . . v 1 315
A fever she Reigns in my blood and will remember'd be . *L. L. Lost* iv 3 96
Marry, well remember'd . . . . . *Mer. of Venice* ii 8 26
Thy sting is not so sharp As friend remember'd not *As Y. Like It* ii 7 189
And, now I am remember'd, scorn'd at me . . . . iii 5 131
But if you be remember'd, I did not bid you mar it *T. of Shrew* iv 3 96
What I saw, to my good use I remembered . . *W. Tale* iv 4 616
Thy ignominy sleep with thee in the grave, But not remember'd in thy epitaph! . . . . 1 *Hen. IV.* v 4 101
As a sullen bell, Remember'd tolling a departing friend . . 2 *Hen. IV.* i 1 103
My humble duty remembered, I will not be your suitor . . . ii 1 137
Your noble and right well remember'd father's . . . iv 1 112
We will accite, As I before remember'd, all our state . . v 2 142
Be in their flowing cups freshly remember'd . . . *Hen. V.* iv 3 55
Shall be remembered; We few, we happy few, we band of brothers . iv 3 59
If your majesties is remembered of it, the Welshmen did good service . iv 7 102
By my troth, if I had been remember'd, I could have given my uncle's grace a flout . . . . *Richard III.* ii 4 23
If I could have remembered a gilt counterfeit . *Troi. and Cres.* ii 3 27
They [my wounds] smart To hear themselves remember'd . *Coriolanus* i 9 29
Be you remember'd, Marcus, she's gone, she's fled *T. Andron.* iv 3 5
Nurse, come back again; I have remember'd me . *Rom. and Jul.* i 3 9
Bid him suppose some good necessity Touches his friend, which craves to be remember'd . . . . *T. of Athens* ii 2 237
Nymph, in thy orisons Be all my sins remember'd . . *Hamlet* iii 1 90
Let our reciprocal vows be remembered . . . . *Lear* iv 6 267
Death remember'd should be like a mirror . . . *Pericles* i 1 45
Rememberest. If thou remember'st aught ere thou camest here, How thou camest here thou mayst . . . . . *Tempest* i 2 51
Thou rememberest Since once I sat upon a promontory . *M. N. Dream* ii 1 148

Rememberest. If thou remember'st not the slightest folly That ever love did make thee run into, Thou hast not loved . . *As Y. Like It* ii 4 34
Thou but rememberest me of mine own conception . . . *Lear* i 4 72
Rememberest thou any that have died on't?—Very many *Ant. and Cleo.* v 2 249
Remembering. Alack, for pity! I, not remembering how I cried out then, Will cry it o'er again . . . . . . *Tempest* i 2 133
Shows Julia but a swarthy Ethiope. I will forget that Julia is alive, Remembering that my love to her is dead . . *T. G. of Ver.* ii 6 28
I count myself in nothing else so happy As in a soul remembering my good friends . . . . *Richard II.* ii 3 47
Myself have play'd The interim, by remembering you 'tis past *Hen. V.* v Prol. 43
Let me stand here till thou remember it.—I shall forget, to have thee still stand there, Remembering how I love thy company *Rom. and Jul.* ii 2 174
Remembrance. Of any thing the image tell me that Hath kept with thy remembrance . . . . *Tempest* i 2 44
Rather like a dream than an assurance That my remembrance warrants i 2 46
The teen that I have turn'd you to, Which is from my remembrance! . i 2 65
This lord of weak remembrance, this, Who shall be of as little memory ii 1 232
How sharp the point of this remembrance is! . . . . v 1 138
Let us not burthen our remembrance with A heaviness that's gone . v 1 199
Keep this remembrance for thy Julia's sake . . *T. G. of Ver.* ii 2 5
The remembrance of my former love Is by a newer object quite forgotten ii 4 194
I pray you now, remembrance to-morrow on the lousy knave *Mer. Wives* iii 3 255
I pray you, have your remembrance, child . . . . iv 1 48
He hath an abstract for the remembrance of such places . . iv 2 63
Lamentation For the remembrance of my father's death . *L. L. Lost* v 2 820
Seems to me now As the remembrance of an idle gawd . *M. N. Dream* iv 1 172
Puts the wretch that lies in woe In remembrance of a shroud . . v 1 385
Take some remembrance of us, as a tribute, Not as a fee *Mer. of Venice* iv 1 422
For your father's remembrance, be at accord . . *As Y. Like It* i 1 67
The remembrance of her father never approaches her heart but the tyranny of her sorrows takes all livelihood from her cheek *All's Well* i 1 56
These great tears grace his remembrance more Than those I shed for him i 1 91
His good remembrance, sir, Lies richer in your thoughts than on his tomb i 2 48
By our remembrances of days foregone, Such were our faults . i 3 140
From the time of his remembrance to this very instant disaster . iv 3 126
Out of a self-gracious remembrance, did first propose . . iv 5 78
Praising what is lost Makes the remembrance dear . . . v 3 20
Which she would keep fresh And lasting in her sad remembrance *T. Night* i 1 32
She is drowned already, sir, with salt water, though I seem to drown her remembrance again with more . . . . ii 1 33
My remembrance is very free and clear from any image of offence . iii 4 248
Extracting frenzy of mine own From my remembrance clearly banish'd his v 1 289
Whose very naming punishes me with the remembrance . *W. Tale* iv 2 24
Grace and remembrance be to you both! . . . . . iv 4 76
You pity not the state, nor the remembrance Of his most sovereign name v 1 25
There's magic in thy majesty, which has My evils conjured to remembrance . . . . v 3 40
Let this be copied out, And keep it safe for our remembrance *K. John* v 2 2
Unkind remembrance! thou and eyeless night Have done me shame . v 6 12
Writ in remembrance more than things long past . *Richard II.* ii 1 14
In the remembrance of a weeping queen . . . . . iii 4 107
So came I a widow; And never shall have length of life enough To rain upon remembrance with mine eyes . . . . 2 *Hen. IV.* ii 3 59
That may repeat and history his loss To new remembrance . . iv 1 204
With this remembrance, that you use the same . . . v 2 115
Awake remembrance of these valiant dead . . . . *Hen. V.* i 2 115
Tombless, with no remembrance over them . . . . i 2 229
All this from my remembrance brutish wrath Sinfully pluck'd *Rich. III.* ii 1 118
So in the Lethe of thy angry soul Thou drown the sad remembrance . iv 4 251
Shall I forget myself to be myself?—Ay, if yourself's remembrance wrong yourself . . . . iv 4 421
My soul is very jocund In the remembrance of so fair a dream . v 3 233
I am joyful To meet the least occasion that may give me Remembrance of my father-in-law . . . . . . *Hen. VIII.* iii 2 8
We did commend To your remembrances . . . *Coriolanus* ii 3 256
More than remembrance of my father's death . . *T. Andron.* iii 1 102
Call me to your remembrances.—What! . . . *T. of Athens* iii 5 92
Let it not cumber your better remembrance . . . . iii 6 52
My young remembrance cannot parallel A fellow to it . *Macbeth* ii 3 67
Let your remembrance apply to Banquo; Present him eminence . . iii 2 30
I will set down what comes from her, to satisfy my remembrance . v 1 37
Think on him, Together with remembrance of ourselves . . *Hamlet* i 2 7
Your visitation shall receive such thanks As fits a king's remembrance ii 2 26
I have remembrances of yours, That I have longed long to re-deliver iii 1 93
There's rosemary, that's for remembrance . . . . iv 5 175
A document in madness, thoughts and remembrance fitted . . iv 5 179
This was her first remembrance from the Moor . . *Othello* iii 3 291
You are jealous now That this is from some mistress, some remembrance iii 4 186
Which seem'd to tell them his remembrance lay In Egypt *Ant. and Cleo.* i 5 57
I must thank him only, Lest my remembrance suffer ill report . . ii 2 159
Some more time Must wear the print of his remembrance out *Cymbeline* ii 3 48
Or look upon our Romans, whose remembrance Is yet fresh in their grief . . . . ii 4 14
Praise Be given to your remembrance . . . . . ii 4 93
Whose remembrance yet Lives in men's eyes . . . . iii 1 2
Many years, Though Cloten then but young, you see, not wore him From my remembrance . . . . iv 4 24
By her own most clear remembrance, she Made known herself my daughter . . . . *Pericles* v 3 12
Remembrancer. Sweet remembrancer! . . . *Macbeth* iii 4 37
And the remembrancer of her to hold The hand-fast to her lord *Cymbeline* i 5 77
Remercimens. Je vous donne mille remercimens . . *Hen. V.* iv 4 58
Remiss. Belike thinking me remiss in mine office . *Meas. for Meas.* iv 2 119
He means, my lord, that we are too remiss . . *Richard II.* iii 2 33
Makes me weep, That thus we die, while remiss traitors sleep 1 *Hen. VI.* iv 3 29
The prince must think me tardy and remiss . . *Troi. and Cres.* iv 4 143
He, being remiss, Most generous and free from all contriving *Hamlet* iv 7 135
Remission. And ask remission for my folly past . . *T. G. of Ver.* i 2 65
I find an apt remission in myself . . . *Meas. for Meas.* v 1 503
What I did, I did in honour, . . . And never shall you see that I will beg A ragged and forestall'd remission . . . . 2 *Hen. IV.* v 2 38
My remission lies In Volscian breasts . . . *Coriolanus* v 2 90
Remissness. Either new, or by remissness new-conceived *Meas. for Meas.* ii 2 96
Remit. As to remit Their saucy sweetness . . . . . ii 4 44
Thy slanders I forgive; and therewithal Remit thy other forfeits . v 1 526
Neither of either; I remit both twain. I see the trick on 't . *L. L. Lost* v 2 459
I do remit these young men's heinous faults . . *T. Andron.* i 1 484
Remnant. I thought the remnant of mine age Should have been cherish'd by her child-like duty . . . . . . *T. G. of Ver.* iii 1 74

Remnant. I may chance have some odd quirks and remnants of wit broken on me *Much Ado* ii 3 245
Away, thou rag, thou quantity, thou remnant *T. of Shrew* iv 3 112
Where I may think the remnant of my thoughts In peace *K. John* v 4 46
The remnant northward, lying off from Trent 1 *Hen. IV.* iii 1 79
Thou bloodless remnant of that royal blood! *Richard III.* i 2 7
Leave those remnants Of fool and feather *Hen. VIII.* i 3 24
Remnants of packthread and old cakes of roses *Rom. and Jul.* v 1 47
Remonstrance. Make rash remonstrance of my hidden power *M. for M.* v 1 397
Remorse. Entertain'd ambition, Expell'd remorse and nature *Tempest* v 1 76
Slighted me into the river with as little remorse as they would have drowned a blind bitch's puppies *Mer. Wives* iii 5 10
But might you do't, and do the world no wrong, If so your heart were touch'd with that remorse As mine is to him? *Meas. for Meas.* ii 2 54
After much debatement, My sisterly remorse confutes mine honour v 1 100
Change slander to remorse; that is some good *Much Ado* iv 1 213
'Tis thought Thou'lt show thy mercy and remorse more strange Than is thy strange apparent cruelty *Mer. of Venice* iv 1 20
It was your pleasure and your own remorse *As Y. Like It* i 3 72
Without any mitigation or remorse of voice *T. Night* ii 3 98
Melted by the windy breath Of soft petitions, pity and remorse *K. John* ii 1 478
The vilest stroke That ever wall-eyed or staring rage Presented to the tears of soft remorse iv 3 50
Makes it seem Like rivers of remorse and innocency iv 3 110
What says Monsieur Remorse? 1 *Hen. IV.* i 2 125
Moved with remorse of these outrageous broils 1 *Hen. VI.* v 4 97
Thy words move rage and not remorse in me 2 *Hen. VI.* iv 1 112
I feel remorse in myself with his words; but I'll bridle it iv 7 111
Nero will be tainted with remorse, To hear and see her plaints 3 *Hen. VI.* iii 1 40
The thought of them would have stirr'd up remorse v 5 64
That word 'judgement' hath bred a kind of remorse in me *Richard III.* i 4 110
We know your tenderness of heart And gentle, kind, effeminate remorse iii 7 211
Thus both are gone with conscience and remorse iv 3 20
Do not these high strains Of divination in our sister work Some touches of remorse? *Troi. and Cres.* ii 2 115
Thy throat shall cut, And mince it sans remorse *T. of Athens* iv 3 122
The abuse of greatness is, when it disjoins Remorse from power *J. Cæsar* ii 1 19
Make thick my blood; Stop up the access and passage to remorse! *Macb.* i 5 45
Never did the Cyclops' hammers fall On Mars's armour forged for proof eterne With less remorse *Hamlet* ii 2 513
A servant that he bred, thrill'd with remorse, Opposed against the act *Lear* iv 2 73
Never pray more; abandon all remorse *Othello* iii 3 369
Let him command, And to obey shall be in me remorse iii 3 468
Remorseful. Valiant, wise, remorseful, well accomplish'd *T. G. of Ver.* iv 3 13
Like a remorseful pardon slowly carried *All's Well* v 3 58
The gaudy, blabbing and remorseful day 2 *Hen. VI.* iv 1 1
These eyes, which never shed remorseful tear *Richard III.* i 2 156
Remorseless have they borne him hence 2 *Hen. VI.* iii 1 213
Thou stern, obdurate, flinty, rough, remorseless 3 *Hen. VI.* i 4 142
Remorseless, treacherous, lecherous, kindless villain! *Hamlet* ii 2 609
Remote from all the pleasures of the world *L. L. Lost* v 2 806
From Athens is her house remote seven leagues *M. N. Dream* i 1 159
Bear it To some remote and desert place *W. Tale* ii 3 176
Places remote enough are in Bohemia iii 3 31
To grace the gentry of a land remote *K. John* v 2 31
New broils To be commenced in strands afar remote 1 *Hen. IV.* i 1 4
Or rudely visit them in parts remote, To fright them *Coriolanus* iv 5 148
Remotion. All thy safety were remotion *T. of Athens* iv 3 346
This remotion of the duke and her Is practice only *Lear* ii 4 115
Remove. It will go near to remove his fit *Tempest* ii 2 79
I must remove Some thousands of these logs and pile them up iii 1 9
In our remove be thou at full ourself *Meas. for Meas.* i 1 44
So shall your loves Woo contrary, deceived by these removes *L. L. Lost* v 2 135
Let us remove: The sight of lovers feedeth those in love *As Y. Like It* iii 4 59
She moves me not, or not removes, at least, Affection's edge *T. of Shrew* i 2 72
Let him that moved you hither Remove you hence ii 1 197
Who hath for four or five removes come short *All's Well* v 3 131
As well Forbid the sea for to obey the moon As or by oath remove or counsel shake The fabric of his folly *W. Tale* i 2 428
And will not . . . once remove The root of his opinion, which is rotten ii 3 88
What, here? O nation, that thou couldst remove! *K. John* v 2 33
The best part of my power, As I upon advantage did remove, Were in the Washes all unwarily Devoured by the unexpected flood v 7 62
I would remove these tedious stumbling-blocks 2 *Hen. VI.* i 2 64
His arms are only to remove from thee The Duke of Somerset iv 9 29
Why I have brought this army hither Is to remove proud Somerset v 1 36
He may gather The ground of your ill-will, and so remove it *Richard III.* i 3 69
The cure is, to Remove these thoughts from you *Hen. VIII.* ii 4 102
If they set down before 's, for the remove Bring up your army *Coriolanus* i 2 28
Which, but their children's end, nought could remove *Rom. and Jul.* Prol. 11
Unless good counsel may the cause remove i 1 148
Away with the joint-stools, remove the court-cupboard, look to the plate i 5 7
You, to remove that siege of grief from her, Betroth'd, and would have married her perforce v 3 237
Good God, betimes remove The means that makes us strangers! *Macbeth* iv 3 162
Remove from her the means of all annoyance, And still keep eyes upon her v 1 84
Till Birnam wood remove to Dunsinane, I cannot taint with fear v 3 2
Once more remove, good friends *Hamlet* i 5 163
And he most violent author Of his own just remove iv 5 81
The night before there was no purpose in them Of this remove *Lear* ii 4 4
Remove your thought; it doth abuse your bosom *Othello* iv 2 14
Cannot remove nor choke the strong conception That I do groan withal v 2 55
Say, our pleasure, To such whose place is under us, requires Our quick remove from hence *Ant. and Cleo.* i 2 203
Come on then, and remove him.—So. Begin *Cymbeline* iv 2 257
Removed. So far from Italy removed I ne'er again shall see her *Tempest* ii 1 110
How I have ever loved the life removed *Meas. for Meas.* i 3 8
See you the fornicatress be removed ii 2 23
Vouchsafe, bright moon, and these thy stars, to shine, Those clouds removed, upon our watery eyne *L. L. Lost* v 2 206
Lysander! what, removed? Lysander! lord! *M. N. Dream* ii 2 151
But mountains may be removed with earthquakes *As Y. Like It* iii 2 195
Something finer than you could purchase in so removed a dwelling iii 2 360
A lie seven times removed v 4 71
Your inclining cannot be removed *All's Well* iii 6 42
He hence removed last night and with more haste Than is his use v 1 23
Grew a twenty years removed thing While one would wink *T. Night* v 1 92
Removed. When he's removed, your highness Will take again your queen *W. Tale* i 2 335
Those that are germane to him, though removed fifty times, shall all come under the hangman iv 4 802
She hath privately twice or thrice a day . . . visited that removed house v 2 116
But the second generation Removed from thy sin-conceiving womb *K. John* ii 1 182
God hath made her sin and her the plague On this removed issue ii 1 186
No plume in any English crest That is removed by a staff of France ii 1 318
The king is moved, and answers not to this.—O, be removed from him! iii 1 218
I have removed Falstaff's horse, and he frets 1 *Hen. IV.* ii 2 1
The rascal hath removed my horse, and tied him I know not where ii 2 11
Nor did he think it meet To lay so dangerous and dear a trust On any soul removed but on his own iv 1 35
Richard thus removed, Leaving no heir 1 *Hen. VI.* ii 5 71
Like a mountain, not to be removed ii 5 103
Deputy of Ireland; who removed, Earl Surrey was sent thither *Hen. VIII.* ii 1 42
She was removed to Kimbolton, Where she remains now sick iv 1 34
Now I have stain'd the childhood of our joy With blood removed but little from her own *Rom. and Jul.* iii 3 96
With what courteous action It waves you to a more removed ground *Ham.* i 4 61
The impediment most profitably removed *Othello* ii 1 287
Removedness. I have eyes under my service which look upon his removedness *W. Tale* iv 2 41
Removing. Now thy uncle is removing hence 1 *Hen. VI.* ii 5 104
None can be so determinate as the removing of Cassio.—How do you mean, removing of him? *Othello* iv 2 232
Remunerate. And will nobly him remunerate *T. Andron.* i 1 398
Remuneration. There is remuneration *L. L. Lost* iii 1 133
Now will I look to his remuneration. Remuneration! O, that's the Latin word for three farthings—remuneration iii 1 137
The price of this inkle?—One penny.—No, I'll give you a remuneration: . . . Remuneration! why, it is a fairer name than French crown iii 1 141
How much carnation ribbon may a man buy for a remuneration? iii 1 147
What is a remuneration?—Marry, sir, halfpenny farthing iii 1 148
O sweet gardon! better than remuneration, a 'leven-pence farthing better iii 1 172
There is the very remuneration I had of thy master v 1 76
O, let not virtue seek Remuneration for the thing it was *Troi. and Cres.* iii 3 170
Rend. I will rend an oak And peg thee in his knotty entrails *Tempest* i 2 294
Thou didst then rend thy faith Into a thousand oaths *T. G. of Ver.* v 4 47
And sleep and snore, and rend apparel out *Mer. of Venice* ii 5 5
There was excellent command,—to charge in with our horse upon our own wings, and to rend our own soldiers! *All's Well* iii 6 53
They supposed I could rend bars of steel 1 *Hen. VI.* i 4 51
From thy burgonet I'll rend thy bear And tread it under foot 2 *Hen. VI.* v 1 208
And so he comes, to rend his limbs asunder 3 *Hen. VI.* i 3 15
Like one lost in a thorny wood, That rends the thorns and is rent iii 2 175
These nails should rend that beauty from my cheeks *Richard III.* i 2 126
We must not rend our subjects from our laws *Hen. VIII.* i 2 93
Rend and deracinate The unity and married calm of states *Troi. and Cres.* i 3 99
Whose rage doth rend Like interrupted waters *Coriolanus* iii 1 248
Rend off thy silver hair, thy other hand Gnawing with thy teeth *T. An.* iii 1 261
Where sighs and groans and shrieks that rend the air Are made *Macbeth* iv 3 168
Anon the dreadful thunder Doth rend the region *Hamlet* ii 2 509
Noble friends, That which combined us was most great, and let not A leaner action rend us *Ant. and Cleo.* ii 2 19
The very principals did seem to rend, And all-to topple *Pericles* iii 2 16
Render. Moe reasons for this action . . . shall I render you *Meas. for Meas.* i 3 49
What have I to give you back, whose worth May counterpoise this rich and precious gift?—Nothing, unless you render her again *Much Ado* iv 1 30
Claudio shall render me a dear account iv 1 337
Nor to their penn'd speech render we no grace *L. L. Lost* v 2 147
He hath my love, And what is mine my love shall render him *M. N. D.* i 1 96
I'll make her render up her page to me ii 1 185
Assume but valour's excrement To render them redoubted *Mer. of Ven.* iii 2 88
See thou render this Into my cousin's hand iii 4 49
We do pray for mercy; And that same prayer doth teach us all to render The deeds of mercy iv 1 201
What mercy can you render him, Antonio?—A halter gratis iv 1 378
To render it, Upon his death, unto the gentleman iv 1 383
I will render thee again in affection *As Y. Like It* i 2 21
I have given him a penny and he renders me the beggarly thanks ii 5 29
He did render him the most unnatural That lived amongst men iv 3 123
Which I presume shall render you no blame *All's Well* v 1 32
That it shall render vengeance and revenge *Richard II.* iv 1 67
That's the dearest grace it renders you 1 *Hen. IV.* iii 1 182
I will call him to so strict account, That he shall render every glory up iii 2 150
Give us leave Freely to render what we have in charge *Hen. V.* i 2 238
Say, if my father render fair return, It is against my will ii 4 127
You know no rules of charity, Which renders good for bad *Richard III.* i 2 69
I Can nothing render but allegiant thanks *Hen. VIII.* iii 2 176
Who commands you To render up the great seal presently Into our hands iii 2 229
If entreaties Will render you no remedy, this ring Deliver them v 1 150
Like a gate of steel Fronting the sun, receives and renders back His figure and his heat *Troi. and Cres.* iii 3 122
And there to render him, For the enfreed Antenor, the fair Cressid iv 1 37
In kissing, do you render or receive?—Both take and give iv 5 36
Of all The treasure . . . We render you the tenth *Coriolanus* i 9 34
He seeks their hate with greater devotion than they can render it him ii 2 22
How many sons of mine hast thou in store, That thou wilt never render to me more! *T. Andron.* i 1 95
Lo, at this tomb my tributary tears I render, for my brethren's obsequies i 1 160
The reason of this?—I could render one.—Do it then *T. of Athens* ii 2 109
Bankrupts, hold fast; Rather than render back, out with your knives! iv 1 9
And send forth us, to make their sorrow'd render v 1 152
O ye gods, Render me worthy of this noble wife! *J. Cæsar* ii 1 303
Let each man render me his bloody hand: First, Marcus Brutus iii 1 184
When I to sulphurous and tormenting flames Must render up myself *Ham.* i 5 4
To Cæsar will I render My legions and my horse *Ant. and Cleo.* iii 10 33
Render to me some corporal sign about her, More evident *Cymbeline* ii 4 119
Yet Report should render him hourly to your ear As truly as he moves iii 4 153
May drive us to a render Where we have lived, and so extort from's that iv 4 11
Take No stricter render of me than my all v 4 17
My boon is, that this gentleman may render Of whom he had this ring v 5 135
Rendered. For whom we render'd up this woe *Much Ado* v 3 33
Some show . . . , to be rendered by our assistants *L. L. Lost* v 1 127

Rendered. There is no firm reason to be render'd . . Mer. of Venice iv 1 53
The desperate languishings whereof The king is render'd lost All's Well i 3 236
Render'd such aspect As cloudy men use to their adversaries 1 Hen. IV. iii 2 82
That freely render'd me these news for true . . 2 Hen. IV. i 1 27
The word of peace is render'd : hark, how they shout ! . . iv 2 87
You shall hear A fearful battle render'd you in music . Hen. V. i 1 44
Nature craves All dues be render'd to their owners . Troi. and Cres. ii 2 174
Shall be render'd to your public laws At heaviest answer T. of Athens v 4 62
Besides, it were a mock Apt to be render'd . . . J. Cæsar ii 2 97
Public reasons shall be rendered Of Cæsar's death . . . iii 2 7
Compare their reasons, When severally we hear them rendered iii 2 10
This way, my lord ; the castle's gently render'd . . Macbeth v 7 24
She render'd life, Thy name so buried in her . . Ant. and Cleo. iv 14 33
Rendering. How shalt thou hope for mercy, rendering none? M. of V. iv 1 88
Mine eyes saw him in bloody state, Rendering faint quittance 2 Hen. IV. i 1 108
Rendezvous. A rendezvous, a home to fly unto . . 1 Hen. IV. iv 1 57
That is my rest, that is the rendezvous of it . . Hen. V. ii 1 18
And there my rendezvous is quite cut off. Old I do wax . v 1 88
You know the rendezvous . . . . . Hamlet iv 4 4
Renegado. Malvolio is turned heathen, a very renegado . T. Night iii 2 74
Renege, affirm, and turn their halcyon beaks With every gale . Lear ii 2 84
His captain's heart . . . reneges all temper . . Ant. and Cleo. i 1 8
Renew. In such a night Medea gather'd the enchanted herbs That did renew old Æson . . . . Mer. of Venice v 1 14
With your puissant arm renew their feats : You are their heir Hen. V. i 2 116
Either renew the fight, Or tear the lions out of England's coat 1 Hen. VI. i 5 27
Long mayst thou live To bear his image and renew his glories ! 3 Hen. VI. v 4 54
With a mind That doth renew swifter than blood decays Troi. and Cres. iii 2 170
Renew, renew ! The fierce Polydamas Hath beat down Menon . v 5 6
Therefore shall he die, And I'll renew me in his fall . Coriolanus v 6 49
And by her presence still renew his sorrows . . T. Andron. v 3 42
Renew I could not, like the moon ; There were no suns . T. of Athens iv 3 68
Could not be so cruel to me, as you, O the dearest of creatures, would even renew me with your eyes . . . . Cymbeline iii 2 42
Renew thy strength : I had rather thou shouldst live while nature will Than die ere I hear more . . . . . v 5 150
Renewed. Let our old acquaintance be renewed . . 2 Hen. IV. iii 2 315
Give renew'd fire to our extincted spirits ! . . . Othello ii 1 81
Gilded pale looks, Part shame, part spirit renew'd . . . Cymbeline v 3 35
Renounce. I renounce all confidence . . . . 1 Hen. VI i 2 97
Renounce your soil, give sheep in lions' stead . . . . i 5 29
To repair my honour lost for him, I here renounce him . 3 Hen. VI. iii 3 194
O you mighty gods ! This world I do renounce . . . Lear iv 6 35
For her To win the Moor—were't to renounce his baptism . Othello ii 3 349
Renouncement. By your renouncement an immortal spirit Meas. for Meas. i 4 35
Renouncing clean The faith they have in tennis . . Hen. VIII. i 3 29
Renown. Of whom so often I have heard renown, But never saw Tempest v 1 193
Honour, high honour and renown, To Hymen ! . . As Y. Like It v 4 151
Of a most chaste renown . . . . . . All's Well iv 3 19
Whate'er the course, the end is the renown . . . . iv 4 36
The memorials and the things of fame That do renown this city T. Night iii 3 24
To win renown Even in the jaws of danger and of death . . K. John v 2 115
This same child of honour and renown, This gallant Hotspur 1 Hen. IV. iii 2 139
If I affect it more Than as your honour and as your renown 2 Hen. IV. iv 5 146
With modesty admiring thy renown . . . . . 1 Hen. VI. ii 2 39
Thou never hadst renown, nor canst not lose it.—Yes, your renowned name . . . . iv 5 40
So am I driven by breath of her renown Either to suffer shipwreck or arrive Where I may have fruition of her love . . . v 5 7
Razing the characters of your renown . . . . 2 Hen. VI. i 1 101
They have demean'd themselves Like men born to renown . 3 Hen. VI. i 4 8
Stay we no longer, dreaming of renown, But sound the trumpets . ii 1 199
She is a theme of honour and renown . . . Troi. and Cres. ii 2 199
That it was no better than picture-like to hang by the wall, if renown made it not stir . . . . Coriolanus i 3 13
All is but toys : renown and grace is dead . . . Macbeth ii 3 99
He was a wight of high renown, And thou art but of low degree Othello ii 3 96
Accumulation of renown, Which he achieved by the minute Ant. and Cleo. iii 1 19
Wounding his belief in her renown With tokens thus, and thus Cymbeline v 5 202
Her thoughts the king Of every virtue gives renown to men ! Pericles i 1 14
As jewels lose their glory if neglected, So princes their renowns if not respected . . . . ii 2 13
Such strong renown as time shall ne'er decay . . . . iii 2 48
I can be modest.—That dignifies the renown of a bawd . . iv 6 42
Renowned. Doctor Caius, the renowned French physician Mer. Wives iii 1 61
There she lost a noble and renowned brother . . Meas. for Meas. iii 1 228
Your most renowned uncle . . . . . Com. of Errors v 1 368
Renowned duke, vouchsafe to take the pains To go with us . . v 1 393
He hath wronged his honour in marrying the renowned Claudio M. Ado ii 2 24
Most rare Pompey !—Renowned Pompey ! . . . L. L. Lost v 2 690
Happy be Theseus, our renowned duke ! . . . M. N. Dream i 1 20
The four winds blow in from every coast Renowned suitors Mer. of Venice i 1 169
Yourself, renowned prince, then stood as fair As any comer . . ii 1 20
Pisa renowned for grave citizens . . . . . T. of Shrew i 1 10 ; iv 2 95
Renown'd in Padua for her scolding tongue . . . . i 2 100
What wilt thou do, renowned Faulconbridge? . . . K. John iv 3 101
Lift up thy brow, renowned Salisbury . . . . . v 2 54
Renowned for their deeds as far from home, For Christian service and true chivalry . . . . Richard II. ii 1 53
What never-dying honour hath he got Against renowned Douglas ! 1 Hen. IV. iii 2 107
Most fine, most honour'd, most renown'd, Hast eat thy bearer up 2 Hen. IV. iv 5 164
The blood and courage that renowned them Runs in your veins Hen. V. i 2 118
Renowned Talbot doth expect my aid . . . 1 Hen. VI. iv 3 12
He, renowned noble gentleman, Yields up his life unto a world of odds iv 4 24
Thou never hadst renown, nor canst not lose it.—Yes, your renowned name . . . . iv 5 41
I have consider'd with myself The title of this most renowned duke 2 Hen. VI. v 1 176
I'll venge thy death, Or die renowned by attempting it . 3 Hen. VI. ii 1 88
Renowned queen, with patience calm the storm . . . iii 3 38
Renowned prince, how shall poor Henry live, Unless thou rescue him? iii 3 214
Three dukes of Somerset, threefold renown'd . . . . v 7 5
My great father-in-law, renowned Warwick . . . Richard III. i 4 49
Sir Walter Herbert, a renowned soldier . . . . iv 5 9
An act that very chance doth throw upon him—Ajax renown'd Troi. and Cres. iii 3 132
Welcome to Rome, renowned Coriolanus ! . . . . Coriolanus ii 1 183
Renowned. Our renowned Rome, whose gratitude Towards her deserved children is enroll'd In Jove's own book . . . Coriolanus iii 1 291
Renowned Titus, flourishing in arms . . . . T. Andron. i 1 38
Renowned Lucius, from our troops I stray'd . . . . v 1 20
O fortune, fortune ! all men call thee fickle : If thou art fickle, what dost thou with him That is renown'd for faith? . Rom. and Jul. iii 5 62
Leave unexecuted Your own renowned knowledge . Ant. and Cleo. iii 7 46
So. Thus then, thou most renown'd . . . . . iii 13 53
Quiet consummation have ; And renowned be thy grave ! . . Cymbeline iv 2 281
A knight of Sparta, my renowned father . . . Pericles ii 2 18
Rent. If this law hold in Vienna ten year, I'll rent the fairest house in it after three-pence a bay . . . . . Meas. for Meas. ii 1 254
What, did these rent lines show some love of thine? L. L. Lost iv 3 220
And will you rent our ancient love asunder? . . M. N. Dream iii 2 215
Lean, rent and beggar'd by the strumpet wind . . Mer. of Venice ii 6 19
My manors, rents, revenues I forego . . . . Richard II. iv 1 212
What are thy rents? what are thy comings in? O ceremony ! Hen. V. iv 1 260
France should have torn and rent my very heart . . 2 Hen. VI. i 1 126
That rends the thorns and is rent with the thorns 3 Hen. VI. iii 2 175
See what a rent the envious Casca made . . J. Cæsar iii 2 179
Tell him, so much the rent of his land comes to . . . Lear i 4 148
Repaid. Demand to have repaid A hundred thousand crowns L. L. Lost ii 1 143
The poorest service is repaid with thanks . . T. of Shrew iv 3 45
For strokes received, and many blows repaid . . 3 Hen. VI. ii 3 3
He is well repaid ; He is frank'd up to fatting for his pains Richard III. i 3 313
Ill art thou repaid For that good hand thou sent'st the emperor T. An. iii 1 235
Repair. Love doth to her eyes repair, To help him . T. G. of Ver. iv 2 46
Repair me with thy presence, Silvia ; Thou gentle nymph ! . v 4 11
Only a repair i' the dark . . . . . Meas. for Meas. iv 1 43
My decayed fair A sunny look of his would soon repair . Com. of Errors ii 1 99
Repair to Leonato's : commend me to him . . . Much Ado i 1 278
All senses to that sense did make their repair . . L. L. Lost ii 1 240
When they repair, Blow like sweet roses in this summer air . . v 2 292
To Athens back again repair And think no more of this . M. N. Dream iv 1 72
Repair thy wit, good youth, or it will fall To cureless ruin Mer. of Ven. iv 1 141
Could I repair what she will wear in me . . . T. of Shrew iii 2 120
It much repairs me To talk of your good father . . All's Well i 2 30
For royalty's repair, For present comfort and for future good W. Tale v 1 31
Some speedy messenger bid her repair To our solemnity K. John ii 1 554
Even in the instant of repair and health, The fit is strongest . . iii 4 113
Bid him repair to us to Ely House To see this business . Richard II. ii 1 216
Then with directions to repair to Ravenspurgh . . . . ii 3 35
Line and new repair our towns of war With men of courage . Hen. V. ii 4 7
Repair to your several dwelling-places . . . 1 Hen. VI. i 3 77
Like a gallant in the brow of youth, Repairs him with occasion 2 Hen. VI. v 3 5
To repair my honour lost for him, I here renounce him 3 Hen. VI. iii 3 193
We must enter in, For hither will our friends repair to us . . iv 7 15
How are they seduced, That we could hear no news of his repair?. . v 1 20
Presently repair to Crosby Place . . . . Richard III. i 2 213
When you have done, repair to Crosby Place . . . . . i 3 345
Times to repair our nature With comforting repose . . Hen. VIII. v 1 3
When that the general is not like the hive To whom the foragers shall all repair, What honey is expected? . . . Troi. and Cres. i 3 82
And, knowing myself again, Repair to the senate-house . Coriolanus ii 3 156
When you have drawn your number, Repair to the Capitol . . ii 3 262
Having read it, Bid them repair to the market-place . . . v 6 3
Bid him repair to me . . . . . . T. Andron. v 2 124
Since it is my father's mind That I repair to Rome, I am content . v 3 2
Mine honest friend, I prithee, but repair to me next morning T. of Athens ii 2 25
If I might beseech you, gentlemen, to repair some other hour . iii 4 69
All this done, Repair to Pompey's porch . . . J. Cæsar i 3 147
That done, repair to Pompey's theatre . . . . . i 3 152
Repair thou to me with as much speed as thou wouldst fly death Hamlet iv 6 23
If your mind dislike any thing, obey it : I will forestal their repair hither v 2 228
I'll repair the misery thou dost bear With something rich . Lear iv 1 79
Let this kiss Repair those violent harms . . . . . iv 7 28
This honest fool Plies Desdemona to repair his fortunes . . Othello ii 3 360
That done, I will be walking on the works ; Repair there to me . iii 2 4
To the ports The discontents repair . . . Ant. and Cleo. i 4 39
O disloyal thing, That shouldst repair my youth, thou heap'st A year's age on me . . . . Cymbeline i 1 132
The crickets sing, and man's o'er-labour'd sense Repairs itself by rest . ii 2 12
Whose repair and franchise Shall, by the power we hold, be our good deed iii 1 57
After all my crosses, Thou givest me somewhat to repair myself Pericles ii 1 128
He brought his disease hither ; here he does but repair it . . iv 2 120
Repaired. Burst and now repaired with knots . . . T. of Shrew iii 2 60
And all the ruins of distressful times Repair'd . . Richard III. iv 4 319
Repairing. Like a German clock, Still a-repairing . . L. L. Lost iii 1 193
'Tis not enough our foes are this time fled, Being opposites of such repairing nature . . . . 2 Hen. VI. v 3 22
Repassed. Well have we pass'd and now repass'd the seas 3 Hen. VI. iv 7 5
Repast. If, before repast, it shall please you to gratify the table with a grace . . . . L. L. Lost iv 2 160
Get me some repast ; I care not what, so it be wholesome T. of Shrew iv 3 15
Like the kind life-rendering pelican, Repast them with my blood Hamlet iv 5 147
If I prove a good repast to the spectators, the dish pays the shot Cymbeline v 4 157
Repasture. Food for his rage, repasture for his den . . L. L. Lost iv 1 95
Repay. I think to repay that money will be a biting affliction Mer. Wives v 5 178
I never heard of it ; And if you prove it, I'll repay it back . L. L. Lost ii 1 159
If you repay me not on such a day, In such a place . . Mer. of Venice i 3 147
'Tis call'd ungrateful, With dull unwillingness to repay a debt Rich. III. ii 2 92
No meed, but he repays Sevenfold above itself . . T. of Athens i 1 288
All that is won and lost ; give me a kiss ; Even this repays me Ant. and Cleo. iii 11 71
Repaying. It might have since been answer'd in repaying What we took from them . . . . T. Night iii 3 33
Repeal. When she for thy repeal was suppliant . T. G. of Ver. iii 1 234
I here forget all former griefs, Cancel all grudge, repeal thee home again v 4 143
The banish'd Bolingbroke repeals himself . . . Richard II. ii 2 49
I will repeal thee, or, be well assured, Adventure to be banished myself : And banished I am, if but from thee . . . 2 Hen. VI. iii 2 349
Repeal daily any wholesome act established against the rich . Coriolanus i 1 84
If the time thrust forth A cause for thy repeal . . . . iv 1 41
Their people Will be as rash in the repeal, as hasty To expel him . iv 7 32
Repeal him with the welcome of his mother . . . . v 5 5
That Publius Cimber may Have an immediate freedom of repeal J. Cæsar iii 1 54
When false opinion, whose wrong thought defiles thee, In thy just proof, repeals and reconciles thee . . . . Lear iii 6 120
That she repeals him for her body's lust . . . . Othello ii 3 363

Repealed. Whose banish'd sense Thou hast repeal'd . . *All's Well* ii 3 55
Provided that my banishment repeal'd And lands restored again be freely granted . . . . *Richard II.* iii 3 40
Here do I throw down this, If he may be repeal'd, to try his honour . iv 1 85
These differences shall all rest under gage Till Norfolk be repeal'd : repeal'd he shall be . . . . iv 1 87
Until that act of parliament be repeal'd . . . . . *3 Hen. VI.* i 1 249
Repealing. For the repealing of my banish'd brother . . *J. Cæsar* iii 1 51
Repeat. Kneel and repeat it ; I will stand . . . *Tempest* iii 2 46
Please you repeat their names, I'll show my mind . . *T. G. of Ver.* i 2 7
Which I had rather seal with my death than repeat over to my shame *Much Ado* v 1 248
The third of the five vowels, if you repeat them ; or the fifth, if I.—I will repeat them . . . . *L. L. Lost* v 1 57
For I the ballad will repeat, Which men full true shall find . *All's Well* i 3 64
Puts on his pretty looks, repeats his words . . . . *K. John* iii 4 95
For what I have I need not to repeat . . . . *Richard II.* iii 4 17
That may repeat and history his loss To new remembrance *2 Hen. IV.* iv 1 203
Repeat their semblance often on the seas . . . . . *1 Hen. VI.* v 3 193
Lo, ere I can repeat this curse again . . . . *Richard III.* iv 1 78
Ere you ask, is given ; Repeat your will and take it . . *Hen. VIII.* i 2 13
I grieve at what I speak, And am right sorry to repeat what follows . v 1 96
And pride so great, The name of help grew odious to repeat . *Pericles* i 4 31
Thou speak'st like him's untutor'd to repeat . . . . i 4 74
'Twould be too tedious to repeat . . . . v 1 28
Repeated. She is too mean To have her name repeated . *All's Well* iii 5 64
My supreme crown of grief! and those repeated Vexations of it! *Cymbeline* i 6 4
Vice repeated is like the wandering wind, Blows dust in others' eyes *Per.* i 1 96
Repeatest. These evils thou repeat'st upon thyself Have banish'd me from Scotland . . . . *Macbeth* iv 3 112
Repeating. This act is as an ancient tale new told, And in the last repeating troublesome . . . . *K. John* iv 2 19
Repel. I did repel his letters and denied His access to me . *Hamlet* ii 1 109
Repent. I kill'd a man, whose death I much repent . *T. G. of Ver.* iv 1 27
Why, ne'er repent it, if it were done so . . . . . iv 1 30
If my wind were but long enough to say my prayers, I would repent *Mer. Wives* iv 5 105
Repent you, fair one, of the sin you carry?—I do . *Meas. for Meas.* ii 3 19
I do confess it, and repent it, father.—'Tis meet so, daughter . . ii 3 29
But lest you do repent, As that the sin hath brought you to this shame, Which sorrow is always towards ourselves, not heaven . . ii 3 30
I do repent me, as it is an evil, And take the shame with joy . . . ii 3 35
Yet did repent me, after more advice . . . . . . v 1 469
I do repent The tedious minutes I with her have spent . *M. N. Dream* ii 2 111
All for your delight We are not here. That you should here repent you v 1 115
I never did repent for doing good, Nor shall not now . *Mer. of Venice* iii 4 10
I'll repent, And wish, for all that, that I had not kill'd them . iii 4 72
Repent but you that you shall lose your friend, And he repents not that he pays your debt . . . . iv 1 278
Indeed, I do marry that I may repent . . . . *All's Well* i 3 39
My state that way is dangerous, since I cannot yet find in my heart to repent . . . . ii 5 13
My offences being many, I would repent out the remainder of nature . iv 3 272
Do not repent these things, for they are heavier Than all thy woes *W. T.* iii 2 209
All faults I make, when I shall come to know them, I do repent . . iii 2 221
Repent each drop of blood That hot rash haste so indirectly shed *K. John* ii 1 48
Look to that, devil ; lest that France repent . . . . iii 1 196
They burn in indignation. I repent. . . . . . . iv 2 103
I do repent me ; read not my name there . . . . *Richard II.* v 3 52
I'll repent, and that suddenly, while I am in some liking *1 Hen. IV.* iii 3 5
I shall be out of heart shortly, and then I shall have no strength to repent . . . . iii 3 8
The young lion repents ; marry, not in ashes and sackcloth . *2 Hen. IV.* i 2 221
Repent at idle times as thou mayest . . . . . . ii 2 140
I repent my fault more than my death . . . . *Hen. V.* ii 2 152
Shall repent his folly, see his weakness, and admire our sufferance . iii 6 131
I must repent. Go therefore, tell thy master here I am . . . . iii 6 161
Clifford, repent in bootless penitence . . . . *3 Hen. VI.* ii 6 70
She hath had too much wrong ; and I repent My part thereof *Richard III.* i 3 307
I repent me that the duke is slain.—So do not I : go, coward as thou art i 4 285
O, now I want the priest that spake to me : I now repent . . . iii 4 90
Men shall deal unadvisedly sometimes, Which after hours give leisure to repent . . . . iv 4 293
As I intend to prosper and repent, So thrive I in my dangerous attempt! iv 4 397
In this rapture I shall surely speak The thing I shall repent *Tr. and Cr.* iii 2 139
Almost all Repent in their election . . . . . . *Coriolanus* ii 3 263
Repent what you have spoke.—For them! I cannot do it to the gods . iii 2 37
Thou and thy faction shall repent this rape . . . *T. Andron.* i 1 404
I am no baby, I, that with base prayers I should repent . . . v 3 186
If one good deed in all my life I did, I do repent it from my very soul . v 3 190
With so strong a fine That you shall all repent the loss . *Rom. and Jul.* iii 1 196
Where I have learn'd me to repent the sin Of disobedient opposition To you . . . . iv 2 17
Are they not Athenians?—Yes.—Then I repent not . . *T. of Athens* i 1 184
O, yet I do repent me of my fury, That I did kill them . . *Macbeth* ii 3 112
Try what repentance can : what can it not? Yet what can it when one can not repent? . . . . *Hamlet* iii 3 66
Confess yourself to heaven ; Repent what's past ; avoid what is to come iii 4 150
For this same lord, I do repent : but heaven hath pleased it so . . iii 4 173
Woe, that too late repents,—O, sir, are you come? . . . *Lear* i 4 279
How malicious is my fortune, that I must repent to be just! . . . iii 5 11
Her will, recoiling to her better judgement, May fall to match you with her country forms And happily repent . . . . . *Othello* iii 3 238
You are eaten up with passion : I do repent me that I put it to you . iii 3 392
I will give over my suit and repent my unlawful solicitation . . . iv 2 202
I can again thy former light restore, Should I repent me . . . . v 2 10
Repent that e'er thy tongue Hath so betray'd thine act . *Ant. and Cleo.* ii 7 83
A proper man.—Indeed, he is so : I repent me much That so I harried him . . . . iii 3 42
If that thy father live, let him repent Thou wast not made his daughter iii 13 134
Be witness to me, . . . poor Enobarbus did Before thy face repent! . iv 9 10
So had you saved The noble Imogen to repent, and struck Me *Cymbeline* v 1 10
Must I repent? I cannot do it better than in gyves . . . v 4 13
He will repent the breadth of his great voyage . . . *Pericles* iv 1 37
Repentance. Who by repentance is not satisfied Is nor of heaven nor earth, for these are pleased . . . . . . *T. G. of Ver.* v 4 79
And then comes repentance and, with his bad legs, falls into the cinque pace faster and faster . . . . *Much Ado* ii 1 81
Pay her the debt . . . , and unpay the villany . . . the one you may do with sterling money, and the other with current repentance *2 Hen. IV.* ii 1 132

Repentance. God of his mercy give You patience to endure, and true repentance! . . . . *Hen. V.* ii 2 180
The constable desires thee thou wilt mind Thy followers of repentance iv 3 85
Full of repentance, Continual meditations, tears, and sorrows *Hen. VIII.* iv 2 27
Implored your highness' pardon and set forth A deep repentance *Macbeth* i 4 7
Try what repentance can : what can it not? Yet what can it when one can not repent? . . . . *Hamlet* iii 3 66
Repentant. And strew'd repentant ashes on his head . . *K. John* iv 1 111
Wet his grave with my repentant tears . . . *Richard III.* i 2 216
Repented. When, after execution, judgement hath Repented . *M. for M.* ii 2 12
It would not seem too dear, Howe'er repented after . . . *All's Well* iii 7 28
Repented The evils she hatch'd were not effected . . . *Cymbeline* v 5 59
Repenting. Wooing, wedding, and repenting, is as a Scotch jig *Much Ado* ii 1 76
Repetition. The first view shall kill All repetition . . . *All's Well* v 3 22
Be more temperate : It ill beseems this presence to cry aim To these ill-tuned repetitions . . . . *K. John* ii 1 197
But repetition of what thou hast marr'd . . . . *Richard III.* iii 3 165
He hath faults, with surplus, to tire in repetition . . . *Coriolanus* i 1 47
Such a name, Whose repetition will be dogg'd with curses . . . v 3 144
Tear the cave where Echo lies, And make her airy tongue more hoarse than mine, With repetition of my Romeo's name . *Rom. and Jul.* ii 2 164
The repetition, in a woman's ear, Would murder as it fell . *Macbeth* ii 3 90
Call And give them repetition to the life . . . . *Pericles* v 1 247
Répétition. Je m'en fais la répétition de tous les mots . . *Hen. V.* iii 4 25
Repine. Let Henry fret and all the world repine . *1 Hen. VI.* v 2 20
Repined. When corn was given them gratis, you repined *Coriolanus* iii 1 43
Repining. What the repining enemy commends, That breath fame blows *Troi. and Cres.* i 3 243
Replant. And replant Henry in his former state . . *3 Hen. VI.* iii 3 198
Replenished. His intellect is not replenished . . . *L. L. Lost* iv 2 27
The most replenish'd villain in the world . . . . *W. Tale* ii 1 79
The most replenished sweet work of nature . . . *Richard III.* iv 3 18
Replete. A man replete with mocks, Full of comparisons . *L. L. Lost* v 2 853
A counterpoise, if not to thy estate A balance more replete . *All's Well* ii 3 183
His sparkling eyes, replete with wrathful fire . . . *1 Hen. VI.* i 1 12
All France will be replete with mirth and joy, When they shall hear . i 6 15
Lend me a heart replete with thankfulness! . . . *2 Hen. VI.* i 1 20
Her looks do argue her replete with modesty . . *3 Hen. VI.* iii 2 84
Replication. Facere, as it were, replication . . . *L. L. Lost* iv 2 15
Tiber trembled underneath her banks, To hear the replication of your sounds Made in her concave shores . . . . *J. Cæsar* i 1 51
What replication should be made by the son of a king? . . *Hamlet* iv 2 13
Replied. How he refell'd me, and how I replied . . *Meas. for Meas.* v 1 94
The boy replied, 'An angel is not evil' . . . . *L. L. Lost* v 2 105
Roundly replied . . . . *T. of Shrew* v 2 21
I replied, Men fear'd the French would prove perfidious . *Hen. VIII.* i 2 155
It tauntingly replied To the discontented members . . . *Coriolanus* i 1 114
He replied, It was a bare petition of a state . . . . . v 1 19
I threaten'd to discover him : he replied, 'Thou unpossessing bastard!' *Lear* ii 1 68
She replied, It should be better he became her guest . *Ant. and Cleo.* ii 2 225
Repliest. Where should she be? How oddly thou repliest! *Rom. and Jul.* ii 5 61
Reply. Or else for want of idle time, could not again reply *T. G. of Ver.* ii 1 172
What reply, ha? What sayest thou? . . . . *Meas. for Meas.* iii 2 50
Expecting thy reply, I profane my lips on thy foot . . *L. L. Lost* iv 1 86
I shall reply amazedly, Half sleep, half waking . . *M. N. Dream* iv 1 151
How begot, how nourished? Reply, reply . . . *Mer. of Venice* iii 2 66
This is called the Reply Churlish . . . . . *As Y. Like It* v 4 80
The third, the Reply Churlish ; the fourth, the Reproof Valiant . . v 4 98
The honour, sir, that flames in your fair eyes, Before I speak, too threateningly replies . . . . *All's Well* ii 3 87
You were straited For a reply . . . . *W. Tale* iv 4 366
Hear me without thine ears, and make reply Without a tongue *K. John* iii 3 49
I must find that title in your tongue, Before I make reply *Richard II.* ii 3 73
Be gone ; We will not now be troubled with reply . . *1 Hen. IV.* v 1 113
I will not undergo this sneap without reply . . . *2 Hen. IV.* ii 1 134
Reply not to me with a fool-born jest . . . . v 5 59
Vouchsafe To give me hearing what I shall reply . . *1 Hen. VI.* iii 1 28
Take leave and stand not to reply . . . . . *3 Hen. VI.* iv 8 23
Why, so I did ; but look'd for no reply . . . . *Richard III.* i 3 237
When I do tell thee, there my hopes lie drown'd, Reply not in how many fathoms deep They lie indrench'd . . . . . *Troi. and Cres.* i 1 50
I said 'Good morrow, Ajax ;' and he replies 'Thanks' . . . . iii 3 262
Speak not, reply not, do not answer me ; My fingers itch *Rom. and Jul.* iii 5 164
Now return, And with their faint reply this answer join *T. of Athens* iii 3 25
If any, speak ; for him have I offended. I pause for a reply . *J. Cæsar* iii 2 37
Why, 'tis a loving and a fair reply : Be as ourself in Denmark *Hamlet* i 2 121
How pregnant sometimes his replies are! . . . . . . ii 2 212
Niggard of question ; but, of our demands, Most free in his reply . . iii 1 14
The Moor replies, That he you hurt is of great fame in Cyprus *Othello* iii 1 47
Why should not we Be there in person?—Well, I could reply *A. and C.* iii 7 7
Look not sad, Nor make replies of loathness : take the hint . . . iii 11 18
Replying. If not to answer, you might haply think Tongue-tied ambition, not replying, yielded . . . . *Richard III.* iii 7 145
The babbling echo mocks the hounds, Replying shrilly . *T. Andron.* ii 3 18
Report. Ay, or very falsely pocket up his report . . . *Tempest* ii 1 67
If in Naples I should report this now, would they believe me? . . iii 3 28
On Valentine's report, You are already Love's firm votary *T. G. of Ver.* iii 2 57
By your own report A linguist . . . . iv 1 56
The report goes she has all the rule of her husband's purse *Mer. Wives* i 3 58
Falling in the flaws of her own youth, Hath blister'd her report *M. for M.* ii 3 12
That you shall stifle in your own report And smell of calumny . . ii 4 158
Some report a sea-maid spawned him . . . . . . iii 2 115
He shall know you better, sir, if I may live to report you . . . iii 2 172
Volumes of report Run with these false and most contrarious quests . iv 1 61
Little beholding to your reports ; but the best is, he lives not in them . iv 3 167
Not better than he, by her own report . . . . . . v 1 274
You must, sir, change persons with me, ere you make that my report . v 1 340
To seek me out By computation and mine host's report . *Com. of Errors* ii 2 4
That is false thou dost report to us . . . . . . v 1 179
For bearing, argument, and valour, Goes foremost in report . *Much Ado* iii 1 97
They have committed false report ; moreover, they have spoken untruths v 1 220
Much too little of that good I saw Is my report . . . *L. L. Lost* ii 1 63
Choughs, many in sort, Rising and cawing at the gun's report *M. N. D.* iii 2 22
Man's hand is not able to taste, his tongue to conceive, nor his heart to report, what my dream was . . . . iv 1 219
If my gossip Report be an honest woman of her word . *Mer. of Venice* iii 1 7
Report speaks goldenly of his profit . . . . . *As Y. Like It* i 1 6
If you like upon report The soil, the profit, and this kind of life . ii 4 97
His uncle, Whom he reports to be a great magician . . . . v 2 33

Report. To make mine eye the witness Of that report . *T. of Shrew* ii 1 53
By report I know him well . . . . ii 1 105
And now I find report a very liar . . . . . . ii 1 246
Why does the world report that Kate doth limp? O slanderous world! ii 1 254
Good report I hear of you . . . . iv 4 28
Say to him, I live; and observe his reports for me . *All's Well* ii 1 46
In every thing I wait upon his will.—I shall report it so . ii 4 56
You shall hear I am run away: know it before the report come . iii 2 25
That pitiful rumour may report my flight, To consolate thine ear . iii 2 130
Let's return again, and suffice ourselves with the report of it . . iii 5 11
There is a gentleman that serves the count Reports but coarsely of her iii 5 60
Not daring the reports of my tongue . . . . . iv 1 34
Made such pestiferous reports of men very nobly held . . . iv 3 340
You are not fallen From the report that goes upon your goodness . v 1 13
Unless it be to report your lord's taking of this . . *T. Night* ii 2 11
No love-broker in the world can more prevail in man's commendation with woman than report of valour . . . . . . iii 2 41
Set upon Aguecheek a notable report of valour . . . . iii 4 210
These wise men that give fools money get themselves a good report . iv 1 24
I shall report, For most it caught me, the celestial habits . *W. Tale* iii 1 3
O sir, I shall be hated to report it! . . . . . . iii 2 144
The report of her is extended more than can be thought . . iv 2 48
I have it Upon his own report and I believe it; He looks like sooth . iv 4 170
Though I report it, That should be silent . . . . . iv 4 177
One three of them, by their own report, sir, hath danced before the king iv 4 345
That which I shall report will bear no credit, Were not the proof so nigh v 1 179
Which lames report to follow it and undoes description to do it . . v 2 62
Give me your good report to the prince . . . . . v 2 162
Ere thou canst report I will be there . . . . *K. John* i 1 25
I'll fill these dogged spies with false reports . . . . iv 1 129
Haste thee to the peers, Throw this report on their incensed rage . iv 2 261
Report of fashions in proud Italy . . . . *Richard II.* ii 1 21
But I shall grieve you to report the rest.—What is't, knave? . ii 2 95
Let not his report Come current for an accusation . . *1 Hen. IV.* i 3 67
This pitch, as ancient writers do report, doth defile . . . ii 4 456
Such as fear the report of a caliver worse than a struck fowl . . iv 2 20
Rumour, . . . Stuffing the ears of men with false reports *2 Hen. IV.* Ind. 8
If he be slain, say so; The tongue offends not that reports his death . i 1 97
Stand my good lord, pray, in your good report . . . . iv 3 89
The man Whose glory fills the world with loud report . *1 Hen. VI.* ii 2 43
Fain would mine eyes be witness with mine ears, To give their censure of these rare reports . . . . ii 3 10
I see report is fabulous and false . . . . . . ii 3 18
Whether it be through force of your report . . . . v 5 79
Let this my sword report what speech forbears . *2 Hen. VI.* iv 10 57
Of Salisbury, who can report of him, That winter lion? . . . v 3 1
Whether 'twas report of her success; Or more than common fear *3 Hen. VI.* ii 1 125
If Warwick be so near as men report . . . . . iv 3 8
If she be accused in true report, Bear with her weakness . *Richard III.* i 3 27
Or with the clamorous report of war, Thus will I drown your exclamations . . . . iv 4 152
Flatter my sorrows with report of it . . . . . . iv 4 245
If . . . you can report, And prove it too, against mine honour *Hen. VIII.* ii 4 38
If he know That I am free of your report, he knows I am not of your wrong . . . . ii 4 99
Who shall report he has A better wife, let him in nought be trusted . ii 4 134
Let him, like an engine Not portable, lie under this report *Troi. and Cres.* ii 3 144
And could be content to give him good report for't, but that he pays himself with being proud . . . . . *Coriolanus* i 1 33
But had he died in the business, madam; how then?—Then his good report should have been my son . . . . i 3 22
Else had I, sir, Half an hour since brought my report . . . i 6 21
If any fear Lesser his person than an ill report . . . . i 6 70
I'll report it Where senators shall mingle tears with smiles . . i 9 2
Too modest are you; More cruel to your good report than grateful To us i 9 54
Of no better report than a horse-drench . . . . . ii 1 129
Without any further deed to have them at all into their estimation and report . . . . ii 2 32
To report otherwise, were a malice . . . . . . ii 2 36
Report A little of that worthy work perform'd By Caius Marcius . . ii 2 48
My mind gave me his clothes made a false report of him . . iv 5 157
There is a slave, whom we have put in prison, Reports . . . iv 6 39
His raising; Nothing but his report . . . . . . iv 6 61
The slave's report is seconded; and more, More fearful, is deliver'd . iv 6 62
Report to the Volscian lords, how plainly I have borne this business . v 3 3
Mercy, if you report him truly.—I paint him in the character . . v 4 27
My scars can witness . . . That my report is just . *T. Andron.* v 3 115
Thou wrong'st it, more than tears, with that report . *Rom. and Jul.* iv 1 32
Men report Thou dost affect my manners, and dost use them *T. of Athens* iv 3 198
That he's so full of gold?—Certain: Alcibiades reports it . . . v 1 5
If it be a just and true report that goes of his having . . . v 1 18
Thou hast painfully discover'd: are his files As full as thy report? . v 2 2
Thrusting this report Into his ears; I may say, thrusting it . *J. Cæsar* v 3 74
What bloody man is that? He can report, As seemeth by his plight *Macb.* i 2 1
I must report they were As cannons overcharged with double cracks . i 2 36
Who did report That very frankly he confess'd his treasons . . i 4 4
I have learned by the perfectest report . . . . . . i 5 2
This report Hath so exasperate the king that he Prepares for some attempt of war . . . . iii 6 37
I have two nights watched with you, but can perceive no truth in your report . . . . v 1 2
What, at any time, have you heard her say?—That, sir, which I will not report after her . . . . v 1 16
Bring me no more reports; let them fly all . . . . . v 3 1
Shadow The numbers of our host and make discovery Err in report of us v 4 7
I should report that which I say I saw, But know not how to do it . v 5 31
Nor shall you do mine ear that violence, To make it truster of your own report Against yourself . . . . *Hamlet* i 2 172
You were better have a bad epitaph than their ill report while you live ii 2 550
Gave you such a masterly report For art and exercise in your defence . iv 7 97
This report of his Did Hamlet so envenom with his envy . . iv 7 103
Report me and my cause aright To the unsatisfied . . . . v 2 350
You shall find Some that will thank you, making just report . *Lear* iii 1 37
I would not take this from report; it is, And my heart breaks at it . iv 6 144
All my reports go with the modest truth; Nor more nor clipp'd, but so iv 7 5
Report is changeable . . . . iv 7 92
In these cases, where the aim reports, 'Tis oft with difference . *Othello* i 3 6
So was I bid report here to the state . . . . . . i 3 15
If you do find me foul in her report, The trust, the office I do hold of you, Not only take away, but let your sentence Even fall upon my life i 3 117
Report. More of this matter cannot I report: But men are men *Othello* ii 3 240
Can you inquire him out, and be edified by report? . . . . . iii 4 15
She said so: I must needs report the truth . . . . . v 2 128
Your reports have set the murder on.—Nay, stare not, masters: it is true . . . . v 2 187
Greater storms and tempests than almanacs can report . *Ant. and Cleo.* i 2 155
Report That I am sudden sick: quick, and return . . . . . i 3 4
Every hour, Most noble Cæsar, shalt thou have report How 'tis abroad i 4 35
And men's reports Give him much wrong'd . . . . . i 4 39
I did inquire it; And have my learning from some true reports . . ii 2 47
I must thank him only, Lest my remembrance suffer ill report . . ii 2 159
She's a most triumphant lady, if report be square to her . . . ii 2 189
Read not my blemishes in the world's report: I have not kept my square ii 3 5
Free, madam! no; I made no such report: He's bound . . . ii 5 57
Bid him Report the feature of Octavia, her years, Her inclination . . ii 5 112
Let me report to him Your sweet dependency . . . . . v 2 25
And would gladly Look him i' the face.—This I'll report . . . v 2 32
How she died of the biting of it, what pain she felt: truly, she makes a very good report o' the worm . . . . v 2 256
Is a thing Too bad for bad report . . . . . *Cymbeline* i 1 17
I honour him Even out of your report . . . . . . i 1 55
A contention in public, which may, without contradiction, suffer the report . . . . i 4 60
That man, who knows By history, report, or his own proof, What woman is . . . . i 6 70
That from my mutest conscience to my tongue Charms this report out . i 6 117
A gentleman, who is as far From thy report as thou from honour . . i 6 146
I have adventured To try your taking of a false report . . . i 6 173
There is gold for you; Sell me your good report.—How! my good name? or to report of you What I shall think is good? . . . . . ii 3 88
Never saw I figures So likely to report themselves . . . . ii 4 83
My report was once First with the best of note . . . . iii 3 57
Report should render him hourly to your ear As truly as he moves . iii 4 153
Am right sorry that I must report ye My master's enemy . . . iii 5 3
Experience, O, thou disprovest report! . . . . . . iv 2 34
Son to the queen, after his own report . . . . . . iv 2 119
Whose father then, as men report Thou orphans' father art . . v 4 39
'Tis now the time To ask of whence you are. Report it . . . v 5 16
Great king! To sour your happiness, I must report The queen is dead . v 5 26
Who worse than a physician Would this report become? . . . v 5 28
What she confess'd I will report, so please you . . . . v 5 34
Drawn by report, adventurous by desire . . . . . *Pericles* i 1 35
When he shall come and find Our paragon to all reports thus blasted . iv 1 36
Report what a sojourner we have; you'll lose nothing . . . iv 2 149
Thou hast the harvest out of thine own report . . . . . iv 2 153
It gives a good report to a number to be chaste . . . . iv 6 43
Report thy parentage . . . . v 1 130
Reported. Nor a temporary meddler, As he's reported *Meas. for Meas.* v 1 146
A fool, and a coward, as you then reported him to be . . . . v 1 338
Is she so hot a shrew as she's reported? . . . *T. of Shrew* iv 1 22
So 'tis reported, sir.—Nay, 'tis most credible . . . *All's Well* i 2 3
It is reported that he has taken their greatest commander . . . iii 5 5
He stole from France, As 'tis reported, for the king had married him . iii 5 56
I have heard her reported to be a woman of an invincible spirit *2 Hen. VI.* i 4 8
It is reported, mighty sovereign, That good Duke Humphrey traitorously is murder'd By Suffolk . . . . iii 2 122
Tyrants themselves wept when it was reported . . *Richard III.* i 3 185
Is it upon record, or else reported Successively from age to age? . . iii 1 72
All is confirm'd, my lord, which was reported . . . . *Macbeth* v 3 31
On the Alps It is reported thou didst eat strange flesh . *Ant. and Cleo.* i 4 67
And oft before gave audience, As 'tis reported, so . . . . iii 6 19
So 'tis reported: But none of 'em can be found . . . *Cymbeline* v 3 87
Reporter. Or my reporter devised well for her . . . *Ant. and Cleo.* ii 2 193
Reportest. Thou, my slave, As thou report'st thyself . . *Tempest* i 2 271
A notable lubber, as thou reportest him to be . . . *T. G. of Ver.* ii 5 47
Priam found the fire ere he his tongue, And I my Percy's death ere thou report'st it . . . . *2 Hen. IV.* i 1 75
Reporting. What course I mean to hold Shall nothing benefit your knowledge, nor Concern me the reporting . . . . . *W. Tale* iv 4 515
It would seem Like lies disdain'd in the reporting . . . . *Pericles* v 1 120
Reportingly. I Believe it better than reportingly . . . *Much Ado* iii 1 116
Reposal. Would the reposal Of any trust, virtue, or worth in thee Make thy words faith'd? No . . . . *Lear* ii 1 70
Repose. A strange repose, to be asleep With eyes wide open . *Tempest* ii 1 213
Whiles we stood here securing your repose, Even now, we heard a hollow burst of bellowing . . . . ii 1 310
If you be pleased, retire into my cell And there repose . . . . iv 1 162
Upon whose faith and honour I repose . . . . *T. G. of Ver.* iv 3 26
That means, Travelling some journey, to repose him here *T. of Shrew* Ind. 1 76
Enter in the castle And there repose you for this night . *Richard II.* ii 3 161
Canst thou, O partial sleep, give thy repose To the wet sea-boy? *2 Hen. IV.* iii 1 26
Thou proud dream, That play'st so subtly with a king's repose *Hen. V.* iv 1 275
For this night we will repose us here . . . . . *2 Hen. VI.* ii 1 201
On thy fortune I repose myself . . . . . . *3 Hen. VI.* iv 6 47
Some day or two Your highness shall repose you at the Tower *Rich. III.* iii 1 65
Times to repair our nature With comforting repose . . *Hen. VIII.* v 1 4
Ere we do repose us, we will write To Rome of our success . *Coriolanus* i 9 74
Repose you here in rest, Secure from worldly chances! . *T. Andron.* i 1 151
Here none but soldiers and Rome's servitors Repose in fame . . . i 1 353
And so repose, sweet gold, for their unrest . . . . . ii 3 8
Good night, good night! as sweet repose and rest Come to thy heart as that within my breast! . . . . *Rom. and Jul.* ii 2 123
Good night, and good repose . . . . *J. Cæsar* iv 3 233
Merciful powers, Restrain in me the cursed thoughts that nature Gives way to in repose! . . . . *Macbeth* ii 1 9
Good repose the while!—Thanks, sir: the like to you! . . . . ii 1 29
Sport and repose lock from me day and night! . . . . *Hamlet* iii 2 227
Repose you there; while I to this hard house . . . . *Lear* iii 2 63
Our foster-nurse of nature is repose . . . . iv 4 12
He that unbuckles this, till we do please To daff't for our repose, shall hear a storm . . . . *Ant. and Cleo.* iv 4 13
At these early hours Shake off the golden slumber of repose *Pericles* iii 2 23
Reposeth. The king reposeth all his confidence in thee . *Richard II.* i 4 6
Reposing too far in his virtue, which he hath not . . *All's Well* iii 6 15
Sorrow breaks seasons and reposing hours . . . . *Richard III.* i 4 76
His right cheek Reposing on a cushion.—Where?—O' the floor *Cymbeline* iv 2 212
Repossess. Her suit is now to repossess those lands . . *3 Hen. VI.* iii 2 4
And pray that I may repossess the crown . . . . . . iv 5 29
Ay, for if Edward repossess the crown, 'Tis like that Richmond with the rest shall down . . . . iv 6 99

Repossess. Went all afoot in summer's scalding heat, That thou mightst repossess the crown in peace . . . . *3 Hen. VI.* v 7 19
Reprehend. I myself reprehend his own person . . . *L. L. Lost* i 1 184
Gentles, do not reprehend: If you pardon, we will mend *M. N. Dream* v 1 436
You come to reprehend my ignorance . . . . *Richard III.* iii 7 113
Reprehended. You should for that have reprehended him *Com. of Errors* v 1 57
She never reprehended him but mildly, When he demean'd himself rough v 1 87
Look'd deadly pale. Which when I saw, I reprehended him *Rich. III.* iii 7 27
Reprehending. Pardon me for reprehending thee . . *T. Andron.* iii 2 69
Represent. The sanguine colour of the leaves Did represent my master's blushing cheeks . . . . *1 Hen. VI.* iv 1 93
The substance Of that great shadow I did represent . . *2 Hen. VI.* i 1 14
And, would you represent our queen aright, It were convenient you had such a devil . . . . *T. Andron.* v 2 89
Reprieve. I have grated upon my good friends for three reprieves for you and your coach-fellow . . . . . . *Mer. Wives* ii 2 6
That in his reprieve, Longer or shorter, he may be so fitted . *M. for M.* ii 4 39
Might but my bending down Reprieve thee from thy fate, it should proceed . . . . iii 1 145
I hope it is some pardon or reprieve For the most gentle Claudio . . iv 2 74
His friends still wrought reprieves for him . . . . . . iv 2 140
Reprieve him from the wrath Of greatest justice . . . *All's Well* iii 4 28
Our general has sworn you out of reprieve and pardon . . *Coriolanus* v 2 53
Who hath the office? send Thy token of reprieve . . . . *Lear* v 3 249
Reprisal. I am on fire To hear this rich reprisal is so nigh *1 Hen. IV.* iv 1 118
Reproach. Might reproach your life And choke your good *Meas. for Meas.* v 1 426
Who can blot that name With any just reproach? . . . *Much Ado* iv 1 82
Myself would, on the rearward of reproaches, Strike at thy life . . iv 1 128
Sir, go: my young master doth expect your reproach . *Mer. of Venice* ii 5 20
Reproach and dissolution hangeth over him . . . *Richard II.* ii 1 258
And let not Bardolph's vital thread be cut With edge of penny cord and vile reproach . . . . *Hen. V.* iii 6 50
Reproach and everlasting shame Sits mocking in our plumes . . . iv 5 4
O, whither shall we fly from this reproach?—We will not fly . *1 Hen. VI.* i 1 97
Or else reproach be Talbot's greatest fame! . . . . . . iii 2 76
In confutation of which rude reproach . . . . iv 1 98
How shall we then dispense with that contract, And not deface your honour with reproach? . . . . v 5 29
Wouldst have me rescue thee from this reproach? . . . *2 Hen. VI.* ii 4 64
I am but reproach: And shall I then be used reproachfully? . . . ii 4 96
And princes' courts be fill'd with my reproach . . . . . iii 2 69
Reproach and beggary Is crept into the palace of our king . . iv 1 101
If black scandal or foul-faced reproach Attend the sequel *Richard III.* iii 7 231
They vent reproaches Most bitterly on you . . . . *Hen. VIII.* i 2 23
O, that her hand, In whose comparison all whites are ink, Writing their own reproach . . . . *Troi. and Cres.* i 1 57
And see their blood, or die with this reproach . . . *T. Andron.* iv 1 94
Many worthy and chaste dames even thus, All guiltless, meet reproach *Othello* iv 1 48
Reproachful. What reproachful words are these? . . . *T. Andron.* i 1 308
And withal Thrust these reproachful speeches down his throat . ii 1 55
Reproachfully. And shall I then be used reproachfully? . . *2 Hen. VI.* ii 4 97
Reprobate. What if we do omit This reprobate? . . *Meas. for Meas.* iv 3 78
Deliver me from the reprobate thought of it . . . *L. L. Lost* i 2 64
Reprobation. Yea, curse his better angel from his side, And fall to reprobation . . . . *Othello* v 2 209
Reproof. And gave such orderly and well-behaved reproof *Mer. Wives* ii 1 59
As you have one eye upon my follies, as you hear them unfolded, turn another into the register of your own; that I may pass with a reproof the easier . . . . ii 2 195
The doubleness of the benefit defends the deceit from reproof *M. for M.* iii 1 269
She did betray me to my own reproof . . . *Com. of Errors* v 1 90
This is called the Reproof Valiant . . . . *As Y. Like It* v 4 82
The third, the Reply Churlish; the fourth, the Reproof Valiant . . v 4 98
Such a headstrong potent fault it is, That it but mocks reproof *T. Night* iii 4 225
In the reproof of this lies the jest . . . . . *1 Hen. IV.* i 2 213
That man is not alive Might so have tempted him as you have done, Without the taste of danger and reproof . . . . iii 1 175
Yet such extenuation let me beg, As, in reproof of many tales devised . iii 2 23
Your reproof is something too round: I should be angry . *Hen. V.* iv 1 216
I know not whether to depart in silence, Or bitterly to speak in your reproof, Best fitteth my degree . . . . . *Richard III.* iii 7 142
I have a touch of your condition, Which cannot brook the accent of reproof . . . . iv 4 158
In the reproof of chance Lies the true proof of men . *Troi. and Cres.* i 3 33
Would pluck reproof and rebuke from every ear that heard it *Coriolanus* ii 2 37
Those enemies of Timon's and mine own Whom you yourselves shall set out for reproof Fall and no more . . . . . . *T. of Athens* v 4 57
Your reproof Were well deserved of rashness . . . *Ant. and Cleo.* ii 2 123
Reproof, obedient and in order, Fits kings, as they are men . *Pericles* i 2 42
It shall no longer grieve without reproof . . . . . . ii 4 19
Reprove. And virtuous; 'tis so, I cannot reprove it . . . *Much Ado* ii 3 241
What grace hast thou, thus to reprove These worms for loving? *L. L. L.* iv 3 153
No railing in a known discreet man, though he do nothing but reprove *T. Night* i 5 104
There's something in me that reproves my fault . . . . . iii 4 223
Reprove my allegation, if you can . . . . *2 Hen. VI.* iii 1 40
If to reprove you for this suit of yours, So season'd with your faithful love to me, Then, on the other side, I check'd my friends *Rich. III.* iii 7 148
My very hairs do mutiny; for the white Reprove the brown for rashness, and they them For fear and doting . . . *Ant. and Cleo.* iii 11 14
Reproveable. A provoking merit, set a-work by a reproveable badness in himself . . . . *Lear* iii 5 9
Reproved. After your highness had reproved the duke . . *Hen. VIII.* i 2 189
Reprovest. Which love to all, of which thyself art one, Who now reprovest me for it . . . . *Pericles* i 2 95
Repugn. When stubbornly he did repugn the truth . . *1 Hen. VI.* iv 1 94
Repugnancy. Sleep upon't, And let the foes quietly cut their throats, Without repugnancy? . . . . *T. of Athens* iii 5 45
Repugnant. Lies where it falls, Repugnant to command . . *Hamlet* ii 2 493
Repulse. Do not, for one repulse, forego the purpose . . *Tempest* iii 3 12
Take no repulse, whatever she doth say . . . *T. G. of Ver.* iii 1 100
Except you mean with obstinate repulse To slay your sovereign *1 Hen. VI.* iii 1 113
He received in the repulse of Tarquin seven hurts i' the body *Coriolanus* ii 1 166
A repulse: though your attempt, as you call it, deserve more *Cymbeline* i 4 128
Repulsed. And he, repulsed—a short tale to make—Fell into a sadness, then into a fast . . . . *Hamlet* ii 2 146
Re-purchased. Once more we sit in England's royal throne, Re-purchased with the blood of enemies . . . . *3 Hen. VI.* v 7 2

Repured. Love's thrice repured nectar . . . . *Troi. and Cres.* iii 2 23
Reputation. Other men, of slender reputation, Put forth their sons to seek preferment out . . . . *T. G. of Ver.* i 3 6
All that is mine I leave at thy dispose, My goods, my lands, my reputation . . . . ii 7 87
I will keep the haviour of reputation . . . . . *Mer. Wives* i 3 86
I could drive her then from the ward of her purity, her reputation . ii 2 258
My coffers ransacked, my reputation gnawn at . . . . . ii 2 307
Defend your reputation, or bid farewell to your good life for ever . . iii 3 126
For that her reputation was disvalued In levity . . *Meas. for Meas.* v 1 221
Herein you war against your reputation . . . *Com. of Errors* iii 1 86
This touches me in reputation . . . . iv 1 71
Of very reverend reputation, sir, Of credit infinite, highly beloved . v 1 5
In love of your brother's honour . . . and his friend's reputation *M. Ado* ii 2 38
You may conceal her, As best befits her wounded reputation . . . iv 1 243
Wrong the reputation of your name, In so unseeming to confess *L. L. L.* ii 1 155
What mean you? You will lose your reputation . . . . v 2 709
Your reputation shall not therefore be misprised . . *As Y. Like It* i 2 191
Seeking the bubble reputation Even in the cannon's mouth . . ii 7 152
And would not put my reputation now In any staining act . *All's Well* iii 7 6
Upon my reputation and credit and as I hope to live . . . iv 3 154
What his reputation is with the duke; what his valour . . . iv 3 201
What is his reputation? . . . . iv 3 223
Your reputation comes too short for my daughter; you are no husband for her . . . . v 3 176
Turn then my freshest reputation to A savour that may strike the dullest nostril Where I arrive! . . . . *W. Tale* i 2 420
The purest treasure mortal times afford Is spotless reputation *Rich. II.* i 1 178
This dear dear land, Dear for her reputation through the world . . ii 1 58
Thy land Wherein thou liest in reputation sick . . . . . ii 1 96
Answer in the effect of your reputation . . . . *2 Hen. IV.* ii 1 142
His reputation is as arrant a villain and a Jacksauce . *Hen. V.* iv 7 148
Spoke like a tall fellow that respects his reputation *Richard III.* i 4 157
Entomb thyself alive And case thy reputation in thy tent *Troi. and Cres.* iii 3 187
I see my reputation is at stake; My fame is shrewdly gored . . iii 3 227
My reputation stain'd With Tybalt's slander . . . *Rom. and Jul.* iii 1 116
Seeing his reputation touch'd to death, He did oppose his foe *T. of A.* iii 5 19
Their residence, both in reputation and profit, was better . *Hamlet* ii 2 344
What's the matter, That you unlace your reputation thus? . *Othello* ii 3 194
Reputation, reputation, reputation! O, I have lost my reputation! . ii 3 262
My reputation, Iago, my reputation! . . . . ii 3 265
I thought you had received some bodily wound; there is more sense in that than in reputation. Reputation is an idle and most false imposition; oft got without merit . . . . ii 3 268
You have lost no reputation at all, unless you repute yourself such a loser . . . . ii 3 271
I have offended reputation, A most unnoble swerving *Ant. and Cleo.* iii 11 49
I make my wager rather against your confidence than her reputation *Cymbeline* i 4 121
For which the pained'st fiend Of hell would not in reputation change *Pericles* iv 6 174
Repute. How will the world repute me? . . . . *T. G. of Ver.* ii 7 59
A man of good repute, carriage, bearing, and estimation . *L. L. Lost* i 1 271
And, sweet my child, let them be men of good repute and carriage . i 2 72
Sweet smoke of rhetoric! He reputes me a cannon . . . iii 1 65
And will repute you ever The patron of my life and liberty *T. of Shrew* iv 2 112
All in England did repute him dead . . . . *1 Hen. IV.* v 1 54
In my conscience do repute his grace The rightful heir . *2 Hen. VI.* v 1 177
The Trojans taste our dear'st repute With their finest palate *Tr. and Cr.* i 3 337
My foes I do repute you every one; So, trouble me no more *T. Andron.* i 1 366
Ingratitude, Which Rome reputes to be a heinous sin . . . i 1 448
Brutus had rather be a villager Than to repute himself a son of Rome Under these hard conditions . . . . *J. Cæsar* i 2 173
Lost no reputation at all, unless you repute yourself such a loser *Othello* ii 3 271
Reputed. Being so reputed In dignity . . . . . . *Tempest* i 2 72
And not without desert so well reputed . . . *T. G. of Ver.* ii 4 57
Yea, but so I am apt to do myself wrong; I am not so reputed *M. Ado* ii 1 214
That therefore only are reputed wise For saying nothing *Mer. of Venice* i 1 96
He excels his brother for a coward, yet his brother is reputed one of the best that is . . . . *All's Well* iv 3 322
The reputed son of Cœur-de-lion, Lord of thy presence . . *K. John* i 1 136
Reputed then In England the most valiant gentleman . *2 Hen. IV.* iv 1 131
The king, your father, was reputed for A prince most prudent *Hen. VIII.* ii 4 45
Reputeless. And left me in reputeless banishment . . *1 Hen. IV.* iii 2 44
Reputing of his high descent, As next the king . . *2 Hen. VI.* iii 1 48
Request. My prime request, Which I do last pronounce, is . *Tempest* i 2 425
At thy request, monster, I will do reason, any reason . . . iii 2 128
And did request me to importune you To let him . . *T. G. of Ver.* i 3 13
You writ them, sir, at my request; But I will none of them . . ii 1 132
I am so far from granting thy request That I despise thee . . iv 2 101
I will do a greater thing than that, upon your request . *Mer. Wives* i 1 249
Can you love the maid?—I will marry her, sir, at your request . . i 1 253
Requests your company . . . . iii 3 25
Tell him yet of Angelo's request, And fit his mind to death . *M. for M.* ii 4 186
Novelty is only in request . . . . iii 2 237
Ginger was not much in request, for the old women were all dead . iv 3 9
Upon his mere request . . . . v 1 152
Were not his requests so far From reason's yielding . . *L. L. Lost* ii 1 150
I am to entreat you, request you, and desire you . *M. N. Dream* i 2 102
I would request you,—or I would entreat you,—not to fear . . iii 1 41
I do wonder, Thou naughty gaoler, that thou art so fond To come abroad with him at his request . . . . . . *Mer. of Venice* iii 3 10
To fill up your grace's request in my stead . . . . . iv 1 161
More at your request than to please myself . . . *As Y. Like It* ii 5 23
This liberty is all that I request . . . . . *T. of Shrew* i 1 95
But did you not request to have it cut?—Thou hast faced many things iv 3 122
Off with 't while 'tis vendible; answer the time of request *All's Well* i 1 169
How do you, Malvolio?—At your request! yes . . . *T. Night* iii 4 38
Grant me another request.—Any thing . . . . v 1 4
So it should now, Were there necessity in your request . . *W. Tale* i 2 22
He'll stay, my lord.—At my request he would not . . . . i 2 87
This your request Is altogether just . . . . iii 2 117
'Tis in request, I can tell you . . . . iv 4 297
At your request My father will grant precious things as trifles . . v 1 221
Willingly I will both hear and grant you your requests . . *K. John* iv 2 46
Heartily request The enfranchisement of Arthur . . . . . iv 2 51
The king by me requests your presence straight . . . . iv 3 22
At whose request the king hath pardon'd them . . . . . v 6 35
But a knave should have some countenance at his friend's request *2 Hen. IV.* v 1 40

Request. At my desires, and my requests, and my petitions . *Hen. V.* v 1 24
Your request shall make me let it pass . . . v 2 372
Ay, if thou wilt say 'ay' to my request; No, if thou dost say 'no' *3 Hen. VI.* iii 2 79
Vouchsafe, at our request, to stand aside, While I use further conference iii 3 110
At my request, See that forthwith Duke Edward be convey'd . . iv 3 51
And be not easily won to our request: Play the maid's part *Richard III.* iii 7 50
Lend favourable ears to our request; And pardon us the interruption . iii 7 101
My desert Unmeritable shuns your high request . . . . . iii 7 155
The king's request that I would visit you; Who grieves much *Hen. VIII.* iv 2 116
Why will he not upon our fair request Untent his person? *Troi. and Cres.* ii 3 177
Things small as nothing, for request's sake only, He makes important . ii 3 179
He holds you well, and will be led At your request a little from himself ii 3 191
At whose request do these men play?— . . . at the request of Paris my lord . . . . iii 1 31
Calchas shall have What he requests of us . . . . . iii 3 32
I request you To give my poor host freedom . . . *Coriolanus* i 9 86
Masters o' the people, We do request your kindest ears . . . ii 2 56
He's to make his requests by particulars . . . . . ii 3 48
The custom of request you have discharged . . . . . ii 3 150
Let deeds express What's like to be their words: 'We did request it' . iii 1 133
I'll try whether my old wit be in request With those that have but little iii 1 251
To both It stands in like request . . . . . . iii 2 51
Coriolanus being now in no request of his country . . . . iv 3 37
I'll watch him Till he be dieted to my request, And then I'll set upon him . . . . v 1 57
If you fail in our request, the blame May hang upon your hardness . v 3 90
Mark; for we'll Hear nought from Rome in private. Your request? . v 3 93
If it were so that our request did tend To save the Romans, thereby to destroy The Volsces whom you serve, you might condemn us . . v 3 132
Say my request's unjust, And spurn me back . . . . . v 3 164
The emperor requests a parley Of warlike Lucius . *T. Andron.* iv 4 101
I gave thee mine before thou didst request it . *Rom. and Jul.* ii 2 128
Hang thyself!—No, I will do nothing at thy bidding: make thy requests to thy friend. . . . . . . *T. of Athens* i 1 279
Let the request be fifty talents.—As you have said, my lord . . ii 2 201
What ill request did Brutus make to thee?—To kill him. *J. Cæsar* v 5 11
We hold a solemn supper, sir, And I'll request your presence *Macbeth* iii 1 15
As you are friends, scholars and soldiers, Give me one poor request *Ham.* i 5 142
Came it by request and such fair question As soul to soul affordeth? *Oth.* i 3 113
My friend is dead; 'tis done at your request . . . . iii 3 474
Let me request you off . . . . *Ant. and Cleo.* ii 7 127
Requires to live in Egypt: which not granted, He lessens his requests . iii 12 13
For Antony, I have no ears to his request . . . . . iii 12 20
A small request, And yet of moment too . . . *Cymbeline* i 6 181
Let his virtue join With my request . . . . . . v 5 89

Requested. He will require them, As if he did contemn what he requested Should be in them to give . . . . . *Coriolanus* ii 2 161
So blessed a disposition, she holds it a vice in her goodness not to do more than she is requested . . . . . . *Othello* ii 3 327
As you requested, Yourself shall go between's . *Ant. and Cleo.* ii 4 24

Requestest. Beg a greater matter; Thou now request'st but moonshine in the water . . . . *L. L. Lost* v 2 208

Requesting your lordship to supply his instant use . *T. of Athens* iii 2 40

Re-quickened. Then straight his doubled spirit Re-quicken'd what in flesh was fatigate . . . . *Coriolanus* ii 2 121

Requiem. We should profane the service of the dead To sing a requiem and such rest to her As to peace-parted souls . . . *Hamlet* v 1 260

Require. And require My dukedom of thee . . . *Tempest* v 1 132
The letter is, to desire and require her . . . *Mer. Wives* i 2 10
The satisfaction I would require is likewise your own benefit. *M. for M.* iii 1 156
Why thou wilt marry.—My poor body, madam, requires it . *All's Well* i 3 30
It requires haste of your lordship . . . . . . iv 3 108
You see My plight requires it . . . . *W. Tale* ii 1 118
Be prosperous In more than this deed does require! . . . ii 3 190
We are lucky, boy; and to be so still requires nothing but secrecy . iii 3 130
You have all kindness at my hand That your estate requires *3 Hen. VI.* iii 3 150
Much more to be thus opposite with heaven, For it requires the royal debt it lent you . . . . . . *Richard III.* ii 2 95
That's the appliance only Which your disease requires . *Hen. VIII.* i 1 125
To climb steep hills Requires slow pace at first . . . . i 1 132
This secret is so weighty, 'twill require A strong faith to conceal it . ii 1 144
In humblest manner I require your highness, That it shall please you . ii 4 144
He, I mean the bishop, did require a respite . . . . ii 4 177
Nature does require Her times of preservation. . . . . iii 2 146
Till further trial in those charges Which will require your answer . . v 1 104
He will require them, As if he did contemn what he requested Should be in them to give . . . . . *Coriolanus* ii 2 160
Once, if he do require our voices, we ought not to deny him . . ii 3 1
Not of a woman's tenderness to be, Requires nor child nor woman's face to see . . . . v 3 130
They have served me to effectless use: Now all the service I require of them Is that the one will help to cut the other. *T. Andron.* iii 1 77
Shed yet some small drops from thy tender spring, Because kind nature doth require it so . . . . v 3 168
The gods require our thanks . . . . *T. of Athens* iii 6 77
It requires swift foot . . . . v 1 231
Always thought That I require a clearness . . . *Macbeth* iii 1 133
Our hostess keeps her state, but in best time We will require her welcome . . . . iii 4 6
What, in the least, Will you require in present dower with her? . *Lear* i 1 195
We do require them of you, so to use them As we shall find their merits v 3 43
The question of Cordelia and her father Requires a fitter place . . v 3 59
He requires your haste-post-haste appearance . . . *Othello* i 2 37
This hand of yours requires A sequester from liberty, fasting and prayer iii 4 39
Say, our pleasure . . . requires Our quick remove from hence *A. and C.* i 2 202
Lord of his fortunes he salutes thee, and Requires to live in Egypt . iii 12 12
Promise, And in our name, what she requires; add more . . iii 12 28
Shall I say to Cæsar What you require of him? for he partly begs To be desired to give . . . . iii 13 66
Give her what comforts The quality of her passion shall require . . v 1 63
If you require a little space for prayer, I grant it . . *Pericles* iv 1 68

Required. When I have required Some heavenly music . . *Tempest* v 1 51
If I let him go, The debt he owes will be required of me . *Com. of Errors* iv 4 121
Nor does The ministration and required office . . *All's Well* ii 5 65
Which hoxes honesty behind, restraining From course required *W. Tale* i 2 245
I do confess I loved him as in honour he required . . . iii 2 64
It is required You do awake your faith . . . . . v 3 94
When there is more better opportunity to be required . . *Hen. V.* iii 2 151
Papers of state he sent me to peruse, As I required. . *Hen. VIII.* iii 2 122
Required. I would dissemble with my nature where My fortunes and my friends at stake required I should do so in honour *Coriolanus* iii 2 63
His personal return was most required and necessary . . . *Lear* iv 3 6
For want of these required conveniences . . . . *Othello* ii 1 234
To lend me arms and aid when I required them . . *Ant. and Cleo.* ii 2 88

Requireth. The time and case requireth haste . . . *3 Hen. VI.* iv 5 18

Requiring. Nor fetch in firing At requiring . . . . *Tempest* ii 2 186
Answer his requiring with a plausible obedience . *Meas. for Meas.* iii 1 253
Like a Jove, That, if requiring fail, he will compel . . *Hen. V.* ii 4 101

Requisite. A good nose is requisite also, to smell out work *W. Tale* iv 4 687
All those requisites in him that folly and green minds look after *Othello* ii 1 251

Requit. Exposed unto the sea, which hath requit it . . . *Tempest* iii 3 71

Requital. In requital whereof, henceforth carry your letters yourself *T. G. of Ver.* i 1 153
I profess requital to a hair's breadth . . . . *Mer. Wives* iv 2 3
In requital of your prophecy, hark you, I advise you . *Meas. for Meas.* ii 1 258
Cannot but yield you forth to public thanks, Forerunning more requital v 1 8
You do so grow in my requital As nothing can unroot you *All's Well* v 1 5
Give him strength To make a more requital to your love. . *K. John* ii 1 34
Make us think Rather our state's defective for requital . *Coriolanus* ii 2 54

Requite. I will requite you with as good a thing . . . *Tempest* v 1 169
Which to requite, command me while I live . . *T. G. of Ver.* iii 1 23
Love on; I will requite thee, Taming my wild heart . *Much Ado* iii 1 111
And I do with an eye of love requite her . . . . . v 4 24
If he love me to madness, I shall never requite him . *Mer. of Venice* i 2 70
Which thou shalt find I will most kindly requite . . *As Y. Like It* i 1 144
And, to requite you further, I will bestow some precepts . *All's Well* iii 5 102
I'll requite it in the highest degree . . . . *T. Night* iv 2 128
Speak, captain, for his life, and I will thee requite . . *Hen. V.* iii 6 51
And I'll requite it With sweet rehearsal of my morning's dream *2 Hen. VI.* i 2 23
I will requite thy forwardness . . . . . *3 Hen. VI.* iv 5 23
Nay, be thou sure I'll well requite thy kindness . . . . iv 6 10
Thanks unto you all: If fortune serve me, I'll requite this kindness . iv 7 78
And see how he requites me! . . . . . *Richard III.* i 4 68
At his return No doubt he will requite it . . . *Hen. VIII.* ii 1 46
More than could My studied purposes requite . . . . . iii 2 168
The hoarded plague o' the gods Requite your love! . . *Coriolanus* iv 2 12
I give thee thanks in part of thy deserts, And will with deeds requite thy gentleness . . . . *T. Andron.* i 1 237
If Lucius live, he will requite your wrongs . . . . . iii 1 297
Whose high exploits . . . Ingrateful Rome requites with foul contempt v 1 12
Does he think . . . That I'll requite it last? . *T. of Athens* iii 3 19
Wish that you had power and wealth To requite me, by making rich yourself. . . . . iv 3 529
How shall I requite you? Can you eat roots, and drink cold water? . v 1 76
I will requite your loves . . . . . . *Hamlet* i 2 251
And in a pass of practice Requite him for your father . . . iv 7 140
Let heaven requite it with the serpent's curse! . . . *Othello* iv 2 16
Besides this treasure for a fee, The gods requite his charity! . *Pericles* iii 2 75

Requited. Love me! why, it must be requited . . . *Much Ado* ii 3 232
Which obloquy set bars before my tongue, Else with the like I had requited him . . . . *1 Hen. VI.* ii 5 50
How earnestly are you set a-work, and how ill requited! *Troi. and Cres.* v 10 38
The drops of blood Shed for my thankless country are requited *Coriol.* iv 5 76
I requited him for his lie . . . . . . *Macbeth* ii 3 44

Rere-mice. War with rere-mice for their leathern wings . *M. N. Dream* ii 2 4

Re-salute. To re-salute his country with his tears . *T. Andron.* i 1 75
I will not re-salute the streets of Rome, Or climb my palace, till from forth this place I lead espoused my bride along with me . . . i 1 326

Rescue. You respect not aught your servant doth, To hazard life and rescue you from him That would have forced your honour *T. G. of Ver.* v 4 21
I would have been a breakfast to the beast, Rather than have false Proteus rescue me . . . . v 4 35
I am thy prisoner: wilt thou suffer them To make a rescue? *Com. of Er.* iv 4 114
How well this yielding rescues thee from shame! . . *L. L. Lost* i 1 118
We are beset with thieves; Rescue thy mistress . *T. of Shrew* iii 2 239
Without rescue in the first assault or ransom afterward . *All's Well* i 3 120
Here comes the man, sir, that did rescue me . . . *T. Night* v 1 53
Rescue those breathing lives to die in beds . . . *K. John* ii 1 419
Where honourable rescue and defence Cries out upon the name of Salisbury! . . . . v 2 18
Thou makest some tender of my life, In this fair rescue . *1 Hen. IV.* v 4 50
A rescue! a rescue!—Good people bring a rescue or two . *2 Hen. IV.* ii 1 61
Spur to the rescue of the noble Talbot . . . . *1 Hen. VI.* iv 3 19
In advantage lingering, looks for rescue . . . . . iv 4 19
Too late comes rescue: he is ta'en or slain . . . . . iv 4 42
Here, purposing the Bastard to destroy, Came in strong rescue . . iv 6 26
Had York and Somerset brought rescue in, We should have found a bloody day of this . . . . iv 7 33
Wouldst have me rescue thee from this reproach? . *2 Hen. VI.* iv 4 64
How shall poor Henry live, Unless thou rescue him? . *3 Hen. VI.* iii 3 215
Rescue, my Lord of Norfolk, rescue, rescue! . . *Richard III.* v 4 1
How comes't that you Have holp to make this rescue? . *Coriolanus* iii 1 277
In the rescue of Lavinia With his own hand did slay his youngest son, In zeal to you . . . . *T. Andron.* i 1 417
Thy weapon drawn?—To rescue my two brothers from their death . iii 1 49
No rescue? What, a prisoner? I am even The natural fool of fortune *Lear* iv 6 194
Death will seize her, but Your comfort makes the rescue *Ant. and Cleo.* iii 11 48

Rescued. Are you his brother?—Was't you he rescued? . *As Y. Like It* iv 3 134
I rescued her; Her highness is in safety . . . *K. John* iii 2 7
Rescued the Black Prince, that young Mars of men . *Richard II.* ii 3 101
Rescued is Orleans from the English . . . . *1 Hen. VI.* i 6 2
I gave thee life and rescued thee from death.—O, twice my father! . iv 6 5
And from the pride of Gallia rescued thee . . . . . iv 6 15
Perhaps I shall be rescued by the French . . . . . v 3 104
And, in the end being rescued, I have seen Him caper upright *2 Hen. VI.* iii 1 364
And from the bishop's huntsmen rescued him . . *3 Hen. VI.* iv 6 84
He rescued me, And said, 'Dear brother, live, and be a king' *Richard III.* ii 1 112
A crew of pirates came and rescued me; Brought me to Mytilene *Pericles* v 1 176

Rescuing. My uncles both are slain in rescuing me . . *3 Hen. VI.* i 4 2

Resemblance. Not a resemblance, but a certainty . . *Meas. for Meas.* iv 2 203
The majesty of the creature in resemblance of the mother . *W. Tale* v 2 39
His resemblance, being not like the duke . . . *Richard III.* iii 7 11

Resemble. If we are like you in the rest, we will resemble you in that *Mer. of Venice* iii 1 70
Sooth to say, In countenance somewhat doth resemble you *T. of Shrew* iv 2 100
If I could make that resemble something in me,—Softly! . *T. Night* ii 5 131
In face, in gait, in speech, he doth resemble . . *2 Hen. VI.* iii 1 373
How well resembles it the prime of youth! . . . *3 Hen. VI.* ii 1 23
The one his purple blood right well resembles; The other his pale cheeks ii 5 99

Resemble. Well mayst thou know her by thy own proportion, For up and down she doth resemble thee . . . *T. Andron.* v 2 107
Would most resemble sweet instruments hung up in cases *T. of Athens* i 2 102
Sith nor the exterior nor the inward man Resembles that it was *Hamlet* ii 2 7
He whose sable arms, Black as his purpose, did the night resemble . ii 2 475
One sand another Not more resembles that sweet rosy lad . *Cymbeline* v 5 121
Resembled. Though it was said she much resembled me, was yet of many accounted beautiful . . . . *T. Night* ii 1 27
I thought King Henry had resembled thee . . . . . 2 *Hen. VI.* i 3 56
Had he not resembled My father as he slept, I had done't *Macbeth* ii 2 13
Resembleth. O, how this spring of love resembleth The uncertain glory of an April day! . . . . *T. G. of Ver.* i 3 84
Resembling. Devils soonest tempt, resembling spirits of light *L. L. Lost* iv 3 257
You have beguiled me with a counterfeit Resembling majesty *K. John* iii 1 100
Re-send. Tokens and letters which she did re-send . *All's Well* iii 6 123
Reservation. He will'd me In heedfull'st reservation to bestow them . i 3 231
I most unfeignedly beseech your lordship to make some reservation of your wrongs . . . . ii 3 260
Making not reservation of yourselves, Still your own foes *Coriolanus* iii 3 130
With reservation of an hundred knights, By you to be sustain'd . *Lear* i 1 135
But kept a reservation to be follow'd With such a number . . ii 4 255
Reserve. These jests are out of season; Reserve them . *Com. of Errors* i 2 69
For what is yours to bestow is not yours to reserve . *T. Night* i 5 201
All lovers swear more performance than they are able and yet reserve an ability that they never perform . . . *Troi. and Cres.* iii 2 92
But reserve still to give, lest your deities be despised . *T. of Athens* iii 6 81
If he covetously reserve it, how shall's get it?—True . . . iv 3 408
Take each man's censure, but reserve thy judgement . . *Hamlet* i 3 69
She reserves it evermore about her To kiss and talk to . *Othello* iii 3 295
No reason I, since of your lives you set So slight a valuation, should reserve My crack'd one to more care . . . . *Cymbeline* iv 4 49
Reserve That excellent complexion, which did steal The eyes *Pericles* iv 1 40
Reserved. One in the prison, That should by private order else have died, I have reserved alive . . . . . . *Meas. for Meas.* iv 2 472
All her deserving Is a reserved honesty . . . . *All's Well* iii 5 65
The other part reserved I by consent . . . . . *Richard II.* i 1 128
Only reserved, you claim no interest . . . . 1 *Hen. VI.* v 4 167
Hell's black intelligencer, Only reserved their factor . *Richard III.* iv 4 72
Lovingly reserved The cordial of mine age to glad my heart! *T. Andron.* i 1 165
The table's full.—Here is a place reserved, sir.—Where? . *Macbeth* iii 4 46
It reserved some quantity of choice, To serve in such a difference *Ham.* iii 4 75
He reserved a blanket, else we had been all shamed . . . *Lear* iii 4 67
This is my treasurer: let him speak, my lord, Upon his peril, that I have reserved To myself nothing . . . . *Ant. and Cleo.* v 2 143
I some lady trifles have reserved, Immoment toys . . . . . v 2 165
Cleopatra, Not what you have reserved, nor what acknowledged, Put we i' the roll of conquest . . . . v 2 180
But nothing—Always reserved my holy duty—what His rage can do on me . . . . *Cymbeline* i 1 87
I will bring from thence that honour of hers which you imagine so reserved . . . . i 4 143
Reside. The very instant that I saw you, did My heart fly to your service; there resides, To make me slave to it . . . *Tempest* iii 1 65
Or to reside In thrilling region of thick-ribbed ice . *Meas. for Meas.* iii 1 122
There, at the moated grange, resides this dejected Mariana . . . iii 1 277
For cogitation Resides not in that man that does not think . *W. Tale* i 2 272
Between our Ilium and where she resides, Let it be call'd the wild and wandering flood, Ourself the merchant . . *Troi. and Cres.* i 1 104
Right and wrong, Between whose endless jar justice resides . . . i 3 117
I have a kind of self resides with you . . . . . . iii 2 155
Come not near him. If thou wouldst not reside But where one villain is, then him abandon . . . . . . *T. of Athens* v 1 113
I would not there reside, To put my father in impatient thoughts *Othello* i 3 242
Residence. A forted residence 'gainst the tooth of time *Meas. for Meas.* v 1 12
You'll run again, rather than suffer question for your residence *All's W.* ii 5 42
God forgive the sin of all those souls That to their everlasting residence, Before the dew of evening fall, shall fleet! . . . *K. John* ii 1 284
Chasing the royal blood With fury from his native residence *Richard II.* ii 1 119
Within the infant rind of this small flower Poison hath residence and medicine power . . . . *Rom. and Jul.* ii 3 24
Whose procreation, residence, and birth, Scarce is dividant *T. of Athens* iv 3 4
Their residence, both in reputation and profit, was better . *Hamlet* ii 2 343
My residence in Rome at one Philario's . . . . *Cymbeline* i 1 97
Haply, near The residence of Posthumus . . . . iii 4 151
Resident. That hath so long been resident in France . 1 *Hen. VI.* iii 4 14
This word 'love' . . . Be resident in men like one another 3 *Hen. VI.* v 6 82
Residing. There residing, the tenderness of her nature became as a prey to her grief . . . . *All's Well* iv 3 60
That thou, residing here, go'st yet with me . . . *Ant. and Cleo.* i 3 103
What was't to you?—No more than my residing here at Rome Might be to you in Egypt . . . . ii 2 37
Residue. The residue of your fortune, Go to my cave and tell me. Good old man, Thou art right welcome . . . . *As Y. Like It* ii 7 196
Resign. Thy dukedom I resign and do entreat Thou pardon me *Tempest* v 1 118
In right of Arthur do I claim of thee: Wilt thou resign them? *K. John* ii 1 154
Take but my shame, And I resign my gage . . . *Richard II.* i 1 176
I thought you had been willing to resign.—My crown I am . . . iv 1 190
Are you contented to resign the crown?—Ay, no; no, ay; for I must nothing be; Therefore no no, for I resign to thee . . . . iv 1 202
He bids you then resign Your crown and kingdom . . . *Hen. V.* ii 4 93
At his pleasure, will resign my place.—Resign it then . . 2 *Hen. VI.* i 3 124
As willingly do I the same resign As e'er thy father Henry made it mine ii 3 33
Be that thou hopest to be, or what thou art Resign to death . . iii 1 334
He rose against him, being his sovereign, And made him to resign 3 *Hen. VI.* i 1 142
He could not so resign his crown But that the next heir should succeed i 1 145
Although my head still wear the crown, I here resign my government . iv 6 24
Resign thy chair, and where I stand kneel thou . . . . . v 5 19
For my part, I'll resign unto your grace The seal I keep *Richard III.* ii 4 70
It is your fault that you resign . . . . iii 7 117
To-morrow yield up rule, resign my life . . . . *T. Andron.* i 1 191
Vile earth, to earth resign; end motion here! . . *Rom. and Jul.* iii 2 59
We will resign, During the life of this old majesty, . . . *Lear* v 3 298
Resignation. Which tired majesty did make thee offer, The resignation of thy state and crown . . . . *Richard II.* iv 1 179
Resigned. Worcester Hath broke his staff, resign'd his stewardship . ii 2 59
Richard, in the view of many lords, Resign'd the crown . 3 *Hen. VI.* i 1 139
Signify to him That thus I have resign'd my charge to you *Richard III.* i 4 98
Resist. I will resist such entertainment . . . . . *Tempest* i 2 465
Stay awhile.—What, resists he? Help him, Lucio . . *Meas. for Meas.* v 1 355
Resist. A woman may be made a fool, If she had not a spirit to resist *T. of Shrew* iii 2 223
Prevent it, resist it, let it not be so . . . . . *Richard II.* iv 1 148
How, my lord, shall we resist it now?—It must be thought on *Hen. V.* i 1 6
It boots not to resist both wind and tide . . . . 3 *Hen. VI.* iv 3 59
If . . . great minds . . . resist the same, There is a law *Troi. and Cres.* ii 2 179
And who resist Are mock'd for valiant ignorance . . *Coriolanus* iv 6 103
Lay hold upon him: if he do resist, Subdue him at his peril . *Othello* i 2 80
Those that would die or ere resist are grown The mortal bugs *Cymbeline* v 3 50
Advise thee to desist For going on death's net, whom none resist *Pericles* i 1 40
Our men be vanquish'd e'er they do resist . . . . i 2 27
Welcome is peace, if he on peace consist; If wars, we are unable to resist i 4 84
These cates resist me, she but thought upon . . . . . . ii 3 29
Resistance. Have vanquish'd the resistance of her youth . *Much Ado* iv 1 47
Unfold to us some warlike resistance.—There is none . . *All's Well* i 1 128
He'll not swagger with a Barbary hen, if her feathers turn back in any show of resistance . . . . 2 *Hen. IV.* ii 4 109
Resisted. Thou that so stoutly hast resisted . . . . 3 *Hen. VI.* ii 5 79
Hath resisted law, And therefore law shall scorn him further trial *Cor.* iii 1 267
Our ædiles smote? ourselves resisted? . . . . iii 1 319
Pompey's name strikes more Than could his war resisted *Ant. and Cleo.* i 4 55
Look For fury not to be resisted. Thus defied, I thank thee *Cymbeline* iii 1 68
Resisting. Our cannon shall be bent Against the brows of this resisting town . . . . *K. John* ii 1 38
Resolute. The resolute acting of your blood Could have attain'd the effect of your own purpose . . . . *Meas. for Meas.* ii 1 12
I'll do it in my shirt.—Most resolute Pompey! . . . *L. L. Lost* v 2 705
Laboured to dissuade him from it, but he is resolute . *As Y. Like It* i 1 147
You are resolute, then?—Not so, neither . . . . . *T. Night* i 5 23
Do what ye dare, we are as resolute . . . . . 1 *Hen. VI.* iii 1 91
But always resolute in most extremes . . . . iv 1 38
'Tis resolutely spoke.—Not resolute, except so much were done 2 *Hen. VI.* iii 1 267
The trust I have is in mine innocence, And therefore am I bold and resolute . . . . iv 4 60
Then leave me not, my lords; be resolute . . . . 3 *Hen. VI.* i 1 43
Edward is at hand, Ready to fight; therefore be resolute . . . v 4 61
I thought thou hadst been resolute . . . . . *Richard III.* i 4 115
Be bloody, bold, and resolute; laugh to scorn The power of man *Macb.* iv 1 79
Shark'd up a list of lawless resolutes, For food and diet . . *Hamlet* i 1 98
Resolutely. The ort is, according to our meaning, 'resolutely' *Mer. Wives* i 1 263
A purse of gold most resolutely snatched on Monday night and most dissolutely spent on Tuesday morning . . . 1 *Hen. IV.* i 2 38
'Tis resolutely spoke.—Not resolute, except so much were done 2 *Hen. VI.* iii 1 266
Resolution. Why give you me this shame? Think you I can a resolution fetch From flowery tenderness? . . . . *Meas. for Meas.* iii 1 82
Do not satisfy your resolution with hopes that are fallible . . . iii 1 170
So I take my leave, In resolution as I swore before . *T. of Shrew* iv 2 43
Your resolution cannot hold, when 'tis Opposed, as it must be *W. Tale* iv 4 36
I must be brief, lest resolution drop Out at mine eyes . *K. John* iv 1 35
Grow great by your example and put on The dauntless spirit of resolution v 1 53
How high a pitch his resolution soars! . . . . *Richard II.* i 1 109
And resolution thus fobbed as it is with the rusty curb of old father antic the law . . . . 1 *Hen. IV.* i 2 67
And withal How terrible in constant resolution . . . *Hen. V.* ii 4 35
Steel thy fearful thoughts, And change misdoubt to resolution 2 *Hen. VI.* iii 1 332
No want of resolution in me, but only my followers' . . . treasons . iv 8 65
I'll stay.—Be it with resolution then to fight . . . 3 *Hen. VI.* ii 2 77
In this resolution, I defy thee . . . . ii 2 170
With resolution, wheresoe'er I meet thee, . . . To plague thee . . v 1 95
In this resolution here we leave you . . . . *Richard III.* iii 7 218
I' the progress of this business, Ere a determinate resolution *Hen. VIII.* ii 4 176
My spritely brethren, I propend to you In resolution . *Troi. and Cres.* ii 2 191
Breaking his oath and resolution like A twist of rotten silk . *Coriolanus* v 6 95
Thy griefs their sports, thy resolution mock'd . . . *T. Andron.* iii 1 239
But call my resolution wise, And with this knife I'll help it *R. and J.* iv 1 53
Let us swear our resolution.—No, not an oath . . . *J. Cæsar* ii 1 113
I pull in resolution, and begin To doubt . . . . . *Macbeth* v 5 42
And thus the native hue of resolution Is sicklied o'er with the pale cast of thought . . . . *Hamlet* iii 1 84
I would unstate myself, to be in a due resolution . . . . *Lear* i 2 108
Think on that, And fix most firm thy resolution . . . *Othello* v 1 5
My resolution and my hands I'll trust; None about Cæsar *A. and C.* iv 15 49
We have no friend But resolution, and the briefest end . . . . iv 15 91
My resolution's placed, and I have nothing Of woman in me . . . v 2 238
I should be sick, But that my resolution helps me . . *Cymbeline* iii 6 4
Resolve. Shortly, single I'll resolve you . . . . . *Tempest* v 1 248
I am now going to resolve him . . . . . . *Meas. for Meas.* iii 1 194
You are amazed; but this shall absolutely resolve you . . . iv 2 225
Suddenly resolve me in my suit . . . . *L. L. Lost* ii 1 110
Shall we resolve to woo these girls of France?—And win them too . iv 3 371
Easy to count atomies as to resolve the propositions of a lover *As Y. L. It* iii 2 245
Continue your resolve To suck the sweets of sweet philosophy *T. of Shrew* i 1 27
Nor is your firm resolve unknown to me . . . . ii 1 93
What, master, read you? first resolve me that . . . . . . iv 2 7
Quit presently the chapel, or resolve you For more amazement *W. Tale* v 3 86
I will resolve for Scotland . . . . 2 *Hen. IV.* ii 3 67
How yet resolves the governor of the town? This is the latest parle *Hen. V.* iii 3 1
Resolve on this, thou shalt be fortunate . . . . . 1 *Hen. VI.* i 2 91
Let us resolve to scale their flinty bulwarks . . . . . . ii 1 27
If with a lady of so high resolve As is fair Margaret he be link'd in love v 5 75
Resolve thee, Richard; claim the English crown . . . 3 *Hen. VI.* i 1 49
Resolve me now; And what your pleasure is, shall satisfy me . . iii 2 19
Let us hear your firm resolve.—Your grant, or your denial, shall be mine . . . . iii 3 129
But, ere I go, Hastings and Montague, Resolve my doubt . . . iv 1 135
I will resolve your grace immediately . . . . *Richard III.* iv 2 26
Darest thou resolve to kill a friend of mine? . . . . . . iv 2 70
Resolve me whether you will or no.—Tut, tut, Thou troublest me . iv 2 120
These letters will resolve him of my mind . . . . . . iv 5 19
So must you resolve, That what you cannot as you would achieve, You must perforce accomplish as you may . . . . *T. Andron.* ii 1 105
Resolve me this: Was it well done? . . . . v 3 35
Get you gone, be strong and prosperous In this resolve . *Rom. and Jul.* iv 1 123
Whose liquid surge resolves The moon into salt tears . *T. of Athens* iv 3 442
Resolve yourselves apart: I'll come to you anon . . . *Macbeth* iii 1 138
O, that this too too solid flesh would melt, Thaw and resolve itself into a dew! . . . . *Hamlet* i 2 130
Resolve me, with all modest haste, which way Thou mightst deserve *Lear* ii 4 25
How they may be, and yet in two, As you will live, resolve it *Pericles* i 1 71

Resolve. Resolve your angry father, if my tongue Did e'er solicit *Pericles* ii 5 68
Where is Lord Helicanus? he can resolve you . . . . . v 1 1
This is the man that can, in aught you would, Resolve you . . . v 1 13
That can From first to last resolve you . . . . . v 3 61
Resolved. Do not, for one repulse, forego the purpose That you resolved to effect . . . . *Tempest* iii 3 13
I am resolved that thou shalt spend some time . . *T. G. of Ver.* i 3 66
He wants wit that wants resolved will . . . . . ii 6 12
I now am full resolved to take a wife . . . . . iii 1 76
And now is he resolved to die . . . . *Meas. for Meas.* iii 2 262
Subscribe to your deep oaths, and keep it too.—I am resolved *L. L. Lost* i 1 24
How I firmly am resolved you know . . . . *T. of Shrew* i 1 49
Gentlemen, content ye; I am resolved . . . . . i 1 90
Well, gentlemen, I am thus resolved . . . . . ii 1 395
I, Thy resolved patient, on thee still rely . . . . *All's Well* ii 1 207
Lays down his wanton siege before her beauty, Resolved to carry her . iii 7 19
But I am resolved on two points . . . . . *T. Night* i 5 24
He's irremoveable, Resolved for flight . . . . *W. Tale* iv 4 519
Until our fears, resolved, Be by some certain king purged . *K. John* ii 1 371
A resolved and honourable war . . . . . . ii 1 585
A resolved villain, Whose bowels suddenly burst out . . . . v 6 29
He was not so resolved when last we spake together . *Richard II.* ii 3 29
Hangs resolved correction in the arm That was uprear'd . 2 *Hen. IV.* iv 1 213
We would be resolved, Before we hear him, of some things . *Hen. V.* i 2 4
Now are we well resolved . . . . i 2 222
Long since we were resolved of your truth, Your faithful service 1 *Hen. VI.* iii 4 20
Therefore are we certainly resolved To draw conditions . . . . v 1 37
I am resolved for death or dignity . . . . . 2 *Hen. VI.* v 1 194
I am resolved to bear a greater storm Than any thou canst conjure up . v 1 198
I cannot joy, until I be resolved . . . . . 3 *Hen. VI.* ii 1 9
By him that made us all, I am resolved . . . . . ii 2 124
At last I firmly am resolved You shall have aid . . . . iii 3 219
Ah, that thy father had been so resolved! . . . . . v 5 22
How now, my hardy, stout resolved mates! . . . *Richard III.* i 3 340
All resolved rather to die than to famish?—Resolved, resolved *Coriolanus* i 1 4
Are you all resolved to give your voices? . . . . . ii 3 40
Stand resolved, but hope withal . . . . . *T. Andron.* i 1 135
And resolved withal To do myself this reason and this right . . . i 1 278
For that I am prepared and full resolved . . . . . . ii 1 57
If he be so resolved, I can o'ersway him . . . . *J. Cæsar* ii 1 202
And be resolved How Cæsar hath deserved to lie in death . . . iii 1 131
To be resolved If Brutus so unkindly knock'd, or no . . . . iii 2 183
How he received you, let me be resolved.—With courtesy . . . iv 2 14
I am fresh of spirit and resolved To meet all perils very constantly . v 1 91
Resolve yourselves apart: I'll come to you anon.—We are resolved *Macb.* iii 1 139
To be once in doubt Is once to be resolved . . . . *Othello* iii 3 180
I have myself resolved upon a course Which has no need of you *Ant. and Cleo.* iii 11 9
Be resolved he lives to govern us, Or dead, give's cause to mourn *Pericles* ii 4 31
Thou art resolved?—I am resolved . . . . . . iv 1 12
Resolvedly. Of that and all the progress, more and less, Resolvedly more leisure shall express . . . . . *All's Well* v 3 332
Resolveth. Bleeds away, even as a form of wax Resolveth from his figure 'gainst the fire . . . . *K. John* v 4 25
Resort. Of all the fair resort of gentlemen That every day with parle encounter me, In thy opinion which is worthiest love? *T. G. of Ver.* i 2 4
Kept severely from resort of men, That no man hath access by day to her.—Why, then, I would resort to her by night . . . . iii 1 108
Doth this Sir Proteus that we talk on Often resort unto this gentlewoman? . . . . iv 2 74
Shall all our houses of resort in the suburbs be pulled down? *Meas. for Meas.* i 2 104
Pity that thou livest To walk where any honest men resort *Com. of Errors* v 1 28
I think it not uneasy to get the cause of my son's resort thither *W. Tale* iv 2 57
What men of name resort to him? . . . . . *Richard III.* iv 5 8
Where, as they say, At some hours in the night spirits resort *R. and J.* iv 3 44
Forbid him her resort; Myself have spoke in vain . . *T. of Athens* i 1 127
Unfold to me . . . what men to-night Have had resort to you *J. Cæsar* ii 1 276
I prescripts gave her, That she should lock herself from his resort *Hamlet* ii 2 143
Know this house to be a place of such resort, and will come into't? *Per.* iv 6 86
Resorted. Men of great worth resorted to this forest . *As Y. Like It* v 4 161
Resorter. 'Tis the better for you that your resorters stand upon sound legs . . . . *Pericles* iv 6 27
Resounds. It resounds As if it felt with Scotland . . . *Macbeth* iv 3 6
Re-speaking. The king's rouse the heavens shall bruit again, Re-speaking earthly thunder . . . . *Hamlet* i 2 128
Respect. If you respect them, best to take them up . *T. G. of Ver.* i 2 134
Win her with gifts, if she respect not words . . . . . iii 1 89
She is not to be kissed fasting, in respect of her breath . . . iii 1 327
I hope my master's suit will be but cold, Since she respects my mistress' love so much . . . . iv 4 187
What should it be that he respects in her But I can make respective? . iv 4 199
I have done for you, Though you respect not aught your servant doth . v 4 20
In love Who respects friend? . . . . v 4 54
If it were not for one trifling respect, I could come to such honour! *Mer. Wives* ii 1 45
A man of his place, gravity and learning, so wide of his own respect . iii 1 58
O powerful love! that, in some respects, makes a beast a man . . v 5 5
Shall we serve heaven With less respect than we do minister To our gross selves? Good, good my lord, bethink you *Meas. for Meas.* ii 2 86
And six or seven winters more respect Than a perpetual honour . . iii 1 76
Do you persuade yourself that I respect you? . . . . . v 1 53
How! know you where you are?—Respect to your great place! . . v 1 294
'Respice finem,' respect your end . . . *Com. of Errors* iv 4 44
I would have daffed all other respects and made her half myself *M. Ado* ii 3 176
But a night-gown in respect of yours . . . . . . iii 4 19
The passado he respects not, the duello he regards not . . *L. L. Lost* i 2 185
That more than all the world I did respect her . . . . . v 2 437
Hector was but a Troyan in respect of this . . . . . . v 2 639
More devout than this in our respects Have we not been . . . v 2 792
Or else misgraffed in respect of years . . . . *M. N. Dream* i 1 137
She respects me as her only son . . . . i 1 160
What worser place can I beg in your love,—And yet a place of high respect with me? . . . . ii 1 209
You in my respect are all the world . . . . ii 1 224
What poor duty cannot do, noble respect Takes it in might, not merit . v 1 91
You have too much respect upon the world . . . *Mer. of Venice* i 1 74
Put on a sober habit, Talk with respect and swear but now and then . ii 2 200
Nothing is good, I see, without respect . . . . . . v 1 99
I attend them with all respect and duty . . . . *As Y. Like It* i 2 177

Respect. In respect of itself, it is a good life; but in respect that it is a shepherd's life, it is naught. In respect that it is solitary, I like it very well; but in respect that it is private, it is a very vile life. Now, in respect it is in the fields, it pleaseth me well; but in respect it is not in the court, it is tedious . . *As Y. Like It* iii 2 13
Thou worms-meat, in respect of a good piece of flesh indeed! . . . iii 2 68
'Fore me, I speak in respect— Nay, 'tis strange . . . *All's Well* ii 3 32
My respects are better than they seem . . . . ii 5 71
If your lordship find him not a hilding, hold me no more in your respect iii 6 4
Indeed he is not for your lordship's respect . . . . . . iii 6 109
Behold this ring, Whose high respect and rich validity Did lack a parallel v 3 192
Is there no respect of place, persons, nor time in you? . . *T. Night* ii 3 98
She uses me with a more exalted respect than any one else . . . ii 5 31
My uncle's will in this respect is mine . . . . . *K. John* ii 1 510
To tread down fair respect of sovereignty . . . . . . iii 1 58
I muse your majesty doth seem so cold, When such profound respects do pull you on . . . . iii 1 318
I am almost ashamed To say what good respect I have of thee . . iii 3 28
You hold too heinous a respect of grief . . . . . . iii 4 90
When perchance it frowns More upon humour than advised respect . iv 2 214
A noble combat hast thou fought Between compulsion and a brave respect! . . . . v 2 44
And this respect besides, For that my grandsire was an Englishman . v 4 41
Such offers of our peace As we with honour and respect may take . . v 7 85
So it be new, there's no respect how vile . . . . *Richard II.* ii 1 25
Throw away respect, Tradition, form and ceremonious duty . . . iii 2 172
Respect Which the proud soul ne'er pays but to the proud . 1 *Hen. IV.* i 3 8
Well contented to be there, in respect of the love I bear your house . ii 3 2
He holds your temper in a high respect . . . . . . iii 1 170
Vouchsafe me hearing and respect . . . . iv 3 31
Before, I loved thee as a brother, John; But now, I do respect thee . v 4 20
The gain proposed Choked the respect of likely peril fear'd . 2 *Hen. IV.* i 1 184
May minister the potion of imprisonment to me in respect of poverty . i 2 146
In some respects, I grant, I cannot go: I cannot tell . . . . i 2 189
There's a letter for you.—Delivered with good respect . . . . ii 2 109
Mock at an ancient tradition, begun upon an honourable respect? *Hen. V.* v 1 75
He was a man; this, in respect, a child . . . . 3 *Hen. VI.* v 5 56
What doth she say . . . ?—Nothing that I respect . . . *Richard III.* i 3 296
Spoke like a tall fellow that respects his reputation . . . . i 4 157
The respects thereof are nice and trivial, All circumstances well considered . . . . iii 7 175
Could do no less, Out of the great respect they bear to beauty *Hen. VIII.* i 4 69
A thousand pounds a year for pure respect! No other obligation! . ii 3 95
As you are truly noble, As you respect the common good . . . iii 2 290
Men so noble, However faulty, yet should find respect For what they have been . . . . v 3 75
Out of dear respect, His royal self in judgement comes to hear . . v 3 119
Respect him; Take him, and use him well, he's worthy of it . . v 3 154
Reason and respect Make livers pale and lustihood deject *Troi. and Cres.* ii 2 49
Carries on the stream of his dispose Without observance or respect of any ii 3 175
You know me dutiful; therefore, dear sir, Let me not shame respect . v 3 73
On both sides more respect . . . . . . *Coriolanus* iii 1 181
With a respect more tender, More holy and profound, than mine own life iii 3 112
He returning to break our necks, they respect not us . . . . v 4 37
In that respect, then, like a loving child, Shed yet some small drops from thy tender spring . . . . *T. Andron.* v 3 166
It is my will, the which if thou respect, Show a fair presence *R. and J.* i 5 74
Come, go with me, In one respect I'll thy assistant be . . . ii 3 90
I think she will be ruled In all respects by me . . . . . iii 4 14
He does deny him, in respect of his . . . . *T. of Athens* iii 2 81
And never learn'd The icy precepts of respect . . . . . iv 3 258
Truly, sir, in respect of a fine workman, I am but, as you would say, a cobbler . . . . *J. Cæsar* i 1 10
Many of the best respect in Rome, Except immortal Cæsar . . . i 2 59
Believe me for mine honour, and have respect to mine honour . . iii 2 15
With respect enough; But not with such familiar instances . . . iv 2 15
They pass by me as the idle wind, Which I respect not . . . . iv 3 69
Thou art a fellow of a good respect . . . . v 5 45
According to his virtue let us use him, With all respect . . . . v 5 77
The malevolence of fortune nothing Takes from his high respect *Macb.* iii 6 29
There's the respect That makes calamity of so long life . . *Hamlet* iii 1 68
The instances that second marriage move Are base respects of thrift . iii 2 193
And yet but yaw neither, in respect of his quick sail . . . . v 2 120
Since that respects of fortune are his love, I shall not be his wife *Lear* i 1 251
'Tis strange that from their cold'st neglect My love should kindle to inflamed respect . . . . i 1 258
In respect of that, I would fain think it were not . . . . . i 2 69
You shall do small respect, show too bold malice Against the grace and person of my master, Stocking his messenger . . . . . . ii 2 137
'Tis worse then murder, To do upon respect such violent outrage . . ii 4 24
Nature's above art in that respect . . . . iv 6 86
My life and education both do learn me How to respect you! . *Othello* i 3 184
With such things else of quality and respect As doth import you . . i 3 283
He is a good one, and his worthiness Does challenge much respect . . ii 1 213
Our general's wife is now the general: I may say so in this respect, for that he hath devoted and given up himself to the contemplation, mark, and denotement of her parts and graces . . . . . . ii 3 321
Returned me expectations and comforts of sudden respect and acquaintance . . . . iv 2 192
And a daughter who He not respects at all . . . . *Cymbeline* i 6 155
His meanest garment, That ever hath but clipp'd his body, is dearer In my respect than all the hairs above thee . . . . ii 3 140
She held the very garment of Posthumus in more respect . . . . iii 5 139
Not a man . . . has respect with him but he . . . . *Pericles* ii 4 18
I have one myself, Who shall not be more dear to my respect Than yours iii 3 33
Respected. The house is a respected house; next, this is a respected fellow; and his mistress is a respected woman . . *Meas. for Meas.* ii 1 169
His wife is a more respected person than any of us all . . . . ii 1 172
The time is yet to come that she was ever respected with man, woman or child.—Sir, she was respected with him before he married with her ii 1 177
I respected with her before I was married to her! If ever I was respected with her, or she with me, let not your worship think me the poor duke's officer . . . . ii 1 183
The service of the foot Being once gangrened, is not then respected For what before it was . . . . *Coriolanus* iii 1 307
Only their ends You have respected . . . . v 3 5
In such a case the gods will not be good unto us. When we banished him, we respected not them . . . . v 4 35
As jewels lose their glory if neglected, So princes their renowns if not respected . . . . *Pericles* ii 2 13

Respectest. Thou respect'st not spilling Edward's blood *Richard II.* ii 1 131
Respecting. I am mean indeed, respecting you *T. of Shrew* v 2 32
There is none worthy, Respecting her that's gone *W. Tale* v 1 35
It is no policy, Respecting what a rancorous mind he bears 2 *Hen. VI.* iii 1 24
Respecting this our marriage with the dowager *Hen. VIII.* ii 4 180
Respective. What should it be that he respects in her But I can make respective in myself? *T. G. of Ver.* iv 4 200
Yet for your vehement oaths, You should have been respective *M. of V.* v 1 156
'Tis too respective and too sociable For your conversion *K. John* i 1 188
Away to heaven, respective lenity! *Rom. and Jul.* iii 1 128
Respectively. You are very respectively welcome *T. of Athens* iii 1 7
'Respice finem,' respect your end *Com. of Errors* iv 4 44
Respite. O injurious love, That respites me a life! *Meas. for Meas.* ii 3 41
I crave but four days' respite iv 2 170
The rest After some respite will return to Calais 1 *Hen. VI.* iv 1 170
All-Souls' day . . . Is the determined respite of my wrongs *Richard III.* v 1 19
He, I mean the bishop, did require a respite *Hen. VIII.* ii 4 177
This respite shook The bosom of my conscience ii 4 181
Forty days longer we do respite you *Pericles* i 1 116
Responsive to the hilts, most delicate carriages *Hamlet* v 2 159
Rest. Of the king's ship The mariners say how thou hast disposed And all the rest o' the fleet *Tempest* i 2 226
For the rest o' the fleet Which I dispersed, they all have met again i 2 232
Sty me In this hard rock, whiles you do keep from me The rest o' the island i 2 344
We two, my lord, Will guard your person while you take your rest ii 1 197
For all the rest, They'll take suggestion as a cat laps milk ii 1 287
Pray, set it down and rest you iii 1 18
Pray now, rest yourself; He's safe for these three hours iii 1 20
By your patience, I needs must rest me.—Old lord, I cannot blame thee iii 3 4
Sit down, and rest iii 3 6
Put some lime upon your fingers, and away with the rest iv 1 247
I have her sovereign aid And rest myself content v 1 144
Every man shift for all the rest, and let no man take care for himself v 1 256
To my poor cell, where you shall take your rest v 1 301
Why not on Proteus, as of all the rest? *T. G. of Ver.* i 2 20
He, of all the rest, hath never moved me.—Yet he, of all the rest, I think, best loves ye i 2 28
There I'll rest, as after much turmoil A blessed soul doth in Elysium ii 7 37
My herald thoughts in thy pure bosom rest them iii 1 144
Therefore, above the rest, we parley to you iv 1 60
Which, with ourselves, all rest at thy dispose iv 1 76
Good rest.—As wretches have o'ernight That wait for execution in the morn iv 2 133
The good humour is to steal at a minute's rest *Mer. Wives* i 3 31
And hath drawn him and the rest of their company from their sport iv 2 34
Now, thus it rests iv 6 34
And here it rests, that you'll procure the vicar iv 6 48
'Twas a commandment to command the captain and all the rest *M. for M.* i 2 13
But two in the dish, . . . this very man having eaten the rest, as I said ii 1 105
I do repent me, as it is an evil, And take the shame with joy.—There rest ii 3 36
Fit his mind to death, for his soul's rest ii 4 187
Thy best of rest is sleep, And that thou oft provokest iii 1 17
Your company is fairer than honest. Rest you well iv 3 186
He that sets up his rest to do more exploits with his mace *Com. of Er.* iv 3 27
One that thinks a man always going to bed and says 'God give you good rest!'—Well, sir, there rest in your foolery iv 3 33
In . . . life-preserving rest To be disturb'd, would mad or man or beast v 1 83
Call the rest of the watch together and thank God *Much Ado* iii 3 30
You swore to that, Biron, and to the rest *L. L. Lost* i 1 53
Endure such public shame as the rest of the court can possibly devise i 1 132
Such short-lived wits do wither as they grow. Who are the rest? ii 1 55
Thou shalt know her, fellow, by the rest that have no heads iv 1 45
For the rest of the Worthies?—I will play three myself v 1 149
To interrupt my purposed rest v 2 91
I make no doubt The rest will ne'er come in, if he be out v 2 152
To flatter up these powers of mine with rest v 2 824
A twelvemonth shall you spend, and never rest v 2 831
Were the world mine, Demetrius being bated, The rest I'ld give to be to you translated *M. N. Dream* i 1 191
To the rest: yet my chief humour is for a tyrant i 2 30
Now name the rest of the players i 2 41
Set your heart at rest ii 1 121
Sing me now asleep; Then to your offices and let me rest ii 2 8
We'll rest us, Hermia, if you think it good ii 2 37
Find you out a bed; For I upon this bank will rest my head ii 2 40
Here is my bed: sleep give thee all his rest!—With half that wish the wisher's eyes be press'd! ii 2 64
Fallen am I in dark uneven way, And here will rest me iii 2 418
Here will I rest me till the break of day iii 2 446
This is the greatest error of all the rest v 1 250
And the owner of it blest Ever shall in safety rest v 1 427
And thankfully rest debtor for the first *Mer. of Venice* i 1 152
Rest you fair, good signior; Your worship was the last man in our mouths i 3 60
Is my boy, God rest his soul, alive or dead? ii 2 75
As I have set up my rest to run away, so I will not rest till I have run ii 2 110
I must to Lorenzo and the rest: But we will visit you at supper-time ii 2 214
There is some ill a-brewing towards my rest ii 5 17
Fie, fie, Gratiano? where are all the rest? 'Tis nine o'clock ii 6 62
If we are like you in the rest, we will resemble you in that iii 1 70
Nerissa and the rest, stand all aloof. Let music sound iii 2 42
No bed shall e'er be guilty of my stay, No rest be interposer 'twixt us iii 2 329
I rest much bounden to you *As Y. Like It* i 2 298
Bring us where we may rest ourselves and feed ii 4 73
You have too courtly a wit for me: I'll rest.—Wilt thou rest damned? iii 2 73
God rest you merry, sir v 1 65
I press in here, sir, amongst the rest of the country copulatives v 4 57
This contents: The rest will comfort *T. of Shrew* i 1 169
One thing more rests, that thyself execute i 1 250
You are the man Must stead us all and me amongst the rest i 2 266
Gratify this gentleman, To whom we all rest generally beholding i 2 274
If that be jest, then all the rest was so ii 1 22
I request, That, upon knowledge of my parentage, I may have welcome 'mongst the rest that woo And free access and favour as the rest ii 1 97
I should be arguing still upon that doubt: But let it rest iii 1 56
Call forth Nathaniel, Joseph, Nicholas, Philip, Walter, Sugarsop and the rest iv 1 92
The rest were ragged, old, and beggarly; Yet, as they are, here are they iv 1 140
Why then, the beef, and let the mustard rest iv 3 26

Rest. I'll in among the rest, Out of hope of all, but my share of the feast *T. of Shrew* v 1 145
The rest have worn me out With several applications *All's Well* i 2 73
Amongst the rest There is a remedy, approved, set down i 3 233
Can do no hurt to try, Since you set up your rest 'gainst remedy ii 1 138
Rest Unquestion'd welcome and undoubted blest ii 1 210
Thanks, sir; all the rest is mute ii 3 83
If thou canst like this creature as a maid, I can create the rest ii 3 150
That you are well restored, my lord, I'm glad: Let the rest go ii 3 155
O, you should not rest Between the elements of air and earth, But you should pity me! *T. Night* i 5 293
Let all the rest give place ii 4 82
And you find so much blood in his liver as will clog the foot of a flea, I'll eat the rest of the anatomy iii 2 67
And willingly, To do you rest, a thousand deaths would die v 1 136
Were you a woman, as the rest goes even, I should my tears let fall v 1 246
Yet shall the oracle Give rest to the minds of others *W. Tale* ii 1 191
Nor night nor day no rest: it is but weakness To bear the matter thus ii 3 1
Say that she were gone, Given to the fire, a moiety of my rest Might come to me again ii 3 8
He took good rest to-night; 'Tis hoped his sickness is discharged ii 3 10
May, if fortune please, both breed thee, pretty, And still rest thine iii 3 49
I would there were no age between sixteen and three-and-twenty, or that youth would sleep out the rest iii 3 61
Wipe not out the rest of thy services by leaving me now iv 2 12
He had both tune and words; which so drew the rest of the herd to me iv 4 620
At the other hill Command the rest to stand *K. John* ii 1 299
You and all the rest so grossly led iii 1 168
An hour, One minute, nay, one quiet breath of rest iii 4 134
If what in rest you have in right you hold iv 2 55
This inundation of mistemper'd humour Rests by you only to be qualified v 1 13
From the organ-pipe of frailty sings His soul and body to their lasting rest v 7 24
The Cardinal Pandulph is within at rest v 7 82
The like tender of our love we make, To rest without a spot for evermore v 7 107
Nought shall make us rue, If England to itself do rest but true v 7 118
For the rest appeal'd, It issues from the rancour of a villain *Richard II.* i 1 142
And all the rest revolted faction traitors ii 2 57
But I shall grieve you to report the rest.—What is't, knave? ii 2 95
These differences shall all rest under gage Till Norfolk be repeal'd iv 1 86
If I turn mine eyes upon myself, I find myself a traitor with the rest iv 1 248
Here let us rest, if this rebellious earth Have any resting v 1 5
Once more, adieu; the rest let sorrow say v 1 102
My lord, you told me you would tell the rest v 2 1
This fester'd joint cut off, the rest rest sound; This let alone will all the rest confound v 3 86
The abbot, With all the rest of that consorted crew v 3 138
Take hence the rest, and give them burial here v 5 119
Amongst the rest, demanded My prisoners 1 *Hen. IV.* i 3 47
With all the rest retold, May reasonably die and never rise i 3 73
Falstaff and the rest of the thieves are at the door: shall we be merry? ii 4 98
Some six or seven fresh men set upon us— And unbound the rest ii 4 201
There is virtue in that Falstaff: him keep with, the rest banish ii 4 473
Hide thee behind the arras: the rest walk up above ii 4 550
Rest your gentle head upon her lap, And she will sing the song iii 1 215
The better part of ours [horses] are full of rest iv 3 27
This to my cousin Scroop, and all the rest To whom they are directed iv 4 3
All his men Upon the foot of fear, fled with the rest v 5 20
All the rest Turn'd on themselves, like dull and heavy lead 2 *Hen. IV.* i 1 117
If ye will needs say I am an old man, you should give me rest i 2 243
Are near at hand: the rest the paper tells ii 1 147
The rest of thy low countries have made a shift to eat up thy holland ii 2 25
Let it be booked with the rest of this day's deeds iv 3 51
As a beacon gives warning to all the rest of this little kingdom, man iv 3 117
Lest rest and lying still might make them look Too near unto my state iv 5 212
I banish thee, on pain of death, As I have done the rest of my misleaders v 5 68
That is my rest, that is the rendezvous of it *Hen. V.* ii 1 17
With a body fill'd and vacant mind Gets him to rest iv 1 287
The rest are princes, barons, lords, knights, squires iv 8 94
In love and dear alliance, Let that one article rank with the rest v 2 374
Cease, cease these jars and rest your minds in peace 1 *Hen. VI.* i 1 44
Most of the rest slaughter'd or took likewise i 1 147
Nought rests for me in this tumultuous strife i 3 70
And now there rests no other shift but this ii 1 75
Let dying Mortimer here rest himself ii 5 2
But, as the rest, so fell that noble earl And was beheaded ii 5 90
Thou art my heir; the rest I wish thee gather: But yet be wary ii 5 96
And what I do imagine let that rest ii 5 119
As will the rest, so willeth Winchester iii 1 162
I speak not to that railing Hecate, But unto thee, Alençon, and the rest iii 2 65
Take away his train, If Dauphin and the rest will be but ruled iii 3 8
Thou wandering lord, Charles and the rest will take thee in their arms iii 3 77
Pardon me, princely Henry, and the rest iv 1 18
Nay, let it rest where it began at first iv 1 121
My lord protector and the rest After some respite will return iv 1 169
But let it rest; Other affairs must now be managed iv 1 180
Shall I, for lucre of the rest unvanquish'd, Detract so much from that? v 4 141
Till you do return, I rest perplexed with a thousand cares v 5 95
So, let her rest: and, madam, list to me 2 *Hen. VI.* i 3 95
Well, to the rest: 'Tell me what fate awaits the Duke of Suffolk?' i 4 66
And what a pitch she flew above the rest! ii 1 6
Kept him in activity till he died. But to the rest ii 2 43
My sovereign lady, with the rest, Causeless have laid disgraces on my head iii 1 161
And charge that no man should disturb your rest iii 2 256
I cannot rest Until the white rose that I wear be dyed Even in the lukewarm blood of Henry's heart 3 *Hen. VI.* i 2 32
Noble Warwick, Cobham, and the rest, Whom we have left protectors i 2 56
Or, with the rest, where is your darling Rutland? i 4 78
The rest stand all aloof, and bark at him ii 1 17
That this my body Might in the ground be closed up in rest! ii 1 76
All the rest is held at such a rate As brings a thousand-fold more care ii 2 51
And spite of spite needs must I rest awhile ii 3 5
So many hours must I take my rest; So many hours must I contemplate ii 5 32
Come, York and Richard, Warwick and the rest ii 6 29
What you command, that rests in me to do iii 2 45

Rest. But for the rest, you tell a pedigree Of threescore and two years *3 Hen. VI.* iii 3 92
He, more incensed against your majesty Than all the rest iv 1 109
You twain, of all the rest, Are near to Warwick by blood and by alliance iv 1 135
I hold it cowardice To rest mistrustful iv 2 8
Now what rests but, in night's coverture, . . . We may surprise and take him? iv 2 13
He hath made a solemn vow Never to lie and take his natural rest iv 3 5
Guess thou the rest; King Edward's friends must down iv 4 28
There shall I rest secure from force and fraud iv 4 33
Brother of Gloucester, Lord Hastings, and the rest, Stand you thus close? iv 5 16
'Tis like that Richmond with the rest shall down iv 6 100
Now, brother Richard, Lord Hastings, and the rest, Yet thus far iv 7 1
And only claim Our dukedom till God please to send the rest iv 7 47
Shall rest in London till we come to him iv 8 22
Here at the palace will I rest awhile iv 8 33
The doubt is that he will seduce the rest.—That's not my fear iv 8 37
O, farewell, Warwick!—Sweet rest his soul! Fly, lords, and save yourselves v 2 48
If the rest be true which I have heard, Thou camest— I'll hear no more v 6 55
Die, prophet, in thy speech: For this, amongst the rest, was I ordain'd v 6 58
Thy turn is next, and then the rest, Counting myself but bad till I be best v 6 90
And now what rests but that we spend the time With stately triumphs? v 7 42
And still, as you are weary of the weight, Rest you *Richard III.* i 2 32
Ill rest betide the chamber where thou liest! i 2 112
God give your grace good rest! Sorrow breaks seasons and reposing hours i 4 75
Look I so pale, Lord Dorset, as the rest? ii 1 83
Like obedient subjects, follow him To his new kingdom of perpetual rest ii 2 46
He is all the mother's, from the top to toe.—Well, let them rest iii 1 157
The rest, that love me, rise and follow me iii 4 81
Which ever since hath kept my eyes from rest iv 1 82
I to my grave, where peace and rest lie with me! iv 1 95
Two deep enemies, Foes to my rest and my sweet sleep's disturbers iv 2 74
Brief abstract and record of tedious days, Rest thy unrest! iv 4 29
Then would I hide my bones, not rest them here iv 4 33
Day, yield me not thy light; nor, night, thy rest! iv 4 401
To Salisbury; the rest march on with me iv 4 540
And so, God give you quiet rest to-night! v 3 43
And sweetly In all the rest show'd a most noble patience *Hen. VIII.* ii 1 36
He to be earl marshal: you may read the rest.—I thank you, sir iv 1 19
All the rest are countesses.—Their coronets say so iv 1 53
Sat down To rest awhile, some half an hour or so iv 1 66
So may he rest; his faults lie gently on him! iv 2 31
Many good nights, my lord: I rest your servant v 1 55
That white hair is my father, and all the rest are his sons *Troi. and Cres.* i 2 176
And all the rest so laughed, that it passed i 2 181
But mark Troilus above the rest i 2 200
My rest and negligence befriends thee now v 6 17
Rest, sword; thou hast thy fill of blood and death v 8 4
He's one honest enough: would all the rest were so! *Coriolanus* i 1 55
Cupboarding the viand, never bearing Like labour with the rest i 1 104
The rest Shall bear the business in some other fight i 6 81
The rest will serve For a short holding i 7 3
I'll follow thee a month, devise with thee Where thou shalt rest iv 1 39
The cruelty and envy of the people . . . hath devour'd the rest iv 5 82
Alarbus goes to rest; and we survive To tremble *T. Andron.* i 1 133
In peace and honour rest you here, my sons! (Repeated) i 1 150
Repose you here in rest, Secure from worldly chances and mishaps! i 1 151
Rest on my word, and let not discontent Daunt all your hopes i 1 267
Traitors, away! he rests not in this tomb i 1 349
Speak thou no more, if all the rest will speed i 1 372
The empress of my soul, Which never hopes more heaven than rests in thee ii 3 41
For love of her that's gone, Perhaps she cull'd it from among the rest iv 1 44
Let her rest in her unrest awhile iv 2 31
Well, God give her good rest! What hath he sent her?—A devil iv 2 63
All the rest depart away: You, Capulet, shall go along *Rom. and Jul.* i 1 105
Ye say honestly: rest you merry! i 2 65
I pray, come and crush a cup of wine. Rest you merry! i 2 86
Susan and she—God rest all Christian souls!—Were of an age i 3 18
It waxes late: I'll to my rest i 5 129
As sweet repose and rest Come to thy heart as that within my breast! ii 2 123
Would I were sleep and peace, so sweet to rest! ii 2 188
Our Romeo hath not been in bed to-night.—That last is true; the sweeter rest was mine ii 3 43
Rests me his minim rest, one, two, and the third in your bosom ii 4 22
And, as you shall use me hereafter, dry-beat the rest of the eight iii 1 83
Good night: Get thee to bed, and rest; for thou hast need iv 3 13
The County Paris hath set up his rest, That you shall rest but little iv 5 6
Here Will I set up my everlasting rest v 3 110
What misadventure is so early up, That calls our person from our morning's rest?—What should it be? v 3 189
With one man beckon'd from the rest below *T. of Athens* i 1 74
It may prove an argument of laughter To the rest iii 3 21
The rest of your fees, O gods—the senators of Athens iii 6 89
And all the rest look like a chidden train *J. Cæsar* i 2 184
I think we are too bold upon your rest ii 1 86
Here, under leave of Brutus and the rest—For Brutus is an honourable man iii 2 86
We, lying still, Are full of rest, defence, and nimbleness iv 3 202
Nature must obey necessity; Which we will niggard with a little rest iv 3 228
I know young bloods look for a time of rest iv 3 262
Since the affairs of men rest still incertain, Let's reason with the worst v 1 96
Come, poor remains of friends, rest on this rock v 5 1
Night hangs upon mine eyes; my bones would rest v 5 41
So call the field to rest; and let's away, To part the glories v 5 80
In viewing o'er the rest o' the selfsame day *Macbeth* i 3 94
The rest is labour, which is not used for you i 4 44
Look up clear; To alter favour ever is to fear: Leave all the rest to me i 5 74
For those of old, And the late dignities . . ., We rest your hermits i 6 20
What, sir, not yet at rest? ii 1 12
Mine eyes are made the fools o' the other senses, Or else worth all the rest ii 1 45
The rest That are within the note of expectation Already are i' the court iii 3 9

Rest. Heaven rest them now! *Macbeth* iv 3 227
She is troubled with thick-coming fancies, That keep her from her rest v 3 39
Rest, rest, perturbed spirit! *Hamlet* i 5 183
That you vouchsafe your rest here in our court Some little time ii 2 13
Go to your rest; at night we'll feast together: Most welcome home! ii 2 84
I will not sort you with the rest of my servants ii 2 275
'Tis well; I'll have thee speak out the rest soon ii 2 546
All but one shall live; the rest shall keep as they are iii 1 156
Confound the rest! Such love must needs be treason in my breast iii 2 187
If the rest of my fortunes turn Turk with me iii 2 287
That spirit upon whose weal depend and rest The lives of many iii 3 14
What then? what rests? Try what repentance can: what can it not? iii 3 64
Are all the rest come back? Or is it some abuse, and no such thing? iv 7 50
One that was a woman, sir; but, rest her soul, she's dead v 1 147
We should profane the service of the dead To sing a requiem and such rest to her As to peace-parted souls v 1 260
The rest is silence.—Now cracks a noble heart v 2 369
Good night, sweet prince; And flights of angels sing thee to thy rest! v 2 371
I loved her most, and thought to set my rest On her kind nursery *Lear* i 1 125
The sway, revenue, execution of the rest, Beloved sons, be yours i 1 139
Some time I shall sleep out, the rest I'll whistle ii 2 163
'Tis his own blame; hath put himself from rest ii 4 293
Like an old lecher's heart; a small spark, all the rest on's body cold iii 4 118
Stand you not so amazed: Will you lie down and rest upon the cushions? iii 6 36
Lie here and rest awhile.—Make no noise, make no noise; draw the curtains iii 6 87
Oppressed nature sleeps: This rest might yet have balm'd thy broken sinews iii 6 105
Do as I bid thee, or rather do thy pleasure; Above the rest, be gone iv 1 50
Sit you down, father; rest you iv 6 260
This sword of mine shall give them instant way, Where they shall rest for ever v 3 150
Hold your hands, Both you of my inclining, and the rest *Othello* i 2 82
My lord shall never rest; I'll watch him tame and talk him out of patience iii 3 22
Close prisoner rest, Till that the nature of your fault be known v 2 335
Rest you happy! *Ant. and Cleo.* i 1 62
Quietness, grown sick of rest, would purge By any desperate change i 3 53
The all-honour'd, honest Roman, Brutus, With the arm'd rest ii 6 17
Our overplus of shipping will we burn; And, with the rest full-mann'd iii 7 52
Canidius and the rest That fell away have entertainment iv 6 16
But even the very middle of my heart Is warm'd by the rest *Cymbeline* i 6 28
Which I, the factor for the rest, have done In France i 6 188
The crickets sing, and man's o'er-labour'd sense Repairs itself by rest ii 2 12
Go in and rest.—We'll not be long away iv 2 43
Three performers are the file when all The rest do nothing v 3 31
Help; Or we poor ghosts will cry To the shining synod of the rest v 4 89
Hence, and rest Upon your never-withering banks of flowers v 4 97
That's an article within our law, As dangerous as the rest *Pericles* i 1 89
Her face was to mine eye beyond all wonder; The rest—hark in thine ear—as black as incest i 2 76
Rest us here, And by relating tales of others' griefs, See if 'twill teach us to forget our own i 4 1
And that in Tarsus was not best Longer for him to make his rest ii Gower 26
I'll pay your bounties; till then rest your debtor ii 1 149
Here take your place: Marshall the rest, as they deserve their grace ii 3 19
Each one betake him to his rest; To-morrow all for speeding do their best ii 3 115
If in his grave he rest, we'll find him there ii 4 30
I nill relate, action may Conveniently the rest convey iii Gower 56
Take from my heart all thankfulness! The gods Make up the rest upon you! iii 3 5
Crack the glass of her virginity, and make the rest malleable iv 6 152
As in the rest you said Thou hast been godlike perfect v 1 207
Let me rest.—A pillow for his head: So, leave him all v 1 236
We do our longing stay To hear the rest untold v 3 84
Rest assured. That I may rest assured Whether yond troops are friend or enemy *J. Cæsar* v 3 17
Rested. It rested in your grace To unloose this *Meas. for Meas.* i 3 31
Thus the Mortimers, In whom the title rested, were suppress'd *1 Hen. VI.* ii 5 92
Some of these Should find a running banquet ere they rested *Hen. VIII.* i 4 12
'Rest. When gentlemen are tired, gives them a sob and 'rests them *Com. of Errors* iv 3 25
'Rested. He is 'rested on the case iv 2 42
He's in a suit of buff which 'rested him iv 2 45
I'll give thee, ere I leave thee, so much money, To warrant thee, as I am 'rested for iv 4 3
Re-stem. Now they do re-stem Their backward course *Othello* i 3 37
Resteth. To strive for that which resteth in my choice *T. of Shrew* iii 1 17
What resteth more, But that I seek occasion how to rise? *3 Hen. VI.* i 2 44
What nobleman is that That with the king here resteth in his tent? iv 3 10
Restful. Is not my arm of length, That reacheth from the restful English court As far as Calais, to mine uncle's head? *Richard II.* iv 1 12
Resting. Here let us rest, if this rebellious earth Have any resting v 1 6
Resting well assured They ne'er did service for't *Coriolanus* iii 1 121
The northern star, Of whose true-fix'd and resting quality There is no fellow in the firmament *J. Cæsar* iii 1 61
Not resting here, accuses him of letters *Ant. and Cleo.* iii 5 10
Restitution. A child of conscience; he makes restitution *Mer. Wives* v 5 33
And never ask'd for restitution *2 Hen. VI.* iii 1 118
He would pawn his fortunes To hopeless restitution *Coriolanus* iii 1 16
He calls me to a restitution large Of gold and jewels *Othello* v 1 15
Restless. Imprison'd in the viewless winds, And blown with restless violence round about The pendent world *Meas. for Meas.* iii 1 125
That goddess blind, That stands upon the rolling restless stone *Hen. V.* iii 6 31
For unfelt imagination, They often feel a world of restless cares *Rich. III.* i 4 81
Than on the torture of the mind to lie In restless ecstasy *Macbeth* iii 2 22
Restoration hang Thy medicine on my lips! *Lear* iv 7 26
Restorative. I will kiss thy lips; Haply some poison yet doth hang on them, To make me die with a restorative *Rom. and Jul.* v 3 166
Lords and ladies in their lives Have read it for restoratives *Pericles* i Gower 8
Restore. My charms I'll break, their senses I'll restore *Tempest* v 1 31
Which perforce, I know, Thou must restore v 1 134
She, Claudio, that you wrong'd, look you restore *Meas. for Meas.* v 1 531
I will but teach them to sing, and restore them to the owner *Much Ado* ii 1 240
I wish your worship well; God restore you to health! v 1 333
If then the king your father will restore But that one half *L. L. Lost* ii 1 138
And Robin shall restore amends *M. N. Dream* v 1 445
Heaven restore thee! *T. Night* iii 4 51

Restore. Thy wits the heavens restore! endeavour thyself to sleep *T. Night* iv 2 104
Restore yourselves Into the good thoughts of the world again 1 *Hen. IV.* i 3 181
Would ye not think his cunning to be great, that could restore this cripple to his legs again? . . . . . . 2 *Hen. VI.* ii 1 133
It [conscience] made me once restore a purse of gold that I found *Rich. III.* i 4 144
Out of all these to restore the king, He counsels a divorce *Hen. VIII.* ii 2 30
I will restore to thee The people's hearts . . . . *T. Andron.* i 1 210
Traitor, restore Lavinia to the emperor.—Dead, if you will . . i 1 296
O heavenly powers, restore him! . . . . . . *Hamlet* iii 1 147
If I quench thee, thou flaming minister, I can again thy former light restore, Should I repent me . . . . . . *Othello* v 2 9
A diminution in our captain's brain Restores his heart . *Ant. and Cleo.* iii 13 199
Art thou mad?—Almost, sir: heaven restore me! . . . *Cymbeline* i 1 148
Restored. And all their lands restored to them again . . *As Y. Like It* v 4 170
Being overjoy'd To see her noble lord restored to health *T. of Shrew* Ind. 1 121
O, how we joy to see your wit restored! . . . . . . Ind. 2 79
Heaven hath through me restored the king to health . . *All's Well* ii 3 70
That you are well restored, my lord, I'm glad: Let the rest go . . ii 3 154
Provided that my banishment repeal'd And lands restored again be freely granted . . . . *Richard II.* iii 3 41
And, though mine enemy, restored again To all his lands and signories iv 1 88
May be restored With good advice and little medicine . 2 *Hen. IV.* iii 1 42
Were you not restored To all the Duke of Norfolk's signories? . . iv 1 110
That all their eyes may bear those tokens home Of our restored love . iv 2 65
Till thou be restored, thou art a yeoman . . . . . 1 *Hen. VI.* ii 4 95
Either to be restored to my blood, Or make my ill the advantage of my good . . . . ii 5 128
Our pleasure is That Richard be restored to his blood . . . iii 1 159
Hast thou been long blind and now restored?—Born blind . 2 *Hen. VI.* ii 1 76
Like a most royal prince, Restored me to my honours . . *Hen. VIII.* ii 1 114
And hundreds call themselves Your creatures, who by you have been restored . . . . *Pericles* iii 2 45
Restoring. What can man's wisdom In the restoring his bereaved sense? He that helps him take all my outward worth . . . *Lear* iv 4 9
Restrain. Such as we see when men restrain their breath . 1 *Hen. IV.* ii 3 64
None of this . . . could restrain The stiff-borne action . . 2 *Hen. IV.* i 1 176
You having lands, and blest with beauteous wives, They would restrain the one, distain the other . . . . *Richard III.* v 3 322
I stand condemn'd for this; They think my little stomach to the war And your great love to me restrains you thus . *Troi. and Cres.* iii 3 221
More piercing statutes daily, to chain up and restrain the poor *Coriolanus* i 1 87
Merciful powers, Restrain in me the cursed thoughts that nature Gives way to in repose! . . . . *Macbeth* ii 1 8
Restrained. As to put metal in restrained means . *Meas. for Meas.* ii 4 48
Thou wert immured, restrained, captivated, bound . *L. L. Lost* iii 1 126
A head-stall of sheep's leather which, being restrained to keep him from stumbling, hath been often burst . . . . *T. of Shrew* iii 2 59
You have restrained yourself within the list of too cold an adieu *All's W.* ii 1 52
If that they . . . Should by the cormorant belly be restrain'd, Who is the sink o' the body,— Well, what then? . . . *Coriolanus* i 1 125
It will be laid to us, whose providence Should have kept short, restrain'd and out of haunt, This mad young man . . *Hamlet* iv 1 18
The king must take it ill, That he's so slightly valued in his messenger, Should have him thus restrain'd . . . . . *Lear* ii 2 154
If, sir, perchance She have restrain'd the riots of your followers, 'Tis on such ground, and to such wholesome end, As clears her from all blame . . . . ii 4 145
Me of my lawful pleasure she restrain'd . . . . *Cymbeline* ii 5 9
Restrainest. The gods will plague thee, That thou restrain'st from me the duty which To a mother's part belongs . . . *Coriolanus* v 3 167
Restraining. Thou art a coward, Which hoxes honesty behind, restraining From course required . . . . . . *W. Tale* i 2 244
Hath sense withal Of it own fail, restraining aid to Timon *T. of Athens* v 1 151
Restraint. Whence comes this restraint?—From too much liberty *Meas. for Meas.* i 2 128
So every scope by the immoderate use Turns to restraint . . i 2 132
I speak not as desiring more; But rather wishing a more strict restraint i 4 4
Perpetual durance, a restraint, Though all the world's vastidity you had iii 1 68
To know the reason of this strange restraint . *Com. of Errors* iii 1 97
He does acknowledge; But puts it off to a compell'd restraint *All's Well* ii 4 44
Madding my eagerness with her restraint . . . . . v 3 213
And did thereto add My love, without retention or restraint . *T. Night* v 1 84
Whose restraint Doth move the murmuring lips of discontent *K. John* iv 2 52
From curb'd license plucks The muzzle of restraint 2 *Hen. IV.* iv 5 132
Put upon you what restraint and grievance The law, with all his might to enforce it on, Will give him cable . . . . . *Othello* i 2 15
Or else break out in peevish jealousies, Throwing restraint upon us iv 3 91
Your gaoler shall deliver you the keys That lock up your restraint *Cymb.* i 1 74
Resty. Weariness Can snore upon the flint, when resty sloth Finds the down pillow hard . . . . iii 6 34
Resume. Nay, mother, Resume that spirit . . . *Coriolanus* iv 1 16
Takes no account How things go from him, nor resumes no care *T. of A.* ii 2 4
Thou shalt find That I'll resume the shape which thou dost think I have cast off for ever . . . . *Lear* i 4 331
That opportunity Which then they had to take from's, to resume We have again. Remember, sir . . . . . *Cymbeline* iii 1 15
Resumed. I have resumed again The part I came in . . . v 3 75
Resurrections. Got deliver to a joyful resurrections! . *Mer. Wives* i 1 54
Re-survey. With better heed To re-survey them . . . *Hen. V.* v 2 81
Retail. He is wit's pedler, and retails his wares At wakes *L. L. Lost* v 2 317
I over-rode him on the way; And he is furnish'd with no certainties More than he haply may retail from me . . 2 *Hen. IV.* i 1 32
To whom I will retail my conquest won . . . *Richard III.* iv 4 335
Retail'd to all posterity, Even to the general all-ending day . iii 1 77
Retain. Thy shape invisible retain thou still . . . *Tempest* iv 1 185
But longer did we not retain much hope . . *Com. of Errors* i 1 66
In substance and authority, Retain but privilege of a private man 1 *Hen. VI.* v 4 136
Retain that dear perfection which he owes Without that title *R. and J.* ii 2 46
May one be pardon'd and retain the offence? . . *Hamlet* iii 3 56
Only we still retain The name, and all the additions to a king . *Lear* i 1 137
Sir, where is the patience now, That you so oft have boasted to retain? iii 6 62
Retained. Reft of his brother, but retain'd his name *Com. of Errors* i 1 129
Being my sworn servant, The duke retain'd him his . *Hen. VIII.* i 2 192
Retainers. Now are mounted Where powers are your retainers . ii 4 113
Retaining but a quantity of life, Which bleeds away . . *K. John* v 4 23
Re-tell. I have told thee often, and I re-tell thee again . *Othello* i 3 372
Retention. No woman's heart So big, to hold so much; they lack retention. Alas, their love may be call'd appetite . . *T. Night* ii 4 99

Retention. And did thereto add My love, without retention or restraint *T. Night* v 1 84
To send the old and miserable king To some retention . . . *Lear* v 3 47
Retentive. Have I been ever free, and must my house Be my retentive enemy, my gaol? . . . . *T. of Athens* iii 4 82
Nor airless dungeon, nor strong links of iron, Can be retentive to the strength of spirit . . . . *J. Cæsar* i 3 95
Retinue. Who, . . . with this retinue, doth any deed of courage 2 *Hen. IV.* iv 3 121
Other of your insolent retinue Do hourly carp and quarrel . *Lear* i 4 221
Retire into my cell And there repose . . . . *Tempest* iv 1 161
Thence retire me to my Milan, where Every third thought shall be my grave . . . . v 1 310
I must advance the colours of my love And not retire . *Mer. Wives* iii 4 86
All his behaviours did make their retire To the court of his eye *L. L. Lost* ii 1 234
You must retire yourself Into some covert . . . . *W. Tale* iv 4 663
With a blessed and unvex'd retire . . . . . . *K. John* ii 1 253
Behold, From first to last, the onset and retire Of both your armies . ii 1 326
The French fight coldly, and retire themselves . . . . v 3 13
When English measure backward their own ground In faint retire . v 5 4
Thou hast talk'd Of sallies and retires, of trenches, tents . 1 *Hen. IV.* ii 3 54
Sickness growing Upon our soldiers, we will retire to Calais . *Hen. V.* iii 3 56
Was have possession of the pridge; but he is enforced to retire . . iii 6 99
That their souls May make a peaceful and a sweet retire . . iv 3 86
Our English troops retire, I cannot stay them . . . 1 *Hen. VI.* i 5 2
It will not be: retire into your trenches . . . . . . i 5 33
If thou retire, the Dauphin, well appointed, Stands with the snares of war to tangle thee . . . . iv 2 21
Retire to Killingworth, Until a power be raised . 2 *Hen. VI.* iv 4 39
When the hardiest warriors did retire, Richard cried 'Charge!' 3 *Hen. VI.* i 4 14
Oft have I heard his praises in pursuit, But ne'er till now his scandal of retire.—Nor now my scandal . . . . ii 1 150
Ne'er may he live to see a sunshine day, That cries 'Retire' . . ii 1 188
Like the selfsame sea Forced to retire by fury of the wind . . ii 5 8
He'll say in Troy when he retires, The Grecian dames are sunburnt and not worth The splinter of a lance . . . *Troi. and Cres.* i 3 281
Who should withhold me? Not fate, obedience, nor the hand of Mars Beckoning with fiery truncheon my retire . . . . . v 3 53
Thou dost miscall retire: I do not fly . . . . . v 4 21
Hark! a retire upon our Grecian part.—The Trojan trumpets sound the like . . . . v 8 15
Give me leave to retire myself.—Indeed, you shall not . *Coriolanus* i 3 30
He that retires, I'll take him for a Volsce, And he shall feel mine edge i 4 28
Come off Like Romans, neither foolish in our stands, Nor cowardly in retire . . . . i 6 3
We have at disadvantage fought and did Retire to win our purpose . i 6 50
Let's retire: The day is hot . . . . *Rom. and Jul.* iii 1 1
Retire we to our chamber: A little water clears us of this deed *Macbeth* ii 2 66
Retire with me to my lodging . . . . *Lear* i 2 183
Retire thee; go where thou art billeted . . . . *Othello* ii 3 386
Man but a rush against Othello's breast, And he retires . . . v 2 271
Please you, retire to your chamber . . . *Ant. and Cleo.* iv 4 35
Retire, we have engaged ourselves too far . . . . . iv 7 1
They do retire.—We'll beat 'em into bench-holes . . . . iv 7 8
Then began A stop i' the chaser, a retire, anon A rout . *Cymbeline* v 3 40
Retired. By being so retired, O'er-prized all popular rate . *Tempest* i 2 91
I have missingly noted, he is of late much retired *W. Tale* iv 2 36
You are retired, As if you were a feasted one and not The hostess . iv 4 62
Like a bated and retired flood . . . . *K. John* v 4 53
That he, our hope, might have retired his power . *Richard II.* ii 2 46
And toil'd with works of war, retired himself To Italy . . . iv 1 96
Whereupon He is retired, to ripe his growing fortunes 2 *Hen. IV.* i 1 13
Or is he but retired to make him strong? . . . 2 *Hen. VI.* iv 9 9
He is retired to Antium.—Spoke he of me? . . . *Coriolanus* iii 1 11
Retired me to a wasteful cock, And set mine eyes at flow *T. of Athens* ii 2 171
Hearing you were retired, your friends fall'n off . . . . v 1 62
Most retired Hath her life been . . . . . . *Cymbeline* iii 5 36
Retirement. For certain words he spake against your grace In your retirement, I had swinged him soundly . . *Meas. for Meas.* v 1 130
A comfort of retirement lives in this . . . . 1 *Hen. IV.* iv 1 56
Make up, Lest your retirement do amaze your friends . . . v 4 6
And never noted in him any study, Any retirement . . *Hen. V.* i 1 58
Is in his retirement marvellous distempered.—With drink? . *Hamlet* iii 2 312
Retiring from the siege of Orleans, Having full scarce six thousand in his troop . . . . 1 *Hen. VI.* i 1 111
Like to the Pontic sea, Whose icy current and compulsive course Ne'er feels retiring ebb . . . . *Othello* iii 3 455
Retold. As may not be Without much shame retold 1 *Hen. IV.* i 1 46
In such a place, At such a time, with all the rest retold . . . i 3 73
Retort. Unjust, Thus to retort your manifest appeal *Meas. for Meas.* v 1 303
This is called the Retort Courteous . . . . *As Y. Like It* v 4 76
The first, the Retort Courteous; the second, the Quip Modest; the third, the Reply Churlish; the fourth, the Reproof Valiant; the fifth, the Countercheck Quarrelsome; the sixth, the Lie with Circumstance; the seventh, the Lie Direct . . . . . v 4 96
I do retort the 'solus' in thy bowels . . . . . *Hen. V.* ii 1 54
In selfsame key Retorts to chiding fortune . . . *Troi. and Cres.* i 3 54
His virtues shining upon others Heat them and they retort that heat again To the first giver . . . . iii 3 101
With one hand beats Cold death aside, and with the other sends It back to Tybalt, whose dexterity Retorts it . . . *Rom. and Jul.* iii 1 169
Retourné. Le chien est retourné à son propre vomissement . *Hen. V.* iii 7 68
Retract. Paris should ne'er retract what he hath done . *Troi. and Cres.* ii 2 141
Retreat. Let us make an honourable retreat . . . . *As Y. Like It* iii 2 170
A coward . . . : in a retreat he outruns any lackey; marry, in coming on he has the cramp . . . . *All's Well* iv 3 323
The trumpet sounds retreat; the day is ours . . . 1 *Hen. IV.* v 4 163
And for a retreat; how swiftly will this Feeble the woman's tailor run off! O, give me the spare men . . . . . . 2 *Hen. IV.* iii 2 286
Have you left pursuit?—Retreat is made and execution stay'd . iv 3 78
The work ish give over, the trumpet sound the retreat . *Hen. V.* iii 2 94
Here sound retreat, and cease our hot pursuit . . . 1 *Hen. VI.* ii 2 3
Dare any be so bold to sound retreat or parley? . . . 2 *Hen. VI.* iv 8 4
Northumberland, Whose warlike ears could never brook retreat 3 *Hen. VI.* i 1 5
Retrograde. When he was predominant.—When he was retrograde, I think . . . . *All's Well* i 1 212
It is most retrograde to our desire . . . . . . *Hamlet* i 2 114
Return. A sweet marriage, and we prosper well in our return *Tempest* ii 1 73
I drink the air before me, and return Or ere your pulse twice beat . v 1 102
See it be return'd; Or else return no more into my sight *T. G. of Ver.* i 1 47
I will return.—If you turn not, you will return the sooner . . ii 2 3

Return. Better forbear till Proteus make return . . . *T. G. of Ver.* ii 7 14
Return, return, and make thy love amends . . . iv 2 99
Find my dog again, Or ne'er return again into my sight . . . iv 4 65
If ever he return and I can speak to him, I will open my lips *M. for M.* iii 1 198
If peradventure he shall ever return to have hearing of this business . iii 1 210
If ever the duke return, as our prayers are he may, let me desire you to make your answer before him . . . . iii 2 164
O, you hope the duke will return no more . . . . iii 2 174
The contents of this is the return of the duke . . . iv 2 211
Make a swift return; For I would commune with you . . iv 3 107
'Tis that he sent me of the duke's return . . . iv 3 143
We are glad to see you.—Happy return be to your royal grace! . . v 1 3
Which consummate, Return him here again . . . v 1 384
Made daily motions for our home return . . . *Com. of Errors* i 1 60
Then return and sleep within mine inn . . . i 2 14
I from my mistress come to you in post; If I return, I shall be post indeed . . . i 2 64
And this thou didst return from him, That he did buffet thee . . ii 2 159
Come to the mart, Where I will walk till thou return to me . . iii 2 156
Have you the chain about you?—An if I have not, sir, I hope you have; Or else you may return without your money . . . iv 1 44
Driven out of doors with it when I go from home; welcomed home with it when I return . . . . iv 4 39
On Saturday we will return to France . . . *L. L. Lost* iv 1 6
But to return to the verses: did they please you? . . . iv 2 156
Will they return?—They will, they will, God knows . . v 2 289
What shall we do, If they return in their own shapes to woo? . . v 2 299
To fetch me trifles, and return again, As from a voyage . *M. N. Dream* ii 1 133
To return to their home and to trouble you with no more suit *Mer. of Ven.* i 2 111
I do expect return Of thrice three times the value of this bond . i 3 160
Return in haste, for I do feast to-night My best-esteem'd acquaintance. ii 2 180
Disguise us at my lodging and return, All in an hour . . ii 4 2
Perhaps I will return immediately: Do as I bid you; shut doors after you . . . . ii 5 52
How like the prodigal doth she return! . . . ii 6 17
Bassanio told him he would make some speed Of his return . . ii 8 38
I commit into your hands The husbandry and manage of my house Until my lord's return . . . . iii 4 26
Attended by Nerissa here, Until her husband and my lord's return . iii 4 30
We will nothing waste till you return . . . *As Y. Like It* ii 7 134
He left a promise to return again Within an hour . . . iv 3 100
And thou return unexperienced to thy grave . . *T. of Shrew* iv 1 85
Now, my honey love, Will we return unto thy father's house . . iv 3 53
What we alone must think, which never Returns us thanks . *All's Well* i 1 200
I will return perfect courtier . . . . . . i 1 221
They may jest Till their own scorn return to them unnoted . . i 2 34
'Tis our hope, sir, . . . to return And find your grace in health . ii 1 6
Return you thither?—Ay, madam, with the swiftest wing of speed . iii 2 75
When haply he shall hear that she is gone, He will return . . iii 4 36
Let's return again, and suffice ourselves with the report of it . . iii 5 10
Return with an invention and clap upon you two or three probable lies iii 6 105
He comes, to beguile two hours in a sleep, and then to return . iv 1 25
Will he travel higher, or return again into France? . . . iv 3 50
My lord your son was upon his return home . . . iv 5 75
Send for your ring, I will return it home, And give me mine again . v 3 223
But from her handmaid do return this answer . . . *T. Night* i 1 25
Be clamorous and leap all civil bounds Rather than make unprofited return . . . . i 4 22
She returns this ring to you, sir: you might have saved me my pains . ii 2 5
I will return again into the house and desire some conduct of the lady . iii 4 264
Stay you by this gentleman till my return . . . iii 4 282
That to my home I will no more return . . . *K. John* ii 1 21
Peace be to England, if that war return From France to England . . ii 1 89
Hither return all gilt with Frenchmen's blood . . . ii 1 316
Our colours do return in those same hands That did display them. . ii 1 319
O fair return of banish'd majesty! . . . . iii 1 321
Deliver him to safety; and return, For I must use thee . . . iv 2 158
Would not my lords return to me again? . . . . v 1 37
Return the precedent to these lords again . . . . v 2 3
I will not return Till my attempt so much be glorified . . . v 2 110
Instantly return with me again, To push destruction . . . v 7 76
And both return back to their chairs again . . . *Richard II.* i 3 120
Let the trumpets sound While we return these dukes what we decree . i 3 122
The hopeless word of 'never to return' Breathe I against thee . . i 3 152
Return again, and take an oath with thee . . . . i 3 178
Six frozen winters spent, Return with welcome home . . . i 3 212
As foil wherein thou art to set The precious jewel of thy home return . i 3 267
The wind sits fair for news to go to Ireland, But none returns . . ii 2 124
O, call back yesterday, bid time return! . . . . iii 2 69
Thus the king returns: His noble cousin is right welcome hither . . iii 3 121
You had rather refuse The offer of an hundred thousand crowns Than Bolingbroke's return . . . . iv 1 17
From whence he intercepted did return To be deposed . . 1 *Hen. IV.* i 3 151
Shall I return this answer to the king?—Not so . . . iv 3 106
Let there be impawn'd Some surety for a safe return again . . iv 3 109
Prove that ever I dress myself handsome till thy return . 2 *Hen. IV.* ii 4 303
At your return visit our house; let our old acquaintance be renewed . iii 2 314
As I return, I will fetch off these justices . . . . iii 2 323
I'll be acquainted with him, if I return . . . . iii 2 354
He might return to vasty Tartar back, And tell the legions . *Hen. V.* ii 2 123
If my father render fair return, It is against my will . . . ii 4 127
Returns us that his powers are yet not ready . . . iii 3 46
Now and then goes to the wars, to grace himself at his return . . iii 6 72
Hot as gunpowder, And quickly will return an injury . . . iv 7 189
Tell her I return great thanks . . . . 1 *Hen. VI.* i 2 51
Return thee therefore with a flood of tears . . . . iii 3 56
Come, come, return; return, thou wandering lord . . . iii 3 76
My lord protector and the rest After some respite will return . . iv 1 170
He that flies so will ne'er return again . . . . iv 5 19
Till you do return, I rest perplexed with a thousand cares . . v 5 94
When from Saint Alban's we do make return, We'll see . 2 *Hen. VI.* i 2 83
But now return we to the false Duke Humphrey.—No more of him . iii 1 322
Stay, Salisbury, With the rude multitude till I return . . . iii 2 135
When I return with victory from the field I'll see your grace 3 *Hen. VI.* i 1 261
I here renounce him and return to Henry . . . . iii 3 194
Return in post, And tell false Edward, thy supposed king . . iii 3 222
I came from Edward as ambassador, But I return his sworn and mortal foe iii 3 257
How could he stay till Warwick made return? . . . iv 1 5
And my son Edward Be sent for, to return from France with speed . iv 6 61
Go, tread the path that thou shalt ne'er return . . *Richard III.* i 1 117
Return. I'll turn yon fellow in his grave; And then return lamenting to my love . . . . . . *Richard III.* i 2 262
Return unto thy lord; Bid him not fear the separated councils . . iii 2 19
Long I shall not stay: I shall return before your lordship . . iii 2 121
Return, good Catesby, to thy lord again; Tell him . . . iii 7 65
I come in perfect love to him; And so once more return and tell his grace . . . . iii 7 91
Proclaim a pardon to the soldiers fled That in submission will return . v 5 17
At his return No doubt he will requite it . . . *Hen. VIII.* ii 1 45
Prayers and wishes Are all I can return . . . . ii 3 70
Pray you, keep your way: When you are call'd, return . . . ii 4 129
Return: with thy approach, I know, My comfort comes along . . ii 4 239
When returns Cranmer?—He is return'd in his opinions . . . iii 2 63
I'll not over the threshold till my lord return from the wars . *Coriolanus* i 3 82
The fourth would return for conscience sake, to help to get thee a wife ii 3 36
Will you hence, Before the tag return? whose rage doth rend . . iii 1 248
You must return and mend it.—There's no remedy . . . iii 2 26
What must I do?—Return to the tribunes.—Well, what then? . . iii 2 36
I'll return consul; Or never trust to what my tongue can do . . iii 2 135
Say that Marcius Return me, as Cominius is return'd, Unheard; what then? . . . . v 1 42
You may not pass, you must return . . . . . v 2 5
He returns, Splitting the air with noise . . . . v 6 51
Laden with honour's spoils, Returns the good Andronicus . *T. Andron.* i 1 37
The bark, that hath discharged her fraught, Returns with precious lading . . . . i 1 72
To re-salute his country with his tears, Tears of true joy for his return i 1 76
We are brought to Rome, To beautify thy triumphs and return . . i 1 110
At thy feet I kneel, with tears of joy, Shed on the earth, for thy return i 1 162
This will I do, and soon return again . . . . v 2 131
Entreat her eyes To twinkle in their spheres till they return *R. and J.* ii 2 17
I did send the nurse; In half an hour she promised to return . . ii 5 2
How shall that faith return again to earth? . . . . iii 5 208
Is the bride ready to go to church?—Ready to go, but never to return . iv 5 34
If thou, jealous, dost return to pry In what I further shall intend to do v 3 33
He drops down The knee before him and returns in peace *T. of Athens* i 1 61
No gift to him, But breeds the giver a return exceeding All use of quittance . . . . i 1 290
I do return those talents, Doubled with thanks and service . . i 2 6
When, for some trifling present, you have bid me Return so much, I have shook my head and wept . . . . . ii 2 146
They do shake their heads, and I am here No richer in return . . ii 2 212
But now return, And with their faint reply this answer join . . iii 3 24
I'll pawn my victories, all My honours to you, upon his good returns . iii 5 82
I will not kiss thee; then the rot returns To thine own lips again . iv 3 64
As rich men deal gifts, Expecting in return twenty for one . . iv 3 517
Therefore, so please thee to return with us . . . . v 1 162
I like this well; he will return again . . . . v 1 207
Let us return, And strain what other means is left unto us . . v 1 229
What should I do? Run to the Capitol, and nothing else? And so return to you, and nothing else? . . . . *J. Cæsar* ii 4 12
Your servants ever Have theirs, themselves and what is theirs, in compt, To make their audit at your highness' pleasure, Still to return your own . . . . *Macbeth* i 6 28
Bloody instructions, which, being taught, return To plague the inventor i 7 9
Hie you to horse: adieu, Till you return at night . . . iii 1 36
Is Banquo gone from court?—Ay, madam, but returns again to-night . iii 2 2
That a swift blessing May soon return to this our suffering country! . iii 6 48
I have seen her rise from her bed . . . and again return to bed; yet all this while in a most fast sleep . . . . . v 1 8
Your leave and favour to return to France . . . *Hamlet* i 2 51
Most fair return of greetings and desires . . . . ii 2 60
The undiscover'd country from whose bourn No traveller returns . . iii 1 80
Your pardon and my return shall be the end of my business . . iii 2 329
Recount the occasion of my sudden and more strange return. . . iv 7 48
To what base uses we may return, Horatio! . . . . v 1 223
You have begot me, bred me, loved me: I Return those duties back *Lear* i 1 99
When he returns from hunting, I will not speak with him . . i 3 7
Get you gone; And hasten your return . . . . i 4 363
I pray you, That to our sister you do make return . . . ii 4 153
Return you to my sister.—Never, Regan . . . . ii 4 160
Return and sojourn with my sister, Dismissing half your train . . ii 4 206
Return to her, and fifty men dismiss'd? No, rather I abjure all roofs . ii 4 210
Return with her? Why, the hot-blooded France, that dowerless took Our youngest born, I could as well be brought To knee his throne ii 4 214
Return with her? Persuade me rather to be slave and sumpter To this detested groom . . . . ii 4 218
Denied me to come in—return, and force Their scanted courtesy . . iii 2 66
The lamentable change is from the best; The worst returns to laughter iv 1 6
His personal return was most required and necessary . . . iv 3 6
There is nothing done, if he return the conqueror . . . iv 6 271
If ever I return to you again, I'll bring you comfort . . . v 2 3
With no money at all and a little more wit, return again . *Othello* ii 3 375
Bade him anon return and here speak with me; The which he promised iv 1 81
I obey the mandate, And will return to Venice . . . iv 1 271
If she will return me my jewels, I will give over my suit . . iv 2 201
Why, then Othello and Desdemona return again to Venice . . iv 2 228
He looks gentler than he did.—He says he will return incontinent . iv 3 12
Report That I am sudden sick: quick, and return . *Ant. and Cleo.* i 3 5
Return it again: you shall have time to wrangle . . . ii 2 105
I begg'd His pardon for return.—Which soon he granted . . iii 6 60
If from the field I shall return once more To kiss these lips . . iii 13 173
If we be not relieved within this hour, We must return . . . iv 9 2
I shall but lend my diamond till your return . . . *Cymbeline* i 4 155
Return he cannot, nor Continue where he is . . . . i 5 53
I shall short my word By lengthening my return . . . i 6 201
I hope the briefness of your answer made The speediness of your return ii 4 31
For the gap That we shall make in time, from our hence-going And our return . . . . iii 2 66
Whereunto I never Purpose return . . . . . iii 4 110
O Imogen, Safe mayst thou wander, safe return again! . . . iii 5 105
I'll stay Till hasty Polydore return, and bring him to dinner . . iv 2 165
His body's hostage For his return . . . . . iv 2 186
I nothing know where she remains, why gone, Nor when she purposes return . . . . iv 3 15
A leg of Rome shall not return to tell What crows have peck'd them here v 3 92
And how you shall speed in your journey's end, I think you'll never return to tell one . . . . v 4 191
So thou ne'er return Unless thou say 'Prince Pericles is dead' *Pericles* i 1 165
Keep your mind, till you return to us Peaceful and comfortable! . . i 2 34

Return. O'erlook What shipping and what lading's in our haven, And then return . . . . *Pericles* i 2 50
My message must return from whence it came . . . . i 3 36
Return them, we are ready . . . . ii 2 4
If in which time expired, he not return, I shall with aged patience bear your yoke . . . . ii 4 47
Whom if you find, and win unto return, You shall like diamonds sit . ii 4 52
Even in his throat . . . That calls me traitor, I return the lie . ii 5 57
Your master will be dead ere you return . . . . . iii 2 7
There's no hope she will return. I'll swear she's dead . . . iv 1 99
Returned. Mars's hot minion is return'd again . . . . *Tempest* iv 1 98
Take the paper: see it be return'd; Or else return no more *T. G. of Ver.* i 2 46
I would the duke we talk of were returned again . *Meas. for Meas.* iii 2 183
He would never bring them to light: would he were returned! . iii 2 189
How chance thou art return'd so soon?—Return'd so soon! *Com. of Er.* i 2 42
Neither my husband nor the slave return'd! . . . . . ii 1 1
And to that end am I returned.—And to that end, sir, I will welcome you iv 4 17
And sent my peasant home For certain ducats: he with none return'd v 1 232
Is Signior Mountanto returned from the wars or no? . . *Much Ado* i 1 30
O, he's returned; and as pleasant as ever he was . . . . i 1 37
Look; Don Pedro is returned to seek you . . . . . i 1 205
Now I am return'd and that war-thoughts Have left their places vacant i 1 303
My herald is return'd.—A wonder, master! . . *L. L. Lost* iii 1 70
My heart to her but as guest-wise sojourn'd, And now to Helen is it home return'd, There to remain . . . . . . *M. N. Dream* iii 2 172
I pray you, is my master yet return'd?—He is not . *Mer. of Venice* v 1 34
Are they return'd?—Madam, they are not yet . . . . . v 1 116
I set forth as soon as you And even but now return'd . . . v 1 272
Shall share the good of our returned fortune . . *As Y. Like It* v 4 180
Her will is, it should be so returned . . . . *T. Night* ii 2 15
The young gentleman of the Count Orsino's is returned . . . iii 4 63
Until it had return'd These terms of treason doubled . *Richard II.* i 1 56
When he's return'd, Against Aumerle we will enforce his trial . iv 1 89
My uncle is return'd: Deliver up my Lord of Westmoreland 1 *Hen. IV.* v 2 28
I hear his majesty is returned with some discomfort . 2 *Hen. IV.* i 2 118
Here is return'd my Lord of Westmoreland . . . . . iv 1 224
Talbot, my life, my joy, again return'd! . . . 1 *Hen. VI.* i 4 23
Answer was return'd that he will come.—Enough . . . . ii 5 20
Are not the speedy scouts return'd again? . . . . . iv 3 1
When returns Cranmer?—He is return'd in his opinions *Hen. VIII.* iii 2 64
Cranmer is return'd with welcome, Install'd lord archbishop . . iii 2 400
Who return'd her thanks In the great'st humbleness . . . v 1 64
Paris is returned home and hurt.—By whom? . . *Troi. and Cres.* i 1 112
These moral laws Of nature and of nations speak aloud To have her back return'd . . . . ii 2 186
From whence he returned, his brows bound with oak . *Coriolanus* i 3 15
Say that Marcius Return me, as Cominius is return'd, Unheard; what then? . . . . v 1 42
I am return'd your soldier, No more infected with my country's love Than when I parted hence . . . . v 6 71
Five times he hath return'd Bleeding to Rome . . . *T. Andron.* i 1 33
With honour and with fortune is return'd . . . . . . i 1 67
Till all these mischiefs be return'd again Even in their throats . . iii 1 274
Was stay'd by accident, and yesternight Return'd my letter *R. and J.* v 3 252
I would have put my wealth into donation, And the best half should have return'd to him . . . . *T. of Athens* iii 2 91
I hope it remains not unkindly with your lordship that I returned you an empty messenger . . . . iii 6 40
Are not Those in commission yet return'd? . . . . *Macbeth* i 4 2
Which had return'd To the inheritance of Fortinbras . *Hamlet* i 1 91
The ambassadors from Norway, my good lord, Are joyfully return'd . ii 2 41
If he be now return'd, As checking at his voyage . . . . iv 7 62
Hamlet return'd shall know you are come home . . . . iv 7 131
Follow'd the old man forth: he is return'd . . . . *Lear* ii 4 298
Was this before the king return'd?—No, since. . . . . iv 3 39
I return'd the rather For that I heard the clink and fall of swords *Othello* ii 3 233
Returned me expectations and comforts of sudden respect and acquaintance . . . . iv 2 191
Get you to bed on the instant; I will be returned forthwith . . iv 3 8
I return'd with simular proof enough . . . . *Cymbeline* v 5 200
Boult's returned. Now, sir, hast thou cried her through the market? *Pericles* iv 2 98
Returnest. To what purpose dost thou hoard thy words, That thou return'st no greeting to thy friends? . . . . . *Richard II.* i 3 254
Returneth. Ne'er returneth To blush and beautify the cheek 2 *Hen. VI.* iii 2 166
Alexander was buried, Alexander returneth into dust . . *Hamlet* v 1 232
Returning. Writ to my lady mother I am returning . . *All's Well* iv 3 103
And, he returning to break our necks, they respect not us . *Coriolanus* v 4 36
The games are done and Cæsar is returning . . . *J. Cæsar* i 2 178
Should I wade no more, Returning were as tedious as go o'er *Macbeth* iii 4 138
Re-united. By the which marriage the line of Charles the Great Was re-united to the crown of France . . . . . . *Hen. V.* i 2 85
Reveal yourself to him . . . . *Meas. for Meas.* v 1 28
Of all treasons, we still see them reveal themselves . . *All's Well* iv 3 27
We intended To keep in darkness what occasion now Reveals *T. Night* v 1 157
Madam, I have a secret to reveal . . . . . . 1 *Hen. VI.* v 3 100
Till the heavens Reveal the damn'd contriver of this deed *T. Andron.* iv 1 36
Good my lord, tell it.—No; you'll reveal it.—Not I, my lord *Hamlet* i 5 119
Reveal how thou at sea didst lose thy wife . . . *Pericles* v 1 245
Revealed. In complete glory she reveal'd herself . . 1 *Hen. VI.* i 2 83
And God in justice hath reveal'd to us The truth and innocence of this poor fellow . . . . 2 *Hen. VI.* ii 3 105
Never,—O fault!—reveal'd myself unto him, Until some half-hour past *Lear* v 3 192
Revel. Be cheerful, sir. Our revels now are ended . . . *Tempest* iv 1 148
Ask him why, that hour of fairy revel, In their so sacred paths he dares to tread In shape profane . . . . . . *Mer. Wives* iv 4 58
Did this companion with the saffron face Revel and feast it at my house to-day? . . . . *Com. of Errors* iv 4 65
Revels, dances, masks and merry hours Forerun fair Love . *L. L. Lost* iv 3 379
The king doth keep his revels here to-night . . *M. N. Dream* ii 1 18
If you will patiently dance in our round And see our moonlight revels ii 1 141
Where is our usual manager of mirth? What revels are in hand? . . v 1 36
A fortnight hold we this solemnity, In nightly revels and new jollity . v 1 377
Go to the feast, revel and domineer, Carouse full measure *T. of Shrew* iii 2 226
Return unto thy father's house And revel it as bravely as the best . iv 3 54
I delight in masques and revels sometimes altogether . . *T. Night* i 3 121
Shall we set about some revels?—What shall we do else? . . . i 3 145
This harness'd masque and unadvised revel . . . . *K. John* v 2 132
Revel the night, rob, murder, and commit The oldest sins 2 *Hen. IV.* iv 5 126
Revel. You cannot revel into dukedoms there . . . *Hen. V.* i 2 253
That Lewis of France is sending over masquers To revel it with him and his new bride . . . . 3 *Hen. VI.* iii 3 225; iv 1 95
To revel in the entrails of my lambs . . . . *Richard III.* iv 4 228
Crave leave to view these ladies and entreat An hour of revels *Hen. VIII.* i 4 72
They will out of their burrows, like conies after rain, and revel *Coriol.* iv 5 227
And revel in Lavinia's treasury . . . . . . *T. Andron.* ii 1 131
Some consequence yet hanging in the stars Shall bitterly begin his fearful date With this night's revels . . . . . *Rom. and Jul.* i 4 109
It may be thought we held him carelessly, Being our kinsman, if we revel much . . . . iii 4 26
Antony, that revels long o' nights, Is notwithstanding up . *J. Cæsar* ii 2 116
This heavy-headed revel east and west Makes us traduced and tax'd of other nations . . . . *Hamlet* i 4 17
Where joy most revels, grief doth most lament; Grief joys, joy grieves iii 2 208
Each man to what sport and revels his addiction leads him . *Othello* ii 2 6
What, man! 'tis a night of revels: the gallants desire it . . . ii 3 45
That we should, with joy, pleasance, revel and applause, transform ourselves into beasts! . . . . ii 3 293
He fishes, drinks, and wastes The lamps of night in revel *Ant. and Cleo.* i 4 5
Comedians Extemporally will stage us, and present Our Alexandrian revels . . . . v 2 218
And waste the time, which looks for other revels . . . *Pericles* ii 3 93
Revelled. Who all this while hath revell'd in the night . *Richard II.* iii 2 48
Was't you that revell'd in our parliament? . . . . 3 *Hen. VI.* i 4 71
His father revell'd in the heart of France, And tamed the king . . ii 2 150
Reveller. You moonshine revellers, and shades of night . *Mer. Wives* v 5 42
The revellers are entering, brother: make good room . . *Much Ado* ii 1 87
A peevish schoolboy, . . . Join'd with a masker and a reveller! *J. Cæsar* v 1 62
So merry and so gamesome: he is call'd The Briton reveller *Cymbeline* i 6 61
Revelling. I know we shall have revelling to-night . . . *Much Ado* i 1 322
With pomp, with triumph and with revelling . . . *M. N. Dream* i 1 19
Still revelling like lords till all be gone . . . . 2 *Hen. VI.* i 1 224
Revelry. And fall into our rustic revelry . . . . *As Y. Like It* v 4 183
Revenge. If thy greatness will Revenge it on him . . . *Tempest* iii 2 62
As in revenge of thy ingratitude . . . . . *T. G. of Ver.* i 2 110
For in revenge of my contempt of love, Love hath chased sleep from my enthralled eyes . . . . ii 4 133
I have operations which be humours of revenge . . . *Mer. Wives* i 3 99
Wilt thou revenge?—By welkin and her star! . . . . . . i 3 100
Let us knog our prains together to be revenge on this same scall . . iii 1 122
May we, with the warrant of womanhood and the witness of a good conscience, pursue him with any further revenge? . . . . . iv 2 222
Revenges to your heart, And general honour . . . *Meas. for Meas.* iv 3 140
With dangerous sense, Might in the times to come have ta'en revenge . iv 4 33
Choose your revenge yourself . . . . *Much Ado* v 1 282
And so dies my revenge.—O noble sir, Your over-kindness! . . . v 1 301
The winds, piping to us in vain, As in revenge. . . . *M. N. Dream* ii 1 89
I'll find Demetrius and revenge this spite . . . . . . iii 2 420
If it will feed nothing else, it will feed my revenge . *Mer. of Venice* iii 1 56
If you poison us, do we not die? and if you wrong us, shall we not revenge? iii 1 69
If a Jew wrong a Christian, what is his humility? Revenge . . . iii 1 72
If a Christian wrong a Jew, what should his sufferance be by Christian example? Why, revenge . . . . iii 1 74
No satisfaction, no revenge: nor no ill luck stirring but what lights on my shoulders . . . . iii 1 98
I should not seek an absent argument Of my revenge, thou present *As Y. Like It* iii 1 4
But kindness, nobler ever than revenge . . . . iv 3 129
I will go sit and weep Till I can find occasion of revenge *T. of Shrew* ii 1 36
Both my revenge and hate Loosing upon thee . . . *All's Well* ii 3 171
I have forgiven and forgotten all; Though my revenges were high bent v 3 10
On that vice in him will my revenge find notable cause to work *T. Night* ii 3 165
May rather pluck on laughter than revenge . . . . . . v 1 374
Thus the whirligig of time brings in his revenges . . . . . v 1 385
His revenges must In that be made more bitter . . . *W. Tale* i 2 456
The very thought of my revenges that way Recoil upon me . . . ii 3 19
See The flatness of my misery, yet with eyes Of pity, not revenge! . iii 2 124
Being transported by my jealousies To bloody thoughts and to revenge iii 2 160
Heaven shall be bribed To do him justice and revenge on you *K. John* ii 1 172
Where revenge did paint The fearful difference of incensed kings . . iii 1 237
Murder, as hating what himself hath done, Doth lay it open to urge on revenge . . . . iv 3 38
I have set a glory to this hand, By giving it the worship of revenge . iv 3 72
I do but stay behind To do the office for thee of revenge . . . v 7 71
If wrongfully, Let heaven revenge . . . . . . *Richard II.* i 2 40
Lament we may, but not revenge thee dead . . . . . . i 3 58
Lie so heavy on my sword, That it shall render vengeance and revenge iv 1 67
Revenge the jeering and disdain'd contempt Of this proud king 1 *Hen. IV.* i 3 183
Thou shalt find a king that will revenge Lord Stafford's death . . v 3 12
Counsel every man The aptest way for safety and revenge . 2 *Hen. IV.* i 1 213
He will drive you out of your revenge and turn all to a merriment . ii 4 324
Rouse up revenge from ebon den with fell Alecto's snake . . . v 5 39
Touching our person seek we no revenge . . . . . *Hen. V.* ii 2 174
By this leek, I will most horribly revenge: I eat and eat, I swear. . v 1 49
I take thy groat in earnest of revenge . . . . v 1 67
You all consented unto Salisbury's death, For none would strike a stroke in his revenge . . . . 1 *Hen. VI.* i 5 35
That hereafter ages may behold What ruin happen'd in revenge of him. ii 2 11
Now shine it like a comet of revenge! . . . . iii 2 31
Fly, to revenge my death, if I be slain . . . . iv 5 18
Fly, to revenge my death when I am dead . . . . . . iv 6 30
In thee thy mother dies, our household's name, My death's revenge . iv 6 39
Like an angry hive of bees That want their leader, scatter up and down And care not who they sting in his revenge . . . 2 *Hen. VI.* iii 2 127
And therefore to revenge it, shalt thou die . . . . . . iv 1 26
Therefore, when merchant-like I sell revenge, Broke be my sword! . iv 1 41
If he revenge it not, yet will his friends . . . . . . iv 1 146
Think therefore on revenge and cease to weep . . . . . . iv 4 3
You both have vow'd revenge On him, his sons, his favourites 3 *Hen. VI.* i 1 55
Such a messenger As shall revenge his death before I stir . . . i 1 100
They seek revenge and therefore will not yield . . . . . i 1 190
Had I thy brethren here, their lives and thine Were not revenge sufficient for me . . . . i 3 26
For his sake pity me, Lest in revenge thereof, sith God is just, He be as miserably slain as I . . . . i 3 41
My ashes, as the phœnix, may bring forth A bird that will revenge . i 4 36
Tears then for babes, blows and revenge for me! . . . . . ii 1 86
Withhold revenge, dear God! 'tis not my fault . . . . . ii 2 7
Warwick, revenge! brother, revenge my death! . . . . . ii 3 19

Revenge. I'll never pause again, never stand still, Till either death hath closed these eyes of mine Or fortune given me measure of revenge *3 Hen. VI.* ii 3 32
Bound to revenge, Wert thou environ'd with a brazen wall ii 4 3
I will revenge his wrong to Lady Bona iii 3 197
Not that I pity Henry's misery, But seek revenge on Edward's mockery iii 3 265
Nor forward of revenge, though they much err'd iv 8 46
O God, which this blood madest, revenge his death! O earth, which this blood drink'st, revenge his death! *Richard III.* i 2 62
No man but prophesied revenge for it i 3 186
God will revenge it ii 1 138; ii 2 14
I am hungry for revenge, And now I cloy me with beholding it iv 4 61
Even for revenge mock my destruction! v 1 9
Then fly. What, from myself? Great reason why: Lest I revenge v 3 186
To whom by oath he menaced Revenge upon the cardinal *Hen. VIII.* i 2 138
Merely to revenge him on the emperor For not bestowing on him ii 1 162
Pleasure and revenge Have ears more deaf than adders *Troi. and Cres.* ii 2 171
With comfort go: Hope of revenge shall hide our inward woe v 10 31
Let us revenge this with our pikes, ere we become rakes *Coriolanus* i 1 23
I speak this in hunger for bread, not in thirst for revenge i 1 25
For thy revenge Wrench up thy power to the highest i 8 10
If thou hast A heart of wreak in thee, that wilt revenge iv 5 91
If thou wilt have The leading of thine own revenges iv 5 143
Vows revenge as spacious as between The young'st and oldest thing iv 6 67
Think to front his revenges with the easy groans of old women? v 2 44
Though I owe My revenge properly, my remission lies In Volscian breasts v 2 90
O, a kiss Long as my exile, sweet as my revenge! v 3 45
Desire not To allay my rages and revenges with Your colder reasons v 3 85
The self-same gods that arm'd the Queen of Troy With opportunity of sharp revenge Upon the Thracian tyrant *T. Andron.* i 1 137
What, madam! be dishonour'd openly, And basely put it up without revenge? i 1 433
Such quarrels may be broach'd Without controlment, justice, or revenge? ii 1 68
Blood and revenge are hammering in my head ii 3 39
Revenge it, as you love your mother's life ii 3 114
Then be joyful, Because the law hath ta'en revenge on them iii 1 117
Then which way shall I find Revenge's cave? iii 1 271
Eat no more Than will preserve just so much strength in us As will revenge these bitter woes of ours iii 2 3
To heaven she heaves them [her arms] for revenge iv 1 40
And here display, at last, What God will have discover'd for revenge iv 1 74
We will prosecute by good advice Mortal revenge upon these iv 1 93
So just that he will not revenge. Revenge, ye heavens, for old Andronicus! iv 1 128
Pluto sends you word, If you will have Revenge from hell, you shall iv 3 38
Threats, in course of this revenge, to do As much as ever Coriolanus did iv 4 67
Say I am Revenge, sent from below To join with him v 2 3
Knock at his study, where, they say, he keeps, To ruminate strange plots of dire revenge; Tell him Revenge is come to join with him v 2 6
I am Revenge; sent from the infernal kingdom, To ease the gnawing vulture of thy mind, By working wreakful vengeance on thy foes v 2 30
Tell them my dreadful name, Revenge, which makes the foul offender quake v 2 40
Art thou Revenge? and art thou sent to me, To be a torment to mine enemies? v 2 41
Now give some surance that thou art Revenge, Stab them, or tear them v 2 46
O sweet Revenge, now do I come to thee v 2 67
For now he firmly takes me for Revenge v 2 73
I'll call my brother back again, And cleave to no revenge but Lucius v 2 136
Revenge now goes To lay a complot to betray thy foes.—I know thou dost; and, sweet Revenge, farewell v 2 146
You know your mother means to feast with me, And calls herself Revenge v 2 186
Now judge what cause had Titus to revenge These wrongs, unspeakable v 3 125
Who had but newly entertain'd revenge *Rom. and Jul.* iii 1 176
He's poor, and that's revenge enough *T. of Athens* iii 4 63
To revenge is no valour, but to bear iii 5 39
If thy revenges hunger for that food Which nature loathes v 4 32
For those that were, it is not square to take On those that are, revenges v 4 37
Cæsar's spirit, ranging for revenge, With Ate by his side *J. Cæsar* iii 1 270
Revenge! About! Seek! Burn! Fire! Kill! Slay! iii 2 208
Most noble Cæsar! We'll revenge his death iii 2 248
Come, Revenge yourselves alone on Cassius iv 3 94
Fly, good Fleance, fly, fly, fly! Thou mayst revenge *Macbeth* iii 3 18
Let's make us medicines of our great revenge, To cure this deadly grief iv 3 214
Revenges burn in them v 2 3
Speak; I am bound to hear.—So art thou to revenge *Hamlet* i 5 7
Revenge his foul and most unnatural murder.—Murder! i 5 25
With wings as swift As meditation . . . May sweep to my revenge i 5 31
Prompted to my revenge by heaven and hell ii 2 613
The croaking raven doth bellow for revenge iii 2 265
O, this is hire and salary, not revenge iii 3 79
How all occasions do inform against me, And spur my dull revenge! iv 5 33
Is't writ in your revenge, That, swoopstake, you will draw both friend and foe, Winner and loser? iv 4 141
Hadst thou thy wits, and didst persuade revenge, It could not move thus iv 5 168
My revenge will come.—Break not your sleeps for that iv 7 29
Revenge should have no bounds iv 7 129
I am satisfied in nature, Whose motive, in this case, should stir me most To my revenge v 2 257
You unnatural hags, I will have such revenges on you both *Lear* ii 4 282
I will have my revenge ere I depart his house iii 5 1
The revenges we are bound to take upon your traitorous father are not fit for your beholding iii 7 7
Gloucester, I live To thank thee for the love thou show'dst the king, And to revenge thine eyes iv 2 97
Let us be conjunctive in our revenge against him *Othello* i 3 375
She that being anger'd, her revenge being nigh, Bade her wrong stay ii 1 153
Partly led to diet my revenge, For that I do suspect the lusty Moor ii 1 303
O, that the slave had forty thousand lives! One is too poor, too weak for my revenge iii 3 443
Till that a capable and wide revenge Swallow them up iii 3 459
We have galls, and though we have some grace, Yet have we some revenge iv 3 94
Had all his hairs been lives, my great revenge Had stomach for them all v 2 74
Then murder's out of tune, And sweet revenge grows harsh v 2 116
Revenge it. I dedicate myself to your sweet pleasure *Cymbeline* i 6 135
Revenges, hers [woman's]; Ambitions, covetings, change of prides, disdain, Nice longing ii 5 24
From proof as strong as my grief and as certain as I expect my revenge iii 4 25
She hath despised me rejoicingly, and I'll be merry in my revenge iii 5 150
Revenge. My revenge is now at Milford: would I had wings to follow it! *Cymbeline* iii 5 160
Would I had done't, So the revenge alone pursued me! iv 2 157
I would revenges, That possible strength might meet, would seek us iv 2 159
With Juno chide, That thy adulteries Rates and revenges v 4 34
The gods revenge it upon me and mine, To the end of generation! *Pericles* iii 3 24
Revenged. I'll after, more to be revenged on Eglamour *T. G. of Ver.* v 2 51
How shall I be revenged on him? for revenged I will be *Mer. Wives* ii 1 30
Let's be revenged on him: let's appoint him a meeting ii 1 96
I will prevent this, detect my wife, be revenged on Falstaff ii 2 326
This knave Ford, on whom to-night I will be revenged v 1 30
Well, I'll be revenged as I may *Much Ado* ii 1 217
Her silence flouts me, and I'll be revenged *T. of Shrew* ii 1 29
But I will in, to be revenged for this villany v 1 139
I'll be revenged on the whole pack of you *T. Night* v 1 386
He does, he does: we'll be revenged on him *1 Hen. IV.* i 3 291
I could tear her: I'll be revenged of her *2 Hen. IV.* ii 4 167
But we will be revenged sufficiently *1 Hen. VI.* i 4 58
How dying Salisbury doth groan! It irks his heart he cannot be revenged i 4 105
If I be not, heavens be revenged on me! *3 Hen. VI.* i 1 57
Revenged may she be on that hateful duke! i 1 266
Be thou revenged on men, and let me live.—In vain thou speak'st i 3 20
How shall Bona be revenged But by thy help to this distressed queen? iii 3 212
I would I were, to be revenged on thee *Richard III.* i 2 133
A quarrel most unnatural, To be revenged on him that loveth you.—It is a quarrel just and reasonable, To be revenged on him that slew my husband i 2 137
And withal whet me To be revenged on Rivers, Vaughan, Grey i 3 333
If God will be revenged for this deed, O, know you yet, he doth it publicly i 4 221
I am joyful To meet the least occasion that may give me Remembrance of my father-in-law, the duke, To be revenged on him *Hen. VIII.* iii 2 9
To the Goths, and raise a power, To be revenged on Rome *T. Andron.* iii 1 301
Show me a villain that hath done a rape, And I am sent to be revenged v 2 95
Show me a thousand that have done thee wrong, And I will be revenged v 2 97
And worse than Progne I will be revenged v 2 196
We will be revenged.—Revenge! About! Seek! Burn! *J. Cæsar* iii 2 207
And so he goes to heaven; And so am I revenged *Hamlet* iii 3 75
Am I then revenged, To take him in the purging of his soul? iii 3 84
Let come what comes; only I'll be revenged Most throughly for my father iv 5 135
These injuries the king now bears will be revenged home *Lear* iii 3 13
When I am revenged upon my charm, I have done all *Ant. and Cleo.* iv 12 16
Be revenged; Or she that bore you was no queen *Cymbeline* i 6 126
Revenged! How should I be revenged? If this be true,—As I have such a heart that both mine ears Must not in haste abuse—if it be true, How should I be revenged? i 6 128
I'll be revenged: 'His meanest garment!' Well ii 3 160
I will conclude to hate her, nay, indeed, To be revenged upon her iii 5 79
I fear 'twill be revenged: Would, Polydore, thou hadst not done't! iv 2 154
Revengeful. And never brandish more revengeful steel! *Richard II.* iv 1 50
Stay thy revengeful hand; thou hast no cause to fear v 3 42
Or shall we on the helmets of our foes Tell our devotion with revengeful arms? If for the last, say ay, and to it *3 Hen. VI.* ii 1 164
If thy revengeful heart cannot forgive *Richard III.* i 2 174
You know his nature, That he's revengeful *Hen. VIII.* i 1 109
My revengeful services may prove As benefits to thee *Coriolanus* iv 5 95
With revengeful war Take wreak on Rome for this ingratitude *T. An.* iv 3 32
I am very proud, revengeful, ambitious *Hamlet* iii 1 126
Revengement. Out of my blood He'll breed revengement *1 Hen. IV.* iii 2 7
Revenger. I do not know Wherefore my father should revengers want, Having a son and friends *Ant. and Cleo.* ii 6 11
And now Pleased fortune does of Marcus Crassus' death Make me revenger iii 1 3
Revenging. Burns with revenging fire *2 Hen. VI.* iv 1 97
The revenging gods 'Gainst parricides did all their thunders bend *Lear* ii 1 47
Revengingly. I have belied a lady, The princess of this country, and the air on't Revengingly enfeebles me *Cymbeline* v 2 4
Revenue. Not only with what my revenue yielded *Tempest* i 2 98
Or a dowager Long withering out a young man's revenue *M. N. Dream* i 1 6
I have a widow aunt, a dowager Of great revenue i 1 158
Whose lands and revenues enrich the new duke *As Y. Like It* i 1 107
Simply your having in beard is a younger brother's revenue iii 2 397
All the revenue that was old Sir Rowland's will I estate upon you v 2 12
I purchased this caparison, and my revenue is the silly cheat *W. Tale* iv 3 28
This juggling witchcraft with revenue cherish *K. John* iii 1 169
We are inforced to farm our royal realm; The revenue whereof shall furnish us For our affairs in hand *Richard II.* i 4 46
We do seize to us The plate, coin, revenues, and moveables ii 1 161
Barely in title, not in revenue.—Richly in both, if justice had her right ii 1 226
My manors, rents, revenues I forego iv 1 212
She bears a duke's revenues on her back *2 Hen. VI.* i 3 83
As my ripe revenue and due by birth *Richard III.* iii 7 158
For the wide world's revenue *Troi. and Cres.* ii 2 206
The common curse of mankind, folly and ignorance, be thine in great revenue! ii 3 31
What advancement may I hope from thee That no revenue hast? *Hamlet* iii 2 63
The sway, revenue, execution of the rest, Beloved sons, be yours *Lear* i 1 139
If our father would sleep till I waked him, you should enjoy half his revenue i 2 56
The father should be as ward to the son, and the son manage his revenue i 2 79
'Tis they have put him on the old man's death, To have the expense and waste of his revenues ii 1 102
And, being, that we detain All his revenue *Ant. and Cleo.* iii 6 30
'Shrew me, If I would lose it for a revenue Of any king's in Europe *Cymbeline* ii 3 148
Reverb. Nor are those empty-hearted whose low sound Reverbs no hollowness *Lear* i 1 156
Reverberate. Halloo your name to the reverberate hills *T. Night* i 5 291
Even at hand a drum is ready braced That shall reverberate all as loud as thine *K. John* v 2 170
Who, like an arch, reverberates The voice again *Troi. and Cres.* iii 3 120
Reverence. Saving your honour's reverence *Meas. for Meas.* ii 1 92
Knavery cannot, sure, hide himself in such reverence *Much Ado* ii 3 125
I think you would have me say, 'saving your reverence, a husband' iii 4 32
Trust not my age, My reverence, calling, nor divinity iv 1 170
That I am forced to lay my reverence by v 1 64
Petty traffickers, That curtsy to them, do them reverence *Mer. of Venice* i 1 13
Who, saving your reverence, is the devil himself ii 2 27

Reverence. His master and he, saving your worship's reverence, are scarce cater-cousins . . . *Mer. of Venice* ii 2 139
I confess, your coming before me is nearer to his reverence *As Y. Like It* i 1 54
With a low submissive reverence Say . . . *T. of Shrew* Ind. 1 53
Father, I charge thee, by thy reverence, Here to unfold . *T. Night* v 1 154
The reverence Of the grave wearers . . . *W. Tale* iii 1 5
So tell the pope, all reverence set apart To him . . *K. John* iii 1 159
The fair reverence of your highness curbs me . . *Richard II.* i 1 54
Which fear, not reverence, makes thee to except . . . i 1 72
What reverence he did throw away on slaves, Wooing poor craftsmen i 4 27
Cover your heads and mock not flesh and blood With solemn reverence iii 2 172
A clergyman Of holy reverence . . . . . iii 3 29
That he is, saving your reverence, a whoremaster . . 1 *Hen. IV.* ii 4 515
To hear with reverence Your exposition on the holy text 2 *Hen. IV.* iv 2 6
O, who shall believe But you misuse the reverence of your place? . iv 2 23
In approbation Of what your reverence shall incite us to *Hen. V.* i 2 20
I am sorry that with reverence I did not entertain thee . 1 *Hen. VI.* ii 3 71
Madam, be still; with reverence may I say . 2 *Hen. VI.* iii 2 207
In thy reverence and thy chair-days . . . . . v 2 48
For reverence to some alive, I give a sparing limit to my tongue *Rich. III.* iii 7 193
You are a saucy fellow: Deserve we no more reverence? *Hen. VIII.* iv 2 101
I could say more, But reverence to your calling makes me modest v 3 69
I ask, that I might waken reverence . . . *Troi. and Cres.* i 3 227
What god soe'er it be, That thou adorest and hast in reverence *T. An.* v 1 83
'Tis thou [gold] that rigg'st the bark and plough'st the foam, Settlest admired reverence in a slave . . . *T. of Athens* v 1 54
With all kind love, good thoughts, and reverence . *J. Cæsar* iii 1 176
Now lies he there, And none so poor to do him reverence iii 2 125
This policy and reverence of age makes the world bitter to the best of our times . . . . . *Lear* i 2 48
You beastly knave, know you no reverence? . . . ii 2 75
Whose reverence even the head-lugg'd bear would lick . . iv 2 42
Let this kiss Repair those violent harms that my two sisters Have in thy reverence made! . . . . . iv 7 29
Do not believe That from the sense of all civility, I thus would play and trifle with your reverence . . . *Othello* i 1 133
In the due reverence of a sacred vow I here engage my words . iii 3 461
Saving reverence of the word . . . *Cymbeline* iv 1 5
Those that I reverence those I fear, the wise: At fools I laugh iv 2 95
Yet reverence, That angel of the world, doth make distinction Of place 'tween high and low . . . . . . iv 2 247
We do not look for reverence, but for love, And harbourage . *Pericles* i 4 99
And he the sun, for them to reverence . . . ii 3 40

Reverenced. We'll set thy statue in some holy place, And have thee reverenced like a blessed saint . . . 1 *Hen. VI.* iii 3 15
Therein reverenced for their lawful king . . . . v 4 140

Reverend. Yonder is a most reverend gentleman *Mer. Wives* iii 1 52
Of very reverend reputation, sir, Of credit infinite . *Com. of Errors* v 1 5
She is a virtuous and a reverend lady . . . . v 1 134
Your worship speaks like a most thankful and reverend youth *Much Ado* v 1 325
There is no staff more reverend than one tipped with horn . v 4 125
Very reverend sport, truly . . . . *L. L. Lost* iv 2 1
I beseech you, let his lack of years be no impediment to let him lack a reverend estimation . . . *Mer. of Venice* iv 1 163
Let me look upon the bond.—Here 'tis, most reverend doctor . iv 1 226
I intend That all is done in reverend care of her *T. of Shrew* iv 1 207
Now I perceive thou art a reverend father . . . iv 5 48
Now by law, as well as reverend age, I may entitle thee my loving father iv 5 60
A sad face, a reverend carriage, a slow tongue . . *T. Night* iii 4 80
Reverend sirs, For you there's rosemary and rue . *W. Tale* iv 4 73
Good reverend father, make my person yours, And tell me *K. John* iii 1 224
Choose out some secret place, some reverend room . *Richard II.* v 6 25
That reverend vice, that grey iniquity, that father ruffian . 1 *Hen. IV.* ii 4 499
Leads ancient lords and reverend bishops on To bloody battles . iii 2 104
I am bound to thee, reverend Feeble . . 2 *Hen. IV.* iii 2 181
You, reverend father, and these noble lords Had not been here . iv 1 38
Their most reverend heads dash'd to the walls. . . *Hen. V.* iii 3 37
Seven earls, twelve barons and twenty reverend bishops . 2 *Hen. VI.* i 1 8
Well accompanied With reverend fathers and well-learned bishops *Richard III.* iii 5 100
He is within, with two right reverend fathers . . . iii 7 61
As mother, And reverend looker on, of two fair queens . . iv 1 31
If ancient sorrow be most reverend, Give mine the benefit of seniory . iv 4 35
The right reverend Cardinal of York.—The devil speed him! *Hen. VIII.* i 1 51
All this business Our reverend cardinal carried . . . i 1 100
You're welcome, Most learned reverend sir, into our kingdom . ii 2 77
You have here, lady, And of your choice, these reverend fathers . ii 4 58
By all the reverend fathers of the land And doctors learn'd . ii 4 205
Unsolicited I left no reverend person in this court . . ii 4 220
What are your pleasures with me, reverend lords? . . . iii 1 26
Holy men I thought ye, Upon my soul, two reverend cardinal virtues . iii 1 103
Come, reverend fathers, Bestow your counsels on me . . iii 1 181
With other Learned and reverend fathers of his order . . iv 1 26
What two reverend bishops Were those that went on each side of the queen? . . . . iv 1 99
The reverend abbot, With all his covent, honourably received him iv 2 18
Thou most reverend for thy stretch'd-out life . *Troi. and Cres.* i 3 61
Most reverend Nestor, I am glad to clasp thee . . . iv 5 204
Though I must be content to bear with those that say you are reverend grave men, yet they lie . . . *Coriolanus* ii 1 66
Therefore, please you, Most reverend and grave elders . . ii 2 46
By my father's reverend tomb, I vow . . *T. Andron.* ii 3 296
O reverend tribunes! O gentle, aged men! Unbind my sons . iii 1 23
Come, thou reverend man of Rome, And bring our emperor . v 3 137
This reverend holy friar, All our whole city is much bound to him *Rom. and Jul.* iv 2 31
For I know your reverend ages love Security . *T. of Athens* iii 5 80
The Athenians, By two of their most reverend senate, greet thee . v 1 132
Declining on the milky head Of reverend Priam . *Hamlet* ii 2 501
As you are old and reverend, you should be wise . *Lear* i 4 261
You stubborn ancient knave, you reverend braggart, We'll teach you . ii 2 133
Most reverend signior, do you know my voice?—Not I . *Othello* i 1 93
The Ottomites, reverend and gracious, Steering with due course . i 3 33
Most potent, grave, and reverend signiors . . . . i 3 76
Hail, reverend sir! the gods preserve you!—And you, sir . *Pericles* v 1 14
This is your wife.—Reverend appearer, no; I threw her overboard . v 3 18
Reverend sir, The gods can have no mortal officer More like a god than you . . . . v 3 61

Reverendest. I do prize it at my love before The reverend'st throat in Athens . . . . *T. of Athens* v 1 185

Reverent. What is she?—A very reverent body . *Com. of Errors* iii 2 91
Beseech your lordship to have a reverent care of your health . 2 *Hen. IV.* i 2 113
Thou art reverent Touching thy spiritual function, not thy life 1 *Hen. VI.* iii 1 49
Do not fear nor fly! For I will touch thee but with reverent hands v 3 47
The reverent care I bear unto my lord Made me . . 2 *Hen. VI.* iii 1 34

Reverently. Chide him for faults, and do it reverently . 2 *Hen. IV.* iv 4 37
How may I reverently worship thee enough? . . 1 *Hen. VI.* i 2 145
Northumberland, I hold thee reverently . . . 3 *Hen. VI.* ii 2 109

Reverse. To see thee pass thy punto, thy stock, thy reverse *Mer. Wives* ii 3 27
Unbind my sons, reverse the doom of death . *T. Andron.* iii 1 24
Unless philosophy can make a Juliet, Displant a town, reverse a prince's doom, It helps not, it prevails not . . *Rom. and Jul.* iii 3 59
Reverse thy doom; And, in thy best consideration, check This *Lear* i 1 151

Reversed. Is Clarence dead? the order was reversed *Richard III.* ii 1 86

Reversion. As were our England in reversion his . . *Richard II.* i 4 35
'Tis in reversion that I do possess . . . . ii 2 38
Where now remains a sweet reversion . . . 1 *Hen. IV.* iv 1 53
No perfection in reversion shall have a praise in present *Troi. and Cres.* iii 2 100

Reverso. The immortal passado! the punto reverso! . *Rom. and Jul.* ii 4 27

Reverted. Armed and reverted, making war against her heir *Com. of Er.* iii 2 126
My arrows, Too slightly timber'd for so loud a wind, Would have reverted to my bow again . . . . . *Hamlet* iv 7 23

Review. In whose company I shall review Sicilia . *W. Tale* iv 4 680

Revile. Did not she herself revile me there? . *Com. of Errors* iv 4 75

Reviled. Did not she herself revile me there?—Sans fable, she herself reviled you there . . . . . . iv 4 76
His eye reviled Me, as his abject object . . *Hen. VIII.* i 1 126

Revisitest. What may this mean, That thou, dead corse, again in complete steel Revisit'st thus the glimpses of the moon? . *Hamlet* i 4 53

Revive. So play the foolish throngs with one that swoons; Come all to help him, and so stop the air By which he should revive *Meas. for Meas.* ii 4 26
Our waggon is prepared, and time revives us . . *All's Well* iv 4 34
With my breath I can revive it . . . . *K. John* iv 1 112
To end one doubt by death Revives two greater in the heirs of life 2 *Hen. IV.* iv 1 200
Henry is dead and never shall revive . . 1 *Hen. VI.* i 1 18
I should revive the soldiers' hearts, Because I ever found them as myself . . . . iii 2 97
He doth revive again: madam, be patient . 2 *Hen. VI.* iii 2 36
O Clifford, how thy words revive my heart! . 3 *Hen. VI.* i 1 163
Those gracious words revive my drooping thoughts . . iii 3 21
My only life, Revive, look up, or I will die with thee! *Rom. and Jul.* iv 5 20
Thus might he pass indeed: yet he revives . . *Lear* iv 6 47
Branches, which, being dead many years, shall after revive *Cymbeline* v 4 142; v 5 439

Revived. What thing, in honour, had my father lost, That need to be revived and breathed in me? . . . . 2 *Hen. IV.* iv 1 114
That Talbot's name might be in thee revived . 1 *Hen. VI.* iv 5 3
How well my comfort is revived by this! . *Rom. and Jul.* iii 3 165
Breathed such life with kisses in my lips, That I revived . . v 1 9
Is not this boy revived from death? . . . *Cymbeline* v 5 120
For many years thought dead, are now revived . . . v 5 456

Reviving. From you great Rome shall suck Reviving blood . *J. Cæsar* ii 2 88
The locking-up the spirits a time, To be more fresh, reviving *Cymbeline* i 5 42
3 *Hen. VI.* ii 6 46

Revoke that doom of mercy . . . . .
And on a safer judgement all revoke Your ignorant election . *Coriolanus* ii 3 226
Revoke Your sudden approbation . . . . . ii 3 258
Revoke thy doom; Or, whilst I can vent clamour from my throat, I'll tell thee thou dost evil . . . . . . *Lear* i 1 167

Revoked. Away! by Jupiter, This shall not be revoked . . . i 1 182

Revokement. Let it be noised That through our intercession this revokement And pardon comes . . . . *Hen. VIII.* i 2 106

Revolt. You are already Love's firm votary And cannot soon revolt and change your mind . . . . . *T. G. of Ver.* iii 2 59
Possess him with yellowness, for the revolt of mine is dangerous *M. W.* i 3 111
The blood of youth burns not with such excess As gravity's revolt to wantonness . . . . . . *L. L. Lost* v 2 74
With well-weighing sums of gold, to corrupt him to a revolt . *All's Well* iv 3 204
I need not to ask you if gold will corrupt him to revolt . . iv 3 310
That suffer surfeit, cloyment and revolt . . *T. Night* ii 4 102
Blessed shall he be that doth revolt From his allegiance to an heretic *K. John* iii 1 174
O foul revolt of French inconstancy! . . . . iii 1 322
The hearts Of all his people shall revolt from him . . iii 4 165
Pick strong matter of revolt and wrath Out of the bloody fingers' ends iii 4 167
The faiths of men ne'er stained with revolt . . . iv 2 6
Our discontented counties do revolt; Our people quarrel with obedience v 1 8
Believe me, prince, I am not glad that such a sore of time Should seek a plaster by contemn'd revolt . . . . . . v 2 13
You degenerate, you ingrate revolts, You bloody Neroes . . v 2 151
Lead me to the revolts of England here . . . . v 4 7
The commons they are cold, And will, I fear, revolt *Richard II.* ii 2 89
Revolt our subjects? that we cannot mend . . . iii 2 100
Let not him be slander'd with revolt . . . 1 *Hen. IV.* i 3 112
How quickly nature falls into revolt When gold becomes her object! 2 *Hen. IV.* iv 5 66
This revolt of thine, methinks, is like Another fall of man *Hen. V.* ii 2 141
What! doth my uncle Burgundy revolt? . . 1 *Hen. VI.* iv 1 64
The stout Parisians do revolt And turn again unto the warlike French v 2 2
The king is merciful, if you revolt . . . 2 *Hen. VI.* iv 2 133
All will revolt from me, and turn to him . . 3 *Hen. VI.* i 1 151
Thou wilt revolt, and fly to him, I fear . . *Richard III.* iv 4 478
If I revolt, off goes young George's head . . . iv 5 4
Bi-fold authority! where reason can revolt Without perdition, and loss assume all reason Without revolt . . . *Troi. and Cres.* v 2 146
Were half to half the world by the ears and he Upon my party, I'ld revolt, to make Only my wars with him . . . *Coriolanus* i 1 238
Their mutinies and revolts, wherein they show'd Most valour . iii 1 126
All the regions Do smilingly revolt; and who resist Are mock'd . iv 6 103
And will revolt from me to succour him . . *T. Andron.* iv 4 80
Revolts from true birth, stumbling on abuse . *Rom. and Jul.* ii 3 20
Or my true heart with treacherous revolt Turn to another . . iv 1 58
I have but little gold of late, brave Timon, The want whereof doth daily make revolt In my penurious band . . . *T. of Athens* iv 3 91
He can report, As seemeth by his plight, of the revolt . *Macbeth* i 2 2
Now minutely revolts upbraid his faith-breach . . . v 2 18
Both more and less have given him the revolt . . . v 4 12
Mere fetches; The images of revolt and flying off . . *Lear* ii 4 91

Revolt. Your daughter, if you have not given her leave, I say again, hath made a gross revolt . . . . . . *Othello* i 1 135
Nor from mine own weak merits will I draw The smallest fear or doubt of her revolt; For she had eyes, and chose me . . . . iii 3 188
And flush youth revolt . . . . . *Ant. and Cleo.* i 4 52
Alexas did revolt; and went to Jewry on Affairs of Antony . . . iv 6 12
O Antony, Nobler than my revolt is infamous, Forgive me . . iv 9 19
All the plagues of hell should at one time Encounter such revolt *Cymb.* i 6 112
All good seeming, By thy revolt, O husband, shall be thought Put on . iii 4 57
Or receive us For barbarous and unnatural revolts . . . iv 4 6
But I must tell you, now my thoughts revolt . . . *Pericles* i 1 78
Revolted. Our revolted wives share damnation together . *Mer. Wives* iii 2 40
Should all despair That have revolted wives, the tenth of mankind Would hang themselves . . . . . . *W. Tale* i 2 199
Why have you not proclaim'd Northumberland And all the rest revolted faction traitors? . . . . . . *Richard II.* ii 2 57
To ransom home revolted Mortimer.—Revolted Mortimer! He never did fall off, my sovereign liege . . . . . 1 *Hen. IV.* i 3 93
Revolted tapsters and ostlers trade-fallen . . . . iv 2 31
France is revolted from the English quite . . . 1 *Hen. VI.* i 1 90
By means whereof the towns each day revolted . . 2 *Hen. VI.* iii 1 63
Farewell, revolted fair! and, Diomed, Stand fast! . *Troi. and Cres.* v 2 186
The kings that have revolted, and the soldier That has this morning left thee, would have still Follow'd thy heels . *Ant. and Cleo.* iv 5 4
Plant those that have revolted in the van, That Antony may seem to spend his fury Upon himself . . . . . . iv 6 9
When men revolted shall upon record Bear hateful memory . . iv 9 8
Revolting. Let the church, our mother, breathe her curse, A mother's curse, on her revolting son . . . . . *K. John* iii 1 257
Our sighs and they shall lodge the summer corn, And make a dearth in this revolting land . . . . . . *Richard II.* iii 3 163
The bad revolting stars That have consented unto Henry's death! 1 *Hen. VI.* i 1 4
The false revolting Normans thorough thee Disdain to call us lord
2 *Hen. VI.* iv 1 87
Revolution. Full of forms, figures, shapes, objects, ideas, apprehensions, motions, revolutions . . . . . *L. L. Lost* iv 2 70
O God! that one might read the book of fate, And see the revolution of the times Make mountains level! . . . . 2 *Hen. IV.* iii 1 46
Here's fine revolution, an we had the trick to see't . . *Hamlet* v 1 98
The present pleasure, By revolution lowering, does become The opposite of itself: she's good, being gone . . . *Ant. and Cleo.* i 2 129
Revolve. If this fall into thy hand, revolve . . . *T. Night* ii 5 155
Where, from company, I may revolve and ruminate my grief 1 *Hen. VI.* v 5 101
And never suffers matter of the world Enter his thoughts, save such as do revolve And ruminate himself . . . *Troi. and Cres.* ii 3 197
You may then revolve what tales I have told you Of courts . *Cymbeline* iii 3 14
Revolving this will teach thee how to curse . . . *Richard III.* iv 4 123
Reward. A most unholy match, Which heaven and fortune still rewards with plagues . . . . . . *T. G. of Ver.* iv 3 31
I desire nothing but the reward of a villain . . . *Much Ado* v 1 250
Is 'old dog' my reward? . . . . . *As Y. Like It* i 1 86
Proffers not took reap thanks for their reward . . *All's Well* ii 1 150
Though I with death and with Reward did threaten and encourage him, Not doing't and being done . . . . . *W. Tale* iii 2 165
God reward me for it! . . . . . . 1 *Hen. IV.* iii 3 54
Let them that should reward valour bear the sin upon their own heads v 4 153
I'll follow, as they say, for reward. He that rewards me, God reward him! . . . . v 4 166
I never knew yet but rebuke and check was the reward of valour
2 *Hen. IV.* iv 3 35
Yet never have you tasted our reward, Or been reguerdon'd with so much as thanks . . . . . . 1 *Hen. VI.* iii 4 22
Here, Hume, take this reward; make merry, man . . 2 *Hen. VI.* i 2 85
Give me leave, my Lord of York, To be the post, in hope of his reward i 4 81
Come, fellow, follow us for thy reward . . . . ii 3 108
I will reward you for this venturous deed . . . . iii 2 9
Thus will I reward thee, the Lent shall be as long again as it is . iv 3 7
Shall have a thousand crowns for his reward . . . iv 8 70
Rise up a knight. We give thee for reward a thousand marks . v 1 79
With promise of high pay and great rewards . . 3 *Hen. VI.* ii 1 134
Promise them such rewards As victors wear at the Olympian games ii 3 52
There's thy reward: be gone . . . . . . iii 3 233
Who finds Edward Shall have a high reward, and he his life . . v 5 10
Remember our reward, when the deed is done.—'Zounds, he dies: I had forgot the reward . . . . . *Richard III.* i 4 126
When he opens his purse to give us our reward, thy conscience flies out i 4 133
Who shall reward you better for my life Than Edward will for tidings of my death.—You are deceived . . . . . . i 4 236
Rewards he my true service With such deep contempt? . . iv 2 123
Hath any well-advised friend proclaim'd Reward? . . . iv 4 518
And, no doubt, In time will find their fit rewards . . *Hen. VIII.* iii 2 245
In sign of what you are, not to reward What you have done *Coriolanus* i 9 26
Rewards His deeds with doing them, and is content . . ii 2 131
These that survive let Rome reward with love . . *T. Andron.* i 1 82
Look for thy reward Among the nettles at the elder-tree . . ii 3 271
Deliver up your pigeons, and then look for your reward . . iv 3 112
His honesty rewards him in itself . . . . *T. of Athens* i 1 130
Let them be received, Not without fair reward . . . . i 2 197
They froze me into silence.—You gods, reward them! . . . ii 2 222
A man that fortune's buffets and rewards Hast ta'en with equal thanks
Hamlet iii 2 72
That soaks up the king's countenance, his rewards, his authorities iv 2 17
Our potency made good, take thy reward . . . . *Lear* i 1 175
The gods reward your kindness! . . . . . . iii 6 5
Love me and reward me, For making him egregiously an ass . *Othello* ii 1 317
To let a fellow that will take rewards And say, 'God quit you!' be familiar with My playfellow, your hand! . . *Ant. and Cleo.* iii 13 123
I will reward thee Once for thy spritely comfort . . . iv 7 14
To my grief, I am The heir of his reward . . . . *Cymbeline* v 5 13
Though This king were great, his greatness was no guard To bar heaven's shaft, but sin had his reward . . . . *Pericles* ii 4 15
You have heard Of monstrous lust the due and just reward . v 3 Gower 86
Rewarded. I am more bound to you than your fellows, for they are but lightly rewarded . . . . . *L. L. Lost* i 2 157
Almost forgot my prayers to content him? And am I thus rewarded?
Hen. VIII. iii 1 133
Rewarder. A liberal rewarder of his friends . . *Richard III.* i 3 124
Rewarding. There is remuneration; for the best ward of mine honour is rewarding my dependents . . . . *L. L. Lost* iii 1 134
Re-word. Bring me to the test, And I the matter will re-word *Hamlet* iii 4 143

Rex Angliæ, et Hæres Franciæ . . . . *Hen. V.* v 2 370
'Ego et Rex meus' Was still inscribed . . . . *Hen. VIII.* iii 2 314
Reynaldo. Give him this money and these notes, Reynaldo *Hamlet* ii 1 1
You shall do marvellous wisely, good Reynaldo . . . . ii 1 3
Do you mark this, Reynaldo?—Ay, very well, my lord . . . ii 1 15
Rhapsody. And sweet religion makes A rhapsody of words . . iii 4 48
Rheims. Hath been long studying at Rheims . . . *T. of Shrew* ii 1 81
Rheims, Orleans, Paris, Guysors, Poictiers, are all quite lost 1 *Hen. VI.* i 1 60
The Dauphin Charles is crowned king in Rheims . . . . i 1 92
Rhenish. For fear of the worst, I pray thee, set a deep glass of rhenish wine on the contrary casket . . . *Mer. of Venice* i 2 104
More [difference] between your bloods than there is between red wine and rhenish . . . . iii 1 44
As he drains his draughts of Rhenish down, The kettle-drum and trumpet thus bray out The triumph of his pledge . . *Hamlet* i 4 10
A mad rogue! a' poured a flagon of Rhenish on my head once . v 1 197
Rhesus. As Ulysses and stout Diomede With sleight and manhood stole to Rhesus' tents . . . . . . 3 *Hen. VI.* iv 2 20
Rhetoric. By the heart's still rhetoric disclosed with eyes *L. L. Lost* ii 1 229
Sweet smoke of rhetoric! He reputes me a cannon . . . iii 1 64
The heavenly rhetoric of thine eye, 'Gainst whom the world cannot hold argument . . . . iv 3 60
Lend me the flourish of all gentle tongues,—Fie, painted rhetoric! . v 2 239
For it is a figure in rhetoric . . . . . *As Y. Like It* v 1 45
And practise rhetoric in your common talk . . *T. of Shrew* i 1 35
Rheum. Do curse the gout, serpigo, and the rheum . *Meas. for Meas.* iii 1 31
I guess it stood in her chin, by the salt rheum that ran *Com. of Errors* iii 2 131
An hour in clamour and a quarter in rheum . . . *Much Ado* v 2 85
You, that did void your rheum upon my beard And foot me *Mer. of Venice* i 3 118
Is he not stupid With age and altering rheums? can he speak? *W. Tale* iv 4 410
Why holds thine eye that lamentable rheum? . . . *K. John* iii 1 22
How now, foolish rheum! Turning dispiteous torture out of door! . iv 1 33
For villany is not without such rheum . . . . . iv 3 108
The north-east wind, Which then blew bitterly against our faces, Awaked the sleeping rheum . . . . . . *Richard II.* i 4 8
Whose low vassal seat The Alps doth spit and void his rheum upon
Hen. V. iii 5 52
I have a rheum in mine eyes too, and such an ache . *Troi. and Cres.* v 3 105
A few drops of women's rheum, which are As cheap as lies *Coriolanus* v 6 46
Run barefoot up and down, threatening the flames With bisson rheum
Hamlet ii 2 529
A salt and sorry rheum offends me; Lend me thy handkerchief *Othello* iii 4 51
That year, indeed, he was troubled with a rheum . *Ant. and Cleo.* iii 2 57
Rheumatic. In your doublet and hose this raw rheumatic day! *M. W.* iii 1 47
That rheumatic diseases do abound . . . . *M. N. Dream* ii 1 105
You are both, i' good truth, as rheumatic as two dry toasts 2 *Hen. IV.* ii 4 62
But then he was rheumatic, and talked of the whore of Babylon *Hen. V.* ii 3 40
Rheumy. And tempt the rheumy and unpurged air . . *J. Cæsar* ii 1 266
Rhinoceros. Like the rugged Russian bear, The arm'd rhinoceros *Macb.* iii 4 101
Rhodes. And I, of whom his eyes had seen the proof At Rhodes *Othello* i 1 29
The Turkish preparation makes for Rhodes . . . . . i 3 14
That as it more concerns the Turk than Rhodes, So may he with more facile question bear it . . . . i 3 22
But altogether lacks the abilities That Rhodes is dress'd in . . i 3 26
In all confidence, he's not for Rhodes . . . . . i 3 31
The Ottomites, reverend and gracious, Steering with due course towards the isle of Rhodes . . . . i 3 34
Rhodope. A statelier pyramis to her I'll rear Than Rhodope's or Memphis' ever was . . . . 1 *Hen. VI.* i 6 22
Rhubarb. What rhubarb, cyme, or what purgative drug, Would scour these English hence? . . . . *Macbeth* v 3 55
Rhyme. Some love of yours hath writ to you in rhyme . *T. G. of Ver.* i 2 79
Whose composed rhymes Should be full-fraught with serviceable vows iii 2 69
Sing a scornful rhyme; And, as you trip, still pinch him *Mer. Wives* v 5 95
In despite of the teeth of all rhyme and reason . . . . v 5 133
In the why and the wherefore is neither rhyme nor reason *Com. of Errors* ii 2 49
Marry, I cannot show it in rhyme; I have tried . . *Much Ado* v 2 36
I can find out no rhyme to 'lady' but 'baby,' an innocent rhyme; for 'scorn,' 'horn,' a hard rhyme; for 'school,' 'fool,' a babbling rhyme . . . . v 2 37
In reason nothing.—Something then in rhyme . . *L. L. Lost* i 1 99
A dangerous rhyme, master, against the reason . . . . i 2 112
Assist me, some extemporal god of rhyme . . . . . i 2 190
I do love: and it hath taught me to rhyme and to be melancholy; and here is part of my rhyme, and here my melancholy . . . iv 3 13
O, rhymes are guards on wanton Cupid's hose . . . . iv 3 58
I heard your guilty rhymes, observed your fashion, Saw sighs reek from you . . . . iv 3 139
When shall you see me write a thing in rhyme? Or groan for love? . iv 3 181
As much love in rhyme As would be cramm'd up in a sheet of paper v 2 6
And spend his prodigal wits in bootless rhymes . . . . v 2 64
Nor woo in rhyme, like a blind harper's song . . . . v 2 405
Thou hast given her rhymes And interchanged love-tokens *M. N. Dream* i 1 28
I'll rhyme you so eight years together . . . *As Y. Like It* iii 2 101
But are you so much in love as your rhymes speak?—Neither rhyme nor reason can express how much . . . . . . iii 2 417
Whipped through the army with this rhyme in's forehead . *All's Well* iv 3 263
To whom he sung, in rude harsh-sounding rhymes . . *K. John* iv 2 150
These fellows of infinite tongue, that can rhyme themselves into ladies' favours, they do always reason themselves out again *Hen. V.* v 2 164
A speaker is but a prater; a rhyme is but a ballad . . . v 2 167
Their rhymes, Full of protest, of oath and big compare *Troi. and Cres.* iii 2 181
There was never a truer rhyme . . . . . . iv 4 22
A rhyme I learn'd even now Of one I danced withal *Rom. and Jul.* i 5 144
Speak but one rhyme, and I am satisfied . . . . . ii 1 9
Ha, ha! how vilely doth this cynic rhyme! . . . . *J. Cæsar* iv 3 133
Will you rhyme upon't, And vent it for a mockery? . *Cymbeline* v 3 55
You have put me into rhyme . . . . v 3 63
If you, born in these latter times, When wit's more ripe, accept my rhymes, And that to hear an old man sing . . *Pericles* i Gower 12
Only I carry winged time Post on the lame feet of my rhyme . iv Gower 48
Rhymed. You might have rhymed . . . . . *Hamlet* iii 2 296
Rhymers. And scald rhymers Ballad us out o' tune . *Ant. and Cleo.* v 2 215
Rhyming. I was rhyming: 'tis you that have the reason *T. G. of Ver.* ii 1 149
I was not born under a rhyming planet . . . . *Much Ado* v 2 40
Rialto. I understand, moreover, upon the Rialto, he hath a third at Mexico, a fourth for England . . . . *Mer. of Venice* i 3 20
What news on the Rialto? . . . . i 3 39
Many a time and oft In the Rialto you have rated me About my moneys i 3 108
Now, what news on the Rialto? . . . . iii 1 1

Rialto. A bankrupt, a prodigal, who dare scarce show his head on the Rialto *Mer. of Venice* iii 1 48
Rib. Confirm'd, confirm'd! O, that is stronger made Which was before barr'd up with ribs of iron! *Much Ado* iv 1 153
Dainty bits Make rich the ribs, but bankrupt quite the wits *L. L. Lost* i 1 27
Vailing her high-top lower than her ribs To kiss her burial *Mer. of Venice* i 1 28
You may tell every finger I have with my ribs ii 2 114
How like the prodigal doth she return, With over-weather'd ribs! ii 6 18
It were too gross To rib her cerecloth in the obscure grave ii 7 51
In a moment threw him and broke three of his ribs *As Y. Like It* i 2 136
It is the first time that ever I heard breaking of ribs was sport for ladies i 2 147
Till their soul-fearing clamours have brawl'd down The flinty ribs of this contemptuous city *K. John* ii 1 384
The fat ribs of peace Must by the hungry now be fed upon iii 3 9
Noble lords, Go to the rude ribs of that ancient castle *Richard II.* iii 3 32
May tear a passage through the flinty ribs Of this hard world v 5 20
Call in ribs, call in tallow *1 Hen. IV.* ii 4 125
Unless you call three fingers on the ribs bare iv 2 80
Then join you with them, like a rib of steel *2 Hen. IV.* ii 3 54
Give me ribs of steel! I shall split all In pleasure *Troi. and Cres.* i 3 177
Unfix my hair And make my seated heart knock at my ribs *Macbeth* i 3 136
I had thought to have yerk'd him here under the ribs *Othello* i 2 5
What ribs of oak, when mountains melt on them, Can hold the mortise? ii 1 8
Ribald. The busy day . . . hath roused the ribald crows *Troi. and Cres.* iv 2 9
Riband. With ribands pendent, flaring 'bout her head *Mer. Wives* iv 6 42
Didst thou not fall out with a tailor for wearing his new doublet before Easter? with another, for tying his new shoes with old riband? *Rom. and Jul.* iii 1 32
A very riband in the cap of youth, Yet needful too *Hamlet* iv 7 78
Ribaudred. Yon ribaudred nag of Egypt *Ant. and Cleo.* iii 10 10
Ribbed and paled in With rocks unscaleable and roaring waters *Cymbeline* iii 1 19
Ribbon. Pray you, sir, how much carnation ribbon may a man buy for a remuneration? *L. L. Lost* iii 1 146
Good strings to your beards, new ribbons to your pumps *M. N. Dream* iv 2 37
He hath ribbons of all the colours i' the rainbow *W. Tale* iv 4 205
It will also be the bondage of certain ribbons and gloves iv 4 236
Not a ribbon, glass, pomander, brooch, table-book, ballad, knife iv 4 609
Rib-breaking. Is there yet another dotes upon rib-breaking? *As Y. Like It* i 2 151
Rice. What will this sister of mine do with rice? *W. Tale* iv 3 42
Rice ap Thomas. Redoubted Pembroke, Sir James Blunt, And Rice ap Thomas *Richard III.* iv 5 12
Rich. Suffer a sea-change Into something rich and strange *Tempest* i 2 401
I as rich in having such a jewel As twenty seas *T. G. of Ver.* ii 4 169
Sure, the match Were rich and honourable iii 1 64
And high and low beguiles the rich and poor *Mer. Wives* i 3 95
He wooes both high and low, both rich and poor, Both young and old ii 1 117
Stones whose rates are either rich or poor As fancy values them *M. for M.* ii 2 150
If thou art rich, thou'rt poor; For, like an ass whose back with ingots bows, Thou bear'st thy heavy riches but a journey, And death unloads thee iii 1 25
When thou art old and rich, Thou hast neither heat, affection, limb, nor beauty, To make thy riches pleasant iii 1 36
Rich she shall be, that's certain; wise, or I'll none *Much Ado* ii 3 32
Rather ask if it were possible any villany should be so rich iii 3 120
What have I to give you back, whose worth May counterpoise this rich and precious gift? iv 1 29
Dainty bits Make rich the ribs, but bankrupt quite the wits *L. L. Lost* i 1 27
We shall be rich ere we depart, If fairings come thus plentifully in v 2 1
Our duty is so rich, so infinite, That we may do it still without accompt v 2 199
This proves you wise and rich, for in my eye,— I am a fool v 2 379
Her womb then rich with my young squire *M. N. Dream* ii 1 131
And return again, As from a voyage, rich with merchandise ii 1 134
Wherefore doth Lysander Deny your love, so rich within his soul? iii 2 229
O sinful thought! Never so rich a gem Was set in worse than gold *Mer. of Venice* ii 7 54
Two rich and precious stones, Stolen by my daughter! ii 8 20
A thousand times more fair, ten thousand times More rich iii 2 156
Art rich?—Faith, sir, so so.—'So so' is good *As Y. Like It* v 1 27
Thinkest thou, Hortensio, though her father be very rich, any man is so very a fool to be married to hell? *T. of Shrew* i 1 128
I'll promise thee she shall be rich And very rich i 2 62
'Tis the mind that makes the body rich iv 3 174
Not so well that I am poor, though many of the rich are damned *All's W.* i 3 18
No legacy is so rich as honesty iii 5 13
How will she love, when the rich golden shaft Hath kill'd the flock of all affections else That live in her! *T. Night* i 1 35
Love-thoughts lie rich when canopied with bowers i 1 41
It was told me I should be rich by the fairies *W. Tale* iii 3 121
Then make your garden rich in gillyvors iv 4 98
His garments are rich, but he wears them not handsomely iv 4 776
And left them More rich for what they yielded v 1 55
Your choice is not so rich in worth as beauty v 1 214
And make her rich In titles, honours and promotions *K. John* ii 1 491
And this rich fair town We make him lord of ii 1 552
My hand, as unattempted yet, Like a poor beggar, raileth on the rich ii 1 592
Whiles I am a beggar, I will rail And say there is no sin but to be rich ii 1 594
Being rich, my virtue then shall be To say there is no vice but beggary ii 1 595
To guard a title that was rich before, To gild refined gold iv 2 10
When they shall know what men are rich, They shall subscribe *Rich. II.* i 4 49
Your presence makes us rich, most noble lord ii 3 63
To rob me of so rich a bottom here *1 Hen. IV.* iii 1 105
What call you rich? let them coin his nose, let them coin his cheeks iii 3 90
To set so rich a main On the nice hazard of one doubtful hour? iv 1 47
And make thee rich for doing me such wrong *2 Hen. IV.* i 1 90
Such are the rich, That have abundance and enjoy it not iv 4 107
'Fore God, you have here a goodly dwelling and a rich v 3 7
As rich with praise As is the ooze and bottom of the sea *Hen. V.* i 2 163
Henry is able to enrich his queen And not to seek a queen to make him rich: So worthless peasants bargain *1 Hen. VI.* v 5 52
If he do, the rich shall have more *Troi. and Cres.* i 2 214
What hath mass or matter, by itself Lies rich in virtue and unmingled i 3 30
Doth think it rich To hear the wooden dialogue and sound i 3 154
Repeal daily any wholesome act established against the rich *Coriolanus* i 1 85
A carbuncle entire, as big as thou art, Were not so rich a jewel i 4 56
O, she is rich in beauty, only poor, That when she dies with beauty dies her store *Rom. and Jul.* i 1 221
Beauty too rich for use, for earth too dear! i 5 49
Conceit, more rich in matter than in words, Brags of his substance ii 6 30
Ah me! how sweet is love itself possess'd, When but love's shadows are so rich in joy! v 1 11
Rich. The world affords no law to make thee rich; Then be not poor, but break it *Rom. and Jul.* v 1 73
As rich shall Romeo's [statue] by his lady's lie v 3 303
'Tis a good form.—And rich: here is a water, look ye *T. of Athens* i 1 18
And returns in peace Most rich in Timon's nod i 1 62
He is gone happy, and has left me rich i 2 4
Faults that are rich are fair i 2 13
Thou art a soldier, therefore seldom rich i 2 228
I myself Rich only in large hurts iii 5 109
Not one word more: Thus part we rich in sorrow, parting poor iv 2 29
My dearest lord, bless'd, to be most accursed, Rich, only to be wretched iv 2 43
This one wish, that you had power and wealth To requite me, by making rich yourself iv 3 529
Go, live rich and happy; But thus condition'd: thou shalt build from men iv 3 532
Swords, made rich With the most noble blood of all this world *J. Cæsar* iii 1 155
Rich, not gaudy; For the apparel oft proclaims the man *Hamlet* i 3 71
Words of so sweet breath composed As made the things more rich iii 1 99
Beyond what can be valued, rich or rare; No less than life *Lear* i 1 58
Most rich, being poor; Most choice, forsaken; and most loved, despised! i 1 253
I'll repair the misery thou dost bear With something rich about me iv 1 80
Poor and content is rich and rich enough *Othello* iii 3 172
Rich in his father's honour *Ant. and Cleo.* i 3 50
All of her that is out of door most rich! *Cymbeline* i 6 15
Plate of rare device, and jewels Of rich and exquisite form i 6 190
A piece of work So bravely done, so rich ii 4 73
You have me, rich; and I will never fail Beginning nor supplyment iii 4 181
This fierce abridgement Hath to it circumstantial branches, which Distinction should be rich in v 5 384
Begin to part their fringes of bright gold; The diamonds of a most praised water Do appear, to make the world twice rich *Pericles* iii 2 103
When She would with rich and constant pen Vail to her mistress iv Gower 28
How achieved you these endowments, which You make more rich to owe? v 1 118
Rich advantage. The rich advantage of good exercise *K. John* iv 2 60
Hector would not lose So rich advantage of a promised glory *T. and C.* ii 2 204
Rich armour. Like a rich armour worn in heat of day *2 Hen. IV.* iv 5 30
Rich aspect. Sapphires, declining their rich aspect to the hot breath of Spain *Com. of Errors* iii 2 139
Rich beholding. Who do, methinks, find out Something not worth in me such rich beholding As they have often given *Troi. and Cres.* iii 3 91
Rich blood. Ha, majesty! how high thy glory towers, When the rich blood of kings is set on fire! *K. John* ii 1 351
Rich burghers. With portly sail, Like signiors and rich burghers on the flood *Mer. of Venice* i 1 10
Rich Capulet. My master is the great rich Capulet *Rom. and Jul.* i 2 84
My heart's dear love is set On the fair daughter of rich Capulet ii 3 58
Rich cardinal. Yet have I gold flies from another coast; I dare not say, from the rich cardinal *2 Hen. VI.* i 2 94
Rich Ceres. Approach, rich Ceres, her to entertain *Tempest* iv 1 75
Rich chair. Sat down To rest . . . In a rich chair of state *Hen. VIII.* iv 1 67
Rich choice. This ring he holds In most rich choice *All's Well* iii 7 26
Rich conceit Taught thee to make vast Neptune weep *T. of Athens* v 4 77
Rich crop. The rich crop Of sea and land *Cymbeline* i 6 33
Rich crown. Thy precious rich crown for a pitiful bald crown! *1 Hen. IV.* ii 4 420
Rich East. And the rich East to boot *Macbeth* iv 3 37
Rich embroidered. A sweeter shade . . . Than doth a rich embroider'd canopy To kings *3 Hen. VI.* ii 5 44
Rich embroidery. Sapphire, pearl and rich embroidery *Mer. Wives* v 5 75
Rich ends. Most poor matters Point to rich ends *Tempest* iii 1 4
Rich enough. If thou know One rich enough to be *T. of Shrew* i 2 67
Poor and content is rich and rich enough *Othello* iii 3 172
Rich expense. Banners sable, trimm'd with rich expense *Pericles* v Gower 19
Rich eyes. To have seen much and to have nothing, is to have rich eyes and poor hands *As Y. Like It* iv 1 24
Rich fellow. And a rich fellow enough, go to *Much Ado* iv 2 86
Rich fields. Sweat drops of gallant youth in our rich fields *Hen. V.* iii 5 25
Rich garments, linens, stuffs and necessaries *Tempest* i 2 164
Rich gift. Here, afore Heaven, I ratify this my rich gift iv 1 8
Rich gifts wax poor when givers prove unkind *Hamlet* iii 1 101
Rich hangings. Like rich hangings in a homely house *2 Hen. VI.* v 3 12
Rich honesty dwells like a miser, sir, in a poor house *As Y. Like It* v 4 62
Rich Jew. Not a poor boy, sir, but the rich Jew's man *Mer. of Venice* ii 2 130
And hath preferr'd thee, if it be preferment To leave a rich Jew's service, to become The follower of so poor a gentleman ii 2 156
From the rich Jew, a special deed of gift v 1 292
Rich jewel. Or play with my—some rich jewel *T. Night* ii 5 67
Like a rich jewel in an Ethiope's ear *Rom. and Jul.* i 5 48
Wear rich jewels, And send for money for 'em *T. of Athens* iii 4 23
I oped the coffin, Found there rich jewels *Pericles* v 3 24
Rich-jeweled. In an urn more precious Than the rich-jewel'd coffer of Darius *1 Hen. VI.* i 6 25
Rich lading. Antonio hath a ship of rich lading wrecked *Mer. of Venice* iii 1 3
Rich leas. Thy rich leas Of wheat, rye, barley *Tempest* iv 1 60
Rich-left. Those rich-left heirs that let their fathers lie Without a monument! *Cymbeline* iv 2 226
Rich legacy. Bequeathing it as a rich legacy *J. Cæsar* iii 2 141
Rich man. A rich man that hath not the gout *As Y. Like It* iii 2 337
Rich men look sad and ruffians dance and leap *Richard II.* ii 4 12
That the gods sent not Corn for the rich men only *Coriolanus* i 1 212
Rich men sin, and I eat root *T. of Athens* i 2 72
As rich men deal gifts, Expecting in return twenty for one iv 3 516
Rich Mercatio. What think'st thou of the rich Mercatio? *T. G. of Ver.* i 2 12
Rich misers. I can compare our rich misers to nothing so fitly as to a whale *Pericles* ii 1 33
Rich music. Let rich music's tongue Unfold the imagined happiness that both Receive *Rom. and Jul.* ii 6 27
Rich offerings. Going to Canterbury with rich offerings *1 Hen. IV.* i 2 140
Rich ones. Will poor folks lie . . . ? Yes; no wonder, When rich ones scarce tell true *Cymbeline* iii 6 12
Rich opinion. And spend your rich opinion for the name Of a night-brawler *Othello* ii 3 195
Rich ornament. Lavinia, Rome's rich ornament *T. Andron.* i 1 52
Rich pearls. I'll set thee in a shower of gold, and hail Rich pearls upon thee *Ant. and Cleo.* ii 5 46
Rich Pisa. Three or four as good, Within rich Pisa walls *T. of Shrew* ii 1 369
Rich place. Like a cipher, Yet standing in rich place *W. Tale* i 2 7
Rich prosperity. Deep Into the purse of rich prosperity *K. John* v 2 61
Rich reprisal. I am on fire To hear this rich reprisal is so nigh And yet not ours *1 Hen. IV.* iv 1 118
Rich scarf. My unshrubb'd down, Rich scarf to my proud earth *Tempest* iv 1 82

Rich stake. Seest a game play'd home, the rich stake drawn . *W. Tale* i 2 248
Rich stream. The rich stream Of lords and ladies . . *Hen. VIII.* iv 1 62
Rich stuffs, and ornaments of household . . . . . iii 2 126
Rich taffeta. Beauties no richer than rich taffeta . . *L. L. Lost* v 2 159
Rich thievery. Injurious time now with a robber's haste Crams his rich thievery up . . . . . *Troi. and Cres.* iv 4 45
Rich things. To your huge store Wise things seem foolish and rich things but poor . . . . . *L. L. Lost* v 2 378
Rich tire. Your lordship, having Rich tire about you . . *Pericles* iii 2 22
Rich validity. Behold this ring, Whose high respect and rich validity Did lack a parallel . . . . *All's Well* v 3 192
Rich value. Besides commends . . . , Gifts of rich value *Mer. of Venice* ii 9 91
Rich villains. When rich villains have need of poor ones, poor ones may make what price they will . . . . *Much Ado* iii 3 121
Rich wisdom. Vouchsafe In your rich wisdom to excuse . *L. L. Lost* v 2 742
Rich words. Sweet air, with admirable rich words . . *Cymbeline* ii 3 19
Rich worth. With the rich worth of your virginity . . *M. N. Dream* ii 1 219
Richard Cœur-de-lion. Mine eye hath well examined his parts And finds them perfect Richard . . . . . *K. John* i 1 90
King Richard Cœur-de-lion was thy father . . . . i 1 253
When Richard me begot, If thou hadst said him nay, it had been sin . i 1 274
Richard, that robb'd the lion of his heart And fought the holy wars . ii 1 3
Richard Conqueror. Look in the chronicles; we came in with Richard Conqueror . . . . . *T. of Shrew* Ind. 1 4
Richard du Champ. Say his name, good friend.—Richard du Champ *Cymbeline* iv 2 377
Richard Earl of Cambridge. Three corrupted men, One, Richard Earl of Cambridge, and the second, Henry Lord Scroop of Masham, and the third, Sir Thomas Grey . . . . *Hen. V.* ii Prol. 23
Then, Richard Earl of Cambridge, there is yours [your commission] . ii 2 66
I arrest thee of high treason, by the name of Richard Earl of Cambridge ii 2 146
Thy father, Richard Earl of Cambridge, For treason executed 1 *Hen. VI.* ii 4 90
Richard Earl of Cambridge; who was son To Edmund Langley 2 *Hen. VI.* ii 2 45
Richard Gloucester (afterwards Richard III.). Well hast thou fought to-day; By the mass, so did we all. I thank you, Richard . . v 3 16
Richard hath best deserved of all my sons . . 3 *Hen. VI.* i 1 17
Richard, enough; I will be king, or die . . . . i 2 35
Thou, Richard, shalt to the Duke of Norfolk, And tell him privily . i 2 38
Edward and Richard, you shall stay with me . . . . i 2 54
Three times did Richard make a lane to me, And thrice cried 'Courage!' i 4 9
And when the hardiest warriors did retire, Richard cried 'Charge!' . i 4 15
Nor now my scandal, Richard, dost thou hear . . . . ii 1 151
Valiant Richard, Montague, Stay we no longer, dreaming of renown . ii 1 198
Now, Richard, I am with thee here alone: This is the hand that stabb'd thy father York . . . . . . ii 4 5
York and Richard, Warwick and the rest; I stabb'd your fathers' bosoms . . . . ii 6 29
Richard mark'd him for the grave: And wheresoe'er he is, he's surely dead . . . . ii 6 40
Richard, I will create thee Duke of Gloucester . . . . ii 6 103
Richard, be Duke of Gloucester. Now to London . . . ii 6 109
Well, say there is no kingdom then for Richard; What other pleasure? iii 2 146
Yea, brother Richard, are you offended too?—Not I . . . iv 1 19
Brother Richard, will you stand by us?—Ay, in despite of all . iv 1 145
What are they that fly there?—Richard and Hastings: let them go . iv 3 28
He was convey'd by Richard Duke of Gloucester And the Lord Hastings iv 6 81
Now, brother Richard, Lord Hastings, and the rest, Yet thus far fortune iv 7 1
And, Richard, do not frown upon my faults, For I will henceforth be no more unconstant . . . . v 1 101
What Clarence but a quicksand of deceit? And Richard but a ragged fatal rock? . . . . v 4 27
Hold, Richard, hold; for we have done too much . . . v 5 43
Where is that devil's butcher, Hard-favour'd Richard? Richard, where art thou? Thou art not here . . . . . . v 5 78
Where's Richard gone?—To London, all in post . . . v 5 83
What's the matter, Clarence? may I know?—Yea, Richard, when I know; for I protest As yet I do not . . . *Richard III.* i 1 52
His minority Is put unto the trust of Richard Gloucester . . i 3 12
Thou detested— Margaret.—Richard!—Ha!—I call thee not . i 3 234
'Twill never stand upright Till Richard wear the garland of the realm . iii 2 40
That I'll give my voice on Richard's side, To bar my master's heirs . iii 2 53
Who, as thou know'st, are dear To princely Richard and to Buckingham iii 2 70
Now Margaret's curse is fall'n upon our heads, For standing by when Richard stabb'd her son . . . . iii 3 16
Then cursed she Buckingham, Then cursed she Richard . . . iii 3 18
O bloody Richard! miserable England! I prophesy the fearfull'st time iii 4 105
Cry 'God save Richard, England's royal king!' . . . iii 7 22
And some ten voices cried 'God save King Richard!' . . iii 7 36
This general applause and loving shout Argues your wisdoms and your love to Richard . . . . iii 7 40
Straight to Westminster, There to be crowned Richard's royal queen . iv 1 33
When, I say, I look'd on Richard's face, This was my wish: 'Be thou,' quoth I, 'accursed!' . . . . iv 1 71
Go thou to Richard, and good angels guard thee! . . . iv 1 93
Thus high, by thy advice And thy assistance, is King Richard seated . iv 2 4
I had an Edward, till a Richard kill'd him; I had a Harry, till a Richard kill'd him: Thou hadst an Edward, till a Richard kill'd him; Thou hadst a Richard, till a Richard kill'd him . . . . . iv 4 40
Thou hadst a Clarence too, and Richard kill'd him . . . iv 4 46
Richard yet lives, hell's black intelligencer . . . . iv 4 71
For my daughters, Richard, They shall be praying nuns, not weeping queens . . . . iv 4 200
Unless thou couldst put on some other shape, And not be Richard . iv 4 287
So long as hell and Richard likes of it . . . . . iv 4 354
Cold friends to Richard: what do they in the north? . . . iv 4 485
Will not King Richard let me speak with him?—No, my good lord . v 1 1
Awake, and think our wrongs in Richard's bosom Will conquer him! . v 3 144
Let us be lead within thy bosom, Richard, And weigh thee down to ruin! . . . . v 3 152
Richard, thy wife, that wretched Anne thy wife, That never slept a quiet hour with thee . . . . v 3 159
And Richard falls in height of all his pride . . . . v 3 176
What do I fear? myself? there's none else by: Richard loves Richard . v 3 183
And every one did threat To-morrow's vengeance on the head of Richard v 3 206
Shadows to-night Have struck more terror to the soul of Richard . v 3 217
Methought their souls, whose bodies Richard murder'd, Came to my tent v 3 230
Richard except, those whom we fight against Had rather have us win . v 3 243
The part my father meant to act upon The usurper Richard *Hen. VIII.* i 2 196
Henry of Buckingham, Who first raised head against usurping Richard ii 1 108
Richard Grey. Sir Richard Grey was slain . . 3 *Hen. VI.* iii 2 2
Richard Ketly. Sir Richard Ketly, Davy Gam, esquire . . *Hen. V.* iv 8 109
Richard of York (son of Edward IV.)! how fares our loving brother? *Richard III.* iii 1 96
Thou hadst a Richard, till a Richard kill'd him . . . iv 4 43
Richard Plantagenet. Kneel thou down Philip, but rise more great, Arise sir Richard and Plantagenet . . . . *K. John* i 1 162
The very spirit of Plantagenet! I am thy grandam, Richard . . i 1 168
Richard, we must speed For France, for France, for it is more than need i 1 178
Now can I make any Joan a lady. 'Good den, sir Richard!' . i 1 185
Sir Richard, what think you? have you beheld, Or have you read or heard? . . . . iv 3 41
This news was brought to Richard but even now: The French fight coldly . . . . v 3 12
Richard Plantagenet (Duke of York). Farewell, ambitious Richard.—How I am braved! . . . . . . 1 *Hen. VI.* ii 4 114
Will my nephew come?—Richard Plantagenet, my lord, will come . ii 5 18
Even since then hath Richard been obscured, Deprived of honour . ii 5 26
Richard Plantagenet, my friend, is he come?—Ay, noble uncle, thus ignobly used, Your nephew, late despised Richard, comes . . ii 5 34
Which in the right of Richard Plantagenet We do exhibit to your majesty iii 1 150
Mark every circumstance, You have great reason to do Richard right . iii 1 154
Our pleasure is That Richard be restored to his blood.—Let Richard be restored to his blood . . . . iii 1 159
If Richard will be true, not that alone But all the whole inheritance I give . . . . iii 1 163
Rise, Richard, like a true Plantagenet . . . . . iii 1 172
And so thrive Richard as thy foes may fall! . . . . iii 1 174
Well didst thou, Richard, to suppress thy voice . . . iv 1 182
Richard Duke of York Was rightful heir unto the English crown 2 *Hen. VI.* i 3 186
Long live our sovereign Richard, England's king!—We thank you, lords. But I am not your king . . . . ii 2 63
Richard shall live to make the Earl of Warwick The greatest man in England but the king . . . . ii 2 81
Resolve thee, Richard; claim the English crown . 3 *Hen. VI.* i 1 49
His natural king?—True, Clifford; and that's Richard Duke of York . i 1 83
Richard, I bear thy name; I'll venge thy death, Or die renowned . ii 1 87
I had a Richard too, and thou didst kill him . . *Richard III.* iv 4 44
Richard Ratcliff. Sir Richard Ratcliff, let me tell thee this . . iii 3 2
Richard the Second. Wherefore comest thou hither, Before King Richard? . . . . *Richard II.* i 3 32
A traitor, foul and dangerous, To God of heaven, King Richard and to me i 3 40
True to King Richard's throne, A loyal, just and upright gentleman . i 3 86
Though Richard my life's counsel would not hear, My death's sad tale may yet undeaf his ear . . . . ii 1 15
O Richard! York is too far gone with grief, Or else he never would compare between . . . . ii 1 184
Save bidding farewell to so sweet a guest As my sweet Richard . ii 2 9
Richard their king is dead.—Ah, Richard, with the eyes of heavy mind ii 4 17
God for his Richard hath in heavenly pay A glorious angel . . iii 2 60
Let them hence away, From Richard's night to Bolingbroke's fair day . iii 2 218
Richard not far from hence hath hid his head.—It would beseem the Lord Northumberland To say 'King Richard' . . . . . iii 3 6
King Richard lies Within the limits of yon lime and stone . . iii 3 25
Henry Bolingbroke On both his knees doth kiss King Richard's hand . iii 3 36
Such crimson tempest should bedrench The fresh green lap of fair King Richard's land . . . . iii 3 47
King Richard and myself should meet With no less terror than the elements Of fire and water . . . . iii 3 54
March on, and mark King Richard how he looks . . . iii 3 61
King Richard doth himself appear, As doth the blushing discontented sun iii 3 62
Will his majesty Give Richard leave to live till Richard die? . . iii 3 174
I come to thee From plume-pluck'd Richard . . . . iv 1 108
Would God that any in this noble presence Were enough noble to be upright judge Of noble Richard! . . . . . . iv 1 119
What subject can give sentence on his king? And who sits here that is not Richard's subject? . . . . iv 1 122
Fetch hither Richard, that in common view He may surrender . . iv 1 155
Long mayst thou live in Richard's seat to sit, And soon lie Richard in an earthy pit! . . . . iv 1 218
Thou map of honour, thou King Richard's tomb, And not King Richard v 1 12
Is my Richard both in shape and mind Transform'd and weaken'd? . v 1 26
From windows' tops Threw dust and rubbish on King Richard's head . v 2 6
Alack, poor Richard! where rode he the whilst? . . . v 2 22
Men's eyes Did scowl on gentle Richard; no man cried 'God save him!' v 2 28
Aumerle that was; But that is lost for being Richard's friend . v 2 42
Love to Richard Is a strange brooch in this all-hating world . v 5 65
Breathless lies The mightiest of thy greatest enemies, Richard of Bordeaux . . . . v 6 33
Was not he proclaim'd By Richard that dead is the next of blood? 1 *Hen. IV.* i 3 146
Did King Richard then Proclaim my brother Edmund Mortimer Heir? . i 3 155
To put down Richard, that sweet lovely rose, And plant this thorn . i 3 175
In Richard's time,—what do you call the place? . . . i 3 242
For all the world As thou art to this hour was Richard then . . iii 2 94
For you my staff of office did I break In Richard's time . . v 1 35
With the blood Of fair King Richard, scraped from Pomfret stones 2 *Hen. IV.* i 1 205
Common dog, didst thou disgorge Thy glutton bosom of the royal Richard i 3 98
They that, when Richard lived, would have him die . . . i 3 101
Richard and Northumberland, great friends, Did feast together . iii 1 58
Even to the eyes of Richard Gave him defiance . . . iii 1 64
Richard, with his eye brimful of tears, Then check'd and rated . iii 1 67
By the necessary form of this King Richard might create a perfect guess iii 1 88
Of which disease Our late king, Richard, being infected, died . iv 1 58
I Richard's body have interred new . . . . *Hen. V.* iv 1 312
Where the sad and solemn priests Sing still for Richard's soul . iv 1 319
Henry the Fourth . . . Deposed his nephew Richard . . 1 *Hen. VI.* ii 5 64
Young King Richard thus removed, Leaving no heir begotten of his body ii 5 71
Edward the Black Prince died before his father And left behind him Richard, his only son . . . . 2 *Hen. VI.* ii 2 19
As all you know, Harmless Richard was murder'd traitorously . ii 2 27
For Richard, the first son's heir, being dead, The issue of the next son should have reign'd . . . . ii 2 31
For Richard, in the view of many lords, Resign'd the crown . 3 *Hen. VI.* i 1 138
Richard the Second here [at Pomfret] was hack'd to death *Richard III.* iii 3 12
Richard (Vernon). My nephew must not know, Sir Richard, The liberal and kind offer . . . . 1 *Hen. IV.* v 2 1
Riched. With champains rich'd, With plenteous rivers . . *Lear* i 1 65
Richer. Furred with fox and lamb-skins too, to signify, that craft, being richer than innocency, stands for the facing . *Meas. for Meas.* iii 2 10

Richer. Beauties no richer than rich taffeta . . . . L. L. Lost v 2 159
His good remembrance, sir, Lies richer in your thoughts than on his tomb ; So in approof lives not his epitaph . . All's Well i 2 49
No richer than his honour : how he glisters Thorough my rust ! W. Tale iii 2 171
Whose veins bound richer blood than Lady Blanch ? K. John ii 1 431
Never king of England Had nobles richer and more loyal subjects Hen. V. i 2 127
Yet I am richer than my base accusers . . . Hen. VIII. ii 1 104
All the Indies in his arms, And more and richer, when he strains that lady iv 1 46
Alas, poor chin ! many a wart is richer . . . Troi. and Cres. i 2 155
Beggar the estimation which you prized Richer than sea and land . ii 2 92
They do shake their heads, and I am here No richer . T. of Athens ii 2 212
A heart Dearer than Plutus' mine, richer than gold . . J. Cæsar iv 3 102
Your wisdom should show itself more richer . . . . Hamlet iii 2 317
Richer than that which four successive kings In Denmark's crown have worn . . . . v 2 284
I am sure, my love's More richer than my tongue . . . . Lear i 1 80
But even for want of that for which I am richer . . . . i 1 233
Threw a pearl away Richer than all his tribe . . . Othello v 2 348
Richer than doing nothing for a bauble . . . . Cymbeline iii 3 23
Poor I am stale, a garment out of fashion ; And, for I am richer than to hang by the walls, I must be ripp'd . . . . . iii 4 54
Riches, poverty, And use of service, none . . . Tempest ii 1 150
The clouds methought would open and show riches Ready to drop upon me . . . . iii 2 150
Honour, riches, marriage-blessing, Long continuance, and increasing . iv 1 106
My riches are these poor habiliments . . . . T. G. of Ver. iv 1 13
'Tis the very riches of thyself That now I aim at . . Mer. Wives iii 4 17
Thou bear'st thy heavy riches but a journey . . Meas. for Meas. iii 1 27
Neither heat, affection, limb, nor beauty, To make thy riches pleasant . iii 1 38
O then, belike, you fancy riches more . . . . T. of Shrew ii 1 16
With too much riches it confound itself . . . Richard II. iii 4 60
That's all the riches I got in his service . . . Hen. V. ii 3 46
Sweet is the country, because full of riches . . 2 Hen. VI. iv 7 67
Repair'd with double riches of content . . . Richard III. iv 4 319
No, not for all the riches under heaven . . . Hen. VIII. ii 3 35
Place, riches, favour, Prizes of accident as oft as merit Troi. and Cres. iii 3 82
We are born to do benefits : and what better or properer can we call our own than the riches of our friends ? . . . . T. of Athens i 2 107
Who would not wish to be from wealth exempt, Since riches point to misery ? . . . . iv 2 32
Behold, The riches of the ship is come on shore ! . . . Othello ii 1 83
Riches fineless is as poor as winter To him that ever fears he shall be poor . . . . iii 3 173
Thy master is not there, who was indeed The riches of it Cymbeline iii 4 73
My riches to the earth from whence they came . . . Pericles i 1 52
For riches strew'd herself even in the streets . . . . i 4 23
Virtue and cunning were endowments greater Than nobleness and riches iii 2 28
Richest. All hail, the richest beauties on the earth ! . . L. L. Lost v 2 158
Love's stories written in love's richest book . . M. N. Dream ii 2 122
Whose beauty did astonish the survey Of richest eyes . All's Well v 3 17
It [my shame] will hang upon my richest robes . . 2 Hen. VI. ii 4 108
Pins Her richest lockram 'bout her reechy neck . . Coriolanus ii 1 225
That which would appear offence in us, His countenance, like richest alchemy, Will change to virtue and to worthiness . . J. Cæsar i 3 159
Richly. Paid me richly for the practice of it . . . Much Ado v 1 255
In Belmont is a lady richly left ; And she is fair . Mer. of Venice i 1 161
There miscarried A vessel of our country richly fraught . . . ii 8 30
Three of your argosies Are richly come to harbour suddenly . . . v 1 277
My house within the city Is richly furnished with plate . T. of Shrew ii 1 349
Out of fashion : richly suited, but unsuitable . . . All's Well i 1 170
Whose worth and honesty Is richly noted . . . . W. Tale v 3 145
Barely in title, not in revenue.—Richly in both . . . Richard II ii 1 227
May see away their shilling Richly in two short hours . Hen. VIII. Prol. 13
That thou depart'st hence safe, Does pay thy labour richly A. and C. iv 14 37
And then myself, I chiefly, That set thee on to this desert, am bound To load thy merit richly . . . . Cymbeline i 5 74
The poor soldier that so richly fought, Whose rags shamed gilded arms v 5 3
Her eyes as jewel-like And cased as richly . . . . Pericles v 1 112
Richmond. Arthur Duke of Bretagne And Earl of Richmond . K. John ii 1 552
Young Henry, earl of Richmond.—Come hither, England's hope 3 Hen. VI. iv 6 67
As Henry's late presaging prophecy Did glad my heart with hope of this young Richmond . . . . iv 6 93
Ay, for if Edward repossess the crown, 'Tis like that Richmond with the rest shall down . . . . iv 6 100
The Countess Richmond, good my Lord of Derby . . Richard III. i 3 20
If thou wilt outstrip death, go cross the seas, And live with Richmond iv 1 43
Go thou to Richmond, and good fortune guide thee ! . . . iv 1 92
Dorset's fled To Richmond, in those parts beyond the sea . . iv 2 47
Well, let that pass. Dorset is fled to Richmond.—I hear that news . iv 2 88
Look to your wife : if she convey Letters to Richmond, you shall answer it . . . . iv 2 96
Henry the Sixth Did prophesy that Richmond should be king, When Richmond was a little peevish boy . . . . . . iv 2 99
Richmond ! When last I was at Exeter, The mayor in courtesy show'd me the castle, And call'd it Rougemont . . . . . iv 2 106
A bard of Ireland told me once, I should not live long after I saw Richmond . . . . iv 2 110
The Breton Richmond aims At young Elizabeth, my brother's daughter iv 3 40
Ely is fled to Richmond ; And Buckingham, back'd with the hardy Welshmen, Is in the field . . . . iv 3 46
Ely with Richmond troubles me more near Than Buckingham . . iv 3 49
'Tis thought that Richmond is their admiral . . . . . iv 4 437
Richmond is on the seas.—There let him sink, and be the seas on him ! iv 4 463
Thou wouldst be gone to join with Richmond : I will not trust you . iv 4 491
Richmond, in Dorsetshire, sent out a boat Unto the shore . . iv 4 524
The Earl of Richmond Is with a mighty power landed at Milford . . iv 4 534
Sir Christopher, tell Richmond this from me . . . . . iv 5 1
Tell me, where is princely Richmond now ?—At Pembroke . . iv 5 6
Bless thee from thy mother, Who prays continually for Richmond's good . . . . v 3 84
Be cheerful, Richmond ; for the wronged souls Of butcher'd princes fight in thy behalf : King Henry's issue, Richmond, comforts thee . v 3 121
Richmond, sleep in peace, and wake in joy ; Good angels guard thee ! . v 3 155
God and good angels fight on Richmond's side ; And Richard falls . v 3 175
Ten thousand soldiers Armed in proof, and led by shallow Richmond . v 3 219
Good morrow, Richmond !—Cry mercy, lords and watchful gentlemen . v 3 223
God and Saint George ! Richmond and victory ! . . . . v 3 270
What said Northumberland as touching Richmond ?—That he was never trained up in arms . . . . v 3 271
Richmond. Not shine to-day ! Why, what is that to me More than to Richmond ? . . . . Richard III. v 3 286
All on foot he fights, Seeking for Richmond in the throat of death . . v 4 5
I think there be six Richmonds in the field . . . . . v 4 11
Courageous Richmond, well hast thou acquit thee . . . . v 5 3
Richmond and Elizabeth, The true succeeders of each royal house . v 5 29
Rid. The red plague rid you For learning me your language ! . . Tempest i 2 364
I am so out of love with life that I will sue to be rid of it . M. for M. iii 1 174
Thank God you are rid of a knave . . . . . Much Ado iii 3 31
He hath rid his prologue like a rough colt . . . M. N. Dream v 1 119
Woo her, wed her and bed her and rid the house of her ! . T. of Shrew i 1 150
Till the father rid his hands of her . . . . i 1 186
Then we are rid of Licio.—I'faith, he'll have a lusty widow now . . iv 2 49
I would we were well rid of this knavery . . . . T. Night iv 2 73
I am glad at heart To be so rid o' the business . . . W. Tale iii 3 15
Why, 'twas my care ; And what loss is it to be rid of care ? Richard II. iii 2 96
Is there no plot To rid the realm of this pernicious blot ? . . . iv 1 325
Have I no friend will rid me of this living fear ? . . . . v 4 2
I am the king's friend, and will rid his foe . . . . . v 4 11
I cannot rid my hands of him . . . . . . 2 Hen. IV. i 2 226
So we be rid of them, do with 'em what thou wilt . . 1 Hen. VI. iv 7 94
This Gloucester should be quickly rid the world, To rid us from the fear we have of him . . . . 2 Hen. VI. iii 1 233
Will thither straight, for willingness rids way . . . 3 Hen. VI. v 3 21
So cut off As, deathsmen, you have rid this sweet young prince ! . . v 5 67
And will, no doubt, shortly be rid of me . . . . Richard III. iv 1 87
Soon I'll rid you from the fear of them.—Thou sing'st sweet music . iv 2 78
As welcome as to one That would be rid of such an enemy Troi. and Cres. iv 5 164
Bid me devise some mean To rid her from this second marriage R. and J. v 3 241
Give it the beasts, to be rid of the men . . . . T. of Athens iv 3 323
I'll give you gold, Rid me these villains from your companies . . v 1 104
Brutus and Cassius Are rid like madmen through the gates . J. Cæsar iii 2 274
I would set my life on any chance, To mend it, or be rid on't Macbeth iii 1 114
Let her who would be rid of him devise His speedy taking off . Lear v 1 64
I must Rid all the sea of pirates . . . . . Ant. and Cleo. ii 6 36
What, of death too, That rids our dogs of languish ? . . . . v 2 42
We must either get her ravished, or be rid of her . . . Pericles iv 6 5
There's no way to be rid on't but by the way to the pox . . . iv 6 16
Riddance. A gentle riddance. Draw the curtains, go . Mer. of Venice ii 7 78
A good riddance . . . . Troi. and Cres. ii 1 132
Ridden. Am I ridden with a Welsh goat too ? . . . Mer. Wives v 5 145
Well chosen, ridden, and furnished . . . . . Hen. VIII. ii 2 3
Riddle. You have not the Book of Riddles about you, have you ?—Book of Riddles ! . . . . Mer. Wives i 1 209
Much upon this riddle runs the wisdom of the world . Meas. for Meas. iii 2 242
No egma, no riddle, no l'envoy ; no salve in the mail, sir . L. L. Lost iii 1 73
Lysander riddles very prettily . . . . . M. N. Dream ii 2 53
So there's my riddle : one that's dead is quick . . . All's Well v 3 304
A fustian riddle ! . . . . T. Night ii 5 119
Let Æsop fable in a winter's night ; His currish riddles sort not with this place . . . . 3 Hen. VI. v 5 26
Hoyday, a riddle ! neither good nor bad ! . . . . Richard III. iv 4 460
How did you dare To trade and traffic with Macbeth In riddles and affairs of death ? . . . . Macbeth iii 5 5
Pray you, go with us.—O, ho, I know the riddle.—I will go . Lear v 1 37
Whoso ask'd her for his wife, His riddle told not, lost his life Per. i Gower 38
Riddle-like lives sweetly where she dies . . . All's Well i 3 223
Riddling. This is a riddling merchant for the nonce . . 1 Hen. VI. ii 3 57
Riddling confession finds but riddling shrift . . . Rom. and Jul. ii 3 56
Ride. To dive into the fire, to ride On the curl'd clouds . . Tempest i 2 191
I saw him beat the surges under him, And ride upon their backs . . ii 1 115
The body public be A horse whereon the governor doth ride . M. for M. i 2 164
She rides me and I long for grass. 'Tis so, I am an ass . Com. of Errors ii 2 202
Disdain and scorn ride sparkling in her eyes . . . Much Ado iii 1 51
An two men ride of a horse, one must ride behind . . . . iii 5 40
Or wilt thou ride ? thy horses shall be trapp'd . . . T. of Shrew Ind. 2 43
Leaden messengers, That ride upon the violent speed of fire . All's Well iii 2 112
I'll ride home to-morrow, Sir Toby.—Pourquoi ? . . . T. Night i 3 94
Marry, I'll ride your horse as well as I ride you . . . . . iii 4 318
Our praises are our wages : you may ride's With one soft kiss a thousand furlongs ere With spur we heat an acre . . . . . W. Tale i 2 94
And most opportune to our need I have A vessel rides fast by . . iv 4 512
I will ride, As far as land will let me, by your side . . Richard II. i 3 251
Though I be old, I doubt not but to ride as fast as York . . . v 2 115
My good sweet honey lord, ride with us to-morrow . . 1 Hen. IV. i 2 179
They ride up and down on her and make her their boots . . . ii 1 90
Come, wilt thou see me ride ? And when I am o' horseback, I will swear ii 3 103
He that rides at high speed and with his pistol kills a sparrow flying . ii 4 379
Heigh, heigh ! the devil rides upon a fiddlestick . . . . ii 4 534
Thou and I have thirty miles to ride yet ere dinner time . . . iii 3 222
If life did ride upon a dial's point . . . . v 2 84
Upon my [Rumour's] tongues continual slanders ride . . 2 Hen. IV. Ind. 6
I will ride thee o' nights like the mare.—I think I am as like to ride the mare, if I have any vantage of ground to get up . . . . . ii 1 83
Rides the wild-mare with the boys . . . . ii 4 268
Get on thy boots : we'll ride all night . . . . . . v 3 138
As it were, to ride day and night ; and not to deliberate . . . v 5 21
For a sovereign's sovereign to ride on . . . . . Hen. V. iii 7 39
They that ride so and ride not warily, fall into foul bogs . . . iii 7 60
Take a trumpet, herald ; Ride thou unto the horsemen on yon hill . iv 7 60
Prepare to ride unto Saint Alban's . . . . . . 2 Hen. VI. i 2 57
Come, Nell, thou wilt ride with us ? . . . . i 2 59
Erst did follow thy proud chariot-wheels When thou didst ride in triumph ii 4 14
Thou dost ride in a foot-cloth, dost thou not ?—What of that ? . . iv 7 51
These borne before us, instead of maces, Will we ride through the streets iv 7 144
Let thy dauntless mind Still ride in triumph over all mischance 3 Hen. VI. iii 3 18
Spur your proud horses hard, and ride in blood . . . Richard III. v 3 340
Strong as the axletree On which heaven rides . . . Troi. and Cres. i 3 67
The prince must think me tardy and remiss, That swore to ride before him iv 4 144
The venom'd vengeance ride upon our swords, Spur them to ruthful work v 3 47
Ride, ride, Messala, ride, and give these bills Unto the legions J. Cæsar v 2 1
Ride, ride, Messala : let them all come down . . . . . . v 2 6
He rides well ; And his great love, sharp as his spur, hath holp him To his home before us . . . . Macbeth i 6 22
Ride you this afternoon ?—Ay, my good lord . . . . . . iii 1 19
Is't far you ride ?—As far, my lord, as will fill up the time 'Twixt this and supper . . . . iii 1 24
Infected be the air whereon they ride ! . . . . iv 1 138
On whose foolish honesty My practices ride easy . . . . . Lear i 2 198
I can keep honest counsel, ride, run, mar a curious tale in telling it . i 4 34

Ride. Ride more than thou goest, Learn more than thou trowest *Lear* i 4 134
Proud of heart, to ride on a bay trotting-horse over four-inched bridges iii 4 57
Hath had three suits to his back, six shirts to his body, horse to ride iii 4 142
Leap thou, attire and all, Through proof of harness to my heart, and there Ride on the pants triumphing! *Ant. and Cleo.* iv 8 16
How many score of miles may we well ride 'Twixt hour and hour?— One score 'twixt sun and sun *Cymbeline* iii 2 69
Slander, . . . whose breath Rides on the posting winds iii 4 38
A tempest, which his mortal vessel tears, And yet he rides it out *Pericles* iv 4 31
Seeing this goodly vessel ride before us, I made to it v 1 18
Rider. Not till it leave the rider in the mire *L. L. Lost* ii 1 121
So doth the hound his master, the ape his keeper, the tired horse his rider iv 2 131
Taught their manage, and to that end riders dearly hired *As Y. Like It* i 1 14
And throw the rider headlong *Richard II.* i 2 52
Mounted upon a hot and fiery steed Which his aspiring rider seem'd to know v 2 9
In patient stillness while his rider mounts him *Hen. V.* iii 7 24
Never bestrid a horse, save one that had A rider like myself *Cymbeline* iv 4 39
Ridest. So ridest thou triumphing in my woe *L. L. Lost* iv 3 35
Rideth. On the western coast Rideth a puissant navy *Richard. III.* iv 4 434
Ridge. I would allow him odds, And meet him, were I tied to run afoot Even to the frozen ridges of the Alps *Richard II.* i 1 64
Now in as low an ebb as the foot of the ladder and by and by in as high a flow as the ridge of the gallows *1 Hen. IV.* i 2 43
Leads fill'd, and ridges horsed With variable complexions *Coriolanus* ii 1 227
Ridiculous. A most ridiculous monster! *Tempest* ii 2 169
The heaving of my lungs provokes me to ridiculous smiling *L. L. Lost* iii 1 78
His general behaviour vain, ridiculous, and thrasonical v 1 13
Ridiculous appears, To check their folly, passion's solemn tears v 2 117
And their rough carriage so ridiculous v 2 306
What in us hath seem'd ridiculous,—As love is full of unbefitting strains v 2 769
How many actions most ridiculous Hast thou been drawn to by thy fantasy?—Into a thousand *As Y. Like It* ii 4 30
Good manners at the court are as ridiculous in the country iii 2 47
Why appear you with this ridiculous boldness? *T. Night* iii 4 40
Thou canst not, cardinal, devise a name So slight, unworthy and ridiculous, To charge me to an answer, as the pope *K. John* iii 1 150
Is wasteful and ridiculous excess iv 2 16
Right ill-disposed in brawl ridiculous *Hen. V.* iv Prol. 51
New customs, Though they be never so ridiculous, Nay, let 'em be unmanly, yet are follow'd *Hen. VIII.* i 3 3
With ridiculous and awkward action *Troi. and Cres.* i 3 149
Our very priests must become mockers, if they shall encounter such ridiculous subjects as you are *Coriolanus* ii 1 94
Riding. Move these eyes? Or whether, riding on the balls of mine, Seem they in motion? *Mer. of Venice* iii 2 117
We came down a foul hill, my master riding behind my mistress *T. of S.* iv 1 69
Traders riding to London with fat purses *1 Hen. IV.* i 2 141
This man was riding From Alcibiades to Timon's cave *T. of Athens* v 2 9
Stay a little: Were you but riding forth to air yourself, Such parting were too petty *Cymbeline* i 1 110
I have heard of riding wagers, Where horses have been nimbler than the sands That run i' the clock's behalf iii 2 73
'Gainst whose shore Riding *Pericles* v 3 11
Riding-robes. Who comes in such haste in riding-robes? *K. John* i 1 217
Riding-rods. If my legs were two such riding-rods i 1 140
Riding-suit. Provide me presently A riding-suit, no costlier than would fit A franklin's housewife *Cymbeline* iii 2 78
Rien puis. Les eaux et la terre.—Rien puis? l'air et le feu *Hen. V.* iv 2 5
Rifle. Throw us that you have about ye: If not, we'll make you sit and rifle you *T. G. of Ver.* iv 1 4
Rift. Within which rift Imprison'd thou didst painfully remain *Tempest* i 2 277
I'ld shriek, that even your ears Should rift to hear me *W. Tale* v 1 66
Wars 'twixt you twain would be As if the world should cleave, and that slain men Should solder up the rift *Ant. and Cleo.* iii 4 32
Rifted. And rifted Jove's stout oak With his own bolt *Tempest* v 1 45
Rig. That is it Hath made me rig my navy *Ant. and Cleo.* ii 6 20
Rigged. They prepared A rotten carcass of a boat, not rigg'd *Tempest* i 2 146
Tight and yare and bravely rigg'd as when We first put out to sea v 1 224
Our great navy 's rigg'd *Ant. and Cleo.* iii 5 20
Riggest. 'Tis thou [gold] that rigg'st the bark *T. of Athens* v 1 53
Riggish. That the holy priests Bless her when she is riggish *Ant. and Cleo.* ii 2 245
Right. Heaven prosper the right! What weapons is he? *Mer. Wives* iii 1 30
You are therein in the right: but to the point *Meas. for Meas.* ii 1 100
He's in the right. Constable what say you to it? ii 1 167
Do him right that, answering one foul wrong, Lives not to act another ii 2 103
Thou'rt i' the right, girl; more o' that ii 2 129
Do me the common right To let me see them ii 3 5
If imprisonment be the due of a bawd, why, 'tis his right iii 2 70
When once our grace we have forgot, Nothing goes right iv 4 37
Right.—It may be right; but you are i' the wrong To speak before your time v 1 85
But, if thou live to see like right bereft, This fool-begg'd patience in thee will be left *Com. of Errors* ii 1 40
Who talks within there? ho, open the door!—Right, sir iii 1 39
He denied you had in him no right.—He meant he did me none iv 2 7
Here begins his morning story right v 1 356
I will do myself the right to trust none *Much Ado* i 1 246
How much might the man deserve of me that would right her! iv 1 264
You say not right, old man v 1 73
Do me right, or I will protest your cowardice v 1 149
Said I, 'a great wit:' 'Right,' says she, 'a great gross one' v 1 163
Give her the right you should have given her cousin v 1 300
God defend the right!—Will you hear this letter? *L. L. Lost* i 1 216
We will give up our right in Aquitaine, And hold fair friendship ii 1 140
Being a watch, But being watch'd that it may still go right! iii 1 195
Your nose says, no, you are not; for it stands too right v 2 568
Most true, 'tis right; you were so v 2 572
I will right myself like a soldier v 2 734
Yield Thy crazed title to my certain right *M. N. Dream* i 1 92
She is mine, and all my right of her I do estate unto Demetrius i 1 97
Why should not I then prosecute my right? i 1 105
To try whose right, Of thine or mine, is most in Helena iii 2 336
I will tell you every thing, right as it fell out iv 2 31
This the cranny is, right and sinister v 1 164
My destiny Bars me the right of voluntary choosing *Mer. of Venice* ii 1 16
How shall I know if I do choose the right? ii 7 10
I could teach you How to choose right, but I am then forsworn iii 2 11
O, these naughty times Put bars between the owners and their rights! iii 2 19

Right. To do a great right, do a little wrong, And curb this cruel devil *Mer. of Venice* iv 1 216
''Tis right:' quoth he 'thus misery doth part The flux of company' *As Y. Like It* ii 1 51
Let me see wherein My tongue hath wrong'd him: if it do him right, Then he hath wrong'd himself ii 7 84
'Many a man knows no end of his goods:' right; many a man has good horns, and knows no end of them iii 3 54
I should have been a woman by right iv 3 177
If you be gentlemen, Do me this right; hear me *T. of Shrew* i 2 239
The base is right; 'tis the base knave that jars iii 1 47
The gown is not for me.—You are i' the right, sir: 'tis for my mistress iv 3 157
A very mean meaning.—Right, I mean you v 2 31
Famous, sir, in his profession, and it was his great right *All's Well* i 1 30
Moderate lamentation is the right of the dead i 1 64
Of all the learned and authentic fellows,— Right; so I say ii 3 15
Not to be helped,— Right; as 'twere, a man assured of a— Uncertain life ii 3 19
Do thine own fortunes that obedient right Which both thy duty owes ii 3 167
And will for ever Do thee all rights of service iv 2 17
Jades' tricks; which are their own right by the law of nature iv 5 64
Thou'rt i' the right. Go, sir, rub your chain with crums *T. Night* ii 3 128
Then think you right: I am not what I am iii 1 153
I doubt not but to do myself much right, or you much shame v 1 317
You scarce can right me throughly then to say You did mistake *W. Tale* ii 1 99
And when I wander here and there, I then do most go right iv 3 18
In right and true behalf Of thy deceased brother *K. John* i 1 7
Fierce and bloody war, To enforce these rights so forcibly withheld i 1 18
Constance would not cease Till she had kindled France and all the world, Upon the right and party of her son i 1 34
Our strong possession and our right for us.—Your strong possession much more than your right, Or else it must go wrong i 1 39
A little from the right, In at the window, or else o'er the hatch i 1 170
Shadowing their right under your wings of war ii 1 14
A noble boy! Who would not do thee right? ii 1 18
The right thou hast in France, Together with that . . . white-faced shore ii 1 22
From England bring That right in peace which here we urge in war ii 1 47
England was Geffrey's right And this is Geffrey's ii 1 105
That stirs good thoughts . . . To look into the blots and stains of right ii 1 114
I'll smoke your skin-coat, an I catch you right ii 1 139
In right of Arthur do I claim of thee: Wilt thou resign them? ii 1 153
The dominations, royalties and rights Of this oppressed boy ii 1 176
For him, and in his right, we hold this town ii 1 268
Till you compound whose right is worthiest, We for the worthiest hold the right from both ii 1 281
Say, shall the current of our right run on? ii 1 335
When we know the king.—Know him in us, that here hold up his right ii 1 364
How may we content This widow lady? In her right we came ii 1 548
Without my wrong There is no tongue hath power to curse him right iii 1 183
When law can do no right, Let it be lawful that law bar no wrong iii 1 185
You, in the right of Lady Blanch your wife, May then make all the claim iii 4 142
If what in rest you have in right you hold iv 2 55
The life, the right and truth of all this realm Is fled to heaven iv 3 144
For the health and physic of our right v 2 21
On our actions set the name of right With holy breath v 2 67
You taught me how to know the face of right v 2 88
New flight; And happy newness, that intends old right v 4 61
As thy cause is right, So be thy fortune in this royal fight! *Richard II.* i 3 55
Receive thy lance; and God defend the right! i 3 101
Right, you say true: as Hereford's love, so his; As theirs, so mine ii 1 145
And gripe into your hands The royalties and rights of banish'd Hereford ii 1 190
Take Hereford's rights away, and take from Time His charters and his customary rights ii 1 195
If justice had her right ii 1 227
Whom the king hath wrong'd, Whom conscience and my kindred bids to right ii 2 115
My rights and royalties Pluck'd from my arms perforce ii 3 120
It stands your grace upon to do him right ii 3 138
Had feeling of my cousin's wrongs And laboured all I could to do him right ii 3 142
To find out right with wrong, it may not be ii 3 145
For the right of that We all have strongly sworn to give him aid ii 3 149
If angels fight, Weak men must fall, for heaven still guards the right iii 2 62
Given my treasures and my rights of thee To thick-eyed musing *1 Hen. IV.* ii 3 48
Shall we divide our right According to our threefold order ta'en? iii 1 70
Of no right, nor colour like to right, He doth fill fields with harness iii 2 100
Nor claim no further than your new-fall'n right, The seat of Gaunt v 1 44
He is not his craft's master; he doth not do it right *2 Hen. IV.* iii 2 298
Therefore let me have right, and let desert mount iv 3 60
Gave it me; Then plain and right must my possession be iv 5 223
You are right, justice, and you weigh this well v 2 102
Now you have done me right.—Do me right, And dub me knight: Samingo v 3 76
O God, that right should thus overcome might! v 4 27
Whose right Suits not in native colours with the truth *Hen. V.* i 2 16
All appear To hold in right and title of the female i 2 89
May I with right and conscience make this claim?—The sin upon my head! i 2 96
With blood and sword and fire to win your right i 2 131
In the right Of your great predecessor, King Edward the Third i 2 247
Thou hast spoke the right; His heart is fracted and corroborate ii 1 129
Nay, that's right; but why wear you your leek to-day? v 1 1
For he perforce must do thee right, because he hath not the gift to woo in other places v 2 162
Now, Salisbury, for thee, and for the right Of English Henry *1 Hen. VI.* ii 1 35
The plot is laid: if all things fall out right ii 3 4
And say withal I think he held the right ii 4 38
In the right of Richard Plantagenet We do exhibit to your majesty iii 1 150
You have great reason to do Richard right iii 1 154
God and Saint George, Talbot and England's right! iv 2 55
Nor shall proud Lancaster usurp my right, Nor hold the sceptre *2 Hen. VI.* i 1 244
Which now they hold by force and not by right ii 2 30
Here let them end it; and God defend the right! ii 3 55
Thou hast prevailed in right! ii 3 102
From Ireland thus comes York to claim his right v 1 1
To wring the widow from her custom'd right v 1 188
As I in justice and true right express it v 2 25
By words or blows here let us win our right *3 Hen. VI.* i 1 37
Be resolute; I mean to take possession of my right i 1 44
His is the right, and therefore pardon me i 1 148
Do right unto this princely Duke of York i 1 166
Your right depends not on his life or death i 2 11

Right. Go boast of this: And if thou tell'st the heavy story right, Upon my soul, the hearers will shed tears . . . . . . *3 Hen. VI.* i 4 160
Here's to right our gentle-hearted king . . . . . i 4 176
Arise a knight; And learn this lesson, draw thy sword in right . . ii 2 62
Say, Henry, shall I have my right, or no? . . . . ii 2 126
If that be right which Warwick says is right, There is no wrong, but every thing is right . . . . ii 2 131
No humble suitors press to speak for right, No, not a man comes . iii 1 19
He, on his right, asking a wife for Edward . . . . iii 1 44
Can Oxford, that did ever fence the right, Now buckler falsehood with a pedigree? For shame! . . . . . . iii 3 98
Did I put Henry from his native right? . . . . iii 3 190
Do me but right, and you must all confess That I was not ignoble of descent . . . . iv 1 69
Unto the sanctuary, To save at least the heir of Edward's right . . iv 4 32
'Tis my right, And Henry but usurps the diadem . . . iv 7 65
Whosoe'er gainsays King Edward's right, By this I challenge him . iv 7 74
With whom an upright zeal to right prevails . . . . v 1 78
Traitors as ye are: And thou usurp'st my father's right and mine . v 5 37
Had I not reason, think ye, to . . . seek their ruin that usurp'd our right? v 6 73
The sorrow that I have, by right is yours . . *Richard III.* i 3 172
So just is God, to right the innocent . . . . . . i 3 182
And see another, as I see thee now, Deck'd in thy rights, as thou art stall'd in mine! . . . . i 3 206
He is kind.—Right, As snow in harvest . . . . . i 4 248
I'll win our ancient right in France again, Or die a soldier . . iii 1 92
Successively from blood to blood, Your right of birth, your empery . iii 7 136
The right and fortune of his happy stars . . . . iii 7 172
Say, that right for right Hath dimm'd your infant morn to aged night . iv 4 15
Where should be graven, if that right were right, The slaughter of the prince . . . . iv 4 141
Then, in the name of God and all these rights, Advance your standards v 3 263
He was in the right; and so indeed it is . . . . . v 3 275
Sir, I desire you do me right and justice . . *Hen. VIII.* ii 4 13
I know a way, if it take right, in spite of fortune Will bring me off . iii 2 219
The citizens, I am sure, have shown at full their royal minds—As, let 'em have their rights, they are ever forward . . . . . iv 1 9
And urge the king To do me this last right . . . . iv 2 158
Force should be right; or rather, right and wrong, Between whose endless jar justice resides, Should lose their names . *Troi. and Cres.* i 3 116
Yet god Achilles still cries 'Excellent!' 'Tis Nestor right' . . . i 3 170
O virtuous fight, When right with right wars who shall be most right! iii 2 179
Ever right.—Menenius ever, ever . . . . *Coriolanus* ii 1 208
'Tis right.—It was his word: O, he would miss it rather . . ii 1 252
You are not right: have you not known The worthiest men have done't? ii 3 54
It shall be so I' the right and strength o' the commons . . . iii 3 14
Rights by rights falter, strengths by strengths do fail . . . iv 7 55
Patrons of my right, Defend the justice of my cause . . *T. Andron.* i 1 1
Romans, friends, followers, favourers of my right . . . . i 1 9
In the Capitol and senate's right, Whom you pretend to honour . . i 1 41
Friends, that have been thus forward in my right, I thank you all . i 1 56
Slain manfully in arms, In right and service of their noble country . i 1 197
Romans, do me right: Patricians, draw your swords . . . i 1 203
And resolved withal To do myself this reason and this right . . i 1 279
Think you not how dangerous It is to jet upon a prince's right? . . ii 1 64
Know, my boys, Your mother's hand shall right your mother's wrong . ii 3 121
And swear unto my soul to right your wrongs. The vow is made . . iii 1 279
Right, you have it . . . . iv 2 24
I am Revenge, sent from below To join with him and right his heinous wrongs . . . . v 2 4
If not so, then here I hit it right . . . *Rom. and Jul.* i 3 41
I am the very pink of courtesy.—Pink for flower.—Right . . . ii 4 63
A deed thou'lt die for.—Right, if doing nothing be death *T. of Athens* i 1 195
That with your other noble parts you'll suit In giving him his right . ii 2 24
Why, this hits right; I dreamt of a silver basin and ewer to-night . iii 1 5
Thus much of this [gold] will make black white, foul fair, Wrong right iv 3 29
By the right and virtue of my place, I ought to know . *J. Cæsar* ii 1 269
I think withal There would be hands uplifted in my right . *Macbeth* iv 3 42
Why, right; you are i' the right . . . . . *Hamlet* i 5 126
The time is out of joint: O cursed spite, That ever I was born to set it right! Nay, come, let's go together . . . . i 5 190
Let me conjure you, by the rights of our fellowship . . . ii 2 294
You say right, sir: o' Monday morning; 'twas so indeed . . . ii 2 406
Am I not i' the right, old Jephthah? . . . . . . ii 2 429
I must commune with your grief, Or you deny me right . . . iv 5 203
It falls right . . . . iv 7 71
I have some rights of memory in this kingdom . . . . v 2 400
When he saw my best alarum'd spirits, Bold in the quarrel's right *Lear* ii 1 56
When every case in law is right; No squire in debt, nor no poor knight iii 2 85
Gave her dear rights To his dog-hearted daughters . . . iv 3 46
No blown ambition doth our arms incite, But love, dear love, and our aged father's right . . . . iv 4 28
Pray that the right may thrive . . . . v 2 2
In my rights, By me invested, he compeers the best . . . v 3 68
Thou hast spoken right, 'tis true; The wheel is come full circle . . v 3 173
To him our absolute power: you, to your rights; With boot . . . v 3 300
I am desperate of my fortunes if they check me here.—You are in the right. Good night . . . . *Othello* ii 3 339
If you dare do yourself a profit and a right . . . . . . iv 2 239
Having the world for your labour, 'tis a wrong in your own world, and you might quickly make it right . . . . iv 3 83
By Hercules, I think I am i' the right.—Soldier, thou art *Ant. and Cleo.* iii 7 68
He is a god, and knows What is most right . . . . . iii 13 61
Our fealty and Tenantius' right With honour to maintain . *Cymbeline* v 4 73
Here's a fish hangs in the net, like a poor man's right in the law *Pericles* ii 1 123
Right and wrong. Hooking both right and wrong to the appetite, To follow as it draws! . . . . *Meas. for Meas.* ii 4 176
A man of complements, whom right and wrong Have chose as umpire . . . . *L. L. Lost* i 1 169
Right and wrong, Between whose endless jar justice resides . *T. and C.* i 3 116
Than to make up a free determination 'Twixt right and wrong . . ii 2 171
Right Anne. Who hath got the right Anne? . . . *Mer. Wives* v 5 225
Right apt. Thy constellation is right apt For this affair . . *T. Night* i 4 35
Right arched. Thou hast the right arched beauty of the brow *M. Wives* iii 3 59
Right arm. His right arm might purchase his own time *T. of Athens* iii 5 77
Right breed. This courtesy is not of the right breed . *Hamlet* iii 2 327
Right butterwomen. It is the right butter-women's rank to market . . . . *As Y. Like It* iii 2 103
Right casket. If he should offer to choose, and choose the right casket, you should refuse . . . . *Mer. of Venice* i 2 100
Right casket. If I fail Of the right casket, never in my life To woo a maid in way of marriage . . . . *Mer. of Venice* ii 9 12
Right cheek. His right cheek is worn bare . . . . *All's Well* iv 5 103
His right cheek Reposing on a cushion . . . . . *Cymbeline* iv 2 211
Right Christian. Pardon us the interruption Of thy devotion and right Christian zeal . . . . *Richard III.* iii 7 103
Right courteous. You are right courteous knights . . . *Pericles* ii 3 27
Right deadly. The time right deadly . . . . *Troi. and Cres.* v 2 39
Right description. A right description of our sport . . *L. L. Lost* v 2 522
Right desires. Grant of our most just and right desires . *2 Hen. IV.* iv 2 40
Right drawn sword. What my tongue speaks my right drawn sword may prove . . . . *Richard II.* i 1 46
Right father. It should here be laid, Either for life or death, upon the earth Of its right father . . . . *W. Tale* iii 3 46
Right fencing grace. This is the right fencing grace . . *2 Hen. IV.* ii 1 206
Right fit. I Return those duties back as are right fit . . . *Lear* i 1 99
Right form. In ranks and squadrons and right form of war . *J. Cæsar* ii 2 20
Right gipsy. Like a right gipsy, hath, at fast and loose, Beguiled me to the very heart of loss . . . . . . *Ant. and Cleo.* iv 12 28
Right glad. I am right glad that he's so out of hope . . *Tempest* iii 3 11
And am right glad to catch this good occasion . . . *Hen. VIII.* v 1 109
Right glad I am he was not at this fray . . . *Rom. and Jul.* i 1 124
I am right glad that his health is well, sir . . *T. of Athens* iii 1 13
Am right glad he is not standing here To tell this tale of mine *Cymbeline* v 5 296
Right good. A right good husband, let him be a noble . *Hen. VIII.* iv 2 146
A right good mark-man! . . . . *Rom. and Jul.* i 1 212
Right gracious lord, I cannot brook delay . . . *3 Hen. VI.* iii 2 18
Right great. Desired my Cressid in right great exchange *Troi. and Cres.* iii 3 21
Right hand. Who should be trusted, when one's own right hand Is perjured to the bosom? . . . . *T. G. of Ver.* v 4 67
It is your brother's right hand . . . . *Much Ado* i 3 51
Turn up on your right hand at the next turning . . *Mer. of Venice* ii 2 42
The murmuring stream Left on your right hand . . *As Y. Like It* iv 3 81
Walk before toward the sea-side; go on the right hand . . *W. Tale* iv 4 856
In this right hand, whose protection Is most divinely vow'd upon the right Of him it holds . . . . *K. John* ii 1 237
This strong right hand of mine Can pluck the diadem . *3 Hen. VI.* ii 1 152
By my soul, If this right hand would buy two hours' life . . . ii 6 80
Still in thy right hand carry gentle peace . . . *Hen. VIII.* iii 2 445
Do you two know how you are censured here in the city, I mean of us o' the right-hand file? . . . . *Coriolanus* ii 1 26
This poor right hand of mine Is left to tyrannize upon my breast *T. An.* iii 2 7
Resolve me this: Was it well done of rash Virginius To slay his daughter with his own right hand? . . . . v 3 37
And the cap Plays in the right hand, thus . . . *T. of Athens* ii 1 19
Come on my right hand, for this ear is deaf . . . *J. Cæsar* i 2 213
Upon the right hand I; keep thou the left . . . . . . v 1 18
This is my right hand, and this is my left: I am not drunk now *Othello* ii 3 118
Right himself. If he could right himself with quarrelling *Much Ado* v 1 51
Right husband. An it be the right husband and the right wife . iii 4 36
Right idea. Being the right idea of your father . . *Richard III.* iii 7 13
Right ill-disposed in brawl ridiculous . . . . *Hen. V.* iv Prol. 51
Right in thine eye. I do see the cruel pangs of death Right in thine eye . . . . *K. John* v 4 60
Right joyful of your reformation . . . . . *L. L. Lost* v 2 879
Right joyous are we to behold your face . . . . . *Hen V.* v 2 9
Right loath. I am right loath to go . . . . *Mer. of Venice* ii 5 16
Right maid. I am a right maid for my cowardice . . *M. N. Dream* iii 2 302
Right master constable. Call up the right master constable *Much Ado* iii 3 178
Right modest. An inviting eye; and yet methinks right modest *Othello* ii 3 24
Right nature. I will make thee Do thy right nature . . *T. of Athens* iv 3 44
Right noble. In the company of the right noble Claudio . . *Much Ado* i 1 84
Be not amazed; right noble is his blood . . . . *T. Night* v 1 271
Shall not be forgot; Right noble is thy merit, well I wot *Richard II.* v 6 18
Doubt you not, right noble princes both . . . *Richard III.* iii 5 64
He's right noble: Let him be call'd for . . . . *Coriolanus* ii 2 133
For his right noble mind, illustrious virtue . . . *T. of Athens* ii 2 87
With my cousin, your right-noble son, Lead our first battle . *Macbeth* v 6 3
Right noble Burgundy, When she was dear to us, we did hold her so *Lear* i 1 198
Right now. Came he right now to sing a raven's note? . *2 Hen. VI.* iii 2 40
Right of it. It is the right of it; it must be so . *Meas. for Meas.* iii 2 60
Right on. I only speak right on; I tell you that which you yourselves do know . . . . *J. Cæsar* iii 2 227
Right opinion. Shall yield the other in the right opinion . *1 Hen. VI.* ii 4 42
Right or wrong. King Henry, be thy title right or wrong, Lord Clifford vows to fight in thy defence . . . . . . *3 Hen. VI.* i 1 159
Right out. And be a boy right out . . . . . . *Tempest* iv 1 101
Right painted. I answer you right painted cloth . . *As Y. Like It* iii 2 290
Right poor. Mean and right poor . . . . . . *1 Hen. VI.* iv 6 23
Right praise. How many things by season season'd are To their right praise and true perfection! . . . . *Mer. of Venice* v 1 108
Right Promethean fire. They [women's eyes] sparkle still the right Promethean fire . . . . *L. L. Lost* iv 3 351
Right proud Of that most delicate lodging . . . . *Cymbeline* ii 4 135
Right reverend. With two right reverend fathers . . *Richard III.* iii 7 61
The right reverend Cardinal of York . . . . . *Hen. VIII.* i 1 51
Right ring. 'Tis no counterfeit.—'Tis the right ring, by heaven . . v 3 103
Right Rosalind. I would not have my right Rosalind of this mind, for, I protest, her frown might kill me . . . . . *As Y. Like It* iv 1 109
Right royal. Thy nephew and right royal sovereign . . . *K. John* i 1 15
Now, by my seat's right royal majesty . . . . *Richard II.* ii 1 120
Young, valiant, wise, and, no doubt, right royal . . *Richard III.* i 2 245
Go on: right royal . . . . *Ant. and Cleo.* iii 13 55
Right sense. Frighted the word out of his right sense . . *Much Ado* v 2 56
Right son to the right Vincentio . . . . . . *T. of Shrew* v 1 118
Right sorry. And am right sorry to repeat what follows . *Hen. VIII.* v 1 96
I must from hence; And am right sorry that I must report ye *Cymbeline* iii 5 3
Right spheres. You stars that move in your right spheres . *K. John* v 7 74
Right suddenly. Buy it with your gold right suddenly . *As Y. Like It* ii 4 100
Right supremacy. Awful rule and right supremacy . . *T. of Shrew* v 2 109
Right true it is, your son Lucentio here Doth love my daughter . . iv 4 40
Right use. I am glad your grace has made that right use of it *Hen. VIII.* iii 2 386
Put your bonnet to his right use; 'tis for the head . . . *Hamlet* v 2 95
Right valiant. I cannot joy, until I be resolved Where our right valiant father is become . . . . *3 Hen. VI.* ii 1 10
This thrice worthy and right valiant lord . . . *Troi. and Cres.* ii 3 200
The right-valiant Banquo walk'd too late . . . . . *Macbeth* iii 6 5
Right Vincento. As if he were the right Vincentio . . *T. of Shrew* iv 2 70
Imagine 'twere the right Vincentio.—Tut, fear not me . . . iv 4 12
Here's Lucentio, Right son to the right Vincentio . . . . . v 1 118

Right virtue. You'll be rotten ere you be half ripe, and that's the right virtue of the medlar . . . . *As Y. Like It* iii 2 127
Right welcome. Thou art right welcome as thy master is . . . ii 7 198
His noble cousin is right welcome hither . . . *Richard II.* iii 3 122
Right welcome, sir! Ere we depart, we'll share a bounteous time *T. of A.* i 1 262
Your lordship is right welcome back to Denmark . . . *Hamlet* v 2 81
Your graces are right welcome . . . . . *Lear* ii 1 131
Right well. O plague right well prevented! . . . *Much Ado* iii 2 136
Your noble and right well remember'd father's . . *2 Hen. IV.* iv 1 112
A hundred almshouses right well supplied . . . *Hen. V.* i 1 17
The one his purple blood right well resembles . . *3 Hen. VI.* ii 5 99
How doth the prince . . . ?—Right well, dear madam . *Richard III.* iv 1 15
Our great need of him You have right well conceited . *J. Cæsar* i 3 162
You know right well you did . . . . . *Hamlet* iii 1 97
Right wife. An it be the right husband and the right wife . *Much Ado* iii 4 36
Right wits. Read i' thy right wits.—So I do, madonna; but to read his right wits is to read thus . . . . . *T. Night* v 1 305
Being in his right wits and his good judgements . . . *Hen. V.* iv 7 49
Right worthy. To thy worth will add right worthy gains *Richard II.* v 6 12
We must follow you; Right worthy you priority . . *Coriolanus* i 1 251
Righteous. I love your daughter In such a righteous fashion *Mer. Wives* iii 4 83
This shall ye do, so help you righteous God! . . . *1 Hen. VI.* iv 1 8
They should be good men; their affairs as righteous . *Hen. VIII.* iii 1 22
Rome and the righteous heavens be my judge! . . . *T. Andron.* i 1 426
Seal with a righteous kiss A dateless bargain! . . *Rom. and Jul.* v 3 114
Let me be recorded by the righteous gods, I am as poor as you *T. of A.* iv 2 4
Righteously. If the truth of thy love to me were so righteously tempered as mine is to thee . . . . . . *As Y. Like It* i 2 14
Rightful. Most rightful judge! . . . . . *Mer. of Venice* iv 1 301
Some will mourn in ashes, some coal-black, For the deposing of a rightful king . . . . *Richard II.* v 1 50
To put forth My rightful hand in a well-hallow'd cause . *Hen. V.* i 2 293
They laboured to plant the rightful heir . . . *1 Hen. VI.* ii 5 80
And join'd with Charles, the rightful King of France . . iv 1 60
Did the Duke of York say he was rightful heir to the crown? *2 Hen. VI.* i 3 32
Poise the cause in justice' equal scales, Whose beam stands sure, whose rightful cause prevails . . . . ii 1 205
Henry the Fourth, Seized on the realm, deposed the rightful king . ii 2 24
Be we the first That shall salute our rightful sovereign . . ii 2 61
In time to come, I hope to reign; For I am rightful heir unto the crown iv 2 139
And in my conscience do repute his grace The rightful heir . . v 1 178
Rightfully. 'Gainst all the world will rightfully maintain *2 Hen. IV.* iv 5 225
Rightly. To be Englished rightly, is . . . . *Mer. Wives* i 3 52
Rightly reasoned, and in his own division . . . *Much Ado* v 1 229
He it was that might rightly say, Veni, vidi, vici . . *L. L. Lost* iv 1 68
Never be chosen by any rightly but one who shall rightly love *M. of V.* i 2 35
If I heard you rightly . . . . . . *As Y. Like It* v 4 186
This thorn Doth to our rose of youth rightly belong . *All's Well* i 3 136
No Christian, that means to be saved by believing rightly . *T. Night* iii 2 76
Perspectives, which rightly gazed upon Show nothing but confusion *Richard II.* ii 2 18
Choler, my lord, if rightly taken.—No, if rightly taken, halter *1 Hen. IV.* ii 4 356
I am assured, if I be measured rightly . . . *2 Hen. IV.* v 2 65
Thy name is Gaultier, being rightly sounded . . . *2 Hen. VI.* iv 1 37
Few men rightly temper with the stars . . . *3 Hen. VI.* iv 6 29
He tells you rightly.—Ye tell me what ye wish for both . *Hen. VIII.* iii 1 97
Digest things rightly Touching the weal o' the common . . *Coriolanus* i 1 154
If thou consider rightly of the matter . . . . *J. Cæsar* iii 2 114
You may be rightly just, Whatever I shall think . . *Macbeth* iv 3 30
Rightly to be great Is not to stir without great argument . *Hamlet* iv 4 53
That justly think'st, and hast most rightly said . . . *Lear* i 1 186
These dispositions, that of late transform you From what you rightly are i 4 243
My title and my perfect soul Shall manifest me rightly . . *Othello* i 2 32
I shall be furnish'd to inform you rightly . . *Ant. and Cleo.* i 4 77
Thou hast been rightly honest;—so hast thou . . . v 2 11
I cannot rightly say . . . . *Pericles* iii 4 8
Rigol. This is a sleep That from this golden rigol hath divorced So many English kings . . . . *2 Hen. IV.* iv 5 36
Rigorous. Seal'd his rigorous statutes with their bloods . *Com. of Errors* i 1 9
Hath ta'en great pains to qualify His rigorous course . *Mer. of Venice* iv 1 8
He shall be thrown down the Tarpeian rock With rigorous hands *Coriol.* iii 1 267
Rigorously. Whose maiden blood, thus rigorously effused, Will cry for vengeance at the gates of heaven . . . . . *1 Hen. VI.* v 4 52
Rigour. Follows close the rigour of the statute . *Meas. for Meas.* i 4 67
I tell you 'Tis rigour and not law . . . . *W. Tale* iii 2 115
As rigour of tempestuous gusts Provokes the mightiest hulk . *1 Hen. VI.* v 5 5
Let him have all the rigour of the law . . . *2 Hen. VI.* i 3 199
Clifford's rigour, Who thunders to his captives blood and death *3 Hen. VI.* ii 1 126
Let my old life Be sacrificed, some hour before his time, Unto the rigour of severest law . . . . *Rom. and Jul.* v 3 269
With others whom the rigour of our state Forced to cry out . *Lear* v 1 22
Rim. Fetch thy rim out at thy throat In drops of crimson blood *Hen. V.* iv 4 15
Rinaldo, you did never lack advice so much . . . *All's Well* iii 4 19
Write, write, Rinaldo, To this unworthy husband of his wife . . iii 4 29
Rind. Sweetest nut has sourest rind . . . . *As Y. Like It* iii 2 115
Within the infant rind of this small flower Poison hath residence and medicine power . . . . *Rom. and Jul.* ii 3 23
Ring. Sea-nymphs hourly ring his knell . . . . *Tempest* i 2 402
Take this ring with thee, Deliver it to Madam Silvia . *T. G. of Ver.* iv 4 76
Well, give her that ring and therewithal This letter . . . iv 4 90
This ring I gave him when he parted from me, To bind him to remember iv 4 102
He sends your ladyship this ring.—The more shame for him . . iv 4 137
Though his false finger have profaned the ring. . . . . iv 4 141
My master charged me to deliver a ring to Madam Silvia, which, out of my neglect, was never done.—Where is that ring? . . . . v 4 89
I pray thee, once to-night Give my sweet Nan this ring . *Mer. Wives* iii 4 104
Meadow-fairies, look you sing, Like to the Garter's compass, in a ring . v 5 70
Do you not hear it ring?—What, the chain?—No, no, the bell *C. of Er.* iv 2 51
Give me the ring of mine you had at dinner . . . . iv 3 69
My ring, or else the chain: I hope you do not mean to cheat me so . iv 3 78
A ring he hath of mine worth forty ducats . . . . iv 3 84
He rush'd into my house and took perforce My ring away . . iv 3 96
And took away my ring—The ring I saw upon his finger . . iv 4 141
Bearing thence Rings, jewels, any thing his rage did like . . v 1 144
And from my finger snatch'd that ring.—'Tis true, my liege; this ring I had of her . . . . v 1 276
He shall live no longer in monument than the bell rings . *Much Ado* v 2 81
A Death's face in a ring.—The face of an old Roman coin . *L. L. Lost* v 2 616
Rings, gawds, conceits, Knacks, trifles, nosegays . . *M. N. Dream* i 1 33
Showed me a ring that he had of your daughter for a monkey *M. of V.* iii 1 123
Ring. Let us all ring fancy's knell: I'll begin it,—Ding, dong, bell *Mer. of Venice* iii 2 70
This house, these servants and this same myself Are yours, my lord: I give them with this ring . . . . iii 2 173
When this ring Parts from this finger, then parts life from hence . . iii 2 185
For your love, I'll take this ring from you . . . . iv 1 427
This ring, good sir, alas, it is a trifle! I will not shame myself to give you this.—I will have nothing else . . . . iv 1 430
The dearest ring in Venice will I give you, And find it out by proclamation . . . . iv 1 435
Good sir, this ring was given me by my wife . . . . iv 1 441
If your wife be not a mad-woman, And know how well I have deserved the ring, She would not hold out enemy for ever, For giving it to me iv 1 446
Let him have the ring: Let his deservings and my love withal Be valued 'gainst your wife's commandment . . . . iv 1 449
Give him the ring, and bring him, if thou canst, Unto Antonio's house iv 1 453
My Lord Bassanio upon more advice Hath sent you here this ring . iv 2 7
His ring I do accept most thankfully: And so, I pray you, tell him . iv 2 9
I'll see if I can get my husband's ring . . . . . iv 2 13
We shall have old swearing That they did give the rings away to men . iv 2 16
About a hoop of gold, a paltry ring That she did give me . . . v 1 147
I gave my love a ring and made him swear Never to part with it . . v 1 170
I were best to cut my left hand off And swear I lost the ring defending it . . . . v 1 178
My Lord Bassanio gave his ring away Unto the judge that begg'd it v 1 179
Neither man nor master would take aught But the two rings.—What ring gave you, my lord? Not that, I hope, which you received of me v 1 184
You see my finger Hath not the ring upon it; it is gone. . . v 1 188
I will ne'er come in your bed Until I see the ring . . . v 1 191
If you did know to whom I gave the ring, If you did know for whom I gave the ring And would conceive for what I gave the ring And how unwillingly I left the ring, When nought would be accepted but the ring . . . . v 1 193
If you had known the virtue of the ring, Or half her worthiness that gave the ring, Or your own honour to contain the ring, You would not then have parted with the ring . . . . v 1 199
I'll die for't but some woman had the ring . . . . v 1 208
No woman had it, but a civil doctor, Which did refuse three thousand ducats of me And begg'd the ring . . . . v 1 212
Had you been there, I think you would have begg'd The ring of me to give the worthy doctor . . . . v 1 222
I once did lend my body for his wealth; Which, but for him that had your husband's ring, Had quite miscarried . . . . . v 1 250
Swear to keep this ring.—By heaven, it is the same I gave the doctor! . v 1 256
Pardon me, Bassanio; For, by this ring, the doctor lay with me . . v 1 259
I'll fear no other thing So sore as keeping safe Nerissa's ring . . v 1 307
You are full of pretty answers. Have you not been acquainted with goldsmiths' wives, and conned them out of rings? . *As Y. Like It* iii 2 289
Wrapp'd in sweet clothes, rings put upon his fingers *T. of Shrew* Ind. 1 38
He that runs fastest gets the ring . . . . . . i 1 145
An you'll not knock, I'll ring it . . . . . . i 2 16
We will have rings and things and fine array . . . . ii 1 325
With silken coats and caps and golden rings . . . . iv 3 55
Ere twice the horses of the sun shall bring Their fiery torcher his diurnal ring . . . . *All's Well* ii 1 165
When thou canst get the ring upon my finger which never shall come off . . . . iii 2 59; v 3 313
A ring the county wears, That downward hath succeeded in his house From son to son . . . : this ring he holds In most rich choice . iii 7 22
No more, But that your daughter, ere she seems as won, Desires this ring . . . . iii 7 32
Give me that ring.—I'll lend it thee, my dear . . . . iv 2 39
Mine honour's such a ring: My chastity's the jewel of our house . iv 2 45
Here, take my ring: My house, mine honour, yea, my life, be thine . iv 2 51
My reasons are most strong; and you shall know them When back again this ring shall be deliver'd . . . . iv 2 60
And on your finger in the night I'll put Another ring . . . iv 2 62
He hath given her his monumental ring, and thinks himself made . iv 3 21
Such a ring as this, The last that e'er I took her leave at court, I saw upon her finger . . . . v 3 78
This ring was mine; and, when I gave it Helen, I bade her, if her fortunes ever stood Necessitied to help, that by this token I would relieve her . . . . v 3 83
Howe'er it pleases you to take it so, The ring was never hers . . v 3 89
She ceased In heavy satisfaction and would never Receive the ring again v 3 101
Not in nature's mystery more science Than I have in this ring . . v 3 104
She is dead; which nothing, but to close Her eyes myself, could win me to believe, More than to see this ring . . . . . . v 3 120
If you shall prove This ring was ever hers . . . . v 3 125
Behold this ring, Whose high respect and rich validity Did lack a parallel v 3 191
This is his wife; That ring's a thousand proofs . . . . v 3 199
She hath that ring of yours.—I think she has . . . . v 3 209
She got the ring; And I had that which any inferior might At market-price have bought . . . . v 3 217
Send for your ring, I will return it home, And give me mine again . v 3 223
What ring was yours, I pray you?—Sir, much like The same upon your finger . . . . v 3 225
Know you this ring? this ring was his of late.—And this was it I gave him . . . . v 3 227
My lord, I do confess the ring was hers.—You boggle shrewdly . . v 3 231
This ring, you say, was yours?—Ay, my good lord.—Where did you buy it? . . . . v 3 271
This ring was mine; I gave it his first wife . . . . v 3 280
Unless thou tell'st me where thou hadst this ring, Thou diest . . v 3 284
The jeweller that owes the ring is sent for, And he shall surety me . v 3 297
There is your ring; And, look you, here's your letter . . . v 3 311
He left this ring behind him, Would I or not . . . *T. Night* i 5 320
She returns this ring to you, sir: you might have saved me my pains . ii 2 5
She took the ring of me: I'll none of it.—Come, sir, you peevishly threw it to her . . . . ii 2 13
I left no ring with her: what means this lady? . . . . ii 2 18
None of my lord's ring! why, he sent her none . . . . ii 2 25
I did send . . . A ring in chase of you . . . . . iii 1 124
The holy close of lips, Strengthen'd by interchangement of your rings . v 1 162
A handkerchief and rings of his that Paulina knows . . *W. Tale* v 2 71
Rejoice, you men of Angiers, ring your bells . . . *K. John* ii 1 312
And ring these fingers with thy household worms . . . iii 4 31
Hold, take my ring . . . . *Richard II.* iii 2 92
He said my ring was copper.—I say 'tis copper . . *1 Hen. IV.* iii 3 162
I will take such order that thy friends shall ring for thee *2 Hen. IV.* iii 2 198

Ring. Bid the merry bells ring to thine ear That thou art crowned 2 *Hen. IV.* iv 5 112
Why ring not out the bells aloud throughout the town? 1 *Hen. VI.* i 6 11
The Dauphin's drum, a warning bell, Sings heavy music to thy timorous soul; And mine shall ring thy dire departure out iv 2 41
Ring, bells, aloud; burn, bonfires, clear and bright 2 *Hen. VI.* v 1 3
Vouchsafe to wear this ring.—To take is not to give *Richard III.* i 2 202
Look, how this ring encompasseth thy finger, Even so thy breast encloseth my poor heart i 2 204
If entreaties Will render you no remedy, this ring Deliver them *Hen. VIII.* v 1 150
By virtue of that ring, I take my cause Out of the gripes of cruel men v 3 99
This is the king's ring.—'Tis no counterfeit.—'Tis the right ring v 3 102
I have seen thee pause and take thy breath, When that a ring of Greeks have hemm'd thee in *Troi. and Cres.* iv 5 193
Ring a hunter's peal, That all the court may echo *T. Andron.* ii 2 5
Upon his bloody finger he doth wear A precious ring ii 3 227
No mournful bell shall ring her burial v 3 197
Thy old groans ring yet in my ancient ears *Rom. and Jul.* ii 3 74
Give this ring to my true knight, And bid him come iii 2 142
Here, sir, a ring she bid me give you, sir iii 3 163
To take thence from her dead finger A precious ring, a ring that I must use In dear employment v 3 31
Make a ring about the corpse of Cæsar *J. Cæsar* iii 2 162
A ring; stand round.—Stand from the hearse iii 2 168
Ring the alarum-bell. Murder and treason! *Macbeth* ii 3 79
Ring the bell.—What's the business? ii 3 85
Now about the cauldron sing, Like elves and fairies in a ring iv 1 42
Ring the alarum-bell! Blow, wind! come, wrack! v 5 51
Pray God, your voice, like a piece of uncurrent gold, be not cracked within the ring *Hamlet* ii 2 448
Is this a prologue, or the posy of a ring?—'Tis brief, my lord iii 2 162
Show her this ring; And she will tell you who your fellow is *Lear* iii 1 47
Met I my father with his bleeding rings, Their precious stones new lost v 3 189
Who's that which rings the bell?—Diablo, ho! The town will rise *Oth.* ii 3 161
Your ring may be stolen too *Cymbeline* i 4 98
You have store of thieves; notwithstanding, I fear not my ring i 4 108
I dare thereupon pawn the moiety of my estate to your ring i 4 119
I will lay you ten thousand ducats to your ring i 4 139
My ring I hold dear as my finger; 'tis part of it i 4 145
I dare you to this match: here's my ring.—I will have it no lay i 4 158
The ring is won.—The stone's too hard to come by ii 4 45
I now Profess myself the winner of her honour, Together with your ring ii 4 54
If you can make't apparent . . . , my hand And ring is yours ii 4 58
Take your ring again; 'tis not yet won: It may be probable she lost it ii 4 114
Back my ring: Render to me some corporal sign about her ii 4 118
Nay, keep the ring—'tis true: I am sure She would not lose it ii 4 123
My boon is, that this gentleman may render Of whom he had this ring v 5 136
By villany I got this ring; 'twas Leonatus' jewel v 5 143
To attain In suit the place of's bed and win this ring v 5 185
He, true knight, No lesser of her honour confident Than I did truly find her, stakes this ring v 5 188
But your ring first; And here the bracelet of the truest princess v 5 415
The king my father gave you such a ring *Pericles* v 3 39
Ring-carrier. Marry, hang you!—And your courtesy, for a ring-carrier! *All's Well* iii 5 95
Ring'd about with bold adversity 1 *Hen. VI.* iv 4 14
Ringing. A cough, sir, which I caught with ringing in the king's affairs upon his coronation-day 2 *Hen. IV.* iii 2 194
Ringleader. The ringleader and head of all this rout 2 *Hen. VI.* ii 1 170
Ringlet. You demi-puppets that By moonshine do the green sour ringlets make *Tempest* v 1 37
To dance our ringlets to the whistling wind *M. N. Dream* ii 1 86
Ring time. Spring time, the only pretty ring time *As Y. Like It* v 3 20
Ringwood. Like Sir Actæon he, with Ringwood at thy heels *Mer. Wives* ii 1 122
Rinsing. And like a glass Did break i' the rinsing *Hen. VIII.* i 1 167
Riot. The council shall hear it; it is a riot.—It is not meet the council hear a riot; there is no fear of Got in a riot: the council, look you, shall desire to hear the fear of Got, and not to hear a riot *Mer. Wives* i 1 35
Other bars he lays before me, My riots past, my wild societies iii 4 8
The riot of the tipsy Bacchanals *M. N. Dream* v 1 48
And make a riot on the gentle brow Of true sincerity *K. John* iii 1 247
His rash fierce blaze of riot cannot last *Richard II.* ii 1 33
Riot and dishonour stain the brow Of my young Harry 1 *Hen. IV.* i 1 85
When his headstrong riot hath no curb 2 *Hen. IV.* iv 4 62
When that my care could not withhold thy riots, What wilt thou do when riot is thy care? iv 5 136
The tutor and the feeder of my riots v 5 66
His hours fill'd up with riots, banquets, sports *Hen. V.* i 1 56
No stop! so senseless of expense, That he will neither know how to maintain it, Nor cease his flow of riot *T. of Athens* ii 2 3
'Gainst the stream of virtue they may strive, And drown themselves in riot! iv 1 28
Thou wouldst have plunged thyself In general riot; melted down thy youth iv 3 256
Breaking forth In rank and not-to-be-endured riots *Lear* i 4 223
If, sir, perchance She have restrain'd the riots of your followers ii 4 145
Let those cities that of plenty's cup And her prosperities so largely taste, With their superfluous riots, hear these tears! *Pericles* i 4 54
Rioter. He's a sworn rioter *T. of Athens* iii 5 68
Rioting. I wrote to you When rioting in Alexandria; you Did pocket up my letters *Ant. and Cleo.* ii 2 72
Riotous. His riotous youth, with dangerous sense, Might in the times to come have ta'en revenge *Meas. for Meas.* iv 4 32
This hand of mine hath writ in thy behalf And therefore shall it charm thy riotous tongue 2 *Hen. VI.* iv 1 64
Who slew to-day a riotous gentleman *Richard III.* ii 1 100
All our offices have been oppress'd With riotous feeders *T. of Athens* ii 2 168
Laertes, in a riotous head, O'erbears your officers *Hamlet* iv 5 101
His knights grow riotous, and himself upbraids us On every trifle *Lear* i 3 6
Our court, infected with their manners, Shows like a riotous inn i 4 265
Was he not companion with the riotous knights That tend upon my father? ii 1 96
The fitchew, nor the soiled horse, goes to't With a more riotous appetite iv 6 125
Riotous madness, To be entangled with those mouth-made vows! *Ant. and Cleo.* i 3 29
Rip. To know our enemies' minds, we'ld rip their hearts *Lear* iv 6 265
I'll have this secret from thy heart, or rip Thy heart to find it *Cymbeline* iii 5 86
Ripe. And Trinculo is reeling ripe *Tempest* v 1 279
His head unmellow'd, but his judgement ripe *T. G. of Ver.* ii 4 70
When the doctor spies his vantage ripe, To pinch her by the hand *M. W.* iv 6 43
Ripe. Ripe as the pomewater, who now hangeth like a jewel *L. L. Lost* iv 2 4
Things growing are not ripe until their season: So I, being young, till now ripe not to reason *M. N. Dream* ii 2 117
O, how ripe in show Thy lips, those kissing cherries, tempting grow! iii 2 139
There is a brief how many sports are ripe v 1 42
So, from hour to hour, we ripe and ripe, And then, form hour to hour, we rot and rot *As Y. Like It* ii 7 26
You'll be rotten ere you be half ripe iii 2 127
My thoughts are ripe in mischief *T. Night* v 1 132
We intended To keep in darkness what occasion now Reveals before 'tis ripe v 1 157
That yon green boy shall have no sun to ripe The bloom that promiseth a mighty fruit *K. John* ii 1 472
His passion is so ripe, it needs must break iv 2 79
When they see the hours ripe on earth, Will rain hot vengeance *Rich. II.* i 2 7
Some unborn sorrow, ripe in fortune's womb, Is coming towards me ii 2 10
When time is ripe, which will be suddenly 1 *Hen. IV.* i 3 294
He is retired, to ripe his growing fortunes 2 *Hen. IV.* iv 1 13
Thou wilt needs invest thee with my honours Before thy hour be ripe iv 5 97
Ripe for exploits and mighty enterprises *Hen. V.* i 2 121
We thought not good to bruise an injury till it were full ripe iii 6 130
Let them keep it till thy sins be ripe *Richard III.* i 3 219
He was a scholar, and a ripe and good one; Exceeding wise *Hen. VIII.* iv 2 51
The strawy Greeks, ripe for his edge, Fall down before him *Troi. and Cres.* v 5 24
Let two more summers wither in their pride, Ere we may think her ripe to be a bride *Rom. and Jul.* i 2 11
Plagues, incident to men, Your potent and infectious fevers heap On Athens, ripe for stroke! *T. of Athens* iv 1 23
Our legions are brim-full, our cause is ripe *J. Cæsar* iv 3 215
Macbeth Is ripe for shaking *Macbeth* iv 3 238
I will work him To an exploit, now ripe in my device *Hamlet* iv 7 65
Yet fruits that blossom first will first be ripe *Othello* ii 3 383
You, born in these latter times, When wit's more ripe *Pericles* i Gower 12
A wench full grown, Even ripe for marriage-rite iv Gower 17
Ripe age. Five and twenty, sir.—A ripe age *As Y. Like It* v 1 22
Ripe aptness. They are in a ripe aptness to take all power from the people *Coriolanus* iv 3 23
Ripe grapes. The tartness of his face sours ripe grapes v 4 18
Ripe lip. Those happy smilets, That play'd on her ripe lip *Lear* iv 3 22
Ripe moving. Give scandal to the blood o' the prince my son, Who I do think is mine and love as mine, Without ripe moving to't? *W. T.* i 1 332
Ripe revenue. My ripe revenue and due by birth *Richard III.* iii 7 158
Ripe sister. Bestows himself Like a ripe sister *As Y. Like It* iv 3 88
Ripe wants. To supply the ripe wants of my friend *Mer. of Venice* i 3 64
Ripely. It fits us therefore ripely Our chariots and our horsemen be in readiness *Cymbeline* iii 5 22
Ripen. Which elder days shall ripen and confirm *Richard II.* ii 3 43
And, as my fortune ripens with thy love, It shall be still thy true love's recompense ii 3 48
And ripens in the sunshine of his favour 2 *Hen. IV.* iv 2 12
And wholesome berries thrive and ripen best Neighbour'd by fruit of baser quality *Hen. V.* i 1 61
And ripen justice in this commonweal *T. Andron.* i 1 227
This is not yet an Alexandrian feast.—It ripens towards it *Ant. and Cleo.* ii 7 103
Ripened. With ripen'd time Unfold the evil which is here wrapt up In countenance! *Meas. for Meas.* v 1 116
Where honeysuckles, ripen'd by the sun, Forbid the sun to enter *M. Ado* iii 1 8
Were growing time once ripen'd to my will 1 *Hen. VI.* ii 4 99
In his full and ripen'd years *Richard III.* ii 3 14
Ripeness. Promises Upon this land a thousand thousand blessings, Which time shall bring to ripeness *Hen. VIII.* v 5 21
Men must endure Their going hence, even as their coming hither: Ripeness is all *Lear* v 2 11
Ripening. This bud of love, by summer's ripening breath, May prove a beauteous flower when next we meet *Rom. and Jul.* ii 2 121
Riper. There was a pretty redness in his lip, A little riper and more lusty red Than that mix'd in his cheek *As Y. Like It* iii 5 121
Ripest. The ripest fruit first falls, and so doth he *Richard II.* ii 1 153
Humble as the ripest mulberry That will not hold the handling *Coriol.* iii 2 79
Riping. But stay the very riping of the time *Mer. of Venice* ii 8 40
Ripped. Macduff was from his mother's womb Untimely ripp'd *Macbeth* v 8 16
Poor I am stale, a garment out of fashion; And, for I am richer than to hang by the walls, I must be ripp'd *Cymbeline* iii 4 55
Ripping. You bloody Neroes, ripping up the womb Of your dear mother England *K. John* v 2 152
Ript. That from me was Posthumus ript, Came crying 'mongst his foes, A thing of pity! *Cymbeline* v 4 45
Rise. The humour rises; it is good *Mer. Wives* i 3 63
Go to bed when she list, rise when she list, all is as she will ii 2 124
Some rise by sin, and some by virtue fall *Meas. for Meas.* ii 1 38
Master Barnardine! you must rise and be hanged! iv 3 23
You must be so good, sir, to rise and be put to death iv 3 29
And never rise until my tears and prayers Have won his grace *C. of Er.* v 1 115
Wake my cousin Beatrice, and desire her to rise *Much Ado* iii 4 2
Rise, Grumio, rise: we will compound this quarrel *T. of Shrew* i 2 27
The marigold, that goes to bed wi' the sun And with him rises weeping *W. Tale* iv 4 106
Kneel thou down Philip, but rise more great, Arise sir Richard *K. John* i 1 161
That rise thus nimbly by a true king's fall *Richard. II.* iv 1 318
Never will I rise up from the ground Till Bolingbroke have pardon'd thee v 2 116
May my knees grow to the earth, . . . Unless a pardon ere I rise or speak v 3 32
Rise up, good aunt.—Not yet, I thee beseech v 3 92
His weary joints would gladly rise, I know v 3 105
May reasonably die and never rise To do him wrong 1 *Hen. IV.* i 3 74
Rise from the ground like feather'd Mercury iv 1 106
Though he be dead: how, if he should counterfeit too and rise? v 4 125
Why may not he rise as well as I? v 4 128
Let me no more from this obedience rise 2 *Hen. IV.* iv 5 147
I will rise there with so full a glory That I will dazzle all *Hen. V.* i 2 278
Like a lackey, from the rise to set Sweats in the eye of Phœbus iv 1 289
Next day after dawn, Doth rise and help Hyperion to his horse iv 1 292
Will make him burst his lead and rise from death 1 *Hen. VI.* i 1 64
If it chance the one of us do fail, The other yet may rise ii 1 32
I gird thee with the valiant sword of York: Rise, Richard, like a true Plantagenet, And rise created princely Duke of York iii 1 172
The commons haply rise, to save his life 2 *Hen. VI.* iii 1 240
I will make myself a knight presently. Rise up Sir John Mortimer iv 2 128
Iden, kneel down. Rise up a knight v 1 78
Lord Cobham, With whom the Kentishmen will willingly rise 3 *Hen. VI.* i 2 41
What resteth more, But that I seek occasion how to rise? i 2 45

Rise. Ere my knee rise from the earth's cold face, I throw my hands, mine eyes, my heart to thee *3 Hen. VI.* ii 3 35
Thou shalt not dread The scatter'd foe that hopes to rise again ii 6 93
Now begins a second storm to rise iii 3 47
I will not rise, unless your highness grant *Richard III.* ii 1 97
Go, bid thy master rise and come to me iii 2 31
The rest, that love me, rise and follow me iii 4 81
Go, by this token: rise, and lend thine ear: There is no more but so iv 2 80
The red wine first must rise In their fair cheeks *Hen. VIII.* i 4 43
Fearing he would rise, he was so virtuous, Kept him a foreign man still ii 2 128
Found thee a way, out of his wreck, to rise in iii 2 437
Who from the sacred ashes of her honour Shall star-like rise v 5 47
I ken the manner of his gait; He rises on the toe *Troi. and Cres.* iv 5 15
Even in the fan and wind of your fair sword, You bid them rise, and live v 3 42
Let Titan rise as early as he dare v 10 25
Who's like to rise, Who thrives and who declines *Coriolanus* i 1 196
I kneel'd before him; 'Twas very faintly he said 'Rise' v 1 66
Rise, Marcus, rise. The dismall'st day is this that e'er I saw *T. Andron.* i 1 383
Rise, Titus, rise; my empress hath prevail'd i 1 459
A crimson river of warm blood, Like to a bubbling fountain stirr'd with wind, Doth rise and fall between thy rosed lips ii 4 24
Rise and stand; Why should you fall into so deep an O? *Rom. and Jul.* iii 3 89
Th' ear, Taste, touch and smell, pleased from thy table rise *T. of Athens* i 2 132
Portia, what mean you? wherefore rise you now? *J. Cæsar* ii 1 234
And put a tongue In every wound of Cæsar that should move The stones of Rome to rise and mutiny iii 2 234
Good night: Early to-morrow will we rise, and hence iv 3 230
Malcolm! Banquo! As from your graves rise up *Macbeth* ii 3 84
Gentlemen, rise: his highness is not well iii 4 52
Now they rise again, With twenty mortal murders on their crowns iii 4 80
What is this That rises like the issue of a king? iv 1 87
Rebellion's head, rise never till the wood Of Birnam rise iv 1 97
I have seen her rise from her bed, throw her nightgown upon her, unlock her closet, take forth paper, fold it, write upon't v 1 5
Foul deeds will rise, Though all the earth o'erwhelm them *Hamlet* i 2 257
The king rises.—What, frighted with false fire! iii 2 276
How abhorred in my imagination it is! my gorge rises at it v 1 207
Lo, here I lie, Never to rise again v 2 330
The younger rises when the old doth fall *Lear* iii 3 26
You rise to play and go to bed to work *Othello* ii 1 116
Who's that which rings the bell?—Diablo, ho! The town will rise ii 3 162
Do not rise yet iii 3 462
Whose fortunes shall rise higher, Cæsar's or mine? *Ant. and Cleo.* ii 3 16
If for the sake of merit thou wilt hear me, Rise from thy stool ii 7 62
To business that we love we rise betime, And go to't with delight iv 4 20
Arise, you shall not kneel: I pray you, rise; rise, Egypt v 2 115
Rise, and fade. He shall be lord of lady Imogen *Cymbeline* v 4 106
Rise, prithee, rise. Sit down: thou art no flatterer *Pericles* i 2 59
Like to groves, being topp'd, they higher rise i 4 9
Arise, I pray you, rise: We do not look for reverence, but for love i 4 98
This day I'll rise, or else add ill to ill ii 1 172
Now, blessing on thee! rise; thou art my child v 1 215
Risen. A holy prophetess new risen up *1 Hen. VI.* i 4 102
The other side o' the city is risen *Coriolanus* i 1 48
Ere I was risen from the place that show'd My duty kneeling *Lear* ii 4 29
Our griefs are risen to the top, And now at length they overflow *Pericles* ii 4 23
Riseth. That ever holds: who riseth from a feast With that keen appetite that he sits down? *Mer. of Venice* ii 6 8
Rising. Their rising senses Begin to chase the ignorant fumes that mantle Their clearer reason *Tempest* v 1 66
Meet with me Upon the rising of the mountain-foot *T. G. of Ver.* v 2 46
Rising and cawing at the gun's report *M. N. Dream* iii 2 22
Though I will not practise to deceive, Yet, to avoid deceit, I mean to learn; For it shall strew the footsteps of my rising *K. John* i 1 216
So he'll die; and, rising so again, When I shall meet him in the court of heaven I shall not know him iii 4 86
Shall see us rising in our throne, the east *Richard II.* iii 2 50
With A rising sigh he wisheth you in heaven *1 Hen. IV.* iii 1 10
Doth enlarge his rising with the blood Of fair King Richard *2 Hen. IV.* i 1 204
From the rising of the lark to the lodging of the lamb *Hen. V.* iii 7 34
As hating thee, are rising up in arms *2 Hen. VI.* iv 1 93
I draw in many a tear And stop the rising of blood-sucking sighs *3 Hen. VI.* iv 4 22
So famous, So excellent in art, and still so rising *Hen. VIII.* iv 2 62
They are rising, they are rising *Coriolanus* iv 5 250
All day long, Even from Hyperion's rising in the east Until his very downfall in the sea *T. Andron.* v 2 56
O me, my heart, my rising heart! but, down! *Lear* ii 4 122
Rite. May With full and holy rite be minister'd *Tempest* iv 1 17
Time goes on crutches till love have all his rites *Much Ado* ii 1 373
Hang mournful epitaphs and do all rites That appertain unto a burial iv 1 209
Now, unto thy bones good night! Yearly will I do this rite v 3 23
After that the holy rites are ended, I'll tell you largely v 4 68
No doubt they rose up early to observe The rite of May *M. N. Dream* iv 1 138
Straight shall our nuptial rites be solemnized *Mer. of Venice* ii 9 6
Proceed, proceed: we will begin these rites, As we do trust they'll end, in true delights *As Y. Like It* v 4 203
The priest attends To speak the ceremonial rites of marriage *T. of Shrew* iii 2 6
The great prerogative and rite of love *All's Well* ii 4 42
Presently The rites of marriage shall be solemnized *K. John* ii 1 539
By that and all the rites of knighthood else, Will I make good *Rich. II.* i 1 75
With mine own breath release all duty's rites iv 1 210
I'll thank myself For doing these fair rites of tenderness *1 Hen. IV.* v 4 98
Do we all holy rites; Let there be sung 'Non nobis' and 'Te Deum' *Hen. V.* iv 8 127
I must not yield to any rites of love *1 Hen. VI.* ii 2 113
God give us leisure for these rites of love! *Richard III.* v 3 101
Stand gracious to the rites that we intend! *T. Andron.* i 1 78
See, lord and father, how we have perform'd Our Roman rites i 1 143
There shall we consummate our spousal rites i 1 337
No funeral rite, nor man in mourning weeds, No mournful bell v 3 196
Where and what time thou wilt perform the rite *Rom. and Jul.* ii 2 146
Lovers can see to do their amorous rites By their own beauties iii 2 8
What cursed foot wanders this way to-night, To cross my obsequies and true love's rite? v 3 20
Cæsar shall Have all true rites and lawful ceremonies *J. Cæsar* iii 1 241
According to his virtue let us use him, With all respect and rites of burial v 5 77
No trophy, sword, nor hatchment o'er his bones, No noble rite *Hamlet* iv 5 215
Who is this they follow? And with such maimed rites? v 1 242
Rite. For his passage, The soldiers' music and the rites of war Speak loudly for him *Hamlet* v 2 410
If I be left behind, A moth of peace, and he go to the war, The rites for which I love him are bereft me *Othello* i 3 258
Rivage. You stand upon the rivage and behold A city on the inconstant billows dancing *Hen. V.* iii Prol. 14
Rival. My foolish rival, that her father likes Only for his possessions are so huge *T. G. of Ver.* ii 4 174
Come, shadow, come, and take this shadow up, For 'tis thy rival iv 4 203
You both are rivals, and love Hermia; And now both rivals, to mock Helena: A trim exploit, a manly enterprise! *M. N. Dream* iii 2 156
Lead these testy rivals so astray As one come not within another's way iii 2 358
I know you two are rival enemies: How comes this gentle concord? iv 1 147
Had I but the means To hold a rival place with one of them *Mer. of Ven.* i 1 174
Again have access to our fair mistress and be happy rivals *T. of Shrew* i 1 119
Her withholds from me and other more, Suitors to her and rivals in my love i 2 122
Who goes there, ha?—Peace, Grumio! it is the rival of my love i 2 142
To present slaves and servants Translates his rivals *T. of Athens* i 1 72
Horatio and Marcellus, The rivals of my watch *Hamlet* i 1 13
Great rivals in our youngest daughter's love *Lear* i 1 47
Rival-hating. With rival-hating envy *Richard II.* i 3 131
Rivality. Cæsar, having made use of him in the wars 'gainst Pompey, presently denied him rivality *Ant. and Cleo.* iii 5 8
Rivalled. Who with this king Hath rivall'd for our daughter *Lear* i 1 194
Rive. Ten thousand French have ta'en the sacrament To rive their dangerous artillery Upon no Christian soul but English Talbot *1 Hen. VI.* iv 2 29
When my heart, As wedged with a sigh, would rive in twain *Tr. and Cr.* i 1 35
Blunt wedges rive hard knots i 3 316
Yet to charge thy sulphur with a bolt That should but rive an oak *Cor.* v 3 153
Close pent-up guilts, Rive your concealing continents *Lear* iii 2 58
Send him word you are dead. The soul and body rive not more in parting Than greatness going off *Ant. and Cleo.* iv 13 5
Rived. When the scolding winds Have rived the knotty oaks *J. Cæsar* i 3 6
Brutus hath rived my heart: A friend should bear his friend's infirmities iv 3 85
Rivelled. The rivelled fee-simple of the tetter *Troi. and Cres.* v 1 26
River. If the river were dry, I am able to fill it with my tears *T. G. of V.* ii 3 58
Shallow rivers, to whose falls Melodious birds sings madrigals *M. Wives* iii 1 17
The rogues slighted me into the river iii 5 10
You say he has been thrown in the rivers iv 4 22
Groping for trouts in a peculiar river *Meas. for Meas.* i 2 91
Which falling in the land Have every pelting river made so proud That they have overborne their continents *M. N. Dream* ii 1 91
Like a proud river peering o'er his bounds *K. John* iii 1 23
Makes it seem Like rivers of remorse and innocency iv 3 110
Nor let my kingdom's rivers take their course Through my burn'd bosom v 7 38
Stormy day, Which makes the silver rivers drown their shores *Rich. II.* iii 2 107
See how this river comes me cranking in, And cuts me from the best of all my land A huge half-moon *1 Hen. IV.* iii 1 98
The river hath thrice flow'd, no ebb between *2 Hen. IV.* iv 4 125
Beyond the river we'll encamp ourselves *Hen. V.* iii 6 180
There is a river in Macedon; and there is also moreover a river at Monmouth iv 7 28
But it is out of my prains what is the name of the other river iv 7 31
A little fire is quickly trodden out; Which, being suffer'd, rivers cannot quench *3 Hen. VI.* iv 8 8
With thy scorns drew'st rivers from his eyes *Richard III.* i 3 176
Should the approach of this wild river break *Hen. VIII.* iii 2 198
The falcon as the tercel, for all the ducks i' the river *Troi. and Cres.* iii 2 56
If you do remember, I send it through the rivers of your blood *Coriolanus* i 1 139
A crimson river of warm blood, Like to a bubbling fountain *T. Andron.* ii 4 22
No, nor the fruitful river in the eye, Nor the dejected 'haviour *Hamlet* i 2 80
With plenteous rivers and wide-skirted meads *Lear* i 1 66
Give me mine angle; we'll to the river *Ant. and Cleo.* ii 5 10
The imperious seas breed monsters, for the dish Poor tributary rivers as sweet fish *Cymbeline* iv 2 36
River Cydnus. She pursed up his heart, upon the river of Cydnus *Ant. and Cleo.* ii 2 192
River Po. Talking of the Alps and Apennines, The Pyrenean and the river Po *K. John* i 1 203
River Sala. And did seat the French Beyond the river Sala *Hen. V.* i 2 63
River Somme. 'Tis certain he hath pass'd the river Somme iii 5 1
River Styx. Fly not; for shouldst thou take the river Styx, I would swim after *Troi. and Cres.* v 4 20
Rivers. Brother Rivers, are you yet to learn What late misfortune is befall'n King Edward? *3 Hen. VI.* iv 4 2
She may, Lord Rivers! why, who knows not so? *Richard III.* i 3 93
You and your husband Grey Were factious for the house of Lancaster; And, Rivers, so were you i 3 129
Rivers and Dorset, you were standers by, And so wast thou i 3 210
And withal whet me To be revenged on Rivers, Vaughan, Grey i 3 333
Rivers and Hastings, take each other's hand ii 1 7
I entreat true peace . . . Of you, Lord Rivers, and, Lord Grey, of you ii 1 66
My uncle Rivers talk'd how I did grow More than my brother ii 4 11
Lord Rivers and Lord Grey are sent to Pomfret ii 4 42
And so falls it out With Rivers, Vaughan, Grey: and so 'twill do With some men else iii 2 67
Rivers, Vaughan, Grey, Untimely smother'd in their dusky graves iv 4 69
Tell her thou madest away her uncle Clarence, Her uncle Rivers iv 4 282
Rivers, Grey, Holy King Henry, and thy fair son Edward v 1 3
Let me sit heavy on thy soul to-morrow, Rivers, that died at Pomfret! v 3 140
Rivet. With busy hammers closing rivets up *Hen. V.* iv Prol. 13
With a palsy-fumbling on his gorget, Shake in and out the rivet *T. and C.* i 3 175
I like thy armour well; I'll frush it and unlock the rivets all v 6 29
Give him heedful note; For I mine eyes will rivet to his face *Hamlet* iii 2 90
Riveted. A thing stuck on with oaths upon your finger And so riveted with faith unto your flesh *Mer. of Venice* v 1 169
A thousand, sir, Early though't be, have on their riveted trim *A. and C.* iv 4 22
Why should I write this down, that's riveted, Screw'd to my memory? *Cymbeline* ii 2 43
Rivo! says the drunkard. Call in ribs, call in tallow *1 Hen. IV.* ii 4 125
Road. Adieu! my father at the road Expects my coming *T. G. of Ver.* i 1 53
I must unto the road, to disembark Some necessaries ii 4 187
Go hie thee presently, post to the road *Com. of Errors* iii 2 152
Whose names yet run smoothly in the even road of a blank verse *M. Ado* v 2 33
Peering in maps for ports and piers and roads *Mer. of Venice* i 1 19
On the outward wall, Even in the force and road of casualty ii 9 30
My ships Are safely come to road v 1 288

Road. Enforce A thievish living on the common road . *As Y. Like It* ii 3 33
Besides an argosy That now is lying in Marseilles' road . *T. of Shrew* ii 1 377
This be the most villanous house in all London road for fleas 1 *Hen. IV.* ii 1 16
This Doll Tearsheet should be some road . . . . . 2 *Hen. IV.* ii 2 183
The Scot, who will make road upon us With all advantages . *Hen. V.* i 2 138
At last, with easy roads, he came to Leicester . *Hen. VIII.* iv 2 17
Ready, when time shall prompt them, to make road Upon's again *Cor.* iii 1 5
You know the very road into his kindness, And cannot lose your way . v 1 59
I am out of the road of rutting for ever . . . . . *Pericles* iv 5 9
Road-way. Never a man's thought in the world keeps the road-way better than thine . 2 *Hen. IV.* ii 2 63
Roam. And lusty lads roam here and there . . . . . v 3 21
Rome shall remedy this.—Roam thither, then. . 1 *Hen. VI.* iii 1 51
Roaming clean through the bounds of Asia . . *Com. of Errors* i 1 134
Daphne roaming through a thorny wood . . . . *T. of Shrew* Ind. 2 59
O mistress mine, where are you roaming? . . . *T. Night* ii 3 40
Roan. When Bolingbroke rode on roan Barbary . *Richard II.* v 5 78
What horse? a roan, a crop-ear, is it not?—It is, my lord.—That roan shall be my throne . . . . . 1 *Hen. IV.* ii 3 72
Give my roan horse a drench . . . . ii 4 120
Roar. If by your art, my dearest father, you have Put the wild waters in this roar, allay them . . . . . *Tempest* i 2 2
Fill all thy bones with aches, make thee roar That beasts shall tremble i 2 370
It was the roar Of a whole herd of lions . . . . . ii 1 315
Hark, they roar!—Let them be hunted soundly . . . . iv 1 262
Thus dost thou hear the Nemean lion roar . . *L. L. Lost* iv 1 90
I will roar, that I will do any man's heart good to hear me *M. N. Dream* i 2 72
I will roar, that I will make the duke say 'Let him roar again' . i 2 74
I will aggravate my voice so that I will roar you as gently as any sucking dove; I will roar you an 'twere any nightingale . . . . i 2 84
Neigh, and bark, and grunt, and roar, and burn . . . . iii 1 113
When lion rough in wildest rage doth roar . . . . . v 1 225
Now the hungry lion roars, And the wolf behowls the moon . . v 1 378
Mock the lion when he roars for prey . . *Mer. of Venice* ii 1 30
Have I not in my time heard lions roar? . . . *T. of Shrew* i 2 201
Peace! no more.—O, tremble, for you hear the lion roar . *K. John* ii 1 294
An if the devil come and roar for them, I will not send them . 1 *Hen. IV.* i 3 125
Let the welkin roar . . . . 2 *Hen. IV.* ii 4 182
Prick me Bullcalf till he roar again.—O Lord! good my lord captain,—What, dost thou roar before thou art pricked? . . . . iii 2 187
And makes him roar these accusations forth . . 1 *Hen. VI.* iii 1 40
But great men tremble when the lion roars . . 2 *Hen. VI.* iii 1 19
Earth gapes, hell burns, fiends roar, saints pray . *Richard III.* iv 4 75
Is this a place to roar in? . . . . . . *Hen. VIII.* v 4 7
Hark, how Troy roars! how Hecuba cries out! . . *Troi. and Cres.* v 3 83
But I fear They'll roar him in again . . . *Coriolanus* iv 6 124
And roars As doth the lion in the Capitol . . . *J. Cæsar* i 3 74
As we shall make our griefs and clamour roar Upon his death *Macbeth* i 7 78
That looks so many fathoms to the sea And hears it roar beneath *Hamlet* i 4 78
Ay me, what act, That roars so loud, and thunders in the index? . iii 4 52
Your flashes of merriment, that were wont to set the table on a roar . v 1 211
Nay, lay thee down and roar; For thou hast kill'd the sweetest innocent That e'er did lift up eye . . . . . *Othello* v 2 198
He did provoke me With language that would make me spurn the sea, If it could so roar to me . . . . . . *Cymbeline* v 5 295
Could I rage and roar As doth the sea she lies in, yet the end Must be as 'tis . . . . *Pericles* iii 3 10
Roared. To cry to the sea that roar'd to us . . . . *Tempest* i 2 149
Well roared, Lion.—Well run, Thisbe . . . *M. N. Dream* v 1 270
Better 'twere I met the ravin lion when he roar'd . . *All's Well* iii 2 120
How the poor souls roared, and the sea mocked them; and how the poor gentleman roared and the bear mocked him . *W. Tale* iii 3 101
How the rogue roar'd! . . . . 1 *Hen. IV.* ii 2 118
Roared for mercy and still run and roared, as ever I heard bull-calf . ii 4 286
There roar'd the sea, and trumpet-clangor sounds . 2 *Hen. IV.* v 5 42
And made the forest tremble when they roar'd . . 3 *Hen. VI.* v 7 12
Your brethren roar'd and ran From the noise of our own drums *Coriol.* ii 3 59
But at his nurse's tears He whined and roar'd away your victory . v 6 98
This torture should be roar'd in dismal hell . . *Rom. and Jul.* iii 2 44
The torrent roar'd, and we did buffet it With lusty sinews . *J. Cæsar* i 2 107
Roarers. What cares these roarers for the name of king? . *Tempest* i 1 18
Roaring. The fire and cracks Of sulphurous roaring the most mighty Neptune Seem to besiege . . . . i 2 204
I will plague them all, Even to roaring . . . . . iv 1 193
'Twixt the green sea and the azured vault Set roaring war . . v 1 44
Strange and several noises Of roaring, shrieking, howling . . v 1 233
You may do it extempore, for it is nothing but roaring . *M. N. Dream* i 2 71
Enrobe the roaring waters with my silks . . *Mer. of Venice* i 1 34
Roaring louder than the sea or weather . . . . *W. Tale* iii 3 103
Whose foot spurns back the ocean's roaring tides . . *K. John* ii 1 24
Talks as familiarly of roaring lions As maids of thirteen do of puppy-dogs! . . . . ii 1 459
By a roaring tempest on the flood, A whole armado . . . Is scatter'd . iii 4 1
As full of peril and adventurous spirit As to o'er-walk a current roaring loud On the unsteadfast footing of a spear . . 1 *Hen. IV.* i 3 192
I fear thee as I fear the roaring of the lion's whelp . . . iii 3 167
Ten times more valour than this roaring devil i' the old play . *Hen. V.* iv 4 75
Haughty words of hers Have batter'd me like roaring cannon-shot 1 *Hen. VI.* iii 3 79
With terms unsquared, Which, from the tongue of roaring Typhon dropp'd, Would seem hyperboles . . . *Troi. and Cres.* i 3 160
He is arm'd and at it, Roaring for Troilus . . . . . v 5 37
And, in roaring for a chamber-pot, dismiss the controversy . *Coriolanus* ii 1 85
Chain me with roaring bears . . . . *Rom. and Jul.* iv 1 80
More inexorable far Than empty tigers or the roaring sea . . v 3 39
With roaring voices . . . . *Lear* ii 3 14
Such groans of roaring wind and rain I never Remember to have heard iii 2 47
He cried almost to roaring . . . . . *Ant. and Cleo.* iii 2 55
Ribbed and paled in With rocks unscaleable and roaring waters *Cymb.* iii 1 20
Scarce made up, I mean, to man, he had not apprehension Of roaring terrors . . . . iv 2 111
Roast. He doth nothing but roast malt-worms . . . . 2 *Hen. IV.* ii 4 361
Suffolk, the new-made duke that rules the roast . . 2 *Hen. VI.* i 1 109
Come in, tailor; here you may roast your goose . . *Macbeth* ii 3 17
Roast me in sulphur! Wash me in steep-down gulfs of liquid fire! *Othello* v 2 279
Roasted Manningtree ox with the pudding in his belly . 1 *Hen. IV.* ii 4 498
Roasted in wrath and fire, And thus o'er-sized with coagulate gore *Ham.* ii 2 483
Eight wild-boars roasted whole at a breakfast . . *Ant. and Cleo.* ii 2 183
Roasted crab. When roasted crabs hiss in the bowl . . *L. L. Lost* v 2 935
In very likeness of a roasted crab . . . . *M. N. Dream* ii 1 48
Roast-meat. She made him roast-meat for worms . . . *Pericles* iv 2 26
Rob. When's god's asleep, he'll rob his bottle . . . *Tempest* ii 2 155
Better . . . disdained of all than to fashion a carriage to rob love *M. Ado* i 3 31
Our house is hell, and thou, a merry devil, Didst rob it of some taste of tediousness . . . . *Mer. of Venice* ii 3 3
Thou art a fool: she robs thee of thy name . . . *As Y. Like It* i 3 82
He that perforce robs lions of their hearts May easily win a woman's *K. John* i 1 268
Must I rob the law?—Your sword is bright, sir; put it up . . iv 3 78
Which robs my tongue from breathing native breath . *Richard II.* i 3 173
Pluck my fair son from mine age, And rob me of a happy mother's name? v 2 93
Stand in narrow lanes, And beat our watch, and rob our passengers . v 3 9
Who, I rob? I a thief? not I . . . . . . 1 *Hen. IV.* i 2 153
Falstaff, Bardolph, Peto and Gadshill shall rob those men . . i 2 182
If you and I do not rob them, cut this head off from my shoulders . i 2 185
I am accursed to rob in that thief's company . . . . . ii 2 10
I'll starve ere I'll rob a foot further . . . . . . ii 2 23
'Zounds, will they not rob us?—What, a coward? . . . . . ii 2 68
Now could thou and I rob the thieves . . . . . . ii 2 99
Francis!—My lord?—Wilt thou rob this leathern jerkin? . . . ii 4 77
It shall not wind with such a deep indent, To rob me of so rich a bottom iii 1 105
Rob me the exchequer the first thing thou doest . . . . iii 3 205
Swear, drink, dance, Revel the night, rob, murder . . 2 *Hen. IV.* iv 5 126
When the dusky sky began to rob My earnest-gaping sight 2 *Hen. VI.* iii 2 104
I should rob the deathsman of his fee . . . . . . iii 2 217
Drones suck not eagles' blood but rob bee-hives . . . . iv 1 109
Like a thief, to come to rob my grounds, Climbing my walls . . iv 10 36
Who can be bound by any solemn vow To do a murderous deed, to rob a man? . . . . v 1 185
And rob his temples of the diadem, Now in his life? 3 *Hen. VI.* i 4 104
Had I so good occasion to lie long As you, Prince Paris, nothing but heavenly business Should rob my bed-mate of my company *Troi. and Cres.* iv 1 5
To use violent thefts, And rob in the behalf of charity . . . v 3 22
If things go well, Opinion that so sticks on Marcius shall Of his demerits rob Cominius . . . . *Coriolanus* i 1 276
A very little thief of occasion will rob you of a great deal of patience . ii 1 32
Andronicus, would thou wert shipp'd to hell, Rather than rob me of the people's hearts! . . . . *T. Andron.* i 1 207
So should I rob my sweet sons of their fee . . . . . ii 3 179
And he [the physician] slays Moe than you rob: . . *T. of Athens* iv 3 436
The sun's a thief, and with his great attraction Robs the vast sea . . iv 3 440
Love not yourselves: away, Rob one another . . . . . iv 3 448
But for your words, they rob the Hybla bees . . . . *J. Cæsar* v 1 34
And yet I know not how conceit may rob The treasury of life, when life itself Yields to the theft . . . . *Lear* iv 6 42
He robs himself that spends a bootless grief . . . . *Othello* i 3 209
Robs me of that which not enriches him And makes me poor indeed . iii 3 160
I'll rob none but myself; and let me die, Stealing so poorly . *Cymbeline* iv 2 15
Purge the land of these drones, that rob the bee of her honey *Pericles* ii 1 51
I will rob Tellus of her weed, To strew thy green with flowers . . iv 1 14
A curse upon him, die he like a thief, That robs thee of thy goodness! . iv 6 122
Robbed. These three have robb'd me; and this demi-devil . *Tempest* v 1 272
A fat woman! the knight may be robbed . . . . *Mer. Wives* iv 5 17
I am robbed, sir, and beaten; my money and apparel ta'en . *W. Tale* iv 3 64
What manner of fellow was he that robbed you? . . . . . iv 3 90
Richard, that robb'd the lion of his heart. . . . . *K. John* ii 1 3
The jewel of life By some damn'd hand was robb'd and ta'en away . v 1 41
If he have robb'd these men, He shall be answerable . 1 *Hen. IV.* ii 4 570
O, Harry, thou hast robb'd me of my youth! . . . . . v 4 77
I never robb'd the soldiers of their pay . . . . 2 *Hen. VI.* iii 1 108
That robb'd my soldiers of their heated spleen . . 3 *Hen. VI.* ii 1 124
Many blows repaid Have robb'd my strong-knit sinews of their strength ii 3 4
For where I am robb'd and bound, There must I be unloosed *Hen. VIII.* ii 4 146
Thy ambition, Thou scarlet sin, robb'd this bewailing land . . iii 2 255
Hath robbed many beasts of their particular additions . *Troi. and Cres.* i 2 19
The incarnate devil That robb'd Andronicus of his good hand *T. Andron.* v 1 41
'Zounds, sir, you're robb'd; for shame, put on your gown . . *Othello* i 1 86
The robb'd that smiles steals something from the thief . . . i 3 208
He that is robb'd, not wanting what is stol'n, Let him not know't, and he's not robb'd at all . . . . iii 3 342
O, thy vile lady! She has robb'd me of my sword . . *Ant. and Cleo.* iv 14 23
This is his sword; I robb'd his wound of it; behold it stain'd . . v 1 25
But envy much Thou hast robb'd me of this deed . . *Cymbeline* iv 2 159
Robber. Then thieves and robbers range abroad unseen . *Richard II.* iii 2 39
Be assailed by robbers and die in many irreconciled iniquities *Hen. V.* iv 1 160
So true men yield, with robbers so o'ermatch'd . . 3 *Hen. VI.* i 4 64
And what makes robbers bold but too much lenity? . . . . ii 6 22
Injurious time now with a robber's haste Crams his rich thievery up, he knows not how . . . . *Troi. and Cres.* iv 4 44
Large-handed robbers your grave masters are, And pill by law *T. of A.* iv 1 11
Shall one of us, That struck the foremost man of all this world But for supporting robbers, shall we now Contaminate our fingers? *J. Cæsar* iv 3 23
With robbers' hands my hospitable favours You should not ruffle thus *Lear* iii 7 40
Thou art a robber, A law-breaker, a villain: yield thee, thief *Cymbeline* iv 2 74
Robbery. Thieves for their robbery have authority When judges steal themselves . . . . *Meas. for Meas.* ii 2 176
Two gentlemen Have in this robbery lost three hundred marks 1 *Hen. IV.* ii 4 569
For the robbery, lad, how is that answered? . . . . . . iii 3 197
He that was in question for the robbery?—He, my lord . 2 *Hen. IV.* i 2 69
Gored the gentle bosom of peace with pillage and robbery . *Hen. V.* iv 1 175
Dost thou think I'll grace thee with that robbery, thy stol'n name Coriolanus in Corioli? . . . . *Coriolanus* v 6 89
A storm or robbery, call it what you will, Shook down my mellow hangings, nay, my leaves . . . . *Cymbeline* iii 3 62
Robbest. If thou engrossest all the griefs are thine, Thou robb'st me of a moiety . . . . *All's Well* iii 2 69
Robbing. To watch, like one that fears robbing . . *T. G. of Ver.* ii 1 26
By the robbing of the banish'd duke. . . . *Richard II.* ii 1 261
One that is like to be executed for robbing a church . . *Hen. V.* iii 6 106
Nor knows he how to live but by the spoil, Unless by robbing 2 *Hen. VI.* iv 8 42
What tell'st thou me of robbing? this is Venice . . *Othello* i 1 105
Robe. Finely attired in a robe of white . . . *Mer. Wives* iv 4 72
The marshal's truncheon, nor the judge's robe . . *Meas. for Meas.* ii 2 61
What shalt thou exchange for rags? robes . . . *L. L. Lost* iv 1 84
Disguised in sober robes . . . . *T. of Shrew* i 2 132
See not your bride in these unreverent robes . . . . . iii 2 114
In pure white robes, Like very sanctity . . . . *W. Tale* iii 3 22
Sure this robe of mine Does change my disposition . . . . iv 4 134

Robe. You were best say these robes are not gentlemen born *W. Tale* v 2 143
O, well did he become that lion's robe That did disrobe the lion of that robe!—It lies as sightly on the back of him *K. John* ii 1 141
And truth suspected, For putting on so new a fashion'd robe iv 2 27
And is not a buff jerkin a most sweet robe of durance? 1 *Hen. IV.* i 2 49
My presence, like a robe pontifical, Ne'er seen but wonder'd at iii 2 56
For there he is in his robes, burning, burning iii 3 37
You have deceived our trust, And made us doff our easy robes of peace v 1 12
Comment appelez-vous le pied et la robe? *Hen. V.* iii 4 53
The crown imperial, The intertissued robe of gold and pearl iv 1 279
My poor soldiers tell me, yet ere night They'll be in fresher robes iv 3 117
Give me my steeled coat. I'll fight for France. Away with these disgraceful wailing robes! 1 *Hen. VI.* i 1 86
Thy scarlet robes as a child's bearing-cloth I'll use to carry thee out i 3 42
My shame will not be shifted with my sheet: No, it will hang upon my richest robes And show itself, attire me how I can 2 *Hen. VI.* ii 4 108
'Tis the king's: my robe, And my integrity to heaven, is all I dare now call mine own *Hen. VIII.* iii 2 452
What should I don this robe, and trouble you? *T. Andron.* i 1 189
So tedious is this day As is the night before some festival To an impatient child that hath new robes And may not wear them *R. and J.* iii 2 30
In thy best robes uncover'd on the bier Thou shalt be borne iv 1 110
Give me my robe, for I will go *J. Cæsar* ii 2 107
Why do you dress me In borrow'd robes? *Macbeth* i 3 109
Lest our old robes sit easier than our new! ii 4 38
His title Hang loose about him, like a giant's robe Upon a dwarfish thief v 2 21
For a robe, About her lank and all o'er-teemed loins, A blanket *Hamlet* ii 2 530
Through tatter'd clothes small vices do appear; Robes and furr'd gowns hide all *Lear* iv 6 169
When old robes are worn out, there are members to make new *A. and C.* i 2 171
Give me my robe, put on my crown; I have Immortal longings in me v 2 283
Give me my robes. I am wild in my beholding *Pericles* v 1 224
Robed. Thou robed man of justice, take thy place *Lear* iii 6 38
Robert. What, John! What, Robert!—Quickly, quickly! *Mer. Wives* iii 3 1
What, John! Robert! John! Go take up these clothes here quickly iii 3 154
Robert Brakenbury, and Sir William Brandon *Richard III.* v 5 14
Robert Faulconbridge. Eldest son, As I suppose, to Robert Faulconbridge, A soldier *K. John* i 1 52
If old sir Robert did beget us both And were our father and this son like him, O old sir Robert, father, on my knee I give heaven thanks I was not like to thee! i 1 80
An if my brother had my shape, And I had his, sir Robert's his, like him; . . . I would not be sir Nob in any case i 1 139
Philip, good old sir Robert's wife's eldest son i 1 159
Blessed be the hour, by night or day, When I was got, sir Robert was away! i 1 166
Robert Shallow. *See* **Shallow**
Robert Waterton and Francis Quoint *Richard II.* ii 1 284
Robin. What, Robin, I say!—Come, come, come *Mer. Wives* iii 3 4
Here comes little Robin.—How now, my eyas-musket! iii 3 21
Hey, Robin, jolly Robin, Tell me how thy lady does *T. Night* iv 2 78
Here, Robin, an if I die, I give thee my apron 2 *Hen. VI.* ii 3 74
For bonny sweet Robin is all my joy *Hamlet* iv 5 187
Robin Goodfellow. Or else you are that shrewd and knavish sprite Call'd Robin Goodfellow *M. N. Dream* ii 1 34
Hie therefore, Robin, overcast the night iii 2 355
Welcome, good Robin. See'st thou this sweet sight? iv 1 51
Robin, take off this head iv 1 85
Give me your hands, if we be friends, And Robin shall restore amends. v 1 445
Robin Hood. By the bare scalp of Robin Hood's fat friar *T. G. of Ver.* iv 1 36
There they live like the old Robin Hood of England *As Y. Like It* i 1 122
Robin Hood, Scarlet, and John 2 *Hen. IV.* v 3 107
Robin Nightwork. Certain she's old; and had Robin Nightwork by old Nightwork iii 2 222
Robin Ostler. This house is turned upside down since Robin Ostler died 1 *Hen. IV.* ii 1 12
Robin-redbreast. To relish a love-song, like a robin-redbreast; to walk alone *T. G. of Ver.* ii 1 21
Robin Starveling, the tailor.—Here, Peter Quince.—Robin Starveling, you must play Thisby's mother *M. N. Dream* i 2 60
Robustious. In robustious and rough coming on *Hen. V.* iii 7 159
It offends me to the soul to hear a robustious periwig-pated fellow *Ham.* iii 2 10
Rochester. Gadshill lies to-night in Rochester 1 *Hen. IV.* i 2 144
Rochford. Sir Thomas Bullen's daughter,—The Viscount Rochford,—one of her highness' women *Hen. VIII.* i 4 93
Rock. And here you sty me In this hard rock *Tempest* i 2 343
Therefore wast thou Deservedly confined into this rock i 2 361
My cellar is in a rock by the sea-side where my wine is hid ii 2 138
I'll get thee Young scamels from the rock ii 2 176
That some whirlwind bear Unto a ragged fearful-hanging rock! *T. G. of V.* i 2 121
If all their sand were pearl, The water nectar and the rocks pure gold ii 4 171
We were encounter'd by a mighty rock *Com. of Errors* i 1 102
I know her spirits are as coy and wild As haggerds of the rock *M. Ado* iii 1 36
The raging rocks And shivering shocks *M. N. Dream* i 2 33
Take hands with me, And rock the ground whereon these sleepers be iv 1 91
Should I go to church And see the holy edifice of stone, And not bethink me straight of dangerous rocks? *Mer. of Venice* i 1 31
Then there is the peril of waters, winds and rocks i 3 26
Not one vessel 'scape the dreadful touch Of merchant-marring rocks? iii 2 274
That's able to breathe life into a stone, Quicken a rock *All's Well* ii 1 77
Mountains and rocks More free from motion *K. John* ii 1 452
A large mouth, indeed, That spits forth death and mountains, rocks and seas! ii 1 458
Then death rock me asleep, abridge my doleful days! 2 *Hen. IV.* ii 4 211
And rock his brains In cradle of the rude imperious surge iii 1 19
As doth a galled rock O'erhang and jutty his confounded base *Hen. V.* iii 1 12
Or turn our stern upon a dreadful rock 2 *Hen. VI.* iii 2 91
The splitting rocks cower'd in the sinking sands iii 2 97
O, I could hew up rocks and fight with flint, I am so angry v 1 24
Ay, as the rocks cheer them that fear their wreck 3 *Hen. VI.* ii 2 5
Whiles, in his moan, the ship splits on the rock v 4 10
Keep our course, though the rough wind say no, From shelves and rocks v 4 23
And Richard but a ragged fatal rock? v 4 27
Bestride the rock; the tide will wash you off, Or else you famish v 4 31
With ruthless waves, with sands and rocks v 4 36
Lo, where comes that rock That I advise your shunning *Hen. VIII.* i 1 113
I'll say't; and make my vouch as strong As shore of rock i 1 158
As doth a rock against the chiding flood iii 2 197
When we vow to weep seas, live in fire, eat rocks *Troi. and Cres.* iii 2 84
To the rock Tarpeian, and from thence Into destruction cast him *Cor.* iii 1 213
Rock. Bear him to the rock.—No, I'll die here *Coriolanus* iii 1 223
He shall be thrown down the Tarpeian rock With rigorous hands iii 1 266
Pile ten hills on the Tarpeian rock iii 2 3
Mark you this, people?—To the rock, to the rock with him! iii 3 75
Banish him our city, In peril of precipitation From off the rock Tarpeian never more To enter our Rome gates iii 3 103
He's the rock, the oak not to be wind-shaken v 2 117
I stand as one upon a rock Environ'd with a wilderness of sea *T. An.* iii 1 93
At once run on The dashing rocks thy sea-sick weary bark! *R. and J.* v 3 118
Come, poor remains of friends, rest on this rock *J. Cæsar* v 5 1
Founded as the rock, As broad and general as the casing air *Macbeth* iii 4 22
Sleep rock thy brain; And never come mischance between us twain! *Hamlet* iii 2 237
Antres vast and deserts idle, Rough quarries, rocks and hills *Othello* i 3 141
Howling winds, The gutter'd rocks and congregated sands ii 1 69
He'll watch the horologe a double set, If drink rock not his cradle ii 3 136
A tower'd citadel, a pendent rock, A forked mountain *Ant. and Cleo.* iv 14 4
As Neptune's park, ribbed and paled in With rocks unscaleable *Cymb.* iii 1 20
On our terrible seas, Like egg-shells moved upon their surges, crack'd As easily 'gainst our rocks iii 1 29
Hail, thou fair heaven! We house i' the rock, yet use thee not so hardly As prouder livers do iii 3 8
This twenty years This rock and these demesnes have been my world iii 3 70
I'll throw't into the creek Behind our rock iv 2 152
I prithee, to our rock iv 2 163
Think that you are upon a rock; and now Throw me again v 5 262
The sea hath cast me on the rocks, Wash'd me from shore to shore *Per.* ii 1 5
Rocky. Whose rocky shore beats back the envious siege *Richard II.* ii 1 62
As firm as rocky mountains 2 *Hen. IV.* iv 1 188
Rush all to pieces on thy rocky bosom *Richard III.* iv 4 234
Rocky-hard. Thy sea-marge, sterile and rocky-hard *Tempest* iv 1 69
Rod. And presently all humbled kiss the rod! *T. G. of Ver.* i 2 59
Not to use, in time the rod Becomes more mock'd than fear'd *M. for M.* i 3 26
Either to make him a garland, as being forsaken, or to bind him up a rod, as being worthy to be whipped *Much Ado* ii 1 227
It had not been amiss the rod had been made, and the garland too ii 1 234
The garland he might have worn himself, and the rod he might have bestowed on you ii 1 236
Come, thou child; I'll whip thee with a rod *M. N. Dream* iii 2 410
Take thy correction mildly, kiss the rod, And fawn on rage *Richard II.* v 1 32
I am whipp'd and scourged with rods, Nettled and stung 1 *Hen. IV.* i 3 239
Thou art only mark'd For the hot vengeance and the rod of heaven iii 2 10
Besides, the king hath wasted all his rods On late offenders 2 *Hen. IV.* iv 1 215
And that the Earl of Surrey, with the rod *Hen. VIII.* iv 1 39
The rod, and bird of peace, and all such emblems Laid nobly on her iv 1 89
Your enigma?—You have been a scourge to her enemies, you have been a rod to her friends *Coriolanus* ii 3 98
Would I had a rod in my mouth, that I might answer thee *T. of Athens* ii 2 79
When thou gavest them the rod, and put'st down thine own breeches *Lear* i 4 189
My messenger He hath whipp'd with rods *Ant. and Cleo.* iv 1 3
Rode. Alack, poor Richard! where rode he the whilst? *Richard II.* v 2 22
Rode he on Barbary? Tell me, gentle friend, How went he under him? v 5 81
There is more news: I learn'd in Worcester, as I rode along 1 *Hen. IV.* iv 1 125
That gentleman that rode by Travers 2 *Hen. IV.* i 1 55
He was some hilding fellow that had stolen The horse he rode on i 1 58
Helter-skelter have I rode to thee, And tidings do I bring v 3 98
You rode, like a kern of Ireland, your French hose off *Hen. V.* iii 7 56
The king himself is rode to view their battle iv 3 2
As I rode from Calais, To haste unto your coronation 1 *Hen. VI.* iv 1 9
The lords at Pomfret, when they rode from London, Were jocund *Richard III.* iii 2 85
The passage and whole carriage of this action Rode on his tide *T. and C.* ii 3 141
My betossed soul Did not attend him as we rode *Rom. and Jul.* v 3 77
You gave Good words the other day of a bay courser I rode on *T. of A.* i 2 218
One that rode to's execution, man, Could never go so slow *Cymbeline* iii 2 72
Roderigo. My name is Sebastian, which I called Roderigo *T. Night* ii 1 17
Sure as you are Roderigo, Were I the Moor, I would not be Iago *Othello* i 1 56
My name is Roderigo.—The worser welcome: I have charged thee not to haunt about my doors i 1 95
This thou shalt answer; I know thee, Roderigo.—Sir, I will answer any thing i 1 120
Now, Roderigo, Where didst thou see her? O unhappy girl! i 1 163
Have you not read, Roderigo, Of some such thing?—Yes, sir, I have indeed i 1 174
On, good Roderigo: I'll deserve your pains i 1 184
You, Roderigo! come, sir, I am for you.—Keep up your bright swords i 2 58
Do you hear, Roderigo?—What say you?—No more of drowning i 3 384
Their breaths embraced together. Villanous thoughts, Roderigo! ii 1 267
My sick fool Roderigo, Whom love hath turn'd almost the wrong side out ii 3 53
How now, Roderigo! I pray you, after the lieutenant; go ii 3 141
How now, Roderigo!—I do follow here in the chase ii 3 368
How now, Roderigo!—I do not find that thou dealest justly with me iv 2 172
Will you hear me, Roderigo?—'Faith, I have heard too much iv 2 183
Thy hand, Roderigo: thou hast taken against me a most just exception iv 2 210
Roderigo, if thou hast that in thee indeed, which I have greater reason to believe now than ever, I mean purpose, courage iv 2 216
Whether he kill Cassio, Or Cassio him, or each do kill the other, Every way makes my gain: live Roderigo, He calls me to a restitution v 1 14
My dear countryman Roderigo! no:—yes, sure:—O heaven! Roderigo v 1 90
Set on in the dark By Roderigo and fellows that are 'scaped: He's almost slain, and Roderigo dead v 1 113
Cassio, my lord, hath kill'd a young Venetian Call'd Roderigo.—Roderigo kill'd! And Cassio kill'd! v 2 113
Here is a letter Found in the pocket of the slain Roderigo v 2 309
The one of them imports The death of Cassio to be undertook By Roderigo v 2 312
And this, it seems, Roderigo meant to have sent this damned villain v 2 316
There is besides in Roderigo's letter, How he upbraids Iago v 2 324
Roe. Whip to our tents, as roes run o'er land *L. L. Lost* v 2 309
As swift As breathed stags, ay, fleeter than the roe *T. of Shrew* Ind. 2 50
A puttock, or a herring without a roe *Troi. and Cres.* v 1 68
Here comes Romeo.—Without his roe, like a dried herring *Rom. and Jul.* ii 4 39
Roger Bolingbroke, the conjurer 2 *Hen. VI.* i 2 76
Roger Earl of March; Roger had issue, Edmund, Anne and Eleanor ii 2 37
Duke of York; Thy grandfather, Roger Mortimer, Earl of March 3 *Hen. VI.* i 1 106
Rogero. The news, Rogero?—Nothing but bonfires *W. Tale* v 2 23
Rogue. Rogues, hence, avaunt! vanish like hailstones *Mer. Wives* i 3 90
French thrift, you rogues; myself and skirted page i 3 93
I never heard such a drawling, affecting rogue ii 1 146
Very rogues, now they be out of service ii 1 182
Hadst thou not fifteen pence?—Reason, you rogue, reason ii 2 15

Rogue. You'll not bear a letter for me, you rogue! you stand upon your honour! . . . *Mer. Wives* ii 2 20
I will use her as the key of the cuckoldy rogue's coffer . . . ii 2 286
Hang him, mechanical salt-butter rogue! . . . ii 2 290
The rogues slighted me into the river . . . iii 5 9
Away, you rogue, away! I am sleepy . . . *Meas. for Meas.* iv 3 30
You rogue, I have been drinking all night; I am not fitted for't . iv 3 46
I'll pheeze you, in faith.—A pair of stocks, you rogue! . *T. of Shrew* Ind. 1 2
The Slys are no rogues; look in the chronicles . . . Ind. 1 3
Here comes the rogue. Sirrah, where have you been? . . . i 1 226
Off with my boots, you rogues! you villains, when? . . . iv 1 147
Out, you rogue! you pluck my foot awry: Take that . . . iv 1 150
Come hither, you rogue. What, have you forgot me?—Forgot you! no v 1 49
And the commanders very poor rogues . . . *All's Well* iv 3 153
Poor rogues, I pray you, say.—Well, that's set down . . . iv 3 176
A truth's a truth, the rogues are marvellous poor . . . iv 3 179
Damnable both-sides rogue! . . . iv 3 251
Peace, you rogue, no more o' that. Here comes my lady . *T. Night* i 5 32
Here's an overweening rogue!—O, peace! . . . ii 5 34
'Slight, I could so beat the rogue!—Peace, I say . . . ii 5 38
Thou killest me like a rogue and a villain . . . iii 4 179
Then he's a rogue, and a passy measures panyn: I hate a drunken rogue v 1 207
Having flown over many knavish professions, he settled only in rogue *W. Tale* iv 3 106
That's the rogue that put me into this apparel.—Not a more cowardly rogue in all Bohemia . . . iv 3 111
An old sheep-whistling rogue, a ram-tender . . . iv 4 805
Let him call me rogue for being so far officious . . . iv 4 871
The incomprehensible lies that this same fat rogue will tell us 1 *Hen. IV.* i 2 210
If I 'scape hanging for killing that rogue . . . ii 2 16
I am bewitched with the rogue's company . . . ii 2 18
As good a deed as drink, to turn true man and to leave these rogues . ii 2 25
Give me my horse, you rogues; give me my horse, and be hanged! . ii 2 32
Out, ye rogue! shall I be your ostler?—Go, hang thyself! . . . ii 2 45
'Tis going to the king's exchequer.—You lie, ye rogue . . . ii 2 58
Were't not for laughing, I should pity him.—How the rogue roar'd! . ii 2 118
What a frosty-spirited rogue is this! . . . ii 3 21
Away, you rogue! dost thou not hear them call? . . . ii 4 88
A plague of all cowards! Give me a cup of sack, rogue . . . ii 4 132
You rogue, here's lime in this sack too: there is nothing but roguery . ii 4 137
Give me a cup of sack: I am a rogue, if I drunk to-day . . . ii 4 168
I am a rogue, if I were not at half-sword with a dozen of them . ii 4 182
They were not bound.—You rogue, they were bound, every man of them ii 4 197
Two I am sure I have paid, two rogues in buckram suits . . . ii 4 213
Four rogues in buckram let drive at me— What, four? thou saidst but two ii 4 216
Out, ye rogue! Play out the play: I have much to say . . . ii 4 531
One or the other plays the rogue with my great toe . 2 *Hen. IV.* i 2 274
Wilt thou? thou bastardly rogue! Murder, murder! . . . ii 1 55
Ah, thou honey-seed rogue! thou art a honey-seed, a man-queller . ii 1 57
Thou wo't, wo't ta? do, do, thou rogue! do, thou hemp-seed! . . ii 1 64
It is the foul-mouthed'st rogue in England . . . ii 4 77
Away, you mouldy rogue, away! I am meat for your master . . ii 4 134
Hang him, rogue! he lives upon mouldy stewed prunes and dried cakes ii 4 158
Ah, you sweet little rogue, you! Alas, poor ape, how thou sweatest! . ii 4 233
Ah, rogue! i' faith, I love thee: thou art as valorous as Hector of Troy ii 4 235
A rascally slave! I will toss the rogue in a blanket . . . ii 4 240
The rogue fled from me like quicksilver . . . ii 4 247
You blue-bottle rogue, you filthy famished correctioner . . . v 4 22
Come, you rogue, come; bring me to a justice . . . v 4 29
Faith, he's very ill.—Away, you rogue! . . . *Hen. V.* ii 1 90
'Tis a gull, a fool, a rogue, that now and then goes to the wars . iii 6 70
Belong to the gallows, and be hanged, ye rogue! . . . *Hen. VIII.* v 4 7
A false-hearted rogue, a most unjust knave . . . *Troi. and Cres.* v 1 96
Would I could meet that rogue Diomed! I would croak like a raven! . v 2 190
No, no, I am a rascal; a scurvy railing knave; a very filthy rogue . v 4 31
What's become of the wenching rogues? . . . v 4 35
What's the matter, you dissentious rogues? . . . *Coriolanus* i 1 167
A braggart, a rogue, a villain, that fights by the book! . *Rom. and Jul.* iii 1 105
Poor rogues, and usurers' men! bawds between gold and want! *T. of Athens* ii 2 61
Put stuff To some she beggar and compounded thee Poor rogue hereditary iv 3 274
Thou tedious rogue! I am sorry I shall lose A stone by thee . . . iv 3 374
Rogue, rogue, rogue! I am sick of this false world . . . iv 3 375
I would I might go to hell among the rogues . . . *J. Cæsar* i 2 271
The satirical rogue says here that old men have grey beards . *Hamlet* ii 2 198
Now I am alone. O, what a rogue and peasant slave am I! . . . ii 2 576
A pestilence on him for a mad rogue! . . . v 1 197
Glass-gazing, superserviceable, finical rogue . . . *Lear* ii 2 20
Draw, you rogue: for, though it be night, yet the moon shines . . ii 2 33
Draw, you rogue, or I'll so carbonado your shanks: draw, you rascal . ii 2 41
Strike, you slave; stand, rogue, stand; you neat slave, strike . . ii 2 44
Such smiling rogues as these, Like rats, oft bite the holy cords a-twain ii 2 79
None of these rogues and cowards But Ajax is their fool . . . ii 2 131
Wast thou fain, poor father, To hovel thee with swine, and rogues forlorn? iv 7 39
And hear poor rogues Talk of court news; and we'll talk with them too v 3 13
You rogue! you rascal!—What's the matter, lieutenant? . *Othello* ii 3 150
Alas, poor rogue! I think, i' faith, she loves me . . . iv 1 112
Some eternal villain, Some busy and insinuating rogue . . . iv 2 131
Rogue, thou hast lived too long . . . *Ant. and Cleo.* ii 5 73
To the choleric fisting of every rogue Thy ear is liable . . *Pericles* iv 6 177

Roguery. Nothing but roguery to be found in villanous man 1 *Hen. IV.* ii 4 138
Tempt me no more to folly.—Roguery! . . . *Troi. and Cres.* v 2 19

Roguing. These roguing thieves serve the great pirate Valdes *Pericles* iv 1 97

Roguish. His roguish madness Allows itself to any thing . . *Lear* iii 7 104

Roi. Have I not heard these islanders shout out 'Vive le roi!'? *K. John* v 2 104
Wilt thou have me?—Dat is as it sall please de roi mon père . *Hen. V.* v 2 267
Notre très-cher fils Henri, Roi d'Angleterre, Héritier de France . v 2 368

Roisting. I have a roisting challenge sent . . . *Troi. and Cres.* ii 2 208

Roll. As the eye doth roll To every varied object . . *L. L. Lost* v 2 774
And make his eyeballs roll with wonted sight . . . *M. N. Dream* iii 2 369
The courses of my life do show I am not in the roll of common men 1 *Hen. IV.* iii 1 43
Where's the roll? where's the roll? Let me see . . 2 *Hen. IV.* iii 2 106
Her [Fortune's] foot, look you, is fixed upon a spherical stone, which rolls, and rolls, and rolls . . . *Hen. V.* iii 6 38
Master O' the rolls, and the king's secretary . . . *Hen. VIII.* v 1 35
Yet I fear you; for you are fatal then When your eyes roll so *Othello* v 2 38
Not what you have reserved, nor what acknowledged, Put we i' the roll of conquest: still be't yours . . . *Ant. and Cleo.* v 2 181

Rolled. Or as the snake roll'd in a flowering bank . . 2 *Hen. VI.* iii 1 228
The snake lies rolled in the cheerful sun . . . *T. Andron.* ii 3 13

Rolling. The poet's eye, in a fine frenzy rolling . . . *M. N. Dream* v 1 12
With wrinkled brows, with nods, with rolling eyes . . . *K. John* iv 2 192
That goddess blind, That stands upon the rolling restless stone *Hen. V.* iii 6 31
I told ye all, When we first put this dangerous stone a-rolling, 'Twould fall upon ourselves . . . *Hen. VIII.* v 3 104

Romage. The source of this our watch and the chief head Of this post-haste and romage in the land . . . *Hamlet* i 1 107

Roman. I will imitate the honourable Romans in brevity . 2 *Hen. IV.* ii 2 135
Look you, of the Roman disciplines . . . *Hen. V.* iii 2 77
In the disciplines of the pristine wars of the Romans . . . iii 2 87
Titus Lartius, a most valiant Roman . . . *Coriolanus* i 2 14
There is the man of my soul's hate, Aufidius, Piercing our Romans . i 5 12
Come off Like Romans, neither foolish in our stands, Nor cowardly in retire . . . i 6 2
I would I were a Roman; for I cannot, Being a Volsce, be that I am . i 10 4
He bestrid An o'er-press'd Roman and i' the consul's view Slew three ii 2 97
Not Romans—as they are not, Though calved i' the porch o' the Capitol iii 1 239
Lest parties . . . break out, And sack great Rome with Romans . . iii 1 316
I am a Roman; and my services are, as you are, against 'em . . iv 3 4
I would not be a Roman, of all nations; I had as lieve be a condemned man iv 5 185
I hope to see Romans as cheap as Volscians. They are rising . . iv 5 249
Do they still fly to the Roman? . . . iv 7 1
You are a Roman, are you?—I am, as thy general is . . . v 2 38
Forgive my tyranny; but do not say For that 'Forgive our Romans' . v 3 44
If it were so that our request did tend To save the Romans . . v 3 133
While the Volsces May say 'This mercy we have show'd;' the Romans, 'This we received' . . . v 3 137
Tabors and cymbals and the shouting Romans, Make the sun dance . v 4 53
Made peace With no less honour to the Antiates Than shame to the Romans . . . v 6 81
Romans, friends, followers, favourers of my right . . *T. Andron.* i 1 9
And, Romans, fight for freedom in your choice . . . i 1 17
Romans, make way: the good Andronicus, Patron of virtue . . i 1 64
Romans, of five and twenty valiant sons . . . Behold the poor remains i 1 79
Romans, do me right: Patricians, draw your swords . . . i 1 203
When I do forget The least of these unspeakable deserts, Romans, forget your fealty to me . . . i 1 257
Romans, let us go: Ransomless here we set our prisoners free . . i 1 273
Thou art a Roman; be not barbarous . . . i 1 378
I am incorporate in Rome, A Roman now adopted happily . . i 1 463
Now you have heard the truth, what say you, Romans? . . . v 3 128
Speak, Romans, speak; and if you say we shall, Lo, hand in hand, Lucius and I will fall . . . v 3 135
All hail, Rome's gracious governor!—Thanks, gentle Romans . . v 3 147
Bade the Romans Mark him and write his speeches in their books *J. Cæsar* i 2 125
He's not dangerous; He is a noble Roman and well given . . i 2 197
Who's there?—A Roman.—Casca, by your voice.—Your ear is good . i 3 41
Those sparks of life That should be in a Roman you do want . . i 3 58
For Romans now Have thews and limbs like to their ancestors . . i 3 80
I know he would not be a wolf, But that he sees the Romans are but sheep . . . i 3 105
He were no lion, were not Romans hinds . . . i 3 106
I have moved already Some certain of the noblest-minded Romans . i 3 122
Every one doth wish You had but that opinion of yourself Which every noble Roman bears of you . . . ii 1 93
Secret Romans, that have spoke the word, And will not palter . . ii 1 125
Every drop of blood That every Roman bears, and nobly bears, Is guilty ii 1 137
Remember What you have said, and show yourselves true Romans . ii 1 223
By all the gods that Romans bow before, I here discard my sickness! . ii 1 320
Pure blood; and many lusty Romans Came smiling, and did bathe their hands in it . . . ii 2 78
Spouting blood in many pipes, In which so many smiling Romans bathed ii 2 86
There is no harm intended to your person, Nor to no Roman else . iii 1 91
Stoop, Romans, stoop, And let us bathe our hands in Cæsar's blood . iii 1 105
Thy master is a wise and valiant Roman; I never thought him worse . iii 1 138
Romans, countrymen, and lovers! hear me for my cause, and be silent iii 2 13
Who is here so rude that would not be a Roman? If any, speak . iii 2 33
You gentle Romans,—Peace, ho! let us hear him . . . iii 2 77
Friends, Romans, countrymen, lend me your ears; I come to bury Cæsar iii 2 78
I had rather be a dog, and bay the moon, Than such a Roman . . iv 3 28
A heart . . . richer than gold: If that thou be'st a Roman, take it forth iv 3 103
Now, as you are a Roman, tell me true.—Then like a Roman bear the truth I tell . . . iv 3 187
Think not, thou noble Roman, That ever Brutus will go bound to Rome v 1 111
Far from this country Pindarus shall run, Where never Roman shall take note of him . . . v 3 50
By your leave, gods:—this is a Roman's part . . . v 3 89
Are yet two Romans living such as these? . . . v 3 98
The last of all the Romans, fare thee well! . . . v 3 99
And, Romans, yet ere night We shall try fortune in a second fight . v 3 109
This was the noblest Roman of them all . . . v 5 68
I am more an antique Roman than a Dane . . . *Hamlet* v 2 352
Ha, ha, ha!—Do you triumph, Roman? do you triumph? . *Othello* iv 1 121
How this Herculean Roman does become The carriage of his chafe *Ant. and Cleo.* i 3 84
Say, the firm Roman to great Egypt sends This treasure of an oyster . i 5 43
The all-honour'd, honest Roman, Brutus, With the arm'd rest . . ii 6 16
The gods keep you, And make the hearts of Romans serve your ends! . ii 2 37
Not cowardly put off my helmet to My countryman,—a Roman by a Roman Valiantly vanquish'd . . . iv 15 57
Who did join his honour Against the Romans with Cassibelan *Cymbeline* i 1 30
Some dozen Romans of us and your lord—The best feather of our wing i 6 185
We shall have need To employ you towards this Roman . . . ii 3 68
Or look upon our Romans, whose remembrance Is yet fresh in their grief ii 4 14
The story Proud Cleopatra, when she met her Roman . . . ii 4 70
Till the injurious Romans did extort This tribute from us, we were free iii 1 48
Swore to Cymbeline I was confederate with the Romans . . . iii 3 68
Lucius the Roman, comes to Milford-Haven To-morrow . . . iii 4 145
Where is our daughter? She hath not appear'd Before the Roman . iii 5 31
This way, the Romans Must or for Britons slay us . . . iv 4 4
The hazard therefore due fall on me by The hands of Romans! . . iv 4 47
We are Romans and will give you that Like beasts which you shun beastly . . . v 3 26
Two boys, an old man twice a boy, a lane, Preserved the Britons, was the Romans' bane . . . v 3 58
Great the slaughter is Here made by the Roman; great the answer be . v 3 79
A Roman, Who had not now been drooping here, if seconds Had answer'd him . . . v 3 89
There are verier knaves desire to live, for all he be a Roman . . v 4 210
You look like Romans, And not o' the court of Britain . . . v 5 24

Roman. A Roman with a Roman's heart can suffer . . *Cymbeline* v 5 81
He hath done no Briton harm, Though he have served a Roman . v 5 91
Is he thy kin? thy friend?—He is a Roman: no more kin to me . . v 5 112
Let A Roman and a British ensign wave Friendly together . . v 5 480
Roman actors. Bear it as our Roman actors do . *J. Cæsar* ii 1 226
Roman boy. The witch shall die: To the young Roman boy she hath sold me, and I fall . . . . . . *Ant. and Cleo.* iv 12 48
Roman brethren. Stay, Roman brethren! . . *T. Andron.* i 1 104
Roman Brutus. But the outside of the Roman Brutus . *Hen. V.* ii 4 37
Roman camp. Our guider, come; to the Roman camp conduct us *Cor.* i 7 7
Roman captive. When came you to serve our Roman captive? *Cymbeline* v 5 385
Roman citizen. To every Roman citizen he gives, To every several man, seventy five drachmas . . . . *J. Cæsar* iii 2 246
Roman coin. The face of an old Roman coin, scarce seen . *L. L. Lost* v 2 617
Roman conqueror. Let's present him to the duke, like a Roman conqueror . . . . . . *As Y. Like It* iv 2 4
Roman courtezan. Some villain . . . Hath done you both this cursed injury.—Some Roman courtezan . . . *Cymbeline* iii 4 126
Roman dames. I would we had a thousand Roman dames At such a bay, by turn to serve our lust . . . *T. Andron.* iv 2 41
Roman disciplines. In the true disciplines of the wars, look you, of the Roman disciplines . . . . . *Hen. V.* iii 2 77
Roman eagle. I saw Jove's bird, the Roman eagle . . *Cymbeline* iv 2 348
The Roman eagle, From south to west on wing soaring aloft, Lessen'd herself . . . . v 5 470
Roman emperor. The Roman emperor's letters, Sent by a consul to me, should not sooner Than thine own worth prefer thee . . iv 2 384
Princes of the Goths, The Roman emperor greets you all by me *T. An.* v 1 157
Roman empery. In election for the Roman empery, Chosen Andronicus i 1 22
Roman empire. Although the victor, we submit to Cæsar, And to the Roman empire . . . . . *Cymbeline* v 5 461
Roman fashion. Let's do it after the high Roman fashion *Ant. and Cleo.* iv 15 87
Roman fool. Why should I play the Roman fool, and die On mine own sword? . . . . *Macbeth* v 8 1
Roman gentlemen. With a supply Of Roman gentlemen . *Cymbeline* iv 3 26
Roman gods! Lead their successes as we wish our own . *Coriolanus* i 6 6
Here I swear by all the Roman gods . . . *T. Andron.* i 1 322
And pray the Roman gods confound you both! . . . iv 2 6
Roman hand. I think we do know the sweet Roman hand . *T. Night* iii 4 31
Roman Hector. Kneel, sweet boy, the Roman Hector's hope *T. Andron.* iv 1 88
Roman honour. One in whom The ancient Roman honour more appears Than any that draws breath . . *Mer. of Venice* iii 2 297
Roman horses. When they hear the Roman horses neigh *Cymbeline* iv 4 17
Roman host. Which portends—Unless my sins abuse my divination—Success to the Roman host. . . . . . iv 2 352
Roman hunting. Madam, now shall ye see Our Roman hunting *T. An.* ii 2 20
Roman justice. 'Suum cuique' is our Roman justice . . . i 1 280
Roman ladies. If The Roman ladies bring not comfort home, They'll give him death . . . . . *Coriolanus* v 4 41
There will the lovely Roman ladies troop . . *T. Andron.* ii 1 113
Roman legions. The Roman legions, all from Gallia drawn, Are landed on your coast . . . . . *Cymbeline* iv 3 24
Roman letters. Carved in Roman letters. . . *T. Andron.* v 1 139
Roman lord. Give signs . . . What Roman lord it was durst do the deed iv 1 62
Roman Lucrece for her chastity . . . . *T. of Shrew* ii 1 298
Roman rites. We have perform'd Our Roman rites . . *T. Andron.* i 1 143
Roman state. You may as well Strike at the heaven with your staves as lift them Against the Roman state . . *Coriolanus* i 1 71
Roman streets. The sheeted dead Did squeak and gibber in the Roman streets . . . . *Hamlet* i 1 116
Roman swords. My body s marked With Roman swords . *Cymbeline* iii 3 57
Roman sworder. A Roman sworder and banditto slave Murder'd sweet Tully . . . . *2 Hen. VI.* iv 1 135
Roman territories. The Volsces with two several powers Are enter'd in the Roman territories . . . *Coriolanus* iv 6 40
Roman thought. A Roman thought hath struck him *Ant. and Cleo.* i 2 87
Roman yoke. Captive to thee and to thy Roman yoke . *T. Andron.* i 1 111
Romano. That rare Italian master, Julio Romano . . *W. Tale* v 2 106
Romanos. Aio te, Æacida, Romanos vincere posse . *2 Hen. VI.* i 4 65
Rome. Some say he is with the Emperor of Russia; other some, he is in Rome: but where is he? . . . *Meas. for Meas.* iii 2 94
It was enjoined him in Rome for want of linen . *L. L. Lost* v 2 719
In loving visitation was with me a young doctor of Rome *Mer. of Venice* iv 1 154
Up farther, and as far as Rome; And so to Tripoli . *T. of Shrew* iv 2 75
O, lawful let it be That I have room with Rome to curse awhile! *K. John* iii 1 180
Raise the power of France upon his head, Unless he do submit himself to Rome . . . . iii 1 194
A heavy curse from Rome, Or the light loss of England for a friend: Forego the easier.—That's the curse of Rome . . . iii 1 205
King John hath reconciled Himself to Rome . . . . v 2 70
Stood out against the holy church, The great metropolis and see of Rome . . . . v 2 72
And come ye now to tell me John hath made His peace with Rome? . v 2 92
Must I back Because that John hath made his peace with Rome? . . v 2 96
Am I Rome's slave? What penny hath Rome borne, What men provided? . . . . v 2 97
That I may justly say, with the hook-nosed fellow of Rome, 'I came, saw, and overcame' . . . . . *2 Hen. IV.* iv 3 45
Like to the senators of the antique Rome . *Hen. V.* v Prol. 26
Exceeding the nine sibyls of old Rome . . . *1 Hen. VI.* i 2 56
Rome shall remedy this.—Roam thither, then. . . . iii 1 51
Carry him to Rome, And set the triple crown upon his head *2 Hen. VI.* i 3 65
Rome, the nurse of judgement . . . . *Hen. VIII.* ii 2 94
The court of Rome commanding . . . . . . ii 2 105
Whilst our commission from Rome is read, Let silence be commanded . ii 4 1
A commission from the consistory, Yea, the whole consistory of Rome ii 4 93
I abhor This dilatory sloth and tricks of Rome . . . ii 4 237
Cardinal Campeius Is stol'n away to Rome; hath ta'en no leave . iii 2 57
Speedily I wish To hear from Rome . . . . . . iii 2 90
To gain the popedom, And fee my friends in Rome . . . iii 2 213
In all you writ to Rome, or else To foreign princes, 'Ego et Rex meus' Was still inscribed . . . . iii 2 313
To furnish Rome, and to prepare the ways You have for dignities . iii 2 328
Rome and her rats are at the point of battle . *Coriolanus* i 1 166
So, your opinion is, Aufidius, That they of Rome are enter'd in our counsels . . . . i 2 2
What ever have been thought on in this state, That could be brought to bodily act ere Rome Had circumvention? . . . . i 2 5
Marcius your old enemy, Who is of Rome worse hated than of you . i 2 13
We never yet made doubt but Rome was ready To answer us . . i 2 18

Rome. Which in the hatching, It seem'd, appear'd to Rome *Coriolanus* i 2 22
To take in many towns ere almost Rome Should know we were afoot . i 2 24
You cowards! you were got in fear, Though you were born in Rome . i 3 37
All the contagion of the south light on you, You shames of Rome! . i 4 31
This will I carry to Rome.—And I this . . . . . i 5 1
Holding Corioli in the name of Rome, Even like a fawning greyhound in the leash, To let him slip at will . . . . . . i 6 37
We thank the gods Our Rome hath such a soldier . . . . i 9 9
Rome must know The value of her own . . . . . i 9 20
Ere we do repose us, we will write To Rome of our success . . i 9 75
Send us to Rome The best, with whom we may articulate . . i 9 76
Learn how 'tis held; and what they are that must Be hostages for Rome . . . . i 10 29
Testy magistrates, alias fools, as any in Rome . . . . ii 1 48
Know, Rome, that all alone Marcius did fight Within Corioli gates . ii 1 179
Welcome to Rome, renowned Coriolanus!—No more of this . . ii 1 184
You are three That Rome should dote on . . . . . ii 1 204
One thing wanting, which I doubt not but Our Rome will cast upon thee . . . . ii 1 218
When Tarquin made a head for Rome, he fought Beyond the mark of others . . . . ii 2 92
This paltering Becomes not Rome . . . . iii 1 59
I would they were barbarians—as they are, Though in Rome litter'd . iii 1 239
Our renowned Rome, whose gratitude Towards her deserved children is enroll'd In Jove's own book . . . . iii 1 291
What has he done to Rome that's worthy death? . . . iii 1 298
Lest parties, as he is beloved, break out, And sack great Rome with Romans . . . . iii 1 316
And come home beloved Of all the trades in Rome . . . . iii 2 134
The honour'd gods Keep Rome in safety, and the chairs of justice Supplied with worthy men! . . . . iii 3 34
You have contrived to take From Rome all season'd office . . iii 3 64
Since he hath Served well for Rome,— What do you prate of service? iii 3 83
From off the rock Tarpeian never more To enter our Rome gates . iii 3 104
I have been consul, and can show for Rome Her enemies' marks upon me . . . . iii 3 110
Now the red pestilence strike all trades in Rome, And occupations perish! . . . . iv 1 13
Banish him that struck more blows for Rome Than thou hast spoken words? . . . . iv 2 19
More noble blows than ever thou wise words; And for Rome's good . iv 2 22
Good man, the wounds that he does bear for Rome! . . . iv 2 28
As far as doth the Capitol exceed The meanest house in Rome . . iv 2 40
Your favour is well approved by your tongue. What's the news in Rome? . . . . iv 3 10
There hath been in Rome strange insurrections . . . . iv 3 13
I shall, between this and supper, tell you most strange things from Rome . . . . iv 3 44
And suffer'd me by the voice of slaves to be Whoop'd out of Rome . iv 5 84
Had we no quarrel else to Rome, but that Thou art thence banish'd . iv 5 133
Pouring war Into the bowels of ungrateful Rome, Like a bold flood o'er-bear . . . . iv 5 136
Who am prepared against your territories, Though not for Rome itself iv 5 141
Whether to knock against the gates of Rome, Or rudely visit them in parts remote, To fright them, ere destroy . . . . . iv 5 147
He'll go, he says, and sowl the porter of Rome gates by the ears . iv 5 214
Rome Sits safe and still without him . . . . . . iv 6 36
Which were inshell'd when Marcius stood for Rome . . . . iv 6 45
Marcius, Join'd with Aufidius, leads a power 'gainst Rome . . iv 6 66
He will shake Your Rome about your ears . . . . . iv 6 99
'Be good to Rome,' they charged him even As those should do that had deserved his hate . . . . iv 6 112
Brought A trembling upon Rome, such as was never So incapable of help . . . . iv 6 119
Desperation Is all the policy, strength and defence, That Rome can make . . . . iv 6 128
Think you he'll carry Rome?—All places yield to him ere he sits down iv 7 27
The nobility of Rome are his: The senators and patricians love him too iv 7 29
I think he'll be to Rome As is the osprey to the fish, who takes it By sovereignty of nature . . . . iv 7 33
When, Caius, Rome is thine, Thou art poor'st of all . . . iv 7 56
Titleless, Till he had forged himself a name o' the fire Of burning Rome v 1 15
A pair of tribunes that have rack'd for Rome, To make coals cheap . v 1 16
What should I do?—Only make trial what your love can do For Rome v 1 41
Yet your good will Must have that thanks from Rome . . . v 1 46
I tell you, he does sit in gold, his eye Red as 'twould burn Rome . v 1 64
From whence?—From Rome.—You may not pass, you must return . v 2 4
You'll see your Rome embraced with fire before You'll speak with Coriolanus . . . . v 2 7
If you have heard your general talk of Rome, And of his friends there . v 2 9
I am, as thy general is.—Then you should hate Rome, as he does . v 2 40
You are deceived; therefore, back to Rome, and prepare for your execution . . . . v 2 51
And conjure thee to pardon Rome, and thy petitionary countrymen . v 2 82
This man, Aufidius, Was my beloved in Rome: yet thou behold'st! . v 2 99
We will before the walls of Rome to-morrow Set down our host . v 3 1
Stopp'd your ears against The general suit of Rome . . . v 3 6
This last old man, Whom with a crack'd heart I have sent to Rome, Loved me . . . . v 3 9
Let the Volsces Plough Rome, and harrow Italy . . . . v 3 34
My lord and husband!—These eyes are not the same I wore in Rome . v 3 38
The moon of Rome, chaste as the icicle That's curdied by the frost . v 3 65
Do not bid me Dismiss my soldiers, or capitulate Again with Rome's mechanics: tell me not Wherein I seem unnatural . . . v 3 83
You Volsces, mark; for we'll Hear nought from Rome in private . v 3 93
If thou conquer Rome, the benefit Which thou shalt thereby reap is such a name, Whose repetition will be dogg'd with curses . . v 3 142
This is the last: so we will home to Rome, And die among our neighbours . . . . v 3 172
O my mother, mother! O! You have won a happy victory to Rome . v 3 186
I'll not to Rome, I'll back with you; and pray you, Stand to me in this v 3 198
Some hope the ladies of Rome, especially his mother, may prevail with him . . . . v 4 6
A merrier day did never yet greet Rome . . . . . v 4 45
Behold our patroness, the life of Rome! . . . . . v 5 1
The army marvell'd at it, and, in the last, When he had carried Rome . v 6 43
And With bloody passage led your wars even to The gates of Rome . v 6 77
He has betray'd your business, and given up, For certain drops of salt, your city Rome . . . . v 6 93
The last That wore the imperial diadem of Rome . . . *T. Andron.* i 1 6

Rome. If ever Bassianus, Cæsar's son, Were gracious in the eyes of royal Rome, Keep then this passage to the Capitol . . *T. Andron.* i 1 11
The people of Rome, for whom we stand A special party . . . i 1 20
Andronicus, surnamed Pius For many good and great deserts to Rome i 1 24
Ten years are spent since first he undertook This cause of Rome . . i 1 32
Five times he hath return'd Bleeding to Rome, bearing his valiant sons i 1 34
At last, laden with honour's spoils, Returns the good Andronicus to Rome . . . . i 1 37
Gracious Lavinia, Rome's rich ornament . . . . i 1 52
Rome, be as just and gracious unto me As I am confident and kind to thee . . . . i 1 60
Rome's best champion, Successful in the battles that he fights . . i 1 65
He circumscribed with his sword, And brought to yoke, the enemies of Rome . . . . i 1 69
Hail, Rome, victorious in thy mourning weeds! . . . . . . i 1 70
Tears of true joy for his return to Rome . . . . i 1 76
These that survive let Rome reward with love . . . . . . i 1 82
Sufficeth not that we are brought to Rome, To beautify thy triumphs? i 1 109
Oppose not Scythia to ambitious Rome . . . . i 1 132
Inter our brethren, And with loud 'larums welcome them to Rome . i 1 147
Rome's readiest champions, repose you here in rest! . . . . . i 1 151
I kneel, with tears of joy, Shed on the earth, for thy return to Rome . i 1 162
Whose fortunes Rome's best citizens applaud . . . . . . i 1 164
Kind Rome, that hast thus lovingly reserved The cordial of mine age! . i 1 165
My beloved brother, Gracious triumpher in the eyes of Rome! . . . i 1 170
The people of Rome, Whose friend in justice thou hast ever been . . i 1 179
Be candidatus then, and put it on, And help to set a head on headless Rome . . . . i 1 186
Rome, I have been thy soldier forty years . . . . . . i 1 193
Draw your swords, and sheathe them not Till Saturninus be Rome's emperor . . . . i 1 205
People of Rome, and people's tribunes here, I ask your voices . . i 1 217
To gratify the good Andronicus, And gratulate his safe return to Rome i 1 221
Whose virtues will, I hope, Reflect on Rome as Titan's rays on earth . i 1 226
We create Lord Saturninus Rome's great emperor . . . . . i 1 232
Lavinia will I make my empress, Rome's royal mistress . . . . i 1 241
Here in sight of Rome to Saturnine . . . do I consecrate My sword . i 1 246
Presents well worthy Rome's imperial lord . . . . i 1 250
How proud I am of thee and of thy gifts Rome shall record . . . i 1 255
Thou comest not to be made a scorn in Rome . . . . . . i 1 265
What, villain boy! Barr'st me my way in Rome? . . . . . . i 1 291
Was there none else in Rome to make a stale, But Saturnine? . . i 1 304
One fit to bandy with thy lawless sons, To ruffle in the commonwealth of Rome . . . . i 1 313
Dost overshine the gallant'st dames of Rome . . . . . . i 1 317
I choose thee, Tamora, for my bride, And will create thee empress of Rome . . . . i 1 320
I will not re-salute the streets of Rome, Or climb my palace, till from forth this place I lead espoused my bride along with me . . . i 1 326
To Rome I swear, If Saturnine advance the Queen of Goths, She will a handmaid be to his desires . . . . i 1 329
Here none but soldiers and Rome's servitors Repose in fame . . . i 1 352
The dismall'st day is this that e'er I saw, To be dishonour'd by my sons in Rome! . . . . i 1 385
How comes it that the subtle Queen of Goths Is of a sudden thus advanced in Rome?—I know not . . . . i 1 393
If Rome have law or we have power, Thou and thy faction shall repent this . . . . i 1 403
Let the laws of Rome determine all; Meanwhile I am possess'd of that is mine . . . . i 1 407
By all the duties that I owe to Rome . . . . i 1 414
In all his deeds A father and a friend to thee and Rome . . . . i 1 423
Rome and the righteous heavens be my judge, How I have loved! . . i 1 426
The gods of Rome forfend I should be author to dishonour you! . . i 1 434
Ingratitude, Which Rome reputes to be a heinous sin . . . . i 1 448
I am incorporate in Rome, A Roman now adopted happily . . . i 1 462
This nymph, This siren, that will charm Rome's Saturnine . . . ii 1 23
Nor would your noble mother for much more Be so dishonour'd in the court of Rome . . . . ii 1 52
Know ye not, in Rome How furious and impatient they be? . . . ii 1 75
Rome's royal empress, Unfurnish'd of her well-beseeming troop . . ii 3 55
For pity of mine age, . . . For all my blood in Rome's great quarrel shed iii 1 4
Were they [the stones] but attired in grave weeds, Rome could afford no tribune like to these . . . . iii 1 44
Dost thou not perceive That Rome is but a wilderness of tigers? Tigers must prey, and Rome affords no prey But me and mine . . . iii 1 54
I'll chop off my hands too; For they have fought for Rome . . . iii 1 73
For hands, to do Rome service, are but vain . . . . . . iii 1 80
Which of your hands hath not defended Rome? . . . . . iii 1 168
The wofull'st man that ever lived in Rome: Farewell, proud Rome . iii 1 290
Now will I to the Goths, and raise a power, To be revenged on Rome . iii 1 301
She loves thee, boy . . . —Ay, when my father was in Rome she did . iv 1 7
Should not be safe For these bad bondmen to the yoke of Rome . . iv 1 109
To gratify your honourable youth, The hope of Rome . . . . iv 2 13
Was't not a happy star Led us to Rome? . . . . iv 2 33
Our empress' shame, and stately Rome's disgrace! . . . . . iv 2 60
Or some of you shall smoke for it in Rome . . . . . . iv 2 111
Our mother is for ever shamed.—Rome will despise her for this foul escape . . . . iv 2 113
Old Andronicus, Shaken with sorrows in ungrateful Rome . . . iv 3 17
Ah, Rome! Well, well; I made thee miserable What time I threw the people's suffrages On him that doth thus tyrannize o'er me . . iv 3 18
And with revengeful war Take wreak on Rome for this ingratitude . iv 3 33
Was ever seen An emperor in Rome thus overborne? . . . . . iv 4 2
Sweet scrolls to fly about the streets of Rome! What's this but libelling? iv 4 16
As who would say, in Rome no justice were . . . . . . iv 4 20
Holp'st to make me great, In hope thyself should govern Rome and me iv 4 60
Arm, arm, my lord;—Rome never had more cause . . . . . iv 4 62
He can at pleasure stint their melody: Even so mayst thou the giddy men of Rome. Then cheer thy spirit . . . . iv 4 87
My faithful friends, I have received letters from great Rome . . v 1 2
Wherein Rome hath done you any scath, Let him make treble satisfaction v 1 7
Whose high exploits and honourable deeds Ingrateful Rome requites with foul contempt . . . . v 1 12
A messenger from Rome Desires to be admitted to your presence . . v 1 152
Look round about the wicked streets of Rome . . . . . . v 2 98
Thy thrice-valiant son, Who leads towards Rome a band of warlike Goths v 2 113
Since it is my father's mind That I repair to Rome, I am content . . v 3 2
Rome's emperor, and nephew, break the parle . . . . . . v 3 19
An honourable end, For peace, for love, for league, and good to Rome . v 3 23

Rome. You sad-faced men, people and sons of Rome . *T. Andron.* v 3 67
Lest Rome herself be bane unto herself . . . . v 3 73
Speak, Rome's dear friend, as erst our ancestor . . . . . v 3 80
That gives our Troy, our Rome, the civil wound . . . . . v 3 87
Basely cozen'd Of that true hand that fought Rome's quarrel out . . v 3 102
Turn'd weeping out, To beg relief among Rome's enemies . . . v 3 106
Come, thou reverend man of Rome, And bring our emperor . . . v 3 137
Lucius, all hail, Rome's royal emperor! . . . . v 3 141
All hail, Rome's gracious governor!—Thanks, gentle Romans . . v 3 146
May I govern so, To heal Rome's harms, and wipe away her woe! . . v 3 148
What tributaries follow him to Rome? . . . . . . *J. Cæsar* i 1 38
You worse than senseless things! O you hard hearts, you cruel men of Rome! . . . . i 1 41
With patient expectation, To see great Pompey pass the streets of Rome i 1 47
Many of the best respect in Rome, Except immortal Cæsar . . . i 2 59
Age, thou art shamed! Rome, thou hast lost the breed of noble bloods! i 2 151
When could they say till now, that talk'd of Rome, That her wide walls encompass'd but one man? . . . . i 2 154
Now is it Rome indeed and room enough, When there is in it but one only man . . . . i 2 156
There was a Brutus once that would have brook'd The eternal devil to keep his state in Rome As easily as a king . . . . i 2 160
Brutus had rather be a villager Than to repute himself a son of Rome Under these hard conditions . . . . i 2 173
Writings all tending to the great opinion That Rome holds of his name i 2 323
What trash is Rome, What rubbish and what offal, when it serves For the base matter to illuminate So vile a thing as Cæsar! . . . . i 3 108
Awake, and see thyself. Shall Rome, &c. Speak, strike, redress! . ii 1 47
Shall Rome stand under one man's awe? What, Rome? . . . . ii 1 52
My ancestors did from the streets of Rome The Tarquin drive . . ii 1 53
Am I entreated To speak and strike? O Rome, I make thee promise! . ii 1 56
Soul of Rome! Brave son, derived from honourable loins! . . . ii 1 321
Signifies that from you great Rome shall suck Reviving blood . . ii 2 87
We will grace his heels With the most boldest and best hearts of Rome iii 1 121
Pity to the general wrong of Rome—As fire drives out fire, so pity pity—Hath done this deed on Cæsar . . . . iii 1 170
Cæsar did write for him to come to Rome.—He did receive his letters . iii 1 278
Is thy master coming?—He lies to-night within seven leagues of Rome . iii 1 286
Here is a mourning Rome, a dangerous Rome, No Rome of safety . . iii 1 288
Not that I loved Cæsar less, but that I loved Rome more . . . iii 2 23
As I slew my best lover for the good of Rome, I have the same dagger for myself, when it shall please my country to need my death . iii 2 50
This Cæsar was a tyrant.— . . . We are blest that Rome is rid of him . iii 2 75
He hath brought many captives home to Rome . . . . . iii 2 93
There's not a nobler man in Rome than Antony . . . . . iii 2 121
That should move The stones of Rome to rise and mutiny . . . iii 2 234
Octavius is already come to Rome.—Where is he? . . . . . iii 2 267
Brutus and Cassius Are rid like madmen through the gates of Rome . iii 2 274
You are contented to be led in triumph Thorough the streets of Rome? v 1 110
Think not, thou noble Roman, That ever Brutus will go bound to Rome v 1 112
The sun of Rome is set! Our day is gone; Clouds, dews, and dangers come; our deeds are done! . . . . v 3 63
It is impossible that ever Rome Should breed thy fellow . . . v 3 100
In the most high and palmy state of Rome . . . . . *Hamlet* i 1 113
When Roscius was an actor in Rome . . . . ii 2 410
News, my good lord, from Rome.—Grates me: the sum . *Ant. and Cleo.* i 1 18
Let Rome in Tiber melt, and the wide arch Of the ranged empire fall! . i 1 33
He approves the common liar, who Thus speaks of him at Rome . . i 1 61
Name Cleopatra as she is call'd in Rome; Rail thou in Fulvia's phrase . i 2 110
Many our contriving friends in Rome Petition us at home . . . i 2 189
Sextus Pompeius Makes his approaches to the port of Rome . . . i 3 46
Let his shames quickly Drive him to Rome . . . . i 4 73
I know they are in Rome together, Looking for Antony . . . . ii 1 19
Mark Antony is every hour in Rome Expected . . . . . . ii 1 29
Welcome to Rome.—Thank you.—Sit . . . . ii 2 28
What was't to you?—No more than my residing here at Rome Might be to you . . . . ii 2 37
The merchandise which thou hast brought from Rome Are all too dear for me . . . . ii 5 104
To scourge the ingratitude that despiteful Rome Cast on my noble father ii 6 22
I must Rid all the sea of pirates; then, to send Measures of wheat to Rome . . . . ii 6 37
Octavia weeps To part from Rome; Cæsar is sad . . . . . iii 2 4
Where?—Madam, in Rome; I look'd her in the face . . . . . iii 3 11
Contemning Rome, he has done all this, and more . . . . . iii 6 1
Let Rome be thus Inform'd . . . . iii 6 19
You are come A market-maid to Rome . . . . iii 6 51
Welcome to Rome; Nothing more dear to me . . . . . . iii 6 85
Welcome, dear madam. Each heart in Rome does love and pity you . iii 6 92
'Tis said in Rome That Photinus an eunuch and your maids Manage this war . . . . iii 7 14
Sink Rome, and their tongues rot That speak against us! . . . iii 7 16
While he was yet in Rome, His power went out in such distractions as Beguiled all spies . . . . iii 7 76
Have I my pillow left unpress'd in Rome? . . . . iii 13 106
Wouldst thou be window'd in great Rome and see Thy master thus? . iv 14 72
Her life in Rome Would be eternal in our triumph . . . . . v 1 65
Shall they hoist me up And show me to the shouting varletry Of censuring Rome? Rather a ditch in Egypt Be gentle grave unto me! v 2 57
Thou, an Egyptian puppet, shalt be shown In Rome, as well as I . . v 2 209
Our army shall In solemn show attend this funeral; And then to Rome v 2 368
My residence in Rome at one Philario's . . . . . . *Cymbeline* i 1 97
A noble gentleman of Rome, Comes from my lord with letters . . i 6 10
Ambassadors from Rome; The one is Caius Lucius . . . . . ii 3 59
For him And his succession granted Rome a tribute . . . . iii 1 8
Be our good deed, Though Rome be therefore angry . . . . iii 1 59
How can she be with him? When was she miss'd? He is in Rome . iii 5 91
But what from Rome?—The senate hath stirr'd up the confiners . . iv 2 336
A leg of Rome shall not return to tell What crows have peck'd them here v 3 92
It was in Rome,—accursed The mansion where!—'twas at a feast . . v 5 154
Good my lord of Rome, Call forth your soothsayer . . . . . v 5 425

Romeo. Where is Romeo? saw you him to-day? . . *Rom. and Jul.* i 1 123
What sadness lengthens Romeo's hours? . . . . i 1 169
I have lost myself; I am not here; This is not Romeo, he's some other where . . . . i 1 204
Why, Romeo, art thou mad?—Not mad, but bound more than a madman i 2 54
Nay, gentle Romeo, we must have you dance.—Not I, believe me . . i 4 13
Young Romeo is it?—'Tis he, that villain Romeo . . . . . i 5 66
His name is Romeo, and a Montague; The only son of your great enemy i 5 138
Now Romeo is beloved and loves again, Alike bewitched . . ii Prol. 5

Romeo. Romeo! my cousin Romeo!—He is wise; And, on my life, hath stol'n him home *Rom. and Jul.* ii 1 3
Romeo! humours! madman! passion! lover! ii 1 7
O, Romeo, that she were, O, that she were An open et cætera, thou a poperin pear! ii 1 37
Romeo, good night: I'll to my truckle-bed; This field-bed is too cold ii 1 39
O Romeo, Romeo! wherefore art thou Romeo? ii 2 33
So Romeo would, were he not Romeo call'd, Retain that dear perfection ii 2 45
Romeo, doff thy name, And for that name which is no part of thee Take all myself.—I take thee at thy word ii 2 47
Call me but love, and I'll be new baptized; Henceforth I never will be Romeo ii 2 51
Art thou not Romeo and a Montague?—Neither, fair saint, if either thee dislike ii 2 60
O gentle Romeo, If thou dost love, pronounce it faithfully ii 2 93
Three words, dear Romeo, and good night indeed ii 2 142
Hist! Romeo, hist! O, for a falconer's voice, To lure this tassel-gentle! ii 2 159
My Romeo's name.—It is my soul that calls upon my name ii 2 164
Romeo!—My dear?—At what o'clock to-morrow Shall I send to thee? ii 2 168
Our Romeo hath not been in bed to-night ii 3 42
Where the devil should this Romeo be? Came he not home to-night? ii 4 1
A challenge, on my life.—Romeo will answer it ii 4 9
Poor Romeo! he is already dead; stabbed with a white wench's black eye ii 4 13
Here comes Romeo.—Without his roe, like a dried herring ii 4 38
Signior Romeo, bon jour! there's a French salutation ii 4 46
Now art thou sociable, now art thou Romeo; now art thou what thou art ii 4 94
Can any of you tell me where I may find the young Romeo?—I can tell you; but young Romeo will be older when you have found him than he was when you sought him ii 4 125
Romeo, will you come to your father's? we'll to dinner, thither ii 4 147
Doth not rosemary and Romeo begin both with a letter?—Ay, nurse ii 4 220
You know not how to choose a man: Romeo! no, not he ii 5 39
Here's such a coil! come, what says Romeo? ii 5 67
Romeo shall thank thee, daughter, for us both.—As much to him ii 6 22
Mercutio, thou consort'st with Romeo,— Consort! what? iii 1 48
Romeo, the hate I bear thee can afford No better term than this,—thou art a villain iii 1 63
O Romeo, Romeo, brave Mercutio's dead! iii 1 121
Romeo, away, be gone! The citizen's are up, and Tybalt slain iii 1 137
There lies the man, slain by young Romeo, That slew thy kinsman iii 1 149
Who began this bloody fray?—Tybalt, here slain, whom Romeo's hand did slay; Romeo that spoke him fair iii 1 157
Romeo he cries aloud, 'Hold, friends! friends, part!' iii 1 169
Then Tybalt fled; But by and by comes back to Romeo iii 1 175
And, as he fell, did Romeo turn and fly. This is the truth iii 1 179
Romeo slew Tybalt, Romeo must not live.—Romeo slew him, he slew Mercutio; Who now the price of his dear blood doth owe?—Not Romeo iii 1 186
Let Romeo hence in haste, Else, when he's found, that hour is his last iii 1 199
And Romeo Leap to these arms, untalk'd of and unseen iii 2 6
Come, night; come, Romeo; come, thou day in night iii 2 17
Gentle night, come, loving, black-brow'd night, Give me my Romeo iii 2 21
Every tongue that speaks But Romeo's name speaks heavenly eloquence iii 2 33
What hast thou there? the cords That Romeo bid thee fetch? iii 2 35
Can heaven be so envious?—Romeo can, Though heaven cannot: O Romeo, Romeo! Who ever would have thought it? Romeo! iii 2 40
Hath Romeo slain himself? say thou but 'I,' And that bare vowel 'I' shall poison more Than the death-darting eye of cockatrice iii 2 45
End motion here; And thou and Romeo press one heavy bier! iii 2 60
Is Romeo slaughter'd, and is Tybalt dead? iii 2 65
Tybalt is gone, and Romeo banished; Romeo that kill'd him, he is banished iii 2 69
O God! did Romeo's hand shed Tybalt's blood?—It did, it did iii 2 71
Shame come to Romeo!—Blister'd be thy tongue For such a wish! iii 2 90
Tybalt is dead, and Romeo—banished; That 'banished' iii 2 112
'Romeo is banished,' to speak that word, Is father, mother, Tybalt, Romeo, Juliet, All slain, all dead iii 2 122
'Romeo is banished!' There is no end, no limit, measure, bound, In that word's death iii 2 124
Wash they his wounds with tears: mine shall be spent, When theirs are dry, for Romeo's banishment iii 2 131
Poor ropes, you are beguiled, Both you and I; for Romeo is exiled iii 2 133
I'll to my wedding-bed; And death, not Romeo, take my maidenhead! iii 2 137
Hie to your chamber: I'll find Romeo To comfort you iii 2 138
Romeo will be here at night: I'll to him; he is hid at Laurence' cell iii 2 140
Romeo, come forth; come forth, thou fearful man iii 3 1
And little mouse, every unworthy thing, Live here in heaven and may look on her; But Romeo may not iii 3 33
More honourable state, more courtship lives In carrion-flies than Romeo iii 3 35
But Romeo may not; he is banished: Flies may do this iii 3 40
Arise; one knocks; good Romeo, hide thyself.—Not I iii 3 71
Who's there? Romeo, arise; Thou wilt be taken. Stay awhile! Stand up iii 3 74
O, tell me, holy friar, Where is my lady's lord, where's Romeo? iii 3 82
Starts up, And Tybalt calls; and then on Romeo cries, And then down falls again iii 3 101
Bid her hasten all the house to bed, Which heavy sorrow makes them apt unto: Romeo is coming iii 3 158
O, by this count I shall be much in years Ere I again behold my Romeo! iii 5 47
That same villain, Romeo.—Villain and he be many miles asunder iii 5 81
Indeed, I never shall be satisfied With Romeo, till I behold him—dead iii 5 95
Romeo should, upon receipt thereof, Soon sleep in quiet iii 5 99
I will not marry yet; and, when I do, I swear, It shall be Romeo iii 5 123
Some comfort, nurse.—Faith, here it is. Romeo is banish'd iii 5 215
O, he's a lovely gentleman! Romeo's a dishclout to him iii 5 221
God join'd my heart and Romeo's, thou our hands iv 1 55
Ere this hand, by thee to Romeo seal'd, Shall be the label to another deed iv 1 56
Mean time, against thou shalt awake, Shall Romeo by my letters know iv 1 114
That very night Shall Romeo bear thee hence to Mantua iv 1 117
Lest in this marriage he should be dishonour'd, Because he married me before to Romeo iv 3 27
How if, when I am laid into the tomb, I wake before the time that Romeo Come to redeem me? iv 3 31
And there die strangled ere my Romeo comes iv 3 35
Methinks I see my cousin's ghost Seeking out Romeo iv 3 56
Romeo, I come! this do I drink to thee iv 3 58
Welcome from Mantua: what says Romeo? v 2 3
Who bare my letter, then, to Romeo?—I could not send it,—here it is again v 2 13
Romeo. She will beshrew me much that Romeo Hath had no notice of these accidents *Rom. and Jul.* v 2 26
I will write again to Mantua, And keep her at my cell till Romeo come v 2 29
There's my master, One that you love.—Who is it?—Romeo v 3 129
Romeo! Alack, alack, what blood is this, which stains The stony entrance of this sepulchre? v 3 139
Romeo! O, pale! Who else? what, Paris too? And steep'd in blood? v 3 144
I do remember well where I should be, And there I am. Where is my Romeo? v 3 150
Here's Romeo's man; we found him in the churchyard.—Hold him in safety v 3 182
The people in the street cry Romeo, Some Juliet, and some Paris v 3 191
Paris slain; And Romeo dead; and Juliet, dead before, Warm and new kill'd v 3 196
Here is a friar, and slaughter'd Romeo's man; With instruments upon them v 3 199
Romeo, there dead, was husband to that Juliet; And she, there dead, that Romeo's faithful wife v 3 231
Meantime I writ to Romeo, That he should hither come v 3 246
To keep her closely at my cell, Till I conveniently could send to Romeo v 3 256
Here untimely lay The noble Paris and true Romeo dead v 3 259
Where's Romeo's man? what can he say in this? v 3 271
As rich shall Romeo's [statue] by his lady's lie; Poor sacrifices! v 3 303
For never was a story of more woe Than this of Juliet and her Romeo v 3 310
Romish. If he shall think it fit, A saucy stranger in his court to mart As in a Romish stew *Cymbeline* i 6 152
Ronyon. You baggage, you polecat, you ronyon! *Mer. Wives* iv 2 195
'Aroint thee, witch!' the rump-fed ronyon cries *Macbeth* i 3 6
Rood. An early stirrer, by the rood! *2 Hen. IV.* iii 2 3
By the holy rood, I do not like these several councils *Richard III.* iii 2 77
By the rood, She could have run and waddled all about *Rom. and Jul.* i 3 36
Have you forgot me?—No, by the rood, not so *Hamlet* iii 4 14
Roof. I have purchased as many diseases under her roof *Meas. for Meas.* i 2 47
My visor is Philemon's roof; within the house is Jove *Much Ado* ii 1 99
The roof of this court is too high to be yours *L. L. Lost* ii 1 92
Swearing till my very roof was dry With oaths of love *Mer. of Venice* iii 2 206
Within this roof The enemy of all your graces lives *As Y. Like It* ii 3 17
My very lips might freeze to my teeth, my tongue to the roof of my mouth, my heart in my belly *T. of Shrew* iv 1 7
Underneath that consecrated roof *T. Night* iv 3 25
Every day under his household roof Did keep ten thousand men *Rich. II.* iv 1 282
May my knees grow to the earth, My tongue cleave to my roof within my mouth v 3 31
The singing masons building roofs of gold *Hen. V.* i 2 198
Your roof were not sufficient to contain't *1 Hen. VI.* ii 3 56
To bring the roof to the foundation, And bury all *Coriolanus* iii 1 205
Thatch your poor thin roofs With burthens of the dead *T. of Athens* iv 3 144
This brave o'erhanging firmament, this majestical roof *Hamlet* ii 2 313
I abjure all roofs, and choose To wage against the enmity o' the air *Lear* ii 4 211
The dust Should have ascended to the roof of heaven *Ant. and Cleo.* iii 6 49
The roof o' the chamber With golden cherubins is fretted *Cymbeline* ii 4 87
A goodly day not to keep house, with such Whose roof's as low as ours! iii 3 2
Though train'd up thus meanly I' the cave wherein they bow, their thoughts do hit The roofs of palaces iii 3 84
The marble pavement closes, he is enter'd His radiant roof v 4 121
Like goodly buildings left without a roof Soon fall to ruin *Pericles* ii 4 36
Roofed. Here had we now our country's honour roof'd, Were the graced person of our Banquo present *Macbeth* iii 4 40
Rook. When turtles tread, and rooks, and daws *L. L. Lost* v 2 915
Augurs and understood relations have By magot-pies and choughs and rooks brought forth The secret'st man of blood *Macbeth* iii 4 125
Rooked. The raven rook'd her on the chimney's top *3 Hen. VI.* v 6 47
Rooky. Light thickens; and the crow Makes wing to the rooky wood *Macbeth* iii 2 51
Room. Blow, till thou burst thy wind, if room enough! *Tempest* i 1 9
Strew good luck, ouphes, on every sacred room *Mer. Wives* v 5 61
It is an open room and good for winter *Meas. for Meas.* ii 1 135
I never come into any room in a taphouse, but I am drawn in ii 1 219
They must be bound and laid in some dark room *Com. of Errors* iv 4 97
In their rooms Come thronging soft and delicate desires *Much Ado* i 1 304
As I was smoking a musty room i 3 61
The revellers are entering, brother: make good room ii 1 88
Room for the incensed Worthies! *L. L. Lost* v 2 703
But, room, fairy! here comes Oberon *M. N. Dream* ii 1 58
Make room, and let him stand before our face *Mer. of Venice* iv 1 16
When a man's verses cannot be understood, . . . it strikes a man more dead than a great reckoning in a little room *As Y. Like It* iii 3 15
Let Bianca take her sister's room *T. of Shrew* iii 2 252
Dissolved from my hive, To give some labourers room *All's Well* i 2 67
We'll have him in a dark room and bound *T. Night* iii 4 148
Please your ladyship To visit the next room *W. Tale* ii 2 47
I was seduced To make room for him in my husband's bed *K. John* i 1 255
O, lawful let it be That I have room with Rome to curse awhile! iii 1 180
Grief fills the room up of my absent child, Lies in his bed iii 4 93
Go thou, and fill another room in hell *Richard II.* v 5 108
This is your doom: Choose out some secret place, some reverend room v 6 25
Come out of that fat room, and lend me thy hand to laugh a little *1 Hen. IV.* ii 4 2
There's no room for faith, truth, nor honesty in this bosom of thine iii 3 174
To fill up the rooms of them that have bought out their services iv 2 35
But now two paces of the vilest earth Is room enough v 4 92
The room where they supped is too hot *2 Hen. IV.* ii 4 14
Call for the music in the other room iv 5 4
Your father is disposed to sleep.—Let us withdraw into the other room iv 5 18
I found the prince in the next room iv 5 83
Pursued the story, In little room confining mighty men *Hen. V.* Epil. 3
Instead whereof let this supply the room *3 Hen. VI.* ii 6 54
And all the unlook'd for issue of their bodies, To take their rooms iii 2 132
I'll throw thy body in another room v 6 92
We will chop him in the malmsey-butt in the next room *Richard III.* i 4 161
We shall have Great store of room, no doubt, left for the ladies *Hen. VIII.* v 4 77
Give room! and foot it, girls. More light, you knaves *Rom. and Jul.* i 5 28
Quench the fire, the room is grown too hot i 5 30
Every room Hath blazed with lights and bray'd with minstrelsy *T. of A.* ii 2 169
But one man? Now is it Rome indeed and room enough, When there is in it but one only man *J. Cæsar* i 2 156
Room for Antony, most noble Antony.—Nay, press not so upon me iii 2 170
Stand far off.—Stand back; room; bear back iii 2 172
I will speak. Must I give way and room to your rash choler? iv 3 39
A noble prisoner!—Room, ho! Tell Antony, Brutus is ta'en v 4 16

Room. I'll lug the guts into the neighbour room . . . . *Hamlet* iii 4 212
In fine withdrew To mine own room again . . . . v 2 16
You must forsake this room, and go with us . . . . *Othello* v 2 330
I have yet Room for six scotches more . . . . *Ant. and Cleo.* iv 7 10
Root. Wither'd roots and husks Wherein the acorn cradled . *Tempest* i 2 463
Growing proud, Disdain to root the summer-swelling flower *T. G. of Ver.* ii 4 162
How oft hast thou with perjury cleft the root! . . . . . . v 4 103
Focative is caret.—And that's a good root . . . *Mer. Wives* iv 1 56
Where it is impossible you should take true root . . . *Much Ado* i 3 25
Under an oak whose antique root peeps out Upon the brook *As Y. L. It* ii 1 31
Once remove The root of his opinion, which is rotten . . *W. Tale* ii 3 89
Seven fair branches springing from one root . . . *Richard II.* i 2 13
One flourishing branch of his most royal root . . . Is hack'd down . i 2 18
I will go root away The noisome weeds . . . . iii 4 37
Pluck'd up root and all by Bolingbroke . . . . iii 4 52
Which should not find a ground to root upon, Unless on you 2 *Hen. IV.* iii 1 91
As gardeners do with ordure hide those roots That shall first spring *Hen. V.* ii 4 39
Her fallow leas The darnel, hemlock and rank fumitory Doth root upon v 2 46
Spring crestless yeomen from so deep a root? . . . 1 *Hen. VI.* ii 4 85
I'll plant Plantagenet, root him up who dares . . . . . 3 *Hen. VI.* i 1 48
Till I root out their accursed line And leave not one alive, I live in hell i 3 32
When we saw our sunshine made thy spring, And that thy summer bred us no increase, We set the axe to thy usurping root . . . . . ii 2 165
But set his murdering knife unto the root . . . . ii 6 49
His love was an eternal plant, Whereof the root was fix'd in virtue's ground . . . . iii 3 125
The thorny wood, Which, by the heavens' assistance and your strength, Must by the roots be hewn up yet ere night . . . . . v 4 69
Why grow the branches now the root is wither'd? . . *Richard III.* ii 2 41
We should take root here where we sit, or sit State-statues only *Hen. VIII.* i 2 87
Though we leave it with a root, thus hack'd, The air will drink the sap i 2 97
Nips his root, And then he falls, as I do . . . . iii 2 357
He's a rank weed, Sir Thomas, And we must root him out . . . v 1 53
Where are my tears? rain, to lay this wind, or my heart will be blown up by the root . . . . *Troi. and Cres.* iv 4 56
A curse begin at very root on's heart, That is not glad to see thee! *Cor.* ii 1 202
Each word thou hast spoke hath weeded from my heart A root of ancient envy . . . . iv 5 109
Rape, I fear, was root of thine annoy . . . . *T. Andron.* iv 1 49
I'll make you feed on berries and on roots, And feed on curds and whey iv 2 177
So fall to't: Rich men sin, and I eat root. . . . *T. of Athens* i 2 72
Like madness is the glory of this life, As this pomp shows to a little oil and root . . . . i 2 140
Earth, yield me roots! Who seeks for better of thee, sauce his palate With thy most operant poison! . . . . iv 3 23
Precious gold? No, gods, I am no idle votarist: roots, you clear heavens! iv 3 27
Yield him, who all thy human sons doth hate, From forth thy plenteous bosom, one poor root! . . . . iv 3 186
O, a root,—dear thanks!—Dry up thy marrows, vines, and plough-torn leas! . . . . iv 3 192
Why should you want? Behold, the earth hath roots . . . . iv 3 420
How shall I requite you? Can you eat roots, and drink cold water? . v 1 77
Be as a cauterizing to the root o' the tongue, Consuming it with speaking! v 1 136
Who, like a boar too savage, doth root up His country's peace . . v 1 168
Or have we eaten on the insane root That takes the reason prisoner? *Macbeth* i 3 84
That myself should be the root and father Of many kings . . . iii 1 5
The ravin'd salt-sea shark, Root of hemlock digg'd i' the dark . . iv 1 25
Who can impress the forest, bid the tree Unfix his earth-bound root? . iv 1 96
This avarice Sticks deeper, grows with more pernicious root . . . iv 3 85
The fat weed That roots itself in ease on Lethe wharf . . *Hamlet* i 5 33
As if he pluck'd up kisses by the roots That grew upon my lips *Othello* iii 3 423
A grief that smites My very heart at root. . . . *Ant. and Cleo.* v 2 105
I cannot delve him to the root . . . . *Cymbeline* i 1 28
He cut our roots In characters, And sauced our broths . . . . iv 2 48
Let the stinking elder, grief, untwine His perishing root! . . . iv 2 60
As the tops of trees, Which fence the roots they grow by . . *Pericles* i 2 30
Your herb-woman; she that sets seeds and roots of shame and iniquity iv 6 93
Rooted. I could not have owed her a more rooted love . . *All's Well* iv 5 13
There rooted betwixt them then such an affection . . . *W. Tale* i 1 25
Thy truth and thy integrity is rooted In us, thy friend . . *Hen. VIII.* v 1 114
Canst thou not . . . Pluck from the memory a rooted sorrow? *Macbeth* v 3 41
I have spoke this, to know if your affiance Were deeply rooted *Cymbeline* i 6 164
Grief and patience, rooted in him both, Mingle their spurs together . iv 2 57
Time hath rooted out my parentage . . . . *Pericles* v 1 93
Rootedly. They all do hate him As rootedly as I . . . . *Tempest* iii 2 103
Rooteth. Underneath the grove of sycamore That westward rooteth from the city's side . . . . *Rom. and Jul.* i 1 129
Rooting. Thou elvish-mark'd, abortive, rooting hog! . . *Richard III.* i 3 228
Rope. We will not hand a rope more . . . . *Tempest* i 1 25
Make the rope of his destiny our cable, for our own doth little advantage i 1 33
Buy thou a rope and bring it home to me.—I buy a thousand pound a year: I buy a rope . . . . *Com. of Errors* iv 1 20
Thou drunken slave, I sent thee for a rope . . . . iv 1 96
I gave the money for the rope.—Five hundred ducats, villain, for a rope? iv 4 12
God and the rope-maker bear me witness That I was sent for nothing but a rope! . . . . iv 4 94
Men make ropes in such a scarre That we'll forsake ourselves *All's Well* iv 2 38
Winchester goose, I cry, a rope! a rope! Now beat them hence 1 *Hen. VI.* i 3 53
Take up those cords: poor ropes, you are beguiled . . *Rom. and Jul.* iii 2 132
Galling His kingly hands, haling ropes . . . . . . *Pericles* iv 1 55
Rope-maker. God and the rope-maker bear me witness! . *Com. of Errors* iv 4 93
Ropery. I pray you, sir, what saucy merchant was this, that was so full of his ropery? . . . . *Rom. and Jul.* ii 4 154
Rope's-end. Go thou And buy a rope's end . . . *Com. of Errors* iv 1 16
To what end did I bid thee hie thee home?—To a rope's-end . . iv 4 16
Rather, the prophecy like the parrot, 'beware the rope's-end' . . iv 4 46
Rope-tricks. An he begin once, he'll rail in his rope-tricks . *T. of Shrew* i 2 112
Roping icicles. Let us not hang like roping icicles Upon our houses' thatch *Hen. V.* iii 5 23
Rosalind. Can you tell if Rosalind, the duke's daughter, be banished with her father? . . . . *As Y. Like It* i 1 110
I pray thee, Rosalind, sweet my coz, be merry . . . . . . i 2 1
Thus must I from the smoke into the smother; From tyrant duke unto a tyrant brother: But heavenly Rosalind! . . . . i 2 301
Why, cousin! why, Rosalind! Cupid have mercy! not a word? . . . i 3 1
O my poor Rosalind, whither wilt thou go? Wilt thou change fathers? i 3 92
Rosalind lacks then the love Which teacheth thee that thou and I am one . . . . i 3 98
Rosalind. O Rosalind! these trees shall be my books . *As Y. Like It* iii 2 5
From the east to western Ind, No jewel is like Rosalind. . . . . iii 2 94
Her worth, being mounted on the wind, Through all the world bears Rosalind . . . . iii 2 96
All the pictures fairest lined Are but black to Rosalind . . . . iii 2 98
Let no fair be kept in mind But the fair of Rosalind . . . . . iii 2 100
If a hart do lack a hind, Let him seek out Rosalind . . . . . iii 2 108
If the cat will after kind, So be sure will Rosalind . . . . . iii 2 110
Winter garments must be lined, So must slender Rosalind . . . . iii 2 112
They that reap must sheaf and bind; Then to cart with Rosalind . . iii 2 114
Sweetest nut hath sourest rind, Such a nut is Rosalind . . . . iii 2 116
He that sweetest rose will find Must find love's prick and Rosalind . iii 2 118
Thus Rosalind of many parts By heavenly synod was devised . . . iii 2 157
Rosalind is your love's name?—Yes, just.—I do not like her name . iii 2 280
Abuses our young plants with carving 'Rosalind' on their barks . . iii 2 379
Hangs odes upon hawthorns and elegies on brambles, all, forsooth, deifying the name of Rosalind . . . . iii 2 381
Are you he that hangs the verses on the trees, wherein Rosalind is so admired?— . . . By the white hand of Rosalind, I am that he . iii 2 412
I would cure you, if you would but call me Rosalind . . . . . iii 2 447
With all my heart, good youth.—Nay, you must call me Rosalind. . iii 2 455
Good day and happiness, dear Rosalind! . . . . iv 1 30
My fair Rosalind, I come within an hour of my promise . . . . iv 1 42
Pardon me, dear Rosalind.—Nay, an you be so tardy, come no more in my sight . . . . iv 1 50
My Rosalind is virtuous.—And I am your Rosalind.—It pleases him to call you so; but he hath a Rosalind of a better leer than you . . iv 1 63
What would you say to me now, an I were your very very Rosalind? . iv 1 71
Am not I your Rosalind?—I take some joy to say you are . . . iv 1 89
I would not have my right Rosalind of this mind . . . . . . iv 1 109
But come, now I will be your Rosalind in a more coming-on disposition iv 1 112
Then love me, Rosalind.—Yes, faith, will I, Fridays and Saturdays and all . . . . iv 1 115
Will you, Orlando, have to wife this Rosalind?—I will.—Ay, but when? iv 1 131
Say 'I take thee, Rosalind, for wife.'—I take thee, Rosalind, for wife iv 1 135
But will my Rosalind do so?—By my life, she will do as I do . . iv 1 158
For these two hours, Rosalind, I will leave thee.—Alas! dear love, I cannot lack thee two hours . . . . iv 1 180
Two o'clock is your hour?—Ay, sweet Rosalind . . . . . . iv 1 191
The most hollow lover and the most unworthy of her you call Rosalind iv 1 198
Keep your promise.—With no less religion than if thou wert indeed my Rosalind . . . . iv 1 202
To that youth he calls his Rosalind He sends this bloody napkin . . iv 3 93
And now he fainted And cried, in fainting, upon Rosalind . . . iv 3 150
Unto the shepherd youth That he in sport doth call his Rosalind . . iv 3 157
I must bear answer back How you excuse my brother, Rosalind . . iv 3 181
Prepare Aliena; for look you, here comes my Rosalind . . . . v 2 18
Why then, to-morrow I cannot serve your turn for Rosalind? . . . v 2 54
If you do love Rosalind so near the heart as your gesture cries it out . v 2 68
If you will be married to-morrow, you shall, and to Rosalind, if you will v 2 81
So am I for Phebe.—And I for Ganymede.—And I for Rosalind . . v 2 93
As you love Rosalind, meet: as you love Phebe, meet . . . . v 2 129
You say, if I bring in your Rosalind, You will bestow her on Orlando?. v 4 6
If there be truth in sight, you are my Rosalind . . . . . . v 4 125
Rosalinda. At every sentence end, Will I Rosalinda write . . iii 2 145
Rosaline. What's her name in the cap?—Rosaline . . . *L. L. Lost* ii 1 210
A gentle lady; When tongues speak sweetly, then they name her name, And Rosaline they call her . . . . iii 1 168
A letter from Monsieur Biron to one Lady Rosaline . . . . . iv 1 53
To a lady of France that he call'd Rosaline . . . . iv 1 107
To the snow-white hand of the most beauteous Lady Rosaline . . . iv 2 137
Who sees the heavenly Rosaline, That . . . Bows not his vassal head?. iv 3 221
But, Rosaline, you have a favour too: Who sent it? . . . . . v 2 30
Rosaline, this favour thou shalt wear, And then the king will court thee v 2 130
And give me thine, So shall Biron take me for Rosaline . . . . v 2 133
Rosaline, What did the Russian whisper in your ear? . . . . . v 2 442
Uncle Capulet, his wife, and daughters; my fair niece Rosaline *R. and J.* i 2 72
At this same ancient feast of Capulet's Sups the fair Rosaline . . . i 2 88
I conjure thee by Rosaline's bright eyes, By her high forehead . . ii 1 17
Wast thou with Rosaline?—With Rosaline, my ghostly father? no . . ii 3 44
Is Rosaline, whom thou didst love so dear, So soon forsaken? . . . ii 3 66
What a deal of brine Hath wash'd thy sallow cheeks for Rosaline! . . ii 3 70
If e'er thou wast thyself and these woes thine, Thou and these woes were all for Rosaline . . . . ii 3 78
Thou chid'st me oft for loving Rosaline.—For doting, not for loving . ii 3 81
That same pale hard-hearted wench, that Rosaline, Torments him so . ii 4 4
Roscius. What scene of death hath Roscius now to act? . . 3 *Hen. VI.* v 6 10
When Roscius was an actor in Rome . . . . *Hamlet* ii 2 410
Rose. The air hath starved the roses in her cheeks . . . *T. G. of Ver.* iv 4 159
Make our peds of roses, And a thousand fragrant posies . *Mer. Wives* iii 1 19
I had rather be a canker in a hedge than a rose in his grace . *Much Ado* i 3 29
At Christmas I no more desire a rose Than wish a snow in May's new-fangled mirth; But like of each thing that in season grows *L. L. Lost* i 1 105
So sweet a kiss the golden sun gives not To those fresh morning drops upon the rose, As thy eye-beams . . . . iv 3 27
Blow like sweet roses in this summer air . . . . v 2 293
Fair ladies mask'd are roses in their bud; Dismask'd, their damask sweet commixture shown, Are angels vailing clouds, or roses blown. . . v 2 295
But earthlier happy is the rose distill'd . . . . . *M. N. Dream* i 1 76
Why is your cheek so pale? How chance the roses there do fade so fast? . . . . i 1 129
Hoary-headed frosts Fall in the fresh lap of the crimson rose. . . ii 1 108
Most lily-white of hue, Of colour like the red rose on triumphant brier. iii 1 96
No doubt they rose up early to observe The rite of May . . . . iv 1 137
My sweet Rose, my dear Rose, be merry . . . . . *As Y. Like It* i 2 24
Slept together, Rose at an instant, learn'd, play'd, eat together . . i 3 76
He that sweetest rose will find Must find love's prick and Rosalind . iii 2 117
She looks as clear As morning roses newly wash'd with dew *T. of Shrew* ii 1 174
What said the wench when he rose again?—Trembled and shook . . iii 2 168
This thorn Doth to our rose of youth rightly belong . . *All's Well* i 3 136
When you have our roses, You barely leave our thorns to prick ourselves iv 2 18
For women are as roses, whose fair flower Being once display'd, doth fall that very hour . . . . *T. Night* ii 4 39
By the roses of the spring, By maidhood, honour, truth and every thing iii 1 161
Gloves as sweet as damask roses . . . . *W. Tale* iv 4 222
My face so thin That in mine ear I durst not stick a rose . . *K. John* i 1 142
Of Nature's gifts thou mayst with lilies boast And with the half-blown rose . . . . iii 1 54
But soft, but see, or rather do not see, My fair rose wither *Richard II.* v 1 8
To put down Richard, that sweet lovely rose . . . . 1 *Hen. IV.* i 3 175

Rose. Never joyed since the price of oats rose; it was the death of him *1 Hen. IV.* ii 1 14
We rose both at an instant and fought a long hour by Shrewsbury clock v 4 150
And your colour, I warrant you, is as red as any rose *2 Hen. IV.* ii 4 28
From off this brier pluck a white rose with me *1 Hen. VI.* ii 4 30
Pluck a red rose from off this thorn with me ii 4 33
I pluck this white rose with Plantagenet.—I pluck this red rose with young Somerset ii 4 36
He upon whose side The fewest roses are cropp'd from the tree Shall yield the other in the right opinion ii 4 41
Giving my verdict on the white rose side.—Prick not your finger as you pluck it off, Lest bleeding you do paint the white rose red ii 4 48
Was wrong in you; In sign whereof I pluck a white rose too ii 4 58
Meditating that Shall dye your white rose in a bloody red ii 4 61
Your cheeks do counterfeit our roses; For pale they look with fear ii 4 62
Thy cheeks Blush for pure shame to counterfeit our roses ii 4 66
Hath not thy rose a canker, Somerset?—Hath not thy rose a thorn, Plantagenet?—Ay, sharp and piercing ii 4 68
Well, I'll find friends to wear my bleeding roses ii 4 72
This pale and angry rose, As cognizance of my blood-drinking hate ii 4 107
I upon thy party wear this rose: And here I prophesy ii 4 123
This brawl to-day, . . . Shall send between the red rose and the white A thousand souls to death ii 4 126
Upbraided me about the rose I wear iv 1 91
I see no reason, if I wear this rose, That any one should therefore be suspicious I more incline to Somerset than York iv 1 152
Then will I raise aloft the milk-white rose, With whose sweet smell the air shall be perfumed *2 Hen. VI.* i 1 254
He rose against him, being his sovereign *3 Hen. VI.* i 1 141
I cannot rest Until the white rose that I wear be dyed Even in the lukewarm blood of Henry's heart i 2 33
The red rose and the white are on his face, The fatal colours ii 5 97
Wither one rose, and let the other flourish ii 5 101
Their lips were four red roses on a stalk *Richard III.* iv 3 12
We will unite the white rose and the red v 5 19
At the Rose, within the parish Saint Lawrence Poultney *Hen. VIII.* i 2 152
At length her grace rose, and with modest paces Came to the altar iv 1 82
Pray'd devoutly. Then rose again and bow'd her to the people iv 1 85
Before the sun rose he was harness'd light *Troi. and Cres.* i 2 8
A rose By any other name would smell as sweet *Rom. and Jul.* ii 2 43
The roses in thy lips and cheeks shall fade To paly ashes iv 1 99
Remnants of packthread and old cakes of roses, Were thinly scatter'd v 1 47
If then that friend demand why Brutus rose against Cæsar, this is my answer *J. Cæsar* iii 2 21
The expectancy and rose of the fair state, The glass of fashion *Hamlet* iii 1 160
With two Provincial roses on my razed shoes iii 2 288
Takes off the rose From the fair forehead of an innocent love iii 4 42
Then up he rose, and donn'd his clothes iv 5 52
O rose of May! Dear maid, kind sister, sweet Ophelia! iv 5 157
When I have pluck'd the rose, I cannot give it vital growth again *Othello* v 2 13
Tell him he wears the rose Of youth upon him *Ant. and Cleo.* iii 13 20
Against the blown rose may they stop their nose iii 13 39
For flesh and blood, sir, white and red, you shall see a rose; and she were a rose indeed *Pericles* iv 6 38
Her art sisters the natural roses; Her inkle, silk v Gower 7
Rose-cheeked. Season the slaves For tubs and baths; bring down rose-cheeked youth To the tub-fast and the diet *T. of Athens* iv 3 86
Rosed. A maid yet rosed over with the virgin crimson of modesty *Hen. V.* v 2 323
Warm blood . . . Doth rise and fall between thy rosed lips *T. Andron.* ii 4 24
Rose-lipped. Patience, thou young and rose-lipp'd cherubin! *Othello* iv 2 63
Rosemary. Reverend sirs, For you there's rosemary and rue *W. Tale* iv 4 74
Doth not rosemary and Romeo begin both with a letter? *Rom. and Jul.* ii 4 219
She hath the prettiest sententious of it, of you and rosemary ii 4 226
Dry up your tears, and stick your rosemary On this fair corse iv 5 79
There's rosemary, that's for remembrance *Hamlet* iv 5 175
Strike in their numb'd and mortified bare arms Pins, wooden pricks, nails, sprigs of rosemary *Lear* ii 3 16
Marry, come up, my dish of chastity with rosemary and bays! *Pericles* iv 6 160
Rosencrantz. Welcome, dear Rosencrantz and Guildenstern! *Hamlet* ii 2 1
Thanks, Rosencrantz and gentle Guildenstern.—Thanks, Guildenstern and gentle Rosencrantz ii 2 33
How dost thou, Guildenstern? Ah, Rosencrantz! Good lads, how do ye both? ii 2 229
Rosencrantz and Guildenstern hold their course for England iv 6 28
So Guildenstern and Rosencrantz go to't v 2 56
His commandment is fulfill'd, That Rosencrantz and Guildenstern are dead v 2 382
Rose-water. Let one attend him with a silver basin Full of rose-water and bestrew'd with flowers *T. of Shrew* Ind. 1 56
Ross. The Lords of Ross, Beaumond, and Willoughby *Richard II.* ii 2 54
I bethink me what a weary way From Ravenspurgh to Cotswold will be found In Ross and Willoughby ii 3 10
Who comes here?—The worthy thane of Ross *Macbeth* i 2 45
Rosy. With A pudency so rosy the sweet view on't Might well have warm'd old Saturn *Cymbeline* ii 5 11
One sand another Not more resembles that sweet rosy lad Who died v 5 121
Rot. Ay, but to die, and go we know not where; To lie in cold obstruction and to rot *Meas. for Meas.* iii 1 119
Shall, Antipholus, Even in the spring of love, thy love-springs rot? *Com. of Errors* iii 2 3
And then, from hour to hour, we rot and rot *As Y. Like It* ii 7 27
Make that thy question, and go rot! *W. Tale* i 2 324
An if I do not, may my hands rot off! *Richard II.* iv 1 49
As fester'd members rot but by degree *1 Hen. VI.* iii 1 192
Like fair fruit in an unwholesome dish, Are like to rot untasted *T. and C.* ii 3 130
Vengeance rot you all! *T. Andron.* v 1 58
Thy lips rot off!—I will not kiss thee; then the rot returns To thine own lips again *T. of Athens* iv 3 63
I'll beat thee, but I should infect my hands.—I would my tongue could rot them off! iv 3 370
How long will a man lie i' the earth ere he rot? *Hamlet* v 1 179
No farther, sir; a man may rot even here *Lear* v 2 8
Let her rot, and perish, and be damned to-night *Othello* iv 1 191
May his pernicious soul Rot half a grain a day! v 2 156
Lackeying the varying tide, To rot itself with motion *Ant. and Cleo.* i 4 47
Sink Rome, and their tongues rot That speak against us! iii 7 16
The south-fog rot him!—He never can meet more mischance than come To be but named of thee *Cymbeline* ii 3 136
Rote. First, rehearse your song by rote *M. N. Dream* v 1 404
And they will learn you by rote where services were done *Hen. V.* iii 6 75
Rote. Thy love did read by rote and could not spell *Rom. and Jul.* ii 3 88
All his faults observed, Set in a note-book, learn'd, and conn'd by rote, To cast into my teeth *J. Cæsar* iv 3 98
Roted. With such words that are but roted in Your tongue *Coriolanus* iii 2 55
Rother. It is the pasture lards the rother's sides *T. of Athens* iv 3 12
Rotted. The ploughman lost his sweat, and the green corn Hath rotted ere his youth attain'd a beard *M. N. Dream* ii 1 95
More sweet, and yet more dangerous, Than baits to fish, or honey-stalks to sheep, When as the one is wounded with the bait, The other rotted with delicious feed *T. Andron.* iv 4 93
Rotten. They prepared A rotten carcass of a boat *Tempest* i 2 146
The air breathes upon us here most sweetly.—As if it had lungs and rotten ones.—Or as 'twere perfumed by a fen ii 1 47
To be detected with a jealous rotten bell-wether *Mer. Wives* iii 5 111
They would else have married me to the rotten medlar *Meas. for Meas.* iv 3 184
Give not this rotten orange to your friend *Much Ado* iv 1 33
The sweet war-man is dead and rotten *L. L. Lost* v 2 666
An evil soul producing holy witness Is like a villain with a smiling cheek, A goodly apple rotten at the heart *Mer. of Venice* i 3 102
But, poor old man, thou prunest a rotten tree *As Y. Like It* ii 3 63
For you'll be rotten ere you be half ripe iii 2 126
Faith, as you say, there's small choice in rotten apples *T. of Shrew* i 1 139
So that the muster-file, rotten and sound, upon my life, amounts not to fifteen thousand poll *All's Well* iv 3 189
Which is rotten As ever oak or stone was sound *W. Tale* ii 3 89
If thou 'lt see a thing to talk on when thou art dead and rotten, come hither iii 3 82
That shakes the rotten carcass of old Death Out of his rags! *K. John* ii 1 456
With inky blots and rotten parchment bonds *Richard II.* ii 1 64
Never did base and rotten policy Colour her working with such deadly wounds *1 Hen. IV.* i 3 108
A rotten case abides no handling *2 Hen. IV.* iv 1 161
The unguided days And rotten times that you shall look upon iv 4 60
To frustrate prophecies and to raze out Rotten opinion v 2 128
And have their heads crushed like rotten apples! *Hen. V.* iii 7 155
If I digg'd up thy forefathers' graves And hung their rotten coffins up in chains, It could not slake mine ire *3 Hen. VI.* i 3 28
Prosperity begins to mellow And drop into the rotten mouth of death *Richard III.* iv 4 2
The rotten diseases of the south, the guts-griping, ruptures *T. and C.* v 1 21
The prayers of priests nor times of sacrifice, Embarquements all of fury, shall lift up Their rotten privilege and custom 'gainst My hate *Coriolanus* i 10 23
Being three parts melted away with rotten dews ii 3 35
Hence, rotten thing! or I shall shake thy bones Out of thy garments iii 1 179
You common cry of curs! whose breath I hate As reek o' the rotten fens iii 3 121
Breaking his oath and resolution like A twist of rotten silk v 6 96
Thus I enforce thy rotten jaws to open *Rom. and Jul.* v 3 47
O blessed breeding sun, draw from the earth Rotten humidity! *T. of A.* iv 3 2
Something is rotten in the state of Denmark *Hamlet* i 4 90
If he be not rotten before he die v 1 180
He'll strike, and quickly too: he's dead and rotten *Lear* v 3 285
Do not fight by sea; Trust not to rotten planks *Ant. and Cleo.* iii 7 63
As good as rotten *Pericles* iv 2 9
Rottenness. Death! Thou odoriferous stench! sound rottenness! *K. John* iii 4 26
Diseased ventures That play with all infirmities for gold Which rottenness can lend nature! *Cymbeline* i 6 125
Rotting. Though mean and mighty, rotting Together, have one dust iv 2 246
Rotundity. And thou, all-shaking thunder, Smite flat the thick rotundity o' the world! *Lear* iii 2 7
Rouen. In a captive chariot into Rouen Bring him our prisoner *Hen. V.* iii 5 54
Prince Dauphin, you shall stay with us in Rouen iii 5 64
Is Paris lost? is Rouen yielded up? *1 Hen. VI.* i 1 65
The gates of Rouen, Through which our policy must make a breach iii 2 1
To sack the city, And we be lords and rulers over Rouen iii 2 11
Now, Rouen, I'll shake thy bulwarks to the ground iii 2 16
And once again we'll sleep secure in Rouen iii 2 19
This is the happy wedding torch That joineth Rouen unto her countrymen iii 2 27
I sit before the walls of Rouen And will be partner of your weal or woe iii 2 91
Rouen hangs her head for grief That such a valiant company are fled iii 2 124
But see his exequies fulfill'd in Rouen iii 2 133
Nor grieve that Rouen is so recovered: Care is no cure iii 3 2
Rougemont. When last I was at Exeter, The mayor in courtesy show'd me the castle, And call'd it Rougemont *Richard III.* iv 2 108
Rough. Till new-born chins Be rough and razorable *Tempest* ii 1 250
A fiend, a fury, pitiless and rough *Com. of Errors* iv 2 35
Ay, but not rough enough.—As roughly as my modesty would let me v 1 58
She never reprehended him but mildly, When he demean'd himself rough v 1 88
When lion rough in wildest rage doth roar *M. N. Dream* v 1 225
My father's rough and envious disposition Sticks me at heart *As Y. L. It* i 2 253
She's too rough for me *T. of Shrew* i 1 55
Were she as rough As are the swelling Adriatic seas i 2 73
I am rough and woo not like a babe ii 1 138
I find you passing gentle. 'Twas told me you were rough and coy and sullen ii 1 245
To a stranger . . . often prove Rough and unhospitable *T. Night* iii 3 11
The fiend is rough, and will not be roughly used iii 4 124
Thou'rt like to have A lullaby too rough *W. Tale* iii 3 55
If it be not too rough for some that know little but bowling iv 4 337
We are but plain fellows, sir.—A lie; you are rough and hairy iv 4 744
We must supplant those rough rug-headed kerns *Richard II.* ii 1 156
These high wild hills and rough uneven ways Draws out our miles ii 3 4
Not all the water in the rough rude sea Can wash the balm off from an anointed king iii 2 54
Are you not ashamed to enforce a poor widow to so rough a course to come by her own? *2 Hen. IV.* ii 1 89
We shall be winnow'd with so rough a wind That even our corn shall seem as light as chaff iv 1 194
The flesh'd soldier, rough and hard of heart *Hen. V.* iii 3 11
Our tongue is rough, coz, and my condition is not smooth v 2 313
With rough and all-unable pen Epil. 1
Confounds the tongue and makes the senses rough *1 Hen. VI.* v 3 71
His well-proportion'd beard made rough and rugged *2 Hen. VI.* iii 2 175
Suffolk's imperial tongue is stern and rough, Used to command iv 1 121
In any case, be not too rough in terms; For he is fierce iv 9 44
Stern, obdurate, flinty, rough, remorseless *3 Hen. VI.* i 4 142
Come, come, you have been too rough, something too rough *Coriolanus* iii 2 25
He bow'd his nature, never known before But to be rough, unswayable v 6 26

Rough. Alas, that love, so gentle in his view, Should be so tyrannous and rough in proof! . . . . *Rom. and Jul.* i 1 176
Is love a tender thing? it is too rough, Too rude, too boisterous . i 4 25
If love be rough with you, be rough with love; Prick love for pricking i 4 27
My nativity was under Ursa major; so that it follows, I am rough *Lear* i 2 142
The tyranny of the open night's too rough For nature to endure . . iii 4 2
Yet as rough, Their royal blood enchafed, as the rudest wind *Cymbeline* iv 2 173
How fresh she looks! They were too rough That threw her in the sea *Pericles* iii 2 79
The rough and woeful music that we have, Cause it to sound, beseech you . . . . iii 2 88
Rough affairs. Give even way unto my rough affairs . 2 *Hen. IV.* ii 3 2
Rough brake. 'Tis but the fate of place, and the rough brake That virtue must go through . . . . . . *Hen. VIII.* i 2 75
Rough carriage. Their rough carriage so ridiculous . *L. L. Lost* v 2 306
Rough-cast. Let him have some plaster, or some loam, or some rough-cast about him, to signify wall . . *M. N. Dream* iii 1 71
This man, with lime and rough-cast, doth present Wall . v 1 132
This rough-cast and this stone doth show That I am that same wall v 1 162
Rough chastisement. For justice and rough chastisement *Richard II.* i 1 106
Rough Clifford. Rutland, by rough Clifford slain . 3 *Hen. VI.* ii 1 63
Rough colt. He hath rid his prologue like a rough colt *M. N. Dream* v 1 119
Rough coming on. In robustious and rough coming on . *Hen. V.* iii 7 159
Rough cradle for such little pretty ones *Richard III.* iv 1 101
Rough deeds of rage and stern impatience . 1 *Hen. VI.* iv 7 8
Rough enforcement. Confess 'twas hers, and by what rough enforcement You got it from her . . . . *All's Well* v 3 107
Rough frown. The grappling vigour and rough frown of war . *K. John* iii 1 104
Rough hearts. Brassy bosoms and rough hearts of flint . *Mer. of Venice* iv 1 31
Rough-hew. There's a divinity that shapes our ends, Rough-hew them how we will . . . . *Hamlet* v 2 11
Rough magic. This rough magic I here abjure . . *Tempest* v 1 50
Rough night. 'Twas a rough night . . . . *Macbeth* ii 3 66
Rough Northumberland, I dare your quenchless fury 3 *Hen. VI.* i 4 27
Rough pash. Thou want'st a rough pash and the shoots that I have, To be full like me . . . . *W. Tale* i 2 128
Rough power. Each thing's a thief: The laws, your curb and whip, in their rough power Have uncheck'd theft *T. of Athens* iv 3 446
Rough quarries, rocks and hills whose heads touch heaven . *Othello* i 3 141
Rough seams. Through the rough seams of the waters . *Pericles* ii 1 155
Rough seas. Till the rough seas, that spare not any man, Took it in rage, though calm'd have given't again . . . . ii 1 137
By the rough seas reft of ships and men . . . . ii 3 84
Rough things. They are very ill-favoured rough things . *Mer. Wives* i 1 311
Rough thistles, kecksies, burs . . . . *Hen. V.* v 2 52
Rough torrent. By the rough torrent of occasion . 2 *Hen. IV.* iv 1 72
Rough touch. To smooth that rough touch with a tender kiss *R. and J.* i 5 98
Rough usage. A little angry for my so rough usage *Cymbeline* iv 1 22
Rough weather. Winter and rough weather . *As Y. Like It* ii 5 8
Rough wind. Keep our course, though the rough wind say no 3 *Hen. VI.* v 4 22
Rough winter. And make rough winter everlastingly *T. G. of Ver.* ii 4 163
Rough work. In this rough work, shaped out a man . *T. of Athens* i 1 43
Rougher. Had a rougher task in hand . . . *Much Ado* i 1 301
Do not take His rougher accents for malicious sounds *Coriolanus* iii 3 55
Roughest. Come what come may, Time and the hour runs through the roughest day . . . . *Macbeth* i 3 147
Did deign The roughest berry on the rudest hedge . *Ant. and Cleo.* i 4 64
Roughly. As roughly as my modesty would let me . *Com. of Errors* v 1 59
The fiend is rough, and will not be roughly used . *T. Night* iii 4 124
And roughly send to prison The immediate heir of England! . 2 *Hen. IV.* v 2 70
Justles roughly by All time of pause. . *Troi. and Cres.* iv 4 36
He might not beteem the winds of heaven Visit her face too roughly *Ham.* i 2 142
What I have done, That might your nature, honour and exception Roughly awake, I here proclaim was madness . . . . v 2 243
Roughness. Doth affect A saucy roughness . . . *Lear* ii 2 103
Round. With rounds of waxen tapers on their heads *Mer. Wives* iv 4 50
So long that nineteen zodiacs have gone round . *Meas. for Meas.* i 2 172
Am I so round with you as you with me, That like a football you do spurn me thus? . . . . *Com. of Errors* ii 1 82
Patiently dance in our round And see our moonlight revels *M. N. Dream* ii 1 140
I'll follow you, I'll lead you about a round . . . iii 1 109
That same dew, . . . like round and orient pearls . . iv 1 59
And hang it round with all my wanton pictures . *T. of Shrew* Ind. 1 47
He that is giddy thinks the world turns round . . . v 2 20
What's the matter, That this distemper'd messenger of wet, The many-colour'd Iris, rounds thine eye? . . . . *All's Well* i 3 158
Water once a day her chamber round With eye-offending brine *T. Night* i 1 29
I must be round with you . . . . ii 3 102
The queen your mother rounds apace . . . *W. Tale* ii 1 16
Within the hollow crown That rounds the mortal temples of a king Keeps Death his court. . . . . . . *Richard II.* iii 2 161
These six dry, round, old, withered knights . 2 *Hen. IV.* ii 4 8
Your reproof is something too round: I should be angry *Hen. V.* iv 1 216
Or as a bear, encompass'd round with dogs . 3 *Hen. VI.* ii 1 15
I would to God that the inclusive verge Of golden metal that must round my brow Were red-hot steel! . . . . *Richard III.* iv 1 60
A health, gentlemen! Let it go round . . . *Hen. VIII.* i 4 97
I am giddy; expectation whirls me round . *Troi. and Cres.* iii 2 19
Not half so big as a round little worm . *Rom. and Jul.* i 4 65
My lord, in heart; and let the health go round . *T. of Athens* i 2 54
What shall be done? he will not hear, till feel: I must be round with him . . . . ii 2 8
But when he once attains the upmost round, He then unto the ladder turns his back, Looks in the clouds . . . . *J Cæsar* ii 1 24
A ring; stand round.—Stand from the hearse . . . iii 2 168
Time is come round, And where I did begin, there shall I end v 3 23
All that impedes thee from the golden round . . *Macbeth* i 5 29
Anon we'll drink a measure The table round . . . iii 4 12
Wears upon his baby-brow the round And top of sovereignty . iv 1 88
I'll charm the air to give a sound, While you perform your antic round iv 1 130
Skirr the country round; Hang those that talk of fear . v 3 35
I went round to work . . . . . . *Hamlet* ii 2 139
Let her be round with him . . . . . . iii 1 191
Full thirty times hath Phœbus' cart gone round Neptune's salt wash iii 2 165
I'll sconce me even here. Pray you, be round with him . iii 4 5
Being thus be-netted round with villanies . . . . v 2 29
I will a round unvarnish'd tale deliver . . . *Othello* i 3 90
Hail to thee, lady! and the grace of heaven, Before, behind thee and on every hand, Enwheel thee round! . . . . . . ii 1 87
Cup us, till the world go round! . . . . *Ant. and Cleo.* ii 7 124

Round. Bear'st thou her face in mind? is't long or round?—Round even to faultiness . . . . *Ant. and Cleo.* iii 3 32
Does the world go round?—How come these staggers on me? *Cymbeline* v 5 232
In our orbs we'll live so round and safe . . . *Pericles* i 2 122
Y-ravished the regions round . . . . . iii Gower 35
Round about. At still midnight, Walk round about an oak *Mer. Wives* iv 4 31
Our dance of custom round about the oak Of Herne the hunter . v 5 79
Glow-worms shall our lanterns be, To guide our measure round about the tree . . . . v 5 83
Blown with restless violence round about The pendent world *M. for M.* iii 1 125
Prolaim it, provost, round about the city, Is any woman wrong'd . v 1 514
With songs of woe, Round about her tomb they go . *Much Ado* v 3 15
Round about Dapples the drowsy east with spots of grey . v 3 26
I'll put a girdle round about the earth In forty minutes. *M. N. Dream* ii 1 175
Empale him with your weapons round about . *Troi. and Cres.* v 7 5
Sit round about some fountain, Looking all downwards . *T. Andron* iii 1 123
What's here? A scroll; and written round about? Let's see . iv 2 18
Look round about the wicked streets of Rome . . . v 2 98
Titinius is enclosed round about With horsemen . *J. Cæsar* v 3 28
Round about the cauldron go . . . . . *Macbeth* iv 1 4
You elements that clip us round about . . . *Othello* iii 3 464
The noise is round about us.—Let us from it . . *Cymbeline* iv 4 1
Round beard. Does he not wear a great round beard? . *Mer. Wives* i 4 20
Round belly. The justice, In fair round belly . *As Y. Like It* ii 7 154
With a white head and something a round belly . 2 *Hen. IV.* i 2 212
Round encompassed and set upon . . . . 1 *Hen. VI.* i 1 114
Round engirt. My body round engirt with misery . 2 *Hen. VI.* iii 1 200
That gold must round engirt these brows of mine . . v 1 99
Round fines. On your heads Clap round fines for neglect *Hen. VIII.* v 4 84
Round haunches. Have their round haunches gored *As Y. Like It* ii 1 25
Round hose. A round hose, madam, now's not worth a pin *T. G. of Ver.* ii 7 55
He bought his doublet in Italy, his round hose in France *Mer. of Venice* i 2 80
Round impaled with a glorious crown . 3 *Hen. VI.* iii 2 171
Round man. You whoreson round man, what's the matter? . 1 *Hen. IV.* ii 4 155
Round nave. Bowl the round nave down the hill of heaven *Hamlet* ii 2 518
Round sum. Tis a good round sum . . . . *Mer. of Venice* i 3 104
Round table. At the round table, by a sea-coal fire . 2 *Hen. IV.* ii 1 95
Round tears. The big round tears Coursed one another down his innocent nose . . . . *As Y. Like It* ii 1 38
Round underborne with a bluish tinsel . . *Much Ado* iii 4 21
Round-wombed. Whereupon she grew round-wombed . *Lear* i 1 14
Round world. The round world Should have shook lions into civil streets, And citizens to their dens . . *Ant. and Cleo.* v 1 15
Rounded. And our little life Is rounded with a sleep . *Tempest* iv 1 158
She his hairy temples then had rounded With coronet of fresh and fragrant flowers . . . . . . *M. N. Dream* iv 1 56
Rounded in the ear With that same purpose-changer . *K. John* ii 1 566
How rank soever rounded in with danger . *Troi. and Cres.* i 3 196
Roundel. Come, now a roundel and a fairy song . *M. N. Dream* ii 2 1
Rounder. I'll wear a boot, to make it somewhat rounder *T. G. of Ver.* v 2 6
Roundest. He answered me in the roundest manner, he would not *Lear* i 4 58
Rounding. Whispering, rounding 'Sicilia is a so-forth' . *W. Tale* i 2 217
Roundly. Shall we clap into 't roundly? . . *As Y. Like It* v 3 11
Shall I then come roundly to thee? . . . *T. of Shrew* i 2 59
'Tis like you'll prove a jolly surly groom, That take it on you at the first so roundly . . . . iii 2 216
Hap what hap may, I'll roundly go about her. . . . iv 4 108
He that is giddy thinks the world turns round.—Roundly replied . v 2 21
This tongue that runs so roundly in thy head Should run thy head from thy unreverent shoulders . . . . . *Richard II.* ii 1 122
Well, how then? come, roundly, roundly . . 1 *Hen. IV.* i 2 24
I would have done any thing indeed too, and roundly too 2 *Hen. IV.* iii 2 21
And fell so roundly to a large confession . *Troi. and Cres.* iii 2 161
Roundure. 'Tis not the roundure of your old-faced walls Can hide you from our messengers of war . . . . . *K. John* ii 1 259
'**Rouse** up a brave mind,' says the fiend, 'and run' . *Mer. of Venice* ii 2 12
Shall we rouse the night-owl in a catch? . . *T. Night* ii 3 60
I shake the world; And rouse from sleep that fell anatomy *K. John* iii 4 40
Rouse up thy youthful blood, be valiant and live . *Richard II.* i 3 83
To rouse his wrongs and chase them to the bay . . ii 3 128
O, the blood more stirs To rouse a lion than to start a hare! . 1 *Hen. IV.* i 3 198
Rouse up fear and trembling, and do observance to my mercy 2 *Hen. IV.* iv 3 15
Rouse up revenge from ebon den with fell Alecto's snake . v 5 39
Rouse yourself, As did the former lions of your blood . *Hen. V.* i 2 123
Show my sail of greatness When I do rouse me in my throne of France i 2 275
Rouse thy vaunting veins: Boy, bristle thy courage up . ii 3 4
And rouse him at the name of Crispian . . . . iv 3 43
We'll quickly rouse the traitors . . . . 3 *Hen. VI.* v 1 65
To rouse a Grecian that is true in love . *Troi. and Cres.* i 3 279
Sweet, rouse yourself . . . . iii 3 222
Rouse him and give him note of our approach . . . iv 1 43
Wake the emperor and his lovely bride And rouse the prince *T. Andron.* ii 2 5
I have dogs, my lord, Will rouse the proudest panther in the chase . ii 2 21
What, rouse thee, man! thy Juliet is alive . . *Rom. and Jul.* iii 3 135
On Thursday early will I rouse ye: Till then, adieu . . iv 1 42
Now, when the bridegroom in the morning comes To rouse thee from thy bed, there art thou dead . . . . iv 1 108
Good things of day begin to droop and drowse; Whiles night's black agents to their preys do rouse . . . . *Macbeth* iii 2 53
My fell of hair Would at a dismal treatise rouse and stir As life were in't . . . . v 5 12
The king's rouse the heavens shall bruit again . *Hamlet* i 2 127
The king doth wake to-night and takes his rouse . . i 4 8
There was a' gaming; there o'ertook in's rouse; There falling out at tennis . . . . ii 1 58
Rouse him: make after him, poison his delight . *Othello* i 1 68
'Fore God, they have given me a rouse already . . . ii 3 66
I see him rouse himself To praise my noble act . *Ant. and Cleo.* v 2 287
Roused up with boisterous untuned drums . *Richard II.* i 3 134
Being mounted and both roused in their seats . 2 *Hen. IV.* iv 1 118
Roused on the sudden from their drowsy beds . 1 *Hen. VI.* ii 2 23
As roused with rage with rage doth sympathize *Troi. and Cres.* i 3 52
The busy day, Waked by the lark, hath roused the ribald crows . iv 2 9
Patroclus' wounds have roused his drowsy blood . . v 5 32
Bold in the quarrel's right, roused to the encounter . *Lear* ii 1 56
Hark, the game is roused! . . . . . *Cymbeline* iii 3 98
Rousillon. It is the Count Rousillon, my good lord . *All's Well* i 2 18
The Count Rousillon cannot be my brother: I am from humble, he from honour'd name . . . . i 3 161
Are you companion to the Count Rousillon?—To any count . . ii 3 200

Rousillon. Until he has no wife! Thou shalt have none, Rousillon, none in France . . . . *All's Well* iii 2 104
Come thou home, Rousillon, Whence honour but of danger wins a scar, As oft it loses all . . . . iii 2 123
Count Rousillon: know you such a one?—But by the ear . iii 5 52
Tell the Count Rousillon, and my brother, We have caught the woodcock iv 1 99
What will Count Rousillon do then? will he travel higher? . . iv 3 49
To take heed of the allurement of one Count Rousillon, a foolish idle boy iv 3 242
Betray the Florentine?—Ay, and the captain of his horse, Count Rousillon . . . . iv 3 328
A copy of the sonnet you writ to Diana in behalf of the Count Rousillon iv 3 356
Whither is he gone?—Marry, as I take it, to Rousillon . . v 1 28
Now is the Count Rousillon a widower: his vows are forfeited to me . v 3 141
Roussi, and Fauconberg, Foix, Lestrale, Bouciqualt . *Hen. V.* iii 5 44; iv 8 104
Rout. And that supposed by the common rout . . *Com. of Errors* iii 1 101
And after me, I know, the rout is coming . . . *T. of Shrew* iii 2 183
Base and abject routs, Led on by bloody youth . . *2 Hen. IV.* iv 1 33
Cheering a rout of rebels with your drum . . . . iv 2 9
Charles, Alençon and that traitorous rout . . . . *1 Hen. VI.* iv 1 173
The ringleader and head of all this rout . . . . *2 Hen. VI.* ii 1 170
Shame and confusion! all is on the rout; Fear frames disorder . v 2 31
Come, damned earth, Thou common whore of mankind, that put'st odds Among the rout of nations . . . . . *T. of Athens* iv 3 43
If you know That I profess myself in banqueting To all the rout, then hold me dangerous . . . . *J. Cæsar* i 2 78
Give me to know How this foul rout began, who set it on . *Othello* ii 3 210
Nothing routs us but The villany of our fears . . . *Cymbeline* v 2 12
Then began A stop i' the chaser, a retire, anon A rout, confusion thick v 3 41
Now sleep yslaked hath the rout; No din but snores . *Pericles* iii Gower 1
Routed. And the shelters whither The routed fly . . *Ant. and Cleo.* iii 1 9
Rove. Thou art too full Of the wars' surfeits, to go rove with one That's yet unbruised . . . . *Coriolanus* iv 1 46
Rover. Next to thyself and my young rover . . . *W. Tale* i 2 176
Row. My wretchedness unto a row of pins, They'll talk of state *Rich. II.* iii 4 26
The first row of the pious chanson will show you more . *Hamlet* ii 2 438
Rowel. Never bestrid a horse, save one that had A rider like myself, who ne'er wore rowel Nor iron on his heel! . . . . *Cymbeline* iv 4 39
Rowel-head. Struck his armed heels Against the panting sides of his poor jade Up to the rowel-head . . . . . . *2 Hen. IV.* i 1 46
Rowland. To Valentinus, Rowland, and to Crassus . *Meas. for Meas.* iv 5 8
Froissart, a countryman of ours, records, England all Olivers and Rowlands bred During the time Edward the Third did reign *1 Hen. VI.* i 2 30
Child Rowland to the dark tower came . . . . *Lear* iii 4 187
Rowland de Boys. The youngest son of Sir Rowland de Boys *As Y. Like It* i 1 60; i 2 235
I am more proud to be Sir Rowland's son, His youngest son . . i 2 245
My father loved Sir Rowland as his soul . . . . . i 2 247
So strong a liking with old Sir Rowland's youngest son . . i 3 28
O my sweet master! O you memory Of old Sir Rowland! . . ii 3 4
If that you were the good Sir Rowland's son, . . . Be truly welcome . ii 7 191
All the revenue that was old Sir Rowland's will I estate upon you . v 2 13
I am the second son of old Sir Rowland . . . . . v 4 158
Roy. What is thy name?—Harry le Roy.—Le Roy! a Cornish name *Hen. V.* iv 1 49
Royal. Our royal, good and gallant ship . . . . *Tempest* v 1 237
Anointed, I implore so much expense of thy royal sweet breath *L. L. L.* v 2 524
Sport royal, I warrant you . . . . *T. Night* ii 3 187
Thou camest not of the blood royal, if thou darest not stand . *1 Hen. IV.* i 2 157
Young, valiant, wise, and, no doubt, right royal . . *Richard III.* i 2 245
What art thou?—A man, as you are.—But not, as I am, royal . i 4 171
The instalment of this noble duke In the seat royal of this famous isle . iii 1 164
A daughter call'd Elizabeth, Virtuous and fair, royal and gracious . iv 4 204
All was royal; To the disposing of it nought rebell'd . . *Hen. VIII.* i 1 42
I minded him how royal 'twas to pardon . . . . *Coriolanus* v 1 18
Cæsar was mighty, bold, royal, and loving . . . *J. Cæsar* iii 1 127
Go on: right royal . . . . *Ant. and Cleo.* iii 13 55
And golden Phœbus never be beheld Of eyes again so royal! . . v 2 321
She levell'd at our purposes, and, being royal, Took her own way . . v 2 339
I love and hate her: for she's fair and royal . . *Cymbeline* ii 5 70
Royal Antiochus—on what cause I know not—Took some displeasure at him . . . . *Pericles* i 3 20
Royal banner. The ear-piercing fife, The royal banner . . *Othello* iii 3 353
Royal bargain. No longer than we well could wash our hands To clap this royal bargain up . . . . *K. John* iii 1 235
Royal battle. Would you and I alone, Without more help, could fight this royal battle! . . . . *Hen. V.* iv 3 75
While we reason here, A royal battle might be won and lost *Rich. III.* iv 4 538
Royal bed. A fellow of the royal bed . . . . *W. Tale* iii 2 39
Broke the possession of a royal bed . . . . *Richard II.* iii 1 13
Let not the royal bed of Denmark be A couch for luxury . *Hamlet* i 5 82
Royal bird. His royal bird Prunes the immortal wing . *Cymbeline* v 4 117
Royal birth. For your royal birth, Inferior to none . *1 Hen. VI.* iii 1 95
Royal blood. Exempted be from me the arrogance To choose from forth the royal blood of France . . . . *All's Well* ii 1 199
Chasing the royal blood With fury from his native residence *Richard II.* ii 1 118
As full of valour as of royal blood: Both have I spill'd . . v 5 114
Thou bloodless remnant of that royal blood! . . . *Richard III.* i 2 7
I have no moe sons of the royal blood For thee to murder . . iv 4 199
She is of royal blood.—To save her life, I'll say she is not so . . iv 4 211
Touch not the boy; he is of royal blood . . . *T. Andron.* iv 1 49
Yet as rough, Their royal blood enchafed, as the rudest wind *Cymbeline* iv 2 174
Royal bones. We'll lay before this town our royal bones . *K. John* ii 1 41
Royal Cæsar. O royal Cæsar! . . . . . . *J. Cæsar* iii 2 249
Royal captain. The royal captain of this ruin'd band . *Hen. V.* iv Prol. 29
Royal Charles. March to Paris, royal Charles of France . *1 Hen. VI.* v 2 4
Royal cheer, I warrant you.—Doubt not that . . . *T. of Athens* iii 6 56
Royal choice. Here I'll make My royal choice . . . *Hen. VIII.* i 4 86
Royal commanders, be in readiness . . . . . *3 Hen. VI.* ii 2 67
Royal company. Grace us with your royal company . . *Macbeth* iii 4 45
Royal couplement. I wish you the peace of mind, most royal couplement! . . . . *L. L. Lost* v 2 535
Royal court. Attends the emperor in his royal court . *T. G. of Ver.* i 3 27
Will give thee time to leave our royal court . . . . iii 1 165
They jointly swear To spoil the city and your royal court *2 Hen. VI.* iv 4 53
Royal cousin, teach you our princess English? . . . *Hen. V.* v 2 307
Royal Cymbeline. The lofty cedar, royal Cymbeline, Personates thee: and thy lopp'd branches point Thy two sons forth . *Cymbeline* v 5 453
Royal Dane. I'll call thee Hamlet, King, father, royal Dane . *Hamlet* i 4 45
Royal day. When is the royal day? . . . . *Richard III.* iii 4 3
Royal debt. Much more to be thus opposite with heaven, For it requires the royal debt it lent you . . . . ii 2 95

Royal dignity. Every word you speak in his behalf Is slander to your royal dignity . . . . *2 Hen. VI.* iii 2 209
Royal disposition. Of his own royal disposition . . *Richard III.* i 3 63
'Tis The royal disposition of that beast . . . *As Y. Like It* iv 3 118
Royal duke. Justice, O royal duke! . . . . *Meas. for Meas.* v 1 20
Royal ear. And I have heard Your royal ear abused . . . v 1 139
Royal Egypt. Madam, madam!—Royal Egypt, Empress! *A. and C.* iv 15 70
Royal emperor. All hail, Rome's royal emperor! . *T. Andron.* v 3 141
Royal empress. Who have we here? Rome's royal empress? . . ii 3 55
Royal excellence. Jesu maintain your royal excellence! *2 Hen. VI.* i 1 161
Royal eye. Face to face and royal eye to eye . . . *Hen. V.* v 2 30
Royal face. Upon his royal face there is no note How dread an army hath enrounded him . . . . iv Prol. 35
Royal faiths. Were our royal faiths martyrs in love . *2 Hen. IV.* iv 1 193
Royal father. She did print your royal father . . . *W. Tale* v 1 125
O my royal father!—My sovereign lord, cheer up yourself *2 Hen. IV.* iv 4 112
Health, peace, and happiness to my royal father! . . . iv 5 227
My royal father, cheer these noble lords . . . *3 Hen. VI.* ii 2 78
Your royal father's murder'd.—O, by whom? . . . *Macbeth* ii 3 105
Thy royal father Was a most sainted king . . . . iv 3 108
It pleaseth you, my royal father, to express My commendations *Pericles* ii 2 8
A prince of Macedon, my royal father . . . . . . ii 2 24
Royal fellowship. A royal fellowship of death! . . . *Hen. V.* iv 8 106
Royal field. That royal field of Shrewsbury . . . *2 Hen. IV.* Ind. 34
Royal fight. As thy cause is right, So be thy fortune in this royal fight! *Richard II.* i 3 56
Royal finger. With his royal finger, thus, dally with my excrement, with my mustachio . . . . *L. L. Lost* v 1 109
I will kiss thy royal finger, and take leave . . . . . v 2 891
Royal fleet. And sail so expeditious that shall catch Your royal fleet far off . . . . *Tempest* v 1 316
Shall waft them over with our royal fleet . . . *3 Hen. VI.* iii 3 253
Royal fool. Must know The royal fool thou copest with . *W. Tale* iv 4 435
Royal fox. O, will you eat no grapes, my royal fox? Yes, but you will my noble grapes, an if My royal fox could reach them . *All's Well* ii 1 73
Royal fronts. Why stand these royal fronts amazed thus? . *K. John* ii 1 356
Royal fruit. The royal tree hath left us royal fruit . *Richard III.* iii 7 167
Royal grace. Happy return be to your royal grace! *Meas. for Meas.* v 1 3
Blessed be your royal grace! . . . . v 1 137
Good time of day unto your royal grace! . . . *Richard III.* i 3 18
Your royal graces, Shower'd on me daily . . . *Hen. VIII.* iii 2 166
To your royal grace, and the good queen, . . . thus pray . . v 5 5
Royal grandsire. By the honourable tomb he swears, That stands upon your royal grandsire's bones . . . . . . *Richard II.* iii 3 106
Royal Hal. God save thy grace, King Hal! my royal Hal! . *2 Hen. IV.* v 5 43
Royal hand. This royal hand and mine are newly knit . *K. John* iii 1 226
Deliver this paper into the royal hand of the king . . *L. L. Lost* iv 2 146
And do thee favours with my royal hands . . . *Richard II.* iii 2 11
And his high sceptre yields To the possession of thy royal hand . iv 1 110
That jade hath eat bread from my royal hand . . . . v 5 85
Royal head. Good angels Fly o'er thy royal head! . . *Hen. VIII.* v 1 160
Royal heart. Let pale-faced fear keep with the mean-born man, And find no harbour in a royal heart . . . . . *2 Hen. VI.* iii 1 336
Royal hope. Prediction Of noble having and of royal hope . *Macbeth* i 3 56
Royal house. The lineal glory of your royal house . *Richard III.* iii 7 121
Richmond and Elizabeth, The true succeeders of each royal house . v 5 30
Royal husband. For ever earn'd a royal husband . . . *W. Tale* i 2 107
Our sovereign lord the king, thy royal husband . . . iii 2 17
Royal image. To spurn at your most royal image . . *2 Hen. IV.* v 2 89
Royal imp. The heavens thee guard and keep, most royal imp of fame! v 5 46
Royal infant. This royal infant—heaven still move about her!—Though in her cradle, yet now promises Upon this land a thousand thousand blessings . . . . *Hen. VIII.* v 5 18
Royal interview. Unto this bar and royal interview . *Hen. V.* v 2 27
Royal king. England, . . . this teeming womb of royal kings *Rich. II.* ii 1 51
You have misled a prince, a royal king, A happy gentleman . . iii 1 8
So shall you, If happy England's royal king be free . *1 Hen. VI.* v 3 115
There to be crowned England's royal king . . . *3 Hen. VI.* ii 6 88
God save Richard, England's royal king! . . . *Richard III.* iii 7 22
Fitting for a princess Descended of so many royal kings . *Ant. and Cleo.* v 2 330
Royal knavery. I found, Horatio,—O royal knavery! . . *Hamlet* v 2 19
Royal lady. Thanks to God for such A royal lady . . *Hen. VIII.* ii 4 153
Royal Lear, Whom I have ever honour'd as my king . . . *Lear* i 1 141
Royal Lear, Give but that portion which yourself proposed . . i 1 244
Royal liege. My royal liege, He is not guilty of her coming hither *W. Tale* ii 3 143
Thus, my most royal liege, Accusing it, I put it on my head *2 Hen. IV.* iv 5 165
Royal lists. Wherefore comest thou hither, Before King Richard in his royal lists? . . . . *Richard II.* i 3 32
Royal lord. My royal lord, You do not give the cheer . *Macbeth* iii 4 32
Royal lover. Like a noble lord in love and one That had a royal lover, took his hint . . . . *Cymbeline* v 5 172
Royal majesty. By my seat's right royal majesty . . *Richard II.* ii 1 120
Jesus preserve your royal majesty! . . . . *2 Hen. VI.* i 2 70
Your royal majesty, Let him have all the rigour of the law . . i 3 198
I humbly thank your royal majesty . . . . . . i 3 215
Most royal majesty, I crave no more than what your highness offer'd *Lear* i 1 196
Royal making. She had all the royal makings of a queen *Hen. VIII.* iv 1 87
Royal man. Give him as much as will make him a royal man *1 Hen. IV.* ii 4 321
Royal master. The king, my ever royal master . . *Hen. VIII.* iii 2 273
To look upon my sometimes royal master's face . . *Richard II.* v 5 75
We are sent To give thee from our royal master thanks . *Macbeth* i 3 101
Our royal master's murder'd!—Woe, alas! What, in our house? . ii 3 92
Royal merchant. That royal merchant, good Antonio . *Mer. of Venice* iii 2 242
Losses . . . Enow to press a royal merchant down . . . . iv 1 29
Royal minds. The citizens, I am sure, have shown at full their royal minds . . . . *Hen. VIII.* iv 1 8
Royal mistress. My empress, Rome's royal mistress . *T. Andron.* i 1 241
Royal name. In Henry's royal name . . . . . *1 Hen. VI.* v 3 160
Royal necessities made separation of their society . . *W. Tale* i 1 28
Royal nephew. My royal nephew, and your name Capucius *Hen. VIII.* iv 2 110
Royal nobleness. Methought thy very gait did prophesy A royal nobleness . . . . *Lear* v 3 176
Royal number. Or add a royal number to the dead . . *K. John* ii 1 347
Royal occupation. O love, That thou couldst see my wars to-day, and knew'st The royal occupation! . . . . . *Ant. and Cleo.* iv 4 17
Royal one. An army ready, say you?—A most royal one *Coriolanus* iv 3 47
I am a king, My masters, know you that?—You are a royal one . *Lear* iv 6 205
Royal party. Which on thy royal party granted once, His glittering arms he will commend to rust . . . . . . *Richard II.* iii 3 115
Royal Pericles. You are, you are—O royal Pericles! . . *Pericles* v 3 14

Royal peril. And drink carouses to the next day's fate, Which promises royal peril . *Ant. and Cleo.* iv 8 35
Royal person. And sends allegiance and true faith of heart To his most royal person . *Richard II.* iii 3 38
You have conspired against our royal person . *Hen. V.* ii 2 167
It is no policy . . . That he should come about your royal person *2 Hen. VI.* iii 1 26
As innocent From meaning treason to our royal person As is the sucking lamb . iii 1 70
In care of your most royal person . iii 2 254
First, to do greetings to thy royal person . *3 Hen. VI.* iii 3 52
The loss of his own royal person.—Then is my sovereign slain? . iv 4 5
Kept an evil diet long, And overmuch consumed his royal person *Rich. III.* i 1 140
His royal person,—Whom God preserve better than you would wish! . i 3 58
Royal piece There's magic in thy majesty . *W. Tale* v 3 38
Royal pleasure. But that your royal pleasure must be done, This act is as an ancient tale new told . *K. John* iv 2 17
We come To know your royal pleasure.—Ye are too bold *Hen. VIII.* ii 2 71
Royal preparation. Ay, my good lord; your royal preparation Makes us hear something . *Macbeth* v 3 57
Royal presence. Your royal presences be ruled by me . *K. John* ii 1 377
Yet of your royal presence I'll adventure The borrow of a week *W. Tale* i 2 38
Worst in this royal presence may I speak . *Richard II.* iv 1 115
Sent to warn them to his royal presence.—Would all were well! *Rich. III.* i 3 39
Have I offer'd love for this, To be so flouted in this royal presence? ii 1 78
Are you merry, knights?—Who can be other in this royal presence? *Pericles* ii 3 49
Royal Priam. Give me leave To take that course by your consent and voice, Which you do here forbid me, royal Priam . *Troi. and Cres.* v 3 75
Royal prince. An arch-villain; believe it, royal prince . *Meas. for Meas.* v 1 57
'Tis shame such wrongs are borne In him, a royal prince *Richard II.* ii 1 239
Hail, royal prince!—Thanks, noble peer . v 5 67
Like a most royal prince, Restored me to my honours . *Hen. VIII.* ii 1 113
Royal queen. That Margaret may be England's royal queen . *1 Hen. VI.* v 5 24
To Westminster, There to be crowned Richard's royal queen *Rich. III.* iv 1 33
Royal queen!—O Cleopatra! thou art taken, queen *Ant. and Cleo.* v 2 37
Royal realm. We are inforced to farm our royal realm . *Richard II.* i 4 45
Royal Richard. So, thou common dog, didst thou disgorge Thy glutton bosom of the royal Richard *2 Hen. IV.* i 3 98
Royal Rome. Were gracious in the eyes of royal Rome . *T. Andron.* i 1 11
Royal root. One flourishing branch of his most royal root *Richard II.* i 2 18
Royal seat. The rightful heir to England's royal seat . *2 Hen. VI.* v 1 178
Royal self. Peace, amity, true love Between our kingdoms and our royal selves . *K. John* iii 1 232
Where shall we sojourn till our coronation?—Where it seems best unto your royal self *Richard III.* iii 1 63
Take to your royal self This proffer'd benefit of dignity . iii 7 195
His royal self in judgement comes to hear The cause . *Hen. VIII.* v 3 120
Royal session. It's fit this royal session do proceed . ii 4 66
Royal siege. I fetch my life and being From men of royal siege, and my demerits May speak unbonneted . *Othello* i 2 22
Royal sir. Mother, fetch my bail. Stay, royal sir . *All's Well* v 3 296
Hail, most royal sir!—What is the news i' the court? . *W. Tale* i 2 366
Royal sir, forgive a foolish woman . iii 2 228
Most royal sir, Fleance is 'scaped . *Macbeth* iii 4 19
Pardon me, royal sir; Election makes not up on such conditions . *Lear* i 1 208
Thus far; and so farewell.—Thanks, royal sir . *Cymbeline* iii 5 1
Sir king, all hail! the gods preserve you! Hail, royal sir! *Pericles* v 1 40
Royal speech. So in approof lives not his epitaph As in your royal speech . *All's Well* i 2 51
Royal state. Up, vanity! Down, royal state . *2 Hen. IV.* iv 5 121
Royal stock. Her royal stock graft with ignoble plants . *Richard III.* iii 7 127
Royal sword. Lay on our royal sword your banish'd hands . *Richard II.* i 3 179
Royal table. At Priam's royal table do I sit . *Troi. and Cres.* i 1 29
Royal tent. Wherefore else guard we his royal tent? *3 Hen. VI.* iv 3 21
Royal thought. Humbly entreating from your royal thoughts A modest one . *All's Well* ii 1 130
Question your royal thoughts, make the case yours . *2 Hen. IV.* v 2 91
Royal throne. This royal throne of kings [England] *Richard II.* ii 1 40
The next degree is England's royal throne . *3 Hen. VI.* ii 1 193
Once more we sit in England's royal throne . v 7 1
Royal time. Are all things fitting for that royal time? . *Richard III.* iii 4 4
Royal Timon. Great Timon, noble, worthy, royal Timon! *T. of Athens* ii 2 177
Royal train. A royal train, believe me . *Hen. VIII.* iv 1 37
Royal tree. The royal tree hath left us royal fruit . *Richard III.* iii 7 167
Royal view. I demand, before this royal view . *Hen. V.* v 2 32
Royal walks. More than to us Wait in your royal walks! *M. N. Dream* v 1 31
Royal wench! She made great Cæsar lay his sword to bed *Ant. and Cleo.* ii 2 231
Royalise. To royalise his blood I spilt mine own . *Richard III.* i 3 125
Royally. The prince your brother is royally entertained . *Much Ado* i 3 45
Have been royally attorneyed with interchange of gifts . *W. Tale* i 1 30
It shall be so my care To have you royally appointed . iv 4 603
The castle royally is mann'd, my lord, Against thy entrance.—Royally! Why, it contains no king? . *Richard II.* iii 3 21
Sorrow so royally in you appears That I will deeply put the fashion on And wear it in my heart . *2 Hen. IV.* v 2 51
Carefully it us concerns To answer royally in our defences . *Hen. V.* ii 4 3
Let us banquet royally, After this golden day of victory . *1 Hen. VI.* i 6 30
He was likely, had he been put on, To have proved most royally *Hamlet* v 2 409
Royalty. Executing the outward face of royalty . *Tempest* i 2 104
Of temporal royalties He thinks me now incapable . i 2 110
Sweet royalty, bestow on me the sense of hearing . *L. L. Lost* v 2 670
I have stay'd To tire your royalty . *W. Tale* i 2 15
For royalty's repair, For present comfort and for future good v 1 31
The dominations, royalties and rights Of this oppressed boy . *K. John* ii 1 176
You were crown'd before, And that high royalty was ne'er pluck'd off . iv 2 5
From forth this morsel of dead royalty, The life, the right and truth of all this realm Is fled to heaven . iv 3 143
Swearing allegiance . . . To stranger blood, to foreign royalty . v 1 11
Thus his royalty doth speak in me . v 2 129
All this thou seest is but a clod And module of confounded royalty . v 7 58
Setting aside his high blood's royalty . *Richard II.* i 1 58
And lay aside my high blood's royalty . i 1 71
Seek you to seize and gripe into your hands The royalties and rights of banish'd Hereford? . ii 1 190
My rights and royalties Pluck'd from my arms perforce and given away ii 3 120
By the royalties of both your bloods . iii 3 107
His coming hither hath no further scope Than for his lineal royalties . iii 3 113
Mingled his royalty with capering fools . *1 Hen. IV.* iii 2 63
My uncle and myself Did give him that same royalty he wears . iv 3 55
Royalty. You have seen The well-appointed king at Hampton pier Embark his royalty . *Hen. V.* iii Prol. 5
As a branch and member of this royalty . v 2 5
Is this . . . the royalty of Albion's king? . *2 Hen. VI.* i 3 48
Ere give consent His master's son, as worshipful he terms it, Shall lose the royalty of England's throne . *Richard III.* iii 4 42
This long-usurped royalty From the dead temples of this bloody wretch Have I pluck'd off, to grace thy brows withal . v 5 4
Whose health and royalty I pray for . *Hen. VIII.* ii 3 73
In his royalty of nature Reigns that which would be fear'd *Macbeth* iii 1 50
'Tis spoken, To the succeeding royalty he leaves The healing benediction iv 3 155
And take vanity the puppet's part against the royalty of her father *Lear* ii 2 40
But that your royalty Holds idleness your subject, I should take you For idleness itself . *Ant. and Cleo.* i 3 91
'Tis wonder That an invisible instinct should frame them To royalty unlearn'd, honour untaught . *Cymbeline* iv 2 178
Married your royalty, was wife to your place; Abhorr'd your person v 5 39
Roynish. The roynish clown, at whom so oft Your grace was wont to laugh, is also missing . *As Y. Like It* ii 2 8
Rub. You rub the sore, When you should bring the plaster *Tempest* ii 1 138
Nay, a' rubs himself with civet: can you smell him out by that? *M. Ado* iii 2 50
Thou 'rt i' the right. Go, sir, rub your chain with crums . *T. Night* ii 3 128
Blow each dust, each straw, each little rub, Out of the path . *K. John* iii 4 128
Play at bowls.—'Twill make me think the world is full of rubs *Rich. II.* iii 4 4
Poor discontents, Which gape and rub the elbow at the news *1 Hen. IV.* v 1 77
We doubt not now But every rub is smoothed on our way *Hen. V.* ii 2 188
I demand, before this royal view, What rub or what impediment there is v 2 33
When they once perceive The least rub in your fortunes, fall away Like water from ye . *Hen. VIII.* ii 1 129
O, this is well; he rubs the vein of him . *Troi. and Cres.* ii 3 210
Rub on, and kiss the mistress . iii 2 52
Nor has Coriolanus Deserved this so dishonour'd rub *Coriolanus* iii 1 60
And with him—To leave no rubs nor botches in the work *Macbeth* iii 1 134
Look, how she rubs her hands.—It is an accustomed action with her v 1 31
To die, to sleep; To sleep: perchance to dream: ay, there's the rub *Hamlet* iii 1 65
Here, Hamlet, take my napkin, rub thy brows . v 2 299
Rub him about the temples.—No, forbear . *Othello* iv 1 53
Rubbed. One rubb'd his elbow thus . *L. L. Lost* v 2 109
Whose disposition, all the world well knows, Will not be rubb'd . *Lear* ii 2 161
I have rubb'd this young quat almost to the sense *Othello* v 1 11
Rubbing. Challenge her to bowl.—I fear too much rubbing *L. L. Lost* iv 1 141
Rubbing the poor itch of your opinion, Make yourselves scabs *Coriolanus* i 1 169
Rubbish. Threw dust and rubbish on King Richard's head *Richard II.* v 2 6
What trash is Rome, What rubbish and what offal! *J. Cæsar* i 3 109
Rubied. Her inkle, silk, twin with the rubied cherry *Pericles* v Gower 8
Rubious. Diana's lip Is not more smooth and rubious . *T. Night* i 4 32
Ruby. The impression of keen whips I'ld wear as rubies . *Meas. for Meas.* ii 4 101
Her nose, all o'er embellished with rubies, carbuncles *Com. of Errors* iii 2 138
Those be rubies, fairy favours . *M. N. Dream* ii 1 12
Over thy wounds now do I prophesy,—Which, like dumb mouths, do ope their ruby lips . *J. Cæsar* iii 1 260
And keep the natural ruby of your cheeks, When mine is blanch'd *Macb.* iii 4 115
But kiss; one kiss! Rubies unparagon'd, How dearly they do't! *Cymb.* ii 2 17
Rudder. The Antoniad, the Egyptian admiral, With all their sixty, fly and turn the rudder *Ant. and Cleo.* iii 10 3
Thou knew'st too well My heart was to thy rudder tied by the strings . iii 11 57
Ruddiness. The ruddiness upon her lip is wet; You'll mar it if you kiss it . *W. Tale* v 3 81
Ruddock. The ruddock would, With charitable bill . *Cymbeline* iv 2 224
Ruddy. You are my true and honourable wife, As dear to me as are the ruddy drops That visit my sad heart . *J. Cæsar* ii 1 289
Rude. Let go that rude uncivil touch . *T. G. of Ver.* v 4 60
When he demean'd himself rough, rude and wildly . *Com. of Errors* v 1 88
Like a rude and savage man of Ind . *L. L. Lost* iv 3 222
Why are you grown so rude? what change is this? . *M. N. Dream* iii 2 262
Thou art too wild, too rude and bold of voice . *Mer. of Venice* ii 2 190
Blow, blow, thou winter wind, . . . Thy tooth is not so keen, Because thou art not seen, Although thy breath be rude *As Y. Like It* ii 7 179
To whom he sung, in rude harsh-sounding rhymes . *K. John* iv 2 150
Which, howsoever rude exteriorly, Is yet the cover of a fairer mind . iv 2 257
Set a form upon that indigest Which he hath left so shapeless and so rude . v 7 27
Rude misgovern'd hands from windows' tops Threw dust *Richard II.* v 2 5
And rock his brains In cradle of the rude imperious surge *2 Hen. IV.* iii 1 20
Canst thou, O partial sleep, give thy repose To the wet sea-boy in an hour so rude? . iii 1 27
His companies unletter'd, rude and shallow . *Hen. V.* i 1 55
'Tis like the commons, rude unpolish'd hinds . *2 Hen. VI.* iii 2 271
A ragged multitude Of hinds and peasants, rude and merciless . iv 4 33
If one so rude and of so mean condition May pass into the presence of a king . v 1 64
Rude ragged nurse, old sullen playfellow For tender princes! *Rich. III.* iv 1 102
Rude, in sooth; in good sooth, very rude . *Troi. and Cres.* iii 1 59
Is love a tender thing? it is too rough, Too rude *Rom. and Jul.* i 4 26
Who is here so rude that would not be a Roman? If any, speak *J. Cæsar* iii 2 33
What have I done, that thou darest wag thy tongue In noise so rude? *Hamlet* iii 4 40
Rude am I in my speech, And little bless'd with the soft phrase . *Othello* i 3 81
Rude assault. What means death in this rude assault? . *Richard II.* v 5 106
Rude beast. Ere this rude beast will profit . *Meas. for Meas.* iii 2 34
Rude behaviour. You are to blame, Knowing she will not lose her wonted greatness, To use so rude behaviour . *Hen. VIII.* iv 2 103
Rude boys. She deserves a lord That twenty such rude boys might tend upon And call her hourly mistress . *All's Well* iii 2 84
Rude brawls. My blood for your rude brawls doth lie a-bleeding; But I'll amerce you . *Rom. and Jul.* iii 1 194
Rude brevity. We two, that with so many thousand sighs Did buy each other, must poorly sell ourselves With the rude brevity and discharge of one . *Troi. and Cres.* iv 4 43
Rude circumference. Harbour'd in their rude circumference. *K. John* ii 1 262
Rude companion, whatsoe'er thou be, I know thee not . *2 Hen. VI.* iv 10 33
Rude despiser. A rude despiser of good manners . *As Y. Like It* ii 7 92
Rude eye. Unthread the rude eye of rebellion . *K. John* v 4 11
Rude fishermen of Corinth . *Com. of Errors* v 1 351
Rude-growing. Cover'd with rude-growing briers . *T. Andron.* ii 3 199
Rude hand. Yea, without stop, didst let thy heart consent, And consequently thy rude hand to act . *K. John* iv 2 240
Was by the rude hands of that Welshman taken . *1 Hen. IV.* i 1 41
And, touching hers, make blessed my rude hand *Rom. and Jul.* i 5 53

Rude impatience. What means this scene of rude impatience?—To make an act of tragic violence . . . . . *Richard III.* ii 2 38
Rude knave. Why does he suffer this rude knave now to knock him about the sconce with a dirty shovel? . . . *Hamlet* v 1 109
Rude man. Out on thee, rude man! . . . . . *K. John* i 1 64
Rude mechanicals, That work for bread . . *M. N. Dream* iii 2 9
Rude melancholy, valour gives thee place . . *L. L. Lost* iii 1 69
Rude multitude. Which the rude multitude call the afternoon v 1 95
Stay, Salisbury, With the rude multitude . . 2 *Hen. VI.* iii 2 135
Rude place. Think us no churls, nor measure our good minds By this rude place we live in . . . . . *Cymbeline* iii 6 66
Rude prince. He gave it like a rude prince . . 2 *Hen. IV.* i 2 219
Rude rascals. Do you look for ale and cakes here, you rude rascals?—Pray, sir, be patient . . . . . *Hen. VIII.* v 4 11
Rude reproach. In confutation of which rude reproach . 1 *Hen. VI.* iv 1 98
Rude ribs. Go to the rude ribs of that ancient castle *Richard II.* iii 3 32
Rude scene. The rude scene may end, And darkness be the burier of the dead! . . . . 2 *Hen. IV.* i 1 159
Rude sea. The rude sea grew civil at her song . . *M. N. Dream* ii 1 152
From the rude sea's enraged and foamy mouth Did I redeem . *T. Night* v 1 81
Not all the water in the rough rude sea Can wash the balm off from an anointed king . . . . . *Richard II.* iii 2 54
Rude slaves. Ye rude slaves, leave your gaping . . *Hen. VIII.* v 4 2
Rude society. Such barren pleasures, rude society . 1 *Hen IV.* iii 2 14
Rude son. And the rude son should strike his father dead *Troi. and Cres.* i 3 115
Rude sounds. Peace, rude sounds! . . . . . . i 1 92
Rude stream. To the mercy Of a rude stream . . *Hen. VIII.* iii 2 364
Rude throats. O you mortal engines, whose rude throats The immortal Jove's dread clamours counterfeit, Farewell! . . *Othello* iii 3 355
Rude tongue. How dares thy harsh rude tongue sound this unpleasing news? . . . . *Richard II.* iii 4 74
Rude transgression. Teach us, sweet madam, for our rude transgression Some fair excuse . . . . . *L. L. Lost* v 2 431
Rude unthankfulness! Thy fault our law calls death . *Rom. and Jul.* iii 3 24
Rude will. Two such opposed kings encamp them still In man as well as herbs, grace and rude will . . . . . . ii 3 28
Rude wind. You are not worth the dust which the rude wind Blows in your face . . . . *Lear* iv 2 30
Rude world. The poor rude world Hath not her fellow . *Mer. of Venice* iii 5 87
Rude wretch. Persuade this rude wretch willingly to die *Meas. for Meas.* iv 3 85
Rudeliest. Thou art the rudeliest welcome to this world That ever was prince's child . . . . . . *Pericles* iii 1 30
Rudely. Yet you began rudely . . . . . *T. Night* i 5 228
Thy place in council thou hast rudely lost . 1 *Hen. IV.* iii 2 32
I, that am rudely stamp'd, and want love's majesty . *Richard III.* i 1 16
Rudely beguiles our lips Of all rejoindure . . *Troi. and Cres.* iv 4 37
Or rudely visit them in parts remote, To fright them . *Coriolanus* iv 5 148
Rudeness. The rudeness that hath appeared in me have I learned from my entertainment . . . . . *T. Night* i 5 230
For the great swing and rudeness of his poise, They place before his hand that made the engine . . . *Troi. and Cres.* i 3 207
Mars his idiot! do, rudeness; do, camel; do, do . . ii 1 58
This rudeness is a sauce to his good wit . . *J. Cæsar* i 2 304
I thought he slept, and put My clouted brogues from off my feet, whose rudeness Answer'd my steps too loud . . *Cymbeline* iv 2 214
Ruder. Makes me the bolder to salute my king With ruder terms 2 *Hen. VI.* i 1 30
Too sharp in sweetness, For the capacity of my ruder powers *T. and C.* iii 2 26
Rudesby. Unto a mad-brain rudesby full of spleen . *T. of Shrew* iii 2 10
Rudesby, be gone! . . . . . . *T. Night* iv 1 55
Rudest. Deign The roughest berry on the rudest hedge *Ant. and Cleo.* i 4 64
As the rudest wind, That by the top doth take the mountain pine *Cymbeline* iv 2 174
Rudiments. Tutor'd in the rudiments Of many desperate studies *As Y. L. It* v 4 31
I must begin with rudiments of art . . . *T. of Shrew* iii 1 66
Rue. Reverend sirs, For you there's rosemary and rue *W. Tale* iv 4 74
Well then, France shall rue . . . . *K. John* iii 1 325
Nought shall make us rue, If England to itself do rest but true . v 7 117
And all too soon, I fear, the king shall rue . *Richard II.* i 3 205
Here in this place I'll set a bank of rue, sour herb of grace . iii 4 105
Rue, even for ruth, here shortly shall be seen . . . iii 4 106
France, thou shalt rue this treason with thy tears 1 *Hen. VI.* iii 2 36
In thy closet pent up, rue my shame, And ban thine enemies! 2 *Hen. VI.* ii 4 24
Thou and thy house shall rue it . . . 3 *Hen. VI.* i 1 94
Shall rue the hour that ever thou wast born . . . v 6 43
That may be determined at the one [council] Which may make you and him to rue at the other . . . . . *Richard III.* iii 2 14
Accept their suit.—Do, good my lord, lest all the land do rue it iii 7 222
Victorious Titus, rue the tears I shed, A mother's tears . *T. Andron.* i 1 105
And what not done, that thou hast cause to rue, Wherein I had no stroke of mischief in it? . . . . . . v 1 109
You'll rue the time That clogs me with this answer . *Macbeth* iii 6 42
There's rue for you; and here's some for me: we may call it herb-grace o' Sundays: O, you must wear your rue with a difference *Ham.* iv 5 181
Rued. Was ever son so rued a father's death? . 3 *Hen. VI.* ii 5 109
Ruff. With ruffs and cuffs and fardingales and things *T. of Shrew* iv 3 56
Mend the ruff and sing; ask questions and sing . *All's Well* iii 2 7
I will murder your ruff for this . . . . 2 *Hen. IV.* ii 4 145
You a captain! you slave, for what? for tearing a poor whore's ruff? . ii 4 157
We shall have him here to-morrow with his best ruff on . *Pericles* iv 2 111
Ruffian, let go that rude uncivil touch . . *T. G. of Ver.* v 4 60
By ruffian lust should be contaminate . *Com. of Errors* ii 2 135
Talk with a ruffian at her chamber-window . . *Much Ado* iv 1 92
A mad-cap ruffian and a swearing Jack . . *T. of Shrew* ii 1 290
How many fruitless pranks This ruffian hath botch'd up *T. Night* iv 1 60
Well, ruffian, I must pocket up these wrongs . *K. John* iii 1 200
Rich men look sad and ruffians dance and leap . *Richard II.* ii 4 12
That grey iniquity, that father ruffian, that vanity in years 1 *Hen. IV.* ii 4 500
The winds, Who take the ruffian billows by the top 2 *Hen. IV.* iii 1 22
Have you a ruffian that will swear, drink, dance? . . iii 2 125
Swear like a ruffian and demean himself Unlike the ruler 2 *Hen. VI.* i 1 188
What, wilt thou on thy death-bed play the ruffian? . . v 1 164
In thy reverence and thy chair-days, thus To die in ruffian battle . v 2 49
Let the ruffian Boreas once enrage The gentle Thetis *Troi. and Cres.* i 3 38
Make curl'd-pate ruffians bald . . . *T. of Athens* iv 3 160
This ancient ruffian, sir, whose life I have spared . *Lear* ii 2 67
Because we come to do you service and you think we are ruffians *Othello* i 1 111
Let the old ruffian know I have many other ways to die *Ant. and Cleo.* iv 1 4
Ruffianed. If it hath ruffian'd so upon the sea, What ribs of oak, when mountains melt on them, Can hold the mortise? . . *Othello* ii 1 7

Ruffle. To ruffle in the commonwealth of Rome . . *T. Andron.* i 1 313
There were an Antony Would ruffle up your spirits . *J. Cæsar* iii 2 232
Alack, the night comes on, and the bleak winds Do sorely ruffle *Lear* ii 4 304
With robbers' hands my hospitable favours You should not ruffle thus iii 7 41
Ruffling. The tailor stays thy leisure, To deck thy body with his ruffling treasure . . . . . . *T. of Shrew* iv 3 60
Rugby. John Rugby! I pray thee, go to the casement, and see *Mer. W.* i 4 1
What, John Rugby! John! what, John, I say! Go, John . . i 4 41
Vere is dat knave Rugby?—What, John Rugby! John! . . i 4 57
You are John Rugby, and you are Jack Rugby . . . i 4 60
Villain! larron! Rugby, my rapier!—Good master, be content . i 4 71
Rugby, baille me some paper. Tarry you a little-a while . i 4 92
Rugby, come to the court with me. Follow my heels, Rugby . i 4 130
Jack Rugby!—Sir?—Vat is de clock? . . Jack Rugby, he is dead already . . . . ii 3 1
Diable! Jack Rugby,—mine host de Jarteer,—have I not stay for him? iii 1 93
Go home, John Rugby; I come anon . . . . . iii 2 87
Rugged. His well-proportion'd beard made rough and rugged 2 *Hen. VI.* iii 2 175
Sleek o'er your rugged looks; Be bright and jovial . *Macbeth* iii 2 27
Approach thou like the rugged Russian bear, The arm'd rhinoceros . iii 4 100
The rugged Pyrrhus, like the Hyrcanian beast . . *Hamlet* ii 2 472
The rugged Pyrrhus, he whose sable arms, Black as his purpose . ii 2 474
Rug-headed. We must supplant those rough rug-headed kerns *Rich. II.* ii 1 156
Ruin. What ruins are in me that can be found, By him not ruin'd? *C. of E.* ii 1 96
Pick'd from the chaff and ruin of the times To be new-varnish'd! *M. of V.* ii 9 48
Let it presage the ruin of your love And be my vantage to exclaim on you . . . . iii 2 175
Repair thy wit, good youth, or it will fall To cureless ruin . iv 1 142
From the whom, I see, There's no disjunction to be made, but by—As heavens forfend!—your ruin; marry her . . *W. Tale* iv 4 541
Kneeling before this ruin of sweet life . . . *K. John* iv 3 65
Cry woe, destruction, ruin and decay; The worst is death *Richard II.* iii 2 102
God knows, whether those that bawl out the ruins of thy linen shall inherit his kingdom . . . . . . 2 *Hen. IV.* ii 2 27
We our kingdom's safety must so tender, Whose ruin you have sought, that to her laws We do deliver you . . . *Hen. V.* ii 2 176
Hereafter ages may behold What ruin happen'd in revenge of him 1 *Hen. VI.* ii 2 11
See the cities and the towns defaced By wasting ruin of the cruel foe iii 3 46
There comes the ruin, there begins confusion . . . iv 1 194
My angry guardant stood alone, Tendering my ruin and assail'd of none iv 7 10
Peace . . . if they turn to us; Else, ruin combat with their palaces! v 2 7
Come, thou new ruin of old Clifford's house . 2 *Hen. VI.* v 2 61
To thy foul disgrace And utter ruin of the house of York . 3 *Hen. VI.* i 1 254
Our ranks are broke, and ruin follows us: What counsel give you? ii 3 10
To make haste, And seek their ruin that usurp'd our right . v 6 73
And all the ruins of distressful times Repair'd with double riches of content . . . . *Richard III.* iv 4 318
Death, desolation, ruin and decay . . . . . iv 4 409
Let us be lead within thy bosom, Richard, And weigh thee down to ruin! v 3 153
And, out of ruins, Made my name once more noble . *Hen. VIII.* ii 1 114
Ye tell me what ye wish for both,—my ruin . . . iii 1 98
He parted frowning from me, as if ruin Leap'd from his eyes . iii 2 205
How sleek and wanton Ye appear in every thing may bring my ruin! iii 2 242
Betwixt that smile . . . , That sweet aspect of princes, and their ruin . iii 2 369
He was never, But where he meant to ruin, pitiful . . iv 2 40
Strew'd with husks And formless ruin of oblivion . *Troi. and Cres.* iv 5 166
Nor you, my brother, with your true sword drawn, Opposed to hinder me, should stop my way, But by my ruin . . . . . v 3 58
They nourish'd disobedience, fed The ruin of the state . *Coriolanus* iii 1 118
And bury all, which yet distinctly ranges, In heaps and piles of ruin iii 1 207
The inheritance of their loves and safeguard Of what that want might ruin . . . . iii 2 69
Come all to ruin; . . . Do as thou list . . . . iii 2 125
Or else Triumphantly tread on thy country's ruin . . v 3 116
And bow this feeble ruin to the earth . . *T. Andron.* iii 1 208
Thou art the ruins of the noblest man That ever lived . *J. Cæsar* iii 1 256
Look'd like a breach in nature For ruin's wasteful entrance *Macbeth* ii 3 120
When it falls, Each small annexment, petty consequence, Attends the boisterous ruin . . . . *Hamlet* iii 3 22
The noble ruin of her magic, Antony . *Ant. and Cleo.* iii 10 19
This mortal house I'll ruin, Do Cæsar what he can . . . v 2 51
The ruin speaks that sometime It was a worthy building . *Cymbeline* iv 2 354
Like goodly buildings left without a roof Soon fall to ruin *Pericles* ii 4 37
Ruinate. I will not ruinate my father's house, Who gave his blood to lime the stones together . . . . 3 *Hen. VI.* v 1 83
Order well the state, That like events may ne'er it ruinate *T. Andron.* v 3 204
Ruined. What ruins are in me that can be found, By him not ruin'd? *Com. of Errors* ii 1 97
Send the breath of parley Into his ruin'd ears . *Richard II.* iii 3 34
Her fruit-trees all unpruned, her hedges ruin'd, Her knots disorder'd iii 4 45
The hope and expectation of thy time Is ruin'd . 1 *Hen. IV.* iii 2 37
O now, who will behold The royal captain of this ruin'd band! *Hen. V.* iv Prol. 29
See the noble ruin'd man you speak of.—Let's stand close *Hen. VIII.* ii 1 54
These shoulders, These ruin'd pillars . . . . . iii 2 382
Mark but my fall, and that that ruin'd me . . . iii 2 439
All broken implements of a ruin'd house . . *T. of Athens* iv 2 16
O ruin'd piece of nature! This great world Shall so wear out . *Lear* iv 6 137
Ruinous. Lest, growing ruinous, the building fall *T. G. of Ver.* v 4 9
Shall love, in building, grow so ruinous? . *Com. of Errors* iii 2 4
You ruinous butt, you whoreson indistinguishable cur *Troi. and Cres.* v 1 32
I stray'd To gaze upon a ruinous monastery . *T. Andron.* v 1 21
Is yond despised and ruinous man my lord? . *T. of Athens* iv 3 465
And all ruinous disorders, follow us disquietly to our graves . *Lear* i 2 123
Rule. There be that can rule Naples As well as he that sleeps *Tempest* ii 1 262
The report goes she has all the rule of her husband's purse *Mer. Wives* i 3 59
By what rule, sir?—Marry, sir, by a rule as plain as the plain bald pate of father Time himself . . . *Com. of Errors* ii 2 69
Yet in such rule that the Venetian law Cannot impugn you *Mer. of Ven.* iv 1 178
I am not so nice, To change true rules for old inventions *T. of Shrew* iii 1 81
Love and quiet life, And awful rule and right supremacy . v 2 109
Or seek for rule, supremacy and sway, When they are bound to serve . v 2 163
Little can be said in 't; 'tis against the rule of nature . *All's Well* i 1 148
You would not give means for this uncivil rule . *T. Night* ii 3 132
You have put me into darkness and given your drunken cousin rule over me . . . . v 1 313
What, canst not rule her? . . . . . *W. Tale* ii 3 46
Trust it, He shall not rule me.—La you now, you hear . ii 3 50
Out of limit and true rule You stand against anointed majesty 1 *Hen. IV.* iv 3 39

Rule. In military rules, humours of blood, He was the mark and glass, copy and book, That fashion'd others . *2 Hen. IV.* ii 3 30
I am passing light in spirit.—So much the worse, if your own rule be true iv 2 86
The honey-bees, Creatures that by a rule in nature teach *Hen. V.* i 2 188
Let senses rule ; the word is 'Pitch and Pay: Trust none ii 3 51
His wickedness, by your rule, should be imposed upon his father . iv 1 157
Good Lord, what madness rules in brainsick men ! . . *1 Hen. VI.* iv 1 111
Margaret shall now be queen, and rule the king ; But I will rule both her, the king and realm . . . . v 5 108
Suffolk, the new-made duke that rules the roast . . *2 Hen. VI.* i 1 109
Whose bookish rule hath pull'd fair England down . . . . i 1 259
Let them obey that know not how to rule . . . . . . v 1 6
Not fit to govern and rule multitudes, Which darest not, no, nor canst not rule a traitor . . . . v 1 95
Thou shalt rule no more O'er him whom heaven created for thy ruler . v 1 104
Though usurpers sway the rule awhile, Yet heavens are just *3 Hen. VI.* iii 3 76
Away with scrupulous wit ! now arms must rule . . . . iv 7 61
Why, what is pomp, rule, reign, but earth and dust? . . . v 2 27
You know no rules of charity, Which renders good for bad *Richard III.* i 2 68
Were they to be ruled, and not to rule, This sickly land might solace as before . . . . ii 3 29
If this rule were true, he should be gracious . . . . . ii 4 20
Ever beloved and loving may his rule be ! . . . *Hen. VIII.* ii 1 92
An army cannot rule 'em . . . . v 4 81
The specialty of rule hath been neglected . . . *Troi. and Cres.* i 3 78
To square the general sex By Cressid's rule . . . . . v 2 133
If there be rule in unity itself, This is not she . . . . v 2 141
You being their mouths, why rule you not their teeth? . *Coriolanus* iii 1 36
Suffer't, and live with such as cannot rule Nor ever will be ruled . iii 1 40
Strive by factions and by friends Ambitiously for rule . *T. Andron.* i 1 19
To-morrow yield up rule, resign my life, And set abroad new business . i 1 191
Where is thy leather apron and thy rule? . . . . *J. Cæsar* i 1 7
Even by the rule of that philosophy By which I did blame Cato . . v 1 101
He cannot buckle his distemper'd cause Within the belt of rule *Macbeth* v 2 16
A vice of kings ; A cutpurse of the empire and the rule . *Hamlet* iii 4 99
Now we will divest us, both of rule, Interest of territory . . *Lear* i 1 50
What safe and nicely I might well delay By rule of knighthood, I disdain v 3 145
You twain Rule in this realm, and the gored state sustain . . v 3 320
Confess perfection so could err Against all rules of nature . . *Othello* i 3 101
Now, by heaven, My blood begins my safer guides to rule . . . ii 3 205
They are close delations, working from the heart That passion cannot rule iii 3 124
Your command is taken off, And Cassio rules in Cyprus . . . v 2 332
Read not my blemishes in the world's report: I have not kept my square ; but that to come Shall all be done by the rule *Ant. and Cleo.* ii 3 7
Mechanic slaves With greasy aprons, rules, and hammers . . v 2 210
Your rule direct to any ; if to me, Day serves not light more faithful than I'll be.—I do not doubt thy faith . . . *Pericles* i 2 109
Your noble self, That best know how to rule and how to reign . ii 4 38
Ruled. We'll do thee homage and be ruled by thee . *T. G. of Ver.* iv 1 66
I beseech you, be ruled by your well-willers . . *Mer. Wives* i 1 72
He says, to veil full purpose.—Be ruled by him . *Meas. for Meas.* iv 6 4
Be ruled by me : depart in patience . . . . *Com. of Errors* iii 1 94
I trust you will be ruled by your father . . . . *Much Ado* ii 1 54
To be ruled by my conscience, I should stay with the Jew *Mer. of Venice* ii 2 23
To run away from the Jew, I should be ruled by the fiend . . . ii 2 26
Would thou'ldst be ruled by me !—Madam, I will . . . *T. Night* iv 1 68
Your royal presences be ruled by me . . . . . *K. John* ii 1 377
Wrath-kindled gentlemen, be ruled by me . . . . *Richard II.* i 1 152
Had they been ruled by me, You should have won them dearer *2 Hen. IV.* ii 3 72
Be thou ruled by me : Chief master-gunner am I . . *1 Hen. VI.* i 4 5
We'll . . . take away his train, If Dauphin and the rest will be but ruled iii 3 8
Yet so he ruled and such a prince he was . . . *2 Hen. VI.* ii 4 44
This lovely face Ruled, like a wandering planet, over me . . . iv 4 16
You shall have four, if you'll be ruled by him . . *3 Hen. VI.* iii 2 30
Why, this it is, when men are ruled by women . . *Richard III.* i 1 62
Were they to be ruled, and not to rule, This sickly land might solace as before . . . . ii 3 29
Shall I call you father?—Ay, my good son.—Be ruled by him *T. and C.* iii 3 268
And live with such as cannot rule Nor ever will be ruled . *Coriolanus* iii 1 41
Prithee now, Go, and be ruled . . . . iii 2 90
My lord, be ruled by me, be won at last . . . . *T. Andron.* i 1 442
Be ruled by me, forget to think of her . . . . *Rom. and Jul.* i 1 231
I think she will be ruled In all respects by me ; nay, more, I doubt it not iii 4 13
Pardon, I beseech you ! Henceforward I am ever ruled by you . . iv 2 22
It shall be said, his judgement ruled our hands . . *J. Cæsar* iii 1 147
This tongue had not offended so to-day, If Cassius might have ruled . v 1 47
Hold off your hands.—Be ruled ; you shall not go . . *Hamlet* i 4 81
Be ruled by me?—Ay, my lord ; So you will not o'errule me to a peace iv 7 60
I will be ruled ; The rather, if you could devise it so That I might be the organ.—It falls right . . . . iv 7 69
You should be ruled and led By some discretion . . . . *Lear* ii 4 150
But, sir, be you ruled by me : I have brought you from Venice *Othello* ii 1 270
Either be ruled by me, or I will make you—Man and wife . *Pericles* ii 5 83
Ruler. And we be lords and rulers over Rouen . . . *1 Hen. VI.* iii 2 11
As doth a ruler with unlawful oaths . . . . v 5 30
And demean himself Unlike the ruler of a commonweal . . *2 Hen. VI.* i 1 189
And he a prince and ruler of the land : Yet so he ruled . . . ii 4 43
'Tis meet that lucky ruler be employ'd ; Witness the fortune he hath had iii 1 291
If, after three days' space, thou here be'st found On any ground that I am ruler of, The world shall not be ransom for thy life . . . . iii 2 296
Thou shalt rule no more O'er him whom heaven created for thy ruler . v 1 105
Ruling. There we'll sit, Ruling in large and ample empery . *Hen. V.* i 2 226
Rumble thy bellyful ! Spit, fire ! spout, rain ! . . . . *Lear* iii 2 14
Ruminat. Fauste, precor gelida quando pecus omne sub umbra Ruminat, —and so forth . . . . *L. L. Lost* iv 2 96
Ruminate. Will ye be gone?—That you may ruminate *T. G. of Ver.* i 2 50
Then she plots, then she ruminates, then she devises . *Mer. Wives* ii 2 321
By their watchful fires Sit patiently and inly ruminate . *Hen. V.* iv Prol. 24
Where, from company, I may revolve and ruminate my grief *1 Hen. VI.* v 5 101
'Twas dangerous for him To ruminate on this so far . . *Hen. VIII.* i 2 180
And never suffers matter of the world Enter his thoughts, save such as do revolve And ruminate himself . . . . *Troi. and Cres.* ii 3 198
Ruminates like an hostess that hath no arithmetic but her brain . . iii 3 252
Knock at his study, where, they say, he keeps, To ruminate strange plots of dire revenge . . . . *T. Andron.* v 2 6
Speak to me as to thy thinkings, As thou dost ruminate . . *Othello* iii 3 132
Ruminated. But what I know Is ruminated, plotted and set down *1 Hen. IV.* i 3 274
'Tis a studied, not a present thought, By duty ruminated *Ant. and Cleo.* ii 2 141
Rumination. Contemplation of my travels, in which my often rumination wraps me in a most humorous sadness . . *As Y. Like It* iv 1 19
Rumour. That pitiful rumour may report my flight . . *All's Well* iii 2 130
To a vision so apparent rumour Cannot be mute . . . *W. Tale* ii 3 270 [sic: ii 1 as printed is unclear]
This from rumour's tongue I idly heard . . . . *K. John* iv 2 123
I find the people strangely fantasied ; Possess'd with rumours . . iv 2 145
Bear me hence From forth the noise and rumour of the field . . v 4 45
Open your ears ; for which of you will stop The vent of hearing when loud Rumour speaks? . . . . *2 Hen. IV.* Ind. 2
Upon my [Rumour's] tongues continual slanders ride . . . . Ind. 6
And who but Rumour, who but only I, Make fearful musters? . . Ind. 11
Rumour is a pipe Blown by surmises, jealousies, conjectures . . Ind. 15
Why is Rumour here? I run before King Harry's victory . . . Ind. 22
From Rumour's tongues They bring smooth comforts false . . . Ind. 39
Rumour doth double, like the voice and echo, The numbers of the fear'd iii 1 97
Great is the rumour of this dreadful knight . . . *1 Hen. VI.* ii 3 7
By holy Paul, they love his grace but lightly That fill his ears with such dissentious rumours . . . . *Richard III.* i 3 46
Rumour it abroad That Anne, my wife, is sick and like to die . . iv 2 51
He sent command to the lord mayor straight To stop the rumour *Hen. VIII.* ii 1 152
Let every feeble rumour shake your hearts . . . *Coriolanus* iii 3 125
Which I hear from common rumours . . . . . *T. of Athens* iii 2 6
Does the rumour hold for true, that he's so full of gold? . . . v 1 4
Prithee, listen well ; I heard a bustling rumour, like a fray . *J. Cæsar* ii 4 18
We hold rumour From what we fear, yet know not what we fear *Macbeth* iv 2 19
There ran a rumour Of many worthy fellows that were out . . . iv 3 182
What news?—Belike 'tis but a rumour . . . *Ant. and Cleo.* iv 3 5
Rumoured. This have I rumour'd through the peasant towns . *2 Hen. IV.* Ind. 33
It is rumour'd . . . These three lead on this preparation *Coriolanus* iv 6 (66)
Rumourer. Go see this rumourer whipp'd . . . . iv 6 47
Rump. How the devil Luxury, with his fat rump and potato-finger, tickles these together ! . . . . *Troi. and Cres.* v 2 56
Rump-fed. 'Aroint thee, witch !' the rump-fed ronyon cries . *Macbeth* i 3 6
Run. Fall to't, yarely, or we run ourselves aground . . . *Tempest* i 1 4
To run upon the sharp wind of the north . . . . . . i 2 254
Ebbing men, indeed, Most often do so near the bottom run . . . ii 1 227
We'll not run, Monsieur Monster.—Nor go neither . . . . iii 2 21
Run into no further danger . . . . iii 3 76
His tears run down his beard, like winter's drops From eaves of reeds v 1 16
Run, boy, run, run, and seek him out . . . *T. G. of Ver.* iii 1 188
And must I go to him?—Thou must run to him . . . . . iii 1 387
That one error Fills him with faults ; makes him run through all the sins . . . . v 4 112
If you run the nuthook's humour on me . . . . . *Mer. Wives* i 1 171
I will run no base humour . . . . i 3 85
Run in here, good young man ; go into this closet . . . . . i 4 38
A woman would run through fire and water for such a kind heart . iii 4 107
Run up, Sir John.—Go, go, sweet Sir John . . . . . . iv 2 81
Where be my horses? . . .—Run away with the cozeners . . . iv 5 67
Fly, run, hue and cry, villain ! I am undone ! . . . . . iv 5 93
When night-dogs run, all sorts of deer are chased . . . . v 5 252
Which have for long run by the hideous law, As mice by lions *M. for M.* i 4 63
Some run from brakes of ice, and answer none . . . . . ii 1 39
Much upon this riddle runs the wisdom of the world . . . . iii 2 242
Volumes of report Run with these false and most contrarious quests . iv 1 62
To make a lamp of her and run from her by her own light *Com. of Errors* iii 2 98
As from a bear a man would run for life, So fly I from her . . . iii 2 159
Fie, now you run this humour out of breath . . . . . . iv 2 (?)
A hound that runs counter and yet draws dry-foot well . . . iv 2 39
Run, master, run ; for God's sake, take a house ! This is some priory v 1 36
And the taker runs presently mad . . . . *Much Ado* i 1 88
You will never run mad, niece.—No, not till a hot January . . . i 1 93
Run thee to the parlour ; There shalt thou find my cousin . . . iii 1 1
Like a lapwing, runs Close by the ground . . . . iii 1 24
Runs not this speech like iron through your blood? . . . . . v 1 252
Whose names yet run smoothly in the even road of a blank verse . . v 2 33
Well run, dice ! . . . . *L. L. Lost* v 2 233
The gallants are at hand.—Whip to our tents, as roes run o'er land . v 2 309
Full merrily Hath this brave manage, this career, been run . . . v 2 482
A conqueror, and afeard to speak ! run away for shame . . . . v 2 582
Rein thy tongue.—I must rather give it the rein, for it runs against Hector . . . . v 2 664
The course of true love never did run smooth . . . *M. N. Dream* i 1 134
I'll run from thee and hide me in the brakes . . . . . . ii 1 227
Run when you will, the story shall be changed . . . . . ii 1 230
I am as ugly as a bear ; For beasts that meet me run away for fear . ii 2 95
And run through fire I will for thy sweet sake . . . . . ii 2 103
Why do they run away? this is a knavery of them to make me afeard iii 1 115
My legs are longer though, to run away . . . . iii 2 343
Well run, Thisbe . . . . v 1 271
We fairies, that do run By the triple Hecate's team . . . . v 1 390
I should not see the sandy hour-glass run, But I should think of shallows and of flats . . . . *Mer. of Venice* i 1 25
Certainly my conscience will serve me to run from this Jew my master ii 2 2
Use your legs, take the start, run away . . . . ii 2 6
Do not run ; scorn running with thy heels . . . . . . ii 2 9
'For the heavens, rouse up a brave mind,' says the fiend, 'and run' ii 2 13
To run away from the Jew, I should be ruled by the fiend . . . ii 2 26
I will run, fiend ; my heels are at your command ; I will run . . ii 2 33
As I have set up my rest to run away, so I will not rest till I have run some ground . . . . ii 2 110
I will run as far as God has any ground . . . . ii 2 117
It is marvel he out-dwells his hour, For lovers ever run before the clock ii 6 4
Run and overtake him ; Give him the ring . . . . . . iv 1 452
And with an unthrift love did run from Venice As far as Belmont . v 1 16
Or brook such disgrace well as he shall run into . . *As Y. Like It* i 1 141
If thou remember'st not the slightest folly That ever love did make thee run into, Thou hast not loved . . . . ii 4 35
We that are true lovers run into strange capers . . . . . ii 4 55
Run, run, Orlando ; carve on every tree . . . . iii 2 9
How brief the life of man Runs his erring pilgrimage . . . . iii 2 138
A woman's thought runs before her actions . . . . iv 1 141
As fast as you pour affection in, it runs out . . . . . . iv 1 215
He that runs fastest gets the ring . . . . . *T. of Shrew* i 1 145
Thou mayst slide from my shoulder to my heel with no greater a run but my head and my neck . . . . iv 1 16
Thus the bowl should run, And not unluckily against the bias . . iv 5 24
Like his greyhound, Which runs himself and catches for his master . v 2 53
I know not how I have deserved to run into my lord's displeasure.—You have made shift to run into't, boots and spurs and all, and out of it you'll run again . . . . *All's Well* ii 5 39

Run. You shall hear I am run away: know it before . . *All's Well* iii 2 25
Why should he be killed?—So say I, madam, if he run away . iii 2 42
For my part, I only hear your son was run away . iii 2 46
Only to seem to deserve well . . . have I run into this danger . iv 3 334
Indeed, he has no pace, but runs where he will . iv 5 71
Run after that same peevish messenger . *T. Night* i 5 319
When the image of it leaves him he must run mad . ii 5 213
How runs the stream? Or I am mad, or else this is a dream . iv 1 64
When she will take the rein I let her run; But she'll not stumble *W. T.* ii 3 51
Think what they have done And then run mad indeed, stark mad! iii 2 184
If you had but looked big and spit at him, he'ld have run . iv 3 114
My desires Run not before mine honour . iv 4 34
Say, shall the current of our right run on? *K. John* ii 1 335
Made to run even upon even ground . ii 1 576
Melancholy Had baked thy blood and made it heavy-thick, Which else runs tickling up and down the veins . iii 3 44
What can go well, when we have run so ill? . iii 4 5
I conjure thee but slowly; run more fast . iv 2 269
Forage, and run To meet displeasure farther from the doors . v 1 59
And calmly run on in obedience . v 4 56
Even so must I run on, and even so stop. What surety of the world? v 7 67
Were I tied to run afoot Even to the frozen ridges of the Alps *Richard II.* i 1 63
This tongue that runs so roundly in thy head Should run thy head from thy unreverent shoulders . ii 1 122
My fortune runs against the bias . iii 4 5
My time Runs posting on . v 5 59
Show it a fair pair of heels and run from it . *1 Hen. IV.* ii 4 53
I would give a thousand pound I could run as fast as thou canst . ii 4 163
And roared for mercy and still run and roared . ii 4 287
'Faith, I ran when I saw others run . ii 4 333
That runs o' horseback up a hill perpendicular . ii 4 377
That rascal hath good mettle in him; he will not run . ii 4 384
Here the smug and silver Trent shall run In a new channel . iii 1 102
He bears his course, and runs me up With like advantage on the other side . iii 1 108
On this north side win this cape of land; And then he runs straight and even . iii 1 114
I am afraid my daughter will run mad, So much she doteth . iii 1 145
Nay, if you melt, then will she run mad . iii 1 212
Why is Rumour here? I run before King Harry's victory *2 Hen. IV.* Ind. 23
Come to my master.—O, run, Doll, run; run, good Doll . ii 4 420
And for a retreat; how swiftly will this Feeble the woman's tailor run off! . iii 2 288
We see which way the stream of time doth run . iv 1 70
Thus runs the bill . *Hen. V.* i 1 19
The blood and courage that renowned them Runs in your veins . i 2 119
We have now no thought in us but France, Save those to God, that run before our business . i 2 303
He that strikes the first stroke, I'll run him up to the hilts . ii 1 68
The king hath run bad humours on the knight . ii 1 127
Coward dogs Most spend their mouths when what they seem to threaten Runs far before them . ii 4 71
If the English had any apprehension, they would run away . iii 7 146
Foolish curs, that run winking into the mouth of a Russian bear! . iii 7 153
O méchante fortune! Do not run away . iv 5 6
If thou spy'st any, run and bring me word . *1 Hen. VI.* i 4 19
Now, like to whelps, we crying run away . i 5 26
Sheep run not half so treacherous from the wolf . i 5 30
Run a tilt at death within a chair . iii 2 51
Before . . . a stroke was given, Like to a trusty squire did run away . iv 1 23
Ere the glass, that now begins to run, Finish the process of his sandy hour . iv 2 35
No hope that ever I will stay, If the first hour I shrink and run away . iv 5 31
The commonwealth hath daily run to wreck . *2 Hen. VI.* i 3 127
To save yourself from whipping, leap me over this stool and run away . ii 1 144
It made me laugh to see the villain run . ii 1 155
Smooth runs the water where the brook is deep . iii 1 53
Runs lowing up and down, Looking the way her harmless young one went . iii 1 214
Run to my Lord of Suffolk; let him know We have dispatch'd the duke iii 2 1
Rear up his body; wring him by the nose.—Run, go, help, help! . iii 2 35
The pissing-conduit run nothing but claret wine this first year . iv 6 4
Oft have I seen a hot o'erweening cur Run back and bite . v 1 152
Beggars mounted run their horse to death . *3 Hen. VI.* i 4 127
Tidings, as swiftly as the posts could run, Were brought me . ii 1 109
Thereby to see the minutes how they run, How many make the hour . ii 5 25
But yet I run before my horse to market . *Richard III.* i 1 160
Why dost thou run so many mile about, When thou mayst tell thy tale a nearer way? Once more, what news? . iv 4 461
We may outrun, By violent swiftness, that which we run at *Hen. VIII.* i 1 142
The fire that mounts the liquor till't run o'er, In seeming to augment it wastes it . i 1 144
I am sorry that the Duke of Buckingham Is run in your displeasure . i 2 110
So run the conditions . i 3 24
When he has run his course and sleeps in blessings . iii 2 398
Did her eyes run o'er too? . *Troi. and Cres.* i 2 161
And those boils did run? say so: did not the general run then? . ii 1 6
My mother's blood Runs on the dexter cheek . iv 5 128
With too much blood and too little brain, these two may run mad . v 1 54
Thou rascal, that art worst in blood to run, Lead'st first to win *Coriol.* i 1 163
I saw him run after a gilded butterfly . i 3 66
How have you run From slaves that apes would beat! . i 4 35
Where he did Run reeking o'er the lives of men . ii 2 123
I'll run away till I am bigger, but then I'll fight . v 3 128
I have horse will follow . . . and run like swallows o'er the plain *T. An.* ii 2 24
That all the tears that thy poor eyes let fall May run into that sink . iii 2 19
Quarrel, I will back thee.—How! turn thy back and run? *Rom. and Jul.* i 1 41
Nay, by the rood, She could have run and waddled all about . i 3 37
Wisely and slow; they stumble that run fast . ii 3 94
That Rosaline, Torments him so, that he will sure run mad . ii 4 5
If thy wits run the wild-goose chase, I have done . ii 4 75
Like a great natural, that runs lolling up and down to hide his bauble . ii 4 96
Run to my study. By and by! God's will, What simpleness is this! . iii 3 76
Presently through all thy veins shall run A cold and drowsy humour . iv 1 95
That living mortals, hearing them, run mad . iv 3 48
You love your child so ill, That you run mad, seeing that she is well . iv 5 76
Live, and hereafter say, A madman's mercy bade thee run away . v 3 67
Now at once run on The dashing rocks thy sea-sick weary bark! . v 3 117
Tell the prince: run to the Capulets: Raise up the Montagues . v 3 177
And all run, With open outcry, toward our monument . v 3 192

Run. Run to your houses, fall upon your knees, Pray to the gods *J. Cæsar* i 1 58
Stand you directly in Antonius' way, When he doth run his course . i 2 4
That what he is, augmented, Would run to these and these extremities . ii 1 31
Now bid me run, And I will strive with things impossible . ii 1 324
Like a fountain with an hundred spouts, Did run pure blood . ii 2 78
I prithee, boy, run to the senate-house; Stay not to answer me . ii 4 1
What should I do? Run to the Capitol, and nothing else? And so return to you, and nothing else? . ii 4 11
Run, Lucius, and commend me to my lord; Say I am merry . ii 4 44
Tyranny is dead! Run hence, proclaim, cry it about the streets . iii 1 79
Men, wives and children stare, cry out and run As it were doomsday . iii 1 97
A creature that I teach to fight, To wind, to stop, to run directly on . iv 1 32
Where I did begin, there shall I end; My life is run his compass . v 3 25
Far from this country Pindarus shall run . v 3 49
Now is that noble vessel full of grief, That it runs over even at his eyes . v 5 14
Hold thou my sword-hilts, whilst I run on it . v 5 28
Turn away thy face, While I do run upon it . v 5 48
I held the sword, and he did run on it . v 5 65
Time and the hour runs through the roughest day . *Macbeth* i 3 147
As little is the wisdom, where the flight So runs against all reason . iv 2 14
He has kill'd me, mother: Run away, I pray you! . iv 2 85
Run barefoot up and down, threatening the flames . *Hamlet* ii 2 528
Our wills and fates do so contrary run . iii 2 221
For some must watch, while some must sleep: So runs the world away iii 2 285
This lapwing runs away with the shell on his head . v 2 193
You shall run a certain course . *Lear* i 2 88
I can keep honest counsel, ride, run, mar a curious tale in telling it . i 4 34
Let go thy hold when a great wheel runs down a hill . ii 4 73
The knave turns fool that runs away; The fool no knave, perdy . ii 4 85
Unbonneted he runs, And bids what will take all . iii 1 14
A farmer's dog bark at a beggar? . . . And the creature run from the cur? iv 6 161
Run, run, O run!—To who, my lord? Who hath the office? . v 3 247
Run from her guardage to the sooty bosom Of such a thing as thou *Oth.* i 2 70
Give't me again: poor lady, she'll run mad When she shall lack it . iii 3 317
The fountain from the which my current runs, Or else dries up . iv 2 59
Run you to the citadel, And tell my lord and lady what hath happ'd . v 1 126
Rogue, thou hast lived too long.—Nay, then I'll run . *Ant. and Cleo.* ii 5 73
Fled myself; and have instructed cowards To run and show their shoulders . iii 11 8
Run one before, And let the queen know of our gests . iv 8 1
I will be A bridegroom in my death, and run into't As to a lover's bed iv 14 100
You have broke his pate with your bowl.—If his wit had been like him that broke it, it would have run all out . *Cymbeline* ii 1 10
Horses have been nimbler than the sands That run i' the clock's behalf iii 2 75
Lads more like to run The country base than to commit such slaughter v 3 19
Since she is living, let the time run on To good or bad . v 5 128
Now our sands are almost run: More a little, and then dumb *Pericles* v 2 266

Runagate. White-liver'd runagate, what doth he there? . *Richard III.* iv 4 465
In Mantua, Where that same banish'd runagate doth live *Rom. and Jul.* iii 5 90
More noble than that runagate to your bed . *Cymbeline* i 6 137
I cannot find those runagates; that villain Hath mock'd me . iv 2 62

Runaway. Thou runaway, thou coward, art thou fled? . *M. N. Dream* iii 2 405
For the close night doth play the runaway . *Mer. of Venice* ii 6 47
Do this suddenly, And let not search and inquisition quail To bring again these foolish runaways . *As Y. Like It* ii 2 21
They bid us to the English dancing-schools, . . . Saying our grace is only in our heels, And that we are most lofty runaways . *Hen. V.* iii 5 35
A sort of vagabonds, rascals, and runaways . *Richard III.* v 3 316
Spread thy close curtain, love-performing night, That runaways' eyes may wink, and Romeo Leap to these arms . *Rom. and Jul.* iii 2 6

Rung. Who call'd here of late?—None, since the curfew rung *M. for M.* iv 2 78
Enter, go in; the market bell is rung . *1 Hen. VI.* iii 2 15
He was brought again to the bar, to hear His knell rung out *Hen. VIII.* ii 1 32
A hunter's peal.—And you have rung it lustily . *T. Andron.* ii 2 14
The second cock hath crow'd, The curfew-bell hath rung *Rom. and Jul.* iv 4 4
Ere to black Hecate's summons The shard-borne beetle with his drowsy hums Hath rung night's yawning peal . *Macbeth* iii 2 43

Runner. Forspent with toil, as runners with a race . *3 Hen. VI.* ii 3 1
'Tis sport to maul a runner . *Ant. and Cleo.* iv 7 14

Runnest. For him [death] thou labour'st by thy flight to shun And yet runn'st toward him still . *Meas. for Meas.* iii 1 13
Where runn'st thou so fast? . *Com. of Errors* iii 2 72
For well I wot Thou runn'st before me . *M. N. Dream* iii 2 423
If thou art moved, thou runn'st away . *Rom. and Jul.* i 1 13

Running. How hast thou lost thy breath?—By running fast *Com. of Er.* iv 2 30
I Costard, running out, that was safely within. . *L. L. Lost* iii 1 117
Do not run; scorn running with thy heels . *Mer. of Venice* ii 2 9
Tongues in trees, books in the running brooks . *As Y. Like It* ii 1 16
Adonis painted by a running brook . *T. of Shrew* Ind. 2 52
That's for advantage.—So is running away . *All's Well* i 1 216
She would not live The running of one glass . *W. Tale* i 2 306
The argument shall be thy running away . *1 Hen. IV.* ii 4 311
What a rascal art thou then, to praise him so for running! . ii 4 386
Starting so He seem'd in running to devour the way . *2 Hen. IV.* i 1 47
That makes a still-stand, running neither way . ii 3 64
The farced title running 'fore the king . *Hen. V.* iv 1 280
When arm in arm they both came swiftly running . *1 Hen. VI.* ii 2 29
Some of these Should find a running banquet ere they rested *Hen. VIII.* i 4 12
And did entreat your highness to this course Which you are running here . ii 4 217
The which You were now running o'er . iii 2 139
Besides the running banquet of two beadles that is to come . v 4 69
Not to crack the wind of the poor phrase, Running it thus . *Hamlet* i 3 109
Nay, if you get it, you shall get it with running. Sa, sa, sa, sa . *Lear* iv 6 207
That tub Both fill'd and running . *Cymbeline* i 6 49

Rupture. It is a rupture that you may easily heal . *Meas. for Meas.* iii 1 244
Ruptures, catarrhs, loads o' gravel i' the back . *Troi. and Cres.* v 1 22

Rural. These rural latches to his entrance open . *W. Tale* iv 4 449
Here is a rural fellow That will not be denied your highness' presence: He brings you figs . *Ant. and Cleo.* v 2 233

Rush. Let them from forth a sawpit rush at once . *Mer. Wives* iv 4 53
Some devils ask but the parings of one's nail, A rush, a hair *Com. of Er.* iv 3 73
Many an error by the same example Will rush into the state *Mer. of Ven.* iv 1 222
In which cage of rushes I am sure you are not prisoner . *As Y. Like It* iii 2 389
Lean but upon a rush, The cicatrice and capable impressure Thy palm some moment keeps . iii 5 22
Were it better, I should rush in thus . *T. of Shrew* ii 1 93
Is supper ready, the house trimmed, rushes strewed? . iv 1 48
As fit . . . as Tib's rush for Tom's forefinger . *All's Well* ii 2 24
Something rare Even then will rush to knowledge . *W. Tale* iii 1 21

Rush. Wide havoc made For bloody power to rush upon your peace *K. John* ii 1 221
When I strike my foot Upon the bosom of the ground, rush forth . iv 1 3
A rush will be a beam To hang thee on . . . . . iv 3 129
She bids you on the wanton rushes lay you down . 1 *Hen. IV.* iii 1 214
More rushes, more rushes . . . . . 2 *Hen. IV.* v 5 1
Rush on his host, as doth the melted snow Upon the valleys. *Hen. V.* iii 5 50
Sound, sound alarum! we will rush on them . . 1 *Hen. VI.* i 2 18
The other lords, like lions wanting food, Do rush upon us . . . i 2 28
Rush all to pieces on thy rocky bosom . . . *Richard III.* iv 4 234
Like to an enter'd tide, they all rush by And leave you . *Troi. and Cres.* iii 3 159
Swims with fins of lead And hews down oaks with rushes . *Coriolanus* i 1 185
Our gates, Which yet seem shut, we have but pinn'd with rushes . . i 4 18
Tickle the senseless rushes with their heels . *Rom. and Jul.* i 4 36
His agile arm beats down their fatal points, And 'twixt them rushes . iii 1 172
Where our fate, Hid in an auger-hole, may rush, and seize us. *Macbeth* ii 3 128
Man but a rush against Othello's breast, And he retires . *Othello* v 2 270
And spurns The rush that lies before him. . . *Ant. and Cleo.* iii 5 18
Is it sin To rush into the secret house of death, Ere death dare come to us? . . . . iv 15 81
Our Tarquin thus Did softly press the rushes . . . *Cymbeline* ii 2 13
Rush-candle. If you please to call it a rush-candle, Henceforth I vow it shall be so for me. . . . . . . *T. of Shrew* iv 5 14
Rushed. He rush'd into my house and took perforce My ring *Com. of Er.* iv 3 95
The king of heaven forbid our lord the king Should so with civil and uncivil arms Be rush'd upon! . . . *Richard II.* iii 3 103
Cried out amain And rush'd into the bowels of the battle 1 *Hen. VI.* i 1 129
With this, my weapon drawn, I rush'd upon him . *T. Andron.* v 1 37
The kind prince, Taking thy part, hath rush'd aside the law *R. and J.* iii 3 26
Rushing in their houses, bearing thence Rings, jewels . *Com. of Errors* v 1 143
What a tide of woes Comes rushing on this woeful land at once! *Rich. II.* ii 2 99
So, rushing in the bowels of the French, He left me proudly 1 *Hen. VI.* iv 7 42
Leave us, Publius; lest that the people, Rushing on us, should do your age some mischief. . . . . . . *J. Cæsar* iii 1 93
Mark how the blood of Cæsar follow'd it, As rushing out of doors . iii 2 183
Lest this great sea of joys rushing upon me O'erbear the shores of my mortality, And drown me . . . . . . *Pericles* v 1 194
Rushling. Smelling so sweetly, all musk, and so rushling *Mer. Wives* ii 2 68
Rushy brook. By paved fountain or by rushy brook . *M. N. Dream* ii 1 84
Russet. Express'd In russet yeas and honest kersey noes . *L. L. Lost* v 2 413
The morn, in russet mantle clad, Walks o'er the dew . *Hamlet* i 1 166
Russet-pated choughs, many in sort . . . *M. N. Dream* iii 2 21
Russia. This will last out a night in Russia . *Meas. for Meas.* ii 1 139
Some say he is with the Emperor of Russia; other some, he is in Rome iii 2 94
The Emperor of Russia was my father: O that he were alive! *W. Tale* iii 2 120
Russian. Apparell'd thus, Like Muscovites or Russians . *L. L. Lost* v 2 121
A mess of Russians left us but of late.—How, madam! Russians! . v 2 361
We four indeed confronted were with four In Russian habit . v 2 368
Wish thee never more to dance, Nor never more in Russian habit wait . v 2 401
What did the Russian whisper in your ear? . . . . v 2 443
Curs, that run winking into the mouth of a Russian bear! . *Hen. V.* iii 7 154
Approach thou like the rugged Russian bear . . . *Macbeth* iii 4 100
Rust. Adieu, valour! rust, rapier! be still, drum! . . *L. L. Lost* i 2 187
Rust, sword! cool, blushes! . . . . . *All's Well* iv 3 373
How he glisters Thorough my rust! . . . . . *W. Tale* iv 2 172
Nay, after that, consume away in rust . . . . *K. John* iv 1 65
His glittering arms he will commend to rust . . *Richard II.* iii 3 116
Better to be eaten to death with a rust than to be scoured to nothing with perpetual motion. . . . . . 2 *Hen. IV.* i 2 246
While that the coulter rusts That should deracinate such savagery *Hen. V.* v 2 46
Thy son's blood cleaving to my blade Shall rust upon my weapon 3 *Hen. VI.* i 3 51
This peace is nothing, but to rust iron, increase tailors . *Coriolanus* iv 5 234
O happy dagger! This is thy sheath; there rust, and let me die *R. and J.* v 3 170
Keep up your bright swords, for the dew will rust them. . *Othello* i 2 59
And on set purpose let his armour rust Until this day . . *Pericles* ii 2 54

Rusted. Here's a vengeful sword, rusted with ease . . 2 *Hen. VI.* iii 2 198
Rustic. And fall into our rustic revelry . . . *As Y. Like It* v 4 183
Of that kind Our rustic garden's barren . . . . *W. Tale* iv 4 84
How now, rustics! whither are you bound? . . . . iv 4 735
Yield, rustic mountaineer . . . . . . *Cymbeline* iv 2 100
Rustically. He keeps me rustically at home . . *As Y. Like It* i 1 7
Rustle. I hear his straw rustle . . . . *Meas. for Meas.* iv 3 38
Rustling. Let not the creaking of shoes nor the rustling of silks betray thy poor heart to woman . . . . *Lear* iii 4 98
Prouder than rustling in unpaid-for silk . . . . *Cymbeline* iii 3 24
Rusty. An old rusty sword ta'en out of the town-armoury *T. of Shrew* iii 2 46
Distaff-women manage rusty bills Against thy seat. . *Richard II.* iii 2 118
With the rusty curb of old father antic the law . 1 *Hen. IV.* i 2 68
And faintly through a rusty beaver peeps . . . *Hen. V.* iv 2 44
In this dull and long-continued truce Is rusty grown *Troi. and Cres.* i 3 263
Quite out of fashion, like a rusty mail In monumental mockery . iii 3 152
Do they grow rusty?—Nay, their endeavour keeps in the wonted pace *Hamlet* ii 2 352
'Tis come at last, and 'tis turned to a rusty armour. . *Pericles* ii 1 125
By his rusty outside he appears To have practised more the whipstock ii 2 50
Ruth. Rue, even for ruth, here shortly shall be seen *Richard II.* iii 4 106
Spur them to ruthful work, rein them from ruth . *Troi. and Cres.* v 3 48
Would the nobility lay aside their ruth, And let me use my sword *Coriolanus* i 1 201
Ruthful. O that my death would stay these ruthful deeds! . 3 *Hen. VI.* ii 5 95
Spur them to ruthful work, rein them from ruth . . *Troi. and Cres.* v 3 48
Villanies Ruthful to hear, yet piteously perform'd . . *T. Andron.* v 1 66
Ruthless. What a ruthless thing is this in him! . *Meas. for Meas.* iii 2 121
Save your subjects from such massacre And ruthless slaughters 1 *Hen. VI.* v 4 161
The ruthless flint doth cut my tender feet . . 2 *Hen. VI.* ii 4 34
Such mercy as his ruthless arm, With downright payment, show'd 3 *Hen. VI.* i 4 31
See, ruthless queen, a hapless father's tears . . . . i 4 156
The ruthless queen gave him to dry his cheeks A napkin . . . ii 1 61
And what is Edward but a ruthless sea? . . . . . v 4 25
No hoped-for mercy with the brothers More than with ruthless waves . v 4 36
Whom I did suborn To do this ruthless piece of butchery *Richard III.* iv 3 5
The woods are ruthless, dreadful, deaf, and dull . . *T. Andron.* ii 1 128
The ruthless, vast, and gloomy woods . . . . . iv 1 53
Rutland. Madam, you must call him Rutland now . . *Richard II.* v 2 43
Until thou bid me joy, By pardoning Rutland, my transgressing boy . v 3 96
Where is your darling Rutland? Look, York . . 3 *Hen. VI.* i 4 78
What, hath thy fiery heart so parch'd thine entrails That not a tear can fall for Rutland's death? . . . . i 4 88
These tears are my sweet Rutland's obsequies . . . . i 4 147
A napkin steeped in the harmless blood Of sweet young Rutland . . ii 1 63
'Twas you that kill'd young Rutland, was it not? . . . . ii 2 98
A treacherous coward, As thou didst kill our tender brother Rutland . ii 2 115
Suppose this arm is for the Duke of York, And this for Rutland . ii 4 3
This is the hand that stabb'd thy father York; And this the hand that slew thy brother Rutland . . . . ii 4 7
Not contented that he lopp'd the branch In hewing Rutland . . ii 6 48
Thou pitied'st Rutland; I will pity thee . . . . . ii 6 74
Whose unstanched thirst York and young Rutland could not satisfy . ii 6 84
To hear the piteous moan that Rutland made When black-faced Clifford shook his sword at him . . . . . *Richard III.* i 2 158
A clout Steep'd in the faultless blood of pretty Rutland . . . i 3 178
I had a Rutland too, thou holp'st to kill him . . . . iv 4 45
Present to her,—as sometime Margaret Did to thy father, steep'd in Rutland's blood,—A handkerchief . . . . . . iv 4 275
Rut-time. Send me a cool rut-time . . . . *Mer. Wives* v 5 15
Rutting. I am out of the road of rutting for ever . *Pericles* iv 5 9
Ruttish. A foolish idle boy, but for all that very ruttish *All's Well* iv 3 243
Rye. Thy rich leas Of wheat, rye, barley, vetches, oats . . *Tempest* iv 1 61
Between the acres of the rye, With a hey, and a ho. . *As Y. Like It* v 3 23
Rye-straw. Make holiday; your rye-straw hats put on . *Tempest* iv 1 136

S

Sa. You shall get it with running. Sa, sa, sa, sa . . *Lear* iv 6 207
Saba was never More covetous of wisdom and fair virtue . . *Hen. VIII.* v 5 24
Sabbath. By our holy Sabbath have I sworn . *Mer. of Venice* iv 1 36
Come the next Sabbath, and I will content you . *Richard III.* iii 2 113
Sable. It was, as I have seen it in his life, A sable silver'd *Hamlet* i 2 242
He whose sable arms, Black as his purpose did the night resemble . ii 2 474
Nay then, let the devil wear black, for I'll have a suit of sables . iii 2 138
Youth no less becomes The light and careless livery that it wears Than settled age his sables and his weeds . . . . . . iv 7 81
His banners sable, trimm'd with rich expense . . *Pericles* v Gower 19
Sable-coloured melancholy . . . . . . *L. L. Lost* i 1 233
Sack. I escaped upon a butt of sack . . . . *Tempest* ii 2 126
My man-monster hath drown'd his tongue in sack . . . iii 2 15
Was there ever man a coward that hath drunk so much sack, as I to-day? iii 2 31
This can sack and drinking do . . . . ii 2 88
You love sack, and so do I. . . . . . *Mer. Wives* ii 1 9
I'll give you a pottle of burnt sack to give me recourse to him . ii 1 223
A morning's draught of sack . . . . ii 2 153
Your hearts are mighty, your skins are whole, and let burnt sack be the issue . . . . iii 1 112
Fetch me a quart of sack; put a toast in't . . . . iii 5 3
Let me pour in some sack to the Thames water . . . iii 5 22
Go brew me a pottle of sack finely.—With eggs, sir?—Simple of itself . iii 5 30
Given to fornications, and to taverns and sack and wine . . v 5 167
More sacks to the mill! O heavens, I have my wish! . *L. L. Lost* iv 3 81
Will't please your lordship drink a cup of sack? . *T. of Shrew* Ind. 2 2
I ne'er drank sack in my life . . . . . . Ind. 2 6
I'll go burn some sack; 'tis too late to go to bed now . *T. Night* ii 3 206
Thou art so fat-witted, with drinking of old sack . 1 *Hen. IV.* i 2 3
Unless hours were cups of sack and minutes capon. . . . i 2 8
What says Sir John Sack and Sugar? Jack! . . . . i 2 125

Sack. Let a cup of sack be my poison . . . . 1 *Hen. IV.* ii 2 49
Give me a cup of sack, boy . . . . ii 4 129
You rogue, here's lime in this sack too . . . . . ii 4 137
Yet a coward is worse than a cup of sack with lime in it . . ii 4 140
O villain, thou stolest a cup of sack eighteen years ago . . ii 4 345
That swollen parcel of dropsies, that huge bombard of sack . . ii 4 497
Wherein is he good, but to taste sack and drink it? . . . ii 4 501
If sack and sugar be a fault, God help the wicked! . . . ii 4 516
Item, Sauce, 4d. Item, Sack, two gallons, 5s. 8d. . . . ii 4 587
O monstrous! but one half-pennyworth of bread to this intolerable deal of sack! . . . . ii 4 592
The sack that thou hast drunk me would have bought me lights . iii 3 50
Get thee before to Coventry; fill me a bottle of sack . . iv 2 2
There's that will sack a city . . . . v 3 56
I'll purge, and leave sack, and live cleanly as a nobleman should do v 4 169
The young lion repents; marry, not in ashes and sackcloth, but in new silk and old sack . . . . 2 *Hen. IV.* i 2 222
I'll steep this letter in sack and make him eat it . . . ii 2 147
I charge you with a cup of sack . . . . . . ii 4 121
Come, give's some sack . . . . ii 4 194
Skill in the weapon is nothing without sack, for that sets it a-work iv 3 124
To forswear thin potations and to addict themselves to sack . iv 3 135
Do you mean to stop any of William's wages, about the sack he lost the other day? . . . . v 1 25
I have drunk too much sack at supper . . . . . v 3 15
They say he cried out of sack . . . . . *Hen. V.* ii 3 29
Shall be engraved the sack of Orleans . . . 1 *Hen. VI.* i 6 25
Our sacks shall be a mean to sack the city . . . . iii 2 10
I'll either make thee stoop and bend thy knee, Or sack this country with a mutiny . . . . v 1 62
I drink to you in a cup of sack . . . . . 2 *Hen. VI.* ii 3 60

Sack. And sack great Rome with Romans *Coriolanus* iii 1 316
Tell me, that I may sack The hateful mansion *Rom. and Jul.* iii 3 107
Sack fair Athens, And take our goodly aged men by the beards *T. of A.* v 1 174
Sackbuts. The trumpets, sackbuts, psalteries, and fifes *Coriolanus* v 4 52
Sackcloth. The young lion repents; marry, not in ashes and sackcloth, but in new silk and old sack 2 *Hen. IV.* i 2 222
He swears Never to wash his face, nor cut his hairs: He puts on sackcloth, and to sea *Pericles* iv 4 29
Sacked. Was this fair face the cause, quoth she, Why the Grecians sacked Troy? *All's Well* i 3 75
Sackerson. I have seen Sackerson loose twenty times, and have taken him by the chain *Mer. Wives* i 1 307
Sacrament. I'll take the sacrament on't *All's Well* iv 3 156
May know wherefore we took the sacrament *K. John* v 2 6
Ere I last received the sacrament I did confess it *Richard II.* i 1 139
You shall not only take the sacrament To bury mine intents iv 1 328
A dozen of them here have ta'en the sacrament v 2 97
Ten thousand French have ta'en the sacrament To rive their dangerous artillery Upon no Christian soul but English Talbot 1 *Hen. VI.* iv 2 28
Thou didst receive the holy sacrament, To fight in quarrel of the house of Lancaster *Richard III.* i 4 208
As we have ta'en the sacrament, We will unite the white rose and the red v 5 18
Sacred. No Valentine, indeed, for sacred Silvia *T. G. of Ver.* iii 1 211
Ask him why, that hour of fairy revel, In their so sacred paths he dares to tread In shape profane *Mer. Wives* iv 4 59
Strew good luck, ouphes, on every sacred room v 5 61
I am combined by a sacred vow And shall be absent *Meas. for Meas.* iv 3 149
In double violation Of sacred chastity and of promise-breach v 1 410
Justice, most sacred duke! *Com. of Errors* v 1 133
He hates our sacred nation, and he rails *Mer. of Venice* i 3 49
Wiped our eyes Of drops that sacred pity hath engender'd *As Y. Like It* ii 7 123
Sacred and sweet was all I saw in her *T. of Shrew* i 1 181
O my most sacred lady! Temptations have since then been born to's *W. Tale* i 2 76
I have dispatch'd in post To sacred Delphos, to Apollo's temple ii 1 183
The sacred honour of himself, his queen's iii 2 84
Their sacred wills be done! iii 3 7
Against whose person, So sacred as it is, I have done sin v 1 172
You gods, look down And from your sacred vials pour your graces Upon my daughter's head! v 3 122
What earthy name to interrogatories Can task the free breath of a sacred king? Thou canst not, cardinal, devise a name *K. John* iii 1 148
Coupled and link'd together With all religious strength of sacred vows iii 1 229
I make a vow, Such neighbour nearness to our sacred blood Should nothing privilege him *Richard II.* i 1 119
One vial full of Edward's sacred blood Is crack'd i 2 17
Alack the heavy day When such a sacred king should hide his head iii 3 8
No hand of blood and bone Can gripe the sacred handle of our sceptre iii 3 80
With mine own tongue deny my sacred state iv 1 209
Dust was thrown upon his sacred head v 2 30
To thy sacred state wish I all happiness v 6 6
God and his angels guard your sacred throne! *Hen. V.* i 2 7
My profession's sacred from above 1 *Hen. VI.* i 2 114
Doth but usurp the sacred name of knight iv 1 40
His weapons holy saws of sacred writ 2 *Hen. VI.* i 3 61
Or my love and duty, Against your sacred person *Hen. VIII.* ii 4 41
To the good of your most sacred person iii 2 173
From the sacred ashes of her honour Shall star-like rise v 5 46
Thy mother, My sacred aunt *Troi. and Cres.* iv 5 134
O sacred receptacle of my joys, Sweet cell of virtue and nobility, How many sons of mine hast thou in store! *T. Andron.* i 1 92
And in the sacred Pantheon her espouse i 1 242
Our empress, with her sacred wit To villany and vengeance consecrate ii 1 120
Make sacred even his stirrup *T. of Athens* i 1 82
They would go and kiss dead Cæsar's wounds And dip their napkins in his sacred blood *J. Cæsar* iii 2 138
The sacred storehouse of his predecessors *Macbeth* ii 4 34
Unite commutual in most sacred bands *Hamlet* iii 2 170
By the sacred radiance of the sun, The mysteries of Hecate *Lear* i 1 111
In the due reverence of a sacred vow I here engage my words *Othello* iii 3 461
O most false love! Where be the sacred vials thou shouldst fill With sorrowful water? Now I see, I see *Ant. and Cleo.* i 3 63
The honour is sacred which he talks on now, Supposing that I lack'd it ii 2 85
Joy and all comfort in your sacred breast! *Pericles* i 2 33
Thy sacred physic shall receive such pay As thy desires can wish v 1 74
Sacrifice. Say that upon the altar of her beauty You sacrifice your tears, your sighs, your heart *T. G. of Ver.* iii 2 74
I stand for sacrifice; The rest aloof are the Dardanian wives *M. of V.* iii 2 57
I would lose all, ay, sacrifice them all Here to this devil, to deliver you iv 1 286
I'll sacrifice the lamb that I do love *T. Night* v 1 133
O, the sacrifice! How ceremonious, solemn and unearthly It was! *W. Tale* iii 1 6
Rescue those breathing lives to die in beds, That here come sacrifices for the field *K. John* ii 1 420
They come like sacrifices in their trim 1 *Hen. IV.* iv 1 113
The poor condemned English, Like sacrifices, by their watchful fires Sit patiently and inly ruminate *Hen. V.* iv Prol. 23
To bear 'em, The back is sacrifice to the load *Hen. VIII.* i 2 50
Make of your prayers one sweet sacrifice, And lift my soul to heaven ii 1 77
Words, vows, gifts, tears, and love's full sacrifice, He offers in another's enterprise *Troi. and Cres.* i 2 308
Ere the first sacrifice, within this hour iv 2 66
More abhorr'd Than spotted livers in the sacrifice v 3 18
May give you thankful sacrifice *Coriolanus* i 6 9
The prayers of priests nor times of sacrifice, Embarquements all of fury i 10 21
And on a pile Ad manes fratrum sacrifice his flesh *T. Andron.* i 1 98
Religiously they ask a sacrifice: To this your son is mark'd i 1 124
I pour'd forth tears in vain, To save your brother from the sacrifice ii 3 164
Poor sacrifices of our enmity! *Rom. and Jul.* v 3 304
Go bid the priests do present sacrifice And bring me their opinions of success.—I will, my lord *J. Cæsar* ii 2 5
Upon such sacrifices, my Cordelia, The gods themselves throw incense *Lear* v 3 20
Thou dost stone my heart, And makest me call what I intend to do A murder, which I thought a sacrifice *Othello* v 2 65
Dead.—Why, sir, give the gods a thankful sacrifice *Ant. and Cleo.* ii 5 167
You reek as a sacrifice: where air comes out, air comes in *Cymbeline* i 2 3
Let's quit this ground, And smoke the temple with our sacrifices v 5 398
And do upon mine altar sacrifice *Pericles* v 1 242
In no wise Till he had done his sacrifice, As Dian bade v 2 277
Sacrificed. To keep that oath were more impiety Than Jephthah's, when he sacrificed his daughter 3 *Hen. VI.* v 1 91
Let my old life Be sacrificed, some hour before his time *Rom. and Jul.* v 3 268
Sacrificers. Let us be sacrificers, but not butchers, Caius *J. Cæsar* ii 1 166
Sacrificial. Rain sacrificial whisperings in his ear *T. of Athens* i 1 81
Sacrificing. Which blood, like sacrificing Abel's, cries *Richard II.* i 1 104
Alarbus' limbs are lopp'd, And entrails feed the sacrificing fire *T. An.* i 1 144
Sacrilegious. Most sacrilegious murder hath broke ope The Lord's anointed temple! *Macbeth* ii 3 72
That kill'd thy daughter:—villain-like, I lie—That caused a lesser villain than myself, A sacrilegious thief, to do't *Cymbeline* v 5 220
Sacring bell. I'll startle you Worse than the sacring bell *Hen. VIII.* iii 2 295
Sad. You are sad.—Indeed, madam, I seem so *T. G. of Ver.* ii 4 8
Where thou shalt find me, sad and solitary iv 4 94
Which is the way? Is it sad, and few words? or how? *Meas. for Meas.* iii 2 53
Look'd he or red or pale, or sad or merrily? *Com. of Errors* iv 2 4
He hath been heavy, sour, sad, And much different from the man he was v 1 45
Why are you thus out of measure sad? *Much Ado* i 3 2
I must be sad when I have cause and smile at no man's jests i 3 14
Wherefore are you sad?—Not sad, my lord.—How then? sick? ii 1 299
The count is neither sad, nor sick, nor merry, nor well; but civil count ii 1 303
She is never sad but when she sleeps, and not ever sad then ii 1 358
If he be sad, he wants money iii 2 20
Let me be: pluck up, my heart, and be sad v 1 208
Prince, thou art sad; get thee a wife, get thee a wife v 4 124
A great sign, sir, that he will look sad *L. L. Lost* i 2 3
He made her melancholy, sad, and heavy; And so she died v 2 14
Amazed, my lord? why looks your highness sad? v 2 391
Here she comes, curst and sad: Cupid is a knavish lad *M. N. Dream* iii 2 439
Then, my queen, in silence sad, Trip we after night's shade iv 1 100
The death of a dear friend would go near to make a man look sad v 1 294
In sooth, I know not why I am so sad: It wearies me *Mer. of Venice* i 1 1
Misfortune to my ventures out of doubt Would make me sad i 1 22
Shall I lack the thought That such a thing bechanced would make me sad? i 1 38
I know, Antonio Is sad to think upon his merchandise i 1 40
My merchandise makes me not sad.—Why, then you are in love i 1 45
Then let us say you are sad, Because you are not merry: and 'twere as easy For you to laugh and leap and say you are merry, Because you are not sad i 1 47
'Tis good to be sad and say nothing.—Why then, 'tis good to be a post.—I have neither the scholar's melancholy *As Y. Like It* iv 1 8
A traveller! By my faith, you have great reason to be sad iv 1 22
I have gained my experience.—And your experience makes you sad iv 1 27
I had rather have a fool to make me merry than experience to make me sad iv 1 29
First were we sad, fearing you would not come; Now sadder *T. of Shrew* iii 2 100
Had a father,—O, that 'had!' how sad a passage 'tis! *All's Well* i 1 20
He is sad and civil, And suits well for a servant with my fortunes *T. Night* iii 4 5
I am as mad as he, If sad and merry madness equal be iii 4 16
Sad, lady! I could be sad: this does make some obstruction in the blood iii 4 21
Tell's a tale.—Merry or sad shall't be? *W. Tale* ii 1 23
A merry heart goes all the day, Your sad tires in a mile-a iv 3 135
She is sad and passionate *K. John* ii 1 544
Cousin, look not sad: Thy grandam loves thee iii 3 2
You are sad.—Indeed, I have been merrier iv 1 11
Mercy on me! Methinks no body should be sad but I iv 1 13
I remember, when I was in France, Young gentlemen would be as sad as night, Only for wantonness iv 1 15
But wherefore do you droop? why look you sad? Be great in act v 1 44
Is't not pity, O my grieved friends, That we, the sons and children of this isle, Were born to see so sad an hour as this? v 2 26
I did not think to be so sad to-night As this hath made me v 5 15
Madam, your majesty is too much sad *Richard II.* ii 2 1
Howe'er it be, I cannot but be sad; so heavy sad As, though on thinking on no thought I think ii 2 30
Rich men look sad and ruffians dance and leap ii 4 12
Where they did spend a sad and bloody hour 1 *Hen. IV.* i 1 56
Yea, there thou makest me sad and makest me sin In envy i 1 78
Look how we can, or sad or merrily, Interpretation will misquote our looks v 2 12
It is not meet that I should be sad, now my father is sick 2 *Hen. IV.* ii 2 43
I could be sad, and sad indeed too.—Very hardly upon such a subject ii 2 45
Yet be sad, good brothers, For, by my faith, it very well becomes you v 2 49
Why then, be sad; But entertain no more of it, good brothers, Than a joint burden v 2 53
Their gesture sad Investing lank-lean cheeks *Hen. V.* iv Prol. 25
Your looks are sad, your cheer appall'd 1 *Hen. VI.* i 2 48
My troublous dream this night doth make me sad 2 *Hen. VI.* i 2 22
With sad unhelpful tears, and with dimm'd eyes iii 1 218
How fares my brother? why is he so sad? 3 *Hen. VI.* ii 1 8
The widow likes it not, for she looks very sad iii 2 110
Why look you so sad?—My heart is ten times lighter than my looks *Richard III.* v 3 2
A serious brow, Sad, high, and working *Hen. VIII.* Prol. 3
Be sad, as we would make ye Prol. 25
You shall hear . . . of him Things to strike honour sad i 2 126
When you would say something that is sad, Speak how I fell ii 1 135
How sad he looks! sure, he is much afflicted ii 2 63
My soul grows sad with troubles; Sing, and disperse 'em iii 1 1
To make a sweet lady sad is a sour offence *Troi. and Cres.* iii 1 79
My lovely Aaron, wherefore look'st thou sad, When every thing doth make a gleeful boast? *T. Andron.* ii 3 10
He did discourse To love-sick Dido's sad attending ear v 3 82
Why look'st thou sad? Though news be sad, yet tell them merrily *Rom. and Jul.* ii 5 21
Prithee, be not sad, Thou art true and honest *T. of Athens* ii 2 229
Tell us what hath chanced to-day, That Cæsar looks so sad *J. Cæsar* i 2 217
And after that, he came, thus sad, away?—Ay i 2 279
If you find him sad, Say I am dancing *Ant. and Cleo.* i 3 3
What, was he sad or merry?—Like to the time o' the year between the extremes Of hot and cold, he was nor sad nor merry i 5 50
He was not sad, for he would shine on those That make their looks by his i 5 55
Be'st thou sad or merry, The violence of either thee becomes i 5 59
Octavia weeps To part from Rome; Cæsar is sad iii 2 4
Pray you, look not sad, Nor make replies of loathness iii 11 17
Look you sad, friends? The gods rebuke me, but it is tidings To wash the eyes of kings v 1 26
I never saw him sad *Cymbeline* i 6 63

Sad and solemn. Where the sad and solemn priests Sing still for Richard's soul — *Hen. V.* iv 1 318
Sad Apollo. At that sight shall sad Apollo weep — *T. of Shrew* Ind. 2 61
Sad aspect. Thy sad aspect Hath from the number of his banish'd years Pluck'd four away — *Richard II.* i 3 209
Sad bosoms. Seek out some desolate shade, and there Weep our sad bosoms empty — *Macbeth* iv 3 2
Sad brow. Speak you this with a sad brow? — *Much Ado* i 1 185
The devil take mocking: speak, sad brow and true maid — *As Y. Like It* iii 2 227
It is much that a lie with a slight oath and a jest with a sad brow will do with a fellow — 2 *Hen. IV.* v 1 92
I will construe to thee All the charactery of my sad brows — *J. Cæsar* ii 1 308
Sad burial feast. Our wedding cheer to a sad burial feast, Our solemn hymns to sullen dirges change — *Rom. and Jul.* iv 5 87
Sad captains. Come, Let's have one other gaudy night: call to me All my sad captains — *Ant. and Cleo.* iii 13 184
Sad companion. The sad companion, dull-eyed melancholy — *Pericles* i 2 2
Sad conference. Hand in hand, in sad conference — *Much Ado* i 3 62
Sad cypress. And in sad cypress let me be laid — *T. Night* ii 4 53
Sad decrees. That so my sad decrees may fly away — *T. Andron.* v 2 11
Sad designs. Leave these sad designs To him that hath more cause to be a mourner — *Richard III.* i 2 211
Sad despair. Our hap is loss, our hope but sad despair — 3 *Hen. VI.* ii 3 9
Sad distrust. Let not the world see fear and sad distrust — *K. John* v 1 46
Sad dog. Where no man never comes but that sad dog — *Richard II.* v 5 70
Sad-eyed. The sad-eyed justice, with his surly hum — *Hen. V.* i 2 202
Sad face. A sad face, a reverend carriage, a slow tongue — *T. Night* iii 4 80
Sad-faced. You sad-faced men, people and sons of Rome — *T. Andron.* v 3 67
Sad fools. This is the rarest dream that e'er dull sleep Did mock sad fools withal — *Pericles* v 1 164
Sad grave. Fidele, I'll sweeten thy sad grave — *Cymbeline* iv 2 220
Sad habiliment. In this strange and sad habiliment — *T. Andron.* v 2 1
Sad heart. As dear to me as are the ruddy drops That visit my sad heart — *J. Cæsar* ii 1 290
Sad-hearted men, much overgone with care, Here sits a king more woful than you are — 3 *Hen. VI.* ii 5 123
Sad hours. Ay me! sad hours seem long — *Rom. and Jul.* i 1 167
Sad invention. If your love Can labour aught in sad invention, Hang her an epitaph — *Much Ado* v 1 292
Sad knot. Sitting, His arms in this sad knot — *Tempest* i 2 224
Sad looks. Counterfeit sad looks, Make mouths upon me — *M. N. Dream* iii 2 237
Sad Lucretia's modesty — *As Y. Like It* iii 2 156
Sad man. Know, thou sad man, I am not Tamora — *T. Andron.* v 2 28
Sad mischance. York's wife, and queen of sad mischance — *Richard III.* iv 4 114
Sad note. Play me that sad note I named my knell — *Hen. VIII.* iv 2 78
Sad occasion. I sent for thee upon a sad occasion — *T. Night* iii 4 20
Sad one. A stage where every man must play a part, And mine a sad one — *Mer. of Venice* i 1 79
Sad ostent. Well studied in a sad ostent To please his grandam — ii 2 205
Sad remembrance. Fresh And lasting in her sad remembrance — *T. Night* ii 1 32
So in the Lethe of thy angry soul Thou drown the sad remembrance of those wrongs — *Richard III.* iv 4 251
Sad sighs. Pure hands held up, Sad sighs, deep groans — *T. G. of Ver.* iii 1 230
Sad signs. Be these sad signs confirmers of thy words? — *K. John* iii 1 24
Sad steps. From your first of difference and decay, Have follow'd your sad steps — *Lear* v 3 289
Sad stop. Where did I leave?—At that sad stop, my lord — *Richard II.* v 2 4
Sad story. Sad stories of my own mishaps — *Com. of Errors* i 1 121
And tell sad stories of the death of kings — *Richard II.* iii 2 156
Told the sad story of my father's death — *Richard III.* i 2 161
Wept like two children in their deaths' sad stories — iv 3 8
Go read with thee Sad stories chanced in the times of old — *T. Andron.* iii 2 83
Sad tale. My death's sad tale may yet undeaf his ear — *Richard II.* ii 1 16
Sad talk. What sad talk was that? — *T. G. of Ver.* i 3 1
My father and the gentlemen are in sad talk — *W. Tale* iv 4 316
Sad tears. My heart's deep languor and my soul's sad tears — *T. Andron.* iii 1 13
Sad things. Go hence, to have more talk of these sad things — *R. and J.* v 3 307
Sad thoughts. Full of sad thoughts and troubles — *Hen. VIII.* ii 2 16
These sad thoughts, that work too much upon him — ii 2 58
Sad tidings bring I to you out of France — 1 *Hen. VI.* i 1 58
Sad time. The weight of this sad time we must obey — *Lear* v 3 323
In that sad time My manly eyes did scorn an humble tear — *Richard III.* i 2 164
Sad Titus. Marcus, my brother! 'tis sad Titus calls — *T. Andron.* v 2 121
Sad true lover. Lay me, O, where Sad true lover never find my grave, To weep there! — *T. Night* ii 4 66
Sad women. Tell these sad women 'Tis fond to wail inevitable strokes, As 'tis to laugh at 'em — *Coriolanus* iv 1 25
Sad wreck. What's thy interest In this sad wreck? — *Cymbeline* iv 2 366
Sadder. Are you sadder than you were before? — *T. G. of Ver.* iv 2 54
I am not as I have been.—So say I: methinks you are sadder — *Much Ado* iii 2 16
First were we sad, fearing you would not come; Now sadder, that you come so unprovided — *T. of Shrew* iii 2 101
Saddest. The wisest aunt, telling the saddest tale — *M. N. Dream* ii 1 51
The saddest spectacle that e'er I view'd — 3 *Hen. VI.* ii 1 67
Saddle. An old mothy saddle and stirrups of no kindred — *T. of Shrew* iii 2 49
Out of their saddles into the dirt — iv 1 59
Who is within there? Saddle my horse — *Richard II.* v 2 74
Tom, beat Cut's saddle, put a few flocks in the point — 1 *Hen. IV.* ii 1 6
Saving your manhoods—to buy a saddle — 2 *Hen. IV.* ii 1 29
Away, Bardolph! saddle my horse — v 3 128
By vaulting into my saddle with my armour on my back — *Hen. V.* v 2 143
Saddle white Surrey for the field to-morrow — *Richard III.* v 3 64
Darkness and devils! Saddle my horses — *Lear* i 4 274
Saddler. To pay the saddler for my mistress' crupper? The saddler had it, sir; I kept it not — *Com. of Errors* i 2 56
Sadly. Bound sadly home for Naples — *Tempest* i 2 235
When you looked sadly, it was for want of money — *T. G. of Ver.* ii 1 31
The conference was sadly borne — *Much Ado* ii 3 229
Wheresoe'er she is, Her heart weighs sadly — *All's Well* iii 5 70
Why dost thou look so sadly on my son? — *K. John* iii 1 20
March sadly after; grace my mournings here — *Richard II.* v 6 51
With his spirit sadly I survive — 2 *Hen. IV.* v 2 125
So part we sadly in this troublous world — 3 *Hen. VI.* v 5 7
The selfsame heaven That frowns on me looks sadly upon him — *Richard III.* v 3 287
Groan! why, no; But sadly tell me who — *Rom. and Jul.* i 1 207
When men come to borrow of your masters, they approach sadly, and go away merry; but they enter my mistress' house merrily, and go away sadly — *T. of Athens* ii 2 106
But, look, where sadly the poor wretch comes reading — *Hamlet* ii 2 168
Though he speak of comfort . . . , yet he looks sadly — *Othello* ii 1 32

Sadly. Why so sadly Greet you our victory? — *Cymbeline* v 5 23
Sitting sadly, Hearing us praise our loves of Italy — v 5 160
Sadness. In good sadness, sir, I am sorry that for my sake you have suffered all this — *Mer. Wives* iii 5 125
But is my husband coming?—Ay, in good sadness, is he — iv 2 93
Therefore the sadness is without limit — *Much Ado* i 3 4
He will look sad.—Why, sadness is one and the self-same thing — *L. L. Lost* i 2 4
How canst thou part sadness and melancholy? — i 2 7
Such a want-wit sadness makes of me — *Mer. of Venice* i 1 6
Being so full of unmannerly sadness in his youth — i 2 54
And there begins my sadness — *As Y. Like It* i 1 5
My often rumination wraps me in a most humorous sadness — iv 1 20
Seeing too much sadness hath congeal'd your blood — *T. of Shrew* Ind. 2 134
In good sadness, son Petruchio, I think thou hast the veriest shrew of all — v 2 63
In good sadness, I do not know — *All's Well* iv 3 230
This league that we have made Will give her sadness very little cure — *K. John* ii 1 546
Brothers, you mix your sadness with some fear — 2 *Hen. IV.* v 2 46
This merry inclination Accords not with the sadness of my suit — 3 *Hen. VI.* iii 2 77
Sorrow, that is couch'd in seeming gladness, Is like that mirth fate turns to sudden sadness — *Troi. and Cres.* i 1 40
What sadness lengthens Romeo's hours? — *Rom. and Jul.* i 1 169
Tell me in sadness, who is that you love.—What, shall I groan and tell thee? — i 1 205
Bid a sick man in sadness make his will — i 1 208
In sadness, cousin, I do love a woman.—I aim'd so near — i 1 210
Fell into a sadness, then into a fast, Thence to a watch — *Hamlet* ii 2 147
When he was here, He did incline to sadness — *Cymbeline* i 6 62
Tavern-bills; which are often the sadness of parting, as the procuring of mirth — v 4 162
Safe. But are they, Ariel, safe? — *Tempest* i 2 217
He's safe for these three hours — iii 1 21
Ay, but the doors be lock'd and keys kept safe — *T. G. of Ver.* iii 1 111
Heaven keep your honour safe! — *Meas. for Meas.* ii 2 157
By this Lord Angelo perceives he's safe — v 1 499
I greatly fear my money is not safe — *Com. of Errors* i 2 105
The gold I gave to Dromio is laid up Safe at the Centaur — ii 2 2
The duke's pleasure is, that you keep Costard safe — *L. L. Lost* i 2 133
I'll fear no other thing So sore as keeping safe Nerissa's ring — *Mer. of Ven.* v 1 307
Baptista is safe, talking with the deceiving father — *T. of Shrew* iv 4 82
Whilst thou liest warm at home, secure and safe — v 2 151
But hold himself safe in his prisonment — *K. John* iii 4 161
Let this be copied out, And keep it safe for our remembrance — v 2 2
All souls that will be safe fly from my side — *Richard II.* iii 2 80
Villain, I'll make thee safe.—Stay thy revengeful hand — v 3 41
To France shall we convey you safe, And bring you back — *Hen. V.* ii Prol. 37
Is the Duke of Exeter safe?—The Duke of Exeter is as magnanimous as Agamemnon; and a man that I love — iii 6 5
And where they would be safe, they perish — iv 1 182
He that outlives this day, and comes safe home, Will stand a tip-toe — iv 3 41
Heavens keep old Bedford safe! And now no more ado — 1 *Hen. VI.* iii 2 100
Set this diamond safe In golden palaces, as it becomes — v 3 169
And yet shalt thou be safe? such safety finds The trembling lamb environed with wolves — 3 *Hen. VI.* i 1 241
Knows not Montague that of itself England is safe, if true within itself? — iv 1 40
Yet will I keep thee safe, And they shall feel the vengeance of my wrath — iv 1 81
We are not safe, Clarence; we are not safe — *Richard III.* i 1 70
So 'twill do With some men else, who think themselves as safe As thou and I — iii 2 68
You sleeping safe, they bring to you unrest — v 3 320
Stanley living?—He is, my lord, and safe in Leicester town — v 5 10
See him safe i' the Tower — *Hen. VIII.* v 3 97
If e'er thou stand at mercy of my sword, Name Cressid, and thy life shall be as safe As Priam is in Ilion — *Troi. and Cres.* iv 4 117
The gods assist you!—And keep your honours safe! — *Coriolanus* i 2 37
And Rome Sits safe and still without him — iv 6 37
With my sword I'll keep this door safe — *T. Andron.* i 1 288
Safe out of fortune's shot — ii 1 2
Their mother's bed-chamber should not be safe For these bad bondmen — iv 1 108
This maugre all the world will I keep safe — iv 2 110
Save thou the child, so we may all be safe — iv 2 131
Then is all safe, the anchor's in the port — iv 4 38
Safe, Antony; Brutus is safe enough — *J. Cæsar* v 4 20
Keep this man safe; Give him all kindness — v 4 27
By doing every thing Safe toward your love and honour — *Macbeth* i 4 27
But Banquo's safe?—Ay, my good lord: safe in a ditch he bides — iii 4 25
I hope the days are near at hand That chambers will be safe — v 4 2
Nor stands it safe with us To let his madness range — *Hamlet* iii 3 1
Most holy and religious fear it is To keep those many many bodies safe That live and feed upon your majesty — iii 3 9
'Tis politic and safe to let him keep At point a hundred knights — *Lear* i 4 346
What will hap more to-night, safe 'scape the king! — iii 6 121
What safe and nicely I might well delay By rule of knighthood, I disdain and spurn — v 3 144
He looks sadly, And prays the Moor be safe — *Othello* ii 1 33
Take note, take note, O world, To be direct and honest is not safe — iii 3 378
Are his wits safe? is he not light of brain?—He's that he is — iv 1 280
My more particular, And that which most with you should safe my going, Is Fulvia's death — *Ant. and Cleo.* i 3 55
That thou depart'st hence safe, Does pay thy labour richly — iv 14 36
If knife, drugs, serpents, have Edge, sting, or operation, I am safe — iv 15 26
Whom in constancy you think stands so safe — *Cymbeline* i 4 138
Send your trunk to me; it shall safe be kept, And truly yielded you — i 6 209
Safe mayst thou wander, safe return again! — iii 5 105
My horse is tied up safe — iv 1 24
In our orbs we'll live so round and safe — *Pericles* i 2 122
That the ship Should house him safe is wreck'd and split — ii Gower 32
Safe and sound. I long that we were safe and sound aboard — *Com. of Er.* iv 4 154
Safe arrived. Soon and safe arrived where I was — iv 1 49
With uplifted arms is safe arrived — *Richard II.* ii 2 50
I would the friends we miss were safe arrived — *Macbeth* v 8 35
Safe conduct. Convey them with safe conduct — *Hen. V.* i 2 297
Procure safe-conduct for his person — *Troi. and Cres.* iii 3 277
Safe-conducting the rebels from their ships — *Richard III.* iv 4 483
Safe conscience. A trade, sir, that, I hope, I may use with a safe conscience — *J. Cæsar* i 1 14
Safe conveyed. See him safe convey'd Home to my house — *Com. of Errors* iv 4 125
Safe discretion. Nor do I think the man of safe discretion That does affect it — *Meas for Meas.* i 1 72

Safe means. By what safe means the crown may be recover'd 3 *Hen. VI.* iv 7 52
Safe off. If the dull brainless Ajax come safe off *Troi. and Cres.* i 3 381
Safe one. A sure and safe one, though thy master miss'd it *Hen. VIII.* iii 2 438
Safe place. Answer me In what safe place you have bestow'd my money *Com. of Errors* i 2 78
Safe reason. In all safe reason He must have some attendants *Cymbeline* iv 2 131
Safe redress. I had thought, by making this well known unto you, To have found a safe redress *Lear* i 4 225
Safe return. Gratulate his safe return to Rome *T. Andron.* i 1 221
Let there be impawn'd Some surety for a safe return again 1 *Hen. IV.* iv 3 109
Safe stowage. And I am something curious, being strange, To have them in safe stowage *Cymbeline* i 6 192
Safed. Best you safed the bringer Out of the host *Ant. and Cleo.* iv 6 26
Safeguard. Consenting to the safeguard of your honour *Meas. for Meas.* v 1 424
To safeguard thine own life, The best way is *Richard II.* i 2 35
We have locks to safeguard necessaries *Hen. V.* i 2 176
And doves will peck in safeguard of their brood 3 *Hen. VI.* ii 2 18
If you do fight in safeguard of your wives, Your wives shall welcome home the conquerors *Richard III.* v 3 259
On safe-guard he came to me *Coriolanus* iii 1 9
The inheritance of their loves and safeguard Of what that want might ruin iii 2 68
Safely. I have with such provision in mine art So safely ordered *Tempest* i 2 29
Safely in harbour Is the king's ship i 2 226
So, king, go safely on to seek thy son ii 1 327
We have safely found Our king and company v 1 221
I Costard, running out, that was safely within, Fell over the threshold, and broke my shin *L. L. Lost* iii 1 117
My ships Are safely come to road *Mer. of Venice* v 1 288
I'll keep him dark and safely lock'd *All's Well* iv 1 104
I was thinking with what manners I might safely be admitted iv 5 94
Be it your charge To keep him safely till his day of trial *Richard II.* iv 1 153
God, and not we, hath safely fought to-day 2 *Hen. IV.* iv 2 121
Had all your quarters been as safely kept 1 *Hen. VI.* ii 1 63
See them guarded And safely brought to Dover v 1 49
I charge thee waft me safely cross the Channel 2 *Hen. VI.* iv 1 114
For how can tyrants safely govern home, Unless abroad they purchase great alliance? 3 *Hen. VI.* iii 3 69
God safely quit her of her burthen! *Hen. VIII.* v 1 70
And the strong course of my authority Might go one way, and safely v 3 36
We'll put you ... in manacles, Then reason safely with you *Coriolanus* i 9 58
Has cluck'd thee to the wars and safely home, Loaden with honour v 3 163
If Brutus will vouchsafe that Antony May safely come to him *J. Cæsar* iii 1 131
To be thus is nothing; But to be safely thus *Macbeth* iii 1 49
Safely stowed *Hamlet* iv 2 1
Subscribed it, gave't the impression, placed it safely v 2 52
Letting go safely by The divine Desdemona *Othello* ii 1 72
Can we, with manners, ask what was the difference?—Safely, I think *Cymbeline* i 4 58
And would so, had it been a carbuncle Of Phœbus' wheel, and might so safely, had it been all the worth of's car v 5 190
O, that the gods Would safely deliver me from this place! *Pericles* iv 6 191
Safer. He bade me store up, as a triple eye, Safer than mine own two, more dear *All's Well* ii 1 112
'Tis safer to Avoid what's grown than question how 'tis born *W. Tale* i 2 432
Nor shall you be safer Than one condemn'd by the king's own mouth i 2 444
Thou mayst hold a serpent by the tongue, A chafed lion by the mortal paw, A fasting tiger safer by the tooth *K. John* iii 1 260
Let him shun castles; Safer shall he be upon the sandy plains 2 *Hen. VI.* i 4 39
The safer when 'tis back'd with France 3 *Hen. VI.* iv 1 41
Blind fear, that seeing reason leads, finds safer footing than blind reason stumbling without fear *Troi. and Cres.* iii 2 77
And on a safer judgement all revoke Your ignorant election *Coriolanus* ii 3 226
But safer triumph is this funeral pomp *T. Andron.* i 1 176
Without knives; Good for their meat, and safer for their lives *T. of A.* i 2 46
Our separated fortune Shall keep us both the safer *Macbeth* ii 3 145
'Tis safer to be that which we destroy Than by destruction dwell in doubtful joy iii 2 6
You may fear too far.—Safer than trust too far *Lear* i 4 351
The safer sense will ne'er accommodate His master thus iv 6 81
Yet opinion, a sovereign mistress of effects, throws a more safer voice on you *Othello* i 3 226
Now, by heaven, My blood begins my safer guides to rule ii 3 205
Often, to our comfort, shall we find The sharded beetle in a safer hold Than is the full-wing'd eagle *Cymbeline* iii 3 20
Safest. Dispatch you with your safest haste *As Y. Like It* i 3 43
Devise the fittest time and safest way To hide us from pursuit i 3 137
And, Parolles, live Safest in shame! *All's Well* iv 3 374
How will she specify Where is the best and safest passage in? 1 *Hen. VI.* ii 2 22
Her life is only safest in her birth *Richard III.* iv 4 213
Our safest way Is to avoid the aim *Macbeth* ii 3 148
To take the safest occasion by the front To bring you in again *Othello* iii 1 52
Safeties. I pray you, Let not my jealousies be your dishonours, But mine own safeties *Macbeth* iv 3 30
Safety. Will guard your person while you take your rest, And watch your safety *Tempest* ii 1 198
The heavens give safety to your purposes! *Meas. for Meas.* i 1 74
You shall find Your safety manifested iv 3 94
As this is true, Let me in safety raise me from my knees! v 1 231
The sailors sought for safety by our boat, And left the ship *Com. of Er.* i 1 77
And the owner of it blest Ever shall in safety rest *M. N. Dream* v 1 427
No further in sport neither than with safety of a pure blush *As Y. L. It* i 2 31
Embrace your own safety and give over this attempt i 2 189
Running away, when fear proposes the safety *All's Well* i 1 217
Unless you undertake that with me which with as much safety you might answer him *T. Night* iii 4 273
I cannot pursue with any safety this sport to the upshot iv 2 76
I must have done no less with wit and safety v 1 218
Didst counsel and aid them, for their better safety, to fly *W. Tale* ii 2 21
My arrival and my wife's in safety v 1 167
Thou Fortune's champion that dost never fight But when her humourous ladyship is by To teach thee safety! *K. John* iii 1 120
Her highness is in safety, fear you not iii 2 8
I will pray, If ever I remember to be holy, For your fair safety iii 3 16
He that steeps his safety in true blood Shall find but bloody safety iii 4 148
Both for myself and them, but, chief of all, Your safety iv 2 50
Deliver him to safety iv 2 158
It is our safety, and we must embrace This gentle offer v 3 12
To seek sweet safety out In vaults and prisons v 2 142
Tendering the precious safety of my prince *Richard II.* i 1 32
Safety. Out of this nettle, danger, we pluck this flower, safety 1 *Hen. IV.* ii 3 11
And shake the peace and safety of our throne iii 2 117
And in conclusion drove us to seek out This head of safety iv 3 103
With nimble wing We were enforced, for safety sake, to fly v 1 65
What I have done my safety urged me to; And I embrace this fortune v 5 11
Covert enmity Under the smile of safety wounds the world 2 *Hen. IV.* Ind. 10
That arrows fled not swifter toward their aim Than did our soldiers, aiming at their safety i 1 124
Counsel every man The aptest way for safety and revenge i 1 213
Crowd us and crush us to this monstrous form, To hold our safety up iv 2 35
Like a rich armour worn in heat of day, That scalds with safety iv 5 31
And blunt the sword That guards the peace and safety of your person v 2 88
But we our kingdom's safety must so tender, Whose ruin you have sought, that to her laws We do deliver you *Hen. V.* ii 2 175
I would give all my fame for a pot of ale and safety iii 2 14
Give us leave, great king, To view the field in safety iv 7 85
And for his safety there I'll best devise 1 *Hen. VI.* i 1 172
I tender so the safety of my liege 2 *Hen. VI.* iii 1 277
I know our safety is to follow them v 3 23
Such safety finds The trembling lamb environed with wolves 3 *Hen. VI.* i 1 241
For strength and safety of our country iii 3 211
In them and in ourselves our safety lies iv 1 46
We were forewarned of your coming, And shut the gates for safety iv 7 18
Hath pass'd in safety through the narrow seas iv 8 3
Tendering my person's safety, hath appointed This conduct *Richard III.* i 1 44
The peace of England and our persons' safety Enforced us to this execution iii 5 45
Only in that safety died her brothers iv 4 214
A heart that wishes towards you Honour and plenteous safety *Hen. VIII.* i 1 104
Make use now, and provide For thine own future safety iii 2 421
In her days every man shall eat in safety, Under his own vine v 5 34
The gods with safety stand about thee! *Troi. and Cres.* v 3 94
The honour'd gods Keep Rome in safety! *Coriolanus* iii 3 34
Now talk at pleasure of your safety *T. Andron.* iv 2 134
If he stand on hostage for his safety, Bid him demand what pledge will please him best iv 4 105
Hold him in safety *Rom. and Jul.* v 3 183
It cannot hold; no reason Can found his state in safety *T. of Athens* ii 1 13
All thy safety were remotion and thy defence absence iv 3 345
Here is a mourning Rome, a dangerous Rome, No Rome of safety *J. C.* iii 1 289
He hath a wisdom that doth guide his valour To act in safety *Macbeth* iii 1 54
On his choice depends The safety and health of this whole state *Hamlet* i 3 21
Be wary then; best safety lies in fear i 3 43
On such regards of safety and allowance As therein are set down ii 2 79
For thine especial safety,—Which we do tender, as we dearly grieve For that which thou hast done iv 3 42
As by your safety, wisdom, all things else, You mainly were stirr'd up iv 7 8
Thy safety being the motive *Lear* i 1 159
As we shall find their merits and our safety May equally determine v 3 44
I do know, the state, However this may gall him with some check, Cannot with safety cast him *Othello* i 1 150
To manage private and domestic quarrel, In night, and on the court and guard of safety! 'Tis monstrous ii 3 216
Something you can deny for your own safety *Ant. and Cleo.* ii 6 96
Of Cæsar seek your honour, with your safety. O!—They do not go together iv 15 46
The worthy Leonatus is in safety *Cymbeline* i 6 12
And pawn mine honour for their safety i 6 194
Saffron. Who with thy saffron wings upon my flowers Diffusest honey-drops, refreshing showers *Tempest* iv 1 78
This companion with the saffron face *Com. of Errors* iv 4 64
Whose villanous saffron would have made all the unbaked and doughy youth of a nation in his colour *All's Well* iv 5 2
I must have saffron to colour the warden pies *W. Tale* iv 3 48
Sag. The heart I bear Shall never sag with doubt nor shake with fear *Macbeth* v 3 10
Sage. We'll whisper o'er a couplet or two of most sage saws *T. Night* iii 4 413
All you sage counsellors, hence! 2 *Hen. IV.* iv 5 121
Enough to deceive de most sage demoiselle dat is en France *Hen. V.* v 2 234
And you sage, grave men *Richard III.* iii 7 227
How's this? how's this? Some more; be sage *Pericles* iv 6 102
Sagittary. The dreadful Sagittary Appals our numbers *Troi. and Cres.* v 5 14
Lead to the Sagittary the raised search *Othello* i 1 159
Send for the lady to the Sagittary, And let her speak of me before her father i 3 115
Said. She said thou wast my daughter *Tempest* i 2 57
Widow Dido!—What if he had said 'widower Æneas' too? ii 1 79
How you take it!—'Widow Dido' said you? you make me study of that ii 1 81
For it hath been said, ... and it shall be said so again ii 1 63
Why, I said nothing.—Mum, then, and no more iii 2 58
Thou hast said well; for some of you there present Are worse than devils iii 3 35
At which time, my lord, You said our work should cease v 1 5
But what said she?—Ay.—Nod—Ay—why, that's noddy *T. G. of Ver.* i 1 117
What said she?—Truly, sir, I think you'll hardly win her i 1 140
What said she? nothing?—No, not so much as 'Take this for thy pains' i 1 150
For all these exercises He said that Proteus your son was meet i 3 12
You have said, sir.—Ay, sir, and done too, for this time ii 4 29
Hide what I have said to thee iv 3 35
He's a good dog, and a fair dog: can there be more said? *Mer. Wives* i 1 99
Said I, 'will you cast away your child on a fool, and a physician?' iii 4 99
Find a maid That, ere she sleep, has thrice her prayers said v 5 54
I think thou never wast where grace was said *Meas. for Meas.* i 2 20
Say that I said so. Farewell iii 2 195
Vail your regard Upon a wrong'd, I would fain have said, a maid! v 1 21
Here's a gentlewoman denies all that you have said v 1 283
Do you remember what you said of the duke?—Most notedly, sir v 1 334
Thou art said to have a stubborn soul v 1 485
Your highness said even now, I made you a duke v 1 521
Then pleaded I for you.—And what said he? *Com. of Errors* iv 2 11
Though I cannot be said to be a flattering honest man *Much Ado* i 3 32
For it is said, 'God sends a curst cow short horns' ii 1 24
When I said I would die a bachelor, I did not think I should live till I were married ii 3 251
I might have said 'No part of it is mine' iv 1 136
I said, thou hadst a fine wit: 'True,' said she, 'a fine little one.' 'No,' said I, 'a great wit' v 1 161
Said I, 'a good wit:' 'Just,' said she, 'it hurts nobody.' 'Nay,' said I, 'the gentleman is wise:' 'Certain,' said she, 'a wise gentleman.' 'Nay,' said I, 'he hath the tongues:' 'That I believe,' said she v 1 164

Said. For the which she wept heartily and said she cared not *Much Ado* v 1 176
Never flout at me for what I have said against it v 4 109
I said the deer was not a haud credo; 'twas a pricket *L. L. Lost* iv 2 21
Set thee down, sorrow! for so they say the fool said, and so say I. iv 3 5
Our parson misdoubts it; 'twas treason, he said iv 3 194
Therefore is Love said to be a child *M. N. Dream* i 1 238
Then how can it be said I am alone, When all the world is here? ii 1 225
As may well be said Becomes a virtuous bachelor and a maid ii 2 58
This is he, my master said, Despised the Athenian maid. ii 2 72
Methought you said you neither lend nor borrow Upon advantage *Mer. of Venice* i 3 70
'Who chooseth me shall get as much as he deserves:' And well said too ii 9 37
Said with weeping tears, 'Wear these for my sake' *As Y. Like It* ii 4 53
You have said; but whether wisely or no, let the forest judge iii 2 129
What did he when thou sawest him? What said he? How looked he? iii 2 233
What they swear in poetry may be said as lovers they do feign iii 3 21
It is said, 'many a man knows no end of his goods' iii 3 53
He said mine eyes were black and my hair black iii 5 130
It may be said of him that Cupid hath clapped him o' the shoulder iv 1 47
If I said his beard was not cut well, he was in the mind it was v 4 74
One of them thought but of an If, as, 'If you said so, then I said so' v 4 106
That I may soon make good What I have said *T. of Shrew* i 1 75
So said, so done, is well i 2 186
What will be said? what mockery will it be? iii 2 4
What said the wench when he rose again?—Trembled and shook iii 2 168
To satisfy you in what I have said, Stand by and mark iv 2 4
The note lies in's throat, if he say I said so iv 3 134
There's little can be said in't; 'tis against the rule of nature *All's Well* i 1 147
When I said 'a mother,' Methought you saw a serpent i 3 146
Just, you say well; so would I have said ii 3 21
That's it; I would have said the very same ii 3 29
Generally thankful.—I would have said it; you say well ii 3 45
What should be said? If thou canst like this creature as a maid ii 3 148
You should have said, sir, before a knave thou'rt a knave ii 4 29
Five or six thousand horse, I said,—I will say true,—or thereabouts iv 3 170
Methought you said You saw one here in court could witness it v 3 199
What is to be said to him, lady? he's fortified against any denial *T. Night* i 5 153
A comfortable doctrine, and much may be said of it. Where lies your text? i 5 240
It was said she much resembled me ii 1 26
You have said, sir. To see this age! iii 1 12
What can be said? Nothing that can be can come between me iii 4 89
I have said too much unto a heart of stone iii 4 221
To be said an honest man and a good housekeeper iv 2 10
Very wittily said to a niece of King Gorboduc, 'That that is is' iv 2 16
Thou hast said to me a thousand times v 1 274
Have I twice said well? when was't before? *W. Tale* i 2 90
When you have said, 'she's goodly,' come between Ere you can say, 'she's honest' ii 1 75
I have said She's an adulteress; I have said with whom ii 1 87
But the last,—O lords, When I have said, cry 'woe!' iii 2 201
How often said, my dignity would last But till 'twere known! iv 4 486
Has not the divine Apollo said, Is't not the tenour of his oracle? v 1 37
You yourself Have said and writ so, but your writing now Is colder v 1 99
And have in vain said many A prayer upon her grave v 3 140
Have I not ever said How that ambitious Constance would not cease? *K. John* i 1 31
If thou hadst said him nay, it had been sin: Who says it was, he lies i 1 275
When I have said, make answer to us both ii 1 235
Fright him there? and make him tremble there? O, let it not be said v 1 59
No, no, on my soul, it never shall be said v 2 108
Who was he that said King John did fly an hour or two before? v 5 16
What said our cousin when you parted with him?—'Farewell' *Rich. II.* i 4 10
All is said: His tongue is now a stringless instrument ii 1 148
Thou hast said enough iii 2 203
Comprising all that may be sworn or said iii 3 111
I say, thou liest, And will maintain what thou hast said is false iv 1 27
That all the walls With painted imagery had said at once 'Jesu preserve thee!' v 2 16
More is to be said and to be done Than out of anger can be uttered *1 Hen. IV.* i 1 106
Said To such a person and in such a place, At such a time i 3 71
Four, Hal; I told thee four.—Ay, ay, he said four ii 4 221
Said he would swear truth out of England but he would make you believe it ii 4 337
So I told him, my lord; and I said I heard your grace say so iii 3 120
And said he would cudgel you.—What! he did not? iii 3 123
He called you Jack, and said he would cudgel you iii 3 159
Indeed, Sir John, you said so.—Yea, if he said my ring was copper iii 3 161
They did me too much injury That ever said I hearken'd for your death v 4 52
Ha! Again: Said he young Harry Percy's spur was cold? *2 Hen. IV.* i 1 49
And summ'd the account of chance, before you said, 'Let us make head' i 1 167
He said, sir, the water itself was a good healthy water i 2 3
My soldiership aside, I had lied in my throat, if I had said so i 2 94
As I am a gentleman.—Faith, you said so before ii 1 149
God send the wench no worse fortune! But I never said so ii 2 153
Putting off his hat, said 'I will now take my leave' ii 4 7
Said he, 'you are in an ill name:' now a' said so, I can tell whereupon ii 4 97
You would bless you to hear what he said ii 4 103
Yes, that a' did; and said they were devils incarnate *Hen. V.* ii 3 33
A' said once, the devil would have him about women ii 3 37
And a' said it was a black soul burning in hell-fire ii 3 43
Ill will never said well iii 7 123
Ay, he said so, to make us fight cheerfully iv 1 204
They have said their prayers, and they stay for death iv 2 56
I said so, dear Katharine; and I must not blush to affirm it v 2 116
Here, said they, is the terror of the French, The scarecrow *1 Hen. VI.* i 4 42
That shall maintain what I have said is true ii 4 73
Must hold his tongue, Lest it be said 'Speak, sirrah, when you should' iii 1 62
My father said A stouter champion never handled sword iii 4 20
Once I encounter'd him, and thus I said iv 7 37
'Tis said the stout Parisians do revolt And turn again v 2 2
That my master was? no, forsooth: my master said that he was *2 Hen. VI.* i 3 34
I never said nor thought any such matter: God is my witness i 3 191
Ask what thou wilt. That I had said and done! i 4 31
Had I but said, I would have kept my word, But when I swear, it is irrevocable iii 2 293
And yet it is said, labour in thy vocation iv 2 17
It shall ne'er be said, while England stands iv 10 45

Said. You said so much before, and yet you fled *3 Hen. VI.* ii 2 106
'Tis better said than done, my gracious lord iii 2 90
What said Lady Bona to my marriage?—These were her words iv 1 97
But what said Henry's queen? For I have heard that she was there in place iv 1 102
Remain the Duke of York.—I thought, at least, he would have said the king v 1 29
And more he would have said, and more he spoke v 2 43
Imagine I have said farewell already *Richard III.* i 2 225
What I have said I will avouch in presence of the king i 3 114
He rescued me, And said, 'Dear brother, live, and be a king' ii 1 113
O, my lord, You said that idle weeds are fast in growth iii 1 103
More than I have said, loving countrymen, The leisure and enforcement of the time Forbids to dwell upon v 3 237
He said the truth: and what said Surrey then?—He smiled and said 'The better for our purpose' v 3 273
Being present both, 'Twas said they saw but one *Hen. VIII.* i 1 32
It's long and, 't may be said, It reaches far i 1 110
No doubt he's noble; He had a black mouth that said other of him i 3 58
You have said well.—And ever may your highness yoke together, As I will lend you cause, my doing well With my well saying! iii 2 149
'Tis well said again; And 'tis a kind of good deed to say well iii 2 152
My father loved you: He said he did; and with his deed did crown His word iii 2 155
Surrey durst better Have burnt that tongue than said so iii 2 254
To pray for her? what, is she crying out?—So said her woman v 1 68
Avoid the gallery. Ha! I have said. Be gone v 1 86
I fear nothing What can be said against me v 1 126
Said I for this, the girl was like to him? I will have more, or else unsay't v 1 174
Who said he came hurt home to-day? he's not hurt *Troi. and Cres.* i 2 232
You have both said well ii 2 163
I have said my prayers and devil Envy say Amen ii 3 22
'Tis said he holds you well, and will be led At your request ii 3 190
When they've said, 'as false As air, as water, wind, or sandy earth' iii 2 198
I said 'Good morrow, Ajax;' and he replies 'Thanks, Agamemnon' iii 3 261
I have said to some my standers by 'Lo, Jupiter is yonder, dealing life!' iv 5 190
Now she sharpens: well said, whetstone! v 2 75
Hang 'em! They said they were an-hungry *Coriolanus* i 1 209
Said to be something imperfect in favouring the first complaint ii 1 53
He said he had wounds, which he could show in private ii 3 174
You should have said That as his worthy deeds did claim no less ii 3 193
Thus to have said, As you were fore-advised ii 3 198
Has said enough.—Has spoken like a traitor, and shall answer As traitors do iii 1 161
In a better hour, Let what is meet be said it must be meet iii 1 170
There's no more to be said, but he is banish'd, As enemy to the people iii 3 117
War, in some sort, may be said to be a ravisher iv 5 243
For mine own part, When I said, banish him, I said, 'twas pity iv 6 140
I ever said we were i' the wrong when we banished him iv 6 155
You hear what he hath said Which was sometime his general v 1 1
He said 'twas folly, For one poor grain or two, to leave unburnt v 1 26
Very faintly he said 'Rise;' dismiss'd me Thus, with his speechless hand v 1 66
I say to you, as I was said to, Away! v 2 114
No more! You have said you will not grant us any thing v 3 87
To wait upon this new-made empress. To wait, said I? *T. Andron.* ii 1 20
Now would she say That to her brother which I said to thee iii 1 145
Two may keep counsel when the third's away: Go to the empress, tell her this I said iv 2 145
What say you to my suit?—But saying o'er what I have said before *Rom. and Jul.* i 2 7
By my holidame, The pretty wretch left crying and said 'Ay' i 3 44
The county will be here with music straight, For so he said he would iv 4 22
To myself I said, 'An if a man did need a poison now' v 1 49
What said my man, when my betossed soul Did not attend him as we rode? v 3 76
Said he not so? or did I dream it so? Or am I mad? v 3 79
Heavens, have I said, the bounty of this lord! *T. of Athens* ii 2 173
Let the request be fifty talents.—As you have said, my lord ii 2 203
True, as you said, Timon is shrunk indeed iii 2 68
'Tis said he gave unto his steward a mighty sum v 1 8
Cæsar said to me 'Darest thou, Cassius, now Leap in with me into this angry flood, And swim to yonder point?' *J. Cæsar* i 2 102
What you have said I will consider i 2 167
What said he when he came unto himself? i 2 264
He said, If he had done or said any thing amiss, he desired their worships to think it was his infirmity i 2 272
It shall be said, his judgement ruled our hands iii 1 147
Remember What you have said, and show yourselves true Romans iii 1 223
I said, an elder soldier, not a better: Did I say 'better'? iv 3 56
You said the enemy would not come down, But keep the hills v 1 2
Much drink may be said to be an equivocator with lechery *Macbeth* ii 3 34
'Tis said they eat each other.—They did so, to the amazement of mine eyes ii 4 18
Yet it was said It should not stand in thy posterity iii 1 3
This is the air-drawn dagger which, you said, Led you to Duncan iii 4 62
My wife kill'd too?—I have said iv 3 213
Remember well What I have said to you.—'Tis in my memory lock'd *Ham.* i 3 85
What is't, Ophelia, he hath said to you? i 3 88
What said he?—He took me by the wrist and held me hard ii 1 86
Hath there been such a time—I'd fain know that—That I have positively said 'Tis so,' When it proved otherwise? ii 2 154
He said I was a fishmonger: he is far gone, far gone ii 2 190
Why did you laugh then, when I said 'man delights not me?' ii 2 326
One said there were no sallets in the lines to make the matter savoury ii 2 462
You need not tell us what Lord Hamlet said; We heard it all iii 1 187
By and by is easily said iii 2 404
And, as you said, and wisely was it said iii 3 30
I have no life to breathe What thou hast said to me iii 4 199
That justly think'st, and hast most rightly said *Lear* i 1 186
Have you nothing said Upon his party? ii 1 27
What, must I come to you With five and twenty, Regan? said you so? ii 4 257
He said it would be thus, poor banish'd man! iii 4 169
Thou shouldst have said, 'Good porter, turn the key' iii 7 64
To say 'ay' and 'no' to every thing that I said! iv 6 101
O, she deceives me Past thought! What said she to you? *Othello* i 1 167
Fled from her wish and yet said 'Now I may' ii 1 152
Nor know I aught By me that's said or done amiss this night ii 3 201
What, If I had said I had seen him do you wrong? Or heard him say iv 1 24
Hath he said any thing?—He hath, my lord; but be you well assured, No more than he'll unswear.—What hath he said? iv 1 29

Said. You have said now.—Ay, and said nothing but what I protest intendment of doing . . . . . . *Othello* iv 2 204
I call'd my love false love; but what said he then? . . . iv 3 55
I have heard it said so. O, these men, these men! . . . iv 3 60
You heard her say herself, it was not I.—She said so . . v 2 128
What shall be said to thee?—Why, any thing: An honourable murderer v 2 293
Give me particulars.—I have said . . . . *Ant. and Cleo.* i 2 58
I was green in judgement: cold in blood, To say as I said then! . i 5 75
You have well deserved ten times as much As I have said you did ii 6 80
He cannot weep't back again.—You've said, sir . . . ii 6 113
Make me not offended In your distrust.—I have said . . iii 2 34
Let me say, Before I strike this bloody stroke, farewell.—'Tis said, man iv 14 92
I swear I love you.—If you but said so, 'twere as deep with me *Cymb.* ii 3 96
Ay, I said so, sir: If you will make't an action, call witness to't . ii 3 155
She gave it me, and said She prized it once . . . ii 4 103
She said upon a time—the bitterness of it I now belch from my heart . iii 5 137
'Tis said a woman's fitness comes by fits . . . . iv 1 6
He said he was gentle, but unfortunate; Dishonestly afflicted, but yet honest . . . . iv 2 39
I ha' strew'd his grave, And on it said a century of prayers . iv 2 391
Said not I as much when I saw the porpus how he bounced? . *Pericles* ii 1 25
My friend; you said you could not beg.—I did but crave . ii 1 89
And it is said For certain in our story . . . iv Gower 18
Remember what I have said.—I warrant you, madam . . . iv 1 47
My father, as nurse said, did never fear, But cried 'Good seamen!' . iv 1 53
What say you?—I said, my lord, if you did know my parentage . v 1 100
Some such thing I said, and said no more but what my thoughts Did warrant me was likely . . . . v 1 134
You said you would believe me . . . . . . v 1 152
As I (have) said *Meas. for Meas.* ii 1; *All's Well* v 3; *W. Tale* i 1; *Richard II.* v 2; 1 *Hen. IV.* i 3; *Hen. V.* i 2; *Rom. and Jul.* i 3; *Cymbeline* iii 1
As I said before . . . . . . *Ant. and Cleo.* ii 6 136
I have heard it said *W. Tale* iv 4; 1 *Hen. VI.* ii 2; *Coriolanus* iv 3
Said I well? *Mer. Wives* i 3; ii 1; ii 3; 2 *Hen. IV.* iii 2
So 'tis said . . . . . . *W. Tale* iv 4 793; *T. of Athens* v 1 81
That's well said *Meas. for Meas.* ii 2; 1 *Hen. IV.* i 2; 2 *Hen. IV.* ii 4; 2 *Hen. VI.* ii 1; iii 2; *Othello* v 1
Well said (occurs throughout the plays)
Said Henry. The said Henry shall espouse the Lady Margaret 2 *Hen. VI.* i 1 46
Saidest. What, four? thou saidst but two even now . . 1 *Hen. IV.* ii 4 218
That said'st I begg'd the empire at thy hands . . . *T. Andron.* i 1 307
Thou said'st—O, it comes o'er my memory, . . . he had my handkerchief . . . . *Othello* iv 1 20
I think thou said'st Thou hadst been toss'd from wrong to injury *Pericles* v 1 130
Sail. Not rigg'd, Nor tackle, sail, nor mast . . . *Tempest* i 2 147
Auspicious gales And sail so expeditious . . . . . v 1 315
Gentle breath of yours my sails Must fill, or else my project fails . Epil. 11
Sail like my pinnace to these golden shores . . . *Mer. Wives* i 3 89
Clap on more sails; pursue; up with your fights: Give fire . . ii 2 142
Had not their bark been very slow of sail . . . *Com. of Errors* i 1 117
Had hoisted sail and put to sea . . . . v 1 21
The ship is under sail, and here she comes amain . . *L. L. Lost* v 2 549
When the false Troyan under sail was seen . . *M. N. Dream* i 1 174
When we have laugh'd to see the sails conceive And grow big-bellied ii 1 128
Would imitate, and sail upon the land . . . . . ii 1 132
Your argosies with portly sail, Like signiors and rich burghers *M. of V.* i 1 9
With over-weather'd ribs and ragged sails . . . . ii 6 18
I desire no more delight Than to be under sail and gone to-night . ii 6 68
I saw Bassanio under sail . . . . ii 8 1
He came too late, the ship was under sail . . . . . ii 8 6
Will you hoist sail, sir? here lies your way . . . *T. Night* i 5 215
A whole armado of convicted sail Is scatter'd . . . *K. John* iii 4 2
And, like a shifted wind unto a sail, It makes the course of thoughts to fetch about . . . . iv 2 23
All the shrouds wherewith my life should sail Are turned to one thread v 7 53
We see the wind sit sore upon our sails, And yet we strike not *Rich. II.* ii 1 265
How many nobles then should hold their places, That must strike sail to spirits of vile sort! . . . . . . 2 *Hen. IV.* v 2 18
The threaden sails, Borne with the invisible and creeping wind *Hen. V.* iii Prol. 10
As doth a sail, fill'd with a fretting gust, Command an argosy 3 *Hen. VI.* ii 6 35
Now Margaret Must strike her sail and learn awhile to serve . . iii 3 5
I had rather chop this hand off at a blow, And with the other fling it at thy face, Than bear so low a sail, to strike to thee . . . v 1 52
Sail how thou canst, have wind and tide thy friend . . . v 1 53
Like a poor bark, of sails and tackling reft, Rush all to pieces *Rich. III.* iv 4 233
He, mistrusting them, Hoised sail and made away for Brittany . iv 4 529
The sea being smooth, How many shallow bauble boats dare sail Upon her patient breast! . . . . . . *Troi. and Cres.* i 3 35
Your breath of full consent bellied his sails . . . . ii 2 74
Light boats sail swift, though greater hulks draw deep . . ii 3 277
As weeds before A vessel under sail, so men obey'd . . *Coriolanus* ii 2 110
But He, that hath the steerage of my course, Direct my sail! *R. and J.* i 4 113
He bestrides the lazy-pacing clouds And sails upon the bosom of the air ii 2 32
Here's goodly gear!—A sail, a sail!—Two, two; a shirt and a smock ii 4 108
But in a sieve I'll thither sail, And, like a rat without a tail, I'll do, I'll do, and I'll do . . . . *Macbeth* i 3 8
The wind sits in the shoulder of your sail, And you are stay'd for *Hamlet* i 3 56
Finding ourselves too slow of sail, we put on a compelled valour . iv 6 17
And yet but yaw neither, in respect of his quick sail . . . v 2 120
How many, as you guess?—Of thirty sail . . . . *Othello* i 3 37
I cannot, 'twixt the heaven and the main, Descry a sail . . ii 1 4
A sail, a sail, a sail! . . . . ii 1 51
On the brow o' the sea Stand ranks of people, and they cry 'A sail!' . ii 1 54
Great Jove, Othello guard, And swell his sail with thine own powerful breath! . . . . ii 1 78
But, hark! a sail.—A sail, a sail! . . . . . . ii 1 93
My boat sails freely, both with wind and stream . . . ii 3 65
Here is my butt, And very sea-mark of my utmost sail . . . v 2 268
Purple the sails, and so perfumed that The winds were love-sick *A. and C.* ii 2 198
Take your time.—Thou canst not fear us, Pompey, with thy sails . ii 6 24
I have sixty sails, Cæsar none better.—Our overplus of shipping will we burn . . . . iii 7 50
The breese upon her, like a cow in June, Hoists sails and flies . iii 10 15
My lord, Forgive my fearful sails! I little thought You would have follow'd . . . . iii 11 55
Swallows have built In Cleopatra's sails their nests . . . iv 12 4
I would thou grew'st unto the shores o' the haven, And question'dst every sail: if he should write . . . . . *Cymbeline* i 3 2
Winds of all the corners kiss'd your sails, To make your vessel nimble . ii 4 28
Sail. That horse and sail and high expense Can stead the quest *Pericles* iii Gower 20
Sail seas in cockles, have an wish but for't . . . . iv 4 2
Toward Ephesus Turn our blown sails . . . . . v 1 256
In feather'd briefness sails are fill'd . . . . . v 2 280
Sailed. A league from Epidamnum had we sail'd . . *Com. of Errors* i 1 63
And you are now sailed into the north of my lady's opinion *T. Night* iii 2 28
How slow his soul sail'd on, How swift his ship . . *Cymbeline* i 3 13
Sailing. There's no more sailing by the star . . . *Much Ado* iii 4 58
This sailing Pandar Our doubtful hope, our convoy . *Troi. and Cres.* i 1 106
The bark thy body is, Sailing in this salt flood . . *Rom. and Jul.* iii 5 135
Sail-maker. He is a sail-maker in Bergamo . . . *T. of Shrew* v 1 80
Sail of greatness. I will keep my state, Be like a king and show my sail of greatness . . . . *Hen. V.* i 2 274
Sail of ships. A portly sail of ships make hitherward . . *Pericles* i 4 61
Sailor. And here was left by the sailors . . . . *Tempest* i 2 270
Every day some sailor's wife, The masters of some merchant and the merchant, Have just our theme of woe . . . . . . ii 1 4
She had a tongue with a tang, Would cry to a sailor, Go hang! . ii 2 53
I escaped upon a butt of sack which the sailors heaved o'erboard . ii 2 127
The sailors sought for safety by our boat, And left the ship *Com. of Er.* i 1 77
Ships are but boards, sailors but men . . . *Mer. of Venice* i 3 23
I spoke with some of the sailors that escaped the wreck . . iii 1 109
Perchance he is not drown'd: what think you, sailors? . *T. Night* i 2 5
They have been grand-jurymen since before Noah was a sailor . iii 2 18
I'll drown more sailors than the mermaid shall . 3 *Hen. VI.* iii 2 186
Half our sailors swallow'd in the flood? Yet lives our pilot still . v 4 5
Lives like a drunken sailor on a mast, Ready, with every nod, to tumble down Into the fatal bowels of the deep . *Richard III.* iii 4 101
He would pun thee into shivers with his fist, as a sailor breaks a biscuit.—You whoreson cur! . . . *Troi. and Cres.* ii 1 43
A sailor's wife had chestnuts in her lap, And munch'd, and munch'd *Macb.* i 3 4
What are they that would speak with me?—Sailors, sir . *Hamlet* iv 6 2
Who brought them?—Sailors, my lord . . . . . iv 7 39
To commix With winds that sailors rail at . . . *Cymbeline* iv 2 56
Cried 'Good seamen!' to the sailors, galling His kingly hands *Pericles* iv 1 54
Sain. An epilogue or discourse, to make plain Some obscure precedence that hath tofore been sain . . . . . *L. L. Lost* iii 1 83
Saint. And is she not a heavenly saint? . . . . *T. G. of Ver.* ii 4 145
To be talk'd with in sincerity, As with a saint . *Meas. for Meas.* i 4 37
Great men may jest with saints; 'tis wit in them . . . ii 2 127
O cunning enemy, that, to catch a saint, With saints dost bait thy hook! ii 2 180
By the saint whom I profess, I will plead against it with my life . iv 2 192
Though they would swear down each particular saint . . . v 1 243
Teach sin the carriage of a holy saint; Be secret-false *Com. of Errors* iii 2 14
I conjure thee by all the saints in heaven! . . . . . iv 4 60
If he have the condition of a saint and the complexion of a devil *M. of V.* i 2 143
They come To kiss this shrine, this mortal-breathing saint . . ii 7 40
Such an injury would vex a very saint, Much more a shrew *T. of Shrew* iii 2 28
She call'd the saints to surety . . . . . . *All's Well* v 3 108
Canonized and worshipp'd as a saint . . . . . *K. John* iii 1 177
My subjects for a pair of carved saints . . . . *Richard II.* iii 3 152
And art indeed able to corrupt a saint . . . . 1 *Hen. IV.* i 2 102
They pray continually to their saint, the commonwealth . . ii 1 88
Joan la Pucelle shall be France's saint . . . . 1 *Hen. VI.* i 6 29
We'll set thy statue in some holy place, And have thee reverenced like a blessed saint . . . . iii 3 15
His loves Are brazen images of canonized saints . . 2 *Hen. VI.* i 3 63
Sweet saint, for charity, be not so curst . . . *Richard III.* i 2 49
And seem a saint, when most I play the devil . . . . i 3 338
My other angel husband And that dead saint which then I weeping follow'd . . . . iv 1 70
Earth gapes, hell burns, fiends roar, saints pray . . . iv 4 75
The prayers of holy saints and wronged souls, Like high-rear'd bulwarks v 3 241
She must die, She must, the saints must have her . . *Hen. VIII.* v 5 61
Saints have hands that pilgrims' hands do touch . . *Rom. and Jul.* i 5 101
Have not saints lips, and holy palmers too?—Ay, pilgrim, lips that they must use in prayer . . . . i 5 103
O, then, dear saint, let lips do what hands do; They pray, grant thou . i 5 105
Saints do not move, though grant for prayers' sake.—Then move not . i 5 107
My name, dear saint, is hateful to myself . . . . . ii 2 55
Neither, fair saint, if either thee dislike . . . . . ii 2 61
Just opposite to what thou justly seem'st, A damned saint! . . iii 2 79
To thee be worship! and thy saints for aye Be crown'd with plagues that thee alone obey! . . . . . . *T. of Athens* v 1 55
Saints in your injuries, devils being offended . . . *Othello* ii 1 112
Saint Alban. Stolen from my host at Saint Alban's . . 1 *Hen. IV.* iv 2 50
As common as the way between Saint Alban's and London 2 *Hen. IV.* ii 2 185
'Tis his highness' pleasure You do prepare to ride unto Saint Alban's 2 *Hen. VI.* i 2 57
When from Saint Alban's we do make return, We'll see these things . i 2 83
The king is now in progress towards Saint Alban's . . . i 4 76
Forsooth, a blind man at Saint Alban's shrine, Within this half-hour, hath received his sight . . . . ii 1 63
Call'd A hundred times and oftener, in my sleep, By good Saint Alban ii 1 91
Yes, master, clear as day, I thank God and Saint Alban . . . ii 1 108
Saint Alban here hath done a miracle . . . . . . ii 1 131
My masters of Saint Alban's, have you not beadles in your town? . ii 1 135
Underneath an alehouse' paltry sign, The Castle in Saint Alban's . v 2 68
Saint Alban's battle won by famous York Shall be eternized in all age to come . . . . v 3 30
March'd toward Saint Alban's to intercept the queen . 3 *Hen. VI.* ii 1 114
Short tale to make, we at Saint Alban's met, Our battles join'd . ii 1 120
When you and I met at Saint Alban's last, Your legs did better service than your hands . . . . ii 2 103
At Saint Alban's field This lady's husband, Sir Richard Grey, was slain iii 2 1
Was not your husband In Margaret's battle at Saint Alban's slain? *Richard III.* i 3 130
Saint Anne. By Saint Anne, and ginger shall be hot i' the mouth too *T. Night* ii 3 126
Saint Bennet. The bells of Saint Bennet, sir, may put you in mind . v 1 42
Saint Charity. By Gis and by Saint Charity . . . *Hamlet* iv 5 59
Saint Clare. The votarists of Saint Clare . . . *Meas. for Meas.* i 4 5
Saint Colme's inch. Till he disbursed at Saint Colme's inch Ten thousand dollars to our general use . . . . . *Macbeth* i 2 61
Saint Crispian. And say 'To-morrow is Saint Crispian' . . *Hen. V.* iv 3 46
Saint Crispin. Whiles any speaks That fought with us upon Saint Crispin's day . . . . iv 3 67
Saint Cupid, then! and soldiers, to the field! . . . *L. L. Lost* iv 3 366
Saint Denis to Saint Cupid! What are they? . . . . . v 2 87

Saint Davy. I'll knock his leek about his pate Upon Saint Davy's day . *Hen. V.* iv 1 55
Saint Denis to Saint Cupid! . . . *L. L. Lost* v 2 87
No longer on Saint Denis will we cry, But Joan la Pucelle shall be France's saint . . . 1 *Hen. VI.* i 6 28
Saint Denis bless this happy stratagem! . . . iii 2 18
Saint Edmundsbury. I will meet him at Saint Edmundsbury *K. John* iv 3 11
Thus hath he sworn . . . Upon the altar at Saint Edmundsbury . v 4 18
Saint George's half-cheek in a brooch . . . *L. L. Lost* v 2 620
Saint George, that swinged the dragon, and e'er since Sits on his horse back at mine hostess' door . . . *K. John* ii 1 288
Since we lay all night in the windmill in Saint George's field 2 *Hen. IV.* iii 2 207
Bonfires in France forthwith I am to make, To keep our great Saint George's feast withal . . . 1 *Hen. VI.* i 1 154
God and Saint George, Talbot and England's right! . . . iv 2 55
Knight of the noble order of Saint George, Worthy Saint Michael . iv 7 68
Saint Gregory. Where meet we?—At Saint Gregory's well *T. G. of Ver.* iv 2 84
Saint Jamy. Nay, by Saint Jamy, I hold you a penny . *T. of Shrew* iii 2 84
Saint Jaques. I am Saint Jaques' pilgrim, thither gone . *All's Well* iii 4 4
Her pretence is a pilgrimage to Saint Jaques le Grand . . iv 3 58
Saint Katharine. In Saint Katharine's churchyard . . 1 *Hen. VI.* i 2 100
Saint-like. And have perform'd A saint-like sorrow . . *W. Tale* v 1 2
Thy meekness saint-like, wife-like government . *Hen. VIII.* ii 4 138
She kneel'd, and saint-like Cast her fair eyes to heaven and pray'd devoutly . . . iv 1 83
Saint Luke. I will presently to Saint Luke's . . *Meas. for Meas.* iii 1 276
Saint Magnus. Up Fish Street! down Saint Magnus' Corner! 2 *Hen. VI.* iv 8 1
Saint Martin. Expect Saint Martin's summer, halcyon days 1 *Hen. VI.* i 2 131
Saint Mary. At Saint Mary's chapel presently The rites of marriage shall be solemnized . . . *K. John* ii 1 538
Saint Michael. Worthy Saint Michael and the Golden Fleece 1 *Hen. VI.* iv 7 69
Saint Nicholas be thy speed! . . . *T. G. of Ver.* iii 1 300
If they meet not with Saint Nicholas' clerks, I'll give thee this neck.—No, I'll none of it . . . 1 *Hen. IV.* ii 1 67
I know thou worshippest Saint Nicholas as truly as a man of falsehood may . . . ii 1 71
Saint Paul. Now, by Saint Paul, this news is bad indeed *Richard III.* i 1 138
Saint Peter. So deliver I up my apes, and away to Saint Peter for the heavens . . . *Much Ado* ii 1 50
You, mistress, That have the office opposite to Saint Peter, And keep the gate of hell! . . . *Othello* iv 2 91
Saint Philip. Helen, the mother of great Constantine, Nor yet Saint Philip's daughters, were like thee . . . 1 *Hen. VI.* i 2 143
Saint-seducing. Nor ope her lap to saint-seducing gold . *Rom. and Jul.* i 1 220
Saint Tavy. I do believe your majesty takes no scorn to wear the leek upon Saint Tavy's day . . . *Hen. V.* iv 7 107
Saint Valentine is past: Begin these wood-birds but to couple now? *M. N. Dream* iv 1 144
To-morrow is Saint Valentine's day, All in the morning betime *Hamlet* iv 5 48
Sainted. I hold you as a thing ensky'd and sainted . *Meas. for Meas.* i 4 34
Barefoot plod I the cold ground upon, With sainted vow . *All's Well* iii 4 7
Would make her sainted spirit Again possess her corpse . *W. Tale* v 1 57
Thy royal father Was a most sainted king: the queen that bore thee, Oftener upon her knees than on her feet . . . *Macbeth* iv 3 109
Saith. Robert Shallow, esquire, saith, he is wronged . *Mer. Wives* i 1 110
As a certain father saith,— Sir, tell not me of the father . *L. L. Lost* iv 2 154
Society, saith the text, is the happiness of life . . . iv 2 167
Death, as the Psalmist saith, is certain to all; all shall die 2 *Hen. IV.* iii 2 41
Thus saith the duke, thus hath the duke inferr'd . *Richard III.* iii 7 32
And as he saith, so say we all with him . . . *T. Andron.* v 1 17
Sake. For your sake Am I this patient log-man . . . *Tempest* iii 1 66
For my sake read it over, And if it please you, so . *T. G. of Ver.* i 1 136
Keep this remembrance for thy Julia's sake . . . ii 2 5
In the day Wherein I sigh not, Julia, for thy sake . . . ii 2 10
Thus, for my duty's sake, I rather chose To cross my friend . iii 1 17
For your friend's sake, will be glad of you . . . iii 2 63
For your sake.—I thank you for your own . . . iv 2 23
I give thee this For thy sweet mistress' sake . . . iv 4 182
I'll use thee kindly for thy mistress' sake . . . iv 4 207
For whose dear sake thou didst then rend thy faith . . v 4 47
I must never trust thee more, But count the world a stranger for thy sake . . . v 4 70
I now beseech you, for your daughter's sake, To grant one boon . v 4 149
Would I were young for your sake! . . . *Mer. Wives* i 1 268
'Pless you from his mercy sake! . . . iii 1 42
I am sorry that for my sake you have suffered all this . . iii 5 126
I have suffered more for their sakes . . . iv 5 110
Her own lamentation, which she yet wears for his sake *Meas. for Meas.* iii 1 238
All great doers in our trade, and are now 'for the Lord's sake' . iv 3 21
This new-married man . . . you must pardon For Mariana's sake . v 1 408
If he be like your brother, for his sake Is he pardon'd . . v 1 495
For your lovely sake, Give me your hand and say you will be mine . v 1 496
For the sake of them thou sorrowest for . . . *Com. of Errors* i 1 122
Let me in.—Can you tell for whose sake? . . . iii 1 57
Then for her wealth's sake use her with more kindness . . iii 2 6
I would you did like me.—So would not I, for your own sake *Much Ado* ii 1 105
O that I were a man for his sake! or that I had any friend would be a man for my sake! . . . iv 1 320
Men grow hard-hearted and will lend nothing for God's sake . v 1 322
Alas, poor heart! If you spite it for my sake, I will spite it for yours . v 2 70
Give him for my sake but one loving kiss . . *L. L. Lost* ii 1 248
When, for fame's sake, for praise, an outward part, We bend to that the working of the heart . . . iv 1 32
Do not curst wives hold that self-sovereignty Only for praise sake? . iv 1 37
Did never sonnet for her sake compile . . . iv 3 134
For wisdom's sake, a word that all men love, Or for love's sake, a word that loves all men, Or for men's sake, the authors of these women, Or women's sake, by whom we men are men, Let us once lose our oaths . . . iv 3 357
For your fair sakes have we neglected time . . . v 2 765
And for her sake do I rear up her boy, And for her sake I will not part with him . . . *M. N. Dream* ii 1 136
Do it for thy true-love take, Love and languish for his sake . . ii 2 29
For my sake, my dear, Lie further off yet, do not lie so near . . ii 2 43
And run through fire I will for thy sweet sake . . . ii 2 103
O, once tell true, tell true, even for my sake! . . . iii 2 68
I no question make To have it of my trust or for my sake *Mer. of Venice* i 1 185
If e'er the Jew her father come to heaven, It will be for his gentle daughter's sake . . . ii 4 35
Slubber not business for my sake . . . ii 8 39
Sake. Give me your gloves, I'll wear them for your sake *Mer. of Venice* iv 1 426
We pray you, for your own sake, to embrace your own safety *As Y. L. It* i 2 189
Pity her for her good father's sake . . . i 2 293
Hate him not, for my sake.—Why should I not? . . . i 3 36
We stay'd her for your sake, Else had she with her father ranged along . i 3 69
Said with weeping tears 'Wear these for my sake' . . ii 4 54
For her sake more than for mine own . . . ii 4 76
For my sake be comfortable; hold death awhile at the arm's end . ii 6 9
For fashion sake, I thank you too for your society . . iii 2 271
Not for my sake, but your master's, I advise You use your manners *T. of Shrew* i 1 246
You're welcome, sir; and he, for your good sake . . ii 1 61
I know him well: you are welcome for his sake . . ii 1 70
All for my master's sake . . . iii 2 150
In this extremity, This favour will I do you for his sake . iv 2 103
Sweet Kate, embrace her for her beauty's sake . . iv 5 34
Then pardon him, sweet father, for my sake . . . v 1 133
For both our sakes, I would that word were true . . v 2 15
Would, for the king's sake, he were living! . . *All's Well* i 1 24
I love him for his sake . . . i 1 110
I hope to have friends for my wife's sake . . . i 3 43
I'll never do you wrong for your own sake . . . ii 3 96
I would it were hell-pains for thy sake, and my poor doing eternal ii 3 245
For the contents' sake are sorry for our pains . . . iii 2 66
We'll strive to bear it for your worthy sake . . . iii 3 5
Which, for traffic's sake, Most of our city did . . *T. Night* iii 3 34
He will fight with you for's oath sake . . . iii 4 326
The gentleman will, for his honour's sake, have one bout with you iii 4 336
For his sake Did I expose myself, pure for his love . . v 1 85
Take again your queen as yours at first, Even for your son's sake *W. Tale* i 2 337
For that England's sake With burden of our armour here we sweat *K. John* ii 1 91
That the true prince may, for recreation sake, prove a false thief 1 *Hen. IV.* i 2 174
And for his sake wear the detested blot Of murderous subornation i 3 162
Which for sport sake are content to do the profession some grace . ii 1 78
For their own credit sake . . . ii 1 80
We were enforced, for safety sake, to fly . . . v 1 65
For my sake, even to the eyes of Richard Gave him defiance 2 *Hen. IV.* iii 1 64
For my old dame's sake, stand my friend . . . iii 2 245
Put me to verses or to dance for your sake, Kate, why you undid me *Hen. V.* v 2 138
For their sake, In your fair minds let this acceptance take . Epil. 13
For my father's sake, In honour of a true Plantagenet, And for alliance sake, declare the cause . . . 1 *Hen. VI.* ii 5 51
A lordly nation That will not trust thee but for profit's sake . iii 3 63
For thy sake have I shed many a tear . . . v 4 19
A little ratsbane for thy sake . . . v 4 29
For his father's sake . . . , I am content he shall reign . 2 *Hen. VI.* iv 2 165
Thou hast one son; for his sake pity me . . 3 *Hen. VI.* i 3 40
Take time to do him dead.—That is my office, for my father's sake i 4 109
I'll wear the willow garland for his sake . . iii 3 228; iv 1 100
Would it were mortal poison, for thy sake! . *Richard III.* i 2 146
I have done those things, Which now bear evidence against my soul, For Edward's sake . . . i 4 68
For whose sake did I that ill deed? For Edward, for my brother, for his sake . . . i 4 216
He for his father's sake so loves the prince, That he will not be won . iii 1 165
And, for her sake, Madest quick conveyance with her good aunt Anne . iv 4 282
Awake! Arm, fight, and conquer, for fair England's sake! . v 3 150
Here are some will thank you . . for their poor mistress' sake *Hen. VIII.* iii 1 47
For her sake that I have been,—for I feel The last fit of my greatness . iii 1 77
And do justice For truth's sake and his conscience . . iii 2 397
And a little To love her for her mother's sake, that loved him . iv 2 137
For your health and your digestion sake . . *Troi. and Cres.* ii 3 120
Things small as nothing, for request's sake only, He makes important . ii 3 179
Why then for Venus' sake, give me a kiss . . . iv 5 49
I cannot Put on the gown, stand naked and entreat them, For my wounds' sake, to give their suffrage . . . *Coriolanus* ii 2 142
The fourth would return for conscience sake . . . ii 3 36
Take this along; I writ it for thy sake, And would have sent it . v 2 96
For thy sake and thy brother's here . . . *T. Andron.* i 1 482
Hadst thou in person ne'er offended me, Even for his sake am I pitiless ii 3 162
For our father's sake and mother's care . . . iii 1 182
Will hold thee dearly for thy mother's sake . . . v 1 36
Saints do not move, though grant for prayers' sake . *Rom. and Jul.* i 5 107
For Juliet's sake, for her sake, rise and stand . . . iii 3 89
Thy Juliet is alive, For whose dear sake thou wast but lately dead . iii 3 136
I'ld rather than the worth of thrice the sum, Had sent to me first, but for my mind's sake . . . *T. of Athens* iii 3 23
With letters of entreaty, . . . In part for his sake moved . . v 2 13
Let me depart alone, And, for my sake, stay here . . *J Cæsar* iii 2 61
For Brutus' sake, I am beholding to you . . . iii 2 70
Did not great Julius bleed for justice' sake? . . . iv 3 19
If, for my sake, Thou wilt o'ertake us, hence a mile or twain . . *Lear* iv 1 43
The one the other poison'd for my sake, And after slew herself . . v 3 240
For your sake, jewel, I am glad at soul I have no other child . . *Othello* i 3 195
Would they were clyster-pipes for your sake! . . . ii 1 179
He desires you, for love's sake, to make no more noise with it . iii 1 13
If for the sake of merit thou wilt hear me . . *Ant. and Cleo.* ii 7 61
For my sake wear this; It is a manacle of love . . *Cymbeline* i 1 121
'Tween man and man they weigh not every stamp; Though light, take pieces for the figure's sake . . . v 4 25
He loved me dearly, And for his sake I wish the having of it . *Pericles* ii 1 145
A little daughter: for the sake of it, Be manly, and take comfort . . iii 1 21
For God's sake *Com. of Errors* i 2; ii 1; v 1; *Mer. of Venice* iv 1; *T. of Shrew* Ind 2; *Richard II.* ii 2; iii 1; v 3; 1 *Hen. IV.* ii 4; iv 3; v 4; 2 *Hen. IV.* ii 3; ii 4; 1 *Hen. VI.* iv 7; 2 *Hen. VI.* i 3; 3 *Hen. VI.* ii 2; v 5; *Richard III.* i 2; i 3; ii 2
For goodness' sake . . . *Hen. VIII.* Prol. 23; iii 1 159
For heaven sake *K. John* iv 1; *Hen. VIII.* iii 1; *Othello* v 1
Sala. That the land Salique is in Germany, Between the floods of Sala and of Elbe . . . *Hen. V.* i 2 45
Which Salique, as I said, 'twixt Elbe and Sala, Is at this day in Germany call'd Meisen . . . i 2 52
Charles the Great Subdued the Saxons, and did seat the French Beyond the river Sala, in the year Eight hundred five . . . i 2 63
Salad. Twas a good lady; we may pick a thousand salads ere we light on such another herb . . . *All's Well* iv 5 15
She was the sweet-marjoram of the salad, or rather, the herb of grace . iv 5 18
My salad days, When I was green in judgement . *Ant. and Cleo.* i 5 73

Salamander. I have maintained that salamander of yours with fire any time this two and thirty years . . . 1 *Hen. IV.* iii 3 53
Salary. O, this is hire and salary, not revenge . . . *Hamlet* iii 3 79
Sale. Beauty is bought by judgement of the eye, Not utter'd by base sale of chapmen's tongues . . . *L. L. Lost* ii 1 16
To things of sale a seller's praise belongs, She passes praise . iv 3 240
His cote, his flocks and bounds of feed Are now on sale . *As Y. Like It* ii 4 84
Who in that sale sells pardon from himself . . *K. John* iii 1 167
Thy sale of offices and towns in France . . 2 *Hen. VI.* i 3 138
If a man did need a poison now, Whose sale is present death *R. and J.* v 1 51
I saw him enter such a house of sale . . . . *Hamlet* ii 1 60
Is not a thing for sale, and only the gift of the gods *Cymbeline* i 4 92
The house you dwell in proclaims you to be a creature of sale *Pericles* iv 6 84
Salerio. My old Venetian friend Salerio . . *Mer. of Venice* iii 2 222
But meeting with Salerio by the way, He did intreat me . . iii 2 231
Your hand, Salerio: what's the news from Venice? . . . iii 2 241
But is it true, Salerio? Have all his ventures fail'd? . . iii 2 269
Sale-work. Why do you look on me? I see no more in you than in the ordinary Of nature's sale-work . . *As Y. Like It* iii 5 43
Salicam. In terram Salicam mulieres ne succedant . . *Hen. V.* i 2 38
Salique. Why the law Salique that they have in France Or should, or should not, bar us in our claim . . . . . i 2 11
'No woman shall succeed in Salique land:' Which Salique land the French unjustly glose To be the realm of France . . . i 2 39
The land Salique is in Germany, Between the floods of Sala and of Elbe i 2 44
No female Should be inheritrix in Salique land . . . i 2 51
The Salique law Was not devised for the realm of France; Nor did the French possess the Salique land . . . . . i 2 54
Howbeit they would hold up this Salique law To bar your highness i 2 91
Salisbury. Stay yet, Lord Salisbury; I'll go with thee . . *K. John* iv 2 96
Lord Salisbury, With eyes as red as new-enkindled fire . . iv 2 162
Stand back, Lord Salisbury, stand back, I say. . . . iv 3 81
Thou wert better gall the devil, Salisbury . . . . iv 3 95
Honourable rescue and defence Cries out upon the name of Salisbury . v 2 19
Lift up thy brow, renowned Salisbury . . . . v 2 54
My Lord of Salisbury, we have stay'd ten days . *Richard II.* ii 4 1
Salisbury Is gone to meet the king, who lately landed . . iii 2 2
With him are the Lord Aumerle, Lord Salisbury, Sir Stephen Scroop . iii 3 27
I have to London sent The heads of Oxford, Salisbury, Blunt, and Kent v 6 8
Farewell, good Salisbury; and good luck go with thee! . . *Hen. V.* iv 3 11
Familiar in his mouth as household words, Harry the king, Bedford and Exeter, Warwick and Talbot, Salisbury and Gloucester . . iv 3 54
Salisbury craveth supply, And hardly keeps his men from mutiny 1 *Hen. VI.* i 1 159
Remaineth none but mad-brain'd Salisbury . . . . i 2 15
Salisbury is a desperate homicide; He fighteth as one weary of his life i 2 25
Speak, Salisbury; at least, if thou canst speak: How farest thou? . i 4 73
In thirteen battles Salisbury o'ercame; Henry the Fifth he first train'd i 4 78
Yet livest thou, Salisbury? though thy speech doth fail, One eye thou hast, to look to heaven for grace . . . . . i 4 82
Heaven, be thou gracious to none alive, If Salisbury wants mercy! . i 4 86
Salisbury, cheer thy spirit with this comfort; Thou shalt not die . i 4 90
How dying Salisbury doth groan! It irks his heart he cannot be revenged. Frenchmen, I'll be a Salisbury to you . . . i 4 104
Convey me Salisbury into his tent . . . . . i 4 110
Help Salisbury to make his testament . . . . . i 5 17
You all consented unto Salisbury's death, For none would strike a stroke in his revenge . . . . i 5 34
O, would I were to die with Salisbury! . . . . . i 5 38
Now, Salisbury, for thee, and for the right Of English Henry . . ii 1 35
Bring forth the body of old Salisbury . . . . . ii 2 4
Somerset, Salisbury, and Warwick; We thank you all . 2 *Hen. VI.* i 1 70
Salisbury, and victorious Warwick, Received deep scars in France . i 1 86
Salisbury and Warwick are no simple peers . . . . i 3 77
Invite my Lords of Salisbury and Warwick To sup with me . . i 4 83
My good Lords of Salisbury and Warwick, Our simple supper ended, give me leave In this close walk to satisfy myself . . . ii 2 1
Then, father Salisbury, kneel we together . . . . ii 2 59
Stay, Salisbury, With the rude multitude till I return . . iii 2 134
An answer from the king, my Lord of Salisbury! . . . iii 2 270
All the honour Salisbury hath won Is, that he was the lord ambassador iii 2 275
Go, Salisbury, and tell them all from me, I thank them . . iii 2 279
Bid Salisbury and Warwick come to me.—Are these thy bears? . v 1 147
Old Salisbury, shame to thy silver hair, Thou mad misleader of thy brain-sick son! . . . . v 1 162
Of Salisbury, who can report of him, That winter lion? . . v 3 1
This happy day Is not itself, nor have we won one foot, If Salisbury be lost . . . . v 3 7
Fly to the duke: Post thou to Salisbury . . . *Richard III* iv 4 443
Meet me presently at Salisbury.—I go.—What is't your highness' pleasure I shall do At Salisbury? . . . . . . iv 4 450
Away towards Salisbury! while we reason here, A royal battle might be won and lost. . . . . iv 4 537
Some one take order Buckingham be brought To Salisbury . . iv 4 540
Who, being at Salisbury, Made suit to come in's presence . *Hen. VIII.* i 2 196
Sallet. I climbed into this garden, to see if I can eat grass, or pick a sallet another while . . . . . . 2 *Hen. VI.* iv 10 9
I think this word 'sallet' was born to do me good: for many a time, but for a sallet, my brain-pan had been cleft with a brown bill . iv 10 11
And now the word 'sallet' must serve me to feed on . . . iv 10 16
There were no sallets in the lines to make the matter savoury *Hamlet* ii 2 462
When the foul fiend rages, eats cow-dung for sallets . . *Lear* iii 4 137
Sallow. What a deal of brine Hath wash'd thy sallow cheeks for Rosaline! *Rom. and Jul.* ii 3 70
Sally. When you sally upon him, speak what terrible language you will: though you understand it not yourselves, no matter . *All's Well* iv 1 2
Thou hast talk'd Of sallies and retires, of trenches . 1 *Hen. IV.* ii 3 54
Too rashly plotted: all our general force Might with a sally of the very town Be buckled with . . . . 1 *Hen. VI.* iv 4 4
No notes of sally, for the heavens, sweet brother . *Troi. and Cres.* v 3 14
Salmon. And there is salmons in both . . . . *Hen. V.* iv 7 32
Never was so frail To change the cod's head for the salmon's tail *Othello* ii 1 156
Salt. When I have deck'd the sea with drops full salt . *Tempest* i 2 155
Thou dost, and think'st it much to tread the ooze Of the salt deep . i 2 253
It may be; I'll prove it. The cover of the salt hides the salt, and therefore it is more than the salt . . . *T. G. of Ver.* iii 1 370
We have some salt of our youth in us . . . *Mer. Wives* ii 3 50
Whose salt imagination yet hath wrong'd Your well defended honour *Meas. for Meas.* v 1 406
By the salt rheum that ran between France and it . *Com. of Errors* iii 2 131
Salt too little which may season give To her foul-tainted flesh! *Much Ado* iv 1 144
Salt. By the salt wave of the Mediterraneum . . . . *L. L. Lost* v 1 61
How came her eyes so bright? Not with salt tears . *M. N. Dream* ii 2 92
Turns into yellow gold his salt green streams . . . . iii 2 393
My fear hath catch'd your fondness: now I see The mystery of your loneliness, and find Your salt tears' head . . . *All's Well* i 3 178
Tempests are kind and salt waves fresh in love . . *T. Night* iii 4 419
The salt in them is hot. Within me is a hell . . . *K. John* v 7 45
As many fresh streams meet in one salt sea . . . *Hen. V.* i 2 209
He is come to me and prings me pread and salt yesterday . . v 1 9
Our isle be made a nourish of salt tears . . . 1 *Hen. VI.* i 1 50
With tears as salt as sea . . . . . . 2 *Hen. VI.* iii 2 96
To drain Upon his face an ocean of salt tears . . . . iii 2 143
Those eyes of thine from mine have drawn salt tears . *Richard III.* i 2 154
Liberality, and such like, the spice and salt that season a man *T. and C.* i 2 277
Better parch in Afric sun Than in the pride and salt scorn of his eyes . i 3 371
A single famish'd kiss, Distasted with the salt of broken tears . . iv 4 50
And given up, For certain drops of salt, your city . . *Coriolanus* v 6 93
The bark thy body is, Sailing in this salt flood . . *Rom. and Jul.* iii 5 135
Make use of thy salt hours . . . . . . *T. of Athens* iv 3 85
The sea's a thief, whose liquid surge resolves The moon into salt tears iv 3 443
Made his everlasting mansion Upon the beached verge of the salt flood v 1 219
Ere yet the salt of most unrighteous tears Had left the flushing in her galled eyes, She married . . . . *Hamlet* i 2 154
Neptune's salt wash and Tellus' orbed ground . . . . iii 2 166
Tears seven times salt, Burn out the sense and virtue of mine eye! . iv 5 154
This would make a man a man of salt . . . . . *Lear* iv 6 199
For the better compassing of his salt and most hidden loose affection *Oth.* ii 1 244
As hot as monkeys, As salt as wolves in pride . . . . iii 3 404
I have a salt and sorry rheum offends me; Lend me thy handkerchief . iii 4 51
Her salt tears fell from her, and soften'd the stones . . . iv 3 47
But all the charms of love, Salt Cleopatra, soften thy waned lip! Let witchcraft join with beauty! . . . . . *Ant. and Cleo.* ii 1 21
Salt-butter. Hang him, mechanical salt-butter rogue! . *Mer. Wives* ii 2 290
Salter. Thy tears are salter than a younger man's . . *Coriolanus* iv 1 22
Salt-fish. The luce is the fresh fish; the salt fish is an old coat *M. Wives* i 1 22
When your diver Did hang a salt-fish on his hook . *Ant. and Cleo.* ii 5 17
Saltiers. They call themselves Saltiers . . . . *W. Tale* iv 4 334
Saltness. Your lordship . . . hath yet some smack of age in you, some relish of the saltness of time . . . . . . 2 *Hen. IV.* i 2 112
Salt-petre. It was great pity, so it was, This villanous salt-petre should be digg'd Out of the bowels of the harmless earth . . 1 *Hen. IV.* i 3 60
Salt-sea. Maw and gulf Of the ravin'd salt-sea shark . . *Macbeth* iv 1 24
Salt-water. Stained with salt water . . . . . *Tempest* ii 1 64
She is drowned already, sir, with salt water . . . *T. Night* ii 1 32
Notable pirate! thou salt-water thief! . . . . . . v 1 72
And yet salt water blinds them not so much . . *Richard II.* iv 1 245
How much salt water thrown away in waste, To season love! *R. and J.* ii 3 71
You shall find us in our salt-water girdle . . . *Cymbeline* iii 1 81
Salutation. Most military sir, salutation . . . . *L. L. Lost* v 1 38
Salutation and greeting to you all! . . . . *As Y. Like It* v 4 39
Loud shouts and salutations from their mouths . . 1 *Hen. IV.* iii 2 53
The early village-cock Hath twice done salutation to the morn *Rich. III.* v 3 210
Bon jour! there's a French salutation to your French slop *Rom. and Jul.* ii 4 47
Pindarus is come To do you salutation from his master . . *J. Cæsar* iv 2 5
Speak my salutation in their minds; Whose voices I desire aloud *Macb.* v 8 57
Panting forth From Goneril his mistress salutations . . *Lear* ii 4 32
Salute. Journeying to salute the emperor . . . . *T. G. of Ver.* i 3 41
There's not a man I meet but doth salute me . . *Com. of Errors* iv 3 1
You told me you salute not at the court, but you kiss your hands *As Y. Like It* iii 2 50
Even till that utmost corner of the west Salute thee for her king *K. John* ii 1 30
When his fair angels would salute my palm . . . . ii 1 590
Dear earth, I do salute thee with my hand . . *Richard II.* iii 2 6
We do salute you, Duke of Burgundy . . . . *Hen. V.* v 2 7
You English princes all, I do salute you . . . . . v 2 22
Makes me the bolder to salute my king With ruder terms . 2 *Hen. VI.* i 1 29
Be we the first That shall salute our rightful sovereign . . ii 2 61
Then I salute you with this kingly title . . . *Richard III.* iii 7 239
I'll salute your grace of York as mother, And reverend looker on . iv 1 30
I was then present, saw them salute on horseback . . *Hen. VIII.* i 1 8
A general welcome from his grace Salutes ye all . . . . i 4 2
Would I had no being, If this salute my blood a jot . . . ii 3 103
Eye to eye opposed Salutes each other with each other's form *T. and C.* iii 3 108
I scarce have leisure to salute you, My matter is so rash . . iv 2 61
Our general doth salute you with a kiss . . . . . iv 5 19
As when the golden sun salutes the morn . . . *T. Andron.* ii 1 5
Lord of his fortunes he salutes thee . . . *Ant. and Cleo.* iii 12 11
Let us salute him, Or know what ground's made happy by his breath *Pericles* ii 4 27
Saluted. By which title, before, these weird sisters saluted me *Macbeth* i 5 9
Saluteth. A soul feminine saluteth us . . . . *L. L. Lost* iv 2 83
What early tongue so sweet saluteth me? . . *Rom. and Jul.* ii 3 32
Salvation. Are you good men and true?—Yea, or else it were pity but they should suffer salvation, body and soul . . . *Much Ado* iii 3 3
In the course of justice, none of us Should see salvation *Mer. of Venice* iv 1 200
For a quart d'écu he will sell the fee-simple of his salvation . *All's Well* iv 3 312
They take it already upon their salvation . . . 1 *Hen. IV.* ii 4 10
About some act That has no relish of salvation in't . . *Hamlet* iii 3 92
Is she to be buried in Christian burial that wilfully seeks her own salvation? . . . . v 1 2
Salve. No riddle, no l'envoy; no salve in the mail, sir . . *L. L. Lost* iii 1 73
No salve, sir, but a plantain! . . . . iii 1 75
Doth the inconsiderate take salve for l'envoy, and the word l'envoy for a salve?—Do the wise think them other? is not l'envoy a salve? . iii 1 79
Some salve for perjury.—'Tis more than need . . . . iv 3 289
I do beseech your majesty may salve The long-grown wounds 1 *Hen. IV.* iii 2 155
To provide A salve for any sore that may betide . . 3 *Hen. VI.* iv 6 88
Speak fair; you may salve so, Not what is dangerous present, but the loss Of what is past . . . . *Coriolanus* iii 2 70
Salved. I would have salved it with a longer treatise . . *Much Ado* i 1 317
Same. Yond same black cloud, yond huge one . . . . *Tempest* ii 2 20
Yond same cloud cannot choose but fall by pailfuls . . . ii 2 24
What is this same?—This is the tune of our catch . . . iii 2 134
Would I were so anger'd with the same! . . . *T. G. of Ver.* i 2 104
What letter is this same? What's here? . . . . . iii 1 137
This is the very same; the very hand, the very words . *Mer. Wives* ii 1 84
The very same man . . . . iv 5 37
Call that same Isabel here once again . . . *Meas. for Meas.* v 1 270
At five o'clock I shall receive the money for the same . *Com. of Errors* iv 1 11
For the same he promised me a chain . . . . . . iv 3 85

Same. O, if thou be'st the same Ægeon, speak, And speak unto the same Æmilia! *Com. of Errors* v 1 344
Which is the lady I must seize upon?—This same is she. *Much Ado* v 4 54
Give me the paper; let me read the same. *L. L. Lost* i 1 116
What lady is that same? ii 1 194
This same shall go iv 3 59
In that same place thou hast appointed me *M. N. Dream* i 1 177
This same progeny of evils comes From our debate ii 1 115
That same cowardly, giant-like ox-beef hath devoured many a gentleman iii 1 197
This is the same Athenian.—This is the woman, but not this the man iii 2 41
I must be one of these same dumb wise men *Mer. of Venice* i 1 106
What lady is the same To whom you swore a secret pilgrimage? i 1 119
There are some shrewd contents in yon same paper iii 2 246
I must freely have the half of any thing That this same paper brings you iii 2 253
Take this same letter, And use thou all the endeavour of a man In speed iii 4 47
A pound of that same merchant's flesh is thine iv 1 299
Yond's that same knave That leads him to these places *All's Well* iii 5 85
What ring was yours? . . . —Sir, much like The same upon your finger v 3 226
Run after that same peevish messenger *T. Night* i 5 319
Get thee to yond same sovereign cruelty ii 4 83
Put the same into young Arthur's hand *K. John* i 1 14
Colbrand the giant, that same mighty man i 1 225
What cracker is this same that deafs our ears? ii 1 147
If this same were a churchyard where we stand iii 3 40
The incomprehensible lies that this same fat rogue will tell us *1 Hen. IV.* i 2 209
That same sword-and-buckler Prince of Wales i 3 230
Secretly into the bosom creep Of that same noble prelate i 3 267
That same mad fellow of the north, Percy ii 4 369
Owen, Owen, the same; and his son-in-law Mortimer ii 4 375
One of these same metre ballad-mongers iii 1 130
That same word, rebellion *2 Hen. IV.* i 1 194
His highness is fallen into this same whoreson apoplexy i 2 123
The same Sir John, the very same iii 2 32
The very same day iii 2 35
This same half-faced fellow, Shadow iii 2 283
This same young sober-blooded boy doth not love me iv 3 94
This same is yours: Read them *Hen. V.* ii 2 68
But, hark! what new alarum is this same? iv 6 35
But prove a chief offender in the same *1 Hen. VI.* iii 1 130
Until thy head be circled with the same *2 Hen. VI.* i 2 10
Whip him till he leap over that same stool ii 1 149
As willingly do I the same resign ii 3 33
Unworthy to behold the same iv 4 18
They took his head, and on the gates of York They set the same *3 Hen. VI.* ii 1 66
We'll quickly rouse the traitors in the same v 1 65
The saying did not hold In him that did object the same to thee *Rich. III.* ii 4 17
This same very day iii 2 49
I will not dine until I see the same iii 4 79
You might well have signified the same iii 5 59
This same Cranmer's A worthy fellow *Hen. VIII.* iii 2 71
Nor fear of bad success in a bad cause, Can qualify the same *Troi. and Cres.* ii 2 118
Great minds, of partial indulgence To their benumbed wills, resist the same ii 2 179
What Trojan is that same that looks so heavy? iv 5 95
He for the same Will send thee hither both thy sons alive *T. Andron.* iii 1 154
That same pale hard-hearted wench *Rom. and Jul.* ii 4 4
Where that same banish'd runagate doth live iii 5 90
This same wayward girl is so reclaim'd iv 2 47
What a pestilent knave is this same! iv 5 148
This same should be the voice of Friar John v 2 2
For all this same, I'll hide me hereabout: His looks I fear v 3 43
Why, this is the world's soul; and just of the same piece Is every flatterer's spirit *T. of Athens* iii 2 71
At all times alike Men are not still the same v 1 125
That same ague which hath made you lean *J. Cæsar* ii 2 113
That every like is not the same, O Cæsar, The heart of Brutus yearns to think upon! ii 2 128
Art thou afeard To be the same in thine own act and valour As thou art in desire? *Macbeth* i 7 40
Yond same star that's westward from the pole Had made his course *Ham.* i 1 36
For this same lord, I do repent iii 4 172
And many more of the same breed that I know the drossy age dotes on v 2 197
Let this same be presently perform'd, Even while men's minds are wild v 2 404
I'll talk a word with this same learned Theban *Lear* iii 4 162
When shall we come to the top of that same hill? iv 6 1
I am old now, And these same crosses spoil me v 3 278
What did you mean by that same handkerchief you gave me? *Othello* iv 1 154
What trumpet is that same? iv 1 226
These same whoreson devils do the gods great harm *Ant. and Cleo.* v 2 277
How far it is To this same blessed Milford *Cymbeline* iii 2 61

Samingo. Do me right, And dub me knight: Samingo *2 Hen. IV.* v 3 79

Samphire. Half way down Hangs one that gathers samphire, dreadful trade! Methinks he seems no bigger than his head *Lear* iv 6 15

Sample. Most praised, most loved, A sample to the youngest *Cymbeline* i 1 48

Sampler. With our needles created both one flower, Both on one sampler, sitting on one cushion *M. N. Dream* iii 2 205
Fair Philomela, she but lost her tongue, And in a tedious sampler sew'd her mind *T. Andron.* ii 4 39

Sampson Stockfish, a fruiterer *2 Hen. IV.* iii 2 35

Samson, master: he was a man of good carriage, great carriage *L. L. Lost* i 2 73
O well-knit Samson! strong-jointed Samson! i 2 77
Who was Samson's love, my dear Moth?—A woman, master i 2 80
To have a love of that colour, methinks Samson had small reason for it i 2 91
Yet was Samson so tempted, and he had an excellent strength i 2 179
None but Samsons and Goliases It sendeth forth to skirmish *1 Hen. VI.* i 2 33
I am not Samson, nor Sir Guy, nor Colbrand, To mow 'em down *Hen. VIII.* v 4 22

Sancta. Ah! sancta majestas, who would not buy thee dear? *2 Hen. VI.* v 1 5

Sanctified. Your virtues, gentle master, Are sanctified and holy traitors to you *As You Like It* ii 3 13
Should be buried in highways out of all sanctified limit *All's Well* i 1 152
His good receipt Shall for my legacy be sanctified i 3 251
Draw no swords but what are sanctified *2 Hen. IV.* iv 4 4
Breathing like sanctified and pious bawds, The better to beguile *Hamlet* i 3 130
So help me every spirit sanctified, As I have spoken for you *Othello* iii 4 126

Sanctify. My idolatrous fancy Must sanctify his reliques *All's Well* i 1 109
Whilst I from far His name with zealous fervour sanctify iii 4 11
Let all the tears that should bedew my hearse Be drops of balm to sanctify thy head *2 Hen. IV.* iv 5 115
After all comparisons of truth, . . . 'As true as Troilus' shall crown up the verse, And sanctify the numbers *Troi. and Cres.* iii 2 190
Sanctifies himself with's hand and turns up the white o' the eye *Coriol.* iv 5 208

Sanctimonious. Before All sanctimonious ceremonies may With full and holy rite be minister'd *Tempest* iv 1 16
Like the sanctimonious pirate, that went to sea with the Ten Commandments, but scraped one out of the table *Meas. for Meas.* i 2 7

Sanctimony. Which holy undertaking with most austere sanctimony she accomplished *All's Well* iv 3 59
If vows be sanctimonies, If sanctimony be the gods' delight *Trio. and Cres.* v 2 140
If sanctimony and a frail vow betwixt an erring barbarian and a super-subtle Venetian be not too hard for my wits *Othello* i 3 362

Sanctity. His kissing is as full of sanctity as the touch of holy bread *As Y. Like It* iii 4 14
Which way is he, in the name of sanctity? *T. Night* iii 4 94
Relieved him with such sanctity of love iii 4 395
In pure white robes, Like very sanctity *W. Tale* iii 3 23
The very opener and intelligencer Between the grace, the sanctities of heaven And our dull workings *2 Hen. IV.* iv 2 21
But at his touch—Such sanctity hath heaven given his hand—They presently amend *Macbeth* iv 3 144
My sanctity Will to my sense bend no licentious ear *Pericles* v 3 29

Sanctuarize. No place, indeed, should murder sanctuarize *Hamlet* iv 7 128

Sanctuary. Having waste ground enough, Shall we desire to raze the sanctuary And pitch our evils there? *Meas. for Meas.* ii 2 171
He took this place for sanctuary *Com. of Errors* v 1 94
While she is here, a man may live as quiet in hell as in a sanctuary *Much Ado* ii 1 266
I'll hence forthwith unto the sanctuary *3 Hen. VI.* iv 4 31
Come, come, my boy; we will to sanctuary *Richard III.* ii 4 66
Come, I'll conduct you to the sanctuary ii 4 73
The queen your mother, and your brother York, Have taken sanctuary iii 1 28
If she be obdurate To mild entreaties, God in heaven forbid We should infringe the holy privilege Of blessed sanctuary! iii 1 42
You break not sanctuary in seizing him iii 1 47
Oft have I heard of sanctuary men; But sanctuary children ne'er till now iii 1 55
Go thou to sanctuary, and good thoughts possess thee! iv 1 94
Nor sleep nor sanctuary, Being naked, sick, nor fane nor Capitol *Coriol.* i 10 19

Sand. Come unto these yellow sands, And then take hands *Tempest* i 2 376
Ye that on the sands with printless foot Do chase the ebbing Neptune v 1 34
If all their sand were pearl, The water nectar *T. G. of Ver.* ii 4 170
Huge leviathans Forsake unsounded deeps to dance on sands iii 2 81
Even from a heart As full of sorrows as the sea of sands iv 3 33
And sat with me on Neptune's yellow sands *M. N. Dream* ii 1 126
Dock'd in sand, Vailing her high-top lower than her ribs *Mer. of Venice* i 1 27
How many cowards, whose hearts are all as false As stairs of sand! iii 2 84
Wreck'd three nights ago on Goodwin Sands *K. John* v 3 11
Cast away and sunk on Goodwin Sands v 5 13
The task he undertakes Is numbering sands and drinking oceans dry *Richard II.* ii 2 146
It is a theme as fluent as the sea: turn the sands into eloquent tongues, and my horse is argument for them all *Hen. V.* iii 7 36
Even as men wrecked upon a sand, that look to be washed off the next tide iv 1 100
The splitting rocks cower'd in the sinking sands *2 Hen. VI.* iii 2 97
Here shall they make their ransom on the sand iv 1 10
The sands are number'd that make up my life *3 Hen. VI.* i 4 25
Tread on the sand; why, there you quickly sink v 4 30
There's no hoped-for mercy with the brothers More than with ruthless waves, with sands and rocks v 4 36
The angry northern wind Will blow these sands, like Sibyl's leaves, abroad, And where's your lesson, then? *T. Andron.* iv 1 105
Here, in the sands, Thee I'll rake up, the post unsanctified Of murderous lechers *Lear* iv 6 280
The gutter'd rocks and congregated sands,—Traitors ensteep'd *Othello* ii 1 69
With sands that will not bear your enemies' boats, But suck them up to the topmast *Cymbeline* iii 1 21
Where horses have been nimbler than the sands That run i' the clock's behalf iii 2 74
One sand another Not more resembles that sweet rosy lad v 5 120
Now our sands are almost run: More a little, and then dumb *Pericles* v 2 1

Sandal. You are come to Sandal in a happy hour *3 Hen. VI.* i 2 63
By his cockle hat and staff, And his sandal shoon *Hamlet* iv 5 26

Sand-blind. More than sand-blind, high-gravel blind *Mer. of Venice* ii 2 37
Do you not know me, father?—Alack, sir, I am sand-blind ii 2 77

Sanded. My hounds are bred out of the Spartan kind, So flew'd, so sanded *M. N. Dream* iv 1 125

Sands. Well said, Lord Sands; Your colt's tooth is not cast yet *Hen. VIII.* i 3 47
My Lord Sands, you are one will keep 'em waking; Pray, sit between these ladies i 4 23
My Lord Sands, I am beholding to you: cheer your neighbours i 4 40

Sandy. I should not see the sandy hour-glass run, But I should think of shallows and of flats *Mer. of Venice* i 1 25
Ere the glass, that now begins to run, Finish the process of his sandy hour, These eyes . . . Shall see thee wither'd *1 Hen. VI.* iv 2 36
Let him shun castles; Safer shall he be upon the sandy plains *2 Hen. VI.* i 4 39
As false As air, as water, wind, or sandy earth *Troi. and Cres.* iii 2 199
This sandy plot is plain; guide, if thou canst, This after me *T. Andron.* iv 1 69

Sandy-bottom'd Severn *1 Hen. IV.* iii 1 66
ii 4 268

Sanguine. This sanguine coward
About the rose I wear; Saying, the sanguine colour of the leaves Did represent my master's blushing cheeks *1 Hen. VI.* iv 1 92
Ye sanguine, shallow-hearted boys! Ye white-limed walls! *T. Andron.* iv 2 97
Upon his neck a mole, a sanguine star; It was a mark of wonder *Cymb.* v 5 364

Sanguis. The deer was, as you know, sanguis, in blood *L. L. Lost* iv 2 3

Sanity. A happiness that often madness hits on, which reason and sanity could not so prosperously be delivered of *Hamlet* ii 2 214

Sans. A confidence sans bound *Tempest* i 2 97
Sans fable, she herself reviled you *Com. of Errors* iv 4 76
I do, sans question *L. L. Lost* v 1 91
My love to thee is sound, sans crack or flaw.—Sans sans, I pray you v 2 415
I did laugh sans intermission An hour by his dial *As Y. Like It* ii 7 32
Sans teeth, sans eyes, sans taste, sans every thing ii 7 166
Sans compliment, what news abroad? *K. John* v 6 16
Sans check to good and bad *Troi. and Cres.* i 3 94
Thy throat shall cut, And mince it sans remorse *T. of Athens* iv 3 122
Eyes without feeling, feeling without sight, Ears without hands or eyes, smelling sans all *Hamlet* iii 4 79
For nature so preposterously to err, Being not deficient, blind, or lame of sense, Sans witchcraft could not *Othello* i 3 64

Santrailles. The brave Lord Ponton de Santrailles *1 Hen. VI.* i 4 28

Sap. All for want of pruning, with intrusion Infect thy sap *Com. of Er.* ii 2 182
There is some sap in this . . . . *W. Tale* iv 4 576
Wound the bark, the skin of our fruit-trees, Lest, being over-proud in sap and blood, With too much riches it confound itself *Richard II.* iii 4 59
Why wither not the leaves the sap being gone? . . *Richard III.* ii 2 42
Did drain The purple sap from her sweet brother's body . . iv 4 277
No English soul More stronger to direct you than yourself, If with the sap of reason you would quench, Or but allay, the fire of passion *Hen. VIII.* i 1 148
Though we leave it with a root, thus hack'd, The air will drink the sap i 2 98
As knots, by the conflux of meeting sap, Infect the sound pine *T. and C.* i 3 7
She that herself will sliver and disbranch From her material sap, perforce must wither And come to deadly use . . . *Lear* iv 2 35
Come on, my queen; There's sap in't yet . . . *Ant. and Cleo.* iii 13 192
Sap-consuming. Hid In sap-consuming winter's drizzled snow *C. of Er.* v 1 312
Sapient. Thou, sapient sir, sit here. Now, you she foxes! . . *Lear* iii 6 24
Sapit. Vir sapit qui pauca loquitur . . . . . *L. L. Lost* iv 2 82
Sapless. That droops his sapless branches to the ground. . 1 *Hen. VI.* ii 5 12
When sapless age and weak unable limbs Should bring thy father to his drooping chair . . . . iv 5 4
Sapling. Mine arm Is, like a blasted sapling, wither'd up *Richard III.* iii 4 71
Peace, tender sapling; thou art made of tears, And tears will quickly melt thy life away . . . . . *T. Andron.* iii 2 50
You're a young foolish sapling, and must be bowed . . *Pericles* iv 2 93
Sapphire. Like sapphire, pearl and rich embroidery . . *Mer. Wives* v 5 75
All o'er embellished with rubies, carbuncles, sapphires . *Com. of Errors* iii 2 138
Saracens. Against black pagans, Turks, and Saracens . *Richard II.* iv 1 95
Sarcenet. And givest such sarcenet surety for thy oaths . 1 *Hen. IV.* iii 1 256
Thou green sarcenet flap for a sore eye . . . *Troi. and Cres.* v 1 36
Sardians. You have condemn'd and noted Lucius Pella For taking bribes here of the Sardians . . . . *J. Cæsar* iv 3 3
Sardinia. You have made me offer Of Sicily, Sardinia *Ant. and Cleo.* ii 6 35
Sardis. They mean this night in Sardis to be quarter'd . *J. Cæsar* iv 2 28
Coming from Sardis, on our former ensign Two mighty eagles fell . v 1 80
At Sardis once, And, this last night, here in Philippi fields . . v 5 18
Sarum plain. Goose, if I had you upon Sarum plain, I'ld drive ye cackling home to Camelot . . . . *Lear* ii 2 89
Sat. I have sat in the stocks for puddings he hath stolen *T. G. of Ver.* iv 4 33
Melodious birds sing madrigals—When as I sat in Pabylon *Mer. Wives* iii 1 24
You have not been inquired after: I have sat here all day *Meas. for Meas.* iv 1 20
O me, with what strict patience have I sat! . . *L. L. Lost* iv 3 165
Sat all day, Playing on pipes of corn and versing love . *M. N. Dream* ii 1 66
And sat with me on Neptune's yellow sands . . . . ii 1 126
Thou rememberest Since once I sat upon a promontory . . ii 1 149
Methought a serpent eat my heart away, And you sat smiling at his cruel prey . . . . ii 2 150
Or if thou hast not sat as I do now, Wearying thy hearer *As Y. Like It* ii 4 37
If ever sat at any good man's feast, If ever from your eyelids wiped a tear ii 7 115
And sat at good men's feasts and wiped our eyes . . . ii 7 122
My mother told me just how he would woo, As if she sat in's heart *All's Well* iv 2 70
Has sat i' the stocks all night, poor gallant knave . . . iv 3 116
She sat like patience on a monument, Smiling at grief . *T. Night* ii 4 117
I myself know well How troublesome it sat upon my head 2 *Hen. IV.* iv 5 187
As if allegiance in their bosoms sat, Crowned with faith . *Hen. V.* ii 2 4
Sat in the council-house Early and late, debating to and fro . 2 *Hen. VI.* i 1 90
Methought I sat in seat of majesty In the cathedral church of Westminster . . . . i 2 36
Think'st thou that I will leave my kingly throne, Wherein my grandsire and my father sat? . . . . . 3 *Hen. VI.* i 1 125
Her grace sat down To rest awhile, some half an hour or so *Hen. VIII.* iv 1 65
Within thine eyes sat twenty thousand deaths . . *Coriolanus* iii 3 70
I have sat too long.—Nay, go not from us thus . . . v 3 131
There have sat The live-long day, with patient expectation . *J. Cæsar* i 1 45
The crowner hath sat on her, and finds it Christian burial . *Hamlet* v 1 4
I sat me down, Devised a new commission, wrote it fair . . v 2 31
Pillicock sat on Pillicock-hill: Halloo, halloo, loo, loo! . . *Lear* iii 4 78
The poor soul sat sighing by a sycamore tree, Sing all a green willow *Oth.* iv 3 41
The barge she sat in, like a burnish'd throne, Burn'd on the water *Ant. and Cleo.* ii 2 196
At the feet sat Cæsarion, whom they call my father's son . . iii 6 5
Satan. As slanderous as Satan?—And as poor as Job? . *Mer. Wives* v 5 163
Satan, avoid! I charge thee, tempt me not . . *Com. of Errors* iv 3 48
Is this Mistress Satan?—It is the devil . . . . . iv 3 49
I charge thee, Satan, housed within this man, To yield possession to my holy prayers . . . . iv 4 57
Talked of Satan and of Limbo and of Furies . . . *All's Well* v 3 261
'Tis not for gravity to play at cherry-pit with Satan . . *T. Night* iii 4 130
Fie, thou dishonest Satan! I call thee by the most modest terms . iv 2 35
Falstaff, that old white-bearded Satan . . . 1 *Hen. IV.* ii 4 509
Satchel. The whining schoolboy, with his satchel And shining morning face, creeping like snail Unwillingly to school . . *As Y. Like It* ii 7 145
Sate. So lust, though to a radiant angel link'd, Will sate itself in a celestial bed, And prey on garbage . . . . . *Hamlet* i 5 56
Sated. She must change for youth: when she is sated with his body, she will find the error of her choice . . . . . *Othello* i 3 356
Satiate. The cloyed will, That satiate yet unsatisfied desire . *Cymbeline* i 6 48
Satiety. And with satiety seeks to quench his thirst . . *T. of Shrew* i 1 24
A mere satiety of commendations . . . . . *T. of Athens* i 1 166
To give satiety a fresh appetite, loveliness in favour . . *Othello* ii 1 231
Satin. Some four suits of peach-coloured satin . . *Meas. for Meas.* iv 3 12
What said Master Dombledon about the satin for my short cloak? 2 *Hen. IV* i 2 34
I looked a' should have sent me two and twenty yards of satin . . i 2 50
Bring me the satin coffer: lay the babe Upon the pillow . *Pericles* iii 1 68
Satire. Dost thou think I care for a satire or an epigram? *Much Ado* v 4 103
That is some satire, keen and critical . . . *M. N. Dream* v 1 54
A satire against the softness of prosperity . . . *T. of Athens* v 1 36
Satirical. Slanders, sir: for the satirical rogue says here that old men have grey beards . . . . *Hamlet* ii 2 198
Satis quod sufficit . . . . *L. L. Lost* v 1 1
Satisfaction. Have you received no promise of satisfaction? *Mer. Wives* ii 2 217
We may soon our satisfaction have Touching that point . *Meas. for Meas.* i 1 83
The satisfaction I would require is likewise your own benefit . . . iii 1 156
Give him promise of satisfaction . . . . iii 1 275
For my better satisfaction . . . . iv 2 125
Therefore make present satisfaction, Or I'll attach you . *Com. of Errors* iv 1 5
Give me ample satisfaction For these deep shames and great indignities v 1 252
We shall make full satisfaction . . . . v 1 399
No satisfaction, no revenge . . . . . *Mer. of Venice* iii 1 98
She ceased In heavy satisfaction . . . . . . *All's Well* v 3 100
Satisfaction can be none but by pangs of death and sepulchre *T. Night* iii 4 261
This satisfaction The by-gone day proclaim'd . . . . *W. Tale* i 2 31
A good conscience will make any possible satisfaction . 2 *Hen. IV.* Epil. 22
King Pepin's title and Hugh Capet's claim, King Lewis his satisfaction, all appear To hold in right and title of the female . . *Hen. V.* i 2 88
And partly for the satisfaction, look you, of my mind . . . iii 2 106
A weak and worthless satisfaction . . . . iii 6 141
How canst thou make me satisfaction? . . . . . . iv 8 48
Nor other satisfaction do I crave . . . . . 1 *Hen. VI.* ii 3 77
What satisfaction canst thou make For bearing arms? . . 3 *Hen. VI.* v 5 14
O, worthy satisfaction! would it were otherwise . . *Troi. and Cres.* ii 3 4
Be . . . Imperious and impatient of your wrongs, And wherein Rome hath done you any scath, Let him make treble satisfaction *T. An.* v 1 8
What satisfaction canst thou have to-night?—The exchange of thy love's faithful vow for mine . . . . *Rom. and Jul.* ii 2 126
But for your private satisfaction, Because I love you . *J. Cæsar* ii 2 73
We will our kingdom give, Our crown, our life, and all that we call ours, To you in satisfaction . . . . *Hamlet* iv 5 209
By an auricular assurance have your satisfaction . . . *Lear* i 2 99
Nor to comply with heat—the young affects In me defunct—and proper satisfaction . . . . *Othello* i 3 265
Why dost thou ask?—But for a satisfaction of my thought . . iii 3 97
What then? how then? What shall I say? Where's satisfaction? . iii 3 401
If imputation and strong circumstances, Which lead directly to the door of truth, Will give you satisfaction, you may have't. . . . iii 3 408
Assure yourself I will seek satisfaction of you . . . . . iv 2 203
I give him satisfaction? Would he had been one of my rank! *Cymbeline* ii 1 16
The satisfaction of her knowledge only In killing creatures vile . v 5 251
Satisfied. Who by repentance is not satisfied Is nor of heaven nor earth *T. G. of Ver.* v 4 79
I cannot be thus satisfied . . . . *Mer. Wives* ii 1 195
Be satisfied; Your brother dies to-morrow; be content . *Meas. for Meas.* ii 2 104
And go well satisfied to France again . . . . *L. L. Lost* ii 1 153
He is well paid that is well satisfied; And I, delivering you, am satisfied And therein do account myself well paid . . *Mer. of Venice* iv 1 415
I am sure you are not satisfied Of these events at full . . . v 1 296
I will satisfy you, if ever I satisfied man . . . *As Y. Like It* v 2 125
I will so excuse As you shall well be satisfied withal . *T. of Shrew* iii 2 111
I am satisfied and need no more Than what I know . . *W. Tale* ii 1 189
The commons will not then be satisfied.—They shall be satisfied *Rich. II.* iv 1 272
I will be satisfied; let me see the writing . . . . . v 2 59
But gladly would be better satisfied . . . . . 2 *Hen. IV.* i 3 6
Wearing the crown of France, till satisfied That fair Queen Isabel, his grandmother, Was lineal of the Lady Ermengare . . . *Hen. V* i 2 80
Enough: my soul shall then be satisfied . . . 1 *Hen. VI.* ii 5 21
Yet so my fancy may be satisfied . . . . v 3 91
And yet not satisfied . . . . 3 *Hen. VI.* ii 2 99
How will my mother for a father's death Take on with me and ne'er be satisfied!—How will my wife for slaughter of my son Shed seas of tears and ne'er be satisfied!—How will the country for these woful chances Misthink the king and not be satisfied! . . . . ii 5 104
Be satisfied, dear God, with our true blood! . . . *Richard III.* iii 3 21
So, I am satisfied. Give me a bowl of wine . . . . . v 3 72
Unloosed, although not there At once and fully satisfied . *Hen. VIII.* ii 4 148
Be pleased yourself to say How far you satisfied me . . . ii 4 211
His opinions; which Have satisfied the king for his divorce . . iii 2 65
In second voice we'll not be satisfied . . . *Troi. and Cres.* iii 3 149
Speak but one rhyme, and I am satisfied . . . *Rom. and Jul.* ii 1 9
I'll stay the circumstance: Let me be satisfied, is't good or bad? . ii 5 37
So, good Capulet,—which name I tender As dearly as my own,—be satisfied . . . . iii 1 75
Then, I hope, thou wilt be satisfied.—Indeed, I never shall be satisfied iii 5 93
Cæsar doth not wrong, nor without cause Will he be satisfied *J. Cæsar* iii 1 48
Tell him, so please him come unto this place, He shall be satisfied . iii 1 141
That were you, Antony, the son of Cæsar, You should be satisfied . iii 1 226
We will be satisfied; let us be satisfied.—Then follow me . . iii 2 1
If he be at hand, I shall be satisfied . . . . . . iv 2 10
I will be satisfied: deny me this, And an eternal curse fall on you! *Macbeth* iv 1 104
I am satisfied in nature, Whose motive, in this case, should stir me most To my revenge . . . . *Hamlet* v 2 255
What if I do obey? How may the duke be therewith satisfied? *Othello* i 2 88
Would I were satisfied!—I see, sir, you are eaten up with passion . iii 3 390
You would be satisfied?—Would! nay, I will.—And may: but, how? how satisfied, my lord? . . . . iii 3 393
I will hear further reason for this.—And you shall be satisfied . iv 2 252
Iago in the interim Came in and satisfied him . . . . v 2 318
I am satisfied. Cæsar sits down in Alexandria . *Ant. and Cleo.* iii 13 167
If further yet you will be satisfied . . . . . *Pericles* i 3 16
Satisfy me once more; once more search with me . *Mer. Wives* iv 2 172
Do not satisfy your resolution with hopes that are fallible *M. for M.* iii 1 170
Satisfy the deputy with the visage Of Ragozine, more like to Claudio iv 3 79
To satisfy this good old man, I would bend under any heavy weight *Much Ado* v 1 286
Satisfy me so . . . . *L. L. Lost* ii 1 163
I will satisfy you, if ever I satisfied man . . . *As Y. Like It* v 2 125
To satisfy you in what I have said, Stand by and mark . *T. of Shrew* v 2 4
Let it satisfy you, you are too old . . . . . *All's Well* ii 3 206
Let us satisfy our eyes With the memorials and the things of fame That do renown this city . . . . *T. Night* iii 3 22
To satisfy your highness and the entreaties Of our most gracious mistress.—Satisfy! The entreaties of your mistress! satisfy! Let that suffice . . . . *W. Tale* i 2 232
Leontes— Shall satisfy your father . . . . iv 4 635
Satisfy her so That we shall stop her exclamation . . *K. John* ii 1 557
Satisfy the poor woman . . . . 2 *Hen. IV.* ii 1 143
Partly to satisfy my opinion, and partly for the satisfaction, look you, of my mind . . . . *Hen. V.* iii 2 105
Give me leave In this close walk to satisfy myself . 2 *Hen. VI.* ii 2 3
Whose unstanched thirst York and young Rutland could not satisfy 3 *Hen. VI.* ii 6 84
Resolve me now; And what your pleasure is, shall satisfy me . . iii 2 20
Let them satisfy their lust on thee . . . . *T. Andron.* ii 3 180
I will not come; That is enough to satisfy the senate . *J. Cæsar* ii 2 72
I will set down what comes from her, to satisfy my remembrance *Macbeth* v 1 37
Straight satisfy yourself: If she be in her chamber or your house *Othello* i 1 138
Of this my letters Before did satisfy you . . . . *Ant. and Cleo.* ii 2 52
Other women cloy The appetites they feed; but she makes hungry Where most she satisfies . . . . ii 2 243

Satisfy. Will this description satisfy him? *Ant. and Cleo.* ii 7 56
No further halting: satisfy me home What is become of her *Cymbeline* iii 5 92
To satisfy, If of my freedom 'tis the main part, take No stricter render of me than my all v 4 15
Why will you kill me?—To satisfy my lady *Pericles* iv 1 72
Satisfying. I have no great devotion to the deed; And yet he hath given me satisfying reasons *Othello* v 1 9
If you seek For further satisfying *Cymbeline* ii 4 134
A doubt In such a time nothing becoming you, Nor satisfying us iv 4 16
Saturday. On Saturday we will return to France *L. L. Lost* iv 1 6
Fridays and Saturdays and all *As Y. Like It* iv 1 116
Saturn. Being, as thou sayest thou art, born under Saturn *Much Ado* i 3 12
Saturn and Venus this year in conjunction! what says the almanac? *2 Hen. IV.* ii 4 286
Though Venus govern your desires, Saturn is dominator over mine *T. Andron.* ii 3 31
Here, to Mercury: To Saturn, Caius, not to Saturnine iv 3 56
The sweet view on't Might well have warm'd old Saturn *Cymbeline* ii 5 12
Saturnine. Proud Saturnine, interrupter of the good That noble-minded Titus means to thee! *T. Andron.* i 1 208
This suit I make, That you create your emperor's eldest son, Lord Saturnine i 1 225
And say 'Long live our Emperor Saturnine!' i 1 233
Saturnine, King and commander of our commonweal, The wide world's emperor i 1 246
Was there none else in Rome to make a stale, But Saturnine? i 1 305
If Saturnine advance the Queen of Goths, She will a handmaid be i 1 330
His lovely bride, Sent by the heavens for Prince Saturnine i 1 335
Receive him, then, to favour, Saturnine i 1 421
Heavens be my judge, How I have loved and honour'd Saturnine! i 1 427
This siren, that will charm Rome's Saturnine, And see his shipwreck ii 1 23
And make proud Saturnine and his empress Beg at the gates iii 1 298
To the Goths, and raise a power, To be revenged on Rome and Saturnine iii 1 301
Or slunk not Saturnine, as Tarquin erst? iv 1 63
Vengeance on the traitor Saturnine iv 3 34
To Saturn, Caius, not to Saturnine iv 3 56
My lovely Saturnine, Lord of my life, commander of my thoughts iv 4 27
Saturninus. Patience, Prince Saturninus.—Romans, do me right i 1 203
Draw your swords, and sheathe them not Till Saturninus be Rome's emperor i 1 205
We create Lord Saturninus Rome's great emperor i 1 232
As good as Saturninus may ii 1 90
He and his shall know that justice lives In Saturninus' health iv 4 24
Satyr. So excellent a king; that was, to this, Hyperion to a satyr *Hamlet* i 2 140
Sauce. I'll make them pay; I'll sauce them *Mer. Wives* iv 3 11
Will you not eat your word?—With no sauce that can be devised *M. Ado* iv 1 281
Honesty coupled to beauty is to have honey a sauce to sugar *As Y. L. It* iii 3 31
As fast as she answers thee with frowning looks, I'll sauce her with bitter words iii 5 69
Item, Sauce, 4d. Item, Sack, two gallons, 5s. 8d. *1 Hen. IV.* ii 4 586
Eat your victuals: come, there is sauce for it *Hen. V.* v 1 36
Will you have some more sauce to your leek? v 1 52
Thy wit is a very bitter sweeting; it is a most sharp sauce *R. and J.* ii 4 84
Sauce his palate With thy most operant poison! *T. of Athens* iv 3 24
Would poison were obedient and knew my mind!—Where wouldst thou send it?—To sauce thy dishes iv 3 299
This rudeness is a sauce to his good wit *J. Cæsar* i 2 304
To feed were best at home; From thence the sauce to meat is ceremony; Meeting were bare without it *Macbeth* iii 4 36
My more-having would be as a sauce To make me hunger more iv 3 81
Epicurean cooks Sharpen with cloyless sauce his appetite *Ant. and Cleo.* ii 1 25
Sauced. Thou say'st his meat was sauced with thy upbraidings *C. of Er.* v 1 73
His folly sauced with discretion *Troi. and Cres.* i 2 24
As if I loved my little should be dieted In praises sauced with lies *Coriol.* i 9 53
Sauced our broths, as Juno had been sick And he her dieter *Cymbeline* iv 2 50
Saucers. Why, then incision Would let her out in saucers *L. L. Lost* iv 3 98
Saucily. Though this knave came something saucily into the world before he was sent for *Lear* i 1 22
The very fellow that of late Display'd so saucily against your highness ii 4 41
Sauciness. Your sauciness will jest upon my love *Com. of Errors* ii 2 28
Which he thinks is a patent for his sauciness *All's Well* iv 5 70
This unhair'd sauciness and boyish troops *K. John* v 2 133
Words that come with such more than impudent sauciness from you *2 Hen. IV.* ii 1 123
You call honourable boldness impudent sauciness ii 1 135
Being intercepted in your sport, Great reason that my noble lord be rated For sauciness *T. Andron.* ii 3 82
Saucy. You, minion, are too saucy *T. G. of Ver.* i 2 92
As to remit Their saucy sweetness that do coin heaven's image In stamps that are forbid *Meas. for Meas.* ii 4 45
A saucy friar, A very scurvy fellow v 1 135
Study is like the heaven's glorious sun, That will not be deep-search'd with saucy looks *L. L. Lost* i 1 85
From the rattling tongue Of saucy and audacious eloquence *M. N. D.* v 1 103
I will speak to him like a saucy lackey *As Y. Like It* iii 2 314
Saucy with lords and honourable personages *All's Well* ii 3 278
When saucy trusting of the cozen'd thoughts Defiles the pitchy night iv 4 23
I heard you were saucy at my gates *T. Night* i 5 209
There's vinegar and pepper in't.—Is't so saucy? iii 4 159
Turn thou the mouth of thy artillery, As we will ours, against these saucy walls *K. John* ii 1 404
By this wine, I'll thrust my knife in your mouldy chaps, an you play the saucy cuttle with me *2 Hen. IV.* ii 4 139
Am I not protector, saucy priest? *1 Hen. VI.* iii 1 45
The envious barking of your saucy tongue iii 4 33
But thou wilt brave me with these saucy terms? *2 Hen. VI.* iv 10 38
You are a saucy fellow: Deserve we no more reverence? *Hen. VIII.* iv 2 100
Where's then the saucy boat Whose weak untimber'd sides but even now Co-rivall'd greatness? *Troi. and Cres.* i 3 42
Saucy controller of our private steps! *T. Andron.* ii 3 60
You are a saucy boy: is't so, indeed? *Rom. and Jul.* i 5 85
What saucy merchant was this, that was so full of his ropery? ii 4 153
What meanest thou by that? mend me, thou saucy fellow! *J. Cæsar* i 1 21
The world, too saucy with the gods, Incenses them to send destruction i 3 12
Saucy fellow, hence!—Bear with him, Brutus; 'tis his fashion iv 3 134
Cabin'd, cribb'd, confined, bound in To saucy doubts and fears *Macbeth* iii 4 25
Beldams as you are, Saucy and overbold iii 5 3
Who, having been praised for bluntness, doth affect A saucy roughness *Lear* ii 2 103
We then have done you bold and saucy wrongs *Othello* i 1 129
Saucy. So saucy with the hand of she here,—what's her name? *Ant. and Cleo.* iii 13 98
Hence, saucy eunuch: peace! She hath betray'd me and shall die iv 14 25
Saucy lictors Will catch at us, like strumpets; and scald rhymers Ballad us v 2 214
A saucy stranger in his court to mart As in a Romish stew *Cymbeline* i 6 151
Ready in gibes, quick-answer'd, saucy and As quarrelous as the weasel iii 4 161
I am too blunt and saucy: here's my knee v 5 325
Sauf votre honneur, en vérité, vous prononcez les mots aussi droit que les natifs d'Angleterre *Hen. V.* iii 4 40
De ilbow.—Sauf votre honneur, de elbow iii 4 51
Oui, vraiment, sauf votre grace, ainsi dit-il v 2 114
Sauf votre honneur, le François que vous parlez, il est meilleur que l'Anglois v 2 199
Saunder Simpcox, an if it please you, master.—Then, Saunder, sit there, the lyingest knave in Christendom *2 Hen. VI.* ii 1 124
Savage. Thou didst not, savage, Know thine own meaning *Tempest* i 2 355
Do you put tricks upon's with savages and men of Ind? ii 2 60
In time the savage bull doth bear the yoke *Much Ado* i 1 263
Those pamper'd animals That rage in savage sensuality iv 1 62
When shall we set the savage bull's horns on the sensible Benedick's head? v 1 183
I think he thinks upon the savage bull v 4 43
Like a rude and savage man of Inde *L. L. Lost* iv 3 222
His lines would ravish savage ears And plant in tyrants mild humility iv 3 348
Show the sunshine of your face, That we, like savages, may worship it. v 2 202
Make a mutual stand, Their savage eyes turn'd to a modest gaze By the sweet power of music *Mer. of Venice* v 1 78
If this uncouth forest yield any thing savage, I will either be food for it or bring it for food to thee *As Y. Like It* ii 6 7
I thought that all things had been savage here ii 7 107
A savage jealousy That sometime savours nobly *T. Night* v 1 122
A savage clamour! *W. Tale* iii 3 56
And tame the savage spirit of wild war *K. John* v 2 74
Thou cruel, Ingrateful, savage and inhuman creature! *Hen. V.* ii 2 95
Our scions, put in wild and savage stock, Spirt up so suddenly iii 5 7
Grow like savages,—as soldiers will That nothing do but meditate on blood v 2 59
Savage islanders [stabbed] Pompey the Great *2 Hen. VI.* iv 1 137
Rather than have made that savage duke thine heir *3 Hen. VI.* i 1 224
Not to relent is beastly, savage, devilish *Richard III.* i 4 265
Even where his lustful eye or savage heart, Without control, listed iii 5 83
Here tend the savage strangeness he puts on *Troi. and Cres.* ii 3 135
Spur them to ruthful work, rein them from ruth.—Fie, savage, fie! v 3 49
Like a boar too savage, doth root up His country's peace *T. of Athens* v 1 168
Else were this a savage spectacle *J. Cæsar* iii 1 223
To fright you thus, methinks, I am too savage *Macbeth* iv 2 70
Most savage and unnatural! *Lear* iii 3 7
He foams at mouth and by and by Breaks out to savage madness *Othello* iv 1 56
With patience more Than savages could suffer *Ant. and Cleo.* i 4 61
I have savage cause iii 13 128
'Tis some savage hold: I were best not call; I dare not call *Cymbeline* iii 6 18
Ho! who's here? If any thing that's civil, speak; if savage, Take or lend iii 6 23
What lies I have heard! Our courtiers say all's savage but at court iv 2 33
She is not dead at Tarsus, as she should have been, By savage Cleon *Per.* v 1 218
Savagely. Your wife and babes Savagely slaughter'd *Macbeth* iv 3 205
Savageness. Wolves and bears, they say, Casting their savageness aside have done Like offices of pity *W. Tale* ii 3 188
A savageness in unreclaimed blood, Of general assault *Hamlet* ii 1 34
O! she will sing the savageness out of a bear *Othello* iv 1 200
Savagery. This is the bloodiest shame, The wildest savagery *K. John* iv 3 48
While that the coulter rusts That should deracinate such savagery *Hen. V.* v 2 47
Savage-wild. The time and my intents are savage-wild *Rom. and Jul.* v 3 37
Save for the son that she did litter here *Tempest* i 2 282
Here is every thing advantageous to life.—True; save means to live ii 1 50
God save his majesty!—Long live Gonzalo! ii 1 168
No woman's face remember, Save, from my glass, mine own iii 1 50
His daughter and I will be king and queen,—save our graces! iii 2 115
Sir Proteus, save you! Saw you my master? *T. G. of Ver.* i 1 70
Be gone, to save your ship from wreck, Which cannot perish having thee aboard i 1 156
A fery discretion answer; save the fall is in the ort 'dissolutely' *M. W.* i 1 261
He has save his soul, dat he is no come ii 3 6
She is fast my wife, Save that we do the denunciation lack Of outward order: this we came not to *Meas. for Meas.* i 2 152
This gentleman, Whom I would save, had a most noble father ii 1 7
God save your honour! ii 2 25
'Save your honour! ii 2 161
Might there not be a charity in sin To save this brother's life? ii 4 64
Admit no other way to save his life ii 4 88
There were No earthly mean to save him ii 4 95
None, but such remedy as, to save a head, To cleave a heart in twain iii 1 62
What sin you do to save a brother's life, Nature dispenses with the deed so far That it becomes a virtue iii 1 134
I'll pray a thousand prayers for thy death, No word to save thee iii 1 147
How will you do to content this substitute, and to save your brother? iii 1 193
The cure of it not only saves your brother, but keeps you from dishonour iii 1 245
To save me from the danger that might come If he were known alive iv 3 89
Save that his riotous youth, with dangerous sense, Might in the times to come have ta'en revenge iv 4 32
You may marvel why I obscured myself, Labouring to save his life v 1 396
Knowing whom it was their hap to save *Com. of Errors* i 1 114
To save the money that he spends in tiring ii 2 98
That labour may you save iv 1 14
Shift and save yourself! v 1 168
And took Deep scars to save thy life v 1 193
Haply I see a friend will save my life v 1 283
Friendship is constant in all other things Save in the office and affairs of love: Therefore all hearts in love use their own tongues *M. Ado* ii 1 183
My lord and brother, God save you! iii 2 82
God save the foundation! v 1 327
I yield upon great persuasion; and partly to save your life v 4 96
Small have continual plodders ever won Save base authority from others' books *L. L. Lost* i 1 87
Now, God save thy life!—And yours from long living! i 1 191
Thus will I save my credit in the shoot iv 1 26
God save your life!—Have with thee, my girl iv 2 149
Fair sir, God save you! v 2 310
Never wrong'd you; Save that, in love unto Demetrius, I told him of your stealth unto this wood *M. N. Dream* iii 2 309

Save. Being blent together, Turns to a wild of nothing, save of joy *Mer. of Venice* iii 2 184
That 'scuse serves many men to save their gifts . . . iv 1 444
He saves my labour by his own approach . . . . *As Y. Like It* ii 7 8
God save you, brother.—And you, fair sister . . . v 2 20
To save my life, Puts my apparel and my countenance on *T. of Shrew* i 1 233
While I make way from hence to save my life . . . i 1 239
Gentlemen, God save you. If I may be bold, Tell me, I beseech you . i 2 219
To save your life in this extremity, This favour will I do you . iv 2 102
Save you, fair queen!—And you, monarch! . . . *All's Well* i 1 117
What impossibility would slay In common sense, sense saves another way ii 1 181
If she be All that is virtuous, save what thou dislikest . ii 3 129
Save that he comes not along with her . . . . iii 2 2
Save you, good madam . . . . iii 2 47
Haply thou mayst inform Something to save thy life . . iv 1 92
In his sleep he does little harm, save to his bed-clothes about him . iv 3 287
Come, you shall ha't; save your word . . . . v 2 40
Unstaid and skittish in all motions else, Save in the constant image of the creature That is beloved . . . . *T. Night* ii 4 19
A thousand thousand sighs to save . . . . . ii 4 64
Save thee, friend, and thy music: dost thou live by thy tabor? . iii 1 1
Save you, gentleman.—And you, sir.—Dieu vous garde, monsieur . iii 1 76
Nor never none Shall mistress be of it, save I alone . . iii 1 172
My stay To you a charge and trouble: to save both, Farewell *W. Tale* i 2 26
You shall pay your fees When you depart, and save your thanks . i 2 54
To save this bastard's life,—for 'tis a bastard, So sure as this beard's grey,—what will you adventure To save this brat's life? . . . ii 3 161
I'll pawn the little blood which I have left To save the innocent . ii 3 167
Save him from danger, do him love and honour . . . iv 4 521
To save unscratch'd your city's threatened cheeks . . *K. John* ii 1 225
Like to a muzzled bear, Save in aspect . . . . ii 1 250
All form is formless, order orderless, Save what is opposite to England's love . . . . iii 1 254
O, save me, Hubert, save me! my eyes are out Even with the fierce looks of these bloody men . . . . iv 1 73
Save back to England, all the world's my way . . *Richard II.* i 3 207
Save bidding farewell to so sweet a guest As my sweet Richard . ii 2 8
He is gone to save far off, Whilst others come to make him lose at home . . . . ii 2 80
Leaving me no sign, Save men's opinions and my living blood . iii 1 26
What can we bequeath Save our deposed bodies to the ground? . iii 2 150
He shall not have a Scot of them; No, if a Scot would save his soul *1 Hen. IV.* i 3 215
All studies here I solemnly defy, Save how to gall and pinch this Bolingbroke . . . . i 3 229
'Tis no little reason bids us speed, To save our heads by raising of a head . . . . i 3 284
Not an eye But is a-weary of thy common sight, Save mine . iii 2 89
To save the blood on either side, Try fortune with him in a single fight v 1 99
Give me life: which if I can save, so; if not, honour comes unlooked for v 3 63
God save your grace!—And yours! . . . . *2 Hen. IV.* ii 2 78
Good morrow; and God save your majesty! . . . . v 2 43
Save that there was not time enough to hear . . . *Hen. V.* i 1 84
So Chrish save me, la! . . . . iii 2 97
What have kings, that privates have not too, Save ceremony? . iv 1 256
Save thou thy labour; Come thou no more for ransom . . iv 3 121
He prays you to save his life: he is a gentleman of a good house . iv 4 47
Are all one reckonings, save the phrase is a little variations . iv 7 18
Do what thou canst to save our honours . . . *1 Hen. VI.* i 2 147
Leave Lord Talbot?—Ay, All the Talbots in the world, to save my life . iii 2 107
God save King Henry, of that name the sixth! . . . iv 1 2
So should we save a valiant gentleman By forfeiting a traitor . iv 3 26
Bought with such a shame, To save a paltry life and slay bright fame . iv 6 45
So doth the swan her downy cygnets save, Keeping them prisoner underneath her wings . . . . v 3 56
It is your policy To save your subjects from such massacre . v 4 160
If you mean to save yourself from whipping, leap me over this stool and run away . . . . *2 Hen. VI.* ii 1 143
The king will labour still to save his life, The commons haply rise, to save his life . . . . iii 1 239
Relent, and save my life . . . . iv 7 124
Chaplain, away! thy priesthood saves thy life . . *3 Hen. VI.* i 3 3
Forthwith unto the sanctuary, To save at least the heir of Edward's right . . . . iv 4 32
Save yourselves; For Warwick bids you all farewell, to meet in heaven v 2 48
What shall we do?—Relent, and save your souls . *Richard III.* i 4 263
God save Richard, England's royal king! . . . . iii 7 22
She is of royal blood.—To save her life, I'll say she is not so . iv 4 212
Of all one pain, save for a night of groans Endured of her . . iv 4 303
Save me so much talking . . . . . . *Hen. VIII.* i 4 40
Whither away so fast?—O, God save ye! Even to the hall . ii 1 1
I'll save you That labour . . . . ii 1 3
When the king knows my truth.—This cannot save you . . iii 2 302
Never suffers matter of the world Enter his thoughts, save such as do revolve And ruminate himself . . . . *Troi. and Cres.* ii 3 197
I do enjoy At ample point all that I did possess, Save these men's looks iii 3 90
Save the thanks this prince expects . . . . . iv 4 119
'Tis not to save labour, nor that I want love . . *Coriolanus* i 3 90
Not one amongst us, save yourself, but says He used us scornfully . ii 3 170
Save you, sir.—And you.—Direct me, if it be your will . . iv 4 6
Not out of hope—Mistake me not—to save my life . . . iv 5 86
Our request did tend To save the Romans, thereby to destroy The Volsces v 3 133
Sir, if you'ld save your life, fly to your house . . . v 4 38
I pour'd forth tears in vain, To save your brother . *T. Andron.* ii 3 164
My youth can better spare my blood than you; And therefore mine shall save my brothers' lives . . . . iii 1 167
Save thou the child, so we may all be safe . . . . iv 2 131
Save the child, And bear it from me to the empress . . . v 1 53
Thou shalt vow . . . To save my boy, to nourish and bring him up . v 1 84
Good thou, save me a piece of marchpane . . *Rom. and Jul.* i 5 9
And all combined, save what thou must combine By holy marriage ii 3 60
Now all are fled, Save only the gods . . . *T. of Athens* iii 3 37
But all, save thee, I fell with curses . . . . . iv 3 507
In every place, save here in Italy . . . . . *J. Cæsar* i 3 88
I do entreat you, not a man depart, Save I alone . . . iii 2 66
All the conspirators save only he Did that they did in envy . v 5 69
And how his audit stands who knows save heaven? . . *Hamlet* iii 3 82
Save me, and hover o'er me with your wings, You heavenly guards! . iii 4 103
What is the matter?—Save yourself, my lord . . . . iv 5 98
Can save the thing from death That is but scratch'd withal . . iv 7 146

Save. The tempest in my mind Doth from my senses take all feeling else Save what beats there . . . . *Lear* iii 4 14
Couldst thou save nothing? Didst thou give them all? . . . iii 4 66
Save him, save him! . . . . v 3 151
Save that, they say, the wars must make examples Out of their best *Oth.* iii 3 65
Save you, friend Cassio!—What make you from home? . . iii 4 169
Save you, worthy general!—With all my heart, sir . . . iv 1 229
His own courses will denote him so That I may save my speech . iv 1 291
Save you your labour . . . . v 1 101
In all obey her, Save when command to your dismission tends *Cymbeline* ii 3 57
'Tis gold Which makes the true man kill'd and saves the thief . ii 3 76
The description Of what is in her chamber nothing saves The wager . ii 4 94
Use like note and words, Save that Euriphile must be Fidele . . iv 2 238
Never bestrid a horse, save one that had A rider like myself . . iv 4 38
Away, boy, from the troops, and save thyself; For friends kill friends . v 2 14
We are Romans and will give you that Like beasts which you shun beastly, and may save . . . . v 3 27
Save him, sir, And spare no blood beside . . . . . v 5 91
The whole world shall not save him . . . . . v 5 321
All o'erjoy'd, Save these in bonds: let them be joyful too . . v 5 402
Without covering, save yon field of stars . . . *Pericles* i 1 37
Come you between, And save poor me, the weaker . . iv 1 91
Saved. One that I saved from drowning . . . *T. G. of Ver.* iv 4 3
By this, is your brother saved, your honour untainted *Meas. for Meas.* iii 1 264
This is another prisoner that I saved, Who should have died . . v 1 492
There's a partridge wing saved, for the fool will eat no supper *Much Ado* ii 1 155
See, see, my beauty will be saved by merit! . . *L. L. Lost* iv 1 21
I shall be saved by my husband; he hath made me a Christian *M. of V.* iii 5 21
The thrifty hire I saved under your father . . *As Y. Like It* ii 3 39
His youthful hose, well saved, a world too wide For his shrunk shank . ii 7 160
If your life be saved, will you undertake to betray the Florentine? *All's Well* iv 3 325
It is perchance that you yourself were saved . . . *T. Night* i 2 6
When you and those poor number saved with you Hung on our driving boat . . . . i 2 10
You might have saved me my pains . . . . . . ii 2 6
No Christian, that means to be saved by believing rightly, can ever believe such . . . . iii 2 7[?]
What shall you ask of me that I'll deny, That honour saved may upon asking give?—Nothing but this . . . . iii 4 23[?]
Thou hast not saved one drop of blood, In this hot trial, more than we *K. John* ii 1 341
O, if men were to be saved by merit, what hole in hell were hot enough for him? This is the most omnipotent villain . . *1 Hen. IV.* i 2 119
Thou hast saved me a thousand marks . . . . . . iii 3 48
And saved the treacherous labour of your son . . . . v 4 57
The better part of valour is discretion; in the which better part I have saved my life . . . . v 4 122
And a many poor men's lives saved . . . . . *Hen. V.* iv 1 128
Part of thy father may be saved in thee . . . *1 Hen. VI.* iv 5 38
All these are saved if thou wilt fly away . . . . iv 6 41
Whiles, in his moan, the ship splits on the rock, Which industry and courage might have saved . . . . . *3 Hen. VI.* v 4 11
A labour saved! . . . . *Troi. and Cres.* iii 3 241
And saved Your husband so much sweat . . . *Coriolanus* iv 1 18
You have well saved me a day's journey . . . . . iv 3 12
Sir, you have saved my longing, and I feed Most hungerly on your sight. —Right welcome, sir! . . . . *T. of Athens* i 1 261
Became his guide, Led him, begg'd for him, saved him from despair *Lear* v 3 191
I might have saved her; now she's gone for ever! Cordelia, Cordelia! v 3 270
God's above all; and there be souls must be saved, and there be souls must not be saved . . . . *Othello* ii 3 106
For mine own part,—no offence to the general, nor any man of quality, —I hope to be saved . . . . ii 3 111
By your leave, not before me; the lieutenant is to be saved before the ancient . . . . ii 3 114
No, as I shall be saved . . . . iv 2 86
But he that will believe all that they [women] say, shall never be saved by half that they do . . . . . . *Ant. and Cleo.* v 2 257
So had you saved The noble Imogen to repent . . . *Cymbeline* v 1 9
How many would have given their honours To have saved their carcases! v 3 67
For that it saved me, keep it . . . . *Pericles* ii 1 134
Saving your honour's reverence . . . . . *Meas. for Meas.* ii 1 92
Saving your merry humour, here's the note . . . *Com. of Errors* iv 1 27
Saving your tale, Petruchio, I pray, Let us . . . speak too *T. of Shrew* ii 1 71
Saving in dialogue of compliment . . . . . *K. John* i 1 201
Saving your manhoods . . . . *2 Hen. IV.* ii 1 29
Saving your majesty's manhood . . . . . . *Hen. V.* iv 8 35
I have a saving faith within me . . . . v 2 217
Which gifts, Saving your mincing, the capacity Of your soft cheveril conscience would receive, If you might please to stretch it *Hen. VIII.* ii 3 31
Standing every flaw, And saving those that eye thee! . *Coriolanus* v 3 75
Then I swore thee, saving of thy life, That whatsoever I did bid thee do, Thou shouldst attempt it . . . . *J. Cæsar* v 3 38
The rather—saving reverence of the word . . . . *Cymbeline* iv 1 5
Saving your reverence *Much Ado* iii 4; *Mer. of Venice* ii 2; *1 Hen. IV.* ii 4
Saviour. Some say that ever 'gainst that season comes Wherein our Saviour's birth is celebrated . . . . *Hamlet* i 1 159
Savory. Hot lavender, mints, savory, marjoram . . *W. Tale* iv 4 104
Savour. She loved not the savour of tar nor of pitch . . *Tempest* ii 2 54
Rubies, fairy favours, In those freckles live their savours *M. N. Dream* ii 1 13
The flowers of odious savours sweet,— Odours, odours. . . iii 1 84
I see, I hear, I speak; I smell sweet savours . . *T. of Shrew* Ind. 2 73
A savage jealousy That sometime savours nobly . . . *T. Night* v 1 123
This savours not much of distraction . . . . . . v 1 322
A savour that may strike the dullest nostril . . . *W. Tale* i 2 421
Something savours Of tyranny . . . . iii 3 119
Rosemary and rue; these keep Seeming and savour all the winter long iv 4 75
The uncleanly savours of a slaughter-house . . . *K. John* iv 3 112
Our master Says that you savour too much of your youth . *Hen. V.* i 2 250
His jest will savour but of shallow wit, When thousands weep . . i 2 295
This admiration, sir, is much o' the savour Of other your new pranks *Lear* i 4 258
Wisdom and goodness to the vile seem vile: Filths savour but themselves . . . . iv 2 39
To me The very doors and windows savour vilely . . . *Pericles* iv 6 117
Savouring. Neither savouring of poetry, wit, nor invention . *L. L. Lost* iv 2 165
Savoury. There were no sallets in the lines to make the matter savoury *Hamlet* ii 2 463
Our stomachs Will make what's homely savoury . . . *Cymbeline* iii 6 33
Savoy. Now go some and pull down the Savoy . . . *2 Hen. VI.* iv 7 2

Saw. O, I have suffer'd With those that I saw suffer . . . *Tempest* i 2 6
Supposing that they saw the king's ship wreck'd . . . i 2 236
A thing divine, for nothing natural I ever saw so noble . . . i 2 419
This Is the third man that e'er I saw, the first That e'er I sigh'd for . i 2 445
I saw him beat the surges under him . . . ii 1 114
As mine eyes open'd, I saw their weapons drawn . . . ii 1 320
The very instant that I saw you, did My heart fly to your service . iii 1 64
I never saw a woman, But only Sycorax my dam and she . . iii 2 108
Would they believe me? If I should say, I saw such islanders . iii 3 29
Never till this day Saw I him touch'd with anger so distemper'd . iv 1 145
Since I saw thee, The affliction of my mind amends . . . v 1 114
Of whom so often I have heard renown, But never saw before . v 1 194
I have been in such a pickle since I saw you last . . . v 1 283
Saw you my master?—But now he parted hence . *T. G. of Ver.* i 1 70
You never saw her since she was deformed . . . ii 1 68
I have loved her ever since I saw her; and still I see her beautiful ii 1 72
Which of you saw Sir Eglamour of late?—Not I.—Nor I.—Saw you my daughter? . . . v 2 32
O, that my husband saw this letter! . . . *Mer. Wives* ii 1 103
I would you knew Ford, sir, that you might avoid him if you saw him ii 2 289
Is at most odds with his own gravity and patience that ever you saw . iii 1 55
I never saw him so gross in his jealousy till now . . . iii 3 201
I saw him arrested, saw him carried away . . *Meas. for Meas.* i 2 67
She and that friar, I saw them at the prison . . . v 1 135
Since which time of five years I never spake with her, saw her . v 1 223
Weeping before for what she saw must come . . *Com. of Errors* i 1 72
I never saw her till this time.—Villain, thou liest . . ii 2 164
I saw it not; but I felt it hot in her breath . . . iii 2 134
And took away my ring—The ring I saw upon his finger . . iv 4 142
You saw they speak us fair, give us gold . . . iv 4 156
The chain, Which, God he knows, I saw not . . . v 1 229
When he ran in here, These people saw the chain about his neck . v 1 258
I never saw the chain, so help me Heaven! And this is false . v 1 267
You know me well.—I never saw you in my life till now . . v 1 296
Grief hath changed me since you saw me last . . . v 1 297
I never saw my father in my life . . . . v 1 319
I ne'er saw Syracusa in my life . . . . v 1 325
Was not Count John here at supper?—I saw him not . *Much Ado* ii 1 2
I never yet saw man, How wise, how noble, young, how rarely featured, But she would spell him backward . . . iii 1 59
Don John saw afar off in the orchard this amiable encounter . . iii 3 160
Before the whole congregation, shame her with what he saw . . iii 3 173
I saw the Duchess of Milan's gown that they praise so . . iii 4 15
Moreover, God saw him when he was hid in the garden . . v 1 181
In Normandy, saw I this Longaville . . . *L. L. Lost* ii 1 43
I saw him at the Duke Alençon's once; And much too little of that good I saw Is my report . . . ii 1 61
What is she in the white?—A woman sometimes, an you saw her in the light . . . . ii 1 198
Such amazes That all eyes saw his eyes enchanted with gazes . ii 1 246
He came, saw, and overcame: he came, one; saw, two; overcame, three iv 1 70
What saw he? the beggar: who overcame he? the beggar . . iv 1 74
Observed your fashion, Saw sighs reek from you, noted well your passion iv 3 140
Oft have I heard of you, my Lord Biron, Before I saw you . v 2 852
And coughing drowns the parson's saw . . . . v 2 932
That very time I saw, but thou couldst not . . *M. N. Dream* ii 1 155
To her, my lord, Was I betroth'd ere I saw Hermia . . iv 1 177
Which, when I saw rehearsed, I must confess, Made mine eyes water . v 1 68
The very best at a beast, my lord, that e'er I saw . . . v 1 233
I am sure he [Dobbin] had more hair of his tail than I have of my face when I last saw him . . *Mer. of Venice* ii 2 105
You saw the mistress, I beheld the maid; You loved, I loved for intermission . . . . iii 2 200
And saw the lion's shadow ere himself And ran dismay'd away . v 1 8
Before ever he saw those pancakes or that mustard . *As Y. Like It* i 2 85
If you saw yourself with your eyes or knew yourself with your judgement i 2 185
Can it be possible that no man saw them? . . . ii 2 1
The ladies, her attendants of her chamber, Saw her a-bed . . ii 2 6
That young swain that you saw here but erewhile . . . ii 4 89
Full of wise saws and modern instances . . . ii 7 156
The shepherd that complain'd of love, Who you saw sitting by me iii 4 52
Now I find thy saw of might, 'Who ever loved that loved not at first sight?' . . . . iii 5 82
I saw her hand: she has a leathern hand, A freestone-colour'd hand iv 3 24
Cæsar's thrasonical brag of 'I came, saw, and overcame' . . v 2 35
The first time that I ever saw him Methought he was a brother . v 4 28
And twenty more such names and men as these Which never were nor no man ever saw . . . *T. of Shrew* Ind. 2 98
I saw sweet beauty in her face, Such as the daughter of Agenor had i 1 172
Saw you no more? mark'd you not how her sister Began to scold? . i 1 176
I saw her coral lips to move . . . . i 1 179
Sacred and sweet was all I saw in her . . . i 1 181
As if they saw some wondrous monument, Some comet . . iii 2 97
I never saw a better-fashion'd gown, More quaint, more pleasing . iv 3 101
You saw my master wink and laugh upon you? . . . iv 4 75
I could not forget you, for I never saw you before in all my life . v 1 52
When I said 'a mother,' Methought you saw a serpent . *All's Well* i 3 147
Such a ring as this, The last that e'er I took her leave at court, I saw upon her finger . . . . . v 3 80
I saw her wear it.—You are deceived, my lord; she never saw it . v 3 91
She never saw it.—Thou speak'st it falsely, as I love mine honour . v 3 112
Methought you said You saw one here in court could witness it . v 3 200
I saw the man to-day, if man he be . . . . v 3 203
I saw your brother, Most provident in peril . . . *T. Night* i 2 11
I saw him hold acquaintance with the waves So long as I could see . i 2 16
I saw him put down the other day with an ordinary fool . . i 5 90
Tell me if this be the lady of the house, for I never saw her . . i 5 183
I saw thee late at the Count Orsino's.— . . . I think I saw your wisdom there . . . . . iii 1 42
I saw your niece do more favours to the count's serving-man . iii 2 6
I saw't i' the orchard.—Did she see thee the while, old boy? . iii 2 8
We'll whisper o'er a couplet or two of most sage saws . . iii 4 413
The old hermit of Prague, that never saw pen and ink . . iv 2 15
That face of his I do remember well; Yet, when I saw it last, it was besmear'd . . . . . v 1 55
I did recoil Twenty-three years, and saw myself unbreech'd . *W. Tale* i 2 155
I do believe thee: I saw his heart in's face. Give me thy hand . i 2 447
Never Saw I men scour so on their way: I eyed them Even to their ships ii 1 35
I never saw a vessel of like sorrow, So fill'd and so becoming . iii 3 21
I never saw The heavens so dim by day. A savage clamour! . iii 3 55

Saw. I have not winked since I saw these sights . . . *W. Tale* iii 3 107
It is fifteen years since I saw my country . . . iv 2 4
It is three days since I saw the prince . . . . iv 2 33
By which means I saw whose purse was best in picture . . iv 4 615
Never saw I Wretches so quake: they kneel, they kiss the earth . v 1 198
We saw not That which my daughter came to look upon . . v 3 12
But how, is to be question'd; for I saw her, As I thought, dead . v 3 139
I saw a smith stand with his hammer, thus . . *K. John* iv 2 193
Let it at least be said They saw we had a purpose of defence . v 1 76
Those baby eyes That never saw the giant world enraged . . v 2 57
Some two days since I saw the prince, And told him . *Richard II.* v 3 13
We two saw you four set on four and bound them . *1 Hen. IV.* ii 4 279
'Faith, I ran when I saw others run . . . . ii 4 333
I saw young Harry, with his beaver on, His cuisses on his thighs . iv 1 104
I saw him hold Lord Percy at the point . . . v 4 21
Why, Percy I killed myself and saw thee dead . . . v 4 147
When he saw The fortune of the day quite turn'd from him . . v 5 17
How is this derived? Saw you the field? . . . *2 Hen. IV.* i 1 24
These mine eyes saw him in bloody state, Rendering faint quittance . i 1 107
I'll be sworn a' ne'er saw him but once . . . . iii 2 346
I saw it, and told John a Gaunt he beat his own name . . iii 2 348
But what of that? he saw me, and yielded . . . iv 3 44
Say, with the hook-nosed fellow of Rome, 'I came, saw, and overcame' iv 3 46
I saw him fumble with the sheets and play with flowers . *Hen. V.* ii 3 14
Do you not remember, a' saw a flea stick upon Bardolph's nose? . ii 3 42
Saw his heroical seed, and smiled to see him, Mangle the work of nature ii 4 59
Never any body saw it but his lackey: 'tis a hooded valour . . iii 7 121
Thrice within this hour I saw him down; thrice up again . . iv 6 5
Till now we never saw your face: Therefore, stand up . *1 Hen. VI.* iii 4 24
I never saw but Humphrey Duke of Gloucester Did bear him like a noble gentleman . . . . . *2 Hen. VI.* i 1 183
His weapons holy saws of sacred writ, His study is his tilt-yard . i 3 61
I saw not better sport these seven years' day . . . ii 1 2
A man that ne'er saw in his life before . . . ii 1 65
I never saw a fellow worse bested, Or more afraid to fight . . ii 3 56
Oft have I struck Those that I never saw and struck them dead . iv 7 87
I saw him in the battle range about . . . *3 Hen. VI.* ii 1 11
When we saw our sunshine made thy spring . . . ii 2 163
Queen Margaret saw Thy murderous falchion smoking in his blood *Richard III.* i 2 93
Methought I saw a thousand fearful wrecks . . . i 4 24
I hope he is much grown since last I saw him.—But I hear, no . ii 4 5
When I was last in Holborn, I saw good strawberries in your garden . iii 4 34
Which when I saw, I reprehended them . . . . iii 7 27
A bard of Ireland told me once, I should not live long after I saw Richmond . . . . iv 2 110
Give me a calendar. Who saw the sun to-day? . . . v 3 277
How have ye done Since last we saw in France? . . *Hen. VIII.* i 1 2
And ever since a fresh admirer Of what I saw there . . . i 1 4
I was then present, saw them salute on horseback . . . i 1 8
Being present both, 'Twas said they saw but one . . . i 1 32
One would take it, That never saw 'em pace before, the spavin Or springhalt reign'd among 'em . . . . . . i 3 12
I saw well chosen, ridden, and furnished . . . . ii 2 2
Subject to your countenance, glad or sorry As I saw it inclined . ii 4 27
Every eye saw 'em, Envy and base opinion set against 'em . . iii 1 35
You saw The ceremony?—That I did.—How was it? . . . iv 1 59
Such joy I never saw before . . . . . iv 1 76
Saw ye none enter since I slept?—None, madam.—No? Saw you not, even now, a blessed troop Invite me to a banquet? . . . iv 2 86
The strangest sight . . . I think your highness saw this many a day v 2 21
She looked yesternight fairer than ever I saw her look . *Troi. and Cres.* i 1 33
Do you know a man if you see him?—Ay, if I ever saw him before . i 2 68
Admirable youth! he ne'er saw three and twenty . . . i 2 255
We saw him at the opening of his tent: He is not sick . . ii 3 91
But this thy countenance, still lock'd in steel, I never saw till now . iv 5 196
There's many a Greek and Trojan dead, Since first I saw yourself . iv 5 215
I saw him run after a gilded butterfly . . . *Coriolanus* i 3 65
I saw our party to their trenches driven, And then I came away . i 6 12
He used me kindly: He cried to me; I saw him prisoner . . i 9 84
Yes, certain, there's a letter for you; I saw't.—A letter for me! . ii 1 124
Our then dictator, Whom with all praise I point at, saw him fight . ii 2 94
No man saw 'em.—He said he had wounds, which he could show in private . . . . ii 3 173
Saw you Aufidius?—On safe-guard he came to me . . . iii 1 8
You had more beard when I last saw you . . . . iv 3 8
More dances my rapt heart Than when I first my wedded mistress saw iv 5 123
The dismall'st day is this that e'er I saw . . . *T. Andron.* i 1 384
How many women saw this child of his? . . . . iv 2 135
Say, again, how many saw the child?—Cornelia the midwife and myself iv 2 140
O, where is Romeo? saw you him to-day? . . *Rom. and Jul.* i 1 123
The all-seeing sun Ne'er saw her match since first the world begun . i 2 98
Tut, you saw her fair, none else being by, Herself poised with herself . i 2 99
Forswear it, sight! For I ne'er saw true beauty till this night . i 5 55
I would not for the world they saw thee here . . . ii 2 74
I saw no man use you at his pleasure . . . . ii 4 165
I saw the wound, I saw it with mine eyes,—God save the mark! . iii 2 52
Most miserable hour that e'er time saw In lasting labour of his pilgrimage! . . . . iv 5 44
I saw her laid low in her kindred's vault . . . . v 1 20
I saw them speak together . . . . . *T. of Athens* i 1 62
When you saw his chariot but appear, Have you not made an universal shout, That Tiber trembled? . . . . *J. Cæsar* i 1 48
I saw Mark Antony offer him a crown;—yet 'twas not a crown neither i 2 237
Why, saw you any thing more wonderful? . . . . i 3 14
Who swore they saw Men all in fire walk up and down the streets . i 3 24
She dreamt to-night she saw my statua, Which . . . Did run pure blood ii 2 76
When the noble Cæsar saw him stab, Ingratitude, more strong than traitors' arms, Quite vanquish'd him . . . . . iii 2 188
Saw you any thing?—No, my lord, I saw nothing . . . iv 3 305
I have spoke With one that saw him die . . . *Macbeth* i 4 4
What, quite unmann'd in folly?—If I stand here, I saw him.—Fie, for shame! . . . . iii 4 74
Saw you the weird sisters?—No, my lord.—Came they not by you? . iv 1 136
The rather, For that I saw the tyrant's power a-foot . . iv 3 185
I should report that which I say I saw, But know not how to do it . v 5 31
I saw him once; he was a goodly king . . . *Hamlet* i 2 186
My lord, I think I saw him yesternight.—Saw? who? . . . i 2 189
Then saw you not his face?—O, yes, my lord; he wore his beaver up . i 2 229
Longer, longer.—Not when I saw't . . . . . i 2 240

Saw. Why the sepulchre, Wherein we saw thee quietly inurn'd, Hath oped his ponderous and marble jaws, To cast thee up again . *Ham.* i 4 49
I'll wipe away all trivial fond records, All saws of books . i 5 100
I know the gentleman; I saw him yesterday, or t' other day . ii 1 56
Or perchance, 'I saw him enter such a house of sale' . ii 1 60
Your ladyship is nearer to heaven than when I saw you last . ii 2 446
If the gods themselves did see her then When she saw Pyrrhus . ii 2 536
Nor do not saw the air too much with your hand, thus . iii 2 5
Who brought them?—Sailors, my lord, they say; I saw them not . iv 7 39
When saw you my father last?—Why, the night gone by *Lear* i 2 166
But when he saw my best alarum'd spirits, . . . Full suddenly he fled ii 1 55
Good king, that must approve the common saw . ii 2 167
I have no way, and therefore want no eyes; I stumbled when I saw . iv 1 21
I' the last night's storm I such a fellow saw . iv 1 34
I saw Othello's visage in his mind . *Othello* i 3 253
I saw't not, thought it not, it harm'd not me . iii 3 339
Is not this man jealous?—I ne'er saw this before . iii 4 100
This would not be believed in Venice, Though I should swear I saw't . iv 1 254
But then I saw no harm, and then I heard Each syllable . iv 2 4
By heaven, I saw my handkerchief in's hand . v 2 62
I saw it in his hand: It was a handkerchief, an antique token . v 2 215
Yet at the first I saw the treasons planted . *Ant. and Cleo.* i 3 26
I saw her once Hop forty paces through the public street . ii 2 233
Since Julius Cæsar . . . There saw you labouring for him . ii 6 14
Since I saw you last, There is a change upon you . ii 6 53
I look'd her in the face, and saw her led Between her brother and Mark Antony . iii 3 12
I never saw an action of such shame . iii 10 22
For when she saw—Which never shall be found—you did suspect . iv 14 121
I do think I saw't this morning . *Cymbeline* ii 3 150
Never saw I figures So likely to report themselves . ii 4 82
Made not here his brag Of 'came' and 'saw' and 'overcame' . iii 1 24
I saw him not these many years, and yet I know 'tis he . iv 2 66
Long is it since I saw him, But time hath nothing blurr'd those lines of favour Which then he wore . iv 2 103
I saw Jove's bird, the Roman eagle, wing'd From the spongy south . iv 2 348
Hath my poor boy done aught but well, Whose face I never saw? . v 4 36
Unless a man would marry a gallows and beget young gibbets, I never saw one so prone . v 4 207
I never saw Such noble fury in so poor a thing . v 5 7
But we saw him dead.—Be silent; let's see further . v 5 126
Said not I as much when I saw the porpus how he bounced? . *Pericles* ii 1 26
I never saw so huge a billow, sir, As toss'd it upon shore . iii 2 58
I saw you lately, When you caught hurt in parting two that fought . iv 1 87
Saw the like. Who ever saw the like? . 1 *Hen. VI.* i 2 22
Caps and shouts: I never saw the like . *Coriolanus* ii 1 284
Sawed. If I were sawed into quantities, I should make four dozen of such bearded hermits' staves . 2 *Hen. IV.* v 1 70
Sawest. Not so much perdition as an hair Betid to any creature in the vessel Which thou heard'st cry, which thou saw'st sink *Tempest* i 2 32
Saw'st thou him enter at the abbey here? . *Com. of Errors* v 1 278
If thou never wast at court, thou never sawest good manners; if thou never sawest good manners, then thy manners must be wicked *As Y. Like It* iii 2 42
What did he when thou sawest him? What said he? How looked he? iii 2 233
Saw'st thou not, boy, how Silver made it good? *T. of Shrew* Ind. 1 19
Say to me, when sawest thou the Prince Florizel, my son? *W. Tale* iv 2 28
How long is't ago, Jack, since thou sawest thine own knee? 1 *Hen. IV.* ii 4 360
Saw'st thou the melancholy Lord Northumberland? . *Richard III.* v 3 68
Cut her hands and trimm'd her as thou saw'st . *T. Andron.* v 1 93
Good boy, wink at me, and say thou sawest me not . *T. of Athens* iii 1 47
I have heard in some sort of thy miseries.—Thou saw'st them, when I had prosperity.—I see them now . iv 3 77
Sawpit. Let them from forth a sawpit rush at once . *Mer. Wives* iv 4 53
Saxons. Where Charles the Great, having subdued the Saxons, There left behind and settled certain French . *Hen. V.* i 2 46
Charles the Great Subdued the Saxons, and did seat the French Beyond the river Sala . i 2 62
Saxony. How like you the young German, the Duke of Saxony's nephew?—Very vilely in the morning . *Mer. of Venice* i 2 91
Say. Out of our way, I say . *Tempest* i 1 29
Of the king's ship The mariners say how thou hast disposed . i 2 225
Caliban her son.—Dull thing, I say so . i 2 285
What shall I do? say what; what shall I do? . i 2 300
Come forth, I say! there's other business for thee . i 2 315
Say what thou seest yond . i 2 409
What? I say, My foot my tutor? . i 2 468
If but one of his pockets could speak, would it not say he lies? . ii 1 66
Thou speak'st Out of thy sleep. What is it thou didst say? . ii 1 212
Say, this were death That now hath seized them . ii 1 260
They'll tell the clock to any business that We say befits the hour . ii 1 290
Weeps when she sees me work, and says, such baseness Had never like executor . iii 1 12
O my father, I have broke your hest to say so! . iii 1 37
You'll lie like dogs and yet say nothing neither . iii 2 23
I say, by sorcery he got this isle; From me he got it . iii 2 60
Didst thou not say he lied?—Thou liest.—Do I so? take thou that . iii 2 82
Let it be to-night . . . —I say, to-night: no more . iii 3 17
Would they believe me? If I should say, I saw such islanders . iii 3 29
Of my instruction hast thou nothing bated In what thou hadst to say . iii 3 86
Before you can say 'come' and 'go,' And breathe twice and cry 'so, so' . iv 1 44
Say again, where didst thou leave these varlets? . iv 1 170
Your fairy, which you say is a harmless fairy . iv 1 196
You said our work should cease.—I did say so . v 1 5
Say, my spirit, How fares the king and 's followers? . v 1 6
Irreparable is the loss, and patience Says it is past her cure . v 1 141
Arise, and say how thou camest here . v 1 181
Mark but the badges of these men, my lords, Then say if they be true . v 1 268
Yet writers say, as in the sweetest bud The eating canker dwells *T. G. of Ver.* i 1 42
I say, she did nod: and you ask me if she did nod; and I say, 'Ay' . i 1 120
Peruse this paper, madam.—'To Julia.' Say, from whom? . i 2 35
Say, say, who gave it thee? . i 2 37
Since maids, in modesty, say 'no' to that Which they would have the profferer construe 'ay' . i 2 55
You may say what sights you see; I see things too . i 2 138
What say you to a letter from your friends Of much good news? . ii 4 51
They say that Love hath not an eye at all . ii 4 96
A worthless mistress.—I'll die on him that says so but yourself . ii 4 114
Say. Nor never welcome to a place till some certain shot be paid and the hostess say 'Welcome!' . *T. G. of Ver.* ii 5 7
Ask my dog: if he say ay, it will; if he say, no, it will; if he shake his tail and say nothing, it will . ii 5 36
May I say to thee, this pride of hers, Upon advice, hath drawn my love from her . iii 1 72
Take no repulse, whatever she doth say . iii 1 100
Though ne'er so black, say they have angels' faces . iii 1 103
I say, is no man, If with his tongue he cannot win a woman . iii 1 104
But say this weed her love from Valentine, It follows not that she will love Sir Thurio . iii 2 49
I am sure she is not buried.—Say that she be . iv 2 109
I have taught him, even as one would say precisely . iv 4 6
'Out with the dog!' says one: 'What cur is that?' says another: 'Whip him out,' says the third: 'Hang him up,' says the duke . iv 4 22
What says she to my little jewel?—Marry, she says your dog was a cur iv 4 51
I have heard him say a thousand times . iv 4 139
What says Silvia to my suit? . v 2 1
What says she to my face?—She says it is a fair one . v 2 8
I heard say . *Mer. Wives* i 1 92; 2 *Hen. IV.* i 2 108
I will say 'marry trap' with you, if you run the nuthook's humour on me . *Mer. Wives* i 1 170
But if you say, 'Marry her,' I will marry her . i 1 258
What says my bully-rook? speak scholarly and wisely . i 3 2
And 'To her, boy,' say I . i 3 62
I will not say, pity me; 'tis not a soldier-like phrase: but I say, love me ii 1 13
He hath not been thrice in my company! What should I say to him? . ii 1 27
Yet I say I could show you to the contrary . ii 1 40
You say,— Your worship says very true . ii 2 48
But what says she to me? be brief . ii 2 81
Do what she will, say what she will, take all, pay all . ii 2 123
Let them say 'tis grossly done; so it be fairly done, no matter . ii 2 148
And that hath taught me to say this: 'Love like a shadow flies' . ii 2 214
They say the jealous wittolly knave hath masses of money . ii 2 283
Who says this is improvident jealousy? . ii 2 302
What say you to young Master Fenton? he capers, he dances . iii 2 67
Thou art a traitor to say so: thou wouldst make an absolute courtier . iii 3 65
I cannot cog and say thou art this and that . iii 3 76
Thou mightst as well say I love to walk by the Counter-gate . iii 3 84
A gentleman that he says is here now in the house . iii 3 115
My husband says my son profits nothing in the world at his book . iv 1 14
Say of me, 'As jealous as Ford, that searched a hollow walnut' . iv 2 170
You say he has been thrown in the rivers . iv 4 21
Say the woman told me so.—May I be bold to say so, sir? . iv 5 52
Do not say they be fled; Germans are honest men . iv 5 73
If my wind were but long enough to say my prayers, I would repent . iv 5 105
Here is a letter will say somewhat. Good hearts, what ado here is! . iv 5 128
They say there is divinity in odd numbers . v 1 3
As one would say . *Meas. for Meas.* i 2 55; *Mer. of Venice* i 2 134
If you live to see this come to pass, say Pompey told you so *M. for M.* ii 1 256
You say, seven years together?—And a half, sir . ii 1 277
I can speak Against the thing I say . ii 4 60
As for you, Say what you can, my false o'erweighs your true . ii 4 170
What says my brother?—Death is a fearful thing . iii 1 116
Say to thyself, From their abominable and beastly touches I drink, I eat iii 2 24
Farewell: go say I sent thee thither . iii 2 66
The duke, I say to thee again, would eat mutton on Fridays . iii 2 192
Say that I said so . iii 2 195
Little have you to say When you depart from him . iv 1 68
I have heard say . iv 2 38
Say it was the desire of the penitent to be so bared before his death . iv 2 188
If you have any thing to say to me, come to my ward . iv 3 66
Mark what I say, which you shall find By every syllable a faithful verity iv 3 130
Say, by this token, I desire his company . iv 3 144
To speak so indirectly I am loath: I would say the truth . iv 6 2
Yet I am advised to do it; He says, to veil full purpose . iv 6 4
What would you say? . v 1 68; *All's Well* ii 5 83
Confess the truth, and say by whose advice Thou camest here to complain . *Meas. for Meas.* v 1 113
You say your husband.—Why, just, my lord, and that is Angelo . v 1 201
Did not you say you knew that Friar Lodowick to be a dishonest person? v 1 261
Not better than he, by her own report.—Say you? . v 1 275
Say, wast thou e'er contracted to this woman?—I was, my lord . v 1 380
Kneel by me; Hold up your hands, say nothing; I'll speak all . v 1 443
They say, best men are moulded out of faults . v 1 444
And, for your lovely sake, Give me your hand and say you will be mine v 1 497
Say in brief the cause . *Com. of Errors* i 1 29
O, let me say no more! Gather the sequel by that went before . i 1 95
But say, sir, is it dinner-time?—No, sir . ii 2 55
If any ask you for your master, Say he dines forth . ii 2 212
I'll say as they say and persever so . ii 2 217
Say that I linger'd with you at your shop . iii 1 3
Say what you will, sir, but I know what I know . iii 1 11
You would say so, master, if your garments were thin . iii 1 70
You wrong me much to say so.—You wrong me more, sir, in denying it iv 1 66
I think him better than I say, And yet would herein others' eyes were worse . iv 2 25
Have you not heard men say, That Time comes stealing on by night and day? . iv 2 59
One that thinks a man always going to bed and says, 'God give you good rest!' . iv 3 33
And thereof comes that the wenches say 'God damn me' . iv 3 53
'Fly pride,' says the peacock: mistress, that you know . iv 3 81
How say you now? . iv 4 48; *As Y. Like It* iv 3 1
Sooth to say *Com. of Errors* iv 4 72; *T. of Shrew* iv 2 99
My liege, I am advised what I say . *Com. of Errors* v 1 214
You say he dined at home; the goldsmith here Denies that saying. Sirrah, what say you? . v 1 273
No; I say nay to that.—And so do I . v 1 371
Is too like an image and says nothing . *Much Ado* ii 1 9
Make curtsy and say 'Father, as it please you' . ii 1 56
So you walk softly and look sweetly and say nothing, I am yours . ii 1 92
I may say so, when I please.—And when please you to say so? . ii 1 95
I say my prayers aloud . ii 1 108
When I know the gentleman, I'll tell him what you say . ii 1 151
You say honestly . ii 1 242
Your grace may well say I have lost it . ii 1 291
His grace hath made the match, and all grace say Amen to it . ii 1 315
I were but little happy, if I could say how much . ii 1 318
I have heard my daughter say, she hath often dreamed of unhappiness ii 1 360

Say. So your daughter says: 'Shall I,' says she, '. . . write to him that I love him?' *Much Ado* ii 3 132
'I measure him,' says she, 'by my own spirit' ii 3 149
She doth indeed; my daughter says so ii 3 156
I pray you, tell Benedick of it, and hear what a' will say ii 3 178
She says she will die, if he love her not ii 3 181
In the managing of quarrels you may say he is wise ii 3 197
Say that thou overheard'st us; And bid her steal into pleached bower iii 1 6
So says the prince and my new-trothed lord iii 1 38
Tell her of it: hear what she will say iii 1 81
Others say thou dost deserve, and I Believe it better than reportingly iii 1 115
I could say she were worse: think you of a worse title iii 2 113
So will you say when you have seen the sequel iii 2 137
You may say they are not the men you took them for iii 3 50
The fashion is the fashion.—Tush! I may as well say the fool's the fool iii 3 130
I warrant your cousin will say so.—My cousin's a fool iii 4 10
I think you would have me say, 'saving your reverence, a husband' iii 4 32
You are tedious.—It pleases your worship to say so iii 5 21
I would fain know what you have to say iii 5 32
I know what you would say: if I have known her, You will say she did embrace me as a husband iv 1 49
It were as possible for me to say I loved nothing so well as you iv 1 272
I will make him eat it that says I love not you iv 1 279
Go, comfort your cousin: I must say she is dead iv 1 339
How answer you for yourselves?—Marry, sir, we say we are none iv 2 26
What heard you him say else? iv 2 48
I say thou hast belied mine innocent child v 1 67
Thine, I say.—You say not right, old man v 1 72
The which if I do not carve most curiously, say my knife's naught v 1 157
Pluck up, my heart, and be sad. Did he not say, my brother was fled? v 1 208
They say he wears a key in his ear and a lock hanging by it v 1 317
I will think nothing to any purpose that the world can say v 4 107
I can but say their protestation over *L. L. Lost* i 1 33
Let me say no, my liege, an if you please i 1 50
Swear me to this, and I will ne'er say no i 1 69
Biron is like an envious sneaping frost . . . —Well, say I am i 1 102
I have for barbarism spoke more Than for that angel knowledge you can say i 1 113
If he say it is so, he is, in telling true, but so i 1 226
Which with,—O, with—but with this I passion to say wherewith i 1 264
I do say thou art quick in answers: thou heatest my blood i 2 31
I love thee.—So I heard you say.—And so, farewell i 2 147
And therefore I will say nothing i 2 169
They say so most that most his humours know ii 1 53
Say that he or we, as neither have, Received that sum ii 1 133
Let it blood.—Would that do it good?—My physic says 'ay' ii 1 188
I say lead is slow.—You are too swift, sir, to say so iii 1 62
Say the moral again iii 1 88
What? first praise me and again say no? O short-lived pride! iv 1 14
He it was that might rightly say, Veni, vidi, vici iv 1 68
A mark! O, mark but that mark! A mark, says my lady! iv 1 133
But omne bene, say I; being of an old father's mind iv 2 33
Or rather, as Horace says in his—What, my soul, verses? iv 2 104
I do invite you too; you shall not say me nay iv 2 171
Well, set thee down, sorrow! for so they say the fool said, and so say I iv 3 5
Ay me! says one; O Jove! the other cries iv 3 141
What will Biron say when that he shall hear Faith so infringed? iv 3 145
Say, can you fast? your stomachs are too young iv 3 294
Such rackers of orthography, as to speak dout, fine, when he should say doubt v 1 23
What are they That charge their breath against us? say, scout, say v 2 88
What would they, say they?—Nothing but peace v 2 180
She says, you have it, and you may be gone v 2 183
Say to her, we have measured many miles To tread a measure with her v 2 184
I say they shall not come.—Nay, my good lord v 2 515
If your ladyship would say, 'Thanks' v 2 559
I am Alisander,— Your nose says, no, you are not v 2 568
O, shall I say, I thank you, gentle wife? v 2 836
I'll mark no words that smooth-faced wooers say v 2 838
And ere a man hath power to say 'Behold!' The jaws of darkness do devour it up: So quick bright things come to confusion *M. N. D.* i 1 147
Say what the play treats on, then read the names of the actors i 2 8
I will roar, that I will make the duke say 'Let him roar again' i 2 74
Beshrew my manners and my pride, If Hermia meant to say Lysander lied ii 2 55
Amen, to that fair prayer, say I; And then end life when I end loyalty! ii 2 62
And reason says you are the worthier maid ii 2 116
Let the prologue seem to say, we will do no harm with our swords iii 1 19
Pyramus and Thisby, says the story, did talk through the chink of a wall iii 1 65
Doth move me On the first view to say, to swear, I love thee iii 1 144
I swear . . . To prove him false that says I love thee not.—I say I love thee more than he can do.—If thou say so, withdraw, and prove it too iii 2 253
Why, then you left me—O, the gods forbid!—In earnest, shall I say? iii 2 277
I am amazed, and know not what to say iii 2 344
Say, sweet love, what thou desirest to eat iv 1 33
But as yet, I swear, I cannot truly say how I came here iv 1 153
I have had a dream, past the wit of man to say what dream it was iv 1 211
Man is but a patched fool, if he will offer to say what methought I had iv 1 216
He is a very paramour for a sweet voice.—You must say 'paragon' iv 2 13
I do not doubt but to hear them say, it is a sweet comedy iv 2 45
Say, what abridgement have you for this evening? v 1 39
He says they can do nothing in this kind v 1 88
All that I have to say, is, to tell you that the lanthorn is the moon v 1 261
It wearies me; you say it wearies you *Mer. of Venice* i 1 2
Let us say you are sad, Because you are not merry: and 'twere as easy For you to laugh and leap and say you are merry, Because you are not sad i 1 47
When shall we laugh? say, when? You grow exceeding strange i 1 66
Say to me what I should do That in your knowledge may by me be done i 1 158
How say you by the French lord? i 2 58
What say you, then, to Falconbridge, the young baron of England?—You know I say nothing to him i 2 71
As you would say i 3 77; ii 2 68; *J. Cæsar* i 1 11
You come to me, and you say, 'Shylock, we would have moneys:' you say so *Mer. of Venice* i 3 116
What should I say to you? Should I not say 'Hath a dog money?' i 3 121
With bated breath and whispering humbleness, Say this i 3 126
I'll seal to such a bond And say there is much kindness in the Jew i 3 154

Say. I say, To buy his favour, I extend this friendship *Mer. of Venice* i 3 168
Take the start, run away.—My conscience says 'No' ii 2 7
'Via!' says the fiend; 'away!' says the fiend; 'for the heavens, rouse up a brave mind,' says the fiend, 'and run' ii 2 11
My conscience, hanging about the neck of my heart, says very wisely to me ii 2 15
My conscience says 'Launcelot, budge not.' 'Budge,' says the fiend. 'Budge not,' says my conscience. 'Conscience,' say I, 'you counsel well;' 'Fiend,' say I, 'you counsel well' ii 2 19
His father, though I say it, is an honest exceeding poor man ii 2 54
And, though I say it, though old man, yet poor man, my father ii 2 148
And sigh and say 'amen' ii 2 203
Why, Jessica, I say!—Why, Jessica!—Who bids thee call? ii 5 6
I will not say you shall see a masque ii 5 23
Go you before me, sirrah; Say I will come.—I will go before, sir ii 5 39
What says that fool of Hagar's offspring, ha? ii 5 44
I will survey the inscriptions back again. What says this leaden casket? ii 7 15
What says the golden chest? ha! let me see ii 9 23
I am half afeard Thou wilt say anon he is some kin to thee ii 9 97
Let me say 'amen' betimes, lest the devil cross my prayer iii 1 22
Then parts life from hence: O, then be bold to say Bassanio's dead! iii 2 187
I'll tell my husband, Launcelot, what you say: here he comes iii 5 30
He says, you are no good member of the commonwealth iii 5 36
And now, good sweet, say thy opinion iii 5 76
I'll not answer that: But, say, it is my humour: is it answer'd? iv 1 43
Shall I say to you, Let them be free, marry them to your heirs? iv 1 93
You stand within his danger, do you not?—Ay, so he says iv 1 181
His breast: So says the bond: doth it not, noble judge? iv 1 253
You, merchant, have you any thing to say?—But little iv 1 263
Say how I loved you, speak me fair in death iv 1 275
A Daniel, still say I, a second Daniel! I thank thee, Jew iv 1 340
In which predicament, I say, thou stand'st iv 1 357
Art thou contented, Jew? what dost thou say?—I am content iv 1 393
He is thrice a villain that says such a father begot villains *As Y. Like It* i 1 61
Can I not say, I thank you? My better parts Are all thrown down i 2 261
Say what thou canst, I'll go along with thee i 3 107
Even till I shrink with cold, I smile and say 'This is no flattery' ii 1 9
Looking on it with lack-lustre eye, Says very wisely, 'It is ten o'clock' ii 7 22
What woman in the city do I name, When that I say the city-woman? ii 7 75
Who can come in and say that I mean her, When such a one as she such is her neighbour? ii 7 77
What is he of basest function That says his bravery is not on my cost? ii 7 80
Forbear, I say: He dies that touches any of this fruit ii 7 97
To say ay and no to these particulars is more than to answer in a catechism iii 2 240
You shall say I'll prove a busy actor in their play iii 4 61
Say that you love me not, but say not so In bitterness iii 5 2
For shame, Lie not, to say mine eyes are murderers! iii 5 19
They say you are a melancholy fellow.—I am so iv 1 3
'Tis good to be sad and say nothing.—Why then, 'tis good to be a post iv 1 8
What would you say to me now, an I were your very very Rosalind? iv 1 70
Am not I your Rosalind?—I take some joy to say you are iv 1 90
In her person I say I will not have you.—Then in mine own person I die iv 1 92
What do you say, sister?—Pray thee, marry us.—I cannot say the words iv 1 126
Then you must say 'I take thee, Rosalind, for wife' iv 1 135
For ever and a day.—Say 'a day,' without the 'ever' iv 1 146
A man that had a wife with such a wit, he might say 'Wit, whither wilt?' iv 1 168
Marry, to say she came to seek you there iv 1 174
She says I am not fair, that I lack manners; She calls me proud iv 3 15
I say she never did invent this letter; This is a man's invention iv 3 28
Say this to her: that if she love me, I charge her to love thee iv 3 71
It is no boast, being ask'd, to say we are iv 3 91
Say with me, I love Aliena; say with her that she loves me v 2 9
Bear a good opinion of my knowledge, insomuch I say I know you are v 2 61
By my life, I do; which I tender dearly, though I say I am a magician v 2 78
And how oft did you say his beard was not well cut? v 4 87
And with a low submissive reverence Say *T. of Shrew* Ind. 1 54
That he hath been lunatic; And when he says he is, say that he dreams Ind. 1 64
If she say I am not fourteen pence on the score for sheer ale, score me up Ind. 2 24
Say thou wilt walk; we will bestrew the ground Ind. 2 42
Yet would you say ye were beaten out of door Ind. 2 87
A husband! a devil.—I say, a husband.—I say, a devil i 1 126
'Con tutto il cuore, ben trovato,' may I say i 2 24
Say that she frown; I'll say she looks as clear As morning roses ii 1 173
Say she be mute and will not speak a word; Then I'll commend her volubility, And say she uttereth piercing eloquence ii 1 175
She says she'll see thee hang'd first.—Is this your speeding? ii 1 302
'Tis a match.—Amen, say we: we will be witnesses ii 1 322
Didst thou not say he comes?— . . . I say his horse comes, with him on his back iii 2 81
Let all the world say no, I'll keep mine own, despite of all the world iii 2 143
A bridegroom say you? 'tis a groom indeed iii 2 154
What say you to a neat's foot?—'Tis passing good iv 3 17
How say you to a fat tripe finely broil'd?—I like it well iv 3 20
What say you to a piece of beef and mustard?—A dish that I do love iv 3 23
Your betters have endured me say my mind iv 3 75
She says your worship means to make a puppet of her iv 3 105
This is true that I say: an I had thee in place where, thou shouldst know it iv 3 150
Ere I do, It shall be what o'clock I say it is iv 3 197
Sir, pardon me in what I have to say iv 4 38
If you say no more than this, . . . The match is made, and all is done iv 4 43
If this be not that you look for, I have no more to say iv 4 96
I say it is the moon that shines so bright.—I know it is the sun iv 5 4
Say as he says, or we shall never go iv 5 11
It is the blessed sun: But sun it is not, when you say it is not iv 5 19
So his mother says, if I may believe her v 1 34
I dare not swear it.—Then thou wert best say that I am not v 1 106
An hasty-witted body Would say your head and butt were head and horn v 2 41
I think thou hast the veriest shrew of all.—Well, I say no v 2 65
She says you have some goodly jest in hand v 2 91
Go to your mistress; Say, I command her come to me v 2 96
When thou hast leisure, say thy prayers *All's Well* i 1 227
He would always say . . . , 'Let me not live' i 2 52
Does it curd thy blood To say I am thy mother? i 3 156
Invention is ashamed, Against the proclamation of thy passion, To say thou dost not i 3 181

Say. Say to him, I live; and observe his reports for me *All's Well* ii 1 45
Come your ways; This is his majesty; say your mind to him ii 1 98
Put off's cap, kiss his hand and say nothing ii 2 11
Such a fellow, to say precisely, were not for the court ii 2 12
Have you, I say, an answer of such fitness for all questions? ii 2 30
They say miracles are past ii 3 1
I may truly say, it is a novelty to the world.—It is, indeed ii 3 22
I may say in the default, he is a man I know ii 3 241
I would she did as you say.—Why, I say nothing ii 4 21
To say nothing, to do nothing, to know nothing, and to have nothing ii 4 25
I am not worthy of the wealth I owe, Nor dare I say 'tis mine ii 5 85
Therefore dare not Say what I think of it iii 1 14
He says he has a stratagem for't iii 6 37
But you say she's honest.—That's all the fault iii 6 119
What shall I say I have done? It must be a very plausive invention iv 1 29
I must give myself some hurts, and say I got them in exploit iv 1 41
They will say, 'Came you off with so little?' and great ones I dare not give iv 1 42
To say it was in stratagem.—'Twould not do.—Or to drown my clothes, and say I was stripped iv 1 54
Say thou art mine, and ever My love as it begins shall so persever iv 2 36
She says all men Have the like oaths iv 2 70
Her death itself, which could not be her office to say is come iv 3 68
He can say nothing of me iv 3 134
He calls for the tortures: what will you say without 'em? iv 3 138
If ye pinch me like a pasty, I can say no more iv 3 140
Five or six thousand horse, I said,—I will say true iv 3 171
A dumb innocent, that could not say him nay iv 3 214
I have but little more to say, sir, of his honesty iv 3 289
What say you to his expertness in war? iv 3 296
This I must say, But first I beg my pardon v 3 11
What says he to your daughter? have you spoke? v 3 28
When his wife was dead, I blush to say it, he won me v 3 140
Thou hast spoken all already, unless thou canst say they are married v 3 269
This ring, you say, was yours?—Ay, my good lord v 3 271
And, look you, here's your letter; this it says v 3 312
They say, she hath abjured the company And sight of men *T. Night* i 2 40
He s a very fool and a prodigal.—Fie, that you'll say so! i 3 26
They are scoundrels and substractors that say so of him i 3 37
Say I do speak with her, my lord, what then? i 4 23
They shall yet belie thy happy years, That say thou art a man i 4 31
That may you be bold to say in your foolery i 5 13
What says Quinapalus? 'Better a witty fool than a foolish wit' i 5 38
As much to say as i 5 63; 2 *Hen. VI.* iv 2 18
How say you to that? *T. Night* i 5 88
Let him be the devil, an he will, I care not: give me faith, say I i 5 137
He says, he'll stand at your door like a sheriff's post i 5 156
I can say little more than I have studied, and that question's out of my part i 5 190
It is heresy. Have you no more to say? i 5 247
So they say ii 3 11
Say that some lady, as perhaps there is, Hath for your love as great a pang of heart ii 4 92
We men may say more, swear more: but indeed Our shows are more than will ii 4 119
Give her this jewel; say, My love can give no place ii 4 126
Did not I say he would work it out? the cur is excellent at faults ii 5 139
Nay, but say true; does it work upon him? ii 5 214
So thou mayst say, the king lies by a beggar, if a beggar dwell near him iii 1 8
Out of my welkin, I might say 'element,' but the word is over-worn iii 1 65
He says he'll come; How shall I feast him? what bestow of him? iii 4 1
'Cast thy humble slough,' says she; 'be opposite with a kinsman' iii 4 76
He's an enemy to mankind.—Do you know what you say? iii 4 110
My lady would not lose him for more than I'll say iii 4 117
Hang him, foul collier!—Get him to say his prayers iii 4 131
Be ruled by me!—Madam, I will.—O, say so, and so be! iv 1 69
As fairly as to say a careful man and a great scholar iv 2 11
Advise you what you say; the minister is here iv 2 102
What say you, sir? I am shent for speaking to you iv 2 111
What do you say? iv 3 31; v 1 109
Or say 'tis not your seal, not your invention: You can say none of this v 1 341
To make us say 'This is put forth too truly' *W. Tale* i 2 13
Say this to him, He's beat from his best ward i 2 32
To tell, he longs to see his son, were strong: But let him say so then i 2 35
But I . . . Should yet say 'Sir, no going.' Verily, You shall not go i 2 49
Of this make no conclusion, lest you say Your queen and I are devils i 2 81
What, hast smutch'd thy nose? They say it is a copy out of mine i 2 122
Yet they say we are Almost as like as eggs; women say so, That will say any thing i 2 129
Then say My wife's a hobby-horse i 2 275
Say't and justify't.—I would not be a stander-by to hear i 2 278
'Tis most dangerous.—Say it be, 'tis true i 2 298
What you do know, you must, And cannot say, you dare not i 2 380
I'ld say he had not, And I'll be sworn you would believe my saying ii 1 62
Be but about To say 'she is a goodly lady' ii 1 66
When you have said 'she's goodly,' come between Ere you can say 'she's honest' ii 1 76
Should a villain say so, . . . He were as much more villain ii 1 78
You scarce can right me throughly then to say You did mistake ii 1 99
The queen receives Much comfort in't; says 'My poor prisoner' ii 2 28
Say that she were gone, Given to the fire, a moiety of my rest Might come to me again ii 3 7
If thou refuse And wilt encounter with my wrath, say so ii 3 138
What I am to say must be but that Which contradicts my accusation iii 2 23
It shall scarce boot me To say 'not guilty' iii 2 27
I say she's dead; I'll swear't. If word nor oath Prevail not, go and see iii 2 204
Take your patience to you, And I'll say nothing iii 2 233
But I am not to say it is a sea, for it is now the sky iii 3 85
Yet that Time himself doth say He wishes earnestly you never may iv 1 31
Say to me, when sawest thou the Prince Florizel, my son? iv 2 28
His vices, you would say; there's no virtue whipped out of the court iv 3 96
How would he look, to see his work so noble Vilely bound up? What would he say? iv 4 22
To this I am most constant, Though destiny say no iv 4 46
Say there be; Yet nature is made better by no mean iv 4 88
Over that art Which you say adds to nature, is an art That nature makes iv 4 91
No more than were I painted I would wish This youth should say 'twere well iv 4 102
He says he loves my daughter: I think so too iv 4 171
A dance which the wenches say is a gallimaufry of gambols iv 4 335

Say. But, my daughter, Say you the like to him?—I cannot speak So well *W. Tale* iv 4 391
The which shall point you forth at every sitting What you must say iv 4 573
I cannot say 'tis pity She lacks instructions iv 4 592
Who, I may say, is no honest man iv 4 718
Advocate's the court-word for a pheasant: say you have none iv 4 769
As I may say iv 4 858; *Hamlet* iii 2 7
I did so: but thou strikest me Sorely, to say I did *W. Tale* v 1 18
His princess, say you, with him?—Ay, the most peerless piece of earth v 1 93
'Tis shrewdly ebb'd, To say you have seen a better v 1 103
Whom he loves—He bade me say so—more than all the sceptres v 1 146
Could not say if the importance were joy or sorrow v 2 19
She did, with an 'Alas,' I would fain say, bleed tears v 2 96
They say one would speak to her and stand in hope of answer v 2 110
See you these clothes? say you see them not and think me still no gentleman born v 2 141
You may say it, but not swear it v 2 171
Let boors and franklins say it, I'll swear it v 2 173
Behold, and say 'tis well. I like your silence v 3 20
Chide me, dear stone, that I may say indeed Thou art Hermione v 3 24
Do not say 'tis superstition, that I kneel and then implore her blessing v 3 43
Now, say, Chatillon, what would France with us? *K. John* i 1 1
Lest men should say 'Look, where three-farthings goes!' i 1 143
At your service, sir: 'No, sir,' says question, 'I, sweet sir, at yours' i 1 199
Who lives and dares but say thou didst not well i 1 271
If thou hadst said him nay, it had been sin: Who says it was, he lies; I say 'twas not i 1 276
What England says, say briefly, gentle lord ii 1 52
Bedlam, have done.—I have but this to say ii 1 183
Say, shall the current of our right run on? ii 1 335
Say, where will you assault? ii 1 408
If not complete of, say he is not she ii 1 434
What say these young ones? What say you, my niece? ii 1 521
She is bound in honour still to do What you in wisdom still vouchsafe to say ii 1 523
Whiles I am a beggar, I will rail And say there is no sin but to be rich ii 1 594
Thou dost but say 'tis so: I trust I may not trust thee iii 1 6
Thou darest not say so, villain, for thy life iii 1 132
What say'st thou to the cardinal?—What should he say, but as the cardinal? iii 1 203
I am perplex'd, and know not what to say.—What canst thou say but will perplex thee more? iii 1 221
I had a thing to say, But I will fit it with some better time iii 3 25
I am almost ashamed To say what good respect I have of thee iii 3 28
Good friend, thou hast no cause to say so yet iii 3 30
I had a thing to say, but let it go iii 3 33
Well, I'll not say what I intend for thee: Remember iii 3 68
Let us go: If you say ay, the king will not say no iii 4 183
Young lad, come forth; I have to say with you iv 1 8
Give me the iron, I say, and bind him here iv 1 75
Now, what says the world To your proceedings? iv 2 132
On that day at noon, whereon he says I shall yield up my crown iv 2 156
Did not the prophet Say that before Ascension-day at noon? v 1 26
He flatly says he'll not lay down his arms v 2 126
Yet can I not of such tame patience boast As to be hush'd and nought at all to say *Richard II.* i 1 53
I say and will in battle prove, Or here or elsewhere i 1 92
Further I say and further will maintain Upon his bad life i 1 98
Our doctors say this is no month to bleed i 1 157
In God's name and the king's, say who thou art i 3 11
Alas, I look'd when some of you should say, I was too strict i 3 243
Go, say I sent thee forth to purchase honour i 3 282
And say, what store of parting tears were shed? i 4 5
He that no more must say is listen'd more Than they whom youth and ease have taught to glose ii 1 9
What says he?—Nay, nothing; all is said ii 1 148
Now, afore God—God forbid I say true! ii 1 200
I must find that title in your tongue, Before I make reply to aught you say iii 3 73
How can you say to me, I am a king? iii 2 177
My tongue hath but a heavier tale to say. I play the torturer iii 2 197
What say you now? what comfort have we now? iii 2 206
It would beseem the Lord Northumberland To say 'King Richard' iii 3 7
You make a leg, and Bolingbroke says ay iii 3 175
Yea, my good lord.—Then I must not say no iii 3 209
Why dost thou say King Richard is deposed? iii 4 77
Little joy have I To breathe this news; yet what I say is true iii 4 82
I heard thee say iv 1 36; *Othello* iii 3 109
And spit upon him, whilst I say he lies, And lies, and lies *Richard II.* iv 1 75
God save the king! Will no man say amen? Am I both priest and clerk? iv 1 172
God save King Harry, unking'd Richard says iv 1 220
Say that again. The shadow of my sorrow! ha! let's see iv 1 293
Once more, adieu; the rest let sorrow say v 1 102
I will be satisfied; let me see it, I say v 2 71
Do not say, 'stand up;' Say 'pardon' first, and afterwards 'stand up' v 3 111
Say 'pardon,' king; let pity teach thee how: The word is short v 3 116
Speak it in French, king; say, 'pardonne moi v 3 119
What my tongue dares not, that my heart shall say v 5 97
The devil, that told me I did well, Says that this deed is chronicled in hell v 5 117
And let men say we be men of good government 1 *Hen. IV.* i 2 30
Therefore, I say,— Peace, cousin, say no more i 3 187
Happy man be his dole, say I: every man to his business ii 2 81
I say unto you again, you are a shallow cowardly hind ii 3 15
Washes his hands, and says to his wife 'Fie upon this quiet life!' ii 4 117
A plague of all cowards, I say still ii 4 147
To hack thy sword as thou hast done, and then say it was in fight! ii 4 289
He says he comes from your father ii 4 318
But to say I know more harm in him than in myself, were to say more than I know ii 4 512
Play out the play: I have much to say in the behalf of that Falstaff ii 4 532
I say the earth did shake when I was born.—And I say the earth was not of my mind, If you suppose as fearing you it shook iii 1 21
Who shall say me nay?—Why, that will I iii 1 117
Others would say 'Where, which is Bolingbroke?' iii 2 49
I would cudgel him like a dog, if he would say so iii 3 101
And I said I heard your grace say so iii 3 121
Why say you so? looks he not for supply? iv 3 3
Say thy prayers, and farewell.—I would 'twere bed-time v 1 124
Deliver what you will: I'll say 'tis so v 2 26
What shall I say you are? 2 *Hen. IV.* i 1 2

Say. This thou wouldst say, 'Your son did thus and thus; Your brother thus' . . . . 2 *Hen. IV.* i 1 76
Yet, for all this, say not that Percy's dead . . . i 1 93
If he be slain, say so; The tongue offends not that reports his death . i 1 96
He doth sin that doth belie the dead, Not he which says the dead is not alive . . . . i 1 99
Yet did you say 'Go forth' . . . . . . i 1 175
You giant, what says the doctor to my water? . . . i 2 1
He will not stick to say his face is a face-royal . . i 2 26
Why, sir, did I say you were an honest man? . . . i 2 92
You lie in your throat, if you say I am any other than an honest man . i 2 98
You hear not what I say to you.—Very well, my lord . i 2 136
All tallow: if I did say of wax, my growth would approve the truth . i 2 180
If ye will needs say I am an old man, you should give me rest . i 2 242
She says up and down the town that her eldest son is like you . ii 1 114
If a man will make courtesy and say nothing, he is virtuous . ii 1 136
The midwives say the children are not in the fault . . ii 2 28
The worst that they can say of me is that I am a second brother . ii 2 71
Never prick their finger but they say, 'There's some of the king's blood' ii 2 122
'How comes that?' says he, that takes upon him not to conceive . ii 2 123
It perfumes the blood ere one can say 'What's this?' . ii 4 31
'Neighbour Quickly,' says he, 'receive those that are civil' . ii 4 96
'Receive,' says he, 'no swaggering companions' . . ii 4 101
I am the worse, when one says swagger . . . ii 4 113
What says the almanac to that? . . . . . ii 4 287
What says your grace?—His grace says that which his flesh rebels against ii 4 378
I may say to you, we knew where the bona-robas were . . iii 2 25
She would always say she could not abide Master Shallow . iii 2 214
'Rah, tah, tah,' would a' say; 'bounce' would a' say . . iii 2 304
You shall say indeed, it is the time, And not the king . iv 1 105
Say you not then our offer is compell'd . . . iv 1 158
Since sudden sorrow Serves to say thus, 'some good thing comes to-morrow' . . . . iv 2 84
That I may justly say, with the hook-nosed fellow of Rome . iv 3 44
The old folk, time's doting chronicles, Say it did so a little time before iv 4 127
No prince nor peer shall have just cause to say, God shorten Harry's happy life one day! . . . . v 2 144
Why then, say an old man can do somewhat . . . v 3 82
'Where is the life that late I led?' say they: Why, here it is . v 3 147
What I have to say is of mine own making; and what indeed I should say will, I doubt, prove mine own marring . . . Epil. 5
You would say it hath been all in all his study . . *Hen. V.* i 1 42
Our master Says that you savour too much of your youth . i 2 250
I say little; but when time shall serve, there shall be smiles . ii 1 5
Hear me, hear me what I say . . . . . ii 1 67
They say he cried out of sack.—Ay, that a' did . . ii 3 29
I say 'tis meet we all go forth To view the sick and feeble parts of France ii 4 21
He scorns to say his prayers, lest a' should be thought a coward . iii 2 40
Our madams mock at us, and plainly say Our mettle is bred out . iii 5 28
Say to England that we send To know what willing ransom he will give iii 5 62
Thus says my king: Say thou to Harry of England . . iii 6 125
To say the sooth, . . . My people are with sickness much enfeebled iii 6 151
We would not seek a battle, as we are; Nor, as we are, we say we will not shun it: So tell your master . . . . . iii 6 174
I will not say so, for fear I should be faced out of my way . iii 7 89
You may as well say, that's a valiant flea that dare eat his breakfast on the lip of a lion . . . . iii 7 155
This lodging likes me better, Since I may say 'Now lie I like a king' . iv 1 17
I myself heard the king say he would not be ransomed . iv 1 202
If ever thou come to me and say, after to-morrow . . iv 1 230
What's to say? A very little little let us do, And all is done . iv 2 32
And say 'To-morrow is Saint Crispian:' Then will he strip his sleeve and show his scars, And say 'These wounds I had on Crispin's day' . iv 3 46
He says his name is Master Fer.—Master Fer! I'll fer him, and firk him iv 4 28
With a feeble gripe, says 'Dear my lord, Commend my service' . . iv 6 22
Your majesty says very true . . . . . iv 7 101
Thou shalt die.—You say very true, scauld knave, when God's will is . v 1 33
I know no ways to mince it in love, but directly to say 'I love you:' then if you urge me farther than to say 'do you in faith?' I wear out my suit . . . . v 2 130
Take me; if not, to say to thee that I shall die, is true . . v 2 158
Take me by the hand, and say 'Harry of England, I am thine' . v 2 255
It is not a fashion for the maids in France to kiss before they are married, would she say? . . . . v 2 291
No, I say, distrustful recreants! Fight till the last gasp . 1 *Hen. VI.* i 2 126
What she says I'll confirm: we'll fight it out . . . i 2 128
A maid, they say.—A maid! and be so martial! . . . ii 1 21
Then say at once if I maintain'd the truth . . . ii 4 5
And say withal I think he held the right . . . ii 4 38
He bears him on the place's privilege, Or durst not, for his craven heart, say thus . . . . ii 4 87
Look to it well and say you are well warn'd . . . ii 4 103
Why didst thou say, of late thou wert despised? . . ii 5 42
If you love me, as you say you do, Let me persuade you to forbear awhile iii 1 104
When Gloucester says the word, King Henry goes . . iii 1 184
Say, gentlemen, what makes you thus exclaim? . . iv 1 83
The world will say, he is not Talbot's blood . . iv 5 16
If I bow, they'll say it was for fear . . . . iv 5 29
Who art thou? say, that I may honour thee . . . v 3 50
My hand would free her, but my heart says no . . v 3 61
Lady, vouchsafe to listen what I say . . . . v 3 103
Such commendations as becomes a maid, A virgin and his servant, say to him . . . . v 3 178
Say, when I am gone, I prophesied France will be lost ere long 2 *Hen. VI.* i 1 145
They say 'A crafty knave does need no broker' . . . i 2 100
Say, man, were these thy words? . . . . . i 3 189
What shall we say to this in law? . . . . . i 3 207
Sometime I'll say, I am Duke Humphrey's wife . . . ii 4 42
I will subscribe and say I wrong'd the duke . . . iii 1 38
It serves you well, my lord, to say so much.—I say no more than truth iii 1 119
Say as you think, and speak it from your souls . . iii 1 247
Say but the word, and I will be his priest . . . iii 1 272
Say you consent and censure well the deed . . . iii 1 275
Say he be taken, rack'd and tortured, I know no pain they can inflict upon him Will make him say I moved him to those arms . . iii 1 376
Say that he thrive, as 'tis great like he will . . . iii 1 379
Say we intend to try his grace to-day, If he be guilty, as 'tis published iii 2 16
Well forewarning wind Did seem to say 'Seek not a scorpion's nest' . iii 2 86
Say, if thou darest, proud Lord of Warwickshire, That I am faulty . iii 2 201
Madam, be still; with reverence may I say . . . . iii 2 207

Say. And say it was thy mother that thou meant'st . . 2 *Hen. VI.* iii 2 222
I say it was never merry world in England since gentlemen came up . iv 2 9
Some say the bee stings: but I say, 'tis the bee's wax . . iv 2 89
That's false.—Ay, there's the question; but I say, 'tis true . . iv 2 149
And furthermore, we'll have the Lord Say's head for selling the dukedom of Maine . . . . iv 2 170
I tell you that Lord Say hath gelded the commonwealth, and made it an eunuch . . . . iv 2 174
Lord Say, Jack Cade hath sworn to have thy head . . iv 4 19
Here's the Lord Say, which sold the towns in France . . iv 7 23
Ah, thou say, thou serge, nay, thou buckram lord! . . iv 7 27
You men of Kent,— What say you of Kent?—Nothing but this . . iv 7 60
Go, take him away, I say, and strike off his head presently . iv 7 116
What say ye, countrymen? will ye relent, And yield to mercy? . iv 8 11
His sons, he says, shall give their words for him . . v 1 137
What says Lord Warwick? shall we after them? . . . v 3 27
My foes will shed fast-falling tears, And say 'Alas!' . . 3 *Hen. VI.* i 4 163
Say how he died, for I will hear it all . . . . ii 1 49
For chair and dukedom, throne and kingdom say; Either that is thine, or else thou wert not his . . . . ii 1 93
If for the last, say ay, and to it, lords . . . . ii 1 165
And long hereafter say unto his child . . . . ii 2 36
If that be right which Warwick says is right, There is no wrong . ii 2 131
He nor sees nor hears us what we say . . . . ii 6 63
Let me embrace thee, sour adversity, For wise men say it is the wisest course . . . . iii 1 25
She weeps, and says her Henry is deposed; He smiles, and says his Edward is install'd . . . . iii 1 45
Say, what art thou that talk'st of kings and queens? . . iii 1 55
Ay, if thou wilt say 'ay' to my request; No, if thou dost say 'no' . iii 2 79
Say that King Edward take thee for his queen? . . . iii 2 89
Well, say there is no kingdom then for Richard; What other pleasure? iii 2 146
Why, say, fair queen, whence springs this deep despair? . . iii 3 12
Often heard him say and swear That this his love was an eternal plant. iii 3 123
I hear, yet say not much, but think the more . . . iv 1 83
I blame not her, she could say little less . . . . iv 1 101
I say not, slaughter him, For I intend but only to surprise him . iv 2 24
And says that once more I shall interchange My waned state . iv 7 3
Say, Somerville, what says my loving son? . . . . v 1 7
Say Warwick was our anchor; what of that? . . . . v 4 13
Keep our course, though the rough wind say no . . . v 4 22
Say you can swim; alas, 'tis but a while! . . . . v 4 29
What I should say My tears gainsay . . . . . v 4 73
Down, down to hell; and say I sent thee thither . . . v 6 67
I have often heard my mother say I came into the world with my legs forward . . . . v 6 70
Which says that G Of Edward's heirs the murderer shall be *Richard III.* i 1 39
And says a wizard told him that by G His issue disinherited should be . i 1 56
You may partake of any thing we say: We speak no treason, man: we say the king Is wise and virtuous . . . . . . i 1 89
Say that I slew them not?—Why, then they are not dead . . i 2 89
Say, then, my peace is made.—That shall you know hereafter . i 2 198
To your good prayers will scarcely say amen . . . i 3 21
What doth she say, my Lord of Buckingham?—Nothing that I respect . i 3 295
Remember this another day, . . . And say poor Margaret was a prophetess! i 3 301
Then he will say 'twas done cowardly, when he wakes . . i 4 103
Why, then he will say we stabbed him sleeping . . . i 4 107
Take thou the fee, and tell him what I say . . . . i 4 284
I say with noble Buckingham, That it is meet so few should fetch the prince . . . . ii 2 138
But say, my lord, it were not register'd, Methinks the truth should live iii 1 75
So wise so young, they say, do never live long . . . iii 1 79
Therefore is he idle?—O, my fair cousin, I must not say so . iii 1 106
In weightier things you'll say a beggar nay . . . iii 1 119
So it should seem by that I have to say . . . . iii 2 7
Besides, he says there are two councils held . . . iii 2 12
I'll tell him what you say . . . . . iii 2 34; iii 7 70
Yet who's so blind, but says he sees it not? Bad is the world . iii 6 12
How now, my lord, what say the citizens? . . . . iii 7 1
If you plead as well for them As I can say nay to thee for myself . iii 7 53
Marry, God forbid his grace should say us nay! . . . iii 7 81
You say that Edward is your brother's son: So say we too . . iii 7 177
We see it, and will say it.—In saying so, you shall but say the truth . iii 7 237
And die, ere men can say, God save the queen! . . . iv 1 63
Say, have I thy consent that they shall die?—Give me some breath . iv 2 23
Say it is done, And I will love thee, and prefer thee too . . iv 2 81
What says your highness to my just demand? . . . iv 2 97
Dear God, I pray, That I may live to say, The dog is dead! . . iv 4 78
Much less spirit to curse Abides in me; I say amen to all . . iv 4 197
She is of royal blood.—To save her life, I'll say she is not so . iv 4 212
A handkerchief; which, say to her, did drain The purple sap from her sweet brother's body . . . . iv 4 276
Say that I did all this for love of her . . . . iv 4 288
What were I best to say? her father's brother Would be her lord? or shall I say, her uncle? . . . . iv 4 338
What shall I say more than I have inferr'd? . . . . v 3 314
What says Lord Stanley? will he bring his power? . . . v 3 342
Peace lives again: That she may long live here, God say amen! . v 5 41
I'll say A man may weep upon his wedding-day . . *Hen. VIII.* Prol. 31
Men might say, Till this time pomp was single . . . i 1 14
Say not 'treasonous.'—To the king I'll say't . . . i 1 156
I say, take heed; Yes, heartily beseech you . . . i 2 175
There's mischief in this man: canst thou say further? . . i 2 187
What say they?—Such a one, they all confess, There is indeed . i 4 82
Hear what I say, and then go home and lose me . . . ii 1 57
I had my trial, And, must needs say, a noble one . . . ii 1 119
And when you would say something that is sad, Speak how I fell . ii 1 135
They will not stick to say you envied him . . . . ii 2 127
Eminence, wealth, sovereignty; Which, to say sooth, are blessings . ii 3 30
I'll to the king, And say I spoke with you . . . . ii 3 80
Say, Are you not stronger than you were? . . . . ii 3 99
To unthink your speaking And to say so no more . . . ii 4 105
That's to say, I meant to rectify my conscience . . . ii 4 202
I have spoke long: be pleased yourself to say How far you satisfied me ii 4 210
Would they speak with me?—They will'd me say so . . . iii 1 18
But say, I warn'd ye; Take heed, for heaven's sake . . iii 1 109
'Tis well said again; And 'tis a kind of good deed to say well . iii 2 153
And, if you may confess it, say withal, If you are bound to us or no . iii 2 165
Say, I taught thee, Say, Wolsey, that once trod the ways of glory . iii 2 434
All the rest are countesses.—Their coronets say so . . . iv 1 54

Say. No man living Could say 'This is my wife' there . *Hen. VIII.* iv 1 80
He would say untruths; and be ever double Both in his words and meaning . . . . . . iv 2 38
Say his long trouble now is passing Out of this world . . . . iv 2 162
Affairs, that walk, As they say spirits do, at midnight . . . v 1 14
And yet my conscience says She's a good creature . . . . v 1 24
Many grievous, I do say, my lord, Grievous complaints of you . v 1 98
Is the queen deliver'd? Say, ay; and of a boy . . . . v 1 163
I could say more, But reverence to your calling makes me modest v 3 68
I cry your honour mercy; you may, worst Of all this table, say so v 3 79
Stay, good my lords, I have a little yet to say . . . . v 3 98
I will say thus much for him, if a prince May be beholding to a subject v 3 156
The common voice, I see, is verified Of thee, which says thus . v 3 177
So, 'tis clear, They'll say 'tis naught . . . . . Epil. 5
If they smile, And say 'twill do, . . . All the best men are ours . Epil. 12
This thou tell'st me, . . . when I say I love her . *Troi. and Cres.* i 1 60
Say I she is not fair?—I do not care whether you do or no . i 1 81
They say he is a very man per se, And stands alone . . . i 2 15
Was he angry?—So he says here.—True, he was so . . . i 2 56
I say Troilus is Troilus.—Then you say as I say . . . i 2 70
To say truth . . . . . . i 2 104; *Rom. and Jul.* i 5 69
At a thousand watches.—Say one of your watches . *Troi. and Cres.* i 2 290
And those boils did run? say so: did not the general run then? . ii 1 5
I'll tell you what I say of him.—What?—I say, this . . . ii 1 81
Thus once again says Nestor from the Greeks: 'Deliver Helen' . ii 2 2
I have said my prayers and devil Envy say Amen . . . . ii 3 23
If she that lays thee out says thou art a fair corse . . . ii 3 35
I shall say so to him . . . . ii 3 90
You shall not sin, If you do say we think him over-proud . . ii 3 132
Will you subscribe his thought, and say he is? . . . . ii 3 157
Jupiter forbid, And say in thunder, 'Achilles go to him' . . ii 3 209
Well said, my lord! well, you say so in fits . . . . . iii 1 61
They say all lovers swear more performance than they are able . iii 2 91
What envy can say worst shall be a mock for his truth . . . iii 2 104
Let them say, to stick the heart of falsehood, 'As false as Cressid' . iii 2 202
To do what? let her say what: what have I brought you to do? . iv 2 28
Is he here, say you? 'tis more than I know, I'll be sworn . . iv 2 53
But 'be thou true,' say I, to fashion in My sequent protestation . iv 4 67
But that you say, 'be't so,' I'll speak it in my spirit and honour, 'no' iv 4 136
Fate, hear me what I say! I reck not though I end my life to-day v 6 25
Come here about me, you my Myrmidons; Mark what I say . . v 7 2
Let him that will a screech-owl aye be call'd, Go in to Troy, and say there, Hector's dead . . . . v 10 17
Hector is dead; there is no more to say . . . . . . v 10 22
I say unto you . . .; soft-conscienced men can be content to say it was for his country . . . . *Coriolanus* i 1 36
You must in no way say he is covetous . . . . . . i 1 44
Whereof, they say, The city is well stored.—Hang 'em! They say! . i 1 194
Shall say against their hearts 'We thank the gods' . . . . i 9 8
I can't say your worships have delivered the matter well . . ii 1 62
I must be content to bear with those that say you are reverend grave men ii 1 66
I had rather have my wounds to heal again Than hear say how I got them ii 2 74
What must I say? 'I pray, sir,'—Plague upon't! I cannot . . ii 3 55
Not one amongst us, save yourself, but says He used us scornfully . ii 3 170
With his hat, thus waving it in scorn, 'I would be consul,' says he . ii 3 176
Say, you chose him More after our commandment . . . . ii 3 237
Say we read lectures to you, How youngly he began to serve his country ii 3 243
Wants not spirit To say he'll turn your current in a ditch . . iii 1 96
False to my nature? Rather say I play The man I am . . . iii 2 15
Say to them, Thou art their soldier, and being bred in broils Hast not the soft way . . . . iii 2 80
He must, and will. Prithee now, say you will, and go about it . iii 2 98
When they hear me say 'It shall be so' . . . . . . iii 3 13
Then let them, If I say fine, cry 'Fine;' if death, cry 'Death' . iii 3 16
First, hear me speak.—Well, say. Peace, ho! . . . . . iii 3 41
I am content.—Lo, citizens, he says he is content . . . . iii 3 48
Answer to us.—Say, then: 'tis true, I ought so . . . . iii 3 62
I would say 'Thou liest' unto thee with a voice as free As I do pray the gods . . . . iii 3 72
I' the people's name, I say it shall be so.—It shall be so . . iii 3 105
You were used To say extremity was the trier of spirits . . . iv 1 4
When you were wont to say, If you had been the wife of Hercules . iv 1 16
Say their great enemy is gone, and they Stand in their ancient strength iv 2 6
They say she's mad . . . . iv 2 9
I would I had the power To say so to my husband . . . . iv 2 16
Have you an army ready, say you?—A most royal one . . . iv 3 46
If Jupiter Should from yond cloud speak divine things, And say 'Tis true,' I'ld not believe them more Than thee . . . . . iv 5 111
Let me commend thee first to those that shall Say yea to thy desires . iv 5 151
Faith, look you, one cannot tell how to say that . . . . iv 5 178
Why do you say 'thwack our general'?—I do not say 'thwack our general' . . . . iv 5 190
He was ever too hard for him; I have heard him say so himself . iv 5 196
To say the troth . . . . iv 5 198
He'll go, he says, and sowl the porter of Rome gates by the ears . iv 5 213
Let me have war, say I; it exceeds peace as far as day does night . iv 5 236
For his best friends, if they Should say, 'Be good to Rome,' they charged him even As those should do that had deserved his hate . . iv 6 112
I have not the face To say 'Beseech you, cease' . . . . iv 6 117
Say not we brought it.—How! Was it we? . . . . . . iv 6 120
Very well: Could he say less? . . . . v 1 22
Say that Marcius Return me, as Cominius is return'd, Unheard; what then? . . . . v 1 41
I am one that, telling true under him, must say, you cannot pass . v 2 34
I'll say an errand for you . . . . v 2 65
I say to you, as I was said to, Away! . . . . v 2 114
Forgive my tyranny; but do not say For that, 'Forgive our Romans' . v 3 43
Say my request's unjust, And spurn me back . . . . . v 3 164
His mother, may prevail with him. But I say there is no hope in't . v 4 7
Ere he express himself, or move the people With what he would say . v 6 56
Given up . . . your city Rome, I say 'your city,' to his wife and mother v 6 94
I say no more, Nor wish no less; and so, I take my leave . *T. Andron.* i 1 401
Had I the power that some say Dian had . . . . . . ii 3 61
O, be to me, though thy hard heart say no, Nothing so kind, but something pitiful! . . . . ii 3 155
Shall I speak for thee? shall I say 'tis so? O, that I knew thy heart! . ii 4 33
O, say thou for her, who hath done this deed? . . . . . iii 1 87
Had she a tongue to speak, now would she say That to her brother which I said to thee . . . . iii 1 144
I'll deceive you in another sort, And that you'll say, ere half an hour pass iii 1 192

Say. Say I account of them As jewels purchased at an easy price *T. An.* iii 1 198
Hark, Marcus, what she says; I can interpret all her martyr'd signs . iii 2 35
She says she drinks no other drink but tears . . . . . iii 2 37
For I have heard my grandsire say full oft, Extremity of griefs would make men mad . . . . iv 1 18
So he bade me say; And so I do . . . . iv 2 13
Here lacks but your mother for to say amen . . . . . iv 2 44
But say, again, how many saw the child? . . . . . . iv 2 140
What says Jupiter?—O, the gibbet-maker! he says that he hath taken them down again . . . . iv 3 79
But what says Jupiter, I ask thee?—Alas, sir, I know not Jupiter . iv 3 83
I could never say grace in all my life . . . . iv 3 100
Myself hath often over-heard them say . . . . iv 4 74
And as he saith, so say we all with him . . . . . . v 1 17
I say thy child shall live.—Swear that he shall . . . . v 1 69
What, canst thou say all this, and never blush? . . . . v 1 121
If you say we shall, Lo, hand in hand, Lucius and I will fall . . v 3 135
Is the law of our side, if I say ay? . . . . . *Rom. and Jul.* i 1 55
He, his own affections' counsellor, Is to himself—I will not say how true i 1 154
What say you to my suit?—But saying o'er what I have said before . i 2 6
To them say, My house and welcome on their pleasure stay . . i 2 36
Ye say honestly: rest you merry! . . . . i 2 65
I cannot choose but laugh, To think it should leave crying and say 'Ay' i 3 51
Stint thou too, I pray thee, nurse, say I . . . . . . i 3 58
I would say thou hadst suck'd wisdom from thy teat . . . . i 3 68
What say you? can you love the gentleman? . . . . . . i 3 79
I say, he shall: go to; Am I the master here, or you? go to . . i 5 79
She speaks, yet she says nothing: what of that? Her eye discourses . ii 2 12
Dost thou love me? I know thou wilt say 'Ay,' And I will take thy word ii 2 90
At lovers' perjuries, They say, Jove laughs . . . . . . ii 2 93
I'll frown and be perverse and say thee nay, So thou wilt woo . . ii 2 96
Too like the lightning, which doth cease to be Ere one can say 'It lightens' . . . . ii 2 120
What she bade me say, I will keep to myself . . . . . ii 4 174
Truly, sir; not a penny.—Go to; I say you shall . . . . ii 4 196
Did you ne'er hear say, Two may keep counsel, putting one away? . ii 4 208
I'll warrant you, when I say so, she looks as pale as any clout . . ii 4 218
How art thou out of breath, when thou hast breath To say to me that thou art out of breath? . . . . ii 5 32
Is thy news good, or bad? answer to that; Say either . . . . ii 5 36
All this did I know before. What says he of our marriage? . . ii 5 48
Your love says, like an honest gentleman, Where is your mother? . . ii 5 62
Claps me his sword upon the table and says 'God send me no need of thee!' . . . . iii 1 7
Say thou but 'I,' And that bare vowel 'I' shall poison more . . iii 2 45
If he be slain, say 'I'; or if not, no: Brief sounds determine of my weal or woe . . . . iii 2 50
Ha, banishment! be merciful, say 'death' . . . . . . iii 3 12
What says My conceal'd lady to our cancell'd love?—O, she says nothing iii 3 97
What say you to Thursday?—My lord, I would that Thursday were to-morrow . . . . iii 4 28
I'll say yon grey is not the morning's eye . . . . . . iii 5 19
You say you do not know the lady's mind . . . . . . iv 1 4
I cry you mercy; you are the singer: I will say for you . . . iv 5 142
What says Romeo? Or, if his mind be writ, give me his letter . . v 2 3
Be gone; live, and hereafter say, A madman's mercy bade thee run away v 3 66
Then say at once what thou dost know in this . . . . . v 3 228
Where's Romeo's man? what can he say in this? . . . . . v 3 271
I will say of it, It tutors nature . . . . . . *T. of Athens* i 1 36
Imprison'd is he, say you?—Ay, my good lord: five talents is his debt . i 1 94
There's none Can truly say he gives, if he receives . . . . i 2 11
I have one word to say to you: look you, my good lord . . . i 2 174
I am proud, say, that my occasions have found time to use 'em . . ii 2 199
La, la! 'nothing doubting,' says he? Alas, good lord! . . . iii 1 22
Good boy, wink at me, and say thou sawest me not . . . . iii 1 47
Say, that I cannot pleasure such an honourable gentleman . . iii 2 62
And say, As 'twere a knell unto our master's fortunes, 'We have seen better days' . . . . iv 2 25
Who dares . . . stand upright, And say 'This man's a flatterer'? . . iv 3 15
Thou flatter'st misery.—I flatter not; but say thou art a caitiff . iv 3 235
I'll say thou'st gold: Thou wilt be throng'd to shortly . . . iv 3 394
I am thinking what I shall say I have provided for him . . . v 1 34
I must needs say you have a little fault . . . . . . v 1 90
Say to Athens, Timon hath made his everlasting mansion . . . v 1 217
Send thy gentle heart before, To say thou'lt enter friendly . . v 4 49
Our elders say, The barren, touched in this holy chase, Shake off their sterile curse . . . . *J. Cæsar* i 2 7
When Cæsar says 'do this,' it is perform'd . . . . . . i 2 10
When could they say till now, that talk'd of Rome, That her wide walls encompass'd but one man? . . . . i 2 154
O, you and I have heard our fathers say . . . . i 2 158
What you have said I will consider; what you have to say I will with patience hear . . . . i 2 168
Did Cicero say any thing?—Ay, he spoke Greek . . . . . i 2 281
Let not men say 'These are their reasons; they are natural' . . i 3 29
They say the senators to-morrow Mean to establish Cæsar as a king . i 3 85
When I tell him he hates flatterers, He says he does . . . . ii 1 208
What say the augurers?—They would not have you to stir forth to-day ii 2 37
Send Mark Antony to the senate-house; And he shall say you are not well . . . . ii 2 53
Antony shall say I am not well; And, for thy humour, I will stay at home . . . . ii 2 55
You well expounded it.—I have, when you have heard what I can say . ii 2 92
It were a mock Apt to be render'd, for some one to say . . . ii 2 97
Commend me to my lord; Say I am merry . . . . . . ii 4 45
Thus he bade me say: Brutus is noble, wise, valiant, and honest . iii 1 125
Say I love Brutus, and I honour him; Say I fear'd Cæsar, honour'd him and loved him . . . . iii 1 128
So says my master Antony.—Thy master is a wise and valiant Roman iii 1 137
The enemies of Cæsar shall say this; Then, in a friend, it is cold modesty iii 1 212
Speak all good you can devise of Cæsar, And say you do't by our permission . . . . iii 1 247
And bid me say to you by word of mouth—O Cæsar! . . . . iii 1 280
To him I say, that Brutus' love to Cæsar was no less than his . . iii 2 19
What does he say of Brutus?—He says, for Brutus' sake, He finds himself beholding to us all . . . . iii 2 71
Peace! let us hear what Antony can say . . . . iii 2 76
But Brutus says he was ambitious; And Brutus is an honourable man . iii 2 91
I heard him say, Brutus and Cassius Are rid like madmen through the gates of Rome . . . . iii 2 273

Say. Wisely and truly: wisely I say, I am a bachelor *J. Cæsar* iii 3 18
I say you are not.—Urge me no more, I shall forget myself iv 3 34
You say you are a better soldier: Let it appear so iv 3 51
I said, an elder soldier, not a better: Did I say 'better'? iv 3 57
There is no more to say?—No more. Good night iv 3 229
What says my general?—Messala, This is my birth-day v 1 71
Nature might stand up And say to all the world 'This was a man!' v 5 75
Say to the king the knowledge of the broil As thou didst leave it *Macbeth* i 2 6
If I say sooth, I must report they were i 2 36
If you can look into the seeds of time, And say which grain will grow i 3 59
Say from whence You owe this strange intelligence? i 3 75
Only I have left to say, More is thy due than more than all can pay i 4 20
The king comes here to-night.—Thou 'rt mad to say it i 5 32
This is a sorry sight.—A foolish thought, to say a sorry sight ii 2 22
But they did say their prayers, and address'd them Again to sleep ii 2 25
Listening their fear, I could not say 'Amen,' When they did say 'God bless us!' ii 2 29
And stole thence The life o' the building!—What is't you say? the life? ii 3 74
If you have a station in the file, Not i' the worst rank of manhood, say't iii 1 103
Say to the king, I would attend his leisure For a few words iii 2 3
Well, let's away, and say how much is done iii 3 22
Thou canst not say I did it: never shake Thy gory locks at me iii 4 49
It will have blood; they say, blood will have blood iii 4 122
Only, I say, Things have been strangely borne iii 6 2
Banquo walk'd too late; Whom, you may say, if't please you, Fleance kill'd iii 6 6
He knows thy thought: Hear his speech, but say thou nought iv 1 70
That this great king may kindly say, Our duties did his welcome pay iv 1 131
Why then, alas, Do I put up that womanly defence, To say I have done no harm? iv 2 79
All my pretty ones? Did you say all? O hell-kite! All? iv 3 217
What, at any time, have you heard her say?—That, sir, which I will not report v 1 15
Make us know What we shall say we have and what we owe v 4 18
I should report that which I say I saw, But know not how to do it v 5 31
He's worth no more: They say he parted well, and paid his score v 8 52
Horatio says 'tis but our fantasy *Hamlet* i 1 23
I would not hear your enemy say so, Nor shall you i 2 170
Arm'd, say you?—Arm'd, my lord.—From top to toe? i 2 226
Then if he says he loves you, It fits your wisdom so far to believe it i 3 24
These men, Carrying, I say, the stamp of one defect i 4 31
Say, why is this? wherefore? what should we do? i 4 57
I say, away! Go on; I'll follow thee.—He waxes desperate i 4 86
How say you, then; would heart of man once think it? But you'll be secret? i 5 121
'I know his father . . . And in part him; but,' you may say 'not well' ii 1 17
And then, sir, does he this—he does—what was I about to say? By the mass, I was about to say something: where did I leave? ii 1 50
Or rather say, the cause of this defect, For this effect defective comes by cause ii 2 102
How say you by that? ii 2 188
The satirical rogue says here that old men have grey beards ii 2 199
What should we say, my lord?—Why, any thing, but to the purpose ii 2 286
Man delights not me: no, nor woman neither, though by your smiling you seem to say so ii 2 323
The lady shall say her mind freely, or the blank verse shall halt for't ii 2 338
Will they not say afterwards, . . . their writers do them wrong? ii 2 364
They say an old man is twice a child ii 2 403
You say right, sir: o' Monday morning; 'twas so indeed ii 2 406
And can say nothing; no, not for a king ii 2 596
And by a sleep to say we end The heart-ache iii 1 61
You played once i' the university, you say?—That did I, my lord iii 2 104
By and by.—I will say so.—By and by is easily said iii 2 403
O, say!—Do not forget: this visitation Is but to whet thy almost blunted purpose iii 4 109
I do not know Why yet I live to say 'This thing's to do' iv 4 44
She speaks much of her father; says she hears There's tricks i' the world iv 5 4
What imports this song?—Say you? nay, pray you, mark iv 5 28
They say the owl was a baker's daughter iv 5 41
But when they ask you what it means, say you this iv 5 47
'Naked!' And in a postscript here, he says 'alone' iv 7 53
Nature her custom holds, Let shame say what it will iv 7 189
The Scripture says 'Adam digged:' could he dig without arms? v 1 42
Thou dost ill to say the gallows is built stronger than the church v 1 54
When you are asked this question next, say 'a grave-maker' v 1 66
A courtier; which could say 'Good morrow, sweet lord!' v 1 90
For my part, I do not lie in't, and yet it is mine.—Thou dost lie in't, to be in't and say it is thine v 1 136
How came he mad?—Very strangely, they say.—How strangely? v 1 172
The interim is mine; And a man's life's no more than to say 'One' v 2 74
I will forestal their repair hither, and say you are not fit v 2 228
Which of you shall we say doth love us most? *Lear* i 1 52
What says our second daughter, Our dearest Regan? i 1 68
What can you say to draw A third more opulent than your sisters? i 1 87
Why have my sisters husbands, if they say They love you all? i 1 101
My lord of Burgundy, What say you to the lady? i 1 241
It is not a little I have to say of what most nearly appertains to us both i 1 286
To converse with him that is wise, and says little i 4 17
What says the fellow there? Call the clotpoll back i 4 50
I will hold my tongue; so your face bids me, though you say nothing i 4 215
Art thou mad, old fellow?—How fell you out? say that ii 2 92
Your son and daughter.—No.—Yes.—No, I say.—I say, yea ii 4 17
Have you no more to say?—Few words, but, to effect, more than all yet iii 1 51
I will be the pattern of all patience; I will say nothing iii 2 38
Most savage and unnatural!—Go to; say you nothing iii 3 8
Who's there?—A spirit, a spirit: he says his name's poor Tom iii 4 42
Through the hawthorn blows the cold wind: Says suum, mun, ha, no, nonny iii 4 103
I do not like the fashion of your garments: you will say they are Persian attire iii 6 85
Might I but live to see thee in my touch, I'ld say I had eyes again! iv 1 26
Who is't can say 'I am at the worst?' I am worse than e'er I was iv 1 27
The worst is not So long as we can say 'This is the worst' iv 1 30
I took it for a man; often 'twould say 'The fiend, the fiend' iv 6 78
To say 'ay' and 'no' to every thing that I said! iv 6 100
None does offend, none, I say, none; I'll able 'em iv 6 172
Your—wife, so I would say—Affectionate servant iv 6 275
They say Edgar, his banished son, is with the Earl of Kent in Germany.—Report is changeable iv 7 90

Say. Either say thou 'lt do't, Or thrive by other means *Lear* v 3 33
Mark, I say, instantly; and carry it so As I have set it down v 3 36
Say thou 'No,' This sword, this arm, and my best spirits, are bent To prove upon thy heart, whereto I speak, Thou liest v 3 138
Thy tongue some say of breeding breathes v 3 143
Say, if I do, the laws are mine, not thine: Who can arraign me for't? v 3 158
Speak you on; You look as you had something more to say v 3 201
He knows not what he says: and vain it is That we present us to him.—Very bootless v 3 293
My master calls me, I must not say no v 3 322
Speak what we feel, not what we ought to say v 3 324
For, 'Certes,' says he, 'I have already chose my officer' *Othello* i 1 16
Heard me say i 1 97; *Pericles* v 3 50
How say you by this change?—This cannot be, By no assay of reason *Oth.* i 3 17
What, in your own part, can you say to this?—Nothing, but this is so i 3 74
Say it, Othello.—Her father loved me; oft invited me i 3 127
Ere I would say, I would drown myself for the love of a guinea-hen i 3 316
I say, put money in thy purse i 3 346
You have little cause to say so ii 1 109
It were an honest action to say So to the Moor ii 3 146
Which till to-night I ne'er might say before ii 3 236
Our general's wife is now the general: I may say so in this respect ii 3 320
Good night, honest Iago.—And what's he then that says I play the villain? ii 3 342
What dost thou say?—Nothing, my lord: or if—I know not what iii 3 35
Utter my thoughts? Why, say they are vile and false? iii 3 136
'Tis not to make me jealous To say my wife is fair, feeds well iii 3 184
Their best conscience Is not to leave't undone, but keep't unknown.—Dost thou say so? iii 3 205
In sleep I heard him say 'Sweet Desdemona, Let us be wary' iii 3 419
Patience, I say; your mind perhaps may change.—Never iii 3 452
Within these three days let me hear thee say That Cassio's not alive iii 3 472
He's a soldier, and for one to say a soldier lies, is stabbing iii 4 5
For me to devise a lodging and say he lies here or he lies there, were to lie in mine own throat iii 4 12
Heaven bless us!—Say you?—It is not lost iii 4 82
Bring me on the way a little, And say if I shall see you soon at night iii 4 198
What, If I had said I had seen him do you wrong? Or heard him say iv 1 25
Lie with her! lie on her! We say lie on her, when they belie her iv 1 35
I say, but mark his gesture. Marry, patience; Or I shall say you are all in all in spleen, And nothing of a man iv 1 88
Prithee, say true.—I am a very villain else iv 1 128
Hang her! I do but say what she is: so delicate with her needle iv 1 198
She says enough; yet she's a simple bawd That cannot say as much iv 2 20
What name, fair lady?—Such as she says my lord did say I was iv 2 119
I cannot say 'whore:' It doth abhor me now I speak the word iv 2 161
He says he will return incontinent: He hath commanded me to go to bed iv 3 12
Say that they slack their duties, . . . or say they strike us iv 3 88
Have mercy on me!—Amen, with all my heart!—If you say so, I hope you will not kill me v 2 35
Lord have mercy on me!—I say, amen.—And have you mercy too! v 2 57
He will not say so.—No, his mouth is stopp'd v 2 71
There is no pause.—But while I say one prayer!—It is too late v 2 83
You heard her say herself, it was not I.—She said so v 2 127
What needs this iteration, woman? I say thy husband v 2 150
My husband say that she was false!—He, woman; I say thy husband v 2 152
If he say so, may his pernicious soul Rot half a grain a day! v 2 155
Disprove this villain, if thou be'st a man: He says thou told'st him that his wife was false v 2 173
A lie, a wicked lie. She false with Cassio!—did you say with Cassio? v 2 182
Set you down this; And say besides v 2 352
Which, you say, must charge his horns with garlands *Ant. and Cleo.* i 2 4
Whilst— Antony, thou wouldst say,— O, my lord! i 2 108
If you find him sad, Say I am dancing i 3 4
There's some good news. What says the married woman? i 3 20
Let her not say 'tis I that keep you here: I have no power upon you i 3 22
Then bid adieu to me, and say the tears Belong to Egypt i 3 77
Say this becomes him, . . . yet must Antony No way excuse his soils i 4 21
Say, the firm Roman to great Egypt sends This treasure of an oyster i 5 43
All the east, Say thou, shall call her mistress i 5 47
When I was green in judgement: cold in blood, To say as I said then! i 5 75
My auguring hope Says it will come to the full ii 1 11
If, or for nothing or a little, I Should say myself offended ii 2 32
For that you must But say, I could not help it ii 2 71
Great Mark Antony Is now a widower.—Say not so ii 2 122
What power is in Agrippa, If I would say, 'Agrippa, be it so,' To make this good? ii 2 144
Say to me, Whose fortunes shall rise higher, Cæsar's or mine? ii 3 15
Get thee gone: Say to Ventidius I would speak with him ii 3 31
I'll think them every one an Antony, And say 'Ah, ha! you're caught' ii 5 15
Antonius dead!—If thou say so, villain, Thou kill'st thy mistress ii 5 26
But, sirrah, mark, we use To say the dead are well ii 5 33
If thou say Antony lives, is well, Or friends with Cæsar ii 5 43
Say 'tis not so, a province I will give thee, And make thy fortunes proud ii 5 68
I cannot hate thee worser than I do, If thou again say 'Yes' ii 5 91
A word.—Say in mine ear: what is't?—Forsake thy seat ii 7 42
Thou hast served me with much faith. What's else to say? ii 7 64
Ho! says a'. There's my cap.—Ho! Noble captain, come ii 7 141
Lepidus, . . . as Menas says, is troubled With the green sickness iii 2 5
Would you praise Cæsar, say 'Cæsar:' go no further iii 2 13
Then does he say, he lent me Some shipping unrestored iii 6 26
What is't you say?—Your presence needs must puzzle Antony iii 7 10
Fall not a tear, I say; one of them rates All that is won and lost iii 11 69
Hear it apart.—None but friends: say boldly iii 13 47
Shall I say to Cæsar What you require of him? iii 13 65
To let a fellow that will take rewards And say 'God quit you!' be familiar with My playfellow, your hand! iii 13 124
Look, thou say He makes me angry with him iii 13 140
He shall not hear thee; or from Cæsar's camp Say 'I am none of thine' iv 5 9
Say that I wish he never find more cause To change a master iv 5 15
They say we shall embattle By the second hour i' the morn iv 9 3
Say, that the last I spoke was 'Antony,' And word it, prithee, piteously iv 13 8
Let me say, Before I strike this bloody stroke, farewell iv 14 90
What is't thou say'st?—I say, O Cæsar, Antony is dead v 1 13
The business of this man looks out of him; We'll hear him what he says v 1 51
Go and say, We purpose her no shame v 1 61
Bring us what she says, And how you find of her v 1 67
Say, good Cæsar, That I some lady trifles have reserved v 2 164
Say, Some nobler token I have kept apart v 2 167

Say. He that will believe all that they [women] say, shall never be saved by half that they do . *Ant. and Cleo.* v 2 257
Dissolve, thick cloud, and rain; that I may say, The gods themselves do weep! . . . . . . v 2 302
I did not take my leave of him, but had Most pretty things to say *Cymb.* i 3 26
Upon my mended judgement—if I offend not to say it is mended . i 4 50
Will my lord say so?—Ay, madam, with his eyes in flood with laughter i 6 73
I was about to say—enjoy your—But It is an office of the gods to venge it, Not mine to speak on't . . . . i 6 91
But that you shall not say I yield being silent, I would not speak . ii 3 99
Now say, what would Augustus Cæsar with us? . . . iii 1 1
I do not say I am one; but I have a hand . . . iii 1 41
Say, then, to Cæsar, Our ancestor was that Mulmutius . . iii 1 54
O, not like me; For mine's beyond beyond—say, and speak thick . iii 2 58
Do as I bid thee: there's no more to say . . . iii 2 83
If it be sin to say so, sir, I yoke me In my good brother's fault iv 2 19
A demand who is't shall die, I'ld say 'My father, not this youth' iv 2 23
What lies I have heard! Our courtiers say all's savage but at court iv 2 33
Say what thou art, Why I should yield to thee? . . iv 2 79
I wish my brother make good time with him, You say he is so fell iv 2 109
To the grave!—Say, where shall's lay him? . . . iv 2 233
If you'll go fetch him, We'll say our song the whilst . . iv 2 254
Say his name, good friend . . . . . iv 2 376
Say you, sir?—Thy name?—Fidele . . . . iv 2 379
I will not say Thou shalt be so well master'd, but, be sure, No less beloved . . . . iv 2 382
That it was folly in me, thou mayst say, And prove it in thy feeling v 5 67
I know not why, wherefore, To say 'live, boy' . . . v 5 96
That diamond upon your finger, say How came it yours? . . v 5 137
O, never say hereafter But I am truest speaker . . . v 5 375
The fairest in all Syria, I tell you what mine authors say *Pericles* i Gower 20
And if Jove stray, who dares say Jove doth ill? . . . i 1 104
It fits thee not to ask the reason why, Because we bid it. Say, is it done? . . . . i 1 158
Nor boots it me to say I honour him, If he suspect I may dishonour him i 2 20
Who wanteth food, and will not say he wants it? . . . i 4 11
To say you're welcome were superfluous . . . . ii 3 2
Here, say we drink this standing-bowl of wine to him . . ii 3 65
Say if you had, Who takes offence at that would make me glad? . ii 5 71
Lay the babe Upon the pillow: hie thee, whiles I say A priestly farewell iii 1 69
Say what coast is this?—We are near Tarsus . . . iii 1 73
Whether there Deliver'd, by the holy gods, I cannot rightly say . iii 4 8
Come, say your prayers.—What mean you? . . . iv 1 66
My masters, you say she's a virgin?—O, sir, we doubt it not . iv 2 45
She meant thee a good turn; therefore say what a paragon she is . iv 2 151
What canst thou say When noble Pericles shall demand his child? iv 3 12
She died at night; I'll say so. Who can cross it? . . iv 3 16
And as for Pericles, What should he say? . . . iv 3 41
If she'ld do the deed of darkness, thou wouldst say.—Your honour knows what 'tis to say well enough . . . . . iv 6 33
I hear say . . . . iv 6 86
Didst thou not say, when I did push thee back? . . . v 1 127
Is it no more to be your daughter than To say my mother's name was Thaisa? . . . . v 1 212
As I say *Meas. for Meas.* ii 1; *Coriolanus* iii 3; *T. of Athens* v 1; *Hamlet* v 2; *Lear* i 2; *Cymbeline* iii 5
As much as to say *T. G. of Ver.* iii 1; *Much Ado* ii 3; iii 2; *2 Hen. IV.* ii 2; *Rom. and Jul.* ii 4; *J. Cæsar* iii 3
As they say. (Repeated through the plays)
As who should say. (Repeated through the plays)
As you say. (Repeated through the plays)
Do not say so *M. N. Dream* ii 2; *All's Well* iii 2; *Ant. and Cleo.* iii 6
How say you? (Repeated through the plays)
I dare not say *T. G. of Ver.* v 4; *All's Well* ii 3; *Richard II.* ii 1; *2 Hen. VI.* i 2; *Othello* iii 4
I dare say *2 Hen. IV.* iii 2; *Hen. V.* iv 1; *1 Hen. VI.* ii 4; *Hen. VIII.* iii 1
I have heard you say *K. John* iii 4; *Coriolanus* iii 2; *Cymbeline* iv 2
I know not what to say *Much Ado* iv 1; *T. of Shrew* ii 1; *W. Tale* ii 1; *3 Hen. VI.* i 1; *Rom. and Jul.* iv 5; *Lear* iv 7
I say again *T. Night* i 5; *K. John* v 4; *Hen. VIII.* i 1; ii 4; *Coriolanus* iii 1; *Othello* i 1; *Ant. and Cleo.* ii 3
I say to you *Meas. for Meas.* iii 2; *Much Ado* iv 2; *T. of Shrew* iv 3; *T. Night* iv 2; *2 Hen. IV.* ii 1; *Coriolanus* i 1
I should say *T. G. of Ver.* ii 1; *1 Hen. IV.* i 2; *3 Hen. VI.* v 6
I would say *Mer. of Venice* iii 2; *W. Tale* iv 3; *Richard II.* ii 2; *Ant. and Cleo.* i 1
Let me say *Hen. VIII.* i 2; *Coriolanus* ii 2; *T. Andron.* iii 1
Say no more *T. of Shrew* iv 3; *W. Tale* iii 2; *Coriolanus* v 6; *Oth.* iv 1
Say on *Tempest* ii 1; *As Y. Like It* iii 2; *2 Hen. IV.* iv 1; *Richard III.* iv 2; *Hamlet* ii 2
Say you so? *Meas. for Meas.* ii 4; *L. L. Lost* v 2; *W. Tale* iv 4; *1 Hen. IV.* ii 3; *3 Hen. VI.* iv 7; *Hamlet* v 2
So I say *All's Well* ii 3; *3 Hen. VI.* iii 2; *Cymbeline* ii 1
So say I *Mer. Wives* iv 2; *Much Ado* iii 2; *All's Well* iii 2; *Richard III.* ii 2; *Cymbeline* iv 4
Some say. (Repeated through the plays)
To say the truth *Meas. for Meas.* i 2; *M. N. Dream* iii 1; *1 Hen. IV.* iv 2; *1 Hen. VI.* v 1; v 4; *3 Hen. VI.* v 7; *Troi. and Cres.* i 2; *Coriolanus* iv 6
What says she? *Mer. Wives* iv 5; *Hen. V.* v 2; *Troi. and Cres.* v 3
What say you? (Repeated through the plays)
What shall I say? *Richard II.* i 2; *Hen. V.* ii 2; *T. Andron.* iv 2; *J. Cæsar* iii 1; *Othello* iii 3
What should I say? *Mer. of Venice* v 1; *1 Hen. VI.* i 1; *Troi. and Cres.* ii 3; *T. of Athens* v 2; *Cymbeline* v 5
You say true *Richard II.* ii 1; *1 Hen. IV.* i 3; *Othello* ii 1
You say well *Mer. Wives* ii 2; *T. of Shrew* i 2; *All's Well* ii 3; *Rom. and Jul.* ii 4; *Pericles* iii 2

Sayed. Of all say'd yet, mayst thou prove prosperous! Of all say'd yet, I wish thee happiness! . . . . . *Pericles* i 1 59

Sayest. By foul play, as thou say'st, were we heaved thence . *Tempest* i 2 62
My staff understands me.—What thou sayest?—Ay, and what I do *T. G. of Ver.* ii 5 29
How sayest thou, that my master is become a notable lover? . ii 5 43
Sayest thou so, old Jack? go thy ways . . *Mer. Wives* ii 2 144
Between nine and ten, sayest thou?—Eight and nine, sir . . iii 5 54
What sayest thou to this tune, matter and method? *Meas. for Meas.* iii 2 50
Thou say'st his sports were hinder'd by thy brawls . *Com. of Errors* v 1 77
Being, as thou sayest thou art, born under Saturn . . *Much Ado* i 3 12
Sayest. As thou sayest, charged my brother, on his blessing, to breed me well . . . . *As Y. Like It* i 1 3
No, say'st me so, friend? . . . . *T. of Shrew* i 2 190
This is a man, old, wrinkled, faded, wither'd, And not a maiden, as thou say'st he is . . . . iv 5 44
What say'st thou to her?—She's impudent, my lord . *All's Well* v 3 187
Sayest thou that house is dark?—As hell . . *T. Night* iv 2 38
Thou, now a-dying, say'st thou flatterest me . *Richard II.* ii 1 90
What sayest thou to a hare, or the melancholy of Moor-ditch? *1 Hen. IV.* i 2 87
What say'st thou, my lady?—What is it carries you away? . ii 3 77
Thou'lt set me a-weeping, an thou sayest so . . *2 Hen. IV.* ii 4 302
What sayest thou then to my love? speak, my fair, and fairly *Hen. V.* v 2 176
What say'st thou, man, before dead Henry's corse? Speak softly *1 Hen. VI.* i 1 62
How say'st thou, Charles? shall our condition stand? . . v 4 165
Your royal majesty!—What say'st thou? majesty! I am but grace *2 Hen. VI.* i 2 71
What sayest thou? speak suddenly; be brief . *Richard III.* iv 2 20
There's something more would out of thee; what say'st? . *Hen. VIII.* i 2 202
What say'st thou, ha? To pray for her? what, is she crying out? v 1 66
I am banished. And say'st thou yet that exile is not death? *R. and J.* iii 3 43
What say'st thou to me now? speak once again . *J. Cæsar* i 2 22
How say'st thou, that Macduff denies his person At our great bidding? *Macbeth* iii 4 128
Ah, ha, boy! say'st thou so? art thou there, truepenny? . *Hamlet* i 5 150
Why, there thou say'st . . . . . . v 1 29
Ha! sayest thou so?—I beseech you, pardon me, my lord . *Lear* i 4 68
Thou say'st the king grows mad; I'll tell thee, friend, I am almost mad myself . . . . iii 4 170
Himself: what say'st thou to him? . . . . iv 3 126
Cordelia, Cordelia! stay a little. Ha! What is't thou say'st? . v 3 272
O unhappy girl! With the Moor, say'st thou? . . *Othello* i 1 165
In state of health thou say'st; and thou say'st free *Ant. and Cleo.* ii 5 56
Thou hast forspoke my being in these wars, And say'st it is not fit iii 7 4
What is't thou say'st?—I say, O Cæsar, Antony is dead . v 1 12
Weeps she still, say'st thou? . . . . *Cymbeline* i 5 46
And you crow, cock, with your comb on.—Sayest thou? . . ii 1 27
Say'st thou me so? . . . *Hen. V.* iv 4 23; *2 Hen. VI.* ii 1 109
Thou sayest true *As Y. Like It* i 2; *T. of Shrew* iv 3; *1 Hen. IV.* i 2; ii 4; iii 3; *2 Hen. IV.* ii 4; *Pericles* iv 2
Thou sayest well . . . *As Y. Like It* v 1 33; *1 Hen. IV.* i 2 34
What sayest thou? (Repeated through the plays)

Saying. The old saying is, Black men are pearls . *T. G. of Ver.* v 2 11
What mean you by that saying? . . . . . v 4 167
Why do you put these sayings upon me? . . *Meas. for Meas.* ii 2 133
You say he dined at home; the goldsmith here Denies that saying *Com. of Errors* v 1 274
Saying, I liked her ere I went to wars . . . *Much Ado* i 1 307
If their singing answer your saying, by my faith, you say honestly ii 1 241
Talk with a man out at a window! A proper saying! . . iv 1 312
I pretty, and my saying apt? or I apt, and my saying pretty? *L. L. Lost* i 2 21
By saying that a costard was broken in a shin . . . iii 1 107
Shall I come upon thee with an old saying? . . . iv 1 121
Saying thus, or to the same defect,—'Ladies,'—or 'Fair ladies' *M. N. D.* iii 1 39
Therefore only are reputed wise For saying nothing *Mer. of Venice* i 1 97
My meaning in saying he is a good man is to have you understand me that he is sufficient . . . . i 3 16
The fiend is at mine elbow and tempts me saying to me . . ii 2 3
According to Fates and Destinies and such odd sayings . . ii 2 66
While grace is saying, hood mine eyes . . . . ii 2 202
Let's see once more this saying graved in gold . . . ii 7 36
The ancient saying is no heresy, Hanging and wiving goes by destiny ii 9 82
He did intreat me, past all saying nay, To come with him along . iii 2 232
Pulled out thy tongue for saying so . . . *As Y. Like It* i 1 64
Tongues I'll hang on every tree, That shall civil sayings show . iii 2 136
The priest was good enough, for all the old gentleman's saying . v 1 4
I do now remember a saying, 'The fool doth think he is wise' . v 1 34
Without hawking or spitting or saying we are hoarse . . v 3 12
For saying so, there's gold . . . . *T. Night* i 2 18
I can tell thee where that saying was born . . . i 5 10
The old saying is, the third pays for all . . . v 1 40
And all those sayings will I over-swear . . . . v 1 276
I'll be sworn you would believe my saying . . *W. Tale* ii 1 63
'Tis a saying, sir, not due to me.—You will not own it . iii 2 59
That give you cause to prove my saying true . . *K. John* iii 1 28
And anon cheer'd up the heavy time, Saying, 'What lack you?' . iv 1 48
Twice saying 'pardon' doth not pardon twain . . *Richard. II.* v 3 134
Thou art an unjust man in saying so . . . *1 Hen. IV.* iii 3 146
Saying that ere long they should call me madam . . *2 Hen. IV.* ii 1 109
There's a saying very old and true . . . . *Hen. V.* i 2 166
Saying our grace is only in our heels, And that we are most lofty runaways . . . . iii 5 34
'Tis a foolish saying . . . . iv 1 215
But the saying is true, 'The empty vessel makes the greatest sound' . iv 4 73
Upbraided me about the rose I wear; Saying, the sanguine colour of the leaves Did represent my master's blushing cheeks . *1 Hen. VI.* iv 1 92
Saying that the Duke of York was rightful heir to the crown *2 Hen. VI.* i 3 29
Chides the sea that sunders him from thence, Saying, he'll lade it dry to have his way . . . . . . *3 Hen. VI.* iii 2 139
The saying did not hold In him that did object the same to thee *Rich. III.* ii 4 16
Only for saying he would make his son Heir to the crown . . iii 5 77
We see it, and will say it.—In saying so, you shall but say the truth iii 7 238
Ever may your highness yoke together, As I will lend you cause, my doing well With my well saying! . . . . *Hen. VIII.* iii 2 152
Saying thus, instead of oil and balm, Thou lay'st in every gash that love hath given me The knife that made it . . *Troi. and Cres.* i 1 61
That he raves in saying nothing . . . . . iii 3 249
'O heart,' as the goodly saying is . . . . . iv 4 15
Yet you must be saying, Marcius is proud . . *Coriolanus* i 1 100
Nor check my courage for what they can give, To have't with saying 'Good morrow' . . . . iii 3 93
Like a black dog, as the saying is . . . . *T. Andron.* v 1 122
What say you to my suit?—But saying o'er what I have said before *Rom. and Jul.* i 2 7
The deed of saying is quite out of use . . . *T. of Athens* v 1 28
Methinks there is much reason in his sayings . . *J. Cæsar* iii 2 113
I thank thee, Brutus, That thou hast proved Lucilius' saying true v 5 59
My father is not dead, for all your saying . . . *Macbeth* iv 2 37
As he in his particular act and place May give his saying deed *Hamlet* i 3 27
I will not have excuse, with saying this Loud music is too harsh *Pericles* ii 3 96
She sent him away as cold as a snowball; saying his prayers too . iv 6 149

'Sblood. I am as melancholy as a gib cat . . . 1 *Hen. IV.* i 2 82
I first bow'd my knee Unto this king of smiles, this Bolingbroke,—
'Sblood! . . . . i 3 247
'Sblood, I'll not bear mine own flesh so far afoot again . . ii 2 37
'Sblood, you starveling, you elf-skin! . . . . ii 4 270
'Sblood, my lord, they are false: nay, I'll tickle ye for a young prince . ii 4 488
'Sblood, I would my face were in your belly! . . . iii 3 56
'Sblood, an he were here, I would cudgel him like a dog . . iii 3 100
'Sblood, 'twas time to counterfeit . . . . . v 4 113
'Sblood! an arrant traitor as any is in the universal world! . *Hen. V.* iv 8 10
'Sblood, there is something in this more than natural . *Hamlet* ii 2 384
'Sblood, do you think I am easier to be played on than a pipe? iii 2 386
'Sblood, but you will not hear me . . . . . *Othello* i 1 4
Scab. My elbow itched; I thought there would a scab follow *Much Ado* iii 3 107
Out, scab!—Nay, patience . . . . . *T. Night* ii 5 82
Thou'rt a good scab: hold, there's a tester for thee . 2 *Hen. IV.* iii 2 296
I would make thee the loathsomest scab in Greece . *Troi. and Cres.* ii 1 31
That, rubbing the poor itch of your opinion, Make yourselves scabs *Cor.* i 1 169
Scabbard. Wilt thou use thy wit?—It is in my scabbard . . *Much Ado* v 1 125
I had a pass with him, rapier, scabbard and all . *T. Night* iii 4 303
Where is your argument?—Here in my scabbard . . 1 *Hen. VI.* ii 4 60
Come, here's my heart. Something's afore't. Soft, soft! we'll no
defence; Obedient as the scabbard . . . *Cymbeline* iii 4 82
Scaffold. That have dared On this unworthy scaffold to bring forth So
great an object . . . . *Hen. V.* Prol. 10
The advancement of your children, gentle lady.—Up to some scaffold,
there to lose their heads? . . . . *Richard III.* iv 4 242
Scaffoldage. And doth think it rich To hear the wooden dialogue and
sound 'Twixt his stretch'd footing and the scaffoldage *Troi. and Cres.* i 3 156
Scald. Thou dost sit Like a rich armour worn in heat of day, That
scalds with safety . . . . . . 2 *Hen. IV.* iv 5 31
She's e'en setting on water to scald such chickens as you *T. of Athens* ii 2 71
May these add to the number that may scald thee! . . . iii 1 54
Mine own tears Do scald like molten lead . . . *Lear* iv 7 48
And scald rhymers Ballad us out o' tune . . *Ant. and Cleo.* v 2 215
Scalded. O, I am scalded with my violent motion! . . *K. John* v 7 49
Scalding. Went all afoot in summer's scalding heat . . 3 *Hen. VI.* v 7 18
There's the sulphurous pit, Burning, scalding . . . *Lear* iv 6 131
Scale. Would serve to scale another Hero's tower . *T. G. of Ver.* iii 1 119
You weigh equally; a feather will turn the scale . *Meas. for Meas.* iv 2 32
Your vows to her and me, put in two scales, Will even weigh *M. N. D.* iii 2 132
If the scale do turn But in the estimation of a hair . *Mer. of Venice* iv 1 330
That canst not dream, We, poising us in her defective scale, Shall weigh
thee to the beam . . . . . . *All's Well* ii 3 161
In your lord's scale is nothing but himself, And some few vanities that
make him light . . . . . . *Richard II.* iii 4 85
The weight of a hair will turn the scales between their avoirdupois
2 *Hen. IV.* ii 4 276
Let us resolve to scale their flinty bulwarks . . . 1 *Hen. VI.* ii 1 27
Poise the cause in justice' equal scales, Whose beam stands sure 2 *Hen. VI.* ii 1 204
In a scale Of common ounces . . . . *Troi. and Cres.* ii 2 27
But in that crystal scales let there be weigh'd Your lady's love against
some other maid . . . . . *Rom. and Jul.* i 2 101
Faith, here's an equivocator, that could swear in both the scales against
either scale . . . . *Macbeth* ii 3 10
Scale of dragon, tooth of wolf, Witches' mummy . . . iv 1 22
In equal scale weighing delight and dole . . . *Hamlet* i 2 13
Thy madness shall be paid with weight, Till our scale turn the beam . iv 5 157
If the balance of our lives had not one scale of reason to poise another
of sensuality . . . . *Othello* i 3 331
They take the flow o' the Nile By certain scales i' the pyramid *A. and C.* ii 7 21
Scaled. And the corrupt deputy scaled . . . *Meas. for Meas.* iii 1 266
They fly or die, like scaled sculls Before the belching whale *T. and C.* v 5 22
I would thou didst, So half my Egypt were submerged and made A cistern
for scaled snakes! . . . . . *Ant. and Cleo.* ii 5 95
Scales. Is took prisoner, And Lord Scales with him . . 1 *Hen. VI.* i 1 146
The heir and daughter of Lord Scales . . . 3 *Hen. VI.* iv 1 52
Scaling his present bearing with his past . . . *Coriolanus* ii 3 257
Scall. To be revenge on this same scall, scurvy, cogging companion
Mer. Wives iii 1 123
Scalp. By the bare scalp of Robin Hood's fat friar . *T. G. of Ver.* iv 1 36
Take this transformed scalp From off the head . *M. N. Dream* iv 1 69
White-beards have arm'd their thin and hairless scalps *Richard II.* iii 2 112
Scaly. Hence, therefore, thou nice crutch! A scaly gauntlet now with
joints of steel Must glove this hand . . . 2 *Hen. IV.* i 1 146
Scamble. And England now is left To tug and scamble . . *K. John* iv 3 146
Scambling, out-facing, fashion-monging boys . . . *Much Ado* v 1 94
The scambling and unquiet time Did push it out of farther question
Hen. V. i 1 4
If ever thou beest mine, Kate, . . . I get thee with scambling . . v 2 218
Scamel. And sometimes I'll get thee Young scamels from the rock *Temp.* ii 2 176
Scan this thing no further; leave it to time . . *Othello* iii 3 245
That makes us scan The outward habit by the inward man . *Pericles* ii 2 56
Scandal. That no particular scandal once can touch . *Meas. for Meas.* iv 4 30
Not without some scandal to yourself . . . *Com. of Errors* v 1 15
In a tomb where never scandal slept . . . . *Much Ado* v 1 70
Your wrongs do set a scandal on my sex . . . *M. N. Dream* ii 1 240
Give scandal to the blood o' the prince my son . . *W. Tale* i 2 330
Ah, would the scandal vanish with my life, How happy then were my
ensuing death! . . . . . . *Richard II.* ii 1 67
O, what a scandal is it to our crown, That two such noble peers as ye
should jar! . . . . 1 *Hen. VI.* iii 1 69
Why, yet thy scandal were not wiped away, But I in danger 2 *Hen. VI.* ii 4 65
Oft have I heard his praises in pursuit, But ne'er till now his scandal of
retire.—Nor now my scandal . . . . 3 *Hen. VI.* ii 1 150
If black scandal or foul-faced reproach Attend the sequel *Richard III.* iii 7 231
If you know That I do fawn on men and hug them hard And after
scandal them, . . . then hold me dangerous . . *J. Cæsar* i 2 76
Take corruption From that particular fault: the dram of eale Doth all
the noble substance of a doubt To his own scandal . *Hamlet* i 4 38
You must not put another scandal on him, That he is open to incontinency ii 1 29
Sinon's weeping Did scandal many a holy tear . . *Cymbeline* iii 4 62
Scandaled. Her and her blind boy's scandal'd company I have forsworn
Tempest iv 1 90
Scandal'd the suppliants for the people, call'd them Time-pleasers *Cor.* iii 1 44
Scandalized. I fear me, it will make me scandalized . *T. G. of Ver.* ii 7 61
We in the world's wide mouth Live scandalized . . 1 *Hen. IV.* i 3 154
Scandalous. Shall we thus permit A blasting and a scandalous breath to
fall On him so near us? . . . . . *Meas. for Meas.* v 1 122
And will ignoble make you, Yea, scandalous to the world . *W. Tale* ii 3 121

Scanned. Who, every word by all my wit being scann'd, Want wit in all
one word to understand . . . . . *Com. of Errors* ii 2 152
Which must be acted ere they may be scann'd . . . *Macbeth* iii 4 140
That would be scann'd: A villain kills my father; and for that, I, his
sole son, do this same villain send To heaven . . . *Hamlet* iii 3 75
Scant. In measure rein thy joy; scant this excess . . *Mer. of Venice* iii 2 113
Welcome to our house: It must appear in other ways than words,
Therefore I scant this breathing courtesy . . . . . v 1 141
Scants us with a single famish'd kiss . . . *Troi. and Cres.* iv 4 49
She shall scant show well that now shows best . . *Rom. and Jul.* i 2 104
Our son shall win.—He's fat, and scant of breath . . *Hamlet* v 2 298
You less know how to value her desert Than she to scant her duty *Lear* ii 4 142
To bandy hasty words, to scant my sizes . . . . ii 4 178
You think I will your serious and great business scant . . *Othello* i 3 268
Or say they strike us, Or scant our former having in despite . . iv 3 92
My good fellows, wait on me to-night: Scant not my cups *Ant. and Cleo.* iv 2 21
Scanted. And what he [Time] hath scanted men in hair he hath given
them in wit . . . . *Com. of Errors* ii 2 81
If my father had not scanted me And hedged me by his wit *Mer. of Ven.* ii 1 17
You have obedience scanted, And well are worth the want . *Lear* i 1 281
Return, and force Their scanted courtesy . . . . . iii 2 67
Scanter. Be somewhat scanter of your maiden presence . *Hamlet* i 3 121
Scanting. Like a miser, spoil his coat with scanting A little cloth *Hen. V.* ii 4 47
Scantling. For the success, Although particular, shall give a scantling
Of good or bad unto the general . . . . *Troi. and Cres.* i 3 341
Scantly. Spoke scantly of me . . . . . *Ant. and Cleo.* iii 4 6
'Scape. What would I do?—'Scape being drunk for want of wine *Tempest* ii 1 146
How didst thou 'scape? How camest thou hither? . . . ii 2 124
The thicket is beset; he cannot 'scape . . . *T. G. of Ver.* v 3 11
It was a miracle to 'scape suffocation . . . *Mer. Wives* iii 5 119
He cannot 'scape me; 'tis impossible he should . . . iii 5 147
No might nor greatness in mortality Can censure 'scape *Meas. for Meas.* iii 2 197
Some gentleman or other shall 'scape a predestinate scratched face
M. Ado i 1 135
Now to 'scape the serpent's tongue . . . . *M. N. Dream* v 1 440
Then to 'scape drowning thrice, and to be in peril of my life with the
edge of a feather-bed; here are simple scapes . *Mer. of Venice* ii 2 172
And not one vessel 'scape the dreadful touch Of merchant-marring rocks? iii 2 273
I cannot see how thou shouldst 'scape . . . *As Y. Like It* iii 2 90
In sooth you 'scape not so . . . . . *T. of Shrew* ii 1 242
Time it is, when raging war is done, To smile at 'scapes and perils over-
blown . . . . v 2 3
Sure, some 'scape: . . . yet I can read waiting-gentlewoman in the 'scape
W. Tale iii 3 73
Should 'scape the true acquaintance of mine ear . . *K. John* v 6 15
If I 'scape hanging for killing that rogue . . 1 *Hen. IV.* ii 2 15
If they 'scape from your encounter, then they light on us . . ii 2 64
How 'scapes he agues, in the devil's name? . . . . iii 1 69
Though I could 'scape shot-free at London, I fear the shot here . v 3 30
Good Master Snare, let him not 'scape . . . 2 *Hen. IV.* ii 1 28
In thy despite shall 'scape mortality . . . . 1 *Hen. VI.* iv 7 22
If we haply 'scape, As well we may, if not through your neglect 2 *Hen. VI.* v 2 79
Whither shall I fly to 'scape their hands? . . . 3 *Hen. VI.* i 3 1
Who 'scapes the lurking serpent's mortal sting? . . . ii 2 15
We were better parch in Afric sun Than in the pride and salt scorn of
his eyes, Should he 'scape Hector fair . . . *Troi. and Cres.* i 3 372
Thou shouldst not 'scape me here . . . . . *Coriolanus* i 8 13
If we meet, we shall not 'scape a brawl . . . *Rom. and Jul.* iii 1 3
That copest with death himself to 'scape from it . . . . iv 1 75
And so 'scape hanging . . . . . . *T. of Athens* iv 3 434
If he 'scape, Heaven forgive him too! . . . . *Macbeth* iv 3 234
Virtue itself 'scapes not calumnious strokes . . . *Hamlet* i 3 38
Use every man after his desert, and who should 'scape whipping? . ii 2 556
If he steal aught the whilst this play is playing, And 'scape detecting,
I will pay the theft . . . . iii 2 94
The fault Would not 'scape censure . . . . . *Lear* i 4 229
All ports I'll bar; the villain shall not 'scape . . . . ii 1 82
Whiles I may 'scape, I will preserve myself . . . . ii 3 5
False justicer, why hast thou let her 'scape? . . . . iii 6 59
What will hap more to-night, safe 'scape the king! . . . iii 6 121
Hair-breadth 'scapes i' the imminent deadly breach . . *Othello* i 3 136
Some innocents 'scape not the thunderbolt . . *Ant. and Cleo.* ii 5 77
I'll turn craver too, and so I shall 'scape whipping . . *Pericles* ii 1 93
The more my fault To 'scape his hands where I was like to die . iv 2 80
Marina thus the brothel 'scapes, and chances Into an honest house v Gower 1
'Scaped. I have not 'scaped drowning to be afeard now . *Tempest* ii 2 61
And art thou living, Stephano? O Stephano, two Neapolitans 'scaped! ii 2 118
What, have I 'scaped love-letters in the holiday-time of my beauty?
Mer. Wives ii 1 1
He could not have 'scaped sixpence a day . . . *M. N. Dream* iv 2 21
I have 'scaped by miracle . . . . . . 1 *Hen. IV.* ii 4 184
What, all unready so?—Unready! ay, and glad we 'scaped so well
1 *Hen. VI.* ii 1 40
Like to a ship that, having 'scaped a tempest, Is straightway calm'd
2 *Hen. VI.* iv 9 32
I wonder how our princely father 'scaped, Or whether he be 'scaped
3 *Hen. VI.* ii 1 2
Had he 'scaped, methinks we should have heard The happy tidings . ii 1 6
How 'scaped I killing when I cross'd you so? . . . *J. Cæsar* iv 3 150
Most royal sir, Fleance is 'scaped.—Then comes my fit again . *Macbeth* iii 4 20
Set on in the dark By Roderigo and fellows that are 'scaped . *Othello* v 1 113
He 'scaped the land, to perish at the sea . . . . *Pericles* i 3 29
Scar. And took Deep scars to save thy life . . *Com. of Errors* v 1 193
Never mole, hare lip, nor scar, Nor mark prodigious . *M. N. Dream* v 1 418
Scratch thee but with a pin, and there remains Some scar of it *As Y. L. It* iii 5 22
Whence honour but of danger wins a scar, As oft it loses all *All's Well* iii 2 124
Whether there be a scar under't or no, the velvet knows . . . iv 5 101
A scar nobly got, or a noble scar, is a good livery of honour . . iv 5 105
You were advised his flesh was capable Of wounds and scars 2 *Hen. IV.* i 1 173
Then will he strip his sleeve and show his scars . . *Hen. V.* iv 3 47
And patches will I get unto these cudgell'd scars, And swear I got them
in the Gallia wars . . . . v 1 93
Victorious Warwick, Received deep scars in France and Normandy
2 *Hen. VI.* i 1 87
Show me one scar character'd on thy skin . . . . iii 1 300
Her face defaced with scars of infamy . . . *Richard III.* iii 7 126
Let Paris bleed: 'tis but a scar to scorn . . . *Troi. and Cres.* i 1 114
To such as boasting show their scars A mock is due . . . iv 5 290
Show them the unaching scars which I should hide, As if I had received
them for the hire Of their breath only! . . . . *Coriolanus* ii 2 152

Scar. Scratches with briers, Scars to move laughter only *Coriolanus* iii 3 52
That hath more scars of sorrow in his heart Than foemen's marks upon his batter'd shield *T. Andron.* iv 1 126
My scars can witness, dumb although they are, That my report is just v 3 114
He jests at scars that never felt a wound . *Rom. and Jul.* ii 2 1
I'll not shed her blood ; Nor scar that whiter skin of hers than snow *Oth.* v 2 4
The scars upon your honour, therefore, he Does pity *Ant. and Cleo.* iii 13 58
To-night I'll force The wine peep through their scars . iii 13 191
Would thou and those thy scars had once prevail'd To make me fight at land ! . . . iv 5 2
More of thee merited than a band of Clotens Had ever scar for *Cymbeline* v 5 305
Scarce. And scarce think Their eyes do offices of truth . *Tempest* v 1 155
I fear me, he will scarce be pleased withal *T. G. of Ver.* ii 7 67
Thou hast stayed so long that going will scarce serve the turn . iii 1 388
His dissolute disease will scarce obey this medicine *Mer. Wives* iii 3 204
Scarce confesses That his blood flows . *Meas. for Meas.* i 3 51
There is scarce truth enough alive to make societies secure . iii 2 240
I scarce could understand it . *Com. of Errors* ii 1 49
A table full of welcome makes scarce one dainty dish . iii 1 23
I would scarce trust myself, though I had sworn the contrary *Much Ado* ii 1 197
She an attending star, scarce seen a light . *L. L. Lost* iv 3 231
Finding barren practisers, Scarce show a harvest of their heavy toil . iv 3 326
The face of an old Roman coin, scarce seen . v 2 617
Where Phœbus' fire scarce thaws the icicles *Mer. of Venice* ii 1 5
Are scarce cater-cousins . ii 2 139
A prodigal, who dare scarce show his head on the Rialto . iii 1 47
Those that she [Fortune] makes fair she scarce makes honest *As Y. L. It* i 2 41
I scarce can speak to thank you for myself . ii 7 170
I will scarce think you have swam in a gondola . iv 1 37
That thou'rt scarce worth . *All's Well* ii 3 219
Something ; and scarce so much : nothing, indeed . ii 5 88
Three great oaths would scarce make that be believed . iv 1 64
One would think his mother's milk were scarce out of him *T. Night* i 5 171
Of such note indeed, That were I ta'en here it would scarce be answer'd iii 3 28
Fabian can scarce hold him yonder . iii 4 310
He finds that now scarce to be worth talking of . iii 4 328
You scarce can right me throughly then to say You did mistake *W. Tale* ii 1 99
It shall scarce boot me To say 'not guilty' . iii 2 26
There's scarce a maid westward but she sings it . iv 4 296
Scarce any joy Did ever so long live . v 3 51
Where words are scarce, they are seldom spent in vain *Richard II.* ii 1 7
Thy lips are scarce wiped since thou drunkest last . *1 Hen. IV.* ii 4 170
Scarce blood enough in all their sickly veins *Hen. V.* iv 2 20
Having full scarce six thousand in his troop *1 Hen. VI.* i 1 112
Duke of Gloucester scarce himself . *2 Hen. VI.* ii 3 40
Scarce can I speak, my choler is so great . v 1 23
I cannot weep ; for all my body's moisture Scarce serves to quench my furnace-burning heart . *3 Hen. VI.* ii 1 80
Scarce I can refrain The execution of my big-swoln heart . ii 2 110
Sent before my time Into this breathing world, scarce half made up *Richard III.* i 1 21
Cannot be quiet scarce a breathing-while . i 3 60
That scarce, some two days since, were worth a noble . i 3 82
Your fire-new stamp of honour is scarce current . i 3 256
When scarce the blood was well wash'd from his hands . iv 1 68
You have scarce time . *Hen. VIII.* iii 2 139
Our issues, Who, if he live, will scarce be gentlemen iii 2 292
Which short-armed ignorance itself knows is so abundant scarce *Troi. and Cres.* ii 3 17
I scarce have leisure to salute you . iv 2 61
The general state, I fear, Can scarce entreat you to be odd with him iv 5 265
I can scarce think there's any, ye're so slight . *Coriolanus* v 2 109
We scarce thought us blest That God had lent us but this only child *Rom. and Jul.* iii 5 165
I scarce know how . *T. of Athens* i 2 186
Whose procreation, residence, and birth, Scarce is dividant . iv 3 5
The dead man's knell Is there scarce ask'd for who. *Macbeth* iv 3 171
Are afraid of goose-quills and dare scarce come thither . *Hamlet* ii 2 360
That will scarce hold the laying in . v 1 182
Speak.—I am scarce in breath . *Lear* ii 2 57
I can scarce speak to thee . ii 4 138
For many miles about There's scarce a bush . ii 4 305
Where the greater malady is fix'd, The lesser is scarce felt iii 4 9
My mind Was then scarce friends with him . iv 1 37
Show scarce so gross as beetles . iv 6 14
He's scarce awake : let him alone awhile . iv 7 51
Poisons, Which at the first are scarce found to distaste *Othello* iii 3 327
I scarce did know you . v 2 201
Thou hast, Ventidius, that Without the which a soldier, and his sword, Grants scarce distinction *Ant. and Cleo.* iii 1 29
I am poor of thanks And scarce can spare them . *Cymbeline* ii 3 95
She can scarce be there yet . iii 5 155
No wonder, When rich ones scarce tell true . iii 6 12
Being scarce made up, I mean, to man . iv 2 109
Scarce ever look'd on blood, But that of coward hares . iv 4 36
The odds Is that we scarce are men and you are gods . v 2 10
Have scarce strength left to give them burial *Pericles* i 4 49
We could scarce help ourselves . ii 1 23
Scarce-bearded. Who knows If the scarce-bearded Cæsar have not sent His powerful mandate to you *Ant. and Cleo.* i 1 21
Scarce-cold. The conquest of our scarce cold conqueror . *1 Hen. VI.* iv 3 50
Ere the stroke Of this yet scarce-cold battle *Cymbeline* v 5 469
Scarcely. They will scarcely believe this without trial *Much Ado* iii 2 41
Scarcely off a mile . *2 Hen. IV.* iv 1 19
My eye will scarcely see it . *Hen. V.* ii 2 104
To your good prayers will scarcely say amen *Richard III.* i 3 21
You scarcely have the hearts to tell me so . i 4 180
Whither away so fast?—I promise you, I scarcely know myself . ii 3 2
I would put mine armour on, Which I can scarcely bear *Coriolanus* iii 2 35
Almost dead for breath, had scarcely more Than would make up his message.—Give him tending *Macbeth* i 5 37
Scarcely have coveted what was mine own . iv 3 127
Impotent and bed-rid, scarcely hears Of this his nephew's purpose *Ham.* i 2 29
With the mischief of your person it would scarcely allay . *Lear* i 2 179
What thou gorgeous wear'st, Which scarcely keeps thee warm ii 4 273
When we our betters see bearing our woes, We scarcely think our miseries our foes . iii 6 110
They yet glance by and scarcely bruise . v 3 148
He'll scarcely look on't . *Cymbeline* iii 6 26
But straight Must cast thee, scarcely coffin'd, in the ooze . *Pericles* iii 1 61

Scarcity and want shall shun you ; Ceres' blessing so is on you *Tempest* iv 1 116
Now heavens forbid such scarcity of youth ! . *Troi. and Cres.* i 3 302
When he was poor, Imprison'd and in scarcity of friends *T. of Athens* ii 2 234
Scare. Did scare away, or rather did affright . *M. N. Dream* v 1 142
The noise of thy cross-bow Will scare the herd *3 Hen. VI.* iii 1 7
In a word, Scare Troy out of itself . *Troi. and Cres.* v 10 21
A noise did scare me from the tomb . *Rom. and Jul.* v 3 262
Scarecrow. We must not make a scarecrow of the law *Meas. for Meas.* ii 1 1
No eye hath seen such scarecrows . *1 Hen. IV.* iv 2 41
The scarecrow that affrights our children so . *1 Hen. VI.* i 4 43
Scared. The spirit of wantonness is, sure, scared out of him *Mer. Wives* iv 2 224
Thy jealous fits Have scared thy husband from the use of wits *C. of Er.* v 1 86
They have scared away two of my best sheep . *W. Tale* iii 3 66
And scared my choughs from the chaff . iv 4 630
I scared the Dauphin and his trull . *1 Hen. VI.* ii 2 28
Poor Tom hath been scared out of his good wits . *Lear* iv 1 59
Scarf. My unshrubb'd down, Rich scarf to my proud earth *Tempest* iv 1 82
Under your arm, like a lieutenant's scarf . *Much Ado* ii 1 198
The beauteous scarf Veiling an Indian beauty . *Mer. of Venice* iii 2 98
How it grieves me to see thee wear thy heart in a scarf ! *As Y. Like It* v 2 23
With scarfs and fans and double change of bravery . *T. of Shrew* iv 3 57
The scarfs and the bannerets about thee did manifoldly dissuade me from believing thee a vessel of too great a burthen *All's Well* ii 3 214
If ever thou be'st bound in thy scarf and beaten, thou shalt find what it is to be proud of thy bondage . ii 3 238
That jack-an-apes with scarfs : why is he melancholy? . iii 5 88
That had the whole theoric of war in the knot of his scarf iv 3 163
You are undone, captain, all but your scarf ; that has a knot on't yet . iv 3 359
Matrons flung gloves, Ladies and maids their scarfs and handkerchers, Upon him as he pass'd *Coriolanus* ii 1 280
We'll have no Cupid hoodwink'd with a scarf . *Rom. and Jul.* i 4 4
I could tell you more news too : Marullus and Flavius, for pulling scarfs off Cæsar's images, are put to silence *J. Cæsar* i 2 289
Come, seeling night, Scarf up the tender eye of pitiful day ! . *Macbeth* iii 2 47
Scarfed. The scarfed bark puts from her native bay *Mer. of Venice* ii 6 15
My sea-gown scarf'd about me, in the dark Groped I . *Hamlet* v 2 13
Scaring the ladies like a crow-keeper . *Rom. and Jul.* i 4 6
Scarlet. What say you, Scarlet and John? . *Mer. Wives* i 1 177
A silken doublet ! a velvet hose ! a scarlet cloak ! *T. of Shrew* v 1 69
Shall ill become the flower of England's face, Change the complexion of her maid-pale peace To scarlet indignation *Richard II.* iii 3 99
They call drinking deep, dyeing scarlet . *1 Hen. IV.* ii 4 17
Robin Hood, Scarlet, and John . *2 Hen. IV.* v 3 107
Thy scarlet robes as a child's bearing-cloth I'll use to carry thee out of this place . *1 Hen. VI.* i 3 42
Out, scarlet hypocrite ! . i 3 56
Thy ambition, Thou scarlet sin, robb'd this bewailing land *Hen. VIII.* iii 2 255
If we live thus tamely, To be thus jaded by a piece of scarlet, Farewell nobility . iii 2 280
By her high forehead and her scarlet lip, By her fine foot *Rom. and Jul.* ii 1 18
Now comes the wanton blood up in your cheeks, They'll be in scarlet straight at any news . ii 5 73
The oaks bear mast, the briers scarlet hips . *T. of Athens* iv 3 422
Scarre. I see that men make ropes in such a scarre That we'll forsake ourselves . *All's Well* iv 2 38
Scarred. England hath long been mad, and scarr'd herself *Richard III.* v 5 23
That body, where against My grained ash an hundred times hath broke, And scarr'd the moon with splinters *Coriolanus* iv 5 115
Whose loss hath pierced him deep and scarr'd his heart *T. Andron.* iv 4 31
Scathe. To do offence and scathe in Christendom . *K. John* ii 1 75
All these could not procure me any scathe, So long as I am loyal *2 Hen. VI.* ii 4 62
To pray for them that have done scathe to us . *Richard III.* i 3 317
Be . . . Imperious and impatient of your wrongs, And wherein Rome hath done you any scathe, Let him make treble satisfaction *T. An.* v 1 7
This trick may chance to scathe you, I know what . *Rom. and Jul.* i 5 86
Scathful. Such scathful grapple did he make With the most noble bottom of our fleet *T. Night* v 1 59
Scatter. Would scatter all her spices on the stream *Mer. of Venice* i 1 33
Such wind as scatters young men through the world . *T. of Shrew* i 2 50
Like an angry hive of bees That want their leader, scatter up and down And care not who they sting in his revenge *2 Hen. VI.* iii 2 126
He dives into the king's soul, and there scatters Dangers, doubts, wringing of the conscience, Fears, and despairs *Hen. VIII.* ii 2 27
Impossible—Unless we sweep 'em from the door with cannons—To scatter 'em . v 4 14
To scatter and disperse the giddy Goths *T. Andron.* v 2 78
The seedsman Upon the slime and ooze scatters his grain *Ant. and Cleo.* ii 7 25
He will come in our shadow, to scatter his crowns in the sun *Pericles* iv 2 121
Scattered. Loose now and then A scatter'd smile . *As Y. Like It* iii 5 104
His plausive words He scatter'd not in ears, but grafted them *All's Well* i 2 54
The troops are all scattered, and the commanders very poor rogues iv 3 152
Whose sons lie scattered on the bleeding ground . *K. John* ii 1 304
A whole armado of convicted sail Is scatter'd and disjoin'd . iii 4 3
The thieves are all scatter'd and possess'd with fear *1 Hen. IV.* ii 2 112
Strike up our drums, pursue the scatter'd stray *2 Hen. IV.* iv 2 120
The French have reinforced their scatter'd men *Hen. V.* iv 6 36
Now there rests no other shift but this ; To gather our soldiers, scatter'd and dispersed . *1 Hen. VI.* ii 1 76
Thou shalt not dread The scatter'd foe that hopes to rise again *3 Hen. VI.* ii 6 93
Unvalued jewels, All scatter'd in the bottom of the sea *Richard III.* i 4 28
And mock'd the dead bones that lay scatter'd by . i 4 33
Buckingham's army is dispersed and scatter'd . iv 4 513
The cockle of rebellion, insolence, sedition, Which we ourselves have plough'd for, sow'd, and scatter'd *Coriolanus* iii 1 71
Like a flight of fowl Scatter'd by winds *T. Andron.* v 3 69
Let me teach you how to knit again This scatter'd corn into one mutual sheaf . v 3 71
Remnants of packthread and old cakes of roses, Were thinly scatter'd, to make up a show *Rom. and Jul.* v 1 48
From France there comes a power Into this scatter'd kingdom *Lear* iii 1 31
Scattering. Take no notice, nor build yourself a trouble Out of his scattering and unsure observance *Othello* iii 3 151
Scauld. The rascally, scauld, beggarly, lousy, pragging knave *Hen. V.* v 1 5
Thou shalt die.—You say very true, scauld knave . v 1 33
Thou dost see I eat.—Much good do you, scauld knave, heartily v 1 55
Scelera. Magni Dominator poli, Tam lentus audis scelera? tam lentus vides?—O, calm thee, gentle lord *T. Andron.* iv 1 82
Scelerisque. Integer vitæ, scelerisque purus, Non eget Mauri jaculis, nec arcu . iv 2 20

Scene. Fat Falstaff Hath a great scene . . . . . *Mer. Wives* iv 6 17
That's the scene that I would see, which will be merely a dumb-show *Much Ado* ii 3 225
What a scene of foolery have I seen, Of sighs, of groans! . *L. L. Lost* iv 3 163
The scene begins to cloud . . . . v 2 730
Forsook his scene and enter'd in a brake . *M. N. Dream* iii 2 15
A tedious brief scene of young Pyramus And his love Thisbe . . v 1 56
This wide and universal theatre Presents more woeful pageants than the scene Wherein we play in . . *As Y. Like It* ii 7 138
Last scene of all, That ends this strange eventful history . . ii 7 163
Your patience this allowing, I turn my glass and give my scene such growing As you had slept between . . *W. Tale* iv 1 16
To have you royally appointed as if The scene you play were mine . iv 4 604
As in a theatre, whence they gape and point At your industrious scenes and acts of death . . . . *K. John* ii 1 376
Allowing him a breath, a little scene, To monarchize *Richard II.* iii 2 164
Our scene is alter'd from a serious thing . . . . v 3 79
The rude scene may end, And darkness be the burier of the dead! 2 *Hen. IV.* i 1 159
All my reign hath been but as a scene Acting that argument . . iv 5 198
A kingdom for a stage, princes to act And monarchs to behold the swelling scene! . . . . *Hen. V.* Prol. 4
The scene is now transported, gentles, to Southampton . . ii Prol. 34
Unto Southampton do we shift our scene . . . . ii Prol. 42
Our swift scene flies In motion of no less celerity Than that of thought iii Prol. 1
And so our scene must to the battle fly . . . . iv Prol. 48
What scene of death hath Roscius now to act? . . . 3 *Hen. VI.* v 6 10
What means this scene of rude impatience?—To make an act of tragic violence: . . our king, is dead . . . . *Richard III.* ii 2 38
Woe's scene, world's shame, grave's due by life usurp'd . . iv 4 27
A queen in jest, only to fill the scene . . . . . iv 4 91
Such noble scenes as draw the eye to flow We now present *Hen. VIII.* Prol. 4
In Troy, there lies the scene . . . . *Troi. and Cres.* Prol. 1
And then, forsooth, the faint defects of age Must be the scene of mirth i 3 173
In that day's feats, When he might act the woman in the scene, He proved best man i' the field . . . . . . *Coriolanus* ii 2 100
The gods look down, and this unnatural scene They laugh at . . v 3 184
In fair Verona, where we lay our scene . . *Rom. and Jul.* Prol. 2
My dismal scene I needs must act alone . . . . iv 3 19
How many ages hence Shall this our lofty scene be acted over! *J. Cæsar* iii 1 112
Scene individable, or poem unlimited . . . . *Hamlet* ii 2 418
An excellent play, well digested in the scenes . . . . ii 2 460
Have by the very cunning of the scene Been struck so to the soul . . ii 2 619
One scene of it comes near the circumstance Which I have told thee of my father's death . . . . iii 2 81
Play one scene Of excellent dissembling . . *Ant. and Cleo.* i 3 78
Whom our fast-growing scene must find At Tarsus *Pericles* iv Gower 6
We commit no crime To use one language in each several clime Where our scenes seem to live . . . . iv 4 7
Our scene must play His daughter's woe . . . . . iv 4 48

Scent. He cried upon it at the merest loss And twice to-day pick'd out the dullest scent . . . . . . *T. of Shrew* Ind. 1 24
He is now at a cold scent . . . . . . *T. Night* ii 5 134
But, soft! methinks I scent the morning air; Brief let me be *Hamlet* i 5 58

Sceptre. His sceptre shows the force of temporal power *Mer. of Venice* iv 1 190
By my sceptre and my hopes of heaven . . . *All's Well* ii 1 195
Thou a sceptre's heir, That thus affect'st a sheep-hook! . *W. Tale* iv 4 430
More than all the sceptres And those that bear them living . . v 1 146
A sceptre snatch'd with an unruly hand Must be as boisterously maintain'd as gain'd . . . . *K. John* iii 4 135
Now, by my sceptre's awe, I make a vow . . *Richard II.* i 1 118
Wipe off the dust that hides our sceptre's gilt . . . . ii 1 294
No hand of blood and bone Can gripe the sacred handle of our sceptre . iii 3 80
My sceptre for a palmer's walking-staff . . . . . iii 3 151
And his high sceptre yields To the possession of thy royal hand . iv 1 109
I will undo myself: I give this heavy weight from off my head And this unwieldy sceptre from my hand . . . . iv 1 205
This chair shall be my state, this dagger my sceptre, and this cushion my crown.—Thy state is taken for a joined-stool, thy golden sceptre for a leaden dagger, and thy precious rich crown for a pitiful bald crown! . . . . 1 *Hen. IV.* ii 4 416
By my sceptre and my soul to boot . . . . . . iii 2 97
She is so idly king'd, Her sceptre so fantastically borne By a vain, giddy, shallow, humorous youth . . . . . . *Hen. V.* ii 4 27
'Tis not the balm, the sceptre and the ball, The sword, the mace . iv 1 277
'Tis much when sceptres are in children's hands 1 *Hen. VI.* iv 1 192
Put a golden sceptre in thy hand And set a precious crown upon thy head . . . . v 3 118
Nor hold the sceptre in his childish fist, Nor wear the diadem 2 *Hen. VI.* i 1 245
I cannot give due action to my words, Except a sword or sceptre balance it . . . . v 1 9
Thy hand is made to grasp a palmer's staff, And not to grace an awful princely sceptre . . . . v 1 98
Here is a hand to hold a sceptre up . . . . . . v 1 102
A sceptre, or an earthly sepulchre! . . . . 3 *Hen. VI.* i 4 17
And wring the awful sceptre from his fist . . . . . ii 1 154
Thy place is fill'd, thy sceptre wrung from thee . . . iii 1 16
His head by nature framed to wear a crown, His hand to wield a sceptre . . . . iv 6 73
Every day It would infect his speech, that if the king Should without issue die, he'll carry it so To make the sceptre his . *Hen. VIII.* i 2 135
Who's that that bears the sceptre?—Marquess Dorset . . iv 1 38
Crowns, sceptres, laurels, But by degree, stand in authentic place *Troi. and Cres.* i 3 107
Give me a staff of honour for mine age, But not a sceptre to control the world: Upright he held it, lords, that held it last . *T. Andron.* i 1 199
And put a barren sceptre in my gripe . . . *Macbeth* iii 1 62
And some I see That two-fold balls and treble sceptres carry . iv 1 121
With a more larger list of sceptres . . *Ant. and Cleo.* iii 6 76
It were for me To throw my sceptre at the injurious gods . . iv 15 76
The sceptre, learning, physic, must All follow this . . *Cymbeline* iv 2 268

Sceptred. But mercy is above this sceptred sway *Mer. of Venice* iv 1 193
This sceptr'd isle, This earth of majesty . . *Richard II.* ii 1 40
The throne majestical, The sceptr'd office of your ancestors *Richard III.* iii 7 119

Schedule. To keep those statutes That are recorded in this schedule here *L. L. Lost* i 1 18
The portrait of a blinking idiot, Presenting me a schedule! *Mer. of Venice* ii 9 55
I will give out divers schedules of my beauty . . *T. Night* i 5 263
This schedule, For this contains our general grievances . 2 *Hen. IV.* iv 1 168
Hail, Cæsar! read this schedule . . . . . *J. Cæsar* iii 1 3

Scholar. I hear you are a scholar,—I will be brief with you *Mer. Wives* ii 2 186
He is a better scholar than I thought he was . . . . iv 1 82
He shall appear to the envious a scholar, a statesman *Meas. for Meas.* iii 2 154
I would to God some scholar would conjure her . . *Much Ado* ii 1 264
The epithets are sweetly varied, like a scholar at the least . *L. L. Lost* iv 2 9
A scholar and a soldier . . . . . . *Mer. of Venice* i 2 124
Neither the scholar's melancholy, which is emulation *As Y. Like It* iv 1 10
Yea, and perhaps with more successful words Than you, unless you were a scholar, sir . . . . *T. of Shrew* i 2 159
This young scholar, that hath been long studying at Rheims . . ii 1 79
I am no breeching scholar in the schools; I'll not be tied to hours . iii 1 18
Thou 'rt a scholar; let us therefore eat and drink . . *T. Night* ii 3 13
To be said an honest man and a good housekeeper goes as fairly as to say a careful man and a great scholar . . . . . . iv 2 12
I dare say my cousin William is become a good scholar . 2 *Hen. IV.* iii 2 11
Never was such a sudden scholar made . . . . *Hen. V.* i 1 32
All scholars, lawyers, courtiers, gentlemen, They call false caterpillars and intend their death . . . . . . 2 *Hen. VI.* iv 4 36
Scholars allow'd freely to argue for her . . . *Hen. VIII.* ii 2 113
He was a scholar, and a ripe and good one; Exceeding wise, fair-spoken iv 2 51
Thou art a scholar; speak to it, Horatio . . . . *Hamlet* i 1 42
As you are friends, scholars and soldiers, Give me one poor request . i 5 141
What a noble mind is here o'erthrown! The courtier's, soldier's, scholar's iii 1 159
You may relish him more in the soldier than in the scholar . *Othello* ii 1 167
Thy master dies thy scholar: to do thus I learn'd of thee *Ant. and Cleo.* iv 14 102
Art hath thus decreed, To make some good, but others to exceed; And you are her labour'd scholar . . . . *Pericles* ii 3 17
You are music's master.—The worst of all her scholars, my good lord . ii 5 31
You must be her master, And she will be your scholar . . . ii 5 39
I doubt not but this populous city will Yield many scholars . . iv 6 198

Scholarly. Speak scholarly and wisely . . . . *Mer. Wives* i 3 2

School. I'll but bring my young man here to school . . . iv 1 8
How now, Sir Hugh! no school to-day? . . . . . . iv 1 10
No rhyme to 'lady' but 'baby,' an innocent rhyme; for 'scorn,' 'horn,' a hard rhyme; for 'school,' 'fool,' a babbling rhyme . *Much Ado* v 2 39
So were there a patch set on learning, to see him in a school . *L. L. Lost* iv 2 32
Folly, in wisdom hatch'd, Hath wisdom's warrant and the help of school . . . . v 2 71
She was a vixen when she went to school . . . *M. N. Dream* iii 2 324
Men shall swear I have discontinued school Above a twelvemonth *Mer. of Venice* iii 4 75
My brother Jaques he keeps at school . . . . *As Y. Like It* i 1 6
Creeping like snail Unwillingly to school . . . . . ii 7 147
I am no breeching scholar in the schools . . . . *T. of Shrew* iii 1 18
As willingly as e'er I came from school . . . . . iii 2 152
When the schools, Embowell'd of their doctrine, have left off The danger to itself . . . . *All's Well* i 3 246
Like a pedant that keeps a school i' the church . . *T. Night* iii 2 81
Like a school broke up, Each hurries toward his home . 2 *Hen. IV.* iv 2 104
I have a whole school of tongues in this belly of mine . . . iv 3 20
Thou hast most traitorously corrupted the youth of the realm in erecting a grammar school . . . . 2 *Hen. VI.* iv 7 37
And set the murderous Machiavel to school . . . 3 *Hen. VI.* iii 2 193
Communities, Degrees in schools and brotherhoods in cities *Tr. and Cr.* i 3 104
Love goes toward love, as schoolboys from their books, But love from love, toward school with heavy looks . . . . *Rom. and Jul.* ii 2 158
Nor are they such That these great towers, trophies and schools should fall For private faults in them . . . . . *T. of Athens* v 4 25
He was quick mettle when he went to school . . . *J. Cæsar* i 2 300
Thou know'st that we two went to school together . . . . v 5 26
My dearest coz, I pray you, school yourself . . . *Macbeth* iv 2 15
For your intent In going back to school in Wittenberg, It is most retrograde to our desire . . . . *Hamlet* i 2 113
We'll set thee to school to an ant, to teach thee there's no labouring i' the winter . . . . *Lear* ii 4 68
His bed shall seem a school, his board a shrift . . . *Othello* iii 3 24

Schoolboy. To sigh, like a schoolboy that had lost his A B C *T. G. of Ver.* ii 1 22
The flat transgression of a schoolboy . . . . *Much Ado* ii 1 229
Never will I trust to speeches penn'd, Nor to the motion of a schoolboy's tongue, Nor never come in vizard to my friend . . *L. L. Lost* v 2 403
Then the whining schoolboy, with his satchel And shining morning face, creeping like snail Unwillingly to school . . *As Y. Like It* ii 7 145
The centre is not big enough to bear A schoolboy's top . . *W. Tale* ii 1 103
Whom, like a schoolboy, you may over-awe . . . 1 *Hen. VI.* i 1 36
And schoolboys' tears take up The glasses of my sight! . *Coriolanus* iii 2 116
Love goes toward love, as schoolboys from their books . *Rom. and Jul.* ii 2 157
A peevish schoolboy, worthless of such honour . . . *J. Cæsar* v 1 61

School-days. Is it all forgot? All school-days' friendship? *M. N. Dream* iii 2 202
In my school-days, when I had lost one shaft, I shot his fellow of the self-same flight The self-same way . . . *Mer. of Venice* i 1 140
Thy school-days frightful, desperate, wild, and furious *Richard III.* iv 4 169

Schooled. Never schooled and yet learned . . . *As Y. Like It* i 1 173
Here comes your boy; 'Twere good he were school'd . *T. of Shrew* iv 4 9
Well, I am school'd: good manners be your speed! . 1 *Hen. IV.* iii 1 190
And is ill school'd In bolted language . . . . *Coriolanus* iii 1 321

Schoolfellows. My two schoolfellows, Whom I will trust as I will adders fang'd . . . . *Hamlet* iii 4 202

Schooling. I have some private schooling for you . . *M. N. Dream* i 1 116

School-maids. Adoptedly; as school-maids change their names By vain though apt affection . . . . . . *Meas. for Meas.* i 4 47

Schoolmaster. Here Have I, thy schoolmaster, made thee more profit Than other princesses . . . . *Tempest* i 2 172
Marry, master schoolmaster, he that is likest to a hogshead . *L. L. Lost* iv 2 87
The schoolmaster is exceeding fantastical . . . . . v 2 531
Schoolmasters will I keep within my house, Fit to instruct her *T. of S.* i 1 94
He took some care To get her cunning schoolmasters to instruct her . i 1 192
You will be schoolmaster And undertake the teaching of the maid . i 1 196
A schoolmaster Well seen in music . . . . . . i 2 133
I promised to inquire carefully About a schoolmaster . . . i 2 167
He had rather see the swords, and hear a drum, than look upon his schoolmaster.—O' my word, the father's son . . *Coriolanus* i 3 61
Keep a schoolmaster that can teach thy fool to lie . . . *Lear* i 4 195
O, sir, to wilful men, The injuries that they themselves procure Must be their schoolmasters . . . . ii 4 307
We sent our schoolmaster; Is he come back? . . *Ant. and Cleo.* iii 11 71
'Tis his schoolmaster: An argument that he is pluck'd, when hither He sends so poor a pinion of his wing . . . . iii 12 2
I am unworthy for her schoolmaster.—She thinks not so . *Pericles* ii 5 40

Sciatica. Which of your hips has the most profound sciatica? *M. for M.* i 2 59
Sciaticas, limekilns i' the palm, incurable bone-ache . *Troi. and Cres.* v 1 25

Sciatica. Thou cold sciatica, Cripple our senators *T. of Athens* iv 1 23
Science. I am put to know that your own science Exceeds, in that, the lists of all advice *Meas. for Meas.* i 1 5
Instruct her fully in those sciences *T. of Shrew* ii 1 57
Plutus himself, That knows the tinct and multiplying medicine, Hath not in nature's mystery more science Than I have in this ring *All's W.* v 3 103
Ourselves and children Have lost, or do not learn for want of time, The sciences that should become our country *Hen. V.* v 2 58
Scimitar. By this scimitar That slew the Sophy *Mer. of Venice* ii 1 24
I'll heat his blood with Greekish wine to-night, Which with my scimitar I'll cool to-morrow *Troi. and Cres.* v 1 2
He dies upon my scimitar's sharp point That touches this my first-born son and heir! *T. Andron.* iv 2 91
Scion. We marry A gentler scion to the wildest stock *W. Tale* iv 4 93
Our scions, put in wild and savage stock, Spirt up so suddenly *Hen. V.* iii 5 7
Our carnal stings, our unbitted lusts, whereof I take this that you call love to be a sect or scion *Othello* i 3 337
Scissors. His man with scissors nicks him like a fool *Com. of Errors* v 1 175
Scoff. All dry-beaten with pure scoff! *L. L. Lost* v 2 263
With scoffs and scorns and contumelious taunts 1 *Hen. VI.* i 4 39
Scoff on, vile fiend and shameless courtezan! iii 2 45
They that of late were daring with their scoffs Are glad and fain by flight to save themselves iii 2 113
I have too long borne Your blunt upbraidings and your bitter scoffs *Richard III.* i 3 104
Scoffer. Foul is most foul, being foul to be a scoffer *As Y. Like It* iii 5 62
Scoffing his state and grinning at his pomp *Richard II.* iii 2 163
Scold. I had rather hear them scold than fight *Mer. Wives* ii 1 240
My very visor began to assume life and scold with her *Much Ado* ii 1 249
Mark'd you not how her sister Began to scold? *T. of Shrew* i 1 177
I know she is an irksome brawling scold i 2 188
Thou unadvised scold *K. John* ii 1 191
Take away this captive scold 3 *Hen. VI.* v 5 29
I will have more, or scold it out of him *Hen. VIII.* v 1 173
'Tis the first time that ever I was forced to scold *Coriolanus* v 6 106
Hoar the flamen, That scolds against the quality of flesh *T. of Athens* iv 3 156
When shrill-tongued Fulvia scolds *Ant. and Cleo.* i 1 32
Scolding. Renown'd in Padua for her scolding tongue *T. of Shrew* i 2 100
Scolding would do little good upon him i 2 109
As famous for a scolding tongue As is the other for beauteous modesty i 2 254
As a scolding quean to a wrangling knave *All's Well* ii 2 27
Nay, take away this scolding crook-back rather 3 *Hen. VI.* v 5 29
When the scolding winds Have rived the knotty oaks *J. Cæsar* i 3 5
Sconce. I shall break that merry sconce of yours *Com. of Errors* i 2 79
Or I will beat this method in your sconce.—Sconce call you it? ii 2 34
I must get a sconce for my head and insconce it too ii 2 37
At such and such a sconce, at such a breach, at such a convoy *Hen. V.* iii 6 76
Must I go show them my unbarbed sconce? *Coriolanus* iii 2 99
I'll sconce me even here. Pray you, be round with him *Hamlet* iii 4 4
Why does he suffer this rude knave now to knock him about the sconce? v 1 110
Scone. He is already named, and gone to Scone To be invested *Macbeth* ii 4 31
Will you to Scone?—No, cousin, I'll to Fife ii 4 35
Whom we invite to see us crown'd at Scone v 8 75
Scope. Your scope is as mine own *Meas. for Meas.* i 1 65
So every scope by the immoderate use Turns to restraint i 2 131
'Twas my fault to give the people scope i 3 35
A restraint, Though all the world's vastidity you had, To a determined scope iii 1 70
Give me the scope of justice; My patience here is touch'd v 1 234
The fated sky Gives us free scope, only doth backward pull *All's Well* i 1 233
No scope of nature, no distemper'd day, No common wind *K. John* iii 4 154
I do know the scope And warrant limited unto my tongue v 2 122
His coming hither hath no further scope *Richard II.* iii 3 112
I'll give thee scope to beat, Since foes have scope to beat both thee and me iii 3 140
He holds your temper in a high respect And curbs himself even of his natural scope When you come 'cross his humour 1 *Hen. IV.* iii 1 171
But, being moody, give him line and scope 2 *Hen. IV.* iv 4 39
And the offender granted scope of speech 2 *Hen. VI.* iii 1 176
O, cut my lace in sunder, that my pent heart May have some scope to beat, or else I swoon! *Richard III.* iv 1 35
Let them have scope iv 4 130
An she agree, within her scope of choice Lies my consent *Rom. and Jul.* i 2 18
'Tis conceived to scope *T. of Athens* i 1 72
With all licentious measure, making your wills The scope of justice v 4 5
Be angry when you will, it shall have scope *J. Cæsar* iv 3 108
In the gross and scope of my opinion *Hamlet* i 1 68
More than the scope Of these delated articles allow i 2 37
An anchor's cheer in prison be my scope! iii 2 229
But let his disposition have that scope That dotage gives it *Lear* i 4 314
Scorch. Her eye did seem to scorch me up like a burning-glass! *M. Wives* i 3 74
To scorch your face and to disfigure you *Com. of Errors* v 1 183
Scorched. As fire cools fire Within the scorched veins of one new-burn'd *K. John* iii 1 278
Thy burning car never had scorch'd the earth! 3 *Hen. VI.* ii 6 13
Score. For a score of kingdoms you should wrangle *Tempest* v 1 174
This boy will carry a letter twenty mile, as easy as a cannon will shoot point-blank twelve score *Mer. Wives* iii 2 34
She will score your fault upon my pate *Com. of Errors* i 2 65
If she say I am not fourteen pence on the score for sheer ale, score me up for the lyingest knave in Christendom *T. of Shrew* Ind. 2 25
She may perhaps call him half a score knaves or so i 2 111
After he scores, he never pays the score *All's Well* iv 3 253
That thou didst love her, strikes some scores away From the great compt v 3 56
Three or four loggerheads amongst three or four score hogsheads 1 *Hen. IV.* ii 4 5
Score a pint of bastard in the Half-moon, or so ii 4 29
He's an infinitive thing upon my score 2 *Hen. IV.* ii 1 26
Dead! a' would have clapped i' the clout at twelve score iii 2 52
How a score of ewes now?—Thereafter as they be: a score of good ewes may be worth ten pounds iii 2 56
There shall be no money; all shall eat and drink on my score 2 *Hen. VI.* iv 2 80
Our forefathers had no other books but the score and the tally iv 7 38
And entertain some score or two of tailors, To study fashions *Richard III.* i 2 257
But a hare that is hoar Is too much for a score *Rom. and Jul.* ii 4 145
Let no assembly of twenty be without a score of villains *T. of Athens* iii 6 87
He parted well, and paid his score: And so, God be with him! *Macbeth* v 8 52
And thou shalt have more Than two tens to a score *Lear* i 4 140
What, keep a week away? seven days and nights? Eight score eight hours? and lovers' absent hours, More tedious than the dial eight score times? O weary reckoning! *Othello* iii 4 174
Score. But I shall, in a more continuate time, Strike off this score of absence *Othello* iii 4 179
Score their backs, And snatch 'em up, as we take hares, behind *A. and C.* iv 7 12
How many score of miles may we well ride 'Twixt hour and hour?—One score 'twixt sun and sun *Cymbeline* iii 2 69
Scored. Have you scored me? Well *Othello* iv 1 130
Scoring. Here's no scoring but upon the pate 1 *Hen. IV.* v 3 31
Scorn. To be in love, where scorn is bought with groans *T. G. of Ver.* i 1 29
She did scorn a present that I sent her iii 1 92
A woman sometimes scorns what best contents her iii 1 93
Never give her o'er; For scorn at first makes after-love the more iii 1 95
If thou scorn our courtesy, thou diest iv 1 68
Whilst man and master laugh my woes to scorn *Com. of Errors* ii 2 207
I would not spare my brother in this case, If he should scorn me so apparently iv 1 78
Did not her kitchen-maid rail, taunt and scorn me? iv 4 77
To make a loathsome abject scorn of me iv 4 106
Become the argument of his own scorn by falling in love *Much Ado* ii 3 12
'Shall I,' says she, 'that have so oft encountered him with scorn, write to him that I love him?' ii 3 133
If she should make tender of her love, 'tis very possible he'll scorn it ii 3 186
Disdain and scorn ride sparkling in her eyes iii 1 51
Stand I condemn'd for pride and scorn so much? Contempt, farewell! iii 1 108
I scorn that with my heels iii 4 50
For 'scorn,' 'horn,' a hard rhyme v 2 38
These oaths and laws will prove an idle scorn *L. L. Lost* i 1 311
I think scorn to sigh i 2 66
How will he scorn! how will he spend his wit! iv 3 147
Dart thy skill at me; Bruise me with scorn, confound me with a flout v 2 397
If sickly ears, Deaf'd with the clamours of their own dear groans, Will hear your idle scorns, continue then v 2 875
When at your hands did I deserve this scorn? *M. N. Dream* ii 2 124
Why should you think that I should woo in scorn? Scorn and derision never come in tears iii 2 122
How can these things in me seem scorn to you, Bearing the badge of faith? iii 2 126
I scorn you not: it seems that you scorn me iii 2 221
Have you not set Lysander, as in scorn, To follow me? iii 2 222
Sweet, do not scorn her so iii 2 247
You are too officious In her behalf that scorns your services iii 2 331
By moonshine did these lovers think no scorn To meet at Ninus' tomb v 1 138
Do not run; scorn running with thy heels *Mer. of Venice* ii 2 9
That is the way to make her scorn you still *As Y. Like It* ii 4 22
The red glow of scorn and proud disdain iii 4 57
Sweet Phebe, do not scorn me; do not, Phebe iii 5 1
Take thou no scorn to wear the horn; It was a crest ere thou wast born iv 2 14
The horn, the lusty horn Is not a thing to laugh to scorn iv 2 19
If the scorn of your bright eyne Have power to raise such love in mine iv 3 50
One that scorn to live in this disguise *T. of Shrew* iv 2 18
They may jest Till their own scorn return to them unnoted *All's Well* i 2 34
That is honour's scorn, Which challenges itself as honour's born ii 3 140
Good beauties, let me sustain no scorn *T. Night* i 5 187
What a deal of scorn looks beautiful In the contempt and anger of his lip! iii 1 157
What means this scorn, thou most untoward knave? *K. John* i 1 243
Which scorns a modern invocation iii 4 42
Your daring tongue Scorns to unsay what once it hath deliver'd *Rich. II.* iv 1 9
Had his great name profaned with their scorns 1 *Hen. IV.* iii 2 64
I will charge you.—Charge me! I scorn you 2 *Hen. IV.* ii 4 132
How, you fat fool! I scorn you ii 4 322
The which hath been with scorn shoved from the court v 2 37
And some are yet ungotten and unborn That shall have cause to curse the Dauphin's scorn *Hen. V.* i 2 288
Base tike, call'st thou me host? Now, by this hand, I swear, I scorn the term ii 1 32
Scorn and defiance; slight regard, contempt, And any thing ii 4 117
He scorns to say his prayers, lest a' should be thought a coward iii 2 40
I do believe your majesty takes no scorn to wear the leek upon Saint Tavy's day iv 7 107
With scoffs and scorns and contumelious taunts 1 *Hen. VI.* i 4 39
O'ertake me, if thou canst; I scorn thy strength i 5 15
I scorn thee and thy fashion, peevish boy ii 4 76
Turn not thy scorns this way, Plantagenet.—Proud Pole, I will, and scorn both him and thee ii 4 77
And take foul scorn to fawn on him iv 4 35
To be shame's scorn and subject of mischance! iv 6 49
Thou antic death, which laugh'st us here to scorn iv 7 18
With a proud majestical high scorn iv 7 39
Yet is he poor, And our nobility will scorn the match v 3 96
In her heart she scorns our poverty 2 *Hen. VI.* i 3 84
The nobility think scorn to go in leather aprons iv 2 13
How I scorn his worthless threats! 3 *Hen. VI.* i 1 101
After many scorns, many foul taunts, They took his head ii 1 64
Dare he presume to scorn us in this manner? iii 3 178
Setting your scorns and your mislike aside, Tell me some reason why iv 1 24
In that sad time My manly eyes did scorn an humble tear *Richard III.* i 2 165
Teach not thy lips such scorn, for they were made For kissing i 2 172
With thy scorns drew'st rivers from his eyes i 3 176
Dallies with the wind and scorns the sun i 3 265
Dost thou scorn me for my gentle counsel? i 3 297
There were crept, As 'twere in scorn of eyes, reflecting gems i 4 31
You do him injury to scorn his corse ii 1 80
To mitigate the scorn he gives his uncle, He prettily and aptly taunts himself iii 1 133
Incensed by his subtle mother To taunt and scorn you iii 1 153
But I disdain'd it, and did scorn to fly iii 4 85
Let Paris bleed: 'tis but a scar to scorn *Troi. and Cres.* i 1 114
This Trojan scorns us; or the men of Troy Are ceremonious courtiers i 3 233
Better parch in Afric sun Than in the pride and salt scorn of his eyes i 3 371
His evasion, wing'd thus swift with scorn, Cannot outfly our apprehensions ii 3 123
Does the cuckold scorn me? iii 3 64
O deadly gall, and theme of all our scorns! iv 5 30
With his hat, thus waving it in scorn *Coriolanus* ii 3 175
He hath resisted law, And therefore law shall scorn him further trial iii 1 268
Thou comest not to be made a scorn in Rome *T. Andron.* i 1 265
Here's thy hand, in scorn to thee sent back iii 1 238
Coal-black is better than another hue, In that it scorns to bear another hue iv 2 100
Cut the winds, Who nothing hurt withal hiss'd him in scorn *R. and J.* i 1 119

Scorn. What dares the slave Come hither, cover'd with an antic face, To fleer and scorn at our solemnity? . . . . *Rom. and Jul.* i 5 59
A villain that is hither come in spite, To scorn at our solemnity . . i 5 65
That gallant spirit hath aspired the clouds, Which too untimely here did scorn the earth . . . . . . iii 1 123
And, with a martial scorn, with one hand beats Cold death aside . iii 1 166
Let my meat make thee silent.—I scorn thy meat . . *T. of Athens* i 2 38
The greater scorns the lesser . . . . . . iv 3 6
He shall spurn fate, scorn death, and bear His hopes 'bove wisdom *Macb.* iii 5 30
Be bloody, bold, and resolute; laugh to scorn The power of man . . iv 1 79
Our castle's strength Will laugh a siege to scorn . . . v 5 3
But swords I smile at, weapons laugh to scorn, Brandish'd by man that's of a woman born . . . . v 7 12
Who would bear the whips and scorns of time, The oppressor's wrong, the proud man's contumely . . . . *Hamlet* iii 1 70
To show virtue her own feature, scorn her own image . . . iii 2 26
The gibes, and notable scorns, That dwell in every region of his face *Oth.* iv 1 83
A fixed figure for the time of scorn To point his slow unmoving finger at! iv 2 54
Let nobody blame him; his scorn I approve,—Nay, that's not next . iv 3 52
Fortune knows We scorn her most when most she offers blows *A. and C.* iii 11 74
Their blood thinks scorn, Till it fly out and show them princes born *Cymbeline* iv 4 53
Knighthoods and honours, borne As I wear mine, are titles but of scorn v 2 7
To become the geck and scorn O' th' other's villany . . . v 4 67
But, O scorn! Gone! they went hence so soon as they were born . v 4 125
The boy disdains me, He leaves me, scorns me . . . . v 5 106
That all those eyes adored them ere their fall Scorn now their hand should give them burial . . . . . . *Pericles* ii 4 12
You scorn: believe me, 'twere best I did give o'er . . . . v 1 168
Scorned. The kitchen-vestal scorn'd you . . *Com. of Errors* iv 4 78
A villain, that hath slandered, scorned, dishonoured my kinswoman *Much Ado* iv 1 304
Mocked at my gains, scorned my nation, thwarted my bargains *M. of V.* iii 1 58
And, now I am remember'd, scorn'd at me . . *As Y. Like It* iii 5 131
Whose words all ears took captive, Whose dear perfection hearts that scorn'd to serve Humbly call'd mistress . . . *All's Well* v 3 18
Scorn'd a fair colour, or express'd it stolen . . . . v 3 50
Which I disdaining scorn'd and craved death . . *1 Hen. VI.* i 4 32
To be thus taunted, scorn'd, and baited at . . . *Richard III.* i 3 109
For one that scorn'd at me, now scorn'd of me . . . . iv 4 102
A woman lost among ye, laugh'd at, scorn'd . . *Hen. VIII.* iii 1 107
How in his suit he scorn'd you . . . . *Coriolanus* ii 3 230
Smiles in such a sort As if he mock'd himself and scorn'd his spirit That could be moved to smile at any thing . . . *J. Cæsar* i 2 206
All poverty was scorn'd, and pride so great . . . *Pericles* i 4 30
Scornedst. Thou abhorr'dst in us our human griefs, Scorn'dst our brain's flow . . . . *T. of Athens* v 4 76
Scornest. Why scorn'st thou at sir Robert? . . . *K. John* i 1 228
Scornful. Sing a scornful rhyme . . . . *Mer. Wives* v 5 95
Scornful Lysander! true, he hath my love . . *M. N. Dream* i 1 95
Dart not scornful glances from those eyes, To wound thy lord *T. of S.* v 2 137
Proud scornful boy, unworthy this good gift . . . *All's Well* ii 3 158
Contempt his scornful perspective did lend me . . . v 3 48
You nimble lightnings, dart your blinding flames Into her scornful eyes! *Lear* ii 4 168
Thou scornful page, There lie thy part . . . *Cymbeline* v 5 228
Scornfully. And our air shakes them passing scornfully . *Hen. V.* iv 2 42
Not one amongst us, save yourself, but says He used us scornfully *Cor.* ii 3 171
Scorning. Will you rent our ancient love asunder, To join with men in scorning your poor friend? . . . . *M. N. Dream* iii 2 216
Scorning whate'er you can afflict me with . . *3 Hen. VI.* i 4 38
Scorning the base degrees By which he did ascend . . *J. Cæsar* ii 1 26
Scorning advice, read the conclusion, then . . . *Pericles* i 1 56
Scorpion. Seek not a scorpion's nest . . . . *2 Hen. VI.* iii 2 86
O, full of scorpions is my mind! . . . . *Macbeth* iii 2 36
She did confess Was as a scorpion to her sight. . *Cymbeline* v 5 45
Scot. Brave Archibald, That ever-valiant and approved Scot *1 Hen. IV.* i 1 54
Ten thousand bold Scots, two and twenty knights, Balk'd in their own blood . . . . i 1 68
Those same noble Scots That are your prisoners,— I'll keep them all . i 3 212
He shall not have a Scot of them; No, if a Scot would save his soul . i 3 214
He that kills me some six or seven dozen of Scots at a breakfast . ii 4 116
That sprightly Scot of Scots, Douglas . . . . . . ii 4 377
Well said, my noble Scot . . . . iv 1 1
I hold as little counsel with weak fear As you, my lord, or any Scot . iv 3 12
I was not born a yielder, thou proud Scot . . . . . v 3 11
O Douglas, hadst thou fought at Holmedon thus, I never had triumph'd upon a Scot.—All's done . . . . v 3 15
Hold up thy head, vile Scot, or thou art like Never to hold it up again! v 4 39
Or that hot termagant Scot had paid me scot and lot too . . . v 4 114
The noble Scot, Lord Douglas . . . . v 5 17
That furious Scot, The bloody Douglas . . . *2 Hen. IV.* i 1 126
With a great power of English and of Scots . . . . iv 4 98
We must not only arm to invade the French, But lay down our proportions to defend Against the Scot. . . . . . *Hen. V.* i 2 138
We do not mean the coursing snatchers only, But fear the main intendment of the Scot, Who hath been still a giddy neighbour to us . i 2 144
The Scot on his unfurnish'd kingdom Came pouring, like the tide . . i 2 148
Taken and impounded as a stray The King of Scots. . . . . i 2 161
To her unguarded nest the weasel Scot Comes sneaking . . . . i 2 170
The Scots captain, Captain Jamy . . . . iii 2 79
As well they may upbraid me with my crown, Because, forsooth, the king of Scots is crown'd . . . . . *1 Hen. VI.* iv 1 157
Scot and lot. 'Twas time to counterfeit, or that hot termagant Scot had paid me scot and lot too . . . . . *1 Hen. IV.* v 4 115
Scotched. He scotched him and notched him like a carbonado *Coriol.* iv 5 198
We have scotch'd the snake, not kill'd it . . . *Macbeth* iii 2 13
Scotches. We'll beat 'em into bench-holes: I have yet Room for six scotches more . . . . . . *Ant. and Cleo.* iv 7 10
Scotch jig. Wooing, wedding, and repenting, is as a Scotch jig, a measure, and a cinque pace: the first suit is hot and hasty, like a Scotch jig *Much Ado* ii 1 77
Scotland. Where Scotland?—I found it by the barrenness *Com. of Errors* iii 2 122
Make the Douglas' son your only mean For powers in Scotland *1 Hen. IV.* i 3 262
Your son in Scotland being thus employ'd . . . . . i 3 265
And then the power of Scotland and of York, To join with Mortimer, ha? i 3 280
Clipp'd in with the sea That chides the banks of England, Scotland, Wales . . . . iii 1 45
Lord Mortimer of Scotland hath sent word . . . . iii 2 164
There is not such a word Spoke of in Scotland as this term of fear . iv 1 85
Scotland. O, fly to Scotland . . . . . . *2 Hen. IV.* ii 3 50
I will resolve for Scotland . . . . ii 3 67
He is retired, to ripe his growing fortunes, To Scotland . . . iv 1 14
If that you will France win, Then with Scotland first begin . *Hen. V.* i 2 168
From Scotland am I stol'n, even of pure love, To greet mine own land with my wishful sight . . . . . *3 Hen. VI.* iii 1 13
A banish'd man, And forced to live in Scotland a forlorn . . iii 3 26
Scotland hath will to help, but cannot help . . . . iii 3 34
Henry now lives in Scotland at his ease . . . . . iii 3 151
Laid open all your victories in Scotland . . . *Richard III.* iii 7 15
Mark, king of Scotland, mark . . . . . *Macbeth* i 2 28
It resounds As if it felt with Scotland and yell'd out Like syllable . iv 3 7
Scotland hath foisons to fill up your will, Of your mere own . . iv 3 88
O Scotland, Scotland! . . . . iv 3 100
These evils thou repeat'st upon thyself Have banish'd me from Scotland iv 3 113
Stands Scotland where it did?—Alas, poor country! . . . iv 3 164
Your eye in Scotland Would create soldiers, make our women fight . iv 3 186
Front to front Bring thou this fiend of Scotland and myself . . iv 3 233
Hail, King of Scotland! . . . . v 8 59
Henceforth be earls, the first that ever Scotland In such an honour named . . . . v 8 63
Scottish. What think you of the Scottish lord? . *Mer. of Venice* i 2 83
Then once more to your Scottish prisoners . . . *1 Hen. IV.* i 3 259
To meet your father and the Scottish power, As is appointed us . . iii 1 85
Scoundrels. They are scoundrels and substractors that say so *T. Night* i 3 36
Scour. She can wash and scour.—A special virtue . *T. G. of Ver.* iii 1 313
I wash, wring, brew, bake, scour, dress meat and drink . *Mer. Wives* i 4 101
Look you scour With juice of balm and every precious flower . v 5 65
Never Saw I men scour so on their way . . . . *W. Tale* ii 1 35
Which, wash'd away, shall scour my shame with it . . *1 Hen. IV.* iii 2 137
I will scour you with my rapier . . . . . *Hen. V.* ii 1 60
What purgative drug Would scour these English hence? . *Macbeth* v 3 56
Let his armour rust Until this day, to scour it in the dust . *Pericles* ii 2 55
Scoured. She can wash and scour.—A special virtue; for then she need not be washed and scoured . . . . . *T. G. of Ver.* iii 1 315
To be scoured to nothing with perpetual motion . . *2 Hen. IV.* i 2 246
But here's a vengeful sword, rusted with ease, That shall be scoured in his rancorous heart . . . . *2 Hen. VI.* iii 2 199
Scourge. Our house, my sovereign liege, little deserves The scourge of greatness to be used on it . . . . . . *1 Hen. IV.* i 3 11
Out of my blood He'll breed revengement and a scourge for me . . iii 2 7
And will scourge With haughty arms this hateful name in us . . v 2 40
Scourge the bad revolting stars! . . . . . *1 Hen. VI.* i 1 4
Assign'd am I to be the English scourge . . . . . i 2 129
Is this the scourge of France? Is this the Talbot, so much fear'd abroad? . . . . ii 3 15
I'll note you in my book of memory, To scourge you for this apprehension . . . . ii 4 102
Fearful owl of death, Our nation's terror and their bloody scourge! . iv 2 16
The Frenchmen's only scourge, Your kingdom's terror and black Nemesis . . . . iv 7 77
Outcast of Naples, England's bloody scourge! . . . *2 Hen. VI.* v 1 118
What scourge for perjury Can this dark monarchy afford? *Richard III.* i 4 50
Your enigma?—You have been a scourge to her enemies, you have been a rod to her friends . . . . *Coriolanus* ii 3 97
See, what a scourge is laid upon your hate, That heaven finds means to kill your joys with love . . . . . *Rom. and Jul.* v 3 292
Heaven hath pleased it so, To punish me with this and this with me, That I must be their scourge and minister . . . *Hamlet* iii 4 175
The offender's scourge is weigh'd, But never the offence . . . iv 3 6
With which I meant To scourge the ingratitude that despiteful Rome Cast on my noble father . . . . . *Ant. and Cleo.* ii 6 22
Scourged. Whipp'd and scourged with rods, Nettled and stung *1 Hen. IV.* i 3 239
Yet nature finds itself scourged by the sequent effects . . *Lear* i 2 115
Scouring. Never came reformation in a flood, With such a heady currance, scouring faults . . . . *Hen. V.* i 1 34
One night, as we were scouring my Lord of York's armour . *2 Hen. VI.* i 3 195
And fearful scouring Doth choke the air with dust . *T. of Athens* v 2 15
Scout. Flout 'em and scout 'em And scout 'em and flout 'em . *Tempest* iii 2 130
What are they That charge their breath against us? say, scout, say *L. L. Lost* v 2 88
Scout me for him at the corner of the orchard like a bum-baily *T. N.* iii 4 193
Are not the speedy scouts return'd again? . . . *1 Hen. VI.* iv 3 1
What tidings send our scouts? . . . . v 2 10
By my scouts I was advertised That she was coming . . *3 Hen. VI.* ii 1 116
Our scouts have found the adventure very easy . . . . iv 2 18
Where slept our scouts, or how are they seduced? . . . . v 1 19
Scowl. Men's eyes Did scowl on gentle Richard . . *Richard II.* v 2 28
Hath a heart that is not Glad at the thing they scowl at . *Cymbeline* i 1 15
Scrap. They have been at a great feast of languages, and stolen the scraps.—O, they have lived long on the alms-basket of words *L. L. Lost* v 1 40
Those scraps are good deeds past; which are devour'd As fast as they are made, forgot as soon As done . . . *Troi. and Cres.* iii 3 148
The fragments, scraps, the bits and greasy relics Of her o'er-eaten faith v 2 159
Foster'd with cold dishes, With scraps o' the court. . . *Cymbeline* ii 3 120
Scrape. Nor scrape trencher, nor wash dish . . . *Tempest* ii 2 187
If it be but to scrape the figures out of your husband's brains *M. Wives* iv 2 231
He shift a trencher? he scrape a trencher! . . *Rom. and Jul.* i 5 2
Scraped. Went to sea with the Ten Commandments, but scraped one out of the table . . . . *Meas. for Meas.* i 2 9
You will be scraped out of the painted cloth for this . *L. L. Lost* v 2 579
With the blood Of fair King Richard, scraped from Pomfret stones *2 Hen. IV.* i 1 205
Scraping. He shall spend mine honour with his shame, As thriftless sons their scraping fathers' gold . . . . . . *Richard II.* v 3 69
Scratch. Yet a tailor might scratch her where'er she did itch . *Tempest* ii 2 55
That, like a testy babe, will scratch the nurse . . *T. G. of Ver.* i 2 58
Scratch my head, Peaseblossom . . . . . *M. N. Dream* iv 1 7
Help Cavalery Cobweb to scratch . . . . . . iv 1 25
I am such a tender ass, if my hair do but tickle me, I must scratch . iv 1 28
Scratch thee but with a pin, and there remains Some scar of it *As Y. Like It* iii 5 21
Wherein have you played the knave with fortune, that she should scratch you, who of herself is a good lady? . . . *All's Well* v 2 33
There is that in this fardel will make him scratch his beard . *W. Tale* iv 4 728
And God forbid a shallow scratch should drive The Prince of Wales from such a field as this! . . . . . . *1 Hen. IV.* v 4 11
I'll scratch your heads . . . . *Hen. VIII.* v 4 9
Tear my bright hair and scratch my praised cheeks . *Troi. and Cres.* iv 2 113

Scratch. I had rather have one scratch my head i' the sun When the alarum were struck than idly sit To hear my nothings monster'd *Coriolanus* ii 2 79
Scratches with briers, Scars to move laughter only iii 3 51
What, art thou hurt?—Ay, ay, a scratch, a scratch *Rom. and Jul.* iii 1 96
'Zounds, a dog, a rat, a mouse, a cat, to scratch a man to death! iii 1 104
You cannot soothsay.—Nay, if an oily palm be not a fruitful prognostication, I cannot scratch mine ear *Ant. and Cleo.* i 2 54
Scratched. I should have scratch'd out your unseeing eyes *T. G. of Ver.* iv 4 209
Some gentleman or other shall 'scape a predestinate scratched face *M. Ado* i 1 136
Priscian! a little scratched, 'twill serve *L. L. Lost* v 1 32
I am a man whom fortune hath cruelly scratched *All's Well* v 2 29
I'll have thy beauty scratch'd with briers *W. Tale* iv 4 436
You scratch'd your head, And too impatiently stamp'd *J. Cæsar* ii 1 243
Can save the thing from death That is but scratch'd withal *Hamlet* iv 7 147
Scratching could not make it worse, an 'twere such a face as yours *M. Ado* i 1 137
Roaming through a thorny wood, Scratching her legs *T. of Shrew* Ind. 2 60
My fingers itch.—I would thou didst itch from head to foot and I had the scratching of thee *Troi. and Cres.* ii 1 30
Scream. I heard the owl scream and the crickets cry *Macbeth* ii 2 16
Lamentings heard i' the air; strange screams of death ii 3 61
Screeching. The screech-owl, screeching loud *M. N. Dream* v 1 383
Screech-owl. Whilst the screech-owl, screeching loud, Puts the wretch that lies in woe In remembrance of a shroud v 1 383
The time when screech-owls cry and ban-dogs howl *2 Hen. VI.* i 4 21
And boding screech-owls make the concert full! iii 2 327
Bring forth that fatal screech-owl to our house, That nothing sung but death to us and ours *3 Hen. VI.* ii 6 56
Let him that will a screech-owl aye be call'd, Go in to Troy, and say there, Hector's dead *Troi. and Cres.* v 10 16
Screen. To have no screen between this part he play'd And him he play'd it for *Tempest* i 2 107
Your leavy screens throw down, And show like those you are *Macbeth* v 6 1
Screened. Hath screen'd and stood between Much heat and him *Hamlet* iii 4 3
Screw. I partly know the instrument That screws me from my true place in your favour *T. Night* v 1 120
But screw your courage to the sticking-place, And we'll not fail *Macbeth* i 7 60
Screwed. To what end? Why should I write this down, that's riveted, Screw'd to my memory? *Cymbeline* ii 2 44
Scribbled. I am a scribbled form, drawn with a pen *K. John* v 7 32
That parchment, being scribbled o'er, should undo a man *2 Hen. VI.* iv 2 88
Scribe. And if thy stumps will let thee play the scribe *T. Andron.* ii 4 4
That my master, being scribe, to himself should write *T. G. of Ver.* ii 1 146
Hearts, tongues, figures, scribes, bards, poets, cannot Think, speak, cast, write, sing, number, ho! His love *Ant. and Cleo.* iii 2 16
Scrimers. The scrimers of their nation, He swore, had neither motion, guard, nor eye, If you opposed them *Hamlet* iv 7 101
Scrip. Call them generally, man by man, according to the scrip *M. N. D.* i 2 3
Not with bag and baggage, yet with scrip and scrippage *As Y. Like It* iii 2 171
Scrippage. Not with bag and baggage, yet with scrip and scrippage iii 2 171
Scripture. The devil can cite Scripture for his purpose *Mer. of Venice* i 3 99
But then I sigh; and, with a piece of scripture, Tell them that God bids us do good for evil *Richard III.* i 3 334
How dost thou understand the Scripture? The Scripture says 'Adam digg'd:' could he dig without arms? *Hamlet* v 1 41
The scriptures of the loyal Leonatus, All turn'd to heresy? *Cymbeline* iii 4 83
Scrivener. My boy shall fetch the scrivener presently *T. of Shrew* iv 4 59
Scroll. Here is the scroll of every man's name *M. N. Dream* i 2 4
Call forth your actors by the scroll. Masters, spread yourselves i 2 16
A carrion Death, within whose empty eye There is a written scroll! I'll read the writing *Mer. of Venice* ii 7 64
Here's the scroll, The continent and summary of my fortune iii 2 130
A gentle scroll. Fair lady, by your leave iii 2 140
Gracing the scroll that tells of this war's loss *K. John* ii 1 348
Do you set down your name in the scroll of youth? *2 Hen. IV.* i 2 202
Accept this scroll, most gracious sovereign *1 Hen. VI.* iii 1 149
And give him from me this most needful scroll *Richard III.* v 3 41
Give the king this fatal-plotted scroll *T. Andron.* ii 3 47
What's here? A scroll; and written round about? iv 2 18
Sweet scrolls to fly about the streets of Rome! What's this but libelling? iv 4 16
Do not exceed The prescript of this scroll *Ant. and Cleo.* iii 8 5
Scroop. Say, Scroop, where lies our uncle with his power? *Richard II.* iii 2 192
Sir Stephen Scroop, besides a clergyman Of holy reverence iii 3 28
Who bears hard His brother's death at Bristol, the Lord Scroop *1 Hen. IV.* i 3 271
This to my cousin Scroop, and all the rest To whom they are directed iv 4 3
With your dearest speed, To meet Northumberland and the prelate Scroop v 5 37
Mowbray, the Bishop Scroop, Hastings and all Are brought to the correction of your law *2 Hen. IV.* iv 4 84
Three corrupted men, One, Richard Earl of Cambridge, and the second, Henry Lord Scroop of Masham *Hen. V.* ii Prol. 24
We'll yet enlarge that man, Though Cambridge, Scroop and Grey ... Would have him punish'd ii 2 58
But, O, What shall I say to thee, Lord Scroop? thou cruel, Ingrateful, savage and inhuman creature! ii 2 94
Scrowl. See, how with signs and tokens she can scrowl *T. Andron.* ii 4 5
Scroyles. These scroyles of Angiers flout you *K. John* ii 1 373
Scrubbed. A little scrubbed boy, No higher than thyself *Mer. of Venice* v 1 162
That same scrubbed boy, the doctor's clerk v 1 261
Scruple. And have given ourselves without scruple to hell *Mer. Wives* v 5 157
Nature never lends The smallest scruple of her excellence *Meas. for Meas.* i 1 38
Nor need you, on mine honour, have to do With any scruple i 1 65
I know them, yea, And what they weigh, even to the utmost scruple *Much Ado* v 1 93
Or the division of the twentieth part Of one poor scruple *Mer. of Venice* iv 1 330
Every dram of it; and I will not bate thee a scruple *All's Well* ii 3 234
If I lose a scruple of this sport, let me be boiled to death *T. Night* ii 5 2
No dram of a scruple, no scruple of a scruple, no obstacle iii 4 87
We do lock Our former scruple in our strong-barr'd gates *K. John* ii 1 370
Uncleanly scruples! fear not you iv 1 7
As thoughts of things divine, are intermix'd With scruples *Richard II.* v 5 13
The wise may make some dram of a scruple, or indeed a scruple itself *2 Hen. IV.* i 2 149
But there remains a scruple in that too *1 Hen. VI.* v 3 93
Possess'd him with a scruple That will undo her *Hen. VIII.* ii 1 158
In committing freely Your scruple to the voice of Christendom ii 2 88
Or Laid any scruple in your way ii 4 150
My conscience first received a tenderness, Scruple, and prick ii 4 171
For not appearance and The king's late scruple iv 1 31
He merits well to have her, that doth seek her, Not making any scruple of her soilure *Troi. and Cres.* iv 1 56
Scruple. For every scruple Of her contaminated carrion weight, A Trojan hath been slain *Troi. and Cres.* iv 1 70
Fears and scruples shake us: In the great hand of God I stand *Macbeth* ii 3 135
Hath from my soul Wiped the black scruples iv 3 116
Whether it be Bestial oblivion, or some craven scruple *Hamlet* iv 4 40
Whereat I, wretch, Made scruple of his praise *Cymbeline* v 5 182
Scrupulous. Away with scrupulous wit! now arms must rule *3 Hen. VI.* iv 7 61
Equality of two domestic powers Breed scrupulous faction *Ant. and Cleo.* i 3 48
Scuffle. His captain's heart, Which in the scuffles of great fights hath burst The buckles on his breast i 1 7
Sculls. They fly or die, like scaled sculls Before the belching whale *Troi. and Cres.* v 5 22
Scullion. Away, you scullion! you rampallian! you fustilarian! *2 Hen. IV.* ii 1 65
And fall a-cursing, like a very drab, A scullion! *Hamlet* ii 2 616
Scum. Word of denial: froth and scum, thou liest! *Mer. Wives* i 1 167
Now, neighbour confines, purge you of your scum *2 Hen. IV.* iv 5 124
Rebellious hinds, the filth and scum of Kent *2 Hen. VI.* iv 2 130
A sort of vagabonds, rascals, and runaways, A scum of Bretons *Rich. III.* v 3 317
Scurril. Upon a lazy bed the livelong day Breaks scurril jests *T. and C.* i 3 148
Scurrility. So it shall please you to abrogate scurrility *L. L. Lost* iv 2 55
Pleasant without scurrility, witty without affection v 1 4
Scurrilous. Forewarn him that he use no scurrilous words *W. Tale* iv 4 215
Scurvy. This is a very scurvy tune to sing at a man's funeral *Tempest* ii 2 46
This is a scurvy tune too ii 2 57
A most scurvy monster! ii 2 159
Thou scurvy patch! iii 2 71
I will teach a scurvy jack-a-nape priest to meddle or make *Mer. Wives* i 4 115
Scurvy jack-dog priest! by gar, me vill cut his ears ii 3 65
This same scall, scurvy, cogging companion iii 1 123
A saucy friar, A very scurvy fellow *Meas. for Meas.* v 1 136
Not scurvy, nor a temporary meddler, As he's reported v 1 145
Scurvy, old, filthy, scurvy lord! *All's Well* ii 3 250
Let thy courtesies alone, they are scurvy ones v 3 324
Whatsoever thou art, thou art but a scurvy fellow *T. Night* iii 4 163
I scorn you, scurvy companion *2 Hen. IV.* ii 4 132
I love thee better than I love e'er a scurvy young boy of them all ii 4 296
You scurvy, lousy knave, God pless you! *Hen. V.* v 1 19
I peseech you heartily, scurvy, lousy knave, at my desires v 1 23
You dog!—You scurvy lord!—You cur! *Troi. and Cres.* ii 1 56
That same scurvy doting foolish young knave's sleeve of Troy v 4 4
I am a rascal; a scurvy railing knave v 4 30
Scurvy knave! I am none of his flirt-gills *Rom. and Jul.* ii 4 161
And, like a scurvy politician, seem To see the things thou dost not *Lear* iv 6 175
He prated, And spoke such scurvy and provoking terms *Othello* i 2 7
Some base notorious knave, some scurvy fellow iv 2 140
I think it is scurvy, and begin to find myself fopped in it iv 2 196
Scurvy-valiant. Thou scurvy-valiant ass! *Troi. and Cres.* ii 1 49
'Scuse. That 'scuse serves many men to save their gifts *Mer. of Venice* iv 1 444
I shifted him away, And laid good 'scuse upon your ecstasy *Othello* iv 1 80
Scut. My doe with the black scut! *Mer. Wives* v 5 20
Scutcheon. My scutcheon plain declares that I am Alisander *L. L. Lost* v 2 567
Honour is a mere scutcheon *1 Hen. IV.* v 1 143
'Tis yours; and we, Your scutcheons and your signs of conquest, shall Hang in what place you please *Ant. and Cleo.* v 2 135
Scylla. Thus when I shun Scylla, your father, I fall into Charybdis, your mother: well, you are gone both ways *Mer. of Venice* iii 5 19
Scythe. That honour which shall bate his scythe's keen edge *L. L. Lost* i 1 6
Burnet and green clover, Wanting the scythe *Hen. V.* v 2 50
The next time I do fight, I'll make death love me; for I will contend Even with his pestilent scythe *Ant. and Cleo.* iii 13 194
Scythia. O cruel, irreligious piety!—Was ever Scythia half so barbarous? —Oppose not Scythia to ambitious Rome *T. Andron.* i 1 131
Scythian. I shall as famous be by this exploit As Scythian Tomyris by Cyrus' death *1 Hen. VI.* ii 3 6
The barbarous Scythian, Or he that makes his generation messes To gorge his appetite, shall to my bosom Be as well neighbour'd *Lear* i 1 118
'Sdeath. And I know not—'Sdeath! *Coriolanus* i 1 221
Sea. Nay, good, be patient.—When the sea is *Tempest* i 1 17
Set her two courses off to sea again; lay her off i 1 53
Now would I give a thousand furlongs of sea for an acre of barren ground i 1 70
The sea, mounting to the welkin's cheek, Dashes the fire out i 2 4
Had I been any god of power, I would Have sunk the sea within the earth or ere It should the good ship so have swallow'd i 2 11
In few, they hurried us aboard a bark, Bore us some leagues to sea i 2 145
There they hoist us, To cry to the sea that roar'd to us i 2 149
When I have deck'd the sea with drops full salt i 2 155
Go make thyself like a nymph o' the sea i 2 301
Our garments, being, as they were, drenched in the sea ii 1 62
And, sowing the kernels of it in the sea, bring forth more islands ii 1 92
I shall no more to sea, to sea, Here shall I die ashore ii 2 44
Then to sea, boys, and let her go hang! ii 2 56
The sea cannot drown me iii 2 15
The sea mocks Our frustrate search on land iii 3 9
The never-surfeited sea Hath caused to belch up you iii 3 55
Exposed unto the sea, which hath requit it, Him and his innocent child iii 3 71
The powers, delaying, not forgetting, have Incensed the seas and shores, yea, all the creatures, Against your peace iii 3 74
And 'twixt the green sea and the azured vault Set roaring war v 1 43
Though the seas threaten, they are merciful v 1 178
Is tight and yare and bravely rigg'd as when We first put out to sea v 1 225
I'll deliver all; And promise you calm seas, auspicious gales v 1 314
Throw it thence into the raging sea! *T. G. of Ver.* i 2 122
Thus have I shunn'd the fire for fear of burning, And drench'd me in the sea, where I am drown'd i 3 79
As rich in having such a jewel As twenty seas, if all their sand were pearl ii 4 170
A sea of melting pearl, which some call tears iii 1 224
What news with your mastership?—With my master's ship? why, it is at sea iii 1 282
Even from a heart As full of sorrows as the sea of sands iv 3 33
If he come under my hatches, I'll never to sea again *Mer. Wives* ii 1 96
Went to sea with the Ten Commandments, but scraped one out *M. for M.* i 2 8
The great soldier who miscarried at sea iii 1 218
Her brother Frederick was wrecked at sea iii 1 225
By the benefit of his wished light, The seas wax'd calm *Com. of Errors* i 1 92
There's nothing situate under heaven's eye But hath his bound, in earth, in sea, in sky ii 1 17
Lords of the wide world and wild watery seas ii 1 21
He is bound to sea iv 1 33

Sea. But for staying on our controversy, Had hoisted sail and put to sea to-day *Com. of Errors* v 1 21
Hath he not lost much wealth by wreck of sea? Buried some dear friend? v 1 49
Besides her urging of her wreck at sea v 1 359
One foot in sea and one on shore, To one thing constant never *Much Ado* ii 3 66
The wide sea Hath drops too few to wash her clean again iv 1 142
The sea will ebb and flow, heaven show his face *L. L. Lost* iv 3 216
By rushy brook, Or in the beached margent of the sea *M. N. Dream* ii 1 85
As in revenge, have suck'd up from the sea Contagious fogs ii 1 89
Such dulcet and harmonious breath That the rude sea grew civil at her song ii 1 152
Or, as it were, the pageants of the sea *Mer. of Venice* i 1 11
When I thought What harm a wind too great at sea might do i 1 24
Thou know'st that all my fortunes are at sea i 1 177
In the narrow seas that part The French and English ii 8 28
Antonio hath a ship of rich lading wrecked on the narrow seas iii 1 4
Do you hear whether Antonio have had any loss at sea or no? iii 1 45
Thus ornament is but the guiled shore To a most dangerous sea iii 2 98
Doth it [pride] not flow as hugely as the sea? *As Y. Like It* ii 7 72
Were she as rough As are the swelling Adriatic seas *T. of Shrew* i 2 74
Have I not heard the sea puff'd up with winds Rage like an angry boar? i 2 202
'Twill bring you gain, or perish on the seas ii 1 331
To painful labour both by sea and land v 2 149
Great floods have flown From simple sources, and great seas have dried When miracles have by the greatest been denied *All's Well* ii 1 143
Notwithstanding thy capacity Receiveth as the sea *T. Night* i 1 11
To a strong mast that lived upon the sea i 2 14
Some hour before you took me from the breach of the sea ii 1 23
Thy mind is a very opal. I would have men of such constancy put to sea ii 4 78
As hungry as the sea, And can digest as much ii 4 103
From the rude sea's enraged and foamy mouth Did I redeem v 1 81
You may as well Forbid the sea for to obey the moon *W. Tale* i 2 427
I have seen two such sights, by sea and by land! but I am not to say it is a sea, for it is now the sky iii 3 84
But to make an end of the ship, to see how the sea flap-dragoned it iii 3 100
How the poor souls roared, and the sea mocked them; and how the poor gentleman roared and the bear mocked him, both roaring louder than the sea or weather iii 3 101
When you do dance, I wish you A wave o' the sea iv 4 141
For all the sun sees or The close earth wombs or the profound seas hide iv 4 501
I am put to sea With her whom here I cannot hold on shore iv 4 509
Large lengths of seas and shores Between my father and my mother lay *K. John* i 1 105
The sea enraged is not half so deaf, Lions more confident ii 1 451
A large mouth, indeed, That spits forth death and mountains, rocks and seas! ii 1 458
All that we upon this side the sea . . . Find liable to our crown ii 1 488
Full of ire, In rage deaf as the sea, hasty as fire *Richard II.* i 1 19
This little world, This precious stone set in the silver sea ii 1 46
England, bound in with the triumphant sea ii 1 61
How brooks your grace the air, After your late tossing on the breaking seas? iii 2 3
Not all the water in the rough rude sea Can wash the balm off from an anointed king iii 2 54
Governed, as the sea is, by our noble and chaste mistress the moon *1 Hen. IV.* i 2 31
Clipp'd in with the sea That chides the banks of England, Scotland, Wales iii 1 44
Knew that we ventured on such dangerous seas *2 Hen. IV.* i 1 181
And the continent, Weary of solid firmness, melt itself Into the sea! iii 1 49
Now doth it turn and ebb back to the sea v 2 131
There roar'd the sea, and trumpet-clangor sounds v 5 42
As is the ooze and bottom of the sea With sunken wreck *Hen. V.* i 2 164
As many fresh streams meet in one salt sea i 2 209
Charming the narrow seas To give you gentle pass ii Prol. 38
Cheerly to sea; the signs of war advance ii 2 192
The threaden sails, Borne with the invisible and creeping wind, Draw the huge bottoms through the furrow'd sea iii Prol. 12
It is a theme as fluent as the sea iii 7 36
Do sinfully miscarry upon the sea iv 1 156
Heave him away upon your winged thoughts Athwart the sea v Prol. 9
Whose shouts and claps out-voice the deep-mouth'd sea v Prol. 11
Now will it best avail your majesty To cross the seas *1 Hen. VI.* iii 1 180
You, that were so hot at sea iii 4 28
Crossing the sea from England into France iv 1 89
In that sea of blood my boy did drench His over-mounting spirit iv 7 14
Commit them to the fortune of the sea v 1 50
Repeat their semblance often on the seas v 3 193
Procure That Lady Margaret do vouchsafe to come To cross the seas v 5 90
The Dauphin hath prevail'd beyond the seas *2 Hen. VI.* i 3 128
Was I for this nigh wreck'd upon the sea? iii 2 82
The pretty-vaulting sea refused to drown me, Knowing that thou wouldst have me drown'd on shore, With tears as salt as sea iii 2 94
The sea received it, And so I wish'd thy body might my heart iii 2 108
The gaudy, blabbing and remorseful day Is crept into the bosom of the sea iv 1 2
The fearful French, whom you late vanquished, Should make a start o'er seas and vanquish you iv 8 45
And I to Norfolk with my followers.—And I unto the sea *3 Hen. VI.* i 1 209
Stern Falconbridge commands the narrow seas i 1 239
As if a channel should be call'd the sea ii 2 141
Now sways it this way, like a mighty sea Forced by the tide to combat with the wind; Now sways it that way, like the selfsame sea Forced to retire by fury of the wind ii 5 5
How will my wife for slaughter of my son Shed seas of tears! ii 5 106
From whence shall Warwick cut the sea to France ii 6 89
I'll cross the sea, To effect this marriage ii 6 97
Chides the sea that sunders him from thence, Saying, he'll lade it dry iii 2 138
Thou and Oxford, with five thousand men, Shall cross the seas iii 3 235
Back'd with God and with the seas Which He hath give for fence impregnable iv 1 43
Well have we pass'd and now repass'd the seas iv 7 5
Hath pass'd in safety through the narrow seas iv 8 3
My sea shall suck them dry, And swell so much the higher by their ebb iv 8 55
With tearful eyes add water to the sea v 4 8
What is Edward but a ruthless sea? What Clarence but a quicksand of deceit? v 4 25
Thyself the sea Whose envious gulf did swallow up his life v 6 24

Sea. Unvalued jewels, All scatter'd in the bottom of the sea *Rich. III.* i 4 28
Smother'd it within my panting bulk, Which almost burst to belch it in the sea i 4 41
I had rather hide me from my greatness, Being a bark to brook no mighty sea iii 7 162
If thou wilt outstrip death, go cross the seas iv 1 42
In those parts beyond the sea Where he abides iv 2 47
Richmond is on the seas.—There let him sink, and be the seas on him! iv 4 463
Tell me, what doth he upon the sea? iv 4 474
Let's whip these stragglers o'er the seas again v 3 327
Thus hulling in The wild sea of my conscience *Hen. VIII.* ii 4 200
Every thing that heard him play, Even the billows of the sea, Hung their heads iii 1 10
In a sea of glory, But far beyond my depth iii 2 360
Such a noise arose As the shrouds make at sea in a stiff tempest iv 1 72
The sea being smooth, How many shallow bauble boats dare sail *T. and C.* i 3 34
What raging of the sea? shaking of earth! Commotion in the winds! i 3 97
The seas and winds, old wranglers, took a truce And did him service ii 2 75
Beggar the estimation which you prized Richer than sea and land ii 2 92
When we vow to weep seas, live in fire, eat rocks, tame tigers iii 2 84
His pupil age Man-enter'd thus, he waxed like a sea *Coriolanus* ii 2 103
When the sea was calm all boats alike Show'd mastership in floating iv 1 6
Of tribunes, such as you, A sea and land full v 4 58
What fool hath added water to the sea? *T. Andron.* iii 1 68
For now I stand as one upon a rock Environ'd with a wilderness of sea iii 1 94
If the winds rage, doth not the sea wax mad, Threatening the welkin? iii 1 223
I am the sea; hark, how her sighs do blow! She is the weeping welkin, I the earth: Then must my sea be moved with her sighs iii 1 226
You may catch her in the sea; Yet there's as little justice as at land iv 3 8
Even from Hyperion's rising in the east Until his very downfall in the sea v 2 57
Being vex'd [love is], a sea nourish'd with lovers' tears *Rom. and Jul.* i 1 198
The fish lives in the sea, and 'tis much pride For fair without the fair within to hide i 3 89
Wert thou as far As that vast shore wash'd with the farthest sea, I would adventure for such merchandise ii 2 83
My bounty is as boundless as the sea, My love as deep ii 2 133
In one little body Thou counterfeit'st a bark, a sea, a wind iii 5 132
Thy eyes, which I may call the sea, Do ebb and flow with tears iii 5 133
More fierce and more inexorable far Than empty tigers or the roaring sea v 3 39
But moves itself In a wide sea of wax *T. of Athens* i 1 47
We must all part Into this sea of air iv 2 22
Lie where the light foam of the sea may beat Thy grave-stone daily iv 3 379
The sun's a thief, and with his great attraction Robs the vast sea iv 3 440
The sea's a thief, whose liquid surge resolves The moon into salt tears iv 3 442
Entomb'd upon the very hem o' the sea; And on his grave-stone this v 4 66
He shall wear his crown by sea and land, In every place *J. Cæsar* i 3 87
On such a full sea are we now afloat; And we must take the current iv 3 222
The weird sisters, hand in hand, Posters of the sea and land *Macbeth* i 3 33
This my hand will rather The multitudinous seas incarnadine ii 2 62
Fear, yet know not what we fear, But float upon a wild and violent sea iv 2 21
Whether in sea or fire, in earth or air, The extravagant and erring spirit hies To his confine *Hamlet* i 1 153
To the dreadful summit of the cliff That beetles o'er his base into the sea i 4 71
The very place puts toys of desperation, Without more motive, into every brain That looks so many fathoms to the sea i 4 77
Or to take arms against a sea of troubles, And by opposing end them iii 1 59
Haply the seas and countries different With variable objects shall expel This something-settled matter in his heart iii 1 179
Mad as the sea and wind, when both contend Which is the mightier iv 1 7
Ere we were two days old at sea, a pirate of very warlike appointment gave us chase iv 6 15
Bids the wind blow the earth into the sea, Or swell the curled waters *Lear* iii 1 5
Thou'ldst shun a bear; But if thy flight lay toward the raging sea, Thou'ldst meet the bear i' the mouth iii 4 10
The sea, with such a storm as his bare head In hell-black night endured, would have buoy'd up, And quench'd the stelled fires iii 7 59
He was met even now As mad as the vex'd sea iv 4 2
Hark, do you hear the sea?—No, truly iv 6 4
He had a thousand noses, Horns whelk'd and waved like the enridged sea iv 6 71
I would not my unhoused free condition Put into circumscription and confine For the sea's worth *Othello* i 2 28
What from the cape can you discern at sea?—Nothing at all ii 1 1
If it hath ruffian'd so upon the sea, What ribs of oak, when mountains melt on them, Can hold the mortise? ii 1 7
O, let the heavens Give him defence against the elements, For I have lost him on a dangerous sea ii 1 46
The town is empty; on the brow o' the sea Stand ranks of people ii 1 53
Tempests themselves, high seas and howling winds, The gutter'd rocks ii 1 68
The great contention of the sea and skies Parted our fellowship ii 1 92
Let the labouring bark climb hills of seas Olympus-high! ii 1 189
Like to the Pontic sea, Whose icy current and compulsive course Ne'er feels retiring ebb iii 3 453
O Spartan dog, More fell than anguish, hunger, or the sea! v 2 362
Sextus Pompeius Hath given the dare to Cæsar, and commands The empire of the sea *Ant. and Cleo.* i 2 192
Pompey is strong at sea i 4 36
Pirates Make the sea serve them, which they ear and wound With keels i 4 49
I shall be furnish'd to inform you rightly Both what by sea and land I can be able To front this present time i 4 78
I shall do well: The people love me, and the sea is mine ii 1 9
By sea He is an absolute master.—So is the fame ii 2 165
We'll speak with thee at sea: at land, thou know'st How much we do o'er-count thee ii 6 25
I must Rid all the sea of pirates; then, to send Measures of wheat to Rome ii 6 36
At sea, I think.—We have, sir.—You have done well by water ii 6 87
You have been a great thief by sea.—And you by land ii 6 96
We should have met you By sea and land iii 6 54
He could so quickly cut the Ionian sea, And take in Toryne iii 7 23
We Will fight with him by sea.—By sea! what else? iii 7 29
No disgrace Shall fall you for refusing him at sea, Being prepared for land iii 7 40
By sea, by sea.—Most worthy sir, you therein throw away The absolute soldiership you have by land iii 7 41
I'll fight at sea.—I have sixty sails, Cæsar none better iii 7 49
O noble emperor, do not fight by sea; Trust not to rotten planks iii 7 62
Octavius, Marcus Justeius, Publicola, and Cælius, are for sea iii 7 74
Strike not by land; keep whole: provoke not battle, Till we have done at sea iii 8 4
Our fortune on the sea is out of breath, And sinks most lamentably iii 10 25
As petty to his ends As is the morn-dew on the myrtle-leaf To his grand sea iii 12 10

Sea To-morrow, soldier, By sea and land I'll fight . . *Ant. and Cleo.* iv 2 5
Their preparation is to-day by sea ; We please them not by land . . iv 10 1
Order for sea is given ; They have put forth the haven . . iv 10 6
Hath nature given them eyes To see this vaulted arch, and the rich crop Of sea and land? . . . . *Cymbeline* i 6 34
From Gallia I cross'd the seas on purpose and on promise To see your grace i 6 202
On our terrible seas, Like egg-shells moved upon their surges iii 1 27
If you are sick at sea, Or stomach-qualm'd at land . . . iii 4 192
The imperious seas breed monsters, for the dish Poor tributary rivers as sweet fish . . . . iv 2 35
I'll throw't into the creek Behind our rock ; and let it to the sea . iv 2 152
The legions garrison'd in Gallia, After your will, have cross'd the sea . iv 2 334
He did provoke me With language that would make me spurn the sea, If it could so roar to me . . . . . . v 5 294
But since he's gone, the king's seas must please : He 'scaped the land, to perish at the sea *Pericles* i 3 28
These mouths, who but of late, earth, sea, and air, Were all to little to content and please . . . . i 4 34
He, doing so, put forth to seas, Where when men been, there's seldom ease . . . . ii Gower 27
Alas, the sea hath cast me on the rocks, Wash'd me from shore to shore ii 1 5
I marvel how the fishes live in the sea.—Why, as men do a-land . ii 1 30
How from the finny subject of the sea These fishers tell the infirmities of men ! . . . . ii 1 52
May see the sea hath cast upon your coast.—What a drunken knave was the sea to cast thee in our way ! . . . . . . ii 1 61
Till the rough seas, that spare not any man, Took it in rage, though calm'd have given't again . . . . . . ii 1 137
Spite of all the rapture of the sea, This jewel holds his building on my arm ii 1 161
Was by the rough seas reft of ships and men . . . . ii 3 84
Only by misfortune of the seas Bereft of ships and men, cast on this shore . . . . ii 3 88
I leap into the seas, Where's hourly trouble for a minute's ease . ii 4 43
Lychorida, her nurse, she takes, And so to sea . . iii Gower 44
The sea works high, the wind is loud, and will not lie till the ship be cleared of the dead . . . . iii 1 48
With us at sea it hath been still observed : and we are strong in custom iii 1 51
Our lodgings, standing bleak upon the sea, Shook as the earth did quake iii 2 14
Even now Did the sea toss upon our shore this chest : 'Tis of some wreck iii 2 50
If the sea's stomach be o'ercharged with gold, 'Tis a good constraint of fortune it belches upon us . . . . iii 2 54
Did the sea cast it up?—I never saw so huge a billow, sir . . iii 2 58
Look how fresh she looks ! They were too rough That threw her in the sea iii 2 80
Could I rage and roar As doth the sea she lies in, yet the end Must be as 'tis . . . . iii 3 11
My gentle babe Marina, whom, For she was born at sea, I have named so iii 3 13
That I was shipp'd at sea, I well remember, Even on my eaning time iii 4 5
Come, give me your flowers, ere the sea mar it . . . iv 1 27
Clasping to the mast, endured a sea That almost burst the deck . iv 1 56
I'll swear she's dead, And thrown into the sea . . . iv 1 100
And longest leagues make short ; Sail seas in cockles, have an wish but for't . . . . iv 4 2
Pericles Is now again thwarting the wayward seas . . iv 4 10
Never to wash his face, nor cut his hairs : He puts on sackcloth, and to sea iv 4 29
She would serve after a long voyage at sea . . . . iv 6 49
Turn our thoughts again, Where we left him, on the sea . v Gower 13
Wherefore call'd Marina?—Call'd Marina For I was born at sea.—At sea ! v 1 158
Lest this great sea of joys rushing upon me O'erbear the shores of my mortality, And drown me with their sweetness . . . v 1 194
Thou that wast born at sea, buried at Tarsus, And found at sea again ! . v 1 198
Before the people all, Reveal how thou at sea didst lose thy wife . v 1 245
At sea in childbed died she, but brought forth A maid-child call'd Marina v 3 5
Thaisa ; Thy burden at the sea, and call'd Marina For she was yielded there . . . . v 3 47
Sea-bank. In such a night Stood Dido with a willow in her hand Upon the wild sea banks . . . . . *Mer. of Venice* v 1 11
I was the other day talking on the sea-bank with certain Venetians *Oth.* iv 1 138
Sea-boy. Canst thou, O partial sleep, give thy repose To the wet sea-boy in an hour so rude ! . . . . . *2 Hen. IV.* iii 1 27
Sea-cap. I know your favour well, Though now you have no sea-cap on your head . . . . *T. Night* iii 4 364
Sea-change. Nothing of him that doth fade But doth suffer a sea-change Into something rich and strange . . . . *Tempest* i 2 400
Sea-coal. At the latter end of a sea-coal fire . *Mer. Wives* i 4 9
In my Dolphin-chamber, at the round table, by a sea-coal fire *2 Hen. IV.* ii 1 95
Seacole. Hugh Otecake, sir, or George Seacole . *Much Ado* iii 3 12
Come hither, neighbour Seacole. God hath blessed you with a good name iii 3 13
Go, get you to Francis Seacole ; bid him bring his pen . . iii 5 63
Sea-farer. For the love Of this poor infant, this fresh-new sea-farer, I would it would be quiet . . . . . . *Pericles* iii 1 41
Seafaring. Such as seafaring men provide for storms *Com. of Errors* i 1 81
Sea-fight. Once, in a sea-fight, 'gainst the count his galleys I did some service . . . . *T. Night* iii 3 26
Now, the next day Was our sea-fight . . . . *Hamlet* v 2 54
Sea-gown. Up from my cabin, My sea-gown scarf'd about me . v 2 13
Seal. O, that our fathers would applaud our loves, To seal our happiness with their consents ! . . . . *T. G. of Ver.* i 3 49
Here, take you this.—And seal the bargain with a holy kiss . ii 2 7
I'll be so bold to break the seal for once . . . . iii 1 139
Seals of love, but seal'd in vain, seal'd in vain . *Meas. for Meas.* iv 1 6
Here is the hand and seal of the duke . . . . iv 2 208
Which with experimental seal doth warrant The tenour of my book *M. Ado* iv 1 168
Which I had rather seal with my death than repeat over to my shame . v 1 247
That he was fain to seal on Cupid's name . . *L. L. Lost* v 2 9
O, let me kiss This princess of pure white, this seal of bliss ! *M. N. D.* iii 2 144
Go with me to a notary, seal me there Your single bond . *Mer. of Venice* i 3 145
I'll seal to such a bond And say there is much kindness in the Jew . i 3 153
You shall not seal to such a bond for me: I'll rather dwell in my necessity . . . . i 3 155
Yes, Shylock, I will seal unto this bond . . . . . i 3 172
O, ten times faster Venus' pigeons fly To seal love's bonds new-made ! . ii 6 6
Till thou canst rail the seal from off my bond, Thou but offend'st thy lungs . . . . iv 1 139
And by him seal up thy mind . . . . *As Y. Like It* iv 3 58
And seal the title with a lovely kiss . . . *T. of Shrew* iii 2 125
It is the show and seal of nature's truth . . *All's Well* i 3 138
And the impressure her Lucrece, with which she uses to seal *T. Night* ii 5 104
Or say 'tis not your seal, not your invention : You can say none of this v 1 341
You have not deigned to break the holy seal . . . *W. Tale* iii 2 130
Break up the seals and read . . . . iii 2 132
Seal. Lay I this zealous kiss, As seal to this indenture of my love *K. John* ii 1 20
Here is your hand and seal for what I did.—O, when the last account 'twixt heaven and earth Is to be made, then shall this hand and seal Witness against us to damnation ! . . . . iv 2 217
My heart this covenant makes, my hand thus seals it . *Richard II.* ii 3 50
There is my gage, the manual seal of death, That marks thee out for hell iv 1 25
What seal is that, that hangs without thy bosom? Yea, look'st thou pale? . . . . v 2 56
We'll but seal, And then to horse immediately . . *1 Hen. IV.* iii 1 270
Wilt thou upon the high and giddy mast Seal up the ship-boy's eyes? *2 Hen. IV.* iii 1 19
Seal this lawless bloody book Of forged rebellion with a seal divine . iv 1 91
Shortly will I seal with him . . . . iv 3 142
Beguiling virgins with the broken seals of perjury . . *Hen. V.* iv 1 172
Seal up your lips, and give no words but mum. . . *2 Hen. VI.* i 2 89
That thou mightst think upon these by the seal, Through whom a thousand sighs are breathed for thee ! . . . . . . iii 2 344
I did but seal once to a thing, and I was never mine own man since iv 2 90
The match is made ; she seals it with a curtsy . . *3 Hen. VI.* iii 2 57
Thus I seal my truth, and bid adieu . . . . . iv 8 29
The duty that I owe unto your majesty I seal upon the lips of this sweet babe . . . . v 7 29
With my hand I seal my true heart's love . . *Richard III.* ii 1 10
Seal thou this league With thy embracements to my wife's allies ii 1 29
I'll resign unto your grace The seal I keep . . . . ii 4 71
Under the confession's seal He solemnly had sworn . *Hen. VIII.* i 2 164
I now seal it ; And with that blood will make 'em one day groan for't ii 1 105
But by particular consent proceeded Under your hands and seals . . ii 4 222
Who commands you To render up the great seal presently Into our hands iii 2 229
That seal, You ask with such a violence, the king, Mine and your master, with his own hand gave me . . . . iii 2 245
You made bold To carry into Flanders the great seal . . iii 2 319
For your stubborn answer About the giving back the great seal to us, The king shall know it . . . . iii 2 347
A bargain made : seal it, seal it ; I'll be the witness . *Troi. and Cres.* iii 2 204
Omission to do what is necessary Seals a commission to a blank of danger . . . . iii 3 231
I will not seal your knowledge with showing them . . *Coriolanus* ii 3 115
What may be sworn by, both divine and human, Seal what I end withal ! iii 1 142
Together with the seal o' the senate . . . . . v 6 83
The empress sends it thee, thy stamp, thy seal . . *T. Andron.* iv 2 69
He is your brother by the surer side, Although my seal be stamped in his face . . . . iv 2 127
Seal with a righteous kiss A dateless bargain . . . *Rom. and Jul.* v 3 114
Seal up the mouth of outrage for a while, Till we can clear these ambiguities . . . . v 3 216
Here's a parchment with the seal of Cæsar . . . . *J. Cæsar* iii 2 133
Here is the will, and under Cæsar's seal . . . . iii 2 245
I have seen her . . . take forth paper, fold it, write upon't, read it, afterwards seal it, and again return to bed . . . *Macbeth* v 1 8
My tongue and soul in this be hypocrites ; How in my words soever she be shent, To give them seals never, my soul, consent ! . *Hamlet* iii 2 417
A combination and a form indeed, Where every god did seem to set his seal, To give the world assurance of a man . . . . iii 4 61
Now must your conscience my acquittance seal . . . iv 7 1
I had my father's signet in my purse, Which was the model of that Danish seal . . . . v 2 50
Take that of me, my friend, who have the power To seal the accuser's lips . . . . *Lear* iv 6 174
Were't to renounce his baptism, All seals and symbols of redeemed sin *Othello* ii 3 350
This kingly seal And plighter of high hearts . . *Ant. and Cleo.* iii 13 125
Yea, very force entangles Itself with strength : seal then, and all is done iv 14 49
I had rather seal my lips, than, to my peril, Speak that which is not . v 2 145
Our peace we'll ratify ; seal it with feasts . . . *Cymbeline* v 5 483
Come, your hands and lips must seal it too . . . *Pericles* ii 5 85
Sealed. Of more value Than stamps in gold or sums in sealed bags *M. W.* iii 4 16
Seals of love, but seal'd in vain, seal'd in vain . *Meas. for Meas.* iv 1 6
Testimonies against his worth and credit That's seal'd in approbation . v 1 245
Have seal'd his rigorous statutes with their bloods . *Com. of Errors* i 1 9
The Frenchman became his surety and sealed under for another *M. of V.* i 2 89
A sealed bag, two sealed bags of ducats, Of double ducats, stolen from me by my daughter ! . . . . ii 8 18
She brought stone jugs and no seal'd quarts . . *T. of Shrew* Ind. 2 90
And all the ceremony of this compact Seal'd in my function . *T. Night* v 1 164
The oracle, Thus by Apollo's great divine seal'd up. . *W. Tale* iii 1 19
Our arms, like to a muzzled bear, Save in aspect, hath all offence seal'd up . . . . *K. John* ii 1 250
Being sealed interchangeably . . . . . *1 Hen. IV.* iii 1 81
Bear this sealed brief With winged haste . . . . iv 4 1
And at my death Thou hast seal'd up my expectation . *2 Hen. IV.* iv 5 104
With blood he seal'd A testament of noble-ending love . . *Hen. V.* iv 6 26
Here had the conquest fully been seal'd up, If Sir John Fastolfe had not play'd the coward . . . . *1 Hen. VI.* i 1 130
Leave the battle, boy, and fly, Now thou art seal'd the son of chivalry iv 6 29
Seal'd in thy nativity The slave of nature and the son of hell ! *Rich. III.* i 3 229
And ere this hand, by thee to Romeo seal'd, Shall be the label to another deed, Or my true heart . . . Turn to another . *Rom. and Jul.* iv 1 56
Seal'd up the doors, and would not let us forth . . . v 2 11
Till we Have seal'd thy full desire . . . . *T. of Athens* v 4 54
I found This paper, thus seal'd up . . . . . *J. Cæsar* ii 1 37
A seal'd compact, Well ratified by law and heraldry . . . *Hamlet* i 1 86
And at last Upon his will I seal'd my hard consent . . . i 2 60
Her election Hath seal'd thee for herself . . . . . iii 2 70
There's letters seal'd . . . . iii 4 202
Away ! for every thing is seal'd and done That else leans on the affair . iv 3 58
How was this seal'd?—Why, even in that was heaven ordinant . v 2 47
I crave our composition may be written, And seal'd between us *A. and C.* ii 6 60
And had the virtue Which their own conscience seal'd them . *Cymbeline* iii 6 85
His seal'd commission, left in trust with me, Doth speak sufficiently he's gone to travel . . . . *Pericles* i 3 13
Sealed-up. And to her white hand see thou do commend This seal'd-up counsel . . . . *L. L. Lost* iii 1 170
And from thence have brought This seal'd-up oracle . . *W. Tale* iii 2 128
Sea-like. Our sever'd navy too Have knit again, and fleet, threatening most sea-like . . . . *Ant. and Cleo.* iii 13 171
Sealing The injury of tongues in courts and kingdoms . . *W. Tale* i 2 337
He is gone ; The other three are sealing . . . *Ant. and Cleo.* iii 2 3
Sealing-day. The sealing-day betwixt my love and me . *M. N. Dream* i 1 84

Seal-ring. I have lost a seal-ring of my grandfather's . 1 *Hen. IV.* iii 3 94
Seam. Bastes his arrogance with his own seam *Troi. and Cres.* ii 3 195
That made up this garment through the rough seams of the waters *Per.* ii 1 156
Sea-maid. Some report a sea-maid spawned him *Meas. for Meas.* iii 2 115
Certain stars shot madly from their spheres, To hear the sea-maid's music *M. N. Dream* ii 1 154
Seaman. But on this day let seamen fear no wreck *K. John* iii 1 92
The seaman's whistle Is as a whisper in the ears of death . *Pericles* iii 1 8
Cried 'Good seamen!' to the sailors, galling His kingly hands . . iv 1 54
Sea-marge. And thy sea-marge, sterile and rocky-hard *Tempest* iv 1 69
Sea-mark. And stick i' the wars Like a great sea-mark, standing every flaw, And saving those that eye thee! . *Coriolanus* v 3 74
Here is my butt, And very sea-mark of my utmost sail *Othello* v 2 268
Sea-monster. When he did redeem The virgin tribute paid by howling Troy To the sea-monster . . . . *Mer. of Venice* iii 2 57
More hideous when thou show'st thee in a child Than the sea-monster! *Lear* i 4 283
Seamy. That turn'd your wit the seamy side without . . *Othello* iv 2 146
Sea-nymphs hourly ring his knell: Ding-dong . . . *Tempest* i 2 402
Sear. For calumny will sear Virtue itself . . . *W. Tale* ii 1 73
Were red-hot steel, to sear me to the brain! . . *Richard III.* iv 1 61
Down! Thy crown does sear mine eye-balls . . . *Macbeth* iv 1 113
My way of life Is fall'n into the sear, the yellow leaf . . v 3 23
Sear up my embracements from a next With bonds of death! *Cymbeline* i 1 116
Search. Let's make further search . . . . *Tempest* ii 1 323
The sea mocks Our frustrate search on land . . . iii 3 10
Thus I search it with a sovereign kiss . . *T. G. of Ver.* i 2 116
The clock gives me my cue, and my assurance bids me search *M. Wives* iii 2 47
To search for a gentleman that he says is here now in the house . iii 3 115
Your husband's coming, with half Windsor at his heels, to search for such a one . . . . iii 3 122
Search, seek, find out: I'll warrant we'll unkennel the fox . . iii 3 173
See the issue of his search . . . . . . iii 3 186
To search his house for his wife's love . . . . iii 5 78
Did he search for you, and could not find you? . . . iii 5 82
On went he for a search, and away went I for foul clothes . . iii 5 107
I will search impossible places . . . . . . iii 5 151
Help to search my house this one time . . . . iv 2 167
Satisfy me once more; once more search with me . . . iv 2 172
About, about; Search Windsor Castle, elves, within and out . . v 5 60
When you have them, they are not worth the search *Mer. of Venice* i 1 118
With outcries raised the duke, Who went with him to search Bassanio's ship . . . . ii 8 5
I know not what's spent in the search: why, thou loss upon loss! . iii 1 96
It is a thing of his own search and altogether against my will *As Y. L. It* i 1 142
Do this suddenly, And let not search and inquisition quail . . ii 2 20
That seeks not to find that her search implies . . *All's Well* i 3 222
Or were you taught to find me? The search, sir, was profitable . ii 4 35
I think I have his letter in my pocket.—Marry, we'll search . . iv 3 229
If zealous love should go in search of virtue, Where should he find it purer than in Blanch? . . . . *K. John* ii 1 428
They are come to search the house. Shall I let them in? . 1 *Hen IV.* ii 4 537
Search his pockets. What hast thou found? . . . . ii 4 580
Search out thy wit for secret policies . . . 1 *Hen. VI.* iii 3 12
These eyes . . . Have been as piercing as the mid-day sun, To search the secret treasons of the world . . . . 3 *Hen. VI.* v 2 18
Modest doubt is call'd The beacon of the wise, the tent that searches To the bottom of the worst. . . . *Troi. and Cres.* ii 2 16
Now to the bottom dost thou search my wound . *T. Andron.* ii 3 262
Hide thyself.—Not I; unless the breath of heart-sick groans, Mist-like, infold me from the search of eyes . . *Rom. and Jul.* iii 3 73
The ground is bloody; search about the churchyard . . . v 3 172
Some others search . . . . v 3 178
Search, seek, and know how this foul murder comes . . . v 3 198
And with this good sword, That ran through Cæsar's bowels, search this bosom. Stand not to answer . . . . *J. Cæsar* v 3 42
What is it ye would see? If aught of woe or wonder, cease your search *Hamlet* v 2 374
Search every acre in the high-grown field, And bring him to our eye *Lear* iv 4 7
Lead to the Sagittary the raised search . . . *Othello* i 1 159
The senate hath sent about three several quests To search you out . i 2 47
The search so slow, That could not trace them! . . *Cymbeline* i 1 64
Bid my woman Search for a jewel that too casually Hath left mine arm ii 3 146
'Twill not be lost.—I hope so: go and search . . . ii 3 154
A pain that only seems to seek out danger I' the name of fame and honour; which dies i' the search . . . . . iii 3 51
Search What companies are near . . . . . iv 2 68
If it be a day fits you, search out of the calendar . *Pericles* ii 1 58
Go search like nobles, like noble subjects, And in your search spend your adventurous worth . . . . ii 4 50
By many a dern and painful perch Of Pericles the careful search . iii Gower 16
Search the market narrowly . . . . . . iv 2 3
But shall I search the market?—What else, man? . . . iv 2 18
Searched. I quaked for fear, lest the lunatic knave would have searched it . . . . *Mer. Wives* iii 5 105
Swears he was carried out, the last time he searched for him, in a basket iv 2 32
Let them say of me, 'As jealous as Ford, that searched a hollow walnut' iv 2 171
Who, inward search'd, have livers white as milk *Mer. of Venice* iii 2 86
I have searched, I have inquired, so has my husband . 1 *Hen. IV.* iii 3 64
He hath been search'd among the dead and living, But no trace of him *Cymbeline* v 5 11
Searchers. The searchers of the town . . . *Rom. and Jul.* v 2 8
Searching of thy wound, I have by hard adventure found mine own *As Y. Like It* ii 4 44
When the searching eye of heaven is hid, Behind the globe *Richard II.* iii 2 37
That's a marvellous searching wine, and it perfumes the blood 2 *Hen. IV.* ii 4 30
But for Achilles, mine own searching eyes Shall find him by his large and portly size . . . . . *Troi. and Cres.* iv 5 161
Searching the window for a flint, I found This paper . *J. Cæsar* ii 1 36
Seared. My maiden's name Sear'd otherwise . . *All's Well* ii 1 176
The sun that sear'd the wings of my sweet boy . 3 *Hen. VI.* v 6 23
In these sear'd hopes, I barely gratify your love . *Cymbeline* iv 4 6
Sea-room. But sea-room, an the brine and cloudy billow kiss the moon, I care not . . . . *Pericles* iii 1 45
Sea-salt. Drown the lamenting fool in sea-salt tears *T. Andron.* iii 2 20
Sea-sick. Why look you pale? Sea-sick, I think *L. L. Lost* v 2 393
Who began to be much sea-sick, and himself little better *W. Tale* v 2 128
Now at once run on The dashing rocks thy sea-sick weary bark! *R. and J.* v 3 118
Sea-side. My cellar is in a rock by the sea-side . *Tempest* ii 2 138
By the sea-side, browsing of ivy . . . *W. Tale* iii 3 68
Thus we set on, Camillo, to the sea-side . . . . . iv 4 682
Sea-side. Walk before toward the sea-side; go on the right hand *W. Tale* iv 4 856
Many carriages he hath dispatch'd To the sea-side . . *K. John* v 7 91
Let's to the sea-side, ho! As well to see the vessel that's come in *Oth.* ii 1 36
To the sea-side straightway: I will possess you of that ship *A. and C.* iii 11 20
Season. What is the time o' the day?—Past the mid season . *Tempest* i 2 239
I warrant you, buck; and of the season too, it shall appear *Mer. Wives* iii 3 169
Even for our kitchens We kill the fowl of season . *Meas. for Meas.* ii 2 85
Do as the carrion does, not as the flower, Corrupt with virtuous season ii 2 168
These jests are out of season; Reserve them till a merrier hour *C. of Er.* i 2 68
Was there ever any man thus beaten out of season? . . . ii 2 48
Time is a very bankrupt and owes more than he's worth to season . iv 2 58
It is needful that you frame the season for your own harvest *Much Ado* i 3 26
And salt too little which may season give To her foul-tainted flesh! . iv 1 144
But like of each thing that in season grows . . *L. L. Lost* i 1 107
How I would make him fawn and beg and seek And wait the season! . v 2 63
Thorough this distemperature we see The seasons alter *M. N. Dream* ii 1 107
Things growing are not ripe until their season: So I, being young, till now ripe not to reason . . . . ii 2 117
It is an attribute to God himself; And earthly power doth then show likest God's When mercy seasons justice . . *Mer. of Venice* iv 1 197
How many things by season season'd are To their right praise! . . v 1 107
Here feel we but the penalty of Adam, The seasons' difference *As Y. L. It* ii 1 6
'Tis the best brine [tears] a maiden can season her praise in *All's Well* i 1 55
I am not a day of season, For thou mayst see a sunshine and a hail In me at once . . . . v 3 32
All this to season A brother's dead love . . . *T. Night* i 1 30
The fairest flowers o' the season Are our carnations . *W. Tale* iv 4 81
Why, so it would have done at the same season, if your mother's cat had but kittened . . . . 1 *Hen. IV.* iii 1 19
As not a soldier of this season's stamp Should go so general current . iv 1 4
You wish me health in very happy season . . 2 *Hen. IV.* iv 2 79
The seasons change their manners, as the year Had found some months asleep . . . . iv 4 123
So cares and joys abound, as seasons fleet . . 2 *Hen. VI.* ii 4 4
And for a season after Could not believe but that I was in hell *Rich. III.* i 4 61
Sorrow breaks seasons and reposing hours, Makes the night morning . i 4 76
In brief,—for so the season bids us be,—Prepare thy battle early . v 3 87
Liberality, and such like, the spice and salt that season a man *T. and C.* i 2 278
Season, form, Office and custom, in all line of order . . i 3 87
How much salt water thrown away in waste, To season love! *R. and J.* ii 3 72
All covered dishes!—Royal cheer, I warrant you.—Doubt not that, if money and the season can yield it . . . *T. of Athens* iii 6 58
Season the slaves For tubs and baths; bring down rose-cheeked youth iv 3 85
Growing on the south, Weighing the youthful season of the year *J. Cæsar* ii 1 108
You lack the season of all natures, sleep . . *Macbeth* iii 4 141
He is noble, wise, judicious, and best knows The fits o' the season . iv 2 17
Ever 'gainst that season comes Wherein our Saviour's birth is celebrated . . . . *Hamlet* i 1 158
Season your admiration for a while With an attent ear . . i 2 192
Farewell: my blessing season this in thee! . . . . i 3 81
It draws near the season Wherein the spirit held his wont to walk . i 4 5
As you may season it in the charge . . . . . ii 1 28
Who in want a hollow friend doth try, Directly seasons him his enemy iii 2 219
Confederate season, else no creature seeing . . . . iii 2 267
Thus out of season, threading dark-eyed night . . *Lear* ii 1 121
How shall your houseless heads and unfed sides, Your loop'd and window'd raggedness, defend you From seasons such as these? . iii 4 32
But I will tell you at some meeter season . *Ant. and Cleo.* v 1 49
Blest be those, How mean soe'er, that have their honest wills, Which seasons comfort . . . . *Cymbeline* i 6 9
And be friended With aptness of the season . . . . ii 3 53
And with what imitation you can borrow From youth of such a season iii 4 175
We'll slip you for a season; but our jealousy Does yet depend . iv 3 22
You are my father too, and did relieve me, To see this gracious season v 5 401
Season'd with a gracious voice, Obscures the show of evil *Mer. of Venice* iii 2 76
Let their palates Be season'd with such viands . . . iv 1 97
How many things by season season'd are To their right praise! . v 1 107
This suit of yours, So season'd with your faithful love to me *Rich. III.* iii 7 149
You have contrived to take From Rome all season'd office *Coriolanus* iii 3 64
Am I then revenged, To take him in the purging of his soul, When he is fit and season'd for his passage? . . . . *Hamlet* iii 3 86
Sea-sorrow. Sit still, and hear the last of our sea-sorrow *Tempest* i 2 170
Sea-storm. Your reason For raising this sea-storm? . . . i 2 177
Sea-swallowed. We all were sea-swallow'd . . . ii 1 251
Seat. Who, newly in the seat, that it may know He can command, lets it straight feel the spur . . . . *Meas. for Meas.* i 2 165
Give us some seats . . . . v 1 165
Let love forbid Sleep his seat on thy eyelid . . *M. N. Dream* ii 2 81
Which makes her seat of Belmont Colchos' strand . *Mer. of Venice* i 1 171
It gives a very echo to the seat Where Love is throned . *T. Night* ii 4 21
This seat of Mars, This other Eden, demi-paradise . *Richard II.* ii 1 41
By my seat's right royal majesty . . . . . . ii 1 120
Distaff-women manage rusty bills Against thy seat . . . iii 2 119
In this seat of peace tumultuous wars Shall kin with kin and kind with kind confound . . . . iv 1 140
Long mayst thou live in Richard's seat to sit! . . . . iv 1 218
Mount, mount, my soul! thy seat is up on high . . . v 5 112
Betwixt that Holmedon and this seat of ours . . 1 *Hen. IV.* i 1 65
Vaulted with such ease into his seat, As if an angel dropp'd down . iv 1 107
Your new-fall'n right, The seat of Gaunt, dukedom of Lancaster . v 1 45
Being mounted and both roused in their seats . . 2 *Hen. IV.* iv 1 118
And struck me in my very seat of judgement . . . . v 2 80
Never Hydra-headed wilfulness So soon did lose his seat . *Hen. V.* i 1 36
And generally to the crown and seat of France . . . . i 1 88
And did seat the French Beyond the river Sala . . . . i 2 62
We never valued this poor seat of England . . . . i 2 269
For your great seats now quit you of great shames . . . iii 5 47
Whose low vassal seat The Alps doth spit and void his rheum upon . iii 5 51
We'll quickly hoise Duke Humphrey from his seat . 2 *Hen. VI.* i 1 169
Methought I sat in seat of majesty . . . . . . i 2 36
The rightful heir to England's royal seat . . . . . v 1 178
This is the palace of the fearful king, And this the regal seat 3 *Hen. VI.* i 1 26
In thy shoulder do I build my seat . . . . . . i 6 100
I must take like seat unto my fortune, And to my humble seat conform myself . . . . iii 3 10
The royal title and the seat Of England's true-anointed lawful king . iii 3 28
And force the tyrant from his seat by war . . . . iii 3 206
God and friends Have shaken Edward from the regal seat . . iv 6 2
Thus have we swept suspicion from our seat And made our footstool of security . . . . v 7 13

Seat. Thy honour, state and seat is due to me . . . *Richard III.* i 3 112
In the seat royal of this famous isle . . . iii 1 164
And, for more slander to thy dismal seat . . . iii 3 13
It is your fault that you resign The supreme seat . . iii 7 118
Will well become the seat of majesty . . . iii 7 169
O, that thou wouldst as well afford a grave As thou canst yield a melancholy seat! . . . iv 4 32
With due observance of thy godlike seat, Great Agamemnon *T. and C.* i 3 31
Even to the court, the heart, to the seat o' the brain . *Coriolanus* i 1 140
Thus we debase The nature of our seats . . . iii 1 136
And suffer not dishonour to approach The imperial seat. *T. Andron.* i 1 14
Alas, kind lord! He's flung in rage from this ingrateful seat Of monstrous friends *T. of Athens* iv 2 45
After this let Cæsar seat him sure; For we will shake him *J. Cæsar* i 2 325
Metellus Cimber throws before thy seat An humble heart . iii 1 34
This castle hath a pleasant seat. . . . *Macbeth* i 6 1
Keep seat; The fit is momentary . . . iii 4 54
While memory holds a seat In this distracted globe . . *Hamlet* i 5 96
But this gallant Had witchcraft in't; he grew unto his seat . iv 7 86
For that I do suspect the lusty Moor Hath leap'd into my seat *Othello* ii 1 305
Forsake thy seat, I do beseech thee, captain, And hear me *Ant. and Cleo.* ii 7 43
Whilst the wheel'd seat Of fortunate Cæsar, drawn before him, branded His baseness that ensued . . . iv 14 75
Wouldst have made my throne A seat for baseness . . *Cymbeline* i 1 142
To be exiled, and thrown From Leonati seat . . . v 4 60
For this from stiller seats we came . . . v 4 69
Antiochus the Great Built up, this city, for his chiefest seat *Pericles* i Gower 18
Seated. It is no mean happiness, therefore, to be seated in the mean *Mer. of Venice* i 2 8
Before I see thee seated in that throne . . *3 Hen. VI.* i 1 22
So would you be again to Henry, If he were seated as King Edward is . iii 1 96
And see him seated in the regal throne . . . iv 3 64
Now am I seated as my soul delights . . . v 7 35
Being seated, and domestic broils Clean over-blown . *Richard III.* ii 4 60
Thus high, by thy advice And thy assistance, is King Richard seated . iv 2 4
So, now you're fairly seated . . . *Hen. VIII.* i 4 31
And make my seated heart knock at my ribs . . *Macbeth* i 3 136
See, what a grace was seated on this brow; Hyperion's curls *Hamlet* iii 4 55
He was seated in a chariot Of an inestimable value. . *Pericles* ii 4 7
Sea-tost. Upon whose deck The sea-tost Pericles appears to speak iii Gower 60
Sea-walled. Our sea-walled garden, the whole land. . *Richard II.* iii 4 43
Sea-water shalt thou drink . . . . *Tempest* i 2 462
Tell me precisely of what complexion.—Of the sea-water green *L. L. Lost* i 2 86
Sea-wing. Antony Claps on his sea-wing, and, like a doting mallard, Leaving the fight in height, flies after her . . *Ant. and Cleo.* iii 10 20
Sebastian, The truth you speak doth lack some gentleness *Tempest* ii 1 136
What might, Worthy Sebastian? O, what might? . . ii 1 205
Noble Sebastian, Thou let'st thy fortune sleep—die, rather . ii 1 215
Keep in Tunis, And let Sebastian wake . . . ii 1 260
Thou art pinch'd for't now, Sebastian . . . v 1 74
With Sebastian, Whose inward pinches therefore are most strong . v 1 76
Sebastian is thy name? I like thee well . . *T. G. of Ver.* iv 4 44
Sebastian, I have entertained thee, Partly that I have need of such a youth . . . . iv 4 68
Spurio, a hundred and fifty; Sebastian, so many . *All's Well* iv 3 184
My name is Sebastian, which I called Roderigo. My father was that Sebastian of Messaline, whom I know you have heard of *T. Night* ii 1 17
Thou hast, Sebastian, done good feature shame . . iii 4 400
He named Sebastian: I my brother know Yet living in my glass . iii 4 414
Sebastian are you?—Fear'st thou that, Antonio? . . v 1 228
An apple, cleft in two, is not more twin Than these two creatures. Which is Sebastian? . . . . v 1 231
Sebastian was my father; Such a Sebastian was my brother too . v 1 239
Second. I'll fight their legions o'er.—I'll be thy second . *Tempest* iii 3 103
Of whom I have Received a second life; and second father This lady makes him to me . . . . v 1 195
I second thee; troop on . . . . *Mer. Wives* i 3 114
Pardon is still the nurse of second woe . . *Meas. for Meas.* ii 1 298
Highly beloved, Second to none that lives here in the city *Com. of Errors* v 1 7
'Tis not wisdom thus to second grief Against yourself . *Much Ado* v 1 2
The first and second cause will not serve my turn . *L. L. Lost* i 2 183
The second, silver, which this promise carries . *Mer. of Venice* ii 7 6
Often known To be the dowry of a second head . . iii 2 95
A second Daniel, a Daniel, Jew! . . . iv 1 333
A Daniel, still say I, a second Daniel! . . . iv 1 340
So he served the second, and so the third. . *As Y. Like It* i 2 137
You shall not entreat him to a second, that have so mightily persuaded him from a first . . . . i 2 218
The first, the Retort Courteous; the second, the Quip Modest . v 4 97
I am the second son of old Sir Rowland . . . v 4 158
For patience she will prove a second Grissel . *T. of Shrew* ii 1 297
In delivering my son from me, I bury a second husband . *All's Well* i 1 2
Here we'll stay To see our widower's second marriage-day . v 3 70
One draught above heat makes him a fool; the second mads him *T. Night* i 5 141
The eldest is eleven; The second and the third, nine, and some five *W. T.* ii 1 145
Good my lords, be second to me . . . . ii 3 27
My second joy And first-fruits of my body . . iii 2 97
Being but the second generation Removed . . *K. John* ii 1 181
Second a villain and a murderer? . . . iv 3 102
What Eve, what serpent, hath suggested thee To make a second fall of cursed man? . . . *Richard II.* iii 4 76
Being the agents, or base second means . . *1 Hen. IV.* i 3 165
The worst that they can say of me is that I am a second brother *2 Hen. IV.* ii 2 71
Him did you leave, Second to none, unseconded by you . . ii 3 34
Though we here fall down, We have supplies to second our attempt: If they miscarry, theirs shall second them . . . iv 2 45
The second property of your excellent sherris is, the warming of the blood . . . . iv 3 110
And mock your workings in a second body . . . v 2 90
Three corrupted men, One, Richard Earl of Cambridge, and the second, Henry Lord Scroop of Masham . . *Hen. V.* ii Prol. 23
And return your mock In second accent of his ordnance . ii 4 126
Like to the bullet's grazing, Break out into a second course of mischief iv 3 106
I thought I should have seen some Hercules, A second Hector *1 Hen. VI.* ii 3 20
Art thou not second woman in the realm? . . *2 Hen. VI.* i 2 43
The second, William of Hatfield, and the third, Lionel . ii 2 12
And now is York in arms to second him . . . iv 9 35
Now begins a second storm to rise . . . *3 Hen. VI.* iii 3 47
Richard the Second here was hack'd to death . *Richard III.* iii 3 12
By the second hour in the morning Desire the earl to see me in my tent v 3 31
Second. The agent of our cardinal, To second all his plot *Hen. VIII.* iii 2 60
Shortly, I believe, His second marriage shall be publish'd . iii 2 68
In second voice we'll not be satisfied; We come to speak with him *Troi. and Cres.* ii 3 149
And on him erect A second hope, as fairly built as Hector . iv 5 109
Now prove good seconds . . . . *Coriolanus* i 4 43
Thy exercise hath been too violent For a second course of fight . i 5 17
Officious, and not valiant, you have shamed me In your condemned seconds . . . . . i 8 15
Rejourn the controversy of three pence to a second day of audience . ii 1 80
Tullus Aufidius, The second name of men . . . iv 6 125
She, poor hen, fond of no second brood . . . v 3 162
Let him feel your sword, Which we will second . . v 6 57
A gentleman of the very first house, of the first and second cause *Rom. and Jul.* ii 4 26
And by the operation of the second cup draws it on the drawer . iii 1 9
I think you are happy in this second match . . . iii 5 224
Bid me devise some mean To rid her from this second marriage . v 3 241
Many so arrive at second masters, Upon their first lord's neck *T. of A.* iv 3 512
What was the second noise for? . . . *J. Cæsar* i 2 224
He is address'd: press near and second him . . . iii 1 29
And, Romans, yet ere night We shall try fortune in a second fight . v 3 110
Who lies i' the second chamber?—Donalbain . . *Macbeth* ii 2 20
Great nature's second course, Chief nourisher in life's feast . ii 2 39
'Faith, sir, we were carousing till the second cock . . ii 3 27
Which is now Our point of second meeting . . . iii 1 86
Occasion smiles upon a second leave . . . *Hamlet* i 3 54
In second husband let me be accurst! None wed the second but who kill'd the first . . . . iii 2 189
The instances that second marriage move Are base respects of thrift, but none of love: A second time I kill my husband dead, When second husband kisses me . . . . iii 2 192
So think thou wilt no second husband wed . . . iii 2 224
This project Should have a back or second, that might hold, If this should blast . . . . . iv 7 154
If Hamlet give the first or second hit, Or quit in answer of the third v 2 279
What says our second daughter, Our dearest Regan? . *Lear* i 1 68
No seconds? all myself? Why, this would make a man a man of salt iv 6 198
Not by old gradation, where each second Stood heir to the first *Othello* i 1 37
Very nature will instruct her in it and compel her to some second choice ii 1 238
'Tis great pity that the noble Moor Should hazard such a place as his own second . . . . . ii 3 144
This is his second fit; he had one yesterday . . . iv 1 52
I will be near to second your attempt, and he shall fall between us iv 2 244
They say we shall embattle By the second hour i' the morn *Ant. and Cleo.* iv 9 4
Where's Dolabella, To second Proculeius? . . . v 1 70
With no more advantage than the opportunity of a second conference *Cymbeline* i 4 141
I'll make a journey twice as far, to enjoy A second night of such sweet shortness . . . . . ii 4 44
That is the second thing that I have commanded thee . . iii 5 157
You some permit To second ills with ills, each elder worse . v 1 14
A Roman, Who had not now been drooping here, if seconds Had answer'd him . . . . . . v 3 90
Who is the second that presents himself?—A prince of Macedon *Pericles* ii 2 23
And cursed be he that will not second it . . . ii 4 20
Second childishness and mere oblivion, Sans teeth, sans eyes *As Y. L. It* ii 7 165
Second edition. These are of the second edition . *Mer. Wives* ii 1 78
Second time. Wherefore,—For urging it the second time *Com. of Errors* ii 2 47
A second time receive The confirmation of my promised gift . *All's Well* ii 3 55
Some of us never shall A second time do such a courtesy . *1 Hen. IV.* v 2 101
I will the second time, As I would buy thee, view thee *Troi. and Cres.* iv 5 237
That great baby you see there is not yet out of his swaddling-clouts.—Happily he's the second time come to them . . *Hamlet* ii 2 402
A second time I kill my husband dead, When second husband kisses me in bed . . . . . . iii 2 194
O, come, be buried A second time within these arms . . *Pericles* v 3 44
Secondarily, they are slanders . . . *Much Ado* v 1 221
Secondary. Escalus, Though first in question, is thy secondary *M. for M.* i 1 47
I am too high-born to be propertied, To be a secondary at control *K. John* v 2 80
Seconded. The slave's report is seconded . . . *Coriolanus* iv 6 62
A man's good wit seconded with the forward child Understanding *As Y. Like It* iii 3 13
Appetite, an universal wolf, So doubly seconded with will and power, Must make perforce an universal prey . *Troi. and Cres.* i 3 122
Secrecy. This secrecy of thine shall be a tailor to thee *Mer. Wives* iii 3 33
Thanks, provost, for thy care and secrecy . *Meas. for Meas.* v 1 536
I do implore secrecy . . . . *L. L. Lost* v 1 116
We are lucky, boy; and to be so still requires nothing but secrecy *W. Tale* iii 3 130
A woman: and for secrecy, No lady closer . . *1 Hen. IV.* ii 3 112
The business asketh silent secrecy . . . *2 Hen. VI.* i 2 90
Not suddenly to be perform'd, But with advice and silent secrecy . ii 2 68
The Lady Anne, Whom the king hath in secrecy long married *Hen. VIII.* iii 2 403
Upon my secrecy, to defend mine honesty . . *Troi. and Cres.* i 2 286
This to me In dreadful secrecy impart they did . . *Hamlet* i 2 207
So shall my anticipation prevent your discovery, and your secrecy to the king and queen moult no feather . . . . ii 2 305
In despite of sense and secrecy, Unpeg the basket on the house's top . iii 4 192
In nature's infinite book of secrecy A little I can read . *Ant. and Cleo.* i 2 9
Our mind partakes Her private actions to your secrecy . . *Pericles* i 1 153
Secret. Being transported And rapt in secret studies . . *Tempest* i 2 77
I have writ your letter Unto the secret nameless friend of yours *T. G. of Ver.* ii 1 111
Thou shalt never get such a secret from me but by a parable . ii 5 40
We have some secrets to confer about . . . iii 1 2
Some affairs That touch me near, wherein thou must be secret . iii 1 60
An unmannerly slave, that will thrust himself into secrets! . iii 1 394
Why I desire thee To give me secret harbour, hath a purpose *M. for M.* i 3 4
'Tis a secret must be locked within the teeth and the lips . iii 2 142
Put them in secret holds . . . . iv 3 91
What secret hath held you here? . . . *Much Ado* i 1 206
I can be secret as a dumb man . . . . i 1 212
The vile encounters they have had A thousand times in secret . iv 1 95
No words!—Of other men's secrets, I beseech you . *L. L. Lost* i 1 232
In faith, secrets! . . . . . iv 3 24
Here sit I in the sky, And wretched fools' secrets heedfully o'er-eye . iv 3 80
One word in secret.—Let it not be sweet . . . v 2 236
What lady is the same To whom you swore a secret pilgrimage? *M. of V.* i 1 120
I have toward heaven breathed a secret vow . . . iii 4 27

Secret. A secret and villanous contriver against me . . . *As Y. Like It* i 1 150
As secret and as dear As Anna to the queen of Carthage was . *T. of Shrew* i 1 158
O, let me live! And all the secrets of our camp I'll show . *All's Well* iv 1 93
You that have so traitorously discovered the secrets of your army . iv 3 339
I have unclasp'd To thee the book even of my secret soul . *T. Night* i 4 14
What I am, and what I would, are as secret as maidenhead . . i 5 232
You have not dared to break the holy seal Nor read the secrets in't *W. Tale* iii 2 131
Is there not milking-time, . . . to whistle off these secrets? . . iv 4 248
It becomes thy oath full well, Thou to me thy secrets tell . . iv 4 307
Show those things you found about her, those secret things . . iv 4 714
Such secrets in this fardel and box, which none must know but the king iv 4 783
The gods Will have fulfill'd their secret purposes . . . v 1 36
Had I been the finder out of this secret, it would not have relished . v 2 132
That takes away by any secret course Thy hateful life . *K. John* iii 1 178
Fearing to do so, Stay and be secret, and myself will go . *Richard II.* ii 1 298
Choose out some secret place, some reverend room, More than thou hast v 6 25
Now I will unclasp a secret book . . . *1 Hen. IV.* i 3 188
In his secret doom, out of my blood He'll breed revengement . iii 2 6
The fix'd sentinels almost receive The secret whispers of each other's watch . . . . . *Hen. V.* iv Prol. 7
Through a secret grate of iron bars In yonder tower . *1 Hen. VI.* i 4 10
Search out thy wit for secret policies . . . . iii 3 12
Madam, I have a secret to reveal . . . . . v 3 100
Hast thou by secret means Used intercession to obtain a league? . . v 4 147
To pry into the secrets of the state . . *2 Hen. VI.* i 1 250
Keep your royal person From treason's secret knife and traitors' rage . iii 1 174
God's secret judgement: I did dream to-night The duke was dumb . iii 2 31
Whispers to his pillow as to him The secrets of his overcharged soul . iii 2 376
In this city will I stay And live alone as secret as I may . . iv 4 48
I have advertised him by secret means . . . *3 Hen. VI.* iv 5 9
If secret powers Suggest but truth to my divining thoughts . . iv 6 68
Attended him In secret ambush on the forest side . . . iv 6 83
Piercing as the mid-day sun, To search the secret treasons of the world v 2 18
Not all so much for love As for another secret close intent *Richard III.* i 1 158
The secret mischiefs that I set abroach I lay unto the grievous charge of others . . . . i 3 325
Had you such leisure in the time of death To gaze upon the secrets of the deep? . . . . i 4 35
Wherein my soul recorded The history of all her secret thoughts . iii 5 28
This secret is so weighty, 'twill require A strong faith to conceal it *Hen. VIII.* ii 1 144
What were't worth to know The secret of your conference? . . ii 3 51
What cross devil Made me put this main secret in the packet? . iii 2 215
I love you; And durst commend a secret to your ear Much weightier than this work . . . . v 1 17
The secrets of nature Have not more gift in taciturnity *Troi. and Cres.* iv 2 74
Drag hence her husband to some secret hole . . *T. Andron.* ii 3 129
I see thou wilt not trust the air With secrets . . . iv 2 170
To himself so secret and so close, So far from sounding . *Rom. and Jul.* i 1 155
Nurse, give leave awhile, We must talk in secret:—nurse, come back again i 3 8
Must be my convoy in the secret night . . . . ii 4 203
Is your man secret? Did you ne'er hear say, Two may keep counsel, putting one away? . . . . ii 4 208
What other bond Than secret Romans, that have spoke the word? *J. C.* ii 1 125
Is it excepted I should know no secrets That appertain to you? . ii 1 281
If this were true, then should I know this secret. I grant I am a woman ii 1 291
Can I bear that with patience, And not my husband's secrets? . ii 1 302
By and by thy bosom shall partake The secrets of my heart . . ii 1 306
You secret, black, and midnight hags! What is't you do? *Macbeth* iv 1 48
Infected minds To their deaf pillows will discharge their secrets . v 1 81
Now does he feel His secret murders sticking on his hands . . v 2 17
I am forbid To tell the secrets of my prison-house . . *Hamlet* i 5 14
But you'll be secret?—Ay, by heaven, my lord . . . i 5 122
'Faith, her privates we.—In the secret parts of fortune? . . ii 2 239
Indeed this counsellor Is now most still, most secret, and most grave iii 4 214
Her brother is in secret come from France . . . iv 5 88
Have secret feet In some of our best ports . . . *Lear* iii 1 32
All blest secrets, All you unpublish'd virtues of the earth . . iv 4 15
A closet lock and key of villanous secrets: And yet she'll kneel *Othello* iv 2 22
Is it sin To rush into the secret house of death? *Ant. and Cleo.* iv 15 81
This secret Will force him think I have pick'd the lock . *Cymbeline* ii 2 40
Maids, matrons, nay, the secrets of the grave This viperous slander enters iii 4 40
I'll have this secret from thy heart, or rip Thy heart to find it . iii 5 86
Some marks Of secret on her person . . . . . v 5 206
Forty days longer . . . ; If by which time our secret be undone *Pericles* i 1 117
That, being bid to ask what he would of the king, desired he might know none of his secrets . . . . i 3 7
Through which secret art, By turning o'er authorities, I have, Together with my practice, made familiar To me . . . . iii 2 32

Secretary. Call Gardiner to me, my new secretary . *Hen. VIII.* ii 2 116
Newly preferr'd from the king's secretary . . . . iv 1 102
Master O' the rolls, and the king's secretary . . . . v 1 35
Speak to the business, master secretary: Why are we met in council? v 3 1

Secretest. Have By magot-pies and choughs and rooks brought forth The secret'st man of blood . . . . . . *Macbeth* iii 4 126

Secret-false. Teach sin the carriage of a holy saint; Be secret-false: what need she be acquainted? . . . *Com. of Errors* iii 2 15

Secretly. What duke should that be comes so secretly? . *Mer. Wives* iv 3 6
Let her awhile be secretly kept in, And publish it that she is dead *Much Ado* iv 1 205
I will deal in this As secretly and justly as your soul Should with your body . . . . iv 1 250
Prince John is this morning secretly stolen away . . . iv 2 63
Pyramus and Thisby Did whisper often very secretly *M. N. Dream* v 1 161
Give him this letter; do it secretly . . . *Mer of Venice* ii 3 7
I am given, sir, secretly to understand . . *As Y. Like. It* i 1 130
Confesses that she secretly o'erheard Your daughter . . . ii 2 11
Shall secretly into the bosom creep Of that same noble prelate *1 Hen. IV.* i 3 266
Were best he do it secretly, alone . . . *Richard III.* i 1 100
A juggling trick,—to be secretly open . . *Troi. and Cres.* v 2 24
And secretly to greet the empress' friends . . *T. Andron.* iv 2 174

Sect. All sects, all ages smack of this vice . *Meas. for Meas.* ii 2 5
Would she begin a sect, might quench the zeal Of all professors else *W. Tale* v 1 107
So is all her sect; an they be once in a calm, they are sick . *2 Hen. IV.* ii 4 41
Do not I know you for a favourer Of this new sect? . *Hen. VIII.* v 3 81
Came into the world When sects and factions were newly born *T. of A.* iii 5 30
And we'll wear out, In a wall'd prison, packs and sects of great ones *Lear* v 3 18
Whereof I take this that you call love to be a sect or scion . *Othello* i 3 336

Sectary. You are a sectary, That's the plain truth . . *Hen. VIII.* v 3 70
How long have you been a sectary astronomical? . . . *Lear* i 2 164

Secundo. Primo, secundo, tertio, is a good play . . *T. Night* v 1 39

Secure. Though Page be a secure fool . . . *Mer. Wives* ii 1 241
Page is an ass, a secure ass: he will trust his wife . . . ii 2 315
Divulge Page himself for a secure and wilful Actæon . . . iii 2 43
There is scarce truth enough alive to make societies secure *Meas. for Meas.* iii 2 240
Whilst thou liest warm at home, secure and safe . *T. of Shrew* v 2 151
Still secure And confident from foreign purposes . . *K. John* ii 1 27
Pretty child, sleep doubtless and secure . . . . iv 1 130
Open the door, secure, fool-hardy king . . . *Richard II.* v 3 43
We may do it as secure as sleep. . . . . *1 Hen. IV.* i 2 145
Proud of their numbers and secure in soul . . *Hen. V.* iv Prol. 17
In iron walls they deem'd me not secure . . *1 Hen. VI.* i 4 49
This happy night the Frenchmen are secure . . . . ii 1 11
Mine was secure.—And so was mine . . . . . ii 1 66
Once again we'll sleep secure in Rouen . . . . iii 2 19
Secure us By what we can, which can no more but fly . *2 Hen. VI.* v 2 76
All which secure and sweetly he enjoys . . . *3 Hen. VI.* ii 5 50
There shall I rest secure from force and fraud . . . iv 4 33
I think there's no man is secure . . . . *Richard III.* ii 1 71
Think you, but that I know our state secure, I would be so triumphant? iii 2 83
And I myself secure in grace and favour . . . . iii 4 93
The wound of peace is surety, Surety secure . *Troi. and Cres.* ii 2 15
Repose you here in rest, Secure from worldly chances! . *T. Andron.* i 1 152
And sits aloft, Secure of thunder's crack or lightning flash . . ii 1 3
To think I shall lack friends? Secure thy heart . *T. of Athens* ii 2 185
Upon my secure hour thy uncle stole, With juice of cursed hebenon *Ham.* i 5 61
Lord Hamlet,— Heaven secure him!—So be it! . . . i 5 114
I stumbled when I saw: full oft 'tis seen, Our means secure us, and our mere defects Prove our commodities . . . . *Lear* iv 1 22
I do not so secure me in the error, But the main article I do approve *Oth.* i 3 10
Wear your eye thus, not jealous nor secure . . . . iii 3 198
To lip a wanton in a secure couch, And to suppose her chaste! . iv 1 72
We'll higher to the mountains; there secure us . . *Cymbeline* iv 4 8
Who has a book of all that monarchs do, He's more secure to keep it shut than shown . . . . *Pericles* i 1 95

Securely. She dwells so securely on the excellency of her honour *M. W.* ii 2 252
And stand securely on their battlements, As in a theatre . *K. John* ii 1 374
Securely I espy Virtue with valour couched in thine eye . *Richard II.* i 3 97
And yet we strike not, but securely perish . . . . ii 1 266
'Tis done like Hector; but securely done, A little proudly *Troi. and Cres.* iv 5 73
Whose youth was spent In dangerous wars, whilst you securely slept *T. Andron.* iii 1 3

Securing. Whiles we stood here securing your repose . . *Tempest* ii 1 310

Security enough to make fellowships accurst . . *Meas. for Meas.* iii 2 241
Bolingbroke, through our security, Grows strong and great *Richard II.* iii 2 34
To bear a gentleman in hand, and then stand upon security! . *2 Hen. IV.* i 2 43
If a man is through with them in honest taking up, then they must stand upon security. I had as lief they would put ratsbane in my mouth as offer to stop it with security . . . . . . i 2 47
I looked a' should have sent me two and twenty yards of satin, as I am a true knight, and he sends me security. Well, he may sleep in security . . . . i 2 51
That's mercy, but too much security . . . . *Hen. V.* ii 2 44
Thus have we swept suspicion from our seat And made our footstool of security . . . . *3 Hen. VI.* v 7 14
Fair leave and large security . . . . *Troi. and Cres.* i 3 223
Thou knowest well enough . . . that this is no time to lend money, especially upon bare friendship, without security . *T. of Athens* iii 1 46
And, for I know your reverend ages love Security, I'll pawn my victories . . . . iii 5 81
Security gives way to conspiracy . . . . . *J. Cæsar* ii 3 8
You all know, security Is mortals' chiefest enemy . . *Macbeth* iii 5 32
Give up yourself merely to chance and hazard, From firm security *Ant. and Cleo.* iii 7 49

Sedge. Giving a gentle kiss to every sedge He overtaketh *T. G. of Ver.* ii 7 29
Alas, poor hurt fowl! now will he creep into sedges . . *Much Ado* ii 1 210
And Cytherea all in sedges hid . . . *T. of Shrew* Ind. 2 53
Even as the waving sedges play with wind . . . Ind. 2 55

Sedged crowns and ever-harmless looks . . . *Tempest* iv 1 129

Sedgy. On the gentle Severn's sedgy bank . . *1 Hen. IV.* i 3 98

Sedition. While the vulture of sedition Feeds in the bosom of such great commanders . . . . *1 Hen. VI.* iv 3 47
And heap'd sedition on his crown at home . . . *3 Hen. VI.* ii 2 158
The cockle of rebellion, insolence, sedition . . *Coriolanus* iii 1 70

Seditious to his grace and to the state . . . *2 Hen. VI.* v 1 37
Mortal and intestine jars 'Twixt thy seditious countrymen and us *C. of E.* i 1 12

Seduce. For me, the gold of France did not seduce . . *Hen. V.* ii 2 155
The doubt is that he will seduce the rest . . . *3 Hen. VI.* iv 8 37
O wicked wit and gifts, that have the power So to seduce! . *Hamlet* i 5 45

Seduced. Think'st thou I am so shallow, so conceitless, To be seduced by thy flattery? . . . . *T. G. of Ver.* iv 2 97
Yet was Solomon so seduced, and he had a very good wit . *L. L. Lost* i 2 180
Many a maid hath been seduced by them . . . *All's Well* iii 5 22
By long and vehement suit I was seduced . . . *K. John* i 1 254
I have seduced a headstrong Kentishman . . . *2 Hen. VI.* iii 1 356
Where slept our scouts, or how are they seduced? . . *3 Hen. VI.* v 1 19
Seduced the pitch and height of all his thoughts To base declension *Richard III.* iii 7 188
For who so firm that cannot be seduced? . . . . *J. Cæsar* i 2 316

Seducer. Otherwise a seducer flourishes . . . . *All's Well* v 3 146

Seducing. He water'd his new plants with dews of flattery, Seducing so my friends . . . . *Coriolanus* v 6 24

See. Would I might But ever see that man! . . . *Tempest* i 2 169
I have no ambition To see a goodlier man. . . . . . i 2 483
She too, Who is so far from Italy removed I ne'er again shall see her . ii 1 111
Methinks I see it in thy face, What thou shouldst be . . . ii 1 206
My strong imagination sees a crown Dropping upon thy head . . ii 1 208
When they will not give a doit to relieve a lame beggar, they will lay out ten to see a dead Indian . . . . ii 2 34
My sweet mistress Weeps when she sees me work . . . . iii 1 12
I would I could see this taborer; he lays it on . . . . iii 2 160
I have hope to see the nuptial Of these our dear-beloved solemnized . v 1 308
Entreat thy company To see the wonders of the world abroad *T. G. of Ver.* i 1 6
My father at the road Expects my coming, there to see me shipp'd . i 1 54
Lord, Lord! to see what folly reigns in us! . . . . i 2 15
See it be return'd; Or else return no more into my sight . . . i 2 46
Let's see your song . . . . i 2 88
I see you have a month's mind to them . . . . . . i 2 137

See. You may say what sights you see ; I see things too, although you judge I wink . . . *T. G. of Ver.* i 2 138
Lend me the letter ; let me see what news.—There is no news . ii 3 55
Not an eye that sees you but is a physician to comment on your malady ii 1 41
I have loved her ever since I saw her ; and still I see her beautiful . ii 1 73
If you love her, you cannot see her.—Why?—Because Love is blind . ii 1 74
What should I see then?—Your own present folly . . . ii 1 80
He, being in love, could not see to garter his hose, and you, being in love, cannot see to put on your hose . . . . ii 1 82
Then, you are in love ; for last morning you could not see to wipe my shoes . . . . ii 1 86
But see how I lay the dust with my tears . . . . ii 3 35
And, being blind, How could he see his way to seek out you? . ii 4 94
They say that Love hath not an eye at all.—To see such lovers . ii 4 97
Let me see thy cloak : I'll get me one of such another length . iii 1 132
Here if thou stay, thou canst not see thy love . . . . iii 1 244
Fellows, stand fast ; I see a passenger.—If there be ten, shrink not iv 1 1
Where you shall hear music and see the gentleman that you asked for . iv 2 31
Didst thou ever see me do such a trick? . . . . iv 4 42
See where she comes. Lady, a happy evening! . . . v 1 7
How like a dream is this I see and hear! . . . . v 4 26
I am glad to see your worships well . . . . *Mer. Wives* i 1 80
You are afraid, if you see the bear loose, are you not? . . . i 1 304
Let me see thee froth and lime : I am at a word ; follow . . i 3 15
Go to the casement, and see if you can see my master . . . i 4 2
Well, I shall see her to-day . . . . . . i 4 166
You are come to see my daughter Anne?—Ay, forsooth . . . ii 1 167
How does good Mistress Anne?—Go in with us and see . . . ii 1 171
Come and see the picture, she says, that you wot of . . . ii 2 90
See the hell of having a false woman! . . . . . ii 2 305
To see thee fight, to see thee foin, to see thee traverse ; to see thee here, to see thee there ; to see thee pass thy punto, thy stock, thy reverse . . . . ii 3 24
If I see a sword out, my finger itches to make one . . . ii 3 47
He is there : see what humour he is in . . . . . ii 3 81
O, you are a flattering boy : now I see you'll be a courtier . . iii 2 8
Whither go you?—Truly, sir, to see your wife . . . . iii 2 11
By your leave, sir : I am sick till I see her . . . . iii 2 29
Will you go, gentles?—Have with you to see this monster . . iii 2 93
I see how thine eye would emulate the diamond . . . . iii 3 58
I see what thou wert, if Fortune thy foe were not, Nature thy friend . iii 3 69
She shall not see me : I will ensconce me behind the arras . . iii 3 96
Let me see't, let me see't, O, let me see't! I'll in, I'll in . . iii 3 144
Up, gentlemen ; you shall see sport anon : follow me . . . iii 3 180
Nay, follow him, gentlemen ; see the issue of his search . . . iii 3 185
By gar, I see 'tis an honest woman . . . . . . iii 3 238
I see I cannot get thy father's love ; Therefore no more turn me to him iii 4 1
She laments, sir, for it, that it would yearn your heart to see it . iii 5 45
'Tis a playing-day, I see. How now, Sir Hugh! no school to-day? . iv 1 9
I see you are obsequious in your love . . . . . iv 2 2
I am glad the knight is not here ; now he shall see his own foolery . iv 2 37
See but the issue of my jealousy . . . . . . iv 2 207
Is beaten black and blue, that you cannot see a white spot about her . iv 5 116
When Slender sees his time To take her by the hand and bid her go, She shall go with him . . . . iv 6 36
Be you in the Park about midnight, at Herne's oak, and you shall see wonders . . . . v 1 13
We'll couch i' the castle-ditch till we see the light of our fairies . v 2 2
When you see your time, take her by the hand . . . . v 3 2
Green let it be, More fertile-fresh than all the field to see . . v 5 72
See you these, husband? do not these fair yokes Become the forest better than the town? . . . . v 5 111
See now how wit may be made a Jack-a-Lent! . . . . v 5 134
Hence shall we see, If power change purpose, what our seemers be *Meas. for Meas.* i 3 53
I'll see what I can do.—But speedily.—I will about it straight . i 4 84
The jewel that we find, we stoop and take't Because we see it ; but what we do not see We tread upon . . . . . . ii 1 25
See that Claudio Be executed by nine to-morrow morning . . ii 1 33
Doth your honour see any harm in his face? . . . . ii 1 159
If you live to see this come to pass, say Pompey told you so . . ii 1 256
See you the fornicatress be removed . . . . . ii 2 23
To let me see them and to make me know The nature of their crimes . iii 3 6
I have kept it myself ; and see how he goes about to abuse me! . iii 2 215
I am a brother Of gracious order, late come from the See . . iii 2 232
What pleasure was he given to?—Rather rejoicing to see another merry iii 2 249
Yet since I see you fearful, . . . I will go further than I meant . iv 2 204
See this be done, And sent according to command . . . iv 3 83
I am pale at mine heart to see thine eyes so red . . . . iv 3 158
Our old and faithful friend, we are glad to see you . . . v 1 2
Give me your hand, And let the subject see . . . . v 1 14
Let's see thy face.—My husband bids me ; now I will unmask . . v 1 205
Give me leave to question ; you shall see how I'll handle her . . v 1 273
Methinks I see a quickening in his eye . . . . . v 1 500
Take him to prison ; And see our pleasure herein executed . . v 1 527
In the quest of him : Whom whilst I labour'd of a love to see, I hazarded the loss of whom I loved . . . *Com. of Errors* i 1 131
Time is their master, and when they see time They'll go or come . ii 1 8
But, if thou live to see like right bereft, This fool-begg'd patience in thee will be left . . . . ii 1 40
I see the jewel best enamelled Will lose his beauty . . . . ii 1 109
I did not see you since you sent me hence . . . . ii 2 15
I am glad to see you in this merry vein . . . . . ii 2 20
I know thou canst ; and therefore see thou do it . . . . ii 2 141
Say that I linger'd with you at your shop To see the making of her carcanet . . . . iii 1 4
I'll knock elsewhere, to see if they'll disdain me . . . . iii 1 121
Receive the money now, For fear you ne'er see chain nor money more . iii 2 182
I see a man here needs not live by shifts . . . . . iii 2 187
See him presently discharged, For he is bound to sea and stays but for it iv 1 32
Come, where's the chain? I pray you, let me see it . . . iv 1 58
Hast thou delight to see a wretched man Do outrage and displeasure to himself? . . . . iv 4 118
Good master doctor, see him safe convey'd Home to my house . . iv 4 125
It may be so, but I did never see it . . . . . . iv 4 144
I see these witches are afraid of swords . . . . . iv 4 151
Upon what cause?—To see a reverend Syracusian merchant . . v 1 124
I tell you true ; I have not breathed almost since I did see it . . v 1 181
Unless the fear of death doth make me dote, I see my son . . v 1 196
As sure, my liege, as I do see your grace . . . . . v 1 279

See. Haply I see a friend will save my life And pay the sum *Com. of Errors* v 1 283
I see thy age and dangers make thee dote . . . . . v 1 329
I see two husbands, or mine eyes deceive me . . . . v 1 331
What then became of them I cannot tell ; I to this fortune that you see me in . . . . v 1 355
If this be not a dream I see and hear . . . . . . v 1 376
I see we still did meet each other's man, And I was ta'en for him . v 1 386
I see by you I am a sweet-faced youth . . . . . v 1 418
Will you walk in to see their gossiping? . . . . . v 1 419
I see, lady, the gentleman is not in your books . . *Much Ado* i 1 78
I can see yet without spectacles and I see no such matter . . i 1 191
Shall I never see a bachelor of threescore again? . . . . i 1 201
I shall see thee, ere I die, look pale with love . . . . i 1 249
Here you may see Benedick the married man . . . . i 1 269
Thou shalt see how apt it is to learn Any hard lesson that may do thee good . . . . i 1 294
I never can see him but I am heart-burned an hour after . . ii 1 4
Well, niece, I hope to see you one day fitted with a husband . . ii 1 60
I have a good eye, uncle ; I can see a church by daylight . . ii 1 85
Now, signior, where's the count? did you see him? . . . ii 1 219
No less likelihood than to see me at her chamber-window . . ii 2 43
And bring them to see this the very night before the intended wedding ii 2 45
He would have walked ten mile a-foot to see a good armour . . ii 3 17
May I be so converted and see with these eyes? I cannot tell . . ii 3 23
See you where Benedick hath hid himself? . . . . . ii 3 42
I could wish he would modestly examine himself, to see how much he is unworthy so good a lady . . . . ii 3 216
That's the scene that I would see, which will be merely a dumb-show . ii 3 226
The pleasant'st angling is to see the fish . . . . . iii 1 26
To-night, you shall see her chamber-window entered . . . iii 2 116
If you dare not trust that you see, confess not that you know . . iii 2 122
If I see any thing to-night why I should not marry her to-morrow . iii 2 126
I cannot see how sleeping should offend . . . . . iii 3 42
All this I see ; and I see that the fashion wears out more apparel than the man . . . . iii 3 148
If your husband have stables enough, you'll see he shall lack no barns iii 4 48
Brief, I pray you ; for you see it is a busy time with me . . iii 5 5
God help us! it is a world to see . . . . iii 5 38
Would you not swear, All you that see her, that she were a maid? . iv 1 40
Myself, my brother and this grieved count Did see her, hear her . iv 1 91
Which is the villain? let me see his eyes . . . . . v 1 269
Sweet, let me see your face.—No, that you shall not . . . v 4 55
Strict observances ; As, not to see a woman in that term . *L. L. Lost* i 1 37
O, these are barren tasks, too hard to keep, Not to see ladies, study, fast! i 1 48
Let's see the penalty. 'On pain of losing her tongue' . . . i 1 123
But I would see his own person in flesh and blood . . . . i 1 185
There did I see that low-spirited swain, that base minnow of thy mirth i 1 250
Well, if ever I do see the merry days of desolation that I have seen, some shall see.—What shall some see? . . . . . . i 2 164
I would be glad to see it.—I would you heard it groan . . . ii 1 182
His tongue, all impatient to speak and not see, Did stumble with haste in his eyesight to be . . . . ii 1 238
What then, do you see?—Ay, our way to be gone . . . . ii 1 256
To her white hand see thou do commend This seal'd-up counsel . . iii 1 169
Why did he come? to see : why did he see? to overcome . . iv 1 72
A most dainty man! To see him walk before a lady and to bear her fan! To see him kiss his hand! . . . . iv 1 147
So were there a patch set on learning, to see him in a school . . iv 2 32
All ignorant that soul that sees thee without wonder . . . iv 2 117
For all the wealth that ever I did see, I would not have him know . iv 3 149
You found his mote ; the king your mote did see . . . . iv 3 161
With what strict patience have I sat, To see a king transformed to a gnat! To see great Hercules whipping a gig! . . . . . . iv 3 166
When shall you see me write a thing in rhyme? . . . . iv 3 181
Who sees the heavenly Rosaline, That . . . Bows not his vassal head? iv 3 221
Look, here's thy love : my foot and her face see . . . . iv 3 277
What upward lies The street should see as she walk'd overhead . iv 3 281
Consider what you first did swear unto, To fast, to study, and to see no woman . . . . iv 3 292
Then when ourselves we see in ladies' eyes, Do we not likewise see our learning there? . . . . iv 3 316
An angel shalt thou see ; Yet fear not thou, but speak audaciously . v 2 103
Not a man of them shall have the grace, Despite of suit, to see a lady's face v 2 129
You are not free, For the Lord's tokens on you do I see . . . v 2 423
I see the trick on't . . . . v 2 460
Alas, you see how 'tis,—a little o'erparted . . . . . v 2 587
Take comfort : he no more shall see my face . . . *M. N. Dream* i 1 202
Before the time I did Lysander see, Seem'd Athens as a paradise to me i 1 204
A proper man, as one shall see in a summer's day . . . . i 2 89
The cowslips tall her pensioners be : In their gold coats spots you see . ii 1 11
And thorough this distemperature we see The seasons alter . . ii 1 106
We have laugh'd to see the sails conceive And grow big-bellied . . ii 1 128
If you will patiently dance in our round And see our moonlight revels . ii 1 141
But I might see young Cupid's fiery shaft Quench'd in the chaste beams of the watery moon . . . . ii 1 161
The juice of it on sleeping eye-lids laid Will make or man or woman madly dote Upon the next live creature that it sees . . . . ii 1 172
It is not night when I do see your face . . . . . . ii 1 221
Nature shows art, That through thy bosom makes me see thy heart . ii 2 105
I'll be an auditor ; An actor too perhaps, if I see cause . . . iii 1 82
He goes but to see a noise that he heard, and is to come again . . iii 1 93
What do I see on thee?—What do you see? you see an ass-head of your own . . . . iii 1 118
I see their knavery : this is to make an ass of me ; to fright me . iii 1 123
What should I get therefore?—A privilege never to see me more . . iii 2 79
See me no more, whether he be dead or no . . . . . iii 2 81
By some illusion see thou bring her here : I'll charm his eyes . . iii 2 98
Shall we their fond pageant see? Lord, what fools these mortals be! . iii 2 114
I see you all are bent To set against me for your merriment . . iii 2 145
In earnest, shall I say?—Ay, by my life ; And never did desire to see thee more . . . . iii 2 278
Let me go : You see how simple and how fond I am . . . iii 2 317
Thou shalt buy this dear, If ever I thy face by daylight see . . iii 2 427
Be as thou wast wont to be ; See as thou wast wont to see . . iv 1 77
Methinks I see these things with parted eye, When every thing seems double . . . . iv 1 194
One sees more devils than vast hell can hold, That is, the madman . v 1 9
The lover, all as frantic, Sees Helen's beauty in a brow of Egypt . v 1 11
Make choice of which your highness will see first . . . . v 1 43

See. I love not to see wretchedness o'ercharged *M. N. Dream* v 1 85
Why, gentle sweet, you shall see no such thing v 1 87
But what see I? No Thisby do I see. O wicked wall, through whom I see no bliss! Cursed be thy stones! v 1 180
You shall see, it will fall pat as I told you v 1 188
I see a voice: now will I to the chink, To spy an I can hear my Thisby's face v 1 194
He dares not come there for the candle; for, you see, it is already in snuff v 1 254
Eyes, do you see? How can it be? O dainty duck! O dear! v 1 284
Will it please you to see the epilogue, or to hear a Bergomask dance? v 1 360
I should not see the sandy hour-glass run, But I should think of shallows and of flats, And see my wealthy Andrew dock'd in sand *Mer. of Venice* i 1 25
Should I go to church And see the holy edifice of stone, And not bethink me straight of dangerous rocks? i 1 30
See to my house, left in the fearful guard Of an unthrifty knave i 3 176
See these letters delivered; put the liveries to making ii 2 123
See it done ii 2 164
Well, we shall see your bearing.—Nay, but I bar to-night ii 2 207
I would not have my father See me in talk with thee ii 3 9
Well, thou shalt see, thy eyes shall be thy judge ii 5 1
I will not say you shall see a masque ii 5 23
Love is blind and lovers cannot see The pretty follies that themselves commit ii 6 36
Cupid himself would blush To see me thus transformed to a boy ii 6 39
Let's see once more this saying graved in gold ii 7 36
But they come, As o'er a brook, to see fair Portia ii 7 47
I long to see Quick Cupid's post that comes so mannerly ii 9 99
I shall never see my gold again: fourscore ducats at a sitting! iii 1 116
Look on beauty, And you shall see 'tis purchased by the weight iii 2 89
But her eyes,—How could he see to do them? iii 2 124
Stand I, even so; As doubtful whether what I see be true iii 2 148
You see me, Lord Bassanio, where I stand, Such as I am iii 2 150
Rating myself at nothing, you shall see How much I was a braggart iii 2 260
All debts are cleared between you and I, if I might but see you at my death iii 2 322
Pray God, Bassanio come To see me pay his debt, and then I care not! iii 3 36
See thou render this Into my cousin's hand iii 4 49
We'll see our husbands Before they think of us.—Shall they see us? iii 4 58
That, in the course of justice, none of us Should see salvation iv 1 200
Is that the law?—Thyself shalt see the act iv 1 314
That thou shalt see the difference of our spirits, I pardon thee thy life iv 1 368
I see, sir, you are liberal in offers: You taught me first to beg iv 1 438
I'll see if I can get my husband's ring iv 2 13
Sola! did you see Master Lorenzo? Master Lorenzo, sola, sola! v 1 41
That light we see is burning in my hall v 1 89
When the moon shone, we did not see the candle v 1 92
Nothing is good, I see, without respect v 1 99
But you see my finger Hath not the ring upon it; it is gone v 1 187
I will ne'er come in your bed Until I see the ring.—Nor I in yours Till I again see mine v 1 191
I swear to thee, even by thine own fair eyes, Wherein I see myself—Mark you but that! In both my eyes he doubly sees himself v 1 243
I hope I shall see an end of him *As Y. Like It* i 1 170
I see thou lovest me not with the full weight that I love thee i 2 8
You may see the end; for the best is yet to do i 2 120
Is there any else longs to see this broken music in his sides? i 2 149
Shall we see this wrestling, cousin?—You must, if you stay here i 2 151
Daughter and cousin! are you crept hither to see the wrestling? i 2 165
Speak to him, ladies; see if you can move him i 2 172
I cannot hear of any that did see her ii 2 4
There is nothing That you will feed on; but what is, come see ii 4 86
Here shall he see No enemy But winter and rough weather ii 5 45
'Thus we may see,' quoth he, 'how the world wags' ii 7 23
What then? Let me see wherein My tongue hath wrong'd him ii 7 83
Not see him since? Sir, sir, that cannot be iii 1 1
That every eye which in this forest looks Shall see thy virtue iii 2 8
The greatest of my pride is to see my ewes graze and my lambs suck iii 2 81
I cannot see else how thou shouldst 'scape iii 2 89
How parted he with thee? and when shalt thou see him again? iii 2 236
Though it be pity to see such a sight, it well becomes the ground iii 2 255
He is drowned in the brook: look but in, and you shall see him.—There I shall see mine own figure iii 2 306
Native of this place?—As the cony that you see dwell where she is kindled iii 2 357
I would fain see this meeting iii 3 46
If you will see a pageant truly play'd, . . . Go hence a little iii 4 55
I see no more in you Than without candle may go dark to bed iii 5 38
'Tis not her glass, but you, that flatters her; And out of you she sees herself more proper Than any of her lineaments can show her iii 5 55
Though all the world could see, None could be so abused in sight as he iii 5 79
I fear you have sold your own lands to see other men's iv 1 23
I see love hath made thee a tame snake iv 3 70
It is meat and drink to me to see a clown v 1 11
How it grieves me to see thee wear thy heart in a scarf! v 2 23
Stay, Jaques, stay.—To see no pastime I v 4 201
It is not the fashion to see the lady the epilogue; but it is no more unhandsome than to see the lord the prologue Epil. 1
Sirrah, go see what trumpet 'tis that sounds *T. of Shrew* Ind. 1 74
And see him dress'd in all suits like a lady Ind. 1 106
Shed tears, as being overjoy'd To see her noble lord restored to health Ind. 1 121
See this dispatch'd with all the haste thou canst Ind. 1 129
I see, I hear, I speak; I smell sweet savours and I feel soft things Ind. 2 72
O, how we joy to see your wit restored! Ind. 2 79
It is a kind of history.—Well, we'll see't Ind. 2 145
To see fair Padua, nursery of arts, I am arrived for fruitful Lombardy i 1 2
But in the other's silence do I see Maid's mild behaviour and sobriety i 1 70
For a while I take my leave, To see my friends i 2 2
And so am come abroad to see the world i 2 58
I will not sleep, Hortensio, till I see her i 2 103
That she shall have no more eyes to see withal than a cat i 2 116
See that at any hand; And see you read no other lectures to her i 2 147
My fortune lives for me; And I do hope good days and long to see i 2 193
Let me be so bold as ask you, Did you yet ever see Baptista's daughter? i 2 252
Tell Whom thou lovest best: see thou dissemble not ii 1 9
Now I see She is your treasure, she must have a husband ii 1 31
I see you do not mean to part with her ii 1 64
You shall go see your pupils presently ii 1 108
O, let me see thee walk: thou dost not halt ii 1 258
By this light, whereby I see thy beauty ii 1 275
I'll see thee hang'd on Sunday first ii 1 301
O, you are novices! 'tis a world to see ii 1 313

See. Now let me see if I can construe it *T. of Shrew* iii 1 41
When will he be here?—When he stands where I am and sees you there iii 2 40
See not your bride in these unreverent robes iii 2 114
I'll after him, and see the event of this iii 2 129
I see a woman may be made a fool, If she had not a spirit to resist iii 2 222
Didst ever see the like?—He kills her in her own humour iv 1 182
Come, tailor, let us see these ornaments; Lay forth the gown iv 3 61
I see she's like to have neither cap nor gown iv 3 93
Say thou wilt see the tailor paid iv 3 166
Wander we to see thy honest son, Who will of thy arrival be full joyous iv 5 69
Come, go along, and see the truth hereof iv 5 75
I'll see the church o' your back; and then come back v 1 5
What, you notorious villain, didst thou never see thy master's father? v 1 55
See where he looks out of the window v 1 57
Let's stand aside and see the end of this controversy v 1 63
I charge you see that he be forthcoming v 1 96
Husband, let's follow, to see the end of this ado v 1 147
But now I see our lances are but straws, Our strength as weak v 2 173
'Twas pretty, though a plague, To see him every hour *All's Well* i 1 104
Withal, full oft we see Cold wisdom waiting on superfluous folly i 1 115
What power is it which mounts my love so high, That makes me see, and cannot feed mine eye? i 1 236
Gentlemen that mean to see The Tuscan service i 2 13
Now I see The mystery of your loneliness i 3 176
Thine eyes See it so grossly shown in thy behaviours That in their kind they speak it i 3 184
See that you come Not to woo honour, but to wed it ii 1 14
There's one arrived, If you will see her ii 1 83
I see things may serve long, but not serve ever ii 2 60
'Twill be two days ere I shall see you, so I leave you to your wisdom ii 5 75
Let me see what he writes, and when he means to come iii 2 11
I will entreat you, when you see my son, To tell him iii 2 95
Here you shall see a countryman of yours That has done worthy service iii 5 50
When your lordship sees the bottom of his success iii 6 38
We have almost embossed him; you shall see his fall to-night iii 6 108
Tell me what a sprat you shall find him; which you shall see this very night iii 6 114
She's a fair creature: Will you go see her? iii 6 125
Now I see The bottom of your purpose.—You see it lawful, then iii 7 28
I see that men make ropes in such a scarre That we'll forsake ourselves iv 2 38
In the common course of all treasons, we still see them reveal themselves iv 3 26
I would gladly have him see his company anatomized iv 3 37
We'll see what may be done, so you confess freely iv 3 275
O Lord, sir, let me live, or let me see my death! iv 3 344
It rejoices me, that I hope I shall see him ere I die iv 5 89
Let us go see your son, I pray you iv 5 108
Since you are like to see the king before me, Commend the paper v 1 30
Thou mayst see a sunshine and a hail In me at once v 3 33
Our own love waking cries to see what's done v 3 65
Here we'll stay To see our widower's second marriage-day v 3 70
Let me see it; for mine eye, While I was speaking, oft was fasten'd to't v 3 81
Which nothing, but to close Her eyes myself, could win me to believe, More than to see this ring v 3 120
Is't real that I see?—No, my lord; 'Tis but the shadow of a wife you see v 3 307
O my dear mother, do I see you living? v 3 320
When mine eyes did see Olivia first, Methought she purged the air *T. Night* i 1 19
I saw him hold acquaintance with the waves So long as I could see i 2 17
When my tongue blabs, then let mine eyes not see i 2 63
When did I see thee so put down?—Never in your life, I think; unless you see canary put me down i 3 86
I hope to see a housewife take thee between her legs and spin it off i 3 109
Let me see thee caper; ha! higher: ha, ha! excellent! i 3 150
He shall see none to fear.—A good lenten answer i 5 8
Now you see, sir, how your fooling grows old, and people dislike it i 5 118
Have you no more to say?—Good madam, let me see your face i 5 248
I see you what you are, you are too proud i 5 269
Else would I very shortly see thee there ii 1 47
My hearts! did you never see the picture of 'we three'? ii 3 17
But first, let me see, let me see, let me see ii 5 122
An you had any eye behind you, you might see more detraction at your heels than fortune before you ii 5 149
And wished to see thee ever cross-gartered ii 5 167; iii 4 55
If not, let me see thee a steward still ii 5 169; iii 4 60
If you will then see the fruits of the sport, mark his first approach ii 5 217
If you will see it, follow me.—To the gates of Tartar ii 5 225
To see this age! A sentence is but a cheveril glove to a good wit iii 1 12
Did she see thee the while, old boy? tell me that.—As plain as I see you now iii 2 9
My desire, More sharp than filed steel, did spur me forth; And not all love to see you iii 3 6
What's to do? Shall we go see the reliques of this town? iii 3 19
First go see your lodging.—I am not weary, and 'tis long to night iii 3 20
Do you not see you move him? let me alone with him iii 4 121
Give ground, if you see him furious iii 4 334
This youth that you see here I snatch'd one half out of the jaws of death iii 4 393
Let's see the event.—I dare lay any money 'twill be nothing yet iii 4 431
He sees thee not.—To him in thine own voice iv 2 70
Nay, I'll ne'er believe a madman till I see his brains iv 2 126
This pearl she gave me, I do feel't and see't iv 3 2
Now, as thou lovest me, let me see his letter v 1 1
Do not desire to see this letter v 1 6
Give me thy hand; And let me see thee in thy woman's weeds v 1 280
You shall see, as I have said, great difference *W. Tale* i 1 3
They that went on crutches ere he was born desire yet their life to see him a man i 1 45
To tell, he longs to see his son, were strong: But let him say so then i 2 34
Canst with thine eyes at once see good and evil, Inclining to them both i 2 303
If I had servants true about me, that bare eyes To see alike mine honour as their profits i 2 310
Who mayst see Plainly as heaven sees earth and earth sees heaven i 2 314
My women may be with me; for you see My plight requires it ii 1 117
I never wish'd to see you sorry; now I trust I shall ii 1 123
Than when I feel and see her no farther trust her ii 1 136
Fourteen they shall not see, To bring false generations ii 1 147
But I do see't and feel't, As you feel doing thus; and see withal The instruments that feel ii 1 152
Is't lawful, pray you, To see her women? any of them? ii 2 12
To see his nobleness! ii 3 12
Leave me solely: go, See how he fares ii 3 18
Take it hence And see it instantly consumed with fire ii 3 134

See. Shall I live on to see this bastard kneel And call me father? *W. Tale* ii 3 155
That he did but see The flatness of my misery, yet with eyes Of pity! . iii 2 122
Look down And see what death is doing . . . . . iii 2 150
If word nor oath Prevail not, go and see . . . . iii 2 205
Thou ne'er shalt see Thy wife Paulina more . . . iii 3 35
If thou'lt see a thing to talk on when thou art dead and rotten, come hither . . . . iii 3 81
I would you did but see how it chafes, how it rages! . . iii 3 89
Sometimes to see 'em, and not to see 'em; now the ship boring the moon iii 3 92
But to make an end of the ship, to see how the sea flap-dragoned it iii 3 100
I'll go see if the bear be gone from the gentleman . . iii 3 133
I should blush To see you so attired . . . . . iv 4 13
How would he look, to see his work so noble Vilely bound up? . iv 4 21
You see, sweet maid, we marry A gentler scion to the wildest stock iv 4 92
Let's first see moe ballads; we'll buy the other things anon . iv 4 277
If I may ever know thou dost but sigh That thou no more shalt see this knack, . . . we'll bar thee from succession . . . iv 4 439
For all the sun sees or The close earth wombs or the profound seas hide iv 4 500
In faith, I mean not To see him any more . . . . iv 4 506
That unhappy king, my master, whom I so much thirst to see . iv 4 524
Enjoy your mistress, from the whom, I see, There's no disjunction to be made . . . . iv 4 539
There present yourself and your fair princess, For so I see she must be iv 4 556
Methinks I see Leontes opening his free arms and weeping His welcomes iv 4 558
It shall take joy To see her in your arms . . . . v 1 81
When I shall see this gentleman, thy speeches Will bring me to consider v 1 121
The stars, I see, will kiss the valleys first . . . . v 1 206
That 'once,' I see by your good father's speed, Will come on very slowly v 1 210
That which you hear you'll swear you see . . . . v 2 35
Did you see the meeting of the two kings? . . . . v 2 43
See you these clothes? say you see them not and think me still no gentleman born . . . . v 2 141
The kings and the princes, our kindred, are going to see the queen's picture . . . . v 2 187
We came To see the statue of our queen . . . . v 3 10
Prepare To see the life as lively mock'd as ever Still sleep mock'd death v 3 19
Do not shun her Until you see her die again . . . v 3 106
I . . . have preserved Myself to see the issue . . . v 3 128
I see a yielding in the looks of France . . . *K. John* ii 1 474
If he see aught in you that makes him like, That any thing he sees, which moves his liking, I can with ease translate it to my will ii 1 511
Further I will not flatter you, my lord, That all I see in you is worthy love, Than this; that nothing do I see in you . . . That I can find should merit any hate . . . . ii 1 517
The yearly course that brings this day about Shall never see it but a holiday . . . . iii 1 82
And force perforce Keep Stephen Langton, chosen archbishop Of Canterbury, from that holy see? . . . . . . iii 1 144
Now shall I see thy love: what motive may Be stronger with thee than the name of wife? . . . . iii 1 313
See thou shake the bags Of hoarding abbots . . . . iii 3 7
Or if that thou couldst see me without eyes, Hear me without thine ears iii 3 48
Lo, now! now see the issue of your peace.—Patience, good lady! . iii 4 21
I have heard you say That we shall see and know our friends in heaven: If that be true, I shall see my boy again . . . iii 4 77
Methinks I see this hurly all on foot . . . . . iii 4 169
See else yourself; There is no malice in this burning coal . iv 1 108
Well, see to live; I will not touch thine eye . . . iv 1 122
Out of my sight, and never see me more! . . . . iv 2 242
Could you think? Or do you almost think, although you see, That you do see? . . . . iv 3 43
Let not the world see fear and sad distrust Govern the motion of a kingly eye . . . . v 1 46
That we, the sons and children of this isle, Were born to see so sad an hour . . . . v 2 26
The great metropolis and see of Rome . . . . . v 2 72
For I do see the cruel pangs of death Right in thine eye . . v 4 59
O, I am scalded with my violent motion, And spleen of speed to see your majesty! . . . . v 7 50
He will the rather do it when he sees Ourselves well sinewed to our defence . . . . v 7 87
We shall see Justice design the victor's chivalry . *Richard II.* i 1 202
Who, when they see the hours ripe on earth, Will rain hot vengeance i 2 7
And what shall good old York there see But empty lodgings? . i 2 67
Even in the glasses of thine eyes I see thy grieved heart . . i 3 209
My inch of taper will be burnt and done, And blindfold death not let me see my son . . . . i 3 224
'Tis doubt . . . Whether our kinsman come to see his friends . i 4 22
I am in health, I breathe, and see thee ill.—Now He that made me knows I see thee ill; Ill in myself to see . . . . ii 1 92
Bid him repair to us to Ely House To see this business . . ii 1 217
We see the wind sit sore upon our sails, And yet we strike not, but securely perish.—We see the very wreck that we must suffer . ii 1 265
Methinks in you I see old Gaunt alive . . . . . ii 3 118
And let him ne'er see joy that breaks that oath! . . . ii 3 151
I see the issue of these arms: I cannot mend it, I must needs confess ii 3 152
I see thy glory like a shooting star Fall to the base earth . ii 4 19
See them deliver'd over To execution and the hand of death . iii 1 29
When this thief, this traitor, . . . Shall see us rising in our throne iii 2 50
Well, well, I see I talk but idly, and you laugh at me . . iii 3 170
Me rather had my heart might feel your love Than my unpleased eye see your courtesy . . . . iii 3 193
Thou darest not, coward, live to see that day . . . iv 1 41
Mine eyes are full of tears, I cannot see: And yet salt water blinds them not so much But they can see a sort of traitors here . iv 1 244
I'll read enough, When I do see the very book indeed Where all my sins are writ, and that's myself . . . . iv 1 274
I see your brows are full of discontent, Your hearts of sorrow . iv 1 331
But soft, but see, or rather do not see, My fair rose wither . v 1 7
Let me see the writing.—My lord, 'tis nothing.—No matter, then, who see it: I will be satisfied; let me see the writing . . v 2 57
Wife, thou art a fool. Boy, let me see the writing . . v 2 69
I may not show it.—I will be satisfied; let me see it, I say . v 2 71
'Tis full three months since I did see him last . . . v 3 2
I see some sparks of better hope, which elder years May happily bring forth . . . . v 3 21
For ever will I walk upon my knees, And never see day that the happy sees . . . . v 3 94
See riot and dishonour stain the brow Of my young Harry . *1 Hen. IV.* i 1 85
I see a good amendment of life in thee . . . . . i 2 114

See. Our horses they shall not see; I'll tie them in the wood *1 Hen. IV.* i 2 198
If he fight longer than he sees reason, I'll forswear arms . i 2 207
Get thee gone; for I do see Danger and disobedience in thine eye . i 3 15
He made me mad To see him shine so brisk and smell so sweet . i 3 54
See already how he doth begin To make us strangers to his looks of love i 3 289
I prithee, lend me thy lantern, to see my gelding in the stable . ii 1 38
Lend me thy lantern, quoth he? marry, I'll see thee hanged first . ii 1 44
Let me see some more. 'The purpose you undertake is dangerous' . ii 3 7
You shall see now in very sincerity of fear and cold heart . ii 3 32
Such as we see when men restrain their breath On some great sudden hest . . . . ii 3 64
Wilt thou see me ride? And when I am o' horseback, I will swear I love thee . . . . ii 3 103
Didst thou never see Titan kiss a dish of butter? . . . ii 4 133
I call thee coward! I'll see thee damned ere I call thee coward . ii 4 161
You are straight enough in the shoulders, you care not who sees your back . . . . ii 4 165
It was so dark, Hal, that thou couldst not see thy hand . . ii 4 248
Do you see these meteors? do you behold these exhalations? . ii 4 351
He doth it as like one of these harlotry players as ever I see! . ii 4 437
I see virtue in his looks . . . . ii 4 470
Nothing but papers, my lord.—Let's see what they be: read them . ii 4 584
O, then the earth shook to see the heavens on fire . . . iii 1 25
Not wind? it shall, it must; you see it doth . . . iii 1 106
Not an eye But is a-weary of thy common sight, Save mine, which hath desired to see thee more . . . . iii 2 89
I never see thy face but I think upon hell-fire and Dives . . iii 3 35
We should on, To see how fortune is disposed to us . . . iv 1 38
I did never see such pitiful rascals.—Tut, tut; good enough to toss iv 2 70
If thou see me down in the battle and bestride me, so . . v 1 121
Why, then I see A very valiant rebel of the name . . . v 4 61
Embowell'd will I see thee by and by . . . . . v 4 109
Nothing confutes me but eyes, and nobody sees me . . . v 4 129
Let us to the highest of the field, To see what friends are living, who are dead . . . . v 4 165
See what a ready tongue suspicion hath! . . . *2 Hen. IV.* i 1 84
I see a strange confession in thine eye: Thou shakest thy head . i 1 94
And yet cannot he see, though he have his own lanthorn to light him i 2 54
Wait close; I will not see him.—What's he that goes there? . i 2 65
I am glad to see your lordship abroad: I heard say your lordship was sick . . . . i 2 107
As in an early spring We see the appearing buds . . . i 3 39
And when we see the figure of the house, Then must we rate the cost i 3 43
How might we see Falstaff bestow himself to-night in his true colours? ii 2 186
My heart's dear Harry Threw many a northward look to see his father ii 3 13
See if thou canst find out Sneak's noise . . . . . ii 4 12
Whether I shall ever see thee again or no, there is nobody cares . ii 4 72
I'll see her damned first; to Pluto's damned lake . . . ii 4 169
See now, whether pure fear and entire cowardice doth not make thee wrong this virtuous gentlewoman? . . . . ii 4 352
You see, my good wenches, how men of merit are sought after . ii 4 404
If I be not sent away post, I will see you again ere I go . . ii 4 408
That one might read the book of fate, And see the revolution of the times! . . . . iii 1 46
To see The beachy girdle of the ocean Too wide for Neptune's hips . iii 1 49
And to see how many of my old acquaintance are dead! . . iii 2 37
It would have done a man's heart good to see . . . . iii 2 54
Let me see, let me see, let me see. So, so, so, so, so, so, so . iii 2 107
You see what a ragged appearance it is . . . . . iii 2 279
I shall ne'er see such a fellow . . . . iii 2 306
I will fetch off these justices: I do see the bottom of Justice Shallow iii 2 324
You, lord archbishop, Whose see is by a civil peace maintain'd . iv 1 42
We see which way the stream of time doth run . . . iv 1 70
Than now to see you here an iron man, Cheering a rout of rebels . iv 2 8
Lead him hence; and see you guard him sure . . . . iv 3 81
Where is he? let me see him: He is not here . . . iv 5 54
I am glad to see your worship.—I thank thee . . . v 1 63
It is a wonderful thing to see the semblable coherence of his men's spirits . . . . v 1 72
O, you shall see him laugh till his face be like a wet cloak ill laid up! . v 1 94
Never shall you see that I will beg A ragged and forestall'd remission v 2 37
See your most dreadful laws so loosely slighted . . . v 2 94
Till you do live to see a son of mine Offend you and obey you . v 2 105
Nay, you shall see my orchard . . . . v 3 1
I hope to see London once ere I die.—An I might see you there . v 3 64
This poor show doth better: this doth infer the zeal I had to see him . v 5 15
Be it your charge, my lord, To see perform'd the tenour of our word . v 5 75
Think, when we talk of horses, that you see them . *Hen. V.* Prol. 26
But see thy fault! . . . . ii Prol. 20
What see you in those papers that you lose So much complexion? . ii 2 72
See you, my princes and my noble peers, These English monsters! . ii 2 84
Though the truth of it stands off as gross As black and white, my eye will scarcely see it . . . . ii 2 104
Saw his heroical seed, and smiled to see him, Mangle the work of nature ii 4 59
You see this chase is hotly follow'd, friends . . . . ii 4 68
Work, work your thoughts, and therein see a seige . . iii Prol. 25
I see you stand like greyhounds in the slips, Straining upon the start iii 1 31
In a moment look to see The blind and bloody soldier . . iii 3 33
When he shall see our army, He'll drop his heart into the sink of fear iii 5 58
But I did see him do as gallant service . . . . . iii 6 16
As you shall see in a summer's day . . . . . . iii 6 67
England shall repent his folly, see his weakness, and admire our sufferance . . . . iii 6 132
Each battle sees the other's umber'd face . . . . iv Prol. 9
Yet sit and see, Minding true things by what their mockeries be . iv Prol. 52
We see yonder the beginning of the day, but I think we shall never see the end of it . . . . iv 1 91
When he sees reason of fears, as we do, his fears, out of doubt, be of the same relish as ours are . . . . iv 1 113
He let him outlive that day to see His greatness and to teach others iv 1 194
If I live to see it, I will never trust his word after . . iv 1 207
If ever I live to see it, I will challenge it . . . . iv 1 233
Never sees horrid night, the child of hell . . . . iv 1 288
He that shall live this day, and see old age . . . . iv 3 44
If I can see my glove in his cap, . . . I will strike it out soundly . iv 7 133
If he be perjured, see you now, his reputation is as arrant a villain iv 7 147
I would fain see the man, that has but two legs . . . iv 7 169
But I would fain see it once, an please God of his grace that I might see iv 7 171
Follow, and see there be no harm between them . . . iv 7 190
So let him land, And solemnly see him set on to London . . v Prol. 14

See. I will be so bold as to wear it in my cap till I see him . *Hen. V.* v 1 13
Quiet thy cudgel; thou dost see I eat.—Much good do you . v 1 54
When you take occasions to see leeks hereafter, I pray you, mock at 'em v 1 58
Augment, or alter, as your wisdom best Shall see advantageable . v 2 88
That never looks in his glass for love of any thing he sees there . v 2 155
Et quand vous avez le possession de moi,—let me see, what then? v 2 193
They are then excused, my lord, when they see not what they do . v 2 330
Who cannot see many a fair French city for one fair French maid . v 2 344
You see them perspectively . v 2 347
Him I forgive my death that killeth me When he sees me go back *1 Hen. VI.* i 2 21
That beauty am I bless'd with which you see . i 2 86
See the coast clear'd . i 3 89
Even these three days have I watch'd, If I could see them . i 4 17
Nay, then, I see our wars Will turn unto a peaceful comic sport . ii 2 44
I see report is fabulous and false . ii 3 18
I laugh to see your ladyship so fond . ii 3 45
For what you see is but the smallest part And least proportion of humanity . ii 3 52
See what cates you have; For soldiers' stomachs always serve them well . ii 3 79
I myself Will see his burial better than his life . ii 5 121
Ay, see the bishop be not overborne . iii 1 53
Plantagenet, I see, must hold his tongue . iii 1 61
You see what mischief and what murder too Hath been enacted . iii 1 115
I would see his heart out, ere the priest Should ever get that privilege of me . iii 1 120
See here, my friends and loving countrymen, This token serveth . iii 1 137
And I will see what physic the tavern affords . iii 1 147
See, noble Charles, the beacon of our friend . iii 2 29
See his exequies fulfill'd in Rouen . iii 2 133
Look on fertile France, And see the cities and the towns defaced . iii 3 45
See, see the pining malady of France; Behold the wounds . iii 3 49
See, then, thou fight'st against thy countrymen . iii 3 74
When thou shalt see I'll meet thee to thy cost . iii 4 43
No simple man that sees This . . . , But that it doth presage some ill event . iv 1 187
These eyes, that see thee now well coloured, Shall see thee wither'd . iv 2 37
This seven years did not Talbot see his son; And now they meet . iv 3 37
See, where he lies inhearsed in the arms Of the most bloody nurser of his harms! . iv 7 45
See them guarded And safely brought to Dover . v 1 48
See, how the ugly witch doth bend her brows! . v 3 34
See, Reignier, see, thy daughter prisoner!—To whom?—To me . v 3 131
And with all speed provide To see her coronation be perform'd *2 Hen. VI.* i 1 74
Rancour will out: proud prelate, in thy face I see thy fury . i 1 143
We'll see these things effected to the full . i 2 84
Are your supplications to his lordship? Let me see them . i 3 17
We'll see thee sent away . i 3 225
My lord protector will, I doubt it not, See you well guerdon'd . i 4 49
We'll see your trinkets here all forthcoming . i 4 56
Now, pray, my lord, let's see the devil's writ . i 4 60
To see how God in all his creatures works! . ii 1 7
Protector, see to't well, protect yourself . ii 1 54
Let me see thine eyes: wink now: now open them: In my opinion yet thou see'st not well . ii 1 105
Thou know'st what colour jet is of?—And yet, I think, jet did he never see . ii 1 114
It made me laugh to see the villain run . ii 1 155
See here the tainture of thy nest, And look thyself be faultless . ii 1 188
Purposely therefore Left I the court, to see this quarrel tried . ii 3 53
See the lists and all things fit: Here let them end it . ii 3 54
See thou thump thy master well . ii 3 85
I'll prepare My tear-stain'd eyes to see her miseries . ii 4 16
Come you, my lord, to see my open shame? Now thou dost penance too ii 4 19
See how the giddy multitude do point, And nod their heads! . ii 4 21
Follow'd with a rabble that rejoice To see my tears . ii 4 33
Go, lead the way; I long to see my prison . ii 4 110
Can you not see? or will ye not observe The strangeness? . iii 1 4
Thou shalt not see me blush Nor change my countenance . iii 1 98
In thy face I see The map of honour, truth and loyalty . iii 1 202
A charge, Lord York, that I will see perform'd . iii 1 321
I'll see it truly done . iii 1 330
View this body.—That is to see how deep my grave is made . iii 2 150
For seeing him I see my life in death . iii 2 152
See how the blood is settled in his face . iii 2 160
Look, on the sheets his hair, you see, is sticking . iii 2 174
Who finds the heifer dead and bleeding fresh And sees fast by a butcher with an axe, But will suspect 'twas he? . iii 2 189
See, how the pangs of death do make him grin! . iii 3 24
I see them! I see them! . iv 2 23
I'll see if his head will stand steadier on a pole, or no . iv 7 100
I see them lording it in London streets . iv 8 47
I see them lay their heads together to surprise me . iv 8 60
I climbed into this garden, to see if I can eat grass, or pick a sallet . iv 10 8
See if thou canst outface me with thy looks . iv 10 49
If you be ta'en, we then should see the bottom Of all our fortunes . v 2 78
And we will live To see their day and them our fortune give . v 2 89
Before I see thee seated in that throne Which now the house of Lancaster usurps, I vow by heaven these eyes shall never close . *3 Hen. VI.* i 1 22
The northern lords that have forsworn thy colours Will follow mine, if once they see them spread . i 1 252
When I return with victory from the field I'll see your grace . i 1 262
Thou wouldst be fee'd, I see, to make me sport . i 4 92
See, ruthless queen, a hapless father's tears . i 4 156
But weep with him, To see how inly sorrow gripes his soul . i 4 171
See how the morning opes her golden gates! . ii 1 21
Dazzle mine eyes, or do I see three suns? . ii 1 25
See, see! they join, embrace, and seem to kiss . ii 1 29
Never henceforth shall I joy again, Never, O never, shall I see more joy! ii 1 78
Ne'er may he live to see a sunshine day, That cries 'Retire' . ii 1 187
To see this sight, it irks my very soul . ii 2 6
To see the minutes how they run, How many make the hour full complete . ii 5 25
See, see what showers arise, Blown with the windy tempest of my heart! ii 5 85
A deadly groan, like life and death's departing.—See who it is . ii 6 44
And he nor sees nor hears us what we say . ii 6 63
First will I see the coronation; And then to Brittany I'll cross the sea ii 6 96
Now to London, To see these honours in possession . ii 6 110
And Nero will be tainted with remorse, To hear and see her plaints . iii 1 41
I see the lady hath a thing to grant . iii 2 12

See. And see where comes the breeder of my sorrow! *3 Hen. VI.* iii 3 43
He dishonours me, But most himself, if he could see his shame . iii 3 185
Art thou here too? Nay, then I see that Edward needs must down iv 3 42
See that forthwith Duke Edward be convey'd Unto my brother . iv 3 52
And see him seated in the regal throne . iv 3 64
Till I see them here, by doubtful fear My joy of liberty is half eclipsed iv 6 62
O cheerful colours! see where Oxford comes!—Oxford, Oxford, for Lancaster! . v 1 58
This cheers my heart, to see your forwardness . v 4 65
For every word I speak, Ye see, I drink the water of mine eyes . v 4 75
Let's away to London And see our gentle queen how well she fares . v 5 89
See how my sword weeps for the poor king's death! . v 6 63
See, see! dead Henry's wounds Open their congeal'd mouths and bleed afresh! . *Richard III.* i 2 55
I will with all expedient duty see you . i 2 217
Much it joys me too, To see you are become so penitent . i 2 221
Shine out, fair sun, till I have bought a glass, That I may see my shadow i 2 264
Northumberland, then present, wept to see it . i 3 187
And see another, as I see thee now, Deck'd in thy rights . i 3 205
And see how he requites me! . i 4 68
That came too lag to see him buried . ii 1 90
And I for comfort have but one false glass, Which grieves me when I see my shame in him . ii 2 54
My mother, I do cry you mercy; I did not see your grace . ii 2 105
Then, masters, look to see a troublous world . ii 3 9
As, by proof, we see The waters swell before a boisterous storm . ii 3 43
I long with all my heart to see the prince . ii 4 4
Ay me, I see the downfall of our house! . ii 4 49
I see, as in a map, the end of all . ii 4 54
O, then, I see, you will part but with light gifts . iii 1 118
To the Tower, Where, he shall see, the boar will use us kindly . iii 2 33
I'll have this crown of mine cut from my shoulders Ere I will see the crown so foul misplaced . iii 2 44
But yet, you see, how soon the day o'ercast . iii 2 88
Well met, my lord; I am glad to see your honour.—I thank thee . iii 2 110
By Saint Paul I swear, I will not dine until I see the same . iii 4 79
The duke would be at dinner: Make a short shrift; he longs to see your head . iii 4 97
Is Catesby gone?—He is; and, see, he brings the mayor along . iii 5 13
Yet had not we determined he should die, Until your lordship came to see his death . iii 5 53
Yet who's so blind, but says he sees it not? . iii 6 12
See, where he stands between two clergymen! . iii 7 95
And, see, a book of prayer in his hand . iii 7 98
God he knows, and you may partly see, How far I am from the desire iii 7 235
God bless your grace! we see it, and will say it . iii 7 237
I am their father's mother; I will see them . iv 1 23
The king is angry: see, he bites the lip . iv 2 27
But didst thou see them dead?—I did, my lord . iv 3 27
See what now thou art: For happy wife, a most distressed widow . iv 4 97
What! we have many goodly days to see . iv 4 320
Desire the earl to see me in my tent . v 3 32
Those that come to see Only a show or two . *Hen. VIII.* Prol. 9
I'll undertake may see away their shilling Richly in two short hours . Prol. 12
Or to see a fellow In a long motley coat guarded with yellow . Prol. 15
Think ye see The very persons of our noble story . Prol. 25
Think you see them great, And follow'd with the general throng . Prol. 27
In a moment, see How soon this mightiness meets misery . Prol. 29
But I can see his pride Peep through each part of him . i 1 68
And proofs as clear as founts in July when We see each grain of gravel i 1 155
Under pretence to see the queen his aunt . i 1 177
I am sorry To see you ta'en from liberty, to look on The business present i 1 205
As far as I see, all the good our English Have got by the late voyage . i 3 5
An English courtier may be wise, And never see the Louvre . i 3 23
Stay there, sir, And see the noble ruin'd man you speak of . ii 1 54
Prepare there, The duke is coming: see the barge be ready . ii 1 98
All that dare Look into these affairs see this main end . ii 2 41
My Wolsey, see it furnish'd . ii 2 141
Why, this it is; see, see! I have been begging sixteen years in court . ii 3 81
We shall see him For it an archbishop.—So I hear.—'Tis so . iii 2 73
I shall fall Like a bright exhalation in the evening, And no man see me more . iii 2 227
If I blush, It is to see a nobleman want manners . iii 2 308
My heart weeps to see him So little of his great self . iii 2 335
There is staying A gentleman, sent from the king, to see you . iv 2 106
But this fellow Let me ne'er see again . iv 2 108
Keep comfort to you; and this morning see You do appear before them v 1 144
You are so merciful: I see your end; 'Tis my undoing . v 3 61
Receive him, And see him safe i' the Tower . v 3 97
Now let me see the proudest He, that dares most, but wag his finger at thee . v 3 130
The common voice, I see, is verified Of thee . v 3 176
As much as one sound cudgel of four foot—You see the poor remainder v 4 20
If I spared any . . . , Let me ne'er hope to see a chine again . v 4 26
I might see from far some forty truncheoners draw to her succour . v 4 54
Our children's children Shall see this, and bless heaven . v 5 56
Many days shall see her, And yet no day without a deed to crown it . v 5 58
When I am in heaven I shall desire To see what this child does . v 5 69
Ye must all see the queen, and she must thank ye, She will be sick else v 5 74
And so I'll tell her the next time I see her *Troi. and Cres.* i 1 84
Up to the eastern tower, . . . To see the battle . i 2 4
Do you know a man if you see him?—Ay, if I ever saw him before . i 2 67
Shall we stand up here, and see them as they pass? . i 2 193
Here's an excellent place; here we may see most bravely . i 2 198
But mark Troilus; you shall see anon . i 2 204
If he see me, you shall see him nod at me.—Will he give you the nod?—You shall see . i 2 210
Look you yonder, do you see? look you there: there's no jesting . i 2 223
Would I could see Troilus now! You shall see Troilus anon . i 2 235
More in Troilus thousand fold I see Than in the glass of Pandar's praise i 2 310
I see them not with my old eyes: what are they? . i 3 366
Then would come some matter from him; I see none now . ii 1 10
You see him there, do you?—Ay; what's the matter? . ii 1 63
I will see you hanged, like clotpoles, ere I come any more . ii 1 128
'Sfoot, I'll learn to conjure and raise devils, but I'll see some issue of my spiteful execrations . ii 3 7
No, you see, he is his argument that has his argument . ii 3 105
Come, draw this curtain, and let's see your picture . iii 2 49
Fears make devils of cherubins; they never see truly . iii 2 75
See, we fools! Why have I blabb'd? . iii 2 131

See. For speculation turns not to itself, Till it hath travell'd and is mirror'd there Where it may see itself *Troi. and Cres.* iii 3 111
Now shall we see to-morrow—An act that very chance doth throw upon him . . . iii 3 130
To see these Grecian lords!—why, even already They clap the lubber Ajax iii 3 138
I see my reputation is at stake; My fame is shrewdly gored . . . iii 3 227
Invite the Trojan lords after the combat To see us here unarm'd . iii 3 237
To see great Hector in his weeds of peace, To talk with him . . . iii 3 239
Let Patroclus make demands to me, you shall see the pageant of Ajax . iii 3 273
My mind is troubled, like a fountain stirr'd; And I myself see not the bottom of it . . . . iii 3 312
Who 's that at door? good uncle, go and see . . . . iv 2 36
We may live to have need of such a verse: we see it, we see it . iv 4 24
A woful Cressid 'mongst the merry Greeks! When shall we see again? iv 4 59
Be thou true, And I will see thee . . . . . . iv 4 69
When shall I see you? . . . . iv 4 73
Great Achilles Doth long to see unarm'd the valiant Hector . . iv 5 153
I will go eat with thee and see your knights . . . . iv 5 158
I beseech you next To feast with me and see me at my tent . . iv 5 229
I pray you, let us see you in the field . . . . . iv 5 266
No, yonder 'tis; There, where we see the lights . . . v 1 75
I will rather leave to see Hector, than not to dog him . . . v 1 103
One eye yet looks on thee; But with my heart the other eye doth see . v 2 108
I would fain see them meet . . . . v 4 5
Now do I see thee, ha! have at thee, Hector!—Pause, if thou wilt . v 6 13
Let one be sent To pray Achilles see us at our tent . . . v 9 8
Did see and hear, devise, instruct, walk, feel . . *Coriolanus* i 1 105
Though all at once cannot See what I do deliver out to each . . i 1 147
Thou Shalt see me once more strike at Tullus' face . . . . i 1 244
See him pluck Aufidius down by the hair . . . . . i 3 33
Methinks I see him stamp thus, and call thus . . . . . i 3 35
Sweet madam.—I am glad to see your ladyship . . . . i 3 53
He had rather see the swords, and hear a drum . . . . i 3 60
See here these movers that do prize their hours At a crack'd drachma! i 5 5
If any such be here—As it were sin to doubt—that love this painting Wherein you see me smear'd . . . . i 6 69
If you see this in the map of my microcosm, follows it that I am known well enough too? . . . . ii 1 68
My gracious silence, hail! Wouldst thou have laugh'd had I come coffin'd home, That weep'st to see me triumph? . . . . . ii 1 194
A curse begin at very root on's heart, That is not glad to see thee! . ii 1 203
I have lived To see inherited my very wishes . . . . . ii 1 215
The bleared sights Are spectacled to see him . . . . . ii 1 222
Variable complexions, all agreeing In earnestness to see him . . ii 1 229
I have seen the dumb men throng to see him and The blind to hear him speak . . . . ii 1 278
And out of his noble carelessness lets them plainly see't . . . ii 2 17
You now see He had rather venture all his limbs for honour . . ii 2 83
You see how he intends to use the people.—May they perceive's intent! ii 2 159
Why either were you ignorant to see't, Or, seeing it, of such childish friendliness To yield your voices? . . . . . . ii 3 182
We shall hardly in our ages see Their banners wave again . . . iii 1 7
See him out at gates, and follow him . . . . . . iii 3 138
The nobility are vex'd, whom we see have sided In his behalf . . iv 2 2
This lady's husband here, this, do you see—Whom you have banish'd iv 2 41
But that I see thee here, Thou noble thing! more dances my rapt heart iv 5 121
But when they shall see, sir, his crest up again, and the man in blood, they will out of their burrows . . . . iv 5 224
I hope to see Romans as cheap as Volscians . . . . . iv 5 249
Who rather had . . . behold Dissentious numbers pestering streets than see Our tradesmen singing in their shops . . . . . . iv 6 7
Go see this rumourer whipp'd . . . . iv 6 47
To see your wives dishonour'd to your noses . . . . . iv 6 83
You'll see your Rome embraced with fire before You'll speak with Coriolanus . . . . v 2 7
'Tis a spell, you see, of much power . . . . . . v 2 102
Making the mother, wife and child to see The son, the husband and the father tearing His country's bowels out . . . . . v 3 101
Not of a woman's tenderness to be, Requires nor child nor woman's face to see . . . . v 3 130
See you yon coign o' the Capitol, yon corner-stone? . . . . v 4 1
And see his shipwreck and his commonweal's . . . *T. Andron.* ii 1 24
Madam, now shall ye see Our Roman hunting . . . . . ii 2 19
A barren detested vale, you see it is . . . . . . ii 3 93
Listen, fair madam: let it be your glory To see her tears . . . ii 3 140
See that you make her sure . . . . ii 3 187
My heart suspects more than mine eye can see . . . . . ii 3 213
Look down into this den, And see a fearful sight of blood and death . ii 3 216
I'll see what hole is here, And what he is that now is leap'd into it . ii 3 246
These bitter tears, which now you see Filling the aged wrinkles in my cheeks . . . . iii 1 6
Come, let me see what task I have to do . . . . . . iii 1 276
The tender boy, in passion moved, Doth weep to see his grandsire's heaviness . . . . iii 2 49
Get thee gone; I see thou art not for my company . . . . iii 2 58
Some book there is that she desires to see.—Which is it, girl, of these? iv 1 31
See how busily she turns the leaves! What would she find? . . . iv 1 45
See, brother, see; note how she quotes the leaves . . . . iv 1 50
And see their blood, or die with this reproach . . . . . iv 1 94
To see so great a lord Basely insinuate and send us gifts . . . iv 2 37
O, tell me, did you see Aaron the Moor? . . . . . . iv 2 52
Hark ye, lords; ye see I have given her physic . . . . . iv 2 162
This done, see that you take no longer days . . . . . iv 2 165
I see thou wilt not trust the air With secrets . . . . . iv 2 169
Let me see your archery; Look ye draw home enough . . . . iv 3 2
Is not this a heavy case, To see thy noble uncle thus distract? . . iv 3 26
I'll be at hand, sir; see you do it bravely . . . . . . iv 3 113
Sirrah, hast thou a knife? come, let me see it . . . . . iv 3 115
First hang the child, that he may see it sprawl . . . . . v 1 51
Thy child shall live, and I will see it nourish'd . . . . . v 1 60
What I mean to do See here in bloody lines I have set down . . . v 2 14
I'll play the cook, And see them ready 'gainst their mother comes . v 2 206
And see the ambush of our friends be strong . . . . . v 3 9
Some stay to see him fasten'd in the earth . . . . . . v 3 183
See justice done on Aaron, that damn'd Moor . . . . . v 3 201
From the city's side, So early walking did I see your son *Rom. and Jul.* i 1 130
Alas, that love, whose view is muffled still, Should, without eyes, see pathways to his will! . . . . i 1 178
Hear all, all see, And like her most whose merit most shall be . . i 2 30
But, I pray, can you read any thing you see?—Ay, if I know the letters i 2 63

See. Pretty fool, To see it tetchy and fall out with the dug! *Rom. and Jul.* i 3 32
To see, now, how a jest shall come about! . . . . . . i 3 45
An I might live to see thee married once, I have my wish . . . i 3 61
Examine every married lineament And see how one another lends content i 3 84
O, then, I see Queen Mab hath been with you. She is the fairies' midwife . . . . i 4 53
See, how she leans her cheek upon her hand! O, that I were a glove! . ii 2 23
If they do see thee, they will murder thee . . . . . ii 2 70
I dare draw as soon as another man, if I see occasion in a good quarrel . ii 4 168
She, good soul, had as lief see a toad, a very toad, as see him . . ii 4 215
Can you not stay awhile? Do you not see that I am out of breath? . ii 5 30
Villain am I none; Therefore farewell; I see thou know'st me not . iii 1 68
Lovers can see to do their amorous rites By their own beauties . . iii 2 8
Honest gentleman! That ever I should live to see thee dead! . . iii 2 63
O, then I see that madmen have no ears . . . . . . iii 3 61
Methinks I see thee, now thou art below, As one dead in the bottom of a tomb . . . . iii 5 55
Tell him so yourself, And see how he will take it at your hands . . iii 5 126
This only child; But now I see this one is one too much . . . iii 5 167
Is there no pity sitting in the clouds, That sees into the bottom of my grief? . . . . iii 5 199
O, look! methinks I see my cousin's ghost Seeking out Romeo . . iv 3 55
She's dead, she's dead!—Ha! let me see her: out, alas! she's cold . iv 5 25
Have I thought long to see this morning's face? . . . . . iv 5 41
Let's see for means . . . . v 1 35
Come hither, man. I see that thou art poor: Hold, there is forty ducats v 1 58
Early in the morning See thou deliver it to my lord and father . . v 3 24
Poison, I see, hath been his timeless end . . . . . . v 3 162
We see the ground whereon these woes do lie . . . . . v 3 179
Thou art early up, To see thy son and heir more early down . . . v 3 209
What further woe conspires against mine age?—Look, and thou shalt see v 3 213
See, what a scourge is laid upon your hate . . . . . v 3 292
I have a jewel here— O, pray, let's see't . . *T. of Athens* i 1 13
Let's see your piece.—'Tis a good piece.—So 'tis . . . . i 1 28
You see this confluence, this great flood of visitors . . . . i 1 42
To see meat fill knaves and wine heat fools . . . . . i 1 271
O you gods, what a number of men eat Timon, and he sees 'em not! . i 2 40
It grieves me to see so many dip their meat in one man's blood . . i 2 41
You see, my lord, how ample you're beloved . . . . . i 2 136
See them well entertain'd . . . . ii 2 45
Would we could see you at Corinth! . . . . ii 2 72
Now I see thou art a fool, and fit for thy master . . . . iii 1 52
See, by good hap, yonder's my lord; I have sweat to see his honour . iii 2 28
O, see the monstrousness of man When he looks out in an ungrateful shape! . . . . iii 2 79
I see no sense for't, But his occasions might have woo'd me first . iii 3 14
Push! did you see my cap?—I have lost my gown . . . . iii 6 119
Yet do our hearts wear Timon's livery; That see I by our faces . . iv 2 18
Thou saw'st them, when I had prosperity.—I see them now . . . iv 3 78
I'll visit thee again.—If I hope well, I'll never see thee more . . iv 3 171
When I know not what else to do, I'll see thee again . . . . iv 3 359
Choler does kill me that thou art alive; I swound to see thee . . iv 3 373
Let us first see peace in Athens . . . . iv 3 461
Ne'er see thou man, and let me ne'er see thee . . . . . iv 3 543
You shall see him a palm in Athens again, and flourish with the highest v 1 12
Have I once lived to see two honest men? . . . . . . v 1 59
Let it [ingratitude] go naked, men may see't the better . . . . v 1 70
You hear him cog, see him dissemble, Know his gross patchery . . v 1 98
We make holiday, to see Cæsar and to rejoice in his triumph *J. Cæsar* i 1 35
To see great Pompey pass the streets of Rome . . . . . i 1 47
See, whether their basest metal be not moved . . . . . i 1 66
Set him before me; let me see his face.—Fellow, come from the throng i 2 20
Will you go see the order of the course?—Not I.—I pray you, do . . i 2 25
Tell me, good Brutus, can you see your face?—No, Cassius; for the eye sees not itself, But by reflection . . . . i 2 51
Turn Your hidden worthiness into your eye, That you might see your shadow . . . . i 2 58
And since you know you cannot see yourself So well as by reflection, I, your glass, Will modestly discover to yourself . . . . . i 2 67
I see, Thy honourable metal may be wrought From that it is disposed . i 2 312
Cast yourself in wonder, To see the strange impatience of the heavens . i 3 61
I know he would not be a wolf, But that he sees the Romans are but sheep . . . . i 3 105
Come, Casca, you and I will yet ere day See Brutus at his house . . i 3 154
Brutus, thou sleep'st: awake, and see thyself . . . . . ii 1 46
'Tis your brother Cassius at the door, Who doth desire to see you . ii 1 71
The things that threaten'd me Ne'er look'd but on my back; when they shall see The face of Cæsar, they are vanished . . . . . ii 2 11
I go to take my stand, To see him pass on to the Capitol . . . ii 4 26
You see we do, yet see you but our hands And this the bleeding business they have done: Our hearts you see not . . . . . . iii 1 167
To see thy Antony making his peace, Shaking the bloody fingers of thy foes iii 1 197
Thy heart is big, get thee apart and weep. Passion, I see, is catching . iii 1 283
You all did see that on the Lupercal I thrice presented him a kingly crown iii 2 100
See what a rent the envious Casca made . . . . . . iii 2 179
I do not like your faults.—A friendly eye could never see such faults . iv 3 90
Let me go in to see the generals; There is some grudge between 'em . iv 3 124
Why comest thou?—To tell thee thou shalt see me at Philippi.—Well; then I shall see thee again?—Ay, at Philippi.—Why, I will see thee at Philippi, then . . . . iv 3 284
I do not know that I did cry.—Yes, that thou didst: didst thou see any thing? . . . . iv 3 298
Behold no more. O, coward that I am, to live so long, To see my best friend ta'en before my face! . . . . v 3 35
Brutus, come apace, And see how I regarded Caius Cassius . . . v 3 88
I owe more tears To this dead man than you shall see me pay . . v 3 102
Go on, And see whether Brutus be alive or dead; And bring us word . v 4 30
With his former title greet Macbeth.—I'll see it done . . *Macbeth* i 2 66
Stars, hide your fires; Let not light see my black and deep desires . i 4 51
Yet let that be, Which the eye fears, when it is done, to see . . i 4 53
That my keen knife see not the wound it makes . . . . . i 5 53
O, never Shall sun that morrow see! . . . . i 5 62
Is this a dagger which I see before me, The handle toward my hand? Come, let me clutch thee. I have thee not, and yet I see thee still ii 1 33
I see thee yet, in form as palpable As this which now I draw . . ii 1 40
I see thee still, And on thy blade and dudgeon gouts of blood . . ii 1 45
Do not bid me speak; See, and then speak yourselves . . . . ii 3 78
Up, up, and see The great doom's image! . . . . . . ii 3 82
How goes the world, sir, now?—Why, see you not? . . . . ii 4 21

See. Well, may you see things well done there: adieu! . . . *Macbeth* ii 4 37
Prithee, see there! behold! look! lo! how say you? . . . ii 4 69
Call 'em; let me see 'em . . . . iv 1 63
Another yet! A seventh! I'll see no more: And yet the eighth appears iv 1 118
And some I see That two-fold balls and treble sceptres carry . . iv 1 120
Horrible sight! Now, I see, 'tis true . . . . . iv 1 122
When shalt thou see thy wholesome days again? . . . . iv 3 105
You see, her eyes are open.—Ay, but their sense is shut . . v 1 28
Within this three mile may you see it coming . . . . v 5 37
Whiles I see lives, the gashes Do better upon them . . . v 8 2
Painted upon a pole, and underwrit, 'Here may you see the tyrant' . v 8 27
Yet, by these I see, So great a day as this is cheaply bought . . v 8 36
Thanks to all at once and to each one, Whom we invite to see us crown'd v 8 75
My lord, I came to see your father's funeral.— . . . I think it was to see my mother's wedding . . . . . *Hamlet* i 2 176
Methinks I see my father.—Where, my lord?—In my mind's eye, Horatio i 2 184
And these few precepts in thy memory See thou character . . i 3 59
See you now; Your bait of falsehood takes this carp of truth . ii 1 62
Moreover that we much did long to see you, The need we have to use you did provoke Our hasty sending . . . . . ii 2 2
That great baby you see there is not yet out of his swaddling-clouts . ii 2 401
We'll e'en to't like French falconers, fly at any thing we see . . ii 2 450
As we often see, against some storm, A silence in the heavens . ii 2 505
But if the gods themselves did see her then When she saw Pyrrhus . ii 2 535
Good my lord, will you see the players well bestowed? . . . ii 2 546
He beseech'd me to entreat your majesties To hear and see the matter . iii 1 23
Now see that noble and most sovereign reason, Like sweet bells jangled iii 1 165
O, woe is me, To have seen what I have seen, see what I see! . iii 1 169
You shall see anon; 'tis a knavish piece of work . . . iii 2 250
I could interpret between you and your love, if I could see the puppets dallying.—You are keen, my lord . . . . iii 2 257
You shall see anon how the murderer gets the love of Gonzago's wife . iii 2 274
O, the recorders! let me see one. To withdraw with you . . iii 2 360
Do you see yonder cloud that's almost in shape of a camel? . . iii 2 393
You go not till I set you up a glass Where you may see the inmost part of you . . . . iii 4 20
See, what a grace was seated on this brow; Hyperion's curls . . iii 4 55
There I see such black and grained spots As will not leave their tinct . iii 4 90
Do you see nothing there?—Nothing at all; yet all that is I see . iii 4 132
Where is Polonius?—In heaven; send thither to see . . . iv 3 35
If thou knew'st our purposes.—I see a cherub that sees them . . iv 3 50
While, to my shame, I see The imminent death of twenty thousand men iv 4 59
God be wi' ye.—Do you see this, O God? . . . . . iv 5 201
To-morrow shall I beg leave to see your kingly eyes . . . iv 7 45
I see, in passages of proof, Time qualifies the spark and fire of it [love] iv 7 113
Here's fine revolution, an we had the trick to see't . . . v 1 99
Yorick's skull, the king's jester.—This?—E'en that.—Let me see . v 1 202
An hour of quiet shortly shall we see; Till then, in patience our proceeding be . . . . v 1 321
So much for this, sir: now shall you see the other . . . v 2 1
By the image of my cause, I see the portraiture of his . . . v 2 77
You shall find in him the continent of what part a gentleman would see v 2 116
This is too heavy, let me see another.—This likes me well . . v 2 275
How does the queen?—She swounds to see them bleed . . . v 2 319
Where is this sight?—What is it ye would see? . . . . v 2 373
Out of my sight!—See better, Lear; and let me still remain The true blank of thine eye . . . . *Lear* i 1 160
We Have no such daughter, nor shall ever see That face of hers again . i 1 266
You see how full of changes his age is . . . . . . i 1 291
I see the business . . . . i 2 198
Shalt see thy other daughter will use thee kindly . . . . i 5 14
And received This hurt you see, striving to apprehend him . . ii 1 110
I have seen better faces in my time Than stands on any shoulder that I see . . . . ii 2 100
Nothing almost sees miracles But misery . . . . . . ii 2 172
But fathers that bear bags Shall see their children kind . . . ii 4 51
I am glad to see your highness—Regan, I think you are . . . ii 4 130
Farewell: We'll no more meet, no more see one another . . . ii 4 223
You see me here, you gods, a poor old man, As full of grief as age . ii 4 275
If you shall see Cordelia,—As fear not but you shall,—show her this ring iii 1 46
Then comes the time, who lives to see't, That going shall be used with feet . . . . iii 2 93
He's a mad yeoman that sees his son a gentleman before him . . iii 6 14
Will you lie down and rest upon the cushions?—I'll see their trial first iii 6 37
Let them anatomize Regan; see what breeds about her heart . . iii 6 80
When we our betters see bearing our woes, We scarcely think our miseries our foes . . . . iii 6 109
I would not see thy cruel nails Pluck out his poor old eyes . . iii 7 56
I shall see The winged vengeance overtake such children.—See't shalt thou never. Fellows, hold the chair. Upon these eyes of thine I'll set my foot . . . . iii 7 65
You have one eye left To see some mischief on him. O!—Lest it see more, prevent it. Out, vile jelly! . . . . iii 7 82
You cannot see your way.—I have no way, and therefore want no eyes . iv 1 19
Might I but live to see thee in my touch, I'ld say I had eyes again! . iv 1 25
That will not see Because he doth not feel . . . . . iv 1 71
See thyself, devil! Proper deformity seems not in the fiend So horrid as in woman . . . . iv 2 59
And by no means Will yield to see his daughter . . . . iv 3 43
Soon may I hear and see him! . . . . iv 4 29
When I do stare, see how the subject quakes . . . . . iv 6 110
Were all the letters suns, I could not see one . . . . . iv 6 143
You see how this world goes.—I see it feelingly . . . . iv 6 151
A man may see how this world goes with no eyes. Look with thine ears iv 6 153
See how yond justice rails upon yond simple thief . . . . iv 6 155
Get thee glass eyes; And, like a scurvy politician, seem To see the things thou dost not . . . . iv 6 176
Let's see these pockets: the letters that he speaks of May be my friends iv 6 261
I should e'en die with pity, To see another thus . . . . iv 7 54
Be comforted, good madam: the great rage, You see, is kill'd in him . iv 7 79
The battle done, and they within our power, Shall never see his pardon v 1 68
Shall we not see these daughters and these sisters? . . . . v 3 7
We'll see 'em starve first . . . . v 3 25
I am the very man,— I'll see that straight . . . . . v 3 287
O, see, see!—And my poor fool is hang'd! No, no, no life! . . v 3 304
Do you see this? Look on her, look, her lips, Look there, look there! v 3 310
We that are young Shall never see so much, nor live so long . . v 3 326
Where didst thou see her? O unhappy girl! With the Moor? . *Othello* i 1 164
Fathers, from hence trust not your daughters' minds By what you see them act . . . . i 1 172

See. I did not see you; welcome, gentle signior; We lack'd your counsel *Othello* i 3 50
Look to her, Moor, if thou hast eyes to see: She has deceived her father i 3 293
It was a violent commencement, and thou shalt see an answerable sequestration . . . . i 3 351
Let's to the seaside, ho! As well to see the vessel that's come in. . ii 1 37
See for the news . . . . ii 1 96
See suitors following and not look behind . . . . . ii 1 158
It gives me wonder great as my content To see you here before me . ii 1 186
Didst thou not see her paddle with the palm of his hand? . . . ii 1 259
You see this fellow that is gone before; He is a soldier fit to stand by Cæsar And give direction: and do but see his vice . . . ii 3 126
It were well The general were put in mind of it. Perhaps he sees it not ii 3 138
This fortification, gentlemen, shall we see't?—We'll wait upon your lordship . . . . iii 2 5
I'll see before I doubt; when I doubt, prove . . . . . iii 3 190
They do let heaven see the pranks They dare not show their husbands . iii 3 202
I see this hath a little dash'd your spirits.—Not a jot, not a jot . iii 3 214
What is spoke Comes from my love. But I do see you're moved . . iii 3 217
Whereto we see in all things nature tends . . . . . iii 3 231
Doubtless Sees and knows more, much more, than he unfolds . . iii 3 243
Make me to see't; or, at the least, so prove it, That the probation bear no hinge nor loop To hang a doubt on . . . . . . iii 3 364
I see, sir, you are eaten up with passion: I do repent me . . iii 3 391
Damn them then, If ever mortal eyes do see them bolster! . . . iii 3 399
Where's satisfaction? It is impossible you should see this . . . iii 3 402
Nay, but be wise: yet we see nothing done; She may be honest yet . iii 3 432
Such a handkerchief . . . did I to-day See Cassio wipe his beard with . iii 3 439
Now do I see 'tis true . . . . iii 3 444
Fetch't, let me see't.—Why, so I can, sir, but I will not now . . iii 4 85
And think it no addition, nor my wish, To have him see me woman'd . iii 4 195
Bring me on the way a little, And say if I shall see you soon at night iii 4 198
I'll see you soon.—'Tis very good; I must be circumstanced . . iii 4 200
O, I see that nose of yours, but not that dog I shall throw it to . iv 1 146
Well, I may chance to see you; for I would very fain speak with you . iv 1 174
And did you see the handkerchief?—Was that mine? . . . . iv 1 183
And to see how he prizes the foolish woman your wife! . . . iv 1 185
I am glad to see you mad.—Why, sweet Othello,— Devil! . . . iv 1 250
What is your pleasure?—Let me see your eyes; Look in my face . . iv 2 25
Why, now I see there's mettle in thee . . . . . . iv 2 207
Let husbands know Their wives have sense like them: they see and smell . . . . iv 3 95
Look upon her: Do you see, gentlemen? nay, guiltiness will speak . v 1 109
Kind gentlemen, let's go see poor Cassio dress'd . . . . v 1 124
Be not afraid, though you do see me weapon'd. . . . . . v 2 266
You shall see in him The triple pillar of the world transform'd Into a strumpet's fool: behold and see. . . . . *Ant. and Cleo.* i 1 11
It is a heart-breaking to see a handsome man loose-wived . . . i 2 74
We kill all our women: we see how mortal an unkindness is to them . i 2 138
Where is he?—I did not see him since.—See where he is . . . i 3 1
See when and where she died . . . . i 3 62
Now I see, I see, In Fulvia's death, how mine received shall be . . i 3 64
You may see, Lepidus, and henceforth know, It is not Cæsar's natural vice . . . . i 4 1
O'er-picturing that Venus where we see The fancy outwork nature . ii 2 205
Your reason?—I see it in My motion, have it not in my tongue . . ii 3 13
We'll follow.—Till I shall see you in your soldier's dress . . . ii 4 4
You see we have burnt our cheeks: strong Enobarb Is weaker than the wine . . . . ii 7 129
To see't mine eyes are blasted . . . . iii 10 4
I'll see you by and by . . . . iii 11 24
See you here, sir?—O fie, fie, fie! . . . . iii 11 30
See, How I convey my shame out of thine eyes . . . . . iii 11 51
I see men's judgements are A parcel of their fortunes . . . iii 13 31
Whip him, fellows, Till, like a boy, you see him cringe his face . iii 13 100
And I see still, A diminution in our captain's brain Restores his heart . iii 13 197
See it done: And feast the army; we have store to do't . . . iv 1 14
Haply you shall not see me more; or if, A mangled shadow . . iv 2 26
Let's see if other watchmen Do hear what we do . . . . iv 3 18
Follow the noise so far as we have quarter; Let's see how it will give off iv 3 23
That thou couldst see my wars to-day, and knew'st The royal occupation! thou shouldst see A workman in't . . . . . . iv 4 16
To-morrow, Before the sun shall see's, we'll spill the blood . . iv 8 3
O sun, thy uprise shall I see no more: Fortune and Antony part here . iv 12 18
Sometime we see a cloud that's dragonish; A vapour sometime like a bear . . . . iv 14 2
When I should see behind me The inevitable prosecution of Disgrace . iv 14 64
Wouldst thou be window'd in great Rome and see Thy master thus? . iv 14 72
I would not see't.—Come, then; for with a wound I must be cured . iv 14 77
O, see, my women, The crown o' the earth doth melt . . . iv 15 62
When such a spacious mirror's set before him, He needs must see himself v 1 35
To my tent; where you shall see How hardly I was drawn into this war v 1 73
Go with me, and see What I can show in this . . . . . v 1 76
You see how easily she may be surprised . . . . . . v 2 35
Let the world see His nobleness well acted . . . . . v 2 44
O, such another sleep, that I might see But such another man! . . v 2 77
See, Cæsar! O, behold, How pomp is follow'd! mine will now be yours v 2 150
And I shall see Some squeaking Cleopatra boy my greatness . . v 2 219
I'll never see't; for, I am sure, my nails Are stronger than mine eyes . v 2 223
I see him rouse himself To praise my noble act . . . . v 2 287
Dost thou not see my baby at my breast, That sucks the nurse asleep? . v 2 312
Thyself art coming To see perform'd the dreaded act . . . . v 2 335
The manner of their deaths? I do not see them bleed . . . v 2 341
Come, Dolabella, see High order in this great solemnity . . . v 2 368
But that there is this jewel in the world That I may see again *Cymbeline* i 1 92
O the gods! When shall we see again? . . . . . . i 1 124
You shall at least Go see my lord aboard: for this time leave me . i 1 178
I see you have some religion in you, that you fear . . . . i 4 148
Hath nature given them eyes To see this vaulted arch? . . . i 6 33
I cross'd the seas on purpose and on promise To see your grace . . i 6 203
I'll go see this Italian: what I have lost to-day at bowls I'll win tonight of him . . . . ii 1 53
The flame o' the taper Bows toward her, and would under-peep her lids, To see the enclosed lights . . . . ii 2 21
I see her yet; Her pretty action did outsell her gift . . . ii 4 101
True Pisanio,—Who long'st, like me, to see thy lord . . . iii 2 55
I see before me, man: nor here, nor here, Nor what ensues, but have a fog in them . . . . iii 2 80
To apprehend thus, Draws us a profit from all things we see . . iii 3 18
Ne'er long'd my mother so To see me first, as I have now . . iii 4 3

See. I see into thy end, and am almost A man already . . *Cymbeline* iii 4 169
This paper is the history of my knowledge Touching her flight.—
Let's see't . . . . iii 5 100
There shall she see my valour, which will then be a torment . . iii 5 143
I see a man's life is a tedious one . . . . . iii 6 1
I see you're angry . . . . iii 6 56
Great griefs, I see, medicine the less . . . . . iv 2 243
Let's see the boy's face.—He's alive, my lord . . . . iv 2 359
Cloten then but young, you see, not wore him From my remembrance . iv 4 23
What thing is it that I never Did see man die! . . . . iv 4 36
That a man should have the best use of eyes to see the way of blindness! v 4 197
I see a thing Bitter to me as death . . . . . v 5 103
See further; he eyes us not; forbear . . . . . v 5 124
But we saw him dead.—Be silent; let's see further . . . v 5 127
Whereupon—Methinks, I see him now— Ay, so thou dost . . v 5 209
You are my father too, and did relieve me, To see this gracious season . v 5 401
See where she comes, apparell'd like the spring . . *Pericles* i 1 12
I'll make my will then, and, as sick men do Who know the world, see heaven . . . . i 1 48
The breath is gone, and the sore eyes see clear To stop the air would hurt them . . . . i 1 99
For wisdom sees, those men Blush not in actions blacker than the night i 1 134
Now do I see he had some reason for't . . . . . i 3 7
By relating tales of others' griefs, See if 'twill teach us to forget our own i 4 3
But see what heaven can do! . . . . i 4 33
Those which see them fall Have scarce strength left to give them burial i 4 48
When I am dead, For that I am a man, pray see me buried . . ii 1 81
An armour, friends! I pray you, let me see it . . . . ii 1 126
A courser, whose delightful steps Shall make the gazer joy to see him tread . . . . ii 1 165
Like beauty's child, whom nature gat For men to see, and seeing wonder at . . . . ii 2 7
Whereby I see that Time's the king of men . . . . . ii 3 45
It pleaseth me so well, that I will see you wed . . . . ii 5 92
See how she gins to blow Into life's flower again! . . . . iii 2 95
My wedded lord I ne'er shall see again, A vestal livery will I take me to iii 4 9
But I'll see further . . . . iv 1 100
I have gone through for this piece, you see . . . . . iv 2 48
He made a groan at it, and swore he would see her to-morrow . . iv 2 118
To see his daughter, all his life's delight . . . . . iv 4 12
Like motes and shadows see them move awhile . . . . iv 4 21
See how belief may suffer by foul show! . . . . . iv 4 23
I am glad to see your honour in good health . . . . iv 6 24
For flesh and blood, sir, white and red, you shall see a rose . . iv 6 38
My authority shall not see thee, or else look friendly upon thee . iv 6 96
Well, I will see what I can do for thee: if I can place thee, I will . iv 6 203
May we not see him?—You may; But bootless is your sight: he will not speak . . . . v 1 31
I will recount it to you: But, see, I am prevented . . . . v 1 64
Who, hearing of your melancholy state, Did come to see you . . v 1 223
At Ephesus, the temple see, Our king and all his company . . v 2 282
May we see them?—Great sir, they shall be brought you to my house . v 3 25
As you see *Mer. Wives* v 1; *J. Cæsar* i 3; iii 2; *Cymbeline* iv 2
For aught I see *Mer. of Venice* i 2; *T. of Shrew* i 2; 1 *Hen. VI.* i 4
I am glad to see you *Mer. Wives* i 1; 2 *Hen. IV.* iii 2; *Othello* v 1
I am glad to see you (thee) well 2 *Hen. IV.* iii 2; *Hamlet* i 2; ii 2
I am very glad to see you *As Y. Like It* iii 3; *Hamlet* i 2; *Othello* iv 1
I see no reason *T. of Shrew* ii 1; 1 *Hen. IV.* i 2; 2 *Hen. IV.* iii 2; 1 *Hen. VI.* iv 1; 2 *Hen. VI.* ii 3
Let me see. (Repeated through the plays)
Let's see *L. L. Lost* v 2; *T. of Shrew* iv 3; *Richard II.* iv 1; *T. Andron.* iv 2; *Lear* i 2; iv 6; iv 7; *Othello* i 3

Seed. They shall stand for seed . . . *Meas. for Meas.* i 2 102
Glean'd from the true seed of honour . . *Mer. of Venice* ii 9 47
And choice breeds A native slip to us from foreign seeds . *All's Well* i 3 152
Let nature crush the sides o' the earth together And mar the seeds within! . . . . *W. Tale* iv 4 490
Which in their seeds And weak beginnings lie intreasured 2 *Hen. IV.* iii 1 84
Would of that seed grow to a greater falseness . . . . . iii 1 90
Saw his heroical seed, and smiled to see him . . . *Hen. V.* ii 4 59
A cousin-german to great Priam's seed . . . *Troi. and Cres.* iv 5 121
Green earthen pots, bladders and musty seeds . . *Rom. and Jul.* v 1 46
If you can look into the seeds of time, And say which grain will grow and which will not . . . . *Macbeth* i 3 58
The seed of Banquo kings! Rather than so, come fate into the list! . iii 1 70
'Tis an unweeded garden, That grows to seed . . . *Hamlet* i 2 136
She that sets seeds and roots of shame and iniquity . *Pericles* iv 6 93

Seeded. The seeded pride That hath to this maturity blown up
Troi. and Cres. i 3 316

Seedness. As blossoming time That from the seedness the bare fallow brings To teeming foison . . . . . *Meas. for Meas.* i 4 42

Seedsman. The seedsman Upon the slime and ooze scatters his grain, And shortly comes to harvest . . . . *Ant. and Cleo.* ii 7 24

Seeing you are beautified With goodly shape . . *T. G. of Ver.* iv 1 55
Master Slender sent to her, seeing her go thorough the streets *M. Wives* iv 5 32
I do much wonder that one man, seeing how much another man is a fool when he dedicates his behaviours to love . . . *Much Ado* ii 3 8
It [love] adds a precious seeing to the eye . . . *L. L. Lost* iv 3 333
When we greet, With eyes best seeing, heaven's fiery eye, By light we lose light . . . . v 2 375
Dark night . . . ; Wherein it doth impair the seeing sense, It pays the hearing double recompense . . . . *M. N. Dream* iii 2 179
But suddenly, Seeing Orlando, it unlink'd itself . *As Y. Like It* iv 3 112
Is't possible . . . that but seeing you should love her? and loving woo? v 2 2
Seeing too much sadness hath congeal'd your blood . *T. of Shrew* Ind. 2 134
And I seeing this came thence for very shame . . . . iii 2 182
That lack'd sight only, nought for approbation But only seeing *W. Tale* ii 1 178
The wisest beholder, that knew no more but seeing, could not say . v 2 19
Now He that made me knows I see thee ill; Ill in myself to see, and in thee seeing ill . . . . *Richard II.* ii 1 94
Seeing thou fall'st on me so luckily, I will assay thee . 1 *Hen. IV.* v 4 33
The appearance of a naked blind boy in her naked seeing self *Hen. V.* v 2 325
Not seeing what is likely to ensue . . . . 1 *Hen. VI.* iii 1 188
My heart accordeth with my tongue, Seeing the deed is meritorious
2 *Hen. VI.* iii 1 270
For seeing him I see my life in death . . . . . iii 2 152
Seeing gentle words will not prevail, Assail them with the army . iv 2 184
Seeing ignorance is the curse of God, Knowledge the wing wherewith we fly to heaven . . . . iv 7 78
Seeing thou hast proved so unnatural a father . . . 3 *Hen. VI.* i 1 218

Seeing. Thou preferr'st thy life before thine honour: And seeing thou dost, I here divorce myself Both from thy table, Henry, and thy bed
3 *Hen. VI.* i 1 247
Seeing 'twas he that made you to depose, Your oath, my lord, is vain i 2 26
How was it?—Well worth the seeing . . . *Hen. VIII.* iv 1 61
You must be seeing christenings? do you look for ale and cakes here? v 4 10
Blind fear, that seeing reason leads, finds safer footing than blind reason stumbling without fear . . . . *Troi. and Cres.* iii 2 76
In first seeing he had proved himself a man . . . *Coriolanus* i 3 18
Why either were you ignorant to see't, Or, seeing it, of such childish friendliness To yield your voices? . . . . . . ii 3 183
Not yet thou knowest me, and, seeing me, dost not Think me for the man I am . . . . iv 5 61
And weep ye now, seeing she is advanced Above the clouds? . *R. and J.* iv 5 73
You love your child so ill, That you run mad, seeing that she is well . iv 5 76
Seeing his reputation touch'd to death, He did oppose his foe *T. of A.* iii 5 19
Seeing that death, a necessary end, Will come when it will come *J. Cæsar* ii 2 36
Mine eyes, Seeing those beads of sorrow stand in thine, Began to water iii 1 284
That you, at such times seeing me, never shall, With arms encumber'd thus, or this head-shake . . . . *Hamlet* i 5 173
Confederate season, else no creature seeing . . . . iii 2 267
Seeing how loathly opposite I stood To his unnatural purpose . *Lear* ii 1 51
When remedies are past, the griefs are ended By seeing the worst . *Othello* i 3 203
I cannot think it, That he would steal away so guilty-like, Seeing you coming . . . . iii 3 40
Seeing these effects will be Both noisome and infectious . . *Cymbeline* i 5 25
Whom nature gat For men to see, and seeing wonder at . . *Pericles* ii 2 7
Seeing this goodly vessel ride before us, I made to it . . . v 1 18
If he be none of mine, my sanctity Will to my sense bend no licentious ear, But curb it, spite of seeing . . . . v 3 31

Seek. Till thou didst seek to violate The honour of my child . *Tempest* i 2 347
Go safely on to seek thy son . . . . ii 1 327
All the more it seeks to hide itself, The bigger bulk it shows . . iii 1 80
I'll seek him deeper than e'er plummet sounded . . . . iii 3 101
I'll be wise hereafter And seek for grace . . . . . v 1 295
The shepherd seeks the sheep, and not the sheep the shepherd *T. G. of V.* i 1 88
I seek my master, and my master seeks not me: therefore I am no sheep i 1 89
Other men, of slender reputation, Put forth their sons to seek preferment out . . . . i 3 7
And, being blind, How could he see his way to seek out you? . . ii 4 94
As soon go kindle fire with snow As seek to quench the fire of love with words.—I do not seek to quench your love's hot fire . . . ii 7 20
Run, boy, run, run, and seek him out . . . . . iii 1 188
Gone to seek his dog . . . . iv 2 78
Trudge, plod away o' the hoof; seek shelter, pack! . . *Mer. Wives* i 3 91
I will seek out Falstaff . . . . ii 1 144
Search, seek, find out: I'll warrant we'll unkennel the fox . . iii 3 173
I seek to heal it only by his wealth . . . . . . iii 4 6
Yet seek my father's love; still seek it, sir . . . . . iii 4 19
I seek you a better husband . . . . iii 4 88
Creep into the kiln-hole.—Where is it?—He will seek there, on my word iv 2 61
He's not here I seek for.—No, nor nowhere else but in your brain . iv 2 165
If I find not what I seek, show no colour for my extremity . . iv 2 168
Doth he so seek his life? . . . . . *Meas. for Meas.* i 4 72
To sue to live, I find I seek to die; And, seeking death, find life . iii 1 42
You bid me seek redemption of the devil: Hear me yourself . . v 1 29
But, O, poor souls, Come you to seek the lamb here of the fox? . v 1 300
Forced me to seek delays for them and me . . *Com. of Errors* i 1 75
I'll limit thee this day To seek thy life by beneficial help . . i 1 152
I to the world am like a drop of water That in the ocean seeks another drop . . . . i 2 36
Go seek this slave: I greatly fear my money is not safe . . . i 2 104
Nor the slave return'd, That in such haste I sent to seek his master! . ii 1 2
Is wander'd forth, in care to seek me out By computation . . . ii 2 3
I must get a sconce for my head and insconce it too; or else I shall seek my wit in my shoulders . . . . ii 2 38
He not coming thither, I went to seek him . . . . . v 1 225
Look; Don Pedro is returned to seek you . . . *Much Ado* i 1 205
Let me be that I am and seek not to alter me . . . . i 3 39
I have brought Count Claudio, whom you sent me to seek . . . ii 1 197
See, see; here comes the man we went to seek . . . . v 1 110
I came to seek you both.—We have been up and down to seek thee . v 1 121
As, painfully to pore upon a book To seek the light of truth . *L. L. Lost* i 1 75
Than seek a dispensation for his oath, To let you enter . . . ii 1 87
What, I! I love! I sue! I seek a wife! . . . . . iii 1 191
As I for praise alone now seek to spill The poor deer's blood . . iv 1 34
Where nothing wants that want itself doth seek . . . . iv 3 237
How I would make him fawn and beg and seek And wait the season! . v 2 62
Our states are forfeit: seek not to undo us . . . . . v 2 425
Never rest, But seek the weary beds of people sick . . . v 2 832
Turn away our eyes, To seek new friends . . . *M. N. Dream* i 1 219
I must go seek some dewdrops here And hang a pearl in every cowslip's ear . . . . ii 1 14
Ere he do leave this grove, Thou shalt fly him and he shall seek thy love ii 1 246
Seek through this grove: A sweet Athenian lady is in love . . ii 1 259
These lovers seek a place to fight: Hie therefore, Robin, overcast the night . . . . iii 2 354
I have a venturous fairy that shall seek The squirrel's hoard . . iv 1 39
You shall seek all day ere you find them, and when you have them, they are not worth the search . . . . *Mer. of Venice* i 1 116
The four strangers seek for you, madam, to take their leave . . i 2 135
I have sent twenty out to seek for you.—I am glad on't . . . ii 6 66
We have been up and down to seek him . . . . . iii 1 79
Since this fortune falls to you, Be content and seek no new . . iii 2 135
He seeks my life; his reason well I know . . . . . iii 3 21
You may as well do any thing most hard, As seek to soften that—than which what's harder?—His Jewish heart . . . . iv 1 79
If it be proved against an alien That by direct or indirect attempts He seek the life of any citizen . . . . iv 1 351
Shall we part, sweet girl? No: let my father seek another heir
As Y. Like It i 3 101
Do not seek to take your change upon you, To bear your griefs yourself i 3 104
Whither shall we go?—To seek my uncle in the forest of Arden . . i 3 109
At seventeen years many their fortunes seek . . . . . ii 3 73
And I'll go seek the duke: his banquet is prepared . . . . ii 5 64
Go, seek him: tell him I would speak with him . . . . ii 7 7
I should not seek an absent argument Of my revenge, thou present . iii 1 3
Seek him with candle; bring him dead or living Within this twelvemonth, or turn thou no more To seek a living in our territory . . iii 1 8
If a hart do lack a hind, Let him seek out Rosalind . . . iii 2 108

Seek. To excuse that?—Marry, to say she came to seek you there *As Y. Like It* iv 1 174
Our master and mistress seeks you; come, away, away! . . . v 1 64
And with satiety seeks to quench his thirst . . . *T. of Shrew* i 1 24
To seek their fortunes farther than at home . . . i 2 51
The gain I seek is, quiet in the match . . . ii 1 332
Seek for rule, supremacy and sway, When they are bound to serve v 2 163
That seeks not to find that her search implies . . . *All's Well* i 3 222
When The bravest questant shrinks, find what you seek . . . ii 1 16
Seek to eke out that Wherein toward me my homely stars have fail'd ii 5 79
Seek these suitors: Go speedily . . . v 3 151
He did seek the love of fair Olivia . . . *T. Night* i 2 34
Go thou and seek the crowner, and let him sit o' my coz . . . i 5 142
Seek him out, and play the tune the while . . . ii 4 14
I found this credit, That he did range the town to seek me out . . . iv 3 7
Though you would seek to unsphere the stars with oaths . . . *W. Tale* i 2 48
If you would seek us, We are yours i' the garden . . . i 2 177
Which if you seek to prove, I dare not stand by . . . i 2 443
Spare your threats: The bug which you would fright me with I seek . iii 2 93
I'll not seek far—For him, I partly know his mind . . . v 3 141
Is it sir Robert's son that you seek so?—Sir Robert's son! . *K. John* i 1 226
Or with taper-light To seek the beauteous eye of heaven to garnish . iv 2 15
Do not seek to stuff My head with more ill news, for it is full . iv 2 133
And others more, going to seek the grave Of Arthur . . . iv 2 164
Bring them before me.—I will seek them out.—Nay, but make haste . iv 2 169
Shall they seek the lion in his den, And fright him there? . . . v 1 57
I am not glad that such a sore of time Should seek a plaster . . . v 2 13
To seek sweet safety out In vaults and prisons . . . v 2 142
Seek out King John and fall before his feet . . . v 4 13
Straight let us seek, or straight we shall be sought . . . v 7 79
Let him not come there, To seek out sorrow that dwells every where *Richard II.* i 2 72
Since thou dost seek to kill my name in me, I mock my name . . . ii 1 86
Seek you to seize and gripe into your hands The royalties? . . . ii 1 189
We hear this fearful tempest sing, Yet seek no shelter to avoid the storm . . . ii 1 264
And I am come to seek that name in England . . . ii 3 71
He is walked up to the top of the hill: I'll go seek him . . 1 *Hen. IV.* ii 2 9
And in conclusion drove us to seek out This head of safety . . . iv 3 102
Thou crossest me? what honour dost thou seek Upon my head? . . . v 3 2
I have two boys Seek Percy and thyself about the field . . . v 4 32
I must go and meet with danger there, Or it will seek me in another place And find me worse provided . . . 2 *Hen. IV.* ii 3 49
Go, seek him out. Is he so hasty that he doth suppose My sleep my death? . . . iv 5 60
And with pale policy Seek to divert the English purposes *Hen. V.* ii Prol. 15
Touching our person seek we no revenge . . . ii 2 174
I must leave them, and seek some better service . . . iii 2 55
Tell thy king I do not seek him now . . . iii 6 149
We would not seek a battle, as we are . . . iii 6 173
That's more than we know.—Ay, or more than we should seek after . iv 1 136
Your nobles, jealous of your absence, Seek through your camp to find you iv 1 303
Pray thee, go seek him, and bring him to my tent . . . iv 7 175
That seeks to overthrow religion . . . 1 *Hen. VI.* i 3 65
How haps it I seek not to advance Or raise myself? . . . iii 1 31
Seek how we may prejudice the foe . . . iii 3 91
Henry is able to enrich his queen And not to seek a queen to make him rich . . . v 5 52
That's the golden mark I seek to hit . . . 2 *Hen. VI.* i 1 243
'Tis that they seek, and they in seeking that Shall find their deaths . ii 2 75
Nor never seek prevention of thy foes . . . ii 4 57
Do seek subversion of thy harmless life . . . iii 1 208
Seek not a scorpion's nest, Nor set no footing on this unkind shore . iii 2 86
Whom have I injured, that ye seek my death? . . . iv 7 107
I seek not to wax great by others' waning, Or gather wealth, I care not iv 10 22
What, wilt thou on thy death-bed play the ruffian, And seek for sorrow with thy spectacles? . . . v 1 165
Seek thee out some other chase, For I myself must hunt this deer . . . v 2 14
In cruelty will I seek out my fame . . . v 2 60
Offer him no violence, Unless he seek to thrust you out perforce 3 *Hen. VI.* i 1 34
They seek revenge and therefore will not yield . . . i 1 190
And neither by treason nor hostility To seek to put me down . . . i 1 200
Accursed be he that seeks to make them foes! . . . i 1 205
What resteth more, But that I seek occasion how to rise? . . . i 2 45
My soul flies through these wounds to seek out Thee . . . i 4 178
Why, therefore Warwick came to seek you out . . . ii 1 166
Is this the alliance that he seeks with France? . . . iii 3 177
Not that I pity Henry's misery, But seek revenge on Edward's mockery iii 3 265
And love thee too, Unless they seek for hatred at my hands . . . iv 1 80
I seek for thee, That Warwick's bones may keep thine company . . . v 2 3
Wise men ne'er sit and wail their loss, But cheerly seek how to redress v 4 2
Had I not reason, think ye, to make haste, And seek their ruin that usurp'd our right? . . . v 6 73
The envious flood Kept in my soul, and would not let it forth To seek the empty, vast and wandering air . . . *Richard III.* i 4 39
And never seek for aid out of himself . . . *Hen. VIII.* i 2 114
If he may Find mercy in the law, 'tis his; if none, Let him not seek't of us . . . i 2 213
If your business Seek me out, and that way I am wife in, Out with it boldly . . . iii 1 38
Seek the king; That sun, I pray, may never set! . . . iii 2 414
A wilder nature than the business That seeks dispatch by day . . . v 1 16
Would you were half so honest! Men's prayers then would seek you, not their fears . . . v 3 83
That seeks his praise more than he fears his peril *Troi. and Cres.* i 3 267
O, let not virtue seek Remuneration for the thing it was . . . iii 3 169
He merits well to have her, that doth seek her . . . iv 1 55
Half heart, half hand, half Hector comes to seek This blended knight . iv 5 85
Go seek thy fortune . . . v 6 19
Strike, fellows, strike; this is the man I seek . . . v 8 10
Till then I'll sweat and seek about for eases . . . v 10 56
Was pleased to let him seek danger where he was like to find fame *Cor.* i 3 14
He seeks their hate with greater devotion than they can render it him ii 2 20
I wish I had a cause to seek him there . . . iii 1 19
We shall not send O'er the vast world to seek a single man . . . iv 1 42
Rather to show a noble grace to both parts Than seek the end of one . v 3 122
Now will I hence to seek my lovely Moor . . . *T. Andron.* ii 3 190
Thou shalt not stir a foot to seek a foe . . . *Rom. and Jul.* i 1 87
Thus then in brief: The valiant Paris seeks you for his love . . . i 3 74

Seek. Go, girl, seek happy nights to happy days *Rom. and Jul.* i 3 106
'Tis in vain To seek him here that means not to be found . . . ii 1 42
Search, seek, and know how this foul murder comes . . . v 3 198
Earth, yield me roots! Who seeks for better of thee, sauce his palate With thy most operant poison! . . . *T. of Athens* iv 3 24
He whose pious breath seeks to convert you . . . iv 3 140
Be thou a flatterer now, and seek to thrive By that which has undone thee iv 3 210
Why dost thou seek me out?—To vex thee . . . iv 3 236
Seek not my name . . . v 4 71
You would have me seek into myself For that which is not in me *J. Cæsar* i 2 64
He's gone To seek you at your house . . . i 3 150
O, then by day Where wilt thou find a cavern dark enough To mask thy monstrous visage? Seek none, conspiracy . . . ii 1 81
You should be satisfied.—That's all I seek . . . iii 1 226
Revenge! About! Seek! Burn! Fire! Kill! Slay! . . . iii 2 208
Away, then! come, seek the conspirators . . . iii 2 237
'Tis better that the enemy seek us: So shall he waste his means . iv 3 199
I will seek for Pindarus the while . . . v 3 79
My plenteous joys . . . seek to hide themselves In drops of sorrow *Macb.* i 4 34
Seek to know no more.—I will be satisfied . . . iv 1 103
Let us seek out some desolate shade, and there Weep our sad bosoms empty . . . iv 3 1
Do not for ever with thy vailed lids Seek for thy noble father in the dust *Hamlet* i 2 71
Come, go with me: I will go seek the king . . . ii 1 101
You go to seek the Lord Hamlet; there he is . . . ii 2 224
With eyes like carbuncles, the hellish Pyrrhus Old grandsire Priam seeks ii 2 486
Go seek him out; speak fair, and bring the body Into the chapel . . iv 1 36
I have sent to seek him, and to find the body . . . iv 3 1
If your messenger find him not there, seek him i' the other place yourself iv 3 36
Go seek him there.—He will stay till you come . . . iv 3 40
Is she to be buried in Christian burial that wilfully seeks her own salvation? . . . v 1 2
They are sheep and calves which seek out assurance in that . . . v 1 125
Ho! let the door be lock'd: Treachery! Seek it out . . . v 2 323
Why so earnestly seek you to put up that letter? . . . *Lear* i 2 28
Seek him out; wind me into him, I pray you . . . i 2 106
I will seek him, sir, presently . . . i 2 109
Very pregnant and potential spurs To make thee seek it [my death] . ii 1 79
What, did my father's godson seek your life? . . . ii 1 93
That sir which serves and seeks for gain, And follows but for form, Will pack when it begins to rain . . . ii 4 79
I will seek him, and privily relieve him . . . iii 3 15
Seek thine own ease: This tempest will not give me leave to ponder . iii 4 23
Who's there? What is't you seek?—What are you there? . . . iii 4 132
Yet have I ventured to come seek you out . . . iii 4 157
Canst thou blame him? His daughters seek his death . . . iii 4 168
It was not altogether your brother's evil disposition made him seek his death . . . iii 5 7
Seek out where thy father is, that he may be ready for our apprehension iii 5 19
Seek, seek for him; Lest his ungovern'd rage dissolve the life That wants the means to lead it . . . iv 4 18
Seek him out Upon the British party: O, untimely death! . . . iv 6 255
Here comes another troop to seek for you . . . *Othello* i 2 54
Seek thou rather to be hanged in compassing thy joy . . . i 3 367
Seek him, bid him come hither: tell him I have moved my lord . iii 4 18
I'll move your suit And seek to effect it to my uttermost . . . iii 4 167
Assure yourself I will seek satisfaction of you . . . iv 2 203
I am sorry to find you thus: I have been to seek you . . . v 1 81
Seek no colour for your going, But bid farewell, and go . *Ant. and Cleo.* i 3 32
Of us must Pompey presently be sought, Or else he seeks out us . . ii 2 162
Who seeks, and will not take when once 'tis offer'd, Shall never find it more . . . ii 7 89
Let your best love draw to that point, which seeks Best to preserve it . iii 4 21
I will seek Some way to leave him . . . iii 13 200
I will go seek Some ditch wherein to die . . . iv 6 37
Of Cæsar seek your honour, with your safety . . . iv 15 46
If you seek To lay on me a cruelty, by taking Antony's course, you shall bereave yourself Of my good purposes . . . v 2 128
To seek through the regions of the earth For one his like, there would be something failing In him that should compare . . . *Cymbeline* i 1 20
If you seek For further satisfying . . . ii 4 133
Which he to seek of me again, perforce, Behoves me keep at utterance . iii 1 72
If you seek us afterwards in other terms, you shall find us in our salt-water girdle . . . iii 1 80
A pain that only seems to seek out danger I' the name of fame and honour . . . iii 3 50
I would revenges, That possible strength might meet, would seek us through And put us to our answer . . . iv 2 160
We'll hunt no more to-day, nor seek for danger Where there's no profit iv 2 162
Let's withdraw; And meet the time as it seeks us . . . iv 3 33
Which directed him To seek her on the mountains near to Milford . v 5 281
Made many princes thither frame, To seek her as a bed-fellow *Per.* i Gower 33
If in the world he live, we'll seek him out; If in his grave he rest, we'll find him there . . . ii 4 29
Seek not to entrap me, gracious lord, A stranger and distressed gentleman ii 5 45
Marina's life Seeks to take off by treason's knife . . . iv Gower 14
Your lady seeks my life; come you between, And save poor me, the weaker . . . iv 1 90
That these pirates . . . had not o'erboard thrown me For to seek my mother! . . . iv 2 71
Till cruel Cleon, with his wicked wife, Did seek to murder me . . . v 1 174

Seekest. Why seek'st thou then to cover with excuse That which appears in proper nakedness? . . . *Much Ado* iv 1 176
Why seek'st thou me? could not this make thee know, The hate I bear thee made me leave thee so? . . . *M. N. Dream* iii 2 189
Thou seek'st the greatness that will overwhelm thee . . . 2 *Hen. IV.* iv 5 98
Hell our prison is. But tell me whom thou seek'st . . . 1 *Hen. VI.* iv 7 59
If thou wert honourable, Thou wouldst have told this tale for virtue, not For such an end thou seek'st . . . *Cymbeline* i 6 144

Seeking. And, seeking death, find life . . . *Meas. for Meas.* iii 1 43
Light seeking light doth light of light beguile . . . *L. L. Lost* i 1 77
Behind the wood, Seeking sweet favours for this hateful fool. *M. N. D.* iv 1 54
Seeking the food he eats And pleased with what he gets. *As Y. Like It* ii 5 42
Seeking the bubble reputation Even in the cannon's mouth . . . ii 7 152
I was seeking for a fool when I found you . . . iii 2 303
This comes with seeking you: But there's no remedy . . . *T. Night* iii 4 366
I am hot with haste in seeking you . . . *K. John* iv 3 74
And they in seeking that Shall find their deaths . . . 2 *Hen. VI.* ii 2 75
Seeking a way and straying from the way. . . . 3 *Hen. VI.* iii 2 176

Seeking. All on foot he fights, Seeking for Richmond in the throat of death *Richard III.* v 4 5
In seeking tales and informations Against this man . *Hen. VIII.* v 3 110
I have been seeking you this hour . . *Troi. and Cres.* v 2 182
What's their seeking?—For corn at their own rates . . *Coriolanus* i 1 192
Envied against the people, seeking means To pluck away their power . iii 3 95
I found her, straying in the park, Seeking to hide herself *T. Andron.* iii 1 89
Methinks I see my cousin's ghost Seeking out Romeo . *Rom. and Jul.* iv 3 56
It shall make honour for you.—So I lose none In seeking to augment it, but still keep My bosom franchised . . . *Macbeth* ii 1 27
Seeking to give Losses their remedies . . . *Lear* ii 2 176
There wants no diligence in seeking him, And will, no doubt, be found *Cymbeline* iv 3 20
Shall, to himself unknown, without seeking find . . . v 4 139
Seel. When light-wing'd toys Of feather'd Cupid seel with wanton dullness My speculative and officed instruments . *Othello* i 3 270
She that, so young, could give out such a seeming, To seel her father's eyes up close as oak . . . . . iii 3 210
But when we in our viciousness grow hard—O misery on't!—the wise gods seel our eyes . . . . *Ant. and Cleo.* iii 13 112
Seely. The heads of Brocas and Sir Bennet Seely, Two of the dangerous consorted traitors . . . . *Richard II.* v 6 14
Seeling night, Scarf up the tender eye of pitiful day! . *Macbeth* iii 2 46
Seem. The sky, it seems, would pour down stinking pitch . *Tempest* i 2 3
Cracks Of sulphurous roaring the most mighty Neptune Seem to besiege i 2 205
Though this island seem to be desert . . . . ii 1 35
Our garments seem now as fresh as when we were at Tunis . . ii 1 97
A space whose every cubit Seems to cry out . . . ii 1 258
Single I'll resolve you, Which to you shall seem probable . . v 1 249
You are sad.—Indeed, madam, I seem so.—Seem you that you are not? *T. G. of Ver.* ii 4 9
What seem I that I am not?—Wise.—What instance of the contrary? ii 4 14
It seems you loved not her, to leave her token . . . iv 4 79
The appetite of her eye did seem to scorch me . . . *Mer. Wives* i 3 74
For the which his wife seems to me well-favoured . . . ii 2 284
Of government the properties to unfold, Would seem in me to affect speech and discourse . . *Meas. for Meas.* i 1 4
Enforce or qualify the laws As to your soul seems good . . i 1 67
'Tis my familiar sin With maids to seem the lapwing and to jest . i 4 32
It seems your most offenceful act Was mutually committed? . . ii 3 26
Either you are ignorant, Or seem so craftily; and that's not good . ii 4 75
Your virtue hath a license in't, Which seems a little fouler than it is . ii 4 146
That we were all, as some would seem to be, From our faults, as faults from seeming, free! . . . . . iii 2 40
How seems he to be touch'd? . . . . . iv 2 148
Make not impossible That which but seems unlike . . . v 1 52
The wicked'st caitiff on the ground May seem as shy, as grave . v 1 54
Let your reason serve To make the truth appear where it seems hid, And hide the false seems true . . . . . v 1 66
Do with your injuries as seems you best, In any chastisement . . v 1 256
It seems he hath great care to please his wife . *Com. of Errors* ii 1 56
It seems thou want'st breaking: out upon thee, hind! . . iii 1 77
It seems his sleeps were hinder'd by thy railing . . . v 1 71
But lest my liking might too sudden seem, I would have salved it with a longer treatise . . . . *Much Ado* i 1 316
The man doth fear God, howsoever it seems not in him . . ii 3 205
They seem to pity the lady: it seems her affections have their full bent ii 3 231
I did never think to marry: I must not seem proud . . ii 3 237
Her wit Values itself so highly that to her All matter else seems weak . iii 1 54
Where his codpiece seems as massy as his club . . . iii 3 146
You seem to me as Dian in her orb . . . . iv 1 58
Meantime let wonder seem familiar, And to the chapel let us presently v 4 70
But that, it seems, he little purposeth . . . *L. L. Lost* ii 1 142
To your huge store Wise things seem foolish and rich things but poor v 2 378
Let the prologue seem to say, we will do no harm . *M. N. Dream* iii 1 19
How can these things in me seem scorn to you? . . . iii 2 126
I scorn you not: it seems that you scorn me . . . iii 2 221
Seem to break loose; take on as you would follow, But yet come not . iii 2 258
All this derision Shall seem a dream and fruitless vision . . iii 2 371
Seems to me now As the remembrance of an idle gawd . . iv 1 171
These things seem small and undistinguishable . . . iv 1 192
Methinks I see these things with parted eye, When every thing seems double . . . . iv 1 195
It seems to me That yet we sleep, we dream . . . iv 1 198
Myself the man i' the moon do seem to be . . . . v 1 249
It should seem, then, that Dobbin's tail grows backward *Mer. of Venice* ii 2 102
An it shall please you to break up this, it shall seem to signify . ii 4 11
Move these eyes? Or whether, riding on the balls of mine, Seem they in motion? . . . . iii 2 118
Besides this nothing that he so plentifully gives me, the something that nature gave me his countenance seems to take from me *As Y. Like It* i 1 19
Thou wilt show more bright and seem more virtuous When she is gone . i 3 83
Doth very foolishly, although he smart, Not to seem senseless of the bob ii 7 55
Time's pace is so hard that it seems the length of seven year . . iii 2 334
He seems to have the quotidian of love upon him . . . iii 2 383
The royal disposition of that beast To prey on nothing that doth seem as dead . . . . iv 3 119
It is my study To seem despiteful and ungentle to you . . v 2 86
It would seem strange unto him when he waked . *T. of Shrew* Ind. 1 43
Cytherea all in sedges hid, Which seem to move and wanton with her breath . . . . Ind. 2 54
Some fifteen year or more.—Ay, and the time seems thirty unto me Ind. 2 116
Who knows not that?—Thou, it seems . . . . iv 1 104
I am not Licio, Nor a musician, as I seem to be . . . iv 2 17
I'll make him glad to seem Vincentio . . . . iv 2 68
You seem a sober ancient gentleman by your habit . . . v 1 75
Wherein our dearest friend Prejudicates the business and would seem To have us make denial . . . . *All's Well* i 2 8
Whose ceremony Shall seem expedient on the now-born brief . ii 3 186
For my respects are better than they seem . . . ii 5 71
Holy seems the quarrel Upon your grace's part . . . iii 1 4
Confidently seems to undertake this business, which he knows is not to be done . . . . iii 6 94
To buy his will, it would not seem too dear, Howe'er repented after . iii 7 27
No more, But that your daughter, ere she seems as won, Desires this ring . . . . iii 7 31
We must not seem to understand him . . . . iv 1 5
So we seem to know, is to know straight our purpose . . iv 1 21
As for you, interpreter, you must seem very politic . . iv 1 23
Only to seem to deserve well, and to beguile the supposition . . iv 3 332
Seem. Though time seem so adverse and means unfit . . *All's Well* v 1 26
All yet seems well . . . . v 3 333
He seems to have a foreknowledge of that too . . . *T. Night* i 5 151
She is drowned already, sir, with salt water, though I seem to drown her remembrance again with more . . . . . . ii 1 32
Come what may, I do adore thee so, That danger shall seem sport . ii 1 49
And she, mistaken, seems to dote on me. What will become of this? . ii 2 36
A murderous guilt shows not itself more soon Than love that would seem hid . . . . iii 1 160
What would my lord . . . Wherein Olivia may seem serviceable? . . v 1 105
If this be so, as yet the glass seems true . . . . v 1 272
He something seems unsettled . . . . . *W. Tale* i 2 147
Are you so fond of your young prince as we Do seem to be of ours? . i 2 165
We have been Deceived in thy integrity, deceived In that which seems so . . . . i 2 241
I will seem friendly, as thou hast advised me . . . . i 2 350
Your most obedient counsellor, yet that dare Less appear so in comforting your evils, Than such as most seem yours . . . . ii 3 57
You, my lord, best know, Who least will seem to do so . . . iii 2 34
And make stale The glistering of this present, as my tale Now seems to it iv 1 15
The fire-robed god, Golden Apollo, a poor humble swain, As I seem now iv 4 31
Nothing she does or seems But smacks of something greater than herself iv 4 157
This ancient sir, who, it should seem, Hath sometime loved . . iv 4 372
How prettily the young swain seems to wash The hand was fair before! iv 4 377
For she seems a mistress To most that teach . . . iv 4 593
He seems to be the more noble in being fantastical . . . iv 4 778
Tell me, for you seem to be honest plain men . . . iv 4 823
He seems to be of great authority: close with him . . . iv 4 830
Whiles he was hastening, in the chase, it seems, Of this fair couple . v 1 189
Who has not only his innocence, which seems much, to justify him . v 2 70
Hermione was not so much wrinkled, nothing So aged as this seems . v 3 29
Masterly done: The very life seems warm upon her lip . . . v 3 66
You came not of one mother then, it seems . . . *K. John* i 1 58
I muse your majesty doth seem so cold . . . . iii 1 317
Your vile intent must needs seem horrible . . . . iv 1 96
Makes it seem Like rivers of remorse and innocency . . . iv 3 109
It seems you know not, then, so much as we . . . . v 7 81
The more fair and crystal is the sky, The uglier seem the clouds *Rich. II.* i 1 42
Shall I seem crest-fall'n in my father's sight? . . . . i 1 188
How he did seem to dive into their hearts With humble and familiar courtesy . . . . i 4 25
By this the weary lords Shall make their way seem short . . ii 3 17
In me it seems it [music] will make wise men mad . . . v 5 63
It seems then that the tidings of this broil Brake off our business *1 Hen. IV.* i 1 47
The foul and ugly mists Of vapours that did seem to strangle him . i 2 227
His present want Seems more than we shall find it . . . iv 1 45
Seems to weep Over his country's wrongs . . . . iv 3 81
Nothing can seem foul to those that win . . . . v 1 8
And my pension shall seem the more reasonable . . *2 Hen. IV.* i 2 276
Past and to come seems best; things present worst . . . i 3 108
Would turn their own perfection to abuse, To seem like him . . ii 3 28
Where nothing but the sound of Hotspur's name Did seem defensible . ii 3 38
That even our corn shall seem as light as chaff . . . iv 1 195
Look you, he must seem thus to the world: fear not your advancements v 5 83
He seems indifferent, Or rather swaying more upon our part . *Hen. V.* i 1 72
How did this offer seem received, my lord? . . . . i 1 82
Seem they grave and learned? Why, so didst thou: . . . seem they religious? Why, so didst thou . . . . ii 2 128
Such and so finely bolted didst thou seem . . . . ii 2 137
In cases of defence 'tis best to weigh The enemy more mighty than he seems . . . . ii 4 44
Coward dogs Most spend their mouths when what they seem to threaten Runs far before them . . . . ii 4 70
And shall our quick blood, spirited with wine, Seem frosty? . . iii 5 22
Big Mars seems bankrupt in their beggar'd host . . . iv 2 43
Which like a mighty whiffler 'fore the king Seems to prepare his way v Prol. 13
Stern looks, defused attire And every thing that seems unnatural . v 2 62
He seem with forged quaint conceit To set a gloss upon his bold intent *1 Hen. VI.* iv 1 102
So seems this gorgeous beauty to mine eyes . . . . v 3 64
He seems a knight, And will not any way dishonour me . . v 3 101
Gazing on that which seems to dim thy sight . . *2 Hen. VI.* i 2 6
Seems he a dove? his feathers are but borrow'd . . . iii 1 75
But well forewarning wind Did seem to say 'Seek not a scorpion's nest' iii 1 86
Ay, every joint should seem to curse and ban . . . iii 2 319
'Tis government that makes them [women] seem divine . *3 Hen. VI.* i 4 132
They join, embrace, and seem to kiss, As if they vow'd some league inviolable . . . . ii 1 29
For the time shall not seem tedious, I'll tell thee what befel me on a day iii 1 9
More than I seem, and less than I was born to . . . iii 1 56
Such it seems As may beseem a monarch like himself . . . iii 3 121
Your grace hath still been famed for virtuous; And now may seem as wise iv 6 27
What youth is that, Of whom you seem to have so tender care? . iv 6 66
And seem a saint, when most I play the devil . . . *Richard III.* i 3 338
Where it seems best unto your royal self . . . . iii 1 63
Cannot thy master sleep these tedious nights?—So it should seem . iii 2 7
I do suspect I have done some offence That seems disgracious . . iii 7 112
Can make seem pleasing to her tender years . . . . iv 4 342
A noble troop of strangers; For so they seem . . . *Hen. VIII.* i 4 54
What's the cause?—It seems the marriage with his brother's wife . ii 2 17
And what expense by the hour Seems to flow from him! . . . iii 2 109
What's the matter? It seems you are in haste . . . v 1 11
The hard and soft, seem all affined and kin . . *Troi. and Cres.* i 3 25
Which, from the tongue of roaring Typhon dropp'd, Would seem hyperboles . . . . i 3 161
But when they would seem soldiers, they have galls, Good arms . i 3 237
It should seem, fellow, that thou hast not seen the Lady Cressida . iii 1 39
Yet that which seems the wound to kill, Doth turn oh! oh! to ha! ha! he! iii 1 132
Why was my Cressid then so hard to win?—Hard to seem won . iii 2 125
Let all untruths stand by thy stained name, And they'll seem glorious v 2 180
Our gates, Which yet seem shut, we have but pinn'd with rushes *Coriol.* i 4 18
Which, to the spire and top of praises vouch'd, Would seem but modest i 9 25
To seem to affect the malice and displeasure of the people is as bad as that which he dislikes, to flatter them . . . . . . ii 2 24
And this shall seem, as partly 'tis, their own, Which we have goaded onward . . . . ii 3 270
Be that you seem, truly your country's friend . . . . iii 1 218
Those cold ways, That seem like prudent helps, are very poisonous . iii 1 221
If it be honour in your wars to seem The same you are not . . iii 2 46
Now we have shown our power, Let us seem humbler after it is done . iv 2 4

Seem. Friends now fast sworn, Whose double bosoms seem to wear one heart *Coriolanus* iv 4 13
A side that would be glad to have This true which they so seem to fear iv 6 152
Although it seems, And so he thinks, and is no less apparent iv 7 19
He would not seem to know me v 1 8
Such a decayed dotant as you seem to be v 2 48
Tell me not Wherein I seem unnatural v 3 84
It seems, some certain snatch or so Would serve your turns *T. Andron.* ii 1 95
A very fatal place it seems to me ii 3 202
They humbly at my feet Receive my tears and seem to weep with me iii 1 42
These two heads do seem to speak to me, And threat me iii 1 272
Ay me! sad hours seem long *Rom. and Jul.* i 1 167
It seems she hangs upon the cheek of night Like a rich jewel in an Ethiope's ear i 5 47
But, as it seems, did violence on herself v 3 264
Or [to trust] a dog, that seems a-sleeping *T. of Athens* i 2 68
It should seem by the sum, Your master's confidence was above mine iii 4 30
I hope it is not so low with him as he made it seem iii 6 6
Our course will seem too bloody, Caius Cassius, To cut the head off and then hack the limbs *J. Cæsar* ii 1 162
Stir up their servants to an act of rage, And after seem to chide 'em ii 1 177
It seems to me most strange that men should fear ii 2 35
How foolish do your fears seem now, Calpurnia! I am ashamed I did yield to them ii 2 105
Did this in Cæsar seem ambitious? When that the poor have cried, Cæsar hath wept iii 2 95
Their shadows seem A canopy most fatal, under which Our army lies v 1 87
So should he look That seems to speak things strange *Macbeth* i 2 47
Are you aught That man may question? You seem to understand me i 3 43
Why do you start; and seem to fear Things that do sound so fair? i 3 51
He seems rapt withal: to me you speak not i 3 57
Which fate and metaphysical aid doth seem To have thee crown'd withal i 5 30
Now o'er the one half-world Nature seems dead ii 1 50
I'll gild the faces of the grooms withal; For it must seem their guilt ii 2 57
Black Macbeth Will seem as pure as snow iv 3 53
Convey your pleasures in a spacious plenty, And yet seem cold iv 3 72
Where violent sorrow seems A modern ecstasy iv 3 169
It is an accustomed action with her, to seem thus washing her hands v 1 33
By this great clatter, one of greatest note Seems bruited v 7 22
It is common.—If it be, Why seems it so particular with thee?—Seems, madam! nay, it is; I know not 'seems' *Hamlet* i 2 76
These indeed seem, For they are actions that a man might play i 2 83
How weary, stale, flat and unprofitable, Seem to me all the uses of this world! i 2 134
But breathe his faults so quaintly That they may seem the taints of liberty ii 1 32
He raised a sigh so piteous and profound As it did seem to shatter all his bulk ii 1 95
This goodly frame, the earth, seems to me a sterile promontory ii 2 310
Man delights not me: no, nor woman neither, though by your smiling you seem to say so ii 2 323
There did seem in him a kind of joy To hear of it iii 1 18
You would play upon me; you would seem to know my stops iii 2 381
A form indeed, Where every god did seem to set his seal iii 4 61
This sudden sending him away must seem Deliberate pause iv 3 8
Each toy seems prologue to some great amiss iv 5 18
For two special reasons; Which may to you, perhaps, seem much unsinew'd iv 7 10
It did always seem so to us *Lear* i 1 3
I do profess to be no less than I seem i 4 14
In cunning I must draw my sword upon you: Draw; seem to defend yourself ii 1 32
I pray you, father, being weak, seem so ii 4 204
Servants, who seem no less, Which are to France the spies iii 1 23
This seems a fair deserving, and must draw me That which my father loses iii 3 24
How light and portable my pain seems now! iii 6 115
What most he should dislike seems pleasant to him; What like, offensive iv 2 10
Wisdom and goodness to the vile seem vile: Filths savour but themselves iv 2 38
Proper deformity seems not in the fiend So horrid as in woman iv 2 60
Methinks he seems no bigger than his head iv 6 16
And, like a scurvy politician, seem To see the things thou dost not iv 6 175
Wretched though I seem, I can produce a champion v 1 42
It seems not meet, nor wholesome to my place, To be produced *Othello* i 1 146
It seems, Your special mandate for the state-affairs Hath hither brought i 3 71
Of a free and open nature, That thinks men honest that but seem to be so i 3 406
The chidden billow seems to pelt the clouds; The wind-shaked surge, with high and monstrous mane, Seems to cast water on the burning bear ii 1 12
Pleasure and action make the hours seem short ii 3 385
If she will stir hither, I shall seem to notify unto her iii 1 31
His bed shall seem a school, his board a shrift iii 3 24
Men should be what they seem; Or those that be not, would they might seem none!—Certain, men should be what they seem iii 3 126
And rather, as it seems to me now, keepest from me all conveniency iv 2 177
And this, it seems, Roderigo meant to have sent this damned villain v 2 315
I'll seem the fool I am not; Antony Will be himself *Ant. and Cleo.* i 1 42
His faults in him seem as the spots of heaven, More fiery by night's blackness i 4 12
All little jealousies, which now seem great, And all great fears ii 2 134
Whose wind did seem To glow the delicate cheeks which they did cool ii 2 208
To punish me for what you make me do Seems much unequal ii 5 101
The band that seems to tie their friendship together will be the very strangler of their amity ii 6 129
You shall not find, Though you be therein curious, the least cause For what you seem to fear iii 2 36
He makes me angry with him; for he seems Proud and disdainful iii 13 141
Plant those that have revolted in the van, That Antony may seem to spend his fury Upon himself iv 6 10
You do not meet a man but frowns: our bloods No more obey the heavens than our courtiers Still seem as does the king *Cymbeline* i 1 3
An eminent monsieur, that, it seems, much loves A Gallian girl at home i 6 65
You do seem to know Something of me, or what concerns me i 6 93
So seem as if You were inspired to do those duties which You tender ii 3 54
How look I, That I should seem to lack humanity? iii 2 16
A pain that only seems to seek out danger I' the name of fame and honour iii 3 50
I' the world's volume Our Britain seems as of it, but not in 't iii 4 141
But not so citizen a wanton as To seem to die ere sick iv 2 9
He made those clothes, Which, as it seems, make thee iv 2 83
That we the horrider may seem to those Which chance to find us iv 2 331

Seem. Inform us of thy fortunes, for it seems They crave to be demanded *Cymbeline* iv 2 361
Who needs must know of her departure and Dost seem so ignorant iv 3 11
The time seems long iv 4 53
How courtesy would seem to cover sin! *Pericles* i 1 121
Whose arm seems far too short to hit me here i 2 8
'Tis time to fear when tyrants seems to kiss i 2 79
He seems to be a stranger ii 2 42
All viands that I eat do seem unsavoury ii 3 31
To me he seems like diamond to glass ii 3 36
The very principals did seem to rend, And all-to topple iii 2 16
And make us weep to hear your fate, fair creature, Rare as you seem to be iii 2 105
You must seem to do that fearfully which you commit willingly iv 2 127
To use one language in each several clime Where our scenes seem to live iv 4 7
If I should tell my history, it would seem Like lies v 1 119
And make my senses credit thy relation To points that seem impossible v 1 125
Tell him O'er, point by point, for yet he seems to doubt v 1 227
It seems You have been noble towards her v 1 263
Seemed but tameness, civility and patience, to this his distemper *M. W.* iv 2 27
It in you more dreadful would have seem'd *Meas. for Meas.* i 3 33
You seem'd of late to make the law a tyrant ii 4 114
Whom she hath in all outward behaviours seemed ever to abhor *M. Ado* ii 3 100
Seem'd I ever otherwise to you?—Out on thee! Seeming! iv 1 56
And what in us hath seem'd ridiculous *L. L. Lost* v 2 769
Seem'd Athens as a paradise to me *M. N. Dream* i 1 205
Every region near Seem'd all one mutual cry iv 1 122
No other reason But that his beard grew thin and hungerly And seem'd to ask him sops as he was drinking *T. of Shrew* iii 2 178
That they have seemed to be together, though absent *W. Tale* i 1 32
They seemed almost, with staring on one another, to tear the cases of their eyes v 2 13
It seemed sorrow wept to take leave of them, for their joy waded in tears v 2 49
Such grief That words seem'd buried in my sorrow's grave *Richard II.* i 4 15
The weeds which his broad-spreading leaves did shelter, That seem'd in eating him to hold him up, Are pluck'd up root and all iii 4 51
Mounted upon a hot and fiery steed Which his aspiring rider seem'd to know v 2 9
Tell me, How show'd his tasking? seem'd it in contempt? *1 Hen. IV.* v 2 51
He seem'd in running to devour the way *2 Hen. IV.* i 1 47
Their weapons only Seem'd on our side i 1 198
It seem'd in me But as an honour snatch'd with boisterous hand iv 5 191
His wildness, mortified in him, Seem'd to die too *Hen. V.* i 1 27
Though we seemed dead, we did but sleep iii 6 126
Which in the hatching, It seem'd, appear'd to Rome *Coriolanus* i 2 22
Till, at the last, I seem'd his follower, not partner v 6 39
The cross blue lightning seem'd to open The breast of heaven *J. Cæsar* i 3 50
Fearing to strengthen that impatience Which seem'd too much enkindled ii 1 249
So from that spring whence comfort seem'd to come Discomfort swells *Macbeth* i 2 27
And what seem'd corporal melted As breath into the wind i 3 81
Those of his chamber, as it seem'd, had done't: Their hands and faces were all badged with blood ii 3 106
He seem'd to find his way without his eyes *Hamlet* ii 1 98
His sword, Which was declining on the milky head Of reverend Priam, seem'd i' the air to stick ii 2 501
It seem'd she was a queen Over her passion *Lear* iv 3 15
Those happy smilets, That play'd on her ripe lip, seem'd not to know What guests were in her eyes iv 3 22
This would have seem'd a period To such as love not sorrow v 3 204
When she seem'd to shake and fear your looks, She loved them most *Oth.* iii 3 207
He was not merry, Which seem'd to tell them his remembrance lay In Egypt with his joy *Ant. and Cleo.* i 5 57
Yet my mother seem'd The Dian of that time *Cymbeline* ii 5 6
The sinful father Seem'd not to strike, but smooth *Pericles* i 2 78
Under the covering of a careful night, Who seem'd my good protector i 2 82
The gods for murder seemed so content To punish them v 3 Gower 98
Seemers. Hence shall we see, If power change purpose, what our seemers be *Meas. for Meas.* i 3 54
Seemest. That in civility thou seem'st so empty *As Y. Like It* ii 7 93
Why at our justice seem'st thou then to lour? *Richard II.* i 3 235
Thou art not what thou seem'st.—No, that's certain *1 Hen. IV.* v 4 140
Thou picture of what thou seemest *Troi. and Cres.* v 1 6
Just opposite to what thou justly seem'st, A damned saint! *R. and J.* iii 2 78
Thou mayst be valiant in a better cause; But now thou seem'st a coward *Cymbeline* iii 4 75
Thou seem'st a palace For the crown'd Truth to dwell in *Pericles* v 1 122
Seemeth. Therefore to 's seemeth it a needful course *L. L. Lost* ii 1 25
So sensible Seemeth their conference v 2 260
Quoniam he seemeth in minority, Ergo I come with this apology v 2 596
So bedazzled with the sun That everything I look on seemeth green *T. of Shrew* iv 5 47
For sorrow ends not when it seemeth done *Richard II.* i 2 61
Me seemeth then it is no policy *2 Hen. VI.* iii 1 23
What to your wisdoms seemeth best, Do or undo, as if ourself were here iii 1 195
Me seemeth good, that, with some little train *Richard III.* ii 2 120
He can report, As seemeth by his plight, of the revolt *Macbeth* i 2 2
Seeming. Pluck the borrowed veil of modesty from the so seeming Mistress Page *Mer. Wives* iii 2 42
How often dost thou with thy case, thy habit, Wrench awe from fools and tie the wiser souls To thy false seeming! *Meas. for Meas.* ii 4 15
Seeming, seeming! I will proclaim thee ii 4 150
That we were all, as some would seem to be, From our faults, as faults from seeming, free! iii 2 41
And showed him a seeming warrant for it iv 2 160
Seeming as burdened With lesser weight but not with lesser woe *C. of Er.* i 1 108
Such seeming truth of Hero's disloyalty *Much Ado* ii 2 49
Seem'd I ever otherwise to you?—Out on thee! Seeming! iv 1 57
So we grew together, Like to a double cherry, seeming parted *M. N. D.* iii 2 209
So, with two seeming bodies, but one heart iii 2 212
The seeming truth which cunning times put on To entrap the wisest *Mer. of Venice* iii 2 100
Every one fault seeming monstrous till his fellow-fault came to match it *As Y. Like It* iii 2 373
As loving yourself than seeming the lover of any other iii 2 403
Bear your body more seeming v 4 72
That seeming to be most which we indeed least are *T. of Shrew* v 2 175
Ensconcing ourselves into seeming knowledge *All's Well* ii 3 5
Or stupified Or seeming so in skill, cannot or will not Relish a truth *W. T.* ii 1 166
These keep Seeming and savour all the winter long iv 4 75
Dismantle you, and, as you can, disliken The truth of your own seeming iv 4 667

Seeming. The father of this seeming lady *W. Tale* v 1 191
Thou art essentially mad, without seeming so *1 Hen. IV.* ii 4 541
By this face, This seeming brow of justice, did he win The hearts of all iv 3 83
The seeming sufferances that you had borne v 1 51
There is no seeming mercy in the king v 2 35
Nor lose the good advantage of his grace By seeming cold *2 Hen. IV.* iv 4 29
I dare swear you borrow not that face Of seeming sorrow v 2 29
To raze out Rotten opinion, who hath writ me down After my seeming v 2 129
Know you not, The fire that mounts the liquor till't run o'er, In seeming to augment it wastes it? *Hen. VIII.* i 1 145
You sign your place and calling, in full seeming, With meekness and humility ii 4 108
Sorrow, that is couch'd in seeming gladness, Is like that mirth fate turns to sudden sadness *Troi. and Cres.* i 1 39
Such to-be-pitied and o'er-wrested seeming He acts thy greatness in i 3 157
This intrusion shall Now seeming sweet convert to bitter gall *R. and J.* i 5 94
Unseemly woman in a seeming man! Or ill-beseeming beast in seeming both! iii 3 112
Then senseless Ilium, Seeming to feel this blow, with flaming top Stoops to his base *Hamlet* ii 2 497
And after we will both our judgements join In censure of his seeming iii 2 92
If aught within that little seeming substance, Or all of it, . . . may fitly like your grace, She's there *Lear* i 1 201
That under covert and convenient seeming Hast practised on man's life iii 2 56
Not I for love and duty, But seeming so, for my peculiar end *Othello* i 1 60
These thin habits and poor likelihoods Of modern seeming i 3 109
I am not merry; but I do beguile The thing I am, by seeming otherwise ii 1 124
Putting on the mere form of civil and humane seeming ii 1 244
She that, so young, could give out such a seeming iii 3 209
Even but now he spake, After long seeming dead, Iago hurt him v 2 328
At the helm A seeming mermaid steers *Ant. and Cleo.* ii 2 214
Bid that welcome Which comes to punish us, and we punish it Seeming to bear it lightly iv 14 138
He hath a kind of honour sets him off, More than a mortal seeming *Cymb.* i 6 171
All good seeming, By thy revolt, O husband, shall be thought Put on iii 4 56
I am sorry for't; not seeming So worthy as thy birth iv 2 93
Thought her like her seeming; it had been vicious To have mistrusted her v 5 65
This hath some seeming v 5 452

Seemingly. She seemingly obedient likewise hath Made promise *M. Wives* iv 6 33

Seeming-virtuous. Won to his shameful lust The will of my most seeming-virtuous queen *Hamlet* i 5 46

Seemly. You know I am a woman, lacking wit To make a seemly answer to such persons *Hen. VIII.* iii 1 178

Seen. Thou think'st there is no more such shapes as he, Having seen but him and Caliban *Tempest* i 2 479
I was the man i' the moon when time was.—I have seen thee in her ii 2 143
Nor have I seen More that I may call men than you, good friend iii 1 50
A Jew would have wept to have seen our parting *T. G. of Ver.* ii 3 13
This love of theirs myself have often seen iii 1 24
What light is light, if Silvia be not seen? iii 1 174
I have seen Sackerson loose twenty times *Mer. Wives* i 1 307
I have seen the time, with my long sword I would have made you four tall fellows skip like rats ii 1 236
A dish of some three-pence; your honours have seen such dishes *Meas. for Meas.* ii 1 96
I have seen, When, after execution, judgement hath Repented o'er his doom ii 2 10
Angelo hath seen them both, and will discover the favour iv 2 184
Here in Vienna, Where I have seen corruption boil and bubble v 1 320
If any born at Ephesus be seen At any Syracusian marts *Com. of Errors* i 1 17
Hath any man seen him at the barber's?—No, but the barber's man hath been seen with him *Much Ado* iii 2 43
And when you have seen more and heard more, proceed accordingly iii 2 124
So will you say when you have seen the sequel iii 2 137
Doth not my wit become me rarely?—It is not seen enough iii 4 71
And not be seen to wink of all the day *L. L. Lost* i 1 43
Item, If any man be seen to talk with a woman i 1 130
I was seen with her in the manor-house, sitting with her upon the form i 1 208
If ever I do see the merry days of desolation that I have seen i 2 165
O, what a scene of foolery have I seen, Of sighs, of groans! iv 3 163
A gracious moon; She an attending star, scarce seen a light iv 3 231
A man of travel, that hath seen the world v 1 114
A smaller hair than may be seen, Above the sense of sense v 2 258
The face of an old Roman coin, scarce seen v 2 617
I have seen the day of wrong through the little hole of discretion v 2 733
When the false Troyan under sail was seen *M. N. Dream* i 1 174
You spotted snakes with double tongue, Thorny hedgehogs, be not seen ii 2 10
Half his face must be seen through the lion's neck iii 1 38
What visions have I seen! Methought I was enamour'd of an ass iv 1 81
The eye of man hath not heard, the ear of man hath not seen iv 1 218
Where I have seen them shiver and look pale v 1 95
In a gondola were seen together Lorenzo and his amorous Jessica *Mer. of Venice* ii 8 8
Yet I have not seen So likely an ambassador of love ii 9 91
It is now our time, That have stood by and seen our wishes prosper iii 2 189
My lord, My purpose was not to have seen you here iii 2 230
You have seen cruel proof of this man's strength *As Y. Like It* i 2 184
We have seen better days ii 7 120; *T. of Athens* iv 2 27
Thy tooth is not so keen, Because thou art not seen *As Y. Like It* ii 7 178
To have seen much and to have nothing, is to have rich eyes and poor hands iv 1 23
This seen, Orlando did approach the man And found it was his brother iv 3 120
We have not yet been seen in any house *T. of Shrew* i 1 204
A schoolmaster Well seen in music i 2 134
Would Katharine had never seen him though! iii 2 26
There to visit A son of mine, which long I have not seen iv 5 57
I have seen them in the church together: God send 'em good shipping! v 1 42
'Tis often seen Adoption strives with nature *All's Well* i 3 150
O, 'tis brave wars!—Most admirable: I have seen those wars ii 1 26
I have seen a medicine That's able to breathe life into a stone ii 1 75
I have seen you in the court of France v 1 10
I have seen her wear it; and she reckon'd it At her life's rate v 3 90
I'll home to-morrow, Sir Toby: your niece will not be seen; or if she be, it's four to one she'll none of me *T. Night* i 3 112
You have not seen such a thing as 'tis iii 2 86
He's a very devil; I have not seen such a firago iii 4 302
I'ld have seen him damned ere I'ld have challenged him iii 4 313
When in other habits you are seen, Orsino's mistress v 1 396
Ha' not you seen, Camillo,—But that's past doubt *W. Tale* i 2 267

Seen. He swears, As he had seen't or been an instrument To vice you to't *W. Tale* i 2 415
I have seen a lady's nose That has been blue, but not her eyebrows ii 1 14
I have drunk, and seen the spider ii 1 45
I have seen two such sights, by sea and by land! iii 3 84
If this be a horseman's coat, it hath seen very hot service iv 3 71
Methinks I play as I have seen them do In Whitsun pastorals iv 4 133
So must thy grave Give way to what's seen now! v 1 98
'Tis shrewdly ebb'd, To say you have seen a better v 1 103
Had our prince, Jewel of children, seen this hour, he had pair'd Well with this lord v 1 116
Then have you lost a sight, which was to be seen, cannot be spoken of v 2 47
If all the world could have seen't, the woe had been universal v 2 100
Where is that blood That I have seen inhabit in those cheeks? *K. John* iv 2 107
My lord, they say five moons were seen to-night iv 2 182
More amazed Than had I seen the vaulty top of heaven Figured quite o'er v 2 52
On some apparent danger seen in him *Richard II.* i 1 13
O, had thy grandsire with a prophet's eye Seen how his son's son should destroy his sons! ii 1 105
More's not seen; Or if it be, 'tis with false sorrow's eye. ii 2 25
Rue, even for ruth, here shortly shall be seen iii 4 106
That honourable day shall ne'er be seen iv 1 91
Thieves are not judged but they are by to hear, Although apparent guilt be seen in them iv 1 124
A matter of small consequence, Which for some reasons I would not have seen v 2 62
High sparks of honour in thee have I seen v 6 29
A virtue that was never seen in you. *1 Hen. IV.* iii 1 126
By being seldom seen, I could not stir But like a comet I was wonder'd at iii 2 46
My presence, like a robe pontifical, Ne'er seen but wonder'd at iii 2 57
So when he had occasion to be seen, He was but as the cuckoo is in June iii 2 74
No eye hath seen such scarecrows. I'll not march through Coventry with them, that's flat iv 2 41
Let it be seen to-morrow in the battle Which of us fears iv 3 13
I am sorry I should force you to believe That which I would to God I had not seen; But these mine eyes saw him *2 Hen. IV.* i 1 106
How might we see Falstaff bestow himself to-night in his true colours, and not ourselves be seen? ii 2 188
You have not seen a hulk better stuffed in the hold ii 4 70
What! we have seen the seven stars ii 4 201
If this were seen, The happiest youth . . . Would shut the book iii 1 53
That thou hadst seen that that this knight and I have seen! iii 2 226
Let's to dinner: Jesus, the days that we have seen! iii 2 234
Which was never seen before in such an assembly Epil. 25
Suppose that you have seen The well-appointed king *Hen. V.* iii Prol. 3
There seen, Heave him away upon your winged thoughts Athwart the sea v Prol. 7
I have seen you gleeking and galling at this gentleman twice or thrice v 1 78
Come from behind; I know thee well, though never seen before *1 Hen. VI.* i 2 67
I thought I should have seen some Hercules ii 3 19
Where false Plantagenet dare not be seen ii 4 74
Depart when heaven please, For I have seen our enemies' overthrow iii 2 111
I fear we should have seen decipher'd there More rancorous spite iv 1 184
Such massacre And ruthless slaughters as are daily seen v 4 161
Her valiant courage and undaunted spirit, More than in women commonly is seen v 5 71
Oft have I seen the haughty cardinal, More like a soldier *2 Hen. VI.* i 1 185
Well hath your highness seen into this duke iii 1 42
In Ireland have I seen this stubborn Cade iii 1 360
I have seen Him caper upright like a wild Morisco iii 1 364
Oft have I seen a timely-parted ghost, Of ashy semblance iii 2 161
You would not feast him like a friend; And 'tis well seen he found an enemy iii 2 185
Were there a serpent seen, with forked tongue iii 2 259
What a sign it is of evil life, Where death's approach is seen so terrible! iii 3 6
I have seen him whipped three market-days together iv 2 62
Oft have I seen a hot o'erweening cur Run back and bite v 1 151
Would I had died a maid, And never seen thee! *3 Hen. VI.* i 1 217
As I have seen a swan With bootless labour swim against the tide i 4 19
And yet be seen to bear a woman's face? i 4 140
In protection of their tender ones, Who hath not seen them? ii 2 29
My crown is in my heart, not on my head; Not deck'd with diamonds and Indian stones, Nor to be seen iii 1 64
Your grace's word shall serve, As well as I had seen and heard him speak *Richard III.* iii 5 63
All will come to nought, When such bad dealing must be seen in thought iii 6 14
Eighty odd years of sorrow have I seen iv 1 96
Lest, being seen, thy brother, tender George, Be executed v 3 95
The sun will not be seen to-day; The sky doth frown and lour v 3 282
That former fabulous story, Being now seen possible enough *Hen. VIII.* i 1 37
In most strange postures We have seen him set himself iii 2 119
He has a loyal breast, For you have seen him open't iii 2 201
There is seen The baby figure of the giant mass *Troi. and Cres.* i 3 344
It should seem, fellow, that thou hast not seen the Lady Cressida iii 1 40
Have you seen my cousin? iii 2 8
I would not for half Troy have you seen here iv 2 42
I have, thou gallant Trojan, seen thee oft Labouring for destiny iv 5 183
I have seen thee, As hot as Perseus, spur thy Phrygian steed iv 5 185
I have seen thee pause and take thy breath, When that a ring of Greeks have hemm'd thee in iv 5 192
This have I seen; But this thy countenance, still lock'd in steel, I never saw iv 5 194
Well, welcome, welcome!—I have seen the time iv 5 210
That you may be abhorr'd Further than seen! *Coriolanus* i 4 33
I have Before-time seen him thus i 6 24
I have seen the dumb men throng to see him and The blind to hear him speak ii 1 278
Battles thrice six I have seen and heard of ii 3 136
Come, try upon yourselves what you have seen me iii 1 225
What you have seen him do and heard him speak iii 3 77
My sometime general, I have seen thee stern iv 1 24
A lonely dragon, that his fen Makes fear'd and talk'd of more than seen iv 1 31
And stop those maims Of shame seen through thy country iv 5 93
O, had the monster seen those lily hands Tremble, like aspen-leaves, upon a lute! *T. Andron.* ii 4 44
Had I but seen thy picture in this plight, It would have madded me iii 1 103
Was ever seen An emperor in Rome thus overborne? iv 4 1

Seen. With twenty popish tricks and ceremonies, Which I have seen thee careful to observe *T. Andron.* v 1 77
Many a morning hath he there been seen *Rom. and Jul.* i 1 137
She hath not seen the change of fourteen years i 2 9
I have seen the day That I have worn a visor i 5 23
Too early seen unknown, and known too late! i 5 141
Never was seen so black a day as this: O woful day, O woful day! iv 5 53
Give me thy torch, boy: hence, and stand aloof: Yet put it out, for I would not be seen v 3 2
I have not seen you long: how goes the world? *T. of Athens* i 1 2
To show Lord Timon that mean eyes have seen The foot above the head i 1 93
Is not my lord seen yet?—Not yet.—I wonder on't iii 4 9
You that are honest, by being what you are, Make them best seen and known v 1 72
I was writing of my epitaph; It will be seen to-morrow v 1 189
And Cicero Looks with such ferret and such fiery eyes As we have seen him in the Capitol *J. Cæsar* i 2 187
I have seen tempests, when the scolding winds Have rived the knotty oaks, and I have seen The ambitious ocean swell and rage and foam i 3 5
There's two or three of us have seen strange sights i 3 138
There is one within, Besides the things that we have heard and seen, Recounts most horrid sights seen by the watch ii 2 15
When beggars die, there are no comets seen ii 2 30
I have seen more days than you iv 1 18
I have seen more years, I'm sure, than ye iv 3 132
So foul and fair a day I have not seen *Macbeth* i 3 38
One cried 'God bless us!' and 'Amen' the other; As they had seen me with these hangman's hands ii 2 28
Within the volume of which time I have seen Hours dreadful and things strange ii 4 2
Which often, since my here-remain in England, I have seen him do iv 3 149
Where nothing, But who knows nothing, is once seen to smile iv 3 167
I have seen her rise from her bed, throw her night-gown upon her v 1 5
Has this thing appear'd again to-night?—I have seen nothing *Hamlet* i 1 22
This dreaded sight, twice seen of us i 1 25
That are so fortified against our story What we have two nights seen i 1 33
By my advice, Let us impart what we have seen to-night i 1 169
Would I had met my dearest foe in heaven Or ever I had seen that day! i 2 183
His beard was grizzled,—no?—It was, as I have seen it in his life i 2 241
Never make known what you have seen to-night i 5 144
Never to speak of this that you have seen i 5 153
Having ever seen in the prenominate crimes The youth you breathe of guilty ii 1 43
But what might you think, When I had seen this hot love on the wing? ii 2 132
But who, O, who had seen the mobled queen— 'The mobled queen?' ii 2 524
Who this had seen, with tongue in venom steep'd ii 2 533
The spirit that I have seen May be the devil ii 2 627
O, woe is me, To have seen what I have seen, see what I see! iii 1 169
O, there be players that I have seen play, and heard others praise iii 2 32
It is a damned ghost that we have seen iii 2 87
And oft 'tis seen the wicked prize itself Buys out the law iii 3 59
Ah, mine own lord, what have I seen to-night! iv 1 5
I've seen myself, and served against, the French iv 7 84
'Twill not be seen in him there; there the men are as mad as he v 1 169
I have seen you both: But since he is better'd, we have therefore odds v 2 273
We have seen the best of our time *Lear* i 2 122
I have told you what I have seen and heard; but faintly i 2 191
Old fools are babes again; and must be used With checks as flatteries, —when they are seen abused i 3 20
Where's my fool? I have not seen him this two days i 4 77
I have seen drunkards Do more than this in sport ii 1 36
I have seen better faces in my time Than stands on any shoulder that I see ii 2 99
What hath been seen, Either in snuffs and packings of the dukes iii 1 25
Full oft 'tis seen, Our means secure us iv 1 21
You have seen Sunshine and rain at once iv 3 19
The shrill-gorged lark so far Cannot be seen or heard iv 6 59
Thou hast seen a farmer's dog bark at a beggar? iv 6 158
Who, having seen me in my worst estate, Shunn'd my abhorr'd society v 3 209
I have seen the day, with my good biting falchion I would have made them skip v 3 276
I, of whom his eyes had seen the proof At Rhodes *Othello* i 1 28
A noble ship of Venice Hath seen a grievous wreck ii 1 23
Knavery's plain face is never seen till used ii 1 321
Much will be seen in that. In the mean time, Let me be thought too busy iii 3 252
Tell me but this, Have you not sometimes seen a handkerchief? iii 3 434
Would to God that I had never seen't! iii 4 77
I have seen the cannon, When it hath blown his ranks into the air iii 4 134
Her honour is an essence that's not seen iv 1 16
What, If I had said I had seen him do you wrong? iv 1 24
It is not honesty in me to speak What I have seen and known iv 1 289
You have seen nothing then?—Nor ever heard, nor ever did suspect iv 2 1
You have seen Cassio and she together iv 2 3
And yet she'll kneel and pray; I have seen her do't iv 2 23
I would you had never seen him!—So would not I: my love doth so approve him iv 3 18
I have seen the day, That, with this little arm and this good sword, I have made my way through more impediments v 2 261
You have seen and proved a fairer former fortune *Ant. and Cleo.* i 2 33
I have seen her die twenty times upon far poorer moment i 2 146
Would I had never seen her!—O, sir, you had then left unseen a wonderful piece of work i 2 158
No vessel can peep forth, but 'tis as soon Taken as seen i 4 54
I have seen thee fight, When I have envied thy behaviour ii 6 76
To be called into a huge sphere, and not to be seen to move in't ii 7 17
The man hath seen some majesty, and should know.—Hath he seen majesty? iii 3 45
Thou hast seen these signs; They are black vesper's pageants iv 14 7
She's a good sign, but I have seen small reflection of her wit *Cymbeline* i 2 33
I have seen him in Britain: he was then of a crescent note i 4 1
I have seen him in France i 4 11
If she went before others I have seen, as that diamond of yours outlustres many I have beheld, I could not but believe she excelled many: but I have not seen the most precious diamond that is, nor you the lady i 4 78
Let it be granted you have seen all this—and praise Be given to your remembrance ii 4 92
How, In this our pinching cave, shall we discourse The freezing hours away? We have seen nothing iii 3 39

Seen. Not seen of late? Grant, heavens, that which I fear Prove false! *Cymbeline* iii 5 52
Her old servant, I have not seen these two days iii 5 55
'Tis wonder That an invisible instinct should frame them To royalty unlearn'd, honour untaught, Civility not seen from other iv 2 179
I had rather Have skipp'd from sixteen years of age to sixty, To have turn'd my leaping-time into a crutch, Than have seen this iv 2 201
The army broken, And but the backs of Britons seen, all flying v 3 6
Your death has eyes in 's head then; I have not seen him so pictured v 4 185
I have surely seen him: His favour is familiar to me v 5 92
Here they're but felt, and seen with mischief's eyes *Pericles* i 4 8
We have heard your miseries as far as Tyre, And seen the desolation of your streets i 4 89
Till when,—the which I hope shall ne'er be seen i 4 105
Here have you seen a mighty king His child, I wis, to incest bring ii Gower 1
That on the touching of her lips I may Melt and no more be seen v 3 43
In Pericles, his queen and daughter, seen . . . Virtue preserved v 3 Gower 87

Seese is not good to give putter; your belly is all putter.—'Seese' and 'putter'! *Mer. Wives* v 5 148

Seest. What seest thou else In the dark backward and abysm of time? *Tempest* i 2 49
The fringed curtains of thine eye advance And say what thou seest yond i 2 409
This gallant which thou seest Was in the wreck i 2 413
See'st thou here, This is the mouth o' the cell iv 1 215
Think on thy Proteus, when thou haply seest Some rare note-worthy object in thy travel *T. G. of Ver.* i 1 12
Forgive me that I do not dream on thee, Because thou see'st me dote ii 4 173
What seest thou?—Him we go to find iii 1 190
If thou seest my boy, Bid him make haste and meet me iii 1 257
If thou seest her before me, commend me *Mer. Wives* i 4 168
Thou seest, thou wicked varlet, now, what's come upon thee *M. for M.* ii 1 199
But seest thou not what a deformed thief this fashion is? *Much Ado* iii 3 131
Thou seest that all the grace that she hath left Is that she will not add to her damnation A sin of perjury iv 1 173
Which here thou viewest, beholdest, surveyest, or seest. *L. L. Lost* i 1 247
What thou seest when thou dost wake, Do it for thy true-love take *M. N. Dream* ii 2 27
Thou see'st these lovers seek a place to fight iii 2 354
Welcome, good Robin. See'st thou this sweet sight? iv 1 51
Thou seest we are not all alone unhappy *As Y. Like It* ii 7 136
Thou see'st how diligent I am To dress thy meat myself *T. of Shrew* iv 3 39
My hair?—Past question; for thou seest it will not curl by nature *T. N.* i 3 104
So soon as ever thou seest him, draw iii 4 195
A fool That seest a game play'd home, the rich stake drawn *W. Tale* i 2 248
Mark and perform it, see'st thou! ii 3 170
Seest thou not the air of the court in these enfoldings? iv 4 755
All this thou seest is but a clod And module of confounded royalty *K. John* v 7 57
In that thou seest thy wretched brother die *Richard II.* i 2 27
Thou seest I have more flesh than another man *1 Hen. IV.* iii 3 188
Thou shalt find me tractable to any honest reason: thou seest I am pacified iii 3 195
All these bold fears Thou see'st with peril I have answered *2 Hen. IV.* iv 5 197
Thou seest that I no issue have *1 Hen. VI.* ii 5 94
What seest thou there? King Henry's diadem? *2 Hen. VI.* i 2 7
In my opinion yet thou see'st not well.—Yes, master, clear as day ii 1 107
O God, seest Thou this, and bearest so long? ii 1 154
The law, thou see'st, hath judged thee ii 3 15
What seest thou in me, York? why dost thou pause? v 2 19
And, as thou seest, ourselves in heavy plight *3 Hen. VI.* iii 3 37
Thou seest what's past, go fear thy king withal iii 3 226
O God, that seest it, do not suffer it! *Richard III.* i 2 271
'Tis not my blood Wherein thou seest me mask'd *Coriolanus* i 8 10
This is dear mercy, and thou seest it not *Rom. and Jul.* iii 3 28
I charge thee, Whate'er thou hear'st or seest, stand all aloof v 3 26
What a beast art thou already, that seest not thy loss! *T. of Athens* iv 3 349
Thou seest the world, Volumnius, how it goes *J. Cæsar* v 5 22
Ah, good father, Thou seest, the heavens, as troubled with man's act, Threaten his bloody stage *Macbeth* ii 4 5
When thou seest that act afoot, Even with the very comment of thy soul Observe mine uncle *Hamlet* iii 2 83
Where's the king? and where's Cordelia? See'st thou this object? *Lear* v 3 238
A' bears the third part of the world, man; see'st not? *Ant. and Cleo.* ii 7 97
Seest thou, my good fellow? Go put on thy defences iv 4 9
When thou see'st him, A little witness my obedience *Cymbeline* iii 4 67
What seest thou in our looks?—An angry brow *Pericles* i 2 51

Seethe. My business seethes.—Sodden business! *Troi. and Cres.* iii 1 43
Go, suck the subtle blood o' the grape, Till the high fever seethe your blood to froth, And so 'scape hanging *T. of Athens* iv 3 433

Seething. Lovers and madmen have such seething brains *M. N. Dream* v 1 4

Segregation. What shall we hear of this?—A segregation of the Turkish fleet *Othello* ii 1 10

Seigneur. O Seigneur Dieu, je m'en oublie! *Hen. V.* iii 4 33
De foot et de coun! O Seigneur Dieu! iii 4 55
Je ne voudrais prononcer ces mots devant les seigneurs de France iii 4 59
O Seigneur Dieu!—O, Signieur Dew should be a gentleman iv 4 6
Vaillant, et très distingué seigneur d'Angleterre iv 4 60
O seigneur! le jour est perdu, tout est perdu! iv 5 2
Laissez, mon seigneur, laissez, laissez v 2 273
Excusez-moi, je vous supplie, mon très-puissant seigneur v 2 277

Seize. What's open made to justice, That justice seizes *Meas. for Meas.* ii 1 22
Which is the lady I must seize upon? *Much Ado* v 4 53
The party 'gainst the which he doth contrive Shall seize one half his goods; the other half Comes to the privy coffer *Mer. of Venice* iv 1 353
All things that thou dost call thine Worth seizure do we seize *As. Y. L. It* iii 1 10
Seize thee that list *T. of Shrew* iii 1 91
Or I'll seize thy life, With what thou else call'st thine *W. Tale* ii 3 136
We do seize to us The plate, coin, revenues and moveables *Richard II.* ii 1 160
Seek you to seize and gripe into your hands The royalties and rights of banish'd Hereford? ii 1 189
If you do wrongfully seize Hereford's rights ii 1 201
Think what you will, we seize into our hands His plate, his goods ii 1 209
Seize it, if thou darest.—An if I do not, may my hands rot off! iv 1 48
Here, cousin, seize the crown iv 1 181
Let vultures vile seize on his lungs! *2 Hen. IV.* v 3 146
Here's the lord of the soil come to seize me for a stray *2 Hen. VI.* iv 10 27
This is the quondam king; let's seize upon him *3 Hen. VI.* iii 1 23
At unawares may beat down Edward's guard And seize himself iv 2 24
Seize on the shame-faced Henry, bear him hence iv 8 53
Seize on him, Furies, take him to your torments! *Richard III.* i 4 57

Seize. Seize him, ædiles!—Down with him! *Coriolanus* iii 1 183
Rape, call you it, my lord, to seize my own? *T. Andron.* i 1 405
Nor great Alcides, nor the god of war, Shall seize this prey iv 2 96
They may seize On the white wonder of dear Juliet's hand *R. and J.* iii 3 35
What should be spoken here, where our fate, Hid in an auger-hole, may rush, and seize us? *Macbeth* ii 3 128
The castle of Macduff I will surprise; Seize upon Fife iv 1 151
Most loved, despised! Thee and thy virtues here I seize upon *Lear* i 1 255
Natures of such deep trust we shall much need; You we first seize on ii 1 118
Swear it, damn thyself; Lest, being like one of heaven, the devils themselves Should fear to seize thee *Othello* iv 2 37
And seize upon the fortunes of the Moor, For they succeed on you v 2 366
Upon his own appeal, seizes him *Ant. and Cleo.* iii 5 12
Her head's declined, and death will seize her, but Your comfort makes the rescue iii 11 47
By medicine life may be prolong'd, yet death Will seize the doctor too *Cymbeline* v 5 30
Dost, with thine angel's face, Seize with thine eagle's talons *Pericles* iv 3 48
Seized. Say, this were death That now hath seized them *Tempest* ii 1 261
There thou mayst brain him, Having first seized his books iii 2 97
Had I been seized by a hungry lion, I would have been a breakfast to the beast, Rather than have false Proteus rescue me *T. G. of Ver.* v 4 33
At length, another ship had seized on us *Com. of Errors* i 1 113
And, but infirmity Which waits upon worn times hath something seized His wish'd ability *W. Tale* v 1 142
John hath seized Arthur *K. John* iii 4 131
Bolingbroke Hath seized the wasteful king *Richard II.* iii 4 55
Henry the Fourth Seized on the realm, deposed the rightful king 2 *Hen. VI.* ii 2 24
Seized upon their towns and provinces 3 *Hen. VI.* i 1 109
Sir Richard Grey was slain, His lands then seized on by the conqueror iii 2 3
Our treasure seized, our soldiers put to flight iii 3 36
The tiger now hath seized the gentle hind *Richard III.* ii 4 50
Wert thou a horse, thou wouldst be seized by the leopard *T. of Athens* iv 3 343
Did forfeit . . . all those his lands Which he stood seized of *Hamlet* i 1 89
Sleep hath seized me wholly *Cymbeline* ii 2 7
Haply, despair hath seized her iii 5 60
They have seized Marina. Let her go *Pericles* iv 1 98
Seizeth. This prince in justice seizeth but his own *T. Andron.* i 1 281
Seizing. You break not sanctuary in seizing him *Richard III.* iii 1 47
Seizure. All things that thou dost call thine Worth seizure do we seize into our hands *As Y. Like It* iii 1 10
Unyoke this seizure and this kind regreet *K. John* iii 1 241
To whose soft seizure The cygnet's down is harsh *Troi. and Cres.* i 1 57
Seld. If I might in entreaties find success—As seld I have the chance iv 5 150
Seldom. It [sleep] seldom visits sorrow *Tempest* ii 1 195
Her husband is seldom from home *Mer. Wives* ii 2 105
Seldom when The steeled gaoler is the friend of men *Meas. for Meas.* iv 2 89
If my observation, which very seldom lies, By the heart's still rhetoric disclosed with eyes, Deceive me not now *L. L. Lost* ii 1 228
Such traitors His majesty seldom fears *All's Well* ii 1 100
The merit of service is seldom attributed to the true and exact performer iii 6 64
I am deceived by him that in such intelligence hath seldom failed iv 5 88
He is seldom from the house of a most homely shepherd *W. Tale* iv 2 43
Now, good now, Say so but seldom v 1 20
Where words are scarce, they are seldom spent in vain *Richard II.* ii 1 7
But when they seldom come, they wish'd for come, And nothing pleaseth but rare accidents 1 *Hen. IV.* i 2 230
By being seldom seen, I could not stir But like a comet I was wonder'd at iii 2 46
And so my state, Seldom but sumptuous, show'd like a feast iii 2 58
Such as is bent on sun-like majesty When it shines seldom in admiring eyes iii 2 80
'Tis seldom when the bee doth leave her comb In the dead carrion 2 *Hen. IV.* iv 4 79
Things are often spoke and seldom meant 2 *Hen. VI.* iii 1 268
Men's flesh preserved so whole do seldom win iii 1 301
My crown is called content: A crown it is that seldom kings enjoy 3 *Hen. VI.* iii 1 65
Hasty marriage seldom proveth well iv 1 18
Bad news, by'r lady; seldom comes the better *Richard III.* ii 3 4
Outward show; which, God he knows, Seldom or never jumpeth with the heart iii 1 11
Thou art a soldier, therefore seldom rich *T. of Athens* i 2 228
I did endure Not seldom, nor no slight checks ii 2 149
Their blood is caked, 'tis cold, it seldom flows ii 2 225
The public body, which doth seldom Play the recanter v 1 148
He hears no music; Seldom he smiles *J. Cæsar* i 2 205
Those that do die of it do seldom or never recover *Ant. and Cleo.* v 2 248
To seas, Where when men been, there's seldom ease *Pericles* ii Gower 28
Seldom but that pity begets you a good opinion iv 2 130
Seld-shown flamens Do press among the popular throngs *Coriolanus* ii 1 229
Select. A certain number, Though thanks to all, must I select from all i 6 81
Are of a most select and generous chief in that *Hamlet* i 3 74
Seleucus. Where's Seleucus?—Here, madam.—This is my treasurer *Ant. and Cleo.* v 2 140
That I have reserved To myself nothing. Speak the truth, Seleucus v 2 144
The ingratitude of this Seleucus does Even make me wild v 2 153
Self. Hurried thence Me and thy crying self *Tempest* i 2 132
Banish'd from her Is self from self: a deadly banishment! *T. G. of Ver.* iii 1 173
Those . . . she tender'd; With them, upon her knees, her humble self iii 1 226
Since the substance of your perfect self Is else devoted, I am but a shadow iv 2 124
For my poor self, I am combined by a sacred vow *Meas. for Meas.* iv 3 148
Better than thy dear self's better part *Com. of Errors* ii 2 125
It is thyself, mine own self's better part, Mine eye's clear eye iii 2 61
They were never so truly turned over and over as my poor self in love *Much Ado* v 2 35
Your fair self should make A yielding 'gainst some reason in my breast *L. L. Lost* ii 1 151
The curate and your sweet self are good at such eruptions v 1 120
Shut My woeful self up in a mourning house v 2 818
Every one doth swear That comes to hazard for my worthless self *Mer. of Venice* ii 9 18
Swear by your double self, And there's an oath of credit v 1 245
To dissever so Our great self and our credit *All's Well* ii 1 126
When your sweet self was got iv 2 10
In those unfledged days was my wife a girl; Your precious self had then not cross'd the eyes Of my young play-fellow *W. Tale* i 2 79

Self. Your high self, The gracious mark o' the land *W. Tale* iv 4 7
What is nearest to him, which is Your gracious self iv 4 534
Happily may your sweet self put on The lineal state! *K. John* v 7 101
Infusing him with self and vain conceit *Richard II.* iii 2 166
So shall the world perceive, That I have turn'd away my former self 2 *Hen. IV.* v 5 62
A naked blind boy in her naked seeing self *Hen. V.* v 2 325
Give me leave, By circumstance, to curse thy cursed self *Richard III.* i 2 80
Outlive thy glory, like my wretched self! i 3 203
My other self, my counsel's consistory, My oracle, my prophet! ii 2 151
Make war upon themselves; blood against blood, Self against self ii 4 63
Where it seems best unto your royal self iii 1 63
We heartily solicit Your gracious self to take on you the charge iii 7 131
Take to your royal self This proffer'd benefit of dignity iii 7 195
The tract of every thing Would by a good discourser lose some life, Which action's self was tongue to *Hen. VIII.* i 1 42
Invited by your noble self ii 2 95
My heart weeps to see him So little of his great self iii 2 336
His royal self in judgement comes to hear The cause v 3 120
I have a kind of self resides with you; But an unkind self, that itself will leave, To be another's fool *Troi. and Cres.* iii 2 155
Tarquin's self he met, And struck him on his knee *Coriolanus* ii 2 98
Swear by thy gracious self, Which is the god of my idolatry *R. and J.* ii 2 113
His poor self, A dedicated beggar to the air, With his disease of all-shunn'd poverty, Walks, like contempt, alone *T. of Athens* iv 2 12
And make thine own self the conquest of thy fury iv 3 340
But, for my single self, I had as lief not be as live to be In awe of such a thing as I myself *J. Cæsar* i 2 94
Which you thought had been Our innocent self *Macbeth* iii 1 79
By self and violent hands Took off her life v 8 70
Your noble self, I am sure, is sent for *Othello* i 2 92
Let me lodge Lichas on the horns o' the moon; And with those hands, that grasp'd the heaviest club, Subdue my worthiest self *A. and C.* iv 12 47
As I my poor self did exchange for you, To your so infinite loss *Cymbeline* i 1 119
Fear and niceness—The handmaids of all women, or, more truly, Woman it pretty self iii 4 160
Your noble self, That best know how to rule and how to reign *Pericles* ii 4 37
Self-abuse. My strange and self-abuse Is the initiate fear that wants hard use: We are yet but young in deed *Macbeth* iii 4 142
Self-admission. In will peculiar and in self-admission *Troi. and Cres.* ii 3 176
Self-affairs. Being over-full of self-affairs, My mind did lose it *M. N. D.* i 1 113
Self-affected. If he were proud,— Or covetous of praise,— Ay, or surly borne,— Or strange, or self-affected! *Troi. and Cres.* ii 3 250
Self-affrighted tremble at his sin *Richard II.* iii 2 53
Self-assumption. Over-proud And under-honest, in self-assumption greater Than in the note of judgement *Troi. and Cres.* ii 3 133
Self bill. I'll tell you; that self bill is urged *Hen. V.* i 1 1
Self-blood. He is your brother, lords, sensibly fed Of that self-blood that first gave life to you *T. Andron.* iv 2 123
Self-born. In one self-born hour To plant and o'erwhelm custom *W. Tale* iv 1 8
And fright our native peace with self-born arms *Richard II.* ii 3 80
Self-bounty. I would not have your free and noble nature, Out of self-bounty, be abused *Othello* iii 3 200
Self-breath. And speaks not to himself but with a pride That quarrels at self-breath *Troi. and Cres.* ii 3 182
Self chain. That self chain about his neck Which he forswore most monstrously to have *Com. of Errors* v 1 10
Self-charity. Unless self-charity be sometimes a vice *Othello* ii 3 202
Self-comparisons. Confronted him with self-comparisons *Macbeth* i 2 55
Self-covered. Thou changed and self-cover'd thing, for shame, Be-monster not thy feature *Lear* iv 2 62
Self-danger. But disguise That which, to appear itself, must not yet be But by self-danger *Cymbeline* iii 4 149
Self-drawing. Spider-like, Out of his self-drawing web *Hen. VIII.* i 1 63
Self-endeared. She cannot love, Nor take no shape nor project of affection, She is so self-endeared *Much Ado* iii 1 56
Self exhibition. To be partner'd With tomboys hired with that self exhibition Which your own coffers yield! *Cymbeline* i 6 122
Self-explication. A thing perplex'd Beyond self-explication iii 4 8
Self-figured. To knit their souls, On whom there is no more dependency But brats and beggary, in self-figured knot ii 3 124
Self-glorious. Free from vainness and self-glorious pride *Hen. V.* v Prol. 20
Self-gracious. Out of a self-gracious remembrance *All's Well* iv 5 78
Self hand. Nor by a hired knife; but that self hand, Which writ his honour in the acts it did *Ant. and Cleo.* v 1 21
Self-harming jealousy! fie, beat it hence! *Com. of Errors* ii 1 102
Self king. And fill'd Her sweet perfections with one self king *T. Night* i 1 39
Self-love. Peevish, proud, idle, made of self-love *All's Well* i 1 157
O, you are sick of self-love, Malvolio *T. Night* i 5 97
Self-love, my liege, is not so vile a sin As self-neglecting *Hen. V.* ii 4 74
He that is truly dedicate to war Hath no self-love 2 *Hen. VI.* v 2 38
Self-loving. Ambitious past all thinking, Self-loving *Coriolanus* iv 6 32
Self mate. The stars above us govern our conditions; Else one self mate and mate could not beget Such different issues *Lear* iv 3 36
Self-mettle. Anger is like A full-hot horse, who being allow'd his way, Self-mettle tires him *Hen. VIII.* i 1 134
Self mould. That metal, that self mould, that fashion'd thee Made him a man *Richard II.* i 2 23
Self-neglecting. Self-love, my liege, is not so vile a sin As self neglecting *Hen. V.* ii 4 75
Self-offence. More nor less to others paying Than by self-offences weighing *Meas. for Meas.* iii 2 280
Self-place. I'll tell thee what befel me on a day In this self-place where now we mean to stand 3 *Hen. VI.* iii 1 11
Self-reproving. He's full of alteration And self-reproving *Lear* v 1 4
Self-same. O perilous mouths, That bear in them one and the self-same tongue, Either of condemnation or approof! *Meas. for Meas.* ii 4 173
She that accuses him . . . In self-same manner doth accuse my husband v 1 196
That very hour and in the self-same inn *Com. of Errors* i 1 54
Why, sadness is one and the self-same thing, dear imp *L. L. Lost* i 2 4
When I had lost one shaft, I shot his fellow of the self-same flight The self-same way *Mer. of Venice* i 1 141
Bid my father welcome, While I with self-same kindness welcome thine *T. of Shrew* v 2 5
The selfsame sun that shines upon his court Hides not his visage from our cottage but Looks on alike *W. Tale* iv 4 455
For selfsame wind that I should speak withal Is kindling coals that fires all my breast, And burns me up 3 *Hen. VI.* ii 1 82
Like the selfsame sea Forced to retire by fury of the wind ii 5 7
For both of you are birds of selfsame feather iii 3 161

Self-same. Kneel thou, Whilst I propose the selfsame words to thee 3 *Hen. VI.* v 5 20
Stabb'd by the selfsame hand that made these wounds! *Richard III.* i 2 11
Why, that was he.—The selfsame name, but one of better nature i 2 143
For the selfsame heaven That frowns on me looks sadly upon him v 3 286
With an accent tuned in selfsame key Retorts to chiding fortune *T. and C.* i 3 53
The self-same gods that arm'd the Queen of Troy *T. Andron.* i 1 136
Whose self-same mettle, Whereof thy proud child, arrogant man, is puff'd, Engenders the black toad *T. of Athens* iv 3 179
Myself have letters of the selfsame tenour *J. Cæsar* iv 3 171
Went it not so?—To the selfsame tune and words *Macbeth* i 3 88
In viewing o'er the rest o' the selfsame day i 3 94
I am made Of the self-same metal that my sister is *Lear* i 1 71
This is a fellow of the self-same colour Our sister speaks of ii 2 145
Self-slaughter. That the Everlasting had not fix'd His canon 'gainst self-slaughter! O God! God! *Hamlet* i 2 132
Against self-slaughter There is a prohibition so divine *Cymbeline* iii 4 78
Self-sovereignty. Do not curst wives hold that self-sovereignty Only for praise sake? *L. L. Lost* iv 1 36
Self-subdued. That worthied him, got praises of the king For him attempting who was self-subdued *Lear* ii 2 129
Self-unable. But like a common and an outward man, That the great figure of a council frames By self-unable motion *All's Well* iii 1 13
Self way. Shoot another arrow that self way *Mer. of Venice* i 1 148
Self-willed. A peevish self-will'd harlotry 1 *Hen. IV.* iii 1 198; *R. and J.* iv 2 14
Ajax is grown self-will'd *Troi. and Cres.* i 3 188
Self-wrong. Lest myself be guilty to self-wrong, I'll stop mine ears against the mermaid's song *Com. of Errors* iii 2 168
Sell. You will needs buy and sell men and women like beasts *M. for M.* iii 2 2
Why, that's spoken like an honest drovier: so they sell bullocks *M. Ado* ii 1 202
To sell a bargain well is as cunning as fast and loose *L. L. Lost* iii 1 104
I will never buy and sell out of this word iii 1 143
We that sell by gross, the Lord doth know, Have not the grace to grace it with such show v 2 319
I will buy with you, sell with you, talk with you, walk with you *M. of V.* i 3 36
She made me vow That I should neither sell nor give nor lose it iv 1 443
Sell when you can: you are not for all markets *As Y. Like It* iii 5 60
For a quart d'écu he will sell the fee-simple of his salvation *All's Well* iv 3 311
When you sing, I'ld have you buy and sell so *W. Tale* iv 4 138
Sell your face for five pence and 'tis dear *K. John* i 1 153
Who in that sale sells pardon from himself iii 1 167
They sell the pasture now to buy the horse *Hen. V.* ii Prol. 5
That he should, for a foreign purse, so sell His sovereign's life to death ii 2 10
I will sell my dukedom, To buy a slobbery and a dirty farm iii 5 12
Bid them achieve me and then sell my bones iv 3 91
The man that once did sell the lion's skin While the beast lived, was kill'd with hunting him iv 3 93
Poor market folks that come to sell their corn 1 *Hen. VI.* iii 2 15
Sell every man his life as dear as mine, And they shall find dear deer of us iv 2 53
Or sell my title for a glorious grave 2 *Hen. VI.* iii 1 92
Therefore, when merchant-like I sell revenge, Broke be my sword! iv 1 41
Thus the cardinal Does buy and sell his honour as he pleases *Hen. VIII.* i 1 192
Let us, like merchants, show our foulest wares, And think, perchance, they'll sell; if not, The lustre of the better *Troi. and Cres.* i 3 360
We'll but commend what we intend to sell iv 1 78
We two, that with so many thousand sighs Did buy each other, must poorly sell ourselves With the rude brevity and discharge of one iv 4 42
When for a day of kings' entreaties a mother should not sell him an hour from her beholding *Coriolanus* i 3 9
I'll nor sell nor give him: lend you him I will For half a hundred years i 4 6
Woollen vassals, things created To buy and sell with groats iii 2 10
An if a man did need a poison now, Whose sale is present death in Mantua, Here lives a caitiff wretch would sell it him *Rom. and Jul.* v 1 52
This same needy man must sell it me v 1 54
There is thy gold, worse poison to men's souls, Doing more murders in this loathsome world, Than these poor compounds that thou mayst not sell. I sell thee poison; thou hast sold me none v 1 82
'Tis rated As those which sell would give *T. of Athens* i 1 169
If I would sell my horse, and buy twenty more Better than he ii 1 7
To sell and mart your offices for gold To undeservers *J. Cæsar* iv 3 11
And sell the mighty space of our large honours For so much trash? iv 3 25
Then you'll buy 'em to sell again *Macbeth* iv 2 41
I am changed: I'll go sell all my land *Othello* i 3 388
There is gold for you; Sell me your good report *Cymbeline* ii 3 88
Seller. To things of sale a seller's praise belongs *L. L. Lost* iv 3 240
Selling. And furthermore, we'll have the Lord Say's head for selling the dukedom of Maine 2 *Hen. VI.* iv 2 170
That by selling her desires Buys herself bread and clothes *Othello* iv 1 95
Selves. I have made you mad; And even with such-like valour men hang and drown Their proper selves *Tempest* iii 3 60
Even for our kitchens We kill the fowl of season: shall we serve heaven With less respect than we do minister To our gross selves? *M. for M.* ii 2 87
True love Between our kingdoms and our royal selves *K. John* iii 1 232
In that nest of spicery they shall breed Selves of themselves *Rich. III.* iv 4 425
As we walk, To our own selves bend we our needful talk *Troi. and Cres.* iv 4 141
Make but an interior survey of your good selves *Coriolanus* ii 1 44
Semblable. It is a wonderful thing to see the semblable coherence of his men's spirits and his 2 *Hen. IV.* v 1 72
Que dit-il? que je suis semblable à les anges? *Hen. V.* v 2 112
His semblable, yea, himself, Timon disdains *T. of Athens* iv 3 22
To make true diction of him, his semblable is his mirror *Hamlet* v 2 124
That were excusable, that, and thousands more Of semblable import *Ant. and Cleo.* iii 4 3
Semblably furnish'd like the king himself 1 *Hen. IV.* v 3 21
Semblance. If you go out in your own semblance, you die *Mer. Wives* iv 2 67
And then another fault in the semblance of a fowl v 5 11
These two Dromios, one in semblance *Com. of Errors* v 1 358
Who is thus like to be cozened with the semblance of a maid *Much Ado* ii 2 39
She's but the sign and semblance of her honour iv 1 34
Now thy image doth appear In the rare semblance that I loved it first v 1 260
How little is the cost I have bestow'd In purchasing the semblance of my soul From out the state of hellish misery! *Mer. of Venice* iii 4 20
A martial outside, As many other mannish cowards have That do outface it with their semblances *As Y. Like It* i 3 124
I have your own letter that induced me to the semblance I put on *T. N.* v 1 315
This ship-boy's semblance hath disguised me quite *K. John* iv 3 4
With forms being fetch'd From glistering semblances of piety *Hen. V.* ii 2 117
But freshly looks and over-bears attaint With cheerful semblance iv Prol. 40
Repeat their semblance often on the seas 1 *Hen. VI.* v 3 193
Semblance. Oft have I seen a timely-parted ghost, Of ashy semblance 2 *Hen. VI.* iii 2 162
But now two mirrors of his princely semblance Are crack'd *Rich. III.* ii 2 51
Which if granted, As he made semblance of his duty *Hen. VIII.* i 2 198
Put off these frowns, An ill-beseeming semblance for a feast *R. and J.* i 5 76
If thou path, thy native semblance on, Not Erebus itself were dim enough To hide thee from prevention *J. Cæsar* ii 1 83
To assume a semblance That very dogs disdain'd *Lear* v 3 187
Let there be no honour Where there is beauty; truth, where semblance; love, Where there's another man *Cymbeline* ii 4 109
Tell thee, with speechless tongues and semblance pale *Pericles* i 1 36
By the semblance Of their white flags display'd, they bring us peace i 4 71
Semblative. And all is semblative a woman's part *T. Night* i 4 34
Semicircle. In a semicircle, Or a half-moon *W. Tale* ii 1 10
Semi-circled. In a semi-circled farthingale *Mer. Wives* iii 3 68
Semiramis. Softer and sweeter than the lustful bed On purpose trimm'd up for Semiramis *T. of Shrew* Ind. 2 41
To wanton with this queen, This goddess, this Semiramis *T. Andron.* ii 1 22
Semiramis, nay, barbarous Tamora, For no name fits thy nature but thy own! ii 3 118
Semper. 'Tis 'semper idem,' for 'obsque hoc nihil est' 2 *Hen. IV.* v 5 30
Sempronius. Publius and Sempronius, you must do it *T. Andron.* iv 3 10
To Lord Lucullus you: I hunted with his honour to-day: you, to Sempronius: commend me to their loves *T. of Athens* ii 2 198
Go, bid all my friends again, Lucius, Lucullus, and Sempronius iii 4 112
Senate. Our business is not unknown to the senate *Coriolanus* i 1 59
The noble senate, who, Under the gods, keep you in awe i 1 190
Is the senate possessed of this? ii 1 145
Yes, yes; the senate has letters from the general ii 1 148
The senate, Coriolanus, are well pleased To make thee consul ii 2 136
Remains That, in the official marks invested, you Anon do meet the senate ii 3 149
In soothing them, we nourish 'gainst our senate The cockle of rebellion iii 1 69
The accusation Which they have often made against the senate iii 1 128
How shall this bisson multitude digest The senate's courtesy? iii 1 132
Break ope the locks o' the senate and bring in The crows to peck the eagles iii 1 138
You are sent for to the senate iv 6 74
Subscribed by the consuls and patricians, Together with the seal o' the senate v 6 83
Please it your honours To call me to your senate v 6 141
He by the senate is accited home From weary wars *T. Andron.* i 1 27
In the Capitol and senate's right, Whom you pretend to honour i 1 41
What's this but libelling against the senate? iv 4 17
There are certain nobles of the senate Newly alighted *T. of Athens* i 2 180
Honour, health, and compassion to the senate! iii 5 5
Banish me! Banish your dotage; banish usury, That makes the senate ugly iii 5 100
Is this the balsam that the usuring senate Pours into captains' wounds? iii 5 110
Slaves and fools, Pluck the grave wrinkled senate from the bench, And minister in their steads! iv 1 5
The Athenians, By two of their most reverend senate, greet thee v 1 132
I will not come; That is enough to satisfy the senate *J. Cæsar* ii 2 72
The senate have concluded To give this day a crown to mighty Cæsar ii 2 93
For some one to say 'Break up the senate till another time, When Cæsar's wife shall meet with better dreams' ii 2 98
What is now amiss That Cæsar and his senate must redress? iii 1 32
The senate hath sent about three several quests To search you *Othello* i 2 46
These letters give, Iago, to the pilot; And by him do my duties to the senate iii 2 2
Is this the noble Moor whom our full senate Call all in all sufficient? iv 1 275
The senate hath stirr'd up the confiners And gentlemen of Italy *Cymb* iv 2 337
A supply Of Roman gentlemen, by the senate sent iv 3 26
Senate-house. At the senate-house?—There, Coriolanus *Coriolanus* ii 3 153
And, knowing myself again, Repair to the senate-house ii 3 156
The nobles in great earnestness are going All to the senate-house iv 6 58
We'll send Mark Antony to the senate-house; And he shall say you are not well to-day *J. Cæsar* ii 2 52
Good morrow, worthy Cæsar: I come to fetch you to the senate-house ii 2 59
I prithee, boy, run to the senate-house; Stay not to answer me ii 4 1
To glad her presence, The senate-house of planets all did sit *Pericles* i 1 10
Senator. Like to the senators of the antique Rome *Hen. V.* v Prol. 26
You malign our senators for that They are not such as you *Coriolanus* i 1 117
The senators of Rome are this good belly i 1 152
It's true; I heard a senator speak it i 3 106
I'll report it Where senators shall mingle tears with smiles i 9 3
You grave but reckless senators iii 1 92
You are plebeians, If they be senators iii 1 102
I am in this, Your wife, your son, these senators, the nobles iii 2 65
Old Menenius, and those senators That always favour'd him iv 3 7
Strange insurrections; the people against the senators iv 3 14
Come, go in, And take our friendly senators by the hands iv 5 138
No question asked him by any of the senators, but they stand bald before him iv 5 206
The nobility of Rome are his: The senators and patricians love him too iv 7 30
This Volumnia Is worth of consuls, senators, patricians, A city full v 4 56
How this lord is follow'd!—The senators of Athens: happy man! *T. of A.* i 1 40
Go you, sir, to the senators—Of whom, even to the state's best health, I have Deserved this hearing ii 2 205
The senators of Athens, together with the common lag of people iii 6 90
Thou cold sciatica, Cripple our senators, that their limbs may halt As lamely as their manners! iv 1 24
The senator shall bear contempt hereditary, The beggar native honour iv 3 10
Place thieves And give them title, knee and approbation With senators iv 3 37
The senators of Athens greet thee, Timon.—I thank them v 1 139
The senators with one consent of love Entreat thee back to Athens v 1 143
I'll beweep these comforts, worthy senators v 1 161
Being cross'd in conference by some senators *J. Cæsar* i 2 188
They say the senators to-morrow Mean to establish Cæsar as a king i 3 85
Bear my greeting to the senators And tell them that I will not come to-day ii 2 61
The throng that follows Cæsar at the heels, Of senators, of prætors ii 4 35
People and senators, be not affrighted; Fly not; stand still iii 1 82
Have put to death an hundred senators iv 3 175
Seventy senators that died By their proscriptions, Cicero being one iv 3 177
Thou art a villain.—You are—a senator *Othello* i 1 119
The tyrant custom, most grave senators i 3 230
Senators of Venice greet you.—I kiss the instrument of their pleasures iv 1 230
The senators alone of this great world, Chief factors for the gods *Ant. and Cleo.* ii 6 9

Send. And sends me forth—For else his project dies . . *Tempest* ii 1 298
I must go send some better messenger . . . . *T. G. of Ver.* i 1 159
Tell me, whither were I best to send him? . . . . . i 3 24
I need not cite him to it: I will send him hither to you presently . ii 4 86
Send her another; never give her o'er . . . . . iii 1 94
Slaves they are to me that send them flying . . . . iii 1 141
Send to me in the morning and I'll send it . . . . iv 2 132
He sends you for a picture . . . . iv 4 120
He sends your ladyship this ring.—The more shame for him that he sends it me . . . . iv 4 137
Heaven send Anne Page no worse fortune! . . *Mer. Wives* i 4 33
Sir Hugh send-a you? Rugby, baille me some paper . . . i 4 92
Mistress Page would desire you to send her your little page, of all loves ii 2 118
You must send her your page; no remedy.—Why, I will . . ii 2 127
Send him by your two men to Datchet-mead . . . . . iii 3 141
Shall we send that foolish carrion, Mistress Quickly, to him? . iii 3 205
Now heaven send thee good fortune! . . . . . . iii 4 105
Behold what honest clothes you send forth to bleaching! . . iii 3 174
Did he send you both these letters at an instant? . . . iv 2 126
Send him word they'll meet him in the park at midnight . . iv 4 3
Go send to Falstaff straight . . . . iv 4 18
Send quickly to Sir John, to know his mind . . . . iv 4 75
Send me a cool rut-time, Jove, or who can blame me to piss my tallow? v 5 83
I would send for certain of my creditors . . *Meas. for Meas.* i 2 136
Send after the duke and appeal to him.—I have done so . . i 2 178
At night I'll send him certain word of my success . . . i 4 89
Quick, dispatch, and send the head to Angelo . . . . iv 3 96
He sends a warrant For my poor brother's head . . . . v 1 102
For God's sake, send some other messenger . *Com. of Errors* ii 1 77
Either send the chain or send me by some token . . . iv 1 56
There is a purse of ducats; let her send it: Tell her I am arrested . iv 1 105
Will you send him, mistress, redemption, the money in his desk? . iv 2 46
And will not suffer us to fetch him out, Nor send him forth . . v 1 158
Unless you send some present help, Between them they will kill the conjurer . . . . v 1 176
I will send for him; and question him yourself . . *Much Ado* i 2 19
'God sends a curst cow short horns;' but to a cow too curst he sends none . . . . ii 1 25
By being too curst, God will send you no horns.—Just, if he send me no husband . . . . ii 1 27
I will go on the slightest errand now to the Antipodes that you can devise to send me on . . . . ii 1 274
Let us send her to call him in to dinner . . . . . ii 3 227
Send her home again without a husband . . . . . iii 3 174
God send every one their heart's desire! . . . . . iii 4 60
When I send for you, come hither mask'd . . . . . v 4 12
Consider who the king your father sends, To whom he sends *L. L. Lost* ii 1 2
And send you many lovers!—Amen, so you be none . . . ii 1 126
You must send the ass upon the horse, for he is very slow-gaited . iii 1 55
By whom shall I send this? . . . . iv 3 77
This will I send and something else more plain . . . . iv 3 121
Madam, this glove.—Did he not send you twain? . . . . v 2 48
How true a gentleman you send relief . . *Mer. of Venice* iii 4 6
Send the deed after me, And I will sign it . . . . . iv 1 396
What should I say, sweet lady? I was enforced to send it after him . v 1 216
Send to his brother; fetch that gallant hither . *As Y. Like It* ii 2 17
But a little beard.—Why, God will send more, if the man will be thankful iii 2 220
To that youth he calls his Rosalind He sends this bloody napkin . iv 3 94
He would send me word, he cut it to please himself . . . v 4 77
Will you go with us, Or shall I send my daughter Kate to you? *T. of S.* ii 1 168
God send you joy, Petruchio! 'tis a match . . . . . ii 1 321
Send for your daughter by your servant here . . . . iv 4 58
God send 'em good shipping! . . . . v 1 43
Let's each one send unto his wife; And he whose wife is most obedient To come at first when he doth send for her, Shall win the wager . v 2 66
My mistress sends you word That she is busy and she cannot come . v 2 80
A kind one too: Pray God, sir, your wife send you not a worse . v 2 84
What is your will, sir, that you send for me? . . . . v 2 100
God send him well! The court's a learning place . . *All's Well* i 1 190
Fair maid, send forth thine eye . . . . ii 3 58
I'd have them whipped; or I would send them to the Turk . . ii 3 94
I'll send her to my house, Acquaint my mother with my hate to her . ii 3 303
I'll send her straight away: to-morrow I'll to the wars . . . ii 3 312
What two things?—One, that she's not in heaven, whither God send her quickly! the other, that she's in earth, from whence God send her quickly! . . . . ii 4 12
I know she will lie at my house; thither they send one another . . iii 5 34
Send forth your amorous token for fair Maudlin . . . . v 3 68
Send for your ring, I will return it home, And give me mine again . v 3 223
God send you, sir, a speedy infirmity! . . . . *T. Night* i 5 84
I cannot love him: let him send no more . . . . . i 5 299
Thou hadst need send for more money . . . . . . ii 3 199
Send for money, knight: if thou hast her not i' the end, call me cut . ii 3 202
Now Jove, in his next commodity of hair, send thee a beard! . . iii 1 51
I did send, After the last enchantment you did here, A ring in chase of you . . . . iii 1 122
She sends him on purpose, that I may appear stubborn to him . . iii 4 73
Keep me in darkness, send ministers to me, asses . . . iv 2 100
Send one presently to Sir Toby.—What's the matter?—He has broke my head . . . . v 1 176
If't please the queen to send the babe . . . . *W. Tale* ii 2 56
Jove send her A better guiding spirit! . . . . . . ii 3 126
Give you all greetings that a king, at friend, Can send his brother . v 1 141
I'll send his soul to hell . . . . *K. John* i 1 272
We from the west will send destruction Into this city's bosom . . ii 1 409
I'll send those powers o'er to your majesty . . . . iii 3 70
Send fair-play orders and make compromise, Insinuation, parley . v 1 67
Send him word by me which way you go . . . . . v 3 7
Send them after to supply our wants . . . . *Richard II.* i 4 51
Bid her send me presently a thousand pound: Hold, take my ring . ii 2 91
Tell her I send to her my kind commends . . . . . iii 1 38
Through brazen trumpet send the breath of parley Into his ruin'd ears iii 3 33
And sends allegiance and true faith of heart . . . . iii 3 37
Send Defiance to the traitor . . . . iii 3 129
Thou, Aumerle, didst send two of thy men To execute the noble duke . iv 1 81
And send him many years of sunshine days! . . . . . iv 1 221
And send the hearers weeping to their beds . . . . . v 1 45
Banish us both and send the king with me . . . . . v 1 83
Sends me word, I shall have none but Mordake . . *1 Hen. IV.* i 1 94
When we need Your use and counsel, we shall send for you . . i 3 21

Send. Send me your prisoners with the speediest means . *1 Hen. IV.* i 3 120
Send us your prisoners, or you will hear of it.—An if the devil come and roar for them, I will not send them . . . . i 3 124
Send danger from the east unto the west, So honour cross it . . i 3 195
For divers reasons Which I shall send you written . . . . i 3 263
Give him as much as will make him a royal man, and send him back again ii 4 321
I'll send him packing . . . . ii 4 328
I will, by to-morrow dinner-time, Send him to answer thee, or any man ii 4 565
A shorter time shall send me to you, lords . . . . . iii 1 91
Did not we send grace, Pardon and terms of love to all of you? . v 5 2
And send you back again to your master, for a jewel . *2 Hen. IV.* i 2 21
I looked a' should have sent me two and twenty yards of satin, as I am a true knight, and he sends me security . . . . . . i 2 51
God send the prince a better companion!—God send the companion a better prince! . . . . i 2 223
God send the wench no worse fortune! . . . . . . ii 2 152
God prosper your affairs! God send us peace! . . . . iii 2 313
Send discoverers forth To know the numbers of our enemies . . iv 1 3
Send Colevile with his confederates To York, to present execution . iv 3 79
What! rate, rebuke, and roughly send to prison The immediate heir of England! . . . . v 2 70
The King of Scots; whom she did send to France . . *Hen. V.* i 2 161
He therefore sends you, meeter for your spirit, This tun of treasure . i 2 254
From the dust of old oblivion raked, He sends you this most memorable line . . . . ii 4 88
We may as bootless spend our vain command Upon the enraged soldiers in their spoil As send precepts to the leviathan To come ashore . iii 3 26
Say to England that we send To know what willing ransom he will give iii 5 62
Shall we go send them dinners and fresh suits? . . . . iv 2 57
This brawl to-day . . . Shall send between the red rose and the white A thousand souls to death . . . . . . *1 Hen. VI.* ii 4 126
O, send some succour to the distress'd lord! . . . . . iv 3 30
It is too late; I cannot send them now . . . . . . iv 4 1
I did send for thee To tutor thee in stratagems of war . . . iv 5 1
What tidings send our scouts? I prithee, speak . . . . v 2 10
A pure unspotted heart, Never yet taint with love, I send the king . v 3 183
I will not so presume To send such peevish tokens to a king . . v 3 186
Take this fellow in, and send for his master with a pursuivant *2 Hen. VI.* i 3 37
Send succours, lords, and stop the rage betime . . . . iii 1 285
'Tis politicly done, To send me packing with an host of men . . iii 1 342
Give thee thy hire and send thy soul to hell, Pernicious blood-sucker! . iii 2 225
Dread lord, the commons send you word by me . . . . iii 2 243
'Tis like the commons, rude unpolish'd hinds, Could send such message iii 2 272
I'll send some holy bishop to entreat . . . . . . iv 4 9
To Smithfield and gather head, And thither I will send you Matthew Goffe . . . . iv 5 11
Tell him I'll send Duke Edmund to the Tower . . . . . iv 9 38
That I have maintains my state And sends the poor well pleased from my gate . . . . iv 10 25
I'll send them all as willing as I live: Lands, goods, horse, armour . v 1 51
I send thee, Warwick, such a messenger As shall revenge his death *3 Hen. VI.* i 1 99
The Duke of Norfolk sends you word by me, The queen is coming . . ii 1 206
To soothe your forgery and his, Sends me a paper to persuade me patience . . . . iii 3 176
I'll follow you, and tell what answer Lewis and the Lady Bona send to him . . . . iv 3 56
We'll send him hence to Brittany, Till storms be past of civil enmity . iv 6 97
And only claim Our dukedom till God please to send the rest . . iv 7 47
'Tis not the king that sends you to the Tower . . *Richard III.* i 1 63
Her brother there, That made him send Lord Hastings to the Tower . i 1 68
I do love thee so, That I will shortly send thy soul to heaven . . i 1 119
Let him thank me, that holp to send him thither . . . . i 2 107
Aiming, belike, at your interior hatred, . . . Makes him to send . . i 3 68
He sends ye not to murder me for this; For in this sin he is as deep as I i 4 219
I will send you to my brother Gloucester, Who shall reward you . . i 4 235
That I, being govern'd by the watery moon, May send forth plenteous tears to drown the world! . . . . ii 2 70
Send straight for him; Let him be crown'd . . . . . ii 2 97
Will your grace Persuade the queen to send the Duke of York? . . iii 1 33
He sends you word He dreamt to-night the boar had razed his helm . iii 2 10
He sends to know your lordship's pleasure . . . . . iii 2 15
And thereupon he sends you this good news . . . . . iii 2 48
I'll send some packing that yet think not on it . . . . iii 2 63
I saw good strawberries . . .: I do beseech you send for some of them iii 4 35
Richard yet lives, hell's black intelligencer, Only reserved their factor, to buy souls And send them thither . . . . iv 4 73
Send to her, by the man that slew her brothers, A pair of bleeding hearts; thereon engrave Edward and York . . . . . . iv 4 271
If this inducement force her not to love, Send her a story of thy noble acts . . . . iv 4 280
Send out a pursuivant at arms To Stanley's regiment . . . v 3 59
Where this is question'd send our letters . . . *Hen. VIII.* i 2 99
And by me Sends you his princely commendations . . . . iv 2 118
Heaven, from thy endless goodness, send prosperous life! . . . v 5 2
Send thy brass voice through all these lazy tents . *Troi. and Cres.* i 3 257
This challenge that the gallant Hector sends . . . . . i 3 321
They were used to bend, To send their smiles before them to Achilles . iii 3 72
I'll send the fool to Ajax and desire him To invite the Trojan lords . iii 3 235
Remember, I send it through the rivers of your blood . *Coriolanus* i 1 139
If I do send, dispatch Those centuries to our aid . . . . i 7 2
Send us to Rome The best, with whom we may articulate . . . i 9 76
Having determined of the Volsces and To send for Titus Lartius . . ii 2 42
We shall not send O'er the vast world to seek a single man . . iv 1 41
Their latest refuge Was to send him . . . . v 3 12
The people of Rome . . . Send thee by me . . . This palliament *T. An.* i 1 181
My lord the emperor Sends thee this word . . . . . iii 1 151
Any one of you, chop off your hand, And send it to the king: he for the same Will send thee hither both thy sons alive . . . . . iii 1 154
With all my heart, I'll send the emperor My hand . . . . iii 1 160
Carry from me to the empress' sons Presents that I intend to send them iv 1 116
And sends them weapons wrapp'd about with lines . . . . iv 2 27
To see so great a lord Basely insinuate and send us gifts . . . iv 2 38
The empress sends it thee, thy stamp, thy seal, And bids thee christen it iv 2 69
See that you take no longer days, But send the midwife presently to me iv 2 166
Pluto sends you word, If you will have Revenge from hell, you shall . iv 3 37
We will solicit heaven and move the gods To send down Justice . . iv 3 51
Being credulous in this mad thought, I'll make him send for Lucius . v 2 75
Send me word to-morrow, By one that I'll procure to come . *R. and J.* ii 2 144
Cease thy suit, and leave me to my grief: To-morrow will I send . . ii 2 154
At what o'clock to-morrow Shall I send to thee? . . . . . ii 2 169

Send. The clock struck nine when I did send the nurse . *Rom. and Jul.* ii 5 1
Send thy man away.—Peter, stay at the gate . . . . ii 5 19
And says 'God send me no need of thee!' . . . . iii 1 7
With one hand beats Cold death aside, and with the other sends It back iii 1 167
I hope thou wilt not keep him long, But send him back . . iii 5 64
I'll send to one in Mantua, Where that same banish'd runagate doth live iii 5 89
How shall that faith return again to earth, Unless that husband send it me from heaven By leaving earth? . . . . . . iii 5 209
I'll send a friar with speed To Mantua, with my letters to thy lord iv 1 123
Send for the county; go tell him of this . . . . iv 2 23
I could not send it,—here it is again . . . . . v 2 14
Till I conveniently could send to Romeo . . . . . v 3 256
Commend me to him: I will send his ransom . . *T. of Athens* i 1 105
Bid 'em send o' the instant A thousand talents to me . . ii 2 207
Does he send to me? Three? hum! It shows but little love or judgement iii 3 9
Your lord sends now for money.—Most true, he does . . iii 4 18
E'en as if your lord should wear rich jewels, And send for money for 'em iii 4 24
Would poison were obedient and knew my mind!—Where wouldst thou send it? . . . . iv 3 298
I thank them; and would send them back the plague . . v 1 140
Send forth us, to make their sorrow'd render . . . v 1 152
So thou wilt send thy gentle heart before . . . . v 4 48
The world, too saucy with the gods, Incenses them to send destruction *J. Cæsar* i 3 13
He did bid Antonius Send word to you he would be there to-morrow . i 3 38
When the most mighty gods by tokens send Such dreadful heralds . i 3 55
Send him but hither, and I'll fashion him . . . . ii 1 220
We'll send Mark Antony to the senate-house . . . . ii 2 52
Say he is sick.—Shall Cæsar send a lie? . . . . ii 2 65
If you shall send them word you will not come, Their minds may change ii 2 95
I did send to you For certain sums of gold, which you denied me . iv 3 69
I did send To you for gold to pay my legions, Which you denied me . iv 3 75
Why didst thou send me forth, brave Cassius? . . . v 3 80
To Thasos send his body: His funerals shall not be in our camp . v 3 104
If charnel-houses and our graves must send Those that we bury back, our monuments Shall be the maws of kites . . . *Macbeth* iii 4 71
Did you send to him, sir?—I hear it by the way; but I will send . . iii 4 129
I'll send my prayers with him . . . . . . iii 6 49
Send out moe horses; skirr the country round; Hang those that talk of fear . . . . v 3 35
Give me my staff. Seyton, send out . . . . . v 3 49
Sends out arrests On Fortinbras; which he, in brief, obeys . *Hamlet* ii 2 67
What have you, my good friends, deserved at the hands of fortune, that she sends you to prison hither? . . . . ii 2 246
If she find him not, To England send him . . . . iii 1 194
Where is Polonius?—In heaven; send thither to see . . . iv 3 35
For that which thou hast done,—must send thee hence With fiery quickness . . . . iv 3 44
Nature is fine in love, and where 'tis fine, It sends some precious instance of itself After the thing it loves . . . . . iv 5 162
He sends to know if your pleasure hold to play . . . v 2 205
His picture I will send far and near . . . . *Lear* ii 1 84
Strange that they should so depart from home, And not send back my messenger . . . . ii 4 2
Make it your cause; send down, and take my part! . . . ii 4 195
If that the heavens do not their visible spirits Send quickly down to tame these vile offences, It will come . . . . . iv 2 47
A century send forth; Search every acre in the high-grown field . iv 4 6
I thought it fit To send the old and miserable king To some retention . v 3 46
Quickly send, Be brief in it, to the castle; for my writ Is on the life of Lear and on Cordelia: Nay, send in time . . . . . v 3 244
Who hath the office? send Thy token of reprieve . . . v 3 248
Send for the lady to the Sagittary, And let her speak of me . *Othello* i 3 115
I have made bold, Iago, To send in to your wife . . . iii 1 36
Procure me some access—I'll send her to you presently . . iii 1 38
Get you away; I'll send for you anon . . . . . iv 1 270
Did they never whisper?—Never, my lord.—Nor send you out o' the way? . . . . iv 2 7
Heaven me such uses send, Not to pick bad from bad, but by bad mend! iv 3 105
No, by my life and soul! Send for the man, and ask him . . v 2 50
I did not send you: if you find him sad, say I am dancing *Ant. and Cleo.* i 3 3
The firm Roman to great Egypt sends This treasure of an oyster . i 5 43
Twenty several messengers: Why do you send so thick? . . i 5 63
To send Measures of wheat to Rome . . . . . ii 6 36
Now I must To the young man send humble treaties . . . iii 11 62
He is pluck'd, when hither He sends so poor a pinion of his wing . iii 12 4
To the boy Cæsar send this grizzled head . . . . iii 13 17
Now I'll set my teeth, And send to darkness all that stop me . iii 13 182
Send his treasure after; do it; Detain no jot, I charge thee . . iv 5 12
Send him word you are dead . . . . . . iv 13 4
My mistress Cleopatra sent me to thee.—When did she send thee? . iv 14 119
Cæsar sends greeting to the Queen of Egypt . . . . v 2 9
I send him The greatness he has got . . . . . v 2 29
Within three days You with your children will he send before . . v 2 202
And with mine eyes I'll drink the words you send . . *Cymbeline* i 1 100
No further service, doctor, Until I send for thee . . . i 5 45
I will make bold To send them to you, only for this night . . i 6 198
Send your trunk to me; it shall safe be kept, And truly yielded you . i 6 209
I think He'll grant the tribute, send the arrearages . . . ii 4 13
May be she pluck'd it off To send it me.—She writes so to you, doth she? ii 4 105
I'll give but notice you are dead and send him Some bloody sign of it . iii 4 127
Thou, king, send out For torturers ingenious . . . . v 5 214
To fulfil his prince' desire, Sends word of all that haps in Tyre *Per.* ii Gower 22
The most just gods For every graff would send a caterpillar . . v 1 60
Sender. Like a remorseful pardon slowly carried, To the great sender turns a sour offence . . . . *All's Well* v 3 59
A merry message.—We hope to make the sender blush at it . *Hen. V.* i 2 299
Any thing that may not misbecome The mighty sender, doth he prize you at . . . . ii 4 119
We must receive him According to the honour of his sender *Cymbeline* ii 3 63
Sendeth. None but Samsons and Goliases It sendeth forth to skirmish. One to ten! Lean raw-boned rascals! . . . . *1 Hen. VI.* i 2 34
Sending. I shall lessen God's sending that way . . . *Much Ado* ii 1 24
Alas! and would you take the letter of her? Might you not know she would do as she has done, By sending me a letter? . . *All's Well* iii 4 3
Lately sending into France, Did claim some certain dukedoms *Hen. V.* i 2 246
And take foul scorn to fawn on him by sending . . *1 Hen. VI.* iv 4 35
Lewis of France is sending over masquers To revel it with him *3 Hen. VI.* iii 3 224
Beshrew your heart for sending me about, To catch my death! *Rom. and Jul.* ii 5 52

Sending. He's ever sending: how shall I thank him, thinkest thou? *T. of Athens* iii 2 36
I was sending to use Lord Timon myself . . . . . iii 2 55
The need we have to use you did provoke Our hasty sending . *Hamlet* ii 2 4
This sudden sending him away must seem Deliberate pause . . iv 3 8
Seneca cannot be too heavy, nor Plautus too light . . . ii 2 419
Senior. We'll draw cuts for the senior . . *Com. of Errors* v 1 422
My tough senior.—Why tough senior? . . . *L. L. Lost* i 2 10
Senior-junior. This senior-junior, giant-dwarf, Dan Cupid . . iii 1 182
Seniory. If ancient sorrow be most reverend, Give mine the benefit of seniory . . . . *Richard III.* iv 4 36
Senis. Hic steterat Priami regia celsa senis . . *T. of Shrew* iii 1 29
'Celsa senis,' that we might beguile the old pantaloon . . . iii 1 36
'Regia,' presume not, 'celsa senis,' despair not . . . . iii 1 45
Senoys. The Florentines and Senoys are by the ears . *All's Well* i 2 1
Sense. It eats and sleeps and hath such senses As we have, such *Tempest* i 2 412
You cram these words into mine ears against The stomach of my sense ii 1 107
My charms I'll break, their senses I'll restore, And they shall be themselves . . . . v 1 31
When I have required Some heavenly music, which even now I do, To work mine end upon their senses . . . . . . v 1 53
Their rising senses Begin to chase the ignorant fumes that mantle Their clearer reason . . . . v 1 66
Howsoe'er you have Been justled from your senses . . . . v 1 158
Were there sense in his idolatry . . . . *T. G. of Ver.* iv 4 205
Out of his five sentences.—It is his five senses . . *Mer. Wives* i 1 181
He speaks sense . . . . i 1 129
Be not amazed; call all your senses to you . . . . iii 3 126
One who never feels The wanton stings and motions of the sense *M. for M.* i 4 59
An act, Under whose heavy sense your brother's life Falls into forfeit . i 4 65
In the beastliest sense . . . . ii 1 229
She speaks, and 'tis Such sense, that my sense breeds with it . ii 2 142
Can it be That modesty may more betray our sense Than woman's lightness? . . . . ii 2 169
Your sense pursues not mine: either you are ignorant, Or seem so craftily . . . . ii 4 74
The sense of death is most in apprehension . . . . iii 1 78
Save that his riotous youth, with dangerous sense, Might in the times to come have ta'en revenge . . . . iv 4 32
Poor soul, She speaks this in the infirmity of sense . . . v 1 47
Her madness hath the oddest frame of sense . . . . v 1 61
As there is sense in truth and truth in virtue . . . . v 1 226
Against all sense you do importune her . . . . . v 1 438
Indued with intellectual sense and souls . . *Com. of Errors* ii 1 22
You are a conjurer; Establish him in his true sense again . . iv 4 51
Thou hast frighted the word out of his right sense . . *Much Ado* v 2 56
Things hid and barr'd, you mean, from common sense? . *L. L. Lost* i 1 57
Where to meet some mistress fine, When mistresses from common sense are hid . . . . i 1 64
All senses to that sense did make their repair . . . . ii 1 240
Methought all his senses were lock'd in his eye, As jewels in crystal . ii 1 242
Warble, child; make passionate my sense of hearing . . . iii 1 2
Cutting a smaller hair than may be seen, Above the sense of sense . v 2 259
Sweet royalty, bestow on me the sense of hearing . . . v 2 670
O, take the sense, sweet, of my innocence! . . *M. N. Dream* ii 2 45
Their sense thus weak, lost with their fears thus strong . . iii 2 27
Wherein it doth impair the seeing sense, It pays the hearing double recompense . . . . iii 2 179
And strike more dead Than common sleep of all these five the sense . iv 1 87
Hath not a Jew hands, organs, dimensions, senses, affections? *Mer. of Venice* iii 1 62
You should in all sense be much bound to him . . . . v 1 136
I think 'twas in another sense . . . . . *T. of Shrew* i 1 220
You are very sensible, and yet you miss my sense . . . v 2 18
And in no sense is meet or amiable . . . . . . v 2 141
Impossible be strange attempts to those That weigh their pains in sense and do suppose What hath been cannot be . . . *All's Well* i 1 240
Whose apprehensive senses All but new things disdain . . . i 2 60
She thought, I dare vow for her, they touched not any stranger sense . i 3 114
Now to all sense 'tis gross You love my son . . . . i 3 178
To esteem A senseless help when help past sense we deem . . ii 1 127
What impossibility would slay In common sense, sense saves another way . . . . ii 1 181
This healthful hand, whose banish'd sense Thou hast repeal'd . . ii 3 54
I have no skill in sense To make distinction . . . . iii 4 39
Your son, As mad in folly, lack'd the sense to know Her estimation home v 3 3
In your denial I would find no sense . . . . . *T. Night* i 5 285
I am mad, or else this is a dream: Let fancy still my sense in Lethe steep! . . . . iv 1 66
My soul disputes well with my sense, That this may be some error . iv 3 9
Yet have I the benefit of my senses as well as your ladyship . . v 1 313
Your senses, unintelligent of our insufficience . . . *W. Tale* i 1 15
You smell this business with a sense as cold As is a dead man's nose . ii 1 151
So surprised my sense, That I was nothing . . . . iii 1 10
My senses, better pleased with madness, Do bid it welcome . . iv 4 495
All their other senses stuck in ears . . . . . . iv 4 621
A good nose is requisite also, to smell out work for the other senses . iv 4 688
No settled senses of the world can match The pleasure of that madness v 3 72
A gnat, a wandering hair, Any annoyance in that precious sense *K. John* iv 1 94
Nor with thy sweets comfort his ravenous sense . . *Richard II.* iii 2 13
O gentle sleep, . . . how have I frighted thee, Thou no more wilt weigh my eyelids down And steep my senses in forgetfulness? *2 Hen. IV.* iii 1 8
The time misorder'd doth, in common sense, Crowd us and crush us . iv 2 33
I spake unto this crown as having sense, And thus upbraided it . . iv 5 158
Let senses rule; the word is 'Pitch and Pay' . . . *Hen. V.* ii 3 51
The king is but a man . . .; all his senses have but human conditions iv 1 108
Every fool, whose sense no more can feel But his own wringing . . iv 1 252
Take from them now The sense of reckoning, if the opposed numbers Pluck their hearts from them . . . . iv 1 308
Confounds the tongue and makes the senses rough . *1 Hen. VI* v 3 71
He'll wrest the sense and hold us here all day. . *2 Hen. VI.* i 1 186
Ay, but, I fear me, in another sense . . . *3 Hen. VI.* iii 2 60
And spirit of sense Hard as the palm of ploughman . *Troi. and Cres.* i 1 58
I bring a trumpet to awake his ear, To set his sense on the attentive bent i 3 252
But, hit or miss, Our project's life this shape of sense assumes . i 3 385
Dost thou think I have no sense, thou strikest me thus? . . ii 1 23
No lady of more softer bowels, More spongy to suck in the sense of fear ii 2 12
The imaginary relish is so sweet That it enchants my sense . . iii 2 21
Nor doth the eye itself, That most pure spirit of sense, behold itself . iii 3 106
Give as soft attachment to thy senses As infants' empty of all thought! iv 2 5

Sense. The grief is fine, full, perfect, that I taste, And violenteth in a sense as strong As that which causeth it . . . *Troi. and Cres.* iv 4 4
A woman of quick sense . . . . iv 5 54
When, by and by, the din of war gan pierce His ready sense . *Coriolanus* ii 2 120
Take it in what sense thou wilt.—They must take it in sense that feel it.—Me they shall feel . . *Rom. and Jul.* i 1 31
Being tasted, slays all senses with the heart . . . ii 3 26
Your worship in that sense may call him 'man' . . iii 1 62
The five best senses Acknowledge thee their patron *T. of Athens* i 2 129
I see no sense for't, But his occasions might have woo'd me first . iii 3 14
Feeling in itself A lack of Timon's aid, hath sense withal Of it own fail v 1 150
Awake your senses, that you may the better judge . *J. Cæsar* iii 2 17
The air Nimbly and sweetly recommends itself Unto our gentle senses *Macbeth* i 6 3
Mine eyes are made the fools o' the other senses, Or else worth all the rest . . . ii 1 44
You see, her eyes are open.—Ay, but their sense is shut. . v 1 29
Who then shall blame His pester'd senses to recoil and start? . v 2 23
The time has been, my senses would have cool'd To hear a night-shriek v 5 10
That palter with us in a double sense ; That keep the word of promise to our ear . . . . . . v 8 20
As common As any the most vulgar thing to sense . *Hamlet* i 2 99
If it be made of penetrable stuff, If damned custom have not brass'd it so That it be proof and bulwark against sense . . iii 4 38
Sense, sure, you have, Else could you not have motion ; but sure, that sense Is apoplex'd ; for madness would not err, Nor sense to ecstasy was ne'er so thrall'd . . . . iii 4 71
Or but a sickly part of one true sense Could not so mope . iii 4 80
That monster, custom, who all sense doth eat, Of habits devil . iii 4 161
In despite of sense and secrecy, Unpeg the basket on the house's top . iii 4 192
As my great power thereof may give thee sense . . iv 3 61
Speaks things in doubt, That carry but half sense . . iv 5 7
Tears seven times salt, Burn out the sense and virtue of mine eye! . iv 5 155
The hand of little employment hath the daintier sense . . v 1 78
Whose wicked deed thy most ingenious sense Deprived thee of . v 1 271
All other joys, Which the most precious square of sense possesses *Lear* i 1 76
The untented woundings of a father's curse Pierce every sense about thee! . . . . i 4 323
The tempest in my mind Doth from my senses take all feeling else . iii 4 13
What can man's wisdom In the restoring his bereaved sense? . iv 4 9
Your other senses grow imperfect By your eyes' anguish . iv 6 5
The safer sense will ne'er accommodate His master thus . . iv 6 81
How stiff is my vile sense, That I stand up, and have ingenious feeling Of my huge sorrows! . . . . iv 6 286
The untuned and jarring senses, O, wind up Of this child-changed father! . . . . iv 7 16
Do not believe That, from the sense of all civility, I thus would play and trifle with your reverence . . . *Othello* i 1 132
I'll refer me to all things of sense, If she in chains of magic were not bound . . . . i 2 64
Judge me the world, if 'tis not gross in sense That thou hast practised . i 2 72
But the main article I do approve In fearful sense . . . i 3 12
So preposterously to err, Being not deficient, blind, or lame of sense . i 3 63
You shall yourself read in the bitter letter After your own sense . i 3 69
As having sense of beauty, do omit Their mortal natures . . ii 1 71
Have you forgot all sense of place and duty? . . . ii 3 167
I thought you had received some bodily wound ; there is more sense in that than in reputation . . . . . . ii 3 268
What sense had I of her stol'n hours of lust? I saw't not, thought it not . . . . iii 3 338
Are you a man? have you a soul or sense? God be wi' you . . iii 3 374
For let our finger ache, and it indues Our other healthful members even to that sense Of pain . . . . . . iii 4 147
Who art so lovely fair and smell'st so sweet That the sense aches at thee! . . . . iv 2 69
Or that mine eyes, mine ears, or any sense, Delighted them in any other form . . . . iv 2 154
Let husbands know Their wives have sense like them . . iv 3 95
I have rubb'd this young quat almost to the sense, And he grows angry v 1 11
That hast such noble sense of thy friend's wrong! . . . v 1 32
I'ld have thee live ; For, in my sense, 'tis happiness to die . . v 2 290
From the barge A strange invisible perfume hits the sense *Ant. and Cleo.* ii 2 217
The conquering wine hath steep'd our sense In soft and delicate Lethe ii 7 113
You take me in too dolorous a sense; For I spake to you for your comfort . . . . iv 2 39
Remain, remain thou here While sense can keep it on . *Cymbeline* i 1 118
Will stupify and dull the sense awhile . . . . . i 5 37
The crickets sing, and man's o'er-labour'd sense Repairs itself by rest . ii 2 11
O sleep, thou ape of death, lie dull upon her! And be her sense but as a monument, Thus in a chapel lying! . . . . . . ii 2 32
Say, and speak thick ; Love's counsellor should fill the bores of hearing, To the smothering of the sense . . . . . iii 2 60
Ere wildness Vanquish my staider senses . . . . . iii 4 10
Have I not found it Murderous to the senses? . . . . iv 2 328
Or senseless speaking or a speaking such As sense cannot untie . v 4 149
Whose containing Is so from sense in hardness, that I can Make no collection of it : let him show His skill . . . . v 5 431
You are a fair viol, and your sense the strings . . *Pericles* i 1 81
It smells most sweetly in my sense.—A delicate odour.—As ever hit my nostril . . . . iii 2 60
I will believe thee, And make my senses credit thy relation . v 1 124
If he be none of mine, my sanctity Will to my sense bend no licentious ear . . . . v 3 30
Senseless. Himself would lodge where senseless they are lying *T. G. of V.* iii 1 143
O thou senseless form, Thou shalt be worshipp'd, kiss'd, loved! . iv 4 203
Thou whoreson, senseless villain!—I would I were senseless, sir, that I might not feel your blows . . . *Com. of Errors* iv 4 25
You are thought here to be the most senseless and fit man . *Much Ado* iii 3 23
Made senseless things begin to do them wrong . *M. N. Dream* iii 2 28
Doth very foolishly, although he smart, Not to seem senseless of the bob . . . . *As Y. Like It* ii 7 55
A senseless villain! Good Hortensio, I bade the rascal knock *T. of Shrew* i 2 36
To esteem A senseless help when help past sense we deem . *All's Well* ii 1 127
Very brief, and to exceeding good sense—less . . *T. Night* iii 4 174
You might have pinched a placket, it was senseless *W. Tale* iv 4 622
Mock not my senseless conjuration . . . *Richard II.* iii 2 23
The senseless brands will sympathize The heavy accent of thy moving tongue . . . . v 1 46
Against the senseless winds shalt grin in vain . . *2 Hen. VI.* iv 1 77
O noble fellow! Who sensibly outdares his senseless sword . *Coriolanus* i 4 53
Senseless. Tickle the senseless rushes with their heels . *Rom. and Jul.* i 4 36
No care, no stop! so senseless of expense . . *T. of Athens* ii 2 1
You blocks, you stones, you worse than senseless things! . *J. Cæsar* i 1 40
Then senseless Ilium, Seeming to feel this blow, with flaming top Stoops to his base . . . . *Hamlet* ii 2 496
Too late : The ears are senseless that should give us hearing . . v 2 380
I am senseless of your wrath ; a touch more rare Subdues all pangs *Cymbeline* i 1 135
And kiss'd it, madam.—Senseless linen! happier therein than I! . i 3 7
In all obey her, Save when command to your dismission tends, And therein you are senseless.—Senseless! not so . . . ii 3 58
Senseless bauble, Art thou a feodary for this act? . . . iii 2 20
Or senseless speaking or a speaking such As sense cannot untie . v 4 148
Senseless-obstinate. You are too senseless-obstinate . *Richard III.* iii 1 44
Sensible. Of such sensible and nimble lungs that they always use to laugh at nothing . . . . . . *Tempest* ii 1 174
'Twas a good sensible fellow . . . . *Mer. Wives* ii 1 151
This sensible warm motion to become A kneaded clod *Meas. for Meas.* iii 1 120
Thou art sensible in nothing but blows, and so is an ass . *Com. of Errors* iv 4 28
The savage bull may; but if ever the sensible Benedick bear it *M. Ado* i 1 265
When shall we set the savage bull's horns on the sensible Benedick's head? . . . . v 1 184
He is only an animal, only sensible in the duller parts . *L. L. Lost* iv 2 28
Love's feeling is more soft and sensible Than are the tender horns of cockled snails ; Love's tongue proves dainty Bacchus gross in taste iv 3 337
So sensible Seemeth their conference . . . . . v 2 259
The wall, methinks, being sensible, should curse again . *M. N. Dream* v 1 183
With affection wondrous sensible He wrung Bassanio's hand *Mer. of Ven.* ii 8 48
From whom he bringeth sensible regreets. . . . . ii 9 89
And therefore 'tis called a sensible tale . . . *T. of Shrew* iv 1 66
You are very sensible, and yet you miss my sense . . . v 2 18
Being not mad but sensible of grief . . . . *K. John* iii 4 53
If thou wert sensible of courtesy, I should not make so dear a show of zeal : But let my favours hide thy mangled face . *1 Hen. IV.* v 4 94
You took it like a sensible lord . . . . *2 Hen. IV.* i 2 220
I would your cambric were sensible as your finger . *Coriolanus* i 3 95
His hand, Not sensible of fire, remain'd unscorch'd . *J. Cæsar* i 3 18
Art thou not, fatal vision, sensible To feeling as to sight? . *Macbeth* ii 1 36
Before my God, I might not this believe Without the sensible and true avouch Of mine own eyes . . . . . . *Hamlet* i 1 57
To be now a sensible man, by and by a fool, and presently a beast! *Oth.* ii 3 309
Sensibly. I will tell you sensibly . . . . *L. L. Lost* iii 1 114
O noble fellow! Who sensibly outdares his senseless sword . *Coriolanus* i 4 53
Sensibly fed Of that self-blood that first gave life to you . *T. Andron.* iv 2 122
I am guiltless of your father's death, And am most sensibly in grief *Ham.* iv 5 150
Sensual. I have begun, And now I give my sensual race the rein *M. for M.* ii 4 160
A libertine, As sensual as the brutish sting itself . *As Y. Like It* ii 7 66
Sensuality. Those pamper'd animals That rage in savage sensuality *Much Ado* iv 1 62
If the balance of our lives had not one scale of reason to poise another of sensuality . . . . *Othello* i 3 331
Sent. I must be here confined by you, Or sent to Naples . *Tempest* Epil. 5
And sent, I think, from Proteus. He would have given it you *T. G. of V.* i 2 38
'Twere good, I think, your lordship sent him thither . . i 3 29
'Tis a word or two Of commendations sent from Valentine . . i 3 53
Look, what thou want'st shall be sent after thee . . . i 3 74
Come, come away, man ; I was sent to call thee . . . ii 3 61
His tears pure messengers sent from his heart. . . . ii 7 77
But she did scorn a present that I sent her . . . . iii 1 92
I curse myself, for they are sent by me . . . . iii 1 148
I was sent to deliver him as a present to Mistress Silvia . . iv 4 7
I do entreat your patience To hear me speak the message I am sent on iv 4 117
O, cry you mercy, sir, I have mistook : This is the ring you sent to Silvia v 4 95
And hath sent your worship a morning's draught of sack *Mer. Wives* ii 2 152
My wife hath sent to him ; the hour is fixed ; the match is made . ii 2 303
Let him be sent for to-morrow, eight o'clock, to have amends . iii 3 209
He sent me word to stay within : I like his money well . . iii 5 59
Master Slender, sent to her, seeing her go thorough the streets . iv 5 31
A strange picklock, which we have sent to the deputy *Meas. for Meas.* iii 2 19
Farewell : go say I sent thee hither . . . . . iii 2 66
My lord hath sent you this note . . . . . . iv 2 105
For my better satisfaction, let me have Claudio's head sent me . iv 2 126
See this be done, And sent according to command . . . iv 3 84
Hath yet the deputy sent my brother's pardon? . . . . iv 3 118
His head is off and sent to Angelo.—Nay, but it is not so . iv 3 120
This letter, then, to Friar Peter give ; 'Tis that he sent me . . iv 3 143
I, in probation of a sisterhood, Was sent to by my brother . v 1 73
Let him be sent for.—Would he were here, my lord! . . . v 1 249
That in such haste I sent to seek his master! . . *Com. of Errors* ii 1 2
I could not speak with Dromio since at first I sent him from the mart . ii 2 6
Your mistress sent to have me home to dinner? . . . ii 2 10
I did not see you since you sent me hence . . . . ii 2 15
She sent for you by Dromio home to dinner.—By Dromio?—By me? . ii 2 156
Who sent whole armadoes of caracks to be ballast at her nose . iii 2 140
A ship you sent me to, to hire waftage.—Thou drunken slave, I sent thee for a rope And told thee to what purpose . . . iv 1 95
You sent me for a rope's end as soon : You sent me to the bay, sir, for a bark . . . . iv 1 98
Master, here's the gold you sent me for . . . . iv 3 12
Here are the angels that you sent for to deliver you . . iv 3 41
Have you that I sent you for? . . . . . . iv 4 9
I sent you money to redeem you, By Dromio here . . . iv 4 86
Bear me witness That I was sent for nothing but a rope! . . iv 4 94
Once did I get him bound and sent him home . . . . v 1 145
I did obey, and sent my peasant home For certain ducats . . v 1 231
I sent you money, sir, to be your bail, By Dromio . . . v 1 382
I have brought Count Claudio, whom you sent me to seek . *Much Ado* ii 1 296
Against my will I am sent to bid you come in to dinner . . ii 3 256
These gloves the count sent me ; they are an excellent perfume . iii 4 62
Him I, as my ever-esteemed duty pricks me on, have sent to thee *L. L. L.* i 1 269
The clown bore it, the fool sent it, and the lady hath it . . iv 3 16
You have a favour too : Who sent it? and what is it? . . v 2 31
What was sent to you from fair Dumain?—Madam, this glove . . v 2 47
This and these pearls to me sent Longaville . . . . v 2 53
And her fairy sent To bear him to my bower in fairy land *M. N. Dream* iv 1 65
Have you sent to Bottom's house? is he come home yet? . . iv 2 1
I am sent with broom before, To sweep the dust behind the door . v 1 396
I have sent twenty out to seek for you . . . *Mer. of Venice* ii 6 66
A learned doctor, Whom I have sent for to determine this . . iv 1 106
My lord Bassanio upon more advice Hath sent you here this ring . . iv 2 7

Sent. Hath not Fortune sent in this fool to cut off the argument? *As Y. Like It* i 2 49
And hath sent this natural for our whetstone i 2 57
Call me not fool till heaven hath sent me fortune ii 7 19
Being strong at heart, He sent me hither, stranger as I am iv 3 153
He sent me word, if I said his beard was not cut well, he was in the mind it was v 4 74
If I sent him word again 'it was not well cut,' he would send me word, he cut it to please himself v 4 76
And sent you hither so unlike yourself *T. of Shrew* iii 2 106
I am sent before to make a fire, and they are coming after to warm them iv 1 4
No duty? Where is the foolish knave I sent before? iv 1 130
I'll slit the villain's nose, that would have sent me to the gaol v 1 135
I have sent you a daughter-in-law *All's Well* iii 2 21
Sent him forth From courtly friends, with camping foes to live iii 4 13
I sent to her, By this same coxcomb that we have i' the wind, Tokens iii 6 121
I have letters sent me That set him high in fame v 3 30
Unless she . . . sent it us Upon her great disaster v 3 111
The jeweller that owes the ring is sent for, And he shall surety me v 3 297
Were you sent hither to praise me?—I see you what you are *T. Night* i 5 268
None of my lord's ring! why, he sent her none ii 2 25
I sent thee sixpence for thy leman: hadst it? ii 3 25
I have sent after him: he says he'll come; How shall I feast him? iii 4 1
Smilest thou? I sent for thee upon a sad occasion iii 4 20
Will you make me believe that I am not sent for you? iv 1 2
I do not know you; nor I am not sent to you by my lady iv 1 6
Posts From those you sent to the oracle are come An hour since *W. Tale* ii 3 194
The penitent king, my master, hath sent for me iv 2 7
Sent by the king your father To greet him and to give him comforts iv 4 567
The king hath sent for you.—O, he is bold and blushes not at death *K. John* iv 3 75
What men provided, what munition sent, To underprop this action? v 2 98
Let me have audience; I am sent to speak v 2 119
Go, say I sent thee forth to purchase honour *Richard II.* i 3 282
And hath sent post haste To entreat your majesty to visit him i 4 55
It is my son, young Harry Percy, Sent from my brother Worcester ii 3 22
And sent me over by Berkeley, to discover ii 3 33
Alack, why am I sent for to a king? iv 1 162
To do what service am I sent for hither? iv 1 176
She came adorned hither like sweet May, Sent back like Hallowmas v 1 80
The next news is, I have to London sent The heads of Oxford, Salisbury v 6 7
But I have sent for him to answer this *1 Hen. IV.* i 1 100
My brother Mortimer doth stir About his title, and hath sent for you i 3 85
Thrice from the banks of Wye And sandy-bottom'd Severn have I sent him iii 1 66
Lord Mortimer of Scotland hath sent word iii 2 164
The king hath sent to know The nature of your griefs iv 3 41
Sir Nicholas Gawsey hath for succour sent, And so hath Clifton v 4 45
Travers, whom I sent On Tuesday last to listen after news *2 Hen. IV.* i 1 28
The king hath won, and hath sent out A speedy power to encounter you i 1 132
I looked a' should have sent me two and twenty yards of satin i 2 49
I sent for you before your expedition to Shrewsbury i 2 115
You would not come when I sent for you i 2 121
I sent for you, when there were matters against you for your life i 2 150
If I be not sent away post, I will see you again ere I go ii 4 408
Have you read o'er the letters that I sent you? iii 1 36
The powers that you already have sent forth Shall bring this prize in iii 1 100
We have sent forth already.—'Tis well done iv 1 5
I sent your grace The parcels and particulars of our grief iv 2 35
Fondly brought here and foolishly sent hence iv 2 119
I'll to the king my master that is dead, And tell him who hath sent me v 2 41
Do not you grieve at this; I shall be sent for in private to him v 5 82
Come, Bardolph: I shall be sent for soon at night v 5 96
Call in the messengers sent from the Dauphin *Hen. V.* i 2 221
Sweeten the bitter mock you sent his majesty ii 4 122
A son that is by his father sent about merchandise iv 1 154
Who hath sent thee now?—The Constable of France iv 3 88
Is this the king we sent to for his ransom? iv 5 9
Hundreds he sent to hell, and none durst stand him *1 Hen. VI.* i 1 123
By a vision sent to her from heaven i 2 52
Slain our citizens And sent our sons and husbands captivate ii 3 42
We sent unto the Temple, unto his chamber ii 5 19
View the letter Sent from our uncle Duke of Burgundy iv 1 49
How now, Sir William! whither were you sent? iv 4 12
York should have sent him aid.—And York as fast upon your grace exclaims iv 4 29
York lies; he might have sent and had the horse iv 4 33
On what submissive message art thou sent?—Submission! iv 7 53
And she sent over of the King of England's own proper cost *2 Hen. VI.* i 1 60
Come, Somerset, we'll see thee sent away i 3 225
Sent his poor queen to France, from whence she came ii 2 25
Did he not, in his protectorship, Levy great sums of money through the realm For soldiers' pay in France, and never sent it? iii 1 62
That Somerset be sent as regent thither: 'Tis meet iii 1 290
He was the lord ambassador Sent from a sort of tinkers to the king iii 2 277
And I am sent to tell his majesty That even now he cries aloud for him iii 2 377
Surprised our forts And sent the ragged soldiers wounded home iv 1 90
The king hath sent him, sure: I must dissemble v 1 13
And for your brother, he was lately sent From your kind aunt *3 Hen. VI.* i 1 145
These letters are for you, Sent from your brother iii 3 164
That Margaret your queen and my son Edward Be sent for iv 6 61
Down, down to hell; and say I sent thee thither v 6 67
And hither have they sent it for her ransom v 7 40
Sent before my time Into this breathing world *Richard III.* i 1 20
And sent to warn them to his royal presence i 3 39
I dare adventure to be sent to the Tower. 'Tis time to speak i 3 116
Why look you pale? Who sent you hither? Wherefore do you come? i 4 176
'Tis he that sent us hither now to slaughter thee i 4 250
We were sent for to the justices.—And so was I ii 3 46
Where is my lord protector? I have sent for these strawberries iii 4 48
The reason we have sent— Look back, defend thee, here are enemies iii 5 18
I in all haste was sent.—And I in all unwillingness will go iv 1 57
Richmond, in Dorsetshire, sent out a boat Unto the shore iv 4 524
There have been commissions Sent down among 'em *Hen. VIII.* i 2 21
Spoke by a holy monk; 'that oft,' says he, 'Hath sent to me' i 2 161
Surrey was sent thither, and in haste too, Lest he should help his father ii 1 43
Out of anger He sent command to the lord mayor straight ii 1 151
The horses your lordship sent for, with all the care I had, I saw well chosen ii 2 2
Excuse me; The king has sent me otherwhere ii 2 60

Sent. Rome, the nurse of judgement, Invited by your noble self, hath sent One general tongue unto us *Hen. VIII.* ii 2 95
They have sent me such a man I would have wish'd for ii 2 101
Who had been hither sent on the debating A marriage ii 4 173
This morning Papers of state he sent me to peruse, As I required iii 2 121
What cross devil Made me put this main secret in the packet I sent the king? iii 2 216
Plague of your policy! You sent me deputy for Ireland iii 2 260
You sent a large commission To Gregory de Cassado iii 2 320
Then that you have sent innumerable substance . . . To furnish Rome iii 2 326
There is staying A gentleman, sent from the king, to see you iv 2 106
Patience, is that letter, I caused you write, yet sent away? iv 2 128
By her woman I sent your message; who return'd her thanks v 1 64
You do desire to know Wherefore I sent for you v 1 90
The gentleman, That was sent to me from the council v 2 2
Have to the port of Athens sent their ships *Troi. and Cres.* Prol. 3
I have a roisting challenge sent amongst The dull and factious nobles ii 2 208
Let him be sent, great princes, And he shall buy my daughter iii 3 27
I was sent for to the king; but why, I know not iv 1 35
Let one be sent To pray Achilles see us at our tent v 9 7
That the gods sent not Corn for the rich men only *Coriolanus* i 1 211
To a cruel war I sent him; from whence he returned, his brows bound with oak i 3 15
What's the matter?—You are sent for to the Capitol ii 1 276
You are sent for to the senate iv 6 74
What he would do, He sent in writing after me v 1 68
Take this along; I writ it for thy sake, And would have sent it v 2 97
This last old man, Whom with a crack'd heart I have sent to Rome v 3 9
His lovely bride, Sent by the heavens *T. Andron.* i 1 335
That noble hand of thine . . . Shall not be sent: my hand will serve iii 1 165
And here's thy hand, in scorn to thee sent back iii 1 238
My grandsire, well advised, hath sent by me The goodliest weapons iv 2 10
God give her good rest! What hath he sent her?—A devil iv 2 63
And say I am Revenge, sent from below To join with him v 2 3
Sent from the infernal kingdom, To ease the gnawing vulture of thy mind v 2 30
Art thou sent to me, To be a torment to mine enemies? v 2 41
And I am sent to be revenged on him v 2 95
Fought Rome's quarrel out, And sent her enemies unto the grave v 3 103
I am sent to find those persons whose names are here writ *Rom. and Jul.* i 2 42
Hath sent a letter to his father's house.—A challenge, on my life ii 4 7
And has sent your honour two brace of greyhounds *T. of Athens* i 2 194
I am sent expressly to your lordship.—Give me breath ii 2 33
Hath sent to your lordship to furnish him iii 1 19
Had he mistook him and sent to me, I should ne'er have denied his occasion iii 2 25
My lord hath sent— Ha! what has he sent? iii 2 34
What has he sent now?—Has only sent his present occasion now iii 2 38
I'ld rather than the worth of thrice the sum, Had sent to me first iii 3 23
He hath sent me an earnest inviting iii 6 10
I am sorry, when he sent to borrow of me, that my provision was out iii 6 17
What of you?—He sent to me, sir,—Here he comes iii 6 26
I am e'en sick of shame, that, when your lordship this other day sent to me, I was so unfortunate a beggar.—Think not on't, sir.—If you had sent but two hours before iii 6 47
The gods out of my misery Have sent thee treasure iv 3 532
We sent to thee, to give thy rages balm v 1 16
A slight unmeritable man, Meet to be sent on errands *J. Cæsar* iv 1 13
We are sent To give thee from our royal master thanks *Macbeth* i 3 100
Sent forth great largess to your offices ii 1 14
Better be with the dead, Whom we, to gain our peace, have sent to peace iii 2 20
Sent he to Macduff?—He did: and with an absolute 'Sir, not I' iii 6 39
Sent to my account With all my imperfections on my head *Hamlet* i 5 78
He sent out to suppress His nephew's levies ii 2 61
Were you not sent for? Is it your own inclining? Is it a free visitation? ii 2 283
You were sent for; and there is a kind of confession in your looks ii 2 288
I know the good king and queen have sent for you ii 2 291
Be even and direct with me, whether you were sent for, or no? ii 2 298
My lord, we were sent for.—I will tell you why ii 2 303
Leave us too; For we have closely sent for Hamlet hither iii 1 29
Your mother, in most great affliction of spirit, hath sent me to you iii 2 324
I have sent to seek him, and to find the body iv 3 1
Let the king have the letters I have sent iv 6 23
He that is mad, and sent into England.—Ay, marry, why was he sent into England?—Why, because he was mad v 1 161
Came something saucily into the world before he was sent for *Lear* i 1 22
I serve the king; On whose employment I was sent to you ii 2 136
To whose hands have you sent the lunatic king? iii 7 46
Where hast thou sent the king?—To Dover iii 7 50
With him I sent the queen; My reason all the same v 3 51
The galleys Have sent a dozen sequent messengers *Othello* i 2 41
The senate hath sent about three several quests To search you out i 2 46
The duke's in council, and your noble self, I am sure, is sent for i 2 93
With what else needful your good grace shall think To be sent after me i 3 288
I have sent to bid Cassio come speak with you iii 4 50
And this, it seems, Roderigo meant to have sent this damned villain v 2 316
Who knows If the scarce-bearded Cæsar have not sent His powerful mandate to you, 'Do this, or this' *Ant. and Cleo.* i 1 21
Upon her landing, Antony sent to her, Invited her to supper ii 2 224
And therefore have we Our written purposes before us sent ii 6 4
Be pleased to tell us . . . how you take The offers we have sent you ii 6 31
We sent our schoolmaster; Is he come back? iii 11 71
Antony Hath after thee sent all thy treasure, with His bounty overplus iv 6 21
My mistress Cleopatra sent me to thee.—When did she send thee? iv 14 118
She sent you word she was dead; But, fearing since how it might work, hath sent Me to proclaim the truth iv 14 124
Cæsar hath sent— Too slow a messenger. O, come apace, dispatch! v 2 324
'The letter That I have sent her . . . Shall give thee opportunity *Cymb.* iii 2 18
I have sent Cloten's clotpoll down the stream, In embassy to his mother iv 2 184
The Roman emperor's letters, Sent by a consul to me iv 2 385
Landed on your coast, with a supply Of Roman gentlemen, by the senate sent iv 3 26
And she sent him away as cold as a snowball *Pericles* iv 6 148
O, here is The lady that I sent for. Welcome, fair one! v 1 65
I am mock'd, And thou by some incensed god sent hither v 1 144

Sentence. Drunk himself out of his five sentences *Mer. Wives* i 1 179
So you must be the first that gives this sentence *Meas. for Meas.* ii 2 106
Yet he must die.—Under your sentence? ii 4 37
I, now the voice of the recorded law, Pronounce a sentence ii 4 62

Sentence. Were not you then as cruel as the sentence That you have slander'd so? . . . . . . *Meas. for Meas.* ii 4 109
Immediate sentence then and sequent death Is all the grace I beg . v 1 378
And passed sentence may not be recall'd . . . . *Com. of Errors* i 1 148
Shall quips and sentences and these paper bullets of the brain awe a man from the career of his humour? . . . . *Much Ado* ii 3 249
Sir, I will pronounce your sentence: yon shall fast a week . *L. L. Lost* i 1 302
Shiver and look pale, Make periods in the midst of sentences *M. N. D.* v 1 96
Good sentences and well pronounced . . . . *Mer. of Venice* i 2 11
This strict court of Venice Must needs give sentence 'gainst the merchant . . . . iv 1 205
We trifle time: I pray thee, pursue sentence . . . . iv 1 298
Most learned judge! A sentence! Come, prepare! . . . iv 1 304
She is banish'd.—Pronounce that sentence then on me . *As Y. Like It* i 3 87
Or at every sentence end, Will I Rosalinda write . . . iii 2 144
With that she sighed as she stood, And gave this sentence then *All's W.* i 3 80
This is a dreadful sentence . . . . iii 2 64
A sentence is but a cheveril glove to a good wit . . *T. Night* iii 1 13
A heavy sentence, my most sovereign liege, And all unlook'd for *Rich. II.* i 3 154
What is thy sentence then but speechless death? . . . i 3 172
After our sentence plaining comes too late . . . . i 3 175
And in the sentence my own life destroy'd . . . . i 3 242
O God! that e'er this tongue of mine, That laid the sentence of dread banishment On yon proud man, should take it off again With words of sooth! . . . . iii 3 134
What subject can give sentence on his king? . . . . iv 1 121
Here is Carlisle living, to abide Thy kingly doom and sentence of his pride . . . . v 6 23
After this cold considerance, sentence me . . . *2 Hen. IV.* v 2 98
To steal his sweet and honey'd sentences . . . . *Hen. V.* i 1 50
God quit you in his mercy! Hear your sentence . . . ii 2 166
Your guilt is great: Receive the sentence of the law for sins Such as by God's book are adjudged to death . . . . *2 Hen. VI.* ii 3 3
Write in the dust this sentence with thy blood . . *3 Hen. VI.* v 1 56
Who pronounced The bitter sentence of poor Clarence' death? *Rich. III.* i 4 191
Enforce the present execution Of what we chance to sentence *Coriolanus* iii 3 22
Give sentence on this execrable wretch . . . . *T. Andron.* v 3 177
Hear the sentence of your moved prince . . . *Rom. and Jul.* i 1 95
And art thou changed? pronounce this sentence then, Women may fall, when there's no strength in men . . . . . . ii 3 79
Prick'd to die, In our black sentence and proscription . *J. Cæsar* iv 1 17
With strain'd pride To come between our sentence and our power . *Lear* i 1 173
The trust, the office I do hold of you, Not only take away, but let your sentence Even fall upon my life . . . . . *Othello* i 3 119
And lay a sentence, Which, as a grise or step, may help these lovers . i 3 199
He bears the sentence well that nothing bears But the free comfort which from thence he hears, But he bears both the sentence and the sorrow That, to pay grief, must of poor patience borrow. These sentences, to sugar, or to gall, Being strong on both sides, are equivocal . . . . i 3 212
'Twere good You lean'd unto his sentence . . . *Cymbeline* i 1 78
I would not thy good deeds should from my lips Pluck a hard sentence v 5 289
Your time's expired: Either expound now, or receive your sentence *Per.* i 1 90
Sentenced. He's sentenced; 'tis to late . . . *Meas. for Meas.* ii 2 55
She is with child; And he that got it, sentenced . . . . ii 3 13
Wherein if he chance to fail, he hath sentenced himself . . . iii 2 271
Is no greater forfeit to the law than Angelo who hath sentenced him . iv 2 168
He's sentenced; no more hearing . . . . . *Coriolanus* iii 3 109
Our throats are sentenced and stay upon execution . . . v 4 8
Sententious. Your reasons at dinner have been sharp and sententious *L. L. Lost* v 1 3
He is very swift and sententious . . . . . *As Y. Like It* v 4 66
She hath the prettiest sententious of it, of you and rosemary *Rom. and Jul.* ii 4 225
Sentest. Ill art thou repaid For that good hand thou sent'st the emperor *T. Andron.* iii 1 236
Sentinel. One aloof stand sentinel . . . . *M. N. Dream* ii 2 26
The hum of either army stilly sounds, That the fix'd sentinels almost receive The secret whispers of each other's watch . *Hen. V.* iv Prol. 6
Passing to and fro, About relieving of the sentinels . *1 Hen. VI.* ii 1 70
Use careful watch, choose trusty sentinels . . . *Richard III.* v 3 54
When shall I see you?—I will corrupt the Grecian sentinels . *T. and C.* iv 4 74
Wither'd murder, Alarum'd by his sentinel, the wolf . . *Macbeth* ii 1 53
Separate. Ill it doth beseem your holiness To separate the husband and the wife.—Be quiet . . . . . . *Com. of Errors* v 1 111
If you can separate yourself and your misdemeanours, you are welcome *T. Night* ii 3 105
A man can no more separate age and covetousness than a' can part young limbs and lechery . . . . . . *2 Hen. IV.* i 2 256
The dragon wing of night o'erspreads the earth, And, stickler-like, the armies separates . . . . *Troi. and Cres.* v 8 18
Separated. Not separated with the racking clouds, But sever'd in a pale clear-shining sky . . . . *3 Hen. VI.* ii 1 27
Bid him not fear the separated councils . . . *Richard III.* iii 2 20
Life and these lips have long been separated . . *Rom. and Jul.* iv 5 27
Our separated fortune Shall keep us both the safer . . *Macbeth* ii 3 144
Separation. Such separation as may well be said Becomes a virtuous bachelor and a maid . . . . *M. N. Dream* ii 2 58
Royal necessities made separation of their society . . *W. Tale* i 1 28
A buzzing of a separation Between the king and Katharine . *Hen. VIII.* ii 1 148
Our separation so abides, and flies, That thou, residing here, go'st yet with me, And I, hence fleeting, here remain with thee *Ant. and Cleo.* i 3 102
Septentrion. Thou art as opposite to every good As the Antipodes are unto us, Or as the south to the septentrion . . . *3 Hen. VI.* i 4 136
Sepulchre. Go to thy lady's grave and call hers thence, Or, at the least, in hers sepulchre thine . . . . . *T. G. of Ver.* iv 2 118
The skull that bred them in the sepulchre . . . *Mer. of Venice* iii 2 96
Satisfaction can be none but by pangs of death and sepulchre *T. Night* iii 4 262
Banish'd this frail sepulchre of our flesh . . . *Richard II.* i 3 196
As is the sepulchre in stubborn Jewry Of the world's ransom . . ii 1 55
As far as to the sepulchre of Christ . . . . *1 Hen. IV.* i 1 19
What is it, but to make thy sepulchre And creep into it? . *3 Hen. VI.* i 1 236
A crown, or else a glorious tomb! A sceptre, or an earthly sepulchre! . i 4 17
My heart, sweet boy, shall be thy sepulchre . . . . ii 5 115
The wrinkles in my brows . . . Were liken'd oft to kingly sepulchres . v 2 20
Alack, alack, what blood is this, which stains The stony entrance of this sepulchre? . . . . *Rom. and Jul.* v 3 141
This sight of death is as a bell, That warns my old age to a sepulchre . v 3 207
Why the sepulchre, Wherein we saw thee quietly inurn'd, Hath oped his ponderous and marble jaws . . . . *Hamlet* i 4 48

Sepulchring. I would divorce me from thy mother's tomb, Sepulchring an adultress . . . . *Lear* ii 4 134
Sequel. I guess the sequel . . . . . . *T. G. of Ver.* ii 1 122
But mark the sequel, Master Brook . . . . *Mer. Wives* iii 5 109
Gather the sequel by that went before . . . *Com. of Errors* i 1 96
So will you say when you have seen the sequel . . . *Much Ado* iii 2 137
Moth, follow.—Like the sequel, I . . . . . *L. L. Lost* iii 1 135
There is no consonancy in the sequel . . . . *T. Night* ii 5 142
His daughter first, and then in sequel all . . . . *Hen. V.* v 2 361
Mark how well the sequel hangs together . . . *Richard III.* iii 6 4
But if black scandal . . Attend the sequel of your imposition . . iii 7 232
But is there no sequel at the heels of this mother's admiration? *Hamlet* iii 2 341
Sequence. Cut off the sequence of posterity . . . *K. John* ii 1 96
How art thou a king But by fair sequence and succession? *Richard II.* ii 1 199
Why lifts she up her arms in sequence thus? . . *T. Andron.* iv 1 37
In the sequence of degree From high to low throughout . *T. of Athens* v 1 211
Sequent. Immediate sentence then and sequent death *Meas. for Meas.* v 1 378
He hath framed a letter to a sequent of the stranger queen's . *L. L. Lost* iv 2 142
Your 'O Lord, sir!' is very sequent to your whipping . *All's Well* ii 2 56
That gem, Conferr'd by testament to the sequent issue . . . v 3 197
'Be thou true,' say I, to fashion in My sequent protestation *Tr. and Cr.* iv 4 68
What to this was sequent Thou know'st already . . . *Hamlet* v 2 54
Though the wisdom of nature can reason it thus and thus, yet nature finds itself scourged by the sequent effects . . . . *Lear* i 2 115
The galleys Have sent a dozen sequent messengers . . . *Othello* i 2 41
Sequester. This hand of yours requires A sequester from liberty . . iii 4 40
Sequestered. A poor sequester'd stag, That from the hunter's aim had ta'en a hurt . . . . *As Y. Like It* ii 1 33
Why are you sequester'd from all your train? . . . *T. Andron.* ii 3 75
Sequestering from me all That time, acquaintance, custom and condition Made tame and most familiar to my nature . . *Troi. and Cres.* iii 3 8
Sequestration. And never noted in him any study, Any retirement, any sequestration From open haunts and popularity . . . *Hen. V.* i 1 58
This loathsome sequestration have I had . . . . *1 Hen. VI.* ii 5 25
Nor he his [love] to her: it was a violent commencement, and thou shalt see an answerable sequestration . . . . . . *Othello* i 3 351
Sere. He is deformed, crooked, old and sere . . *Com. of Errors* iv 2 19
The clown shall make those laugh whose lungs are tickle o' the sere *Ham.* ii 2 337
Serenissima. Tanta est erga te mentis integritas, regina serenissima,—O, good my lord, no Latin . . . . *Hen. VIII.* iii 1 41
Serge. Ah, thou say, thou serge, nay, thou buckram lord! *2 Hen. VI.* iv 7 27
Sergeant. If any hour meet a sergeant, a' turns back for very fear *Com. of Errors* iv 2 56
If Time be in debt and theft, and a sergeant in the way, Hath he not reason to turn back an hour in a day? . . . . iv 2 61
The sergeant of the band; he that brings any man to answer it . . iv 3 30
Then were you hindered by the sergeant, to tarry for the hoy Delay . iv 3 40
Let us have knowledge at the court of guard.—Sergeant, you shall *1 Hen. VI.* ii 1 5
Your office, sergeant; execute it . . . . . *Hen. VIII.* i 1 198
This is the sergeant Who like a good and hardy soldier fought *Macbeth* i 2 3
This fell sergeant, death, Is strict in his arrest . . . *Hamlet* v 2 347
Serious. I am more serious than my custom: you Must be so too *Tempest* ii 1 219
And make a common of my serious hours . . . . *Com. of Errors* ii 2 29
Serious business, craving quick dispatch . . . . *L. L. Lost* ii 1 31
Among other important and most serious designs . . . . v 1 105
A very serious business calls on him . . . . . *All's Well* ii 4 41
Our rash faults Make trivial price of serious things we have . . v 3 61
A servant grafted in my serious trust And therein negligent . *W. Tale* i 2 246
If thou beest capable of things serious . . . . . . iv 4 791
Our scene is alter'd from a serious thing . . . *Richard II.* v 3 79
I'll hence to London on a serious matter . . . *3 Hen. VI.* v 5 47
Things now, That bear a weighty and a serious brow *Hen. VIII.* Prol. 2
He did it with a serious mind; a heed Was in his countenance . . iii 2 80
His thinkings are below the moon, not worth His serious considering . iii 2 135
O heavy lightness! serious vanity! Mis-shapen chaos! . *Rom. and Jul.* i 1 184
Intending other serious matters . . . . . *T. of Athens* ii 2 219
From this instant, There's nothing serious in mortality . . *Macbeth* ii 3 98
Pity me not, but lend thy serious hearing To what I shall unfold *Hamlet* i 5 5
What serious contemplation are you in? . . . . . *Lear* i 2 150
He is posted hence on serious matter . . . . . . iv 5 8
You think I will your serious and great business scant . . *Othello* i 3 268
Her length of sickness, with what else more serious . *Ant. and Cleo.* i 2 124
I should have cause to use thee with a serious industry . *Cymbeline* iii 5 111
Have done; And do not play in wench-like words with that Which is so serious . . . . iv 2 231
And so stand aloof for more serious wooing . . . . *Pericles* iv 6 95
Seriously. Juno and Ceres whisper seriously . . . . *Tempest* iv 1 125
Now, by my faith and honour, If seriously I may convey my thoughts In this my light deliverance . . . . *All's Well* ii 1 84
Do you think he will make no deed at all of this that so seriously he does address himself unto? . . . . iii 6 103
Dost thou speak seriously? . . . . . . *T. of Athens* iii 2 47
This to hear Would Desdemona seriously incline . . . *Othello* i 3 146
Sermons in stones and good in every thing . . . *As Y. Like It* ii 1 17
In her chamber, making a sermon of continency to her . *T. of Shrew* iv 1 185
Come, sermon me no further . . . . . . *T. of Athens* ii 2 181
Serpent. As I dare take a serpent by the tongue . . . *Much Ado* v 1 90
And when he was a babe, a child, a shrimp, Thus did he strangle serpents in his manus . . . . *L. L. Lost* v 2 595
Do thy best To pluck this crawling serpent from my breast! *M. N. Dream* ii 2 146
Methought a serpent eat my heart away, And you sat smiling . . ii 2 149
With doubler tongue Than thine, thou serpent, never adder stung . iii 2 73
Vile thing, let loose, Or I will shake thee from me like a serpent! . . iii 2 261
Now to 'scape the serpent's tongue, We will make amends ere long . v 1 440
What, wouldst thou have a serpent sting thee twice? . *Mer. of Venice* iv 1 69
When I said 'a mother,' Methought you saw a serpent . . *All's Well* i 3 147
France, thou mayst hold a serpent by the tongue . . . *K. John* iii 1 258
I'll tell thee what, my friend, He is a very serpent in my way . . iii 3 61
What Eve, what serpent, hath suggested thee To make a second fall of cursed man? . . . . *Richard II.* iii 4 75
Forget to pity him, lest thy pity prove A serpent that will sting thee . v 3 58
Their touch affrights me as a serpent's sting . . . *2 Hen. VI.* iii 2 47
Were there a serpent seen, with forked tongue, That slily glided towards your majesty, It were but necessary you were waked . . . . iii 2 259
They will guard you, whether you will or no, From such fell serpents . iii 2 266
Their music frightful as the serpent's hiss! . . . . . iii 2 326
Who 'scapes the lurking serpent's mortal sting? . . . *3 Hen. VI.* ii 2 15
A most unjust knave; I will no more trust him when he leers than I will a serpent when he hisses . . . . *Troi. and Cres.* v 1 97

Serpent. Not Afric owns a serpent I abhor More than thy fame and envy . . . *Coriolanus* i 8 3
O serpent heart, hid with a flowering face! . . . *Rom. and Jul.* iii 2 73
Or bid me lurk Where serpents are; chain me with roaring bears . . . iv 1 80
Therefore think him as a serpent's egg Which, hatch'd, would, as his kind, grow mischievous . . . *J. Cæsar* ii 1 32
Look like the innocent flower, But be the serpent under't *Macbeth* i 5 67
There the grown serpent lies; the worm that's fled Hath nature that in time will venom breed . . . iii 4 29
'Tis given out that, sleeping in my orchard, A serpent stung me *Hamlet* i 5 36
The serpent that did sting thy father's life Now wears his crown . . . i 5 39
How sharper than a serpent's tooth it is To have a thankless child! *Lear* i 4 310
I arrest thee On capital treason; and, in thine attaint, This gilded serpent . . . v 3 84
Let heaven requite it with the serpent's curse! *Othello* iv 2 16
Much is breeding, Which, like the courser's hair, hath yet but life, And not a serpent's poison . . . *Ant. and Cleo.* i 2 201
Murmuring 'Where's my serpent of old Nile?' For so he calls me . . . i 5 25
Melt Egypt into Nile! and kindly creatures Turn all to serpents! . . . ii 5 79
You've strange serpents there . . . ii 7 27
Your serpent of Egypt is bred now of your mud by the operation of your sun . . . ii 7 29
'Tis a strange serpent.—'Tis so. And the tears of it are wet . . . ii 7 54
If knife, drugs, serpents, have Edge, sting, or operation, I am safe . iv 15 25
And both like serpents are, who though they feed On sweetest flowers, yet they poison breed . . . *Pericles* i 1 132
Serpentine. And, Mercury, lose all the serpentine craft of thy caduceus! *Troi. and Cres.* ii 3 13
Serpent-like. Struck me with her tongue, Most serpent-like, upon the very heart . . . *Lear* ii 4 163
Serpigo. Do curse the gout, serpigo, and the rheum. *Meas. for Meas.* iii 1 31
Now, the dry serpigo on the subject! *Troi. and Cres.* ii 3 81
Servant. Come away, servant, come. I am ready now . . . *Tempest* i 2 187
Thou, my slave, As thou report'st thyself, wast then her servant . . . i 2 271
My brother's servants Were then my fellows; now they are my men . ii 1 273
To be your fellow You may deny me; but I'll be your servant, Whether you will or no . . . iii 1 85
My industrious servant, Ariel!—What would myp otent master? . iv 1 33
Sir Valentine and servant, to you two thousand *T. G. of Ver.* ii 1 106
I thank you, gentle servant: 'tis very clerkly done . . . ii 1 114
If it please you, take it for your labour: And so, good morrow, servant ii 1 140
Servant!—Mistress?— . . . Servant, you are sad.—Indeed, madam, I seem so . . . ii 4 1
We thank the giver.—Who is that, servant?—Yourself, sweet lady . ii 4 36
Too low a mistress for so high a servant . . . ii 4 106
Too mean a servant To have a look of such a worthy mistress . . . ii 4 107
Sweet lady, entertain him for your servant . . . ii 4 110
Servant, you are welcome to a worthless mistress . . . ii 4 113
Once more, new servant, welcome . . . ii 4 118
All these are servants to deceitful men . . . ii 7 72
Myself do want my servants' fortune . . . iii 1 147
Sir Proteus, as I take it.—Sir Proteus, gentle lady, and your servant . iv 2 91
Who calls?—Your servant and your friend . . . iv 3 4
When a man's servant shall play the cur with him, look you, it goes hard iv 4 1
How many masters would do this for his servant? . . . iv 4 32
Cannot be true servant to my master, Unless I prove false traitor to myself . . . iv 4 109
This service I have done for you, Though you respect not aught your servant doth . . . v 4 20
Kind fellow, as ever servant shall come in house withal . *Mer. Wives* i 4 11
God bless them and make them his servants! . . . ii 2 54
I shall be glad to be your servant . . . ii 2 185
I have a servant comes with me along, That stays upon me *M. for M.* iv 1 46
Go bid the servants spread for dinner *Com. of Errors* ii 2 189
Servants must their masters' minds fulfil . . . iv 1 113
Let your servants bring my husband forth . . . v 1 93
My servant straight was mute *L. L. Lost* v 2 277
Fear not, my lord, your servant shall do so *M. N. Dream* ii 1 268
Master of my servants, Queen o'er myself *Mer. of Venice* iii 2 170
But now, This house, these servants and this same myself Are yours iii 2 172
Give order to my servants that they take No note at all of our being absent . . . v 1 119
Let me be your servant: Though I look old, yet I am strong *As Y. Like It* ii 3 46
O, this is it that makes your servants droop! *T. of Shrew* Ind. 2 29
Thy servants do attend on thee, Each in his office ready at thy beck Ind. 2 35
Servants, leave me and her alone. Madam, undress you and come now to bed . . . Ind. 2 118
My trusty servant, well approved in all . . . i 1 7
In my stead, Keep house and port and servants, as I should . . . i 1 208
Was it fit for a servant to use his master so? . . . i 2 32
Your ancient, trusty, pleasant servant Grumio . . . i 2 47
You know, Pitchers have ears, and I have many servants . . . iv 4 52
Send for your daughter by your servant here . . . iv 4 58
Sir, what are you that offer to beat my servant? . . . v 1 66
I am undone! while I play the good husband at home, my son and my servant spend all at the university . . . v 1 72
The best wishes that can be forged in your thoughts be servants to you! *All's Well* i 1 85
My dear lord he is; and I His servant live, and will his vassal die . i 3 165
Dost make hose of thy sleeves? do other servants so? . . . ii 3 266
I can nothing say, But that I am your most obedient servant . . . ii 5 77
Who was with him?—A servant only, and a gentleman . . . iii 2 86
You never had a servant to whose trust Your business was more welcome . . . iv 4 15
Be opposite with a kinsman, surly with servants . *T. Night* ii 5 163; iii 4 77
The fellow of servants, and not worthy to touch Fortune's fingers . . . ii 5 170
What is your name?—Cesario is your servant's name . . . iii 1 108
My servant, sir! 'Twas never merry world Since lowly feigning was call'd compliment: You're servant to the Count Orsino . . . iii 1 109
Your servant's servant is your servant, madam . . . iii 1 113
So did I abuse Myself, my servant and, I fear me, you . . . iii 1 125
He is sad and civil, And suits well for a servant with my fortunes . iii 4 6
If not, let me see thee a servant still . . . iii 4 60
A servant grafted in my serious trust And therein negligent . *W. Tale* i 2 246
If I Had servants true about me, that bare eyes To see alike mine honour as their profits, Their own particular thrifts . . . i 2 309
If from me he have wholesome beverage, Account me not your servant . i 2 347
Hear me, who profess Myself your loyal servant . . . ii 3 54
I knew him once a servant of the prince . . . iv 3 93
She was both pantler, butler, cook, Both dame and servant . . . iv 4 57
Servant. And then my soul shall wait on thee to heaven, As it on earth hath been thy servant still . . . *K. John* v 7 73
And all the household servants fled with him . . . *Richard II.* ii 2 60
Man by man, boy by boy, servant by servant . . . *1 Hen. IV.* iii 3 66
Love thy husband, look to thy servants, cherish thy guests . . . iii 3 193
My servant Travers, whom I sent On Tuesday last to listen after news *2 Hen. IV.* i 1 28
No man could better command his servants . . . v 1 83
If a servant, under his master's command transporting a sum of money, be assailed by robbers and die in many irreconciled iniquities, you may call the business of the master the author of the servant's damnation . . . *Hen. V.* iv 1 158
The king is not bound to answer the particular endings of his soldiers, the father of his son, nor the master of his servant . . . iv 1 165
Let me thy servant and not sovereign be . . . *1 Hen. VI.* i 2 111
Thy humble servant vows obedience And humble service . . . iii 1 167
This is my servant: hear him, noble prince.—And this is mine . . . iv 1 80
Servant in arms to Harry King of England . . . iv 2 4
Such commendations as becomes a maid, A virgin and his servant . v 3 178
He hath witness of his servant's malice . . . *2 Hen. VI.* i 3 213
The appellant, The servant of this armourer . . . ii 3 58
Thou demand'st.—The forfeit, sovereign, of my servant's life *Richard III.* ii 1 99
Of lust; Which stretched to their servants, daughters, wives . . . iii 5 82
Being my sworn servant, The duke retain'd him his . . . *Hen. VIII.* i 2 191
Flying for succour to his servant . . ., was by that wretch betray'd ii 1 109
Yet thus far we are one in fortunes: both Fell by our servants . ii 1 122
Join'd with me their servant In the unpartial judging of this business . ii 2 106
My learn'd and well-beloved servant, Cranmer . . . ii 4 238
Think us Those we profess, peace-makers, friends, and servants . . . iii 1 167
In which you brought the king To be your servant . . . iii 2 316
And your name Capucius.—Madam, the same; your servant . . . iv 2 111
I rest your servant . . . v 1 55
The servants to this chosen infant Shall then be his . . . v 5 49
'Twill make us proud to be his servant *Troi. and Cres.* iii 1 168
I tell thee, lord of Greece, She is as far high-soaring o'er thy praises As thou unworthy to be call'd her servant . . . iv 4 127
I had rather be their servant in my way Than sway with them in theirs *Coriolanus* ii 1 219
A petty servant to the state . . . ii 3 186
He was A noble servant to them; but he could not Carry his honours even . . . iv 7 36
I'll deliver Myself your loyal servant, or endure Your heaviest censure v 6 142
The servants of your adversary, And yours, close fighting *Rom. and Jul.* i 1 113
To present slaves and servants Translates his rivals *T. of Athens* i 1 71
Thou hast a servant named Lucilius.—I have so: what of him? . . . i 1 111
One Varro's servant, my good lord . . . ii 2 27
I think no usurer but has a fool to his servant: my mistress is one . ii 2 104
Bound servants, steal! Large-handed robbers your grave masters are . iv 1 10
This [gold] Will lug your priests and servants from your sides . . . iv 3 31
I have forgot thee.—An honest poor servant of yours . . . iv 3 482
Let our hearts, as subtle masters do, Stir up their servants to an act of rage, And after seem to chide 'em . . . *J. Cæsar* ii 1 176
Our duties Are to your throne and state children and servants *Macbeth* i 4 25
Your servants ever Have theirs, themselves and what is theirs, in compt, To make their audit . . . i 6 25
Being unprepared, Our will became the servant to defect . . . ii 1 18
There's not a one of them but in his house I keep a servant fee'd . . . iii 4 132
My children too?—Wife, children, servants, all That could be found . iv 3 211
Your poor servant ever.—Sir, my good friend; I'll change that name with you . . . *Hamlet* i 2 162
The time invites you; go; your servants tend . . . i 3 83
I will not sort you with the rest of my servants . . . ii 2 275
And your disorder'd rabble Make servants of their betters . . . *Lear* i 4 278
Give me my servant forth. Go tell the duke and's wife I'ld speak with them . . . ii 4 116
Who stock'd my servant? Regan, I have good hope Thou didst not know on't . . . ii 4 191
Why might not you, my lord, receive attendance From those that she calls servants? . . . ii 4 247
Servants, who seem no less, Which are to France the spies . . . iii 1 23
This trusty servant Shall pass between us . . . iv 2 18
Slain by his servant, going to put out The other eye of Gloucester . iv 2 71
A servant that he bred, thrill'd with remorse, Opposed against the act, bending his sword To his great master . . . iv 2 73
Your—wife, so I would say—Affectionate servant, GONERIL . . . iv 6 276
Are you not Kent?—The same, Your servant Kent. Where is your servant Caius? . . . v 3 283
The servants of the duke, and my lieutenant . . . *Othello* i 2 34
Whatever shall become of Michael Cassio, He's never any thing but your true servant.—I know't; I thank you . . . iii 3 9
I go from hence Thy soldier, servant . . . *Ant. and Cleo.* i 3 70
Call forth my household servants: let's to-night Be bounteous at our meal . . . iv 2 9
That mine own servant should Parcel the sum of my disgraces! . . . v 2 162
I shall remain your debtor.—I your servant. Adieu, good queen . . . v 2 205
Here is your servant. How now, sir! What news? . . . *Cymbeline* i 1 159
This hath been Your faithful servant: I dare lay mine honour He will remain so . . . i 1 174
Cæsar, that hath more kings his servants than Thyself domestic officers iii 1 64
I must die; And if I do not by thy hand, thou art No servant of thy master's . . . iii 4 78
Pisanio, her old servant, I have not seen these two days . . . iii 5 54
Cadwal and I Will play the cook and servant; 'tis our match . . . iii 6 30
Beseech your highness, Hold me your loyal servant . . . iv 3 16
Every good servant does not all commands: No bond but to do just ones v 1 6
Our brother; Joy'd are we that you are.—Your servant, princes . . . v 5 425
Be my helps, As I am son and servant to your will . . . *Pericles* i 1 23
Fit counsellor and servant for a prince, Who by thy wisdom makest a prince thy servant . . . i 2 63
I'll not bereave you of your servant . . . iv 1 32
Servant brow. Majesty might never yet endure The moody frontier of a servant brow . . . *1 Hen. IV.* i 3 19
Servanted. My affairs Are servanted to others . . . *Coriolanus* v 2 89
Servant-maid. I had rather be a country servant-maid Than a great queen, with this condition . . . *Richard III.* i 3 107
Servant-monster, drink to me.—Servant-monster! . . . *Tempest* iii 2 3
Drink, servant-monster, when I bid thee . . . iii 2 9
Serve. He does make our fire, Fetch in our wood and serves in offices . i 2 312
A plague upon the tyrant that I serve! . . . ii 2 166
The mistress which I serve quickens what's dead . . . iii 1 6

Serve. Let me lick thy shoe. I'll not serve him ; he is not valiant *Tempest* iii 2 27
Thou shalt be lord of it and I'll serve thee . . . . iii 2 65
Less than a pound shall serve me for carrying your letter *T. G. of Ver.* i 1 111
With a pair of anchoring hooks, Would serve to scale another Hero's tower . . . . iii 1 119
The time now serves not to expostulate . . . . iii 1 251
She is her master's maid, and serves for wages . . . iii 1 270
On my word, it will serve him ; she's as big as he is *Mer. Wives* iv 2 79
Sure, one of you does not serve heaven well, that you are so crossed . iv 5 130
Serve Got, and leave your desires, and fairies will not pinse you . . v 5 136
One that serves a bad woman . . . . . . *Meas. for Meas.* ii 1 64
Are there not men in your ward sufficient to serve it? . . . ii 1 281
Even for our kitchens We kill the fowl of season : shall we serve heaven With less respect than we do minister To our gross selves? . . ii 2 85
Are you agreed?—Sir, I will serve him . . . . . iv 2 52
Let your reason serve To make the truth appear where it seems hid . v 1 65
When I serve him so, he takes it ill . . *Com. of Errors* ii 1 12
How many fond fools serve mad jealousy! . . . . ii 1 116
I'll serve you, sir, five hundred at the rate . . . . iv 4 14
The fairest grant is the necessity. Look, what will serve is fit *Much Ado* i 1 320
Will it serve for any model to build mischief on? . . . i 3 48
Masters, do you serve God?—Yea, sir, we hope.—Write down, that they hope they serve God : and write God first . . . . iv 2 18
Do not forget to specify, when time and place shall serve, that I am an ass v 1 264
And how do you?—Very ill too.—Serve God, love me, and mend . v 2 95
It would neither serve for the writing nor the tune . . *L. L. Lost* i 2 119
Boyet, you can carve ; Break up this capon.—I am bound to serve . iv 1 56
Priscian! a little scratch'd, 'twill serve . . . . v 1 32
Doth this man serve God?—Why ask you? . . . . v 2 526
I'll serve thee true and faithfully till then . . . . v 2 841
I serve the fairy queen, To dew her orbs upon the green *M. N. Dream* ii 1 8
One turf shall serve as pillow for us both . . . . . ii 2 41
I have enough to serve mine own turn . . . . . iii 1 153
My conscience will serve me to run from this Jew . *Mer. of Venice* ii 2 1
If I serve not him, I will run as far as God has any ground . . ii 2 117
For I am a Jew, if I serve the Jew any longer . . . . ii 2 120
He hath a great infection, sir, as one would say, to serve,— Indeed, the short and the long is, I serve the Jew . . . . . ii 2 134
What would you?—Serve you, sir.—That is the very defect of the matter ii 2 151
Bid them cover the table, serve in the meat, and we will come in to dinner . . . . iii 5 64
Pray thee, let it serve for table-talk . . . . . . iii 5 93
I am sorry that your leisure serves you not . . . . iv 1 405
That 'scuse serves many men to save their gifts . . . . iv 1 444
To some kind of men Their graces serve them but as enemies *As Y. L. It* ii 3 11
An you serve me such another trick, never come in my sight more . iv 1 40
It shall become to serve all hopes conceived . . . *T. of Shrew* i 1 15
Fall to them as you find your stomach serves you . . . i 1 38
And while I pause, serve in your harmony . . . . iii 1 14
How durst you, villains, bring it from the dresser, And serve it thus to me? . . . . iv 1 167
They are bound to serve, love and obey . . . . . v 2 164
In the which, my instruction shall serve to naturalize thee . *All's Well* i 1 222
It well may serve A nursery to our gentry . . . . . i 2 15
Would God would serve the world so all the year! . . . . i 3 88
Health, at your bidding, serve your majesty! . . . . . ii 1 18
Beware of being captives, Before you serve . . . . . ii 1 22
But for me, I have an answer will serve all men . . . . ii 2 14
Will your answer serve fit to all questions? . . . . . ii 2 20
I see things may serve long, but not serve ever . . . . ii 2 60
There't serves well again . . . . ii 2 64
Whom I serve above is my master.—Who? God?—Ay, sir . . ii 3 261
Madam, he's gone to serve the duke of Florence . . . . iii 2 54
We serve you, madam, In that and all your worthiest affairs . . iii 2 98
A gentleman that serves the count Reports but coarsely of her . . iii 5 59
Drown my clothes, and say I was stripped.—Hardly serve . . iv 1 59
Ay, so you serve us Till we serve you . . . . . . iv 2 17
Can serve the world for no honest use . . . . . . iv 3 341
If I cannot serve you, I can serve as great a prince as you are . . iv 5 38
There's my purse: I give thee not this to suggest thee from thy master thou talkest of; serve him still . . . . iv 5 48
Whose dear perfection hearts that scorn'd to serve Humbly call'd mistress v 3 18
Whereto thy speech serves for authority . . . . *T. Night* i 2 20
I'll serve this duke . . . . i 2 55
If that this simple syllogism will serve, so; if it will not, what remedy? i 5 55
She may command me : I serve her ; she is my lady . . . ii 5 127
I was preserved to serve this noble count . . . . . v 1 263
Let him be Until a time may serve . . . . . *W. Tale* ii 3 22
I'll serve you As I would do the gods . . . . . . iii 2 207
If thou want'st a cord, the smallest thread That ever spider twisted from her womb Will serve to strangle thee . . . *K. John* iv 3 129
Must I not serve a long apprenticehood To foreign passages? *Richard II.* i 3 271
Which serves it in the office of a wall Or as a moat . . . . ii 1 47
If he serve God, We'll serve Him too and be his fellow so . . iii 2 98
Which serves as paste and cover to our bones . . . . . iii 2 154
O, thou think'st To serve me last, that I may longest keep Thy sorrow in my breast . . . . iii 4 95
Not so much as will serve to be prologue to an egg and butter 1 *Hen. IV.* i 2 23
Yet time serves wherein you may redeem Your banish'd honours . . i 3 180
How long hast thou to serve? . . . . ii 4 45
The powers of us may serve so great a day . . . . . iv 1 132
And made her serve your uses both in purse and in person 2 *Hen. IV.* ii 1 126
It shall serve among wits of no higher breeding than thine . . ii 2 38
To serve bravely is to come halting off . . . . . . ii 4 54
Shadow will serve for summer . . . . iii 2 144
No man is too good to serve's prince . . . . . . iii 2 253
Have the summary of all our griefs, When time shall serve, to show in articles . . . . iv 1 74
Sudden sorrow Serves to say thus, 'some good thing comes to-morrow' iv 2 84
There is no excuse shall serve ; you shall not be excused . . v 1 7
This Davy serves you for good uses ; he is your serving-man and your husband . . . . v 3 11
I say little ; but when time shall serve, there shall be smiles *Hen. V.* ii 1 6
Your father's enemies Have steep'd their galls in honey and do serve you ii 2 30
But all they three, though they would serve me, could not be man to me iii 2 31
What he has spoke to me, that is well, I warrant you, when time is serve iii 6 69
Under what captain serve you? . . . . iv 1 95
Ayez pitié de moi!—Moy shall not serve . . . . . . iv 4 14
I pray you to serve God, and keep you out of prawls, and prabbles . iv 8 68

Serve. I can tell you, it will serve you to mend your shoes . . *Hen. V.* iv 8 74
The cry of Talbot serves me for a sword . . . . . 1 *Hen. VI.* ii 1 79
Soldiers' stomachs always serve them well . . . . . ii 3 80
Although you break it when your pleasure serves . . . . v 4 164
Be still awhile, till time do serve . . . . . 2 *Hen. VI.* i 1 248
A subtle knave! but yet it shall not serve . . . . . ii 1 104
It serves you well, my lord, to say so much.—I say no more than truth iii 1 119
And now the word 'sallet' must serve me to feed on . . . iv 10 17
If our words will serve.—And if words will not, then our weapons shall v 1 139
I cannot weep ; for all my body's moisture Scarce serves to quench my furnace-burning heart . . . . 3 *Hen. VI.* ii 1 80
Now Margaret Must strike her sail and learn awhile to serve . . iii 3 5
As occasion serves . . . . iii 3 236
I will hence again : I came to serve a king and not a duke . . iv 7 49
If fortune serve me, I'll requite this kindness . . . . iv 7 78
To serve me well, you all should do me duty . . . *Richard III.* i 3 251
O, serve me well, and teach yourselves that duty! . . . . i 3 253
Your grace's word shall serve, As well as I had seen and heard him speak iii 5 62
Shame serves thy life and doth thy death attend . . . . iv 4 195
What do they in the north, When they should serve their sovereign in the west? . . . . iv 4 486
Are all in uproar, And danger serves among them . . *Hen. VIII.* i 2 37
Your words, Domestics to you, serve your will as't please Yourself . ii 4 114
Serve the king ; And,—prithee, lead me in . . . . . iii 2 449
What is or is not, serves As stuff for these two to make paradoxes *Troi. and Cres.* i 3 183
I serve thee not, Well, go to, go to.—I serve here voluntary . . ii 1 101
Thersites is a fool to serve such a fool, and Patroclus is a fool positive ii 3 70
Will the time serve to tell? I do not think . . . *Coriolanus* i 6 46
The rest will serve For a short holding . . . . . . i 7 3
To make us no better thought of, a little help will serve . . . ii 3 16
How youngly he began to serve his country, How long continued . ii 3 244
I think 'twill serve, if he Can thereto frame his spirit . . . iii 2 96
The day serves well for them now . . . . iv 3 32
Then thou dwellest with daws too?—No, I serve not thy master . . iv 5 49
Thou pratest, and pratest ; serve with thy trencher, hence! . . iv 5 54
To save the Romans, thereby to destroy The Volsces whom you serve . v 3 134
I am as able and as fit as thou to serve . . . *T. Andron.* ii 1 34
There serve your lusts, shadow'd from heaven's eye . . . . ii 1 130
Let it serve To ransom my two nephews from their death . . . iii 1 172
Would we had a thousand Roman dames At such a bay, by turn to serve our lust . . . . iv 2 42
That is as fit as can be to serve for your oration . . . . iv 3 96
I serve as good a man as you.—No better.—Well, sir *Rom. and Jul.* i 1 61
What doth her beauty serve, but as a note Where I may read who pass'd that passing fair? . . . . i 1 241
Go thy ways, wench ; serve God . . . . ii 5 45
Nor so wide as a church-door ; but 'tis enough, 'twill serve . . iii 1 101
All these woes shall serve For sweet discourses in our time to come . iii 5 52
My leisure serves me, pensive daughter, now . . . . . iv 1 39
Our bridal flowers serve for a buried corse . . . . . iv 5 89
Time to be honest.—That time serves still . . . *T. of Athens* i 1 267
You three serve three usurers?—Ay ; would they served us! . . ii 2 97
This answer will not serve.—If 'twill not serve, 'tis not so base as you ; For you serve knaves . . . . iii 4 57
I'll ever serve his mind with my best will . . . . . iv 2 49
And, as my lord, Still serve him with my life. My dearest master! . iv 3 478
I never had honest man about me, I ; all I kept were knaves, to serve in meat to villains . . . . iv 3 485
I must serve him so too, tell him of an intent that's coming toward him v 1 22
When the day serves, before black-corner'd night, Find what thou want'st v 1 47
What trash is Rome, What rubbish, and what offal, when it serves For the base matter to illuminate So vile a thing as Cæsar . . *J. Cæsar* i 3 109
You serve Octavius Cæsar, do you not?—I do, Mark Antony . . iii 1 276
And we must take the current when it serves, Or lose our ventures . iv 3 223
When we can entreat an hour to serve . . . . . *Macbeth* ii 1 22
None serve with him but constrained things Whose hearts are absent too v 4 13
Whereto serves mercy But to confront the visage of offence? *Hamlet* iii 3 46
But it reserved some quantity of choice, To serve in such a difference . iii 4 76
Our indiscretion sometimes serves us well, When our deep plots do pall v 2 8
Shall I hear from you anon?—I do serve you in this business . *Lear* i 2 194
If thou canst serve where thou dost stand condemn'd . . . . i 4 5
I do profess . . . to serve him truly that will put me in trust . . i 4 15
What wouldst thou?—Service.—Who wouldst thou serve?—You . . i 4 26
Follow me ; thou shalt serve me : if I like thee no worse after dinner . i 4 43
I shall serve you, sir, Truly, however else . . . . . ii 1 118
I serve you, madam ; Your graces are right welcome . . . . ii 1 130
I serve the king ; On whose employment I was sent to you . . ii 2 135
That sir which serves and seeks for gain, And follows but for form, Will pack when it begins to rain . . . . ii 4 79
When time shall serve, let but the herald cry, And I'll appear again . v 1 48
You are one of those that will not serve God, if the devil bid you *Othello* i 1 109
Are there no stones in heaven But what serve for the thunder? . . v 2 235
You shall outlive the lady whom you serve . . *Ant. and Cleo.* i 2 31
Famous pirates Make the sea serve them . . . . . . i 4 49
Every time Serves for the matter that is then born in't . . . ii 2 10
Better to leave undone, than by our deed Acquire too high a fame when him we serve's away . . . . iii 1 15
So, the gods keep you, And make the hearts of Romans serve your ends! . . . . iii 2 37
If we should serve with horse and mares together, The horse were merely lost . . . . iii 7 8
These offers, Which serve not for his vantage, he shakes off; And so should you . . . . iii 7 34
Perchance to-morrow You'll serve another master . . . . iv 2 28
They are beaten, sir ; and our advantage serves For a fair victory . iv 7 11
Wilt thou serve me?—Sir, I will.—Give me thy hand . . *Cymbeline* iii 5 122
How fit his garments serve me! . . . . iv 1 3
Try many, all good, serve truly, never Find such another master . . iv 2 373
She is served As I would serve a rat . . . . v 5 248
How lived you? And when came you to serve our Roman captive? . v 5 385
Nor the time nor place Will serve our long inter'gatories . . . v 5 392
Day serves not light more faithful than I'll be . . . *Pericles* i 2 110
These roguing thieves serve the great pirate Valdes . . . . iv 1 97
'Faith, she would serve after a long voyage at sea . . . . iv 6 48
Go to the wars, would you? where a man may serve seven years for the loss of a leg? . . . . iv 6 181
Serve by indenture to the common hangman : Any of these ways are yet better than this . . . . iv 6 187

Serve my purpose. It serves my purpose . . . . *Coriolanus* i 1 94

Serve my turn. This maid will not serve your turn, sir.—This maid will serve my turn, sir *L. L. Lost* i 1 301
The first and second cause will not serve my turn . . i 2 184
Now were I happy, if His going I could frame to serve my turn *W. Tale* iv 4 520
My uses cry to me, I must serve my turn Out of mine own *T. of Athens* ii 1 20
But, O, what form of prayer Can serve my turn? . . *Hamlet* iii 3 52
O, sir, content you; I follow him to serve my turn upon him *Othello* i 1 42
Serve our turn. Power enough to serve our turn . *Richard II.* iii 2 90
Serve the turn. A cloak as long as thine will serve the turn? *T. G. of V.* iii 1 131
Why, any cloak will serve the turn . . . . iii 1 134
Thou hast stayed so long that going will scarce serve the turn . iii 1 388
I have a sonnet that will serve the turn . . . . iii 2 93
I spied An ancient angel coming down the hill, Will serve the turn *T. of Shrew* iv 2 62
I would the cutting of my garments would serve the turn . *All's Well* iv 1 51
My hand will serve the turn . . . . *T. Andron.* iii 1 165
Serve thy turn. And make my misery serve thy turn . *Coriolanus* iv 5 94
Serve your turn. This maid will not serve your turn . *L. L. Lost* i 1 300
Will none but Herne the hunter serve your turn? . . *Mer. Wives* v 5 108
Why then, to-morrow I cannot serve your turn? . . *As Y. Like It* v 2 53
Nay, that shall not serve your turn; that shall it not . *Troi. and Cres.* iii 1 81
It seems, some certain snatch or so Would serve your turns *T. Andron.* ii 1 96
Served Without or grudge or grumblings . . . *Tempest* i 2 248
I remember the trick you served me . . . *T. G. of Ver.* iv 4 38
Madam Julia's gown, Which served me as fit, by all men's judgements . iv 4 167
If I be served such another trick, I'll have my brains ta'en out *Mer. Wives* iii 5 6
Shall we tell our husbands how we have served him? . . iv 2 229
I have served him from the hour of my nativity to this instant *C. of Er.* iv 4 31
Long since thy husband served me in my wars . . . v 1 161
Did you think the prince would have served you thus? . *Much Ado* ii 1 203
If your leisure served, I would speak with you . . . iii 2 84
This was a venture, sir, that Jacob served for . . *Mer. of Venice* i 3 92
For the table, sir, it shall be served in; for the meat, sir, it shall be covered . . . . iii 5 66
So he served the second, and so the third . . *As Y. Like It* i 2 137
I have eat none yet.—Nor shalt not, till necessity be served . ii 7 89
Thy will by my performance shall be served . . *All's Well* ii 1 205
O that I served that lady! . . . . *T. Night* i 2 41
We have always truly served you, and beseech you So to esteem of us *W. Tale* ii 3 148
I have served Prince Florizel and in my time wore three-pile . iv 3 13
Welcomed all, served all; Would sing her song and dance her turn iv 4 57
I would have you served with the best . . *2 Hen. IV.* iii 2 274
Those precepts cannot be served . . . . v 1 15
I have served your worship truly, sir, this eight years . . v 1 51
It [sallet] hath served me instead of a quart pot to drink in *2 Hen. VI.* iv 10 15
Were you well served, you would be taught your duty *Richard III.* i 3 250
His master would be served before a subject, if not before the king; which stopped our mouths . . . . . . *Hen. VIII.* ii 2 8
Had I but served my God with half the zeal I served my king . iii 2 456
Why hast thou not served thyself in to my table so many meals? *Troi. and Cres.* iii 3 45
Since he hath Served well for Rome,— What do you prate of service? *Cor.* iii 3 83
Served his designments In mine own person . . . v 6 35
Why, then, it seems, some certain snatch or so Would serve your turns. —Ay, so the turn were served . . . . *T. Andron.* ii 1 96
And they have served me to effectless use . . . iii 1 76
The guests are come, supper served up, you called *Rom. and Jul.* i 3 101
It is a most sharp sauce.—And is it not well served in to a sweet goose? ii 4 85
This gentleman of mine hath served me long: To build his fortune I will strain a little, For 'tis a bond in men . *T. of Athens* i 1 142
You three serve three usurers?—Ay; would they served us!—So would I,—as good a trick as ever hangman served thief . . . ii 2 98
What touches us ourself shall be last served . . *J. Cæsar* iii 1 8
All that served Brutus, I will entertain them . . . v 5 60
And let the angel whom thou still hast served Tell thee . *Macbeth* v 8 14
I've seen myself, and served against, the French . *Hamlet* iv 7 84
He is justly served; It is a poison temper'd by himself . . v 2 338
Served the lust of my mistress' heart, and did the act of darkness. *Lear* iii 4 89
I have served you ever since I was a child; But better service have I never done you Than now to bid you hold . . . iii 7 73
I have served him, and the man commands Like a full soldier *Othello* ii 1 35
Thou hast served me with much faith. What's else to say? . *A. and C.* ii 7 64
Within our files there are, Of those that served Mark Antony but late . iv 1 13
You have served me well, And kings have been your fellows . iv 2 12
Doughty-handed are you, and have fought Not as you served the cause iv 8 6
Mark Antony I served, who best was worthy Best to be served . v 1 6
He served with glory and admired success . . *Cymbeline* i 1 32
He hath done no Briton harm, Though he have served a Roman . v 5 91
She is served As I would serve a rat . . . . v 5 247
Servest. Who servest thou under? . . . *Hen. V.* iv 7 154
Thou art a witch, And straightway give thy soul to him thou servest *1 Hen. VI.* i 5 7
I thank thee, fellow; thou servest me, and I'll love thee . *Lear* i 4 97
Serveth. This token serveth for a flag of truce . *1 Hen. VI.* iii 1 138
Service. Remember I have done thee worthy service . *Tempest* i 2 247
Whom now I keep in service . . . . i 2 286
Letters should not be known; riches, poverty, And use of service, none ii 1 151
The very instant that I saw you, did My heart fly to your service . iii 1 65
Thou and thy meaner fellows your last service Did worthily perform . iv 1 35
For a little Follow, and do me service . . . iv 1 267
All this service Have I done since I went . . . v 1 225
To commend their service to his will . . *T. G. of Ver.* i 3 42
Lose thy master, and, in losing thy master, lose thy service . ii 3 49
Lose the tide, and the voyage, and the master, and the service, and the tied! . . . . ii 3 57
There is no woe to his correction Nor to his service no such joy on earth ii 4 139
Wilt thou go?—At thy service . . . . ii 5 63
For you know that love Will creep in service where it cannot go . iv 2 20
To know what service It is your pleasure to command me in . . iv 3 9
I like thee well And will employ thee in some service presently . iv 4 45
Madam, this service I have done for you . . . v 4 19
Very rogues, now they be out of service . . *Mer. Wives* ii 1 183
It hath done meritorious service . . . . iv 2 218
You that have worn your eyes almost out in the service *Meas. for Meas.* i 2 114
Do me this kind service . . . . . i 2 181
He knew the service, and that instructed him to mercy . . iv 2 127
I am still Attorney'd at your service . . . . v 1 390
All my life to come I'll lend you all my life to do you service . v 1 437
If I last in this service, you must case me in leather *Com. of Errors* ii 1 85
Service. And have nothing at his hands for my service but blows *Com. of Errors* iv 4 33
O, grant me justice! Even for the service that long since I did thee v 1 191
He hath done good service, lady, in these wars . . *Much Ado* i 1 48
Will your grace command me any service to the world's end? . ii 1 271
And shape his service wholly to my hests . . *L. L. Lost* v 2 65
Dumain was at my service, and his sword . . . v 2 276
And Longaville was for my service born . . . v 2 284
Please it your majesty Command me any service to her thither? . v 2 312
Impose some service on me for thy love . . . v 2 850
You are too officious In her behalf that scorns your services *M. N. Dream* iii 2 331
Conn'd with cruel pain, To do you service . . . v 1 81
I love not to see wretchedness o'ercharged And duty in his service perishing . . . . v 1 86
I am famished in his service . . . *Mer. of Venice* ii 2 113
If it be preferment To leave a rich Jew's service . . ii 2 156
I cannot get a service, no; I have ne'er a tongue in my head . ii 2 165
And stand indebted, over and above, In love and service to you evermore . . . . v 1 414
Most true, I have lost my teeth in your service . *As Y. Like It* i 1 87
Turning these jests out of service, let us talk in good earnest . i 3 26
To be my foster-nurse When service should in my old limbs lie lame . ii 3 41
I'll do the service of a younger man In all your business and necessities ii 3 54
The constant service of the antique world, When service sweat for duty . . . . ii 3 57
These times, Where none will sweat but for promotion, And having that, do choke their service up Even with the having . . ii 3 61
It [to love] is to be all made of faith and service . . . v 2 95
Players That offer service to your lordship . . *T. of Shrew* Ind. 1 78
If this be not a lawful cause for me to leave his service . . i 2 30
Pray, accept his service.—A thousand thanks . . . ii 1 84
The poorest service is repaid with thanks . . . iv 3 45
Gentlemen that mean to see The Tuscan service . . *All's Well* i 2 14
He did look far Into the service of the time . . . i 2 27
Service is no heritage . . . . . . i 3 25
I give Me and my service, ever whilst I live, Into your guiding power . ii 3 110
They say the French count has done most honourable service . iii 5 4
You shall see a countryman of yours That has done worthy service . iii 5 51
That was not to be blamed in the command of the service . . iii 6 55
The merit of service is seldom attributed to the true and exact performer iii 6 64
And will for ever Do thee all rights of service . . . iv 2 17
A knave or a fool?—A fool, sir, at a woman's service, and a knave at a man's . . . . iv 5 25
I would cozen the man of his wife and do his service.—So you were a knave at his service, indeed . . . . . iv 5 29
I would give his wife my bauble, sir, to do her service . . iv 5 33
Thou art both knave and fool.—At your service . . . iv 5 36
That will allow me very worth his service . . . *T. Night* i 2 59
Here, madam, at your service . . . . . i 5 318
She that would alter services with thee, THE FORTUNATE-UNHAPPY . ii 5 172
Give me your hand, sir.—My duty, madam, and most humble service . iii 1 106
'Gainst the count his galleys I did some service . . . iii 3 27
His counsel now might do me golden service . . . iv 3 8
For your service done him, So much against the mettle of your sex . v 1 329
On the like occasion whereon my services are now on foot . *W. Tale* i 1 3
For myself, I'll put My fortunes to your service . . . i 2 440
We shall Present our services to a fine new prince One of these days . ii 1 17
We beg, As recompense of our dear services Past and to come . . ii 3 150
Wipe not out the rest of thy services by leaving me now . . iv 2 12
Or take away with thee the very services thou hast done . . iv 2 18
I have eyes under my service which look upon his removedness . iv 2 41
But now I am out of service . . . . . iv 3 14
If this be a horseman's coat, it hath seen very hot service . . iv 3 71
Commend them and condemn them to her service Or to their own perdition . . . . iv 4 388
I think You have heard of my poor services . . . . iv 4 527
All my services You have paid home . . . . . v 3 3
At your employment; at your service, sir . . . *K. John* i 1 198
But you at your sick service had a prince . . . . iv 1 52
Remember well, Upon your oath of service to the pope . . . v 1 23
Your nobles will not hear you, but are gone To offer service to your enemy . . . . v 1 34
I do bequeath my faithful services And true subjection everlastingly . v 7 104
Renowned for their deeds as far from home, For Christian service *Richard II.* ii 1 54
Gone to Ravenspurgh, To offer service to the Duke of Hereford . ii 3 32
I tender you my service, Such as it is, being tender, raw and young . ii 3 41
Which elder days shall ripen and confirm To more approved service . ii 3 44
And his heart To faithful service of your majesty . . . iii 3 118
So far be mine . . . As my true service shall deserve your love . iii 3 199
To do what service am I sent for hither? . . . . iv 1 176
I know not whether God will have it so, For some displeasing service I have done . . . . *1 Hen. IV.* iii 2 5
They have bought out their services . . . . . iv 2 24
If the prince put thee into my service for any other reason than to set me off, why then I have no judgement . . . *2 Hen. IV.* i 2 15
He hath since done good service at Shrewsbury . . . i 2 71
Your day's service at Shrewsbury hath a little gilded over your night's exploit on Gad's-hill . . . . i 2 168
Stay at home till you are past service . . . . iii 2 269
The service that I truly did his life Hath left me open to all injuries . v 2 7
Owe yourselves, your lives and services To this imperial throne *Hen. V.* i 2 34
So service shall with steeled sinews toil, And labour shall refresh itself with hope, To do your grace incessant services . . . . ii 2 36
That's all the riches I got in his service . . . . ii 3 46
I knew by that piece of service the men would carry coals . . iii 2 49
I must leave them, and seek some better service . . . iii 2 56
Ay'll de gud service, or ay'll lig i' the grund for it . . iii 2 123
There is very excellent services committed at the bridge . . iii 6 4
He is as valiant a man as Mark Antony; and he is a man of no estimation in the world; but I did see him do as gallant service . . . iii 6 17
And they will learn you by rote where services were done . . iii 6 75
They purpose not their death, when they purpose their services . iv 1 166
Hark, how our steeds for present service neigh! . . . iv 2 8
Turn them out of service . . . . . . iv 3 119
Commend my service to my sovereign . . . . . iv 6 23
The Welshmen did good service in a garden where leeks did grow . iv 7 103
Is an honourable badge of the service . . . . . iv 7 106
Thy humble servant vows obedience And humble service . *1 Hen. VI.* iii 1 168
Long since we were resolved of your truth, Your faithful service . . iii 4 21

Service. I'll cope with thee And do some service to Duke Humphrey's ghost — *2 Hen. VI.* iii 2 231
'Twere not amiss He were created knight for his good service — v 1 77
And such a piece of service will you do, If you oppose yourselves — v 1 155
Your legs did better service than your hands — *3 Hen. VI.* ii 2 104
So shall you bind me to your highness' service.—What service wilt thou do me? — iii 2 43
I'll do thee service for so good a gift — v 1 33
First, madam, I entreat true peace of you, Which I will purchase with my duteous service — *Richard III.* ii 1 63
A boon, my sovereign, for my service done! — ii 1 95
Ghastly looks Are at my service, like enforced smiles — iii 5 9
Earnest in the service of my God, Neglect the visitation of my friends — iii 7 106
Rewards he my true service With such deep contempt? — iv 2 123
A most unnatural and faithless service! — *Hen. VIII.* ii 1 123
I am sorry my integrity should breed, And service to his majesty and you, So deep suspicion — iii 1 52
Offers, as I do, in a sign of peace, His service and his counsel — iii 1 67
We are ready To use our utmost studies in your service — iii 1 174
Pray, do my service to his majesty: He has my heart yet — iii 1 179
Left me, Weary and old with service, to the mercy Of a rude stream — iii 2 363
I know his noble nature—not to let Thy hopeful service perish too — iii 2 419
The king shall have my service; but my prayers For ever and for ever shall be yours — iii 2 426
Noble lady, First, mine own service to your grace — iv 2 115
If a prince May be beholding to a subject, I Am, for his love and service — v 3 158
And here ye lie baiting of bombards, when Ye should do service — v 4 86
Your last service was sufferance, 'twas not voluntary — *Troi. and Cres.* ii 1 104
'Tis mad idolatry To make the service greater than the god — ii 2 57
The seas and winds, old wranglers, took a truce And did him service — ii 2 76
For the service I have done you, The advantage of the time prompts me aloud To call for recompense — iii 3 1
And here, to do you service, am become As new into the world — iii 3 11
Shall quite strike off all service I have done, In most accepted pain — iii 3 29
Desert in service, Love, friendship, charity, are subjects all To envious and calumniating time — iii 3 172
Commend my service to her beauty — v 5 3
Consider you what services he has done for his country? — *Coriolanus* i 1 30
To gratify his noble service that Hath thus stood for his country — ii 2 44
I do owe them still My life and services — ii 2 138
My wounds! I got them in my country's service — ii 3 58
But your loves, Thinking upon his services, took from you The apprehension of his present portance — ii 3 231
Resting well assured They ne'er did service for't — iii 1 122
This kind of service Did not deserve corn gratis — iii 1 124
The service of the foot Being once gangrened, is not then respected For what before it was — iii 1 306
The warlike service he has done, consider; think Upon the wounds his body bears — iii 3 49
What do you prate of service?—I talk of that, that know it.—You? — iii 3 83
I am a Roman; and my services are, as you are, against 'em — iv 3 4
If he give me way, I'll do his country service — iv 4 26
What service is here! I think our fellows are asleep — iv 5 1
'Tis an honester service than to meddle with thy mistress — iv 5 52
The painful service, The extreme dangers and the drops of blood Shed for my thankless country are requited — iv 5 74
My revengeful services may prove As benefits to thee — iv 5 95
And cannot live but to thy shame, unless It be to do thee service — iv 5 107
Fair lords, your fortunes are alike in all, That in your country's service drew your swords — *T. Andron.* i 1 175
Slain manfully in arms, In right and service of their noble country — i 1 197
All the service I require of them Is that the one will help to cut the other — iii 1 77
For hands, to do Rome service, are but vain — iii 1 80
His napkin . . . Can do no service on her sorrowful cheeks — iii 1 147
Come down, and welcome me.—Do me some service, ere I come to thee — v 2 44
Of grave and austere quality, tender down Their services — *T. of Athens* i 1 55
Attends he here, or no? Lucilius!—Here, at your lordship's service — i 1 115
I do return those talents, Doubled with thanks and service — i 2 7
Your heart's in the field now.—My heart is ever at your service — i 2 76
His service done At Lacedæmon and Byzantium Were a sufficient briber for his life.—What's that?—I say, my lords, he has done fair service — iii 5 59
By oppressing and betraying me, Thou mightst have sooner got another service — iv 3 511
We are hither come to offer you our service — v 1 75
What we can do, we'll do, to do you service — v 1 78
Take him to follow thee, That did the latest service to my master — *J. C.* v 5 67
The service and the loyalty I owe, In doing it, pays itself — *Macbeth* i 4 22
All our service In every point twice done and then done double Were poor and single business — i 6 14
I'll make so bold to call, For 'tis my limited service — ii 3 57
But, as this temple waxes, The inward service of the mind and soul Grows wide withal — *Hamlet* i 3 13
Give up ourselves, in the full bent To lay our service freely at your feet — ii 2 31
Hither are they coming, to offer you service — ii 2 331
What ho! Horatio!—Here, sweet lord, at your service — iii 2 58
Such officers do the king best service in the end — iv 2 18
Your fat king and your lean beggar is but variable service — iv 3 25
We should profane the service of the dead To sing a requiem . . . to her — v 1 259
Now It did me yeoman's service — v 2 36
My services to your lordship — *Lear* i 1 29
Thou, nature, art my goddess; to thy law My services are bound — i 2 2
If you come slack of former services, You shall do well — i 3 9
What wouldst thou?—Service.—Who wouldst thou serve?—You — i 4 25
What services canst thou do?—I can keep honest counsel, ride, run — i 4 33
Now, my friendly knave, I thank thee: there's earnest of thy service — i 4 104
One that wouldst be a bawd, in way of good service — ii 2 21
The dear father Would with his daughter speak, commands her service — ii 4 103
But better service have I never done you Than now to bid you hold — iii 7 74
Of the loyal service of his son, When I inform'd him, then he call'd me sot — iv 2 7
O, the difference of man and man! To thee a woman's services are due — iv 2 27
And did him service Improper for a slave — v 3 220
'Tis the curse of service, Preferment goes by letter and affection — *Othello* i 1 35
Throwing but shows of service on their lords, Do well thrive by them — i 1 52
We come to do you service and you think we are ruffians — i 1 110
I lack iniquity Sometimes to do me service — i 2 4
My services which I have done the signiory Shall out-tongue his complaints — i 2 18
My place supplied, My general will forget my love and service — iii 3 18

Service. Witness that here Iago doth give up The execution of his wit, hands, heart, To wrong'd Othello's service! — *Othello* iii 3 467
Nor my service past, nor present sorrows, Nor purposed merit in futurity — iii 4 116
I have done the state some service, and they know't. No more of that — v 2 339
Where's Alexas?—Here, at your service — *Ant. and Cleo.* i 2 90
The strong necessity of time commands Our services awhile — i 3 43
There I deny my land service — ii 6 98
I had as lief have a reed that will do me no service as a partisan I could not heave — ii 7 14
In me 'tis villany; In thee 't had been good service — ii 7 81
Would prevail Under the service of a child as soon As i' the command of Cæsar — iii 13 24
I wish I could be made so many men, And all of you clapp'd up together in An Antony, that I might do you service — iv 2 18
But, like a master Married to your good service, stay till death — iv 2 31
How wouldst thou have paid My better service, when my turpitude Thou dost so crown with gold! — iv 6 33
Do it at once; Or thy precedent services are all But accidents unpurposed — iv 14 83
Bear me, good friends, where Cleopatra bides; 'Tis the last service that I shall command you — iv 14 132
Doctor, your service for this time is ended; Take your own way — *Cymb.* i 5 30
No further service, doctor, Until I send for thee — i 5 44
Let me my service tender on your lips — i 6 140
He cannot choose but take this service I have done fatherly — ii 3 39
Make denials Increase your services — ii 3 54
If it be so to do good service, never Let me be counted serviceable — iii 2 14
This service is not service, so being done, But being so allow'd — iii 3 16
Desire his service, tell him Wherein you're happy — iii 4 176
If thou wouldst not be a villain, but do me true service — iii 5 110
The first service thou dost me, fetch that suit hither: let it be thy first service — iii 5 130
Above him in birth, alike conversant in general services — iv 1 14
Most willing spirits, That promise noble service — iv 2 339
I may wander From east to occident, cry out for service, Try many, all good, serve truly, never Find such another master — iv 2 372
I'll weep and sigh; And leaving so his service, follow you — iv 2 393
The king Hath not deserved my service nor your loves — iv 4 25
He brags his service As if he were of note — v 3 93
The service that you three have done is more Unlike than this thou tell'st — v 5 353
My good master, I will yet do you service — v 5 404
His daughter's woe and heavy well-a-day In her unholy service — *Pericles* iv 4 50
But I am For other service first — v 1 255
Serviceable. Should be full-fraught with serviceable vows — *T. G. of Ver.* iii 2 70
Be serviceable to my son — *T. of Shrew* i 1 219
What would my lord . . . Wherein Olivia may seem serviceable? — *T. Night* v 1 105
I know thee well: a serviceable villain — *Lear* iv 6 257
If it be so to do good service, never Let me be counted serviceable — *Cymbeline* iii 2 15
Servile. A breath thou art, Servile to all the skyey influences — *M. for M.* iii 1 9
Where fearing dying pays death servile breath — *Richard II.* iii 2 185
If this servile usage once offend, Go and be free again — *1 Hen. VI.* v 3 58
Shoot forth thunder Upon these paltry, servile, abject drudges — *2 Hen. VI.* iv 1 105
Away with slavish weeds and servile thoughts! — *T. Andron.* ii 1 18
By the waggon-wheel Trot, like a servile footman, all day long — v 2 55
And keep us all in servile fearfulness — *J. Cæsar* i 1 80
But yet I call you servile ministers — *Lear* iii 2 21
Servility. More vile Than is a slave in base servility — *1 Hen. VI.* v 3 113
Servilius! you are kindly met, sir. Fare thee well — *T. of Athens* iii 2 30
Dost thou speak seriously, Servilius?—Upon my soul, 'tis true, sir — iii 2 47
I'll look you out a good turn, Servilius — iii 2 67
O, here's Servilius; now we shall know some answer — iii 4 66
Serving. What a coil's here! Serving of becks and jutting-out of bums! — i 2 237
We are fellows still, Serving alike in sorrow — iv 2 19
Hath he seen majesty? Isis else defend, And serving you so long! — *Ant. and Cleo.* iii 3 47
In their serving, And with what imitation you can borrow — *Cymbeline* iii 4 173
Serving-creature. Then will I lay the serving creature's dagger on your pate — *Rom. and Jul.* iv 5 119
Serving-man. A withered serving-man [makes] a fresh tapster — *Mer. Wives* i 3 19
Good Master Slender's serving-man, and friend Simple by your name — iii 1 2
The serving-men in their new fustian — *T. of Shrew* iv 1 49
I saw your niece do more favours to the count's serving-man than ever she bestowed upon me — *T. Night* iii 2 7
A secondary at control, Or useful serving-man — *K. John* v 2 81
Indeed were never soldiers, but discarded unjust serving-men — *1 Hen. IV.* iv 2 30
He, by conversing with them, is turned into a justice-like serving-man — *2 Hen. IV.* v 1 76
He is your serving-man and your husband — v 3 12
A serving-man, proud in heart and mind; that curled my hair — *Lear* iii 4 87
Serviteur. Votre serviteur.—I hope, sir, you are — *T. Night* iii 1 79
Baisant la main d'une de votre seigneurie indigne serviteur — *Hen. V.* v 2 276
Servitor. Thus are poor servitors, When others sleep upon their quiet beds, Constrain'd to watch in darkness, rain and cold — *1 Hen. VI.* ii 1 5
Let former grudges pass, And henceforth I am thy true servitor — *3 Hen. VI.* iii 3 196
Fearful commenting Is leaden servitor to dull delay — *Richard III.* iv 3 52
Here none but soldiers and Rome's servitors Repose in fame — *T. Andron.* i 1 352
Your trusty and most valiant servitor — *Othello* i 3 40
Servitude. This servitude makes you to keep unwed — *Com. of Errors* ii 1 26
The spirit of my father, which I think is within me, begins to mutiny against this servitude — *As Y. Like It* i 1 25
Sold your king to slaughter, His princes and his peers to servitude — *Hen. V.* ii 2 171
And to the world and awkward casualties Bound me in servitude — *Pericles* v 1 95
Sessa. Let the world slide: sessa! — *T. of Shrew* Ind. 1 6
Dolphin my boy, my boy, sessa! let him trot by — *Lear* iii 4 104
Do de, de, de. Sessa! Come, march to wakes and fairs — iii 6 77
Session. No longer session hold upon my shame — *Meas. for Meas.* v 1 376
Summon a session, that we may arraign Our most disloyal lady — *W. Tale* ii 3 202
This sessions, to our great grief we pronounce, Even pushes 'gainst our heart — iii 2 1
The sessions shall proceed: this is mere falsehood — iii 2 142
Every shop, church, session, hanging, yields a careful man work — iv 4 701
It's fit this royal session do proceed — *Hen. VIII.* ii 4 66
And they are ready To-morrow, or at further space, to appear Where you shall hold your session — *Lear* v 3 54
To prison, till fit time Of law and course of direct session Call thee to answer.—What if I do obey? — *Othello* i 2 86
But some uncleanly apprehensions Keep leets and law-days and in session sit With meditations lawful — iii 3 140
Sestos. Found it was 'Hero of Sestos' — *As Y. Like It* iv 1 106

Set her two courses off to sea again; lay her off . . . *Tempest* i 1 52
Set all hearts i' the state To what tune pleased his ear . . . i 2 84
Nor set A mark so bloody on the business . . . i 2 141
I'll set thee free for this . . . i 2 442
Set it down and rest you . . . iii 1 18
The sun will set before I shall discharge What I must strive to do . iii 1 22
Beseech you—Chiefly that I might set it in my prayers—What is your name? . . . iii 1 35
Thy eyes are almost set in thy head.—Where should they be set else? he were a brave monster indeed, if they were set in his tail iii 2 10
'Twixt the green sea and the azured vault Set roaring war . v 1 44
Set it down With gold on lasting pillars . . . v 1 207
Set Caliban and his companions free; Untie the spell . v 1 252
As you from crimes would pardon'd be, Let your indulgence set me free Epil. 20
War with good counsel, set the world at nought . *T. G. of Ver.* i 1 68
Now you have taken the pains to set it together, take it for your pains i 1 123
Give me a note: your ladyship can set.—As little by such toys i 2 81
I stand affected to her.—I would you were set, so your affection would cease . . . ii 1 91
Then may I set the world on wheels, when she can spin for her living . iii 1 317
O villain, that set this down among her vices! . . . iii 1 337
Here, set it down.—Give your men the charge. *Mer. Wives* iii 3 6
I had rather be set quick i' the earth And bowl'd to death with turnips! iii 4 90
If he bid you set it down, obey him . . . iv 2 112
Set spurs and away, like three German devils . . . iv 5 70
The knave constable had set me i' the stocks, i' the common stocks . iv 5 123
Lest the oil that's in me should set hell on fire . . . v 5 39
Lock hand in hand; yourselves in order set . . . v 5 81
One fruitful meal would set me to't . . *Meas. for Meas.* iv 3 161
In brief, to set the needless process by . . . v 1 92
Some one hath set you on: Confess the truth . . . v 1 112
Instruments of some more mightier member That sets them on . v 1 238
He indeed Hath set the women on to this complaint . . v 1 251
Did you set these women on to slander Lord Angelo? . . v 1 289
Ere the weary sun set in the west . . *Com. of Errors* i 2 7
Have at you with a proverb—Shall I set in my staff? . iii 1 51
Pluck off the bull's horns and set them in my forehead *Much Ado* i 1 266
Cloth o' gold, and cuts, and laced with silver, set with pearls . iii 4 20
When shall we set the savage bull's horns on the sensible Benedick's head? . . . v 1 183
But did my brother set thee on to this? . . . v 1 254
I give thee thy liberty, set thee from durance . *L. L. Lost* iii 1 129
Such barren plants are set before us . . . iv 2 29
So were there a patch set on learning, to see him in a school . . iv 2 32
Set thee down, sorrow! for so they say the fool said . . iv 3 4
An odorous chaplet of sweet summer buds Is, as in mockery, set *M. N. Dream* ii 1 111
Set your heart at rest . . . ii 1 121
Your wrongs do set a scandal on my sex . . . ii 1 240
Who would set his wit to so foolish a bird? . . . iii 1 137
Have you not set Lysander, as in scorn, To follow me? . . iii 2 222
Set a deep glass of rhenish wine on the contrary casket . *Mer. of Venice* i 2 104
Never so rich a gem Was set in worse than gold . . . ii 7 55
I'll set you forth. . . . iii 5 95
I set him every day to woo me . . . *As Y. Like It* iii 2 428
To set her before your eyes to-morrow human as she is . . v 2 73
For a night or two, Or, if not so, until the sun be set . *T. of Shrew* Ind. 2 122
By helping Baptista's eldest daughter to a husband we set his youngest free . . . i 1 142
Achieve the elder, set the younger free For our access . . i 2 268
Here comes Baptista: set your countenance, sir . . . iv 4 18
Thou wert best set thy lower part where thy nose stands . *All's Well* ii 3 267
Whoever shoots at him, I set him there . . . iii 2 115
Whom [death] I myself embrace, to set him free . . . iii 4 17
His own judgements, wherein so curiously he had set this counterfeit . iv 3 39
I have letters sent me That set him high in fame . . v 3 31
In women's waxen hearts to set their forms . . *T. Night* ii 2 31
Wilt thou set thy foot o' my neck?—Or o' mine either? . . ii 5 206
Have you not set mine honour at the stake? . . . iii 1 129
Set 'em down: go, about it . . . iii 2 51
Set upon Aguecheek a notable report of valour . . . iii 4 209
His eyes were set at eight i' the morning . . . v 1 205
Myself and Toby Set this device against Malvolio here . . v 1 368
Doth set my pugging tooth on edge . . . *W. Tale* iv 3 7
I'll not put The dibble in earth to set one slip of them . . iv 4 100
'Nointed over with honey, set on the head of a wasp's nest . . iv 4 813
Set against a brick-wall, the sun looking with a southward eye upon him . . . iv 4 818
The heaven sets spies upon us . . . v 1 203
I would set an ox-head to your lion's hide . . *K. John* ii 1 292
It in golden letters should be set Among the high tides in the calendar iii 1 85
But, ere sunset, Set armed discord 'twixt these perjured kings! . iii 1 111
As patches set upon a little breach Discredit more in hiding of the fault iv 2 32
Like heralds 'twixt two dreadful battles set . . . iv 2 78
There is no sure foundation set on blood . . . iv 2 104
Be Mercury, set feathers to thy heels, And fly like thought . iv 2 174
Till I have set a glory to this hand, By giving it the worship of revenge iv 3 71
And on our actions set the name of right With holy breath . v 2 67
And shall I now give o'er the yielded set? . . . v 2 107
The sun of heaven methought was loath to set . . . v 5 1
You are born To set a form upon that indigest . . . v 7 26
O cousin, thou art come to set mine eye . . . v 7 51
Where ever Englishman durst set his foot . . *Richard II.* i 1 66
Esteem as foil wherein thou art to set The precious jewel of thy home return . . . i 3 266
Sorrow hath less power to bite The man that mocks at it and sets it light . . . i 3 293
This little world, This precious stone set in the silver sea . ii 1 46
Thy sun sets weeping in the lowly west, Witnessing storms to come . ii 4 21
Time hath set a blot upon my pride . . . iii 2 81
Thou, old Adam's likeness, set to dress this garden . . iii 4 73
Here in this place I'll set a bank of rue, sour herb of grace . iii 4 105
Set before my face the Lord Aumerle.—Cousin, stand forth . iv 1 6
Who sets me else? by heaven, I'll throw at all . . . iv 1 57
My heart is not confederate with my hand.—It was, villain, ere thy hand did set it down . . . v 3 54
Thine eye begins to speak; set thy tongue there . . . v 3 125
And do set the word itself Against the word . . . v 5 13
Now shall we know if Gadshill have set a match . *1 Hen. IV.* i 2 119
Attract more eyes Than that which hath no foil to set it off . i 2 239

Set. You, that set the crown Upon the head of this forgetful man *1 Hen. IV.* i 3 160
Well, here I am set.—And here I stand: judge, my masters . ii 4 482
And that would set my teeth nothing on edge, Nothing so much . iii 1 133
Were it good To set the exact wealth of all our states All at one cast? to set so rich a main On the nice hazard of one doubtful hour? iv 1 46
Each heart being set On bloody courses, the rude scene may end *2 Hen. IV.* i 1 158
For any other reason than to set me off . . . i 2 15
Set your knighthood and your soldiership aside . . . i 2 95
Which is almost to pluck a kingdom down And set another up . i 3 50
The prince once set a dish of apple-johns before him . . ii 4 5
Cover, and set them down . . . ii 4 11
Thou 'lt set me a-weeping, an thou sayest so . . . ii 4 301
All their prayers and love Were set on Hereford . . . iv 1 138
Skill in the weapon is nothing without sack, for that sets it a-work . iv 3 124
Sack commences it and sets it in act and use . . . iv 3 126
Set me the crown upon my pillow here . . . iv 5 5
To have a son set your decrees at nought . . . v 2 85
Play a set Shall strike his father's crown into the hazard . *Hen. V.* i 2 262
The king is set from London . . . ii Prol. 34
We consider It was excess of wine that set him on . . ii 2 42
Now set the teeth and stretch the nostril wide, Hold hard the breath . iii 1 15
Like a lackey, from the rise to set Sweats in the eye of Phœbus . iv 1 289
The French are bravely in their battles set . . . iv 3 69
He wanted pikes to set before his archers . . *1 Hen. VI.* i 1 116
Their arms are set like clocks, still to strike on . . . i 2 42
Which obloquy set bars before my tongue . . . ii 5 49
Leave this peevish broil And set this unaccustom'd fight aside . iii 1 93
Stoop then and set your knee against my foot . . . iii 1 169
We'll set thy statue in some holy place, And have thee reverenced . iii 3 14
When they heard he was thine enemy, They set him free . . iii 3 72
Lord bishop, set the crown upon his head . . . iv 1 1
With forged quaint conceit To set a gloss upon his bold intent . iv 1 103
York set him on to fight and die in shame . . . iv 4 8
Who with me Set from our o'ermatch'd forces forth for aid . iv 4 11
York set him on; York should have sent him aid . . . iv 4 29
Put a golden sceptre in thy hand And set a precious crown upon thy head . . . v 3 119
Set this diamond safe In golden palaces, as it becomes . . v 3 169
Kneel'd to me And on my head did set the diadem . *2 Hen. VI.* i 2 40
Carry him to Rome, And set the triple crown upon his head . i 3 66
I'ld set my ten commandments in your face . . . i 3 145
Were't not all one, an empty eagle were set To guard the chicken? . iii 1 248
Seek not a scorpion's nest, Nor set no footing on this unkind shore . iii 2 87
The traitorous Warwick with the men of Bury Set all upon me . iii 2 241
Like lime-twigs set to catch my winged soul . . . iii 3 16
As for these whose ransom we have set, It is our pleasure one of them depart . . . iv 1 139
Turn it, and set a new nap upon it . . . iv 2 7
But first, go and set London bridge on fire . . . iv 6 16
Set limb to limb, and thou art far the lesser . . . iv 10 50
But that my heart's on future mischief set, I would speak blasphemy . v 2 84
Sweet father, do so; set it on your head . . *3 Hen. VI.* i 1 115
'Tis not thy southern power . . . Can set the duke up in despite of me i 1 158
Let's set our men in order, And issue forth and bid them battle straight i 2 70
Hold you his hands, whilst I do set it on . . . i 4 95
Off with his head, and set it on York gates . . . i 4 179
They took his head, and on the gates of York They set the same . ii 1 66
Who 'scapes the lurking serpent's mortal sting? Not he that sets his foot upon her back . . . ii 2 16
Kneel for grace, And set thy diadem upon my head . . ii 2 82
We set the axe to thy usurping root . . . ii 2 165
But set his murdering knife unto the root . . . ii 6 49
And set the murderous Machiavel to school . . . iii 2 193
The king by this is set him down to sleep . . . iv 3 2
He comes towards London, To set the crown once more on Henry's head iv 4 27
He shall here find his friends with horse and men To set him free. iv 5 13
Confess who set thee up and pluck'd thee down . . . v 1 26
To set my brother Clarence and the king In deadly hate . *Richard III.* i 1 34
Stay, you that bear the corse, and set it down . . . i 2 33
'Twas thy heavenly face that set me on . . . i 2 183
Sin, death, and hell have set their marks on him . . . i 3 293
He that set you on To do this deed will hate you for the deed . i 4 261
And now in peace my soul shall part to heaven, Since I have set my friends at peace on earth . . . ii 1 6
When the sun sets, who doth not look for night? . . . ii 3 34
Hath he set bounds betwixt their love and me? I am their mother . iv 1 21
The weary sun hath made a golden set . . . v 3 19
A base foul stone, made precious by the foil Of England's chair, where he is falsely set . . . v 3 251
I have set my life upon a cast, And I will stand the hazard of the die . v 4 9
Who set the body and the limbs Of this great sport together? *Hen. VIII.* i 1 46
Men of his way should be most liberal; They are set here for examples i 3 62
In most strange postures We have seen him set himself . . iii 2 119
Seek the king; That sun, I pray, may never set! . . . iii 2 415
Patience, be near me still; and set me lower . . . iv 2 76
On one and other side, Trojan and Greek, Sets all on hazard *T. and C.* Prol. 22
What grief hath set the jaundice on your cheeks? . . . i 3 2
And sets Thersites . . . To match us in comparisons with dirt . i 3 192
To awake his ear, To set his sense on the attentive bent . . i 3 252
Will you set your wit to a fool's? . . . ii 1 94
If he do set The very wings of reason to his heels And fly . . ii 2 43
Set them down For sluttish spoils of opportunity . . . iv 5 61
They set me up, in policy, that mongrel cur, Ajax, against that dog . v 4 13
Look, Hector, how the sun begins to set; How ugly night comes . . v 8 5
Good traders in the flesh, set this in your painted cloths . . v 10 46
He did so set his teeth and tear it . . . *Coriolanus* i 3 70
Set me against Aufidius and his Antiates . . . i 6 59
Keep your duties, As I have set them down . . . i 7 2
That's as easy As to set dogs on sheep . . . ii 1 273
In his person wrought To be set high in place . . . ii 3 255
Why rule you not their teeth? Have you not set them on? . . iii 1 37
The man, I think, that shall set them in present action . . iv 3 52
Set at upper end o' the table; no question asked him . . iv 5 204
I am glad thou hast set thy mercy and thy honour At difference in thee v 3 200
Help to set a head on headless Rome . . . *T. Andron.* i 1 186
Ransomless here we set our prisoners free . . . i 1 274
As sure a card as ever won the set . . . v 1 100
Set deadly enmity between two friends . . . v 1 131

Set. Oft have I digg'd up dead men from their graves, And set them upright at their dear friends' doors *T. Andron.* v 1 136
Set him breast-deep in earth, and famish him v 3 179
Who set this ancient quarrel new abroach? *Rom. and Jul.* i 1 111
You will set cock-a-hoop! you'll be the man! i 5 83
My heart's dear love is set On the fair daughter of rich Capulet: As mine on hers, so hers is set on mine ii 3 57
Look thou stay not till the watch be set iii 3 148
Either be gone before the watch be set, Or by the break of day iii 3 167
When the sun sets, the air doth drizzle dew iii 5 127
There shall no figure at such rate be set As that of true and faithful Juliet v 3 301
Ceremony was but devised at first To set a gloss on faint deeds *T. of A.* i 2 16
You have . . . , fair ladies, Set a fair fashion on our entertainment i 2 152
Call me before the exactest auditors And set me on the proof ii 2 166
I have retired me to a wasteful cock, And set mine eyes at flow ii 2 172
I cannot think but, in the end, the villanies of man will set him clear iii 3 31
Like those that under hot ardent zeal would set whole realms on fire iii 3 34
To bring manslaughter into form and set quarrelling Upon the head of valour iii 5 27
Set them down horrible traitors iv 3 118
By thy virtue Set them into confounding odds iv 3 392
He is set so only to himself That nothing but himself which looks like man Is friendly with him v 1 120
Set but thy foot Against our rampired gates, and they shall ope v 4 46
Set him before me; let me see his face *J. Cæsar* i 2 20
Set honour in one eye and death i' the other i 2 86
And I will set this foot of mine as far As who goes farthest i 3 119
Set this up with wax Upon old Brutus' statue i 3 145
Set a huge mountain 'tween my heart and tongue! ii 4 7
All his faults observed, Set in a note-book iv 3 98
As Pompey was, am I compell'd to set Upon one battle all our liberties v 1 75
O setting sun, As in thy red rays thou dost sink to night, So in his red blood Cassius' day is set; The sun of Rome is set! v 3 62
Set our battles on: 'Tis three o'clock v 3 108
It [drink] sets him on, and it takes him off *Macbeth* ii 3 36
May they not be my oracles as well, And set me up in hope? iii 1 10
I would set my life on any chance, To mend it, or be rid on't iii 1 113
Thou'ldst never fear the net nor lime, The pitfall nor the gin.—Why should I, mother? Poor birds they are not set for iv 2 36
Within my sword's length set him; if he 'scape, Heaven forgive him too! iv 3 234
Set your entreatments at a higher rate Than a command to parley *Ham.* i 3 122
I do not set my life at a pin's fee i 4 65
My tables,—meet it is I set it down, That one may smile, and smile, and be a villain i 5 107
The time is out of joint: O cursed spite, That ever I was born to set it right! i 5 190
Aroused vengeance sets him new a-work ii 2 510
I have in quick determination Thus set it down iii 1 177
Nay, then, I'll set those to you that can speak iii 4 17
You go not till I set you up a glass Where you may see the inmost part of you iii 4 19
Calls virtue hypocrite, takes off the rose From the fair forehead of an innocent love And sets a blister there iii 4 44
A form indeed, Where every god did seem to set his seal iii 4 61
This man shall set me packing iii 4 211
Thou mayst not coldly set Our sovereign process iv 3 64
You shall know I am set naked on your kingdom iv 7 44
And set a double varnish on the fame The Frenchman gave you iv 7 133
Your flashes of merriment, that were wont to set the table on a roar v 1 210
Good Gertrude, set some watch over your son v 1 319
Set me the stoups of wine upon that table v 2 278
Give him the cup.—I'll play this bout first; set it by awhile v 2 295
I loved her most, and thought to set my rest On her kind nursery *Lear* i 1 125
He flashes into one gross crime or other, That sets us all at odds i 3 5
Learn more than thou trowest, Set less than thou throwest i 4 136
My father hath set guard to take my brother ii 1 18
Where may we set our horses?—I' the mire ii 2 4
What's he that hath so much thy place mistook To set thee here? ii 4 13
An thou hadst been set i' the stocks for that question, thou hadst well deserved it ii 4 65
We'll set thee to school to an ant ii 4 68
How came my man i' the stocks?—I set him there, sir ii 4 202
That their great stars Throned and set high iii 1 23
Set ratsbane by his porridge iii 4 55
Set not thy sweet heart on proud array iii 4 84
Upon these eyes of thine I'll set my foot iii 7 68
Set me where you stand.—Give me your hand iv 6 24
Mark, I say, instantly; and carry it so As I have set it down v 3 37
That never set a squadron in the field *Othello* i 1 22
Sow lettuce, set hyssop, and weed up thyme i 3 325
Come, let's set the watch ii 3 125
He'll watch the horologe a double set, If drink rock not his cradle ii 3 135
Give me to know How this foul rout began, who set it on ii 3 210
My wife must move for Cassio to her mistress; I'll set her on ii 3 390
Avaunt! be gone! thou hast set me on the rack iii 3 335
Your reports have set the murder on v 2 187
He spake, After long seeming dead, Iago hurt him, Iago set him on v 2 329
Set you down this; And say besides v 2 351
I'll set a bourn how far to be beloved *Ant. and Cleo.* i 1 16
I'll set thee in a shower of gold, and hail Rich pearls upon thee ii 5 45
Thy grand captain Antony Shall set thee on triumphant chariots iii 1 10
The piece of virtue, which is set Betwixt us as the cement of our love iii 2 28
Set we our squadrons on yond side o' the hill, In eye of Cæsar's battle iii 9 1
Now I'll set my teeth, And send to darkness all that stop me iii 13 181
The strong-wing'd Mercury should fetch thee up, And set thee by Jove's side iv 15 36
When such a spacious mirror's set before him, He needs must see himself v 1 34
That parting kiss which I had set Betwixt two charming words *Cymb.* i 3 34
I chiefly, That set thee on to this desert, am bound To load thy merit richly i 5 73
He hath a kind of honour sets him off, More than a mortal seeming i 6 170
Thus mine enemy fell, And thus I set my foot on's neck iii 1 92
And on the gates of Lud's-town set your heads iv 2 99; 123
My life is yours; I humbly set it at your will iv 3 13
Since of your lives you set So slight a valuation iv 4 48
Cast mire upon me, set The dogs o' the street to bay me v 5 222
Set we forward: let A Roman and a British ensign wave Friendly together v 5 479
Set't down, let's look upon't.—'Tis like a coffin *Pericles* iii 2 51

Set. She that sets seeds and roots of shame and iniquity *Pericles* iv 6 92
O, that the gods Would set me free from this unhallow'd place! iv 6 107
Set about. Shall we set about some revels? *T. Night* i 3 145
Set abroach. Alack, what mischiefs might he set abroach! 2 *Hen. IV.* iv 2 14
I do the wrong, and first begin to brawl. The secret mischiefs that I set abroach I lay unto the grievous charge of others *Richard III.* i 3 325
Set abroad new business for you all *T. Andron.* i 1 192
Set a-fire. Like powder in a skilless soldier's flask, Is set a-fire by thine own ignorance *Rom. and Jul.* iii 3 133
Set against. You all are bent To set against me *M. N. Dream* iii 2 146
Envy and base opinion set against 'em *Hen. VIII.* iii 1 36
Set apart. All reverence set apart To him *K. John* iii 1 159
Set aside. Our purposed hunting shall be set aside *M. N. Dream* iv 1 188
All dissembling set aside, Tell me for truth 3 *Hen. VI.* iii 3 119
Set at liberty. Imprisoned angels Set at liberty *K. John* iii 3 9
Set at nought. The public power Which he so sets at nought *Coriol.* iii 1 270
Set at work. I was set at work Among my maids *Hen. VIII.* iii 1 74
Set a-work. How earnestly are you set a-work! *Troi. and Cres.* v 10 38
A provoking merit, set a-work by a reproveable badness in himself *Lear* iii 5 8
Set down the basket, villain! Somebody call my wife *Mer. Wives* iv 2 120
'Tis set down so in heaven, but not in earth *Meas. for Meas.* ii 4 50
Only get the learned writer to set down our excommunication *Much Ado* iii 5 68
You, Nick Bottom, are set down for Pyramus *M. N. Dream* i 2 22
Set down your venerable burden And let him feed *As Y. Like It* ii 7 167
Which hath two letters for her name fairly set down in studs *T. of Shrew* iii 2 63
Amongst the rest There is a remedy, approved, set down *All's Well* i 3 234
My greatest grief, Though little he do feel it, set down sharply iii 4 33
Shall I set down your answer so?—Do: I'll take the sacrament on't iv 3 155
Set down, for I'll speak truth iv 3 171
Poor rogues, I pray you, say.—Well, that's set down iv 3 177
And consequently sets down the manner how *T. Night* iii 4 79
Convey what I will set down to my lady iv 2 118
Thou dost advise me Even so as I mine own course have set down *W. Tale* i 2 340
Hast thou read truth?—Ay, my lord; even so As it is here set down iii 2 140
I love a ballad but even too well, if it be doleful matter merrily set down iv 4 189
On Wednesday next we solemnly set down Our coronation *Richard II.* iv 1 319
And interchangeably set down their hands, To kill the king v 2 98
Many limits of the charge set down But yesternight 1 *Hen. IV.* i 1 35
What I know Is ruminated, plotted and set down i 3 274
Do you set down your name in the scroll of youth 2 *Hen. IV.* i 2 201
Set down, set down your honourable load *Richard III.* i 2 1
Villains, set down the corse i 2 36
His wit set down to make his valour live iii 1 86
We have not yet set down this day of triumph iii 4 44
Hath no arithmetic but her brain to set down her reckoning *Tr. and Cr.* iii 3 254
If they set down before's, for the remove Bring up your army *Coriolanus* i 2 28
Your lord and Titus Lartius are set down before their city Corioli i 3 110
A catalogue Of all the voices that we have procured Set down by the poll iii 3 10
And set down—As best thou art experienced iv 5 144
We will before the walls of Rome to-morrow Set down our host v 3 2
What I mean to do See here in bloody lines I have set down *T. Andron.* v 2 14
Before proud Athens he's set down by this *T. of Athens* v 3 9
I will set down what comes from her, to satisfy my remembrance *Macbeth* v 1 36
On such regards of safety and allowance As therein are set down *Hamlet* ii 2 80
Though I most powerfully and potently believe, yet I hold it not honesty to have it thus set down ii 2 205
Set down with as much modesty as cunning ii 2 460
Some dozen or sixteen lines, which I would set down and insert in't ii 2 567
Let those that play your clowns speak no more than is set down for them iii 2 43
I have a letter guessingly set down *Lear* iii 7 47
I'll set down the pegs that make this music, As honest as I am *Othello* ii 1 202
Speak of me as I am; nothing extenuate, Nor set down aught in malice v 2 343
We will have these things set down by lawful counsel *Cymbeline* i 4 178
Set eye on (upon). King Cophetua set eye upon the pernicious and indubitate beggar Zenelophon *L. L. Lost* iv 1 66
No single soul Can we set eye on *Cymbeline* iv 2 131
Set fire on barns and hay-stacks in the night *T. Andron.* v 1 133
Set foot. In his waning age Set foot under thy table *T. of Shrew* ii 1 404
When I from France set foot at Ravenspurgh 1 *Hen. IV.* iii 2 95
Set footing. Who strongly hath set footing in this land *Richard II.* ii 2 48
When Talbot hath set footing once in France 1 *Hen. VI.* iii 3 64
That little thought, when she set footing here, She should have bought her dignities so dear *Hen. VIII.* iii 1 183
Can it be That so degenerate a strain as this Should once set footing in your generous bosoms? *Troi. and Cres.* ii 2 155
Set forth. It is meet I presently set forth *Mer. of Venice* iv 1 404
I set forth as soon as you And even but now return'd v 1 271
By these arguments of fear, Set forth in your pursuit *T. Night* iii 3 13
Where we'll set forth In best appointment all our regiments *K. John* ii 1 295
From whence, set forth in pomp, She came adorned hither *Richard II.* v 1 78
We will set forth before or after them 1 *Hen. IV.* i 2 189
Did set forth Upon his Irish expedition i 3 149
To-day will I set forth, to-morrow you. Will this content you? ii 3 119
You and I And my good Lord of Worcester will set forth iii 1 84
The Earl of Westmoreland set forth to-day; With him my son iii 2 170
The king himself in person is set forth, Or hitherwards intended iv 1 91
Implored your highness' pardon and set forth A deep repentance *Macbeth* i 4 6
But are my brother's powers set forth? *Lear* iv 5 1
Our troops set forth to-morrow: stay with us; The ways are dangerous iv 5 16
Set forward. Let us meet him then.—Or rather then set forward *K. John* iv 3 19
And dares him to set forward to the fight *Richard II.* i 3 109
Sound, trumpets; and set forward, combatants i 3 117
Are they not some of them set forward already? 1 *Hen. IV.* ii 3 30
We are prepared. I will set forward to-night ii 3 38
On Wednesday next, Harry, you shall set forward iii 2 173
In God's name, then, set forward 2 *Hen. IV.* i 1 227
Set hand. Which in a set hand fairly is engross'd *Richard III.* iii 6 2
Set in order. After that things are set in order here 1 *Hen. VI.* ii 2 32
Set kind. These set kind of fools *T. Night* i 5 95
Set nothing by. I think you set nothing by a bloody coxcomb v 1 194
Set of beads. I'll give my jewels for a set of beads *Richard II.* iii 3 147
Set of books. Take you the lute, and you the set of books *T. of Shrew* iii 1 107
Set of sun. When the battle's lost and won.—That will be ere the set of sun *Macbeth* i 1 5
Set of wit. A set of wit well play'd *L. L. Lost* v 2 29
Set off. There be some sports are painful, and their labour Delight in them sets off *Tempest* iii 1 2
By my hopes, This present enterprise set off his head 1 *Hen. IV.* v 1 88
Every thing set off That might so much as think you enemies 2 *Hen. IV.* iv 1 145
Consider . . . That it is place which lessens and sets off *Cymbeline* iii 3 13

Set on. Love set on thy horns *Mer. Wives* v 5 4
Your best appointment make with speed; To-morrow you set on *Meas. for Meas.* iii 1 61
To set on this wretched woman here Against our substitute! v 1 132
And that that I did, I was set on to do't *T. Night* v 1 189
Thou, traitor, hast set on thy wife to this *W. Tale* ii 3 131
Fortune speed us! Thus we set on iv 4 682
Set on toward Swinstead: to my litter straight *K. John* v 3 16
Set on you To wake our peace *Richard II.* i 3 131
Set on towards London, cousin, is it so? iii 3 208
We two saw you four set on four and bound them 1 *Hen. IV.* ii 4 279
Then did we two set on you four ii 4 282
On their answer, will we set on them: And God befriend us! v 1 119
Now, Esperance! Percy! and set on v 2 97
Shall we go draw our numbers and set on? 2 *Hen. IV.* i 3 109
Come, come, I know thou wast set on to this ii 1 165
See perform'd the tenour of our word. Set on v 5 76
So let him land, And solemnly see him set on to London *Hen. V.* v Prol. 14
Break up the court: I say, set on *Hen. VIII.* ii 4 241
The people are abused; set on. This paltering Becomes not Rome *Cor.* iii 1 58
Set on; and leave no ceremony out *J. Cæsar* i 2 11
Set on your foot, And with a heart new-fired I follow you ii 1 331
Bid him set on his powers betimes before, And we will follow iv 3 308
Let them set on at once; for I perceive But cold demeanour v 2 3
Laugh, to set on some quantity of barren spectators to laugh too *Ham.* iii 2 45
Let me know more; Set on thy wife to observe *Othello* iii 3 240
Cassio hath here been set on in the dark v 1 112
Our peace we'll ratify; seal it with feasts. Set on there! *Cymbeline* v 5 484
The men of Tyrus on the head Of Helicanus would set on The crown of Tyre *Pericles* iii Gower 27
Set on fire. When the rich blood of kings is set on fire *K. John* ii 1 351
The time of night when Troy was set on fire 2 *Hen. VI.* i 4 20
Set ope. Then, heaven, set ope thy everlasting gates! iv 9 13
Set out. When they were ready to set out for London *Hen. VIII.* ii 2 5
Whom you yourselves shall set out for reproof *T. of Athens* v 4 57
Set purpose. And on set purpose let his armour rust *Pericles* ii 2 54
Set terms. Rail'd on Lady Fortune in good terms, In good set terms and yet a motley fool *As Y. Like It* ii 7 17
Set to. Can honour set to a leg? 1 *Hen. IV.* v 1 133
Set together. You ask me if she did nod; and I say, 'Ay.'—And that set together is noddy *T. G. of Ver.* i 1 122
Set up. He that sets up his rest to do more exploits with his mace than a morris-pike *Com. of Errors* iv 3 27
He set up his bills here *Much Ado* i 1 39
I have set up my rest to run away *Mer. of Venice* ii 2 110
If knowledge could be set up against mortality *All's Well* i 1 35
No hurt to try, Since you set up your rest 'gainst remedy ii 1 138
Your cares set up do not pluck my cares down *Richard II.* iv 1 195
Gave his blood to lime the stones together, And set up Lancaster 3 *Hen. VI.* v 1 85
O madness of discourse, That cause sets up with and against itself! *Troi. and Cres.* v 2 143
Set up the bloody flag against all patience *Coriolanus* ii 1 84
He turned me about with his finger and his thumb, as one would set up a top iv 5 161
Paris hath set up his rest, That you shall rest but little. *Rom. and Jul.* iv 5 6
O, here Will I set up my everlasting rest v 3 110
Thou that didst set up My disobedience 'gainst the king my father *Cymb.* iii 4 90
The heavens, through you, increase our wonder and set up Your fame for ever *Pericles* iii 2 97
Set upon. For every trifle are they set upon me *Tempest* ii 2 8
Which they shall have no sooner achieved, but we'll set upon them 1 *Hen. IV.* i 2 194
We four set upon some dozen— Sixteen at least, my lord ii 4 193
As we were sharing, some six or seven fresh men set upon us ii 4 200
Was round encompassed and set upon. No leisure had he 1 *Hen. VI.* i 1 114
Gather we our forces out of hand And set upon our boasting enemy iii 2 103
So other foes may set upon our backs 3 *Hen. VI.* v 1 61
Advance our standards, set upon our foes *Richard III.* v 3 348
Till he be dieted to my request, And then I'll set upon him *Coriolanus* v 1 58
Setebos. His art is of such power, It would control my dam's god, Setebos, And make a vassal of him *Tempest* i 2 373
O Setebos, these be brave spirits indeed! How fine my master is! v 1 261
Setter. 'Tis our setter: I know his voice 1 *Hen. IV.* ii 2 53
Setter up. Thou setter up and plucker down of kings 3 *Hen. VI.* ii 3 37
Warwick, peace, Proud setter up and puller down of kings! iii 3 157
Settest. Thou set'st on thy wife. *W. Tale* ii 3 141
Like a civil war set'st oath to oath *K. John* iii 1 264
Base-hearted lord, That set'st the word itself against the word! *Rich. II.* v 3 122
But, Warwick, after God, thou set'st me free 3 *Hen. VI.* iv 6 16
Setting. The setting of thine eye and cheek proclaim A matter *Tempest* ii 1 229
Setting the attraction of my good parts aside I have no other charms *M. Wives* ii 2 109
Make a scarecrow . . . , Setting it up to fear the birds of prey *M. for M.* ii 1 2
I mean setting thee at liberty, enfreedoming thy person *L. L. Lost* iii 1 124
By your setting on, by your consent *M. N. Dream* iii 2 231
Therefore, setting all this chat aside, Thus in plain terms *T. of Shrew* ii 1 270
To this very instant disaster of his setting i' the stocks *All's Well* iv 3 127
Setting aside his high blood's royalty *Richard II.* i 1 58
The setting sun, and music at the close, As the last taste of sweets ii 1 12
How shall we part with them in setting forth? 1 *Hen. IV.* i 2 187
Setting thy knighthood aside, thou art a knave iii 3 137
Setting thy womanhood aside, thou art a beast to say otherwise iii 3 139
Setting my knighthood and my soldiership aside, I had lied 2 *Hen. IV.* i 2 93
Setting endeavour in continual motion *Hen. V.* i 2 185
We took him setting of boys' copies.—Here 's a villain! 2 *Hen. VI.* iv 2 95
Setting your scorns and your mislike aside, Tell me some reason 3 *Hen. VI.* iv 1 24
From that full meridian of my glory, I haste now to my setting *Hen. VIII.* iii 2 225
Men shut their doors against a setting sun *T. of Athens* i 2 150
She's e'en setting on water to scald such chickens as you are ii 2 71
He is a man, setting his fate aside, Of comely virtues iii 5 14
O setting sun, As in thy red rays thou dost sink to-night, So in his red blood Cassius' day is set! *J. Cæsar* v 3 60
Already at a point, was setting forth *Macbeth* iv 3 135
Keeps still in Dunsinane, and will endure Our setting down before 't v 4 10
Settle. All the honours that can fly from us Shall on them settle *All's W.* iii 1 21
Till the fury of his highness settle, Come not before him *W. Tale* iv 4 482
If beauty, wisdom, modesty, can settle The heart of Antony, Octavia is A blessed lottery to him *Ant. and Cleo.* ii 2 246

Settled. Whose settled visage and deliberate word Nips youth i' the head *Meas. for Meas.* iii 1 90
We'll light upon some settled low content *As Y. Like It* ii 3 68
Having flown over many knavish professions, he settled only in rogue *W. Tale* iv 3 106
If your more ponderous and settled project May suffer alteration iv 4 535
No settled senses of the world can match The pleasure of that madness v 3 72
The swelling difference of your settled hate *Richard II.* i 1 201
The blood; which, before cold and settled, left the liver white and pale 2 *Hen. IV.* iv 3 112
There left behind and settled certain French *Hen. V.* i 2 47
They are cloy'd With long continuance in a settled place 1 *Hen. VI.* ii 5 106
Breed love's settled passions in my heart v 5 4
See how the blood is settled in his face 2 *Hen. VI.* iii 2 160
No, he's settled, Not to come off, in his displeasure *Hen. VIII.* iii 2 22
Her blood is settled, and her joints are stiff *Rom. and Jul.* iv 5 26
I am settled, and bend up Each corporal agent to this terrible feat *Macb.* i 7 79
Youth no less becomes The light and careless livery that it wears Than settled age his sables and his weeds *Hamlet* iv 7 81
Welcomed and settled to his own desire *Pericles* iv Gower 2
Settlest. 'Tis thou [gold] that rigg'st the bark and plough'st the foam, Settlest admired reverence in a slave *T. of Athens* v 1 54
Settling. Trouble him no more Till further settling *Lear* iv 7 82
Seven. By seven o'clock I'll get you such a ladder *T. G. of Ver.* iii 1 126
Did her grandsire leave her seven hundred pound? *Mer. Wives* i 1 59
Seven hundred pounds and possibilities is goot gifts i 1 65
Seven groats in mill-sixpences, and two Edward shovel-boards i 1 158
Me have stay six or seven, two, tree hours for him ii 3 37
How long have you been in this place of constable?—Seven year and a half *Meas. for Meas.* ii 1 274
You say, seven years together?—And a half, sir ii 1 277
Bring me in the names of some six or seven, the most sufficient ii 1 287
And six or seven winters more respect Than a perpetual honour iii 1 76
Sure, it is no sin; Or of the deadly seven it is the least iii 1 111
So crack'd and splitted my poor tongue In seven short years *Com. of Er.* v 1 309
But seven years since, in Syracusa, boy, Thou know'st we parted v 1 320
A' has been a vile thief this seven year *Much Ado* iii 3 134
From Athens is her house remote seven leagues *M. N. Dream* i 1 159
The fire seven times tried this: Seven times tried that judgement is, That did never choose amiss *Mer. of Venice* ii 9 63
One man in his time plays many parts, His acts being seven ages *As Y. Like It* ii 7 143
I was seven of the nine days out of the wonder before you came iii 2 184
Time's pace is so hard that it seems the length of seven year iii 2 335
Upon a lie seven times removed v 4 71
I knew when seven justices could not take up a quarrel v 4 103
Who for this seven years hath esteemed him No better *T. of Shrew* Ind. 1 122
'Tis now some seven o'clock, And well we may come there by dinner-time iv 3 189
It shall be seven ere I go to horse iv 3 193
Till seven years' heat, Shall not behold her face at ample view *T. Night* i 1 26
Seven of my people, with an obedient start, make out for him ii 5 64
Nutmegs, seven; a race or two of ginger *W. Tale* iv 3 50
There shall not at your father's house these seven years Be born another such iv 4 589
Edward's seven sons, whereof thyself art one, Were as seven vials of his sacred blood, Or seven fair branches springing from one root: Some of those seven are dried by nature's course *Richard II.* i 2 11
All is uneven, And every thing is left at six and seven ii 2 122
He that kills me some six or seven dozen of Scots at a breakfast 1 *Hen. IV.* ii 4 115
Some six or seven fresh men set upon us ii 4 199
Took all their seven points in my target, thus.—Seven? why, there were but four even now.— . . . Seven, by these hilts ii 4 224
With a thought seven of the eleven I paid ii 4 242
I did that I did not this seven year before, I blushed ii 4 343
Swore little; diced not above seven times a week iii 3 18
The Earl of Westmoreland, seven thousand strong, Is marching hitherwards iv 1 88
What money is in my purse?—Seven groats and two pence 2 *Hen. IV.* i 2 263
Twelve cities and seven walled towns of strength 1 *Hen. VI.* iii 4 7
This seven years did not Talbot see his son; And now they meet v 3 37
Seven earls, twelve barons, and twenty reverend bishops 2 *Hen. VI.* i 1 8
I saw not better sport these seven years' day ii 1 2
Edward the Third, my lords, had seven sons ii 2 10
There shall be in England seven halfpenny loaves sold for a penny iv 2 71
Six or seven thousand is their utmost power *Richard III.* v 3 10
After seven years' siege yet Troy walls stand *Troi. and Cres.* i 3 12
A letter for me! it gives me an estate of seven years' health *Coriolanus* ii 1 126
He received in the repulse of Tarquin seven hurts i' the body ii 1 166
If I could shake off but one seven years From these old arms and legs iv 1 55
He was wont to shine at seven *T. of Athens* iii 4 10
Some six or seven, who did hide their faces Even from darkness *J. Cæsar* ii 1 277
He lies to-night within seven leagues of Rome iii 1 286
Let every man be master of his time Till seven at night *Macbeth* iii 1 42
Tears seven times salt, Burn out the sense and virtue of mine eye! *Ham.* iv 5 154
But mice and rats, and such small deer, Have been Tom's food for seven long year *Lear* iii 4 145
My letters say a hundred and seven galleys *Othello* i 3 3
Since these arms of mine had seven years' pith, Till now some nine moons wasted i 3 83
I have looked upon the world for four times seven years i 3 313
What, keep a week away? seven days and nights? Eight score eight hours? iii 4 173
Were you a gamester at five or at seven? *Pericles* iv 6 81
Go to the wars, would you? where a man may serve seven years for the loss of a leg? iv 6 182
Sevenfold. No meed, but he repays Sevenfold above itself *T. of Athens* i 1 289
Off, pluck off: The seven-fold shield of Ajax cannot keep The battery from my heart *Ant. and Cleo.* iv 14 38
Seven-night. A just seven-night; and a time too brief, too *Much Ado* ii 1 375
If the interim be but a se'nnight, Time's pace is so hard that it seems the length of seven year *As Y. Like It* iii 2 333
No longer stay.—One seven-night longer *W. Tale* i 2 17
Weary se'nnights nine times nine Shall he dwindle, peak and pine *Macb.* i 3 22
Whose footing here anticipates our thoughts A se'nnight's speed *Othello* ii 1 77
Seven stars. We that take purses go by the moon and the seven stars, and not by Phœbus 1 *Hen. IV.* i 2 16
What! we have seen the seven stars 2 *Hen. IV.* ii 4 201
The reason why the seven stars are no more than seven is a pretty reason *Lear* i 5 38

Seventeen. When she is able to overtake seventeen years old . *Mer. Wives* i 1 55
Of brown paper and old ginger, nine-score and seventeen pounds
Meas. for Meas. iv 3 6
From seventeen years till now almost fourscore Here lived I *As Y. Like It* ii 3 71
At seventeen years many their fortunes seek; But at fourscore it is too late a week . . . . ii 3 73
Betake thee to thy faith, for seventeen poniards are at thy bosom
All's Well iv 1 83
In the brunt of seventeen battles . . . . . . *Coriolanus* ii 2 104
Seventh. There's half-a-dozen sweets.—Seventh sweet, adieu *L. L. Lost* v 2 234
The quarrel was upon the seventh cause.—How seventh cause?
As Y. Like It v 4 52
But, for the seventh cause; how did you find the quarrel on the seventh cause? . . . . v 4 69
William of Windsor was the seventh and last . . 2 *Hen. VI.* ii 2 17
Henry the Seventh succeeding, truly pitying My father's loss *Hen. VIII.* ii 1 112
Another yet! A seventh! I'll see no more . . . *Macbeth* iv 1 118
Seventy. We would muster all From twelve to seventy *Coriolanus* iv 5 135
Seventy senators that died By their proscriptions . . *J. Cæsar* iv 3 177
Seventy five. To every several man, seventy five drachmas . iii 2 247
Sever. And who can sever love from charity? . . . *L. L. Lost* iv 3 365
Sever themselves and madly sweep the sky . . . *M. N. Dream* iii 2 23
The fire That severs day from night . . . . . *T. Night* v 1 279
Several. For several virtues Have I liked several women *Tempest* iii 1 42
My meaner ministers Their several kinds have done . . . iii 3 88
Strange and several noises Of roaring, shrieking, howling, jingling chains v 1 232
I'll kiss each several paper for amends . . . *T. G. of Ver.* i 2 108
I do protest That I have wept a hundred several times . . iv 4 150
I suffered the pangs of three several deaths . . *Mer. Wives* iii 5 110
The several chairs of order look you scour . . . . v 5 65
Each fair instalment, coat, and several crest . . . . v 5 67
When I would pray and think, I think and pray To several subjects
Meas. for Meas. ii 4 2
Each his several way . . . . *Much Ado* v 3 29
My lips are no common, though several they be . . *L. L. Lost* ii 1 223
In her fair cheek, Where several worthies make one dignity . iv 3 236
Every one his love-feat will advance Unto his several mistress, which they'll know By favours several which they did bestow . . . v 2 124
Their several counsels they unbosom shall To loves mistook . . v 2 141
Each several chamber bless, Through this palace . . *M. N. Dream* v 1 424
Draw aside the curtains and discover The several caskets *Mer. of Venice* ii 7 2
The rest have worn me out With several applications . . *All's Well* i 2 74
By some severals Of head-piece extraordinary . . . *W. Tale* i 2 226
By twos and threes at several posterns Clear them o' the city . i 2 438
He sings several tunes faster than you'll tell money . . . iv 4 184
Lay aside the sword Which sways usurpingly these several titles *K. John* i 1 13
Let us take a . . . loving farewell of our several friends . *Richard II.* i 3 51
Good uncle, help to order several powers To Oxford . . . v 3 140
In reckoning up the several devils' names That were his lackeys 1 *Hen. IV.* iii 1 157
He should draw his several strengths together . . 2 *Hen. IV.* i 3 76
Each several article herein redress'd. . . . . . . iv 1 170
Discharge your powers unto their several counties, As we will ours . iv 2 61
The severals and unhidden passages Of his true titles . . *Hen. V.* i 1 86
As many arrows, loosed several ways, Come to one mark . . . i 2 207
This is muttered, That here you maintain several factions . 1 *Hen. VI.* i 1 71
Repair to your several dwelling-places . . . . . . i 3 77
Better far, I guess, That we do make our entrance several ways . ii 1 30
Your several suits Have been consider'd and debated on . . . v 1 34
As thus to name the several colours we do wear . . 2 *Hen. VI.* ii 1 128
Where thou art, there is the world itself, With every several pleasure . iii 2 363
I do dismiss you to your several countries . . . . . iv 9 21
I do not like these several councils, I . . . *Richard III.* iii 2 78
Limit each leader to his several charge . . . . . . v 3 25
My conscience hath a thousand several tongues, And every tongue brings in a several tale, And every tale condemns me . . . . . v 3 193
All several sins, all used in each degree, Throng to the bar . . v 3 198
An inventory, thus importing; The several parcels of his plate *Hen. VIII.* iii 2 125
Gifts, natures, shapes, Severals and generals of grace exact *Troi. and Cres.* i 3 180
A quarrel Which hath our several honours all engaged . . . ii 2 124
A cause that hath no mean dependance Upon our joint and several dignities . . . . ii 2 193
In these several places of the city You cry against the noble senate *Cor.* i 1 189
Thou hast beat me out Twelve several times . . . . . iv 5 128
Two several powers Are enter'd in the Roman territories . . . iv 6 39
I take all and your several visitations So kind to heart . *T. of Athens* i 2 224
I hope it is not so low with him as he made it seem in the trial of his several friends . . . . iii 6 7
Touch them with several fortunes . . . . iv 3 5
I will this night, In several hands, in at his windows throw, As if they came from several citizens, Writings . . . . . *J. Cæsar* i 2 320
Every drop of blood That every Roman bears, and nobly bears, Is guilty of a several bastardy . . . . ii 1 138
He gives, To every several man, seventy five drachmas . . . iii 2 247
The ghost of Cæsar hath appear'd to me Two several times by night . v 5 18
Abound In the division of each several crime, Acting it many ways *Macb.* iv 3 96
Before we reckon with your several loves, And make us even with you v 8 61
An exact command, Larded with many several sorts of reasons *Hamlet* v 2 20
We have this hour a constant will to publish Our daughters' several dowers . . . . *Lear* i 1 45
The several messengers From hence attend dispatch . . . ii 1 126
The senate hath sent about three several quests To search you out *Othello* i 2 46
Twenty several messengers: Why do you send so thick? *Ant. and Cleo.* i 5 62
He shall have every day a several greeting . . . . . i 5 77
That great face of war, whose several ranges Frighted each other . . iii 13 5
Gather Their several virtues and effects . . . . *Cymbeline* i 5 23
I'll then discourse our woes, felt several years . . . *Pericles* i 4 18
Conduct These knights unto their several lodgings . . . . ii 3 110
We commit no crime To use one language in each several clime . . iv 4 6
Severally entreat him . . . . *Troi. and Cres.* iv 5 274
I will dispatch you severally . . . . . . *T. of Athens* ii 2 196
Compare their reasons, When severally we hear them rendered *J. Cæsar* iii 2 10
The counterchange Is severally in all . . . . . *Cymbeline* v 5 397
Severe. Lord Angelo is severe.—It is but needful . *Meas. for Meas.* i 1 296
O just but severe law! . . . . ii 2 41
My brother justice have I found so severe, that he hath forced me to tell him he is indeed Justice . . . . iii 2 267
He who the sword of heaven will bear Should be as holy as severe . iii 2 276
With eyes severe and beard of formal cut . . . *As Y. Like It* ii 7 155
If we conclude a peace, It shall be with such strict and severe covenants As little shall the Frenchmen gain thereby . . . 1 *Hen. VI.* v 4 114
Severe. Come, you are too severe a moraler . . . . *Othello* ii 3 301
Severed. Is she the goddess that hath sever'd us? . . . *Tempest* v 1 187
Thus have you heard me sever'd from my bliss . . *Com. of Errors* i 1 119
Here are sever'd lips, Parted with sugar breath . . *Mer. of Venice* iii 2 118
The puritan and . . . the papist, howsome'er their hearts are severed in religion, their heads are both one . . . . . *All's Well* i 3 57
Well, the king hath severed you and Prince Harry . . . 2 *Hen. IV.* i 2 227
No more can I be sever'd from your side, Than can yourself yourself in twain divide: Stay, go, do what you will, the like do I 1 *Hen. VI.* iv 5 48
But sever'd in a pale clear-shining sky . . . . 3 *Hen. VI.* ii 1 28
God forbid that I should wish them sever'd Whom God hath join'd together . . . . iv 1 21
By uproar sever'd, like a flight of fowl Scatter'd by winds *T. Andron.* v 3 68
Better I were distract: So should my thoughts be sever'd from my griefs . . . . *Lear* iv 6 289
Our sever'd navy too Have knit again . . . . *Ant. and Cleo.* iii 13 170
Severely. And kept severely from resort of men . . *T. G. of Ver.* iii 1 108
That will the king severely prosecute 'Gainst us . . . *Richard II.* ii 1 244
Severest. Unto the rigour of severest law. . . . *Rom. and Jul.* v 3 269
Severing. A sufferance panging As soul and body's severing *Hen. VIII.* ii 3 16
Envious streaks Do lace the severing clouds in yonder east *R. and J.* iii 5 8
Severity. It is too general a vice, and severity must cure it *M. for M.* iii 2 106
Whereon to practise your severity . . . . . . 1 *Hen. VI.* ii 3 47
Scorn him further trial Than the severity of the public power *Coriolanus* iii 1 269
Beauty starved with her severity Cuts beauty off from all posterity
Rom. and Jul. i 1 225
Severn. On the gentle Severn's sedgy bank . . . . 1 *Hen. IV.* i 3 98
Three times did they drink, Upon agreement, of swift Severn's flood . i 3 103
Thrice from the banks of Wye And sandy-bottom'd Severn have I sent him iii 1 66
England, from Trent and Severn hitherto, By south and east is to my part assign'd: All westward, Wales beyond the Severn shore, . . . To Owen Glendower . . . . iii 1 74
Till he have cross'd the Severn . . . . *Cymbeline* iii 5 17
Sew. She can sew.—That's as much as to say, Can she so? *T. G. of V.* iii 1 307
If ever I said loose-bodied gown, sew me in the skirts of it *T. of Shrew* iv 3 137
Ere I lead this life long, I'll sew nether stocks . . . 1 *Hen. IV.* ii 4 130
I can sing, weave, sew, and dance, With other virtues . . *Pericles* iv 6 194
Sewed. I commanded the sleeves should be cut out and sewed up
T. of Shrew iv 3 148
Lost her tongue, And in a tedious sampler sew'd her mind *T. Andron.* ii 4 39
Cut those pretty fingers off, That could have better sew'd than Philomel ii 4 43
A sibyl . . . In her prophetic fury sew'd the work . . . *Othello* iii 4 72
Sewer. 'Sweet' quoth 'a! sweet sink, sweet sewer . . *Troi. and Cres.* v 1 83
Sewing. You are manifest house-keepers. What are you sewing here?
Coriolanus i 3 55
As I was sewing in my closet, Lord Hamlet, with his doublet all unbraced, . . . comes before me . . . . *Hamlet* ii 1 77
Sex. I do not know One of my sex; no woman's face remember *Tempest* iii 1 49
From this testimony of your own sex . . . . *Meas. for Meas.* ii 4 131
A professed tyrant to their sex . . . . *Much Ado* i 1 170
Your wrongs do set a scandal on my sex . . . . *M. N. Dream* ii 1 240
'Tis not maidenly: Our sex, as well as I, may chide you for it . . iii 2 218
I thank God I am not a woman, to be touched with so many giddy offences as he hath generally taxed their whole sex withal *As Y. L. It* iii 2 368
You have simply misused our sex in your love-prate . . . . iv 1 205
In her sex, her years, profession, . . . hath amazed me . . *All's Well* ii 1 86
So much against the mettle of your sex . . . . . *T. Night* v 1 330
I am not prone to weeping, as our sex Commonly are . . *W. Tale* ii 1 108
My courage try by combat, if thou darest, And thou shalt find that I exceed my sex . . . . 1 *Hen. VI.* i 2 90
How ill-beseeming is it in thy sex! . . . . . 3 *Hen. VI.* i 4 113
Ah, poor our sex! this fault in us I find, The error of our eye directs our mind: What error leads must err . . . . *Troi. and Cres.* v 2 109
To square the general sex By Cressid's rule . . . . . . v 2 132
Think you I am no stronger than my sex, Being so father'd? . *J. Cæsar* ii 1 296
Follow his chariot, like the greatest spot Of all thy sex *Ant. and Cleo.* iv 12 36
Laden with like frailties which before Have often shamed our sex . v 2 124
I'ld change my sex to be companion with them . . . *Cymbeline* iii 6 88
Sexton. A stool and a cushion for the sexton . . . *Much Ado* iv 2 2
God's my life, where's the sexton? . . . . iv 2 72
By this time our sexton hath reformed Signior Leonato of the matter . v 1 262
Here comes master Signior Leonato, and the sexton too . . . v 1 267
And threw the sops all in the sexton's face . . . *T. of Shrew* iii 2 175
Old Time the clock-setter, that bald sexton Time . . *K. John* iii 1 324
Chapless, and knocked about the mazzard with a sexton's spade *Hamlet* v 1 98
I have been sexton here, man and boy, thirty years . . . . v 1 177
If I had been the sexton, I would have been that day in the belfry *Per.* ii 1 41
Sextus Pompeius Hath given the dare to Cæsar . . *Ant. and Cleo.* i 2 190
Sextus Pompeius Makes his approaches to the port of Rome . . . i 3 45
Having in Sicily Sextus Pompeius spoil'd, we had not rated him His part iii 6 25
Seymour. Lords of York, Berkeley, and Seymour; None else of name
Richard II. ii 3 55
Seyton!—I am sick at heart, When I behold—Seyton, I say! . *Macbeth* v 3 20
Seyton!—What is your gracious pleasure?—What news more? . . v 3 29
Come, put mine armour on; give me my staff. Seyton, send out . . v 3 49
'Sfoot, I'll learn to conjure and raise devils . . *Troi. and Cres.* ii 3 6
Shackle. That dost in vile misprision shackle up My love *All's Well* ii 3 159
Bolts and shackles!—O peace, peace, peace! . . . . *T. Night* ii 5 62
Which shackles accidents and bolts up change . . *Ant. and Cleo.* v 2 6
Shade. You moonshine revellers, and shades of night *Mer. Wives* v 5 42
I'll drop the paper: Sweet leaves, shade folly . . . *L. L. Lost* iv 3 44
Under the cool shade of a sycamore I thought to close mine eyes . . v 2 89
To interrupt my purposed rest, Toward that shade I might behold addrest v 2 92
In silence sad, Trip we after night's shade . . . *M. N. Dream* iv 1 101
And Thisby, tarrying in mulberry shade, His dagger drew, and died . v 1 149
Under the shade of melancholy boughs . . . . *As Y. Like It* ii 7 111
Under which bush's shade A lioness, with udders all drawn dry, Lay couching . . . . iv 3 114
To dwell in solemn shades of endless night . . . . *Richard II.* i 3 177
With Cain go wander thorough shades of night . . . . . v 6 43
Diana's foresters, gentlemen of the shade, minions of the moon 1 *Hen. IV.* i 2 28
Under the sweet shade of your government . . . . *Hen. V.* ii 2 28
But darkness and the gloomy shade of death Environ you! . 1 *Hen. VI.* v 4 89
In the shade of death I shall find joy . . . . . 2 *Hen. VI.* ii 2 54
Their sweetest shade a grove of cypress trees! . . . . . iii 2 323
Gives not the hawthorn-bush a sweeter shade To shepherds? 3 *Hen. VI.* ii 5 42
His wonted sleep under a fresh tree's shade . . . . . . ii 5 49
Under whose shade the ramping lion slept . . . . v 2 13
And scorns the sun.—And turns the sun to shade; alas! alas! Witness my son, now in the shade of death . . . . . *Richard III.* i 3 266

Shade. Now, good angels Fly o'er thy royal head, and shade thy person Under their blessed wings! . . . . . . *Hen. VIII.* v 1 160
And flies fled under shade . . . . . . *Troi. and Cres.* i 3 51
Your hand, and yours: Ere in our own house I do shade my head, The good patricians must be visited . . . . *Coriolanus* ii 1 211
Under their sweet shade, Aaron, let us sit . . . . *T. Andron.* ii 3 16
Let us seek out some desolate shade, and there Weep . . *Macbeth* iv 3 1
To some shade, And fit you to your manhood . . . *Cymbeline* iii 4 194
Shadow. Broom-groves, Whose shadow the dismissed bachelor loves *Tempest* iv 1 67
Think that she is by And feed upon the shadow of perfection *T. G. of V.* iii 1 177
I am but a shadow; And to your shadow will I make true love . . iv 2 125
Your falsehood shall become you well To worship shadows . . . iv 2 131
One Julia . . . Would better fit his chamber than this shadow . . iv 4 125
Come, shadow, come, and take this shadow up, For 'tis thy rival . iv 4 202
Love like a shadow flies when substance love pursues . *Mer. Wives* ii 2 215
That the time may have all shadow and silence in it *Meas. for Meas.* iii 1 257
Momentany as a sound, Swift as a shadow . . . *M. N. Dream* i 1 144
Believe me, king of shadows, I mistook . . . . . iii 2 347
The best in this kind are but shadows; and the worst are no worse . v 1 213
If we shadows have offended, Think but this, and all is mended . . v 1 430
He will fence with his own shadow . . . . *Mer. of Venice* i 2 66
Some there be that shadows kiss; Such have but a shadow's bliss . . ii 9 66
The substance of my praise doth wrong this shadow In underprizing it, so far this shadow Doth limp behind the substance . . . iii 2 128
And saw the lion's shadow ere himself And ran dismay'd away . . v 1 8
I'll go find a shadow and sigh till he come . . . *As Y. Like It* iv 1 222
'Tis but the shadow of a wife you see, The name and not the thing *All's Well* v 3 308
Yonder i' the sun practising behaviour to his own shadow . *T. Night* ii 5 21
'Tis such as you, That creep like shadows by him and do sigh *W. Tale* ii 3 34
The shadow of myself form'd in her eye; Which, being but the shadow of your son, Becomes a sun and makes your son a shadow *K. John* ii 1 498
Each substance of a grief hath twenty shadows . . *Richard II.* ii 2 14
Which, look'd on as it is, is nought but shadows Of what it is not. . ii 2 23
Let's step into the shadow of these trees . . . . . iii 4 25
The shadow of your sorrow hath destroy'd The shadow of your face.—Say that again. The shadow of my sorrow! ha! let's see . . . iv 1 292
These external manners of laments Are merely shadows to the unseen grief . . . . iv 1 297
By my sceptre and my soul to boot, He hath more worthy interest to the state Than thou the shadow of succession . 1 *Hen. IV.* iii 2 99
Grieves at heart So many of his shadows thou hast met And not the very king . . . . v 4 30
Had only but the corpse, But shadows and the shows of men, to fight 2 *Hen. IV.* i 1 193
I am your shadow, my lord; I'll follow you . . . . . ii 2 174
Simon Shadow!—Yea, marry, let me have him to sit under: he's like to be a cold soldier . . . . iii 2 132
Shadow, whose son art thou?—My mother's son, sir.—Thy mother's son! like enough, and thy father's shadow. . . . . . iii 2 137
The son of the female is the shadow of the male . . . . iii 2 141
Shadow will serve for summer; prick him, for we have a number of shadows to fill up the muster-book . . . . iii 2 144
Choose for me.—Marry, then, Mouldy, Bullcalf, Feeble and Shadow . iii 2 267
This same half-faced fellow, Shadow; give me this man . . . iii 2 283
Alack, what mischiefs might he set abroach In shadow of such greatness! iv 2 15
Long time thy shadow hath been thrall to me . . . 1 *Hen. VI.* ii 3 36
I laugh to see your ladyship so fond To think that you have aught but Talbot's shadow Whereon to practise your severity . . . ii 3 46
I am but shadow of myself: You are deceived, my substance is not here ii 3 50
Are you now persuaded That Talbot is but shadow of himself? . . ii 3 62
Must he be then as shadow of himself? . . . . . . v 4 133
That are the substance Of that great shadow I did represent . 2 *Hen. VI.* i 1 14
That raught at mountains with outstretched arms, Yet parted but the shadow with his hand . . . . 3 *Hen. VI.* i 4 69
Wear the English crown, And be true king indeed, thou but the shadow iv 3 50
We'll yoke together, like a double shadow . . . . . . iv 6 49
Have no delight to pass away the time, Unless to spy my shadow in the sun And descant on mine own deformity . . *Richard III.* i 1 26
Shine out, fair sun, till I have bought a glass, That I may see my shadow i 2 264
Then came wandering by A shadow like an angel . . . . i 4 53
I call'd thee then poor shadow, painted queen . . . . iv 4 83
Nay, good my lord, be not afraid of shadows . . . . v 3 215
Shadows to-night Have struck more terror to the soul of Richard Than can the substance of ten thousand soldiers Armed in proof . . v 3 216
I am the shadow of poor Buckingham, Whose figure even this instant cloud puts on, By darkening my clear sun . . *Hen. VIII.* i 1 224
Disdains the shadow Which he treads on at noon . . . *Coriolanus* i 1 264
That so the shadows be not unappeased . . . . *T. Andron.* i 1 100
And die he must, To appease their groaning shadows that are gone . i 1 126
The green leaves quiver with the cooling wind And make a chequer'd shadow on the ground . . . . ii 3 15
Those sweet ornaments, Whose circling shadows kings have sought to sleep in . . . . ii 4 19
Grief has so wrought on him, He takes false shadows for true substances iii 2 80
With the shadow of his wings He can at pleasure stint their melody iv 4 85
The sun's beams, Driving back shadows over louring hills *Rom. and Jul.* ii 5 6
How sweet is love itself possess'd, When but love's shadows are so rich! v 1 11
How dost, fool?—Dost dialogue with thy shadow? . . *T. of Athens* ii 2 52
Myself and such As slept within the shadow of your power . . v 4 6
You have no such mirrors as will turn Your hidden worthiness into your eye, That you might see your shadow . . . *J. Cæsar* i 2 58
Their shadows seem A canopy most fatal, under which Our army lies v 1 87
Hence, horrible shadow! Unreal mockery, hence! . . . *Macbeth* iii 4 106
Show his eyes, and grieve his heart; Come like shadows, so depart! . iv 1 111
Thereby shall we shadow The numbers of our host and make discovery Err in report of us . . . . v 4 5
Out, out, brief candle! Life's but a walking shadow, a poor player . v 5 24
Dreams indeed are ambition, for the very substance of the ambitious is merely the shadow of a dream . . . . . . *Hamlet* ii 2 265
A dream itself is but a shadow.—Truly, and I hold ambition of so airy and light a quality that it is but a shadow's shadow.—Then are our beggars bodies, and our monarchs and outstretched heroes the beggars' shadows . . . . ii 2 266
Who is it that can tell me who I am?—Lear's shadow . . . *Lear* i 4 251
To course his own shadow for a traitor . . . . . . iii 4 58
Here, father, take the shadow of this tree For your good host . . v 2 1
Swagger? swear? and discourse fustian with one's own shadow? *Othello* ii 3 282
Haply you shall not see me more; or if, A mangled shadow *A. and C.* iv 2 27
Shadow. To imagine An Antony, were nature's piece 'gainst fancy, Condemning shadows . . . . *Ant. and Cleo.* v 2 100
Poor shadows of Elysium, hence, and rest . . . *Cymbeline* v 4 97
I know he will come in our shadow, to scatter his crowns in the sun *Per.* iv 2 121
Like motes and shadows see them move awhile . . . . . iv 4 21
Shadowed. The shadow'd livery of the burnish'd sun . *Mer. of Venice* ii 1 2
There serve your lusts, shadow'd from heaven's eye . *T. Andron.* ii 1 130
Shadowing their right under your wings of war . . . *K. John* ii 1 14
Nature would not invest herself in such shadowing passion . *Othello* iv 1 41
Shadowy. This shadowy desert, unfrequented woods . *T. G. of Ver.* v 4 2
With shadowy forests and with champains rich'd . . . . *Lear* i 1 65
Shady. For aye to be in shady cloister mew'd . . . *M. N. Dream* i 1 71
To draw The shady curtains from Aurora's bed . . *Rom. and Jul.* i 1 142
Shafalus. Not Shafalus to Procrus was so true.—As Shafalus to Procrus, I to you . . . . *M. N. Dream* v 1 200
Shaft. I'll make a shaft or a bolt on't: 'slid, 'tis but venturing *Mer. W.* iii 4 24
But I might see young Cupid's fiery shaft Quench'd in the chaste beams of the watery moon . . . . *M. N. Dream* ii 1 161
In my school-days, when I had lost one shaft, I shot his fellow of the self-same flight The self-same way . . . . *Mer. of Venice* i 1 140
How will she love, when the rich golden shaft Hath kill'd the flock of all affections else That live in her! . . . . . *T. Night* i 1 35
Carried you a forehand shaft a fourteen and fourteen and a half 2 *Hen. IV.* iii 2 52
For, O, love's bow Shoots buck and doe: The shaft confounds *T. and C.* iii 1 128
Kinsmen, shoot all your shafts into the court . . . *T. Andron.* iv 3 61
I am too sore enpierced with his [Cupid's] shaft To soar. *Rom. and Jul.* i 4 19
This murderous shaft that's shot Hath not yet lighted . . *Macbeth* ii 3 147
The bow is bent and drawn, make from the shaft . . . . *Lear* i 1 145
His greatness was no guard To bar heaven's shaft . . . *Pericles* ii 4 15
Your shafts of fortune, though they hurt you mortally, Yet glance full wanderingly on us . . . . iii 3 6
Shag-haired. Like a shag-hair'd crafty kern . . . 2 *Hen. VI.* iii 1 367
Thou liest, thou shag-hair'd villain!—What, you egg! . *Macbeth* iv 2 83
Shake. His bold waves tremble, Yea, his dread trident shake . *Tempest* i 2 206
Your story put Heaviness in me.—Shake it off . . . . . i 2 307
If of life you keep a care, Shake off slumber, and beware . . . ii 1 304
This will shake your shaking, I can tell you, and that soundly . . ii 2 87
The strong-based promontory Have I made shake . . . . v 1 47
Ask my dog: if he say ay, it will; if he say, no, it will; if he shake his tail and say nothing, it will . . . . . *T. G. of Ver.* ii 5 37
And shakes a chain In a most hideous and dreadful manner *Mer. Wives* iv 4 33
We are made to be no stronger Than faults may shake our frames *M. for M.* ii 4 133
The devil will shake her chain and fright us with it . *Com. of Errors* iv 3 77
You shake the head at so long a breathing . . . *Much Ado* ii 1 377
A wither'd hermit, five-score winters worn, Might shake off fifty, looking in her eye . . . . *L. L. Lost* iv 3 243
Let loose, Or I will shake thee from me like a serpent! . *M. N. Dream* iii 2 261
To shake the head, relent, and sigh, and yield . . *Mer. of Venice* iii 3 15
Thou shalt hear how he will shake me up . . . *As Y. Like It* i 1 30
I could shake them off my coat: these burs are in my heart . . i 3 16
Ay, to the proof; as mountains are for winds, That shake not, though they blow perpetually . . . . *T. of Shrew* ii 1 142
Confounds thy fame as whirlwinds shake fair buds . . . . v 2 140
Many a man's tongue shakes out his master's undoing . *All's Well* ii 4 24
Where I will never come Whilst I can shake my sword or hear the drum ii 5 96
Half of the which dare not shake the snow from off their cassocks, lest they shake themselves to pieces . . . . iv 3 191
Till the pangs of death shake him . . . . . . *T. Night* i 5 82
Go shake your ears . . . . ii 3 134
Be pleased that I shake off these names you give me . . . . v 1 76
As or by oath remove or counsel shake The fabric of his folly *W. Tale* i 2 428
Miseries enough; no hope to help you, But as you shake off one to take another . . . . iv 4 580
That shakes the rotten carcass of old Death Out of his rags! . *K. John* ii 1 456
Our curses light on thee So heavy as thou shalt not shake them off . iii 1 296
Shake the bags Of hoarding abbots; imprisoned angels Set at liberty . iii 3 7
Then with a passion would I shake the world . . . . . iii 4 39
They shake their heads And whisper one another in the ear . . . iv 2 188
To thrill and shake Even at the crying of your nation's crow . . v 2 143
If then we shall shake off our slavish yoke . . . *Richard II.* ii 1 291
I say the earth did shake when I was born . . . 1 *Hen. IV.* iii 1 21
Shakes the old beldam earth and topples down Steeples . . . iii 1 32
Shake the peace and safety of our throne . . . . . . iii 2 117
Feel, masters, how I shake . . . . 2 *Hen. IV.* ii 4 114
Plucking to unfix an enemy, He doth unfasten so and shake a friend . iv 1 209
You withal shall make all Gallia shake . . . . . *Hen. V.* i 2 216
Shake in their fear . . . . ii Prol. 14
He'll make your Paris Louvre shake for it . . . . . . ii 4 132
And our air shakes them passing scornfully . . . . . . iv 2 42
I'll shake thy bulwarks to the ground . . . . 1 *Hen. VI.* iii 2 17
Wrings his hapless hands And shakes his head . . . 2 *Hen. VI.* i 1 227
Shake he his weapon at us and pass by . . . . iv 8 18
Thus do I hope to shake King Henry's head . . . . 3 *Hen. VI.* i 1 20
Nor . . . The proudest he . . . Dares stir a wing, if Warwick shake his bells i 1 47
They that stand high have many blasts to shake them *Richard III.* i 3 259
Why do you look on us, and shake your head? . . . . . ii 2 5
Like rams In the old time of war, would shake the press *Hen. VIII.* iv 1 78
Her foes shake like a field of beaten corn, And hang their heads . . v 5 32
With a palsy-fumbling on his gorget, Shake in and out the rivet *T. and C.* i 3 175
And either greet him not, Or else disdainfully, which shall shake him more Than if not look'd on . . . . iii 3 53
Like a fashionable host That slightly shakes his parting guest by the hand iii 3 166
You shake, my lord, at something: will you go? You will break out . v 2 50
Thou madest thine enemies shake, as if the world Were feverous *Coriol.* i 4 60
Hence, rotten thing! or I shall shake thy bones Out of thy garments . iii 1 179
Let every feeble rumour shake your hearts! . . . . . . iii 3 125
If I could shake off but one seven years From these old arms and legs . iv 1 55
He will shake Your Rome about your ears.—As Hercules Did shake down mellow fruit. You have made fair work! . . . . . iv 6 98
Constrains them weep and shake with fear and sorrow . . . . v 3 100
A better head her glorious body fits Than his that shakes for age *T. An.* i 1 188
Sitting in the sun under the dove-house wall; . . . 'Shake,' quoth the dove-house; 'twas no need, I trow, To bid me trudge *Rom. and Jul.* i 3 33
And shake the yoke of inauspicious stars From this world-wearied flesh v 3 111
I am not of that feather to shake off My friend when he must need me. I do know him A gentleman that well deserves . . . *T. of Athens* i 1 100
They do shake their heads, and I am here No richer in return . . . ii 2 211
Let's shake our heads, and say, As 'twere a knell unto our master's fortunes . . . . iv 2 25

Shake. And shakes his threatening sword Against the walls of Athens *T. of Athens* v 1 169
Our elders say, The barren, touched in this holy chase, Shake off their sterile curse *J. Cæsar* i 2 9
I did mark How he did shake: 'tis true, this god did shake . i 2 121
Let Cæsar seat him sure; For we will shake him, or worse days endure i 2 326
Are not you moved, when all the sway of earth Shakes like a thing unfirm? . i 3 4
That part of tyranny that I do bear I can shake off at pleasure . i 3 100
Let each man render me his bloody hand: First, Marcus Brutus, will I shake with you.; Next, Caius Cassius . iii 1 185
Turn him off, Like to the empty ass, to shake his ears, And graze . iv 1 26
My thought . . . Shakes so my single state of man *Macbeth* i 3 140
That no compunctious visitings of nature Shake my fell purpose . i 5 47
Some say, the earth Was feverous and did shake.—'Twas a rough night ii 3 66
Shake off this downy sleep, death's counterfeit, And look on death itself! ii 3 81
Fears and scruples shake us: In the great hand of God I stand . ii 3 135
And sleep In the affliction of these terrible dreams That shake us nightly iii 2 19
Thou canst not say I did it: never shake Thy gory locks at me . iii 4 50
The heart I bear Shall never sag with doubt nor shake with fear . v 3 10
And we fools of nature So horridly to shake our disposition With thoughts beyond the reaches of our souls . *Hamlet* i 4 55
'Tis our fast intent To shake all cares and business from our age *Lear* i 1 40
And shake in pieces the heart of his obedience . . . . . i 2 91
I am ashamed That thou hast power to shake my manhood thus . i 4 319
Caitiff, to pieces shake . . . . iii 2 55
Feel what wretches feel, That thou mayst shake the superflux to them iii 4 35
If you did wear a beard upon your chin, I'd shake it on this quarrel . iii 7 77
And, in your sights, Shake patiently my great affliction off . iv 6 36
That minces virtue, and does shake the head To hear of pleasure's name iv 6 122
I fear the trust Othello puts him in, On some odd time of his infirmity, Will shake this island . . . . *Othello* ii 3 133
And when she seem'd to shake and fear your looks, She loved them most iii 3 207
It is not words that shake me thus . . . . . . iv 1 42
Is this the nature Whom passion could not shake? . . . . iv 1 277
Though he do shake me off To beggarly divorcement—love him dearly . iv 2 157
Go know of Cassio where he supp'd to-night. What, do you shake at that?—He supp'd at my house; but I therefore shake not . v 1 118
Some bloody passion shakes your very frame . . . . v 2 44
Though you in swearing shake the throned gods . *Ant. and Cleo.* i 3 28
Let me shake thy hand; I never hated thee . . . . ii 6 75
These offers, Which serve not for his vantage, he shakes off . . iii 7 34
Wisdom and fortune combating together, If that the former dare but what it can, No chance may shake it . . . . . iii 13 81
Henceforth The white hand of a lady fever thee, Shake thou to look on 't iii 13 139
But when he meant to quail and shake the orb, He was as rattling thunder v 2 85
The tyrannous breathing of the north Shakes all our buds from growing *Cymbeline* i 3 37
Did put the yoke upon 's; which to shake off Becomes a warlike people iii 1 52
Their vessel shakes On Neptune's billow . . . *Pericles* iii Gower 44
Should at these early hours Shake off the golden slumber of repose . iii 2 23
Shaked. I shaked you, sir, and cried . . . . . *Tempest* ii 1 319
At my birth The frame and huge foundation of the earth Shaked 1 *Hen. IV.* iii 1 17
He is so shaked of a burning quotidian tertian . . *Hen. V.* ii 1 124
O, when degree is shaked, Which is the ladder to all high designs, Then enterprise is sick! . . . . *Troi. and Cres.* i 3 101
A sly and constant knave, Not to be shaked . . . *Cymbeline* i 5 76
Shake hands. I hold it fit that we shake hands and part *Hamlet* i 5 128
Fortune and Antony part here; Even here Do we shake hands *A. and C.* iv 12 20
Shaken. So shaken as we are, so wan with care . 1 *Hen. IV.* i 1 1
Now that God and friends Have shaken Edward from the regal seat 3 *Hen. VI.* iv 6 2
Old Andronicus, Shaken with sorrows in ungrateful Rome *T. Andron.* iv 3 17
Shakest. Why shakest thou so? Fear not, man . . . *W. Tale* iv 4 641
Thou shakest thy head and hold'st it fear or sin To speak a truth 2 *Hen. IV.* i 1 95
Shaking. This will shake your shaking, I can tell you *Tempest* ii 2 87
He has much worthy blame laid upon him for shaking off so good a wife and so sweet a lady . . . . . . *All's Well* iv 3 8
Bullets wrapp'd in fire, To make a shaking fever in your walls *K. John* ii 1 228
What dost thou mean by shaking of thy head? Why dost thou look so sadly? . . . . iii 1 19
Like a wild Morisco, Shaking the bloody darts as he his bells 2 *Hen. VI.* iii 1 366
That with the very shaking of their chains They may astonish these fell-lurking curs . . . . v 1 145
What raging of the sea! shaking of earth! . . *Troi. and Cres.* i 3 97
Making his peace, Shaking the bloody fingers of thy foes *J. Cæsar* iii 1 198
Is ripe for shaking, and the powers above Put on their instruments *Macb.* iv 3 238
A little shaking of mine arm And thrice his head thus waving *Hamlet* ii 1 92
Shale. And your fair show shall suck away their souls, Leaving them but the shales and husks of men . . . *Hen. V.* iv 2 18
Shall. Shall we give o'er and drown? . . . . *Tempest* i 1 41
My noble master! What shall I do? say what; what shall I do? . i 2 300
Hark in thine ear.—My lord, it shall be done . . . . i 2 318
For this, be sure, to-night thou shalt have cramps . . . i 2 325
Make thee roar That beasts shall tremble at thy din . . . i 2 371
Sea-water shalt thou drink; thy food shall be The fresh-brook muscles i 2 462
One word more Shall make me chide thee, if not hate thee . . i 2 476
Follow me. Hark what thou else shalt do me . . . . i 2 495
Who shall be of as little memory When he is earth'd . . . ii 1 233
How shall that Claribel Measure us back to Naples? . . . ii 1 258
Thy case, dear friend, Shall be my precedent . . . . ii 1 291
One stroke Shall free thee from the tribute which thou payest . ii 1 293
I shall no more to sea, to sea, Here shall I die ashore . . ii 2 44
He shall taste of my bottle: if he have never drunk wine afore, it will go near to remove his fit . . . . ii 2 77
He shall pay for him that hath him, and that soundly . . ii 2 81
Than of Our human generation you shall find Many, nay, almost any . iii 3 33
I'll waste With such discourse as, I not doubt, shall make it Go quick away . . . . v 1 303
It shall go hard but I'll prove it . . . . *T. G. of Ver.* i 1 86
My bosom as a bed Shall lodge thee till thy wound be throughly heal'd i 2 115
There shall he practise tilts and tournaments, Hear sweet discourse . i 3 30
Thou shalt never get such a secret from me . . . . ii 5 40
Much less shall she that hath Love's wings to fly . . . ii 7 11
Time will melt her frozen thoughts And worthless Valentine shall be forgot iii 2 10
When a man's servant shall play the cur with him, look you, it goes hard iv 4 1
Watch the door with pistols, that none shall issue out *Mer. Wives* iv 2 53
What shall I do? I'll creep up into the chimney . . . iv 2 56
They are fairies; he that speaks to them shall die . . . v 5 51
We shall write to you . . . . *Meas. for Meas.* i 1 57
Shall. I shall follow it as the flesh and fortune shall better determine *Meas. for Meas.* ii 1 268
What shall be done, sir, with the groaning Juliet? . . . ii 2 15
Be absolute for death; either death or life Shall thereby be the sweeter iii 1 6
That shall not be much amiss . . . . iii 1 200
If peradventure he shall ever return to have hearing of this business . iii 1 210
Give notice to such men of sort and suit as are to meet him.—I shall, sir iv 4 21
This jest shall cost me some expense . . . *Com. of Errors* iii 1 123
In despite of his quick wit . . . , he shall fall in love *Much Ado* ii 1 399
When he shall hear she died upon his words, The idea of her life shall sweetly creep Into his study of imagination . . . . iv 1 226
Every lovely organ of her life Shall come apparell'd in more precious habit . . . . iv 1 229
Then shall he mourn, If ever love had interest in his liver . . iv 1 232
Do not forget to specify, when time and place shall serve, that I am an ass . . . . v 1 264
Some shall see.—What shall some see?—Nay, nothing . *L. L. Lost* i 2 165
Then the moon . . . shall behold the night Of our solemnities *M. N. D.* i 1 11
A proper man, as one shall see in a summer's day . . . i 2 89
Thou shalt not from this grove Till I torment thee for this injury . ii 1 146
Thou shalt know the man By the Athenian garments he hath on . . ii 1 268
Fair Jessica shall be my torch-bearer . . *Mer. of Venice* ii 4 40
Let good Antonio look he keep his day, Or he shall pay for this . . ii 8 26
Come, away! For you shall hence upon your wedding-day . . iii 2 313
Your grace shall understand that at the receipt of your letter I am very sick . . . . iv 1 150
That thou shalt see the difference of our spirits, I pardon thee thy life iv 1 368
You shall perceive them make a mutual stand . . . . v 1 77
Come see, And in my voice most welcome shall you be . *As Y. Like It* ii 4 87
What is he that shall buy his flock and pasture? . . . . ii 4 88
Inform him So 'tis our will he should.—I shall, my liege . *All's Well* v 3 27
Then shall we have a match. I have letters sent me That set him high v 3 30
Sir, shall I to this lady?—Ay, that's the theme . . . *T. Night* ii 4 125
Haply your eye shall light upon some toy You have desire to purchase iii 3 44
Back you shall not to the house . . . . iii 4 271
If you tarry longer, I shall give worse payment . . . . iv 1 21
You say That we shall see and know our friends in heaven *K. John* iii 4 78
When I shall meet him in the court of heaven I shall not know him . iii 4 87
When he shall hear of your approach . . . , Even at that news he dies iii 4 162
And then the hearts Of all his people shall revolt from him . . iii 4 165
We three here part that ne'er shall meet again . . *Richard II.* ii 2 143
Will you permit that I shall stand condemn'd A wandering vagabond? ii 3 119
I fear we shall stay too long . . . . . . 1 *Hen. IV.* iv 2 83
By cock and pie, sir, you shall not away to-night . . . 2 *Hen. IV.* v 1 1
They shall be aprehended by and by . . . . *Hen. V.* ii 2 2
When he shall see our army, He 'll drop his heart into the sink of fear . iii 5 58
Desire them all to my pavilion.—We shall, my liege.—Shall I attend? . iv 1 28
Collect them all together at my tent: I'll be before thee.—I shall do't iv 1 305
If they do this,—As, if God please, they shall,—my ransom then Will soon be levied . . . . iv 3 120
My joints; Which if they have as I will leave 'em them, Shall yield them little, tell the constable.—I shall . . . . iv 3 125
Your request shall make me let it pass . . . . . . v 2 372
When they shall hear how we have play'd the men . 1 *Hen. VI.* i 6 16
What madness rules in brainsick men, When for so slight and frivolous a cause Such factious emulations shall arise! . . . . . iv 1 113
A day will come when York shall claim his own . 2 *Hen. VI.* i 1 239
You, madam, shall with us. Stafford, take her to thee . . . i 4 54
Shall we after them?—After them! nay, before them, if we can . v 3 27
Thou shalt to London presently, And whet on Warwick 3 *Hen. VI.* i 2 36
Your horse stands ready at the park-corner.—But whither shall we then? iv 5 20
Richmond with the rest shall down.—It shall be so; he shall to Brittany iv 6 100
When the morning sun shall raise his car Above the border of this horizon . . . . iv 7 80
Come, shall we to this gear? . . . . . . *Richard III.* i 4 157
Men shall deal unadvisedly sometimes . . . . . . iv 4 292
I shall despair. There is no creature loves me; And if I die, no soul shall pity me . . . . v 3 201
When these so noble benefits shall prove Not well disposed . *Hen. VIII.* i 2 115
I yet remember Some of these articles; and out they shall . . iii 2 304
That thou shalt know, Trojan, he is awake, He tells thee so himself *Troi. and Cres.* i 3 255
Ready, when time shall prompt them, to make road Upon's *Coriolanus* iii 1 5
Hear you this Triton of the minnows? mark you His absolute 'shall'? iii 1 90
With his peremptory 'shall,' being but The horn and noise o' the monster's . . . . iii 1 94
Puts his 'shall,' His popular 'shall,' against a graver bench Than ever frown'd . . . . iii 1 105
He must be buried with his brethren.—And shall, or him we will accompany.—'And shall!' what villain was it spake that word? *T. Andron.* i 1 358
Pluto sends you word, If you will have Revenge from hell, you shall . iv 3 38
Where shall we dine? O me! What fray was here? . *Rom. and Jul.* i 1 179
I have remember'd me, thou's hear our counsel . . . . i 3 9
We shall to't presently . . . . *T. of Athens* iii 6 37
He shall wear his crown by sea and land, In every place . *J. Cæsar* i 3 87
You shall not stir out of your house to day.—Cæsar shall forth . ii 2 10
If much you note him, You shall offend him . . . *Macbeth* iii 4 57
Yet my poor country Shall have more vices than it had before . iv 3 45
Do you consent we shall acquaint him with it? . . . . *Hamlet* i 1 172
Shall we to the court? for, by my fay, I cannot reason . . . ii 2 271
And he to England shall along with you . . . . . iii 3 4
Refrain to-night, And that shall lend a kind of easiness To the next . iii 4 166
Keep out, che vor ye, or ise try whether your costard or my ballow be the harder: chill be plain with you . . . . . . *Lear* iv 6 246
When time shall serve, let but the herald cry, And I'll appear again . v 1 48
He that parts us shall bring a brand from heaven, And fire us hence . v 3 22
The good-years shall devour them, flesh and fell, Ere they shall make us weep: we'll see 'em starve first . . . . v 3 24
You shall mark Many a duteous and knee-crooking knave . . *Othello* i 1 44
That you shall surely find him, Lead to the Sagittary the raised search i 1 158
This fortification, gentlemen, shall we see't? . . . . . ii 2 5
You shall find there A man who is the abstract of all faults *Ant. and Cleo.* i 4 8
If the great gods be just, they shall assist The deeds of justest men . ii 1 1
I cannot hope Cæsar and Antony shall well greet together . . ii 1 39
He shall to Parthia. Be it art or hap, He hath spoken true . . ii 3 32
Thou shalt bring him to me Where I will write . . . . iii 3 49
Observe how Antony becomes his flaw . . . —Cæsar, I shall . . iii 12 36
Make it so known.—Cæsar, I shall . . . . iv 6 4
The three-nook'd world Shall bear the olive freely . . . . iv 6 7

Shall. To-morrow, Before the sun shall see's, we'll spill the blood That has to-day escaped . . . . *Ant. and Cleo.* iv 8 3
Tell him he mocks The pauses that he makes.—Cæsar, I shall . . v 1 3
Bring us what she says, And how you find of her.—Cæsar, I shall . . v 1 68
To Cæsar I will speak what you shall please . . . . . . v 2 69
He was here: I dare be bound he's true and shall perform All parts of his subjection loyally . . . . . . *Cymbeline* iv 3 18
Shallenge. It is a shallenge: I will cut his troat . . . *Mer. Wives* i 4 114
Shallow. This is a very shallow monster! . . . . *Tempest* ii 2 147
On some shallow story of deep love . . . . *T. G. of Ver.* i 1 21
I'll show my mind According to my shallow simple skill . . . i 2 8
Think'st thou I am so shallow, so conceitless, To be seduced by thy flattery? . . . . iv 2 96
He shall not abuse Robert Shallow, esquire . . . . *Mer. Wives* i 1 4
Here is Got's plessing, and your friend, and Justice Shallow . . . i 1 77
I thank you for my venison, Master Shallow . . . . . i 1 81
Robert Shallow, esquire, saith, he is wronged . . . . . i 1 110
Now, Master Shallow, you'll complain of me to the king? . . . i 1 112
I will do as my cousin Shallow says: . . . he's a justice of peace . i 1 224
For all you are my man, go wait upon my cousin Shallow . . . i 1 282
Master Shallow, you have yourself been a great fighter . . . ii 3 43
To shallow rivers, to whose falls Melodious birds sings madrigals . iii 1 17
There comes my master, Master Shallow, and another gentleman . iii 1 32
Good Master Shallow, let him woo for himself . . . . . iii 4 51
I had been drowned, but that the shore was shelvy and shallow . . iii 5 15
Smother'd in errors, feeble, shallow, weak . . *Com. of Errors* iii 2 35
After he hath laughed at such shallow follies in others . *Much Ado* ii 3 10
What your wisdoms could not discover, these shallow fools have brought to light . . . . v 1 240
'That shallow vassal,'— Still me? . . . . . *L. L. Lost* i 1 256
To what end Their shallow shows and prologue vilely penn'd . . v 2 305
That loose grace Which shallow laughing hearers give to fools . . v 2 870
I should not see the sandy hour-glass run, But I should think of shallows and of flats . . . . *Mer. of Venice* i 1 26
Let not the sound of shallow foppery enter My sober house . . ii 5 35
Shallow, shallow. A better instance, I say . . *As Y. Like It* iii 2 58
Shallow again. A more sounder instance, come . . . . . iii 2 62
Most shallow man! . . . . iii 2 67
God help thee, shallow man! God make incision in thee! thou art raw iii 2 75
Fantastical, apish, shallow, inconstant, full of tears . . . . iii 2 432
As he that leaves A shallow plash to plunge him in the deep . *T. of Shrew* i 1 23
You're shallow, madam, in great friends . . . . *All's Well* i 3 45
You are idle shallow things: I am not of your element . *T. Night* iii 4 137
A bawbling vessel was he captain of, For shallow draught and bulk unprizable . . . . v 1 58
You are a shallow cowardly hind, and you lie . . . *1 Hen. IV.* ii 3 16
He ambled up and down With shallow jesters . . . . . iii 2 61
God forbid a shallow scratch should drive The Prince of Wales from such a field as this! . . . . v 4 11
A good shallow young fellow: a' would have made a good pantler *2 Hen. IV.* ii 4 257
They will talk of mad Shallow yet.—You were called 'lusty Shallow' then . . . . iii 2 16
Which is Justice Shallow?—I am Robert Shallow, sir; a poor esquire . iii 2 62
Well, Master Shallow; deep, Master Shallow . . . . . iii 2 172
I am glad to see you, by my troth, Master Shallow . . . . iii 2 205
She would always say she could not abide Master Shallow . . . iii 2 215
Doth she hold her own well?—Old, old, Master Shallow . . . iii 2 219
We have heard the chimes at midnight, Master Shallow . . . iii 2 229
Will you tell me, Master Shallow, how to choose a man? . . . iii 2 275
Give me the spirit, Master Shallow . . . . iii 2 278
I do see the bottom of Justice Shallow . . . . . . iii 2 325
You are too shallow, Hastings, much too shallow, To sound the bottom of the after-times . . . . iv 2 50
I'll through Gloucestershire; and there will I visit Master Robert Shallow . . . . iv 3 139
You must excuse me, Master Robert Shallow.—I will not excuse you . v 1 4
If I were sawed into quantities, I should make four dozen of such bearded hermits' staves as Master Shallow . . . . . v 1 72
If I had a suit to Master Shallow, I would humour his men with the imputation of being near their master: if to his men, I would curry with Master Shallow . . . . v 1 80
I will devise matter enough out of this Shallow to keep Prince Harry in continual laughter . . . . v 1 88
Sir John!—I come, Master Shallow; I come, Master Shallow . . v 1 97
Master Robert Shallow, choose what office thou wilt in the land . v 3 129
Master Shallow, my Lord Shallow,—be what thou wilt . . . . v 3 136
Master Robert Shallow; I will make the king do you grace . . . v 5 5
Master Shallow, I owe you a thousand pound . . . . . v 5 77
His companies unletter'd, rude and shallow . . . . *Hen. V.* i 1 55
His jest will savour but of shallow wit, When thousands weep more than did laugh at it . . . . i 2 295
Fantastically borne By a vain, giddy, shallow, humorous youth . . ii 4 28
I have perhaps some shallow spirit of judgement . . . *1 Hen. VI.* ii 4 16
You show'd your judgement, Which being shallow, you shall give me leave To play the broker in mine own behalf . . *3 Hen. VI.* iv 1 62
Incapable and shallow innocents . . . . . *Richard III.* ii 2 18
Tell him his fears are shallow, wanting instance . . . . iii 2 25
Your reasons are too shallow and too quick . . . . . iv 4 361
Relenting fool, and shallow, changing woman! . . . . . iv 4 431
Armed in proof, and led by shallow Richmond . . . . . v 3 219
The sea being smooth, How many shallow bauble boats dare sail! *Troi. and Cres.* i 3 35
All the voyage of their life Is bound in shallows and in miseries *J. Cæsar* iv 3 221
Shallow, beggarly, three-suited, . . . worsted-stocking knave . *Lear* ii 2 16
Shallowest. The shallowest thick-skin of that barren sort *M. N. Dream* iii 2 13
Shallow-hearted. Ye sanguine, shallow-hearted boys! Ye white-limed walls! ye alehouse painted signs . . . . *T. Andron.* iv 2 97
Shallowly. Most shallowly did you these arms commence *2 Hen. IV.* iv 2 118
Shallow-rooted. Now 'tis the spring, and weeds are shallow-rooted *2 Hen. VI.* iii 1 31
Shambles. To make a shambles of the parliament-house! . *3 Hen. VI.* i 1 71
Honest.—O, ay; as summer flies are in the shambles . . *Othello* iv 2 66
Shame. 'Tis a passing shame That I, unworthy body as I am, Should censure thus on lovely gentlemen . . . . *T. G. of Ver.* i 2 17
It were a shame to call her back again And pray her to a fault for which I chid her . . . . i 2 51
A slave, that still an end turns me to shame! . . . . . iv 4 67
He sends your ladyship this ring.—The more shame for him . . iv 4 138
My shame and guilt confounds me . . . . v 4 73
Shame. Be thou ashamed that I have took upon me Such an immodest raiment, if shame live In a disguise of love . . *T. G. of Ver.* v 4 106
I fear not mine own shame so much as his peril . *Mer. Wives* iii 3 130
For shame! never stand 'you had rather' and 'you had rather' . . iii 3 133
Never name her, child, if she be a whore.—For shame, 'oman . . iv 1 66
Away with him! better shame than murder . . . . . iv 2 46
Repent you, fair one, of the sin you carry?—I do; and bear the shame most patiently . . . . *Meas. for Meas.* ii 3 20
But lest you do repent, As that the sin hath brought you to this shame ii 3 31
I do repent me, as it is an evil, And take the shame with joy . . . ii 3 36
And strip myself to death, . . . ere I'ld yield My body up to shame . ii 4 104
Why give you me this shame? . . . . iii 1 81
Is't not a kind of incest, to take life From thine own sister's shame? . iii 1 140
Shame to him whose cruel striking Kills for faults of his own liking! . iii 2 281
Twice treble shame on Angelo, To weed my vice and let his grow! . iii 2 283
But that her tender shame Will not proclaim against her maiden loss, How might she tongue me! . . . . iv 4 26
By so receiving a dishonour'd life With ransom of such shame . . iv 4 35
The vile conclusion I now begin with grief and shame to utter . . v 1 96
No longer session hold upon my shame . . . . . . v 1 376
No man that hath a name, By falsehood and corruption doth it shame *Com. of Errors* ii 1 113
Be not thy tongue thy own shame's orator; Look sweet, speak fair . iii 2 10
Shame hath a bastard fame, well managed . . . . . iii 2 19
I shall have law in Ephesus, To your notorious shame . . . . iv 1 84
Free from these slanders and this open shame . . . . . iv 4 70
Is't good to soothe him in these contraries?—It is no shame . . iv 4 83
I wonder much That you would put me to this shame and trouble . v 1 14
Beside the charge, the shame, imprisonment, You have done wrong . v 1 18
Give me ample satisfaction For these deep shames and great indignities v 1 253
My cunning shall not shame me . . . . . . *Much Ado* ii 2 56
In the congregation, where I should wed, there will I shame her . . iii 2 128
And there, before the whole congregation, shame her . . . . iii 3 173
Death is the fairest cover for her shame That may be wish'd for . iv 1 117
Doth not every earthly thing Cry shame upon her? . . . . iv 1 123
Thought I thy spirits were stronger than thy shames . . . . iv 1 127
This shame derives itself from unknown loins . . . . . iv 1 137
A thousand innocent shames In angel whiteness beat away those blushes iv 1 162
Which I had rather seal with my death than repeat over to my shame . v 1 248
So the life that died with shame Lives in death with glorious fame . v 3 7
How well this yielding rescues thee from shame! . . *L. L. Lost* i 1 118
Such public shame as the rest of the court can possibly devise . . i 1 132
Stands in attainder of eternal shame . . . . i 1 158
She hath but one [name] for herself; to desire that were a shame . . ii 1 200
Sweet fellowship in shame!—One drunkard loves another of the name . iv 3 49
You whoreson loggerhead! you were born to do me shame . . . iv 3 204
And they, well mock'd, depart away with shame . . . . . v 2 156
You have lived in desolation here, Unseen, unvisited, much to our shame v 2 358
They will shame us: let them not approach.—We are shame-proof . v 2 512
A conqueror, and afeard to speak! run away for shame . . . . v 2 583
The more shame for you (ye) . . . v 2 606; *Hen. VIII.* iii 1 102
How canst thou thus for shame, Titania, Glance at my credit? *M. N. Dream* ii 1 74
Have you no modesty, no maiden shame, No touch of bashfulness? . iii 2 285
For fear lest day should look their shames upon . . . . . iii 2 385
Forget the shames that you have stain'd me with . . *Mer. of Venice* i 3 140
What, must I hold a candle to my shames? They in themselves, good sooth, are too too light . . . . ii 6 41
But of force Must yield to such inevitable shame As to offend . . iv 1 57
Alas, it is a trifle! I will not shame myself to give you this . . . iv 1 431
I was beset with shame and courtesy . . . . v 1 217
For shame, Lie not, to say mine eyes are murderers! . *As Y. Like It* iii 5 18
What must we understand by this?—Some of my shame . . . . iv 3 96
'Twas I; but 'tis not I: I do not shame To tell you what I was . . iv 3 136
For shame, thou hilding of a devilish spirit . . . *T. of Shrew* ii 1 26
What says Lucentio to this shame of ours?—No shame but mine . . iii 2 7
Doff this habit, shame to your estate, An eye-sore to our solemn festival! iii 2 102
And I seeing this came thence for very shame . . . . . iii 2 182
If thou account'st it shame, lay it on me; And therefore frolic . . iv 3 183
A divulged shame Traduced by odious ballads . . . . *All's Well* ii 1 174
Shall at home be encountered with a shame as ample . . . . iv 3 81
Find out a country where but women were that had received so much shame . . . . iv 3 363
Rust, sword! cool, blushes! and, Parolles, live, Safest in shame! . . iv 3 374
While shame full late sleeps out the afternoon . . . . . v 3 66
Glad to have the . . . sheep-biter come by some notable shame *T. Night* ii 5 7
Thou hast, Sebastian, done good feature shame . . . . . iii 4 400
Desperate of shame and state, In private brabble did we apprehend him v 1 67
With the which I doubt not but to do myself much right, or you much shame . . . . v 1 317
Wherein our entertainment shall shame us we will be justified in our loves . . . . *W. Tale* i 1 9
One that knows What she should shame to know herself . . . . ii 1 91
Took it deeply, Fasten'd and fix'd the shame on't in himself . . . ii 3 15
As you were past all shame,—Those of your fact are so—so past all truth iii 2 85
Upon them shall The causes of their death appear, unto Our shame perpetual . . . . iii 2 239
May be, he has paid you more, which will shame you to give him again iv 4 242
I am proof against that title and what shame else belongs to't . . iv 4 872
Thou dost shame thy mother And wound her honour . . . *K. John* i 1 64
Where how he did prevail I shame to speak, But truth is truth . . i 1 104
His mother shames him so, poor boy, he weeps.—Now shame upon you! ii 1 166
His grandam's wrongs, and not his mother's shames, Draws those heaven-moving pearls from his poor eyes . . . . ii 1 168
Rather turn this day out of the week, This day of shame, oppression . iii 1 88
O Lymoges! O Austria! thou dost shame That bloody spoil . . . iii 1 114
Thou wear a lion's hide! doff it for shame, And hang a calf's-skin . iii 1 128
Well could I bear that England had this praise, So we could find some pattern of our shame . . . . iii 4 16
And bitter shame hath spoil'd the sweet world's taste, That it yields nought but shame . . . . iii 4 110
You will but make it blush And glow with shame of your proceedings . iv 1 114
Apparent foul play; and 'tis shame That greatness should so grossly offer it . . . . iv 2 93
A fellow by the hand of nature mark'd, Quoted and sign'd to do a deed of shame . . . . iv 2 222
Deep shame hath struck me dumb . . . . iv 2 235
This is the bloodiest shame, The wildest savagery, the vilest stroke . iv 3 47
If thou but frown on me, or stir thy foot, Or teach thy hasty spleen to do me shame, I'll strike thee dead . . . . iv 3 97

Shame. You ingrate revolts, You bloody Neroes, ripping up the womb Of your dear mother England, blush for shame . . . *K. John* v 2 153
Unkind remembrance! thou and eyeless night Have done me shame . v 6 13
Return with me again, To push destruction and perpetual shame Out . v 7 77
My life thou shalt command, but not my shame . . *Richard II.* i 1 166
Take but my shame, And I resign my gage . . . . . i 1 175
Where shame doth harbour, even in Mowbray's face . . . i 1 195
Bound in with shame, With inky blots and rotten parchment bonds . ii 1 63
From forth thy reach he would have laid thy shame . . . ii 1 106
Wert thou regent of the world, It were a shame to let this land by lease; But for thy world enjoying but this land, Is it not more than shame to shame it so? . . . . ii 1 110
Live in thy shame, but die not shame with thee! . . . . ii 1 135
'Tis shame such wrongs are borne In him, a royal prince . . ii 1 238
Would it not shame thee in so fair a troop To read a lecture of them? . iv 1 231
And he shall spend mine honour with his shame . . . . v 3 68
In the stocks refuge their shame, That many have and others must sit there . . . . v 5 26
As may not be Without much shame retold or spoken of . *1 Hen. IV.* i 1 46
Shall it for shame be spoken in these days, Or fill up chronicles? . i 3 170
And shall it in more shame be further spoken, That you are fool'd, discarded and shook off By him for whom these shames ye underwent? i 3 177
What device, what starting-hole, canst thou now find out to hide thee from this open and apparent shame? . . . . . . ii 4 292
To shame the devil By telling truth: tell truth and shame the devil . iii 1 59
Bring him hither, and I'll be sworn I have power to shame him hence . iii 1 61
O, while you live, tell truth and shame the devil! . . . iii 1 62
A bloody mask, Which, wash'd away, shall scour my shame with it . iii 2 137
For every honour sitting on his helm, Would they were multitudes, and on my head My shames redoubled! . . . . iii 2 144
For my part, I may speak it to my shame, I have a truant been . v 1 93
And did grace the shame Of those that turn'd their backs . *2 Hen. IV.* i 1 129
Though it be a shame to be on any side but one, it is worse shame to beg than to be on the worst side . . . . i 2 87
It is a shame to be thought on . . . . ii 1 38
That argues but the shame of your offence: A rotten case abides no handling . . . . iv 1 160
You must not dare, for shame, to talk of mercy . . . *Hen. V.* ii 2 81
Witness our too much memorable shame When Cressy battle fatally was struck . . . . ii 4 53
'Tis shame for us all: so God sa' me, 'tis shame to stand still; it is shame iii 2 117
For your great seats now quit you of great shames . . . . iii 5 47
Reproach and everlasting shame Sits mocking in our plumes . . . iv 5 4
O perdurable shame! let's stab ourselves . . . . . . iv 5 7
Shame and eternal shame, nothing but shame! Let us die in honour . iv 5 10
Let life be short; else shame will be too long . . . . . iv 5 23
And with my nails digg'd stones out of the ground, To hurl at the beholders of my shame . . . . *1 Hen. VI.* i 4 46
The shame hereof will make me hide my head . . . . . i 5 39
Thy cheeks Blush for pure shame to counterfeit our roses . . . ii 4 66
For shame, my lord of Winchester, relent! . . . . . . iii 1 132
I'll have a bout with you again, Or else let Talbot perish with this shame iii 2 57
Shame to the Duke of Burgundy and thee! . . . . . . iv 1 13
York set him on to fight and die in shame . . . . . . iv 4 8
His fame lives in the world, his shame in you . . . . . . iv 4 46
Rather than I'll shame my mother's womb . . . . . . iv 5 35
Part of thy father may be saved in thee.—No part of him but will be shame in me . . . . iv 5 39
My age was never tainted with such shame.—And shall my youth be? . iv 5 46
Bought with such a shame, To save a paltry life . . . . . iv 6 44
To be shame's scorn and subject of mischance! . . . . . iv 6 49
I banish her my bed and company And give her as a prey to law and shame . . . . *2 Hen. VI.* ii 1 198
Gazing on thy face, With envious looks, laughing at thy shame . . ii 4 12
Come you, my lord, to see my open shame? . . . . . . ii 4 19
In thy closet pent up, rue my shame, And ban thine enemies . . . ii 4 24
Methinks I should not thus be led along, Mail'd up in shame . . ii 4 31
But be thou mild and blush not at my shame . . . . . . ii 4 48
Thou hast been conduct of my shame.—It is my office . . . . ii 4 101
My shame will not be shifted with my sheet . . . . . . ii 4 107
Nay, then, a shame take all!—And, in the number, thee that wishest shame! . . . . iii 1 307
Rob the deathsman of his fee, Quitting thee thereby of ten thousand shames . . . . iii 2 218
Were't not a shame, that whilst you live at jar, The fearful French . . . Should make a start o'er seas and vanquish you? . . . . iv 8 43
Shame to thy silver hair, Thou mad misleader of thy brain-sick son! . v 1 162
And shame thine honourable age with blood? . . . . . . v 1 170
For shame! in duty bend thy knee to me That bows unto the grave . v 1 173
Fie! charity, for shame! speak not in spite . . . . . . v 1 213
Shame and confusion! all is on the rout; Fear frames disorder . . v 2 31
Away, my lord! you are slow; for shame, away! . . . . . v 2 72
I am thy sovereign.—I am thine.—For shame, come down . *3 Hen. VI.* i 1 77
I shame to hear thee speak. Ah, timorous wretch! . . . . i 1 231
Were shame enough to shame thee, wert thou not shameless . . . i 4 120
For shame, my liege, make them your precedent! . . . . . ii 2 33
Ah, what a shame were this! Look on the boy . . . . . ii 2 39
For shame! leave Henry, and call Edward king.—Call him my king? . iii 3 100
He dishonours me, But most himself, if he could see his shame . . iii 3 185
And am I guerdon'd at the last with shame? Shame on himself! . . iii 3 191
Ah, what a shame! ah, what a fault were this! . . . . . v 4 12
And warriors faint! why, 'twere perpetual shame . . . . . v 4 51
Hie thee to hell for shame, and leave the world! . . *Richard III.* i 3 143
Thou move our patience.—Foul shame upon you! you have all moved mine . . . . i 3 249
Have done! for shame, if not for charity.—Urge neither charity nor shame to me . . . . i 3 273
My charity is outrage, life my shame; And in that shame still live my sorrow's rage! . . . . i 3 277
He is my son; yea, and therein my shame . . . . . . ii 2 29
And I for comfort have but one false glass, Which grieves me when I see my shame in him . . . . ii 2 54
Woe's scene, world's shame, grave's due by life usurp'd . . . iv 4 27
Bloody will be thy end; Shame serves thy life and doth thy death attend iv 4 195
Convey me to the block of shame; Wrong hath but wrong . . . v 1 28
Let us be lead within thy bosom, Richard, And weigh thee down to ruin, shame, and death! . . . . v 3 153
And in record, left them the heirs of shame . . . . . . v 3 335
But cardinal sins and hollow hearts I fear ye: Mend 'em, for shame *Hen. VIII.* iii 1 105

Shame. They would shame to make me Wait else at door, a fellow-counsellor . . . . *Hen. VIII.* v 2 16
This is too much; Forbear, for shame, my lords . . . . . v 3 86
What a shame was this! Did my commission Bid ye so far forget yourselves? . . . . v 3 141
Embrace him: Be friends, for shame, my lords! . . . . . . v 3 160
And struck him down, the disdain and shame whereof hath ever since kept Hector fasting and waking . . . . . *Troi. and Cres.* i 2 36
Peace, for shame, peace!—Mark him; note him . . . . . i 2 250
Do you with cheeks abash'd behold our works, And call them shames? . i 3 19
Both our honour and our shame in this Are dogg'd with two strange followers . . . . i 3 364
Will you set your wit to a fool's?—No, I warrant you; for a fool's will shame it . . . . ii 1 96
Fears and reasons? fie, for godly shame! . . . . ii 2 32
Disgrace to your great worths and shame to me . . . . . ii 2 151
Come, come, what need you blush? shame's a baby . . . . iii 2 43
Thou dost not use me courteously, To shame the zeal of my petition to thee . . . . iv 4 124
You know me dutiful; therefore, dear sir, Let me not shame respect . v 3 73
Bid the snail-paced Ajax arm for shame . . . . v 5 18
Ignomy and shame Pursue thy life, and live aye with thy name! . . v 10 33
All the contagion of the south light on you, You shames of Rome! *Coriol.* i 4 31
Never shame to hear What you have nobly done . . . . . ii 2 71
Are you mankind?—Ay, fool; is that a shame? . . . . . iv 2 17
And stop those maims Of shame seen through thy country . . . iv 5 93
And cannot live but to thy shame, unless It be to do thee service . iv 5 106
Who shall ask it? The tribunes cannot do't for shame . . . . iv 6 109
That thou mayst prove To shame unvulnerable . . . . . . v 3 73
Down, ladies; let us shame him with our knees . . . . . . v 3 169
Made peace With no less honour to the Antiates Than shame to the Romans . . . . v 6 81
Will you be put in mind of his blind fortune, Which was your shame? . v 6 119
For shame, put up.—Not I, till I have sheathed My rapier in his bosom *T. Andron.* ii 1 53
For shame, be friends, and join for that you jar . . . . . ii 1 103
Were't not for shame, Well could I leave our sport to sleep awhile . ii 3 196
Ah, now thou turn'st away thy face for shame! . . . . . . ii 4 28
My sons' sweet blood will make it shame and blush . . . . iii 1 15
That which I would hide from heaven's eye, Our empress' shame . iv 2 60
Let you speak? Villains, for shame you could not beg for grace . v 2 180
The girl should not survive her shame . . . . v 3 41
Die, die, Lavinia, and thy shame with thee; And, with thy shame, thy father's sorrow die! . . . . v 3 46
Why, uncle, 'tis a shame.—Go to, go to; You are a saucy boy *R. and J.* i 5 84
Be quiet, or—More light, more light! For shame! I'll make you quiet i 5 89
The brightness of her cheek would shame those stars, As daylight doth a lamp . . . . ii 2 19
Beat down their weapons. Gentlemen, for shame, forbear this outrage! iii 1 90
Shame come to Romeo!—Blister'd be thy tongue For such a wish! . iii 2 90
He was not born to shame: Upon his brow shame is ashamed to sit . iii 2 91
Likely thou wilt undertake A thing like death to chide away this shame iv 1 74
And this shall free thee from this present shame . . . . . iv 1 118
For shame, bring Juliet forth; her lord is come . . . . . iv 5 22
Peace, ho, for shame! confusion's cure lives not In these confusions . iv 5 65
And here is come to do some villanous shame To the dead bodies . . v 3 52
My most honourable lord, I am e'en sick of shame . . *T. of Athens* iii 6 46
Shame not these woods, By putting on the cunning of a carper . . iv 3 208
Shame that they wanted cunning, in excess Hath broke their hearts . v 4 28
The gods do this in shame of cowardice . . . . . . *J. Cæsar* ii 2 41
For shame, you generals! what do you mean? Love, and be friends . iv 3 130
The gods defend him from so great a shame! . . . . . . v 4 23
My hands are of your colour; but I shame To wear a heart so white *Macb.* ii 2 64
Is't night's predominance, or the day's shame, That darkness does the face of earth entomb, When living light should kiss it? . . . . ii 4 8
Shame itself! Why do you make such faces? . . . . . . iii 4 66
If I stand here, I saw him.—Fie, for shame! . . . . . . iii 4 74
Aboard, for shame! The wind sits in the shoulder of your sail *Hamlet* i 3 55
Be not you ashamed to show, he'll not shame to tell you what it means iii 2 155
O shame! where is thy blush? . . . . iii 4 82
Proclaim no shame When the compulsive ardour gives the charge . . iii 4 85
While, to my shame, I see The imminent death of twenty thousand men iv 4 59
By Gis and by Saint Charity, Alack, and fie for shame! . . . . iv 5 60
Nature her custom holds, Let shame say what it will . . . . iv 7 189
I will gain nothing but my shame and the odd hits . . . . . v 2 185
Who cover faults, at last shame them derides . . . . . . *Lear* i 1 284
Which else were shame, that then necessity Will call discreet proceeding i 4 232
The shame itself doth speak For instant remedy . . . . . i 4 267
O, lady, lady, shame would have it hid! . . . . ii 1 95
Makest thou this shame thy pastime? . . . . ii 4 6
Your son and daughter found this trespass worth The shame which here it suffers . . . . ii 4 45
I'll not chide thee; Let shame come when it will, I do not call it . . ii 4 229
Self-cover'd thing, for shame, Be-monster not thy feature . . . iv 2 62
Cried 'Sisters! sisters! Shame of ladies! sisters! Kent! father! sisters!' . . . . iv 3 29
A sovereign shame so elbows him . . . . iv 3 44
That burning shame Detains him from Cordelia . . . . . . iv 3 48
'Zounds, sir, you're robb'd; for shame, put on your gown . . *Othello* i 1 86
It is my shame to be so fond; but it is not in my virtue to amend it . i 3 320
Hold! the general speaks to you; hold, hold, for shame! . . . ii 3 168
For Christian shame, put by this barbarous brawl . . . . . ii 3 172
Had they rain'd All kinds of sores and shames on my bare head . . iv 2 49
That she with Cassio hath the act of shame A thousand times committed v 2 211
Let heaven and men and devils, let them all, All, all, cry shame against me, yet I'll speak . . . . v 2 222
Else so thy cheek pays shame When shrill-tongued Fulvia scolds *A. and C.* i 1 31
'Tis pity of him.—Let his shames quickly Drive him to Rome . . i 4 72
I never saw an action of such shame . . . . iii 10 22
Speak to him: He is unqualitied with very shame . . . . . iii 11 44
See, How I convey my shame out of thine eyes By looking back . . iii 11 52
'Twas a shame no less Than was his loss, to course your flying flags, And leave his navy gazing . . . . iii 13 10
And I, an ass, am onion-eyed: for shame, Transform us not to women . iv 2 35
Bending down His corrigible neck, his face subdued To penetrative shame . . . . iv 14 75
Go and say, We purpose her no shame . . . . v 1 62
O Cæsar, what a wounding shame is this! . . . . v 2 159
With shame—The first that ever touch'd him [Cæsar]—he was carried From off our coast, twice beaten . . . . . *Cymbeline* iii 1 24

Shame. To shame the guise o' the world, I will begin The fashion *Cymb.* v 1 32
And cowards living To die with lengthen'd shame v 3 13
With faces fit for masks, or rather fairer Than those for preservation cased, or shame v 3 22
Gilded pale looks, Part shame, part spirit renew'd v 3 35
Poison and treason are the hands of sin, Ay, and the targets, to put off the shame *Pericles* i 1 140
Is it a shame to get when we are old? iv 2 32
Your bride goes to that with shame which is her way to go with warrant iv 2 138
I do shame To think of what a noble strain you are, And of how coward a spirit iv 3 23
She that sets seeds and roots of shame and iniquity iv 6 93
Shamed. You're shamed, you're overthrown, you're undone! *Mer. Wives* iii 3 102
Why then you are utterly shamed, and he's but a dead man iv 2 43
Now shall the devil be shamed iv 2 124
I'll warrant they'll have him publicly shamed iv 2 236
There would be no period to the jest, should he not be publicly shamed iv 2 238
Death is a fearful thing.—And shamed life a hateful *Meas. for Meas.* iii 1 117
If I be foiled, there is but one shamed that was never gracious *As Y. L. It* i 2 200
My shamed life in his dishonour lies *Richard II.* v 3 71
Those eyes of thine from mine have drawn salt tears, Shamed their aspect with store of childish drops *Richard III.* i 2 155
You have shamed me In your condemned seconds *Coriolanus* i 8 14
By this our mother is for ever shamed *T. Andron.* iv 2 112
Age, thou art shamed! *J. Cæsar* i 2 150
He reserved a blanket, else we had been all shamed *Lear* iii 4 68
God's will, lieutenant, hold! You will be shamed for ever *Othello* ii 3 163
Frailties which before Have often shamed our sex *Ant. and Cleo.* v 2 124
The poor soldier that so richly fought, Whose rags shamed gilded arms *Cymbeline* v 5 4
Shame-faced. Seize on the shame-faced Henry *3 Hen. VI.* iv 8 53
Shamefast. A blushing shamefast spirit [conscience] that mutinies in a man's bosom *Richard III.* i 4 142
Shameful. I'll pluck out these false eyes That would behold in me this shameful sport *Com. of Errors* iv 4 108
To force that on you, in a shameful cunning, Which you knew none of yours: what might you think? *T. Night* iii 1 127
It is the shameful work of Hubert's hand *K. John* iv 3 62
That England, that was wont to conquer others, Hath made a shameful conquest of itself *Richard II.* ii 1 66
Shameful is this league! Fatal this marriage! *2 Hen. VI.* i 1 98
Can I bear this shameful yoke? ii 4 37
Thrust from the crown By shameful murder of a guiltless king iv 1 95
My lord, you do me shameful injury *Richard III.* i 3 88
In beastly sort, dragg'd through the shameful field *Troi. and Cres.* v 10 5
And make two pasties of your shameful heads *T. Andron.* v 2 190
Do shameful execution on herself v 3 76
Won to his shameful lust The will of my most seeming-virtuous queen *Hamlet* i 5 45
Take vantage, heavy eyes, not to behold This shameful lodging *Lear* ii 2 179
Rebukeable And worthy shameful check it were *Ant. and Cleo.* iv 4 31
Shamefully. You would have married her most shamefully *Mer. Wives* v 5 234
We had not been thus shamefully surprised *1 Hen. VI.* ii 1 65
They say, is shamefully bereft of life *2 Hen. VI.* iii 2 269
And shamefully by you my hopes are butcher'd *Richard III.* i 3 276
Shameless. Beyond imagination is the wrong That she this day hath shameless thrown on me *Com. of Errors* v 1 202
Such misuse, Such beastly shameless transformation *1 Hen. IV.* i 1 44
Scoff on, vile fiend and shameless courtezan! *1 Hen. VI.* iii 2 45
Were shame enough to shame thee, wert thou not shameless *3 Hen. VI.* i 4 120
To make this shameless callet know herself ii 2 145
Peace, impudent and shameless Warwick, peace! iii 3 156
Shameless-desperate. Failing of her end by his strange absence, Grew shameless-desperate *Cymbeline* v 5 58
Shame-proof. We are shame-proof, my lord *L. L. Lost* v 2 513
Shamest. Thou shamest to acknowledge me in misery *Com. of Errors* v 1 322
Shamest thou not, knowing whence thou art extraught? *3 Hen. VI.* ii 2 142
If good, thou shamest the music of sweet news By playing it to me with so sour a face *Rom. and Jul.* ii 5 23
Fie, fie, thou shamest thy shape, thy love, thy wit iii 3 122
O conspiracy, Shamest thou to show thy dangerous brow by night? *J. C.* ii 1 78
Shank. Spectacles on nose and pouch on side, His youthful hose, well saved, a world too wide For his shrunk shank *As Y. Like It* ii 7 161
With dead men's rattling bones, With reeky shanks *Rom. and Jul.* iv 1 83
Draw, you rogue, or I'll so carbonado your shanks *Lear* ii 2 41
My conscience, thou art fetter'd More than my shanks and wrists *Cymb.* v 4 9
Shape. Not honour'd with A human shape *Tempest* i 2 284
Go take this shape And hither come in't i 2 303
Thou think'st there is no more such shapes as he i 2 478
Nor can imagination form a shape, Besides yourself, to like of iii 1 56
Though they are of monstrous shape, . . . Their manners are more gentle-kind iii 3 31
I cannot too much muse Such shapes, such gesture and such sound iii 3 37
Thy shape invisible retain thou still iv 1 185
He is as disproportion'd in his manners As in his shape v 1 291
Seeing you are beautified With goodly shape *T. G. of Ver.* iv 1 56
To worship shadows and adore false shapes iv 2 131
It is the lesser blot, modesty finds, Women to change their shapes than men their minds.—Than men their minds! v 4 109
I would my husband would meet him in this shape *Mer. Wives* iv 2 87
To the forge with it then; shape it: I would not have things cool iv 2 240
In this shape when you have brought him thither, What shall be done with him? iv 4 44
In their so sacred paths he dares to tread In shape profane iv 4 60
He beat me grievously, in the shape of a woman; for in the shape of man, Master Brook, I fear not Goliath with a weaver's beam v 1 22
Let it keep one shape, till custom make it Their perch *Meas. for Meas.* ii 1 3
I am transformed . . . both in mind and in my shape *Com. of Errors* ii 2 199
She cannot love, Nor take no shape nor project of affection *Much Ado* iii 1 55
For shape, for bearing, argument and valour, Goes foremost in report iii 1 96
A Frenchman to-morrow, or in the shape of two countries at once iii 2 34
And doubt not but success Will fashion the event in better shape iv 1 237
In every lineament, branch, shape and form v 1 14
For he hath wit to make an ill shape good, And shape to win grace though he had no wit *L. L. Lost* ii 1 59
A foolish extravagant spirit, full of forms, figures, shapes, objects, ideas iv 2 69
The shape of Love's Tyburn that hangs up simplicity iv 3 54
We will with some strange pastime solace them, Such as the shortness of the time can shape iv 3 378
And shape his service wholly to my hests v 2 65
Shape. Immediately they will again be here In their own shapes *L. L. Lost* v 2 288
What shall we do, If they return in their own shapes to woo? v 2 299
Like the eye, Full of strange shapes, of habits and of forms v 2 773
I mistake your shape and making quite *M. N. Dream* ii 1 32
In the shape of Corin sat all day, Playing on pipes of corn ii 1 66
Gentle mortal, sing again: Mine ear is much enamour'd of thy note: So is mine eye enthralled to thy shape iii 1 142
The poet's pen Turns them to shapes v 1 16
Never did I know A creature, that did bear the shape of man, So keen and greedy to confound a man *Mer. of Venice* iii 2 277
If sight and shape be true, Why then, my love adieu! *As Y. Like It* v 4 126
And succeed thy father In manners, as in shape! *All's Well* i 1 71
So full of shapes is fancy That it alone is high fantastical *T. Night* i 1 14
Only shape thou thy silence to my wit i 2 61
In dimension and the shape of nature A gracious person i 5 280
By the colour of his beard, the shape of his leg, the manner of his gait ii 3 170
Humbling their deities to love, have taken The shapes of beasts *W. Tale* iv 4 27
An if my brother had my shape, And I had his, sir Robert's his, like him; . . . And, to his shape, were heir to all this land *K. John* i 1 138
Find shapes of grief, more than himself, to wail *Richard II.* ii 2 22
What, is my Richard both in shape and mind Transform'd and weaken'd? v 1 26
A sad and bloody hour; As by discharge of their artillery, And shape of likelihood, the news was told *1 Hen. IV.* i 1 58
At my nativity The front of heaven was full of fiery shapes iii 1 14
All the other gifts appertinent to man, as the malice of this age shapes them, are not worth a gooseberry *2 Hen. IV.* i 2 195
Let time shape, and there an end iii 2 358
If damn'd commotion so appear'd, In his true, native and most proper shape iv 1 37
Quick, forgetive, full of nimble fiery and delectable shapes iv 3 108
When I do shape In forms imaginary the unguided days iv 4 58
What your highness suffered under that shape, I beseech you take it for your own fault and not mine *Hen. V.* iv 8 56
I find thou art no less than fame hath bruited And more than may be gather'd by thy shape *1 Hen. VI.* ii 3 69
Doth bend her brows, As if with Circe she would change my shape! v 3 35
Changed to a worser shape thou canst not be v 3 36
No shape but his can please your dainty eye v 3 38
Who cannot steal a shape that means deceit? *2 Hen. VI.* iii 1 79
Foul indigested lump, As crooked in thy manners as thy shape! v 1 158
To shape my legs of an unequal size; To disproportion me *3 Hen. VI.* iii 2 159
I can add colours to the chameleon, Change shapes with Proteus iii 2 192
Oh, that deceit should steal such gentle shapes! *Richard III.* ii 2 27
There is no other way; Unless thou couldst put on some other shape iv 4 286
I do pronounce him in that very shape He shall appear in proof *Hen. VIII.* i 1 196
Birth, beauty, good shape, discourse, manhood, learning *Troi. and Cres.* i 2 275
And that unbodied figure of the thought That gave't surmised shape i 3 17
All our abilities, gifts, natures, shapes, Severals and generals of grace exact i 3 179
I have a young conception in my brain; Be you my time to bring it to some shape i 3 313
Hit or miss, Our project's life this shape of sense assumes i 3 385
And this whole night Hath nothing been but shapes and forms of slaughter v 3 12
You souls of geese, That bear the shapes of men! *Coriolanus* i 4 35
Made by some other deity than nature, That shapes man better iv 6 92
Nor age nor honour shall shape privilege *T. Andron.* iv 4 57
She comes In shape no bigger than an agate-stone *Rom. and Jul.* i 4 55
Fie, fie, thou shamest thy shape, thy love, thy wit iii 3 122
And usest none in that true use indeed Which should bedeck thy shape iii 3 125
Thy noble shape is but a form of wax, Digressing from the valour of a man iii 3 126
Thy wit, that ornament to shape and love, Mis-shapen in the conduct of them both iii 3 130
In all shapes that man goes up and down in from fourscore to thirteen, this spirit walks in *T. of Athens* ii 2 119
O, see the monstrousness of man When he looks out in an ungrateful shape! iii 2 80
Yet thanks I must you con That you are thieves profess'd, that you work not In holier shapes iv 3 430
Could it work so much upon your shape As it hath much prevail'd on your condition, I should not know you *J. Cæsar* ii 1 253
It is the weakness of mine eyes That shapes this monstrous apparition iv 3 277
Take any shape but that, and my firm nerves Shall never tremble *Macb.* iii 4 102
With all forms, moods, shapes of grief, That can denote me truly *Hamlet* i 2 82
Thou comest in such a questionable shape That I will speak to thee i 4 43
Virtue, as it never will be moved, Though lewdness court it in a shape of heaven i 5 54
The devil hath power To assume a pleasing shape ii 2 629
Imagination to give them shape, or time to act them in iii 1 129
Do you see yonder cloud that's almost in shape of a camel? iii 2 394
I, in forgery of shapes and tricks, Come short of what he did iv 7 90
Weigh what convenience both of time and means May fit us to our shape iv 7 151
There's a divinity that shapes our ends, Rough-hew them how we will v 2 10
He'll shape his old course in a country new *Lear* i 1 190
My dimensions are as well compact, My mind as generous, and my shape as true i 2 8
I'll resume the shape which thou dost think I have cast off for ever i 4 331
Poorest shape That ever penury, in contempt of man, Brought near to beast ii 3 7
Howe'er thou art a fiend, A woman's shape doth shield thee iv 2 67
My hopes do shape him for the governor *Othello* ii 1 55
Oft my jealousy Shapes faults that are not iii 3 148
He hath fought to-day As if a god, in hate of mankind, had Destroy'd in such a shape *Ant. and Cleo.* iv 8 26
Here I am Antony; Yet cannot hold this visible shape, my knave iv 14 14
I'll move the king To any shape of thy preferment *Cymbeline* i 5 71
I know the shape of's leg: this is his hand; His foot Mercurial iv 2 309
With her neeld composes Nature's own shape, of bud, bird, branch, or berry *Pericles* v Gower 6
Shaped. Then, since the heavens have shaped my body so, Let hell make crook'd my mind to answer it *3 Hen. VI.* v 6 78
I, that am not shaped for sportive tricks *Richard III.* i 1 14
I have, in this rough work, shaped out a man *T. of Athens* i 1 43
It is shaped, sir, like itself: and it is as broad as it hath breadth: it is just so high as it is *Ant. and Cleo.* ii 7 47
The more of you 'twas felt, the more it shaped Unto my end *Cymbeline* v 5 346
Shapeless. Wear out thy youth with shapeless idleness *T. G. of Ver.* i 1 8
Ill-faced, worse bodied, shapeless everywhere *Com. of Errors* iv 2 20

Shapeless. Disguised like Muscovites, in shapeless gear *L. L. Lost* v 2 303
To set a form upon that indigest Which he hath left so shapeless *K. John* v 7 27
Shaping. Such seething brains, Such shaping fantasies *M. N. Dream* v 1 5
Shard. For charitable prayers, Shards, flints and pebbles should be thrown on her *Hamlet* v 1 254
They are his shards, and he their beetle *Ant. and Cleo.* iii 2 19
Shard-borne. The shard-borne beetle with his drowsy hums *Macbeth* iii 2 42
Sharded. Often, to our comfort, shall we find The sharded beetle in a safer hold Than is the full-wing'd eagle *Cymbeline* iii 3 20
Share. Didst not thou share? hadst thou not fifteen pence? *Mer. Wives* ii 2 14
Good plots, they are laid; and our revolted wives share damnation together iii 2 40
With such gifts that heaven shall share with you *Meas. for Meas.* ii 2 147
Share the good of our returned fortune *As Y. Like It* v 4 180
I'll in among the rest, Out of hope of all, but my share of the feast *T. of S.* v 1 146
Thy goodness Share with thy birthright! *All's Well* i 1 73
Share the advice betwixt you ii 1 3
My part of death, no one so true Did share it *T. Night* ii 4 59
I shall have share in this most happy wreck v 1 273
An art which in their piedness shares With great creating nature *W. Tale* iv 4 87
Nay, let us share thy thoughts, as thou dost ours *Richard II.* ii 1 273
Thou shalt have a share in our purchase *1 Hen. IV.* ii 1 101
Let us share, and then to horse before day ii 2 104
Think not, Percy, To share with me in glory any more v 4 64
The fewer men, the greater share of honour *Hen. V.* iv 3 22
I would not lose so great an honour As one man more, methinks, would share from me For the best hope I have iv 3 32
Make boot of this; The other, Walter Whitmore, is thy share *2 Hen. VI.* iv 1 14
'Tis beauty that doth oft make women proud; But, God he knows, thy share thereof is small *3 Hen. VI.* i 4 129
The least of you shall share his part thereof *Richard III.* v 3 268
What glory our Achilles shares from Hector, Were he not proud, we all should share with him *Troi. and Cres.* i 3 368
Will he not upon our fair request Untent his person and share the air with us? ii 3 178
Shall pride carry it?—An 'twould, you'ld carry half.—A' would have ten shares ii 3 230
That book in many's eyes doth share the glory, That in gold clasps locks in the golden story *Rom. and Jul.* i 3 91
So shall you share all that he doth possess, By having him, making yourself no less i 3 93
We'll share a bounteous time In different pleasures *T. of Athens* i 1 263
Good fellows all, The latest of my wealth I'll share amongst you iv 2 23
Is it fit, The three-fold world divided, he should stand One of the three to share it?—So you thought him *J. Cæsar* iv 1 15
I commend your pains; And every one shall share i' the gains *Macbeth* iv 1 40
No mind that's honest But in it shares some woe iv 3 198
Half a share.—A whole one, I *Hamlet* iii 2 290
Shared. All the counsel that we two have shared *M. N. Dream* iii 2 198
Stands aloof, While all is shared and all is borne away *2 Hen. VI.* i 1 228
Founded his good fortunes on your love, Shared dangers with you *Oth.* iii 4 95
Sharing. As we were sharing, some six or seven fresh men set upon us—And unbound the rest *1 Hen. IV.* ii 4 199
Hear me, you wrangling pirates, that fall out In sharing that which you have pill'd from me! *Richard III.* i 3 159
Shark. Maw and gulf Of the ravin'd salt-sea shark *Macbeth* iv 1 24
Sharked. Here and there Shark'd up a list of lawless resolutes *Hamlet* i 1 98
Sharp. To run upon the sharp wind of the north *Tempest* i 2 254
Sharp furzes, pricking goss and thorns, Which enter'd their frail shins iv 1 180
How sharp the point of this remembrance is! v 1 138
It is too sharp.—You, minion, are too saucy *T. G. of Ver.* i 2 91
But you, Sir Thurio, are not sharp enough; You must lay lime iii 2 67
What he gets more of her than sharp words, let it lie on my head *M. W.* ii 1 191
With thy sharp and sulphurous bolt *Meas. for Meas.* ii 2 115
Fit thy consent to my sharp appetite; Lay by all nicety ii 4 161
If voluble and sharp discourse be marr'd, Unkindness blunts it *C. of Er.* ii 1 92
How fiery and how sharp he looks!—Mark how he trembles in his ecstasy! iv 4 53
A good sharp fellow: I will send for him *Much Ado* i 2 19
A sharp wit match'd with too blunt a will *L. L. Lost* ii 1 49
Your reasons at dinner have been sharp and sententious v 1 3
Look, how you butt yourself in these sharp mocks! v 2 251
Thrust thy sharp wit quite through my ignorance; Cut me to pieces v 2 398
To that place the sharp Athenian law Cannot pursue us *M. N. Dream* i 1 162
No metal can . . . bear half the keenness Of thy sharp envy *M. of Ven.* iv 1 126
Thy sting is not so sharp As friend remember'd not *As Y. Like It* ii 7 188
My falcon now is sharp and passing empty *T. of Shrew* iv 1 193
When he roar'd With sharp constraint of hunger *All's Well* iii 2 121
Ah, what sharp stings are in her mildest words! iii 4 18
When briers shall have leaves as well as thorns, And be as sweet as sharp iv 4 33
Goaded with most sharp occasions, Which lay nice manners by v 1 14
My desire, More sharp than filed steel, did spur me forth *T. Night* iii 3 5
By heaven, I think my sword's as sharp as yours *K. John* iv 3 82
Children yet unborn Shall feel this day as sharp to them as thorn *Rich. II.* iv 1 323
His nose was as sharp as a pen, and a' babbled of green fields *Hen. V.* ii 3 17
Speed him hence: Let him greet England with our sharp defiance iii 5 37
Sharp stakes pluck'd out of hedges They pitched in the ground *1 Hen. VI.* i 1 117
In these nice sharp quillets of the law, Good faith, I am no wiser than a daw ii 4 17
Hath not thy rose a thorn, Plantagenet?—Ay, sharp and piercing ii 4 70
I feel such sharp dissension in my breast, Such fierce alarums v 5 84
Sharp Buckingham unburthens with his tongue The envious load that lies upon his heart *2 Hen. VI.* iii 1 156
Yet be well assured You put sharp weapons in a madman's hands iii 1 347
My words are dull; O, quicken them with thine!—Thy woes will make them sharp, and pierce like mine *Richard III.* iv 4 125
By this one bloody trial of sharp war v 2 16
I know his sword Hath a sharp edge *Hen. VIII.* i 1 110
Alleged Many sharp reasons to defeat the law ii 1 14
The sharp thorny points Of my alleged reasons, drive this forward ii 4 224
The king Does whet his anger to him.—Sharp enough, Lord, for thy justice! iii 2 92
You are a little, By your good favour, too sharp v 3 74
Though you bite so sharp at reasons, You are so empty of them *T. and C.* ii 2 33
Tuned too sharp in sweetness, For the capacity of my ruder powers iii 2 25
Great Troy is ours, and our sharp wars are ended v 9 10
With opportunity of sharp revenge *T. Andron.* i 1 137
You are very short with us; But, if we live, we'll be as sharp with you i 1 410
He dies upon my scimitar's sharp point That touches this iv 2 91
'Tis true, 'tis true; witness my knife's sharp point v 3 63

Sharp. Thy wit is a very bitter sweeting; it is a most sharp sauce *Rom. and Jul.* ii 4 84
So out of tune, Straining harsh discords and unpleasing sharps iii 5 28
Meagre were his looks, Sharp misery had worn him to the bones v 1 41
Strike their sharp shins, And mar men's spurring *T. of Athens* iv 3 152
His great love, sharp as his spur, hath holp him To his home *Macbeth* i 6 23
Pray can I not, Though inclination be as sharp as will *Hamlet* iii 3 39
Here stood he in the dark, his sharp sword out *Lear* ii 1 40
To be a comrade with the wolf and owl,—Necessity's sharp pinch! ii 4 214
Through the sharp hawthorn blows the cold wind iii 4 47
Do not please sharp fate To grace it with your sorrows *Ant. and Cleo.* iv 14 135
With thy sharp teeth this knot intrinsicate Of life at once untie v 2 307
There cannot be a pinch in death More sharp than this is *Cymbeline* i 1 131
Till the diminution Of space had pointed him sharp as my needle i 3 19
Forbear sharp speeches to her: she's a lady So tender of rebukes iii 5 39
We'll enforce it from thee By a sharp torture iv 3 12
Sharp physic is the last *Pericles* i 1 72
So sharp are hunger's teeth, that man and wife Draw lots who first shall die to lengthen life i 4 45
She would with sharp needle wound The cambric iv Gower 23
If fires be hot, knives sharp, or waters deep iv 2 159
Sharpen. Now she sharpens: well said, whetstone! *Troi. and Cres.* v 2 75
Epicurean cooks Sharpen with cloyless sauce his appetite *Ant. and Cleo.* ii 1 25
The air is quick there, And it pierces and sharpens the stomach *Pericles* iv 1 29
Sharper. Slander, Whose sting is sharper than the sword's *W. Tale* ii 3 86
Finds brotherhood in thee no sharper spur? *Richard II.* i 2 9
With spirit of honour edged More sharper than your swords *Hen. V.* iii 5 39
How sharper than a serpent's tooth it is To have a thankless child! *Lear* i 4 310
Haply this life is best, If quiet life be best; sweeter to you That have a sharper known; well corresponding With your stiff age *Cymbeline* iii 3 31
'Tis slander, Whose edge is sharper than the sword iii 4 36
Sharpest. All deaths are too few, the sharpest too easy *W. Tale* iv 4 809
Both conjointly bend Your sharpest deeds of malice on this town *K. John* ii 1 380
And so give me up To the sharp'st kind of justice *Hen. VIII.* ii 4 44
Ready for the way of life or death, I wait the sharpest blow *Pericles* i 1 55
Sharp-ground. Hadst thou no poison mix'd, no sharp-ground knife, No sudden mean of death? *Rom. and Jul.* iii 3 44
Sharp-looking. A needy, hollow-eyed, sharp-looking wretch *Com. of Er.* v 1 240
Sharply. One of their kind, that relish all as sharply *Tempest* v 1 23
My greatest grief, Though little he do feel it, set down sharply *All's W.* iii 4 33
With a swaggering accent sharply twanged off *T. Night* iii 4 198
Though those that are betray'd Do feel the treason sharply, yet the traitor Stands in worse case of woe *Cymbeline* iii 4 88
Sharpness. Contempt nor bitterness Were in his pride or sharpness *All's Well* i 2 37
The friend hath lost his friend; And the best quarrels, in the heat, are cursed By those that feel their sharpness *Lear* v 3 57
Thou must not take my former sharpness ill *Ant. and Cleo.* iii 3 38
Sharp-pointed. If thy revengeful heart cannot forgive, Lo, here I lend thee this sharp-pointed sword *Richard III.* i 2 175
Sharp-provided. With what a sharp-provided wit he reasons! iii 1 132
Sharp-quilled. Till that his thighs with darts Were almost like a sharp-quill'd porpentine *2 Hen. VI.* iii 1 363
Sharp-toothed. O Regan, she hath tied Sharp-tooth'd unkindness, like a vulture, here *Lear* ii 4 137
Shatter. He raised a sigh so piteous and profound As it did seem to shatter all his bulk *Hamlet* ii 1 95
Shave the head, and tie the beard *Meas. for Meas.* iv 2 187
Now, by God's mother, priest, I'll shave your crown for this *2 Hen. VI.* i 1 51
Were I the wearer of Antonius' beard, I would not shave't to-day *Ant. and Cleo.* ii 2 8
Shaved. Bardolph was shaved and lost many a hair *1 Hen. IV.* iii 3 68
Shaven. Sometime like the shaven Hercules *Much Ado* iii 3 145
Shaw. Go, Lovel, with all speed to Doctor Shaw *Richard III.* iii 5 103
She. I never saw a woman, But only Sycorax my dam and she *Tempest* iii 2 109
Dost thou know my lady Silvia?—She that you gaze on so? *T. G. of Ver.* ii 1 46
Much less shall she that hath Love's wings to fly ii 7 11
Thou art not ignorant How she opposes her against my will iii 2 26
I say, sir, I will detest myself also, as well as she *Meas. for Meas.* ii 1 76
She should this Angelo have married; was affianced to her iii 1 221
There will she hide her, To listen our purpose *Much Ado* iii 1 11
Then we, Following the signs, woo'd but the sign of she *L. L. Lost* v 2 469
The fair, the chaste and unexpressive she *As Y. Like It* iii 2 10
What 'her' is this?—Why, Doctor She *All's Well* ii 1 82
You are the cruell'st she alive *T. Night* i 5 259
Go to, go to! How she holds up the neb, the bill to him! *W. Tale* i 2 183
But she I can hook to me: say that she were gone, Given to the fire ii 3 6
Sooth, when I was young And handed love as you do, I was wont To load my she with knacks iv 4 360
Doll Tearsheet she by name *Hen. V.* ii 1 81
I have, and I will hold, the quondam Quickly For the only she ii 1 83
I made no spare, sir . . . If I spared any That had a head to hit, either young or old, He or she *Hen. VIII.* v 4 25
That she beloved knows nought that knows not this *Troi. and Cres.* i 2 314
That she was never yet that ever knew Love got so sweet as when desire did sue i 2 316
Praise him that got thee, she that gave thee suck ii 3 252
The earth hath swallow'd all my hopes but she *Rom. and Jul.* i 2 14
She whom I love now Doth grace for grace and love for love allow ii 3 85
How! will she none? doth she not give us thanks? Is she not proud? doth she not count her blest, Unworthy as she is? iii 5 143
You have seen Cassio and she together *Othello* iv 2 3
So saucy with the hand of she here,—what's her name? *Ant. and Cleo.* iii 13 98
Make him swear The shes of Italy should not betray Mine interest and his honour *Cymbeline* i 3 29
Apes and monkeys 'Twixt two such shes would chatter this way and Contemn with mows the other i 6 40
The temple Of virtue was she; yea, and she herself v 5 221
She-angel. You would think a smock were a she-angel *W. Tale* iv 4 211
She-bear. Pluck the young sucking cubs from the she-bear *Mer. of Venice* ii 1 29
She beggar. Who in spite put stuff To some she beggar *T. of Athens* iv 3 273
She foxes. Thou, sapient sir, sit here. Now, you she foxes! *Lear* iii 6 24
She knight-errant. Come, you she knight-errant, come *2 Hen. IV.* v 4 25
She-lamb. To betray a she-lamb of a twelvemonth *As Y. Like It* iii 2 86
She-Mercury. Be brief, my good she-Mercury *Mer. Wives* ii 2 82
She-wolf of France, but worse than wolves of France! *3 Hen. VI.* i 4 111
Sheaf. They that reap must sheaf and bind *As Y. Like It* iii 2 113
O, let me teach you how to knit again This scatter'd corn into one mutual sheaf, These broken limbs again into one body *T. Andron.* v 3 71
Shealed. That's a shealed peascod *Lear* i 4 219

Shear. I am shepherd to another man And do not shear the fleeces that I graze . . . *As Y. Like It* ii 4 79
So many years ere I shall shear the fleece . . . *3 Hen. VI.* ii 5 37
Shearer. She hath made me four and twenty nosegays for the shearers *W. Tale* iv 3 44
If I make not this cheat bring out another and the shearers prove sheep iv 3 130
Shearing. Welcome to our shearing! . . . iv 4 77
Shearman. Villain, thy father was a plasterer; And thou thyself a shearman, art thou not? *2 Hen. VI.* iv 2 141
Shears. There went but a pair of shears between us . *Meas. for Meas.* i 2 29
Since you have shore With shears his thread of silk *M. N. Dream* v 1 348
Think you I bear the shears of destiny? . . . *K. John* iv 2 91
With his shears and measure in his hand, Standing on slippers . iv 2 196
Sheath. You tailor's-yard, you sheath, you bow-case . *1 Hen. IV.* ii 4 273
Ere thou sleep in thy sheath . . . *2 Hen. VI.* iv 10 61
Go to; have your lath glued within your sheath Till you know better how to handle it . . . *T. Andron.* ii 1 41
O happy dagger! This is thy sheath; there rust, and let me die *Rom. and Jul.* v 3 170
Sheathe thy impatience, throw cold water on thy choler . *Mer. Wives* ii 3 88
Put it up again.—Not till I sheathe it in a murderer's skin . *K. John* iv 3 80
And sheathe for lack of sport . . . *Hen. V.* iv 2 23
Here sheathe thy sword, I'll pardon thee my death . *3 Hen. VI.* v 5 70
There's his period, To sheathe his knife in us . . *Hen. VIII.* i 2 210
Here Goths have given me leave to sheathe my sword . *T. Andron.* i 1 85
Draw your swords, and sheathe them not Till Saturninus be Rome's emperor . . . i 1 204
Sheathe your dagger: Be angry when you will, it shall have scope *J. C.* iv 3 107
Either thou, Macbeth, Or else my sword with an unbatter'd edge I sheathe again undeeded . . . *Macbeth* v 7 20
Sheathed. And sheathed their swords for lack of argument . *Hen. V.* iii 1 21
Put up.—Not I, till I have sheathed My rapier in his bosom *T. Andron.* ii 1 53
Sheathing. Walter's dagger was not come from sheathing *T. of Shrew* iv 1 138
Sheathing the steel in my adventurous body . . *T. Andron.* v 3 112
Shed. Like a foul bombard that would shed his liquor . *Tempest* ii 2 22
Yet did not this cruel-hearted cur shed one tear . *T. G. of Ver.* ii 3 10
The dog all this while sheds not a tear nor speaks a word . . ii 3 34
But more merry tears The passion of loud laughter never shed *M. N. D.* v 1 70
If thou dost shed One drop of Christian blood, thy lands and goods Are, by the laws of Venice, confiscate . . *Mer. of Venice* iv 1 309
Shed thou no blood, nor cut thou less nor more But just a pound of flesh iv 1 325
Bid him shed tears, as being overjoy'd . . *T. of Shrew* Ind. 1 120
The tears that she hath shed for thee Like envious floods . Ind. 2 66
These great tears grace his remembrance more Than those I shed *All's W.* i 1 92
He weeps like a wench that had shed her milk . . iv 3 124
A devil Would have shed water out of fire ere done't . *W. Tale* iii 2 194
Tears shed there Shall be my recreation . . . iii 2 240
And so we wept, and there was the first gentleman-like tears that ever we shed.—We may live, son, to shed many more . . v 2 156
We shall repent each drop of blood That hot rash haste so indirectly shed . . . *K. John* ii 1 49
Farewell, my blood; which if to-day thou shed, Lament we may, but not revenge thee dead . . . *Richard II.* i 3 57
What store of parting tears were shed?—Faith, none for me . i 4 5
On his part I'll empty all these veins, And shed my dear blood drop by drop in the dust . . . *1 Hen. IV.* i 3 134
There will be a world of water shed Upon the parting of your wives and you . . . iii 1 94
He to-day that sheds his blood with me Shall be my brother *Hen. V.* iv 3 61
Interchanging blows I quickly shed Some of his bastard blood *1 Hen. VI.* iv 6 19
For thy sake have I shed many a tear . . . v 4 19
My sword should shed hot blood, mine eyes no tears . *2 Hen. VI.* i 1 118
Thou shalt be waking while I shed thy blood . . . iii 2 227
The honourable blood of Lancaster Must not be shed by such a jaded groom . . . iv 1 52
Upon my soul, the hearers will shed tears; Yea even my foes will shed fast-falling tears . . . *3 Hen. VI.* i 4 161
How will my wife for slaughter of my son Shed seas of tears! . ii 5 106
O traitors! murderers! They that stabb'd Cæsar shed no blood at all v 5 53
O, may such purple tears be alway shed From those that wish the downfall of our house! . . . v 6 64
These eyes, which never shed remorseful tear . . *Richard III.* i 2 156
By Christ's dear blood shed for our grievous sins . . i 4 195
The liquid drops of tears that you have shed Shall come again . iv 4 321
The brother blindly shed the brother's blood . . . v 5 24
I did not think to shed a tear In all my miseries *Hen. VIII.* iii 2 428
By the blood we have shed together, by the vows We have made *Coriol.* i 6 57
As for my country I have shed my blood, Not fearing outward force . iii 1 76
The extreme dangers and the drops of blood Shed for my thankless country . . . iv 5 76
And bear the palm for having bravely shed Thy wife and children's blood v 3 117
Rue the tears I shed, A mother's tears in passion for her son *T. Andron.* i 1 105
At thy feet I kneel, with tears of joy, Shed on the earth . . i 1 162
No man shed tears for noble Mutius; He lives in fame . . i 1 389
Upon my feeble knee I beg this boon, with tears not lightly shed . ii 3 289
For all my blood in Rome's great quarrel shed . . . iii 1 4
I have not another tear to shed . . . iii 1 267
Draw you near, To shed obsequious tears upon this trunk . . v 3 152
Like a loving child, Shed yet some small drops from thy tender spring v 3 167
As thou art true, For blood of ours, shed blood of Montague *R. and J.* iii 1 154
O God! did Romeo's hand shed Tybalt's blood? . . . iii 2 71
Woe to the hand that shed this costly blood! . . *J. Cæsar* iii 1 258
If you have tears, prepare to shed them now . . . iii 2 173
Blood hath been shed ere now, i' the olden time . . *Macbeth* iii 4 75
I'll not shed her blood; Nor scar that whiter skin of hers than snow *Othello* v 2 3
How many worthy princes' bloods were shed . . *Pericles* i 2 88
Shedding. No tears but of my shedding . . *Mer. of Venice* iii 1 101
Make some pretty match with shedding tears . . *Richard II.* iii 3 165
Achilles must or now be cropp'd, Or, shedding, breed a nursery of like evil, To overbulk us all . . . *Troi. and Cres.* i 3 319
Sheen. By fountain clear, or spangled starlight sheen . *M. N. Dream* ii 1 29
Thirty dozen moons with borrow'd sheen . . . *Hamlet* iii 2 167
Sheep. Turfy mountains, where live nibbling sheep . . *Tempest* iv 1 62
I have play'd the sheep in losing him . . . *T. G. of Ver.* i 1 73
Indeed, a sheep doth very often stray, An if the shepherd be a while away i 1 74
You conclude that my master is a shepherd then and I a sheep?—I do . i 1 77
A silly answer and fitting well a sheep.—This proves me still a sheep . i 1 81
The shepherd seeks the sheep, and not the sheep the shepherd . i 1 88
I seek my master, and my master seeks not me: therefore I am no sheep i 1 91
Sheep. The sheep for fodder follow the shepherd; the shepherd for food follows not the sheep: . . . therefore thou art a sheep.—Such another proof will make me cry 'baa' . . *T. G. of Ver.* i 1 92
Thou peevish sheep, What ship of Epidamnum stays for me? *Com. of Er.* iv 1 93
Two hot sheeps, marry.—And wherefore not ships? No sheep, sweet lamb, unless we feed on your lips.—You sheep, and I pasture *L. L. L.* ii 1 220
This love is as mad as Ajax: it kills sheep; it kills me, I a sheep . . iv 3 8
Ba, pueritia, with a horn added.—Ba, most silly sheep with a horn . v 1 53
I will repeat them,—a, e, i,— The sheep: the other two concludes it,—o, u v 1 59
When Jacob grazed his uncle Laban's sheep . . *Mer. of Venice* i 3 72
That good pasture makes fat sheep . . . *As Y. Like It* iii 2 29
They [our hands] are often tarred over with the surgery of our sheep . iii 2 64
To wash your liver as clean as a sound sheep's heart . . iii 2 444
They have scared away two of my best sheep . . *W. Tale* iii 3 66
Let my sheep go: come, good boy, the next way home . . iii 3 131
If I make not this cheat bring out another and the shearers prove sheep iv 3 130
By my christendom, So I were out of prison and kept sheep, I should be as merry as the day is long . . . *K. John* iv 1 17
Thee I'll chase hence, thou wolf in sheep's array . . *1 Hen. VI.* i 3 55
Renounce your soil, give sheep in lions' stead . . . i 5 29
Sheep run not half so treacherous from the wolf . . . i 5 30
So worthless peasants bargain for their wives, As market-men for oxen, sheep, or horse . . . v 5 54
Being burnt i' the hand for stealing of sheep . . . *2 Hen. VI.* iv 2 68
They fell before thee like sheep and oxen, and thou behavedst thyself as if thou hadst been in thine own slaughter-house . . iv 3 4
Now, like Ajax Telamonius, On sheep or oxen could I spend my fury . v 1 27
Shepherds looking on their silly sheep . . . *3 Hen. VI.* ii 5 43
So first the harmless sheep doth yield his fleece And next his throat . v 6 8
I had rather be a tick in a sheep than such a valiant ignorance *T. and C.* iii 3 315
And that's as easy As to set dogs on sheep . . *Coriolanus* ii 1 273
With words more sweet, and yet more dangerous, Than baits to fish, or honey-stalks to sheep . . . *T. Andron.* iv 4 91
He would not be a wolf, But that he sees the Romans are but sheep *J. Cæsar* i 3 105
They are sheep and calves which seek out assurance in that . *Hamlet* v 1 125
Thou owest the worm no silk, the beast no hide, the sheep no wool *Lear* iii 4 109
Thy sheep be in the corn; And for one blast of thy minikin mouth, Thy sheep shall take no harm . . . iii 6 44
Sheep-biter. The niggardly rascally sheep-biter . . *T. Night* ii 5 6
Sheep-biting. Show your sheep-biting face, and be hanged! *M. for M.* v 1 359
Sheep-cote. At our sheep-cote now, By reason of his absence, there is nothing That you will feed on . . *As Y. Like It* ii 4 84
A sheep-cote fenced about with olive-trees . . . iv 3 78
Draw our throne into a sheep-cote! . . . *W. Tale* iv 4 808
From low farms, Poor pelting villages, sheep-cotes, and mills . *Lear* ii 3 18
Sheep-hook. Thou a sceptre's heir, That thus affect'st a sheep-hook! *W. Tale* iv 4 431
Sheeps' guts. Is it not strange that sheeps' guts should hale souls out of men's bodies? . . . *Much Ado* ii 3 61
Sheep-shearing. What am I to buy for our sheep-shearing feast? *W. Tale* iv 3 39
I must go buy spices for our sheep-shearing . . . iv 3 125
I'll be with you at your sheep-shearing too . . . iv 3 130
Your sheep-shearing Is as a meeting of the petty gods, And you the queen iv 4 3
Bid us welcome to your sheep-shearing, As your good flock shall prosper iv 4 69
Sheep-skin. Is not parchment made of sheep-skins? . . *Hamlet* v 1 123
Sheep's leather. A head-stall of sheep's leather . . *T. of Shrew* iii 2 58
Sheep-whistling. An old sheep-whistling rogue . . *W. Tale* iv 4 805
Sheer. If she say I am not fourteen pence on the score for sheer ale, score me up for the lyingest knave . . . *T. of Shrew* Ind. 2 25
Thou sheer, immaculate and silver fountain! . . *Richard II.* v 3 61
Sheet. Sit in her smock till she have writ a sheet of paper . *Much Ado* ii 3 138
Now you talk of a sheet of paper, I remember a pretty jest . . ii 3 140
Reading it over, she found Benedick and Beatrice between the sheet . ii 3 144
As much love in rhyme As would be cramm'd up in a sheet of paper *L. L. Lost* v 2 7
And here I'll fling the pillow, there the bolster, This way the coverlet, another way the sheets . . . *T. of Shrew* iv 1 205
As many lies as will lie in thy sheet of paper, although the sheet were big enough for the bed of Ware in England . . *T. Night* iii 2 50
Sully The purity and whiteness of my sheets . . *W. Tale* i 2 327
The white sheet bleaching on the hedge . . . iv 3 5
My traffic is sheets; when the kite builds, look to lesser linen . iv 3 23
I'll canvass thee between a pair of sheets . . . *2 Hen. IV.* ii 4 244
Put thy face between his sheets, and do the office of a warming-pan *Hen. V.* ii 1 88
I saw him fumble with the sheets and play with flowers . . ii 3 15
Throw off this sheet, And go we to attire you for our journey *2 Hen. VI.* ii 4 105
My shame will not be shifted with my sheet . . . ii 4 107
On the sheets his hair, you see, is sticking . . . iii 2 174
Tybalt, liest thou there in thy bloody sheet? . . *Rom. and Jul.* v 3 97
Most wicked speed, to post With such dexterity to incestuous sheets! *Hamlet* 2 157
A pick-axe, and a spade, a spade, For and a shrouding sheet . . v 1 103
Such sheets of fire, such bursts of horrid thunder . . *Lear* iii 2 46
Gloucester's bastard son Was kinder to his father than my daughters Got 'tween the lawful sheets . . . iv 6 118
It is thought abroad, that 'twixt my sheets He has done my office *Othello* i 3 393
Well, happiness to their sheets! . . . ii 3 29
Prithee, to-night Lay on my bed my wedding sheets: remember . iv 2 105
I have laid those sheets you bade me on the bed.—All's one . . iv 3 22
If I do die before thee, prithee, shroud me In one of those same sheets iv 3 25
You think none but your sheets are privy to your wishes *Ant. and Cleo.* i 2 41
When snow the pasture sheets . . . i 4 65
Should he make me Live, like Diana's priest, betwixt cold sheets? *Cymb.* i 6 133
How bravely thou becomest thy bed, fresh lily, And whiter than the sheets! . . . ii 2 16
Sheeted. The graves stood tenantless and the sheeted dead Did squeak and gibber in the Roman streets . . . *Hamlet* i 1 115
Sheffield. Lord Furnival of Sheffield, The thrice-victorious Lord of Falconbridge . . . *1 Hen. VI.* iv 7 66
Shekels. Not with fond shekels of the tested gold . *Meas. for Meas.* ii 2 149
Shelf. That from a shelf the precious diadem stole . . *Hamlet* iii 4 100
Shell. You would eat chickens i' the shell. . . *Troi. and Cres.* i 2 148
Think him as a serpent's egg Which, hatch'd, would, as his kind, grow mischievous, And kill him in the shell . . *J. Cæsar* ii 1 34
This lapwing runs away with the shell on his head . . *Hamlet* v 2 193
Canst tell how an oyster makes his shell? . . . *Lear* i 5 27
Humming water must o'erwhelm thy corpse, Lying with simple shells *Pericles* iii 1 65

Shelter. There is no other shelter hereabout . . . *Tempest* ii 2 40
Trudge, plod away o' the hoof; seek shelter, pack! . . . *Mer. Wives* i 3 91
Under the shelter of your honour! You will not do it, you! . ii 2 29
Let there come a tempest of provocation, I will shelter me here . v 5 24
I will bear thee to some shelter; and thou shalt not die *As Y. Like It* ii 6 17
We hear this fearful tempest sing, Yet seek no shelter . *Richard II.* ii 1 264
The weeds which his broad-spreading leaves did shelter . . iii 4 50
Come, shelter, shelter . . . . *1 Hen. IV.* ii 2 1
Thou shalt prove a shelter to thy friends . . *2 Hen. IV.* iv 4 42
Thus yields the cedar to the axe's edge, Whose arms gave shelter to the princely eagle . . . . *3 Hen. VI.* v 2 12
His feigned ecstasies Shall be no shelter to these outrages *T. Andron.* iv 4 22
The gods to their dear shelter take thee! . . . . *Lear* i 1 185
The shelters whither The routed fly . . . *Ant. and Cleo.* iii 1 8
Upon The leafy shelter that abuts against The island's side . *Pericles* v 1 51
Sheltered. The covert'st shelter'd traitor That ever lived *Richard III.* iii 5 33
Shelves. From shelves and rocks that threaten us with wreck *3 Hen. VI.* v 4 23
About his shelves A beggarly account of empty boxes *Rom. and Jul.* v 1 44
Shelving. And built so shelving that one cannot climb it *T. G. of Ver.* iii 1 115
Shelvy. The shore was shelvy and shallow . . . *Mer. Wives* iii 5 15
Shent. We shall all be shent . . . . i 4 38
I am shent for speaking to you . . . . . *T. Night* iv 2 112
He shent our messengers . . . . . *Troi. and Cres.* ii 3 86
Do you hear how we are shent for keeping your greatness back? *Coriol.* v 2 104
My tongue and soul in this be hypocrites; How in my words soever she be shent, To give them seals never, my soul, consent! *Hamlet* iii 2 416
Shepherd. Indeed, a sheep doth very often stray, An if the shepherd be a while away . . . . *T. G. of Ver.* i 1 75
You conclude that my master is a shepherd then and I a sheep?—I do. i 1 76
This proves me still a sheep.—True; and thy master a shepherd . i 1 83
The shepherd seeks the sheep, and not the sheep the shepherd . i 1 88
The sheep for fodder follow the shepherd; the shepherd for food follows not the sheep: thou for wages followest thy master . . i 1 92
Thou hast entertain'd A fox to be the shepherd of thy lambs . . iv 4 97
Look, the unfolding star calls up the shepherd . *Meas. for Meas.* iv 2 219
When shepherds pipe on oaten straws . . . . *L. L. Lost* v 2 913
And Dick the shepherd blows his nail And Tom bears logs into the hall v 2 923
More tuneable than lark to shepherd's ear . . *M. N. Dream* i 1 184
The skilful shepherd peel'd me certain wands . *Mer. of Venice* i 3 85
Alas, poor shepherd! searching of thy wound, I have by hard adventure found mine own . . . . *As Y. Like It* ii 4 44
Jove, Jove! this shepherd's passion Is much upon my fashion . ii 4 61
I prithee, shepherd, if that love or gold Can . . . buy entertainment . ii 4 71
I am shepherd to another man And do not shear the fleeces that I graze ii 4 78
And how like you this shepherd's life, Master Touchstone?—Truly, shepherd, in respect of itself, it is a good life; but in respect that it is a shepherd's life, it is naught . . . . . . iii 2 11
Hast any philosophy in thee, shepherd? . . . . . . iii 2 23
Wast ever in court, shepherd?—No, truly.—Then thou art damned . iii 2 34
Thou art in a parlous state, shepherd . . . . . . iii 2 45
You kiss your hands: that courtesy would be uncleanly, if courtiers were shepherds . . . . iii 2 52
Mend the instance, shepherd.—You have too courtly a wit for me . iii 2 71
If thou beest not damned for this, the devil himself will have no shepherds . . . . iii 2 89
Shepherd, go off a little . . . . iii 2 167
Come, shepherd, let us make an honourable retreat . . . iii 2 169
You have oft inquired After the shepherd that complain'd of love . iii 4 51
You foolish shepherd, wherefore do you follow her? . . . iii 5 49
So take her to thee, shepherd . . . . iii 5 63
Shepherd, ply her hard . . . . iii 5 77
Dead shepherd, now I find thy saw of might . . . . iii 5 82
Well, shepherd, well, This is a letter of your own device . . iv 3 19
Art thou god to shepherd turn'd, That a maiden's heart hath burn'd? . iv 3 40
Alas, poor shepherd!—Do you pity him? no, he deserves no pity . iv 3 65
Give this napkin Dyed in his blood unto the shepherd youth . iv 3 156
Here live and die a shepherd . . . . v 2 14
You are there followed by a faithful shepherd; Look upon him, love him v 2 87
Good shepherd, tell this youth what 'tis to love . . . . v 2 89
You'll give yourself to this most faithful shepherd?—So is the bargain v 4 14
That you'll marry me, Or else refusing me, to wed this shepherd . v 4 22
I do remember in this shepherd boy Some lively touches of my daughter's favour . . . . v 4 26
Nine changes of the watery star hath been The shepherd's note *W. Tale* i 2 2
A shepherd's daughter, And what to her adheres, which follows after, Is the argument of Time . . . . iv 1 27
He is seldom from the house of a most homely shepherd . . iv 2 43
We will, not appearing what we are, have some question with the shepherd . . . . iv 2 55
Your youth, And the true blood which peepeth fairly through't, Do plainly give you out an unstain'd shepherd . . . . . iv 4 149
Pray, good shepherd, what fair swain is this Which dances with your daughter? . . . . iv 4 166
There is three carters, three shepherds, three neat-herds . . iv 4 332
How now, fair shepherd! Your heart is full of something that does take Your mind from feasting . . . . iv 4 356
About his son, that should have married a shepherd's daughter.—If that shepherd be not in hand-fast, let him fly . . . . iv 4 794
Though my case be a pitiful one, I hope I shall not be flayed out of it.—O, that's the case of the shepherd's son . . . . iv 4 846
Fled from his father, from his hopes, and with A shepherd's daughter . v 1 185
I was by at the opening of the fardel, heard the old shepherd . v 2 4
Methought I heard the shepherd say, he found the child . . v 2 7
Now he thanks the old shepherd, which stands by like a weather-bitten conduit of many kings' reigns . . . . v 2 59
He was torn to pieces with a bear: this avouches the shepherd's son . v 2 69
Wrecked the same instant of their master's death and in the view of the shepherd . . . . v 2 77
He at that time, over-fond of the shepherd's daughter . . . v 2 127
I am by birth a shepherd's daughter, My wit untrain'd *1 Hen. VI.* i 2 72
Not me begotten of a shepherd swain, But issued from the progeny of kings . . . . v 4 37
Till they have snared the shepherd of the flock . . *2 Hen. VI.* ii 2 73
Thus is the shepherd beaten from thy side And wolves are gnarling who shall gnaw thee first . . . . iii 1 191
Growing light, What time the shepherd, blowing of his nails, Can neither call it perfect day nor night . . . *3 Hen. VI.* ii 5 3
Gives not the hawthorn-bush a sweeter shade To shepherds looking on their silly sheep? . . . . ii 5 43
The shepherd's homely curds, His cold thin drink out of his leather bottle ii 5 47
Shepherd. So flies the reckless shepherd from the wolf . *3 Hen. VI.* v 6 7
The shepherd knows not thunder from a tabor More than I know the sound of Marcius' tongue From every meaner man . *Coriolanus* i 6 25
Deserve such pity of him as the wolf Does of the shepherds . . iv 6 111
Like a shepherd, Approach the fold and cull the infected forth *T. of Athens* v 4 42
Crow-flowers, nettles, daisies, and long purples That liberal shepherds give a grosser name . . . . *Hamlet* iv 7 171
Sleepest or wakest thou, jolly shepherd? Thy sheep be in the corn *Lear* iii 6 43
Would I were A neat-herd's daughter, and my Leonatus Our neighbour shepherd's son!—Thou foolish thing! . . . *Cymbeline* i 1 150
Shepherdess. Where dwell you, pretty youth?—With this shepherdess, my sister . . . . *As Y. Like It* iii 2 353
Praising the proud disdainful shepherdess . . . . . iii 4 53
Shepherdess, look on him better, And be not proud . . . iii 5 78
No shepherdess, but Flora Peering in April's front . . *W. Tale* iv 4 2
Shepherdess,—A fair one are you—well you fit our ages With flowers of winter . . . . iv 4 77
Sheriff. He says, he'll stand at your door like a sheriff's post *T. Night* i 5 157
Hath Butler brought those horses from the sheriff? . *1 Hen. IV.* ii 3 70
The sheriff with a most monstrous watch is at the door . . . ii 4 529
I deny your major: if you will deny the sheriff, so . . . ii 4 545
Call in the sheriff. Now, master sheriff, what is your will with me? . ii 4 554
And, sheriff, I will engage my word to thee . . . . ii 4 563
Are by the sheriff of Yorkshire overthrown . . *2 Hen. IV.* iv 4 99
Please your grace, we'll take her from the sheriff.—No, stir not *2 Hen. VI.* ii 4 17
Master sheriff, Let not her penance exceed the king's commission . ii 4 74
Sheriff, farewell, and better than I fare, Although thou hast been conduct of my shame.—It is my office . . . . . . ii 4 100
Sherris. The second property of your excellent sherris is, the warming of the blood; . . . the sherris warms it and makes it course from the inwards to the parts extreme . . . . . . *2 Hen. IV.* iv 3 111
This valour comes of sherris . . . . iv 3 122
Drinking good and good store of fertile sherris . . . . iv 3 131
Sherris-sack. A good sherris-sack hath a two-fold operation in it . iv 3 104
Shield. Heaven shield my mother play'd my father fair! *Meas. for Meas.* iii 1 141
Heaven shield your grace from woe! . . . . v 1 118
Oft in field, with targe and shield, did make my foe to sweat *L. L. Lost* v 2 556
To bring in—God shield us!—a lion among ladies . *M. N. Dream* iii 1 31
Heavens shield Lysander, if they mean a fray! . . . . iii 2 447
Thanks, courteous wall: Jove shield thee well for this! . . . v 1 179
God shield you mean it not! . . . . *All's Well* i 3 174
Sword and shield, In bloody field, Doth win immortal fame *Hen. V.* iii 2 9
Bishop, farewell: shield thee from Warwick's frown . *3 Hen. VI.* iv 5 28
Come, muster men: my counsel is my shield . . *Richard III.* iv 3 56
Whose honour heaven shield from soil! . . . . *Hen. VIII.* i 2 26
Now put your shields before your hearts, and fight With hearts more proof than shields . . . . *Coriolanus* i 4 24
None of you but is Able to bear against the great Aufidius A shield as hard as his . . . . i 6 80
In a violent popular ignorance, given your enemy your shield . . v 2 44
Jove shield your husband from his hounds to-day! . . *T. Andron.* ii 3 70
More scars of sorrow in his heart Than foemen's marks upon his batter'd shield . . . . iv 1 127
God shield I should disturb devotion! . . . . *Rom. and Jul.* iv 1 41
Before my body I throw my warlike shield. Lay on, Macduff *Macbeth* v 8 33
Five days we do allot thee, for provision To shield thee from diseases of the world; And on the sixth to turn thy hated back . . *Lear* i 1 177
Howe'er thou art a fiend, A woman's shape doth shield thee . . iv 2 67
O, he is more mad Than Telamon for his shield . *Ant. and Cleo.* iv 13 2
The seven-fold shield of Ajax cannot keep The battery from my heart iv 14 38
It hath been a shield 'Twixt me and death . . . . *Pericles* ii 1 132
The device he bears upon his shield Is a black Ethiope reaching at the sun . . . . ii 2 19
The device he bears upon his shield Is an arm'd knight that's conquer'd by a lady . . . . ii 2 25
Shielded him From this earth-vexing smart . . . *Cymbeline* v 4 41
Shift. Every man shift for all the rest . . . . . *Tempest* v 1 256
There is no remedy; I must cony-catch; I must shift *Mer. Wives* i 3 37
Thy complexion shifts to strange effects, After the moon *Meas. for Meas.* iii 1 24
I see a man here needs not live by shifts, When in the streets he meets such golden gifts . . . . *Com. of Errors* iii 2 187
Shift and save yourself! . . . . v 1 168
Thou singest well enough for a shift . . . . . *Much Ado* ii 3 80
I hope I shall make shift to go without him . . *Mer. of Venice* i 2 97
The sixth age shifts Into the lean and slipper'd pantaloon *As Y. Like It* ii 7 157
For lovers lacking—God warn us!—matter, the cleanliest shift is to kiss . . . . iv 1 78
An onion will do well for such a shift . . . *T. of Shrew* Ind. 1 126
Am I your bird? I mean to shift my bush . . . . . v 2 46
You have made shift to run into't, boots and spurs and all *All's Well* ii 5 39
If I get down, and do not break my limbs, I'll find a thousand shifts to get away . . . . *K. John* iv 3 7
Let it alone; I'll make other shift . . . . . *2 Hen. IV.* ii 1 169
The rest of thy low countries have made a shift to eat up thy holland ii 2 25
Not to deliberate, not to remember, not to have patience to shift me v 5 23
Unto Southampton do we shift our scene . . . . *Hen. V.* ii Prol. 42
And now there rests no other shift but this . . . *1 Hen. VI.* ii 1 75
For me, I will make shift for one . . . . . *2 Hen. VI.* iv 8 33
When he was made a shriver, 'twas for shift . . . *3 Hen. VI.* iii 2 108
Cursed be that heart that forced us to this shift! . *T. Andron.* iv 1 72
I'll bear you hence; For it is you that puts us to our shifts . iv 2 176
Where's Potpan, that he helps not to take away? He shift a trencher? he scrape a trencher! . . . . *Rom. and Jul.* i 5 2
When Fortune in her shift and change of mood . *T. of Athens* i 1 84
He took up my legs sometime, yet I made a shift to cast him *Macbeth* ii 3 46
Let us not be dainty of leave-taking, But shift away . . . ii 3 151
Hic et ubique? then we'll shift our ground . . . . *Hamlet* i 5 156
Taught me to shift Into a madman's rags . . . . . *Lear* v 3 186
Dodge And palter in the shifts of lowness . . *Ant. and Cleo.* iii 11 63
O, behold, How pomp is follow'd! mine will now be yours; And, should we shift estates, yours would be mine . . . . . . v 2 152
Sir, I would advise you to shift a shirt . . . . *Cymbeline* i 2 1
If my shirt were bloody, then to shift it . . . . . i 2 6
Return he cannot, nor Continue where he is: to shift his being Is to exchange one misery with another . . . . i 5 54
Shifted. Thou hast shifted out of thy tale into telling me of the fashion *Much Ado* iii 3 151
And, like a shifted wind unto a sail, It makes the course of thoughts to fetch about . . . . *K. John* iv 2 23

Shifted. My shame will not be shifted with my sheet . . 2 *Hen. VI.* ii 4 107
I shifted him away, And laid good 'scuse upon your ecstasy *Othello* iv 1 79
Shifting. Thou runn'st before me, shifting every place *M. N. Dream* iii 2 423
Shilling. That cost me two shilling and two pence a-piece *Mer. Wives* i 1 160
I had rather than forty shillings I had my Book of Songs and Sonnets . i 1 205
Five shillings to one on 't . . . . *Much Ado* iii 3 84
I had rather than forty shillings I had such a leg . . . *T. Night* ii 3 20
Every tod yields pound and odd shilling . . . . *W. Tale* iv 3 34
Who, I rob? I a thief? not I, by my faith.— . . . Thou camest not of the blood royal, if thou darest not stand for ten shillings . 1 *Hen. IV.* i 2 158
Never spake other English in his life than 'Eight shillings and sixpence' ii 4 27
Holland of eight shillings an ell . . . . iii 3 83
Didst thou not kiss me and bid me fetch thee thirty shillings? 2 *Hen. IV.* ii 1 111
Quoit him down, Bardolph, like a shove-groat shilling . . . ii 4 207
Here's four Harry ten shillings in French crowns for you . . iii 2 236
You'll pay me the eight shillings I won of you at betting? . *Hen. V.* ii 1 98
One shilling to the pound, the last subsidy . . 2 *Hen. VI.* iv 7 25
May see away their shilling Richly in two short hours . *Hen. VIII.* Prol. 12
Shin. Pricking goss and thorns, Which enter'd their frail shins *Tempest* iv 1 181
I bruised my shin th' other day with playing at sword and dagger *M. W.* i 1 294
Pinch them, arms, legs, backs, shoulders, sides, and shins . . v 5 58
A wonder, master! here's a costard broken in a shin . *L. L. Lost* iii 1 71
How did this argument begin?—By saying that a costard was broken in a shin . . . . iii 1 107
How was there a costard broken in a shin?—I will tell you sensibly . iii 1 113
Fell over the threshold, and broke my shin . . . . . iii 1 118
We will talk no more of this matter.—Till there be more matter in the shin . . . . iii 1 120
Thou speakest wiser than thou art ware of.—Nay, I shall ne'er be ware of mine own wit till I break my shins against it . *As Y. Like It* ii 4 60
Your plaintain-leaf is excellent for that.—For what, I pray thee?—For your broken shin . . . . . . *Rom. and Jul.* i 2 53
Strike their sharp shins, And mar men's spurring . . *T. of Athens* iv 3 152
Shine. These follies are within you and shine through you *T. G. of Ver.* ii 1 40
Wilt thou reach stars, because they shine on thee? . . . iii 1 156
Then did the sun on dunghill shine . . . . *Mer. Wives* i 3 70
When the sun shines let foolish gnats make sport . *Com. of Errors* ii 2 30
Nor shines the silver moon one half so bright . . *L. L. Lost* iv 3 30
Then thou, fair sun, which on my earth dost shine, Exhalest this vapour-vow . . . . iv 3 69
As fair as day.—Ay, as some days; but then no sun must shine . . iv 3 91
O, 'tis the sun that maketh all things shine . . . . iv 3 246
Vouchsafe, bright moon, and these thy stars, to shine . . . v 2 205
And Phibbus' car Shall shine from far . . . *M. N. Dream* i 2 38
Doth the moon shine that night we play our play? . . . iii 1 52
Find out moonshine, find out moonshine.—Yes, it doth shine that night iii 1 56
The moon may shine in at the casement . . . . . iii 1 59
Let her shine as gloriously As the Venus of the sky . . . iii 2 106
Yonder shines Aurora's harbinger . . . . iii 2 380
Shine comforts from the east, That I may back to Athens by daylight . iii 2 432
Truly, the moon shines with a good grace . . . . . v 1 273
The moon shines bright: in such a night as this . *Mer. of Venice* v 1 1
So shines a good deed in a naughty world . . . . . v 1 91
A substitute shines brightly as a king Until a king be by . . v 1 94
How bright and goodly shines the moon!—The moon! the sun: it is not moonlight now.—I say it is the moon that shines so bright.—I know it is the sun that shines so bright . . *T. of Shrew* iv 5 2
My stars shine darkly over me . . . . . . *T. Night* ii 1 3
Foolery, sir, does walk about the orb like the sun, it shines every where iii 1 44
Heavens so shine, That they may fairly note this act of mine! . iv 3 34
The pale moon shines by night . . . . . . *W. Tale* iv 3 16
The selfsame sun that shines upon his court Hides not his visage from our cottage . . . . iv 4 455
That sun that warms you here shall shine on me . *Richard II.* i 3 145
He made me mad To see him shine so brisk and smell so sweet 1 *Hen. IV.* i 3 54
The moon shines fair; you may away by night . . . . iii 1 142
Such as is bent on sun-like majesty When it shines seldom in admiring eyes iii 2 80
He hath the horn of abundance, and the lightness of his wife shines through it: and yet cannot he see . . . 2 *Hen. IV.* i 2 53
Let desert mount.—Thine's too heavy to mount.—Let it shine, then.—Thine's too thick to shine . . . . iv 3 63
The sun and not the moon; for it shines bright and never changes *Hen. V.* v 2 172
Late did he shine upon the English side; Now we are victors 1 *Hen. VI.* i 2 3
Our Lady gracious hath it pleased To shine on my contemptible estate i 2 75
Now shine it like a comet of revenge! . . . . . . iii 2 31
Whose hopeful colours Advance our half-faced sun, striving to shine 2 *Hen. VI.* iv 1 98
And who shines now but Henry's enemies? . 3 *Hen. VI.* ii 6 10
The sun shines hot; and, if we use delay, Cold biting winter mars our hoped-for hay . . . . iv 8 60
Shine out, fair sun, till I have bought a glass, That I may see my shadow as I pass . . . . *Richard III.* i 2 263
Who saw the sun to-day?—Not I, my lord.—Then he disdains to shine v 3 278
Not shine to-day! Why, what is that to me More than to Richmond? v 3 285
This heaven of beauty Shall shine at full upon them . *Hen. VIII.* i 4 60
Wherever the bright sun of heaven shall shine . . . . v 5 51
Let desert in pure election shine . . . . *T. Andron.* i 1 16
I will be bright, and shine in pearl and gold . . . . ii 1 19
Here never shines the sun; here nothing breeds, Unless the nightly owl ii 3 96
Which, like a taper in some monument, Doth shine . . . ii 3 229
So pale did shine the moon on Pyramus . . . . . ii 3 231
I wonder on't; he was wont to shine at seven . *T. of Athens* iii 4 10
If, after two days' shine, Athens contain thee . . . . iii 5 101
Whereon Hyperion's quickening fire doth shine . . . . iv 3 184
The skies are painted with unnumber'd sparks, They are all fire and every one doth shine . . . . *J. Cæsar* iii 1 64
Signs of nobleness, like stars, shall shine On all deservers . *Macbeth* i 4 41
If there come truth from them—As upon thee, Macbeth, their speeches shine . . . . iii 1 7
Your spirits shine through you . . . . iii 1 128
For a quality Wherein, they say, you shine . . . *Hamlet* iv 7 74
Though it be night, yet the moon shines . . . . *Lear* ii 2 34
Our Italy Shines o'er with civil swords . . . *Ant. and Cleo.* i 3 45
He would shine on those That make their looks by his . . . i 5 55
Thy lustre thickens, When he shines by . . . . . . ii 3 28
She shines not upon fools, lest the reflection should hurt her. *Cymbeline* i 2 34
Hath Britain all the sun that shines? . . . . . . iii 4 139
By this sun that shines, I'll thither . . . . . . iv 4 34
The radiant Cymbeline, Which shines here in the west . . . v 5 476
Thou show'dst a subject's shine, I a true prince . . . *Pericles* i 2 124
Shinest. Thou shinest in every tear that I do weep . . *L. L. Lost* iv 3 33
Shineth. A brittle glory shineth in this face . . *Richard II.* iv 1 287
Shining. Have no more profit of their shining nights Than those that walk and wot not what they are . . . . . *L. L. Lost* i 1 90
I thank thee, Moon, for shining now so bright . . *M. N. Dream* v 1 278
With his satchel And shining morning face . . . *As Y. Like It* ii 7 146
So well apparell'd, So clear, so shining and so evident That it will glimmer through a blind man's eye . . . . . . 1 *Hen. VI.* ii 4 23
As the snake roll'd in a flowering bank, With shining checker'd slough, doth sting a child . . . . 2 *Hen. VI.* iii 1 229
All of us have cause To wail the dimming of our shining star *Richard III.* ii 2 102
As when his virtues shining upon others Heat them and they retort that heat again To the first giver . . . . . *Troi. and Cres.* iii 3 100
Some other maid That I will show you shining at this feast *Rom. and Jul.* i 2 103
We poor ghosts will cry To the shining synod of the rest . *Cymbeline* v 4 89
Shiny. The night Is shiny; and they say we shall embattle By the second hour i' the morn . . . . *Ant. and Cleo.* iv 9 3
Ship. Though the ship were no stronger than a nutshell . . *Tempest* i 1 50
I would Have sunk the sea within the earth or ere It should the good ship so have swallow'd and The fraughting souls within her . . i 2 12
I boarded the king's ship; now on the beak, Now in the waist . . i 2 196
Of the king's ship The mariners say how thou hast disposed . . i 2 224
Safely in harbour Is the king's ship; in the deep nook . . i 2 227
They saw the king's ship wreck'd And his great person perish . i 2 236
To the king's ship, invisible as thou art . . . . . v 1 97
Our ship—Which, but three glasses since, we gave out split—Is tight and yare . . . . v 1 222
Where we, in all her trim, freshly beheld Our royal, good and gallant ship . . . . v 1 237
In the morn I'll bring you to your ship and so to Naples . . v 1 307
Go, go, be gone, to save your ship from wreck . *T. G. of Ver.* i 1 156
What news with your mastership?—With my master's ship? . . iii 1 281
And left the ship, then sinking-ripe, to us . . *Com. of Errors* i 1 78
We discovered Two ships from far making amain to us . . . i 1 93
For, ere the ships could meet by twice five leagues, We were encounter'd by a mighty rock . . . . i 1 101
Our helpful ship was splitted in the midst . . . . . i 1 104
At length, another ship had seized on us . . . . . . i 1 113
If any ship put out, then straight away . . . . . iii 2 190
The ship is in her trim; the merry wind Blows fair from land . iv 1 90
What ship of Epidamnum stays for me?—A ship you sent me to . iv 1 94
Is there any ship puts forth to-night? may we be gone? . . . iv 3 35
Two hot sheeps, marry.—And wherefore not ships? . *L. L. Lost* ii 1 219
The ship is under sail, and here she comes amain . . . . v 2 549
But ships are but boards, sailors but men . . *Mer. of Venice* i 3 22
There can be no dismay; My ships come home a month before the day i 3 182
In their ship I am sure Lorenzo is not . . . . . . ii 8 3
Raised the duke, Who went with him to search Bassanio's ship.—He came too late, the ship was under sail . . . . ii 8 5
Antonio certified the duke They were not with Bassanio in his ship . ii 8 11
Antonio hath a ship of rich lading wrecked on the narrow seas . . iii 1 3
Where the carcases of many a tall ship lie buried . . . . iii 1 6
Ha! what sayest thou? Why, the end is, he hath lost a ship . . iii 1 19
My ships have all miscarried, my creditors grow cruel . . . iii 2 317
Here I read for certain that my ships Are safely come to road . v 1 287
Your ships are stay'd at Venice . . . . . . *T. of Shrew* iv 2 83
After our ship did split, . . . I saw your brother . . *T. Night* i 2 9
My ships are ready and My people did expect my hence departure *W. Tale* i 2 449
I eyed them Even to their ships . . . . ii 1 36
Thou art perfect then, our ship hath touch'd upon The deserts of Bohemia? . . . . iii 3 1
Now the ship boring the moon with her main-mast, and anon swallowed iii 3 93
But to make an end of the ship, to see how the sea flap-dragoned it . iii 3 99
I would you had been by the ship side, to have helped her . . iii 3 112
He is gone aboard a new ship to purge melancholy and air himself . iv 4 790
Eight tall ships, three thousand men of war . . . *Richard II.* ii 1 286
This grace of kings must die . . . Ere he take ship for France *Hen. V.* ii Prol. 30
Now am I like that proud insulting ship Which Cæsar and his fortune bare at once . . . . 1 *Hen. VI.* i 2 138
Your ships already are in readiness . . . . . . iii 1 186
I expect my soldiers; For there I'll ship them all for Ireland 2 *Hen. VI.* iii 1 329
Like to a ship that, having 'scaped a tempest, Is straightway calm'd . iv 9 32
Turn back and fly, like ships before the wind . . . 3 *Hen. VI.* i 4 4
To Lynn, my lord, And ship from thence to Flanders . . . iv 5 21
Whiles, in his moan, the ship splits on the rock, Which industry and courage might have saved . . . . v 4 10
Safe-conducting the rebels from their ships . . . *Richard III.* iv 4 483
Ships, Fraught with the ministers and instruments Of cruel war *T. and C.* Prol. 3
She is a pearl, Whose price hath launch'd above a thousand ships . . ii 2 82
The sun no sooner shall the mountains touch, But we will ship him hence . . . . *Hamlet* iv 1 30
In the grapple I boarded them: on the instant they got clear of our ship iv 6 19
A noble ship of Venice Hath seen a grievous wreck and sufferance On most part of their fleet . . . . *Othello* ii 1 22
The ship is here put in, A Veronesa . . . . . . ii 1 25
That he may bless this bay with his tall ship . . . . ii 1 79
O, behold, The riches of the ship is come on shore! . . . ii 1 83
Your ships are not well mann'd; Your mariners are muleters *A. and C.* iii 7 35
Their ships are yare; yours, heavy: no disgrace Shall fall you for refusing him at sea, Being prepared for land . . . . . iii 7 39
We'll to our ship: Away, my Thetis! . . . . . . iii 7 60
From which place We may the number of the ships behold . . iii 9 3
I have a ship Laden with gold; take that, divide it; fly . . iii 11 4
To the sea-side straightway: I will possess you of that ship and treasure iii 11 21
His coin, ships, legions, May be a coward's . . . . iii 13 22
And o'er green Neptune's back With ships made cities . . . iv 14 59
How slow his soul sail'd on, How swift his ship . . *Cymbeline* i 3 14
Attending You here at Milford-Haven with your ships . . . iv 2 335
Upon our neighbouring shore, A portly sale of ships make hitherward *Per.* i 4 61
Let not our ships and number of our men Be like a beacon fired to amaze your eyes . . . . i 4 86
Our ships, you happily may think Are like the Trojan horse was stuff'd within With bloody veins . . . . i 4 92
And harbourage for ourself, our ships, and men . . . . i 4 100
Thunder above and deeps below Make such unquiet, that the ship Should house him safe is wreck'd and split . . . . . ii Gower 31
Was by the rough seas reft of ships and men . . . . . ii 3 84
By misfortune of the seas Bereft of ships and men, cast on this shore . ii 3 89
As a duck for life that dives, So up and down the poor ship drives iii Gower 50
In your imagination hold This stage the ship . . . . iii Gower 59

Ship. The sea works high, the wind is loud, and will not lie till the ship be cleared of the dead . *Pericles* iii 1 49
Well-sailing ships and bounteous winds have brought This king to Tarsus iv 4 17
Our Tyrian ship espies, His banners sable, trimm'd with rich expense v Gower 18
Shipboard. Shall I fetch your stuff from shipboard? *Com. of Errors* v 1 408
To shipboard Get undescried . . . . *W. Tale* iv 4 668
Ship-boy. This ship-boy's semblance hath disguised me quite . *K. John* iv 3 4
Upon the high and giddy mast Seal up the ship-boy's eyes 2 *Hen. IV.* iii 1 19
Behold Upon the hempen tackle ship-boys climbing *Hen. V.* iii Prol. 8
Shipman. The dreadful spout Which shipmen do the hurricano call *Troi. and Cres.* v 2 172
And the very ports they blow, All the quarters that they know I' the shipman's card . . . . *Macbeth* i 3 17
The shipman's toil, With whom each minute threatens life or death *Per.* i 3 24
Shipped. Once more adieu! my father at the road Expects my coming, there to see me shipp'd . . . . . . *T. G. of Ver.* i 1 54
He is shipp'd already, And I have play'd the sheep in losing him . i 1 72
Thy master is shipped and thou art to post after with oars ii 3 37
I hope the king is not yet shipp'd for Ireland . *Richard II.* ii 2 42
Would thou wert shipp'd to hell! . . . . *T. Andron.* i 1 206
This wicked emperor may have shipp'd her hence iv 3 23
And hath shipped me intil the land, As if I had never been such *Hamlet* v 1 81
Is he well shipp'd?—His bark is stoutly timber'd *Othello* ii 1 47
That I was shipp'd at sea, I well remember, Even on my eaning time *Per.* iii 4 5
Shipping. I have seen them in the church together: God send 'em good shipping! . . . . *T. of Shrew* v 1 43
Take, therefore, shipping; post, my lord, to France . 1 *Hen. VI.* v 5 87
Then does he say, he lent me Some shipping unrestored . *Ant. and Cleo.* iii 6 27
Our overplus of shipping will we burn; And, with the rest full-mann'd iii 7 51
His shipping—Poor ignorant baubles!—on our terrible seas, Like egg-shells moved upon their surges, crack'd As easily . *Cymbeline* iii 1 26
O'erlook What shipping and what lading's in our haven . *Pericles* i 2 49
Ship-tire. Thou hast the right arched beauty of the brow that becomes the ship-tire . . . . *Mer. Wives* iii 3 60
Shipwreck. So am I driven by breath of her renown Either to suffer shipwreck or arrive Where I may have fruition of her love 1 *Hen. VI.* v 5 8
This siren, that will charm Rome's Saturnine, And see his shipwreck and his commonweal's . . . . . . *T. Andron.* ii 1 24
My shipwreck now's no ill, Since I have here my father's gift *Pericles* ii 1 139
Reft of ships and men, And after shipwreck driven upon this shore ii 3 85
Shipwreck'd upon a kingdom, where no pity, No friends . *Hen. VIII.* iii 1 149
Gave healthful welcome to their shipwreck'd guests *Com. of Errors* i 1 115
Shipwrecking. As whence the sun 'gins his reflection Shipwrecking storms and direful thunders break . . . *Macbeth* i 2 26
Shipwright. Why such impress of shipwrights, whose sore task Does not divide the Sunday from the week? *Hamlet* i 1 75
What is he that builds stronger than either the mason, the shipwright, or the carpenter?—The gallows-maker . . . v 1 47
Who builds stronger than a mason, a shipwright, or a carpenter? . v 1 58
Shire. Let there be letters writ to every shire . . *Hen. VIII.* i 2 103
Shirley. The spirits Of valiant Shirley, Stafford, Blunt, are in my arms: It is the Prince of Wales that threatens thee . . . 1 *Hen. IV.* v 4 41
Shirt. Rammed me in with foul shirts and smocks *Mer. Wives* iii 5 91
I'll do it in my shirt.—Most resolute Pompey! . *L. L. Lost* v 2 704
Gentlemen and soldiers, pardon me; I will not combat in my shirt v 2 711
The naked truth of it is, I have no shirt . . v 2 717
I bought you a dozen of shirts to your back . . 1 *Hen. IV.* iii 3 77
There's but a shirt and a half in all my company; and the half shirt is two napkins tacked together . . . ; and the shirt, to say the truth, stolen from my host at Saint Alban's . . . . iv 2 47
I take but two shirts out with me, and I mean not to sweat extraordinarily 2 *Hen. IV.* i 2 234
The inventory of thy shirts, as, one for superfluity, and another for use ii 2 20
Go in their hose and doublets.—And work in their shirt too 2 *Hen. VI.* iv 7 57
A sail, a sail!—Two, two; a shirt and a smock . *Rom. and Jul.* ii 4 109
What, think'st That the bleak air, thy boisterous chamberlain, Will put thy shirt on warm? . . . . . . *T. of Athens* iv 3 223
Pale as his shirt; his knees knocking each other . *Hamlet* ii 1 81
Who hath had three suits to his back, six shirts to his body . *Lear* iii 4 142
Here's one comes in his shirt, with light and weapons . *Othello* v 1 47
My leg is cut in two.—Marry, heaven forbid! Light, gentlemen: I'll bind it with my shirt . . . . v 1 73
The shirt of Nessus is upon me . . . . . *Ant. and Cleo.* iv 12 43
Sir, I would advise you to shift a shirt . . *Cymbeline* i 2 2
If my shirt were bloody, then to shift it . . . i 2 6
Shive. Easy it is Of a cut loaf to steal a shive, we know . *T. Andron.* ii 1 87
Shiver and look pale, Make periods in the midst of sentences *M. N. Dream* v 1 95
There it is, crack'd in a hundred shivers . . *Richard II.* iv 1 289
He would pun thee into shivers with his fist . . *Troi. and Cres.* ii 1 42
Shivered. Thou'dst shiver'd like an egg . . . *Lear* iv 6 51
Shivering. The raging rocks And shivering shocks . *M. N. Dream* i 2 34
The north, Where shivering cold and sickness pines the clime *Rich. II.* v 1 77
Shoal. And sounded all the depths and shoals of honour . *Hen. VIII.* iii 2 436
Here, upon this bank and shoal of time . . . *Macbeth* i 7 6
Shock. The raging rocks And shivering shocks . . *M. N. Dream* i 2 34
Come the three corners of the world in arms, And we shall shock them *K. John* v 7 117
Grating shock of wrathful iron arms . . . . *Richard II.* i 3 136
The elements Of fire and water, when their thundering shock At meeting tears the cloudy cheeks of heaven . . . . i 3 56
In the intestine shock And furious close of civil butchery . 1 *Hen. IV.* i 1 12
Without stratagem, But in plain shock and even play of battle *Hen. V.* iv 8 114
And aid thee in this doubtful shock of arms . . *Richard III.* v 3 93
The thousand natural shocks That flesh is heir to . . *Hamlet* iii 1 62
Shoe. How does thy honour? Let me lick thy shoe . . *Tempest* iii 2 26
He was more than over shoes in love . . . *T. G. of Ver.* i 1 24
You are in love; for last morning you could not see to wipe my shoes ii 1 86
This shoe is my father: no, this left shoe is my father: no, no, this left shoe is my mother: nay, that cannot be so neither . . ii 3 16
This shoe, with the hole in it, is my mother, and this my father . ii 3 19
Now should not the shoe speak a word for weeping . . ii 3 27
Swart, like my shoe, but her face nothing like so clean kept *Com. of Er.* iii 2 104
A man may go over shoes in the grime of it . . . iii 2 106
I do affect the very ground, which is base, where her shoe, which is baser, guided by her foot, which is basest, doth tread . *L. L. Lost* i 2 173
Being o'er shoes in blood, plunge in the deep, And kill me too *M. N. D.* iii 2 48
He can shoe him himself . . . . . . *Mer. of Venice* i 2 47
Your sleeve unbuttoned, your shoe untied . . . *As Y. Like It* iii 2 399
No more shoes than feet; nay, sometime more feet than shoes, or such shoes as my toes look through the over-leather . *T. of Shrew* Ind. 2 10

Shoe. Creaking my shoes on the plain masonry . . *All's Well* ii 1 31
The whoreson smooth-pates do now wear nothing but high shoes 2 *Hen. IV.* i 2 44
I kiss his dirty shoe, and from heart-string I love the lovely bully *Hen. V.* iv 1 47
His reputation is as arrant a villain and a Jacksauce, as ever his black shoe trod upon God's ground . . . . . . iv 7 149
It will serve you to mend your shoes: come, wherefore should you be so pashful? your shoes is not so good . . . . iv 8 74
One that never in his life Felt so much cold as over shoes in snow *Richard III.* v 3 326
Feebling such as stand not in their liking Below their cobbled shoes *Coriolanus* i 1 200
You have dancing shoes With nimble soles: I have a soul of lead *R. and J.* i 4 14
Didst thou not fall out with a tailor for wearing his new doublet before Easter? with another, for tying his new shoes with old riband? . iii 1 31
I am, indeed, sir, a surgeon to old shoes . . . *J. Cæsar* i 1 27
Why dost thou lead these men about the streets?—Truly, sir, to wear out their shoes, to get myself into more work . . . . i 1 33
A little month, or ere those shoes were old . . . *Hamlet* i 2 147
On fortune's cap we are not the very button.—Nor the soles of her shoe? . . . . ii 2 234
With two Provincial roses on my razed shoes . . . iii 2 288
Let not the creaking of shoes nor the rustling of silks betray thy poor heart to woman . . . . *Lear* iii 4 98
It were a delicate stratagem, to shoe A troop of horse with felt iv 6 188
Shoeing. The smith's note for shoeing and plough-irons . 2 *Hen. IV.* v 1 20
Shoeing-horn. A thrifty shoeing-horn in a chain . *Troi. and Cres.* v 1 61
Shoemaker. The shoemaker should meddle with his yard *Rom. and Jul.* i 2 39
Shoe-tie. Tape, glove, shoe-tie, bracelet, horn-ring . . *W. Tale* iv 4 611
Shog. Will you shog off? I would have you solus . . *Hen. V.* ii 1 47
Shall we shog? the king will be gone from Southampton . ii 3 47
Shone. Well shone, Moon. Truly, the moon shines with a good grace *M. N. Dream* v 1 272
When the moon shone, we did not see the candle . *Mer. of Venice* v 1 92
His princess, say you, with him?—Ay, the most peerless piece of earth, I think, That e'er the sun shone bright on . . *W. Tale* v 1 95
All in gold, like heathen gods, Shone down the English . *Hen. VIII.* i 1 20
Now, by the burning tapers of the sky, That shone so brightly when this boy was got, He dies . . . . . *T. Andron.* iv 2 90
Shook. What said the wench when he rose again?—Trembled and shook *T. of Shrew* iii 2 169
Hadst thou but shook thy head or made a pause When I spake darkly what I purposed . . . . *K. John* iv 2 231
Alack, why am I sent for to a king, Before I have shook off the regal thoughts Wherewith I reign'd? . . . . *Richard II.* iv 1 163
But dust was thrown upon his sacred head; Which with such gentle sorrow he shook off, His face still combating with tears and smiles v 2 31
You are fool'd, discarded and shook off By him . . 1 *Hen. IV.* i 3 178
I say the earth was not of my mind, If you suppose as fearing you it shook . . . . iii 1 23
The earth shook to see the heavens on fire, And not in fear of your nativity . . . . iii 1 25
Our grandam earth, having this distemperature, In passion shook . iii 1 35
That England, being empty of defence, Hath shook and trembled *Hen. V.* i 2 154
Yesterday your mistress shrewdly shook your back.—So perhaps did yours . . . . iii 7 52
Like a new-married wife about her husband's neck, hardly to be shook off v 2 191
And thought thee happy when I shook my head . 2 *Hen. VI.* iv 1 55
Dogs howl'd, and hideous tempest shook down trees . 3 *Hen. VI.* v 6 46
When black-faced Clifford shook his sword at him . *Richard III.* i 2 159
This respite shook The bosom of my conscience . . *Hen. VIII.* ii 4 181
Like a dew-drop from the lion's mane, Be shook to air . *Troi. and Cres.* iii 3 225
When, for some trifling present, you have bid me Return so much, I have shook my head and wept . . . *T. of Athens* ii 2 146
Those that understood him smiled at one another and shook their heads *J. Cæsar* i 2 286
That we can let our beard be shook with danger And think it pastime *Hamlet* iv 7 32
She shook The holy water from her heavenly eyes . . . *Lear* iv 3 31
A fuller blast ne'er shook our battlements . . . *Othello* ii 1 6
His conquering banner shook from Syria To Lydia . *Ant. and Cleo.* i 2 106
The round world Should have shook lions into civil streets . v 1 16
A storm or robbery, call it what you will, Shook down my mellow hangings, nay, my leaves, And left me bare . . *Cymbeline* iii 3 63
Our lodgings, standing bleak upon the sea, Shook as the earth did quake *Pericles* iii 2 15
Shook hands. They shook hands and swore brothers . *As Y. Like It* v 4 107
Though absent, shook hands, as over a vast . . . *W. Tale* i 1 32
As I bethink me, you should not be king Till our King Henry had shook hands with death . . . . . . 3 *Hen. VI.* i 4 102
Which ne'er shook hands, nor bade farewell to him, Till he unseam'd him from the nave to the chaps . . . . . *Macbeth* i 2 21
Shoon. Spare none but such as go in clouted shoon . 2 *Hen. VI.* iv 2 195
By his cockle hat and staff, And his sandal shoon . . . *Hamlet* iv 5 26
Shoot. Swears he will shoot no more but play with sparrows *Tempest* iv 1 100
This boy will carry a letter twenty mile, as easy as a cannon will shoot point-blank twelve score . . . . . *Mer. Wives* iii 2 34
If I do, hang me in a bottle like a cat and shoot at me . . *Much Ado* i 1 260
Thrice cut Cupid's bow-string and the little hangman dare not shoot at him . . . . iii 2 12
Sweet smoke of rhetoric! He reputes me a cannon; and the bullet, that's he: I shoot thee at the swain . . *L. L. Lost* iii 1 66
A stand where you may make the fairest shoot.—I thank my beauty, I am fair that shoot, And thereupon thou speak'st the fairest shoot . iv 1 10
Thus will I save my credit in the shoot . . . iv 1 26
Indeed, a' must shoot nearer, or he'll ne'er hit the clout . iv 1 136
If you please To shoot another arrow that self way Which you did shoot the first . . . . . . *Mer. of Venice* i 1 148
Under the presentation of that he shoots his wit . . *As Y. Like It* v 4 112
Whoever shoots at him, I set him there . . . *All's Well* iii 2 115
My revenges were high bent upon him, And watch'd the time to shoot v 3 11
Thou want'st a rough pash and the shoots that I have . *W. Tale* i 2 128
They shoot but calm words folded up in smoke . . *K. John* ii 1 229
From north to south: Austria and France shoot in each other's mouth ii 1 414
Who's there? speak, ho! speak quickly, or I shoot . . v 6 1
A' drew a good bow; and dead! a' shot a fine shoot . 2 *Hen. IV.* iii 2 49
Ready they were to shoot me to the heart . . . 1 *Hen. VI.* i 4 56
O, were mine eye-balls into bullets turn'd, That I in rage might shoot them at your faces! . . . . iv 7 80
O that I were a god, to shoot forth thunder! . . . 2 *Hen. VI.* iv 1 104

Shoot. I'll stay above the hill, so both may shoot . *3 Hen. VI.* iii 1 5
The noise of thy cross-bow Will scare the herd, and so my shoot is lost iii 1 7
For, O, love's bow Shoots buck and doe . *Troi. and Cres.* iii 1 127
You were as good to shoot against the wind . *T. Andron.* iv 3 57
Kinsmen, shoot all your shafts into the court . iv 3 61
What a mental power This eye shoots forth! . *T. of Athens* i 1 32
Go, bid the soldiers shoot . *Hamlet* v 2 414
I do not call it: I do not bid the thunder-bearer shoot . *Lear* ii 4 230
'Tis one of those odd tricks which sorrow shoots Out of the mind *Ant. and Cleo.* iv 2 14
Shooter. I am the shooter.—And who is your deer? *L. L. Lost* iv 1 116
Shooting. I stood like a man at a mark, with a whole army shooting at me . *Much Ado* ii 1 254
Now mercy goes to kill, And shooting well is then accounted ill *L. L. L.* iv 1 25
Some say a sore; but not a sore, till now made sore with shooting iv 2 59
I see thy glory like a shooting star Fall to the base earth *Richard II.* ii 4 19
Shooty. Brave Master Shooty the great traveller *Meas. for Meas.* iv 3 18
Shop. Stand like the forfeits in a barber's shop, As much in mock as mark . v 1 323
Say that I linger'd with you at your shop *Com. of Errors* iii 1 3
You shall buy this sport as dear As all the metal in your shop . iv 1 82
Even now a tailor call'd me in his shop And show'd me silks iv 3 7
With your hat penthouse-like o'er the shop of your eyes *L. L. Lost* iii 1 18
Cut and slish and slash, Like to a censer in a barber's shop *T. of Shrew* iv 3 91
Every shop, church, session, hanging, yields a careful man work *W. T.* iv 4 700
And we for fear compell'd to shut our shops . *1 Hen. VI.* iii 1 85
I am the storehouse and the shop Of the whole body . *Coriolanus* i 1 137
Our tradesmen singing in their shops and going About their functions . iv 6 8
In his needy shop a tortoise hung, An alligator stuff'd *Rom. and Jul.* v 1 42
Being holiday, the beggar's shop is shut. What, ho! apothecary! . v 1 56
Break open shops; nothing can you steal, But thieves do lose it *T. of A.* iv 3 450
Wherefore art not in thy shop to-day? . *J. Cæsar* i 1 31
A shop of all the qualities that man Loves woman for . *Cymbeline* v 5 166
Shore. Fortune . . . hath mine enemies Brought to this shore *Tempest* i 2 180
But was not this nigh shore?—Close by . i 2 216
And oar'd Himself with his good arms in lusty stroke To the shore ii 1 120
I swam, ere I could recover the shore, five and thirty leagues off and on iii 2 16
The powers, delaying, not forgetting, have Incensed the seas and shores iii 3 74
The approaching tide Will shortly fill the reasonable shore v 1 81
Who three hours since Were wreck'd upon this shore . v 1 137
Who most strangely Upon this shore, where you were wreck'd, was landed . v 1 161
Now, blasphemy, That swear'st grace o'erboard, not an oath on shore? v 1 219
Being destined to a drier death on shore . *T. G. of Ver.* i 1 158
Sail like my pinnace to these golden shores *Mer. Wives* i 3 89
I had been drowned, but that the shore was shelvy and shallow iii 5 15
To the extremest shore of my modesty *Meas. for Meas.* iii 2 266
Post to the road: An if the wind blow any way from shore, I will not harbour in this town to-night *Com. of Errors* iii 2 153
One foot in sea and one on shore, To one thing constant never *Much Ado* ii 3 66
Since you have shore With shears his thread of silk *M. N. Dream* v 1 347
Ornament is but the guiled shore To a most dangerous sea *Mer. of Venice* iii 2 97
The captain that did bring me first on shore Hath my maid's garments *T. Night* v 1 281
How it rages, how it takes up the shore! *W. Tale* iii 3 90
I am put to sea With her whom here I cannot hold on shore . iv 4 510
To unpath'd waters, undream'd shores iv 4 578
I will bring these . . . aboard him: if he think it fit to shore them again iv 4 869
My best train I have from your Sicilian shores dismiss'd v 1 164
Large lengths of seas and shores Between my father and my mother lay, As I have heard my father speak *K. John* i 1 105
That white-faced shore, Whose foot spurns back the ocean's roaring tides ii 1 23
And o'erswell With course disturb'd even thy confining shores ii 1 338
Two such shores to two such streams made one, Two such controlling bounds shall you be ii 1 443
Bear thee from the knowledge of thyself, And grapple thee unto a pagan shore v 2 36
Whose rocky shore beats back the envious siege Of watery Neptune *Richard II.* ii 1 62
And shortly mean to touch our northern shore ii 1 288
An unseasonable stormy day, Which makes the silver rivers drown their shores . iii 2 107
All westward, Wales beyond the Severn shore *1 Hen. IV.* iii 1 76
Sneaking home, My father gave him welcome to the shore iv 3 59
Upon the naked shore at Ravenspurgh iv 3 77
The tide of pomp That beats upon the high shore of this world *Hen. V.* iv 1 282
The contending kingdoms Of France and England, whose very shores look pale With envy of each other's happiness v 2 378
Seek not a scorpion's nest, Nor set no footing on this unkind shore *2 Hen. VI.* iii 2 87
Bid them blow towards England's blessed shore iii 2 90
The pretty-vaulting sea refused to drown me, Knowing that thou wouldst have me drown'd on shore iii 2 95
When from thy shore the tempest beat us back, I stood upon the hatches iii 2 102
Here shall they make their ransom on the sand, Or with their blood stain this discolour'd shore iv 1 11
Like one that stands upon a promontory, And spies a far-off shore *3 Hen. VI.* iii 2 136
Heralds That trudge betwixt the king and Mistress Shore *Richard III.* i 1 73
We say that Shore's wife hath a pretty foot, A cherry lip, a bonny eye i 1 93
Naught to do with Mistress Shore! I tell thee, fellow, He that doth naught with her, excepting one, Were best he do it secretly, alone i 1 98
For joy of this good news, Give Mistress Shore one gentle kiss the more iii 1 185
That monstrous witch, Consorted with that harlot strumpet Shore iii 4 73
His apparent open guilt omitted, I mean, his conversation with Shore's wife, He lived from all attainder of suspect iii 5 31
I never look'd for better at his hands, After he once fell in with Mistress Shore iii 5 51
To the shore Throng many doubtful hollow-hearted friends iv 4 434
Upon the western shore, Safe-conducting the rebels from their ships iv 4 482
Sent out a boat Unto the shore . iv 4 525
And make my vouch as strong As shore of rock . *Hen. VIII.* i 1 158
Peaceful commerce from dividable shores *Troi. and Cres.* i 3 105
The bounded waters Should lift their bosoms higher than the shores i 3 112
Two traded pilots 'twixt the dangerous shores Of will and judgement ii 2 64
Like a bourn, a pale, a shore, confines Thy spacious and dilated parts ii 3 260
Unkind and careless of thine own, Why suffer'st thou thy sons, unburied yet, To hover on the dreadful shore of Styx? *T. Andron.* i 1 88
Wert thou as far As that vast shore wash'd with the farthest sea, I would adventure for such merchandise *Rom. and Jul.* ii 2 83
Shore. Tiber trembled underneath her banks, To hear the replication of your sounds Made in her concave shores *J. Cæsar* i 1 51
Till the lowest stream Do kiss the most exalted shores of all . i 1 65
Once, upon a raw and gusty day, The troubled Tiber chafing with her shores i 2 101
Do but stand upon the foaming shore *Othello* ii 1 11
Cassio, Lieutenant to the warlike Moor Othello, Is come on shore ii 1 28
O, behold, The riches of the ship is come on shore! ii 1 83
Pure grief Shore his old thread in twain v 2 206
I'll try you on the shore.—And shall, sir: give's your hand *Ant. and Cleo.* ii 7 133
Take heed you fall not. Menas, I'll not on shore.—No, to my cabin ii 7 137
O sun, Burn the great sphere thou movest in! darkling stand The varying shore o' the world iv 15 11
I would thou grew'st unto the shores o' the haven *Cymbeline* i 3 1
Upon our neighbouring shore, A portly sail of ships make hitherward *Pericles* i 4 60
Alas, the sea hath cast me on the rocks, Wash'd me from shore to shore ii 1 6
How far is his court distant from this shore? ii 1 111
And after shipwreck driven upon this shore ii 3 85
By misfortune of the seas Bereft of ships and men, cast on this shore ii 3 89
Even now Did the sea toss upon our shore this chest iii 2 50
I never saw so huge a billow, sir, As toss'd it upon shore iii 2 59
We'll bring your grace e'en to the edge o' the shore iii 3 35
And swears she'll never stint, Make raging battery upon shores of flint iv 4 43
Being on shore, honouring of Neptune's triumphs v 1 17
What countrywoman? Here of these shores?—No, nor of any shores v 1 104
Lest this great sea of joys rushing upon me O'erbear the shores of my mortality v 1 195
Shall we refresh us, sir, upon your shore? v 1 257
Early in blustering morn this lady was Thrown upon this shore v 3 23
Shorn. Fifteen hundred shorn, what comes the wool to? *W. Tale* iv 3 35
Short. He loves your wife; there's the short and the long *Mer. Wives* ii 1 137
This is the short and the long of it ii 2 60
Speak, breathe, discuss; brief, short, quick, snap iv 5 2
Her promised proportions Came short of composition *Meas. for Meas.* v 1 220
Mark how short his answer is;—With Hero, Leonato's short daughter *Much Ado* i 1 215
He comes too short of you.—Gifts that God gives iii 5 45
And so to study, three years is but short *L. L. Lost* i 1 181
The way is but short: away!—As swift as lead, sir. iii 1 57
She passes praise; then praise too short doth blot iv 3 241
Dost thou not wish in heart The chain were longer and the letter short? v 2 56
Excuse me so, coming too short of thanks v 2 748
A time, methinks, too short To make a world-without-end bargain in v 2 798
Swift as a shadow, short as any dream *M. N. Dream* i 1 144
For the short and the long is, our play is preferred iv 2 39
The short and the long is, I serve the Jew *Mer. of Venice* ii 2 135
I will be bitter with him and passing short *As Y. Like It* iii 5 138
And, to be short, what not, that's sweet and happy? *T. of Shrew* v 2 110
For four or five removes come short To tender it herself *All's Well* v 3 131
Your reputation comes too short for my daughter; you are no husband for her v 3 176
He makes a July's day short as December *W. Tale* i 2 169
The revenue whereof shall furnish us . . .: if that come short, Our substitutes at home shall have blank charters *Richard II.* i 4 47
Small showers last long, but sudden storms are short ii 1 35
To-morrow must we part; Be merry, for our time of stay is short ii 1 223
By this the weary lords Shall make their way seem short ii 3 17
Twice for one step I'll groan, the way being short v 1 91
The word is short, but not so short as sweet v 3 117
Uncle, adieu: O, let the hours be short Till fields and blows and groans applaud our sport! *1 Hen. IV.* i 3 301
The time of life is short! To spend that shortness basely were too long v 2 82
Is not your voice broken? your wind short? *2 Hen. IV.* i 2 206
For women are shrews, both short and tall v 3 36
Good my sovereign, Take up the English short *Hen. V.* ii 4 72
Let life be short; else shame will be too long iv 5 23
Put forth thy hand, reach at the glorious gold. What, is't too short? *2 Hen. VI.* i 2 12
The welfare of us all Hangs on the cutting short that fraudful man iii 1 81
I myself, Rather than bloody war shall cut them short, Will parley iv 4 12
Even in so short a space, my woman's heart Grossly grew captive to his honey words *Richard III.* iv 1 79
My endeavours Have ever come too short of my desires *Hen. VIII.* iii 2 170
And, to be short, for not appearance and The king's late scruple iv 1 30
Because we have business of more moment, We will be short with you . v 3 52
That we come short of our suppose so far *Troi. and Cres.* i 3 11
She does so blush, and fetches her wind so short, as if she were frayed iii 2 33
She fetches her breath as short as a new-ta'en sparrow iii 2 36
Is't possible that so short a time can alter the condition of a man? *Coriolanus* v 4 9
'Tis good, sir: you are very short with us; But, if we live, we'll be as sharp with you *T. Andron.* i 1 409
What sadness lengthens Romeo's hours?—Not having that, which, having, makes them short.—In love? *Rom. and Jul.* i 1 170
Thou wouldst else have made thy tale large.— . . . I would have made it short ii 4 104
On Thursday, sir? the time is very short . iv 1 1
We shall be short in our provision: 'Tis now near night . iv 2 38
His means most short, his creditors most strait *T. of Athens* i 1 96
But, gentle heavens, Cut short all intermission *Macbeth* iv 3 232
Anon he finds him Striking too short at Greeks *Hamlet* ii 2 491
Should have kept short, restrain'd, and out of haunt, This mad young man iv 1 18
I, in forgery of shapes and tricks, Come short of what he did iv 7 91
It will be short: the interim is mine; And a man's life's no more than to say 'One' v 2 73
I find she names my very deed of love; Only she comes too short *Lear* i 1 74
All vengeance comes too short Which can pursue the offender ii 1 90
To match thy goodness? My life will be too short iv 7 2
To hovel thee with swine, and rogues forlorn, In short and musty straw iv 7 40
'Tis morning; Pleasure and action make the hours seem short *Othello* ii 3 385
He comes too short of that great property *Ant. and Cleo.* i 1 58
When good will is show'd, though't come too short, The actor may plead pardon ii 5 8
I shall short my word By lengthening my return *Cymbeline* i 6 200
Danger, which I fear'd, is at Antioch, Whose arm seems far too short to hit me here *Pericles* i 2 8
Thus time we waste, and longest leagues make short iv 4 1

Short-armed. Which short-armed ignorance itself knows is so abundant scarce . . . . *Troi. and Cres.* ii 3 15
Short banishment. Would the word 'farewell' have lengthen'd hours And added years to his short banishment . . . . *Richard II.* i 4 17
Short blistered breeches. Tall stockings, Short blister'd breeches, and those types of travel . . . *Hen. VIII.* i 3 31
Short breath. That no man might draw short breath to-day But I and Harry Monmouth! . . . . . . 1 *Hen. IV.* v 2 49
Short cloak. What said Master Dombledon about the satin for my short cloak and my slops? . . . . . . 2 *Hen. IV.* i 2 34
Short date. I will be brief, for my short date of breath Is not so long as is a tedious tale . . . *Rom. and Jul.* v 3 229
Short daughter. With Hero, Leonato's short daughter . . *Much Ado* i 1 216
Short farewell. We must take a short farewell . . *Cymbeline* iii 4 188
Short-grassed. Why hath thy queen Summon'd me hither, to this short-grass'd green? . . . . *Tempest* iv 1 83
Short holding. The rest will serve For a short holding . . *Coriolanus* i 7 4
Short horns. God sends a curst cow short horns . . *Much Ado* ii 1 25
Short hours. If they be still and willing, I'll undertake may see away their shilling Richly in two short hours . . . *Hen. VIII.* Prol. 13
Short knife. A short knife and a throng! . . . *Mer. Wives* ii 2 18
Short-legged. A couple of short-legged hens . . . 2 *Hen. IV.* v 1 28
Short-lived. Such short-lived wits do wither as they grow . *L. L. Lost* iv 1 54
O short-lived pride! Not fair? alack for woe! . . . . iv 1 15
Short minute. It cannot countervail the exchange of joy That one short minute gives me in her sight . . *Rom. and Jul.* ii 6 5
Short shrift. Make a short shrift . . . . *Richard III.* iii 4 97
Short space. In short space It rain'd down fortune . . 1 *Hen. IV.* v 1 46
Short summers lightly have a forward spring . . *Richard III.* iii 1 94
Short tale to make, we at Saint Alban's met . . 3 *Hen. VI.* ii 1 120
And he, repulsed—a short tale to make—Fell into a sadness . *Hamlet* ii 2 146
Short time. In short time after, he deposed the king . 1 *Hen. IV.* iv 3 90
Would cease The present power of life, but in short time All offices of nature should again Do their due functions . . *Cymbeline* v 5 256
Short-winded accents of new broils To be commenced . . 1 *Hen. IV.* i 1 3
He sure means brevity in breath, short-winded . . . 2 *Hen. IV.* ii 2 136
Short work. Come with me, and we will make short work *Rom. and Jul.* ii 6 35
Short years. O time's extremity, Hast thou so crack'd and splitted my poor tongue In seven short years? . . . *Com. of Errors* v 1 309
Shortcake. Why, did you not lend it to Alice Shortcake? *Mer. Wives* i 1 211
Shorten up their sinews With aged cramps . . . . *Tempest* iv 1 260
I am sorry that by hanging thee I can But shorten thy life one week *W. Tale* iv 4 433
In regard of me He shortens four years of my son's exile *Richard II.* i 3 217
Shorten my days thou canst with sullen sorrow, And pluck nights from me . . . . i 3 227
To shorten you, For taking so the head, your whole head's length . iii 3 12
No prince nor peer shall have just cause to say, God shorten Harry's happy life one day! . . . . 2 *Hen. IV.* v 2 145
He that is not guilty of his own death shortens not his own life *Hamlet* v 1 22
Yet to be known shortens my made intent . . . *Lear* iv 7 9
Shortened. Circumstances shortened, for she has been too long a talking of, the lady is disloyal . . . . *Much Ado* iii 2 106
Let there be enow: Place barrels of pitch upon the fatal stake, That so her torture may be shortened . . . . 1 *Hen. VI.* v 4 58
By the discovery We shall be shorten'd in our aim . . . *Coriolanus* i 2 23
Shortening. 'Tis but the shortening of my life one day . 1 *Hen. VI.* iv 6 37
Shorter. That in his reprieve, Longer or shorter, he may be so fitted That his soul sicken not . . . . . *Meas. for Meas.* ii 4 40
A shorter time shall send me to you . . . 1 *Hen. IV.* iii 1 91
Ay, but the days are wax'd shorter with him . . *T. of Athens* iii 4 11
Shall not be a maid long, unless things be cut shorter . . *Lear* i 5 56
So shall you have a shorter journey to your desires by the means I shall then have to prefer them . . . . . . *Othello* ii 1 284
Your way is shorter; My purposes do draw me much about . *A. and C.* ii 4 7
Shortest. Sent back like Hallowmas or short'st of day . *Richard II.* v 1 80
Shortly shall all my labours end . . . . . *Tempest* iv 1 265
The approaching tide Will shortly fill the reasonable shore . . v 1 81
At pick'd leisure Which shall be shortly, single I'll resolve you . v 1 248
A very virtuous maid, And to be shortly of a sisterhood *Meas. for Meas.* ii 2 21
If my passion change not shortly, God forbid it should be otherwise *Much Ado* i 1 221
Thou wilt quake for this shortly.—I look for an earthquake too, then . i 1 274
False knaves; and it will go near to be thought so shortly . . iv 2 25
Either I must shortly hear from him, or I will subscribe him a coward . v 2 58
We shall not shortly have a rasher on the coals for money *Mer. of Venice* iii 5 27
I shall grow jealous of you shortly . . . . . . iii 5 31
The best grace of wit will shortly turn into silence . . . . iii 5 49
We shall have shortly discord in the spheres . . *As Y. Like It* ii 7 6
Her brother, Who shortly also died . . . . *T. Night* i 2 39
Else would I very shortly see thee there . . . . . ii 1 47
And shortly mean to touch our northern shore . . *Richard II.* ii 1 288
Rue, even for ruth, here shortly shall be seen . . . . iii 4 106
He intercepted did return To be deposed and shortly murdered 1 *Hen. IV.* i 3 152
I shall be out of heart shortly . . . . iii 3 7
A' must, then, to the inns o' court shortly . . . 2 *Hen. IV.* iii 2 14
Shortly will I seal with him . . . . iv 3 141
Open the gates, or I'll shut thee out shortly . . . 1 *Hen. VI.* i 3 26
Till the axe of death Hang over thee, as, sure, it shortly will . 2 *Hen. VI.* ii 4 50
In hope he'll prove a widower shortly . . 3 *Hen. VI.* iii 3 227; iv 1 99
To that end I shortly mind to leave you . . . . . iv 1 64
I do love thee so, That I will shortly send thy soul to heaven *Rich. III.* i 1 119
They smile at me that shortly shall be dead . . . . iii 4 106
And will, no doubt, shortly be rid of me . . . . . iv 1 87
Write to me very shortly, And you shall understand from me her mind iv 4 428
Shortly after This world had air'd them . . . . *Hen. VIII.* iii 4 192
Shortly, I believe, His second marriage shall be publish'd . . iii 2 67
Then shortly art thou mine . . . . . . *Coriolanus* iv 7 57
We should have none shortly, for one would kill the other *Rom. and Jul.* iii 1 17
Thou wilt give away thyself in paper shortly . . . *T. of Athens* i 2 248
I'll say thou'st gold: Thou wilt be throng'd to shortly . . . iv 3 395
That mine own use invites me to cut down, And shortly must I fell it . v 1 210
I must leave thee, love, and shortly too . . . . *Hamlet* iii 2 183
You shortly shall hear more . . . . iv 7 33
An hour of quiet shortly shall we see; Till then, in patience . . v 1 321
It must be shortly known to him . . . . . . v 2 71
An thou canst not smile as the wind sits, thou'lt catch cold shortly *Lear* i 4 113
I have a journey, sir, shortly to go; My master calls me . . v 3 321
Shall be to him shortly as bitter as coloquintida . . *Othello* i 3 355
Nor know I aught But that he's well and will be shortly here . ii 1 90

Shortly. Some other time.—But shall't be shortly?—The sooner, sweet, for you . . . . *Othello* iii 3 56
As it ebbs, the seedsman Upon the slime and ooze scatters his grain, And shortly comes to harvest . . . . . *Ant. and Cleo.* ii 7 26
Shortness. Such as the shortness of the time can shape . . *L. L. Lost* iv 3 378
Your plainness and your shortness please me well . *T. of Shrew* iv 4 39
The time of life is short! To spend that shortness basely were too long 1 *Hen. IV.* v 2 83
I'll make a journey twice as far, to enjoy A second night of such sweet shortness which Was mine in Britain . . . . . *Cymbeline* ii 4 44
Shot. A fine volley of words, gentlemen, and quickly shot off *T. G. of Ver.* ii 4 34
Never welcome to a place till some certain shot be paid . . . ii 5 7
Where, for one shot of five pence, thou shalt have five thousand welcomes . . . . ii 5 10
A mark marvellous well shot . . . . . . *L. L. Lost* iv 1 132
Shot, by heaven! Proceed, sweet Cupid . . . . . . iv 3 22
And certain stars shot madly from their spheres . *M. N. Dream* ii 1 153
When I had lost one shaft, I shot his fellow . . *Mer. of Venice* i 1 141
Therefore a health to all that shot and miss'd . . . *T. of Shrew* v 2 51
'Tis the rarest argument of wonder that hath shot out . . *All's Well* ii 3 8
Where thou Wast shot at with fair eyes, to be the mark Of smoky muskets . . . . iii 2 110
Near or far off, well won is still well shot . . . . *K. John* i 1 174
With a volley of our needless shot, After such bloody toil, we bid good night . . . . v 5 5
Though I could 'scape shot-free at London, I fear the shot here 1 *Hen. IV.* v 3 30
A' drew a good bow; and dead! a' shot a fine shoot . . 2 *Hen. IV.* iii 2 49
O, give me always a little, lean, old, chapt, bald shot . . . iii 2 295
Who was shot, who disgraced, what terms the enemy stood on *Hen. V.* iii 6 77
'A fool's bolt is soon shot.'—You have shot over . . . . iii 7 132
That's a perilous shot out of an elder-gun . . . . . iv 1 210
And oft have shot at them, Howe'er unfortunate I miss'd my aim 1 *Hen. VI.* i 4 3
How with most advantage They may vex us with shot or with assault . i 4 13
A guard of chosen shot I had That walk'd about me every minute while i 4 53
I am your butt, and I abide your shot . . . 3 *Hen. VI.* i 4 29
A garish flag, To be the aim of every dangerous shot . *Richard III.* iv 4 90
A file of boys behind 'em, loose shot . . . . *Hen. VIII.* v 4 59
Safe out of fortune's shot; And sits aloft, Secure . . *T. Andron.* ii 1 2
See, see, thou hast shot off one of Taurus' horns . . . . iv 3 69
When Publius shot, The Bull, being gall'd, gave Aries such a knock That down fell both the Ram's horns . . . . iv 3 70
He that shot so trim, When King Cophetua loved the beggar-maid! *Rom. and Jul.* ii 1 13
Stabbed with a white wench's black eye; shot thorough the ear with a love-song . . . . ii 4 14
As if that name, Shot from the deadly level of a gun, Did murder her . iii 3 103
This murderous shaft that's shot Hath not yet lighted . *Macbeth* ii 3 147
Keep you in the rear of your affection, Out of the shot and danger of desire . . . . *Hamlet* i 3 35
As level as the cannon to his blank, Transports his poison'd shot . . iv 1 43
That I have shot mine arrow o'er the house, And hurt my brother . v 2 254
That thou so many princes at a shot So bloodily hast struck . . . v 2 377
They do discharge their shot of courtesy: Our friends at least *Othello* ii 1 56
The shot of accident, nor dart of chance, Could neither graze nor pierce iv 1 278
My good stars, that were my former guides, Have empty left their orbs, and shot their fires Into the abysm of hell . . *Ant. and Cleo.* iii 13 146
I shall here abide the hourly shot Of angry eyes . . . *Cymbeline* i 1 89
But a bolt of nothing, shot at nothing, Which the brain makes of fumes iv 2 300
If I prove a good repast to the spectators, the dish pays the shot . v 4 158
Like an arrow shot From a well-experienced archer hits the mark *Pericles* i 1 163
In sorrow all devour'd, With sighs shot through, and biggest tears o'er-shower'd . . . . iv 4 26
Shot-free. Though I could 'scape shot-free at London, I fear the shot here; here's no scoring but upon the pate . . . 1 *Hen. IV.* v 3 30
Shotten. Then am I a shotten herring . . . . . . ii 4 143
Shough. Mongrels, spaniels, curs, Shoughs, water-rugs, and demi-wolves are clept All by the name of dogs . . . . *Macbeth* iii 1 94
Should. I would Have sunk the sea within the earth or ere It should the good ship so have swallow'd . . . . . . *Tempest* i 2 12
'Tis time I should inform thee farther . . . . . . i 2 23
Mark me—that a brother should Be so perfidious! . . . . i 2 67
I should sin To think but nobly of my grandmother . . . . i 2 118
That he . . . Should presently extirpate me and mine . . . i 2 125
An undergoing stomach, to bear up Against what should ensue . . i 2 158
Where should this music be? i' the air or the earth? . . . i 2 387
You have taken it wiselier than I meant you should . . . . ii 1 21
You rub the sore, When you should bring the plaster . . . ii 1 139
Letters should not be known; riches, poverty, And use of service, none ii 1 150
Methinks I see it in thy face, What thou shouldst be . . . ii 1 207
If it should thunder as it did before, I know not where to hide my head ii 2 22
Where the devil should he learn our language? . . . . ii 2 69
I should know that voice: it should be—but he is drowned . . ii 2 90
I had rather crack my sinews, break my back, Than you should such dishonour undergo . . . . iii 1 27
Thy eyes are almost set in thy head.—Where should they be set else? . iii 2 11
That a monster should be such a natural! . . . . . iii 2 37
If I should take a displeasure against you, look you . . . . iv 1 202
But how should Prospero Be living and be here? . . . . v 1 119
For a score of kingdoms you should wrangle, And I would call it fair play v 1 174
Where should they Find this grand liquor that hath gilded 'em? . . v 1 279
And he . . . , Methinks, should not be chronicled for wise *T. G. of Ver.* i 1 41
That I, unworthy body as I am, Should censure thus . . . . i 2 19
By a figure.—What figure?—By a letter, I should say . . . ii 1 156
Now should not the shoe speak a word for weeping: now should I kiss my father; well, he weeps on . . . . ii 3 27
Why dost thou stop my mouth?—For fear thou shouldst lose thy tongue ii 3 52
But there I leave to love where I should love . . . . . ii 6 18
Should she thus be stol'n away from you, It would be much vexation . iii 1 15
If you should here disfurnish me, You take the sum and substance that I have . . . . iv 1 14
I cannot choose But pity her.—Wherefore shouldst thou pity her? . iv 4 83
What should it be that he respects in her But I can make respective in myself? . . . . iv 4 199
O time most accurst, 'Mongst all foes that a friend should be the worst! v 4 72
O, I should remember him: does he not hold up his head? *Mer. Wives* i 4 29
I have been content, sir, you should lay my countenance to pawn . ii 2 5
'Tis not good that children should know any wickedness . . . ii 2 134
If the bottom were as deep as hell, I should down . . . . iii 5 14
What a thing should I have been when I had been swelled! . . . iii 5 17

Should. Which way should he go? how should I bestow him? *Mer. Wives* iv 2 47
Alas, what noise?—Heaven forgive our sins!—What should this be? v 5 36
This day my sister should the cloister enter *Meas. for Meas.* i 2 182
What should I think? Heaven shield my mother play'd my father fair! iii 1 140
He who the sword of heaven will bear Should be as holy as severe iii 2 276
Put not yourself into amazement how these things should be iv 2 220
Why should we proclaim it in an hour before his entering, that if any crave redress of injustice, they should exhibit their petitions in the street? iv 4 9
He should have lived, Save that his riotous youth, with dangerous sense, Might . . . have ta'en revenge iv 4 31
Why should their [men's] liberty than ours be more? *Com. of Errors* ii 1 10
I should kick, being kick'd iii 1 17
I would not spare my brother in this case, If he should scorn me so iv 1 78
This I wonder at, That he, unknown to me, should be in debt iv 2 48
That I should be attach'd in Ephesus, I tell you, 'twill sound harshly iv 4 6
You should for that have reprehended him.—Why, so I did v 1 57
Thou singest well enough for a shift.—An he had been a dog that should have howled thus, they would have hanged him *Much Ado* ii 3 81
A' brushes his hat o' mornings; what should that bode? iii 2 42
One o' these maids' girdles for your waist should be fit *L. L. Lost* iv 1 50
What upward lies The street should see as she walk'd overhead iv 3 281
To what end Their shallow shows . . . Should be presented at our tent to us v 2 307
Be advised, fair maid: To you your father should be as a god *M. N. D.* i 1 47
We should be woo'd and were not made to woo ii 1 242
O, that a lady, of one man refused, Should of another therefore be abused! ii 2 134
So should a murderer look, so dead, so grim.—So should the murder'd look, and so should I iii 2 57
Why should you think that I should woo in scorn? iii 2 122
As who should say 'I am Sir Oracle' *Mer. of Venice* i 1 93
As who should say 'If you will not have me, choose' i 2 51
If he should offer to choose, and choose the right casket, you should refuse to perform your father's will, if you should refuse to accept him i 2 99
It should seem, then, that Dobbin's tail grows backward ii 2 102
'Tis an office of discovery, love; And I should be obscured ii 6 44
Besides, it should appear, that if he had The present money to discharge the Jew, He would not take it iii 2 275
If I had a thunderbolt in mine eye, I can tell who should down *As Y. L. It* i 2 227
Thou shouldst have better pleased me with this deed, Hadst thou descended from another house i 2 240
Of what kind should this cock come of? ii 7 90
But didst thou hear without wondering how thy name should be hanged and carved upon these trees? iii 2 182
With catlike watch, When that the sleeping man should stir iv 3 117
I should knock you first, And then I know after who comes by the worst.—Will it not be? *T. of Shrew* i 2 13
When the priest Should ask, if Katharine should be his wife iii 2 161
As who should say, if I should sleep or eat, 'Twere deadly sickness iv 3 13
Would have made nature immortal, and death should have play *All's W.* i 1 23
I should believe you; For you have show'd me that which well approves iii 7 12
To be your prisoner should import offending *W. Tale* i 2 57
How should this grow?—I know not i 2 431
But be't known, From him that has most cause to grieve it should be, She's an adulteress.—Should a villain say so ii 1 77
This ancient sir, who, it should seem, Hath sometime loved! iv 4 372
They throng who should buy first, as if my trinkets had been hallowed iv 4 612
His son, that should have married a shepherd's daughter iv 4 794
If lusty love should go in quest of beauty, Where should he find it fairer than in Blanch? *K. John* ii 1 427
It cannot be That, whiles warm life plays in that infant's veins, The misplaced John should entertain an hour . . . of rest iii 4 133
If an angel should have come to me And told me Hubert should put out mine eyes, I would not have believed him iv 1 68
That, ere the next Ascension-day at noon, Your highness should deliver up your crown iv 2 152
I am not glad that such a sore of time Should seek a plaster v 2 13
'Tis strange that death should sing v 7 20
I should to Plashy too; But time will not permit *Richard II.* ii 2 120
Alack the heavy day When such a sacred king should hide his head iii 3 8
Alack, for woe, That any harm should stain so fair a show! iii 3 71
As who should say, 'I would thou wert the man' v 4 8
That with our small conjunction we should on *1 Hen. IV.* iv 1 37
'Tis not well That you and I should meet upon such terms v 1 10
Why should that gentleman that rode by Travers Give then such instances of loss? *2 Hen. IV.* i 1 55
I looked a' should have sent me two and twenty yards of satin i 2 49
Who is it like should lead his forces hither? ii 3 81
This Doll Tearsheet should be some road ii 2 182
Is it not strange that desire should so many years outlive performance? ii 4 283
And wherefore should these good news make me sick? iv 4 102
I should rejoice now at this happy news; And now my sight fails iv 4 109
O God, that right should thus overcome might! v 4 27
Which is a wonder how his grace should glean it *Hen. V.* i 1 53
What should I say? his deeds exceed all speech *1 Hen. VI.* i 1 15
That you, being supreme magistrates, Thus contumeliously should break the peace! i 3 58
Good God, these nobles should such stomachs bear! i 3 90
As who should say 'When I am dead and gone, Remember to avenge me' i 4 93
Then how or which way should they first break in? ii 1 71
I thought I should have seen some Hercules ii 3 19
What a scandal is it to our crown, That two such noble peers as ye should jar! iii 1 70
As who should say, Had death been French, then death had died to-day iv 7 27
That Suffolk should demand a whole fifteenth For costs! *2 Hen. VI.* i 1 133
It is no policy . . . That he should come about your royal person iii 1 26
Whiles I was protector, Pity was all the fault that was in me; For I should melt at an offender's tears iii 1 126
That he should die is worthy policy iii 1 235
He nods at us, as who should say, I'll be even with you iv 7 99
Why should you sigh, my lord?—Not for myself *3 Hen. VI.* i 1 191
Now melt with woe That winter should cut off our spring-time so ii 3 47
Less than I was born to: A man at least, for less I should not be iii 1 57
'Twill grieve your grace my sons should call you father iii 2 100
It ill befits thy state And birth, that thou shouldst stand iii 3 3
Oh, that deceit should steal such gentle shapes! *Richard III.* ii 2 27
Cannot thy master sleep these tedious nights?—So it should seem iii 2 7
There should be one amongst 'em, by his person, More worthy *Hen. VIII.* i 4 78
What should this mean? What sudden anger's this? iii 2 203
That should be The Duke of Suffolk?—'Tis the same iv 1 40
Should. If my sight fail not, You should be lord ambassador *Hen. VIII.* iv 2 109
The bounded waters Should lift their bosoms higher than the shores *Troi. and Cres.* i 3 112
Strength should be lord of imbecility i 3 114
Force should be right; or rather, right and wrong, Between whose endless jar justice resides, Should lose their names, and so should justice too i 3 116
What should I say? He is so plaguy proud ii 3 186
What then?—Should by the cormorant belly by restrain'd *Coriolanus* i 1 125
Then his good report should have been my son i 3 22
So shall my lungs Coin words till their decay against those measles, Which we disdain should tetter us iii 1 79
As any mortal body hearing it Should straight fall mad *T. Andron.* ii 3 104
O, why should nature build so foul a den? iv 1 59
As who should say 'Old lad, I am thine own' iv 2 121
And who should find them but the empress' villain? iv 3 73
But all so soon as the all-cheering sun Should in the furthest east begin to draw The shady curtains from Aurora's bed *Rom. and Jul.* i 1 141
Alas, that love, so gentle in his view, Should be so tyrannous! i 1 176
Alas, that love, whose view is muffled still, Should, without eyes, see pathways to his will! i 1 178
Where the devil should this Romeo be? Came he not home to-night? ii 4 1
Madmen have no ears.—How should they, when that wise men have no eyes? iii 3 62
I fear it is: and yet, methinks, it should not iv 3 28
As I remember, this should be the house v 1 55
This same should be the voice of Friar John v 2 2
What should it be, that they so shriek abroad? v 3 190
I hope it is not so low with him.—It should not be, by the persuasion of his new feasting.—I should think so *T. of Athens* iii 6 8
That nature, being sick of man's unkindness, Should yet be hungry! iv 3 177
Where should he have this gold? iv 3 399
Brutus and Cæsar: what should be in that 'Cæsar'? Why should that name be sounded more than yours? *J. Cæsar* i 2 142
It seems to me most strange that men should fear ii 2 35
So should he look That seems to speak things strange *Macbeth* i 2 46
You should be women, And yet your beards forbid i 3 45
Hums, as who should say 'You'll rue the time' iii 6 42
I should report that which I say I saw, But know not how to do it v 5 31
There thou shouldst be v 7 20
What it should be, More than his father's death, . . . I cannot dream of *Hamlet* ii 2 7
What should we say, my lord?—Why, any thing, but to the purpose ii 2 286
Your wisdom should show itself more richer to signify this to his doctor iii 2 316
That we would do, We should do when we would; for this 'would' changes iv 7 120
This 'should' is like a spendthrift sigh, That hurts by easing iv 7 123
And the more pity that great folk should have countenance in this world to drown or hang themselves v 1 30
Thou shouldst be honest.—I should be wise, for honesty's a fool *Othello* iii 3 381
Where should I lose that handkerchief? iii 4 23
By heaven, that should be my handkerchief! iv 1 164
May you suspect Who they should be that have thus mangled you? v 1 79
Why, how should she be murder'd?—Alas, who knows? v 2 126
I should have known no less *Ant. and Cleo.* i 4 40
She replied, It should be better he became her guest ii 2 226
And in his offence Should my performance perish iii 1 27
Thou knew'st too well My heart was to thy rudder tied by the strings, And thou shouldst tow me after iii 11 58
Peace, I say! What should this mean? iv 3 15
That such a crafty devil . . . Should yield the world this ass! *Cymb.* ii 1 58
Report should render him hourly to your ear As truly as he moves iii 4 153
How should this be? iv 2 323
If you Should have ta'en vengeance on my faults, I never Had lived v 1 8
Which, being took, Should by the minute feed on life v 5 51
What should I say? he was too good to be Where ill men were v 5 158
Shoulder. Take this basket on your shoulders *Mer. Wives* iii 3 13
They took me on their shoulders iii 5 102
Take the basket again on your shoulders: your master is hard at door iv 2 111
I will keep my sides to myself, my shoulders for the fellow of this walk v 5 29
Pinch them, arms, legs, backs, shoulders, sides and shins v 5 58
We would have thrust virtue out of our hearts by the head and shoulders v 5 156
Thy head stands so tickle on thy shoulders *Meas. for Meas.* i 2 177
Some of my mistress' marks upon my shoulders *Com. of Errors* i 2 83
My errand, due unto my tongue, I thank him, I bare home upon my shoulders ii 1 73
Or else I shall seek my wit in my shoulders ii 2 39
The mark of my shoulder, the mole in my neck iii 2 147
I bear it on my shoulders, as a beggar wont her brat iv 4 39
If Signior Leonato be her father, she would not have his head on her shoulders for all Messina, as like him as she is *Much Ado* i 1 115
Let him be clapped on the shoulder, and called Adam i 1 261
Stoop, I say; Her shoulder is with child *L. L. Lost* iv 3 90
Sometime to lean upon my poor shoulder v 1 108
With that, all laugh'd and clapp'd him on the shoulder v 2 107
No ill luck stirring but what lights on my shoulders *Mer. of Venice* iii 1 99
The city-woman bears The cost of princes on unworthy shoulders *As Y. Like It* ii 7 76
It may be said of him that Cupid hath clapp'd him o' the shoulder iv 1 48
Thou mayst slide from my shoulder to my heel with no greater a run but my head and my neck *T. of Shrew* iv 1 15
Now here, At upper end o' the table, now i' the middle; On his shoulder, and his; her face o' fire With labour *W. Tale* iv 4 60
What! I am dubb'd! I have it on my shoulder *K. John* i 1 245
Lay on that shall make your shoulders crack ii 1 146
Which gently laid my knighthood on my shoulder *Richard II.* i 1 79
This tongue that runs so roundly in thy head Should run thy head from thy unreverent shoulders ii 1 123
If you and I do not rob them, cut this head off from my shoulders *1 Hen. IV.* i 2 186
You are straight enough in the shoulders, you care not who sees your back ii 4 164
Thrown over the shoulders like an herald's coat without sleeves iv 2 48
With two points on your shoulder? much! *2 Hen. IV.* ii 4 143
The rascal's drunk: you have hurt him, sir, i' the shoulder ii 4 231
A fellow that never had the ache in his shoulders! v 1 94
Thou hast drawn my shoulder out of joint v 4 3
The French may lay twenty French crowns to one, they will beat us; for they bear them on their shoulders *Hen. V.* iv 1 244

Shoulder. My breast I'll burst with straining of my courage And from my shoulders crack my arms asunder . . . 1 *Hen. VI.* i 5 11
Weak shoulders, overborne with burthening grief, And pithless arms . ii 5 10
Shall not wear a head on his shoulders, unless he pay me tribute 2 *Hen. VI.* iv 7 128
As did Æneas old Anchises bear, So bear I thee upon my manly shoulders v 2 63
On thy shoulder will I lean . . . . 3 *Hen. VI.* ii 1 189
In thy shoulder do I build my seat . . . . . . ii 6 100
This shoulder was ordain'd so thick to heave; And heave it shall . . v 7 23
Which laid their guilt upon my guiltless shoulders . *Richard III.* i 2 98
Because that I am little, like an ape, He thinks that you should bear me on your shoulders . . . . iii 1 131
I'll have this crown of mine cut from my shoulders . . . iii 2 43
And from these shoulders, These ruin'd pillars, out of pity, taken A load would sink a navy, too much honour . . . *Hen. VIII.* iii 2 381
From Cupid's shoulder pluck his painted wings . *Troi. and Cres.* iii 2 15
Even already They clap the lubber Ajax on the shoulder . . . iii 3 139
Where is he wounded?—I' the shoulder and i' the left arm . *Coriolanus* ii 1 163
As Æneas, our great ancestor, Did from the flames of Troy upon his shoulder The old Anchises bear . . . *J. Cæsar* i 2 113
The wind sits in the shoulder of your sail, And you are stay'd for *Hamlet* i 3 56
His head over his shoulder turn'd, He seem'd to find his way without his eyes . . . . ii 1 97
I have seen better faces in my time Than stands on any shoulder that I see Before me at this instant . . . . . . *Lear* ii 2 100
Men whose heads Do grow beneath their shoulders . . . *Othello* i 3 145
And have instructed cowards To run and show their shoulders *A. and C.* iii 11 8
What mortality is! Posthumus, thy head, which now is growing upon thy shoulders, shall within this hour be off . . *Cymbeline* iv 1 17
But yield me to the veriest hind that shall Once touch my shoulder . v 3 78
Shoulder-blade. My shoulder-blade is out . . . *W. Tale* iv 3 77
Shoulder-bone. To see how the bear tore out his shoulder-bone . . iii 3 97
Shoulder-clapper. A back-friend, a shoulder-clapper . *Com. of Errors* iv 2 37
Shoulder'd in the swallowing gulf Of blind forgetfulness . *Richard III.* iii 7 128
Shouldering. This shouldering of each other in the court . 1 *Hen. VI.* iv 1 189
Shoulder-shotten. Swayed in the back and shoulder-shotten *T. of Shrew* iii 2 56
Shout. Hearing applause and universal shout, Giddy in spirit *M. of Ven.* iii 2 144
Have I not heard these islanders shout out 'Vive le roi!' . *K. John* v 2 103
That I did pluck allegiance from men's hearts, Loud shouts and salutations from their mouths . . . . 1 *Hen. IV.* iii 2 53
The word of peace is render'd: hark, how they shout! . . 2 *Hen. IV.* iv 2 87
Whose shouts and claps out-voice the deep-mouth'd sea . *Hen. V.* v Prol. 11
Hark, hark, my lord! what shouts are these? . . . 3 *Hen. VI.* iv 8 52
This general applause and loving shout Argues your wisdoms *Rich. III.* iii 7 39
Hark! hark! what shout is that?—Peace, drums! . . *Troi. and Cres.* v 9 1
What shouts are these? The other side o' the city is risen . *Coriolanus* i 1 47
You shout me forth In acclamations hyperbolical . . . . i 9 50
The commons made A shower and thunder with their caps and shouts . ii 1 283
Ha! what shout is this? Shall I be tempted to infringe my vow? . v 3 19
Have you not made an universal shout, That Tiber trembled? *J. Cæsar* i 1 49
Another general shout! . . . . i 2 132
We'll bring him to his house With shouts and clamours . . . iii 2 58
Hark! they shout for joy.—Come down, behold no more . . . v 3 32
Didst thou not hear their shouts? Alas, thou hast misconstrued every thing! . . . . v 3 83
Shouted. They shouted thrice: what was the last cry for? . . . i 2 226
At every putting-by mine honest neighbours shouted . . . i 2 231
Shouting their emulation . . . . . . *Coriolanus* i 1 218
Tabors and cymbals and the shouting Romans Make the sun dance . v 4 53
What means this shouting? I do fear, the people Choose Cæsar *J. Cæsar* i 2 79
And then the people fell a-shouting . . . . . . i 2 223
Let him take thee, And hoist thee up to the shouting plebeians *A. and C.* iv 12 34
Shall they hoist me up And show me to the shouting varletry? . . v 2 56
Shove. Offence's gilded hand may shove by justice . . . *Hamlet* iii 3 58
Shoved. The which hath been with scorn shoved from the court 2 *Hen. IV.* iv 2 37
The hand could pluck her back that shoved her on. *Ant. and Cleo.* i 2 131
Shove-groat. Like a shove-groat shilling . . . . 2 *Hen. IV.* ii 4 206
Shovel. And lay me Where no priest shovels in dust . . *W. Tale* iv 4 469
Why does he suffer this rude knave now to knock him about the sconce with a dirty shovel? . . . . *Hamlet* v 1 110
Shovel-board. Two Edward shovel-boards, that cost me two shilling and two pence a-piece . . . . *Mer. Wives* i 1 159
Show. Who makest a show but darest not strike . . . *Tempest* i 2 470
I'll show thee every fertile inch o' th' island . . . . . ii 2 152
I'll show thee the best springs . . . . ii 2 164
Show thee a jay's nest and instruct thee how To snare the nimble marmoset . . . . ii 2 173
Poor worm, thou art infected! This visitation shows it . . . iii 1 32
All the more it seeks to hide itself, The bigger bulk it shows . . iii 1 81
I'll not show him Where the quick freshes are . . . . iii 2 74
If thou beest a man, show thyself in thy likeness . . . . iii 2 137
The clouds methought would open and show riches . . . . iii 2 150
Mine eyes, even sociable to the show of thine, Fall fellowly drops . v 1 63
I'll show my mind According to my shallow simple skill *T. G. of Ver.* i 2 7
His little speaking shows his love but small . . . . . i 2 29
They do not love that do not show their love . . . . . i 2 31
Say, from whom?—That the contents will show . . . . . i 2 36
I fear'd to show my father Julia's letter . . . . . . i 3 80
An April day, Which now shows all the beauty of the sun . . . i 3 86
I'll show you the manner of it . . . . ii 3 15
And Silvia . . . Shows Julia but a swarthy Ethiope . . . . ii 6 26
To be fantastic may become a youth Of greater time than I shall show to be . . . . ii 7 48
This discipline shows thou hast been in love . . . . . iii 2 88
We'll bring thee to our crews, And show thee all the treasure we have got iv 1 75
O wicked, wicked world! One that is well-nigh worn to pieces with age to show himself a young gallant! . . . *Mer. Wives* ii 1 22
I'll ne'er believe that; I have to show to the contrary . . . ii 1 38
I say I could show you to the contrary . . . . . . ii 1 41
Give him a show of comfort in his suit . . . . . . ii 1 98
He is de coward Jack priest of de vorld; he is not show his face . ii 3 33
You shall have sport; I will show you a monster . . . . iii 2 82
A pitiful lady!—Let the court of France show me such another . . iii 3 57
Show me now, William, some declensions of your pronouns . . iv 1 76
If I find not what I seek, show no colour for my extremity . . . iv 2 168
That neither singly can be manifested, Without the show of both . . iv 6 16
The image of the jest I'll show you here at large . . . . iv 6 18
Why dost thou show me thus to the world? . . *Meas. for Meas.* i 2 120
Then, if you speak, you must not show your face, Or, if you show your face, you must not speak . . . . i 4 12
Like a prophet, Looks in a glass, that shows what future evils . . ii 2 95
Show. Yet show some pity.—I show it most of all when I show justice *Meas. for Meas.* ii 2 99
Show it now, By putting on the destined livery . . . . ii 4 137
Show me how, good father . . . . iii 1 247
In action all of precept, he did show me The way twice o'er . . iv 1 40
It is not so.—It is no other: show your wisdom, daughter . . iv 3 122
His actions show much like to madness . . . . . . iv 4 4
He shows his reason for that . . . . iv 4 13
Is this the witness, friar? First, let her show her face, and after speak v 1 168
I will not show my face Until my husband bid me . . . . v 1 169
Show your knave's visage, with a pox to you! show your sheep-biting face v 1 358
We'll show What's yet behind, that's meet you all should know . v 1 544
That you beat me at the mart, I have your hand to show *Com. of Errors* iii 1 12
Muffle your false love with some show of blindness . . . . iii 2 8
Though others have the arm, show us the sleeve . . . . . iii 2 23
Less in your knowledge and your grace you show not Than our earth's wonder . . . . iii 2 31
Joy could not show itself modest enough without a badge of bitterness *Much Ado* i 1 22
They have a good cover; they show well outward . . . . i 2 8
You must not make the full show of this till you may do it without controlment . . . . i 3 21
He shows me where the bachelors sit, and there live we as merry as the day is long . . . . ii 1 50
Finding a birds' nest, shows it his companion, and he steals it . . ii 1 231
That no dishonesty shall appear in me.—Show me briefly how . . ii 2 11
Why, what effects of passion shows she? . . . . . . ii 3 112
He doth indeed show some sparks that are like wit . . . . ii 3 193
I'll show thee some attires, and have thy counsel Which is the best . iii 1 102
As to show a child his new coat and forbid him to wear it . . . iii 2 6
If you will follow me, I will show you enough . . . . . iii 2 124
Bear it coldly but till midnight, and let the issue show itself . . iii 2 133
Let him show himself what he is and steal out of your company . . iii 3 62
I wonder at it.—That shows thou art unconfirmed . . . . iii 3 124
O, what authority and show of truth Can cunning sin cover itself withal! . . . . iv 1 36
Would you not swear, All you that see her, that she were a maid, By these exterior shows? . . . . iv 1 41
Then we find The virtue that possession would not show us . . iv 1 223
Is there any way to show such friendship?—A very even way . . iv 1 265
I will go before and show him their examination . . . . iv 2 68
Boys, That lie and cog and flout, deprave and slander, Go anticly, show outward hideousness . . . . v 1 96
Marry, I cannot show it in rhyme; I have tried . . . . . v 2 36
If wounding, then it was to show my skill . . . *L. L. Lost* iv 1 28
Ostentare, to show, as it were, his inclination . . . . . iv 2 16
Do but behold the tears that swell in me, And they thy glory through my grief will show . . . . iv 3 38
The sea will ebb and flow, heaven show his face . . . . iv 3 216
What, did these rent lines show some love of thine? . . . . iv 3 220
Finding barren practisers, Scarce show a harvest of their heavy toil . iv 3 326
The arts, the academes, That show, contain and nourish all the world . iv 3 353
Some delightful ostentation, or show, or pageant, or antique, or firework v 1 118
Some entertainment of time, some show in the posterior of this day . v 1 126
Vouchsafe to show the sunshine of your face . . . . . v 2 201
Or ever, but in vizards, show their faces . . . . . . v 2 271
To what end Their shallow shows and prologue vilely penn'd . . v 2 305
Have not the grace to grace it with such show . . . . . v 2 320
Smiles on every one, To show his teeth as white as whale's bone . . v 2 332
'Tis some policy To have one show worse than the king's and his company v 2 514
If these four Worthies in their first show thrive, These four will change habits . . . . v 2 541
There is five in the first show.—You are deceived; 'tis not so . . v 2 543
It should have followed in the end of our show . . . . . v 2 898
Nature shows art, That through thy bosom makes me see thy heart *M. N. Dream* ii 2 104
O, how ripe in show Thy lips, those kissing cherries, tempting grow! . iii 2 139
If you were men, as men you are in show, You would not use a gentle lady so . . . . iii 2 151
If thou dost intend Never so little show of love to her, Thou shalt aby it iii 2 334
For if but once thou show me thy grey light, I'll find Demetrius . . iii 2 419
To show our simple skill, That is the true beginning of our end . . v 1 110
By their show You shall know all that you are like to know . . . v 1 116
Gentles, perchance you wonder at this show; But wonder on . . . v 1 128
This rough-cast and this stone doth show That I am that same wall . v 1 162
O sweet and lovely wall, Show me thy chink, to blink through with mine eyne! . . . . v 1 178
They'll not show their teeth in way of smile . . *Mer. of Venice* i 1 55
This kindness will I show. Go with me to a notary . . . . i 3 144
Where thou art not known, why, there they show Something too liberal ii 2 193
A golden mind stoops not to shows of dross . . . . . . ii 7 20
That choose by show, Not learning more than the fond eye doth teach . ii 9 26
A day in April never came so sweet, To show how costly summer was at hand . . . . ii 9 94
A prodigal, who dare scarce show his head on the Rialto . . . iii 1 47
So may the outward shows be least themselves . . . . . iii 2 73
Being season'd with a gracious voice, Obscures the show of evil . . iii 2 77
His letter there Will show you his estate . . . . . . iii 2 239
Bid your friends welcome, show a merry cheer . . . . . iii 2 314
If you knew to whom you show this honour, How true a gentleman . iii 4 5
Wilt thou show the whole wealth of thy wit in an instant? . . . iii 5 61
'Tis thought Thou'lt show thy mercy and remorse more strange Than is thy strange apparent cruelty . . . . iv 1 20
His sceptre shows the force of temporal power . . . . . iv 1 190
Earthly power doth then show likest God's When mercy seasons justice iv 1 196
Herein Fortune shows herself more kind Than is her custom . . . iv 1 267
I pray you, show my youth old Shylock's house . . . . . iv 2 11
Will you show me to this house? . . . . iv 2 19
Dear Celia, I show more mirth than I am mistress of . . *As Y. Like It* i 2 3
The little foolery that wise men have makes a great show . . . i 2 97
Thou wilt show more bright and seem more virtuous When she is gone . i 3 83
Show me the place: I love to cope him in these sullen fits . . . ii 1 66
Doublet and hose ought to show itself courageous to petticoat . . ii 4 7
Bare distress hath ta'en from me the show Of smooth civility . . . ii 7 95
Tongues I'll hang on every tree, That shall civil sayings show . . iii 2 136
The quintessence of every sprite Heaven would in little show . . iii 2 148
Tell me where it is.—Go with me to it and I'll show it you . . . iii 2 451
Now show the wound mine eye hath made in thee . . . . . iii 5 20
Out of you she sees herself more proper Than any of her lineaments can show her . . . . iii 5 56

Show. And show the world what the bird hath done to her own nest *As Y. Like It* iv 1 207
You have done me much ungentleness, To show the letter that I writ to you v 2 84
Wherein your lady and your humble wife May show her duty *T. of S.* Ind. 1 117
We'll show thee Io as she was a maid, And how she was beguiled Ind. 2 56
What company is this?—Master, some show to welcome us to town i 1 47
Am bold to show myself a forward guest Within your house ii 1 51
Then show it me.—Had I a glass, I would ii 1 233
'D sol re,' one clef, two notes have I: 'E la mi,' show pity, or I die iii 1 78
He that knows better how to tame a shrew, Now let him speak: 'tis charity to show iv 1 214
A sober ancient gentleman by your habit, but your words show you a madman v 1 76
I will win my wager better yet And show more sign of her obedience v 2 117
Show what we alone must think, which never Returns us thanks *All's W.* i 1 199
Who ever strove To show her merit, that did miss her love? i 1 242
It is the show and seal of nature's truth i 3 138
It is not so with Him that all things knows As 'tis with us that square our guess by shows ii 1 153
I will show myself highly fed and lowly taught ii 2 3
A need Greater than shows itself at the first view ii 5 73
Show me a child begotten of thy body that I am father to, then call me husband iii 2 60
The misery is, example, that so terrible shows in the wreck of maidenhood iii 5 24
Now will I lead you to the house, and show you The lass I spoke of iii 6 118
All the secrets of our camp I'll show, Their force, their purposes iv 1 93
And then show you the heart of my message *T. Night* i 5 203
We will draw the curtain and show you the picture i 5 251
Fate, show thy force: ourselves we do not owe i 5 329
His eyes do show his days are almost done ii 3 112
We men may say more, swear more: but indeed Our shows are more than will ii 4 120
Full of labour as a wise man's art: For folly that he wisely shows is fit iii 1 74
A murderous guilt shows not itself more soon Than love that would seem hid iii 1 159
She did show favour to the youth in your sight only to exasperate you iii 2 19
I will show thee no reason for't. iii 4 166
Stand here, make a good show on't iii 4 317
Sicilia cannot show himself over-kind to Bohemia *W. Tale* i 1 23
How thou lovest us, show in our brother's welcome i 2 174
Your changed complexions are to me a mirror Which shows me mine changed too i 2 382
If she dares trust me with her little babe, I'll show't the king ii 2 38
I should blush To see you so attired, sworn, I think, To show myself a glass iv 4 14
Fairly offer'd.—This shows a sound affection iv 4 390
Happy be you! All that you speak shows fair iv 4 636
Show those things you found about her, those secret things iv 4 713
Show the inside of your purse to the outside of his hand, and no more ado iv 4 833
We must to the king and show our strange sights iv 4 849
The affection of nobleness which nature shows above her breeding v 2 41
I like your silence, it the more shows off Your wonder v 3 21
Come, lady, I will show thee to my kin *K. John* i 1 273
Stay, And I shall show you peace and fair-faced league ii 1 417
Evils that take leave, On their departure most of all show evil iii 4 115
That close aspect of his Does show the mood of a much troubled breast iv 2 73
Show boldness and aspiring confidence v 1 56
A noble temper dost thou show in this v 2 40
Lie gently at the foot of peace, And be no further harmful than in show v 2 77
Show me the very wound of this ill news: I am no woman, I'll not swoon v 6 21
Show now your mended faiths, And instantly return with me again v 7 75
From where you do remain let paper show *Richard II.* i 3 250
Each substance of a grief hath twenty shadows, Which shows like grief itself ii 2 15
Like perspectives, which rightly gazed upon Show nothing but confusion ii 2 19
Show me thy humble heart, and not thy knee, Whose duty is deceiveable ii 3 83
To show the world I am a gentleman iii 1 27
My stooping duty tenderly shall show iii 3 48
Alack, alack, for woe, That any harm should stain so fair a show! iii 3 71
Show us the hand of God That hath dismiss'd us from our stewardship iii 3 77
Stand all apart, And show fair duty to his majesty iii 3 188
Dry your eyes; Tears show their love, but want their remedies iii 3 203
By that fair sun which shows me where thou stand'st iv 1 35
That . . . souls refined Should show so heinous, black, obscene a deed! iv 1 131
Command a mirror hither straight, That it may show me what a face I have iv 1 266
I'll lay A plot shall show us all a merry day iv 1 334
The truth of what we are Shows us but this v 1 20
Let me see the writing.—I do beseech you, pardon me; I may not show it v 2 70
Thou shalt know The treason that my haste forbids me show v 3 50
So sighs and tears and groans Show minutes, times, and hours v 5 58
With Cain go wander thorough shades of night, And never show thy head v 6 44
Shall show more goodly and attract more eyes *1 Hen. IV.* i 2 238
Pardon me that I descend so low, To show the line and the predicament Wherein you range i 3 168
He shows in this, he loves his own barn better than he loves our house ii 3 5
Step aside, and I'll show thee a precedent ii 4 36
Show it a fair pair of heels and run from it ii 4 53
And have it; yea, and can show it you here in the house ii 4 284
All the courses of my life do show I am not in the roll of common men iii 1 42
Amend this fault: Though sometimes it show greatness, courage, blood iii 1 181
Curtsy at his frowns, To show how much thou art degenerate iii 2 128
Draws a curtain, That shows the ignorant a kind of fear iv 1 74
If thou wert sensible of courtesy, I should not make so dear a show of zeal v 4 95
But the corpse, But shadows and the shows of men, to fight *2 Hen. IV.* i 1 193
Doth it not show vilely in me to desire small beer? ii 2 7
He'll not swagger with a Barbary hen, if her feathers turn back in any show of resistance ii 4 109
Faculties a' has, that show a weak mind and an able body ii 4 273
I was then Sir Dagonet in Arthur's show iii 2 300
Rather show awhile like fearful war, To diet rank minds sick of happiness iv 1 63
Have the summary of all our griefs, When time shall serve, to show in articles iv 1 74
This will I show the general iv 1 178

Show. My love to ye Shall show itself more openly hereafter *2 Hen. IV.* iv 2 76
If you do not all show like gilt two-pences to me iv 3 55
O'ershine you as much as the full moon doth the cinders of the element, which show like pins' heads to her iv 3 58
And never live to show the incredulous world The noble change iv 5 154
This poor show doth better: this doth infer the zeal I had v 5 14
It shows my earnestness of affection,— It doth so v 5 17
With some shows of truth, Though, in pure truth, it was corrupt *Hen. V.* i 2 72
Shall we sparingly show you far off The Dauphin's meaning? i 2 239
I will keep my state, Be like a king and show my sail of greatness i 2 274
Good Corporal Nym, show thy valour, and put up your sword ii 1 45
You show great mercy, if you give him life ii 2 50
Show men dutiful? Why, so didst thou: seem they grave and learned? ii 2 127
Let us do it with no show of fear ii 4 23
You, good yeomen, Whose limbs were made in England, show us here The mettle of your pasture iii 1 26
He is not the man that he would gladly make show to the world he is iii 6 88
The element shows to him as it doth to me iv 1 107
He may show what outward courage he will; but I believe iv 1 118
O ceremony, show me but thy worth! What is thy soul of adoration? iv 1 261
Your fair show shall suck away their souls iv 2 17
Description cannot suit itself in words To demonstrate the life of such a battle In life so lifeless as it shows itself iv 2 55
Then will he strip his sleeve and show his scars iv 3 47
As I suck blood, I will some mercy show iv 4 68
So the maid that stood in the way for my wish shall show me the way to my will v 2 355
How can these contrarieties agree?—That will I show you *1 Hen. VI.* ii 3 60
Which, once discern'd, shows that her meaning is, No way to that iii 2 24
Make a show of love to proud Duke Humphrey *2 Hen. VI.* i 1 241
To show your highness A spirit raised from depth of under-ground i 2 78
Show some reason, Buckingham, Why Somerset should be preferr'd in this i 3 116
Give me leave To show some reason, of no little force i 3 166
It will hang upon my richest robes And show itself, attire me how I can ii 4 109
He knits his brow and shows an angry eye And passeth by iii 1 15
In his simple show he harbours treason iii 1 54
Gloucester's show Beguiles him as the mournful crocodile iii 1 225
We have but trivial argument, More than mistrust, that shows him worthy death iii 1 242
Show me one scar character'd on thy skin iii 1 300
You, my lord, were glad to be employ'd, To show how quaint an orator you are iii 2 274
Show me where he is: I'll give a thousand pound to look upon him iii 3 12
Soldiers, show what cruelty ye can, That this my death may never be forgot! iv 1 132
Follow me. Now show yourselves men; 'tis for liberty iv 2 193
As on a mountain top the cedar shows v 1 205
Will you we show our title to the crown? *3 Hen. VI.* i 1 102
Nay, if thou be that princely eagle's bird, Show thy descent by gazing 'gainst the sun ii 1 92
Her words do show her wit incomparable iii 2 85
My mangled body shows, My blood, my want of strength, my sick heart shows, That I must yield my body to the earth v 2 7
Mirthful comic shows, Such as befits the pleasure of the court v 7 43
Your interior hatred, Which in your outward actions shows itself *Richard III.* i 3 66
Nor more can you distinguish of a man Than of his outward show iii 1 10
So smooth he daub'd his vice with show of virtue iii 5 29
Those that come to see Only a show or two *Hen. VIII.* Prol. 10
To rank our chosen truth with such a show As fool and fight is Prol. 18
Only to show his pomp as well in France As here at home i 1 163
In him Sparing would show a worse sin than ill doctrine i 3 60
For 'tis to such a thing,— You cannot show me i 4 48
If you can blush and cry 'guilty,' cardinal, You'll show a little honesty iii 2 306
In celebration of this day with shows, Pageants and sights of honour iv 1 10
I'll show your grace the strangest sight v 2 20
Those joyful tears show thy true heart v 3 175
I'll show you Troilus anon: if he see me, you shall see him nod *T. and C.* i 2 210
Even so Doth valour's show and valour's worth divide In storms of fortune i 3 46
Degree being vizarded, The unworthiest shows as fairly in the mask i 3 84
Like merchants, show our foulest wares, And think, perchance, they'll sell; if not, The lustre of the better yet to show, Shall show the better i 3 359
By my head, 'tis pride: but why, why? let him show us the cause ii 3 96
Perchance, my lord, I show more craft than love iii 2 160
Whereupon I will show you a chamber with a bed iii 2 215
Pride hath no other glass To show itself but pride iii 3 48
Men, like butterflies, Show not their mealy wings but to the summer iii 3 79
It lies as coldly in him as fire in a flint, which will not show without knocking iii 3 258
For what he has he gives, what thinks he shows iv 5 101
To such as boasting show their scars A mock is due iv 5 290
Come, come, thou boy-queller, show thy face v 5 45
Troilus, thou coward Troilus, show thy head! v 6 1
They have had inkling this fortnight what we intend to do, which now we'll show 'em in deeds *Coriolanus* i 1 60
Keep your great pretences veil'd till when They needs must show themselves i 2 21
In the embracements of his bed where he would show most love i 3 5
If these shows be not outward, which of you But is four Volsces? i 6 77
There will be large cicatrices to show the people ii 1 164
Show them the unaching scars which I should hide ii 2 152
If he show us his wounds and tell us his deeds, we are to put our tongues into those wounds and speak for them ii 3 6
I have wounds to show you, which shall be yours in private ii 3 83
He said he had wounds, which he could show in private ii 3 174
You show too much of that For which the people stir iii 1 52
To show bare heads In congregations, to yawn iii 2 10
Rather show our general louts How you can frown than spend a fawn upon 'em iii 2 66
Must I go show them my unbarbed sconce? iii 2 99
Plant love among's! Throng our large temples with the shows of peace! iii 3 36
The wounds his body bears, which show Like graves i' the holy churchyard iii 3 50
I have been consul, and can show for Rome Her enemies' marks upon me iii 3 110
Present My throat to thee and to thy ancient malice; Which not to cut would show thee but a fool iv 5 103
Durst not, look you, sir, show themselves, as we term it, his friends iv 5 221

Show. Go home, And show no sign of fear . . . . *Coriolanus* iv 6 153
He bears all things fairly, And shows good husbandry . . . iv 7 22
Of thy deep duty more impression show Than that of common sons . v 3 51
Unproperly Show duty, as mistaken all this while Between the child and parent . . . . v 3 55
Which by the interpretation of full time May show like all yourself v 3 70
If I cannot persuade thee Rather to show a noble grace . . v 3 121
And this for me, struck home to show my strength *T. Andron.* ii 3 117
Do thou entreat her show a woman pity . . . . . ii 3 147
A precious ring, that lightens all the hole, . . . Doth shine upon the dead man's earthy cheeks, And shows the ragged entrails of the pit ii 3 230
And in dumb shows Pass the remainder of our hateful days . . iii 1 131
Now let me show a brother's love to thee . . . . iii 1 183
I'll show thee wondrous things, That highly may advantage thee to hear v 1 55
Show me a murderer, I'll deal with him.—Show me a villain that hath done a rape . . . . v 2 93
Show me a thousand that have done thee wrong, And I will be revenged on them all . . . . v 2 96
The trumpets show the emperor is at hand . . . . v 3 16
What say you, Romans? Have we done aught amiss,—show us wherein v 3 129
That shows thee a weak slave; for the weakest goes to the wall *R. and J.* i 1 17
'Tis all one, I will show myself a tyrant . . . . . i 1 25
Show me a mistress that is passing fair, What doth her beauty serve? . i 1 240
Compare her face with some that I shall show . . . . i 2 91
Let there be weigh'd Your lady's love against some other maid That I will show you shining at this feast, And she shall scant show well that now shows best . . . . i 2 103
Beauty too rich for use, for earth too dear! So shows a snowy dove trooping with crows, As yonder lady o'er her fellows shows . i 5 50
Which if thou respect, Show a fair presence and put off these frowns . i 5 75
You do wrong your hand too much, Which mannerly devotion shows in this . . . . i 5 100
Wolvish-ravening lamb! Despised substance of divinest show! . . iii 2 77
Some grief shows much of love; But much of grief shows still some want of wit . . . . iii 5 73
Fetch drier logs: Call Peter, he will show thee where they are . iv 4 16
And old cakes of roses, Were thinly scatter'd, to make up a show . v 1 48
I will be gone, sir, and not trouble you.—So shalt thou show me friendship . . . . v 3 41
The sun, for sorrow, will not show his head . . . . v 3 306
The fire i' the flint Shows not till it be struck . *T. of Athens* i 1 23
A thousand moral paintings I can show . . . . . i 1 90
To show Lord Timon that mean eyes have seen The foot above the head i 1 93
When dinner's done, Show me this piece . . . . . i 1 255
Like madness is the glory of this life, As this pomp shows to a little oil and root. We make ourselves fools . . . . . . i 2 140
I prithee, let's be provided to show them entertainment . . . i 2 185
Nor will he . . . yield me this, To show him what a beggar his heart is i 2 201
It shows but little love or judgement in him: Must I be his last refuge? iii 3 10
I'll show you how to observe a strange event . . . . iii 4 17
Mark, how strange it shows, Timon in this should pay more than he owes . . . . iii 4 21
The place which I have feasted, does it now, Like all mankind, show me an iron heart? . . . . iii 4 84
That which I show, heaven knows, is merely love, Duty and zeal . iv 3 522
Thou shalt build from men; Hate all, curse all, show charity to none . iv 3 534
It will show honestly in us; and is very likely to load our purposes . v 1 15
That gentleness And show of love as I was wont to have *J. Cæsar* i 2 34
With himself at war, Forgets the shows of love to other men . . i 2 47
I am glad that my weak words Have struck but thus much show of fire i 2 177
Our yoke and sufferance show us womanish . . . . . i 3 84
O conspiracy, Shamest thou to show thy dangerous brow by night? . ii 1 78
All remember What you have said, and show yourselves true Romans . ii 1 223
And that I am he, Let me a little show it, even in this . . iii 1 71
I will myself into the pulpit first, And show the reason of our Cæsar's death . . . . iii 1 237
Then make a ring about the corpse of Cæsar, And let me show you him that made the will . . . . iii 2 163
Show you sweet Cæsar's wounds, poor poor dumb mouths, And bid them speak for me . . . . iii 2 229
But hollow men, like horses hot at hand, Make gallant show and promise iv 2 24
Go show your slaves how choleric you are, And make your bondmen tremble . . . . iv 3 43
Who, much enforced, shows a hasty spark, And straight is cold again . iv 3 112
Prepare you, generals: The enemy comes on in gallant show . . v 1 13
O hateful error, melancholy's child, Why dost thou show to the apt thoughts of men The things that are not? . . . . . . v 3 68
Look what I have.—Show me, show me . . . . *Macbeth* i 3 27
Are ye fantastical, or that indeed Which outwardly ye show? . . i 3 54
Away, and mock the time with fairest show . . . . . i 7 81
Get on your nightgown, lest occasion call us, And show us to be watchers ii 2 71
To show an unfelt sorrow is an office Which the false man does easy . ii 3 142
Was never call'd to bear my part, Or show the glory of our art . iii 5 9
Come, high or low; Thyself and office deftly show! . . . iv 1 68
Show!—Show!—Show!—Show his eyes, and grieve his heart . . iv 1 110
Filthy hags! Why do you show me this? . . . . . iv 1 116
The eighth appears, who bears a glass Which shows me many more . iv 1 120
Come, sisters, cheer we up his sprites, And show the best of our delights iv 1 128
Now near enough: your leavy screens throw down, And show like those you are . . . . v 6 2
That way the noise is. Tyrant, show thy face! . . . . v 7 14
Then yield thee, coward, And live to be the show and gaze o' the time . v 8 24
We do it wrong, being so majestical, To offer it the show of violence *Hamlet* i 1 144
In that and all things will we show our duty.—We doubt it nothing . i 2 40
I came to Denmark, To show my duty in your coronation . . i 2 53
But I have that within which passeth show; These but the trappings and the suits of woe . . . . i 2 85
It shows a will most incorrect to heaven, A heart unfortified . . i 2 95
Do not, as some ungracious pastors do, Show me the steep and thorny way to heaven . . . . i 3 48
They are brokers, Not of that dye which their investments show . . i 3 128
Fare thee well at once! The glow-worm shows the matin to be near . i 5 89
Show us so much gentry and good will As to expend your time with us awhile . . . . ii 2 22
Which, I tell you, must show fairly outward . . . . ii 2 391
The first row of the pious chanson will show you more . . . ii 2 438
Read on this book; That show of such an exercise may colour Your loneliness . . . . iii 1 45
Let his queen mother all alone entreat him To show his grief . . iii 1 191

Show. To hold, as 'twere, the mirror up to nature; to show virtue her own feature . . . . *Hamlet* iii 2 25
That's villanous, and shows a most pitiful ambition in the fool that uses it . . . . iii 2 49
Belike this show imports the argument of the play . . . iii 2 149
Will he tell us what this show meant?—Ay, or any show that you'll show him: be not you ashamed to show, he'll not shame to tell you what it means . . . . iii 2 153
Your wisdom should show itself more richer to signify this to his doctor iii 2 316
Like some ore Among a mineral of metals base, Shows itself pure . iv 1 27
To show you how a king may go a progress through the guts of a beggar iv 3 32
That inward breaks, and shows no cause without Why the man dies . iv 4 28
What would you undertake, To show yourself your father's son in deed More than in words? . . . . iv 7 126
That shows his hoar leaves in the glassy stream . . . . iv 7 168
'Swounds, show me what thou'lt do: Woo't weep? woo't fight? . . v 1 297
Such a sight as this Becomes the field, but here shows much amiss . v 2 413
Our court, infected with their manners, Shows like a riotous inn . *Lear* i 4 265
O most small fault, How ugly didst thou in Cordelia show! . . i 4 289
You shall do small respect, show too bold malice . . . . ii 2 137
And are at point To show their open banner . . . . iii 1 34
Show her this ring; And she will tell you who your fellow is . . iii 1 47
That thou mayest shake the superflux to them, And show the heavens more just . . . . iii 4 36
Suffers most i' the mind, Leaving free things and happy shows behind . iii 6 112
Post speedily to my lord your husband; show him this letter . . iii 7 2
This shows you are above, You justicers, that these our nether crimes So speedily can venge! . . . . iv 2 78
Would I could meet him, madam! I should show What party I do follow iv 5 39
Choughs that wing the midway air Show scarce so gross as beetles . iv 6 14
Throwing but shows of service on their lords, Do well thrive by them *Othello* i 1 52
Yet, for necessity of present life, I must show out a flag and sign of love i 1 157
'Tis my breeding That gives me this bold show of courtesy . . ii 1 100
One unperfectness shows me another, to make me frankly despise myself ii 3 299
Divinity of hell! When devils will the blackest sins put on, They do suggest at first with heavenly shows . . . . ii 3 358
If thou dost love me, Show me thy thought.—My lord, you know I love you . . . . iii 3 116
Now I shall have reason To show the love and duty that I bear you . iii 3 194
They do let heaven see the pranks They dare not show their husbands . iii 3 203
'Tis not a year or two shows us a man . . . . . iii 4 103
If thou hast that in thee . . . , I mean purpose, courage and valour, this night show it . . . . iv 2 219
I will show you such a necessity in his death that you shall think yourself bound to put it on him . . . . iv 2 247
I know this act shows horrible and grim . . . . . v 2 203
A little I can read.—Show him your hand . . *Ant. and Cleo.* i 2 10
When it pleaseth their deities to take the wife of a man from him, it shows to man the tailors of the earth . . . . i 2 169
'Tis time we twain Did show ourselves i' the field . . . . i 4 74
May I never To this good purpose, that so fairly shows, Dream of impediment! . . . . ii 2 147
Show us the way, sir . . . . ii 6 83
Show me which way . . . . ii 7 75
She shows a body rather than a life, A statue than a breather . . iii 3 23
Six kings already Show me the way of yielding . . . . iii 10 35
I have fled myself; and have instructed cowards To run and show their shoulders . . . . iii 11 8
Like enough, high-battled Cæsar will Unstate his happiness, and be staged to the show, Against a sworder! . . . . . . iii 13 30
I dare not, Lest I be taken: not the imperious show Of the full-fortuned Cæsar ever shall Be brooch'd with me . . . . . . iv 15 23
Go with me, and see What I can show in this . . . . . v 1 77
Shall they hoist me up And show me to the shouting varletry Of censuring Rome? . . . . v 2 56
Or I shall show the cinders of my spirits Through the ashes of my chance v 2 173
Show me, my women, like a queen: go fetch My best attires . . v 2 227
Our army shall In solemn show attend this funeral; And then to Rome v 2 367
There is No danger in what show of death it makes, More than the locking-up the spirits a time . . . . . . *Cymbeline* i 5 40
A precedent Which not to read would show the Britons cold . . iii 1 76
Strikes life into my speech and shows much more His own conceiving . iii 3 97
For ourself To show less sovereignty than they, must needs Appear unkinglike . . . . iii 5 6
O melancholy! Who ever yet could sound thy bottom? find The ooze, to show what coast thy sluggish crare Might easiliest harbour in? . iv 2 205
Their blood thinks scorn, Till it fly out and show them princes born . iv 4 54
Let me make men know More valour in me than my habits show . . v 1 30
No more, thou thunder-master, show Thy spite on mortal flies . . v 4 30
By watching, weeping, tendance, kissing, to O'ercome you with her show v 5 54
Appear'd to me, with other spritely shows Of mine own kindred . . v 5 428
Let him show His skill in the construction . . . . . v 5 432
This mercy shows we'll joy in such a son . . . . *Pericles* i 1 118
To show his sorrow, he'ld correct himself . . . . . i 3 23
Who makes the fairest show means most deceit . . . . i 4 75
I'll show you those in troubles reign, Losing a mite, a mountain gain ii Gower 7
I'll show the virtue I have borne in arms . . . . . ii 1 151
Which shows that beauty hath his power and will, Which can as well inflame as it can kill . . . . ii 2 34
He had need mean better than his outward show Can any way speak . ii 2 48
More than 's fit, Since every worth in show commends itself . . ii 3 6
Yon knight doth sit too melancholy, As if the entertainment in our court Had not a show might countervail his worth . . . . . ii 3 56
What's dumb in show I'll plain with speech . . . . iii Gower 14
Unscissar'd shall this hair of mine remain, Though I show ill in't . . iii 3 30
See how belief may suffer by foul show! . . . . . iv 4 23
If you were born to honour, show it now . . . . . iv 6 99
What shows, What minstrelsy, and pretty din, The regent made . . v 2 271

Showed. I loved thee And show'd thee all the qualities o' the isle *Tempest* i 2 337
My mistress show'd me thee and thy dog and thy bush . . . ii 2 144
You have showed yourself a wise physician . . . *Mer. Wives* ii 3 56
Showed him a seeming warrant for it . . . . *Meas. for Meas.* iv 2 160
And show'd me silks that he had bought for me . . *Com. of Errors* iv 3 8
As a brother to his sister, show'd Bashful sincerity and comely love *Much Ado* iv 1 54
Whoe'er a' was, a' show'd a mounting mind . . . *L. L. Lost* iv 1 4
Behaviour, what wert thou Till this madman show'd thee? . . v 2 338
That superfluous case That hid the worse and show'd the better face . v 2 388
Our letters, madam, show'd much more than jest.—So did our looks . v 2 795

Showed. Fetch me that flower; the herb I shew'd thee once *M. N. Dream* ii 1 169
Showed me a ring that he had of your daughter for a monkey *M. of V.* iii 1 123
Did your brother tell you how I counterfeited to swoon when he showed me your handkercher? . . . *As Y. Like It* v 2 29
I promise you You have show'd a tender fatherly regard *T. of Shrew* ii 1 288
You have show'd me that which well approves You're great in fortune *All's Well* iii 7 13
For the fair kindness you have show'd me here . . . *T. Night* iii 4 376
Alas! I have show'd too much The rashness of a woman *W. Tale* iii 2 221
If I had thought the sight of my poor image Would thus have wrought you,—for the stone is mine—I'ld not have show'd it . . v 3 59
He show'd his warrant to a friend of mine *K. John* iv 2 70
His chin new reap'd Show'd like a stubble-land at harvest-home 1 *Hen. IV.* i 3 35
I am now of all humours that have showed themselves humours . ii 4 105
And so my state, Seldom but sumptuous, showed like a feast . . iii 2 58
Tell me, tell me, How show'd his tasking? seem'd it in contempt? v 2 51
Redeem'd thy lost opinion, And show'd thou makest some tender of my life . . . v 4 49
It better show'd with you When that your flock, assembled by the bell, Encircled you to hear with reverence . . . 2 *Hen. IV.* iv 2 4
And show'd how well you love your prince and country . 2 *Hen. VI.* iv 9 16
Ay, to such mercy as his ruthless arm, With downright payment, show'd unto my father . . . 3 *Hen. VI.* i 4 32
In choosing for yourself, you show'd your judgement . . iv 1 61
By his face straight shall you know his heart.—What of his heart perceive you in his face By any likelihood he show'd to-day? *Rich. III.* iii 4 57
The mayor in courtesy show'd me the castle, And call'd it Rougemont . iv 2 107
Every man that stood Show'd like a mine *Hen. VIII.* i 1 22
My surveyor is false; the o'er-great cardinal Hath show'd him gold . i 1 223
Sweetly In all the rest show'd a most noble patience . . . ii 1 36
In The merciful construction of good women; For such a one we show'd 'em . . . . . . Epil. 11
He should have show'd us His marks of merit . . . *Coriolanus* ii 3 171
Their mutinies and revolts, wherein they show'd Most valour . . iii 1 126
Lesser had been The thwartings of your dispositions, if You had not show'd them how ye were disposed . . . . iii 2 22
That when the sea was calm all boats alike Show'd mastership in floating iv 1 7
And therein show'd like enemies . . . iv 6 114
Though I show'd sourly to him, once more offer'd The first conditions . v 3 13
The Volsces May say 'This mercy we have show'd;' the Romans, 'This we received' . . . . . . v 3 137
Thou hast never in thy life Show'd thy dear mother any courtesy . v 3 161
When they show'd me this abhorred pit, They told me *T. Andron.* ii 3 98
Urged extremely for 't and showed what necessity belonged to't *T. of A.* iii 2 14
There was very little honour showed in't . . . iii 2 21
You show'd your teeth like apes, and fawn'd like hounds *J. Cæsar* v 1 41
Statilius show'd the torch-light, but, my lord, He came not back . v 5 2
Fortune, on his damned quarrel smiling, Show'd like a rebel's whore *Macb.* i 2 15
The three weird sisters: To you they have show'd some truth . ii 1 21
I have show'd the unfitness . . . *Lear* i 4 356
Ere I was risen from the place that show'd My duty kneeling . ii 4 29
So much duty as my mother show'd To you . . *Othello* i 3 186
As well as I can, madam.—And when good will is show'd, though't come too short, The actor may plead pardon *Ant. and Cleo.* ii 5 8
Dolphin-like; they show'd his back above The element they lived in v 2 89
Milford, When from the mountain-top Pisanio show'd thee, Thou wast within a ken: O Jove! I think Foundations fly the wretched *Cymb.* iii 6 5
Last night the very gods show'd me a vision . . . iv 2 346
It show'd well in you: do so now . . . *Pericles* iv 1 89
Showedst. I live To thank thee for the love thou show'dst the king *Lear* iv 2 96
Thou show'dst a subject's shine, I a true prince . . *Pericles* i 2 124
Shower. Upon my flowers Diffusest honey-drops, refreshing showers *Temp.* iv 1 79
A man may hear this shower sing in the wind . *Mer. Wives* iii 2 38
So he dissolved, and showers of oaths did melt *M. N. Dream* i 1 245
A woman's gift To rain a shower of commanded tears . *T. of Shrew* Ind. 1 125
This shower, blown up by tempest of the soul, Startles mine eyes *K. John* v 2 50
Small showers last long, but sudden storms are short *Richard II.* ii 1 35
And lay the summer's dust with showers of blood . . iii 3 43
Faster than spring-time showers comes thought on thought 2 *Hen. VI.* iii 1 337
For raging wind blows up incessant showers . . 3 *Hen. VI.* i 4 145
Even then that sunshine brew'd a shower for him . . ii 2 156
See what showers arise, Blown with the windy tempest of my heart! . ii 5 85
Once more I shower a welcome on ye; welcome all . . *Hen. VIII.* i 4 63
As sun and showers There had made a lasting spring . . iii 1 7
Delivered such a shower of pebbles, that I was fain to draw mine honour in v 4 60
The commons made A shower and thunder with their caps and shouts *Coriolanus* ii 1 283
Than youthful April shall with all his showers . . *T. Andron.* iii 1 18
Come hither, boy; come, come, and learn of us To melt in showers . v 3 161
One cloud of winter showers, These flies are couch'd . *T. of Athens* ii 2 180
He and myself Have travail'd in the great shower of your gifts . v 1 73
Which bewept to the grave did go With true-love showers . *Hamlet* iv 5 39
She makes a shower of rain as well as Jove . . *Ant. and Cleo.* i 2 156
I'll set thee in a shower of gold, and hail Rich pearls upon thee . ii 5 45
The April's in her eyes: it is love's spring, And these the showers to bring it on. Be cheerful . . . . . iii 2 44
Showered. Your royal graces, Shower'd on me daily, have been more than could My studied purposes requite . . *Hen. VIII.* iii 2 167
Showering. It rain'd down fortune showering on your head . 1 *Hen. IV.* v 1 47
A conduit, girl? what, still in tears? Evermore showering? . *R. and J.* iii 5 131
Showest. Thou showest the naked pathway to thy life . . *Richard II.* i 2 31
Though thy tackle's torn, Thou show'st a noble vessel . *Coriolanus* iv 5 68
Have more than thou showest, Speak less than thou knowest . *Lear* i 4 131
More hideous when thou show'st thee in a child Than the sea-monster! . i 4 282
Showing we would not spare heaven as we love it . . *Meas. for Meas.* ii 3 33
By something showing a more swelling port . *Mer. of Venice* i 1 124
If you will have it in showing, you shall read it in—what do ye call there?—A showing of a heavenly effect in an earthly actor *All's Well* ii 3 25
Showing, as in a model, our firm estate . . *Richard II.* iii 4 42
Though some of you with Pilate wash your hands Showing an outward pity . . . . iv 1 240
No man should possess him with any appearance of fear, lest he, by showing it, should dishearten his army . . *Hen. V.* iv 1 116
Nor, showing, as the manner is, his wounds To the people . *Coriolanus* ii 1 251
I will not seal your knowledge with showing them . . . ii 3 116
The canker gnaw thy heart, For showing me again the eyes of man! *T. of Athens* iv 3 50
Of very soft society and great showing . . . *Hamlet* v 2 113
Shown. Thou hast shown some sign of good desert . *T. G. of Ver.* iii 2 18
Sir Hugh hath shown himself a wise and patient churchman *Mer. Wives* ii 3 57
Shown. Blushing cheeks by faults are bred And fears by pale white shown *L. L. Lost* i 2 107
Dismask'd, their damask sweet commixture shown, Are angels vailing clouds . . . . v 2 296
That every man should take his own, In your waking shall be shown *M. N. Dream* iii 2 460
And thine eyes See it so grossly shown in thy behaviours That in their kind they speak it . . . . . *All's Well* i 3 184
So holy writ in babes hath judgement shown . . . ii 1 141
To one of your receiving Enough is shown . . . *T. Night* iii 1 132
His valour shown upon our crests to-day Hath taught us how to cherish such high deeds Even in the bosom of our adversaries 1 *Hen. IV.* v 5 29
Which oft our stage hath shown . . . . *Hen. V.* Epil. 13
Nor should thy prowess want praise and esteem, But that 'tis shown ignobly and in treason . . . . . 2 *Hen. VI.* v 2 23
Were thy heart as hard as steel, As thou hast shown it flinty by thy deeds, I come to pierce it . . . . 3 *Hen. VI.* ii 1 202
With no man here he is offended; For, were he, he had shown it in his looks.—I pray God he be not . . . *Richard III.* iii 4 59
The citizens, I am sure, have shown at full their royal minds *Hen. VIII.* iv 1 8
Now we have shown our power, Let us seem humbler *Coriolanus* iv 2 3
I'll go along, no such sight to be shown . . *Rom. and Jul.* i 2 105
Hollow welcomes, Recanting goodness, sorry ere 'tis shown *T. of Athens* i 2 17
When I might ha' shown myself honourable! how unluckily it happened! . . . . iii 2 51
With an entreaty, herein further shown, That it might please you *Hamlet* ii 2 76
This, in obedience, hath my daughter shown me . . ii 2 125
I hear that you have shown your father A child-like office . *Lear* ii 1 107
Sir, you have shown to-day your valiant strain . . v 3 40
As if there were some monster in his thought Too hideous to be shown *Othello* iii 3 108
You have shown all Hectors . . . *Ant. and Cleo.* iv 8 7
Most monster-like, be shown For poor'st diminutives, for doits . iv 12 36
This sword but shown to Cæsar, with this tidings, Shall enter me with him . . . . iv 14 112
I must perforce Have shown to thee such a declining day, Or look on thine . . . . v 1 38
Thou, an Egyptian puppet, shalt be shown In Rome, as well as I . . v 2 208
Who has a book of all that monarchs do, He's more secure to keep it shut than shown . . . . . . *Pericles* i 1 95
This man, Through whom the gods have shown their power . v 3 60
Go with me to my house, Where shall be shown you all was found with her . . . . v 3 66
Show-place. I' the common show-place, where they exercise *Ant. and Cleo.* iii 6 12
Shred. With these shreds They vented their complainings *Coriolanus* i 1 212
A king of shreds and patches . . . *Hamlet* iii 4 102
Shrew. But, like a shrew, you first begin to brawl . *Com. of Errors* iv 1 51
A pox of that jest! and I beshrew all shrows . *L. L. Lost* v 2 46
In such a night Did pretty Jessica, like a little shrew, Slander her love, and he forgave it her . . . *Mer. of Venice* v 1 21
A meacock wretch can make the curstest shrew . *T. of Shrew* ii 1 315
Such an injury would vex a very saint, Much more a shrew . iii 2 29
Is she so hot a shrew as she's reported? . . . iv 1 22
By this reckoning he is more shrew than she . . . iv 1 87
He that knows better how to tame a shrew, Now let him speak . iv 1 213
To tame a shrew and charm her chattering tongue . . iv 2 58
Your husband, being troubled with a shrew, Measures my husband's sorrow by his woe . . . . v 2 28
I think thou hast the veriest shrew of all.—Well, I say no . v 2 64
Now, go thy ways; thou hast tamed a curst shrew . . v 2 188
Bless you, fair shrew . . . . . *T. Night* i 3 50
'Shrew my heart, You never spoke what did become you less *W. Tale* i 2 281
For women are shrews, both short and tall . . 2 *Hen. IV.* v 3 36
'Shrew me, If I would lose it for a revenue Of any king's . *Cymbeline* ii 3 147
Shrewd. There is shrewd construction made of her . *Mer. Wives* ii 2 232
I shall beat you to your tent, and prove a shrewd Cæsar to you *M. for M.* ii 1 263
Thou wilt never get thee a husband, if thou be so shrewd of thy tongue . . . . *Much Ado* ii 1 20
A shrewd unhappy gallows . . . . *L. L. Lost* v 2 12
That shrewd and knavish sprite Call'd Robin Goodfellow *M. N. Dream* ii 1 33
O, when she's angry, she is keen and shrewd! . . . iii 2 323
There are some shrewd contents in yon same paper . *Mer. of Venice* iii 2 246
Every of this happy number That have endured shrewd days and nights with us Shall share the good . *As Y. Like It* v 4 179
Her eldest sister is so curst and shrewd . . . *T. of Shrew* i 1 185
Shall I then come roundly to thee And wish thee to a shrewd ill-favour'd wife? . . . . i 2 60
As curst and shrewd As Socrates' Xanthippe, or a worse . . i 2 70
She is intolerable curst And shrewd and froward . . . i 2 90
This young maid might do her A shrewd turn, if she pleased *All's Well* iii 5 71
A shrewd knave and an unhappy.—So he is . . . iv 5 66
Ah, foul shrewd news! beshrew thy very heart! . . *K. John* v 5 14
To lift shrewd steel against our golden crown . *Richard II.* iii 2 59
Methought a' made a shrewd thrust at your belly . 2 *Hen. IV.* ii 4 228
These women are shrewd tempters with their tongues . 1 *Hen. VI.* i 2 123
Gloucester scarce himself, That bears so shrewd a maim . 2 *Hen. VI.* ii 3 41
A parlous boy: go to, you are too shrewd . . *Richard III.* ii 4 35
But they are shrewd ones . . . . . *Hen. VIII.* i 3 7
Do my Lord of Canterbury A shrewd turn, and he is your friend for ever v 3 178
He has a shrewd wit, I can tell you . . *Troi. and Cres.* i 2 206
We shall find of him A shrewd contriver . . . *J. Cæsar* ii 1 158
'Tis a shrewd doubt, though it be but a dream . . *Othello* iii 3 429
This last day was A shrewd one to 's . . . *Ant. and Cleo.* iv 9 5
Shrewdly. You apprehend passing shrewdly . . . *Much Ado* ii 1 84
He's shrewdly vexed at something . . . *All's Well* iii 5 92
You boggle shrewdly, every feather starts you . . . v 3 232
This practice hath most shrewdly pass'd upon thee . . *T. Night* v 1 360
Your verse Flow'd with her beauty once: 'tis shrewdly ebb'd *W. Tale* v 1 102
Methought yesterday your mistress shrewdly shook your back *Hen. V.* iii 7 52
Ay, but these English are shrewdly out of beef . . iii 7 163
My fame is shrewdly gored . . . *Troi. and Cres.* iii 3 228
My misgiving still Falls shrewdly to the purpose . *J. Cæsar* iii 1 146
The air bites shrewdly; it is very cold . . . *Hamlet* i 4 1
Shrewdness. Out of her impatience, which not wanted Shrewdness of policy too, I grieving grant Did you too much disquiet *Ant. and Cleo.* ii 2 69
Shrewish. My wife is shrewish when I keep not hours . *Com. of Errors* iii 1 2
Shrewishly. He speaks very shrewishly; one would think his mother's milk were scarce out of him . . . . *T. Night* i 5 170
Shrewishness. I have no gift at all in shrewishness . *M. N. Dream* iii 2 301

Shrewsbury. As is appointed us, at Shrewsbury . . 1 *Hen. IV.* iii 1 86
The English rebels met The eleventh of this month at Shrewsbury . iii 2 166
I thought your honour had already been at Shrewsbury . iv 2 58
At Shrewsbury, As I am truly given to understand . . . . iv 4 10
Fought a long hour by Shrewsbury clock . . . . . v 4 151
In a bloody field by Shrewsbury Hath beaten down young Hotspur 2 *Hen. IV.* Ind. 24
Between that royal field of Shrewsbury And this worm-eaten hold . Ind. 34
I bring you certain news from Shrewsbury.—Good, an God will! . i 1 12
How is this derived? Saw you the field? came you from Shrewsbury? i 1 24
Of him I did demand what news from Shrewsbury . . . i 1 40
Didst thou come from Shrewsbury?—I ran from Shrewsbury, my noble lord . . . . i 1 64
He hath since done good service at Shrewsbury . . . . i 2 71
I sent for you before your expedition to Shrewsbury . . . i 2 116
Your day's service at Shrewsbury hath a little gilded over your night's exploit on Gad's-hill . . . . i 2 167
It was young Hotspur's case at Shrewsbury . . . . i 3 26
For these good deserts, We here create you Earl of Shrewsbury 1 *Hen. VI.* iii 4 26
Lord Talbot, Earl of Shrewsbury, Created, for his rare success in arms iv 7 61
Shriek. You would fright the duchess and the ladies, that they would shriek; and that were enough to hang us all . *M. N. Dream* i 2 78
And so, with shrieks, She melted into air . . *W. Tale* iii 3 36
Then I'ld shriek, that even your ears Should rift to hear me . v 1 65
For night-owls shriek where mounting larks should sing *Richard II.* iii 3 183
What noise? what shriek is this?—'Tis our mad sister *Troi. and Cres.* ii 2 97
Shrieks like mandrakes' torn out of the earth, That living mortals, hearing them, run mad . . . . . *Rom. and Jul.* iv 3 47
What should it be, that they so shriek abroad? . . . v 3 190
And ghosts did shriek and squeal about the streets . *J. Cæsar* ii 2 24
Sighs and groans and shrieks that rend the air Are made, not mark'd *Macbeth* iv 3 168
The lady shrieks, and well-a-near Does fall in travail . *Pericles* iii Gower 51
Shrieked. The women have so cried and shrieked at it . *Mer. Wives* i 1 309
The owl shriek'd at thy birth,—an evil sign . . 3 *Hen. VI.* v 6 44
It was the owl that shriek'd, the fatal bellman . . *Macbeth* ii 2 3
Shrieking. Several noises Of roaring, shrieking, howling *Tempest* v 1 233
They clap the lubber Ajax on the shoulder, As if his foot were on brave Hector's breast And great Troy shrieking . *Troi. and Cres.* iii 3 141
Yesterday the bird of night did sit Even at noon-day upon the market-place, Hooting and shrieking . . . . . *J. Cæsar* i 3 28
Shrieve. He was whipped for getting the shrieve's fool with child *A. W.* iv 3 213
Shrift. I will give him a present shrift and advise him for a better place *Meas. for Meas.* iv 2 223
The ghostly father now hath done his shrift . 3 *Hen. VI.* iii 2 107
Make a short shrift; he longs to see your head *Richard III.* iii 4 97
I would thou wert so happy by thy stay, To hear true shrift *Rom. and Jul.* i 1 165
Riddling confession finds but riddling shrift . . . ii 3 56
Bid her devise Some means to come to shrift this afternoon . ii 4 192
Have you got leave to go to shrift to-day?—I have . . . ii 5 68
See where she comes from shrift with merry look . . . iv 2 15
His bed shall seem a school, his board a shrift . *Othello* iii 3 24
Shrill. And fetch shrill echoes from the hollow earth *T. of Shrew* Ind. 2 48
Thy small pipe Is as the maiden's organ, shrill and sound . *T. Night* i 4 33
With this shrill addition, 'Anon, anon, sir!' . . 1 *Hen. IV.* ii 4 29
Hear the shrill whistle which doth order give To sounds confused *Hen. V.* iii Prol. 9
How poor Andromache shrills her dolours forth! . *Troi. and Cres.* v 3 84
Farewell the neighing steed, and the shrill trump! . *Othello* iii 3 351
Shriller. I hear a tongue, shriller than all the music . *J. Cæsar* i 2 16
Shrill-gorged. Look up a-height; the shrill-gorged lark so far Cannot be seen or heard . . . . *Lear* iv 6 58
Shrill-shrieking. Your shrill-shrieking daughters . *Hen. V.* iii 3 35
Shrill-sounding. The cock, that is the trumpet to the morn, Doth with his lofty and shrill-sounding throat Awake the god of day *Hamlet* i 1 151
Shrill-tongued. Else so thy cheek pays shame When shrill-tongued Fulvia scolds . . . . *Ant. and Cleo.* i 1 32
Is she shrill-tongued or low?—Madam, I heard her speak; she is low-voiced . . . . iii 3 15
Shrill-voiced. What shrill-voiced suppliant makes this eager cry? *Rich. II.* v 3 75
Shrilly. Whilst the babbling echo mocks the hounds, Replying shrilly to the well-tuned horns . . . . . *T. Andron.* ii 3 18
Crack the lawyer's voice, That he may never more false title plead, Nor sound his quillets shrilly . . . . . *T. of Athens* iv 3 155
Shrimp. When he was a babe, a child, a shrimp, Thus did he strangle serpents in his manus . . . . . . *L. L. Lost* v 2 594
It cannot be this weak and writhled shrimp Should strike such terror to his enemies . . . . 1 *Hen. VI.* ii 3 23
Shrine. From the four corners of the earth they come, To kiss this shrine, this mortal-breathing saint . . *Mer. of Venice* ii 7 40
A blind man at Saint Alban's shrine, Within this half-hour, hath received his sight . . . . . . 2 *Hen. VI.* ii 1 63
Camest thou here by chance, Or of devotion, to this holy shrine? . ii 1 88
Who said, 'Simpcox, come, Come, offer at my shrine, and I will help thee' ii 1 92
If I profane with my unworthiest hand This holy shrine *Rom. and Jul.* i 5 96
For feature, laming The shrine of Venus, or straight-pight Minerva *Cymb.* v 5 164
Shrink. If there be ten, shrink not, but down with 'em *T. G. of Ver.* iv 1 2
It bites and blows upon my body, Even till I shrink with cold *As Y. L. It* ii 1 9
When The bravest questant shrinks, find what you seek . *All's Well* ii 1 16
Against this fire Do I shrink up . . . . *K. John* v 7 34
Makes me with heavy nothing faint and shrink . *Richard II.* ii 2 32
Yet once ere night I will embrace him with a soldier's arm, That he shall shrink under my courtesy . . . . . 1 *Hen. IV.* v 2 75
There is no hope that ever I will stay, If the first hour I shrink 1 *Hen. VI.* iv 5 31
When he perceived me shrink and on my knee, His bloody sword he brandish'd over me . . . . iv 7 5
She did corrupt frail nature with some bribe, To shrink mine arm up like a wither'd shrub . . . . . . 3 *Hen. VI.* iii 2 156
He hath no friends but who are friends for fear, Which in his greatest need will shrink from him . . . . . *Richard III.* v 2 21
I'll play the eaves-dropper, To see if any mean to shrink from me . v 3 222
Cranmer will find a friend will not shrink from him . *Hen. VIII.* v 1 107
He moves like an engine, and the ground shrinks before his treading *Coriolanus* v 4 20
Ah, that this sight should make so deep a wound, And yet detested life not shrink thereat! . . . . . . *T. Andron.* iii 1 248
His estate shrinks from him . . . . *T. of Athens* iii 2 7
Shrinking. Not fearing death, nor shrinking for distress 1 *Hen. VI.* i 1 37
To be still hot summer's tanlings and The shrinking slaves of winter *Cymbeline* iv 4 30
Shrive. And shrive you of a thousand idle pranks . . *Com. of Errors* ii 2 210
I had rather he should shrive me than wive me . . *Mer. of Venice* i 2 144
Doubtless he shrives this woman to her smock . . 1 *Hen. VI.* i 2 119
Shrived. And there she shall at Friar Laurence' cell Be shrived and married . . . . *Rom. and Jul.* ii 4 194
Shrivelled. A fire from heaven came and shrivell'd up Their bodies, even to loathing . . . . *Pericles* ii 4 9
Shriver. When he was made a shriver, 'twas for shift . 3 *Hen. VI.* iii 2 108
Shriving. Your honour hath no shriving work in hand *Richard III.* iii 2 116
Shriving-time. He should the bearers put to sudden death, Not shriving-time allow'd . . . . *Hamlet* v 2 47
Shroud. I will here shroud till the dregs of the storm be past *Tempest* ii 2 42
Die when you will, a smock shall be your shroud . . *L. L. Lost* v 2 479
Puts the wretch that lies in woe In remembrance of a shroud *M. N. D.* v 1 385
My shroud of white, stuck all with yew, O, prepare it! . . *T. Night* ii 4 56
But now Some hangman must put on my shroud and lay me Where no priest shovels in dust . . . . *W. Tale* iv 4 468
All the shrouds wherewith my life should sail Are turned to one thread, one little hair . . . . *K. John* v 7 53
Under this thick-grown brake we'll shroud ourselves 3 *Hen. VI.* iii 1 1
Nor how to shroud yourself from enemies . . . . iv 3 40
The friends of France our shrouds and tacklings . . . v 4 18
Such a noise arose As the shrouds make at sea in a stiff tempest *Hen. VIII.* iv 1 72
And hide me with a dead man in his shroud *Rom. and Jul.* iv 1 85
Where bloody Tybalt, yet but green in earth, Lies festering in his shroud . . . . iv 3 43
And pluck the mangled Tybalt from his shroud . . . . iv 3 52
White his shroud as the mountain snow . . . *Hamlet* iv 5 35
How foolish are our minds! If I do die before thee, prithee, shroud me In one of those same sheets . . . . . . *Othello* iv 3 25
And put yourself under his shroud, The universal landlord *Ant. and Cleo.* iii 13 71
Shrouded. I have been closely shrouded in this bush . *L. L. Lost* iv 3 137
Set down, set down your honourable load, If honour may be shrouded in a hearse . . . . *Richard III.* i 2 2
I'll be sworn and sworn upon't she never shrouded any but lazars *Troi. and Cres.* ii 3 36
What's here? a corse!—Most strange!—Shrouded in cloth of state! *Per.* iii 2 65
Shrouding. A pick-axe, and a spade, a spade, For and a shrouding sheet: O, a pit of clay for to be made . . . . . . *Hamlet* v 1 103
Shrove-tide. And welcome merry Shrove-tide . . 2 *Hen. IV.* v 3 38
Shrove Tuesday. As a pancake for Shrove Tuesday . . *All's Well* ii 2 25
Shrub. Here's neither bush nor shrub, to bear off any weather *Tempest* ii 2 18
To shrink mine arm up like a wither'd shrub . . 3 *Hen. VI.* iii 2 156
And kept low shrubs from winter's powerful wind . . . . v 2 15
We are but shrubs, no cedars we, No big-boned men . *T. Andron.* iv 3 45
Shrug. Still have I borne it with a patient shrug . *Mer. of Venice* i 3 110
The shrug, the hum or ha, these petty brands That calumny doth use *W. Tale* ii 1 71
These shrugs, these hums and ha's . . . . . . ii 1 74
Where great patricians shall attend and shrug . . . *Coriolanus* i 9 4
Shrug'st thou, malice? . . . . *Tempest* i 2 367
Shrunk. His youthful hose, well saved, a world too wide For his shrunk shank . . . . *As Y. Like It* ii 7 161
One of you will prove a shrunk panel and, like green timber, warp . iii 3 89
Ill-weaved ambition, how much art thou shrunk! . . . 1 *Hen. V.* v 4 88
In this borrow'd likeness of shrunk death . . *Rom. and Jul.* iv 1 104
True, as you said, Timon is shrunk indeed . . *T. of Athens* iii 2 68
Dost thou lie so low? Are all thy conquests, glories, triumphs, spoils, Shrunk to this little measure? . . . . . . *J. Cæsar* iii 1 150
The morning cock crew loud, And at the sound it shrunk in haste away *Hamlet* i 2 219
Shudder. I know, you'll swear, terribly swear Into strong shudders and to heavenly agues The immortal gods that hear you *T. of Athens* iv 3 137
Shuddering fear, and green-eyed jealousy . . *Mer. of Venice* iii 2 110
Shuffle. Am fain to shuffle, to hedge and to lurch . *Mer. Wives* ii 2 25
Hath appointed That he shall likewise shuffle her away . . iv 6 29
Your life, good master, Must shuffle for itself . . . *Cymbeline* v 5 105
Shuffled. Oft good turns Are shuffled off with such uncurrent pay *T. N.* iii 3 16
What dreams may come When we have shuffled off this mortal coil *Ham.* iii 1 67
Shuffling. 'Tis like the forced gait of a shuffling nag 1 *Hen. IV.* iii 1 135
'Tis not so above; There is no shuffling, there the action lies In his true nature . . . . *Hamlet* iii 3 61
With ease, Or with a little shuffling, you may choose . . . iv 7 138
Shun. Scarcity and want shall shun you . . . . *Tempest* iv 1 116
Therein she doth evitate and shun A thousand irreligious cursed hours *Mer. Wives* v 5 241
Thou art death's fool; For him thou labour'st by thy flight to shun And yet runn'st toward him still . . . . . *Meas. for Meas.* iii 1 12
Shun me, and I will spare your haunts . . . *M. N. Dream* ii 1 142
When I shun Scylla, your father, I fall into Charybdis, your mother *Mer. of Venice* iii 5 18
Who doth ambition shun And loves to live i' the sun . *As Y. Like It* ii 5 40
Hence comes it that your kindred shuns your house . *T. of Shrew* Ind. 2 30
Who shuns thy love shuns all his love in me . . . *All's Well* iii 3 79
Do not shun her Until you see her die again . . . *W. Tale* v 3 105
We would not seek a battle as we are; Nor, as we are, we say we will not shun it: So tell your master . . . . *Hen. V.* iii 6 174
Let him shun castles; Safer shall he be upon the sandy plains 2 *Hen. VI.* i 4 38
And I am faint and cannot fly their fury: And were I strong, I would not shun their fury . . . . 3 *Hen. VI.* i 4 24
They follow us with wings; And weak we are and cannot shun pursuit ii 3 13
To shun the danger that his soul divines . . . *Richard III.* iii 2 18
My desert Unmeritable shuns your high request . . . . iii 7 155
You cannot shun Yourself.—Let me go and try . *Troi. and Cres.* iii 2 152
Thou'ldst shun a bear; But if thy flight lay toward the raging sea, Thou'ldst meet the bear i' the mouth . . . . . *Lear* iii 4 9
O, that way madness lies; let me shun that; No more of that . . iii 4 21
And will give you that Like beasts which you shun beastly . *Cymbeline* v 3 27
Those men Blush not in actions blacker than the night, Will shun no course to keep them from the light . . . . . *Pericles* i 1 136
By flight I'll shun the danger which I fear . . . . . i 1 142
Here pleasures court mine eyes, and mine eyes shun them . . i 2 6
I'll take thy word for faith, not ask thine oath: Who shuns not to break one will sure crack both . . . . i 2 121
Shunless. Alone he enter'd The mortal gate of the city, which he painted With shunless destiny . . . . *Coriolanus* ii 2 116
Shunned. Thus have I shunn'd the fire for fear of burning *T. G. of Ver.* i 3 78
A rashness that I ever yet have shunn'd . . . . . . iii 1 30
And my approach be shunn'd, Nay, hated too . . . *W. Tale* i 2 422
The mouse ne'er shunn'd the cat as they did budge . . *Coriolanus* i 6 44

Shunned. And gladly shunn'd who gladly fled from me . *Rom. and Jul.* i 1 136
Having seen me in my worst estate, Shunn'd my abhorr'd society . *Lear* v 3 210
She shunn'd The wealthy curled darlings of our nation . *Othello* i 2 67
Rather shunned to go even with what I heard than in my every action to be guided by others' experiences . *Cymbeline* i 4 47
Shunning. As children from a bear, the Volsces shunning him *Coriolanus* i 3 34
Lo, where comes that rock That I advise your shunning . *Hen. VIII.* i 1 114
Shut. I wish mine eyes Would, with themselves, shut up my thoughts *Tempest* ii 1 192
Of her purse she shall not, for that I'll keep shut . *T. G. of Ver.* iii 1 358
His own doors being shut against his entrance *Com. of Errors* iv 3 90
Acquainted with his fits, On purpose shut the doors against his way . iv 3 92
Upon me the guilty doors were shut And I denied to enter in my house iv 4 66
Were not my doors lock'd up and I shut out?—Perdie, your doors were lock'd and you shut out . iv 4 73
And here the abbess shuts the gates on us . v 1 156
She shut the doors upon me, While she with harlots feasted in my house . v 1 204
Take away this villain; shut him up *L. L. Lost* i 2 158
Till that instant shut My woeful self up in a mourning house v 2 817
Sleep, that sometimes shuts up sorrow's eye *M. N. Dream* iii 2 435
Whiles we shut the gates upon one wooer, another knocks at the door *Mer. of Venice* i 2 147
Perhaps I will return immediately: Do as I bid you; shut doors after you . ii 5 53
Eyes, . . . Who shut their coward gates on atomies *As Y. Like It* iii 5 13
It will out at the casement; shut that and 'twill out at the key-hole iv 1 164
We, the poorer born, Whose baser stars do shut us up in wishes *All's Well* i 1 197
Shut his bosom Against our borrowing prayers . iii 1 8
And makest conjectural fears to come into me, Which I would fain shut out . v 3 115
Let the garden door be shut, and leave me to my hearing . *T. Night* iii 1 103
'Gainst knaves and thieves men shut their gate . v 1 404
The effects of his fond jealousies so grieving That he shuts up himself *W. Tale* iv 1 19
Shut the door; there comes no swaggerers here . 2 *Hen. IV.* ii 4 82
Would shut the book, and sit him down and die . iii 1 56
The gates of mercy shall be all shut up . *Hen. V.* iii 3 10
Open the gates, or I'll shut thee out shortly . 1 *Hen. VI.* i 3 26
Peel'd priest, dost thou command me to be shut out? . i 3 30
And we for fear compell'd to shut our shops . iii 1 85
Is all thy comfort shut in Gloucester's tomb? . 2 *Hen. VI.* iii 2 78
Unless our halberds did shut up his passage . 3 *Hen. VI.* iv 3 20
Shut the gates for safety of ourselves . iv 7 18
These gates must not be shut But in the night or in the time of war . iv 7 35
Let the foul'st contempt Shut door upon me . *Hen. VIII.* ii 4 43
In whom the tempers and the minds of all Should be shut up *T. and C.* i 3 58
If we talk of reason, Let's shut our gates and sleep . ii 2 47
Our gates, Which yet seem shut, we have but pinn'd with rushes *Coriol.* i 4 18
They have shut him in.—To the pot, I warrant him . i 4 47
Hence, and shut your gates upon's. Our guider, come . i 7 6
Myself unkindly banished, The gates shut on me . *T. Andron.* v 3 105
Shuts up his windows, locks fair daylight out . *Rom. and Jul.* i 1 145
Shut up in prison, kept without my food, Whipp'd and tormented . i 2 56
Or those eyes shut, that make thee answer 'I' . iii 2 49
O, shut the door! and when thou hast done so, Come weep with me . iv 1 44
Chain me with roaring bears; Or shut me nightly in a charnel-house . iv 1 81
Like death, when he shuts up the day of life . iv 1 101
Being holiday, the beggar's shop is shut . v 1 56
Your honourable letter he desires To those have shut him up *T. of Athens* i 1 98
Men shut their doors against a setting sun . i 2 150
Were all the wealth I have shut up in thee, I'ld give thee leave to hang it iv 3 279
As his host, Who should against his murderer shut the door *Macbeth* i 7 15
And shut up In measureless content. . ii 1 16
You see, her eyes are open.—Ay, but their sense is shut. . v 1 29
Where's your father?—At home, my lord.—Let the doors be shut *Hamlet* iii 1 135
Shut up your doors, my lord; 'tis a wild night . *Lear* ii 4 311
In such a night To shut me out! Pour on; I will endure. In such a night as this! . iii 4 18
Shut your mouth, dame, Or with this paper shall I stop it . v 3 154
Didst contract and purse thy brow together, As if thou then hadst shut up in thy brain Some horrible conceit . *Othello* iii 3 114
And shut myself up in some other course, To fortune's alms . iii 4 121
Leave procreants alone and shut the door . iv 2 28
I have enough: To the trunk again, and shut the spring of it *Cymbeline* ii 2 47
Who has a book of all that monarchs do, He's more secure to keep it shut than shown . *Pericles* i 1 95
Shuttle. Because I know also life is a shuttle . *Mer. Wives* v 1 25
Shy. A shy fellow was the duke . *Meas. for Meas.* iii 2 138
The wicked'st caitiff on the ground May seem as shy, as grave . v 1 54
Shylock, do you hear?—I am debating of my present store *Mer. of Venice* i 3 53
Shylock, although I neither lend nor borrow . . . , I'll break a custom i 3 62
Well, Shylock, shall we be beholding to you? . i 3 106
You come to me, and you say 'Shylock, we would have moneys' . i 3 117
Yes, Shylock, I will seal unto this bond . i 3 172
Shylock thy master spoke with me this day, And hath preferr'd thee ii 2 154
The old proverb is very well parted between my master Shylock and you, sir . ii 2 159
Thy eyes shall be thy judge, The difference of old Shylock and Bassanio ii 5 2
How now, Shylock! what news among the merchants? . iii 1 25
And Shylock, for his own part, knew the bird was fledged . iii 1 31
Hear me yet, good Shylock.—I'll have my bond; speak not against my bond . iii 3 3
Shylock, the world thinks, and I think so too . iv 1 17
Which the Jew?—Antonio and old Shylock, both stand forth.—Is your name Shylock?—Shylock is my name . iv 1 175
Shylock, there's thrice thy money offer'd thee . iv 1 227
Have by some surgeon, Shylock, on your charge, To stop his wounds . iv 1 257
Furthermore, I pray you, show my youth old Shylock's house . iv 2 11
Sibyl. As old as Sibyl . *T. of Shrew* i 2 70
The spirit of deep prophecy she hath, Exceeding the nine sibyls of old Rome: What's past and what's to come she can descry . 1 *Hen. VI.* i 2 56
The angry northern wind Will blow these sands, like Sibyl's leaves, abroad, And where's your lesson, then? . *T. Andron.* iv 1 105
A sibyl, that had number'd in the world The sun to course two hundred compasses, In her prophetic fury sew'd the work . *Othello* iii 4 70
Sibylla. If I live to be as old as Sibylla, I will die as chaste as Diana, unless I be obtained by the manner of my father's will *Mer. of Venice* i 2 116
Sic. The motto thus, 'Sic spectanda fides' . *Pericles* ii 2 38

Sicil. In presence of the Kings of France and Sicil . 2 *Hen. VI* i 1 6
King of Naples, Of both the Sicils and Jerusalem . 3 *Hen. VI.* i 4 122
Reignier, her father, to the king of France Hath pawn'd the Sicils . v 7 39
Sicilia. Great difference betwixt our Bohemia and your Sicilia *W. Tale* i 1 5
Sicilia means to pay Bohemia the visitation which he justly owes him . i 1 7
Sicilia cannot show himself over-kind to Bohemia . i 1 23
What means Sicilia?—He something seems unsettled . i 2 146
They're here with me already, whispering, rounding 'Sicilia is a so-forth' . i 2 218
Hermione, queen to the worthy Leontes, king of Sicilia . iii 2 13
Of that fatal country, Sicilia, prithee speak no more . iv 2 23
Lay aside the thoughts of Sicilia.—I willingly obey your command . iv 2 59
Purchase the sight again of dear Sicilia . iv 4 522
If you will not change your purpose But undergo this flight, make for Sicilia . iv 4 554
We are not furnish'd like Bohemia's son, Nor shall appear in Sicilia . iv 4 600
I shall review Sicilia, for whose sight I have a woman's longing . iv 4 680
By his command Have I here touch'd Sicilia . v 1 139
Daughter unto Reignier King of Sicilia and Jerusalem 2 *Hen. VI.* i 1 48
Sicilian. My best train I have from your Sicilian shores dismiss'd *W. Tale* v 1 164
Sicilius. His father Was call'd Sicilius, who did join his honour Against the Romans with Cassibelan . *Cymbeline* i 1 29
That he deserved the praise o' the world, As great Sicilius' heir . v 4 51
Sicily. Let what is dear in Sicily be cheap . *W. Tale* i 2 175
Now let hot Ætna cool in Sicily! . *T. Andron.* iii 1 242
Carry back to Sicily much tall youth That else must perish *A. and C.* ii 6 7
You have made me offer Of Sicily, Sardinia . ii 6 35
When Cæsar and your brother were at blows, Your mother came to Sicily ii 6 46
Having in Sicily Sextus Pompeius spoil'd, we had not rated him His part iii 6 24
Sicinius. Five tribunes . . . : one's Junius Brutus, Sicinius Velutus, and I know not—'Sdeath! . *Coriolanus* i 1 221
What, ho! Sicinius! Brutus! Coriolanus! Citizens! . iii 1 187
Coriolanus, patience! Speak, good Sicinius . iii 1 192
Sick. Made wit with musing weak, heart sick with thought *T. G. of Ver.* i 1 69
When I was sick, you gave me bitter pills, And I must minister the like to you . ii 4 149
I am sick till I see her . *Mer. Wives* iii 2 28
Strip myself to death, as to a bed That longing have been sick for *Meas. for Meas.* ii 4 103
At this instant he is sick, my lord, Of a strange fever . v 1 151
Are you sad?—Not sad, my lord.—How then? sick?—Neither *Much Ado* ii 1 301
The count is neither sad, nor sick, nor merry, nor well . ii 1 303
I am sick in displeasure to him . ii 2 5
Benedick Is sick in love with Beatrice . iii 1 21
By my troth, I am sick.—Get you some of this distilled Carduus Benedictus . iii 4 72
He looks pale. Art thou sick, or angry? . v 1 131
They swore that you were almost sick for me . v 4 80
To her decrepit, sick and bedrid father . *L. L. Lost* i 1 139
Is the fool sick?—Sick at the heart.—Alack, let it blood . ii 1 184
Bear with me, I am sick; I'll leave it by degrees . v 2 417
Never rest, But seek the weary beds of people sick . v 2 832
Visit the speechless sick and still converse With groaning wretches . v 2 861
I am sick when I do look on thee.—And I am sick when I look not on you . *M. N. Dream* ii 1 212
They are as sick that surfeit with too much as they that starve with nothing . *Mer. of Venice* i 2 6
Not sick, my lord, unless it be in mind; Nor well, unless in mind . iii 2 237
Honourable ladies sought my love, Which I denying, they fell sick and died . iii 4 71
Understand that at the receipt of your letter I am very sick . iv 1 151
This night methinks is but the daylight sick; It looks a little paler . v 1 124
I will not cast away my physic but on those that are sick *As Y. Like It* iii 2 377
Who are sick For breathing and exploit . *All's Well* i 2 16
Her eye is sick on't: I observe her now . i 3 142
O, you are sick of self-love, Malvolio . *T. Night* i 5 97
If it be a suit from the count, I am sick, or not at home . i 5 117
I told him you were sick; he takes on him to understand so much . i 5 148
I am almost sick for one [a beard]; though I would not have it grow on my chin . iii 1 53
I am sick and capable of fears, Oppress'd with wrongs . *K. John* iii 1 12
Are you sick, Hubert? you look pale to-day: In sooth, I would you were a little sick, That I might sit all night and watch with you . iv 1 28
Makes sound opinion sick and truth suspected . iv 2 26
We heard how near his death he was Before the child himself felt he was sick . iv 2 88
The present time's so sick, That present medicine must be minister'd . v 1 14
This fever . . . Lies heavy on me; O, my heart is sick! . v 3 4
They say King John sore sick hath left the field . v 4 6
Not sick, although I have to do with death . *Richard II.* i 3 65
Old John of Gaunt is grievous sick, my lord, Suddenly taken . i 4 54
Thy death-bed is no lesser than thy land Wherein thou liest in reputation sick . ii 1 96
Yet am I sick for fear: speak it again . v 3 133
Seen, but with such eyes As, sick and blunted with community, Afford no extraordinary gaze . 1 *Hen. IV.* iii 2 77
He is grievous sick.—'Zounds! how has he the leisure to be sick? iv 1 16
Sick now! droop now! this sickness doth infect The very life-blood of our enterprise; 'Tis catching hither, even to our camp . iv 1 28
Sick in the world's regard, wretched and low . iv 3 57
These news, Having been well, that would have made me sick, Being sick, have in some measure made me well . 2 *Hen. IV.* i 1 138
I am glad to see your lordship abroad: I heard say your lordship was sick . i 2 108
The commonwealth is sick of their own choice . i 3 87
How many good young princes would do so, their fathers being so sick? ii 2 34
It is not meet that I should be sad, now my father is sick . ii 2 43
My heart bleeds inwardly that my father is so sick . ii 2 52
The immortal part needs a physician; but that moves not him: though that be sick, it dies not . ii 2 114
Sick of a calm; yea, good faith.—So is all her sect; an they be once in a calm, they are sick . ii 4 40
To diet rank minds sick of happiness . iv 1 64
Toward the court, my lords: I hear the king my father is sore sick . iv 3 83
Wherefore should these good news make me sick? . iv 4 102
If he be sick with joy, he'll recover without physic . iv 5 14
O my poor kingdom, sick with civil blows! . iv 5 134
I know the young king is sick for me . v 3 142
He is very sick, and would to bed . *Hen. V.* ii 1 86
'Tis meet we all go forth To view the sick and feeble parts of France . ii 4 22

Sick. His numbers are so few, His soldiers sick and famish'd *Hen. V.* iii 5 57
O, be sick, great greatness, And bid thy ceremony give thee cure! iv 1 268
For once I read That stout Pendragon in his litter sick Came to the field and vanquished his foes *1 Hen. VI.* iii 2 95
I am sick with working of my thoughts v 5 86
I would be blind with weeping, sick with groans *2 Hen. VI.* iii 2 62
Rumour it abroad That Anne, my wife, is sick and like to die *Rich. III.* iv 2 52
I would not be so sick though for his place *Hen. VIII.* ii 2 83
To rectify my conscience,—which I then did feel full sick, and yet not well ii 4 204
Since which she was removed to Kimbolton, Where she remains now sick iv 1 35
He fell sick suddenly, and grew so ill He could not sit his mule iv 2 15
Ye must all see the queen, and she must thank ye, She will be sick else v 5 75
He is a very man per se, And stands alone.—So do all men, unless they are drunk, sick, or have no legs *Troi. and Cres.* i 2 18
O, when degree is shaked, Which is the ladder to all high designs, Then enterprise is sick! i 3 103
So every step, Exampled by the first pace that is sick Of his superior, grows to an envious fever i 3 132
The fever whereof all our power is sick i 3 139
He is not sick.—Yes, lion-sick, sick of proud heart ii 3 92
Your poor disposer's sick.—I spy.—You spy! what do you spy? iii 1 101
I have a woman's longing, An appetite that I am sick withal iii 3 238
Nor sleep nor sanctuary, Being naked, sick, nor fane nor Capitol, shall lift up Their rotten privilege *Coriolanus* i 10 20
The envious moon, Who is already sick and pale with grief *Rom. and Jul.* ii 2 5
Her vestal livery is but sick and green And none but fools do wear it ii 2 8
You'll be sick to-morrow For this night's watching iv 4 7
I have watch'd ere now All night for lesser cause, and ne'er been sick iv 4 10
To associate me, Here in this city visiting the sick v 2 7
He's much out of health, and keeps his chamber.—Many do keep their chambers are not sick *T. of Athens* iii 4 74
I am sick of that grief too, as I understand how all things go iii 6 19
My most honourable lord, I am e'en sick of shame iii 6 46
That nature, being sick of man's unkindness, Should yet be hungry! iv 3 176
I am sick of this false world iv 3 376
Is Brutus sick? and is it physical To walk unbraced and suck up the humours Of the dank morning? *J. Cæsar* ii 1 261
What, is Brutus sick, And will he steal out of his wholesome bed, To dare the vile contagion of the night? ii 1 263
O, what a time have you chose out, brave Caius, To wear a kerchief! Would you were not sick! ii 1 315
I am not sick, if Brutus have in hand Any exploit worthy the name of honour ii 1 316
But are not some whole that we must make sick?—That must we also ii 1 328
I will not come to-day: tell them so, Decius.—Say he is sick ii 2 65
I am sick of many griefs.—Of your philosophy you make no use, If you give place to accidental evils iv 3 144
Not so sick, my lord, As she is troubled with thick-coming fancies *Macb.* v 3 37
Was sick almost to doomsday with eclipse *Hamlet* i 1 120
You are so sick of late, So far from cheer and from your former state iii 2 173
When we are sick in fortune,—often the surfeit of our behaviour *Lear* i 2 129
I will not speak with him; say I am sick i 3 8
Deny to speak with me? They are sick? they are weary? ii 4 89
Sick, O, sick!—If not, I'll ne'er trust medicine v 3 95
If you find him sad, Say I am dancing; if in mirth, report That I am sudden sick: quick, and return *Ant. and Cleo.* i 3 5
I am sick and sullen.—I am sorry to give breathing to my purpose i 3 13
Quietness, grown sick of rest, would purge By any desperate change i 3 53
Your cause doth strike my heart With pity, that doth make me sick *Cymbeline* i 6 119
If your are sick at sea, Or stomach-qualm'd at land, a dram of this Will drive away distemper iii 4 192
I should be sick, But that my resolution helps me iii 6 3
I am very sick.—Go you to hunting; I'll abide with him iv 2 5
So sick I am not, yet I am not well; But not so citizen a wanton as To seem to die ere sick iv 2 7
I am not very sick, Since I can reason of it iv 2 13
I am sick still; heart-sick. Pisanio, I'll now taste of thy drug iv 2 37
Pray, be not sick, For you must be our housewife iv 2 44
And sauced our broths, as Juno had been sick And he her dieter iv 2 50
Yet am I better Than one that's sick o' the gout v 4 5
Sick air. When Jove Will o'er some high-viced city hang his poison In the sick air *T. of Athens* iv 3 110
Sick at heart. I am sick at heart, When I behold *Macbeth* v 3 19
'Tis bitter cold, And I am sick at heart *Hamlet* i 1 9
Sick cause. Put my sick cause into his hands that hates me? *Hen. VIII.* iii 1 118
Sick desires. Stand no more off, But give thyself unto my sick desires, Who then recover *All's Well* iv 2 35
Sick-fall'n. As doth a raven on a sick-fall'n beast *K. John* iv 3 153
Sick fool. My sick fool Roderigo, Whom love hath turn'd almost the wrong side out *Othello* ii 3 53
Sick girl. That tongue of his that bade the Romans Mark him, . . . Alas, it cried 'Give me some drink, Titinius,' As a sick girl *J. Cæsar* i 2 128
Sick health. Bright smoke, cold fire, sick health! *Rom. and Jul.* i 1 186
Sick heart. My want of strength, my sick heart shows, That I must yield my body to the earth *3 Hen. VI.* v 2 8
Sick hour. Now comes the sick hour that his surfeit made *Richard II.* ii 2 84
Sick interpreters. What we oft do best, By sick interpreters, once weak ones, is Not ours, or not allow'd *Hen. VIII.* i 2 82
Sick man. Can sick men play so nicely with their names? *Richard II.* ii 1 84
Do as every sick man in his bed, wash every mote out of his conscience *Hen. V.* iv 1 188
Your affections are A sick man's appetite, who desires most that Which would increase his evil *Coriolanus* i 1 182
Bid a sick man in sadness make his will: Ah, word ill urged! *R. and J.* i 1 208
Here is a sick man that would speak with you *J. Cæsar* ii 1 310
What's to do?—A piece of work that will make sick men whole ii 1 327
As sick men do Who know the world, see heaven, but, feeling woe, Gripe not at earthly joys as erst they did *Pericles* i 1 47
Sick offence. You have some sick offence within your mind *J. Cæsar* ii 1 268
Sick service. You at your sick service had a prince *K. John* iv 1 52
Sick soul. To my sick soul, as sin's true nature is, Each toy seems prologue to some great amiss *Hamlet* iv 5 17
Sick to death. That the lover, sick to death, Wish himself the heaven's breath *L. L. Lost* iv 3 107
How does your grace?—O Griffith, sick to death! *Hen. VIII.* iv 2 1
And, when he's sick to death, let not that part of nature, Which my lord paid for, be of any power To expel sickness, but prolong his hour! *T. of Athens* iii 1 64

Sick tune. How now? do you speak in the sick tune? *Much Ado* iii 4 42
Sicked. It did so a little time before That our great-grandsire, Edward, sick'd and died *2 Hen. IV.* iv 4 128
Sicken. So fitted That his soul sicken not *Meas. for Meas.* ii 4 41
I know the more one sickens the worse at ease he is *As Y. Like It* iii 2 25
Whose nature sickens but to speak a truth *All's Well* v 3 207
That, surfeiting, The appetite may sicken, and so die *T. Night* i 1 3
When love begins to sicken and decay, It useth an enforced ceremony *J. Cæsar* iv 2 20
Though castles topple . . . ; though the treasure Of nature's germens tumble all together, Even till destruction sicken *Macbeth* iv 1 60
The dead man's knell Is there scarce ask'd for who; and good men's lives Expire before the flowers in their caps, Dying or ere they sicken iv 3 173
Mine eyes did sicken at the sight *Ant. and Cleo.* iii 10 17
Sickened. That have By this so sicken'd their estates, that never They shall abound as formerly *Hen. VIII.* i 1 82
Sicker. Thou diest, though I the sicker be.—I am in health *Richard II.* ii 1 91
Sicklemen. You sunburnt sicklemen, of August weary *Tempest* iv 1 134
Sicklied. Thus the native hue of resolution Is sicklied o'er with the pale cast of thought *Hamlet* iii 1 85
Sickliness. Impute his words To wayward sickliness and age *Richard II.* ii 1 142
Sickly. I am not such a sickly creature, I give heaven praise *Mer. Wives* iii 4 61
Sickly ears, Deaf'd with the clamours of their own dear groans *L. L. Lost* v 2 873
Thou know'st she has raised me from my sickly bed *All's Well* iii 4 118
Hence, thou sickly quoif! *2 Hen. IV.* i 1 147
My army but a weak and sickly guard *Hen. V.* iii 6 164
Scarce blood enough in all their sickly veins To give each naked curtle-axe a stain, That our French gallants shall to-day draw out iv 2 20
The king is sickly, weak and melancholy *Richard III.* i 1 136
A pleasing cordial . . . Is this thy vow unto my sickly heart ii 1 42
This sickly land might solace as before ii 3 30
And nothing else?—Yes, bring me word, boy, if thy lord look well, For he went sickly forth *J. Cæsar* ii 4 14
And downward look on us, As we were sickly prey v 1 87
Who wear our health but sickly in his life *Macbeth* iii 1 107
Meet we the medicine of the sickly weal, And with him pour we in our country's purge Each drop of us v 2 27
This physic but prolongs thy sickly days *Hamlet* iii 3 96
Or but a sickly part of one true sense Could not so mope iii 4 80
To take the indisposed and sickly fit For the sound man *Lear* ii 4 112
When perforce he could not But pay me terms of honour, cold and sickly He vented them *Ant. and Cleo.* iii 4 7
Sickness. Go, sickness as thou art! *L. L. Lost* v 2 280
I will attend my husband, be his nurse, Diet his sickness *Com. of Errors* v 1 99
With anger, with sickness, or with hunger, my lord, not with love *M. Ado* i 1 251
War, death, or sickness did lay siege to it *M. N. Dream* i 1 142
Sickness is catching: O, were favour so, Yours would I catch i 1 186
But, like in sickness, did I loathe this food iv 1 178
As who should say, if I should sleep or eat, 'Twere deadly sickness or else present death *T. of Shrew* iv 3 14
Nature and sickness Debate it at their leisure *All's Well* i 2 74
Health shall live free and sickness freely die ii 1 171
There is a sickness Which puts some of us in distemper *W. Tale* i 2 384
A sickness caught of me, and yet I well! i 2 398
He took good rest to-night; 'Tis hoped his sickness is discharged iii 3 11
'Tis a sickness denying thee any thing; a death to grant this iv 2 2
Indeed we fear'd his sickness was past cure *K. John* iv 2 86
Even now he sung.—O vanity of sickness! v 7 13
Join with the present sickness that I have *Richard II.* ii 1 132
I towards the north, Where shivering cold and sickness pines the clime v 1 77
I would the state of time had first been whole Ere he by sickness had been visited: His health was never better worth than now *1 Hen. IV.* iv 1 26
This sickness doth infect The very life-blood of our enterprise iv 1 28
That inward sickness—And that his friends by deputation could not So soon be drawn iv 1 31
Your father's sickness is a maim to us.—A perilous gash iv 1 42
What with the sickness of Northumberland iv 4 14
These unseason'd hours perforce must add Unto your sickness *2 Hen. IV.* iii 1 106
That will not stay so long Till his friend sickness hath determined me iv 5 82
The winter coming on and sickness growing *Hen. V.* iii 3 55
My people are with sickness much enfeebled, My numbers lessened iii 6 154
Some better place, Fitter for sickness and for crazy age *1 Hen. VI.* iii 2 89
Suddenly a grievous sickness took him, That makes him gasp *2 Hen. VI.* iii 2 370
Long sitting to determine poor men's causes Hath made me full of sickness iv 7 94
Bear with her weakness, which, I think, proceeds From wayward sickness, and no grounded malice *Richard III.* i 3 29
I do lament the sickness of the king, As loath to lose him ii 2 9
Had the king in his last sickness fail'd, The cardinal's and Sir Thomas Lovell's heads Should have gone off *Hen. VIII.* i 2 184
So went to bed; where eagerly his sickness Pursued him still iv 2 24
If we suffer, Out of our easiness and childish pity To one man's honour, this contagious sickness, Farewell all physic v 3 26
The nature of the sickness found, Ulysses, What is the remedy? *T. and C.* i 3 140
Let not that part of nature Which my lord paid for, be of any power To expel sickness, but prolong his hour! *T. of Athens* iii 1 66
Performance is a kind of will or testament which argues a great sickness in his judgement that makes it v 1 31
My long sickness Of health and living now begins to mend v 1 189
He hath the falling sickness.—No, Cæsar hath it not; but you and I And honest Casca, we have the falling sickness *J. Cæsar* i 2 256
And tempt the rheumy and unpurged air To add unto his sickness ii 1 267
By all the gods that Romans bow before, I here discard my sickness! ii 1 321
O insupportable and touching loss! Upon what sickness? iv 3 152
That so his sickness, age and impotence Was falsely borne in hand *Hamlet* ii 2 66
It warms the very sickness in my heart iv 7 56
My sickness grows upon me *Lear* v 3 105
Where died she?—In Sicyon: Her length of sickness, with what else more serious Importeth thee to know, this bears *Ant. and Cleo.* i 2 124
Not sickness should detain me i 2 173
Lepidus, since Pompey's feast . . . is troubled With the green sickness iii 2 6
Go bid my woman feign a sickness *Cymbeline* iii 2 76
The boy Fidele's sickness Did make my way long forth iv 2 148
Sicyon. From Sicyon, ho, the news! Speak there!—The man from Sicyon,—is there such an one? *Ant. and Cleo.* i 2 117
Fulvia thy wife is dead.—Where died she?—In Sicyon i 2 123
Side. And by my side wear steel *Mer. Wives* i 3 84
Empty it in the muddy ditch close by the Thames side iii 3 16
Each a haunch: I will keep my sides to myself v 5 28
Pinch them, arms, legs, backs, shoulders, sides and shins v 5 58

Side. O, what may man within him hide, Though angel on the outward side! . . . *Meas. for Meas.* iii 2 286
Whose western side is with a vineyard back'd . . . iv 1 29
He tells me that, if peradventure He speak against me on the adverse side, I should not think it strange . . . iv 6 6
Poor fool, it keeps on the windy side of care . . . . *Much Ado* ii 1 327
So turns she every man the wrong side out . . . iii 1 68
Dost thou wear thy wit by thy side?—Never any did so, though very many have been beside their wit . . . v 1 126
The conclusion is victory: on whose side? the king's. The captive is enriched: on whose side? the beggar's. The catastrophe is a nuptial: on whose side? the king's: no, on both in one *L. L. Lost* iv 1 76
Armado o' th' one side,—O, a most dainty man! To see him walk before a lady! . . . And his page o' t' other side . . . . . iv 1 146
Well proved again o' my side! . . . . iv 3 8
Writ o' both sides the leaf, margent and all . . . v 2 8
This side is Hiems, Winter, this Ver, the Spring . . . v 2 901
By night, Full often hath she gossip'd by my side . . *M. N. Dream* ii 1 125
Then by your side no bed-room me deny . . . . ii 2 51
I took him sleeping, . . . And the Athenian woman by his side . . iii 2 39
What love could press Lysander from my side?—Lysander's love . . iii 2 185
As if our hands, our sides, voices and minds, Had been incorporate . iii 2 207
Dangerous rocks, Which touching but my gentle vessel's side, Would scatter all her spices on the stream . . *Mer. of Venice* i 1 32
Never shall you lie by Portia's side With an unquiet soul . . iii 2 307
Is there any else longs to see this broken music in his sides? *As Y. L. It* i 2 150
With spectacles on nose and pouch on side . . . . ii 7 159
Thou art damned like an ill-roasted egg, all on one side . . . iii 2 39
A puisny tilter, that spurs his horse but on one side . . . iii 4 47
Come, madam wife, sit by my side and let the world slip *T. of Shrew* Ind. 2 146
Our cake's dough on both sides . . . . . i 1 110
Sit, my preserver, by thy patient's side . . . *All's Well* ii 3 53
Taurus! That's sides and heart.—No, sir; it is legs and thighs *T. Night* i 3 148
No woman's sides Can bide the beating of so strong a passion . . ii 4 96
How quickly the wrong side may be turned outward! . . . iii 1 14
Still you keep o' the windy side of the law . . . iii 4 181
He did me kindness, sir, drew on my side . . . . v 1 69
That most ingrateful boy there by your side . . . v 1 80
If that the injuries be justly weigh'd That have on both sides pass'd v 1 376
He cracks his gorge, his sides, With violent hefts . . *W. Tale* ii 1 44
And blessing Against this cruelty fight on thy side, Poor thing! . . ii 3 191
To me comes a creature, Sometimes her head on one side, some another iii 3 20
I would you had been by the ship side, to have helped her . . iii 3 112
Let nature crush the sides o' the earth together And mar the seeds within! . . . . iv 4 489
The pennyworth on his side be the worst, yet hold thee, there's some boot . . . . iv 4 650
Brother by the mother's side, give me your hand . . *K. John* i 1 163
In a moment, Fortune shall cull forth Out of one side her happy minion ii 1 392
And all that we upon this side the sea . . . Find liable to our crown . ii 1 488
Thou ever strong upon the stronger side! Thou Fortune's champion! . iii 1 117
Cold-blooded slave, Hast thou not spoke like thunder on my side? . iii 1 124
Which is the side that I must go withal? I am with both . . iii 1 327
Whoever wins, on that side shall I lose . . . . iii 1 335
They would be as a call To train ten thousand English to their side . iii 4 175
Upon our sides it never shall be broken . . . . v 2 8
That I must draw this metal from my side To be a widow-maker! . . v 2 16
I will ride, As far as land will let me, by your side . . *Richard II.* i 3 252
The commons they are cold, And will, I fear, revolt on Hereford's side ii 2 89
Where one on his side fights, thousands will fly . . . ii 2 147
All souls that will be safe fly from my side . . . iii 2 80
On this side my hand, and on that side yours . . . . iv 1 183
He, from the one side to the other turning, Bareheaded . . v 2 18
Thou hadst fire and sword on thy side, and yet thou rannest away 1 *Hen. IV.* ii 4 348
And runs me up With like advantage on the other side; Gelding the opposed continent as much As on the other side it takes from you iii 1 109
Trench him here And on this north side win this cape of land . . iii 1 113
We of the offering side Must keep aloof from strict arbitrement . iv 1 69
To save the blood on either side, Try fortune with him in a single fight v 1 99
Struck his armed heels Against the panting sides of his poor jade 2 *Hen. IV.* i 1 45
Their weapons only Seem'd on our side . . . . i 1 198
Though it be a shame to be on any side but one, it is worse shame to beg than to be on the worst side . . . . . . i 2 88
By his bloody side, Yoke-fellow to his honour-owing wounds *Hen. V.* iv 6 8
The Duke of Alençon flieth to his side . . . 1 *Hen. VI.* i 1 95
Late did he shine upon the English side; Now we are victors . . i 2 3
Here is my keen-edged sword, Deck'd with five flower-de-luces on each side . . . . i 2 99
One of thy eyes and thy cheek's side struck off! . . . i 4 75
The truth appears so naked on my side That any purblind eye may find it out.—And on my side it is so well apparell'd, So clear . . ii 4 20
He upon whose side The fewest roses are cropp'd from the tree Shall yield the other in the right opinion . . . . . ii 4 40
Giving my verdict on the white rose side . . . . ii 4 48
And fall on my side so, against your will . . . . ii 4 51
Opinion shall be surgeon to my hurt And keep me on the side where still I am . . . . ii 4 54
Pale they look with fear, as witnessing The truth on our side . . ii 4 64
No more can I be sever'd from your side, Than can yourself yourself in twain divide: Stay, go, do what you will, the like do I . . . iv 5 48
If thou wilt fight, fight by thy father's side . . . iv 6 56
Great rage of heart Suddenly made him from my side to start . . iv 7 12
And stablish quietness on every side . . . . . v 1 10
I kiss these fingers for eternal peace, And lay them gently on thy tender side . . . . v 3 49
If thou darest, This evening, on the east side of the grove . 2 *Hen. VI.* ii 1 43
Are ye advised? the east side of the grove?—Cardinal, I am with you . ii 1 48
Thus is the shepherd beaten from thy side And wolves are gnarling . iii 1 191
The splitting rocks cower'd in the sinking sands And would not dash me with their ragged sides . . . . iii 2 98
Sometime he talks as if Duke Humphrey's ghost Were by his side . iii 2 374
On our long-boat's side Strike off his head . . . . iv 1 68
God on our side, doubt not of victory . . . . . iv 8 54
And full as oft came Edward to my side . . . 3 *Hen. VI.* i 4 11
Our battles join'd, and both sides fiercely fought . . . ii 1 121
She, on his left side, craving aid for Henry, He, on his right . . iii 1 43
Be thou still like thyself, And sit thee by our side . . . iii 3 16
Who attended him In secret ambush on the forest side . . . iv 6 83
Come thou on my side, and entreat for me . . . *Richard III.* i 4 272
Side. I'll give my voice on Richard's side, To bar my master's heirs *Richard III.* iii 2 53
Pry on every side, Tremble and start at wagging of a straw . . iii 5 6
Then, on the other side, I check'd my friends . . . . iii 7 150
But on thy side I may not be too forward . . . . v 3 94
God and good angels fight on Richmond's side . . . . v 3 175
Yet remember this, God and our good cause fight upon our side . v 3 240
Whose puissance on either side Shall be well winged with our chiefest horse . . . . v 3 299
What men of name are slain on either side? . . . . v 5 12
Language unmannerly, yea, such which breaks The sides of loyalty *Hen. VIII.* i 2 28
Will it please you sit? Sir Harry, Place you that side . . . . i 4 20
To the water side I must conduct your grace . . . . ii 1 95
On all sides the authority allow'd . . . . . . ii 4 4
What two reverend bishops Were those that went on each side of the queen? . . . . iv 1 100
On one and other side, Trojan and Greek, Sets all on hazard *T. and C.* Prol. 21
Peace, you ungracious clamours! peace, rude sounds! Fools on both sides! . . . . i 1 93
Where's then the saucy boat Whose weak untimber'd sides but even now Co-rivall'd greatness? . . . . i 3 43
A plague of opinion! a man may wear it on both sides, like a leather jerkin . . . . iii 3 266
There is expectance here from both the sides, What further you will do iv 5 146
O' the t'other side, the policy of those crafty swearing rascals . . . is not proved worth a blackberry . . . . v 4 10
The other side o' the city is risen: why stay we prating here? *Coriolanus* i 1 48
Rome and her rats are at the point of battle; The one side must have bale . . . . i 1 167
Side factions and give out Conjectural marriages . . . . i 1 197
Know you on which side They have placed their men of trust? . . i 6 51
On both sides more respect . . . . iii 1 181
A side that would be glad to have This true which they so seem to fear iv 6 151
An evident calamity, though we had Our wish, which side should win v 3 113
Each in either side Give the all-hail to thee . . . . v 3 138
Our mother, unadvised, Gave you a dancing-rapier by your side *T. An.* ii 1 39
At the lodge Upon the north side of this pleasant chase . . . ii 3 255
He is your brother by the surer side . . . . . iv 2 126
Hang him on this tree, And by his side his fruit of bastardy . . v 1 48
Lo, by thy side where Rape and Murder stands . . . . v 2 45
Let us take the law of our sides; let them begin *Rom. and Jul.* i 1 44
Do you bite your thumb at us, sir?—Is the law of our side, if I say ay? i 1 54
The grove of sycamore That westward rooteth from the city's side . i 1 129
If I see occasion in a good quarrel, and the law on my side . . ii 4 169
What a head have I! It beats as it would fall in twenty pieces. My back o' t' other side,—O, my back, my back! . . . . . ii 5 51
As he was coming from this churchyard side . . . . v 3 186
It is the pasture lards the rother's sides . . . *T. of Athens* iv 3 12
This [gold] Will lug your priests and servants from your sides . iv 3 31
O constancy, be strong upon my side! . . . *J. Cæsar* ii 4 6
Ranging for revenge, With Ate by his side come hot from hell . . iii 1 271
His private arbours and new-planted orchards, On this side Tiber . iii 2 254
My letters, praying on his side, Because I knew the man, were slighted off iv 3 4
When your vile daggers Hack'd one another in the sides of Cæsar . v 1 40
Give these bills Unto the legions on the other side . . . v 2 2
I have no spur To prick the sides of my intent . . . *Macbeth* i 7 26
Both sides are even: here I'll sit i' the midst . . . . iii 4 10
The tyrant's people on both sides do fight . . . . . v 7 25
So this side of our known world esteem'd him . . . *Hamlet* i 1 85
There has been much to do on both sides . . . . . ii 2 370
The carriages, sir, are the hangers.—The phrase would be more german to the matter, if we could carry cannon by our sides . . . v 2 166
Your grace hath laid the odds o' the weaker side . . . v 2 272
They bleed on both sides. How is it, my lord? . . . . v 2 315
Thou hast pared thy wit o' both sides, and left nothing i' the middle *Lear* i 4 205
To keep one's eyes of either side's nose . . . . . i 5 22
O sides, you are too tough; Will you yet hold? . . . . ii 4 200
Your houseless heads and unfed sides, Your loop'd and window'd raggedness . . . . iii 4 30
Take thy place; And thou, his yoke-fellow of equity, Bench by his side iii 6 40
One side will mock another; the other too . . . . . iii 7 71
Then he call'd me sot, And told me I had turn'd the wrong side out . iv 2 9
Hardly shall I carry out my side, Her husband being alive . . v 1 61
Whose age has charms in it, whose title more, To pluck the common bosom on his side . . . . v 3 49
Whose messengers are here about my side . . . . *Othello* i 2 89
These sentences, to sugar, or to gall, Being strong on both sides, are equivocal . . . . i 3 217
Whom love hath turn'd almost the wrong side out . . . . ii 3 54
She might lie by an emperor's side and command him tasks . . iv 1 195
Some such squire he was That turn'd your wit the seamy side without . iv 2 146
I have much to do, But to go hang my head all at one side, And sing it iv 3 32
Curse his better angel from his side, And fall to reprobation . . v 2 208
O, lay me by my mistress' side . . . . . . v 2 237
Whose quality, going on, The sides o' the world may danger *Ant. and Cleo.* i 2 199
It cannot be thus long, the sides of nature Will not sustain it . . i 3 16
Thou hast a sister by the mother's side . . . . . ii 2 120
On each side her Stood pretty dimpled boys, like smiling Cupids . . ii 2 206
Therefore, O Antony, stay not by his side . . . . . ii 3 18
The holding every man shall bear as loud As his strong sides can volley ii 7 118
Set we our squadrons on yond side o' the hill, In eye of Cæsar's battle . iii 9 1
How appears the fight?—On our side like the token'd pestilence . . iii 10 9
O, cleave, my sides! Heart, once be stronger than thy continent . iv 14 39
Look out o' the other side your monument . . . . . iv 15 8
Strong-wing'd Mercury should fetch thee up, And set thee by Jove's side iv 15 36
Though the catalogue of his endowments had been tabled by his side *Cymbeline* i 4 6
Can my sides hold, to think that man, who knows By history, report, or his own proof, What woman is, yea, what she cannot choose But must be, will his free hours languish for Assured bondage? . . i 6 69
Cæsar's ambition, Which swell'd so much that it did almost stretch The sides o' the world . . . . iii 1 51
For me, my ransom's death; On either side I come to spend my breath v 3 81
Stand by my side, you whom the gods have made Preservers of my throne . . . . v 5 1
The leafy shelter that abuts against The island's side . . *Pericles* v 1 52
Side by side. Come, side by side together live and die . . 1 *Hen. VI.* iv 5 54
Sided. The nobility are vex'd, whom we see have sided In his behalf *Cor.* iv 2 2
Side-piercing. O thou side-piercing sight! . . . . . *Lear* iv 6 85

Side sleeves. Down sleeves, side sleeves, and skirts *Much Ado* iii 4 21
Side-stitches that shall pen thy breath up *Tempest* i 2 326
Siege. How camest thou to be the siege of this moon-calf? ii 2 110
As to lay an amiable siege to the honesty of this Ford's wife *Mer. Wives* ii 2 243
Besides, upon the very siege of justice Lord Angelo hath to the public ear Profess'd the contrary *Meas. for Meas.* iv 2 101
War, death, or sickness did lay siege to it *M. N. Dream* i 1 142
Lays down his wanton siege before her beauty *All's Well* iii 7 18
Then turn your forces from this paltry siege *K. John* ii 1 54
All preparation for a bloody siege And merciless proceeding ii 1 213
Death, having prey'd upon the outward parts, Leaves them invisible, and his siege is now Against the mind v 7 16
Whose rocky shore beats back the envious siege Of watery Neptune *Richard II.* ii 1 62
Girding with grievous siege castles and towns *Hen. V.* i 2 152
Work, work your thoughts, and therein see a siege iii Prol. 25
The Duke of Gloucester, to whom the order of the siege is given iii 2 70
His powers are yet not ready To raise so great a siege iii 3 47
This dreadful lord, Retiring from the siege of Orleans 1 *Hen. VI.* i 1 111
Let's raise the siege: why live we idly here? i 2 13
Rather with their teeth The walls they'll tear down than forsake the siege i 2 40
By a vision sent to her from heaven Ordained is to raise this tedious siege i 2 53
This night the siege assuredly I'll raise i 2 130
Leave off delays, and let us raise the siege.—Woman, do what thou canst i 2 146
A holy prophetess . . . Is come with a great power to raise the siege i 4 103
Delays my promised supply Of horsemen, that were levied for this siege iv 3 11
O, beat away the busy meddling fiend That lays strong siege unto this wretch's soul And from his bosom purge this black despair! 2 *Hen. VI.* iii 3 22
After seven years' siege yet Troy walls stand *Troi. and Cres.* i 3 12
She will not stay the siege of loving terms *Rom. and Jul.* i 1 218
You, to remove that siege of grief from her, Betroth'd and would have married her perforce To County Paris v 3 237
Not nature, To whom all sores lay siege, can bear great fortune *T. of A.* iv 3 7
Our castle's strength Will laugh a siege to scorn *Macbeth* v 5 3
And that, in my regard, Of the unworthiest siege *Hamlet* iv 7 77
I fetch my life and being From men of royal siege *Othello* i 2 22
The battles, sieges, fortunes, That I have pass'd i 3 130
Whose love-suit hath been to me As fearful as a siege *Cymbeline* iii 4 137
Sieve. Falls into mine ears as profitless As water in a sieve *Much Ado* v 1 5
In this captious and intenible sieve I still pour in the waters of my love And lack not to lose still *All's Well* i 3 208
The remainder viands We do not throw in unrespective sieve *Tr. and Cr.* ii 2 71
In a sieve I'll thither sail, And, like a rat without a tail, I'll do, I'll do, and I'll do *Macbeth* i 3 8
Sift. We'll sift this matter further *All's Well* v 3 124
As near as I could sift him on that argument *Richard II.* i 1 12
Well, we shall sift him *Hamlet* ii 2 58
Sifted. If thy thoughts were sifted 1 *Hen. VI.* iii 1 24
Sigeia. Hic ibat Simois; hic est Sigeia tellus *T. of Shrew* iii 1 28
'Sigeia tellus,' disguised thus to get your love iii 1 33
Sigh. To cry to the sea that roar'd to us, to sigh To the winds *Tempest* i 2 149
Whom I left cooling of the air with sighs ii 1 222
Scorn is bought with groans; Coy looks with heart-sore sighs *T. G. of Ver.* i 1 30
To sigh, like a schoolboy that had lost his A B C ii 1 22
When that hour o'erslips me in the day Wherein I sigh not, Julia ii 2 10
If the wind were down, I could drive the boat with my sighs ii 3 60
With penitential groans, With nightly tears and daily heart-sore sighs ii 4 132
Pure hands held up, Sad sighs, deep groans, nor silver-shedding tears iii 1 230
Say that upon the altar of her beauty You sacrifice your tears, your sighs iii 2 74
To that [your picture] I'll speak, to that I'll sigh and weep iv 2 123
That a milkmaid, if she be in love, may sigh it off *Meas. for Meas.* i 2 178
An thou wilt needs thrust thy neck into a yoke, wear the print of it and sigh away Sundays *Much Ado* i 1 204
Sigh no more, ladies, sigh no more, Men were deceivers ever ii 3 64
Then sigh not so, but let them go, And be you blithe and bonny ii 3 68
Like cover'd fire, Consume away in sighs, waste inwardly iii 1 78
What! sigh for the toothache? iii 2 26
At last she concluded with a sigh, thou wast the properest man in Italy v 1 173
Midnight, assist our moan; Help us to sigh and groan, Heavily, heavily v 3 17
I think scorn to sigh: methinks I should outswear Cupid *L. L. Lost* i 2 67
Sigh a note and sing a note, sometime through the throat iii 1 13
By thy favour, sweet welkin, I must sigh in thy face iii 1 68
I, that have been love's whip; A very beadle to a humorous sigh iii 1 177
The anointed sovereign of sighs and groans, Liege of all loiterers iii 1 184
And I to sigh for her! to watch for her! To pray for her! iii 1 202
Well, I will love, write, sigh, pray, sue and groan iii 1 206
Observed your fashion, Saw sighs reek from you, noted well your passion iv 3 140
What a scene of foolery have I seen, Of sighs, of groans, of sorrow! iv 3 164
Until his ink were temper'd with Love's sighs iv 3 347
As due to love as thoughts and dreams and sighs *M. N. Dream* i 1 154
Pale of cheer, With sighs of love, that costs the fresh blood dear iii 2 97
Hood mine eyes Thus with my hat, and sigh and say 'amen' *M. of Ven.* ii 2 203
No sighs but of my breathing; no tears but of my shedding iii 1 100
A soft and dull-eyed fool, To shake the head, relent, and sigh iii 3 15
I'll go find a shadow and sigh till he come *As Y. Like It* iv 1 222
Tell this youth what 'tis to love.—It is to be all made of sighs and tears v 2 90
Let me never have a cause to sigh, Till I be brought to such a silly pass! —Fie! what a foolish duty call you this? *T. of Shrew* v 2 123
To imperial Love, that god most high, Do my sighs stream *All's Well* ii 3 82
With groans that thunder love, with sighs of fire *T. Night* i 5 275
What thriftless sighs shall poor Olivia breathe! ii 2 40
A thousand thousand sighs to save ii 4 64
She thus advises thee that sighs for thee ii 5 165
And then to sigh, as t'were The mort o' the deer *W. Tale* i 2 117
Kissing with inside lip? stopping the career Of laughter with a sigh? i 2 287
Do sigh At each his needless heavings ii 3 34
For thee, fond boy, If I may ever know thou dost but sigh iv 4 438
My heart will sigh when I miscall it so *Richard II.* i 3 263
With despised tears; Our sighs and they shall lodge the summer corn iii 3 162
Go, count thy way with sighs; I mine with groans v 1 89
With sighs they jar Their watches on unto mine eyes v 5 51
So sighs and tears and groans Show minutes, times, and hours v 5 57
And with A rising sigh he wisheth you in heaven 1 *Hen. IV.* iii 1 10
To stop my ear indeed, Thou hast a sigh to blow away this praise 2 *Hen. IV.* i 1 80
Behold My sighs and tears and will not once relent? 1 *Hen. VI.* iii 1 108
Heart-offending groans Or blood-consuming sighs 2 *Hen. VI.* iii 2 61
Look pale as primrose with blood-drinking sighs iii 2 63

Sigh. Through whom a thousand sighs are breathed for thee 2 *Hen. VI.* iii 2 345
Why should you sigh, my lord?—Not for myself 3 *Hen. VI.* i 1 191
Her sighs will make a battery in his breast iii 1 37
For this I draw in many a tear And stop the rising of blood-sucking sighs iv 4 22
Many an old man's sigh and many a widow's, And many an orphan's v 6 39
But then I sigh; and, with a piece of scripture, Tell them that God bids us do good for evil *Richard III.* i 3 334
Believe him not: he would insinuate with thee but to make thee sigh i 4 153
When my heart, As wedged with a sigh, would rive in twain *Troi. and Cres.* i 1 35
As when the sun doth light a storm, Buried this sigh in wrinkle of a smile i 1 38
Why sigh you so profoundly? iv 2 83
We two, that with so many thousand sighs Did buy each other iv 4 41
Sighs, and takes my glove, And gives memorial dainty kisses to it v 2 79
I have been blown out of your gates with sighs *Coriolanus* v 2 81
With our sighs we'll breathe the welkin dim *T. Andron.* iii 1 212
I am the sea; hark, how her sighs do blow! She is the weeping welkin, I the earth: Then must my sea be moved with her sighs iii 1 226
Thou shalt not sigh, nor hold thy stumps to heaven iii 2 42
Adding to clouds more clouds with his deep sighs *Rom. and Jul.* i 1 139
Love is a smoke raised with the fume of sighs i 1 196
Appear thou in the likeness of a sigh: Speak but one rhyme ii 1 8
The sun not yet thy sighs from heaven clears ii 3 73
The bark thy body is, Sailing in this salt flood; the winds, thy sighs iii 5 135
Here is a friar, that trembles, sighs, and weeps v 3 184
Sighs and groans and shrieks that rend the air Are made, not mark'd *Macbeth* iv 3 168
What a sigh is there! The heart is sorely charged v 1 59
He raised a sigh so piteous and profound As it did seem to shatter all his bulk And end his being *Hamlet* ii 1 94
The lover shall not sigh gratis; the humorous man shall end his part in peace ii 2 335
Never alone Did the king sigh, but with a general groan iii 3 23
There's matter in these sighs, these profound heaves iv 1 1
This 'should' is like a spendthrift sigh, That hurts by easing iv 7 123
My cue is villanous melancholy, with a sigh like Tom o' Bedlam *Lear* i 2 148
My story being done, She gave me for my pains a world of sighs *Othello* i 3 159
We cannot call her winds and waters sighs and tears *Ant. and Cleo.* i 2 153
Then shall the sighs of Octavia blow the fire up in Cæsar ii 6 135
He furnaces The thick sighs from him *Cymbeline* i 6 67
Wherefore breaks that sigh From the inward of thee? iii 4 5
Nobly he yokes A smiling with a sigh, as if the sigh Was that it was, for not being such a smile; The smile mocking the sigh, that it would fly From so divine a temple, to commix With winds that sailors rail at iv 2 52
I'll weep and sigh; And leaving so his service, follow you iv 2 392
In sorrow all devour'd, With sighs shot through *Pericles* iv 4 26
Sighed. This Is the third man that e'er I saw, the first That e'er I sigh'd for *Tempest* i 2 446
And sigh'd his soul toward the Grecian tents, Where Cressid lay *M. of V.* v 1 5
As true a lover As ever sigh'd upon a midnight pillow *As Y. Like It* ii 4 27
No sooner looked but they loved, no sooner loved but they sighed, no sooner sighed but they asked one another the reason v 2 38
With that she sighed as she stood, And gave this sentence *All's Well* i 3 79
And sigh'd my English breath in foreign clouds *Richard II.* iii 1 20
Sigh'd forth proverbs, That hunger broke stone walls *Coriolanus* i 1 209
Never man Sigh'd truer breath iv 5 121
And sigh'd, and kiss'd; and then Cried 'Cursed fate!' *Othello* iii 3 425
Sighest. O heart, heavy heart, Why sigh'st thou without breaking? Because thou canst not ease thy smart *Troi. and Cres.* iv 4 18
Sighing. To sigh To the winds whose pity, sighing back again, Did us but loving wrong *Tempest* i 2 150
And then the lover, Sighing like furnace *As Y. Like It* ii 7 148
Sighing every minute and groaning every hour would detect the lazy foot of Time as well as a clock iii 2 321
A plague of sighing and grief! it blows a man up like a bladder 1 *Hen. IV.* ii 4 365
He came sighing on After the admired heels of Bolingbroke 2 *Hen. IV.* i 3 104
My sighing breast shall be thy funeral bell 3 *Hen. VI.* ii 5 117
Welcome ever smiles, And farewell goes out sighing *Troi. and Cres.* iii 3 169
Wound it with sighing, girl, kill it with groans *T. Andron.* iii 2 15
And walk'd about, Musing and sighing, with your arms across *J. Cæsar* ii 1 240
The poor soul sat sighing by a sycamore tree, Sing all a green willow *Othello* iv 3 41
Sight. Be subject To no sight but thine and mine *Tempest* i 2 302
At the first sight They have changed eyes i 2 440
If these be true spies which I wear in my head, here's a goodly sight v 1 260
See it be return'd; Or else return no more into my sight *T. G. of Ver.* i 2 47
You may say what sights you see; I see things too, although you judge I wink i 2 138
She will love you, Now Valentine is banish'd from her sight iii 2 2
Find my dog again, Or ne'er return again into my sight iv 4 65
Engrossed opportunities to meet her; fee'd every slight occasion that could but niggardly give me sight of her *Mer. Wives* ii 2 205
Upon their sight, We two in great amazedness will fly iv 4 54
Stick it in their children's sight For terror, not to use *Meas. for Meas.* i 3 25
Can you so stead me As bring me to the sight of Isabella? i 4 18
You shall not be admitted to his sight iv 3 125
In our sight they three were taken up By fishermen *Com. of Errors* i 1 111
Gaze where you should, and that will clear your sight iii 2 57
God keep him out of my sight when the dance is done! *Much Ado* ii 1 113
The sight whereof I think you had from me v 4 25
To-morrow you shall have a sight of them.—It shall suffice me *L. L. Lost* ii 1 166
Come on, then; wear the favours most in sight v 2 136
We must starve our sight From lovers' food till morrow. *M. N. Dream* i 1 222
Herein mean I to enrich my pain, To have his sight thither and back again i 1 251
Take heed the queen come not within his sight ii 1 19
Ere I take this charm from off her sight, As I can take it ii 1 183
So, at his sight, away his fellows fly iii 2 24
Thou hast mistaken quite And laid the love-juice on some true-love's sight iii 2 89
And make his eyeballs roll with wonted sight iii 2 369
Thou takest True delight In the sight Of thy former lady's eye iii 2 456
See'st thou this sweet sight? Her dotage now I do begin to pity iv 1 51
By thy . . . glittering gleams, I trust to take of truest Thisby sight v 1 280
Good wrestling, which you have lost the sight of *As Y. Like It* i 2 117
Though it be pity to see such a sight, it well becomes the ground iii 2 255
The sight of lovers feedeth those in love. Bring us to this sight iii 4 61

Sight. The common executioner, Whose heart the accustom'd sight of death makes hard *As Y. Like It* iii 5 4

Though all the world could see, None could be so abused in sight as he iii 5 80

Who ever loved that loved not at first sight? iii 5 83

An you serve me such another trick, never come in my sight more iv 1 41

An you be so tardy, come no more in my sight iv 1 52

I cannot be out of the sight of Orlando iv 1 221

If there be truth in sight, you are my daughter v 4 124

If there be truth in sight, you are my Rosalind v 4 125

If sight and shape be true, Why then, my love adieu! v 4 126

At that sight shall sad Apollo weep *T. of Shrew* Ind. 2 61

Bring our lady hither to our sight Ind. 2 76

Whose sudden sight hath thrall'd my wounded eye i 1 225

Her silence flouts me, and I'll be revenged.—What, in my sight? ii 1 30

If they do approach the city, we shall lose all the sight *All's Well* iii 5 2

She hath abjured the company And sight of men *T. Night* i 2 41

She did show favour to the youth in your sight only to exasperate you iii 2 20

In my sight she uses thee kindly iii 4 171

Will it be ever thus? Ungracious wretch, . . . out of my sight! iv 1 53

As gross as ever touch'd conjecture, That lack'd sight only *W. Tale* ii 1 177

We do not know How he may soften at the sight o' the child ii 2 40

I have seen two such sights, by sea and by land! iii 3 84

I have not winked since I saw these sights iii 3 107

Here's a sight for thee; look thee, a bearing-cloth for a squire's child! iii 3 118

Fetch me to the sight of him.—Marry, will I iii 3 139

Hardly Will he endure your sight as yet, I fear iv 4 481

Do him love and honour, Purchase the sight again of dear Sicilia iv 4 522

I shall review Sicilia, for whose sight I have a woman's longing iv 4 680

We must to the king and show our strange sights iv 4 849

You lost a sight, which was to be seen, cannot be spoken of v 2 46

If I had thought the sight of my poor image Would thus have wrought you v 3 57

On the sight of us your lawful king, . . . Behold, the French amazed vouchsafe a parle *K. John* ii 1 222

I cannot brook thy sight: This news hath made thee a most ugly man iii 1 36

How oft the sight of means to do ill deeds Make deeds ill done! iv 2 219

Out of my sight, and never see me more! iv 2 242

Shall I seem crest-fall'n in my father's sight? *Richard II.* i 1 188

God's substitute, His deputy anointed in His sight, Hath caused his death i 2 38

Make their way seem short, as mine hath done By sight of what I have ii 3 18

Sit blushing in his face, Not able to endure the sight of day iii 2 52

Whither?—Whither you will, so I were from your sights iv 1 315

Hence, villain! never more come in my sight.—Give me my boots v 2 86

Not an eye But is a-weary of thy common sight *1 Hen. IV.* iii 2 88

Even our love durst not come near your sight For fear of swallowing v 1 63

We were enforced, for safety sake, to fly Out of your sight v 1 66

His dimensions to any thick sight were invincible *2 Hen. IV.* iii 2 336

Their eyes of fire sparkling through sights of steel iv 1 121

In sight of both our battles we may meet; And either end in peace iv 1 179

Now my sight fails, and my brain is giddy: O me! come near me iv 4 110

Upon thy sight My worldly business makes a period iv 5 230

Bid them come down, Or void the field; they do offend our sight *Hen. V.* iv 7 62

The dreadful judgement-day So dreadful will not be as was his sight *1 Hen. VI.* i 1 30

Let us look in; the sight will much delight thee i 4 62

Wilt thou be daunted at a woman's sight? v 3 69

Boiling choler chokes The hollow passage of my poison'd voice, By sight of these our baleful enemies v 4 122

Upon my bended knee, In sight of England and her lordly peers *2 Hen. VI.* i 1 11

Her sight did ravish; but her grace in speech, Her words y-clad with wisdom's majesty, Makes me from wondering fall to weeping joys i 1 32

Why are thine eyes fix'd to the sullen earth, Gazing on that which seems to dim thy sight? i 2 6

Never more abase our sight so low As to vouchsafe one glance unto the ground i 2 15

A blind man at Saint Alban's shrine . . . hath received his sight ii 1 64

Great is his comfort in this earthly vale, Although by his sight his sin be multiplied ii 1 71

Sight may distinguish of colours, but suddenly to nominate them all, it is impossible ii 1 129

In sight of God and us, your guilt is great ii 3 2

Go, take hence that traitor from our sight ii 3 103

Thou baleful messenger, out of my sight! iii 2 48

Come, basilisk, And kill the innocent gazer with thy sight iii 2 53

The dusky sky began to rob My earnest-gaping sight of thy land's view iii 2 105

In thy sight to die, what were it else But like a pleasant slumber in thy lap? iii 2 389

From thy sight, I should be raging mad iii 2 394

Even in their wives' and children's sight, Be hang'd up for example iv 2 189

The sight of me is odious in their eyes iv 4 46

Shall I endure the sight of Somerset? False king! v 1 90

Even at this sight My heart is turn'd to stone v 2 49

The sight of any of the house of York Is as a fury to torment my soul; And till I root out their accursed line . . . , I live in hell *3 Hen. VI.* i 3 30

To see this sight, it irks my very soul. Withhold revenge, dear God! ii 2 6

Like a brace of greyhounds Having the fearful flying hare in sight ii 5 130

To greet mine own land with my wishful sight iii 1 14

I here protest, in sight of heaven, And by the hope I have of heavenly bliss iii 3 181

Out of my sight! thou dost infect my eyes *Richard III.* i 2 149

Foul wrinkled witch, what makest thou in my sight? i 3 164

I have pass'd a miserable night, So full of ugly sights! i 4 3

What ugly sights of death within mine eyes! i 4 23

Take some privy order, To draw the brats of Clarence out of sight iii 5 107

Bring me to their sights; I'll bear thy blame iv 1 25

Blind sight, dead life, poor mortal living ghost iv 4 26

If I be so disgracious in your sight, Let me march on iv 4 177

Lest, being seen, thy brother . . . Be executed in his father's sight v 3 96

With shows, Pageants and sights of honour *Hen. VIII.* iv 1 11

If my sight fail not, You should be lord ambassador iv 2 108

I'll show your grace the strangest sight— What's that, Butts? v 2 20

Purblind Argus, all eyes and no sight *Troi. and Cres.* i 2 31

That, through the sight I bear in things to love, I have abandon'd Troy iii 3 4

Yea, so familiar!—She will sing any man at first sight v 2 9

And the bleared sights Are spectacled to see him *Coriolanus* ii 1 221

That the precipitation might down stretch Below the beam of sight iii 2 5

And schoolboys' tears take up The glasses of my sight! iii 2 117

Thy sight, which should Make our eyes flow with joy, hearts dance with comforts, Constrains them weep v 3 98

Here in sight of Rome . . . do I consecrate My sword *T. Andron.* i 1 246

Here, in sight of heaven, to Rome I swear i 1 329

Sight. My sight is very dull, whate'er it bodes *T. Andron.* ii 3 195

With the dismall'st object hurt That ever eye with sight made heart lament! ii 3 205

Look down into this den, And see a fearful sight of blood and death ii 3 216

Go, and make thy father blind; For such a sight will blind a father's eye ii 4 53

What accursed hand Hath made thee handless in thy father's sight? iii 1 67

Ah, that this sight should make so deep a wound, And yet detested life not shrink thereat! iii 1 247

With this dear sight Struck pale and bloodless iii 1 257

And be this dismal sight The closing up of our most wretched eyes iii 1 262

Go get thee from my sight; Thou art an exile, and thou must not stay iii 1 284

Thy sight is young, And thou shalt read when mine begin to dazzle iii 2 84

Letters . . . Which signify . . . how desirous of our sight they are v 1 4

A sight to vex the father's soul withal v 1 52

I'll go along, no such sight to be shown *Rom. and Jul.* i 2 105

Forswear it, sight! For I ne'er saw true beauty till this night i 5 54

I have night's cloak to hide me from their sight ii 2 75

Come what sorrow can, It cannot countervail the exchange of joy That one short minute gives me in her sight ii 6 5

All bedaub'd in blood, All in gore-blood; I swounded at the sight iii 2 56

Have I thought long to see this morning's face, And doth it give me such a sight as this? iv 5 42

One poor and loving child, But one thing to rejoice and solace in, And cruel death hath catch'd it from my sight! iv 5 48

Pitiful sight! here lies the county slain; And Juliet bleeding v 3 174

This sight of death is as a bell, That warns my old age to a sepulchre v 3 206

I am joyful of your sights *T. of Athens* i 1 255

Sir, you have saved my longing, and I feed Most hungerly on your sight i 1 262

Nor sight of priests in holy vestments bleeding, Shall pierce a jot iv 3 125

You know him well by sight *J. Cæsar* i 3 15

There's two or three of us have seen strange sights i 3 138

Recounts most horrid sights seen by the watch ii 2 16

O most bloody sight!—We will be revenged iii 2 206

Get higher on that hill; My sight was ever thick v 3 21

Piercing steel and darts envenomed Shall be as welcome to the ears of Brutus As tidings of this sight v 3 78

Only to herald thee into his sight, Not pay thee *Macbeth* i 3 102

Art thou not, fatal vision, sensible To feeling as to sight? ii 1 37

This is a sorry sight.—A foolish thought, to say a sorry sight ii 2 21

Approach the chamber, and destroy your sight With a new Gorgon ii 3 76

Though I could With barefaced power sweep him from my sight iii 1 119

Avaunt! and quit my sight! let the earth hide thee! iii 4 93

You can behold such sights, And keep the natural ruby of your cheeks, When mine is blanch'd with fear.—What sights, my lord? iii 4 114

Horrible sight! Now, I see, 'tis true iv 1 122

This deed I'll do before this purpose cool. But no more sights! iv 1 155

My mind she has mated, and amazed my sight v 1 86

Will not let belief take hold of him Touching this dreaded sight *Hamlet* i 1 25

At the sound it shrunk in haste away, And vanish'd from our sight i 2 220

If you have hitherto conceal'd this sight, Let it be tenable in your silence i 2 247

Or look'd upon this love with idle sight ii 2 138

Eyes without feeling, feeling without sight, Ears without hands or eyes iii 4 78

'Twould be a sight indeed, If one could match you iv 7 100

Where is this sight?—What is it ye would see? v 2 373

The sight is dismal; And our affairs from England come too late v 2 378

Such a sight as this Becomes the field, but here shows much amiss v 2 412

Hence, and avoid my sight! So be my grave my peace, as here I give Her father's heart from her! *Lear* i 1 126

Out of my sight!—See better, Lear; and let me still remain i 1 159

Out, varlet, from my sight!—What means your grace? ii 4 190

Yond tall anchoring bark, Diminish'd to her cock; her cock, a buoy Almost too small for sight iv 6 20

I'll look no more; Lest my brain turn, and the deficient sight Topple down headlong iv 6 23

And, in your sights, Shake patiently my great affliction off iv 6 35

I am the king himself.—O thou side-piercing sight! iv 6 85

The small gilded fly Does lecher in my sight iv 6 115

A sight most pitiful in the meanest wretch, Past speaking of in a king! iv 6 208

With this ungracious paper strike the sight Of the death-practised duke iv 6 283

This is a dull sight. Are you not Kent?—The same v 3 282

Out of my sight!—I will not stay to offend you *Othello* iv 1 258

Did he live now, This sight would make him do a desperate turn v 2 207

Whip me, ye devils, From the possession of this heavenly sight! v 2 278

This is thy work: the object poisons sight; Let it be hid v 2 364

Mine eyes did sicken at the sight *Ant. and Cleo.* iii 10 17

A heavy sight!—I am dying, Egypt, dying iv 15 40

Thou basest thing, avoid! hence, from my sight! *Cymbeline* i 1 125

Your daughter . . . she did confess Was as a scorpion to her sight v 5 45

O, get thee from my sight; Thou gavest me poison v 5 236

O you powers That give heaven countless eyes to view men's acts, Why cloud they not their sights perpetually? *Pericles* i 1 74

Like an hypocrite, The which is good in nothing but in sight i 1 123

Their tables were stored full, to glad the sight, And not so much to feed on as delight i 4 28

In your supposing once more put your sight Of heavy Pericles v Gower 21

But bootless is your sight: he will not speak To any v 1 33

Sighted. Make me not sighted like the basilisk *W. Tale* i 2 388

Sight-hole. And stop all sight-holes, every loop from whence The eye of reason may pry in upon us *1 Hen. IV.* iv 1 71

Sightless. Full of unpleasing blots and sightless stains *K. John* iii 1 45

You murdering ministers, Wherever in your sightless substances You wait on nature's mischief! *Macbeth* i 5 50

Heaven's cherubim, horsed Upon the sightless couriers of the air i 7 23

Sightly. It lies as sightly on the back of him As great Alcides' shows upon an ass *K. John* ii 1 143

Sight-outrunning. Jove's lightnings, . . . more momentary And sight-outrunning were not *Tempest* i 2 203

Sign. Thou hast shown some sign of good desert *T. G. of Ver.* iii 2 18

Sign me a present pardon for my brother *Meas. for Meas.* ii 4 152

For the sign of blind Cupid *Much Ado* i 1 256

Let them signify under my sign 'Here you may see Benedick the married man' i 1 269

She will rather die than give any sign of affection ii 3 236

If he be not in love with some woman, there is no believing old signs iii 2 41

She's but the sign and semblance of her honour iv 1 34

What sign is it when a man of great spirit grows melancholy?—A great sign, sir, that he will look sad *L. L. Lost* i 2 1

We, Following the signs, woo'd but the sign of she v 2 469

Sign. Until the twelve celestial signs Have brought about the annual reckoning . . . *L. L. Lost* v 2 807
Send the deed after me, And I will sign it . . . *Mer. of Venice* iv 1 397
Give him this deed And let him sign it . . . iv 2 2
In sign whereof, Please ye we may contrive this afternoon . *T. of Shrew* i 2 275
Expound the meaning or moral of his signs and tokens . . . iv 4 80
I will win my wager better yet And show more sign of her obedience . v 2 117
He does bear some signs of me, yet you Have too much blood in him *W. T.* ii 1 57
From one sign of dolour to another . . . . . . v 2 95
Be these sad signs confirmers of thy words? . . *K. John* iii 1 24
Prodigies and signs, Abortives, presages and tongues of heaven . iii 4 157
Thou didst understand me by my signs And didst in signs again parley with sin . . . iv 2 237
With signs of war about his aged neck . . . *Richard II.* ii 2 74
These signs forerun the death or fall of kings . . . ii 4 15
Leaving me no sign, Save men's opinions and my living blood . iii 1 25
Yet blessing on his heart that gives it me! For 'tis a sign of love . v 5 65
And dials the signs of leaping-houses . . . *1 Hen. IV.* i 2 9
These signs have mark'd me extraordinary . . . . iii 1 41
Wears his boots very smooth, like unto the sign of the leg . *2 Hen. IV.* ii 4 271
Cheerly to sea; the signs of war advance . . . *Hen. V.* ii 2 192
By some apparent sign Let us have knowledge at the court of guard *1 Hen. VI.* ii 1 3
In sign whereof I pluck a white rose too . . . . . ii 4 58
I'll by a sign give notice to our friends . . . . . iii 2 8
Choice spirits that admonish me And give me signs of future accidents v 3 4
And I again . . . Give thee her hand, for sign of plighted faith . v 3 162
It's sign she hath been liberal and free . . . . . v 4 82
I can express no kinder sign of love Than this kind kiss . . *2 Hen. VI.* i 1 18
And make my image but an alehouse sign . . . . . iii 2 81
He was murder'd here; The least of all these signs were probable . iii 2 178
With full as many signs of deadly hate, As lean-faced Envy . . iii 2 314
What a sign it is of evil life, Where death's approach is seen so terrible! iii 3 5
He dies, and makes no sign. O God, forgive him! . . . . iii 3 29
There's no better sign of a brave mind than a hard hand . . iv 2 22
Underneath an alehouse' paltry sign . . . . . . v 2 67
Hath pawn'd an open hand in sign of love . . *3 Hen. VI.* iv 2 9
In sign of truth, I kiss your highness' hand . . . . iv 8 26
The owl shriek'd at thy birth,—an evil sign; The night-crow cried v 6 44
I'll kiss thy hand, In sign of league and amity with thee *Richard III.* i 3 281
Meaning indeed his house, Which, by the sign thereof, was termed so . iii 5 79
A sign of dignity, a garish flag, To be the aim of every dangerous shot . iv 4 89
You sign your place and calling, in full seeming, With meekness *Hen. VIII.* ii 4 108
Offers, as I do, in a sign of peace, His service and his counsel . . iii 1 66
In sign of what you are, not to reward What you have done . *Coriolanus* i 9 26
Go home, And show no sign of fear . . . . . . iv 6 153
These are no venereal signs: Vengeance is in my heart *T. Andron.* ii 3 37
See, how with signs and tokens she can scrowl . . . . ii 4 5
Let me kiss thy lips; Or make some sign how I may do thee ease . . iii 1 121
Marcus, mark! I understand her signs . . . . . iii 1 143
Thou map of woe, that thus dost talk in signs! . . . . iii 2 12
Hark, Marcus, what she says; I can interpret all her martyr'd signs . iii 2 36
Nor nod, nor kneel, nor make a sign, But I of these will wrest an alphabet . . . . . . iii 2 43
What means my niece Lavinia by these signs?—Fear her not . . iv 1 8
Give signs, sweet girl, for here are none but friends . . . iv 1 61
Shallow-hearted boys! Ye white-limed walls! ye alehouse painted signs! iv 2 98
My frosty signs and chaps of age, Grave witnesses of true experience . v 3 77
Being mechanical, you ought not walk Upon a labouring day without the sign Of your profession . . . . . . *J. Cæsar* i 1 4
But, with an angry wafture of your hand, Gave sign for me to leave you ii 1 247
Their bloody sign of battle is hung out, And something to be done immediately . . . . v 1 14
Mark Antony, shall we give sign of battle?—No, Cæsar . . . v 1 23
Signs of nobleness, like stars, shall shine On all deservers . *Macbeth* i 4 41
It were a good sign that I should quickly have a new father . . iv 2 62
Yet, for necessity of present life, I must show out a flag and sign of love, Which is indeed but sign . . . . . *Othello* i 1 158
Music i' the air.—Under the earth.—It signs well, does it not? *A. and C.* iv 3 15
Thou hast seen these signs; They are black vesper's pageants . . iv 14 7
We, Your scutcheons and your signs of conquest . . . . v 2 135
She's a good sign, but I have seen small reflection of her wit . *Cymbeline* i 2 33
Render to me some corporal sign about her, More evident than this . ii 4 119
I'll give but notice you are dead and send him Some bloody sign of it . iii 4 128
If we had of every nation a traveller, we should lodge them with this sign . . . . *Pericles* iv 2 124
Signal. Shall we give the signal to our rage? . . *K. John* ii 1 265
Courageously and with a free desire Attending but the signal *Richard II.* i 3 116
Giving full trophy signal and ostent Quite from himself to God *Hen. V.* v Prol. 21
In signal of my love to thee . . . . . . *1 Hen. VI.* ii 4 121
If thou think'st on heaven's bliss, Hold up thy hand, make signal of thy hope. He dies, and makes no sign . . *2 Hen. VI.* iii 3 28
For God's sake, lords, give signal to the fight . *3 Hen. VI.* ii 2 100; v 4 72; 82
Gives signal of a goodly day to-morrow . . . *Richard III.* v 3 21
Whistle then to me, As signal that thou hear'st something approach *Rom. and Jul.* v 3 8
Stir not until the signal.—Words before blows . . *J. Cæsar* v 1 26
Signed. As doubtful whether what I see be true, Until confirm'd, sign'd, ratified by you . . . . . *Mer. of Venice* iii 2 149
Mark'd, Quoted and sign'd to do a deed of shame . . *K. John* iv 2 222
Here didst thou fall; and here thy hunters stand, Sign'd in thy spoil, and crimson'd in thy lethe . . . . . . *J. Cæsar* iii 1 206
Signet. The signet is not strange to you . . *Meas. for Meas.* iv 2 209
I have been bold . . . To them to use your signet and your name *T. of A.* ii 2 210
In that was heaven ordinant. I had my father's signet in my purse *Ham.* v 2 49
Signieur. O Seigneur Dieu!—O, Signieur Dew should be a gentleman: Perpend my words, O Signieur Dew, and mark; O Signieur Dew, thou diest on point of fox, Except, O signieur, thou do give to me Egregious ransom . . . . *Hen. V.* iv 4 6
Most brave, valorous, and thrice-worthy signieur of England . . iv 4 67
Significant. Bear this significant to the country maid . *L. L. Lost* iii 1 131
In dumb significants proclaim your thoughts . . . *1 Hen. VI.* ii 4 26
Signified. Plainly signified That I should snarl and bite . *3 Hen. VI.* v 6 76
You might well have signified the same . . *Richard III.* iii 5 59
This by Calpurnia's dream is signified . . . *J. Cæsar* ii 2 90
Signify. The tenour of them doth but signify My health and happy being at your court . . . . *T. G. of Ver.* iii 1 56
It is a familiar beast to man, and signifies love . . . *Mer. Wives* i 1 21
Signify. Furred with fox and lamb-skins too, to signify, that craft, being richer than innocency, stands for the facing . *Meas. for Meas.* iii 2 10
Signify under my sign, 'Here you may see Benedick the married man' *Much Ado* i 1 268
Haste, signify so much; while we attend . . . *L. L. Lost* ii 1 33
Some man or other must present Wall: and let him have some plaster, or some loam, or some rough-cast about him, to signify wall *M. N. Dream* iii 1 71
Please you to break up this, it shall seem to signify . *Mer. of Venice* ii 4 11
One that comes before To signify the approaching of his lord . . ii 9 88
Signify, I pray you, Within the house, your mistress is at hand . v 1 51
There is come a messenger before, To signify their coming . . v 1 118
To signify Not only my success in Libya, sir, But my arrival *W. Tale* v 1 165
Go, signify as much, while here we march Upon the grassy carpet *Richard II.* iii 3 49
Fortune is painted blind, with a muffler afore her eyes, to signify to you that Fortune is blind . . . . *Hen V.* iii 6 34
From Ireland am I come amain, To signify that rebels there are up *2 Hen. VI.* iii 1 283
Signify unto his majesty That Cardinal Beaufort is at point of death . iii 2 368
Teeth hadst thou in thy head when thou wast born, To signify thou camest to bite the world . . . . . *3 Hen. VI.* v 6 54
And signify to him That thus I have resign'd my charge to you *Rich. III.* i 4 97
Signify this loving interview To the expecters of our Trojan part *T. and C.* iv 5 155
What signifies my deadly-standing eye, My silence? . . *T. Andron.* ii 3 32
Letters . . . Which signify what hate they bear . . . . v 1 3
He shall signify from time to time Every good hap to you *Rom. and Jul.* iii 3 170
Which bears that office, to signify their pleasures . . *T. of Athens* i 2 125
We attend his lordship; pray, signify so much . . . . iii 4 37
Signifies that from you great Rome shall suck Reviving blood *J. Cæsar* ii 2 87
Your wisdom should show itself more richer to signify this to his doctor *Hamlet* iii 2 317
His majesty bade me signify to you that he has laid a great wager . v 2 105
Thou wilt write to Antony?—I'll humbly signify what in his name, That magical word of war, we have effected . . *Ant. and Cleo.* iii 1 30
Signifying. Full of sound and fury, Signifying nothing . *Macbeth* v 5 28
Signior. Good signior, take the stranger to my house . *Com. of Errors* iv 1 36
Signior, you are very near my brother in his love . . *Much Ado* ii 1 169
Now, signior, where's the count? did you see him? . . . ii 1 218
Boy!—Signior?—In my chamber-window lies a book: bring it . . ii 3 2
You have no stomach, signior: fare you well . . . . ii 3 265
Old signior, walk aside with me: I have studied eight or nine wise words to speak to you . . . . iii 2 73
Here comes the man we went to seek.—Now, signior, what news? . v 1 111
Welcome, signior: you are almost come to part almost a fray . . v 1 113
Wouldst thou come when I called thee?—Yea, signior . . . v 2 44
Will you go hear this news, signior?—I will live in thy heart . . v 2 103
I must entreat your pains, I think.—To do what, signior? . . v 4 19
Truth it is, good signior, Your niece regards me with an eye of favour . v 4 21
I would be loath to have you overflown with a honey-bag, signior *M. N. Dream* iv 1 17
With portly sail, Like signiors and rich burghers on the flood *M. of Ven.* i 1 10
Good signiors both, when shall we laugh? say, when? . . . . i 1 66
Rest you fair, good signior; Your worship was the last man in our mouths . . . . i 3 60
I cannot tell; I make it breed as fast: But note me, signior . . . i 3 98
Come and fight it out?—Signior, no.—Signior, hang! . *1 Hen. VI.* iii 2 67
Signior, is all your family within?—Are your doors lock'd? . *Othello* i 1 84
Most reverend signior, do you know my voice?—Not I . . . . i 1 93
Signior, it is the Moor.—Down with him, thief! . . . . i 2 57
Good signior, you shall more command with years Than with your weapons . . . . i 2 60
'Tis true, most worthy signior; The duke's in council . . . i 2 91
I did not see you; welcome, gentle signior; We lack'd your counsel . i 3 50
Most potent, grave, and reverend signiors . . . . . i 3 76
Noble signior, If virtue no delighted beauty lack, Your son-in-law is far more fair than black . . . . i 3 289
I am very glad to see you, signior; Welcome to Cyprus . . iv 1 233
This worthy signior, I thank him, makes no stranger of me . *Cymbeline* i 4 111
Signiory. My services which I have done the signiory Shall out-tongue his complaints . . . . *Othello* i 2 18
Signories. Through all the signories it was the first . *Tempest* i 2 71
You have fed upon my signories, Dispark'd my parks . *Richard II.* iii 1 22
Though mine enemy, restored again To all his lands and signories . iv 1 89
Were you not restored To all the Duke of Norfolk's signories? *2 Hen. IV.* iv 1 111
Signum. My sword hacked like a hand-saw—ecce signum! . *1 Hen. IV.* ii 4 187
Silence. To cabin: silence! trouble us not . . . *Tempest* i 1 19
If you can command these elements to silence . . . . . i 1 24
Silence! one word more Shall make me chide thee, if not hate thee . i 2 475
Sweet, now, silence! Juno and Ceres whisper seriously . . iv 1 124
In dumb silence will I bury mine [news] . . *T. G. of Ver.* iii 1 207
The night's dead silence Will well become such sweet-complaining grievance . . . . iii 2 85
Elves, list your names; silence, you airy toys . . *Mer. Wives* v 5 46
That the time may have all shadow and silence in it *Meas. for Meas.* iii 1 257
Silence that fellow: I would he had some cause To prattle for himself . v 1 181
He was drunk then my lord: it can be no better.—For the benefit of silence, would thou wert so too! . . . . v 1 190
Silence is the perfectest herald of joy . . . . *Much Ado* ii 1 317
Your silence most offends me, and to be merry best becomes you . . ii 1 345
Night and silence.—Who is here? . . . . *M. N. Dream* ii 2 70
Silence awhile. Robin, take off this head. Titania, music call . iv 1 85
Then, my queen, in silence sad, Trip we after night's shade . . iv 1 100
Out of this silence yet I pick'd a welcome . . . . . v 1 100
But, silence! here comes Thisbe.—This is old Ninny's tomb . . v 1 266
Silence is only commendable In a neat's tongue dried and a maid not vendible.—Is that any thing now? . . . *Mer. of Venice* i 1 111
And wish'd in silence that it were not his . . . . . ii 8 32
The best grace of wit will shortly turn into silence . . . . iii 5 50
Who comes so fast in silence of the night?—A friend . . . v 1 25
It sounds much sweeter than by day.—Silence bestows that virtue on it v 1 101
Her very silence and her patience Speak to the people . *As Y. Like It* i 3 80
In the other's silence do I see Maid's mild behaviour . *T. of Shrew* i 1 70
Her silence flouts me, and I'll be revenged . . . . ii 1 29
Be check'd for silence, But never tax'd for speech . . *All's Well* i 1 76
Only shape thou thy silence to my wit . . . . *T. Night* i 2 61
Though our silence be drawn from us with cars, yet peace . . ii 5 70
Silence, like a Lucrece knife, With bloodless stroke my heart doth gore ii 5 116
The silence often of pure innocence Persuades when speaking fails *W. T.* ii 2 41
Appear in person here in court. Silence!—Read the indictment . . iii 2 10

Silence. I like your silence, it the more shows off Your wonder: but yet speak . . . *W. Tale* v 3 21
Silence, good mother; hear the embassy . . . *K. John* i 1 6
Silence; no more: go closely in with me: Much danger do I undergo for thee . . . iv 1 133
My heart is great; but it must break with silence . . . *Richard II.* ii 1 228
The unseen grief That swells with silence in the tortured soul . . . iv 1 298
There's for your silence.—I have no tongue, sir . . . *2 Hen. IV.* ii 2 178
And how doth my good cousin Silence? . . . iii 2 4
Master Surecard, as I think?—No, Sir John; it is my cousin Silence . . . iii 2 96
Good Master Silence, it well befits you should be of the peace . . . iii 2 98
Cousin Silence, that thou hadst seen that that this knight and I have seen! . . . iii 2 225
God keep you, Master Silence: I will not use many words with you . . . iii 2 308
Come, cousin Silence: and then to bed . . . v 3 4
There's a merry heart! Good Master Silence, I'll give you a health . . . v 3 25
I did not think Master Silence had been a man of this mettle . . . v 3 40
And a merry heart lives long-a.—Well said, Master Silence . . . v 3 51
Health and long life to you, Master Silence . . . v 3 55
Carry Master Silence to bed . . . v 3 135
What means this silence? Dare no man answer? . . . *1 Hen. VI.* ii 4 1
It is well objected: If I have fewest, I subscribe in silence . . . ii 4 44
With silence, nephew, be thou politic . . . ii 5 101
O, hold me not with silence over-long! . . . v 3 13
Command silence.—Silence! . . . *2 Hen. VI.* iv 2 39
Silence!—Widow, we will consider of your suit . . . *3 Hen. VI.* iii 2 15
And ask'd the mayor what meant this wilful silence . . . *Richard III.* iii 7 28
I know not whether to depart in silence, Or bitterly to speak in your reproof . . . iii 7 141
Then we shall have 'em Talk us to silence . . . *Hen. VIII.* i 4 45
Let silence be commanded.—What's the need? . . . ii 4 2
Still in thy right hand carry gentle peace, To silence envious tongues . . . iii 2 446
How his silence drinks up this applause! . . . *Troi. and Cres.* ii 3 211
Your silence, Cunning in dumbness, from my weakness draws My very soul . . . iii 2 139
We in silence hold this virtue well, We'll but commend what we intend to sell . . . iv 1 77
And to silence that, Which, to the spire and top of praises vouch'd, Would seem but modest . . . *Coriolanus* i 9 23
My gracious silence, hail! Wouldst thou have laugh'd had I come coffin'd home? . . . ii 1 192
There greet in silence, as the dead are wont . . . *T. Andron.* i 1 90
Here are no storms, No noise, but silence and eternal sleep . . . i 1 155
What signifies my deadly-standing eye, My silence and my cloudy melancholy? . . . ii 3 33
With . . . cold-moving nods They froze me into silence . . . *T. of Athens* ii 2 222
More news too: Marullus and Flavius, for pulling scarfs off Cæsar's images, are put to silence . . . *J. Cæsar* i 2 290
The noble Brutus is ascended: silence! . . . iii 2 11
My countrymen,— Peace, silence! Brutus speaks . . . iii 2 59
I pray you all, If you have hitherto conceal'd this sight, Let it be tenable in your silence still . . . *Hamlet* i 2 248
As we often see, against some storm, A silence in the heavens . . . ii 2 506
His silence will sit drooping . . . v 1 311
The rest is silence.—Now cracks a noble heart . . . v 2 369
Silence that dreadful bell: it frights the isle From her propriety . . . *Othello* ii 3 175
Silence those whom this vile brawl distracted . . . ii 3 256
Speak, or thy silence on the instant is Thy condemnation . . . *Cymbeline* iii 5 97
O Imogen! I'll speak to thee in silence . . . v 4 29
Will think me speaking, though I swear to silence . . . *Pericles* i 2 19
Silenced. Since the little wit that fools have was silenced, the little foolery that wise men have makes a great show . . . *As Y. Like It* i 2 95
Is it therefore The ambassador is silenced?—Marry, is't . . . *Hen. VIII.* i 1 97
Silenced their pleaders and Dispropertied their freedoms . . . *Coriolanus* ii 1 263
Nor then silenced when—'Commend me to your master'—and the cap Plays in the right hand, thus . . . *T. of Athens* ii 1 17
Silenced with that, In viewing o'er the rest o' the selfsame day . . . *Macbeth* i 3 93
Silencing. And in your power soft silencing your son . . . *2 Hen. IV.* v 2 97
Silent. No tongue! all eyes! be silent . . . *Tempest* iv 1 59
Dumb jewels often in their silent kind More than quick words do move a woman's mind . . . *T. G. of Ver.* iii 1 90
If speaking, why, a vane blown with all winds; If silent, why, a block moved with none . . . *Much Ado* iii 1 67
Hear me a little; for I have only been Silent so long . . . iv 1 158
It is not for prisoners to be too silent in their words . . . *L. L. Lost* i 2 169
No woman may approach his silent court . . . ii 1 24
I wish, my liege, You had only in your silent judgment tried it . . . *W. Tale* ii 1 171
Though I report it, That should be silent . . . iv 4 178
Mark, silent king, the moral of this sport . . . *Richard II.* iv 1 290
Give no words but mum: The business asketh silent secrecy . . . *2 Hen. VI.* i 2 90
Deep night, dark night, the silent of the night . . . i 4 19
That's not suddenly to be perform'd, But with advice and silent secrecy . . . ii 2 68
Hear him, lords; And be you silent and attentive too, For he that interrupts him shall not live . . . *3 Hen. VI.* i 1 122
Why, then, let's on our way in silent sort . . . iv 2 28
The sweet silent hours of marriage joys . . . *Richard III.* iv 4 330
The silent hours steal on, And flaky darkness breaks within the east . . . v 3 85
Here is a man—but 'tis before his face; I will be silent . . . *Troi. and Cres.* ii 3 241
Be silent, boy; I profit not by thy talk . . . v 1 16
That for their tongues to be silent, and not confess so much, were a kind of ingrateful injury . . . *Coriolanus* ii 2 34
That's off, that's off; I would you rather had been silent . . . ii 2 65
Should we be silent and not speak, our raiment And state of bodies would bewray what life We have led since thy exile . . . v 3 94
Let's leave her to her silent walks . . . *T. Andron* ii 4 8
A stone is silent, and offendeth not . . . iii 1 46
Let my meat make thee silent.—I scorn thy meat . . . *T. of Athens* i 2 37
Hear me for my cause, and be silent, that you may hear . . . *J. Cæsar* iii 2 14
Why are you silent?—Such welcome and unwelcome things at once 'Tis hard to reconcile . . . *Macbeth* iv 3 137
What shall Cordelia do? Love, and be silent . . . *Lear* i 1 63
My duty cannot be silent when I think your highness wronged . . . i 4 70
How silent is this town!—Ho! murder! murder!—What may you be? . . . *Othello* v 1 64
Speak no more.—That truth should be silent I had almost forgot . . . *Ant. and Cleo.* ii 2 109
But that you shall not say I yield being silent, I would not speak . . . *Cymbeline* ii 3 99
But we saw him dead.—Be silent; let's see further . . . v 5 127
Silently. Tie up my love's tongue, bring him silently . . . *M. N. Dream* iii 1 206

Silius. O Silius, Silius, I have done enough . . . *Ant. and Cleo.* iii 1 11
For learn this, Silius; Better to leave undone, than by our deed Acquire too high a fame when him we serve's away . . . iii 1 13
Silk. So rushling, I warrant you, in silk and gold . . . *Mer. Wives* ii 2 68
In a robe of white.—That silk will I go buy . . . iv 4 73
Even now a tailor call'd me in his shop And show'd me silks . . . *C. of Er.* iv 3 8
Three-farthing worth of silk . . . *L. L. Lost* iii 1 150
Since you have shore With shears his thread of silk . . . *M. N. Dream* v 1 348
Enrobe the roaring waters with my silks . . . *Mer. of Venice* i 1 34
Your black silk hair, Your bugle eyeballs . . . *As Y. Like It* iii 5 46
Any silk, any thread, Any toys for your head . . . *W. Tale* iv 4 325
Not in ashes and sackcloth, but in new silk and old sack . . . *2 Hen. IV.* i 2 222
Take note how many pair of silk stockings thou hast . . . ii 2 17
Stand firm by honour: We turn not back the silks upon the merchant, When we have soil'd them . . . *Troi. and Cres.* ii 2 69
When steel grows soft as the parasite's silk . . . *Coriolanus* i 9 45
Breaking his oath and resolution like A twist of rotten silk . . . v 6 96
And with a silk thread plucks it back again . . . *Rom. and Jul.* ii 2 181
The very butcher of a silk button, a duellist . . . ii 4 24
Thy flatterers yet wear silk, drink wine, lie soft . . . *T. of Athens* iv 3 206
Let not the creaking of shoes nor the rustling of silks betray thy poor heart to woman . . . *Lear* iii 4 98
Thou owest the worm no silk, the beast no hide, the sheep no wool . . . iii 4 108
The worms were hallow'd that did breed the silk . . . *Othello* iii 4 73
It was hang'd With tapestry of silk and silver . . . *Cymbeline* ii 4 69
Prouder than rustling in unpaid-for silk . . . iii 3 24
She weaved the sleided silk With fingers long, small, white as milk . . . *Pericles* iv Gower 21
Her inkle, silk, twin with the rubied cherry . . . v Gower 8
Silken. I'll knit it up in silken strings . . . *T. G. of Ver.* ii 7 45
Fetter strong madness in a silken thread . . . *Much Ado* v 1 25
Taffeta phrases, silken terms precise, Three-piled hyperboles . . . *L. L. Lost* v 2 406
With silken coats and caps and golden rings . . . *T. of Shrew* iv 3 55
It is a paltry cap, A custard-coffin, a bauble, a silken pie . . . iv 3 82
O fine villain! A silken doublet! a velvet hose! a scarlet cloak! . . . v 1 68
I would have ransack'd The pedlar's silken treasury . . . *W. Tale* iv 4 361
A beardless boy, A cocker'd silken wanton . . . *K. John* v 1 70
For a silken point I'll give my barony . . . *2 Hen IV.* i 1 53
And silken dalliance in the wardrobe lies . . . *Hen. V.* ii Prol. 2
His brave fleet With silken streamers the young Phœbus fanning . . . iii Prol. 6
Abused By silken, sly, insinuating Jacks . . . *Richard III.* i 3 53
Upon a lute, And make the silken strings delight to kiss them . . . *T. An.* ii 4 46
The silken tackle Swell with the touches of those flower-soft hands . . . *Ant. and Cleo.* ii 2 214
Or tie my treasure up in silken bags, To please the fool and death . . . *Per.* iii 2 41
Silken-coated. As for these silken-coated slaves, I pass not . . . *2 Hen. VI.* iv 2 136
Silkman. To Master Smooth's the silkman . . . *2 Hen. IV.* ii 1 31
Silliest. This is the silliest stuff that ever I heard . . . *M. N. Dream* v 1 212
Silliness. It is silliness to live when to live is torment . . . *Othello* i 3 309
Silling. 'Tis a good silling, I warrant you, or I will change it . . . *Hen. V.* iv 8 76
Silly. A silly answer and fitting well a sheep . . . *T. G. of Ver.* i 1 81
Provided that you do no outrages On silly women or poor passengers . . . iv 1 72
Thou enforcest laughter; thy silly thought my spleen . . . *L. L. Lost* iii 1 77
Ba, most silly sheep with a horn . . . v 1 53
Till I be brought to such a silly pass! . . . *T. of Shrew* v 2 124
It is silly sooth, And dallies with the innocence of love . . . *T. Night* ii 4 47
I purchased this caparison, and my revenue is the silly cheat . . . *W. Tale* iv 3 28
Like silly beggars Who sitting in the stocks refuge their shame, That many have and others must sit there . . . *Richard II.* v 5 25
Alas, this is a child, a silly dwarf! . . . *1 Hen. VI.* ii 3 22
Here is a silly stately style indeed! . . . iv 7 72
While as the silly owner of the goods Weeps over them . . . *2 Hen. VI.* i 1 225
Had I been there, which am a silly woman . . . *3 Hen. VI.* i 1 243
Shepherds looking on their silly sheep . . . ii 5 43
A silly time To make prescription for a kingdom's worth . . . iii 3 93
Harbour more craft . . . Than twenty silly ducking observants . . . *Lear* ii 2 109
I will incontinently drown myself.— . . . Why, thou silly gentleman! . . . *Othello* i 3 308
A fourth man, in a silly habit, That gave the affront with them . . . *Cymbeline* v 3 86
Silver. Not a holiday fool there but would give a piece of silver . . . *Tempest* ii 2 31
Hey, Mountain, hey!—Silver! there it goes, Silver! . . . iv 1 257
Seven hundred pounds of moneys, and gold and silver . . . *Mer. Wives* i 1 52
Spread o'er the silver waves thy golden hairs . . . *Com. of Errors* iii 2 48
To see the fish Cut with her golden oars the silver stream . . . *Much Ado* iii 1 27
Cloth o' gold, and cuts, and laced with silver, set with pearls . . . iii 4 20
Nor shines the silver moon one half so bright . . . *L. L. Lost* iv 3 30
The moon, like to a silver bow New-bent in heaven . . . *M. N. Dream* i 1 10
When Phœbe doth behold Her silver visage in the watery glass . . . i 1 210
The lottery . . . in these three chests of gold, silver and lead . . . *Mer. of Ven.* i 2 33
Is your gold and silver ewes and rams?—I cannot tell . . . i 3 96
The second, silver, which this promise carries, 'Who chooseth me shall get as much as he deserves' . . . ii 7 6
What says the silver with her virgin hue? . . . ii 7 22
Shall I think in silver she's immured, Being ten times undervalued to tried gold? O sinful thought! . . . ii 7 52
Fortune now To my heart's hope! Gold; silver; and base lead . . . ii 9 20
Why, then to thee, thou silver treasure-house . . . ii 9 34
Saw'st thou not, boy, how Silver made it good At the hedge-corner, in the coldest fault? . . . *T. of Shrew* Ind. 1 19
Let one attend him with a silver basin Full of rose-water . . . Ind. 1 55
Let his silver water keep A peaceful progress to the ocean . . . *K. John* ii 1 339
Two such silver currents, when they join, Do glorify the banks . . . ii 1 441
Bell, book, and candle shall not drive me back, When gold and silver becks me to come on . . . iii 3 13
Where but by chance a silver drop hath fallen . . . iii 4 63
This little world, This precious stone set in the silver sea . . . *Richard II.* ii 1 46
Unseasonable stormy day, Which makes the silver rivers drown their shores . . . iii 2 107
Thou sheer, immaculate and silver fountain! . . . v 3 61
Here the smug and silver Trent shall run In a new channel . . . *1 Hen. IV.* iii 1 102
I will inset you neither in gold nor silver, but in vile apparel . . . *2 Hen. IV.* i 2 20
Whose beard the silver hand of peace hath touch'd . . . iv 1 43
Your fathers taken by the silver beards . . . *Hen. V.* iii 3 36
Troubles the silver spring where England drinks . . . *2 Hen. VI.* i 1 72
Shame to thy silver hair, Thou mad misleader of thy brain-sick son! . . . v 1 162
And to achieve The silver livery of advised age . . . v 2 47
Venerable Nestor, hatch'd in silver . . . *Troi. and Cres.* i 3 65
Tell him from me I'll hide my silver beard in a gold beaver . . . i 3 296
A murrain on't! I took this for silver . . . *Coriolanus* i 5 4
Rend off thy silver hair, thy other hand Gnawing with thy teeth . . . *T. An.* iii 1 261

Silver. By yonder blessed moon I swear That tips with silver all these fruit-tree tops— O, swear not by the moon . . . *Rom. and Jul.* ii 2 108
'Then music with her silver sound'—why 'silver sound'? why 'music with her silver sound'? . . . . . . iv 5 130
Marry, sir, because silver hath a sweet sound . . . . iv 5 133
I say 'silver sound,' because musicians sound for silver . . iv 5 136
'Music with her silver sound,' because musicians have no gold for sounding . . . . iv 5 142
'Then music with her silver sound With speedy help doth lend redress' iv 5 145
Four milk-white horses, trapp'd in silver . . . *T. of Athens* i 2 189
Why, this hits right; I dreamt of a silver basin and ewer to-night . iii 1 6
He ne'er drinks, But Timon's silver treads upon his lip . . iii 2 78
His silver hairs Will purchase us a good opinion . . *J. Cæsar* ii 1 144
Here lay Duncan, His silver skin laced with his golden blood *Macbeth* ii 3 118
The oars were silver, Which to the tune of flutes kept stroke *A. and C.* ii 2 199
It was hang'd With tapestry of silk and silver . . . *Cymbeline* ii 4 69
Her andirons—I had forgot them—were two winking Cupids Of silver . ii 4 90
Money, youth?—All gold and silver rather turn to dirt! . . iii 6 54
Do it, and happy; by my silver bow! . . . . . *Pericles* v 1 249
Who, O goddess, Wears yet thy silver livery . . . . v 3 7
Silver-bright. Their armours, that march'd hence so silver-bright, Hither return all gilt with Frenchmen's blood . . . *K. John* ii 1 315
Silvered. There be fools alive, I wis, Silver'd o'er . *Mer. of Venice* ii 9 69
His beard was grizzled,—no?—It was, as I have seen it in his life, A sable silver'd . . . . *Hamlet* i 2 242
On a tribunal silver'd, Cleopatra and himself in chairs of gold *A. and C.* iii 6 3
Silverly. Let me wipe off this honourable dew, That silverly doth progress on thy cheeks . . . . *K. John* v 2 46
Silver-shedding. Nor silver-shedding, tears Could penetrate *T. G. of Ver.* iii 1 230
Silver sweet. How silver-sweet sound lovers' tongues by night, Like softest music to attending ears! . . . . *Rom. and Jul.* ii 2 166
Silver-voiced. As wand-like straight; As silver-voiced . . *Pericles* v 1 111
Silver-white. Violets blue And lady-smocks all silver-white . *L. L. Lost* v 2 905
Silvia. Ah, Silvia, Silvia!—Madam Silvia! Madam Silvia! *T. G. of Ver.* ii 1 5
Do you know Madam Silvia?—She that your worship loves? . . ii 1 15
But tell me, dost thou know my lady Silvia?—She that you gaze on so? ii 1 45
To do what?—To be a spokesman from Madam Silvia . . . ii 1 152
Here comes my father.—Now, daughter Silvia, you are hard beset . ii 4 49
Welcome him then according to his worth. Silvia, I speak to you . ii 4 84
To love fair Silvia, shall I be forsworn . . . . . ii 6 2
Thus find I by their loss For Valentine myself, for Julia Silvia . . ii 6 22
And Silvia—witness Heaven, that made her fair!—Shows Julia but a swarthy Ethiope . . . . ii 6 25
Valentine I'll hold an enemy, Aiming at Silvia as a sweeter friend . ii 6 30
He meaneth with a corded ladder To climb celestial Silvia's chamber-window . . . . ii 6 34
What letter is this same? What's here? 'To Silvia'! . . . iii 1 137
My thoughts do harbour with my Silvia nightly . . . . iii 1 140
Silvia, this night I will enfranchise thee . . . . . iii 1 151
To die is to be banish'd from myself; And Silvia is myself . . . iii 1 172
What light is light, if Silvia be not seen? What joy is joy, if Silvia be not by? Unless it be to think that she is by . . . . iii 1 174
Except I be by Silvia in the night, There is no music in the nightingale iii 1 178
Unless I look on Silvia in the day, There is no day for me to look upon iii 1 180
Is Silvia dead?—No, Valentine.—No Valentine, indeed, for sacred Silvia iii 1 209
No Valentine, if Silvia have forsworn me. What is your news? . iii 1 214
That thou art banished—O, that's the news!—From hence, from Silvia iii 1 218
Doth Silvia know that I am banished?—Ay, ay . . . . iii 1 221
As thou lovest Silvia, though not for thyself, Regard thy danger . . iii 1 255
O my dear Silvia! Hapless Valentine! . . . . . . iii 1 260
Upon this warrant shall you have access Where you with Silvia may confer iii 2 61
But Silvia is too fair, too true, too holy, To be corrupted with my worthless gifts . . . . iv 2 5
I hope, sir, that you love not here.—Sir, but I do; or else I would be hence.—Who? Silvia?—Ay, Silvia; for your sake . . . iv 2 23
Who is Silvia? what is she, That all our swains commend her? . iv 2 39
Then to Silvia let us sing, That Silvia is excelling . . . . iv 2 49
This is the hour that Madam Silvia Entreated me to call . . . iv 3 1
I was sent to deliver him as a present to Mistress Silvia from my master iv 4 8
I remember the trick you served me when I took my leave of Madam Silvia . . . . iv 4 39
I carried Mistress Silvia the dog you bade me . . . . iv 4 49
Go presently and take this ring with thee, Deliver it to Madam Silvia . iv 4 77
Methinks that she loved you as well As you do love your lady Silvia . iv 4 85
I pray you, be my mean To bring me where to speak with Madam Silvia iv 4 114
The very hour That Silvia, at Friar Patrick's cell, should meet me . v 1 3
What says Silvia to my suit?—O, sir, I find her milder than she was . v 2 1
More to be revenged on Eglamour Than for the love of reckless Silvia . v 2 52
I will follow, more for Silvia's love Than hate of Eglamour . . v 2 53
I will follow, more to cross that love Than hate for Silvia . . v 2 56
Repair me with thy presence, Silvia; Thou gentle nymph, cherish thy forlorn swain! . . . . v 4 11
And, that my love may appear plain and free, All that was mine in Silvia I give thee . . . . v 4 83
My master charged me to deliver a ring to Madam Silvia . . . v 4 89
Cry you mercy, sir, I have mistook: This is the ring you sent to Silvia v 4 95
What is in Silvia's face, but I may spy More fresh in Julia's? . . v 4 114
Yonder is Silvia; and Silvia's mine.—Thurio, give back . . . v 4 125
Do not name Silvia thine; if once again, Verona shall not hold thee . v 4 128
Take thou thy Silvia, for thou hast deserved her.—I thank your grace . v 4 147
Silvius. What say'st thou, Silvius?—Sweet Phebe, pity me.—Why, I am sorry for thee, gentle Silvius . . . . . *As Y. Like It* iii 5 84
Silvius, the time was that I hated thee . . . . . iii 5 92
Some women, Silvius, . . . would have gone near To fall in love with him iii 5 124
I'll write to him a very taunting letter, And thou shalt bear it: wilt thou, Silvius?—Phebe, with all my heart . . . . . iii 5 135
Keep your word, Silvius, that you'll marry her, If she refuse me . . v 4 23
Where have you this? 'tis false.—From Silvius, sir . . *Ant. and Cleo.* ii 1 18
Simile. Into a thousand similes . . . . . *As Y. Like It* ii 1 45
A good swift simile, but something currish . . . . *T. of Shrew.* v 2 54
I do pity his distress in my similes of comfort. . . . *All's Well* v 2 26
Thou hast the most unsavoury similes . . . . *1 Hen. IV.* i 2 89
When their rhymes, Full of protest, of oath and big compare, Want similes, truth tired with iteration . . . . *Troi. and Cres.* iii 2 183
Simois. Hic ibat Simois; hic est Sigeia tellus . . . *T. of Shrew* iii 1 28
'Hic ibat,' as I told you before, 'Simois,' I am Lucentio . . . iii 1 31
Simon Shadow!—Yea, marry, let me have him to sit under *2 Hen. IV.* iii 2 132
What say you, Simon Catling? . . . . . *Rom. and Jul.* iv 5 132
Simonides. If the good King Simonides were of my mind . *Pericles* ii 1 48
This is called Pentapolis, and our king the good Simonides . . . ii 1 104
Simonides. We are honour'd much by good Simonides.—Your presence glads our days . . . . *Pericles* ii 3 20
Good morrow to the good Simonides . . . . ii 5 1
To the court of King Simonides Are letters brought, the tenour these iii Gower 23
Simony was fair-play; His own opinion was his law . . *Hen. VIII.* iv 2 36
Simpcox, come, Come, offer at my shrine, and I will help thee *2 Hen. VI.* ii 1 91
What's thine own name?—Saunder Simpcox, an if it please you . . ii 1 124
Simpering. As I perceive by your simpering . . . . *As Y. Like It* Epil. 16
Behold yond simpering dame, Whose face between her forks presages snow . . . . *Lear* iv 6 120
Simple. According to my shallow simple skill . . . *T. G. of Ver.* i 2 8
Without you were so simple, none else would . . . . . ii 1 38
In my simple conjectures . . . . *Mer. Wives* i 1 30
Where's Simple, my man? Can you tell? . . . . . . i 1 136
How now, Simple! where have you been? I must wait on myself, must I? . . . . i 1 207
He's a justice of peace in his country, simple though I stand here . i 1 226
Peter Simple, you say your name is?—Ay, for fault of a better . . i 4 15
Qu'ai-j'oublie! dere is some simples in my closet . . . . i 4 65
Master Slender's serving-man, and friend Simple by your name . . iii 1 2
And smell like Bucklersbury in simple time . . . . . iii 3 79
With eggs, sir?—Simple of itself; I'll no pullet-sperm in my brewage . iii 5 32
Not only . . . in the simple office of love, but in all the accoutrement iv 2 4
We are simple men; we do not know what's brought to pass under the profession of fortune-telling . . . . iv 2 182
What simple thief brags of his own attaint? . . . *Com. of Errors* iii 2 16
She tells to your highness simple truth . . . . . . v 1 211
Do you question me, as an honest man should do, for my simple true judgement; or would you have me speak after my custom? *Much Ado* i 1 168
Comes not that blood as modest evidence To witness simple virtue? . iv 1 39
A swain! a most simple clown! . . . . . . *L. L. Lost* iv 1 142
This is a gift that I have, simple, simple; a foolish extravagant spirit . iv 2 67
Farewell, mad wenches; you have simple wits . . . . . v 2 264
You see how simple and how fond I am . . . . *M. N. Dream* iii 2 317
To show our simple skill, That is the true beginning of our end . . v 1 110
Here's a simple line of life: here's a small trifle of wives *Mer. of Venice* ii 2 169
Eleven widows and nine maids is a simple coming-in for one man . . ii 2 171
In peril of my life with the edge of a feather-bed; here are simple scapes ii 2 174
There is no vice so simple but assumes Some mark of virtue . . iii 2 81
That is another simple sin in you . . . . . *As Y. Like It* iii 2 82
Am I the man yet? doth my simple feature content you? . . . iii 3 3
It is a melancholy of mine own, compounded of many simples . . iv 1 16
When they do homage to this simple peasant . . . *T. of Shrew* Ind. 1 135
Toward the education of your daughters, I here bestow a simple instrument . . . . ii 1 100
I am ashamed that women are so simple . . . . . . v 2 161
Whose simple touch Is powerful to araise King Pepin . . *All's Well* ii 1 78
Great floods have flown From simple sources, and great seas have dried ii 1 143
O Lord, sir! There's a simple putting off . . . . . . ii 2 43
I am a simple maid, and therein wealthiest, That I protest I simply am a maid . . . . ii 3 72
If that this simple syllogism will serve, so . . . . *T. Night* i 5 55
'Tis time to part them. He's simple and tells much . . *W. Tale* iv 4 355
What a fool Honesty is! and Trust, his sworn brother, a very simple gentleman! . . . . iv 4 607
How blessed are we that are not simple men! . . . . . iv 4 772
I dare not fight; but I will wink and hold out mine iron: it is a simple one; but what though? . . . . *Hen. V.* ii 1 8
No simple man that sees This jarring discord of nobility *1 Hen. VI.* iv 1 187
Salisbury and Warwick are no simple peers . . . *2 Hen. VI.* i 3 77
Our simple supper ended, give me leave In this close walk to satisfy myself . . . . ii 2 2
In his simple show he harbours treason . . . . . . iii 1 54
God forbid so many simple souls Should perish by the sword! . . iv 4 10
Trust not simple Henry nor his oaths . . . . *3 Hen. VI.* i 2 59
Ah, simple men, you know not what you swear! . . . . iii 1 83
But attended by a simple guard, We may surprise and take him . . iv 2 16
Go, tread the path that thou shalt ne'er return, Simple, plain Clarence! I do love thee so . . . . *Richard III.* i 1 118
Cannot a plain man live and think no harm, But thus his simple truth must be abused? . . . . i 3 52
I do beweep to many simple gulls . . . . i 3 328
I am a simple woman, much too weak To oppose your cunning *Hen. VIII.* ii 4 106
You have made a simple choice; you know not how to choose a man *Rom. and Jul.* ii 5 38
The fee-simple! O simple! . . . . iii 1 37
Till strange love, grown bold, Think true love acted simple modesty . iii 2 16
In tatter'd weeds, with overwhelming brows, Culling of simples . . v 1 40
There are no tricks in plain and simple faith . . . *J. Cæsar* iv 2 22
A mind impatient, An understanding simple and unschool'd . . *Hamlet* i 2 97
Collected from all simples that have virtue Under the moon . . . iv 7 145
Be simple answerer, for we know the truth . . . . *Lear* iii 7 43
Many simples operative, whose power Will close the eye of anguish . iv 4 14
Look with thine ears: see how yond justice rails upon yond simple thief iv 6 155
In simple and pure soul I come to you . . . . . *Othello* i 1 107
She says enough; yet she's a simple bawd That cannot say as much . iv 2 20
Will it eat me?—You must not think I am so simple but I know the devil himself will not eat a woman . . . . *Ant. and Cleo.* v 2 273
A simple countryman, that brought her figs: This was his basket . v 2 342
Nature prompts them In simple and low things to prince it much *Cymb.* iii 3 85
No more ado With that harsh, noble, simple nothing, That Cloten . iii 4 135
Thy corpse, Lying with simple shells . . . . . *Pericles* iii 1 65
Simpleness. That Which simpleness and merit purchaseth . *Much Ado* iv 1 70
Never anything can be amiss, When simpleness and duty tender it *M. N. Dream* v 1 83
In her they are the better for their simpleness . . . *All's Well* i 1 51
God's will, What simpleness is this! . . . . *Rom. and Jul.* iii 3 77
Let me find a charter in your voice, To assist my simpleness . . *Othello* i 3 247
Simpler. But, alas! I am as true as truth's simplicity And simpler than the infancy of truth . . . . . . *Troi. and Cres.* iii 2 177
In the plainer and simpler kind of people, the deed of saying is quite out of use. To promise is most courtly . . . *T. of Athens* v 1 27
Simplicity. You are a very simplicity 'oman: I pray you, peace *M. W.* iv 1 31
Such is the simplicity of man to hearken after the flesh . . *L. L. Lost* i 1 219
Twice-sod simplicity, bis coctus! O thou monster Ignorance! . . iv 2 23
The shape of Love's Tyburn that hangs up simplicity . . . . iv 3 54
A huge translation of hypocrisy, Vilely compiled, profound simplicity v 2 52
All the power thereof it doth apply To prove, by wit, worth in simplicity v 2 78
By the simplicity of Venus' doves . . . . . . *M. N. Dream* i 1 171
Love, therefore, and tongue-tied simplicity In least speak most . . v 1 104

Simplicity. But more for that in low simplicity He lends out money gratis *Mer. of Venice* i 3 44
From whose simplicity I think it not uneasy to get the cause *W. Tale* iv 2 55
I am as true as truth's simplicity *Troi. and Cres.* iii 2 176
Alas, it is my vice, my fault: Whiles others fish with craft for great opinion, I with great truth catch mere simplicity iv 4 106
Simply. If he take her, let him take her simply *Mer. Wives* iii 2 78
He hath simply the best wit of any handicraft man in Athens *M. N. Dream* iv 2 9
Simply your having in beard is a younger brother's revenue *As Y. Like It* iii 2 396
You have simply misused our sex in your love-prate iv 1 205
And therein wealthiest, That I protest I simply am a maid *All's Well* ii 3 73
Simply the thing I am Shall make me live iv 3 369
I have the back-trick simply as strong as any man in Illyria *T. Night* i 3 132
An I had but a belly of any indifferency, I were simply the most active fellow in Europe *2 Hen. IV.* iv 3 24
He is simply the most active gentleman of France *Hen. V.* iii 7 105
Not a man, for being simply man, Hath any honour *Troi. and Cres.* iii 3 80
He is simply the rarest man i' the world *Coriolanus* iv 5 168
Simular. Thou perjured, and thou simular man of virtue *Lear* iii 2 54
My practice so prevail'd, That I return'd with simular proof *Cymbeline* v 5 200
Simulation. This simulation is not as the former *T. Night* ii 5 151
Sin. I should sin To think but nobly of my grandmother *Tempest* i 2 118
O, forgive me my sins!—He that dies pays all debts iii 2 139
You are three men of sin iii 3 53
Were man But constant, he were perfect. That one error Fills him with faults; makes him run through all the sins *T. G. of Ver.* v 4 112
Now shall I sin in my wish: I would thy husband were dead *Mer. Wives* iii 3 51
Heaven forgive my sins at the day of judgement! iii 3 226
Alas, what noise?—Heaven forgive our sins!—What should this be? v 5 35
But those as sleep and think not on their sins, Pinch them, arms, legs, backs, shoulders, sides and shins v 5 57
'Tis my familiar sin With maids to seem the lapwing and to jest *M. for M.* i 4 31
Some rise by sin, and some by virtue fall: Some run from brakes of ice ii 1 38
Is this her fault or mine? The tempter or the tempted, who sins most? ii 2 163
Most dangerous Is that temptation that doth goad us on To sin in loving virtue ii 2 183
Repent you, fair one, of the sin you carry?—I do; and bear the shame most patiently ii 3 19
Mutually committed?—Mutually.—Then was your sin of heavier kind than his ii 3 28
But lest you do repent, As that the sin hath brought you to this shame ii 3 31
Our compell'd sins Stand more for number than for accompt ii 4 57
Might there not be a charity in sin To save this brother's life? ii 4 63
I'll take it as a peril to my soul, It is no sin at all, but charity ii 4 66
To do't at peril of your soul, Were equal poise of sin and charity ii 4 68
That I do beg his life, if it be sin, Heaven let me bear it! ii 4 69
If that be sin, I'll make it my morn prayer To have it added to the faults of mine, And nothing of your answer ii 4 71
Sure, it is no sin; Or of the deadly seven it is the least iii 1 110
What sin you do to save a brother's life, Nature dispenses with the deed so far That it becomes a virtue iii 1 134
Thy sin's not accidental, but a trade iii 1 149
Nay, if the devil have given thee proofs for sin, Thou wilt prove his iii 2 31
To bring you thus together, 'tis no sin iv 1 73
This is his pardon, purchased by such sin For which the pardoner himself is in iv 2 111
Prating mountebanks, And many such-like liberties of sin *Com. of Errors* i 2 102
Teach sin the carriage of a holy saint; Be secret-false iii 2 14
A sin prevailing much in youthful men v 1 52
Truly, I hold it a sin to match in my kindred *Much Ado* ii 1 67
As quiet in hell as in a sanctuary: and people sin upon purpose, because they would go thither ii 1 266
O, what authority and show of truth Can cunning sin cover itself withal! iv 1 37
And so extenuate the 'forehand sin iv 1 51
She will not add to her damnation A sin of perjury iv 1 175
Let all my sins lack mercy! iv 1 182
Impose me to what penance your invention Can lay upon my sin v 1 284
'Tis deadly sin to keep that oath, my lord, And sin to break it *L. L. Lost* ii 1 105
Do not call it sin in me, That I am forsworn for thee iv 3 115
I, that am honest; I, that hold it sin To break the vow I am engaged in iv 3 177
Even that falsehood, in itself a sin, Thus purifies itself and turns to grace v 2 785
You must be purged too, your sins are rack'd, You are attaint with faults v 2 828
In truth, I know it is a sin to be a mocker *Mer. of Venice* i 2 61
What heinous sin is it in me To be ashamed to be my father's child! ii 3 16
You'll make me wish a sin, That I had been forsworn iii 2 13
The sins of the father are to be laid upon the children iii 5 1
So the sins of my mother should be visited upon me iii 5 15
Most mischievous foul sin, in chiding sin *As Y. Like It* ii 7 64
Thy manners must be wicked; and wickedness is sin, and sin is damnation iii 2 41
That is another simple sin in you iii 2 82
Self-love, which is the most inhibited sin in the canon *All's Well* i 1 158
Only sin And hellish obstinacy tie thy tongue i 3 185
Lawful meaning in a lawful act, Where both not sin, and yet a sinful fact iii 7 47
In this disguise I think't no sin To cozen him that would unjustly win iv 2 75
Virtue that trangesses is but patched with sin; and sin that amends is but patched with virtue *T. Night* i 5 53
I would not have you to think that my desire of having is the sin of covetousness v 1 50
Which to reiterate were sin As deep as that, though true *W. Tale* i 2 283
If the sins of your youth are forgiven you, you're well to live iii 3 124
Against whose person, So sacred as it is, I have done sin v 1 172
Some sins do bear their privilege on earth, And so doth yours *K. John* i 1 261
If thou hadst said him nay, it had been sin: Who says it was, he lies i 1 275
Thy sins are visited in this poor child ii 1 179
He is not only plagued for her sin, But God hath made her sin and her the plague On this removed issue ii 1 184
Her sin his injury, Her injury the beadle to her sin ii 1 187
God forgive the sin of all those souls! ii 1 283
Whiles I am a beggar, I will rail And say there is no sin but to be rich ii 1 594
Thou didst understand me by my signs And didst in signs again parley with sin iv 2 238
Shall give a holiness, a purity, To the yet unbegotten sin of times iv 3 54
I am stifled with this smell of sin iv 3 113
If I in act, consent, or sin of thought, Be guilty iv 3 135
O, God defend my soul from such deep sin! *Richard II.* i 1 187
Be Mowbray's sins so heavy in his bosom, That they may break his foaming courser's back! i 2 50
Murders, treasons and detested sins iii 2 44
But self-affrighted tremble at his sin iii 2 53
Sin. You Pilates Have here deliver'd me to my sour cross, And water cannot wash away your sin *Richard II.* iv 1 242
The very book indeed Where all my sins are writ, and that's myself iv 1 275
Ere foul sin gathering head Shall break into corruption v 1 58
Let your mother in: I know she is come to pray for your foul sin v 3 82
If thou do pardon, whosoever pray, More sins for this forgiveness prosper may v 3 84
There thou makest me sad and makest me sin In envy *1 Hen. IV.* i 1 78
'Tis my vocation, Hal; 'tis no sin for a man to labour in his vocation i 2 117
I'll be no longer guilty of this sin ii 4 267
If to be old and merry be a sin ii 4 518
Let them that should reward valour bear the sin upon their own heads v 4 153
Shakest thy head and hold'st fear or sin To speak a truth *2 Hen. IV.* i 1 95
He doth sin that doth belie the dead, Not he which says the dead is not alive i 1 98
Foul sin, gathering head, Shall break into corruption iii 1 76
Rob, murder, and commit The oldest sins the newest kind of ways iv 5 127
Is in your conscience wash'd As pure as sin with baptism *Hen. V.* i 2 32
The sin upon my head, dread sovereign! i 2 97
Self-love, my liege, is not so vile a sin As self-neglecting ii 4 74
Et le menton?—De chin.—De sin. Le col, de nick; le menton, de sin iii 4 38
It were not sin to think that, making God so free an offer, He let him outlive that day to see His greatness iv 1 193
Our debts, our careful wives, Our children and our sins lay on the king! iv 1 249
If it be a sin to covet honour, I am the most offending soul alive iv 3 28
Thou that givest whores indulgences to sin *1 Hen. VI.* i 3 35
I have heard you preach That malice was a great and grievous sin iii 1 128
So should I give consent to flatter sin v 5 25
Great is his comfort in this earthly vale, Although by his sight his sin be multiplied *2 Hen. VI.* ii 1 71
Sins Such as by God's book are adjudged to death ii 3 3
Murder, indeed, that bloody sin, I tortured Above the felon iii 1 131
Then is sin struck down like an ox, and iniquity's throat cut like a calf iv 2 28
It is great sin to swear unto a sin, But greater sin to keep a sinful oath v 1 182
But do not break your oaths; for of that sin My mild entreaty shall not make you guilty *3 Hen. VI.* iii 1 90
In devotion spend my latter days, To sin's rebuke and my Creator's praise iv 6 44
'Twas sin before, but now 'tis charity v 5 76
My good lord:—my lord, I should say rather; 'Tis sin to flatter v 6 3
O, God forgive my sins, and pardon thee! v 6 60
O, let them keep it till thy sins be ripe! *Richard III.* i 3 219
Sin, death, and hell have set their marks on him i 3 293
By Christ's dear blood shed for our grievous sins i 4 195
In this sin he is as deep as I i 4 220
Not for all this land Would I be guilty of so deep a sin iii 1 43
I am in So far in blood that sin will pluck on sin iv 2 65
All several sins, all used in each degree, Throng to the bar, crying all, Guilty! guilty! I shall despair v 3 198
Sparing would show a worse sin than ill doctrine *Hen. VIII.* i 3 60
The willing'st sin I ever yet committed May be absolved in English iii 1 49
But cardinal sins and hollow hearts I fear ye iii 1 104
Thy ambition, Thou scarlet sin, robb'd this bewailing land iii 2 255
Produce the grand sum of his sins, the articles Collected from his life iii 2 293
I charge thee, fling away ambition: By that sin fell the angels iii 2 441
Though he were unsatisfied in getting, Which was a sin, yet in bestowing, madam, He was most princely iv 2 56
You shall not sin, If you do say we think him over-proud *Troi. and Cres.* ii 3 131
A kind of godly jealousy—Which, I beseech you, call a virtuous sin iv 4 83
I sin in envying his nobility *Coriolanus* i 1 234
If any such be here—As it were sin to doubt—that love this painting i 6 68
Ingratitude, Which Rome reputes to be a heinous sin *T. Andron.* i 1 448
As Tarquin erst, That left the camp to sin in Lucrece' bed iv 1 64
To strike him dead I hold it not a sin *Rom. and Jul.* i 5 61
Thus from my lips, by yours, my sin is purged.—Then have my lips the sin that they have took.—Sin from my lips? O trespass sweetly urged! Give me my sin again i 5 109
God pardon sin! wast thou with Rosaline?—With Rosaline? ii 3 44
O deadly sin! O rude unthankfulness! Thy fault our law calls death iii 3 24
In pure and vestal modesty, Still blush, as thinking their own kisses sin iii 3 39
Is it more sin to wish me thus forsworn, Or to dispraise my lord with that same tongue Which she hath praised him with above compare So many thousand times? iii 5 236
Where I have learn'd me to repent the sin Of disobedient opposition iv 2 17
My state, Which, well thou know'st, is cross and full of sin iv 3 5
Put not another sin upon my head, By urging me to fury v 3 62
Rich men sin, and I eat root. Much good dich thy good heart! *T. of A.* i 2 72
If I should be bribed too, there would be none left to rail upon thee, and then thou wouldst sin the faster i 2 246
Nothing emboldens sin so much as mercy iii 5 3
You cannot make gross sins look clear iii 5 38
To kill, I grant, is sin's extremest gust iii 5 54
He has a sin that often Drowns him, and takes his valour prisoner iii 5 68
Strange, unusual blood, When man's worst sin is, he does too much good! iv 2 39
We sin against our own estate, When we may profit meet, and come too late v 1 44
The sin of my ingratitude even now Was heavy on me *Macbeth* i 4 15
Sudden, malicious, smacking of every sin That has a name iv 3 59
Cut off even in the blossoms of my sin, Unhousel'd, disappointed *Hamlet* i 5 76
And the nation holds it no sin to tarre them to controversy ii 2 370
Nymph, in thy orisons Be all my sins remember'd iii 1 90
To my sick soul, as sin's true nature is, Each toy seems prologue to some great amiss: So full of artless jealousy is guilt iv 5 17
Plate sin with gold, And the strong lance of justice hurtless breaks *Lear* iv 6 169
I do love her too; Not out of absolute lust, though peradventure I stand accountant for as great a sin *Othello* ii 1 302
Forgive us our sins!—Gentlemen, let's look to our business ii 3 116
Unless self-charity be sometimes a vice, And to defend ourselves it be a sin ii 3 203
Were't to renounce his baptism, All seals and symbols of redeemed sin ii 3 350
Divinity of hell! When devils will the blackest sins put on, They do suggest at first with heavenly shows ii 3 357
Alas, what ignorant sin have I committed? iv 2 70
Think on thy sins.—They are loves I bear to you v 2 40
Not yet to die.—Yes, presently: Therefore confess thee freely of thy sin v 2 53
Impatience does Become a dog that's mad: then is it sin To rush into the secret house of death, Ere death dare come to us? *A. and C.* iv 15 80
If it be a sin to make a true election, she is damned *Cymbeline* i 2 29
To leave you in your madness, 'twere my sin: I will not i 3 104
You sin against Obedience, which you owe your father ii 3 116
If it be sin to say so, sir, I yoke me In my good brother's fault iv 2 19

Sin. Which portends—Unless my sins abuse my divination—Success *Cymbeline* iv 2 351
Some, turn'd coward But by example—O, a sin in war! . . . . v 3 36
But custom what they did begin Was with long use account no sin *Pericles* i Gower 30
For he's no man on whom perfections wait That, knowing sin within, will touch the gate . . . . i 1 80
Few love to hear the sins they love to act . . . . . . i 1 92
How courtesy would seem to cover sin, When what is done is like an hypocrite! . . . . i 1 121
One sin, I know, another doth provoke; Murder's as near to lust as flame to smoke: Poison and treason are the hands of sin . . . i 1 137
Nor tell the world Antiochus doth sin In such a loathed manner . . i 1 146
For flattery is the bellows blows up sin . . . . . . i 2 39
How Thaliard came full bent with sin And had intent to murder him ii Gower 23
His greatness was no guard To bar heaven's shaft, but sin had his reward ii 4 15
Sin-absolver. A ghostly confessor, A sin-absolver . *Rom. and Jul.* iii 3 50
Since. Twelve year since, Miranda, twelve year since . *Tempest* i 2 53
Linens, stuffs and necessaries, Which since have steaded much . . i 2 165
Since thou dost give me pains, Let me remember thee what thou hast promised . . . . i 2 242
Who with mine eyes, never since at ebb, beheld The king my father wreck'd . . . . i 2 435
Not since widow Dido's time.—Widow! a pox o' that! . . . ii 1 76
I made of the bark of a tree with mine own hands since I was cast ashore ii 2 129
No matter, since They have left their viands behind . . . iii 3 40
No matter, since I feel The best is past . . . . . iii 3 50
Since they did plot The means that dusky Dis my daughter got . iv 1 88
Since I saw thee, The affliction of my mind amends . . . . v 1 114
Who three hours since Were wreck'd upon this shore . . . . v 1 136
Our ship—Which, but three glasses since, we gave out split . . v 1 223
All this service Have I done since I went. . . . . . v 1 226
I have been in such a pickle since I saw you last . . . . v 1 282
Let me not, Since I have my dukedom got . . . , dwell In this bare island Epil. 6
But since thou lovest, love still and thrive therein . *T. G. of Ver.* i 1 9
Since maids, in modesty, say 'no' to that Which they would have the profferer construe 'ay' . . . . i 2 55
The lines are very quaintly writ; But since unwillingly, take them again ii 1 129
Since his exile she hath despised me most . . . . . iii 2 3
Since the substance of your perfect self Is else devoted, I am but a shadow . . . . iv 2 124
Since your falsehood shall become you well To worship shadows and adore false shapes, Send to me in the morning . . . . iv 2 130
But since she did neglect her looking-glass And threw her sun-expelling mask away, The air hath starved the roses in her cheeks . . iv 4 157
By my troth, I cannot abide the smell of hot meat since . *Mer. Wives* i 1 297
I never prospered since I forswore myself at primero . . . iv 5 103
She and I, long since contracted, Are now so sure . . . . v 5 236
Since I am put to know that your own science Exceeds . *Meas. for Meas.* i 1 5
He promised to meet me two hours since, and he was ever precise . i 2 76
And five years since there was some speech of marriage . . . . v 1 217
Since which time of five years I never spake with her . . . v 1 222
Since the mortal and intestine jars 'Twixt thy seditious countrymen and us, It hath in solemn synods been decreed . *Com. of Errors* i 1 11
Since that my beauty cannot please his eye, I'll weep what's left away ii 1 114
I could not speak with Dromio since at first I sent him from the mart . ii 2 5
When spake I such a word?—Even now, even here, not half an hour since ii 2 14
Since mine own doors refuse to entertain me, I'll knock elsewhere . iii 1 120
Since Pentecost the sum is due, And since I have not much importuned you . . . . iv 1 1
You know I gave it you half an hour since.—You gave me none . . iv 1 65
Why, sir, I brought you word an hour since . . . . . iv 3 38
My bones bear witness, That since have felt the vigour of his rage . iv 4 81
Long since thy husband served me in my wars . . . . . v 1 161
O, grant me justice! Even for the service that long since I did thee . v 1 191
But seven years since, in Syracusa, boy, Thou know'st we parted . v 1 320
I think I told your lordship a year since . . . *Much Ado* ii 2 13
How long have you professed apprehension?—Ever since you left it . iii 4 69
The world was very guilty of such a ballad some three ages since *L. L. L.* i 2 117
Never, since the middle summer's spring, Met we on hill *M. N. Dream* ii 1 82
Thou rememberest Since once I sat upon a promontory . . . ii 1 149
Since night you loved me; yet since night you left me . . . iii 2 275
Will much impeach the justice of his state; Since that the trade and profit of the city Consisteth of all nations . . *Mer. of Venice* iii 3 30
But since that thou canst talk of love so well, Thy company, which erst was irksome to me, I will endure . . . *As Y. Like It* iii 5 94
I remember, Since once he play'd a farmer's eldest son . *T. of Shrew* Ind. 1 84
How long is't, count, Since the physician at your father's died? *All's W.* i 2 70
His wife some two months since fled from his house . . . iv 3 57
My desires, like fell and cruel hounds, E'er since pursue me . *T. Night* i 1 23
A virtuous maid, the daughter of a count That died some twelvemonth since . . . . i 2 37
Since the youth of the count's was to-day with my lady, she is much out of quiet . . . . ii 3 143
They have been grand-jurymen since before Noah was a sailor . . iii 2 18
Posts From those you sent to the oracle are come An hour since *W. Tale* ii 3 195
Remember since you owed no more to time Than I do now . . . v 1 219
Saint George, that swinged the dragon, and e'er since Sits on his horse back at mine hostess' door . . . . . . *K. John* ii 1 288
Who half an hour since came from the Dauphin . . . . . v 7 83
I know you, Mistress Dorothy.— . . . Since when, I pray you, sir? *2 Hen. IV.* ii 4 141
It is but eight years since This Percy was the man nearest my soul . iii 1 60
Do you remember since we lay all night in the windmill? . . . iii 2 206
Is nothing worth, Since that my penitence comes after all . *Hen. V.* iv 1 321
I was not angry since I came to France Until this instant . . iv 7 58
Long since we were resolved of your truth . . *1 Hen. VI.* iii 4 20
Who two hours since I met in travel toward his warlike father . . iv 3 35
We know the time since he was mild and affable . *2 Hen. VI.* iii 1 9
Against that monstrous rebel Cade, Who since I heard to be discomfited v 1 63
And fled, as he hears since, to Burgundy . . . *3 Hen. VI.* iv 6 79
Since that our brother dubb'd them gentlewomen, Are mighty gossips *Richard III.* i 1 82
Whom I, some three months since, Stabb'd in my angry mood . . i 2 241
And since, methinks, I would not grow so fast . . . . . ii 4 14
Which, since, succeeding ages have re-edified . . . . . iii 1 71
Since that I myself Find in myself no pity to myself . . . . v 3 202
How long is't since?—Above an hour my lord . . *Coriolanus* i 6 14
Else had I, sir, Half an hour since brought my report . . . i 6 21
Since that to both It stands in like request . . . . . iii 2 50
Since. Since that thy sight, which should Make our eyes flow with joy, hearts dance with comforts, Constrains them weep . . *Coriolanus* v 3 98
Ay, and since too, murders have been perform'd . . . *Macbeth* iii 4 77
When shalt thou see thy wholesome days again, Since that the truest issue of thy throne By his own interdiction stands accursed? . . iv 3 106
How long is that since?—Cannot you tell that? . . . *Hamlet* v 1 158
Since that respects of fortune are his love, I shall not be his wife *Lear* i 1 251
Since it is as it is, mend it for your own good . . . *Othello* ii 3 304
Where is he?—I did not see him since . . . *Ant. and Cleo.* i 3 1
Since death of my dear'st mother It did not speak before . *Cymbeline* iv 2 190
Sincere. His oaths are oracles, His love sincere . . *T. G. of Ver.* ii 7 76
Supposed sincere and holy in his thoughts . . . *2 Hen. IV.* i 1 202
From sincere motions, by intelligence, And proofs . . . *Hen. VIII.* i 1 153
In sincere verity, Under the allowance of your great aspect . *Lear* ii 2 111
Sincerely. And hath challenged thee.—Most sincerely . . *Much Ado* v 1 201
That you may, fair lady, Perceive I speak sincerely . . *Hen. VIII.* ii 3 59
Hear me profess sincerely . . . . *Coriolanus* i 3 24
Sincerity. To be talk'd with in sincerity, As with a saint *Meas. for Meas.* i 4 36
I partly think A due sincerity govern'd his deeds . . . . v 1 451
As a brother to his sister, show'd Bashful sincerity and comely love *Much Ado* iv 1 55
And make a riot on the gentle brow Of true sincerity . . *K. John* ii 1 248
You shall see now in very sincerity of fear and cold heart . *1 Hen. IV.* ii 3 32
You advise me well.—I protest, in the sincerity of love . . *Othello* ii 3 333
Sin-conceiving. Being but the second generation Removed from thy sin-conceiving womb . . . . *K. John* ii 1 182
Sinel. By Sinel's death I know I am thane of Glamis . . *Macbeth* i 3 71
Sinew. I had rather crack my sinews, break my back . . *Tempest* iii 1 26
Shorten up their sinews With aged cramps . . . . . . iv 1 260
For Orpheus' lute was strung with poets' sinews . . *T. G. of Ver.* iii 2 78
With him, the portion and sinew of her fortune . . *Meas. for Meas.* iii 1 230
Nay, patience, or we break the sinews of our plot . . . *T. Night* ii 5 83
That knit your sinews to the strength of mine. . . . *K. John* v 2 63
Who with them was a rated sinew too And comes not in . . *1 Hen. IV.* iv 4 17
By God's help, And yours, the noble sinews of our power . . *Hen. V.* i 2 223
So service shall with steeled sinews toil . . . . . . ii 2 36
Stiffen the sinews, summon up the blood, Disguise fair nature . . iii 1 7
These are his substance, sinews, arms and strength . . *1 Hen. VI.* ii 3 63
Fester'd members rot but by degree, Till bones and flesh and sinews fall away . . . . iii 1 193
For strokes received, and many blows repaid, Have robb'd my strong-knit sinews of their strength . . . . . . *3 Hen. VI.* ii 3 4
So shalt thou sinew both these lands together . . . . . ii 6 91
'Tis this fever that keeps Troy on foot, Not her own sinews *Tr. and Cr.* i 3 136
Whom opinion crowns The sinew and the forehand of our host . . i 3 143
A great deal of your wit, too, lies in your sinews . . . . ii 1 109
Shall more obey than to the edge of steel Or force of Greekish sinews . iii 1 166
Unless the fiddler Apollo get his sinews to make catlings on . . . iii 3 305
The sinews of this leg All Greek, and this all Troy . . . . iv 5 126
Let grow thy sinews till their knots be strong . . . . . v 3 33
Now, Troy, sink down! Here lies thy heart, thy sinews, and thy bone . v 8 12
There was it: For which my sinews shall be stretch'd upon him *Coriol.* v 6 45
The torrent roar'd, and we did buffet it With lusty sinews . *J. Cæsar* i 2 108
And you, my sinews, grow not instant old, But bear me stiffly up *Hamlet* i 5 94
Heart with strings of steel, Be soft as sinews of the new-born babe! . iii 3 71
This rest might yet have balm'd thy broken sinews. . . . *Lear* iii 6 105
Sinewed. To leave this war.—He will the rather do it when he sees Ourselves well sinewed to our defence . . . . . . *K. John* v 7 88
Sinewy. As motion and long-during action tires The sinewy vigour of the traveller . . . . *L. L. Lost* iv 3 308
The wrestler That did but lately foil the sinewy Charles. *As Y. Like It* ii 2 14
Worthy fellows; and like to prove most sinewy sword-men . *All's Well* ii 1 62
Bull-bearing Milo his addition yield To sinewy Ajax . *Troi. and Cres.* ii 3 259
Sinful. Fie on sinful fantasy! . . . . *Mer. Wives* v 5 97
Shall I think in silver she's immured . . . ? O sinful thought! *M. of V.* ii 7 54
Where both not sin, and yet a sinful fact . . . . *All's Well* iii 7 47
With your sinful hours Made a divorce betwixt his queen and him *Richard II.* iii 1 11
Why, thou globe of sinful continents, what a life dost thou lead! *2 Hen. IV.* ii 4 309
Canst thou dispense with heaven for such an oath?—It is great sin to swear unto a sin, But greater sin to keep a sinful oath . *2 Hen. VI.* v 1 183
Yet that thy brazen gates of heaven may ope, And give sweet passage to my sinful soul! . . . . *3 Hen. VI.* ii 3 41
Sinful Macduff, They were all struck for thee! . . . *Macbeth* iv 3 224
The beauty of this sinful dame Made many princes thither frame *Per.* i Gower 31
The sinful father Seem'd not to strike, but smooth . . . . . i 2 77
Sinfully. So, if a son that is by his father sent about merchandise do sinfully miscarry upon the sea . . . . . . *Hen. V.* iv 1 155
All this from my remembrance brutish wrath Sinfully pluck'd *Rich. III.* ii 1 119
Sing. Another storm brewing; I hear it sing i' the wind . . *Tempest* ii 2 20
A very scurvy time to sing at a man's funeral . . . . . ii 2 46
Let us sing. 'Flout 'em and scout 'em' . . . . . . iii 2 129
The billows spoke and told me of it; The winds did sing it to me . . iii 3 97
Hourly joys be still upon you! Juno sings her blessings on you . . iv 1 109
Some love of yours hath writ to you in rhyme.—That I might sing it, madam, to a tune. Give me a note . . . . *T. G. of Ver.* i 2 80
Best sing it to the tune of 'Light o' love' . . . . . i 2 83
Melodious were it, would you sing it.—And why not you? . . . i 2 86
Keep tune there still, so you will sing it out . . . . . i 2 89
Then to Silvia let us sing, That Silvia is excelling . . . . iv 2 49
Vat is you sing? I do not like des toys . . . . *Mer. Wives* i 4 45
Take heed, ere summer comes or cuckoo-birds do sing . . . . ii 1 127
To shallow rivers, to whose falls Melodious birds sings madrigals . . iii 1 18
A man may hear this shower sing in the wind . . . . . iii 2 38
Meadow-fairies, look you sing, Like to the Garter's compass, in a ring . v 5 69
Sing a scornful rhyme; And, as you trip, still pinch him to your time . v 5 95
Sing, siren, for thyself and I will dote . . . *Com. of Errors* iii 2 47
I have decreed not to sing in my cage . . . . . *Much Ado* i 3 36
Stolen his birds' nest.—I will but teach them to sing, and restore them ii 1 239
Sing, and let me woo no more.—Because you talk of wooing, I will sing ii 3 50
Sing no more ditties, sing no moe, Of dumps so dull and heavy . . ii 3 72
Do you sing it, and I'll dance it . . . . iii 4 45
Hang her an epitaph upon her tomb And sing it to her bones . . v 1 294
Now, music, sound, and sing your solemn hymn . . . . . v 3 11
Why should proud summer boast Before the birds have any cause to sing? . . . . *L. L. Lost* i 1 103
Sing, boy; my spirit grows heavy in love . . . . . . i 2 127
I say, sing.—Forbear till this company be past . . . . . i 2 130
Sigh a note and sing a note, sometime through the throat . . . iii 1 14

Sing. That sings heaven's praise with such an earthly tongue . *L. L. Lost* iv 2 122
He can sing A mean most meanly; and in ushering Mend him who can v 2 327
Thus sings he, Cuckoo; Cuckoo, cuckoo: O word of fear! v 2 909
Then nightly sings the staring owl, Tu-whit; Tu-who, a merry note v 2 927
Sing me now asleep; Then to your offices and let me rest *M. N. Dream* ii 2 7
Philomel, with melody Sing in our sweet lullaby ii 2 14
I will sing, that they shall hear I am not afraid iii 1 126
Gentle mortal, sing again: Mine ear is much enamour'd of thy note iii 1 140
Sing while thou on pressed flowers dost sleep iii 1 162
And I will sing it in the latter end of a play, before the duke iv 1 223
Peradventure, to make it the more gracious, I shall sing it at her death iv 1 225
And this ditty, after me, Sing, and dance it trippingly v 1 403
Hand in hand, with fairy grace, Will we sing, and bless this place v 1 407
If a throstle sing, he falls straight a capering *Mer. of Venice* i 2 65
When the bagpipe sings i' the nose iv 1 49
There's not the smallest orb which thou behold'st But in his motion like an angel sings, Still quiring to the young-eyed cherubins v 1 61
The crow doth sing as sweetly as the lark When neither is attended, and I think The nightingale, if she should sing by day, . . . would be thought No better a musician than the wren v 1 102
I do not desire you to please me; I do desire you to sing *As Y. Like It* ii 5 18
Will you sing?—More at your request than to please myself ii 5 22
Come, sing; and you that will not, hold your tongues ii 5 30
And I'll sing it.—Thus it goes:—If it do come to pass ii 5 50
Give us some music; and, good cousin, sing ii 7 173
Heigh-ho! sing, heigh-ho! unto the green holly ii 7 180
I would sing my song without a burden: thou bringest me out of tune iii 2 261
Sing it: 'tis no matter how it be in tune, so it make noise enough. iv 2 9
Then sing him home; Take thou no scorn to wear the horn iv 2 13
When birds do sing, hey ding a ding, ding: Sweet lovers love the spring v 3 21
Whiles a wedlock-hymn we sing, Feed yourselves with questioning v 4 143
Apollo plays And twenty caged nightingales do sing *T. of Shrew* Ind. 2 38
I'll try how you can sol, fa, and sing it i 2 17
I'll tell her plain She sings as sweetly as a nightingale ii 1 172
Your marriage comes by destiny, Your cuckoo sings by kind *All's Well* i 3 67
He will look upon his boot and sing; mend the ruff and sing; ask questions and sing; pick his teeth and sing iii 2 7
Move the still-peering air, That sings with piercing iii 2 114
Who had even tuned his bounty to sing happiness to him iv 3 12
In fine, made a groan of her last breath, and now she sings in heaven iv 3 63
I can sing And speak to him in many sorts of music *T. Night* i 2 57
Sing them loud even in the dead of night i 5 290
Such a leg, and so sweet a breath to sing ii 3 21
Your true love's coming, That can sing both high and low ii 3 42
He is not here, so please your lordship, that should sing it ii 4 9
Are you ready, sir?—Ay; prithee, sing ii 4 51
With heigh! the sweet birds, O, how they sing! *W. Tale* iv 3 6
But one puritan amongst them, and he sings psalms to hornpipes iv 3 47
Welcomed all, served all; Would sing her song and dance her turn iv 4 58
When you sing, I'ld have you buy and sell so, so give alms, Pray so; and, for the ordering your affairs, To sing them too iv 4 137
He sings several tunes faster than you'll tell money iv 4 184
He sings 'em over as they were gods or goddesses iv 4 209
There's scarce a maid westward but she sings it; 'tis in request, I can tell you iv 4 296
We can both sing it: if thou'lt bear a part, thou shalt hear iv 4 298
'Tis strange that death should sing *K. John* v 7 20
From the organ-pipe of frailty sings His soul and body to their lasting rest v 7 23
We hear this fearful tempest sing *Richard II.* ii 1 263
For night-owls shriek where mounting larks should sing iii 3 183
Madam, I'll sing.—'Tis well that thou hast cause iii 4 19
I could sing, would weeping do me good iii 4 22
I would I were a weaver; I could sing psalms or any thing 1 *Hen. IV.* ii 4 146
She will sing the song that pleaseth you iii 1 216
With all my heart I'll sit and hear her sing iii 1 223
Lie still, ye thief, and hear the lady sing in Welsh iii 1 239
What's that?—Peace! she sings.—Come, Kate, I'll have your song too iii 1 249
Come, sing.—I will not sing.—'Tis the next way to turn tailor iii 1 262
Come sing me a bawdy song; make me merry iii 3 15
O Westmoreland, thou art a summer bird, Which ever in the haunch of winter sings The lifting up of day 2 *Hen. IV.* iv 4 92
I heard a bird so sing, Whose music, to my thinking, pleased the king v 5 113
As duly, but not as truly, As bird doth sing on bough *Hen. V.* iii 2 20
He trots the air; the earth sings when he touches it iii 7 17
Where the sad and solemn priests Sing still for Richard's soul iv 1 319
I will divide my crown with her, And all the priests and friars in my realm Shall in procession sing her endless praise 1 *Hen. VI.* i 6 20
A warning bell, Sings heavy music to thy timorous soul iv 2 40
Came he right now to sing a raven's note? 2 *Hen. VI.* iii 2 40
Stamp, rave, and fret, that I may sing and dance 3 *Hen. VI.* i 4 91
My soul grows sad with troubles; Sing, and disperse 'em *Hen. VIII.* iii 1 2
Orpheus with his lute made trees, And the mountain tops that freeze, Bow themselves when he did sing iii 1 5
And sing The merry songs of peace to all his neighbours v 5 35
This shall not hedge us out: we'll hear you sing *Troi. and Cres.* iii 1 66
Come, come, I'll hear no more of this; I'll sing you a song now iii 1 115
And all the Greekish girls shall tripping sing iii 3 211
I cannot sing, Nor heel the high lavolt, nor sweeten talk iv 4 87
She will sing any man at first sight.—And any man may sing her v 2 9
Full merrily the humble-bee doth sing, Till he hath lost his honey and his sting v 10 42
Daughter, sing; or express yourself in a more comfortable sort *Coriolanus* i 3 1
Did ever raven sing so like a lark? *T. Andron.* iii 1 158
The eagle suffers little birds to sing, And is not careful what they mean iv 4 83
So bright That birds would sing and think it were not night *R. and J.* ii 2 22
He fights as you sing prick-song, keeps time, distance, and proportion ii 4 21
Nightly she sings on yon pomegranate-tree iii 5 4
It is the lark that sings so out of tune, Straining harsh discords iii 5 27
When we for recompense have praised the vile, It stains the glory in that happy verse Which aptly sings the good *T. of Athens* i 1 17
Now about the cauldron sing, Like elves and fairies in a ring *Macbeth* iv 1 41
Will they pursue the quality no longer than they can sing? *Hamlet* ii 2 363
You must sing a-down a-down, An you call him a-down-a iv 5 170
Has this fellow no feeling of his business, that he sings at grave-making? v 1 74
That skull had a tongue in it, and could sing once v 1 84
To sing a requiem and such rest to her As to peace-parted souls v 1 260
Good night, sweet prince; And flights of angels sing thee to thy rest! v 2 371
We two alone will sing like birds i' the cage *Lear* v 3 9
So we'll live, And pray, and sing, and tell old tales v 3 12

Sing. Loves company, Is free of speech, sings, plays and dances well *Othello* iii 3 185
An admirable musician: O! she will sing the savageness out of a bear iv 1 200
I have much to do, But to go hang my head all at one side, And sing it like poor Barbara iv 3 33
The poor soul sat sighing by a sycamore tree, Sing all a green willow iv 3 42
What's your highness' pleasure?—Not now to hear thee sing *A. and C.* i 5 9
By your most gracious pardon, I sing but after you i 5 73
Make battery to our ears with the loud music: The while I'll place you: then the boy shall sing ii 7 116
Scribes, bards, poets, cannot Think, speak, cast, write, sing, number iii 2 17
The crickets sing, and man's o'er-labour'd sense Repairs itself *Cymbeline* ii 2 11
Hark, hark! the lark at heaven's gate sings, And Phœbus 'gins arise ii 3 22
Our cage We make a quire, as doth the prison'd bird, And sing our bondage freely iii 3 44
How angel-like he sings!—But his neat cookery! iv 2 47
Though now our voices Have got the mannish crack, sing him to the ground iv 2 236
I cannot sing: I'll weep, and word it with thee iv 2 240
To sing a song that old was sung *Pericles* i Gower 1
And that to hear an old man sing May to your wishes pleasure bring i Gower 13
And crickets sing at the oven's mouth, E'er the blither for their drouth iii Gower 7
Shall's go hear the vestals sing?—I'll do any thing now that is virtuous iv 5 7
I can sing, weave, sew, and dance, With other virtues iv 6 194
She sings like one immortal, and she dances As goddess-like v Gower 3
Singe. Be advised; Heat not a furnace for your foe so hot That it do singe yourself *Hen. VIII.* i 1 141
Vaunt-couriers to oak-cleaving thunder-bolts, Singe my white head! *Lear* iii 2 6
Singed. Whose beard they have singed off with brands of fire *Com. of Er.* v 1 171
Thus hath the candle singed the moth. O, these deliberate fools! *Mer. of Venice* ii 9 79
Singeing. Till our ground, Singeing his pate against the burning zone, Make Ossa like a wart! *Hamlet* v 1 305
Singer. His filching was like an unskilful singer; he kept not time *M. W.* i 3 29
A good song.—And an ill singer *Much Ado* ii 3 78
The riot of the tipsy Bacchanals, Tearing the Thracian singer *M. N. D.* v 1 49
I cry you mercy; you are the singer *Rom. and Jul.* iv 5 141
Singest. Thou singest well enough for a shift *Much Ado* ii 3 79
I'll rid you from the fear of them.—Thou sing'st sweet music *Rich. III.* iv 2 79
Singeth. The bird of dawning singeth all night long *Hamlet* i 1 160
Singing. If their singing answer your saying, by my faith, you say honestly *Much Ado* ii 1 241
How pitiful I deserve,—I mean in singing v 2 30
As if you swallowed love with singing love *L. L. Lost* iii 1 15
No pains, sir; I take pleasure in singing, sir *T. Night* ii 4 69
Prithee bring him in; and let him approach singing *W. Tale* iv 4 214
Suppose the singing birds musicians *Richard II.* i 3 288
For my voice, I have lost it with halloing and singing of anthems 2 *Hen. IV.* i 2 213
Surveys The singing masons building roofs of gold *Hen. V.* i 2 198
Our tradesmen singing in their shops *Coriolanus* iv 6 8
Not so young, sir, to love a woman for singing *Lear* i 4 41
He was met even now As mad as the vex'd sea; singing aloud iv 4 2
She had a song of 'willow;' An old thing 'twas, but it express'd her fortune, And she died singing it *Othello* iv 3 30
Singing-man. The prince broke thy head for liking his father to a singing-man of Windsor 2 *Hen. IV.* ii 1 98
Single. What wert thou . . . ?—A single thing, as I am now *Tempest* i 2 432
At pick'd leisure Which shall be shortly, single I'll resolve you v 1 248
A double heart for his single one *Much Ado* ii 1 289
I might have cudgelled thee out of thy single life v 4 116
We single you As our best-moving fair solicitor *L. L. Lost* ii 1 28
Grows, lives and dies in single blessedness *M. N. Dream* i 1 78
Or on Diana's altar to protest For aye austerity and single life i 1 90
To death, or to a vow of single life i 1 121
Two bosoms interchained with an oath; So then two bosoms and a single troth ii 2 50
Go with me to a notary, seal me there Your single bond *Mer. of Venice* i 3 146
Is the single man therefore blessed? No *As Y. Like It* iii 3 58
I'll to the wars, she to her single sorrow *All's Well* ii 3 313
The plain single vow that is vow'd true iv 2 22
Hear me one single word.—You beg a single penny more v 2 38
In single opposition, hand to hand 1 *Hen. IV.* i 3 99
To save the blood on either side, Try fortune with him in a single fight v 1 100
Challenged you to single fight.—O, would the quarrel lay upon our heads! v 2 47
Your wind short? your chin double? your wit single? 2 *Hen. IV.* i 2 207
In single combat thou shalt buckle with me 1 *Hen. VI.* i 2 95
Let these have a day appointed them For single combat 2 *Hen. VI.* i 3 212
Single out some other chase; For I myself will hunt this wolf 3 *Hen. VI.* ii 4 12
By this I challenge him to single fight iv 7 75
But, whiles he thought to steal the single ten, The king was slily finger'd from the deck! v 1 43
Men might say, Till this time pomp was single, but now married *Hen. VIII.* i 1 15
I know but of a single part, in aught Pertains to the state i 2 41
I have no further gone in this than by A single voice i 2 70
I speak it with a single heart, my lords v 3 38
For what, alas, can these my single arms? *Troi. and Cres.* ii 2 135
Scants us with a single famish'd kiss iv 4 49
The glory of our Troy doth this day lie On his fair worth and single chivalry iv 4 150
You can do very little alone; for your helps are many, or else your actions would grow wondrous single *Coriolanus* ii 1 40
Wherein every one of us has a single honour ii 3 49
Yet, were there but this single plot to lose, This mould of Marcius iii 2 102
We shall not send O'er the vast world to seek a single man iv 1 42
Single you thither then this dainty doe *T. Andron.* ii 1 117
That when the single sole of it is worn, the jest may remain after the wearing sole singular *Rom. and Jul.* ii 4 66
The fool hangs on your back already.—No, thou stand'st single *T. of A.* ii 2 58
Perchance some single vantages you took iii 2 138
All single and alone, Yet an arch-villain keeps him company v 1 110
But, for my single self, I had as lief not be as live to be In awe of such a thing as I myself *J. Cæsar* i 2 97
My thought . . . Shakes so my single state of man *Macbeth* i 3 140
All our service In every point twice done and then done double Were poor and single business to contend Against those honours deep and broad i 6 16

Single. What concern they? The general cause? or is it a fee-grief Due to some single breast? Macbeth iv 3 197
The single and peculiar life is bound, With all the strength and armour of the mind, To keep itself from noyance Hamlet iii 3 11
When sorrows come, they come not single spies, But in battalions iv 5 78
Trust to thy single virtue Lear v 3 103
So hath my lord dared him to single fight Ant. and Cleo. iii 7 31
That he and Cæsar might Determine this great war in single fight! iv 4 37
The death of Antony Is not a single doom v 1 18
More remarkable in single oppositions Cymbeline iv 1 14
And swore With his own single hand he'ld take us in iv 2 121
No single soul Can we set eye on iv 2 130
Yet a princess To equal any single crown o' the earth Pericles iv 3 8
Singled. And watch'd him how he singled Clifford forth 3 Hen. VI. ii 1 12
Now, Clifford, I have singled thee alone ii 4 1
Singled forth to try experiments T. Andron. ii 3 69
Singleness. Solely singular for the singleness! Rom. and Jul. ii 4 70
Single-soled. O single-soled jest, solely singular for the singleness! ii 4 69
Singly. Neither singly can be manifested, Without the show of both Mer. Wives iv 6 15
Demand them singly.—Do you know this Captain? All's Well iv 3 208
He must fight singly to-morrow with Hector Troi. and Cres. iii 3 247
The man I speak of cannot in the world Be singly counterpoised Coriol. ii 2 91
Thou singly honest man T. of Athens iv 3 530
Singular. A most singular and choice epithet L. L. Lost v 1 17
Each your doing, So singular in each particular W. Tale iv 4 144
Very singular good! in faith, well said 2 Hen. IV. iii 2 119
Men of singular integrity and learning Hen. VIII. ii 4 59
That when the single sole of it is worn, the jest may remain after the wearing sole singular Rom. and Jul. ii 4 68
O single-soled jest, solely singular for the singleness! ii 4 69
Some villain, ay, and singular in his art Cymbeline iii 4 124
Singulariter, nominativo, hic, hæc, hoc Mer. Wives iv 1 42
Singularity. Put thyself into the trick of singularity T. Night ii 5 164; iii 4 79
Your gallery Have we pass'd through, not without much content In many singularities W. Tale v 3 12
In what fashion, More than his singularity, he goes Coriolanus i 1 282
Singuled. We will be singuled from the barbarous L. L. Lost v 1 85
Sinister. He professes to have received no sinister measure M. for M. iii 2 256
This the cranny is, right and sinister M. N. Dream v 1 164
An emblem of war, here on his sinister cheek All's Well ii 1 44
I am very comptible, even to the least sinister usage T. Night i 5 188
'Tis no sinister nor no awkward claim Hen. V. ii 4 85
My mother's blood Runs on the dexter cheek, and this sinister Bounds in my father's Troi. and Cres. iv 5 128
Sink. Shall we give o'er and drown? Have you a mind to sink? Tempest i 1 42
Let's all sink with the king.—Let's take leave of him i 1 67
Not so much perdition as an hair Betid to any creature in the vessel Which thou heard'st cry, which thou saw'st sink i 2 32
Why Doth it not then our eyelids sink? ii 1 201
Let Love, being light, be drowned if she sink! Com. of Errors iii 2 52
Faster and faster, till he sink into his grave Much Ado ii 1 83
Why, how now, cousin! wherefore sink you down? iv 1 111
Hit with Cupid's archery, Sink in apple of his eye M. N. Dream iii 2 104
Lay a more noble thought upon mine honour Than for to think that I would sink it here All's Well v 3 181
My gross flesh sinks downward, here to die Richard II. v 5 113
If he fall in, good night! or sink or swim 1 Hen. IV. i 3 194
He'll drop his heart into the sink of fear Hen. V. iii 5 59
Sir Pool! lord! Ay, kennel, puddle, sink 2 Hen. VI. iv 1 71
Tread on the sand; why, there you quickly sink 3 Hen. VI. v 4 30
Will the aspiring blood of Lancaster Sink in the ground? v 6 62
There let him sink, and be the seas on him! Richard III. iv 4 464
Heaven bear witness, And if I have a conscience, let it sink me, Even as the axe falls, if I be not faithful! Hen. VIII. ii 1 60
When they once perceive The least rub in your fortunes, fall away Like water from ye, never found again But where they mean to sink ye ii 1 131
A load would sink a navy, too much honour iii 2 383
Sweet draught: 'sweet' quoth 'a! sweet sink, sweet sewer T. and C. v 1 83
So, Ilion, fall thou next! now, Troy, sink down! v 8 11
The cormorant belly ..., Who is the sink o' the body Coriolanus i 1 126
Sink, my knee, i' the earth v 3 50
Against thy heart make thou a hole; That all the tears that thy poor eyes let fall May run into that sink T. Andron. iii 2 19
Under love's heavy burden do I sink.—And, to sink in it, should you burden love; Too great oppression Rom. and Jul. i 4 22
Ne'er speak, or think, That Timon's fortunes 'mong his friends can sink. —I would I could not think it T. of Athens ii 2 240
Burn, house! sink, Athens! henceforth hated be! iii 6 114
Cæsar cried 'Help me, Cassius, or I sink!' J. Cæsar i 2 111
They fall their crests, and, like deceitful jades, Sink in the trial iv 2 27
O setting sun, As in thy red rays thou dost sink to night, So in his red blood Cassius' day is set! v 3 61
Why sinks that cauldron? and what noise is this? Macbeth iv 1 106
I think our country sinks beneath the yoke; It weeps, it bleeds iv 3 39
The best of you Shall sink in my rebuke Othello ii 3 209
These quick-sands, Lepidus, Keep off them, for you sink Ant. and Cleo. ii 7 66
Sink Rome, and their tongues rot That speak against us! iii 7 16
Our fortune on the sea is out of breath, And sinks most lamentably iii 10 26
But even before, I was At point to sink for food Cymbeline iii 6 17
Now my heavy conscience sinks my knee, As then your force did v 5 413
Here many sink, yet those which see them fall Have scarce strength left to give them burial Pericles i 4 48
Your house, but for this virgin that doth prop it, Would sink and overwhelm you iv 6 128
Sink-a-pace. My very walk should be a jig; I would not so much as make water but in a sink-a-pace T. Night i 3 139
Sinking. Know by my size that I have a kind of alacrity in sinking M. W. iii 5 13
The splitting rocks cower'd in the sinking sands 2 Hen. VI. iii 2 97
Than camels in the war, who have their provand Only for bearing burdens, and sore blows For sinking under them Coriolanus ii 1 269
Thou art so leaky, That we must leave thee to thy sinking A. and C. iii 13 64
Sinking-ripe. And left the ship, then sinking-ripe, to us Com. of Errors i 1 78
Sinned. O sweet-suggesting Love, if thou hast sinn'd, Teach me, thy tempted subject, to excuse it! T. G. of Ver. ii 6 7
Yet sinn'd I not But in mistaking Much Ado v 1 284
I have then sinned against his experience All's Well ii 5 10
We'll answer, If you first sinn'd with us W. Tale i 2 84
I am a man More sinn'd against than sinning Lear iii 2 60
Doubting lest that he had err'd or sinn'd Pericles i 3 22
Sinner. Made such a sinner of his memory, To credit his own lie Tempest i 2 101
O, for my beads! I cross me for a sinner Com. of Errors ii 2 190
I will be so much a sinner, to be a double-dealer T. Night v 1 37
O Lord, have mercy on us, wretched sinners! 1 Hen. VI. i 4 70
Forbear to judge, for we are sinners all 2 Hen. VI. iii 3 31
I would forget it fain; But, O, it presses to my memory, Like damned guilty deeds to sinners' minds Rom. and Jul. iii 2 111
Here's that which is too weak to be a sinner, honest water T. of Athens i 2 59
Get thee to a nunnery: why wouldst thou be a breeder of sinners? Hamlet iii 1 123
Sinning. I am a man More sinn'd against than sinning Lear iii 2 60
Sinon. And, like a Sinon, take another Troy 3 Hen. VI. iii 2 190
Tell us what Sinon hath bewitch'd our ears T. Andron. v 3 85
Sinon's weeping Did scandal many a holy tear Cymbeline iii 4 61
Sip. I warrant you, they could never get her so much as sip on a cup with the proudest of them all Mer. Wives ii 2 77
None so dry or thirsty Will deign to sip or touch one drop of it T. of S. v 2 145
On his shoulder, and his; her face o' fire With labour and the thing she took to quench it, She would to each one sip W. Tale iv 4 62
Sipping. Whereon but sipping, If he by chance escape your venom'd stuck, Our purpose may hold there Hamlet iv 7 161
Sir. A loyal sir To him thou follow'st! Tempest v 1 69
Most wicked sir, whom to call brother Would even infect my mouth v 1 130
How fares my gracious sir? v 1 253
Most military sir, salutation L. L. Lost v 1 38
Fair sir, and you my merry mistress T. of Shrew iv 5 53
In the habit of some sir of note T. Night iii 4 81
This great sir will yet stay longer W. Tale i 2 212
O, hear me breathe my life Before this ancient sir! iv 4 372
No hearing, no feeling, but my sir's song iv 4 625
'At your service, sir:' 'No, sir,' says question, 'I, sweet sir, at yours' K. John i 1 198
Worthy sir, thou bleed'st; Thy exercise hath been too violent Coriol. i 5 15
Most absolute sir, if thou wilt have The leading iv 5 142
That sir which serves and seeks for gain, And follows but for form, Will pack when it begins to rain Lear ii 4 79
Which now again you are most apt to play the sir in Othello ii 1 176
Good sirs, take heart: We'll bury him Ant. and Cleo. iv 15 85
Sole sir o' the world, I cannot project mine own cause so well v 2 120
O brave sir! I would they were in Afric both together Cymbeline i 1 166
A lady to the worthiest sir that ever Country call'd his! i 6 160
Your great judgement In the election of a sir so rare i 6 175
A nobler sir ne'er lived 'Twixt sky and ground v 5 145
Sir Alice Ford! These nights will hack Mer. Wives ii 1 51
Sir boy, come, follow me: Sir boy, I'll whip you Much Ado v 1 83
Sir boy, now let me see your archery T. Andron. iv 3 2
Sir Oracle. As who should say 'I am Sir Oracle, And when I ope my lips let no dog bark!' Mer. of Venice i 1 93
Sir page, Look on me with your welkin eye: sweet villain! W. Tale i 2 135
Sir priest. Had rather go with sir priest than sir knight T. Night iii 4 298
Sir Prudence. This ancient morsel, this Sir Prudence Tempest ii 1 286
Sir-reverence. A very reverent body; ay, such a one as a man may not speak of without he say 'Sir-reverence' Com. of Errors iii 2 93
We'll draw thee from the mire Of this sir-reverence love Rom. and Jul. i 4 42
Sir Smile. By his next neighbour, by Sir Smile, his neighbour W. Tale i 2 196
Sir Valour. And at this sport Sir Valour dies Troi. and Cres. i 3 176
Sire. Could penetrate her uncompassionate sire T. G. of Ver. iii 1 231
Thine own bowels, which do call thee sire Meas. for Meas. iii 1 29
A child shall get a sire, if I fail not of my cunning T. of Shrew ii 1 413
These breed honour: that is honour's scorn, Which challenges itself as honour's born And is not like the sire All's Well ii 3 142
A gross and foolish sire Blemish'd his gracious dam W. Tale iii 2 198
Like unruly children, make their sire Stoop with oppression Richard II. iii 4 30
Whiles that his mountain sire, on mountain standing Hen. V. ii 4 57
Then follow thou thy desperate sire of Crete, Thou Icarus 1 Hen. VI. iv 6 54
And raise his issue, like a loving sire 3 Hen. VI. ii 2 22
Thou art neither like thy sire nor dam ii 2 135
And graced thy poor sire with his bridal-day ii 2 155
And cheers these hands that slew thy sire and brother ii 4 9
The son, compell'd, been butcher to the sire Richard III. v 5 26
Too like the sire for ever being good T. Andron. v 1 50
Son of sixteen, Pluck the lined crutch from thy old limping sire, With it beat out his brains! T. of Athens iv 1 14
Sweet king-killer [gold], and dear divorce 'Twixt natural son and sire! iv 3 383
Cowards father cowards and base things sire base Cymbeline iv 2 26
Siren. Sing, siren, for thyself and I will dote Com. of Errors iii 2 47
This siren, that will charm Rome's Saturnine T. Andron. ii 1 23
Sirrah. You'ld be king o' the isle, sirrah? Tempest v 1 287
Go, sirrah, to my cell; Take with you your companions v 1 291
But, sirrah, how did thy master part with Madam Julia? T. G. of Ver. ii 5 11
Sirrah, for all you are my man, go wait upon my cousin Shallow M. W. i 1 281
Hold, sirrah, bear you these letters tightly i 3 88
What do you call your knight's name, sirrah? iii 2 21
Come on, sirrah; hold up your head; answer your master iv 1 19
Well said, brazen-face! hold it out. Come forth, sirrah! iv 2 142
Come hither, sirrah. Can you cut off a man's head? Meas. for Meas. iv 2 1
Sirrah, here's a fellow will help you to-morrow in your execution iv 2 23
Sirrah, no more!—Enough, my lord v 1 214
You, sirrah, that knew me for a fool, a coward, One all of luxury v 1 505
Sirrah, if any ask you for your master, Say he dines forth Com. of Errors ii 2 211
If a crow help us in, sirrah, we'll pluck a crow together iii 1 83
Sirrah, you shall buy this sport as dear As all the metal in your shop iv 1 81
The goldsmith here Denies that saying. Sirrah, what say you? v 1 274
But, sirrah, what say you to this?—Sir, I confess L. L. Lost i 1 283
Sirrah Costard, I will enfranchise thee.—O, marry me to one Frances iii 1 121
Chirrah!—Quare chirrah, not sirrah? v 1 36
Go you before me, sirrah; Say I will come Mer. of Venice ii 5 38
Go in, sirrah; bid them prepare for dinner.—That is done, sir iii 5 51
Ah, sirrah, a body would think this was well counterfeited! As Y. L. It iv 3 166
Sirrah, where have you been?—Where have I been! T. of Shrew i 1 226
Sirrah, come hither: 'tis no time to jest i 1 231
Sirrah, not for my sake, but your master's, I advise You use your manners i 1 246
Faith, sirrah, an you'll not knock, I'll ring it i 2 16
Now, knock when I bid you, sirrah villain! i 2 19
Sirrah, lead these gentlemen To my daughters ii 1 109
Sirrah young gamester, your father were a fool To give thee all ii 1 402
Sirrah, I will not bear these braves of thine iii 1 15
Sirrah, get you hence, And bid my cousin Ferdinand come hither iv 1 153
Sirrah Biondello, Now do your duty throughly, I advise you iv 4 10
Why, then let's home again. Come, sirrah, let's away v 1 152

Sirrah. Sirrah Biondello, go and entreat my wife To come to me forthwith *T. of Shrew* v 2 86
What does this knave here? Get you gone, sirrah *All's Well* i 3 9
Sirrah, tell my gentlewoman I would speak with her i 3 72
What, one good in ten? you corrupt the song, sirrah i 3 85
I must tell thee, sirrah, I write man; to which title age cannot bring thee ii 3 208
Sirrah, your lord and master's married; there's news for you ii 3 257
Sirrah, inquire further after me; I had talk of you last night v 2 55
Tell me, sirrah, but tell me true, I charge you v 3 234
Ay, husband: can he that deny?—Her husband, sirrah! *T. Night* v 1 148
Sirrah, speak, What doth move you to claim your brother's land? *K. John* i 1 90
Sirrah, your brother is legitimate i 1 116
I'll smoke your skin-coat, an I catch you right; Sirrah, look to't ii 1 140
Sirrah, were I at home, At your den, sirrah, with your lioness ii 1 290
And, sirrah, I have cases of buckram for the nonce *1 Hen. IV.* i 2 200
But, sirrah, henceforth Let me not hear you speak of Mortimer i 3 118
Sirrah carrier, what time do you mean to come to London? ii 1 46
Sirrah, if they meet not with Saint Nicholas' clerks, I'll give thee this neck ii 1 67
Sirrah Jack, thy horse stands behind the hedge ii 2 73
Sirrah, I am sworn brother to a leash of drawers ii 4 6
Sirrah, Falstaff and the rest of the thieves are at the door ii 4 98
Sirrah, do I owe you a thousand pound? iii 3 153
But, sirrah, there's no room for faith, truth, nor honesty in this bosom of thine iii 3 173
But, sirrah, make haste: Percy is already in the field iv 2 80
Therefore, sirrah, with a new wound in your thigh, come you along with me v 4 130
Sirrah, you giant, what says the doctor to my water? *2 Hen. IV.* i 2 1
Sirrah, where's Snare?—O Lord, ay! good Master Snare ii 1 6
Sirrah, you boy, and Bardolph, no word to your master ii 2 176
Pay the musicians, sirrah. Farewell, hostess; farewell, Doll ii 4 403
Ah, sirrah! quoth-a, we shall Do nothing but eat v 3 17
Then keep thy vow, sirrah, when thou meetest the fellow *Hen. V.* iv 7 151
Sirrah, thou know'st how Orleans is besieged *1 Hen. VI.* i 4 1
Must hold his tongue, Lest it be said, 'Speak, sirrah, when you should' iii 1 62
Sirrah, thy lord I honour as he is.—Why, what is he? iii 4 35
Sirrah, or you must fight, or else be hang'd *2 Hen. VI.* i 3 222
Tell me, sirrah, what's my name?—Alas, master, I know not ii 1 117
Sirrah, go fetch the beadle hither straight ii 1 140
Now, sirrah, if you mean to save yourself from whipping ii 1 143
Sirrah beadle, whip him till he leap over that same stool ii 1 148
Sirrah, what's thy name?—Peter, forsooth ii 3 81
Come hither, sirrah, I must examine thee: what is thy name? iv 2 104
Sirrah, call in my sons to be my bail v 1 111
Sirrah, leave us to ourselves: we must confer *3 Hen. VI.* v 6 6
How now, sirrah! how goes the world with thee? *Richard III.* iii 2 98
Keep the door close, sirrah.—What would you have me do? *Hen. VIII.* v 4 30
How now, how now!—Sirrah, walk off *Troi. and Cres.* iii 2 7
Sirrah, if thy captain knew I were here, he would use me with estimation *Coriolanus* v 2 55
Your knee, sirrah.—That's my brave boy! v 3 75
There's for thyself, and that's for Tamora. Ah, sirrah! *T. Andron.* iii 2 75
Sirrah, what tidings? have you any letters? Shall I have justice? iv 3 78
Come, sirrah, you must be hanged.—Hanged! iv 4 47
Go, sirrah, trudge about Through fair Verona *Rom. and Jul.* i 2 34
Ah, sirrah, this unlook'd-for sport comes well i 5 31
Sirrah, go hire me twenty cunning cooks.—You shall have none ill iv 2 2
Make haste, make haste. Sirrah, fetch drier logs iv 4 15
Sirrah, what made your master in this place? v 3 280
Get you gone, sirrah. Draw nearer, honest Flaminius *T. of Athens* iii 1 41
What, is the fellow mad?—Sirrah, give place *J. Cæsar* iii 1 10
Get you hence, sirrah; saucy fellow, hence!—Bear with him, Brutus iv 3 134
My life is run his compass.—Sirrah, what news?—O my lord! v 3 25
Come hither, sirrah: In Parthia did I take thee prisoner v 3 36
Sirrah, a word with you: attend those men Our pleasure? *Macbeth* iii 1 45
Sirrah, your father's dead: And what will you do now? iv 2 30
Whose grave's this, sirrah?—Mine, sir *Hamlet* v 1 127
Go, sirrah, seek him; I'll apprehend him *Lear* i 2 83
You, you, sirrah, where's my daughter? i 4 48
Sirrah, you were best take my coxcomb.—Why, fool? i 4 109
Take heed, sirrah; the whip.—Truth's a dog must to kennel i 4 123
Sirrah, I'll teach thee a speech.—Do.—Mark it, nuncle i 4 128
When were you wont to be so full of songs, sirrah? i 4 186
An you lie, sirrah, we'll have you whipped i 4 197
Peace, sirrah! You beastly knave, know you no reverence? ii 2 74
Take him you on.—Sirrah, come on; go along with us iii 4 184
Sirrah, naked fellow,— Poor Tom's a-cold iv 1 53
Do you know, sirrah, where Lieutenant Cassio lies? *Othello* iii 4 1
Now, sirrah; you do wish yourself in Egypt? *Ant. and Cleo.* ii 3 10
But, sirrah, mark, we use To say the dead are well ii 5 32
I am again for Cydnus, To meet Mark Antony: sirrah Iras, go v 2 229
Who is here? What, are you packing, sirrah? Come hither *Cymbeline* iii 5 80
Sirrah, if thou wouldst not be a villain, but do me true service iii 5 108

Sister. How does my bounteous sister? *Tempest* iv 1 103
My father wailing, my sister crying, our maid howling *T. G. of Ver.* ii 3 7
This staff is my sister, for, look you, she is as white as a lily ii 3 22
Now come I to my sister; mark the moan she makes ii 3 33
When three or four of his blind brothers and sisters went to it iv 4 5
This day my sister should the cloister enter *Meas. for Meas.* i 2 182
The fair sister To her unhappy brother Claudio i 4 19
I am that Isabella and his sister i 4 23
The sister of the man condemn'd Desires access to you.—Hath he a sister? ii 2 18
Who's there?—One Isabel, a sister, desires access to you ii 4 18
That you, his sister, Finding yourself desired of such a person ii 4 90
Better it were a brother died at once, Than that a sister, by redeeming him, Should die for ever ii 4 107
Before his sister should her body stoop To such abhorr'd pollution ii 4 182
Look, signior, here's your sister iii 1 49
Now, sister, what's the comfort?—Why, As all comforts are iii 1 54
Sweet sister, let me live iii 1 133
Is't not a kind of incest, to take life From thine own sister's shame? iii 1 140
Vouchsafe a word, young sister, but one word iii 1 152
I have overheard what hath passed between you and your sister iii 1 162
Go to your knees and make ready.—Let me ask my sister pardon iii 1 173
Have you not heard speak of Mariana, the sister of Frederick? iii 1 217
Wrecked at sea, having in that perished vessel the dowry of his sister iii 1 226
What would you say?—I am the sister of one Claudio v 1 69

Sister. Sir, to dinner: My mistress and her sister stays for you. *Com. of Errors* i 2 76
Good sister, let us dine and never fret: A man is master of his liberty ii 1 6
When they see time They'll go or come: if so, be patient, sister ii 1 9
Sister, you know he promised me a chain ii 1 106
When were you wont to use my sister thus? ii 2 155
If you did wed my sister for her wealth, Then for her wealth's sake use her with more kindness iii 2 5
Muffle your false love ...: Let not my sister read it in your eye iii 2 9
Get you in again; Comfort my sister, cheer her, call her wife iii 2 26
Your weeping sister is no wife of mine, Nor to her bed no homage do I owe iii 2 42
Train me not, sweet mermaid, with thy note, To drown me in thy sister's flood of tears: Sing, siren, for thyself iii 2 46
Why call you me love? call my sister so.—Thy sister's sister.—That's my sister.—No; It is thyself iii 2 59
All this my sister is, or else should be.—Call thyself sister, sweet iii 2 65
Sir! hold you still: I'll fetch my sister, to get her good will iii 2 70
Her fair sister, Possess'd with such a gentle sovereign grace iii 2 164
Send him, mistress, redemption, the money in his desk?—Go fetch it, sister iv 2 47
Bring thy master home immediately. Come, sister iv 2 65
Go bear him hence. Sister, go you with me iv 4 133
Myself, he and my sister To-day did dine together v 1 207
By the way we met My wife, her sister, and a rabble more v 1 236
This fair gentlewoman, her sister here, Did call me brother v 1 373
She now shall be my sister, not my wife v 1 416
If fair-faced, She would swear the gentleman should be her sister *M. Ado* iii 1 62
But, as a brother to his sister, show'd Bashful sincerity and comely love iv 1 54
You'll ne'er be friends with him; a' kill'd your sister *L. L. Lost* v 2 13
To live a barren sister all your life, Chanting faint hymns *M. N. Dream* i 1 72
The sisters' vows, the hours that we have spent iii 2 199
O Sisters Three, Come, come to me, With hands as pale as milk v 1 343
The Sisters Three and such branches of learning *Mer. of Venice* ii 2 66
Whose loves Are dearer than the natural bond of sisters *As Y. Like It* i 2 288
Here comes my sister, reading: stand aside iii 2 132
Where dwell you, pretty youth?—With this shepherdess, my sister iii 2 353
Come, sister, will you go? iii 2 456; iii 5 78
Come, sister, you shall be the priest and marry us iv 1 124
What do you say, sister?—Pray thee, marry us.—I cannot say the words iv 1 126
Of female favour, and bestows himself Like a ripe sister iv 3 88
God save you, brother.—And you, fair sister v 2 21
Your brother and my sister no sooner met but they looked v 2 36
Sister, content you in my discontent *T. of Shrew* i 1 80
Mark'd you not how her sister Began to scold? i 1 176
Her eldest sister is so curst and shrewd i 1 185
Good sister, wrong me not, nor wrong yourself ii 1 1
Believe me, sister, of all the men alive I never yet beheld that special face Which I could fancy more than any other ii 1 10
If you affect him, sister, here I swear I'll plead for you myself ii 1 14
I prithee, sister Kate, untie my hands ii 1 21
Nor is your firm resolve unknown to me, In the preferment of the eldest sister ii 1 94
You grow too forward, sir: Have you so soon forgot the entertainment Her sister Katharine welcomed you withal? iii 1 3
Leave your books And help to dress your sister's chamber up iii 1 83
Mistress, what's your opinion of your sister? iii 2 245
Supply the bridegroom's place; And let Bianca take her sister's room iii 2 252
The sister to my wife, this gentlewoman, Thy son by this hath married iv 5 62
Brother Petruchio, sister Katharina, And thou, Hortensio v 2 6
Where is your sister, and Hortensio's wife? v 2 101
I care no more for than I do for heaven, So I were not his sister *All's W.* i 3 171
He left behind him myself and a sister, both born in an hour *T. Night* ii 1 20
Before you took me from the breach of the sea was my sister drowned ii 1 24
But died thy sister of her love? ii 4 122
I would, therefore, my sister had had no name, sir.—Why, man?—Why, sir, her name's a word; and to dally with that word might make my sister wanton iii 1 19
I had a sister, Whom the blind waves and surges have devour'd v 1 235
That day that made my sister thirteen years v 1 255
Think me as well a sister as a wife v 1 325
A sister! you are she v 1 334
Meantime, sweet sister, We will not part from hence v 1 393
What was my first? it has an elder sister, Or I mistake you *W. Tale* i 2 98
What will this sister of mine do with rice? iv 3 41
These pedlars, that have more in them than you'ld think, sister iv 4 218
He must know 'tis none of your daughter nor my sister iv 4 850
Then the prince my brother and the princess my sister called my father father v 2 154
Sister, farewell; I must to Coventry *Richard II.* i 2 56
Sirrah, get thee to Plashy, to my sister Gloucester ii 2 90
Come, sister,—cousin, I would say,—pray, pardon me ii 2 105
That he swears thou art to marry his sister Nell *2 Hen. IV.* ii 2 140
John with my brothers and sister, and Sir John with all Europe ii 2 145
But do you use me thus, Ned? must I marry your sister? ii 2 151
Why, then, let grievous, ghastly, gaping wounds Untwine the Sisters Three! ii 4 213
Unto our brother France, and to our sister, Health and fair time of day *Hen. V.* v 2 2
Will you, fair sister, Go with the princes, or stay here with us? v 2 90
Duke of York, Marrying my sister that thy mother was *1 Hen. VI.* ii 5 86
His eldest sister, Anne, My mother, being heir unto the crown *2 Hen. VI.* ii 2 43
To crave the French king's sister To wife for Edward *3 Hen. VI.* iii 1 30
And in conclusion wins the king from her, With promise of his sister iii 1 51
Lady Bona, thy fair sister, To England's king in lawful marriage iii 3 56
Tell me for truth the measure of his love Unto our sister Bona iii 3 121
Now, sister, let us hear your firm resolve iii 3 129
Then, Warwick, thus: our sister shall be Edward's iii 3 134
Were it to call King Edward's widow sister, I will perform it *Rich. III.* i 1 109
And for my sister and her princely sons, Be satisfied, dear God iii 3 20
By substitute betroth'd To Bona, sister to the King of France iii 7 182
A joyful time of day!—As much to you, good sister! iv 1 7
Kind sister, thanks: we'll enter all together iv 1 11
Every true heart weeps for't: all that dare Look into these affairs see this main end, The French king's sister *Hen. VIII.* ii 2 42
It shall be to the Duchess of Alençon, The French king's sister iii 2 86
I will not dispraise your sister Cassandra's wit, but *Troi. and Cres.* i 1 47
Had I a sister were a grace, or a daughter a goddess, he should take his choice i 2 257

Sister. What shriek is this?—'Tis our mad sister, I do know her voice . *Troi. and Cres.* ii 2 98
Peace, sister, peace! . . . . . . ii 2 103
Do not these high strains Of divination in our sister work Some touches of remorse? or is your blood So madly hot? . . . ii 2 114
Greekish girls shall tripping sing, 'Great Hector's sister did Achilles win' iii 3 212
Thou art, great lord, my father's sister's son . . . iv 5 120
Where is my brother Hector?—Here, sister; arm'd, and bloody in intent v 3 8
Brethren and sisters of the hold-door trade . . . v 10 52
The noble sister of Publicola, The moon of Rome . . *Coriolanus* v 3 64
Tendering our sister's honour and our own . . *T. Andron.* i 1 476
Speak, gentle sister, who hath martyr'd thee? . . . . iii 1 81
Witness the sorrow that their sister makes . . . . iii 1 119
At your grief, See how my wretched sister sobs and weeps . . iii 1 137
Farewell, Lavinia, my noble sister . . . . . iii 1 293
They cut thy sister's tongue and ravish'd her And cut her hands . v 1 92
They it were that ravished our sister . . . . v 3 99
County Anselme and his beauteous sisters . . . *Rom. and Jul.* i 2 68
Below thy sister's orb Infect the air! . . . *T. of Athens* iv 3 2
Publius shall not live, Who is your sister's son . . *J. Cæsar* iv 1 5
Where hast thou been, sister?—Killing swine . . . *Macbeth* i 3 1
The weird sisters, hand in hand, Posters of the sea and land . i 3 32
These weird sisters saluted me, and referred me to the coming on of time i 5 9
I dreamt last night of the three weird sisters . . . . ii 1 20
He chid the sisters When first they put the name of king upon me . iii 1 57
I will to-morrow, And betimes I will, to the weird sisters . . iii 4 133
Come, sisters, cheer we up his sprites, And show the best of our delights iv 1 127
Saw you the weird sisters?—No, my lord . . . . . iv 1 136
Our sometime sister, now our queen . . . . *Hamlet* i 2 8
Sister, . . . do not sleep, But let me hear from you . . . i 3 2
Fear it, Ophelia, fear it, my dear sister . . . . i 3 33
Dear maid, kind sister, sweet Ophelia! O heavens! . . . iv 5 158
A noble father lost; A sister driven into desperate terms . . iv 7 26
Your sister's drown'd, Laertes.—Drown'd! O, where? . . . iv 7 165
A ministering angel shall my sister be, When thou liest howling . v 1 264
I am made Of the self-same metal that my sister is . . . *Lear* i 1 71
What can you say to draw A third more opulent than your sisters? . i 1 88
Why have my sisters husbands, if they say They love you all? . . i 1 101
Sure, I shall never marry like my sisters, To love my father all . . i 1 105
Bid farewell to your sisters.—The jewels of our father . . . i 1 270
Like a sister am most loath to call Your faults as they are named . i 1 273
Sister, it is not a little I have to say of what most nearly appertains to us both . . . . i 1 286
He always loved our sister most; and with what poor judgement he hath now cast her off appears too grossly . . . . . i 1 293
Let him to our sister, Whose mind and mine, I know, in that are one . i 3 14
I'll write straight to my sister, To hold my very course . . . i 3 25
What he hath utter'd I have writ my sister . . . . . i 4 354
What, have you writ that letter to my sister? . . . . . i 4 357
I have this present evening from my sister Been well inform'd of them ii 1 103
Our father he hath writ, so hath our sister, Of differences . . ii 1 124
The messengers from our sister and the king . . . . . ii 2 54
This is a fellow of the self-same colour Our sister speaks of . . ii 2 146
My sister may receive it much more worse . . . . . ii 2 155
Thy sister's naught: O Regan, she hath tied Sharp-tooth'd unkindness, like a vulture, here . . . . ii 4 136
I cannot think my sister in the least Would fail her obligation . . ii 4 143
I pray you, That to our sister you do make return; Say you have wrong'd her . . . . ii 4 153
These are unsightly tricks: Return you to my sister . . . ii 4 160
What trumpet's that?—I know't, my sister's . . . . . ii 4 186
You will return and sojourn with my sister . . . . . ii 4 206
Give ear, sir, to my sister . . . . ii 4 236
Keep you our sister company . . . . iii 7 7
Our posts shall be swift and intelligent betwixt us. Farewell, dear sister . . . . iii 7 13
I would not see thy cruel nails Pluck out his poor old eyes; nor thy fierce sister In his anointed flesh stick boarish fangs . . . iii 7 57
This letter, madam, craves a speedy answer; 'Tis from your sister . iv 2 83
Cried 'Sisters! sisters! Shame of ladies! sisters! Kent! father! sisters!' . . . . iv 3 29
With much ado: Your sister is the better soldier . . . . iv 5 3
What might import my sister's letter to him?—I know not . . . iv 5 6
Let this kiss Repair those violent harms that my two sisters Have in thy reverence made!—Kind and dear princess! . . . . . iv 7 28
I know you do not love me; for your sisters Have, as I do remember, done me wrong: You have some cause, they have not . . . iv 7 73
Our sister's man is certainly miscarried.—'Tis to be doubted . . v 1 5
Speak the truth, Do you not love my sister? . . . . . v 1 9
I had rather lose the battle than that sister Should loosen him and me v 1 18
Our very loving sister, well be met . . . . . . v 1 20
Sister, you'll go with us?—No.—'Tis most convenient . . . v 1 34
To both these sisters have I sworn my love . . . . . v 1 55
Shall we not see these daughters and these sisters? . . . v 3 7
For your claim, fair sister, I bar it in the interest of my wife . . v 3 84
And her sister By her is poisoned; she hath confess'd it . . . v 3 226
Thou hast a sister by the mother's side . . *Ant. and Cleo.* ii 2 120
A sister I bequeath you, whom no brother Did ever love so dearly . ii 2 152
And do invite you to my sister's view, Whither straight I'll lead you . ii 2 170
Cæsar's sister is called Octavia . . . . ii 6 116
Sister, prove such a wife As my thoughts make thee . . . iii 2 25
Farewell, my dearest sister, fare thee well . . . . . iii 2 39
Why have you stol'n upon us thus? You come not Like Cæsar's sister iii 6 43
No, my most wronged sister; Cleopatra Hath nodded him to her . . iii 6 65
Sister, welcome: pray you, Be ever known to patience: my dear'st sister! . . . . iii 6 97
Good morrow, fairest: sister, your sweet hand . . *Cymbeline* ii 3 91
You call'd me brother, When I was but your sister; I you brothers, When ye were so indeed . . . . v 5 377
That even her art sisters the natural roses . . . *Pericles* v Gower 7

Sisterhood. I speak not as desiring more; But rather wishing a more strict restraint Upon the sisterhood . . . *Meas. for Meas.* i 4 5
A very virtuous maid, And to be shortly of a sisterhood, If not already ii 2 21
I, in probation of a sisterhood, Was sent to by my brother . . . v 1 72
A nun of winter's sisterhood kisses not more religiously *As Y. Like It* iii 4 17
I'll dispose of thee Among a sisterhood of holy nuns . *Rom. and Jul.* v 3 157

Sisterly. My sisterly remorse confutes mine honour . *Meas. for Meas.* v 1 100

Sit. Look how well my garments sit upon me . . . *Tempest* ii 1 272
While I sit lazy by . . . . iii 1 28
Sit then and talk with her; she is thine own . . . . . iv 1 32
Sit. If not, we'll make you sit and rifle you . . . *T. G. of Ver.* iv 1 4
Here can I sit alone, unseen of any . . . . v 4 4
They will not sit till you come . . . . . . *Mer. Wives* i 1 289
I sit at ten pounds a week . . . . i 3 8
Where indeed you have a delight to sit, have you not? *Meas. for Meas.* ii 1 134
Sit with my cousin; lend him your kind pains . . . . . v 1 246
Your brother's death, I know, sits at your heart . . . . v 1 394
Waked with it when I sleep; raised with it when I sit *Com. of Errors* iv 4 37
He shows me where the bachelors sit . . . . . *Much Ado* ii 1 51
I may sit in a corner and cry heigh-ho for a husband! . . . . ii 1 332
Stalk on, stalk on; the fowl sits . . . . ii 3 96
Sits the wind in that corner? . . . . ii 3 102
She will sit you, you heard my daughter tell you how . . . ii 3 115
There will she sit in her smock till she have writ a sheet of paper . ii 3 137
Let us go sit here upon the church-bench till two . . . . iii 3 95
The god of love, That sits above, And knows me . . . . . v 2 27
Like a demigod here sit I in the sky . . . . . *L. L. Lost* iv 3 79
Birds sit brooding in the snow And Marian's nose looks red . . v 2 933
Plucking the grass, to know where sits the wind . *Mer. of Venice* i 1 18
Why should a man, whose blood is warm within, Sit like his grandsire cut in alabaster? . . . . i 1 84
Wherein doth sit the dread and fear of kings . . . . . iv 1 192
Here will we sit and let the sounds of music Creep in our ears . . v 1 55
Sit, Jessica. Look how the floor of heaven Is thick inlaid . . . v 1 58
Let us sit and mock the good housewife Fortune . *As Y. Like It* i 2 34
Come, sit, sit, and a song.—We are for you: sit i' the middle . . v 3 8
Come, madam wife, sit by my side and let the world slip *T. of Shrew* Ind. 2 146
I will go sit and weep Till I can find occasion of revenge . . . ii 1 35
A join'd-stool.—Thou hast hit it: come, sit on me . . . . . ii 1 199
And sits as one new-risen from a dream . . . . . . iv 1 189
Nothing but sit and sit, and eat and eat! . . . . . . v 2 12
They sit conferring by the parlour fire.—Go, fetch them hither . . v 2 102
To see him every hour; to sit and draw His arched brows . *All's Well* i 1 104
Yet these fix'd evils sit so fit in him . . . . i 1 113
Sit, my preserver, by thy patient's side . . . . . . ii 3 53
Let the white death sit on thy cheek for ever . . . . . ii 3 77
Seek the crowner, and let him sit o' my coz . . . *T. Night* i 5 143
Under your hard construction must I sit . . . . . . iii 1 126
Where he sits crowned in his master's spite . . . . . v 1 131
Pray you, sit by us, And tell's a tale . . . . . *W. Tale* ii 1 22
Sits on his horse back at mine hostess' door . . . *K. John* ii 1 289
Here I and sorrows sit; Here is my throne, bid kings come bow to it . iii 1 73
I would you were a little sick, That I might sit all night and watch with you . . . . iv 1 30
Drive these men away, And I will sit as quite as a lamb . . . iv 1 80
Here once again we sit, once again crown'd . . . . . . iv 2 1
And in his forehead sits A bare-ribb'd death . . . . . v 2 176
O, sit my husband's wrongs on Hereford's spear! . . . *Richard II.* i 2 47
Woe doth the heavier sit, Where it perceives it is but faintly borne . i 3 280
A thousand flatterers sit within thy crown . . . . . . ii 1 100
We see the wind sit sore upon our sails . . . . . . ii 1 265
The wind sits fair for news to go to Ireland, But none returns . . ii 2 123
His treasons will sit blushing in his face . . . . . . iii 2 51
Let us sit upon the ground And tell sad stories of the death of kings . iii 2 155
Within the hollow crown That rounds the mortal temples of a king Keeps Death his court and there the antic sits . . . . . iii 2 162
And who sits here that is not Richard's subject? . . . . . iv 1 122
Long mayst thou live in Richard's seat to sit! . . . . . iv 1 218
In winter's tedious nights sit by the fire With good old folks . . v 1 40
Like silly beggars Who sitting in the stocks refuge their shame, That many have and others must sit there . . . . v 5 27
Sit, cousin Percy; sit, good cousin Hotspur . . . 1 *Hen. IV.* iii 1 7
With all my heart I'll sit and hear her sing . . . . . iii 1 223
The mailed Mars shall on his altar sit Up to the ears in blood . . iv 1 116
And the spirits of the wise sit in the clouds and mock us . 2 *Hen. IV.* ii 2 155
Let them play. Play, sirs. Sit on my knee, Doll . . . . ii 4 246
Simon Shadow!—Yea, marry, let me have him to sit under . . . iii 2 133
That man that sits within a monarch's heart . . . . . iv 2 11
I will sit and watch here by the king . . . . . . iv 5 20
Thou dost sit Like a rich armour worn in heat of day . . . iv 5 29
Lo, here it sits, Which God shall guard . . . . . . iv 5 43
Who undertook to sit and watch by you . . . . . . iv 5 53
Sit thou by my bed; And hear, I think, the very latest counsel . . iv 5 182
This new and gorgeous garment, majesty, Sits not so easy on me as you think . . . . v 2 45
Sweet sir, sit; I'll be with you anon; most sweet sir, sit . . . v 3 28
You are their heir; you sit upon their throne . . . *Hen. V.* i 2 117
There we'll sit, Ruling in large and ample empery . . . . i 2 225
For now sits Expectation in the air . . . . . . ii Prol. 8
There is the playhouse now, there must you sit . . . . ii Prol. 36
Now sits the wind fair, and we will aboard . . . . . ii 2 12
There's not, I think, a subject That sits in heart-grief and uneasiness ii 2 27
By their watchful fires Sit patiently and inly ruminate . . . iv Prol. 24
Yet sit and see, Minding true things by what their mockeries be . iv Prol. 52
The farced title running 'fore the king, The throne he sits on . . iv 1 281
The horsemen sit like fixed candlesticks, With torch-staves in their hand . . . . iv 2 45
Reproach and everlasting shame Sits mocking in our plumes . . iv 5 5
Appoint some of your council presently To sit with us once more . . v 2 80
I could lay on like a butcher and sit like a jack-an-apes, never off . v 2 147
And sit at chiefest stern of public weal . . . 1 *Hen. VI.* i 1 177
Do not so dishonour me: Here will I sit before the walls of Rouen . iii 2 91
So York must sit and fret and bite his tongue . . 2 *Hen. VI.* i 1 230
Madam, sit you and fear not: whom we raise, We will make fast . i 4 24
Sit there, the lyingest knave in Christendom . . . . . ii 1 125
Upon thy eye-balls murderous tyranny Sits in grim majesty . . . iii 2 50
To sit and witch me, as Ascanius did . . . . . . iii 2 116
Look where the sturdy rebel sits, Even in the chair of state . 3 *Hen. VI.* i 1 50
He durst not sit there, had your father lived . . . . . i 1 63
Shall I stand, and thou sit in my throne?—It must and shall be so . i 1 84
Over the chair of state, where now he sits, Write up his title . . i 1 168
Di faciant laudis summa sit ista tuæ! . . . . i 3 48
To be no better than a homely swain; To sit upon a hill, as I do now . ii 5 23
Sad-hearted men, much overgone with care, Here sits a king more woful ii 5 124
An envious mountain on my back, Where sits deformity to mock my body . . . . iii 2 158
It ill befits . . . that thou shouldst stand while Lewis doth sit . . iii 3 3
Be thou still like thyself, And sit thee by our side . . . . iii 3 16
Now, brother king, farewell, and sit you fast, For I will hence . . iv 1 119
Now, Montague, sit fast; I seek for thee . . . . v 2 3

Sit. We will not from the helm to sit and weep, But keep our course *3 Hen. VI.* v 4 21
Once more we sit in England's royal throne . . . v 7 1
Here are the keys, there sits the duke asleep . . . *Richard III.* i 4 96
Summon him to-morrow to the Tower, To sit about the coronation . iii 1 173
Fortune and victory sit on thy helm! . . . . . v 3 79
Let me sit heavy on thy soul to-morrow! (Repeated) . . . . v 3 118
Upon them! Victory sits on our helms . . . . . v 3 351
We should take root here where we sit, or sit State-statues only *Hen. VIII.* i 2 87
Sit by us; you shall hear—This was his gentleman in trust . . . i 2 124
Sweet ladies, will it please you sit? Sir Harry, Place you that side i 4 19
Pray, sit between these ladies.—By my faith, And thank your lordship i 4 24
Heaven is above all yet; there sits a judge That no king can corrupt . iii 1 100
Grew so ill He could not sit his mule . . . . iv 2 16
Whilst I sit meditating On that celestial harmony I go to . . . iv 2 79
I'm very sorry To sit here at this present, and behold That chair stand empty . . . . v 3 9
At Priam's royal table do I sit . . . . . . *Troi. and Cres.* i 1 29
Danger, like an ague, subtly taints Even then when we sit idly in the sun . . . . iii 3 233
Sit, gods, upon your thrones, and smile at Troy! . . . . . v 10 7
They'll sit by the fire, and presume to know What's done i' the Capitol *Coriolanus* i 1 195
Nay, keep your place.—Sit, Coriolanus . . . . . ii 2 71
Than idly sit To hear my nothings monster'd . . . . ii 2 80
Rome Sits safe and still without him . . . . . iv 6 37
I tell you, he does sit in gold, his eye Red as 'twould burn Rome . v 1 63
The glorious gods sit in hourly synod about thy particular prosperity! v 2 74
He sits in his state, as a thing made for Alexander . . . . v 4 22
Sits aloft, Secure of thunder's crack or lightning flash *T. Andron.* ii 1 2
Sit fas aut nefas, till I find the stream To cool this heat . . . ii 1 133
Under their sweet shade, Aaron, let us sit . . . . ii 3 16
And thou, and I, sit round about some fountain, Looking all downwards iii 1 123
Sit: and look you eat no more Than will preserve just so much strength iii 2 1
Empress I am, but yonder sits the emperor . . . . iv 4 41
Take our good meaning, for our judgement sits Five times in that ere once in our five wits . . . . . . *Rom. and Jul.* i 4 46
Nay, sit, nay, sit, good cousin Capulet; For you and I are past our dancing days: How long is't now since? . . . . . i 5 32
Now will he sit under a medlar tree, And wish his mistress were that kind of fruit As maids call medlars . . . . . . ii 1 34
Here upon thy cheek the stain doth sit Of an old tear . . . ii 3 75
Stand so much on the new form, that they cannot sit at ease on the old bench . . . . ii 4 36
My bosom's lord sits lightly in his throne . . . . . v 1 3
Sit; more welcome are ye to my fortunes Than my fortunes to me *T. of A.* i 2 19
The fellow that sits next him now, parts bread with him . . . i 2 47
Men must learn now with pity to dispense; For policy sits above conscience . . . . iii 2 94
Make not a city feast of it, to let the meat cool ere we can agree upon the first place: sit, sit . . . . iii 6 77
If there sit twelve women at the table, let a dozen of them be—as they are iii 6 87
Now breathless wrong Shall sit and pant in your great chairs of ease . v 4 11
The bird of night did sit Even at noon-day upon the market-place *J. C.* i 3 26
O, he sits high in all the people's hearts . . . . . i 3 157
Let us presently go sit in council . . . . . . iv 1 45
Now sit we close about this taper here, And call in question our necessities . . . . iv 3 164
Adieu! Lest our old robes sit easier than our new! . . . *Macbeth* ii 4 38
Here I'll sit i' the midst: Be large in mirth; anon we'll drink a measure iii 4 10
May't please your highness sit . . . . . . iii 4 39
Sit, worthy friends: my lord is often thus, And hath been from his youth iii 4 53
My little spirit, see, Sits in a foggy cloud, and stays for me . . iii 5 35
This gentle and unforced accord of Hamlet Sits smiling to my heart *Ham.* i 2 124
The wind sits in the shoulder of your sail . . . . i 3 56
There's something in his soul, O'er which his melancholy sits on brood iii 1 173
Come hither, my dear Hamlet, sit by me.—No, good mother . . iii 2 114
But, look, amazement on thy mother sits . . . . . iii 4 112
His silence will sit drooping . . . . v 1 311
An thou canst not smile as the wind sits, thou'lt catch cold shortly *Lear* i 4 113
The stocks! As I have life and honour, There shall he sit till noon . ii 2 141
Death on my state! wherefore Should he sit here? . . . . ii 4 114
Come, sit thou here, most learned justicer; Thou, sapient sir, sit here . iii 6 23
You are o' the commission, Sit you too . . . . . iii 6 41
In session sit With meditations lawful . . . . *Othello* iii 3 140
Upon your sword Sit laurel victory! . . . . *Ant. and Cleo.* i 3 100
To sit And keep the turn of tippling with a slave . . . . i 4 18
Stands he, or sits he? Or does he walk? or is he on his horse? . . i 5 19
Sit.—Sit, sir.—Nay, then.—I learn, you take things ill . . . ii 2 28
Antony, Enthroned i' the market-place, did sit alone . . . ii 2 220
Sit,—and some wine! A health to Lepidus! . . . . . ii 7 33
Though my reason Sits in the wind against me . . . . iii 10 37
He sits 'mongst men like a descended god . . . . *Cymbeline* i 6 169
When on my three-foot stool I sit and tell The warlike feats I have done iii 3 89
To glad her presence, The senate-house of planets all did sit . *Pericles* i 1 10
Our daughter . . . Sits here, like beauty's child . . . . ii 2 6
Had princes sit, like stars, about his throne, And he the sun . . . ii 3 39
Yet pause awhile: Yon knight doth sit too melancholy . . . ii 3 54
Come, gentlemen, we sit too long on trifles, And waste the time . . ii 3 92
You shall like diamonds sit about his crown . . . . . ii 4 53
More, if might, Shall be discover'd; please you, sit and hark . v Gower 24
Thy name, my most kind virgin? Recount, I do beseech thee: come, sit by me . . . . v 1 142
Sit at dinner. Jest, sir, as you sit at dinner . . . *Com. of Errors* i 2 62
Mark Antony In Egypt sits at dinner . . . *Ant. and Cleo.* ii 1 12
Sit at supper. She that you gaze on so as she sits at supper? *T. G. of V.* ii 1 46
One night, as we did sit at supper . . . . *Richard III.* ii 4 10
Sit down; For thou must now know farther . . . . *Tempest* i 2 32
If you'll sit down, I'll bear your logs the while . . . . iii 1 23
Sit down, and rest. Even here I will put off my hope . . . iii 3 6
Either get thee from the door or sit down at the hatch *Com. of Errors* iii 1 33
And men sit down to that nourishment which is called supper *L. L. Lost* i 1 239
Come, sit down, every mother's son . . . . *M. N. Dream* iii 1 75
Who riseth from a feast With that keen appetite that he sits down? *Mer. of Venice* ii 6 9
Sit down and feed, and welcome to our table . . . *As Y. Like It* ii 7 105
Where are those—Sit down, Kate, and welcome . . . *T. of Shrew* iv 1 144
Come, Kate, sit down; I know you have a stomach . . . . iv 1 161
Sit down; For now we sit to chat as well as eat . . . . v 2 10
There was a man— Nay, come, sit down; then on . . . *W. Tale* ii 1 29

Sit down. Cousin Glendower, Will you sit down? . . . *1 Hen. IV.* iii 1 4
Now sit down, now sit down: come, cousin . . . . *2 Hen. IV.* v 3 16
Sit down with us: it ill befits thy state And birth, that thou shouldst stand while Lewis doth sit . . . . . . *3 Hen. VI.* iii 3 2
Let's sit down quiet, For fear we wake her . . . . *Hen. VIII.* iv 2 81
Good man, sit down . . . . v 3 130
All places yield to him ere he sits down . . . . *Coriolanus* iv 7 28
Let us sit down and mark their yelping noise . . . . *T. Andron.* ii 3 20
Sit down, sweet niece: brother, sit down by me . . . . . iv 1 65
You know your own degrees; sit down . . . . . *Macbeth* iii 4 1
Come, love and health to all; Then I'll sit down . . . . iii 4 88
Sit down awhile; And let us once again assail your ears . . *Hamlet* i 1 30
Let me sit down. O Juno! . . . . . . *Ant. and Cleo.* iii 11 28
Cæsar sits down in Alexandria; where I will oppose his fate . . iii 13 168
Sit down: thou art no flatterer: I thank thee for it . . . *Pericles* i 2 60
Sit him down. Would shut the book, and sit him down and die *2 Hen. IV.* iii 1 56
Sit me down. Here on this molehill will I sit me down . . *3 Hen. VI.* ii 5 14
Sit still, and hear the last of our sea-sorrow . . . . *Tempest* i 2 170
Being gone, I am a man again. Pray you, sit still . . . *Macbeth* iii 4 108
Would the night were come! Till then sit still, my soul . . *Hamlet* i 2 257
Being demanded that, She would sit still and weep . . . *Pericles* v 1 191
Sit thee down. Till then, sit thee down, sorrow! . . . *L. L. Lost* i 1 317
Come, sit thee down upon this flowery bed . . . *M. N. Dream* iv 1 1
Sit thee down, Clitus: slaying is the word . . . . *J. Cæsar* v 5 4
Sit up. Let the nurse this night sit up with you . . *Rom. and Jul.* iv 3 10
Sit we down. And, to cut off all strife, here sit we down *T. of Shrew* iii 1 21
Then sit we down, and let us all consult . . . . *T. Andron.* iv 2 132
Sit we down, And let us hear Bernardo speak of this . . . *Hamlet* i 1 33
Sit you down: We'll borrow place of him . . . . *Meas. for Meas.* v 1 366
Sit you down in gentleness . . . . . . *As Y. Like It* ii 7 124
Peace! sit you down, And let me wring your heart . . . . *Hamlet* iii 4 34
Sit you down, father; rest you. Let's see these pockets . . *Lear* iv 6 260
Sit you out. Well, sit you out: go home, Biron: adieu . . *L. L. Lost* v 2 110
Sith so prettily He couples it to his complaining names . *T. G. of Ver.* i 2 126
Sith you yourself know how easy it is to be such an offender *Mer. Wives* ii 2 195
Sith 'twas my fault to give the people scope . . *Meas. for Meas.* i 3 35
Sith that the justice of your title to him Doth flourish the deceit . . iv 1 74
Sith it your pleasure is, And I am tied to be obedient . . *T. of Shrew* i 1 216
Talk not of France, sith thou hast lost it all . . . . *3 Hen. VI.* i 1 110
Lest in revenge thereof, sith God is just, He be as miserably slain as I . i 3 41
I come to tell you things sith then befall'n . . . . . ii 1 106
Sith every action that hath gone before, Whereof we have record, trial did draw Bias and thwart . . . . . . *Troi. and Cres.* i 3 13
Sith yet there is a credence in my heart . . . . . . v 2 120
Sith true nobility Warrants these words in princely courtesy *T. Andron.* i 1 271
Sith priest and holy water are so near And tapers burn so bright . . i 1 323
Sith there's no justice in earth nor hell, We will solicit heaven . . iv 3 49
Sith nor the exterior nor the inward man Resembles that it was *Hamlet* ii 2 6
Brought up with him, And sith so neighbour'd to his youth and haviour ii 2 12
'This thing's to do;' Sith I have cause and will and strength and means To do't . . . . iv 4 45
Sith you have heard, and with a knowing ear . . . . . iv 7 3
Sith thus thou wilt appear, Freedom lives hence . . . . *Lear* i 1 183
Sith that both charge and danger Speak 'gainst so great a number . ii 4 242
But, sith I am enter'd in this cause so far, . . . I will go on . *Othello* iii 3 411
Sithence. To acquaint you withal; sithence, in the loss that may happen, it concerns you something to know it . . . *All's Well* i 3 124
Have you inform'd them sithence? . . . . . *Coriolanus* iii 1 47
Sittest. And start so often when thou sit'st alone . . *1 Hen. IV.* ii 3 46
Whiles thou, a moral fool, sit'st still, and criest 'Alack' . . *Lear* iv 2 58
Sitting, His arms in this sad knot . . . . . *Tempest* i 2 223
Sitting on a bank, Weeping . . . . i 2 389
He, sir, sitting, as I say, in a lower chair . . . *Meas. for Meas.* ii 1 132
In the manor-house, sitting with her upon the form . . *L. L. Lost* i 1 209
Your lion, that holds his poll-axe sitting on a close-stool . . . v 2 580
Both on one sampler, sitting on one cushion . . . *M. N. Dream* iii 2 205
Fourscore ducats at a sitting! fourscore ducats! . . *Mer. of Venice* iii 1 117
The shepherd . . . Who you saw sitting by me on the turf *As Y. Like It* ii 4 52
Man, sitting down before you, will undermine you . . . *All's Well* i 1 129
Having been three months married to her, sitting in my state *T. Night* ii 5 50
Which shall point you forth at every sitting What you must say *W. Tale* iv 4 572
Like silly beggars Who sitting in the stocks refuge their shame, That many have and others must sit there . . . . . *Richard II.* v 5 26
For every honour sitting on his helm, Would they were multitudes! *1 Hen. IV.* iii 2 142
Sitting in my Dolphin-chamber, at the round table . . *2 Hen. IV.* ii 1 94
Here, sitting upon London-stone, I charge and command . *2 Hen. VI.* iv 6 2
Long sitting to determine poor men's causes Hath made me full of sickness . . . . iv 7 93
Sitting in the sun under the dove-house wall . . . *Rom. and Jul.* i 3 27
Is there no pity sitting in the clouds? . . . . . . iii 5 198
I have heard That guilty creatures sitting at a play Have by the very cunning of the scene Been struck so to the soul . . . *Hamlet* ii 2 618
Sitting sadly, Hearing us praise our loves of Italy . . . *Cymbeline* v 5 160
Situate. There's nothing situate under heaven's eye But hath his bound, in earth, in sea, in sky . . . . . . *Com. of Errors* ii 1 16
I know where it is situate.—Lord, how wise you are! . *L. L. Lost* i 2 142
Situation. We survey The plot of situation and the model *2 Hen. IV.* i 3 51
The situations, look you, is both alike . . . . *Hen. V.* iv 7 27
Siward. Is gone to pray the holy king, upon his aid To wake Northumberland and warlike Siward . . . . *Macbeth* iii 6 31
Old Siward, with ten thousand warlike men, Already at a point . . iv 3 134
Gracious England hath Lent us good Siward and ten thousand men . iv 3 190
Led on by Malcolm, His uncle Siward and the good Macduff . . v 2 2
There is Siward's son, And many unrough youths . . . . v 2 9
Six. The time 'twixt six and now Must by us both be spent most preciously . . . . *Tempest* i 2 240
From whom my absence was not six months old . . *Com. of Errors* i 1 45
It shall be written in eight and six . . . . . *M. N. Dream* iii 1 25
On Black-Monday last at six o'clock i' the morning . *Mer. of Venice* ii 5 25
Pay him six thousand, and deface the bond; Double six thousand . iii 2 301
For thy three thousand ducats here is six.—If every ducat in six thousand ducats Were in six parts and every part a ducat, I would not draw them . . . . iv 1 84
The poor world is almost six thousand years old . . *As Y. Like It* iv 1 95
Repaired with knots; one girth six times pieced . . *T. of Shrew* iii 2 61
How long is't, count, Since the physician at your father's died? He was much famed.—Some six months since . . . . *All's Well* i 2 71
Five or six thousand horse, I said . . . . iv 3 170
Of six preceding ancestors, that gem, . . . Hath it been owed and worn v 3 196

Six. Five or six honest wives that were present . . . *W. Tale* iv 4 273
Six frozen winters spent, Return with welcome home . . *Richard II.* i 3 211
Ere the six years that he hath to spend Can change their moons . . i 3 219
Six years we banish him, and he shall go . . . . . i 3 248
What is six winters? they are quickly gone.—To men in joy . . i 3 260
When he was not six and twenty strong . . . . *1 Hen. IV.* iv 3 56
These six dry, round, old, withered knights . *2 Hen. IV.* ii 4 8
The wearing out of six fashions, which is four terms, or two actions . v 1 89
Six thousand and two hundred good esquires . . . *Hen. V.* i 1 14
Having full scarce six thousand in his troop . . *1 Hen. VI.* i 1 112
When but in all I was six thousand strong . . . . iv 1 20
Within six hours they will be at his aid.—Too late comes rescue . iv 4 41
Some six miles off the duke is with the soldiers . . . *3 Hen. VI.* ii 1 144
Whom thou obeyed'st thirty and six years . . . . iii 3 96
I think there be six Richmonds in the field . . *Richard III.* v 4 11
At Dunstable, six miles off From Ampthill . . *Hen. VIII.* iv 1 27
Battles thrice six I have seen and heard of . . *Coriolanus* ii 3 135
If you had been the wife of Hercules, Six of his labours you'ld have done . . . . iv 1 18
Worth six on him . . . . iv 5 174
O that I had him, With six Aufidiuses, or more! . . . . v 6 130
'Twas due on forfeiture, my lord, six weeks And past . *T. of Athens* ii 2 30
Yet may your pains, six months, Be quite contrary . . . iv 3 143
Six French rapiers and poniards, with their assigns . . *Hamlet* v 2 156
Six Barbary horses against six French swords . . . . . v 2 168
Who hath had three suits to his back, six shirts to his body . . *Lear* iii 4 142
Some five or six and thirty of his knights, Hot questrists after him . iii 7 16
Six kings already Show me the way of yielding . . *Ant. and Cleo.* iii 10 34
I have yet Room for six scotches more . . . . . iv 7 10
Can it be six mile yet?—I have gone all night . . . *Cymbeline* iv 2 293
If King Pericles Come not home in twice six moons . . *Pericles* iii Gower 31
Six and seven. And every thing is left at six and seven . *Richard II.* ii 2 122
Six-gated. Priam's six-gated city . . . . *Troi. and Cres.* Prol. 15
Six or seven. Me have stay six or seven, two, tree hours . *Mer. Wives* ii 3 37
Bring me in the names of some six or seven, the most sufficient . *M. for M.* ii 1 287
Six or seven winters more respect Than a perpetual honour . . iii 1 76
He that kills me some six or seven dozen of Scots at a breakfast *1 Hen. IV.* ii 4 115
As we were sharing, some six or seven fresh men set upon us . . . ii 4 199
Six or seven thousand is their utmost power . . *Richard III.* v 3 10
Some six or seven, who did hide their faces Even from darkness *J. Cæsar* ii 1 277
Six-or-seven-times-honoured captain-general . *Troi. and Cres.* iii 3 278
Sixpence. O,—sixpence, that I had o' Wednesday last . *Com. of Errors* i 2 55
I will even take sixpence in earnest . . . . . *Much Ado* ii 1 42
Thus hath he lost sixpence a day during his life; he could not have 'scaped sixpence a day: an the duke had not given him sixpence a day for playing Pyramus, I'll be hanged; he would have deserved it: sixpence a day in Pyramus, or nothing . . . *M. N. Dream* iv 2 20
I sent thee sixpence for thy leman: hadst it? . . . . *T. Night* ii 3 26
There is sixpence for you: let's have a song . . . . . ii 3 32
An under-skinker, one that never spake other English in his life than 'Eight shillings and sixpence' . . . . . . *1 Hen. IV.* ii 4 28
A face-royal, for a barber shall never earn sixpence out of it . *2 Hen. IV.* i 2 29
There is sixpence to preserve thee . . . . ii 2 102
His breeches cost him but a crown; He held them sixpence all too dear *Othello* ii 3 94
Sixpenny. No long-staff sixpenny strikers . . . *1 Hen. IV.* ii 1 82
Sixscore fat oxen standing in my stalls . . . *T. of Shrew* ii 1 360
Sixteen. Some sixteen months, and longer might have stay'd *T. G. of V.* iv 1 21
I have to-night dispatched sixteen businesses . . . *All's Well* iv 3 98
I would there were no age between sixteen and three-and-twenty *W. T.* iii 3 60
I slide O'er sixteen years . . . . iv 1 6
Which lets go by some sixteen years and makes her As she lived now . v 3 31
We four set upon some dozen— Sixteen at least . . *1 Hen. IV.* ii 4 194
There are but sixteen hundred mercenaries; The rest are princes *Hen. V.* iv 8 93
I have been begging sixteen years in court . . *Hen. VIII.* ii 3 82
At sixteen years, When Tarquin made a head for Rome . *Coriolanus* ii 2 91
Son of sixteen, Pluck the lined crutch from thy old limping sire, With it beat out his brains! . . . . *T. of Athens* iv 1 13
You could, for a need, study a speech of some dozen or sixteen lines? *Hamlet* ii 2 567
I had rather Have skipp'd from sixteen years of age to sixty . *Cymbeline* iv 2 199
Sixth. How's the day?—On the sixth hour . . . . *Tempest* v 1 4
The sixth of July: Your loving friend, Benedick . . . *Much Ado* i 1 285
Sixth and lastly, they have belied a lady . . . . . v 1 221
About the sixth hour; when beasts most graze . . . *L. L. Lost* i 1 238
The sixth age shifts Into the lean and slipper'd pantaloon *As Y. Like It* ii 7 157
The sixth, the Lie with Circumstance; the seventh, the Lie Direct . v 4 100
God save King Henry, of that name the sixth! . . . *1 Hen. VI.* iv 1 2
Which compel from each The sixth part of his substance . *Hen. VIII.* i 2 58
Sixth part of each? A trembling contribution! . . . . i 2 94
And on the sixth to turn thy hated back Upon our kingdom . . *Lear* i 1 178
At the sixth hour of morn, at noon, at midnight, To encounter me *Cymb.* i 3 31
Vile men, Who of their broken debtors take a third, A sixth, a tenth . v 4 20
And what's The sixth and last, the which the knight himself With such a graceful courtesy deliver'd? . . . . . . *Pericles* ii 2 40
Sixty and nine, that wore Their crownets regal . *Troi. and Cres.* Prol. 5
I have sixty sails, Cæsar none better . . . *Ant. and Cleo.* iii 7 50
The Egyptian admiral, With all their sixty, fly and turn the rudder . iii 10 3
I had rather Have skipp'd from sixteen years of age to sixty . *Cymbeline* iv 2 199
Size. Know by my size that I have a kind of alacrity in sinking *M. Wives* iii 5 12
'Tis a word too great for any mouth of this age's size . *As Y. Like It* iii 2 240
An answer of most monstrous size that must fit all demands . *All's Well* ii 2 35
He hath songs for man or woman, of all sizes . . . *W. Tale* iv 4 192
To shape my legs of an unequal size; To disproportion me . *3 Hen. VI.* iii 2 159
You are potently opposed; and with a malice Of as great size *Hen. VIII.* v 1 135
But for Achilles, mine own searching eyes Shall find him by his large and portly size . . . . *Troi. and Cres.* iv 5 162
With all the size that verity Would without lapsing suffer . *Coriolanus* v 2 18
No cedars we, No big-boned men framed of the Cyclops' size *T. Andron.* iv 3 46
I am rapt and cannot cover The monstrous bulk of this ingratitude With any size of words . . . . *T. of Athens* v 1 69
To bandy hasty words, to scant my sizes . . . . . *Lear* ii 4 178
Comforts we dispise; our size of sorrow, Proportion'd to our cause, must be as great As that which makes it . . *Ant. and Cleo.* iv 15 4
But, if there be, or ever were, one such, It's past the size of dreaming . v 2 97
Sized. What my love is, proof hath made you know; And as my love is sized, my fear is so . . . . *Hamlet* iii 2 180
Skains-mates. Scurvy knave! I am none of his flirt-gills; I am none of his skains-mates . . . . . . *Rom. and Jul.* ii 4 162

Skein. Braved in mine own house with a skein of thread? *T. of Shrew* iv 3 111
Thou idle immaterial skein of sleave-silk . . . *Troi. and Cres.* v 1 35
Skies. The skies, the fountains, every region near Seem'd all one mutual cry *M. N. Dream* iv 1 121
And heaven's artillery thunder in the skies . . . *T. of Shrew* i 2 205
The skies look grimly And threaten present blusters . . *W. Tale* iii 3 3
The skies are painted with unnumber'd sparks . . . *J. Cæsar* iii 1 63
The wrathful skies Gallow the very wanderers of the dark . *Lear* iii 2 43
Why, thou wert better in thy grave than to answer with thy uncovered body this extremity of the skies . . . . iii 4 107
The great contention of the sea and skies Parted our fellowship *Othello* ii 1 92
Skilful. The skilful shepherd peel'd me certain wands . *Mer. of Venice* i 3 85
He was skilful enough to have lived still . . . . *All's Well* i 1 34
Thy assailant is quick, skilful and deadly . . . *T. Night* iii 4 245
The most skilful, bloody and fatal opposite that you could possibly have found . . . . iii 4 293
For once allow'd the skilful pilot's charge . . . . *3 Hen. VI.* v 4 20
Skilful to their strength, Fierce to their skill . . . *Troi. and Cres.* i 1 7
Dyed in mummy which the skilful Conserved of maidens' hearts *Othello* iii 4 74
Skilfully. Thou art an old love-monger and speakest skilfully *L. L. Lost* ii 1 253
Skill. I'll show my mind According to my shallow simple skill *T. G. of V.* i 2 8
If not, to compass her I'll use my skill . . . . . ii 4 214
The Frenchman hath good skill in his rapier . . . *Mer. Wives* ii 1 231
If I read it not truly, my ancient skill beguiles me . *Meas. for Meas.* iv 2 164
Go you with me, and I will use your skill . . . . *Much Ado* i 2 28
If wounding, then it was to show my skill . . . . *L. L. Lost* iv 1 28
Dart thy skill at me; Bruise me with scorn, confound me with a flout . v 2 396
O that your frowns would teach my smiles such skill! . *M. N. Dream* i 1 195
Touching now the point of human skill, Reason becomes the marshal to my will . . . . ii 2 119
To show our simple skill, That is the true beginning of our end . . v 1 110
And by how much defence is better than no skill . . *As Y. Like It* iii 3 63
Whate'er he be, It skills not much, we'll fit him to our turn *T. of Shrew* iii 2 134
Whose skill was almost as great as his honesty . . . *All's Well* i 1 21
There's something in't, More than my father's skill . . . . i 3 249
This to hazard needs must intimate Skill infinite or monstrous desperate ii 1 187
I have no skill in sense To make distinction . . . . . iii 4 39
I am no great Nebuchadnezzar, sir; I have not much skill in grass . iv 5 22
Into a most hideous opinion of his rage, skill, fury . . *T. Night* iii 4 213
Hath in him what youth, strength, skill and wrath can furnish man withal . . . . iii 4 254
It skills not much when they are delivered . . . . . v 1 295
Or stupified Or seeming so in skill, cannot or will not . . *W. Tale* ii 1 166
You have As little skill to fear as I have purpose To put you to't . iv 4 152
They do confound their skill in covetousness . . . *K. John* iv 2 29
I would my skill were subject to thy curse . . . *Richard II.* iii 4 103
I'll so offend to make offence a skill . . . . . *1 Hen. IV.* i 2 240
Honour hath no skill in surgery, then? no. What is honour? a word . v 1 135
Skill in the weapon is nothing without sack . . . *2 Hen. IV.* iv 3 123
Go, call her in. But first, to try her skill . . . . *1 Hen. VI.* i 2 60
Let thy looks be stern: By this means shall we sound what skill she hath i 2 63
Had I sufficient skill to utter them, Would make a volume . . . v 5 13
It skills not greatly who impugns our doom . . . *2 Hen. VI.* iii 1 281
Skilful to their strength, Fierce to their skill . . . *Troi. and Cres.* i 1 8
Were it a casque composed by Vulcan's skill, My sword should bite it . v 2 170
Meanwhile, sir, with the little skill I have, Full well shalt thou perceive how much I dare . . . . *T. Andron.* ii 1 43
If the measure of thy joy Be heap'd like mine and that thy skill be more To blazon it . . . . *Rom. and Jul.* ii 6 25
Our captain hath in every figure skill, An aged interpreter *T. of Athens* v 3 7
These are the stops.—But these cannot I command to any utterance of harmony; I have not the skill . . . . *Hamlet* iii 2 378
We must, with all our majesty and skill, Both countenance and excuse iv 1 31
Your skill shall, like a star i' the darkest night, Stick fiery off indeed . v 2 267
All the skill I have Remembers not these garments . . . *Lear* iv 7 66
When Julius Cæsar Smiled at their lack of skill, but found their courage Worthy his frowning at . . . . *Cymbeline* ii 4 22
'Tis greater skill In a true hate, to pray they have their will . . ii 5 33
Let him show His skill in the construction . . . . . v 5 433
This Philoten contends in skill With absolute Marina . *Pericles* iv Gower 30
I will use My utmost skill in his recovery . . . . . . v 1 76
Skilled. Gentlemen well skill'd in music . . . . *T. G. of Ver.* iii 2 92
Well skill'd in curses, stay awhile, And teach me how to curse! *Rich. III.* iv 4 116
Thou art deeper read, and better skill'd . . . . *T. Andron.* iv 1 33
Skilless. How features are abroad, I am skilless of . . . *Tempest* iii 1 53
Being skilless in these parts . . . . . . *T. Night* iii 3 9
And skilless as unpractised infancy . . . . *Troi and Cres.* i 1 12
Like powder in a skilless soldier's flask, Is set a-fire *Rom. and Jul.* iii 3 132
Skillet. Let housewives make a skillet of my helm! . . . *Othello* i 3 273
Skim milk, and sometimes labour in the quern . . *M. N. Dream* ii 1 36
O, I could divide myself and go to buffets, for moving such a dish of skim milk! . . . . *1 Hen. IV.* ii 3 36
Skimble-skamble. Such a deal of skimble-skamble stuff . . . iii 1 154
Skin. He'll fill our skins with pinches, Make us strange stuff . *Tempest* iv 1 233
Your hearts are mighty, your skins are whole . . . *Mer. Wives* iii 1 111
A kind of medicine in itself, That skins the vice o' the top *Meas. for Meas.* ii 2 136
Tear the stain'd skin off my harlot-brow . . . *Com. of Errors* ii 2 138
If the skin were parchment and the blows you gave were ink . iii 1 13
He that goes in the calf's skin that was killed for the Prodigal . iv 3 18
Honest as the skin between his brows . . . . . *Much Ado* iii 5 13
There the snake throws her enamell'd skin . . . *M. N. Dream* ii 1 255
What shall he have that kill'd the deer? His leather skin *As Y. Like It* iv 2 12
Is the adder better than the eel, Because his painted skin contents the eye? O, no, good Kate . . . . *T. of Shrew* iv 3 180
As the pudding to his skin . . . . *All's Well* ii 2 29
Put it up again.—Not till I sheathe it in a murderer's skin . *K. John* iv 3 80
We at time of year Do wound the bark, the skin of our fruit-trees *Rich. II.* iii 4 58
My skin hangs about me like an old lady's loose gown . *1 Hen IV.* iii 3 3
The man that once did sell the lion's skin While the beast lived, was killed with hunting him . . . . *Hen. V.* iv 3 93
Throw none away; the skin is good for your broken coxcomb . . v 1 56
Is he a lamb? his skin is surely lent him . . . *2 Hen. VI.* iii 1 77
Show me one scar character'd on thy skin . . . . . iii 1 300
He shall have the skins of our enemies, to make dog's-leather of . iv 2 25
That of the skin of an innocent lamb should be made parchment . . iv 2 86
Here's a deer whose skin's a keeper's fee . . . *3 Hen. VI.* iii 1 22
Digg'd up dead men . . . , And on their skins, as on the bark of trees, Have with my knife carved in Roman letters . . . *T. Andron.* v 1 138
An alligator stuff'd, and other skins Of ill-shaped fishes . *Rom. and Jul.* v 1 43
Here lay Duncan, His silver skin laced with his golden blood *Macbeth* ii 3 118

Skin. It will but skin and film the ulcerous place *Hamlet* iii 4 147
This contentious storm Invades us to the skin *Lear* iii 4 7
That whiter skin of hers than snow, And smooth as monumental alabaster *Othello* v 2 4
Skin-coat. I'll smoke your skin-coat, an I catch you right *K. John* ii 1 139
Skinny. You seem to understand me, By each at once her choppy finger laying Upon her skinny lips *Macbeth* i 3 45
Skip. I would have made you four tall fellows skip like rats *Mer. Wives* ii 1 237
Fairies, skip hence : I have forsworn his bed *M. N. Dream* ii 1 61
A hot temper leaps o'er a cold decree : such a hare is madness the youth, to skip o'er the meshes of good counsel the cripple *Mer. of Venice* i 2 21
Let not thy sword skip one : Pity not honour'd age *T. of Athens* iv 3 110
Will these moss'd trees, That have outlived the eagle, page thy heels, And skip where thou point'st out? iv 3 225
With my good biting falchion, I would have made them skip *Lear* v 3 277
And with a dropping industry they skip From stem to stern *Pericles* iv 1 63
Skipped. I had rather Have skipp'd from sixteen years of age to sixty, To have turn'd my leaping-time into a crutch *Cymbeline* iv 2 199
Skipper, stand back : 'tis age that nourisheth *T. of Shrew* ii 1 341
Skipping. As love is full of unbefitting strains, All wanton as a child, skipping and vain *L. L. Lost* v 2 771
Allay with some cold drops of modesty Thy skipping spirit *Mer. of Ven.* ii 2 196
If you have reason, be brief : 'tis not that time of moon with me to make one in so skipping a dialogue *T. Night* i 5 214
The skipping king, he ambled up and down With shallow jesters 1 *Hen. IV.* iii 2 60
Compell'd these skipping kerns to trust their heels *Macbeth* i 2 30
Skirmish. They never meet but there's a skirmish of wit *Much Ado* i 1 64
None but Samsons and Goliases It sendeth forth to skirmish 1 *Hen. VI.* i 2 34
This city must be famish'd Or with light skirmishes enfeebled i 4 69
Skirr. And make them skirr away, as swift as stones *Hen. V.* iv 7 64
Send out moe horses ; skirr the country round *Macbeth* v 3 35
Skirt. There is but three skirts for yourself *Mer Wives* i 1 29
Skirts, round underborne with a bluish tinsel *Much Ado* iii 4 21
Here in the skirts of the forest, like fringe upon a petticoat *As Y. Like It* iii 2 354
To the skirts of this wild wood he came v 4 165
If ever I said loose-bodied gown, sew me in the skirts of it *T. of Shrew* iv 3 137
Hath in the skirts of Norway here and there Shark'd up a list of lawless resolutes, For food and diet *Hamlet* i 1 97
Skirted. French thrift, you rogues ; myself and skirted page *Mer. Wives* i 3 93
Skittish. Such as I am all true lovers are, Unstaid and skittish *T. Night* ii 4 18
Now expectation, tickling skittish spirits *Troi. and Cres.* Prol. 20
How some men creep in skittish fortune's hall, Whiles others play the idiots! iii 3 134
Skogan. I see him break Skogan's head at the court-gate 2 *Hen. IV.* iii 2 33
Skulking in corners? wishing clocks more swift? *W. Tale* i 2 289
Skull. With a log Batter his skull, or paunch him with a stake *Tempest* iii 2 98
Cure thy brains, Now useless, boil'd within thy skull! v 1 60
The skull that bred them in the sepulchre *Mer. of Venice* iii 2 96
Whose skull Jove cram with brains! *T. Night* i 5 121
Do lie In earth as quiet as thy father's skull *Richard II.* iv 1 69
And this land be call'd The field of Golgotha and dead men's skulls iv 1 144
Some lay in dead men's skulls *Richard III.* i 4 29
And truly I think if all our wits were to issue out of one skull, they would fly east, west, north, south *Coriolanus* ii 3 23
With reeky shanks and yellow chapless skulls *Rom. and Jul.* iv 1 83
What torch is yond, that vainly lends his light To grubs and eyeless skulls? v 3 126
That skull had a tongue in it, and could sing once *Hamlet* v 1 83
Why may not that be the skull of a lawyer? v 1 107
Here's a skull now ; this skull has lain in the earth three and twenty years v 1 190
This same skull, sir, was Yorick's skull, the king's jester v 1 198
Sky. The sky, it seems, would pour down stinking pitch *Tempest* i 2 3
The queen o' the sky, Whose watery arch and messenger am I iv 1 70
The sun begins to gild the western sky *T. G. of Ver.* v 1 1
Let the sky rain potatoes *Mer. Wives* v 5 21
There's nothing situate under heaven's eye But hath his bound, in earth, in sea, in sky *Com. of Errors* ii 1 17
Like a jewel in the ear of caelo, the sky *L. L. Lost* iv 2 5
Like a demigod here sit I in the sky iv 3 79
At the gun's report, Sever themselves and madly sweep the sky *M. N. D.* iii 2 23
Let her shine as gloriously As the Venus of the sky iii 2 107
Now am I dead, Now am I fled ; My soul is in the sky v 1 308
Freeze, freeze, thou bitter sky, That dost not bite so nigh As benefits forgot : Though thou the waters warp *As Y. Like It* ii 7 184
Maids are May when they are maids, but the sky changes when they are wives iv 1 149
The fated sky Gives us free scope, only doth backward pull *All's Well* i 1 232
To your own bents dispose you : you'll be found, Be you beneath the sky *W. Tale* i 2 180
Then the world and all that's in't is nothing ; The covering sky is nothing i 2 294
I am not to say it is a sea, for it is now the sky iii 3 86
Now, by the sky that hangs above our heads, I like it well *K. John* ii 1 397
Some airy devil hovers in the sky And pours down mischief iii 2 2
No natural exhalation in the sky, No scope of nature, no distemper'd day iii 4 153
So foul a sky clears not without a storm iv 2 108
The more fair and crystal is the sky, The uglier seem the clouds *Rich. II.* i 1 41
Men judge by the complexion of the sky The state and inclination of the day iii 2 194
I in the clear sky of fame o'ershine you 2 *Hen. IV.* iv 3 56
Are those stars or suns upon it?—Stars, my lord.—Some of them will fall to-morrow, I hope.—And yet my sky shall not want. *Hen. V.* iii 7 78
Comets, importing change of times and states, Brandish your crystal tresses in the sky! 1 *Hen. VI.* i 1 3
Two Talbots, winged through the lither sky, . . . shall 'scape mortality iv 7 21
When the dusky sky began to rob My earnest-gaping sight 2 *Hen. VI.* iii 2 104
Sever'd in a pale clear-shining sky 3 *Hen. VI.* ii 1 28
Ascend the sky, And there awake God's gentle-sleeping peace *Rich. III.* i 3 287
The sun will not be seen to-day ; The sky doth frown and lour v 3 283
Divides more wider than the sky and earth *Troi. and Cres.* v 2 149
Whose smoke, like incense, doth perfume the sky *T. Andron.* i 1 145
Now, by the burning tapers of the sky, That shone so brightly iv 2 89
This disturb'd sky Is not to walk in *J. Cæsar* i 3 39
The Norweyan banners flout the sky And fan our people cold *Macbeth* i 2 49
With presented nakedness outface The winds and persecutions of the sky *Lear* ii 3 12
Whate'er the ocean pales, or sky inclips, Is thine *Ant. and Cleo.* ii 7 74
A nobler sir ne'er lived 'Twixt sky and ground *Cymbeline* v 5 146
Sky-aspiring and ambitious thoughts *Richard II.* i 3 130

Skyey. A breath thou art, Servile to all the skyey influences *M. for M.* iii 1 9
Skyish. To o'ertop old Pelion, or the skyish head Of blue Olympus *Ham.* v 1 276
Sky-planted. The thunderer, whose bolt, you know, Sky-planted batters all rebelling coasts *Cymbeline* v 4 96
Slab. Make the gruel thick and slab *Macbeth* iv 1 32
Slack. What a beast am I to slack it! *Mer. Wives* iii 4 115
Sir, I shall not be slack *T. of Shrew* i 2 275
If thou be slack, I'll fight it out 1 *Hen. VI.* i 1 99
Being a woman, I will not be slack To play my part in Fortune's pageant 2 *Hen. VI.* i 2 66
The duke shall know how slack thou art *Richard III.* i 4 282
Their negotiations all must slack, Wanting his manage *Troi. and Cres.* iii 3 24
And I am nothing slow to slack his haste *Rom. and Jul.* iv 1 3
If you come slack of former services, You shall do well *Lear* i 3 9
If then they chanced to slack you, We could control them ii 4 248
Husbands' faults If wives do fall : say that they slack their duties *Oth.* iv 3 88
Slack the bolins there! Thou wilt not, wilt thou? *Pericles* iii 1 43
Alack that Leonine was so slack, so slow! He should have struck, not spoke iv 2 68
Slackly. So slackly guarded, and the search so slow *Cymbeline* i 1 64
Slackness. Are as interpreters Of my behind-hand slackness *W. Tale* v 1 151
A good rebuke, Which might have well becomed the best of men, To taunt at slackness *Ant. and Cleo.* iii 7 28
Slain. If thou hast slain Lysander in his sleep, . . . kill me too *M. N. D.* iii 2 47
Hast thou slain him, then? Henceforth be never number'd among men! iii 2 66
And finds his trusty Thisby's mantle slain v 1 146
I am slain by a fair cruel maid *T. Night* ii 4 55
Arthur ta'en prisoner? divers dear friends slain? *K. John* iii 4 7
Here : what news?—The Count Melun is slain v 5 10
Though thou livest and breathest, Yet art thou slain in him *Richard II.* i 2 25
The death of kings : How some have been deposed ; some slain in war iii 2 157
Fear, and be slain ; no worse can come to fight iii 2 183
Whether they be ta'en or slain we hear not v 6 4
Of prisoners' ransom and of soldiers slain 1 *Hen. IV.* ii 3 57
Three knights upon our party slain to-day, A noble earl v 5 6
The noble Percy slain, and all his men Upon the foot of fear v 5 19
Prince Harry slain outright ; and both the Blunts Kill'd 2 *Hen. IV.* i 1 16
If he be slain, say so ; The tongue offends not that reports his death i 1 96
Had three times slain the appearance of the king i 1 128
Ten thousand French That in the field lie slain *Hen. V.* iv 8 86
Is Talbot slain? then I will slay myself, For living idly here 1 *Hen. VI.* i 1 141
Slain our citizens And sent our sons and husbands captivate ii 3 41
Too late comes rescue : he is ta'en or slain ; For fly he could not iv 4 42
Fly, to revenge my death, if I be slain.—He that flies so will ne'er return iv 5 18
You cannot witness for me, being slain iv 5 43
Is Talbot slain, the Frenchmen's only scourge, Your kingdom's terror? iv 7 77
All will be ours, now bloody Talbot's slain iv 7 96
I meant Maine, Which I will win from France, or else be slain 2 *Hen. VI.* i 1 213
But Jove was never slain, as thou shalt be iv 1 49
Picardy Hath slain their governors, surprised our forts iv 1 89
Is Jack Cade slain?—No, my lord, nor likely to be slain iv 5 1
O, I am slain! famine and no other hath slain me iv 10 64
Is't Cade that I have slain, that monstrous traitor? iv 10 71
Were by the swords of common soldiers slain 3 *Hen. VI.* i 1 9
Buckingham Is either slain or wounded dangerously i 1 11
But when the duke is slain, they'll quickly fly i 1 69
Lest in revenge thereof, sith God is just, He be as miserably slain as I i 3 42
My uncles both are slain in rescuing me i 4 2
Had he been slain, we should have heard the news ii 1 5
One that was a woful looker-on When as the noble Duke of York was slain ii 1 46
In the harmless blood Of sweet young Rutland, by rough Clifford slain ii 1 63
Boisterous Clifford! thou hast slain The flower of Europe for his chivalry ii 1 70
The Duke of York is slain!—O Warwick, Warwick! ii 1 100
Sir Richard Grey was slain, His lands then seized on by the conqueror iii 2 2
Then is my sovereign slain?—Ay, almost slain, for he is taken prisoner iv 4 6
His subjects slain, His statutes cancell'd and his treasure spent v 4 78
Then he is alive.—Nay, he is dead ; and slain by Edward's hand *Rich. III.* i 2 92
Was not your husband In Margaret's battle at Saint Alban's slain? i 3 130
Tell him what I say ; For I repent me that the duke is slain i 4 285
You speak as if that I had slain my cousins.—Cousins, indeed iv 4 221
If thou hadst fear'd to break an oath by Him, The unity the king thy brother made Had not been broken, nor my brother slain iv 4 380
You sleep in peace, the tyrant being slain v 3 256
His horse is slain, and all on foot he fights, Seeking for Richmond v 4 4
I think there be six Richmonds in the field ; Five have I slain to-day v 4 12
What men of name are slain on either side? v 5 12
For every scruple Of her [Helen's] contaminated carrion weight, A Trojan hath been slain *Troi. and Cres.* iv 1 72
Polyxenes is slain, Amphimachus and Thoas deadly hurt, Patroclus, ta'en or slain, and Palamedes Sore hurt v 5 11
And cry you all amain, 'Achilles hath the mighty Hector slain' v 8 14
Hector's slain! Achilles!—The bruit is, Hector's slain v 9 3
Hector is slain.—Hector! the gods forbid!—He's dead v 10 3
What is become of Marcius?—Slain, sir, doubtless *Coriolanus* i 4 48
As with a man by his own alms empoison'd, And with his charity slain v 6 12
And patient fools, Whose children he hath slain, their base throats tear With giving him glory v 6 53
And sleep in peace, slain in your country's wars! *T. Andron.* i 1 91
And for their brethren slain Religiously they ask a sacrifice i 1 123
Slain manfully in arms, In right and service of their noble country i 1 196
In wrongful quarrel you have slain your son i 1 293
O, see what thou hast done! In a bad quarrel slain a virtuous son i 1 342
Here none but soldiers . . . Repose in fame : none basely slain in brawls i 1 353
'Tis not life that I have begg'd so long ; Poor I was slain when Bassianus died ii 3 171
Why hast thou slain thine only daughter thus? v 3 55
Alive, in triumph! and Mercutio slain! Away to heaven! *Rom. and Jul.* iii 1 127
Away, be gone! The citizens are up, and Tybalt slain iii 1 138
There lies the man, slain by young Romeo, That slew thy kinsman iii 1 149
Ere I Could draw to part them, was stout Tybalt slain iii 1 178
Hath Romeo slain himself? say thou but 'I' iii 2 45
If he be slain, say 'I'; or if not, no : Brief sounds determine of my weal or woe iii 2 50
My husband lives, that Tybalt would have slain ; And Tybalt's dead, that would have slain my husband iii 2 105
That one word 'banished' Hath slain ten thousand Tybalts iii 2 114
'Romeo is banished,' to speak that word, Is father, mother, Tybalt, Romeo, Juliet, All slain, all dead iii 2 124

Slain. Hast thou slain Tybalt? wilt thou slay thyself? And slay thy lady too? . . . . *Rom. and Jul.* iii 3 116
Tybalt being slain so late, It may be thought we held him carelessly . iii 4 24
Beguiled, divorced, wronged, spited, slain! . . . . iv 5 55
O, I am slain! If thou be merciful, Open the tomb, lay me with Juliet v 3 72
Here lies the County Paris slain; And Romeo dead . . . v 3 195
And slain in fight many of your enemies . . . . *T. of Athens* iii 5 64
Titinius' face is upward.—He is slain . . . . *J. Cæsar* v 3 93
But, my lord, He came not back: he is or ta'en or slain . . v 5 3
Who did this . . . ?—Those that Macbeth hath slain . *Macbeth* ii 4 23
This avarice . . . hath been The sword of our slain kings . . iv 3 87
If thou be'st slain and with no stroke of mine, My wife and children's ghosts will haunt me still . . . . v 7 15
O, I am slain!—O me, what hast thou done? . . . *Hamlet* iii 4 24
Hamlet in madness hath Polonius slain . . . . . iv 1 34
Fight for a plot . . . Which is not tomb enough and continent To hide the slain . . . . iv 4 65
First, her father slain: Next, your son gone . . . . iv 5 79
He which hath your noble father slain Pursued my life . . . iv 7 4
Hamlet, thou art slain; No medicine in the world can do thee good . v 2 324
O, I am slain! My lord, you have one eye left . . . *Lear* iii 7 81
The Duke of Cornwall's dead; Slain by his servant . . . iv 2 71
Slave, thou hast slain me: villain, take my purse . . . iv 6 252
Holds it true, sir, that the Duke of Cornwall was so slain? . . iv 7 86
Though in the trade of war I have slain men, Yet do I hold it very stuff o' the conscience To do no contrived murder . *Othello* i 2 1
O, I am slain!—I am maim'd for ever. Help, ho! murder! . . v 1 26
He that lies slain here, Cassio, Was my dear friend . . . v 1 101
He's almost slain, and Roderigo dead.—Alas, good gentleman! . . v 1 114
Here is a letter Found in the pocket of the slain Roderigo . . v 2 309
And he wept When at Philippi he found Brutus slain . *Ant. and Cleo.* iii 2 56
Wars 'twixt you twain would be As if the world should cleave, and that slain men Should solder up the rift . . . . . iii 4 31
Go tell him I have slain myself . . . . iv 13 7
When I have slain thee with my proper hand, I'll follow those *Cymb.* iv 2 97
A very valiant Briton and a good, That here by mountaineers lies slain iv 2 370
I heard no letter from my master since I wrote him Imogen was slain . iv 3 37
Some slain before; some dying; some their friends O'er-borne . . v 3 47
That striking in our country's cause Fell bravely and were slain . v 4 72
Here they stand martyrs, slain in Cupid's wars . . *Pericles* i 1 38
If she remain, Whom they have ravish'd must by me be slain . . iv 1 103
Slake. It could not slake mine ire, nor ease my heart . 3 *Hen. VI.* i 3 29
Slander. The best way is to slander Valentine . . *T. G. of Ver.* iii 2 31
Then you must undertake to slander him . . . . . iii 2 38
Where your good word cannot advantage him, Your slander never can endamage him; Therefore the office is indifferent . . . iii 2 43
And yet my nature never in the fight To do in slander . *Meas. for Meas.* i 3 43
If he took you a box o' the ear, you might have your action of slander . ii 1 190
Did you set these women on to slander Lord Angelo? . . . v 1 290
Slander to the state! Away with him to prison! . . . . v 1 325
Thy slanders I forgive; and therewithal Remit thy other forfeits . . v 1 525
Slander lives upon succession, For ever housed where it gets possession *Com. of Errors* iii 1 105
Free from these slanders and this open shame . . . . . iv 4 70
A very dull fool; only his gift is in devising impossible slanders *M. Ado* ii 1 144
Tax not so bad a voice To slander music any more than once . . ii 3 47
I'll devise some honest slanders To stain my cousin with . . . iii 1 84
My villany, which did confirm any slander . . . . . iii 3 169
This well carried shall on her behalf Change slander to remorse . . iv 1 213
With public accusation, uncovered slander, unmitigated rancour . . iv 1 307
Thy slander hath gone through and through her heart . . . v 1 68
Fashion-monging boys, That lie and cog and flout, deprave and slander . v 1 95
Moreover, they have spoken untruths; secondarily, they are slanders . v 1 221
Your brother incensed me to slander the Lady Hero . . . . v 1 243
She died, my lord, but whiles her slander lived . . . . v 4 66
Did pretty Jessica, like a little shrew, Slander her love . *Mer. of Venice* v 1 22
Such as you are fain to be beholding to your wives for: but he comes armed in his fortune and prevents the slander of his wife *As Y. L. It* iv 1 61
There is no slander in an allowed fool . . . *T. Night* i 5 101
Slander, Whose sting is sharper than the sword's . . *W. Tale* ii 3 85
Bid his ears a little while be deaf, Till I have told this slander *Rich. II.* i 1 113
Pierced to the soul with slander's venom'd spear . . . . i 1 171
A partial slander sought I to avoid . . . . . . i 3 241
Thou hast wrought A deed of slander with thy fatal hand Upon my head v 6 35
He slanders thee most grossly.—So he doth you . 1 *Hen. IV.* iii 3 150
You speak it out of fear and cold heart.—Do me no slander, Douglas . iv 3 8
Upon my [Rumour's] tongues continual slanders ride . 2 *Hen. IV.* Ind. 6
You must learn to know such slanders of the age . . *Hen. V.* iii 6 84
So shall my name with slander's tongue be wounded . 2 *Hen. VI.* iii 2 68
That slanders me with murder's crimson badge . . . . iii 2 200
Every word you speak in his behalf Is slander to your royal dignity . iii 2 209
And bite thy tongue, that slanders him with cowardice . 3 *Hen. VI.* i 4 47
Either not believe The envious slanders of her false accusers *Richard III.* i 3 26
Thou slander of thy mother's heavy womb! . . . . . i 3 231
Do not slander him, for he is kind.—Right, As snow in harvest . . i 4 247
For more slander to thy dismal seat, We give thee up our guiltless blood iii 3 13
Slander myself as false to Edward's bed . . . . . iv 4 207
That slander, sir, Is found a truth now . . . *Hen. VIII.* ii 1 153
Whose gall coins slanders like a mint . . . *Troi. and Cres.* i 3 193
You slander The helms o' the state, who care for you like fathers, When you curse them as enemies . . . . . *Coriolanus* i 1 78
My reputation stain'd With Tybalt's slander . . *Rom. and Jul.* iii 1 117
That is no slander, sir, which is a truth . . . . . iv 1 33
I would not, in plain terms, from this time forth, Have you so slander any moment leisure . . . . *Hamlet* i 3 133
Slanders, sir: for the satirical rogue says here that old men have grey beards ii 2 198
When slanders do not live in tongues . . . . . *Lear* iii 2 87
If thou dost slander her and torture me, Never pray more . *Othello* iii 3 368
The purest of their wives Is foul as slander . . . . iv 2 19
If some . . . cozening slave, to get some office, Have not devised this slander . . . . iv 2 133
There is never a fair woman has a true face.—No slander *Ant. and Cleo.* ii 6 106
No, be assured you shall not find me, daughter, After the slander of most stepmothers . . . . *Cymbeline* i 1 71
Revenges, hers [woman's]; Ambitions, covetings, . . . slanders, mutability . . . . ii 5 26
'Tis slander, Whose edge is sharper than the sword . . . . iii 4 35
Maids, matrons, nay, the secrets of the grave This viperous slander enters iii 4 41
Slanders so her judgement That what's else rare is choked . . iii 5 76
The leaf of eglantine, whom not to slander, Out-sweeten'd not thy breath iv 2 223

Slander. Fear not slander, censure rash;—Thou hast finish'd joy and moan . . . . *Cymbeline* iv 2 272
Slandered. Cruel as the sentence That you have slander'd so . *M. for M.* ii 4 110
A villain, that hath slandered, scorned, dishonoured my kinswoman *Much Ado* iv 1 304
She is wronged, she is slandered, she is undone . . . . iv 1 315
She is dead, slander'd to death by villains . . . . . v 1 88
But once he slander'd me with bastardy . . . . *K. John* i 1 74
And you have slander'd nature in my form . . . . . iv 2 256
Let not him be slander'd with revolt . . . . 1 *Hen. IV.* i 3 112
Thy face is mine, and thou hast slander'd it . . *Rom. and Jul.* iv 1 35
Slanderer. Stir not you till you have well determined Upon these slanderers . . . . *Meas. for Meas.* v 1 259
Thou monstrous slanderer of heaven and earth!—Thou monstrous injurer of heaven and earth! Call not me slanderer . . *K. John* ii 1 173
Awkward action, Which, slanderer, he imitation calls . *Troi. and Cres.* i 3 150
O, fie upon thee, slanderer!—Nay, it is true . . . *Othello* ii 1 114
Slandering a prince deserves it [hanging] . . . *Meas. for Meas.* v 1 530
Slanderous. And one that is as slanderous as Satan? . *Mer. Wives* v 5 163
What king so strong Can tie the gall up in the slanderous tongue? *Meas. for Meas.* iii 2 199
Done to death by slanderous tongues . . . . . *Much Ado* v 3 3
O slanderous world! . . . . *T. of Shrew* ii 1 255
Ugly and slanderous to thy mother's womb . . . . *K. John* iii 1 44
I spit at him; Call him a slanderous coward and a villain . *Richard II.* i 1 61
Mine honour soil'd With the attainder of his slanderous lips . . iv 1 24
I was provoked by her slanderous tongue . . . . *Richard III.* i 2 97
To ease ourselves of divers slanderous loads . . . *J. Cæsar* iv 1 20
Hath as oft a slanderous epitaph As record of fair act . *Cymbeline* iii 3 52
Slash. I'll slash; I'll do it by the sword . . . . *L. L. Lost* v 2 701
Here's snip and nip and cut and slish and slash . . *T. of Shrew* iv 3 90
Slaughter. Hang'd for human slaughter . . . *Mer. of Venice* iv 1 134
One good deed dying tongueless Slaughters a thousand waiting *W. Tale* i 2 93
With purpled hands, Dyed in the dying slaughter of their foes *K. John* ii 1 323
With slaughter coupled to the name of kings . . . . ii 1 349
They were besmear'd and overstain'd With slaughter's pencil . . iii 1 237
Wherein you would have sold your king to slaughter . . *Hen. V.* ii 2 170
The cowardly rascals that ran from the battle ha' done this slaughter . iv 7 7
Sad tidings bring I to you out of France, Of loss, of slaughter 1 *Hen. VI.* i 1 59
After the slaughter of so many peers, So many captains . . . v 4 103
Such massacre And ruthless slaughters as are daily seen . . . v 4 161
Will suspect 'twas he that made the slaughter . . 2 *Hen. VI.* iii 2 190
I wear no knife to slaughter sleeping men . . . . . iii 2 197
How will my wife for slaughter of my son Shed seas of tears! 3 *Hen. VI.* ii 5 105
I say not, slaughter him, For I intend but only to surprise him . . iv 2 24
For this, amongst the rest, was I ordain'd.—Ay, and for much more slaughter after this . . . . v 6 59
By despairing, shouldst thou stand excused; For doing worthy vengeance on thyself, Which didst unworthy slaughter upon others *Richard III.* i 2 88
Our duty, and thy fault, Provoke us hither now to slaughter thee . . i 4 231
'Tis he that sent us hither now to slaughter thee.—It cannot be . . i 4 250
Your carters or your waiting-vassals Have done a drunken slaughter . ii 1 122
From all the slaughters, wretch, that thou hast done! . . . iv 4 139
The slaughter of the prince that owed that crown . . . . iv 4 142
So she may live unscarr'd of bleeding slaughter . . . . iv 4 209
I have dream'd Of bloody turbulence, and this whole night Hath nothing been but shapes and forms of slaughter . . . *Troi. and Cres.* v 3 12
Till another Cæsar Have added slaughter to the sword of traitors . *J. C.* v 1 55
Naught that I am, Not for their own demerits, but for mine, Fell slaughter on their souls . . . . *Macbeth* iv 3 227
Thereabout of it especially, where he speaks of Priam's slaughter *Hamlet* ii 2 469
Accidental judgements, casual slaughters . . . . . . v 2 393
And such a daughter, Should sure to the slaughter . . . *Lear* i 4 342
Lads more like to run The country base than to commit such slaughter *Cymbeline* v 3 20
Great the slaughter is Here made by the Roman; great the answer be . v 3 78
Their good souls may be appeased with slaughter . . . . v 5 72
That her daughter Might stand peerless by this slaughter *Pericles* iv Gower 40
Such a piece of slaughter The sun and moon ne'er look'd upon! . . iv 3 2
She was of Tyrus the king's daughter, On whom foul death hath made this slaughter . . . . iv 4 37
Slaughtered. What, shall our feast be kept with slaughter'd men? *K. John* iii 1 302
In suffering thus thy brother to be slaughter'd, Thou showest the naked pathway to thy life . . . . *Richard II.* i 2 30
Showers of blood Rain'd from the wounds of slaughter'd Englishmen . iii 3 44
Here is the number of the slaughter'd French . . . . *Hen. V.* iv 8 79
Most of the rest slaughter'd or took likewise . . . 1 *Hen. VI.* i 1 147
All will fight And have our bodies slaughter'd by thy foes . . . iii 1 101
Slaughter'd by the ireful arm Of unrelenting Clifford . . 3 *Hen. VI.* ii 1 57
What of him? Our slaughter'd friends the tackles; what of these? . v 4 15
Poor Anne, Wife to thy Edward, to thy slaughter'd son . *Richard III.* i 2 10
The children live, whose parents thou hast slaughter'd, Ungovern'd youth . . . . iv 4 391
And slaughter'd those that were the means to help him . . . v 3 249
The father rashly slaughter'd his own son . . . . . . v 5 25
But must my sons be slaughter'd in the streets, For valiant doings in their country's cause? . . . . *T. Andron.* i 1 112
All on a heap, like to a slaughter'd lamb . . . . . . ii 3 223
Is Romeo slaughter'd, and is Tybalt dead? . . . *Rom. and Jul.* iii 2 65
Well, girl, thou weep'st not so much for his death, As that the villain lives which slaughter'd him . . . . iii 5 80
To wreak the love I bore my cousin Upon his body that hath slaughter'd him . . . . iii 5 103
I'll bury thee in a triumphant grave; A grave? O, no! a lantern, slaughter'd youth, For here lies Juliet . . . . v 3 84
Here is a friar, and slaughter'd Romeo's man; With instruments upon them . . . . v 3 199
Your castle is surprised; your wife and babes Savagely slaughter'd *Macbeth* iv 3 205
Slaughterer. Thou dost then wrong me, as that slaughterer doth Which giveth many wounds when one will kill . . . 1 *Hen. VI.* ii 5 109
Slaughter-house. The uncleanly savours of a slaughter-house *K. John* iv 3 112
Bearing it to the bloody slaughter-house . . . 2 *Hen. VI.* iii 1 212
Thou behavedst thyself as if thou hadst been in thine own slaughter-house . . . . iv 3 6
His state usurp'd, His realm a slaughter-house . . 3 *Hen. VI.* v 4 78
As loath to bear me to the slaughter-house . . . *Richard III.* iii 4 88
Hie thee from this slaughter-house, Lest thou increase the number of the dead . . . . iv 1 44

Slaughtering. Hold your slaughtering hands and keep the peace *1 Hen. VI.* iii 1 87
To be adjudged some direful slaughtering death, As punishment *T. An.* v 3 144
The enemy full-hearted, Lolling the tongue with slaughtering *Cymbeline* v 3 8
Slaughter-man. Herod's bloody-hunting slaughtermen *Hen. V.* iii 3 41
Had he been slaughter-man to all my kin, I should not for my life but weep with him *3 Hen. VI.* i 4 169
For this proud mock I'll be thy slaughter-man *T. Andron.* iv 4 58
Ten, chased by one, Are now each one the slaughter-man of twenty *Cymbeline* v 3 49
And join'st with them will be thy slaughter-men *1 Hen. VI.* iii 3 75
Slaughterous. Direness, familiar to my slaughterous thoughts, Cannot once start me *Macbeth* v 5 14
Slave. Thou, my slave, As thou report'st thyself, wast then her servant *Tempest* i 2 270
We'll visit Caliban my slave, who never Yields us kind answer . i 2 308
What, ho! slave! Caliban! Thou earth, thou! speak . i 2 313
Thou poisonous slave, got by the devil himself Upon thy wicked dam! i 2 319
Thou most lying slave, Whom stripes may move, not kindness! . i 2 344
Abhorred slave, Which any print of goodness wilt not take! . i 2 351
The very instant that I saw you, did My heart fly to your service; there resides, To make me slave to it . iii 1 66
And slaves they are to me that send them flying *T. G. of Ver.* iii 1 141
Go, base intruder! overweening slave! . iii 1 157
An unmannerly slave, that will thrust himself into secrets! . iii 1 393
A slave, that still an end turns me to shame! . iv 4 67
Do you think there is truth in them?—Hang 'em, slaves! *Mer. Wives* ii 1 179
Thy mistress' marks? what mistress, slave, hast thou? *Com. of Errors* i 2 87
Go seek this slave: I greatly fear my money is not safe . i 2 104
Neither my husband nor the slave return'd! . ii 1 1
Go back again, thou slave, and fetch him home . ii 1 75
Back, slave, or I will break thy pate across . ii 1 78
The heedful slave Is wander'd forth, in care to seek me out . ii 2 2
How ill agrees it with your gravity To counterfeit thus grossly with your slave! . ii 2 171
Thou drunken slave, I sent thee for a rope . iv 1 96
Hie thee, slave, be gone! On, officer, to prison till it come . iv 1 107
This pernicious slave, Forsooth, took on him as a conjurer . v 1 241
Art thou the slave that with thy breath hast kill'd Mine innocent child?—Yea, even I alone *Much Ado* v 1 273
He throws upon the gross world's baser slaves *L. L. Lost* i 1 30
Come, you transgressing slave; away!—Let me not be pent up, sir . i 2 159
Stay, slave; I must employ thee . iii 1 152
It must be done this afternoon. Hark, slave, it is but this . iii 1 164
Many a purchased slave, Which, like your asses and your dogs and mules, You use in abject and in slavish parts *Mer. of Venice* iv 1 90
You will answer 'The slaves are ours:' so do I answer you . iv 1 98
And I to live and die her slave *As Y. Like It* iii 2 162
Let me be a slave, to achieve that maid *T. of Shrew* i 1 224
Wrong me not, nor wrong yourself, To make a bondmaid and a slave of me . ii 1 2
You heedless joltheads and unmanner'd slaves! . iv 1 169
Get thee gone, thou false deluding slave . iv 3 31
The mere word's a slave Debosh'd on every tomb *All's Well* ii 3 144
What a past-saving slave is this! . iv 3 159
What of him? He's quoted for a most perfidious slave . v 3 205
I hate thee, Pronounce thee a gross lout, a mindless slave *W. Tale* i 2 301
We profess Ourselves to be the slaves of chance . iv 4 551
Where is that slave, thy brother? *K. John* i 1 222
Thou slave, thou wretch, thou coward! Thou little valiant! . iii 1 115
Thou cold-blooded slave, Hast thou not spoke like thunder on my side? iii 1 123
It is the curse of kings to be attended By slaves . iv 2 209
Am I Rome's slave? What penny hath Rome borne? . v 2 97
What reverence he did throw away on slaves *Richard II.* i 4 27
There I'll pine away; A king, woe's slave, shall kingly woe obey . iii 2 210
Made glory base and sovereignty a slave, Proud majesty a subject . iv 1 251
Treason! foul treason! Villain! traitor! slave!—What is the matter? v 2 72
They are not the first of fortune's slaves, Nor shall not be the last . v 5 24
What a slave art thou, to hack thy sword as thou hast done, and then say it was in fight! *1 Hen. IV.* ii 4 288
Such a commodity of warm slaves, as had as lieve hear the devil as a drum . iv 2 19
Slaves as ragged as Lazarus in the painted cloth . iv 2 27
But thought's the slave of life, and life time's fool . v 4 81
You a captain! you slave, for what? *2 Hen. IV.* ii 4 156
A rascally slave! I will toss the rogue in a blanket . ii 4 240
A rascal bragging slave! the rogue fled from me like quicksilver . ii 4 247
Base is the slave that pays *Hen. V.* ii 1 100
Not all these, laid in bed majestical, Can sleep so soundly as the wretched slave, Who with a body fill'd and vacant mind Gets him to rest . iv 1 285
The slave, a member of the country's peace, Enjoys it . iv 1 298
Come hither, boy: ask me this slave in French What is his name . iv 4 24
Whilst by a slave, no gentler than my dog, His fairest daughter is contaminated . iv 5 15
Let's leave this town; for they are hare-brain'd slaves *1 Hen. VI.* i 2 37
You fly from your oft-subdued slaves . i 5 32
To make a bastard and a slave of me! . iv 5 15
To be a queen in bondage is more vile Than is a slave in base servility . v 3 113
Base slave, thy words are blunt and so art thou *2 Hen. VI.* iv 1 67
A Roman sworder and banditto slave Murder'd sweet Tully . iv 1 135
As for these silken-coated slaves, I pass not . iv 2 136
Dead they are, and, devilish slave, by thee *Richard III.* i 2 90
Seal'd in thy nativity The slave of nature and the son of hell! . i 3 230
Have I a tongue to doom my brother's death, And shall the same give pardon to a slave? . ii 1 103
Tell me, thou villain slave, where are my children? . iv 4 144
Slave, I have set my life upon a cast, And I will stand the hazard . v 4 9
This tractable obedience is a slave To each incensed will *Hen. VIII.* i 2 64
Ye rude slaves, leave your gaping . v 4 3
A slave whose gall coins slanders like a mint *Troi. and Cres.* i 3 193
Thou art bought and sold among those of any wit, like a barbarian slave ii 1 52
The desire is boundless and the act a slave to limit . iii 2 90
Turn, slave, and fight.—What art thou? . v 7 13
I'ld make a quarry With thousands of these quarter'd slaves *Coriolanus* i 1 203
How have you run From slaves that apes would beat! . i 4 36
These base slaves, Ere yet the fight be done, pack up . i 5 8
Where is that slave Which told me they had beat you to your trenches? i 6 39
Let the first budger die the other's slave, And the gods doom him after! i 8 5
And suffer'd me by the voice of slaves to be Whoop'd out of Rome . iv 5 83
Slave. O slaves, I can tell you news,—news, you rascals! *Coriolanus* iv 5 181
Worthy tribunes, There is a slave, whom we have put in prison . iv 6 38
'Tis this slave;—Go whip him 'fore the people's eyes . iv 6 59
The slave's report is seconded; and more, More fearful, is deliver'd iv 6 62
Boy! O slave! Pardon me, lords, 'tis the first time that ever I was forced to scold . v 6 104
Look, how the black slave smiles upon the father *T. Andron.* iv 2 120
Come on, you thick-lipp'd slave, I'll bear you hence . iv 2 175
Peace, tawny slave, half me and half thy dam! . v 1 27
Say, wall-eyed slave, whither wouldst thou convey This growing image of thy fiend-like face? . v 1 44
Away, inhuman dog! unhallow'd slave! . v 3 14
That shows thee a weak slave; for the weakest goes to the wall *R. and J.* i 1 17
What dares the slave Come hither, cover'd with an antic face? . i 5 57
Meantime forbear, And let mischance be slave to patience . v 3 221
To present slaves and servants Translates his rivals *T. of Athens* i 1 71
How many prodigal bits have slaves and peasants This night englutted! ii 2 174
This slave, Unto his honour, has my lord's meat in him . iii 1 59
They have e'en put my breath from me, the slaves. Creditors? devils! iii 4 104
You fools of fortune, trencher-friends, time's flies, Cap and knee slaves! iii 6 107
Slaves and fools, Pluck the grave wrinkled senate from the bench! . iv 1 4
This yellow slave [gold] Will knit and break religions, bless the accursed . iv 3 33
Season the slaves For tubs and baths; bring down rose-cheeked youth iv 3 85
Thou art a slave, whom Fortune's tender arm With favour never clasp'd iv 3 250
Beast!—Slave!—Toad!—Rogue, rogue, rogue! . iv 3 375
O thou touch of hearts [gold]! Think, thy slave man rebels . iv 3 391
'Tis thou [gold] that . . . Settlest admired reverence in a slave . v 1 54
Hence, pack! there's gold; you came for gold, ye slaves . v 1 115
A common slave—you know him well by sight *J. Cæsar* i 3 15
Had you rather Cæsar were living and die all slaves, than that Cæsar were dead, to live all free men? . iii 2 25
Go show your slaves how choleric you are, And make your bondmen tremble . iv 3 43
Carved out his passage Till he faced the slave *Macbeth* i 2 20
Fly, good Fleance, fly, fly, fly! Thou mayst revenge. O slave! . iii 3 18
That were the slaves of drink and thralls of sleep . iii 6 13
Liar and slave!—Let me endure your wrath, if't be not so . v 5 35
Now I am alone. O, what a rogue and peasant slave am I! *Hamlet* ii 2 576
Ere this I should have fatted all the region kites With this slave's offal . ii 2 608
Give me that man That is not passion's slave, and I will wear him In my heart's core, ay, in my heart of heart . iii 2 77
Purpose is but the slave to memory, Of violent birth, but poor validity iii 2 198
A slave that is not twentieth part the tithe Of your precedent lord . iii 4 97
Why came not the slave back to me when I called him? *Lear* i 4 56
You whoreson dog! you slave! you cur!—I am none of these, my lord i 4 89
Superserviceable, finical rogue; one-trunk-inheriting slave . ii 2 20
Strike, you slave; stand, rogue, stand; you neat slave, strike . ii 2 45
That such a slave as this should wear a sword, Who wears no honesty . ii 2 78
This is a slave, whose easy-borrow'd pride Dwells in the fickle grace of her he follows . ii 4 188
Persuade me rather to be slave and sumpter To this detested groom . ii 4 219
Here I stand, your slave, A poor, infirm, weak, and despised old man . iii 2 19
Turn out that eyeless villain; throw this slave Upon the dunghill . iii 7 96
The superfluous and lust-dieted man, That slaves your ordinance . iv 1 71
Let go, slave, or thou diest!—Good gentleman, go your gait . iv 6 241
Slave, thou hast slain me: villain, take my purse . iv 6 252
And did him service Improper for a slave . v 3 221
I kill'd the slave that was a-hanging thee . v 3 274
Pardon me: Though I am bound to every act of duty, I am not bound to that all slaves are free to *Othello* iii 3 135
'Twas mine, 'tis his, and has been slave to thousands . iii 3 158
O, that the slave had forty thousand lives! One is too poor, too weak iii 3 442
Some cogging, cozening slave, to get some office . iv 2 132
O murderous slave! O villain!—O damn'd Iago! O inhuman dog! . v 1 61
I'll after that same villain, For 'tis a damn'd slave . v 2 243
O cursed slave! Whip me, ye devils, From the possession of this heavenly sight! . v 2 276
O thou Othello, that wert once so good, Fall'n in the practice of a damned slave, What shall be said to thee? . v 2 292
For this slave, If there be any cunning cruelty That can torment him v 2 332
To sit And keep the turn of tippling with a slave *Ant. and Cleo.* i 4 19
Call the slave again: Though I am mad, I will not bite him . ii 5 79
O slave, of no more trust Than love that's hired! . v 2 154
Slave, soulless villain, dog! O rarely base! . v 2 157
Mechanic slaves With greasy aprons, rules, and hammers . v 2 209
A base slave, A hilding for a livery, a squire's cloth *Cymbeline* ii 3 127
What slave art thou?—A thing More slavish did I ne'er than answering A slave without a knock . iv 2 72
To be still hot summer's tanlings and The shrinking slaves of winter . iv 4 30
Forthwith they fly . . . slaves, The strides they victors made . v 3 42
Slave-like. Why this spade? this place? This slave-like habit? and these looks of care? *T. of Athens* iv 3 205
Slaver with lips as common as the stairs That mount the Capitol *Cymbeline* i 6 105
Slavery. Would no more endure This wooden slavery . *Tempest* iii 1 62
Dastards, and delight to live in slavery to the nobility *2 Hen. VI.* iv 8 29
And free us from his slavery.—We had need pray *Hen. VIII.* ii 2 44
Of being taken by the insolent foe And sold to slavery . *Othello* i 3 138
Slavish. You use in abject and in slavish parts . *Mer. of Venice* iv 1 92
My teeth shall tear The slavish motive of recanting fear . *Richard II.* i 1 193
If then we shall shake off our slavish yoke . ii 1 291
Away with slavish weeds and servile thoughts! *T. Andron.* ii 1 18
What slave art thou?—A thing More slavish did I ne'er than answering A slave without a knock . *Cymbeline* iv 2 73
Slay. The one I'll slay, the other slayeth me *M. N. Dream* ii 1 190
What impossibility would slay In common sense, sense saves another way *All's Well* ii 1 180
Then I will slay myself, For living idly here in pomp and ease *1 Hen. VI.* i 1 141
Be thou cursed Cain, To slay thy brother Abel, if thou wilt . i 3 40
I will not slay thee, but I'll drive thee back . i 5 3
Except you mean with obstinate repulse To slay your sovereign . iii 1 114
To save a paltry life and slay bright fame . iv 6 45
And do not stand on quillets how to slay him . *2 Hen. VI.* iii 1 261
I never did thee harm: why wilt thou slay me? . *3 Hen. VI.* i 3 38
I'll slay more gazers than the basilisk . iii 2 187
O, 'twas the foulest deed to slay that babe! *Richard III.* i 3 183
Are you call'd forth from out a world of men To slay the innocent? . i 4 187
Then know me not, Lest that thy wives with spits and boys with stones In puny battle slay me . *Coriolanus* iv 4 6

Slay. I'll enter: if he slay me, He does fair justice . . . *Coriolanus* iv 4 24
With his own hand did slay his youngest son . . . *T. Andron.* i 1 418
Resolve me this: Was it well done of rash Virginius To slay his daughter with his own right hand? . . . . . . v 3 37
Being tasted, slays all senses with the heart . . *Rom. and Jul.* ii 3 26
Who began this bloody fray?—Tybalt, here slain, whom Romeo's hand did slay. . . . . . iii 1 157
Wilt thou slay thyself? And slay thy lady too that lives in thee? . iii 3 116
Ere this hand, by thee to Romeo seal'd, Shall be the label to another deed, Or my true heart with treacherous revolt Turn to another, this shall slay them both . . . . . iv 1 59
If, rather than to marry County Paris, Thou hast the strength of will to slay thyself . . . . . iv 1 72
Trust not the physician; His antidotes are poison, and he slays Moe than you rob: take wealth and lives together . *T. of Athens* iv 3 435
Cassius or Cæsar never shall turn back, For I will slay myself *J. Cæsar* iii 1 22
Revenge! About! Seek! Burn! Fire! Kill! Slay! . . . iii 2 209
Our valiant Hamlet . . . Did slay this Fortinbras . *Hamlet* i 1 86
This way, the Romans Must or for Britons slay us, or receive us For barbarous and unnatural revolts During their use, and slay us after *Cymbeline* iv 4 5
Slayeth. The one I'll slay, the other slayeth me . . *M. N. Dream* ii 1 190
Slaying is the word; It is a deed in fashion . . . *J. Cæsar* v 5 4
Sleave. Sleep that knits up the ravell'd sleave of care . *Macbeth* ii 2 37
Sleave-silk. Thou idle immaterial skein of sleave-silk *Troi. and Cres.* v 1 35
Sledded. He smote the sledded Polacks on the ice . . *Hamlet* i 1 63
Sleek. Stick musk-roses in thy sleek smooth head . *M. N. Dream* iv 1 3
How sleek and wanton Ye appear in every thing may bring my ruin! *Hen. VIII.* iii 2 241
Sleek o'er your rugged looks; Be bright and jovial . . *Macbeth* iii 2 27
Sleek-headed men and such as sleep o' nights . *J. Cæsar* i 2 193
Sleekly. Let their heads be sleekly combed . . *T. of Shrew* iv 1 93
Sleep. Thou art inclined to sleep; 'tis a good dulness . *Tempest* i 2 185
It eats and sleeps and hath such senses As we have, such . . i 2 412
Will you laugh me asleep, for I am very heavy?—Go sleep, and hear us ii 1 190
I find not Myself disposed to sleep.—Nor I; my spirits are nimble . ii 1 202
It is a sleepy language and thou speak'st Out of thy sleep . . ii 1 212
Thou let'st thy fortune sleep—die, rather; wink'st Whiles thou art waking . . . . . . ii 1 216
'Tis as impossible that he's undrown'd As he that sleeps here swims . ii 1 238
There be that can rule Naples As well as he that sleeps . . . ii 1 263
That you bore The mind that I do! what a sleep were this For your advancement! . . . . . . ii 1 267
'Tis a custom with him, I' th' afternoon to sleep . . . iii 2 96
Voices That, if I then had waked after long sleep, Will make me sleep again . . . . . . iii 2 148
We are such stuff As dreams are made on, and our little life Is rounded with a sleep . . . . . . iv 1 158
We were dead of sleep, And—how we know not—all clapp'd under hatches . . . . . . v 1 230
My horns are his horns, whether I wake or sleep . *T. G. of Ver.* i 1 80
Love hath chased sleep from my enthralled eyes . . . ii 4 134
Dine, sup and sleep, Upon the very naked name of love . . ii 4 141
'She doth talk in her sleep.'—It's no matter for that, so she sleep not in her talk . . . . . . iii 1 333
Hath he any eyes? hath he any thinking? Sure, they sleep *Mer. Wives* iii 2 31
Is this a vision? is this a dream? do I sleep? . . . iii 5 142
A maid That, ere she sleep, has thrice her prayers said . . v 5 54
Raise up the organs of her fantasy; Sleep she as sound as careless infancy . . . . . . v 5 56
Those as sleep and think not on their sins, Pinch them, arms, legs, backs v 5 57
Thy best of rest is sleep, And that thou oft provokest *Meas. for Meas.* iii 1 17
Thou hast nor youth nor age, But, as it were, an after-dinner's sleep . iii 1 33
As fast lock'd up in sleep as guiltless labour When it lies starkly in the traveller's bones: He will not wake . . . . iv 2 69
A man that apprehends death no more dreadfully but as a drunken sleep iv 2 150
Awake till you are executed, and sleep afterwards . . . iv 3 35
He that drinks all night, and is hanged betimes in the morning, may sleep the sounder all the next day . . . . . iv 3 50
Then return and sleep within mine inn . . *Com. of Errors* i 2 14
Or sleep I now and think I hear all this? . . . . ii 2 185
I am waked with it when I sleep; raised with it when I sit . . iv 4 36
It seems his sleeps were hinder'd by thy railing, And thereof comes it that his head is light . . . . . v 1 71
Ne'er may I look on day, nor sleep on night, But she tells to your highness simple truth! . . . . . . v 1 210
Sleep when I am drowsy and tend on no man's business. . *Much Ado* i 3 17
She is never sad but when she sleeps, and not ever sad then . . ii 1 359
We will rather sleep than talk: we know what belongs to a watch . iii 3 39
And then, to sleep but three hours in the night . . *L. L. Lost* i 1 42
Barren tasks, too hard to keep, Not to see ladies, study, fast, not sleep! i 1 48
There sleeps Titania sometime of the night . . *M. N. Dream* ii 1 253
Here is my bed: sleep give thee all his rest!—With half that wish the wisher's eyes be press'd! . . . . . . ii 2 64
When thou wakest, let love forbid Sleep his seat on thy eyelid . . ii 2 81
Hermia, sleep thou there: And never mayst thou come Lysander near! ii 2 135
And sing while thou on pressed flowers dost sleep . . . iii 1 162
If thou hast slain Lysander in his sleep, . . . kill me too . . iii 2 47
So sorrow's heaviness doth heavier grow For debt that bankrupt sleep doth sorrow owe . . . . . . iii 2 85
Death-counterfeiting sleep With leaden legs and batty wings doth creep iii 2 364
Sleep, that sometimes shuts up sorrow's eye, Steal me awhile . . iii 2 435
On the ground Sleep sound: I'll apply To your eye, Gentle lover, remedy . . . . . . iii 2 449
I have an exposition of sleep come upon me.—Sleep thou, and I will wind thee in my arms . . . . . iv 1 43
And strike more dead Than common sleep of all these five the sense . iv 1 87
Music, ho! music, such as charmeth sleep! . . . . iv 1 88
To sleep by hate, and fear no enmity? . . . . . iv 1 150
I shall reply amazedly, Half sleep, half waking . . . iv 1 152
Are you sure That we are awake? It seems to me That yet we sleep, we dream . . . . . . iv 1 199
Sleep when he wakes and creep into the jaundice By being peevish? *Mer. of Venice* i 1 85
And sleep and snore, and rend apparel out . . . . ii 5 5
Snail-slow in profit, and he sleeps by day More than the wild-cat . ii 5 47
How sweet the moonlight sleeps upon this bank! Here will we sit . v 1 54
The moon sleeps with Endymion And would not be awaked . . v 1 109
I'll go sleep, if I can; if I cannot, I'll rail . *As Y. Like It* ii 5 62
Sleeps easily because he cannot study . . . . . iii 2 338

Sleep. Who stays it [Time] still withal?—With lawyers in the vacation; for they sleep between term and term . . *As Y. Like It* iii 2 350
I will laugh like a hyen, and that when thou art inclined to sleep . iv 1 157
I'll go find a shadow and sigh till he come.—And I'll sleep . . iv 1 224
He hath ta'en his bow and arrows and is gone forth to sleep . . iv 3 5
This were a bed but cold to sleep so soundly . *T. of Shrew* Ind. 1 33
Wilt thou sleep? we'll have thee to a couch Softer and sweeter than the lustful bed On purpose trimm'd up for Semiramis . . Ind. 2 39
Do I dream? or have I dream'd till now? I do not sleep: I see, I hear Ind. 2 72
I will not sleep, Hortensio, till I see her . . . . . i 2 103
Am starved for meat, giddy for lack of sleep . . . . iv 3 9
As who should say, if I should sleep or eat, 'Twere deadly sickness . iv 3 13
Hath that awaken'd you?—Ay, but not frighted me; therefore I'll sleep again . . . . . . v 2 43
Here he comes, to beguile two hours in a sleep . . *All's Well* iv 1 25
In his sleep he does little harm, save to his bed-clothes about him . iv 3 286
But I will eat and drink, and sleep as soft As captain shall . . iv 3 368
While shame full late sleeps out the afternoon . . . . v 3 66
If it be thus to dream, still let me sleep! . . . *T. Night* iv 1 67
Endeavour thyself to sleep, and leave thy vain bibble babble . . iv 2 104
The purity and whiteness of my sheets, Which to preserve is sleep *W. T.* i 2 328
Threw off his spirit, his appetite, his sleep, And downright languish'd . ii 3 16
Not so hot, good sir: I come to bring him sleep . . . ii 3 33
Purge him of that humour That presses him from sleep . . . ii 3 39
I would there were no age between sixteen and three-and-twenty, or that youth would sleep out the rest . . . . . iii 3 61
For the life to come, I sleep out the thought of it . . . iv 3 31
Life as lively mock'd as ever Still sleep mock'd death . . . v 3 20
Then with a passion would I shake the world; And rouse from sleep that fell anatomy . . . . . *K. John* iii 4 40
And, pretty child, sleep doubtless and secure . . . . iv 1 130
Draws the sweet infant breath of gentle sleep . . *Richard II.* i 3 133
Peace shall go sleep with Turks and infidels . . . . iv 1 139
We may do it as secure as sleep . . . . *1 Hen. IV.* i 2 146
'Tis dangerous to take a cold, to sleep, to drink . . . ii 3 9
What is't that takes from thee Thy stomach, pleasure and thy golden sleep? . . . . . . ii 3 44
So bestirr'd thee in thy sleep, That beads of sweat have stood upon thy brow . . . . . . ii 3 60
There let him sleep till day . . . . . . ii 4 594
Sing the song that pleaseth you And on your eyelids crown the god of sleep . . . . . . iii 1 217
Such difference 'twixt wake and sleep As is the difference betwixt day and night . . . . . . iii 1 219
Thy ignominy sleep with thee in the grave! . . . . v 4 100
He may sleep in security; for he hath the horn of abundance *2 Hen. IV.* i 2 51
The undeserver may sleep, when the man of action is called on . ii 4 406
O sleep, O gentle sleep, Nature's soft nurse, how have I frighted thee? iii 1 5
Why rather, sleep, liest thou in smoky cribs, Upon uneasy pallets stretching thee And hush'd with buzzing night-flies to thy slumber? iii 1 9
Canst thou, O partial sleep, give thy repose To the wet sea-boy? . . iii 1 26
Speak low; The king your father is disposed to sleep . . . iv 5 17
Sleep with it now! Yet not so sound and half so deeply sweet As he whose brow with homely biggen bound . . . . iv 5 25
This sleep is sound indeed; this is a sleep That from this golden rigol hath divorced So many English kings . . . . . iv 5 35
Is he so hasty that he doth suppose My sleep my death? . . . iv 5 62
Have broke their sleep with thoughts, their brains with care . . iv 5 69
Men may sleep, and they may have their throats about them *Hen. V.* ii 1 23
Though we seemed dead, we did but sleep . . . . . iii 6 127
Not all these, laid in bed majestical, Can sleep so soundly as the wretched slave . . . . . . iv 1 285
Sweats in the eye of Phœbus and all night Sleeps in Elysium . . iv 1 291
Winding up days with toil and nights with sleep . . . . iv 1 296
When others sleep upon their quiet beds . . . *1 Hen. VI.* ii 1 6
And once again we'll sleep secure in Rouen . . . . . iii 2 19
Wrathful fury makes me weep, That thus we die, while remiss traitors sleep . . . . . . iv 3 29
Being call'd A hundred times and oftener, in my sleep . . *2 Hen. VI.* ii 1 90
They say, . . . That if your highness should intend to sleep And charge that no man should disturb your rest . . . . . iii 2 255
The mortal worm might make the sleep eternal . . . . . iii 2 263
They have been up these two days.—They have the more need to sleep now . . . . . . iv 2 3
Steel, if thou turn the edge, . . . ere thou sleep in thy sheath . . iv 10 61
His wonted sleep under a fresh tree's shade . . . *3 Hen. VI.* ii 5 49
The king by this is set him down to sleep.—What, will he not to bed? . iv 3 2
Your beauty, which did haunt me in my sleep . . *Richard III.* i 2 122
No sleep close up that deadly eye of thine! . . . . . i 3 225
Stay by me; My soul is heavy, and I fain would sleep . . . i 4 74
What, shall we stab him as he sleeps? . . . . . i 4 102
I shall not sleep in quiet at the Tower.—Why, what should you fear? iii 1 142
Shall we hear from you, Catesby, ere we sleep?—You shall, my lord . iii 1 188
Cannot thy master sleep these tedious nights?—So it should seem . iii 2 6
Never yet one hour in his bed Have I enjoy'd the golden dew of sleep . iv 1 84
Foes to my rest and my sweet sleep's disturbers . . . . iv 2 74
The sons of Edward sleep in Abraham's bosom . . . . iv 3 38
When didst thou sleep when such a deed was done? . . . iv 4 24
Forbear to sleep the nights, and fast the days . . . . iv 4 118
Harry, that prophesied thou shouldst be king, Doth comfort thee in thy sleep . . . . . . v 3 130
Sleep, Richmond, sleep in peace, and wake in joy; Good angels guard thee! . . . . . . v 3 155
That wretched Anne thy wife, That never slept a quiet hour with thee, Now fills thy sleep with perturbations . . . . v 3 161
Thou quiet soul, sleep thou a quiet sleep; Dream of success! . . v 3 164
Sweetest sleep, and fairest-boding dreams That ever enter'd in a drowsy head . . . . . . v 3 227
If you do sweat to put a tyrant down, You sleep in peace . . . v 3 256
When he has run his course and sleeps in blessings . *Hen. VIII.* iii 2 398
When I am forgotten, as I shall be, And sleep in dull cold marble . iii 2 433
Till Cranmer, Cromwell, her two hands, and she, Sleep in their graves v 1 32
Impossible . . . To scatter 'em, as 'tis to make 'em sleep On May-day morning . . . . . . v 4 14
Nor shall this peace sleep with her . . . . . . v 5 40
Some come to take their ease, And sleep an act or two . . . Epil. 3
Helen, Menelaus' queen, With wanton Paris sleeps . *Troi. and Cres.* Prol. 10
Weaker than a woman's tear, Tamer than sleep, fonder than ignorance . i 1 10
If we talk of reason, Let's shut our gates and sleep . . . ii 2 47
Go we to council. Let Achilles sleep: Light boats sail swift . . ii 3 276

Sleep. Sleep kill those pretty eyes, And give as soft attachment to thy senses As infants' empty of all thought! . . . *Troi. and Cres.* iv 2 4
Hast not slept to-night? would he not, a naughty man, let it sleep? . iv 2 33
Nor sleep nor sanctuary, Being naked, sick, nor fane nor Capitol *Coriol.* i 10 19
I warrant him consul.—Then our office may, During his power, go sleep ii 1 239
Were I as patient as the midnight sleep, By Jove, 'twould be my mind! iii 1 85
Whose passions and whose plots have broke their sleep . . . . iv 4 19
We have been down together in my sleep, Unbuckling helms . . iv 5 130
And sleep in peace, slain in your country's wars! . . . *T. Andron.* i 1 91
Here are no storms, No noise, but silence and eternal sleep . . . i 1 155
And welcome, nephews, from successful wars, You that survive, and you that sleep in fame! . . . . i 1 173
I have been troubled in my sleep this night, But dawning day new comfort hath inspired . . . . ii 2 9
Were't not for shame, Well could I leave our sport to sleep awhile . ii 3 197
If I do wake, some planet strike me down, That I may slumber in eternal sleep! . . . . ii 4 15
Those sweet ornaments, Whose circling shadows kings have sought to sleep in . . . . ii 4 19
And when he sleeps will she do what she list . . . . . . iv 1 100
Justice lives In Saturninus' health, whom, if she sleep, He'll so awake as she in fury shall Cut off the proud'st conspirator that lives . iv 4 24
Still-waking sleep, that is not what it is! . . . *Rom. and Jul.* i 1 187
And being thus frighted swears a prayer or two And sleeps again . . i 4 88
I'll to my truckle-bed; This field-bed is too cold for me to sleep . . ii 1 40
Sleep dwell upon thine eyes, peace in thy breast! Would I were sleep and peace, so sweet to rest! . . . . ii 2 187
And where care lodges, sleep will never lie . . . . . . ii 3 36
Where unbruised youth with unstuff'd brain Doth couch his limbs, there golden sleep doth reign . . . . ii 3 38
That Romeo should, upon receipt thereof, Soon sleep in quiet . . iii 5 100
Thou shalt continue two and forty hours, And then awake as from a pleasant sleep . . . . iv 1 106
You take your pennyworths now; Sleep for a week . . . . iv 5 5
If I may trust the flattering truth of sleep, My dreams presage some joyful news at hand . . . . v 1 1
Her body sleeps in Capel's monument . . . . v 1 18
As I did sleep under this yew-tree here, I dreamt . . . . v 3 137
Lady, come from that nest Of death, contagion, and unnatural sleep . v 3 152
Sleep upon't, And let the foes quietly cut their throats? *T. of Athens* iii 5 43
Here is no use for gold.—The best and truest; For here it sleeps, and does no hired harm . . . . iv 3 291
Sleek-headed men and such as sleep o' nights . . . . *J. Cæsar* i 2 193
I would it were my fault to sleep so soundly . . . . . . ii 1 4
It will not let you eat, nor talk, nor sleep . . . . . . ii 1 252
Thrice hath Calpurnia in her sleep cried out, 'Help, ho! they murder Cæsar!' . . . . ii 2 2
I'll have them sleep on cushions in my tent . . . . . . iv 3 243
Lie in my tent and sleep; It may be I shall raise you by and by . iv 3 246
Thou shalt sleep again; I will not hold thee long . . . . . iv 3 264
Didst thou see any thing?—Nothing, my lord.—Sleep again, Lucius . iv 3 300
Why did you so cry out, sirs, in your sleep?—Did we, my lord? . . iv 3 304
Sleep shall neither night nor day Hang upon his pent-house lid *Macbeth* i 3 19
When in swinish sleep Their drenched natures lie as in a death . . i 7 67
A heavy summons lies like lead upon me, And yet I would not sleep . ii 1 7
Nature seems dead, and wicked dreams abuse The curtain'd sleep . . ii 1 51
There's one did laugh in's sleep, and one cried 'Murder!' . . . ii 2 23
They did say their prayers, and address'd them Again to sleep . . ii 2 26
Methought I heard a voice cry 'Sleep no more! Macbeth does murder sleep' . . . . ii 2 35
The innocent sleep, Sleep that knits up the ravell'd sleave of care. . ii 2 36
Still it cried 'Sleep no more!' to all the house: 'Glamis hath murder'd sleep, and therefore Cawdor Shall sleep no more; Macbeth shall sleep no more' . . . . ii 2 41
[Drink provokes] nose-painting, sleep, and urine . . . . . ii 3 31
Equivocates him in a sleep, and, giving him the lie, leaves him . . ii 3 39
Shake off this downy sleep, death's counterfeit, And look on death itself! ii 3 81
Eat our meal in fear and sleep In the affliction of these terrible dreams iii 2 17
Duncan is in his grave; After life's fitful fever he sleeps well . . iii 2 23
You lack the season of all natures, sleep.—Come, we'll to sleep . . iii 4 141
That were the slaves of drink and thralls of sleep . . . . . iii 6 13
We may again Give to our tables meat, sleep to our nights . . . iii 6 34
That I may tell pale-hearted fear it lies, And sleep in spite of thunder . iv 1 86
Yet all this while in a most fast sleep . . . . v 1 9
A great perturbation in nature, to receive at once the benefit of sleep, and do the effects of watching! . . . . v 1 11
Yet I have known those which have walked in their sleep who have died holily in their beds . . . . v 1 67
Do not sleep, But let me hear from you . . . . . . *Hamlet* i 3 3
Prithee, say on: he's for a jig or a tale of bawdry, or he sleeps: say on ii 2 523
To die: to sleep; No more; and by a sleep to say we end The heart-ache iii 1 60
To die, to sleep; To sleep: perchance to dream: ay, there's the rub; For in that sleep of death what dreams may come . . . . . iii 1 66
My spirits grow dull, and fain I would beguile The tedious day with sleep . . . . iii 2 237
Sleep rock thy brain; And never come mischance between us twain! . iii 2 237
For some must watch, while some must sleep: So runs the world away iii 2 284
A knavish speech sleeps in a foolish ear . . . . iv 2 25
What is a man, If his chief good and market of his time Be but to sleep and feed? a beast, no more . . . . iv 4 35
How stand I then, That have a father kill'd, a mother stain'd, Excitements of my reason and my blood, And let all sleep? . . . . iv 4 59
My revenge will come.—Break not your sleeps for that . . . . iv 7 30
In my heart there was a kind of fighting, That would not let me sleep . v 2 5
If our father would sleep till I waked him, you should enjoy half his revenue for ever . . . . *Lear* i 2 55
The fault Would not 'scape censure, nor the redresses sleep . . . i 4 229
I will not sleep, my lord, till I have delivered your letter . . . i 5 6
Some time I shall sleep out, the rest I'll whistle . . . . . ii 2 163
Or at their chamber-door I'll beat the drum Till it cry sleep to death . ii 4 120
Shall of a corn cry woe, And turn his sleep to wake . . . . iii 2 34
I'll pray, and then I'll sleep . . . . iii 4 27
Oppressed nature sleeps: This rest might yet have balm'd thy broken sinews . . . . iii 6 104
How does the king?—Madam, sleeps still . . . . iv 7 13
In the heaviness of his sleep We put fresh garments on him . . . iv 7 21
What will I do, thinkest thou?—Why, go to bed, and sleep . . *Othello* i 3 305
Alas, she has no speech.—In faith, too much; I find it still, when I have list to sleep . . . . ii 1 105
But is he often thus?—'Tis evermore the prologue to his sleep . . ii 3 134
Sleep. Nor all the drowsy syrups of the world Shall ever medicine thee to that sweet sleep Which thou owedst yesterday . . *Othello* iii 3 332
Being troubled with a raging tooth, I could not sleep . . . . iii 3 415
There are a kind of men so loose of soul, That in their sleeps will mutter their affairs . . . . iii 3 417
In sleep I heard him say 'Sweet Desdemona, Let us be wary' . . . iii 3 419
That I might sleep out this great gap of time . . . *Ant. and Cleo.* i 5 5
That sleep and feeding may prorogue his honour Even till a Lethe'd dulness! . . . . ii 1 26
We did sleep day out of countenance, and made the night light . . ii 2 181
Sleep a little.—No, my chuck. Eros, come; mine armour, Eros! . . iv 4 1
He sleeps.—Swoons rather; for so bad a prayer as his Was never yet for sleep . . . . iv 9 26
The long day's task is done, And we must sleep . . . . . iv 14 36
Which sleeps, and never palates more the dug, The beggar's nurse and Cæsar's . . . . v 2 7
If idle talk will once be necessary, I'll not sleep neither . . . v 2 51
O, such another sleep, that I might see But such another man! . . . v 2 77
Feed, and sleep: Our care and pity is so much upon you . . . v 2 187
But she looks like sleep, As she would catch another Antony . . . v 2 349
Sleep hath seized me wholly. To your protection I commend me, gods *Cymbeline* ii 2 7
O sleep, thou ape of death, lie dull upon her! . . . . . . ii 2 31
If sleep charge nature, To break it with a fearful dream of him . . iii 4 44
Why, he but sleeps: If he be gone, he'll make his grave a bed . . iv 2 215
'Faith, I'll lie down and sleep. But, soft! no bedfellow! . . . . iv 2 294
Nature doth abhor to make his bed With the defunct, or sleep upon the dead . . . . iv 2 358
Sleep, thou hast been a grandsire, and begot A father to me . . . v 4 123
He that sleeps feels not the tooth-ache . . . . v 4 177
A man that were to sleep your sleep, and a hangman to help him to bed, I think he would change places with his officer . . . . . v 4 178
Peaceful night, The tomb where grief should sleep . . . . *Pericles* i 2 5
Drew sleep out of mine eyes, blood from my cheeks, Musings into my mind . . . . i 2 96
Now sleep yslaked hath the rout; No din but snores the house about iii Gower 1
This is the rarest dream that e'er dull sleep Did mock sad fools withal. v 1 163
Truth can never be confirm'd enough, Though doubts did ever sleep . v 1 204
Sleeper. Graves at my command Have waked their sleepers . *Tempest* v 1 49
And rock the ground whereon these sleepers be . . . *M. N. Dream* iv 1 91
Good morrow. I have been long a sleeper . . . . *Richard III.* iv 4 24
What's the business, That such a hideous trumpet calls to parley The sleepers of the house? . . . . *Macbeth* ii 3 88
Hark! the drums Demurely wake the sleepers . . . *Ant. and Cleo.* iv 9 31
Sleepest. Awake, thou coward majesty! thou sleepest . *Richard II.* iii 2 84
Hector, thou sleep'st; Awake thee! . . . . . *Troi. and Cres.* iv 5 114
Brutus, thou sleep'st: awake, and see thyself . . . . *J. Cæsar* ii 1 46
Therefore thou sleep'st so sound . . . . ii 1 233
Sleepest or wakest thou, jolly shepherd? Thy sheep be in the corn *Lear* iii 6 43
Sleeping. Am I in earth, in heaven, or in hell? Sleeping or waking? *Com. of Errors* ii 2 215
I cannot see how sleeping should offend . . . . . . *Much Ado* iii 3 42
The juice of it on sleeping eye-lids laid Will make or man or woman madly dote Upon the next live creature . . . . *M. N. Dream* ii 1 170
Here the maiden, sleeping sound, On the dank and dirty ground . . ii 2 74
Painted butterflies To fan the moonbeams from his sleeping eyes . . iii 1 176
I took him sleeping,—that is finish'd too . . . . . . iii 2 38
Would he have stolen away From sleeping Hermia? . . . . . iii 2 52
Hast thou kill'd him sleeping? O brave touch! . . . . . . iii 2 70
That I sleeping here was found With these mortals on the ground. . iv 1 106
A wretched ragged man, o'ergrown with hair, Lay sleeping *As Y. Like It* iv 3 108
With catlike watch, When that the sleeping man should stir . . . iv 3 117
Having come from a day-bed, where I have left Olivia sleeping *T. Night* ii 5 55
All proofs sleeping else But what your jealousies awake. . *W. Tale* iii 2 113
Those sleeping stones, That as a waist doth girdle you about. *K. John* ii 1 216
The northeast wind, Which then blew bitterly against our faces, Awaked the sleeping rheum . . . . *Richard II.* i 4 8
For sleeping England long time have I watch'd . . . . . ii 1 77
Some poison'd by their wives; some sleeping kill'd. . . . . iii 2 159
Unbuttoning thee after supper and sleeping upon benches after noon *1 Hen. IV.* i 2 4
This apoplexy is, as I take it, a kind of lethargy, an't please your lordship; a kind of sleeping in the blood . . . . *2 Hen. IV.* i 2 128
But since all is well, keep it so: wake not a sleeping wolf . . . i 2 174
The unguided days And rotten times that you shall look upon When I am sleeping with my ancestors . . . . iv 4 61
Take heed . . . How you awake our sleeping sword of war . *Hen. V.* i 2 22
Sleeping or waking must I still prevail? . . . . . *1 Hen. VI.* ii 1 56
Sleeping neglection doth betray to loss The conquest . . . . iv 3 49
May ye both be suddenly surprised By bloody hands, in sleeping on your beds! . . . . v 3 41
Sleeping or waking, 'tis no matter how, So he be dead . *2 Hen. VI.* iii 1 263
I wear no knife to slaughter sleeping men . . . . iii 2 197
Why, then he will say we stabbed him sleeping . . *Richard III.* i 4 108
Not sleeping, to engross his idle body, But praying . . . . . iii 7 76
Sleeping and waking, O, defend me still! . . . . v 3 117
You sleeping safe, they bring to you unrest . . . . . . v 3 320
You ever Have wish'd the sleeping of this business . . . *Hen. VIII.* ii 4 163
A stirring dwarf we do allowance give Before a sleeping giant *T. and C.* ii 3 147
Then gave I her, so tutor'd by my art, A sleeping potion *Rom. and Jul.* v 3 244
Or a dog, that seems a-sleeping . . . . *T. of Athens* i 2 68
Pity's sleeping: Strange times, that weep with laughing, not with weeping! . . . . iv 3 492
The sleeping and the dead Are but as pictures . . . . *Macbeth* ii 2 53
Toad, that under cold stone . . . has . . . Swelter'd venom sleeping got iv 1 8
'Tis given out that, sleeping in my orchard, A serpent stung me *Hamlet* i 5 35
Sleeping within my orchard, My custom always of the afternoon . . i 5 59
Thus was I, sleeping, by a brother's hand Of life, of crown, of queen, at once dispatch'd . . . . i 5 74
As the sleeping soldiers in the alarm, Your bedded hair, like life in excrements, Start up, and stand an end . . . . iii 4 120
How! a page! Or dead, or sleeping on him? But dead rather *Cymb.* iv 2 356
Sleeping-hour. She was in her dull and sleeping hour *M. N. Dream* iii 2 8
Dinners and suppers and sleeping-hours excepted . . *As Y. Like It* iii 2 102
It is not Agamemnon's sleeping hour . . . . . *Troi. and Cres.* i 3 254
Sleepy. It is a sleepy language and thou speak'st Out of thy sleep *Tempest* ii 1 211
Away, you rogue, away! I am sleepy . . . . . *Meas. for Meas.* iv 3 31
Moist Hesperus hath quench'd his sleepy lamp . . . . *All's Well* ii 1 167
We will give you sleepy drinks . . . . *W. Tale* i 1 15
In the mildness of your sleepy thoughts, Which here we waken *Rich. III.* iii 7 123

Sleepy. Peace is a very apoplexy, lethargy; mulled, deaf, sleepy *Coriol.* iv 5 239
This is a sleepy tune. O murderous slumber, Lay'st thou thy leaden mace upon my boy, That plays thee music? *J. Cæsar* iv 3 267
When we have mark'd with blood those sleepy two Of his own chamber and used their very daggers, That they have done't *Macbeth* i 7 75
Go carry them; and smear The sleepy grooms with blood.—I'll go no more ii 2 50
'Tis not sleepy business; But must be look'd to speedily *Cymbeline* iii 5 26
Sleeve. The Hundredth Psalm to the tune of 'Green Sleeves' *Mer. Wives* ii 1 64
Let it thunder to the tune of Green Sleeves v 5 22
I will fasten on this sleeve of thine *Com. of Errors* ii 2 175
Though others have the arm, show us the sleeve iii 2 23
Down sleeves, side sleeves, and skirts *Much Ado* iii 4 20
This gallant pins the wenches on his sleeve *L. L. Lost* v 2 321
I knew her by this jewel on her sleeve v 2 455
Some sleeves, some hats, from yielders all things catch *M. N. Dream* iii 2 30
Your sleeve unbuttoned, your shoe untied *As Y. Like It* iii 2 398
What's this? a sleeve? 'tis like a demi-cannon *T. of Shrew* iv 3 88
'With a trunk sleeve:'—I confess two sleeves.—'The sleeves curiously cut' iv 3 142
I commanded the sleeves should be cut out and sewed up again iv 3 147
Dost make hose of thy sleeves? do other servants so? *All's Well* ii 3 266
Thrown over the shoulders like an herald's coat without sleeves 1 *Hen. IV.* iv 2 49
Then will he strip his sleeve and show his scars *Hen. V.* iv 3 47
Wear this sleeve.—And you this glove *Troi. and Cres.* iv 4 72
Now the pledge; now, now, now!—Here, Diomed, keep this sleeve v 2 66
You look upon that sleeve; behold it well. He loved me v 2 69
That sleeve is mine that he'll bear on his helm v 2 169
Believe, I come to lose my arm, or win my sleeve v 3 96
That same scurvy doting foolish young knave's sleeve of Troy v 4 4
Send that Greekish whoremasterly villain, with the sleeve, back v 4 8
Soft! here comes sleeve, and t'other v 4 19
Trojan!—now the sleeve, now the sleeve! v 4 26
As they pass by, pluck Casca by the sleeve *J. Cæsar* i 2 179
I will wear my heart upon my sleeve For daws to peck at *Othello* i 1 64
Sleeve-hand. He so chants to the sleeve-hand and the work about the square on't *W. Tale* iv 4 211
Sleeveless. Of a sleeveless errand *Troi. and Cres.* v 4 9
Sleided. She weaved the sleided silk With fingers long *Pericles* iv Gower 21
Sleight. As Ulysses and stout Diomede With sleight and manhood stole to Rhesus' tents 3 *Hen. VI.* iv 2 20
Distill'd by magic sleights Shall raise such artificial sprites *Macbeth* iii 5 26
Slender. While other men, of slender reputation, Put forth their sons to seek preferment out *T. G. of Ver.* i 3 6
Ay, cousin Slender, and 'Custalorum' *Mer. Wives* i 1 7
Here young Master Slender, that peradventures shall tell you another tale i 1 78
Slender, I broke your head: what matter have you against me? i 1 124
Pistol, did you pick Master Slender's purse? i 1 154
Give ear to his motions, Master Slender: I will description the matter to you i 1 221
Cousin Abraham Slender, can you love her?—I hope, sir i 1 239
Master Slender, come; we stay for you.—I'll eat nothing, I thank you i 1 313
And Master Slender's your master?—Ay, forsooth i 4 18
Master guest, and Master Page, and eke Cavaleiro Slender ii 3 78
Good Master Slender's serving-man, and friend Simple by your name iii 1 1
About a match between Anne Page and my cousin Slender iii 2 59
I hope I have your good will, father Page.—You have, Master Slender iii 2 62
Hark ye; Master Slender would speak a word with you iii 4 29
Now, Master Slender,— Now, good Mistress Anne,— What is your will? iii 4 56
I mean, Master Slender, what would you with me? iii 4 63
Now, Master Slender: love him, daughter Anne iii 4 71
I would Master Slender had her; or, in sooth, I would Master Fenton had her iii 4 109
Master Slender is let the boys leave to play.—Blessing of his heart! iv 1 11
In that time Shall Master Slender steal my Nan away iv 4 74
Slender, though well landed, is an idiot; And he my husband best of all affects iv 4 86
I come to speak with Sir John Falstaff from Master Slender iv 5 5
Master Slender, sent to her, seeing her go thorough the streets iv 5 31
The very same man that beguiled Master Slender of his chain iv 5 38
Her father hath commanded her to slip Away with Slender iv 6 24
When Slender sees his time To take her by the hand and bid her go iv 6 36
Remember, son Slender, my daughter v 2 3
Tell her Master Slender hath married her daughter v 5 182
Now, mistress, how chance you went not with Master Slender? v 5 231
An your waist, mistress, were as slender as my wit *L. L. Lost* iv 1 49
Winter garments must be lined, So must slender Rosalind *As Y. Like It* iii 2 112
Kate like the hazel-twig Is straight and slender *T. of Shrew* ii 1 256
At so slender warning, You are like to have a thin and slender pittance iv 4 61
Your means are very slender, and your waste is great 2 *Hen. IV.* i 2 159
How would he hang his slender gilded wings! *T. Andron.* iii 2 61
It is some poor fragment, some slender ort of his remainder *T. of Athens* iv 3 400
Grief joys, joy grieves, on slender accident *Hamlet* iii 2 209
Slenderer. I would it were otherwise; I would my means were greater, and my waist slenderer 2 *Hen. IV.* i 2 162
Slenderly. He hath ever but slenderly known himself *Lear* i 1 297
Slept. Awake, dear heart, awake! thou hast slept well; Awake! *Tempest* i 2 305
The law hath not been dead, though it hath slept *Meas. for Meas.* ii 2 90
In bed he slept not for my urging it *Com. of Errors* v 1 63
In a tomb where never scandal slept *Much Ado* v 1 70
We still have slept together, Rose at an instant *As Y. Like It* i 3 75
Or when you waked, so waked as if you slept *T. of Shrew* Ind. 2 82
They say that I have dream'd And slept above some fifteen year Ind. 2 115
Last night she slept not, nor to-night she shall not iv 1 201
Madam, he hath not slept to-night *W. Tale* ii 3 31
Give my scene such growing As you had slept between iv 1 17
O, where hath our intelligence been drunk? Where hath it slept? *K. John* iv 2 117
Hung their eyelids down, Slept in his face 1 *Hen. IV.* iii 2 82
Hadst thou been meek, our title still had slept 3 *Hen. VI.* ii 2 160
Where slept our scouts, or how are they seduced? v 1 19
Under whose shade the ramping lion slept v 2 13
Thy wife, That never slept a quiet hour with thee *Richard III.* v 3 160
How have you slept, my lord?—The sweetest sleep v 3 226
Eyes, that so long have slept upon This bold bad man *Hen. VIII.* ii 2 43
He gave his honours to the world again, His blessed part to heaven, and slept in peace.—So may he rest! iv 2 30
It is not you I call for: Saw ye none enter since I slept?—None, madam iv 2 86
Their great general slept, Whilst emulation in the army crept *Tr. and Cr.* ii 2 211
Slept. Hast not slept to-night? would he not, a naughty man, let it sleep? *Troi. and Cres.* iv 2 33
Whose youth was spent In dangerous wars, whilst you securely slept *T. Andron.* iii 1 3
Myself and such As slept within the shadow of your power *T. of Athens* v 4 6
Since Cassius first did whet me against Cæsar, I have not slept *J. Cæsar* ii 1 62
I have slept, my lord, already.—It was well done iv 3 263
Hath it slept since? And wakes it now, to look so green and pale? *Macb.* i 7 36
Had he not resembled My father as he slept, I had done't ii 2 14
One that slept in the contriving of lust, and waked to do it *Lear* iii 4 92
So please your majesty That we may wake the king: he hath slept long iv 7 18
It harm'd not me: I slept the next night well *Othello* iii 3 340
Not till you have slept; I fear me you'll be in till then *Ant. and Cleo.* ii 7 37
First, her bedchamber,—Where, I confess, I slept not *Cymbeline* ii 4 67
Since I received command to do this business I have not slept one wink iii 4 103
I thought he slept, and put My clouted brogues from off my feet iv 2 213
As I slept, methought Great Jupiter, upon his eagle back'd, Appear'd to me v 5 426
Slew. But yet I slew him manfully in fight *T. G. of Ver.* iv 1 28
Pardon, goddess of the night, Those that slew thy virgin knight *M. Ado* v 3 13
By this scimitar That slew the Sophy *Mer. of Venice* ii 1 25
With his own hand he slew the duke's brother *All's Well* iii 5 7
Belike you slew great number of his people *T. Night* iii 3 29
For Gloucester's death, I slew him not *Richard II.* i 1 133
A traitor's head, The head of Cade, whom I in combat slew 2 *Hen. VI.* v 1 67
Tell me, my friend, art thou the man that slew him? v 1 71
What, all afoot?—The deadly-handed Clifford slew my steed v 2 9
He slew thy father, And thine, Lord Clifford 3 *Hen. VI.* i 1 54
We are those which chased you from the field And slew your fathers i 1 91
May that ground gape and swallow me alive, Where I shall kneel to him that slew my father! i 1 162
As for the brat of this accursed duke, Whose father slew my father, he shall die i 3 5
Cruel child-killer.—I slew thy father, call'st thou him a child? ii 2 113
And this the hand that slew thy brother Rutland ii 4 7
And cheers these hands that slew thy sire and brother ii 4 9
This man, whom hand to hand I slew in fight ii 5 56
Say that I slew them not?—Why, then they are not dead *Richard III.* i 2 89
Who slew to-day a riotous gentleman ii 1 100
Think that thy babes were fairer than they were, And he that slew them fouler iv 4 121
Send to her, by the man that slew her brothers, A pair of bleeding hearts iv 4 271
Shall I say, her uncle? Or, he that slew her brothers and her uncles? iv 4 339
And i' the consul's view Slew three opposers *Coriolanus* ii 2 98
The Greeks upon advice did bury Ajax That slew himself *T. Andron.* i 1 380
There lies the man, slain by young Romeo, That slew thy kinsman *Rom. and Jul.* iii 1 150
Romeo slew Tybalt, Romeo must not live.—Romeo slew him, he slew Mercutio; Who now the price of his dear blood doth owe? iii 1 186
I dreamt my master and another fought, And that my master slew him v 3 139
I honour him: but, as he was ambitious, I slew him *J. Cæsar* iii 2 28
As I slew my best lover for the good of Rome, I have the same dagger for myself, when it shall please my country iii 2 49
This ensign here of mine was turning back; I slew the coward v 3 4
The one the other poison'd for my sake, And after slew herself *Lear* v 3 241
I slew him there.—Marry, the gods forfend! *Cymbeline* v 5 287
This man is better than the man he slew, As well descended as thyself v 5 302
Slewest. Tybalt would kill thee, But thou slew'st Tybalt *Rom. and Jul.* iii 3 138
From Modena, where thou slew'st Hirtius and Pansa *Ant. and Cleo.* i 4 57
Slice, I say! pauca, pauca: slice! that's my humour *Mer. Wives* i 1 134
'Slid. I'll make a shaft or a bolt on't: 'slid, 'tis but venturing iii 4 24
'Slid, I'll after him again and beat him *T. Night* iii 4 426
Slide. Therefore paucas pallabris; let the world slide *T. of Shrew* Ind. 1 6
Thou mayst slide from my shoulder to my heel iv 1 15
I slide O'er sixteen years and leave the growth untried *W. Tale* iv 1 5
The fool slides o'er the ice that you should break *Troi. and Cres.* iii 3 215
Let the famish'd flesh slide from the bone *T. of Athens* iv 3 535
Sliding. And rather proved the sliding of your brother A merriment than a vice *Meas. for Meas.* ii 4 115
Slight. And leave her on such slight conditions *T. G. of Ver.* v 4 138
Engrossed opportunities to meet her; fee'd every slight occasion that could but niggardly give me sight of her *Mer. Wives* ii 2 204
Some please-man, some slight zany, Some mumble-news *L. L. Lost* v 2 463
In some slight measure it will pay *M. N. Dream* iii 2 86
If thou dost him any slight disgrace *As Y. Like It* i 1 155
I must give myself some hurts, and say I got them in exploit: yet slight ones will not carry it *All's Well* iv 1 41
Puts him off, slights him, with 'Whoop, do me no harm' *W. Tale* iv 4 200
A name So slight, unworthy and ridiculous, . . . as the pope *K. John* iii 1 150
For thy walls, a pretty slight drollery 2 *Hen. IV.* ii 1 156
I muse you make so slight a question iv 1 167
Every slight and false-derived cause iv 1 190
It is much that a lie with a slight oath and a jest with a sad brow will do v 1 92
Slight regard, contempt, And any thing that may not misbecome *Hen. V.* ii 4 117
For so slight and frivolous a cause 1 *Hen. VI.* iv 1 112
No quarrel, but a slight contention 3 *Hen. VI.* i 2 6
I can scarce think there's any, ye're so slight *Coriolanus* v 2 110
Murdering impossibility, to make What cannot be, slight work v 3 62
Be not ceased With slight denial *T. of Athens* ii 1 17
I did endure Not seldom, nor no slight checks ii 2 149
A slight unmeritable man, Meet to be sent on errands *J. Cæsar* iv 1 12
Have mind upon your health, tempt me no farther.—Away, slight man! iv 3 37
You laying these slight sullies on my son *Hamlet* ii 1 39
So slight, so drunken, and so indiscreet an officer *Othello* ii 3 279
Is Cæsar with Antonius prized so slight? *Ant. and Cleo.* i 1 56
Upon importance of so slight and trivial a nature *Cymbeline* i 4 45
My quarrel was not altogether slight i 4 51
We have been too slight in sufferance iii 5 35
Since of your lives you set So slight a valuation iv 4 49
Iachimo, Slight thing of Italy v 4 64
'Slight, I could so beat the rogue! *T. Night* ii 5 38
'Slight, will you make an ass o' me? iii 2 14
Slighted. The rogues slighted me into the river with as little remorse as they would have drowned a blind bitch's puppies *Mer. Wives* iii 5 9
Your most dreadful laws so loosely slighted 2 *Hen. IV.* v 2 94
My letters, praying on his side, . . . were slighted off *J. Cæsar* iv 3 5
Slightest. I will go on the slightest errand *Much Ado* ii 1 272
If thou remember'st not the slightest folly That ever love did make thee run into, Thou hast not loved *As Y. Like It* ii 4 34
Even the slightest worship of his time 1 *Hen. IV.* iii 2 151

Slightly. The guards are but slightly basted on neither . . *Much Ado* i 1 289
To part so slightly with your wife's first gift . *Mer. of Venice* v 1 167
Left nothing fitting for the purpose Untouch'd, or slightly handled, in discourse . . . . *Richard III.* iii 7 19
Gone slightly o'er low steps and now are mounted . *Hen. VIII.* ii 4 112
For time is like a fashionable host That slightly shakes his parting guest by the hand . . . . *Troi. and Cres.* iii 3 166
My arrows, Too slightly timber'd for so loud a wind . *Hamlet* iv 7 22
If I gall him slightly, It may be death . . . . . . iv 7 148
The king must take it ill, That he's so slightly valued in his messenger *Lear* ii 2 153
Struck down Some mortally, some slightly touch'd . . *Cymbeline* v 3 10
Slightness. And give way the while To unstable slightness *Coriolanus* iii 1 148
Slily. A serpent . . . , That slily glided towards your majesty 2 *Hen. VI.* iii 2 260
He slily stole away and left his men . . . . . 3 *Hen. VI.* i 1 3
Deceive more slily than Ulysses could . . . . . . iii 2 189
The king was slily finger'd from the deck . . . . . v 1 44
Here in these confines slily have I lurk'd . . . . *Richard III.* iv 4 3
As if that whatsoever god who leads him Were slily crept into his human powers And gave him graceful posture . . . *Coriolanus* ii 1 236
Slime. With miry slime left on them by a flood . . *T. Andron.* iii 1 126
An honest man he is, and hates the slime That sticks on filthy deeds *Oth.* v 2 148
By the fire That quickens Nilus' slime . . . *Ant. and Cleo.* i 3 69
The higher Nilus swells, The more it promises: as it ebbs, the seedsman Upon the slime and ooze scatters his grain . . . . ii 7 25
These fig-leaves Have slime upon them, such as the aspic leaves . v 2 355
Slimy. Reflecting gems, Which woo'd the slimy bottom of the deep *Richard III.* i 4 32
My bended hook shall pierce Their slimy jaws. . . *Ant. and Cleo.* ii 5 13
Sling. Swift as stones Enforced from the old Assyrian slings . *Hen. V.* iv 7 65
Whether 'tis nobler in the mind to suffer The slings and arrows of outrageous fortune, Or to take arms against a sea of troubles *Hamlet* iii 1 58
Slink. We will slink away in supper-time . . . . *Mer. of Venice* ii 4 1
'Tis he: slink by, and note him . . . . . *As Y. Like It* iii 2 267
So his familiars to his buried fortunes Slink all away . *T. of Athens* iv 2 11
Slip. Otherwise you might slip away . . . . . *Mer. Wives* iv 2 54
Her father hath commanded her to slip Away with Slender . . iv 6 23
Which for this nineteen years we have let slip. . *Meas. for Meas.* i 3 21
Such a warped slip of wilderness Ne'er issued from his blood . . . iii 1 142
I am sorry, one so learned and so wise As you, Lord Angelo, have still appear'd, Should slip so grossly . . . . v 1 477
Then slip I from her bum, down topples she . . . . *M. N. Dream* ii 1 53
It is true, without any slips of prolixity . . . *Mer. of Venice* iii 1 12
And with indented glides did slip away Into a bush . *As Y. Like It* iv 3 113
Sit by my side and let the world slip: we shall ne'er be younger *T. of Shrew* Ind. 2 146
And choice breeds A native slip to us from foreign seeds . *All's Well* i 3 152
Let him let the matter slip, and I'll give him my horse . . *T. Night* iii 4 314
Of that kind Our rustic garden's barren; and I care not To get slips of them . . . . *W. Tale* iv 4 85
I'll not put The dibble in earth to set one slip of them . . . . iv 4 100
Before the game is afoot, thou still let'st slip . . . 1 *Hen. IV.* i 3 278
You stand like greyhounds in the slips, Straining upon the start *Hen. V.* iii 1 31
Thy sons, fair slips of such a stock . . . . . 2 *Hen. VI.* ii 2 58
And noble stock Was graft with crab-tree slip. . . . . . . iii 2 214
From which even here I slip my weary neck . . . *Richard III.* iv 4 112
Like a fawning greyhound in the leash, To let him slip at will *Coriolanus* i 6 39
These slips have made him noted long . . . . *T. Andron.* ii 3 86
Brave slip, sprung from the great Andronicus . . . . . . v 1 9
What counterfeit did I give you?—The slip, sir, the slip . *Rom. and Jul.* ii 4 51
Let him slip down, Not one accompanying his declining foot *T. of Athens* i 1 87
Greases his pure mind, That from it all consideration slips! . . . iv 3 196
With a monarch's voice Cry 'Havoc,' and let slip the dogs of war *J. C.* iii 1 273
Gall of goat, and slips of yew Sliver'd in the moon's eclipse . *Macbeth* iv 1 27
Such wanton, wild and usual slips As are companions noted . *Hamlet* ii 1 22
So they do nothing, 'tis a venial slip. . . . . . *Othello* iv 1 9
We'll slip you for a season; but our jealousy Does yet depend *Cymbeline* iv 3 22
Slipped. Lucentio slipp'd me like his greyhound . . *T. of Shrew* v 2 52
You slipp'd not With any but with us . . . . . *W. Tale* i 2 85
Had slipp'd our claim until another age . . . . 3 *Hen. VI.* ii 2 162
If I could have remembered a gilt counterfeit, thou wouldst not have slipped out of my contemplation . . . . *Troi. and Cres.* ii 3 28
The bonds of heaven are slipp'd, dissolved, and loosed . . . v 2 156
A thing slipp'd idly from me. Our poesy is as a gum . *T. of Athens* i 1 20
He did command me to call timely on him: I have almost slipp'd the hour . . . . *Macbeth* ii 3 52
Slipper. If 'twere a kibe, 'Twould put me to my slipper . . *Tempest* ii 1 277
I do adore thy sweet grace's slipper . . . . . *L. L. Lost* v 2 672
Where are my slippers? . . . . *T. of Shrew* iv 1 156
Standing on slippers, which his nimble haste Had falsely thrust upon contrary feet . . . . *K. John* iv 2 197
A slipper and subtle knave, a finder of occasions . . *Othello* ii 1 246
Slippered. The sixth age shifts Into the lean and slipper'd pantaloon, With spectacles on nose . . . . *As Y. Like It* ii 7 158
Slippery. Ha' not you seen, . . . My wife is slippery? . . *W. Tale* i 2 273
He that stands upon a slippery place Makes nice of no vile hold *K. John* iii 4 137
Hanging them With deafening clamour in the slippery clouds 2 *Hen. IV.* iii 1 24
Slippery standers, The love that lean'd on them as slippery too *T. and C.* iii 3 84
O world, thy slippery turns! . . . . *Coriolanus* iv 4 12
As well of glib and slippery creatures as Of grave . . *T. of Athens* i 1 53
What shall I say? My credit now stands on such slippery ground *J. C.* iii 1 191
Our slippery people, Whose love is never link'd to the deserver Till his deserts are past . . . . *Ant. and Cleo.* i 2 192
As slippery as the Gordian knot was hard! . . . . *Cymbeline* ii 2 34
Is certain falling, or so slippery that The fear's as bad as falling . . iii 3 48
Slip-shod. Thy wit shall ne'er go slip-shod . . . . . . *Lear* i 5 12
Slipt. If he had been as you and you as he, You would have slipt like him; but he, like you, Would not have been so stern *Meas. for Meas.* ii 2 65
Slish. Here's snip and nip and cut and slish and slash . *T. of Shrew* iv 3 90
Slit. I'll slit the villain's nose, that would have sent me to the gaol . v 1 134
Sliver. There, on the pendent boughs her coronet weeds Clambering to hang, an envious sliver broke . . . . *Hamlet* iv 7 174
She that herself will sliver and disbranch From her material sap . *Lear* iv 2 34
Slivered. Slips of yew Sliver'd in the moon's eclipse . . . *Macbeth* iv 1 28
Slobbery. To buy a slobbery and a dirty farm . . . . *Hen. V.* iii 5 13
Slop. A German from the waist downward, all slops . . *Much Ado* iii 2 36
O, rhymes are guards on wanton Cupid's hose: Disfigure not his slop *L. L. Lost* iv 3 59
About the satin for my short cloak and my slops . . 2 *Hen. IV.* i 2 34
Bon jour! there's a French salutation to your French slop *Rom. and Jul.* ii 4 47

Slope. Though castles topple on their warders' heads; Though palaces and pyramids do slope Their heads to their foundations . *Macbeth* iv 1 57
Sloth. To ebb Hereditary sloth instructs me . . . . . *Tempest* ii 1 223
Ebbing men, indeed, Most often do so near the bottom run By their own fear or sloth.—Prithee, say on . . . . ii 1 228
Let not sloth dim your honours new-begot . . . . . 1 *Hen. VI.* i 1 79
I abhor This dilatory sloth and tricks of Rome . . . *Hen. VIII.* ii 4 237
Hog in sloth, fox in stealth, wolf in greediness, dog in madness . *Lear* iii 4 96
Weariness Can snore upon the flint, when resty sloth Finds the down pillow hard. Now peace be here! . . . . . . *Cymbeline* iii 6 34
Slothful. The slothful watch but weak . . . . . 1 *Hen. VI.* iii 2 7
Slough. They threw me off . . . in a slough of mire . . *Mer. Wives* iv 5 69
Cast thy humble slough . . . . *T. Night* ii 5 161; iii 4 76
And newly move, With casted slough and fresh legerity . . *Hen. V.* iv 1 23
Or as the snake roll'd in a flowering bank, With shining checker'd slough, doth sting a child . . . . 2 *Hen. VI.* iii 1 229
Slovenly. A slovenly unhandsome corse . . . . . 1 *Hen. IV.* i 3 44
Slovenry. Time hath worn us into slovenry . . . . *Hen. V.* iv 3 114
Slow. The man i' the moon's too slow . . . . . . *Tempest* ii 1 249
A quick wit.—And yet it cannot overtake your slow purse *T. G. of Ver.* i 1 133
You'll still be too forward.—And yet I was last chidden for being too slow ii 1 13
She is slow in words.—O villain, that set this down among her vices! To be slow in words is a woman's only virtue . . . . iii 1 338
Too liberal.—Of her tongue she cannot, for that's writ down she is slow of iii 1 357
A quick ear.—Ay, I would I were deaf; it makes me have a slow heart iv 2 65
Had not their bark been very slow of sail . . . *Com. of Errors* i 1 117
Is not lead a metal heavy, dull, and slow? . . . . *L. L. Lost* iii 1 60
I say lead is slow.—You are too swift, sir, to say so: Is that lead slow which is fired from a gun? . . . . iii 1 62
Other slow arts entirely keep the brain . . . . iv 3 324
But, O, methinks, how slow This old moon wanes! . . *M. N. Dream* i 1 3
Give it me, for I am slow of study . . . . i 2 69
Slow in pursuit, but match'd in mouth like bells, Each under each . iv 1 128
Slow in speech, yet sweet as spring-time flowers . . *T. of Shrew* ii 1 248
Thou shalt soon feel, to thy cold comfort, for being slow in thy hot office iv 1 34
Only doth backward pull Our slow designs . . . . . *All's Well* i 1 234
A sad face, a reverend carriage, a slow tongue . . . . *T. Night* iii 4 81
Creep time ne'er so slow, Yet it shall come for me to do thee good *K. John* iii 3 31
For thee remains a heavier doom . . . The sly slow hours shall not determinate The dateless limit of thy dear exile . . . *Richard II.* i 3 150
With slow but stately pace kept on his course . . . . . v 2 10
You are as slow As hot Lord Percy is on fire to go . . 1 *Hen. IV.* iii 1 68
With their drowsy, slow and flagging wings . . . 2 *Hen. VI.* iv 1 5
You are slow; for shame, away!—Can we outrun the heavens? . . . v 2 72
Nor posted off their suits with slow delays . . . 3 *Hen. VI.* iv 8 40
I would not grow so fast, Because sweet flowers are slow *Richard III.* ii 4 15
To climb steep hills Requires slow pace at first . . . *Hen. VIII.* i 1 132
Churlish as the bear, slow as the elephant . . . *Troi. and Cres.* i 2 21
Thou strikest as slow as another . . . . ii 1 33
Wisely and slow; they stumble that run fast . . . . *Rom. and Jul.* ii 3 94
But old folks, many feign as they were dead; Unwieldy, slow, heavy . ii 5 17
Too swift arrives as tardy as too slow . . . . ii 6 15
And I am nothing slow to slack his haste . . . . iv 1 3
That swiftest wing of recompense is slow To overtake thee . *Macbeth* i 4 17
The valued file Distinguishes the swift, the slow, the subtle . . . iii 1 96
He hath, my lord, wrung from me my slow leave . . . . *Hamlet* i 2 58
With solemn march Goes slow and stately by them . . . . i 2 202
Finding ourselves too slow of sail, we put on a compelled valour . . iv 6 17
But, alas, to make me A fixed figure for the time of scorn To point his slow unmoving finger at! . . . . *Othello* iv 2 55
Cæsar hath sent— Too slow a messenger . . . *Ant. and Cleo.* v 2 324
The search so slow, That could not trace them! . . . . *Cymbeline* i 1 64
Could best express how slow his soul sail'd on, How swift his ship . i 3 13
Which are the movers of a languishing death; But though slow, deadly i 5 10
Why, one that rode to's execution, man, Could never go so slow . . . iii 2 73
Thou art too slow to do thy master's bidding, When I desire it too . iii 4 100
Alack that Leonine was so slack, so slow! . . . . *Pericles* iv 2 68
Slowed. I would I knew not why it should be slow'd . *Rom. and Jul.* iv 1 16
Slower. It was the swift celerity of his death, Which I did think with slower foot came on . . . . *Meas. for Meas.* v 1 400
Fall somewhat into a slower method . . . . . *Richard III.* i 2 116
Have a continent forbearance till the speed of his rage goes slower *Lear* i 2 183
Slow-gaited. He is very slow-gaited . . . . . . *L. L. Lost* iii 1 56
Slowly. To torment me For bringing wood in slowly . . . *Tempest* ii 2 16
A snail; for though he comes slowly, he carries his house *As Y. Like It* iv 1 55
Like a remorseful pardon slowly carried . . . . . *All's Well* v 3 58
That 'once,' I see by your good father's speed, Will come on very slowly *W. Tale* v 1 211
I conjure thee but slowly; run more fast. . . . . . . *K. John* iv 2 269
Slowness. I do not all believe: 'tis my slowness that I do not *All's Well* i 3 10
This fool's speed Be cross'd with slowness; labour be his meed! *Cymb.* iii 5 168
Slow-winged. O slow-wing'd turtle! shall a buzzard take thee? *T. of S.* ii 1 208
Slubber not business for my sake . . . . . . *Mer. of Venice* ii 8 39
Be content to slubber the gloss of your new fortunes . . . *Othello* i 3 227
Slug. Thou drone, thou snail, thou slug, thou sot! . . *Com. of Errors* ii 2 196
Fie, what a slug is Hastings, that he comes not! . . *Richard III.* iii 1 22
Slug-a-bed. Why, lamb! why, lady, fie, you slug-a-bed! . *Rom. and Jul.* iv 5 2
Sluggard. You have ta'en a tardy sluggard here . . . *Richard III.* v 3 225
Sluggardized. Living dully sluggardized at home . . . *T. G. of Ver.* i 1 7
Sluggish. Find The ooze, to show what coast thy sluggish crare Might easiliest harbour in . . . . *Cymbeline* iv 2 205
Sluiced. Holds his wife by the arm, That little thinks she has been sluiced in's absence . . . . *W. Tale* i 2 194
Sluiced out his innocent soul through streams of blood . . *Richard II.* i 1 103
Slumber. If of life you keep a care, Shake off slumber . . *Tempest* ii 1 304
In which hurtling From miserable slumber I awaked . . *As Y. Like It* iv 3 133
But you must not now slumber in it. . . . . . *All's Well* iii 6 78
I did in time collect myself and thought This was so and no slumber *W. Tale* iii 3 39
In thy faint slumbers I by thee have watch'd, And heard thee murmur tales of iron wars . . . . 1 *Hen. IV.* ii 3 50
And hush'd with buzzing night-flies to thy slumber . . 2 *Hen. IV.* iii 1 11
Golden care! That keep'st the ports of slumber open wide! . . . iv 5 24
Ere theise eyes of mine take themselves to slomber. . . . *Hen. V.* iii 2 123
Being suffer'd in that harmful slumber . . . . . 2 *Hen. VI.* iii 2 262
In thy sight to die, what were it else But like a pleasant slumber? . . iii 2 390
I wonder he is so fond To trust the mockery of unquiet slumbers *Richard III.* iii 2 27
To take a nap, Lest leaden slumber peise me down to-morrow . . v 3 105

Slumber. Therefore best Not wake him in his slumber . . . *Hen. VIII.* i 1 122
You are for dreams and slumbers, brother priest . . *Troi. and Cres.* ii 2 37
We may, each wreathed in the other's arms, Our pastimes done, possess a golden slumber . . . . . . *T. Andron.* ii 3 26
If I do wake, some planet strike me down, That I may slumber in eternal sleep! . . . . ii 4 15
When will this fearful slumber have an end?—Now, farewell, flattery: die, Andronicus; Thou dost not slumber . . . . iii 1 253
Fast asleep? It is no matter; Enjoy the honey-heavy dew of slumber *J. Cæsar* ii 1 230
O murderous slumber, Lay'st thou thy leaden mace upon my boy? . iv 3 267
'Tis the soldiers' life To have their balmy slumbers waked with strife *Othello* ii 3 258
Thus smiling, as some fly had tickled slumber, Not as death's dart *Cymb.* iv 2 210
If heaven slumber while their creatures want . . . *Pericles* i 4 16
Should at these early hours Shake off the golden slumber of repose . iii 2 23
It nips me unto listening, and thick slumber Hangs upon mine eyes . v 1 235
Slumbered. Think but this, and all is mended, That you have but slumber'd here While these visions did appear . . *M. N. Dream* v 1 432
Slumbery. In this slumbery agitation, besides her walking and other actual performances . . . . *Macbeth* v 1 12
Slunk. Or slunk not Saturnine, as Tarquin erst, That left the camp to sin in Lucrece' bed? . . . . . . *T. Andron.* iv 1 63
Slut. Our radiant queen hates sluts and sluttery . . *Mer. Wives* v 5 50
To cast away honesty upon a foul slut were to put good meat into an unclean dish.—I am not a slut, though I thank the gods I am foul *As Y. Like It* iii 3 36
Hold up, you sluts, Your aprons mountant . . . *T. of Athens* iv 3 134
Sluttery. Our radiant queen hates sluts and sluttery . *Mer. Wives* v 5 50
Sluttery to such neat excellence opposed Should make desire vomit emptiness, Not so allured to feed . . . . *Cymbeline* i 6 44
Sluttish. Fortune's displeasure is but sluttish . . . *All's Well* v 2 7
Set them down For sluttish spoils of opportunity . . *Troi. and Cres.* iv 5 62
And bakes the elf-locks in foul sluttish hairs . . *Rom. and Jul.* i 4 90
Sluttishness. Praised be the gods for thy foulness! sluttishness may come hereafter . . . . *As Y. Like It* iii 3 41
Sly. I'll quickly cross By some sly trick . . . . *T. G. of Ver.* ii 6 41
The Slys are no rogues; look in the chronicles . . *T. of Shrew* Ind. 1 3
I am Christophero Sly; call not me 'honour' nor 'lordship' . . Ind. 2 5
Am not I Christopher Sly, old Sly's son of Burtonheath, by birth a pedlar? . . . . Ind. 2 19
Stephen Sly and old John Naps of Greece And Peter Turph . . Ind. 2 95
That sly devil, That broker, that still breaks the pate of faith *K. John* ii 1 567
For thee remains a heavier doom . . . : The sly slow hours shall not determinate The dateless limit of thy dear exile . . *Richard II.* i 3 150
Behold Thy sly conveyance and thy lord's false love . . *3 Hen. VI.* iii 3 160
Silken, sly, insinuating Jacks . . . . . *Richard III.* i 3 53
The sly whoresons Have got a speeding trick to lay down ladies *Hen. VIII.* i 3 39
Sly frantic wretch, that holp'st to make me great . *T. Andron.* iv 4 59
A sly and constant knave, Not to be shaked . . . *Cymbeline* i 5 75
Smack. All sects, all ages smack of this vice . . *Meas. for Meas.* ii 2 5
My father did something smack, something grow to . *Mer. of Venice* ii 2 18
Kiss'd her lips with such a clamorous smack . . . *T. of Shrew* iii 2 180
For thou hast to pull at a smack o' the contrary . . *All's Well* iii 3 237
He hath a smack of all neighbouring languages . . . . iv 1 18
Nothing she does or seems But smacks of something greater . *W. Tale* iv 4 158
He is but a bastard to the time That doth not smack of observation; And so am I, whether I smack or no . . . . . . *K. John* i 1 208
Smacks it not something of the policy? . . . . . . ii 1 396
Hath yet some smack of age in you . . . . *2 Hen. IV.* i 2 111
Thy words become thee as thy wounds; They smack of honour both *Macbeth* i 2 44
Smacking. Sudden, malicious, smacking of every sin That has a name . iv 3 59
Small. Too small a pasture for such store of muttons . *T. G. of Ver.* i 1 105
His little speaking shows his love but small . . . . . i 2 29
She is as white as a lily and as small as a wand . . . . ii 3 23
But were you banish'd for so small a fault? . . . . . iv 1 31
She has brown hair, and speaks small like a woman . . *Mer. Wives* i 1 49
A small spare mast, Such as seafaring men provide for storms *Com. of Er.* i 1 80
Small cheer and great welcome makes a merry feast . . . . iii 1 26
Small have continual plodders ever won Save base authority from others' books . . . . *L. L. Lost* i 1 86
But to have a love of that colour, methinks Samson had small reason for it . . . . i 2 92
More calf, certain.—No; he is best indued in the small . . . v 2 646
Play it in a mask, and you may speak as small as you will *M. N. Dream* i 2 52
Leathern wings, To make my small elves coats . . . . ii 2 5
These things seem small and undistinguishable, Like far-off mountains iv 1 192
It appears, by his small light of discretion, that he is in the wane . . v 1 257
Here's a small trifle of wives: alas, fifteen wives is nothing! *Mer. of Ven.* ii 2 169
After some small space, being strong at heart, He sent me *As Y. Like It* iv 3 152
The small acquaintance, my sudden wooing . . . . . . v 2 7
For God's sake, a pot of small ale . . . . *T. of Shrew* Ind. 2 1
As you say, there's small choice in rotten apples . . . . i 1 138
To seek their fortunes farther than at home Where small experience grows . . . . i 2 52
This small packet of Greek and Latin books . . . . . ii 1 101
With a small compassed cape . . . . iv 3 140
Thy small pipe Is as the maiden's organ, shrill and sound . *T. Night* i 4 32
That none so small advantage shall step forth . . . *K. John* iii 4 151
Feeling what small things are boisterous there [in the eye] . . . iv 1 95
Small showers last long, but sudden storms are short . *Richard II.* ii 1 35
Incaged in so small a verge, The waste is no whit lesser than thy land . ii 1 102
Nothing can we call our own but death And that small model of the barren earth Which serves as paste and cover to our bones . . iii 2 153
I play the torturer, by small and small To lengthen out the worst . iii 2 198
A matter of small consequence, Which for some reasons I would not have seen . . . . v 2 61
As hard to come as for a camel To thread the postern of a small needle's eye . . . . v 5 17
With our small conjunction we should on . . . *1 Hen. IV.* iv 1 37
When that this body did contain a spirit, A kingdom for it was too small a bound . . . . v 4 90
Doth it not show vilely in me to desire small beer? . *2 Hen. IV.* ii 2 7
I do now remember the poor creature, small beer . . . . ii 2 13
A night is but small breath and little pause To answer matters of this consequence . . . . *Hen. V.* ii 4 145
Small time, but in that small most greatly lived This star of England . Epil. 5
To hazard all our lives in one small boat! . . . *1 Hen. VI.* iv 6 33
Small curs are not regarded when they grin . . . *2 Hen. VI.* iii 1 18
Small. Did he not, contrary to form of law, Devise strange deaths for small offences done? . . . . *2 Hen. VI.* iii 1 59
Small things make base men proud . . . . iv 1 106
And I will make it felony to drink small beer . . . . . iv 2 73
This small inheritance my father left me Contenteth me . . . iv 10 20
'Tis beauty that doth oft make women proud; But, God he knows, thy share thereof is small . . . . *3 Hen. VI.* i 4 129
You are the fount that makes small brooks to flow . . . . iv 8 55
The city being but of small defence, We'll quickly rouse the traitors . v 1 64
Small joy have I in being England's queen.—And lessen'd be that small, God, I beseech thee! . . . . *Richard III.* i 3 110
Small herbs have grace, great weeds do grow apace . . . . ii 4 13
And part in just proportion our small strength . . . . . v 3 26
Your enemies are many, and not small . . . . *Hen. VIII.* v 1 128
A haberdasher's wife of small wit . . . . v 4 49
But small thanks for my labour . . . . . *Troi. and Cres.* i 1 72
In such indexes, although small pricks To their subsequent volumes . i 3 343
Things small as nothing, for request's sake only, He makes important . ii 3 179
If you'll bestow a small—of what you have little—Patience awhile *Coriol.* i 1 129
The strongest nerves and small inferior veins . . . . . i 1 142
Into a pipe Small as an eunuch, or the virgin voice . . . . iii 2 114
The main blaze of it is past, but a small thing would make it flame again iv 3 21
Let me go grind their bones to powder small . . . *T. Andron.* v 2 199
Like a loving child, Shed yet some small drops from thy tender spring v 3 167
Her waggoner a small grey-coated gnat . . . . *Rom. and Jul.* i 4 64
Thy face is much abused with tears.—The tears have got small victory iv 1 30
Small love 'mongst these sweet knaves, And all this courtesy! *T. of A.* i 1 258
I have received some small kindnesses from him . . . . . iii 2 22
When it falls, Each small annexment, petty consequence, Attends the boisterous ruin . . . . *Hamlet* iii 3 21
O most small fault, How ugly didst thou in Cordelia show! . . *Lear* i 4 288
You shall do small respect, show too bold malice . . . . ii 2 137
How chance the king comes with so small a train? . . . . ii 4 64
Like an old lecher's heart; a small spark, all the rest on's body cold . iii 4 117
Mice and rats, and such small deer, Have been Tom's food for seven long year . . . . iii 4 144
Her cock, a buoy Almost too small for sight . . . . . iv 6 20
The small gilded fly Does lecher in my sight . . . . . iv 6 114
Through tatter'd clothes small vices do appear . . . . . iv 6 168
To do what?—To suckle fools and chronicle small beer . . *Othello* ii 1 161
And thou, by that small hurt, hast cashier'd Cassio . . . . ii 3 381
The world's a huge thing: it is a great price For a small vice . . iv 3 70
Every time Serves for the matter that is then born in't.—But small to greater matters must give way.—Not if the small come first *Ant. and Cleo.* ii 2 11
She's a good sign, but I have seen small reflection of her wit . *Cymbeline* i 2 33
A small request, And yet of moment too . . . . . . i 6 181
If there be Yet left in heaven as small a drop of pity As a wren's eye . iv 2 304
Yet my good will is great, though the gift small . . . *Pericles* iii 4 18
With fingers long, small, white as milk . . . . . . iv Gower 22
Smaller. A smaller boon than this I cannot beg . . . *T. G. of Ver.* v 4 24
Cutting a smaller hair than may be seen . . . . *L. L. Lost* v 2 258
A power Much smaller than the smallest of his thoughts . *2 Hen. IV.* i 3 30
Smallest. Nature never lends The smallest scruple of her excellence *Meas. for Meas.* i 1 38
Swerve not from the smallest article of it . . . . . . iv 2 107
I may make my case as Claudio's, to cross this in the smallest . . iv 2 179
Being that I flow in grief, The smallest twine may lead me . *Much Ado* iv 1 252
Strike his honour down That violates the smallest branch . *L. L. Lost* i 1 21
Ladies, you, whose gentle hearts do fear The smallest monstrous mouse that creeps on floor . . . . *M. N. Dream* v 1 223
There's not the smallest orb which thou behold'st But in his motion like an angel sings . . . . *Mer. of Venice* v 1 60
And once again, a pot o' the smallest ale . . . . *T. of Shrew* Ind 2 77
The smallest thread That ever spider twisted . . . . *K. John* iv 3 127
Ere break the smallest parcel of this vow . . . . *1 Hen. IV.* iii 2 159
A power Much smaller than the smallest of his thoughts . *2 Hen. IV.* i 3 30
What you see is but the smallest part . . . . . *1 Hen. VI.* ii 3 52
The smallest worm will turn being trodden on . . . *3 Hen. VI.* ii 2 17
The traces of the smallest spider's web . . . . *Rom. and Jul.* i 4 61
If he do break the smallest particle Of any promise . . . *J. Cæsar* ii 1 139
Nor from mine own weak merits will I draw The smallest fear or doubt of her revolt; For she had eyes, and chose me . . . . *Othello* iii 3 188
How have I been behaved, that he might stick The small'st opinion on my least misuse? . . . . iv 2 109
Small-knowing. That unlettered small-knowing soul . . . *L. L. Lost* i 1 253
Smallness. Nay, follow'd him, till he had melted from The smallness of a gnat to air . . . . *Cymbeline* i 3 21
Smalus. Where the warlike Smalus, That noble honour'd lord, is fear'd and loved . . . . *W. Tale* v 1 157
Smart. Some of us will smart for it . . . . . . *Much Ado* v 1 109
Doth very foolishly, although he smart, Not to seem senseless *As Y. L. It* ii 7 54
The sword of Orleans hath not made me smart . . . *1 Hen. VI.* iv 6 42
Their softest touch as smart as lizards' stings! . . . *2 Hen. VI.* iii 2 325
But is't not cruel That she should feel the smart of this? *Hen. VIII.* ii 1 166
Thou canst not ease thy smart By friendship nor by speaking *T. and C.* iv 4 20
I have some wounds upon me, and they smart To hear themselves remember'd.—Should they not, Well might they fester . *Coriolanus* i 9 28
How smart a lash that speech doth give my conscience! . . *Hamlet* iii 1 50
And shielded him From this earth-vexing smart . . . *Cymbeline* v 4 42
Smarting. All smarting with my wounds being cold . . . *1 Hen. IV.* i 3 49
Stew'd in brine, Smarting in lingering pickle . . . *Ant. and Cleo.* ii 5 66
Smartly. And loosed his love-shaft smartly from his bow *M. N. Dream* ii 1 159
Smatch. Thy life hath had some smatch of honour in it . . *J. Cæsar* v 5 46
Smatter with your gossips, go . . . . . . *Rom. and Jul.* iii 5 172
Smear. Go carry them; and smear The sleepy grooms with blood *Macb.* ii 2 49
Smeared. Triumphant death, smear'd with captivity . . *1 Hen. VI.* iv 7 3
Lo, now my glory smear'd in dust and blood! . . . *3 Hen. VI.* v 2 23
If any such be here—As it were sin to doubt—that love this painting Wherein you see me smear'd . . . . *Coriolanus* i 6 69
This dread and black complexion smear'd With heraldry more dismal *Hamlet* ii 2 477
Smell. He smells like a fish; a very ancient and fish-like smell *Tempest* ii 2 26
I do smell all horse-piss; at which my nose is in great indignation . iv 1 199
I, having been acquainted with the smell before . . *T. G. of Ver.* iv 4 25
By my troth, I cannot abide the smell of hot meat since . *Mer. Wives* i 1 297
He writes verses, he speaks holiday, he smells April and May . . iii 2 69
And smell like Bucklersbury in simple time . . . . . . iii 3 79
The rankest compound of villanous smell that ever offended nostril . iii 5 94
But, stay; I smell a man of middle-earth . . . . v 5 84

Smell. You shall stifle in your own report And smell of calumny *M. for M.* ii 4 159
A' rubs himself with civet: can you smell him out by that? *Much Ado* iii 2 51
I am stuffed, cousin; I cannot smell iii 4 64
I smell some l'envoy, some goose, in this *L. L. Lost* iii 1 122
I smell false Latin; dunghill for unguem v 1 83
Your nose smells 'no' in this, most tender-smelling knight v 2 569
If it please you to dine with us.—Yes, to smell pork *Mer. of Venice* i 3 34
If I keep not my rank,— Thou losest thy old smell *As Y. Like It* i 2 114
I see, I hear, I speak; I smell sweet savours *T. of Shrew* Ind. 2 73
I am now, sir, muddied in fortune's mood, and smell somewhat strong of her strong displeasure *All's Well* v 2 5
Fortune's displeasure is but sluttish, if it smell so strongly v 2 8
Mine eyes smell onions; I shall weep anon v 3 321
I smell a device.—I have't in my nose too *T. Night* ii 3 176
You smell this business with a sense as cold As is a dead man's nose *W. T.* ii 1 151
I smell the trick on't iv 4 657
A good nose is requisite also, to smell out work for the other senses iv 4 687
I am stifled with this smell of sin *K. John* iv 3 113
He made me mad To see him shine so brisk and smell so sweet *1 Hen. IV.* i 3 54
I smell it: upon my life, it will do well i 3 277
To wake a wolf is as bad as to smell a fox *2 Hen. IV.* i 2 175
The violet smells to him as it doth to me *Hen. V.* iv 1 106
The smell whereof shall breed a plague in France iv 3 103
Hence! I am qualmish at the smell of leek v 1 22
With whose sweet smell the air shall be perfumed *2 Hen. VI.* i 1 255
A goodly house: the feast smells well *Coriolanus* iv 5 5
Thy counsel, lad, smells of no cowardice *T. Andron.* ii 1 132
What's in a name? that which we call a rose By any other name would smell as sweet *Rom. and Jul.* ii 2 44
With loathsome smells, And shrieks like mandrakes' torn out of the earth iv 3 46
Th' ear, Taste, touch and smell, pleased from thy table rise *T. of Athens* i 2 132
Of him that, his particular to foresee, Smells from the general weal iv 3 160
That this foul deed shall smell above the earth *J. Cæsar* iii 1 274
The heaven's breath Smells wooingly here *Macbeth* i 6 6
Here's the smell of the blood still: all the perfumes of Arabia will not sweeten this little hand v 1 56
O, my offence is rank, it smells to heaven *Hamlet* iii 3 36
Do you smell a fault?—I cannot wish the fault undone *Lear* i 1 16
What a man cannot smell out, he may spy into i 5 23
There's not a nose among twenty but can smell him that's stinking ii 4 72
Fie, foh, and fum, I smell the blood of a British man iii 4 189
Go thrust him out at gates, and let him smell His way to Dover iii 7 93
O, let me kiss that hand!—Let me wipe it first; it smells of mortality iv 6 136
Thou know'st, the first time that we smell the air, We wawl and cry iv 6 183
Foh! one may smell in such a will most rank, Foul disproportion *Othello* iii 3 232
They see and smell And have their palates both for sweet and sour, As husbands iv 3 95
When I have pluck'd the rose, I cannot give it vital growth again, It must needs wither: I'll smell it on the tree v 2 15
Villany! I think upon't, I think: I smell't: O villany! v 2 191
And stand the buffet With knaves that smell of sweat *Ant. and Cleo.* i 4 21
His celestial breath Was sulphurous to smell *Cymbeline* v 4 115
It smells most sweetly in my sense.—A delicate odour *Pericles* iii 2 60

Smellest. O thou weed, Who art so lovely fair and smell'st so sweet That the sense aches at thee! *Othello* iv 2 68

Smelling so sweetly, all musk, and so rushling *Mer. Wives* ii 2 67
Through the nose, as if you snuffed up love by smelling love *L. L. Lost* iii 1 17
And why, indeed, Naso, but for smelling out the odoriferous flowers of fancy? iv 2 128
Sometime she gallops o'er a courtier's nose, And then dreams he of smelling out a suit *Rom. and Jul.* i 4 78
Ears without hands or eyes, smelling sans all *Hamlet* iii 4 79

Smelt. Lifted up their noses As they smelt music *Tempest* iv 1 178
All the chamber smelt him *T. G. of Ver.* iv 4 22
Though she smelt brown bread and garlic *Meas. for Meas.* iii 2 194
You are the musty chaff; and you are smelt Above the moon *Coriolanus* v 1 31
For this, being smelt, with that part cheers each part *Rom. and Jul.* ii 3 25
E'en so.—And smelt so? pah!—E'en so, my lord *Hamlet* v 1 221
There I found 'em, there I smelt 'em out *Lear* iv 6 105
Would he had been one of my rank!—To have smelt like a fool *Cymbeline* ii 1 18

Smile. Thou didst smile, Infused with a fortitude from heaven *Tempest* i 2 153
Do not smile at me that I boast her off iv 1 9
How angerly I taught my brow to frown, When inward joy enforced my heart to smile! *T. G. of Ver.* i 2 63
Overweening slave! Bestow thy fawning smiles on equal mates iii 1 158
I dare be bold With our discourse to make your grace to smile v 4 163
Do you not smile at this? *Meas. for Meas.* v 1 163
I did but smile till now: Now, good my lord, give me the scope of justice v 1 233
I must be sad when I have cause and smile at no man's jests *Much Ado* i 3 15
If such a one will smile and stroke his beard, Bid sorrow wag v 1 15
Affliction may one day smile again *L. L. Lost* i 1 316
This is the flower that smiles on every one, To show his teeth v 2 331
That smiles his cheek in years and knows the trick To make my lady laugh v 2 465
To enforce the pained impotent to smile v 2 864
O that your frowns would teach my smiles such skill! *M. N. Dream* i 1 195
I jest to Oberon and make him smile ii 1 44
Of such vinegar aspect That they'll not show their teeth in way of smile, Though Nestor swear the jest be laughable *Mer. of Venice* i 1 55
He hears merry tales and smiles not i 2 52
I smile and say, 'This is no flattery' *As Y. Like It* ii 1 9
And bid him take that for coming a-night to Jane Smile ii 4 49
Shallow, inconstant, full of tears, full of smiles iii 2 433
Loose now and then A scatter'd smile, and that I'll live upon iii 5 104
If you should smile he grows impatient *T. of Shrew* Ind. 1 99
Time it is, when raging war is done, To smile at scapes and perils overblown v 2 3
Good fortune and the favour of the king Smile upon this contract *All's W.* ii 3 185
Quenching my familiar smile with an austere regard of control *T. Night* ii 5 73
Thy smiles become thee well; therefore in my presence still smile, dear my sweet ii 5 191
I will smile; I will do everything that thou wilt have me ii 5 194
He will smile upon her, which will now be so unsuitable to her disposition ii 5 221
Why, then, methinks 'tis time to smile again iii 1 137
He does smile his face into more lines than is in the new map iii 2 84
My lady will strike him: if she do, he'll smile and take't for a great favour iii 2 89

Smile. He does nothing but smile: your ladyship were best to have some guard about you *T. Night* iii 4 11
Why dost thou smile so and kiss thy hand so oft? iii 4 35
That thou thereby Mayst smile at this iv 1 61
Why laugh you at such a barren rascal? an you smile not, he's gagged v 1 384
Making practised smiles, As in a looking-glass *W. Tale* i 2 116
And his pond fish'd by his next neighbour, by Sir Smile, his neighbour i 2 196
The pretty dimples of his chin and cheek, His smiles ii 3 102
This unhair'd sauciness and boyish troops The king doth smile at *K. John* v 2 134
Wooing poor craftsmen with the craft of smiles *Richard II.* i 4 28
As a long-parted mother with her child Plays fondly with her tears and smiles in meeting iii 2 9
His face still combating with tears and smiles v 2 32
Where I first bow'd my knee Unto this king of smiles *1 Hen. IV.* i 3 246
While covert enmity Under the smile of safety wounds the world *2 Hen. IV.* Ind. 10
When time shall serve, there shall be smiles *Hen. V.* ii 1 6
I saw him fumble with the sheets and play with flowers and smile upon his fingers' ends ii 3 15
Bids them good morrow with a modest smile And calls them brothers iv Prol. 33
Now we are victors; upon us he smiles *1 Hen. VI.* i 2 4
He beckons with his hand and smiles on me i 4 92
We mourn, France smiles; we lose, they daily get iv 3 32
Young Talbot's valour makes me smile at thee iv 7 4
Poor boy! he smiles, methinks, as who should say, Had death been French, then death had died to-day iv 7 27
Whose smile and frown, like to Achilles' spear, Is able with the change to kill and cure *2 Hen. VI.* v 1 100
Smile, gentle heaven! or strike, ungentle death! *3 Hen. VI.* ii 3 6
She weeps, and says her Henry is deposed; He smiles, and says his Edward is install'd iii 1 46
Why, I can smile, and murder whiles I smile iii 2 182
Methinks these peers of France should smile at that iii 3 91
I like it well that our fair queen and mistress Smiles at her news iii 3 168
And who durst smile when Warwick bent his brow? v 2 22
Speak fair, Smile in men's faces, smooth, deceive and cog *Richard III.* i 3 48
They smile at me that shortly shall be dead iii 4 109
Ghastly looks Are at my service, like enforced smiles iii 5 9
These English woes will make me smile in France iv 4 115
Smile heaven upon this fair conjunction, That long have frown'd! v 5 20
First, methought I stood not in the smile of heaven *Hen. VIII.* ii 4 187
There is, betwixt that smile we would aspire to, That sweet aspect of princes, and their ruin, More pangs and fears iii 2 368
No sun shall ever usher forth mine honours, Or gild again the noble troops that waited Upon my smiles iii 2 412
If they [women] smile, And say 'twill do, I know, within a while All the best men are ours Epil. 11
I have, as when the sun doth light a storm, Buried this sigh in wrinkle of a smile *Troi. and Cres.* i 1 38
But how should this man, that makes me smile, make Hector angry? i 2 33
O, he smiles valiantly.—Does he not?—O yes, an 'twere a cloud in autumn i 2 137
Would not lose So rich advantage of a promised glory As smiles upon the forehead of this action ii 2 205
They were used to bend, To send their smiles before them to Achilles iii 3 72
Welcome ever smiles, And farewell goes out sighing iii 3 168
You smile and mock me, as if I meant naughtily iv 2 38
Sit, gods, upon your thrones, and smile at Troy! v 10 7
With a kind of smile, Which ne'er came from the lungs *Coriolanus* i 1 111
For, look you, I may make the belly smile As well as speak i 1 113
But I'll report it Where senators shall mingle tears with smiles i 9 3
The smiles of knaves Tent in my cheeks! iii 2 115
When I am forth, Bid me farewell, and smile iv 1 50
And wonder greatly that man's face can fold In pleasing smiles such murderous tyranny *T. Andron.* ii 3 267
Look, how the black slave smiles upon the father iv 2 120
The grey-eyed morn smiles on the frowning night *Rom. and Jul.* ii 3 1
So smile the heavens upon this holy act, That after hours with sorrow chide us not!—Amen, amen! ii 6 1
I little talk'd of love; For Venus smiles not in a house of tears iv 1 8
I have need of many orisons To move the heavens to smile upon my state iv 3 4
No porter at his gate, But rather one that smiles and still invites All that pass by. It cannot hold *T. of Athens* ii 1 11
Then they could smile and fawn upon his debts iii 4 51
Spare not the babe, Whose dimpled smiles from fools exhaust their mercy iv 3 119
Thou rather shalt enforce it with thy smile Than hew to't with thy sword v 4 45
Seldom he smiles, and smiles in such a sort As if he mock'd himself and scorn'd his spirit That could be moved to smile at any thing *J. C.* i 2 205
Hide it in smiles and affability ii 1 82
Popilius Lena speaks not of our purposes; For, look, he smiles iii 1 24
That mothers shall but smile when they behold Their infants quarter'd with the hands of war iii 1 267
Some that smile have in their hearts, I fear, Millions of mischiefs iv 1 50
If we do meet again, why, we shall smile; If not, why then, this parting was well made v 1 118
If we do meet again, we'll smile indeed; If not, 'tis true this parting was well made v 1 121
Where we are, There's daggers in men's smiles *Macbeth* ii 3 146
The blood-bolter'd Banquo smiles upon me iv 1 123
Where nothing, But who knows nothing, is once seen to smile iv 3 167
But swords I smile at, weapons laugh to scorn, Brandish'd by man that's of a woman born v 7 12
Occasion smiles upon a second leave *Hamlet* i 3 54
Meet it is I set it down, That one may smile, and smile, and be a villain i 5 108
An thou canst not smile as the wind sits, thou'lt catch cold shortly *Lear* i 4 112
Smile you my speeches, as I were a fool? ii 2 88
Fortune, good night: smile once more; turn thy wheel! ii 2 180
Her smiles and tears Were like a better way iv 3 20
The robb'd that smiles steals something from the thief *Othello* i 3 208
We lose it not, so long as we can smile i 3 211
Ay, smile upon her, do; I will gyve thee in thine own courtship ii 1 170
Here he comes: As he shall smile, Othello shall go mad iv 1 101
His unbookish jealousy must construe Poor Cassio's smiles, gestures and light behaviour, Quite in the wrong iv 1 103
If't be summer news, Smile to't before *Cymbeline* iii 4 13

Smile. Nobly he yokes A smiling with a sigh, as if the sigh Was that it was, for not being such a smile; The smile mocking the sigh *Cymb.* iv 2 53
Feast here awhile, Until our stars that frown lend us a smile *Pericles* i 4 108
Smiled. When men were fond, I smiled and wonder'd how . *M. for M.* ii 2 187
These traitorly rascals, whose miseries are to be smiled at . *W. Tale* iv 4 822
And still he smiled and talk'd . . . . 1 *Hen. IV.* i 3 41
Who knows on whom fortune would then have smiled? . 2 *Hen. IV.* iv 1 133
And smiled to see him Mangle the work of nature . . *Hen. V.* ii 4 59
I came and cheer'd him up: He smiled me in the face, raught me his hand . . . . iv 6 21
He smiled and said 'The better for our purpose' . . *Richard III.* v 3 274
Those that understood him smiled at one another . . . *J. Cæsar* i 2 286
I told him of the army that was landed; He smiled at it . . *Lear* iv 2 5
When Julius Cæsar Smiled at their lack of skill, but found their courage Worthy his frowning at . . . . *Cymbeline* ii 4 22
Smiledst. Thou that smiledst at good Duke Humphrey's death 2 *Hen. VI.* iv 1 76
Smilest thou? I sent for thee upon a sad occasion . . *T. Night* iii 4 19
And I will think thou smilest And buss thee as thy wife . *K. John* iii 4 34
Thou cutt'st my head off with a golden axe, And smilest upon the stroke that murders me . . . . *Rom. and Jul.* iii 3 23
Smilets. Those happy smilets, That play'd on her ripe lip . *Lear* iv 3 21
Smiling. The heaving of my lungs provokes me to ridiculous smiling *L. L. Lost* iii 1 78
Though the mourning brow of progeny Forbid the smiling courtesy of love . . . . v 2 755
Methought a serpent eat my heart away, And you sat smiling *M. N. D.* ii 2 150
Like a villain with a smiling cheek, A goodly apple rotten at the heart *Mer. of Venice* i 3 101
She sat like patience on a monument, Smiling at grief . . *T. Night* ii 4 118
If thou entertainest my love, let it appear in thy smiling . . . ii 5 191
Bade me come smiling and cross-garter'd to you . . . . v 1 345
Then camest in smiling, And in such forms which here were presupposed v 1 357
And on the marriage-bed Of smiling peace to march a bloody host *K. John* iii 1 246
So, weeping, smiling, greet I thee, my earth . . . *Richard II.* iii 2 10
By smiling pick-thanks and base newsmongers . . 1 *Hen. IV.* iii 2 25
Stood smiling to behold his lion's whelp Forage in blood . *Hen. V.* i 2 109
Thou smiling while he knit his angry brows . . . . 3 *Hen. VI.* ii 2 20
With smiling plenty and fair prosperous days! . . *Richard III.* v 5 34
I think his smiling becomes him better than any man . *Troi. and Cres.* i 2 135
Both our powers, with smiling fronts encountering . . *Coriolanus* i 6 8
Most smiling, smooth, detested parasites, Courteous destroyers! *T. of Athens* iii 6 104
Many lusty Romans Came smiling, and did bathe their hands in it *J. C.* ii 2 79
Spouting blood in many pipes, In which so many smiling Romans bathed ii 2 86
Fortune, on his damned quarrel smiling, Show'd like a rebel's whore *Macbeth* i 2 14
I would, while it was smiling in my face, Have pluck'd my nipple from his boneless gums, And dash'd the brains out . . . . . i 7 56
This gentle and unforced accord of Hamlet Sits smiling to my heart *Ham.* i 2 124
O villain, villain, smiling, damned villain! . . . . . i 5 106
Man delights not me: no, nor woman neither, though by your smiling you seem to say so . . . . ii 2 323
Such smiling rogues as these, Like rats, oft bite the holy cords a-twain Which are too intrinse t' unloose . . . . . . *Lear* ii 2 79
Pretty dimpled boys, like smiling Cupids . . . *Ant. and Cleo.* ii 2 207
Comest thou smiling from The world's great snare uncaught? . . iv 8 17
Nobly he yokes A smiling with a sigh . . . . . *Cymbeline* iv 2 52
Thus smiling, as some fly had tickled slumber, Not as death's dart, being laugh'd at . . . . iv 2 210
Patience gazing on kings' graves, and smiling Extremity out of act *Per.* v 1 139
Smilingly. All the regions Do smilingly revolt . . *Coriolanus* iv 6 103
'Twixt two extremes of passion, joy and grief, Burst smilingly . *Lear* v 3 199
Smirch. With a kind of umber smirch my face. . . *As Y. Like It* i 3 114
Smirched. In the smirched worm-eaten tapestry . . . *M. Ado* iii 3 145
Smirched thus and mired with infamy . . . . . . iv 1 135
Do, with his smirch'd complexion, all fell feats . . . *Hen. V.* iii 3 17
Smit. My reliances on his fracted dates Have smit my credit *T. of Athens* ii 1 23
Smite. I will smite his noddles . . . . . *Mer. Wives* iii 1 128
All-shaking thunder, Smite flat the thick rotundity o' the world! *Lear* iii 2 7
The first stone Drop in my neck: as it determines, so Dissolve my life! The next Cæsarion smite! . . . . . . *Ant. and Cleo.* iii 13 162
I do feel, By the rebound of yours, a grief that smites My very heart . v 2 104
The gods! it smites me Beneath the fall I have . . . . . v 2 171
Smith. His mother played false with a smith . . *Mer. of Venice* i 2 48
I saw a smith stand with his hammer, thus . . . . *K. John* iv 2 193
Here is now the smith's note for shoeing and plough-irons . 2 *Hen. IV.* v 1 19
And Dick the Butcher, . . . And Smith the weaver . 2 *Hen. VI.* iv 2 30
Smithfield. He's gone into Smithfield to buy your worship a horse.—I bought him in Paul's, and he'll buy me a horse in Smithfield 2 *Hen. IV.* i 2 56
The witch in Smithfield shall be burn'd to ashes . . 2 *Hen. VI.* ii 3 7
Get you to Smithfield and gather head . . . . . . iv 5 10
There's an army gathered together in Smithfield . . . . iv 6 14
Smock. Foul shirts and smocks, socks, foul stockings . *Mer. Wives* iii 5 91
There will she sit in her smock till she have writ a sheet of paper *M. Ado* ii 3 137
Die when you will, a smock shall be your shroud . . . *L. L. Lost* v 2 479
And maidens bleach their summer smocks . . . . . . v 2 916
I shall stay here the forehorse to a smock . . . *All's Well* ii 1 30
You would think a smock were a she-angel . . . *W. Tale* iv 4 210
Doubtless he shrives this woman to her smock . . 1 *Hen. VI.* i 2 119
A sail, a sail!—Two, two; a shirt and a smock . *Rom. and Jul.* ii 4 109
How dost thou look now? O ill-starr'd wench! Pale as thy smock! *Oth.* v 2 273
Your old smock brings forth a new petticoat . . *Ant. and Cleo.* i 2 175
Smoke. Sweet smoke of rhetoric! He reputes me a cannon . *L. L. Lost* iii 1 64
Thus must I from the smoke into the smother . . *As Y. Like It* i 2 299
Out at the key-hole; stop that, 'twill fly with the smoke out at the chimney . . . . iv 1 165
They begin to smoke me . . . . *All's Well* iv 1 30
It was besmear'd As black as Vulcan in the smoke of war . *T. Night* v 1 56
I'll smoke your skin-coat, an I catch you right . . . *K. John* ii 1 139
They shoot but calm words folded up in smoke . . . . . ii 1 229
He speaks plain cannon fire, and smoke and bounce . . . ii 1 462
This night, whose black contagious breath Already smokes . . v 4 34
So bees with smoke and doves with noisome stench Are from their hives and houses driven away . . . . 1 *Hen. VI.* i 5 23
Far as I could well discern For smoke and dusky vapours of the night ii 2 27
And entrails feed the sacrificing fire, Whose smoke, like incense, doth perfume the sky . . . . *T. Andron.* i 1 145
This maugre all the world will I keep safe, Or some of you shall smoke for it . . . . iv 2 111

Smoke. Feather of lead, bright smoke, cold fire, sick health! *Rom. and Jul.* i 1 186
Love is a smoke raised with the fume of sighs . . . . . . i 1 196
Mouth-friends! smoke and luke-warm water Is your perfection *T. of A.* iii 6 99
Burn him up; Let your close fire predominate his smoke . . . iv 3 142
Now, whilst your purpled hands do reek and smoke . . *J. Cæsar* iii 1 158
Come, thick night, And pall thee in the dunnest smoke of hell *Macbeth* i 5 52
What means that bloody knife?—'Tis hot, it smokes . . *Lear* v 3 223
Let's quit this ground, And smoke the temple with our sacrifices . *Cymb.* v 5 398
And let our crooked smokes climb to their nostrils From our blest altars v 5 477
Murder's as near to lust as flame to smoke . . . . *Pericles* i 1 138
Smoked. He was first smoked by the old lord Lafeu . . *All's Well* iii 6 111
His brandish'd steel, Which smoked with bloody execution . *Macbeth* i 2 18
Smoking. I was smoking a musty room . . . . *Much Ado* i 3 61
Their steeds, That stain'd their fetlocks in his smoking blood 3 *Hen. VI.* ii 3 21
Queen Margaret saw Thy murderous falchion smoking in his blood *Richard III.* i 2 94
That we with smoking swords may march from hence . . *Coriolanus* i 4 11
Smoky. To be the mark Of smoky muskets . . . . *All's Well* iii 2 111
Worse than a smoky house. . . . . 1 *Hen. IV.* iii 1 161
To the fire-eyed maid of smoky war All hot and bleeding will we offer them . . . . iv 1 114
Why rather, sleep, liest thou in smoky cribs, Upon uneasy pallets? 2 *Hen. IV.* iii 1 9
Unlustrous as the smoky light That's fed with stinking tallow *Cymbeline* i 6 109
Smooth. The course of true love never did run smooth . *M. N. Dream* i 1 134
And stick musk-roses in thy sleek smooth head . . . . . iv 1 3
Bare distress hath ta'en from me the show Of smooth civility *As Y. L. It* ii 7 96
I have been politic with my friend, smooth with mine enemy . . v 4 47
Why are our bodies soft and weak and smooth? . . . *T. of Shrew* v 2 165
Diana's lip Is not more smooth and rubious . . . . *T. Night* i 4 32
With such a smooth, discreet, and stable bearing . . . . . iv 3 19
To smooth the ice, or add another hue Unto the rainbow . . *K. John* iv 2 13
To smooth his fault I should have been more mild . . . *Richard II.* i 3 240
He hath brought us smooth and welcome news . . . 1 *Hen. IV.* i 1 66
Which hath been smooth as oil, soft as young down . . . . i 3 7
They bring smooth comforts false, worse than true wrongs 2 *Hen. IV.* Ind. 40
To Master Smooth's the silkman . . . . ii 1 31
Swears with a good grace, and wears his boots very smooth . . . ii 4 270
How smooth and even they do bear themselves! . . . *Hen. V.* ii 2 3
Our tongue is rough, coz, and my condition is not smooth . . . v 2 314
And smooth my way upon their headless necks . . . 2 *Hen. VI.* i 2 65
Smooth runs the water where the brook is deep . . . . . iii 1 53
Faults unknown, Which time will bring to light in smooth Duke Humphrey . . . . iii 1 65
And smooth the frowns of war with peaceful looks . . . 3 *Hen. VI.* ii 6 32
Smooths the wrong, Inferreth arguments of mighty strength . . . iii 1 48
How haps it, in this smooth discourse, You told not? . . . . iii 3 88
Smile in men's faces, smooth, deceive and cog . . . *Richard III.* i 3 48
His grace looks cheerfully and smooth to-day . . . . . . iii 4 50
So smooth he daub'd his vice with show of virtue . . . . . iii 5 29
The sea being smooth, How many shallow bauble boats dare sail! *T. and C.* i 3 34
I can smooth and fill his aged ear With golden promises . *T. Andron.* iv 4 96
Yield to his humour, smooth, and speak him fair . . . . v 2 140
To smooth that rough touch with a tender kiss . . *Rom. and Jul.* i 5 98
Ah, poor my lord, what tongue shall smooth thy name? . . . iii 2 98
Most smiling, smooth, detested parasites! . . . *T. of Athens* iii 6 104
Thy verse swells with stuff so fine and smooth That thou art even natural in thine art . . . . v 1 87
A most instant tetter bark'd about, Most lazar-like, with vile and loathsome crust, All my smooth body . . . . . . *Hamlet* i 5 73
To bear all smooth and even, This sudden sending him away must seem Deliberate pause . . . . iv 3 7
Smooth every passion That in the natures of their lords rebel . *Lear* ii 2 81
He hath a person and a smooth dispose To be suspected . . *Othello* i 3 403
That whiter skin of hers than snow, And smooth as monumental alabaster v 2 5
And smooth success Be strew'd before your feet! . . *Ant. and Cleo.* i 3 100
The sinful father Seem'd not to strike, but smooth . . *Pericles* i 2 78
Smoothed. We doubt not now But every rub is smoothed on our way *Hen. V.* ii 2 188
As by his smoothed brows it doth appear. . . . 1 *Hen. VI.* iii 1 124
Grim-visaged war hath smooth'd his wrinkled front . *Richard III.* i 1 9
Every grise of fortune Is smooth'd by that below . . *T. of Athens* iv 3 17
Smoothest. Pernicious protector, dangerous peer, That smooth'st it so with king and commonweal! . . . . 2 *Hen. VI.* i 1 22
Smooth-faced. I'll mark no words that smooth-faced wooers say *L. L. Lost* v 2 838
That smooth-faced gentleman, tickling Commodity . . . *K. John* ii 1 573
With smooth-faced peace, With smiling plenty . . *Richard III.* v 5 33
Smoothing. Let not his smoothing words Bewitch your hearts 2 *Hen. VI.* i 1 156
My tongue could never learn sweet smoothing words . . *Richard III.* i 2 169
Smoothly. Run smoothly in the even road of a blank verse . *Much Ado* v 2 33
Most incony vulgar wit! When it comes so smoothly off . *L. L. Lost* iv 1 145
Smoothness. Her smoothness, Her very silence . . *As Y. Like It* i 3 79
You must acquire and beget a temperance that may give it smoothness *Hamlet* iii 2 9
Smooth-pates do now wear nothing but high shoes . . 2 *Hen. IV.* i 2 43
Smooth-tongue. Puke-stocking, caddis-garter, smooth-tongue 1 *Hen. IV.* ii 4 79
Smote. So full of valour that they smote the air . . . *Tempest* iv 1 172
As thy eye-beams, when their fresh rays have smote The night of dew that on my cheeks down flows . . . . . . *L. L. Lost* iv 3 28
Our ædiles smote? ourselves resisted? . . . . . *Coriolanus* iii 1 319
When, in an angry parle, He smote the sledded Polacks on the ice *Ham.* i 1 63
I took by the throat the circumcised dog, And smote him, thus *Othello* v 2 356
Smother. These things, come thus to light, Smother her spirits up *M. Ado* iv 1 113
Thus must I from the smoke into the smother . . . *As Y. Like It* i 2 299
To smother up his beauty . . . . 1 *Hen. IV.* i 2 223
We are enow yet living in the field To smother up the English *Hen. V.* iv 5 20
Your private grudge, my Lord of York, will out, Though ne'er so cunningly you smother it . . . . 1 *Hen. VI.* iv 1 110
In the breath of bitter words let's smother My damned son *Richard III.* iv 4 133
It is fit, What being more known grows worse, to smother it . *Pericles* i 1 106
Smother'd in errors, feeble, shallow, weak . . *Com. of Errors* iii 2 35
Smother'd it within my panting bulk, Which almost burst *Richard III.* i 4 40
And in the vapour of my glory smother'd . . . . . . iii 7 164
We smothered The most replenished sweet work of nature . . . iv 3 17
Untimely smother'd in their dusky graves . . . . . . iv 4 70
In the breath of bitter words let's smother My damned son, which thy two sweet sons smother'd . . . . iv 4 133
Dream on thy cousins smother'd in the Tower . . . . . v 3 151
Stalls, bulks, windows, Are smother'd up, leads fill'd . *Coriolanus* ii 1 227
Function Is smother'd in surmise, and nothing is But what is not *Macb.* i 3 141

Smothering. Love's counsellor should fill the bores of hearing, To the smothering of the sense . . . . *Cymbeline* iii 2 60
Smug. A beggar, that was used to come so smug upon the mart *M. of V.* iii 1 49
Here the smug and silver Trent shall run In a new channel 1 *Hen. IV.* iii 1 102
Smulkin. Peace, Smulkin; peace, thou fiend! . . . . . *Lear* iii 4 146
Smutched. What, hast smutch'd thy nose? . . . . . *W. Tale* i 2 121
Snaffle. Which with a snaffle You may pace easy . . *Ant. and Cleo.* ii 2 63
Snail. Thou drone, thou snail, thou slug, thou sot! . . *Com. of Errors* ii 2 196
Love's feeling is more soft and sensible Than are the tender horns of cockled snails . . . . *L. L. Lost* iv 3 338
Worm nor snail, do no offence . . . . *M. N. Dream* ii 2 23
Creeping like snail Unwillingly to school . . . *As Y. Like It* ii 7 146
I had as lief be wooed of a snail.—Of a snail?—Ay, of a snail; for though he comes slowly, he carries his house on his head . . iv 1 52
I can tell why a snail has a house.—Why?—Why, to put his head in *Lear* i 5 29
Snail-paced. Delay leads impotent and snail-paced beggary *Rich. III.* iv 3 53
Bid the snail-paced Ajax arm for shame . . . . *Troi. and Cres.* v 5 18
Snail-slow. A huge feeder; Snail-slow in profit . . *Mer. of Venice* ii 5 47
Snake. His enter and exit shall be strangling a snake . *L. L. Lost* v 1 142
Well done, Hercules! now thou crushest the snake! . . . v 1 146
There the snake throws her enamell'd skin . . . *M. N. Dream* ii 1 255
You spotted snakes with double tongue, Thorny hedgehogs, be not seen ii 2 9
I see love hath made thee a tame snake . . . *As Y. Like It* iv 3 71
About his neck A green and gilded snake had wreathed itself . iv 3 109
Snakes, in my heart-blood warm'd, that sting my heart! *Richard II.* iii 2 131
Rouse up revenge from ebon den with fell Alecto's snake 2 *Hen. IV.* v 5 39
Or as the snake roll'd in a flowering bank . . . 2 *Hen. VI.* iii 1 228
I fear me you but warm the starved snake . . . . . iii 1 343
The snake lies rolled in the cheerful sun . . . *T. Andron.* ii 3 13
A thousand hissing snakes, Ten thousand swelling toads . . . ii 3 100
That kiss is comfortless As frozen water to a starved snake . . . iii 1 252
We have scotch'd the snake, not kill'd it . . . . *Macbeth* iii 2 13
Fillet of a fenny snake, In the cauldron boil and bake . . . iv 1 12
If not well, Thou shouldst come like a Fury crown'd with snakes *Ant. and Cleo.* ii 5 40
So half my Egypt were submerged and made A cistern for scaled snakes! ii 5 95
Snaky. Crisped snaky golden locks . . . . . *Mer. of Venice* iii 2 92
Snap. Speak, breathe, discuss; brief, short, quick, snap *Mer. Wives* iv 5 3
A sweet touch, a quick venue of wit! snip, snap, quick and home! *L. L. Lost* v 1 63
I see no reason in the law of nature but I may snap at him 2 *Hen. IV.* iii 2 357
Snapped. We had like to have had our two noses snapped off *Much Ado* v 1 116
Snapper-up. A snapper-up of unconsidered trifles . . . *W. Tale* iv 3 26
Snare. And instruct thee how To snare the nimble marmoset *Tempest* ii 2 174
Sirrah, where's Snare?—O Lord, ay! good Master Snare . 2 *Hen. IV.* ii 1 6
Snare, we must arrest Sir John Falstaff.—Yea, good Master Snare . ii 1 9
Master Fang, hold him sure: good Master Snare, let him not 'scape . ii 1 27
Master Fang and Master Snare, do me, do me, do me your offices . ii 1 44
Well appointed, Stands with the snares of war to tangle thee 1 *Hen. VI.* iv 2 22
Beguiles him as the mournful crocodile With sorrow snares relenting passengers . . . . 2 *Hen. VI.* iii 1 227
Be it by gins, by snares, by subtlety, Sleeping or waking, 'tis no matter how . . . . iii 1 262
My brain more busy than the labouring spider Weaves tedious snares . iii 1 340
In, and prepare: Ours is the fall, I fear; our foes the snare *T. of Athens* v 2 17
Our exiled friends abroad That fled the snares of watchful tyranny *Macb.* v 8 67
Comest thou smiling from The world's great snare uncaught? *A. and C.* iv 8 18
Snared. Till they have snared the shepherd of the flock . . 2 *Hen. VI.* ii 2 73
But fear not thou, until thy foot be snared . . . . . ii 4 56
Snarl. Which plainly signified That I should snarl and bite 3 *Hen. VI.* v 6 77
Snarleth. And snarleth in the gentle eyes of peace . . *K. John* iv 3 150
Snarling. What! were you snarling all before I came? . *Richard III.* i 3 188
Snatch. Leave me your snatches, and yield me a direct answer *M. for M.* iv 2 6
It were a fault to snatch words from my tongue . . . *L. L. Lost* v 2 382
Briers and thorns at their apparel snatch . . . *M. N. Dream* iii 2 29
To snatch our palm from palm, Unswear faith sworn . . *K. John* iii 1 244
Like a dog that is compell'd to fight, Snatch at his master . . . iv 1 117
Do not snatch it from me; He that takes that doth take my heart *Troi. and Cres.* v 2 81
It seems, some certain snatch or so Would serve your turns *T. Andron.* ii 1 95
And her pale fire she snatches from the sun . . . *T. of Athens* iv 3 441
Which time she chanted snatches of old tunes . . . *Hamlet* iv 7 178
When we shall meet at compt, This look of thine will hurl my soul from heaven, And fiends will snatch at it . . . . . *Othello* v 2 275
Score their backs And snatch 'em up, as we take hares, behind *A. and C.* iv 7 13
The snatches in his voice, And burst of speaking, were as his *Cymbeline* iv 2 105
You snatch some hence for little faults; that's love, To have them fall no more . . . . v 1 12
O you gods! Why do you make us love your goodly gifts, And snatch them straight away? . . . . *Pericles* iii 1 24
Snatched. From my finger snatch'd that ring . . . *Com. of Errors* v 1 276
I am afeard the life of Helen, lady, Was foully snatch'd . *All's Well* v 3 154
This youth . . . I snatch'd one half out of the jaws of death *T. Night* iii 4 394
A sceptre snatch'd with an unruly hand . . . . *K. John* iii 4 135
A purse of gold most resolutely snatched on Monday night . 1 *Hen. IV.* i 2 38
It seem'd in me But as an honour snatch'd with boisterous hand 2 *Hen. IV.* iv 5 192
Death hath snatch'd my husband from mine arms . *Richard III.* ii 2 57
Snatchers. We do not mean the coursing snatchers only . *Hen. V.* i 2 143
Snatching. And ladies too, they will not let me have all fool to myself; they'll be snatching . . . . *Lear* i 4 169
Sneak not away, sir; for the friar and you Must have a word *Meas. for Meas.* v 1 363
See if thou canst find out Sneak's noise . . . 2 *Hen. IV.* ii 4 12
Sneak-cup. How! the prince is a Jack, a sneak-cup . 1 *Hen. IV.* iii 3 99
Sneaking. A poor unminded outlaw sneaking home . . . . iv 3 58
To her unguarded nest the weasel Scot Comes sneaking . *Hen. V.* i 2 171
What sneaking fellow comes yonder? . . . . *Troi. and Cres.* i 2 246
Sneap. I will not undergo this sneap without reply . . 2 *Hen. IV.* ii 1 133
Sneaping. Like an envious sneaping frost That bites the first-born infants of the spring . . . . *L. L. Lost* i 1 100
That may blow No sneaping winds at home . . . . *W. Tale* i 2 13
Sneck up. We did keep time, sir, in our catches. Sneck up! *T. Night* ii 3 101
Snip. Keep not too long in one tune, but a snip and away . *L. L. Lost* iii 1 22
A sweet touch, a quick venue of wit! snip, snap, quick and home! . v 1 63
Here's snip and nip and cut and slish and slash . . *T. of Shrew* iv 3 90
Snipe. If I would time expend with such a snipe, But for my sport *Oth.* i 3 391
Snipt-taffeta. Misled with a snipt-taffeta fellow . . . *All's Well* iv 5 2
Snore. Thou dost snore distinctly; There's meaning in thy snores *Temp.* ii 1 217
Whilst the heavy ploughman snores . . . . . *M. N. Dream* v 1 380
Sleep and snore, and rend apparel out . . . *Mer. of Venice* ii 5 5
Snore. Not so sound and half so deeply sweet As he whose brow with homely biggen bound Snores out the watch of night 2 *Hen. IV.* iv 5 28
And the surfeited grooms Do mock their charge with snores *Macbeth* ii 2 6
Weariness Can snore upon the flint . . . . . . *Cymbeline* iii 6 34
Now sleep yslaked hath the rout; No din but snores the house about *Pericles* iii Gower 2
Snoring. While you here do snoring lie, Open-eyed conspiracy His time doth take . . . . *Tempest* ii 1 300
Snorting. Fast asleep behind the arras, and snorting like a horse 1 *Hen. IV.* ii 4 578
Arise, arise; Awake the snorting citizens with the bell . . *Othello* i 1 90
Snout, the tinker.—Here, Peter Quince.—You, Pyramus' father *M. N. D.* i 2 63
Heigh-ho! Peter Quince! Flute, the bellows-mender! Snout, the tinker! . . . . iv 1 208
It doth befall That I, one Snout by name, present a wall . . . v 1 157
Snow. I warrant you, sir; The white cold virgin snow upon my heart Abates the ardour of my liver . . . . *Tempest* iv 1 55
Thou wouldst as soon go kindle fire with snow As seek to quench the fire of love with words . . . . *T. G. of Ver.* ii 7 19
Hail kissing-comfits and snow eringoes . . . . *Mer. Wives* v 5 22
Though now this grained face of mine be hid In sap-consuming winter's drizzled snow . . . . *Com. of Errors* v 1 312
At Christmas I no more desire a rose Than wish a snow in May's new-fangled mirth; But like of each thing that in season grows *L. L. L.* i 1 106
Coughing drowns the parson's saw And birds sit brooding in the snow . v 2 933
That pure congealed white, high Taurus' snow . . *M. N. Dream* iii 2 141
My love to Hermia, Melted as the snow . . . . . . iv 1 171
Tedious and brief! That is, hot ice and wondrous strange snow . . v 1 59
There may as well be amity and life 'Tween snow and fire *Mer. of Ven.* iii 2 31
Half of the which dare not shake the snow from off their cassocks, lest they shake themselves to pieces . . . . *All's Well* iv 3 191
Lawn as white as driven snow; Cyprus black as e'er was crow *W. Tale* iv 4 220
Or the fann'd snow that's bolted By the northern blasts twice o'er . iv 4 375
As a little snow, tumbled about, Anon becomes a mountain *K. John* iii 4 176
Or wallow naked in December snow By thinking on fantastic summer's heat . . . . *Richard II.* i 3 298
O that I were a mockery king of snow! . . . . iv 1 260
Rush on his host, as doth the melted snow Upon the valleys *Hen. V.* iii 5 50
Cold snow melts with the sun's hot beams . . . 2 *Hen. VI.* iii 1 223
He is kind.—Right, As snow in harvest . . . . *Richard III.* i 4 249
One that never in his life Felt so much cold as over shoes in snow . v 3 326
Chaste as the icicle That's curdied by the frost from purest snow *Coriol.* v 3 66
In winter with warm tears I'll melt the snow . . . *T. Andron.* iii 1 20
Whiter than new snow on a raven's back . . . *Rom. and Jul.* iii 2 19
Doth thaw the consecrated snow That lies on Dian's lap *T. of Athens* iv 3 386
Black Macbeth Will seem as pure as snow . . . . *Macbeth* iv 3 53
Be thou as chaste as ice, as pure as snow, thou shalt not escape calumny . . . . *Hamlet* iii 1 141
Is there not rain enough in the sweet heavens To wash it white as snow? iii 3 46
White his shroud as the mountain snow . . . . . . iv 5 35
His beard was as white as snow, All flaxen was his poll . . . iv 5 195
Bring oil to fire, snow to their colder moods . . . . *Lear* ii 2 83
Behold yond simpering dame, Whose face between her forks presages snow . . . . iv 6 121
That whiter skin of hers than snow, And smooth as monumental alabaster . . . . *Othello* v 2 4
Yea, like the stag, when snow the pasture sheets, The barks of trees thou browsed'st . . . . *Ant. and Cleo.* i 4 65
I thought her As chaste as unsunn'd snow . . . . *Cymbeline* ii 5 13
Snowball. My belly's as cold as if I had swallowed snowballs *Mer. W.* iii 5 24
She sent him away as cold as a snowball; saying his prayers too *Per.* iv 6 149
Snow-broth. A man whose blood Is very snow-broth *Meas. for Meas.* i 4 58
Snow-white. That draweth from my snow-white pen the ebon-coloured ink . . . . *L. L. Lost* i 1 245
To the snow-white hand of the most beauteous Lady Rosaline . iv 2 136
Dismounted from your snow-white goodly steed . . *T. Andron.* ii 3 76
Snowy. So shows a snowy dove trooping with crows . *Rom. and Jul.* i 5 50
Snuff. You'll mar the light by taking it in snuff . . *L. L. Lost* v 2 22
You see, it is already in snuff . . . . . . *M. N. Dream* v 1 254
'Let me not live,' quoth he, 'After my flame lacks oil, to be the snuff Of younger spirits' . . . . *All's Well* i 2 59
Who therewith angry, when it next came there, Took it in snuff 1 *Hen. IV.* i 3 41
This candle burns not clear: 'tis I must snuff it . . *Hen. VIII.* iii 2 96
There lives within the very flame of love A kind of wick or snuff that will abate it; And nothing is at a like goodness still *Hamlet* iv 7 116
What hath been seen, Either in snuffs and packings of the dukes *Lear* iii 1 26
My snuff and loathed part of nature should Burn itself out . . iv 6 39
Lamentable! What, To hide me from the radiant sun and solace I' the dungeon by a snuff? . . . . *Cymbeline* i 6 87
Snuffed. As if you snuffed up love by smelling love . . *L. L. Lost* iii 1 16
Snug, the joiner; you, the lion's part . . . . *M. N. Dream* i 2 66
Tell them plainly he is Snug the joiner . . . . . . iii 1 47
Then know that I, one Snug the joiner, am A lion-fell . . . v 1 226
So. Where was she born? . . . —Sir, in Argier.—O, was she so? *Tempest* i 2 261
You have cause, So have we all, of joy . . . . . . ii 1 2
The visitor will not give him o'er so . . . . ii 1 11
The fault's your own.—So is the dear'st o' the loss . . . . ii 1 135
I am more serious than my custom: you Must be so too . . . ii 1 220
So, king, go safely on to seek thy son . . . . ii 1 327
Didst thou not say he lied?—Thou liest.—Do I so? . . . . iii 2 84
So I charm'd their ears That calf-like they my lowing follow'd . iv 1 178
My nose is in great indignation.—So is mine . . . . . iv 1 201
Wish you joy!—Be it so! Amen! . . . . v 1 215
So, by your circumstance, you call me fool . . . *T. G. of Ver.* i 1 36
And so, sir, I'll commend you to my master . . . . . . i 1 154
No other but a woman's reason; I think him so because I think him so i 2 24
Keep tune there still, so you will sing it out . . . . . . i 2 89
She that you gaze on so as she sits at supper? . . . . . ii 1 46
I would you were set, so your affection would cease . . . . ii 1 91
You think too much of so much pains?—No, madam; so it stead you . ii 1 119
For my sake read it over, And if it please you, so; if not, why, so . ii 1 137
Take it for your labour: And so, good morrow, servant . . . ii 1 140
That cannot be so neither: yes, it is so, it is so . . . . . ii 3 18
Besides, her intercession chafed him so . . . . iii 1 233
My friends,— That's not so, sir: we are your enemies . . . . iv 1 8
If I would but go to hell for an eternal moment or so . . *Mer. Wives* ii 1 50
If it be my luck, so; if not, happy man be his dole! . . . . iii 4 67
And as I find her, so am I affected . . . . iii 4 95
He shall have no desires.—So think I too . . . . . . iv 4 26

So. I am not yet instructed.—'Tis so with me *Meas. for Meas.* i 1 82
On whom it will, it will; On whom it will not, so; yet still 'tis just i 2 127
So I have strew'd it in the common ear, And so it is received i 3 15
You may not so extenuate his offence For I have had such faults ii 1 27
If it please your honour, this is not so.—Prove it ii 1 87
If so your heart were touch'd with that remorse As mine is ii 2 54
So play the foolish throngs with one that swoons ii 4 24
Can this be so? did Angelo so leave her? iii 1 233
We may pity, though not pardon thee.—O, had the gods done so! *C. of Er.* i 1 99
As you love strokes, so jest with me again ii 2 8
Am I not?—I think thou art in mind, and so am I ii 2 198
I long for grass. 'Tis so, I am an ass ii 2 203
Let it not be so! Herein you war against your reputation iii 1 85
One of these men is Genius to the other; And so of these v 1 333
If this were so, so were it uttered *Much Ado* i 1 217
It is not so, nor 'twas not so, but, indeed, God forbid it should be so i 1 219
Brave conquerors,—for so you are *L. L. Lost* i 1 8
'So it is,'— It may be so: but if he say it is so, he is, in telling true, but so i 1 225
And send you many lovers!—Amen, so you be none ii 1 127
Is she wedded or no?—To her will, sir, or so ii 1 212
I'll make one in a dance, or so; or I will play On the tabor v 1 160
They'll know By favours several which they did bestow.—And will they so? v 2 126
Do you not jest?—Yes, sooth; and so do you *M. N. Dream* iii 2 265
I extend this friendship: If he will take it, so *Mer. of Venice* i 3 170
So he served the second, and so the third *As Y. Like It* i 2 136
'Tis no matter how it be in tune, so it make noise enough iv 2 10
If love have touch'd you, nought remains but so *T. of Shrew* i 1 166
She may perhaps call him half a score knaves or so i 2 111
Alas! sir, it is worse for me than so v 2 88
His eyes do show his days are almost done.—Is't even so? *T. Night* ii 3 114
Nor this is not my nose neither. Nothing that is so is so iv 1 9
And would by combat make her good, so were I A man *W. Tale* ii 3 60
Never, Paulina; so be blest my spirit! v 1 71
Cousin, farewell; and, uncle, bid him so *Richard II.* i 3 247
I would to God, So my untruth had not provoked him to it ii 2 101
To shorten you, For taking so the head, your whole head's length iii 3 13
Or any way impeach What then he said, so he unsay it now *1 Hen. IV.* i 3 76
Give me life: which if I can save, so v 3 64
So we be rid of them, do with 'em what thou wilt *1 Hen. VI.* iv 7 94
In earnest of a further benefit, So you do condescend to help me now v 3 17
Sleeping or waking, 'tis no matter how, So he be dead *2 Hen. VI.* iii 1 264
Would fain that all were well, So 'twere not 'long of him *3 Hen. VI.* iv 7 32
Why, so: now have I done a good day's work *Richard III.* ii 1 1
Her grace sat down To rest awhile, some half an hour or so *Hen. VIII.* iv 1 66
Reach a chair: So; now, methinks, I feel a little ease iv 2 4
So I grow stronger, you more honour gain v 3 182
Why, so: you have made good work! *Coriolanus* v 1 15
Thou dost over-ween in all; And so in this *T. Andron.* ii 1 30
I'll frown and be perverse and say thee nay, So thou wilt woo *R. and J.* ii 2 97
Good morrow, Antony.—So to most noble Cæsar *J. Cæsar* ii 2 118
Why, so: being gone, I am a man again *Macbeth* iii 4 107
What, is this so?—Ay, sir, all this is so iv 1 124
Those foresaid lands So by his father lost *Hamlet* i 1 104
The perfume and suppliance of a minute; No more.—No more but so? i 3 10
'Good sir,' or so, or 'friend,' or 'gentleman' ii 1 46
So by your companies To draw him on to pleasures ii 2 14
And as my love's sized, my fear is so iii 2 180
But 'tis not so above; There is no shuffling, there the action lies iii 3 60
If it be so, Laertes—As how should it be so? how otherwise? iv 7 58
So may it come, thy master . . . Shall find thee full of labours *Lear* i 4 6
But to know so must be my benefit *Othello* iii 4 119
And oft before gave audience, As 'tis reported, so *Ant. and Cleo.* iii 6 29
This if she perform, She shall not sue unheard. So to them both iii 12 24
The queen shall then have courtesy, so she Will yield us up.—He says so iii 13 15
We intend so to dispose you as Yourself shall give us counsel v 2 186
This service is not service, so being done, But being so allow'd *Cymbeline* iii 3 16
Yet is't not probable To come alone, either he so undertaking, Or they so suffering iv 2 142
So able. Now or whensoever, provided I be so able as now *Hamlet* v 2 211
So above. He is so above me: In his bright radiance *All's Well* i 1 98
So and so. He's very wild; Addicted so and so *Hamlet* ii 1 19
So as thou livest in peace, die free from strife *Richard II.* v 6 27
So base. Who is here so base that would be a bondman? *J. Cæsar* iii 2 31
So be it, for it cannot be but so *K. John* iii 4 140
So big. No woman's heart So big, to hold so much *T. Night* ii 4 99
So blind. Who's so blind, but says he sees it not? *Richard III.* iii 6 12
So bold. I'll be so bold as stay, sir, till she come down *Mer. Wives* iv 5 13
I'll make so bold to call, For 'tis my limited service *Macbeth* ii 3 56
So brave. Is it so brave a lass? *Tempest* iii 2 111
So brief. Would you have been so brief with him, he would Have been so brief with you *Richard II.* iii 3 11
So dear. They durst not, So dear the love my people bore me *Tempest* i 2 141
So defend thee heaven! *Richard II.* i 3 34
So dry. None so dry or thirsty Will deign to sip *T. of Shrew* v 2 144
So far as. And elsewhere, so far as my coin would stretch *1 Hen. IV.* i 2 61
So far As thou hast power and person *Coriolanus* iii 2 85
Follow the noise so far as we have quarter *Ant. and Cleo.* iv 3 22
So firm. Who was so firm, so constant, that this coil Would not infect his reason? *Tempest* i 2 207
For who so firm that cannot be seduced? *J. Cæsar* i 2 316
So flood-gate. Of so flood-gate and o'erbearing nature *Othello* i 3 56
So fond. Thou art so fond To come abroad *Mer. of Venice* iii 3 9
He is so fond To trust the mockery of unquiet slumbers *Richard III.* iii 2 26
So forth. Quando pecus omne sub umbra Ruminat,—and so forth *L. L. L.* iv 2 96
Item, one neck, one chin, and so forth *T. Night* i 5 267
A slow tongue, in the habit of some sir of note, and so forth iii 4 82
Whispering, rounding, 'Sicilia is a so-forth' *W. Tale* i 2 218
With a dish of caraways, and so forth *2 Hen. IV.* v 3 4
'Such a house of sale,' Videlicet, a brothel, or so forth *Hamlet* ii 1 61
So full. Never any With so full soul *Tempest* iii 1 44
So glad of this as they I cannot be, Who are surprised withal iii 1 92
So good. You must be so good, sir, to rise *Meas. for Meas.* iv 3 29
Will you be so good, scauld knave, as eat it? *Hen. V.* v 1 31
That I might do you service So good as you have done *Ant. and Cleo.* iv 2 19
So gross. Who's so gross, That seeth not this palpable device? *Rich. III.* iii 6 10
So happy. I would thou wert so happy by thy stay *Rom. and Jul.* i 1 164
This alliance may so happy prove ii 3 91
So help me. I never saw the chain, so help me Heaven! *Com. of Errors* v 1 267
So help me every spirit sanctified! *Othello* iii 4 126

So high. Too low a mistress for so high a servant *T. G. of Ver.* ii 4 106
So is on you. Ceres' blessing so is on you *Tempest* iv 1 117
So long. Give thanks you have lived so long i 1 27
So long as. He shall need none, so long as I live *T. of Shrew* v 1 25
So long as I could see *T. Night* i 2 17
So long as nature Will bear up with this exercise, so long I daily vow to use it *W. Tale* iii 2 241
So long as out of limit and true rule You stand *1 Hen. IV.* iv 3 39
I will live so long as I may, that's the certain of it *Hen. V.* ii 1 15
All these could not procure me any scathe, So long as I am loyal *2 Hen. VI.* ii 4 63
So long as heaven and nature lengthens it.—So long as hell and Richard likes of it *Richard III.* iv 4 353
So much. So safely ordered that there is no soul—No, not so much perdition as an hair Betid to any creature *Tempest* i 2 30
Was there ever man a coward that hath drunk so much sack as I to-day? iii 2 31
I'll venture so much of my hawk or hound, But twenty times so much upon my wife *T. of Shrew* v 2 72
Shall I so much dishonour my fair stars? *Richard II.* iv 1 21
That now our loss might be ten times so much *1 Hen. VI.* ii 1 53
And so much shall you give, or off goes yours [your head] *2 Hen. VI.* iv 1 17
To be more than what you were, you would Be so much more the man *Macbeth* i 7 51
So much as you may take upon a knife's point *Much Ado* ii 3 263
Never so much as in a thought unborn Did I offend *As Y. Like It* i 3 53
To gather, So much as from occasion you may glean *Hamlet* ii 2 16
So noble. For nothing natural I ever saw so noble *Tempest* i 2 419
So oft as that shall be, So often shall the knot of us be call'd The men that gave their country liberty *J. Cæsar* iii 1 116
So out of. I am right glad that he's so out of hope *Tempest* iii 3 11
I am so out of love with life *Meas. for Meas.* iii 1 174
So perfidious. That a brother should Be so perfidious! *Tempest* i 2 68
So possessed. Thy conscience Is so possess'd with guilt i 2 471
So prosper I, as I swear perfect love! *Richard III.* ii 1 16
So quick. Our haste from hence is of so quick condition *Meas. for Meas.* i 1 54
So rare. No cataplasm so rare, Collected from all simples *Hamlet* iv 7 144
So sacred as. Against whose person, So sacred as it is, I have done sin *W. Tale* v 1 172
So say I. This is not well, indeed.—So say I too, sir *Mer. Wives* iv 2 134
I am not as I have been.—So say I: methinks you are sadder *Much Ado* iii 2 16
So simple. Without you were so simple, none else would *T. G. of Ver.* ii 1 38
So slow. The search so slow, That could not trace them! *Cymbeline* i 1 64
So so. Before you can say 'come' and 'go,' And breathe twice and cry 'so, so' *Tempest* iv 1 45
But yet thou shalt have freedom: so, so, so v 1 96
What think'st thou of the rich Mercatio?—Well of his wealth; but of himself, so so *T. G. of Ver.* i 2 13
The dog is me, and I am myself; ay, so, so ii 3 26
He's tall: His leg is but so so; and yet 'tis well *As Y. Like It* iii 5 119
Art rich?—Faith, sir, so so.—'So so' is good, very good, very excellent good; and yet it is not; it is but so so v 1 28
So, so; These are the limbs o' the plot: no more, I hope *Hen. VIII.* i 1 219
Thou counterfeit'st most lively.—So, so, my lord.—E'en so, sir, *T. of A.* v 1 85
Make no noise; draw the curtains: so, so, so *Lear* iii 6 90
Ha, ha, ha!—So, so, so, so: they laugh that win *Othello* iv 1 124
I would not have thee linger in thy pain: So, so v 2 88
So soon as ever thou seest him, draw *T. Night* iii 4 194
My letters, by this means being there So soon as you arrive *W. Tale* iv 4 633
The day shall not be up so soon as I *K. John* v 5 21
So soon as dinner's done, we'll forth again *T. of Athens* ii 2 14
So soon as I can win the offended king, I will be known *Cymbeline* i 1 75
I would have left it on the board so soon As I had made my meal iii 6 51
They went hence so soon as they were born v 4 126
And let it be confiscate all, so soon As I have received it v 5 323
So stead me As bring me to the sight of Isabella *Meas. for Meas.* i 4 17
So strong. One so strong That could control the moon *Tempest* v 1 269
What king so strong Can tie the gall up in the slanderous tongue? *M. for M.* iii 2 198
A jealousy so strong That judgement cannot cure *Othello* ii 1 310
So tempered. Were your days As green as Ajax' and your brain so temper'd *Troi. and Cres.* ii 3 265
So thrive I, as I truly swear the like! *Richard III.* ii 1 11
So thrive I in my dangerous attempt Of hostile arms! iv 4 398
So well thy words become thee as thy wounds *Macbeth* i 2 43
So without. But you are so without these follies *T. G. of Ver.* ii 1 39
So won. 'Tis won as towns with fire, so won, so lost *L. L. Lost* i 1 147
So worthy as. Expected to prove so worthy as since he hath been allowed the name of *Cymbeline* i 4 3
Soaked. Lie drown'd and soak'd in mercenary blood *Hen. V.* iv 7 79
Soaking. Thy conceit is soaking, will draw in More than the common blocks *W. Tale* i 2 224
Soaking in Drown the lamenting fool in sea-salt tears *T. Andron.* iii 2 19
Soaks. That soaks up the king's countenance, his rewards, *Hamlet* iv 2 16
Soar. Thou hast hawks will soar Above the morning lark *T. of Shrew* Ind. 2 45
How high a pitch his resolution soars! *Richard II.* i 1 109
When I bestride him, I soar, I am a hawk: he trots the air *Hen. V.* iii 7 16
'Tis but a base ignoble mind That mounts no higher than a bird can soar.—I thought as much *2 Hen. VI.* ii 1 14
Although the kite soar with unbloodied beak iii 2 193
Borrow Cupid's wings, And soar with them above a common bound.—I am too sore enpierced with his shaft To soar with his light feathers *Rom. and Jul.* i 4 18
Who else would soar above the view of men *J. Cæsar* i 1 79
Soaring. When his soaring insolence Shall touch the people *Coriolanus* ii 1 270
The Roman eagle, From south to west on wing soaring aloft *Cymbeline* v 5 471
Sob. When gentlemen are tired, gives them a sob and 'rests them *C. of Er.* iv 3 25
Weeps, sobs, beats her heart, tears her hair, prays, curses *Much Ado* ii 3 153
And twenty times made pause to sob and weep *Richard III.* i 2 162
He hugg'd me in his arms, and swore, with sobs, That he would labour my delivery i 4 252
Crack my clear voice with sobs and break my heart *Troi. and Cres.* iv 2 114
See how my wretched sister sobs and weeps *T. Andron.* iii 1 137
Sobbing. Weeping and commenting Upon the sobbing deer *As Y. Like It* ii 1 66
Sober. Her sober virtue, years and modesty *Com. of Errors* iii 1 90
I pray thee speak in sober judgement *Much Ado* i 1 171
Let them alone till they are sober: if they make you not then the better answer iii 3 49
In the morning, when he is sober *Mer. of Venice* i 2 93
Put on a sober habit, Talk with respect and swear but now and then ii 2 199
Let not the sound of shallow foppery enter My sober house ii 5 36
In religion, What damned error, but some sober brow Will bless it? iii 2 78
Speakest thou in sober meanings?—By my life, I do *As Y. Like It* v 2 76

Sober. Do me grace, And offer me disguised in sober robes *T. of Shrew* i 2 132
You seem a sober ancient gentleman by your habit, but your words show you a madman v 1 75
And we with sober speed will follow you *2 Hen. IV.* iv 3 86
With such sober and unnoted passion He did behave his anger *T. of A.* iii 5 21
This sober form of yours hides wrongs *J. Cæsar* iv 2 40
For who, that's but a queen, fair, sober, wise, Would from a paddock, from a bat, a gib, Such dear concernings hide? *Hamlet* iii 4 189
Nor once be chastised with the sober eye Of dull Octavia *Ant. and Cleo.* v 2 54
Sober-blooded. This same young sober-blooded boy *2 Hen. IV.* iv 3 94
Soberly. And soberly did mount an arm-gaunt steed *Ant. and Cleo.* i 5 48
Sober-suited. Civil night, Thou sober-suited matron *Rom. and Jul.* iii 2 11
Sobriety. Maid's mild behaviour and sobriety *T. of Shrew* i 1 71
And the cares of it, and the forms of it, and the sobriety of it *Hen. V.* iv 1 74
Sociable. Mine eyes, even sociable to the show of thine, Fall fellowly drops *Tempest* v 1 63
'Tis too respective and too sociable For your conversion *K. John* i 1 188
Ten thousand wiry friends Do glue themselves in sociable grief iii 4 65
Can he not be sociable?—The raven chides blackness *Troi. and Cres.* ii 3 220
Is not this better now than groaning for love? now art thou sociable, now art thou Romeo *Rom. and Jul.* ii 4 93
Society is no comfort To one not sociable *Cymbeline* iv 2 13
Society. Of her society Be not afraid *Tempest* iv 1 91
He lays before me, My riots past, my wild societies *Mer. Wives* iii 4 8
There is scarce truth enough alive to make societies secure *M. for M.* iii 2 240
I beseech your society.—And thank you too *L. L. Lost* iv 2 166
Society, saith the text, is the happiness of life iv 2 167
Thou makest the triumviry, the corner-cap of society iv 3 53
Thy love is far from charity, That in love's grief desirest society iv 3 128
Either to die the death or to abjure For ever the society of men *M. N. D.* i 1 66
But yet, for fashion sake, I thank you too for your society *As Y. L. It* iii 2 272
You clown, abandon,—which is in the vulgar leave,—the society v 1 53
Abandon the society of this female, or, clown, thou perishest v 1 56
Since their more mature dignities and royal necessities made separation of their society *W. Tale* i 1 29
I lost—All mine own folly—the society, Amity too, of your brave father v 1 135
This is worshipful society And fits the mounting spirit *K. John* i 1 205
Such barren pleasures, rude society, As thou art match'd withal *1 Hen. IV.* iii 2 14
Their spirits are so married in conjunction with the participation of society that they flock together in consent *2 Hen. IV.* v 1 78
If sorrow can admit society, Tell o'er your woes again *Richard III.* iv 4 38
By my life, They are a sweet society of fair ones *Hen. VIII.* i 4 14
To stop the inundation of her tears; Which, too much minded by herself alone, May be put from her by society *Rom. and Jul.* iv 1 14
Nay, an you begin to rail on society once, I am sworn not to give regard to you. Farewell *T. of Athens* i 2 250
You great benefactors, sprinkle our society with thankfulness iii 6 79
That their society, as their friendship, may Be merely poison! iv 1 31
Therefore, be abhorr'd All feasts, societies, and throngs of men! iv 3 21
To make society The sweeter welcome, we will keep ourself Till supper-time alone: while then, God be with you! *Macbeth* iii 1 42
Ourself will mingle with society, And play the humble host iii 4 3
Of very soft society and great showing *Hamlet* v 2 112
Having seen me in my worst estate, Shunn'd my abhorr'd society *Lear* v 3 210
He enchants societies into him; Half all men's hearts are his *Cymbeline* i 6 167
Society is no comfort To one not sociable iv 2 12
Sock. Foul shirts and smocks, socks, foul stockings *Mer. Wives* iii 5 91
Socrates. As curst and shrewd As Socrates' Xanthippe *T. of Shrew* i 2 71
Sodden water, A drench for sur-rein'd jades *Hen. V.* iii 5 18
Sodden business! there's a stewed phrase indeed! *Troi. and Cres.* iii 1 44
A strong wind will blow it to pieces, they are so pitifully sodden *Pericles* iv 2 21
Sodden-witted lord! thou hast no more brain than I have in mine elbows; an assinego may tutor thee *Troi. and Cres.* ii 1 47
Soever. So curses all Eve's daughters, of what complexion soever *Mer. W.* iv 2 25
How low soever the matter, I hope in God for high words *L. L. Lost* i 1 194
Nought enters there, Of what validity and pitch soe'er *T. Night* i 1 12
Whose tongue soe'er speaks false, Not truly speaks *K. John* iv 3 91
No man shall have private conference, Of what degree soever *Richard III.* i 1 87
Whose hand soever lanced their tender hearts, Thy head, all indirectly, gave direction iv 4 224
How rank soever rounded in with danger *Troi. and Cres.* i 3 196
Thou shalt vow By that same god, what god soe'er it be *T. Andron.* v 1 82
How strange or odd soe'er I bear myself *Hamlet* i 5 170
How in my words soever she be shent, To give them seals never, my soul, consent! iii 2 416
Blest be those, How mean soe'er, that have their honest wills *Cymbeline* i 6 8
What villany soe'er I bid thee do, to perform it directly and truly iii 5 112
Soft, sir! one word more *Tempest* i 2 449
For we are soft as our complexions are *Meas. for Meas.* ii 4 129
For thou dost fear the soft and tender fork Of a poor worm iii 1 16
Soft and low, 'Remember now my brother' iv 1 69
But, soft! who wafts us yonder? *Com. of Errors* ii 2 111
But, soft! my door is lock'd. Go bid them let us in iii 1 30
O, soft, sir! hold you still: I'll fetch my sister iii 2 69
But, soft! I see the goldsmith. Get thee gone; Buy thou a rope iv 1 19
In their rooms Come thronging soft and delicate desires *Much Ado* i 1 305
But, soft you, let me be: pluck up, my heart, and be sad v 1 207
Soft and fair, friar. Which is Beatrice?—I answer to that name v 4 72
Soft! whither away so fast? *L. L. Lost* iv 3 186
Love's feeling is more soft and sensible Than are the tender horns of cockled snails iv 3 337
Soft, let us see: Write, 'Lord have mercy on us' on those three v 2 418
But, soft! what nymphs are these? *M. N. Dream* iv 1 132
But soft! how many months Do you desire? *Mer. of Venice* i 3 59
I'll not be made a soft and dull-eyed fool, To shake the head, relent iii 3 14
Let their beds Be made as soft as yours iv 1 96
Soft! The Jew shall have all justice; soft! no haste iv 1 320
With soft low tongue and lowly courtesy *T. of Shrew* Ind. 1 114
Entertain'st thy wooers With gentle conference, soft and affable ii 1 253
Soft, son! Sir, by your leave iv 4 23
But, soft! company is coming here iv 5 26
Why are our bodies soft and weak and smooth, Unapt to toil and trouble? v 2 165
I will eat and drink, and sleep as soft As captain shall *All's Well* iv 3 368
Not too fast: soft, soft! *T. Night* i 5 312
By your leave, wax. Soft! and the impressure her Lucrece ii 5 103
Soft! here follows prose ii 5 154
So far beneath your soft and tender breeding v 1 331
This hand, As soft as dove's down and as white as it *W. Tale* iv 4 374
Soft, swain, awhile, beseech you; Have you a father? iv 4 402
Soft. Some say he shall be stoned; but that death is too soft for him *W. Tale* iv 4 807
But soft, but see, or rather do not see, My fair rose wither *Richard II.* v 1 7
Which hath been smooth as oil, soft as young down *1 Hen. IV.* i 3 7
But, soft, I pray you; did King Richard then Proclaim my brother? i 3 155
By God, soft; I know a trick worth two of that ii 1 40
But, soft! whom have we here? Did you not tell me this fat man was dead? v 4 134
But, soft! I think she comes; and I'll prepare *2 Hen. VI.* ii 4 15
Women are soft, mild, pitiful and flexible *3 Hen. VI.* i 4 141
I would to God my heart were flint, like Edward's; Or Edward's soft and pitiful, like mine *Richard III.* i 3 141
But, soft! here come my executioners i 3 339
Soft! I did but dream. O coward conscience, how dost thou afflict me! v 3 178
The capacity Of your soft cheveril conscience would receive *Hen. VIII.* ii 3 32
The artist and unread, The hard and soft, seem all affined *Troi. and Cres.* i 3 25
Farewell: yet, soft! Hector, I take my leave v 3 89
Soft! here comes sleeve, and t'other v 4 19
When steel grows soft as the parasite's silk *Coriolanus* i 9 45
A stone is soft as wax,—tribunes more hard than stones *T. Andron.* iii 1 45
Soft! see how busily she turns the leaves! What would she find? iv 1 45
But, soft! methinks I do digress too much, Citing my worthless praise v 3 116
Farewell, my coz.—Soft! I will go along *Rom. and Jul.* i 1 201
But, soft! what light through yonder window breaks? It is the east ii 2 2
Alack, that heaven should practise stratagems Upon so soft a subject as myself! iii 5 212
What, dost thou go? Soft! take thy physic first *T. of Athens* iii 6 110
Let not the virgin's cheek Make soft thy trenchant sword iv 3 115
Thy flatterers yet wear silk, drink wine, lie soft iv 3 206
But, soft, I pray you: what, did Cæsar swound? *J. Cæsar* i 2 253
But soft, behold! lo, where it comes again! *Hamlet* i 1 126
But, soft! methinks I scent the morning air; Brief let me be i 5 58
Soft you now! The fair Ophelia! iii 1 88
Soft! now to my mother. O heart, lose not thy nature iii 2 410
And, heart with strings of steel, Be soft as sinews of the new-born babe! iii 3 71
But soft, what noise? who calls on Hamlet? O, here they come iv 2 3
But soft! but soft! aside: here comes the king v 1 240
Her voice was ever soft, Gentle, and low, an excellent thing in woman *Lear* v 3 272
O, come in, Emilia: Soft; by and by *Othello* v 2 104
Soft you; a word or two before you go v 2 338
Entreat your captain To soft and gentle speech *Ant. and Cleo.* ii 2 3
Soft, Cæsar!—No, Lepidus, let him speak ii 2 83
The beds i' the east are soft ii 6 51
The conquering wine hath steep'd our sense In soft and delicate Lethe ii 7 114
As sweet as balm, as soft as air, as gentle,—O Antony! v 2 314
Soft, soft! we'll no defence; Obedient as the scabbard *Cymbeline* iii 4 81
But, soft! no bedfellow!—O gods and goddesses! iv 2 295
Soft, ho! what trunk is here Without his top? iv 2 353
Soft! here he comes: I must dissemble it *Pericles* ii 5 23
Soft! it smells most sweetly in my sense.—A delicate odour iii 2 60
No visor does become black villany So well as soft and tender flattery iv 4 45
Soft! who comes here? *Coriolanus* i 1; *T. Andron.* iv 2; *J. Cæsar* iii 1
Soft attachment. Sleep kill those pretty eyes, And give as soft attachment to thy senses As infants'! *Troi. and Cres.* iv 2 5
Soft beds. 'Tis strange he [death] hides him in fresh cups, soft beds, Sweet words *Cymbeline* v 3 71
Soft conditions. Our soft conditions and our hearts Should well agree with our external parts *T. of Shrew* v 2 167
Soft-conscienced men can be content to say *Coriolanus* i 1 37
Soft couch. His gold will hold, And his soft couch defile *Mer. Wives* i 3 108
Soft courage. This soft courage makes your followers faint *3 Hen. VI.* ii 2 57
Soft grace. Of whose soft grace For the like loss I have her sovereign aid And rest myself content *Tempest* v 1 142
Soft-hearted. Fie, coward woman and soft-hearted wretch! *2 Hen. VI.* ii 2 307
Why stand we like soft-hearted women here, Wailing our losses? *3 Hen. VI.* ii 3 25
Soft hours. Now, for the love of Love and her soft hours *Ant. and Cleo.* i 1 44
Soft impression. With wax I brought away, whose soft impression Interprets for my poor ignorance *T. of Athens* v 4 68
Soft infancy, that nothing canst but cry *Troi. and Cres.* ii 2 105
Soft kiss. You may ride's With one soft kiss a thousand furlongs ere With spur we heat an acre *W. Tale* i 2 95
Soft laws. I should not deal in her [love's] soft laws *3 Hen. VI.* iii 2 154
Soft mercy. We yield our town and lives to thy soft mercy *Hen. V.* iii 3 48
Soft mouth. Touch her soft mouth, and march ii 3 61
Soft myrtle. Thy sharp and sulphurous bolt Split'st the unwedgeable and gnarled oak Than the soft myrtle *Meas. for Meas.* ii 2 117
Soft nurse. O sleep, O gentle sleep, Nature's soft nurse *2 Hen. IV.* iii 1 6
Soft parts. And have not those soft parts of conversation *Othello* iii 3 264
Soft petitions. Melted by the windy breath Of soft petitions *K. John* ii 1 478
Soft phrase. Little bless'd with the soft phrase of peace *Othello* i 3 82
Soft pillow. A good soft pillow for that good white head *Hen. V.* iv 1 14
Soft remorse. The vilest stroke, That ever wall-eyed wrath or staring rage Presented to the tears of soft remorse *K. John* iv 3 50
Soft seizure. Her hand, . . . to whose soft seizure The cygnet's down is harsh *Troi. and Cres.* i 1 57
Soft silencing. In your power soft silencing your son *2 Hen. IV.* v 2 97
Soft society. Of very soft society and great showing *Hamlet* v 2 112
Soft stillness and the night Become the touches of sweet harmony *M. of V.* v 1 56
Soft things. I smell sweet savours and I feel soft things *T. of Shrew* Ind. 2 73
Soft way. Say to them, Thou art their soldier, and being bred in broils Hast not the soft way *Coriolanus* iii 2 82
Soften. Whose golden touch could soften steel and stones *T. G. of Ver.* iii 2 79
Unless you have the grace by your fair prayer To soften Angelo *M. for M.* i 4 70
You may as well do any thing most hard, As seek to soften that—than which what's harder?—His Jewish heart *Mer. of Venice* iv 1 79
We do not know How he may soften at the sight o' the child *W. Tale* ii 2 40
Oft have I heard that grief softens the mind *2 Hen. VI.* iv 4 1
All the charms of love, Salt Cleopatra, soften thy waned lip! *A. and C.* ii 1 21
Softened. Thy beauty hath made me effeminate And in my temper soften'd valour's steel *Rom. and Jul.* iii 1 120
Her salt tears fell from her, and soften'd the stones *Othello* iv 3 47
Softer. A couch Softer and sweeter than the lustful bed On purpose trimm'd up for Semiramis *T. of Shrew* Ind. 2 40
There is no lady of more softer bowels *Troi. and Cres.* ii 2 11
With no softer cushion than the flint, I kneel before thee *Coriolanus* v 3 53
Softest. Eyes, that are the frail'st and softest things *As Y. Like It* iii 5 12
Their softest touch as smart as lizards' stings! *2 Hen. VI.* iii 2 325
Like softest music to attending ears *Rom. and Jul.* ii 2 167

Softly. Tread softly, that the blind mole may not Hear a foot fall *Temp.* iv 1 194
Speak softly. All's hush'd as midnight yet . . . . . . iv 1 206
Speak softly: yonder, as I think, he walks . . . *Com. of Errors* v 1 9
So you walk softly and look sweetly and say nothing, I am yours *M. Ado* ii 1 91
Bleat softly then; the butcher hears you cry . . . *L. L. Lost* v 2 255
With a thief to the gallows, for though he go as softly as foot can fall, he thinks himself too soon there . . . *As Y. Like It* iii 2 346
Softly, my masters! if you be gentlemen, Do me this right . *T. of Shrew* i 2 238
Softly and swiftly, sir; for the priest is ready . . . . . v 1 1
If I could make that resemble something in me,—Softly! . *T. Night* ii 5 132
There was a man . . . Dwelt by a churchyard: I will tell it softly *W. T.* ii 1 30
O, good sir, softly, good sir! I fear, sir, my shoulder-blade is out.— How now! canst stand?—Softly, dear sir; good sir, softly . . iv 3 76
I will even take my leave of you, and pace softly towards my kinsman's iv 3 121
Bear me hence Into some other chamber: softly, pray . 2 *Hen. IV.* iv 4 132
Speak softly, or the loss of those great towns Will make him burst his lead and rise from death . . . . . 1 *Hen. VI.* i 1 63
Let's sit down quiet, For fear we wake her: softly . . *Hen. VIII.* iv 2 82
Speak your griefs softly: I do know you well . . *J. Cæsar* iv 2 42
Lead your battle softly on, Upon the left hand of the even field v 1 16
I will do't, my lord.—Go softly on . . . . *Hamlet* iv 4 8
Where is the queen?—Speak softly, wake her not . . *Ant. and Cleo.* v 2 323
Our Tarquin thus Did softly press the rushes . . . *Cymbeline* ii 2 13
Walk softly, do not heat your blood . . . . *Pericles* iv 1 49
Softly-sprighted. A softly-sprighted man, is he not? . *Mer. Wives* i 4 25
Softness. A satire against the softness of prosperity . *T. of Athens* v 1 36
Soho. Seek him out.—Soho, soho! . . . . *T. G. of Ver.* iii 1 189
Soil. As free from touch or soil with her As she from one ungot *M. for M.* v 1 141
That would be as great a soil in the new gloss of your marriage *M. Ado* iii 2 5
The only soil of his fair virtue's gloss, If virtue's gloss will stain with any soil, Is a sharp wit . . . . *L. L. Lost* ii 1 47
On the face of terra, the soil, the land, the earth . . . iv 2 7
If you like upon report The soil, the profit . . *As Y. Like It* ii 4 98
And flesh his spirit in a warlike soil . . . . *K. John* v 1 71
Sweet soil, adieu; My mother, and my nurse, that bears me yet! *Rich. II.* i 3 306
The noisome weeds, which without profit suck The soil's fertility . iii 4 39
No more the thirsty entrance of this soil Shall daub her lips with her own children's blood . . . . . . 1 *Hen. IV.* i 1 5
Stain'd with the variation of each soil Betwixt that Holmedon and this seat of ours . . . . i 1 64
Most subject is the fattest soil to weeds . . . 2 *Hen. IV.* iv 4 54
For all the soil of the achievement goes With me into the earth . iv 5 190
Renounce your soil, give sheep in lions' stead . . 1 *Hen. VI.* i 5 29
I had hope of France, Even as I have of fertile England's soil 2 *Hen. VI.* i 1 238
Here's the lord of the soil come to seize me for a stray . . iv 10 26
Leads discontented steps in foreign soil . . . *Richard III.* iv 4 312
Whose honour heaven shield from soil! . . . . *Hen. VIII.* i 2 26
I would have the soil of her fair rape Wiped off . *Troi. and Cres.* ii 2 148
What hath she done, prince, that can soil our mothers? . . . v 2 134
Nor did he soil the fact with cowardice . . . *T. of Athens* iii 5 16
Which give some soil perhaps to my behaviours . . . *J. Cæsar* i 2 42
No soil nor cautel doth besmirch The virtue of his will . *Hamlet* i 3 15
They clepe us drunkards, and with swinish phrase Soil our addition . i 4 20
Yet must Antony No way excuse his soils . . *Ant. and Cleo.* i 4 24
You are curb'd from that enlargement by The consequence o' the crown, and must not soil The precious note of it . . . . *Cymbeline* ii 3 126
Soil'd With that dear blood which it hath fostered . . *Richard II.* i 3 125
Or have mine honour soil'd With the attainder of his slanderous lips . iv 1 23
Stand firm by honour: We turn not back the silks upon the merchant, When we have soil'd them . . . . . *Troi. and Cres.* ii 2 70
As 'twere a thing a little soil'd i' the working . . *Hamlet* ii 1 40
Nor the soiled horse, goes to't With a more riotous appetite . *Lear* iv 6 124
Soilure. Not making any scruple of her soilure . *Troi. and Cres.* iv 1 56
Sojourn. Where shall we sojourn till our coronation? *Richard III.* iii 1 62
Be gone . . . , disguised from hence: Sojourn in Mantua *Rom. and Jul.* iii 3 169
Long in our court have made their amorous sojourn . . . *Lear* i 1 48
If they come to sojourn at my house, I'll not be there . . . ii 1 105
You will return and sojourn with my sister . . . . ii 4 206
How comes it he is to sojourn with you? How creeps acquaintance? *Cymbeline* i 4 24
Sojourned. Have you long sojourned there? . . *T. G. of Ver.* iv 1 20
My heart to her but as guest-wise sojourn'd . . *M. N. Dream* iii 2 171
In the mean time sojourn'd at my father's . . . *K. John* i 1 103
Sojourner. Report what a sojourner we have . . . *Pericles* iv 2 149
Sol. Ut, re, sol, la, mi, fa . . . . . *L. L. Lost* iv 2 102
I'll try how you can sol, fa, and sing it . . . *T. of Shrew* i 2 17
'D sol re,' one clef, two notes have I: 'E la mi,' show pity, or I die . iii 1 77
And therefore is the glorious planet Sol In noble eminence enthroned and sphered Amidst the other . . . . *Troi. and Cres.* i 3 89
O, these eclipses do portend these divisions! fa, sol, la, mi . *Lear* i 2 149
Sola. Ah, heavens, it is a most pathetical nit! Sola, sola! . *L. L. Lost* iv 1 151
Sola, sola! wo ha, ho! sola, sola!—Who calls?—Sola! . *Mer. of Venice* v 1 39
Solace. We will with some strange pastime solace them . . *L. L. Lost* iv 3 377
Sorrow would solace and mine age would ease . . 2 *Hen. VI.* ii 3 21
For with his soul fled all my worldly solace . . . . iii 2 151
This sickly land might solace as before . . . *Richard III.* ii 3 30
My mother, you wot well My hazards still have been your solace *Cor.* iv 1 28
One poor and loving child, But one thing to rejoice and solace in, And cruel death hath catch'd it from my sight! . *Rom. and Jul.* iv 5 47
Lamentable! What, To hide me from the radiant sun and solace I' the dungeon by a snuff? . . . . . . *Cymbeline* i 6 86
Sold. Money buys lands, and wives are sold by fate *Mer. Wives* v 5 246
It would make a man mad as a buck, to be so bought and sold *C. of Er.* iii 1 72
The boy hath sold him a bargain, a goose, that's flat . *L. L. Lost* iii 1 102
Assuredly the thing is to be sold . . . *As Y. Like It* ii 4 96
I fear you have sold your own lands to see other men's . . iv 1 22
I know a man that had this trick of melancholy sold a goodly manor for a song . . . . *All's Well* iii 2 9
I have sold all my trumpery . . . . . *W. Tale* iv 4 608
Have sold their fortunes at their native homes . . *K. John* ii 1 69
Fly, noble English, you are bought and sold . . . . v 4 10
My father's goods are all distrain'd and sold . . *Richard II.* ii 3 131
They sold themselves: but thou, like a kind fellow, gavest thyself away gratis; and I thank thee . . . . 2 *Hen. IV.* iv 3 74
Wherein you would have sold your king to slaughter . . *Hen. V.* ii 2 170
Bore it twelve leagues, and sold it for three half-pence . . . iii 2 46
Thou wouldst think I had sold my farm to buy my crown . . . v 2 129
Whither, my lord? from bought and sold Lord Talbot . 1 *Hen. VI.* iv 4 13
And sold their bodies for their country's benefit . . . v 4 106
While his own lands are bargain'd for and sold . . 2 *Hen. VI.* i 1 231
Sold. By thee Anjou and Maine were sold to France . 2 *Hen. VI.* iv 1 86
She was, indeed, a pedler's daughter, and sold many laces . . iv 2 49
There shall be in England seven halfpenny loaves sold for a penny . iv 2 71
Here's the Lord Say, which sold the towns in France . . . iv 7 23
I sold not Maine, I lost not Normandy . . . . . iv 7 70
Two of thy name, both Dukes of Somerset, Have sold their lives unto the house of York . . . . . . 3 *Hen. VI.* v 1 74
Be not too bold, For Dickon thy master is bought and sold *Richard III.* v 3 305
And thou art bought and sold among those of any wit . *Troi. and Cres.* ii 1 51
He sold the blood and labour Of our great action . . *Coriolanus* v 6 47
And, though I am sold, Not yet enjoy'd . . . *Rom. and Jul.* iii 2 27
I sell thee poison; thou hast sold me none . . . . v 1 83
Let all my land be sold.—'Tis all engaged, some forfeited *T. of Athens* ii 2 154
The feast is sold That is not often vouch'd, while 'tis a-making *Macbeth* iii 4 33
Nor will it yield . . . A ranker rate, should it be sold in fee . *Hamlet* iv 4 22
Of being taken by the insolent foe And sold to slavery . . *Othello* i 3 138
If heaven would make me such another world Of one entire and perfect chrysolite, I'ld not have sold her for it . . . . . v 2 146
'Tis thou Hast sold me to this novice . . . *Ant. and Cleo.* iv 12 14
The witch shall die: To the young Roman boy she hath sold me, and I fall . . . . iv 12 48
Cæsar's no merchant, to make prize with you Of things that merchants sold . . . . v 2 184
The one may be sold, or given, if there were wealth enough for the purchase, or merit for the gift . . . . *Cymbeline* i 4 90
Since I came, Diseases have been sold dearer than physic . *Pericles* iv 6 105
Soldat. Faites vous prêt; car ce soldat ici est disposé tout à cette heure de couper votre gorge . . . . . . *Hen. V.* iv 4 37
Solder. Wars 'twixt you twain would be As if the world should cleave, and that slain men Should solder up the rift . . *Ant. and Cleo.* iii 4 32
Solderest. Thou visible god [gold], That solder'st close impossibilities, And makest them kiss! . . . . *T. of Athens* iv 3 388
Soldier. I'll woo you like a soldier, at arms' end . . *T. G. of Ver.* v 4 57
If the love of soldier can suffice . . . . . *Mer. Wives* ii 1 12
You were good soldiers and tall fellows . . . . . . ii 2 10
Money is a good soldier, sir, and will on . . . . . . ii 2 176
There's not a soldier of us all . . . do relish the petition *Meas. for Meas.* i 2 15
I never heard any soldier dislike it . . . . i 2 18
That in the captain's but a choleric word, Which in the soldier is flat blasphemy.—Art avised o' that? . . . . ii 2 131
The great soldier who miscarried at sea . . . . . . iii 1 217
He shall appear to the envious a scholar, a statesman and a soldier . iii 2 155
A good soldier too, lady.—And a good soldier to a lady . *Much Ado* i 1 53
I look'd upon her with a soldier's eye, That liked, but had a rougher task i 1 300
He was wont to speak plain and to the purpose, like an honest man and a soldier . . . . ii 3 20
Like Pharaoh's soldiers in the reechy painting . . . . . iii 3 143
As it is base for a soldier to love . . . . . *L. L. Lost* i 2 61
Saint Cupid, then! and, soldiers, to the field! . . . . . iv 3 366
A soldier, a man of travel, that hath seen the world . . . v 1 113
Gentlemen and soldiers, pardon me; I will not combat in my shirt . v 2 710
I will right myself like a soldier . . . . v 2 735
A Venetian, a scholar and a soldier . . . . *Mer. of Venice* i 2 124
Then a soldier, Full of strange oaths and bearded like the pard *As Y. L. It* ii 7 149
Nor the courtier's, which is proud, nor the soldier's, which is ambitious iv 1 13
Will my daughter prove a good musician?—I think she'll sooner prove a soldier: Iron may hold with her, but never lutes . *T. of Shrew* ii 1 146
You have some stain of soldier in you . . . . *All's Well* i 1 122
'Tis our hope, sir, After well enter'd soldiers, to return . . . ii 1 6
But I hope your lordship thinks not him a soldier . . . . ii 5 2
Yonder is heavy news within between two soldiers and my young lady! iii 2 36
And to be a soldier?—Such is his noble purpose . . . . iii 2 72
There was excellent command,— . . to rend our own soldiers! . . iii 6 53
By the hand of a soldier, I will undertake it . . . . . iii 6 76
Shall we have this dialogue between the fool and the soldier? . . iv 3 113
And say a soldier, Dian, told thee this, Men are to mell with . . iv 3 256
The manifold linguist and the armipotent soldier . . . . iv 3 265
I long to talk with the young noble soldier . . . . . iv 5 109
He has promised me, as he is a gentleman and a soldier . *T. Night* iii 4 339
My young soldier, put up your iron: you are well fleshed . . . iv 1 42
Mine enemy, My parasite, my soldier, statesman, all . . *W. Tale* i 2 168
Let me have no lying: it becomes none but tradesmen, and they often give us soldiers the lie . . . . iv 4 746
A soldier, by the honour-giving hand Of Cœur-de-lion knighted *K. John* i 1 53
Wilt thou . . . follow me? I am a soldier and now bound to France . i 1 150
His forces strong, his soldiers confident . . . . . . ii 1 61
The swords of soldiers are his teeth, his fangs . . . . . ii 1 353
Whom zeal and charity brought to the field As God's own soldier . . ii 1 566
Hast thou not spoke like thunder on my side, Been sworn my soldier? iii 1 125
Brave soldier, pardon me, That any accent breaking from thy tongue Should 'scape the true acquaintance of mine ear . . . . . v 6 13
In name of lendings for your highness' soldiers . . . . *Richard II.* i 1 89
Three parts of that receipt I had for Calais Disbursed I duly to his highness' soldiers . . . . i 1 127
The lining of his coffers shall make coats To deck our soldiers . . i 4 62
This earth shall have a feeling and these stones Prove armed soldiers . iii 2 25
To the sepulchre of Christ, Whose soldier now, under whose blessed cross We are impressed . . . . 1 *Hen. IV.* i 1 20
As the soldiers bore dead bodies by, He call'd them untaught knaves . i 3 42
And but for these vile guns, He would himself have been a soldier . i 3 64
Of prisoners' ransom and of soldiers slain . . . . . . ii 3 57
She will not part with you; She'll be a soldier too, she'll to the wars . iii 1 195
Holds from all soldiers chief majority And military title capital . . iii 2 109
As not a soldier of this season's stamp Should go so general current . iv 1 4
Our soldiers shall march through; we'll to Sutton Co'fil' to-night . iv 2 2
If I be not ashamed of my soldiers, I am a soused gurnet . . . iv 2 12
In exchange of a hundred and fifty soldiers, three hundred and odd pounds . . . . iv 2 15
Such as indeed were never soldiers, but discarded unjust serving-men . iv 2 29
Yet once ere night I will embrace him with a soldier's arm . . v 2 74
Fellows, soldiers, friends, Better consider what you have to do . . v 2 76
Up, and away! Our soldiers stand full fairly for the day . . v 3 29
Arrows fled not swifter toward their aim Than did our soldiers 2 *Hen. IV.* i 1 124
Doth not the king lack subjects? do not the rebels need soldiers? . i 2 87
You are to take soldiers up in counties as you go . . . . ii 1 199
This Sir John, cousin, that comes hither anon about soldiers? . . iii 2 31
A soldier is better accommodated than with a wife . . . . iii 2 72
Shadow! . . . let me have him to sit under: he's like to be a cold soldier iii 2 134
I cannot put him to a private soldier that is the leader of so many thousands . . . . iii 2 177

Soldier. My little soldier there, be merry . . . *2 Hen. IV.* v 3 34
Others, like soldiers, armed in their stings, Make boot upon the summer's velvet buds . . . *Hen. V.* i 2 193
I'll run him up to the hilts, as I am a soldier . . . ii 1 69
As I am a soldier, A name that in my thoughts becomes me best . . iii 3 5
The flesh'd soldier, rough and hard of heart . . . iii 3 11
As bootless spend our vain command Upon the enraged soldiers in their spoil . . . iii 3 25
Take pity of your town and of your people, Whiles yet my soldiers are in my command . . . iii 3 29
In a moment look to see The blind and bloody soldier with foul hand . iii 3 34
The winter coming on and sickness growing Upon our soldiers . . iii 3 56
His soldiers sick and famish'd in their march . . . iii 5 57
A soldier, firm and sound of heart, And of buxom valour . . . iii 6 27
To grace himself at his return into London under the form of a soldier . iii 6 73
We did but sleep: advantage is a better soldier than rashness . . iii 6 127
The king is not bound to answer the particular endings of his soldiers . iv 1 164
There is no king, be his cause never so spotless, if it come to the arbitrement of swords, can try it out with all unspotted soldiers . . iv 1 169
Therefore should every soldier in the wars do as every sick man in his bed . . . iv 1 188
O God of battles! steel my soldiers' hearts; Possess them not with fear iv 1 306
My poor soldiers tell me, yet ere night They'll be in fresher robes, or they will pluck The gay new coats o'er the French soldiers' heads . iv 3 116
Now, soldiers, march away: And how thou pleasest, God, dispose the day! . . . iv 3 131
In which array, brave soldier, doth he lie, Larding the plain . . . iv 6 7
Then every soldier kill his prisoners; Give the word through . . iv 6 37
The king, most worthily, hath caused every soldier to cut his prisoner's throat . . . iv 7 10
Soldier, you must come to the king.—Soldier, why wearest thou that glove? . . . iv 7 124
Which he swore, as he was a soldier, he would wear if alive . . . iv 7 135
Is it fit this soldier keep his oath?—He is a craven and a villain else . iv 7 138
Call him hither to me, soldier.—I will, my liege . . . iv 7 158
The glove which I have given him for a favour May haply purchase him a box o' th' ear; It is the soldier's . . . iv 7 182
If that the soldier strike him, as I judge By his blunt bearing he will . iv 7 184
Give me thy glove, soldier; look, here is the fellow of it . . . iv 8 41
Grow like savages,—as soldiers will That nothing do but meditate on blood . . . v 2 59
Vouchsafe to teach a soldier terms Such as will enter at a lady's ear . v 2 99
I speak to thee plain soldier: if thou canst love me for this, take me . v 2 156
Take me; and take me, take a soldier; take a soldier, take a king . v 2 175
Amongst the soldiers this is muttered . . . *1 Hen. VI.* i 1 70
His soldiers spying his undaunted spirit A Talbot! a Talbot! cried out amain . . . i 1 127
Ten thousand soldiers with me I will take . . . i 1 155
Be vigilant: If any noise or soldier you perceive . . . ii 1 2
Improvident soldiers! had your watch been good, This sudden mischief never could have fall'n . . . ii 1 58
Now there rests no other shift but this; To gather our soldiers . . ii 1 76
See what cates you have; For soldiers' stomachs always serve them well ii 3 80
Will ye, like soldiers, come and fight it out? . . . iii 2 66
I should revive the soldiers' hearts, Because I ever found them as myself iii 2 97
A braver soldier never couched lance, A gentler heart did never sway in court . . . iii 2 134
Saint George and victory! fight, soldiers, fight . . . iv 6 1
My spirit can no longer bear these harms. Soldiers, adieu! . . . iv 7 31
I am a soldier and unapt to weep Or to exclaim on fortune's fickleness . v 3 133
The slaughter of so many peers, So many captains, gentlemen and soldiers . . . v 4 104
Oft have I seen the haughty cardinal, More like a soldier than a man o' the church . . . *2 Hen. VI.* i 1 186
Levy great sums of money through the realm For soldiers' pay in France iii 1 62
You took bribes of France, And, being protector, stay'd the soldiers' pay iii 1 105
I never robb'd the soldiers of their pay, Nor ever had one penny bribe . iii 1 108
Provide me soldiers, lords, Whiles I take order for mine own affairs . iii 1 319
Within fourteen days At Bristol I expect my soldiers . . . iii 1 328
Bring forth the soldiers of our prize . . . iv 1 8
Surprised our forts And sent the ragged soldiers wounded home . . iv 1 90
Come, soldiers, show what cruelty ye can . . . iv 1 132
Soldiers, defer the spoil of the city until night . . . iv 7 142
Follow me, soldiers: we'll devise a mean To reconcile you all unto the king . . . iv 8 71
Soldiers, this day have you redeem'd your lives . . . iv 9 15
I do dismiss my powers. Soldiers, I thank you all. . . . v 1 45
Let no soldier fly. He that is truly dedicate to war Hath no self-love . v 2 36
And breaking in Were by the swords of common soldiers slain *3 Hen. VI.* i 1 9
Stay by me, my lords; And, soldiers, stay and lodge by me this night . i 1 32
The city favours them, And they have troops of soldiers at their beck . i 1 68
I'll keep London with my soldiers.—And I to Norfolk with my followers i 1 207
The soldiers should have toss'd me on their pikes Before I would have granted to that act . . . i 1 244
They are soldiers, Witty, courteous, liberal, full of spirit . . . i 2 42
Soldiers, away with him!—Ah, Clifford, murder not this innocent child! i 3 7
I, then in London, keeper of the king, Muster'd my soldiers . . ii 1 112
That robb'd my soldiers of their heated spleen . . . ii 1 124
Their weapons like to lightning came and went; Our soldiers', like the night-owl's lazy flight, . . . Fell gently down . . . ii 1 130
Some six miles off the duke is with the soldiers . . . ii 1 144
He was lately sent . . . With aid of soldiers to this needful war . . ii 1 147
Our soldiers put to flight, And, as thou seest, ourselves in heavy plight iii 3 36
With some few bands of chosen soldiers, I'll undertake to land them . iii 3 204
Why stay we now? These soldiers shall be levied . . . iii 3 251
His soldiers lurking in the towns about . . . iv 2 15
What now remains . . . to do But march to London with our soldiers? iv 3 61
For well I wot that Henry is no soldier . . . iv 7 83
Come on, brave soldiers: doubt not of the day, And, that once gotten, doubt not of large pay . . . iv 7 87
I'll win our ancient right in France again, Or die a soldier *Richard III.* iii 1 93
Sir Walter Herbert, a renowned soldier . . . iv 5 9
From troop to troop Went through the army, cheering up the soldiers . v 3 71
Than can the substance of ten thousand soldiers Armed in proof . . v 3 218
If you fight against God's enemy, God will in justice ward you as his soldiers . . . v 3 254
I will lead forth my soldiers to the plain, And thus my battle shall be ordered . . . v 3 291
Proclaim a pardon to the soldiers fled That in submission will return . v 5 16
But when they would seem soldiers, they have galls, Good arms *T. and C.* i 3 237

Soldier. But we are soldiers; And may that soldier a mere recreant prove, That means not, hath not, or is not in love! . *Troi. and Cres.* i 3 286
I knew thy grandsire, And once fought with him: he was a soldier good iv 5 197
Let the trumpets blow, That this great soldier may his welcome know iv 5 276
The counsellor heart, the arm our soldier, Our steed the leg . *Coriolanus* i 1 120
A soldier Even to Cato's wish, not fierce and terrible Only in strokes . i 4 56
We thank the gods Our Rome hath such a soldier . . . i 9 9
Nay, my good soldier, up; My gentle Marcius, worthy Caius. . . ii 1 188
Thou art their soldier, and being bred in broils Hast not the soft way . iii 2 81
Thou hast said My praises made thee first a soldier . . . iii 2 108
When he speaks not like a citizen, You find him like a soldier . . iii 3 54
Do not take His rougher accents for malicious sounds, But, as I say, such as become a soldier . . . iii 3 56
But a greater soldier than he, you wot one . . . iv 5 170
Worth six on him.—Nay, not so neither: but I take him to be the greater soldier . . . iv 5 176
And not a hair upon a soldier's head Which will not prove a whip. . iv 6 133
Your soldiers use him as the grace 'fore meat, Their talk at table . iv 7 3
The tribunes are no soldiers . . . iv 7 31
The god of soldiers, With the consent of supreme Jove . . . v 3 70
Do not bid me Dismiss my soldiers, or capitulate Again with Rome's mechanics . . . v 3 82
I am return'd your soldier . . . v 6 71
Take him up. Help, three o' the chiefest soldiers; I'll be one . . v 6 150
Rome, I have been thy soldier forty years . . . *T. Andron.* i 1 193
Here none but soldiers and Rome's servitors Repose in fame . . . i 1 352
A halter, soldiers! hang him on this tree . . . v 1 47
Bid him encamp his soldiers where they are . . . v 2 126
Sometime she driveth o'er a soldier's neck . . . *Rom. and Jul.* i 4 82
Like powder in a skilless soldier's flask, Is set a-fire by thine own ignorance . . . iii 3 132
Thou art a soldier, therefore seldom rich . . . *T. of Athens* i 2 228
Soldiers should brook as little wrongs as gods . . . iii 5 117
There's gold to pay thy soldiers: Make large confusion . . . iv 3 126
Thieves?—Soldiers, not thieves.—Both too; and women's sons . . iv 3 416
He likewise enriched poor straggling soldiers . . . v 1 7
Do your will; But he's a tried and valiant soldier . . *J. Cæsar* iv 1 28
I am a soldier, I, Older in practice, abler than yourself . . . iv 3 30
You say you are a better soldier: Let it appear so . . . iv 3 51
I said, an elder soldier, not a better: Did I say 'better?' . . . iv 3 56
So shall he waste his means, weary his soldiers, Doing himself offence . iv 3 200
There they perch'd, Gorging and feeding from our soldiers' hands . . v 1 82
His soldiers fell to spoil, Whilst we by Antony are all enclosed . . v 3 7
His bones to-night shall lie, Most like a soldier, order'd honourably . v 5 79
Who like a good and hardy soldier fought 'Gainst my captivity *Macbeth* i 2 4
Your eye in Scotland Would create soldiers, make our women fight . iv 3 187
An older and a better soldier none That Christendom gives out . . iv 3 191
Fie, my lord, fie! a soldier, and afeard? . . . v 1 41
There is ten thousand— Geese, villain?—Soldiers, sir . . . v 3 13
Thou lily-liver'd boy. What soldiers, patch? Death of thy soul! . . v 3 15
Let every soldier hew him down a bough And bear't before him . . v 4 4
Your son, my lord, has paid a soldier's debt . . . v 8 39
Had he his hurts before?—Ay, on the front.—Why then, God's soldier be he! . . . v 8 47
O, farewell, honest soldier: Who hath relieved you? . . . *Hamlet* i 1 16
As you are friends, scholars and soldiers, Give me one poor request . i 5 141
Gives him three thousand crowns in annual fee, And his commission to employ those soldiers . . . ii 2 74
O, what a noble mind is here o'erthrown! The courtier's, soldier's, scholar's, eye, tongue, sword . . . iii 1 159
As the sleeping soldiers in the alarm, Your bedded hair, like life in excrements, Start up, and stand an end . . . iii 4 120
Let four captains Bear Hamlet, like a soldier, to the stage . . v 2 407
The soldiers' music and the rites of war Speak loudly for him . . v 2 410
Such a sight as this Becomes the field, but here shows much amiss. Go, bid the soldiers shoot . . . v 2 414
Madam, with much ado: Your sister is the better soldier . . *Lear* iv 5 3
To't, luxury, pell-mell! for I lack soldiers . . . iv 6 119
Take thou my soldiers, prisoners, patrimony; Dispose of them, of me . v 3 75
Thy soldiers, All levied in my name, have in my name Took their discharge . . . v 3 103
I have served him, and the man commands Like a full soldier *Othello* ii 1 36
You may relish him more in the soldier than in the scholar . . . ii 1 167
Not past a pint, as I am a soldier . . . ii 3 69
A soldier's a man; A life's but a span; Why, then, let a soldier drink . ii 3 73
He is a soldier fit to stand by Cæsar And give direction . . . ii 3 127
If partially affined, or leagued in office, Thou dost deliver more or less than truth, Thou art no soldier . . . ii 3 220
'Tis the soldiers' life To have their balmy slumbers waked with strife . ii 3 257
He's a soldier, and for one to say a soldier lies, is stabbing . . iii 4 5
I have a weapon; A better never did itself sustain Upon a soldier's thigh . . . v 2 261
Who, high in name and power, Higher than both in blood and life, stands up For the main soldier . . . *Ant. and Cleo.* i 2 198
Thou, the greatest soldier of the world, Art turn'd the greatest liar . i 3 38
I go from hence Thy soldier, servant; making peace or war . . i 3 70
Was borne so like a soldier, that thy cheek So much as lank'd not . i 4 70
Thou art a soldier only: speak no more . . . ii 2 108
Till I shall see you in your soldier's dress, Which will become you both, farewell . . . ii 4 4
I know thee now: how farest thou, soldier?—Well; And well am like to do . . . ii 6 72
Celebrate our drink?—Let's ha't, good soldier . . . ii 7 111
And ambition, The soldier's virtue, rather makes choice of loss . . iii 1 23
That Without the which a soldier, and his sword, Grants scarce distinction . . . iii 1 28
Adieu, noble Agrippa.—Good fortune, worthy soldier; and farewell . iii 2 22
The mares would bear A soldier and his horse . . . iii 7 10
How now, worthy soldier!—O noble emperor, do not fight by sea . . iii 7 61
I think I am i' the right.—Soldier, thou art . . . iii 7 69
To-morrow, soldier, By sea and land I'll fight . . . iv 2 4
Soldiers, have careful watch.—And you. Good night . . . iv 3 7
Fare thee well, dame, whate'er becomes of me: This is a soldier's kiss . iv 4 30
The soldier That has this morning left thee would have still Follow'd thy heels.—Who's gone this morning? . . . iv 5 4
No more a soldier: bruised pieces, go; You have been nobly borne . iv 14 42
The soldier's pole is fall'n: young boys and girls Are level now with men iv 15 65
Ah, soldier!—How goes it here?—All dead . . . v 2 331
His father and I were soldiers together; to whom I have been often bound for no less than my life . . . *Cymbeline* i 4 26

Soldier. When a soldier was the theme, my name Was not far off *Cymb.* iii 3 59
This attempt I am soldier to, and will abide it with A prince's courage iii 4 186
He shall be interr'd As soldiers can . . . . iv 2 402
Which gave advantage to an ancient soldier, An honest one, I warrant. v 3 15
The poor soldier that so richly fought, Whose rags shamed gilded arms v 5 3
Why, old soldier, Wilt thou undo the worth thou art unpaid for? . v 5 306
The forlorn soldier, that so nobly fought . . . . . v 5 405
I am, sir, The soldier that did company these three In poor beseeming . v 5 408
Even in your armours, as you are address'd, Will very well become a
soldier's dance. I will not have excuse . . . . *Pericles* ii 3 95
Nor let pity, which Even women have cast off, melt thee, but be A soldier
to thy purpose . . . . iv 1 8
Soldier-breeder. And thou must therefore needs prove a good soldier-
breeder . . . . *Hen. V.* v 2 219
Soldier-like. I will not say, pity me; 'tis not a soldier-like phrase: but
I say, love me . . . . *Mer. Wives* ii 1 13
A soldier-like word, and a word of exceeding good command 2 *Hen. IV.* iii 2 83
Soldiership. When thy father and myself in friendship First tried our
soldiership . . . . *All's Well* i 2 26
And, to the possibility of thy soldiership, will subscribe for thee . iii 6 89
More of his soldiership I know not . . . . . . iv 3 300
Setting my knighthood and my soldiership aside . . . 2 *Hen. IV.* i 2 93
And put we on Industrious soldiership . . . . *Macbeth* v 4 16
Mere prattle, without practice, Is all his soldiership . *Othello* i 1 27
His soldiership Is twice the other twain . . . *Ant. and Cleo.* ii 1 34
You therein throw away The absolute soldiership you have by land . iii 7 43
Soldest. How agrees the devil and thee about thy soul, that thou soldest
him on Good-Friday last for a cup of Madeira? . . . 1 *Hen. IV.* i 2 127
Sole. The sole drift of my purpose doth extend Not a frown further *Temp.* v 1 29
This left shoe is my mother . . . , it hath the worser sole *T. G. of Ver.* ii 3 19
My sole earth's heaven and my heaven's claim. . *Com. of Errors* iii 2 64
From the crown of his head to the sole of his foot, he is all mirth *M. Ado* iii 2 10
The welkin's vicegerent and sole dominator of Navarre . . *L. L. Lost* i 1 222
The sole inheritor Of all perfections that a man may owe . . . ii 1 5
Sole imperator and great general Of trotting 'paritors . . . iii 1 187
Not on thy sole, but on thy soul, harsh Jew, Thou makest thy knife
keen; . . . Can no prayers pierce thee? . . *Mer. of Venice* iv 1 123
His sole child, my lord, and bequeathed to my overlooking . *All's Well* i 1 44
This, so sole and so unmatchable . . . . . *K. John* iv 3 52
Sole heir male Of the true line and stock . . . . *Hen. V.* i 2 70
King Lewis the Tenth, Who was sole heir to the usurper Capet . . i 2 78
Philippe, Sole daughter unto Lionel Duke of Clarence . 2 *Hen. VI.* ii 2 50
Henry, sole possessor of my love . . . . . 3 *Hen. VI.* iii 3 24
She shall be sole victress, Cæsar's Cæsar . . . *Richard III.* iv 4 336
That praise, sole pure, transcends . . . . *Troi. and Cres.* i 3 244
Affecting one sole throne, Without assistance . . . *Coriolanus* iv 6 32
You have dancing shoes With nimble soles: I have a soul of lead *R. and J.* i 4 15
That when the single sole of it is worn, the jest may remain after the
wearing sole singular.—O single-soled jest! . . . . . ii 4 67
A throne where honour may be crown'd Sole monarch of the universal
earth . . . . iii 2 94
A trade, sir, that, I hope, I may use with a safe conscience; which is,
indeed, sir, a mender of bad soles . . . . *J. Cæsar* i 1 15
This tyrant, whose sole name blisters our tongues . . . *Macbeth* iv 3 12
We are not over-happy; On fortune's cap we are not the very button.—
Nor the soles of her shoe? . . . . . . *Hamlet* ii 2 234
And for that, I, his sole son, do this same villain send To heaven . . iii 3 77
Sole sir o' the world, I cannot project mine own cause so well
Ant. and Cleo. v 2 120
His wife's sole son—a widow That late he married . . *Cymbeline* i 1 5
Is she sole child to the king?—His only child . . . . . i 1 56
That mightst have had the sole son of my queen! . . . . . i 1 138
An enterprise of kindness Perform'd to your sole daughter . *Pericles* iv 3 39
Solely. I am not solely led By nice direction of a maiden's eyes *M. of V.* ii 1 13
Left solely heir to all his lands and goods . . *T. of Shrew* ii 1 118
Think him a great way fool, solely a coward . . . *All's Well* i 1 112
Leave me solely: go, See how he fares . . . . *W. Tale* ii 3 17
Honour's thought Reigns solely in the breast of every man *Hen. V.* ii Prol. 4
Had borne the action of yourself, or else To him had left it solely *Coriol.* iv. 7 16
O single-soled jest, solely singular for the singleness! . *Rom. and Jul.* ii 4 69
Which shall to all our nights and days to come Give solely sovereign
sway and masterdom . . . . *Macbeth* i 5 71
Solemn. The solemn temples, the great globe itself . . . *Tempest* iv 1 153
That rejoice To hear the solemn curfew . . . . . . v 1 40
A solemn air and the best comforter To an unsettled fancy . . . v 1 58
It hath in solemn synods been decreed . . . *Com. of Errors* i 1 13
Now, music, sound, and sing your solemn hymn . . *Much Ado* v 3 11
Ridiculous appears, To check their folly, passion's solemn tears
L. L. Lost v 2 118
A young man and an old in solemn talk . . . *As Y. Like It* ii 4 21
An eye-sore to our solemn festival! . . . . *T. of Shrew* iii 2 103
The solemn feast Shall more attend upon the coming space . *All's Well* ii 3 187
Although before the solemn priest I have sworn . . . . . ii 3 286
Of whom he hath taken a solemn leave . . . . . . iv 3 90
A solemn combination shall be made Of our dear souls . . *T. Night* v 1 392
How ceremonious, solemn and unearthly It was! . . . *W. Tale* iii 1 7
Why do you bend such solemn brows on me? . . . . *K. John* iv 2 90
To dwell in solemn shades of endless night . . . *Richard II.* i 3 177
Cover your heads and mock not flesh and blood With solemn reverence iii 2 172
Where the sad and solemn priests Sing still . . . . *Hen. V.* iv 1 318
Let your drums be still, For here we entertain a solemn peace 1 *Hen. VI.* v 4 175
A dreadful oath, sworn with a solemn tongue! . . 2 *Hen. VI.* iii 2 158
Who can be bound by any solemn vow To do a murderous deed, . . .
And have no other reason for this wrong But that he was bound
by a solemn oath? . . . . v 1 184
Crown'd so soon, and broke his solemn oath? . . . 3 *Hen. VI.* i 4 100
He hath made a solemn vow Never to lie and take his natural rest . iv 3 4
A solemn hunting is in hand . . . . . *T. Andron.* ii 1 112
When he is here, even at thy solemn feast . . . . . v 2 115
With his solemn tongue he did discourse . . . . . . v 3 81
Our solemn hymns to sullen dirges change . . *Rom. and Jul.* iv 5 88
To-night we hold a solemn supper, sir . . . . *Macbeth* iii 1 14
Nor customary suits of solemn black . . . . . *Hamlet* i 2 78
With solemn march Goes slow and stately by them . . . . i 2 201
We'll make a solemn wager on your cunnings . . . . . iv 7 156
With a solemn earnestness, More than indeed belong'd to such a trifle *Oth.* v 2 227
Our army shall In solemn show attend this funeral . *Ant. and Cleo.* v 2 367
All solemn things Should answer solemn accidents . . *Cymbeline* iv 2 191
Solemness. Turn thy solemness out o' door . . . *Coriolanus* i 3 120
Solemnity. With triumphs, mirth and rare solemnity . . *T. G. of Ver.* v 4 161

Solemnity. Between which time of the contract and limit of the solemnity
Meas. for Meas. iii 1 224
Shall behold the night Of our solemnities . . . *M. N. Dream* i 1 12
Hearing our intent, Came here in grace of our solemnity . . . iv 1 139
We'll hold a feast in great solemnity . . . . iv 1 190
A fortnight hold we this solemnity, In nightly revels and new jollity . v 1 376
Some speedy messenger bid her repair To our solemnity . . *K. John* ii 1 555
Showed like a feast And won by rareness such solemnity . 1 *Hen. IV.* iii 2 59
What dares the slave Come hither, cover'd with an antic face, To fleer
and scorn at our solemnity? . . . . . . *Rom. and Jul.* i 5 59
A villain that is hither come in spite, To scorn at our solemnity . i 5 65
Uncomfortable time, why camest thou now To murder, murder our
solemnity? . . . . iv 5 61
Dolabella, see High order in this great solemnity . *Ant. and Cleo.* v 2 369
Solemnize. To solemnize The bargain of your faith . . *Mer. of Venice* iii 2 194
To solemnize this day the glorious sun Stays in his course . *K. John* iii 1 77
Solemnized. I have hope to see the nuptial Of these our dear-beloved
solemnized . . . . *Tempest* v 1 309
At a marriage-feast, . . . solemnized In Normandy . . *L. L. Lost* ii 1 42
Straight shall our nuptial rites be solemnized . . . *Mer. of Venice* ii 9 6
He [Time] trots hard with a young maid between the contract of her
marriage and the day it is solemnized . . *As Y. Like It* iii 2 333
Presently The rites of marriage shall be solemnized . . *K. John* ii 1 539
And make this marriage to be solemnized . . . . 1 *Hen. VI.* v 3 168
Solemnly. And will to-morrow midnight solemnly Dance *M. N. Dream* iv 1 93
On Wednesday next we solemnly set down Our coronation *Richard II.* iv 1 319
All studies here I solemnly defy . . . . . 1 *Hen. IV.* i 3 228
Let him land, And solemnly see him set on to London . *Hen. V.* v Prol. 14
Solemnly interr'd At Chertsey monastery . . . *Richard III.* i 2 214
Under the confession's seal He solemnly had sworn . . *Hen. VIII.* i 2 165
Solicit. Be gone; solicit me no more . . . . *T. G. of Ver.* iv 4 40
To desire and require her to solicit your master's desires . *Mer. Wives* i 2 10
If the prince do solicit you in that kind, you know your answer *M. Ado* ii 1 70
May be the amorous count solicits her In the unlawful purpose *All's W.* iii 5 72
I had rather hear you to solicit that Than music from the spheres *T. N.* iii 1 120
Alas, the part I had in Woodstock's blood Doth more solicit me than
your exclaims! . . . . *Richard II.* i 2 2
Solicit Henry with her wondrous praise . . . . 1 *Hen. VI.* v 3 190
We heartily solicit Your gracious self to take on you the charge *Rich. III.* iii 7 130
Did you perceive He did solicit you in free contempt? . . *Coriolanus* ii 3 208
Who, as I hear, mean to solicit him For mercy to his country . . v 1 72
Sith there's no justice in earth nor hell, We will solicit heaven *T. An.* iv 3 50
How he solicits heaven, Himself best knows . . . *Macbeth* iv 3 149
If you bethink yourself of any crime Unreconciled as yet to heaven and
grace, Solicit for it straight . . . . . . *Othello* v 2 28
Resolve your angry father, if my tongue Did e'er solicit, or my hand
subscribe To any syllable that made love to you . . . *Pericles* ii 5 69
Solicitation. If she will return me my jewels, I will give over my suit
and repent my unlawful solicitation . . . . . *Othello* iv 2 202
Solicited. I have told my neighbour how you have been solicited by a
gentleman his companion . . . . . . *All's Well* iii 5 16
I am solicited, not by a few, And those of true condition . *Hen. VIII.* i 2 18
So tell him, with the occurrents, more and less, Which have solicited
Hamlet v 2 369
Solicit'st here a lady that disdains Thee and the devil alike . *Cymbeline* i 6 147
Soliciting. This supernatural soliciting Cannot be ill . . *Macbeth* i 3 130
And more above, hath his solicitings, As they fell out by time, by means
and place, All given to mine ear . . . . . . *Hamlet* ii 2 126
And bring him jump when he may Cassio find Soliciting his wife *Othello* ii 3 393
Frame yourself To orderly soliciting . . . . . *Cymbeline* ii 3 52
Solicitor. We single you As our best-moving fair solicitor . *L. L. Lost* ii 1 29
Thy solicitor shall rather die Than give thy cause away . . *Othello* iii 3 27
Solid. Make mountains level, and the continent, Weary of solid firmness,
melt itself Into the sea! . . . . 2 *Hen. IV.* iii 1 48
And make a sop of all this solid globe . . . *Troi. and Cres.* i 3 113
O, that this too too solid flesh would melt, Thaw! . . . *Hamlet* i 2 129
Whose solid virtue The shot of accident, nor dart of chance, Could
neither graze nor pierce . . . . *Othello* iv 1 277
Solidares. Here's three solidares for thee . . . *T. of Athens* iii 1 46
Solidity. This solidity and compound mass, With tristful visage . *Ham.* iii 4 49
Solinus. Proceed, Solinus, to procure my fall . . *Com. of Errors* i 1 1
Solitary. Where thou shalt find me, sad and solitary . *T. G. of Ver.* iv 4 94
In respect that it is solitary, I like it very well . . *As Y. Like It* iii 2 16
Solomon. Yet was Solomon so seduced, and he had a very good wit *L. L. L.* i 2 180
Profound Solomon to tune a jig, And Nestor play at push-pin . . iv 3 168
Solon. But safer triumph is this funeral pomp, That hath aspired to
Solon's happiness And triumphs over chance in honour's bed *T. An.* i 1 177
Solum. Cum privilegio ad imprimendum solum . . *T. of Shrew* iv 4 93
Solus. Will you shog off? I would have you solus . . . *Hen. V.* ii 1 48
'Solus,' egregious dog? O viper vile! The 'solus' in thy most
mervailous face; The 'solus' in thy teeth, and in thy throat! . ii 1 49
I do retort the 'solus' in thy bowels . . . . ii 1 54
Solyman. That won three fields of Sultan Solyman . . *Mer. of Venice* ii 1 26
Some. We all were sea-swallow'd, though some cast again . *Tempest* ii 1 251
I must remove Some thousands of these logs and pile them up . . iii 1 10
How if your husband start some other where? . . *Com. of Errors* ii 1 30
Some tender money to me; some invite me; Some other give me thanks
for kindnesses; Some offer me commodities to buy . . . . iv 3 4
Some of us will smart for it . . . . *Much Ado* v 1 109
Some such strange bull leap'd your father's cow . . . . . v 4 49
Some say a sore; but not a sore, till now made sore with shooting *L. L. L.* iv 2 59
How happy some o'er other some can be! . . . *M. N. Dream* i 1 226
Some there be that shadows kiss; Such have but a shadow's bliss
Mer. of Venice ii 9 66
Let's see; I think 'tis now some seven o'clock . . . *T. of Shrew* iv 3 189
To me comes a creature, Sometimes her head on one side, some another
W. Tale iii 3 20
Go some of you and fetch a looking-glass . . . . *Richard II.* iv 1 268
Let me see some more . . . . 1 *Hen. IV.* ii 3 7
For what sum?—It is more than for some, my lord; it is for all 2 *Hen. IV.* ii 1 79
Bate me some and I will pay you some . . . . Epil. 16
For reverence to some alive, I give a sparing limit to my tongue *Rich. III.* iii 7 193
I have said to some my standers by 'Lo, Jupiter is yonder!' *T. and C.* iv 5 190
I am not here; This is not Romeo, he's some other where *Rom. and Jul.* i 1 204
When I came, some minute ere the time Of her awaking . . . . v 3 257
Some of your function, mistress; Leave procreants alone . *Othello* iv 2 27
But end it by some means for Imogen . . . . . *Cymbeline* v 3 83
Somebody call my wife. . . . . *Mer. Wives* iv 2 121
Didst thou not hear somebody?—No; 'twas the vane . *Much Ado* iii 3 137
I believe a' means to cozen somebody in this city . . *T. of Shrew* iv 2 40

Somebody. He would make this a bloody day to somebody . 2 *Hen. IV.* v 4 14
I was too hot to do somebody good, That is too cold in thinking of it now . . . . *Richard III.* i 3 311
A black day will it be to somebody . . . . v 3 280
I would somebody had heard her talk yesterday, as I did *Troi. and Cres.* i 1 45
Go to the gate; somebody knocks . . . *J. Cæsar* ii 1 60
Some one with child by him? My cousin Juliet? *Meas. for Meas.* i 4 45
Some one hath set you on: Confess the truth . . . . . v 1 112
Some one among us whom we must produce for an interpreter *All's Well* iv 1 5
To let you understand, If case some one of you would fly from us 3 *Hen. VI.* v 4 34
Some one take order Buckingham be brought To Salisbury *Richard III.* iv 4 539
For some one to say 'Break up the senate till another time' *J. Cæsar* ii 2 97
Somerset. Else was wrangling Somerset in the error? . 1 *Hen. VI.* ii 4 6
I pluck this red rose with young Somerset . . . ii 4 37
Now, Somerset, where is your argument? . . . . ii 4 59
Hath not thy rose a canker, Somerset?—Hath not thy rose a thorn? . ii 4 68
Now, by God's will, thou wrong'st him, Somerset . . ii 4 82
But no traitor; And that I'll prove on better men than Somerset . ii 4 98
Against proud Somerset and William Pole, Will I . . . wear this rose . ii 4 122
Some words there grew 'twixt Somerset and me . . ii 5 46
Those bitter injuries, Which Somerset hath offer'd to my house . ii 5 125
The envious barking of your saucy tongue Against my lord the Duke of Somerset . . . . iii 4 34
Will not this malice, Somerset, be left? . . . . iv 1 108
Good cousins both, of York and Somerset, Quiet yourselves . . iv 1 114
There is my pledge; accept it, Somerset.—Nay, let it rest . iv 1 120
I see no reason, if I wear this rose, That any one should therefore be suspicious I more incline to Somerset than York . iv 1 154
And, good my Lord of Somerset, unite Your troops of horsemen . iv 1 164
Yet I like it not, In that he wears the badge of Somerset . iv 1 177
A plague upon that villain Somerset, That thus delays! . . iv 3 9
O God, that Somerset, who in proud heart Doth stop my cornets, were in Talbot's place! . . . . iv 3 24
We lose, they daily get; All 'long of this vile traitor Somerset iv 3 33
Maine, Blois, Poictiers, and Tours, are won away, 'Long all of Somerset iv 3 46
Ring'd about with bold adversity, Cries out for noble York and Somerset iv 4 15
Had York and Somerset brought rescue in, We should have found a bloody day of this . . . . iv 7 33
Buckingham, Somerset, Salisbury, and Warwick . . . 2 *Hen. VI.* i 1 69
Cousin of Somerset, join you with me, And all together . . i 1 167
Or thou or I, Somerset, will be protector, Despite Duke Humphrey i 1 178
On the pieces of the broken wand Were placed the heads of Edmund Duke of Somerset, And William de la Pole . . . i 2 29
Beaufort The imperious churchman, Somerset, Buckingham . i 3 72
I care not which; Or Somerset or York, all's one to me . i 3 105
If Somerset be unworthy of the place, Let York be regent . i 3 108
Show some reason, Buckingham, Why Somerset should be preferr'd . i 3 117
My Lord of Somerset will keep me here, Without discharge . i 3 171
If I may judge: Let Somerset be regent o'er the French . i 3 209
Come, Somerset, we'll see thee sent away . . . i 3 225
What shall betide the Duke of Somerset?—Let him shun castles . i 4 69
Suffolk's insolence, At Beaufort's pride, at Somerset's ambition . ii 2 71
Welcome, Lord Somerset. What news from France? . . iii 1 83
Cold news, Lord Somerset: but God's will be done! . . iii 1 86
What counsel give you in this weighty cause?—That Somerset be sent as regent . . . . iii 1 290
No more, good York; sweet Somerset, be still . . . iii 1 304
The Duke of Somerset, whom he terms a traitor . . iv 9 30
Send Duke Edmund to the Tower; And, Somerset, we will commit thee thither . . . . iv 9 39
Why I have brought this army hither Is to remove proud Somerset . v 1 36
The king hath yielded unto thy demand: . . . Somerset is in the Tower v 1 41
Any thing I have Is his to use, so Somerset may die . . v 1 53
What intends these forces thou dost bring?—To heave the traitor Somerset . . . . v 1 61
See, Buckingham, Somerset comes with the queen . . . v 1 83
Is Somerset at liberty? Then, York, unloose thy long-imprison'd thoughts . . . . v 1 87
Shall I endure the sight of Somerset? False king! . . . v 1 90
Somerset Hath made the wizard famous in his death . . v 2 68
But is your grace dead, my Lord of Somerset? . . 3 *Hen. VI.* i 1 18
And you too, Somerset and Montague, Speak freely what you think . iv 1 27
Clarence and Somerset both gone to Warwick! . . . iv 1 127
But see where Somerset and Clarence comes! Speak suddenly, my lords, are we all friends? . . . . iv 2 3
Then, gentle Clarence, welcome unto Warwick; And welcome, Somerset iv 2 7
Somerset, at my request, See that forthwith Duke Edward be convey'd iv 3 51
Somerset, what youth is that, Of whom you seem to have so tender care? . . . . iv 6 65
Somerset, Somerset, for Lancaster!—Two of thy name, both Dukes of Somerset, Have sold their lives unto the house of York . . v 1 72
The queen is valued thirty thousand strong, And Somerset, with Oxford, fled to her . . . . v 3 15
Is not Oxford here another anchor? And Somerset another goodly mast? v 4 17
Thanks, gentle Somerset; sweet Oxford, thanks . . . v 4 58
For Somerset, off with his guilty head . . . . v 5 3
Three Dukes of Somerset, threefold renown'd For hardy and undoubted champions . . . . v 7 5
Somerville. Say, Somerville, what says my loving son? . . v 1 7
Something. Suffer a sea-change Into something rich and strange *Tempest* i 2 401
He's something stain'd With grief, that's beauty's canker . i 2 414
But I prattle Something too wildly . . . . . iii 1 58
I' the name of something holy, sir, why stand you In this strange stare? iii 3 94
There's something else to do: hush, and be mute . . iv 1 126
My will is something sorted with his wish . *T. G. of Ver.* i 3 63
He is given to prayer: he is something peevish that way *Mer. Wives* i 4 14
The which hath something emboldened me to this unseasoned intrusion ii 2 173
What made me love thee? let that persuade thee there's something extraordinary in thee . . . . iii 3 75
Good hearts, devise something: any extremity rather than a mischief . iv 2 75
Other jests are something rank on foot . . . . iv 6 22
Give leave, my lord, That we may bring you something on the way *Meas. for Meas.* i 1 62
It draws something near to the speech we had to such a purpose . i 2 78
I something do excuse the thing I hate . . . . ii 4 119
Something too crabbed that way . . . . . iii 2 104
Happily You something know . . . . . . iv 2 99
This something that you gave me for nothing.—I'll make you amends next, to give you nothing for something . . *Com. of Errors* ii 2 52
Something. There is something in the wind, that we cannot get in *Com. of Errors* iii 1 69
Go fetch me something: I'll break ope the gate . . . iii 1 73
Civil as an orange, and something of that jealous complexion *Much Ado* ii 1 305
In reason nothing.—Something then in rhyme . . *L. L. Lost* i 1 99
I will something affect the letter, for it argues facility . iv 2 56
This will I send and something else more plain . . iv 3 121
Confer with you Of something nearly that concerns yourselves *M. N. D.* i 1 126
She is something lower than myself . . . . . iii 2 304
For the morning now is something worn . . . . iv 1 187
And grows to something of great constancy . . . v 1 26
By something showing a more swelling port . . *Mer. of Venice* i 1 124
Wherein my time something too prodigal Hath left me gaged . i 1 129
My father did something smack, something grow to, he had a kind of taste . . . . ii 2 18
Where thou art not known, why, there they show Something too liberal ii 2 194
These foolish drops do something drown my manly spirit . ii 3 14
There's something tells me, but it is not love, I would not lose you iii 2 4
The full sum of me Is sum of something . . . . iii 2 160
Where every something, being blent together, Turns to a wild of nothing iii 2 183
There must be something else Pawn'd with the other . . iii 5 86
Tarry a little; there is something else . . . . iv 1 305
Besides this nothing that he so plentifully gives me, the something that nature gave me his countenance seems to take from me *As Y. Like It* i 1 18
Thou art overthrown! Or Charles or something weaker masters thee . i 2 272
Something that hath a reference to my state . . . i 3 129
It grows something stale with me . . . . . ii 4 63
If I bring thee not something to eat, I will give thee leave to die . ii 6 12
Something finer than you could purchase in so removed a dwelling . iii 2 359
For every passion something and for no passion truly any thing . iii 2 433
Something browner than Judas's . . . . . iii 4 9
I shall devise something . . . . iv 3 182
Well have you heard, but something hard of hearing *T. of Shrew* ii 1 184
A good swift simile, but something currish . . . v 2 54
It concerns you something to know it . . . *All's Well* i 3 125
There's something in't, More than my father's skill . . i 3 248
A good traveller is something at the latter end of a dinner . ii 5 30
What would you have?—Something; and scarce so much: nothing, indeed . . . . ii 5 88
He's shrewdly vexed at something . . . . . ii 5 92
Haply thou mayst inform Something to save thy life . . iv 1 92
There is something in't that stings his nature . . . iv 3 4
Under my poor instructions yet must suffer Something in my behalf . iv 4 28
Possess us; tell us something of him . . . *T. Night* ii 3 149
If I could make that resemble something in me,—Softly! . . ii 5 131
I do care for something; but in my conscience, sir, I do not care for you iii 1 32
There's something in me that reproves my fault . . . iii 4 223
It is something of my negligence, nothing of my purpose . . iii 4 279
Out of my lean and low ability I'll lend you something . . iii 4 379
There's something in't That is deceiveable . . . . iv 3 20
Then 'tis very credent Thou mayst co-join with something . *W. Tale* i 2 143
He something seems unsettled . . . . . . i 2 147
She is something before her time deliver'd . . . . ii 2 25
Please you, come something nearer . . . . . ii 2 55
Something savours Of tyranny and will ignoble make you . . ii 3 119
Something rare Even then will rush to knowledge . . . iii 1 20
Nothing she does or seems But smacks of something greater than herself iv 4 158
He tells her something That makes her blood look out . . iv 4 159
Your heart is full of something that does take Your mind from feasting iv 4 357
You offer him, if this be so, a wrong Something unfilial . . iv 4 417
That I may call thee something more than man . . . iv 4 546
Who wants but something to be a reasonable man . . . iv 4 617
Being something gently considered . . . . . iv 4 825
From the all that are took something good, To make a perfect woman . v 1 14
And speak of something wildly By us perform'd before . . v 1 129
Infirmity Which waits upon worn times hath something seized His wish'd ability . . . . v 1 142
Comes it not something near?—Her natural posture! . . v 3 23
Something about, a little from the right, In at the window . *K. John* i 1 170
Smacks it not something of the policy? . . . . ii 1 396
At some thing it grieves, More than with parting from my lord *Rich. II.* ii 2 12
Nothing hath begot my something grief; Or something hath the nothing ii 2 36
With a white head and something a round belly . 2 *Hen. IV.* i 2 212
I am, on the sudden, something ill . . . . . iv 2 80
Let it do something, my good lord, that may do me good . . iv 3 65
Utter more to me; and withal devise something to do thyself good . v 3 140
Your reproof is something too round . . . *Hen. V.* iv 1 216
Bawd I'll turn, And something lean to cutpurse of quick hand . v 1 91
Something I must do to procure me grace . . . 1 *Hen. VI.* i 4 7
Though the edge hath something hit ourselves . . 3 *Hen. VI.* i 2 166
If something thou wilt swear to be believed, Swear then by something that thou hast not wrong'd . . . . . . *Richard III.* iv 4 373
I am sorry to hear this of him; and could wish he were Something mistaken in't . . . . *Hen. VIII.* i 1 195
There's something more would out of thee; what say'st? . . i 2 202
He sweat extremely, And something spoke in choler . . ii 1 34
And when you would say something that is sad, Speak how I fell . ii 1 135
He is vex'd at something.—I would 'twere something that would fret the string, The master-cord on's heart! . . . . . . iii 2 104
Ye shall be my guests: Something I can command . . . iv 2 116
That they may have their wages duly paid 'em, And something over . v 2 151
He hangs the lip at something: you know all . . *Troi. and Cres.* iii 1 152
Find out Something not worth in me such rich beholding . . iii 3 91
But something may be done that we will not . . . iv 4 96
You shake, my lord, at something: will you go? . . . v 2 50
I'll give you something else.—I will have this . . . v 2 86
Said to be something imperfect in favouring the first complaint *Coriol.* ii 1 54
But this is something odd . . . . ii 3 88
You have been too rough, something too rough . . . iii 2 25
I knew by his face that there was something in him . . iv 5 163
Who is't can blame him? Your enemies and his find something in him iv 6 106
O, be to me . . . Nothing so kind, but something pitiful! *T. Andron.* ii 3 156
A hare, sir, in a lenten pie, that is something stale and hoar *R. and J.* ii 4 139
Couple it with something; make it a word and a blow . . iii 1 43
Whistle then to me, As signal that thou hear'st something approach v 3 8
The boy gives warning something doth approach . . . v 3 18
A fool in good clothes, and something like thee . . *T. of Athens* ii 2 114
They could have wish'd—they know not—Something hath been amiss . ii 2 217
I do wish thou wert a dog, That I might love thee something . iv 3 55

Something. I have no will to wander forth of doors, Yet something leads me forth . . . *J. Cæsar* iii 3 4
Their bloody sign of battle is hung out, And something to be done immediately . . . v 1 15
For't must be done to-night, And something from the palace . *Macbeth* iii 1 132
By the pricking of my thumbs, Something wicked this way comes . iv 1 45
I am young; but something You may deserve of him through me . iv 3 14
Your royal preparation Makes us hear something . . . v 3 58
Is not this something more than fantasy? What think you on't? *Hamlet* i 1 54
What is't, Ophelia, he hath said to you?—So please you, something touching the Lord Hamlet . . . i 3 89
Something is rotten in the state of Denmark . . . i 4 90
I was about to say something: where did I leave? . . . ii 1 51
Something have you heard Of Hamlet's transformation . . . ii 2 4
There is something in this more than natural, if philosophy could find it out . . . ii 2 384
I'll have these players Play something like the murder of my father ii 2 624
But that the dread of something after death, The undiscover'd country iii 1 78
There's something in his soul, O'er which his melancholy sits on brood iii 1 172
Something too much of this . . . iii 2 79
Ay, sir, but, 'While the grass grows,'—the proverb is something musty iii 2 359
Hearing something stir, Whips out his rapier, cries, 'A rat, a rat!' . iv 1 9
I am not splenitive and rash, Yet have I something in me dangerous . v 1 285
Came something saucily into the world before he was sent for . *Lear* i 1 21
That's something yet: Edgar I nothing am . . . ii 3 21
Something deeper, Whereof perchance these are but furnishings . iii 1 28
That nature thus gives way to loyalty, something fears me to think of . iii 5 4
I'll repair the misery thou dost bear With something rich about me . iv 1 80
Know you the reason?—Something he left imperfect in the state . iv 3 3
Transport her purposes by word? Belike, Something—I know not what iv 5 21
Speak you on; You look as you had something more to say . . v 3 201
What is the matter, think you?—Something from Cyprus *Othello* i 2 39
Whereof by parcels she had something heard, But not intentively . i 3 154
The robb'd that smiles steals something from the thief . . . i 3 208
While I spare speech, which something now offends me . . . ii 3 199
I will content your pains; Something that's brief . . . iii 1 2
Thou dost mean something: I heard thee say even now, thou likedst not that . . . iii 3 108
Who steals my purse steals trash; 'tis something, nothing; 'Twas mine, 'tis his . . . iii 3 157
This may do something. The Moor already changes with my poison . iii 3 324
And can he be angry? Something of moment then . . iii 4 138
Something, sure, of state, Either from Venice, or some unhatch'd practice . . . iii 4 140
What trumpet is that same?—Something from Venice, sure . iv 1 227
Something it is I would,—O, my oblivion is a very Antony *Ant. and Cleo.* i 3 89
Yes, something you can deny for your own safety . . . ii 6 95
From which the world should note Something particular . . iii 13 22
Though grey Do something mingle with our younger brown . . iv 8 20
A very honest woman, but something given to lie . . . v 2 252
Here, on her breast, There is a vent of blood and something blown . v 2 352
There would be something failing In him that should compare *Cymbeline* i 1 21
My dearest husband, I something fear my father's wrath . . i 1 86
A kind of hand-in hand comparison—had been something too fair . . i 4 76
My estate to your ring; which, in my opinion, o'ervalues it something . i 4 120
You do seem to know Something of me, or what concerns me . . i 6 94
And I am something curious, being strange . . . i 6 191
I'll do something— Quite besides The government of patience! . ii 4 149
Come, here's my heart. Something's afore't . . . iii 4 81
Who, being born your vassal, Am something nearer . . . v 5 114
I think I shall have something to do with you. . *Pericles* iv 2 92
You have heard something of my power, and so stand aloof . . iv 6 94
But there is something glows upon my cheek, And whispers in mine ear v 1 96
You are like something that—What countrywoman? . . . v 1 103
Something-settled. Variable objects shall expel This something-settled matter in his heart . . . *Hamlet* iii 1 181
Sometime I'ld divide, And burn in many places . . *Tempest* i 2 198
Sometime like apes that mow and chatter at me . . . ii 2 9
Sometime am I All wound with adders . . . ii 2 12
Sometimes I'll get thee Young scamels from the rock . . ii 2 175
Sometimes a thousand twangling instruments Will hum about mine ears iii 2 146
I will discase me, and myself present As I was sometime Milan . . v 1 86
A woman sometimes scorns what best contents her *T. G. of Ver.* iii 1 93
A justice of peace sometime may be beholding to his friend *Mer. Wives* i 1 283
Sometimes the beam of her view gilded my foot, sometimes my portly belly . . . i 3 68
I myself sometimes, leaving the fear of God on the left hand . . ii 2 23
Herne the hunter, Sometime a keeper here . . . iv 4 29
Whether you had not sometime in your life Err'd in this point *M. for M.* ii 1 14
Though sometimes you do blench from this to that, As cause doth minister . . . iv 5 5
Let the devil Be sometime honour'd for his burning throne! . . . v 1 295
Because that I familiarly sometimes Do use you for my fool *Com. of Er.* ii 2 26
The body of your discourse is sometime guarded with fragments *M. Ado* i 1 288
My daughter is sometime afeard she will do a desperate outrage to herself . . . ii 3 158
Sometimes fashioning them like Pharaoh's soldiers in the reechy painting, sometime like god Bel's priests in the old church-window, sometime like the shaven Hercules . . . iii 3 142
What is she in the white?—A woman sometimes . . *L. L. Lost* ii 1 198
Sometime through the throat, as if you swallowed love with singing love, sometime through the nose, as if you snuffed up love . iii 1 14
Out of question so it is sometimes, Glory grows guilty . . iv 1 30
Sometime to lean upon my poor shoulder . . . v 1 108
Skim milk, and sometimes labour in the quern . *M. N. Dream* ii 1 36
And sometime make the drink to bear no barm . . . ii 1 38
Sometime lurk I in a gossip's bowl, In very likeness of a roasted crab . ii 1 47
Sometime for three-foot stool mistaketh me . . . ii 1 52
There sleeps Titania sometime of the night, Lull'd in these flowers . ii 1 253
Sometime a horse I'll be, sometime a hound, A hog, a headless bear, sometime a fire . . . iii 1 111
Like to Lysander sometime frame thy tongue . . . iii 2 360
And sometime rail thou like Demetrius . . . iii 2 362
Sleep, that sometimes shuts up sorrow's eye, Steal me awhile . . iii 2 435
That same dew, which sometime on the buds Was wont to swell . iv 1 58
Sometimes from her eyes I did receive fair speechless messages *M. of V.* i 1 163
I sometimes do believe, and sometimes do not . *As Y. Like It* v 4 3
No more shoes than feet; nay, sometime more feet than shoes *T. of S.* Ind. 2 11
Sometimes you would call out for Cicely Hacket . . Ind. 2 91
Call'd plain Kate, And bonny Kate and sometimes Kate the curst . ii 1 187

Sometime. A gentleman Which I have sometime known . . *All's Well* iii 2 87
How mightily sometimes we make us comforts of our losses!—And how mightily some other times we drown our gain in tears! . . . iv 3 76
I have been sometimes there . . . v 1 11
A fond and desperate creature, Whom sometime I have laugh'd with . v 3 179
Methinks sometimes I have no more wit than a Christian . *T. Night* i 3 88
I delight in masques and revels sometimes altogether . . . i 3 121
Sometimes he is a kind of puritan.—O, if I thought that! . . . ii 3 151
Kill what I love?—a savage jealousy That sometime savours nobly . v 1 123
How sometimes nature will betray its folly . . *W. Tale* i 2 151
No man is free, But that his negligence, his folly, fear, Among the infinite doings of the world, Sometime puts forth . . . i 2 254
To me comes a creature, Sometimes her head on one side, some another iii 3 20
Sometimes to see 'em, and not to see 'em . . . iii 3 92
This ancient sir, who, it should seem, Hath sometime loved . . iv 4 373
Though I am not naturally honest, I am so sometimes by chance . iv 4 733
Thy sometimes brother's wife . . . *Richard II.* i 2 54
Did they not sometime cry, 'all hail!' to me? So Judas did to Christ iv 1 169
Good sometime queen, prepare thee hence for France . . v 1 37
Sometimes am I king; Then treasons make me wish myself a beggar . v 5 32
Have gotten leave To look upon my sometimes royal master's face . v 5 75
Sometime he angers me With telling me of the moldwarp 1 *Hen. IV.* iii 1 148
Amend this fault: Though sometimes it show greatness, courage, blood iii 1 181
His nose, . . . sometimes plue and sometimes red . . *Hen. V.* iii 6 110
That will be verified Henry the Fifth did sometime prophesy 1 *Hen. VI.* v 1 31
Thus sometimes hath the brightest day a cloud . 2 *Hen. VI.* ii 4 1
Sometime I'll say, I am Duke Humphrey's wife, And he a prince . . i 4 42
Sometime he talks as if Duke Humphrey's ghost Were by his side; sometime he calls the king And whispers to his pillow as to him . iii 2 374
Jove sometime went disguised, and why not I? . . . iv 1 48
Even with those wings Which sometime they have used with fearful flight, Make war with him . . . 3 *Hen. VI.* i 2 30
Sometime the flood prevails, and then the wind; Now one the better . ii 5 9
Present to her,—as sometime Margaret Did to thy father, steep'd in Rutland's blood,—A handkerchief . . *Richard III.* iv 4 274
Men shall deal unadvisedly sometimes . . . iv 4 292
The dowager, Sometimes our brother's wife . . *Hen. VIII.* ii 4 181
These are stars indeed; And sometimes falling ones . . iv 1 55
Sometime, great Agamemnon, Thy topless deputation he puts on *Troi. and Cres.* i 3 151
Sometimes we are devils to ourselves . . . iv 4 97
I sometime lay here in Corioli At a poor man's house . *Coriolanus* i 9 82
To give forth The corn o' the storehouse gratis, as 'twas used Sometime in Greece . . . iii 1 115
My sometime general, I have seen thee stern . . . iv 1 23
You hear what he hath said Which was sometime his general . . v 1 2
Stain the sun with fog, as sometime clouds When they do hug him *T. An.* iii 1 213
Sometime she gallops o'er a courtier's nose . *Rom. and Jul* i 4 77
Sometime comes she with a tithe-pig's tail Tickling a parson's nose . i 4 79
Sometime she driveth o'er a soldier's neck . . . i 4 82
And vice sometimes by action dignified . . . ii 3 22
I anger her sometimes and tell her that Paris is the properer man . ii 4 216
'Tis a spirit: sometime't appears like a lord; sometime like a lawyer; sometime like a philosopher . . . *T. of Athens* ii 2 115
I do not always follow lover, elder brother and woman; sometime the philosopher . . . ii 2 131
An effect of humour, Which sometime hath his hour with every man *J. C.* ii 1 251
To keep with you at meals, comfort your bed, And talk to you sometimes ii 1 285
The love that follows us sometime is our trouble . . *Macbeth* i 6 11
Though he took up my legs sometime, yet I made a shift to cast him . ii 3 46
To do harm Is often laudable, to do good sometime Accounted dangerous folly . . . iv 2 76
In which the majesty of buried Denmark Did sometimes march *Hamlet* i 1 49
Our sometime sister, now our queen . . . i 2 8
Sometimes he walks four hours together Here in the lobby . . ii 2 160
How pregnant sometimes his replies are! . . . ii 2 212
This was sometime a paradox, but now the time gives it proof . iii 1 114
Our indiscretion sometimes serves us well, When our deep plots do pall v 2 8
The barbarous Scythian . . . shall to my bosom Be as well neighbour'd, pitied, and relieved, As thou my sometime daughter . . *Lear* i 1 122
Sometimes I am whipped for holding my peace . . . i 4 202
Sometime with lunatic bans, sometime with prayers, Enforce their charity . . . ii 3 19
Who sometime, in his better tune, remembers What we are come about iv 3 41
I lack iniquity Sometimes to do me service . . *Othello* i 2 4
Unless self-charity be sometimes a vice . . . ii 3 202
But men are men; the best sometimes forget . . . ii 3 241
Where's that palace whereinto foul things Sometimes intrude not? . iii 3 138
Have you not sometimes seen a handkerchief Spotted with strawberries? iii 3 434
Sometimes, when he is not Antony, He comes too short *Ant. and Cleo.* i 1 57
The world and my great office will sometimes Divide me from your bosom . . . ii 3 1
Sometime we see a cloud that's dragonish; A vapour sometime like a bear or lion . . . iv 14 2
Nay, sometime hangs both thief and true man . . *Cymbeline* ii 3 77
Our very eyes Are sometimes like our judgements, blind . . iv 2 302
The ruin speaks that sometime It was a worthy building . . iv 2 354
That Belarius whom you sometime banish'd . . . v 5 333
Yon sometimes famous princes, like thyself, Drawn by report *Pericles* i 1 34
It was sometime target to a king; I know it by this mark . . ii 1 143
Somewhat. I'll wear a boot, to make it somewhat rounder *T. G. of Ver.* v 2 6
Here is a letter will say somewhat . . *Mer. Wives* iv 5 128
This gentleman told somewhat of my tale . *Meas. for Meas.* v 1 84
That's somewhat madly spoken.—Pardon it . . . v 1 89
In countenance somewhat doth resemble you . . *T. of Shrew* iv 2 100
And smell somewhat strong of her strong displeasure . *All's Well* v 2 5
Our coffers . . . are grown somewhat light . . *Richard II.* i 4 44
Well, somewhat we must do. Come, cousin, I'll Dispose of you . ii 2 116
Is't so? Why then, say an old man can do somewhat . 2 *Hen. IV.* v 3 83
Somewhat too sudden, sirs, the warning is . . 1 *Hen. VI.* v 2 14
Fall somewhat into a slower method . . *Richard III.* i 2 116
Chop off his head, man; somewhat we will do. . . . iii 1 193
The loving haste of these our friends, Somewhat against our meaning . iii 5 55
That's somewhat sudden . . . *Hen. VIII.* iii 2 394
There is a fellow somewhat near the door, he should be a brazier . v 4 41
An her hair were not somewhat darker than Helen's . *Troi. and Cres.* i 1 41
Somewhat too early for new-married ladies . . *T. Andron.* ii 2 15
Fear her not, Lucius: somewhat doth she mean . . . iv 1 9
From this time Be somewhat scanter of your maiden presence *Hamlet* i 3 121
Thou givest me somewhat to repair myself . . . *Pericles* ii 1 128

Somewhere. He's somewhere gone to dinner *Com. of Errors* ii 1 5
I prithee, vent thy folly somewhere else *T. Night* iv 1 10
Marry, for Justice, she is so employ'd, He thinks, with Jove in heaven, or somewhere else *T. Andron* iv 3 40
Somewhither would she have thee go with her iv 1 11
Somme. 'Tis certain he hath pass'd the river Somme *Hen. V.* iii 5 1
Son. Good wombs have borne bad sons *Tempest* i 2 120
The king's son, Ferdinand, With hair up-staring,—then like reeds i 2 212
The king's son have I landed by himself i 2 221
The son that she did litter here, A freckled whelp hag-born i 2 282
Not honour'd with A human shape.—Yes, Caliban her son i 2 284
The duke of Milan And his brave son being twain i 2 438
He will carry this island home in his pocket and give it his son for an apple ii 1 91
For, coming thence, My son is lost ii 1 109
We have lost your son, I fear, for ever ii 1 131
Hath here almost persuaded . . . the king his son's alive ii 1 236
Lead off this ground; and let's make further search For my poor son ii 1 324
So, king, go safely on to seek thy son ii 1 327
Thee of thy son, Alonso, They have bereft iii 3 75
Therefore my son i' the ooze is bedded iii 3 100
Tell me, heavenly bow, If Venus or her son, as thou dost know, Do now attend the queen? iv 1 87
Cutting the clouds towards Paphos and her son Dove-drawn with her iv 1 93
Her waspish-headed son has broke his arrows iv 1 99
You do look, my son, in a moved sort, As if you were dismay'd iv 1 146
I have lost—How sharp the point of this remembrance is!—My dear son v 1 139
I wish Myself were mudded in that oozy bed Where my son lies v 1 152
If this prove A vision of the Island, one dear son Shall I twice lose v 1 176
While other men, of slender reputation, Put forth their sons to seek preferment out: Some to the wars *T. G. of Ver.* i 3 7
For all these exercises He said that Proteus your son was meet i 3 12
I have received my proportion, like the prodigious son ii 3 4
A son that well deserves The honour and regard of such a father ii 4 59
Why, Phaëthon,—for thou art Merops' son,—Wilt thou aspire to guide the heavenly car? iii 1 153
Who begot thee?—Marry, the son of my grandfather.—O illiterate loiterer! it was the son of thy grandmother iii 1 295
We are the sons of women *Mer. Wives* ii 3 51
Come, Master Shallow; come, son Slender, in iii 4 79
My son profits nothing in the world at his book iv 1 15
My daughter and my little son And three or four more of their growth iv 4 47
Remember, son Slender, my daughter.—Ay, forsooth v 2 3
Son, how now! how now, son! have you dispatched? v 5 188
Were he my kinsman, brother, or my son, It should be thus with him *Meas. for Meas.* ii 2 81
Son, I have overheard what hath passed between you and your sister iii 1 161
I had rather my brother die by the law than my son should be unlawfully born iii 1 195
She became A joyful mother of two goodly sons *Com. of Errors* i 1 51
Those . . . I bought and brought up to attend my sons i 1 58
Unless the fear of death doth make me dote, I see my son v 1 196
My only son Knows not my feeble key of untuned cares v 1 309
A wife once call'd Æmilia That bore thee at a burden two fair sons v 1 343
Tell me where is that son That floated with thee on the fatal raft? v 1 347
Rude fishermen of Corinth By force took Dromio and my son v 1 352
Thirty-three years have I but gone in travail Of you, my sons v 1 401
Hath Leonato any son, my lord?—No child but Hero *Much Ado* i 1 296
Where is my cousin, your son? hath he provided this music? i 2 2
Like my lady's eldest son, evermore tattling ii 1 11
Adam's sons are my brethren ii 1 66
Not till Monday, my dear son, which is hence a just seven-night ii 1 374
Give me this maid, your daughter?—As freely, son, as God did give her me iv 1 27
Their sons are well tutored by you, and their daughters profit *L. L. Lost* iv 2 76
If their sons be ingenuous, they shall want no instruction iv 2 80
She respects me as her only son *M. N. Dream* i 1 160
That would hang us, every mother's son i 2 80
Come, sit down, every mother's son, and rehearse your parts iii 1 75
Being an honest man's son, or rather an honest woman's son *Mer. of Ven.* ii 2 16
No master, sir, but a poor man's son ii 2 53
Well, old man, I will tell you news of your son: give me your blessing ii 2 82
Murder cannot be hid long; a man's son may, but at the length truth will out ii 2 84
Your boy that was, your son that is, your child that shall be ii 2 90
I cannot think you are my son ii 2 92
Here's my son, sir, a poor boy,— Not a poor boy, sir, but the rich Jew's man ii 2 129
Go, father, with thy son. Take leave of thy old master ii 2 161
Record a gift, Here in the court, of all he dies possess'd, Unto his son iv 1 390
The youngest son of Sir Rowland de Boys *As Y. Like It* i 1 59; i 2 234
There comes an old man and his three sons i 2 126
I would thou hadst been son to some man else i 2 237
I am more proud to be Sir Rowland's son, His youngest son i 2 245
Had I before known this young man his son, I should have given him tears i 2 249
Is it possible, on such a sudden, you should fall into so strong a liking with old Sir Rowland's youngest son i 3 29
Doth it therefore ensue that you should love his son dearly? i 3 33
Your brother—no, no brother; yet the son—Yet not the son, I will not call him son Of him I was about to call his father ii 3 19
If that you were the good Sir Rowland's son, . . . Be truly welcome ii 7 191
I am the second son of old Sir Rowland v 4 158
I remember, Since once he play'd a farmer's eldest son *T. of Shrew* Ind. 1 84
Vincentio's son brought up in Florence i 1 14
Who shall bear your part, And be in Padua here Vincentio's son? i 1 200
'Be serviceable to my son,' quoth he, Although I think 'twas in another sense i 1 219
Old Antonio's son: My father dead, my fortune lives for me i 2 191
Antonio's son, A man well known throughout all Italy ii 1 68
Son to Vincentio.—A mighty man of Pisa; by report I know him ii 1 104
From my mother-wit.—A witty mother! witless else her son ii 1 266
'Simois,' I am Lucentio, 'hic est,' son unto Vincentio of Pisa iii 1 32
Give me Bianca for my patrimony.—Soft, son! iv 4 23
My son Lucentio Made me acquainted with a weighty cause iv 4 25
Your son Lucentio here Doth love my daughter and she loveth him iv 4 40
Your son shall have my daughter with consent.—I thank you, sir iv 4 47
Talking with the deceiving father of a deceitful son iv 4 83
By my mother's son, and that's myself iv 5 6
There to visit A son of mine, which long I have not seen iv 5 57
Gentle sir.—Happily met; the happier for thy son iv 5 59
Son. The sister to my wife, this gentlewoman, Thy son by this hath married *T. of Shrew* iv 5 63
Let me embrace with old Vincentio, And wander we to see thy honest son iv 5 69
Nay, I told you your son was well beloved v 1 26
While I play the good husband at home, my son and my servant spend all at the university v 1 71
He is mine only son, and heir to the lands of me v 1 88
O, my son, my son! Tell me, thou villain, where is my son? v 1 92
Pardon, sweet father.—Lives my sweet son? v 1 115
Here's Lucentio, Right son to the right Vincentio v 1 118
In delivering my son from me, I bury a second husband *All's Well* i 1 1
Welcome, count; My son's no dearer.—Thank your majesty i 2 76
Her matter was, she loved your son i 3 115
You are my mother, madam; would you were,—So that my lord your son were not my brother,—Indeed my mother! i 3 168
Love you my son?—Do not you love him, madam?—Go not about i 3 193
My lord your son made me to think of this i 3 238
Whether I live or die, be you the sons Of worthy Frenchmen ii 1 11
Commend me to my kinsmen and my son: This is not much ii 2 68
An they were sons of mine, I'd have them whipped ii 3 93
You are too young, too happy, and too good, To make yourself a son out of my blood ii 3 103
Well, thou hast a son shall take this disgrace off me ii 3 249
My duty to you. Your unfortunate son iii 2 28
Your son will not be killed so soon as I thought he would iii 2 39
For my part, I only hear your son was run away iii 2 46
Where is my son, I pray you?—Madam, he's gone to serve the duke iii 2 53
He was my son; But I do wash his name out of my blood iii 2 69
My son corrupts a well-derived nature With his inducement iii 2 90
I will entreat you, when you see my son, To tell him that his sword can never win The honour that he loses iii 2 95
That from the bloody course of war My dearest master, your dear son, may hie iii 4 9
That is Antonio, the duke's eldest son iii 5 79
That downward hath succeeded in his house From son to son iii 7 24
Your son was misled with a snipt-taffeta fellow there iv 5 1
Your daughter-in-law had been alive at this hour, and your son here at home iv 5 5
And that my lord your son was upon his return home iv 5 74
To stop up the displeasure he hath conceived against your son iv 5 81
I have letters that my son will be here to-night iv 5 90
Yonder's my lord your son with a patch of velvet on's face iv 5 99
Your son, As mad in folly, lack'd the sense to know Her estimation v 3 2
Come on, my son, in whom my house's name Must be digested v 3 73
The ring was never hers.—Son, on my life, I have seen her wear it v 3 89
Leaving her In the protection of his son, her brother *T. Night* i 2 38
Thou hast spoke for us, madonna, as if thy eldest son should be a fool i 5 121
Journeys end in lovers meeting, Every wise man's son doth know ii 3 45
If the king had no son, they would desire to live on crutches till he had one *W. Tale* i 1 49
Give scandal to the blood o' the prince my son, Who I do think is mine i 2 330
Take again your queen as yours at first, Even for your son's sake i 2 337
In the which three great ones suffer, Yourself, your queen, your son ii 1 129
The sacred honour of himself, his queen's, His hopeful son's ii 3 85
The prince your son, with mere conceit and fear Of the queen's speed, is gone iii 2 145
Bring me To the dead bodies of my queen and son iii 2 236
I'll tarry till my son come; he hallooed but even now iii 3 78
And remember well, I mentioned a son o' the king's iv 1 22
Say to me, when sawest thou the Prince Florizel, my son? iv 2 29
But, I fear, the angle that plucks our son thither iv 2 52
I think it not uneasy to get the cause of my son's resort thither iv 2 57
He compassed a motion of the Prodigal Son, and married a tinker's wife iv 3 103
A father Is at the nuptial of his son a guest That best becomes the table iv 4 406
Reason my son Should choose himself a wife iv 4 417
My son: he shall not need to grieve At knowing of thy choice iv 4 426
Mark your divorce, young sir, Whom son I dare not call iv 4 429
Asks thee the son forgiveness, As 'twere i' the father's person iv 4 560
We are not furnish'd like Bohemia's son, Nor shall appear in Sicilia iv 4 599
The old man come in with a whoo-bub against his daughter and the king's son iv 4 630
Should I now meet my father, He would not call me son iv 4 672
I will tell the king all, every word, yea, and his son's pranks too iv 4 718
About his son, that should have married a shepherd's daughter iv 4 793
Has the old man e'er a son, sir, do you hear, an't like you, sir?—He has a son, who shall be flayed alive iv 4 810
O, that's the case of the shepherd's son: hang him, he'll be made an example iv 4 846
One that gives out himself Prince Florizel, Son of Polixenes v 1 86
What might I have been, Might I a son and daughter now have look'd on! v 1 177
He was torn to pieces with a bear: this avouches the shepherd's son v 2 69
I brought the old man and his son aboard the prince v 2 124
Thy sons and daughters will be all gentlemen born v 2 138
The king's son took me by the hand, and called me brother v 2 151
There was the first gentleman-like tears that ever we shed.—We may live, son, to shed many more v 2 157
Prithee, son, do; for we must be gentle, now we are gentlemen v 2 164
Let boors and franklins say it, I'll swear it.—How if it be false, son? v 2 174
This is your son-in-law And son unto the king v 3 150
In right and true behalf Of thy deceased brother Geffrey's son *K. John* i 1 8
My son! have I not ever said How that ambitious Constance would not cease Till she had kindled France and all the world, Upon the right and party of her son? i 1 31
Born in Northamptonshire and eldest son, As I suppose i 1 51
What art thou?—The son and heir to that same Faulconbridge i 1 56
If old sir Robert did beget us both and were our father and this son like him, O old sir Robert, father, on my knee I give heaven thanks I was not like to thee! i 1 81
Do you not read some tokens of my son In the large composition of this man? i 1 87
And took it on his death That this my mother's son was none of his i 1 111
How if my brother, Who, as you say, took pains to get this son, Had of your father claim'd this son for his? i 1 121
My mother's son did get your father's heir i 1 128
The reputed son of Cœur-de-lion, Lord of thy presence and no land beside i 1 136
So is my name begun; Philip, good old sir Robert's wife's eldest son i 1 159
Is it sir Robert's son that you seek so?—Sir Robert's son! Ay, thou unreverend boy, Sir Robert's son: why scorn'st thou at sir Robert? He is sir Robert's son, and so art thou i 1 226
That Geffrey was thy elder brother born, And this his son ii 1 105

Son. Who is it thou dost call usurper, France?—Let me make answer; thy usurping son *K. John* ii 1 121
My bed was ever to thy son as true As thine was to thy husband ii 1 124
This is thy eld'st son's son, Infortunate in nothing but in thee ii 1 177
I can produce A will that bars the title of thy son ii 1 192
Young Plantagenet, Son to the elder brother of this man ii 1 239
Whose sons lie scattered on the bleeding ground ii 1 304
Son, list to this conjunction, make this match ii 1 468
If . . . thy princely son Can in this book of beauty read 'I love' ii 1 484
Being but the shadow of your son, Becomes a sun and makes your son a shadow ii 1 499
If thou be pleased withal, Command thy son and daughter to join hands ii 1 532
Where is she and her son? tell me, who knows ii 1 543
Why dost thou look so sadly on my son? iii 1 20
Let the church, our mother, breathe her curse, A mother's curse, on her revolting son iii 1 257
Young Arthur is my son, and he is lost: I am not mad iii 4 47
If I were mad, I should forget my son, Or madly think a babe of clouts were he iii 4 57
O that these hands could so redeem my son, As they have given these hairs their liberty! iii 4 71
He talks to me that never had a son iii 4 91
My boy, my Arthur, my fair son! My life, my joy, my food! iii 4 103
Is it my fault that I was Geffrey's son? No, indeed, is't not; and I would to heaven I were your son iv 1 22
Many a poor man's son would have lien still iv 1 50
That we, the sons and children of this isle, Were born to see so sad an hour v 2 25
Hast thou . . . Brought hither Henry Hereford thy bold son? *Richard II.* i 1 3
As he is but my father's brother's son i 1 117
We'll calm the Duke of Norfolk, you your son i 1 159
Throw down, my son, the Duke of Norfolk's gage i 1 161
Edward's seven sons, whereof thyself art one, Were as seven vials of his sacred blood, Or seven fair branches i 2 11
Furbish new the name of John a Gaunt, Even in the lusty haviour of his son i 3 77
In regard of me He shortens four years of my son's exile i 3 217
And blindfold death not let me see my son i 3 224
Thy son is banish'd upon good advice, Whereto thy tongue a party-verdict gave i 3 233
Come, come, my son, I'll bring thee on thy way i 3 304
Of the world's ransom, blessed Mary's Son ii 1 56
O, had thy grandsire with a prophet's eye Seen how his son's son should destroy his sons ii 1 105
Wert thou not brother to great Edward's son ii 1 124
O, spare me not, my brother Edward's son, For that I was his father Edward's son ii 1 124
I am the last of noble Edward's sons ii 1 171
Is not his heir a well-deserving son? ii 1 194
The Duke of Lancaster is dead.—And living too; for now his son is duke ii 1 225
The Lord Northumberland, his son young Henry Percy ii 2 53
My lord, your son was gone before I came.—He was? Why, so! ii 2 86
My son, young Harry Percy, Sent from my brother Worcester ii 3 21
You have a son, Aumerle, my noble cousin ii 3 125
Ten thousand bloody crowns of mothers' sons iii 3 96
Here comes my son Aumerle.—Aumerle that was v 2 41
Welcome, my son: who are the violets now? v 2 46
Have we more sons? or are we like to have? Is not my teeming date drunk up with time? And wilt thou pluck my fair son from mine age? v 2 90
Were he twenty times my son, I would appeach him v 2 101
Thou dost suspect That I have been disloyal to thy bed, And that he is a bastard, not thy son v 2 106
Can no man tell me of my unthrifty son? v 3 1
O loyal father of a treacherous son! v 3 60
Thy abundant goodness shall excuse This deadly blot in thy digressing son v 3 66
He shall spend mine honour with his shame, As thriftless sons their scraping fathers' gold v 3 69
Come, my old son: I pray God make thee new v 3 146
Earl of Fife, and eldest son To beaten Douglas *1 Hen. IV.* i 1 71
So blest a son, A son who is the theme of honour's tongue i 1 80
I'll be damned for never a king's son in Christendom i 2 109
Either envy, therefore, or misprision Is guilty of this fault and not my son i 3 28
We license your departure with your son i 3 123
And make the Douglas' son your only mean For powers in Scotland i 3 261
Your son in Scotland being thus employ'd i 3 265
Help me to my horse, good king's son.—Out, ye rogue! shall I be your ostler? ii 2 44
That ever this fellow should have fewer words than a parrot, and yet the son of a woman! ii 4 111
A king's son! If I do not beat thee out of thy kingdom with a dagger of lath ii 4 150
They are villains and the sons of darkness ii 4 191
That thou art my son, I have partly thy mother's word ii 4 444
If then thou be son to me, here lies the point; why, being son to me, art thou so pointed at? ii 4 448
Shall the son of England prove a thief and take purses? ii 4 451
In the closing of some glorious day Be bold to tell you that I am your son iii 2 134
The Earl of Westmoreland set forth to-day; With him my son iii 2 171
The son of utter darkness iii 3 42
Where is his son, The nimble-footed madcap Prince of Wales? iv 1 94
I press me none but good householders, yeomen's sons iv 2 17
Unjust serving-men, younger sons to younger brothers iv 2 30
It was myself, my brother and his son, That brought you home v 1 39
And saved the treacherous labour of your son v 4 57
And, in the fortune of my lord your son, Prince Harry slain *2 Hen. IV.* i 1 15
The hulk Sir John, Is prisoner to your son i 1 20
If my young lord your son have not the day, Upon mine honour, for a silken point I'll give my barony i 1 52
How doth my son and brother? Thou tremblest i 1 67
This thou wouldst say, 'Your son did thus and thus; Your brother thus' i 1 76
Ending with 'Brother, son, and all are dead' i 1 81
Your son,— Why, he is dead. See what a ready tongue suspicion hath! i 1 83
I cannot think, my lord, your son is dead i 1 104
It was your presurmise, That, in the dole of blows, your son might drop i 1 169
Your son had only but the corpse, But shadows and the shows of men, to fight i 1 192
She says up and down the town that her eldest son is like you ii 1 115
To the son of the king, nearest his father, Harry Prince of Wales ii 2 130
There were two honours lost, yours and your son's ii 3 16
So did your son; He was so suffer'd: so came I a widow ii 3 56
Ha! a bastard son of the king's? And art not thou Poins his brother? ii 4 307

Son. Shadow, whose son art thou?—My mother's son, sir.—Thy mother's son! like enough, and thy father's shadow: so the son of the female is the shadow of the male *2 Hen. IV.* iii 2 137
Whereon this Hydra son of war is born iv 2 38
If I had a thousand sons, the first humane principle I would teach them should be, to forswear thin potations iv 3 133
Humphrey, my son of Gloucester, Where is the prince your brother? iv 4 12
Prince John your son doth kiss your grace's hand iv 4 83
See, sons, what things you are! How quickly nature falls into revolt! iv 5 65
For this they have been thoughtful to invest Their sons with arts iv 5 74
O my son, God put it in thy mind to take it hence! iv 5 178
God knows, my son, By what by-paths and indirect crook'd ways I met this crown iv 5 184
Thou bring'st me happiness and peace, son John iv 5 228
To have a son set your decrees at nought v 2 85
Make the case yours; Be now the father and propose a son v 2 92
Behold yourself so by a son disdain'd v 2 95
Imagine me taking your part And in your power soft silencing your son v 2 97
I do wish your honours may increase, Till you do live to see a son of mine Offend you and obey you, as I did v 2 105
Happy am I, that have a man so bold, That dares do justice on my proper son; And not less happy, having such a son, That would deliver up his greatness so v 2 109
Son To Lewis the emperor, and Lewis the son Of Charles the Great *Hen. V.* i 2 75
Mock mothers from their sons, mock castles down i 2 286
Ce sont mots de son mauvais, corruptible, gros, et impudique iii 4 56
So, if a son that is by his father sent about merchandise do sinfully miscarry iv 1 154
The king is not bound to answer the particular endings of his soldiers, the father of his son iv 1 164
This story shall the good man teach his son iv 3 56
Take her, fair son, and from her blood raise up Issue to me v 2 376
The world's best garden he achieved, And of it left his son imperial lord Epil. 8
Slain our citizens And sent our sons and husbands captivate *1 Hen. VI.* ii 3 42
Third son to the third Edward King of England ii 4 84; ii 5 75
Edward's son, The first-begotten and the lawful heir Of Edward king ii 5 64
Like true subjects, sons of your progenitors, Go cheerfully together iv 1 166
God take mercy on brave Talbot's soul; And on his son young John! iv 3 35
This seven years did not Talbot see his son iv 3 37
What joy shall noble Talbot have To bid his young son welcome to his grave? iv 3 40
Is my name Talbot? and am I your son? And shall I fly? iv 5 12
I take my leave of thee, fair son, Born to eclipse thy life this afternoon iv 5 52
O, twice my father, twice am I thy son! iv 6 6
Fly, Now thou art seal'd the son of chivalry? iv 6 29
An if I fly, I am not Talbot's son: Then talk no more of flight, it is no boot; If son to Talbot, die at Talbot's foot iv 6 51
O my dear lord, lo, where your son is borne! iv 7 17
For Henry, son unto a conqueror, Is likely to beget more conquerors v 5 73
But wherefore weeps Warwick, my valiant son? *2 Hen. VI.* i 1 115
My son, the comfort of my age i 1 190
Edward the Third, my lords, had seven sons ii 2 10
Edward the Black Prince died before his father And left behind him Richard, his only son ii 2 19
Duke of Lancaster, The eldest son and heir of John of Gaunt ii 2 22
The first son's heir, being dead, The issue of the next son should have reign'd ii 2 31
The third son, Duke of Clarence, from whose line I claim the crown ii 2 34
Richard Earl of Cambridge; who was son To Edmund Langley, Edward the Third's fifth son ii 2 45
Roger Earl of March, who was the son Of Edmund Mortimer ii 2 48
So, if the issue of the elder son Succeed before the younger, I am king ii 2 51
Henry doth claim the crown from John of Gaunt, The fourth son ii 2 55
But flourishes in thee And in thy sons, fair slips of such a stock ii 2 58
There's Best's son, the tanner of Wingham iv 2 24
His son am I; deny it, if you can.—Nay, 'tis too true iv 2 154
Is Cade the son of Henry the Fifth, That thus you do exclaim? iv 8 36
Command my eldest son, nay, all my sons, As pledges of my fealty v 1 49
Sirrah, call in my sons to be my bail v 1 111
The sons of York, thy betters in their birth, Shall be their father's bail v 1 119
His sons, he says, shall give their words for him.—Will you not, sons? v 1 137
Shame to thy silver hair, Thou mad misleader of thy brain-sick son! v 1 163
O war, thou son of hell, Whom angry heavens do make their minister! v 2 33
Richard hath best deserved of all my sons *3 Hen. VI.* i 1 17
You both have vow'd revenge On him, his sons, his favourites and his friends i 1 56
Of thee and these thy sons, Thy kinsmen and thy friends, I'll have more lives i 1 95
I am the son of Henry the Fifth, Who made the Dauphin and the French to stoop And seized upon their towns i 1 107
Sons, peace!—Peace, thou! and give King Henry leave to speak i 1 119
What wrong is this unto the prince your son! i 1 176
My son, Whom I unnaturally shall disinherit i 1 192
And long live thou and these thy forward sons! i 1 203
Would I had died a maid, And never seen thee, never borne thee son! i 1 217
And disinherited thine only son.—Father, you cannot disinherit me i 1 225
Pardon me, sweet son: The Earl of Warwick and the duke enforced me i 1 228
Timorous wretch! Thou hast undone thyself, thy son and me i 1 232
Until that act of parliament be repeal'd Whereby my son is disinherited i 1 250
Come, son, let's away; Our army is ready; come, we'll after them i 1 255
Gentle son Edward, thou wilt stay with me?—Ay, to be murder'd i 1 259
Come, son, away; we may not linger thus i 1 263
Poor queen! how love to me and to her son Hath made her break out into terms of rage! i 1 264
And like an empty eagle Tire on the flesh of me and of my son! i 1 269
Why, how now, sons and brother! at a strife? What is your quarrel? i 2 4
I'll prove the contrary, if you'll hear me speak.—Thou canst not, son i 2 21
Thou hast one son; for his sake pity me i 3 40
And this thy son's blood cleaving to my blade Shall rust upon my weapon, till thy blood, Congeal'd with this, do make me wipe off both i 3 50
My sons, God knows what hath bechanced them i 4 6
Where are your mess of sons to back you now? i 4 73
Methinks, 'tis prize enough to be his son ii 1 20
We, the sons of brave Plantagenet, Each one already blazing by our meeds ii 1 35
He, but a duke, would have his son a king, And raise his issue, like a loving sire; Thou, being a king, blest with a goodly son, Didst yield consent to disinherit him ii 2 21

Son. Happy always was it for that son Whose father for his hoarding went to hell? I'll leave my son my virtuous deeds behind 3 *Hen. VI.* ii 2 47
You promised knighthood to our forward son: Unsheathe your sword. ii 2 58
Caused him, by new act of parliament, To blot out me, and put his own son in ii 2 92
Who should succeed the father but the son? ii 2 94
Is this our foeman's face? Ah, no, no, no, it is mine only son! ii 5 83
How will my wife for slaughter of my son Shed seas of tears! ii 5 105
Was ever son so rued a father's death?—Was ever father so bemoan'd his son? ii 5 109
So obsequious will thy father be, Even for the loss of thee, having no more, As Priam was for all his valiant sons ii 5 120
Thou didst love York, and I am son to York ii 6 73
My queen and son are gone to France for aid iii 1 28
If this news be true, Poor queen and son, your labour is but lost iii 1 32
'Twill grieve your grace my sons should call you father iii 2 100
'Tis a happy thing To be the father unto many sons iii 2 105
Between my soul's desire and me . . . Is Clarence, Henry, and his son iii 2 130
I, poor Margaret, With this my son, Prince Edward, Henry's heir iii 3 31
Bestow'd the heir Of the Lord Bonville on your new wife's son iv 1 57
And thou, son Clarence, Shalt stir up in Suffolk, Norfolk and in Kent iv 8 11
Say, Somerville, what says my loving son? v 1 7
See . . . how well she fares: By this, I hope, she hath a son for me v 5 90
A peevish fool was that of Crete, That taught his son the office of a fowl! v 6 19
Thy son I kill'd for his presumption.—Hadst thou been kill'd when first thou didst presume, Thou hadst not lived to kill a son of mine v 6 34
Men for their sons, wives for their husbands, And orphans for their parents' timeless death—Shall rue the hour that ever thou wast born v 6 41
King Henry and the prince his son are gone: Clarence, thy turn is next v 6 89
Two Cliffords, as the father and the son, And two Northumberlands v 7 7
Poor Anne, Wife to thy Edward, to thy slaughter'd son. *Richard III.* i 2 10
The heavens have bless'd you with a goodly son, To be your comforter i 3 9
Thou slewest my husband Henry in the Tower, And Edward, my poor son i 3 120
A husband and a son thou owest to me; And thou a kingdom i 3 170
Edward thy son, which now is Prince of Wales, For Edward my son, which was Prince of Wales i 3 199
When my son Was stabb'd with bloody daggers i 3 211
The slave of nature and the son of hell! i 3 230
Witness my son, now in the shade of death! i 3 267
And with thy treacherous blade Unrip'dst the bowels of thy sovereign's son i 4 212
Our princely father York Bless'd his three sons with his victorious arm i 4 242
If you were a prince's son, Being pent from liberty, as I am now i 4 266
And cry 'O Clarence, my unhappy son!' ii 2 4
He is my son; yea, and therein my shame ii 2 29
Edward, my lord, your son, our king, is dead ii 2 40
Bethink you, like a careful mother, Of the young prince your son ii 2 97
Though we have spent our harvest of this king, We are to reap the harvest of his son ii 2 116
By God's good grace his son shall reign ii 3 10
O, full of danger is the Duke of Gloucester! And the queen's sons and brothers haught and proud ii 3 28
They say my son of York Hath almost overta'en him in his growth ii 4 6
Up and down my sons were toss'd, For me to joy and weep their gain and loss ii 4 58
Now Margaret's curse is fall'n upon our heads, For standing by when Richard stabb'd her son iii 3 16
And for my sister and her princely sons, Be satisfied, dear God, with our true blood iii 3 20
Put to death a citizen, Only for saying he would make his son Heir to the crown iii 5 77
Edward is your brother's son; So say we too, but not by Edward's wife iii 7 177
As, in love and zeal, Loath to depose the child, your brother's son iii 7 209
Your brother's son shall never reign our king iii 7 215
How doth the prince, and my young son of York?—Right well iv 1 14
You shall have letters from me to my son To meet you on the way iv 1 50
Stanley, he is your wife's son: well, look to it iv 2 90
The son of Clarence have I pent up close; His daughter meanly have I match'd iv 3 36
The sons of Edward sleep in Abraham's bosom iv 3 38
When holy Harry died, and my sweet son iv 4 25
In the breath of bitter words let's smother My damned son, which thy two sweet sons smother'd iv 4 134
And the dire death of my two sons and brothers iv 4 143
Where is thy brother Clarence? And little Ned Plantagenet, his son? iv 4 146
Art thou my son?—Ay, I thank God, my father, and yourself iv 4 154
I have no moe sons of the royal blood For thee to murder iv 4 199
If I did take the kingdom from your sons, To make amends, I'll give it to your daughter iv 4 294
The loss you have is but a son being king, And by that loss your daughter is made queen iv 4 307
Your son, that with a fearful soul Leads discontented steps in foreign soil iv 4 311
But, hear you, leave behind Your son, George Stanley iv 4 497
In the sty of this most bloody boar My son George Stanley is frank'd up iv 5 3
Rivers, Grey, Holy King Henry, and thy fair son Edward v 1 4
Lest his son George fall Into the blind cave of eternal night v 3 61
Edward's unhappy sons do bid thee flourish v 3 158
The father rashly slaughter'd his own son, The son, compell'd, been butcher to the sire v 5 25
That blind priest, like the eldest son of fortune, Turns what he list *Hen. VIII.* ii 2 21
I, her frail son, amongst my brethren mortal, Must give my tendance to iii 2 148
Sperr up the sons of Troy *Troi. and Cres.* Prol. 19
Strength should be lord of imbecility, And the rude son should strike his father dead: Force should be right i 3 115
Achilles' horse Makes many Thetis' sons i 3 212
Thou bitch-wolf's son, canst thou not hear? ii 1 11
For my private part, I am no more touch'd than all Priam's sons ii 2 126
Shall I call you father?—Ay, my good son ii 3 268
As wolf to heifer's calf, Pard to the hind, or stepdame to her son iii 2 201
They will almost Give us a prince of blood, a son of Priam iii 3 26
How now, Ulysses!—Now, great Thetis' son! iii 3 94
For emulation hath a thousand sons That one by one pursue iii 3 156
The youngest son of Priam, a true knight, Not yet mature iv 5 96
My father's sister's son, A cousin-german to great Priam's seed iv 5 120
What art thou?—A bastard son of Priam's v 7 15
If the son of a whore fight for a whore, he tempts judgement v 7 21

Son. If my son were my husband, I should freelier rejoice in that absence wherein he won honour than in the embracements of his bed *Coriol.* i 3 2
When yet he was but tender-bodied and the only son i 3 7
But had he died in the business, madam; how then?—Then his good report should have been my son i 3 23
Had I a dozen sons, each in my love alike and none less dear than thine and my good Marcius, I had rather had eleven die nobly for their country than one voluptuously surfeit out of action i 3 24
How does your little son?—I thank your ladyship; well i 3 57
O' my word, the father's son: I'll swear, 'tis a very pretty boy i 3 62
O, well begg'd! Were he the butcher of my son, he should Be free i 9 88
He gives my son the whole name of the war ii 1 149
Such eyes the widows in Corioli wear, And mothers that lack sons ii 1 196
Numa's daughter's son, Who, after great Hostilius, here was king ii 3 247
I am in this, Your wife, your son, these senators, the nobles iii 2 65
Now, my son, Go to them, with this bonnet in thy hand iii 2 72
Your son Will or exceed the common or be caught With cautelous baits iv 1 31
My first son, Whither wilt thou go? iv 1 33
I would my son Were in Arabia, and thy tribe before him iv 2 23
As far as doth the Capitol exceed The meanest house in Rome, so far my son, . . . Whom you have banish'd, does exceed you all iv 2 40
Why, he is so made on here within, as if he were son and heir to Mars iv 5 204
You shall perceive that a Jack guardant cannot office me from my son v 2 68
O my son, my son! thou art preparing fire for us v 2 76
Of thy deep duty more impression show Than that of common sons v 3 52
What is this? Your knees to me? to your corrected son? v 3 57
The son, the husband and the father tearing His country's bowels out v 3 102
For myself, son, I purpose not to wait on fortune v 3 118
Thou know'st, great son, The end of war's uncertain v 3 140
Speak to me, son: Thou hast affected the fine strains of honour v 3 148
But, for your son,—believe it, O, believe it, Most dangerously you have with him prevail'd, If not most mortal to him v 3 187
He killed my son. My daughter. He killed my cousin Marcus v 6 122
I am his first-born son, that was the last That wore the imperial diadem of Rome; Then let my father's honours live in me *T. Andron.* i 1 5
If ever Bassianus, Cæsar's son, Were gracious in the eyes of royal Rome i 1 10
With his sons, a terror to our foes, Hath yoked a nation strong i 1 29
Five times he hath return'd Bleeding to Rome, bearing his valiant sons In coffins from the field i 1 34
Of five and twenty valiant sons, Half of the number that King Priam had, Behold the poor remains, alive and dead! i 1 79
Unkind and careless of thine own, Why suffer'st thou thy sons, unburied yet, To hover on the dreadful shore of Styx? i 1 87
How many sons of mine hast thou in store, That thou wilt never render to me more! i 1 94
The noblest that survives, The eldest son of this distressed queen i 1 103
Rue the tears I shed, A mother's tears in passion for her son: And if thy sons were ever dear to thee, O, think my son to be as dear to me! i 1 106
Must my sons be slaughter'd in the streets, For valiant doings? i 1 112
Thrice noble Titus, spare my first-born son.—Patient yourself, madam. i 1 120
To this your son is mark'd, and die he must i 1 125
In peace and honour rest you here, my sons! i 1 150; 156
With these our late-deceased emperor's sons i 1 184
And buried one and twenty valiant sons, Knighted in field i 1 195
Create your emperor's eldest son, Lord Saturnine i 1 224
In wrongful quarrel you have slain your son.—Nor thou, nor he, are any sons of mine; My sons would never so dishonour me i 1 293
Nor thy traitorous haughty sons, Confederates all thus to dishonour me i 1 302
One fit to bandy with thy lawless sons, To ruffle in the commonwealth i 1 312
See what thou hast done! In a bad quarrel slain a virtuous son.—No, foolish tribune, no; no son of mine i 1 342
Unworthy brother, and unworthy sons! i 1 346
The Greeks upon advice did bury Ajax That slew himself; and wise Laertes' son Did graciously plead for his funerals i 1 380
The dismall'st day is this that e'er I saw, To be dishonour'd by my sons! i 1 385
In the rescue of Lavinia With his own hand did slay his youngest son i 1 418
The cruel father and his traitorous sons, To whom I sued for my dear son's life i 1 452
Sons, let it be your charge, as it is ours, To attend the emperor's person ii 2 7
Thy sons make pillage of her chastity ii 3 44
I'll go fetch thy sons To back thy quarrels, whatsoe'er they be ii 3 53
This is a witness that I am thy son ii 3 116
Yet every mother breeds not sons alike ii 3 146
So should I rob my sweet sons of their fee ii 3 179
Farewell, my sons: see that you make her sure ii 3 187
And let my spleenful sons this trull deflour ii 3 191
The unhappy son of old Andronicus; Brought hither in a most unlucky hour ii 3 250
This fell fault of my accursed sons, Accursed, if the fault be proved ii 3 290
Fear not thy sons; they shall do well enough ii 3 305
Be pitiful to my condemned sons, Whose souls are not corrupted iii 1 8
For two and twenty sons I never wept, Because they died in honour's lofty bed iii 1 10
My sons' sweet blood will make it shame and blush iii 1 15
With warm tears I'll melt the snow, And keep eternal spring-time on thy face, So thou refuse to drink my dear sons' blood iii 1 22
O gentle, aged men! Unbind my sons, reverse the doom of death iii 1 24
This way to death my wretched sons are gone iii 1 98
Here stands my other son, a banish'd man, And here my brother iii 1 99
If thou love thy sons, Let Marcus, Lucius, or thyself, old Titus, Or any one of you, chop off your hand, And send it to the king: he for the same Will send thee hither both thy sons alive iii 1 151
As for my sons, say I account of them As jewels purchased at an easy price iii 1 198
And for thy hand Look by and by to have thy sons with thee iii 1 202
Here are the heads of thy two noble sons iii 1 237
See, thy two sons' heads, Thy warlike hand, thy mangled daughter here; Thy other banish'd son, with this dear sight Struck pale and bloodless iii 1 255
Cornelia never with more care Read to her sons than she hath read to thee iv 1 13
What! the lustful sons of Tamora Performers of this heinous, bloody deed? iv 1 79
My boy, Shalt carry from me to the empress' sons Presents iv 1 115
Here's the son of Lucius; He hath some message to deliver us iv 2 1
Why do the emperor's trumpets flourish thus?—Belike, for joy the emperor hath a son iv 2 50
He dies upon my scimitar's sharp point That touches this my first-born son! iv 2 92
My son and I will have the wind of you: Keep there iv 2 133
Even with law, against the wilful sons Of old Andronicus iv 4 8
Bear the faults of Titus' age, The effects of sorrow for his valiant sons iv 4 30

Son. As if his traitorous sons . . . Have by my means been butcher'd wrongfully! *T. Andron.* iv 4 53
They hither march amain, under conduct Of Lucius, son to old Andronicus iv 4 66
But he will not entreat his son for us iv 4 94
'Twas her two sons that murder'd Bassianus v 1 91
When, for his hand, he had his two sons' heads v 1 115
How like the empress' sons they are! v 2 64
In this mad thought, I'll make him send for Lucius his son v 2 75
Can the son's eye behold his father bleed? There's meed for meed! v 3 65
You sad-faced men, people and sons of Rome, By uproar sever'd v 3 67
These sorrowful drops upon thy blood-stain'd face, The last true duties of thy noble son! v 3 155
From the city's side, So early walking did I see your son *Rom. and Jul.* i 1 130
Steals home my heavy son, And private in his chamber pens himself i 1 143
His son is elder, sir; His son is thirty.—Will you tell me that? His son was but a ward two years ago i 5 40
What is yond gentleman?—The son and heir of old Tiberio i 5 131
A Montague; The only son of your great enemy i 5 139
Speak to my gossip Venus one fair word, One nickname for her purblind son ii 1 12
Young son, it argues a distemper'd head So soon to bid good morrow to thy bed ii 3 33
That's my good son: but where hast thou been, then? ii 3 47
Be plain, good son, and homely in thy drift ii 3 55
Too familiar Is my dear son with such sour company iii 3 7
Acquaint her here of my son Paris' love iii 4 16
But for the sunset of my brother's son It rains downright iii 5 128
O son! the night before thy wedding-day Hath Death lain with thy wife iv 5 35
Thou art early up, To see thy son and heir more early down v 3 209
My wife is dead to-night; Grief of my son's exile hath stopp'd her breath v 3 211
Son of sixteen, Pluck the lined crutch from thy old limping sire, With it beat out his brains! *T. of Athens* iv 1 13
Yield him, who all thy human sons doth hate, From forth thy plenteous bosom, one poor root! iv 3 185
O thou sweet king-killer [gold], and dear divorce 'Twixt natural son and sire! iv 3 383
Thieves?—Soldiers, not thieves.—Both too; and women's sons iv 3 417
Brutus had rather be a villager Than to repute himself a son of Rome Under these hard conditions *J. Cæsar* i 2 173
Brave son, derived from honourable loins! ii 1 322
Our reasons are so full of good regard That were you, Antony, the son of Cæsar, You should be satisfied iii 1 225
Publius shall not live, Who is your sister's son, Mark Antony iv 1 5
I am the son of Marcus Cato, ho! A foe to tyrants v 4 4
Thou diest as bravely as Titinius; And mayst be honour'd, being Cato's son v 4 11
Sons, kinsmen, thanes, And you whose places are the nearest *Macbeth* i 4 35
The king's two sons, Are stol'n away and fled ii 4 25
Thence to be wrench'd with an unlineal hand, No son of mine succeeding iii 1 64
Fleance his son . . . must embrace the fate Of that dark hour iii 1 135
There's but one down; the son is fled.—We have lost Best half iii 3 20
All you have done Hath been but for a wayward son iii 5 11
Had he Duncan's sons under his key—As, an't please heaven, he shall not—they should find What 'twere to kill a father iii 6 18
The son of Duncan, From whom this tyrant holds the due of birth iii 6 24
There is Siward's son, And many unrough youths v 2 9
Macduff is missing, and your noble son.—Your son, my lord, has paid a soldier's debt v 8 38
Had I as many sons as I have hairs, I would not wish them to a fairer death v 8 48
My cousin Hamlet, and my son,— A little more than kin *Hamlet* i 2 64
With no less nobility of love Than that which dearest father bears his son i 2 111
Our chiefest courtier, cousin, and our son i 2 117
Finding By this . . . drift of question That they do know my son ii 1 11
Laying these slight sullies on my son, As 'twere a thing a little soil'd ii 1 39
I beseech you instantly to visit My too much changed son ii 2 36
He hath found The head and source of all your son's distemper ii 2 55
I will be brief: your noble son is mad: Mad call I it ii 2 92
Horridly trick'd With blood of fathers, mothers, daughters, sons ii 2 480
I, the son of a dear father murder'd, Prompted to my revenge by heaven and hell ii 2 612
O wonderful son, that can so astonish a mother! iii 2 340
And for that, I, his sole son, do this same villain send To heaven iii 3 77
Do you not come your tardy son to chide? iii 4 106
O gentle son, Upon the heat and flame of thy distemper Sprinkle cool patience iii 4 122
Where is your son?—Bestow this place on us a little while iv 1 3
What replication should be made by the son of a king? iv 2 13
Your son gone; and he most violent author Of his own just remove iv 5 80
What would you undertake, To show yourself your father's son in deed? iv 7 126
I will fight with him upon this theme . . .—O my son, what theme? v 1 291
Good Gertrude, set some watch over your son v 1 319
Our son shall win.—He's fat, and scant of breath v 2 298
Is not this your son, my lord?—His breeding, sir, hath been at my charge *Lear* i 1 8
Had, indeed, sir, a son for her cradle ere she had a husband for her bed i 1 15
I have, sir, a son by order of law, some year elder than this i 1 19
Our son of Cornwall, And you, our no less loving son of Albany i 1 42
The sway, revenue, execution of the rest, Beloved sons, be yours i 1 140
My son Edgar! Had he a hand to write this? i 2 59
That, sons at perfect age, and fathers declining, the father should be as ward to the son, and the son manage his revenue i 2 77
In palaces, treason; and the bond cracked 'twixt son and father i 2 118
This villain of mine comes under the prediction; there's son against father i 2 120
Coward, pandar, and the son and heir of a mongrel bitch ii 2 23
It is both he and she; Your son and daughter ii 4 14
Your son and daughter found this trespass worth The shame ii 4 44
I had a son, Now outlaw'd from my blood; he sought my life, But lately, very late: I loved him, friend; No father his son dearer: truth to tell thee, The grief hath crazed my wits iii 4 171
He's a yeoman that has a gentleman to his son; for he's a mad yeoman that sees his son a gentleman before him iii 6 14
All dark and comfortless. Where's my son Edmund? iii 7 85
O dear son Edgar, The food of thy abused father's wrath! iv 1 23
Which made me think a man a worm: my son Came then into my mind iv 1 35
Bless thee, good man's son, from the foul fiend! iv 1 60
Son. Of the loyal service of his son, When I inform'd him, then he call'd me sot *Lear* iv 2 7
Where was his son when they did take his eyes? iv 2 89
Gloucester's bastard son Was kinder to his father than my daughters iv 6 116
The bastard son of Gloucester.—They say Edgar, his banished son, is with the Earl of Kent in Germany iv 7 89
My name is Edgar, and thy father's son v 3 169
Yea, though our proper son Stood in your action *Othello* i 3 69
Our slippery people . . . begin to throw Pompey the Great and all his dignities Upon his son *Ant. and Cleo.* i 2 196
I do not know Wherefore my father should revengers want, Having a son and friends ii 6 12
Bear the king's son's body Before our army iii 1 3
Cæsarion, whom they call my father's son iii 6 6
His sons he there proclaim'd the kings of kings iii 6 13
If he please To give me conquered Egypt for my son v 2 19
The heir of's kingdom, whom He purposed to his wife's sole son *Cymb.* i 1 5
Two other sons, who in the wars o' the time Died with their swords in hand i 1 35
Is she sole child to the king?—His only child. He had two sons i 1 57
That mightst have had the sole son of my queen! i 1 138
Would I were a neat-herd's daughter, and my Leonatus Our neighbour shepherd's son!—Thou foolish thing! i 1 150
My lord your son drew on my master.—Ha! No harm, I trust, is done? i 1 160
Your son's my father's friend; he takes his part i 1 165
He's for his master, And enemy to my son i 5 29
When thou shalt bring me word she loves my son i 5 49
But think Thou hast thy mistress still, to boot, my son i 5 69
Her son Cannot take two from twenty, for his heart, And leave eighteen ii 1 59
Our dear son, . . . Attend the queen and us ii 3 65
A gentleman.—No more?—Yes, and a gentlewoman's son ii 3 83
Wert thou the son of Jupiter and no more But what thou art besides, thou wert too base To be his groom ii 3 130
Son, let your mother end iii 1 39
These boys know little they are sons to the king iii 3 80
Son, I say, follow the king iii 5 53
How now, my son!—'Tis certain she is fled iii 5 66
Would it had been so, that they Had been my father's sons! iii 6 77
I partly know him: 'tis Cloten, the son o' the queen iv 2 65
To thy mere confusion, thou shalt know I am son to the queen iv 2 93
Cut off one Cloten's head, Son to the queen, after his own report iv 2 119
Let it to the sea, And tell the fishes he's the queen's son, Cloten iv 2 153
He was a queen's son, boys; And though he came our enemy, remember iv 2 244
A fever with the absence of her son, A madness, of which her life's in danger iv 3 2
Her son gone, So needful for this present: it strikes me iv 3 7
Now for the counsel of my son and queen! I am amazed with matter iv 3 27
Sons, We'll higher to the mountains; there secure us iv 4 7
'Tis thought the old man and his sons were angels v 3 85
Since, Jupiter, our son is good, Take off his miseries v 4 85
Be content; Your low-laid son our godhead will uplift v 4 103
In time, When she had fitted you with her craft, to work Her son into the adoption of the crown v 5 56
But her son Is gone, we know not how nor where v 5 272
My sons, I must, For mine own part, unfold a dangerous speech v 5 312
First pay me for the nursing of thy sons . . . —Nursing of my sons! v 5 322
I will prefer my sons; Then spare not the old father v 5 326
These two young gentlemen, that call me father And think they are my sons, are none of mine v 5 329
But, gracious sir, Here are your sons again v 5 348
I know not how to wish A pair of worthier sons v 5 356
This gentleman, my Cadwal, Arviragus, Your younger princely son v 5 360
Thy lopp'd branches point Thy two sons forth v 5 455
Be my helps, As I am son and servant to your will! *Pericles* i 1 23
Prince Pericles,— That would be son to great Antiochus i 1 26
He's father, son, and husband mild; I mother, wife, and yet his child i 1 68
This mercy shows we'll joy in such a son i 1 118
Where now you're both a father and a son i 1 127
Now his son's like a glow-worm in the night, The which hath fire in darkness ii 3 43
Our son and daughter shall in Tyrus reign v 3 82
Sonance. Let the trumpets sound The tucket sonance *Hen. V.* iv 2 35
Song. Let's see your song *T. G. of Ver.* i 2 88
There wanteth but a mean to fill your song.—The mean is drown'd i 2 95
I had rather than forty shillings I had my Book of Songs *Mer. Wives* i 1 206
Rush at once With some diffused song iv 4 54
Break off thy song, and haste thee quick away *Meas. for Meas.* iv 1 7
I'll stop mine ears against the mermaid's song *Com. of Errors* iii 2 169
In what key shall a man take you, to go in the song? *Much Ado* i 1 188
We'll hear that song again.—O, good my lord, tax not so bad a voice ii 3 46
By my troth, a good song.—And an ill singer ii 3 77
For the which, with songs of woe, Round about her tomb they go v 3 14
Nor woo in rhyme, like a blind harper's song! *L. L. Lost* v 2 405
The words of Mercury are harsh after the songs of Apollo v 2 941
That the rude sea grew civil at her song *M. N. Dream* ii 1 152
Come, now a roundel and a fairy song ii 2 1
Both warbling of one song, both in one key iii 2 206
First, rehearse your song by rote, To each word a warbling note v 1 404
I can suck melancholy out of a song, as a weasel sucks eggs *As Y. Like It* ii 5 13
Hold your tongues.—Well, I'll end the song ii 5 32
Here was he merry, hearing of a song ii 7 4
I would sing my song without a burden: thou bringest me out of tune iii 2 261
Have you no song, forester, for this purpose? iv 2 6
Come, sit, sit, and a song.—We are for you v 3 9
I count it but time lost to hear such a foolish song v 3 41
What, one good in ten? you corrupt the song, sirrah.—One good woman in ten, madam; which is a purifying o' the song *All's Well* i 3 85
Sold a goodly manor for a song iii 2 10
Every night he comes With musics of all sorts and songs iii 7 40
This is the best fooling, when all is done. Now, a song *T. Night* ii 3 31
There is a sixpence for you: let's have a song ii 3 33
Would you have a love-song, or a song of good life?—A love-song ii 3 36
That piece of song, That old and antique song we heard last night ii 4 2
O, fellow, come, the song we had last night ii 4 43
The thrush and the jay, Are summer songs for me and my aunts *W. Tale* iv 3 11
Welcomed all, served all; Would sing her song and dance her turn iv 4 58
He hath songs for man or woman, of all sizes iv 4 191
We'll have this song out anon by ourselves iv 4 315
Grew so in love with the wenches' song, that he would not stir iv 4 618
No hearing, no feeling, but my sir's song iv 4 625

Song. Rest your gentle head upon her lap, And she will sing the song that pleaseth you And on your eyelids crown the god of sleep *1 Hen. IV.* iii 1 216
Come, Kate, I'll have your song too.—Not mine, in good sooth . . iii 1 250
Come sing me a bawdy song; make me merry . . . . . iii 3 16
A merry song, come: it grows late . . . . *2 Hen. IV.* ii 4 299
Out on you, owls! nothing but songs of death? . . *Richard III.* iv 4 509
A French song and a fiddle has no fellow . . . . *Hen. VIII.* i 3 41
And sing The merry songs of peace to all his neighbours . . . v 5 36
I'll hear no more of this; I'll sing you a song now . *Troi. and Cres.* iii 1 115
Let thy song be love: this love will undo us all . . . . iii 1 119
Be unto us as is a nurse's song Of lullaby . . . *T. Andron.* ii 3 28
Then weigh what loss your honour may sustain, If with too credent ear you list his songs . . . . *Hamlet* i 3 30
Alas, sweet lady, what imports this song? . . . . . iv 5 27
Where be your gibes now? your gambols? your songs? . . . v 1 209
When were you wont to be so full of songs? . . . . *Lear* i 4 186
An excellent song.—I learned it in England . . . *Othello* ii 3 77
Why, this is a more exquisite song than the other.—Will you hear't again? . . . . ii 3 101
She had a song of 'willow;' An old thing 'twas, but it express'd her fortune, And she died singing it: that song to-night Will not go from my mind . . . . iv 3 28
What did thy song bode, lady? Hark, canst thou hear me? I will play the swan, And die in music . . . . v 2 246
If you'll go fetch him, We'll say our song the whilst . . *Cymbeline* iv 2 254
To sing a song that old was sung, From ashes ancient Gower is come *Pericles* i Gower 1
Son-in-law. Since you could not be my son-in-law, Be yet my nephew *Much Ado* v 1 296
And yet we hear not of our son-in-law . . . *T. of Shrew* iii 2 3
I will buy me a son-in-law in a fair, and toll for this . *All's Well* v 3 148
Embraces his son-in-law; then again worries he his daughter *W. Tale* v 2 57
This is your son-in-law And son unto the king. . . . . v 3 149
Owen, the same; and his son-in-law Mortimer . . *1 Hen. IV.* iii 4 375
Break into his son-in-law's house . . . . *2 Hen. VI.* iv 7 117
These very words I've heard him utter to his son-in-law . *Hen. VIII.* i 2 136
A valiant son-in-law thou shalt enjoy . . . . *T. Andron.* i 1 311
Death is my son-in-law, Death is my heir; My daughter he hath wedded *Rom. and Jul.* iv 5 38
And when I have stol'n upon these sons-in-law, Then, kill, kill, kill! *Lear* iv 6 190
Your son-in-law is far more fair than black . . . . *Othello* i 3 291
We'll learn our freeness of a son-in-law . . . . *Cymbeline* v 5 421
Sonnet. Tangle her desires By wailful sonnets . . . *T. G. of Ver.* iii 2 69
I have a sonnet that will serve the turn To give the onset . . iii 2 93
I had rather than forty shillings I had my Book of Songs and Sonnets here *Mer. Wives* i 1 206
Will you then write me a sonnet in praise of my beauty? . *Much Ado* v 2 4
A halting sonnet of his own pure brain . . . . . v 4 87
Assist me, some extemporal god of rhyme, for I am sure I shall turn sonnet. Devise, wit; write, pen . . . . *L. L. Lost* i 2 190
She hath one o' my sonnets already . . . . . . iv 3 15
Did never sonnet for her sake compile . . . . . . iv 3 134
Give me a copy of the sonnet you writ . . . . *All's Well* iv 3 355
It is with me as the very true sonnet is, 'Please one, and please all' *T. Night* iii 4 24
I once writ a sonnet in his praise and began thus: 'Wonder of nature,'— I have heard a sonnet begin so to one's mistress . . *Hen. V.* iii 7 42
Sonneting. None but minstrels like of sonneting! . *L. L. Lost* iv 3 158
Sonties. By God's sonties, 'twill be a hard way to hit . *Mer. of Venice* ii 2 47
Soon. What, all so soon asleep! . . . . . *Tempest* ii 1 191
I cannot be so soon provided: Please you, deliberate a day or two *T. G. of Ver.* i 3 72
Thou wouldst as soon go kindle fire with snow . . . . ii 7 19
You are already Love's firm votary And cannot soon revolt . . iii 2 59
If any man may, you may as soon as any . . . *Mer. Wives* ii 2 246
Better three hours too soon than a minute too late . . . . ii 2 327
So soon as I came beyond Eton, they threw me off . . . iv 5 68
We may soon our satisfaction have Touching that point . *Meas. for Meas.* i 1 83
And soon and safe arrived where I was . . . *Com. of Errors* i 1 49
Unwilling I agreed; alas! too soon We came aboard . . . i 1 61
Lest that your goods too soon be confiscate . . . . . i 2 2
Soon at five o'clock, Please you, I'll meet with you upon the mart . i 2 26
My decayed fair A sunny look of his would soon repair . . . ii 1 99
Soon at supper-time I'll visit you And then receive my money . iii 2 179
I sent thee for a rope . . . —You sent me for a rope's end as soon . iv 1 98
I'll believe as soon This whole earth may be bored . *M. N. Dream* iii 2 52
Soon at supper shalt thou see Lorenzo . . . *Mer. of Venice* ii 3 5
A murderous guilt shows not itself more soon Than love that would seem hid: love's night is noon . . . . . *T. Night* iii 1 159
So soon as ever thou seest him, draw . . . . . . iii 4 195
Come to me, Tyrrel, soon at after supper . . . *Richard III.* iv 3 31
All so soon as the all-cheering sun Should in the furthest east begin to draw The shady curtains . . . . . *Rom. and Jul.* i 1 140
I do not know the man I should avoid So soon as that spare Cassius *J. Cæsar* i 2 201
Whose ministers would prevail Under the service of a child as soon As i' the command of Cæsar . . . . . *Ant. and Cleo.* iii 13 24
'Tis but a blow, which never shall be known. Thou canst not do a thing in the world so soon, To yield thee so much profit . . *Pericles* iv 1 3
Soon at night. We'll have a posset for't soon at night . *Mer. Wives* i 4 8
Come to me soon at night . . . . ii 2 295
Soon at night I'll send him certain word of my success . *Meas. for Meas.* i 4 88
Come, Bardolph: I shall be sent for soon at night . . *2 Hen. IV.* v 5 96
But you shall bear the burden soon at night . . *Rom. and Jul.* ii 5 78
Bring me on the way a little, And say if I shall see you soon at night *Othello* iii 4 198
Soon-believing. Suggest his soon-believing adversaries . *Richard II.* iv 1 101
Sooner. If you turn not, you will return the sooner . . *T. G. of Ver.* ii 2 4
Why didst not tell me sooner? pox of your love-letters! . . . iii 1 390
I came no sooner into the dining-chamber but he steps me to her trencher iv 4 9
Curse the gout, serpigo, and the rheum, For ending thee no sooner *Meas. for Meas.* iii 1 32
If you handled her privately, she would sooner confess . . . v 1 277
If it prove so, I will be gone the sooner . . *Com. of Errors* i 2 103
I will, if suddenly I may.—You will the sooner, that I were away *L. L. L.* ii 1 112
Superfluity comes sooner by white hairs . . . *Mer. of Venice* i 2 9
Beauty provoketh thieves sooner than gold . . . *As Y. Like It* i 3 112
Our hands are hard.—Your lips will feel them the sooner . . . iii 2 61

Sooner. No sooner met but they looked, no sooner looked but they loved, no sooner loved but they sighed, no sooner sighed but they asked one another the reason, no sooner knew the reason but they sought the remedy . . . . *As Y. Like It* v 2 36
What, will my daughter prove a good musician?—I think she'll sooner prove a soldier . . . . *T. of Shrew* ii 1 146
And, indeed, I do marry that I may repent.—Thy marriage, sooner than thy wickedness . . . . *All's Well* i 3 40
Such as will strike sooner than speak, and speak sooner than drink, and drink sooner than pray . . . . . . *1 Hen. IV.* ii 1 86
The breath no sooner left his father's body, But that his wildness, mortified in him, Seem'd to die too . . . . . *Hen. V.* i 1 25
Forget the office of our hand, Sooner than quittance of desert and merit ii 2 34
Which word thou shalt no sooner bless mine ear withal . . . v 2 257
The sooner to effect And surer bind this knot . . . *1 Hen. VI.* v 1 15
A liberal dower, Where Reignier sooner will receive than give . . v 5 47
To this gear the sooner the better . . . . *2 Hen. VI.* i 4 17
And sooner dance upon a bloody pole Than stand uncover'd . . iv 1 127
No sooner was I crept out of my cradle But I was made a king . . iv 9 3
I shall sooner rail thee into wit and holiness . *Troi. and Cres.* ii 1 17
Thy horse will sooner con an oration than thou learn a prayer without book . . . . ii 1 18
No sooner justice had with valour arm'd . . . *Macbeth* i 2 29
The which no sooner had his prowess confirm'd . . . . v 8 41
The power of beauty will sooner transform honesty from what it is *Ham.* iii 1 112
The sun no sooner shall the mountains touch, But we will ship him . iv 1 29
Soonest. Devils soonest tempt, resembling spirits of light . *L. L. Lost* iv 3 257
The gentler gamester is the soonest winner . . . . *Hen. V.* iii 6 120
And fearless minds climb soonest unto crowns . . *3 Hen. VI.* iv 7 62
Your grace, we think, should soonest know his mind . *Richard III.* iii 4 9
A right fair mark, fair coz, is soonest hit . . . *Rom. and Jul.* i 1 213
Make your soonest haste; So your desires are yours . *Ant. and Cleo.* iii 4 27
Soon-speeding. Let me have A dram of poison, such soon-speeding gear As will disperse itself through all the veins . . *Rom. and Jul.* v 1 60
Sooth. Well drawn, monster, in good sooth! . . . *Tempest* ii 2 151
Or, in sooth, I would Master Fenton had her . . *Mer. Wives* iii 4 110
Yes, in good sooth, the vice is of a great kindred . *Meas. for Meas.* iii 2 108
Sooth to say, you did not dine at home . . . *Com. of Errors* iv 4 72
Good troth, you do me wrong, good sooth, you do . *M. N. Dream* ii 2 129
Do you not jest?—Yes, sooth; and so do you . . . . . iii 2 265
In sooth, I know not why I am so sad . . . . *Mer. of Venice* i 1 1
They in themselves, good sooth, are too too light . . . . ii 6 42
But, in good sooth, are you he that hangs the verses on the trees? *As Y. Like It* iii 2 410
Understand you this of me in sooth . . . . . *T. of Shrew* i 2 259
Nay, hear you, Kate: in sooth you 'scape not so . . . . ii 1 242
But thus, I trust, you will not marry her.—Good sooth, even thus . iii 2 118
And, sooth to say, In countenance somewhat doth resemble you . . iv 2 99
You were the first that found me!—Was I, in sooth? . *All's Well* v 2 47
Let me yet know of you whither you are bound.—No, sooth, sir *T. Night* ii 1 11
In sooth, thou wast in very gracious fooling last night . . . ii 3 22
It is silly sooth, And dallies with the innocence of love . . . ii 4 47
I cannot be so answer'd.—Sooth, but you must . . . . ii 4 91
One seven-night longer.—Very sooth, to-morrow . . . *W. Tale* i 2 17
Good sooth, she is The queen of curds and cream . . . . iv 4 160
I have it Upon his own report and I believe it; He looks like sooth . iv 4 171
Sooth, when I was young And handed love as you do . . . iv 4 358
In sooth, good friend, your father might have kept This calf . *K. John* i 1 123
In sooth, I would you were a little sick . . . . . iv 1 29
I can heat it, boy.—No, in good sooth; the fire is dead with grief . iv 1 106
Take it off again With words of sooth! . . . . *Richard II.* iii 3 136
Not mine, in good sooth.—Not yours, in good sooth! Heart! you swear like a comfit-maker's wife. 'Not you, in good sooth,' and 'as true as I live,' and 'as God shall mend me' . . . *1 Hen. IV.* iii 1 251
Swear me, Kate, like a lady as thou art, A good mouth-filling oath, and leave 'in sooth,' And such protest of pepper-gingerbread . . iii 1 259
To say the sooth, Though 'tis no wisdom to confess so much . *Hen. V.* iii 6 151
Which, to say sooth, are blessings . . . . . *Hen. VIII.* ii 3 30
Yes, good sooth: to, Achilles! to, Ajax! to! . . *Troi. and Cres.* ii 1 119
Rude, in sooth; in good sooth, very rude . . . . . iii 1 59
Sooth, madam, I hear nothing . . . . . . *J. Cæsar* ii 4 20
If I say sooth, I must report they were As cannons overcharged *Macbeth* i 2 36
If thy speech be sooth, I care not if thou dost for me as much . . v 5 40
In good sooth, in sincere verity . . . . . . *Lear* ii 2 111
Went he hence now?—Ay, sooth . . . . . *Othello* iii 3 52
In sooth, you are to blame . . . . iii 4 97
Sooth, la, I'll help: thus it must be . . . . *Ant. and Cleo.* iv 4 8
Good sooth, I care not for you . . . . *Pericles* i 1 86
When Signior Sooth here does proclaim a peace, He flatters you . . i 2 44
Good sooth, it show'd well in you: do so now . . . . . iv 1 89
Soothe. Is't good to soothe him in these contraries? *Com. of Errors* iv 4 82
And now, to soothe your forgery and his, Sends me a paper *3 Hen. VI.* iii 3 175
What, dost thou scorn me for my gentle counsel? And soothe the devil that I warn thee from? . . . . *Richard III.* i 3 298
Good my lord, soothe him; let him take the fellow . . *Lear* iii 4 182
Soothed. You soothed not, therefore hurt not . . . . *Coriolanus* ii 2 77
Soother. I do defy The tongues of soothers . . . *1 Hen. IV.* iv 1 7
Soothest. Thou art perjured too, And soothest up greatness . *K. John* iii 1 121
Soothing. Let courts and cities be Made all of false-faced soothing! *Coriol.* i 9 44
In soothing them, we nourish 'gainst our senate The cockle of rebellion iii 1 69
Soothsay. Go, you wild bedfellow, you cannot soothsay . *Ant. and Cleo.* i 2 52
Soothsayer. A soothsayer bids you beware the ides of March.—Set him before me . . . . *J. Cæsar* i 2 19
Where's the soothsayer that you praised so to the queen? *Ant. and Cleo.* i 2 3
Call forth your soothsayer . . . . *Cymbeline* v 5 426
Sooty. Run from her guardage to the sooty bosom Of such a thing as thou, to fear, not to delight . . . . *Othello* i 2 70
Sop. Threw the sops all in the sexton's face; Having no other reason But that his beard grew thin and hungerly And seem'd to ask him sops as he was drinking . . . . *T. of Shrew* iii 2 175
O excellent device! make a sop of him . . . . *Richard III.* i 4 162
And make a sop of all this solid globe . . . *Troi. and Cres.* i 3 113
I'll make a sop o' the moonshine of you . . . . . *Lear* ii 2 35
Sophister. A subtle traitor needs no sophister . . . *2 Hen. VI.* v 1 191
Sophisticated. Ha! here's three on's are sophisticated! . . *Lear* iii 4 110
Sophy. By this scimitar That slew the Sophy . . . *Mer. of Venice* ii 1 25
A pension of thousands to be paid from the Sophy . . . *T. Night* ii 5 198
They say he has been fencer to the Sophy . . . . . . iii 4 307
Sorcerer. I am subject to a tyrant, a sorcerer . . . . *Tempest* iii 2 49
Dark-working sorcerers that change the mind . . . *Com. of Errors* i 2 99

Sorcerer. And Lapland sorcerers inhabit here . . . *Com. of Errors* iv 3 11
Shall we think the subtle-witted French Conjurers and sorcerers? 1 *Hen. VI.* i 1 26
Sorceress. Thou art, as you are all, a sorceress . . . *Com. of Errors* iv 3 67
Pucelle, that witch, that damned sorceress, Hath wrought this 1 *Hen. VI.* iii 2 38
Bring forth that sorceress condemn'd to burn . . . v 4 1
Sorcery. For mischiefs manifold and sorceries terrible . . *Tempest* i 2 264
I say, by sorcery he got this isle . . . iii 2 60
To quittance their deceit Contrived by art and baleful sorcery 1 *Hen. VI.* ii 1 15
Sore. You rub the sore, When you should bring the plaster . *Tempest* ii 1 138
Upon a sore injunction . . . iii 1 11
You'ld be king o' the isle, sirrah?—I should have been a sore one then v 1 288
If you went in pain, master, this 'knave' would go sore *Com. of Errors* iii 1 65
To strange sores strangely they strain the cure . . . *Much Ado* iv 1 254
Some say a sore; but not a sore, till now made sore with shooting *L. L. L.* iv 2 59
Put L to sore, then sorel jumps from thicket; Or pricket sore, or else sorel; the people fall a-hooting. If sore be sore, then L to sore makes fifty sores one sorel. Of one sore I an hundred make by adding but one more L . . . iv 2 60
I'll fear no other thing So sore as keeping safe Nerissa's ring *M. of Ven.* v 1 307
All the embossed sores and headed evils . . . *As Y. Like It* ii 7 67
Your sorrow was too sore laid on . . . *W. Tale* v 3 49
I am not glad that such a sore of time Should seek a plaster . *K. John* v 2 12
King John sore sick hath left the field . . . v 4 6
Fell sorrow's tooth doth never rankle more Than when he bites, but lanceth not the sore . . . *Richard II.* i 3 303
We see the wind sit sore upon our sails, And yet we strike not . . ii 1 265
Slaves as ragged as Lazarus in the painted cloth, where the glutton's dogs licked his sores . . . 1 *Hen. IV.* iv 2 29
I hear the king my father is sore sick . . . 2 *Hen. IV.* iv 3 83
A sore complaint 'Gainst him whose wrongs give edge unto the swords *Hen. V.* i 2 26
His soul Shall stand sore charged for the wasteful vengeance . . i 2 283
'Twill be sore law, then . . . 2 *Hen. VI.* iv 7 9
To provide A salve for any sore that may betide . . 3 *Hen. VI.* iv 6 88
Awaked you not with this sore agony? . . . *Richard III.* i 4 42
Not that it wounds, But tickles still the sore . . *Troi. and Cres.* iii 1 130
Thou green sarcenet flap for a sore eye . . . v 1 36
And Palamedes Sore hurt and bruised . . . v 5 14
Who have their provand Only for bearing burdens, and sore blows For sinking under them . . . *Coriolanus* ii 1 268
'Tis a sore upon us, You cannot tent yourself . . . iii 1 235
I am too sore enpierced with his shaft To soar . . *Rom. and Jul.* i 4 19
Not nature, To whom all sores lay siege, can bear great fortune *T. of A.* iv 3 7
She, whom the spital-house and ulcerous sores Would cast the gorge at iv 3 39
Sore labour's bath, Balm of hurt minds . . . *Macbeth* ii 2 38
This sore night Hath trifled former knowings . . . ii 4 3
Whose sore task Does not divide the Sunday from the week . *Hamlet* i 1 75
Your water is a sore decayer of your whoreson dead body . . v 1 188
How I am punish'd With sore distraction . . . v 2 241
Though the conflict be sore between that and my blood . . . *Lear* iii 5 24
Had they rain'd All kinds of sores and shames on my bare head *Othello* iv 2 49
Let's to billiards: come, Charmian.—My arm is sore . *Ant. and Cleo.* ii 5 4
My horse is tied up safe: out, sword, and to a sore purpose! *Cymbeline* iv 1 25
The breath is gone, and the sore eyes see clear . . . *Pericles* i 1 99
The sore terms we stand upon with the gods will be strong with us . iv 2 37
Sorel. Put L to sore, then sorel jumps from thicket; Or pricket sore, or else sorel; the people fall a-hooting. If sore be sore, then L to sore makes fifty sores one sorel . . . *L. L. Lost* iv 2 60
Sorely. This drum sticks sorely in your disposition . . *All's Well* iii 6 47
Thou strikest me Sorely, to say I did . . . *W. Tale* v 1 18
Brought him forward, As a man sorely tainted, to his answer *Hen. VIII.* iv 2 14
What a sigh is there! The heart is sorely charged . . . *Macbeth* v 1 60
The bleak winds Do sorely ruffle . . . *Lear* ii 4 304
Of which I do accuse myself so sorely, That I will joy no more *A. and C.* iv 6 19
Sorer. To lapse in fulness Is sorer than to lie for need . . *Cymbeline* iii 6 13
Sore-shaming. O bill, sore-shaming Those rich-left heirs that let their fathers lie Without a monument! . . . iv 2 225
Sorrier. I am the sorrier; would 'twere otherwise . . . 2 *Hen. IV.* v 2 32
Sorriest. Of sorriest fancies your companions making . . *Macbeth* iii 2 9
Sorrow. Wisely, good sir, weigh Our sorrow with our comfort *Tempest* ii 1 9
It [sleep] seldom visits sorrow; when it doth, It is a comforter . . ii 1 195
Mourning over them, Brimful of sorrow and dismay . . . v 1 14
Let grief and sorrow still embrace his heart That doth not wish you joy! . . . v 1 214
Watchers of mine own heart's sorrow . . . *T. G. of Ver.* ii 4 135
Heap on your head A pack of sorrows which would press you down . iii 1 20
Even from a heart As full of sorrows as the sea of sands . . iv 3 33
That's her cause of sorrow.—Is she not passing fair? . . . iv 4 152
Would I might be dead If I in thought felt not her very sorrow! . iv 4 177
If hearty sorrow Be a sufficient ransom for offence, I tender't here . v 4 74
Your sorrow hath eaten up my sufferance . . . *Mer. Wives* iv 2 1
Which sorrow is always toward ourselves, not heaven . *Meas. for Meas.* ii 3 32
I am sorry that such sorrow I procure . . . v 1 479
I'll utter what my sorrow gives me leave . . . *Com. of Errors* i 1 36
Fortune had left to both of us alike What to delight in, what to sorrow for . . . i 1 107
Which of these sorrows is he subject to?—To none of these . . v 1 54
When you depart from me, sorrow abides and happiness takes his leave *Much Ado* i 1 102
Bid sorrow wag, cry 'hem!' when he should groan . . . v 1 16
'Tis all men's office to speak patience To those that wring under the load of sorrow, But no man's virtue nor sufficiency To be so moral v 1 28
Welcome the sour cup of prosperity! Affliction may one day smile again; and till then, sit thee down, sorrow! . . *L. L. Lost* i 1 317
Set thee down, sorrow! for so they say the fool said, and so say I . iv 3 4
O, what a scene of foolery have I seen, Of sighs, of groans, of sorrow! . iv 3 164
Since love's argument was first on foot, Let not the cloud of sorrow justle it . . . v 2 758
So sorrow's heaviness doth heavier grow For debt that bankrupt sleep doth sorrow owe . . . *M. N. Dream* iii 2 84
Sleep, that sometimes shuts up sorrow's eye, Steal me awhile from mine own company . . . iii 2 435
By this heaven, now at our sorrows pale . . . *As Y. Like It* i 3 106
Wherever sorrow is, relief would be: If you do sorrow at my grief in love, By giving love your sorrow and my grief Were both extermined iii 5 87
Sorrow on thee and all the pack of you! . . . *T. of Shrew* iv 3 33
Measures my husband's sorrow by his woe . . . v 2 29
The tyranny of her sorrows takes all livelihood from her cheek *All's W.* i 1 58
Lest it be rather thought you affect a sorrow than have it.—I do affect a sorrow indeed, but I have it too . . . i 1 60

Sorrow. This she delivered in the most bitter touch of sorrow that e'er I heard . . . *All's Well* i 3 122
To-morrow I'll to the wars, she to her single sorrow . . . ii 3 313
Grief would have tears, and sorrow bids me speak . . . iii 4 42
If she be so abandon'd to her sorrow As it is spoke . . *T. Night* i 4 19
Laugh at me, make their pastime at my sorrow . . . *W. Tale* ii 3 24
Come and lead me Unto these sorrows . . . iii 2 244
I never saw a vessel of like sorrow, So fill'd and so becoming . . iii 3 21
To whose feeling sorrows I might be some allay, or I o'erween to think so iv 2 8
You have done enough, and have perform'd A saint-like sorrow . . v 1 2
The wisest beholder, that knew no more but seeing, could not say if the importance were joy or sorrow . . . v 2 20
Sorrow wept to take leave of them, for their joy waded in tears . v 2 49
But O, the noble combat that 'twixt joy and sorrow was fought in Paulina! . . . v 2 80
Your sorrow was too sore laid on, Which sixteen winters cannot blow away . . . v 3 49
Scarce any joy Did ever so long live; no sorrow But kill'd itself much sooner . . . v 3 52
If thou teach me to believe this sorrow, Teach thou this sorrow how to make me die . . . *K. John* iii 1 29
I will instruct my sorrows to be proud; For grief is proud . . . iii 1 68
Here I and sorrows sit; Here is my throne, bid kings come bow to it . iii 1 73
You utter madness, and not sorrow.—Thou art not holy to belie me so iii 4 43
Now will canker sorrow eat my bud And chase the native beauty from his cheek . . . iii 4 82
My food, my all the world! My widow-comfort, and my sorrows' cure! . . . iii 4 105
This must not be thus borne: this will break out To all our sorrows . iv 2 102
For sorrow ends not when it seemeth done . . . *Richard II.* i 2 61
Let him not come there, To seek out sorrow that dwells every where . i 2 72
Shorten my days thou canst with sullen sorrow . . . i 3 227
Gnarling sorrow hath less power to bite The man that mocks at it . i 3 292
Fell sorrow's tooth doth never rankle more than when he bites, but lanceth not the sore . . . i 3 302
Such grief That words seem'd buried in my sorrow's grave . . . i 4 15
Methinks, Some unborn sorrow, ripe in fortune's womb, Is coming towards me . . . ii 2 10
For sorrow's eye, glazed with blinding tears, Divides one thing entire to many objects . . . ii 2 16
'Tis with false sorrow's eye, Which for things true weeps things imaginary . . . ii 2 26
A gasping new-deliver'd mother, Have woe to woe, sorrow to sorrow join'd . . . ii 2 66
With rainy eyes Write sorrow on the bosom of the earth . . . iii 2 147
Sorrow and grief of heart Makes him speak fondly, like a frantic man . iii 3 184
We'll tell tales.—Of sorrow or of joy?—Of either, madam.—Of neither, girl: For if of joy, being altogether wanting, It doth remember me the more of sorrow; Or if of grief, being altogether had, It adds more sorrow to my want of joy . . . iii 4 11
Give sorrow leave awhile to tutor me To this submission . . . iv 1 166
No deeper wrinkles yet? hath sorrow struck So many blows upon this face of mine, And made no deeper wounds? . . . iv 1 277
How soon my sorrow hath destroy'd my face.—The shadow of your sorrow hath destroy'd The shadow of your face . . . iv 1 291
I see your brows are full of discontent, Your hearts of sorrow . . iv 1 332
In wooing sorrow let's be brief, Since, wedding it, there is such length in grief . . . v 1 93
Once more, adieu; the rest let sorrow say . . . v 1 102
But dust was thrown upon his sacred head; Which with such gentle sorrow he shook off . . . v 2 31
Hath in reason taken from me all ostentation of sorrow . . 2 *Hen. IV.* ii 2 54
Since sudden sorrow Serves to say thus, 'some good thing comes tomorrow' . . . iv 2 83
Thy due from me Is tears and heavy sorrows of the blood . . . iv 5 38
With such a deep demeanour in great sorrow . . . iv 5 85
I dare swear you borrow not that face Of seeming sorrow, it is sure your own . . . v 2 29
Sorrow so royally in you appears That I will deeply put the fashion on v 2 51
Mourn not, except thou sorrow for my good . . . 1 *Hen. VI.* ii 5 111
Sorrow and grief have vanquish'd all my powers . . 2 *Hen. VI.* ii 1 183
This dishonour in thine age Will bring thy head with sorrow to the ground! . . . ii 3 19
Give me leave to go; Sorrow would solace and mine age would ease . ii 3 21
As the mournful crocodile With sorrow snares relenting passengers . iii 1 227
And to survey his dead and earthy image, What were it but to make my sorrow greater? . . . iii 2 148
Mischance and sorrow go along with you! . . . iii 2 300
And with the southern clouds contend in tears, Theirs for the earth's increase, mine for my sorrows . . . iii 2 385
And seek for sorrow with thy spectacles . . . v 1 165
To our heart's great sorrow . . . 3 *Hen. VI.* i 1 128
And I, with grief and sorrow, to the court . . . i 1 210
To see how inly sorrow gripes his soul . . . i 4 171
Much is your sorrow; mine ten times so much . . . ii 5 112
Give my tongue-tied sorrows leave to speak . . . iii 3 22
O, but impatience waiteth on true sorrow. And see where comes the breeder of my sorrow! . . . iii 3 43
Full of sorrow and heart's discontent . . . iii 3 173
Then none but I shall turn his jest to sorrow . . . iii 3 261
Your dislike, to whom I would be pleasing, Doth cloud my joys with danger and with sorrow . . . iv 1 74
What danger or what sorrow can befall thee? . . . iv 1 76
Turn'd my captive state to liberty, My fear to hope, my sorrows unto joys . . . iv 6 4
What these sorrows could not thence exhale, Thy beauty hath *Rich. III.* i 2 166
The sorrow that I have, by right is yours . . . i 3 172
Life my shame; And in that shame still live my sorrow's rage! . . i 3 278
Remember this another day, When he shall split thy very heart with sorrow . . . i 3 300; v 1 26
Sorrow breaks seasons and reposing hours, Makes the night morning . i 4 76
I pray thee, peace: my soul is full of sorrow . . . ii 1 96
It were lost sorrow to wail one that's lost . . . ii 2 11
So much interest have I in thy sorrow As I had title in thy noble husband! . . . ii 2 47
I am your sorrow's nurse, And I will pamper it with lamentations . ii 2 87
In him your comfort lives: Drown desperate sorrow in dead Edward's grave . . . ii 2 99
And, when thou wed'st, let sorrow haunt thy bed! . . . iv 1 74
Eighty odd years of sorrow have I seen . . . iv 1 96

Sorrow. You ancient stones, . . . use my babies well! So foolish sorrow bids your stones farewell *Richard III.* iv 1 104
If ancient sorrow be most reverend, Give mine the benefit of seniory iv 4 35
If sorrow can admit society, Tell o'er your woes again by viewing mine iv 4 38
Thou didst usurp my place, and dost thou not Usurp the just proportion of my sorrow? iv 4 110
Flatter my sorrows with report of it iv 4 245
Save for a night of groans Endured of her, for whom you bid like sorrow iv 4 304
Than to be perk'd up in a glistering grief, And wear a golden sorrow *Hen. VIII.* ii 3 22
Our mistress' sorrows we were pitying ii 3 53
Nor to betray you any way to sorrow, You have too much iii 1 56
Take heed, lest at once The burthen of my sorrows fall upon ye iii 1 111
We are to cure such sorrows, not to sow 'em iii 1 158
Bear witness . . . With what a sorrow Cromwell leaves his lord iii 2 425
That time offer'd sorrow; This, general joy iv 1 6
Full of repentance, Continual meditations, tears, and sorrows iv 2 28
Her foes shake like a field of beaten corn, And hang their heads with sorrow v 5 33
Sorrow, that is couch'd in seeming gladness, Is like that mirth fate turns to sudden sadness *Troi. and Cres.* i 1 39
The sorrow that delivers us thus changed Makes you think so *Coriolanus* v 3 39
Constrains them weep and shake with fear and sorrow v 3 100
My rage is gone; And I am struck with sorrow v 6 149
Sorrow concealed, like an oven stopp'd, Doth burn the heart to cinders where it is *T. Andron.* ii 4 36
No man is by; And you recount your sorrows to a stone iii 1 29
I bring consuming sorrow to thine age.—Will it consume me? iii 1 61
Witness the sorrow that their sister makes iii 1 119
Is not my sorrow deep, having no bottom? Then be my passions bottomless iii 1 217
To weep with them that weep doth ease some deal; But sorrow flouted at is double death iii 1 246
This sorrow is an enemy, And would usurp upon my watery eyes iii 1 268
How now! has sorrow made thee dote already? iii 2 23
She says she drinks no other drink but tears, Brew'd with her sorrow iii 2 38
And I have read that Hecuba of Troy Ran mad for sorrow iv 1 21
Come, and take choice of all my library, And so beguile thy sorrow iv 1 35
Heaven guide thy pen to print thy sorrows plain! iv 1 75
That hath more scars of sorrow in his heart Than foemen's marks upon his batter'd shield iv 1 126
Old Andronicus, Shaken with sorrows in ungrateful Rome iv 3 17
Kinsmen, his sorrows are past remedy iv 3 31
And what an if His sorrows have so overwhelm'd his wits? iv 4 10
Calm thee, and bear the faults of Titus' age, The effects of sorrow iv 4 30
Ay, now begin our sorrows to approach iv 4 72
Even when their sorrows almost were forgot v 1 137
Let not your sorrow die, though I am dead v 1 140
Witness the tiring day and heavy night; Witness all sorrow v 2 25
Because the girl should not survive her shame, And by her presence still renew his sorrows v 3 42
Die, die, Lavinia, and thy shame with thee; And, with thy shame, thy father's sorrow die! v 3 47
Could we but learn from whence his sorrows grow, We would as willingly give cure as know *Rom. and Jul.* i 1 160
Parting is such sweet sorrow, That I shall say good night till it be morrow ii 2 185
So smile the heavens upon this holy act, That after hours with sorrow chide us not!—Amen, amen! but come what sorrow can, It cannot countervail the exchange of joy That one short minute gives me in her sight ii 6 2
These griefs, these woes, these sorrows make me old iii 2 89
What sorrow craves acquaintance at my hand, That I yet know not? iii 3 5
Hasten all the house to bed, Which heavy sorrow makes them apt unto iii 3 157
Dry sorrow drinks our blood iii 5 59
Her father counts it dangerous That she doth give her sorrow so much sway iv 1 10
The sun, for sorrow, will not show his head v 3 306
We are fellows still, Serving alike in sorrow *T. of Athens* iv 2 19
Thus part we rich in sorrow, parting poor iv 2 29
Passion, I see, is catching; for mine eyes, Seeing those beads of sorrow stand in thine, Began to water *J. Cæsar* iii 1 284
No man bears sorrow better. Portia is dead.—Ha! Portia!—She is dead iv 3 147
My plenteous joys, Wanton in fulness, seek to hide themselves In drops of sorrow *Macbeth* i 4 35
Our tears are not yet brew'd.—Nor our strong sorrow Upon the foot of motion ii 3 130
To show an unfelt sorrow is an office Which the false man does easy ii 3 142
New sorrows Strike heaven on the face, that it resounds iv 3 5
Where violent sorrow seems A modern ecstasy iv 3 169
Give sorrow words: the grief that does not speak Whispers the o'er-fraught heart and bids it break iv 3 209
Canst thou not . . . Pluck from the memory a rooted sorrow? v 3 41
Your cause of sorrow Must not be measured by his worth v 8 44
He's worth more sorrow, And that I'll spend for him v 8 50
We with wisest sorrow think on him *Hamlet* i 2 6
Bound In filial obligation for some term To do obsequious sorrow i 2 92
Look'd he frowningly?—A countenance more in sorrow than in anger i 2 232
When sorrows come, they come not single spies, But in battalions iv 5 78
Are you like the painting of a sorrow, A face without a heart? iv 7 109
Whose phrase of sorrow Conjures the wandering stars v 1 278
For me, with sorrow I embrace my fortune v 2 399
Then they for sudden joy did weep, And I for sorrow sung *Lear* i 4 192
Down, thou climbing sorrow, Thy element's below! ii 4 57
Of how unnatural and bemadding sorrow The king hath cause to plain iii 1 38
Bad is the trade that must play fool to sorrow, Angering itself and others iv 1 40
Patience and sorrow strove Who should express her goodliest iv 3 18
Sorrow would be a rarity most beloved, If all could so become it iv 3 25
Who, by the art of known and feeling sorrows, Am pregnant to good pity iv 6 226
I stand up, and have ingenious feeling Of my huge sorrows iv 6 288
Let sorrow split my heart, if ever I Did hate thee! v 3 177
This would have seem'd a period To such as love not sorrow v 3 205
It is a chance which does redeem all sorrows That ever I have felt v 3 266
It engluts and swallows other sorrows And it is still itself *Othello* i 3 57
But he bears both the sentence and the sorrow That, to pay grief, must of poor patience borrow i 3 214
This hand is moist, my lady.—It yet hath felt no age nor known no sorrow iii 4 37

Sorrow. Nor my service past, nor present sorrows, Nor purposed merit in futurity *Othello* iii 4 116
This sorrow's heavenly; It strikes where it doth love v 2 21
It is a deadly sorrow to behold a foul knave uncuckolded *Ant. and Cleo.* i 2 76
The tears live in an onion that should water this sorrow i 2 177
'Tis one of those odd tricks which sorrow shoots Out of the mind iv 2 14
There then: thus I do escape the sorrow Of Antony's death iv 14 94
Do not please sharp fate To grace it with your sorrows iv 14 136
Comforts we despise; our size of sorrow, Proportion'd to our cause, must be as great As that which makes it iv 15 4
The miserable change now at my end Lament nor sorrow at iv 15 52
All Is outward sorrow; though I think the king Be touch'd *Cymbeline* i 1 9
For which their father . . . took such sorrow That he quit being i 1 37
Notes of sorrow out of tune are worse Than priests and fanes that lie iv 2 241
As from thence Sorrow were ever razed *Pericles* i 1 17
Lest that he had err'd or sinn'd, To show his sorrow, he'ld correct himself i 3 23
Our tongues and sorrows do sound deep Our woes into the air i 4 13
Speak out thy sorrows which thou bring'st in haste i 4 58
One sorrow never comes but brings an heir, That may succeed as his inheritor i 4 63
Nor come we to add sorrow to your tears, But to relieve them i 4 90
In sorrow all devour'd, With sighs shot through iv 4 25
Let me entreat to know at large the cause Of your king's sorrow v 1 63

Sorrowed. Some swooned, all sorrowed *W. Tale* v 2 99
And send forth us, to make their sorrow'd render *T. of Athens* v 1 152

Sorrowest. For the sake of them thou sorrowest for *Com. of Errors* i 1 122

Sorrowful. His napkin, with his true tears all bewet, Can do no service on her sorrowful cheeks *T. Andron.* iii 1 147
A joyless, dismal, black, and sorrowful issue iv 2 66
Go, go into old Titus' sorrowful house v 3 142
O, take . . . These sorrowful drops upon thy blood-stain'd face! v 3 154
O most false love! Where be the sacred vials thou shouldst fill With sorrowful water? *Ant. and Cleo.* i 3 64

Sorrowing. Do not Consume your blood with sorrowing *Pericles* iv 1 24

Sorrow-wreathen. Unknit that sorrow-wreathen knot *T. Andron.* iii 2 4

Sorry. I am sorry I beat thee *Tempest* iii 2 119
I am sorry I must never trust thee more *T. G. of Ver.* v 4 69
I am sorry that for my sake you have suffered all this *Mer. Wives* iii 5 125
Who I would be sorry should be thus foolishly lost *Meas. for Meas.* i 2 195
I am sorry, one so learned and so wise . . . Should slip so grossly v 1 475
I am sorry that such sorrow I procure v 1 479
I am sorry, sir, that I have hinder'd you *Com. of Errors* v 1 1
I am sorry now that I did draw on him v 1 43
I am sorry for her, as I have just cause, being her uncle *Much Ado* ii 3 172
Well, I am sorry for your niece iii 3 206
I am sorry you must hear iv 1 89
Pretty lady, I am sorry for thy much misgovernment iv 1 100
I confess nothing, nor I deny nothing. I am sorry for my cousin iv 1 275
My heart is sorry for your daughter's death v 1 103
I am sorry, madam; for the news I bring Is heavy in my tongue *L. L. L.* v 2 726
I am sorry thou wilt leave my father so *Mer. of Venice* ii 3 1
I am sorry for thee: thou art come to answer A stony adversary iv 1 3
I am sorry that your leisure serves you not iv 1 405
Sweet Phebe, pity me.—Why, I am sorry for thee *As Y. Like It* iii 5 86
Sorry am I that our good will effects Bianca's grief *T. of Shrew* i 1 86
And for the contents' sake are sorry for our pains *All's Well* iii 2 66
I am heartily sorry that he'll be glad of this iii 3 74
I would be sorry, sir, but the fool should be as oft with your master as with my mistress *T. Night* iii 1 45
I am sorry, madam, I have hurt your kinsman v 1 216
I never wish'd to see you sorry; now I trust I shall *W. Tale* ii 1 123
I am sorry for't: All faults I make, when I shall come to know them, I do repent iii 2 219
I am sorry that by hanging thee I can But shorten thy life one week iv 4 432
I am but sorry, not afeard; delay'd, But nothing alter'd iv 4 474
I am sorry, Most sorry, you have broken from his liking v 1 211
And as sorry Your choice is not so rich in worth as beauty v 1 213
I am sorry, sir, I have thus far stirr'd you v 3 74
I am sorry I should force you to believe That which I would to God I had not seen; But these mine eyes saw him *2 Hen. IV.* i 1 105
I would be sorry, my lord, but it should be thus iv 3 33
Sorry am I his numbers are so few *Hen. V.* iii 5 56
I am sorry that with reverence I did not entertain thee *1 Hen. VI.* ii 3 71
Sorry am I to hear what I have heard *2 Hen. VI.* ii 1 193
He can make obligations, and write court-hand.—I am sorry for't iv 2 102
I am so sorry for my trespass *3 Hen. VI.* v 1 92
Sorry I am my noble cousin should Suspect me *Richard III.* iii 7 88
I am sorry To hear this of him *Hen. VIII.* i 1 193
I am sorry To see you ta'en from liberty i 1 204
I am sorry that the Duke of Buckingham Is run in your displeasure i 2 109
Truly is he, and condemn'd upon't.—I am sorry for't ii 1 9
Subject to your countenance, glad or sorry As I saw it inclined ii 4 26
I am sorry my integrity should breed . . . So deep suspicion iii 1 51
I grieve at what I speak, And am right sorry to repeat what follows v 1 96
I'm very sorry To sit here at this present, and behold That chair stand empty v 3 8
He is much sorry, If any thing more than your sport and pleasure Did move your greatness *Troi. and Cres.* ii 3 116
Art thou not sorry for these heinous deeds?—Ay, that I had not done a thousand more *T. Andron.* v 1 123
I' faith, I am sorry that thou art not well *Rom. and Jul.* ii 5 54
Hollow welcomes, Recanting goodness, sorry ere 'tis shown *T. of Athens* i 2 17
Are sorry—you are honourable,—But yet they could have wish'd ii 2 215
I am sorry, when he sent to borrow of me, that my provision was out iii 6 17
Thou tedious rogue! I am sorry I shall lose A stone by thee iv 3 374
O, forget What we are sorry for ourselves in thee v 1 142
Do not presume too much upon my love; I may do that I shall be sorry for.—You have done that you should be sorry for *J. Cæsar* iv 3 64
I'm sorry they offend you, heartily; Yes, 'faith, heartily *Hamlet* i 5 134
I am sorry. What, have you given him any hard words of late? ii 1 106
I am sorry that with better heed and judgement I had not quoted him ii 1 111
But I am very sorry, good Horatio, That to Laertes I forgot myself v 2 75
I am sorry, then, you have so lost a father *Lear* i 1 249
I am sorry for thee, friend; 'tis the duke's pleasure ii 2 159
I have one part in my heart That's sorry yet for thee iii 2 73
He's dead; I am only sorry He had no other death's-man iv 6 262
We are very sorry for't.—What, in your own part, can you say? *Othello* ii 3 73
I am sorry For your displeasure; but all will sure be well iii 1 44
I am very sorry that you are not well iii 3 289
I am sorry to hear this iii 3 344

Sorry. I am sorry that I am deceived in him . . . *Othello* iv 1 293
I am sorry to find you thus . . . . . . v 1 81
I bleed, sir; but not kill'd.—I am not sorry neither . . v 2 289
I am full sorry That he approves the common liar . *Ant. and Cleo.* i 1 59
I am sorry to give breathing to my purpose . . . i 3 14
For my part, I am sorry it is turned to a drinking . . ii 6 108
Be thou sorry To follow Cæsar in his triumph . . . . iii 13 135
I am much sorry, sir, You put me to forget a lady's manners *Cymbeline* ii 3 109
I am sorry, Cymbeline, That I am to pronounce Augustus Cæsar thine enemy . . . . iii 1 62
Am right sorry that I must report ye My master's enemy . . iii 5 3
Thou shalt know I am son to the queen.—I am sorry for't . iv 2 93
Is't enough I am sorry? So children temporal fathers do appease . v 4 11
Sorry that you have paid too much, and sorry that you are paid too much v 4 164
Thy mother's dead.—I am sorry for't . . . . . v 5 270
I am sorry for thee: By thine own tongue thou art condemn'd . v 5 297
Sorry breakfast. A sorry breakfast for my lord protector . 2 *Hen. VI.* i 4 79
Sorry execution. The place of death and sorry execution *Com. of Errors* v 1 121
Sorry rheum. I have a salt and sorry rheum offends me . *Othello* iii 4 51
Sorry sight. This is a sorry sight.—A foolish thought, to say a sorry sight . . . . *Macbeth* ii 2 21
Sort. I mean, in a sort.—That sort was well fished for . *Tempest* ii 1 104
You do look, my son, in a moved sort, As if you were dismay'd . iv 1 146
To sort some gentlemen well skill'd in music . *T. G. of Ver.* iii 2 92
He doth in some sort confess it . . . . *Mer. Wives* i 1 106
I defy all angels, in any such sort, as they say, but in the way of honesty ii 2 74
When night-dogs run, all sorts of deer are chased . . . v 5 252
It does stink in some sort . . . . *Meas. for Meas.* iii 2 29
Give notice to such men of sort and suit as are to meet him . iv 4 19
But few of any sort, and none of name . . *Much Ado* i 1 7
There was none such in the army of any sort . . . i 1 33
If it sort not well, you may conceal her . . . iv 1 242
Well, I am glad that all things sort so well . . . v 4 7
There are Worthies a-coming will speak their mind in some other sort *L. L. Lost* v 2 590
The shallowest thick-skin of that barren sort . *M. N. Dream* iii 2 13
Russet-pated choughs, many in sort, Rising and cawing . . iii 2 21
None of noble sort Would so offend a virgin . . . iii 2 159
So far am I glad it so did sort . . . . . iii 2 352
But we are spirits of another sort . . . . . iii 2 388
There are a sort of men whose visages Do cream and mantle like a standing pond . . . . . . *Mer. of Venice* i 1 88
Unless you may be won by some other sort than your father's imposition i 2 113
But God sort all! You are welcome home, my lord . . v 1 132
Full of noble device, of all sorts enchantingly beloved . *As Y. Like It* i 1 174
To teach you gamut in a briefer sort . . . *T. of Shrew* iii 1 67
Every night he comes With musics of all sorts . . *All's Well* iii 7 40
I can sing And speak to him in many sorts of music . *T. Night* i 2 58
Are you a party in this business?—In some sort, sir . *W. Tale* iv 4 844
But they can see a sort of traitors here . . *Richard II.* iv 1 246
The better sort, As thoughts of things divine, are intermix'd With scruples . . . . v 5 11
In some sort it jumps with my humour . . . 1 *Hen. IV.* i 2 77
Men of all sorts take a pride to gird at me . . 2 *Hen. IV.* i 2 6
What in me was purchased, Falls upon thee in a more fairer sort . iv 5 201
That must strike sail to spirits of vile sort . . . . v 2 18
They have a king and officers of sorts . . . *Hen. V.* i 2 190
A' did in some sort, indeed, handle women . . . . ii 3 39
My name is Pistol call'd.—It sorts well with your fierceness . iv 1 63
Sort our nobles from our common men . . . . . iv 7 77
It may be his enemy is a gentleman of great sort . . . iv 7 142
What prisoners of good sort are taken? . . . . . iv 8 80
The mayor and all his brethren in best sort . . . . v Prol. 25
I'll sort some other time to visit you . . 1 *Hen. VI.* ii 3 27
Choked with ambition of the meaner sort . . . . ii 5 123
Talk like the vulgar sort of market man . . . . iii 2 4
He then that is not furnish'd in this sort Doth but usurp . iv 1 34
Sort how it will, I shall have gold for all . . 2 *Hen. VI.* i 2 107
A sort of naughty persons, lewdly bent . . . . ii 1 167
I pray thee, sort thy heart to patience . . . . ii 4 68
Lord ambassador Sent from a sort of tinkers to the king . . iii 2 277
Why then it sorts, brave warriors, let's away . 3 *Hen. VI.* ii 1 209
Here I stand to answer thee, Or any he the proudest of thy sort . ii 2 97
Let's on our way in silent sort . . . . . iv 2 28
His currish riddles sort not with this place . . . . v 5 26
Discharge the common sort With pay and thanks . . . v 5 87
Thou keep'st me from the light: But I will sort a pitchy day for thee . v 6 85
I'll sort occasion, As index to the story we late talk'd of *Richard III.* ii 2 148
All may be well; but, if God sort it so, 'Tis more than we deserve . ii 3 36
A sort of vagabonds, rascals, and runaways . . . . v 3 316
Because not there: this woman's answer sorts . *Troi. and Cres.* i 1 109
Let blockish Ajax draw The sort to fight with Hector . . i 3 376
No man alive can love in such a sort The thing he means to kill . iv 1 23
Yet, in a sort, lechery eats itself . . . . . v 4 37
In beastly sort, dragg'd through the shameful field . . . v 10 5
Sing; or express yourself in a more comfortable sort . *Coriolanus* i 3 2
War, in some sort, may be said to be a ravisher . . . iv 5 242
That the weaker sort may wish Good Marcius home again . . iv 6 69
With voices and applause of every sort . . *T. Andron.* i 1 230
In some sort they are better . . . . . . iii 1 39
I'll deceive you in another sort . . . . . . iii 1 191
Help me sort such needful ornaments As you think fit . *Rom. and Jul.* iv 2 34
Properties to his love and tendance All sorts of hearts . *T. of Athens* i 1 58
In some sort, these wants of mine are crown'd, That I account them blessings . . . . ii 2 190
I have heard in some sort of thy miseries.—Thou saw'st them . iv 3 76
For this fault, Assemble all the poor men of your sort . *J. Cæsar* i 1 62
Seldom he smiles, and smiles in such a sort As if he mock'd himself . i 2 205
Am I yourself But, as it were, in sort or limitation? . . ii 1 283
I have bought Golden opinions from all sorts of people . . *Macbeth* i 7 33
Well may it sort that this portentous figure Comes armed . *Hamlet* i 1 109
It is common for the younger sort To lack discretion . . . ii 1 116
I will not sort you with the rest of my servants . . . ii 2 274
An exact command, Larded with many several sorts of reasons . v 2 20
Other sorts offend as well as we . . . . *Pericles* iv 2 40
How dost thou find the inclination of the people, especially of the younger sort? . . . . iv 2 105
Sortance. Such powers As might hold sortance with his quality 2 *Hen. IV.* iv 1 11
Sorted. My will is something sorted with his wish . *T. G. of Ver.* i 3 63
Sorted and consorted, contrary to thy established proclaimed edict *L. L. L.* i 1 261
Sorted. All my pains is sorted to no proof . . . *T. of Shrew* iv 3 43
'Occupy;' which was an excellent good word before it was ill sorted 2 *Hen. IV.* ii 4 162
Hath sorted out a sudden day of joy . . . *Rom. and Jul.* iii 5 110
Sorting. Not sorting with a nuptial ceremony . . *M. N. Dream* v 1 55
Sossius, One of my place in Syria . . . . *Ant. and Cleo.* iii 1 17
Sot. Possess his books; for without them He's but a sot . *Tempest* iii 2 101
Have you make-a de sot of us? . . . . *Mer. Wives* iii 1 119
Thou drone, thou snail, thou slug, thou sot! . *Com. of Errors* ii 2 196
A plague o' these pickle-herring! How now, sot! . . . *T. Night* i 5 129
Sot, didst see Dick surgeon, sot?—O, he's drunk . . . v 1 202
Then he call'd me sot, And told me I had turn'd the wrong side out *Lear* iv 2 8
Or his description Proved us unspeaking sots . . . *Cymbeline* v 5 178
Soto. I think 'twas Soto that your honour means . *T. of Shrew* Ind. 1 88
Sottish. All's but naught; Patience is sottish . *Ant. and Cleo.* iv 15 79
Soud, soud, soud, soud! . . . . . *T. of Shrew* iv 1 145
Sought. I rather think You have not sought her help . *Tempest* v 1 142
I have sought To match my friend Sir Thurio to my daughter *T. G. of V.* iii 1 61
The sailors sought for safety by our boat, And left the ship *Com. of Errors* i 1 77
And tell quaint lies, How honourable ladies sought my love *Mer. of Ven.* iii 4 70
No sooner knew the reason but they sought the remedy . *As Y. Like It* v 2 40
Love sought is good, but given unsought is better . . *T. Night* iii 1 168
If love ambitious sought a match of birth . . . *K. John* ii 1 430
Straight let us seek, or straight we shall be sought . . . v 7 79
A partial slander sought I to avoid . . . . *Richard II.* i 3 241
Dangerous consorted traitors That sought at Oxford thy dire overthrow v 6 16
Sought to entrap me by intelligence . . . 1 *Hen. IV.* iv 3 98
I have not sought the day of this dislike.—You have not sought it! . v 1 26
Men of merit are sought after . . . . 2 *Hen. IV.* ii 4 405
Whose ruin you have sought . . . . . *Hen. V.* ii 2 176
Have I sought every country far and near, And, now it is my chance to find thee out, Must I behold thy timeless cruel death? . 1 *Hen. VI.* v 4 3
That sought to be encompass'd with your crown . . 3 *Hen. VI.* ii 2 3
But those that sought it I could wish more Christians . . *Hen. VIII.* ii 1 64
To those men that sought him sweet as summer . . . . iv 2 54
God turn their hearts! I never sought their malice . . . v 2 15
Yet sought The very way to catch them . . . *Coriolanus* iii 1 79
Whose circling shadows kings have sought to sleep in . *T. Andron.* ii 4 19
You are looked for and called for, asked for and sought for *Rom. and Jul.* i 5 14
Romeo will be older when you have found him than he was when you sought him . . . . ii 4 128
The most you sought was her promotion . . . . . iv 5 71
Here's the book I sought for so . . . . . *J. Cæsar* iv 3 252
By many of these trains hath sought to win me Into his power *Macbeth* iv 3 118
Thou hast sought to make us break our vow, Which we durst never yet *Lear* i 1 171
He sought my life, But lately, very late . . . . iii 4 172
Who, most rebel-like, Sought to be king o'er her . . . iv 3 17
Of us must Pompey presently be sought, Or else he seeks out us *A. and C.* ii 2 161
I sought a husband, in which labour I found that kindness in a father *Pericles* i 1 66
Against the face of death, I sought the purchase of a glorious beauty . i 1 72
Who at fourteen years He sought to murder . . . . v 3 9
Soughtest. The dreaded act which thou So sought'st to hinder *A. and C.* v 2 335
Soul. Poor souls, they perish'd . . . . . *Tempest* i 2 9
I would Have sunk the sea within the earth or ere It should the good ship so have swallow'd and The fraughting souls within her . i 2 13
There is no soul—No, not so much perdition as an hair Betid to any creature in the vessel . . . . i 2 29
Not a soul But felt a fever of the mad . . . . . i 2 208
It goes on, I see, As my soul prompts it . . . . . i 2 420
The fair soul herself Weigh'd between loathness and obedience . ii 1 129
Have I liked several women; never any With so full soul . . iii 1 44
Hear my soul speak: The very instant that I saw you, did My heart fly to your service; there resides . . . . iii 1 63
O, know'st thou not his looks are my soul's food? . *T. G. of Ver.* ii 7 15
There I'll rest, as after much turmoil A blessed soul doth in Elysium . ii 7 38
Whom my very soul abhors . . . . iv 3 17
Whose life's as tender to me as my soul . . . . . v 4 37
Think'st thou I'll endanger my soul gratis? . . *Mer. Wives* ii 2 16
The folly of my soul dares not present itself . . . . ii 2 253
By gar, he has save his soul, dat he is no come . . . ii 3 6
He is a curer of souls, and you a curer of bodies . . . ii 3 40
'Pless my soul, how full of chollors I am! . . . . iii 1 11
As I am a Christians soul now, look you, this is the place appointed . iii 1 96
We have with special soul Elected him our absence to supply *M. for M.* i 1 18
So to enforce or qualify the laws As to your soul seems good . . i 1 67
Why, all the souls that were were forfeit once . . . . ii 2 73
Prayers from preserved souls, From fasting maids . . . ii 2 153
Wrench awe from fools and tie the wiser souls To thy false seeming! . ii 4 14
Longer or shorter, he may be so fitted That his soul sicken not . ii 4 41
Sir, believe this, I had rather give my body than my soul.—I talk not of your soul: our compell'd sins Stand more for number than for accompt . . . . ii 4 56
I'll take it as a peril to my soul, It is no sin at all, but charity.—Pleased you to do't at peril of your soul, Were equal poise of sin and charity ii 4 65
And fit his mind to death, for his soul's rest . . . . ii 4 187
Grace, being the soul of your complexion, shall keep the body of it ever fair . . . . iii 1 187
Our soul Cannot but yield you forth to public thanks . . . v 1 6
Poor soul, She speaks this in the infirmity of sense . . . v 1 46
O, poor souls, Come you to seek the lamb here of the fox? . . v 1 299
A stubborn soul, That apprehends no further than this world . . v 1 485
Her part, poor soul! seeming as burdened With lesser weight *C. of Er.* ii 1 108
My soul should sue as advocate for thee . . . . . i 1 146
Indued with intellectual sense and souls, Of more pre-eminence than fish . . . . ii 1 22
A wretched soul, bruised with adversity, We bid be quiet . . ii 1 34
Against my soul's pure truth why labour you To make it wander? . iii 2 37
She that doth call me husband, even my soul Doth for a wife abhor . iii 2 163
One that before the judgement carries poor souls to hell . . iv 2 40
I am not mad.—O, that thou wert not, poor distressed soul! . . iv 4 62
God help, poor souls, how idly do they talk! . . . . iv 4 132
So befall my soul As this is false he burdens me withal! . . v 1 208
Now, divine air! now is his soul ravished! . . . *Much Ado* ii 3 60
Is it not strange that sheeps' guts should hale souls out of men's bodies? ii 3 62
Or else it were pity but they should suffer salvation, body and soul . iii 3 3
An honest soul, i' faith, sir; by my troth he is, as ever broke bread . iii 5 41
I charge you, on your souls, to utter it . . . . . iv 1 14
Will you with free and unconstrained soul Give me this maid? . . iv 1 25

Soul. Not to knit my soul to an approved wanton . . . *Much Ado* iv 1 45

On my soul, my cousin is belied! . . . iv 1 148

More moving-delicate and full of life, Into the eye and prospect of his soul . . . iv 1 231

I will deal in this As secretly and justly as your soul Should with your body . . . iv 1 250

Think you in your soul the Count Claudio hath wronged Hero?—Yea, as sure as I have a thought or a soul . . . iv 1 331

My soul doth tell me Hero is belied . . . v 1 42

Yet sinn'd I not But in mistaking.—By my soul, nor I . . . v 1 285

My soul's earth's god, and body's fostering patron . . . *L. L. Lost* i 1 223

That unlettered small-knowing soul . . . i 1 254

By my sweet soul, I mean setting thee at liberty . . . iii 1 124

But if thou strive, poor soul, what art thou then? . . . iv 1 94

By my soul, a swain! a most simple clown! . . . iv 1 142

A soul feminine saluteth us . . . iv 2 83

As Horace says in his—What, my soul, verses? . . . iv 2 104

All ignorant that soul that sees thee without wonder . . . iv 2 117

And entreat, Out of a new-sad soul . . . v 2 741

Mirth cannot move a soul in agony . . . v 2 867

Whose unwished yoke My soul consents not to give sovereignty *M. N. D.* i 1 82

Made love to Nedar's daughter, Helena, And won her soul . . . i 1 108

By the simplicity of Venus' doves, By that which knitteth souls . . . i 1 172

She shall pursue it with the soul of love . . . ii 1 182

Pretty soul! she durst not lie Near this lack-love . . . ii 2 76

You must join in souls to mock me too . . . iii 2 150

And extort A poor soul's patience, all to make you sport . . . iii 2 161

Wherefore doth Lysander Deny your love, so rich within his soul? . . . iii 2 229

Hear my excuse: My love, my life, my soul, fair Helena! . . . iii 2 246

Poor souls, they are content To whisper . . . v 1 134

Now am I dead, Now am I fled; My soul is in the sky . . . v 1 308

An evil soul producing holy witness Is like a villain with a smiling cheek, A goodly apple rotten at the heart . . . *Mer. of Venice* i 3 100

Tell me, is my boy, God rest his soul, alive or dead? . . . ii 2 75

Like herself, wise, fair, and true, Shall she be placed in my constant soul . . . ii 6 57

Never shall you lie by Portia's side With an unquiet soul . . . iii 2 308

Whose souls do bear an equal yoke of love . . . iii 4 13

How little is the cost I have bestow'd In purchasing the semblance of my soul From out the state of hellish misery! . . . iii 4 20

Not on thy sole, but on thy soul, harsh Jew, Thou makest thy knife keen . . . iv 1 123

That souls of animals infuse themselves Into the trunks of men . . . iv 1 132

Even from the gallows did his fell soul fleet . . . iv 1 135

I have an oath in heaven: Shall I lay perjury upon my soul? . . . iv 1 229

By my soul I swear There is no power in the tongue of man To alter me iv 1 240

Mounted the Troyan walls And sigh'd his soul toward the Grecian tents v 1 5

Stealing her soul with many vows of faith And ne'er a true one . . . v 1 19

Sweet soul, let's in, and there expect their coming . . . v 1 49

Such harmony is in immortal souls . . . v 1 63

No, by my honour, madam, by my soul, No woman had it . . . v 1 209

By my soul I swear I never more will break an oath with thee . . . v 1 247

My soul upon the forfeit, that your lord Will never more break faith . . . v 1 252

For my soul, yet I know not why, hates nothing more than he *As Y. L. It* i 1 171

My father loved Sir Rowland as his soul . . . i 2 247

Violated vows 'Twixt the souls of friend and friend . . . iii 2 142

She, poor soul, Knows not which way to stand, to look, to speak *T. of S.* iv 1 187

The soul of this man is his clothes . . . *All's Well* ii 5 48

With the divine forfeit of his soul upon oath . . . iii 6 34

But, fair soul, In your fine frame hath love no quality? . . . iv 2 3

I have unclasp'd To thee the book even of my secret soul . . . *T. Night* i 4 14

I think his soul is in hell, madonna.—I know his soul is in heaven, fool.—The more fool, madonna, to mourn for your brother's soul being in heaven . . . i 5 74

Call upon my soul within the house . . . i 5 288

Rouse the night-owl in a catch that will draw three souls out of one weaver . . . ii 3 61

That miracle and queen of gems That nature pranks her in attracts my soul . . . ii 4 89

Fare thee well; and God have mercy upon one of our souls! . . . iii 4 184

A fiend like thee might bear my soul to hell . . . iii 4 237

A devil in private brawl: souls and bodies hath he divorced three . . . iii 4 259

This shall end without the perdition of souls . . . iii 4 318

Beshrew his soul for me, He started one poor heart of mine in thee . . . iv 1 62

What is the opinion of Pythagoras concerning wild fowl?—That the soul of our grandam might haply inhabit a bird . . . iv 2 56

I think nobly of the soul, and no way approve his opinion . . . iv 2 59

Fear to kill a woodcock, lest thou dispossess the soul of thy grandam . . . iv 2 64

My soul disputes well with my sense, That this may be some error . . . iv 3 9

That my most jealous and too doubtful soul May live at peace . . . iv 3 27

My soul the faithfull'st offerings hath breathed out . . . v 1 117

O, that record is lively in my soul! . . . v 1 253

Will I over-swear; And all those swearings keep as true in soul . . . v 1 277

A solemn combination shall be made Of our dear souls . . . v 1 393

A gracious innocent soul, More free than he is jealous . . . *W. Tale* ii 3 29

I do in justice charge thee, On thy soul's peril and thy body's torture . . . ii 3 181

O, the most piteous cry of the poor souls! . . . iii 3 92

How the poor souls roared, and the sea mock'd them . . . iii 3 101

Alack, poor soul! thou hast need of more rags to lay on thee . . . iv 3 57

So much to my good comfort, as it is Now piercing to my soul . . . v 3 34

Who lives and dares but say thou didst not well When I was got, I'll send his soul to hell . . . *K. John* i 1 272

By my soul, I think His father never was so true begot . . . ii 1 129

Then God forgive the sin of all those souls! . . . ii 1 283

Urge them while their souls Are capable of this ambition . . . ii 1 475

Lest that France repent, And by disjoining hands, hell lose a soul . . . iii 1 197

The conjunction of our inward souls Married in league . . . iii 1 227

Within this wall of flesh There is a soul counts thee her creditor . . . iii 3 21

Look, who comes here! a grave unto a soul . . . iii 4 17

Now that their souls are topfull of offence . . . iii 4 180

Heaven take my soul, and England keep my bones! . . . iv 3 10

From whose obedience I forbid my soul, Kneeling before this ruin . . . iv 3 64

Our souls religiously confirm thy words . . . iv 3 73

Away with me, all you whose souls abhor The uncleanly savours . . . iv 3 111

Upon my soul— If thou didst but consent To this most cruel act . . . iv 3 125

Swearing allegiance and the love of soul To stranger blood . . . v 1 10

So, on my soul, he did, for aught he knew . . . v 1 43

It grieves my soul, That I must draw this metal from my side . . . v 2 15

This shower, blown up by tempest of the soul, Startles mine eyes . . . v 2 50

No, no, on my soul, it never shall be said . . . v 2 108

Soul. And part this body and my soul With contemplation and devout desires . . . *K. John* v 4 47

Beshrew my soul But I do love the favour and the form Of this . . . v 4 49

His pure brain, Which some suppose the soul's frail dwelling-house . . . v 7 3

From the organ-pipe of frailty sings His soul and body to their lasting rest . . . v 7 24

Now my soul hath elbow-room; It would not out at windows nor at doors v 7 28

My soul shall wait on thee to heaven, As it on earth hath been thy servant v 7 72

I have a kind soul that would give you thanks And knows not how to do it v 7 108

What I speak My body shall make good upon this earth, Or my divine soul answer it in heaven . . . *Richard II.* i 1 38

Sluiced out his innocent soul through streams of blood . . . i 1 103

Nor partialize The unstooping firmness of my upright soul . . . i 1 121

I lay an ambush for your life, A trespass that doth vex my grieved soul i 1 138

Pierced to the soul with slander's venom'd spear . . . i 1 171

God defend my soul from such deep sin! Shall I seem crest-fall'n? . . . i 1 187

My dancing soul doth celebrate This feast of battle with mine adversary i 3 91

Had the king permitted us, One of our souls had wander'd in the air . . . i 3 195

Bear not along The clogging burthen of a guilty soul . . . i 3 200

What thy soul holds dear, imagine it To lie that way thou go'st . . . i 3 286

This land of such dear souls, this dear dear land, Dear for her reputation ii 1 57

Plain well-meaning soul, Whom fair befal in heaven 'mongst happy souls! ii 1 128

My inward soul With nothing trembles: at some thing it grieves . . . ii 2 11

It may be so; but yet my inward soul Persuades me it is otherwise . . . ii 2 28

Now hath my soul brought forth her prodigy . . . ii 2 64

In nothing else so happy As in a soul remembering my good friends . . . ii 3 47

I will not vex your souls—Since presently your souls must part your bodies . . . iii 1 2

My comfort is that heaven will take our souls And plague injustice . . . iii 1 33

All souls that will be safe fly from my side . . . iii 2 80

Terrible hell make war Upon their spotted souls for this offence! . . . iii 2 134

Again uncurse their souls; their peace is made With heads . . . iii 2 137

Have torn their souls by turning them from us . . . iii 3 83

Now, by my soul, I would it were this hour . . . iv 1 42

There at Venice gave His body to that pleasant country's earth, And his pure soul unto his captain Christ . . . iv 1 99

Sweet peace conduct his sweet soul to the bosom Of good old Abraham! iv 1 103

Who with willing soul Adopts thee heir . . . iv 1 108

O, forfend it, God, That in a Christian climate souls refined Should show so heinous, black, obscene a deed! . . . iv 1 130

The souls of men May deem that you are worthily deposed . . . iv 1 226

I have given here my soul's consent To undeck the pompous body of a king . . . iv 1 249

Shadows to the unseen grief That swells with silence in the tortured soul iv 1 298

Learn, good soul, To think our former state a happy dream . . . v 1 17

We pray with heart and soul and all beside . . . v 3 104

My brain I'll prove the female to my soul, My soul the father . . . v 5 6

Mount, mount, my soul! thy seat is up on high . . . v 5 112

My soul is full of woe, That blood should sprinkle me to make me grow v 6 45

How agrees the devil and thee about thy soul? . . . *1 Hen. IV.* i 2 127

Lost that title of respect Which the proud soul ne'er pays but to the proud . . . i 3 9

Who, on my soul, hath wilfully betray'd The lives of those that he did lead to fight . . . i 3 81

And let my soul Want mercy, if I do not join with him . . . i 3 131

He shall not have a Scot of them; No, if a Scot would save his soul . . . i 3 215

The soul of every man Prophetically doth forethink thy fall . . . iii 2 37

By my sceptre and my soul to boot . . . iii 2 97

Nor did he think it meet To lay so dangerous and dear a trust On any soul removed but on his own . . . iv 1 35

Therein should we read The very bottom and the soul of hope . . . iv 1 50

Welcome, by my soul.—Pray God my news be worth a welcome . . . iv 1 86

There is many a soul Shall pay full dearly for this encounter . . . v 1 83

How show'd his tasking? seem'd it in contempt?—No, by my soul . . . v 2 52

A fool go with thy soul, whither it goes! . . . v 3 22

Before, I loved thee as a brother, John; But now, I do respect thee as my soul . . . v 4 20

Rebellion, did divide The action of their bodies from their souls *2 Hen. IV.* i 1 195

But, for their spirits and souls, This word, rebellion, it had froze them up i 1 198

My lord, this is a poor mad soul . . . ii 1 113

She is in hell already, and burns poor souls . . . ii 4 366

The man nearest my soul, Who like a brother toil'd in my affairs . . . iii 1 61

These griefs shall be with speed redress'd; Upon my soul, they shall . . . iv 2 60

What I did, I did in honour, Led by the impartial conduct of my soul . . . v 2 36

To relief of lazars and weak age, Of indigent faint souls . . . *Hen. V.* i 1 16

Or bow your reading, Or nicely charge your understanding soul . . . i 2 15

His soul Shall stand sore charged for the wasteful vengeance . . . i 2 282

That knew'st the very bottom of my soul . . . ii 2 97

I can never win A soul so easy as that Englishman's . . . ii 2 125

And a' said it was a black soul burning in hell-fire . . . ii 3 44

To take mercy On the poor souls . . . ii 4 104

By my hand, I swear, and my father's soul . . . iii 2 95

A man that I love and honour with my soul, and my heart, and my duty iii 6 8

Proud of their numbers and secure in soul . . . iv Prol. 17

Some soul of goodness in things evil, Would men observingly distil it out iv 1 4

Every subject's duty is the king's; but every subject's soul is his own iv 1 187

Let us our lives, our souls, Our debts, our careful wives, Our children and our sins lay on the king! . . . iv 1 247

What is thy soul of adoration? Art thou aught else but place, degree? iv 1 262

Where the sad and solemn priests Sing still for Richard's soul . . . iv 1 319

Shall suck away their souls, Leaving them but the shales and husks of men . . . iv 2 17

If it be a sin to covet honour, I am the most offending soul alive . . . iv 3 29

That their souls May make a peacefu and a sweet retire . . . iv 3 85

My soul shall thine keep company to heaven; Tarry, sweet soul, for mine iv 6 16

A far more glorious star thy soul will make Than Julius Cæsar *1 Hen. VI.* i 1 55

Blood will I draw on thee, thou art a witch, And straightway give thy soul to him thou servest . . . i 5 7

Now have I paid my vow unto his soul . . . ii 2 7

Send between the red rose and the white A thousand souls to death . . . ii 4 127

Enough: my soul shall then be satisfied . . . ii 5 21

And peace, no war, befall thy parting soul! . . . ii 5 115

O, how this discord doth afflict my soul! . . . iii 1 106

Now, quiet soul, depart when heaven please . . . iii 2 110

Upon no Christian soul but English Talbot . . . iv 2 30

A warning bell, Sings heavy music to thy timorous soul . . . iv 2 40

Then God take mercy on brave Talbot's soul! . . . iv 3 34

Side by side together live and die; And soul with soul from France to heaven fly . . . iv 5 55

Then take my soul, my body, soul and all . . . v 3 22

Soul. For thou hast given me in this beauteous face A world of earthly blessings to my soul . . . . *2 Hen. VI.* i 1 22
But God in mercy so deal with my soul, As I in duty love my king! . i 3 160
God be praised, that to believing souls Gives light in darkness! . ii 1 66
Poor soul, God's goodness hath been great to thee . . . . . ii 1 84
Say as you think, and speak it from your souls . . . . . iii 1 247
I will stir up in England some black storm Shall blow ten thousand souls to heaven or hell . . . . iii 1 350
Stay my thoughts, My thoughts, that labour to persuade my soul! . iii 2 137
With his soul fled all my worldly solace . . . . . . iii 2 151
As surely as my soul intends to live With that dread King . . iii 2 153
And send thy soul to hell, Pernicious blood-sucker of sleeping men! . iii 2 225
Whispers to his pillow as to him The secrets of his overcharged soul . iii 2 376
Grieve I at an hour's poor loss, Omitting Suffolk's exile, my soul's treasure? . . . . iii 2 382
In thy lap? Here could I breathe my soul into the air, As mild and gentle as the cradle-babe . . . . iii 2 391
Stop my mouth; So shouldst thou either turn my flying soul, Or I should breathe it so into thy body . . . . . . iii 2 397
Comb down his hair; look, look! it stands upright, Like lime-twigs set to catch my winged soul . . . . iii 3 16
O, beat away the busy meddling fiend That lays strong siege unto this wretch's soul! . . . . iii 3 22
Peace to his soul, if God's good pleasure be! . . . . . . iii 3 26
God forbid so many simple souls Should perish by the sword! . . iv 4 10
If when you make your prayers, God should be so obdurate as yourselves, How would it fare with your departed souls? . . . iv 7 123
The unconquered soul of Cade is fled . . . . iv 10 69
And as I thrust thy body in with my sword, So wish I, I might thrust thy soul to hell . . . . iv 10 85
A sceptre shall it have, have I a soul . . . . v 1 10
It grieves my soul to leave thee unassail'd . . . . . . v 2 18
My soul and body on the action both!—A dreadful lay! . . . v 2 26
Peace with his soul, heaven, if it be thy will! . . . . . v 2 30
And, by his soul, thou and thy house shall rue it . . . *3 Hen. VI.* i 1 94
The sight of any of the house of York Is as a fury to torment my soul . i 3 31
Upon my soul, the hearers will shed tears . . . . i 4 161
Take me from the world: My soul to heaven, my blood upon your heads! . . . . i 4 168
Weep with him, To see how inly sorrow gripes his soul . . . . i 4 171
Open Thy gate of mercy, gracious God! My soul flies through these wounds to seek out Thee . . . . i 4 178
Now my soul's palace is become a prison: Ah, would she break from hence! . . . . ii 1 74
That Plantagenet, Which held thee dearly as his soul's redemption . ii 1 102
To see this sight, it irks my very soul . . . . ii 2 6
And in this vow do chain my soul to thine! . . . . . . ii 3 34
Yet that thy brazen gates of heaven may ope, And give sweet passage to my sinful soul! . . . . ii 3 41
I fear thy overthrow More than my body's parting with my soul! . . ii 6 4
Whose soul is that which takes her heavy leave? . . . . . ii 6 42
And thou, poor soul, Art then forsaken, as thou went'st forlorn! . . iii 1 53
I swear to thee I speak no more than what my soul intends . . . iii 2 94
And yet, between my soul's desire and me . . . Is Clarence, Henry . iii 2 128
Take my hand, And with thy lips keep in my soul awhile! . . . v 2 35
Sweet rest his soul! Fly, lords, and save yourselves . . . . v 2 48
Now am I seated as my soul delights, Having my country's peace . v 7 35
Instead of mounting barbed steeds To fright the souls of fearful adversaries . . . . *Richard III.* i 1 11
Dive, thoughts, down to my soul: here Clarence comes . . . . i 1 41
I will shortly send thy soul to heaven, If heaven will take the present . i 1 119
Thou hadst but power over his mortal body, His soul thou canst not have . . . . i 2 48
And let the soul forth that adoreth thee . . . . i 2 177
From bitterness of soul Denounced against thee . . . . . i 3 179
The worm of conscience still begnaw thy soul! . . . . . . i 3 222
Still the envious flood Kept in my soul, and would not let it forth . i 4 38
My dream was lengthen'd after life; O, then began the tempest to my soul . . . . i 4 44
The first that there did greet my stranger soul, Was my great father-in-law . . . . i 4 48
I have done those things, Which now bear evidence against my soul . i 4 67
My soul is heavy, and I fain would sleep . . . . i 4 74
And charged us from his soul to love each other . . . . . i 4 243
Hast thou that holy feeling in thy soul, To counsel me to make my peace with God, And art thou yet to thy own soul so blind, That thou wilt war with God? . . . . i 4 257
What shall we do?—Relent, and save your souls . . . . . i 4 263
Now in peace my soul shall part to heaven, Since I have set my friends at peace on earth . . . . ii 1 5
I do not know that Englishman alive With whom my soul is any jot at odds . . . . ii 1 70
But he, poor soul, by your first order died . . . . . . ii 1 87
I pray thee, peace: my soul is full of sorrow . . . . . . ii 1 96
How the poor soul did forsake The mighty Warwick, and did fight for me . . . . ii 1 109
Nor I, ungracious, speak unto myself For him, poor soul . . . ii 1 128
I'll join with black despair against my soul . . . . . . ii 2 36
Be brief, That our swift-winged souls may catch the king's . . . ii 2 44
Truly, the souls of men are full of dread . . . . ii 3 38
To shun the danger that his soul divines . . . . iii 2 18
Wherein my soul recorded The history of all her secret thoughts . . iii 5 27
Not sleeping, to engross his idle body, But praying, to enrich his watchful soul . . . . iii 7 77
Albeit against my conscience and my soul . . . . iii 7 226
Go, go, poor soul, I envy not thy glory . . . . iv 1 64
And proved the subject of my own soul's curse . . . . . iv 1 81
I pity thy complaining.—No more than from my soul I mourn for yours . . . . iv 1 89
Woful welcomer of glory!—Adieu, poor soul, that takest thy leave of it! . . . . iv 1 91
If yet your gentle souls fly in the air And be not fix'd in doom perpetual iv 4 11
Grand tyrant of the earth, That reigns in galled eyes of weeping souls . iv 4 53
The little souls of Edward's children Whisper the spirits of thine enemies . . . . iv 4 191
So in the Lethe of thy angry soul Thou drown the sad remembrance . iv 4 250
Then know, that from my soul I love thy daughter.—My daughter's mother thinks it with her soul.—What do you think?—That thou dost love my daughter from thy soul: So from thy soul's love didst thou love her brothers . . . . iv 4 255

Soul. I mean, that with my soul I love thy daughter, And mean to make her queen . . . . *Richard III.* iv 4 262
With a fearful soul Leads discontented steps in foreign soil . . . iv 4 311
To thee, herself, and many a Christian soul, Death, desolation, ruin . iv 4 408
If that your moody discontented souls Do through the clouds behold this present hour, Even for revenge mock my destruction! . . . v 1 7
All-Souls' day to my fearful soul Is the determined respite of my wrongs v 1 18
To thee I do commend my watchful soul . . . . v 3 115
Let me sit heavy on thy soul to-morrow! . . . . . v 3 118; 131; 139
For the wronged souls Of butcher'd princes fight in thy behalf . . v 3 121
Think upon Grey, and let thy soul despair! . . . . . . v 3 141
Quiet untroubled soul, awake, awake! Arm, fight, and conquer! . . v 3 149
Thy nephews' souls bid thee despair and die! . . . . . . v 3 154
Thou quiet soul, sleep thou a quiet sleep; Dream of success! . . v 3 164
There is no creature loves me; And if I die, no soul shall pity me . v 3 201
Methought the souls of all that I had murder'd Came to my tent . . v 3 204
Shadows to-night Have struck more terror to the soul of Richard . . v 3 217
Methought their souls, whose bodies Richard murder'd, Came to my tent v 3 230
My soul is very jocund In the remembrance of so fair a dream . . v 3 232
The prayers of holy saints and wronged souls, Like high-rear'd bulwarks v 3 241
Let not our babbling dreams affright our souls . . . . . v 3 308
There is no English soul More stronger to direct you than yourself *Hen. VIII.* i 1 146
Charge not in your spleen a noble person And spoil your nobler soul . i 2 175
On my soul, I'll speak but truth . . . . i 2 177
Make of your prayers one sweet sacrifice, And lift my soul to heaven . ii 1 78
And, till my soul forsake, Shall cry for blessings on him . . . ii 1 89
He dives into the king's soul, and there scatters Dangers, doubts . ii 2 27
'Tis a sufferance panging As soul and body's severing . . . . ii 3 16
I utterly abhor, yea, from my soul Refuse you for my judge . . . ii 4 81
My soul grows sad with troubles; Sing, and disperse 'em, if thou canst iii 1 1
Would all other women Could speak this with as free a soul as I do! . iii 1 32
Holy men I thought ye, Upon my soul, two reverend cardinal virtues . iii 1 103
I know you have a gentle, noble temper, A soul as even as a calm . . iii 1 166
Crack their duty to you, And throw it from their soul . . . . iii 2 194
By my soul, Your long coat, priest, protects you . . . . . iii 2 275
I am able now, methinks, Out of a fortitude of soul I feel, To endure . iii 2 388
Sir, as I have a soul, she is an angel . . . . iv 1 44
For virtue and true beauty of the soul, For honesty and decent carriage iv 2 144
As you wish Christian peace to souls departed . . . . . iv 2 156
I swear he is true-hearted; and a soul None better in my kingdom . v 1 154
Win straying souls with modesty again, Cast none away . . . . v 3 64
Saba was never More covetous of wisdom and fair virtue Than this pure soul shall be . . . . v 5 26
Things won are done; joy's soul lies in the doing . *Troi. and Cres.* i 2 313
Nerve and bone of Greece, Heart of our numbers, soul and only spirit . i 3 56
Or those that with the fineness of their souls By reason guide . . i 3 209
If none of them have soul in such a kind, We left them all at home . i 3 285
Choice, being mutual act of all our souls, Makes merit her election . i 3 348
Every tithe soul, 'mongst many thousand dismes, Hath been as dear . ii 2 19
The mortal Venus, the heart-blood of beauty, love's invisible soul . . iii 1 35
Like a strange soul upon the Stygian banks Staying for waftage . . iii 2 10
See, see, your silence, Cunning in dumbness, from my weakness draws My very soul of counsel! . . . . iii 2 141
There is a mystery—with whom relation Durst never meddle—in the soul of state . . . . iii 3 202
Tell me true, Even in the soul of sound good-fellowship . . . . iv 1 52
No kin, no love, no blood, no soul so near me As the sweet Troilus . iv 2 104
And with private soul Did in great Ilion thus translate him to me . iv 5 111
To make a recordation to my soul Of every syllable that here was spoke v 2 116
If beauty have a soul, this is not she; If souls guide vows . . . v 2 138
Within my soul there doth conduce a fight Of this strange nature . . v 2 147
Never did young man fancy With so eternal and so fix'd a soul . . v 2 166
You souls of geese, That bear the shapes of men . . . *Coriolanus* i 4 34
There is the man of my soul's hate, Aufidius, Piercing our Romans . i 5 11
Of no more soul nor fitness for the world Than camels in the war . . ii 1 266
And my soul aches To know . . . . iii 1 108
With wine and feeding, we have suppler souls Than in our priest-like fasts . . . . v 1 55
Let Andronicus Make this his latest farewell to their souls . *T. Andron.* i 1 149
Titus, more than half my soul,— Dear father, soul and substance of us all i 1 373
The empress of my soul, Which never hopes more heaven than rests in thee . . . . ii 3 40
Be pitiful to my condemned sons, Whose souls are not corrupted . . iii 1 9
In the dust I write My heart's deep languor and my soul's sad tears . iii 1 13
That which gives my soul the greatest spurn, is dear Lavinia, dearer than my soul . . . . iii 1 101
Aaron will have his soul black like his face . . . . . . iii 1 206
Swear unto my soul to right your wrongs . . . . iii 1 279
'Twill vex thy soul to hear what I shall speak . . . . . . v 1 62
If one good deed in all my life I did, I do repent it from my very soul v 3 190
Susan and she—God rest all Christian souls!—Were of an age *R. and J.* i 3 18
My husband—God be with his soul! A' was a merry man . . . . i 3 39
I have a soul of lead So stakes me to the ground I cannot move . . i 4 15
God shall mend my soul! You'll make a mutiny among my guests! . i 5 81
So thrive my soul . . . . ii 2 154
It is my soul that calls upon my name . . . . ii 2 165
But she, good soul, had as lief see a toad, a very toad, as see him . ii 4 215
Mercutio's soul Is but a little way above our heads, Staying for thine . iii 1 131
How is't, my soul? let's talk; it is not day . . . . . . iii 5 25
O God, I have an ill-divining soul! . . . . iii 5 54
Die in the streets, For, by my soul, I'll ne'er acknowledge thee . . iii 5 195
Speakest thou from thy heart?—And from my soul too . . . . iii 5 228
Poor soul, thy face is much abused with tears . . . . . . iv 1 29
O child! O child! my soul, and not my child! Dead art thou! . . iv 5 62
There is thy gold, worse poison to men's souls, Doing more murders in this loathsome world, Than these poor compounds that thou mayst not sell . . . . v 1 80
What said my man, when my betossed soul Did not attend him as we rode? . . . . v 3 76
O, he's the very soul of bounty! . . . . *T. of Athens* i 2 215
This is the world's soul; and just of the same piece Is every flatterer's spirit . . . . iii 2 71
Take't of my soul, my lord leans wondrously to discontent . . . iii 4 70
You only speak from your distracted soul . . . . iii 4 115
Here lies a wretched corse, of wretched soul bereft: Seek not my name v 4 70
Cried 'Alas, good soul!' and forgave him with all their hearts *J. Cæsar* i 2 275
The sufferance of our souls, the time's abuse,—If these be motives weak ii 1 115
Old feeble carrions and such suffering souls That welcome wrongs . ii 1 130
Soul of Rome! Brave son, derived from honourable loins! . . . ii 1 321

Soul. Poor soul! his eyes are red as fire with weeping . . *J. Cæsar* iii 2 120
Kind souls, what, weep you when you but behold Our Cæsar's vesture wounded? . . . . iii 2 199
Never come such division 'tween our souls! Let it not, Brutus . iv 3 235
And all things else that might To half a soul and to a notion crazed *Macbeth* iii 1 83
Thy soul's flight, If it find heaven, must find it out to-night . . iii 1 141
His wife, his babes, and all unfortunate souls That trace him in his line iv 1 152
Hath from my soul Wiped the black scruples . . . . . iv 3 115
There are a crew of wretched souls That stay his cure . . . iv 3 141
Not for their own demerits, but for mine, Fell slaughter on their souls iv 3 227
Death of thy soul! those linen cheeks of thine Are counsellors to fear . v 3 16
Get thee back; my soul is too much charged With blood of thine already v 8 5
Would the night were come! Till then sit still, my soul *Hamlet* i 2 257
As this temple waxes, The inward service of the mind and soul Grows wide . . . . i 3 13
Those friends thou hast, and their adoption tried, Grapple them to thy soul with hoops of steel . . . . i 3 63
When the blood burns, how prodigal the soul Lends the tongue vows . i 3 116
With thoughts beyond the reaches of our souls . . . . i 4 56
And for my soul, what can it do to that, Being a thing immortal as itself? i 4 66
I could a tale unfold whose lightest word Would harrow up thy soul . i 5 16
O my prophetic soul! My uncle! . . . . i 5 40
Taint not thy mind, nor let thy soul contrive Against thy mother aught i 5 85
I hold my duty, as I hold my soul, Both to my God and to my gracious king . . . . ii 2 44
Brevity is the soul of wit, And tediousness the limbs and outward flourishes . . . . ii 2 90
To the celestial and my soul's idol, the most beautified Ophelia . ii 2 109
In a dream of passion, Could force his soul so to his own conceit . . ii 2 579
Struck so to the soul that presently They have proclaim'd their malefactions . . . . ii 2 620
There's something in his soul, O'er which his melancholy sits on brood iii 1 172
O, it offends me to the soul to hear a robustious periwig-pated fellow . iii 2 10
Since my dear soul was mistress of her choice And could of men distinguish . . . . iii 2 68
Even with the very comment of thy soul Observe mine uncle . . iii 2 84
We that have free souls, it touches us not: let the galled jade wince . iii 2 252
Let not ever The soul of Nero enter this firm bosom . . . iii 2 412
My tongue and soul in this be hypocrites; How in my words soever she be shent, To give them seals never, my soul, consent! . . . iii 2 415
O limed soul, that, struggling to be free, Art more engaged! . . . iii 3 68
To take him in the purging of his soul, When he is fit and season'd . iii 3 85
And that his soul may be as damn'd and black As hell, whereto it goes iii 3 94
O, such a deed As from the body of contraction plucks The very soul . iii 4 47
Speak no more: Thou turn'st mine eyes into my very soul . . iii 4 89
Amazement on thy mother sits: O, step between her and her fighting soul . . . . iii 4 113
For love of grace, Lay not that flattering unction to your soul . iii 4 145
O, come away! My soul is full of discord and dismay . . . iv 1 45
Two thousand souls and twenty thousand ducats Will not debate the question . . . . iv 4 25
To my sick soul, as sin's true nature is, Each toy seems prologue to some great amiss: So full of artless jealousy is guilt . . . iv 5 17
God ha' mercy on his soul! And of all Christian souls . . . iv 5 199
We shall jointly labour with your soul To give it due content . . iv 5 211
She's so conjunctive to my life and soul . . . . . iv 7 14
One that was a woman, sir; but, rest her soul, she's dead . . v 1 147
We should profane the service of the dead To sing a requiem and such rest to her As to peace-parted souls . . . . . . v 1 261
The devil take thy soul!—Thou pray'st not well . . . . v 1 281
In the verity of extolment, I take him to be a soul of great article . v 2 122
Bring some covering for this naked soul . . . . *Lear* iv 1 46
Thou art a soul in bliss; but I am bound Upon a wheel of fire . iv 7 46
Friends of my soul, you twain Rule in this realm . . . v 3 319
These fellows have some soul: And such a one do I profess myself *Othello* i 1 54
Your heart is burst, you have lost half your soul . . . . i 1 87
In simple and pure soul I come to you . . . . . i 1 107
That, for their souls, Another of his fathom they have none . . i 1 152
My parts, my title, and my perfect soul Shall manifest me rightly . i 2 31
Came it by request and such fair question As soul to soul affordeth? . i 3 114
I am glad at soul I have no other child . . . . . i 3 196
To his honours . . . Did I my soul and fortunes consecrate . . i 3 255
Heaven defend your good souls, that you think I will . . . i 3 267
O my soul's joy! . . . . ii 1 186
My soul hath her content so absolute . . . . . . ii 1 193
Lay thy finger thus, and let thy soul be instructed . . . . ii 1 223
Nothing can or shall content my soul Till I am even'd with him . . ii 1 307
There be souls must be saved, and there be souls must not be saved . ii 3 106
He that stirs next to carve for his own rage Holds his soul light . ii 3 174
His soul is so enfetter'd to her love, That she may make, unmake . ii 3 351
I wonder in my soul, What you would ask me, that I should deny. . iii 3 68
Excellent wretch! Perdition catch my soul, But I do love thee! . . iii 3 90
Good name in man and woman, dear my lord, Is the immediate jewel of their souls: Who steals my purse steals trash . . . . iii 3 156
Good heaven, the souls of all my tribe defend From jealousy! . . iii 3 175
Exchange me for a goat, When I shall turn the business of my soul To such exsufflicate and blown surmises . . . . . . iii 3 181
By the worth of man's eternal soul, Thou hadst been better have been born a dog Than answer my waked wrath! . . . . . iii 3 361
Are you a man? have you a soul or sense? God be wi' you . . iii 3 374
There are a kind of men so loose of soul, That in their sleeps will mutter iii 3 416
I was . . . Arraigning his unkindness with my soul . . . iii 4 152
I never gave him cause.—But jealous souls will not be answer'd so . iii 4 159
I durst, my lord, to wager she is honest, Lay down my soul at stake . iv 2 13
I should have found in some place of my soul A drop of patience . iv 2 52
The poor soul sat sighing by a sycamore tree, Sing all a green willow . iv 3 41
It is the cause, it is the cause, my soul,—Let me not name it to you . v 2 1
I would not kill thy unprepared spirit; No; heaven forfend! I would not kill thy soul.—Talk you of killing? . . . . . . v 2 32
No, by my life and soul! Send for the man, and ask him . . v 2 49
Sweet soul, take heed, Take heed of perjury; thou art on thy death-bed v 2 50
May his pernicious soul Rot half a grain a day! . . . . v 2 155
Upon my soul, a lie, a wicked lie . . . . . . v 2 181
So come my soul to bliss, as I speak true; So speaking as I think, I die v 2 250
This look of thine will hurl my soul from heaven . . . . v 2 274
Demand that demi-devil Why he hath thus ensnared my soul and body? v 2 302
Betray'd I am: O this false soul of Egypt! . *Ant. and Cleo.* iv 12 25
The soul and body rive not more in parting Than greatness going off . iv 13 5
Where souls do couch on flowers, we'll hand in hand . . . iv 14 51
Soul. How slow his soul sail'd on, How swift his ship . . *Cymbeline* i 3 13
Whose every touch would force the feeler's soul To the oath of loyalty. i 6 101
O dearest soul! your cause doth strike my heart With pity . . . i 6 118
To knit their souls, On whom there is no more dependency But brats and beggary, in self-figured knot . . . . . . ii 3 122
No single soul Can we set eye on . . . . iv 2 130
To darkness fleet souls that fly backwards . . . . . v 3 25
Hang there like fruit, my soul, Till the tree die! . . . . v 5 263
With a soul Embolden'd with the glory of her praise . . *Pericles* i 1 3
You were not so bad As with foul incest to abuse your soul . . . i 1 126
Makes both my body pine and soul to languish . . . . . i 2 31
Poor souls, it grieved my heart to hear what pitiful cries they made . ii 1 21
What a man cannot get, he may lawfully deal for—his wife's soul . . ii 1 121
Soul-confirming. Twenty thousand soul-confirming oaths *T. G. of Ver.* ii 6 16
Soul-curer. French and Welsh, soul-curer and body-curer *Mer. Wives* iii 1 100
Soul-fearing. Their soul-fearing clamours . . . . *K. John* ii 1 383
Soul-killing witches that deform the body . . *Com. of Errors* i 2 100
Soulless. Slave, soulless villain, dog! O rarely base! . *Ant. and Cleo.* v 2 157
Soul-vexed. On this stage, Where we're offenders now, appear soul-vex'd, And begin, 'Why to me?' . . . . *W. Tale* v 1 59
Sound. Where should this music be? i' the air or the earth? It sounds no more . . . . *Tempest* i 2 388
This is no mortal business, nor no sound That the earth owes . . i 2 406
O heaven, O earth, bear witness to this sound! . . . . iii 1 68
Sounds and sweet airs, that give delight and hurt not . . . iii 2 145
The sound is going away; let's follow it . . . . . iii 2 157
I cannot too much muse Such shapes, such gesture and such sound . iii 3 37
And deeper than did ever plummet sound I'll drown my book . . v 1 56
How oddly will it sound that I Must ask my child forgiveness! . . v 1 197
Howling, jingling chains, And moe diversity of sounds, all horrible . v 1 234
I have a disguise to sound Falstaff . . . . . *Mer. Wives* ii 1 246
Terms! names! Amaimon sounds well; Lucifer, well . . . ii 2 311
Let the supposed fairies pinch him sound . . . . . iv 4 61
Sleep she as sound as careless infancy . . . . . v 5 56
Thou art full of error; I am sound.—Nay, not as one would say, healthy; but so sound as things that are hollow *Meas. for Meas.* i 2 54
Let it not sound a thought upon your tongue Against my brother's life ii 2 140
Try your penitence, if it be sound, Or hollowly put on . . . ii 3 22
I remember you, sir, by the sound of your voice . . . . iv 1 330
I tell you, 'twill sound harshly in her ears . . *Com. of Errors* iv 4 7
I long that we were safe and sound aboard . . . . . iv 4 154
Converting all your sounds of woe Into Hey nonny, nonny . *Much Ado* ii 3 70
He hath a heart as sound as a bell . . . . . . iii 2 13
Now, music, sound, and sing your solemn hymn . . . . v 3 11
A lover's ear will hear the lowest sound . . . *L. L. Lost* iv 3 335
The trumpet sounds: be mask'd; the maskers come . . . v 2 157
My love to thee is sound, sans crack or flaw . . . . v 2 415
Making it momentany as a sound, Swift as a shadow . *M. N. Dream* i 1 143
Sleeping sound, On the dank and dirty ground . . . . ii 2 74
What, out of hearing? gone? no sound, no word? Alack, where are you? ii 2 152
Mine ear, I thank it, brought me to thy sound . . . . iii 2 182
On the ground Sleep sound . . . . iii 2 449
Sound, music! Come, my queen, take hands with me . . . iv 1 90
Like a child on a recorder; a sound, but not in government . . v 1 123
Thou shalt not know the sound of thine own tongue *Mer. of Venice* i 1 109
Let not the sound of shallow foppery enter My sober house . . ii 5 35
Let music sound while he doth make his choice . . . . iii 2 43
Those dulcet sounds in break of day . . . . . . iii 2 51
Your exposition Hath been most sound . . . . . . iv 1 238
Here will we sit and let the sounds of music Creep in our ears . . v 1 55
If they but hear perchance a trumpet sound, Or any air of music . . v 1 75
Nor is not moved with concord of sweet sounds . . . . . v 1 84
Methinks it sounds much sweeter than by day . . . . . v 1 100
His big manly voice, Turning again toward childish treble, pipes And whistles in his sound . . . . . . *As Y. Like It* ii 7 163
Ready when he wakes, To make a dulcet and a heavenly sound *T. of S.* Ind. 1 51
Go see what trumpet 'tis that sounds . . . . . . Ind. 1 74
This contents: The rest will comfort, for thy counsel's sound . . i 1 169
To sound the depth of this knavery . . . . v 1 141
Methinks in thee some blessed spirit doth speak His powerful sound within an organ weak . . . . *All's Well* ii 1 179
The muster-file, rotten and sound, upon my life, amounts not to fifteen thousand poll . . . . iv 3 189
Like the sweet sound, That breathes upon a bank of violets . *T. Night* i 1 5
Thy small pipe Is as the maiden's organ, shrill and sound . . . i 4 33
Rotten As ever oak or stone was sound . . . . . *W. Tale* ii 3 90
The latest breath that gave the sound of words Was deep-sworn faith *K. John* iii 1 230
Sound on into the drowsy race of night . . . . . . iii 3 39
Using conceit alone, Without eyes, ears and harmful sound of words . iii 3 51
To sound the purposes of all their hearts . . . . . . iv 2 48
Sound but another, and another shall As loud as thine rattle . . v 2 171
Ere my tongue Shall . . . sound so base a parle . . *Richard II.* i 1 192
Sound, trumpets; and set forward, combatants . . . . . i 3 117
Let the trumpets sound While we return these dukes what we decree . i 3 121
Flattering sounds, As praises, of whose taste the wise are fond, Lascivious metres, to whose venom sound The open ear of youth doth always listen . . . . ii 1 17
How dares thy harsh rude tongue sound this unpleasing news? . . iii 4 74
This fester'd joint cut off, the rest rest sound . . . . . v 3 85
The sound that tells what hour it is Are clamorous groans . . . v 5 55
This music mads me; let it sound no more . . . . . v 5 61
That bears a frosty sound . . . . *1 Hen. IV.* iv 1 128
Sound all the lofty instruments of war . . . . . . v 2 98
The trumpet sounds retreat; the day is ours . . . . . v 4 163
And his tongue Sounds ever after as a sullen bell . . *2 Hen. IV.* i 1 102
His coffers sound With hollow poverty and emptiness . . . . i 3 74
Where nothing but the sound of Hotspur's name Did seem defensible . ii 3 37
Lull'd with sound of sweetest melody . . . . iii 1 14
Much too shallow, To sound the bottom of the after-times . . . iv 2 51
Sleep with it now! Yet not so sound and half so deeply sweet . . iv 5 26
This sleep is sound indeed; this is a sleep . . . . . iv 5 35
My voice shall sound as you do prompt mine ear . . . . v 2 119
There roar'd the sea, and trumpet-clangor sounds . . . . v 5 42
Hear the shrill whistle which doth order give To sounds confused *Hen. V.* iii Prol. 10
The work ish give over, the trompet sound the retreat . . . iii 2 94
A soldier, firm and sound of heart, And of buxom valour . . . iii 6 27
Through the foul womb of night The hum of either army stilly sounds iv Prol. 5
Let the trumpets sound The tucket sonance and the note to mount . iv 2 34

Sound. The saying is true, 'The empty vessel makes the greatest sound' *Hen. V.* iv 4 74
Sound, sound alarum! we will rush on them 1 *Hen. VI.* i 2 18
Let thy looks be stern: By this means shall we sound what skill she hath i 2 63
Whilst any trump did sound, or drum struck up, His sword did ne'er leave striking in the field i 4 80
Here sound retreat, and cease our hot pursuit ii 2 3
By the sound of drum you may perceive Their powers are marching iii 3 29
Sound, trumpets, alarum to the combatants! 2 *Hen. VI.* ii 3 95
Can chase away the first-conceived sound iii 2 44
Thy name affrights me, in whose sound is death iv 1 33
Dare any be so bold to sound retreat or parley? iv 8 4
Now let the general trumpet blow his blast, Particularities and petty sounds To cease! v 2 44
Sound drums and trumpets, and to London all v 3 32
Sound drums and trumpets, and the king will fly 3 *Hen. VI.* i 1 118
Stay we no longer, dreaming of renown, But sound the trumpets ii 1 200
Sound trumpets! let our bloody colours wave! ii 2 173
Now death shall stop his dismal threatening sound ii 6 58
Sound trumpet; Edward shall be here proclaim'd iv 7 69
Go, trumpet, to the walls, and sound a parle v 1 16
Two braver men Ne'er spurr'd their coursers at the trumpet's sound v 7 9
Sound drums and trumpets! farewell sour annoy! v 7 45
Sound thou Lord Hastings, How he doth stand affected *Richard III.* iii 1 170
I have consider'd in my mind The late demand that you did sound me in iv 2 87
Look that my staves be sound, and not too heavy v 3 65
Sound drums and trumpets boldly and cheerfully; God and Saint George! v 3 269
The trumpets sound: stand close, the queen is coming *Hen. VIII.* iv 1 36
He cast his eyes upon me! Pray heaven, he sound not my disgrace! v 2 13
Ye are not sound.—Not sound?—Not sound, I say. v 3 81
Hark! the trumpets sound; They're come already from the christening v 4 86
Peace, you ungracious clamours! peace, rude sounds! *Troi. and Cres.* i 1 92
Doth think it rich to hear the wooden dialogue and sound i 3 155
When fame shall in our islands sound her trump iii 3 210
Ho! bid my trumpet sound.—No notes of sally, for the heavens v 3 13
A retire upon our Grecian part.—The Trojan trumpets sound the like v 8 16
Thy grim looks and The thunder-like percussion of thy sounds *Coriolanus* i 4 59
Go, sound thy trumpet in the market-place i 5 27
I know the sound of Marcius' tongue From every meaner man i 6 26
O, let me clip ye In arms as sound as when I woo'd! i 6 30
May these same instruments, which you profane, Never sound more! i 9 42
And will deny him: I'll have five hundred voices of that sound ii 3 219
Do not take His rougher accents for malicious sounds iii 3 55
A name unmusical to the Volscians' ears, And harsh in sound to thine iv 5 65
Go sound the ocean, and cast your nets *T. Andron.* iv 3 7
My ears have not yet drunk a hundred words Of that tongue's utterance, yet I know the sound *Rom. and Jul.* ii 2 59
How silver-sweet sound lovers' tongues by night, Like softest music! ii 2 166
If he be slain, say 'I;' or if not, no: Brief sounds determine of my weal or woe iii 2 51
Then, dreadful trumpet, sound the general doom! iii 2 67
No limit, measure, bound, In that word's death; no words can that woe sound iii 2 126
Marry, and amen, how sound is she asleep! I must needs wake her iv 5 8
'Then music with her silver sound'—why 'silver sound?' iv 5 130
Marry, sir, because silver hath a sweet sound iv 5 134
I say 'silver sound,' because musicians sound for silver iv 5 136
'Music with her silver sound,' because musicians have no gold for sounding iv 5 143
Then music with her silver sound With speedy help doth lend redress iv 5 144
Most resemble sweet instruments hung up in cases that keep their sounds to themselves *T. of Athens* i 2 103
Feast your ears with the music awhile, if they will fare so harshly o' the trumpet's sound iii 6 37
Crack the lawyer's voice, That he may never more false title plead, Nor sound his quillets shrilly iv 3 155
Sound to this coward and lascivious town Our terrible approach v 4 1
That Tiber trembled underneath her banks, To hear the replication of your sounds Made in her concave shores *J. Cæsar* i 1 51
Sound them, it doth become the mouth as well; Weigh them, it is as heavy i 2 145
Shall we sound him? I think he will stand very strong with us ii 1 141
Therefore thou sleep'st so sound ii 1 233
Is there no voice more worthy than my own, To sound more sweetly? iii 1 50
Why do you start; and seem to fear Things that do sound so fair? *Macbeth* i 3 52
I'll charm the air to give a sound, While you perform your antic round iv 1 129
Let not your ears despise my tongue for ever, Which shall possess them with the heaviest sound That ever yet they heard iv 3 202
Find her disease, And purge it to a sound and pristine health v 3 52
It is a tale Told by an idiot, full of sound and fury, Signifying nothing v 5 27
If thou hast any sound, or use of voice, Speak to me *Hamlet* i 1 128
The morning cock crew loud, And at the sound it shrunk in haste away i 2 219
Your party in converse, him you would sound ii 1 42
They are not a pipe for fortune's finger To sound what stop she please iii 2 76
You would sound me from my lowest note to the top of my compass iii 2 383
Nor are those empty-hearted whose low sound Reverbs no hollowness *Lear* i 1 155
Hast heavy substance; bleed'st not; speak'st; art sound iv 6 52
Most sure and vulgar: every one hears that, Which can distinguish sound iv 6 215
If you have victory, let the trumpet sound v 1 41
Come hither, herald,—Let the trumpet sound,—And read out this v 3 107
Let him appear by the third sound of the trumpet v 3 114
What an eye she has! methinks it sounds a parley of provocation *Othello* ii 3 23
When to sound your name It not concern'd me *Ant. and Cleo.* ii 2 34
Bid a loud farewell To these great fellows: sound and be hang'd, sound out! ii 7 140
That heaven and earth may strike their sounds together, Applauding our approach iv 8 38
My ingenious instrument! Hark, Polydore, it sounds! *Cymbeline* iv 2 187
O melancholy! Who ever yet could sound thy bottom? iv 2 204
Our tongues and sorrows do sound deep Our woes into the air *Pericles* i 4 13
Like to gnats, Which make a sound, but kill'd are wonder'd at ii 3 63
And every one with claps can sound, 'Our heir-apparent is a king!' iii Gower 36
The rough and woeful music that we have, Cause it to sound, beseech you iii 2 89
Wound The cambric, which she made more sound By hurting it iv Gower 24
Rarest sounds! Do ye not hear? v 1 233
Sound affection. This shows a sound affection *W. Tale* iv 4 390
Sound cudgel. As much as one sound cudgel of four foot *Hen. VIII.* v 4 19
Sound direction. Call for some men of sound direction *Richard III.* v 3 16
Sound good-fellowship. Tell me true, Even in the soul of sound good-fellowship *Troi. and Cres.* iv 1 52
Sound jest. Here's no sound jest! *T. Andron.* iv 2 26
Sound legs. False hearts should never have sound legs *T. of Athens* i 2 240
'Tis the better for you that your resorters stand upon sound legs *Pericles* iv 6 27
Sound man. To take the indisposed and sickly fit For the sound man *Lear* ii 4 113
Sound ones. For what reason?—For two; and sound ones too *Com. of Er.* ii 2 92
Sound opinion. Makes sound opinion sick and truth suspected *K. John* iv 2 26
Sound parts. What is infirm from your sound parts shall fly *All's Well* ii 1 170
Sound pine. Infect the sound pine and divert his grain *Troi. and Cres.* i 3 8
Sound rottenness. Thou odoriferous stench! sound rottenness! *K. John* iii 4 26
Sound sheep's heart. I take upon me to wash your liver as clean as a sound sheep's heart *As Y. Like It* iii 2 443
Sounded. I'll seek him deeper than e'er plummet sounded *Tempest* iii 3 101
Twice have the trumpets sounded *Meas. for Meas.* iv 6 12
How many fathom deep I am in love! But it cannot be sounded *As Y. Like It* iv 1 211
Thy virtues spoke of, and thy beauty sounded *T. of Shrew* ii 1 193
Tell me, moreover, hast thou sounded him? *Richard II.* i 1 8
I have sounded the very base-string of humility 1 *Hen. IV.* ii 4 6
The trumpets have sounded twice 2 *Hen. IV.* v 5 2
Thy name is Gaultier, being rightly sounded 2 *Hen. VI.* iv 1 37
Which sounded like a clamour in a vault 3 *Hen. VI.* v 2 44
I have not sounded him, nor he deliver'd His gracious pleasure *Rich. III.* iii 4 17
Catesby hath sounded Hastings in our business iii 4 38
And sounded all the depths and shoals of honour *Hen. VIII.* iii 2 436
Why should that name be sounded more than yours? *J. Cæsar* i 2 143
Nor do we find him forward to be sounded *Hamlet* iii 1 7
Hath he never heretofore sounded you in this business? *Lear* i 2 74
Twice then the trumpets sounded, And there I left him tranced v 3 217
Sounder. May sleep the sounder all the next day *Meas. for Meas.* iv 3 50
Shallow again. A more sounder instance, come *As Y. Like It* iii 2 62
Dare mate a sounder man than Surrey can be *Hen. VIII.* iii 2 274
Soundest. He's one o' the soundest judgements in Troy *Troi. and Cres.* i 2 208
The best and soundest of his time hath been but rash *Lear* i 1 298
Sounding. And break my heart With sounding Troilus *Troi. and Cres.* iv 2 115
So close, So far from sounding and discovery, As is the bud bit with an envious worm *Rom. and Jul.* i 1 156
'Music with her silver sound,' because musicians have no gold for sounding iv 5 143
Soundless. Not stingless too.—O, yes, and soundless too *J. Cæsar* v 1 36
Soundly. He shall pay for him that hath him, and that soundly *Tempest* ii 2 81
This will shake your shaking, I can tell you, and that soundly ii 2 88
Let them be hunted soundly iv 1 263
I had swinged him soundly *Meas. for Meas.* v 1 130
This were a bed but cold to sleep so soundly *T. of Shrew* Ind. 1 33
Knock me here soundly.—Knock you here, sir! i 2 8
He bid me knock him and rap him soundly i 2 31
Knock me here, rap me here, knock me well, and knock me soundly i 2 42
Swinge me them soundly forth unto their husbands v 2 104
Cuff him soundly, but never draw thy sword *T. Night* iii 4 428
I will have you as soundly swinged for this 2 *Hen. IV.* v 4 21
Not all these . . . Can sleep so soundly as the wretched slave *Hen. V.* iv 1 285
I will strike it out soundly iv 7 136
If you will love me soundly v 2 105
I mean to tug it and to cuff you soundly 1 *Hen. VI.* i 3 48
Good Catesby, go, effect this business soundly *Richard III.* iii 1 186
Has he disciplined Aufidius soundly? *Coriolanus* ii 1 139
I have it, And soundly too *Rom. and Jul.* iii 1 113
I will then give it you soundly.—What will you give us? iv 5 113
I would it were my fault to sleep so soundly *J. Cæsar* ii 1 4
When Duncan is asleep—Whereto the rather shall his day's hard journey Soundly invite him *Macbeth* i 7 63
Is he whipp'd?—Soundly, my lord *Ant. and Cleo.* iii 13 132
Soundness. I would I had that corporal soundness now *All's Well* i 2 24
Soundpost. What say you, James Soundpost? *Rom. and Jul.* iv 5 138
Sour. That By moonshine do the green sour ringlets make *Tempest* v 1 37
She hath a sweet mouth.—That makes amends for her sour breath *T. G. of Ver.* iii 1 331
This week he hath been heavy, sour, sad *Com. of Errors* v 1 45
Welcome the sour cup of prosperity! *L. L. Lost* i 1 315
You must not look so sour.—It is my fashion, when I see a crab.—Why, here's no crab; and therefore look not sour *T. of Shrew* ii 1 229
When she is froward, peevish, sullen, sour, And not obedient v 2 157
Love that comes too late, Like a remorseful pardon slowly carried, To the great sender turns a sour offence *All's Well* v 3 59
Things sweet to taste prove in digestion sour *Richard II.* i 3 236
Have ever made me sour my patient cheek, Or bend one wrinkle ii 1 169
Speak sweetly, man, although thy looks be sour iii 2 193
Here in this place I'll set a bank of rue, sour herb of grace iii 4 105
Yet you Pilates Have here deliver'd me to my sour cross iv 1 241
Ah, my sour husband, my hard-hearted lord! v 3 121
How sour sweet music is, When time is broke and no proportion kept! v 5 42
With clog of conscience and sour melancholy v 6 20
Heart's discontent and sour affliction Be playfellows to keep you company! There's two of you 2 *Hen. VI.* iii 2 301
Let me embrace thee, sour adversity 3 *Hen. VI.* iii 1 24
Farewell sour annoy! For here, I hope, begins our lasting joy v 7 45
Lofty and sour to them that loved him not *Hen. VIII.* iv 2 53
To make a sweet lady sad is a sour offence *Troi. and Cres.* iii 1 80
The tartness of his face sours ripe grapes *Coriolanus* v 4 18
Nor with sour looks afflict his gentle heart *T. Andron.* i 1 441
If good, thou shamest the music of sweet news By playing it to me with so sour a face *Rom. and Jul.* ii 5 24
If sour woe delights in fellowship And needly will be rank'd with other griefs iii 2 116
Too familiar Is my dear son with such sour company iii 3 7
O, give me thy hand, One writ with me in sour misfortune's book! v 3 82
Lips, let sour words go by and language end *T. of Athens* v 1 223
He will, after his sour fashion, tell you What hath proceeded *J. Cæsar* i 2 180
They see and smell And have their palates both for sweet and sour *Oth.* iv 3 96
To sour your happiness, I must report The queen is dead *Cymbeline* v 5 26
Source. Great floods have flown From simple sources *All's Well* ii 1 143
A little gale will soon disperse that cloud And blow it to the source from whence it came 3 *Hen. VI.* v 3 11
That your activity may defeat and quell The source of all erection *T. of Athens* iv 3 164
The spring, the head, the fountain of your blood Is stopp'd; the very source of it is stopp'd *Macbeth* ii 3 104
The source of this our watch and the chief head Of this post-haste *Ham.* i 1 106

Source. He hath found The head and source of all your son's distemper *Hamlet* ii 2 55
Ah, dear, if I be so, From my cold heart let heaven engender hail, And poison it in the source . . . *Ant. and Cleo.* iii 13 160
Who ever but his approbation added, Though not his prime consent, he did not flow From honourable sources *Pericles* iv 3 28
Sour-cold. If thou didst put this sour-cold habit on To castigate thy pride, 'twere well. . . . *T. of Athens* iv 3 239
Soured. Three crabbed months had sour'd themselves to death *W. Tale* i 2 102
Sourest. Sweetest nut hath sourest rind . . . *As Y. Like It* iii 2 115
Sweet love . . . Turns to the sourest and most deadly hate *Richard II.* iii 2 136
Touch you the sourest points with sweetest terms . *Ant. and Cleo.* ii 2 24
Sourest-natured. I think Crab my dog be the sourest-natured dog that lives *T. G. of Ver.* ii 3 6
Sour-eyed. Barren hate, Sour-eyed disdain, and discord . *Tempest* iv 1 20
Sourly. Though I show'd sourly to him . . . *Coriolanus* v 3 13
Souse. Like an eagle o'er his aery towers, To souse annoyance that comes near his nest . . . *K. John* v 2 150
Soused. If I be not ashamed of my soldiers, I am a soused gurnet 1 *Hen. IV.* iv 2 13
South. By east, west, north, and south, I spread my conquering might *L. L. Lost* v 2 566
Like foggy south puffing with wind and rain . *As Y. Like It* iii 5 50
In the south suburbs, at the Elephant, Is best to lodge . *T. Night* iii 3 39
'Tis powerful, think it, From east, west, north and south *W. Tale* i 2 203
Our thunder from the south Shall rain their drift of bullets . *K. John* ii 1 411
From north to south: Austria and France shoot in each other's mouth ii 1 413
Send danger from the east unto the west, So honour cross it from the north to south, And let them grapple . . 1 *Hen. IV.* i 3 196
By south and east is to my part assign'd . . . iii 1 75
Like the south Borne with black vapour . . 2 *Hen. IV.* ii 4 392
Like youthful steers unyoked, they take their courses East, west, north, south . . . iv 2 104
Thou art as opposite to every good As the Antipodes are unto us, Or as the south to the septentrion . . . 3 *Hen. VI.* i 4 136
His regiment lies half a mile at least South . . *Richard III.* v 3 38
The rotten diseases of the south . . . *Troi. and Cres.* v 1 21
All the contagion of the south light on you! . . *Coriolanus* i 4 30
'Tis south the city mills . . . i 10 31
They would fly east, west, north, south . . . ii 3 24
Turning his face to the dew-dropping south *Rom. and Jul.* i 4 103
The sun arises, Which is a great way growing on the south . *J. Cæsar* ii 1 107
I hear a knocking At the south entry . . *Macbeth* ii 2 66
The chimney Is south the chamber . . . *Cymbeline* ii 4 81
The Roman eagle, wing'd From the spongy south to this part of the west iv 2 349
The Roman eagle, From south to west on wing soaring aloft . v 5 471
Southam. At Southam I did leave him with his forces 3 *Hen. VI.* v 1 9
Here Southam lies: The drum your honour hears marcheth from Warwick . . . v 1 12
Southampton. If hell and treason hold their promises, Ere he take ship for France, and in Southampton . . *Hen. V.* ii Prol. 30
The scene Is now transported, gentles, to Southampton . ii Prol. 35
Unto Southampton do we shift our scene . ii Prol. 42
Southerly. I am but mad north-north-west: when the wind is southerly I know a hawk from a handsaw . . *Hamlet* ii 2 397
Southern. All your southern gentlemen in arms *Richard II.* iii 2 202
The southern wind Doth play the trumpet to his purposes . 1 *Hen. IV.* v 1 3
And with the southern clouds contend in tears . 2 *Hen. VI.* iii 2 384
Thou art deceived: 'tis not thy southern power 3 *Hen. VI.* i 1 155
South-fog. The south-fog rot him! . . . *Cymbeline* ii 3 136
South north. The clearstores toward the south north are as lustrous as ebony . . . *T. Night* iv 2 42
South-sea. One inch of delay more is a South-sea of discovery *As Y. L. It* iii 2 207
Southward. The sun looking with a southward eye upon him *W. Tale* iv 4 819
If it were at liberty, 'twould, sure, southward. . . *Coriolanus* ii 3 32
Southwark. The rebels are in Southwark . . 2 *Hen. VI.* iv 4 27
Leave me at the White Hart in Southwark . . . iv 8 25
Southwell. John Southwell, read you; and let us to our work . i 4 14
South-west. A south-west blow on ye And blister you all o'er! *Tempest* i 2 323
Is this wind westerly that blows?—South-west . *Pericles* iv 1 51
South-wind. A prosperous south-wind friendly . *W. Tale* v 1 161
Souviendrai. Ma foi, j'oublie les doigts; mais je me souviendrai *Hen. V.* iii 4 10
Sovereign. With her sovereign grace, Here on this grass-plot *Tempest* iv 1 72
I have her sovereign aid And rest myself content . . v 1 143
And thus I search it with a sovereign kiss *T. G. of Ver.* ii 2 116
Sovereign to all the creatures on the earth.—Except my mistress . ii 4 153
Her fair sister, Possess'd with such a gentle sovereign grace *Com. of Er.* iii 2 165
A man of sovereign parts he is esteem'd; Well fitted in arts *L. L. Lost* ii 1 44
The anointed sovereign of sighs and groans, Liege of all loiterers . iii 1 184
Dear sovereign, hear me speak . . *As Y. Like It* i 3 68
Thy husband is thy lord, thy life, thy keeper, Thy head, thy sovereign *T. of Shrew* v 2 147
A guide, a goddess, and a sovereign . . . *All's Well* i 1 183
O'er whom both sovereign power and father's voice I have to use . ii 3 60
My high-repented blames, Dear sovereign, pardon to me . v 3 37
Liver, brain and heart, These sovereign thrones . . *T. Night* i 1 38
Get thee to yond same sovereign cruelty . . . ii 4 83
I would not be a stander-by to hear My sovereign mistress clouded so *W. Tale* i 2 280
To take away the life of our sovereign lord the king, thy royal husband iii 2 17
Nor the remembrance Of his most sovereign name . . v 1 26
What, sovereign sir, I did not well I meant well . . v 3 2
Thy nephew and right royal sovereign . . *K. John* i 1 15
As holding of the pope Your sovereign greatness and authority . v 1 4
Useful serving-man and instrument, To any sovereign state . v 2 82
Many years of happy days befal My gracious sovereign! . *Richard II.* i 1 21
And wish, so please my sovereign, ere I move, What my tongue speaks my right drawn sword may prove . . . i 1 45
Let my sovereign turn away his face And bid his ears a little while be deaf . . . i 1 111
My sovereign liege was in my debt Upon remainder of a dear account i 1 129
Myself I throw, dread sovereign, at thy foot . . i 1 165
Let me kiss my sovereign's hand, And bow my knee before his majesty i 3 46
Harry of Hereford . . . Stands here for God, his sovereign and himself i 3 105
A heavy sentence, my most sovereign liege . . . i 3 154
Or bend one wrinkle on my sovereign's face . . . ii 1 170
My sovereign, whom both my oath And duty bids defend . . ii 2 112
In braving arms against thy sovereign . . . ii 3 112
And make you stoop Unto the sovereign mercy of the king . ii 3 157
Feed not thy sovereign's foe, my gentle earth . . iii 2 12

Sovereign. With a mortal touch Throw death upon thy sovereign's enemies . . *Richard II.* iii 2 22
Where subjects' feet May hourly trample on their sovereign's head . iii 3 157
Our house, my sovereign liege, little deserves The scourge of greatness 1 *Hen. IV.* i 3 10
Thou shalt have charge and sovereign trust herein . . iii 2 161
Health to my sovereign, and new happiness! . . 2 *Hen. IV.* iv 4 81
My sovereign lord, cheer up yourself, look up . . . iv 4 113
Then hear me, gracious sovereign, and you peers . *Hen. V.* i 2 33
The sin upon my head, dread sovereign! . . . i 2 97
That he should, for a foreign purse, so sell His sovereign's life . ii 2 11
Let him be punish'd, sovereign, lest example Breed, by his sufferance . ii 2 45
My fault, but not my body, pardon, sovereign. . . ii 2 165
Good my sovereign, Take up the English short . . ii 4 71
'Tis a subject for a sovereign to reason on, and for a sovereign's sovereign to ride on . . . iii 7 38
My sovereign lord, bestow yourself with speed . . iv 3 68
Dear my lord, Commend my service to my sovereign . . iv 6 23
Bear me witness all, That here I kiss her as my sovereign queen v 2 386
Let me thy servant and not sovereign be . . 1 *Hen. VI.* i 2 111
That haughty prelate, Whom Henry, our late sovereign, ne'er could brook . . . i 3 24
Thy sovereign, is not quite exempt From envious malice . iii 1 25
Except you mean with obstinate repulse To slay your sovereign . iii 1 114
Accept this scroll, most gracious sovereign . . iii 1 149
I have awhile given truce unto my wars, To do my duty to my sovereign . . . iii 4 4
Hath he forgot he is his sovereign? . . . iv 1 52
Grant me the combat, gracious sovereign.—And me, my lord iv 1 78
Call my sovereign yours, And do him homage as obedient subjects iv 2 6
With you, mine alder-liefest sovereign . . 2 *Hen. VI.* i 1 28
Articles of contracted peace Between our sovereign and the French king i 1 41
Why should he, then, protect our sovereign, He being of age? i 1 165
Exploits done in the heart of France, When thou wert regent for our sovereign . . . i 1 197
My sovereign, York is meetest man To be your regent . i 3 163
Be we the first That shall salute our rightful sovereign . ii 2 61
Long live our sovereign Richard, England's king! . . ii 2 63
By wicked means to frame our sovereign's fall . . iii 1 52
I am clear from treason to my sovereign: Who can accuse me? . iii 1 102
And you, my sovereign lady, with the rest . . iii 1 161
Hath he not twit our sovereign lady here With ignominious words? . iii 1 178
And to preserve my sovereign from his foe, Say but the word, and I will be his priest . . . iii 1 271
Comfort, my sovereign! gracious Henry, comfort! . . iii 2 38
It is reported, mighty sovereign, That good Duke Humphrey traitorously is murder'd. . . . iii 2 122
Come hither, gracious sovereign, view this body . . iii 2 149
And that my sovereign's presence makes me mild . . iii 2 219
'Tis like the commons, rude unpolish'd hinds, Could send such message to their sovereign . . . iii 2 272
How fares my lord? speak, Beaufort, to thy sovereign . iii 3 1
Beaufort, it is thy sovereign speaks to thee . . . iii 3 7
Let my sovereign, virtuous Henry, Command my eldest son . v 1 48
We are thy sovereign, Clifford, kneel again; For thy mistaking so, we pardon thee.—This is my king, York. . . v 1 127
Kneel for grace and mercy at my feet; I am thy sovereign 3 *Hen. VI.* i 1 76
He rose against him, being his sovereign, And made him to resign . i 1 141
Whilst I live, To honour me as thy king and sovereign . i 1 198
Becomes it thee to be thus bold in terms Before thy sovereign? . ii 2 86
I am a subject fit to jest withal, But far unfit to be a sovereign . iii 2 92
King of Albion, My lord and sovereign, and thy vowed friend . iii 3 50
And with my tongue To tell the passion of my sovereign's heart . iii 3 62
So long as Edward is thy constant friend, And their true sovereign iv 1 78
What letters or what news From France?—My sovereign liege, no letters . . . iv 1 86
Then is my sovereign slain?—Ay, almost slain . . iv 4 6
Subjects may challenge nothing of their sovereigns . . iv 6 6
What answers Clarence to his sovereign's will?—That he consents . iv 6 45
It shall be done, my sovereign, with all speed . . iv 6 64
But let us hence, my sovereign, to provide A salve for any sore . iv 6 87
Ay, now my sovereign speaketh like himself . . iv 7 67
My sovereign, with the loving citizens . . . Shall rest in London . iv 8 19
Fair lords, take leave and stand not to reply. Farewell, my sovereign iv 8 24
No more but this: Henry, your sovereign, Is prisoner to the foe . v 4 76
Unrip'dst the bowels of thy sovereign's son . *Richard III.* i 4 212
Good morrow to my sovereign king and queen! . . ii 1 46
A blessed labour, my most sovereign liege . . . ii 1 52
A boon, my sovereign, for my service done!—I pray thee, peace . ii 1 95
What is it thou demand'st?—The forfeit, sovereign, of my servant's life ii 1 99
My thoughts' sovereign: The weary way hath made you melancholy . iii 1 2
He may command me as my sovereign; But you have power in me as in a kinsman . . . iii 1 108
All hail, my sovereign liege! . . . iv 3 23
Say, I, her sovereign, am her subject love.—But she, your subject, loathes such sovereignty . . . iv 4 355
First, mighty sovereign, let me know your mind . . iv 4 446
What doth he there?—I know not, mighty sovereign, but by guess iv 4 466
What do they in the north, When they should serve their sovereign in the west?—They have not been commanded, mighty sovereign . iv 4 486
Most mighty sovereign, You have no cause to hold my friendship doubtful . . . iv 4 492
In the name Of our most sovereign king . . *Hen. VIII.* i 1 202
These exactions, Whereof my sovereign would have note . i 2 48
Obeying in commanding, and thy parts Sovereign and pious else . ii 4 140
My sovereign, I confess your royal graces, Shower'd on me daily . iii 2 166
Dread sovereign, how much are we bound to heaven In daily thanks, that gave us such a prince . . . v 3 114
Dread sovereign, may it like your grace To let my tongue excuse all v 3 148
The most sovereign prescription in Galen is but empiricutic *Coriolanus* ii 1 127
How now, dear sovereign, and our gracious mother! *T. Andron.* ii 3 89
Sovereign, here lies the County Paris slain; And Romeo dead *R. and J.* v 3 195
Whose eyes are on this sovereign lady fix'd . *T. of Athens* i 1 68
Shall to all our nights and days to come Give solely sovereign sway and masterdom . . . *Macbeth* i 5 71
To dew the sovereign flower and drown the weeds . . v 2 30
Both your majesties Might, by the sovereign power you have of us *Ham.* ii 2 27
Now see that noble and most sovereign reason, Like sweet bells jangled iii 1 165
Thou mayst not coldly set Our sovereign process . . iv 3 65
A sovereign shame so elbows him . . . *Lear* iv 3 44

Sovereign. Opinion, a sovereign mistress of effects — *Othello* i 3 225
At thy sovereign leisure read The garboils she awaked — *Ant. and Cleo.* i 3 60
Sovereign of Egypt, hail! — i 5 34
O sovereign mistress of true melancholy, The poisonous damp of night disponge upon me — iv 9 12
She is dead too, our sovereign — iv 15 69
But yet let me lament, With tears as sovereign as the blood of hearts — v 1 41
Most sovereign creature — v 2 81
Daughter, peace! Sweet sovereign, Leave us to ourselves — *Cymbeline* i 1 154
Guide me to your sovereign's court — *Pericles* ii 1 146
Your noble self, That best know how to rule and how to reign, We thus submit unto,—our sovereign — ii 4 39
Sovereignest. Telling me the sovereign'st thing on earth Was parmaceti for an inward bruise — *1 Hen. IV.* i 3 57
Sovereignly. I cannot Believe this crack to be in my dread mistress, So sovereignly being honourable — *W. Tale* i 2 323
Sovereignty. No sovereignty;—Yet he would be king — *Tempest* ii 1 156
To call her bad, Whose sovereignty so oft thou hast preferr'd — *T. G. of V.* ii 6 15
O, give me pardon, That I, your vassal, have employ'd and pain'd Your unknown sovereignty! — *Meas. for Meas.* v 1 392
Of all complexions the cull'd sovereignty — *L. L. Lost* iv 3 234
Whose unwished yoke My soul consents not to give sovereignty — *M. N. D.* i 1 82
Some prescriptions . . . such as his reading And manifest experience had collected For general sovereignty — *All's Well* i 3 230
To tread down fair respect of sovereignty — *K. John* iii 1 58
Made glory base and sovereignty a slave — *Richard II.* iv 1 251
Speak in your state What I have done that misbecame my place, My person, or my liege's sovereignty — *2 Hen. IV.* v 2 101
All the peers . . . Have been as bondmen to thy sovereignty — *2 Hen. VI.* i 3 130
All her perfections challenge sovereignty — *3 Hen. VI.* iii 2 86
I do but dream on sovereignty — iii 2 134
Would this gracious prince Take on himself the sovereignty thereof — *Richard III.* iii 7 79
Yielded To bear the golden yoke of sovereignty — iii 7 146
Put in her tender heart the aspiring flame Of golden sovereignty — iv 4 329
But she, your subject, loathes such sovereignty — iv 4 356
Who fed him every minute With words of sovereignty — *Hen. VIII.* ii 2 150
A woman's heart; which ever yet Affected eminence, wealth, sovereignty — ii 3 29
As is the osprey to the fish, who takes it By sovereignty of nature — *Coriol.* iv 7 35
Then 'tis most like The sovereignty will fall upon Macbeth — *Macbeth* ii 4 30
And wears upon his baby-brow the round And top of sovereignty — iv 1 89
Some other horrible form, Which might deprive your sovereignty of reason And draw you into madness — *Hamlet* i 4 73
By the marks of sovereignty, knowledge, and reason, I should be false persuaded I had daughters — *Lear* i 4 253
To show less sovereignty than they, must needs Appear unkinglike — *Cymbeline* iii 5 6
Sow. He'ld sow't with nettle-seed — *Tempest* ii 1 144
Our corn's to reap, for yet our tithe's to sow — *Meas. for Meas.* iv 1 76
Like a sow that hath overwhelmed all her litter but one — *2 Hen. IV.* i 2 13
Shall we sow the headland with wheat?—With red wheat, Davy — v 1 15
I could make as true a boast as that, if I had a sow to my mistress — *Hen. V.* iii 7 67
We are to cure such sorrows, not to sow 'em — *Hen. VIII.* iii 1 158
Itches, blains, Sow all the Athenian bosoms! — *T. of Athens* iv 1 29
Consumptions sow In hollow bones of man — iv 3 151
Pour in sow's blood, that hath eaten Her nine farrow — *Macbeth* iv 1 64
If we will plant nettles, or sow lettuce, set hyssop — *Othello* i 3 325
Sow'd cockle reap'd no corn — *L. L. Lost* iv 3 383
What wilt thou be When time hath sow'd a grizzle on thy case? — *T. Night* v 1 168
And reap the harvest which that rascal sow'd — *2 Hen. VI.* iii 1 381
Which we ourselves have plough'd for, sow'd, and scatter'd — *Coriolanus* iii 1 71
Civility not seen from other, valour That wildly grows in them, but yields a crop As if it had been sow'd — *Cymbline* iv 2 181
Sowing the kernels of it in the sea, bring forth more islands — *Tempest* ii 1 92
Sowl. He'll go, he says, and sowl the porter of Rome gates by the ears — *Coriolanus* iv 5 213
Sow-skin. If tinkers may have leave to live, And bear the sow-skin budget — *W. Tale* iv 3 20
Sowter. He is now at a cold scent.—Sowter will cry upon 't — *T. Night* ii 5 135
Space. A dozen years; within which space she died — *Tempest* i 2 279
Space enough Have I in such a prison — i 2 492
Queen of Tunis; So is she heir of Naples; 'twixt which regions There is some space.—A space whose every cubit Seems to cry out — ii 1 257
I warrant he hath a thousand of these letters, writ with blank space for different names — *Mer. Wives* ii 1 77
Stay here in your court for three years' space — *L. L. Lost* i 1 52
All forsworn Three thousand times within this three years' space — i 1 151
After some small space, being strong at heart, He sent me — *As Y. Like It* iv 3 152
The mightiest space in fortune nature brings To join like likes — *All's Well* i 1 237
Art thou so confident? within what space Hopest thou my cure? — ii 1 162
The solemn feast Shall more attend upon the coming space — ii 3 188
Come on; thou art granted space — iv 1 98
Within that space you may have drawn together Your tenants — *1 Hen. IV.* iii 1 89
But in short space It rain'd down fortune showering on your head — v 1 46
If, after three days' space, thou here be'st found — *2 Hen. VI.* iii 2 295
Even in so short a space, my woman's heart Grossly grew captive to his honey words — *Richard III.* iv 1 79
Whom, we know well, The world's large spaces cannot parallel — *T. and C.* ii 2 162
Thou great-sized coward, No space of earth shall sunder our two hates — v 10 27
Sell the mighty space of our large honours For so much trash? — *J. Cæsar* iv 3 25
For the whole space that's in the tyrant's grasp — *Macbeth* iv 3 36
I could be bounded in a nut-shell and count myself a king of infinite space, were it not that I have bad dreams — *Hamlet* ii 2 261
Dearer than eye-sight, space, and liberty — *Lear* i 1 57
No less in space, validity, and pleasure, Than that conferr'd on Goneril — i 1 83
O undistinguish'd space of woman's will! — iv 6 278
They are ready To-morrow, or at further space, to appear — v 3 53
The wide arch Of the ranged empire fall! Here is my space — *A. and C.* i 1 34
Since he went from Egypt 'tis A space for further travel — ii 1 31
Therefore Make space enough between you — ii 3 23
Till the diminution Of space had pointed him sharp as my needle — *Cymb.* i 3 19
If you require a little space for prayer, I grant it — *Pericles* iv 1 68
Spacious. Use a more spacious ceremony — *All's Well* ii 1 51
Of such a spacious lofty pitch, Your roof were not sufficient — *1 Hen. VI.* ii 3 55
The spacious world cannot again afford — *Richard III.* i 2 246
Like a bourn, . . . confines Thy spacious and dilated parts — *T. and C.* ii 3 261
The spacious breadth of this division Admits no orifex — v 2 150
As spacious as between The young'st and oldest thing — *Coriolanus* iv 6 67
The forest walks are wide and spacious — *T. Andron.* ii 1 114
Spacious. Do you dare our anger? 'Tis in few words, but spacious in effect — *T. of Athens* iii 5 97
Convey your pleasures in a spacious plenty, And yet seem cold — *Macbeth* iv 3 71
'Tis a chough; but, as I say, spacious in the possession of dirt — *Hamlet* v 2 90
Cæsar is touch'd.—When such a spacious mirror's set before him, He needs must see himself — *Ant. and Cleo.* v 1 34
Were I chief lord of all this spacious world, I'ld give it to undo the deed — *Pericles* iv 3 5
Spade. 'Tis you must dig with mattock and with spade — *T. Andron.* iv 3 11
We took this mattock and this spade from him — *Rom. and Jul.* v 3 185
Why this spade? this place? This slave-like habit? — *T. of Athens* iv 3 204
Come, my spade. There is no ancient gentlemen but gardeners — *Hamlet* v 1 33
Chapless, and knocked about the mazzard with a sexton's spade — v 1 98
A pick-axe, and a spade, a spade, For and a shrouding sheet — v 1 102
Spain Where Spain?—Faith, I saw it not; but I felt it hot — *Com. of Errors* iii 2 133
Sapphires, declining their rich aspect to the hot breath of Spain — iii 2 140
A refined traveller of Spain — *L. L. Lost* i 1 164
Many a knight From tawny Spain — i 1 174
With her her niece, the Lady Blanch of Spain — *K. John* ii 1 64
That daughter there of Spain, the Lady Blanch, Is niece to England — ii 1 423
It is well.—The fig of Spain! — *Hen. V.* iii 6 62
Great John of Gaunt, Which did subdue the greatest part of Spain — *3 Hen. VI.* iii 3 82
Ferdinand, My father, king of Spain, was reckon'd one The wisest prince that there had reign'd — *Hen. VIII.* ii 4 48
Spare me, till I may Be by my friends in Spain advised — ii 4 55
He had a fever when he was in Spain — *J. Cæsar* i 2 119
It is a sword of Spain, the ice-brook's temper — *Othello* v 2 253
Spake Who is that that spake? — *T. G. of Ver.* iv 2 87
You spake in Latin then too; but 'tis no matter — *Mer. Wives* i 1 185
I spake with the old woman about it.—And what says she? — iv 5 35
There spake my brother; there my father's grave Did utter forth a voice — *Meas. for Meas.* iii 1 86
For certain words he spake against your grace In your retirement — v 1 129
Since which time of five years I never spake with her — v 1 223
Spake he so doubtfully, thou couldst not feel his meaning? — *Com. of Er.* ii 1 50
When spake I such a word?—Even now, even here — ii 2 13
That never words were music to thine ear, . . . Unless I spake — ii 2 120
I never spake with her in all my life — ii 2 167
He would answer, I spake not true — *As Y. Like It* v 4 82
Spake you not these words plain? — *T. of Shrew* iv 2 39
You need not to stop your nose, sir; I spake but by a metaphor — *All's W.* v 2 12
I spake with him; who now Has these poor men in question — *W. Tale* v 1 197
Hadst thou but shook thy head or made a pause When I spake darkly what I purposed — *K. John* iv 2 232
And even there, methinks, an angel spake — v 2 64
He was not so resolved when last we spake together — *Richard II.* ii 3 29
You would have thought the very windows spake — v 2 12
Didst thou not mark the king, what words he spake? — v 4 1
'Have I no friend?' quoth he: he spake it twice, and urged it twice — v 4 4
One that never spake other English in his life — *1 Hen. IV.* ii 4 26
I spake with one, my lord, that came from thence — *2 Hen. IV.* i 1 25
I spake unto this crown as having sense — iv 5 158
Hang me, if ever I spake the words — *2 Hen. VI.* i 3 200
Who spake of brotherhood? who spake of love? — *Richard III.* ii 1 108
O, now I want the priest that spake to me — iii 4 89
And did they so?—No, so God help me, they spake not a word — iii 7 24
Thus hath the duke inferr'd; But nothing spake in warrant from himself — iii 7 33
Spake one the least word that might Be to the prejudice of her — *Hen. VIII.* ii 4 153
This is about that which the bishop spake — v 1 84
Ever spake against Your liberties and the charters that you bear — *Coriol.* ii 3 187
'And shall!' what villain was it spake that word? — *T. Andron.* i 1 359
And what I spake, I spake it to my face — *Rom. and Jul.* iv 1 34
Caius Ligarius, that Metellus spake of — *J. Cæsar* ii 1 311
What he spake, though it lack'd form a little, Was not like madness — *Ham.* iii 1 171
Spake you with him?—Ay, two hours together — *Lear* i 2 169
Swore as many oaths as I spake words — iii 4 91
Lord Edmund spake not with your lord at home? — iv 5 4
Wherein I spake of most disastrous chances, Of moving accidents — *Othello* i 3 134
Upon this hint I spake: She loved me for the dangers I had pass'd — i 3 166
What is she?—She that I spake of, our great captain's captain — ii 1 74
Even but now he spake, After long seeming dead — v 2 327
Spake you of Cæsar? How! the nonpareil! — *Ant. and Cleo.* iii 2 11
I spake to you for your comfort — iv 2 40
The last she spake Was 'Antony! most noble Antony!' — iv 14 29
O Cæsar, This Charmian lived but now; she stood and spake — v 2 344
What was the last That he spake to thee?—It was his queen, his queen! — *Cymbeline* i 3 5
He spake of her, as Dian had hot dreams, And she alone were cold — v 5 180
In that he spake too far.—And thou shalt die for't — v 5 309
I never spake bad word, nor did ill turn To any living creature — *Pericles* iv 1 76
Are you not Pericles? Like him you spake, Like him you are — v 3 32
Spakest. I heard thee say, and vauntingly thou spakest it — *Richard II.* iv 1 36
Darest thou maintain the former words thou spakest? — *1 Hen. VI.* ii 4 31
Spakest thou of Juliet? how is it with her? — *Rom. and Jul.* iii 3 93
Span. The stretching of a span Buckles in his sum of age — *As Y. Like It* iii 2 139
You have scarce time To steal from spiritual leisure a brief span — *Hen. VIII.* iii 2 140
With spans and inches so diminutive As fears and reasons — *Troi. and Cres.* ii 2 31
Timon is dead, who hath outstretch'd his span — *T. of Athens* v 3 3
A soldier's a man; A life's but a span — *Othello* ii 3 74
Span-counter. Henry the Fifth, in whose time boys went to span-counter for French crowns — *2 Hen. VI.* iv 2 166
Spangle. What stars do spangle heaven with such beauty? — *T. of Shrew* iv 5 31
Spangled. By fountain clear, or spangled starlight sheen — *M. N. Dream* ii 1 29
Who, stuck and spangled with your flatteries, Washes it off — *T. of Athens* iii 6 101
Spaniard. A Spaniard from the hip upward, no doublet — *Much Ado* iii 2 36
Too much odds for a Spaniard's rapier — *L. L. Lost* i 2 183
This Armado is a Spaniard, that keeps here in court — iv 1 100
And fig me, like The bragging Spaniard — *2 Hen. IV.* v 3 125
The Spaniard, tied by blood and favour to her, Must now confess — *Hen. VIII.* ii 2 90
There was a Spaniard's mouth so watered — *Pericles* iv 2 108
Spaniel. I am your spaniel; and, Demetrius, The more you beat me, I will fawn on you: Use me but as your spaniel, spurn me, strike me, Neglect me, lose me — *M. N. Dream* ii 1 203
What, ho! Where's my spaniel Troilus? — *T. of Shrew* iv 1 153
You play the spaniel, And think with wagging of your tongue to win me; But . . . I'm sure Thou hast a cruel nature — *Hen. VIII.* v 3 126
Hounds and greyhounds, mongrels, spaniels, curs, Shoughs — *Macbeth* iii 1 93
Hound or spaniel, brach or lym, Or bobtail tike or trundle-tail — *Lear* iii 6 72
Let me be gelded like a spaniel — *Pericles* iv 6 133

Spanieled. The hearts That spaniel'd me at heels, to whom I gave Their wishes, do discandy, melt their sweets . . . *Ant. and Cleo.* iv 12 21
Spaniel-fawning. Court'sies and base spaniel-fawning . . *J. Cæsar* iii 1 43
Spaniel-like, the more she spurns my love, The more it grows and fawneth on her still . . . . *T. G. of Ver.* iv 2 14
Spanish. The breaking of my Spanish sword . . . *All's Well* iv 1 52
Of breaches, ambuscadoes, Spanish blades . . . *Rom. and Jul.* i 4 84
The motto thus, in Spanish, 'Piu por dulzura que por fuerza' *Pericles* ii 2 27
Spanish-pouch. Caddis-garter, smooth-tongue, Spanish-pouch 1 *Hen. IV.* ii 4 79
Spanned. My life is spann'd already . . . . . *Hen. VIII.* i 1 223
Spare. I prithee, spare.—Well, I have done . . . . *Tempest* ii 1 24
Spare him, spare him! He's not prepared for death . *Meas. for Meas.* ii 2 83
Showing we would not spare heaven as we love it, But as we stand in fear . . . . ii 3 33
A small spare mast, Such as seafaring men provide for storms *C. of Er.* i 1 80
I would not spare my brother in this case, If he should scorn me so . iv 1 77
Spare not to tell him . . . . *Much Ado* ii 2 22
We will spare for no wit, I warrant you . . . . . . iii 5 66
It should none spare that come within his power . . *L. L. Lost* ii 1 51
Shun me, and I will spare your haunts . . . *M. N. Dream* ii 1 142
I shall hardly spare a pound of flesh To-morrow . . *Mer. of Venice* iii 3 33
As it is a spare life, look you, it fits my humour well . *As Y. Like It* iii 2 20
Give me thy mete-yard, and spare not me . . . . *T. of Shrew* iv 3 153
He that ears my land spares my team . . . . *All's Well* i 3 47
The rather will I spare my praises towards him; Knowing him is enough ii 1 106
Thick, thick, spare not me . . . . ii 2 47
O Lord, sir! spare not me.—Do you cry, 'O Lord, sir!' at your whipping, and 'spare not me?' . . . . ii 2 53
The general is content to spare thee yet . . . . . . iv 1 89
Shall I bid him go, and spare not? . . . . . . *T. Night* ii 3 120
For life, I prize it As I weigh grief, Which I would spare *W. Tale* iii 2 44
Spare your threats: The bug which you would fright me with I seek . iii 2 92
O, spare mine eyes, Though to no use but still to look on you! *K. John* iv 1 102
O, spare me not, my brother Edward's son . . . *Richard II.* ii 1 124
He will spare neither man, woman, nor child . . . 2 *Hen. IV.* ii 1 18
O, give me the spare men, and spare me the great ones . . . iii 2 288
Spare in diet, Free from gross passion . . . . . *Hen. V.* ii 2 131
Spare for no faggots, let there be enow . . . . 1 *Hen. VI.* v 4 56
Such a petty sum!—I'll give it, sir; and therefore spare my life 2 *Hen. VI.* iv 1 23
Spare none but such as go in clouted shoon . . . . . . iv 2 195
Such aid as I can spare you shall command . . . . . iv 5 7
Spare England, for it is your native coast . . . . . iv 8 52
York not our old men spares; No more will I their babes . . . v 2 51
The world goes hard When Clifford cannot spare his friends an oath 3 *Hen. VI.* ii 6 78
Threat you me with telling of the king? Tell him, and spare not *Rich. III.* i 3 114
O, spare my guiltless wife and my poor children! . . . . . i 4 72
You may, then, spare that time. . . . . . . *Hen. VIII.* ii 4 5
Spare me, till I may Be by my friends in Spain advised . . . . ii 4 54
Come, come, my lord, you'ld spare your spoons . . . . . v 3 167
I made no spare, sir.—You did nothing, sir . . . . . . v 4 21
Being moved, he will not spare to gird the gods . . *Coriolanus* i 1 260
Lay the fault on us.—Ay, spare us not . . . . ii 3 243
Thrice noble Titus, spare my first-born son . . . *T. Andron.* i 1 120
My youth can better spare my blood than you. . . . . . iii 1 166
Agree between you; I will spare my hand . . . . . . iii 1 184
Spare not for cost . . . . *Rom. and Jul.* iv 4 6
We'll bear, with your lordship.—He'll spare none . . *T. of Athens* i 1 177
Spare not the babe, Whose dimpled smiles from fools exhaust their mercy . . . . iv 3 118
Spare your oaths, I'll trust to your conditions . . . . . . iv 3 138
Spare thy Athenian cradle and those kin Which in the bluster of thy wrath must fall With those that have offended . . . . . . v 4 40
I do not know the man I should avoid So soon as that spare Cassius *J. C.* i 2 201
Spare my gray beard, you wagtail? . . . . *Lear* ii 2 72
Wear this; spare speech; Decline your head . . . . . . iv 2 21
Iago can inform you,—While I spare speech . . . . *Othello* ii 3 199
I am poor of thanks And scarce can spare them . . . *Cymbeline* ii 3 95
I would not speak. I pray you, spare me . . . . . . ii 3 100
You'll give me leave to spare, when you shall find You need it not . ii 4 65
Spare your arithmetic: never count the turns; Once, and a million! . ii 4 142
Save him, sir, And spare no blood beside . . . . v 5 92
I will prefer my sons; Then spare not the old father . . . . v 5 327
The power that I have on you is to spare you . . . . . . v 5 418
Must feel war's blow, who spares not innocence . . . *Pericles* i 2 93
Till the rough seas, that spare not any man, Took it in rage . . ii 1 137
Spared. You shall well be spared . . . . . . *Meas. for Meas.* ii 2 14
My noble prince, With other princes that may best be spared Shall wait upon your father's funeral . . . . *K. John* v 7 97
Farewell! I could have better spared a better man . . . 1 *Hen. IV.* v 4 104
If I spared any That had a head to hit, either young or old . *Hen. VIII.* v 4 23
Whose life I have spared at suit of his gray beard . . . *Lear* ii 2 68
Take from his heart, take from his brain, from's time, What should not then be spared . . . . *Ant. and Cleo.* iii 7 13
Sparing. To a niggardly host and more sparing guest . *Com. of Errors* iii 1 27
For reverence to some alive, I give a sparing limit to my tongue *Richard III.* iii 7 194
In him Sparing would show a worse sin than ill doctrine . *Hen. VIII.* i 3 60
And in that sparing makes huge waste . . . . *Rom. and Jul.* i 1 224
Sparingly. Or shall we sparingly show you far off? . . . *Hen. V.* i 2 239
But touch this sparingly, as 'twere far off. . . . *Richard III.* iii 5 93
Spark. He doth indeed show some sparks that are like wit . *Much Ado* ii 3 193
'Tis not his fault, the spark . . . . *All's Well* ii 1 25
Good sparks and lustrous, a word, good metals . . . . . ii 1 41
Yet through both I see some sparks of better hope . . *Richard II.* v 3 21
High sparks of honour in thee have I seen . . . . . . v 6 29
Could out of thee extract one spark of evil . . . . *Hen. V.* ii 2 101
This spark will prove a raging fire, If wind and fuel be brought 2 *Hen. VI.* iii 1 302
In whose cold blood no spark of honour bides . . . 3 *Hen. VI.* i 1 184
If any spark of life be yet remaining, Down, down to hell . . . v 6 66
My drops of tears I'll turn to sparks of fire . . . *Hen. VIII.* ii 4 73
One noble man that hath one spark of fire, To answer for his love *T. and C.* i 3 294
Those sparks of life That should be in a Roman you do want . *J. Cæsar* i 3 57
The skies are painted with unnumber'd sparks, They are all fire . . iii 1 63
Who, much enforced, shows a hasty spark, And straight is cold again . iv 3 112
In passages of proof, Time qualifies the spark and fire of it [love] *Hamlet* iv 7 114
Like an old lecher's heart; a small spark, all the rest on's body cold *Lear* iii 4 118
Enkindle all the sparks of nature, To quit this horrid act . . . iii 7 86
How hard it is to hide the sparks of nature! . . . . *Cymbeline* iii 3 79

Spark. The thing the which is flatter'd, but a spark, To which that blast gives heat and stronger glowing . . . . *Pericles* i 2 40
Sparkle. From women's eyes this doctrine I derive: They sparkle still the right Promethean fire . . . . *L. L. Lost* iv 3 351
Give a favour from you To sparkle in the spirits of my daughter *All's W.* v 3 75
Nay, it perchance will sparkle in your eyes . . . . *K. John* iv 1 115
Mine eyes should sparkle like the beaten flint . . . 2 *Hen. VI.* iii 2 317
Sparkles this stone as it was wont? or is't not Too dull? . *Cymbeline* ii 4 40
Sparkling. Disdain and scorn ride sparkling in her eyes . . *Much Ado* iii 1 51
Their eyes of fire sparkling through sights of steel . . . 2 *Hen. IV.* iv 1 121
His sparkling eyes, replete with wrathful fire . . . . 1 *Hen. VI.* i 1 12
Beaufort's red sparkling eyes blab his heart's malice . . 2 *Hen. VI.* iii 1 154
His viands sparkling in a golden cup . . . . . 3 *Hen. VI.* ii 5 52
With fiery eyes sparkling for very wrath . . . . ii 5 131
Love is a smoke raised with the fume of sighs; Being purged, a fire sparkling in lovers' eyes . . . . *Rom. and Jul.* i 1 197
Sparrow. Swears he will shoot no more but play with sparrows *Tempest* iv 1 100
Sparrows must not build in his house-caves . . *Meas. for Meas.* iii 2 185
The finch, the sparrow, and the lark . . . . . *M. N. Dream* iii 1 133
He that doth the ravens feed, Yea, providently caters for the sparrow, Be comfort to my age! . . . . *As Y. Like It* ii 3 44
Philip! sparrow: James, There's toys abroad . . . . *K. John* i 1 231
Rides at high speed and with his pistol kills a sparrow flying 1 *Hen. IV.* ii 4 380
You have hit it.—So did he never the sparrow. . . . . . . ii 4 382
As that ungentle gull, the cuckoo's bird, Useth the sparrow . . . v 1 61
I will buy nine sparrows for a penny, and his pia mater is not worth the ninth part of a sparrow . . . . *Troi. and Cres.* ii 1 77
She fetches her breath as short as a new-ta'en sparrow . . . . iii 2 36
Now my double-henned sparrow! . . . . v 7 11
Dismay'd not this Our captains, Macbeth and Banquo?—Yes; As sparrows eagles, or the hare the lion . . . . *Macbeth* i 2 35
There's a special providence in the fall of a sparrow . . . *Hamlet* v 2 231
Sparta. They bay'd the bear With hounds of Sparta . . *M. N. Dream* iv 1 119
Nor cheer'd with horn, In Crete, in Sparta, nor in Thessaly . . . iv 1 131
If Helen then be wife to Sparta's king, As it is known she is *Tr. and Cr.* ii 2 183
A knight of Sparta, my renowned father . . . . . *Pericles* ii 2 18
Spartan. My hounds are bred out of the Spartan kind . *M. N. Dream* iv 1 124
O Spartan dog, More fell than anguish, hunger, or the sea! . *Othello* v 2 361
Spavin. Full of windgalls, sped with spavins . . . *T. of Shrew* iii 2 53
The spavin Or springhalt reign'd among 'em . . . . *Hen. VIII.* i 3 12
Spawn. Your multiplying spawn how can he flatter? . . . *Coriolanus* ii 2 82
Spawned. Some report a sea-maid spawned him . . *Meas. for Meas.* iii 2 115
Spe. The motto, 'In hac spe vivo' . . . . *Pericles* ii 2 44
Speak to the mariners: fall to't, yarely . . . . . . *Tempest* i 1 3
Where was she born? speak; tell me . . . . i 2 260
Thou earth, thou! speak . . . . i 2 314
I pitied thee, Took pains to make thee speak . . . . i 2 354
I am the best of them that speak this speech, Were I but where 'tis spoken . . . . i 2 429
That wonders To hear thee speak of Naples . . . . i 2 433
Why speaks my father so ungently? . . . . i 2 444
Speak not you for him; he's a traitor . . . . i 2 460
For the miracle, I mean our preservation, few in millions Can speak like us ii 1 8
If but one of his pockets could speak, would it not say he lies? . . . ii 1 65
The truth you speak doth lack some gentleness And time to speak it in ii 1 137
The occasion speaks thee . . . . ii 1 207
What, art thou waking?—Do you not hear me speak? . . . . . ii 1 210
His forward voice now is to speak well of his friend . . . . . ii 2 94
If thou beest Stephano, touch me and speak to me . . . . . . ii 2 105
Hear my soul speak . . . . iii 1 63
And crown what I profess with kind event If I speak true! . . . . iii 1 70
Moon-calf, speak once in thy life, if thou beest a good moon-calf . iii 2 24
Therefore speak softly. All's hush'd as midnight yet . . . . . iv 1 206
For more assurance that a living prince Does now speak to thee . . v 1 109
The devil speaks in him . . . . v 1 129
To speak puling, like a beggar at Hallowmas . . . *T. G. of Ver.* ii 1 26
All this I speak in print, for in print I found it . . . . . . ii 1 175
What, gone without a word? Ay, so true love should do: it cannot speak ii 2 17
Now should not the shoe speak a word for weeping . . . . . . ii 3 28
Now come I to my mother: O, that she could speak now like a wood woman! . . . . ii 3 30
The dog all this while sheds not a tear nor speaks a word . . . . ii 3 34
I speak to you, and you, Sir Thurio; For Valentine, I need not cite him to it . . . . ii 4 84
Your father would speak with you . . . . ii 4 116
Then speak the truth by her . . . . ii 4 151
What then?—Nothing.—Can nothing speak? . . . . iii 1 199
If I can do it By aught that I can speak in his dispraise. . . . . iii 2 47
Shall I hear him speak?—Ay, that you shall.—That will be music . . iv 2 33
She is dead.—'Twere false, if I should speak it . . . . . . iv 2 107
To that I'll speak, to that I'll sigh and weep . . . . iv 2 123
Be my mean To bring me where to speak with Madam Silvia . . . iv 4 114
I do entreat your patience To hear me speak the message I am sent on iv 4 117
Why, wag! how now! what's the matter? Look up; speak . . . . v 4 87
She has brown hair, and speaks small like a woman . . . *Mer. Wives* i 1 49
It is spoke as a Christians ought to speak . . . . i 1 104
You must speak possitable, if you can carry her your desires towards her . . . . i 1 244
What says my bully-rook? speak scholarly and wisely . . . . . i 3 2
A box, a green-a box; do intend vat I speak? a green-a box . . . i 4 48
Peace-a your tongue. Speak-a your tale . . . . i 4 85
Desire this honest gentlewoman, your maid, to speak a good word . i 4 88
Alas, he speaks but for his friend . . . . i 4 120
He speaks sense.—I will be patient . . . . ii 1 129
My name is Corporal Nym; I speak and I avouch . . . . ii 1 138
Here's a woman would speak with you . . . . ii 2 32
One Master Brook below would fain speak with you . . . . . . ii 2 151
And you, sir! Would you speak with me? . . . . ii 2 161
If you will give me the hearing.—Speak, good Master Brook . . . ii 2 184
Me vill kill de priest; for he speak for a jack-an-ape to Anne Page . ii 3 87
I pray you, let-a me speak a word with your ear . . . . . . iii 1 81
He writes verses, he speaks holiday, he smells April and May . . . iii 2 69
I'll speak it before the best lord . . . . iii 3 53
Looking wildly, and would needs speak with you presently . . . . iii 3 95
My kinsman shall speak for himself . . . . iii 4 23
Hark ye; Master Slender would speak a word with you. . . . . . iii 4 29
Here's Mistress Quickly, sir, to speak with you . . . . iii 5 20
Let me speak with the gentlemen: they speak English? . . . . . iv 3 7
Speak, breathe, discuss; brief, short, quick, snap . . . . . . iv 5 –
I come to speak with Sir John Falstaff from Master Slender . . . . iv 5 4

Speak. He'll speak like an Anthropophaginian unto thee *Mer. Wives* iv 5 9
I'll be so bold as stay, sir, till she come down; I come to speak with her iv 5 14
Speak from thy lungs military: art thou there? iv 5 18
Where be my horses? speak well of them iv 5 65
Let me speak with you in your chamber: you shall hear how things go iv 5 125
Yet hear me speak. Assist me in my purpose iv 6 3
Am I a woodman, ha? Speak I like Herne the hunter? v 5 31
They are fairies; he that speaks to them shall die v 5 51
Do I speak feelingly now?—I think thou dost. *Meas. for Meas.* i 2 36
If I could speak so wisely under an arrest i 2 135
May your grace speak of it? i 3 6
I speak not as desiring more; But rather wishing a more strict restraint i 4 3
You must not speak with men But in the presence of the prioress: Then, if you speak, you must not show your face, Or, if you show your face, you must not speak i 4 10
Why dost thou not speak, Elbow?—He cannot, sir; he's out at elbow ii 1 60
Too late? why, no; I, that do speak a word, May call it back again ii 2 57
She speaks, and 'tis Such sense, that my sense breeds with it ii 2 141
What, do I love her, That I desire to hear her speak again? ii 2 178
Nay, I'll not warrant that; for I can speak Against the thing I say ii 4 59
To be received plain, I'll speak more gross: Your brother is to die ii 4 82
It oft falls out, To have what we would have, we speak not what we mean ii 4 118
Let me entreat you speak the former language ii 4 140
Bring me to hear them speak, where I may be concealed iii 1 52
If ever he return and I can speak to him, I will open my lips in vain, or discover his government iii 1 198
Let me hear you speak farther iii 1 212
Have you not heard speak of Mariana, the sister of Frederick? iii 1 216
You are pleasant, sir, and speak apace iii 2 120
You speak unskilfully; or if your knowledge be more it is much darkened in your malice iii 2 155
I can hardly believe that, since you know not what you speak iii 2 163
To speak so indirectly I am loath: I would say the truth iv 6 1
He tells me that, if peradventure He speak against me on the adverse side, I should not think it strange iv 6 6
Your desert speaks loud v 1 9
Now is your time: speak loud v 1 19
That which I must speak Must either punish me, not being believed, Or wring redress from you v 1 30
She will speak most bitterly and strange.—Most strange, but yet most truly, will I speak v 1 36
Poor soul, She speaks this in the infirmity of sense v 1 47
You were not bid to speak.—No, my good lord v 1 78
But you are i' the wrong To speak before your time v 1 87
Came I hither, To speak, as from his mouth, what he doth know v 1 155
First, let her show her face, and after speak v 1 168
Call that same Isabel here once again: I would speak with her v 1 271
Speak not you to him till we call upon you.—Mum v 1 286
Where is the duke? 'tis he should hear me speak v 1 296
We will hear you speak: Look you speak justly v 1 297
Lay bolts enough upon him: let him speak no more v 1 351
Kneel by me; Hold up your hands, say nothing; I'll speak all v 1 443
A heavier task could not have been imposed Than I to speak my griefs unspeakable *Com. of Errors* i 1 33
Didst thou speak with him? know'st thou his mind? ii 1 47
I could not speak with Dromio since at first I sent him from the mart ii 2 5
To me she speaks; she moves me for her theme ii 2 183
Look sweet, speak fair, become disloyalty iii 2 11
Teach me, dear creature, how to think and speak iii 2 33
Didst speak him fair?—Have patience, I beseech iv 2 16
They will surely do us no harm: you saw they speak us fair iv 4 156
Speak softly: yonder, as I think, he walks v 1 9
Good sir, draw near to me, I'll speak to him v 1 12
Most mighty duke, vouchsafe me speak a word v 1 282
Speak freely, Syracusian, what thou wilt v 1 285
Speak, old Ægeon, if thou be'st the man That hadst a wife once call'd Æmilia . . . : O, if thou be'st the same Ægeon, speak, And speak unto the same Æmilia! v 1 341
He speaks to me. I am your master, Dromio v 1 411
Would you have me speak after my custom? *Much Ado* i 1 169
I pray thee speak in sober judgement i 1 171
Speak you this with a sad brow? or do you play the flouting Jack? i 1 185
You speak this to fetch me in, my lord.—By my troth, I speak my thought i 1 225
Speak low, if you speak love ii 1 103
She speaks poniards, and every word stabs ii 1 255
Speak, count, 'tis your cue.—Silence is the perfectest herald of joy ii 1 316
Speak, cousin; or, if you cannot, stop his mouth with a kiss, and let not him speak neither ii 1 322
I was born to speak all mirth and no matter ii 1 343
He was wont to speak plain and to the purpose, like an honest man ii 3 19
These are very crotchets that he speaks; Note, notes, forsooth, and nothing ii 3 58
I should think this a gull, but that the white-bearded fellow speaks it ii 3 124
It were not good She knew his love, lest she make sport at it.—Why, you speak truth iii 1 59
If I should speak, She would mock me into air iii 1 74
For what his heart thinks his tongue speaks iii 2 14
I have studied eight or nine wise words to speak to you iii 2 74
If your leisure served, I would speak with you iii 2 85
You speak like an ancient and most quiet watchman iii 3 41
Never speak: we charge you let us obey you to go with us iii 3 188
How now? do you speak in the sick tune? iii 4 41
Speaks a little off the matter iii 5 10
Is my lord well, that he doth speak so wide?—Sweet prince, why speak not you?—What should I speak? iv 1 63
If they speak but truth of her, These hands shall tear her iv 1 192
Bring me a father that so loved his child, Whose joy of her is overwhelm'd like mine, And bid him speak of patience v 1 10
Men Can counsel and speak comfort to that grief Which they themselves not feel v 1 21
'Tis all men's office to speak patience To those that wring under the load of sorrow, But no man's virtue nor sufficiency To be so moral v 1 27
I speak not like a dotard nor a fool, As under privilege of age to brag v 1 59
Show outward hideousness, And speak off half a dozen dangerous words v 1 97
Shall I speak a word in your ear? v 1 144
I know not how to pray your patience; Yet I must speak v 1 282
Your worship speaks like a most thankful and reverend youth v 1 324
Comes in embassy The French king's daughter with yourself to speak *L. L. Lost* i 1 136

Speak. If I break faith, this word shall speak for me *L. L. Lost* i 1 154
It is the manner of a man to speak to a woman i 1 212
Speak you this in my praise, master?—In thy condign praise i 2 26
He speaks the mere contrary; crosses love not him i 2 35
His tongue, all impatient to speak and not see, Did stumble with haste ii 1 238
Boyet is disposed.—But to speak that in words which his eye hath disclosed ii 1 250
Thou hast no feeling of it, Moth: I will speak that l'envoy iii 1 116
When tongues speak sweetly, then they name her name iii 1 167
I may speak of thee as the traveller doth of Venice iv 2 97
When Love speaks, the voice of all the gods Make heaven drowsy iv 3 344
To speak dout, fine, when he should say doubt v 1 22
They teach him there; 'Thus must thou speak,' and, 'thus thy body bear' v 2 100
An angel shalt thou see; Yet fear not thou, but speak audaciously v 2 104
If they do speak our language, 'tis our will That some plain man recount their purposes: Know what they would v 2 175
How blow? how blow? speak to be understood v 2 294
Madam, speak true. It is not so, my lord v 2 364
Speak for yourselves; my wit is at an end v 2 430
He speaks not like a man of God's making v 2 528
A conqueror, and afeard to speak! run away for shame v 2 582
There are Worthies a-coming will speak their mind in some other sort v 2 589
Speak, brave Hector: we are much delighted v 2 671
You may speak as small as you will *M. N. Dream* i 2 52
I'll speak in a monstrous little voice i 2 54
Do I entice you? do I speak you fair? ii 1 199
To speak troth, I have forgot our way: We'll rest us ii 2 36
Where are you? speak, an if you hear; Speak, of all loves! ii 2 153
Half his face must be seen through the lion's neck: and he himself must speak iii 1 39
Must I speak now?—Ay, marry, must you iii 1 91
'Ninus' tomb,' man: why, you must not speak that yet iii 1 101
You speak all your part at once, cues and all iii 1 102
You speak not as you think: it cannot be iii 2 191
Wherefore speaks he this To her he hates? iii 2 227
How low am I, thou painted maypole? speak; How low am I? iii 2 296
Let her alone: speak not of Helena; Take not her part iii 2 332
Where art thou, proud Demetrius? speak thou now iii 2 401
Lysander! speak again: Thou runaway, thou coward, art thou fled? Speak! iii 2 404
As I think,—for truly would I speak, And now I do bethink me, so it is iv 1 154
Love, therefore, and tongue-tied simplicity In least speak most v 1 105
It is not enough to speak, but to speak true v 1 121
I wonder if the lion be to speak.—No wonder, my lord v 1 153
Would you desire lime and hair to speak better? v 1 166
O Pyramus, arise! Speak, speak. Quite dumb? Dead, dead? v 1 334
I love thee, and it is my love that speaks *Mer. of Venice* i 1 87
If they should speak, would almost damn those ears Which, hearing them, would call their brothers fools i 1 98
I must be one of these same dumb wise men, For Gratiano never lets me speak i 1 107
Gratiano speaks an infinite deal of nothing, more than any man i 1 113
Say to me what I should do That in your knowledge may by me be done, And I am prest unto it: therefore, speak i 1 160
I will bethink me. May I speak with Antonio? i 3 31
Never to speak to lady afterward In way of marriage ii 1 41
One speak for both. What would you? ii 2 150
Tell gentle Jessica I will not fail her; speak it privately ii 4 21
Master Antonio is at his house and desires to speak with you both iii 1 78
I speak too long; but 'tis to peize the time, To eke it and to draw it out iii 2 22
You speak upon the rack, Where men enforced do speak any thing iii 2 32
You have bereft me of all words, Only my blood speaks to you in my veins iii 2 178
I'll have my bond; speak not against my bond iii 3 4
I pray thee, hear me speak.—I'll have my bond; I will not hear thee speak: I'll have my bond; and therefore speak no more iii 3 11
Although I speak it in your presence, You have a noble and a true conceit iii 4 1
And speak between the change of man and boy With a reed voice iii 4 66
And speak of frays Like a fine bragging youth, and tell quaint lies iii 4 68
I was always plain with you, and so now I speak my agitation of the matter iii 5 4
Thou but offend'st thy lungs to speak so loud iv 1 140
Say how I loved you, speak me fair in death iv 1 275
Sir, I would speak with you iv 2 12
Speak not so grossly. You are all amazed v 1 266
He keeps at school, and report speaks goldenly of his profit *As Y. L. It* i 1 6
Or, to speak more properly, stays me here at home unkept i 1 8
Was not Charles, the duke's wrestler, here to speak with me? i 1 95
Almost with tears I speak it, there is not one so young and so villanous this day living. I speak but brotherly of him i 1 160
Speak no more of him; you'll be whipped for taxation one of these days i 2 90
The more pity, that fools may not speak wisely what wise men do foolishly i 2 93
Speak to him, ladies; see if you can move him i 2 171
How dost thou, Charles?—He cannot speak, my lord i 2 232
What passion hangs these weights upon my tongue? I cannot speak to her i 2 270
Dear sovereign, hear me speak i 3 68
Her very silence and her patience Speak to the people i 3 81
Go, seek him: tell him I would speak with him ii 7 7
Invest me in my motley; give me leave To speak my mind ii 7 59
Sit down and feed, and welcome to our table.—Speak you so gently? ii 7 106
I scarce can speak to thank you for myself ii 7 170
I prithee, tell me who is it quickly, and speak apace iii 2 208
The devil take mocking: speak, sad brow and true maid iii 2 226
Do you not know I am a woman? when I think, I must speak iii 2 264
I will speak to him like a saucy lackey iii 2 313
An old religious uncle of mine taught me to speak iii 2 362
But are you so much in love as your rhymes speak? iii 2 417
He writes brave verses, speaks brave words, swears brave oaths iii 4 44
Yet words do well When he that speaks them pleases those that hear iii 5 112
I would kiss before I spoke.—Nay, you were better speak first iv 1 73
O, I have heard him speak of that same brother iv 3 122
Know of me then, for now I speak to some purpose v 2 57
I speak not this that you should bear a good opinion of my knowledge v 2 59
Who do you speak to, 'Why blame you me to love you?' v 2 115

Speak. If he chance to speak, be ready straight And with a low submissive reverence Say 'What is it?' *T. of Shrew* Ind. 1 52
Have I dream'd till now? I do not sleep: I see, I hear, I speak Ind. 2 72
But did I never speak of all that time?—O, yes, my lord Ind. 2 84
Hark, Tranio! thou may'st hear Minerva speak i 1 84
If you speak me fair, I'll tell you news indifferent good for either i 2 180
You like not of my company.—Mistake me not; I speak but as I find ii 1 66
I pray, Let us, that are poor petitioners, speak too ii 1 72
Say she be mute and will not speak a word; Then I'll commend her volubility ii 1 175
The priest attends To speak the ceremonial rites of marriage iii 2 6
She, poor soul, Knows not which way to stand, to look, to speak iv 1 188
He that knows better how to tame a shrew, Now let him speak iv 1 214
I trust I may have leave to speak; And speak I will iv 3 73
Look, what I speak, or do, or think to do, You are still crossing it iv 3 194
His father is come from Pisa and is here at the door to speak with him v 1 30
To speak on the part of virginity, is to accuse your mothers *All's Well* i 1 148
Knew the true minute when Exception bid him speak i 2 40
A prophet I, madam; and I speak the truth the next way i 3 62
He bid Helen come to you: of her I am to speak i 3 71
Tell my gentlewoman I would speak with her i 3 73
I thank you for your honest care: I will speak with you further anon i 3 132
Thine eyes See it so grossly shown in thy behaviours That in their kind they speak it i 3 185
Speak, is't so? If it be so, you have wound a goodly clew i 3 187
Had you not lately an intent,—speak truly,—To go to Paris? i 3 224
Eat, speak, and move under the influence of the most received star ii 1 56
In thee some blessed spirit doth speak His powerful sound within an organ weak ii 1 178
A trifle neither, in good faith, if the learned should speak truth of it ii 2 37
'Fore me, I speak in respect— Nay, 'tis strange, 'tis very strange ii 3 32
The honour, sir, that flames in your fair eyes, Before I speak, too threateningly replies ii 3 87
Speak; thine answer.—Pardon, my gracious lord ii 3 173
Is it not a language I speak?—A most harsh one ii 3 197
Write to the king That which I durst not speak ii 3 306
Grief would have tears, and sorrow bids me speak iii 4 42
But to speak of him as my kinsman, he's a most notable coward iii 6 10
The duke shall both speak of it, and extend to you what further becomes iii 6 73
When you sally upon him, speak what terrible language you will iv 1 3
What linsey-woolsey hast thou to speak to us again?—E'en such as you speak to me iv 1 14
We must every one be a man of his own fancy, not to know what we speak iv 1 20
If there be here German, or Dane, low Dutch, Italian, or French, let him speak to me iv 1 79
I understand thee, and can speak thy tongue iv 1 82
Nay, I'll speak that Which you will wonder at iv 1 94
Remain there but an hour, nor speak to me iv 2 58
I will say true,—or thereabouts, set down, for I'll speak truth iv 3 172
Fare ye well, sir; I am for France too: we shall speak of you there iv 3 365
I moved the king my master to speak in the behalf of my daughter iv 5 76
Whose nature sickens but to speak a truth. Am I or that or this for what he'll utter, That will speak any thing? v 3 207
I know more than I'll speak.—But wilt thou not speak all thou knowest? v 3 256
I can sing And speak to him in many sorts of music *T. Night* i 2 58
Speaks three or four languages word for word without book i 3 27
Say I do speak with her, my lord, what then? i 4 23
There is at the gate a young gentleman much desires to speak with you i 5 108
He speaks nothing but madman i 5 114
Madam, yond young fellow swears he will speak with you. I told him you were sick; he takes on him to understand so much, and therefore comes to speak with you i 5 148
Tell him he shall not speak with me.—Has been told so i 5 155
But he'll speak with you.—What kind o' man is he? i 5 158
He'll speak with you, will you or no.—Of what personage and years is he? i 5 162
He is very well-favoured and he speaks very shrewishly i 5 169
Which is she?—Speak to me; I shall answer for her. Your will? i 5 179
Speak your office.—It alone concerns your ear i 5 223
Methought her eyes had lost her tongue, For she did speak in starts ii 2 22
Thou dost speak masterly: My life upon't, young though thou art ii 4 23
I bade you never speak again of him iii 1 118
A cypress, not a bosom, Hideth my heart. So, let me hear you speak iii 1 133
Youth is bought more oft than begg'd or borrow'd. I speak too loud iii 4 4
If all the devils of hell be drawn in little, and Legion himself possessed him, yet I'll speak to him iii 4 96
Lo, how hollow the fiend speaks within him! iii 4 101
An you speak ill of the devil, how he takes it at heart! iii 4 111
Come, sir, I pray you, go.—Let me speak a little iii 4 393
I am not sent to you by my lady, to bid you come speak with her iv 1 7
Let your lady know I am here to speak with her v 1 46
My lord would speak; my duty hushes me v 1 110
Why do you speak to me? I never hurt you v 1 190
I leave my duty a little unthought of and speak out of my injury v 1 319
Hear me speak, And let no quarrel nor no brawl to come v 1 363
I speak it in the freedom of my knowledge *W. Tale* i 1 12
I speak as my understanding instructs me i 1 20
Speak you.—I had thought, sir, to have held my peace i 2 27
Even at this present, Now while I speak this i 2 193
This is strange: methinks My favour here begins to warp. Not speak? i 2 365
You'll kiss me hard and speak to me as if I were a baby still ii 1 5
He who shall speak for her is afar off guilty But that he speaks ii 1 104
It is for you we speak, not for ourselves: You are abused ii 1 140
We are to speak in public; for this business Will raise us all ii 1 197
Whose love had spoke, Even since it could speak, from an infant iii 2 71
You speak a language that I understand not iii 2 81
Go on: Thou canst not speak too much iii 2 216
Fool again!—I'll speak of her no more, nor of your children iii 2 230
Thou didst speak but well When most the truth iii 2 233
And with speed so pace To speak of Perdita, now grown in grace iv 1 24
Of that fatal country, Sicilia, prithee speak no more iv 2 23
One of these two must be necessities, Which then will speak iv 4 39
When you speak, sweet, I'ld have you do it ever iv 4 136
I cannot speak So well, nothing so well; no, nor mean better iv 4 391
Can he speak? hear? Know man from man? dispute his own estate? iv 4 410
Once or twice I was about to speak and tell him plainly iv 4 454
Speak ere thou diest.—I cannot speak, nor think, Nor dare to know that which I know iv 4 462
It is my father's music To speak your deeds iv 4 530
You have your father's bosom there And speak his very heart iv 4 575

Speak. Happy be you! All that you speak shows fair *W. Tale* iv 4 636
And speak of something wildly By us perform'd before v 1 129
Where's Bohemia? speak.—Here in your city v 1 185
I speak amazedly; and it becomes My marvel and my message v 1 187
They kiss the earth; Forswear themselves as often as they speak v 1 200
They say one would speak to her and stand in hope of answer v 2 110
I like your silence, it the more shows off Your wonder: but yet speak v 3 22
What you can make her do, I am content to look on: what to speak, I am content to hear; for 'tis as easy To make her speak as move v 3 92
She hangs about his neck: If she pertain to life let her speak too v 3 113
But it appears she lives, Though yet she speak not v 3 118
Thus, after greeting, speaks the King of France *K. John* i 1 2
Sirrah, speak, What doth move you to claim your brother's land? i 1 90
How he did prevail I shame to speak, But truth is truth i 1 104
As I have heard my father speak himself i 1 107
We coldly pause for thee; Chatillon, speak ii 1 53
Let us hear them speak Whose title they admit ii 1 199
Speak, citizens, for England: who's your king?—The king of England ii 1 362
Hear me, mighty kings.—Speak on with favour; we are bent to hear ii 1 422
He speaks plain cannon fire, and smoke and bounce ii 1 462
Speak England first, that hath been forward first To speak unto this city ii 1 482
Or if you will, to speak more properly, I will enforce it easily ii 1 514
Speak then, prince Dauphin; can you love this lady? ii 1 524
Then speak again; not all thy former tale, But this one word, whether thy tale be true iii 1 25
Itself so heinous is As it makes harmful all that speak of it iii 1 41
O, that a man should speak those words to me! iii 1 130
Speaks not from her faith, But from her need iii 1 210
Now hear me speak with a prophetic spirit iii 4 126
What I mean to speak Shall blow each dust ... Out of the path iii 4 127
I will not stir, nor wince, nor speak a word iv 1 81
And can give audience To any tongue, speak it of what it will iv 2 140
He that speaks doth gripe the hearer's wrist iv 2 190
Whose tongue soe'er speaks false, Not truly speaks; who speaks not truly, lies iv 3 91
Let me have audience; I am sent to speak v 2 119
Now hear our English king; For thus his royalty doth speak in me v 2 129
Give me leave to speak.—No, I will speak.—We will attend to neither v 2 162
Who's there? speak, ho! speak quickly, or I shoot.—A friend v 6 1
The king Yet speaks and peradventure may recover v 6 31
His highness yet doth speak, and holds belief That, being brought into the open air, It would allay the burning quality Of that fell poison v 7 6
Ourselves will hear The accuser and the accused freely speak *Richard II.* i 1 17
For what I speak My body shall make good upon this earth i 1 36
What my tongue speaks my right drawn sword may prove i 1 46
What I speak, my life shall prove it true i 1 87
Speak truly, on thy knighthood and thy oath i 3 14
Speak like a true knight, so defend thee heaven! i 3 34
Nay, speak thy mind; and let him ne'er speak more That speaks thy words again to do thee harm! ii 1 230
Be confident to speak, Northumberland: We three are but thyself ii 1 274
For God's sake, speak comfortable words ii 2 76
Discomfort guides my tongue And bids me speak of nothing but despair iii 2 66
Boys, with women's voices, Strive to speak big iii 2 114
Of comfort no man speak: Let's talk of graves, of worms and epitaphs iii 2 144
Speak sweetly, man, although thy looks be sour iii 2 193
Let no man speak again To alter this, for counsel is but vain iii 2 213
Speak to his gentle hearing kind commends iii 3 126
To look so poorly and to speak so fair iii 3 128
In the base court he doth attend To speak with you iii 3 177
Sorrow and grief of heart Makes him speak fondly iii 3 185
When, and how, Camest thou by this ill tidings? speak, thou wretch iii 4 80
I speak no more than every one doth know iii 4 91
Call forth Bagot. Now, Bagot, freely speak thy mind iv 1 2
Worst in this royal presence may I speak, Yet best beseeming me to speak the truth iv 1 115
I speak to subjects, and a subject speaks, Stirr'd up by God iv 1 132
Before I freely speak my mind herein iv 1 327
For ever may my knees grow to the earth, My tongue cleave to my roof within my mouth, Unless a pardon ere I rise or speak v 3 32
Shall I for love speak treason to thy face? v 3 44
Speak with me, pity me, open the door v 3 77
Speak it in French, king; say, 'pardonne moi' v 3 119
Speak 'pardon' as 'tis current in our land; The chopping French we do not understand. Thine eye begins to speak v 3 123
Speak it again; Twice saying 'pardon' doth not pardon twain v 3 133
Now am I, if a man should speak truly, little better than one of the wicked *1 Hen. IV.* i 2 105
You were about to speak.—Yea, my good lord i 3 22
But, sirrah, henceforth Let me not hear you speak of Mortimer i 3 119
Speak of Mortimer! 'Zounds, I will speak of him i 3 130
He would not ransom Mortimer; Forbad my tongue to speak of Mortimer i 3 220
I'll have a starling shall be taught to speak Nothing but 'Mortimer' i 3 224
I speak not this in estimation, As what I think might be i 3 272
Strike sooner than speak, and speak sooner than drink ii 1 86
And heard thee murmur tales of iron wars; Speak terms of manage ii 3 52
Do you not love me? Nay, tell me if you speak in jest or no ii 3 102
Let them speak: if they speak more or less than truth, they are villains ii 4 190
Speak, sirs; how was it?—We four set upon some dozen ii 4 192
When thou hast tired thyself in base comparisons, hear me speak but this ii 4 277
There is a nobleman of the court at door would speak with you ii 4 318
I must speak in passion, and I will do it in King Cambyses' vein ii 4 424
Now I do not speak to thee in drink but in tears ii 4 457
Then, peremptorily I speak it, there is virtue in that Falstaff ii 4 472
Dost thou speak like a king? Do thou stand for me, and I'll play my father ii 4 476
As oft as Lancaster Doth speak of you, his cheek looks pale iii 1 9
I think there's no man speaks better Welsh iii 1 49
Speak it in Welsh.—I can speak English, lord, as well as you iii 1 121
My wife can speak no English, I no Welsh iii 1 193
He speaks most vilely of you, like a foul-mouthed man as he is iii 3 122
You do not counsel well: You speak it out of fear and cold heart iv 3 7
I may speak it to my shame, I have a truant been to chivalry v 1 93
I prithee, speak; we will not trust our eyes Without our ears v 4 139
Which of you will stop The vent of hearing when loud Rumour speaks? *2 Hen. IV.* Ind. 2
I [Rumour] speak of peace, while covert enmity Under the smile of safety wounds the world Ind. 9
But what mean I To speak so true at first? Ind. 28
Speak, Morton; Tell thou an earl his divination lies i 1 87

Speak. Thou shakest thy head and hold'st it fear or sin To speak a truth *2 Hen. IV.* i 1 96
I hear for certain, and do speak the truth i 1 188
You must speak louder; my master is deaf i 2 78
Go, pluck him by the elbow; I must speak with him i 2 82
Sir, my lord would speak with you i 2 104
Well, God mend him! I pray you, let me speak with you i 2 125
I sent for you, when there were matters against you for your life, to come speak with me i 2 150
Speak plainly your opinions of our hopes i 3 3
You speak as having power to do wrong ii 1 141
I have given over, I will speak no more: Do what you will ii 3 5
Those that could speak low and tardily Would turn their own perfection to abuse, To seem like him ii 3 26
Ancient Pistol's below, and would speak with you.—Hang him! ii 4 75
Nay, an a' do nothing but speak nothing, a' shall be nothing here ii 4 207
Do not speak like a death's-head; do not bid me remember mine end ii 4 254
How vilely did you speak of me even now! ii 4 327
I cannot speak; if my heart be not ready to burst ii 4 409
When Richard . . . Did speak these words, now proved a prophecy iii 1 69
You speak, Lord Mowbray, now you know not what iv 1 130
The leaders, having charge from you to stand, Will not go off until they hear you speak iv 2 100
Not a tongue of them all speaks any other word but my name iv 3 22
I, in my condition, Shall better speak of you than you deserve iv 3 91
Speak lower, princes, for the king recovers iv 4 129
Not so much noise, my lords: sweet prince, speak low iv 5 16
I never thought to hear you speak again iv 5 92
An honest man, sir, is able to speak for himself, when a knave is not v 1 50
We meet like men that had forgot to speak v 2 22
Well, you must now speak Sir John Falstaff fair v 2 33
Speak in your state What I have done that misbecame my place v 2 99
So shall I live to speak my father's words v 2 107
I speak of Africa and golden joys v 3 104
Under which king, Bezonian? speak, or die v 3 119
I speak the truth: When Pistol lies, do this; and fig me v 3 123
Is the old king dead?—As nail in door: the things I speak are just v 3 127
Pistol speaks nought but truth v 5 40
Speak to that vain man.—Have you your wits? know you what 'tis you speak? v 5 48
My king! my Jove! I speak to thee, my heart! v 5 50
I cannot now speak: I will hear you soon v 5 100
That, when he speaks, The air, a charter'd libertine, is still *Hen. V.* i 1 47
I could with a ready guess declare, Before the Frenchman speak a word i 1 97
Speak, my lord; For we will hear, note, and believe in heart That what you speak is in your conscience wash'd i 2 29
Either our history shall with full mouth Speak freely of our acts i 2 231
The Duke of Gloucester would speak with you iii 2 60
Therefore, go speak: the duke will hear thy voice iii 6 48
Speak, captain, for his life, and I will thee requite iii 6 51
The king is coming, and I must speak with him from the pridge iii 6 90
Now we speak upon our cue, and our voice is imperial iii 6 130
So! in the name of Jesu Christ, speak iv 1 65
I will speak lower.—I pray you and beseech you that you will iv 1 82
Though I speak it to you, I think the king is but a man, as I am iv 1 105
I will speak my conscience of the king iv 1 123
Howsoever you speak this to feel other men's minds iv 1 130
And hold their manhoods cheap whiles any speaks That fought with us iv 3 66
Let me speak proudly: tell the constable We are but warriors iv 3 108
I speak but in the figures and comparisons of it iv 7 46
You thought, because he could not speak English in the native garb, he could not therefore handle an English cudgel v 1 80
Your majesty shall mock at me; I cannot speak your England v 2 103
I am glad thou canst speak no better English v 2 126
I speak to thee plain soldier: if thou canst love me for this, take me v 2 156
What sayest thou then to my love? speak, my fair, and fairly v 2 177
It is as easy for me, Kate, to conquer the kingdom as to speak so much more French v 2 196
Who, though I speak it before his face, if he be not fellow with the best king, thou shalt find the best king of good fellows v 2 260
God speak this Amen! v 2 396
Speak softly, or the loss of those great towns Will make him burst his lead and rise from death *1 Hen. VI.* i 1 63
What's past and what's to come she can descry. Speak, shall I call her in? i 2 58
Speak, Salisbury; at least, if thou canst speak: How farest thou? i 4 73
Hast thou any life? Speak unto Talbot; nay, look up to him i 4 89
Here is the Talbot: who would speak with him? ii 2 37
Since you are tongue-tied and so loath to speak, In dumb significants proclaim your thoughts ii 4 25
Plantagenet, I see, must hold his tongue, Lest it be said 'Speak, sirrah, when you should' iii 1 62
I speak not to that railing Hecate, But unto thee, Alençon iii 2 64
Speak, Pucelle, and enchant him with thy words iii 3 40
Stay, let thy humble handmaid speak to thee.—Speak on iii 3 42
Give them leave to speak. Say, gentlemen, what makes you thus exclaim? iv 1 82
Speak, thy father's care, Art thou not weary, John? iv 6 26
Speak to thy father ere thou yield thy breath! iv 7 24
He speaks with such a proud commanding spirit iv 7 88
What tidings send our scouts? I prithee, speak v 2 10
Fain would I woo her, yet I dare not speak: I'll call for pen and ink v 3 65
Speaks Suffolk as he thinks?—Fair Margaret knows That Suffolk doth not flatter v 3 141
Speak, Winchester; for boiling choler chokes The hollow passage of my poison'd voice, By sight of these v 4 120
Let thy betters speak.—The cardinal's not my better *2 Hen. VI.* i 3 112
He did speak them to me in the garret one night i 3 194
Answer that I shall ask; For, till thou speak, thou shalt not pass i 4 30
Witness my tears, I cannot stay to speak ii 4 86
Had I first been put to speak my mind, I think I should have told iii 1 43
Shall I speak my conscience, Our kinsman Gloucester is as innocent iii 1 68
They play'd me false! And well such losers may have leave to speak iii 1 185
Say as you think, and speak it from your souls iii 1 247
I did dream to-night The duke was dumb and could not speak a word iii 2 32
Every word you speak in his behalf Is slander to your royal dignity iii 2 208
Go; speak not to me; even now be gone. O, go not yet! iii 2 352
How fares my lord? speak, Beaufort, to thy sovereign iii 3 1
Beaufort, it is thy sovereign speaks to thee iii 3 7
Speak, captain, shall I stab the forlorn swain? iv 1 65
My gracious lord, entreat him, speak him fair iv 1 120

Speak. It is to you, good people, that I speak *2 Hen. VI.* iv 2 137
Will you credit this base drudge's words, That speaks he knows not what? iv 2 160
And more than that, he can speak French; and therefore he is a traitor iv 2 176
Can he that speaks with the tongue of an enemy be a good counsellor, or no? iv 2 181
I desire no more.—And, to speak truth, thou deservest no less iv 3 11
He speaks Latin.—Hear me but speak, and bear me where you will iv 7 63
Wherein have I offended most? Have I affected wealth or honour? speak iv 7 104
He has a familiar under his tongue; he speaks not o' God's name iv 7 115
Scarce can I speak, my choler is so great v 1 23
Speak not in spite, For you shall sup with Jesu Christ to-night v 1 213
I would speak blasphemy ere bid you fly: But fly you must v 2 85
Speak thou for me and tell them what I did *3 Hen. VI.* i 1 16
Peace, thou! and give King Henry leave to speak.—Plantagenet shall speak first i 1 120
Art thou king, and wilt be forced? I shame to hear thee speak i 1 231
Hear me speak.—Thou hast spoke too much already i 1 257
I'll prove the contrary, if you'll hear me speak i 2 20
Sweet Clifford, hear me speak before I die i 3 18
Wrath makes him deaf: speak thou, Northumberland i 4 53
York cannot speak, unless he wear a crown i 4 93
By your leave I speak it, You love the breeder better than the male ii 1 41
O, speak no more, for I have heard too much ii 1 48
For selfsame wind that I should speak withal Is kindling coals that fires all my breast, And burns me up ii 1 82
Blame me not: 'Tis love I bear thy glories makes me speak ii 1 158
Ay, now methinks I hear great Warwick speak ii 1 186
Are you there, butcher? O, I cannot speak! ii 2 95
Why, how now, long-tongued Warwick! dare you speak? ii 2 102
Have done with words, my lords, and hear me speak ii 2 117
Give no limits to my tongue: I am a king, and privileged to speak ii 2 120
I defy thee; Not willing any longer conference, Since thou deniest the gentle king to speak ii 2 172
For, though before his face I speak the words, Your brother Richard mark'd him for the grave ii 6 39
His ill-boding tongue no more shall speak ii 6 59
Speak, Clifford, dost thou know who speaks to thee? ii 6 61
No humble suitors press to speak for right, No, not a man iii 1 19
She, poor wretch, for grief can speak no more iii 1 47
I swear to thee I speak no more than what my soul intends iii 2 94
Those gracious words revive my drooping thoughts And give my tongue-tied sorrows leave to speak iii 3 22
Lady Bona, hear me speak, Before you answer Warwick iii 3 65
Canst thou speak against thy liege, Whom thou obeyed'st thirty and six years? iii 3 95
And you too, Somerset and Montague, Speak freely what you think iv 1 28
Speak suddenly, my lords, are we all friends? iv 2 4
Hence with him to the Tower; let him not speak iv 8 57
Speak gentle words and humbly bend thy knee v 1 22
That glues my lips and will not let me speak v 2 38
As good to chide the waves as speak them fair v 4 24
This speak I, lords, to let you understand v 4 33
A woman of this valiant spirit Should, if a coward heard her speak these words, Infuse his breast with magnanimity v 4 40
I speak not this as doubting any here v 4 43
For every word I speak, Ye see, I drink the water of mine eyes v 4 74
Go, bear them hence; I will not hear them speak v 5 4
Bring forth the gallant, let us hear him speak v 5 12
Speak like a subject, proud ambitious York! v 5 17
Sweet Ned! speak to thy mother, boy! Canst thou not speak? v 5 51
No, no, my heart will burst, an if I speak: And I will speak, that so my heart may burst v 5 59
You may partake of any thing we say: We speak no treason *Richard III.* i 1 90
My proud heart sues and prompts my tongue to speak i 2 171
That was in thy rage: Speak it again, and, even with the word i 2 189
His grace speaks cheerfully.—God grant him health! i 3 34
Because I cannot flatter and speak fair, Smile in men's faces i 3 47
To whom in all this presence speaks your grace? i 3 54
'Tis time to speak; my pains are quite forgot i 3 117
I would speak with Clarence, and I came hither on my legs i 4 86
How darkly and how deadly dost thou speak! Your eyes do menace me i 4 175
Speak at once what is it thou demand'st ii 1 98
But for my brother not a man would speak, Nor I, ungracious, speak unto myself For him, poor soul ii 1 126
In God's name, speak: when is the royal day? iii 4 3
Speak and look back, and pry on every side iii 5 6
We would have had you heard The traitor speak iii 5 57
Your grace's word shall serve, As well as I had seen and heard him speak iii 5 63
What tongueless blocks were they! would they not speak? iii 7 42
I know not whether to depart in silence, Or bitterly to speak iii 7 142
To speak, and to avoid the first, And then, in speaking, not to incur the last iii 7 151
O Dorset, speak not to me, get thee hence! iv 1 39
What sayest thou? speak suddenly; be brief iv 2 20
Give me some breath, some little pause, my lord, Before I positively speak iv 2 25
Thus both are gone with conscience and remorse; They could not speak iv 3 21
O, let me speak!—Do then; but I'll not hear.—I will be mild iv 4 159
I prithee, hear me speak.—You speak too bitterly.—Hear me a word; For I shall never speak to thee again iv 4 179
I say amen to all.—Stay, madam; I must speak a word with you iv 4 198
You speak as if that I had slain my cousins.—Cousins, indeed iv 4 221
Will not King Richard let me speak with him?—No, my good lord v 1 1
Fool, of thyself speak well: fool, do not flatter v 3 192
Speak freely.—First, it was usual with him *Hen. VIII.* i 2 131
To this point hast thou heard him At any time speak aught? i 2 146
Go forward.—On my soul, I'll speak but truth i 2 177
Go, give 'em welcome; you can speak the French tongue i 4 57
Because they speak no English, thus they pray'd i 4 65
Pray, speak what has happen'd.—You may guess quickly what ii 1 6
If he speak of Buckingham, pray, tell him You met him half in heaven ii 1 87
And when you would say something that is sad, Speak how I fell ii 1 136
These news are every where; every tongue speaks 'em ii 2 39
Perceive I speak sincerely, and high note's Ta'en of your many virtues ii 3 59
Speak my thanks and my obedience, As from a blushing handmaid ii 3 71
Lord cardinal, To you I speak.—Your pleasure, madam? ii 4 69
I do profess You speak not like yourself ii 4 85
The which before His highness shall speak in, I do beseech You, gracious madam, to unthink your speaking ii 4 103

Speak. Thy parts Sovereign and pious else, could speak thee out, The queen of earthly queens *Hen. VIII.* ii 4 140
I speak my good lord cardinal to this point, And thus far clear him . ii 4 166
Would they speak with me?—They will'd me say so, madam . iii 1 17
We shall give you The full cause of our coming.—Speak it here . iii 1 29
Would all other women Could speak this with as free a soul as I do! . iii 1 32
Pray, speak in English: here are some will thank you, If you speak truth . iii 1 46
Ye speak like honest men; pray God, ye prove so! . iii 1 69
Let me speak myself, Since virtue finds no friends . iii 1 125
You speak your pleasures: What he deserves of you and me I know . iii 2 13
I have no power to speak, sir.—What, amazed At my misfortunes? . iii 2 373
Speak it to us.—As well as I am able . iv 1 61
Yet thus far, Griffith, give me leave to speak him, And yet with charity iv 2 32
May it please your highness To hear me speak his good now? . iv 2 47
Christendom shall ever speak his virtue . iv 2 63
Now, sir, you speak of two The most remark'd i' the kingdom . v 1 32
Who dare speak One syllable against him?—Yes, yes, Sir Thomas, There are that dare; and I myself have ventured To speak my mind of him v 1 38
I grieve at what I speak, And am right sorry to repeat what follows . v 1 95
Speak to the business, master secretary: Why are we met in council? . v 3 1
I speak it with a single heart . v 3 38
Let me speak, sir, For heaven now bids me . v 5 15
I speak no more than truth.—Thou dost not speak so much *Tr. and Cr.* i 1 64
Pray you, speak no more to me: I will leave all as I found it . i 1 90
But mark Troilus above the rest.—Speak not so loud . i 2 201
Sir, my lord would instantly speak with you . i 2 297
Yet let it please both, Thou great, and wise, to hear Ulysses speak.—Speak, Prince of Ithaca . i 3 69
And when he speaks, 'Tis like a chime a-mending; with terms unsquared i 3 158
To set his sense on the attentive bent, And then to speak.—Speak frankly as the wind . i 3 253
He bade me take a trumpet, And to this purpose speak . i 3 264
Speak then, thou vinewedst leaven, speak . ii 1 15
I shall cut out your tongue.—'Tis no matter; I shall speak as much as thou afterwards.—No more words . ii 1 122
You speak Like one besotted on your sweet delights . ii 2 142
These moral laws Of nature and of nations speak aloud . ii 2 185
Who comes here?—Patroclus, I'll speak with nobody . ii 3 75
In second voice we'll not be satisfied; We come to speak with him . ii 3 150
Possess'd he is with greatness, And speaks not to himself but with a pride . ii 3 181
I come to speak with Paris from the Prince Troilus . iii 1 40
You speak your fair pleasure, sweet queen . iii 1 51
An you draw backward, we'll put you i' the fills. Why do you not speak to her? . iii 2 48
And what truth can speak truest not truer than Troilus . iii 2 105
Sweet, bid me hold my tongue, For in this rapture I shall surely speak The thing I shall repent . iii 2 138
Where is my wit? I know not what I speak.—Well know they what they speak that speak so wisely . iii 2 158
Because it shall not speak of your pretty encounters, press it to death . iii 2 217
Comes the general to speak with me? You know my mind . iii 3 55
I as your lover speak; The fool slides o'er the ice that you should break iii 3 214
Since she could speak, She hath not given so many good words breath . iv 1 72
Do not deny him: It doth import him much to speak with me . iv 2 52
I speak not 'be thou true,' as fearing thee . iv 4 64
O heavens! 'be true' again!—Hear why I speak it, love . iv 4 77
But that you say 'be't so,' I'll speak it in my spirit and honour, 'no' . iv 4 137
There's language in her eye, her cheek, her lip, Nay, her foot speaks . iv 5 56
What, are you up here, ho? speak.—Who calls? . v 2 1
By hell and all hell's torments, I will not speak a word! . v 2 44
You shall not go: one cannot speak a word, But it straight starts you . v 2 100
I do not speak of flight, of fear, of death . v 10 12
Before we proceed any further, hear me speak.—Speak, speak *Coriolanus* i 1 2
The gods know I speak this in hunger for bread . i 1 24
He pays himself with being proud.—Nay, but speak not maliciously . i 1 35
Where go you With bats and clubs? The matter? speak, I pray you . i 1 57
For, look you, I may make the belly smile As well as speak . i 1 114
What then? 'Fore me, this fellow speaks! What then? what then? . i 1 124
O, doubt not that; I speak from certainties . i 2 31
It's true; I heard a senator speak it . i 3 107
When you speak best unto the purpose, it is not worth the wagging of your beards . ii 1 95
All tongues speak of him, and the bleared sights Are spectacled to see him . ii 1 221
I have seen the dumb men throng to see him and The blind to hear him speak . ii 1 279
Speak, good Cominius: Leave nothing out for length . ii 2 52
I would you rather had been silent. Please you To hear Cominius speak? . ii 2 66
For this last, Before and in Corioli, let me say, I cannot speak him home ii 2 107
It then remains That you do speak to the people . ii 2 139
We are to put our tongues into those wounds and speak for them . ii 3 8
You must not speak of that: you must desire them To think upon you ii 3 61
Pray you, speak to 'em, I pray you, In wholesome manner . ii 3 65
Tell me of corn! This was my speech, and I will speak't again . iii 1 62
You speak o' the people, As if you were a god to punish . iii 1 80
Why, shall the people give One that speaks thus their voice? . iii 1 119
What is about to be? I am out of breath; Confusion's near; I cannot speak . iii 1 190
Speak, speak, speak.—You are at point to lose your liberties . iii 1 193
What the vengeance! Could he not speak 'em fair? . iii 1 263
Hear me speak: As I do know the consul's worthiness . iii 1 277
Speak briefly then; For we are peremptory to dispatch This viperous traitor . iii 1 285
And wonder, When one but of my ordinance stood up To speak of peace or war . iii 2 13
Therein you can never be too noble, But when extremities speak . iii 2 41
Why force you this?—Because that now it lies you on to speak . iii 2 52
Speak fair: you may salve so, Not what is dangerous present, but the loss Of what is past . iii 2 70
This but done, Even as she speaks, why, their hearts were yours . iii 2 87
Then he speaks What's in his heart; and that is there which looks With us to break his neck . iii 3 28
Peace, I say!—First, hear me speak.—Well, say. Peace, ho! . iii 3 41
When he speaks not like a citizen, You find him like a soldier . iii 3 53
What you have seen him do and heard him speak, . . . Deserves the extremest death . iii 3 77
Then if I would Speak that,— We know your drift: speak what? . iii 3 116

Speak. Thy name? Why speak'st not? speak, man: what's thy name? *Coriolanus* iv 5 59
If Jupiter Should from yond cloud speak divine things, And say ''Tis true' . iv 5 110
Nay, if he coy'd To hear Cominius speak, I'll keep at home . v 1 7
I am an officer of state, and come To speak with Coriolanus . v 2 4
You'll see your Rome embraced with fire before You'll speak with Coriolanus . v 2 8
I would not speak with him till after dinner . v 2 37
Another word, Menenius, I will not hear thee speak . v 2 98
Should we be silent and not speak, our raiment And state of bodies would bewray what life We have led . v 3 94
Speak to me, son: Thou hast affected the fine strains of honour . v 3 148
Why dost not speak? Think'st thou it honourable for a noble man Still to remember wrongs? Daughter, speak you . v 3 153
Speak thou, boy: Perhaps thy childishness will move him more . v 3 156
I am hush'd until our city be afire, And then I'll speak a little . v 3 182
Peace, both, and hear me speak . v 6 111
Beat thou the drum, that it speak mournfully: Trail your steel pikes . v 6 151
How fair the tribune speaks to calm my thoughts! . *T. Andron.* i 1 46
Speak, Queen of Goths, dost thou applaud my choice? . i 1 321
Father, and in that name doth nature speak,— Speak thou no more . i 1 371
Then hear me speak indifferently for all; And at my suit, sweet, pardon i 1 430
Whose fury not dissembled speaks his griefs . i 1 438
There speak, and strike, brave boys, and take your turns . ii 1 129
I will not hear her speak; away with her!—Sweet lords, entreat her hear me . ii 3 137
Speak, brother, hast thou hurt thee with the fall? . ii 3 203
Some bring the murder'd body, some the murderers: Let them not speak . ii 3 301
Now go tell, an if thy tongue can speak, Who 'twas that cut thy tongue ii 4 1
Why dost not speak to me? Alas, a crimson river of warm blood . ii 4 21
Shall I speak for thee? shall I say 'tis so? O, that I knew thy heart! . ii 4 33
My gracious lord, no tribune hears you speak.—Why, 'tis no matter . iii 1 32
Speak, Lavinia, what accursed hand Hath made thee handless? . iii 1 66
Speak, gentle sister, who hath martyr'd thee? . iii 1 81
Had she a tongue to speak, now would she say That to her brother . iii 1 144
Speak with possibilities, And do not break into these deep extremes . iii 1 215
These two heads do seem to speak to me, And threat me . iii 1 272
How now, good fellow! wouldst thou speak with us? . iv 4 39
Why dost not speak? what, deaf? not a word? A halter, soldiers! hang him . v 1 46
Befall what may befall, I'll speak no more but 'Vengeance rot you all!' v 1 58
'Twill vex thy soul to hear what I shall speak; For I must talk of murders . v 1 62
Sirs, stop his mouth, and let him speak no more . v 1 151
Yield to his humour, smooth and speak him fair, And tarry with him . v 2 140
Stop close their mouths, let them not speak a word . v 2 165
Let them not speak to me; But let them hear what fearful words I utter . v 2 168
What would you say, if I should let you speak? . v 2 179
Speak, Rome's dear friend, as erst our ancestor . v 3 80
Let him tell the tale; Your hearts will throb and weep to hear him speak v 3 95
Now is my turn to speak . v 3 119
Speak, Romans, speak; and if you say we shall, Lo, hand in hand, Lucius and I will fall . v 3 135
I cannot speak to him for weeping; My tears will choke me . v 3 174
Who set this ancient quarrel new abroach? Speak, nephew *Rom. and Jul.* i 1 112
Speak briefly, can you like of Paris' love? . i 3 96
Speak but one rhyme, and I am satisfied . ii 1 9
Speak to my gossip Venus one fair word, One nick-name for her purblind son . ii 1 11
She speaks, yet she says nothing: what of that? Her eye discourses . ii 2 12
I am too bold, 'tis not to me she speaks . ii 2 14
She speaks: O, speak again, bright angel! . ii 2 25
Shall I hear more, or shall I speak at this? . ii 2 37
Else would a maiden blush bepaint my cheek For that which thou hast heard me speak to-night . ii 2 87
Bondage is hoarse, and may not speak aloud . ii 2 161
Will speak more in a minute than he will stand to in a month . ii 4 156
An a' speak any thing against me, I'll take him down . ii 4 158
Nay, come, I pray thee, speak; good, good nurse, speak . ii 5 28
Follow me close, for I will speak to them. Gentlemen, good den . iii 1 40
Affection makes him false; he speaks not true . iii 1 182
Every tongue that speaks But Romeo's name speaks heavenly eloquence iii 2 32
Will you speak well of him that kill'd your cousin?—Shall I speak ill of him that is my husband? . iii 2 96
'Romeo is banished,' to speak that word, Is father, mother, Tybalt, Romeo, Juliet, All slain, all dead . iii 2 122
Hear me but speak a word.—O, thou wilt speak again of banishment . iii 3 52
Thou canst not speak of that thou dost not feel . iii 3 64
Then mightst thou speak, then mightst thou tear thy hair . iii 3 68
I beseech you on my knees, Hear me with patience but to speak a word iii 5 160
Speak not, reply not, do not answer me; My fingers itch . iii 5 164
Smatter with your gossips, go.—I speak no treason . iii 5 173
May not one speak?—Peace, you mumbling fool! . iii 5 174
Talk not to me, for I'll not speak a word: Do as thou wilt . iii 5 204
Be not so long to speak; I long to die, If what thou speak'st speak not of remedy.—Hold, daughter . iv 1 66
Death, that hath ta'en her hence to make me wail, Ties up my tongue, and will not let me speak . iv 5 32
How this grace Speaks his own standing! *T. of Athens* i 1 31
I saw them speak together . i 1 62
Hear me speak.—Freely, good father . i 1 110
He speaks the common tongue, Which all men speak with him . i 1 174
I have told more of you to myself than you can with modesty speak in your own behalf . i 2 97
His promises fly so beyond his state That what he speaks is all in debt i 2 204
Dost dialogue with thy shadow?—I speak not to thee . ii 2 53
Speak to 'em, fool.—How do you, gentlemen? . ii 2 67
Pray you, walk near: I'll speak with you anon . ii 2 132
Men and men's fortunes could I frankly use As I can bid thee speak . ii 2 189
Thou art true and honest; ingeniously I speak, No blame belongs to thee . ii 2 230
Ne'er speak, or think, That Timon's fortunes 'mong his friends can sink ii 2 239
Your lordship speaks your pleasure . iii 1 35
Dost thou speak seriously, Servilius?—Upon my soul, 'tis true . iii 2 47
Who can speak broader than he that has no house to put his head in? . iii 4 63
O my lord, You only speak from your distracted soul . iii 4 115
Under favour, pardon me, If I speak like a captain . iii 5 41

Speak. What art thou there? speak.—A beast, as thou art *T. of Athens* iv 3 48
And, thy fury spent, Confounded be thyself! Speak not, be gone iv 3 128
Ye've heard that I have gold; I am sure you have: speak truth v 1 80
It is in vain that you would speak with Timon v 1 119
It is our part and promise to the Athenians To speak with Timon v 1 124
Look out, and speak to friends v 1 131
Speak, and be hang'd: For each true word, a blister! v 1 134
Then let him know, and tell him Timon speaks it v 1 178
We speak in vain v 1 193
Our old love made a particular force, And made us speak like friends v 2 9
This should be the place. Who's here? speak, ho! No answer! What is this? v 3 2
Speak, what trade art thou?—Why, sir, a carpenter *J. Cæsar* i 1 5
Calpurnia!—Peace, ho! Cæsar speaks.—Calpurnia!—Here, my lord i 2 1
Speak; Cæsar is turn'd to hear.—Beware the ides of March i 2 17
What say'st thou to me now? speak once again i 2 22
You pull'd me by the cloak; would you speak with me? i 2 215
To-morrow, if you please to speak with me, I will come home to you i 2 308
I perhaps speak this Before a willing bondman i 3 112
You speak to Casca, and to such a man That is no fleering tell-tale i 3 116
To speak truth of Cæsar, I have not known when his affections sway'd More than his reason ii 1 19
'Speak, strike, redress!' Am I entreated To speak and strike? ii 1 55
Here is a sick man that would speak with you ii 1 310
I'll get me to a place more void, and there Speak to great Cæsar ii 4 38
Popilius Lena speaks not of our purposes; For, look, he smiles iii 1 23
Speak, hands, for me!—Et tu, Brute! Then fall, Cæsar! iii 1 76
In the pulpit, as becomes a friend, Speak in the order of his funeral iii 1 230
You know not what you do: do not consent That Antony speak in his funeral iii 1 233
What Antony shall speak, I will protest He speaks by leave iii 1 238
Speak all good you can devise of Cæsar iii 1 246
You shall speak In the same pulpit whereto I am going, After my speech iii 1 249
Those that will hear me speak, let 'em stay here; Those that will follow Cassius, go with him iii 2 5
I will hear Brutus speak.—I will hear Cassius; and compare their reasons iii 2 8
If any, speak; for him have I offended. I pause for a reply iii 2 32; 36
My countrymen,— Peace, silence! Brutus speaks.—Peace, ho! iii 2 59
'Twere best he speak no harm of Brutus here iii 2 73
Come I to speak in Cæsar's funeral. He was my friend iii 2 89
I speak not to disprove what Brutus spoke, But here I am to speak what I do know iii 2 105
Now mark him, he begins again to speak iii 2 122
And that they know full well That gave me public leave to speak of him iii 2 224
I only speak right on; I tell you that which you yourselves do know; Show you sweet Cæsar's wounds, poor poor dumb mouths, And bid them speak for me iii 2 227
Yet hear me, countrymen; yet hear me speak.—Peace, ho! Hear Antony iii 2 238
Stand, ho! Speak the word along iv 2 33
Speak your griefs softly: I do know you well iv 2 42
You know that you are Brutus that speak this, Or, by the gods, this speech were else your last iv 3 13
Hear me, for I will speak. Must I give way and room to your rash choler? iv 3 38
Therein our letters do not well agree; Mine speak of seventy senators iv 3 177
Speak to me what thou art?—Thy evil spirit, Brutus.—Why comest thou? iv 3 281
If we do lose this battle, then is this The very last time we shall speak together v 1 99
So should he look That seems to speak things strange *Macbeth* i 2 47
Speak, if you can: what are you? i 3 47
My noble partner You greet . . . : to me you speak not. i 3 57
Speak then to me, who neither beg nor fear Your favours nor your hate i 3 60
Why Upon this blasted heath you stop our way With such prophetic greeting? Speak, I charge you i 3 78
Would they had stay'd!—Were such things here as we do speak about? i 3 83
What, can the devil speak true? i 3 107
Let us speak Our free hearts each to other i 3 154
We will speak further.—Only look up clear; To alter favour ever is to fear i 5 72
Did not you speak?—When?—Now.—As I descended? ii 2 17
Do not bid me speak; See, and then speak yourselves ii 3 77
O gentle lady, 'Tis not for you to hear what I can speak ii 3 89
He chid the sisters When first they put the name of king upon me, And bade them speak to him iii 1 59
My heart speaks they are welcome iii 4 8
Look! lo! how say you? Why, what care I? If thou canst nod, speak too iii 4 70
Speak not; he grows worse and worse; Question enrages him iii 4 117
Blood will have blood: Stones have been known to move and trees to speak iii 4 123
More shall they speak; for now I am bent to know, By the worst means, the worst iii 4 134
Answer me To what I ask you.—Speak.—Demand iv 1 61
Listen, but speak not to't iv 1 89
I dare not speak much further; But cruel are the times iv 2 17
I speak not as in absolute fear of you iv 3 38
If such a one be fit to govern, speak: I am as I have spoken iv 3 101
Sundry blessings hang about his throne, That speak him full of grace iv 3 159
The grief that does not speak Whispers the o'er-fraught heart iv 3 209
Hark! she speaks: I will set down what comes from her v 1 36
My mind she has mated, and amazed my sight. I think, but dare not speak v 1 87
Make all our trumpets speak; give them all breath v 6 9
That speak my salutation in their minds; Whose voices I desire aloud v 8 57
That if again this apparition come, He may . . . speak to it. *Hamlet* i 1 29
Well, sit we down, And let us hear Bernardo speak of this i 1 34
Thou art a scholar; speak to it, Horatio.—Looks it not like the king? i 1 42
By heaven I charge thee, speak!—It is offended i 1 49
Stay! speak, speak! I charge thee, speak!—'Tis gone i 1 51
Stay, illusion! If thou hast any sound, or use of voice, Speak to me i 1 129
If there be any good thing to be done, That may to thee do ease and grace to me, Speak to me i 1 132
If thou art privy to thy country's fate, Which, happily, foreknowing may avoid, O, speak! i 1 135
Speak of it: stay, and speak! i 1 139
It was about to speak, when the cock crew i 1 147
Upon my life, This spirit, dumb to us, will speak to him i 1 171
You cannot speak of reason to the Dane, And lose your voice i 2 44
Distill'd Almost to jelly with the act of fear, Stand dumb and speak not i 2 206

Speak. Did you not speak to it?—My lord, I did; But answer made it none: yet once methought It lifted up its head and did address Itself to motion, like as it would speak *Hamlet* i 2 214
I'll speak to it, though hell itself should gape And bid me hold my peace i 2 245
You speak like a green girl, Unsifted in such perilous circumstance i 3 101
Thou comest in such a questionable shape That I will speak to thee i 4 44
It will not speak; then I will follow it.—Do not, my lord i 4 63
Where wilt thou lead me? speak; I'll go no further i 5 1
Speak; I am bound to hear.—So art thou to revenge, when thou shalt hear i 5 6
Never to speak of this that you have seen, Swear by my sword i 5 153
Never to speak of this that you have heard, Swear by my sword i 5 159
Or 'If we list to speak,' or 'There be, an if they might,' Or such i 5 177
With a look so piteous in purport As if he had been loosed out of hell To speak of horrors ii 1 84
O, speak of that; that do I long to hear ii 2 50
I'll speak to him again. What do you read, my lord? ii 2 192
For, to speak to you like an honest man, I am most dreadfully attended ii 2 275
Come, deal justly with me: come, come; nay, speak ii 2 285
I heard thee speak me a speech once, but it was never acted ii 2 454
'Twas Æneas' tale to Dido; and thereabout of it especially, where he speaks of Priam's slaughter ii 2 469
Murder, though it have no tongue, will speak With most miraculous organ ii 2 622
He does confess he feels himself distracted; But from what cause he will by no means speak iii 1 6
Speak the speech, I pray you, as I pronounced it to you iii 2 1
Not to speak it profanely iii 2 34
Let those that play your clowns speak no more than is set down for them iii 2 43
You think what now you speak; But what we do determine oft we break iii 2 196
She desires to speak with you in her closet, ere you go to bed iii 2 343
There is much music, excellent voice, in this little organ; yet cannot you make it speak iii 2 386
The queen would speak with you, and presently iii 2 391
I will speak daggers to her, but use none iii 2 414
Nay, then, I'll set those to you that can speak iii 4 17
O Hamlet, speak no more: Thou turn'st mine eyes into my very soul iii 4 88
O, speak to me no more; These words, like daggers, enter in mine ears iii 4 94
Speak to her, Hamlet.—How is it with you, lady? iii 4 115
To whom do you speak this?—Do you see nothing there? iii 4 131
Lay not that flattering unction to your soul, That not your trespass, but my madness speaks iii 4 146
Go seek him out; speak fair, and bring the body Into the chapel iv 1 36
Truly to speak, and with no addition, We go to gain a little patch of ground iv 4 17
I will not speak with her.—She is importunate, indeed distract iv 5 1
She speaks much of her father; says she hears There's tricks i' the world iv 5 4
Speaks things in doubt, That carry but half sense iv 5 6
Let him go, Gertrude. Speak, man.—Where is my father? iv 5 127
Why, now you speak Like a good child and a true gentleman iv 5 147
What are they that would speak with me?—Sailors, sir iv 6 1
I have words to speak in thine ear will make thee dumb iv 6 25
I will speak to this fellow. Whose grave's this, sirrah? v 1 126
We must speak by the card, or equivocation will undo us v 1 149
Indeed, to speak feelingly of him, he is the card or calendar of gentry v 2 113
Your lordship speaks most infallibly of him v 2 126
If his fitness speaks, mine is ready; now or whensoever v 2 209
Let the kettle to the trumpet speak, The trumpet to the cannoneer without. v 2 286
Let me speak to the yet unknowing world How these things came about v 2 390
Of that I shall have also cause to speak, And from his mouth whose voice will draw on more v 2 402
The soldiers' music and the rites of war Speak loudly for him v 2 411
Goneril, Our eldest-born, speak first.—Sir, I love you more than words can wield the matter *Lear* i 1 55
What says our second daughter, Our dearest Regan, wife to Cornwall? Speak i 1 69
What wilt thou do, old man? Think'st thou that duty shall have dread to speak, When power to flattery bows? i 1 149
If for I want that glib and oily art, To speak and purpose not; since what I well intend, I'll do't before I speak i 1 228
Come to me, that of this I may speak more i 2 54
From whence I will fitly bring you to hear my lord speak i 2 185
When he returns from hunting, I will not speak with him; say I am sick i 3 8
I would breed from hence occasions, and I shall, That I may speak i 3 25
Go you, and tell my daughter I would speak with her i 4 82
Speak less than thou knowest, Lend less than thou owest i 4 132
If I speak like myself in this, let him be whipped that first finds it so i 4 179
Doth Lear walk thus? speak thus? Where are his eyes? i 4 247
The shame itself doth speak For instant remedy i 4 267
Woe, that too late repents,—O, sir, are you come? Is it your will? Speak i 4 280
What is your difference? speak.—I am scarce in breath, my lord ii 2 56
Speak yet, how grew your quarrel? ii 2 66
He cannot flatter, he, An honest mind and plain, he must speak truth! ii 2 105
Deny to speak with me? They are sick? they are weary? ii 4 89
I'ld speak with the Duke of Cornwall and his wife.—Well, my good lord, I have inform'd them so ii 4 98
The king would speak with Cornwall; the dear father Would with his daughter speak, commands her service ii 4 102
Go tell the duke and 's wife I'ld speak with them, Now, presently ii 4 117
I can scarce speak to thee; thou'lt not believe With how depraved a quality—O Regan! ii 4 138
Sith that both charge and danger Speak 'gainst so great a number ii 4 243
With five and twenty, Regan? said you so?—And speak 't again, my lord ii 4 258
I'll speak a prophecy ere I go iii 2 80
Neither to speak of him, entreat for him, nor any way sustain him iii 3 5
Her boat hath a leak, And she must not speak iii 6 29
To whose hands have you sent the lunatic king? Speak iii 7 47
This kiss, if it durst speak, Would stretch thy spirits up into the air iv 2 22
I know you are of her bosom.—I, madam?—I speak in understanding iv 5 28
Hear you, sir! speak! Thus might he pass indeed; yet he revives iv 6 46
Thy life's a miracle. Speak yet again.—But have I fall'n, or no? iv 6 55
He wakes; speak to him.—Madam, do you; 'tis fittest iv 7 42
Tell me—but truly—but then speak the truth, Do you not love my sister? v 1 8
Sir, you speak nobly.—Why is this reason'd? v 1 28
What's he that speaks for Edmund Earl of Gloucester?—Himself v 3 125

Speak. To prove upon thy heart, whereto I speak, Thou liest. *Lear* v 3 140
Where they shall rest for ever. Trumpets, speak! v 3 150
Speak you on; You look as you had something more to say v 3 200
Help, help, O, help!—What kind of help?—Speak, man v 3 222
Great thing of us forgot! Speak, Edmund, where's the king? v 3 237
Speak what we feel, not what we ought to say v 3 324
My demerits May speak unbonneted to as proud a fortune *Othello* i 2 23
Little of this great world can I speak, More than pertains to feats of broil and battle i 3 86
But, Othello, speak: Did you by indirect and forced courses Subdue and poison this young maid's affections? i 3 110
Send for the lady . . . , And let her speak of me before her father i 3 116
It was my hint to speak,—such was the process i 3 142
And often did beguile her of her tears, When I did speak of some distressful stroke That my youth suffer'd i 3 157
Hear her speak: If she confess that she was half the wooer i 3 175
Let me speak like yourself, and lay a sentence, Which, as a grise or step, may help these lovers Into your favour i 3 199
Though he speak of comfort Touching the Turkish loss, yet he looks sadly ii 1 31
He speaks home, madam: you may relish him more in the soldier than in the scholar ii 1 166
I cannot speak enough of this content; It stops me here ii 1 198
When she speaks, is it not an alarum to love? ii 3 26
I am not drunk now; I can stand well enough, and speak well enough ii 3 120
Have you forgot all sense of place and duty? Hold! the general speaks ii 3 168
Speak, who began this? on thy love, I charge thee ii 3 178
I cannot speak Any beginning to this peevish odds ii 3 184
How comes it, Michael, you are thus forgot?—I pray you, pardon me; I cannot speak ii 3 189
Yet, I persuade myself, to speak the truth Shall nothing wrong him ii 3 223
Drunk? and speak parrot? and squabble? swagger? swear? ii 3 281
Have your instruments been in Naples, that they speak i' the nose thus? iii 1 4
The general and his wife are talking of it; And she speaks for you stoutly iii 1 47
I will bestow you where you shall have time To speak your bosom freely iii 1 58
Stay, and hear me speak.—Madam, not now: I am very ill at ease iii 3 31
Nay, yet there's more in this: I prithee, speak to me as to thy thinkings iii 3 131
I speak not yet of proof. Look to your wife; observe her well with Cassio iii 3 196
I do not in position Distinctly speak of her; though I may fear Her will iii 3 235
Why do you speak so faintly? Are you not well? iii 3 282
It speaks against her with the other proofs iii 3 441
I cannot speak of this. Come now, your promise.—What promise, chuck?—I have sent to bid Cassio come speak with you iii 4 48
Why do you speak so startingly and rash?—Is't lost? is't gone? speak iii 4 79
When he is gone, I would on great occasion speak with you iv 1 59
Bade him anon return and here speak with me; The which he promised iv 1 81
Well, I may chance to see you; for I would very fain speak with you iv 1 175
It is not honesty in me to speak What I have seen and known iv 1 288
I should make very forges of my cheeks, That would to cinders burn up modesty, Did I but speak thy deeds iv 2 76
Speak within door.—O, fie upon them! Some such squire he was iv 2 144
It doth abhor me now I speak the word iv 2 162
A proper man.—A very handsome man.—He speaks well iv 3 37
Nay, guiltiness will speak, Though tongues were out of use v 1 109
O, good my lord, I would speak a word with you!—Yes: 'tis Emilia. By and by. She's dead. 'Tis like she comes to speak of Cassio's death v 2 90
What's best to do? If she come in, she'll sure speak to my wife: My wife! v 2 96
I do beseech you That I may speak with you, O, good my lord! v 2 102
O lady, speak again! Sweet Desdemona! O sweet mistress, speak! v 2 120
I know thou didst not, thou 'rt not such a villain: Speak, for my heart is full v 2 175
Charm your tongue.—I will not charm my tongue; I am bound to speak v 2 184
Let me have leave to speak: 'Tis proper I obey him, but not now v 2 195
'Twill out, 'twill out: I peace! No, I will speak as liberal as the north v 2 220
Let heaven and men and devils, let them all, All, all, cry shame against me, yet I'll speak v 2 222
So come my soul to bliss, as I speak true; So speaking as I think v 2 250
Speak with me, Or, naked as I am, I will assault thee v 2 257
What you know, you know: From this time forth I never will speak word v 2 304
Speak of me as I am; nothing extenuate, Nor set down aught in malice: then must you speak Of one that loved not wisely but too well v 2 342
Come, my queen; Last night you did desire it: Speak not to us *A. and C.* i 1 55
I am full sorry That he approves the common liar, who Thus speaks of him i 1 61
Speak to me home, mince not the general tongue i 2 109
The death of Fulvia, with more urgent touches, Do strongly speak to us i 2 188
And speaks as loud As his own state and ours i 4 29
And all this—It wounds thine honour that I speak it now i 4 69
Let Antony look over Cæsar's head And speak as loud as Mars ii 2 6
Let him speak: The honour is sacred which he talks on now ii 2 84
The present need Speaks to atone you ii 2 102
Thou art a soldier only: speak no more.—That truth should be silent I had almost forgot ii 2 108
You wrong this presence; therefore speak no more ii 2 111
I am not married, Cæsar: let me hear Agrippa further speak ii 2 126
And whose general graces speak That which none else can utter ii 2 132
Will Cæsar speak?—Not till he hears how Antony is touch'd With what is spoke already ii 2 141
Our courteous Antony, Whom ne'er the word of 'No' woman heard speak ii 2 228
Speak this no more.—To none but thee; no more, but when to thee ii 3 23
Say to Ventidius I would speak with him; He shall to Parthia ii 3 31
Pity me, Charmian, But do not speak to me ii 5 119
We'll speak with thee at sea ii 6 25
Forsake thy seat, I do beseech thee, captain, And hear me speak a word ii 7 44
And mine own tongue Splits what it speaks ii 7 131
Scribes, bards, poets, cannot Think, speak, cast, write, sing, number, ho! iii 2 17
Didst hear her speak? is she shrill-tongued or low?—Madam, I heard her speak; she is low-voiced iii 3 15
Sink Rome, and their tongues rot That speak against us! iii 7 17
Speak not against it; I will not stay behind iii 7 19
Go to him, madam, speak to him: He is unqualitied with very shame iii 11 43
Approach, and speak.—Such as I am, I come from Antony iii 12 6
What thou think'st his very action speaks In every power that moves iii 12 35
We'll speak to them; and to-night I'll force The wine peep through their scars iii 13 190

Speak. Let's speak To him.—Let's hear him, for the things he speaks May concern Cæsar.—Let's do so *Ant. and Cleo.* iv 9 23
Awake; speak to us.—Hear you, sir?—The hand of death hath raught him iv 9 29
The augurers Say they know not, they cannot tell; look grimly, And dare not speak their knowledge iv 12 6
I am dying, Egypt, dying: Give me some wine, and let me speak a little.—No, let me speak iv 15 42
To Cæsar I will speak what you shall please, If you'll employ me to him v 2 69
Let him speak, my lord, Upon his peril, that I have reserved To myself nothing. Speak the truth, Seleucus v 2 142
I had rather seal my lips, than, to my peril, Speak that which is not v 2 147
O, couldst thou speak, That I might hear thee call great Cæsar ass! v 2 309
Where is the queen?—Speak softly, wake her not v 2 323
You speak him far.—I do extend him, sir, within himself *Cymbeline* i 1 24
The king Hath charged you should not speak together i 1 83
About some half-hour hence, I pray you, speak with me i 1 177
You speak of him when he was less furnished than now he is i 4 8
It is an office of the gods to venge it, Not mine to speak on't i 6 93
If she be up, I'll speak with her; if not, Let her lie still and dream ii 3 69
But that you shall not say I yield being silent, I would not speak ii 3 100
Let proof speak iii 1 77
Say, and speak thick; Love's counsellor should fill the bores of hearing iii 2 58
Speak, How many score of miles may we well ride 'Twixt hour and hour? iii 2 68
No life to ours.—Out of your proof you speak iii 3 27
How you speak! Did you but know the city's usuries And felt them iii 3 44
Speak, man: thy tongue May take off some extremity, which to read Would be even mortal to me iii 4 16
I speak not out of weak surmises, but from proof as strong as my grief iii 4 23
Good lady, Hear me with patience.—Talk thy tongue weary; speak iii 4 115
But speak.—Then, madam, I thought you would not back again iii 4 118
Speak, or thy silence on the instant is Thy condemnation and thy death iii 5 97
Ho! who's here? If any thing that's civil, speak; if savage, Take or lend iii 6 23
We'll mannerly demand thee of thy story, So far as thou wilt speak it iii 6 93
I dare speak it to myself—for it is not vain-glory iv 1 7
Since death of my dear'st mother It did not speak before iv 2 191
I cannot sing: I'll weep, and word it with thee . . . —We'll speak it, then iv 2 242
The rain speaks that sometime It was a worthy building iv 2 354
O Imogen! I'll speak to thee in silence v 4 29
I speak against my present profit, but my wish hath a preferment in't v 4 214
Know'st him thou look'st on? speak, Wilt have him live? v 5 110
My good youth, my page; I'll be thy master: walk with me; speak freely v 5 119
Bitter torture shall Winnow the truth from falsehood. On, speak to him v 5 134
Strive, man, and speak v 5 152
For beauty that made barren the swell'd boast Of him that best could speak v 5 163
What, makest thou me a dullard in this act? Wilt thou not speak to me? v 5 266
My lord, Now fear is from me, I'll speak troth v 5 274
That I was he, Speak, Iachimo: I had you down v 5 411
Since you have given me leave to speak, Freely will I speak *Pericles* i 2 101
His seal'd commission, left in trust with me, Doth speak sufficiently i 3 14
I'll then discourse our woes, felt several years, And wanting breath to speak help me with tears i 4 19
But tidings to the contrary Are brought your eyes; what need speak I? ii Gower 16
He had need mean better than his outward show Can any way speak in his just commend ii 2 49
The ship, upon whose deck The sea-tost Pericles appears to speak iii Gower 60
I can speak of the disturbances That nature works, and of her cures iii 2 37
If this you purpose as ye speak, Diana's temple is not distant far iii 4 12
She has a good face, speaks well, and has excellent good clothes iv 2 51
For what thou professest, a baboon, could he speak, Would own a name too dear iv 6 189
May we not see him?—You may; But bootless is your sight: he will not speak To any v 1 33
Hail, royal sir!—It is in vain; he will not speak to you v 1 41
See, she will speak to him.—Hail, sir! my lord, lend ear v 1 82
She speaks My lord, that, may be, hath endured a grief Might equal yours v 1 87
But there is something glows upon my cheek, And whispers in mine ear, 'Go not till he speak' v 1 97
Prithee, speak: Falseness cannot come from thee v 1 120
Speaks nobly of her.—She would never tell Her parentage v 1 189

Speak of. I would not break with her for more money than I'll speak of *Mer. Wives* iii 2 57
What but to speak of would offend again *Meas. for Meas.* i 2 140
Know you that Friar Lodowick that she speaks of?—I know him v 1 143
A very reverent body; ay, such a one as a man may not speak of without he say 'Sir-reverence' *Com. of Errors* iii 2 92
What I would speak of concerns him *Much Ado* iii 2 88
'Tis strange, my Theseus, that these lovers speak of *M. N. Dream* v 1 1
But what is the sport, monsieur, that the ladies have lost?—Why, this that I speak of *As Y. Like It* i 2 144
What he is indeed, More suits you to conceive than I to speak of i 2 279
How called you the man you speak of, madam? *All's Well* i 1 27
More advanced by the king than by that red-tailed humble-bee I speak of iv 5 7
The master I speak of ever keeps a good fire iv 5 50
Is this the man you speak of?—Ay, my lord v 3 233
Things which would derive me ill will to speak of; therefore I will not speak v 3 266
How now, good Blunt? thy looks are full of speed.—So hath the business that I come to speak of *1 Hen. IV.* iii 2 163
See the noble ruin'd man you speak of.—Let's stand close *Hen. VIII.* ii 1 54
This priest has no pride in him?—Not to speak of ii 2 83
The man I speak of cannot in the world Be singly counterpoised *Coriol.* ii 2 90
This is a fellow of the self-same colour Our sister speaks of *Lear* ii 2 146
Made you no more offence but what you speak of? ii 4 62
That thing you speak of, I took it for a man iv 6 77
Let's see these pockets: the letters that he speaks of May be my friends iv 6 261
What should we speak of When we are old as you? *Cymbeline* iii 3 35
Can you teach all this you speak of?—Prove that I cannot *Pericles* iv 6 199

Speak on; but be not over-tedious *1 Hen. VI.* iii 3 43
Speak on: How grounded he his title to the crown? *Hen. VIII.* i 2 143
Speak on, sir; I dare your worst objections iii 2 306
Well; speak on. Where were you born? *Pericles* v 1 156

Speak out. I'll have thee speak out the rest soon *Hamlet* ii 2 545
Speak out thy sorrows which thou bring'st in haste *Pericles* i 4 58

Speaker. That contempt will kill the speaker's heart *L. L. Lost* v 2 149
To us the speaker in his parliament; To us the imagined voice of God himself; The very opener and intelligencer *2 Hen. IV.* iv 2 18

Speaker. A speaker is but a prater; a rhyme is but a ballad . *Hen. V.* v 2 166
God speed the parliament! who shall be the speaker? 1 *Hen. VI.* iii 2 60
The gentleman is learn'd, and a most rare speaker . . . *Hen. VIII.* i 2 111
After my death I wish no other herald, No other speaker of my living actions . . . iv 2 70
O, be not moved, Prince Troilus: Let me be privileged by my place and message, To be a speaker free . . . *Troi. and Cres.* iv 4 133
Stay, you imperfect speakers, tell me more *Macbeth* i 3 70
What's the newest grief?—That of an hour's age doth hiss the speaker . iv 3 175
O, never say hereafter But I am truest speaker *Cymbeline* v 5 376
Speakest. It is a sleepy language and thou speak'st Out of thy sleep *Temp.* ii 1 211
No more; unless the next word that thou speak'st Have some malignant power upon my life . . . *T. G. of Ver.* iii 1 237
Fond wretch, thou know'st not what thou speak'st. . *Meas. for Meas.* v 1 105
Dissembling villain, thou speak'st false in both . *Com. of Errors* iv 4 103
Make those that do offend you suffer too.—There thou speak'st reason *Much Ado* v 1 41
Thou art an old love-monger and speakest skilfully . *L. L. Lost* ii 1 253
I am fair that shoot, And thereupon thou speak'st the fairest shoot . iv 1 12
Thou speak'st aright; I am that merry wanderer of the night *M. N. D.* ii 1 42
He hath enough.—Thou speak'st it well . . . *Mer. of Venice* ii 2 161
Howsoe'er thou speak'st, 'mong other things I shall digest it . . iii 5 94
Thou speakest wiser than thou art ware of . . *As Y. Like It* ii 4 58
Speakest thou in sober meanings?—By my life, I do . . v 2 76
Is but sluttish, if it smell so strongly as thou speakest of . *All's Well* v 2 8
Thou speak'st it falsely, as I love mine honour . . v 3 113
Mercury endue thee with leasing, for thou speakest well of fools! *T. Night* i 5 106
Thou speak'st truth. No more such wives; therefore, no wife *W. Tale* v 1 55
That what thou speakest may move and what he hears may be believed 1 *Hen. IV.* i 2 172
Thou speak'st as if I would deny my name . . . v 4 60
God-a-mercy, old heart! thou speak'st cheerfully . . *Hen. V.* iv 1 34
Why speak'st thou not? what ransom must I pay? . 1 *Hen. VI.* iv 3 76
Let me live.—In vain thou speak'st, poor boy . . 3 *Hen. VI.* i 3 21
Thou speakest wonders . . . *Hen. VIII.* v 5 56
Though thou speak'st truth, Methinks thou speak'st not well *Coriolanus* i 6 13
Thy name? Why speak'st not? speak, man: what's thy name? . iv 5 59
An if it please me which thou speak'st, Thy child shall live *T. Andron.* v 1 59
Speakest thou from thy heart?—And from my soul too . *Rom. and Jul.* iii 5 228
I long to die, If what thou speak'st speak not of remedy . iv 1 67
There is no leprosy but what thou speak'st . . *T. of Athens* iv 3 367
[Gold] that speak'st with every tongue, To every purpose! O thou touch of hearts! . . iv 3 389
What, thou speak'st drowsily? Poor knave, I blame thee not *J. Cæsar* iv 3 240
Thou speak'st with all thy wit; and yet, i' faith, With wit enough *Macb.* iv 2 42
If thou speak'st false, Upon the next tree shalt thou hang alive . v 5 38
With my sword I'll prove the lie thou speak'st . . v 7 11
Thou speak'st In better phrase and matter than thou didst . *Lear* iv 6 7
Thou dost breathe; Hast heavy substance; bleed'st not; speak'st . iv 6 52
That handkerchief thou speak'st of I found by fortune . *Othello* v 2 225
I have a mind to strike thee ere thou speak'st . . *Ant. and Cleo.* ii 5 42
Thou weep'st, and speak'st. The service that you three have done is more Unlike than this thou tell'st . . . *Cymbeline* v 5 352
Thou speak'st like a physician, Helicanus, That minister'st a potion *Per.* i 2 67
Thou speak'st like him's untutor'd to repeat . . . i 4 74
Speaketh. Ay, now my sovereign speaketh like himself . 3 *Hen. VI.* iv 7 67
Speaking. Standing, speaking, moving, And yet so fast asleep *Tempest* ii 1 214
His little speaking shows his love but small . *T. G. of Ver.* i 2 29
If speaking, why, a vane blown with all winds . . *Much Ado* iii 1 66
I pray you, be not angry with me, madam, Speaking my fancy . . iii 1 95
Art not ashamed?—Of what, lady? of speaking honourably! . iii 4 29
An bad thinking do not wrest true speaking, I'll offend nobody . iii 4 34
Who loved her so, that, speaking of her foulness, Wash'd it with tears . iv 1 155
Follow not; I'll have no speaking: I will have my bond *Mer. of Venice* iii 3 17
Let me see it; for mine eye, While I was speaking, oft was fasten'd to't *All's Well* v 3 82
What say you, sir? I am shent for speaking to you . *T. Night* iv 2 112
The silence often of pure innocence Persuades when speaking fails *W. Tale* ii 2 42
We three are but thyself; and, speaking so, Thy words are but as thoughts; therefore, be bold . . *Richard II.* ii 1 275
O, I am press'd to death through want of speaking! . iii 4 72
And speaking it, he wistly look'd on me . . . v 4 7
If speaking truth In this fine age were not thought flattery 1 *Hen. IV.* iv 1 1
Speaking thick, which nature made his blemish . 2 *Hen. IV.* ii 3 24
But thy speaking of my tongue, and I thine, most truly-falsely, must needs be granted to be much at one . . . *Hen. V.* v 2 203
Brave death by speaking, whether he will or no 1 *Hen. VI.* iv 7 25
Therefore, to speak, and to avoid the first, And then, in speaking, not to incur the last, Definitively thus I answer you *Richard III.* iii 7 152
To unthink your speaking And to say so no more . *Hen. VIII.* ii 4 104
Let him in nought be trusted, For speaking false in that . . ii 4 136
Yet, good faith, I wish'd myself a man, Or that we women had men's privilege Of speaking first . . . *Troi. and Cres.* iii 2 137
Speaking is for beggars; he wears his tongue in's arms . . iii 3 270
Because thou canst not ease thy smart By friendship nor by speaking . iv 4 21
Matchless, firm of word, Speaking in deeds and deedless in his tongue . iv 5 98
If thou couldst please me with speaking to me, thou mightst have hit upon it here . . . *T. of Athens* iv 3 350
For each true word, a blister! and each false Be as a cauterizing to the root o' the tongue, Consuming it with speaking! . v 1 137
Many of the best respect in Rome, Except immortal Cæsar, speaking of Brutus . . . , Have wish'd that noble Brutus had his eyes *J. Cæsar* i 2 60
Ligarius doth bear Cæsar hard, Who rated him for speaking well of Pompey . . . ii 1 216
My first false speaking Was this upon myself . . *Macbeth* iv 3 130
They'll have me whipped for speaking true, thou'lt have me whipped for lying; and sometimes I am whipped for holding my peace *Lear* i 4 200
She gave strange œillades and most speaking looks. . iv 5 25
A sight most pitiful in the meanest wretch, Past speaking of in a king! iv 6 209
Little shall I grace my cause In speaking for myself . . *Othello* i 3 89
Find some occasion to anger Cassio, either by speaking too loud or tainting his discipline . . . ii 1 275
So come my soul to bliss, as I speak true; So speaking as I think, I die v 2 251
He's speaking now, Or murmuring 'Where's my serpent of old Nile?' *Ant. and Cleo.* i 5 24
The snatches in his voice, And burst of speaking, were as his *Cymbeline* iv 2 106
Or senseless speaking or a speaking such As sense cannot untie . v 4 148
Will think me speaking, though I swear to silence . *Pericles* i 2 19
Spear. Pierced to the soul with slander's venom'd spear . *Richard II.* i 1 171
O, sit my husband's wrongs on Hereford's spear! . . . i 2 47

Spear. Let no noble eye profane a tear For me, if I be gored with Mowbray's spear . . . *Richard II.* i 3 60
Let them lay by their helmets and their spears, And both return . i 3 119
As full of peril and adventurous spirit As to o'er-walk a current roaring loud On the unsteadfast footing of a spear . 1 *Hen. IV.* i 3 193
A base Walloon, . . . Thrust Talbot with a spear . . 1 *Hen. VI.* i 1 138
He was thrust in the mouth with a spear, and 'tis not whole yet 2 *Hen. VI.* iv 7 10
Like to Achilles' spear, Is able with the change to kill and cure . v 1 100
Spear-grass. Yea, and to tickle our noses with spear-grass . 1 *Hen. IV.* ii 4 340
Special. Why, how know you that I am in love?—Marry, by these special marks . . . *T. G. of Ver.* ii 1 18
Confirm his welcome with some special favour . . . ii 4 101
She can wash and scour.—A special virtue . . . iii 1 314
My husband hath some special suspicion of Falstaff's being here *M. W.* iii 3 200
Though you have ta'en a special stand to strike at me . . v 5 248
We have with special soul Elected him . . *Meas. for Meas.* i 1 18
I do it not in evil disposition, But from Lord Angelo by special charge i 2 123
In special business from his holiness . . . iii 2 233
And hold you ever to our special drift . . . iv 5 4
Had you a special warrant for the deed? . . . v 1 464
Not by might master'd but by special grace . . *L. L. Lost* i 1 153
You can produce acquittances For such a sum from special officers . ii 1 162
Some certain special honours it pleaseth his greatness to impart . v 1 112
Of all the men alive I never yet beheld that special face Which I could fancy more than any other . . *T. of Shrew* ii 1 11
When the special thing is well obtain'd, That is, her love . iv 1 129
Thus he his special nothing ever prologues . . *All's Well* ii 1 95
What place make you special, when you put off that with such contempt? ii 2 6
Let some of my people have a special care of him . . *T. Night* iii 4 69
Take special care my greetings be deliver'd *Richard II.* iii 1 39
Hath drawn The special head of all the land together . 1 *Hen. IV.* iv 4 28
Being ordain'd his special governor . . 1 *Hen. VI.* iii 1 171
The special watchmen of our English weal . . . iii 1 66
'Tis my special hope That you will clear yourself . 2 *Hen. VI.* iii 1 139
Such as I, without your special pardon, Dare not relate . 3 *Hen. VI.* iv 1 87
The people of Rome, for whom we stand A special party . *T. Andron.* i 1 21
For nought so vile that on the earth doth live But to the earth some special good doth give . . . *Rom. and Jul.* ii 3 18
Special dignities, which vacant lie For thy best use . *T. of Athens* v 1 145
Can such things be, And overcome us like a summer's cloud, Without our special wonder? . . . *Macbeth* iii 4 112
With this special observance, that you o'erstep not the modesty of nature . . . *Hamlet* iii 2 20
For two special reasons; Which may to you, perhaps, seem much unsinew'd . . . iv 7 9
There's a special providence in the fall of a sparrow . . v 2 231
The queen on special cause is here, Her army is moved on . *Lear* iv 6 219
Raise some special officers of night . . . *Othello* i 1 183
Your special mandate for the state-affairs Hath hither brought . i 3 72
There he dropp'd it for a special purpose Which wrought to his desire . v 2 322
Specially. By virtue specially to be achieved . . *T. of Shrew* i 2 20
To labour and effect one thing specially . . . i 1 121
Specialties. Where that and other specialties are bound . *L. L. Lost* ii 1 165
Let specialties be therefore drawn between us . *T. of Shrew* ii 1 127
Specialty. The specialty of rule hath been neglected *Troi. and Cres.* i 3 78
Specify. Masters, do not forget to specify, when time and place shall serve, that I am an ass . . . *Much Ado* v 1 264
As my father shall specify . . . *Mer. of Venice* ii 2 131; 137
How will she specify Where is the best and safest passage in? 1 *Hen. VI.* iii 2 21
Speciously. But speciously for Master Fenton . . *Mer. Wives* iii 4 113
Have not they suffered? Yes, I warrant; speciously one of them. . iv 5 114
Spectacle. The direful spectacle of the wreck . . *Tempest* i 2 26
I can see yet without spectacles and I see no such matter *Much Ado* i 1 191
But what said Jaques? Did he not moralize this spectacle? *As Y. Like It* ii 1 44
With spectacles on nose and pouch on side . . . ii 7 159
And prove a deadly bloodshed but a jest, Exampled by this heinous spectacle . . . *K. John* iv 3 56
In open market-place produced they me, To be a public spectacle 1 *Hen. VI.* i 4 41
And bid mine eyes be packing with my heart And call'd them blind and dusky spectacles, For losing ken 2 *Hen. VI.* iii 2 112
O barbarous and bloody spectacle! . . . iv 1 144
Wilt thou on thy death-bed play the ruffian, And seek for sorrow with thy spectacles? . . . v 1 165
There it doth remain, The saddest spectacle that e'er I view'd . 3 *Hen. VI.* ii 1 67
O piteous spectacle! O bloody times! . . . ii 5 73
What a pair of spectacles is here! . . *Troi. and Cres.* iv 4 14
Thou hast oft beheld Heart-hardening spectacles *Coriolanus* iv 1 25
Give me reasons Why and wherein Cæsar was dangerous.—Or else were this a savage spectacle . . *J. Cæsar* iii 1 223
O piteous spectacle!—O noble Cæsar!—O woful day!—O traitors, villains! . . . iii 2 202
If it be nothing, I shall not need spectacles . . *Lear* i 2 36
And can we not Partition make with spectacles so precious 'Twixt fair and foul? . . . *Cymbeline* i 6 37
Spectacled. The bleared sights Are spectacled to see him . *Coriolanus* ii 1 222
Spectanda. The motto thus, 'Sic spectanda fides' . . *Pericles* ii 2 38
Spectator. Though devised And play'd to take spectators . *W. Tale* iii 2 38
Imagine me, Gentle spectators, that I now may be In fair Bohemia . iv 1 20
Laugh, to set on some quantity of barren spectators to laugh too *Hamlet* iii 2 46
If I prove a good repast to the spectators, the dish pays the shot *Cymb.* v 4 158
Spectatorship. The state of hanging, or of some death more long in spectatorship, and crueller in suffering . *Coriolanus* v 2 71
Speculation. Took stand for idle speculation . . *Hen. V.* iv 2 31
Speculation turns not to itself, Till it hath travell'd *Troi. and Cres.* iii 3 109
Thou hast no speculation in those eyes Which thou dost glare with! *Macbeth* iii 4 95
The spies and speculations Intelligent of our state . . *Lear* iii 1 24
Speculative. Thoughts speculative their unsure hopes relate . *Macbeth* v 4 19
Seel with wanton dullness My speculative and officed instruments *Oth.* i 3 271
Sped. And sped you, sir?—Very ill-favouredly . . *Mer. Wives* iii 5 67
I will ever be your head: So be gone: you are sped *Mer. of Venice* ii 9 72
Sped with spavins, rayed with the yellows . . *T. of Shrew* iii 2 53
We three are married, but you two are sped . . . v 2 185
I have look'd on thousands, who have sped the better By my regard *W. T.* i 2 389
How I have sped among the clergymen . . *K. John* iv 2 141
I marvel how he sped . . . 1 *Hen. VI.* ii 1 48
Not long before your highness sped to France . . *Hen. VIII.* i 2 151
I long to hear how they sped to-day . . . *Troi. and Cres.* iii 1 155
I am hurt. A plague o' both your houses! I am sped . *Rom. and Jul.* iii 1 94

Speech. I am the best of them that speak this speech . . *Tempest* i 2 429
My father's of a better nature, sir, Than he appears by speech . . i 2 497
His backward voice is to utter foul speeches and to detract . . ii 2 96
Would seem in me to affect speech and discourse . . *Meas. for Meas.* i 1 4
I do bend my speech To one that can my part in him advertise . . i 1 41
Give me leave To have free speech with you . . . . . i 1 78
With most painful feeling of thy speech . . . . . . i 2 38
It draws something near to the speech we had to such a purpose . . i 2 79
I would by and by have some speech with you . . . . iii 1 155
There was some speech of marriage Betwixt myself and her . . . v 1 217
One that hath spoke most villanous speeches . . . . . . v 1 265
Did not I pluck thee by the nose for thy speeches? . . . . v 1 343
First he did praise my beauty, then my speech . . *Com. of Errors* iv 2 15
Runs not this speech like iron through your blood? . . *Much Ado* v 1 252
Deserve well at my hands by helping me to the speech of Beatrice . v 2 3
A better speech was never spoke before . . . . . *L. L. Lost* v 2 110
To their penn'd speech render we no grace . . . . . v 2 147
Construe my speeches better, if you may . . . . . . v 2 341
Never will I trust to speeches penn'd . . . . . . v 2 402
When you have spoken your speech, enter into that brake *M. N. Dream* iii 1 77
His speech was like a tangled chain; nothing impaired, but all disordered . . . . v 1 125
Without more speech, my lord, You must be gone . . *Mer. of Venice* ii 9 7
Therein suits His folly to the mettle of my speech . . *As Y. Like It* ii 7 82
Slow in speech, yet sweet as spring-time flowers . . *T. of Shrew* ii 1 248
Where did you study all this goodly speech? . . . . . ii 1 264
Be check'd for silence, But never tax'd for speech . . *All's Well* i 1 77
So in approof lives not his epitaph As in your royal speech . . . i 2 51
I do know him well, and common speech Gives him a worthy pass . ii 5 57
Only he desires Some private speech with you . . . . . ii 5 62
Vanquish'd thereto by the fair grace and speech Of the poor suppliant . v 3 133
Thy speech serves for authority . . . . . . *T. Night* i 2 20
I would be loath to cast away my speech. . . . . . . i 5 184
Give me modest assurance if you be the lady of the house, that I may proceed in my speech . . . . i 5 193
But this is from my commission: I will on with my speech in your praise . . . . i 5 202
My fortunes having cast me on your niece give me this prerogative of speech . . . . ii 5 79
Put strange speech upon me: I know not what 'twas but distraction . v 1 70
Her without-door form, Which on my faith deserves high speech *W. Tale* ii 1 70
You have made fault I' the boldness of your speech . . . . iii 2 219
And gasping to begin some speech, her eyes Became two spouts . . iii 3 25
You know your father's temper: at this time He will allow no speech . iv 4 479
He shall know within this hour, if I may come to the speech of him . iv 4 786
When I shall see this gentleman, thy speeches Will bring me to consider that which may Unfurnish me of reason . . . . v 1 121
There was speech in their dumbness, language in their very gesture . v 2 14
Heaven be the record to my speech! . . . . . *Richard II.* i 1 30
Curbs me From giving reins and spurs to my free speech . . . i 1 55
Free speech and fearless I to thee allow . . . . . . i 1 123
'Pardon' should be the first word of thy speech . . . . . v 3 114
Here is my leg.—And here is my speech . . . . . *1 Hen. IV.* ii 4 428
In speech, in gait, In diet, . . . He was the mark . . . *2 Hen. IV.* ii 3 28
Unto your grace do I in chief address The substance of my speech . iv 1 32
Wherefore do you so ill translate yourself Out of the speech of peace? . iv 1 48
But for my tears, The moist impediments unto my speech . . . iv 5 140
My lungs are wasted so That strength of speech is utterly denied me . iv 5 218
First my fear; then my courtesy; last my speech . . . . . Epil. 2
If you look for a good speech now, you undo me . . . . . Epil. 4
And my speech entreats That I may know the let . . . *Hen. V.* v 2 64
What should I say? his deeds exceed all speech . . . *1 Hen. VI.* i 1 15
Else ne'er could he so long protract his speech . . . . . i 2 120
Though thy speech doth fail, One eye thou hast, to look to heaven for grace . . . . i 4 82
I with sudden and extemporal speech Purpose to answer . . . . iii 1 6
Her grace in speech, Her words y-clad with wisdom's majesty *2 Hen. VI.* i 1 32
'Tis not my speeches that you do mislike, But 'tis my presence . . i 1 140
I'll have thy head for this thy traitor's speech . . . . . i 3 197
And the offender granted scope of speech . . . . . . iii 1 176
In face, in gait, in speech, he doth resemble . . . . . iii 1 373
On thy knee Make thee beg pardon for thy passed speech . . . iii 2 221
Let this my sword report what speech forbears . . . . . iv 10 57
For this one speech Lord Hastings well deserves To have the heir of the Lord Hungerford . . . . *3 Hen. VI.* iv 1 47
I'll hear no more: die, prophet, in thy speech . . . . . v 6 57
I will be mild and gentle in my speech . . . . . *Richard III.* iv 4 160
When we, Almost with ravish'd listening, could not find His hour of speech a minute . . . . *Hen. VIII.* i 2 121
It was usual with him, every day It would infect his speech . . . i 2 133
Did of me demand What was the speech among the Londoners Concerning the French journey . . . . i 2 154
On certain speeches utter'd By the Bishop of Bayonne . . . . ii 4 171
Applause and approbation . . . I give to both your speeches *T. and C.* i 3 62
Excitements to the field, or speech for truce, Success or loss . . i 3 182
Give pardon to my speech: Therefore 'tis meet Achilles meet not Hector i 3 357
After so many hours, lives, speeches spent, Thus once again says Nestor ii 2 1
Should not our father Bear the great sway of his affairs with reasons, Because your speech hath none that tells him so? . . . . . ii 2 36
Witness the process of your speech . . . . iv 1 8
No, 'tis his kind of speech: he did not mock us . . . *Coriolanus* ii 3 169
Tell me of corn! This was my speech, and I will speak 't again . iii 1 62
All's in anger.—Only fair speech . . . . iii 2 96
Thrust these reproachful speeches down his throat . . . *T. Andron.* ii 1 55
Whate'er I forge . . . , Do you uphold and maintain in your speeches . v 2 72
Shall this speech be spoke for our excuse? Or shall we on? *Rom. and Jul.* i 4 1
Mark him and write his speeches in their books . . . *J. Cæsar* i 2 126
You shall not in your funeral speech blame us, But speak all good . iii 1 245
You shall speak In the same pulpit whereto I am going, After my speech iii 1 251
Do grace to Cæsar's corpse, and grace his speech Tending to Cæsar's glories . . . . iii 2 62
Action, nor utterance, nor the power of speech, To stir men's blood . iii 2 226
You know that you are Brutus that speak this, Or, by the gods, this speech were else your last . . . . iv 3 14
As upon thee, Macbeth, their speeches shine . . . . *Macbeth* iii 1 7
Have you consider'd of my speeches? . . . . iii 1 76
My former speeches have but hit your thoughts, Which can interpret further . . . . iii 6 1
He knows thy thought: Hear his speech, but say thou nought . . iv 1 70
Be not a niggard of your speech: how goes 't? . . . . . . iv 3 180

Speech. Having no witness to confirm my speech . . . *Macbeth* v 1 21
If thy speech be sooth, I care not if thou dost for me as much . . v 5 40
And hath given countenance to his speech, my lord, With almost all the holy vows of heaven . . . . *Hamlet* i 3 113
We'll have a speech straight: come, give us a taste of your quality; come, a passionate speech.—What speech, my lord? . . . . ii 2 451
I heard thee speak me a speech once, but it was never acted . . . ii 2 454
One speech in it I chiefly loved: 'twas Æneas' tale to Dido . . . ii 2 467
You could, for a need, study a speech of some dozen or sixteen lines? . ii 2 566
He would drown the stage with tears And cleave the general ear with horrid speech . . . . ii 2 589
How smart a lash that speech doth give my conscience! . . . . iii 1 50
Speak the speech, I pray you, as I pronounced it to you, trippingly . iii 2 1
If his occulted guilt Do not itself unkennel in one speech . . . iii 2 86
'Tis meet that some more audience than a mother, Since nature makes them partial, should o'erhear The speech, of vantage . . . . iii 3 33
A knavish speech sleeps in a foolish ear . . . . . . iv 2 25
Her speech is nothing, Yet the unshaped use of it doth move The hearers iv 5 7
Wants not buzzers to infect his ear With pestilent speeches . . . iv 5 91
I have a speech of fire, that fain would blaze, But that this folly douts it iv 7 191
Strengthen your patience in our last night's speech . . . . . v 1 317
A love that makes breath poor, and speech unable . . . . *Lear* i 1 61
Mend your speech a little, Lest it may mar your fortunes . . . i 1 96
Your large speeches may your deeds approve . . . . . . i 1 187
If but as well I other accents borrow, That can my speech defuse . . i 4 2
Sirrah, I'll teach thee a speech.—Do.—Mark it, nuncle . . . i 4 128
With curst speech I threaten'd to discover him . . . . . ii 1 67
Smile you my speeches, as I were a fool? . . . . . . ii 2 88
Wear this; spare speech; Decline your head: this kiss . . . iv 2 21
If e'er your grace had speech with man so poor . . . . . v 1 38
If my speech offend a noble heart, Thy arm may do thee justice . . v 3 127
This speech of yours hath moved me, And shall perchance do good . v 3 199
Rude am I in my speech, And little bless'd with the soft phrase of peace *Othello* i 3 81
Alas, she has no speech.—In faith, too much; I find it still, when I have list to sleep . . . . ii 1 103
With your earliest Let me have speech with you . . . . . ii 3 8
Iago, can inform you,—While I spare speech, which something now offends me . . . . ii 3 199
Montano and myself being in speech, There comes a fellow crying out . ii 3 225
Tell her there's one Cassio entreats her a little favour of speech . . iii 1 29
Loves company, Is free of speech, sings, plays, and dances well . . iii 3 185
I am to pray you not to strain my speech To grosser issues . . . iii 3 218
My speech should fall into such vile success As my thoughts aim not at iii 3 222
And stood within the blank of his displeasure For my free speech! . iii 4 129
And his own courses will denote him so That I may save my speech . iv 1 291
Upon my knees, what doth your speech import? . . . . . iv 2 31
His speech sticks in my heart.—Mine ear must pluck it thence *A. and C.* i 5 41
Entreat your captain To soft and gentle speech . . . . . ii 2 3
Your speech is passion: But, pray you, stir no embers up . . . ii 2 12
I do not much dislike the matter, but The manner of his speech . . ii 2 114
If he mislike My speech and what is done, tell him he has Hipparchus, my enfranched bondman . . . . iii 13 148
I am the master of my speeches, and would undergo what's spoken *Cymb.* i 4 152
Strikes life into my speech and shows much more His own conceiving . iii 3 97
Forbear sharp speeches to her: she's a lady So tender of rebukes . . iii 5 39
He on the ground, my speech of insultment ended on his dead body . iii 5 145
I must, For mine own part, unfold a dangerous speech . . . v 5 313
What's dumb in show I'll plain with speech . . *Pericles* iii Gower 14
Had I brought hither a corrupted mind, Thy speech had alter'd it . iv 6 112
Who starves the ears she feeds, and makes them hungry, The more she gives them speech . . . . v 1 114
Speechless. In her youth There is a prone and speechless dialect *M. for M.* i 2 188
You have a double tongue within your mask, And would afford my speechless vizard half . . . . *L. L. Lost* v 2 246
From day to day Visit the speechless sick . . . . . . v 2 861
Sometimes from her eyes I did receive fair speechless messages *M. of V.* i 1 164
I left him almost speechless . . . . *K. John* v 6 24
What is thy sentence then but speechless death? . . . *Richard II.* i 3 172
Dismiss'd me Thus, with his speechless hand . . . *Coriolanus* v 1 67
Speechless complainer, I will learn thy thought . . *T. Andron.* iii 2 39
He fell down in the market-place, and foamed at mouth, and was speechless . . . . *J. Cæsar* i 2 255
The bold winds speechless and the orb below As hush as death *Hamlet* ii 2 507
His fortunes all lie speechless and his name Is at last gasp *Cymbeline* i 5 52
Tell thee, with speechless tongues and semblance pale . . *Pericles* i 1 36
Speed. As thou lovest thy life, make speed from hence . *T. G. of Ver.* iii 1 169
There; and Saint Nicholas be thy speed! . . . . . . iii 1 301
Heaven it knows, I would not have him speed . . . . . iv 4 112
Come you to me at night; you shall know how I speed . *Mer. Wives* ii 2 278
May be he tells you true.—No, heaven so speed me in my time to come! iii 4 12
Come to me at your convenient leisure, and you shall know how I speed iii 5 137
Dispose of her To some more fitter place, and that with speed *M. for M.* i 2 17
Your best appointment make with speed; To-morrow you set on . . iii 1 60
I'll make all speed . . . . iv 3 109
Was carried with more speed before the wind . . . *Com. of Errors* i 1 110
I would my horse had the speed of your tongue . . . *Much Ado* i 1 142
Hymen now with luckier issue speed's . . . . v 3 32
Your wit's too hot, it speeds too fast, 'twill tire . . *L. L. Lost* ii 1 120
The extreme parts of time extremely forms All causes to the purpose of his speed . . . . v 2 751
Go with speed To some forlorn and naked hermitage . . . . v 2 804
God speed fair Helena! whither away? . . . . . *M. N. Dream* i 1 180
The mild hind Makes speed to catch the tiger; bootless speed, When cowardice pursues and valour flies . . . . ii 1 233
Told him he would make some speed Of his return . . *Mer. of Venice* ii 8 37
Use thou all the endeavour of a man In speed to Padua . . . . iii 4 49
Bring them, I pray thee, with imagined speed. . . . . . iii 4 52
Madam, I go with all convenient speed . . . . iii 4 56
Praying for our husbands' healths, Which speed, we hope, the better . v 1 115
Now Hercules be thy speed, young man! . . . . *As Y. Like It* i 2 222
Though Paris came in hope to speed alone . . . . *T. of Shrew* i 2 247
Well mayst thou woo, and happy be thy speed! . . . . . ii 1 139
How speed you with my daughter?—How but well, sir? how but well? It were impossible I should speed amiss . . . . ii 1 283
With the swiftest wing of speed . . . . . . *All's Well* iii 2 76
O you leaden messengers, That ride upon the violent speed of fire . iii 2 112
And hope I may that she, Hearing so much, will speed her foot again . iii 4 37
A worthy exploit: if you speed well in it . . . . . . iii 6 72
Which, if it speed, Is wicked meaning in a lawful deed . . . . iii 7 44

Speed. I will come after you with what good speed Our means will make us means *All's Well* v 1 34
Speeds from me and So leaves me to consider what is breeding *W. Tale* i 2 373
Their speed Hath been beyond account.—Twenty three days They have been absent: 'tis good speed ii 3 197
Your son, with mere conceit and fear Of the queen's speed, is gone iii 2 146
Blossom, speed thee well! There lie, and there thy character iii 3 46
And with speed so pace To speak of Perdita iv 1 23
Fortune speed us! Thus we set on . . . —The swifter speed the better iv 4 681
That 'once,' I see by your good father's speed, Will come on very slowly v 1 210
We must speed For France, for France *K. John* i 1 178
Forwearied in this action of swift speed ii 1 233
Speed then, to take advantage of the field ii 1 297
So hot a speed with such advice disposed, Such temperate order iii 4 11
The copy of your speed is learn'd by them iv 2 113
Withhold thy speed, dreadful occasion! iv 2 125
The spirit of the time shall teach me speed iv 2 176
Bear away that child And follow me with speed iv 3 157
O, I am scalded with my violent motion, And spleen of speed! v 7 50
Bid him—ah, what?—With all good speed at Plashy visit me *Richard II.* i 2 66
A brace of draymen bid God speed him well i 4 32
With all swift speed you must away to France v 1 54
Come yourself with speed to us again; For more is to be said *1 Hen. IV.* i 1 105
'Tis no little reason bids us speed, To save our heads i 3 283
He that rides at high speed and with his pistol kills a sparrow flying ii 4 379
Good manners be your speed! iii 1 190
Thy looks are full of speed.—So hath the business that I come to speak of iii 2 162
With all speed You shall have your desires with interest iv 3 48
And, to prevent the worst, Sir Michael, speed iv 4 35
Arm, arm with speed: and, fellows, soldiers, friends, Better consider v 2 76
Bend you with your dearest speed v 5 36
Came spurring hard A gentleman, almost forspent with speed *2 Hen. IV.* i 1 37
As the thing that's heavy in itself Upon enforcement flies with greatest speed i 1 120
Make friends with speed: Never so few, and never yet more need i 1 214
O'er-read these letters, And well consider of them: make good speed iii 1 3
These griefs shall be with speed redress'd iv 2 59
You shall bear to comfort him, And we with sober speed will follow you iv 3 86
Dispatch us with all speed *Hen. V.* ii 4 141
Speed him hence: Let him greet England with our sharp defiance iii 5 36
Bestow yourself with speed iv 3 68
Let me see, what then? Saint Denis be my speed! v 2 194
God speed the parliament! who shall be the speaker? *1 Hen. VI.* iii 2 60
With all speed provide To see her coronation be perform'd *2 Hen. VI.* i 1 73
Stay not to expostulate, make speed *3 Hen. VI.* ii 5 135
And leave your brothers to go speed elsewhere iv 1 58
Return from France with speed iv 6 61
It shall be done, my sovereign, with all speed iv 6 64
Neighbours, God speed!—Give you good morrow, sir *Richard III.* ii 3 6
Take horse with him, And with all speed post iii 2 17
Go, Lovel, with all speed to Doctor Shaw iii 5 103
An honest tale speeds best being plainly told iv 4 358
Once more, adieu: be valiant, and speed well! v 3 102
The devil speed him! no man's pie is freed From his ambitious finger *Hen. VIII.* i 1 52
With great speed of judgement, Ay, with celerity *Troi. and Cres.* i 3 329
Frown on, you heavens, effect your rage with speed! v 10 6
Speed thee straight, And make my misery serve thy turn *Coriolanus* iv 5 93
I'll prove him, Speed how it will v 1 61
Speak thou no more, if all the rest will speed *T. Andron.* i 1 372
Would it offend you, then, That both should speed?—Faith, not me ii 1 101
I'll send a friar with speed To Mantua *Rom. and Jul.* iv 1 123
My speed to Mantua there was stay'd.—Who bare my letter, then? v 2 12
Saint Francis be my speed! how oft to-night Have my old feet stumbled! v 3 121
Shrunk indeed; And he that's once denied will hardly speed *T. of Athens* iii 2 69
Forget not, in your speed, Antonius, To touch Calpurnia *J. Cæsar* i 2 6
Let the gods so speed me as I love The name of honour more than I fear death i 2 88
O Brutus, The heavens speed thee in thine enterprise! ii 4 41
Post back with speed, and tell him what hath chanced iii 1 287
One of my fellows had the speed of him *Macbeth* i 5 36
Most wicked speed, to post With such dexterity to incestuous sheets! *Hamlet* i 2 156
He shall with speed to England iii 1 177
Tempt him with speed aboard; Delay it not; I'll have him hence to-night iv 3 56
Repair thou to me with as much speed as thou wouldst fly death iv 6 24
If this letter speed, And my invention thrive *Lear* i 2 19
Have a continent forbearance till the speed of his rage goes slower i 2 182
Make your speed to Dover, you shall find Some that will thank you iii 1 36
Hail, gentle sir.—Sir, speed you: what's your will? iv 6 212
The affair cries haste, And speed must answer it *Othello* i 3 278
Has had most favourable and happy speed ii 1 67
Whose footing here anticipates our thoughts A se'nnight's speed ii 1 77
If this suit lay in Bianca's power, How quickly should you speed! iv 1 109
If we draw lots, he speeds *Ant. and Cleo.* ii 3 35
This speed of Cæsar's Carries beyond belief iii 7 75
This fool's speed Be cross'd with slowness; labour be his meed! *Cymb.* iii 5 167
How you shall speed in your journey's end, I think you'll never return to tell v 4 190
Speeded. It shall be speeded well *Meas. for Meas.* iv 5 10
I have speeded hither with the very extremest inch of possibility *2 Hen. IV.* iv 3 38
Speedier. A speedier course than lingering languishment Must we pursue, and I have found the path *T. Andron.* ii 1 110
I will make you way for these your letters; And do't the speedier *Ham.* iv 6 33
Speediest. With the speediest expedition I will dispatch him *T. G. of Ver.* i 3 37
Send me your prisoners with the speediest means *1 Hen. IV.* i 3 120
With your speediest bring us what she says *Ant. and Cleo.* v 1 67
Speedily. I'll see what I can do.—But speedily *Meas. for Meas.* i 4 84
It lies much in your holding up. Haste you speedily to Angelo iii 1 274
Which I held my duty speedily to acquaint you withal *All's Well* i 3 124
Seek these suitors: Go speedily v 3 152
She and my aunt Percy Shall follow in your conduct speedily *1 Hen. IV.* iii 1 197
In person is set forth, Or hitherwards intended speedily iv 1 92
Let us take a muster speedily: Doomsday is near iv 1 133
Come, therefore, let's about it speedily *3 Hen. VI.* iv 6 102
Speedily I wish To hear from Rome *Hen. VIII.* ii 2 89
Post speedily to my lord your husband; show him this letter *Lear* iii 7 1
You justicers, that these our nether crimes So speedily can venge! iv 2 80
Speedily. 'Tis not sleepy business; But must be look'd to speedily and strongly *Cymbeline* iii 5 27
Speediness. I hope the briefness of your answer made The speediness of your return ii 4 31
Speeding. Is this your speeding? nay, then, good night our part! *T. of S.* ii 1 303
A speeding trick to lay down ladies *Hen. VIII.* i 3 40
To-morrow all for speeding do their best *Pericles* ii 3 116
Speedy. Will move us For speedy aid *All's Well* i 2 7
God send you, sir, a speedy infirmity! *T. Night* i 5 84
As it hath been to us rare, pleasant, speedy, The time is worth *W. Tale* iii 1 13
Some speedy messenger bid her repair To our solemnity *K. John* ii 1 554
As speedy in your end As all the poisonous potions in the world *1 Hen. IV.* v 4 55
The king hath won, and hath sent out A speedy power to encounter you *2 Hen. IV.* i 1 133
Are not the speedy scouts return'd again? *1 Hen. VI.* iv 3 1
You speedy helpers, that are substitutes Under the lordly monarch of the north, Appear and aid me v 3 5
This speedy and quick appearance argues proof Of your accustom'd diligence v 3 8
And craves your company for speedy counsel *3 Hen. VI.* ii 1 208
Make all the speedy haste you may *Richard III.* iii 1 60
I will wish her speedy strength, and visit her with my prayers *Coriol.* i 3 87
Music with her silver sound With speedy help doth lend redress *Rom. and Jul.* iv 5 146
He humbly prays your speedy payment *T. of Athens* ii 2 28
Arm you, I pray you, to this speedy voyage *Hamlet* iii 3 24
If your diligence be not speedy, I shall be there afore you *Lear* i 5 4
This letter, madam, craves a speedy answer iv 2 82
How near's the other army?—Near and on speedy foot iv 6 217
Let her who would be rid of him devise His speedy taking off v 1 65
Speken. Where each man Thinks all is writ he speken can *Pericles* ii Gower 12
Spell. Hush, and be mute, Or else our spell is marr'd *Tempest* iv 1 127
Set Caliban and his companions free; Untie the spell v 1 253
Let me not . . . dwell In this bare island by your spell Epil. 8
She works by charms, by spells, by the figure, and such daubery *M. Wives* iv 2 185
I never yet saw man . . . But she would spell him backward *Much Ado* iii 1 61
Never harm, Nor spell nor charm, Come our lovely lady nigh *M. N. D.* ii 2 17
Her actions shall be holy as You hear my spell is lawful *W. Tale* v 3 105
Now help, ye charming spells and periapts; *1 Hen. VI.* v 3 2
Is't possible the spells of France should juggle Men? *Hen. VIII.* i 3 1
O, fear him not; His spell in that is out iii 2 20
'Tis a spell, you see, of much power *Coriolanus* v 2 102
Thy love did read by rote and could not spell *Rom. and Jul.* ii 3 88
Your vessels and your spells provide, Your charms *Macbeth* iii 5 18
Corrupted By spells and medicines bought of mountebanks *Othello* i 3 61
Ah, thou spell! Avaunt!—Why is my lord enraged? *Ant. and Cleo.* iv 12 30
Spelling. Unchain your spirits now with spelling charms *1 Hen. VI.* v 3 31
Spell-stopped. There stand, For you are spell-stopp'd *Tempest* v 1 61
Spelt. What is a, b, spelt backward, with the horn on his head? *L. L. L.* v 1 50
Spend. What of him?—He wonder'd that your lordship Would suffer him to spend his youth at home *T. G. of Ver.* i 3 5
Did request me to importune you To let him spend his time no more at home i 3 14
I am resolved that thou shalt spend some time With Valentinus i 3 66
And spends what he borrows kindly in your company ii 4 39
If you spend word for word with me, I shall make your wit bankrupt ii 4 41
And here he means to spend his time awhile ii 4 80
Intend to chide myself Even for this time I spend in talking to thee iv 2 104
There is money; spend it, spend it; spend more; spend all I have *Mer. Wives* ii 2 241
To save the money that he spends in tiring *Com. of Errors* ii 2 99
How will he spend his wit! How will he triumph! *L. L. Lost* iv 3 147
Or spend a minute's time In pruning me iv 3 182
Observe the times And spend his prodigal wits in bootless rhymes v 2 64
We number nothing that we spend for you: Our duty is so rich v 2 198
A twelvemonth shall you spend, and never rest v 2 831
You spend your passion on a misprised mood *M. N. Dream* iii 2 74
Spend but time To wind about my love with circumstance *Mer. of Ven.* i 1 153
My son and my servant spend all at the university *T. of Shrew* v 1 72
That we with thee May spend our wonder *All's Well* ii 1 92
This man may help me to his majesty's ear, If he would spend his power v 1 8
Spend this for me.—I am no fee'd post, lady *T. Night* i 5 302
Not to spend it so unneighbourly *K. John* v 2 39
Ere the six years that he hath to spend Can change their moons *Rich. II.* i 3 219
His noble hand Did win what he did spend ii 1 180
And he shall spend mine honour with his shame, As thriftless sons v 3 68
Where they did spend a sad and bloody hour *1 Hen. IV.* i 1 56
We may boldly spend upon the hope of what Is to come in iv 1 54
The time of life is short! To spend that shortness basely were too long v 2 83
For coward dogs Most spend their mouths when what they seem to threaten Runs far before them *Hen. V.* ii 4 70
We may as bootless spend our vain command Upon the enraged soldiers iii 3 24
He may well in fretting spend his gall *1 Hen. VI.* i 2 16
And in his bosom spend my latter gasp ii 5 38
What! did my brother Henry spend his youth, His valour, coin, and people, in the wars? *2 Hen. VI.* i 1 78
On sheep or oxen could I spend my fury v 1 27
As I have seen a swan With bootless labour swim against the tide And spend her strength with over-matching waves *3 Hen. VI.* i 4 21
In devotion spend my latter days, To sin's rebuke iv 6 43
Men ne'er spend their fury on a child v 5 57
And now what rests but that we spend the time With stately triumphs? v 7 42
As I am a Christian faithful man, I would not spend another such a night, Though 'twere to buy a world of happy days *Richard III.* i 4 5
He will spend his mouth, and promise, like Brabbler the hound *T. and C.* v 1 98
What I think I utter, and spend my malice in my breath *Coriolanus* ii 1 58
And is content To spend the time to end it ii 2 133
Show our general louts How you can frown than spend a fawn upon 'em iii 2 67
And spend our flatteries, to drink those men Upon whose age we void it up again, With poisonous spite and envy *T. of Athens* i 2 142
And come again to supper to him, of purpose to have him spend less iii 1 27
My lord and I have made an end; I have no more to reckon, he to spend iii 4 56
When we can entreat an hour to serve, We would spend it in some words upon that business *Macbeth* ii 1 23
This night I'll spend Unto a dismal and a fatal end iii 5 20
He's worth more sorrow, And that I'll spend for him v 8 51
We shall not spend a large expense of time Before we reckon v 8 60
Time be thine, And thy best graces spend it at thy will! *Hamlet* i 2 63
I will but spend a word here in the house, And go with you *Othello* i 2 48

Spend. He robs himself that spends a bootless grief *Othello* i 3 209
I have but an hour Of love, of worldly matters, and direction, To spend with thee i 3 301
And spend your rich opinion for the name Of a night-brawler ii 3 195
Plant those that have revolted in the van, That Antony may seem to spend his fury Upon himself *Ant. and Cleo.* iv 6 10
He was my master; and I wore my life To spend upon his haters v 1 9
He'll make demand of her, and spend that kiss Which is my heaven to have v 2 305
Must take me up for swearing; as if I borrowed mine oaths of him and might not spend them at my pleasure *Cymbeline* ii 1 6
On either side I come to spend my breath v 3 81
And in your search spend your adventurous worth *Pericles* ii 4 51
Spend thou that in the town: report what a sojourner we have iv 2 148
And ourselves Will in that kingdom spend our following days v 3 81
Spendest. Thou spend'st such high-day wit in praising him *Mer. of Ven.* ii 9 98
I do not only marvel where thou spendest thy time 1 *Hen. IV.* ii 4 440
Spending. In spending your wit in the praise of mine *L. L. Lost* ii 1 19
Spending his manly marrow in her arms *All's Well* ii 3 298
Spendthrift. What a spendthrift is he of his tongue! *Tempest* ii 1 23
This 'should' is like a spendthrift sigh, That hurts by easing *Hamlet* iv 7 123
Spent. The time 'twixt six and now Must by us both be spent most preciously *Tempest* i 2 241
We have conversed and spent our hours together *T. G. of Ver.* ii 4 63
I am a gentleman that have spent much *Mer. Wives* ii 2 166
Five summers have I spent in furthest Greece *Com. of Errors* i 1 133
If Cupid have not spent all his quiver in Venice *Much Ado* i 1 273
Surely suit ill spent and labour ill bestowed iii 2 103
A merrier man . . . I never spent an hour's talk withal *L. L. Lost* ii 1 68
I do repent The tedious minutes I with her have spent *M. N. Dream* ii 2 112
The hours that we have spent, When we have chid the hasty-footed time iii 2 199
I know not what's spent in the search *Mer. of Venice* iii 1 96
Your daughter spent in Genoa, as I heard, in one night fourscore ducats iii 1 113
What prodigal portion have I spent? *As Y. Like It* i 1 41
And what wilt thou do? beg, when that is spent? i 1 80
And ere we have thy youthful wages spent, We'll light upon some settled low content ii 3 67
And when in music we have spent an hour, Your lecture shall have leisure for as much *T. of Shrew* iii 1 7
The fury spent, anon Did this break from her *W. Tale* iii 3 26
Of this allow, If ever you have spent time worse ere now iv 1 30
Our cannons' malice vainly shall be spent *K. John* ii 1 251
We hold our time too precious to be spent With such a brabbler v 2 161
This arm shall do it, or this life be spent *Richard II.* i 1 108
Six frozen winters spent, Return with welcome home i 3 211
Where words are scarce, they are seldom spent in vain ii 1 7
Words, life, and all, old Lancaster hath spent ii 1 150
The ripest fruit first falls, and so doth he; His time is spent ii 1 154
His noble hand Did win what he did spend and spent not that Which his triumphant father's hand had won ii 1 180
More hath he spent in peace than they in wars ii 1 255
A purse of gold most resolutely snatched on Monday night and most dissolutely spent on Tuesday morning; got with swearing 'Lay by' and spent with crying 'Bring in' 1 *Hen. IV.* i 2 39
The mad days that I have spent! 2 *Hen. IV.* iii 2 37
Mouldy, it is time you were spent.—Spent! iii 2 128
These eyes, like lamps whose wasting oil is spent, Wax dim 1 *Hen. VI.* ii 5 8
In prison hast thou spent a pilgrimage ii 5 116
And so break off; the day is almost spent 2 *Hen. VI.* iii 1 325
And think it but a minute spent in sport iii 2 338
His statutes cancell'd and his treasure spent 3 *Hen. VI.* v 4 79
A happy time of day!—Happy, indeed, as we have spent the day *Richard III.* ii 1 48
Though we have spent our harvest of this king, We are to reap the harvest of his son ii 2 115
What, shall we toward the Tower? the day is spent iii 2 91
Eleven hours I spent to write it over iii 6 5
After so many hours, lives, speeches spent *Troi. and Cres.* ii 2 1
I would not wish a drop of Trojan blood Spent more in her defence ii 2 198
How have we spent this morning! The prince must think me tardy iv 4 142
This night in banqueting must all be spent v 1 51
Ten years are spent since first he undertook This cause *T. Andron.* i 1 31
For pity of mine age, whose youth was spent In dangerous wars iii 1 2
No hare, sir; unless a hare, sir, in a lenten pie, that is something stale and hoar ere it be spent *Rom. and Jul.* ii 4 140
A hare that is hoar Is too much for a score, When it hoars ere it be spent ii 4 146
Wash they his wounds with tears: mine shall be spent, When theirs are dry iii 2 130
When all's spent, he'ld be cross'd then, an he could *T. of Athens* i 2 168
I know my lord hath spent of Timon's wealth iii 4 26
With such sober and unnoted passion He did behave his anger, ere 'twas spent iii 5 22
And, thy fury spent, Confounded be thyself! iv 3 127
As two spent swimmers, that do cling together And choke their art *Macb.* i 2 8
Nought's had, all's spent, Where our desire is got without content iii 2 4
His purse is empty already; all's golden words are spent *Hamlet* v 2 137
My money is almost spent *Othello* ii 3 371
Our lamp is spent, it's out! *Ant. and Cleo.* iv 15 85
My youth I spent Much under him; of him I gather'd honour *Cymbeline* iii 1 70
Almost spent with hunger, I am fall'n in this offence iii 6 63
His comforts thrive, his trials well are spent v 4 104
Time that is so briefly spent With your fine fancies quaintly eche *Pericles* iii Gower 12
Sperato. Si fortune me tormente, sperato me contento 2 *Hen. IV.* ii 4 195
Spero. Si fortuna me tormenta, spero contenta v 5 102
Sperr up the sons of Troy *Troi. and Cres.* Prol. 19
Sphere. You would lift the moon out of her sphere *Tempest* ii 1 183
I do wander every where, Swifter than the moon's sphere *M. N. Dream* ii 1 7
Certain stars shot madly from their spheres, To hear the sea-maid's music ii 1 153
As bright, as clear, As yonder Venus in her glimmering sphere iii 2 61
We shall have shortly discord in the spheres *As Y. Like It* ii 7 6
Survey With thy chaste eye, from thy pale sphere above iii 2 3
He is so above me: In his bright radiance and collateral light Must I be comforted, not in his sphere *All's Well* i 1 100
I had rather hear you to solicit that Than music from the spheres *T. N.* iii 1 121
You stars that move in your right spheres, Where be your powers? *K. John* v 7 74
Two stars keep not their motion in one sphere 1 *Hen. IV.* v 4 65
Do entreat her eyes To twinkle in their spheres till they return *R. and J.* ii 2 17
Sphere. All kind of natures, That labour on the bosom of this sphere *T. of Athens* i 1 66
Make thy two eyes, like stars, start from their spheres *Hamlet* i 5 17
That, as the star moves not but in his sphere, I could not but by her iv 7 15
To be called into a huge sphere, and not to be seen to move in't *A. and C.* ii 7 16
O sun, Burn the great sphere thou movest in! iv 15 10
His voice was propertied As all the tuned spheres, and that to friends v 2 84
The music of the spheres! *Pericles* v 1 231
Sphered. And therefore is the glorious planet Sol In noble eminence enthroned and sphered Amidst the other *Troi. and Cres.* i 3 90
Till thy sphered bias cheek Outswell the colic of puff'd Aquilon iv 5 8
Spherical. She is spherical, like a globe *Com. of Errors* iii 2 116
Her [Fortune's] foot, look you, is fixed upon a spherical stone *Hen. V.* iii 6 37
Knaves, thieves, and treachers, by spherical predominance *Lear* i 2 134
Sphery. What wicked and dissembling glass of mine Made me compare with Hermia's sphery eyne? *M. N. Dream* ii 2 99
Sphinx. Subtle as Sphinx *L. L. Lost* iv 3 342
Spice. Rocks, Which touching but my gentle vessel's side, Would scatter all her spices on the stream *Mer. of Venice* i 1 33
Stark mad! for all Thy by-gone fooleries were but spices of it *W. Tale* iii 2 185
I must go buy spices for our sheep-shearing iv 3 125
Your purse is not hot enough to purchase your spice iv 3 128
And so would you, For all this spice of your hypocrisy *Hen. VIII.* ii 3 26
Liberality, and such like, the spice and salt that season a man *T. and C.* i 2 277
He hath spices of them all, not all *Coriolanus* iv 7 46
Take these keys, and fetch more spices, nurse *Rom. and Jul.* iv 4 1
This embalms and spices To the April day again *T. of Athens* iv 3 40
Bid Nestor bring me spices, ink and paper, My casket *Pericles* iii 1 66
Balm'd and entreasured With full bags of spices! iii 2 66
Spiced. In the spiced Indian air by night *M. N. Dream* ii 1 124
Spicery. In that nest of spicery they shall breed *Richard III.* iv 4 424
Spider. To draw with idle spiders' strings Most ponderous and substantial things! *Meas. for Meas.* iii 2 289
Weaving spiders, come not here; Hence, you long-legg'd spinners! *M. N. Dream* ii 2 20
Here in her hairs The painter plays the spider *Mer. of Venice* iii 2 121
There may be in the cup A spider steep'd, and one may drink *W. Tale* ii 1 40
I have drunk, and seen the spider ii 1 45
The smallest thread That ever spider twisted *K. John* iv 3 128
Let thy spiders, that suck up thy venom, And heavy-gaited toads lie in their way, Doing annoyance *Richard II.* iii 2 14
My brain more busy than the labouring spider Weaves tedious snares 2 *Hen. VI.* iii 1 339
Adders, spiders, toads, Or any creeping venom'd thing *Richard III.* i 2 19
Why strew'st thou sugar on that bottled spider? i 3 242
Help me curse That bottled spider, that foul bunch-back'd toad! iv 4 81
It will not in circumvention deliver a fly from a spider *Troi. and Cres.* ii 3 18
The traces of the smallest spider's web *Rom. and Jul.* i 4 61
Were it Toad, or Adder, Spider, 'Twould move me sooner *Cymbeline* iv 2 90
Spider-like, Out of his self-drawing web, he gives us note *Hen. VIII.* i 1 62
Spied a blossom passing fair Playing in the wanton air *L. L. Lost* iv 3 103
She hath spied him already with those sweet eyes *M. N. Dream* v 1 328
At last I spied An ancient angel coming down the hill *T. of Shrew* iv 2 60
He's shrewdly vexed at something: look, he has spied us *All's Well* iii 5 93
At last I spied his eyes 2 *Hen. IV.* ii 2 87
The white hair that Helen spied on Troilus' chin *Troi. and Cres.* i 2 165
As when, by night and negligence, the fire Is spied in populous cities *Oth.* i 1 77
Spies. If these be true spies which I wear in my head, here's a goodly sight *Tempest* v 1 259
I fear I am attended by some spies *T. G. of Ver.* v 1 10
When the doctor spies his vantage ripe, To pinch her by the hand *M. W.* iv 6 43
The heaven sets spies upon us *W. Tale* v 1 203
I'll fill these dogged spies with false reports *K. John* iv 1 129
Like one that stands upon a promontory, And spies a far-off shore 3 *Hen. VI.* iii 2 136
Spies of the Volsces Held me in chase *Coriolanus* i 6 18
When sorrows come, they come not single spies, But in battalions *Ham.* iv 5 78
The spies and speculations Intelligent of our state *Lear* iii 1 24
And take upon's the mystery of things, As if we were God's spies v 3 17
His power went out in such distractions as Beguiled all spies *A. and C.* iii 7 78
Spigot. O base Hungarian wight! wilt thou the spigot wield? *Mer. Wives* i 3 24
Spill. I for praise alone now seek to spill The poor deer's blood *L. L. Lost* iv 1 34
You came in arms to spill mine enemies' blood *K. John* iii 1 102
Contaminated, base, And misbegotten blood I spill of thine 1 *Hen. VI.* iv 6 22
He forfeits his own blood that spills another *T. of Athens* iii 5 88
So full of artless jealousy is guilt, It spills itself in fearing to be spilt *Hamlet* iv 5 20
Crack nature's moulds, all germens spill at once, That make ingrateful man! *Lear* iii 2 8
To-morrow . . . we'll spill the blood That has to-day escaped *A. and C.* iv 8 3
Spilled. As full of valour as of royal blood: Both have I spill'd *Rich. II.* v 5 115
Spilling. Thou respect'st not spilling Edward's blood iii 1 131
Spilt. Is crack'd, and all the precious liquor spilt i 2 19
There's some of the king's blood spilt 2 *Hen. IV.* ii 2 122
To royalise his blood I spilt mine own *Richard III.* i 3 125
Be satisfied, dear God, with our true blood, Which, as thou know'st, unjustly must be spilt iii 3 22
O, the blood is spilt Of my dear kinsman! *Rom. and Jul.* iii 1 152
So full of artless jealousy is guilt, It spills itself in fearing to be spilt *Hamlet* iv 5 20
Spilth. Our vaults have wept With drunken spilth of wine *T. of Athens* ii 2 169
Spin. She can spin.—Then may I set the world on wheels, when she can spin for her living *T. G. of Ver.* iii 1 316
It [your hair] hangs like flax on a distaff; and I hope to see a housewife take thee between her legs and spin it off *T. Night* i 3 110
That their hot blood may spin in English eyes *Hen. V.* iv 2 10
Spinii. In the regiment of the Spinii one Captain Spurio *All's Well* ii 1 43
Spinner. Hence, you long-legg'd spinners, hence! *M. N. Dream* ii 2 21
Her waggon-spokes made of long spinners' legs *Rom. and Jul.* i 4 59
Spinster. The spinsters and the knitters in the sun *T. Night* ii 4 45
The spinsters, carders, fullers, weavers *Hen. VIII.* i 2 33
Nor the division of a battle knows More than a spinster *Othello* i 1 24
Spire. Which, to the spire and top of praises vouch'd *Coriolanus* i 9 24
Spirit. Hast thou, spirit, Perform'd to point the tempest? *Tempest* i 2 193
My brave spirit! Who was so firm, so constant, that this coil Would not infect his reason?—Not a soul i 2 206
Cried, 'Hell is empty, And all the devils are here.'—Why, that's my spirit! i 2 215
Thou wast a spirit too delicate To act her earthy and abhorr'd commands i 2 272

Spirit. What is't? a spirit? Lord, how it looks about! *Tempest* i 2 409
It carries a brave form. But 'tis a spirit.—No, wench; it eats and sleeps i 2 411
Spirit, fine spirit! I'll free thee Within two days for this i 2 420
If the ill spirit have so fair a house, Good things will strive to dwell with't i 2 458
My spirits, as in a dream, are all bound up i 2 486
I find not Myself disposed to sleep.—Nor I; my spirits are nimble ii 1 202
He's a spirit of persuasion, only Professes to persuade ii 1 235
His spirits hear me And yet I needs must curse ii 2 3
Lo, now, lo! Here comes a spirit of his, and to torment me ii 2 15
The spirit torments me; Oh! ii 2 66
He's but a sot, as I am, nor hath not One spirit to command iii 2 102
Who am myself attach'd with weariness, To the dulling of my spirits iii 3 6
Their great guilt, Like poison given to work a great time after, Now 'gins to bite the spirits iii 3 106
Bring a corollary, Rather than want a spirit iv 1 58
May I be bold To think these spirits?—Spirits, which by mine art I have from their confines call'd to enact My present fancies iv 1 120
Our actors, As I foretold you, were all spirits and Are melted into air iv 1 149
Spirit, We must prepare to meet with Caliban.—Ay, my commander iv 1 165
My charms crack not; my spirits obey; and time Goes upright v 1 2
Say, my spirit, How fares the king and 's followers? v 1 6
Your affections Would become tender.—Dost thou think so, spirit? v 1 19
Quickly, spirit; Thou shalt ere long be free v 1 86
All this service Have I done since I went.—My tricksy spirit! v 1 226
Come hither, spirit: Set Caliban and his companions free; Untie the spell v 1 251
These be brave spirits indeed! v 1 261
Now I want Spirits to enforce, art to enchant Epil. 14
Who then? his spirit?—Neither.—What then?—Nothing *T. G. of Ver.* iii 1 195
If the gentle spirit of moving words Can no way change you v 4 55
By the honour of my ancestry, I do applaud thy spirit v 4 140
What spirit, what devil suggests this imagination? *Mer. Wives* iii 3 230
The spirit of wantonness is, sure, scared out of him iv 2 223
You have heard of such a spirit iv 4 35
Dis-horn the spirit, And mock him home iv 4 63
The night is dark; light and spirits will become it well v 2 13
As I am a true spirit, welcome! v 5 33
Spirits are not finely touch'd But to fine issues *Meas. for Meas.* i 1 36
I hold you as a thing ensky'd and sainted, By your renouncement an immortal spirit, And to be talk'd with in sincerity i 4 35
Bound by my charity and my blest order, I come to visit the afflicted spirits ii 3 4
And the delighted spirit To bathe in fiery floods iii 1 121
I have spirit to do any thing that appears not foul in the truth of my spirit iii 1 213
Heaven give your spirits comfort! iv 2 73
The best and wholesomest spirits of the night Envelope you! iv 2 76
That spirit's possess'd with haste That wounds the unsisting postern with these strokes iv 2 91
Which is the natural man, And which the spirit? *Com. of Errors* v 1 334
I would have thought her spirit had been invincible *Much Ado* ii 3 119
'I measure him,' says she, 'by my own spirit' ii 3 149
The man, as you know all, hath a contemptible spirit ii 3 188
Her spirits are as coy and wild As haggerds of the rock iii 1 35
Nay, but his jesting spirit iii 2 60
These things, come thus to light, Smother her spirits up iv 1 113
Thought I thy spirits were stronger than thy shames iv 1 127
Whose spirits toil in frame of villanies iv 1 191
What sign is it when a man of great spirit grows melancholy? *L. L. Lost* i 2 2
I am ill at reckoning; it fitteth the spirit of a tapster i 2 43
My spirit grows heavy in love i 2 127
Now, madam, summon up your dearest spirits ii 1 1
A foolish extravagant spirit, full of forms, figures, shapes, objects iv 2 68
Devils soonest tempt, resembling spirits of light iv 3 257
Universal plodding poisons up The nimble spirits in the arteries iv 3 306
Such a merry, nimble, stirring spirit, She might ha' been a grandam v 2 16
Out of your favours, heavenly spirits, vouchsafe Not to behold v 2 166
Excuse or hide The liberal opposition of our spirits v 2 743
Why, that's the way to choke a gibing spirit v 2 868
Throw away that spirit, And I shall find you empty of that fault v 2 877
Awake the pert and nimble spirit of mirth *M. N. Dream* i 1 14
How now, spirit! whither wander you?—Over hill, over dale ii 1 1
Farewell, thou lob of spirits; I'll be gone ii 1 16
Tempt not too much the hatred of my spirit ii 1 211
The clamorous owl that nightly hoots and wonders At our quaint spirits ii 2 7
I am a spirit of no common rate iii 1 157
I will purge thy mortal grossness so That thou shalt like an airy spirit go iii 1 164
How now, mad spirit! What night-rule now about this haunted grove? iii 2 4
Damned spirits all, That in crossways and floods have burial iii 2 382
But we are spirits of another sort iii 2 388
Allay with some cold drops of modesty Thy skipping spirit *Mer. of Ven.* ii 2 196
These foolish drops do something drown my manly spirit ii 3 14
All things that are, Are with more spirit chased than enjoy'd ii 6 13
The watery kingdom . . . is no bar To stop the foreign spirits ii 7 46
I will not jump with common spirits ii 9 32
Hearing applause and universal shout, Giddy in spirit iii 2 145
Her gentle spirit Commits itself to yours to be directed iii 2 165
The best-condition'd and unwearied spirit In doing courtesies iii 2 295
There must be needs a like proportion Of lineaments, of manners, and of spirit iii 4 15
Am arm'd To suffer with a quietness of spirit iv 1 12
Thy currish spirit Govern'd a wolf iv 1 133
Thou shalt see the difference of our spirits iv 1 368
I am never merry when I hear sweet music.—The reason is, your spirits are attentive v 1 70
The motions of his spirit are dull as night And his affections dark v 1 86
The spirit of my father, which I think is within me, begins to mutiny against this servitude *As Y. Like It* i 1 23
The spirit of my father grows strong in me, and I will no longer endure it i 1 73
Young gentleman, your spirits are too bold for your years i 2 183
O Jupiter, how weary are my spirits!—I care not for my spirits, if my legs were not weary ii 4 1
An unquestionable spirit, which you have not, a beard neglected iii 2 394
Nor your cheek of cream, That can entame my spirits to your worship iii 5 48
O, that a mighty man of such descent, Of such possessions, and so high esteem, Should be infused with so foul a spirit! *T. of Shrew* Ind. 2 17
Thou hilding of a devilish spirit, Why dost thou wrong her? ii 1 26

Spirit. Woo her with some spirit when she comes *T. of Shrew* ii 1 170
I see a woman may be made a fool, If she had not a spirit to resist iii 2 223
Pluck up thy spirits; look cheerfully upon me iv 3 38
Let me not live . . . to be the snuff Of younger spirits *All's Well* i 2 60
In thee some blessed spirit doth speak His powerful sound ii 1 178
He's of a most facinerious spirit that will not acknowledge it ii 3 35
This exceeding posting day and night Must wear your spirits low v 1 2
Give a favour from you To sparkle in the spirits of my daughter v 3 75
O spirit of love! how quick and fresh art thou *T. Night* i 1 9
Thy limbs, actions, and spirit, Do give thee five-fold blazon i 5 311
The spirit of humours intimate reading aloud to him! ii 5 93
Thy Fates open their hands; let thy blood and spirit embrace them ii 5 160
If spirits can assume both form and suit You come to fright us v 1 242
A spirit I am indeed; But am in that dimension grossly clad v 1 243
And our weak spirits ne'er been higher rear'd With stronger blood *W. T.* i 2 72
Threw off his spirit, his appetite, his sleep, And downright languish'd ii 3 16
Jove send her A better guiding spirit! ii 3 127
Some powerful spirit instruct the kites and ravens To be thy nurses! ii 3 186
I have heard, but not believed, the spirits o' the dead May walk again iii 3 16
I would your spirit were easier for advice, Or stronger for your need iv 4 516
Would make her sainted spirit Again possess her corpse v 1 57
So be blest my spirit! v 1 71
From thy admiring daughter took the spirits, Standing like stone v 3 41
The very spirit of Plantagenet! I am thy grandam, Richard *K. John* i 1 167
This is worshipful society And fits the mounting spirit like myself i 1 206
A braver choice of dauntless spirits . . . Did never float ii 1 72
Whose labour'd spirits, Forwearied in this action of swift speed ii 1 232
Back to the stained field, You equal potents, fiery kindled spirits! ii 1 358
With my vex'd spirits I cannot take a truce iii 1 17
If that surly spirit, melancholy, Had baked thy blood iii 3 42
A grave unto a soul; Holding the eternal spirit, against her will iii 4 18
Now hear me speak with a prophetic spirit iii 4 126
The breath of heaven hath blown his spirit out iv 1 110
The spirit of the time shall teach me speed iv 2 176
O me! my uncle's spirit is in these stones iv 3 9
Put on The dauntless spirit of resolution v 1 53
Brave our fields, And flesh his spirit in a warlike soil v 1 71
His spirit is come in, That so stood out against the holy church v 2 70
Tame the savage spirit of wild war v 2 74
And cull'd these fiery spirits from the world v 2 114
Up once again; put spirit in the French v 4 2
A jewel in a ten-times-barr'd-up chest Is a bold spirit in a loyal breast Mine honour is my life *Richard II.* i 1 181
O thou, the earthly author of my blood, Whose youthful spirit, in me regenerate i 3 70
I have a thousand spirits in one breast, To answer twenty thousand iv 1 58
Well, God give thee the spirit of persuasion 1 *Hen. IV.* i 2 170
As full of peril and adventurous spirit As to o'er-walk a current roaring i 3 191
Thy spirit within thee hath been so at war ii 3 59
That spirit Percy, and that devil Glendower ii 4 405
I can call spirits from the vasty deep.—Why, so can I, or so can any man iii 1 52
As full of spirit as the month of May, And gorgeous as the sun iv 1 101
As if he master'd there a double spirit Of teaching and of learning v 2 64
I did not think thee lord of such a spirit v 4 18
The spirits Of valiant Shirley, Stafford, Blunt, are in my arms v 4 40
When that this body did contain a spirit, A kingdom for it was too small v 4 89
Your spirit is too true, your fears too certain 2 *Hen. IV.* i 1 92
Whose spirit lent a fire Even to the dullest peasant in his camp i 1 112
Let one spirit of the first-born Cain Reign in all bosoms! i 1 157
His forward spirit Would lift him where most trade of danger ranged i 1 173
For their spirits and souls, This word, rebellion, it had froze them up i 1 198
You have . . . practised upon the easy-yielding spirit of this woman ii 1 126
Thus we play the fools with the time, and the spirits of the wise sit in the clouds and mock us ii 2 155
You do draw my spirits from me With new lamenting ancient oversights ii 3 46
Care I for the limb, the thewes? . . . Give me the spirit iii 2 278
The dove and very blessed spirit of peace iv 1 46
Believe me, I am passing light in spirit iv 2 85
The vital commoners and inland petty spirits iv 3 119
Unless some dull and favourable hand Will whisper music to my weary spirit iv 5 3
Which my most inward true and duteous spirit Teacheth iv 5 148
If any rebel or vain spirit of mine Did with the least affection of a welcome Give entertainment iv 5 172
It is a wonderful thing to see the semblable coherence of his men's spirits and his v 1 73
Their spirits are so married in conjunction with the participation of society v 1 76
How many nobles then should hold their places, That must strike sail to spirits of vile sort! v 2 18
Use the same With the like bold, just, and impartial spirit v 2 116
With his spirit sadly I survive, To mock the expectation of the world v 2 125
Pardon, gentles all, The flat unraised spirits *Hen. V.* Prol. 9
Leaving his body as a paradise, To envelope and contain celestial spirits i 1 31
Invoke his warlike spirit, And your great-uncle's i 2 104
He therefore sends you, meeter for your spirit, This tun of treasure i 2 254
Give me thy fist, thy fore-foot to me give: Thy spirits are most tall ii 1 72
Constant in spirit, not swerving with the blood ii 2 133
Hold hard the breath and bend up every spirit To his full height iii 1 16
Follow your spirit, and upon this charge Cry 'God for Harry, England!' iii 1 33
With spirit of honour edged More sharper than your swords iii 5 38
'Tis good for men to love their present pains Upon example; so the spirit is eased iv 1 19
My horse! varlet! laquais! ha!—O brave spirit! iv 2 3
I cannot so conjure up the spirit of love in her v 2 316
His soldiers spying his undaunted spirit 1 *Hen. VI.* i 1 127
The spirit of deep prophecy she hath, Exceeding the nine sibyls i 2 55
Salisbury, cheer thy spirit with this comfort i 4 90
Well, let them practise and converse with spirits ii 1 25
I have perhaps some shallow spirit of judgement ii 4 16
Undaunted spirit in a dying breast! iii 2 99
A breathing valiant man, Of an invincible unconquer'd spirit! iv 2 32
In that sea of blood my boy did drench His over-mounting spirit iv 7 15
My spirit can no longer bear these harms iv 7 30
He speaks with such a proud commanding spirit iv 7 88
These news, my lords, may cheer our drooping spirits v 2 1
Ye choice spirits that admonish me And give me signs of future accidents v 3 3
Ye familiar spirits, that are cull'd Out of the powerful regions under earth, Help me this once v 3 10
Unchain your spirits now with spelling charms v 3 31

Spirit. I never had to do with wicked spirits . . . . 1 *Hen. VI.* v 4 42
Her . . . undaunted spirit, More than in women commonly is seen . v 5 70
This they have promised, to show your highness A spirit raised from depth of under-ground . . . . 2 *Hen. VI.* i 2 79
I have heard her reported to be a woman of an invincible spirit . . i 4 9
The time when screech-owls cry and ban-dogs howl And spirits walk . i 4 22
Raising up wicked spirits from under ground . . . . . . ii 1 174
He dares not calm his contumelious spirit . . . . . . iii 2 204
Soft-hearted wretch! Hast thou not spirit to curse thine enemy? . . iii 2 308
Inspired with the spirit of putting down kings and princes . . . iv 2 38
Unless you be possess'd with devilish spirits, You cannot but forbear . iv 7 80
Whose haughty spirit, winged with desire, Will cost my crown 3 *Hen. VI.* i 1 267
They are soldiers, Witty, courteous, liberal, full of spirit . . . i 2 43
Cheer up your spirits: our foes are nigh . . . . ii 2 56
A woman of this valiant spirit Should, if a coward heard her speak these words, Infuse his breast with magnanimity . . . . . . v 4 39
He might infect another And make him of like spirit to himself . . v 4 47
'Tis [conscience] a blushing shamefast spirit that mutinies in a man's bosom; it fills one full of obstacles . . . . *Richard III.* i 4 142
There's some conceit or other likes him well, When he doth bid good morrow with such a spirit . . . . iii 4 52
So much is my poverty of spirit, So mighty and so many my defects . iii 7 159
The little souls of Edward's children Whisper the spirits of thine enemies iv 4 192
Though far more cause, yet much less spirit to curse Abides in me . iv 4 196
I have not that alacrity of spirit, Nor cheer of mind, that I was wont to have . . . . v 3 73
By their heralds challenged The noble spirits to arms . . *Hen. VIII.* i 1 35
Stand forth, and with bold spirit relate . . . . i 2 129
To stubborn spirits They swell, and grow as terrible as storms . . iii 1 163
A noble spirit, As yours was put into you, ever casts Such doubts, as false coin, from it . . . . iii 1 169
Some spirit put this paper in the packet, To bless your eye withal . iii 2 129
Can thy spirit wonder A great man should decline? . . . . . iii 2 374
Spirits of peace, where are ye? are ye all gone, And leave me here in wretchedness behind ye? . . . . iv 2 83
Affairs that walk, As they say spirits do, at midnight . . . . v 1 14
Now expectation, tickling skittish spirits . . . *Troi. and Cres.* Prol. 20
And spirit of sense Hard as the palm of ploughman . . . . . i 1 58
Nerve and bone of Greece, Heart of our numbers, soul and only spirit . i 3 56
There's not the meanest spirit on our party Without a heart to dare or sword to draw When Helen is defended . . . . ii 2 156
Will strike amazement to their drowsy spirits . . . . . . ii 2 210
Nor doth the eye itself, That most pure spirit of sense, behold itself . iii 3 106
But that you say, 'be't so,' I'll speak it in my spirit and honour, 'no' . iv 4 137
That spirit of his In aspiration lifts him from the earth . . . . iv 5 15
Her wanton spirits look out At every joint and motive of her body . iv 5 56
And make distinct the very breach whereout Hector's great spirit flew iv 5 246
Hoy-day! spirits and fires! . . . . v 1 73
Will I wear it on my helm, And grieve his spirit that dares not challenge it . . . . v 2 94
Whilst I, with those that have the spirit, will haste . . *Coriolanus* i 5 14
Death, that dark spirit, in's nervy arm doth lie . . . . . ii 1 177
Straight his doubled spirit Re-quicken'd what in flesh was fatigate . ii 2 120
Thus to have said, As you were fore-advised, had touch'd his spirit . ii 3 199
You must inquire your way, Which you are out of, with a gentler spirit iii 1 55
Wants not spirit To say he'll turn your current in a ditch . . . iii 1 95
I think 'twill serve, if he Can thereto frame his spirit . . . . iii 2 97
Well, I must do't: Away, my disposition, and possess me Some harlot's spirit! . . . . iii 2 112
You were used To say extremity was the trier of spirits . . . . iv 1 4
Resume that spirit, when you were wont to say, If you had been the wife of Hercules, Six of his labours you'ld have done, and saved Your husband so much sweat . . . . iv 1 16
Even so mayst thou . . . Then cheer thy spirit . . *T. Andron.* iv 4 88
That codding spirit had they from their mother . . . . . v 1 99
'Twould anger him To raise a spirit in his mistress' circle *Rom. and Jul.* ii 1 24
That gallant spirit hath aspired the clouds . . . . iii 1 122
What hadst thou to do in hell, When thou didst bower the spirit of a fiend In mortal paradise of such sweet flesh? . . . . . . iii 2 81
Where, as they say, At some hours in the night spirits resort . . iv 3 44
All this day an unaccustom'd spirit Lifts me above the ground . . v 1 4
Magic of bounty! all these spirits thy power Hath conjured *T. of Athens* i 1 6
Faults that are rich are fair.—A noble spirit! . . . . . . i 2 14
'Tis a spirit: sometime 't appears like a lord; sometime like a lawyer . ii 2 115
In all shapes that man goes up and down in from fourscore to thirteen, this spirit walks in . . . . ii 2 120
I have observed thee always for a towardly prompt spirit . . . . iii 1 37
And just of the same piece Is every flatterer's spirit . . . . . iii 2 72
With a noble fury and fair spirit, Seeing his reputation touch'd . . iii 5 18
And, not to swell our spirit, He shall be executed presently . . . iii 5 102
O abhorred spirits!—Not all the whips of heaven are large enough . v 1 63
These well express in thee thy latter spirits . . . . . . v 4 74
I do lack some part Of that quick spirit that is in Antony . . *J. Cæsar* i 2 29
Brutus will start a spirit as soon as Cæsar . . . . i 2 147
Scorn'd his spirit That could be moved to smile at any thing . . . i 2 206
Heaven hath infused them with these spirits, To make them instruments of fear . . . . i 3 69
Our fathers' minds are dead, And we are govern'd with our mothers' spirits . . . . i 3 83
Nor walls of beaten brass, Nor airless dungeon, nor strong links of iron, Can be retentive to the strength of spirit . . . . i 3 95
To kindle cowards and to steel with valour The melting spirits of women ii 1 122
Nor the insuppressive mettle of our spirits . . . . ii 1 134
We all stand up against the spirit of Cæsar; And in the spirit of men there is no blood: O, that we then could come by Cæsar's spirit, And not dismember Cæsar! . . . . ii 1 167
Bear it as our Roman actors do, With untired spirits and formal constancy . . . . ii 1 227
Thou, like an exorcist, hast conjured up My mortified spirit . . . ii 1 324
The choice and master spirits of this age . . . . iii 1 163
If then thy spirit look upon us now, Shall it not grieve thee? . . . iii 1 195
And Cæsar's spirit, ranging for revenge, With Ate by his side . . . iii 1 270
But were I Brutus, And Brutus Antony, there were an Antony Would ruffle up your spirits . . . . iii 2 232
His corporal motion govern'd by my spirit . . . . iv 1 33
O, I could weep My spirit from mine eyes! . . . . iv 3 100
Speak to me what thou art.—Thy evil spirit, Brutus.—Why comest thou? . . . . iv 3 282
Ill spirit, I would hold more talk with thee . . . . . . iv 3 289
I am fresh of spirit and resolved To meet all perils very constantly . v 1 91

Spirit. O Julius Cæsar, thou art mighty yet! Thy spirit walks abroad *J. C.* v 3 95
Arm 'gainst arm, Curbing his lavish spirit . . . . . *Macbeth* i 2 57
Hie thee hither, That I may pour my spirits in thine ear . . . . i 5 27
Come, you spirits That tend on mortal thoughts, unsex me here! . . i 5 41
Your spirits shine through you . . . . iii 1 128
My little spirit, see, Sits in a foggy cloud, and stays for me . . . iii 5 34
Black spirits and white, Red spirits and grey . . . . . . iv 1 43
Thou art too like the spirit of Banquo; down! . . . . . . iv 1 112
The spirits that know All mortal consequences have pronounced me thus v 3 4
For which, they say, you spirits oft walk in death . . . . *Hamlet* i 1 138
The extravagant and erring spirit hies To his confine . . . . i 1 154
And then, they say, no spirit dare stir abroad; The nights are wholesome, then no planets strike . . . . i 1 161
Upon my life, This spirit, dumb to us, will speak to him . . . . i 1 171
My father's spirit in arms! all is not well; I doubt some foul play . i 2 255
It draws near the season Wherein the spirit held his wont to walk . i 4 6
Be thou a spirit of health or goblin damn'd . . . . i 4 40
I am thy father's spirit, Doom'd for a certain term to walk the night . i 5 9
Rest, rest, perturbed spirit! . . . . i 5 183
The spirit that I have seen May be the devil . . . . . . ii 2 627
As he is very potent with such spirits, Abuses me to damn me . . ii 2 631
That no revenue hast but thy good spirits, To feed and clothe thee . iii 2 63
My spirits grow dull, and fain I would beguile The tedious day with sleep iii 2 236
Your mother, in most great affliction of spirit, hath sent me to you . iii 2 324
That spirit upon whose weal depend and rest The lives of many . . iii 3 14
Forth at your eyes your spirits wildly peep . . . . iii 4 119
Whose spirit with divine ambition puff'd Makes mouths at the invisible event . . . . iv 4 49
I will receive it, sir, with all diligence of spirit . . . . . v 2 95
The potent poison quite o'er-crows my spirit . . . . v 2 364
When he saw my best alarum'd spirits, Bold in the quarrel's right *Lear* ii 1 55
Come not in here, nuncle, here's a spirit. Help me, help me! . . iii 4 39
Who's there?—A spirit, a spirit: he says his name's poor Tom . . iii 4 42
It is the cowish terror of his spirit, That dares not undertake . . iv 2 12
This kiss, if it durst speak, Would stretch thy spirits up into the air . iv 2 23
If that the heavens do not their visible spirits Send quickly down . iv 2 46
Let not my worser spirit tempt me again To die before you please! . iv 6 222
Do you know me?—You are a spirit, I know: when did you die? . . iv 7 49
This sword, this arm, and my best spirits, are bent To prove upon thy heart . . . . v 3 139
My spirit and my place have in them power To make this bitter to thee *Othello* i 1 103
Of spirit so still and quiet, that her motion Blush'd at herself . . i 3 95
That he may . . . Give renew'd fire to our extincted spirits . . . ii 1 81
Noble swelling spirits, That hold their honours in a wary distance . ii 3 57
O thou invisible spirit of wine, if thou hast no name to be known by, let us call thee devil! . . . . ii 3 283
To show the love and duty that I bear you With franker spirit . . iii 3 195
I see this hath a little dash'd your spirits.—Not a jot, not a jot . . iii 3 214
And knows all qualities, with a learned spirit, Of human dealings . . iii 3 259
Should hold her loathed and his spirits should hunt After new fancies . iii 4 62
So help me every spirit sanctified, As I have spoken for you all my best iii 4 126
Or some unhatch'd practice . . . Hath puddled his clear spirit . . iii 4 143
I would not kill thy unprepared spirit; No; heaven forfend! . . . v 2 31
There's a great spirit gone! . . . . *Ant. and Cleo.* i 2 126
As for my wife, I would you had her spirit in such another . . . ii 2 62
Thy demon, that's thy spirit which keeps thee, is Noble, courageous . ii 3 19
Thy spirit Is all afraid to govern thee near him; But, he away, 'tis noble ii 3 28
The elements be kind to thee, and make Thy spirits all of comfort! . iii 2 41
O'er my spirit Thy full supremacy thou knew'st . . . . . . iii 11 58
It would warm his spirits, To hear from me you had left Antony . . iii 13 69
This morning, like the spirit of a youth That means to be of note, begins betimes . . . . iv 4 26
Now my spirit is going; I can no more.—Noblest of men, woo't die? . iv 15 58
Come, away: This case of that huge spirit now is cold . . . . iv 15 89
A rarer spirit never Did steer humanity . . . . v 1 31
I shall show the cinders of my spirits Through the ashes of my chance v 2 173
I do know her spirit, And will not trust one of her malice . *Cymbeline* i 5 34
There is No danger in what show of death it makes, More than the locking-up the spirits a time . . . . i 5 41
When on my three-foot stool I sit and tell The warlike feats I have done, his spirits fly out Into my story . . . . iii 3 90
Most willing spirits, That promise noble service . . . . . . iv 2 338
Gilded pale looks, Part shame, part spirit renew'd . . . . . v 3 35
No more, you petty spirits of region low, Offend our hearing . . . v 4 93
For whom my heart drops blood, and my false spirits Quail to remember v 5 148
Yet neither pleasure's art can joy my spirits . . . . . *Pericles* i 2 9
And yet the fire of life kindle again The o'erpress'd spirits . . . iii 2 84
To think of what a noble strain you are, And of how coward a spirit . iv 3 25
Spirited. Shall our quick blood, spirited with wine, Seem frosty? *Hen. V.* iii 5 21
Spiriting. Pardon, master; I will be correspondent to command And do my spiriting gently . . . . *Tempest* i 2 298
Spiritless. Even such a man, so faint, so spiritless, So dull . 2 *Hen. IV.* i 1 70
Spirit-stirring. The spirit-stirring drum, the ear-piercing fife *Othello* iii 3 352
Spiritual. Whose spiritual counsel had, Shall stop or spur me *W. Tale* ii 1 186
Upon our spiritual convocation . . . . *Hen. V.* i 1 76
Thou art reverent Touching thy spiritual function, not thy life 1 *Hen. VI.* iii 1 50
I must tell you, You tender more your person's honour than Your high profession spiritual . . . . *Hen. VIII.* ii 4 117
His contemplation were above the earth, And fix'd on spiritual object . iii 2 132
You have scarce time To steal from spiritual leisure a brief span . . iii 2 140
Spiritualty. We of the spiritualty Will raise your highness such a mighty sum . . . . *Hen. V.* i 2 132
Spirt. Our scions, put in wild and savage stock, Spirt up so suddenly . iii 5 8
Spit. As she spit in his face, so she defied him . . *Meas. for Meas.* ii 1 86
The capon burns, the pig falls from the spit . . *Com. of Errors* i 2 44
Wouldst thou not spit at me and spurn at me? . . . . . . ii 2 136
She would have made Hercules have turned spit . . . *Much Ado* ii 1 261
Your arms crossed on your thin-belly doublet like a rabbit on a spit *L. L. Lost* iii 1 20
And spit upon my Jewish gaberdine . . . . . *Mer. of Venice* i 3 113
You spit on me on Wednesday last; You spurn'd me such a day . . i 3 127
I am as like to call thee so again, To spit on thee again, to spurn thee too i 3 132
The watery kingdom, whose ambitious head Spits in the face of heaven ii 7 45
Now weep for him, then spit at him . . . . . *As Y. Like It* iii 2 438
Very good orators, when they are out, they will spit . . . . iv 1 76
Spit in the hole, man, and tune again . . . . . *T. of Shrew* iii 1 40
If you had but looked big and spit at him, he'ld have run . *W. Tale* iv 3 113
Ready mounted are they to spit forth Their iron indignation . . *K. John* ii 1 211
Here's a large mouth, indeed, That spits forth death and mountains . ii 1 458

Spit. I do defy him, and I spit at him ; Call him a slanderous coward and villain . . . *Richard II.* i 1 60
Spit it bleeding in his high disgrace . i 1 194
Spit upon him, whilst I say he lies, And lies, and lies . iv 1 75
If I tell thee a lie, spit in my face, call me horse . *1 Hen. IV.* ii 4 214
If it be a hot day, and I brandish any thing but a bottle, I would I might never spit white again . *2 Hen. IV.* i 2 237
Whose low vassal seat The Alps doth spit and void his rheum upon *Hen. V.* iii 5 52
Why dost thou spit at me?—Would it were mortal poison ! *Richard III.* i 2 145
Tongues spit their duties out, and cold hearts freeze . *Hen. VIII.* i 2 61
The faint defects of age . . . ; to cough and spit . *Troi. and Cres.* i 3 173
Look'd not lovelier Than Hector's forehead when it spit forth blood *Cor.* i 3 45
Lest that thy wives with spits and boys with stones In puny battle slay me . iv 4 5
Weke, weke! so cries a pig prepared to the spit . *T. Andron.* iv 2 146
That did spit his body Upon a rapier's point . *Rom. and Jul.* iv 3 56
Would thou wert clean enough to spit upon ! . *T. of Athens* iv 3 364
Rumble thy bellyful ! Spit, fire ! spout, rain ! . *Lear* iii 2 14
To have a thousand with red burning spits Come hissing in upon 'em iii 6 16
Spit, and throw stones, cast mire upon me . *Cymbeline* v 5 222
Thou stormest venomously ; Wilt thou spit all thyself? . *Pericles* iii 1 8
Thou mayst cut a morsel off the spit . iv 2 142
Spital. To the spital go, And from the powdering-tub of infamy Fetch forth the lazar kite of Cressid's kind . *Hen. V.* ii 1 78
News have I, that my Nell is dead i' the spital . v 1 86
Spital-house. She, whom the spital-house and ulcerous sores Would cast the gorge at . *T. of Athens* iv 3 39
Spite. Hark, what fine change is in the music !—Ay, that change is the spite . *T. G. of Ver.* iv 2 69
O spite of spites ! We talk with goblins, owls, and sprites *Com. of Errors* ii 2 191
Be it for nothing but to spite my wife . iii 1 118
You had in him no right.—He meant he did me none ; the more my spite iv 2 8
In spite of your heart, I think ; alas, poor heart ! If you spite it for my sake, I will spite it for yours . *Much Ado* v 2 69
Spite of cormorant devouring Time . *L. L. Lost* i 1 4
O spite ! too old to be engaged to young . *M. N. Dream* i 1 138
O spite ! O hell ! I see you all are bent To set against me . iii 2 145
To fashion this false sport, in spite of me . iii 2 194
I'll find Demetrius and revenge this spite . iii 2 420
But stay, O spite ! But mark, poor knight ! . v 1 281
The more my wrong, the more his spite appears *T. of Shrew* iv 3 2
And that which spites me more than all these wants, He does it under name of perfect love . iv 3 11
Where he sits crowned in his master's spite . *T. Night* v 1 131
I'll sacrifice the lamb that I do love, To spite a raven's heart . v 1 134
O'erbearing interruption, spite of France . *K. John* iii 4 9
Faulconbridge, In spite of spite, alone upholds the day . v 4 5
Fear not, my lord : that Power that made you king Hath power to keep you king in spite of all . *Richard II.* iii 2 28
This is the deadly spite that angers me . *1 Hen. IV.* iii 1 192
And approach The ragged'st hour that time and spite dare bring ! *2 Hen. IV.* i 1 151
In spite of pope or dignities of church . *1 Hen. VI.* i 3 50
In spite of us or aught that we could do . i 5 37
These my friends in spite of thee shall wear . ii 4 106
They set him free . . . , In spite of Burgundy and all his friends . iii 3 73
We should have seen decipher'd there More rancorous spite . iv 1 185
The spite of man prevaileth against me. O Lord, have mercy ! *2 Hen. VI.* i 3 218
Climbing my walls in spite of me the owner . iv 10 37
That keeps his leaves in spite of any storm . v 1 206
Speak not in spite, For you shall sup with Jesu Christ to-night . v 1 213
And spite of spite needs must I rest awhile . *3 Hen. VI.* ii 3 5
I may conquer fortune's spite By living low, where fortune cannot hurt me . iv 6 19
O unbid spite ! is sportful Edward come? . v 1 18
I know A way, if it take right, in spite of fortune . *Hen. VIII.* iii 2 219
As if that luck, in very spite of cunning, Bade him win all *Tr. and Cr.* v 5 41
In mere spite, To be full quit of those my banishers *Coriolanus* iv 5 88
Flourishes his blade in spite of me . *Rom. and Jul.* i 1 85
A villain that is hither come in spite, To scorn at our solemnity . i 5 64
That were some spite . ii 1 27
It was bad enough before their spite . iv 1 31
And spend our flatteries, to drink those men Upon whose age we void it up again, With poisonous spite and envy . *T. of Athens* i 2 144
Creatures Whose naked natures live in all the spite Of wreakful heaven iv 3 228
Who in spite put stuff To some she beggar and compounded thee . iv 3 272
I am reckless what I do to spite the world . *Macbeth* iii 1 111
That I may tell pale-hearted fear it lies, And sleep in spite of thunder . iv 1 86
The time is out of joint : O cursed spite, That ever I was born to set it right ! Nay, come, let's go together . *Hamlet* i 5 189
Deliver'd letters, spite of intermission . *Lear* ii 4 33
Let him do his spite . *Othello* i 2 17
In spite of nature, Of years, of country, credit, every thing . i 3 96
O, 'tis the spite of hell, the fiend's arch-mock ! . iv 1 71
No more, thou thunder-master, show Thy spite on mortal flies *Cymbeline* v 4 31
Spite of all the rapture of the sea, This jewel holds his building *Pericles* ii 1 161
Will to my sense bend no licentious ear, But curb it, spite of seeing . v 3 31
Spited. Beguiled, divorced, wronged, spited, slain ! . *Rom. and Jul.* iv 5 55
Spiteful. As for your spiteful false objections, Prove them . *2 Hen. VI.* i 3 158
I'll see some issue of my spiteful execrations . *Troi. and Cres.* ii 3 7
Spiteful and wrathful, who, as others do, Loves for his own ends *Macb.* iii 5 12
Spitted. Your naked infants spitted upon pikes . *Hen. V.* iii 3 38
Spitting. Without hawking or spitting or saying we are hoarse *As Y. L. It* v 3 12
Splay. Mean to geld and splay all the youth of the city? *Meas. for Meas.* ii 1 243
Spleen. Who, with our spleens, Would all themselves laugh mortal . ii 2 122
Thou enforcest laughter ; thy silly thought my spleen . *L. L. Lost* iii 1 77
In this spleen ridiculous appears, To check their folly . v 2 117
Brief as the lightning in the collied night, That, in a spleen, unfolds both heaven and earth . *M. N. Dream* i 1 146
Begot of thought, conceived of spleen, and born of madness *As Y. L. It* iv 1 217
Haply my presence May well abate the over-merry spleen *T. of Shrew* Ind. 1 137
Unto a mad-brain rudesby full of spleen . iii 2 10
If you desire the spleen, and will laugh yourselves into stitches, follow me . *T. Night* iii 2 72
Fiery voluntaries, With ladies' faces and fierce dragons' spleens *K. John* ii 1 68
With swifter spleen than powder can enforce . ii 1 448
Or teach thy hasty spleen to do me shame, I'll strike thee dead . iv 3 97
O, I am scalded with my violent motion, And spleen of speed ! . v 7 50
A weasel hath not such a deal of spleen As you are toss'd with *1 Hen. IV.* ii 3 81
Through vassal fear, Base inclination, and the start of spleen . iii 2 125

Spleen. A hare-brain'd Hotspur, govern'd by a spleen . *1 Hen. IV.* v 2 19
Leaden age, Quicken'd with youthful spleen and warlike rage *1 Hen. VI.* iv 6 13
That robb'd my soldiers of their heated spleen . *3 Hen. VI.* ii 1 124
O, preposterous And frantic outrage, end thy damned spleen ! *Rich. III.* ii 4 64
Inspire us with the spleen of fiery dragons ! Upon them ! . v 3 350
Take good heed You charge not in your spleen a noble person *Hen. VIII.* i 2 174
I have no spleen against you ; nor injustice For you or any . ii 4 89
Your heart Is cramm'd with arrogancy, spleen, and pride . ii 4 110
Give me ribs of steel ! I shall split all In pleasure of my spleen *T. and C.* i 3 178
Such things as might offend the weakest spleen To fight for and maintain ! ii 2 128
Were it not glory that we more affected Than the performance of our heaving spleens . ii 2 196
With the spleen Of all the under fiends . *Coriolanus* iv 5 97
Could not take truce with the unruly spleen Of Tybalt . *Rom. and Jul.* iii 1 162
It is a cause worthy my spleen and fury, That I may strike *T. of Athens* iii 5 113
You shall digest the venom of your spleen, Though it do split you *J. C.* iv 3 47
If she must teem, Create her child of spleen . *Lear* i 4 304
Or I shall say you are all in all in spleen, And nothing of a man *Othello* iv 1 89
Spleenful. Myself have calm'd their spleenful mutiny . *2 Hen. VI.* iii 2 128
And let my spleenful sons this trull deflour . *T. Andron.* ii 3 191
Spleeny. Yet I know her for A spleeny Lutheran . *Hen. VIII.* iii 2 99
Splendour. The glorious sun Stays in his course and plays the alchemist, Turning with splendour of his precious eye The meagre cloddy earth to glittering gold . *K. John* iii 1 79
But to rejoice in splendour of mine own . *Rom. and Jul.* i 2 106
Splenitive. Though I am not splenitive and rash, Yet have I something in me dangerous . *Hamlet* v 1 284
Splinter. The Grecian dames are sunburnt and not worth The splinter of a lance . *Troi. and Cres.* i 3 283
Where against My grained ash an hundred times hath broke, And scarr'd the moon with splinters . *Coriolanus* iv 5 115
This broken joint between you and her husband entreat her to splinter *Othello* ii 3 329
Splintered. The broken rancour of your high-swoln hearts, but lately splinter'd . *Richard III.* ii 2 118
Split. Mercy on us !—We split, we split !—Farewell my wife and children ! —Farewell, brother !—We split, we split, we split ! . *Tempest* i 1 65
Our ship—Which, but three glasses since, we gave out split—Is tight . v 1 223
My chief humour is for a tyrant : I could play Ercles rarely, or a part to tear a cat in, to make all split . *M. N. Dream* i 2 32
After our ship did split, . . . I saw your brother . *T. Night* i 2 9
I stabb'd your fathers' bosoms, split my breast . *3 Hen. VI.* ii 6 30
The ship splits on the rock, Which industry and courage might have saved . v 4 10
O, but remember this another day, When he shall split thy very heart with sorrow ! . *Richard III.* i 3 300
'When he,' quoth she, 'shall split thy heart with sorrow' . v 1 26
I shall split all In pleasure of my spleen . *Troi. and Cres.* i 3 177
Now crack thy lungs, and split thy brazen pipe . iv 5 7
You shall digest the venom of your spleen, Though it do split you *J. C.* iv 3 48
To split the ears of the groundlings . *Hamlet* iii 2 12
Let sorrow split my heart, if ever I Did hate thee ! . *Lear* v 3 177
And mine own tongue Splits what it speaks . *Ant. and Cleo.* ii 7 131
The ship Should house him safe is wreck'd and split . *Pericles* ii Gower 32
Slack the bolins there ! Thou wilt not, wilt thou? Blow, and split thyself iii 1 44
Splitted. Our helpful ship was splitted in the midst . *Com. of Errors* i 1 104
O time's extremity, Hast thou so crack'd and splitted my poor tongue? v 1 308
Even as a splitted bark, so sunder we : This way fall I to death *2 Hen. VI.* iii 2 411
That self hand, Which writ his honour in the acts it did, Hath, with the courage which the heart did lend it, Splitted the heart *Ant. and Cleo.* v 1 24
Splittest. Thou rather with thy sharp and sulphurous bolt Split'st the unwedgeable and gnarled oak Than the soft myrtle *Meas. for Meas.* ii 2 116
This is all : Do't and thou hast the one half of my heart ; Do't not, thou split'st thine own . *W. Tale* i 2 349
Splitting. The splitting rocks cower'd in the sinking sands *2 Hen. VI.* iii 2 97
Enter'd me, Yea, with a splitting power . *Hen. VIII.* ii 4 183
The splitting wind Makes flexible the knees of knotted oaks *T. and C.* i 3 49
He returns Splitting the air with noise . *Coriolanus* v 6 52
Spoil. Is fit for treasons, stratagems, and spoils *Mer. of Venice* v 1 85
He fleshes his will in the spoil of her honour . *All's Well* iv 3 20
Thou dost shame That bloody spoil . *K. John* iii 1 115
Is not this an honourable spoil? A gallant prize? . *1 Hen. IV.* i 1 74
Company, villanous company, hath been the spoil of me . iii 3 11
Doth, like a miser, spoil his coat with scanting A little cloth *Hen. V.* ii 4 47
As bootless spend our vain command Upon the enraged soldiers in their spoil . iii 3 25
Contagious clouds Of heady murder, spoil, and villany . iii 3 32
Old age, that ill layer up of beauty, can do no more spoil upon my face v 2 249
I have loaden me with many spoils . *1 Hen. VI.* ii 1 80
Death doth front thee with apparent spoil . iv 2 26
They jointly swear To spoil the city and your royal court *2 Hen. VI.* iv 4 53
Soldiers, defer the spoil of the city until night . iv 7 142
Nor knows he how to live but by the spoil, Unless by robbing . iv 8 41
Whose hand is that the forest bear doth lick? Not his that spoils her young before her face . *3 Hen. VI.* ii 2 14
And yonder is the wolf that makes this spoil . v 4 80
Nay, then indeed she cannot choose but hate thee, Having bought love with such a bloody spoil . *Richard III.* iv 4 290
Take good heed You charge not in your spleen a noble person And spoil your nobler soul . *Hen. VIII.* i 2 175
Set them down For sluttish spoils of opportunity . *Troi. and Cres.* iv 5 62
To the wanton spoil Of Phœbus' burning kisses . *Coriolanus* ii 1 233
He did Run reeking o'er the lives of men, as if 'Twere a perpetual spoil ii 2 124
Our spoils he kick'd at . ii 2 128
And that the spoil got on the Antiates Was ne'er distributed . iii 3 4
We look'd For no less spoil than glory . v 6 44
Our spoils we have brought home Do more than counterpoise a full third part The charges of the action . v 6 77
And now at last, laden with honour's spoils, Returns the good Andronicus to Rome . *T. Andron.* i 1 36
With a power Of high-resolved men, bent to the spoil . iv 4 64
Dost thou lie so low? Are all thy conquests, glories, triumphs, spoils, Shrunk to this little measure? . *J. Cæsar* iii 1 149
Here thy hunters stand, Sign'd in thy spoil, and crimson'd in thy lethe iii 1 206
His soldiers fell to spoil . v 3 7
A thing of custom : 'tis no other ; Only it spoils the pleasure *Macbeth* iii 4 98
I am old now, And these same crosses spoil me . *Lear* v 3 278
Spoiled. In, or we are spoil'd ! . *Com. of Errors* v 1 37
Stark spoiled with the staggers . *T. of Shrew* iii 2 55
O ! we are spoiled and—yonder he is . v 1 113

Spoiled. Bitter shame hath spoil'd the sweet world's taste . *K. John* iii 4 110
Disorder, that hath spoil'd us, friend us now! . . . . *Hen. V.* iv 5 17
The . . . usurping boar, That spoil'd your summer fields *Richard III.* v 2 8
O, I am spoil'd, undone by villains! Give me some help. . *Othello* v 1 54
Having in Sicily Sextus Pompeius spoil'd. . . . *Ant. and Cleo.* iii 6 25
Spoke. Methought the billows spoke and told me of it . . *Tempest* iii 3 96
Fairly spoke. Sit then and talk with her . . . . . iv 1 31
I have inly wept, Or should have spoke ere this . . . . v 1 201
She'll think that it is spoke in hate . . . . *T. G. of Ver.* iii 2 34
It is spoke as a Christians ought to speak . . . *Mer. Wives* i 1 103
I have spoke; let him follow . . . . i 3 14
As it were, spoke the prologue of our comedy . . . . . iii 5 75
I have spoke with her and we have a nay-word how to know one another v 2 4
If it be honest you have spoke, you have courage to maintain it *M. for M.* iii 2 166
One that hath spoke most villanous speeches . . . . . v 1 265
You, indeed, spoke so of him; and much more, much worse . . v 1 340
What you have spoke I pardon: sit you down . . . . . v 1 366
'Faith, my lord, I spoke it but according to the trick . . . v 1 509
I speak my thought.—And, in faith, my lord, I spoke mine.—And, by my two faiths and troths, my lord, I spoke mine *Much Ado* i 1 227
Nor knew not what she did when she spoke to me . . . . v 1 310
And though I have for barbarism spoke more Than for that angel knowledge you can say. . . . . . . *L. L. Lost* i 1 112
I spoke it, tender juvenal, as a congruent epitheton . . . i 2 14
Fleer'd and swore A better speech was never spoke before . . v 2 110
While 'tis spoke each turn away her face . . . . . v 2 148
You nickname virtue; vice you should have spoke . . . . v 2 349
I have heard so much, And with Demetrius thought to have spoke *M. N. D.* i 1 112
By all the vows that ever men have broke, In number more than ever women spoke . . . . i 1 176
Thy master spoke with me this day . . . . *Mer. of Venice* ii 2 154
We have not spoke us yet of torch-bearers . . . . ii 4 5
I spoke with some of the sailors that escaped the wreck . . . iii 1 109
As, after some oration fairly spoke By a beloved prince . . . iii 2 180
I have spoke thus much To mitigate the justice of thy plea . . iv 1 202
My old master! he would not have spoke such a word *As Y. Like It* i 1 88
Know'st thou the youth that spoke to me erewhile?—Not very well iii 5 105
I would kiss before I spoke.—Nay, you were better speak first . iv 1 72
That's my office.—Spoke like an officer . . *T. of Shrew* v 2 37
The king very lately spoke of him admiringly . . *All's Well* i 1 33
I have spoke With one that, in her sex, her years, . . . hath amazed me ii 1 85
If I break time, or flinch in property Of what I spoke, unpitied let me die . . . . ii 1 191
I have, sir, as I was commanded from you Spoke with the king . ii 5 60
Had I spoke with her, I could have well diverted her intents . iii 4 20
I spoke with her but once And found her wondrous cold . . iii 6 120
What says he to your daughter? have you spoke? . . . . v 3 28
I have spoke the truth . . . . v 3 230
If she be so abandon'd to her sorrow As it is spoke . . *T. Night* i 4 20
Thou hast spoke for us, madonna, as if thy eldest son should be a fool . i 5 120
But once before I spoke to the purpose: when? Nay, let me have't *W. Tale* i 2 100
Why, lo you now, I have spoke to the purpose twice . . . . i 2 106
You never spoke what did become you less Than this . . . i 2 282
Whose love had spoke, Even since it could speak, from an infant . iii 2 70
This news hath made thee a most ugly man.—What other harm have I, good lady, done, But spoke the harm that is by others done? *K. John* iii 1 39
Hast thou not spoke like thunder on my side? . . . . iii 1 124
Many a poor man's son would have lien still And ne'er have spoke a loving word . . . . iv 1 51
Spoke like a sprightful noble gentleman . . . . . iv 2 177
Whoever spoke it, it is true . . . . v 5 19
What I have spoke, or thou canst worse devise . . *Richard II.* i 1 77
Spoke your deservings like a chronicle, Making you ever better than his praise . . . . *1 Hen. IV.* v 2 58
Upon my life, Spoke at a venture . . . . . . *2 Hen. IV.* i 1 59
You knew I was at your back, and spoke it on purpose to try my patience . . . . ii 4 334
Go to; I have spoke at a word. God keep you . . . . iii 2 319
Ere you with grief had spoke and I had heard . . . . iv 5 142
Why, there spoke a king. Lack nothing: be merry . . . . v 3 73
Thou hast spoke the right; His heart is fracted and corroborate *Hen. V.* ii 1 129
What he has spoke to me, that is well, I warrant you, when time is serve iii 6 68
Far truer spoke than meant . . . . . . *2 Hen. VI.* iii 1 183
'Tis resolutely spoke.—Not resolute, except so much were done . iii 1 266
Things are often spoke and seldom meant . . . . . iii 1 268
Now we three have spoke it, It skills not greatly who impugns our doom iii 1 280
Thou hast spoke too much already: get thee gone . . *3 Hen. VI.* i 1 258
More he would have said, and more he spoke . . . . v 2 43
Spoke like a tall fellow that respects his reputation . *Richard III.* i 4 156
Be not you spoke with, but by mighty suit . . . . . iii 7 46
I think the duke will not be spoke withal . . . . . iii 7 57
'Twould prove the verity of certain words Spoke by a holy monk *Hen. VIII.* i 2 160
He solemnly had sworn, that what he spoke My chaplain to no creature living, but To me, should utter . . . . i 2 165
Much He spoke, and learnedly, for life . . . . . ii 1 28
He sweat extremely, And something spoke in choler . . . ii 1 34
I'll to the king, And say I spoke with you . . . . . ii 3 80
I have spoke long: be pleased yourself to say How far you satisfied me ii 4 210
What Troy means fairly shall be spoke aloud . . *Troi. and Cres.* i 3 259
To make a recordation to my soul Of every syllable that here was spoke v 2 117
They lie in view; but have not spoke as yet . . . *Coriolanus* i 4 4
There's wondrous things spoke of him . . . . . . ii 1 152
Spoke he of me?—He did, my lord.—How? what? . . . . iii 1 12
Their mutinies and revolts, wherein they show'd Most valour, spoke not for them . . . . iii 1 127
Repent what you have spoke.—For them! I cannot do it to the gods . iii 2 37
Each word thou hast spoke hath weeded from my heart A root of ancient envy. . . . . iv 5 108
It is spoke freely out of many mouths—How probable I do not know . iv 6 64
What, shall this speech be spoke for our excuse? . . *Rom. and Jul.* i 4 1
Nor no without-book prologue, faintly spoke After the prompter . i 4 7
Fain would I dwell on form, fain, fain deny What I have spoke . ii 2 89
Came he not home to-night?—Not to his father's; I spoke with his man ii 4 3
Romeo that spoke him fair, bade him bethink How nice the quarrel was iii 1 158
It will be of more price, Being spoke behind your back, than to your face . . . . iv 1 28
Forbid him her resort; Myself have spoke in vain . . *T. of Athens* i 1 128
Spoke. That's well spoke . . . . *T. of Athens* v 1 196
Are his files As full as thy report?—I have spoke the least . . v 2 2
Did Cicero say any thing?—Ay, he spoke Greek . . . *J. Cæsar* i 2 282
Secret Romans, that have spoke the word, And will not palter . . ii 1 125
I do entreat you, not a man depart, Save I alone, till Antony have spoke iii 2 66
I speak not to disprove what Brutus spoke . . . . . iii 2 105
When I spoke that, I was ill-temper'd too . . . . . iv 3 116
But I have spoke With one that saw him die . . . . *Macbeth* i 4 3
Was it not yesterday we spoke together?—It was, so please your highness . . . . iii 1 74
What you have spoke, it may be so perchance . . . . . iv 3 11
She has spoke what she should not, I am sure of that . . . . v 1 53
Break all the spokes and fellies from her [Fortune's] wheel . *Hamlet* ii 2 517
I had as lief the town-crier spoke my lines . . . . . iii 2 4
To whose huge spokes ten thousand lesser things Are mortised . . iii 3 19
By what yourself too late have spoke and done . . . . *Lear* i 4 226
Spoke, with how manifold and strong a bond The child was bound to the father . . . . ii 1 49
You spoke not with her since? . . . . iv 3 37
Methinks our pleasure might have been demanded, Ere you had spoke so far . . . . v 3 63
He prated, And spoke such scurvy and provoking terms . *Othello* i 2 7
Methinks the wind hath spoke aloud at land . . . . . ii 1 5
Many a time, When I have spoke of you dispraisingly, Hath ta'en your part . . . . iii 3 72
I hope you will consider what is spoke Comes from my love . . iii 3 216
O bloody period!—All that's spoke is marr'd . . . . . v 2 357
An arm-gaunt steed, Who neigh'd so high, that what I would have spoke Was beastly dumb'd . . . . *Ant. and Cleo.* i 5 49
Pardon what I have spoke; For 'tis a studied, not a present thought . ii 2 139
Not till he hears how Antony is touch'd With what is spoke already . ii 2 143
Would we had spoke together! . . . . ii 2 167
She spoke, and panted, That she did make defect perfection . . ii 2 235
Made his will, and read it To public ear: Spoke scantly of me . . iii 4 6
Tell him I have slain myself; Say, that the last I spoke was 'Antony' iv 13 8
Whilst he stood up and spoke, He was my master . . . . v 1 7
I have spoke already, and it is provided; Go put it to the haste . v 2 195
Would I had put my estate and my neighbour's on the approbation of what I have spoke! . . . . *Cymbeline* i 4 135
I have spoke this, to know if your affiance Were deeply rooted . . i 6 163
In an hour,—was't not?—Or less,—at first?—perchance he spoke not . ii 5 15
I love thee; I have spoke it . . . . iv 2 16
And, but she spoke it dying, I would not Believe her lips in opening it v 5 41
Were't he, I am sure He would have spoke to us . . . . v 5 126
Thou'lt torture me to leave unspoken that Which, to be spoke, would torture thee . . . . v 5 140
Deny't again.—I have spoke it, and I did it . . . . . v 5 290
He should have struck, not spoke . . . . . . *Pericles* iv 2 69
I did not think Thou couldst have spoke so well; ne'er dream'd thou couldst . . . . iv 6 110
Spoke of. There is no better way than that they spoke of *Mer. Wives* iv 4 17
Here comes the rascal I spoke of . . . . *Meas. for Meas.* v 1 284
This is the rascal; this is he I spoke of . . . . . . v 1 306
They are not to be named, my lord, Not to be spoke of . . *Much Ado* iv 1 97
Thy mildness praised in every town, Thy virtues spoke of *T. of Shrew* ii 1 193
Now will I lead you to the house, and show you The lass I spoke of *All's Well* iii 6 119
With A rising sigh he wisheth you in heaven.—And you in hell, as oft as he hears Owen Glendower spoke of . . . . *1 Hen. IV.* iii 1 12
There is not such a word Spoke of in Scotland as this term of fear . iv 1 85
That I would have spoke of . . . . *Coriolanus* v 6 29
This is the letter he spoke of . . . . *Lear* iii 5 11
With those legions Which I have spoke of . . . . *Cymbeline* iii 7 13
Spoke on. I am well spoke on: I can hear it with mine own ears *2 Hen. IV.* ii 2 69
Ah, this thou shouldst have done, And not have spoke on't! . *A. and C.* ii 7 80
Spoke to. His answer was, the people were not wont To be spoke to but by the recorder . . . . *Richard III.* iii 7 30
Which I would not be, For I was spoke to, with Sir Henry Guildford This night to be comptrollers . . . . *Hen. VIII.* i 3 66
It would be spoke to.—Question it, Horatio . . . . *Hamlet* i 1 45
Spoken. I am the best of them that speak this speech, Were I but where 'tis spoken . . . . *Tempest* i 2 430
You have spoken truer than you purposed . . . . . . ii 1 20
It must with circumstance be spoken By one whom she esteemeth *T. G. of Ver.* iii 2 36
I would I could have spoken with the woman herself; I had other things to have spoken with her too from him . . . . *Mer. Wives* iv 5 40
That's somewhat madly spoken. . . . . . *Meas. for Meas.* v 1 89
Why, that's spoken like an honest drovier . . . . *Much Ado* ii 1 201
Are these things spoken, or do I but dream?—Sir, they are spoken . iv 1 67
Moreover, they have spoken untruths; secondarily, they are slanders . v 1 220
O, stay but till then!—'Then' is spoken . . . . . . v 2 46
Thou hast spoken no word all this while . . . . *L. L. Lost* v 1 156
When you have spoken your speech, enter into that brake *M. N. Dream* iii 1 77
He's within, sir, but not to be spoken withal . . . *T. of Shrew* v 1 20
I have spoken better of you than you have or will to deserve. *All's Well* ii 5 51
What to your sworn counsel I have spoken Is so from word to word . iii 7 9
When you have spoken it, 'tis dead, and I am the grave of it . . iv 3 15
I will not speak what I know.—Thou hast spoken all already . . v 3 268
You might have spoken a thousand things that would Have done the time more benefit and graced Your kindness better . . . *W. Tale* v 1 21
Then have you lost a sight, which was to be seen, cannot be spoken of. v 2 47
To lengthen out the worst that must be spoken . . *Richard II.* iii 2 199
As may not be Without much shame retold or spoken of . *1 Hen. IV.* i 1 46
In the world's wide mouth Live scandalized and foully spoken of . . i 3 154
Shall it for shame be spoken in these days, Or fill up chronicles? . . i 3 170
Shall it in more shame be further spoken, That you are fool'd? . . i 3 177
Who hath not heard it spoken How deep you were within the books of God? To us the speaker in his parliament . . . . *2 Hen. IV.* iv 2 16
Under the correction of bragging be it spoken . . . . *Hen. V.* v 2 144
Well hast thou spoken, cousin: be it so . . . . *3 Hen. VI.* i 1 66
That is spoken like a toward prince . . . . ii 2 66
His grace Hath spoken well and justly . . . . . *Hen. VIII.* ii 4 65
'Tis nobly spoken: Take notice, lords, he has a loyal breast . . iii 2 199
Has spoken like a traitor, and shall answer As traitors do *Coriolanus* iii 1 162
That struck more blows for Rome Than thou hast spoken words . . iv 2 20
I'll lay fourteen of my teeth,—And yet, to my teen be it spoken, I have but four,—She is not fourteen . . . . . . *Rom. and Jul.* i 3 13
'Tis most nobly spoken . . . . *T. of Athens* v 4 63

Spoken. What should be spoken here, where our fate, Hid in an auger-hole, may rush, and seize us? Let's away. *Macbeth* ii 3 127
I am as I have spoken iv 3 102
'Tis spoken, To the succeeding royalty he leaves The healing benediction iv 3 154
Well spoken, with good accent and good discretion *Hamlet* ii 2 488
'Twere good she were spoken with; for she may strew Dangerous conjectures iv 5 14
Have you not spoken 'gainst the Duke of Cornwall? He's coming *Lear* ii 1 25
Is this well spoken!—I dare avouch it ii 4 239
I have received a letter this night; 'tis dangerous to be spoken iii 3 11
Methinks you're better spoken iv 6 10
Thou hast spoken right, 'tis true; The wheel is come full circle v 3 173
I have spoken for you all my best And stood within the blank of his displeasure For my free speech *Othello* iii 4 127
'Tis noble spoken *Ant. and Cleo.* ii 2 98
Worthily spoken, Mecænas ii 2 102
Be it art or hap, He hath spoken true ii 3 33
I am the master of my speeches, and would undergo what's spoken *Cymbeline* i 4 153
Worse and worse, mistress; she has here spoken holy words. *Pericles* iv 6 142
A man who for this three months hath not spoken To any one v 1 24
Spokesman. To do what?—To be a spokesman. *T. G. of Ver.* ii 1 152
Spokest. When thou spokest of Pigrogromitus. *T. Night* ii 3 23
Thou never spokest To better purpose *W. Tale* i 2 88
I never did thee harm.—Yes, thou spokest well of me *T. of Athens* iv 3 173
Sponge. I will do any thing, Nerissa, ere I'll be married to a sponge *Mer. of Venice* i 2 108
Besides, to be demanded of a sponge! . . . —Take you me for a sponge, my lord?—Ay, sir, that soaks up the king's countenance. *Hamlet* iv 2 12
It is but squeezing you, and, sponge, you shall be dry again iv 2 22
Spongy. Which spongy April at thy hest betrims *Tempest* iv 1 65
There is no lady of more softer bowels, More spongy to suck in the sense of fear *Troi. and Cres.* ii 2 12
What not put upon His spongy officers, who shall bear the guilt? *Macbeth* i 7 71
Wing'd From the spongy south to this part of the west. *Cymbeline* iv 2 349
Spoon. Mercy, mercy! This is a devil, and no monster: I will leave him; I have no long spoon *Tempest* ii 2 103
If you do, expect spoon-meat; or bespeak a long spoon *Com. of Errors* iv 3 62
He must have a long spoon that must eat with the devil iv 3 64
Wouldst thou drown thyself, Put but a little water in a spoon *K. John* iv 3 131
Come, my lord, you'ld spare your spoons *Hen. VIII.* v 3 168
The spoons will be the bigger v 4 40
Cushions, leaden spoons, Irons of a doit *Coriolanus* i 5 6
Spoon-meat. Expect spoon meat; or bespeak a long spoon *Com. of Errors* iv 3 61
Sport. There be some sports are painful, and their labour Delight in them sets off *Tempest* iii 1 1
Here on this grass-plot, in this very place, To come and sport iv 1 74
He strays With willing sport to the wild ocean *T. G. of Ver.* ii 7 32
I love the sport well; but I shall as soon quarrel at it as any man *M. W.* i 1 302
Will you go with us? we have sport in hand ii 1 204
Hark, I will tell you what our sport shall be ii 1 219
Besides your cheer, you shall have sport iii 2 82
If I suspect without cause, why then make sport at me iii 3 160
Up, gentlemen; you shall see sport anon iii 3 180
Hath drawn him and the rest of their company from their sport iv 2 35
To make us public sport, Appoint a meeting with this old fat fellow iv 4 14
Shuffle her away, While other sports are tasking of their minds iv 6 30
Heaven prosper our sport! v 2 14
Let us every one go home, And laugh this sport o'er by a country fire v 5 256
He had some feeling of the sport; he knew the service *Meas. for Meas.* iii 2 127
When the sun shines let foolish gnats make sport *Com. of Errors* ii 2 30
'Tis holy sport to be a little vain iii 2 27
You shall buy this sport as dear As all the metal in your shop iv 1 81
I'll pluck out these false eyes That would behold in me this shameful sport iv 4 108
Thou say'st his sports were hinder'd by thy brawls v 1 77
In sport and life-preserving rest To be disturb'd, would mad or man or beast v 1 83
Thou thinkest I am in sport *Much Ado* i 1 179
He would make but a sport of it and torment the poor lady worse. ii 3 163
The sport will be, when they hold one an opinion of another's dotage ii 3 223
It were not good She knew his love, lest she make sport at it. iii 1 58
Costard the swain and he shall be our sport *L. L. Lost* i 1 180
One that makes sport To the prince and his bookmates iv 1 101
Very reverend sport, truly iv 2 1
Honest Dull! To our sport, away! v 1 162
There's no such sport as sport by sport o'erthrown v 2 153
Might not you Forestall our sport, to make us thus untrue? v 2 473
That sport best pleases that doth least know how v 2 517
A right description of our sport, my lord v 2 522
These ladies' courtesy Might well have made our sport a comedy v 2 886
With thy brawls thou hast disturb'd our sport *M. N. Dream* ii 1 87
In their sport Forsook his scene and enter'd in a brake iii 2 14
Then will two at once woo one; That must needs be sport alone iii 2 119
And extort A poor soul's patience, all to make you sport iii 2 161
They have conjoin'd all three To fashion this false sport, in spite of me iii 2 194
Hold the sweet jest up: This sport, well carried, shall be chronicled iii 2 240
This their jangling I esteem a sport iii 2 353
I with the morning's love have oft made sport iii 2 389
If our sport had gone forward, we had all been made men iv 2 17
There is a brief how many sports are ripe v 1 42
Unless you can find sport in their intents v 1 79
Our sport shall be to take what they mistake v 1 90
In a merry sport, If you repay me not on such a day *Mer. of Venice* i 3 146
We shall ne'er win at that sport, and stake down iii 2 219
Devise sports. Let me see; what think you of falling in love?—Marry, I prithee, do, to make sport withal *As Y. Like It* i 2 27
Nor no further in sport neither than with safety of a pure blush thou mayst in honour come off again.—What shall be our sport, then? i 2 31
You have lost much good sport.—Sport! of what colour? i 2 106
But what is the sport, monsieur, that the ladies have lost? i 2 142
It is the first time that ever I heard breaking of ribs was sport for ladies i 2 147
The shepherd youth That he in sport doth call his Rosalind iv 3 157
I have some sport in hand Wherein your cunning can assist me *T. of S.* Ind. 1 91
We will hence forthwith, To feast and sport us at thy father's house iv 3 185
We'll make you some sport with the fox ere we case him *All's Well* iii 6 110
My lord that's gone made himself much sport out of him iv 5 68
Wait on me home, I'll make sport with thee v 3 323
I do adore thee so, That danger shall seem sport *T. Night* ii 1 49
Admirable!—Sport royal, I warrant you ii 3 187
If I lose a scruple of this sport, let me be boiled to death with melancholy *T. Night* ii 5 3
I will not give my part of this sport for a pension of thousands ii 5 196
If you will then see the fruits of the sport, mark his first approach ii 5 218
I cannot pursue with any safety this sport to the upshot iv 2 76
What is this? sport?—Bear the boy hence *W. Tale* ii 1 58
Let her sport herself With that she's big with ii 1 60
Whom he hath used rather for sport than need *K. John* v 2 175
Misery makes sport to mock itself *Richard II.* ii 1 85
What sport shall we devise here in this garden, To drive away the heavy thought of care? iii 4 1
No dancing, girl; some other sport iii 4 9
Mark, silent king, the moral of this sport. iv 1 290
If all the year were playing holidays, To sport would be as tedious as to work; But when they seldom come, they wish'd for come *1 Hen. IV.* i 2 229
O, let the hours be short Till fields and blows and groans applaud our sport! i 3 302
Which for sport sake are content to do the profession some grace ii 1 78
This is excellent sport, i' faith! ii 4 430
His hours fill'd up with riots, banquets, sports *Hen. V.* i 1 56
And sheathe for lack of sport iv 2 23
Then, I see our wars Will turn unto a peaceful comic sport *1 Hen. VI.* ii 2 45
I saw not better sport these seven years' day *2 Hen. VI.* ii 1 2
Had not your man put up the fowl so suddenly, We had had more sport ii 1 46
And think it but a minute spent in sport iii 2 338
Thou wouldst be fee'd, I see, to make me sport *3 Hen. VI.* i 4 92
So many hours must I contemplate; So many hours must I sport myself ii 5 34
Who set the body and the limbs Of this great sport together? *Hen. VIII.* i 1 47
Hark, what good sport is out of town to-day! *Troi. and Cres.* i 1 116
But to the sport abroad: are you bound thither?—In all swift haste i 1 118
And at this sport Sir Valour dies; cries 'O, enough, Patroclus!' i 3 175
Bids me say, he is much sorry, If any thing more than your sport and pleasure Did move your greatness ii 3 117
Like a book of sport thou'lt read me o'er iv 5 239
By his rare example made the coward Turn terror into sport *Coriolanus* ii 2 109
Horse and chariots let us have, And to our sport *T. Andron.* ii 2 19
Being intercepted in your sport, Great reason that my noble lord be rated ii 3 80
Were't not for shame, Well could I leave our sport to sleep awhile ii 3 197
Thy griefs their sports, thy resolution mock'd iii 1 239
This was the sport, my lord iv 3 70
'Twas Trim sport for them that had the doing of it v 1 96
When I told the empress of this sport, She swooned almost v 1 118
Ah, sirrah, this unlook'd-for sport comes well *Rom. and Jul.* i 5 31
The sport is at the best.—Ay, so I fear; the more is my unrest i 5 121
Let's ha' some sport with 'em *T. of Athens* ii 2 48
He is given To sports, to wildness, and much company *J. Cæsar* ii 1 189
How many times shall Cæsar bleed in sport! iii 1 114
When she saw Pyrrhus make malicious sport In mincing with his sword her husband's limbs *Hamlet* ii 2 536
Sport and repose lock from me day and night! iii 2 227
'Tis the sport to have the enginer Hoist with his own petar iii 4 206
There was good sport at his making *Lear* i 1 23
I have seen drunkards Do more than this in sport ii 1 37
As flies to wanton boys, are we to the gods, They kill us for their sport iv 1 39
If thou canst cuckold him, thou dost thyself a pleasure, me a sport *Othello* i 3 376
If I would time expend with such a snipe, But for my sport and profit. i 3 392
When the blood is made dull with the act of sport ii 1 230
Each man to what sport and revels his addiction leads him ii 2 6
She is sport for Jove ii 3 17
Is it sport? I think it is: and doth affection breed it? I think it doth iv 3 98
And have not we affections, Desires for sport, and frailty, as men have? iv 3 102
What sport to-night?—Hear the ambassadors *Ant. and Cleo.* i 1 47
But to confound such time, That drums him from his sport i 4 29
In our sports my better cunning faints Under his chance ii 3 34
Snatch 'em up, as we take hares, behind: 'Tis sport to maul a runner iv 7 14
O, quick, or I am gone.—Here's sport indeed! iv 15 32
Make not, sir, Your loss your sport *Cymbeline* ii 4 48
Now for our mountain sport: up to yond hill; Your legs are young iii 3 10
I wish ye sport.—You health iv 2 31
Your present kindness Makes my past miseries sports *Pericles* ii 3 41
Sportful. And then let Kate be chaste and Dian sportful! *T. of Shrew* ii 1 263
How with a sportful malice it was follow'd *T. Night* v 1 373
O unbid spite! is sportful Edward come? *3 Hen. VI.* v 1 18
Though't be a sportful combat, Yet in the trial much opinion dwells *Troi. and Cres.* i 3 335
Sporting-place. Like a school broke up, Each hurries toward his home and sporting-place *2 Hen. IV.* iv 2 105
Sportive. I am not in a sportive humour now *Com. of Errors* i 2 58
Is it I That drive thee from the sportive court? *All's Well* iii 2 109
I, that am not shaped for sportive tricks *Richard III.* i 1 14
Spot. Beaten black and blue, that you cannot see a white spot about her *Mer. Wives* iv 5 116
Round about Dapples the drowsy east with spots of grey *Much Ado* v 3 27
In their gold coats spots you see *M. N. Dream* ii 1 11
There shall not be one spot of love in't *As Y. Like It* iii 2 443
With all the spots o' the world tax'd and debosh'd *All's Well* v 3 206
An innocent hand, Not painted with the crimson spots of blood *K. John* iv 2 253
I must withdraw and weep Upon the spot of this enforced cause v 2 30
The like tender of our love we make, To rest without a spot for evermore v 7 107
Lions make leopards tame.—Yea, but not change his spots *Richard II.* i 1 175
And wash away thy country's stained spots *1 Hen. VI.* iii 3 57
What are you sewing here? A fine spot, in good faith *Coriolanus* i 3 56
Wert thou a leopard, thou wert german to the lion and the spots of thy kindred were jurors on thy life *T. of Athens* iv 3 344
The angry spot doth glow on Cæsar's brow *J. Cæsar* i 2 183
He shall not live; look, with a spot I damn him ii 1 6
Yet here's a spot . . . Out, damned spot! out, I say! *Macbeth* v 1 35
There I see such black and grained spots As will not leave their tinct *Hamlet* iii 4 90
His faults in him seem as the spots of heaven *Ant. and Cleo.* i 4 12
Follow his chariot, like the greatest spot Of all thy sex iv 12 35
Spotless I' the eyes of heaven and to you *W. Tale* ii 1 131
The purest treasure mortal times afford Is spotless reputation *Richard II.* i 1 178
There is no king, be his cause never so spotless, if it come to the arbitrement of swords, can try it out with all unspotted soldiers *Hen. V.* iv 1 168
To force a spotless virgin's chastity *2 Hen. VI.* v 1 186
So much fairer And spotless shall mine innocence arise *Hen. VIII.* iii 2 301
This palliament of white and spotless hue *T. Andron.* i 1 182
And that more dear Than hands or tongue, her spotless chastity v 2 177

Spotted. Dotes in idolatry Upon this spotted and inconstant man *M. N. D.* i 1 110
You spotted snakes with double tongue . . . ii 2 9
Which being spotted Is goads, thorns, nettles *W. Tale* i 2 328
Terrible hell make war Upon their spotted souls for this! *Richard II.* iii 2 134
Thy garments are not spotted with our blood *Richard III.* i 3 283
More abhorr'd Than spotted livers in the sacrifice *Troi. and Cres.* v 3 18
Doth make your honour of his body's hue, Spotted, detested *T. Andron.* ii 3 74
And by the hazard of the spotted Let die the spotted *T. of Athens* v 4 34
A handkerchief Spotted with strawberries *Othello* iii 3 435
Thy bed, lust-stain'd, shall with lust's blood be spotted v 1 36
Spousal. So be there 'twixt your kingdoms such a spousal *Hen. V.* v 2 390
There shall we consummate our spousal rites *T. Andron.* i 1 337
Spouse. Drew me from kind embracements of my spouse *Com. of Errors* i 1 44
So qualified as may beseem The spouse of any noble gentleman *T. of S.* iv 5 67
O hound of Crete, think'st thou my spouse to get? *Hen. V.* ii 1 77
Commit not with man's sworn spouse *Lear* iii 4 84
Spout. Gasping to begin some speech, her eyes Became two spouts *W. T.* iii 3 26
We will bear home that lusty blood again Which here we came to spout against your town *K. John* ii 1 256
Come, stretch thy chest, and let thy eyes spout blood *Troi. and Cres.* iv 5 10
Not the dreadful spout Which shipmen do the hurricano call v 2 171
As from a conduit with three issuing spouts *T. Andron.* ii 4 30
Like a fountain with an hundred spouts, Did run pure blood *J. Cæsar* ii 2 77
Cataracts and hurricanoes, spout Till you have drench'd our steeples! *Lear* iii 2 2
Rumble thy bellyful! Spit, fire! spout, rain! iii 2 14
Spouting. Your statue spouting blood in many pipes *J. Cæsar* ii 2 85
Sprag. He is a good sprag memory *Mer. Wives* iv 1 84
Sprang. I sprang not more in joy at first hearing he was a man-child *Cor.* i 3 17
Sprangest. That I love the tree from whence thou sprang'st, Witness the loving kiss I give the fruit *3 Hen. VI.* v 7 31
Sprat. When his disguise and he is parted, tell me what a sprat you shall find him *All's Well* iii 6 113
Sprawl. First hang the child, that he may see it sprawl *T. Andron.* v 1 51
Sprawl'st thou? take that, to end thy agony *3 Hen. VI.* v 5 39
Spray. Cut off the heads of too fast growing sprays *Richard II.* iii 4 34
A few sprays of us, The emptying of our fathers' luxury *Hen. V.* iii 5 5
Thus droops this lofty pine and hangs his sprays *2 Hen. VI.* ii 3 45
The root From whence that tender spray did sweetly spring *3 Hen. VI.* ii 6 50
Spread. Go bid the servants spread for dinner *Com. of Errors* ii 2 189
Spread o'er the silver waves thy golden hairs, And as a bed I'll take them iii 2 48
Let there be the same net spread for her *Much Ado* iii 3 221
By east, west, north, and south, I spread my conquering might *L. L. Lost* v 2 566
Masters, spread yourselves.—Answer as I call you *M. N. Dream* i 2 16
She is spread of late Into a goodly bulk *W. Tale* ii 1 19
Hither is he come, To spread his colours *K. John* ii 1 8
Mocking the air with colours idly spread, And find no check v 1 72
Spread, Davy; spread, Davy *2 Hen. IV.* v 3 9
His arms spread wider than a dragon's wings *1 Hen. VI.* i 1 11
So great fear of my name 'mongst them was spread i 4 50
There goes the Talbot, with his colours spread iii 3 31
With colours spread March'd through the city *3 Hen. VI.* i 1 91
The northern lords that have forsworn thy colours Will follow mine, if once they see them spread; And spread they shall be i 1 252
With one hand on his dagger, Another spread on 's breast *Hen. VIII.* i 2 205
There's an ill opinion spread then Even of yourself ii 2 125
However it is spread in general name *Troi. and Cres.* i 3 322
Lest his infection, being of catching nature, Spread further *Coriolanus* iii 1 311
Ere he can spread his sweet leaves to the air *Rom. and Jul.* i 1 158
Spread thy close curtain, love-performing night iii 2 5
March, noble lord, Into our city with thy banners spread *T. of Athens* v 4 30
Do not spread the compost on the weeds, To make them ranker *Hamlet* iii 4 151
Her clothes spread wide; And, mermaid-like, awhile they bore her up iv 7 176
France spreads his banners in our noiseless land *Lear* iv 2 56
Like the wandering wind, Blows dust in others' eyes, to spread itself *Pericles* i 1 97
When fame Had spread their cursed deed v 3 Gower 96
Spreading. Till by broad spreading it disperse to nought *1 Hen. VI.* i 2 135
Whose top-branch overpeer'd Jove's spreading tree *3 Hen. VI.* v 2 14
Sprightful. Spoke like a sprightful noble gentleman *K. John* iv 2 177
Sprightfully and bold, Stays but the summons *Richard II.* i 3 3
Sprightly. Entertain them sprightly, And let's be red with mirth *W. T.* iv 4 53
Northumberland, and that sprightly Scot of Scots, Douglas *1 Hen. IV.* ii 4 377
And with our sprightly port make the ghosts gaze *Ant. and Cleo.* iv 14 52
Most welcome! Be sprightly, for you fall 'mongst friends *Cymbeline* iii 6 75
Sprigs. Strike in their numb'd and mortified bare arms Pins, wooden pricks, nails, sprigs of rosemary *Lear* ii 3 16
Spring. The fresh springs, brine-pits, barren place and fertile *Tempest* i 2 338
I'll show thee the best springs; I'll pluck thee berries ii 2 164
Spring come to you at the farthest In the very end of harvest! iv 1 114
How this spring of love resembleth The uncertain glory of an April day, Which now shows all the beauty of the sun! *T. G. of Ver.* i 3 84
Shall, Antipholus, Even in the spring of love, thy love-springs rot? *Com. of Errors* iii 2 3
The spring is near when green geese are a-breeding *L. L. Lost* i 1 97
An envious sneaping frost That bites the first-born infants of the spring i 1 101
From whence doth spring the true Promethean fire iv 3 304
This side is Hiems, Winter, this Ver, the Spring v 2 901
Never, since the middle summer's spring, Met we *M. N. Dream* ii 1 82
The spring, the summer, The childing autumn, angry winter, change Their wonted liveries ii 1 111
Sweet lovers love the spring *As Y. Like It* v 3 22
By the roses of the spring, By maidhood, honour, truth *T. Night* iii 1 161
Would I had some flowers o' the spring that might Become your time of day *W. Tale* iv 4 113
Welcome hither, As is the spring to the earth v 1 152
Fetch from false Mowbray their first head and spring *Richard II.* i 1 97
Four lagging winters and four wanton springs End in a word i 3 214
Currents that spring from one most gracious head iii 3 108
He that hath suffer'd this disorder'd spring Hath now himself met with the fall of leaf iii 4 48
Who are the violets now That strew the green lap of the new come spring? v 2 47
Bear you well in this new spring of time v 2 50
Farewell, thou latter spring! farewell, All-hallown summer! *1 Hen. IV.* i 2 177
We, as the spring of all, shall pay for all v 2 23
As in an early spring We see the appearing buds *2 Hen. IV.* i 3 38
As sudden As flaws congealed in the spring of day iv 4 35
As gardeners do with ordure hide those roots That shall first spring *Hen. V.* ii 4 40
Spring. Spring crestless yeomen from so deep a root? *1 Hen. VI.* ii 4 85
From whence you spring by lineal descent iii 1 166
As my duty springs, so perish they That grudge one thought! iii 1 175
Now 'tis the spring, and weeds are shallow-rooted *2 Hen. VI.* iii 1 31
The purest spring is not so free from mud As I am clear from treason iii 1 101
Whose filth and dirt Troubles the silver spring where England drinks iv 1 72
When we saw our sunshine made thy spring *3 Hen. VI.* ii 2 163
The root From whence that tender spray did sweetly spring ii 6 50
That from his loins no hopeful branch may spring, To cross me! iii 2 126
Whence springs this deep despair?—From such a cause as fills mine eyes with tears iii 3 12
His demand Springs not from Edward's well-meant honest love iii 3 67
Now stops thy spring; my sea shall suck them dry iv 8 55
All springs reduce their currents to mine eyes *Richard III.* ii 2 68
Short summers lightly have a forward spring iii 1 94
As sun and showers There had made a lasting spring *Hen. VIII.* iii 1 8
Straight Springs out into fast gait iii 2 116
I'll spring up in his tears, an 'twere a nettle against May *Troi. and Cres.* i 2 190
What stock he springs of, The noble house o' the Marcians *Coriolanus* ii 3 245
Here stands the spring whom you have stain'd with mud *T. Andron.* v 2 171
Like a loving child, Shed yet some small drops from thy tender spring v 3 167
Back, foolish tears, back to your native spring *Rom. and Jul.* iii 2 102
Till we can clear these ambiguities, And know their spring v 3 218
Within this mile break forth a hundred springs *T. of Athens* iv 3 421
From that spring whence comfort seem'd to come Discomfort swells *Macb.* i 2 27
The spring, the head, the fountain of your blood Is stopp'd ii 3 103
The canker galls the infants of the spring *Hamlet* i 3 39
This is the poison of deep grief; it springs All from her father's death iv 5 76
Like the spring that turneth wood to stone, Convert his gyves to graces iv 7 20
And from her fair and unpolluted flesh May violets spring! v 1 263
That good effects may spring from words of love *Lear* i 1 188
And from her derogate body never spring A babe to honour her! i 4 302
All you unpublish'd virtues of the earth, Spring with my tears! iv 4 17
The April's in her eyes: it is love's spring *Ant. and Cleo.* iii 2 43
And in's spring became a harvest *Cymbeline* i 1 46
I have enough: To the trunk again, and shut the spring of it ii 2 47
Phœbus 'gins arise, His steeds to water at those springs ii 3 23
See where she comes, apparell'd like the spring *Pericles* i 1 12
The fairest, sweet'st, and best lies here, Who wither'd in her spring of year iv 4 35
The main grief springs from the loss Of a beloved daughter and a wife v 1 29
Springe. If the springe hold, the cock 's mine *W. Tale* iv 3 36
Springes to catch woodcocks *Hamlet* i 3 115
As a woodcock to mine own springe, Osric; I am justly kill'd v 2 317
Springeth. It is a fault that springeth from your eye *Com. of Errors* iii 2 55
Springhalt. The spavin Or springhalt reign'd among 'em *Hen. VIII.* i 3 13
Springing. Seven fair branches springing from one root *Richard II.* i 2 13
Spring-time. In the spring time, the only pretty ring time *As Y. Like It* v 3 20
Slow in speech, yet sweet as spring-time flowers *T. of Shrew* ii 1 248
Faster than spring-time showers comes thought on thought *2 Hen. VI.* iii 1 337
Now melt with woe That winter should cut off our spring-time so *3 Hen. VI.* ii 3 47
And keep eternal spring-time on thy face *T. Andron.* iii 1 21
Sprinkle. I protest, my soul is full of woe, That blood should sprinkle me to make me grow *Richard II.* v 6 46
You great benefactors, sprinkle our society with thankfulness *T. of A.* iii 6 79
Washes it off, and sprinkles in your faces Your reeking villany iii 6 102
Upon the heat and flame of thy distemper Sprinkle cool patience *Hamlet* iii 4 124
Sprite. And, sweet sprites, the burthen bear *Tempest* i 2 381
These be fine things, an if they be not sprites ii 2 121
O spite of spites! We talk with goblins, owls, and sprites *Com. of Errors* ii 2 192
That shrewd and knavish sprite Call'd Robin Goodfellow *M. N. Dream* ii 1 33
The graves all gaping wide, Every one lets forth his sprite v 1 388
Every elf and fairy sprite Hop as light as bird from brier v 1 400
Teaching all that read to know The quintessence of every sprite *As Y. Like It* iii 2 147
A sad tale 's best for winter: I have one Of sprites and goblins *W. Tale* ii 1 26
Do your best To fright me with your sprites; you're powerful at it ii 1 28
And fetches her wind so short, as if she were frayed with a sprite *Troi. and Cres.* iii 2 34
Rise up, and walk like sprites, To countenance this horror! *Macbeth* ii 3 84
Distill'd by magic sleights Shall raise such artificial sprites iii 5 27
Come, sisters, cheer we up his sprites, And show the best of our delights iv 1 127
Sprited. I am sprited with a fool, Frighted, and anger'd worse *Cymbeline* ii 3 144
Spritely. And make you dance canary With spritely fire *All's Well* ii 1 78
My spritely brethren, I propend to you In resolution *Troi. and Cres.* ii 2 190
Let me have war . . . ; it's spritely, waking, audible *Coriolanus* iv 5 237
I will reward thee Once for thy spritely comfort *Ant. and Cleo.* iv 7 15
Great Jupiter, upon his eagle back'd, Appear'd to me, with other spritely shows Of mine own kindred *Cymbeline* v 5 428
Sprout. That it may grow and sprout as high as heaven *2 Hen. IV.* ii 3 60
Spruce. He is too picked, too spruce, too affected, too odd *L. L. Lost* v 1 14
Three-piled hyperboles, spruce affectation, Figures pedantical v 2 407
Now, my spruce companions, is all ready, and all things neat? *T. of S.* iv 1 116
Sprung. The enmity and discord which of late Sprung *Com. of Errors* i 1 6
From whence with life he never more sprung up *2 Hen. IV.* i 1 111
They never then had sprung like summer flies *3 Hen. VI.* ii 6 17
To his music plants and flowers Ever sprung *Hen. VIII.* iii 1 7
Again, there is sprung up An heretic, an arch one, Cranmer iii 2 101
Brave slip, sprung from the great Andronicus *T. Andron.* v 1 9
My only love sprung from my only hate! *Rom. and Jul.* i 5 140
Joy had the like conception in our eyes And at that instant like a babe sprung up *T. of Athens* i 2 116
A poor unmanly melancholy sprung From change of fortune iv 3 203
The origin and commencement of his grief Sprung from neglected love *Hamlet* iii 1 186
Spun. Argo, their thread of life is spun *2 Hen. VI.* iv 2 31
You would be another Penelope: yet, they say, all the yarn she spun in Ulysses' absence did but fill Ithaca full of moths *Coriolanus* i 3 93
Spur. And by the spurs pluck'd up The pine and cedar *Tempest* v 1 47
So much they spur their expedition *T. G. of Ver.* v 1 6
And set spurs and away, like three German devils *Mer. Wives* iv 5 70
That it may know He can command, lets it straight feel the spur *M. for M.* i 2 166
Which he spurs on his power To qualify in others iv 2 85
'Tis 'long of you that spur me with such questions *L. L. Lost* ii 1 119
As a puisny tilter, that spurs his horse but on one side *As Y. Like It* iii 4 47
You have made shift to run into't, boots and spurs and all *All's Well* ii 1 30
His heels have deserved it, in usurping his spurs so long iv 3 119
My desire, More sharp than filed steel, did spur me forth *T. Night* iii 3 5
Our praises are our wages: you may ride's With one soft kiss a thousand furlongs ere With spur we heat an acre *W. Tale* i 2 96

Spur. Whose spiritual counsel had, Shall stop or spur me . *W. Tale* ii 1 187
Which is another spur to my departure . iv 2 10
Curbs me From giving reins and spurs to my free speech . *Richard II.* i 1 55
Finds brotherhood in thee no sharper spur? . i 2 9
He tires betimes that spurs too fast betimes . ii 1 36
Spur thee on with full as many lies As may be holloa'd . iv 1 53
How fondly dost thou spur a forward horse! . iv 1 72
Mount thee upon his horse; Spur post, and get before him . v 2 112
He told me . . . that young Harry Percy's spur was cold *2 Hen. IV.* i 1 42
Said he young Harry Percy's spur was cold? Of Hotspur Coldspur? . i 1 49
Their neighing coursers daring of the spur . iv 1 119
From helmet to the spur all blood he was . *Hen. V.* iv 6 6
Spur to the rescue of the noble Talbot . *1 Hen. VI.* iv 3 19
Her fume needs no spurs, She'll gallop far enough to her destruction *2 Hen. VI.* i 3 153
Spur your proud horses hard, and ride in blood . *Richard III.* v 3 340
Stop their mouths with stubborn bits, and spur 'em, Till they obey *Hen. VIII.* v 3 23
She is . . . A spur to valiant and magnanimous deeds . *Troi. and Cres.* ii 2 200
I have seen thee, As hot as Perseus, spur thy Phrygian steed . iv 5 186
Spur them to ruthful work, rein them from ruth . v 3 48
Bring me word thither How the world goes, that to the pace of it I may spur on my journey . *Coriolanus* i 10 33
Switch and spurs, switch and spurs; or I'll cry a match *Rom. and Jul.* ii 4 73
With that spur as he would to the lip of his mistress *T. of Athens* iii 6 73
What need we any spur but our own cause? . *J. Cæsar* ii 1 123
But when they should endure the bloody spur, They fall their crests . iv 2 25
Mount thou my horse, and hide thy spurs in him, Till he have brought thee up . v 3 15
Enclosed round about With horsemen, that make to him on the spur . v 3 29
His great love, sharp as his spur, hath holp him To his home before us *Macbeth* i 6 23
I have no spur To prick the sides of my intent . i 7 25
Now spurs the lated traveller apace To gain the timely inn . iii 3 6
How all occasions do inform against me, And spur my dull revenge! *Ham.* iv 4 33
The profits of my death Were very pregnant and potential spurs . *Lear* ii 1 78
Spur through Media, Mesopotamia . *Ant. and Cleo.* iii 1 7
Discover to me What both you spur and stop . *Cymbeline* i 6 99
Grief and patience, rooted in him both, Mingle their spurs together . iv 2 58
But if to that my nature need a spur, The gods revenge it! . *Pericles* iii 3 23
Spurio. In the regiment of the Spinii one Captain Spurio . *All's Well* ii 1 43
Let me see: Spurio, a hundred and fifty; Sebastian, so many . iv 3 184
Spurn. The more she spurns my love, The more it grows . *T. G. of Ver.* iv 2 14
You spurn me hence, and he will spurn me hither . *Com. of Errors* ii 1 84
Wouldst thou not spit at me and spurn at me? . ii 2 136
Use me but as your spaniel, spurn me, strike me . *M. N. Dream* ii 1 205
Who even but now did spurn me with his foot, To call me goddess . iii 2 225
Threaten'd me To strike me, spurn me, nay, to kill me too . iii 2 313
And foot me as you spurn a stranger cur Over your threshold *M. of Ven.* i 3 119
I am as like to call thee so again, To spit on thee again, to spurn thee too i 3 132
Whose foot spurns back the ocean's roaring tides . *K. John* ii 1 24
Why thou against the church, our holy mother, So wilfully dost spurn iii 1 142
Nay, more, to spurn at your most royal image . *2 Hen. IV.* v 2 89
Rend bars of steel And spurn in pieces posts of adamant . *1 Hen. VI.* i 4 52
When he might spurn him with his foot away . *3 Hen. VI.* i 4 58
I'll strike thee to my foot, And spurn upon thee, beggar . *Richard III.* i 2 42
And wilt thou, then, Spurn at his edict and fulfil a man's? . i 4 203
Say my request's unjust, And spurn me back . *Coriolanus* v 3 165
But that which gives my soul the greatest spurn, Is dear Lavinia *T. An.* iii 1 101
When Fortune in her shift and change of mood Spurns down her late beloved, all his dependants . . . let him slip down . *T. of Athens* i 1 85
Away, unpeaceable dog, or I'll spurn thee hence! . i 1 281
Who dies, that bears not one spurn to their graves Of their friends' gift? i 2 146
I know no personal cause to spurn at him, But for the general *J. Cæsar* ii 1 11
I spurn thee like a cur out of my way . iii 1 46
He shall spurn fate, scorn death, and bear His hopes 'bove wisdom *Macb.* iii 5 30
The spurns That patient merit of the unworthy takes . *Hamlet* iii 1 73
Beats her heart; Spurns enviously at straws; speaks things in doubt . iv 5 6
What safe and nicely I might well delay By rule of knighthood, I disdain and spurn . *Lear* v 3 145
I'll spurn thine eyes Like balls before me . *Ant. and Cleo.* ii 5 63
He's walking in the garden—thus; and spurns The rush that lies before him . iii 5 17
And all this done, spurn her home to her father . *Cymbeline* iv 1 20
He did provoke me With language that would make me spurn the sea . v 5 294
Spurned. You spurn'd me such a day . *Mer. of Venice* i 3 128
Spurred. But love will not be spurr'd to what it loathes . *T. G. of Ver.* v 2 7
Was that the king, that spurred his horse so hard? . *L. L. Lost* iv 1 1
And yet I bear a burthen like an ass, Spurr'd, gall'd, and tired *Rich. II.* v 5 94
Two braver men Ne'er spurr'd their coursers at the trumpet's sound *3 Hen. VI.* v 7 9
Spurring. Bloody with spurring, fiery-red with haste . *Richard II.* ii 3 58
After him came spurring hard A gentleman, almost forspent with speed *2 Hen. IV.* i 1 36
Strike their sharp shins, And mar men's spurring . *T. of Athens* iv 3 153
Spy. And hast put thyself Upon this island as a spy . *Tempest* i 2 455
What is in Silvia's face, but I may spy More fresh in Julia's? *T. G. of Ver.* v 4 114
I spy entertainment in her; she discourses, she carves . *Mer. Wives* i 3 48
I spy a great peard under his muffler . iv 2 204
I spy comfort; I cry bail . *Meas. for Meas.* iii 2 43
I do spy some marks of love in her . *Much Ado* ii 3 254
When they him spy, As wild geese that the creeping fowler eye *M. N. D.* iii 2 19
I am to spy her through the wall . v 1 187
Now will I to the chink, To spy an I can hear my Thisby's face . v 1 195
Even through the hollow eyes of death I spy life peering *Richard II.* ii 1 271
Take you no care; I'll never trouble you, if I may spy them . *1 Hen. VI.* i 4 22
And, when I spy advantage, claim the crown . *2 Hen. VI.* i 1 242
I spy a black, suspicious, threatening cloud . *3 Hen. VI.* v 3 4
Have no delight . . ., Unless to spy my shadow in the sun *Richard III.* i 1 26
My friend, I spy some pity in thy looks . i 4 270
She takes upon her to spy a white hair on his chin *Troi. and Cres.* i 2 153
I spy.—You spy! what do you spy? . iii 1 102
What eye but such an eye would spy out such a quarrel? *Rom. and Jul.* iii 1 23
I do spy a kind of hope, Which craves as desperate an execution . iv 1 68
If I were a huge man, I should fear to drink at meals; Lest they should spy my windpipe's dangerous notes . *T. of Athens* i 2 52
Acquaint you with the perfect spy o' the time, The moment on't *Macbeth* iii 1 130
That what a man cannot smell out, he may spy into . *Lear* i 5 24
If you will come to me,—For now I spy a danger . ii 4 250
I confess, it is my nature's plague To spy into abuses . *Othello* iii 3 147

Spyest. If thou spy'st any, run and bring me word . *1 Hen. VI.* i 4 19
Spying. His soldiers spying his undaunted spirit . i 1 127
By spying and avoiding fortune's malice . *3 Hen. VI.* iv 6 28
Squabble. Drunk? and speak parrot? and squabble? swagger? *Othello* ii 3 281
Squadron. On either hand thee there are squadrons pitch'd *1 Hen. VI.* iv 2 23
Fiery warriors fought upon the clouds, In ranks and squadrons *J. Cæsar* ii 2 20
That never set a squadron in the field . *Othello* i 1 22
Set we our squadrons on yond side o' the hill . *Ant. and Cleo.* iii 9 1
Squandered. And other ventures he hath, squandered abroad *Mer. of Ven.* i 3 22
Squandering. The wise man's folly is anatomized Even by the squandering glances of the fool . *As Y. Like It* ii 7 57
Square. They never meet . . . But they do square . *M. N. Dream* ii 1 30
It is not so with Him that all things knows As 'tis with us that square our guess by shows . *All's Well* ii 1 153
He so chants to the sleeve-hand and the work about the square on't *W. Tale* iv 4 212
Peasants, Who in unnecessary action swarm About our squares of battle . *Hen. V.* iv 2 28
For depravation, to square the general sex By Cressid's rule . *T. and C.* v 2 132
Are you such fools To square for this? . *T. Andron.* ii 1 100
That will not suffer you to square yourselves . ii 1 124
Fie, fie, how franticly I square my talk! . iii 2 31
All have not offended; For those that were, it is not square to take On those that are, revenges . *T. of Athens* v 4 36
All other joys, Which the most precious square of sense possesses *Lear* i 1 76
Were't not that we stand up against them all, 'Twere pregnant they should square between themselves . *Ant. and Cleo.* ii 1 45
She's a most triumphant lady, if report be square to her . ii 2 190
I have not kept my square; but that to come Shall all be done by the rule . ii 3 6
Dealt on lieutenantry, and no practice had In the brave squares of war iii 11 40
Mine honesty and I begin to square . iii 13 41
My queen's square brows; Her stature to an inch . *Pericles* v 1 109
Squared. Dreams are toys: Yet for this once, yea, superstitiously, I will be squared by this . *W. Tale* iii 3 41
O, that ever I Had squared me to thy counsel! . v 1 52
Squarer. Is there no young squarer now that will make a voyage with him to the devil? . *Much Ado* i 1 82
Squarest. That apprehends no further than this world, And squarest thy life according . *Meas. for Meas.* v 1 487
Squash. Commend me to Mistress Squash, your mother . *M. N. Dream* iii 1 191
As a squash is before 'tis a peascod, . *T. Night* i 5 166
How like, methought, I then was to this kernel, This squash *W. Tale* i 2 160
Squeak. Ye squeak out your coziers' catches . *T. Night* ii 3 97
The sheeted dead Did squeak and gibber in the Roman streets *Hamlet* i 1 116
Squeaked. And he squeak'd out aloud, 'Clarence is come' *Richard III.* i 4 54
Squeaking. And I shall see Some squeaking Cleopatra boy my greatness I' the posture of a whore . *Ant. and Cleo.* v 2 220
Squeal. And ghosts did shriek and squeal about the streets . *J. Cæsar* ii 2 24
Squealing. The vile squealing of the wry-neck'd fife *Mer. of Venice* ii 5 30
Squeezing. It is but squeezing you, and, sponge, you shall be dry *Hamlet* iv 2 22
Squele. Francis Pickbone, and Will Squele, a Cotswold man *2 Hen. IV.* iii 2 23
Squier. Do not you know my lady's foot by the squier? . *L. L. Lost* v 2 474
But jumps twelve foot and a half by the squier . *W. Tale* iv 4 348
If I travel but four foot by the squier further afoot . *1 Hen. IV.* ii 2 13
Squint. He gives the web and the pin, squints the eye . *Lear* iii 4 122
Squiny. I remember thine eyes well enough. Dost thou squiny at me? iv 6 140
Squire. Come cut and long-tail, under the degree of a squire *Mer. Wives* iii 4 48
Even he.—A proper squire! . *Much Ado* i 3 54
Her womb then rich with my young squire . *M. N. Dream* ii 1 131
So stands this squire Officed with me . *W. Tale* i 2 171
A bearing-cloth for a squire's child! look thee here . iii 3 119
A landless knight makes thee a landed squire . *K. John* i 1 177
Let not us that are squires of the night's body be called thieves of the day's beauty: let us be Diana's foresters . *1 Hen. IV.* i 2 27
And now is this Vice's dagger become a squire . *2 Hen. IV.* iii 2 344
Knights and squires, Full fifteen hundred, besides common men *Hen. V.* iv 8 83
Knights, squires, And gentlemen of blood and quality . iv 8 94
I will make you to-day a squire of low degree . v 1 38
Like to a trusty squire did run away . *1 Hen. VI.* iv 1 23
Here do you keep a hundred knights and squires . *Lear* i 4 262
When every case in law is right; No squire in debt, nor no poor knight iii 2 86
Some such squire he was That turn'd your wit the seamy side without *Othello* iv 2 145
My queen's a squire More tight at this than thou . *Ant. and Cleo.* iv 4 14
A hilding for a livery, a squire's cloth, A pantler . *Cymbeline* ii 3 128
Squire-like, pension beg To keep base life afoot . *Lear* ii 4 217
Squirrel. The other squirrel was stolen from me . *T. G. of Ver.* iv 4 59
I have a venturous fairy that shall seek The squirrel's hoard *M. N. Dream* iv 1 40
Her chariot is an empty hazel-nut Made by the joiner squirrel *R. and J.* i 4 68
Stab. Or with bemock'd-at stabs Kill the still-closing waters . *Tempest* iii 3 63
She speaks poniards, and every word stabs . *Much Ado* ii 1 255
Affection! thy intention stabs the centre . *W. Tale* i 2 138
An ye call me coward, by the Lord, I'll stab thee . *1 Hen. IV.* ii 4 160
It may chance cost some of us our lives, for he will stab . *2 Hen. IV.* ii 1 13
Thou hast whetted on thy stony heart, To stab at half an hour of my life iv 5 109
O perdurable shame! let's stab ourselves . *Hen. V.* iv 5 7
Shall I stab the forlorn swain?—First let my words stab him *2 Hen. VI.* iv 1 65
At each word's deliverance Stab poniards in our flesh . *3 Hen. VI.* ii 1 98
Shall we stab him as he sleeps?—No; then he will say 'twas done cowardly, when he wakes.—When he wakes! . *Richard III.* i 4 101
This sudden stab of rancour I misdoubt . iii 2 89
Stab them, or tear them on thy chariot-wheels . *T. Andron.* v 2 47
When thou find'st a man that's like thyself, Good Murder, stab him; he's a murderer. Go thou with him; and when it is thy hap To find another that is like to thee, Good Rapine, stab him. . v 2 100
Hang them or stab them, drown them in a draught . *T. of Athens* v 1 105
When the noble Cæsar saw him stab, Ingratitude, more strong than traitors' arms, Quite vanquish'd him . *J. Cæsar* iii 2 188
What villain touch'd his body, that did stab, And not for justice? . iv 3 20
His gash'd stabs look'd like a breach in nature . *Macbeth* ii 3 119
Stabbed. Who, in my mood, I stabb'd unto the heart . *T. G. of Ver.* iv 1 51
Wild Half-can that stabbed Pots, and, I think, forty more . *M. for M.* iv 3 19
O, I am stabb'd with laughter! . *L. L. Lost* v 2 80
He stabbed me in mine own house, and that most beastly . *2 Hen. IV.* ii 1 15
Brutus' bastard hand Stabb'd Julius Cæsar . *2 Hen. VI.* iv 1 137
This is the hand that stabb'd thy father York . *3 Hen. VI.* ii 4 6
I stabb'd your fathers' bosoms, split my breast . ii 6 30
They that stabb'd Cæsar shed no blood at all . v 5 53
Stabb'd by the selfsame hand that made these wounds! . *Richard III.* i 2 11

Stabbed. 'Twas I that stabb'd young Edward, But 'twas thy heavenly face that set me on *Richard III.* i 2 182
Her lord, whom I, some three months since, Stabb'd in my angry mood i 2 242
When my son Was stabb'd with bloody daggers i 3 212
False, fleeting, perjured Clarence, That stabb'd me in the field i 4 56
Why, then he will say we stabb'd him sleeping i 4 108
For standing by when Richard stabb'd her son iii 3 16
Thy Edward he is dead, that stabb'd my Edward iv 4 63
He is already dead; stabbed with a white wench's black eye *R. and J.* ii 4 14
If Cæsar had stabbed their mothers, they would have done no less *J. C.* i 2 277
I fear I wrong the honourable men Whose daggers have stabb'd Cæsar iii 2 156
Through this the well-beloved Brutus stabb'd iii 2 180
Stabbedst. Think, how thou stab'dst me in my prime of youth *Rich. III.* v 3 119
Stabbing. We pay them for it with stamped coin, not stabbing steel *W. Tale* iv 4 748
He's a soldier, and for one to say a soldier lies, is stabbing *Othello* iii 4 6
Stable. Then, if your husband have stables enough, you'll see he shall lack no barns *Much Ado* iii 4 48
To other regions France is a stable *All's Well* ii 3 301
With such a smooth, discreet, and stable bearing *T. Night* iv 3 19
Prove She's otherwise, I'll keep my stables where I lodge my wife *W. T.* ii 1 134
To crouch in litter of your stable planks *K. John* v 2 140
He will commend . . . His barbed steeds to stables *Richard II.* iii 3 117
I was a poor groom of thy stable, king, When thou wert king v 5 72
Lend me thy lantern, to see my gelding in the stable 1 *Hen. IV.* ii 1 39
Bid the ostler bring my gelding out of the stable ii 1 106
Stableness. The king-becoming graces, As justice, verity, temperance, stableness, Bounty, perseverance, mercy, lowliness *Macbeth* iv 3 92
Stablish. And stablish quietness on every side 1 *Hen. VI.* v 1 10
Stablishment. Unto her He gave the stablishment of Egypt *A. and C.* iii 6 9
Staff. I'll break my staff, Bury it certain fathoms in the earth *Tempest* v 1 54
This staff is my sister, for, look you, she is as white as a lily *T. G. of Ver.* ii 3 21
My staff understands me.—What thou sayest? ii 5 28
I'll but lean, and my staff understands me ii 5 31
Hope is a lover's staff; walk hence with that iii 1 246
Have at you with a proverb—Shall I set in my staff? *Com. of Errors* iii 1 51
Give him another staff: this last was broke cross *Much Ado* v 1 138
There is no staff more reverend than one tipped with horn v 4 125
Let me hear a staff, a stanze, a verse *L. L. Lost* iv 2 107
The boy was the very staff of my age, my very prop.—Do I look like a cudgel or a hovel-post, a staff or a prop? *Mer. of Venice* ii 2 70
By Jacob's staff, I swear, I have no mind of feasting forth to-night ii 5 36
Breaks his staff like a noble goose *As Y. Like It* iii 4 47
There stuck no plume . . . That is removed by a staff of France *K. John* ii 1 318
Hath broke his staff, resign'd his stewardship *Richard II.* ii 2 59
Broken his staff of office and dispersed The household of the king ii 3 27
For you my staff of office did I break In Richard's time 1 *Hen. IV.* v 1 34
His own life hung upon the staff he threw 2 *Hen. IV.* iv 1 126
Methought this staff, mine office-badge in court, Was broke 2 *Hen. VI.* i 2 25
Ere thou go, Give up thy staff ii 3 23
Give up your staff, sir, and the king his realm.—My staff? here, noble Henry, is my staff ii 3 31
This staff of honour raught, there let it stand Where it best fits to be ii 3 43
A staff is quickly found to beat a dog iii 1 171
Thereby is England mained, and fain to go with a staff iv 2 172
Thy hand is made to grasp a palmer's staff v 1 97
Old Nevil's crest, The rampant bear chain'd to the ragged staff v 1 203
Now thou art gone, we have no staff, no stay 3 *Hen. VI.* ii 1 69
Give me a staff of honour for mine age, But not a sceptre *T. Andron.* i 1 198
Come, put mine armour on; give me my staff *Macbeth* v 3 48
By his cockle hat and staff, And his sandal shoon *Hamlet* iv 5 25
Of his fortunes you should make a staff To lean upon *Ant. and Cleo.* iii 13 68
Has done no more than other knights have done; Has broken a staff or so *Pericles* ii 3 35
Stafford dear to-day hath bought Thy likeness 1 *Hen. IV.* v 3 7
Thou shalt find a king that will revenge Lord Stafford's death v 3 13
The spirits Of valiant Shirley, Stafford, Blunt, are in my arms v 4 41
Prince John And Westmoreland and Stafford fled the field 2 *Hen. IV.* i 1 18
You, madam, shall with us. Stafford, take her to thee 2 *Hen. VI.* i 4 55
Stafford and his brother are hard by, with the king's forces iv 2 120
Stafford and his brother's death Hath given them heart and courage iv 4 34
Himself, Lord Clifford, and Lord Stafford, all abreast 3 *Hen. VI.* i 1 7
Lord Stafford's father, Duke of Buckingham, Is either slain or wounded i 1 10
Pembroke and Stafford, you in our behalf Go levy men iv 1 130
Duke of Buckingham, and Earl Of Hereford, Stafford, and Northampton, I Arrest thee of high treason *Hen. VIII.* i 1 200
Staffordshire. Little John Doit of Staffordshire 2 *Hen. IV.* iii 2 22
Stag. For me, I am here a Windsor stag *Mer. Wives* v 5 14
A poor sequester'd stag, That from the hunter's aim hath ta'en a hurt, Did come to languish *As Y. Like It* ii 1 33
Thy greyhounds are as swift As breathed stags *T. of Shrew* Ind. 2 50
Moody-mad and desperate stags 1 *Hen. VI.* iv 2 50
Jove shield your husband from his hounds to-day! 'Tis pity they should take him for a stag *T. Andron.* ii 3 71
Yea, like the stag, when snow the pasture sheets, The barks of trees thou browsed'st *Ant. and Cleo.* i 4 65
Stage. I love the people, But do not like to stage me to their eyes *Meas. for Meas.* i 1 69
This green plot shall be our stage *M. N. Dream* iii 1 4
A stage where every man must play a part, And mine a sad one *M. of V.* i 1 78
All the world's a stage, And all the men and women merely players: They have their exits and their entrances *As Y. Like It* ii 7 139
If this were played upon a stage now, I could condemn it *T. Night* iii 4 140
On this stage, Where we're offenders now *W. Tale* v 1 58
After a well-graced actor leaves the stage *Richard II.* v 2 24
Let order die! And let this world no longer be a stage To feed contention in a lingering act! 2 *Hen. IV.* i 1 155
A kingdom for a stage, princes to act, And monarchs to behold *Hen. V.* Prol. 3
Which oft our stage hath shown Epil. 13
Is now the two hours' traffic of our stage *Rom. and Jul.* Prol. 12
The heavens, as troubled with man's act, Threaten his bloody stage *Macb.* ii 4 6
A poor player That struts and frets his hour upon the stage v 5 25
These are now the fashion, and so berattle the common stages *Hamlet* ii 2 358
He would drown the stage with tears And cleave the general ear ii 2 588
Give order that these bodies High on a stage be placed to the view v 2 389
Let four captains Bear Hamlet, like a soldier, to the stage v 2 407
When we are born, we cry that we are come To this great stage of fools *Lear* iv 6 187
Supplying every stage With an augmented greeting *Ant. and Cleo.* iii 6 54
The quick comedians Extemporally will stage us v 2 217
Stage. In your imagination hold This stage the ship *Pericles* iii Gower 59
Learn of me, who stand i' the gaps to teach you, The stages of our story iv 4 9
Staged. And be staged to the show, Against a sworder! *Ant. and Cleo.* iii 13 30
Stagger. Whether the tyranny be in his place, Or in his eminence that fills it up, I stagger in *Meas. for Meas.* i 2 169
A man may, if he were of a fearful heart, stagger in this attempt *As Y. Like It* iii 3 49
Stark spoiled with the staggers, begnawn with the bots *T. of Shrew* iii 2 55
Into the staggers and the careless lapse Of youth and ignorance *All's W.* ii 3 170
Go thou, and fill another room in hell. That hand shall burn in never-quenching fire That staggers thus my person *Richard II.* v 5 110
The question did at first so stagger me *Hen. VIII.* ii 4 212
Does the world go round?—How come these staggers on me? *Cymbeline* v 5 233
Staggering. Without any pause or staggering take this basket on your shoulders *Mer. Wives* iii 3 12
Staider. Ere wildness Vanquish my staider senses *Cymbeline* iii 4 10
Stain. Do no stain to your own gracious person *Meas. for Meas.* iii 1 208
I'll devise some honest slanders To stain my cousin with *Much Ado* iii 1 85
If virtue's gloss will stain with any soil *L. L. Lost* ii 1 48
As she fled, her mantle she did fall, Which Lion vile with bloody mouth did stain *M. N. Dream* v 1 144
You have some stain of soldier in you *All's Well* i 1 122
We must not So stain our judgement, or corrupt our hope ii 1 123
Here's such ado to make no stain a stain As passes colouring *W. Tale* ii 2 19
You'll mar it if you kiss it, stain your own With oily painting v 3 82
Lest unadvised you stain your swords with blood *K. John* ii 1 45
To look into the blots and stains of right ii 1 114
Full of unpleasing blots and sightless stains iii 1 45
To stain the track Of his bright passage to the occident *Richard II.* iii 3 66
Alack, for woe, That any harm should stain so fair a show! iii 3 71
Being all too base To stain the temper of my knightly sword iv 1 29
See riot and dishonour stain the brow Of my young Harry 1 *Hen. IV.* i 1 85
Leaves behind a stain Upon the beauty of all parts besides iii 1 187
I will wear a garment all of blood And stain my favours in a bloody mask iii 2 136
A sword, whose temper I intend to stain With the best blood that I can meet v 2 94
There is not work enough for all our hands; Scarce blood enough in all their sickly veins To give each naked curtle-axe a stain *Hen. V.* iv 2 21
Stain to thy countrymen, thou hear'st thy doom! 1 *Hen. VI.* iv 1 45
Flight cannot stain the honour you have won; But mine it will iv 5 26
Thy father's charge shall clear thee from that stain iv 5 42
Or with their blood stain this discolour'd shore 2 *Hen. VI.* iv 1 11
Your mere enforcement shall acquittance me From all the impure blots and stains thereof *Richard III.* iii 7 234
O, let her live, And I'll corrupt her manners, stain her beauty iv 4 206
Nor any man an attaint but he carries some stain of it *Troi. and Cres.* i 2 26
My valour's poison'd With only suffering stain by him *Coriolanus* i 10 18
Cut me to pieces, Volsces; men and lads, Stain all your edges on me v 6 113
Stain not thy tomb with blood *T. Andron.* i 1 116
With our sighs we'll breathe the welkin dim, And stain the sun with fog iii 1 213
Lo, here upon thy cheek the stain doth sit Of an old tear *Rom. and Jul.* ii 3 75
What blood is this, which stains The stony entrance of this sepulchre? v 3 140
When we for recompense have praised the vile, It stains the glory in that happy verse Which aptly sings the good *T. of Athens* i 1 16
Giving our holy virgins to the stain Of contumelious, beastly, mad-brain'd war v 1 176
Do not stain The even virtue of our enterprise *J. Cæsar* ii 1 132
Great men shall press For tinctures, stains, relics, and cognizance ii 2 89
Let not women's weapons, water-drops, Stain my man's cheeks! *Lear* ii 4 281
If that her breath will mist or stain the stone, Why, then she lives v 3 262
I'll raise the preparation of a war Shall stain your brother *Ant. and Cleo.* iii 4 27
You do remember This stain upon her?—Ay, and it doth confirm Another stain, as big as hell can hold *Cymbeline* ii 4 139
Stained. He's something stain'd With grief that's beauty's canker *Temp.* i 2 414
Being rather new-dyed than stained with salt water ii 1 64
Or, to redeem him, Give up your body to such sweet uncleanness As she that he hath stain'd *Meas. for Meas.* ii 4 55
Tear the stain'd skin off my harlot-brow *Com. of Errors* ii 2 138
Thy mantle good, What, stain'd with blood! *M. N. Dream* v 1 288
Forget the shames that you have stain'd me with *Mer. of Venice* i 3 140
How, and why, and where This handkercher was stain'd *As Y. Like It* iv 3 98
Back to the stained field, You equal potents, fiery kindled spirits! *K. John* ii 1 357
The faiths of men ne'er stained with revolt iv 2 6
And stain'd the beauty of a fair queen's cheeks With tears *Richard II.* iii 1 14
Thy fierce hand Hath with the king's blood stain'd the king's own land v 5 111
Lighted from his horse, Stain'd with the variation of each soil 1 *Hen. IV.* i 1 64
Such a field as this, Where stain'd nobility lies trodden on v 4 13
Stand stained with travel, and sweating with desire to see him 2 *Hen. IV.* v 5 25
And wash away thy country's stained spots 1 *Hen. VI.* iii 3 57
Stain'd with the guiltless blood of innocents v 4 44
I am not your king Till I be crown'd and that my sword be stain'd 2 *Hen. VI.* ii 2 65
An enemy to the flock, Before his chaps be stain'd with crimson blood. iii 1 259
I stain'd this napkin with the blood 3 *Hen VI.* i 4 79
That face of his the hungry cannibals Would not have touch'd, would not have stain'd with blood i 4 153
Their steeds, That stain'd their fetlocks in his smoking blood ii 3 21
Let all untruths stand by thy stained name *Troi. and Cres.* v 2 179
Behold our cheeks How they are stain'd, as meadows, yet not dry *T. Andron.* iii 1 125
Here stands the spring whom you have stain'd with mud v 2 171
To slay his daughter with his own right hand, Because she was enforced, stain'd, and deflower'd? v 3 38
My reputation stain'd With Tybalt's slander *Rom. and Jul.* iii 1 116
Now I have stain'd the childhood of our joy With blood iii 3 95
How stand I then, That have a father kill'd, a mother stain'd? *Hamlet* iv 4 57
This is his sword; I robb'd his wound of it; behold it stain'd With his most noble blood *Ant. and Cleo.* v 1 25
Staines. Honey-sweet husband, let me bring thee to Staines *Hen. V.* ii 3 2
Staining. Would not put my reputation now In any staining act *A. W.* iii 7 7
Stainless. Of great estate, of fresh and stainless youth *T. Night* i 5 278
A winning match, Play'd for a pair of stainless maidenhoods *R. and J.* iii 2 13
Stair. Shall I always keep below stairs? *Much Ado* v 2 10
The stairs, as he treads on them, kiss his feet *L. L. Lost* v 2 330
Cowards, whose hearts are all as false As stairs of sand *Mer. of Venice* iii 2 84
In these degrees have they made a pair of stairs to marriage *As Y. Like It* v 2 41
Didst thou not, when she was gone down stairs, desire me to be no more so familiarity with such poor people? 2 *Hen. IV.* ii 1 107

Stair. Thrust him down stairs: I cannot endure such a fustian rascal *2 Hen. IV.* ii 4 202
Thrust him down stairs! know we not Galloway nags? ii 4 204
Within this hour my man shall be with thee, And bring thee cords made like a tackled stair *Rom. and Jul.* ii 4 201
You shall nose him as you go up the stairs into the lobby *Hamlet* iv 3 39
Slaver with lips as common as the stairs That mount the Capitol *Cymb.* i 6 105
Stair-work. Some stair-work, some trunk-work *W. Tale* iii 3 75
Stake. Paunch him with a stake, Or cut his wezand with thy knife *Temp.* iii 2 98
That fire cannot melt out of me: I will die in it at the stake *Much Ado* i 1 235
For a thousand ducats.—What, and stake down?—No; we shall ne'er win at that sport, and stake down *Mer. of Venice* iii 2 218
Let the rest go.—My honour's at the stake *All's Well* ii 3 156
Have you not set mine honour at the stake? *T. Night* iii 1 129
A fool That seest a game play'd home, the rich stake drawn *W. Tale* i 2 248
Sharp stakes pluck'd out of hedges They pitched in the ground *1 Hen. VI.* i 1 117
I prithee, give me leave to curse awhile.—Curse, miscreant, when thou comest to the stake v 3 44
Place barrels of pitch upon the fatal stake v 4 57
Call hither to the stake my two brave bears *2 Hen. VI.* v 1 144
I see my reputation is at stake; My fame is shrewdly gored *Tr. and Cr.* iii 3 227
I would dissemble with my nature where My fortunes and my friends at stake required I should do so in honour *Coriolanus* iii 2 63
I have a soul of lead So stakes me to the ground I cannot move *R. and J.* i 4 16
We are at the stake, And bay'd about with many enemies *J. Cæsar* iv 1 48
They have tied me to a stake; I cannot fly *Macbeth* v 7 1
Greatly to find quarrel in a straw When honour's at the stake *Hamlet* iv 4 56
He which finds him shall deserve our thanks, Bringing the murderous coward to the stake *Lear* ii 1 64
I am tied to the stake, and I must stand the course iii 7 54
I durst, my lord, to wager she is honest, Lay down my soul at stake *Oth.* iv 2 13
He, true knight, No lesser of her honour confident Than I did truly find her, stakes this ring *Cymbeline* v 5 188
Stale. Go bring it hither, For stale to catch these thieves *Tempest* iv 1 187
Is he dead, bully stale? is he dead? *Mer. Wives* ii 3 30
Poor I am but his stale.—Self-harming jealousy! *Com. of Errors* ii 1 101
A contaminated stale *Much Ado* ii 2 26
That have gone about To link my dear friend to a common stale iv 1 66
Fast bind, fast find; A proverb never stale in thrifty mind *Mer. of Ven.* ii 5 55
It grows something stale with me *As Y. Like It* ii 4 63
Is it your will To make a stale of me amongst these mates? *T. of Shrew* i 1 58
Be so humble To cast thy wandering eyes on every stale iii 1 90
And make stale The glistering of this present *W. Tale* iv 1 13
Patience is stale, and I am weary of it *Richard II.* v 5 104
So common-hackney'd in the eyes of men, So stale and cheap *1 Hen. IV.* iii 2 41
You bottle-ale rascal! you basket-hilt stale juggler, you! *2 Hen. IV.* ii 4 141
Had he none else to make a stale but me? *3 Hen. VI.* iii 3 260
A Grecian queen, whose youth and freshness Wrinkles Apollo's, and makes stale the morning *Troi. and Cres.* ii 2 79
This thrice worthy and right valiant lord Must not so stale his palm ii 3 201
That stale old mouse-eaten dry cheese, Nestor v 4 11
Since it serves my purpose, I will venture To stale 't a little more *Coriol.* i 1 95
Was there none else in Rome to make a stale, But Saturnine? *T. Andron.* i 1 304
A lenten pie, that is something stale and hoar *Rom. and Jul.* ii 4 139
To stale with ordinary oaths my love To every new protester *J. Cæsar* i 2 73
How weary, stale, flat, and unprofitable, Seem to me all the uses of this world! Fie on 't! ah fie! *Hamlet* i 2 133
Within a dull, stale, tired bed *Lear* i 2 13
Thou didst drink The stale of horses, and the gilded puddle *Ant. and Cleo.* i 4 62
Age cannot wither her, nor custom stale Her infinite variety ii 2 240
Poor I am stale, a garment out of fashion *Cymbeline* iii 4 53
Staled. Which, out of use and staled by other men, Begin his fashion *J. Cæsar* iv 1 38
Staleness. We are not destitute for want, But weary for the staleness *Pericles* v 1 58
Stalk. O, ay: stalk on, stalk on; the fowl sits *Much Ado* ii 3 95
Or shall we . . . stalk in blood to our possession? *K. John* ii 1 266
Their lips were four red roses on a stalk *Richard III.* iv 3 12
I stalk about her door, Like a strange soul upon the Stygian banks *Troi. and Cres.* iii 2 9
He stalks up and down like a peacock,—a stride and a stand iii 3 251
See, it stalks away!—Stay! speak, speak! I charge thee, speak! *Hamlet* i 1 50
Jump at this dead hour, With martial stalk hath he gone by our watch i 1 66
Here comes that which grows to the stalk; never plucked yet *Pericles* iv 6 46
Stalking-horse. He uses his folly like a stalking-horse *As Y. Like It* v 4 111
Stall. Rude mechanicals, That work for bread upon Athenian stalls *M. N. Dream* iii 2 10
Sixscore fat oxen standing in my stalls *T. of Shrew* ii 1 360
Stall this in your bosom; and I thank you for your honest care *All's W.* i 3 131
We shall feed like oxen at a stall *1 Hen. IV.* v 2 14
Stalls, bulks, windows, Are smother'd up, leads fill'd *Coriolanus* ii 1 226
Turn'd wild in nature, broke their stalls, flung out *Macbeth* ii 4 16
We could not stall together In the whole world *Ant. and Cleo.* v 1 39
Stalled. Deck'd in thy rights, as thou art stall'd in mine! *Richard III.* i 3 206
Stalling. Call you that keeping for a gentleman of my birth, that differs not from the stalling of an ox? *As Y. Like It* i 1 11
Stamford. How a good yoke of bullocks at Stamford fair? *2 Hen. IV.* iii 2 43
Stammer. I would thou couldst stammer *As Y. Like It* iii 2 209
Stamp. I found thee of more value Than stamps in gold *Mer. Wives* iii 4 16
Do coin heaven's image In stamps that are forbid *Meas. for Meas.* ii 4 46
Are they good?—As the event stamps them *Much Ado* i 2 7
And, at our stamp, here o'er and o'er one falls *M. N. Dream* iii 2 25
To cozen fortune and be honourable Without the stamp of merit *Mer. of Venice* ii 9 39
Nay, look not big, nor stamp, nor stare, nor fret *T. of Shrew* iii 2 230
What a fool art thou, A ramping fool, to brag and stamp and swear! *K. John* iii 1 122
Not a soldier of this season's stamp Should go so general current *1 Hen. IV.* iv 1 4
Under my feet I stamp thy cardinal's hat *1 Hen. VI.* i 3 49
Your hearts I'll stamp out with my horse's heels i 4 108
Stamp, rave, and fret, that I may sing and dance *3 Hen. VI.* i 4 91
Stamps, as he were nettled: I hope all's for the best iii 3 169
Your fire-new stamp of honour is scarce current *Richard III.* i 3 256
Strangely neglected? when did he regard The stamp of nobleness in any person Out of himself? *Hen. VIII.* iii 2 12
Methinks I see him stamp thus, and call thus: 'Come on, you cowards!' *Coriolanus* i 3 35
He has the stamp of Marcius; and I have Before-time seen him thus i 6 23
His sword, death's stamp, Where it did mark, it took ii 2 111
Stamp. The empress sends it thee, thy stamp, thy seal *T. Andron.* iv 2 69
I should fear those that dance before me now Would one day stamp upon me: 't has been done *T. of Athens* i 2 149
He cures, Hanging a golden stamp about their necks *Macbeth* iv 3 153
These men, Carrying, I say, the stamp of one defect *Hamlet* i 4 31
For use almost can change the stamp of nature iii 4 168
Let it stamp wrinkles in her brow of youth! *Lear* i 4 306
That has an eye can stamp and counterfeit advantages *Othello* ii 1 247
'Tween man and man they weigh not every stamp *Cymbeline* v 4 24
This is he; Who hath upon him still that natural stamp v 5 366
Stamped. Let there be some more test made of my metal, Before so noble and so great a figure Be stamp'd upon it *Meas. for Meas.* i 1 51
A coin that bears the figure of an angel Stamped in gold *Mer. of Venice* ii 7 57
He stamp'd and swore, As if the vicar meant to cozen him *T. of Shrew* iii 2 169
We pay them for it with stamped coin, not stabbing steel *W. Tale* iv 4 747
I, that am rudely stamp'd, and want love's majesty *Richard III.* i 1 16
You have caused Your holy hat to be stamp'd on the king's coin *Hen. VIII.* iii 2 325
And in his praise Have almost stamp'd the leasing *Coriolanus* v 2 22
Nay, he is your brother by the surer side, Although my seal be stamped in his face *T. Andron.* iv 2 127
You scratch'd your head, And too impatiently stamp'd *J. Cæsar* ii 1 244
That most venerable man which I Did call my father, was I know not where When I was stamp'd *Cymbeline* ii 5 5
Stanch. Let my tears stanch the earth's dry appetite *T. Andron.* iii 1 14
Yet, if I knew What hoop should hold us stanch, from edge to edge O' the world I would pursue it *Ant. and Cleo.* ii 2 117
Stanchless. Such A stanchless avarice that, were I king, I should cut off the nobles for their lands *Macbeth* iv 3 78
Stand. Twenty consciences, That stand 'twixt me and Milan *Tempest* ii 1 279
Kneel and repeat it; I will stand iii 2 47
Now, forward with your tale. Prithee, stand farther off iii 2 92
Why stand you In this strange stare? iii 3 94
There stand, For you are spell-stopp'd v 1 60
And how stand you affected to his wish? *T. G. of Ver.* i 3 60
Why, then, how stands the matter with them?—Marry, thus; when it stands well with him, it stands well with her ii 5 21
The doom—Which, unreversed, stands in effectual force iii 1 223
Stand, sir, and throw us that you have about ye iv 1 3
I pray you, stand not to discourse v 2 44
Here she stands: Take but possession of her with a touch v 4 129
Simple though I stand here *Mer. Wives* i 1 226
In these times you stand on distance, your passes ii 1 233
And stands so firmly on his wife's frailty ii 1 242
I stand wholly for you: but my wife, master doctor, is for you iii 2 62
Never stand 'you had rather' and 'you had rather' iii 3 133
Now doth thy honour stand, In him that was of late an heretic, As firm as faith iv 4 8
That it may stand till the perpetual doom v 5 62
Have I lived to stand at the taunt of one that makes fritters of English? v 5 151
Stand not amazed; here is no remedy v 5 244
I am glad, though you have ta'en a special stand to strike at me, that your arrow hath glanced v 5 248
Thus stands it with me *Meas. for Meas.* i 2 149
Thy head stands so tickle on thy shoulders i 2 176
Stands at a guard with envy; scarce confesses That his blood flows i 3 51
To fine the faults whose fine stands in record, And let go by the actor ii 2 40
Our compell'd sins Stand more for number than for accompt ii 4 58
As the matter now stands, he will avoid your accusation iii 1 201
Pattern in himself to know, Grace to stand, and virtue go iii 2 278
I have found you out a stand most fit iv 6 10
His integrity Stands without blemish v 1 108
The strong statutes Stand like the forfeits in a barber's shop v 1 323
I shall break that merry sconce of yours That stands on tricks *Com. of Er.* i 2 80
They stand at the door, master; bid them welcome hither iii 1 68
Your cake there is warm within; you stand here in the cold iii 1 71
In what part of her body stands Ireland? iii 2 118
I'll prove mine honour and mine honesty Against thee presently, if thou darest stand.—I dare v 1 31
Come, stand by me; fear nothing v 1 185
Stand I condemn'd for pride and scorn so much? *Much Ado* iii 1 108
You are to bid any man stand, in the prince's name.—How if a' will not stand? iii 3 28
If he will not stand when he is bidden, he is none of the prince's subjects iii 3 32
Stand thee close, then, under this pent-house, for it drizzles rain iii 3 110
Stand thee by, friar. Father, by your leave iv 1 24
Stand I here? Is this the prince? is this the prince's brother? iv 1 70
Here stand a pair of honourable men; A third is fled v 1 276
But, for my will, my will is your good will May stand with ours v 4 29
Our late edict shall strongly stand in force *L. L. Lost* i 1 11
Stands in attainder of eternal shame i 1 158
Where is the bush That we must stand and play the murderer in? iv 1 8
A stand where you may make the fairest shoot iv 1 10
So stands the comparison iv 1 80
Stand in your own defence; Or hide your heads like cowards v 2 85
Here stand I: lady, dart thy skill at me; Bruise me with scorn v 2 396
Stand between her back, sir, and the fire, Holding a trencher, jesting merrily v 2 476
Your nose says, no, you are not; for it stands too right v 2 568
It stands as an edict in destiny *M. N. Dream* i 1 151
And darest not stand, nor look me in the face iii 2 424
And the blots of Nature's hand Shall not in their issue stand v 1 417
If it stand, as you yourself still do, Within the eye of honour *Mer. of Ven.* i 1 136
This is the pent-house under which Lorenzo Desired us to make stand ii 6 2
There stand the caskets, noble prince ii 9 4
That the comparison May stand more proper iii 2 46
So, thrice-fair lady, stand I, even so; As doubtful whether what I see be true iii 2 147
You see me, Lord Bassanio, where I stand, Such as I am iii 2 150
I do know A many fools, that stand in better place iii 5 73
He stands obdurate iv 1 8
Make room, and let him stand before our face iv 1 16
As well go stand upon the beach And bid the main flood bate iv 1 71
I stand here for law iv 1 142
You stand within his danger, do you not?—Ay, so he says iv 1 180
You shall perceive them make a mutual stand v 1 77
Here he stands; I dare be sworn for him he would not leave it v 1 171
Stand you both forth now: stroke your chins *As Y. Like It* i 2 75
If it stand with honesty, Buy thou the cottage ii 4 91
In the purlieus of this forest stands A sheep-cote iv 3 77

Stand. Thus it stands . . . . *T. of Shrew* i 1 184
Thus it stands with me . . . . i 2 53
An she stand him but a little, he will throw a figure in her face . . i 2 113
I'll plead for you As for my patron, stand you so assured . . . i 2 156
When will he be here?—When he stands where I am and sees you there iii 2 40
And here she stands, touch her whoever dare . . . . . . iii 2 235
She, poor soul, Knows not which way to stand, to look, to speak . iv 1 188
Take away this dish.—I pray you, let it stand . . . . . . iv 3 44
I pray you, stand good father to me now . . . . iv 4 21
And such assurance ta'en As shall with either part's agreement stand . iv 4 50
Freely have they leave To stand on either part . . . *All's Well* i 2 15
Then here's a man stands, that has brought his pardon . . . . ii 1 65
The honour Of my dear father's gift stands chief in power . . . ii 1 115
This youthful parcel Of noble bachelors stand at my bestowing . . ii 3 59
Thou wert best set thy lower part where thy nose stands . . . ii 3 268
Stand no more off, But give thyself unto my sick desires . . . iv 2 34
So stand thou forth; The time is fair again . . . . . . v 3 35
Stand you a while aloof . . . . *T. Night* i 4 12
Stand at her doors, And tell them, there thy fixed foot shall grow . i 4 16
He says, he'll stand at your door like a sheriff's post . . . . i 5 157
My house doth stand by the church . . . . iii 1 7
Or, the church stands by thy tabor, if thy tabor stand by the church . iii 1 10
I'll make the motion: stand here, make a good show on't . . . iii 4 316
Do I stand there? I never had a brother . . . . v 1 233
So stands this squire Officed with me . . . . . *W. Tale* i 2 171
But, for me, What case stand I in? . . . . i 2 352
Upon mine honour, I Will stand betwixt you and danger . . . ii 2 66
For, as the case now stands, it is a curse He cannot be compell'd to't . ii 3 87
My life stands in the level of your dreams, Which I'll lay down . . iii 2 82
My shoulder-blade is out.—How now! canst stand? . . . . . iv 3 78
I can stand and walk: I will even take my leave of you . . . . iv 3 120
O lady Fortune, Stand you auspicious! . . . . iv 4 52
Never gazed the moon Upon the water as he'll stand and read As 'twere my daughter's eyes . . . . iv 4 173
Then stand till he be three quarters and a dram dead . . . . iv 4 814
One would speak to her and stand in hope of answer . . . . v 2 110
O, thus she stood, Even with such life of majesty, warm life, As now it coldly stands! . . . . v 3 36
In this right hand, whose protection Is most divinely vow'd upon the right Of him it holds, stands young Plantagenet . . . *K. John* ii 1 238
Some bastards too.—Stand in his face to contradict his claim . . ii 1 280
And at the other hill Command the rest to stand . . . . . ii 1 299
Why stand these royal fronts amazed thus? . . . . ii 1 356
And stand securely on their battlements, As in a theatre . . . . ii 1 374
Turn this day out of the week, . . . Or, if it must stand still, let wives with child Pray that their burthens may not fall this day . . . iii 1 89
If this same were a churchyard where we stand . . . . . iii 3 40
He that stands upon a slippery place Makes nice of no vile hold to stay him up: That John may stand, then Arthur needs must fall . . iii 4 137
Heat me these irons hot; and look thou stand Within the arras . . iv 1 1
Go, stand within; let me alone with him . . . . iv 1 85
Every part of what we would Doth make a stand at what your highness will . . . . iv 2 39
I saw a smith stand with his hammer, thus . . . . iv 2 193
Who ready here do stand in arms . . . . . . *Richard II.* i 3 36
Stands here for God, his sovereign, and himself . . . . . . i 3 105
Wherein the king stands generally condemn'd . . . . . . ii 2 132
There stands the castle, by yon tuft of trees . . . . . . ii 3 53
Let me know my fault: On what condition stands it and wherein? . ii 3 107
It stands your grace upon to do him right . . . . ii 3 138
By the honourable tomb he swears, That stands upon your royal grandsire's bones . . . . iii 3 106
If that thy valour stand on sympathy . . . . iv 1 33
That stand and look upon, Whilst that my wretchedness doth bait myself iv 1 237
Ah, thou, the model where old Troy did stand . . . . . . v 1 11
Loose companions, Even such, they say, as stand in narrow lanes . . v 3 8
I do not sue to stand; Pardon is all the suit I have in hand . . . v 3 129
While I stand fooling here, his Jack o' the clock . . . . . v 5 60
The most omnipotent villain that ever cried 'Stand' to a true man 1 *Hen. IV.* i 2 122
Stand.—So I do, against my will.—O, 'tis our setter . . . . ii 2 51
Thy horse stands behind the hedge . . . . ii 2 73
Do thou stand in some by-room, while I question my puny drawer . . ii 4 32
Here I am set.—And here I stand: judge, my masters . . . . ii 4 483
Percy stands on high; And either we or they must lower lie . . . iii 3 227
Our soldiers stand full fairly for the day . . . . v 3 29
Stand from him, fellow: wherefore hang'st upon him? . . 2 *Hen. IV.* ii 1 74
His apparel is built upon his back and the whole frame stands upon pins iii 2 155
Good Master Corporate Bardolph, stand my friend . . . . . iii 2 235
Here stand, my lords; and send discoverers forth . . . . . iv 1 3
Wherefore do I this? so the question stands . . . . . . iv 1 53
My bosom tells me That no conditions of our peace can stand . . iv 1 184
Our peace shall stand as firm as rocky mountains . . . . . iv 1 188
Wherefore stands our army still?—The leaders, having charge from you to stand, Will not go off . . . . iv 2 98
Stand my good lord, pray, in your good report . . . . . iv 3 89
Stand from him, give him air; he'll straight be well . . . . iv 4 116
Though no man be assured what grace to find, You stand in coldest expectation: I am the sorrier . . . . v 2 31
Stand here by me, Master Robert Shallow . . . . v 5 5
Stand behind me. O, if I had had time to have made new liveries . v 5 10
But to stand stained with travel, and sweating with desire to see him . v 5 25
Let another half stand laughing by, All out of work . . . *Hen. V.* i 2 113
His soul Shall stand sore charged for the wasteful vengeance . . i 2 283
I stand here for him: what to him from England? . . . . . ii 4 116
You stand upon the rivage and behold A city on the inconstant billows dancing . . . . iii Prol. 14
I see you stand like greyhounds in the slips, Straining upon the start . iii 1 31
That goddess blind, That stands upon the rolling restless stone . . iii 6 31
Though France himself and such another neighbour Stand in our way . iii 6 167
Well placed: there stands your friend for the devil . . . . iii 7 128
Though we upon this mountain's basis by Took stand for idle speculation . . . . iv 2 31
What is this castle call'd that stands hard by? . . . . . . iv 7 91
Who cannot see many a fair French city for one fair French maid that stands in my way . . . . v 2 346
Hundreds he sent to hell, and none durst stand him . . 1 *Hen. VI.* i 1 123
To try her skill, Reignier, stand thou as Dauphin in my place . . i 2 61
Who willed you? or whose will stands but mine? . . . . . . i 3 11
There stand lords.—And I, here, at the bulwark of the bridge . . i 4 66

Stand. The burning torch in yonder turret stands . . 1 *Hen. VI.* iii 2 30
The Dauphin, well appointed, Stands with the snares of war to tangle thee . . . . iv 2 22
The help of one stands me in little stead . . . . iv 6 31
Shall our condition stand?—It shall . . . . v 4 165
Paris is lost; the state of Normandy Stands on a tickle point 2 *Hen. VI.* i 1 216
Well, so it stands . . . . i 2 104
Safer shall he be upon the sandy plains Than where castles mounted stand . . . . i 4 40; 72
Alas, master, what shall I do? I am not able to stand . . . . ii 1 153
And, for my wife, I know not how it stands . . . . . . ii 1 192
Poise the cause in justice' equal scales, Whose beam stands sure . . ii 1 205
There let it stand Where it best fits to be . . . . ii 3 43
Do not stand on quillets how to slay him . . . . iii 1 261
Sooner dance upon a bloody pole Than stand uncover'd to the vulgar groom . . . . iv 1 128
Stand, villain, stand, or I'll fell thee down . . . . . . iv 2 123
I'll see if his head will stand steadier on a pole, or no . . . iv 7 101
Thus stands my state, 'twixt Cade and York distress'd . . . . iv 9 31
It shall ne'er be said, while England stands . . . . . . iv 10 45
He shall not hide his head, But boldly stand and front him to his face . v 1 86
And shall I stand, and thou sit in my throne? . . . . 3 *Hen. VI.* i 1 84
Let's fight it out and not stand cavilling thus . . . . . . ii 1 117
Make him stand upon this molehill here, That raught at mountains . i 4 67
I cannot speak!—Ay, crook-back, here I stand to answer thee . . ii 2 96
Whoever got thee, there thy mother stands . . . . ii 2 133
Why stand we like soft-hearted women here, Wailing our losses? . . ii 3 25
If with thy will it stands That to my foes this body must be prey . . ii 3 38
Off with the traitor's head, And rear it in the place your father's stands ii 6 86
In this covert will we make our stand, Culling the principal of all the deer . . . . iii 1 3
In this self-place where now we mean to stand . . . . . . iii 1 11
Like one that stands upon a promontory, And spies a far-off shore . iii 2 135
Many lives stand between me and home . . . . iii 2 173
It ill befits thy state And birth, that thou shouldst stand . . . iii 3 3
But were he dead, Yet here Prince Edward stands, King Henry's son . iii 3 73
How like you our choice, That you stand pensive? . . . . . iv 1 10
Come on, my masters, each man take his stand . . . . . . iv 3 1
If Warwick knew in what estate he stands, 'Tis to be doubted he would waken him . . . . iv 3 18
This is his tent; and see where stand his guard . . . . . iv 3 23
Thus stands the case . . . . iv 5 4
Nay, this way, man: see where the huntsmen stand . . . . . iv 5 15
And the rest, Stand you thus close, to steal the bishop's deer? . . iv 5 17
Your horse stands ready at the park-corner.—But whither shall we then? . . . . iv 5 19
Why, master mayor, why stand you in a doubt? Open the gates . . iv 7 27
Why, brother, wherefore stand you on nice points? . . . . . iv 7 58
Take leave and stand not to reply . . . . iv 8 23
Stand we in good array; for they no doubt Will issue out again . . v 1 62
Yonder stands the thorny wood . . . . v 4 67
Resign thy chair, and where I stand kneel thou . . . . . . v 5 19
Unmanner'd dog! stand thou, when I command . . . *Richard III.* i 2 39
We will not stand to prate; Talkers are no good doers . . . . i 3 351
Get a prayer-book in your hand, And stand betwixt two churchmen . iii 7 48
See, where he stands between two clergymen! . . . . . . iii 7 95
It stands me much upon, To stop all hopes whose growth may damage me . . . . iv 2 59
My kingdom stands on brittle glass . . . . iv 2 62
Cold fearful drops stand on my trembling flesh . . . . . . v 3 181
Prayers of holy saints and wronged souls, Like high-rear'd bulwarks, stand before our faces . . . . v 3 242
I have set my life upon a cast, And I will stand the hazard of the die . v 4 10
As I am made without him, so I'll stand, If the king please . *Hen. VIII.* ii 2 52
And stand unshaken yours . . . . iii 2 199
You come to take your stand here . . . . iv 1 2
Stand these poor people's friend . . . . iv 2 157
Stands in the gap and trade of moe preferments . . . . . v 1 36
The good I stand on is my truth and honesty . . . . . . v 1 122
Know you not How your state stands i' the world, with the whole world? v 1 127
All that stand about him are under the line . . . . . . v 4 44
He stands there, like a mortar-piece, to blow us . . . . . v 4 47
After seven years' siege yet Troy walls stand . . *Troi. and Cres.* i 3 12
How many Grecian tents do stand Hollow upon this plain . . . . i 3 79
Crowns, sceptres, laurels, But by degree, stand in authentic place . i 3 108
Troy in our weakness stands, not in her strength . . . . . i 3 137
Practise your eyes with tears! Troy must not be, nor goodly Ilion stand ii 2 109
The walls will stand till they fall of themselves . . . . . ii 3 10
Achilles stands i' the entrance of his tent . . . . . . iii 3 38
He stalks up and down like a peacock,—a stride and a stand . . iii 3 252
If e'er thou stand at mercy of my sword, Name Cressid . . . . iv 4 116
I wonder now how yonder city stands When we have here her base and pillar . . . . iv 5 211
There they stand yet, and modestly I think . . . . iv 5 222
Stand again: Think'st thou to catch my life so pleasantly? . . . iv 5 248
Stand where the torch may not discover us . . . . v 2 5
Let all untruths stand by thy stained name, And they'll seem glorious v 2 179
I'll stand to-day for thee and me and Troy . . . . . . v 3 36
Farewell: the gods with safety stand about thee! . . . . . v 3 94
Stands colossus-wise, waving his beam, Upon the pashed corses . . v 5 9
Stand, stand, thou Greek; thou art a goodly mark . . . . . v 6 27
Stand, ho! yet are we masters of the field: Never go home . . . v 10 1
Feebling such as stand not in their liking . . . . . *Coriolanus* i 1 199
Come off Like Romans, neither foolish in our stands, Nor cowardly in retire . . . . i 6 2
Doubt not The commoners, for whom we stand . . . . . . ii 1 243
Come by him where he stands, by ones, by twos, and by threes . . ii 3 46
If it may stand with the tune of your voices that I may be consul . ii 3 91
Why in this woolvish toge should I stand here, To beg of Hob and Dick? ii 3 122
So then the Volsces stand but as at first . . . . iii 1 4
Since that to both It stands in like request . . . . . . iii 2 51
They Stand in their ancient strength . . . . iv 2 7
Let me but stand; I will not hurt your hearth . . . . . . iv 5 26
To be full quit of those my banishers, Stand I before thee here . . iv 5 90
The commonwealth doth stand, and so would do, Were he more angry at it iv 6 14
Whence are you?—Stand, and go back.—You guard like men . . v 2 1
But stand, As if a man were author of himself And knew no other kin . v 3 35
Stand, Aufidius, And trouble not the peace . . . . . . v 6 128
For whom we stand A special party . . . . *T. Andron.* i 1 20
Every thing In readiness for Hymenæus stand . . . . . . i 1 325

Stand. This way, or not at all, stand you in hope *T. Andron.* ii 1 119
Now I stand as one upon a rock Environ'd with a wilderness of sea iii 1 93
Here stands my other son, a banish'd man, And here my brother, weeping iii 1 99
Stand by me, Lucius; do not fear thine aunt iv 1 5
If he stand on hostage for his safety, Bid him demand what pledge iv 4 105
Lo, by thy side where Rape and Murder stands v 2 45
Here stands the spring whom you have stain'd with mud v 2 171
There let him stand, and rave, and cry for food v 3 180
To move is to stir; and to be valiant is to stand *Rom. and Jul.* i 1 12
A dog of that house shall move me to stand i 1 15
Me they shall feel while I am able to stand i 1 34
May stand in number, though in reckoning none i 2 33
Tell me, daughter Juliet, How stands your disposition to be married? i 3 65
The measure done, I'll watch her place of stand i 5 52
My lips, two blushing pilgrims, ready stand To smooth that rough touch i 5 97
Letting it there stand Till she had laid it and conjured it down ii 1 25
I have forgot why I did call thee back.—Let me stand here till thou remember it.—I shall forget, to have thee still stand there ii 2 172
I stand on sudden haste.—Wisely and slow; they stumble that run fast ii 3 93
Who stand so much on the new form, that they cannot sit at ease on the old bench ii 4 35
Stand not amazed: the prince will doom thee death, If thou art taken iii 1 139
For Juliet's sake, for her sake, rise and stand iii 3 89
Here stands all your state iii 3 166
Since the case so stands as now it doth, I think it best you married iii 5 218
Here I stand, both to impeach and purge Myself condemned and myself excused v 3 226
And we, poor mates, stand on the dying deck *T. of Athens* iv 2 20
Thou'lt go, strong thief [gold], When gouty keepers of thee cannot stand iv 3 46
All villains that do stand by thee are pure iv 3 366
We stand much hazard, if they bring not Timon v 2 5
Stand you directly in Antonius' way, When he doth run his course *J. C.* i 2 3
The high east Stands, as the Capitol, directly here ii 1 111
Shall we sound him? I think he will stand very strong with us ii 1 142
Here will I stand till Cæsar pass along ii 3 11
I go to take my stand, To see him pass ii 4 25
My credit now stands on such slippery ground iii 1 191
Here thy hunters stand, Sign'd in thy spoil, and crimson'd in thy lethe iii 1 205
Mine eyes, Seeing those beads of sorrow stand in thine, Began to water iii 1 284
A ring; stand round.—Stand from the hearse, stand from the body iii 2 168
He should stand One of the three to share it iv 1 14
Stand, ho!—Give the word, ho! and stand iv 2 1
Must I observe you? must I stand and crouch Under your testy humour? iv 3 45
Stand but in a forced affection iv 3 205
So please you, we will stand and watch your pleasure iv 3 249
They stand, and would have parley v 1 21
Stand not to answer v 3 43
And to be king Stands not within the prospect of belief *Macbeth* i 3 74
Fears and scruples shake us: In the great hand of God I stand ii 3 136
Yet it was said It should not stand in thy posterity iii 1 4
Then stand with us iii 3 4
What, quite unmann'd in folly?—If I stand here, I saw him.—Fie! iii 4 74
Stand not upon the order of your going, But go at once iii 4 119
Why Stands Macbeth thus amazedly? iv 1 126
Let this pernicious hour Stand aye accursed in the calendar! iv 1 134
Stands Scotland where it did?—Alas, poor country! iv 3 164
As I did stand my watch upon the hill v 5 33
Hail, king! for so thou art: behold, where stands The usurper's cursed head v 8 54
Nay, answer me: stand, and unfold yourself *Hamlet* i 1 2
I think I hear them. Stand, ho! Who's there? i 1 14
The moist star Upon whose influence Neptune's empire stands i 1 119
Shall I strike at it with my partisan?—Do, if it will not stand i 1 141
Each particular hair to stand an end i 5 19
Nor stands it safe with us To let his madness range iii 3 1
Like a man to double business bound, I stand in pause where I shall first begin, And both neglect iii 3 42
And how his audit stands who knows save heaven? iii 3 82
Your bedded hair, like life in excrements, Start up, and stand an end iii 4 122
How stand I then, That have a father kill'd, a mother stain'd? iv 4 56
Where is this king? Sirs, stand you all without.—No, let's come in iv 5 112
To this point I stand, That both the worlds I give to negligence iv 5 133
Here lies the water; good: here stands the man; good v 1 17
And makes them stand Like wonder-wounded hearers v 1 279
And stand a comma 'tween their amities v 2 42
Does it not, thinks't thee, stand me now upon? v 2 63
Let a beast be lord of beasts, and his crib shall stand at the king's mess v 2 89
There she stands: If aught within that little seeming substance, Or all of it, with our displeasure pieced, And nothing more, may fitly like your grace, She's there, and she is yours *Lear* i 1 200
Wherefore should I Stand in the plague of custom? i 2 3
He must be whipped out, when Lady the brach may stand by the fire i 4 125
Come place him here by me, Do thou for him stand i 4 157
Thou canst tell why one's nose stands i' the middle on's face? i 5 19
Conjuring the moon To stand auspicious mistress ii 1 42
Strike, you slave; stand, rogue, stand; you neat slave, strike ii 2 44
I have seen better faces in my time Than stands on any shoulder that I see Before me at this instant ii 2 100
Nature in you stands on the very verge Of her confine ii 4 149
Not being the worst Stands in some rank of praise ii 4 261
Here I stand, your slave, A poor, infirm, weak, and despised old man iii 2 19
Look, where he stands and glares! Wantest thou eyes at trial, madam? iii 6 25
Stand you not so amazed: Will you lie down and rest? iii 6 35
If thou shouldst dally half an hour, his life, With thine, and all that offer to defend him, Stand in assured loss iii 6 102
Which, if convenience will not allow, Stand in hard cure iii 6 107
I am tied to the stake, and I must stand the course iii 7 54
The lowest and most dejected thing of fortune Stands still in esperance iv 1 4
Set me where you stand.—Give me your hand iv 6 24
How is't? Feel you your legs? You stand.—Too well, too well iv 6 65
The main descry Stands on the hourly thought iv 6 218
My state Stands on me to defend, not to debate v 1 69
The Cyprus wars, Which even now stand in act *Othello* i 1 152
Holla! stand there!—Signior, it is the Moor.—Down with him, thief! i 2 56
It stands not in such warlike brace, But altogether lacks the abilities i 3 24
Stand upon the foaming shore, The chidden billow seems to pelt the clouds ii 1 11
Therefore my hopes, not surfeited to death, Stand in bold cure ii 1 51
The town is empty; on the brow o' the sea Stand ranks of people ii 1 54
Who stands so eminent in the degree of this fortune? ii 1 240
Stand. If this poor trash of Venice . . . stand the putting on *Othello* ii 1 313
I am not drunk now; I can stand well enough, and speak well enough ii 3 120
He is a soldier fit to stand by Cæsar And give direction ii 3 127
As the time, the place, and the condition of this country stands ii 3 303
He shall in strangeness stand no further off Than in a politic distance iii 3 12
I wonder in my soul, What you would ask me, that I should deny, Or stand so mammering on iii 3 70
Stand you awhile apart; Confine yourself but in a patient list iv 1 75
Come, stand not amazed at it, but go along with me iv 2 246
Here, stand behind this bulk; straight will he come v 1 1
Be bold, and take thy stand.—I have no great devotion to the deed v 1 7
The Moor May unfold me to him; there stand I in much peril v 1 21
Pray you, stand farther from me.—What's the matter? *Ant. and Cleo.* i 3 18
And give true evidence to his love, which stands An honourable trial i 3 74
And stand the buffet With knaves that smell of sweat i 4 20
Stands he, or sits he? Or does he walk? or is he on his horse? i 5 19
Great Pompey Would stand and make his eyes grow in my brow i 5 32
It only stands Our lives upon to use our strongest hands ii 1 50
The swan's down-feather, That stands upon the swell at full of tide iii 2 49
Worthy shameful check it were, to stand On more mechanic compliment iv 4 31
Yet they are not join'd: where yond pine does stand, I shall discover all iv 12 1
Darkling stand The varying shore o' the world iv 15 10
The villain would not stand me *Cymbeline* i 2 15
Stand you! You have land enough of your own i 2 18
What lady would you choose to assail?—Yours; whom in constancy you think stands so safe i 4 138
Tell thy mistress how The case stands with her; do't as from thyself i 5 67
That thou mayst stand, To enjoy thy banish'd lord and this great land! ii 1 69
And makes Diana's rangers false themselves, yield up Their deer to the stand o' the stealer ii 3 75
Your isle, which stands As Neptune's park iii 1 18
Yet the traitor Stands in worse case of woe iii 4 89
Why hast thou gone so far, To be unbent when thou hast ta'en thy stand? iii 4 111
Stand, stand! We have the advantage of the ground v 2 11
Stand, stand, and fight! v 2 13
Camest thou from where they made the stand?—I did v 3 1
Stand; Or we are Romans and will give you that Like beasts which you shun beastly v 3 25
With this word 'Stand, stand,' Accommodated by the place v 3 31
Who dares not stand his foe, I'll be his friend v 3 60
Stand by my side, you whom the gods have made Preservers of my throne v 5 1
Why stands he so perplex'd?—What wouldst thou, boy? v 5 108
Stand thou by our side; Make thy demand aloud v 5 129
I stand on fire: Come to the matter v 5 168
Before thee stands this fair Hesperides, With golden fruit *Pericles* i 1 27
Without covering, save yon field of stars, Here they stand martyrs i 1 38
Here stands a lord, and there a lady weeping; Here many sink i 4 47
When peers thus knit, a kingdom ever stands ii 4 58
Tyrus stands In a litigious peace iii 3 2
That her daughter Might stand peerless by this slaughter iv Gower 40
Learn of me, who stand i' the gaps to teach you, The stages of our story iv 4 8
'Tis the better for you that your resorters stand upon sound legs iv 6 27
My temple stands in Ephesus: hie thee thither v 1 241
Stand accountant. I stand accountant for as great a sin *Othello* ii 1 302
Stand accursed. By his own interdiction stands accursed *Macbeth* iv 3 107
Stand affected. In conclusion, I stand affected to her *T. G. of Ver.* ii 1 90
Sound thou Lord Hastings, How he doth stand affected *Richard III.* iii 1 171
Stand against. Which shall then have no power to stand against us *Meas. for Meas.* iv 4 16
You are not of our quality, But stand against us like an enemy *1 Hen. IV.* iv 3 37
When they stand against you, may they fall! *2 Hen. IV.* iv 4 95
Manhood is call'd foolery, when it stands Against a falling fabric *Coriol.* iii 1 246
If I would stand against thee, would the reposal Of any trust, virtue, or worth in thee Make thy words faith'd? *Lear* ii 1 70
To stand against the deep dread-bolted thunder iv 7 33
Stand agreed. It stands agreed, I take it, by all voices *Hen. VIII.* v 3 87
Stand all aloof. Nerissa and the rest, stand all aloof *Mer. of Venice* iii 2 42
The rest stand all aloof, and bark at him *3 Hen. VI.* ii 1 17
Stand all aloof: but, uncle, draw you near *T. Andron.* v 3 151
Whate'er thou hear'st or seest, stand all aloof *Rom. and Jul.* v 3 26
Stand all apart, And show fair duty *Richard II.* iii 3 187
Stand all apart. Cousin of Buckingham!—My gracious sovereign? *Richard III.* iv 2 1
Stand alone. Alas, master, I am not able to stand alone *2 Hen. VI.* ii 1 145
Stands alone.—So do all men, unless they are drunk, sick *Troi. and Cres.* i 2 16
It is eleven years; For then she could stand alone *Rom. and Jul.* i 3 36
I am almost afraid to stand alone Here in the churchyard v 3 10
Stand aloof. And make the cowards stand aloof at bay *1 Hen. VI.* iv 2 52
Give me thy torch, boy: hence, and stand aloof *Rom. and Jul.* v 3 1
In my terms of honour I stand aloof; and will no reconcilement *Hamlet* v 2 258
Love's not love When it is mingled with regards that stand Aloof from the entire point *Lear* i 1 242
And so stand aloof for more serious wooing *Pericles* v 6 94
Stand amazed. You stand amazed; But be of comfort *T. Night* iii 4 371
Stand apart; I know not which is which *Com. of Errors* v 1 364
Stand apart; the king shall know your mind *2 Hen. VI.* iii 2 242
Stand aside. Peace! stand aside: the company parts *T. G. of Ver.* iv 2 81
Sir, I say to you we are none.—Well, stand aside *Much Ado* iv 2 32
Thy letter! he's a good friend of mine: Stand aside *L. L. Lost* iv 1 55
Stand aside: the noise they make Will cause Demetrius to awake *M. N. Dream* iii 2 116
Peace! Here comes my sister, reading: stand aside *As Y. Like It* iii 2 132
Bianca, stand aside. Poor girl! she weeps. Go ply thy needle *T. of S.* ii 1 24
Let's stand aside and see the end of this controversy v 1 63
Thou art too fine in thy evidence; therefore stand aside *All's Well* v 3 270
Here is my speech. Stand aside, nobility *1 Hen. IV.* ii 4 428
Peace, fellow, peace; stand aside: know you where you are? *2 Hen. IV.* iii 2 130
I did not care, for mine own part, so much.—Go to; stand aside iii 2 243
Vouchsafe, at our request, to stand aside *3 Hen. VI.* iii 3 110
Stand away. Deliver me this paper.—Foh! prithee, stand away *All's W.* v 2 17
Stand away, Captain Gower; I will give treason his payment *Hen. V.* iv 8 14
Stand back. Skipper, stand back: 'tis age that nourisheth *T. of Shrew* ii 1 341
Stand back, Lord Salisbury, stand back, I say *K. John* iv 3 81
Stand back, you lords, and give us leave awhile *1 Hen. VI.* i 2 70
Stand back, thou manifest conspirator i 3 33
Nay, stand thou back; I will not budge a foot i 3 38
My lord, stand back, and let the coffin pass *Richard III.* i 2 38
Stand far off.—Stand back; room; bear back *J. Cæsar* iii 2 172

Stand bald. They stand bald before him *Coriolanus* iv 5 206
Stand bare. How many then should cover that stand bare! *Mer. of Venice* ii 9 44
The cloak of night being pluck'd from off their backs, Stand bare *Rich. II.* iii 2 46
Stand by a while.—A proper stripling! *T. of Shrew* i 2 143
Stand by and mark the manner of his teaching iv 2 5
I Have utter'd truth: which if you seek to prove, I dare not stand by *W. Tale* i 2 444
Now he thanks the old shepherd, which stands by v 2 60
So long could I Stand by, a looker on v 3 85
Stand by, or I shall gall you, Faulconbridge *K. John* iv 3 94
Stand by, my masters: bring him near the king *2 Hen. VI.* ii 1 72
Now, brother Richard, will you stand by us? *3 Hen. VI.* iv 1 145
Go, gentle knight, Stand by our Ajax *Troi. and Cres.* iv 5 89
And thou must stand by too, and suffer every knave to use me at his pleasure?—I saw no man use you *Rom. and Jul.* ii 4 163
Yet now—No matter.—Ah, stand by *Ant. and Cleo.* iii 11 41
Stand close. Some treason, masters: yet stand close *Much Ado* iii 3 114
Stand close: this is the same Athenian *M. N. Dream* iii 2 41
Where are our disguises?—Here, hard by: stand close *1 Hen. IV.* ii 2 79
Stand close; I hear them coming ii 2 103
Stand close: my lord protector will come this way by and by *2 Hen. VI.* i 3 1
See the noble ruin'd man you speak of.—Let's stand close *Hen. VIII.* ii 1 55
The trumpets sound: stand close, the queen is coming iv 1 36
You great fellow, Stand close up, or I'll make your head ache v 4 92
Stand close awhile, for here comes one in haste *J. Cæsar* i 3 131
Upon my life, fast asleep. Observe her; stand close *Macbeth* v 1 24
What man is this?—Stand close, and list him *Ant. and Cleo.* iv 9 6
Stand condemned. Will you permit that I shall stand condemn'd A wandering vagabond? *Richard II.* ii 3 119
I stand condemn'd for this *Troi. and Cres.* iii 3 219
If thou canst serve where thou dost stand condemn'd *Lear* i 4 5
Stand cursed. Thou shalt stand cursed and excommunicate *K. John* iii 1 173
Stand debted. I stand debted to this gentleman *Com. of Errors* iv 1 31
Stand dishonoured. What should I speak? I stand dishonour'd *M. Ado* iv 1 65
Stand dumb. Whilst they, distill'd Almost to jelly with the act of fear, Stand dumb *Hamlet* i 2 206
Stand empty. The fold stands empty in the drowned field *M. N. Dream* ii 1 96
To sit here at this present, and behold That chair stand empty *Hen. VIII.* v 3 10
Stand engaged. I do stand engaged to many Greeks *Troi. and Cres.* v 3 68
Stand excused. All murders past do stand excused in this *K. John* iv 3 51
And, by despairing, shouldst thou stand excused *Richard III.* i 2 86
Stand fair, I pray thee: let me look on thee.—Behold thy fill *Tr. and Cr.* iv 5 235
Stand fast, good Fate, to his hanging *Tempest* i 1 32
Fellows, stand fast; I see a passenger *T. G. of Ver.* iv 1 1
Stand fast! the devil tempts thee *K. John* iii 1 208
Farewell, and stand fast.—Now cannot I strike him *1 Hen. IV.* ii 2 75
To-morrow We must with all our main of power stand fast *Troi. and Cres.* ii 3 273
Stand fast, and wear a castle on thy head! v 2 187
If you'll stand fast, we'll beat them to their wives *Coriolanus* i 4 41
Stand fast; We have as many friends as enemies iii 1 231
Stand fast together, lest some friend of Cæsar's Should chance— Talk not of standing *J. Cæsar* iii 1 87
They stand, and would have parley.—Stand fast v 1 22
Stand firm. There can be no evasion To blench from this and to stand firm by honour *Troi. and Cres.* ii 2 68
Stand fixed. Shall star-like rise, as great in fame as she was, And so stand fix'd *Hen. VIII.* v 5 48
Stand for. They shall stand for seed *Meas. for Meas.* i 2 102
To signify, that craft, being richer than innocency, stands for the facing iii 2 11
I am to stand for him *L. L. Lost* v 2 508
I stand for sacrifice *Mer. of Venice* iii 2 57
I stand for judgement: answer; shall I have it? iv 1 103
I hope this reason stands for my excuse.—Ay, it stands so that I may hardly tarry so long *T. of Shrew* Ind. 2 126
I will stand for't a little, though therefore I die a virgin *All's Well* i 1 145
'Tis a derivative from me to mine, And only that I stand for *W. Tale* iii 2 46
Which, till my infant fortune comes to years, Stands for my bounty *Richard II.* ii 3 67
Nor thou camest not of the blood royal, if thou darest not stand for ten shillings *1 Hen. IV.* i 2 157
Do thou stand for my father, and examine me ii 4 413
Do thou stand for me, and I'll play my father ii 4 477
Stand for your own; unwind your bloody flag *Hen. V.* i 2 101
And for this once my will shall stand for law *3 Hen. VI.* iv 1 50
When he shall stand for his place *Coriolanus* ii 1 165
Were he to stand for consul, never would he Appear i' the market-place ii 1 248
How many stand for consulships?—Three, they say ii 2 2
His stoutness When he did stand for consul v 6 28
Must thou needs stand for a villain in thine own work? *T. of Athens* v 1 39
This borrow'd passion stands for true old woe *Pericles* iv 4 24
Stand forfeit. How can this be true, That you stand forfeit? *L. L. Lost* v 2 427
Stand forth, Demetrius. My noble lord, This man hath my consent to marry her. Stand forth, Lysander *M. N. Dream* i 1 24
Speak, Pyramus. Thisby, stand forth iii 1 83
Antonio and old Shylock, both stand forth *Mer. of Venice* iv 1 175
Cousin, stand forth, and look upon that man *Richard II.* iv 1 7
Stand forth, Dame Eleanor Cobham, Gloucester's wife *2 Hen. VI.* ii 3 1
Stand forth, and with bold spirit relate *Hen. VIII.* i 2 129
Stand forth face to face, And freely urge against me v 3 47
Stand friendly. The gods to-day stand friendly! *J. Cæsar* v 1 94
Stand gracious to the rites that we intend! *T. Andron.* i 1 78
Stand high. Only to stand high in your account *Mer. of Venice* iii 2 157
They that stand high have many blasts to shake them *Richard III.* i 3 259
Stand indebted, over and above, In love and service to you evermore *Mer. of Venice* iv 1 413
Stand in fear. Showing we would not spare heaven as we love it, But as we stand in fear *Meas. for Meas.* ii 3 34
He should stand in fear of fire, being burnt i' the hand *2 Hen. VI.* iv 2 66
Stand in need. Take a note of what I stand in need of *T. G. of Ver.* ii 7 84
Stand minded. But to know How you stand minded *Hen. VIII.* iii 1 58
Stand naked. Put on the gown, stand naked, and entreat them *Coriol.* ii 2 141
Stand off. Yet stand off In differences so mighty *All's Well* ii 3 127
Though the truth of it stands off as gross As black and white *Hen. V.* ii 2 103
Stand on end. My hair doth stand on end to hear her curses *Richard III.* i 3 304
Stand opposed by such means As you yourself have forged *1 Hen. IV.* v 1 67
Stand out. Now for the rebels which stand out in Ireland *Richard II.* i 4 38
Stand pleased. So you stand pleased withal *Mer. of Venice* iii 2 211
Stand possessed. Whereof . . . Gaunt did stand possess'd *Richard II.* ii 1 162
Stand resolved, but hope withal *T. Andron.* i 1 135
Stand sentinel. One aloof stand sentinel *M. N. Dream* ii 2 26
Stand still. Who Time gallops withal and who he stands still withal *As Y. Like It* iii 2 329
Then all stand still; On *W. Tale* v 3 95
'Tis shame for us all: so God sa' me, 'tis shame to stand still *Hen. V.* iii 2 118
I'll never pause again, never stand still *3 Hen. VI.* ii 3 30
If we shall stand still, In fear our motion will be mock'd or carp'd at, We should take root here *Hen. VIII.* i 2 85
Be not affrighted; Fly not; stand still: ambition's debt is paid *J. C.* iii 1 83
A silence in the heavens, the rack stand still *Hamlet* ii 2 506
Come on, sir; here's the place: stand still *Lear* iv 6 11
Stand stone-still. What need you be so boisterous-rough? I will not struggle, I will stand stone-still *K. John* iv 1 77
Stand the push Of every beardless vain comparative *1 Hen. IV.* iii 2 66
I stand the push of your one thing that you will tell *2 Hen. IV.* ii 2 40
What propugnation is in one man's valour, To stand the push and enmity of those This quarrel would excite? *Troi. and Cres.* ii 2 137
Stand tiptoe. Will stand a tip-toe when this day is named *Hen. V.* iv 3 42
And jocund day Stands tiptoe on the misty mountain tops *Rom. and Jul.* iii 5 10
Stand to. I will stand to and feed, Although my last *Tempest* iii 3 49
Brother, my lord the duke, Stand to and do as we iii 3 52
Sir John stands to his word *1 Hen. IV.* i 2 130
Be good to me. I beseech you, stand to me *2 Hen. IV.* ii 1 70
Call them pillars that will stand to us *3 Hen. VI.* ii 3 51
Troilus will stand to the proof, if you'll prove it so *Troi. and Cres.* i 2 142
Or let us stand to our authority, Or let us lose it *Coriolanus* iii 1 208
Pray you, Stand to me in this cause v 3 199
Will speak more in a minute than he will stand to in a month *R. and J.* ii 4 157
[Drink] makes him stand to, and not stand to *Macbeth* ii 3 38
Stand to it. I'll stand to it, the pancakes were naught *As Y. Like It* i 2 69
An thy mind stand to't, boy, steal away bravely *All's Well* ii 1 29
Yet you will stand to it; you will not pocket up wrong *1 Hen. IV.* iii 3 183
Is't a lusty yeoman? will a' stand to't? *2 Hen. IV.* ii 1 5
'Tis he.—Stand to't.—It will be rain to-night *Macbeth* iii 3 15
Stand under. It stands under thee, indeed.—Why, stand-under and under-stand is all one *T. G. of Ver.* ii 5 33
But stand under the adoption of abominable terms *Mer. Wives* ii 2 308
Which else would stand under grievous imposition *Meas. for Meas.* i 2 193
The cardinal Cannot stand under them *Hen. VIII.* iii 2 3
There's none stands under more calumnious tongues Than I myself v 1 113
Shall Rome stand under one man's awe? What, Rome? *J. Cæsar* ii 1 52
Stand up. Your suit's unprofitable; stand up, I say *Meas. for Meas.* v 1 460
I pray you all, stand up. I know you two are rival enemies *M. N. Dream* iv 1 146
Pray you, sir, stand up: I am sure you are not Launcelot *Mer. of Venice* ii 2 86
That which here stands up Is but a quintain, a mere lifeless block *As Y. Like It* i 2 262
I'll fee thee to stand up *All's Well* ii 1 64
That at my bidding you could so stand up ii 1 67
Good aunt, stand up.—Nay, do not say, 'stand up;' Say 'pardon' first, and afterwards 'stand up'. *Richard II.* v 3 111
Stand up.—I do not sue to stand; Pardon is all the suit I have in hand v 3 129
He that temper'd thee bade thee stand up *Hen. V.* ii 2 118
Stand up; and, for these good deserts, We here create you Earl *1 Hen. VI.* iii 4 25
Stand up, good Canterbury: . . . give me thy hand, stand up *Hen. VIII.* v 1 113
Stand up, lord. With this kiss take my blessing: God protect thee! v 5 10
Shall we stand up here, and see them as they pass? *Troi. and Cres.* i 2 193
Outdares his senseless sword, And, when it bows, stands up *Coriolanus* i 4 54
O, stand up blest! Whilst . . . I kneel before thee v 3 52
I do remit these young men's heinous faults: Stand up *T. Andron.* i 1 485
Arise; Thou wilt be taken. Stay awhile! Stand up *Rom. and Jul.* iii 3 75
Stand up, stand up; stand, an you be a man iii 3 88
This is well: stand up: This is as't should be iv 2 28
We all stand up against the spirit of Cæsar *J. Cæsar* ii 1 167
That Nature might stand up And say to all the world, 'This was a man!' v 5 74
Now, gods, stand up for bastards! *Lear* i 2 22
A peasant stand up thus! iii 7 80
The king is mad: how stiff is my vile sense, That I stand up! iv 6 287
The which immediacy may well stand up, And call itself your brother v 3 65
In which I bind, On pain of punishment, the world to weet We stand up peerless *Ant. and Cleo.* i 1 40
Higher than both in blood and life, stands up For the main soldier i 2 197
Were't not that we stand up against them all, 'Twere pregnant they should square between themselves ii 1 44
If to-morrow Our navy thrive, I have an absolute hope Our landmen will stand up iv 3 11
In Britain where was he That could stand up his parallel? *Cymbeline* v 4 54
Stand upon. 'Tis best we stand upon our guard *Tempest* ii 1 321
You rogue! you stand upon your honour! *Mer. Wives* ii 2 20
Consider how it stands upon my credit *Com. of Errors* iv 1 68
This fellow doth not stand upon points *M. N. Dream* v 1 118
Not a word, a word; we stand upon our manners *W. Tale* iv 4 164
But O, the thorns we stand upon! iv 4 596
To bear a gentleman in hand, and then stand upon security! *2 Hen. IV.* i 2 42
Then they must stand upon security i 2 47
To determine Of what conditions we shall stand upon iv 1 165
A true-born gentleman And stands upon the honour of his birth *1 Hen. VI.* ii 4 28
I do refuse it; And stand upon my common part with those *Coriolanus* i 9 39
Do not stand upon't ii 2 154
'Tis but the time And drawing days out, that men stand upon *J. Cæsar* iii 1 100
The sore terms we stand upon with the gods will be strong with us *Per.* iv 2 38
Stand upright. It stands upright, Like lime-twigs *2 Hen. VI.* iii 3 15
It is a reeling world, indeed, my lord; And I believe 'twill never stand upright Till Richard wear the garland *Richard III.* iii 2 39
Who dares, In purity of manhood stand upright? *T. of Athens* iv 3 14
Standard. Thou shalt be my lieutenant, monster, or my standard.—Your lieutenant, if you list; he's no standard *Tempest* iii 2 19
Advance your standards, and upon them *L. L. Lost* iv 3 367
Pray God she prove not masculine ere long, If underneath the standard of the French She carry armour *1 Hen. VI.* ii 1 23
And in my standard bear the arms of York *2 Hen. VI.* v 1 256
Sir William Brandon, you shall bear my standard *Richard III.* v 3 22
Advance your standards, draw your willing swords v 3 264
A thousand hearts are great within my bosom: Advance our standards v 3 348
Standers. They fall, as being slippery standers *Troi. and Cres.* iii 3 84
Stander-by. I would not be a stander-by to hear My sovereign mistress clouded so *W. Tale* i 2 279
That all the standers-by had wet their cheeks *Richard III.* i 2 163
You were standers by, And so wast thou, Lord Hastings, when my son Was stabb'd with bloody daggers i 3 210
I have said to some my standers by 'Lo, Jupiter is yonder!' *T. and C.* iv 5 190

Stander-by. When a gentleman is disposed to swear, it is not for any standers-by to curtail his oaths *Cymbeline* ii 1 12
Standest. Thus dost thou hear the Nemean lion roar 'Gainst thee, thou lamb, that standest as his prey *L. L. Lost* iv 1 91
O lovely wall, That stand'st between her father's ground and mine! *M. N. Dream* v 1 176
In which predicament, I say, thou stand'st *Mer. of Venice* iv 1 357
By that fair sun which shows me where thou stand'st *Richard II.* iv 1 35
Standest thou still, and hearest such a calling? 1 *Hen. IV.* ii 4 90
And in that very line, Harry, standest thou iii 2 85
What, stand'st thou idle here? lend me thy sword v 3 41
Though thou stand'st more sure than I could do, Thou art not firm enough, since griefs are green 2 *Hen. IV.* iv 5 203
By his treason, stand'st not thou attainted? 1 *Hen. VI.* ii 4 92
Lo, there thou stand'st, a breathing valiant man iv 2 31
Stand'st thou aloof upon comparison? v 4 150
Dull, unmindful villain, Why stand'st thou still, and go'st not? *Rich. III.* iv 4 445
Art thou stiff? stand'st out? *Coriolanus* i 1 245
If thou standest not i' the state of hanging v 2 70
But wherefore stand'st thou with thy weapon drawn? *T. Andron.* iii 1 48
The fool hangs on your back already.—No, thou stand'st single *T. of A.* ii 2 58
Cæsar entreats, Not to consider in what case thou stand'st *A. and C.* iii 13 54
Thou that stand'st so for Posthumus! *Cymbeline* iii 5 56
Standeth. It standeth north-north-east and by east *L. L. Lost* i 1 248
Here standeth Thomas Mowbray, Duke of Norfolk *Richard II.* i 3 110
The question then, Lord Hastings, standeth thus 2 *Hen. IV.* i 3 15
Standing, speaking, moving, And yet so fast asleep *Tempest* ii 1 214
Well, I am standing water.—I'll teach you how to flow ii 1 221
Ye elves of hills, brooks, standing lakes, and groves v 1 33
Whose visages Do cream and mantle like a standing pond *Mer. of Venice* i 1 89
Sixscore fat oxen standing in my stalls *T. of Shrew* ii 1 360
The danger is in standing to 't *All's Well* iii 2 43
'Tis with him in standing water, between boy and man *T. Night* i 5 168
Like a cipher, Yet standing in rich place, I multiply With one *W. Tale* i 2 7
His folly, whose foundation Is piled upon his faith and will continue The standing of his body i 2 431
Standing To prate and talk for life and honour 'fore Who please to come iii 2 41
Poor trespasses, More monstrous standing by iii 2 191
From thy admiring daughter took the spirits, Standing like stone with thee v 3 42
With his shears and measure in his hand, Standing on slippers *K. John* iv 2 197
O that I were a mockery king of snow, Standing before the sun of Bolingbroke, To melt myself away in water-drops! *Richard II.* iv 1 261
Shall there be gallows standing in England when thou art king? 1 *Hen. IV.* i 2 66
His mountain sire, on mountain standing, Up in the air *Hen. V.* ii 4 57
Well could I curse away a winter's night, Though standing naked on a mountain top 2 *Hen. VI.* iii 2 336
'Tis but surmised whiles thou art standing by iii 2 347
Now Margaret's curse is fall'n upon our heads, For standing by when Richard stabb'd her son *Richard III.* iii 3 16
You know the cause, sir, of my standing here *Coriolanus* ii 3 68
Standing your friendly lord ii 3 198
Like a great sea-mark, standing every flaw v 3 74
How this grace Speaks his own standing! *T. of Athens* i 1 31
Talk not of standing. Publius, good cheer *J. Cæsar* iii 1 89
What a wounded name, Things standing thus unknown, shall live behind me! *Hamlet* v 2 356
Drinks the green mantle of the standing pool *Lear* iii 4 139
We Have used to conquer, standing on the earth, And fighting *A. and C.* iii 7 66
Two winking Cupids Of silver, each on one foot standing *Cymbeline* ii 4 90
Am right glad he is not standing here To tell this tale of mine v 5 296
Our lodgings, standing bleak upon the sea *Pericles* iii 2 14
Standing-bed. His castle, his standing-bed, and truckle-bed *Mer. Wives* iv 5 7
Standing-bowl. We drink this standing-bowl of wine to him *Pericles* ii 3 65
Standing-tuck. You tailor's-yard, you sheath, you bow-case, you vile standing-tuck 1 *Hen. IV.* ii 4 274
Staniel. And with what wing the staniel checks at it! *T. Night* ii 5 124
Stanley. With Sir John Stanley, in the Isle of Man 2 *Hen. VI.* ii 3 13
Sir John Stanley is appointed now To take her with him to the Isle of Man ii 4 77
Thy office is discharged. Come, Stanley, shall we go? ii 4 104
Sir William Stanley, Leave off to wonder why I drew you hither 3 *Hen. VI.* iv 5 1
Stanley, I will requite thy forwardness iv 5 23
What think'st thou, then, of Stanley? what will he? *Richard III.* iii 1 167
Who knocks at the door?—A messenger from the Lord Stanley iii 2 3
Stanley did dream the boar did raze his helm; But I disdain'd it iii 4 84
Stanley, he is your wife's son: well, look to it iv 2 90
Stanley, look to your wife: if she convey Letters to Richmond, you shall answer it iv 2 95
But, hear you, leave behind Your son, George Stanley iv 4 497
In the sty of this most bloody boar My son George Stanley is frank'd up iv 5 3
Sir Gilbert Talbot, Sir William Stanley; Oxford, redoubted Pembroke iv 5 10
And here receive we from our father Stanley Lines of fair comfort v 2 5
Where is Lord Stanley quarter'd, dost thou know? v 3 34
Send out a pursuivant at arms To Stanley's regiment v 3 60
Call up Lord Stanley, bid him bring his power v 3 290
What says Lord Stanley? will he bring his power? v 3 342
After the battle let George Stanley die v 3 346
Tell me, is young George Stanley living?—He is, my lord v 5 9
Stanze. Let me hear a staff, a stanze, a verse; lege, domine *L. L. Lost* iv 2 107
Stanzo. Come, more; another stanzo: call you 'em stanzos? *As Y. L. It* ii 5 18
Staple. He draweth out the thread of his verbosity finer than the staple of his argument *L. L. Lost* v 1 19
Massy staples And corresponsive and fulfilling bolts *Troi. and Cres.* Prol. 17
Star. I find my zenith doth depend upon A most auspicious star *Tempest* i 2 182
I did adore a twinkling star, But now I worship a celestial sun *T. G. of V.* ii 6 9
But truer stars did govern Proteus' birth ii 7 74
Wilt thou reach stars, because they shine on thee? iii 1 156
Wilt thou revenge?—By welkin and her star! *Mer. Wives* i 3 101
Look, the unfolding star calls up the shepherd *Meas. for Meas.* iv 2 219
There were no living near her; she would infect to the north star *M. Ado* ii 1 258
There was a star danced, and under that was I born ii 1 349
An you be not turned Turk, there's no more sailing by the star iii 4 58
These earthly godfathers of heaven's lights That give a name to every fixed star Have no more profit of their shining nights *L. L. Lost* i 1 89
O, pardon me, my stars! iii 1 79
My love, her mistress, is a gracious moon; She an attending star iv 3 231
Vouchsafe, bright moon, and these thy stars, to shine v 2 205
Thus pour the stars down plagues for perjury v 2 394
Certain stars shot madly from their spheres *M. N. Dream* ii 1 153
Star. Thou coward, art thou bragging to the stars? *M. N. Dream* iii 2 407
It shall be moon, or star, or what I list, Or ere I journey *T. of Shrew* iv 5 7
What stars do spangle heaven with such beauty, As those two eyes become that heavenly face? iv 5 31
Happier the man, whom favourable stars Allot thee for his lovely bed-fellow! iv 5 40
'Twere all one That I should love a bright particular star *All's Well* i 1 97
We, the poorer born, Whose baser stars do shut us up in wishes i 1 197
You were born under a charitable star.—Under Mars, I i 1 205
An we might have a good woman born but one every blazing star i 3 91
My legacy be sanctified By the luckiest stars in heaven i 3 252
Eat, speak, and move under the influence of the most received star ii 1 57
Wherein toward me my homely stars have fail'd To equal my great fortune ii 5 80
Thy leg, it was formed under the star of a galliard *T. Night* i 3 142
My stars shine darkly over me ii 1 3
In my stars I am above thee; but be not afraid of greatness ii 5 156
I thank my stars I am happy ii 5 185
Jove and my stars be praised! ii 5 188
Nine changes of the watery star hath been The shepherd's note *W. Tale* i 2 1
Though you would seek to unsphere the stars with oaths i 2 48
Happy star reign now! i 2 363
Swear his thought over By each particular star in heaven i 2 425
Stars, stars, And all eyes else dead coals! v 1 67
The stars, I see, will kiss the valleys first v 1 206
Bidding me depend Upon thy stars, thy fortune, and thy strength *K. John* iii 1 126
Now, you stars that move in your right spheres, Where be your powers? v 7 74
And meteors fright the fixed stars of heaven *Richard II.* ii 4 9
I see thy glory like a shooting star Fall to the base earth ii 4 19
Shall I so much dishonour my fair stars? iv 1 21
For we that take purses go by the moon and the seven stars 1 *Hen. IV.* i 2 16
Two stars keep not their motion in one sphere v 4 65
We have seen the seven stars 2 *Hen. IV.* ii 4 201
The armour that I saw in your tent to-night, are those stars or suns upon it?—Stars, my lord.—Some of them will fall to-morrow *Hen. V.* iii 7 74
Small time, but in that small most greatly lived This star of England Epil. 6
And with them scourge the bad revolting stars 1 *Hen. VI.* i 1 4
A far more glorious star thy soul will make Than Julius Cæsar i 1 55
Bright star of Venus, fall'n down on the earth i 2 144
O malignant and ill-boding stars! Now thou art come unto a feast of death iv 5 6
What louring star now envies thy estate? 2 *Hen. VI.* iii 1 206
That the people of this blessed land May not be punish'd with my thwarting stars, . . . I here resign my government 3 *Hen. VI.* iv 6 22
For few men rightly temper with the stars iv 6 29
All of us have cause To wail the dimming of our shining star *Richard III.* ii 2 102
I lay what you would lay on me, The right and fortune of his happy stars iii 7 172
At their births good stars were opposite iv 4 215
These are stars indeed; And sometimes falling ones *Hen. VIII.* iv 1 54
Fly like chidden Mercury from Jove, Or like a star disorb'd *T. and C.* ii 2 46
As many farewells as be stars in heaven iv 4 46
Let the pebbles on the hungry beach Fillip the stars *Coriolanus* v 3 59
Was't not a happy star Led us to Rome? *T. Andron.* iv 2 32
Earth-treading stars that make dark heaven light *Rom. and Jul.* i 2 25
My mind misgives Some consequence yet hanging in the stars i 4 107
Two of the fairest stars in all the heaven, Having some business, do entreat her eyes To twinkle in their spheres ii 2 15
The brightness of her cheek would shame those stars ii 2 19
When he shall die, Take him and cut him out in little stars iii 2 22
Is it even so? then I defy you, stars! v 1 24
And shake the yoke of inauspicious stars From this world-wearied flesh v 3 111
The fault, dear Brutus, is not in our stars, But in ourselves *J. Cæsar* i 2 140
I cannot, by the progress of the stars, Give guess how near to day ii 1 2
I am constant as the northern star iii 1 60
But signs of nobleness, like stars, shall shine On all deservers *Macbeth* i 4 41
Stars, hide your fires; Let not light see my black and deep desires i 4 50
Yond same star that's westward from the pole *Hamlet* i 1 36
As stars with trains of fire and dews of blood, Disasters in the sun i 1 117
The moist star Upon whose influence Neptune's empire stands i 1 118
The stamp of one defect, Being nature's livery, or fortune's star i 4 32
Make thy two eyes, like stars, start from their spheres i 5 17
Doubt thou the stars are fire; Doubt that the sun doth move ii 2 116
Lord Hamlet is a prince, out of thy star ii 2 141
As the star moves not but in his sphere, I could not but by her iv 7 15
Whose phrase of sorrow Conjures the wandering stars v 1 279
Your skill shall, like a star i' the darkest night, Stick fiery off indeed v 2 267
We make guilty of our disasters the sun, the moon, and the stars *Lear* i 2 131
An admirable evasion of whore-master man, to lay his goatish disposition to the charge of a star! i 2 139
I should have been that I am, had the maidenliest star in the firmament twinkled on my bastardizing i 2 143
The reason why the seven stars are no more than seven is a pretty reason i 5 38
Who have—as who have not, that their great stars Throned and set high? iii 1 22
It is the stars, The stars above us, govern our conditions iv 3 35
Let me not name it to you, you chaste stars! *Othello* v 2 2
Let all the number of the stars give light To thy fair way! *A. and C.* iii 2 65
Moon and stars! Whip him iii 13 95
My good stars, that were my former guides, Have empty left their orbs iii 13 145
The star is fall'n.—And time is at his period iv 14 106
That our stars, Unreconciliable, should divide Our equalness to this v 1 46
O eastern star!—Peace, peace! v 2 311
Learn'd indeed were that astronomer That knew the stars as I his characters; He'ld lay the future open *Cymbeline* iii 2 28
Our Jovial star reign'd at his birth, and in Our temple was he married v 4 105
For they are worthy To inlay heaven with stars v 5 352
Upon his neck a mole, a sanguine star; It was a mark of wonder v 5 364
Without covering, save yon field of stars, Here they stand martyrs *Per.* i 1 37
Feast here awhile, Until our stars that frown lend us a smile i 4 108
Yet cease your ire, you angry stars of heaven! ii 1 1
Had princes sit, like stars, about his throne, And he the sun ii 3 39
But her better stars Brought her to Mytilene v 3 9
My father's dead.—Heavens make a star of him! v 3 79
Star-blasting. Bless thee from whirlwinds, star-blasting! *Lear* iii 4 60
Star-chamber. I will make a Star-chamber matter of it *Mer. Wives* i 1 2
Star-crossed. A pair of star-cross'd lovers take their life *Rom. and Jul.* Prol. 6
Stare. Why stand you In this strange stare? *Tempest* iii 3 95
I will stare him out of his wits *Mer. Wives* ii 2 291
Nay, look not big, nor stamp, nor stare, nor fret *T. of Shrew* iii 2 230
What means our cousin, that he stares and looks So wildly? *Richard II.* v 3 24
That makes him gasp and stare and catch the air 2 *Hen. VI.* iii 2 371

Stare. Why are you breathless? and why stare you so?—Are not you moved? . . . . *J. Cæsar* i 3 2
Men, wives, and children stare, cry out and run As it were doomsday iii 1 97
Shall I be frighted when a madman stares? . . . . . iv 3 40
Art thou some god, some angel, or some devil, That makest my blood cold and my hair to stare? . . . . iv 3 280
When I do stare, see how the subject quakes . . *Lear* iv 6 110
Nay, if you stare, we shall hear more anon . . *Othello* v 1 107
Nay, stare not, masters: it is true, indeed.—'Tis a strange truth . v 2 188
What is in thy mind, That makes thee stare thus? . . *Cymbeline* iii 4 5
Stared. You stared upon me with ungentle looks . . *J. Cæsar* ii 1 242
They stared, and were distracted . . . *Macbeth* ii 3 110
Staring. To drinkings and swearings and starings . . *Mer. Wives* v 5 168
Then nightly sings the staring owl, Tu-whit . . *L. L. Lost* v 2 927
They seemed almost, with staring on one another, to tear the cases of their eyes; there was speech in their dumbness . . *W. Tale* v 2 13
Wall-eyed wrath or staring rage . . . . *K. John* iv 3 49
Staring full ghastly like a strangled man; His hair uprear'd 2 *Hen. VI.* iii 2 170
Stark. But, sure, he is stark mad . . . *Com. of Errors* ii 1 59
I think you are all mated or stark mad . . . . . v 1 281
That wench is stark mad or wonderful froward . *T. of Shrew* i 1 69
Stark spoiled with the staggers, begnawn with the bots . . iii 2 55
Strip your sword stark naked; for meddle you must . *T. Night* iii 4 274
O, think what they have done And then run mad indeed, stark mad! *W. T.* iii 2 184
Many a nobleman lies stark and stiff . . . 1 *Hen. IV.* v 3 42
Shall, stiff and stark and cold, appear like death . . *Rom. and Jul.* iv 1 103
Rather on Nilus' mud Lay me stark naked! . . . *Ant. and Cleo.* v 2 59
How found you him?—Stark, as you see . . . *Cymbeline* iv 2 209
Starkly. As fast lock'd up in sleep as guiltless labour When it lies starkly in the traveller's bones . . . . . *Meas. for Meas.* iv 2 70
Starlight. Till candles and starlight and moonshine be out *Mer. Wives* v 5 106
By fountain clear, or spangled starlight sheen . . *M. N. Dream* ii 1 29
She will find him by starlight . . . . v 1 320
Star-like. Shall star-like rise, as great in fame . *Hen. VIII.* v 5 47
What! to you, Whose star-like nobleness gave life and influence To their whole being! . . . . . . *T. of Athens* v 1 66
Starling. I'll have a starling shall be taught to speak Nothing but 'Mortimer,' and give it him . . . . 1 *Hen. IV.* i 3 224
Starred. My third comfort, Starr'd most unluckily . . *W. Tale* iii 2 100
Starry. The starry welkin cover thou anon With drooping fog *M. N. D.* iii 2 356
Start. But if he start, It is the flesh of a corrupted heart *Mer. Wives* v 5 90
Well, I am your theme: you have the start of me . . . v 5 171
How if your husband start some other where? *Com. of Errors* ii 1 30
I have mark'd A thousand blushing apparitions To start into her face *Much Ado* iv 1 162
Use your legs, take the start, run away . . *Mer. of Venice* ii 2 6
What's in 'mother,' That you start at it? . . . *All's Well* i 3 148
I have felt so many quirks of joy and grief, That the first face of neither, on the start, Can woman me unto't . . . . . iii 2 52
You boggle shrewdly, every feather starts you . . . . v 3 232
For she did speak in starts distractedly . . . *T. Night* ii 2 22
Seven of my people, with an obedient start, make out for him . ii 5 65
You perceive she stirs: Start not . . . . *W. Tale* v 3 104
Do but start An echo with the clamour of thy drum . *K. John* v 2 167
O, the blood more stirs To rouse a lion than to start a hare! . 1 *Hen. IV.* i 3 198
You start away And lend no ear unto my purposes . . . . i 3 216
Why dost thou bend thine eyes upon the earth, And start so often . ii 3 46
Through vassal fear, Base inclination, and the start of spleen . iii 2 125
You stand like greyhounds in the slips, Straining upon the start *Hen. V.* iii 1 32
Mangling by starts the full course of their glory . . . Epil. 4
Great rage of heart Suddenly made him from my side to start 1 *Hen. VI.* iv 7 12
When I start, the envious people laugh And bid me be advised 2 *Hen. VI.* ii 4 35
The fearful French, whom you late vanquished, Should make a start o'er seas and vanquish you . . . . iv 8 45
Tremble and start at wagging of a straw . . *Richard III.* iii 5 7
He bites his lip, and starts; Stops on a sudden . . *Hen. VIII.* iii 2 113
One cannot speak a word, But it straight starts you . *Troi. and Cres.* v 2 101
A wild exposture to each chance That starts i' the way before thee *Cor.* iv 1 37
At which he starts and wakes, And being thus frighted swears a prayer or two And sleeps again . . . . . *Rom. and Jul.* i 4 86
Then starts up, And Tybalt calls; and then on Romeo cries . iii 3 100
So get the start of the majestic world And bear the palm alone *J. Cæsar* i 2 130
Brutus will start a spirit as soon as Cæsar . . . . i 2 147
Why do you start; and seem to fear Things that do sound so fair? *Macb.* i 3 51
These flaws and starts, Impostors to true fear . . . iii 4 63
Start, eyes! What, will the line stretch out to the crack of doom? iv 1 116
Who then shall blame His pester'd senses to recoil and start? . v 2 23
Direness, familiar to my slaughterous thoughts, Cannot once start me . v 5 15
Make thy two eyes, like stars, start from their spheres *Hamlet* i 5 17
Put your discourse into some frame and start not so wildly from my affair . . . . iii 2 321
Your bedded hair, like life in excrements, Start up, and stand an end . iii 4 122
How much I had to do to calm his rage! Now fear I this will give it start again . . . . iv 7 194
Such unconstant starts are we like to have from him . . *Lear* i 1 304
Upon malicious bravery, dost thou come To start my quiet . *Othello* i 1 101
Of late, when I cried 'Ho!' Like boys unto a muss, kings would start forth, And cry 'Your will?' . . . . *Ant. and Cleo.* iii 13 91
By starts, His fretted fortunes give him hope, and fear . . iv 12 7
Started. He started one poor heart of mine in thee . . *T. Night* iv 1 63
Rougemont: at which name I started, Because a bard of Ireland told me once, I should not live long after I saw Richmond *Richard III.* iv 2 108
And then it started like a guilty thing Upon a fearful summons *Hamlet* i 1 148
Then away she started To deal with grief alone . . . *Lear* iv 3 33
Startest. Why start'st thou? what, doth death affright? 2 *Hen. VI.* iv 1 32
Starting so He seem'd in running to devour the way . . 2 *Hen. IV.* i 1 46
Starting thence away To what may be digested in a play *Troi. and Cres.* Prol. 28
Fresh and fair, Anticipating time with starting courage . . . iv 5 2
No more o' that: you mar all with this starting . . *Macbeth* v 1 50
Blest pray you be, That, after this strange starting from your orbs, You may reign in them now! . . . . . . *Cymbeline* v 5 371
Starting-hole. What trick, what device, what starting-hole, canst thou now find out to hide thee? . . . . . . 1 *Hen. IV.* ii 4 290
Startingly. Why do you speak so startingly and rash? . *Othello* iii 4 79
Startle. Patience herself would startle at this letter . *As Y. Like It* iv 3 13
Startles and frights consideration, Makes sound opinion sick *K. John* iv 2 25
This shower, blown up by tempest of the soul, Startles mine eyes . . v 2 51
I'll startle you Worse than the sacring bell . . *Hen. VIII.* iii 2 294
What fear is this which startles in our ears? . . *Rom. and Jul.* v 3 194
Thou little know'st how thou dost startle me . . . *Pericles* v 1 147

Startled. Three times to-day my foot-cloth horse did stumble, And startled, when he look'd upon the Tower . . . *Richard III.* iii 4 87
Start-up. That young start-up hath all the glory of my overthrow *M. Ado* i 3 69
Starve. Whilst I at home starve for a merry look . *Com. of Errors* ii 1 88
She did starve the general world beside . . . *L. L. Lost* ii 1 11
We must starve our sight From lovers' food till morrow *M. N. Dream* i 1 222
For aught I see, they are as sick that surfeit with too much as they that starve with nothing . . . . *Mer. of Venice* i 2 7
On the barren mountains let him starve . . . . 1 *Hen. IV.* i 3 89
I cannot blame his cousin king, That wish'd him on the barren mountains starve . . . . i 3 159
I'll starve ere I'll rob a foot further . . . . . . ii 2 22
Your grace may starve perhaps before that time . . 1 *Hen. VI.* iii 2 48
Ready to starve and dare not touch his own . . 2 *Hen. VI.* i 1 229
By all that's holy, he had better starve . . . *Hen. VIII.* v 3 132
Never go home; here starve we out the night . . *Troi. and Cres.* v 10 2
Better to starve, Than crave the hire which first we do deserve *Coriol.* ii 3 120
Anger's my meat; I sup upon myself, And so shall starve with feeding iv 2 51
An you be not, hang, beg, starve, die in the streets . *Rom. and Jul.* iii 5 194
Aches contract and starve your supple joints! . . . *T. of Athens* i 1 257
Ere they shall make us weep: we'll see 'em starve first . . *Lear* v 3 25
Lest the bargain should catch cold and starve . . *Cymbeline* i 4 180
Thou wilt starve, sure; for here's nothing to be got now-a-days *Pericles* ii 1 72
Who starves the ears she feeds, and makes them hungry . . v 1 113
Starved. The air hath starved the roses in her cheeks . *T. G. of Ver.* iv 4 159
Thy desires Are wolvish, bloody, starved, and ravenous *Mer. of Venice* iv 1 138
Fair ladies, you drop manna in the way Of starved people . . v 1 295
Starved for meat, giddy for lack of sleep . . . *T. of Shrew* iv 3 9
The turkeys in my pannier are quite starved . . . 1 *Hen. IV.* ii 1 30
This same starved justice hath done nothing but prate to me 2 *Hen. IV.* iii 2 327
Ay, come, you starved blood-hound . . . . v 4 31
Do but behold yon poor and starved band . . . *Hen. V.* iv 2 16
She should have stayed in France and starved in France . 2 *Hen. VI.* i 1 135
I fear me you but warm the starved snake . . . . . iii 1 343
It is too starved a subject for my sword . . . *Troi. and Cres.* i 1 96
That kiss is comfortless As frozen water to a starved snake *T. Andron.* iii 1 252
In that sparing makes huge waste, For beauty starved with her severity Cuts beauty off from all posterity . . . . . *Rom. and Jul.* i 1 225
They are now starved for want of exercise . . . *Pericles* i 4 38
Make your needy bread, And give them life whom hunger starved half dead . . . . i 4 96
Starve-lackey. Master Starve-lackey the rapier and dagger man *M. for M.* iv 3 15
Starveling. Robin Starveling, you must play Thisby's mother *M. N. D.* i 2 62
Starveling! God's my life, stolen hence, and left me asleep! . . iv 1 208
Old Sir John hangs with me, and thou knowest he is no starveling 1 *Hen. IV.* ii 1 76
'Sblood, you starveling, you elf-skin, you dried neat's tongue! . ii 4 270
Starveth. Need and oppression starveth in thine eyes . *Rom. and Jul.* v 1 70
Starving. Moody beggars, starving for a time Of pellmell havoc 1 *Hen. IV.* v 1 81
State. Whom . . . I loved and to him put The manage of my state *Temp.* i 2 70
The government I cast upon my brother And to my state grew stranger i 2 76
Set all hearts i' the state To what tune pleased his ear . . i 2 84
If th' other two be brained like us, the state totters . . . iii 2 8
High'st queen of state, Great Juno, comes; I know her by her gait . iv 1 101
Plead a new state in thy unrival'd merit . . . *T. G. of Ver.* v 4 144
My state being gall'd with my expense, I seek to heal it *Mer. Wives* iii 4 5
In state as wholesome as in state 'tis fit, Worthy the owner . v 5 63
In love the heavens themselves do guide the state . . . v 5 245
Acquaint her with the danger of my state . . *Meas. for Meas.* i 2 184
We do learn By those that know the very nerves of state . . i 4 53
The state, whereon I studied, Is like a good thing, being often read, Grown fear'd and tedious . . . . ii 4 7
My place i' the state Will so your accusation overweigh . . ii 4 156
It was a mad fantastical trick of him to steal from the state . . iii 2 99
My business in this state Made me a looker on here in Vienna . v 1 318
Slander to the state! Away with him to prison! . . . . v 1 325
That's not my fault: he's master of my state . . *Com. of Errors* ii 1 95
Whose weakness married to thy stronger state Makes me with thy strength to communicate . . . . ii 2 177
To thy state of darkness hie thee straight . . . . . iv 4 59
Mannerly-modest, as a measure, full of state and ancientry . *Much Ado* ii 1 80
So politic a state of evil that they will not admit any good part . v 2 63
Conjoin'd In the state of honourable marriage . . . . . v 4 30
A gait, a state, a brow, a breast, a waist, A leg, a limb . *L. L. Lost* iv 3 185
Flat treason 'gainst the kingly state of youth . . . . iv 3 293
So perttaunt-like would I o'ersway his state That he should be my fool v 2 67
Trim gallants, full of courtship and of state . . . . v 2 363
Our states are forfeit: seek not to undo us . . . . . v 2 425
Keep some state in thy exit, and vanish . . . . . . v 2 598
The summer still doth tend upon my state . . . *M. N. Dream* iii 1 158
When I told you My state was nothing, I should then have told you That I was worse than nothing . . . . *Mer. of Venice* iii 2 262
Doth impeach the freedom of the state, If they deny him justice . iii 2 280
If it be denied, Will much impeach the justice of his state . . iii 3 29
Purchasing the semblance of my soul From out the state of hellish misery! . . . . iii 4 21
And pluck commiseration of his state From brassy bosoms . . iv 1 30
Many an error by the same example Will rush into the state . . iv 1 222
Thy lands and goods Are, by the laws of Venice, confiscate Unto the state . . . . iv 1 312
The other half Comes to the privy coffer of the state . . . iv 1 354
Thy wealth being forfeit to the state, Thou hast not left the value of a cord; Therefore thou must be hang'd at the state's charge . . iv 1 365
Half thy wealth, it is Antonio's; The other half comes to the general state . . . . iv 1 371
Ay, for the state, not for Antonio . . . . iv 1 373
Then his state Empties itself, as doth an inland brook . . . v 1 95
Something that hath a reference to my state . . . *As Y. Like It* i 3 129
Thou art in a parlous state, shepherd . . . . iii 2 45
Shall share the good of our returned fortune, According to the measure of their states . . . . v 4 181
Were my state far worser than it is, I would not wed her . *T. of Shrew* i 2 91
Bianca's love Made me exchange my state with Tranio . . . v 1 128
Come, come, disclose The state of your affection . . *All's Well* i 3 196
Give pity To her, whose state is such that cannot choose . . i 3 220
My low and humble name to propagate With any branch or image of thy state . . . . ii 1 201
My state that way is dangerous . . . . ii 5 12
The reasons of our state I cannot yield . . . . . . iii 1 10
What is your parentage?—Above my fortunes, yet my state is well *T. N.* i 5 297

State. My state is desperate for my master's love *T. Night* ii 2 38
An affectioned ass, that cons state without book ii 3 161
Having been three months married to her, sitting in my state ii 5 50
And then to have the humour of state ii 5 58
Let thy tongue tang arguments of state ii 5 164; iii 4 78
Desperate of shame and state, In private brabble did we apprehend him v 1 67
Thy beauty scratch'd with briers, and made More homely than thy state *W. Tale* iv 4 437
Beseech you, Of your own state take care iv 4 459
You pity not the state, nor the remembrance Of his most sovereign name v 1 25
Cut off the sequence of posterity, Out-faced infant state *K. John* ii 1 97
How like you this wild counsel, mighty states? ii 1 395
To me and to the state of my great grief Let kings assemble iii 1 70
Troubled not the land With any long'd-for change or better state iv 2 8
My state is braved, Even at my gates, with ranks of foreign powers iv 2 243
The unowed interest of proud-swelling state iv 3 147
Useful serving-man and instrument, To any sovereign state v 2 82
May your sweet self put on The lineal state and glory of the land! v 7 102
'Gainst us, our state, our subjects, or our land *Richard II.* i 3 190
Thy state of law is bondslave to the law ii 1 114
Unhappy day, too late, O'erthrows thy joys, friends, fortune, and thy state iii 2 72
Thy very beadsmen learn to bend their bows . . . against thy state iii 2 117
Scoffing his state and grinning at his pomp iii 2 163
Men judge by the complexion of the sky The state and inclination of the day iii 2 195
My wretchedness unto a row of pins, They'll talk of state iii 4 27
Poor queen! so that thy state might be no worse, I would my skill were subject to thy curse iii 4 102
Which tired majesty did make thee offer, The resignation of thy state iv 1 179
You may my glories and my state depose, But not my griefs iv 1 192
With mine own tongue deny my sacred state iv 1 209
Against the state and profit of this land iv 1 225
Sovereignty a slave, Proud majesty a subject, state a peasant iv 1 252
Learn, good soul, To think our former state a happy dream v 1 18
Whose state and honour I for aye allow v 2 40
The concord of my state and time Had not an ear to hear my true time broke v 5 47
To thy sacred state wish I all happiness v 6 6
This chair shall be my state, this dagger my sceptre *1 Hen. IV.* ii 4 416
Thy state is taken for a joined-stool, thy golden sceptre for a leaden dagger ii 4 418
And so my state, Seldom but sumptuous, showed like a feast iii 2 57
Carded his state, Mingled his royalty with capering fools iii 2 62
He hath more worthy interest to the state Than thou the shadow of succession iii 2 98
As ever offer'd foul play in a state iii 2 169
Thou knowest in the state of innocency Adam fell iii 3 186
I would the state of time had first been whole iv 1 25
Were it good To set the exact wealth of all our states All at one cast? iv 1 46
And in the neck of that, task'd the whole state iv 3 92
You did swear . . . That you did nothing purpose 'gainst the state v 1 43
But these mine eyes saw him in bloody state *2 Hen. IV.* i 1 107
Under the canopies of costly state iii 1 13
Necessity so bow'd the state That I and greatness were compell'd to kiss iii 1 73
The king that loved him, as the state stood then, Was force perforce compell'd to banish him iv 1 115
Up, vanity! Down, royal state! iv 5 121
And lying still might make them look Too near unto my state iv 5 213
As you are a king, speak in your state What I have done v 2 99
Back to the sea, Where it shall mingle with the state of floods v 2 132
Our state may go In equal rank with the best govern'd nation v 2 136
We will accite, As I before remember'd, all our state v 2 142
Therefore doth heaven divide The state of man in divers functions *Hen. V.* i 2 184
Tell the Dauphin I will keep my state, Be like a king i 2 273
With what great state he heard their embassy ii 4 32
Whose state so many had the managing, That they lost France Epil. 11
Comets, importing change of times and states *1 Hen. VI.* i 1 2
More blessed hap did ne'er befall our state i 6 10
When his holy state is touch'd so near.—State holy or unhallow'd, what of that? iii 1 58
Such as shall pretend Malicious practices against his state iv 1 7
The states of Christendom, Moved with remorse v 4 96
Brave peers of England, pillars of the state *2 Hen. VI.* i 1 75
The state of Normandy Stands on a tickle point i 1 215
Wake when others be asleep, To pry into the secrets of the state i 1 250
Set the triple crown upon his head: That were a state fit for his holiness i 3 67
Have practised dangerously against your state ii 1 171
There to be used according to your state.—That's bad enough ii 4 95
Like to a duchess . . . ; According to that state you shall be used ii 4 99
Suborned some to swear False allegations to o'erthrow his state iii 1 181
That dread King that took our state upon him To free us iii 2 154
My thoughts do hourly prophesy Mischance unto my state iii 2 284
Thus stands my state, 'twixt Cade and York distress'd iv 9 31
Sufficeth that I have maintains my state iv 10 24
Seditious to his grace and to the state v 1 37
Look where the sturdy rebel sits, Even in the chair of state *3 Hen. VI.* i 1 51
And over the chair of state, where now he sits, Write up his title i 1 168
But that I hate thee deadly, I should lament thy miserable state i 4 85
Had he match'd according to his state, He might have kept that glory ii 2 152
By my state I swear to thee I speak no more than what my soul intends iii 2 93
It ill befits thy state And birth, that thou shouldst stand iii 3 2
Replant Henry in his former state iii 3 198
Before it pleased his majesty To raise my state to title of a queen iv 1 68
Though fortune's malice overthrow my state, My mind exceeds the compass of her wheel iv 3 46
And turn'd my captive state to liberty, My fear to hope iv 6 3
I shall interchange My waned state for Henry's regal crown iv 7 4
His state usurp'd, His realm a slaughter-house v 4 77
Thy honour, state, and seat is due to me *Richard III.* i 3 112
So stood the state when Henry the Sixth Was crown'd in Paris but at nine months old.—Stood the state so? No, no, good friends, God wot ii 3 16
What news, what news, in this our tottering state? iii 2 37
Think you, but that I know our state secure, I would be so triumphant? iii 2 83
Were jocund, and supposed their state was sure iii 2 86
And I in better state than e'er I was iii 2 106
Your state of fortune and your due of birth iii 7 120
Alas, why would you heap these cares on me? I am unfit for state iii 7 205

State. What state, what dignity, what honour, Canst thou demise to any child of mine? *Richard III.* iv 4 246
Urge the necessity and state of times, And be not peevish-fond iv 4 416
A serious brow, Sad, high, and working, full of state and woe *Hen. VIII.* Prol. 3
The state takes notice of the private difference Betwixt you i 1 101
I know but of a single part, in aught Pertains to the state i 2 42
You would swear directly Their very noses had been counsellors To Pepin or Clotharius, they keep state so i 3 10
That trick of state Was a deep envious one ii 1 44
Let it alone; my state now will but mock me ii 1 101
The least word that might Be to the prejudice of her present state ii 4 154
The question did at first so stagger me, Bearing a state of mighty moment in't ii 4 213
We are contented To wear our mortal state to come with her ii 4 228
Papers of state he sent me to peruse, As I required iii 2 121
A time To think upon the part of business which I bear i' the state iii 2 146
Have I not made you The prime man of the state? iii 2 162
Mine own ends Have been mine so that evermore they pointed To the good of your most sacred person and The profit of the state iii 2 174
As you respect the common good, the state Of our despised nobility iii 2 290
Without the king's will or the state's allowance iii 2 322
This is the state of man: to-day he puts forth The tender leaves of hopes iii 2 352
In a rich chair of state iv 1 67
So she parted, And with the same full state paced back again iv 1 93
An old man, broken with the storms of state iv 2 21
Know you not How your state stands i' the world, with the whole world? v 1 127
Who holds his state at door, 'mongst pursuivants, Pages, and footboys v 2 24
Commotions, uproars, with a general taint Of the whole state v 3 29
For kindling such a combustion in the state v 4 52
Rend and deracinate The unity and married calm of states *Troi. and Cres.* i 3 100
Makes factious feasts; rails on our state of war i 3 191
Did move your greatness and this noble state To call upon him ii 3 118
Please it our great general To call together all his state of war ii 3 271
You are in the state of grace.—Grace! not so, friend iii 1 15
And mighty states characterless are grated To dusty nothing iii 2 195
Is that a wonder? The providence that's in a watchful state Knows almost every grain of Plutus' gold iii 3 196
There is a mystery—with whom relation Durst never meddle—in the soul of state; Which hath an operation more divine iii 3 202
Is it so concluded?—By Priam and the general state of Troy iv 2 69
Hail, all you state of Greece! what shall be done? iv 5 65
The general state, I fear, Can scarce entreat you to be odd with him iv 5 264
You may as well Strike at the heaven with your staves as lift them Against the Roman state *Coriolanus* i 1 71
You slander The helms o' the state, who care for you like fathers i 1 79
What ever have been thought on in this state, That could be brought to bodily act ere Rome Had circumvention? i 2 4
Here's a letter from him: the state hath another ii 1 118
Make us think Rather our state's defective for requital ii 2 54
When he had no power, But was a petty servant to the state ii 3 186
Arriving A place of potency and sway o' the state ii 3 190
They nourish'd disobedience, fed The ruin of the state iii 1 118
Even when the navel of the state was touch'd iii 1 123
That love the fundamental part of state More than you doubt the change on't iii 1 151
Your dishonour Mangles true judgement and bereaves the state iii 1 158
The violent fit o' the time craves it as physic For the whole state iii 2 34
I have a note from the Volscian state, to find you out there iv 3 11
Hath been! is it ended, then? Our state thinks not so iv 3 17
Is he in Antium?—He is, and feasts the nobles of the state iv 4 9
He bears all things fairly, And shows good husbandry for the Volscian state iv 7 22
It was a bare petition of a state To one whom they had punish'd v 1 20
By your leave, I am an officer of state v 2 3
If thou standest not i' the state of hanging v 2 70
Suits, Nor from the state nor private friends, hereafter Will I lend ear to v 3 18
Our raiment And state of bodies would bewray what life We have led v 3 95
He sits in his state, as a thing made for Alexander v 4 22
You lords and heads o' the state, perfidiously He has betray'd your business v 6 91
For your honour and your state, Will use you nobly *T. Andron.* i 1 259
Afterwards, to order well the state, That like events may ne'er it ruinate v 3 203
In this state she gallops night by night Through lovers' brains *R. and J.* i 4 70
More honourable state, more courtship lives In carrion-flies than Romeo iii 3 34
Here stands all your state iii 3 166
I have need of many orisons To move the heavens to smile upon my state iv 3 4
We have cull'd such necessaries As are behoveful for our state to-morrow iv 3 8
All deserts, all kind of natures, That labour on the bosom of this sphere To propagate their states *T. of Athens* i 1 67
I thank your lordship: never may That state or fortune fall into my keeping, Which is not owed to you! i 1 150
Those healths will make thee and thy state look ill i 2 58
His promises fly so beyond his state That what he speaks is all in debt i 2 203
It cannot hold; no reason Can found his state in safety ii 1 13
Wherefore ere this time Had you not fully laid my state before me? ii 2 134
Even to the state's best health, I have Deserved this hearing ii 2 206
To have his pomp and all what state compounds But only painted iv 2 35
When neighbour states, But for thy sword and fortune, trod upon them iv 3 94
Best state, contentless, Hath a distracted and most wretched being iv 3 245
Would have brook'd The eternal devil to keep his state in Rome *J. Cæsar* i 2 160
Make them instruments of fear and warning Unto some monstrous state i 3 71
The state of man, Like to a little kingdom, suffers then ii 1 67
Acted over In states unborn and accents yet unknown iii 1 113
Thorough the hazards of this untrod state iii 1 136
Thou shalt discourse To young Octavius of the state of things iii 1 296
He can report . . . of the revolt The newest state *Macbeth* i 2 3
Shakes so my single state of man that function Is smother'd in surmise i 3 140
Our duties Are to your throne and state children and servants i 4 25
When therewithal we shall have cause of state Craving us jointly iii 1 34
Our hostess keeps her state, but in best time We will require her welcome iii 4 5
I am not to you known, Though in your state of honour I am perfect iv 2 66
Will seem as pure as snow, and the poor state Esteem him as a lamb iv 3 53
This bodes some strange eruption to our state *Hamlet* i 1 69
As it doth well appear unto our state i 1 101
In the most high and palmy state of Rome i 1 113
Our queen, The imperial jointress to this warlike state i 2 9
Or thinking by our late dear brother's death Our state to be disjoint i 2 20
On his choice depends The safety and health of this whole state i 3 21

State. Something is rotten in the state of Denmark . . . *Hamlet* i 4 90
Let me be no assistant for a state, But keep a farm and carters . . ii 2 166
'Gainst Fortune's state would treason have pronounced . . ii 2 534
With a crafty madness, keeps aloof, When we would bring him on to some confession Of his true state . . . . iii 1 10
The expectancy and rose of the fair state, The glass of fashion . . iii 1 160
So far from cheer and from your former state, That I distrust you . iii 2 174
O wretched state! O bosom black as death! O limed soul! . . iii 3 67
Thy state is the more gracious; for 'tis a vice to know him . . v 2 86
Divest us, both of rule, Interest of territory, cares of state . *Lear* i 1 51
Divisions in state, menaces and maledictions against king and nobles . i 2 159
And shall find time From this enormous state . . . . . ii 2 176
Death on my state! wherefore Should he sit here? . . . . ii 4 113
You should be ruled and led By some discretion, that discerns your state Better than you yourself . . . . ii 4 151
The spies and speculations Intelligent of our state . . . . iii 1 25
With plumed helm thy state begins to threat . . . . . iv 2 57
Something he left imperfect in the state . . . . . . iv 3 3
With others whom the rigour of our state Forced to cry out . . v 1 22
My state Stands on me to defend, not to debate . . . . v 1 68
You twain Rule in this realm, and the gored state sustain . . v 3 320
Let loose on me the justice of the state For thus deluding you . *Othello* i 1 140
I do know, the state, However this may gall him with some check, Cannot with safety cast him . . . . i 1 148
Upon some present business of the state . . . . . . i 2 90
Any of my brothers of the state Cannot but feel this wrong as 'twere their own . . . . i 2 96
So was I bid report here to the state. . . . . . . i 3 15
Most humbly therefore bending to your state . . . . . i 3 236
Something, sure, of state . . . . iii 4 140
The business of the state does him offence, And he does chide with you iv 2 166
You shall close prisoner rest, Till that the nature of your fault be known To the Venetian state . . . . v 2 337
I have done the state some service, and they know't . . . . v 2 339
In Aleppo once, Where a malignant and a turban'd Turk Beat a Venetian and traduced the state. . . . . v 2 354
And to the state This heavy act with heavy heart relate. . . . v 2 370
That war had end, and the time's state Made friends of them . *A. and C.* i 2 95
The business she hath broached in the state Cannot endure my absence i 2 178
Into the hearts of such as have not thrived Upon the present state . i 3 52
And speaks as loud As his own state and ours . . . . . i 4 30
It hath been taught us from the primal state, That he which is was wish'd until he were . . . . i 4 41
Yet, if you there Did practise on my state, your being in Egypt Might be my question . . . . ii 2 39
In state of health thou say'st; and thou say'st free . . . . ii 5 56
Quake in the present winter's state . . . . . *Cymbeline* ii 4 5
And we will fear no poison, which attends In place of greater state . iii 3 78
Kings, queens, and states, Maids, matrons, nay, the secrets of the grave This viperous slander enters . . . . iii 4 39
Ask of Cymbeline what boon thou wilt, Fitting my bounty and thy state v 5 98
Will look so huge, Amazement shall drive courage from the state *Pericles* i 2 26
A pretty moral; From the dejected state wherein he is, He hopes by you his fortunes yet may flourish . . . . ii 2 46
I came unto your court for honour's cause, And not to be a rebel to her state . . . . ii 5 62
Shrouded in cloth of state; balm'd and entreasured With full bags of spices! . . . . iii 2 65
Though wayward fortune did malign my state . . . . . . v 1 90
State-affairs. Your special mandate for the state-affairs . . . *Othello* i 3 72
I have done. Please it your grace, on to the state-affairs . . . i 3 190
Statelier. A statelier pyramis to her I'll rear Than Rhodope's or Memphis' ever was . . . . *1 Hen. VI.* i 6 21
Stately. With slow but stately pace kept on his course . *Richard II.* v 2 10
Death's dishonourable victory We with our stately presence glorify *1 Hen. VI.* i 1 21
Even with the earth Shall lay your stately and air-braving towers . iv 2 13
Here is a silly stately style indeed! . . . . iv 7 72
What rests but that we spend the time With stately triumphs? *3 Hen. VI.* v 7 43
Like the stately Phœbe 'mongst her nymphs . . . *T. Andron.* i 1 316
Our empress' shame, and stately Rome's disgrace! . . . . iv 2 60
And with solemn march Goes slow and stately by them . . *Hamlet* i 2 202
When from a stately cedar shall be lopped branches *Cymbeline* v 4 140; v 5 438
State-matters. Pray heaven it be state-matters, as you think *Othello* iii 4 155
Statesman. He shall appear to the envious a scholar, a statesman, and a soldier . . . . *Meas. for Meas.* iii 2 155
My parasite, my soldier, statesman, all . . . *W. Tale* i 2 168
Statesmen. If such actions may have passage free, Bond-slaves and pagans shall our statesmen be . . . . *Othello* i 2 99
State-statue. Or sit State-statues only . . . . *Hen. VIII.* i 2 88
Statilius show'd the torch-light, but, my lord, He came not back *J. Cæsar* v 5 2
Station. And puff To win a vulgar station . . . *Coriolanus* ii 1 231
Poor gentleman, take up some other station; here's no place for you iv 5 33
If you have a station in the file, Not i' the worst rank of manhood *Macb.* iii 1 102
The which no sooner had his prowess confirm'd In the unshrinking station where he fought, But like a man he died . . . . . v 8 42
They in France of the best rank and station Are of a most select and generous chief in that . . . . *Hamlet* i 3 73
A station like the herald Mercury New-lighted on a heaven-kissing hill iii 4 58
She creeps: Her motion and her station are as one . *Ant. and Cleo.* iii 3 22
Statist. Hold it, as our statists do, A baseness to write fair . *Hamlet* v 2 33
I do believe, Statist though I am none, nor like to be . . *Cymbeline* ii 4 16
Statua. Erect his statua and worship it . . . . *2 Hen. VI.* iii 2 80
Like dumb statuas or breathing stones, Gazed each on other *Rich. III.* iii 7 25
She dreamt to-night she saw my statua, Which, like a fountain with an hundred spouts, Did run pure blood . . . . . . *J. Cæsar* ii 2 76
At the base of Pompey's statua, Which all the while ran blood . . iii 2 192
Statue. My substance should be statue in thy stead . *T. G. of Ver.* iv 4 206
With any man that knows the statues, he may stay him *Much Ado* iii 3 85
Her mother's statue, which is in the keeping of Paulina . . *W. Tale* v 2 103
We came To see the statue of our queen . . . . . . v 3 10
That which my daughter came to look upon, The statue of her mother . v 3 14
The statue is but newly fix'd, the colour's Not dry . . . . v 3 47
I'll make the statue move indeed, descend, And take you by the hand . v 3 88
We'll set thy statue in some holy place, And have thee reverenced *1 Hen. VI.* iii 3 14
The primitive statue, and oblique memorial of cuckolds *Troi. and Cres.* v 1 60
Make wells and Niobes of the maids and wives, Cold statues of the youth . . . . v 10 20
The nobles bended, As to Jove's statue . . . . *Coriolanus* ii 1 282
Statue. I will raise her statue in pure gold . . . *Rom. and Jul.* v 3 299
Set this up with wax Upon old Brutus' statue . . . . *J. Cæsar* i 3 146
Your statue spouting blood in many pipes . . . . . . ii 2 85
Give him a statue with his ancestors . . . . iii 2 55
She shows a body rather than a life, A statue than a breather *A. and C.* iii 3 24
To remember what he does, Build his statue to make him glorious *Pericles* ii Gower 14
Stature. How tall was she?—About my stature . . *T. G. of Ver.* iv 4 163
If he be of any reasonable stature, he may creep in here *Mer. Wives* iii 3 138
I perceive that she hath made compare Between our statures *M. N. D.* iii 2 291
What stature is she of?—Just as high as my heart . *As Y. Like It* iii 2 285
Care I for the limb, the thewes, the stature, bulk, and big assemblance of a man! Give me the spirit . . . . . . *2 Hen. IV.* iii 2 277
Her stature to an inch; as wand-like straight; As silver-voiced *Pericles* v 1 110
Statute. We have strict statutes and most biting laws *Meas. for Meas.* i 3 19
Follows close the rigour of the statute, To make him an example . . i 4 67
The strong statutes Stand like the forfeits in a barber's shop . . v 1 322
Have seal'd his rigorous statutes with their bloods . . *Com. of Errors* i 1 9
According to the statute of the town . . . . i 2 6
Against the laws and statutes of this town . . . . . . v 1 126
Keep those statutes That are recorded in this schedule here *L. L. Lost* i 1 17
My acts, decrees, and statutes I deny . . . . *Richard II.* iv 1 213
We are like to have biting statutes, unless his teeth be pulled out *2 Hen. VI.* iv 7 19
His statutes cancell'd and his treasure spent . . . *3 Hen. VI.* v 4 79
More piercing statutes daily, to chain up and restrain the poor *Coriol.* i 1 86
I' the olden time, Ere humane statute purged the gentle weal *Macbeth* iii 4 76
With his statutes, his recognizances, his fines, his double vouchers *Ham.* v 1 113
Statute-caps. Better wits have worn plain statute-caps . *L. L. Lost* v 2 281
Staves. He holds Belzebub at the staves' end . . . . *T. Night* v 1 292
Their armed staves in charge, their beavers down . *2 Hen. IV.* iv 1 120
If I were sawed into quantities, I should make four dozen of such bearded hermits' staves . . . . v 1 71
Look that my staves be sound, and not too heavy . . *Richard III.* v 3 65
Amaze the welkin with your broken staves! . . . . . . v 3 341
Fetch me a dozen crab-tree staves, and strong ones . . *Hen. VIII.* v 4 8
You may as well Strike at the heaven with your staves as lift them Against the Roman state . . . . *Coriolanus* i 1 70
I cannot strike at wretched kerns, whose arms Are hired to bear their staves . . . . *Macbeth* v 7 18
Stay. Left me to a bootless inquisition, Concluding 'Stay: not yet' *Tempest* i 2 36
Dinner is ready, and your father stays.—Well, let us go *T. G. of Ver.* i 2 131
No more of stay! to-morrow thou must go . . . . . . i 3 75
My father stays my coming; answer not . . . . ii 2 13
Nay, not thy tide of tears; That tide will stay me longer than I should ii 2 15
If you think so, then stay at home and go not . . . . . . ii 7 62
There is a messenger That stays to bear my letters . . . . iii 1 53
No matter; stay with me awhile . . . . iii 1 58
Here if thou stay, thou canst not see thy love . . . . . iii 1 244
Thy master stays for thee at the North-gate.—For me? . . . . iii 1 382
Come, coz; we stay for you. A word with you, coz . . *Mer. Wives* i 1 213
We stay for you.—I'll eat nothing, I thank you, sir . . . . i 1 314
Go into this closet: he will not stay long . . . . . . i 4 40
Bear vitness that me have stay six or seven, two, tree hours for him . ii 3 37
Have I not stay for him to kill him? have I not? . . . . iii 1 94
He sent me word to stay within: I like his money well . . . . iii 5 59
Come, we stay too long . . . . iv 1 87
I'll be so bold as stay, sir, till she come down. . . . . . iv 5 13
Procure the vicar To stay for me at church 'twixt twelve and one . iv 6 49
But, stay; I smell a man of middle-earth . . . . v 5 84
Stay a little while. You're welcome . . . . *Meas. for Meas.* ii 2 26
Stay awhile, And you shall be conducted. . . . . ii 3 17
My stay must be stolen out of other affairs . . . . . . iii 1 158
Your stay with him may not be long . . . . iii 1 256
I have possess'd him my most stay Can be but brief . . . . iv 1 44
I have a servant comes with me along, That stays upon me . . . iv 1 47
There he must stay until the officer Arise to let him in . . . . iv 2 93
Call at Flavius' house, And tell him where I stay . . . . . iv 5 7
Stay, sir; stay awhile.—What, resists he? . . . . v 1 354
Go bear it to the Centaur, where we host, And stay there *Com. of Errors* i 2 10
My mistress and her sister stays for you . . . . i 2 76
What patch is made our porter? My master stays in the street . . iii 1 36
The chain unfinish'd made me stay thus long . . . . . . iii 2 173
I'll to the mart and there for Dromio stay . . . . . . iii 2 189
See him presently discharged, For he is bound to sea and stays but for it iv 1 33
A bark of Epidamnum That stays but till her owner comes aboard . . iv 1 86
They stay for nought at all But for their owner . . . . . iv 1 91
Thou peevish sheep, What ship of Epidamnum stays for me? . . . iv 1 94
Faith, stay here this night; they will surely do us no harm . . . iv 4 155
I could find in my heart to stay here still and turn witch . . . iv 4 160
I will not stay to-night for all the town; Therefore away . . . iv 4 161
I, sir, am Dromio: pray, let me stay . . . . v 1 336
Stay, stand apart; I know not which is which . . . . . . v 1 364
I tell him we shall stay here at the least a month . . *Much Ado* i 1 150
I do but stay till your marriage be consummate . . . . . iii 2 1
If you meet the prince in the night, you may stay him . . . . iii 3 81
With any man that knows the statues, he may stay him . . . . iii 3 85
It is an offence to stay a man against his will . . . . . . iii 3 88
They stay for you to give your daughter to her husband . . . . iii 5 59
And depart when you bid me.—O, stay but till then! . . . . . v 2 45
And stay here in your court for three years' space . . *L. L. Lost* i 1 52
I have sworn to stay with you . . . . i 1 111
For you'll prove perjured if you make me stay . . . . . . ii 1 113
I cannot stay thanksgiving . . . . ii 1 193
Stay, slave; I must employ thee . . . . iii 1 152
Stay not thy compliment; I forgive thy duty: adieu . . . . . iv 2 147
By whom shall I send this?—Company! stay . . . . iv 3 77
Walk aside the true folk, and let the traitors stay . . . . . iv 3 213
So shall we stay, mocking intended game . . . . v 2 155
Sweet Jude! nay, why dost thou stay?—For the latter end of his name v 2 629
I will away to-night.—Madam, not so; I do beseech you, stay . . . v 2 738
I'll stay with patience; but the time is long . . . . v 2 845
There will I stay for thee.—My good Lysander! . . . *M. N. Dream* i 1 168
How long within this wood intend you stay? . . . . ii 1 138
We shall chide downright, if I longer stay . . . . ii 1 145
I will not stay thy questions; let me go . . . . ii 1 235
Stay, though thou kill me . . . . ii 2 84
Stay, on thy peril: I alone will go . . . . ii 2 87
Stay thou but here awhile, And by and by I will to thee appear . . iii 1 88

Stay. In some slight measure it will pay, If for his tender here I make some stay . . . . *M. N. Dream* iii 2 87
Why should he stay, whom love doth press to go? . . . iii 2 184
Stay, gentle Helena; hear my excuse: My love, my life, my soul! iii 2 245
I will not trust you, I, Nor longer stay in your curst company iii 2 341
In courtesy, in all reason, we must stay the time . . . . v 1 259
But stay, O spite! But mark, poor knight! . . . . . v 1 281
Trip away; make no stay; Meet me all by break of day. . . v 1 428
To be ruled by my conscience, I should stay with the Jew *Mer. of Venice* ii 2 24
My conscience is but a kind of hard conscience, to offer to counsel me to stay . . . . ii 2 31
On, gentlemen; away! Our masquing mates by this time for us stay . ii 6 59
Where are all the rest? 'Tis nine o'clock: our friends all stay for you . ii 6 63
But stay the very riping of the time . . . . . . ii 8 40
To peize the time, To eke it and to draw it out in length, To stay you . iii 2 24
Till I come again, No bed shall e'er be guilty of my stay. . . iii 2 328
My coach, which stays for us At the park gate . . . iii 4 82
Here stays without A messenger with letters from the doctor . iv 1 107
I stay here on my bond . . . . iv 1 242
Why, then the devil give him good of it! I'll stay no longer question . iv 1 346
Whether till the next night she had rather stay, Or go to bed now . v 1 302
For my part, he keeps me rustically at home, or, to speak more properly, stays me here at home unkept . . . *As Y. Like It* i 1 8
She would have followed her exile, or have died to stay behind her . i 1 115
You might stay him from his intendment. . . . . i 1 139
Shall we see this wrestling, cousin?—You must, if you stay here . i 2 153
Yonder, sure, they are coming: let us now stay and see it . . i 2 157
I did not then entreat to have her stay; It was your pleasure . i 3 71
Jumps along by him And never stays to greet him . . . ii 1 54
Let me stay the growth of his beard . . . . . . iii 2 221
Who stays it [Time] still withal?—With lawyers in the vacation . iii 2 348
Stay, Jaques, stay.—To see no pastime I: what you would have I'll stay to know at your abandon'd cave . . . . . . v 4 202
Do you intend to stay with me to-night?—So please your lordship *T. of Shrew* Ind. 1 81
And how my men will stay themselves from laughter . . Ind. 1 134
But stay a while: what company is this? . . . . i 1 46
Katharina, you may stay; For I have more to commune with Bianca . i 1 100
I'll give her thanks, As though she bid me stay by her a week . ii 1 179
I must be gone.—Faith, mistress, then I have no cause to stay . iii 1 86
Means but well, Whatever fortune stays him from his word . . iii 2 23
But where is Kate? I stay too long from her: The morning wears . iii 2 112
If you knew my business, You would entreat me rather go than stay . iii 2 194
Let us entreat you stay till after dinner . . . . . iii 2 199
Are you content to stay?—I am content you shall entreat me stay; But yet not stay, entreat me how you can . . . . . iii 2 202
Father, be quiet: he shall stay my leisure . . . . iii 2 219
So shall you stay Till you have done your business in the city . iv 2 109
The tailor stays thy leisure, To deck thy body . . . iv 3 59
To stay him not too long, I am content . . . . . iv 4 30
Carry me to the gaol!—Stay, officer: he shall not go to prison . v 1 98
Let's away.—Nay, I will give thee a kiss: now pray thee, love, stay v 1 153
I'll stay at home And pray God's blessing into thy attempt . *All's Well* i 3 259
O my sweet lord, that you will stay behind us!—'Tis not his fault . ii 1 24
I shall stay here the forehorse to a smock, Creaking my shoes . ii 1 30
What will ye do?—Stay: the king . . . . . . ii 1 50
I pray you, stay not, but in haste to horse . . . . ii 5 92
My being here it is that holds thee hence: Shall I stay here to do't? . iii 2 127
I thank you, and will stay upon your leisure . . . . iii 5 48
And here we'll stay To see our widower's second marriage-day . v 3 69
I'll stay a month longer . . . . *T. Night* i 3 119
Will you stay no longer? nor will you not that I go with you? . . ii 1 1
Where are you roaming? O, stay and hear; your true love's coming . ii 3 41
Stay: I prithee, tell me what thou think'st of me . . . iii 1 149
I'll not stay a jot longer.—Thy reason, dear venom, give thy reason iii 2 1
I could not stay behind you . . . . iii 3 4
Stay you by this gentleman till my return . . . . iii 4 281
Come, away!—Whither, my lord? Cesario, husband, stay . . v 1 146
Stay your thanks a while; And pay them when you part . *W. Tale* i 2 9
No longer stay.—One seven-night longer . . . . . i 2 16
My stay To you a charge and trouble: to save both, Farewell . i 2 25
I had thought, sir, to have held my peace until You had drawn oaths from him not to stay . . . . i 2 29
He shall not stay, We'll thwack him hence with distaffs . . i 2 36
You'll stay?—No, madam.—Nay, but you will? . . . . i 2 44
Is he won yet?—He'll stay, my lord.—At my request he would not . i 2 87
My last good deed was to entreat his stay . . . . . i 2 97
This great sir will yet stay longer.—You had much ado to make his anchor hold . . . . i 2 212
He would not stay at your petitions; made His business more material i 2 215
How came't, Camillo, That he did stay?—At the good queen's entreaty i 2 220
Bohemia stays here longer.—Ha!—Stays here longer . . . i 2 230
Thou art worthy to be hang'd, That wilt not stay her tongue . . ii 3 110
Stay to execute them thyself . . . . iv 2 17
They cherish it [virtue] to make it stay there . . . . iv 3 98
Let them come in; but quickly now.—Why, they stay at door, sir . iv 4 352
Nothing so certain as your anchors, who Do their best office, if they can but stay you Where you'll be loath to be . . . . . . iv 4 582
Stay for an answer to your embassy . . . . . . *K. John* ii 1 44
Vouchsafe awhile to stay, And I shall show you peace and fair-faced league . . . . ii 1 416
Here's a stay That shakes the rotten carcass of old Death Out of his rags! ii 1 455
The glorious sun Stays in his course and plays the alchemist . . iii 1 78
Your grace shall stay behind So strongly guarded . . . . iii 3 1
And he that stands upon a slippery place Makes nice of no vile hold to stay him up . . . . iii 4 138
And so, farewell.—Stay yet, Lord Salisbury; I'll go with thee . iv 2 96
As good to die and go, as die and stay . . . . . iv 3 8
My heart hath one poor string to stay it by . . . . v 7 55
What surety of the world, what hope, what stay? . . . v 7 68
I do but stay behind To do the office for thee of revenge . . v 7 70
As much good stay with thee as go with me! . . . *Richard II.* i 2 57
Sprightfully and bold, Stays but the summons of the appellant's trumpet i 3 4
The champions are prepared, and stay For nothing but his majesty's approach . . . . i 3 5
Stay, the king hath thrown his warder down . . . . i 3 118
I'll bring thee on thy way: Had I thy youth and cause, I would not stay i 3 305
Be merry, for our time of stay is short . . . . . ii 1 223
They stay The first departing of the king for Ireland . . . ii 1 289
But if you faint, as fearing to do so, Stay and be secret . . . ii 1 298
Stay. Stay yet another day, thou trusty Welshman . *Richard II.* ii 4 5
'Tis thought the king is dead; we will not stay . . . . ii 4 7
But stay, here come the gardeners: Let's step into the shadow . iii 4 24
They tend the crown, yet still with me they stay . . . iv 1 199
Stay thy revengeful hand; thou hast no cause to fear . . v 3 42
Give place; here is no longer stay . . . . . . v 5 95
What, drunk with choler? stay and pause awhile . *1 Hen. IV.* i 3 129
We will stay your leisure.—I have done, i' faith . . . i 3 258
Only stays but to behold the face Of that occasion that shall bring it on i 3 275
Pray stay a little, my lord . . . . ii 4 63
I fear we shall stay too long . . . . iv 2 83
For God's sake, cousin, stay till all come in . . . . iv 3 29
Stay, and breathe awhile: Thou hast redeem'd thy lost opinion . v 4 47
But he did long in vain. Who then persuaded you to stay at home? *2 Hen. IV.* ii 3 15
A dozen captains stay at door for you . . . . . ii 4 402
And, for mine own part, have a desire to stay with my friends . iii 2 241
For you, Mouldy, stay at home till you are past service . . iii 2 269
Now, where is he that will not stay so long Till his friend sickness hath determined me? . . . . iv 5 81
I stay too long by thee, I weary thee . . . . . . iv 5 94
Thou seek'st the greatness that will overwhelm thee. Stay but a little iv 5 99
Doth the man of war stay all night, sir? . . . . . v 1 31
It follows then the cat must stay at home . . . . *Hen. V.* i 2 174
That you shall read In your own losses, if he stay in France . ii 4 139
Stay: the knocks are too hot . . . . iii 2 3
You shall stay with us in Rouen.—Not so, I do beseech your majesty . iii 5 64
I will go with thee: The day, my friends, and all things stay for me . iv 1 326
Why do you stay so long, my lords of France? . . . . iv 2 38
They have said their prayers, and they stay for death . . iv 2 56
I stay but for my guidon: to the field! . . . . . iv 2 60
I must stay with the lackeys, with the luggage of our camp . . iv 4 79
The lamentation of the French Invites the King of England's stay at home . . . . v Prol. 37
Will you, fair sister, Go with the princes, or stay here with us? . v 2 91
Stay, stay thy hands! thou art an Amazon . . *1 Hen. VI.* i 2 104
A rope! a rope! Now beat them hence; why do you let them stay? . i 3 54
Now do thou watch, for I can stay no longer . . . . i 4 18
Our English troops retire, I cannot stay them . . . . i 5 2
Stay, lords and gentlemen, and pluck no more . . . . ii 4 39
These feet, whose strengthless stay is numb . . . . . ii 5 13
Stay, stay, I say! And if you love me, as you say you do . . iii 1 103
Stay, let thy humble handmaid speak to thee.—Speak on . . iii 3 42
If we both stay, we both are sure to die.—Then let me stay . iv 5 20
There is no hope that ever I will stay, If the first hour I shrink . iv 5 30
Stay, go, do what you will, the like do I . . . . . iv 5 50
By me they nothing gain an if I stay . . . . . . iv 6 36
All these and more we hazard by thy stay . . . . . iv 6 40
O, stay! I have no power to let her pass . . . . . v 3 60
But, Suffolk, stay; Thou mayst not wander in that labyrinth . v 3 187
If I longer stay, We shall begin our ancient bickerings . *2 Hen. VI.* i 1 143
God shall be my hope, My stay, my guide, and lantern to my feet . ii 3 25
Please your grace, here my commission stays . . . . ii 4 76
Witness my tears, I cannot stay to speak.—Art thou gone too? . ii 4 86
Stay, Salisbury, With the rude multitude till I return . . iii 2 134
O Thou that judgest all things, stay my thoughts! . . . . iii 2 136
O, let me stay, befall what may befall! . . . . . . iii 2 402
But stay, I'll read it over once again . . . . . . iv 4 14
In this city will I stay And live alone as secret as I may . . iv 4 47
Now am I so hungry that if I might have a lease of my life for a thousand years I could stay no longer . . . . iv 10 7
Good Margaret, stay.—What are you made of? you'll nor fight nor fly . v 2 73
Stay by me, my lords; And, soldiers, stay and lodge by me . *3 Hen. VI.* i 1 31
Arm'd as we are, let's stay within this house . . . . . i 1 38
I cannot stay to hear these articles.—Nor I . . . . . i 1 180
Be patient, gentle queen, and I will stay.—Who can be patient? . i 1 214
Stay, gentle Margaret, and hear me speak.—Thou hast spoke too much i 1 257
Gentle son Edward, thou wilt stay with me?—Ay, to be murder'd . i 1 259
But, stay: what news? Why comest thou in such post? . . . i 2 48
You shall stay with me; My brother Montague shall post to London . i 2 54
Here must I stay, and here my life must end . . . . i 4 26
Nay, stay; let's hear the orisons he makes . . . . . i 4 110
Now thou art gone, we have no staff, no stay . . . . . ii 1 69
Ne'er may he live to see a sunshine day, That cries 'Retire,' if Warwick bid him stay . . . . ii 1 188
Stay we no longer, dreaming of renown, But sound the trumpets . ii 1 199
Leave us to our fortune.—Why, that's my fortune too; therefore I'll stay ii 2 76
No, nor your manhood that durst make you stay . . . . ii 2 108
Stay, Edward.—No, wrangling woman, we'll no longer stay . . ii 2 175
Give them leave to fly that will not stay . . . . . ii 3 50
O that my death would stay these ruthful deeds! . . . . ii 5 95
Stay not to expostulate, make speed; Or else come after . . ii 5 135
Not that I fear to stay, but love to go . . . . . . ii 5 138
I'll stay above the hill, so both may shoot . . . . . iii 1 5
Here comes a man; let's stay till he be past . . . . . iii 1 12
But stay thee, 'tis the fruits of love I mean . . . . iii 2 58
The more we stay, the stronger grows our foe . . . . iii 3 40
The more I stay, the more I'll succour thee . . . . iii 3 41
Why stay we now? These soldiers shall be levied . . . . iii 3 251
How could he stay till Warwick made return? . . . . . iv 1 5
I Stay not for the love of Edward, but the crown . . . . iv 1 126
Who goes there?—Stay, or thou diest! . . . . . . iv 3 27
But wherefore stay we? 'tis no time to talk . . . . . iv 5 24
Nay, stay, Sir John, awhile, and we'll debate . . . . iv 7 51
Stay, you that bear the corse, and set it down . . *Richard III.* i 2 33
And leave out thee? stay, dog, for thou shalt hear me . . i 3 216
In falling, Struck me, that thought to stay him, overboard . . i 4 19
I pray thee, gentle keeper, stay by me; My soul is heavy . . i 4 73
I pray thee, stay a while: I hope my holy humour will change . i 4 120
I must away; For this will out, and here I must not stay . . i 4 290
What stay had I but Edward? and he's gone.—What stay had we but Clarence? and he's gone.—What stays had I but they? and they are gone . . . . ii 2 74
Towards Ludlow then, for we'll not stay behind . . . . ii 2 154
But long I shall not stay: I shall return before your lordship . iii 2 120
I stay dinner there.—And supper too, although thou know'st it not . iii 2 122
To stay him from the fall of vanity . . . . iii 7 97
Stay, yet look back with me unto the Tower . . . . . iv 1 98
O thou well skill'd in curses, stay awhile, And teach me how to curse! iv 4 116
I say amen to all.—Stay, madam; I must speak a word with you . iv 4 198

Stay. Stay with me. The Earl of Pembroke keeps his regiment *Rich. III.* v 3 28
Stay, my lord, And let your reason with your choler question *Hen. VIII.* i 1 129
My barge stays; Your lordship shall along . . . i 3 63
Stay there, sir, And see the noble ruin'd man you speak of . . . ii 1 53
The cardinal did entreat his holiness To stay the judgement o' the divorce iii 2 33
Stay, good my lords, I have a little yet to say . . . v 3 97
This day, no man think Has business at his house; for all shall stay . v 5 76
Stay the cooling too, or you may chance to burn your lips *Troi. and Cres.* i 1 25
She's a fool to stay behind her father; let her to the Greeks . i 1 83
He stays for you to conduct him thither.—O, here he comes . iii 2 3
Beshrew the witch! with venomous wights she stays As tediously as hell iv 2 12
This Ajax is half made of Hector's blood: In love whereof, half Hector stays at home . . . iv 5 84
Fail fame; honour or go or stay; My major vow lies here, this I'll obey v 1 48
I pray you, stay; by hell and all hell's torments, I will not speak a word! v 2 43
Nay, stay; by Jove, I will not speak a word . . . v 2 54
Why stay we, then?—To make a recordation to my soul . . v 2 115
Ajax, your guard, stays to conduct you home . . . v 2 184
He is thy crutch; now if thou lose thy stay, Thou on him leaning . v 3 60
Hector is dead; there is no more to say. Stay yet. . v 10 23
The other side o' the city is risen: why stay we prating here? *Coriolanus* i 1 49
I'll lean upon one crutch and fight with t'other, Ere stay behind . i 1 247
Yet oft, When blows have made me stay, I fled from words . ii 2 76
We are not to stay all together . . . ii 3 45
Will you along?—We stay here for the people . . . ii 3 158
This mutiny were better put in hazard, Than stay, past doubt, for greater ii 3 265
Peace! Stay, hold, peace!—What is about to be? I am out of breath iii 1 188
You shall stay too: I would I had the power To say so to my husband iv 2 15
I'll tell thee what; yet go: Nay, but thou shalt stay too . iv 2 23
Why stay we to be baited With one that wants her wits? . iv 2 43
He could not stay to pick them in a pile Of noisome musty chaff v 1 25
Stay: whence are you?—Stand, and go back . . . v 2 1
Our throats are sentenced and stay upon execution . . v 4 8
Stay not to talk with them . . . *T. Andron.* ii 3 306
Hear me, grave fathers! noble tribunes, stay! For pity of mine age iii 1 1
My hand: Good Aaron, wilt thou help to chop it off?—Stay, father! . iii 1 163
Now stay your strife: what shall be is dispatch'd . . iii 1 193
Thou art an exile, and thou must not stay: Hie to the Goths . iii 1 285
Stay, murderous villains! will you kill your brother? . . iv 2 88
So that perforce you must needs stay a time . . . iv 3 41
Let Rape and Murder stay with me; Or else I'll call my brother back v 2 134
This is our doom: Some stay to see him fasten'd in the earth . v 3 183
I would thou wert so happy by thy stay, To hear true shrift *Rom. and Jul.* i 1 164
She will not stay the siege of loving terms . . . i 1 218
To them say, My house and welcome on their pleasure stay . i 2 37
Ye say honestly: rest you merry!—Stay, fellow; I can read . i 2 66
Juliet, the county stays.—Go, girl, seek happy nights to happy days i 3 105
Sweet Montague, be true. Stay but a little, I will come again . ii 2 138
I'll still stay, to have thee still forget, Forgetting any other home but this ii 2 175
And stay, good nurse, behind the abbey wall . . . ii 4 199
Hast thou met with him? Send thy man away.—Peter, stay at the gate ii 5 20
Can you not stay awhile? Do you not see that I am out of breath? ii 5 29
Is thy news good, or bad? answer to that; Say either, and I'll stay the circumstance: Let me be satisfied . . . ii 5 36
Hence to Friar Laurence' cell; There stays a husband to make you a wife ii 5 71
You shall not stay alone Till holy church incorporate two in one . ii 6 36
Hence, be gone, away!—O, I am fortune's fool!—Why dost thou stay? iii 1 141
Romeo, arise; Thou wilt be taken. Stay awhile! Stand up . iii 3 75
Look thou stay not till the watch be set, For then thou canst not pass iii 3 148
I must be gone and live, or stay and die . . . iii 5 11
Therefore stay yet; thou need'st not to be gone . . iii 5 16
I have more care to stay than will to go: Come, death, and welcome! iii 5 23
Stay, Tybalt, stay! Romeo, I come! this do I drink to thee . iv 3 57
Tarry for the mourners, and stay dinner . . . iv 5 150
Stay not, be gone; live, and hereafter say, A madman's mercy bade thee run away . . . v 3 66
For fear of that, I still will stay with thee . . . v 3 106
Did menace me with death, If I did stay to look on his intents.—Stay, then . . . v 3 134
Stay not to question, for the watch is coming; Come, go, good Juliet, I dare no longer stay . . . v 3 158
A great suspicion: stay the friar too . . . v 3 187
Till I be gentle, stay thou for thy good morrow *T. of Athens* i 1 179
Let me stay at thine apperil, Timon: I come to observe . . i 2 32
Stay, stay, here comes the fool with Apemantus: let's ha' some sport . ii 2 47
Will you leave me there?—If Timon stay at home . . ii 2 96
Why then, women are more valiant That stay at home . . iii 5 48
Gentlemen, our dinner will not recompense this long stay . iii 6 35
Take thy physic first—thou too—and thou;—Stay, I will lend thee money iii 6 111
Let's make no stay . . . iii 6 128
Nay, stay thou out for earnest . . . iv 3 47
O, let me stay, And comfort you, my master . . . iv 3 540
Stay not, all's in vain . . . v 1 187
Pass by and curse thy fill, but pass and stay not here thy gait . v 4 73
I do know, by this, they stay for me In Pompey's porch . *J. Cæsar* i 3 125
Cæsar should be a beast without a heart, If he should stay at home to-day ii 2 43
Antony shall say I am not well; And, for thy humour, I will stay at home ii 2 56
I will let you know; Calpurnia here, my wife, stays me at home . ii 2 75
On her knee Hath begg'd that I will stay at home to-day . ii 2 82
Stay not to answer me, but get thee gone: Why dost thou stay?—To know my errand . . . ii 4 2
Yet, stay awhile; Thou shalt not back till I have borne this corse Into the market-place . . . iii 1 290
Those that will hear me speak, let 'em stay here . . iii 2 5
Let me depart alone, And, for my sake, stay here with Antony . iii 2 61
Stay, countrymen.—Peace there! hear the noble Antony . . iii 2 210
The will! Let's stay and hear the will . . . iii 2 244
You shall not come to them.—Nothing but death shall stay me . iv 3 128
Arming myself with patience To stay the providence of some high powers v 1 107
I prithee, Strato, stay thou by thy lord . . . v 5 44
Stay, you imperfect speakers, tell me more . . . *Macbeth* i 3 70
Worthy Macbeth, we stay upon your leisure . . . i 3 148
Now go to the door, and stay there till we call . . . iii 1 73
I am call'd; my little spirit, see, Sits in a foggy cloud, and stays for me iii 5 35
I am so much a fool, should I stay longer, It would be my disgrace . iv 2 28
There are a crew of wretched souls That stay his cure . . iv 3 142
See, it stalks away!—Stay! speak! speak . . . *Hamlet* i 1 51
Stay, illusion! If thou hast any sound, or use of voice, Speak to me i 1 127
Let not thy mother lose her prayers, Hamlet: I pray thee, stay with us i 2 119
O, fear me not. I stay too long: but here my father comes . i 3 52

Stay. Good madam, stay awhile; I will be faithful . . . *Hamlet* ii 2 115
They stay upon your patience . . . iii 2 112
My mother stays: This physic but prolongs thy sickly days . . iii 3 95
Go seek him there.—He will stay till you come . . . iv 3 41
Who shall stay you?—My will, not all the world . . . iv 5 136
No leisure bated, No, not to stay the grinding of the axe . . v 2 24
Stay; give me drink. Hamlet, this pearl is thine; Here's to thy health v 2 293
Let me not stay a jot for dinner; go get it ready . . . *Lear* i 4 8
Follow me not; Stay here . . . ii 4 60
But I will tarry; the fool will stay, And let the wise man fly . ii 4 83
I can be patient; I can stay with Regan, I and my hundred knights . ii 4 233
Entreat him by no means to stay.—Alack, the night comes on . ii 4 302
Thou must not stay behind . . . iii 6 108
Our troops set forth to-morrow: stay with us; The ways are dangerous iv 5 16
Stay till I have read the letter.—I was forbid it . . v 1 47
Let the drum strike, and prove my title thine.—Stay yet; hear reason v 3 82
Now she's gone for ever! Cordelia, Cordelia! stay a little . . v 3 271
It seems not meet, nor wholesome to my place, To be produced—as, if I stay, I shall—Against the Moor . . . *Othello* i 1 147
Be it as you shall privately determine, Either for her stay or going . i 3 277
She that being anger'd, her revenge being nigh, Bade her wrong stay . ii 1 154
Out of my sight!—I will not stay to offend you . . . iv 1 258
The messengers of Venice stay the meat: Go in, and weep not . iv 2 170
O, bear him out o' the air. Stay you, good gentlemen . . v 1 105
You must not stay here longer, your dismission Is come *Ant. and Cleo.* i 1 26
He stays upon your will.—Let him appear . . . i 2 119
Whose fortunes shall rise higher, Cæsar's or mine?—Cæsar's. Therefore, O Antony, stay not by his side . . . ii 3 18
Speak not against it; I will not stay behind.—Nay, I have done . iii 7 20
I must stay his time . . . iii 13 155
I turn you not away; but, like a master Married to your good service, stay till death . . . iv 2 31
Our foot upon the hills adjoining to the city Shall stay with us . iv 10 6
All is done. Eros!—I come, my queen:—Eros!—Stay for me . iv 14 50
Nay, I will take thee too: What should I stay— In this vile world? v 2 316
Nay, stay a little: Were you but riding forth to air yourself, Such parting were too petty . . . *Cymbeline* i 1 109
Stay; come not in. But that it eats our victuals, I should think Here were a fairy . . . iii 6 40
You shall have better cheer Ere you depart; and thanks to stay and eat it . . . iii 6 68
Brother, stay here: Are we not brothers?—So man and man should be iv 2 2
I'll stay Till hasty Polydore return, and bring him To dinner . iv 2 164
Stay, sir king: This man is better than the man he slew . . v 5 301
And stay your coming to present themselves . . . *Pericles* ii 2 3
But stay, the knights are coming: we will withdraw Into the gallery . ii 2 58
We do our longing stay To hear the rest untold . . . v 3 83
Stayed. You are stay'd for.—Go; I come, I come . *T. G. of Ver.* ii 2 19
He hath stayed for a better man than thee . . . iii 1 385
Thou hast stayed so long that going will scarce serve the turn . iii 1 388
And longer might have stay'd, If crooked fortune had not thwarted me iv 1 21
You have stayed me in a happy hour . . . *Much Ado* iv 1 285
Until the goose came out of door, And stay'd the odds by adding four *L. L. Lost* iii 1 93
Here they stay'd an hour, And talk'd apace . . . v 2 368
I would have stay'd till I had made you merry . *Mer. of Venice* i 1 60
We are stay'd for at Bassanio's feast . . . ii 6 48
We stay'd her for your sake . . . *As Y. Like It* i 3 69
Your ships are stay'd at Venice . . . *T. of Shrew* iv 2 83
Thine eye Hath stay'd upon some favour that it loves . *T. Night* ii 4 25
I have stay'd To tire your royalty . . . *W. Tale* i 2 14
The adverse winds, Whose leisure I have stay'd, have given him time *K. John* ii 1 58
The sun of heaven methought was loath to set, But stay'd and made the western welkin blush . . . v 5 2
We have stay'd ten days, And hardly kept our countrymen together *Richard II.* ii 4 1
When there was nothing could have stay'd My father . *2 Hen. IV.* iv 1 123
Retreat is made and execution stay'd . . . iv 3 78
He came not through the chamber where we stay'd . . iv 5 57
She should have stayed in France and starved in France . *2 Hen. VI.* i 1 135
Pardon, my liege, that I have stay'd so long . . . iii 1 94
Being protector, stay'd the soldiers' pay . . . iii 1 105
He never would have stay'd in France so long . . . iii 1 295
I have stay'd for thee, God knows, in anguish, pain, and agony *Rich. III.* iv 4 162
An untimely ague Stay'd me a prisoner in my chamber . *Hen. VIII.* i 1 5
An he had stayed by him, I would not have been so fidiused . *Coriolanus* ii 1 143
Thou hast stay'd us here too long . . . *T. Andron.* ii 3 181
I could have stay'd here all the night To hear good counsel *Rom. and Jul.* iii 3 159
My speed to Mantua there was stay'd . . . v 2 12
Friar John Was stay'd by accident, and yesternight Return'd my letter v 3 251
Am I not stay'd for, Cinna?—I am glad on't . . . *J. Cæsar* i 3 136
Am I not stay'd for? tell me.—Yes, you are . . . i 3 139
Whither are they vanish'd?—Into the air; and what seem'd corporal melted As breath into the wind. Would they had stay'd! *Macbeth* i 3 82
Stay'd it long?—While one with moderate haste might tell a hundred *Hamlet* i 2 237
The wind sits in the shoulder of your sail, And you are stay'd for . i 3 57
He falls to such perusal of my face As he would draw it. Long stay'd he so . . . ii 1 91
You stayed well by't in Egypt . . . *Ant. and Cleo.* ii 2 179
I died whilst in the womb he stay'd Attending nature's law *Cymbeline* v 4 37
Good Helicane, that stay'd at home, Not to eat honey like a drone *Pericles* ii Gower 17
Stayest. Away, I say! stay'st thou to vex me here? . *T. G. of Ver.* iv 4 66
Staying. Besides, thy staying will abridge thy life . . . iii 1 245
No longer staying but to give the mother Notice of my affair *M. for M.* i 4 86
Who, but for staying on our controversy, Had hoisted sail *Com. of Errors* v 1 20
Until the goose came out of door, Staying the odds by adding four *L. L. Lost* iii 1 99
He seem'd in running to devour the way, Staying no longer question *2 Hen. IV.* i 1 48
By staying there so long till all were lost . . . *2 Hen. VI.* i 1 299
My sword make way for me, for here is no staying . . iv 8 62
There is staying A gentleman, sent from the king, to see you *Hen. VIII.* iv 2 105
Like a strange soul upon the Stygian banks Staying for waftage *T. and C.* iii 2 11
For Mercutio's soul Is but a little way above our heads, Staying for thine to keep him company . . . *Rom. and Jul.* iii 1 133
When you sued staying, Then was the time for words *Ant. and Cleo.* iii 3 33
Stead. So it stead you, I will write . . . *T. G. of Ver.* ii 1 119
My substance should be statue in thy stead . . . iv 4 206

Stead. Can you so stead me As bring me to the sight of Isabella? *Meas. for Meas.* i 4 17
We shall advise this wronged maid to stead up your appointment . . . iii 1 260
May you stead me? will you pleasure me? . . *Mer. of Venice* i 3 7
To fill up your grace's request in my stead . . . iv 1 161
In my stead, Keep house and port and servants, as I should *T. of Shrew* i 1 207
You are the man Must stead us all and me amongst the rest . . . i 2 266
It nothing steads us To chide him from our eaves . *All's Well* iii 7 41
Had you that craft, to reave her Of what should stead her most? . v 3 87
Renounce your soil, give sheep in lions' stead . . 1 *Hen. VI.* i 5 29
The help of one stands me in little stead . . . . iv 6 31
Were you in my stead, would you have heard A mother less? *Coriolanus* v 3 192
For, lo, My intercession likewise steads my foe . . *Rom. and Jul.* ii 3 54
Slaves and fools, Pluck the grave wrinkled senate from the bench, And minister in their steads! . . . . . *T. of Athens* iv 1 6
In their steads do ravens, crows, and kites Fly o'er our heads *J. Cæsar* v 1 85
In their stead, Curses, not loud but deep . . . *Macbeth* v 3 26
I could never better stead thee than now . . . . *Othello* i 3 344
With all due diligence That horse and sail and high expense Can stead the quest . . . . . . *Pericles* iii Gower 21
The sooner her vile thoughts to stead, Lychorida, our nurse, is dead iv Gower 41
Steaded. Stuffs and necessaries, Which since have steaded much *Tempest* i 2 165
Steadfast-gazing. Oppose thy steadfast-gazing eyes to mine 2 *Hen. VI.* iv 10 48
Steadier. I'll see if his head will stand steadier on a pole, or no iv 7 101
Steal. We steal by line and level, an't like your grace . *Tempest* iv 1 239
'Steal by line and level' is an excellent pass of pate . . . iv 1 243
As the morning steals upon the night, Melting the darkness . . v 1 65
Lest the bare earth Should from her vesture chance to steal a kiss *T. G. of Ver.* ii 4 160
My friend This night intends to steal away your daughter . . iii 1 11
Myself was from Verona banished For practising to steal away a lady . iv 1 48
He steps me to her trencher and steals her capon's leg . . . iv 4 10
The good humour is to steal at a minute's rest . *Mer. Wives* i 3 30
'Convey,' the wise it call. 'Steal!' foh! a fico for the phrase! . . i 3 32
In that time Shall Master Slender steal my Nan away . . iv 4 74
'Thou shalt not steal?'—Ay, that he razed . *Meas. for Meas.* i 2 10
They put forth to steal . . . . i 2 14
Thieves for their robbery have authority When judges steal themselves ii 2 177
It was a mad fantastical trick of him to steal from the state . . iii 2 99
The hour steals on; I pray you, sir, dispatch . *Com. of Errors* iv 1 52
Finding a birds' nest, shows it his companion, and he steals it *Much Ado* ii 1 231
Bid her steal into the pleached bower . . . . . iii 1 7
Let him show himself what he is and steal out of your company . iii 3 63
If thou lovest me then, Steal forth thy father's house *M. N. Dream* i 1 164
Through Athens' gates have we devised to steal . . . i 1 213
The honey-bags steal from the humble-bees . . . . iii 1 171
And sleep . . . Steal me awhile from mine own company . . iii 2 436
Thrift is blessing, if men steal it not . . . *Mer. of Venice* i 3 91
I would not change this hue, Except to steal your thoughts . ii 1 12
But her eyes,—How could he see to do them? having made one, Methinks it should have power to steal both his . . . . . iii 2 125
There are some shrewd contents in yon same paper, That steals the colour from Bassanio's cheek . . . . iii 2 247
In such a night Did Jessica steal from the wealthy Jew . . . v 1 15
What if we assay'd to steal The clownish fool? *As Y. Like It* i 3 131
My Lord of Amiens and myself Did steal behind him as he lay along ii 1 30
'Twere good, methinks, to steal our marriage . *T. of Shrew* iii 2 142
But on us both did haggish age steal on And wore us out of act *All's W.* i 2 29
An thy mind stand to't, boy, steal away bravely . . . ii 1 29
I'll steal away.—There's honour in the theft . . . . ii 1 33
Most fain would steal What law does vouch mine own . . . ii 5 86
With the dark, poor thief, I'll steal away . . . . iii 2 132
Certain it is, that he will steal himself into a man's favour . . iii 6 98
He will steal, sir, an egg out of a cloister . . . . iv 3 280
On our quick'st decrees The inaudible and noiseless foot of Time Steals ere we can effect them . . . . v 3 42
Here's nobody will steal that from thee . . . . *W. Tale* iv 4 646
Still, 'tis strange He thus should steal upon us . . . v 1 115
Unless he do profane, steal, or usurp . . *Richard II.* iii 3 81
The moon, under whose countenance we steal . 1 *Hen. IV.* i 2 33
When time is ripe, which will be suddenly, I'll steal to Glendower . i 3 295
We steal as in a castle, cock-sure; we have the receipt of fern-seed ii 1 95
From whom you now must steal and take no leave . . . iii 1 93
Where shall I find one that can steal well? . . . . iii 3 211
I am as vigilant as a cat to steal cream.—I think, to steal cream indeed iv 2 65
Shall we steal upon them, Ned, at supper? . . 2 *Hen. IV.* ii 2 172
To steal his sweet and honey'd sentences . . . *Hen. V.* i 1 50
They will steal any thing, and call it purchase . . . iii 2 44
They are both hanged; and so would this be, if he durst steal . iv 4 78
To England will I steal, and there I'll steal . . . . v 1 92
The fox barks not when he would steal the lamb . 2 *Hen. VI.* iii 1 55
Who cannot steal a shape that means deceit? . . . . iii 1 79
I'll steal away.—Exeter, so will I . . . . 3 *Hen. VI.* i 1 212
Stand you thus close, to steal the bishop's deer? . . . iv 5 17
But, whiles he thought to steal the single ten, The king was slily finger'd from the deck! . . . . v 1 43
A man cannot steal, but it [conscience] accuseth him . *Richard III.* i 4 139
Oh, that deceit should steal such gentle shapes! . . . . ii 2 27
The silent hours steal on, And flaky darkness breaks within the east . v 3 85
Scarce time To steal from spiritual leisure a brief span . *Hen. VIII.* iii 2 140
And easy it is Of a cut loaf to steal a shive, we know . *T. Andron.* ii 1 87
Away from light steals home my heavy son . *Rom. and Jul.* i 1 143
Steal love's sweet bait from fearful hooks . . . ii Prol. 8
And steal immortal blessing from her lips . . . . iii 3 37
If I want gold, steal but a beggar's dog, And give it Timon *T. of Athens* ii 1 5
Bound servants, steal! Large-handed robbers your grave masters are . iv 1 10
Break open shops; nothing can you steal, But thieves do lose it . iv 3 450
Steal no less for this I give you; and gold confound you howsoe'er! . iv 3 451
What, is Brutus sick, And will he steal out of his wholesome bed? *J. Cæsar* ii 1 264
I come not, friends, to steal away your hearts: I am no orator . iii 2 220
There's warrant in that theft Which steals itself . . . *Macbeth* ii 3 152
If he steal aught the whilst this play is playing, And 'scape detecting, I will pay the theft . . . . *Hamlet* iii 2 93
Why, look you there! look, how it steals away! . . . . iii 4 134
The robb'd that smiles steals something from the thief . . *Othello* i 3 208
O God, that men should put an enemy in their mouths to steal away their brains! . . . . ii 3 292
No, sure, I cannot think it, That he would steal away so guilty-like . iii 3 39
Who steals my purse steals trash; 'tis something, nothing; 'Twas mine, 'tis his, and has been slave to thousands . . . . . . iii 3 157
Steal. My wayward husband hath a hundred times Woo'd me to steal it *Othello* iii 3 293
What handkerchief! . . . That which so often you did bid me steal . iii 3 309
With a solemn earnestness, More than indeed belong'd to such a trifle, He begg'd of me to steal it . . . . v 2 229
But there is never a fair woman has a true face.—No slander; they steal hearts . . . . *Ant. and Cleo.* ii 6 106
They induced to steal it! And by a stranger!—No . *Cymbeline* ii 4 125
But first of all, How we may steal from hence . . . . iii 2 64
That excellent complexion, which did steal The eyes of young and old *Pericles* iv 1 41
Stealer. The transgression is in the stealer . . . *Much Ado* ii 1 233
You once did love me.—So I do still, by these pickers and stealers *Ham.* iii 2 349
Yield up Their deer to the stand o' the stealer . . *Cymbeline* iii 3 75
Stealing. Time comes stealing on by night and day . *Com. of Errors* iv 2 60
Stealing her soul with many vows of faith And ne'er a true one *M. of Ven.* v 1 19
Upon a bank of violets, Stealing and giving odour! . . *T. Night* i 1 7
Wronging the ancientry, stealing, fighting . . . *W. Tale* iii 3 63
Stealing away from his father with his clog at his heels . . . iv 4 694
If I . . . Be guilty of the stealing that sweet breath . *K. John* iv 3 136
Stealing a cade of herrings . . . . . 2 *Hen. VI.* iv 2 35
Being burnt i' the hand for stealing of sheep . . . . iv 2 67
Mellow'd by the stealing hours of time . . . *Richard III.* iii 7 168
Here's an English tailor come hither, for stealing out of a French hose *Macbeth* ii 3 15
But age, with his stealing steps, Hath claw'd me in his clutch *Hamlet* v 1 79
Hobbididance, prince of dumbness; Mahu, of stealing . . . *Lear* iv 1 63
I'll rob none but myself; and let me die, Stealing so poorly *Cymbeline* iv 2 16
The more it shaped Unto my end of stealing them . . . . v 5 347
Stealth. The stealth of our most mutual entertainment *Meas. for Meas.* i 2 158
If you like elsewhere, do it by stealth . . *Com. of Errors* iii 2 7
I told him of your stealth unto this wood . . *M. N. Dream* iii 2 310
Fair Helen told me of their stealth, Of this their purpose hither . iv 1 165
I feel this youth's perfections With an invisible and subtle stealth To creep in at mine eyes . . . . *T. Night* i 5 316
If he do, it needs must be by stealth . . . *Rom. and Jul.* iii 5 217
I know my lord hath spent of Timon's wealth, And now ingratitude makes it worse than stealth . . . . . . *T. of Athens* iii 4 27
Who, in the lusty stealth of nature, take More composition . . *Lear* i 2 11
Fox in stealth, wolf in greediness, dog in madness, lion in prey . iii 4 96
Stealthy. With his stealthy pace, With Tarquin's ravishing strides, towards his design Moves like a ghost . . . . . *Macbeth* ii 1 54
Steed. Or Phœbus' steeds are founder'd, Or Night kept chain'd below *Tempest* iv 1 30
Loud 'larums, neighing steeds, and trumpets' clang . *T. of Shrew* i 2 207
The bound and high curvet Of Mars's fiery steed . . *All's Well* ii 3 300
He will commend . . . His barbed steeds to stables . . *Richard II.* iii 3 117
Upon a hot and fiery steed Which his aspiring rider seem'd to know . v 2 8
Turning, Bareheaded, lower than his proud steed's neck . . . v 2 19
Speak terms of manage to thy bounding steed . . . 1 *Hen. IV.* ii 3 52
Steed threatens steed, in high and boastful neighs . *Hen. V.* iv Prol. 10
Hark, how our steeds for present service neigh! . . . . iv 2 8
Their wounded steeds Fret fetlock deep in gore . . . . iv 7 81
The deadly-handed Clifford slew my steed . . . . 2 *Hen. VI.* v 2 9
And once again bestride our foaming steeds . . . 3 *Hen. VI.* ii 1 183
Underneath the belly of their steeds . . . . . . ii 3 20
O Phœbus, hadst thou never given consent That Phaëthon should check thy fiery steeds! . . . . ii 6 12
And brought from thence the Thracian fatal steeds . . . iv 2 21
Instead of mounting barbed steeds To fright the souls . *Richard III.* i 1 10
As hot as Perseus, spur thy Phrygian steed . . *Troi. and Cres.* iv 5 186
Take thou Troilus' horse; Present the fair steed to my lady Cressid . v 5 2
The counsellor heart, the arm our soldier, Our steed the leg *Coriolanus* i 1 121
Here is the steed, we the caparison . . . . . . i 9 12
In token of the which, My noble steed, known to the camp, I give him i 9 61
I mean to stride your steed, and at all times To undercrest your good addition To the fairness of my power . . . . i 9 71
Dismounted from your snow-white goodly steed . . *T. Andron.* ii 3 76
Gallop apace, you fiery-footed steeds, Towards Phœbus' lodging *Rom. and Jul.* iii 2 1
O, farewell! Farewell the neighing steed, and the shrill trump! *Othello* iii 3 351
So he nodded, And soberly did mount an arm-gaunt steed *Ant. and Cleo.* i 5 48
Phœbus 'gins arise, His steeds to water at those springs . *Cymbeline* ii 3 24
Steel. Whom I, with this obedient steel, three inches of it, Can lay to bed for ever . . . . *Tempest* ii 1 283
Give her no token but stones; for she's as hard as steel *T. G. of Ver.* i 1 149
Whose golden touch could soften steel and stones, Make tigers tame . iii 2 79
And by my side wear steel . . . . *Mer. Wives* i 3 84
With wit or steel?—With both the humours, I . . . . . i 3 102
If my breast had not been made of faith and my heart of steel *Com. of Errors* iii 2 150
One whose hard heart is button'd up with steel . . . . iv 2 34
For my heart Is true as steel . . . . *M. N. Dream* ii 1 197
I will deal in poison with thee, or in bastinado, or in steel *As Y. Like It* v 1 60
My desire, More sharp than filed steel, did spur me forth *T. Night* iii 3 5
Pins and poking-sticks of steel, What maids lack from head to heel *W. Tale* iv 4 228
We pay them for it with stamped coin, not stabbing steel . . iv 4 748
Now doth Death line his dead chaps with steel . . *K. John* ii 1 352
With thy blessings steel my lance's point . . *Richard II.* i 3 74
To lift shrewd steel against our golden crown . . . . iii 2 59
With hard bright steel and hearts harder than steel . . . . iii 2 111
May my hands rot off And never brandish more revengeful steel! . . iv 1 50
To crush our old limbs in ungentle steel . . . 1 *Hen. IV.* v 1 13
A scaly gauntlet now with joints of steel Must glove this hand 2 *Hen. IV.* i 1 146
Then join you with them, like a rib of steel, To make strength stronger ii 3 54
Their eyes of fire sparkling through sights of steel . . . . iv 1 121
Give them great meals of beef and iron and steel . . . *Hen. V.* iii 7 161
O God of battles! steel my soldiers' hearts; Possess them not with fear iv 1 306
They supposed I could rend bars of steel . . . . 1 *Hen. VI.* i 4 51
My three attendants, Lean famine, quartering steel, and climbing fire . iv 2 11
Turn on the bloody hounds with heads of steel . . . . iv 2 51
Steel thy fearful thoughts, And change misdoubt to resolution 2 *Hen. VI.* iii 1 331
And he but naked, though lock'd up in steel, Whose conscience with injustice is corrupted . . . . iii 2 234
Steel, if thou turn the edge, or cut not out the burly-boned clown in chines of beef ere thou sleep in thy sheath, I beseech God on my knees thou mayst be turned to hobnails . . . . . . iv 10 59
The hope thereof makes Clifford mourn in steel . . . 3 *Hen. VI.* i 1 58
Shall we go throw away our coats of steel? . . . . . ii 1 160

Steel. Were thy heart as hard as steel, As thou hast shown it flinty by thy deeds, I come to pierce it . 3 *Hen. VI.* ii 1 201
Steel thy melting heart To hold thine own . . . ii 2 41
And bloody steel grasp'd in their ireful hands . . . ii 5 132
I would to God that the inclusive verge Of golden metal that must round my brow Were red-hot steel! . *Richard III.* iv 1 61
As the long divorce of steel falls on me . . *Hen. VIII.* ii 1 76
Give me ribs of steel! I shall split all In pleasure of my spleen *T. and C.* i 3 177
To steel a strong opinion to themselves . . . i 3 353
With these your white enchanting fingers touch'd, Shall more obey than to the edge of steel . . . . iii 1 165
As true as steel, as plantage to the moon, As sun to day . iii 2 184
Like a gate of steel Fronting the sun, receives and renders back . iii 3 121
But this thy countenance, still lock'd in steel, I never saw till now . iv 5 195
When steel grows soft as the parasite's silk . *Coriolanus* i 9 45
Beat thou the drum, that it speak mournfully: Trail your steel pikes . v 6 152
I will go get a leaf of brass, And with a gad of steel will write *T. An.* iv 1 103
Steel to the very back, Yet wrung with wrongs more than our backs can bear . . . . iv 3 47
My heart is not compact of flint nor steel . . . v 3 88
Sheathing the steel in my adventurous body . . . v 3 112
Enemies to peace, Profaners of this neighbour-stained steel *Rom. and Jul.* i 1 89
I warrant thee, my man's as true as steel . . . ii 4 210
Made me effeminate And in my temper soften'd valour's steel . iii 1 120
He tilts With piercing steel at bold Mercutio's breast . . iii 1 164
And to steel with valour The melting spirits of women . *J. Cæsar* ii 1 121
As he pluck'd his cursed steel away, Mark how the blood of Cæsar follow'd it . . . . . . iii 2 181
Piercing steel and darts envenomed Shall be as welcome . . v 3 76
His brandish'd steel, Which smoked with bloody execution . *Macbeth* i 2 17
Treason has done his worst: nor steel, nor poison, Malice domestic, foreign levy, nothing, Can touch him further . . . iii 2 24
Grapple them to thy soul with hoops of steel . . *Hamlet* i 3 63
Again in complete steel Revisit'st thus the glimpses of the moon . i 4 52
Heart with strings of steel, Be soft as sinews of the new-born babe! . iii 3 70
Hath made the flinty and steel couch of war My thrice-driven bed of down . . . . *Othello* i 3 231
I'll leave thee Now, like a man of steel . . *Ant. and Cleo.* iv 4 33
His body's a passable carcass, if he be not hurt: it is a throughfare for steel, if it be not hurt.—His steel was in debt . *Cymbeline* i 2 12
By your furtherance I am clothed in steel . . *Pericles* ii 1 160
Steeled. Seldom when The steeled gaoler is the friend of men *Meas. for Meas.* iv 2 90
Had not God, for some strong purpose, steel'd The hearts of men *Richard II.* v 2 34
For from his metal was his party steel'd . . . 2 *Hen. IV.* i 1 116
So service shall with steeled sinews toil . . . *Hen. V.* ii 2 36
Give me my steeled coat. I'll fight for France . . 1 *Hen. VI.* i 1 85
With lies well steel'd with weighty arguments . . *Richard III.* i 1 148
Steely. When virtue's steely bones Look bleak i' the cold wind *All's W.* i 1 114
Broach'd with the steely point of Clifford's lance . . 3 *Hen. VI.* ii 3 16
Steep. Against the steep uprising of the hill . . *L. L. Lost* iv 1 2
Four days will quickly steep themselves in night . *M. N. Dream* i 1 8
Let fancy still my sense in Lethe steep . . . *T. Night* iv 1 66
He that steeps his safety in true blood Shall find but bloody safety *K. John* iii 4 147
I'll steep this letter in sack and make him eat it . . 2 *Hen. IV.* ii 2 147
Thou no more wilt weigh my eyelids down And steep my senses in forgetfulness . . . . iii 1 8
To climb steep hills Requires slow pace at first . . *Hen. VIII.* i 1 131
Let them pronounce the steep Tarpeian death . . *Coriolanus* iii 3 88
Show me the steep and thorny way to heaven . . *Hamlet* i 3 48
Methinks the ground is even.—Horrible steep . . . *Lear* iv 6 3
Steep-down. Wash me in steep-down gulfs of liquid fire! . *Othello* v 2 280
Steeped. There may be in the cup A spider steep'd . . *W. Tale* ii 1 40
Your father's enemies Have steep'd their galls in honey . *Hen. V.* ii 2 30
A napkin steeped in the harmless blood Of sweet young Rutland 3 *Hen. VI.* ii 1 62
A clout Steep'd in the faultless blood of pretty Rutland *Richard III.* i 3 178
To thy father, steep'd in Rutland's blood,—A handkerchief . . iv 4 275
Who else? what, Paris too? And steep'd in blood? . *Rom. and Jul.* v 3 145
There, the murderers, Steep'd in the colours of their trade . *Macbeth* ii 3 121
With tongue in venom steep'd . . . . . *Hamlet* ii 2 533
Steep'd me in poverty to the very lips . . . *Othello* iv 2 50
Wine hath steep'd our sense In soft and delicate Lethe . *Ant. and Cleo.* ii 7 113
Many dream not to find, neither deserve, And yet are steep'd in favours *Cymbeline* v 4 131
Steeple. Inscrutable, invisible, As a nose on a man's face, or a weather-cock on a steeple! . . . . . *T. G. of Ver.* ii 1 142
Topples down Steeples and moss-grown towers . . 1 *Hen. IV.* iii 1 33
Spout Till you have drench'd our steeples, drown'd the cocks! . *Lear* iii 2 3
Never leave gaping till they've swallowed the whole parish, church, steeple, bells, and all . . . . . *Pericles* ii 1 38
He should never have left, till he cast bells, steeple, church, and parish, up again . . . . ii 1 47
Steepy. Bowing his head against the steepy mount . . *T. of Athens* i 1 75
Steer. The steer, the heifer, and the calf Are all call'd neat *W. Tale* i 2 124
Like youthful steers unyoked, they take their courses 2 *Hen. IV.* iv 2 103
And you yourself shall steer the happy helm . . 2 *Hen. VI.* i 3 103
I did steer Toward this remedy . . . . *Hen. VIII.* ii 4 200
At the helm A seeming mermaid steers . . *Ant. and Cleo.* ii 2 214
A rarer spirit never Did steer humanity . . . . v 1 32
Steerage. He, that hath the steerage of my course, Direct my sail! *Rom. and Jul.* i 4 112
So with his steerage shall your thoughts grow . . . *Pericles* iv 4 19
Steered. Fortune brings in some boats that are not steer'd . *Cymbeline* iv 3 46
Steering with due course towards the isle of Rhodes . . *Othello* i 3 34
Stelled. Would have buoy'd up, And quench'd the stelled fires . *Lear* iii 7 61
Stem. Two lovely berries moulded on one stem . . *M. N. Dream* iii 2 211
This is a stem Of that victorious stock . . . *Hen. V.* ii 4 62
Sweet stem from York's great stock . . . . 1 *Hen. VI.* ii 5 41
As doth a sail . . . Command an argosy to stem the waves . 3 *Hen. VI.* ii 6 36
As weeds before A vessel under sail, so men obey'd And fell below his stem: his sword, death's stamp . . . . . *Coriolanus* ii 2 111
And with a dropping industry they skip From stem to stern . *Pericles* iv 1 64
Stemming it with hearts of controversy . . . *J. Cæsar* i 2 109
Stench! O amiable lovely death! Thou odoriferous stench! . *K. John* iii 4 26
So bees with smoke and doves with noisome stench Are from their hives and houses driven away . . . . . 1 *Hen. VI.* i 5 23
There's the sulphurous pit, Burning, scalding, stench, consumption *Lear* iv 6 131

Step. Shall step by step attend You and your ways . . . *Tempest* iii 3 78
A true-devoted pilgrim is not weary To measure kingdoms with his feeble steps; Much less shall she . . . . *T. G. of Ver.* ii 7 10
And make a pastime of each weary step, Till the last step have brought me to my love; And there I'll rest . . . . . ii 7 35
He steps me to her trencher and steals her capon's leg . . iv 4 9
Step into the chamber, Sir John . . . . *Mer. Wives* iv 2 11
Now step I forth to whip hypocrisy . . . . *L. L. Lost* iv 3 151
We measure them by weary steps . . . . . v 2 194
How many weary steps, Of many weary miles you have o'ergone, Are number'd in the travel of one mile? . . . . . v 2 195
And turn two mincing steps Into a manly stride . *Mer. of Venice* iii 4 67
Who after me hath many a weary step Limp'd in pure love *As Y. Like It* ii 7 130
My fellow-schoolmaster Doth watch Bianca's steps so narrowly *T. of S.* iii 2 141
Deadly divorce step between me and you! . . . *All's Well* v 3 319
As surely as your feet hit the ground they step on . . *T. Night* iii 4 306
We two will walk, my lord, And leave you to your graver steps *W. Tale* i 2 173
With thought of such affections, Step forth mine advocate . . v 1 221
None so small advantage shall step forth To check his reign . *K. John* iii 4 151
Your fears, which, as they say, attend The steps of wrong, should move you . . . . iv 2 57
Wherein we step after a stranger march Upon her gentle bosom . . v 2 27
We will untread the steps of damned flight . . . . v 4 52
The sullen passage of thy weary steps Esteem as foil . *Richard II.* i 3 265
And thy steps no more Than a delightful measure or a dance . . i 3 290
The treacherous feet Which with usurping steps do trample thee . iii 2 17
Where is Green? That they have let the dangerous enemy Measure our confines with such peaceful steps? . . . . . . iii 2 125
Let's step into the shadow of these trees . . . . iii 4 25
Twice for one step I'll groan, the way being short . . . v 1 91
Step aside, and I'll show thee a precedent . . . 1 *Hen. IV.* ii 4 36
He presently, as greatness knows itself, Steps me a little higher . iv 3 75
My judgement is, we should not step too far . . 2 *Hen. IV.* i 3 20
Threefold vengeance tend upon your steps! . . . 2 *Hen. VI.* iii 2 304
They are as children but one step below . . . *Richard III.* iv 4 301
That with a fearful soul Leads discontented steps in foreign soil . iv 4 312
And front but in that file Where others tell steps with me *Hen. VIII.* i 2 43
You have, by fortune and his highness' favours, Gone slightly o'er low steps . . . . ii 4 112
The general's disdain'd By him one step below, he by the next, That next by him beneath; so every step, Exampled by the first pace *Troi. and Cres.* i 3 131
We'll consecrate the steps that Ajax makes When they go from Achilles ii 3 193
Step out of these dreary dumps . . . . *T. Andron.* i 1 391
Saucy controller of our private steps! . . . . ii 3 60
Step aside; I'll know his grievance, or be much denied . *Rom. and Jul.* i 1 162
That is a step On which I must fall down, or else o'erleap *Macbeth* i 4 48
Thou sure and firm-set earth, Hear not my steps . . . ii 1 57
What judgement Would step from this to this? . . *Hamlet* iii 4 71
Amazement on thy mother sits: O, step between her and her fighting soul . . . . iii 4 113
But age, with his stealing steps, Hath claw'd me in his clutch . v 1 79
It is no vicious blot, . . . No unchaste action, or dishonour'd step *Lear* i 1 231
One step I have advanced thee . . . . . . v 3 28
That, from your first of difference and decay, Have follow'd your sad steps . . . . v 3 289
And lay a sentence, Which, as a grise or step, may help these lovers *Oth.* i 3 200
Sir, this gentleman Steps in to Cassio, and entreats his pause . ii 3 229
And put My clouted brogues from off my feet, whose rudeness Answer'd my steps too loud . . . . *Cymbeline* iv 2 215
Step you forth; Give answer to this boy . . . . v 5 130
A courser, whose delightful steps Shall make the gazer joy *Pericles* ii 1 164
Step-dame. She lingers my desires, Like to a step-dame . *M. N. Dream* i 1 5
Pard to the hind, or stepdame to her son . . *Troi. and Cres.* iii 2 201
A father cruel, and a step-dame false . . . *Cymbeline* i 6 1
A father by thy step-dame govern'd, A mother hourly coining plots . ii 1 63
Stephano. It shall be said so again while Stephano breathes *Tempest* ii 2 65
If thou beest Stephano, touch me and speak to me . . . ii 2 104
But art thou not drowned, Stephano? . . . . . ii 2 113
Art thou living, Stephano? O Stephano, two Neapolitans 'scaped! . ii 2 117
O king Stephano! O peer! O worthy Stephano! . . . iv 1 221
O king Stephano! . . . . iv 1 225
Is not this Stephano, my drunken butler? . . . . v 1 277
Why, how now, Stephano!— . . . I am not Stephano, but a cramp . v 1 285
Stephano is my name; and I bring word . . *Mer. of Venice* v 1 28
Why should we go in? My friend Stephano, signify, I pray you . v 1 51
Stephen Sly and old John Naps of Greece . . . *T. of Shrew* Ind. 2 95
Stephen Langton, chosen archbishop Of Canterbury . *K. John* iii 1 143
Sir Stephen Scroop, besides a clergyman Of holy reverence *Richard II.* iii 3 28
God and Saint Stephen give you good den . . . *T. Andron.* iv 4 42
King Stephen was a worthy peer, His breeches cost him but a crown *Oth.* ii 3 92
Stepmothers. You shall not find me, daughter, After the slander of most stepmothers, Evil-eyed unto you . . . . . *Cymbeline* i 1 71
Steppe. Come from the farthest steppe of India . . *M. N. Dream* ii 1 69
Stepped. Since we are stepp'd thus far in, I will continue . *T. of Shrew* i 2 83
The Prince of Wales stepp'd forth before the king . . 1 *Hen. IV.* v 2 46
Tell me how he died: If well, he stepp'd before me, happily *Hen. VIII.* iv 2 10
By whose death he's stepp'd Into a great estate . . *T. of Athens* i 2 232
A friend of mine, who, in hot blood, Hath stepp'd into the law . iii 5 12
I am in blood Stepp'd in so far that, should I wade no more, Returning were as tedious as go o'er . . . . . . *Macbeth* iii 4 137
Whose naked breast Stepp'd before targes of proof . . *Cymbeline* v 5 5
Stepping. Not stepping o'er the bounds of modesty . *Rom. and Jul.* iv 2 27
Sterile. Thy sea-marge, sterile and rocky-hard . . . *Tempest* iv 1 69
Like lean, sterile, and bare land, manured, husbanded . 2 *Hen. IV.* iv 3 129
Our elders say, The barren, touched in this holy chase, Shake off their sterile curse . . . . *J. Cæsar* i 2 9
This goodly frame, the earth, seems to me a sterile promontory *Hamlet* ii 2 310
Sterile with idleness, or manured with industry . . . *Othello* i 3 330
Sterility. Into her womb convey sterility! . . . . *Lear* i 4 300
Sterling. An if my word be sterling yet in England, Let it command a mirror hither straight . . . . . . *Richard II.* iv 1 264
The one you may do with sterling money . . . . 2 *Hen. IV.* i 1 131
You have ta'en these tenders for true pay, Which are not sterling *Hamlet* i 3 107
Stern. He, like you, Would not have been so stern . *Meas. for Meas.* ii 2 66
Pierced through the heart with your stern cruelty . . *M. N. Dream* iii 2 59
Therefore put I on the countenance Of stern commandment *As Y. Like It* ii 7 109
As I guess By the stern brow and waspish action . . . iv 3 9
You are cold and stern . . . . *All's Well* iv 2 8
He hath a stern look, but a gentle heart . . . . *K. John* iv 1 88

Stern. We cannot deal but with the very hand Of stern injustice *K. John* v 2 23
Teaching stern murder how to butcher thee *Richard II.* i 2 32
By the stern tyrant war 2 *Hen. IV.* Ind. 14
Grow like savages,—as soldiers will That nothing do but meditate on blood,—To swearing and stern looks *Hen. V.* v 2 61
And sit at chiefest stern of public weal 1 *Hen. VI.* i 1 177
Let thy looks be stern : By this means shall we sound what skill she hath i 2 62
Why look you still so stern and tragical? iii 1 125
Like a hungry lion, did commence Rough deeds of rage and stern impatience iv 7 8
Turn our stern upon a dreadful rock. 2 *Hen. VI.* iii 2 91
Thy mother took into her blameful bed Some stern untutor'd churl iii 2 213
Stern and rough, Used to command, untaught to plead for favour iv 1 121
Stern Falconbridge commands the narrow seas 3 *Hen. VI.* i 1 239
Stern, obdurate, flinty, rough, remorseless i 4 142
Plantagenet . . . Is by the stern Lord Clifford done to death ii 1 103
Our stern alarums changed to merry meetings *Richard III.* i 1 7
That I, forsooth, am stern and love them not? i 3 44
Murder, stern murder, in the direst degree v 3 197
My sometime general, I have seen thee stern *Coriolanus* iv 1 24
What stern ungentle hands Have lopp'd and hew'd and made thy body bare Of her two branches? *T. Andron.* ii 4 16
Which I wish may prove More stern and bloody than the Centaurs' feast v 2 204
Lest with this piteous action you convert My stern effects *Hamlet* iii 4 129
If wolves had at thy gate howl'd that stern time, Thou shouldst have said 'Good porter, turn the key' *Lear* iii 7 63
Attend you here the door of our stern daughter? *Cymbeline* ii 3 42
And with a dropping industry they skip From stem to stern. *Pericles* iv 1 64
Sternage. Grapple your minds to sternage of this navy *Hen. V.* iii Prol. 18
Sterner. Will you sterner be Than he that dies and lives by bloody drops? *As Y. Like It* iii 5 6
Ambition should be made of sterner stuff *J. Cæsar* iii 2 97
Sternest. I would outstare the sternest eyes that look *Mer. of Venice* ii 1 27
The fatal bellman, Which gives the stern'st good-night *Macbeth* ii 2 4
Sternness. Behold The sternness of his presence *W. Tale* iv 4 24
Steterat. Hic steterat Priami regia celsa senis *T. of Shrew* iii 1 29
'Hic steterat,' and that Lucentio that comes a-wooing iii 1 34
'Hic steterat Priami,' take heed he hear us not iii 1 43
Stew. Where I have seen corruption boil and bubble Till it o'er-run the stew *Meas for Meas.* v 1 321
He would unto the stews, And from the common'st creature pluck a glove *Richard II.* v 3 16
An I could get me but a wife in the stews 2 *Hen. IV.* i 2 60
A saucy stranger in his court to mart As in a Romish stew *Cymbeline* i 6 152
Steward. If my lady have not called up her steward *T. Night* ii 3 77
Art any more than a steward? ii 3 123
Let me see thee a steward still, the fellow of servants ii 5 169
Here comes the Lady Paulina's steward : he can deliver you more *W. Tale* v 2 28
The figure of God's majesty, His captain, steward *Richard II.* iv 1 126
I am fortune's steward—get on thy boots 2 *Hen. IV.* v 3 137
Not as protector, steward, substitute, Or lowly factor *Richard III.* iii 7 133
Plutus, the god of gold, Is but his steward *T. of Athens* i 1 288
Go to my steward.—Please it your lordship, he hath put me off ii 2 18
Your steward puts me off, my lord ii 2 32
Is not that his steward muffled so? He goes away in a cloud iii 4 41
I'll have it so. My steward!—Here, my lord.—So fitly? iii 4 109
Hear you, master steward, where's our master? Are we undone? iv 2 1
Whilst I have gold, I'll be his steward still iv 2 50
Ne'er did poor steward wear a truer grief For his undone lord iv 3 487
And whilst this poor wealth lasts To entertain me as your steward still iv 3 496
Had I a steward So true, so just, and now so comfortable? iv 3 497
I do proclaim One honest man—mistake me not—but one ; No more, I pray,—and he's a steward iv 3 505
'Tis said he gave unto his steward a mighty sum v 1 8
It is the false steward, that stole his master's daughter *Hamlet* iv 5 173
Stewardship. Hath broke his staff, resign'd his stewardship *Richard II.* ii 2 59
Show us the hand of God That hath dismiss'd us from our stewardship iii 3 78
Stewed. Three veneys for a dish of stewed prunes *Mer. Wives* i 1 296
More than half stewed in grease, like a Dutch dish iii 5 121
Longing, saving your honour's reverence, for stewed prunes *M. for M.* ii 1 92
There's no more faith in thee than in a stewed prune 1 *Hen. IV.* iii 3 128
He lives upon mouldy stewed prunes and dried cakes 2 *Hen. IV.* ii 4 158
Sodden business! there's a stewed phrase indeed! *Troi. and Cres.* iii 1 44
Stew'd in corruption, honeying and making love Over the nasty sty *Ham.* iii 4 93
Came there a reeking post, Stew'd in his haste, half breathless *Lear* ii 4 31
Thou shalt be whipp'd with wire, and stew'd in brine *Ant. and Cleo.* ii 5 65
Stick. I can here disarm thee with this stick *Tempest* i 2 472
A plague upon the tyrant that I serve! I'll bear him no more sticks ii 2 167
A devil, a born devil, on whose nature Nurture can never stick iv 1 189
If the ground be overcharged, you were best stick her *T. G. of Ver.* i 1 108
Unless you have a codpiece to stick pins on ii 7 56
Stick it in their children's sight For terror, not to use *Meas. for Meas.* i 3 25
I am a kind of burr ; I shall stick iv 3 190
So deep sticks it in my penitent heart That I crave death v 1 480
Stick musk-roses in thy sleek smooth head *M. N. Dream* iv 1 3
My father's rough and envious disposition Sticks me at heart *As Y. L. It* i 2 254
This drum sticks sorely in your disposition *All's Well* iii 6 46
My face so thin That in mine ear I durst not stick a rose *K. John* i 1 142
He will not stick to say his face is a face-royal 2 *Hen. IV.* i 2 26
The knave will stick by thee . . . —And I'll stick by him v 3 70
A' saw a flea stick upon Bardolph's nose *Hen. V.* ii 3 43
Wear thou this favour for me and stick it in thy cap iv 7 161
He that breaks a stick of Gloucester's grove Shall lose his head 2 *Hen. VI.* i 2 33
Thy leg a stick compared with this truncheon. iv 10 52
Have you a precedent . . . ? We must not rend our subjects from our laws, And stick them in our will *Hen. VIII.* i 2 94
They will not stick to say you envied him ii 2 127
They'll stick where they are thrown *Troi. and Cres.* iii 2 120
'Yea,' let them say, to stick the heart of falsehood, 'As false as Cressid' iii 2 202
If things go well, Opinion that so sticks on Marcius shall Of his demerits rob Cominius *Coriolanus* i 1 275
And stick i' the wars Like a great sea-mark, standing every flaw v 3 73
Stick your rosemary On this fair corse *Rom. and Jul.* iv 5 79
I do fear, When every feather sticks in his own wing, Lord Timon will be left a naked gull *T. of Athens* ii 1 30
Our fears in Banquo Stick deep. *Macbeth* iii 1 50
This avarice Sticks deeper, grows with more pernicious root iv 3 85
His sword, Which was declining on the milky head Of reverend Priam, seem'd i' the air to stick *Hamlet* ii 2 501

Stick. Like fruit unripe, sticks on the tree *Hamlet* iii 2 200
Necessity, of matter beggar'd, Will nothing stick our person to arraign iv 5 93
Your skill shall, like a star i' the darkest night, Stick fiery off indeed v 2 268
She knapped 'em o' the coxcombs with a stick *Lear* ii 4 125
In his anointed flesh stick boarish fangs iii 7 58
That he might stick The small'st opinion on my least misuse *Othello* iv 2 108
An honest man he is, and hates the slime That sticks on filthy deeds v 2 149
His speech sticks in my heart.—Mine ear must pluck it thence *A. and C.* i 5 41
Stick to your journal course : the breach of custom Is breach of all *Cymbeline* iv 2 10
Stickest. Thou stickest a dagger in me *Mer. of Venice* iii 1 115
We'll draw thee from the mire Of this sir-reverence love, wherein thou stick'st Up to the ears *Rom. and Jul.* i 4 42
Sticking. Faithful loves, Sticking together in calamity *K. John* iii 4 67
On the sheets his hair, you see, is sticking 2 *Hen. VI.* iii 2 174
Now does he feel His secret murders sticking on his hands *Macbeth* v 2 17
Sticking-place. But screw your courage to the sticking-place i 7 60
Stickler-like, the armies separates *Troi. and Cres.* v 8 18
Stiff. With long travel I am stiff and weary *Com. of Errors* i 2 15
Speak big and clap their female joints In stiff unwieldy arms *Richard II.* iii 2 115
Many a nobleman lies stark and stiff 1 *Hen. IV.* v 3 42
Passeth by with stiff unbowed knee, Disdaining duty 2 *Hen. VI.* iii 1 16
Such a noise arose As the shrouds make at sea in a stiff tempest *Hen. VIII.* iv 1 72
Make you ready your stiff bats and clubs *Coriolanus* i 1 165
What, art thou stiff? stand'st out? i 1 245
Shall, stiff and stark and cold, appear like death *Rom. and Jul.* iv 1 103
Her blood is settled, and her joints are stiff iv 5 26
How stiff is my vile sense, That I stand up! *Lear* iv 6 286
This is stiff news *Ant. and Cleo.* i 2 104
Well corresponding With your stiff age *Cymbeline* iii 3 32
Stiff-borne. And none of this, Though strongly apprehended, could restrain The stiff-borne action 2 *Hen. IV.* i 1 177
Stiffen the sinews, summon up the blood *Hen. V.* iii 1 7
Stiffly. Hold, hold, my heart ; And you, my sinews, grow not instant old, But bear me stiffly up *Hamlet* i 5 95
Stifle. You shall stifle in your own report *Meas. for Meas.* ii 4 158
With the issuing blood Stifle the villain 3 *Hen. VI.* ii 6 83
Stifled. I am stifled with this smell of sin *K. John* iv 3 113
I am stifled With the mere rankness of their joy *Hen. VIII.* iv 1 58
Shall I not, then, be stifled in the vault? *Rom. and Jul.* iv 3 33
Stigmatic. Foul stigmatic, that's more than thou canst tell 2 *Hen. VI.* v 1 215
A foul mis-shapen stigmatic, Mark'd by the destinies to be avoided 3 *Hen. VI.* ii 2 136
Stigmatical. Blunt, unkind, Stigmatical in making *Com. of Errors* iv 2 22
Stile. Over the stile, this way *Mer. Wives* iii 1 33
Jog on, jog on, the foot-path way, And merrily hent the stile-a *W. Tale* iv 3 133
Know'st thou the way to Dover?—Both stile and gate *Lear* iv 1 58
Still. Sit still, and hear the last of our sea-sorrow *Tempest* i 2 170
Still 'tis beating in my mind, your reason For raising this sea-storm i 2 176
So you may continue and laugh at nothing still ii 1 179
Hourly joys be still upon you! Juno sings her blessings on you iv 1 108
A turn or two I'll walk, To still my beating mind iv 1 163
This was well done, my bird. Thy shape invisible retain thou still iv 1 185
Give me thy favour still. Be patient, for the prize I'll bring thee to iv 1 204
Let grief and sorrow still embrace his heart That doth not wish you joy! v 1 214
Since thou lovest, love still and thrive therein *T. G. of Ver.* i 1 9
This proves me still a sheep.—True i 1 82
Keep tune there still, so you will sing it out i 2 89
You'll still be too forward ii 1 11
I have loved her ever since I saw her ; and still I see her beautiful ii 1 73
Nay, sure, I think she holds them prisoners still ii 4 92
Love is still most precious in itself ii 6 24
Well, your old vice still ; mistake the word iii 1 283
The more she spurns my love, The more it grows and fawneth on her still iv 2 15
A most unholy match, Which heaven and fortune still rewards with plagues iv 3 31
Did not I bid thee still mark me and do as I do? iv 4 39
A slave, that still an end turns me to shame! iv 4 67
'Tis the curse in love, and still approved v 4 43
Youthful still! in your doublet and hose this raw rheumatic day! *Mer. Wives* iii 1 46
Yet seek my father's love ; still seek it, sir iii 4 19
We two will still be the ministers iv 2 234
Sing a scornful rhyme ; And, as you trip, still pinch him to your time v 5 96
The words of heaven ; on whom it will, it will ; On whom it will not, so ; yet still 'tis just *Meas. for Meas.* i 2 127
Pardon is still the nurse of second woe ii 1 298
Respites me a life, whose very comfort Is still a dying horror! ii 3 42
Him thou labour'st by thy flight to shun And yet runn'st toward him still iii 1 13
He would give't thee, from this rank offence, So to offend him still iii 1 101
Double and treble admonition, and still forfeit in the same kind! iii 2 206
His friends still wrought reprieves for him iv 2 140
You make my bonds still greater.—O, your desert speaks loud v 1 8
Not changing heart with habit, I am still Attorney'd at your service v 1 389
Like doth quit like, and MEASURE still FOR MEASURE v 1 416
I am sorry, one so learned and so wise As you, Lord Angelo, have still appear'd, Should slip so grossly v 1 476
Because their business still lies out o' door *Com. of Errors* ii 1 11
Yet the gold bides still, That others touch ii 1 110
O, soft, sir! hold you still : I'll fetch my sister, to get her good will iii 2 69
Have patience, I beseech.—I cannot, nor I will not, hold me still iv 2 17
Wilt thou still talk? iv 4 47
I could find in my heart to stay here still and turn witch iv 4 160
Still did I tell him it was vile and bad v 1 67
I see we still did meet each other's man v 1 386
How still the evening is, As hush'd on purpose to grace harmony! *Much Ado* ii 3 40
If you hear a child cry in the night, you must call to the nurse and bid her still it iii 3 70
A little Academe, Still and contemplative in living art *L. L. Lost* i 1 14
Adieu, valour! rust, rapier! be still, drum! i 2 188
Let's mock them still, as well known as disguised v 2 301
I frown upon him, yet he loves me still *M. N. Dream* i 1 194
What though? Yet Hermia still loves you : then be content ii 2 110
The summer still doth tend upon my state iii 1 158
If it stand, as you yourself still do, Within the eye of honour *Mer. of Ven.* i 1 136
As I have ever found thee honest-true, So let me find thee still iii 4 47
Who Time gallops withal and who he stands still withal *As Y. Like It* iii 2 329

Still. Who stays it [Time] still withal?—With lawyers in the vacation; for they sleep between term and term . . . *As Y. Like It* iii 2 348
What you do Still betters what is done . . . *W. Tale* iv 4 136
Then all stand still; On . . . . v 3 95
That still I lay upon my mother's head . . . *K. John* i 1 76
Many a poor man's son would have lien still And ne'er have spoke . iv 1 50
Lie still, ye thief, and hear the lady sing . . . *1 Hen. IV.* iii 1 238
Wouldst thou have thy head broken?—No.—Then be still . . iii 1 244
Thou seest I am pacified still . . . . iii 3 196
O, my sweet beef, I must still be good angel to thee . . . iii 3 199
Wherefore stands our army still? . . . *2 Hen. IV.* iv 2 98
Lest rest and lying still might make them look Too near unto my state iv 5 212
When he speaks, The air, a charter'd libertine, is still . . *Hen. V.* i 1 48
And leave your England, as dead midnight still . . . iii Prol. 19
The gimmal bit Lies foul with chew'd grass, still and motionless . . iv 2 50
That with his name the mothers still their babes . . *1 Hen. VI.* ii 3 17
Be placed as viceroy under him, And still enjoy thy regal dignity . . v 4 132
Let your drums be still, For here we entertain a solemn peace . . v 4 174
For France, 'tis ours; and we will keep it still . . *2 Hen. VI.* i 1 106
Then, York, be still awhile, till time do serve . . . . i 1 248
No more, good York; sweet Somerset, be still . . . . iii 1 304
Madam, be still; with reverence may I say . . . . iii 2 207
Thus war hath given thee peace, for thou art still. Peace with his soul! v 2 29
This meeting here Cannot be cured by words; therefore be still *3 Hen. VI.* ii 2 122
I'll never pause again, never stand still . . . . . ii 3 30
That still use of grief makes wild grief tame . . . *Richard III.* iv 4 229
Which she shall purchase with still lasting war . . . . iv 4 344
Unmindful villain, Why stand'st thou still, and go'st not? . . iv 4 445
If they be still and willing, I'll undertake may see away their shilling *Hen. VIII.* Prol. 11
A peace above all earthly dignities, A still and quiet conscience . . iii 2 380
The still and mental parts, That do contrive how many hands shall strike, When fitness calls them on . . *Troi. and Cres.* i 3 200
A still and dumb-discoursive devil That tempts most cunningly . . iv 4 92
Yet will I still Be thus to them.—You do the nobler . . *Coriolanus* iii 2 5
Be still and wonder, When one but of my ordinance stood up To speak iii 2 11
Rome Sits safe and still without him . . . . . . iv 6 37
Now is a time to storm; why art thou still? . . *T. Andron.* iii 1 264
Thou canst not strike it [thy heart] thus to make it still . . . iii 2 14
I shall forget, to have thee still stand there, Remembering how I love thy company.—And I'll still stay, to have thee still forget *R. and J.* ii 2 173
Two such opposed kings encamp them still In man as well as herbs . ii 3 27
This is the old man still.—Will't hold? will't hold?—It does *T. of Athens* iii 6 69
We are fellows still, Serving alike in sorrow . . . . iv 2 18
Suspect still comes where an estate is least . . . . iv 3 521
At all times alike Men are not still the same . . . . v 1 125
Trouble him no further; thus you still shall find him . . . v 1 216
Bid every noise be still: peace yet again! . . . *J. Cæsar* i 2 14
Whilst we, lying still, Are full of rest, defence, and nimbleness . iv 3 201
Cæsar, now be still: I kill'd not thee with half so good a will . . v 5 50
But in these cases We still have judgement here . . . *Macbeth* i 7 8
Come, let me clutch thee. I have thee not, and yet I see thee still . ii 1 35
I see thee still, And on thy blade and dudgeon gouts of blood . . ii 1 45
Though all things foul would wear the brows of grace, Yet grace must still look so . . . . iv 3 24
Hang out our banners on the outward walls; The cry is still 'They come' . . . . v 5 2
Thou still hast been the father of good news . . . *Hamlet* ii 2 42
A silence in the heavens, the rack stand still . . . . ii 2 506
This counsellor Is now most still, most secret, and most grave . . iii 4 214
And nothing is at a like goodness still . . . . . iv 7 117
To be worst . . . Stands still in esperance, lives not in fear . . *Lear* iv 1 4
Of spirit so still and quiet, that her motion Blush'd at herself . *Othello* i 3 95
But still the house-affairs would draw her thence . . . i 3 147
Peace, and be still!—I will so. What's the matter? . . . v 2 46
Ha! no more moving? Still as the grave . . . . . v 2 94
We bring forth weeds, When our quick minds lie still *Ant. and Cleo.* i 2 114
You shall hear from me still; the time shall not Out-go my thinking on you iii 2 60
Being charged, we will be still by land, Which, as I take't, we shall . iv 11 1
Dost thou lie still? . . . . v 2 299
Our bloods No more obey the heavens than our courtiers Still seem as does the king . . . . *Cymbeline* i 1 3
And will continue fast to your affection, Still close as sure . . i 6 139
Let her lie still and dream . . . . ii 3 70
Still, I swear I love you.—If you but said so, 'twere as deep with me: If you swear still, your recompense is still That I regard it not . ii 3 95
He made a law, To keep her still, and men in awe . . *Pericles* i Gower 36
O, still Thy deafening, dreadful thunders! . . . . . iii 1 4
Still-born. Grant that our hopes, yet likely of fair birth, Should be still-born . . . . *2 Hen. IV.* i 3 64
Still-breeding. A generation of still-breeding thoughts . *Richard II.* v 5 8
Still-closing. Wound the loud winds, or with bemock'd-at stabs Kill the still-closing waters . . . . *Tempest* iii 3 64
Still conclusion. With her modest eyes And still conclusion *A. and C.* iv 15 28
Still conversation. Of a holy, cold, and still conversation . . ii 6 131
Still-discordant. The still-discordant wavering multitude *2 Hen. IV.* Ind. 19
Still midnight. At still midnight, Walk round about an oak *Mer. Wives* iv 4 30
Still-peering. Move the still-peering air . . . *All's Well* iii 2 113
Still practice. By still practice learn to know thy meaning *T. Andron.* iii 2 45
Still rhetoric. By the heart's still rhetoric . . . *L. L. Lost* ii 1 229
Still sleep. Prepare To see the life as lively mock'd as ever Still sleep mock'd death . . . . *W. Tale* v 3 20
Still-soliciting. A still-soliciting eye, and such a tongue As I am glad I have not . . . . *Lear* i 1 234
Still-stand. As with the tide swell'd up unto his height, That makes a still-stand, running neither way . . . *2 Hen. IV.* ii 3 64
Still swine eats all the draff . . . . . *Mer. Wives* iv 2 109
Still-vexed. To fetch dew From the still-vex'd Bermoothes *Tempest* i 2 229
Still-waking sleep, that is not what it is! . . . *Rom. and Jul.* i 1 187
Stilled. Whose advice Hath often still'd my brawling discontent *Meas. for Meas.* iv 1 9
Stiller. For this from stiller seats we came . . . *Cymbeline* v 4 69
Stillest. In the calmest and most stillest night . . *2 Hen. IV.* iii 1 28
Stillness. A wilful stillness entertain, With purpose to be dress'd in an opinion Of wisdom, gravity . . . . . *Mer. of Venice* i 1 90
Soft stillness and the night Become the touches of sweet harmony . v 1 56
In peace there's nothing so becomes a man As modest stillness *Hen. V.* iii 1 4
In patient stillness while his rider mounts him . . . . iii 7 24
The gravity and stillness of your youth The world hath noted *Othello* ii 3 191
Stilly. The hum of either army stilly sounds . . . *Hen. V.* iv Prol. 5

Sting. Injurious wasps, to feed on such sweet honey And kill the bees that yield it with your stings! . . . . . *T. G. of Ver.* i 2 107
One who never feels The wanton stings and motions of the sense *M. for M.* i 4 59
What, wouldst thou have a serpent sting thee twice? *Mer. of Venice* iv 1 69
A libertine, As sensual as the brutish sting itself . *As Y. Like It* ii 7 66
Thy sting is not so sharp As friend remember'd not . . . ii 7 188
If I be waspish, best beware my sting . . . *T. of Shrew* ii 1 211
Who knows not where a wasp does wear his sting? . . . . ii 1 215
What sharp stings are in her mildest words! . . . *All's Well* iii 4 18
There is something in't that stings his nature . . . . iv 3 4
Betrays to slander, Whose sting is sharper than the sword's . *W. Tale* ii 3 86
Snakes, in my heart-blood warm'd, that sting my heart! *Richard II.* iii 2 131
Lest thy pity prove A serpent that will sting thee to the heart . v 3 58
Thy friends, Have but their stings and teeth newly ta'en out *2 Hen. IV.* iv 5 206
Armed in their stings, Make boot upon the summer's velvet buds *Hen. V.* i 2 193
As the snake roll'd in a flowering bank, With shining checker'd slough, doth sting a child . . . . *2 Hen. VI.* iii 1 229
The starved snake, Who, cherish'd in your breasts, will sting your hearts iii 1 344
Their touch affrights me as a serpent's sting . . . . iii 2 47
Scatter up and down And care not who they sting . . . . iii 2 127
With whose envenomed and fatal sting, Your loving uncle, twenty times his worth, They say, is shamefully bereft of life . . . . iii 2 267
Their softest touch as smart as lizards' stings! . . . . iii 2 325
Some say the bee stings: but I say, 'tis the bee's wax . . . iv 2 89
Who 'scapes the lurking serpent's mortal sting? . . *3 Hen. VI.* ii 2 15
To be avoided, As venom toads, or lizards' dreadful stings . . ii 2 138
They cannot greatly sting to hurt, Yet look to have them buzz . . ii 6 94
Wasps that buzz about his nose Will make this sting the sooner *Hen. VIII.* iii 2 56
Full merrily the humble-bee doth sing, Till he hath lost his honey and his sting . . . . *Troi. and Cres.* v 10 43
But when ye have the honey ye desire, Let not this wasp outlive, us both to sting.—I warrant you . . . . . *T. Andron.* ii 3 132
We put a sting in him, That at his will he may do danger with *J. Cæsar* ii 1 16
Very wisely threat before you sting . . . . v 1 38
Adder's fork and blind-worm's sting, Lizard's leg and howlet's wing *Macbeth* iv 1 16
The serpent that did sting thy father's life Now wears his crown . *Ham.* i 5 39
To those thorns that in her bosom lodge, To prick and sting her . . i 5 88
These things sting His mind so venomously . . . . *Lear* iv 3 47
We have reason to cool our raging motions, our carnal stings . *Othello* i 3 335
If knife, drugs, serpents, have Edge, sting, or operation *Ant. and Cleo.* iv 15 26
Stinging. Each pinch more stinging Than bees that made 'em *Tempest* i 2 329
Yield stinging nettles to mine enemies . . . *Richard II.* iii 2 18
Like stinging bees in hottest summer's day . . *T. Andron.* v 1 14
Stingless. Leave them honeyless.—Not stingless too . . *J. Cæsar* v 1 35
Stink. Indeed, it does stink in some sort . . . *Meas. for Meas.* iii 2 29
If your metaphor stink, I will stop my nose . . . *All's Well* v 2 13
They would but stink, and putrefy the air . . . *1 Hen. VI.* iv 7 90
His breath stinks with eating toasted cheese . . *2 Hen. VI.* iv 7 13
When Lady the brach may stand by the fire and stink . . . *Lear* i 4 126
She makes our profession as it were to stink afore the face of the gods *Pericles* iv 6 145
Stinking. The sky, it seems, would pour down stinking pitch *Tempest* i 2 3
Stinking clothes that fretted in their own grease . . *Mer. Wives* iii 5 115
You may buy land now as cheap as stinking mackerel . *1 Hen. IV.* ii 4 394
Him that thou magnifiest with all these titles Stinking and fly-blown lies here at our feet . . . . *1 Hen. VI.* iv 7 76
It will be stinking law; for his breath stinks . . *2 Hen. VI.* iv 7 12
Showing . . . his wounds To the people, beg their stinking breaths *Cor.* ii 1 252
When you cast Your stinking greasy caps . . . . . . iv 6 131
And threw up their sweaty night-caps and uttered such a deal of stinking breath . . . . *J. Cæsar* i 2 248
There's not a nose among twenty but can smell him that's stinking *Lear* ii 4 72
Unlustrous as the smoky light That's fed with stinking tallow *Cymbeline* i 6 110
Let the stinking elder, grief, untwine His perishing root! . . . iv 2 59
Stinkingly. Canst thou believe thy living is a life, So stinkingly depending? . . . . *Meas. for Meas.* iii 2 28
Stint. We must not stint Our necessary actions, in the fear To cope malicious censurers . . . . *Hen. VIII.* i 2 76
The combatants being kin Half stints their strife . *Troi. and Cres.* iv 5 93
With the shadow of his wings He can at pleasure stint their melody *T. An.* iv 4 86
It stinted and said 'Ay.'—And stint thou too, I pray thee *Rom. and Jul.* i 3 58
Make war breed peace, make peace stint war . . *T. of Athens* v 4 83
Swears she'll never stint, Make raging battery upon shores of flint *Per.* iv 4 42
Stinted. And, pretty fool, it stinted and said 'Ay' . *Rom. and Jul.* i 3 48; 57
Stir. What halloing and what stir is this to-day? . . *T. G. of Ver.* v 4 13
If I did not think it had been Anne Page, would I might never stir! *M. W.* v 5 199
Never could the strumpet, With all her double vigour, art, and nature, Once stir my temper . . . . *Meas. for Meas.* ii 2 185
Stir not you till you have well determined . . . . . v 1 258
I will not let him stir Till I have used the approved means *Com. of Er.* v 1 102
I will determine this before I stir . . . . v 1 167
What, Conrade!—Peace! stir not.—Conrade, I say! . *Much Ado* iii 3 103
More Ates! stir them on! stir them on! . . . . *L. L. Lost* v 2 695
Stir up the Athenian youth to merriments . . . *M. N. Dream* i 1 13
I will not stir from this place, do what they can . . . . iii 1 125
Stir Demetrius up with bitter wrong . . . . iii 2 361
Let none of your people stir me: I have an exposition of sleep . . iv 1 43
Now will I stir this gamester . . . . . . *As Y. Like It* i 1 170
So shall we pass along And never stir assailants . . . . . i 3 116
With catlike watch, When that the sleeping man should stir . . . iv 3 117
'Tis time to stir him from his trance. . . . . *T. of Shrew* i 1 182
Whose worthiness would stir it up where it wanted . . *All's Well* i 1 10
By all means stir on the youth to an answer . . . *T. Night* iii 2 63
What wisdom stirs amongst you? . . . . *W. Tale* ii 1 21
They are heavier Than all thy woes can stir . . . . . iii 2 210
He would not stir his pettitoes till he had both tune and words . . iv 4 619
The wrongs I have done thee stir Afresh within me . . . . v 1 148
Proceed: No foot shall stir . . . . v 3 98
Stir, nay, come away, Bequeath to death your numbness . . . . v 3 101
You perceive she stirs: Start not . . . . v 3 103
Would I might never stir from off this place . . . *K. John* i 1 145
Who dares not stir by day must walk by night . . . . . i 1 172
Stir them up against a mightier task . . . . ii 1 55
From that supernal judge, that stirs good thoughts . . . . ii 1 112
I'll stir them to it . . . . ii 1 415
I will sit as quiet as a lamb; I will not stir, nor wince, nor speak a word iv 1 81
If thou but frown on me, or stir thy foot, . . . I'll strike thee dead . iv 3 96
To stir against the butchers of his life . . . . *Richard II.* i 2 3
What stir Keeps good old York there with his men of war? . . . ii 3 51

Stir. My blood hath been too cold and temperate, Unapt to stir 1 *Hen. IV.* i 3 2
O, the blood more stirs To rouse a lion than to start a hare! . . . i 3 197
I fear my brother Mortimer doth stir About his title . . . ii 3 84
I could not stir But like a comet I was wonder'd at . . . iii 2 46
Be advised; stir not to-night . . . . iv 3 5
By his gates of breath There lies a downy feather which stirs not 2 *Hen. IV.* iv 5 32
All hell shall stir for this . . . . . . *Hen. V.* v 1 72
If I did but stir out of my bed, Ready they were to shoot me 1 *Hen. VI.* i 4 55
What stir is this? what tumult's in the heavens? . . . . i 4 98
Stir not, for your lives; let her pass by . . . 2 *Hen. VI.* ii 4 18
Nor stir at nothing till the axe of death Hang over thee . . ii 4 49
I will stir up in England some black storm . . . . iii 1 349
Dares stir a wing, if Warwick shake his bells . . 3 *Hen. VI.* i 1 47
Such a messenger As shall revenge his death before I stir . . i 1 100
And thou, son Clarence, Shalt stir up in Suffolk, Norfolk, and in Kent iv 8 12
Wheresoe'er I meet thee—As I will meet thee, if thou stir abroad . v 1 96
Say it is the queen and her allies That stir the king *Richard III.* i 3 331
He stirs: shall I strike?—No, first let's reason with him . . i 4 164
Stir with the lark to-morrow, gentle Norfolk . . . . v 3 56
I know 'twill stir him strongly . . . . *Hen. VIII.* iii 2 218
He will advance thee; Some little memory of me will stir him . iii 2 417
A man that more detests, more stirs against, Both in his private conscience and his place, Defacers of a public peace . . . v 3 39
We may as well push against Powle's, as stir 'em . . . v 4 16
Things in motion sooner catch the eye Than what not stirs *Troi. and Cres.* iii 3 184
Picture-like to hang by the wall, if renown made it not stir *Coriolanus* i 3 13
You show too much of that For which the people stir . . . iii 1 53
To stir a mutiny in the mildest thoughts . . *T. Andron.* iv 1 85
To move is to stir; and to be valiant is to stand . . *Rom. and Jul.* i 1 11
Thou shalt not stir a foot to seek a foe . . . . . i 1 87
Tush, I will stir about, And all things shall be well . . . iv 2 39
Come, stir, stir, stir! the second cock hath crow'd, The curfew-bell hath rung, 'tis three o'clock . . . . iv 4 3
The lady stirs . . . . v 3 147
You do yourselves but wrong to stir me up; Let me pass *T. of Athens* iii 4 53
This fearful night, There is no stir or walking in the streets *J. Cæsar* i 3 127
Stir up their servants to an act of rage, And after seem to chide 'em . ii 1 176
Think you to walk forth? You shall not stir out of your house to-day . ii 2 9
What say the augurers?—They would not have you to stir forth to-day ii 2 38
O masters, if I were disposed to stir Your hearts and minds to mutiny and rage, I should do Brutus wrong . . . . . . iii 2 126
Sweet friends, let me not stir you up To such a sudden flood of mutiny iii 2 214
I have neither wit, nor words, nor worth, Action, nor utterance, nor the power of speech, To stir men's blood . . . . . . iii 2 227
Stir not until the signal.—Words before blows . . . . v 1 26
If chance will have me king, why, chance may crown me, Without my stir . . . . *Macbeth* i 3 144
My fell of hair Would at a dismal treatise rouse and stir . . v 5 12
And then, they say, no spirit dare stir abroad . . . *Hamlet* i 1 161
Duller shouldst thou be than the fat weed That roots itself in ease on Lethe wharf, Wouldst thou not stir in this . . . . . i 5 34
Behind the arras hearing something stir, Whips out his rapier . . iv 1 9
Rightly to be great Is not to stir without great argument . . iv 4 54
I am satisfied in nature, Whose motive, in this case, should stir me most v 2 256
Call France; who stirs? Call Burgundy . . . . . *Lear* i 1 128
If you do stir abroad, go armed.—Armed, brother! . . . i 2 186
If it be you that stir these daughters' hearts Against their father . ii 4 277
This feather stirs: she lives! . . . . v 3 265
He that stirs next to carve for his own rage Holds his soul light *Othello* ii 3 173
If I once stir, Or do but lift this arm, the best of you Shall sink . ii 3 207
She is stirring, sir: if she will stir hither, I shall seem to notify unto her iii 1 30
Look, he stirs: Do you withdraw yourself a little while . . iv 1 56
Shall she come in? were't good?—I think she stirs again:—no . v 2 95
Of stirs abroad, I shall beseech you, sir, To let me be partaker *A. and C.* i 4 82
Your speech is passion: But, pray you, stir no embers up . . ii 2 13
As the fits and stirs of's mind Could best express . . *Cymbeline* i 6 38
I could not stir him: He said he was gentle, but unfortunate . iv 2 38
No further with your din Express impatience, lest you stir up mine v 4 112
Why do you stir so early? . . . . . . *Pericles* iii 2 12
Men must feed you, men must stir you up . . . . iv 2 98
Thunder shall not so awake the beds of eels as my giving out her beauty stir up the lewdly-inclined . . . . iv 2 156
Stirred. I am sorry, sir, I have thus far stirr'd you . . *W. Tale* v 3 74
A subject speaks, Stirr'd up by God . . . . *Richard II.* iv 1 133
Have stirr'd up My liefest liege to be mine enemy . 2 *Hen. VI.* iii 1 163
The thought of them would have stirr'd up remorse . 3 *Hen. VI.* v 5 64
Stirr'd up by Dorset, Buckingham, and Ely . *Richard III.* iv 4 468
He was stirr'd With such an agony, he sweat extremely. *Hen. VIII.* ii 1 32
Never desired It to be stirr'd; but oft have hinder'd, oft . . ii 4 164
My mind is troubled, like a fountain stirr'd . *Troi. and Cres.* iii 3 311
Like to a bubbling fountain stirr'd with wind . . *T. Andron.* ii 4 23
What, Brutus, are you stirr'd so early too? . . . *J. Cæsar* ii 2 110
As by your safety, wisdom, all things else, You mainly were stirr'd up *Hamlet* iv 7 9
Antony Will be himself.—But stirr'd by Cleopatra . . *Ant. and Cleo.* i 1 43
The senate hath stirr'd up the confiners . . . *Cymbeline* iv 2 337
Stirrer. An early stirrer, by the rood! . . . 2 *Hen. IV.* iii 2 3
Our bad neighbour makes us early stirrers . . . *Hen. V.* iv 1 6
Stirrest. How thou stirrest now! come away, or I'll fetch thee *Pericles* ii 1 16
How thou stirr'st, thou block! . . . . . . ii 2 90
Stirreth. He heareth not, he stirreth not, he moveth not *Rom. and Jul.* ii 1 15
Stirring. In the stirring passage of the day . *Com. of Errors* iii 1 99
Such a merry, nimble, stirring spirit . . . *L. L. Lost* v 2 16
I might approve This flower's force in stirring love . . *M. N. Dream* ii 2 69
No ill luck stirring but what lights on my shoulders . *Mer. of Venice* iii 1 99
The mother-queen, An Ate, stirring him to blood and strife . *K. John* ii 1 63
Be stirring as the time; be fire with fire . . . . . v 1 48
There's no equity stirring . . . . . . 1 *Hen. IV.* ii 2 106
What satisfaction canst thou make For bearing arms, for stirring up my subjects? . . . . 3 *Hen. VI.* v 5 15
You are early stirring: What news, what news? . . *Richard III.* iii 2 36
E'en so: Hector was stirring early . . . *Troi. and Cres.* i 2 52
I will keep where there is wit stirring . . . . . ii 1 130
A stirring dwarf we do allowance give Before a sleeping giant . . ii 3 146
Then we shall have a stirring world again . . . *Coriolanus* iv 5 233
For now, these hot days, is the mad blood stirring . *Rom. and Jul.* iii 1 4
Is thy master stirring? Our knocking has awaked him . . *Macbeth* ii 3 47
Is the king stirring, worthy thane?—Not yet . . . . ii 3 50
Have you had quiet guard?—Not a mouse stirring . . . *Hamlet* i 1 10
Stirring. If the gentlewoman that attends the general's wife be stirring . . . ?—She is stirring, sir: if she will stir hither *Othello* iii 1 27
That our stirring Can from the lap of Egypt's widow pluck The ne'er-lust-wearied Antony . . . . *Ant. and Cleo.* ii 1 36
Stirrup. An old mothy saddle and stirrups of no kindred *T. of Shrew* iii 2 50
What, no man at door To hold my stirrup nor to take my horse! . iv 1 124
Hast thou not kiss'd thy hand and held my stirrup? 2 *Hen. VI.* iv 1 53
And my arm'd knees, Who bow'd but in my stirrup, bend like his That hath received an alms! . . . . *Coriolanus* iii 2 119
Make sacred even his stirrup . . . . . *T. of Athens* i 1 82
Stitchery. Come, lay aside your stitchery . . . *Coriolanus* i 3 75
Stitches. And will laugh yourselves into stitches . . *T. Night* iii 2 73
Stithied. By the forge that stithied Mars his helm . *Troi. and Cres.* iv 5 255
Stithy. And my imaginations are as foul As Vulcan's stithy . *Hamlet* iii 2 89
Stoccadoes. Your passes, stoccadoes, and I know not what *Mer. Wives* ii 1 234
Stoccata. Alla stoccata carries it away . . . *Rom. and Jul.* iii 1 77
Stock. What need a man care for a stock with a wench, when she can knit him a stock? . . . . *T. G. of Ver.* iii 1 311
I have sat in the stocks for puddings he hath stolen . . . iv 4 33
Thy stock, thy reverse, thy distance, thy montant . *Mer. Wives* ii 3 26
Set me i' the stocks, i' the common stocks, for a witch . . iv 5 123
What needs all that, and a pair of stocks in the town? . *Com. of Errors* iii 1 60
Would any of the stock of Barrabas Had been her husband! *Mer. of Ven.* iv 1 296
I'll pheeze you, in faith.—A pair of stocks, you rogue! . *T. of Shrew* Ind. 1 2
Let's be no stoics nor no stocks, I pray . . . . . i 1 31
With a linen stock on one leg and a kersey boot-hose on the other . iii 2 67
Bring him forth: has sat i' the stocks all night . . *All's Well* iv 3 117
I have told your lordship already, the stocks carry him . . . iv 3 122
To this very instant disaster of his setting i' the stocks . . iv 3 127
Let me live, sir, in a dungeon, i' the stocks, or any where, so I may live iv 3 273
It does indifferent well in a flame-coloured stock . . *T. Night* i 3 144
My account I well may give, And in the stocks avouch it . *W. Tale* iv 3 22
We marry A gentler scion to the wildest stock . . . . iv 4 93
Like silly beggars Who sitting in the stocks refuge their shame, That many have and others must sit there . . . . *Richard II.* v 5 26
Ere I lead this life long, I'll sew nether stocks . . 1 *Hen. IV.* ii 4 130
Of the true line and stock of Charles the Great . . *Hen. V.* i 2 71
This is a stem Of that victorious stock . . . . . i 4 63
Our scions, put in wild and savage stock, Spirt up so suddenly . . iii 5 7
Sweet stem from York's great stock . . . . 1 *Hen. VI.* ii 5 41
Thy sons, fair slips of such a stock . . . . 2 *Hen. VI.* ii 2 58
And noble stock Was graft with crab-tree slip . . . . iii 2 213
To the corruption of a blemish'd stock . . . *Richard III.* iii 7 122
Her royal stock graft with ignoble plants . . . . . iii 7 127
Though from an humble stock, undoubtedly Was fashion'd to much honour from his cradle . . . . *Hen. VIII.* iv 2 49
But for the stock, Sir Thomas, I wish it grubb'd up now . . . v 1 22
How long continued, and what stock he springs of . . *Coriolanus* ii 3 245
Yet here he lets me prate Like one i' the stocks . . . . v 3 160
The emperor needs her not, Not her, nor thee, nor any of thy stock *T. An.* i 1 300
Now, by the stock and honour of my kin, To strike him dead I hold it not a sin . . . . *Rom. and Jul.* i 5 60
Virtue cannot so inoculate our old stock but we shall relish of it *Ham.* iii 1 119
Fetch forth the stocks! . . . We'll teach you— Sir, I am too old to learn: Call not your stocks for me . . . . . . *Lear* ii 2 132
Fetch forth the stocks! As I have life and honour, There shall he sit till noon . . . . ii 2 140
Bring away the stocks!—Let me beseech your grace not to do so . . ii 2 146
An thou hadst been set i' the stocks for that question, thou hadst well deserved it . . . . ii 4 65
Where learned you this, fool?—Not i' the stocks, fool . . . ii 4 88
How came my man i' the stocks?—I set him there, sir . . . ii 4 201
Be revenged; Or she that bore you was no queen, and you Recoil from your great stock . . . . *Cymbeline* i 6 128
Be jointed to the old stock and freshly grow . . . v 4 143; v 5 440
Were I well assured Came of a gentle kind and noble stock . *Pericles* v 1 68
Stocked. Who stock'd my servant? . . . . . *Lear* ii 4 191
Stock-fish. By this hand, I'll turn my mercy out o' doors and make a stock-fish of thee . . . . *Tempest* iii 2 79
He was begot between two stock-fishes . . . *Meas. for Meas.* iii 2 116
You stock-fish! O for breath to utter what is like thee! 1 *Hen. IV.* ii 4 271
One Sampson Stockfish, a fruiterer, behind Gray's Inn 2 *Hen. IV.* iii 2 35
Stocking. Foul stockings, greasy napkins . . . *Mer. Wives* iii 5 92
No more stockings than legs, nor no more shoes than feet *T. of Shrew* Ind. 2 10
The serving-men in their new fustian, their white stockings . . iv 1 50
Remember who commended thy yellow stockings . *T. Night* ii 5 166; iii 4 53
I will be strange, stout, in yellow stockings, and cross-gartered . ii 5 186
He will come to her in yellow stockings, and 'tis a colour she abhors . ii 5 219
He's in yellow stockings.—And cross-gartered?—Most villanously . iii 2 78
To put on yellow stockings and to frown . . . . . . v 1 346
Take note how many pair of silk stockings thou hast . 2 *Hen. IV.* ii 2 18
Tennis, and tall stockings, Short blister'd breeches . . *Hen. VIII.* i 3 30
His stockings foul'd, Ungarter'd, and down-gyved to his ancle *Hamlet* ii 1 79
You shall do small respect, show too bold malice Against the grace and person of my master, Stocking his messenger . . . . *Lear* ii 2 139
Stockish. Nought so stockish, hard, and full of rage, But music for the time doth change his nature . . . . . *Mer. of Venice* v 1 81
Stock-punished. Who is whipped from tithing to tithing, and stock-punished, and imprisoned . . . . *Lear* iii 4 140
Stoics. Let's be no stoics nor no stocks, I pray . . *T. of Shrew* i 1 31
Stokesly and Gardiner; the one of Winchester, Newly preferr'd from the king's secretary, The other, London . . . . *Hen. VIII.* iv 1 101
Stole. Bestow your luggage where you found it.—Or stole it, rather *Temp.* v 1 300
Tell Mistress Anne the jest, how my father stole two geese *Mer. Wives* iii 4 40
'Twas the boy that stole your meat, and you'll beat the post *Much Ado* ii 1 206
Warily I stole into a neighbour thicket by . . . *L. L. Lost* v 2 94
Unto the gentleman That lately stole his daughter . . *Mer. of Venice* iv 1 385
He stole from France, As 'tis reported, for the king had married him against his liking . . . . *All's Well* iii 5 55
He stole from Florence, taking no leave, and I follow him . . . v 3 143
Then I stole all courtesy from heaven . . . . 1 *Hen. IV.* iii 2 50
Bardolph stole a lute-case, bore it twelve leagues, and sold it *Hen. V.* iii 2 45
Sworn brothers in filching, and in Calais they stole a fire-shovel . iii 2 48
He slily stole away and left his men . . . . 3 *Hen. VI.* i 1 3
As Ulysses and stout Diomede With sleight and manhood stole to Rhesus' tents . . . . iv 2 20
He was ware of me And stole into the covert of the wood *Rom. and Jul.* i 1 132
You've ungently, Brutus, Stole from my bed . . . *J. Cæsar* ii 1 238
Most sacrilegious murder hath broke ope The Lord's anointed temple, and stole thence The life o' the building! . . . . . *Macbeth* ii 3 73

Stole. Upon my secure hour thy uncle stole, With juice of cursed hebenon in a vial . . . *Hamlet* i 5 61
That from a shelf the precious diadem stole, And put it in his pocket . iii 4 100
It is the false steward, that stole his master's daughter . . . iv 5 173
At three and two years old, I stole these babes . . *Cymbeline* iii 3 101
Their nurse, Euriphile, Whom for the theft I wedded, stole these children v 5 341
Stolen. Should she thus be stol'n away from you, It would be much vexation to your age . . . *T. G. of Ver.* iii 1 15
I have sat in the stocks for puddings he hath stolen . . . iv 4 34
The other squirrel was stolen from me by the hangman boys . . iv 4 59
These filthy vices! It were as good To pardon him that hath from nature stolen A man already made . . *Meas. for Meas.* ii 4 43
My stay must be stolen out of other affairs . . . . iii 1 159
Thou hast stolen both mine office and my name . . *Com. of Errors* iii 1 44
Who, as I take it, have stolen his birds' nest . . . *Much Ado* ii 1 238
Have a care that your bills be not stolen . . . . . iii 3 44
Prince John is this morning secretly stolen away . . . iv 2 64
Writ in my cousin's hand, stolen from her pocket . . . v 4 89
They have been at a great feast of languages, and stolen the scraps *L. L. L.* v 1 40
And stolen the impression of her fantasy . . *M. N. Dream* i 1 32
As her attendant hath A lovely boy, stolen from an Indian king . ii 1 22
I know When thou hast stolen away from fairy land . . . ii 1 65
Thou told'st me they were stolen unto this wood . . . ii 1 191
Would he have stolen away From sleeping Hermia? . . . iii 2 51
Have you come by night And stolen my love's heart from him? . iii 2 284
They would have stolen away; they would . . . . iv 1 161
Stolen hence, and left me asleep! . . . . . . iv 1 209
Two sealed bags of ducats, Of double ducats, stolen from me by my daughter! And jewels, two stones, two rich and precious stones, Stolen by my daughter! . . . . *Mer. of Venice* ii 8 19
Has my fellow Tranio stolen your clothes? Or you stolen his? *T. of Shrew* i 1 229
Scorn'd a fair colour, or express'd it stolen . . *All's Well* v 3 50
Where she has lived, Or how stolen from the dead . . *W. Tale* v 3 115
Worcester is stolen away to-night . . . . *1 Hen. IV.* ii 4 392
And the shirt, to say the truth, stolen from my host . . . iv 2 50
Some hilding fellow that had stolen The horse he rode on . *2 Hen. IV.* i 1 57
Thou hast stolen that which after some few hours Were thine without offence . . . . iv 5 102
He hath stolen a pax, and hanged must a' be . . . *Hen. V.* iii 6 42
Being put to nurse, Was by a beggar-woman stolen away . *2 Hen. VI.* iv 2 151
From Scotland am I stol'n, even of pure love . . *3 Hen. VI.* iii 1 13
That you might still have worn the petticoat, And ne'er have stol'n the breech from Lancaster . . . . v 5 24
With old odd ends stolen out of holy writ . . . *Richard III.* i 3 337
Cardinal Campeius Is stol'n away to Rome . . . *Hen. VIII.* iii 2 57
O, theft most base, That we have stol'n what we do fear to keep! But, thieves, unworthy of a thing so stol'n . . . *Troi. and Cres.* ii 2 93
Dost thou think I'll grace thee with that robbery, thy stol'n name Coriolanus in Corioli? . . . . . . *Coriolanus* v 6 89
He is wise; And, on my life, hath stol'n him home to bed *Rom. and Jul.* ii 1 4
Their stol'n marriage-day Was Tybalt's dooms-day . . . v 3 233
A composture stolen From general excrement . . *T. of Athens* iv 3 444
Soundless too; For you have stol'n their buzzing, Antony . *J. Cæsar* v 1 37
The king's two sons, Are stol'n away and fled . . . *Macbeth* ii 4 26
When I have stol'n upon these sons-in-law, Then, kill, kill, kill! *Lear* iv 6 190
Stol'n from me, and corrupted By spells and medicines . . *Othello* i 3 60
Hast stol'n it from her?—No, 'faith; she let it drop by negligence . iii 3 310
What sense had I of her stol'n hours of lust? I saw 't not, thought it not iii 3 338
He that is robb'd, not wanting what is stol'n, Let him not know 't, and he's not robb'd at all . . . . iii 3 342
Why have you stol'n upon us thus? You come not Like Cæsar's sister *Ant. and Cleo.* iii 6 42
To tell them that this world did equal theirs Till they had stol'n our jewel . . . . iv 15 78
From their nursery Were stol'n . . . . . *Cymbeline* i 1 60
Your ring may be stolen too: so your brace of unprizable estimations . i 4 98
Who knows if one of her women, being corrupted, Hath stol'n it from her? . . . . ii 4 117
This was stolen.—By Jupiter, I had it from her arm . . . ii 4 120
I have stol'n nought, nor would not, though I had found Gold strew'd i' the floor . . . . iii 6 49
You shall not now be stol'n, you have locks upon you . . . v 4 1
Who, by Belarius stol'n, For many years thought dead . . . v 5 455
Stolest. O villain, thou stolest a cup of sack eighteen years ago *1 Hen. IV.* ii 4 345
And stolest away the ladies' hearts of France . . *2 Hen. VI.* i 3 55
Stomach. Which raised in me An undergoing stomach, to bear up *Tempest* i 2 157
You cram these words into mine ears against The stomach of my sense . ii 1 107
Do not turn me about; my stomach is not constant . . . ii 2 118
No matter, since They have left their viands behind; for we have stomachs . . . . iii 3 41
I would it were, That you might kill your stomach on your meat *T. G. of V.* i 2 68
You come not home because you have no stomach; You have no stomach having broke your fast . . . . *Com. of Errors* i 2 49
He is a very valiant trencher-man; he hath an excellent stomach *M. Ado* i 1 52
Eat when I have stomach and wait for no man's leisure . . . i 3 16
Despite of his quick wit and his queasy stomach . . . . ii 1 399
You have no stomach, signior: fare you well . . . . ii 3 265
I hope, when I do it, I shall do it on a full stomach . . *L. L. Lost* i 2 154
Say, can you fast? your stomachs are too young . . . . iv 3 294
For as a surfeit of the sweetest things The deepest loathing to the stomach brings . . . . *M. N. Dream* ii 2 138
Prepare for dinner.—That is done, sir; they have all stomachs *M. of V.* iii 5 54
Let me praise you while I have a stomach . . . . . iii 5 92
As there is no more plenty in it, it goes much against my stomach *As Y. Like It* iii 2 22
Fall to them as you find your stomach serves you . . *T. of Shrew* i 1 38
But if you have a stomach, to 't i' God's name . . . . i 2 195
Sit down; I know you have a stomach . . . . . iv 1 161
My banquet is to close our stomachs up, After our great good cheer . v 2 9
Then vail your stomachs, for it is no boot . . . . . v 2 176
And so dies with feeding his own stomach . . . *All's Well* i 1 156
I begin to love, as an old man loves money, with no stomach . . ii 1 18
If you have a stomach, to 't . . . . iii 6 67
When my knightly stomach is sufficed, Why then I suck my teeth *K. John* i 1 191
What is 't that takes from thee Thy stomach, pleasure? . *1 Hen. IV.* ii 3 44
That furious Scot . . . 'Gan vail his stomach . . *2 Hen. IV.* i 1 129
She either gives a stomach and no food; Such are the poor, in health . iv 4 105
For, if we may, We'll not offend one stomach with our play *Hen. V.* ii Prol. 40
Their villany goes against my weak stomach, and therefore I must cast it up . . . . iii 2 57

Stomach. They have only stomachs to eat and none to fight . *Hen. V.* iii 7 166
He which hath no stomach to this fight, Let him depart . . . iv 3 35
Good God, these nobles should such stomachs bear! . *1 Hen. VI.* i 3 90
For soldiers' stomachs always serve them well . . . . . ii 3 80
How will their grudging stomachs be provoked To wilful disobedience! iv 1 141
The winds grow high; so do your stomachs, lords . *2 Hen. VI.* ii 1 55
Which is not amiss to cool a man's stomach this hot weather . . iv 10 10
All goodness Is poison to thy stomach . . . *Hen. VIII.* iii 2 283
He was a man Of an unbounded stomach . . . . . . iv 2 34
Call some knight to arms That hath a stomach . . *Troi. and Cres.* ii 1 137
They think my little stomach to the war And your great love to me restrains you thus . . . . iii 3 220
You may have every day enough of Hector, If you have stomach . iv 5 264
Then give me leave, for losers will have leave To ease their stomachs with their bitter tongues . . . . . *T. Andron.* iii 1 234
Although the cheer be poor, 'Twill fill your stomachs . . . v 3 29
Where feed'st thou o' days, Apemantus?—Where my stomach finds meat; or, rather, where I eat it . . . . . *T. of Athens* iv 3 294
Gives men stomach to digest his words With better appetite . *J. Cæsar* i 2 305
If you dare fight to-day, come to the field; If not, when you have stomachs . . . . v 1 66
To some enterprise That hath a stomach in't . . . . *Hamlet* i 1 100
I am not well; else I should answer From a full-flowing stomach *Lear* v 3 74
'Tis not a year or two shows us a man: They are all but stomachs *Oth.* iii 4 104
Had all his hairs been lives, my great revenge Had stomach for them all v 2 75
Make the wars alike against my stomach, Having alike your cause *Ant. and Cleo.* ii 2 50
Believe not all; or, if you must believe, Stomach not all . . iii 4 12
Our stomachs Will make what's homely savoury . . . *Cymbeline* iii 6 32
So graze as you find pasture.—Ay, or a stomach . . . . v 4 2
If the sea's stomach be o'ercharged with gold, 'Tis a good constraint of fortune it belches upon us . . . . . . *Pericles* iii 2 54
The air is quick there, And it pierces and sharpens the stomach . . iv 1 29
Stomachers. Golden quoifs and stomachers . . . *W. Tale* iv 4 226
Corrupters of my faith! you shall no more Be stomachers to my heart *Cymbeline* iii 4 86
Stomaching. 'Tis not a time For private stomaching . *Ant. and Cleo.* ii 2 9
Stomach-qualmed. If you are sick at sea, Or stomach-qualm'd at land, a dram of this Will drive away distemper . . . . *Cymbeline* iii 4 193
Stone. Give her no token but stones; for she's as hard as steel *T. G. of V.* i 1 149
In revenge of thy ingratitude, I throw thy name against the bruising stones . . . . i 2 111
He is a stone, a very pebble stone, and has no more pity in him than a dog . . . . ii 3 11
He makes sweet music with the enamell'd stones . . . . ii 7 28
Whose golden touch could soften steel and stones . . . . iii 2 79
By gar, I will cut all his two stones; by gar, he shall not have a stone to throw at his dog . . . . *Mer. Wives* i 4 118
What is 'lapis,' William?—A stone.—And what is 'a stone,' William? —A pebble . . . . iv 1 33
Or that his appetite Is more to bread than stone . *Meas. for Meas.* i 3 53
Cracking the stones of the foresaid prunes . . . . . ii 1 110
Stones whose rates are either rich or poor As fancy values them . . ii 2 150
This stone doth show That I am that same wall . . *M. N. Dream* v 1 162
Cursed be thy stones for thus deceiving me! . . . . . v 1 182
My cherry lips have often kiss'd thy stones, Thy stones with lime and hair knit up in thee . . . . v 1 192
Should I go to church And see the holy edifice of stone? *Mer. of Venice* i 1 30
Two stones, two rich and precious stones, Stolen by my daughter! . ii 8 20
Find the girl; She hath the stones upon her, and the ducats . . ii 8 22
All the boys in Venice follow him, Crying, his stones, his daughter . ii 8 24
Therefore the poet Did feign that Orpheus drew trees, stones, and floods . . . . v 1 80
Books in the running brooks, Sermons in stones . . *As Y. Like It* ii 1 17
When I was in love I broke my sword upon a stone . . . ii 4 47
She brought stone jugs and no seal'd quarts . . *T. of Shrew* Ind. 2 90
I have seen a medicine That's able to breathe life into a stone *All's Well* ii 1 76
An ordinary fool that has no more brain than a stone . . *T. Night* i 5 92
I have said too much unto a heart of stone . . . . . iii 4 221
Nor brass nor stone nor parchment bears not one [example] . *W. Tale* i 2 360
Is rotten As ever oak or stone was sound . . . . . ii 3 90
Not a counterfeit stone, not a ribbon, glass, pomander . . . iv 4 609
Chide me, dear stone, that I may say indeed Thou art Hermione . . v 3 24
Does not the stone rebuke me For being more stone than it? . . . v 3 37
From thy admiring daughter took the spirits, Standing like stone with thee . . . . v 3 42
If I had thought the sight of my poor image Would thus have wrought you,—for the stone is mine—I'ld not have show'd it . . . v 3 58
Those sleeping stones, That as a waist doth girdle you about . *K. John* ii 1 216
O me! my uncle's spirit is in these stones: Heaven take my soul! . iv 3 9
Unfurnish'd walls, Unpeopled offices, untrodden stones . *Richard II.* i 2 69
This little world, This precious stone set in the silver sea . . ii 1 46
This earth shall have a feeling and these stones Prove armed soldiers . iii 2 24
King Richard lies Within the limits of yon lime and stone . . iii 3 26
This worm-eaten hold of ragged stone . . . *2 Hen. IV.* Ind. 35
The blood Of fair King Richard, scraped from Pomfret stones . . i 1 205
It shall go hard but I will make him a philosopher's two stones to me . iii 2 355
His feet . . . were as cold as any stone; then I felt to his knees, and they were as cold as any stone, and so upward and upward, and all was as cold as any stone . . . . *Hen. V.* ii 3 26
That goddess blind, That stands upon the rolling restless stone . . iii 6 31
Fixed upon a spherical stone, which rolls, and rolls, and rolls . . iii 6 38
As swift as stones Enforced from the old Assyrian slings . . . iv 7 64
And with my nails digg'd stones out of the ground, To hurl at the beholders of my shame . . . . *1 Hen. VI.* i 4 45
An uproar, I dare warrant, Begun through malice . . . 'Stones! stones!' . . . . iii 1 76
Have fill'd their pockets full of pebble stones . . . . . iii 1 80
If we be forbidden stones, we'll fall to it with our teeth . . . iii 1 89
Even at this sight My heart is turn'd to stone . . *2 Hen. VI.* v 2 50
Not deck'd with diamonds and Indian stones, Nor to be seen *3 Hen. VI.* iii 1 63
I will not ruinate my father's house, Who gave his blood to lime the stones together . . . . v 1 84
Leave the town and fight? Or shall we beat the stones about thine ears? v 1 108
Heaps of pearl, Inestimable stones, unvalued jewels . *Richard III.* i 4 27
Like dumb statuas or breathing stones, Gazed each on other . . iii 7 25
I am not made of stones, But penetrable to your kind entreats . . iii 7 224
Pity, you ancient stones, those tender babes! . . . . . iv 1 99
So foolish sorrow bids your stones farewell . . . . . iv 1 104
A base foul stone, made precious by the foil Of England's chair . . v 3 250

Stone. I told ye all, When we first put this dangerous stone a-rolling, 'Twould fall upon ourselves . . . *Hen. VIII.* v 3 104
When waterdrops have worn the stones of Troy . . *Troi. and Cres.* iii 2 193
The fall of every Phrygian stone will cost A drop of Grecian blood . iv 5 223
Hector's dead: There is a word will Priam turn to stone . v 10 18
Thy knee bussing the stones—for in such business Action is eloquence *Coriolanus* iii 2 75
Lest that thy wives with spits and boys with stones In puny battle slay me . . . . iv 4 5
No man is by; And you recount your sorrows to a stone *T. Andron.* iii 1 29
And bootless unto them . . . Therefore I tell my sorrows to the stones iii 1 37
A stone is soft as wax,—tribunes more hard than stones; A stone is silent, and offendeth not . . . . . . iii 1 45
And on the ragged stones beat forth our brains . . v 3 133
It had upon its brow A bump as big as a young cockerel's stone *R. and J.* i 3 53
O, mickle is the powerful grace that lies In herbs, plants, stones . ii 3 16
Thy canopy is dust and stones;—Which with sweet water nightly I will dew . . . . v 3 13
Sometime like a philosopher, with two stones moe than 's artificial one *T. of Athens* ii 2 117
One day he gives us diamonds, next day stones . . iii 6 131
Thou tedious rogue! I am sorry I shall lose a stone by thee . iv 3 375
You blocks, you stones, you worse than senseless things! *J. Cæsar* i 1 40
You are not wood, you are not stones, but men . . iii 2 147
That should move The stones of Rome to rise and mutiny . iii 2 234
For fear Thy very stones prate of my whereabout . *Macbeth* ii 1 58
Stones have been known to move and trees to speak . . iii 4 123
Toad, that under cold stone Days and nights has thirty one iv 1 6
How pale he glares! His form and cause conjoin'd, preaching to stones, Would make them capable . . . . . *Hamlet* iii 4 126
At his head a grass-green turf, At his heels a stone . . iv 5 32
Like the spring that turneth wood to stone, Convert his gyves to graces iv 7 20
This hard house—More harder than the stones whereof 'tis raised *Lear* iii 2 64
Met I my father with his bleeding rings, Their precious stones new lost v 3 190
Howl, howl, howl, howl! O, you are men of stones . . v 3 257
If that her breath will mist or stain the stone, Why, then she lives . v 3 262
My heart is turned to stone; I strike it, and it hurts my hand *Othello* iv 1 193
Her salt tears fell from her, and soften'd the stones . iv 3 47
Thou dost stone my heart, And makest me call what I intend to do A murder . . . . v 2 63
Are there no stones in heaven But what serve for the thunder? . v 2 234
Go to, then; your considerate stone . . . . *Ant. and Cleo.* ii 2 112
The first stone Drop in my neck: as it determines, so Dissolve my life! iii 13 160
I praised her as I rated her: so do I my stone . . *Cymbeline* i 4 84
The twinn'd stones Upon the number'd beach . . . i 6 35
Sparkles this stone as it was wont? or is't not Too dull? . ii 4 40
The stone's too hard to come by.—Not a whit, Your lady being so easy ii 4 46
Spit, and throw stones, cast mire upon me . . . v 5 222
The gods throw stones of sulphur on me . . . . v 5 240
The blest infusions That dwell in vegetives, in metals, stones *Pericles* iii 2 36
Stone-bow. O, for a stone-bow, to hit him in the eye! . *T. Night* ii 5 51
Stone-cutter. A stone-cutter or a painter could not have made him so ill, though he had been but two hours at the trade . *Lear* ii 2 63
Stoned. Some say he shall be stoned; but that death is too soft *W. Tale* iv 4 807
Remember 'stoned,' and 'flayed alive' . . . . iv 4 835
Stone-hard. The murderous knife was dull and blunt Till it was whetted on thy stone-hard heart . . . *Richard III.* iv 4 227
Stone-still. I will not struggle, I will stand stone-still . *K. John* iv 1 77
Stone walls. Sigh'd forth proverbs, That hunger broke stone walls *Coriol.* i 1 210
Stony. Thou art come to answer A stony adversary . *Mer. of Venice* iv 1 4
Which thou hast whetted on thy stony heart . . *2 Hen. IV.* iv 5 108
My heart is turn'd to stone: and while 'tis mine, It shall be stony *2 Hen. VI.* v 2 51
Thy brother, I, Even like a stony image, cold and numb *T. Andron.* iii 1 259
For stony limits cannot hold love out . . *Rom. and Jul.* ii 2 67
What blood is this, which stains The stony entrance of this sepulchre? v 3 141
Nor stony tower, nor walls of beaten brass, Nor airless dungeon *J. Cæsar* i 3 93
Stony-hearted. The stony-hearted villains know it well enough *1 Hen. IV.* ii 2 28
Stony-Stratford. At Stony-Stratford will they be to-night *Richard III.* ii 4 2
Stood. Whiles we stood here securing your repose . . *Tempest* ii 1 310
Such men Whose heads stood in their breasts . . . iii 3 47
Thou Hast strangely stood the test . . . . . iv 1 7
I have stood on the pillory for geese he hath killed *T. G. of Ver.* iv 4 35
What dangerous action, stood it next to death, Would I not undergo! . v 4 41
Stood, as it were, in a fruit-dish, a dish of some three-pence *M. for M.* ii 1 94
I have stood by, my lord, and I have heard Your royal ear abused . v 1 138
Where England?— . . . I guess it stood in her chin, by the salt rheum that ran between France and it . . *Com. of Errors* iii 2 131
Where stood Belgia, the Netherlands?—Oh, sir, I did not look so low iii 2 142
You have of late stood out against your brother . *Much Ado* i 3 22
I stood like a man at a mark, with a whole army shooting at me . ii 1 253
Or else it stood upon the choice of friends . *M. N. Dream* i 1 139
And that same dew . . . Stood now within the pretty flowerets' eyes . iv 1 60
Stood as fair As any comer I have look'd on yet *Mer. of Venice* ii 1 20
Your fortune stood upon the casket there, And so did mine . iii 2 203
In such a night Stood Dido with a willow in her hand . . v 1 10
Stood on the extremest verge of the swift brook . *As Y. Like It* ii 1 42
The feet were lame and could not bear themselves without the verse and therefore stood lamely in the verse . . . . . iii 2 180
While idly I stood looking on, I found the effect of love in idleness *T. of Shrew* i 1 155
There I stood amazed for a while, As on a pillory . . . ii 1 156
With that she sighed as she stood, And gave this sentence then *All's Well* i 3 79
I bade her, if her fortunes ever stood Necessitied to help, that by this token I would relieve her . . . . v 3 84
Noble she was, and thought I stood engaged . . . . v 3 96
Most of our city did: only myself stood out . . . *T. Night* iii 3 35
I lost a couple that 'twixt heaven and earth Might thus have stood begetting wonder . . . . *W. Tale* v 1 133
O, thus she stood, Even with such life of majesty! . . . v 3 34
His spirit is come in, That so stood out against the holy church *K. John* v 2 71
Thus long have we stood To watch the fearful bending of thy knee *Richard II.* iii 3 72
That beads of sweat have stood upon thy brow . *1 Hen. IV.* ii 3 61
Attended him on bridges, stood in lanes, Laid gifts before him . iv 3 70
As the state stood then, Was force perforce compell'd to banish him *2 Hen. IV.* iv 1 115
Whiles his most mighty father on a hill Stood smiling . *Hen. V.* ii 2 109
Who was shot, who disgraced, what terms the enemy stood on . . iii 6 78
When articles too nicely urged be stood on . . . . v 2 94

Stood. So the maid that stood in the way for my wish shall show me the way to my will . . . . *Hen. V.* v 2 355
All the whole army stood agazed on him . . . . *1 Hen. VI.* i 1 126
He is not Talbot's blood, That basely fled when noble Talbot stood . iv 5 17
My angry guardant stood alone, Tendering my ruin and assail'd of none iv 7 9
He stood by whilst I, his forlorn duchess, Was made a wonder *2 Hen. VI.* ii 4 45
I stood upon the hatches in the storm . . . . . iii 2 103
In our voiding lobby hast thou stood And duly waited for my coming forth? . . . . iv 1 61
And stood against them, as the hope of Troy . . *3 Hen. VI.* ii 1 51
You should not blemish it, if I stood by . . *Richard III.* i 2 128
So stood the state when Henry the Sixth Was crown'd . . . —Stood the state so? No, no, good friends, God wot . . . ii 3 16
The moveables Whereof the king my brother stood possess'd . iii 1 196
Every man that stood Show'd like a mine . . . *Hen. VIII.* i 1 21
I stood i' the level Of a full-charged confederacy . . . i 2 2
You speak not like yourself; who ever yet Have stood to charity . ii 4 86
First, methought I stood not in the smile of heaven . . ii 4 187
I weigh'd the danger which my realms stood in By this my issue's fail . ii 4 197
We have Stood here observing him: some strange commotion Is in his brain . . . . iii 2 112
To gratify his noble service that Hath thus stood for his country *Coriol.* ii 2 45
He never stood To ease his breast with panting . . . ii 2 125
We stood up about the corn . . . . ii 3 16
You have stood your limitation . . . . ii 3 146
His worthy deeds did claim no less Than what he stood for . . ii 3 195
To yawn, be still, and wonder, When one but of my ordinance stood up iii 2 12
We stood to't in good time . . . . iv 6 10
His horns . . .; Which were inshell'd when Marcius stood for Rome . iv 6 45
Your franchises, whereon you stood, confined Into an auger's bore . iv 6 86
You that stood so much Upon the voice of occupation . . . iv 6 96
This monument five hundred years hath stood . . *T. Andron.* i 1 350
This minion stood upon her chastity, Upon her nuptial vow . ii 3 124
When I did name her brothers, then fresh tears Stood on her cheeks . iii 1 112
Three or four wenches, where I stood, cried 'Alas, good soul!' *J. Cæsar* i 2 275
I never stood on ceremonies, Yet now they fright me . . ii 2 13
But yesterday the word of Cæsar might Have stood against the world . iii 2 124
Doubtful it stood; As two spent swimmers, that do cling together *Macb.* i 2 7
Whiles I stood rapt in the wonder of it . . . . . i 5 6
One cried 'Murder!' That they did wake each other: I stood and heard them . . . . ii 2 24
How came she by that light?—Why, it stood by her . . . v 1 26
Did forfeit, with his life, all those his lands Which he stood seized of *Ham.* i 1 89
A little ere the mightiest Julius fell, The graves stood tenantless . i 1 115
So, as a painted tyrant, Pyrrhus stood . . . . . ii 2 502
A clout upon that head Where late the diadem stood . . . ii 2 530
Your grace hath screen'd and stood between Much heat and him . iii 4 3
Stood challenger on mount of all the age For her perfections . iv 7 28
Stood I within his grace, I would prefer him to a better place *Lear* i 1 276
Here stood he in the dark, his sharp sword out, Mumbling of wicked charms . . . . ii 1 40
Seeing how loathly opposite I stood To his unnatural purpose . ii 1 51
As I stood here below, methought his eyes Were two full moons . iv 6 69
Mine enemy's dog, Though he had bit me, should have stood that night Against my fire . . . . iv 7 37
Not by old gradation, where each second Stood heir to the first . *Othello* i 1 38
Yea, though our proper son Stood in your action . . . i 3 70
And stood within the blank of his displeasure For my free speech . iii 4 128
On each side her Stood pretty dimpled boys . *Ant. and Cleo.* ii 2 207
A more unhappy lady, If this division chance, ne'er stood between . iii 4 13
Whilst he stood up and spoke, He was my master . . . v 1 7
This Charmian lived but now; she stood and spake: . . . tremblingly she stood And on the sudden dropp'd . . . . . . v 2 344
She did distain my child, and stood between Her and her fortunes *Per.* iv 3 31
My derivation was from ancestors Who stood equivalent with mighty kings . . . . v 1 92
Stool. A stool and a cushion for the sexton . . *Much Ado* iv 2 2
Sometime for three-foot stool mistaketh me . . *M. N. Dream* ii 1 52
To comb your noddle with a three-legg'd stool . . *T. of Shrew* i 1 64
Now fetch me a stool hither by and by . . . *2 Hen. VI.* ii 1 142
Leap me over this stool and run away . . . . . ii 1 144
Beadle, whip him till he leap over that same stool . . . ii 1 149
Thou stool for a witch! . . . . . . *Troi. and Cres.* ii 1 46
Each man to his stool, with that spur as he would to the lip of his mistress: your diet shall be in all places alike . *T. of Athens* iii 6 73
Why do you make such faces? When all 's done, You look but on a stool *Macbeth* iii 4 68
Now they rise again, With twenty mortal murders on their crowns, And push us from our stools . . . . iii 4 82
If for the sake of merit thou wilt hear me, Rise from thy stool *A. and C.* ii 7 62
When on my three-foot stool I sit and tell The warlike feats . *Cymbeline* iii 3 89
Stoop. Why didst thou stoop, then?—To take a paper up *T. G. of Ver.* i 2 72
The jewel that we find, we stoop and take't . . *Meas. for Meas.* ii 1 24
Before his sister should her body stoop To such abhorr'd pollution . ii 4 182
Stoop, I say; Her shoulder is with child . . . *L. L. Lost* iv 3 89
A golden mind stoops not to shows of dross . . *Mer. of Venice* ii 7 20
Till she stoop she must not be full-gorged . . . *T. of Shrew* iv 1 194
For grief is proud and makes his owner stoop . . *K. John* iii 1 69
Stoop low within those bounds we have o'erlook'd . . . v 4 55
If guilty dread have left thee so much strength As to take up mine honour's pawn, then stoop . . . . . . *Richard II.* i 1 74
I would attach you all and make you stoop . . . . ii 3 156
Like unruly children, make their sire Stoop with oppression . . iii 4 31
Of this madness cured, Stoop tamely to the foot of majesty *2 Hen. IV.* iv 1 42
I will stoop and humble my intents To your well-practised wise directions . . . . v 2 120
When they stoop, they stoop with the like wing . . *Hen. V.* iv 1 112
A straight back will stoop; a black beard will turn white . . v 2 168
Compassion on the king commands me stoop . . *1 Hen. VI.* iii 1 119
Stoop then and set your knee against my foot . . . iii 1 169
I'll either make thee stoop and bend thy knee, Or sack this country . v 1 61
Kneel down and take my blessing, good my girl. Wilt thou not stoop? v 4 26
What, are ye daunted now? now will ye stoop? . *2 Hen. VI.* iv 1 119
Rather let my head Stoop to the block than these knees bow to any . iv 1 125
Than you should stoop unto a Frenchman's mercy . . . iv 8 50
Henry the Fifth, Who made the Dauphin and the French to stoop *3 Hen. VI.* i 1 108
Tamed the king, and made the dauphin stoop . . . ii 2 151
But stoop with patience to my fortune . . . . . v 5 6
Before he should thus stoop to the herd . . . . *Coriolanus* iii 2 32

Stoop. And virtue stoops and trembles at her frown . *T. Andron.* ii 1 11
At thy mercy shall they stoop and kneel . . . v 2 118
Stoop, Romans, stoop, And let us bathe our hands in Cæsar's blood *J. C.* iii 1 105
With flaming top Stoops to his base, and with a hideous crash *Hamlet* ii 2 498
To plainness honour's bound, When majesty stoops to folly . *Lear* i 1 151
Do So far ask pardon as befits mine honour To stoop . *Ant. and Cleo.* ii 2 98
Stoop, boys; this gate Instructs you how to adore the heavens *Cymbeline* iii 3 2
As the rudest wind, That by the top doth take the mountain pine, And make him stoop to the vale . . . . . iv 2 176
Stooped. We do condemn thee to the very block Where Claudio stoop'd to death, and with like haste . . *Meas. for Meas.* v 1 420
The priest let fall the book; And, as he stoop'd again to take it up, The mad-brain'd bridegroom took him such a cuff . *T. of Shrew* iii 2 164
Have stoop'd my neck under your injuries . *Richard II.* iii 1 19
Stoop'd his anointed head as low as death . 2 *Hen. IV.* Ind. 32
Forthwith they fly Chickens, the way which they stoop'd eagles *Cymb.* v 3 42
The holy eagle Stoop'd, as to foot us . . . . v 4 116
Stooping. To most ignoble stooping . . . *Tempest* i 2 116
The shore, that o'er his wave-worn basis bow'd, As stooping to relieve him . . . . ii 1 121
If it be worth stooping for, there it lies in your eye . *T. Night* ii 2 16
My stooping duty tenderly shall show . . *Richard II.* iii 3 48
Which he lost By lack of stooping . . . . . *Coriolanus* v 6 29
Here stooping to your clemency, We beg your hearing patiently *Hamlet* iii 2 160
Stop: Let us not burthen our remembrance with A heaviness that's gone *Tempest* v 1 198
Why dost thou stop my mouth?—For fear thou shouldst lose thy tongue *T. G. of Ver.* ii 3 50
Stop there; I'll have her . . . . iii 1 364
We'll unkennel the fox. Let me stop this way first *Mer. Wives* iii 3 174
Come all to help him, and so stop the air By which he should revive *Meas. for Meas.* ii 4 25
Stop in your wind, sir: tell me this, I pray . *Com. of Errors* i 2 53
I'll stop mine ears against the mermaid's song . . iii 2 169
Stop his mouth with a kiss, and let not him speak . *Much Ado* ii 1 321
Now crept into a lute-string and now governed by stops . . iii 2 62
Peace! I will stop your mouth . . . . . . v 4 98
These be the stops that hinder study quite . . *L. L. Lost* i 1 70
Proceeded well, to stop all good proceeding! . . . . i 1 95
Rid his prologue like a rough colt; he knows not the stop *M. N. Dream* v 1 120
Stop my house's ears, I mean my casements . *Mer. of Venice* ii 5 34
The watery kingdom . . . is no bar To stop the foreign spirits . ii 7 46
Come, the full stop.—Ha! what sayest thou? Why, the end is . iii 1 17
Have by some surgeon, Shylock, on your charge, To stop his wounds iv 1 258
Stop that, 'twill fly with the smoke out at the chimney . *As Y. Like It* iv 1 165
I'll bring mine action on the proudest he That stops my way *T. of S.* iii 2 237
If you cannot, best you stop your ears . . . . . v 3 76
And, to stop up the displeasure he hath conceived . *All's Well* iv 5 79
Nay, you need not to stop your nose, sir; I spake but by a metaphor.— Indeed, sir, if your metaphor stink, I will stop my nose . . v 2 11
Whose spiritual counsel had, Shall stop or spur me . *W. Tale* ii 1 187
Stops his ears, and threatens them With divers deaths in death . v 1 201
Satisfy her so That we shall stop her exclamation . *K. John* ii 1 558
John, to stop Arthur's title in the whole, Hath willingly departed with a part . . . . ii 1 562
Will not a calf's-skin stop that mouth of thine? . . . iii 1 299
And stop this gap of breath with fulsome dust . . . iii 4 32
Without stop, didst let thy heart consent . . . . iv 2 239
Use all your power To stop their marches . . . . v 1 7
But now a king, now thus.—Even so must I run on, and even so stop . v 7 67
Thou canst help time to furrow me with age, But stop no wrinkle *Richard II.* i 3 230
One kiss shall stop our mouths, and dumbly part . . . v 1 95
Where did I leave?—At that sad stop . . . . . v 2 4
Tears do stop the flood-gates of her eyes . . 1 *Hen. IV.* ii 4 435
Stop all sight-holes, every loop . . . . . . iv 1 71
And time, that takes survey of all the world, Must have a stop . v 4 83
Which of you will stop The vent of hearing when loud Rumour speaks? 2 *Hen. IV.* Ind. 1
Of so easy and so plain a stop . . . . . . Ind. 17
To stop my ear indeed, Thou hast a sigh to blow away this praise . i 1 79
I had as lief they would put ratsbane in my mouth as offer to stop it . i 2 48
Purge the obstructions which begin to stop Our very veins of life . iv 1 65
Do you mean to stop any of William's wages, about the sack he lost? . v 1 24
Turn head, and stop pursuit . . . . . *Hen. V.* ii 4 69
The liberty that follows our places stops the mouth of all find-faults . v 2 297
O God, that Somerset, who in proud heart Doth stop my cornets, were in Talbot's place! . . . . . . 1 *Hen. VI.* iv 3 25
Vexation almost stops my breath . . . . . . iv 3 41
As the only means To stop effusion of our Christian blood . . v 1 9
Stop the rage betime, Before the wound do grow uncurable 2 *Hen. VI.* iii 1 285
A breach that craves a quick expedient stop! . . . . iii 1 288
To have thee with thy lips to stop my mouth . . . . iii 2 396
Now death shall stop his dismal threatening sound . 3 *Hen. VI.* ii 6 58
Why stops my lord? shall I not hear my task? . . . iii 2 52
Fills mine eyes with tears And stops my tongue . . . iii 3 14
I draw in many a tear And stop the rising of blood-sucking sighs . iv 4 22
Now stops thy spring; my sea shall suck them dry . . iv 8 55
To stop devoted charitable deeds . . . *Richard III.* i 2 35
Murder thy breath in middle of a word, And then begin again, and stop again . . . . iii 5 3
Hath he so long held out with me untired, And stops he now for breath? iv 2 45
It stands me much upon, To stop all hopes whose growth may damage me . . . . iv 2 60
Stop the rumour, and allay those tongues That durst disperse it *Hen. VIII.* ii 1 152
Stops on a sudden, looks upon the ground, Then lays his finger on his temple; straight Springs out into fast gait; then stops again . . iii 2 114
Stop their mouths with stubborn bits, and spur 'em, Till they obey . v 3 23
As will stop the eye of Helen's needle . . *Troi. and Cres.* ii 1 87
Stop my mouth.—And shall, albeit sweet music issues thence . iii 2 141
To stop his ears against admonishment . . . . v 3 2
Nor you, my brother, with your true sword drawn, Opposed to hinder me, should stop my way, But by my ruin . . . . . v 3 57
Stop, Or all will fall in broil . . . . *Coriolanus* iii 1 32
Stop those maims Of shame seen through thy country . . iv 5 92
Your good tongue, More than the instant army we can make, Might stop our countryman . . . . v 1 38
Confusion fall— Nay, then I'll stop your mouth . *T. Andron.* ii 3 185
Sirs, stop his mouth, and let him speak no more . . . v 1 151
Bind them sure, And stop their mouths, if they begin to cry . . v 2 162

Stop. Stop close their mouths, let them not speak a word *T. Andron.* v 2 165
Stop his mouths, let them not speak to me; But let them hear . . v 2 168
Stop there.—Thou desirest me to stop in my tale against the hair *Rom. and Jul.* ii 4 98
Hastes our marriage, To stop the inundation of her tears . . iv 1 12
Stop thy unhallow'd toil! . . . . v 3 54
No care, no stop! so senseless of expense . . *T. of Athens* ii 2 1
And what remains will hardly stop the mouth Of present dues . ii 2 156
Whoso please To stop affliction, let him take his haste . . v 1 213
It is a creature that I teach to fight, To wind, to stop . *J. Cæsar* iv 1 32
Or why Upon this blasted heath you stop our way? . . *Macbeth* i 3 77
Make thick my blood; Stop up the access and passage to remorse! . i 5 45
Speak of it: stay, and speak! Stop it, Marcellus . . *Hamlet* i 1 139
They are not a pipe for fortune's finger To sound what stop she please . iii 2 76
Look you, these are the stops.—But these cannot I command . . iii 2 376
You would play upon me; you would seem to know my stops . . iii 2 381
Why of that loam, whereto he was converted, might they not stop a beer-barrel? . . . . v 1 235
Imperious Cæsar, dead and turn'd to clay, Might stop a hole . . v 1 237
Father, father! Stop, stop! No help? . . . . *Lear* ii 1 38
Stop her there! Arms, arms, sword, fire! Corruption in the place! . iii 6 57
Shut your mouth, dame, Or with this paper shall I stop it . . v 3 155
I cannot speak enough of this content; It stops me here . *Othello* ii 1 199
Let's teach ourselves that honourable stop, Not to outsport discretion ii 3 2
Had I as many mouths as Hydra, such an answer would stop them all . ii 3 308
Therefore these stops of thine fright me the more . . . iii 3 120
Heaven stops the nose at it and the moon winks . . . . iv 2 77
I have made my way through more impediments Than twenty times your stop . . . . v 2 264
Against the blown rose may they stop their nose . *Ant. and Cleo.* iii 13 39
Now I'll set my teeth, And send to darkness all that stop me . iii 13 182
Discover to me What both you spur and stop . . . *Cymbeline* i 6 99
Then began A stop i' the chaser, a retire, anon A rout, confusion thick v 3 40
The sore eyes see clear To stop the air would hurt them . . *Pericles* i 1 100
What may make him blush in being known, He'll stop the course by which it might be known . . . . i 2 23
With thousand doubts How I might stop this tempest ere it came . i 2 98
What! do you stop your ears? . . . . iv 2 86
O, stop there a little! This is the rarest dream . . . v 1 162
Stopped. But stopp'd And left me to a bootless inquisition . *Tempest* i 2 34
Being stopp'd, impatiently doth rage . . *T. G. of Ver.* ii 7 26
And then, to be stopped in, like a strong distillation . *Mer. Wives* iii 5 114
When the suspicious head of theft is stopp'd . . *L. L. Lost* iv 3 336
Her ear Is stopp'd with dust . . . . . *K. John* iv 2 120
It is stopp'd with other flattering sounds, As praises . *Richard II.* ii 1 17
That stopp'd by me to breathe his bloodied horse . 2 *Hen. IV.* i 1 38
Forced Those waters from me which I would have stopp'd . *Hen. V.* iv 6 29
This breach now in our fortunes made May readily be stopp'd 2 *Hen. VI.* v 2 83
In vain thou speak'st, poor boy; my father's blood Hath stopp'd the passage where thy words should enter . . . 3 *Hen. VI.* i 3 22
I have not stopp'd mine ears to their demands . . . . iv 8 39
'But O! the devil'—there the villain stopp'd . . *Richard III.* iv 3 16
Now civil wounds are stopp'd, peace lives again . . . v 5 40
Which stopped our mouths . . . . . . *Hen. VIII.* ii 2 9
I cannot speak him home: he stopp'd the fliers . *Coriolanus* ii 2 107
Stopp'd your ears against The general suit of Rome . . . v 3 5
Sorrow concealed, like an oven stopp'd, Doth burn the heart to cinders where it is . . . . *T. Andron.* ii 4 36
Grief of my son's exile hath stopp'd her breath *Rom. and Jul.* v 3 211
The fountain of your blood Is stopp'd; the very source of it is stopp'd *Macbeth* ii 3 104
Whose disposition, all the world well knows, Will not be rubb'd nor stopp'd . . . . *Lear* ii 2 161
He will not say so.—No, his mouth is stopp'd . . *Othello* v 2 71
There lies your niece, Whose breath, indeed, these hands have newly stopp'd . . . . v 2 202
Make a battery through his deafen'd parts, Which now are midway stopp'd . . . . *Pericles* v 1 48
Stopping the career Of laughter with a sigh . . *W. Tale* i 2 286
Stopping my greedy ear with their bold deeds . 2 *Hen. IV.* i 2 78
Trace the noble dust of Alexander, till he find it stopping a bung-hole *Hamlet* v 1 225
Stopt. My ears are stopt and cannot hear good news *T. G. of Ver.* iii 1 205
Store. Here's too small a pasture for such store of muttons . i 1 105
Thou call'st for such store, When one is one too many? *Com. of Errors* iii 1 31
To your huge store Wise things seem foolish . *L. L. Lost* v 2 377
I am debating of my present store . . . *M. of Venice* i 3 54
I have better news in store for you Than you expect . . v 1 274
Which I did store to be my foster-nurse . . *As Y. Like It* ii 3 40
Have prepared great store of wedding cheer . *T. of Shrew* iii 2 188
He bade me store up, as a triple eye, Safer than mine own two *All's Well* ii 1 111
Aid me with that store of power you have To come into his presence . v 1 20
Your store, I think, is not for idle markets . . *T. Night* iii 3 45
And say, what store of parting tears were shed? . *Richard II.* i 4 5
I would your store were here! . . . . . . 1 *Hen. IV.* ii 2 94
Of drinking good and good store of fertile sherris . 2 *Hen. IV.* iv 3 131
Many a pound of mine own proper store . . . Have I dispursed 2 *Hen. VI.* iii 1 115
I shall not want false witness to condemn me, Nor store of treasons . iii 1 169
May be possessed with some store of crowns . . 3 *Hen. VI.* ii 5 57
Those eyes of thine from mine have drawn salt tears, Shamed their aspect with store of childish drops . . . . *Richard III.* i 2 155
If heaven have any grievous plague in store . . . . i 3 217
We shall have Great store of room, no doubt, left for the ladies *Hen. VIII.* v 4 77
Whereof we have ta'en good and good store, of all The treasure *Coriolanus* i 9 32
How many sons of mine hast thou in store! . . . *T. Andron.* i 1 94
Only poor, That when she dies with beauty dies her store *Rom. and Jul.* i 1 222
And you, among the store, One more, most welcome, makes my number more . . . . i 2 22
I have an hour's talk in store for you . . . . *J. Cæsar* ii 2 121
For that I do appoint him store of provender . . . . iv 1 30
Whose warp'd looks proclaim What store her heart is made on . *Lear* iii 6 57
As many to the vantage as would store the world they played for *Othello* iv 3 86
Feast the army; we have store to do't . . . *Ant. and Cleo.* iv 1 15
I do nothing doubt you have store of thieves . . . *Cymbeline* i 4 107
For which, the most high gods not minding longer To withhold the vengeance that they had in store . . . . . . *Pericles* ii 4 4
Stored. I did not think the king so stored with friends . . *K. John* v 4 1
Whereof, they say, The city is well stored . . . *Coriolanus* i 1 194
He's poor in no one fault, but stored with all.—Especially in pride . ii 1 20
All the stored vengeances of heaven fall On her ingrateful top! . *Lear* ii 4 164

Stored. Fair glass of light, I loved you, and could still, Were not this glorious casket stored with ill . . . *Pericles* i 1 77
Their tables were stored full, to glad the sight, And not so much to feed on . . . . i 4 28
These our ships . . . Are stored with corn to make your needy bread . i 4 95
Here, with a cup that's stored unto the brim . . . . . ii 3 50
Store-house. Suffer us to famish, and their store-houses crammed with grain . . . . *Coriolanus* i 1 83
I am the store-house and the shop Of the whole body . . . i 1 137
Whoever gave that counsel, to give forth The corn o' the storehouse gratis iii 1 114
The sacred storehouse of his predecessors . . . *Macbeth* ii 4 34
Storm. Keep your cabins: you do assist the storm . . *Tempest* i 1 15
Another storm brewing; I hear it sing i' the wind . . . ii 2 19
Alas, the storm is come again! . . . . ii 2 39
I will here shroud till the dregs of the storm be past . . ii 2 43
Is the storm overblown? I hid me under the dead moon-calf's gaberdine for fear of the storm . . . . ii 2 114
A small spare mast, Such as seafaring men provide for storms *Com. of Er.* i 1 81
Such a February face, So full of frost, of storm, and cloudiness *M. Ado* v 4 42
I will move storms, I will condole in some measure . *M. N. Dream* i 2 29
Why, look you, how you storm! I would be friends with you *M. of Ven.* i 3 138
Such a storm That mortal ears might hardly endure the din *T. of Shrew* i 1 177
Carousing to his mates After a storm . . . . . iii 2 174
To watch the night in storms, the day in cold . . . . v 2 150
Upon a barren mountain, and still winter In storm perpetual *W. Tale* iii 2 214
The storm begins: poor wretch, That for thy mother's fault art thus exposed! . . . . iii 3 49
So foul a sky clears not without a storm . . . *K. John* iv 2 108
My tongue shall hush again this storm of war . . . . v 1 20
With a great heart heave away this storm . . . . . v 2 55
Small showers last long, but sudden storms are short . *Richard II.* ii 1 35
We hear this fearful tempest sing, Yet seek no shelter to avoid the storm ii 1 264
Thy sun sets weeping in the lowly west, Witnessing storms to come . ii 4 22
I will stir up in England some black storm . . *2 Hen. VI.* iii 1 349
I stood upon the hatches in the storm . . . . . iii 2 103
I am resolved to bear a greater storm Than any thou canst conjure up . v 1 198
The cedar shows That keeps his leaves in spite of any storm . . v 1 206
With patience calm the storm, While we bethink a means *3 Hen. VI.* iii 3 38
Ay, now begins a second storm to rise . . . . . iii 3 47
Would more have strengthen'd this our commonwealth 'Gainst foreign storms . . . . iv 1 38
Till storms be past of civil enmity . . . . . . iv 6 98
To help King Edward in his time of storm . . . . iv 7 43
For every cloud engenders not a storm . . . . . v 3 13
Untimely storms make men expect a dearth . . *Richard III.* ii 3 35
We see The waters swell before a boisterous storm . . . ii 3 44
Every man, After the hideous storm that follow'd, was A thing inspired; and, not consulting, broke Into a general prophecy . . *Hen. VIII.* i 1 90
To stubborn spirits They swell, and grow as terrible as storms . iii 1 164
An old man, broken with the storms of state, Is come to lay his weary bones among ye . . . . iv 2 21
Lest Hector or my father should perceive me, I have, as when the sun doth light a storm, Buried this sigh in wrinkle of a smile *T. and C.* i 1 37
So Doth valour's show and valour's worth divide In storms of fortune . i 3 47
Here are no storms, No noise, but silence and eternal sleep . *T. Andron.* i 1 154
Holloa! what storm is this? . . . . ii 1 25
When with a happy storm they were surprised . . . . ii 3 23
One hour's storm will drown the fragrant meads; What will whole months of tears thy father's eyes? . . . . iii 1 54
Now is a time to storm; why art thou still? . . . . iii 1 264
The ocean swells not so as Aaron storms . . . . . iv 2 139
I hang the head As flowers with frost or grass beat down with storms . iv 4 71
Wherefore storm you so? . . . . . *Rom. and Jul.* i 5 62
What storm is this that blows so contrary? . . . . . iii 2 64
Left me open, bare For every storm that blows . . *T. of Athens* iv 3 266
Blow wind, swell billow, and swim bark! The storm is up . *J. Cæsar* v 1 68
As whence the sun 'gins his reflection Shipwrecking storms and direful thunders break . . . . *Macbeth* i 2 26
As we often see, against some storm, A silence in the heavens *Hamlet* ii 2 505
Will pack when it begins to rain, And leave thee in the storm . *Lear* ii 4 82
Let us withdraw; 'twill be a storm . . . . . . ii 4 290
'Tis a wild night: My Regan counsels well: come out o' the storm . ii 4 312
Fie on this storm! I will go seek the king . . . . . iii 1 49
This contentious storm Invades us to the skin . . . . iii 4 6
Whereso'er you are, That bide the pelting of this pitiless storm . iii 4 29
The sea, with such a storm as his bare head In hell-black night endured, would have buoy'd up, And quench'd the stelled fires . . . iii 7 59
I' the last night's storm I such a fellow saw . . . . iv 1 34
What, i' the storm? i' the night? Let pity not be believed! . . iv 3 30
My downright violence and storm of fortunes May trumpet to the world *Othello* i 3 250
Greater storms and tempests than almanacs can report . *Ant. and Cleo.* i 2 154
By the discandying of this pelleted storm, Lie graveless . . . iii 13 165
He that unbuckles this, till we do please To daff't for our repose, shall hear a storm . . . . iv 4 13
A storm or robbery, call it what you will, Shook down my mellow hangings, nay, my leaves . . . . . *Cymbeline* iii 3 62
What ensues in this fell storm Shall for itself itself perform *Pericles* iii Gower 53
Patience, good sir; do not assist the storm . . . . . iii 1 19
This world to me is like a lasting storm, Whirring me from my friends . iv 1 20
Stormest. Thou stormest venomously; Wilt thou spit all thyself? . . iii 1 7
Stormy. Like an unseasonable stormy day . . . *Richard II.* iii 2 106
Which, if you give o'er To stormy passion, must perforce decay *2 Hen. IV.* i 1 165
Beaufort's red sparkling eyes blab his heart's malice, And Suffolk's cloudy brow his stormy hate . . . . . . *2 Hen. VI.* iii 1 155
'T has been a turbulent and stormy night . . . *Pericles* iii 2 4
Story. Without the which this story Were most impertinent . *Tempest* i 2 137
The strangeness of your story put Heaviness in me. . . . i 2 306
That shall be by and by: I remember the story . . . . iii 2 156
This must crave, An if this be at all, a most strange story . . v 1 117
The story of my life And the particular accidents gone by . . v 1 304
I long To hear the story of your life, which must Take the ear strangely v 1 312
Some shallow story of deep love: How young Leander cross'd the Hellespont.—That's a deep story of a deeper love . . *T. G. of Ver.* i 1 21
'Tis your penance but to hear The story of your loves discovered . . v 4 171
Painted about with the story of the Prodigal . . *Mer. Wives* iv 5 8
Make me not your story.—It is true . . . *Meas. for Meas.* i 4 30
Who hath a story ready for your ear . . . . . . iv 1 56
To tell sad stories of my own mishaps . . . *Com. of Errors* i 1 121
Here must end the story of my life . . . . . . i 1 138
Story. Here begins his morning story right . . . *Com. of Errors* v 1 356
Was't not to this end That thou began'st to twist so fine a story? *M. Ado* i 1 313
Could she here deny The story that is printed in her blood? . . iv 1 124
Run when you will, the story shall be changed . . *M. N. Dream* ii 1 230
Love's stories written in love's richest book . . . . ii 2 122
Pyramus and Thisby, says the story, did talk through the chink of a wall . . . . iii 1 65
All the story of the night told over . . . . . . v 1 23
He sent me hither, stranger as I am, To tell this story . *As Y. Like It* iv 3 154
Her own letters, which makes her story true . . *All's Well* iv 3 66
The story then goes false, you threw it him Out of a casement . . v 3 229
Let us from point to point this story know . . . . . v 3 325
Sit upon the ground And tell sad stories of the death of kings *Rich. II.* iii 2 156
Weeping made you break the story off . . . . . . v 2 2
You picked my pocket?—It appears so by the story . *1 Hen. IV.* iii 3 191
A pretty slight drollery, or the story of the Prodigal . *2 Hen. IV.* ii 1 157
And breeds no bate with telling of discreet stories . . . ii 4 272
Our humble author will continue the story . . . . . Epil. 29
This story shall the good man teach his son . . . *Hen. V.* iv 3 56
Vouchsafe to those that have not read the story, That I may prompt them . . . . v Prol. 1
With rough and all-unable pen, Our bending author hath pursued the story . . . . Epil. 2
If thou tell'st the heavy story right, Upon my soul, the hearers will shed tears; Yea even my foes . . . . . *3 Hen. VI.* i 4 160
Whose heavy looks foretell Some dreadful story hanging on thy tongue ii 1 44
Like a child, Told the sad story of my father's death . *Richard III.* i 2 161
I'll sort occasion, As index to the story we late talk'd of . . . ii 2 149
Wept like two children in their deaths' sad stories . . . . iv 3 8
If this inducement force her not to love, Send her a story of thy noble acts . . . . iv 4 280
Think ye see The very persons of our noble story . . *Hen. VIII.* Prol. 26
That former fabulous story, Being now seen possible enough, got credit i 1 36
There was a lady once, 'tis an old story, That would not be a queen . ii 3 90
I must read this paper; I fear, the story of his anger . . . iii 2 209
And go read with thee Sad stories chanced in the times of old *T. Andron.* iii 2 83
The story of that baleful burning night When subtle Greeks surprised King Priam's Troy . . . . v 3 83
That in gold clasps locks in the golden story . . *Rom. and Jul.* i 3 92
For never was a story of more woe Than this of Juliet and her Romeo . v 3 309
Honour is the subject of my story . . . . . *J. Cæsar* i 2 92
Would well become A woman's story at a winter's fire . . *Macbeth* iii 4 65
Thou comest to use thy tongue; thy story quickly . . . . v 5 29
Let us once again assail your ears, That are so fortified against our story *Hamlet* i 1 32
The story is extant, and writ in choice Italian . . . . . iii 2 273
And in this harsh world draw thy breath in pain, To tell my story . . v 2 360
Still question'd me the story of my life, From year to year . . *Othello* i 3 129
My story being done, She gave me for my pains a world of sighs . . i 3 158
I should but teach him how to tell my story, And that would woo her . i 3 165
Now he begins the story . . . . iv 1 135
And earns a place i' the story . . . . . *Ant. and Cleo.* iii 13 46
Their story is No less in pity than his glory . . . . . v 2 364
How worthy he is I will leave to appear hereafter, rather than story him in his own hearing . . . . *Cymbeline* i 4 34
The arras; figures, Why, such and such; and the contents o' the story ii 2 27
The story Proud Cleopatra, when she met her Roman . . . . ii 4 69
This story The world may read in me . . . . . . iii 3 55
When on my three-foot stool I sit and tell The warlike feats I have done, his spirits fly out Into my story . . . . iii 3 91
When we have supp'd, We'll mannerly demand thee of thy story . . iii 6 92
What became of him I further know not.—Let me end the story . . v 5 286
It is said For certain in our story . . . . . *Pericles* iv Gower 19
Learn of me, who stand i' the gaps to teach you, The stages of our story iv 4 9
Tell thy story; If thine consider'd prove the thousandth part Of my endurance, thou art a man . . . . v 1 135
I'll hear you more, to the bottom of your story, And never interrupt you v 1 166
Stoup. Marian, I say! a stoup of wine! . . . . *T. Night* ii 3 14
Fetch me a stoup of liquor . . . . *Hamlet* v 1 68
Set me the stoups of wine upon that table . . . . . . v 2 278
Come, lieutenant, I have a stoup of wine . . . . *Othello* ii 3 30
Stout. And rifted Jove's stout oak With his own bolt . . *Tempest* v 1 45
I will be strange, stout, in yellow stockings . . . *T. Night* ii 5 186
With dreadful pomp of stout invasion! . . . . . *K. John* iv 2 173
This earth that bears thee dead Bears not alive so stout a gentleman *1 Hen. IV.* v 4 93
A dismal fight Betwixt the stout Lord Talbot and the French *1 Hen. VI.* i 1 106
Stout Pendragon in his litter sick Came to the field . . . . iii 2 95
The stout Parisians do revolt . . . . v 2 2
As stout and proud as he were lord of all . . . *2 Hen. VI.* i 1 187
A mighty power Of gallowglasses and stout kerns . . . . iv 9 26
Stout Diomede With sleight and manhood stole to Rhesus' tents *3 Hen. VI.* iv 2 19
A wise stout captain, and soon persuaded! . . . . . . iv 7 30
How now, my hardy, stout resolved mates! . . . *Richard III.* i 3 340
The stout Earl Northumberland Arrested him . . . *Hen. VIII.* iv 2 12
Correcting thy stout heart, Now humble as the ripest mulberry *Coriol.* iii 2 78
An envious thrust from Tybalt hit the life Of stout Mercutio *Rom. and Jul.* iii 1 174
Ere I Could draw to part them, was stout Tybalt slain . . . iii 1 178
Pluck stout men's pillows from below their heads . . *T. of Athens* iv 3 32
He finds thee in the stout Norweyan ranks . . . . *Macbeth* i 3 95
Stouter. A stouter champion never handled sword . . *1 Hen. VI.* iii 4 19
Stoutly. Thou that so stoutly hast resisted me . . . *3 Hen. VI.* ii 5 79
Is he well shipp'd?—His bark is stoutly timber'd . . . *Othello* ii 1 48
And she speaks for you stoutly . . . . iii 1 47
Stoutness. Let Thy mother rather feel thy pride than fear Thy dangerous stoutness . . . . *Coriolanus* iii 2 127
His stoutness When he did stand for consul, which he lost By lack of stooping . . . . v 6 27
Stover. Nibbling sheep, And flat meads thatch'd with stover . *Tempest* iv 1 63
Stowage. And I am something curious, being strange, To have them in safe stowage . . . . *Cymbeline* i 6 192
Stowed. The mariners all under hatches stow'd . . . *Tempest* i 2 230
Safely stowed . . . . *Hamlet* iv 2 1
O thou foul thief, where hast thou stow'd my daughter? . *Othello* i 2 62
Strachy. The lady of the Strachy married the yeoman of the wardrobe *T. Night* ii 5 45
Stragglers. Let's whip these stragglers o'er the seas again *Richard III.* v 3 327
Straggling. He likewise enriched poor straggling soldiers *T. of Athens* v 1 7

Straight. This shall be answered.—I will answer it straight *Mer. Wives* i 1 118
We'll come dress you straight: put on the gown the while . . . iv 2 85
I'll bring linen for him straight . . . . iv 2 103
Go send to Falstaff straight.—Nay, I'll to him again . . . . iv 4 75
At the deanery, where a priest attends, Straight marry her . . . iv 6 32
Lets it straight feel the spur . . . . . . *Meas. for Meas.* i 2 166
I'll see what I can do.—But speedily.—I will about it straight . i 4 85
He's hearing of a cause; he will come straight: I'll tell him of you . ii 2 1
Floating straight, obedient to the stream . . . . *Com. of Errors* i 1 87
If any ship put out, then straight away . . . . iii 2 190
Villain, hie thee straight: Give her this key . . . . . iv 1 102
There's the money, bear it straight, And bring thy master home . iv 2 63
To thy state of darkness hie thee straight . . . . . iv 4 59
Straight after did I meet him with a chain . . . . . iv 4 143
No point, quoth I; my servant straight was mute . . . *L. L. Lost* v 2 277
Lo, he is tilting straight! . . . . v 2 483
Where art thou?—I will be with thee straight . . . *M. N. Dream* iii 2 403
I then did ask of her her changeling child; Which straight she gave me iv 1 65
Bethink me straight of dangerous rocks . . . *Mer. of Venice* i 1 31
If a throstle sing, he falls straight a capering . . . . i 2 65
I will go and purse the ducats straight . . . . . . i 3 175
I'll be gone about it straight.—And so will I . . . . ii 4 25
And gild myself With some more ducats, and be with you straight . ii 6 50
Quick, quick, I pray thee; draw the curtain straight . . . ii 9 1
Straight shall our nuptial rites be solemnized . . . . ii 9 6
I'll bring you to him straight . . . . . . *As Y. Like It* ii 1 69
I'll write it straight; The matter's in my head and in my heart . iii 5 136
Be ready straight And with a low submissive reverence *T. of Shrew* Ind. 1 52
Dost thou love pictures? we will fetch thee straight Adonis painted Ind. 2 51
Kate like the hazel-twig Is straight and slender . . . . ii 1 256
What, do you grumble? I'll be with you straight . . . iv 1 170
I am for thee straight: take thou the bill . . . . . iv 3 152
Go, call my men, and let us straight to him . . . . . iv 3 186
Hie you home, And bid Bianca make her ready straight . . . iv 4 63
Away, I say, and bring them hither straight . . . . . v 2 105
I'll send her straight away: to-morrow I'll to the wars . *All's Well* ii 3 312
So we seem to know, is to know straight our purpose . . . iv 1 21
Do not think I have wit enough to lie straight in my bed *T. Night* ii 3 148
This will I tell my lady straight: I would not be in some of your coats iv 1 32
And straight The shrug, the hum or ha, these petty brands *W. Tale* ii 1 70
He straight declined, droop'd, took it deeply . . . . ii 3 14
Take it up straight: Within this hour bring me word 'tis done . . ii 3 135
Determine what we shall do straight . . . . . *K. John* ii 1 149
Distemper'd lords! The king by me requests your presence straight . iv 3 22
To my litter straight; Weakness possesseth me, and I am faint . . v 3 16
Straight let us seek, or straight we shall be sought . . . v 7 79
To the Earl of Wiltshire straight: Bid him repair to us *Richard II.* ii 1 215
Well, I will for refuge straight to Bristol castle . . . . ii 2 135
If my word be sterling yet in England, Let it command a mirror hither straight . . . . iv 1 265
Destruction straight shall dog them at the heels . . . . v 3 139
Think that I am unking'd by Bolingbroke, And straight am nothing . v 5 38
We at our own charge shall ransom straight His brother-in-law 1 *Hen. IV.* i 3 79
I will after straight And tell him so; for I will ease my heart . i 3 126
To your Scottish prisoners. Deliver them up without their ransom straight . . . . i 3 260
That roan shall be my throne. Well, I will back him straight . . ii 3 74
You are straight enough in the shoulders, you care not who sees your back . . . . ii 4 164
Win this cape of land; And then he runs straight and even . . iii 1 114
Straight they shall be here: sit, and attend . . . . . iii 1 228
I'll to Clifton straight.—Stay, and breathe awhile . . . . v 4 46
The room where they supped is too hot; they'll come in straight 2 *Hen. IV.* ii 4 15
Stand from him, give him air; he'll straight be well . . . iv 4 116
Your worship! I'll be with you straight. A cup of wine, sir? . . v 3 47
It will be thought we keep a bawdy house straight . . *Hen. V.* ii 1 38
Let us deliver Our puissance into the hand of God, Putting it straight in expedition . . . . ii 2 191
To horse, you gallant princes! straight to horse! . . . . iv 2 15
Your eyes advance, After your thoughts, straight back again to France v Prol. 45
Then gather strength and march unto him straight 1 *Hen. VI.* iv 1 73
I will dispatch the horsemen straight . . . . . . iv 4 40
You judge it straight a thing impossible . . . . . v 4 47
Sirrah, go fetch the beadle hither straight . . . 2 *Hen. VI.* ii 1 141
Go, call our uncle to our presence straight . . . . . iii 2 15
Unless Lord Suffolk straight be done to death . . . . iii 2 244
I'll give it, sir . . . . —And so will I and write home for it straight iv 1 24
Issue forth and bid them battle straight . . . 3 *Hen. VI.* i 2 71
Myself in person will straight follow you . . . . . iv 1 133
We, having now the best at Barnet field, Will thither straight . . v 3 21
Away with Oxford to Hames Castle straight . . . . . v 5 2
About your business straight; Go, go, dispatch . . *Richard III.* i 3 355
You straight are on your knees for pardon, pardon . . . . ii 1 124
Send straight for him; Let him be crown'd; in him your comfort lives ii 2 97
Go we to determine Who they shall be that straight shall post to Ludlow ii 2 142
For by his face straight shall you know his heart . . . iii 4 55
You must straight to Westminster, There to be crowned . . . iv 1 32
Some mean-born gentleman, Whom I will marry straight to Clarence' daughter . . . . iv 2 55
Bid him levy straight The greatest strength and power he can make . iv 4 448
He sent command to the lord mayor straight To stop the rumour *Hen. VIII.* ii 1 151
Straight Springs out into fast gait; then stops again . . . iii 2 115
Go we to him straight. Two curs shall tame each other *Troi. and Cres.* i 3 390
Walk here i' the orchard, I'll bring her straight . . . . iii 2 18
She's making her ready, she'll come straight: you must be witty now . iii 2 32
Thou shalt bear a letter to him straight.—Let me bear another to his horse . . . . iii 3 308
Let us make ready straight.—Yea, with a bridegroom's fresh alacrity iv 4 146
One cannot speak a word, But it straight starts you . . . v 2 101
Straight his doubled spirit Re-quicken'd what in flesh was fatigate *Coriol.* ii 2 120
That I'll straight do; and, knowing myself again, Repair to the senate-house . . . . ii 3 155
Must these have voices, that can yield them now And straight disclaim? iii 1 35
Put him to choler straight: he hath been used Ever to conquer . iii 3 25
Speed thee straight, And make my misery serve thy turn . . . iv 5 93
Away with him! and make a fire straight . . . *T. Andron.* i 1 127
As any mortal body hearing it Should straight fall mad, or else die . ii 3 104

Straight. Straight they told me they would bind me here *T. Andron.* ii 3 106
Straight will I bring you to the loathsome pit Where I espied the panther ii 3 193
Let me see your archery; Look ye draw home enough, and 'tis there straight . . . . iv 3 3
I beseech you, follow straight.—We follow thee *Rom. and Jul.* i 3 104
O'er courtiers' knees, that dream on court'sies straight, O'er lawyers' fingers, who straight dream on fees, O'er ladies' lips, who straight on kisses dream . . . . i 4 73
Now comes the wanton blood up in your cheeks, They'll be in scarlet straight at any news . . . . ii 5 73
The county will be here with music straight, For so he said he would . iv 4 21
Get thee gone, And hire those horses; I'll be with thee straight . . v 1 33
If you had the strength Of twenty men, it would dispatch you straight v 1 79
Get me an iron crow, and bring it straight Unto my cell . . v 2 21
Ask nothing, give it him, it foals me, straight, And able horses *T. of A.* ii 1 9
Thither will I straight to visit him: He comes upon a wish . *J. Cæsar* iii 2 270
We must straight make head: Therefore let our alliance be combined . iv 1 42
Who, much enforced, shows a hasty spark, And straight is cold again . iv 3 113
Only I yield to die: There is so much that thou wilt kill me straight . v 4 13
I'll call upon you straight: abide within . . . . *Macbeth* iii 1 140
Did he not straight In pious rage the two delinquents tear? . . iii 6 11
We'll have a speech straight . . . . *Hamlet* ii 2 451
He will come straight. Look you lay home to him . . . iii 4 1
I'll be with you straight. Go a little before . . . . iv 4 31
Make her grave straight: the crowner hath sat on her . . . v 1 4
I'll write straight to my sister, To hold my very course . . . *Lear* i 3 25
They summon'd up their meiny, straight took horse . . . ii 4 35
I will arraign them straight. Come, sit thou here, most learned justicer iii 6 22
Mine eyes are not o' the best: I'll tell you straight . . . v 3 279
I am the very man,— I'll see that straight . . . . . v 3 287
Straight satisfy yourself: If she be in her chamber or your house . *Othello* i 1 138
Valiant Othello, we must straight employ you Against the general enemy i 3 48
Farewell, my Desdemona: I'll come to thee straight . . . iii 3 87
Withdraw yourself a little while, He will recover straight . . iv 1 58
Straight will he come: Wear thy good rapier bare, and put it home . v 1 1
If you bethink yourself of any crime Unreconciled as yet to heaven and grace, Solicit for it straight . . . . v 2 28
The place, the torture: O, enforce it! Myself will straight aboard . v 2 370
Invite you to my sister's view, Whither straight I'll lead you *A. and C.* ii 2 171
I'll bring thee word Straight, how 'tis like to go . . . . iv 12 3
Straight away for Britain, lest the bargain should catch cold . *Cymbeline* i 4 179
O you gods! Why do you make us love your goodly gifts, And snatch them straight away? . . . . *Pericles* iii 1 24
Briefly yield her; for she must overboard straight . . . . . iii 1 54
Nor have I time To give thee hallow'd to thy grave, but straight Must cast thee, scarcely coffin'd, in the ooze . . . . iii 1 60
Whate'er it be, 'Tis wondrous heavy. Wrench it open straight . . iii 2 53
Her stature to an inch; as wand-like straight; As silver-voiced . . v 1 110
Straight arms. Other of them may have crook'd noses, but to owe such straight arms, none . . . . *Cymbeline* iii 1 38
Straight back. A straight back will stoop . . . . *Hen. V.* v 2 168
Straight leg. By her fine foot, straight leg, and quivering thigh, And the demesnes that there adjacent lie . . . . *Rom. and Jul.* ii 1 19
Straight-pight. The shrine of Venus, or straight-pight Minerva *Cymbeline* v 5 164
Straightest. Amongst a grove, the very straightest plant . 1 *Hen. IV.* i 1 82
Straightway. We were awaked; straightway, at liberty . . . *Tempest* v 1 235
Titania waked and straightway loved an ass . . . *M. N. Dream* iii 2 34
Wilt thou at Ninny's tomb meet me straightway? . . . . . v 1 204
Straightway give thy soul to him thou servest . . . 1 *Hen. VI.* i 5 7
Like to a ship that, having 'scaped a tempest, Is straightway calm'd and boarded with a pirate . . . . 2 *Hen. VI.* iv 9 33
We, like friends, will straightway go together . . . *J. Cæsar* ii 2 127
To the sea-side straightway . . . . *Ant. and Cleo.* iii 11 20
In a word; or else Thou art straightway with the fiends . *Cymbeline* iii 5 83
Strain. Hark, hark! I hear The strain of strutting chanticleer *Tempest* i 2 385
Unless he know some strain in me, that I know not myself *Mer. Wives* ii 1 91
I would all of the same strain were in the same distress . . . iii 3 197
He is of a noble strain, of approved valour . . . *Much Ado* ii 1 394
To strange sores strangely they strain the cure . . . . iv 1 254
Let it answer every strain for strain, As thus for thus . . . v 1 12
Love is full of unbefitting strains, All wanton as a child . *L. L. Lost* v 2 770
What, to make thee an instrument and play false strains upon thee! not to be endured! . . . . *As Y. Like It* iv 3 68
That strain again! it had a dying fall . . . . . *T. Night* i 1 4
And strain their cheeks to idle merriment . . . . *K. John* iii 3 46
You strain too far. I rather of his absence make this use 1 *Hen. IV.* iv 1 75
Or swell my thoughts to any strain of pride . . . 2 *Hen. IV.* iv 5 171
He is bred out of that bloody strain That haunted us . . *Hen. V.* ii 4 51
She is an angel; Our king has all the Indies in his arms, And more and richer, when he strains that lady . . . . . . *Hen. VIII.* iv 1 46
And, in the publication, make no strain . . . . *Troi. and Cres.* i 3 326
Do not these high strains Of divination in our sister work Some touches of remorse? or is your blood So madly hot? . . . . . . ii 2 113
Can it be that so degenerate a strain as this Should once set footing in your generous bosoms? . . . . ii 2 154
I do not strain at the position,—It is familiar . . . . iii 3 112
Thou hast affected the fine strains of honour . . . . *Coriolanus* v 3 149
In such a case as mine a man may strain courtesy . . *Rom. and Jul.* ii 4 55
I already know thy grief; It strains me past the compass of my wits . iv 1 47
To build his fortune I will strain a little . . . . *T. of Athens* i 1 143
The strain of man's bred out Into baboon and monkey . . . i 1 259
Praise his most vicious strain, And call it excellent . . . iv 3 213
Let us return, And strain what other means is left unto us . . v 1 230
Touch thy instrument a strain or two . . . . . *J. Cæsar* iv 3 257
If thou wert the noblest of thy strain, Young man, thou couldst not die more honourable . . . . v 1 59
Sir, you have shown to-day your valiant strain . . . . *Lear* v 3 40
I am to pray you not to strain my speech To grosser issues . *Othello* iii 3 218
Note, if your lady strain his entertainment With any strong or vehement importunity; Much will be seen in that . . . . iii 3 250
He sweats, Strains his young nerves, and puts himself in posture *Cymb.* iii 3 94
It is no act of common passage, but A strain of rareness . . . iii 4 95
O noble strain! O worthiness of nature! breed of greatness! . . iv 2 24
I do shame To think of what a noble strain you are, And of how coward a spirit . . . . *Pericles* iv 3 24
Strained. The quality of mercy is not strain'd . . *Mer. of Venice* iv 1 184
I Have strain'd to appear thus . . . . *W. Tale* iii 2 51
This strained passion doth you wrong, my lord . . . 2 *Hen. IV.* i 1 161
I love thee in so strain'd a purity . . . . . *Troi. and Cres.* iv 4 26
Faith and troth, Strain'd purely from all hollow bias-drawing . . iv 5 169

Strained. Nor aught so good but strain'd from that fair use Revolts from true birth *Rom. and Jul.* ii 3 19
With strain'd pride To come between our sentence and our power *Lear* i 1 172
Straining. More straining on for plucking back *W. Tale* iv 4 476
You stand like greyhounds in the slips, Straining upon the start *Hen. V.* iii 1 32
My breast I'll burst with straining of my courage 1 *Hen. VI.* i 5 10
Out of tune, Straining harsh discords and unpleasing sharps *R. and J.* iii 5 28
Strait. Whom I believe to be most strait in virtue *Meas. for Meas.* ii 1 9
I know into what straits of fortune she is driven *As Y. Like It* v 2 71
I do not ask you much, I beg cold comfort; and you are so strait And so ingrateful, you deny me that *K. John* v 7 42
Some certain edicts and some strait decrees That lie too heavy 1 *Hen. IV.* iv 3 79
Your French hose off, and in your strait strossers *Hen. V.* iii 7 57
Notwithstanding such a strait edict 2 *Hen. VI.* iii 2 258
Take the instant way; For honour travels in a strait so narrow, Where one but goes abreast *Troi. and Cres.* iii 3 154
His means most short, his creditors most strait *T. of Athens* i 1 96
All flying Through a strait lane *Cymbeline* v 3 7
The strait pass was damm'd With dead men hurt behind v 3 11
Straited. You were straited For a reply *W. Tale* iv 4 365
Straiter. Proceed no straiter 'gainst our uncle Gloucester 2 *Hen. VI.* iii 2 20
Straitly. His majesty hath straitly given in charge *Richard III.* i 1 85
The king hath straitly charged the contrary iv 1 17
Straitness. If his own life answer the straitness of his proceeding, it shall become him well *Meas. for Meas.* iii 2 269
Strand. Which makes her seat of Belmont Colchos' strand *Mer. of Venice* i 1 171
When with his knees he kiss'd the Cretan strand *T. of Shrew* i 1 175
New broils To be commenced in strands afar remote 1 *Hen. IV.* i 1 4
So looks the strand whereon the imperious flood Hath left a witness'd usurpation 2 *Hen. IV.* i 1 62
Which were the hope o' the Strand, where she was quartered *Hen. VIII.* v 4 55
Strange. By accident most strange *Tempest* i 2 178
Doth suffer a sea-change Into something rich and strange i 2 401
With good life And observation strange iii 3 87
This is strange: your father's in some passion iv 1 143
These are not natural events; they strengthen From strange to stranger v 1 228
With strange and several noises Of roaring, shrieking, howling v 1 232
This is as strange a maze as e'er men trod v 1 242
She makes it strange; but she would be best pleased To be so anger'd with another letter *T. G. of Ver.* i 2 102
This is strange. Who hath got the right Anne? *Mer. Wives* v 5 224
The signet is not strange to you *Meas. for Meas.* iv 2 209
He tells me that, if peradventure He speak against me on the adverse side, I should not think it strange iv 6 7
She will speak most bitterly and strange.—Most strange, but yet most truly v 1 36
That Angelo's forsworn; is it not strange? That Angelo's a murderer; is't not strange? v 1 38
Is it not strange and strange?—Nay, it is ten times strange v 1 42
This is all as true as it is strange: Nay, it is ten times true v 1 44
And, which was strange, the one so like the other As could not be distinguish'd but by names *Com. of Errors* i 1 52
Look strange and frown: Some other mistress hath thy sweet aspects ii 2 112
Estranged from thyself? Thyself I call it, being strange to me ii 2 123
As strange unto your town as to your talk ii 2 151
Why, this is strange. Go call the abbess hither v 1 280
Why look you strange on me? you know me well.—I never saw you v 1 295
Now is his soul ravished! Is it not strange that sheeps' guts should hale souls out of men's bodies? *Much Ado* ii 3 61
Is not that strange?—As strange as the thing I know not iv 1 270
Learned without opinion, and strange without heresy *L. L. Lost* v 1 6
Thou bid'st me beg: this begging is not strange v 2 210
O monstrous! O strange! we are haunted. Pray, masters! *M. N. D.* iii 1 107
'Tis strange, my Theseus, that these lovers speak of.—More strange than true v 1 1
Something of great constancy; But, howsoever, strange and admirable v 1 27
When shall we laugh? say, when? You grow exceeding strange *M. of V.* i 1 67
I never heard a passion so confused, So strange, outrageous ii 8 13
'Tis thought Thou'lt show thy mercy and remorse more strange Than is thy strange apparent cruelty iv 1 20
Last scene of all, That ends this strange eventful history *As Y. Like It* ii 7 164
It would seem strange unto him when he waked *T. of Shrew* Ind. 1 43
Will you be so strange? Sorry am I i 1 85
Such a life, with such a wife, were strange! But if you have a stomach, to't i 2 194
Tis strange, tis very strange, that is the brief and the tedious of it *All's Well* ii 3 33
Strange is it that our bloods, Of colour, weight, and heat, pour'd all together, Would quite confound distinction ii 3 125
Why do you look so strange upon your wife? v 3 168
I will be strange, stout, in yellow stockings *T. Night* ii 5 185
This is as uncivil as strange iii 4 277
This is strange: methinks My favour here begins to warp *W. Tale* i 2 364
The prettiest love-songs for maids; so without bawdry, which is strange iv 4 194
'Tis strange He thus should steal upon us v 1 114
'Tis strange to think how much King John hath lost *K. John* iii 4 121
'Tis strange that death should sing v 7 20
Strange that desire should so many years outlive performance 2 *Hen. IV.* ii 4 283
'Tis so strange, That, though the truth of it stands off as gross As black and white, my eye will scarcely see it *Hen. V.* ii 2 102
Lord Strange of Blackmere, Lord Verdun of Alton 1 *Hen. VI.* iv 7 65
'Tis wondrous strange, the like yet never heard of 3 *Hen. VI.* ii 1 33
You'd think it strange if I should marry her iii 2 111
'Tis strange: a three-pence bow'd would hire me, Old as I am *Hen. VIII.* ii 3 36
This is strange to me.—How tastes it? is it bitter? ii 3 88
A strange tongue makes my cause more strange, suspicious iii 1 45
Yet he loves himself: is't not strange? *Troi. and Cres.* ii 3 171
If he were proud,— Or covetous of praise,— Ay, or surly borne,— Or strange, or self-affected! ii 3 250
Am become As new into the world, strange, unacquainted iii 3 12
This is not strange at all iii 3 111
Topping all others in boasting.—This is strange now *Coriolanus* ii 1 24
To achieve her! how?—Why makest thou it so strange? *T. Andron.* ii 1 81
In this strange and sad habiliment, I will encounter with Andronicus v 2 1
I'll prove more true Than those that have more cunning to be strange. I should have been more strange, I must confess, But that thou overheard'st, ere I was ware *Rom. and Jul.* ii 2 101
What particular rarity? what strange? *T. of Athens* i 1 4
Mark, how strange it shows, Timon in this should pay more than he owes iii 4 21
Strange, unusual blood, When man's worst sin is, he does too much good! iv 2 38

Strange. I know thee well; But in thy fortunes am unlearn'd and strange *T. of Athens* iv 3 56
You bear too stubborn and too strange a hand Over your friend that loves you *J. Cæsar* i 2 35
It seems to me most strange that men should fear ii 2 35
That, methinks, is strange.—Why ask you? hear you aught of her? iv 3 184
So should he look That seems to speak things strange *Macbeth* i 2 47
'Tis strange: And oftentimes, to win us to our harm i 3 122
I have seen Hours dreadful and things strange ii 4 3
A thing most strange and certain ii 4 14
This is more strange Than such a murder is iii 4 82
You make me strange Even to the disposition that I owe iii 4 112
My strange and self-abuse Is the initiate fear that wants hard use iii 4 142
'Tis strange.—Thus twice before . . . hath he gone by our watch *Hamlet* i 1 64
'Tis very strange.—As I do live, my honour'd lord, 'tis true i 2 220
Murder most foul, as in the best it is; But this most foul, strange i 5 28
O day and night, but this is wondrous strange! i 5 164
Never, so help you mercy, How strange or odd soe'er I bear myself i 5 170
It is not very strange; for mine uncle is king of Denmark ii 2 380
'Tis not strange That even our loves should with our fortunes change iii 2 210
This is most strange, That she, that even but now was your best object, . . . should . . . Commit a thing so monstrous *Lear* i 1 216
'Tis strange that from their cold'st neglect My love should kindle i 1 257
True-hearted Kent banished! his offence, honesty! 'Tis strange i 2 127
'Tis strange that they should so depart from home ii 4 1
The art of our necessities is strange, That can make vile things precious iii 2 70
She swore, in faith, 'twas strange, 'twas passing strange, 'Twas pitiful, 'twas wondrous pitiful *Othello* i 3 160
To be now a sensible man, by and by a fool, and presently a beast! O strange! ii 3 310
That's strange.—I durst, my lord, to wager she is honest iv 2 11
A strange invisible perfume hits the sense *Ant. and Cleo.* ii 2 217
Is it not strange, Canidius, . . . He could so quickly cut the Ionian sea? iii 7 21
Can he be there in person? 'tis impossible; Strange that his power should be iii 7 58
Heard you of nothing strange about the streets? iv 3 3
How now! do you hear this?—Ay; is't not strange? iv 3 20
Let's see how it will give off.—Content. 'Tis strange iv 3 23
All strange and terrible events are welcome, But comforts we despise iv 15 3
Strange it is, That nature must compel us to lament Our most persisted deeds v 1 28
Howsoe'er 'tis strange, Or that the negligence may well be laughed at, Yet is it true *Cymbeline* i 1 65
She doth think she has Strange lingering poisons i 5 34
He Is strange and peevish i 6 54
I am something curious, being strange, To have them in safe stowage i 6 191
Yet still it's strange What Cloten's being here to us portends iv 2 181
No letter from my master since I wrote him Imogen was slain: 'tis strange iv 3 37
'Tis strange he [death] hides him in fresh cups, soft beds, Sweet words v 3 71
'Twas very strange.—And yet but justice *Pericles* ii 4 13
'Tis most strange, Nature should be so conversant with pain iii 2 24
O you most potent gods! what's here? a corse!—Most strange! iii 2 64
What world is this?—Is not this strange?—Most rare iii 2 107
Strange absence. Failing of her end by his strange absence *Cymbeline* v 5 57
Strange abuse. This is a strange abuse *Meas. for Meas.* v 1 205
Strange accident. You shall not know by what strange accident I chanced on this letter *Mer. of Venice* v 1 278
Strange-achieved. For this they have engross'd and piled up The canker'd heaps of strange-achieved gold 2 *Hen. IV.* iv 5 72
Strange alteration. Here's a strange alteration! *Coriolanus* iv 5 154
Strange attempts. Impossible be strange attempts to those That weigh their pains in sense *All's Well* i 1 239
Strange beast. Any strange beast there makes a man *Tempest* ii 2 32
Strange beasts, which in all tongues are called fools *As Y. Like It* v 4 37
Strange bed-fellows. Misery acquaints a man with strange bed-fellows *Tempest* ii 2 41
Strange beginning. A strange beginning: 'borrow'd majesty!' *K. John* i 1 5
Strange brooch. Love to Richard Is a strange brooch in this all-hating world *Richard II.* v 5 66
Strange bull. Some such strange bull leap'd your father's cow *M. Ado* v 4 49
Strange capers. We that are true lovers run into strange capers *As Y. L. It* ii 4 55
Strange case. What a strange case was that! *T. of Athens* iii 2 18
Strange chance: A narrow lane, an old man, and two boys *Cymbeline* v 3 51
Strange commotion Is in his brain: he bites his lip *Hen. VIII.* iii 2 112
Strange concealments. Exceedingly well read, and profited In strange concealments 1 *Hen. IV.* iii 1 167
Strange confession. I see a strange confession in thine eye 2 *Hen. IV.* i 1 94
Strange course. Not for that dream I on this strange course *Much Ado* iv 1 214
Strange courtesies. He hath laid strange courtesies and great Of late upon me *Ant. and Cleo.* ii 2 157
Strange deaths. Devise strange deaths for small offences done 2 *Hen. VI.* iii 1 59
Strange defeatures. Careful hours with time's deformed hand Have written strange defeatures in my face *Com. of Errors* v 1 299
Strange disguises. A fancy that he hath to strange disguises *M. Ado* iii 2 32
Strange dishes. A very fantastical banquet, just so many strange dishes ii 3 22
Strange-disposed. Indeed, it is a strange-disposed time *J. Cæsar* i 3 33
Strange dream, that gives a dead man leave to think! *Rom. and Jul.* v 1 7
Strange drowsiness. What a strange drowsiness possesses them! *Temp.* ii 1 199
Strange effect. Thy complexion shifts to strange effects, After the moon *Meas. for Meas.* iii 1 24
Alack, in me what strange effect! *As Y. Like It* iv 3 52
Strange encounter. That with your strange encounter much amazed me *T. of Shrew* iv 5 54
Strange eruption. Diseased nature oftentimes breaks forth In strange eruptions 1 *Hen. IV.* iii 1 28
Fearful, as these strange eruptions are *J. Cæsar* i 3 78
This bodes some strange eruption to our state *Hamlet* i 1 69
Strange event. 'Tis I must make conclusion Of these most strange events *As Y. Like It* v 4 133
I'll show you how to observe a strange event *T. of Athens* iii 4 17
Strange face. It is the witness still of excellency To put a strange face on his own perfection *Much Ado* ii 3 49
Strange fantasies. With many legions of strange fantasies *K. John* v 7 18
Strange fellow. Now, by two-headed Janus, Nature hath framed strange fellows in her time *Mer. of Venice* i 1 51
Is not this a strange fellow, my lord? *All's Well* ii 6 93
A strange fellow here Writes me *Troi. and Cres.* iii 3 95
A tailor made thee.—Thou art a strange fellow: a tailor make a man? *Lear* ii 2 61
A stranger, and I not know on't!—He's a strange fellow himself, and knows it not *Cymbeline* ii 1 38

Strange fever. He is sick, my lord, Of a strange fever *Meas. for Meas.* v 1 152
Strange fish. What strange fish Hath made his meal on thee? *Tempest* ii 1 112
A kind of not of the newest Poor-John. A strange fish! ii 2 28
Strange flesh. On the Alps It is reported thou didst eat strange flesh, Which some did die to look on *Ant. and Cleo.* i 4 67
Strange flies. Afflicted with these strange flies *Rom. and Jul.* ii 4 34
Strange followers. Our honour and our shame in this Are dogg'd with two strange followers *Troi. and Cres.* i 3 365
Strange forms. It's past the size of dreaming: nature wants stuff To vie strange forms with fancy *Ant. and Cleo.* v 2 98
Strange fortune. As by strange fortune It came to us *W. Tale* ii 3 179
Strange fowl light upon neighbouring ponds *Cymbeline* i 4 97
Strange garments. New honours come upon him, Like our strange garments, cleave not to their mould But with the aid of use *Macbeth* i 3 145
Strange guest. Tell my master what a strange guest he has *Coriolanus* iv 5 38
Strange images. Nothing afeard of what thyself didst make, Strange images of death *Macbeth* i 3 97
Strange impatience. To see the strange impatience of the heavens *J. C.* i 3 61
Strange Indian. Some strange Indian with the great tool *Hen. VIII.* v 4 34
Strange indignity. Some strange indignity, Which patience could not pass *Othello* ii 3 245
Strange infection. What a strange infection Is fall'n into thy ear! *Cymb.* iii 2 3
Strange infirmity. I have a strange infirmity, which is nothing To those that know me *Macbeth* iii 4 86
Strange inquire. Fame answering the most strange inquire *Pericles* iii Gower 22
Strange insurrections. In Rome strange insurrections *Coriolanus* iv 3 13
Strange intelligence. Say from whence You owe this strange intelligence? *Macbeth* i 3 76
Strange invention. Filling their hearers With strange invention iii 1 33
Strange love. Till strange love, grown bold, Think true love acted simple modesty *Rom. and Jul.* iii 2 15
Strange lunacy. Beaten hence by your strange lunacy *T. of Shrew* Ind. 2 31
Strange manner. He's coming, madam; but in very strange manner *T. Night* iii 4 9
For certain she is dead, and by strange manner *J. Cæsar* iv 3 189
Strange matters. Your face, my thane, is as a book where men May read strange matters *Macbeth* i 5 64
Strange men. But, O strange men! *All's Well* iv 4 21
Strange misprision. There is some strange misprision in the princes *Much Ado* iv 1 187
Strange motions. In thy face strange motions have appear'd *1 Hen. IV.* ii 3 63
Strange mutations. O world! But that thy strange mutations make us hate thee, Life would not yield to age *Lear* iv 1 11
Strange mysteries. Is't possible the spells of France should juggle Men into such strange mysteries? *Hen. VIII.* i 3 2
Strange nature. Of a strange nature is the suit you follow *M. of Ven.* iv 1 177
Within my soul there doth conduce a fight Of this strange nature *Troi. and Cres.* v 2 148
'Twould anger him To raise a spirit in his mistress' circle Of some strange nature *Rom. and Jul.* ii 1 25
Strange news. I can tell you strange news *Much Ado* i 2 4
Strange news.—If it be true, all vengeance comes too short *Lear* ii 1 89
There's strange news come, sir.—What, man? *Ant. and Cleo.* iii 5 2
Strange oaths. Then a soldier, Full of strange oaths *As Y. Like It* ii 7 150
Strange œillades and most speaking looks *Lear* iv 5 25
Strange one. I heard a humming, And that a strange one too *Tempest* ii 1 318
And a petition granted them, a strange one *Coriolanus* i 1 214
You are a pair of strange ones ii 1 89
What fellow's this?—A strange one as ever I looked on iv 5 21
Strange pastime. We will with some strange pastime solace them *L. L. L.* iv 3 377
Strange picklock. We have found upon him, sir, a strange picklock *Meas. for Meas.* iii 2 18
Strange places. He hath strange places cramm'd With observation, the which he vents In mangled forms *As Y. Like It* ii 7 40
Strange plots. To ruminate strange plots of dire revenge *T. Andron.* v 2 6
Strange postures. In most strange postures We have seen him set himself *Hen. VIII.* iii 2 118
Strange queen. One of the strange queen's lords *L. L. Lost* iv 2 134
Strange regard. You throw a strange regard upon me *T. Night* v 1 219
Strange repose. This is a strange repose, to be asleep With eyes wide open *Tempest* ii 1 213
Strange restraint. Come yourself alone To know the reason of this strange restraint *Com. of Errors* iii 1 97
Strange return. The occasion of my sudden and more strange return *Hamlet* iv 7 48
Strange screams of death, And prophesying *Macbeth* ii 3 61
Strange serpent. You've strange serpents there *Ant. and Cleo.* ii 7 27
'Tis a strange serpent.—'Tis so. And the tears of it are wet ii 7 54
Strange shapes. Like the eye, Full of strange shapes *L. L. Lost* v 2 773
Strange sight. To the king and show our strange sights *W. Tale* iv 4 849
There's two or three of us have seen strange sights *J. Cæsar* i 3 138
Strange snow. That is, hot ice and wondrous strange snow *M. N. Dream* v 1 59
Strange sores. To strange sores strangely they strain the cure *M. Ado* iv 1 254
Strange soul. Like a strange soul upon the Stygian banks *Tr. and Cr.* iii 2 10
Strange speech. In conclusion put strange speech upon me *T. Night* v 1 70
Strange stare. Why stand you In this strange stare? *Tempest* iii 3 95
Strange starting. Blest pray you be, That, after this strange starting from your orbs, You may reign in them now! *Cymbeline* v 5 371
Strange story. This must crave, An if this be at all, a most strange story *Tempest* v 1 117
Strange stuff. He'll fill our skins with pinches, Make us strange stuff iv 1 234
Strange suits. You lisp and wear strange suits *As Y. Like It* iv 1 34
Strange tenour. Receives letters of strange tenour *Meas. for Meas.* iv 2 216
Strange thing. This is a strange thing as e'er I look'd on *Tempest* v 1 289
Follow me: I'll tell you strange things of this knave *Mer. Wives* v 1 29
Follow. Strange things in hand, Master Brook! Follow v 1 32
Believe then, if you please, that I can do strange things *As Y. Like It* v 2 65
I shall, between this and supper, tell you most strange things *Coriolanus* iv 3 44
Strange things I have in head, that will to hand *Macbeth* iii 4 139
There is some strange thing toward *Lear* iii 3 20
Strange times, that weep with laughing, not with weeping! *T. of Athens* iv 3 493
Strange tongue. The prince but studies his companions Like a strange tongue *2 Hen. IV.* iv 4 69
A strange tongue makes my cause more strange, suspicious *Hen. VIII.* iii 1 45
Strange tortures for offenders never heard of *2 Hen. VI.* iii 1 122
Strange truth. It is true, indeed.—'Tis a strange truth *Othello* v 2 189
Strange unquietness. He went hence but now, And certainly in strange unquietness iii 4 133
Strange virtue. With this strange virtue, He hath a heavenly gift of prophecy *Macbeth* iv 3 156

Strangely. They vanish'd strangely.—No matter *Tempest* iii 3 40
Thou Hast strangely stood the test iv 1 7
Most strangely Upon this shore, where you were wreck'd, was landed v 1 160
The story of your life, which must Take the ear strangely v 1 313
The duke is very strangely gone from hence *Meas. for Meas.* i 4 50
Awakens me with this unwonted putting-on; methinks strangely iv 2 120
O day untowardly turned!—O mischief strangely thwarting! *Much Ado* iii 2 135
To strange sores strangely they strain the cure iv 1 254
Commend it strangely to some place Where chance may nurse or end it *W. Tale* ii 3 182
I find the people strangely fantasied; Possess'd with rumours *K. John* iv 2 144
The herds Were strangely clamorous to the frighted fields *1 Hen. IV.* iii 1 40
You all look strangely on me: and you most *2 Hen. IV.* v 2 63
Uncontemn'd gone by him, or at least Strangely neglected *Hen. VIII.* iii 2 11
How came His practices to light?—Most strangely iii 2 29
All were woven So strangely in one piece iv 1 81
The times and titles now are alter'd strangely With me iv 2 112
What other Would you expect? you are strangely troublesome v 3 94
Pass strangely by him, As if he were forgot *Troi. and Cres.* iii 3 39
They pass by strangely: they were used to bend iii 3 71
Only, I say, Things have been strangely borne *Macbeth* iii 6 3
How came he mad?—Very strangely, they say.—How strangely? *Hamlet* v 1 172
It is a day turn'd strangely: or betimes Let's re-inforce, or fly *Cymbeline* v 2 17
And long of her it was That we meet here so strangely v 5 272
To earn To an honour'd triumph strangely furnished *Pericles* ii 2 53
Strangely-visited people, All swoln and ulcerous *Macbeth* iv 3 150
Strangeness. The strangeness of your story put Heaviness in me *Tempest* i 2 306
Do not infest your mind with beating on The strangeness of this business v 1 247
I am more amazed at his dishonour Than at the strangeness of it *M. for M.* v 1 386
I prithee now, ungird thy strangeness *T. Night* iv 1 16
Will ye not observe The strangeness of his alter'd countenance? *2 Hen. VI.* iii 1 5
Here tend the savage strangeness he puts on *Troi. and Cres.* ii 3 135
I have derision medicinable, To use between your strangeness and his pride iii 3 45
Put on A form of strangeness as we pass along iii 3 51
This is above all strangeness *Lear* iv 6 66
In strangeness stand no further off Than in a politic distance *Othello* iii 3 12
Stranger. The government I cast upon my brother And to my state grew stranger *Tempest* i 2 76
These are not natural events; they strengthen From strange to stranger v 1 228
But count the world a stranger for thy sake *T. G. of Ver.* v 4 70
We being strangers here, how darest thou trust So great a charge from thine own custody? *Com. of Errors* i 2 60
Signior, take the stranger to my house iv 1 36
Then swore he that he was a stranger here iv 2 9
He hath framed a letter to a sequent of the stranger queen's *L. L. Lost* iv 2 143
What would these strangers? know their minds v 2 174
Since you are strangers and come here by chance, We'll not be nice v 2 218
To seek new friends and stranger companies *M. N. Dream* i 1 219
A stranger Pyramus than e'er played here iii 1 90
The four strangers seek for you, madam, to take their leave *Mer. of Venice* i 2 135
And foot me as you spurn a stranger cur Over your threshold i 3 119
Cheer yon stranger; bid her welcome iii 2 240
The commodity that strangers have With us in Venice, if it be denied, Will much impeach the justice of his state iii 3 27
I do desire we may be better strangers *As Y. Like It* iii 2 275
He sent me hither, stranger as I am, To tell this story iv 3 153
Gentle sir, methinks you walk like a stranger *T. of Shrew* i 1 87
That, being a stranger in this city here, Do make myself a suitor ii 1 90
Thus strangers may be haled and abused iv 1 111
She thought, I dare vow for her, they touched not any stranger sense *All's Well* i 3 114
Strangers and foes do sunder, and not kiss ii 5 91
Some band of strangers i' the adversary's entertainment iv 1 17
Let him approach, A stranger, no offender v 3 26
He hath known you but three days, and already you are no stranger *T. N.* i 4 4
Which to a stranger, Unguided and unfriended, often prove Rough iii 3 9
Swearing allegiance and the love of soul To stranger blood *K. John* v 1 11
Wherein we step after a stranger march Upon her gentle bosom v 2 27
But tread the stranger paths of banishment *Richard II.* i 3 143
O, had it been a stranger, not my child, To smooth his fault I should have been more mild i 3 239
Believe me, noble lord, I am a stranger here in Gloucestershire ii 3 3
He doth begin To make us strangers to his looks of love *1 Hen. IV.* i 3 290
Strangers in court do take her for the queen *2 Hen. VI.* i 3 82
The first that there did greet my stranger soul *Richard III.* i 4 48
What is't?—A noble troop of strangers; For so they seem *Hen. VIII.* i 4 53
Your grace must needs deserve all strangers' loves, You are so noble ii 2 102
Alas, poor lady! She's a stranger now again ii 3 17
I am a most poor woman, and a stranger, Born out of your dominions ii 4 15
Your queen Desires your visitation, and to be Acquainted with this stranger v 1 168
How may A stranger to those most imperial looks Know them from eyes of other mortals? *Troi. and Cres.* i 3 224
Led us to Rome, strangers, and more than so, Captives *T. Andron.* iv 2 33
My child is yet a stranger in the world *Rom. and Jul.* i 2 8
Anon, anon! Come, let's away; the strangers all are gone i 5 146
We know him for no less, though we are but strangers to him *T. of A.* iii 2 4
Here abjure The taints and blames I laid upon myself, For strangers to my nature *Macbeth* iv 3 125
Good God, betimes remove The means that makes us strangers! iv 3 163
Wondrous strange!—And therefore as a stranger give it welcome *Hamlet* i 5 165
As a stranger to my heart and me Hold thee, from this, for ever *Lear* i 1 117
An extravagant and wheeling stranger Of here and every where *Othello* i 1 137
Thou dost conspire against thy friend, Iago, If thou but think'st him wrong'd and makest his ear A stranger to thy thoughts iii 3 144
Let him be so entertained amongst you as suits, with gentlemen of your knowing, to a stranger of his quality *Cymbeline* i 4 30
Makes no stranger of me; we are familiar at first i 4 111
None a stranger there So merry and so gamesome i 6 59
A saucy stranger in his court to mart As in a Romish stew i 6 151
Did you hear of a stranger that's come to court to-night?—A stranger, and I not know on't!—He's a strange fellow himself, and knows it not ii 1 35
Who told you of this stranger? ii 1 44
Her attendants are All sworn and honourable:—they induced to steal it! And by a stranger!—No ii 4 126
And strangers ne'er beheld but wonder'd at *Pericles* i 4 25
He seems to be a stranger ii 2 42

Stranger. He well may be a stranger, for he comes To an honour'd triumph strangely furnished *Pericles* ii 2 52
It befits not me Unto a stranger knight to be so bold ii 3 67
She'll wed the stranger knight, Or never more to view nor day nor light ii 5 16
A stranger and distressed gentleman ii 5 46
Will you, not having my consent, Bestow your love and your affections Upon a stranger? ii 5 78
Where do you live?—Where I am but a stranger v 1 115
Strangered. Dower'd with our curse, and stranger'd with our oath *Lear* i 1 207
Strangest. I am a fellow o' the strangest mind i' the world *T. Night* i 3 120
Here is the strangest controversy Come from the country *K. John* i 1 44
This is the strangest tale that ever I heard.—This is the strangest fellow, brother John 1 *Hen. IV.* v 4 158
I'll show your grace the strangest sight— What's that? *Hen. VIII.* v 2 19
Strangle. When he was a babe, a child, a shrimp, Thus did he strangle serpents in his manus *L. L. Lost* v 2 595
It is . . . thy fear That makes thee strangle thy propriety *T. Night* v 1 150
Strangle such thoughts as these *W. Tale* iv 4 47
If thou want'st a cord, the smallest thread That ever spider twisted from her womb Will serve to strangle thee *K. John* iv 3 129
Vapours that did seem to strangle him 1 *Hen. IV.* i 2 227
Strangles our dear vows Even in the birth *Troi. and Cres.* iv 4 39
'Tis day, And yet dark night strangles the travelling lamp *Macbeth* ii 4 7
Do it not with poison, strangle her in her bed *Othello* iv 1 220
Strangled. I hope I shall as soon be strangled with a halter 1 *Hen. IV.* ii 4 547
You three shall be strangled on the gallows 2 *Hen. VI.* ii 3 8
Staring full ghastly like a strangled man iii 2 170
He has strangled His language in his tears *Hen. VIII.* v 1 156
And there die strangled ere my Romeo comes *Rom. and Jul.* iv 3 35
Strangler. The band that seems to tie their friendship together will be the very strangler of their amity *Ant. and Cleo.* ii 6 130
Strangling. His enter and exit shall be strangling a snake *L. L. Lost* v 1 142
Who intercepts my expedition?—O, she that might have intercepted thee, By strangling thee in her accursed womb *Richard III.* iv 4 138
Strappado. An I were at the strappado, or all the racks in the world, I would not tell you on compulsion 1 *Hen. IV.* ii 4 262
Straps. Let them hang themselves in their own straps *T. Night* i 3 13
Stratagem. Is fit for treasons, stratagems, and spoils *Mer. of Venice* v 1 85
He says he has a stratagem for't *All's Well* iii 6 37
If you think your mystery in stratagem can bring this iii 6 68
Say it was in stratagem.—'Twould not do. iv 1 55
Every minute now Should be the father of some stratagem 2 *Hen. IV.* i 1 8
It will be an excellent stratagem iv 4 22
Without stratagem, But in plain shock and even play of battle *Hen. V.* iv 8 113
Saint Denis bless this happy stratagem! 1 *Hen. VI.* iii 2 18
I did send for thee To tutor thee in stratagems of war iv 5 2
What stratagems, how fell, how butcherly! 3 *Hen. VI.* ii 5 89
Ready in their offices, At any time, to grace my stratagems *Richard III.* iii 5 11
'Tis policy and stratagem must do That you affect *T. Andron.* ii 1 104
Know that this gold must coin a stratagem ii 3 5
Alack, that heaven should practise stratagems! *Rom. and Jul.* iii 5 211
It were a delicate stratagem, to shoe A troop of horse with felt *Lear* iv 6 188
Strato, thou hast been all this while asleep; Farewell to thee too, Strato *J. Cæsar* v 5 32
Strato, stay thou by thy lord: Thou art a fellow of a good respect v 5 44
Hold then my sword, and turn away thy face, While I do run upon it. Wilt thou, Strato? v 5 48
Farewell, good Strato. Cæsar, now be still v 5 50
Strato, where is thy master?—Free from the bondage you are in v 5 53
Straw. The strongest oaths are straw To the fire i' the blood *Tempest* iv 1 52
He is coming; I hear his straw rustle *Meas. for Meas.* iv 3 38
When shepherds pipe on oaten straws *L. L. Lost* v 2 913
Now I see our lances are but straws *T. of Shrew* v 2 173
They know his conditions and lay him in straw *All's Well* iv 3 289
No life, I prize it not a straw, but for mine honour *W. Tale* iii 2 111
Shall blow each dust, each straw, each little rub, Out of the path *K. John* iii 4 128
Give me your doublet and stuff me out with straw 2 *Hen. IV.* v 5 88
For oaths are straws, men's faiths are wafer-cakes *Hen. V.* ii 3 53
A wisp of straw were worth a thousand crowns 3 *Hen. VI.* ii 2 144
Tremble and start at wagging of a straw *Richard III.* iii 5 7
First thrash the corn, then after burn the straw *T. Andron.* ii 3 123
Those that with haste will make a mighty fire Begin it with weak straws: what trash is Rome, What rubbish! *J. Cæsar* i 3 108
Twenty thousand ducats Will not debate the question of this straw *Ham.* iv 4 26
Greatly to find quarrel in a straw When honour's at the stake iv 4 55
Hems, and beats her heart; Spurns enviously at straws iv 5 6
Where is this straw, my fellow? The art of our necessities is strange, That can make vile things precious *Lear* iii 2 69
What art thou that dost grumble there i' the straw? Come forth iii 4 45
Arm it in rags, a pigmy's straw does pierce it iv 6 171
To hovel thee with swine, and rogues forlorn, In short and musty straw iv 7 40
Strawberry. The strawberry grows underneath the nettle *Hen. V.* i 1 60
I saw good strawberries in your garden *Richard III.* iii 4 34
I have sent for these strawberries iii 4 49
A handkerchief Spotted with strawberries *Othello* iii 3 435
Straw-colour beard, your orange-tawny beard *M. N. Dream* i 2 95
Strawy. And there the strawy Greeks, ripe for his edge, Fall down before him, like the mower's swath *Troi. and Cres.* v 5 24
Stray. He hath lost his fellows, And strays about to find 'em *Tempest* i 2 417
He is drown'd Whom thus we stray to find iii 3 9
A sheep doth very often stray, An if the shepherd be a while away *T. G. of Ver.* i 1 74
By many winding nooks he strays With willing sport to the wild ocean ii 7 31
Until the break of day, Through this house each fairy stray *M. N. Dream* v 1 409
She doth stray about By holy crosses, where she kneels *Mer. of Venice* v 1 30
Now no way can I stray; Save back to England, all the world's my way *Richard II.* i 3 206
Strike up our drums, pursue the scatter'd stray 2 *Hen. IV.* iv 2 120
Taken and impounded as a stray *Hen. V.* i 2 160
And as the butcher takes away the calf And binds the wretch and beats it when it strays 2 *Hen. VI.* iii 1 211
Here's the lord of the soil come to seize me for a stray iv 10 27
I would not from your love make such a stray *Lear* i 1 212
Since the torch is out, Lie down, and stray no farther *Ant. and Cleo.* iv 14 47
If Jove stray, who dares say Jove doth ill? It is enough you know *Per.* i 1 104
Strayed. Hath not else his eye Stray'd his affection? *Com. of Errors* v 1 51
What if I stray'd no further, but chose here? *Mer. of Venice* ii 7 35
From our troops I stray'd To gaze upon a ruinous monastery *T. Andron.* v 1 20
Straying. Seeking a way and straying from the way 3 *Hen. VI.* iii 2 176
Win straying souls with modesty again, Cast none away *Hen. VIII.* v 3 64
Straying. O, thus I found her, straying in the park *T. Andron.* iii 1 88
Streak. With the juice of this I'll streak her eyes *M. N. Dream* ii 1 257
Chequering the eastern clouds with streaks of light *Rom. and Jul.* ii 3 2
What envious streaks Do lace the severing clouds in yonder east iii 5 7
The west yet glimmers with some streaks of day *Macbeth* iii 3 5
Streaked. All the eanlings which were streak'd and pied Should fall as Jacob's hire *Mer. of Venice* i 3 80
Streak'd gillyvors, Which some call nature's bastards *W. Tale* iv 4 82
Stream. I'll be as patient as a gentle stream *T. G. of Ver.* ii 7 34
The very stream of his life and the business he hath helmed *M. for M.* iii 2 150
Floating straight, obedient to the stream *Com. of Errors* i 1 87
To see the fish Cut with her golden oars the silver stream *Much Ado* iii 1 27
Turns into yellow gold his salt green streams *M. N. Dream* iii 2 393
Would scatter all her spices on the stream *Mer. of Venice* i 1 33
My eye shall be the stream And watery death-bed for him iii 2 46
Weeping into the needless stream *As Y. Like It* ii 1 46
To forswear the full stream of the world and to live in a nook iii 2 439
The rank of osiers by the murmuring stream iv 3 80
To imperial Love, that god most high, Do my sighs stream *All's Well* ii 3 82
Contrives against his own nobility, In his proper stream o'erflows himself iv 3 29
What relish is in this? how runs the stream? *T. Night* iv 1 64
And two such shores to two such streams made one *K. John* ii 1 443
Sluiced out his innocent soul through streams of blood *Richard II.* i 1 103
From whence this stream through muddy passages Hath held his current v 3 62
Like bubbles in a late-disturbed stream 1 *Hen. IV.* ii 3 62
We see which way the stream of time doth run 2 *Hen. IV.* iv 1 70
Which swims against your stream of quality v 2 34
As many fresh streams meet in one salt sea *Hen. V.* i 2 209
One drop of blood drawn from thy country's bosom Should grieve thee more than streams of foreign gore 1 *Hen. VI.* iii 3 55
As plays the sun upon the glassy streams v 3 62
And make poor England weep in streams of blood! *Richard III.* v 5 37
To the mercy Of a rude stream, that must for ever hide me *Hen. VIII.* iii 2 364
The rich stream Of lords and ladies iv 1 62
Carries on the stream of his dispose Without observance *Troi. and Cres.* ii 3 174
We will be there before the stream o' the people *Coriolanus* ii 3 269
Sit fas aut nefas, till I find the stream To cool this heat *T. Andron.* ii 1 133
Her eyes in heaven Would through the airy region stream so bright That birds would sing and think it were not night *Rom. and Jul.* ii 2 21
That 'gainst the stream of virtue they may strive *T. of Athens* iv 1 27
Not a man Shall pass his quarter, or offend the stream Of regular justice v 4 60
Weep your tears Into the channel, till the lowest stream Do kiss the most exalted shores of all *J. Cæsar* i 1 64
Had I as many eyes as thou hast wounds, Weeping as fast as they stream forth thy blood iii 1 201
Unsafe the while, that we Must lave our honours in these flattering streams, And make our faces vizards *Macbeth* iii 2 33
That shows his hoar leaves in the glassy stream *Hamlet* iv 7 168
My boat sails freely, both with wind and stream *Othello* ii 3 65
If there be cords, or knives, Poison, or fire, or suffocating streams, I'll not endure it iii 3 389
The fresh streams ran by her, and murmur'd her moans; Sing willow iv 3 45
Like to a vagabond flag upon the stream, Goes to and back *Ant. and Cleo.* i 4 45
I have sent Cloten's clotpoll down the stream *Cymbeline* iv 2 184
Streamers. His brave fleet With silken streamers *Hen. V.* iii Prol. 6
Streaming the ensign of the Christian cross Against black pagans *Rich. II.* iv 1 94
Street. Hard by; at street end; he will be here anon *Mer. Wives* iv 2 40
Sent to her, seeing her go thorough the streets iv 5 32
They should exhibit their petitions in the street *Meas. for Meas.* iv 4 12
My master stays in the street *Com. of Errors* iii 1 36
I see a man here needs not live by shifts, When in the streets he meets such golden gifts iii 2 188
Tell her I am arrested in the street iv 1 106
Desperately he hurried through the street v 1 140
In the street I met him And in his company that gentleman v 1 225
You shall also make no noise in the streets *Much Ado* iii 3 36
O, if the streets were paved with thine eyes, Her feet were much too dainty for such tread! *L. L. Lost* iv 3 278
As she goes, what upward lies The street should see as she walk'd overhead iv 3 281
Nor thrust your head into the public street *Mer. of Venice* ii 5 32
The dog Jew did utter in the streets: 'My daughter! O my ducats!' ii 8 14
Are not the streets as free For me as for you? *T. of Shrew.* i 2 233
First kiss me, Kate, and we will.—What, in the midst of the street? v 1 149
Where's your master?—He met the duke in the street *All's Well* iv 3 89
I do not without danger walk these streets *T. Night* iii 3 25
In the streets, desperate of shame and state, In private brabble v 1 67
Here's a prophet, that I brought with me From forth the streets of Pomfret *K. John* iv 2 148
Old men and beldams in the streets Do prophesy upon it dangerously iv 2 185
They found him dead and cast into the streets v 1 39
When I beheld In London streets, that coronation-day *Richard II.* v 5 77
An old lord of the council rated me the other day in the street 1 *Hen. IV.* i 2 95
I regarded him not; and yet he talked wisely, and in the street too i 2 98
Wisdom cries out in the streets, and no man regards it i 2 100
Grew a companion to the common streets iii 2 68
And the feats he hath done about Turnbull Street 2 *Hen. IV.* iii 2 329
Make bonfires And feast and banquet in the open streets 1 *Hen. VI.* i 6 13
Our windows are broke down in every street iii 1 84
Uneath may she endure the flinty streets, To tread them 2 *Hen. VI.* ii 4 8
When thou didst ride in triumph through the streets ii 4 14
Ride through the streets; and at every corner have them kiss iv 7 144
Up Fish Street! down Saint Magnus' Corner! iv 8 1
I see them lording it in London streets, Crying 'Villiago!' iv 8 47
Plant love among's! Throng our large temples with the shows of peace, And not our streets with war! *Coriolanus* iii 3 37
Behold Dissentious numbers pestering streets iv 6 7
These fellows ran about the streets, Crying confusion iv 6 28
As a foreign recreant, be led With manacles thorough our streets v 3 115
Must my sons be slaughter'd in the streets, For valiant doings? *T. An.* i 1 112
I will not re-salute the streets of Rome, Or climb my palace, till from forth this place I lead espoused my bride i 1 326
And make them know what 'tis to let a queen Kneel in the streets i 1 455
Sweet scrolls to fly about the streets of Rome! What's this but libelling? iv 4 16
Look round about the wicked streets of Rome v 2 98
Have thrice disturb'd the quiet of our streets *Rom. and Jul.* i 1 98
If ever you disturb our streets again, Your lives shall pay the forfeit i 1 103
Thou hast quarrelled with a man for coughing in the street iii 1 27
The prince expressly hath Forbidden bandying in Verona streets iii 1 92

Street. Beg, starve, die in the streets, For, by my soul, I'll ne'er acknowledge thee . *Rom. and Jul.* iii 5 194
The people in the street cry Romeo, Some Juliet, and some Paris . v 3 191
Why dost thou lead these men about the streets? *J. Cæsar* i 1 32
To see great Pompey pass the streets of Rome . . . i 1 47
I'll about, And drive away the vulgar from the streets . . i 1 75
Who swore they saw Men all in fire walk up and down the streets . i 3 25
I have walk'd about the streets, Submitting me unto the perilous night i 3 46
This fearful night, There is no stir or walking in the streets . . . i 3 127
My ancestors did from the streets of Rome The Tarquin drive . . ii 1 53
A lioness hath whelped in the streets; And graves have yawn'd . ii 2 17
Dying men did groan, And ghosts did shriek and squeal about the streets . . . . ii 2 24
Here the street is narrow: The throng . . . Will crowd a feeble man almost to death . . . . ii 4 33
What, urge you your petitions in the street? Come to the Capitol . iii 1 11
Tyranny is dead! Run hence, proclaim, cry it about the streets . iii 1 79
Go you into the other street, And part the numbers . . iii 2 3
You are contented to be led in triumph Thorough the streets of Rome? v 1 110
The sheeted dead Did squeak and gibber in the Roman streets *Hamlet* i 1 116
Baked and impasted with the parching streets. . . . . ii 2 481
Make after him, poison his delight, Proclaim him in the streets . *Othello* i 1 69
After her, after her.—'Faith, I must; she'll rail in the street else . iv 1 170
And all alone To-night we'll wander through the streets and note The qualities of people . . . . *Ant. and Cleo.* i 1 53
To reel the streets at noon, and stand the buffet With knaves . i 4 20
I saw her once Hop forty paces through the public street . . ii 2 234
Heard you of nothing strange about the streets? . . iv 3 3
The round world Should have shook lions into civil streets . v 1 16
Cast mire upon me, set The dogs o' the street to bay me . *Cymbeline* v 5 223
A city on whom plenty held full hand, For riches strew'd herself even in the streets . . . . . *Pericles* i 4 23
We have heard your miseries as far as Tyre, And seen the desolation of your streets . . . . i 4 89
Strength. Your swords are now too massy for your strengths *Tempest* iii 3 67
What strength I have's mine own . . . . . Epil. 2
As one nail by strength drives out another *T. G. of Ver.* ii 4 193
All advice My strength can give you. . *Meas. for Meas.* i 1 7
A power I have, but of what strength and nature I am not yet instructed . . . . i 1 80
O, it is excellent To have a giant's strength . . . ii 2 108
Makes me with thy strength to communicate . . *Com. of Errors* ii 2 178
Abused and dishonour'd me Even in the strength and height of injury! v 1 200
Both strength of limb and policy of mind, Ability in means *Much Ado* iv 1 200
Yet was Samson so tempted, and he had an excellent strength *L. L. Lost* i 2 180
Thy threats have no more strength than her weak prayers *M. N. Dream* iii 2 250
Abate the strength of your displeasure . . *Mer. of Venice* v 1 198
To try with him the strength of my youth . . . *As Y. Like It* i 2 182
You have seen cruel proof of this man's strength . . . i 2 185
The little strength that I have, I would it were with you . . i 2 206
Our strength as weak, our weakness past compare . *T. of Shrew* v 2 174
It is A charge too heavy for my strength . . . *All's Well* iii 3 4
Demand of him, of what strength they are a-foot . . . iv 3 181
What youth, strength, skill, and wrath can furnish man withal *T. Night* iii 4 254
I' the open air, before I have got strength of limit . *W. Tale* iii 2 107
Ere they can behold Bright Phœbus in his strength . . . iv 4 124
He has his health and ampler strength indeed Than most have of his age iv 4 414
Till your strong hand shall help to give him strength . *K. John* ii 1 33
Strength match'd with strength, and power confronted power . ii 1 330
Dissever your united strengths, And part your mingled colours . ii 1 388
Bidding me depend Upon thy stars, thy fortune, and thy strength . iii 1 126
Coupled and link'd together With all religious strength of sacred vows . iii 1 229
So, nobles, shall you all, That knit your sinews to the strength of mine . . . . v 2 63
That hand which had the strength, even at your door, To cudgel you v 2 137
If guilty dread have left thee so much strength . *Richard II.* i 1 73
To fear the foe, since fear oppresseth strength, Gives in your weakness strength unto your foe . . . . iii 2 180
Not with such strength denied As is deliver'd . . 1 *Hen. IV.* i 3 25
I shall be out of heart shortly, and then I shall have no strength to repent . . . . iii 3 7
He should draw his several strengths together . 2 *Hen. IV.* i 3 76
Then join you with them, like a rib of steel, To make strength stronger ii 3 55
To his former strength may be restored With good advice and little medicine . . . . iii 1 42
Every thing lies level to our wish: Only, we want a little personal strength . . . . iv 4 8
Put the world's whole strength Into one giant arm . . . iv 5 44
My lungs are wasted so That strength of speech is utterly denied me . iv 5 218
We will, according to your strengths and qualities, Give you advancement . . . . v 5 73
Praised be God, and not our strength, for it! . . *Hen. V.* iv 7 90
I have no strength in measure, yet a reasonable measure in strength . v 2 140
Whom all France with their chief assembled strength Durst not presume to look once in the face . . . . 1 *Hen. VI.* i 1 139
Where is my strength, my valour, and my force? . . . i 5 1
O'ertake me, if thou canst; I scorn thy strength . . . i 5 15
These are his substance, sinews, arms, and strength . . . ii 3 63
What is the trust or strength of foolish man? . . . . iii 2 112
Twelve cities and seven walled towns of strength . . . iii 4 7
Then gather strength and march unto him straight . . . iv 1 73
Thou princely leader of our English strength . . . . iv 3 17
Or one that, at a triumph having vow'd To try his strength . . v 5 32
Why, then from Ireland come I with my strength . 2 *Hen. VI.* iii 1 380
Tugg'd for life and was by strength subdued . . . . iii 2 173
My foot shall fight with all the strength thou hast . . . iv 10 53
And spend her strength with over-matching waves . . 3 *Hen. VI.* i 4 21
Many blows repaid, Have robb'd my strong-knit sinews of their strength ii 3 4
No way to fly, nor strength to hold out flight . . . . ii 6 24
Inferreth arguments of mighty strength . . . . . iii 1 49
My eye's too quick, my heart o'erweens too much, Unless my hand and strength could equal them . . . . iii 2 145
He's very likely now to fall from him, For matching more for wanton lust than honour, Or than for strength and safety . . . iii 3 211
My want of strength, my sick heart shows, That I must yield my body to the earth . . . . v 2 8
Our strength will be augmented In every county . . . v 3 22
And give more strength to that which hath too much . . . v 4 9
By the heavens' assistance and your strength, Must by the roots be hewn up . . . . v 4 68
Strength. Bid him levy straight The greatest strength and power he can make . . . . *Richard III.* iv 4 449
Besides, the king's name is a tower of strength . . . . v 3 12
Part in just proportion our small strength . . . . . v 3 26
Skilful to their strength, Fierce to their skill . *Troi. and Cres.* i 1 7
Strength should be lord of imbecility . . . . . i 3 114
Troy in our weakness stands, not in her strength . . . i 3 137
Disguise the holy strength of their command . . . . ii 3 136
A proof of strength she could not publish more . . . v 2 113
I will wish her speedy strength, and visit her with my prayers *Coriolanus* i 3 87
It shall be so I' the right and strength o' the commons . . iii 3 14
Say their great enemy is gone, and they Stand in their ancient strength iv 2 7
As ever in ambitious strength I did Contend against thy valour . iv 5 118
Thou know'st Thy country's strength and weakness,—thine own ways . iv 5 146
Desperation Is all the policy, strength, and defence, That Rome can make . . . . iv 6 127
Rights by rights falter, strengths by strengths do fail . . . . iv 7 55
Does reason our petition with more strength Than thou hast to deny't v 3 176
Withdraw you and abate your strength . . . *T. Andron.* i 1 43
I have been thy soldier forty years, And led my country's strength successfully . . . . i 1 194
Or, wanting strength to do thee so much good, I may be pluck'd into the swallowing womb Of this deep pit . . . . ii 3 238
I have no strength to pluck thee to the brink.—Nor I no strength to climb without thy help . . . . . . ii 3 241
Eat no more Than will preserve just so much strength in us As will revenge these bitter woes of ours . . . . iii 2 2
No more deep will I endart mine eye Than your consent gives strength to make it fly . . . . *Rom. and Jul.* i 3 99
Women may fall, when there's no strength in men . . . ii 3 80
If, rather than to marry County Paris, Thou hast the strength of will to slay thyself . . . . iv 1 72
Love give me strength! and strength shall help afford . . iv 1 125
If you had the strength Of twenty men, it would dispatch you straight v 1 78
Nor strong links of iron, Can be retentive to the strength of spirit *J. C.* i 3 95
Our arms, in strength of malice, and our hearts Of brothers' temper . iii 1 174
You do unbend your noble strength, to think So brainsickly . *Macbeth* ii 2 45
By the strength of their illusion Shall draw him on to his confusion . iii 5 28
Our castle's strength Will laugh a siege to scorn . . . v 5 2
With all the strength and armour of the mind . . *Hamlet* iii 3 12
'This thing's to do;' Sith I have cause and will and strength and means iv 4 45
Conferring them on younger strengths . . . . *Lear* i 1 41
Make your own purpose, How in my strength you please . . ii 1 114
Moreover, to descry The strength o' the enemy . . . iv 5 14
Now let thy friendly hand Put strength enough to't . . . iv 6 235
Here is the guess of their true strength and forces By diligent discovery v 1 52
I protest, Maugre thy strength, youth, place, and eminence . v 3 131
The hated, grown to strength, Are newly grown to love . *Ant. and Cleo.* i 3 48
Cæsar and Lepidus Are in the field: a mighty strength they carry . ii 1 17
What is his strength by land?—Great and increasing . . ii 2 164
That which is the strength of their amity shall prove the immediate author of their variance . . . . ii 6 137
I'll wrestle with you in my strength of love . . . . iii 2 62
Yea, very force entangles Itself with strength . . . . . iv 14 49
Our strength is all gone into heaviness, That makes the weight . iv 15 33
Whose strength I will confirm with oath . . . *Cymbeline* ii 4 63
I would revenges, That possible strength might meet, would seek us . iv 2 160
Gods, put the strength o' the Leonati in me! . . . . v 1 31
Give me leave; I faint.—My daughter! what of her? Renew thy strength v 5 150
The care I had and have of subjects' good On thee I lay, whose wisdom's strength can bear it . . . . . . *Pericles* i 2 119
Those which see them fall Have scarce strength left to give them burial i 4 49
Strengthen. They strengthen From strange to stranger . *Tempest* v 1 227
You came in arms to spill mine enemies' blood, But now in arms you strengthen it with yours . . . . . . *K. John* iii 1 103
With powerful policy strengthen themselves . . 3 *Hen. VI.* i 2 58
To strengthen and support King Edward's place . . . iii 1 52
To strengthen That holy duty, out of dear respect . . *Hen. VIII.* v 3 118
My faction if thou strengthen with thy friends, I will most thankful be *T. Andron.* i 1 214
Fearing to strengthen that impatience Which seem'd too much enkindled *J. Cæsar* ii 1 248
Strengthen your patience in our last night's speech . *Hamlet* v 1 317
Persever in that clear way thou goest, And the gods strengthen thee! *Pericles* iv 6 114
Strengthen'd with what apology you think . . *All's Well* ii 4 51
Strengthen'd by interchangement of your rings . . *T. Night* v 1 162
The world increases, and kindreds are mightily strengthened 2 *Hen. IV.* ii 2 30
Such alliance Would more have strengthen'd this our commonwealth 3 *Hen. VI.* iv 1 37
Strengthening. Impairing Henry, strengthening misproud York . ii 6 7
Strengthless. Fever-weaken'd joints, Like strengthless hinges 2 *Hen. IV.* i 1 141
These feet, whose strengthless stay is numb . . . 1 *Hen. VI.* ii 5 13
Stretch. The duke Dare no more stretch this finger of mine than he Dare rack his own. . . . . . . *Meas. for Meas.* v 1 316
Such groans That their discharge did stretch his leathern coat *As Y. L. It* ii 1 37
The gift doth stretch itself as 'tis received . . . *All's Well* ii 1 4
So far as my coin would stretch . . . . . 1 *Hen. IV.* i 2 62
My grief Stretches itself beyond the hour of death . 2 *Hen. IV.* iv 4 57
How shall we stretch our eye When capital crimes, chew'd, swallow'd, and digested, Appear before us? . . . . . *Hen. V.* ii 2 55
Now set the teeth and stretch the nostril wide, Hold hard the breath . iii 1 15
His will is most malignant; and it stretches Beyond you . *Hen. VIII.* i 2 141
The capacity Of your soft cheveril conscience would receive, If you might please to stretch it . . . . ii 3 33
Come, stretch thy chest, and let thy eyes spout blood *Troi. and Cres.* iv 5 10
Leave nothing out for length, and make us think Rather our state's defective for requital Than we to stretch it out . . *Coriolanus* ii 2 55
That the precipitation might down stretch Below the beam of sight . iii 2 4
Here's a wit of cheveril, that stretches from an inch narrow to an ell broad!—I stretch it out for that word 'broad' . *Rom. and Jul.* ii 4 87
You know, his means, If he improve them, may well stretch so far As to annoy us all . . . . *J. Cæsar* ii 1 159
What, will the line stretch out to the crack of doom? . . *Macbeth* iv 1 117
Twenty silly ducking observants That stretch their duties nicely *Lear* ii 2 110
This kiss, if it durst speak, Would stretch thy spirits up into the air . iv 2 23
That would upon the rack of this tough world Stretch him out longer . v 3 315
Not a minute of our lives should stretch Without some pleasure *Ant. and Cleo.* i 1 46
Swell'd so much that it did almost stretch The sides o' the world *Cymb.* iii 1 50

Stretched. The ox hath therefore stretch'd his yoke in vain *M. N. Dream* ii 1 93
Extremely stretch'd and conn'd with cruel pain . . . . v 1 80
There lay he, stretched along, like a wounded knight *As Y. Like It* iii 2 253
Had it stretched so far, would have made nature immortal . *All's Well* i 1 22
His hair uprear'd, his nostrils stretched with struggling *2 Hen. VI.* iii 2 171
Which stretched to their servants, daughters, wives *Richard III.* iii 5 82
He stretch'd him, and, with one hand on his dagger . *Hen. VIII.* i 2 204
'Twixt his stretch'd footing and the scaffoldage *Troi. and Cres.* i 3 156
And thus far having stretch'd it—here be with them *Coriolanus* iii 2 74
There was it: For which my sinews shall be stretch'd upon him . v 6 45
Have I in conquest stretch'd mine arm so far, To be afeard to tell gray-beards the truth? . . . . *J. Cæsar* ii 2 66
Let our alliance be combined, Our best friends made, our means stretch'd iv 1 44
Since your kindness We have stretch'd thus far . *Pericles* v 1 55
Stretched-out. Most reverend for thy stretch'd-out life . *Troi. and Cres.* i 3 61
Stretching. The stretching of a span Buckles in his sum of age *As Y. Like It* iii 2 139
Upon uneasy pallets stretching thee . . *2 Hen. IV.* iii 1 10
Stretch-mouthed. Some stretch-mouthed rascal . . *W. Tale* iv 4 196
Strew good luck, ouphes, on every sacred room . . *Mer. Wives* v 5 61
O, these I lack, To make you garlands of, and my sweet friend, To strew him o'er and o'er! . . . . *W. Tale* iv 4 129
For it [deceit] shall strew the footsteps of my rising . *K. John* i 1 216
Violets now That strew the green lap of the new come spring *Richard II.* v 2 47
Strew me over With maiden flowers, that all the world may know I was a chaste wife to my grave . . . . *Hen. VIII.* iv 2 168
Strew flowers before them . . . . *Coriolanus* v 5 3
Sweet flower, with flowers thy bridal bed I strew . *Rom. and Jul.* v 3 12
The obsequies that I for thee will keep Nightly shall be to strew thy grave and weep . . . . v 3 17
And strew this hungry churchyard with thy limbs . . . . . v 3 36
He came with flowers to strew his lady's grave . . . . v 3 281
Do you now strew flowers in his way That comes in triumph? *J. Cæsar* i 1 55
She may strew Dangerous conjectures in ill-breeding minds *Hamlet* iv 5 14
Even so These herblets shall, which we upon you strew. *Cymbeline* iv 2 287
I will rob Tellus of her weed, To strew thy green with flowers *Pericles* iv 1 15
Strewed. So I have strew'd it in the common ear *Meas. for Meas.* i 3 15
Is supper ready, the house trimmed, rushes strewed? . *T. of Shrew* iv 1 48
Whose want, and whose delay, is strew'd with sweets . *All's Well* ii 4 45
And strew'd repentant ashes on his head . . . *K. John* iv 1 111
The grass whereon thou tread'st the presence strew'd . *Richard II.* i 3 289
What's past and what's to come is strew'd with husks *Troi. and Cres.* iv 5 166
I thought thy bride-bed to have deck'd, sweet maid, And not have strew'd thy grave . . . . *Hamlet* v 1 269
And smooth success Be strew'd before your feet! *Ant. and Cleo.* i 3 101
Good troth, I have stol'n nought, nor would not, though I had found Gold strew'd i' the floor . . . . . *Cymbeline* iii 6 50
With wild wood-leaves and weeds I ha' strew'd his grave . iv 2 390
For riches strew'd herself even in the streets . *Pericles* i 4 23
Strewest. Why strew'st thou sugar on that bottled spider? *Richard III.* i 3 242
Strewing. Dances, masks, and merry hours Forerun fair Love, strewing her way with flowers . . . . . *L. L. Lost* iv 3 380
The herbs that have on them cold dew o' the night Are strewings fitt'st for graves . . . . *Cymbeline* iv 2 285
Strewment. She is allow'd her virgin crants, Her maiden strewments and the bringing home Of bell and burial . . *Hamlet* v 1 256
Stricken. Our holy lives must win a new world's crown, Which our profane hours here have stricken down . *Richard II.* v 1 25
Count the clock.—The clock hath stricken three . *J. Cæsar* ii 1 192
Why, let the stricken deer go weep, The hart ungalled play . *Hamlet* iii 2 282
Strict. That she make friends To the strict deputy . . *Meas. for Meas.* i 2 186
We have strict statutes and most biting laws . . . . i 3 19
I speak not as desiring more; But rather wishing a more strict restraint i 4 4
But there are other strict observances . . . *L. L. Lost* i 1 36
With what strict patience have I sat! . . . . . iv 3 165
This strict court of Venice Must needs give sentence *Mer. of Venice* iv 1 204
I was too strict to make mine own away . . . *Richard II.* i 3 244
The pleasure that some fathers feed upon, Is my strict fast . ii 1 80
I will call him to so strict account . . . *1 Hen. IV.* iii 2 149
We of the offering side Must keep aloof from strict arbitrement . iv 1 70
Is all your strict preciseness come to this? . . *1 Hen. VI.* v 4 67
If we conclude a peace, It shall be with such strict and severe covenants . v 4 114
You undergo too strict a paradox . . . . *T. of Athens* iii 5 24
Law is strict, and war is nothing more . . . . . iii 5 85
Why this same strict and most observant watch So nightly toils? *Hamlet* i 1 71
This fell sergeant, death, Is strict in his arrest . . . v 2 348
By the tenour of our strict edict, Your exposition misinterpreting *Pericles* i 1 111
With this strict charge, even as he left his life . . . ii 1 131
That the strict fates had pleased you had brought him hither! . iii 3 8
Stricter. Take No stricter render of me than my all . . *Cymbeline* v 4 17
Strictest. To the strict'st decrees I'll write my name . . *L. L. Lost* i 1 117
Strictly. She hath so strictly tied Her to her chamber . *Pericles* ii 5 8
Stricture. A man of stricture and firm abstinence . *Meas. for Meas.* i 3 12
Stride. Turn two mincing steps into a manly stride . *Mer. of Venice* iii 4 68
Every tedious stride I make Will but remember me . *Richard II.* i 3 268
Every stride he makes upon my land Is dangerous treason . . iii 3 92
He stalks up and down like a peacock,—a stride and a stand *Tr. and Cr.* iii 3 252
I mean to stride your steed . . . . . *Coriolanus* i 9 71
On the moment Follow his strides . . . *T. of Athens* i 1 80
With his stealthy pace, With Tarquin's ravishing strides . *Macbeth* ii 1 55
A prison for a debtor, that not dares To stride a limit . *Cymbeline* iii 3 35
Forthwith they fly . . . slaves, The strides they victors made . v 3 43
Striding. Pity, like a naked new-born babe, Striding the blast *Macbeth* i 7 22
Strife. One that, above all other strifes, contended especially to know himself . . . . *Meas. for Meas.* iii 2 246
Cheer her, call her wife: 'Tis holy sport to be a little vain, When the sweet breath of flattery conquers strife . *Com. of Errors* iii 2 28
If I should as lion come in strife Into this place . *M. N. Dream* v 1 228
If thou keep promise, I shall end this strife . *Mer. of Venice* iii 2 20
I will compound this strife: 'Tis deeds must win the prize *T. of Shrew* ii 1 343
To cut off all strife, here sit we down . . . . iii 1 21
War is no strife To the dark house and the detested wife . *All's Well* ii 3 308
Which we will pay, With strife to please you, day exceeding day . Epil. 4
A barful strife! Whoe'er I woo, myself would be his wife . *T. Night* i 4 41
An Ate, stirring him to blood and strife . . . *K. John* ii 1 63
So as thou livest in peace, die free from strife . *Richard II.* v 6 27
Nought rests for me in this tumultuous strife . . . *1 Hen. VI.* i 3 70
Pray, uncle Gloucester, mitigate this strife . . . . iii 1 88
Confounded be your strife! And perish ye, with your audacious prate! iv 1 123
Let me be umpire in this doubtful strife . . . . . iv 1 151

Strife. But dies, betray'd to fortune by your strife . . *1 Hen. VI.* iv 4 39
It was both impious and unnatural That such immanity and bloody strife Should reign among professors of one faith . . . . v 1 13
What is wedlock forced but a hell, An age of discord and continual strife? v 5 63
I pray, my lords, let me compound this strife . . *2 Hen. VI.* ii 1 58
Sons and brother! at a strife? What is your quarrel? . . *3 Hen. VI.* i 2 4
I would to God all strifes were well compounded . *Richard III.* ii 1 74
The combatants being kin Half stints their strife . *Troi. and Cres.* iv 5 93
Now stay your strife: what shall be is dispatch'd . . *T. Andron.* ii 1 193
Do with their death bury their parents' strife . . *Rom. and Jul.* Prol. 8
Some twenty of them fought in this black strife . . . iii 1 183
Artificial strife Lives in these touches, livelier than life . *T. of Athens* i 1 37
Either there is a civil strife in heaven, Or else the world, too saucy with the gods, Incenses them to send destruction . . *J. Cæsar* i 3 11
Domestic fury and fierce civil strife Shall cumber all the parts of Italy iii 1 263
Pursue me lasting strife, If, once a widow, ever I be wife! . *Hamlet* iii 2 232
We have this hour a constant will to publish Our daughters' several dowers, that future strife May be prevented now . . . *Lear* i 1 45
You have the captives That were the opposites of this day's strife . v 3 42
'Tis the soldiers' life To have their balmy slumbers waked with strife *Othello* ii 3 258
Let this fellow Be nothing of our strife . . *Ant. and Cleo.* ii 2 80
Strike. As fast as mill-wheels strike . . . . *Tempest* i 2 281
Who makest a show but darest not strike . . . . . i 2 470
He's winding up the watch of his wit; by and by it will strike . ii 1 13
Alas! this parting strikes poor lovers dumb . *T. G. of Ver.* ii 2 21
Shall I strike?—Who wouldst thou strike?—Nothing.—Villain, forbear. —Why, sir, I'll strike nothing . . . . iii 1 199
Good gentlemen, let him not strike the old woman . *Mer. Wives* iv 2 190
I am glad, though you have ta'en a special stand to strike at me, that your arrow hath glanced . . . . v 5 248
Sith 'twas my fault to give the people scope, 'Twould be my tyranny to strike and gall them . . . . *Meas. for Meas.* i 3 36
Back-wounding calumny The whitest virtue strikes . . . iii 2 198
Your maw, like mine, should be your clock And strike you home without a messenger . . . . . *Com. of Errors* i 2 67
It was two ere I left him, and now the clock strikes one . . iv 2 54
Not marked or not laughed at, strikes him into melancholy . *Much Ado* ii 1 154
Now you strike like the blind man . . . . . ii 1 205
Myself would, on the rearward of reproaches, Strike at thy life . iv 1 129
That his own hand may strike his honour down . *L. L. Lost* i 1 20
She strikes at the brow.—But she herself is hit lower . . iv 1 119
Use me but as your spaniel, spurn me, strike me, Neglect me *M. N. D.* ii 1 205
What, should I hurt her, strike her, kill her dead? . . . iii 2 269
I am a right maid for my cowardice: Let her not strike me . iii 2 303
And strike more dead Than common sleep of all these five the sense iv 1 86
It strikes a man more dead than a great reckoning in a little room *As Y. Like It* iii 3 14
I'll cuff you, if you strike again . . . *T. of Shrew* ii 1 221
If you strike me, you are no gentleman . . . . . ii 1 223
To those Italian fields, Where noble fellows strike . *All's Well* iii 3 308
That thou didst love her, strikes some scores away From the great compt v 3 56
I know my lady will strike him: if she do, he'll smile . *T. Night* iii 2 88
It is a bawdy planet, that will strike Where 'tis predominant *W. Tale* i 2 201
A savour that may strike the dullest nostril . . . . i 2 421
The heavens themselves Do strike at my injustice . . . iii 2 148
Music, awake her; strike! . . . . v 3 98
Strike all that look upon with marvel . . . . . v 3 100
When I strike my foot Upon the bosom of the ground, rush forth *K. John* iv 1 2
If thou but frown on me, or stir thy foot, . . . I'll strike thee dead . iv 3 98
We see the wind sit sore upon our sails, And yet we strike not *Rich. II.* ii 1 266
A puny subject strikes At thy great glory . . . . . iii 2 86
Armies of pestilence; and they shall strike Your children yet unborn . iii 3 87
Strike him, Aumerle. Poor boy, thou art amazed . . . v 2 85
Clamorous groans, which strike upon my heart, Which is the bell . v 5 56
Such as will strike sooner than speak, and speak sooner than drink *1 Hen. IV.* ii 1 85
Now cannot I strike him, if I should be hanged . . . . ii 2 76
Strike; down with them; cut the villains' throats . . . ii 2 87
Play a set Shall strike his father's crown into the hazard *Hen. V.* i 2 263
I will dazzle all the eyes of France, Yea, strike the Dauphin blind . i 2 280
He that strikes the first stroke, I'll run him up to the hilts . ii 1 68
God's arm strike with us! 'tis a fearful odds . . . . iv 3 5
I will strike it out soundly . . . . iv 7 135
If that the soldier strike him, as I judge By his blunt bearing he will . iv 7 184
I promised to strike him, if he did . . . . . iv 8 32
'Twas I, indeed, thou promised'st to strike . . . . iv 8 43
Their arms are set like clocks, still to strike on . . *1 Hen. VI.* i 2 42
For none would strike a stroke in his revenge . . . . i 5 35
It cannot be this weak and writhled shrimp Should strike such terror . ii 3 24
Strike those that hurt, and hurt not those that help . . . iii 3 53
She shall not strike Dame Eleanor unrevenged . . *2 Hen. VI.* i 3 150
Since we have begun to strike, We'll never leave . . *3 Hen. VI.* i 2 167
Smile, gentle heaven! or strike, ungentle death! . . . . ii 3 6
Now Margaret Must strike her sail and learn awhile to serve . . iii 3 5
Strike now, or else the iron cools.—I had rather chop this hand off at a blow, And with the other fling it at thy face, Than bear so low a sail, to strike to thee . . . . v 1 49
I'll strike thee to my foot, And spurn upon thee, beggar *Richard III.* i 2 41
Either heaven with lightning strike the murderer dead, Or earth, gape open wide and eat him quick! . . . . i 2 64
Would they were basilisks, to strike thee dead! . . . . i 2 151
He stirs: shall I strike?—No, first let's reason with him . . i 4 164
Upon the stroke of ten.—Well, let it strike.—Why let it strike? iv 2 115
A flourish, trumpets! strike alarum, drums! . . . . iv 4 148
Things to strike honour sad . . . . . *Hen. VIII.* i 2 126
Strikes his breast hard, and anon he casts His eye against the moon . iii 2 117
And the rude son should strike his father dead . *Troi. and Cres.* i 3 115
The still and mental parts, That do contrive how many hands shall strike i 3 201
Thou canst strike, canst thou? . . . . . . ii 1 50
Thou shouldst strike him . . . . ii 1 40
Will strike amazement to their drowsy spirits . . . . ii 2 210
Strike not a stroke, but keep yourselves in breath . . . v 7 3
Strike, fellows, strike; this is the man I seek . . . . v 8 10
Strike a free march to Troy! . . . . v 10 30
You may as well Strike at the heaven with your staves . *Coriolanus* i 1 70
Thou Shalt see me once more strike at Tullus' face . . . i 1 244
'Tis sworn between us we shall ever strike Till one can do no more . i 2 35
Now the red pestilence strike all trades in Rome! . . . iv 1 13
Let the mutinous winds Strike the proud cedars 'gainst the fiery sun . v 3 60

Strike. My pretext to strike at him admits A good construction *Coriol.* v 6 20
And strike her home by force, if not by words *T. Andron.* ii 1 118
There speak, and strike, brave boys, and take your turns ii 1 129
Some planet strike me down, That I may slumber in eternal sleep! ii 4 14
When thy poor heart beats with outrageous beating, Thou canst not strike it thus to make it still iii 2 14
What dost thou strike at, Marcus, with thy knife? iii 2 52
I strike quickly, being moved.—But thou art not quickly moved to strike *Rom. and Jul.* i 1 8
Strike! beat them down! Down with the Capulets! i 1 80
On, lusty gentlemen.—Strike, drum i 4 114
By the stock and honour of my kin, To strike him dead I hold it not a sin i 5 61
It is a cause worthy my spleen and fury, That I may strike at Athens *T. of Athens* iii 5 114
Strike me the counterfeit matron; It is her habit only that is honest iv 3 112
Consumptions sow In hollow bones of man; strike their sharp shins iv 3 152
Take Thy beagles with thee.—We but offend him. Strike! iv 3 175
Each Prescribe to other as each other's leech. Let our drums strike v 4 85
Speak, strike, redress! Brutus, thou sleep'st: awake! *J. Cæsar* ii 1 47
'Speak, strike, redress!' Am I entreated To speak and strike? ii 1 55
Strike, as thou didst at Cæsar iv 3 105
Bid thy mistress, when my drink is ready, She strike upon the bell *Macb.* ii 1 32
New widows howl, new orphans cry, new sorrows Strike heaven on the face iv 3 6
I cannot strike at wretched kerns, whose arms Are hired to bear their staves v 7 17
We have met with foes That strike beside us v 7 29
Shall I strike at it with my partisan?—Do, if it will not stand *Hamlet* i 1 140
Then no planets strike, No fairy takes, nor witch hath power to charm i 1 162
In rage strikes wide ii 2 494
Did my father strike my gentleman for chiding of his fool? *Lear* i 3 1
You strike my people; and your disorder'd rabble Make servants of their betters i 4 277
Strike, you slave; stand, rogue, stand; you neat slave, strike ii 2 44
Keep peace, upon your lives: He dies that strikes again ii 2 53
It pleased the king his master very late To strike at me ii 2 124
Strike in their numb'd and mortified bare arms Pins, wooden pricks, nails ii 3 15
Strike her young bones, You taking airs, with lameness! ii 4 165
With this ungracious paper strike the sight Of the death-practised duke iv 6 283
Let the drum strike, and prove my title thine v 3 81
He's a good fellow, I can tell you that; He'll strike, and quickly too v 3 285
Strike on the tinder, ho! Give me a taper! call up all my people! *Othello* i 1 141
He is rash and very sudden in choler, and haply may strike at you ii 1 280
As men in rage strike those that wish them best ii 3 243
My heart is turned to stone; I strike it, and it hurts my hand iv 1 193
What, strike his wife!—'Faith, that was not so well; yet would I knew That stroke would prove the worst! iv 1 283
Or say they strike us, Or scant our former having in despite iv 3 91
This sorrow's heavenly; It strikes where it doth love v 2 22
Pompey's name strikes more Than could his war resisted *Ant. and Cleo.* i 4 54
Will't please you hear me?—I have a mind to strike thee ere thou speak'st ii 5 42
These hands do lack nobility, that they strike A meaner than myself ii 5 82
Strike the vessels, ho! Here is to Cæsar! ii 7 103
Strike not by land; keep whole: provoke not battle, Till we have done at sea iii 8 3
I'll strike, and cry 'Take all.'—Well said; come on iv 2 8
That heaven and earth may strike their sounds together iv 8 38
Let me say, Before I strike this bloody stroke, farewell iv 14 91
Farewell, great chief. Shall I strike now?—Now, Eros.—Why, there then iv 14 93
Let him that loves me strike me dead.—Not I.—Nor I iv 14 108
High events as these Strike those that make them v 2 364
Your cause doth strike my heart With pity *Cymbeline* i 6 118
He that strikes The venison first shall be the lord o' the feast iii 3 74
Strikes life into my speech and shows much more His own conceiving iii 3 97
If thou fear to strike and to make me certain it is done, thou art the pandar to her dishonour iii 4 31
Do his bidding; strike; Thou mayst be valiant in a better cause iii 4 73
It strikes me, past The hope of comfort iv 3 8
That hook of wiving, Fairness which strikes the eye v 5 168
If this be so, the gods do mean to strike me To death with mortal joy v 5 234
Pardon me, or strike me, if you please; I cannot be much lower *Pericles* i 2 46
I have ground the axe myself; Do you but strike the blow i 2 59
The sinful father Seem'd not to strike, but smooth i 2 78
Strike me, honour'd sir; Give me a gash, put me to present pain v 1 192
Strike home. May, in the ambush of my name, strike home *M. for M.* i 3 41
Strike off. And on our long-boat's side Strike off his head 2 *Hen. VI.* iv 1 69
Take him away, I say, and strike off his head presently iv 7 116
Strike off his head, and bring them both upon two poles hither iv 7 118
Her presence Shall quite strike off all service I have done *Troi. and Cres.* iii 3 29
I shall, in a more continuate time, Strike off this score of absence *Othello* iii 4 179
Strike out. Who did strike out the light? *Macbeth* iii 3 19
Strike sail. How many nobles then should hold their places, That must strike sail to spirits of vile sort! 2 *Hen. IV.* v 2 18
Strike up, pipers *Much Ado* v 4 130
Come on, strike up! *W. Tale* iv 4 161
Drummer, strike up, and let us march away 3 *Hen. VI.* iv 7 50
Strike up the drums *K. John* v 2; 2 *Hen. IV.* iv 2; 3 *Hen. VI.* ii 1; v 3; *Richard III.* iv 4; *T. of Athens* iv 3
Strikers. No foot-land rakers, no long-staff sixpenny strikers 1 *Hen. IV.* ii 1 82
Strikest. Thou strikest me Sorely, to say I did *W. Tale* v 1 17
Dost thou think I have no sense, thou strikest me thus? *Troi. and Cres.* ii 1 24
Thou strikest as slow as another ii 1 32
Thou strikest not me, 'tis Cæsar thou defeat'st *Ant. and Cleo.* iv 14 68
Striking. Shame to him whose cruel striking Kills for faults of his own liking! *Meas. for Meas.* iii 2 281
The nobleman that committed the prince for striking him 2 *Hen. IV.* i 2 63
As he is striking, holds his infant up iv 1 212
His sword did ne'er leave striking in the field 1 *Hen. VI.* i 4 81
Anon he finds him Striking too short at Greeks *Hamlet* ii 2 491
Striking in our country's cause Fell bravely and were slain *Cymbeline* v 4 71
String. I'll knit it up in silken strings *T. G. of Ver.* ii 7 45
He plays false, father.—How? out of tune on the strings? iv 2 60
Making practice on the times, To draw with idle spiders' strings Most ponderous and substantial things! *Meas. for Meas.* iii 2 289
Get your apparel together, good strings to your beards *M. N. Dream* iv 2 36
My heart hath one poor string to stay it by *K. John* v 7 55
The daintiness of ear To check time broke in a disorder'd string *Rich. II.* v 5 46
When such strings jar, what hope of harmony? 2 *Hen. VI.* ii 1 57
String. Harp not on that string, madam; that is past *Richard III.* iv 4 364
Something that would fret the string, The master-cord on's heart *Hen. VIII.* iii 2 105
Untune that string, And, hark, what discord follows! *Troi. and Cres.* i 3 109
Those lily hands Tremble, like aspen-leaves, upon a lute, And make the silken strings delight to kiss them *T. Andron.* ii 4 46
The strings, my lord, are false *J. Cæsar* iv 3 292
Heart with strings of steel, Be soft as sinews of the new-born babe! *Ham.* iii 3 70
His grief grew puissant, and the strings of life Began to crack *Lear* v 3 216
Thou, Iago, who hast had my purse As if the strings were thine *Othello* i 1 3
Egypt, thou knew'st too well My heart was to thy rudder tied by the strings, And thou shouldst tow me after *Ant. and Cleo.* iii 11 57
You are a fair viol, and your sense the strings *Pericles* i 1 81
Stringless. His tongue is now a stringless instrument *Richard II.* ii 1 149
Strip. And strip myself to death, as to a bed *Meas. for Meas.* ii 4 102
Strip your sword stark naked *T. Night* iii 4 274
All the temporal lands which men devout By testament have given to the church Would they strip from us *Hen. V.* i 1 11
Then will he strip his sleeve and show his scars iv 3 47
Why dost thou lash that whore? Strip thine own back *Lear* iv 6 165
If such tricks as these strip you out of your lieutenantry, it had been better you had not kissed your three fingers so oft *Othello* ii 1 173
Stripe. Most lying slave, Whom stripes may move, not kindness! *Tempest* i 2 345
The loathsomeness of them offends me more than the stripes. *W. Tale* iv 3 60
Who wears my stripes impress'd upon him *Coriolanus* v 6 108
Hence with thy stripes, begone! *Ant. and Cleo.* iii 13 152
Stripling. A proper stripling and an amorous! *T. of Shrew* i 2 144
A bachelor, a handsome stripling too *Richard III.* i 3 101
Two striplings—lads more like to run The country base *Cymbeline* v 3 19
Stripped. Who led me instantly unto his cave, There stripp'd himself *As Y. L. It* iv 3 147
Drown my clothes, and say I was stripped *All's Well* iv 1 58
His own unkindness, That stripp'd her from his benediction *Lear* iv 3 45
She stripp'd it from her arm; I see her yet *Cymbeline* ii 4 101
Stripping. How, in stripping it, You more invest it! *Tempest* ii 1 225
Strive. If the ill spirit have so fair a house, Good things will strive to dwell with't i 2 459
The sun will set before I shall discharge What I must strive to do iii 1 23
If I did think, sir, I were well awake, I'ld strive to tell you v 1 230
They strive to be Lords o'er their lords *L. L. Lost* iv 1 37
But if thou strive, poor soul, what art thou then? Food for his rage iv 1 94
Where zeal strives to content, and the contents Dies in the zeal v 2 518
Strive mightily, but eat and drink as friends *T. of Shrew* i 2 279
You do me double wrong, To strive for that which resteth in my choice iii 1 17
'Tis often seen Adoption strives with nature *All's Well* i 3 151
Daughter and mother So strive upon your pulse i 3 175
I know I love in vain, strive against hope i 3 207
I cannot love her, nor will strive to do't.—Thou wrong'st thyself, if thou shouldst strive to choose ii 3 153
We'll strive to bear it for your worthy sake iii 3 5
Do not strive against my vows iv 2 14
We'll strive to please you every day *T. Night* v 1 417
Your discontenting father strive to qualify *W. Tale* iv 4 543
When workmen strive to do better than well, They do confound their skill in covetousness *K. John* iv 2 28
Strive not with your breath; For all in vain comes counsel *Richard II.* ii 1 3
Strives Bolingbroke to be as great as we? Greater he shall not be iii 2 97
Boys, with women's voices, Strive to speak big iii 2 114
Now I have mine own again, be gone, That I may strive to kill it with a groan v 1 100
So strives the woodcock with the gin 3 *Hen. VI.* i 4 61
Often did I strive To yield the ghost *Richard III.* i 4 36
I'll strive, with troubled thoughts, to take a nap v 3 104
Bid him strive To gain the love o' the commonalty *Hen. VIII.* i 2 169
That strive by factions and by friends Ambitiously for rule *T. Andron.* i 1 18
Strive no more: such wither'd herbs as these Are meet for plucking up iii 1 178
What here shall miss, our toil shall strive to mend *Rom. and Jul.* Prol. 14
How fairly this lord strives to appear foul! *T. of Athens* iii 3 32
'Gainst the stream of virtue they may strive, And drown themselves in riot! iv 1 27
I will strive with things impossible; Yea, get the better of them *J. Cæsar* ii 1 325
To whose young love The vines of France and milk of Burgundy Strive to be interess'd *Lear* i 1 87
Strives in his little world of man to out-scorn The to-and-fro-conflicting wind and rain iii 1 10
By how much she strives to do him good, She shall undo her credit *Oth.* ii 3 364
Let me live to-night!—Nay, if you strive,— But half an hour! v 2 81
Whom every thing becomes . . . ; whose every passion fully strives To make itself, in thee, fair and admired! *Ant. and Cleo.* i 1 50
So bravely done, so rich, that it did strive In workmanship and value *Cymbeline* ii 4 73
Strive, man, and speak v 5 152
For though he strive To killen bad, keep good alive *Pericles* ii Gower 19
Strived. The city strived God Neptune's annual feast to keep v Gower 16
Strivest. What thou hast not, still thou strivest to get *Meas. for Meas.* iii 1 22
Striving. For enlargement striving, Shakes the old beldam earth 1 *Hen. IV.* iii 1 31
Our half-faced sun, striving to shine 2 *Hen. VI.* ii 1 98
The fatal colours of our striving houses 3 *Hen. VI.* ii 5 98
You might have been enough the man you are, With striving less to be so *Coriolanus* iii 2 19
Striving to make an ugly deed look fair *T. of Athens* iii 5 25
Striving to better, oft we mar what's well *Lear* i 4 369
Received This hurt you see, striving to apprehend him ii 1 110
Stroke. And oar'd Himself with his good arms in lusty stroke *Tempest* ii 1 119
Draw thy sword: one stroke Shall free thee from the tribute which thou payest ii 1 292
Not so, not so; his life is parallel'd Even with the stroke and line of his great justice *Meas. for Meas.* iv 2 83
What noise? That spirit's possess'd with haste That wounds the unsisting postern with these strokes iv 2 92
As you love strokes, so jest with me again *Com. of Errors* ii 2 8
If such a one will smile and stroke his beard *Much Ado* v 1 15
Stroke your chins, and swear by your beards that I am a knave *As Y. L. It* i 2 75
But silence, . . With bloodless stroke my heart doth gore *T. Night* ii 5 117
Win you this city without stroke or wound *K. John* ii 1 418
This is the bloodiest shame, The wildest savagery, the vilest stroke iv 3 48
More welcome is the stroke of death to me *Richard II.* iii 1 31
You may stroke him as gently as a puppy greyhound 2 *Hen. IV.* ii 4 106
Like an offensive wife That hath enraged him on to offer strokes iv 1 211
He that strikes the first stroke, I'll run him up to the hilts *Hen. V.* ii 1 68

Stroke. Cowardly fled, not having struck one stroke . . . 1 *Hen. VI.* i 1 134
For none would strike a stroke in his revenge . . . i 5 35
Before we met or that a stroke was given, . . . did run away . . . iv 1 22
Free from oppression or the stroke of war . . . v 3 155
And many strokes, though with a little axe, Hew down and fell the hardest-timber'd oak . . . . . . 3 *Hen. VI.* ii 1 54
For strokes received, and many blows repaid, Have robb'd my strong-knit sinews of their strength . . . . ii 3 3
I lay it naked to the deadly stroke, And humbly beg the death *Rich. III.* i 2 178
What is't o'clock?—Upon the stroke of four.—Cannot thy master sleep? iii 2 5
But what's o'clock?—Upon the stroke of ten.—Well, let it strike . iv 2 115
Like a Jack, thou keep'st the stroke Betwixt thy begging and my meditation . . . . iv 2 117
And put thy fortune to the arbitrement Of bloody strokes . . v 3 90
How far into the morning is it, lords?—Upon the stroke of four . v 3 235
Life, honour, name, and all That made me happy at one stroke has taken For ever from the world . . . *Hen. VIII.* ii 1 117
When the greatest stroke of fortune falls, Will bless the king . . ii 2 36
Play me Nestor; hem, and stroke thy beard, As he . *Troi. and Cres.* i 3 165
The combatants being kin Half stints their strife before their strokes begin . . . . iv 5 93
She strokes his cheek! . . . . . . v 2 51
Strike not a stroke, but keep yourselves in breath . . . v 7 3
Not fierce and terrible Only in strokes . . . *Coriolanus* i 4 58
Cursing yourselves, Opposing laws with strokes . . . iii 3 79
Now at last Given hostile strokes . . . . iii 3 97
'Tis fond to wail inevitable strokes, As 'tis to laugh at 'em . iv 1 26
And what not done, that thou hast cause to rue, Wherein I had no stroke of mischief in it? . . . . *T. Andron.* v 1 110
Thou cutt'st my head off with a golden axe, And smilest upon the stroke that murders me . . . . . *Rom. and Jul.* iii 3 23
Plagues, incident to men, Your potent and infectious fevers heap On Athens, ripe for stroke! . . . *T. of Athens* iv 1 23
To ease them of their griefs, Their fears of hostile strokes, their aches, losses, Their pangs of love . . . . . v 1 202
We were not all unkind, nor all deserve The common stroke of war . v 4 22
Good words are better than bad strokes, Octavius.—In your bad strokes, Brutus, you give good words . . . *J. Cæsar* v 1 29
So they Doubly redoubled strokes upon the foe . . *Macbeth* i 2 38
Certain issue strokes must arbitrate . . . . v 4 20
If thou be'st slain and with no stroke of mine, My wife and children's ghosts will haunt me still . . . . . v 7 15
Virtue itself 'scapes not calumnious strokes . . . *Hamlet* i 3 38
Thou whom the heavens' plagues Have humbled to all strokes . *Lear* iv 1 68
But not without that harmful stroke, which since Hath pluck'd him after iv 2 77
In the most terrible and nimble stroke Of quick, cross lightning . . iv 7 34
Some distressful stroke That my youth suffer'd . . . *Othello* i 3 157
Yet would I knew That stroke would prove the worst! . . . iv 1 285
The oars were silver, Which to the tune of flutes kept stroke, and made The water which they beat to follow faster, As amorous of their strokes . . . . . . *Ant. and Cleo.* ii 2 200
Let me say, Before I strike this bloody stroke, farewell . . iv 14 91
Draw thy sword, and give me Sufficing strokes for death . . iv 14 117
Lest, in her greatness, by some mortal stroke She do defeat us . v 1 64
The stroke of death is as a lover's pinch, Which hurts, and is desired . v 2 298
So tender of rebukes that words are strokes And strokes death to her *Cymbeline* iii 5 40
Fear no more the frown o' the great; Thou art past the tyrant's stroke iv 2 265
Ere the stroke Of this yet scarce-cold battle . . . v 5 468
Strokedst. Thou strokedst me and madest much of me . . *Tempest* i 2 333
Strong. Whose inward pinches therefore are most strong . . v 1 77
One so strong That could control the moon . . . . v 1 269
Her mother, ever strong against that match . . *Mer. Wives* iv 6 27
In my heart the strong and swelling evil Of my conception *M. for M.* ii 4 6
What king so strong Can tie the gall up in the slanderous tongue? . iii 2 198
The fiend is strong within him.—Ay me, poor man! . *Com. of Errors* iv 4 110
Folly in fools bears not so strong a note As foolery in the wise *L. L. Lost* v 2 75
Their sense thus weak, lost with their fears thus strong *M. N. Dream* iii 2 27
The spirit of my father grows strong in me . . *As Y. Like It* i 1 74
Is it possible, on such a sudden, you should fall into so strong a liking? i 3 28
Wherefore are you gentle, strong, and valiant? . . . ii 3 6
Though I look old, yet I am strong and lusty . . . ii 3 47
Being strong at heart, He sent me hither . . . . iv 3 152
My reasons are most strong; and you shall know them . *All's Well* iv 2 59
Demand of him how many horse the duke is strong . . . iv 3 149
I am now, sir, muddied in fortune's mood, and smell somewhat strong of her strong displeasure . . . . v 2 5
When oil and fire, too strong for reason's force, O'erbears it and burns on v 3 7
I have the back-trick simply as strong as any man in Illyria *T. Night* i 3 132
'Tis strong, and it does indifferent well . . . . i 3 143
There is no woman's sides Can bide the beating of so strong a passion . ii 4 97
I have been dear to him, lad, some two thousand strong, or so . iii 2 59
To tell, he longs to see his son, were strong . . *W. Tale* i 2 34
His forces strong, his soldiers confident . . . *K. John* ii 1 61
Thou little valiant, great in villany! Thou ever strong upon the stronger side! . . . . iii 1 117
So lately purged of blood, So newly join'd in love, so strong in both . iii 1 240
Some reasons of this double coronation I have possess'd you with and think them strong; And more, more strong, then lesser is my fear, I shall indue you with . . . . iv 2 41
Strong as a tower in hope, I cry amen . . *Richard II.* i 3 102
Bolingbroke, through our security, Grows strong and great in substance and in power . . . . iii 2 35
O heinous, strong, and bold conspiracy! . . . . v 3 59
Twice saying 'pardon' doth not pardon twain, But makes one pardon strong . . . . v 3 135
Westmoreland, seven thousand strong, Is marching hitherwards 1 *Hen. IV.* iv 1 88
With strong and mighty preparation . . . . . iv 1 93
When he was not six and twenty strong, Sick in the world's regard . iv 3 56
'Tis but wisdom to make strong against him . . . . iv 4 39
In place and in account Nothing so strong and fortunate as I . . v 1 38
Let them alone: The marshal and the archbishop are strong 2 *Hen. IV.* ii 3 42
They say the bishop and Northumberland Are fifty thousand strong . iii 1 96
A good-limbed fellow; young, strong, and of good friends . . iii 2 114
Our men more perfect in the use of arms, Our armour all as strong . iv 1 156
Though it do work as strong As aconitum or rash gunpowder . . iv 4 47
Think we King Harry strong . . . . . *Hen. V.* ii 4 48
At the battle of Patay, When but in all I was six thousand strong 1 *Hen. VI.* iv 1 20

Strong. And hell too strong for me to buckle with . . . 1 *Hen. VI.* v 3 28
Threatens more Than Bargulus the strong Illyrian pirate 2 *Hen. VI.* iv 1 108
You are strong and manly; God on our side, doubt not of victory . iv 8 53
Or is he but retired to make him strong? . . . . . iv 9 9
But I must make fair weather yet a while, Till Henry be more weak and I more strong . . . . v 1 31
I have reasons strong and forcible . . . . 3 *Hen. VI.* i 2 3
I am faint and cannot fly their fury: And were I strong, I would not . i 4 24
Their power, I think, is thirty thousand strong . . . . ii 1 177
The queen is valued thirty thousand strong . . . . . v 3 14
Be well assured Her faction will be full as strong as ours . . v 3 17
Conscience is but a word that cowards use, Devised at first to keep the strong in awe: Our strong arms be our conscience . *Richard III.* v 3 310
And make my vouch as strong As shore of rock . . . *Hen. VIII.* i 1 157
The Greeks are strong and skilful to their strength *Troi. and Cres.* i 1 7
Strong as the axletree On which heaven rides . . . . i 3 66
You are as strong, as valiant, as wise, no less noble, much more gentle ii 3 158
And violenteth in a sense as strong As that which causeth it . iv 4 4
An esperance so obstinately strong, That doth invert the attest of eyes and ears . . . . v 2 121
Instance, O instance! strong as Pluto's gates . . . . v 2 153
Instance, O instance! strong as heaven itself . . . . v 2 155
It is the purpose that makes strong the vow . . . . v 3 23
Let grow thy sinews till their knots be strong, And tempt not yet the brushes of the war . . . . v 3 33
Making parties strong And feebling such as stand not in their liking Below their cobbled shoes . . . . . *Coriolanus* i 1 198
With accusations, as I hear, more strong Than are upon you yet . . iii 2 140
Be strong and ready for this hint, When we shall hap to give't them . iii 3 23
With his sons, a terror to our foes, Hath yoked a nation strong *T. An.* i 1 30
Why should you fear? is not your city strong? . . . iv 4 78
And see the ambush of our friends be strong . . . . v 3 9
A reason mighty, strong, and effectual; A pattern, precedent . . v 3 43
But I'll amerce you with so strong a fine . . . *Rom. and Jul.* iii 1 195
Be strong and prosperous In this resolve . . . . . iv 1 122
Be strong in whore, allure him, burn him up . . *T. of Athens* iv 3 141
When crouching marrow in the bearer strong Cries of itself 'No more' v 4 9
Cassius from bondage will deliver Cassius: Therein, ye gods, you make the weak most strong . . . . *J. Cæsar* i 3 91
Shall we sound him? I think he will stand very strong with us . . ii 1 142
O constancy, be strong upon my side! . . . . . ii 4 6
Your voice shall be as strong as any man's In the disposing of new dignities . . . . iii 1 177
Ingratitude, more strong than traitors' arms, Quite vanquish'd him . iii 2 189
I am arm'd so strong in honesty That they pass by me as the idle wind iv 3 67
Impatient of my absence, And grief that young Octavius with Mark Antony Have made themselves so strong . . . . . . iv 3 154
I held Epicurus strong And his opinion . . . . . v 1 77
I am his kinsman and his subject, Strong both against the deed *Macbeth* i 7 14
Being too strong for him, though he took up my legs sometime, yet I made a shift to cast him . . . . ii 3 45
Things bad begun make strong themselves by ill . . . . iii 2 55
For two special reasons; Which may to you, perhaps, seem much unsinew'd, But yet to me they are strong . . . . . *Hamlet* iv 7 11
Spoke, with how manifold and strong a bond The child was bound to the father . . . . *Lear* ii 1 49
Strong and fasten'd villain! Would he deny his letter? . . . . ii 1 79
These sentences, to sugar, or to gall, Being strong on both sides, are equivocal: But words are words . . . . . . *Othello* i 3 217
Into a jealousy so strong That judgement cannot cure . . . ii 1 310
Note, if your lady strain his entertainment With any strong or vehement importunity; Much will be seen in that . . . . . iii 3 251
Trifles light as air Are to the jealous confirmations strong As proofs of holy writ: this may do something . . . . . . iii 3 323
These strong Egyptian fetters I must break, Or lose myself *Ant. and Cleo.* i 2 120
Pompey is strong at sea; And it appears he is beloved . . . i 4 36
Women are not In their best fortunes strong; but want will perjure The ne'er-touch'd vestal . . . . iii 12 30
From proof as strong as my grief . . . . . *Cymbeline* iii 4 24
I am weak with toil, yet strong in appetite . . . . iii 6 37
The lines of my body are as well drawn as his; no less young, more strong iv 1 11
We are strong in custom . . . . *Pericles* iii 1 52
The sore terms we stand upon with the gods will be strong with us for giving over . . . . iv 2 38
Strong actions. Strong reasons make strong actions . . *K. John* iii 4 182
Strong arms. To bear our fortunes in our own strong arms 1 *Hen. IV.* i 3 298
Our strong arms be our conscience, swords our law *Richard III.* v 3 311
They shall know we have strong arms too . . . *Coriolanus* i 1 62
With his strong arms He fasten'd on my neck, and bellow'd out *Lear* v 3 211
Strong authority. In any breast of strong authority . . *K. John* ii 1 113
Strong-barred. We do lock Our former scruple in our strong-barr'd gates ii 1 370
Strong base. The strong base and building of my love Is as the very centre of the earth . . . . *Troi. and Cres.* iv 2 109
Strong-based. The strong-based promontory Have I made shake *Tempest* v 1 46
Strong bidding. To thy strong bidding task Ariel and all his quality . i 2 192
Strong breaths. They say poor suitors have strong breaths . *Coriolanus* i 1 61
Strong circumstances, Which lead directly to the door of truth *Othello* iii 3 406
Strong composure. It was a strong composure a fool could disunite *Troi. and Cres.* ii 3 108
Strong conception. Cannot remove nor choke the strong conception That I do groan withal . . . . *Othello* v 2 55
Strong correction. To tie thee to my strong correction . *Richard II.* iv 1 77
Strong corruption. Or any taint of vice whose strong corruption Inhabits our frail blood . . . . *T. Night* iii 4 390
Strong course. The strong course of my authority . . *Hen. VIII.* v 3 35
Strong disease. Before the curing of a strong disease, Even in the instant of repair and health, The fit is strongest . . . . *K. John* iii 4 112
Strong displeasure. I am now, sir, muddied in fortune's mood, and smell somewhat strong of her strong displeasure . . . *All's Well* v 2 6
Strong distillation. To be stopped in, like a strong distillation *M. W.* iii 5 114
Strong encounter. With the force And strong encounter . . *Much Ado* i 1 327
Strong endeavours. I have labour'd, With all my wits, my pains, and strong endeavours . . . . *Hen. V.* v 2 25
Strong enforcement. Let gentleness my strong enforcement be *As Y. L. It* ii 7 118
Strong Enobarb Is weaker than the wine . . . *Ant. and Cleo.* ii 7 129
Strong enough. I think we are a body strong enough . 2 *Hen. IV.* i 3 66
We are well fortified And strong enough to issue out and fight 1 *Hen. VI.* v 2 20
This is not strong enough to be believed Of one persuaded well of *Cymb.* ii 4 131
Strong escape. I wot not by what strong escape, He broke from those that had the guard of him . . . . *Com. of Errors* v 1 148

Strong faith. This secret is so weighty, 'twill require A strong faith to conceal it . . . . *Hen. VIII.* ii 1 145
Strong fellow. I would I were invisible, to catch the strong fellow by the leg . . . . *As Y. Like It* i 2 224
Fill till the cup be hid.—There's a strong fellow . . *Ant. and Cleo.* ii 7 94
Strong-fixed is the house of Lancaster . . . . . 1 *Hen. VI.* ii 5 102
Strong-framed. I am strong-framed, he cannot prevail with me *Rich. III.* i 4 154
Strong hand. If by strong hand you offer to break in . *Com. of Errors* iii 1 98
Your strong hand shall help to give him strength . . *K. John* ii 1 33
We cannot hold mortality's strong hand . . . . . iv 2 82
To recover of us, by strong hand And terms compulsatory . *Hamlet* i 1 102
Strong imagination. My strong imagination sees a crown . *Tempest* ii 1 208
Such tricks hath strong imagination . . . . *M. N. Dream* v 1 18
Strong immures. Within whose strong immures The ravish'd Helen, Menelaus' queen, With wanton Paris sleeps . *Troi. and Cres.* Prol. 8
Strong intent. My stronger guilt defeats my strong intent . *Hamlet* iii 3 40
Strong-jointed. O well-knit Samson! strong-jointed Samson! *L. L. Lost* i 2 77
Strong joints. They have galls, Good arms, strong joints *Troi. and Cres.* i 3 238
Strong-knit. And large proportion of his strong-knit limbs . 1 *Hen. VI.* ii 3 21
Many blows repaid Have robb'd my strong-knit sinews of their strength 3 *Hen. VI.* ii 3 4
Strong knots. Wife and child, . . . those strong knots of love *Macbeth* iv 3 27
Strong lance. Plate sin with gold, And the strong lance of justice hurtless breaks . . . . *Lear* iv 6 170
Strong law. Yet must not we put the strong law on him . *Hamlet* iv 3 3
Strong link. Cracking ten thousand curbs Of more strong link asunder *Coriolanus* i 1 73
Nor airless dungeon, nor strong links of iron, Can be retentive to the strength of spirit . . . . *J. Cæsar* i 3 94
Strong madness. Fetter strong madness in a silken thread . *Much Ado* v 1 25
Strong mast. To a strong mast that lived upon the sea . *T. Night* i 2 14
Strong matter. And pick strong matter of revolt and wrath . *K. John* iii 4 167
Strong necessity. The strong necessity of time commands Our services awhile . . . . *Ant. and Cleo.* i 3 42
Which drives O'er your content these strong necessities . . . iii 6 83
Strong ones. Fetch me a dozen crab-tree staves, and strong ones *Hen. VIII.* v 4 8
Strong opinion. To steel a strong opinion to themselves *Troi. and Cres.* i 3 353
Strong party. Make strong party, or defend yourself By calmness *Cor.* iii 2 94
Strong passion. Love's strong passion is impress'd in youth *All's Well* i 3 139
Strong poison. Bid the apothecary Bring the strong poison 2 *Hen. VI.* iii 3 18
Strong possession. Our strong possession and our right for us.—Your strong possession much more than your right . . *K. John* i 1 40
Strong prevailment. Nosegays, sweetmeats, messengers Of strong prevailment . . . . *M. N. Dream* i 1 35
Strong proof. In strong proof of chastity well arm'd . *Rom. and Jul.* i 1 216
I have made strong proof of my constancy . . . *J. Cæsar* ii 1 299
Strong purpose. Had not God, for some strong purpose, steel'd The hearts of men . . . . *Richard II.* v 2 34
Strong reasons make strong actions . . . . *K. John* iii 4 182
Of this my privacy I have strong reasons . . *Troi. and Cres.* iii 3 191
Strong renown. Such strong renown as time shall ne'er decay *Pericles* iii 2 48
Strong rescue. Here . . . Came in strong rescue . . 1 *Hen. VI.* iv 6 26
Strong-ribbed. And anon behold The strong-ribb'd bark through liquid mountains cut . . . . *Troi. and Cres.* i 3 40
Strong right hand. This strong right hand of mine Can pluck the diadem from faint Henry's head . . 3 *Hen. VI.* ii 1 152
Strong shudders. Terribly swear Into strong shudders . *T. of Athens* iv 3 137
Strong sides. As loud As his strong sides can volley . *Ant. and Cleo.* ii 7 119
Strong siege. O, beat away the busy meddling fiend That lays strong siege unto this wretch's soul! . . . . . 2 *Hen. VI.* iii 3 22
Strong sorrow. Our tears are not yet brew'd.—Nor our strong sorrow Upon the foot of motion . . . . . . *Macbeth* ii 3 130
Strong statutes. The strong statutes Stand like the forfeits in a barber's shop . . . . *Meas. for Meas.* v 1 322
Strong suspicion. The verity of it is in strong suspicion *W. Tale* v 2 31
Strong thief. Thou 'lt go, strong thief [gold], When gouty keepers of thee cannot stand . . . . *T. of Athens* iv 3 45
Strong toil. She looks like sleep, As she would catch another Antony In her strong toil of grace . . . . . *Ant. and Cleo.* v 2 351
Strong warrant. Cracking the strong warrant of an oath *Richard II.* iv 1 235
Strong wind. A strong wind will blow it to pieces . . *Pericles* ii 2 20
Strong-wing'd Mercury should fetch thee up . . *Ant. and Cleo.* iv 15 35
Stronger. Though the ship were no stronger than a nutshell . *Tempest* i 1 50
We are made to be no stronger Than faults may shake our frames *Meas. for Meas.* ii 4 132
Whose weakness married to thy stronger state Makes me with thy strength to communicate . . . . . *Com. of Errors* ii 2 177
Not on a band, but on a stronger thing; A chain, a chain! . . iv 2 50
Thought I thy spirits were stronger than thy shames . *Much Ado* iv 1 127
O, that is stronger made Which was before barr'd up with ribs of iron! iv 1 152
The oath of a lover is no stronger than the word of a tapster *As Y. L. It* iii 4 34
And nature, stronger than his just occasion, Made him give battle . iv 3 130
How is this justified?—The stronger part of it by her own letters *All's Well* iv 3 65
In breaking 'em [oaths] he is stronger than Hercules . . . iv 3 283
And our weak spirits ne'er been higher rear'd With stronger blood *W. T.* i 2 73
I would your spirit were easier for advice, Or stronger for your need . iv 4 517
Thou ever strong upon the stronger side! . . . *K. John* iii 1 117
What motive may Be stronger with thee than the name of wife? . . iii 1 314
Join you with them, like a rib of steel, To make strength stronger 2 *Hen. IV.* ii 3 55
Like a broken limb united, Grow stronger for the breaking . . . iv 1 223
What stronger breastplate than a heart untainted! . . 2 *Hen. VI.* iii 2 232
The more we stay, the stronger grows our foe . . 3 *Hen. VI.* iii 3 40
When we grow stronger, then we'll make our claim . . . iv 7 59
There is no English soul More stronger to direct you than yourself *Hen. VIII.* i 1 147
Say, Are you not stronger than you were? . . . . . . ii 3 100
As I have made ye one, lords, one remain; So I grow stronger . . v 3 182
With surety stronger than Achilles' arm . . . *Troi. and Cres.* i 3 220
Therefore, be gone. Mine ears against your suits are stronger than Your gates against my force . . . . . . *Coriolanus* v 2 94
I melt, and am not Of stronger earth than others . . . v 3 29
A woman well-reputed, Cato's daughter. Think you I am no stronger than my sex, Being so father'd and so husbanded? . *J. Cæsar* ii 1 296
My stronger guilt defeats my strong intent . . . *Hamlet* iii 3 40
What is he that builds stronger than either the mason, the shipwright, or the carpenter? . . . . v 1 46
Thou dost ill to say the gallows is built stronger than the church . v 1 54
Stronger. Who builds stronger than a mason, a shipwright, or a carpenter? . . . . *Hamlet* v 1 57
This crack of your love shall grow stronger than it was before *Othello* ii 3 331
Heart, once be stronger than thy continent, Crack thy frail case! *Ant. and Cleo.* iv 14 40
I'll never see't; for, I am sure, my nails Are stronger than mine eyes v 2 224
Here's a voucher, Stronger than ever law could make . *Cymbeline* ii 2 40
Our kingdom is stronger than it was at that time . . . iii 1 35
Are outlaws, and in time May make some stronger head . . . iv 2 139
A spark, To which that blast gives heat and stronger glowing *Pericles* i 2 41
Strongest. The most opportune place, the strong'st suggestion *Tempest* iv 1 26
The strongest oaths are straw To the fire i' the blood . . . iv 1 52
I swear to thee, by Cupid's strongest bow . . *M. N. Dream* i 1 169
Even in the instant of repair and health, The fit is strongest . *K. John* iii 4 114
Well you deserve: they well deserve to have, That know the strong'st and surest way to get . . . . . . *Richard II.* iii 3 201
The strongest nerves and small inferior veins From me receive *Coriolanus* i 1 142
Conceit in weakest bodies strongest works . . . . *Hamlet* iii 4 114
It only stands Our lives upon to use our strongest hands *Ant. and Cleo.* ii 1 51
Whose death indeed's the strongest in our censure . . . *Pericles* ii 4 34
Strongly. Your father's in some passion That works him strongly *Temp.* iv 1 144
Your charm so strongly works 'em . . . . v 1 17
Which now are too too strongly embattled against me . *Mer. Wives* ii 2 260
As strongly As words could make up vows . . *Meas. for Meas.* v 1 227
Our late edict shall strongly stand in force . . . *L. L. Lost* i 1 11
Put in practice that Which each to other hath so strongly sworn . . i 1 309
A true conceit Of god-like amity; which appears most strongly In bearing thus the absence of your lord . . . *Mer. of Venice* iii 4 3
Fortune's displeasure is but sluttish, if it smell so strongly . *All's Well* v 2 8
Which was so strongly urged past my defence . . . *K. John* i 1 258
Your grace shall stay behind So strongly guarded . . . . iii 3 2
Who strongly hath set footing in this land . . . *Richard II.* ii 2 48
We all have strongly sworn to give him aid . . . . . ii 3 150
The thieves are all scattered and possess'd with fear So strongly that they dare not meet each other . . . . . . 1 *Hen. IV.* ii 2 113
None of this, Though strongly apprehended, could restrain . 2 *Hen. IV.* i 1 176
Look you strongly arm to meet him . . . . . *Hen. V.* ii 4 49
There remain, And fortify it strongly 'gainst the French . . . iii 3 53
Deliver'd strongly through my fixed teeth . . . 2 *Hen. VI.* iii 2 313
All these accused him strongly . . . . . . *Hen. VIII.* ii 1 24
I know 'twill stir him strongly . . . . v 2 218
'Tis strongly wedged up in a block-head . . . . *Coriolanus* ii 3 30
Hark! she speaks: I will set down what comes from her, to satisfy my remembrance the more strongly . . . . *Macbeth* v 1 38
What does the tyrant?—Great Dunsinane he strongly fortifies . . v 2 12
And she for him pleads strongly to the Moor . . . *Othello* ii 3 361
But, O, what damned minutes tells he o'er Who dotes, yet doubts, suspects, yet strongly loves! . . . . iii 3 170
With more urgent touches, Do strongly speak to us . . *Ant. and Cleo.* i 2 188
This will witness outwardly, As strongly as the conscience does within *Cymbeline* ii 2 36
'Tis not sleepy business; But must be look'd to speedily and strongly iii 5 27
Strossers. Your French hose off, and in your strait strossers *Hen. V.* iii 7 57
Strove. Who ever strove To show her merit, that did miss her love? *All's Well* i 1 241
Which of your friends Have I not strove to love? . . *Hen. VIII.* ii 4 30
Patience and sorrow strove Who should express her goodliest . *Lear* iv 3 18
Strown. Not a flower sweet, On my black coffin let there be strown *T. N.* ii 4 61
'Stroyed. What I have left behind 'Stroy'd in dishonour *Ant. and Cleo.* iii 11 54
Struck. It struck mine ear most terribly . . . . . *Tempest* ii 1 313
With their high wrongs I am struck to the quick . . . . v 1 25
It hath struck ten o'clock.—The night is dark. . . *Mer. Wives* v 2 11
The Windsor bell hath struck twelve; the minute draws on . . . v 5 1
He struck so plainly, I could too well feel his blows . *Com. of Errors* ii 1 52
Well struck! there was blow for blow . . . . . . iii 1 56
And, with that word, she struck me on the head . . *T. of Shrew* iii 2 154
Myself am struck in years, I must confess . . . . . ii 1 362
Though I struck him first, yet it's no matter for that . . *T. Night* iv 1 38
If I could find example Of thousands that had struck anointed kings And flourish'd after, I'ld not do't . . . . . *W. Tale* i 2 358
Deep shame had struck me dumb, made me break off . . *K. John* iv 2 235
No deeper wrinkles yet? hath sorrow struck So many blows upon this face of mine, And made no deeper wounds? . . . *Richard II.* iv 1 277
Who struck this heat up after I was gone? . . . 1 *Hen. IV.* iii 3 139
Such as fear the report of a caliver worse than a struck fowl . . iv 2 21
Death hath not struck so fat a deer to-day, Though many dearer . . v 4 107
Struck his armed heels Against the panting sides of his poor jade Up to the rowel-head . . . . 2 *Hen. IV.* i 1 44
How cold it struck my heart! . . . . iv 5 152
Struck me in my very seat of judgement . . . . . . v 2 80
Thou wert better thou hadst struck thy mother . . . . . v 4 11
Much memorable shame When Cressy battle fatally was struck *Hen. V.* ii 4 54
Struck the glove which your majesty is take out of the helmet of Alençon . . . . iv 8 27
Cowardly fled, not having struck one stroke . . . 1 *Hen. VI.* i 1 134
One of thy eyes and thy cheek's side struck off! . . . . . i 4 75
Whilst any trump did sound, or drum struck up, His sword did ne'er leave . . . . i 4 80
When from the Dauphin's crest thy sword struck fire . . . iv 6 10
Some sudden qualm hath struck me at the heart . . 2 *Hen. VI.* i 1 54
Then is sin struck down like an ox, and iniquity's throat cut like a calf iv 2 28
Oft have I struck Those that I never saw and struck them dead . iv 7 87
Fell gently down, as if they struck their friends . . . 3 *Hen. VI.* ii 1 132
Well struck in years, fair, and not jealous . . . *Richard III.* i 1 92
In falling, Struck me, that thought to stay him, overboard . . . i 4 19
Brave Plantagenet, That princely novice, was struck dead by thee . i 4 228
Shadows to-night Have struck more terror to the soul of Richard . v 3 217
It's one o'clock, boy, is't not?—It hath struck . . *Hen. VIII.* v 1 1
He chid Andromache and struck his armorer . . *Troi. and Cres.* i 2 6
He yesterday coped Hector in the battle and struck him down . . i 2 35
All damage else—As honour, loss of time, travail, . . . Shall be struck off . . . . ii 2 7
Whiles we have struck, By interims and conveying gusts we have heard The charges of our friends . . . . . . *Coriolanus* i 6 4
I had rather have one scratch my head i' the sun When the alarum were struck . . . . ii 2 80
Tarquin's self he met, And struck him on his knee . . . . ii 2 99
And with a sudden re-inforcement struck Corioli like a planet . . ii 2 117
Fortune's blows, When most struck home, being gentle wounded, craves A noble cunning . . . . iv 1 8

Struck. Him that struck more blows for Rome Than thou hast spoken words *Coriolanus* iv 2 19
You shall have the drum struck up this afternoon iv 5 230
My rage is gone; And I am struck with sorrow v 6 149
Even thou hast struck upon my crest *T. Andron.* i 1 364
Full often struck a doe, And borne her cleanly by the keeper's nose ii 1 93
And this for me, struck home to show my strength ii 3 117
With this dear sight Struck pale and bloodless iii 1 258
Is the day so young?—But new struck nine *Rom. and Jul.* i 1 167
The clock struck nine when I did send the nurse ii 5 1
The fire i' the flint Shows not till it be struck *T. of Athens* i 1 23
My weak words Have struck but thus much show of fire *J. Cæsar* i 2 177
I, that did love Cæsar when I struck him iii 1 182
One of us, That struck the foremost man of all this world iv 3 22
Whilst damned Casca, like a cur, behind Struck Cæsar on the neck v 1 44
But wail his fall Who I myself struck down *Macbeth* iii 1 123
Sinful Macduff, They were all struck for thee! naught that I am iv 3 225
'Tis now struck twelve; get thee to bed *Hamlet* i 1 7
I think it lacks of twelve.—No, it is struck i 4 4
Struck so to the soul that presently They have proclaim'd their malefactions ii 2 620
Your behaviour hath struck her into amazement and admiration iii 2 339
Not to stay the grinding of the axe, My head should be struck off v 2 25
That thou so many princes at a shot So bloodily hast struck v 2 378
I'll not be struck, my lord.—Nor tripped neither *Lear* i 4 94
Struck me with her tongue, Most serpent-like, upon the very heart ii 4 162
But on the sudden A Roman thought hath struck him *Ant. and Cleo.* i 2 87
Now, darting Parthia, art thou struck iii 1 1
While I struck The lean and wrinkled Cassius iii 11 36
And mine ear, Therein false struck, can take no greater wound *Cymb.* iii 4 117
From this most bravest vessel of the world Struck the main-top! iv 2 320
So had you saved The noble Imogen to repent, and struck Me, wretch v 1 10
Struck down Some mortally, some slightly touch'd v 3 9
Could not find death where I did hear him groan, Nor feel him where he struck v 3 70
Upon a time,—unhappy was the clock That struck the hour! v 5 154
So slack, so slow! He should have struck, not spoke *Pericles* iv 2 69
Strucken. The clock hath strucken twelve upon the bell *Com. of Errors* i 2 45
Strucken blind Kisses the base ground with obedient breast *L. L. Lost* iv 3 224
I had thought to have strucken him with a cudgel *Coriolanus* iv 5 156
He that is strucken blind cannot forget The precious treasure *R. and J.* i 1 238
What is't o'clock?—Cæsar, 'tis strucken eight *J. Cæsar* ii 2 114
How like a deer, strucken by many princes, Dost thou here lie! iii 1 209
Struckest. When struck'st thou one blow in the field? 2 *Hen. VI.* iv 7 84
Struggle. I will not struggle, I will stand stone-still *K. John* iv 1 77
So doth the cony struggle in the net 3 *Hen. VI.* i 4 62
Struggling. His nostrils stretch'd with struggling 2 *Hen. VI.* iii 2 171
O limed soul, that, struggling to be free, Art more engaged! *Hamlet* iii 3 68
Strumpet. Never could the strumpet, With all her double vigour, art, and nature, Once stir my temper *Meas. for Meas.* ii 2 183
O most unhappy day!—O most unhappy strumpet! *Com. of Errors* iv 4 127
Hugg'd and embraced by the strumpet wind *Mer of Venice* ii 6 16
Lean, rent, and beggar'd by the strumpet wind ii 6 19
Tax of impudence, A strumpet's boldness *All's Well* ii 1 174
Great king, I am no strumpet, by my life v 3 293
Myself on every post Proclaim'd a strumpet *W. Tale* iii 2 103
That strumpet Fortune, that usurping John! *K. John* iii 1 61
I will chastise this high-minded strumpet 1 *Hen. VI.* i 5 12
Strumpet, thy words condemn thy brat and thee v 4 84
Consorted with that harlot strumpet Shore *Richard III.* iii 4 73
If! thou protector of this damned strumpet, Tellest thou me of 'ifs'? iii 4 76
That strumpet, your unhallow'd dam *T. Andron.* v 2 191
Fortune? O, most true; she is a strumpet *Hamlet* ii 2 240
Out, out, thou strumpet, Fortune! ii 2 515
'Tis the strumpet's plague To beguile many and be beguiled by one *Oth.* iv 1 97
What committed! Impudent strumpet!—By heaven, you do me wrong iv 2 81
Are not you a strumpet?—No, as I am a Christian iv 2 82
If to preserve this vessel for my lord From any other foul unlawful touch Be not to be a strumpet, I am none iv 2 85
Minion, your dear lies dead, And your unblest fate hies: strumpet, I come v 1 34
My sweet Cassio! O Cassio, Cassio, Cassio!—O notable strumpet! v 1 78
Fie, fie upon thee, strumpet!—I am no strumpet v 1 121
Out, strumpet! weep'st thou for him to my face? v 2 77
Down, strumpet!—Kill me to-morrow: let me live to-night! v 2 79
The triple pillar of the world transform'd Into a strumpet's fool *A. and C.* i 1 13
Saucy lictors Will catch at us, like strumpets; and scald rhymers Ballad us v 2 215
Thy mistress, Pisanio, hath played the strumpet in my bed *Cymbeline* iii 4 22
I have heard I am a strumpet; and mine ear, Therein false struck, can take no greater wound iii 4 116
Strumpeted. Being strumpeted by thy contagion *Com. of Errors* ii 2 146
Strung. Orpheus' lute was strung with poets' sinews *T. G. of Ver.* iii 2 78
As sweet and musical As bright Apollo's lute, strung with his hair *L. L. L.* iv 3 343
Strut. Does he not hold up his head, as it were, and strut? *Mer. Wives* i 4 31
Want love's majesty To strut before a wanton ambling nymph *Richard III.* i 1 17
A poor player That struts and frets his hour upon the stage *Macbeth* v 5 25
Laugh at's, while we strut To our confusion *Ant. and Cleo.* iii 13 114
The famed Cassibelan . . . Made Lud's town with rejoicing fires bright And Britons strut with courage *Cymbeline* iii 1 33
Strutted. So strutted and bellowed that I have thought some of nature's journeymen had made men and not made them well *Hamlet* iii 2 36
Strutting. I hear The strain of strutting chanticleer *Tempest* i 2 385
Like a strutting player, whose conceit Lies in his hamstring *Tr. and Cr.* i 3 153
Stubble. Will be his fire To kindle their dry stubble *Coriolanus* ii 1 274
Stubble-land. Fresh as a bridegroom; and his chin new reap'd Show'd like a stubble-land at harvest-home 1 *Hen. IV.* i 3 35
Stubborn. Proud, disobedient, stubborn, lacking duty *T. G. of Ver.* iii 1 69
A stubborn soul, That apprehends no further than this world *M. for M.* v 1 485
I fear these stubborn lines lack power to move *L. L. Lost* iv 3 55
Turn'd her obedience, which is due to me, To stubborn harshness *M. N. D.* i 1 38
From stubborn Turks and Tartars, never train'd To offices of tender courtesy *Mer. of Venice* iv 1 32
Leaving his wealth and ease, A stubborn will to please *As Y. Like It* ii 5 55
She sends him on purpose, that I may appear stubborn to him *T. Night* iii 4 74
Upon some stubborn and uncourteous parts v 1 369
Though authority be a stubborn bear, yet he is oft led by the nose *W. T.* iv 4 832
Upon your stubborn usage of the pope *K. John* v 1 18
As is the sepulchre in stubborn Jewry Of the world's ransom *Richard II.* ii 1 55
Created with a stubborn outside, with an aspect of iron *Hen. V.* v 2 244
Stubborn. In Ireland have I seen this stubborn Cade Oppose himself against a troop of kerns 2 *Hen. VI.* iii 1 360
Free from a stubborn opposite intent iii 2 251
Stubborn to justice, apt to accuse it, and Disdainful *Hen. VIII.* ii 4 122
To stubborn spirits They swell, and grow as terrible as storms iii 1 163
For your stubborn answer About the giving back the great seal to us iii 2 346
Stop their mouths with stubborn bits, and spur 'em, Till they obey the manage v 3 23
His stubborn buckles, With these your white enchanting fingers touch'd, Shall more obey than to the edge of steel *Troi. and Cres.* iii 1 163
Do not give advantage To stubborn critics v 2 131
You bear too stubborn and too strange a hand Over your friend *J. Cæsar* i 2 35
Help, angels! Make assay! Bow, stubborn knees! *Hamlet* iii 3 70
You stubborn ancient knave, you reverend braggart *Lear* ii 2 133
Be content to slubber the gloss of your new fortunes with this more stubborn and boisterous expedition *Othello* i 3 228
Stubborn-chaste. She is stubborn-chaste against all suit *Troi. and Cres.* i 1 100
Stubbornest. It is the stubbornest young fellow of France *As Y. Like It* i 1 148
Stubborn-hard. Are you more stubborn-hard than hammer'd iron? *K. John* iv 1 67
Stubbornly he did repugn the truth 1 *Hen. VI.* iv 1 94
Stubbornness. Happy is your grace, That can translate the stubbornness of fortune Into so quiet and so sweet a style *As Y. Like It* ii 1 19
To persever In obstinate condolement is a course Of impious stubbornness; 'tis unmanly grief *Hamlet* i 2 94
Even his stubbornness, his checks, his frowns,—Prithee, unpin me,—have grace and favour in them *Othello* iv 3 20
Stuck. Millions of false eyes Are stuck upon thee *Meas. for Meas.* iv 1 61
With two pitch-balls stuck in her face for eyes *L. L. Lost* iii 1 199
A lemon.—Stuck with cloves v 2 654
He stuck them up before the fulsome ewes *Mer. of Venice* i 3 87
A thing stuck on with oaths upon your finger v 1 168
Admiringly, my liege, at first I stuck my choice upon her *All's Well* v 3 45
My shroud of white, stuck all with yew, O, prepare it! *T. Night* ii 4 56
All their other senses stuck in ears *W. Tale* iv 4 621
There stuck no plume in any English crest That is removed *K. John* ii 1 317
Suspicion all our lives shall be stuck full of eyes 1 *Hen. IV.* v 2 8
It stuck upon him as the sun In the grey vault of heaven 2 *Hen. IV.* ii 3 18
He himself stuck not to call us the many-headed multitude *Coriolanus* ii 3 17
Who, stuck and spangled with your flatteries, Washes it off *T. of Athens* ii 6 101
That numberless upon me stuck as leaves Do on the oak iv 3 263
I had most need of blessing, and 'Amen' Stuck in my throat *Macbeth* ii 2 33
If he by chance escape your venom'd stuck, Our purpose may hold there *Hamlet* iv 7 162
His face was as the heavens; and therein stuck A sun and moon *A. and C.* v 2 79
Constantly thou hast stuck to the bare fortune of that beggar *Cymbeline* iii 5 119
Stuck in. He gives me the stuck in with such a mortal motion *T. Night* iii 4 303
Studded. Their harness studded all with gold and pearl *T. of Shrew* Ind. 2 44
Student. Keep a gamester from the dice, and a good student from his book, and it is wonderful *Mer. Wives* iii 1 38
Another of these students at that time Was there with him *L. L. Lost* ii 1 64
Negligent student! learn her by heart.—By heart and in heart iii 1 36
Nor lean enough to be thought a good student *T. Night* iv 2 9
Studied. He hath studied her will, and translated her will *Mer. Wives* i 3 54
The state, whereon I studied, Is like a good thing, being often read *Meas. for Meas.* ii 4 7
I have studied eight or nine wise words to speak to you *Much Ado* iii 2 73
Now here is three studied, ere ye'll thrice wink *L. L. Lost* i 2 54
Like one well studied in a sad ostent To please his grandam *Mer. of Ven.* ii 2 205
Not so; but I answer you right painted cloth, from whence you have studied your questions *As Y. Like It* iii 2 291
Twenty such vile terms, As had she studied to misuse me so *T. of Shrew* ii 1 160
I can say little more than I have studied *T. Night* i 5 190
What studied torments, tyrant, hast for me? *W. Tale* iii 2 176
Why, a prince should not be so loosely studied as to remember so weak a composition 2 *Hen. IV.* ii 2 10
Studied so long, sat in the council-house Early and late 2 *Hen. VI.* i 1 90
Your royal graces, Shower'd on me daily, have been more than could My studied purposes requite *Hen. VIII.* iii 2 168
He died as one that had been studied in his death *Macbeth* i 4 9
'Tis a studied, not a present thought, By duty ruminated *Ant. and Cleo.* ii 2 140
And am well studied for a liberal thanks Which I do owe you ii 6 48
'Tis known, I ever Have studied physic *Pericles* iii 2 32
Studious. Some to the studious universities *T. G. of Ver.* i 3 10
Yet be wary in thy studious care 1 *Hen. VI.* ii 5 97
Studiously. Written pamphlets studiously devised iii 1 2
Studs. Hath two letters for her name fairly set down in studs *T. of Shrew* iii 2 63
Study. Those being all my study *Tempest* i 2 74
Being transported And rapt in secret studies i 2 77
You make me study of that ii 1 82
My father Is hard at study; . . . He's safe for these three hours iii 1 20
Thou hast metamorphosed me, Made me neglect my studies *T. G. of Ver.* i 1 67
Study help for that which thou lament'st iii 1 242
What, the sword and the word! do you study them both, master parson? *Mer. Wives* iii 1 45
Blunt his natural edge With profits of the mind, study and fast *Meas. for Meas.* i 4 61
I see, lady, the gentleman is not in your books.—No; an he were, I would burn my study *Much Ado* i 1 81
The idea of her life shall sweetly creep Into his study of imagination iv 1 227
To live and study here three years *L. L. Lost* i 1 35
Barren tasks, too hard to keep, Not to see ladies, study, fast, not sleep! i 1 48
I only swore to study with your grace i 1 51
What is the end of study? let me know i 1 55
That is study's god-like recompense i 1 58
I will swear to study so, To know the thing I am forbid to know i 1 59
To study where I well may dine, When I to feast expressly am forbid; Or study where to meet some mistress fine i 1 61
Having sworn too hard a keeping oath, Study to break it i 1 66
If study's gain be thus and this be so, Study knows that which yet it doth not know i 1 67
These be the stops that hinder study quite i 1 70
Study me how to please the eye indeed By fixing it upon a fairer eye i 1 80
Study is like the heaven's glorious sun That will not be deep-search'd i 1 84
To study now it is too late, Climb o'er the house to unlock the little gate i 1 108
So study evermore is overshot: While it doth study to have what it would It doth forget to do the thing it should i 1 143
For interim to our studies shall relate i 1 172
And so to study, three years is but short i 1 181
I have promised to study three years i 2 37

Study. Is this such a piece of study? *L. L. Lost* i 2 53
Till painful study shall outwear three years, No woman may approach. ii 1 23
Study his bias leaves and makes his book thine eyes iv 2 113
Consider what you first did swear unto, To fast, to study, and to see no woman iv 3 292
When would you, my lord, or you, or you, Have found the ground of study's excellence Without the beauty of a woman's face? iv 3 300
You have in that forsworn the use of eyes And study too iv 3 311
O, we have made a vow to study, lords, And in that vow we have forsworn our books iv 3 318
Studies my lady? mistress, look on me v 2 847
I am slow of study *M. N. Dream* i 2 69
Sleeps easily because he cannot study *As Y. Like It* iii 2 339
My love deny, And then I'll study how to die iv 3 63
It is my study To seem despiteful and ungentle to you v 2 85
Tutor'd in the rudiments Of many desperate studies v 4 32
Institute A course of learning and ingenious studies *T. of Shrew* i 1 9
For the time I study, Virtue and that part of philosophy Will I apply that treats of happiness i 1 17
In brief, sir, study what you most affect i 1 40
Where did you study all this goodly speech? ii 1 264
Was it [music] not to refresh the mind of man After his studies? iii 1 12
To be more thankful to thee shall be my study *W. Tale* iv 2 21
For the which myself and them Bend their best studies *K. John* iv 2 51
Who studies day and night To answer all the debt he owes to you *1 Hen. IV.* i 3 184
All studies here I solemnly defy i 3 228
It hath it original from much grief, from study *2 Hen. IV.* i 2 132
The prince but studies his companions Like a strange tongue iv 4 68
You would say it hath been all in all his study *Hen. V.* i 1 42
And never noted in him any study, Any retirement i 1 57
Unless my study and my books be false *1 Hen. VI.* ii 4 56
Or who should study to prefer a peace? iii 1 110
And fitter is my study and my books Than wanton dalliance v 1 22
His study is his tilt-yard, and his loves Are brazen images *2 Hen. VI.* i 3 62
Nor how to study for the people's welfare *3 Hen. VI.* iv 3 39
To study fashions to adorn my body *Richard III.* i 2 258
All your studies Make me a curse like this *Hen. VIII.* iii 1 123
We are ready To use our utmost studies in your service iii 1 174
I have labour'd, And with no little study, that my teaching And the strong course of my authority Might go one way v 3 34
Knock at his study, where, they say, he keeps, To ruminate *T. Andron.* v 2 5
My sad decrees may fly away, And all my study be to no effect v 2 12
Stand up; Run to my study *Rom. and Jul.* iii 3 76
Get me a taper in my study, Lucius *J. Cæsar* ii 1 7
You could, for a need, study a speech of some dozen or sixteen lines? *Hamlet* ii 2 566
I must love you, and sue to know you better.—Sir, I shall study deserving *Lear* i 1 32
Let your study Be to content your lord i 1 279
What is your study?—How to prevent the fiend, and to kill vermin iii 4 163
Study on what fair demands Thou mean'st to have him grant thee *Ant. and Cleo.* v 2 10
Studying. This young scholar, that hath been long studying *T. of Shrew* ii 1 80
Studying how I may compare This prison where I live unto the world *Richard II.* v 5 1
So help me God, as I have watch'd the night, Ay, night by night, in studying good for England *2 Hen. VI.* iii 1 111
Stuff. Rich garments, linens, stuffs, and necessaries *Tempest* i 2 164
What stuff is this! how say you? ii 1 254
We are such stuff As dreams are made on iv 1 156
He'll fill our skins with pinches, Make us strange stuff iv 1 234
O heavens! what stuff is here? *Meas. for Meas.* iii 2 5
Fetch our stuff from thence *Com. of Errors* iv 4 153
Therefore away, to get our stuff aboard iv 4 162
Shall I fetch your stuff from shipboard?—Dromio, what stuff of mine hast thou embark'd? v 1 408
Nature never framed a woman's heart Of prouder stuff *Much Ado* iii 1 50
I never knew man hold vile stuff so dear *L. L. Lost* iv 3 276
This is the silliest stuff that ever I heard *M. N. Dream* v 1 212
What stuff 'tis made of, whereof it is born, I am to learn *Mer. of Venice* i 1 4
It is more pleasing stuff.—What, household stuff? *T. of Shrew* Ind. 2 142
She is my house, My household stuff, my field, my barn iii 2 233
O mercy, God! what masquing stuff is here? What's this? a sleeve? iv 3 87
I gave him no order; I gave him the stuff iv 3 119
As she went to the garden for parsley to stuff a rabbit iv 4 101
Youth's a stuff will not endure *T. Night* ii 3 53
Stuffs out his vacant garments with his form *K. John* iii 4 97
Do not seek to stuff My head with more ill news, for it is full iv 2 133
With a foul traitor's name stuff I thy throat *Richard II.* i 1 44
If you will go, I will stuff your purses full of crowns *1 Hen. IV.* i 2 146
Such a deal of skimble-skamble stuff As puts me from my faith iii 1 154
There's a whole merchant's venture of Bourdeaux stuff in him *2 Hen. IV.* ii 4 69
Here's goodly stuff toward! ii 4 214
What stuff wilt have a kirtle of? I shall receive money o' Thursday ii 4 297
Give me your doublet and stuff me out with straw v 5 87
There's in him stuff that puts him to these ends *Hen. VIII.* i 1 58
His treasure, Rich stuffs, and ornaments of household iii 2 126
You are full of heavenly stuff iii 2 137
At this fusty stuff The large Achilles, on his press'd bed lolling, From his deep chest laughs out a loud applause *Troi. and Cres.* i 3 161
What is or is not, serves As stuff for these two to make paradoxes i 3 184
Deserve not so honourable a grave as to stuff a botcher's cushion *Coriol.* ii 1 98
In spite put stuff To some she beggar and compounded thee *T. of Athens* iv 3 272
Thy verse swells with stuff so fine and smooth That thou art even natural v 1 87
Ambition should be made of sterner stuff *J. Cæsar* iii 2 97
O proper stuff! This is the very painting of your fear *Macbeth* iii 4 60
Cleanse the stuff'd bosom of that perilous stuff Which weighs upon the heart v 3 44
There was no such stuff in my thoughts.—Why did you laugh then? *Hamlet* ii 2 324
Let me wring your heart; for so I shall, If it be made of penetrable stuff iii 4 36
You must not think That we are made of stuff so flat and dull iv 7 31
It will stuff his suspicion more fully *Lear* iii 5 22
I hold it very stuff o' the conscience To do no contrived murder *Othello* i 2 2
Nature wants stuff To vie strange forms with fancy *Ant. and Cleo.* v 2 97
So fair an outward and such stuff within *Cymbeline* i 1 23
Such boil'd stuff As well might poison poison! i 6 125
Moulded the stuff so fair, That he deserved the praise o' the world v 4 49
'Tis still a dream, or else such stuff as madmen Tongue and brain not v 4 146

Stuff. A certain stuff, which, being ta'en, would cease The present power of life *Cymbeline* v 5 255
The stuff we have, a strong wind will blow it to pieces *Pericles* iv 2 19
Stuffed. They are stuff'd with protestations *T. G. of Ver.* iv 4 134
Stuffed with all honourable virtues *Much Ado* i 1 56
A stuffed man: but for the stuffing,—well, we are all mortal i 1 59
The old ornament of his cheek hath already stuffed tennis-balls iii 2 47
I am stuffed, cousin; I cannot smell.—A maid, and stuffed! iii 4 64
In ivory coffers I have stuff'd my crowns *T. of Shrew* ii 1 352
Whom you know Of stuff'd sufficiency *W. Tale* ii 1 185
My arms such eel-skins stuff'd, my face so thin *K. John* i 1 141
That huge bombard of sack, that stuffed cloak-bag of guts *1 Hen. IV.* ii 4 497
You have not seen a hulk better stuffed in the hold *2 Hen. IV.* ii 4 70
When we have stuff'd These pipes and these conveyances of our blood With wine and feeding, we have suppler souls *Coriolanus* v 1 53
Nobly train'd, Stuff'd, as they say, with honourable parts *Rom. and Jul.* iii 5 183
In his needy shop a tortoise hung, An alligator stuff'd v 1 43
Cleanse the stuff'd bosom of that perilous stuff *Macbeth* v 3 44
A bombast circumstance Horribly stuff'd with epithets of war *Othello* i 1 14
Hath stuff'd these hollow vessels with their power, To beat us down *Per.* i 4 67
Like the Trojan horse was stuff'd within With bloody veins i 4 93
Stuffing. He is no less than a stuffed man: but for the stuffing,—well, we are all mortal *Much Ado* i 1 59
Stuffing the ears of men with false reports *2 Hen. IV.* Ind. 8
Stumble. Wouldst thou then counsel me to fall in love?—Ay, madam, so you stumble not unheedfully *T. G. of Ver.* i 2 3
His tongue, all impatient to speak and not see, Did stumble with haste in his eyesight to be *L. L. Lost* ii 1 239
It grows dark, he may stumble v 2 633
When she will take the rein I let her run; But she'll not stumble *W. T.* ii 3 52
Would he not stumble? would he not fall down? *Richard II.* v 5 87
My tongue should stumble in mine earnest words *2 Hen. VI.* iii 2 316
For many men that stumble at the threshold Are well foretold that danger lurks within *3 Hen. VI.* iv 7 11
Three times to-day my foot-cloth horse did stumble *Richard III.* iii 4 86
Wisely and slow; they stumble that run fast *Rom. and Jul.* ii 3 94
Stumbled. How he beat me because her horse stumbled *T. of Shrew* iv 1 79
Methought that Gloucester stumbled; and, in falling, Struck me *Richard III.* i 4 18
How oft to-night Have my old feet stumbled at graves! *Rom. and Jul.* v 3 122
I have no way, and therefore want no eyes; I stumbled when I saw *Lear* iv 1 21
Stumblest. What man art thou that thus bescreen'd in night So stumblest on my counsel? *Rom. and Jul.* ii 2 53
Stumbling. Being restrained to keep him from stumbling *T. of Shrew* iii 2 59
The stumbling night did part our weary powers *K. John* v 5 18
In his flight, Stumbling in fear, was took *2 Hen. IV.* i 1 131
Blind fear, that seeing reason leads, finds safer footing than blind reason stumbling without fear *Troi. and Cres.* iii 2 77
Revolts from true birth, stumbling on abuse *Rom. and Jul.* ii 3 20
Stumbling-blocks. Were I a man, a duke, and next of blood, I would remove these tedious stumbling-blocks *2 Hen. VI.* i 2 64
Stump. Your colt's tooth is not cast yet.—No, my lord; Nor shall not, while I have a stump *Hen. VIII.* i 3 49
An if thy stumps will let thee play the scribe *T. Andron.* ii 4 4
Thou shalt not sigh, nor hold thy stumps to heaven, Nor wink iii 2 42
Witness this wretched stump, witness these crimson lines v 2 22
Whilst that Lavinia 'tween her stumps doth hold The basin v 2 183
Stung. With doubler tongue Than thine, thou serpent, never adder stung *M. N. Dream* iii 2 73
Scourged with rods, Nettled and stung with pismires *1 Hen. IV.* i 3 240
I am stung like a tench ii 1 16
'Tis given out that, sleeping in my orchard, A serpent stung me *Hamlet* i 5 36
Each jealous of the other, as the stung Are of the adder *Lear* v 1 56
Stunk. They so stunk, That all those eyes adored them ere their fall Scorn now their hand should give them burial *Pericles* ii 4 10
Stupid. Is he not stupid With age and altering rheums? *W. Tale* iv 4 409
Stupified Or seeming so in skill ii 1 165
Stupify. Will stupify and dull the sense awhile *Cymbeline* i 5 37
Stuprum. Do ye read, my lord, what she hath writ? 'Stuprum. Chiron. Demetrius' *T. Andron.* iv 1 78
Sturdy. Look where the sturdy rebel sits *3 Hen. VI.* i 1 50
Sty. And here you sty me In this hard rock *Tempest* i 2 342
In the sty of this most bloody boar My son George Stanley is frank'd up in hold *Richard III.* iv 5 2
Stew'd in corruption, honeying and making love Over the nasty sty *Ham.* iii 4 94
This dull world, which in thy absence is No better than a sty *A. and C.* iv 15 62
Though most ungentle fortune Have placed me in this sty *Pericles* iv 6 104
Styga. Till I find the stream To cool this heat, a charm to calm these fits, Per Styga, per manes vehor *T. Andron.* ii 1 135
Stygian. I stalk about her door, Like a strange soul upon the Stygian banks Staying for waftage *Troi. and Cres.* iii 2 10
Style. I can construe the action of her familiar style *Mer. Wives* i 3 51
I will aggravate his style ii 2 297
They have writ the style of gods And made a push at chance *Much Ado* v 1 37
In so high a style, Margaret, that no man living shall come over it v 2 6
Be it as the style shall give us cause to climb in the merriness *L. L. Lost* i 1 201
I am much deceived but I remember the style iv 1 98
Into so quiet and so sweet a style *As Y. Like It* ii 1 20
'Tis a boisterous and a cruel style, A style for challengers iv 3 32
To what is count's man: count's master is of another style *All's Well* ii 3 205
What means his grace, that he hath changed his style? *1 Hen. VI.* iv 1 50
Here is a silly stately style indeed! The Turk, that two and fifty kingdoms hath, Writes not so tedious a style as this iv 7 72
Whose large style Agrees not with the leanness of his purse *2 Hen. VI.* i 1 111
Am I a queen in title and in style, And must be made a subject to a duke? i 3 51
Plain and not honest is too harsh a style *Richard III.* iv 4 360
Styled The under-hangman of his kingdom, and hated *Cymbeline* ii 3 134
Styx. Shouldst thou take the river Styx, I would swim after *Tr. and Cr.* v 4 20
Unkind and careless of thine own, Why suffer'st thou thy sons, unburied yet, To hover on the dreadful shore of Styx? *T. Andron.* i 1 88
Sub. Precor gelida quando pecus omne sub umbra Ruminat *L. L. Lost* iv 2 96
Sub-contracted. She is sub-contracted to this lord *Lear* v 3 86
Subdue. This virtuous maid Subdues me quite *Meas. for Meas.* ii 2 186
He doth with holy abstinence subdue That in himself which he spurs on his power To qualify in others iv 2 84
His glory is to subdue men *L. L. Lost* i 2 187
Praise we may afford To any lady that subdues a lord iv 1 40
I think affliction may subdue the cheek, But not take in the mind *W. T.* iv 4 587
John of Gaunt, Which did subdue the greatest part of Spain *3 Hen. VI.* iii 3 82

Subdue. Your virtue is To make him worthy whose offence subdues him *Coriolanus* i 1 179
Subdues and properties to his love and tendance All sorts of hearts *T. of A.* i 1 57
Lay hold upon him: if he do resist, Subdue him at his peril . *Othello* i 2 81
Did you by indirect and forced courses Subdue and poison this young maid's affections? . i 3 112
'Tis most easy The inclining Desdemona to subdue In any honest suit . ii 3 346
'Twould make her amiable and subdue my father Entirely to her love . iii 4 59
And with those hands, that grasp'd the heaviest club, Subdue my worthiest self . . . . . *Ant. and Cleo.* iv 12 47
A touch more rare Subdues all pangs, all fears . . . *Cymbeline* i 1 136
Subdued. This man's threats, To whom I am subdued, are but light to me *Tempest* i 2 489
Their cheer is the greater that I am subdued . . *Much Ado* i 3 74
Her infinite cunning, with her modern grace, Subdued me . *All's Well* v 3 217
A peace is of the nature of a conquest; For then both parties nobly are subdued, And neither party loser . . 2 *Hen. IV.* iv 2 90
Charles the Great, having subdued the Saxons . . *Hen. V.* i 2 46; 62
My heart and hands thou hast at once subdued . . 1 *Hen. VI.* i 2 109
Tugg'd for life and was by strength subdued . 2 *Hen. VI.* iii 2 173
By many hands your father was subdued . . 3 *Hen. VI.* ii 1 56
And being once subdued in armed tail, Sweet honey and sweet notes together fail . . . . . . *Troi. and Cres.* v 10 44
He hath no daughters, sir.—Death, traitor! nothing could have subdued nature To such a lowness but his unkind daughters . *Lear* iii 4 72
My heart's subdued Even to the very quality of my lord . *Othello* i 3 251
Whose subdued eyes, Albeit unused to the melting mood, Drop tears . v 2 348
Cæsar, thou hast subdued His judgement too . . *Ant. and Cleo.* iii 13 36
Bending down His corrigible neck, his face subdued To penetrative shame . . . . iv 14 74
Or could this carl, A very drudge of nature's, have subdued me? . *Cymb.* v 2 5
Subduements. Despising many forfeits and subduements *Troi. and Cres.* iv 5 187
Subject his coronet to his crown and bend The dukedom *Tempest* i 2 114
Be subject To no sight but thine and mine . . . . i 2 301
I am all the subjects that you have, Which first was mine own king . i 2 341
No marrying 'mong his subjects?—None, man; all idle . . ii 1 165
I'll swear upon that bottle to be thy true subject . . . ii 2 131
I'll kiss thy foot; I'll swear myself thy subject . . . ii 2 156
The poor monster's my subject and he shall not suffer indignity . . iii 2 41
I am subject to a tyrant, a sorcerer . . . . . iii 2 48
Here have I few attendants And subjects none abroad . . . v 1 167
O sweet-suggesting Love, if thou hast sinn'd, Teach me, thy tempted subject, to excuse it! . . . . . *T. G. of Ver.* ii 6 8
Have I 'scaped love-letters in the holiday-time of my beauty, and am I now a subject for them? . . . . . *Mer. Wives* ii 1 3
As subject to heat as butter; a man of continual dissolution and thaw . iii 5 117
When I would pray and think, I think and pray To several subjects *Meas. for Meas.* ii 4 2
Even so The general, subject to a well-wish'd king, Quit their own part ii 4 27
The greater file of the subject held the duke to be wise . . iii 2 145
Give me your hand, And let the subject see, to make them know That outward courtesies would fain proclaim Favours that keep within . v 1 14
His subject am I not, Nor here provincial . . . . v 1 317
Thoughts are no subjects; Intents but merely thoughts . . v 1 458
The fishes and the winged fowls Are their males' subjects *Com. of Errors* ii 1 19
Which of these sorrows is he subject to?—To none of these . . v 1 54
Alone, it was the subject of my theme; In company I often glanced it v 1 65
If he will not stand when he is bidden, he is none of the prince's subjects.—True, and they are to meddle with none but the prince's subjects *Much Ado* iii 3 33
I pray you choose another subject . . . . . . v 1 137
I will have that subject newly writ o'er . . . *L. L. Lost* i 2 120
Varying in subjects as the eye doth roll To every varied object . v 2 774
Subject to the same diseases, healed by the same means *Mer. of Venice* iii 1 64
Even as the flourish when true subjects bow To a new-crowned monarch iii 2 49
I am the unhappy subject of these quarrels . . . . v 1 238
I rather will subject me to the malice Of a diverted blood *As Y. Like It* ii 3 36
Such duty as the subject owes the prince, Even such a woman oweth to her husband . . . . . . *T. of Shrew* v 2 155
One that indeed physics the subject, makes old hearts fresh . *W. Tale* i 1 43
Stay her tongue.—Hang all the husbands That cannot do that feat, you'll leave yourself Hardly one subject . . . . ii 3 112
Contrary to the faith and allegiance of a true subject . . . iii 2 20
Camillo a true subject; Leontes a jealous tyrant . . . iii 2 134
Your faithful subject I, a gentleman Born in Northamptonshire *K. John* i 1 50
Wade to the market-place in Frenchmen's blood, But we will make it subject to this boy . . . . ii 1 43
You men of Angiers, and my loving subjects,— You loving men of Angiers, Arthur's subjects . . . . ii 1 204
We are the king of England's subjects: For him, and in his right, we hold this town . . . . ii 1 267
A widow, husbandless, subject to fears . . . . iii 1 14
Let me have no subject enemies, When adverse foreigners affright my towns . . . . iv 2 171
Or worthily, as a good subject should . . . *Richard II.* i 1 10
A subject's love, Tendering the precious safety of my prince . . i 1 31
He is our subject, Mowbray; so art thou: Free speech and fearless I to thee allow . . . . i 1 122
Or complot any ill 'Gainst us, our state, our subjects, or our land . i 3 190
And he our subjects' next degree in hope . . . . i 4 36
I am a subject, And I challenge law: attorneys are denied me . ii 3 133
Arm, arm, my name! a puny subject strikes At thy great glory . iii 2 86
Revolt our subjects? that we cannot mend; They break their faith to God as well as us . . . . iii 2 100
I'll give . . . My subjects for a pair of carved saints . . iii 3 152
Where subjects' feet May hourly trample on their sovereign's head . iii 3 156
I would my skill were subject to thy curse . . . . iii 4 103
What subject can give sentence on his king? . . . . iv 1 121
I speak to subjects, and a subject speaks, Stirr'd up by God, thus boldly for his king . . . . iv 1 132
Made glory base and sovereignty a slave, Proud majesty a subject . iv 1 252
When I was a king, my flatterers Were then but subjects; being now a subject, I have a king here to my flatterer . . . . iv 1 307
To Bolingbroke are we sworn subjects now . . . . v 2 39
And drive all thy subjects afore thee like a flock of wild-geese 1 *Hen. IV.* ii 4 152
Doth not the king lack subjects? do not the rebels need soldiers? 2 *Hen. IV.* i 2 86
Leaves his part-created cost A naked subject to the weeping clouds . i 3 61
We are time's subjects, and time bids be gone . . . . i 3 110
I could be sad, and sad indeed too.—Very hardly upon such a subject . ii 2 47
I have done the part of a careful friend and a true subject . . ii 4 349

Subject. How many thousand of my poorest subjects Are at this hour asleep? . . . . 2 *Hen. IV.* iii 1 4
Lord, Lord, how subject we old men are to this vice of lying! . iii 2 325
You have ta'en up, Under the counterfeited zeal of God, The subjects of his substitute, my father . . . . iv 2 28
A famous rebel art thou, Colevile.—And a famous true subject took him iv 3 70
Most subject is the fattest soil to weeds . . . . . iv 4 54
Never king of England Had nobles richer and more loyal subjects *Hen. V.* i 2 127
Unto whose grace our passion is as subject As are our wretches fetter'd in our prisons . . . . i 2 242
There's not, I think, a subject That sits in heart-grief and uneasiness Under the sweet shade of your government . . . . ii 2 26
Never did faithful subject more rejoice At the discovery of most dangerous treason Than I do . . . . ii 2 161
You would have sold your king to slaughter, His princes and his peers to servitude, His subjects to oppression . . . . ii 2 172
You'll find a difference, As we his subjects have in wonder found . ii 4 135
The subjects we have lost, the disgrace we have digested . . iii 6 135
'Tis a subject for a sovereign to reason on . . . . iii 7 38
Every subject's duty is the king's; but every subject's soul is his own . iv 1 186
Subject to the breath Of every fool . . . . . . iv 1 251
Doo's me as great honours as can be desired in the hearts of his subjects iv 7 168
The presence of a king engenders love Amongst his subjects 1 *Hen. VI.* iii 1 182
Like true subjects, sons of your progenitors, Go cheerfully together . iv 1 166
Call my sovereign yours, And do him homage as obedient subjects . iv 2 7
To be shame's scorn and subject of mischance! . . . . iv 6 49
It is your policy To save your subjects from such massacre . . v 4 160
Am I a queen in title and in style, And must be made a subject to a duke? . . . . 2 *Hen. VI.* i 3 52
If thy claim be good, The Nevils are thy subjects to command . ii 2 8
Daughter of a worthless king, Having neither subject, wealth, nor diadem iv 1 82
Never subject long'd to be a king As I do long and wish to be a subject iv 9 6
Or why thou, being a subject as I am, Against thy oath and true allegiance sworn, Should raise so great a power . . . . v 1 19
I am too mean a subject for thy wrath: Be thou revenged on men 3 *Hen. VI.* i 3 19
To kings that fear their subjects' treachery . . . . ii 5 45
Was ever king so grieved for subjects' woe? . . . . . ii 5 111
You are the king King Edward hath deposed; And we his subjects . iii 1 70
You were sworn true subjects unto me . . . . . . iii 1 78
We were subjects but while you were king . . . . . iii 1 81
We are true subjects to the king, King Edward.—So would you be again to Henry, If he were seated . . . . iii 1 94
'Tis but to love a king.—That's soon perform'd, because I am a subject iii 2 54
I am a subject fit to jest withal, But far unfit to be a sovereign . iii 2 91
Subjects may challenge nothing of their sovereigns . . . . iv 6 6
To help King Edward in his time of storm, As every loyal subject ought to do . . . . iv 7 44
Henry is my king, Warwick his subject . . . . . . v 1 38
His state usurp'd, His realm a slaughter-house, his subjects slain . v 4 78
What satisfaction canst thou make For bearing arms, for stirring up my subjects? . . . . v 5 15
Speak like a subject, proud ambitious York! . . . . . v 5 17
If not, that, I being queen, you bow like subjects . . *Richard III.* i 3 161
Teach me to be your queen, and you my subjects . . . . i 3 252
Live each of you the subjects to his hate, And he to yours, and all of you to God's! . . . . i 3 302
Like obedient subjects, follow him To his new kingdom of perpetual rest ii 2 45
And proved the subject of my own soul's curse . . . . iv 1 81
Is thy name Tyrrel?—James Tyrrel, and your most obedient subject . iv 2 68
Say, I, her sovereign, am her subject love.—But she, your subject, loathes such sovereignty . . . . iv 4 355
Let fall a tear; The subject will deserve it . . . *Hen. VIII.* Prol. 7
Your subjects Are in great grievance . . . . . . i 2 19
The subjects' grief Comes through commissions . . . . i 2 56
We must not rend our subjects from our laws, And stick them in our will i 2 93
Relate what you, Most like a careful subject, have collected . . i 2 130
His master would be served before a subject, if not before the king . i 2 8
Subject to your countenance, glad or sorry As I saw it inclined . ii 4 26
Though he be grown so desperate to be honest, And live a subject . iii 1 87
At such proud rate, that it out-speaks Possession of a subject . . iii 2 128
A loyal and obedient subject is Therein illustrated . . . iii 2 180
If a prince May be beholding to a subject, I Am, for his love and service v 3 157
How may I deserve it, That am a poor and humble subject to you? . v 3 166
It is too starved a subject for my sword . . . *Troi. and Cres.* i 1 96
The eastern tower, Whose height commands as subject all the vale . i 2 3
Nor none so noble Whose life were ill bestow'd or death unfamed Where Helen is the subject . . . . ii 2 160
Now, the dry serpigo on the subject! . . . . . . ii 3 81
Love, friendship, charity, are subjects all To envious and calumniating time . . . . iii 3 173
Our very priests must become mockers, if they shall encounter such ridiculous subjects as you are . . . . . *Coriolanus* ii 1 94
Rebellious subjects, enemies to peace . . . . *Rom. and Jul.* i 1 88
Alack, that heaven should practise stratagems Upon so soft a subject! iii 5 212
If thou wilt curse, thy father, that poor rag, Must be thy subject *T. of A.* iv 3 272
What beast couldst thou be, that were not subject to a beast? . iv 3 347
Honour is the subject of my story . . . . . *J. Cæsar* i 2 92
He's here in double trust; First, as I am his kinsman and his subject *Macb.* i 7 13
Near approaches The subject of our watch . . . . . iii 3 8
This . . . observant watch So nightly toils the subject of the land *Hamlet* i 1 72
The lists and full proportions, are all made Out of his subject . . i 2 33
His will is not his own; For he himself is subject to his birth . i 3 18
If thou be as poor for a subject as he is for a king, thou art poor enough *Lear* i 4 22
When I do stare, see how the subject quakes . . . . iv 6 110
By your patience, I hold you but a subject of this war, Not as a brother v 3 60
But that your royalty Holds idleness your subject, I should take you For idleness itself . . . . . . *Ant. and Cleo.* i 3 92
Left these notes Of what commands I should be subject to . *Cymbeline* i 1 172
Our subjects, sir, Will not endure his yoke . . . . . iii 5 4
Thou hadst, great king, a subject who Was call'd Belarius . . v 5 316
Publish we this peace To all our subjects . . . . . v 5 479
Graces her subjects, and her thoughts the king Of every virtue *Pericles* i 1 13
And subjects punish'd that ne'er thought offence . . . . i 2 27
An issue I might propagate, Are arms to princes, and bring joys to subjects . . . . i 2 74
The care I had and have of subjects' good On thee I lay . . . i 2 118
Thou show'dst a subject's shine, I a true prince . . . . i 2 124
How from the finny subject of the sea These fishers tell the infirmities of men! . . . . ii 1 52

Subject. He is a happy king, since he gains from his subjects the name of good . . . . *Pericles* ii 1 110
Go search like nobles, like noble subjects . . . . . . ii 4 50
Subjected. Needs must you lay your heart at his dispose, Subjected tribute to commanding love . . . . *K. John* i 1 264
Subjected thus, How can you say to me, I am a king? *Richard II.* iii 2 176
Subjection. I am now in ward, evermore in subjection . . *All's Well* i 1 6
I do bequeath my faithful services And true subjection . . *K. John* v 7 105
Whom to disobey were against all proportion of subjection . *Hen. V.* iv 1 153
He's true and shall perform All parts of his subjection loyally . *Cymb.* iv 3 19
I'll tame you; I'll bring you in subjection . . *Pericles* ii 5 75
Submerged. So half my Egypt were submerged and made A cistern for scaled snakes! . . . . . . *Ant. and Cleo.* ii 5 94
Submission. Be not as extreme in submission As in offence *Mer. Wives* iv 4 11
With all submission, on my knee I do bequeath my faithful services *K. John* v 7 103
Give sorrow leave awhile to tutor me To this submission *Richard II.* iv 1 167
Find pardon on my true submission . . . . 1 *Hen. IV.* iii 2 28
Tell her I return great thanks, And in submission will attend on her 1 *Hen. VI.* ii 2 52
Submission, Dauphin! 'tis a mere French word; We English warriors wot not what it means . . . . iv 7 54
All the court admired him for submission . . . . 2 *Hen. VI.* iii 1 12
I commend this kind submission . . . . v 1 54
In all submission and humility . . . . v 1 58
Proclaim a pardon to the soldiers fled That in submission will return to us . . . . *Richard III.* v 5 17
O calm, dishonourable, vile submission! . . *Rom. and Jul.* iii 1 76
Submissive fall his princely feet before . . . *L. L. Lost* iv 1 92
With a low submissive reverence Say 'What is it?'. *T. of Shrew* Ind. 1 53
With submissive loyalty of heart Ascribes the glory of his conquest got First to my God and next unto your grace . 1 *Hen. VI.* iii 4 10
On what submissive message art thou sent?—Submission! . . . iv 7 53
Submit. We should submit ourselves to an unknown fear *All's Well* ii 3 6
I submit My fancy to your eyes . . . . ii 3 174
Submit thee, boy.—Come to thy grandam, child . . *K. John* ii 1 159
Raise the power of France upon his head, Unless he do submit himself to Rome . . . . iii 1 194
What must the king do now? must he submit? . . *Richard II.* iii 3 143
I do confess my fault; And do submit me to your highness' mercy *Hen. V.* ii 2 77
He shall submit, or I will never yield . . . . 1 *Hen. VI.* iii 1 118
Winchester will not submit, I trow, Or be inferior to the proudest peer v 1 56
Upon condition thou wilt swear To pay him tribute, and submit thyself v 4 130
I do demand, If you submit you to the people's voices? . *Coriolanus* iii 3 44
Cleopatra does confess thy greatness; Submits her to thy might *Ant. and Cleo.* iii 12 17
We submit to Cæsar, And to the Roman empire . . . *Cymbeline* v 5 460
Your noble self, That best know how to rule and how to reign, We thus submit unto,—our sovereign . . . . . *Pericles* ii 4 39
Submitting me unto the perilous night . . . . *J. Cæsar* i 3 47
Suborn. Whom I did suborn To do this ruthless piece of butchery *Richard III.* iv 3 4
Subornation. And for his sake wear the detested blot Of murderous subornation . . . . 1 *Hen. IV.* i 3 163
By his subornation, Upon my life, began her devilish practices 2 *Hen. VI.* iii 1 45
Foul subornation is predominant And equity exiled . . . . iii 1 145
Suborned. Thou art suborn'd against his honour . . *Meas. for Meas.* v 1 106
Is't not enough thou hast suborn'd these women To accuse this worthy man? . . . . v 1 308
Thou hast suborn'd the goldsmith to arrest me . . *Com. of Errors* iv 4 85
What peer hath been suborn'd to grate on you? . 2 *Hen. IV.* iv 1 90
You have suborn'd this man, Of purpose to obscure my noble birth 1 *Hen. VI.* v 4 21
As if she had suborned some to swear False allegations . 2 *Hen. VI.* iii 1 180
Alas, the day! What good could they pretend?—They were suborn'd *Macbeth* ii 4 24
Now I find I had suborn'd the witness, And he's indicted falsely *Othello* iii 4 153
Subscribe. Plead a new state in thy unrival'd merit, To which I thus subscribe . . . . *T. G. of Ver.* v 4 145
I subscribe not that, nor any other . . . . . *Meas. for Meas.* ii 4 89
I will subscribe him a coward . . . . *Much Ado* v 2 59
Your oaths are pass'd; and now subscribe your names . . *L. L. Lost* i 1 19
As sworn to do, Subscribe to your deep oaths, and keep it too . . i 1 23
Sir, to your pleasure humbly I subscribe . . . *T. of Shrew* i 1 81
And, to the possibility of thy soldiership, will subscribe for thee *All's W.* iii 6 89
I will subscribe for thee, thou art both knave and fool . . . iv 5 34
When they shall know what men are rich, They shall subscribe them for large sums of gold . . . . *Richard II.* i 4 50
I subscribe in silence . . . . 1 *Hen VI.* ii 4 44
I will subscribe and say I wrong'd the duke . . . 2 *Hen. VI.* iii 1 38
Will you subscribe his thought, and say he is? . *Troi. and Cres.* ii 3 156
In his blaze of wrath subscribes To tender objects . . . . iv 5 105
And we will all subscribe to thy advice . . . *T. Andron.* iv 2 130
Write to him—I will subscribe—gentle adieus and greetings *A. and C.* iv 5 14
Resolve your angry father, if my tongue Did e'er solicit, or my hand subscribe To any syllable that made love to you . . *Pericles* ii 5 69
Subscribed. Reading the challenge, subscribed for Cupid . *Much Ado* i 1 41
When I had subscribed To mine own fortune and inform'd her fully I could not answer in that course of honour . . . *All's Well* v 3 96
Only he hath not yet subscribed this . . . . . *Hen. V.* v 2 363
Subscribed by the consuls and patricians . . . . *Coriolanus* v 6 82
Folded the writ up in form of the other, Subscribed it . . *Hamlet* v 2 52
And the king gone to-night! subscribed his power! . . . *Lear* i 2 24
Thou shouldst have said 'Good porter, turn the key,' All cruels else subscribed . . . . iii 7 65
Subscription. You owe me no subscription . . . . . . iii 2 18
Subsequent. In such indexes, although small pricks To their subsequent volumes . . . . *Troi. and Cres.* i 3 344
Subsidy. He that made us pay one and twenty fifteens, and one shilling to the pound, the last subsidy . . . . 2 *Hen. VI.* iv 7 25
Nor much oppress'd them with great subsidies . . 3 *Hen. VI.* iv 8 45
Subsisting. Still subsisting Under your great command . . *Coriolanus* v 6 73
Substance. You take the sum and substance that I have *T. G. of Ver.* iv 1 15
Since the substance of your perfect self Is else devoted, I am but a shadow . . . . iv 2 124
If 'twere a substance, you would, sure, deceive it, And make it but a shadow . . . . iv 2 127
Were there sense in his idolatry, My substance should be statue in thy stead . . . . iv 4 206
Substance. I ken the wight: he is of substance good . . *Mer. Wives* i 3 40
Love like a shadow flies when substance love pursues . . . ii 2 215
He shall not knit a knot in his fortunes with the finger of my substance iii 2 77
Thy substance, valued at the highest rate, Cannot amount unto a hundred marks . . . . *Com. of Errors* i 1 24
The substance of my praise doth wrong this shadow In underprizing it, so far this shadow Doth limp behind the substance *Mer. of Venice* iii 2 128
Be it but so much As makes it light or heavy in the substance . iv 1 328
Each substance of a grief hath twenty shadows . . *Richard II.* ii 2 14
Through our security, Grows strong and great in substance and in power iii 2 35
Merely shadows to the unseen grief . . . ; There lies the substance . iv 1 299
All of one nature, of one substance bred . . . . . 1 *Hen. IV.* i 1 11
He hath put all my substance into that fat belly of his . 2 *Hen. IV.* ii 1 81
So the son of the female is the shadow of the male: it is often so, indeed; but much of the father's substance! . . . . . iii 2 142
Their cold intent, tenour, and substance, thus . . . . . iv 1 9
Unto your grace do I in chief address The substance of my speech . iv 1 32
Now the substance shall endure the like . . . . 1 *Hen. VI.* ii 3 38
Then have I substance too.—No, no, I am but shadow of myself: You are deceived, my substance is not here . . . . ii 3 49
These are his substance, sinews, arms, and strength . . . . ii 3 63
Yet, in substance and authority, Retain but privilege of a private man v 4 135
The substance Of that great shadow I did represent . 2 *Hen. VI.* i 1 13
Shadows to-night Have struck more terror to the soul of Richard Than can the substance of ten thousand soldiers *Richard III.* v 3 218
Which compel from each The sixth part of his substance *Hen. VIII.* i 2 58
Innumerable substance—By what means got, I leave to your own conscience . . . . iii 2 326
Perspicuous even as substance . . . . . . *Troi. and Cres.* i 3 324
Dear father, soul and substance of us all . . . . *T. Andron.* i 1 374
Grief has so wrought on him, He takes false shadows for true substances iii 2 80
As thin of substance as the air And more inconstant . *Rom. and Jul.* i 4 99
Conceit, more rich in matter than in words, Brags of his substance . ii 6 31
Wolvish-ravening lamb! Despised substance of divinest show! . . iii 2 77
You murdering ministers, Wherever in your sightless substances You wait on nature's mischief! . . . . *Macbeth* i 5 50
Doth all the noble substance of a doubt To his own scandal . *Hamlet* i 4 37
The very substance of the ambitious is merely the shadow of a dream ii 2 264
There she stands: If aught within that little seeming substance, Or all of it, with our displeasure pieced, And nothing more, may fitly like your grace, She's there, and she is yours . . . *Lear* i 1 201
Thou dost breathe; Hast heavy substance; bleed'st not; speak'st; art sound . . . . iv 6 52
Wind, rain, and thunder, remember, earthly man Is but a substance that must yield to you . . . . *Pericles* ii 1 3
Substantial. To draw with idle spiders' strings Most ponderous and substantial things! . . . . . . *Meas. for Meas.* iii 2 290
Your reason was not substantial . . . . . *Com. of Errors* ii 2 105
Acquitted by a true substantial form . . . . 2 *Hen. IV.* iv 1 173
A dream, Too flattering-sweet to be substantial . *Rom. and Jul.* ii 2 141
Substitute. How will you do to content this substitute? *Meas. for Meas.* iii 1 192
Were you sworn to the duke, or to the deputy?—To him, and to his substitutes . . . . iv 2 198
To set on this wretched woman here Against our substitute! . . . v 1 133
First, hath this woman Most wrongfully accused your substitute . . v 1 140
A substitute shines brightly as a king Until a king be by *Mer. of Venice* v 1 94
God's substitute, His deputy anointed in His sight . *Richard II.* i 2 37
If that come short, Our substitutes at home shall have blank charters . i 4 48
You have ta'en up, Under the counterfeited zeal of God, The subjects of his substitute, my father . . . . . 2 *Hen. IV.* iv 2 28
Our power collected, Our substitutes in absence well invested . . iv 4 6
That are substitutes Under the lordly monarch of the north . 1 *Hen. VI.* v 3 5
This devil here shall be my substitute . . . 2 *Hen. VI.* iii 1 371
Not as protector, steward, substitute, Or lowly factor . *Richard III.* iii 7 133
And afterward by substitute betroth'd To Bona . . . . . iii 7 181
We have there a substitute of most allowed sufficiency . . *Othello* i 3 224
I left behind an ancient substitute . . . . . . *Pericles* v 3 51
Substituted. Who is substituted 'gainst the French, I have no certain notice . . . . 2 *Hen. IV.* i 3 84
Substituted in the place of mine . . . . . . *T. Andron.* iv 2 159
Substitution. Out o' the substitution, And executing the outward face of royalty, With all prerogative . . . . *Tempest* i 2 103
Substractors. They are scoundrels and substractors that say so *T. Night* i 3 37
Subtilty. You do yet taste Some subtilties o' the isle . . *Tempest* v 1 124
'Tis the king's subtilty to have my life . . . . . *Pericles* i 5 44
Subtle. It must needs be of subtle, tender, and delicate temperance.—Temperance was a delicate wench.—Ay, and a subtle . *Tempest* ii 1 41
Thou subtle, perjured, false, disloyal man! . . . . *T. G. of Ver.* iv 2 95
Am I politic? am I subtle? am I a Machiavel? . . . *Mer. Wives* iii 1 103
Subtle as Sphinx; as sweet and musical As bright Apollo's lute *L. L. L.* iv 3 342
She is too subtle for thee . . . . *As Y. Like It* i 3 79
I feel this youth's perfections With an invisible and subtle stealth To creep in at mine eyes . . . . *T. Night* i 5 316
The predicament Wherein you range under this subtle king . 1 *Hen. IV.* i 3 169
A subtle knave! but yet it shall not serve . . . 2 *Hen. VI.* ii 1 104
A subtle traitor needs no sophister . . . . v 1 191
Warwick is a subtle orator . . . . 3 *Hen. VI.* iii 1 33
As true and just As I am subtle, false, and treacherous . *Richard III.* i 1 37
Incensed by his subtle mother To taunt and scorn you . . . . iii 1 152
The subtle traitor This day had plotted, in the council-house To murder me . . . . iii 5 37
Thy age confirm'd, proud, subtle, bloody, treacherous . . . iv 4 171
He is equal ravenous As he is subtle . . . . . . *Hen. VIII.* i 1 160
Nor sweeten talk, Nor play at subtle games . . *Troi. and Cres.* iv 4 89
Admits no orifex for a point as subtle As Ariachne's broken woof . v 2 151
He's the devil.—Bolder, though not so subtle . . . *Coriolanus* i 10 17
Like to a bowl upon a subtle ground, I have tumbled past the throw . v 2 20
How comes it that the subtle Queen of Goths Is of a sudden thus advanced in Rome?—I know not . . . . . . *T. Andron.* i 1 392
What subtle hole is this, Whose mouth is cover'd with rude-growing briers? . . . . ii 3 198
When subtle Greeks surprised King Priam's Troy . . . . . v 3 84
Go, suck the subtle blood o' the grape . . . . *T. of Athens* iv 3 432
Is not thy kindness subtle, covetous, If not a usuring kindness? . . iv 3 515
Let our hearts, as subtle masters do, Stir up their servants to an act of rage, And after seem to chide 'em . . . . *J. Cæsar* ii 1 175
The valued file Distinguishes the swift, the slow, the subtle . *Macbeth* iii 1 96
A slipper and subtle knave, a finder of occasions . . . *Othello* ii 1 246
This is a subtle whore, A closet lock and key of villanous secrets . iv 2 21
We are beastly, subtle as the fox for prey . . . . *Cymbeline* iii 3 40

Subtle-potent. Or some joy too fine, Too subtle-potent, tuned too sharp in sweetness . . . *Troi. and Cres.* iii 2 25
Subtlety. Be it by gins, by snares, by subtlety . . . 2 *Hen. VI.* iii 1 262
Subtle-witted. Or shall we think the subtle-witted French Conjurers and sorcerers? . . . 1 *Hen. VI.* i 1 25
Subtly. Thou proud dream, That play'st so subtly with a king's repose *Hen. V.* iv 1 275
Danger, like an ague, subtly taints . . . *Troi. and Cres.* iii 3 232
What if it be a poison, which the friar Subtly hath minister'd to have me dead? . . . *Rom. and Jul.* iv 3 25
Suburbs. All houses in the suburbs of Vienna must be plucked down *Meas. for Meas.* i 2 98
But shall all our houses of resort in the suburbs be pulled down? . . . i 2 105
Whose house, sir, was, as they say, plucked down in the suburbs . . . ii 1 65
In the south suburbs, at the Elephant, Is best to lodge . . . *T. Night* iii 3 39
Thou know'st how Orleans is besieged, And how the English have the suburbs won . . . 1 *Hen. VI.* i 4 2
The English, in the suburbs close intrench'd . . . i 4 9
Are all these Your faithful friends o' the suburbs? . . . *Hen. VIII.* v 4 76
Dwell I but in the suburbs Of your good pleasure? . . . *J. Cæsar* ii 1 285
Subversion. Do seek subversion of thy harmless life . . . 2 *Hen. VI.* iii 1 208
Subverts. Razeth your cities and subverts your towns . . . 1 *Hen. VI.* ii 3 65
Succedant. In terram Salicam mulieres ne succedant . . . *Hen. V.* i 2 38
Succeed. Only he Owe and succeed thy weakness . . . *Meas. for Meas.* ii 4 123
Succeed thy father In manners, as in shape! . . . *All's Well* i 1 70
Not Amurath an Amurath succeeds, But Harry Harry . . . 2 *Hen. IV.* v 2 48
No woman shall succeed in Salique land . . . *Hen. V.* i 2 39
Henry the Sixth, in infant bands crown'd King Of France and England, did this king succeed . . . Epil. 10
If the issue of the elder son Succeed before the younger, I am king 2 *Hen. VI.* ii 2 52
After summer evermore succeeds Barren winter . . . ii 4 2
For he could not so resign his crown But that the next heir should succeed and reign . . . 3 *Hen. VI.* i 1 146
You cannot disinherit me: If you be king, why should not I succeed? . . . i 1 227
Who should succeed the father but the son? . . . ii 2 94
She shall be—But few now living can behold that goodness—A pattern to all princes living with her, And all that shall succeed *Hen. VIII.* v 5 24
By honour of his name, Whom worthily you would have now succeed *T. Andron.* i 1 40
More vices than it had before, More suffer and more sundry ways than ever, By him that shall succeed . . . *Macbeth* iv 3 49
The effects he writes of succeed unhappily . . . *Lear* i 2 157
That not another comfort like to this Succeeds in unknown fate *Othello* ii 1 195
Seize upon the fortunes of the Moor, For they succeed on you . . . v 2 367
Being here, Bethought me what was past, what might succeed *Pericles* i 2 83
One sorrow never comes but brings an heir, That may succeed . . . i 4 64
The curse of heaven and men succeed their evils! . . . i 4 104
Succeeded. A ring the county wears, That downward hath succeeded in his house From son to son . . . *All's Well* iii 7 23
Succeeder. Airy succeeders of intestate joys! . . . *Richard III.* iv 4 128
Richmond and Elizabeth, The true succeeders of each royal house . . . v 5 30
Succeeding. Is it not a language I speak?—A most harsh one, and not to be understood without bloody succeeding . . . *All's Well* ii 3 199
Engaged by my oath . . . Both to defend my loyalty and truth To God, my king, and my succeeding issue . . . *Richard II.* i 3 20
Henry the Fifth, Succeeding his father Bolingbroke, did reign 1 *Hen. VI.* ii 5 83
Which, since, succeeding ages have re-edified . . . *Richard III.* iii 1 71
Henry the Seventh succeeding, truly pitying My father's loss *Hen. VIII.* ii 1 112
To be wrench'd with an unlineal hand, No son of mine succeeding *Macb.* iii 1 64
'Tis spoken, To the succeeding royalty he leaves The healing benediction iv 3 155
Hope, succeeding from so fair a tree As your fair self . . . *Pericles* i 1 114
Success. On a love-book pray for my success . . . *T. G. of Ver.* i 1 19
Let me hear from thee by letters Of thy success in love . . . i 1 58
Soon at night I'll send him certain word of my success . . . *Meas. for Meas.* i 4 89
Doubt not but success Will fashion the event in better shape *Much Ado* iv 1 236
I know he will be glad of our success . . . *Mer. of Venice* iii 2 243
But give me leave to try success, I'ld venture The well-lost life of mine on his grace's cure . . . *All's Well* i 3 253
When your lordship sees the bottom of his success . . . iii 6 39
We cannot greatly condemn our success . . . iii 6 59
I know not what the success will be, my lord; but the attempt I vow . . . iii 6 86
By an abstract of success . . . iv 3 100
Our parents' noble names, In whose success we are gentle . . . *W. Tale* i 2 394
To signify Not only my success in Libya, sir, But my arrival . . . v 1 166
And so success of mischief shall be born . . . 2 *Hen. IV.* iv 2 47
Leave not one behind that doth not wish Success and Conquest to attend on us . . . *Hen. V.* ii 2 24
Her aid she promised and assured success . . . 1 *Hen. VI.* i 2 82
How shall I honour thee for this success? . . . i 6 5
Created, for his rare success in arms, Great Earl of Washford . . . iv 7 62
Success unto our valiant general, And happiness to his accomplices! . . . v 2 8
Why should I not now have the like success? . . . 3 *Hen. VI.* i 2 76
Whether 'twas report of her success; Or more than common fear . . . ii 1 125
Didst thou never hear That things ill-got had ever bad success? . . . ii 2 46
The queen hath best success when you are absent . . . ii 2 74
If your title to the crown be weak, As may appear by Edward's good success . . . iii 3 146
Promise them success and victory . . . *Richard III.* iv 4 193
So thrive I in my enterprise And dangerous success of bloody wars! . . . iv 4 236
Dream of success and happy victory! . . . v 3 165
Success or loss, what is or is not, serves As stuff for these two to make paradoxes . . . *Troi. and Cres.* i 3 183
For the success, Although particular, shall give a scantling Of good or bad unto the general . . . i 3 340
Nor fear of bad success in a bad cause Can qualify the same . . . ii 2 117
If I might in entreaties find success—As seld I have the chance . . . iv 5 149
Such a nature, Tickled with good success, disdains the shadow Which he treads on at noon . . . *Coriolanus* i 1 264
Ye Roman gods! Lead their successes as we wish our own . . . i 6 7
Ere we do repose us, we will write To Rome of our success . . . i 9 75
The present consul, and last general In our well-found successes . . . ii 2 48
I shall ere long have knowledge Of my success . . . v 1 62
Go bid the priests do present sacrifice And bring me their opinions of success.—I will, my lord . . . *J. Cæsar* ii 2 6
Mistrust of my success hath done this deed.—Mistrust of good success hath done this deed . . . v 3 65
The king hath happily received, Macbeth, The news of thy success *Macb.* i 3 90
Why hath it given me earnest of success, Commencing in a truth? . . . i 3 132
They met me in the day of success . . . i 5 1
Success. If the assassination Could trammel up the consequence, and catch With his surcease success . . . *Macbeth* i 7 4
Not sure, though hoping of this good success . . . *Lear* v 3 194
Should you do so, my lord, My speech should fall into such vile success As my thoughts aim not at . . . *Othello* iii 3 222
And smooth success Be strew'd before your feet! . . . *Ant. and Cleo.* i 3 100
Sir, good success!—Farewell . . . ii 4 9
This is old: what is the success? . . . iii 5 6
Would I might never O'ertake pursued success, but I do feel, By the rebound of yours, a grief that smites My very heart at root . . . v 2 103
He served with glory and admired success . . . *Cymbeline* i 1 32
Which portends—Unless my sins abuse my divination—Success . . . iv 2 352
Successantly. Then go successantly, and plead to him . . . *T. Andron.* iv 4 113
Successful. Perhaps with more successful words Than you . . . *T. of Shrew* i 2 158
If the event o' the journey Prove as successful to the queen . . . *W. Tale* iii 1 12
If God doth give successful end To this debate . . . 2 *Hen. IV.* iv 4 1
His manly face, which promiseth Successful fortune . . . 3 *Hen. VI.* ii 2 41
Rome's best champion, Successful in the battles that he fights *T. An.* i 1 66
Welcome, nephews, from successful wars, You that survive! . . . i 1 172
Successfully. Alas, he is too young! yet he looks successfully *As Y. L. It* i 2 162
And 'tis my hope to end successfully . . . *T. of Shrew* iv 1 192
And led my country's strength successfully . . . *T. Andron.* i 1 194
Succession, Bourn, bound of land, tilth, vineyard, none . . . *Tempest* ii 1 151
Slander lives upon succession, For ever housed where it gets possession *Com. of Errors* iii 1 105
Cannot for all that dissuade succession . . . *All's Well* iii 5 25
A perpetual succession for it perpetually . . . iv 3 314
We'll bar thee from succession; Not hold thee of our blood . . . *W. Tale* iv 4 440
From my succession wipe me, father; I Am heir to my affection . . . iv 4 491
How art thou a king But by fair sequence and succession? *Richard II.* ii 1 199
By my sceptre and my soul to boot, He hath more worthy interest to the state Than thou the shadow of succession . . . 1 *Hen. IV.* iii 2 99
Touching King Henry's oath and your succession . . . 3 *Hen. VI.* ii 1 119
He swore consent to your succession, His oath enrolled in the parliament ii 1 172
What else? and that succession be determined . . . iv 6 56
He hath put me off To the succession of new days this month *T. of A.* ii 2 20
Their writers do them wrong, to make them exclaim against their own succession . . . *Hamlet* ii 2 368
You have the voice of the king himself for your succession in Denmark . . . iii 2 356
For him And his succession granted Rome a tribute . . . *Cymbeline* iii 1 8
Thinking to bar thee of succession, as Thou reft'st me of my lands . . . iii 3 102
Successive. To have no successive degrees, But, ere they live, to end *Meas. for Meas.* ii 2 98
As next the king he was successive heir . . . 2 *Hen. VI.* iii 1 49
My loving followers, Plead my successive title with your swords *T. An.* i 1 4
An union shall he throw, Richer than that which four successive kings In Denmark's crown have worn . . . *Hamlet* v 2 284
Successively. So thou the garland wear'st successively . . . 2 *Hen. IV.* iv 5 202
Is it upon record, or else reported Successively from age to age? *Rich. III.* iii 1 73
Successively from blood to blood, Your right of birth, your empery . . . iii 7 135
Successor. All his successors gone before him hath done't . . . *Mer. Wives* i 1 14
So his successor Was like to be the best . . . *W. Tale* v 1 48
Not propp'd by ancestry, whose grace Chalks successors their way *Hen. VIII.* i 1 60
Succour. With travel much oppress'd And faints for succour *As Y. L. It* ii 4 75
Heaven's offer we refuse, The proffer'd means of succour *Richard II.* iii 2 32
Sir Nicholas Gawsey hath for succour sent, And so hath Clifton 1 *Hen. IV.* v 4 45
The Dauphin, whom of succours we entreated, Returns us that his powers are yet not ready . . . *Hen. V.* iii 3 45
Be not dismay'd, for succour is at hand . . . 1 *Hen. VI.* i 2 30
O, send some succour to the distress'd lord! . . . iv 3 30
Let not your private discord keep away The levied succours . . . iv 4 23
Send succours, lords, and stop the rage betime . . . 2 *Hen. VI.* iii 1 285
God, our hope, will succour us.—My hope is gone . . . iv 4 55
The more I stay, the more I'll succour thee . . . 3 *Hen. VI.* iii 3 41
'Tis not his new-made bride shall succour him . . . iii 3 207
I'll leave you to your fortune and be gone To keep them back that come to succour you . . . iv 7 56
Flying for succour to his servant Banister, Being distress'd *Hen. VIII.* ii 1 109
Far from his succour, from the king, from all That might have mercy . . . ii 2 261
When I might see from far some forty truncheoners draw to her succour v 4 55
The citizens favour Lucius, And will revolt from me to succour him *T. Andron.* iv 4 80
Till Pericles be dead, My heart can lend no succour to my head *Pericles* i 1 171
Such. Made such a sinner of his memory, To credit his own lie *Tempest* i 2 101
Nothing ill can dwell in such a temple . . . i 2 457
Space enough Have I in such a prison . . . i 2 493
Tunis was never graced before with such a paragon to their queen . . . ii 1 74
Of such sensible and nimble lungs that they always use to laugh at nothing . . . ii 1 174
That a monster should be such a natural! . . . iii 2 37
I fear my Julia would not deign my lines, Receiving them from such a worthless post . . . *T. G. of Ver.* i 1 161
Such as the fury of ungovern'd youth Thrust from the company of awful men . . . iv 1 45
Such a youth That can with some discretion do my business . . . iv 4 69
If that be all the difference in his love, I'll get me such a colour'd periwig iv 4 196
That such a one and such a one were past cure . . . *Meas. for Meas.* ii 1 114
A meaner woman was delivered Of such a burden, male twins, both alike *Com. of Errors* i 1 56
A small spare mast, Such as seafaring men provide for storms . . . i 1 81
Nor let no comforter delight mine ear But such a one . . . *Much Ado* v 1 7
Such is the simplicity of man to hearken after the flesh . . . *L. L. Lost* i 1 219
Come, sir, you blush; as his your case is such . . . iv 3 131
You spurn'd me such a day . . . *Mer. of Venice* i 3 128
If you repay me not on such a day, In such a place, such sum or sums i 3 147
According to Fates and Destinies and such odd sayings, the Sisters Three, and such branches of learning . . . ii 2 65
In such a night as this, When the sweet wind did gently kiss the trees v 1 1
In such a night Troilus methinks mounted the Troyan walls . . . v 1 3
In such a night Did Thisbe fearfully o'ertrip the dew . . . v 1 6
In such a night Stood Dido with a willow in her hand . . . v 1 9
In such a night Medea gather'd the enchanted herbs . . . v 1 12
In such a night Did Jessica steal from the wealthy Jew . . . v 1 14
In such a night Did young Lorenzo swear he loved her well . . . v 1 17
In such a night Did pretty Jessica, like a little shrew, Slander her love v 1 20
I have other holy reasons, such as they are . . . *All's Well* i 3 35
O, then, give pity To her, whose state is such that cannot choose! . . . i 3 220
I'ld venture The well-lost life of mine on his grace's cure By such a day and hour . . . i 3 255

Such. Though the devil lead the measure, such are to be followed *All's Well* ii 1 58

Such I will have, whom I am sure he knows not . . . . iii 6 24

For such as we are made of, such we be . . . *T. Night* ii 2 33

Such an affection, which cannot choose but branch now *W. Tale* i 1 26

Such allow'd infirmities that honesty Is never free of . . i 1 263

Who else but I, And such as to my claim are liable? *K. John* v 2 101

Had said To such a person and in such a place, At such a time *1 Hen. IV.* i 3 72

There is not such a word Spoke of in Scotland as this term of fear . iv 1 84

I did never see such pitiful rascals . . . . . iv 2 70

Being men of such great leading as you are . . . . iv 3 17

Chid his truant youth with such a grace . . . . . v 2 63

I did not think thee lord of such a spirit . . . . . v 4 18

A stomach and no food; Such are the poor, in health; or else a feast And takes away the stomach; such are the rich *2 Hen. IV.* iv 4 106

Shall join together at the latter day and cry all 'We died at such a place' *Hen. V.* iv 1 144

If thou would have such a one, take me . . . . . v 2 174

Will fast Before he'll buy again at such a rate . *1 Hen. VI.* iii 2 43

Beauty's princely majesty is such, Confounds the tongue . . v 3 70

I feel such sharp dissension in my breast, Such fierce alarums . v 5 84

Such as my wit affords And over-joy of heart doth minister . *2 Hen. VI.* i 1 30

Such as my heart doth tremble to unfold . . . . ii 1 166

Thy sons, fair slips of such a stock . . . . . ii 2 58

Far be it we should honour such as these With humble suit . iv 1 123

Spare none but such as go in clouted shoon . . . . iv 2 195

Patience is for poltroons, such as he . . . *3 Hen. VI.* i 1 62

Such is the lightness of you common men . . . . iii 1 89

I would not spend another such a night, Though 'twere to buy a world of happy days, So full of dismal terror was the time! *Richard III.* i 4 5

For the most part such To whom as great a charge as little honour He meant to lay upon *Hen. VIII.* i 1 76

His training such, That he may furnish and instruct great teachers . i 2 112

What say they?—Such a one, they all confess, There is indeed . . i 4 82

He was stirr'd With such an agony, he sweat extremely . . . ii 1 33

No man alive can love in such a sort The thing he means to kill more excellently . . . *Troi. and Cres.* iv 1 23

I shall have such a life! . . . . . . iv 2 22

As welcome as to one That would be rid of such an enemy . . iv 5 164

If any such be here—As it were sin to doubt . *Coriolanus* i 6 67

They choose their magistrate, And such a one as he . . . iii 1 105

You have put me now to such a part which never I shall discharge to the life . . . . iii 2 105

Ay, such a place there is, where we did hunt—O, had we never, never hunted there! . . . . *T. Andron.* iv 1 55

In such a case as mine a man may strain courtesy . *Rom. and Jul.* ii 4 54

Such a case as yours constrains a man to bow in the hams . . ii 4 56

Nay, an there were two such, we should have none shortly, for one would kill the other . . . . . . iii 1 16

Find thou the means, and I'll find such a man . . . . iii 5 104

I'll tell thee joyful tidings, girl.—And joy comes well in such a needy time . . . . iii 5 106

These pencill'd figures are Even such as they give out *T. of Athens* i 1 160

Such a house broke! So noble a master fall'n! All gone! . iv 2 5

I had as lief not be as live to be In awe of such a thing as I myself *J. C.* i 2 96

It doth amaze me A man of such a feeble temper should So get the start of the majestic world . . . . . . i 2 129

Sleek-headed men and such as sleep o' nights . . . . i 2 193

Uttered such a deal of stinking breath . . . . . i 2 247

You speak to Casca, and to such a man That is no fleering tell-tale . i 3 116

Old feeble carrions and such suffering souls That welcome wrongs . ii 1 130

In such a time as this it is not meet That every nice offence should bear his comment . . . . iv 3 7

In no place so unsanctified Where such as thou mayst find him *Macbeth* iv 2 82

What's he That was not born of woman? Such a one Am I to fear, or none . . . . v 7 3

Every man has business and desire, Such as it is . . . *Hamlet* i 5 131

I saw him yesterday, or t' other day, Or then, or then; with such, or such ii 1 57

My lord such-a-one, that praised my lord such-a-one's horse . v 1 92

Such a sight as this Becomes the field, but here shows much amiss . v 2 412

Her offence Must be of such unnatural degree, That monsters it . *Lear* i 1 222

Such smiling rogues as these, Like rats, oft bite the holy cords a-twain ii 2 79

And put upon him such a deal of man, That worthied him . . ii 2 127

It was my hint to speak,—such was the process . . . *Othello* i 3 142

She wish'd That heaven had made her such a man . . . i 3 163

'Tis great pity that the noble Moor Should hazard such a place . ii 3 144

If you have any music that may not be heard, to't again . . . —We have none such . . . . iii 1 19

I gave her such a one; 'twas my first gift . . . . iii 3 436

What name, fair lady?—Such as she says my lord did say I was . iv 2 119

Why did he so?—I do not know; I am sure I am none such . . iv 2 123

There be some such, no question . . . . . . iv 3 63

Wouldst thou do such a deed for all the world? . . . iv 3 64; 68

I would not do such a thing for a joint-ring . . . . iv 3 72

Beshrew me, if I would do such a wrong For the whole world . . iv 3 78

What should such a fool Do with so good a woman? . . . v 2 233

Prove such a wife As my thoughts make thee . . *Ant. and Cleo.* iii 2 25

Approach, and speak.—Such as I am, I come from Antony . . iii 12 7

I must perforce Have shown to thee such a declining day, Or look on thine . . . . v 1 38

Think you there was, or might be, such a man? . . . . v 2 93

If there be, or ever were, one such, It's past the size of dreaming . v 2 96

Sluttery to such neat excellence opposed . . . *Cymbeline* i 6 44

To their approvers they are people such That mend upon the world . ii 4 25

Such a welcome as I'ld give to him After long absence . . . iii 6 73

Some villain mountaineers? I have heard of such . . . iv 2 72

I ha' strew'd his grave, And on it said a century of prayers, Such as I can iv 2 392

Or senseless speaking or a speaking such As sense cannot untie . v 4 148

These gentle princes—For such and so they are . . . v 5 337

If there be such a dart in princes' frowns . . . *Pericles* i 2 53

Even such our griefs are; Here they're but felt . . . . i 4 7

My ears were never better fed With such delightful pleasing harmony . ii 5 28

But such a night as this, Till now, I ne'er endured . . . iii 2 5

Did you ever dream of such a thing? . . . . . iv 5 5

She's such a one, that, were I well assured Came of a gentle kind and noble stock, I'ld wish no better choice . . . . . v 1 67

My dearest wife was like this maid, and such a one My daughter might have been . . . . v 1 108

Such and such. At such and such a sconce, at such a breach, at such a convoy . . . . *Hen. V.* iii 6 75

Such and such. Such and such pictures; there the window; such The adornment of her bed; the arras; figures, Why, such and such *Cymbeline* ii 2 25

Such another proof will make me cry 'baa' . . . *T. G. of Ver.* i 1 97

Treasure, Enough to purchase such another island . *2 Hen. VI.* iii 3 3

If heaven would make me such another world Of one entire and perfect chrysolite, I'ld not have sold her for it . . . *Othello* v 2 144

O, such another sleep, that I might see But such another man! *A. and C.* v 2 77

Such apology. There needs no such apology . *Richard III.* iii 7 104

Such business. You are like to do such business . *Coriolanus* iii 1 48

Such daughter. Let her be thine; for we Have no such daughter *Lear* i 1 266

Such deeds. Turk Gregory never did such deeds in arms . *1 Hen. IV.* v 3 46

Such despite. Thrown such despite and heavy terms upon her *Othello* iv 2 116

Such dignity. Things of such dignity As we greet modern friends withal *Ant. and Cleo.* v 2 166

Such entertainment. I will resist such entertainment . . *Tempest* i 2 465

Such extremes. Who can be patient in such extremes? . *3 Hen. VI.* i 1 215

Such faults. A friendly eye could never see such faults . *J. Cæsar* iv 3 90

Such forms which here were presupposed Upon thee in the letter *T. Night* v 1 358

Such furniture as suits The greatness of his person . *Hen. VIII.* ii 1 99

Such gifts that heaven shall share with you . . *Meas. for Meas.* ii 2 147

Such head. Given unto the house of York such head . *3 Hen. VI.* ii 1 233

Such honour. If it were not for one trifling respect, I could come to such honour! . . . . *Mer. Wives* ii 1 45

Such integrity. And frame some feeling line That may discover such integrity . . . . . . *T. G. of Ver.* iii 2 77

Your daughter, whom she bore in hand to love With such integrity *Cymbeline* v 5 44

Such intent. Though then, God knows, I had no such intent *2 Hen. IV.* iii 1 72

Such juggling and such knavery! . . . . *Troi. and Cres.* ii 3 77

Such leisure. Had you such leisure in the time of death? *Richard III.* i 4 34

Such like. And even with such-like valour men hang and drown Their proper selves . . . . *Tempest* iii 3 59

And I for such like petty crimes as these. . . *T. G. of Ver.* iv 1 52

Prating mountebanks, And many such-like liberties of sin *Com. of Errors* i 2 102

Such like toys as these Have moved his highness to commit me *Rich. III.* i 1 60

Gentleness, virtue, youth, liberality, and such like. . *Troi. and Cres.* i 2 277

As money, plate, jewels, and such-like trifles . . *T. of Athens* iii 2 23

And many such-like 'As'es of great charge . . . *Hamlet* v 2 43

Such matter. We'll wait upon you.—No such matter . . . ii 2 274

Such means As you yourself have forged . . . *1 Hen. IV.* v 1 67

Such men. He thinks too much: such men are dangerous . *J. Cæsar* i 2 195

Such men as he be never at heart's ease Whiles they behold a greater . i 2 208

Such offence. A young man More fit to do another such offence Than die for this . . . . . . *Meas. for Meas.* ii 3 14

Such patchery, such juggling, and such knavery! . *Troi. and Cres.* ii 3 77

Such pay. Shall receive such pay As thy desires can wish . *Pericles* v 1 74

Such people. O brave new world, That has such people in't! *Tempest* v 1 184

Such perfection. I would with such perfection govern, sir, To excel the golden age . . . . ii 1 167

Such pity. Pity me!—Such pity as my rapier's point affords . *3 Hen. VI.* i 3 37

Such power. His art is of such power, It would control my dam's god, Setebos . . . . *Tempest* i 2 372

Such provision. I have with such provision in mine art So safely ordered . . . . i 2 28

Such report. I made no such report . . . *Ant. and Cleo.* ii 5 57

Such resort. Do you know this house to be a place of such resort? *Per.* iv 6 86

Such sanctity. Relieved him with such sanctity of love. . *T. Night* iii 4 395

Such senses. And hath such senses As we have, such . . *Tempest* i 2 412

Such shes. For apes and monkeys 'Twixt two such shes would chatter this way and Contemn with mows the other . . . *Cymbeline* i 6 40

Such sights. You can behold such sights, And keep the natural ruby of your cheeks . . . . *Macbeth* iii 4 114

Such sin. This is his pardon, purchased by such sin For which the pardoner himself is in . . . . . *Meas. for Meas.* iv 2 111

Such strings. When such strings jar, what hope of harmony? *2 Hen. VI.* ii 1 57

Such terms. 'Tis not well That you and I should meet upon such terms As now we meet . . . . *1 Hen. IV.* v 1 10

Such thing. For I would commune with you of such things That want no ear but yours . . . . . *Meas. for Meas.* iv 3 108

Can such things be, And overcome us like a summer's cloud? *Macbeth* iii 4 110

Have you not read, Roderigo, Of some such thing? . . *Othello* i 1 175

Why, methinks, by him, This creature's no such thing . *Ant. and Cleo.* iii 3 44

Some such thing I said, and said no more but what my thoughts Did warrant me was likely . . . . . . *Pericles* v 1 133

Such thoughts. There was no need to trouble himself with any such thoughts yet . . . . *Hen. V.* ii 3 23

How I would think on him at certain hours Such thoughts and such *Cymbeline* i 3 28

Such time. And when such time they have begun to cry, Let them not cease . . . . *Coriolanus* iii 3 19

To confound such time, That drums him from his sport *Ant. and Cleo.* i 4 28

Such two that would by all likelihood have confounded one the other *Cymbeline* i 4 53

Such uses. Heaven me such uses send, Not to pick bad from bad, but by bad mend! . . . . *Othello* iv 3 105

Such viands. Let their beds Be made as soft as yours and let their palates Be season'd with such viands . . . *Mer. of Venice* iv 1 97

Such vigilance. They Will not, nor cannot, use such vigilance As when they are fresh . . . . *Tempest* iii 3 16

Such whales have I heard on o' the land . . . *Pericles* ii 1 36

Such woman. I do not think there is any such woman . . *Othello* iv 3 84

Such words that are but roted in Your tongue . *Coriolanus* iii 2 55

Such wrong. And make thee rich for doing me such wrong . *2 Hen. IV.* i 1 90

Do not yourself such wrong, who are in this Relieved *Ant. and Cleo.* v 2 40

Suck. All the infections that the sun sucks up From bogs, fens *Tempest* ii 2 1

Where the bee sucks, there suck I: In a cowslip's bell I lie . v 1 88

They'll suck our breath or pinch us black and blue . *Com. of Errors* ii 2 194

I can suck melancholy out of a song, as a weasel sucks eggs *As Y. Like It* ii 5 13

My pride is to see my ewes graze and my lambs suck . . . iii 2 81

Continue your resolve To suck the sweets of sweet philosophy *T. of Shrew* i 1 28

When my knightly stomach is sufficed, Why then I suck my teeth *K. John* i 1 192

Spiders, that suck up thy venom, And heavy-gaited toads *Richard II.* iii 2 14

The noisome weeds, which without profit suck The soil's fertility . iii 4 38

The weasel Scot Comes sneaking and so sucks her princely eggs *Hen. V.* i 2 171

Like horse-leeches, my boys, To suck, to suck, the very blood to suck! ii 3 59

Your fair show shall suck away their souls . . . . iv 2 17

As I suck blood, I will some mercy show . . . . iv 4 68

When at their mothers' moist eyes babes shall suck . *1 Hen. VI.* i 1 49

Drones suck not eagles' blood but rob bee-hives . *2 Hen. VI.* iv 1 109

Suck. Now stops thy spring: my sea shall suck them dry 3 *Hen. VI.* iv 8 55
There is no lady . . . More spongy to suck in the sense of fear *T. and C.* ii 2 12
Praise him that got thee, she that gave thee suck . . . ii 3 252
And feed on curds and whey, and suck the goat . . *T. Andron.* iv 2 178
Go, suck the subtle blood o' the grape . . *T. of Athens* iv 3 432
Is Brutus sick? and is it physical To walk unbraced and suck up the humours Of the dank morning? . . . . *J. Cæsar* ii 1 262
From you great Rome shall suck Reviving blood . . . ii 2 87
I have given suck, and know How tender 'tis to love the babe that milks me . . . . *Macbeth* i 7 54
See my baby at my breast, That sucks the nurse asleep? *Ant. and Cleo.* v 2 313
With sands that will not bear your enemies' boats, But suck them up to the topmast . . . . *Cymbeline* iii 1 22
Sucked. He was The ivy which had hid my princely trunk, And suck'd my verdure out on't . . . . *Tempest* i 2 87
As in revenge, have suck'd up from the sea Contagious fogs *M. N. Dream* ii 1 89
Food to the suck'd and hungry lioness . . . *As Y. Like It* iv 3 127
One that was a man When Hector's grandsire suck'd . *Troi. and Cres.* i 3 292
Were not I thine only nurse, I would say thou hadst suck'd wisdom from thy teat . . . . *Rom. and Jul.* i 3 68
Death, that hath suck'd the honey of thy breath . . . v 3 92
That suck'd the honey of his music vows . . . . *Hamlet* iii 1 164
He did comply with his dug, before he sucked it . . . . v 2 196
Suckedst. I would the milk Thy mother gave thee when thou suck'dst her breast Had been a little ratsbane! . . . . 1 *Hen. VI.* v 4 28
Thy valiantness was mine, thou suck'dst it from me . *Coriolanus* iii 2 129
The milk thou suck'dst from her did turn to marble . *T. Andron.* ii 3 144
Sucking. I will roar you as gently as any sucking dove . *M. N. Dream* i 2 85
Pluck the young sucking cubs from the she-bear . *Mer. of Venice* ii 1 29
His approaches makes as fierce As waters to the sucking of a gulf *Hen. V.* ii 4 10
Was in the mouth of every sucking babe . . . 1 *Hen. VI.* iii 1 197
As is the sucking lamb or harmless dove . . . 2 *Hen. VI.* iii 1 71
And from her womb children of divers kind We sucking on her natural bosom find . . . . *Rom. and Jul.* ii 3 12
Suckle. The breasts of Hecuba, When she did suckle Hector, look'd not lovelier . . . . *Coriolanus* i 3 44
To do what?—To suckle fools and chronicle small beer . *Othello* ii 1 161
Sudden. Then let us both be sudden . . . . . *Tempest* ii 1 306
Notwithstanding all her sudden quips . . . *T. G. of Ver.* iv 2 12
Upon a sudden, As Falstaff, she, and I, are newly met *Mer. Wives* iv 4 51
The guiltiness of my mind, the sudden surprise of my powers . . v 5 130
To-morrow! O, that's sudden! Spare him! . . . *Meas for Meas.* ii 2 83
But lest my liking might too sudden seem, I would have salved it with a longer treatise . . . . *Much Ado* i 1 316
Such eruptions and sudden breaking out of mirth . . *L. L. Lost* v 1 121
The sudden hand of death close up mine eye! . . . . v 2 825
Let us talk in good earnest: is it possible, on such a sudden, you should fall into so strong a liking? . . . . . *As Y. Like It* i 3 27
Jealous in honour, sudden and quick in quarrel . . . ii 7 151
The small acquaintance, my sudden wooing, nor her sudden consenting v 2 8
There was never any thing so sudden but the fight of two rams . v 2 33
Is it possible That love should of a sudden take such hold? *T. of Shrew* i 1 152
That maid Whose sudden sight hath thrall'd my wounded eye . . i 1 225
His approach, So out of circumstance and sudden . . . *W. Tale* v 1 90
I will be sudden and dispatch . . . . *K. John* iv 1 27
That you might The better arm you to the sudden time . . . v 6 26
Sudden storms are short; He tires betimes that spurs too fast betimes *Richard II.* ii 1 35
Join not with grief, fair woman, do not so, To make my end too sudden v 1 17
When men restrain their breath On some great sudden hest 1 *Hen. IV.* ii 3 65
For I am, on the sudden, something ill . . . 2 *Hen. IV.* iv 2 80
Since sudden sorrow Serves to say thus, 'some good thing comes to-morrow' . . . . iv 2 83
As sudden As flaws congealed in the spring of day . . . . iv 4 34
Never was such a sudden scholar made . . . . *Hen. V.* i 1 32
Some sudden mischief may arise of it . . . . . . iv 7 186
None durst come near for fear of sudden death . . 1 *Hen. VI.* i 4 48
Had your watch been good, This sudden mischief never could have fall'n . . . . ii 1 59
Roused on the sudden from their drowsy beds . . . . . ii 2 23
I with sudden and extemporal speech Purpose to answer . . iii 1 6
One sudden foil shall never breed distrust . . . . . iii 3 11
I'll direct thee how thou shalt escape By sudden flight . . iv 5 11
Somewhat too sudden, sirs, the warning is . . . . . v 2 14
I know it will excuse This sudden execution of my will . . . v 5 99
Some sudden qualm hath struck me at the heart . 2 *Hen. VI.* i 1 54
View his breathless corpse, And comment then upon his sudden death iii 2 133
Madam, what makes you in this sudden change? . . 3 *Hen. VI.* iv 4 1
He's sudden, if a thing comes in his head . . . . . . v 5 86
Be sudden in the execution, Withal obdurate . . . *Richard III.* i 3 346
This sudden stab of rancour I misdoubt . . . . . . iii 2 89
To-morrow, in mine opinion, is too sudden . . . . . iii 4 45
By sudden floods and fall of waters, Buckingham's army is dispersed . iv 4 512
Dashing the garment of this peace, aboded The sudden breach on't *Hen. VIII.* i 1 94
He bites his lip, and starts; Stops on a sudden, looks upon the ground iii 2 114
What should this mean? What sudden anger's this? how have I reap'd it? . . . . iii 2 204
That's somewhat sudden: But he's a learned man . . . . iii 2 394
Do you note How much her grace is alter'd on the sudden? . iv 2 96
Which reformation must be sudden . . . . v 3 20
You were ever good at sudden commendations . . . . . v 3 122
But sorrow, that is couch'd in seeming gladness, Is like that mirth fate turns to sudden sadness . . . . . . *Troi. and Cres.* i 1 40
Who, upon the sudden, Clapp'd to their gates . . . *Coriolanus* i 4 50
On the sudden, I warrant him consul . . . . . . ii 1 237
With a sudden re-inforcement struck Corioli like a planet . . ii 2 117
Revoke Your sudden approbation . . . . ii 3 259
If thou be pleased with this my sudden choice, Behold, I choose thee *T. Andron.* i 1 318
The subtle Queen of Goths Is of a sudden thus advanced in Rome . i 1 393
Too rash, too unadvised, too sudden; Too like the lightning *R. and J.* ii 2 118
Where on a sudden one hath wounded me That's by me wounded . ii 3 50
I stand on sudden haste.—Wisely and slow; they stumble that run fast ii 3 93
Hadst thou no poison mix'd, no sharp-ground knife, No sudden mean of death? . . . . iii 3 45
A sudden day of joy, That thou expect st not nor I look'd not for . iii 5 110
Without a sudden calm, will overset Thy tempest-tossed body . . iii 5 137
You have your hands full all, In this so sudden business . . iv 3 12
Casca, be sudden, for we fear prevention . . . . . *J. Cæsar* iii 1 19
Sudden. Let me not stir you up To such a sudden flood of mutiny *J. C.* iii 2 215
Sudden push gives them the overthrow . . . . v 2 5
Sudden, malicious, smacking of every sin That has a name . *Macbeth* iv 3 59
With a sudden vigour it doth posset And curd . . . . *Hamlet* i 5 68
This sudden sending him away must seem Deliberate pause . . iv 3 8
Recount the occasion of my sudden and more strange return . . iv 7 47
He could nothing do but wish and beg Your sudden coming o'er . iv 7 106
Put to sudden death, Not shriving-time allow'd . . . . . v 2 46
They for sudden joy did weep, And I for sorrow sung . . . *Lear* i 4 191
He is rash and very sudden in choler . . . . . *Othello* ii 1 279
Returned me expectations and comforts of sudden respect and acquaintance . . . . iv 2 192
On the sudden A Roman thought hath struck him . . *Ant. and Cleo.* i 2 86
Report that I am sudden sick: quick, and return . . . . i 3 5
Tremblingly she stood And on the sudden dropp'd . . . . v 2 347
Sudden-bold. But pardon me, I am too sudden-bold . . *L. L. Lost* ii 1 107
Suddenly. Muse not that I thus suddenly proceed . . *T. G. of Ver.* i 3 64
When I suddenly call you, come forth . . . . *Mer. Wives* iii 3 11
Mistress Ford desires you to come suddenly.—I'll be with her by and by iv 1 6
And upon the grief of this suddenly died . . . . *Much Ado* iv 2 66
Suddenly resolve me in my suit.—Madam, I will, if suddenly I may *L. L. Lost* ii 1 110
Yet do not suddenly, for it may grieve him . . *Mer. of Venice* ii 8 34
Three of your argosies Are richly come to harbour suddenly . . v 1 277
His malice 'gainst the lady Will suddenly break forth . *As Y. Like It* i 2 295
Do this suddenly, And let not search and inquisition quail . . ii 2 19
Buy it with your gold right suddenly . . . . . . ii 4 100
Suddenly, Seeing Orlando, it unlink'd itself . . . . . iv 3 111
Was ever match clapp'd up so suddenly? . . . *T. of Shrew* ii 1 327
I, with a troop of Florentines, will suddenly surprise him *All's Well* iii 6 24
The great Apollo suddenly will have The truth of this appear *W. Tale* ii 3 200
A resolved villain, Whose bowels suddenly burst out . . *K. John* v 6 30
Grievous sick, my lord, Suddenly taken . . . . *Richard II.* i 4 55
When time is ripe, which will be suddenly . . . 1 *Hen. IV.* i 3 294
I'll repent, and that suddenly, while I am in some liking . . iii 3 5
Our scions, put in wild and savage stock, Spirt up so suddenly *Hen. V.* iii 5 8
We will suddenly Pass our accept and peremptory answer . . . v 2 81
What chance is this that suddenly hath cross'd us? . . 1 *Hen. VI.* i 4 72
Do it without invention, suddenly . . . . iii 1 5
Nature makes me suddenly relent . . . . iii 3 59
Great rage of heart Suddenly made him from my side to start . iv 7 12
May ye both be suddenly surprised! . . . . v 3 40
Had not your man put up the fowl so suddenly, We had had more sport 2 *Hen. VI.* ii 1 45
Sight may distinguish of colours, but suddenly to nominate them all, it is impossible . . . . ii 1 129
That's not suddenly to be perform'd, But with advice . . . ii 2 67
Suddenly a grievous sickness took him, That makes him gasp . iii 2 370
Speak suddenly, my lords, are we all friends? . . . 3 *Hen. VI.* iv 2 4
I would have it suddenly perform'd. What sayest thou? speak suddenly *Richard III.* iv 2 19
Fiends roar, saints pray, To have him suddenly convey'd away . . iv 4 76
How to make ye suddenly an answer, In such a point of weight *Hen. VIII.* iii 1 70
He fell sick suddenly, and grew so ill He could not sit his mule . iv 2 15
I defied 'em still: when suddenly a file of boys behind 'em, loose shot, delivered such a shower of pebbles . . . . v 4 58
I'll lay ye all By the heels, and suddenly . . . . . v 4 83
And suddenly; where injury of chance Puts back leave-taking *T. and C.* iv 4 35
I myself Am like a prophet suddenly enrapt . . . . . v 3 65
Hearing it Should straight fall mad, or else die suddenly *T. Andron.* ii 3 104
Suddenly I heard a child cry underneath a wall . . . . v 1 23
I rush'd upon him, Surprised him suddenly . . . . . v 1 38
Suddenly arose, and walk'd about, Musing and sighing . *J. Cæsar* ii 1 239
Suddenly contrive the means of meeting between him and my daughter *Hamlet* ii 2 215
Gasted by the noise I made, Full suddenly he fled . . *Lear* ii 1 58
Why the King of France is so suddenly gone back know you the reason? iv 3 1
It came in too suddenly; let it die as it was born . . *Cymbeline* i 4 131
Hie thee, whiles I say A priestly farewell to her: suddenly, woman *Per.* iii 1 70
Come, let's have her aboard suddenly . . . . . . iv 1 96
Sue. My master sues to her, and she hath taught her suitor *T. G. of Ver.* ii 1 143
I desire more acquaintance of you.—Good Sir John, I sue for yours *M. W.* ii 2 170
When maidens sue, Men give like gods . . . *Meas. for Meas.* i 4 80
Lay by all nicety and prolixious blushes, That banish what they sue for ii 4 163
To sue to live, I find I seek to die; And, seeking death, find life . iii 1 42
I am so out of love with life that I will sue to be rid of it . . iii 1 174
My soul should sue as advocate for thee . . . *Com. of Errors* i 1 146
What, I! I love! I sue! I seek a wife! . . . . *L. L. Lost* iii 1 191
Well, I will love, write, sigh, pray, sue, and groan . . . iii 1 206
How can this be true, That you stand forfeit, being those that sue? . v 2 427
We were not born to sue, but to command . . . . *Richard II.* i 1 196
Call in the letters patents that he hath By his attorneys-general to sue His livery . . . . ii 1 203
I am denied to sue my livery here . . . . ii 3 129
Stand up.—I do not sue to stand . . . . v 3 129
To sue his livery and beg his peace, With tears of innocency 1 *Hen. IV.* iv 3 62
They humbly sue unto your excellence To have a godly peace 1 *Hen. VI.* v 1 4
Begin your suits anew, and sue to him . . . . 2 *Hen. VI.* i 3 42
What love, think'st thou, I sue so much to get? . . 3 *Hen. VI.* iii 2 61
My proud heart sues and prompts my tongue to speak . *Richard III.* i 2 171
Who sues to thee and cries 'God save the queen'? . . . . iv 4 94
For one being sued to, one that humbly sues . . . . . iv 4 101
For further life in this world I ne'er hope, Nor will I sue . *Hen. VIII.* ii 1 70
Men prize the thing ungain'd more than it is: That she was never yet that ever knew Love got so sweet as when desire did sue *Tr. and Cr.* i 2 317
To sue, and be denied such common grace . . . *T. of Athens* iii 5 95
I must love you, and sue to know you better . . . . *Lear* i 1 30
Sue to him again, and he's yours.—I will rather sue to be despised *Othello* ii 3 276
Or sue to you to do a peculiar profit To your own person . . . iii 3 79
Whiles we are suitors to their throne, decays The thing we sue for *Ant. and Cleo.* ii 1 5
Sues To let him breathe between the heavens and earth, A private man iii 12 13
This if she perform, She shall not sue unheard . . . . . iii 12 24
Sued. I never sued to friend nor enemy . . . . *Richard III.* i 2 168
Who sued to me for him? who, in my rage, Kneel'd at my feet? . . ii 1 106
For one being sued to, one that humbly sues . . . . . iv 4 101
That therefore such a writ be sued against you . . *Hen. VIII.* iii 2 341
To whom I sued for my dear son's life . . . . *T. Andron.* i 1 453
When you sued staying, Then was the time for words . *Ant. and Cleo.* i 3 33

Sued-for. Bestow Your sued-for tongues . . . . . *Coriolanus* ii 3 216
Suerly. That sall I suerly do, that is the breff and the long *Hen. V.* iii 2 126
Sueth. 'Tis the French Dauphin sueth to thee thus . 1 *Hen. VI.* i 2 112
Suffer. O, I have suffer'd With those that I saw suffer . *Tempest* i 2 6
Nothing of him that doth fade But doth suffer a sea-change . i 2 400
Than to suffer The flesh-fly blow my mouth . . . iii 1 62
The poor monster's my subject and he shall not suffer indignity . iii 2 42
Why, what of him?—He wonder'd that your lordship Would suffer him
to spend his youth at home . . . . . . *T. G. of Ver.* i 3 5
I do as truly suffer As e'er I did commit . . . . v 4 76
'Tis my fault, Master Page : I suffer for it.—You suffer for a pad conscience
Mer. Wives iii 3 233
So you must be the first that gives this sentence, And he, that suffers.
O, it is excellent To have a giant's strength . *Meas. for Meas.* ii 2 107
Either You must lay down the treasures of your body To this supposed,
or else to let him suffer . . . . ii 4 97
An ass.—Marry, so it doth appear By the wrongs I suffer *Com. of Errors* iii 1 16
I am thy prisoner : wilt thou suffer them To make a rescue? . . iv 4 113
The abbess shuts the gates on us And will not suffer us to fetch him out v 1 157
It were pity but they should suffer salvation, body and soul *Much Ado* iii 3 3
Make those that do offend you suffer too . . . . . v 1 40
For which of my good parts did you first suffer love for me?—Suffer
love ! a good epithet ! I do suffer love indeed . . . . v 2 65
I suffer for the truth . . . . *L. L. Lost* i 1 313
You must suffer him to take no delight nor no penance . . . i 2 133
Why will you suffer her to flout me thus? . . . *M. N. Dream* iii 2 327
Am arm'd To suffer, with a quietness of spirit . . *Mer. of Venice* iv 1 12
What, will you not suffer me? . . . . . . *T. of Shrew* ii 1 31
Dian no queen of virgins, that would suffer her poor knight surprised
All's Well i 3 119
You'll run again, rather than suffer question for your residence . ii 5 42
You, Diana, Under my poor instructions yet must suffer Something . iv 4 27
I am yours Upon your will to suffer . . . . . . iv 4 30
Whose age and honour Both suffer under this complaint. . . v 3 163
The palate, That suffer surfeit, cloyment, and revolt . *T. Night* ii 4 102
That suffers under probation . . . . ii 5 142
In the which three great ones suffer . . . . . *W. Tale* ii 1 128
If your more ponderous and settled project May suffer alteration . iv 4 536
Not he alone shall suffer what wit can make heavy and vengeance bitter iv 4 800
If I had a mind to be honest, I see Fortune would not suffer me . iv 4 863
Go we, as well as haste will suffer us . . . . *K. John* iv 1 559
How long Shall tender duty make me suffer wrong? . . *Richard II.* ii 1 164
We see the very wreck that we must suffer . . . . . ii 1 267
Detraction will not suffer it . . . . . . 1 *Hen. IV.* v 1 142
What wrongs our arms may do, what wrongs we suffer . 2 *Hen. IV.* iv 1 68
And suffer the condition of these times . . . . . iv 1 101
Heavens, can you suffer hell so to prevail? . . . 1 *Hen. VI.* i 5 9
Ere that we will suffer such a prince . . . To be disgraced . . iii 1 97
And suffer you to breathe in fruitful peace . . . . . v 4 127
Either to suffer shipwreck or arrive Where I may have fruition of her
love . . . . v 5 8
Suffer them now, and they'll o'ergrow the garden . . 2 *Hen. VI.* iii 1 32
Shall we suffer this? let's pluck him down . . . . 3 *Hen. VI.* i 1 59
O God, that seest it, do not suffer it! . . . . *Richard III.* i 3 271
By your patience, I may not suffer you to visit them . . . iv 1 16
You suffer Too hard an exclamation . . . . . *Hen. VIII.* i 2 51
As not thus to suffer A man of his place . . . To dance attendance . v 2 29
If we suffer, Out of our easiness and childish pity To one man's honour v 3 24
Do you think, my lords, The king will suffer but the little finger Of this
man to be vex'd? . . . . v 3 106
Never suffers matter of the world Enter his thoughts . *Troi. and Cres.* ii 3 196
You'll ne'er be good, Nor suffer others . . . . . iv 2 31
Suffer us to famish, and their store-houses crammed with grain *Coriolanus* i 1 82
Suffer't, and live with such as cannot rule Nor ever will be ruled . iii 1 40
To us all, that do't and suffer it, A brand to the end o' the world . iii 1 303
And are content To suffer lawful censure for such faults . . . iii 3 46
Who rather had, Though they themselves did suffer by't, behold Dis-
sentious numbers pestering streets . . . . . . iv 6 6
With all the size that verity Would without lapsing suffer . . v 2 19
Suffer thy brother Marcus to inter His noble nephew . . *T. Andron.* i 1 375
She shall file our engines with advice, That will not suffer you to square ii 1 124
The eagle suffers little birds to sing, And is not careful what they mean iv 4 83
And thou must stand by too, and suffer every knave to use me? *R. and J.* ii 4 163
He's truly valiant that can wisely suffer The worst that man can breathe,
and make his wrongs His outsides . . . *T. of Athens* iii 5 31
The state of man, Like to a little kingdom, suffers then The nature of
an insurrection . . . . *J. Cæsar* ii 1 68
When we have our naked frailties hid, That suffer in exposure *Macbeth* ii 3 133
Let the frame of things disjoint, both the worlds suffer, Ere we will eat
our meal in fear . . . . iii 2 16
My poor country Shall have more vices than it had before, More suffer iv 3 48
If't be the affliction of his love or no That thus he suffers for. *Hamlet* iii 1 37
Whether 'tis nobler in the mind to suffer The slings and arrows of out-
rageous fortune, Or to take arms against a sea of troubles . . iii 1 57
For thou hast been As one, in suffering all, that suffers nothing . . iii 2 71
Or else shall he suffer not thinking on, with the hobby-horse. . . iii 2 142
Why does he suffer this rude knave now to knock him about the sconce? v 1 109
His definement suffers no perdition in you . . . . . v 2 117
Found this trespass worth The shame which here it suffers . *Lear* ii 4 45
Nature, being oppress'd, commands the mind To suffer with the body . ii 4 110
My duty cannot suffer To obey in all your daughters' hard commands . iii 4 153
Who alone suffers suffers most i' the mind . . . . . iii 6 111
Could my good brother suffer you to do it? . . . . . iv 2 44
That he hath left part of his grief with me, To suffer with him *Othello* iii 3 54
Thou hast no weapon, and perforce must suffer . . . . v 2 256
If they suffer our departure, death's the word . . *Ant. and Cleo.* i 2 139
With patience more Than savages could suffer . . . . . i 4 61
I must thank him only, Lest my remembrance suffer ill report . ii 2 159
Things outward Do draw the inward quality after them, To suffer all
alike . . . . iii 13 34
He would not suffer me To bring him to the haven . . *Cymbeline* i 1 170
A contention in public, which may, without contradiction, suffer the
report . . . . i 4 59
Why did you suffer Iachimo, Slight thing of Italy, To taint his nobler
heart and brain With needless jealousy? . . . . . v 4 63
Sufficeth A Roman with a Roman's heart can suffer . . . . v 5 81
See how belief may suffer by foul show! . . . . *Pericles* iv 4 23
Sufferance. Your sorrow hath eaten up my sufferance *Mer. Wives* iv 2 2
Shall his death draw out To lingering sufferance . . *Meas. for Meas.* ii 4 167
In corporal sufferance finds a pang as great As when a gaint dies . iii 1 80
Sufferance. If not a present remedy, at least a patient sufferance *M. Ado* i 3 10
Writ the style of gods And made a push at chance and sufferance . v 1 38
Sufferance is the badge of all our tribe . . . *Mer. of Venice* i 3 111
What should his sufferance be by Christian example? Why, revenge . iii 1 73
Some villains of my court Are of consent and sufferance in this *As Y. L. It* ii 2 3
The seeming sufferances that you had borne . . . 1 *Hen. IV.* v 1 51
Well, of sufferance comes ease . . . . . . 2 *Hen. IV.* v 4 28
Lest example Breed, by his sufferance, more of such a kind . *Hen. V.* ii 2 46
I in sufferance heartily will rejoice, Beseeching God and you to pardon me ii 2 159
England shall repent his folly, see his weakness, and admire our suffer-
ance . . . . iii 6 132
Thou shalt reign but by their sufferance . . . . . 3 *Hen. VI.* i 1 234
'Tis a sufferance panging As soul and body's severing . *Hen. VIII.* ii 3 15
Her sufferance made Almost each pang a death . . . . . v 1 68
Patience herself, what goddess e'er she be, Doth lesser blench at suffer-
ance than I do . . . . *Troi. and Cres.* i 1 28
Your last service was sufferance, 'twas not voluntary . . . ii 1 104
Our sufferance is a gain to them . . . . . *Coriolanus* i 1 22
They do prank them in authority, Against all noble sufferance . iii 1 24
Thy nature did commence in sufferance, time Hath made thee hard in't.
Why shouldst thou hate men? . . . . . . *T. of Athens* iv 3 268
Have wander'd with our traversed arms and breathed Our sufferance
vainly . . . . v 4 8
Our yoke and sufferance show us womanish . . . *J. Cæsar* i 3 84
The sufferance of our souls, the time's abuse,—If these be motives weak ii 1 115
The mind much sufferance doth o'erskip, When grief hath mates *Lear* iii 6 113
A noble ship of Venice Hath seen a grievous wreck and sufferance *Othello* ii 1 23
Call her before us ; for We have been too slight in sufferance *Cymbeline* iii 5 35
Suffered. O, I have suffer'd With those that I saw suffer . . *Tempest* i 2 5
Who, with a charm join'd to their suffer'd labour, I have left asleep . i 2 231
An islander, that hath lately suffered by a thunderbolt . . . ii 2 38
Sure as I live, he had suffered for't . . . . *T. G. of Ver.* iv 4 17
I have stood on the pillory for geese he hath killed, otherwise he had
suffered for't . . . . iv 4 36
You shall hear, Master Brook, what I have suffered . *Mer. Wives* iii 5 97
I suffered the pangs of three several deaths . . . . . iii 5 109
I am sorry that for my sake you have suffered all this . . . iii 5 126
I have suffered more for their sakes . . . . . . iv 5 110
And have not they suffered? Yes, I warrant ; speciously one of them . iv 5 113
Over and above that you have suffered . . . . . . v 5 177
That by this sympathized one day's error Have suffer'd wrong *C. of Er.* v 1 398
I did deny him And suffer'd him to go displeased away *Mer. of Venice* v 1 213
Why have you suffer'd me to be imprison'd? . . . . *T. Night* v 1 349
I do believe Hermione hath suffer'd death . . . . *W. Tale* iii 3 42
He that hath suffer'd this disorder'd spring Hath now himself met with
the fall of leaf . . . . *Richard II.* iii 4 48
Suffer'd his kinsman March, Who is, if every owner were well placed,
Indeed his king, to be engaged in Wales . . . 1 *Hen. IV.* iv 3 93
So did your son ; He was so suffer'd : so came I a widow . 2 *Hen. IV.* ii 3 57
And what your highness suffered under that shape . . . *Hen. V.* iv 8 56
Lest, being suffer'd in that harmful slumber, The mortal worm might
make the sleep eternal . . . . 2 *Hen. VI.* iii 2 262
Who, being suffer'd with the bear's fell paw, Hath clapp'd his tail be-
tween his legs and cried . . . . v 1 153
A little fire is quickly trodden out ; Which, being suffer'd, rivers cannot
quench . . . . 3 *Hen. VI.* iv 8 8
I think your grace, Out of the pain you suffer'd, gave no ear to't
Hen. VIII. iv 2 8
As for her Greeks and Trojans suffer'd death . . *Troi. and Cres.* iv 1 74
I am half through ; The one part suffer'd, the other will I do *Coriolanus* ii 3 131
Suffer'd me by the voice of slaves to be Whoop'd out of Rome . . iv 5 83
Your jewel Hath suffer'd under praise . . . *T. of Athens* i 1 165
Nor his offences enforced, for which he suffered death . . *J. Cæsar* iii 2 44
Truly in my youth I suffered much extremity for love . . *Hamlet* ii 2 191
Who sways, not as it hath power, but as it is suffered . . . *Lear* i 2 54
Some distressful stroke That my youth suffer'd . . . . *Othello* i 3 158
I will indeed no longer endure it, nor am I yet persuaded to put up in
peace what already I have foolishly suffered . . . . . iv 2 182
Make as much of me As when mine empire was your fellow too, And
suffer'd my command . . . . *Ant. and Cleo.* iv 2 23
That I suffer'd Was all the harm I did . . . . . *Cymbeline* v 5 335
Provided That none but I and my companion maid Be suffer'd to come
near him . . . . *Pericles* v 1 79
Thou art a man, and I Have suffer'd like a girl . . . . v 1 138
Sufferest. What kind of god art thou, that suffer'st more Of mortal griefs
than do thy worshippers? . . . . *Hen. V.* iv 1 258
Unkind and careless of thine own, Why suffer'st thou thy sons, unburied
yet, To hover on the dreadful shore of Styx? . . *T. Andron.* i 1 87
Suffering. If I did love you in my master's flame, With such a suffering,
such a deadly life . . . . *T. Night* i 5 284
In suffering thus thy brother to be slaughter'd, Thou showest the naked
pathway to thy life . . . . *Richard II.* i 2 30
Unavoided is the danger now, For suffering so the causes of our wreck ii 1 269
For suffering flesh to be eaten in thy house, contrary to the law 2 *Hen. IV.* ii 4 372
For your wants, Your suffering in this dearth, you may as well Strike
at the heaven with your staves . . . . . *Coriolanus* i 1 69
My valour's poison'd With only suffering stain by him . . . i 10 18
Some death more long in spectatorship, and crueller in suffering . . v 2 72
The felon . . . wiser than the judge, If wisdom be in suffering *T. of A.* iii 5 51
Old feeble carrions and such suffering souls That welcome wrongs *J. C.* ii 1 130
That a swift blessing May soon return to this our suffering country *Macb.* iii 6 48
For thou hast been As one, in suffering all, that suffers nothing *Hamlet* iii 2 71
Who hast not in thy brows an eye discerning Thine honour from thy
suffering . . . . *Lear* iv 2 53
Either he so undertaking, Or they so suffering . . . *Cymbeline* iv 2 143
Suffice. Let it suffice thee, Mistress Page,—at the least, if the love of
soldier can suffice,—that I love thee . . . . *Mer. Wives* ii 1 10
You shall have a sight of them.—It shall suffice me . *L. L. Lost* ii 1 167
If knowledge be the mark, to know thee shall suffice . . . iv 2 115
If that will not suffice, I will be bound to pay it ten times o'er *M. of Ven.* iv 1 210
If this will not suffice, it must appear That malice bears down truth . iv 1 213
Let it suffice thee that I trust thee not . . . *As Y. Like It* i 3 57
'Twixt such friends as we Few words suffice . . . . *T. of Shrew* i 2 66
Let's return again, and suffice ourselves with the report of it *All's Well* iii 5 10
The entreaties of your mistress ! satisfy ! Let that suffice . *W. Tale* i 2 235
Let that suffice, most forcible Feeble.—It shall suffice, sir 2 *Hen. IV.* iii 2 178
To prove him tyrant this reason may suffice . . . 3 *Hen. VI.* iii 3 71
Patroclus is a fool positive.—Why am I a fool?—Make that demand of
the prover. It suffices me thou art . . . . . *Troi. and Cres.* ii 3 73
And more I will Than for myself I dare : let that suffice you *Othello* iii 4 131

Suffice. Let it suffice the greatness of your powers To have bereft a prince of all his fortunes *Pericles* ii 1 8
My veins are chill, And have no more of life than may suffice To give my tongue that heat to ask your help ii 1 78
Sufficed. Till he be first sufficed, Oppress'd with two weak evils, age and hunger, I will not touch a bit *As Y. Like It* ii 7 131
When my knightly stomach is sufficed, Why then I suck my teeth *K. John* i 1 191
Sufficeth, my reasons are both good and weighty *T. of Shrew* i 1 252
Sufficeth, I am come to keep my word iii 2 108
Sufficeth that I have maintains my state *2 Hen. VI.* iv 10 24
Sufficeth not that we are brought to Rome, To beautify thy triumphs? *T. Andron.* i 1 109
To do I know not what: but it sufficeth That Brutus leads me on *J. C.* ii 1 333
But it sufficeth that the day will end, And then the end is known v 1 125
Sufficeth A Roman with a Roman's heart can suffer *Cymbeline* v 5 80
Sufficiency. No more remains, But that to your sufficiency *Meas. for Meas.* i 1 8
But no man's virtue nor sufficiency To be so moral *Much Ado* v 1 29
Whom you know Of stuff'd sufficiency *W. Tale* ii 1 185
We have there a substitute of most allowed sufficiency *Othello* i 3 224
Sufficient. If hearty sorrow Be a sufficient ransom for offence, I tender't here *T. G. of Ver.* v 4 75
Are there not men in your ward sufficient to serve it? *Meas. for Meas.* ii 1 281
Bring me in the names of some six or seven, the most sufficient ii 1 287
My meaning in saying he is a good man is to have you understand me that he is sufficient *Mer. of Venice* i 3 17
The man is, notwithstanding, sufficient i 3 27
Pass my daughter a sufficient dower, The match is made *T. of Shrew* iv 4 45
Take the priest, clerk, and some sufficient honest witnesses iv 4 95
Have you provided me here half a dozen sufficient men? *2 Hen. IV.* iii 2 102
A wall sufficient to defend Our inland from the pilfering borderers *Hen. V.* i 2 141
The concavities of it is not sufficient iii 2 64
Your roof were not sufficient to contain't *1 Hen. VI.* ii 3 56
Had I sufficient skill to utter them, Would make a volume v 5 13
For your expenses and sufficient charge, Among the people gather up a tenth v 5 92
Their lives and thine Were not revenge sufficient for me *3 Hen. VI.* i 3 26
A sufficient briber for his life *T. of Athens* iii 5 61
You'll never meet a more sufficient man *Othello* iii 4 91
Whom our full senate Call all in all sufficient iv 1 276
If I bring you no sufficient testimony *Cymbeline* i 4 161
Sufficiently. Which none without thee can sufficiently manage *W. Tale* iv 2 16
But we will be revenged sufficiently *1 Hen. VI.* i 4 58
His seal'd commission, left in trust with me, Doth speak sufficiently he's gone to travel *Pericles* i 3 14
Sufficing. Give me Sufficing strokes for death *Ant. and Cleo.* iv 14 117
Sufficit. Satis quod sufficit *L. L. Lost* v 1 1
Suffigance. It shall be suffigance *Much Ado* iii 5 56
Suffocate. Let man go free And let not hemp his wind-pipe suffocate *Hen. V.* iii 6 45
May he be suffocate, That dims the honour of this warlike isle! *2 Hen. VI.* i 1 124
This chaos, when degree is suffocate, Follows the choking *Troi. and Cres.* i 3 125
Suffocating. If there be cords, or knives, Poison, or fire, or suffocating streams, I'll not endure it *Othello* iii 3 389
Suffocation. It was a miracle to 'scape suffocation *Mer. Wives* iii 5 119
Suffolk. Yoke-fellow to his honour-owing wounds, The noble Earl of Suffolk also lies. Suffolk first died *Hen. V.* iv 6 10
Tarry, dear cousin Suffolk! My soul shall thine keep company to heaven iv 6 15
Over Suffolk's neck He threw his wounded arm and kiss'd his lips iv 6 24
The Earl of Suffolk, Sir Richard Ketly, Davy Gam, esquire iv 8 108
An earl I am, and Suffolk am I call'd *1 Hen. VI.* v 3 53
Go and be free again as Suffolk's friend v 3 59
Say, Earl of Suffolk—if thy name be so—What ransom must I pay? v 3 72
Speaks Suffolk as he thinks?—Fair Margaret knows That Suffolk doth not flatter, face, or feign v 3 141
Good wishes, praise, and prayers Shall Suffolk ever have of Margaret v 3 174
O, wert thou for myself! But, Suffolk, stay v 3 187
Whether it be through force of your report, My noble Lord of Suffolk v 5 80
Thus Suffolk hath prevail'd; and thus he goes, As did the youthful Paris once to Greece v 5 103
Suffolk, arise. Welcome, Queen Margaret *2 Hen. VI.* i 1 17
Marquess of Suffolk, ambassador for Henry King of England i 1 45
We here create thee the first duke of Suffolk i 1 64
Suffolk, the new-made duke that rules the roast i 1 109
For Suffolk's duke, may he be suffocate! i 1 124
A proper jest, and never heard before, That Suffolk should demand a whole fifteenth For costs and charges! i 1 133
With the Duke of Suffolk, We'll quickly hoise Duke Humphrey i 1 168
In what we can, to bridle and suppress The pride of Suffolk i 1 201
Suffolk concluded on the articles, The peers agreed i 1 217
From the rich cardinal And from the great and new-made Duke of Suffolk i 2 95
Yet am I Suffolk and the cardinal's broker i 2 101
This is the Duke of Suffolk, and not my lord protector i 3 10
Against the Duke of Suffolk, for enclosing the commons of Melford i 3 24
Away, base cullions! Suffolk, let them go i 3 43
Suffolk, say, is this the guise, Is this the fashion in the court of England? i 3 45
Till Suffolk gave two dukedoms for his daughter i 3 90
I'll tell thee, Suffolk, why I am unmeet: First, for I cannot flatter thee i 3 168
What mean'st thou, Suffolk? tell me, what are these? i 3 183
What fates await the Duke of Suffolk? i 4 35; 67
Why, Suffolk, England knows thine insolence.—And thy ambition ii 1 31
Wink at the Duke of Suffolk's insolence ii 2 70
For Suffolk, he that can do all in all With her that hateth thee ii 4 51
Suffolk, Buckingham, and York, Reprove my allegation, if you can iii 1 39
Suffolk, thou shalt not see me blush, Nor change my countenance iii 1 98
Beaufort's red sparkling eyes blab his heart's malice, And Suffolk's cloudy brow his stormy hate iii 1 155
My lord cardinal, and you, my Lord of Suffolk, Say as you think iii 1 246
Thrice-noble Suffolk, 'tis resolutely spoke iii 1 266
The day is almost spent: Lord Suffolk, you and I must talk of that event iii 1 326
Suffolk, within fourteen days At Bristol I expect my soldiers iii 1 327
Run to my Lord of Suffolk; let him know We have dispatch'd the duke iii 2 1
Where is our uncle? what's the matter, Suffolk?—Dead in his bed iii 2 28
What, doth my Lord of Suffolk comfort me? iii 2 39
Why do you rate my Lord of Suffolk thus? iii 2 56
How often have I tempted Suffolk's tongue! iii 2 114
Good Duke Humphrey traitorously is murder'd By Suffolk iii 2 124
Suffolk. Are you the butcher, Suffolk? Where's your knife? *2 Hen. VI.* iii 2 195
What dares not Warwick, if false Suffolk dare him? iii 2 203
Though Suffolk dare him twenty thousand times iii 2 206
Unless Lord Suffolk straight be done to death, Or banished iii 2 244
They will guard you ... From such fell serpents as false Suffolk is iii 2 266
My thoughts do hourly prophesy Mischance unto my state by Suffolk's means iii 2 284
Let me plead for gentle Suffolk!—Ungentle queen, to call him gentle Suffolk! iii 2 289
Let thy Suffolk take his heavy leave iii 2 306
Enough, sweet Suffolk; thou torment'st thyself iii 2 329
Thus is poor Suffolk ten times banished iii 2 357
A wilderness is populous enough, So Suffolk had thy heavenly company iii 2 361
Suffolk's exile, my soul's treasure? Why only, Suffolk, mourn I not for thee? iii 2 382
To France, sweet Suffolk: let me hear from thee iii 2 405
Thy prisoner is a prince, The Duke of Suffolk, William de la Pole.—The Duke of Suffolk muffled up in rags! iv 1 45
Come, Suffolk, I must waft thee to thy death iv 1 116
Suffolk's imperial tongue is stern and rough, Used to command iv 1 121
And Suffolk dies by pirates iv 1 138
Still lamenting and mourning for Suffolk's death? iv 4 22
Ah, were the Duke of Suffolk now alive, These Kentish rebels would be soon appeased! iv 4 41
My hope is gone, now Suffolk is deceased iv 4 56
'Tis not thy southern power, Of Essex, Norfolk, Suffolk *3 Hen. VI.* i 1 156
Thou, son Clarence, Shalt stir up in Suffolk, Norfolk, and in Kent iv 8 12
The Duke of Suffolk is the first, and claims To be high-steward *Hen. VIII.* iv 1 17
Left him at primero With the Duke of Suffolk v 1 8
Suffrage. I cannot Put on the gown, stand naked, and entreat them, For my wounds' sake, to give their suffrage *Coriolanus* ii 2 142
People of Rome, ... I ask your voices and your suffrages *T. Andron.* i 1 218
I threw the people's suffrages On him that thus doth tyrannize o'er me iv 3 19
For honour's cause, forbear your suffrages *Pericles* ii 4 41
Sugar. In such wine and sugar of the best and the fairest *Mer. Wives* ii 2 70
One sweet word with thee.—Honey, and milk, and sugar *L. L. Lost* v 2 231
Here are sever'd lips, Parted with sugar breath *Mer. of Venice* iii 2 119
Honesty coupled to beauty is to have honey a sauce to sugar *As Y. L. It* iii 3 31
Three pound of sugar, five pound of currants *W. Tale* iv 3 40
Your fair discourse hath been as sugar, Making the hard way sweet and delectable *Richard II.* ii 3 6
What says Sir John Sack and Sugar? *1 Hen. IV.* i 2 126
I give thee this pennyworth of sugar ii 4 25
The sugar thou gavest me, 'twas a pennyworth, wast't not? ii 4 65
If sack and sugar be a fault, God help the wicked! ii 4 517
You have witchcraft in your lips, Kate: there is more eloquence in a sugar touch of them *Hen. V.* v 2 303
Why strew'st thou sugar on that bottled spider? *Richard III.* i 3 242
With devotion's visage And pious action we do sugar o'er The devil *Ham.* iii 1 48
These sentences, to sugar, or to gall, Being strong on both sides, are equivocal: But words are words *Othello* i 3 216
Sugar-candy. One poor penny-worth of sugar-candy to make thee long-winded *1 Hen. IV.* iii 3 180
Sugared. By fair persuasions mix'd with sugar'd words *1 Hen. VI.* iii 3 18
Hide not thy poison with such sugar'd words *2 Hen. VI.* iii 2 45
Your grace attended to their sugar'd words, But look'd not on the poison of their hearts *Richard III.* iii 1 13
And never learn'd The icy precepts of respect, but follow'd The sugar'd game before thee *T. of Athens* iv 3 259
Sugarsop. Philip, Walter, Sugarsop, and the rest *T. of Shrew* iv 1 92
Suggest. What spirit, what devil suggests this imagination? *Mer. Wives* iii 3 230
I give thee not this to suggest thee from thy master *All's Well* iv 5 47
Suggest his soon-believing adversaries *Richard II.* i 1 101
All other devils that suggest by treasons Do botch and bungle *Hen. V.* ii 2 114
If secret powers Suggest but truth to my divining thoughts *3 Hen. VI.* iv 6 69
Suggests the king our master To this last costly treaty *Hen. VIII.* i 1 164
Suggest the people in what hatred He still hath held them *Coriolanus* ii 1 261
Divinity of hell! When devils will the blackest sins put on, They do suggest at first with heavenly shows *Othello* ii 3 358
Suggested. Knowing that tender youth is soon suggested *T. G. of Ver.* iii 1 34
Those heavenly eyes, that look into these faults, Suggested us to make *L. L. Lost* v 2 780
What Eve, what serpent, hath suggested thee? *Richard II.* iii 4 75
This, as you say, suggested At some time when his soaring insolence Shall touch the people *Coriolanus* ii 1 269
Suggestion. They'll take suggestion as a cat laps milk *Tempest* ii 1 288
The most opportune place, the strong'st suggestion Our worser genius can iv 1 26
Suggestions are to other as to me; But I believe *L. L. Lost* i 1 159
A filthy officer he is in those suggestions *All's Well* iii 5 18
Better conquest never canst thou make Than arm thy constant and thy nobler parts Against these giddy loose suggestions *K. John* iii 1 292
Arthur, whom they say is kill'd to-night On your suggestion iv 2 166
Herein misled by your suggestion *1 Hen. IV.* iv 3 51
Mingled with venom of suggestion *2 Hen. IV.* iv 4 45
Then was I going prisoner to the Tower, By the suggestion of the queen's allies *Richard III.* iii 2 103
One that, by suggestion, Tied all the kingdom *Hen. VIII.* iv 2 35
If good, why do I yield to that suggestion Whose horrid image doth unfix my hair? *Macbeth* i 3 134
I'ld turn it all To thy suggestion, plot, and damned practice *Lear* ii 1 75
Suit. Being once perfected how to grant suits, How to deny them *Tempest* i 2 79
Being an enemy To me inveterate, hearkens my brother's suit i 2 122
Wilt thou be pleased to hearken once again to the suit I made to thee? iii 2 44
I despise thee for thy wrongful suit *T. G. of Ver.* iv 2 102
I hope my master's suit will be but cold iv 4 186
What says Silvia to my suit?—O, sir, I find her milder v 2 1
Shall I not lose my suit?—Troth, sir, all is in his hands above *Mer. Wives* i 4 153
Give him a show of comfort in his suit ii 1 98
Hast thou no suit against my knight? ii 1 220
If opportunity and humblest suit Cannot attain it, why, then iii 4 20
My suit then is desperate; you'll undertake her no more iii 5 126
Please but your honour hear me.—Well; what's your suit? *M. for M.* ii 2 28
Heaven let me bear it! you granting of my suit ii 4 70
Then is there here one Master Caper, at the suit of Master Three-pile the mercer, for some four suits of peach-coloured satin iv 3 10
Give notice to such men of sort and suit as are to meet him iv 4 19
Your suit's unprofitable; stand up, I say v 1 460
Officer, arrest him at my suit *Com. of Errors* iv 1 69
I do arrest you, sir: you hear the suit iv 1 79

Suit. With words that in an honest suit might move . *Com. of Errors* iv 2 14
Is he arrested? Tell me at whose suit.—I know not at whose suit he is arrested well ; But he's in a suit of buff which 'rested him . iv 2 43
He, sir, that takes pity on decayed men and gives them suits of durance iv 3 26
Say now, whose suit is he arrested at? . iv 4 134
The first suit is hot and hasty, like a Scotch jig . *Much Ado* ii 1 78
She mocks all her wooers out of suit . ii 1 365
Many a wooer doth commence his suit To her he thinks not worthy . ii 3 52
Surely suit ill spent and labour ill bestowed . iii 2 103
No comforter delight mine ear But such a one whose wrongs do suit with mine . v 1 7
Suddenly resolve me in my suit . *L. L. Lost* ii 1 110
Black is the badge of hell, The hue of dungeons, and the suit of night . iv 3 255
Not a man of them shall have the grace, Despite of suit, to see a lady's face . v 2 129
Did swear himself out of all suit . v 2 275
Coming too short of thanks For my great suit so easily obtain'd . v 2 749
The holy suit which fain it would convince . v 2 756
Behold . . . mine eye, What humble suit attends thy answer there . v 2 849
To return to their home and to trouble you with no more suit *Mer. of Venice* i 2 113
Moneys is your suit. What should I say to you? . i 3 120
My suit is— In very brief, the suit is impertinent to myself . ii 2 145
I know thee well ; thou hast obtain'd thy suit . ii 2 153
I have a suit to you.— You have obtain'd it . ii 2 186
I would entreat you rather to put on Your boldest suit of mirth . ii 2 211
What page's suit she hath in readiness . ii 4 33
Your suit is cold.—Cold, indeed ; and labour lost . ii 7 73
I follow thus A losing suit against him . iv 1 62
Of a strange nature is the suit you follow . iv 1 177
We will make it our suit to the duke . *As Y. Like It* i 2 192
Wear this for me, one out of suits with fortune . i 2 258
What he is indeed, More suits you to conceive than I to speak of . i 2 279
Were it not better, Because that I am more than common tall, That I did suit me all points like a man? . i 3 118
It is my only suit . ii 7 44
Therein suits His folly to the mettle of my speech . ii 7 81
You lisp and wear strange suits, disable all the benefits of your own country . iv 1 34
What, of my suit?—Not out of your apparel, and yet out of your suit . iv 1 87
Some one be ready with a costly suit And ask him what apparel he will wear . *T. of Shrew* Ind. 1 59
Go you to . . . my page, And see him dress'd in all suits like a lady Ind. 1 106
I follow him not By any token of presumptuous suit . *All's Well* i 3 204
Will you hear my suit?—And grant it . ii 3 82
That can in such a suit Corrupt the tender honour of a maid . iii 5 74
All is well ended, if this suit be won, That you express content . Epil. 2
She will admit no kind of suit . *T. Night* i 2 45
Thou hast a mind that suits With this thy fair and outward character . i 2 50
If it be a suit from the count, I am sick, or not at home . i 5 116
But, would you undertake another suit, I had rather hear you . iii 1 119
He is sad and civil, And suits well for a servant with my fortunes . iii 4 6
Antonio, I arrest thee at the suit of Count Orsino . iii 4 360
If spirits can assume both form and suit You come to fright us . v 1 242
He upon some action Is now in durance, at Malvolio's suit . v 1 283
Whereof the least Is not this suit of mine . *W. Tale* i 2 402
If it be in man besides the king to effect your suits, here is man shall do it . iv 4 828
By long and vehement suit I was seduced . *K. John* i 1 254
Let it be our suit That you have bid us ask his liberty . iv 2 62
Although my will to give is living, The suit which you demand is gone and dead . iv 2 84
May it please you, lords, to grant the commons' suit *Richard II.* iv 1 154
Pardon is all the suit I have in hand . v 3 130
For obtaining of suits, whereof the hangman hath no lean wardrobe *1 Hen. IV.* i 2 81
Two I am sure I have paid, two rogues in buckram suits . ii 4 213
In buckram?—Ay, four, in buckram suits . ii 4 228
I arrest you at the suit of Mistress Quickly . *2 Hen. IV.* ii 1 48
I am a poor widow of Eastcheap, and he is arrested at my suit . ii 1 77
And might by no suit gain our audience . iv 1 76
If I had a suit to Master Shallow, I would humour his men with the imputation of being near their master . v 1 79
Whose right Suits not in native colours with the truth . *Hen. V.* i 2 17
A horrid suit of the camp . iii 6 81
Description cannot suit itself in words . iv 2 53
Shall we go send them dinners and fresh suits? . iv 2 57
If you urge me farther than to say 'do you in faith?' I wear out my suit . v 2 132
You may not, my lord, despise her gentle suit . *1 Hen. VI.* ii 2 47
Your several suits Have been consider'd and debated on . v 1 34
My body shall Pay recompense, if you will grant my suit . v 3 19
How canst thou tell she will deny thy suit, Before thou make a trial? . v 3 75
What answer makes your grace unto my suit? . v 3 150
Begin your suits anew, and sue to him . *2 Hen. VI.* i 3 42
Far be it we should honour such as these With humble suit . iv 1 124
I have a suit unto your lordship.—Be it a lordship, thou shalt have it. iv 7 4
Her suit is now to repossess those lands . *3 Hen. VI.* iii 1 4
Grant her suit ; It were dishonour to deny it her . iii 2 8
The lady hath a thing to grant, Before the king will grant her humble suit . iii 2 13
Widow, we will consider of your suit ; And come some other time . iii 2 16
This merry inclination Accords not with the sadness of my suit . iii 2 77
My suit is at an end . iii 2 81
Her suit is granted for her husband's lands . iii 2 117
It was thy device By this alliance to make void my suit . iii 3 142
Nor posted off their suits with slow delays . iv 8 40
And I nothing to back my suit at all, But the plain devil *Richard III.* i 2 236
Be not you spoke with, but by mighty suit . iii 7 46
Bent to meditation ; And in no worldly suit would he be moved . iii 7 63
In this just suit come I to move your grace . iii 7 140
To reprove you for this suit of yours . iii 7 148
O, make them joyful, grant their lawful suit! . iii 7 203
Whether you accept our suit or no, Your brother's son shall never reign iii 7 214
Call them again, my lord, and accept their suit . iii 7 221
His suit was granted Ere it was ask'd . *Hen. VIII.* i 1 186
Half your suit Never name to us ; you have half our power : The other moiety, ere you ask, is given . i 2 10
Made suit to come in's presence . i 2 197
Fit it with such furniture as suits The greatness of his person . ii 1 99

Suit. Nor could Come pat betwixt too early and too late For any suit of pounds . *Hen. VIII.* ii 3 85
I have a suit which you must not deny me . v 3 161
She is stubborn-chaste against all suit . *Troi. and Cres.* i 1 100
He would miss it rather Than carry it but by the suit of the gentry to him *Coriolanus* ii 1 254
Forget not . . . How in his suit he scorn'd you . ii 3 230
Mine ears against your suits are stronger than Your gates against my force . v 2 94
Stopp'd your ears against The general suit of Rome . v 3 6
Fresh embassies and suits, Nor from the state nor private friends, hereafter Will I lend ear to . v 3 17
Our suit Is, that you reconcile them . v 3 135
This suit I make, That you create your emperor's eldest son, Lord Saturnine . *T. Andron.* i 1 223
And at my suit, sweet, pardon what is past . i 1 431
Then, at my suit, look graciously on him . i 1 439
What say you to my suit?—But saying o'er what I have said . *R. and J.* i 2 6
She gallops o'er a courtier's nose, And then dreams he of smelling out a suit . i 4 78
Cease thy suit, and leave me to my grief : To-morrow will I send . ii 2 153
Humbly prays you That with your other noble parts you'll suit In giving him his right . *T. of Athens* ii 2 23
Thou hast some suit to Cæsar, hast thou not? . *J. Cæsar* ii 4 27
Brutus hath a suit That Cæsar will not grant . ii 4 42
O'er-read, At your best leisure, this his humble suit.—O Cæsar, read mine first ; for mine's a suit That touches Cæsar nearer . iii 1 5
Let him go, And presently prefer his suit to Cæsar . iii 1 28
And take the present horror from the time, Which now suits with it *Macbeth* ii 1 60
You told us of some suit ; what is't, Laertes? . *Hamlet* i 2 43
Nor customary suits of solemn black, Nor windy suspiration . i 2 78
These but the trappings and the suits of woe . i 2 86
Mere implorators of unholy suits . i 3 129
Suit the action to the word, the word to the action . iii 2 19
Nay then, let the devil wear black, for I'll have a suit of sables . iii 2 138
Whose life I have spared at suit of his gray beard . *Lear* ii 2 68
Who hath had three suits to his back, six shirts to his body . iii 4 141
In personal suit to make me his lieutenant, Off-capp'd to him . *Othello* i 1 9
'Tis most easy The inclining Desdemona to subdue In any honest suit . ii 3 347
My suit to her Is, that she will . . . Procure me some access . iii 1 36
I'll intermingle every thing he does With Cassio's suit . iii 3 26
When I have a suit Wherein I mean to touch your love indeed, It shall be full of poise and difficult weight . iii 3 80
This is a trick to put me from my suit . iii 4 87
If I do find him fit, I'll move your suit And seek to effect it . iii 4 166
By their own importunate suit, Or voluntary dotage of some mistress . iv 1 26
If this suit lay in Bianca's power, How quickly should you speed! . iv 1 108
If she will return me my jewels, I will give over my suit . iv 2 201
Let him be so entertained amongst you as suits, with gentlemen *Cymb.* i 4 29
And make me put into contempt the suits Of princely fellows . iii 4 92
The same suit he wore when he took leave of my lady . iii 5 128
The first service thou dost me, fetch that suit hither . iii 5 131
With that suit upon my back, will I ravish her : first kill him . iii 5 141
And suit myself As does a Briton peasant . v 1 23
Whose kinsmen have made suit That their good souls may be appeased with slaughter Of you . v 5 71
To attain In suit the place of's bed and win this ring . v 5 185
When you come ashore, I have another suit . *Pericles* v 1 262

Suitable. The common lag of people—what is amiss in them, you gods, make suitable for destruction . *T. of Athens* iii 6 92

Suited. There's one meaning well suited . *Much Ado* v 1 231
How oddly he is suited! . *Mer. of Venice* i 2 79
O dear discretion, how his words are suited! . iii 5 70
Out of fashion : richly suited, but unsuitable . *All's Well* i 1 170
So went he suited to his watery tomb . *T. Night* v 1 241
Suited In like conditions as our argument . *Troi. and Cres.* Prol. 24
Be better suited : These weeds are memories of those worser hours *Lear* iv 7 6

Suiting. His whole function suiting With forms to his conceit *Hamlet* ii 2 582

Suitor. My master sues to her, and she hath taught her suitor *T. G. of V.* ii 1 143
I am a woeful suitor to your honour . *Meas. for Meas.* ii 2 27
She hath been a suitor to me for her brother . v 1 34
They would else have been troubled with a pernicious suitor *Much Ado* i 1 130
We attend, Like humble-visaged suitors . *L. L. Lost* ii 1 34
Who is the suitor?—Shall I teach you to know? . iv 1 110
The four winds blow in from every coast Renowned suitors *Mer. of Ven.* i 1 169
What warmth is there in your affection towards any of these princely suitors? . i 2 38
I drave my suitor from his mad humour of love . *As Y. Like It* iii 2 438
She will not be annoy'd with suitors . *T. of Shrew* i 1 189
Suitors to her and rivals in my love . i 2 122
Are you a suitor to the maid you talk of, yea or no? . i 2 230
She may more suitors have and me for one . i 2 243
The youngest daughter . . . Her father keeps from all access of suitors i 2 261
Since you do profess to be a suitor, You must, as we do, gratify this gentleman . i 2 272
Of all thy suitors, here I charge thee, tell Whom thou lovest best . ii 1 8
That, being a stranger in this city here, Do make myself a suitor . ii 1 91
I am your neighbour, and was suitor first . ii 1 336
When she was young you woo'd her ; now in age Is she become the suitor? . *W. Tale* v 3 109
My humble duty remembered, I will not be your suitor . *2 Hen. IV.* ii 1 138
No humble suitors press to speak for right . *3 Hen. VI.* iii 1 19
Of his own royal disposition, And not provoked by any suitor else *Richard III.* i 3 64
Nay, we must longer kneel : I am a suitor . *Hen. VIII.* i 2 9
They say poor suitors have strong breaths . *Coriolanus* i 1 61
Your wife, this lady, and myself, Are suitors to you . v 3 78
As suitors should, Plead your deserts in peace and humbleness *T. An.* i 1 44
I am an humble suitor to your virtues . *T. of Athens* iii 5 7
Here will I stand till Cæsar pass along, And as a suitor will I give him this . *J. Cæsar* ii 3 12
Take good note What Cæsar doth, what suitors press to him . ii 4 15
The throng that follows Cæsar at the heels, Of senators, of prætors, common suitors, Will crowd a feeble man . ii 4 35
And am moreover suitor that I may Produce his body to the market-place . iii 1 227
No heretics burn'd, but wenches' suitors . *Lear* iii 2 84
She that could think and ne'er disclose her mind, See suitors following and not look behind . *Othello* ii 1 158

Suitor. And needs no other suitor but his likings . . . . *Othello* iii 1 51
Talking with a suitor here, A man that languishes in your displeasure . iii 3 42
Whiles we are suitors to their throne, decays The thing we sue for *A. and C.* ii 1 4
A foolish suitor to a wedded lady . . . . *Cymbeline* i 6 2
Suivez-vous le grand capitaine . . . . . *Hen. V.* iv 4 70
Sullen. She is peevish, sullen, froward, Proud . . *T. G. of Ver.* iii 1 68
I love to cope him in these sullen fits . . . *As Y. Like It* ii 1 67
'Twas told me you were rough and coy and sullen . . *T. of Shrew* ii 1 245
Sullen, sour, And not obedient to his honest will . . . . v 2 157
And sullen presage of your own decay . . . . *K. John* i 1 28
Shorten my days thou canst with sullen sorrow . *Richard II.* i 3 227
The sullen passage of thy weary steps Esteem as foil . . . i 3 265
Let them die that age and sullens have; For both hast thou . . ii 1 139
Mourn with me for that I do lament, And put on sullen black incontinent v 6 48
Like bright metal on a sullen ground . . . . *1 Hen. IV.* i 2 236
His tongue Sounds ever after as a sullen bell . . *2 Hen. IV.* i 1 102
Why are thine eyes fix'd to the sullen earth? . . *2 Hen. VI.* i 2 5
Rude ragged nurse, old sullen playfellow For tender princes! *Rich. III.* iv 1 102
Like a misbehaved and sullen wench, Thou pout'st . *Rom. and Jul.* iii 3 143
Our solemn hymns to sullen dirges change . . . . . iv 5 88
If thou wert not sullen, I would be good to thee . . *T. of Athens* i 2 242
But here comes Antony.—I am sick and sullen . *Ant. and Cleo.* i 3 13
Sullied. Hath sullied all his gloss of former honour . . *1 Hen. VI.* iv 4 6
Sullies. Laying these slight sullies on my son, As 'twere a thing a little soil'd i' the working . . . . . . *Hamlet* ii 1 39
Sully. I will consent to act any villany against him, that may not sully the chariness of our honesty . . . . *Mer. Wives* ii 1 102
Sully The purity and whiteness of my sheets . . . *W. Tale* i 2 326
Your white canvas doublet will sully . . . *1 Hen. IV.* ii 4 84
Sulphur. And yet to charge thy sulphur with a bolt That should but rive an oak . . . . *Coriolanus* v 3 152
With a little act upon the blood, Burn like the mines of sulphur *Othello* iii 3 329
Roast me in sulphur! Wash me in steep-down gulfs of liquid fire! . . v 2 279
The gods throw stones of sulphur on me . . . *Cymbeline* v 5 240
Sulphurous. The fire and cracks Of sulphurous roaring . *Tempest* i 2 204
Merciful Heaven, Thou rather with thy sharp and sulphurous bolt Split'st the unwedgeable and gnarled oak . . *Meas. for Meas.* ii 2 115
My hour is almost come, When I to sulphurous and tormenting flames Must render up myself . . . . . . *Hamlet* i 5 3
You sulphurous and thought-executing fires . . . *Lear* iii 2 4
There's hell, there's darkness, there's the sulphurous pit, Burning, scalding . . . . iv 6 130
He came in thunder; his celestial breath Was sulphurous to smell *Cymb.* v 4 115
Gently quench Thy nimble, sulphurous flashes! . . . *Pericles* iii 1 6
Sultan. A Persian prince That won three fields of Sultan Solyman *M. of V.* ii 1 26
Sultry. But yet methinks it is very sultry and hot for my complexion.—Exceedingly, my lord; it is very sultry,—as 'twere,—I cannot tell how . . . . *Hamlet* v 2 101
Sum. You take the sum and substance that I have . *T. G. of Ver.* iv 1 15
Of more value Than stamps in gold or sums in sealed bags *Mer. Wives* iii 4 16
Beg thou, or borrow, to make up the sum . . *Com. of Errors* i 1 154
Since Pentecost the sum is due, And since I have not much importuned you . . . . iv 1 1
Even just the sum that I do owe to you Is growing to me by Antipholus iv 1 7
Take the chain and bid my wife Disburse the sum on the receipt thereof iv 1 38
Either consent to pay this sum for me Or I attach you by this officer . iv 1 72
I know the man. What is the sum he owes?—Two hundred ducats . iv 4 136
If any friend will pay the sum for him, He shall not die . . . v 1 131
Haply I see a friend will save my life And pay the sum . . . . v 1 284
That is the sum of all . . . . *Much Ado* ii 1 147
You know how much the gross sum of deuce-ace amounts to . *L. L. Lost* i 2 49
One half of an entire sum Disbursed by my father in his wars . . ii 1 131
Say that he or we, as neither have, Received that sum . . . ii 1 134
You can produce acquittances For such a sum . . . . . ii 1 162
Neither have I money nor commodity To raise a present sum *Mer. of Ven.* i 1 179
Three thousand ducats; 'tis a good round sum . . . . i 3 104
Such sum or sums as are Express'd in the condition . . . . i 3 148
'Confess' and 'love' Had been the very sum of my confession . . iii 2 36
The full sum of me Is sum of something . . . . . . iii 2 160
He would rather have Antonio's flesh Than twenty times the value of the sum That he did owe him . . . . iii 2 289
What sum owes he the Jew?—For me three thousand ducats . . . iii 2 299
Here I tender it for him in the court; Yea, twice the sum . . iv 1 210
Giving thy sum of more To that which had too much *As Y. Like It* ii 1 48
That the stretching of a span Buckles in his sum of age . . . iii 2 140
Make assurance . . . Of greater sums than I have promised *T. of Shrew* iii 2 137
With well-weighing sums of gold, to corrupt him to a revolt . *All's Well* iv 3 204
This is the very sum of all . . . . *K. John* ii 1 151
How I have sped among the clergymen, The sums I have collected shall express . . . . iv 2 142
When they shall know what men are rich, They shall subscribe them for large sums of gold . . . . *Richard II.* i 4 50
The sum of all Is that the king hath won . . . *2 Hen. IV.* i 1 131
For what sum?—It is more than for some, my lord; it is for all . . ii 1 78
What is the gross sum that I owe thee? . . . . . ii 1 91
To give a greater sum Than ever at one time the clergy yet Did *Hen. V.* i 1 79
Such a mighty sum As never did the clergy at one time Bring in . . i 2 133
The sum is paid; the traitors are agreed . . . . ii Prol. 33
The sum of all our answer is but this . . . . . . iii 6 172
A servant, under his master's command transporting a sum of money . iv 1 159
You shall first receive The sum of money which I promised . *1 Hen. VI.* v 1 52
I never read but England's kings have had Large sums of gold and dowries with their wives . . . . . . *2 Hen. VI.* i 1 129
Levy great sums of money through the realm For soldiers' pay . . iii 1 61
The lives of those which we have lost in fight Be counterpoised with such a petty sum! . . . . iv 1 22
The sum of all I can, I have disclosed . . . *Richard III.* ii 4 46
Produce the grand sum of his sins . . . . *Hen. VIII.* iii 2 293
Whose grossness little characters sum up . . *Troi. and Cres.* i 3 325
Will you with counters sum The past proportion of his infinite? . ii 2 28
O, were the sum of these that I should pay Countless and infinite, yet would I pay them! . . . . *T. Andron.* v 3 158
I cannot sum up sum of half my wealth . . . *Rom. and Jul.* ii 6 34
I doubt whether their legs be worth the sums That are given for 'em *T. of Athens* i 2 238
He owes nine thousand; besides my former sum . . . . . ii 2 2
I'ld rather than the worth of thrice the sum, Had sent to me first . iii 3 22
It should seem by the sum, Your master's confidence was above mine . iii 4 30
Why then preferr'd you not your sums and bills, When your false masters eat of my lord's meat? . . . . iii 4 49

Sum. Cut my heart in sums.—Mine, fifty talents.—Tell out my blood *T. of Athens* iii 4 93
'Tis said he gave unto his steward a mighty sum . . . . . v 1 9
Even such heaps and sums of love and wealth As shall to thee blot out what wrongs were theirs . . . . v 1 155
I did send to you For certain sums of gold, which you denied me . *J. C.* iv 3 70
Your sum of parts Did not together pluck such envy from him *Hamlet* iv 7 74
I loved Ophelia: forty thousand brothers Could not, with all their quantity of love, Make up my sum . . . . v 1 294
News, my good lord, from Rome.—Grates me: the sum . *Ant. and Cleo.* i 1 18
Parcel the sum of my disgraces by Addition of his envy! . . . v 2 163
A man worth any woman, overbuys me Almost the sum he pays . *Cymb.* i 1 147
Have mingled sums To buy a present . . . . i 6 186
O, the charity of a penny cord! it sums up thousands in a trice . . v 4 170
The sum of this, Brought hither to Pentapolis . . *Pericles* iii Gower 33
Sumless. With sunken wreck and sumless treasuries . . *Hen. V.* i 2 165
Summa. Di faciant laudis summa sit ista tuæ! . . . . *3 Hen. VI.* i 3 48
Summary. The continent and summary of my fortune *Mer. of Venice* iii 2 131
And have the summary of all our griefs, When time shall serve *2 Hen. IV.* iv 1 73
Summed. You cast the event of war, my noble lord, And summ'd the account of chance . . . . i 1 167
Summer. On the bat's back I do fly After summer merrily *Tempest* v 1 92
Take heed, ere summer comes or cuckoo-birds do sing . *Mer. Wives* ii 1 127
Five summers have I spent in furthest Greece . *Com. of Errors* i 1 133
The fraud of men was ever so, Since summer first was leavy . *Much Ado* ii 3 75
Why should proud summer boast Before the birds have any cause to sing? . . . . *L. L. Lost* i 1 102
Blow like sweet roses in this summer air . . . . . . v 2 293
And maidens bleach their summer smocks . . . . . . v 2 916
A sweet-faced man; a proper man, as one shall see in a summer's day *M. N. Dream* i 2 89
Never, since the middle summer's spring, Met we on hill, in dale . . ii 1 82
An odorous chaplet of sweet summer buds . . . . . ii 1 110
The spring, the summer, The childing autumn, angry winter, change Their wonted liveries . . . . ii 1 111
The summer still doth tend upon my state . . . . . iii 1 158
A day in April never came so sweet, To show how costly summer was at hand, As this fore-spurrer comes . . . *Mer. of Venice* ii 9 94
Warmed and cooled by the same winter and summer as a Christian is . iii 1 66
Like the mending of highways In summer, where the ways are fair enough v 1 264
But with the word the time will bring on summer . . *All's Well* iv 4 31
Let summer bear it out . . . . *T. Night* i 5 21
This coming summer, the King of Sicilia means to pay Bohemia the visitation which he justly owes him . . . . . *W. Tale* i 1 6
The thrush and the jay Are summer songs for me and my aunts . . iv 3 11
The year growing ancient, Not yet on summer's death . . . . iv 4 80
These are flowers Of middle summer, and I think they are given To men of middle age . . . . iv 4 107
Which sixteen winters cannot blow away, So many summers dry . . v 3 51
There is so hot a summer in my bosom, That all my bowels crumble up to dust . . . . *K. John* v 7 30
Is hack'd down, and his summer leaves all faded, By envy's hand and murder's bloody axe . . . . *Richard II.* i 2 20
Till twice five summers have enrich'd our fields . . . . . i 3 141
Wallow naked in December snow By thinking on fantastic summer's heat i 3 299
And lay the summer's dust with showers of blood . . . . . iii 3 43
Our sighs and they shall lodge the summer corn . . . . . iii 3 162
Farewell, thou latter spring! farewell, All-hallown summer! *1 Hen. IV.* i 2 178
Sung by a fair queen in a summer's bower, With ravishing division . iii 1 210
Shadow will serve for summer . . . . . *2 Hen. IV.* iii 2 144
Grew like the summer grass, fastest by night, Unseen, yet crescive *Hen. V.* i 1 65
As clear as is the summer's sun . . . . i 2 86
Armed in their stings, Make boot upon the summer's velvet buds . . i 2 194
Uttered as prave words at the pridge as you shall see in a summer's day iii 6 67
As you shall desire in a summer's day . . . . iv 8 23
This moral ties me over to time and a hot summer . . . . . v 2 340
Expect Saint Martin's summer, halcyon days . . . *1 Hen. VI.* i 2 131
In open field, In winter's cold and summer's parching heat . *2 Hen. VI.* i 1 81
After summer evermore succeeds Barren winter . . . . . ii 4 2
Like to the summer's corn by tempest lodged . . . . . iii 2 176
When we saw our sunshine made thy spring, And that thy summer bred us no increase . . . . *3 Hen. VI.* ii 2 164
Watch'd the winter's night, Went all afoot in summer's scalding heat . v 7 18
Now is the winter of our discontent Made glorious summer *Richard III.* i 1 2
Short summers lightly have a forward spring . . . . . iii 1 94
Their lips were four red roses on a stalk, Which in their summer beauty kiss'd each other . . . . iv 3 13
The wretched, bloody, and usurping boar, That spoil'd your summer fields . . . . v 2 8
This many summers in a sea of glory, But far beyond my depth *Hen. VIII.* iii 2 360
But to those men that sought him sweet as summer . . . . iv 2 54
Men, like butterflies, Show not their mealy wings but to the summer *Troi. and Cres.* iii 3 79
With no less confidence Than boys pursuing summer butterflies, Or butchers killing flies . . . . *Coriolanus* iv 6 94
The trees, though summer, yet forlorn and lean . . *T. Andron.* ii 3 94
In summer's drought I'll drop upon thee still . . . . . iii 1 19
We'll follow where thou lead'st, Like stinging bees in hottest summer's day . . . . v 1 14
This goodly summer with your winter mix'd . . . . . . v 2 172
Let two more summers wither in their pride, Ere we may think her ripe to be a bride . . . . *Rom. and Jul.* i 2 10
Verona's summer hath not such a flower . . . . . . i 3 77
This bud of love, by summer's ripening breath, May prove a beauteous flower . . . . ii 2 121
A lover may bestride the gossamer That idles in the wanton summer air ii 6 19
The swallow follows not summer more willing than we your lordship.—Nor more willingly leaves winter . . . *T. of Athens* iii 6 31
'Twas on a summer's evening, in his tent . . . *J. Cæsar* iii 2 176
This guest of summer, The temple-haunting martlet . . *Macbeth* i 6 3
Can such things be, And overcome us like a summer's cloud? . . iii 4 111
If't be summer news, Smile to't before . . . . *Cymbeline* iii 4 12
Whilst summer lasts and I live here, Fidele I'll sweeten thy sad grave iv 2 219
To be still hot summer's tanlings and The shrinking slaves of winter . iv 4 29
Those palates who, not yet two summers younger, Must have inventions *Pericles* i 4 39
And she is fair too, is she not?—As a fair day in summer, wondrous fair ii 5 36
Summer-bird. Thou art a summer bird, Which ever in the haunch of winter sings The lifting up of day . . . . . *2 Hen. IV.* iv 4 91
Willingly leaves winter; such summer-birds are men *T. of Athens* iii 6 34

Summer-days. Purple violets, and marigolds, Shall as a carpet hang upon thy grave, While summer-days do last . . . . *Pericles* iv 1 18

Summered. Maids, well summered and warm kept, are like flies at Bartholomew-tide . . . . *Hen. V.* v 2 335

Summer-flies. These summer-flies Have blown me full of maggot ostentation . . . . *L. L. Lost* v 2 408

The common people swarm like summer flies . . . . 3 *Hen. VI.* ii 6 8

They never then had sprung like summer flies . . . ii 6 17

As summer flies are in the shambles, That quicken even with blowing *Othello* iv 2 66

Summer-house. In any summer-house in Christendom . 1 *Hen. IV.* iii 1 164

Summer-seeming. Sticks deeper, grows with more pernicious root Than summer-seeming lust . . . . *Macbeth* iv 3 86

Summer-swelling. To root the summer-swelling flower *T. G. of Ver.* ii 4 162

Summit. What if it tempt you toward the flood, my lord, Or to the dreadful summit of the cliff? . . . *Hamlet* i 4 70

It is a massy wheel, Fix'd on the summit of the highest mount . iii 3 18

From the dread summit of this chalky bourn . . *Lear* iv 6 57

Summon. On this green land Answer your summons . . *Tempest* iv 1 131

Summon up your dearest spirits . . . *L. L. Lost* ii 1 1

Those dulcet sounds in break of day That creep into the dreaming bride-groom's ear And summon him to marriage . *Mer. of Venice* iii 2 53

Summon a session, that we may arraign Our most disloyal lady *W. Tale* iii 2 202

Some trumpet summon hither to the walls These men of Angiers *K. John* ii 1 198

What lusty trumpet thus doth summon us? . . . v 2 117

Stays but the summons of the appellant's trumpet . *Richard II.* i 3 4

Stiffen the sinews, summon up the blood . . *Hen. V.* iii 1 7

Summon a parley; we will talk with him . . 1 *Hen. VI.* iii 3 35

Summon their general unto the wall . . . iv 2 2

I summon your grace to his majesty's parliament . . 2 *Hen. VI.* ii 4 70

I'll knock once more to summon them . . 3 *Hen. VI.* iv 7 16

Summon him to-morrow to the Tower . . *Richard III.* iii 1 172

And got your leave To make this present summons . *Hen. VIII.* ii 4 219

Summon the town.—How far off lie these armies? *Coriolanus* i 4 7

A heavy summons lies like lead upon me, And yet I would not sleep *Macbeth* ii 1 6

Hear it not, Duncan; for it is a knell That summons thee to heaven or to hell . . . ii 1 64

Ere to black Hecate's summons The shard-borne beetle with his drowsy hums Hath rung night's yawning peal . . iii 2 41

And then it started like a guilty thing Upon a fearful summons *Hamlet* i 1 149

Your name, your quality? and why you answer This present summons? *Lear* v 3 121

What is the reason of this terrible summons? . . *Othello* i 1 82

Hark, how these instruments summon to supper! . . iv 2 169

Summoned. Why hath thy queen Summon'd me hither? . *Tempest* iv 1 83

The people do admit you, and are summon'd To meet anon *Coriolanus* ii 3 151

They summon'd up their meiny, straight took horse *Lear* ii 4 35

Summoners. Close pent-up guilts, Rive your concealing continents, and cry These dreadful summoners grace . . iii 2 59

Sumpter. Return with her? Persuade me rather to be slave and sumpter To this detested groom . . ii 4 219

Sumptuous. My state, Seldom but sumptuous, show'd like a feast 1 *Hen. IV.* iii 2 58

With a large and sumptuous dowry . . 1 *Hen. VI.* v 1 20

Thy sumptuous buildings and thy wife's attire Have cost a mass of public treasury . . . 2 *Hen. VI.* i 3 133

Is my apparel sumptuous to behold? . . iv 7 106

Sumptuously. This monument five hundred years hath stood, Which I have sumptuously re-edified . . . *T. Andron.* i 1 351

Sun. She that from Naples Can have no note, unless the sun were post —The man i' the moon's too slow *Tempest* ii 1 248

All the infections that the sun sucks up From bogs, fens, flats ii 2 1

The sun will set before I shall discharge What I must strive to do iii 1 22

I have bedimm'd The noontide sun, call'd forth the mutinous winds v 1 42

An April day, Which now shows all the beauty of the sun, And by and by a cloud takes all away! . . . *T. G. of Ver.* i 3 86

At first I did adore a twinkling star, But now I worship a celestial sun ii 6 10

The sun begins to gild the western sky . . v 1 1

Then did the sun on dunghill shine . . *Mer. Wives* i 3 70

I rather will suspect the sun with cold Than thee with wantonness iv 4 7

Have I laid my brain in the sun and dried it, that it wants matter? v 5 143

Lying by the violet in the sun, Do as the carrion does *Meas. for Meas.* ii 2 166

Ere twice the sun hath made his journal greeting To the under generation iv 3 92

My woes end likewise with the evening sun *Com. of Errors* i 1 28

At length the sun, gazing upon the earth, Dispersed those vapours i 1 89

Ere the weary sun set in the west . . . i 2 7

When the sun shines let foolish gnats make sport . . ii 2 30

For gazing on your beams, fair sun, being by . . iii 2 56

Where honeysuckles, ripen'd by the sun, Forbid the sun to enter *M. Ado* iii 1 8

Study is like the heaven's glorious sun That will not be deep-search'd with saucy looks . . . *L. L. Lost* i 1 84

So sweet a kiss the golden sun gives not To those fresh morning drops . iv 3 26

Then thou, fair sun, which on my earth dost shine, Exhalest this vapour-vow . . . iv 3 69

As fair as day.—Ay, as some days; but then no sun must shine . iv 3 91

O, 'tis the sun that maketh all things shine . . iv 3 246

But be first advised, In conflict that you get the sun of them iv 3 369

The sun was not so true unto the day As he to me . *M. N. Dream* iii 2 50

From the presence of the sun, Following darkness like a dream v 1 392

Mislike me not for my complexion, The shadow'd livery of the burnish'd sun, To whom I am a neighbour . . *Mer. of Venice* ii 1 2

'Tis a day, Such as the day is when the sun is hid . . v 1 126

We should hold day with the Antipodes, If you would walk in absence of the sun . . . v 1 128

Who doth ambition shun And loves to live i' the sun *As Y. Like It* ii 5 41

I met a fool; Who laid him down and bask'd him in the sun . ii 7 15

That a great cause of the night is lack of the sun . . iii 2 30

Let me entreat of you To pardon me yet for a night or two, Or, if not so, until the sun be set *T. of Shrew* Ind. 2 122

And as the sun breaks through the darkest clouds, So honour peereth in the meanest habit . . . iv 3 175

Why, so this gallant will command the sun . . iv 3 198

How bright and goodly shines the moon!—The moon! the sun . iv 5 3

I say it is the moon that shines so bright.—I know it is the sun iv 5 5

Be it moon, or sun, or what you please: An if you please to call it a rush-candle, Henceforth I vow it shall be so for me . iv 5 13

I know it is the moon.—Nay, then you lie: it is the blessed sun.—Then, God be bless'd, it is the blessed sun: But sun it is not, when you say it is not . . . iv 5 17

Sun. My mistaking eyes, That have been so bedazzled with the sun *T. of Shrew* iv 5 46

I adore The sun, that looks upon his worshipper *All's Well* i 3 212

Ere twice the horses of the sun shall bring Their fiery torcher his diurnal ring . . . ii 1 164

The spinsters and the knitters in the sun . . *T. Night* ii 4 45

He has been yonder i' the sun practising behaviour to his own shadow . ii 5 20

Foolery, sir, does walk about the orb like the sun, it shines every where iii 1 44

This is the air; that is the glorious sun; This pearl she gave me . iv 3 1

We were as twinn'd lambs that did frisk i' the sun . *W. Tale* i 2 67

Four pound of prunes, and as many of raisins o' the sun . iv 3 52

The marigold, that goes to bed wi' the sun And with him rises weeping iv 4 105

The selfsame sun that shines upon his court Hides not his visage from our cottage but Looks on alike . . . iv 4 455

For all the sun sees or The close earth wombs or the profound seas hide iv 4 500

The sun looking with a southward eye upon him . . iv 4 819

The most peerless piece of earth, I think, That e'er the sun shone bright on . . . v 1 95

No sun to ripe The bloom that promiseth a mighty fruit *K. John* ii 1 472

Being but the shadow of your son, Becomes a sun and makes your son a shadow . . . ii 1 500

The glorious sun Stays in his course and plays the alchemist . iii 1 77

The sun's o'ercast with blood: fair day, adieu! . . iii 1 326

I had a thing to say, but let it go: The sun is in the heaven . iii 3 34

The burning crest Of the old, feeble, and day-wearied sun . v 4 35

The sun of heaven methought was loath to set, But stay'd and made the western welkin blush . . . v 5 1

That sun that warms you here shall shine on me *Richard II.* i 3 145

The setting sun, and music at the close, As the last taste of sweets ii 1 12

Thy sun sets weeping in the lowly west, Witnessing storms to come ii 4 21

As doth the blushing discontented sun From out the fiery portal of the east . . . iii 3 63

By that fair sun which shows me where thou stand'st, I heard thee say iv 1 35

As many lies As may be holloa'd in thy treacherous ear From sun to sun iv 1 55

A mockery king of snow, Standing before the sun of Bolingbroke iv 1 261

Was this the face That, like the sun, did make beholders wink? . iv 1 284

The blessed sun himself a fair hot wench in flame-coloured taffeta 1 *Hen. IV.* i 2 10

Herein will I imitate the sun, Who doth permit the base contagious clouds To smother up his beauty from the world . i 2 221

Pitiful-hearted Titan, that melted at the sweet tale of the sun's! . ii 4 135

Shall the blessed sun of heaven prove a micher and eat blackberries? . ii 4 449

As full of spirit as the month of May, And gorgeous as the sun at mid-summer . . . iv 1 102

Worse than the sun in March, This praise doth nourish agues . iv 1 111

How bloodily the sun begins to peer Above yon busky hill! . v 1 1

It stuck upon him as the sun In the grey vault of heaven . 2 *Hen. IV.* ii 3 18

As clear as is the summer's sun . . *Hen. V.* i 2 86

On mountain standing, Up in the air, crown'd with the golden sun ii 4 58

On whom, as in despite, the sun looks pale, Killing their fruit iii 5 17

The armour that I saw in your tent to-night, are those stars or suns upon it? . . . iii 7 74

A largess universal like the sun His liberal eye doth give to every one iv Prol. 43

You may as well go about to turn the sun to ice with fanning . iv 1 212

The sun doth gild our armour; up, my lords! . . iv 2 1

Come, come, away! The sun is high, and we outwear the day . iv 2 63

There the sun shall greet them, And draw their honours reeking up to heaven . . . iv 3 100

A good heart, Kate, is the sun and the moon; or rather the sun v 2 171

More dazzled and drove back his enemies Than mid-day sun 1 *Hen. VI.* i 1 14

I waited on my tender lambs, And to sun's parching heat display'd my cheeks . . . i 2 77

The sun with one eye vieweth all the world . . i 4 84

As plays the sun upon the glassy streams . . v 3 62

May never glorious sun reflex his beams Upon the country where you make abode! . . . v 4 87

Trow'st thou that e'er I'll look upon the world, Or count them happy that enjoy the sun? No; dark shall be my light . 2 *Hen. VI.* ii 4 39

Cold snow melts with the sun's hot beams . . iii 1 223

The golden circuit on my head, Like to the glorious sun's transparent beams . . . iii 1 353

Like the sun 'gainst glass, Or like an overcharged gun, recoil iii 2 330

Whose hopeful colours Advance our half-faced sun, striving to shine iv 1 98

See how the morning opes her golden gates, And takes her farewell of the glorious sun! . 3 *Hen. VI.* ii 1 22

Dazzle mine eyes, or do I see three suns?—Three glorious suns, each one a perfect sun . . . ii 1 25

Now are they but one lamp, one light, one sun . . ii 1 31

Henceforward will I bear Upon my target three fair-shining suns . ii 1 40

Nay, if thou be that princely eagle's bird, Show thy descent by gazing 'gainst the sun . . . ii 1 92

This world frowns, and Edward's sun is clouded . . ii 3 7

Swarm like summer flies; And whither fly the gnats but to the sun? ii 6 9

The leaves and fruit maintain'd with beauty's sun, Exempt from envy iii 3 126

When the morning sun shall raise his car Above the border of this horizon iv 7 80

The sun shines hot; and, if we use delay, Cold biting winter mars our hoped-for hay . . . iv 8 60

These eyes, that now are dimm'd with death's black veil, Have been as piercing as the mid-day sun . . v 2 17

A . . . threatening cloud, That will encounter with our glorious sun . v 3 5

The sun that sear'd the wings of my sweet boy Thy brother Edward v 6 23

Now is the winter of our discontent Made glorious summer by this sun of York . . . *Richard III.* i 1 2

Have no delight to pass away the time, Unless to spy my shadow in the sun . . . i 1 26

As all the world is cheered by the sun, So I by that; it is my day i 2 129

Shine out, fair sun, till I have bought a glass, That I may see my shadow i 2 263

Dallies with the wind and scorns the sun.—And turns the sun to shade i 3 265

When the sun sets, who doth not look for night? . ii 3 34

The weary sun hath made a golden set . . v 3 19

Give me a calendar. Who saw the sun to-day? . . v 3 277

The sun will not be seen to-day; The sky doth frown and lour v 3 282

When Those suns of glory, those two lights of men, Met *Hen. VIII.* i 1 6

These suns—For so they phrase 'em . . . i 1 33

I wonder That such a keech can with his very bulk Take up the rays o' the beneficial sun And keep it from the earth . . i 1 56

I am the shadow of poor Buckingham, Whose figure even this instant cloud puts on, By darkening my clear sun. . . i 1 226

After So many courses of the sun enthroned, Still growing in a majesty ii 3 6

As sun and showers There had made a lasting spring . . iii 1 7

Sun. No sun shall ever usher forth mine honours . . *Hen. VIII.* iii 2 410
Seek the king; That sun, I pray, may never set! . . . . iii 2 415
Whose bright faces Cast thousand beams upon me, like the sun . iv 2 89
Wherever the bright sun of heaven shall shine, His honour and the greatness of his name Shall be, and make new nations . . . v 5 51
I have, as when the sun doth light a storm, Buried this sigh in wrinkle of a smile . . . . *Troi. and Cres.* i 1 37
Before the sun rose he was harness'd light, And to the field goes he . i 2 8
Better parch in Afric sun Than in the pride and salt scorn of his eyes . i 3 370
By the fifth hour of the sun . . . . ii 1 134
As true as steel, as plantage to the moon, As sun to day . . iii 2 185
Like a gate of steel Fronting the sun, receives and renders back . iii 3 122
Danger, like an ague, subtly taints Even then when we sit idly in the sun . . . . iii 3 233
Jove, let Æneas live . . . A thousand complete courses of the sun! . iv 1 27
The sun borrows of the moon, when Diomed keeps his word . . . v 1 101
Which shipmen do the hurricano call, Constringed in mass by the almighty sun . . . . v 2 173
How the sun begins to set; How ugly night comes breathing at his heels v 8 5
Even with the vail and darking of the sun, To close the day up, Hector's life is done . . . . v 8 7
You are no surer, no, Than is the coal of fire upon the ice, Or hailstone in the sun . . . . *Coriolanus* i 1 178
I had rather have one scratch my head i' the sun When the alarum were struck . . . . ii 2 79
Then let the mutinous winds Strike the proud cedars 'gainst the fiery sun v 3 60
Is it most certain?—As certain as I know the sun is fire . . v 4 48
Tabors and cymbals and the shouting Romans Make the sun dance . v 4* 54
As when the golden sun salutes the morn . . . . *T. Andron.* ii 1 5
The snake lies rolled in the cheerful sun, The green leaves quiver . ii 3 13
Here never shines the sun; here nothing breeds, Unless the nightly owl ii 3 96
Sing so like a lark, That gives sweet tidings of the sun's uprise . iii 1 159
And stain the sun with fog, as sometime clouds When they do hug him in their melting bosoms . . . . iii 1 213
Is the sun dimm'd, that gnats do fly in it? . . . . . iv 4 82
What, hath the firmament more suns than one?—What boots it thee to call thyself a sun? . . . . v 3 17
The worshipp'd sun Peer'd forth the golden window of the east *R. and J.* i 1 125
Soon as the all-cheering sun Should in the furthest east begin to draw The shady curtains from Aurora's bed . . . . . . i 1 140
Ere he can spread his sweet leaves to the air, Or dedicate his beauty to the sun . . . . i 1 159
The all-seeing sun Ne'er saw her match since first the world begun . i 2 97
Sitting in the sun under the dove-house wall . . . . . i 3 27
What light through yonder window breaks? It is the east, and Juliet is the sun. Arise, fair sun, and kill the envious moon . . ii 2 3
Ere the sun advance his burning eye, The day to cheer . . . ii 3 5
The sun not yet thy sighs from heaven clears, Thy old groans ring yet . ii 3 73
Thoughts, Which ten times faster glide than the sun's beams . . ii 5 5
Now is the sun upon the highmost hill Of this day's journey . . ii 5 9
He hath wakened thy dog that hath lain asleep in the sun . . iii 1 29
The world will be in love with night And pay no worship to the garish sun . . . . iii 2 25
Some meteor that the sun exhales, To be to thee this night a torch-bearer . . . . iii 5 13
When the sun sets, the air doth drizzle dew . . . . . iii 5 127
The sun, for sorrow, will not show his head . . . . . v 3 306
Men shut their doors against a setting sun . . . *T. of Athens* i 2 150
You must consider that a prodigal course Is like the sun's . . . iii 4 13
O blessed breeding sun, draw from the earth Rotten humidity! . . iv 3 1
Renew I could not, like the moon; There were no suns to borrow of . iv 3 69
The sun's a thief, and with his great attraction Robs the vast sea . iv 3 439
The moon's an arrant thief, And her pale fire she snatches from the sun iv 3 441
Thou sun, that comfort'st, burn! Speak, and be hang'd . . . v 1 134
Graves only be men's works and death their gain! Sun, hide thy beams! v 1 226
The sun arises, Which is a great way growing on the south . *J. Cæsar* ii 1 106
O setting sun, As in thy red rays thou dost sink to night, So in his red blood Cassius' day is set; The sun of Rome is set! . . . . v 3 60
That will be ere the set of sun . . . . . . *Macbeth* i 1 5
As whence the sun 'gins his reflection Shipwrecking storms and direful thunders break . . . . i 2 25
O, never Shall sun that morrow see! . . . . i 5 62
I gin to be aweary of the sun . . . . v 5 49
As stars with trains of fire and dews of blood, Disasters in the sun *Ham.* i 1 118
I am too much i' the sun . . . . i 2 67
Doubt thou the stars are fire; Doubt that the sun doth move . . ii 2 117
If the sun breed maggots in a dead dog, being a god kissing carrion . ii 2 181
Let her not walk i' the sun: conception is a blessing; but not as your daughter may conceive . . . . ii 2 185
So many journeys may the sun and moon Make us again count o'er ere love be done! . . . . iii 2 171
The sun no sooner shall the mountains touch . . . . . iv 1 29
So would I ha' done, by yonder sun . . . . iv 5 65
By the sacred radiance of the sun, The mysteries of Hecate . . *Lear* i 1 111
These late eclipses in the sun and moon portend no good to us . . i 2 112
We make guilty of our disasters the sun, the moon, and the stars . . i 2 131
Thou out of heaven's benediction comest To the warm sun! . . . ii 2 169
Infect her beauty, You fen-suck'd fogs, drawn by the powerful sun! . ii 4 169
Were all the letters suns, I could not see one . . . . . iv 6 143
Though other things grow fair against the sun, Yet fruits that blossom first will first be ripe . . . . *Othello* ii 3 382
I think the sun where he was born Drew all such humours from him . iii 4 30
A sibyl, that had number'd in the world The sun to course two hundred compasses . . . . iii 4 71
Methinks it should be now a huge eclipse Of sun and moon . . . v 2 100
Your serpent of Egypt is bred now of your mud by the operation of your sun: so is your crocodile . . . . . . *Ant. and Cleo.* ii 7 30
To-morrow, Before the sun shall see's, we'll spill the blood . . . iv 8 3
O sun, thy uprise shall I see no more: Fortune and Antony part here . iv 12 18
O sun, Burn the great sphere thou movest in! . . . . . iv 15 9
His face was as the heavens; and therein stuck A sun and moon . . v 2 80
Very many there could behold the sun with as firm eyes as he *Cymbeline* i 4 12
What, To hide me from the radiant sun and solace I' the dungeon by a snuff? . . . . i 6 86
If Cæsar can hide the sun from us with a blanket . . . . . iii 1 43
One score [of miles] 'twixt sun and sun, Madam,'s enough for you . . iii 2 70
So high that giants may jet through And keep their impious turbans on, without Good morrow to the sun . . . . iii 3 7
Hath Britain all the sun that shines? Day, night, Are they not but in Britain? . . . . iii 4 139

Sun. Fear no more the heat o' the sun, Nor the furious winter's rages *Cymbeline* iv 2 258
By this sun that shines, I'll thither . . . . iv 4 34
I am ashamed To look upon the holy sun . . . . iv 4 41
Soaring aloft, Lessen'd herself, and in the beams o' the sun So vanish'd v 5 472
Upon his shield Is a black Ethiope reaching at the sun . . *Pericles* ii 2 20
Had princes sit, like stars, about his throne, And he the sun . . . ii 3 40
I know he will come in our shadow, to scatter his crowns in the sun . iv 2 122
Such a piece of slaughter The sun and moon ne'er look'd upon! . . iv 3 3
Sun-beamed. Once to behold with your sun-beamed eyes . . *L. L. Lost* v 2 168
Sunbeams. The Roman eagle, wing'd From the spongy south to this part of the west, There vanish'd in the sunbeams . . . *Cymbeline* iv 2 350
Sun-bright. To be regarded in her sun-bright eye . . *T. G. of Ver.* iii 1 88
Sun-burning. Whose face is not worth sun-burning . . . *Hen. V.* v 2 154
Sunburnt. You sunburnt sicklemen, of August weary . . *Tempest* iv 1 134
Thus goes every one to the world but I, and I am sunburnt . *Much Ado* ii 1 331
He'll say in Troy . . . , The Grecian dames are sunburnt *Troi. and Cres.* i 3 282
Sunday. Wear the print of it and sigh away Sundays . . *Much Ado* i 1 204
We have 'greed so well together, That upon Sunday is the wedding-day. —I'll see the hang'd on Sunday first . . . *T. of Shrew* ii 1 300
Sunday comes apace: We will have rings and things and fine array . ii 1 324
Kiss me, Kate, we will be married o' Sunday . . . . . ii 1 326
On Sunday next you know My daughter Katharine is to be married . ii 1 395
On the Sunday following, shall Bianca Be bride to you . . . ii 1 397
She would be as fair on Friday as Helen is on Sunday . *Troi. and Cres.* i 1 79
Whose sore task Does not divide the Sunday from the week . . *Hamlet* i 1 76
We may call it herb-grace o' Sundays . . . . iv 5 182
Sunday-citizens. And leave 'in sooth,' And such protest of pepper-gingerbread, To velvet-guards and Sunday-citizens . . 1 *Hen. IV.* iii 1 261
Sunder. Gnawing with my teeth my bonds in sunder . . *Com. of Errors* v 1 249
Wall, that vile Wall which did these lovers sunder . . *M. N. Dream* v 1 133
So sweet a bar Should sunder such sweet friends . . *Mer. of Venice* iii 2 120
Strangers and foes do sunder, and not kiss . . . . *All's Well* ii 5 91
Even as a splitted bark, so sunder we . . . . 2 *Hen. VI.* iii 2 411
Chides the sea that sunders him from thence, Saying, he'll lade it dry 3 *Hen. VI.* iii 2 138
'Twere pity To sunder them that yoke so well together . . . iv 1 23
O, cut my lace in sunder, that my pent heart May have some scope to beat, or else I swoon! . . . . *Richard III.* iv 1 34
No space of earth shall sunder our two hates . . *Troi. and Cres.* v 10 27
With that hand that cut thy youth in twain To sunder his *Rom. and Jul.* v 3 100
Sundered. Shall we be sunder'd? shall we part, sweet girl? *As Y. Like It* i 3 100
Away! vexation almost stops my breath, That sunder'd friends greet in the hour of death . . . . 1 *Hen. VI.* iv 3 42
Sweet discourse, Which so long sunder'd friends should dwell upon *Richard III.* v 3 100
Sundry. The sundry contemplation of my travels . . *As Y. Like It* iv 1 17
For sundry weighty reasons . . . . *Macbeth* iii 1 126
My poor country Shall have more vices than it had before, More suffer and more sundry ways than ever . . . . iv 3 48
Sundry blessings hang about his throne, That speak him full of grace . iv 3 158
Sun-expelling. And threw her sun-expelling mask away . *T. G. of Ver.* iv 4 158
Sung. Thou hast by moonlight at her window sung . . *M. N. Dream* i 1 30
To be sung By an Athenian eunuch to the harp . . . . . v 1 44
A very pleasant thing indeed and sung lamentably . . . *W. Tale* iv 4 190
And sung this ballad against the hard hearts of maids . . . iv 4 282
To whom he sung, in rude harsh-sounding rhymes . . . *K. John* iv 2 150
He is more patient Than when you left him; even now he sung . . v 7 12
An I have not ballads made on you all and sung to filthy tunes 1 *Hen. IV.* ii 2 48
Ditties highly penn'd, Sung by a fair queen in a summer's bower . . iii 1 210
And sung those tunes to the over-scutched huswives . . 2 *Hen. IV.* iii 2 340
Let there be sung 'Non nobis' and 'Te Deum' . . . *Hen. V.* iv 8 128
That nothing sung but death to us and ours . . . 3 *Hen. VI.* ii 6 57
And chattering pies in dismal discords sung . . . . . v 6 48
With all the choicest music of the kingdom, Together sung 'Te Deum' *Hen. VIII.* iv 1 92
Like a sweet melodious bird, it sung Sweet varied notes . *T. Andron.* iii 1 85
Many a time he danced thee on his knee, Sung thee asleep . . . v 3 163
Then they for sudden joy did weep, And I for sorrow sung . . *Lear* i 4 192
To sing a song that old was sung, From ashes ancient Gower is come *Pericles* i Gower 1
It hath been sung at festivals, On ember-eves and holy-ales . . i Gower 5
When to the lute She sung, and made the night-bird mute . . iv Gower 26
Sunk. I would Have sunk the sea within the earth . . . *Tempest* i 2 11
Cast away and sunk on Goodwin Sands . . . . . *K. John* v 5 13
For every false drop in her bawdy veins A Grecian's life hath sunk *Troi. and Cres.* iv 1 70
Sunken. A blue eye and sunken . . . . . . *As Y. Like It* iii 2 393
As is the ooze and bottom of the sea With sunken wreck . . *Hen. V.* i 2 165
Sun-like. Afford no extraordinary gaze, Such as is bent on sun-like majesty When it shines seldom . . . . . . 1 *Hen. IV.* iii 2 79
Sunny. My decayed fair A sunny look of his would soon repair *C. of Er.* ii 1 99
Sweet Moon, I thank thee for thy sunny beams . . *M. N. Dream* v 1 277
Her sunny locks Hang on her temples like a golden fleece *Mer. of Venice* i 1 169
Sun-rise. With true prayers That shall be up at heaven and enter there Ere sun-rise . . . . *Meas. for Meas.* ii 2 153
Sunrising. Bid him bring his power Before sunrising . *Richard III.* v 3 61
Sunset. Ere sunset, Set armed discord 'twixt these perjured kings! *K. John* iii 1 110
But ere sunset I'll make thee curse the deed . . 3 *Hen. VI.* ii 1 116
But for the sunset of my brother's son It rains downright *Rom. and Jul.* iii 5 128
Sunshine. Vouchsafe to show the sunshine of your face . *L. L. Lost* v 2 201
Thou mayst see a sunshine and a hail In me at once . . *All's Well* v 3 33
And send him many years of sunshine days! . . . *Richard II.* iv 1 221
And ripens in the sunshine of his favour . . . 2 *Hen. IV.* iv 2 12
Ne'er may he live to see a sunshine day . . . 3 *Hen. VI.* ii 1 187
Even then that sunshine brew'd a shower for him . . . . ii 2 156
When we saw our sunshine made thy spring . . . . . ii 2 163
You have seen Sunshine and rain at once: her smiles and tears Were like a better way . . . . *Lear* iv 3 20
Sup. Dine, sup, and sleep, Upon the very naked name of love *T. G. of V.* ii 4 141
I am fain to dine and sup with water and bran . . *Meas. for Meas.* iv 3 159
If a' have no more man's blood in's belly than will sup a flea . *L. L. Lost* v 2 698
To bid my old master the Jew to sup to-night with my new master *Mer. of Venice* ii 4 18
But sup them well and look unto them all . . . *T. of Shrew* Ind. 1 28
Thither with all greediness of affection are they gone, and there they intend to sup . . . . *W. Tale* v 2 112
Meet me to-morrow night in Eastcheap; there I'll sup . . 1 *Hen. IV.* i 2 217

Sup. Will you sup with me, Master Gower? *2 Hen. IV.* ii 1 201
Where sups he? doth the old boar feed in the old frank? ii 2 159
Sup any women with him? ii 2 165
Invite my Lords of Salisbury and Warwick To sup with me *2 Hen. VI.* i 4 84
Speak not in spite, For you shall sup with Jesu Christ to-night v 1 214
If not in heaven, you'll surely sup in hell v 1 216
Let us sup betimes, that afterwards We may digest our complots *Richard III.* iii 1 199
It's supper-time, my lord; It's nine o'clock.—I will not sup to-night v 3 48
What exploit's in hand? where sups he to-night? *Troi. and Cres.* iii 1 89
You must not know where he sups iii 1 94
You'll sup with me?—Anger's my meat; I sup upon myself *Coriolanus* iv 2 49
At this same ancient feast of Capulet's Sups the fair Rosaline *R. and J.* i 2 88
Will you sup with me to-night, Casca?—No, I am promised forth *J. Cæsar* i 2 292
Will you sup there?—'Faith, I intend so *Othello* iv 1 172
Sir, to-night, I do entreat that we may sup together: You are welcome, sir iv 1 273
He sups to-night with a harlotry, and thither will I go to him iv 2 239
Had our great palace the capacity To camp this host, we all would sup together, And drink carouses *Ant. and Cleo.* iv 8 33
Super-dainty Kate, For dainties are all Kates *T. of Shrew* ii 1 189
Superficial. A very superficial, ignorant, unweighing fellow *M. for M.* iii 2 147
This superficial tale Is but a preface of her worthy praise *1 Hen. VI.* v 5 10
Superficially. And on the cause and question now in hand Have glozed, but superficially *Troi. and Cres.* ii 2 165
You know me, do you not?—Faith, sir, superficially iii 1 10
Superfluity comes sooner by white hairs *Mer. of Venice* i 2 8
Or to bear the inventory of thy shirts, as, one for superfluity, and another for use! *2 Hen. IV.* ii 2 20
If they would yield us but the superfluity, while it were wholesome *Cor.* i 1 17
Then we shall ha' means to vent Our musty superfluity i 1 230
Superfluous. I have no superfluous leisure *Meas. for Meas.* iii 1 158
That superfluous case That hid the worse and show'd the better face *L. L. Lost* v 2 387
Full oft we see Cold wisdom waiting on superfluous folly *All's Well* i 1 116
Deafs our ears With this abundance of superfluous breath *K. John* ii 1 148
This 'once again,' but that your highness pleased, Was once superfluous iv 2 4
Superfluous branches We lop away, that bearing boughs may live *Richard II.* iii 4 63
I see no reason why thou shouldst be so superfluous to demand the time of the day *1 Hen. IV.* i 2 12
Shall I prick him down, Sir John?—It were superfluous *2 Hen. IV.* iii 2 154
And dout them with superfluous courage, ha! *Hen. V.* iv 2 11
Our superfluous lackeys and our peasants iv 2 26
Purchased At a superfluous rate! *Hen. VIII.* i 1 99
In many places Gives me superfluous death *Hamlet* iv 5 96
Our basest beggars Are in the poorest thing superfluous *Lear* ii 4 268
The superfluous and lust-dieted man, That slaves your ordinance iv 1 70
Had superfluous kings for messengers Not many moons gone by *Ant. and Cleo.* iii 12 5
With their superfluous riots *Pericles* i 4 54
To say you're welcome were superfluous ii 3 2
Superfluously. You bear a many superfluously *Hen. V.* iii 7 80
Superflux. Expose thyself to feel what wretches feel, That thou mayst shake the superflux to them *Lear* iii 4 35
Superior. So every step, Exampled by the first pace that is sick Of his superior, grows to an envious fever *Troi. and Cres.* i 3 133
Supernal. From that supernal judge, that stirs good thoughts *K. John* ii 1 112
Supernatural. We have our philosophical persons, to make modern and familiar, things supernatural and causeless *All's Well* ii 3 3
This supernatural soliciting Cannot be ill, cannot be good *Macbeth* i 3 130
Superpraise. To vow, and swear, and superpraise my parts *M. N. Dream* iii 2 153
Superscript. I will overglance the superscript *L. L. Lost* iv 2 135
Superscription. Doth this churlish superscription Pretend some alteration in good will? *1 Hen. VI.* iv 1 53
Read me the superscription of these letters *T. of Athens* ii 2 81
Superserviceable, finical rogue; one-trunk-inheriting slave *Lear* ii 2 19
Superstition. Do not say 'tis superstition *W. Tale* v 3 43
That's your superstition.—Pardon us, sir *Pericles* iii 1 50
Superstitious. The superstitious idle-headed eld *Mer. Wives* iv 4 36
Been, out of fondness, superstitious to him *Hen. VIII.* iii 1 131
This foolish, dreaming, superstitious girl *Troi. and Cres.* v 3 79
He is superstitious grown of late *J. Cæsar* ii 1 195
Superstitiously. For this once, yea, superstitiously, I will be squared by this *W. Tale* iii 3 40
You are like one that superstitiously Doth swear to the gods that winter kills the flies *Pericles* iv 3 49
Supersubtle. A frail vow betwixt an erring barbarian and a supersubtle Venetian *Othello* i 3 363
Supervise. Let me supervise the canzonet *L. L. Lost* iv 2 124
On the supervise, no leisure bated *Hamlet* v 2 23
Supervisor. Would you, the supervisor, grossly gape on? *Othello* iii 3 395
Supped. The room where they supped is too hot *2 Hen. IV.* ii 4 14
He has almost supp'd: why have you left the chamber? *Macbeth* i 7 29
I have supp'd full with horrors v 5 13
Go know of Cassio where he supp'd to-night. What, do you shake at that?—He supp'd at my house; but I therefore shake not *Othello* v 1 117
When we have supp'd, We'll mannerly demand thee of thy story *Cymb.* iii 6 91
Supper. She that you gaze on so as she sits at supper? *T. G. of Ver.* ii 1 47
We'll wait upon your grace till after supper iii 2 96
Tell him I will not fail him at supper *Much Ado* i 1 279
I came yonder from a great supper i 3 44
Let us to the great supper i 3 73
Was not Count John here at supper?—I saw him not ii 1 1
There's a partridge wing saved, for the fool will eat no supper that night ii 1 156
And men sit down to that nourishment which is called supper *L. L. Lost* i 1 240
That supper be ready at the farthest by five of the clock *Mer. of Venice* ii 2 122
Soon at supper shalt thou see Lorenzo, who is thy new master's guest ii 3 5
I am bid forth to supper, Jessica: There are my keys ii 5 11
Dinners and suppers and sleeping-hours excepted *As Y. Like It* iii 2 102
Is supper ready, the house trimmed, rushes strewed? *T. of Shrew* iv 1 47
Go, rascals, go, and fetch my supper in iv 1 142
His daughter is to be brought by you to the supper iv 4 86
It draws toward supper in conclusion so *K. John* i 1 204
Come home with me to supper *Richard II.* iv 1 333
With drinking of old sack and unbuttoning thee after supper and sleeping upon benches after noon *1 Hen. IV.* i 2 3
I have bespoke supper to-morrow night in Eastcheap i 2 144
The incomprehensible lies that this same fat rogue will tell us when we meet at supper i 2 211
Supper. I heard him tell it to one of his company last night at supper *1 Hen. IV.* ii 1 62
Item, Anchovies and sack after supper, 2s. 6d. ii 4 589
I hope you'll come to supper *2 Hen. IV.* ii 1 172
Will you have Doll Tearsheet meet you at supper? ii 1 177
Shall we steal upon them, Ned, at supper? ii 2 173
Like a man made after supper of a cheese-paring iii 2 332
By the mass, I have drunk too much sack at supper v 3 15
Our simple supper ended, give me leave In this close walk *2 Hen. VI.* ii 2 2
To make a bloody supper in the Tower *3 Hen. VI.* v 5 85
As we did sit at supper, My uncle Rivers talk'd how I did grow *Rich. III.* ii 4 10
I stay dinner there.—And supper too, although thou know'st it not iii 2 123
Come to me, Tyrrel, soon at after supper iv 3 31
This night he makes a supper, and a great one *Hen. VIII.* i 3 52
If the king call for him at supper, you will make his excuse *T. and C.* iii 1 84
I shall, between this and supper, tell you most strange things *Coriol.* iv 3 43
Whither should they come?—Up.—Whither?—To supper *Rom. and Jul.* i 2 78
The guests are come, supper served up, you called, my young lady asked for i 3 100
Supper is done, and we shall come too late.—I fear, too early i 4 105
She will indite him to some supper ii 4 135
Come again to supper to him, of purpose to have him spend less *T. of A.* iii 1 26
At supper, You suddenly arose, and walk'd about *J. Cæsar* ii 1 238
We hold a solemn supper, sir, And I'll request your presence *Macbeth* iii 1 14
As will fill up the time 'Twixt this and supper iii 1 26
Where's Polonius?—At supper.—At supper! where?—Not where he eats, but where he is eaten *Hamlet* iv 3 18
We'll go to supper i' the morning. So, so, so *Lear* iii 6 90
Being full of supper and distempering draughts *Othello* i 1 99
Shall't be to-night at supper?—No, not to-night.—To-morrow dinner, then? iii 3 57
An you'll come to supper to-night, you may; an you will not, come when you are next prepared for iv 1 166
Hark, how these instruments summon to supper! iv 2 169
Antony sent to her, Invited her to supper *Ant. and Cleo.* ii 2 225
Let's to supper, come, And drown consideration iv 2 44
Supper-time. Ere supper-time must I perform Much business *Tempest* iii 1 95
At supper-time I'll visit you And then receive my money *Com. of Errors* iii 2 179
We will visit you at supper-time *Mer. of Venice* ii 2 215
Nay, we will slink away in supper-time ii 4 1
'Tis almost two; And 'twill be supper-time ere you come there *T. of S.* iv 3 192
Bianca Hath cost me an hundred crowns since supper-time v 2 128
Now it is supper-time in Orleans *1 Hen. VI.* i 4 59
It's supper-time, my lord; It's nine o'clock.—I will not sup to-night *Richard III.* v 3 47
We will keep ourself Till supper-time alone *Macbeth* iii 1 44
It is now high supper-time, and the night grows to waste *Othello* iv 2 249
Supping. What tell'st thou me of supping? *Com. of Errors* v 3 66
Supplant. I remember You did supplant your brother *Tempest* ii 1 271
By this hand, I will supplant some of your teeth iii 2 56
You three From Milan did supplant good Prospero iii 3 70
We must supplant those rough rug-headed kerns *Richard II.* ii 1 156
Which fear if better reasons can supplant, I will subscribe *2 Hen. VI.* iii 1 37
And so supplant you for ingratitude *T. Andron.* i 1 447
Supple. And had the tribute of his supple knee *Richard II.* i 4 33
I will knead him; I'll make him supple *Troi. and Cres.* ii 3 231
Supple knees Feed arrogance and are the proud man's fees iii 3 48
Supple and courteous to the people *Coriolanus* iii 2 29
Each part, deprived of supple government *Rom. and Jul.* iv 1 102
Aches contract and starve your supple joints! *T. of Athens* i 1 257
Suppler. You That are of suppler joints, follow them swiftly *Tempest* iii 3 107
We have suppler souls Than in our priest-like fasts *Coriolanus* v 1 55
Suppliance. The perfume and suppliance of a minute *Hamlet* i 3 9
Suppliant. When she for thy repeal was suppliant *T. G. of Ver.* iii 1 234
Vanquish'd thereto by the fair grace and speech Of the poor suppliant *All's Well* v 3 134
What shrill-voiced suppliant makes this eager cry? *Richard II.* v 3 75
Heard ye not what an humble suppliant Lord Hastings was to her? *Richard III.* i 1 74
If thy poor devoted suppliant may But beg one favour i 2 207
Scandal'd the suppliants for the people, call'd them Time-pleasers *Coriol.* iii 1 44
Thou hast made it like an humble suppliant *T. Andron.* iv 3 117
Supplication. Than we may deliver our supplications in the quill *2 Hen. VI.* i 3 3
Are your supplications to his lordship? Let me see them i 3 16
What answer makes your grace to the rebels' supplication? iv 4 8
As if Olympus to a molehill should In supplication nod *Coriolanus* v 3 31
Can you with a grace deliver a supplication? *T. Andron.* iv 3 107
Here is a supplication for you iv 3 110
Supplie. O, je vous supplie, pour l'amour de Dieu, me pardonner? *Hen. V.* iv 4 42
Excusez-moi, je vous supplie, mon très-puissant seigneur v 2 277
Supplied. I fill up a place, which may be better supplied when I have made it empty *As Y. Like It* i 2 205
When liver, brain, and heart, These sovereign thrones, are all supplied *T. Night* i 1 38
Thy place in council thou hast rudely lost, Which by thy younger brother is supplied *1 Hen. IV.* iii 2 33
A hundred almshouses right well supplied *Hen. V.* i 1 17
How well supplied with noble counsellors, How modest in exception ii 4 33
Keep . . . the chairs of justice Supplied with worthy men! *Coriolanus* iii 3 35
From the western isles Of kerns and gallowglasses is supplied *Macbeth* i 2 13
I being absent and my place supplied, My general will forget my love *Oth.* iii 3 17
By their own importunate suit, Or voluntary dotage of some mistress, Convinced or supplied them iv 1 28
Supplies. 'Tis their fresh supplies *Cymbeline* v 2 16
Our supplies live largely in the hope Of great Northumberland *2 Hen. IV.* i 3 12
Though we here fall down, We have supplies to second our attempt iv 2 45
With furbish'd arms and new supplies of men Began a fresh assault *Macb.* i 2 32
Suppliest. Keepest from me all conveniency than suppliest me with the least advantage of hope *Othello* iv 2 178
Supply. Elected him our absence to supply *Meas. for Meas.* i 1 19
Supply me with the habit and instruct me i 3 46
And did supply thee at thy garden-house In her imagined person v 1 212
To supply the ripe wants of my friend, I'll break a custom *Mer. of Venice* i 3 64
Supply your present wants and take no doit Of usance i 3 141
Bride and bridegroom wants For to supply the places at the table *T. of S.* iii 2 249
You shall supply the bridegroom's place iii 2 251
The great supply That was expected by the Dauphin here, Are wreck'd three nights ago on Goodwin Sands *K. John* v 3 9
Your supply, which you have wish'd so long, Are cast away v 5 12
And send them after to supply our wants *Richard II.* i 4 51

Supply. Looks he not for supply?—So do we . . 1 *Hen. IV.* iv 3 3
Lined himself with hope, Eating the air on promise of supply 2 *Hen. IV.* i 3 28
For the which supply, Admit me Chorus to this history . . *Hen. V.* Prol. 31
The Earl of Salisbury craveth supply . . . 1 *Hen. VI.* i 1 159
A plague upon that villain Somerset, That thus delays my promised supply ! . . . . . . iv 3 10
Instead whereof let this supply the room . . 3 *Hen. VI.* ii 6 54
This noble queen And prince shall follow with a fresh supply . . iii 3 237
And supply his place ; I mean, in bearing weight of government . iv 6 50
Immediate are my needs, and my relief Must not be toss'd and turn'd to me in words, But find supply immediate . . *T. of Athens* ii 1 27
My occasions have found time to use 'em toward a supply of money ii 2 201
An empty box, sir ; which . . . I come to entreat your honour to supply iii 1 18
Requesting your lordship to supply his instant use with so many talents iii 2 40
Nor has he with him to Supply his life, or that which can command it . iv 2 47
If he care not for't, he will supply us easily . . . v 3 407
For the supply and profit of our hope . . . *Hamlet* ii 2 24
From the loathed warmth whereof deliver me, and supply the place *Lear* iv 6 273
Supply it with one gender of herbs, or distract it with many . . *Othello* i 3 326
With a supply Of Roman gentlemen, by the senate sent . *Cymbeline* iv 3 25
Supplyant. Whereunto your levy Must be supplyant . . . iii 7 14
Supplying every stage With an augmented greeting . *Ant. and Cleo.* iii 6 55
Supplyment. I will never fail Beginning nor supplyment . *Cymbeline* iii 4 182
Support him by the arm . . . . *As Y. L. It* ii 7 199
Who, weak with age, cannot support myself . *Richard II.* ii 2 83
Takes on the point of honour to support So dissolute a crew . . v 3 11
Yet are these feet, whose strengthless stay is numb, Unable to support this lump of clay . . . . . 1 *Hen. VI.* ii 5 14
To strengthen and support King Edward's place . 3 *Hen. VI.* iii 1 52
A thousand pound a year, annual support, Out of his grace he adds *Hen. VIII.* ii 3 64
Make edicts for usury, to support usurers . . *Coriolanus* i 1 84
'Tis not enough to help the feeble up, But to support him after *T. of Athens* i 1 108
And in the most exact regard support The worships of their name *Lear* i 4 287
Wherefore, bold peasant, Darest thou support a publish'd traitor? . iv 6 236
But his flaw'd heart, Alack, too weak the conflict to support ! . . v 3 197
I a heavy interim shall support By his dear absence . . *Othello* i 3 259
Supportable To make the dear loss, have I means much weaker Than you may call to comfort you . . . . *Tempest* v 1 145
Supportance. Therefore draw, for the supportance of his vow *T. Night* iii 4 329
Give some supportance to the bending twigs . . *Richard II.* iii 4 32
Supported. Timon has been this lord's father, And kept his credit with his purse, Supported his estate . . . *T. of Athens* iii 2 76
Supporter. Good supporters are you . . . *Meas. for Meas.* v 1 18
He says, he'll stand at your door like a sheriff's post, and be the supporter to a bench . . . . . *T. Night* i 5 158
My grief's so great That no supporter but the huge firm earth Can hold it up : here I and sorrows sit . . *K. John* iii 1 72
Supporting. Struck the foremost man of all this world But for supporting robbers . . . . . *J. Cæsar* iv 3 23
Supposal. Holding a weak supposal of our worth . . *Hamlet* i 2 18
Suppose. Ferdinand, whom they suppose is drown'd . *Tempest* iii 3 92
I likewise hear that Valentine is dead.—And so suppose am I *T. G. of V.* iv 2 114
He supposes me travell'd to Poland . . *Meas. for Meas.* i 3 14
I suppose we are made to be no stronger Than faults may shake our frames . . . . ii 4 132
While counterfeit supposes blear'd thine eyne . . *T. of Shrew* v 1 120
And do suppose What hath been cannot be . . *All's Well* i 1 240
Hoodwink him so, that he shall suppose no other . . . iii 6 26
He hath confessed himself to Morgan, whom he supposes to be a friar . iv 3 125
I suppose him virtuous, know him noble . . . *T. Night* i 5 277
Eldest son, As I suppose, to Robert Faulconbridge . . *K. John* i 1 52
I did suppose it should be on constraint . . . . v 1 28
His pure brain, Which some suppose the soul's frail dwelling-house . v 7 3
Or suppose Devouring pestilence hangs in our air . . *Richard II.* i 3 283
Suppose the singing birds musicians . . . . . i 3 288
And I say the earth was not of my mind, If you suppose as fearing you it shook . . . . . . 1 *Hen. IV.* iii 1 23
Is he so hasty that he doth suppose My sleep my death? 2 *Hen. IV.* iv 5 61
Suppose within the girdle of these walls Are now confined two mighty monarchies . . . . . . *Hen. V.* Prol. 19
Suppose that you have seen The well-appointed king . . iii Prol. 3
Suppose the ambassador from the French comes back . . iii Prol. 28
Who would e'er suppose They had such courage and audacity? 1 *Hen. VI.* i 2 35
If he suppose that I have pleaded truth, . . . pluck a white rose with me ii 4 29
Would you not suppose Your bondage happy, to be made a queen? . v 3 110
Suppose, my lords, he did it unconstrain'd . . 3 *Hen. VI.* i 1 143
Suppose this arm is for the Duke of York, And this for Rutland . . ii 4 2
Suppose they take offence without a cause . . . . iv 1 14
Suppose that I am now my father's mouth . . . . v 5 18
As little joy, my lord, as you suppose You should enjoy, were you this country's king, As little joy may you suppose in me *Richard III.* i 3 151
We come short of our suppose so far . . . *Troi. and Cres.* i 3 11
Lose not so noble a friend on vain suppose . . . *T. Andron.* i 1 440
I know them all, though they suppose me mad . . . v 2 142
Bid him suppose some good necessity Touches his friend *T. of Athens* ii 2 236
To lip a wanton in a secure couch, And to suppose her chaste! *Othello* iv 1 73
And on this coast Suppose him now at anchor . . *Pericles* v Gower 16
You aptly will suppose What pageantry, what feats, what shows . . v 2 270
Supposed. Let the supposed fairies pinch him sound *Mer. Wives* iv 4 61
I'll be supposed upon a book, his face is the worst thing *Meas. for Meas.* ii 1 162
You must lay down the treasures of your body To this supposed . . ii 4 97
Supposed by the common rout Against your yet ungalled estimation *Com. of Errors* iii 1 101
How easy is a bush supposed a bear ! . . . *M. N. Dream* v 1 22
Make such wanton gambols with the wind, Upon supposed fairness *Mer. of Venice* iii 2 94
Supposed Lucentio Must get a father, call'd 'supposed Vincentio' *T. of Shrew* ii 1 409
If you should tender your supposed aid, He would receive it . *All's Well* i 3 242
You must know, I am supposed dead . . . . iv 4 11
Supposed sincere and holy in his thoughts, He's followed 2 *Hen. IV.* i 1 202
Which daily grew to quarrel and to bloodshed, Wounding supposed peace iv 5 196
Jerusalem ; Which vainly I supposed the Holy Land . . iv 5 239
King Pharamond, Idly supposed the founder of this law . *Hen. V.* i 2 59
They supposed I could rend bars of steel . . . 1 *Hen. VI.* i 4 51
More furious raging broils Than yet can be imagined or supposed . iv 1 186
We John Cade, so termed of our supposed father . 2 *Hen. VI.* iv 2 33
Return in post, And tell false Edward, thy supposed king 3 *Hen. VI.* iii 3 223 ; iv 1 93

Supposed. Vouchsafe . . . , Of these supposed evils, to give me leave, By circumstance, but to acquit myself . . *Richard III.* i 2 76
Were jocund, and supposed their state was sure . . . iii 2 86
It is supposed He that meets Hector issues from our choice *Tr. and Cr.* i 3 346
Such as was supposed The wandering prince and Dido once enjoy'd *T. An.* ii 3 21
I aim'd so near, when I supposed you loved . *Rom. and Jul.* i 1 211
But to his foe supposed he must complain . . . ii Prol. 7
With which grief, It is supposed, the fair creature died . . . v 3 51
Tender our loves to him, in this supposed distress of his *T. of Athens* v 1 15
Edmund, supposed Earl of Gloucester . . . . *Lear* v 3 112
That Thaisa am I, supposed dead And drown'd . . *Pericles* v 3 35
Supposest. Drown the sad remembrance of those wrongs Which thou supposest I have done to thee . . . *Richard III.* iv 4 252
Supposing that they saw the king's ship wreck'd . . *Tempest* i 2 236
Supposing it a thing impossible . . . . *T. of Shrew* i 2 123
Let him speak : The honour is sacred which he talks on now, Supposing that I lack'd it . . . . . . *Ant. and Cleo.* ii 2 86
In your supposing once more put your sight Of heavy Pericles *Per.* v Gower 21
Supposition. And in that glorious supposition think He gains by death *Com. of Errors* iii 2 50
The supposition of the lady's death Will quench the wonder of her infamy *Much Ado* iv 1 240
Yet his means are in supposition . . . . *Mer. of Venice* i 3 18
Only to seem to deserve well, and to beguile the supposition . *All's Well* iv 3 333
Suppress. To crown himself king and suppress the prince . 1 *Hen. VI.* i 3 68
Well didst thou, Richard, to suppress thy voice . . . iv 1 182
In what we can, to bridle and suppress The pride of Suffolk . 2 *Hen. VI.* i 1 200
To suppress His further gait herein . . . *Hamlet* i 2 30
He sent out to suppress His nephew's levies . . . . ii 2 61
Suppressed. The mercy that was quick in us but late, By your own counsel is suppress'd and kill'd . . . *Hen. V.* ii 2 80
Thus the Mortimers, In whom the title rested, were suppress'd 1 *Hen. VI.* ii 5 92
He hath made a solemn vow Never to lie and take his natural rest Till Warwick or himself be quite suppress'd . 3 *Hen. VI.* iv 3 6
Suppresseth. Yet heavens are just, and time suppresseth wrongs . iii 3 77
Supremacy. Peace it bodes, and love and quiet life, And awful rule and right supremacy . . . . . *T. of Shrew* v 2 109
Or seek for rule, supremacy, and sway, When they are bound to serve . v 2 163
As we, under heaven, are supreme head, So under Him that great supremacy, Where we do reign, we will alone uphold *K. John* iii 1 156
O'er my spirit Thy full supremacy thou knew'st . *Ant. and Cleo.* iii 11 59
Like lesser lights, Did vail their crowns to his supremacy . *Pericles* ii 3 42
Supreme. We, under heaven, are supreme head . . *K. John* iii 1 155
Fie, lords ! that you, being supreme magistrates, Thus contumeliously should break the peace ! . . . . . 1 *Hen. VI.* i 3 57
Take heed you dally not before your king ; Lest he that is the supreme King of kings Confound your hidden falsehood . *Richard III.* ii 1 13
It is your fault that you resign The supreme seat . . . iii 7 118
My soul aches To know, when two authorities are up, Neither supreme, how soon confusion May enter 'twixt the gap of both *Coriolanus* iii 1 110
The god of soldiers, With the consent of supreme Jove, inform Thy thoughts with nobleness ! . . . . . . v 3 71
O, that husband ! My supreme crown of grief ! . . *Cymbeline* i 6 4
Sur-addition. He served with glory and admired success, So gain'd the sur-addition Leonatus . . . . . . i 1 33
Surance. Now give some surance that thou art Revenge . *T. Andron.* v 2 46
Surcease. Lest I surcease to honour mine own truth *Coriolanus* iii 2 121
No pulse Shall keep his native progress, but surcease . *Rom. and Jul.* iv 1 97
And catch With his surcease success . . . . *Macbeth* i 7 4
Sure. For this, be sure, to-night thou shalt have cramps . *Tempest* i 2 325
It sounds no more : and, sure, it waits upon Some god o' the island . i 2 388
Most sure, the goddess On whom these airs attend ! . . . i 2 421
Sure, it was the roar Of a whole herd of lions . . . ii 1 315
Heavens keep him from these beasts ! For he is, sure, i' the island . ii 1 325
Nay, sure, I think she holds them prisoners still . *T. G. of Ver.* ii 4 92
And, sure, the match Were rich and honourable . . . . iii 1 63
I am sure she is not buried.—Say that she be . . . iv 2 108
If 'twere a substance, you would, sure, deceive it . . iv 2 127
Guess'd that it was she, But, being mask'd, he was not sure of it . v 2 40
Less than this, I am sure, you cannot give . . . . v 4 25
Revenged I will be, as sure as his guts are made of puddings . *Mer. Wives* ii 1 31
I warrant he hath a thousand of these letters, writ with blank space for different names,—sure, more . . . . . . ii 1 77
For, sure, unless he know some strain in me, that I know not myself . ii 1 90
I'll be sure to keep him above deck . . . . . ii 1 94
Meed, I am sure, I have received none . . . . ii 2 212
If your husbands were dead, you two would marry.—Be sure of that . iii 2 16
Hath he any eyes? hath he any thinking? Sure, they sleep . . iii 2 31
Sure he is by this, or will be presently . . . . iv 1 3
There are fairer things than polecats, sure . . . . iv 1 30
But are you sure of your husband now? . . . . iv 2 6
In my house I am sure he is . . . . . . iv 2 154
The spirit of wantonness is, sure, scared out of him . . . iv 2 223
Sure, he'll come.—Fear not you that . . . . iv 4 77
Sure, one of you does not serve heaven well, that you are so crossed . iv 5 129
She and I, long since contracted, Are now so sure that nothing can dissolve us . . . . v 5 237
Art thou sure of this?—I am too sure of it . . *Meas. for Meas.* i 2 72
Precise villains they are, that I am sure of . . . . ii 1 55
Sure, it is no sin ; Or of the deadly seven it is the least . . iii 1 110
Many that are not mad Have, sure, more lack of reason . . v 1 68
Sure, Luciana, it is two o'clock . . . *Com. of Errors* ii 1 3
Why, mistress, sure my master is horn-mad . . . . ii 1 57
I mean not cuckold-mad ; But, sure, he is stark mad . . . ii 1 59
Sure ones then.—Nay, not sure, in a thing falsing.—Certain ones then . ii 2 94
Sure, these are but imaginary wiles And Lapland sorcerers inhabit here iv 3 10
Anon, I'm sure, the duke himself in person Comes this way . . v 1 119
As sure, my liege, as I do see your grace . . . . v 1 279
I am sure you both of you remember me . . . . v 1 291
I am sure thou dost.—Ay, sir, but I am sure I do not . . v 1 303
You are both sure, and will assist me?—To the death . *Much Ado* i 3 71
I am sure you know him well enough.—Not I, believe me . . ii 1 138
I am sure he is in the fleet . . . . . . ii 1 148
Sure my brother is amorous on Hero . . . . . ii 1 161
You were born in a merry hour.—No, sure, my lord, my mother cried . ii 1 348
Knavery cannot, sure, hide himself in such reverence . . . ii 3 125
But are you sure That Benedick loves Beatrice so entirely? . . iii 1 36
She is so self-endeared.—Sure, I think so . . . . . iii 1 56
Sure, sure, such carping is not commendable . . . . iii 1 71
As sure as I have a thought or a soul . . . . . iv 1 333

Sure. Come, cousin, I am sure you love the gentleman . . . *Much Ado* v 4 84
I am sure you know how much the gross sum of deuce-ace amounts to
L. L. Lost i 2 48
I am sure I shall turn sonnet. Devise, wit; write, pen . . i 2 190
Are we not all in love?—Nothing so sure . . . iv 3 283
Mine, as sure as bark on tree . . . v 2 285
I am sure you hate me with your hearts . . *M. N. Dream* iii 2 154
Are you sure That we are awake? . . . iv 1 197
His discretion, I am sure, cannot carry his valour . . v 1 239
I am very sure, If they should speak, would almost damn those ears
Mer. of Venice i 1 97
I am sure you are not Launcelot, my boy . . . ii 2 86
I am sure he had more hair of his tail than I have of my face . ii 2 103
And in their ship I am sure Lorenzo is not . . . ii 8 3
I am sure, if he forfeit, thou wilt not take his flesh . . iii 1 53
I wish you all the joy that you can wish; For I am sure you can wish
none from me . . . iii 2 193
I am sure the duke Will never grant this forfeiture to hold . iii 3 24
Know him I shall, I am well sure of it . . . v 1 229
I am sure you are not satisfied Of these events at full . . v 1 296
Yonder, sure, they are coming: let us now stay *As Y. Like It* i 2 156
As sure I think did never man love so . . . ii 4 29
If the cat will after kind, So be sure will Rosalind . . iii 2 110
In which cage of rushes I am sure you are not prisoner . . iii 2 389
'Tis pretty, sure, and very probable! . . . iii 5 11
I am sure there is no force in eyes That can do hurt . . iii 5 26
But, sure, he's proud, and yet his pride becomes him . . iii 5 114
This is a man's invention and his hand.—Sure, it is hers . iv 3 30
There is, sure, another flood toward . . . v 4 35
You and you are sure together, As the winter to foul weather . v 4 141
I am sure, . . . will, for my kind offer, when I make curtsy, bid me
farewell . . . Epil. 21
But, sure, that part Was aptly fitted and naturally perform'd *T. of Shrew* Ind. 1 86
I would I were as sure of a good dinner . . . i 2 218
This is a gift very grateful, I am sure of it . . . ii 1 76
I will be sure my Katharine shall be fine . . . ii 1 319
Mistrust it not; for, sure, Æacides Was Ajax . . . iii 1 52
I am sure, sweet Kate, this kindness merits thanks. What, not a word? iv 3 41
Cannot choose But lend and give where she is sure to lose . *All's Well* i 3 221
Be sure of this, What I can help thee to thou shalt not miss . i 3 261
I know most sure My art is not past power nor you past cure . ii 1 160
Sure, they are bastards to the English; the French ne'er got 'em . ii 3 100
I am sure thy father drunk wine . . . ii 3 105
Will this capriccio hold in thee? art sure? . . . ii 3 310
I am sure the younger of our nature, That surfeit on their ease, will day
by day Come here for physic . . . iii 1 17
Whom I am sure he knows not from the enemy . . . iii 6 25
But, sure, he is the prince of the world; let his nobility remain in's court iv 5 51
I am sure I saw her wear it.—You are deceived, my lord . . v 3 91
I am sure care's an enemy to life . . *T. Night* i 3 2
Sure, my noble lord, . . . she never will admit me . . i 4 18
I, that am sure I lack thee, may pass for a wise man . . i 5 37
Sure, you have some hideous matter to deliver . . . i 5 221
Sure methought her eyes had lost her tongue, For she did speak in
starts distractedly. She loves me, sure . . . ii 2 21
He is, sure, possessed, madam . . . iii 4 9
For, sure, the man is tainted in's wits . . . iii 4 13
I am sure no man hath any quarrel to me . . . iii 4 247
Tell him, you are sure All in Bohemia's well . . *W. Tale* i 2 30
I am sure 'tis safer to Avoid what's grown than question how 'tis born i 2 432
'Tis a bastard, So sure as this beard's grey . . . ii 3 162
A pretty one; a very pretty one: sure, some 'scape . . iii 3 72
Sure this robe of mine Does change my disposition . . iv 4 134
I love a ballad in print o' life, for then we are sure they are true . iv 4 264
Sure the gods do this year connive at us, and we may do any thing
extempore . . . iv 4 691
Sure, When I shall see this gentleman, thy speeches Will bring me to
consider that which may Unfurnish me of reason . . v 1 120
I would fain say, bleed tears, for I am sure my heart wept blood . v 2 97
Be sure I count myself in nothing else so happy . *Richard II.* ii 3 45
Two I am sure I have paid, two rogues in buckram suits *1 Hen. IV.* ii 4 212
These promises are fair, the parties sure . . . iii 1 1
So should I be sure to be heart-burned . . . iii 3 58
And for their bareness, I am sure they never learned that of me . iv 2 78
I have paid Percy, I have made him sure . . . v 3 48
Mine I am sure thou art, whoe'er thou be . . . v 4 37
I'll make him sure; yea, and I'll swear I killed him . . v 4 127
My master is deaf.—I am sure he is, to the hearing of any thing good
2 Hen. IV. i 2 80
Good Master Fang, hold him sure . . . ii 1 27
He sure means brevity in breath, short-winded . . . i 2 135
Certain, 'tis certain; very sure, very sure . . . iii 2 40
Lead him hence; and see you guard him sure . . . iv 3 81
Though thou stand'st more sure than I could do, Thou art not firm
enough . . . iv 5 203
You borrow not that face Of seeming sorrow, it is sure your own . v 2 29
God and his angels guard your sacred throne And make you long be-
come it!—Sure, we thank you . . . *Hen. V.* i 2 8
Nay, sure, he's not in hell: he's in Arthur's bosom . . ii 3 9
For I am sure, when he shall see our army, He'll drop his heart . iii 5 58
So should he be sure to be ransomed, and a many poor men's lives
saved . . . iv 1 127
Which I am sure will hang upon my tongue like a new-married wife . v 2 189
We will meet; to thy cost, be sure: Thy heart-blood I will have *1 Hen. VI.* i 3 82
If not of hell, the heavens, sure, favour him . . . i 1 47
'Tis sure they found some place But weakly guarded . . ii 1 73
Am sure I scared the Dauphin . . . ii 2 28
As sure as English Henry lives And as his father here was conqueror,
As sure as in this late-betrayed town Great Cœur-de-lion's heart
was buried, So sure I swear to get the town or die . . iii 2 80
If we both stay, we both are sure to die . . . iv 5 20
He talks at random; sure, the man is mad . . . v 3 84
I'll be the first, sure.—Come back, fool . . *2 Hen. VI.* i 3 8
Poise the cause in justice' equal scales, Whose beam stands sure . ii 1 205
Till the axe of death Hang over thee, as, sure, it shortly will . ii 4 50
Take away the duke, and guard him sure . . . iii 1 188
So the poor chicken should be sure of death . . . iii 1 251
For, sure, my thoughts do hourly prophesy Mischance unto my state . iii 2 283
The king hath sent him, sure: I must dissemble . . . v 1 13
Why, so! then am I sure of victory . . . *3 Hen. VI.* iv 1 147

Sure. If Warwick take us we are sure to die . . *3 Hen. VI.* iv 4 35
Be thou sure I'll well requite thy kindness . . . iv 6 10
Ere ye come there, be sure to hear some news . . . v 5 48
A persecutor, I am sure, thou art . . . v 6 31
Were jocund, and supposed their state was sure . . *Richard III.* iii 2 86
But, sure, I fear, we shall ne'er win him to it . . . iii 7 80
For I am sure the emperor Paid ere he promised . . *Hen. VIII.* i 1 185
That, sure, they've worn out Christendom . . . i 3 15
I am glad they are going, For, sure, there's no converting of 'em . i 3 43
I do not think he fears death.—Sure, he does not: He never was so
womanish . . . ii 1 37
Where you are liberal of your loves and counsels Be sure you be not
loose . . . ii 1 127
How sad he looks! sure, he is much afflicted . . . ii 2 63
Sure, in that I deem you an ill husband . . . iii 2 141
Found thee a way, out of his wreck, to rise in; A sure and safe one . iii 2 438
The citizens, I am sure, have shown at full their royal minds . iv 1 8
And, sure, those men are happy that shall have 'em . . iv 2 147
Sure, you know me?—Yes, my lord; But yet I cannot help you . v 2 4
I'm sure Thou hast a cruel nature and a bloody . . . v 3 128
Meant for his trial, And fair purgation to the world, than malice, I'm
sure . . . v 3 153
You say as I say; for, I am sure, he is not Hector . *Troi. and Cres.* i 2 71
I think Helen loves him better than Paris . . Nay, I am sure she does i 2 119
She was not, sure.—Most sure she was . . . v 2 126
My dreams will, sure, prove ominous to the day . . . v 3 6
If it were at liberty, 'twould, sure, southward . . *Coriolanus* ii 3 32
Why, so he did, I am sure.—No, no; no man saw 'em . . ii 3 173
Wish To jump a body with a dangerous physic That's sure of death
without it . . . iii 1 155
He shall, sure on't.—Sir, sir,— Peace! . . . iii 1 273
Be thou sure, When he shall come to his account, he knows not What
I can urge against him . . . iv 7 17
But, sure, if you Would be your country's pleader . . . v 1 35
Not with such friends That thought them sure of you . . v 3 8
I warrant you, madam, we will make that sure . *T. Andron.* ii 3 133
See that you make her sure . . . ii 3 187
But, sure, some Tereus hath deflowered thee . . . ii 4 26
Sweet blowse, you are a beauteous blossom, sure . . iv 2 72
As sure a card as ever won the set . . . v 1 100
Whilst I at a banquet hold him sure . . . v 2 76
Bind them sure, And stop their mouths . . . v 2 161
Is he sure bound? look that you bind them fast . . . v 2 166
Because I would be sure to have all well . . . v 3 31
That Rosaline Torments him so, that he will sure run mad *Rom. and Jul.* ii 4 5
Thou hast more of the wild-goose in one of thy wits than, I am sure, I
have in my whole five . . . ii 4 77
I will confess to you that I love him.—So will ye, I am sure, that you
love me . . . iv 1 26
I am sure you have your hands full all, In this so sudden business . iv 3 11
Must be employ'd Now to guard sure their master . *T. of Athens* iii 3 40
Banished!—'Tis so, be sure of it.—How! how! . . . iii 6 63
Tell me true—For I must ever doubt, though ne'er so sure . . iv 3 514
Ye've heard that I have gold; I am sure you have . . . v 1 80
Dead, sure; and this his grave. What's on this tomb I cannot read . v 3 5
But, I am sure, Cæsar fell down . . . *J. Cæsar* i 2 260
And after this let Cæsar seat him sure; For we will shake him . i 2 325
Ere day We will awake him and be sure of him . . . i 3 164
I am sure, It did not lie there when I went to bed . . . ii 1 37
If these, As I am sure they do, bear fire enough To kindle cowards . ii 1 120
Sure, the boy heard me: Brutus hath a suit That Cæsar will not grant ii 4 42
Yet Brutus says he was ambitious; And, sure, he is an honourable man iii 2 104
For I have seen more years, I'm sure, than ye . . . iv 3 132
I was sure your lordship did not give it me . . . iv 3 254
I know my hour is come.—Not so, my lord.—Nay, I am sure it is . v 5 21
Thou sure and firm-set earth, Hear not my steps . . *Macbeth* ii 1 56
I'll make assurance double sure, And take a bond of fate . . iv 1 83
Lay thou thy basis sure, For goodness dare not check thee . . iv 3 32
She has spoke what she should not, I am sure of that . . v 1 54
At least I'm sure it may be so in Denmark . . *Hamlet* i 5 109
Sure I am two men there are not living To whom he more adheres . ii 2 20
This brain of mine Hunts not the trail of policy so sure As it hath used
to do . . . ii 2 47
And sure, dear friends, my thanks are too dear a halfpenny . . ii 2 281
Sense, sure, you have, Else could you not have motion; but sure, that
sense Is apoplex'd . . . iii 4 71
Sure, he that made us with such large discourse, Looking before and
after . . . iv 4 36
There might be thought, Though nothing sure, yet much unhappily . iv 5 13
But, sure, the bravery of his grief did put me Into a towering passion . v 2 79
Since, I am sure, my love's More richer than my tongue . . *Lear* i 1 79
Sure, I shall never marry like my sisters, To love my father all . i 1 105
Sure, her offence Must be of such unnatural degree, That monsters it . i 1 221
Yet have I left a daughter, Who, I am sure, is kind and comfortable . i 4 328
And such a daughter Should sure to the slaughter . . . i 4 342
Advise yourself.—I am sure on't, not a word . . . ii 1 29
I know your lady does not love her husband; I am sure of that . iv 5 24
Most sure and vulgar: every one hears that, Which can distinguish
sound . . . iv 6 214
Not sure, though hoping, of this good success, I ask'd his blessing . v 3 194
As sure as you are Roderigo, Were I the Moor, I would not be Iago *Oth.* i 1 56
Be sure My spirit and my place have in them power To make this bitter i 1 102
The duke's in council, and your noble self, I am sure, is sent for . i 2 93
Thou art sure of me:—go, make money . . . i 3 371
I am sorry For your displeasure; but all will sure be well . . iii 1 45
Was not that Cassio parted from my wife?—Cassio, my lord! No, sure iii 3 36
For, sure, he fills it up with great ability . . . iii 3 245
Villain, be sure thou prove my love a whore, Be sure of it . . iii 3 359
But such a handkerchief—I am sure it was your wife's—did I to-day
See Cassio wipe his beard with . . . iii 3 438
Sure, there's some wonder in this handkerchief: I am most unhappy in
the loss . . . iii 4 101
Something, sure, of state, Either from Venice, or some unhatch'd
practice . . . iii 4 140
Ply Desdemona well, and you are sure on't . . . iv 1 107
What trumpet is that same?—Something from Venice, sure . . iv 1 227
But you shall make all well.—Are you sure of that? . . . iv 1 238
Why did he so?—I do not know; I am sure I am none such . . iv 2 123
My friend and my dear countryman Roderigo! no:—yes, sure:—O
heaven! . . . v 1 90

Sure. What's best to do? If she come in, she'll sure speak to my wife *Othello* v 2 96
Sure, he hath kill'd his wife.—Ay, ay: O, lay me by my mistress' side. v 2 236
If thou dost play with him at any game, Thou art sure to lose *Ant. and Cleo.* ii 3 26
O, that his fault should make a knave of thee, That art not what thou'rt sure of! ii 5 103
Pompey doth this day laugh away his fortune.—If he do, sure, he cannot weep't back again ii 6 111
How appears the fight?—On our side like the token'd pestilence, Where death is sure iii 10 10
To be sure of that, I will ask Antony iii 13 62
I am sure, Though you can guess what temperance should be, You know not what it is iii 13 120
I am sure, my nails Are stronger than mine eyes v 2 223
You are too sure an augurer v 2 337
Doubting things go ill often hurts more Than to be sure they do *Cymb.* i 6 96
And will continue fast to your affection, Still close as sure i 6 139
I would I were so sure To win the king as I am bold her honour Will remain hers ii 4 1
No companies abroad?—None in the world: you did mistake him, sure iv 2 102
I will not say Thou shalt be so well master'd, but, be sure, No less beloved iv 2 383
Or to take upon yourself that which I am sure you do not know v 4 188
I am sure hanging's the way of winking v 4 197
Were't he, I am sure He would have spoke to us v 5 125
There was our error.—This is, sure, Fidele v 5 260
How! my issue!—So sure as you your father's v 5 332
Who shuns not to break one will sure crack both *Pericles* i 2 121
If I do it not, I am sure to be hanged at home i 3 3
Thou wilt starve, sure; for here's nothing to be got now-a-days ii 1 72
I yet am unprovided Of a pair of bases.—We'll sure provide ii 1 168
Sure, he's a gallant gentleman.—He's but a country gentleman ii 3 32
Sure, all's effectless; yet nothing we'll omit That bears recovery's name v 1 53
For yet he seems to doubt, How sure you are my daughter v 1 228
Sure as day. 'As God shall mend me,' and 'as sure as day' *1 Hen. IV.* iii 1 255
Sure as death I swore I would not part a bachelor from the priest *T. Andron.* i 1 487
Sure as I live, he had suffered for't *T. G. of Ver.* iv 4 17
Sure death. Uncertain life, and sure death *All's Well* ii 3 20
Sure destruction. Linger not our sure destructions on! *Troi. and Cres.* v 10 9
It shall be to him then as our good wills, A sure destruction *Coriolanus* ii 1 259
Sure enough. If we recover that, we are sure enough *T. G. of Ver.* v 1 12
'Tis sure enough, an you knew how *T. Andron.* iv 1 95
If money were as certain as your waiting, 'Twere sure enough *T. of A.* iii 4 48
If I can get him within my pistol's length, I'll make him sure enough *Pericles* i 1 169
Sure foundation. There is no sure foundation set on blood *K. John* iv 2 104
Consent upon a sure foundation *2 Hen. IV.* i 3 52
Sure of foot. I wish your horses swift and sure of foot *Macbeth* iii 1 38
Sure ones then.—Nay, not sure, in a thing falsing *Com. of Errors* ii 2 94
Sure physician. He had rather Groan so in perpetuity than be cured By the sure physician, death *Cymbeline* v 4 7
Sure uncertainty. Until I know this sure uncertainty, I'll entertain the offer'd fallacy *Com. of Errors* ii 2 187
Surecard. Master Surecard, as I think? *2 Hen. IV.* iii 2 95
Surely It is a sleepy language *Tempest* ii 1 210
Surely I think you have charms, la; yes, in truth *Mer. Wives* ii 2 107
'Tis surely for a name.—I warrant it is *Meas. for Meas.* i 2 175
You do him wrong, surely iii 2 137
Surely, sir, a good favour you have, but that you have a hanging look iv 2 34
Surely, master, not a rag of money *Com. of Errors* iv 4 89
They will surely do us no harm: you saw they speak us fair iv 4 156
Hero thinks surely she will die *Much Ado* ii 3 180
Surely suit ill spent and labour ill bestowed iii 2 103
Surely I do believe your fair cousin is wronged iv 1 261
Surely, a princely testimony! iv 1 317
A sweet gallant, surely! iv 1 319
I do live, And surely as I live, I am a maid v 4 64
He surely affected her for her wit *L. L. Lost* i 2 92
None are so surely caught, when they are catch'd, As wit turn'd fool v 2 69
Wherever they are gone, That youth is surely in their company *As Y. Like It* ii 2 16
For me, that I may surely keep mine oath, I will be married *T. of Shrew* iv 2 36
In gait and countenance surely like a father iv 2 65
Think you it is so?—Ay, surely, mere the truth *All's Well* iii 5 58
Surely as your feet hit the ground they step on *T. Night* iii 4 305
By this knot thou shalt so surely tie Thy now unsured assurance *K. John* ii 1 470
Is Norfolk dead?—As surely as I live, my lord *Richard II.* iv 1 102
Good phrases are surely, and ever were, very commendable *2 Hen. IV.* iii 2 77
Surely, by all the glory you have won *1 Hen. VI.* iv 6 50
Is he a lamb? his skin is surely lent him *2 Hen. VI.* iii 1 77
As surely as my soul intends to live With that dread King iii 2 153
If not in heaven, you'll surely sup in hell v 1 216
Wheresoe'er he is, he's surely dead *3 Hen. VI.* ii 6 41
Surely, sir, There's in him stuff that puts him to these ends *Hen. VIII.* i 1 57
Was he not held a learned man?—Yes, surely ii 2 124
When he thinks, good easy man, full surely His greatness is a-ripening iii 2 356
The devil was amongst 'em, I think, surely v 4 62
In this rapture I shall surely speak The thing I shall repent *T. and C.* iii 2 138
Else, surely, his had equall'd *T. of Athens* iii 4 32
Let me behold thy face. Surely, this man Was born of woman iv 3 500
You do, surely, bar the door upon your own liberty *Hamlet* iii 2 351
That you shall surely find him, Lead to the Sagittary the raised search *Othello* i 1 158
Surely Cassio, I believe, received From him that fled some strange indignity ii 3 244
I have surely seen him: His favour is familiar to me *Cymbeline* v 5 92
Surer. The sooner to effect And surer bind this knot of amity *1 Hen. VI.* v 1 16
You are no surer, no, Than is the coal of fire upon the ice *Coriolanus* i 1 176
He is your brother by the surer side *T. Andron.* iv 2 126
Surest. They well deserve to have, That know the strong'st and surest way to get *Richard II.* iii 3 201
Go sit in council, How covert matters may be best disclosed, And open perils surest answered *J. Cæsar* iv 1 47
Surety. Have pity; I'll be his surety *Tempest* i 2 475
In surety of the which, One part of Aquitaine is bound to us *L. L. Lost* ii 1 135
I think the Frenchman became his surety *Mer. of Venice* i 2 89
You shall be his surety. Give him this And bid him keep it v 1 254
One of the greatest in the Christian world Shall be my surety *All's Well* iv 4 3
Surety. She call'd the saints to surety *All's Well* v 3 108
The jeweller that owes the ring is sent for, And he shall surety me v 3 298
And makest an oath the surety for thy truth Against an oath *K. John* iii 1 282
What surety of the world, what hope, what stay? v 7 68
Procure your sureties for your days of answer *Richard II.* iv 1 159
And givest such sarcenet surety for thy oaths *1 Hen. IV.* iii 1 256
Let there be impawn'd Some surety for a safe return again iv 3 109
He is a man Who with a double surety binds his followers *2 Hen. IV.* i 1 191
We'll take your oath, And all the peers', for surety of our leagues *Hen. V.* v 2 400
The bastard boys of York Shall be the surety for their traitor father *2 Hen. VI.* v 1 116
Bane to those That for my surety will refuse the boys! v 1 121
With surety stronger than Achilles' arm *Troi. and Cres.* i 3 220
The wound of peace is surety, Surety secure ii 2 14
Give me some token for the surety of it v 2 60
We'll surety him.—Aged sir, hands off *Coriolanus* iii 1 178
But I, for mere suspicion in that kind, Will do as if for surety *Othello* i 3 396
Surfeit. O, I have fed upon this woe already, And now excess of it will make me surfeit *T. G. of Ver.* iii 1 220
Surfeit is the father of much fast *Meas. for Meas.* i 2 130
As a surfeit of the sweetest things The deepest loathing to the stomach brings *M. N. Dream* ii 2 137
So thou, my surfeit and my heresy, Of all he hated! ii 2 141
For aught I see, they are as sick that surfeit with too much as they that starve with nothing *Mer. of Venice* i 2 6
I feel too much thy blessing: make it less, For fear I surfeit iii 2 115
The younger of our nature, That surfeit on their ease *All's Well* iii 1 18
Their love may be call'd appetite, No motion of the liver, but the palate, That suffer surfeit, cloyment, and revolt *T. Night* ii 4 102
Now comes the sick hour that his surfeit made *Richard II.* ii 2 84
As one that surfeits thinking on a want *2 Hen. VI.* iii 2 348
If not by war, by surfeit die your king, As ours by murder! *Richard III.* i 3 197
What authority surfeits on would relieve us *Coriolanus* i 1 16
I had rather had eleven die nobly for their country than one voluptuously surfeit out of action i 3 28
Thou art too full Of the wars' surfeits, to go rove iv 1 46
And this the banquet she shall surfeit on *T. Andron.* v 2 194
Will the cold brook, Candied with ice, caudle thy morning taste, To cure thy o'er-night's surfeit? *T. of Athens* iv 3 227
When we are sick in fortune,—often the surfeit of our own behaviour *Lear* i 2 130
Full surfeits, and the dryness of his bones, Call on him for't *Ant. and Cleo.* i 4 27
Surfeited. They surfeited with honey and began To loathe the taste of sweetness *1 Hen. IV.* iii 2 71
Their over-greedy love hath surfeited *2 Hen. IV.* i 3 88
The surfeited grooms Do mock their charge with snores *Macbeth* ii 2 5
My hopes, not surfeited to death, Stand in bold cure *Othello* ii 1 50
Surfeiter. I did not think This amorous surfeiter would have donn'd his helm For such a petty war *Ant. and Cleo.* ii 1 33
Surfeiting. His purpose surfeiting, he sends a warrant *Meas. for Meas.* v 1 102
That, surfeiting, The appetite may sicken, and so die *T. Night* i 1 2
We are all diseased, And with our surfeiting and wanton hours Have brought ourselves into a burning fever *2 Hen. IV.* iv 1 55
Henry, surfeiting in joys of love, With his new bride *2 Hen. VI.* i 1 251
Surfeit-swelled. So surfeit-swell'd, so old, and so profane *2 Hen. IV.* v 5 54
Surge. I saw him beat the surges under him, And ride upon their backs; he trod the water, Whose enmity he flung aside, and breasted The surge most swoln that met him *Tempest* ii 1 114
Thrown into the Thames, and cooled, glowing hot, in that surge *Mer. Wives* iii 5 123
I had a sister, Whom the blind waves and surges have devour'd *T. Night* v 1 236
And rock his brains In cradle of the rude imperious surge *2 Hen. IV.* iii 1 20
Through the furrow'd sea, Breasting the lofty surge *Hen. V.* iii Prol. 13
Marks the waxing tide grow wave by wave, Expecting ever when some envious surge Will in his brinish bowels swallow him *T. Andron.* iii 1 96
Stand on the dying deck, Hearing the surges threat *T. of Athens* iv 2 21
The sea's a thief, whose liquid surge resolves The moon into salt tears iv 3 442
Who once a day with his embossed froth The turbulent surge shall cover v 1 221
The murmuring surge, That on the unnumber'd idle pebbles chafes *Lear* iv 6 20
The wind-shaked surge, with high and monstrous mane *Othello* ii 1 13
On our terrible seas, Like egg-shells moved upon their surges *Cymbeline* iii 1 28
Thou god of this great vast, rebuke these surges! *Pericles* iii 1 1
Surgeon. With the help of a surgeon he might yet recover *M. N. Dream* v 1 316
Have by some surgeon, Shylock, on your charge, To stop his wounds *Mer. of Venice* iv 1 257
For the love of God, a surgeon! *T. Night* v 1 175
Sot, didst see Dick surgeon, sot? v 1 202
Some swearing, some crying for a surgeon *Hen. V.* iv 1 145
Opinion shall be surgeon to my hurt *1 Hen. VI.* ii 4 53
I'll to the surgeon's.—And so will I iii 1 146
Who keeps the tent now?—The surgeon's box *Troi. and Cres.* v 1 12
Where is my page? Go, villain, fetch a surgeon *Rom. and Jul.* iii 1 97
I am, indeed, sir, a surgeon to old shoes *J. Cæsar* i 1 27
Go get him surgeons *Macbeth* i 2 44
Let me have surgeons; I am cut to the brains *Lear* iv 6 196
Sir, for your hurts, myself will be your surgeon *Othello* ii 3 253
O, help, ho! light! a surgeon! v 1 30
I'll fetch the general's surgeon v 1 100
Have you that a man may deal withal, and defy the surgeon? *Pericles* iv 6 29
Surgere. 'Diluculo surgere,' thou know'st *T. Night* ii 3 3
Surgery. Tarred over with the surgery of our sheep *As Y. Like It* iii 2 64
Honour hath no skill in surgery, then? no. What is honour? *1 Hen. IV.* v 1 135
To come halting off, you know: to come off the breach with his pike bent bravely, and to surgery bravely *2 Hen. IV.* ii 4 56
Pitiful to the eye, The mere despair of surgery *Macbeth* iv 3 152
Are you hurt, lieutenant?—Ay, past all surgery *Othello* ii 3 260
Surly. 'Tis like you'll prove a jolly surly groom *T. of Shrew* iii 2 215
Be opposite with a kinsman, surly with servants *T. Night* ii 5 163; iii 4 77
If that surly spirit, melancholy, Had baked thy blood *K. John* iii 3 42
The sad-eyed justice, with his surly hum *Hen. V.* i 2 202
Be a pupil still Under the surly Gloucester's governance *2 Hen. VI.* i 3 50
See how the surly Warwick mans the wall! *3 Hen. VI.* v 1 17
Covetous of praise,— Ay, or surly borne,— Or strange *Troi. and Cres.* ii 3 249
It would have gall'd his surly nature *Coriolanus* ii 3 203
I met a lion, Who glared upon me, and went surly by *J. Cæsar* i 3 21
Surmise. If I shall be condemn'd Upon surmises *W. Tale* iii 2 113
Rumour is a pipe Blown by surmises, jealousies, conjectures *2 Hen. IV.* Ind. 16
Surmise Of aids incertain should not be admitted i 3 23
By false intelligence, or wrong surmise *Richard III.* i 2 54
My compassionate heart Will not permit mine eyes once to behold The thing whereat it trembles by surmise *T. Andron.* ii 3 219

Surmise. Shakes so my single state of man that function Is smother'd in surmise *Macbeth* i 3 141
Now gather, and surmise *Hamlet* ii 2 108
Exchange me for a goat, When I shall turn the business of my soul To such exsufflicate and blown surmises *Othello* iii 3 182
I speak not out of weak surmises, but from proof *Cymbeline* iii 4 24
Surmised. 'Tis but surmised whiles thou art standing by 2 *Hen. VI.* iii 2 347
That unbodied figure of the thought That gave 't surmised shape *T. and C.* i 3 17
Surmount. And far surmounts our labour to attain it *Richard II.* ii 3 64
Bethink thee on her virtues that surmount, And natural graces 1 *Hen. VI.* v 3 191
Surmounted. This Hector far surmounted Hannibal *L. L. Lost* v 2 677
Surname. Thereto witness may My surname, Coriolanus *Coriolanus* iv 5 74
The extreme dangers and the drops of blood Shed for my thankless country are requited But with that surname iv 5 77
To his surname Coriolanus 'longs more pride Than pity to our prayers v 3 170
Surnamed. Pompey surnamed the Big,— The Great *L. L. Lost* v 2 553
Andronicus, surnamed Pius For many good and great deserts *T. Andron.* i 1 23
Surpasseth. She as far surpasseth Sycorax As great'st does least *Tempest* iii 2 110
Surpassing. Much surpassing The common praise it bears *W. Tale* iii 1 2
Surplice. It will do no hurt; it will wear the surplice of humility over the black gown of a big heart *All's Well* i 3 99
Surplus. It is a surplus of your grace *W. Tale* v 3 7
He hath faults, with surplus, to tire in repetition *Coriolanus* i 1 46
Surprise. The guiltiness of my mind, the sudden surprise *Mer. Wives* v 5 131
I, with a troop of Florentines, will suddenly surprise him *All's Well* iii 6 24
Surprise her with discourse of my dear faith *T. Night* i 4 25
I see them lay their heads together to surprise me 2 *Hen. VI.* iv 8 61
We may surprise and take him at our pleasure 3 *Hen. VI.* iv 2 17
I say not, slaughter him, For I intend but only to surprise him iv 2 25
You witch me in it; Surprise me to the very brink of tears *T. of Athens* v 1 159
The castle of Macduff I will surprise; Seize upon Fife *Macbeth* iv 1 150
Pure surprise and fear Made me to quit the house *Pericles* iii 2 17
Surprised. So glad of this as they I cannot be, Who are surprised withal *Tempest* iii 1 93
You'll be surprised: Muster your wits *L. L. Lost* v 2 84
We'll show thee Io as she was a maid, And how she was beguiled and surprised, As lively painted as the deed *T. of Shrew* Ind. 2 57
Dian no queen of virgins, that would suffer her poor knight surprised *All's Well* i 3 120
So surprised my sense, That I was nothing *W. Tale* iii 1 10
The prisoners, Which he in this adventure hath surprised 1 *Hen. IV.* i 1 93
We had not been thus shamefully surprised 1 *Hen. VI.* ii 1 65
Myself and divers gentlemen beside Were there surprised and taken iv 1 26
And may ye both be suddenly surprised By bloody hands, in sleeping on your beds! v 3 40
Picardy Hath slain their governors, surprised our forts 2 *Hen. VI.* iv 1 89
Is the traitor Cade surprised? Or is he but retired to make him strong? iv 9 8
Either betray'd by falsehood of his guard Or by his foe surprised 3 *Hen. VI.* iv 4 9
Lavinia is surprised!—Surprised! by whom? *T. Andron.* i 1 284
When with a happy storm they were surprised ii 3 23
I am surprised with an uncouth fear ii 3 211
Wert thou thus surprised, sweet girl? iv 1 51
I rush'd upon him, Surprised him suddenly v 1 38
When subtle Greeks surprised King Priam's Troy v 3 84
Your castle is surprised; your wife and babes Savagely slaughter'd *Macb.* iv 3 204
You see how easily she may be surprised *Ant. and Cleo.* v 2 35
Sur-reined. Sodden water, A drench for sur-rein'd jades *Hen. V.* iii 5 19
Surrender. About surrender up of Aquitaine *L. L. Lost* i 1 138
Fetch hither Richard, that in common view He may surrender *Richard II.* iv 1 156
If I but knew him, with my love and duty I would surrender it *Hen. VIII.* i 4 81
Importing the surrender of those lands Lost by his father *Hamlet* i 2 23
This last surrender of his will but offend us *Lear* i 1 309
Surrey, thou liest.—Dishonourable boy! *Richard II.* iv 1 65
I dare meet Surrey in a wilderness, And spit upon him iv 1 74
Go call the Earls of Surrey and of Warwick 2 *Hen IV.* iii 1 1
My Lord of Surrey, why look you so sad? *Richard III.* v 3 2
Saddle white Surrey for the field to-morrow v 3 64
The Earl of Surrey, and himself, Much about cock-shut time, from troop to troop Went through the army v 3 69
He said the truth: and what said Surrey then?—He smiled v 3 273
Thomas Earl of Surrey Shall have the leading of this foot and horse v 3 296
Earl Surrey was sent thither, and in haste too *Hen. VIII.* ii 1 43
Surrey durst better Have burnt that tongue than said so iii 2 253
Dare mate a sounder man than Surrey can be, And all that love his follies iii 2 274
The Earl of Surrey, with the rod.—A bold brave gentleman iv 1 39
Survey. I will survey the inscriptions back again *Mer. of Venice* ii 7 14
Thrice-crowned queen of night, survey With thy chaste eye *As Y. L. It* iii 2 2
Whose beauty did astonish the survey Of richest eyes *All's Well* v 3 16
And time, that takes survey of all the world, Must have a stop 1 *Hen. IV.* v 4 82
When we mean to build, We first survey the plot 2 *Hen. IV.* i 3 42
Survey The plot of situation and the model, Consent upon a sure foundation i 3 51
Busied in his majesty, surveys The singing masons *Hen. V.* i 2 197
I am come to survey the Tower this day 1 *Hen. VI.* i 3 1
To know what prisoners thou hast ta'en And to survey the bodies of the dead iv 7 57
And to survey his dead and earthly image, What were it but to make my sorrow greater? 2 *Hen. VI.* iii 2 147
Let us survey the vantage of the field *Richard III.* v 3 15
Make but an interior survey of your good selves *Coriolanus* ii 1 44
Upon a just survey, take Titus' part *T. Andron.* i 1 446
Surveyed. Or here or elsewhere to the furthest verge That ever was survey'd by English eye *Richard II.* i 1 94
Surveyest. Which here thou viewest, beholdest, surveyest, or seest *L. L. L.* i 1 247
Surveying. The Norweyan lord surveying vantage *Macbeth* i 2 31
Surveyor. Question surveyors, know our own estate 2 *Hen. IV.* i 3 53
Were't not madness, then, To make the fox surveyor of the fold? 2 *Hen. VI.* iii 1 253
The Duke of Buckingham's surveyor, ha? Where's his examination? *Hen. VIII.* i 1 115
My surveyor is false; the o'er-great cardinal Hath show'd him gold i 1 222
If I know you well, You were the duke's surveyor i 2 172
At which appear'd against him his surveyor ii 1 19
Survive. Yet Valentine thy friend Survives *T. G. of Ver.* iv 2 110
I'll assure her of Her widowhood, be it that she survive me *T. of Shrew* ii 1 125
Sadly I survive, To mock the expectation of the world 2 *Hen. IV.* v 2 125
Thou shalt not die this treason with thy tears, If Talbot but survive 1 *Hen. VI.* iii 2 37
These that survive let Rome reward with love *T. Andron.* i 1 82
I give him you, the noblest that survives i 1 102
We survive To tremble under Titus' threatening looks i 1 133

Survive. Welcome, nephews, from successful wars, You that survive! *T. Andron.* i 1 173
The girl should not survive her shame v 3 41
Survivor. The fall of either Makes the survivor heir of all *Coriolanus* v 6 19
That father lost, lost his, and the survivor bound In filial obligation for some term To do obsequious sorrow *Hamlet* i 2 90
Susan and she—God rest all Christian souls!—Were of an age: well, Susan is with God; She was too good for me *Rom. and Jul.* i 3 18
As thou lovest me, let the porter let in Susan Grindstone and Nell i 5 10
Suspect. If I suspect without cause, why then make sport at me *Mer. Wives* iii 3 159
I suspect without cause, mistress, do I?—Heaven be my witness you do, if you suspect me in any dishonesty iv 2 138
I rather will suspect the sun with cold Than thee with wantonness iv 4 7
And draw within the compass of suspect *Com. of Errors* iii 1 87
You may suspect him, by virtue of your office, to be no true man *M. Ado* iii 3 53
Dost thou not suspect my place? dost thou not suspect my years? iv 2 76
What these Christians are, Whose own hard dealings teaches them suspect The thoughts of others! *Mer. of Venice* i 3 163
Lest she suspect, as he does, Her children not her husband's *W. Tale* ii 3 107
I do suspect thee very grievously *K. John* iv 3 134
Thou dost suspect That I have been disloyal *Richard II.* v 2 104
He will suspect us still and find a time To punish this offence 1 *Hen. IV.* v 2 6
If they were known, as the suspect is great, Would make thee quickly hop without thy head 2 *Hen. VI.* i 3 139
'Tis my special hope That you will clear yourself from all suspect iii 1 140
Thousands more, that yet suspect no peril, Will not conclude iii 1 152
If my suspect be false, forgive me, God iii 2 139
Then you, belike, suspect these noblemen As guilty iii 2 186
Who ... But will suspect 'twas he that made the slaughter? iii 2 190
If you mind to hold your true obedience, Give me assurance with some friendly vow, That I may never have you in suspect 3 *Hen. VI.* iv 1 142
Did I but suspect a fearful man, He should have leave to go away betimes v 4 44
Falsely to draw me in these vile suspects *Richard III.* i 3 89
Thy friends suspect for traitors while thou livest! i 3 223
He lived from all attainder of suspect iii 5 32
Sorry I am my noble cousin should Suspect me, that I mean no good to him iii 7 89
I do suspect I have done some offence That seems disgracious iii 7 111
My heart suspects more than mine eye can see *T. Andron.* ii 3 213
If you suspect my husbandry or falsehood, Call me before the exactest auditors And set me on the proof *T. of Athens* ii 2 164
If thou wert the fox, the lion would suspect thee iv 3 333
In whose breast Doubt and suspect, alas, are placed too late iv 3 519
Suspect still comes where an estate is least iv 3 521
Whose nature is so far from doing harms, That he suspects none *Lear* i 2 197
I do suspect the lusty Moor hath leap'd into my seat *Othello* ii 1 304
But, O, what damned minutes tells he o'er Who dotes, yet doubts, suspects, yet strongly loves! iii 3 170
You have seen nothing then?—Nor ever heard, nor ever did suspect iv 2 2
If haply you my father do suspect An instrument of this your calling back, Lay not your blame on me iv 2 44
Turn'd your wit the seamy side without, And made you to suspect me iv 2 147
Cassio, may you suspect Who they should be that have thus mangled you? v 1 78
I do suspect this trash To be a party in this injury v 1 85
You did suspect She had disposed with Cæsar *Ant. and Cleo.* iv 14 122
I do suspect you, madam; But you shall do no harm *Cymbeline* i 5 31
Nor boots it me to say I honour him, If he suspect I may dishonour him *Pericles* i 2 21
Suspected. Only sin And hellish obstinacy tie thy tongue, That truth should be suspected *All's Well* i 3 187
Who would have suspected an ambush where I was taken? iv 3 335
Makes sound opinion sick and truth suspected *K. John* iv 2 26
I am the greatest, able to do least, Yet most suspected *Rom. and Jul.* v 3 224
He hath a person and a smooth dispose To be suspected *Othello* i 3 404
Weep no more, lest I give cause To be suspected of more tenderness Than doth become a man *Cymbeline* i 1 94
Lest, being miss'd, I be suspected of Your carriage from the court iii 4 189
Suspecting that we both were in a house Where the infectious pestilence did reign, Seal'd up the doors *Rom. and Jul.* v 2 9
Suspend your indignation against my brother *Lear* i 2 86
Suspend thy purpose, if thou didst intend To make this creature fruitful! i 4 298
Suspicion. To give him such cause of suspicion!—What cause of suspicion?—What cause of suspicion! *Mer. Wives* iii 3 108
I think my husband hath some special suspicion iii 3 200
To make another experiment of his suspicion iv 2 36
Hath not the world one man but he will wear his cap with suspicion? *Much Ado* i 1 201
Out of all suspicion, she is virtuous ii 3 166
Nothing Of his ill-ta'en suspicion *W. Tale* i 2 460
More it would content me To have her honour true than your suspicion ii 1 160
I have too much believed mine own suspicion iii 2 152
The verity of it is in strong suspicion v 2 31
Your pardons, That e'er I put between your holy looks My ill suspicion v 3 149
So we shall proceed Without suspicion *Richard II.* iv 1 157
Suspicion all our lives shall be stuck full of eyes 1 *Hen. IV.* v 2 8
See what a ready tongue suspicion hath! 2 *Hen. IV.* i 1 84
To mark the full-fraught man and best indued With some suspicion *Hen. V.* ii 2 140
In York this breeds suspicion 2 *Hen. VI.* i 3 210
Pray God he may acquit him of suspicion! iii 2 25
Suspicion always haunts the guilty mind 3 *Hen. VI.* v 6 11
Thus have we swept suspicion from our seat v 7 13
And yet go current from suspicion! *Richard III.* ii 1 94
Tremble and start at wagging of a straw, Intending deep suspicion iii 5 8
I am sorry my integrity should breed, And service to his majesty and you, So deep suspicion *Hen. VIII.* iii 1 53
A woman, I dare say without vain-glory, Never yet branded with suspicion iii 1 128
They shall be ready at your highness' will To answer their suspicion with their lives *T. Andron.* ii 3 298
A great suspicion: stay the friar too *Rom. and Jul.* v 3 187
Bring forth the parties of suspicion v 3 222
The king's two sons Are stol'n away and fled; which puts upon them Suspicion of the deed *Macbeth* ii 4 27
It will stuff his suspicion more fully *Lear* iii 5 22
But I, for mere suspicion in that kind, Will do as if for surety *Othello* i 3 395

Suspicion. Think'st thou I'ld make a life of jealousy, To follow still the changes of the moon With fresh suspicions? *Othello* iii 3 179
I am to pray you not to strain my speech To grosser issues nor to larger reach Than to suspicion iii 3 220
Your suspicion is not without wit and judgement iv 2 215
Suspicious. When the suspicious head of theft is stopp'd *L. L. Lost* iv 3 336
I see no reason, if I wear this rose, That any one should therefore be suspicious I more incline to Somerset than York *1 Hen. VI.* iv 1 153
Even so suspicious is this tragedy *2 Hen. VI.* iii 2 194
I spy a black, suspicious, threatening cloud *3 Hen. VI.* v 3 4
A strange tongue makes my cause more strange, suspicious *Hen. VIII.* iii 1 45
Suspiration. Nor windy suspiration of forced breath *Hamlet* i 2 79
Suspire. Since the birth of Cain, the first male child, To him that did but yesterday suspire *K. John* iii 4 80
There lies a downy feather which stirs not: Did he suspire, that light and weightless down Perforce must move *2 Hen. IV.* iv 5 33
Sustain. You take my house when you do take the prop That doth sustain my house *Mer. of Venice* iv 1 376
Should sustain the bound and high curvet Of Mars's fiery steed *All's Well* ii 3 299
Good beauties, let me sustain no scorn *T. Night* i 5 186
In a trice, Like to the old Vice, Your need to sustain iv 2 135
To do them good, I would sustain some harm *3 Hen. VI.* iii 2 39
I cannot promise But that you shall sustain moe new disgraces *Hen. VIII.* iii 2 5
With other incident throes That nature's fragile vessel doth sustain In life's uncertain voyage *T. of Athens* v 1 204
Then weigh what loss your honour may sustain *Hamlet* i 3 29
If she sustain him and his hundred knights *Lear* i 4 355
Neither to speak of him, entreat for him, nor any way sustain him iii 3 6
You twain Rule in this realm, and the gored state sustain v 3 320
Behold, I have a weapon; A better never did itself sustain Upon a soldier's thigh *Othello* v 2 260
It cannot be thus long, the sides of nature Will not sustain it *A. and C.* i 3 17
Well then, sustain me: O! iii 11 45
I doubt not you sustain what you're worthy of by your attempt *Cymb.* i 4 125
Sustained. Prick'd on by public wrongs sustain'd in France *1 Hen. VI.* iii 2 78
An hundred knights, By you to be sustain'd *Lear* i 1 136
Sustaining. On their sustaining garments not a blemish *Tempest* i 2 218
Darnel, and all the idle weeds that grow In our sustaining corn *Lear* iv 4 6
Sustenance. This accursed devil; Let him receive no sustenance *T. An.* v 3 6
Nor taken sustenance But to prorogue his grief *Pericles* v 1 25
Sutler. I shall sutler be Unto the camp, and profits will accrue *Hen. V.* ii 1 116
Sutton Co'fil'. We'll to Sutton Co'fil' to-night *1 Hen. IV.* iv 2 3
'Suum cuique' is our Roman justice *T. Andron.* i 1 280
Says suum, mun, ha, no, nonny. Dolphin my boy, my boy, sessa! *Lear* iii 4 103
Swabber. The master, the swabber, the boatswain, and I *Tempest* ii 2 48
No, good swabber; I am to hull here a little longer. *T. Night* i 5 217
Swaddling-clouts. Is not yet out of his swaddling-clouts *Hamlet* ii 2 401
Swag-bellied. Your swag-bellied Hollander—Drink, ho! *Othello* ii 3 80
Swagger. If he swagger, let him not come here *2 Hen. IV.* ii 4 79
He'll not swagger with a Barbary hen, if her feathers turn back ii 4 107
I am the worse, when one says swagger: feel, masters, how I shake ii 4 113
Will he swagger himself out on's own eyes? *Troi. and Cres.* v 2 136
Drunk? and speak parrot? and squabble? swagger? swear? *Othello* ii 3 281
Swaggered. A rascal that swaggered with me last night *Hen. V.* iv 7 131
Swaggerer. Patience herself would startle at this letter And play the swaggerer; bear this, bear all *As Y. Like It* iv 3 14
I must live among my neighbours; I'll no swaggerers *2 Hen. IV.* ii 4 81
Shut the door; there comes no swaggerers here ii 4 83
Your ancient swaggerer comes not in my doors ii 4 91
No, I'll no swaggerers.—He's no swaggerer, hostess; a tame cheater, i' faith ii 4 104
I cannot abide swaggerers ii 4 117
Swaggering. What hempen home-spuns have we swaggering here? *M. N. Dream* iii 1 79
With a swaggering accent sharply twanged off *T. Night* iii 4 197
By swaggering could I never thrive v 1 408
Hang him, swaggering rascal! let him not come hither *2 Hen. IV.* ii 4 76
I have not lived all this while, to have swaggering now ii 4 84
'Receive,' says he, 'no swaggering companions' ii 4 102
I do not love swaggering, by my troth ii 4 112
Keeps wassail, and the swaggering up-spring reels *Hamlet* i 4 9
Swain. What is she, That all our swains commend her? *T. G. of Ver.* iv 2 40
Thou gentle nymph, cherish thy forlorn swain? v 4 12
Costard the swain and he shall be our sport *L. L. Lost* i 1 180
That low-spirited swain, that base minnow of thy mirth i 1 250
So is the weaker vessel called which I apprehended with the aforesaid swain i 1 277
Give enlargement to the swain, bring him festinately hither iii 1 5
Fetch hither the swain: he must carry me a letter iii 1 50
I shoot thee at the swain.—Thump then and I flee iii 1 66
By my soul, a swain! a most simple clown! iv 1 142
This swain, because of his great limb or joint, shall pass Pompey the Great v 1 134
He presents Hector of Troy; the swain, Pompey the Great v 2 538
And, gentle Puck, take this transformed scalp From off the head of this Athenian swain *M. N. Dream* iv 1 70
That young swain that you saw here but erewhile *As Y. Like It* ii 4 89
Too light for such a swain as you to catch *T. of Shrew* ii 1 205
As foolish as I was before.—You peasant swain! iv 1 132
Your high self . . . you have obscured With a swain's wearing *W. Tale* iv 4 9
The fire-robed god, Golden Apollo, a poor humble swain, As I seem iv 4 30
What fair swain is this Which dances with your daughter? iv 4 166
How prettily the young swain seems to wash The hand was fair before! iv 4 377
Soft, swain, awhile, beseech you; Have you a father? iv 4 402
Like a hedge-born swain That doth presume to boast of gentle blood *1 Hen. VI.* iv 1 43
Not me begotten of a shepherd swain, But issued from the progeny of kings v 4 37
Obscure and lowly swain *2 Hen. VI.* iv 1 50
Speak, captain, shall I stab the forlorn swain? iv 1 65
It were a happy life, To be no better than a homely swain *3 Hen. VI.* ii 5 22
True swains in love shall in the world to come Approve their truths by Troilus *Troi. and Cres.* iii 2 180
Swallow. Daffodils, That come before the swallow dares *W. Tale* iv 4 119
Now swallow down that lie *Richard II.* i 1 132
Do you think me a swallow, an arrow, or a bullet? *2 Hen. IV.* iv 3 36
I'll make thee . . . swallow my sword like a great pin *2 Hen. VI.* iv 10 31
May that ground gape and swallow me alive, Where I shall kneel to him that slew my father! *3 Hen. VI.* i 1 161
Thyself the sea Whose envious gulf did swallow up his life v 6 25
Swallow. Or earth, gape open wide and eat him quick, As thou dost swallow up this good king's blood! *Richard III.* i 2 66
True hope is swift, and flies with swallow's wings v 2 23
And run like swallows o'er the plain *T. Andron.* ii 2 24
Expecting ever when some envious surge Will in his brinish bowels swallow him iii 1 97
Now to the Goths, as swift as swallow flies iv 2 172
Like to the earth swallow her own increase v 2 192
The swallow follows not summer more willing than we *T. of Athens* iii 6 31
Let prisons swallow 'em, Debts wither 'em to nothing! iv 3 537
Though the yesty waves Confound and swallow navigation up *Macbeth* iv 1 54
Swallows the old rat and the ditch-dog *Lear* iii 4 137
That it engluts and swallows other sorrows *Othello* i 3 57
Till that a capable and wide revenge Swallow them up iii 3 460
Swallows have built In Cleopatra's sails their nests *Ant. and Cleo.* iv 12 3
Swallowed. I would Have sunk the sea within the earth or ere It should the good ship so have swallow'd *Tempest* i 2 12
My belly's as cold as if I had swallowed snowballs *Mer. Wives* iii 5 24
Swallowed his vows whole *Meas. for Meas.* iii 1 235
As if you swallowed love with singing love *L. L. Lost* iii 1 15
Thou art easier swallowed than a flap-dragon v 1 45
Swallowed with yest and froth, as you'ld thrust a cork into a hogshead *W. Tale* iii 3 94
Being daily swallow'd by men's eyes, They surfeited with honey *1 Hen. IV.* iii 2 70
Capital crimes, chew'd, swallow'd, and digested, Appear before us *Hen. V.* ii 2 56
Fathers and betrothed lovers, That shall be swallow'd in this controversy ii 4 109
The holding-anchor lost, And half our sailors swallow'd in the flood *3 Hen. VI.* v 4 5
The interview, That swallow'd so much treasure *Hen. VIII.* i 1 166
And blind oblivion swallow'd cities up *Troi. and Cres.* iii 2 194
I think they have swallowed one another: I would laugh at that miracle v 4 36
The earth hath swallow'd all my hopes but she *Rom. and Jul.* i 2 14
She fell distract, And, her attendants absent, swallow'd fire *J. Cæsar* iv 3 156
First mouthed, to be last swallow'd *Hamlet* iv 2 20
If they had swallow'd poison, 'twould appear By external swelling *Ant. and Cleo.* v 2 348
We thought he died.—By the queen's dram she swallow'd *Cymbeline* v 5 381
Never leave gaping till they've swallowed the whole parish *Pericles* ii 1 37
Because he should have swallowed me too ii 1 43
At her birth, Thetis, being proud, swallow'd some part o' the earth iv 4 39
Swallowing. With open mouth swallowing a tailor's news *K. John* iv 2 195
Our love durst not come near your sight For fear of swallowing *1 Hen. IV.* v 1 64
Now will I dam up this thy yawning mouth For swallowing the treasure of the realm *2 Hen. VI.* iv 1 74
Almost shoulder'd in the swallowing gulf Of blind forgetfulness *Richard III.* iii 7 128
I may be pluck'd into the swallowing womb Of this deep pit *T. Andron.* ii 3 239
He hath a drug of mine; I pray his absence Proceed by swallowing that *Cymbeline* iii 5 58
Swam. I swam, ere I could recover the shore, five and thirty leagues *Tempest* iii 2 16
I will scarce think you have swam in a gondola *As Y. Like It* iv 1 38
Swan. You were also, Jupiter, a swan for the love of Leda *Mer. Wives* v 5 7
Like Juno's swans, Still we went coupled and inseparable *As Y. Like It* i 3 77
I am the cygnet to this pale faint swan *K. John* v 7 21
So doth the swan her downy cygnets save *1 Hen. VI.* v 3 56
I have seen a swan With bootless labour swim against the tide *3 Hen. VI.* i 4 19
For all the water in the ocean Can never turn the swan's black legs to white, Although she lave them hourly *T. Andron.* iv 2 102
I will make thee think thy swan a crow *Rom. and Jul.* i 2 92
I will play the swan, And die in music *Othello* v 2 247
The swan's down-feather, That stands upon the swell at full of tide, And neither way inclines *Ant. and Cleo.* iii 2 48
Britain seems as of it, but not in't; In a great pool a swan's nest *Cymb.* iii 4 142
Swan-like. He makes a swan-like end, Fading in music *Mer. of Venice* iii 2 44
Sware. And sware they were his fancies or his good-nights *2 Hen. IV.* iii 2 342
Lord Junius Brutus sware for Lucrece' rape *T. Andron.* iv 1 91
Swarm. And from this swarm of fair advantages You took occasion to be quickly woo'd *1 Hen. IV.* v 1 55
Peasants, Who in unnecessary action swarm About our squares of battle *Hen. V.* iv 2 27
The common people swarm like summer flies *3 Hen. VI.* ii 6 8
The common people by numbers swarm to us iv 2 2
The multiplying villanies of nature Do swarm upon him *Macbeth* i 2 12
Swarming. Her wholesome herbs Swarming with caterpillars *Richard II.* iii 4 47
With the plebeians swarming at their heels *Hen. V.* v Prol. 27
Swart, like my shoe, but her face nothing like so clean kept *Com. of Er.* iii 2 104
Lame, foolish, crooked, swart, prodigious *K. John* iii 1 46
And, whereas I was black and swart before, With those clear rays which she infused on me That beauty am I bless'd with which you see *1 Hen. VI.* i 2 84
Swarth. An affectioned ass, that cons state without book and utters it by great swarths *T. Night* ii 3 162
Your swarth Cimmerian Doth make your honour of his body's hue *T. Andron.* ii 3 72
Swarthy. Silvia . . . Shows Julia but a swarthy Ethiope *T. G. of Ver.* ii 6 26
Swasher. Young as I am, I have observed these three swashers *Hen. V.* iii 2 30
Swashing. We'll have a swashing and a martial outside *As Y. Like It* i 3 122
Gregory, remember thy swashing blow *Rom. and Jul.* i 1 70
Swath. Fall down before him, like the mower's swath *Troi. and Cres.* v 5 25
Hadst thou, like us from our first swath, proceeded The sweet degrees that this brief world affords *T. of Athens* iv 3 252
Swathing-clothes. The eldest of them at three years old, I' the swathing-clothes the other *Cymbeline* i 1 59
Swathling clothes. This Hotspur, Mars in swathling clothes *1 Hen. IV.* iii 2 112
Sway. So dry he was for sway *Tempest* i 2 112
To behold his sway, I will, as 'twere a brother of your order, Visit both prince and people *Meas. for Meas.* i 3 43
Were you wedded, you would bear some sway *Com. of Errors* ii 1 28
Pause awhile, And let my counsel sway you in this case *Much Ado* iv 1 203
With what art You sway the motion of Demetrius' heart *M. N. Dream* i 1 193
For affection, Mistress of passion, sways it *Mer. of Venice* iv 1 51
But mercy is above this sceptred sway iv 1 193
Thy huntress' name that my full life doth sway *As Y. Like It* iii 2 4
Or seek for rule, supremacy and sway *T. of Shrew* v 2 163
So wears she to him, So sways she level in her husband's heart *T. Night* ii 4 32
M, O, A, I, doth sway my life ii 5 118
Gentle friend, Let thy fair wisdom, not thy passion, sway v 1 56
If 'twere so, She could not sway her house iv 3 17
Lay aside the sword Which sways usurpingly these several titles *K. John* i 1 13

Sway. By this hand I swear, That sways the earth this climate overlooks *K. John* ii 1 344
This vile-drawing bias, This sway of motion, this Commodity ii 1 578
The pride of kingly sway from out my heart *Richard II.* iv 1 206
You took occasion to be quickly woo'd To gripe the general sway *1 Hen. IV.* v 1 57
Rebellion in this land shall lose his sway v 5 41
Let us sway on and face them in the field *2 Hen. IV.* iv 1 24
No one should sway but he; No one but he *1 Hen. VI.* iii 1 37
A gentler heart did never sway in court iii 2 135
Now sways it this way, like a mighty sea Forced by the tide to combat with the wind; Now sways it that way, like selfsame sea Forced to retire by fury of the wind *3 Hen. VI.* ii 5 5
Though usurpers sway the rule awhile, Yet heavens are just iii 3 76
Thou art worthy of the sway iv 6 32
Most mighty for thy place and sway *Troi. and Cres.* i 3 60
Should not our father Bear the great sway of his affairs with reasons? ii 2 35
Know, good mother, I had rather be their servant in my way, Than sway with them in theirs *Coriolanus* ii 1 220
Now, arriving A place of potency and sway o' the state iii 3 190
Dangerous That she doth give her sorrow so much sway *Rom. and Jul.* iv 1 10
He's but a mad lord, and nought but humour sways him *T. of Athens* iii 6 122
Are not you moved, when all the sway of earth Shakes? *J. Cæsar* i 3 3
Shall to all our nights and days to come Give solely sovereign sway *Macb.* i 5 71
The mind I sway by and the heart I bear Shall never sag with doubt v 3 9
The sway, revenue, execution of the rest, Beloved sons, be yours *Lear* i 1 139
Who sways, not as it hath power, but as it is suffered i 2 53
If your sweet sway Allow obedience, if yourselves are old ii 4 193
Be govern'd by your knowledge, and proceed I' the sway of your own will iv 7 20
From this hour The heart of brothers govern in our loves And sway our great designs! *Ant. and Cleo.* ii 2 151
You gods that made me man, and sway in love *Pericles* i 1 19
Swayed. The will of man is by his reason sway'd *M. N. Dream* ii 2 115
Sway'd and fashion'd by the hand of heaven *Mer. of Venice* i 3 94
Swayed in the back and shoulder-shotten *T. of Shrew* iii 2 56
And God forgive them that so much have sway'd Your majesty's good thoughts away from me! *1 Hen. IV.* iii 2 130
Hadst thou sway'd as kings should do, Or as thy father and his father *3 Hen. VI.* ii 6 14
Minds sway'd by eyes are full of turpitude *Troi. and Cres.* v 2 112
I have not known when his affections sway'd More than his reason *J. Cæsar* ii 1 20
Therefore I took your hands, but was, indeed, Sway'd from the point iii 1 219
Swaying. He seems indifferent, Or rather swaying more upon our part *Hen. V.* i 1 73
Swear. He'll be hang'd yet, Though every drop of water swear against it *Tempest* i 1 62
Swear by this bottle how thou camest hither ii 2 125
I'll swear upon that bottle to be thy true subject ii 2 130
Swear then how thou escapedst.—Swum ashore, man ii 2 132
Swear to that; kiss the book: I will furnish it anon with new contents: swear ii 2 145
I'll swear myself thy subject.—Come on then; down, and swear ii 2 156
Swears he will shoot no more but play with sparrows And be a boy iv 1 100
Whether this be Or be not, I'll not swear v 1 123
Love bade me swear and Love bids me forswear *T. G. of Ver.* ii 6 6
By this pale queen of night I swear iv 2 100
Think not I flatter, for I swear I do not iv 3 12
He would not swear; praised women's modesty *Mer. Wives* ii 1 58
He swears he'll turn me away iii 3 32
Swears he was carried out, the last time he searched for him, in a basket iv 2 31
He swears she's a witch iv 2 88
This would make mercy swear and play the tyrant *Meas. for Meas.* iii 2 207
I swear I will not die to-day for any man's persuasion iv 3 62
Though they would swear down each particular saint v 1 243
As I have heard him swear himself v 1 516
There did this perjured goldsmith swear me down *Com. of Errors* v 1 227
I had rather hear my dog bark at a crow than a man swear he loves me *Much Ado* i 1 133
I dare swear he is no hypocrite, but prays from his heart i 1 152
If you swear, my lord, you shall not be forsworn i 1 154
I heard him swear his affection i 1 175
Yet he wooes, Yet will he swear he loves ii 3 54
Swears she never will: that's her torment ii 3 129
She would swear the gentleman should be her sister iii 1 62
Would you not swear, All you that see her, that she were a maid? iv 1 39
By my sword, Beatrice, thou lovest me.—Do not swear, and eat it.—I will swear by it that you love me iv 1 277
He is now as valiant as Hercules that only tells a lie and swears it iv 1 325
Take her hand Before this friar and swear to marry her v 4 57
Margaret and Ursula Are much deceived; for they did swear you did v 4 79
I will swear to study so, To know the thing I am forbid to know *L. L. L.* i 1 59
Swear me to this, and I will ne'er say no i 1 69
We will read it, I swear. Break the neck of the wax iv 1 58
To see him kiss his hand! and how most sweetly a' will swear! iv 1 148
If love make me forsworn, how shall I swear to love? iv 2 109
Thou for whom Jove would swear Juno but an Ethiope were iv 3 117
Faith so infringed, which such zeal did swear iv 3 146
Where is a book? That I may swear beauty doth beauty lack iv 3 251
Consider what you first did swear unto, To fast, to study iv 3 291
Biron did swear himself out of all suit v 2 275
Not so, my lord; it is not so, I swear v 2 359
Yet swear not, lest ye be forsworn again v 2 842
I swear to thee, by Cupid's strongest bow, By his best arrow *M. N. Dream* i 1 169
Neeze and swear A merrier hour was never wasted there ii 1 56
Thy fair virtue's force perforce doth move me On the first view to say, to swear, I love thee iii 1 144
To vow, and swear, and superpraise my parts iii 2 153
I love thee; by my life, I do: I swear by that which I will lose for thee iii 2 252
But as yet, I swear, I cannot truly say how I came here iv 1 152
Though Nestor swear the jest be laughable *Mer. of Venice* i 1 56
You will come into the court and swear that I have a poor pennyworth i 2 76
I swear The best-regarded virgins of our clime Have loved it too ii 1 9
Either not attempt to choose at all Or swear before you choose ii 1 40
If any man in Italy have a fairer table which doth offer to swear upon a book ii 2 168
Put on a sober habit, Talk with respect, and swear but now and then ii 2 200
By Jacob's staff, I swear, I have no mind of feasting forth to-night ii 5 36
Tell me, for more certainty, Albeit I'll swear that I do know your tongue ii 6 27
Swear. To these injunctions every one doth swear That comes to hazard *Mer. of Venice* ii 9 17
That swear he cannot choose but break iii 1 119
I have heard him swear To Tubal and to Chus, his countrymen iii 2 286
That men shall swear I have discontinued school Above a twelvemonth iii 4 75
Which I did make him swear to keep for ever iv 2 14
In such a night Did young Lorenzo swear he loved her well v 1 18
By yonder moon I swear you do me wrong v 1 142
I gave my love a ring and made him swear Never to part with it v 1 170
I were best to cut my left hand off And swear I lost the ring defending it v 1 178
He hath got the jewel that I loved, And that which you did swear to keep v 1 225
I swear to thee, even by thine own fair eyes v 1 242
Swear by your double self, And there's an oath of credit v 1 245
Pardon this fault, and by my soul I swear I never more will break an oath v 1 247
Swear to keep this ring.—By heaven, it is the same I gave the doctor! v 1 256
Stroke your chins, and swear by your beards *As Y. Like It* i 2 76
If you swear by that that is not, you are not forsworn i 2 81
And, in that kind, swears you do more usurp Than doth your brother ii 1 27
I swear to thee, youth, by the white hand of Rosalind iii 2 413
What they swear in poetry may be said as lovers they do feign iii 3 21
But why did he swear he would come this morning, and comes not? iii 4 20
You have heard him swear downright he was iii 4 31
He writes brave verses, speaks brave words, swears brave oaths iii 4 44
He hath been a courtier, he swears v 4 43
To swear and to forswear; according as marriage binds and blood breaks v 4 58
Scratching her legs that one shall swear she bleeds *T. of Shrew* Ind. 2 60
Here I swear I'll plead for you myself, but you shall have him ii 1 14
I swear I'll cuff you, if you strike again ii 1 221
Rails, and swears, and rates, that she, poor soul, Knows not which way to stand iv 1 187
Now, tell me, I pray, You that durst swear iv 2 12
I dare swear this is the right Vincentio.—Swear, if thou darest.—Nay, I dare not swear it v 1 102
I will tell truth; by grace itself I swear *All's Well* i 3 226
An idle lord, I swear.—I think so ii 5 54
Then to return and swear the lies he forges iv 1 26
I would I had any drum of the enemy's: I would swear I recovered it iv 1 67
What is not holy, that we swear not by, But take the High'st to witness iv 2 23
If I should swear by God's great attributes, I loved you dearly, would you believe my oaths, When I did love you ill? iv 2 25
This has no holding, To swear by him whom I protest to love iv 2 28
When he swears oaths, bid him drop gold, and take it iv 3 252
Sith wives are monsters to you, And that you fly them as you swear them lordship v 3 156
He knows I am no maid, and he'll swear to't; I'll swear I am a maid, and he knows not v 3 291
I have heard her swear't. Tut, there's life in't, man *T. Night* i 3 117
Yond young fellow swears he will speak with you i 5 147
By the very fangs of malice I swear, I am not that I play i 5 196
We men may say more, swear more: but indeed Our shows are more than will ii 4 119
By innocence I swear, and by my youth, I have one heart, one bosom iii 1 169
So soon as ever thou seest him, draw; and, as thou drawest, swear horrible iii 4 196
And whom, by heaven I swear, I tender dearly v 1 129
O, do not swear! Hold little faith, though thou hast too much fear v 1 173
Let him swear so, and he shall not stay, We'll thwack him hence *W. Tale* i 2 36
He thinks, nay, with all confidence he swears, As he had seen't i 2 414
Swear his thought over By each particular star in heaven i 2 424
Swear by this sword Thou wilt perform my bidding ii 3 168
I swear to do this, though a present death Had been more merciful ii 3 184
You here shall swear upon this sword of justice iii 2 125
All this we swear.—Break up the seals and read iii 2 131
I say she's dead; I'll swear't. If word nor oath Prevail not, go and see iii 2 204
So turtles pair, That never mean to part.—I'll swear for 'em iv 4 155
Will you swear Never to marry but by my free leave? v 1 69
That which you hear you'll swear you see, there is such unity v 2 35
I will swear to the prince thou art as honest a true fellow as any is v 2 168
You may say it, but not swear it.—Not swear it, now I am a gentleman? Let boors and franklins say it, I'll swear it v 2 171
If it be ne'er so false, a true gentleman may swear it in the behalf of his friend v 2 176
By this hand I swear, That sways the earth this climate overlooks *K. John* ii 1 343
Gone to be married! gone to swear a peace! False blood to false blood join'd! iii 1 1
What a fool art thou, A ramping fool, to brag and stamp and swear! iii 1 122
The truth thou art unsure To swear, swears only not to be forsworn; Else what a mockery should it be to swear! But thou dost swear only to be forsworn; And most forsworn, to keep what thou dost swear iii 1 284
We swear A voluntary zeal and an unurged faith To your proceedings v 2 9
By that sword I swear, Which gently laid my knighthood on my shoulder, I'll answer thee *Richard II.* i 1 78
Ask him his name and orderly proceed To swear him i 3 10
Swear by the duty that you owe to God i 3 180
I swear.—And I, to keep all this i 3 191
By the honourable tomb he swears, That stands upon your royal grandsire's bones iii 3 105
This swears he, as he is a prince, is just iii 3 119
God keep all vows unbroke that swear to thee! iv 1 215
They shall not live within this world, I swear v 3 142
When I am o' horseback, I will swear I love thee infinitely *1 Hen. IV.* ii 3 104
He would swear truth out of England but he would make you believe it ii 4 337
Swear it was the blood of true men ii 4 342
You swear like a comfit-maker's wife iii 1 253
Swear me, Kate, like a lady as thou art, A good mouth-filling oath iii 1 258
If thou wert any way given to virtue, I would swear by thy face iii 3 38
When he heard him swear and vow to God iv 3 60
You swore to us, And you did swear that oath at Doncaster v 1 42
Therefore I'll make him sure; yea, and I'll swear I killed him v 4 127
Thou didst swear to me upon a parcel-gilt goblet *2 Hen. IV.* ii 1 93
Thou didst swear to me then, as I was washing thy wound, to marry me ii 1 98
He swears thou art to marry his sister Nell ii 2 139
Swears with a good grace, and wears his boots very smooth ii 4 269
And swear here, by the honour of my blood iv 2 55
Have you a ruffian that will swear, drink, dance, Revel the night? iv 5 125

Swear. I dare swear you borrow not that face Of seeming sorrow 2 *Hen. IV.* v 2 28
Call'st thou me host? Now, by this hand, I swear, I scorn the term *Hen. V.* ii 1 32
Let us swear That you are worth your breeding . . . iii 1 27
Swear by her foot, that she may tread out the oath . . iii 7 103
Come thou no more for ransom, gentle herald: They shall have none, I swear . . . . iv 3 123
By this leek, I will most horribly revenge: I eat and eat, I swear . v 1 50
Have some more sauce to your leek? there is not enough leek to swear by v 1 53
Patches will I get unto these cudgell'd scars, And swear I got them in the Gallia wars . . . . v 1 94
I dare not swear thou lovest me; yet my blood begins to flatter me . v 2 238
Then shall I swear to Kate, and you to me; And may our oaths well kept and prosperous be! . . . . . . v 2 401
So sure I swear to get the town or die . . 1 *Hen. VI.* iii 2 84
You fled for vantage, every one will swear . . . iv 5 28
Upon condition thou wilt swear To pay him tribute . . v 4 129
Then swear allegiance to his majesty, As thou art knight . . v 4 169
Oft have I seen the haughty cardinal . . . Swear like a ruffian 2 *Hen. VI.* i 1 188
As if she had suborned some to swear False allegations . . iii 1 180
Therefore, by His majesty I swear, Whose far unworthy deputy I am . iii 2 285
Had I but said, I would have kept my word, But when I swear, it is irrevocable . . . . iii 2 294
They jointly swear To spoil the city and your royal court . iv 4 52
It is great sin to swear unto a sin, But greater sin to keep a sinful oath v 1 182
An oath is of no moment, being not took Before a true and lawful magistrate, That hath authority over him that swears . 3 *Hen. VI.* i 2 24
Swear as thou wast wont.—What, not an oath? . . . ii 6 76
Did you never swear, and break an oath?—No, never such an oath . iii 1 72
Ah, simple men, you know not what you swear! . . . iii 1 83
By my state I swear to thee I speak no more than what my soul intends iii 2 93
Often heard him say and swear That this his love was an eternal plant . iii 3 123
Didst thou not hear me swear I would not do it? . . . v 5 74
He cannot swear, but it [conscience] checks him *Richard III.* i 4 140
Dissemble not your hatred, swear your love . . . ii 1 8
So thrive I, as I truly swear the like!—Take heed you dally not . ii 1 11
So prosper I, as I swear perfect love! . . . . ii 1 16
Upon my part shall be unviolable.—And so swear I . . ii 1 28
Now, by Saint Paul I swear, I will not dine until I see the same . iii 4 78
I swear— By nothing; for this is no oath . . . iv 4 368
If something thou wilt swear to be believed, Swear then by something that thou hast not wrong'd . . . . . iv 4 372
What canst thou swear by now?—The time to come . . iv 4 387
Swear not by time to come; for that thou hast Misused ere used . iv 4 395
You would swear directly Their very noses had been counsellors *Hen. VIII.* i 3 8
Verily, I swear, 'tis better to be lowly born . . . ii 3 19
I swear again, I would not be a queen For all the world . . ii 3 45
Might corrupt minds procure knaves as corrupt To swear against you? v 1 133
I swear he is true-hearted; and a soul None better in my kingdom v 1 154
I swear to you, I think Helen loves him better than Paris *Troi. and Cres.* i 2 116
Swear the oaths now to her that you have sworn to me . . iii 2 43
All lovers swear more performance than they are able . . iii 2 91
By Venus' hand I swear, No man alive can love in such a sort . iv 1 22
Your quondam wife swears still by Venus' glove . . . iv 5 179
What did you swear you would bestow on me? . . . v 2 25
I had your heart before, this follows it.—I did swear patience . v 2 84
The gods have heard me swear.—The gods are deaf to hot and peevish vows . . . . v 3 15
The father's son: I'll swear, 'tis a very pretty boy . . *Coriolanus* i 3 62
I heard him swear, Were he to stand for consul, never would he Appear i' the market-place . . . . . . ii 1 247
And here I swear by all the Roman gods . . . *T. Andron.* i 1 322
And here, in sight of heaven, to Rome I swear . . . i 1 329
Turn me to each one of you, And swear unto my soul to right your wrongs . . . . iii 1 279
And swear with me, as, with the woful fere And father of that chaste dishonour'd dame, Lord Junius Brutus sware for Lucrece' rape iv 1 89
And this shall all be buried by my death, Unless thou swear to me my child shall live . . . . v 1 68
Swear that he shall, and then I will begin.—Who should I swear by? . v 1 70
I know An idiot holds his bauble for a god And keeps the oath which by that god he swears . . . . . . v 1 80
Even by my god I swear to thee I will . . . . v 1 86
Being thus frighted swears a prayer or two And sleeps again *R. and J.* i 4 87
Which of you all Will now deny to dance? she that makes dainty, She, I'll swear, hath corns . . . . i 5 22
He may not have access To breathe such vows as lovers use to swear ii Prol. 10
By yonder blessed moon I swear That tips with silver all these fruit-tree tops— O, swear not by the moon, the inconstant moon, That monthly changes . . . . ii 2 109
What shall I swear by?—Do not swear at all; Or, if thou wilt, swear by thy gracious self . . . . . . ii 2 112
If my heart's dear love— Well, do not swear . . . ii 2 116
I will not marry yet; and, when I do, I swear, It shall be Romeo . iii 5 122
Swear against objects; Put armour on thine ears . *T. of Athens* iv 3 122
I know, you'll swear, terribly swear Into strong shudders and to heavenly agues The immortal gods . . . . . iv 3 136
Let us swear our resolution.—No, not an oath . . *J. Cæsar* ii 1 113
Swear priests and cowards and men cautelous, Old feeble carrions . ii 1 129
Unto bad causes swear Such creatures as men doubt . . ii 1 131
Here's an equivocator, that could swear in both the scales *Macbeth* ii 3 10
What is a traitor?—Why, one that swears and lies . . iv 2 47
Must they all be hanged that swear and lie?—Every one . . iv 2 51
Nay, but swear't.—In faith, My lord, not I.—Nor I, my lord *Hamlet* i 5 145
We have sworn, my lord, already.—Indeed, upon my sword, indeed.—Swear . . . . i 5 149
Consent to swear.—Propose the oath, my lord.—Never to speak of this that you have seen, Swear by my sword.—Swear . . . i 5 152
Never to speak of this that you have heard, Swear by my sword.—Swear i 5 160
So grace and mercy at your most need help you, Swear.—Swear . i 5 181
Madam, I swear I use no art at all. That he is mad, 'tis true . ii 2 96
If the matter were good, my lord, I durst swear it were his . *Lear* i 2 69
By Jupiter, I swear, no.—By Juno, I swear, ay . . . ii 4 21
Obey thy parents; keep thy word justly; swear not . . iii 4 83
I will not swear these are my hands: let's see; I feel this pin prick . iv 7 55
Drunk? and speak parrot? and squabble? swagger? swear? *Othello* ii 3 281
I swear 'tis better to be much abused Than but to know't a little . iii 3 336
Nightly lie in those unproper beds Which they dare swear peculiar . iv 1 70
This would not be believed in Venice, Though I should swear I saw't . iv 1 254

Swear. Your wife, my lord; your true And loyal wife.—Come, swear it, damn thyself . . . . *Othello* iv 2 35
Swear thou art honest.—Heaven doth truly know it . . . iv 2 38
I could make him swear The shes of Italy should not betray Mine interest and his honour . . . . . . *Cymbeline* i 3 28
I am the master of my speeches, and would undergo what's spoken, I swear . . . . i 4 153
When a gentleman is disposed to swear, it is not for any standers-by to curtail his oaths . . . . ii 1 11
Still, I swear I love you.—If you but said so, 'twere as deep with me: If you swear still, your recompense is still That I regard it not . ii 3 95
Hark you, he swears; by Jupiter he swears. 'Tis true . . ii 4 122
I'll be sworn— No swearing. If you will swear you have not done't, you lie . . . . ii 4 144
As it is like him—might break out, and swear He'ld fetch us in . . iv 2 140
Will think me speaking, though I swear to silence . *Pericles* i 2 19
I'll swear she's dead, And thrown into the sea . . . iv 1 99
Superstitiously Doth swear to the gods that winter kills the flies . iv 3 50
He swears Never to wash his face, nor cut his hairs . . iv 4 27
And swears she'll never stint, Make raging battery upon shores of flint iv 4 42

Swearer. I do believe the swearer . . . *Mer. Wives* ii 2 40
Then the liars and swearers are fools, for there are liars and swearers enow to beat the honest men and hang up them *Macbeth* iv 2 56
She'll disfurnish us of all our cavaliers, and make our swearers priests *Pericles* iv 6 13

Swearest. Now, blasphemy, That swear'st grace o'erboard, not an oath on shore . . . . *Tempest* v 1 219
Thou swearest to me thou art honest . . *As Y. Like It* iii 3 25
But thou hast sworn against religion, By what thou swear'st against the thing thou swear'st . . . . . *K. John* iii 1 281
Swearest thou, ungracious boy? henceforth ne'er look on me 1 *Hen. IV.* ii 4 490
Yet, if thou swear'st, Thou mayst prove false . . *Rom. and Jul.* ii 2 91
Thou swear'st thy gods in vain . . . . . *Lear* i 1 163

Swearing. I am damned in hell for swearing to gentlemen *Mer. Wives* ii 2 9
Drinkings and swearings and starings, pribbles and prabbles . . v 5 168
Use it for my love some other way than swearing by it . *Much Ado* iv 1 330
Swearing till my very roof was dry With oaths of love . *Mer. of Venice* iii 2 206
We shall have old swearing . . . . . . iv 2 15
Swearing by his honour, for he never had any . *As Y. Like It* i 2 83
Swearing that we Are mere usurpers, tyrants . . . . ii 1 60
A mad-cap ruffian and a swearing Jack . . *T. of Shrew* ii 1 290
Nay, let me alone for swearing . . . . *T. Night* iii 4 201
I over-swear; And all those swearings keep as true in soul . . v 1 277
Swearing allegiance and the love of soul To stranger blood *K. John* v 1 10
Got with swearing 'Lay by' and spent with crying 'Bring in' 1 *Hen. IV.* i 2 40
Some swearing, some crying for a surgeon, some upon their wives *Hen. V.* iv 1 144
To swearing and stern looks, defused attire . . . . v 2 61
Swearing that you withhold his levied host . . 1 *Hen. VI.* iv 4 31
Swearing both They prosper best of all when I am thence . 3 *Hen. VI.* ii 5 17
O' the t'other side, the policy of those crafty swearing rascals *T. and C.* v 4 11
Swearing, if The Roman ladies bring not comfort home, They'll give him death by inches . . . . *Coriolanus* v 4 40
Or drinking, fencing, swearing, quarrelling, Drabbing . *Hamlet* ii 1 25
At gaming, swearing, or about some act That has no relish of salvation in't iii 3 91
Though you in swearing shake the throned gods . *Ant. and Cleo.* i 3 28
Those mouth-made vows, Which break themselves in swearing! . . i 3 31
And then a whoreson jackanapes must take me up for swearing *Cymb.* ii 1 5
No swearing. If you will swear you have not done't, you lie . ii 4 143

Sweat. All things in common nature should produce Without sweat or endeavour . . . . *Tempest* ii 1 160
What with the war, what with the sweat, what with the gallows *M. for M.* i 2 84
Her face nothing like so clean kept: for why, she sweats *Com. of Er.* iii 2 105
Oft in field, with targe and shield, did make my foe to sweat *L. L. Lost* v 2 556
The ox hath therefore stretch'd his yoke in vain, The ploughman lost his sweat . . . . *M. N. Dream* ii 1 94
For wooing here until I sweat again, And swearing till my very roof was dry With oaths of love . . . . . *Mer. of Venice* iii 2 205
Why sweat they under burthens? . . . . . . iv 1 95
When service sweat for duty, not for meed . . *As Y. Like It* ii 3 58
The fashion of these times, Where none will sweat but for promotion . ii 3 60
Do not your courtier's hands sweat? and is not the grease of a mutton as wholesome as the sweat of a man? . . . . iii 2 58
Rage like an angry boar chafed with sweat . . *T. of Shrew* i 2 203
For that England's sake With burden of our armour here we sweat *K. John* ii 1 92
Who else but I, And such as to my claim are liable, Sweat in this business? v 2 102
Falstaff sweats to death, And lards the lean earth as he walks along 1 *Hen. IV.* ii 2 115
Beads of sweat have stood upon thy brow, Like bubbles . . ii 3 61
I take but two shirts out with me, and I mean not to sweat extra-ordinarily . . . . 2 *Hen. IV.* i 2 235
Shall I sweat for you? If I do sweat, they are the drops of thy lovers iv 3 13
For any thing I know, Falstaff shall die of a sweat . . . Epil. 32
Sweat drops of gallant youth in our rich fields . . *Hen. V.* iii 5 25
Like a lackey, from the rise to set Sweats in the eye of Phœbus . iv 1 290
Drops bloody sweat from his war-wearied limbs . 1 *Hen. VI.* iv 4 18
If you do sweat to put a tyrant down, You sleep in peace *Richard III.* v 3 255
Follow'd with the general throng and sweat Of thousand friends *Hen. VIII.* Prol. 28
The madams too, Not used to toil, did almost sweat to bear The pride . i 1 24
He was stirr'd With such an agony, he sweat extremely . . ii 1 33
Till then I'll sweat and seek about for eases . *Troi. and Cres.* v 10 56
They do disdain us . . . , Which makes me sweat with wrath *Coriolanus* i 4 27
If you had been the wife of Hercules, Six of his labours you'ld have done, and saved Your husband so much sweat . . . . iv 1 19
It is no little thing to make Mine eyes to sweat compassion . . v 3 196
A chilling sweat o'er-runs my trembling joints . . *T. Andron.* ii 3 212
I have sweat to see his honour . . . . *T. of Athens* iii 2 28
He shall but bear them as the ass bears gold, To groan and sweat *J. C.* iv 1 22
If arguing make us sweat, The proof of it will turn to redder drops . v 1 48
Come in time; have napkins enow about you; here you'll sweat for't *Macbeth* ii 3 7
Who would fardels bear, To grunt and sweat under a weary life? *Hamlet* iii 1 77
Nay, but to live In the rank sweat of an enseamed bed . . iii 4 92
At this time We sweat and bleed . . . . . *Lear* v 3 55
He sweats not to overthrow your Almain . . . *Othello* ii 3 85
And stand the buffet With knaves that smell of sweat . *Ant. and Cleo.* i 4 21
He sweats, Strains his young nerves, and puts himself in posture *Cymb.* iii 3 93
The sweat of industry would dry and die, But for the end it works to . iii 6 31

Sweaten. Grease that's sweaten From the murderer's gibbet throw Into the flame . . . . *Macbeth* iv 1 65

Sweatest. Alas, poor ape, how thou sweatest! . 2 *Hen. IV.* ii 4 234
Sweating. Here's Mistress Page at the door, sweating and blowing *M. W.* iii 3 93
A dozen captains, Bare-headed, sweating, knocking at the taverns 2 *Hen. IV.* ii 4 388
To stand stained with travel, and sweating with desire to see him v 5 26
And, in good time, here comes the sweating lord . . *Richard III.* iii 1 24
'Tis sweating labour To bear such idleness so near the heart . *A. and C.* i 3 93
Here's a young and sweating devil here, That commonly rebels *Othello* iii 4 42
Sweaty. The rabblement hooted and clapped their chopped hands and threw up their sweaty night-caps . . . *J. Cæsar* i 2 247
This sweaty haste Doth make the night joint-labourer with the day *Ham.* i 1 77
Sweep. Sever themselves and madly sweep the sky . . *M. N. Dream* iii 2 23
Their heads are hung With ears that sweep away the morning dew . iv 1 126
I am sent with broom before, To sweep the dust behind the door v 1 397
Sweep on, you fat and greasy citizens; 'Tis just the fashion *As Y. L. It* ii 1 55
Bar Harry England, that sweeps through our land With pennons painted in the blood of Harfleur . . . . . *Hen. V.* iii 5 48
Let frantic Talbot triumph for a while And like a peacock sweep along his tail; We'll pull his plumes . . . . 1 *Hen. VI.* iii 3 6
She sweeps it through the court with troops of ladies . . 2 *Hen. VI.* i 3 80
Thy lips that kiss'd the queen shall sweep the ground . . . . iv 1 75
I am the besom that must sweep the court clean . . . . iv 7 34
Lo, where George of Clarence sweeps along . . 3 *Hen. VI.* v 1 76
Impossible—Unless we sweep 'em from the door with cannons *Hen. VIII.* v 4 13
What a sweep of vanity comes this way! . . . *T. of Athens* i 2 137
Though I could With barefaced power sweep him from my sight *Macbeth* iii 1 119
That I, with wings as swift As meditation or the thoughts of love, May sweep to my revenge . . . . *Hamlet* i 5 31
They must sweep my way, And marshal me to knavery . . . iii 4 204
You shall Have letters from me to some friends that will Sweep your way for you. Pray you, look not sad . . . *Ant. and Cleo.* iii 11 17
Sweet, now, silence! . . . . *Tempest* iv 1 124
Sweet, except not any; Except thou wilt except against my love *T. G. of Ver.* ii 4 154
Look sweet, speak fair, become disloyalty . . . *Com. of Errors* iii 2 11
Call thyself sister, sweet, for I am thee. Thee will I love . . iii 2 66
The desk, the purse! sweet, now, make haste . . . . iv 2 29
You have among you killed a sweet and innocent lady . *Much Ado* v 1 194
Sweet, let me see your face.—No, that you shall not . . . v 4 55
So sweet and voluble is his discourse . . . . . *L. L. Lost* ii 1 76
Here, sweet, put up this: 'twill be thine another day . . . iv 1 109
Trip and go, my sweet; deliver this paper . . . . . iv 2 145
So sweet a kiss the golden sun gives not . . . . . iv 3 25
Vow, alack, for youth unmeet, Youth so apt to pluck a sweet! . iv 3 114
As sweet and musical As bright Apollo's lute, strung with his hair iv 3 342
The word is well culled, chose, sweet, and apt . . . . v 1 98
Hold, take thou this, my sweet, and give me thine . . . v 2 132
There's half-a-dozen sweets.—Seventh sweet, adieu! . . . v 2 234
One word in secret.—Let it not be sweet . . . . . v 2 236
The ladies call him sweet; The stairs, as he treads on them, kiss his feet v 2 329
Fair gentle sweet, Your wit makes wise things foolish . . v 2 373
That is all one, my fair, sweet, honey monarch . . . . v 2 530
Emptying our bosoms of their counsel sweet . . . *M. N. Dream* i 1 216
She never had so sweet a changeling . . . . . . ii 1 23
A sweet Athenian lady is in love With a disdainful youth . . ii 1 260
O, take the sense, sweet, of my innocence! . . . . . ii 2 45
The flowers of odious savours sweet,— Odours, odours . . . iii 1 84
Sweet, do not scorn her so.—If she cannot entreat, I can compel . iii 2 247
Why, gentle sweet, you shall see no such thing . . . . v 1 87
Trust me, sweet, Out of this silence yet I pick'd a welcome . . v 1 99
And thou, O wall, O sweet, O lovely wall! . . . . . v 1 175
O sweet and lovely wall, Show me thy chink, to blink through with mine eyne! . . . . v 1 177
I should be obscured.—So are you, sweet . . . *M. of Venice* ii 6 44
Sweet, adieu. I'll keep my oath, Patiently to bear my wroth . ii 9 77
A day in April never came so sweet . . . . . . ii 9 93
So sweet a bar Should sunder such sweet friends . . . . iii 2 119
And now, good sweet, say thy opinion . . . . . iii 5 76
How sweet the moonlight sleeps upon this bank! . . . . v 1 54
This life more sweet Than that of painted pomp . . *As Y. Like It* ii 1 2
Sweet are the uses of adversity . . . . ii 1 12
That can translate the stubbornness of fortune Into so quiet and so sweet a style . . . . ii 1 20
Sweet, say on.—You bring me out . . . . . . iii 2 264
Pacing through the forest, Chewing the food of sweet and bitter fancy . iv 3 102
Burn sweet wood to make the lodging sweet . . *T. of Shrew* Ind. 1 49
Continue your resolve To suck the sweets of sweet philosophy . . i 1 28
Sacred and sweet was all I saw in her . . . . . . i 1 181
Slow in speech, yet sweet as spring-time flowers . . . . ii 1 248
Give away myself To this most patient, sweet, and virtuous wife . iii 2 196
Young budding virgin, fair and fresh and sweet, Whither away? . iv 5 37
And, to be short, what not, that's sweet and happy? . . . v 2 110
Whose want, and whose delay, is strew'd with sweets . . *All's Well* ii 4 45
So good a wife and so sweet a lady . . . . . . iv 3 9
They cannot be too sweet for the king's tartness . . . . iv 3 95
When briers shall have leaves as well as thorns, And be as sweet as sharp iv 4 33
If it end so meet, The bitter past, more welcome is the sweet . . v 3 334
Enough; no more: 'Tis not so sweet now as it was before . *T. Night* i 1 8
Whose red and white Nature's own sweet and cunning hand laid on . i 5 258
So sweet a breath to sing . . . . ii 3 21
A contagious breath.—Very sweet and contagious, i' faith . . ii 3 57
Not a flower, not a flower sweet, On my black coffin let there be strown ii 4 60
In my presence still smile, dear my sweet . . . . . ii 5 193
We do know the sweet Roman hand . . . . iii 4 31
The climate's delicate, the air most sweet, Fertile the isle . *W. Tale* iii 1 1
When you speak, sweet, I'ld have you do it ever . . . . iv 4 136
Gloves as sweet as damask roses; Masks for faces and for noses . iv 4 222
This affliction has a taste as sweet As any cordial comfort . . v 3 76
The daintiest last, to make the end most sweet . . *Richard II.* i 3 68
Draws the sweet infant breath of gentle sleep . . . . . i 3 133
Things sweet to taste prove in digestion sour . . . . . i 3 236
The setting sun, and music at the close, As the last taste of sweets, is sweetest last . . . . ii 1 13
Save bidding farewell to so sweet a guest . . . . . . ii 2 8
Your fair discourse hath been as sugar, Making the hard way sweet . ii 3 7
Feed not thy sovereign's foe, my gentle earth, Nor with thy sweets comfort his ravenous sense . . . . iii 2 13
I am sworn brother, sweet, To grim Necessity . . . . . v 1 20
The word is short, but not so short as sweet . . . . . v 3 117
The most comparative, rascalliest, sweet young prince . . 1 *Hen. IV.* i 2 91
Sweet. For he made me mad To see him shine so brisk and smell so sweet . . . . 1 *Hen. IV.* i 3 54
Richard, that sweet lovely rose . . . . i 3 175
Thy tongue Makes Welsh as sweet as ditties highly penn'd . . . iii 1 209
England did never owe so sweet a hope . . . . . . v 2 68
You sweet little rogue, you! . . . . 2 *Hen. IV.* ii 4 233
Sleep with it now! Yet not so sound and half so deeply sweet . iv 5 26
Like the bee, culling from every flower The virtuous sweets . . iv 5 76
To steal his sweet and honey'd sentences . . . . . *Hen. V.* i 1 50
What drink'st thou oft, instead of homage sweet, But poison'd flattery? iv 1 267
Thy life to me is sweet . . . . 1 *Hen. VI.* iv 6 55
Happy for so sweet a child . . . . v 3 148
Sweet is the country, because full of riches; The people liberal 2 *Hen. VI.* iv 7 67
How sweet a thing it is to wear a crown . . . . 3 *Hen. VI.* i 2 29
Steeped in the harmless blood Of sweet young Rutland . . . ii 1 63
Ah, what a life were this! how sweet! how lovely! . . . . ii 5 41
Sweet rest his soul! Fly, lords, and save yourselves . . . . v 2 48
How sweet a plant have you untimely cropp'd! . . . . . v 5 62
As, deathsmen, you have rid this sweet young prince . . . . v 5 67
Never came poison from so sweet a place . . . . *Richard III.* i 2 147
My tongue could never learn sweet smoothing words . . . . i 2 169
So sweet is zealous contemplation . . . . iii 7 94
My tender babes! My unblown flowers, new-appearing sweets! . . iv 4 10
Acquaint the princess With the sweet silent hours of marriage joys iv 4 330
Would it not grieve an able man to leave So sweet a bedfellow? *Hen. VIII.* ii 2 143
Majesty and pomp, the which To leave a thousand-fold more bitter than 'Tis sweet at first to acquire . . . . ii 3 9
But to those men that sought him sweet as summer . . . . iv 2 54
Men prize the thing ungain'd more than it is: That she was never yet that ever knew Love got so sweet as when desire did sue *Troi. and Cres.* i 2 317
Sweet, above thought I love thee . . . . iii 1 172
The imaginary relish is so sweet That it enchants my sense . . . iii 2 20
Build there, carpenter; the air is sweet . . . . iii 2 54
Sweet, bid me hold my tongue, For in this rapture I shall surely speak The thing I shall repent . . . . iii 2 137
Your great love to me restrains you thus: Sweet, rouse yourself . iii 3 222
Let them not lick The sweet which is their poison . . *Coriolanus* iii 1 157
O, a kiss Long as my exile, sweet as my revenge! . . . . v 3 45
At my suit, sweet, pardon what is past . . . . *T. Andron.* i 1 431
Sweet melodious birds Be unto us as is a nurse's song Of lullaby . ii 3 27
Like a sweet melodious bird, it sung Sweet varied notes . . . iii 1 86
With words more sweet, and yet more dangerous, Than baits to fish . iv 4 90
He must not die So sweet a death as hanging . . . . . v 1 146
A madness most discreet, A choking gall, and a preserving sweet *R. and J.* i 1 200
This intrusion shall Now seeming sweet convert to bitter gall . . i 5 94
Tempering extremities with extreme sweet . . . . . . ii Prol. 14
That which we call a rose By any other name would smell as sweet . ii 2 44
Look thou but sweet, And I am proof against their enmity . . . ii 2 72
Sweet, good night! This bud of love, by summer's ripening breath, May prove a beauteous flower when next we meet . . . . ii 2 120
I would I were thy bird.—Sweet, so would I . . . . . ii 2 183
Would I were sleep and peace, so sweet to rest! . . . . . ii 2 188
What early tongue so sweet saluteth me? . . . . . . ii 3 32
I'll tell my lady you will come.—Do so, and bid my sweet prepare to chide iii 3 162
How sweet is love itself possess'd, When but love's shadows are so rich! v 1 10
With some sweet oblivious antidote Cleanse the stuff'd bosom *Macbeth* v 3 43
'Tis sweet and commendable in your nature, Hamlet . . . *Hamlet* i 2 87
Forward, not permanent, sweet, not lasting . . . . . . i 3 8
As wholesome as sweet, and by very much more handsome than fine . ii 2 466
Sweet, leave me here awhile; My spirits grow dull . . . . iii 2 235
O, 'tis most sweet, When in one line two crafts directly meet . . iii 4 209
In youth, when I did love, did love, Methought it was very sweet . v 1 70
Sweets to the sweet: farewell! . . . . v 1 266
O my sweet, I prattle out of fashion, and I dote In mine own comforts *Oth.* ii 1 207
Shall't be shortly?—The sooner, sweet, for you . . . . . iii 3 56
Whose is it?—I know not, sweet: I found it in my chamber . . iii 4 188
O thou weed, Who art so lovely fair and smell'st so sweet! . . . iv 2 68
They see and smell And have their palates both for sweet and sour . iv 3 96
One more, and this the last: So sweet was ne'er so fatal . . . v 2 19
You have heard on't, sweet? . . . . . . *Ant. and Cleo.* iii 7 24
Do discandy, melt their sweets On blossoming Cæsar . . . . iv 12 22
As sweet as balm, as soft as air, as gentle,—O Antony! . . . v 2 314
Shall quite unpeople her Of liegers for her sweet . . . *Cymbeline* i 5 80
With every thing that pretty is, My lady sweet, arise . . . . ii 3 29
His ascension is More sweet than our blest fields . . . . . v 4 117
One sand another Not more resembles that sweet rosy lad Who died . v 5 121
Therefore to make his entrance more sweet, Here, say we drink this standing-bowl of wine to him . . . . *Pericles* ii 3 64
Sweet air. Allaying both their fury and my passion With its sweet air *Tempest* i 2 393
The isle is full of noises, Sounds, and sweet airs . . . . . iii 2 145
Sweet air! Go, tenderness of years . . . . . . *L. L. Lost* iii 1 4
Your tongue's sweet air More tuneable than lark to shepherd's ear *M. N. D.* i 1 183
A wonderful sweet air, with admirable rich words to it . . . *Cymbeline* ii 3 19
Sweet Alexas, most any thing Alexas . . . . *Ant. and Cleo.* i 2 1
Sweet and twenty. Then come kiss me, sweet and twenty . . *T. Night* ii 3 52
Sweet Anne Page! . . . . *Mer. Wives* iii 1 72; 117
Sweet aspect. Some other mistress hath thy sweet aspects *Com. of Er.* ii 2 113
That smile we would aspire to, That sweet aspect of princes *Hen. VIII.* iii 2 369
Sweet aspersion. No sweet aspersion shall the heavens let fall *Tempest* iv 1 18
Sweet Audrey. Come, sweet Audrey: We must be married *As Y. Like It* iii 3 98
Sweet aunt, be quiet; 'twas against her will . . . 2 *Hen. VI.* i 3 146
Alas, sweet aunt, I know not what you mean . . . *T. Andron.* iv 1 4
Sweet babe. The duty that I owe unto your majesty I seal upon the lips of this sweet babe . . . . 3 *Hen. VI.* v 7 29
Sweet bait. That her ear lose nothing Of the false sweet bait *Much Ado* iii 1 33
And she steal love's sweet bait from fearful hooks . *Rom. and Jul.* ii Prol. 8
Sweet Bassanio, my ships have all miscarried . . . *Mer. of Venice* iii 2 317
Sweet Beatrice. God forgive me!—What offence, sweet Beatrice? *M. Ado* iv 1 284
Tarry, sweet Beatrice.—I am gone, though I am here . . . . iv 1 294
Sweet Beatrice, wouldst thou come when I called thee? . . . . v 2 42
Sweet beauty. I saw sweet beauty in her face . . . . *T. of Shrew* i 1 172
Sweet beds. Away before me to sweet beds of flowers . . . *T. Night* i 1 40
Sweet beef, I must still be good angel to thee . . . 1 *Hen. IV.* iii 3 199
Sweet bells. Like sweet bells jangled, out of tune and harsh *Hamlet* iii 1 166
Sweet Benedick. O sweet Benedick! God give me patience! *Much Ado* ii 3 154
Sweet benefit. Omitting the sweet benefit of time . . . *T. G. of Ver.* ii 4 65
Sweet Bianca. Yet, for the love I bear my sweet Bianca . . *T. of Shrew* i 1 111
Sweet Bianca! Happy man be his dole! . . . . i 1 144
So shall you quietly enjoy your hope, And marry sweet Bianca . . iii 2 139

Sweet Bianca. Shall sweet Bianca practise how to bride it? *T. of Shrew* iii 2 253
Sweet Bianca, Take me this work out . . . . . *Othello* iii 4 179
How now, my sweet Bianca! how now! how now! . . . iv 1 162
Sweet bird. Turn his merry note Unto the sweet bird's throat *As Y. L. It* ii 5 4
With heigh! the sweet birds, O, how they sing! . . *W. Tale* iv 3 6
The hapless male to one sweet bird . . . . . . *3 Hen. VI.* v 6 15
Sweet bloods, I both may and will . . . . . . *L. L. Lost* v 2 714
My sons' sweet blood will make it shame and blush *T. Andron.* iii 1 15
Sweet blowse, you are a beauteous blossom, sure . . . iv 2 72
Sweet bodements! good! Rebellion's head, rise never . *Macbeth* iv 1 96
Sweet body. I had been happy, if the general camp, Pioners and all, had tasted her sweet body . . . . *Othello* iii 3 346
Sweet bosom. Plant neighbourhood and Christian-like accord In their sweet bosoms . . . . *Hen. V.* v 2 382
So I might live one hour in your sweet bosom . . *Richard III.* i 2 124
Sweet Bottom. Let us hear, sweet Bottom.—Not a word *M. N. Dream* iv 2 33
Sweet boy. God save thee, my sweet boy! . . . *2 Hen. IV.* v 5 47
This cloth thou dip'dst in blood of my sweet boy . . *3 Hen. VI.* i 4 157
My heart, sweet boy, shall be thy sepulchre . . . . ii 5 115
The sun that sear'd the wings of my sweet boy . . . v 6 23
Kneel, sweet boy, the Roman Hector's hope . . *T. Andron.* iv 1 88
Sweet breath. 'Tis holy sport to be a little vain, When the sweet breath of flattery conquers strife . . . . . . *Com. of Errors* iii 2 28
Tapers they are, with your sweet breaths puff'd out *L. L. Lost* v 2 267
I implore so much expense of thy royal sweet breath . . v 2 524
Eat no onions nor garlic, for we are to utter sweet breath *M. N. Dream* iv 2 44
As many as have good beards or good faces or sweet breaths *As Y. L. It* Epil. 22
That sweet breath Which was embounded in this beauteous clay *K. John* iv 3 136
Sweet brother. If thou be there, sweet brother, take my hand *3 Hen. VI.* v 2 34
Did drain The purple sap from her sweet brother's body *Richard III.* iv 4 277
No notes of sally, for the heavens, sweet brother *Troi. and Cres.* v 3 14
Sweet bully. O sweet bully Bottom! . . . . *M. N. Dream* iv 2 19
Sweet Cæsar's wounds, poor poor dumb mouths . . *J. Cæsar* iii 2 229
Sweet captain. No, good Captain Pistol; not here, sweet captain *2 Hen. IV.* ii 4 150
Sweet Cassio. O my dear Cassio! my sweet Cassio! . . *Othello* v 1 76
Sweet cell of virtue and nobility . . . . . *T. Andron.* i 1 93
Sweet child. The foul corruption of a sweet child's death *K. John* iv 2 81
Sweet chuck. Present the princess, sweet chuck, with some delightful ostentation . . . . *L. L. Lost* v 1 117
Sweet chucks, beat not the bones of the buried . . . v 2 667
Use lenity, sweet chuck! . . . . *Hen. V.* iii 2 26
Sweet Clarence, do thou do it . . . . . . *3 Hen. VI.* v 5 73
Sweet Clifford, hear me speak before I die . . . . . i 3 18
Sweet Clifford, pity me!—Such pity as my rapier's point affords . i 3 36
Sweet clothes. What think you, if he were convey'd to bed, Wrapp'd in sweet clothes? . . . . *T. of Shrew* Ind. 1 38
Sweet clown, sweeter fool, sweetest lady! . . . *L. L. Lost* iv 3 17
Sweet comedy. It is a sweet comedy. No more words *M. N. Dream* iv 2 45
Sweet commixture. Their damask sweet commixture shown *L. L. Lost* v 2 296
Sweet-complaining. Such sweet-complaining grievance . *T. G. of Ver.* iii 2 86
Sweet complexion. And Ethiopes of their sweet complexion crack *L. L. Lost* iv 3 268
Sweet composure. Thou art of sweet composure . . *Troi. and Cres.* ii 3 251
Sweet concert. Visit by night your lady's chamber-window With some sweet concert . . . . *T. G. of Ver.* iii 2 84
Sweet constraint. I love thee By love's own sweet constraint *All's Well* iv 2 16
Sweet countrymen. Forgive me, country, and sweet countrymen *1 Hen. VI.* iii 3 81
Sweet coz. Conceive me, sweet coz: what I do is to pleasure you *M. W.* i 1 250
Sweet creature. Helen, that's dead, Was a sweet creature . *All's Well* v 3 78
How now, my sweet creature of bombast! . . . *1 Hen. IV.* ii 4 359
Then, sir, would he gripe and wring my hand, Cry 'O sweet creature!' *Othello* iii 3 422
Sweet Cressid. For this time will I take my leave, my lord.—Your leave, sweet Cressid! . . . . *Troi. and Cres.* iii 2 148
Sweet Cupid. Shot, by heaven! Proceed, sweet Cupid . *L. L. Lost* iv 3 23
Sweet daughter Joan, I'll die with thee! . . . . *1 Hen. VI.* v 4 6
Sweet dear. While you, sweet dear, prove mistress of my heart! *T. of S.* iv 2 10
Sweet degrees. The sweet degrees that this brief world affords *T. of A.* iv 3 253
Sweet delights. You speak Like one besotted on your sweet delights: You have the honey still . . . . *Troi. and Cres.* ii 2 143
Sweet Demetrius. Stay, though thou kill me, sweet Demetrius *M. N. D.* ii 2 84
Sweet dependency. Let me report to him Your sweet dependency *Ant. and Cleo.* v 2 26
Sweet Desdemona. Not now, sweet Desdemona; some other time *Othello* iii 3 55
Sweet Desdemona, Let us be wary, let us hide our loves . . . iii 3 419
Sweet Desdemona! O sweet mistress, speak! . . . . . v 2 121
Sweet disaster. His faith, his sweet disaster . . . . *All's Well* i 1 187
Sweet discourse. Hear sweet discourse, converse with noblemen *T. G. of V.* i 3 31
Ample interchange of sweet discourse . . . . *Richard III.* v 3 99
These woes shall serve For sweet discourses in our time to come *R. and J.* iii 5 53
Sweet disgrace. I will take it as a sweet disgrace . . . *2 Hen. IV.* i 1 89
Sweet division. Some say the lark makes sweet division *Rom. and Jul.* iii 5 29
Sweet doctor, you shall be my bed-fellow . . . . *Mer of Venice* v 1 284
Sweet draught: 'sweet' quoth 'a! sweet sink, sweet sewer *Tr. and Cr.* v 1 82
Sweet ducks!—O Troilus! Troilus!—What a pair of spectacles! . . iv 4 12
Sweet duke. List to me, my Humphrey, my sweet duke . *2 Hen. VI.* i 2 35
Sweet Duke of York, our prop to lean upon . . . *3 Hen. VI.* ii 1 68
Sweet earl, divorce not wisdom from your honour . *2 Hen. IV.* i 1 162
Sweet Elysium. And then it lived in sweet Elysium . *2 Hen. VI.* iii 2 399
Sweet emperor. Come, sweet emperor; come, Andronicus . *T. Andron.* i 1 456
Nay, nay, sweet emperor, we must all be friends . . . . i 1 479
Sweet emperor, be blithe again, And bury all thy fear in my devices . iv 4 111
Sweet end. 'Tis a physic That's bitter to sweet end . *Meas. for Meas.* iv 6 8
Sweet England! King Stephen was a worthy peer . . *Othello* ii 3 91
Sweet enlargement. Just death, kind umpire of men's miseries, With sweet enlargement doth dismiss me hence . . . . . *1 Hen. VI.* ii 5 30
Sweet Exeter. Nay, take me with thee, good sweet Exeter . *3 Hen. VI.* ii 5 137
Sweet eyes. She hath spied him already with those sweet eyes *M. N. D.* v 1 329
A tomb Must cover thy sweet eyes . . . . v 1 336
Bless thy sweet eyes, they bleed . . . . *Lear* iv 1 56
Sweet face. The Lord bless that sweet face of thine! . . *2 Hen. IV.* ii 4 317
And broke them in the sweet face of heaven . . . . *Lear* iii 4 91
Sweet-faced. I am a sweet-faced youth . . . . *Com. of Errors* v 1 418
A sweet-faced man; a proper man, as one shall see in a summer's day *M. N. Dream* i 2 88
Sweet father. Pardon, sweet father.—Lives my sweet son? *T. of Shrew* v 1 115
Then pardon him, sweet father, for my sake . . . . . v 1 133
Tear the crown from the usurper's head.—Sweet father, do so *3 Hen. VI.* i 1 115
Sweet father, cease your tears . . . . . . *T. Andron.* iii 1 136
Sweet father, if I shall be thought thy son, Let me redeem my brothers iii 1 180
Sweet favour. Seeking sweet favours for this hateful fool *M. N. Dream* iv 1 54
Heart too capable Of every line and trick of his sweet favour . *All's Well* i 1 107
Sweet fellow. For future good, To bless the bed of majesty again With a sweet fellow to't . . . . *W. Tale* v 1 34
Sweet fellowship in shame!—One drunkard loves another . *L. L. Lost* iv 3 49
Sweet fire. Which, not to anger bent, is music and sweet fire . . iv 2 120
Sweet fish. The imperious seas breed monsters, for the dish Poor tributary rivers as sweet fish . . . . *Cymbeline* iv 2 36
Sweet flesh. When thou didst bower the spirit of a fiend In mortal paradise of such sweet flesh . . . . *Rom. and Jul.* iii 2 82
Sweet flowers are slow and weeds make haste . . *Richard III.* ii 4 15
Sweet flower, with flowers thy bridal bed I strew . . *Rom. and Jul.* v 3 12
Larded with sweet flowers . . . . *Hamlet* iv 5 37
Sweet fool. Dost thou know the difference, my boy, between a bitter fool and a sweet fool? . . . . *Lear* i 4 152
The sweet and bitter fool Will presently appear; The one in motley here i 4 158
Sweet Fortune. Who is sweet Fortune's minion and her pride *1 Hen. IV.* i 1 83
Sweet Frank! why art thou melancholy? . . . . *Mer. Wives* ii 1 155
Sweet friend. Good night, sweet friend . . . . *M. N. Dream* ii 2 60
Sweet friends, to bed. A fortnight hold we this solemnity . . . v 1 375
Sweet friends, your patience for my long abode . . *Mer. of Venice* ii 6 21
So sweet a bar Should sunder such sweet friends . . . . iii 2 120
Sweet friend, what happy gale Blows you to Padua? . . *T. of Shrew* i 2 48
O, these I lack, To make you garlands of, and my sweet friend, To strew him o'er and o'er! . . . . *W. Tale* iv 4 128
Good friends, sweet friends, let me not stir you up . . . *J. Cæsar* iii 2 214
Sweet gallant. Count Comfect; a sweet gallant, surely! . *Much Ado* iv 1 319
Sweet Ganymede. How now, Ganymede! sweet Ganymede! *As Y. L. It* iv 3 158
Sweet gardon. O sweet gardon! better than remuneration . *L. L. Lost* iii 1 171
Sweet gentlemen. Dispatch, sweet gentlemen, and follow me *T. G. of V.* v 2 48
Sweet gentleness. Thy rare qualities, sweet gentleness . . *Hen. VIII.* ii 4 137
Sweet Gertrude, leave us too; For we have closely sent for Hamlet *Ham.* iii 1 28
Sweet girl. Shall we be sunder'd? shall we part, sweet girl? *As Y. Like It* i 3 100
Wert thou thus surprised, sweet girl? . . . . . *T. Andron.* iv 1 51
Give signs, sweet girl, for here are none but friends . . . . iv 1 61
Sweet glances. To the sweet glances of thy honour'd love *T. G. of Ver.* i 1 4
Sweet gloves. Come, you promised me a tawdry-lace and a pair of sweet gloves . . . . *W. Tale* iv 4 253
Sweet gold. And so repose, sweet gold, for their unrest . *T. Andron.* ii 3 8
Sweet goose. Is it not well served in to a sweet goose? . *Rom. and Jul.* ii 4 85
Sweet grace. By thy sweet grace's officer, Anthony Dull . *L. L. Lost* i 1 270
I do adore thy sweet grace's slipper.—Loves her by the foot . . v 2 672
Sweet Greek. Bid me do any thing but that, sweet Greek *Troi. and Cres.* v 2 27
Sweet guardian. My sweet guardian! Hark, a word with you . . v 2 7
Sweet Hal. Good morrow, sweet Hal. What says Monsieur Remorse? *1 Hen. IV.* i 2 124
Sweet Hamlet. These words, like daggers, enter in mine ears; No more, sweet Hamlet! . . . . *Hamlet* iii 4 96
Sweet hand. Good morrow, fairest: sister, your sweet hand . *Cymbeline* ii 3 91
My hand cut off and made a merry jest; Both her sweet hands *T. An.* v 2 176
Sweet harmony. Soft stillness and the night Become the touches of sweet harmony . . . . *Mer. of Venice* v 1 57
With her sweet harmony And other chosen attractions . . *Pericles* v 1 45
'Sweet Harry,' says she, 'how many hast thou killed to-day?' *1 Hen. IV.* ii 4 118
Had my sweet Harry had but half their numbers . . . *2 Hen. IV.* ii 3 43
Sweet hay. Good hay, sweet hay, hath no fellow . . *M. N. Dream* iv 1 37
Sweet head. They are as gentle As zephyrs blowing below the violet, Not wagging his sweet head . . . . *Cymbeline* iv 2 173
Sweet health and fair desires consort your grace! . . . *L. L. Lost* ii 1 178
Sweetheart. How now, sweetheart! who's at home besides yourself? *Mer. Wives* iv 2 12
Mistress Page is come with me, sweetheart . . . . . . v 5 26
But, sweet heart, let that pass . . . . *L. L. Lost* v 1 110
Sweet heart, I do implore secrecy . . . . v 1 115
Sweet hearts, we shall be rich ere we depart . . . . . v 2 1
Curtsy, sweet hearts; and so the measure ends . . . . v 2 221
What's the matter, sweet-heart? . . . . *All's Well* ii 3 285
What, what, sweet-heart?—O my Parolles, they have married me! . ii 3 288
Wherefore, sweet-heart? what's your metaphor? . . . . *T. Night* i 3 75
To bed! ay, sweet-heart, and I'll come to thee . . . . . iii 4 33
Take your sweetheart's hat And pluck it o'er your brows . *W. Tale* iv 4 664
Sweetheart, methinks now you are in an excellent good temperality *2 Hen. IV.* ii 4 24
Sweetheart, lie thou there . . . . ii 4 197
Sweetheart, I were unmannerly, to take you out, And not to kiss you *Hen. VIII.* i 4 94
Why, love, I say! madam! sweet-heart! why, bride! . *Rom. and Jul.* iv 5 3
Set not thy sweet heart on proud array . . . . . . *Lear* iii 4 85
Tray, Blanch, and Sweet-heart, see, they bark at me . . . iii 6 66
Sweet heaven. O, help him, you sweet heavens! . . . . *Hamlet* iii 1 138
Is there not rain enough in the sweet heavens To wash it white as snow? iii 3 45
O, let me not be mad, not mad, sweet heaven! . . . . . *Lear* i 5 50
Sweet Hector. Unarm, sweet Hector.—Hold you still, I say *Tr. and Cr.* v 3 25
Sweet Helen. Be this sweet Helen's knell, and now forget her *All's Well* v 3 67
Sweet Helen, I must woo you To help unarm our Hector *Troi. and Cres.* iii 1 162
Sweet Henry, favour him.—Be patient, lords . . . . *1 Hen. VI.* iv 1 81
Sweet Hercules. Most sweet Hercules! More authority . . *L. L. Lost* i 2 70
Sweet Hermia. Relent, sweet Hermia . . . . . *M. N. Dream* i 1 91
Sweet Hero. Good morrow, sweet Hero.—Why, how now? . *Much Ado* iii 4 40
Sweet Hero! She is wronged, she is slandered, she is undone . . iv 1 314
Sweet Hero! now thy image doth appear In the rare semblance that I loved it first . . . . v 1 259
Sweet honey. Injurious wasps, to feed on such sweet honey! *T. G. of V.* i 2 106
Sweet honey and sweet notes together fail . . *Troi. and Cres.* v 10 45
Sweet honey Greek, tempt me no more to folly . . . . v 2 18
Sweet honey lord. My good sweet honey lord, ride with us . *1 Hen. IV.* i 2 179
Sweet honeysuckle. So doth the woodbine the sweet honeysuckle Gently entwist . . . . *M. N. Dream* iv 1 47
Sweet hope. My food, my fortune, and my sweet hope's aim *Com. of Er.* iii 2 63
Sweet huntsman, Bassianus 'tis we mean . . . . *T. Andron.* ii 3 269
Sweet husband. Come down, I say!—Nay, good, sweet husband! *M. W.* iv 2 189
Sweet York, sweet husband, be not of that mind . . *Richard II.* v 2 107
Sweet Imogen. Cast From her his dearest one, Sweet Imogen *Cymbeline* v 4 62
Sweet instruments. Would most resemble sweet instruments hung up in cases . . . . *T. of Athens* i 2 102
Sweet invocation of a child; most pretty and pathetical! . *L. L. Lost* i 2 102
Sweet Isabel, take my part; Lend me your knees . . *Meas. for Meas.* v 1 435
Isabel, Sweet Isabel, do yet but kneel by me . . . . . . v 1 442

Sweet Isis. Let him marry a woman that cannot go, sweet Isis! *Ant. and Cleo.* i 2 66
Sweet Jack Falstaff, kind Jack Falstaff, true Jack Falstaff 1 *Hen. IV.* ii 4 522
Well, sweet Jack, have a care of thyself 2 *Hen. IV.* ii 4 410
Sweet Jerusalem. To meet with joy in sweet Jerusalem 3 *Hen. VI.* v 5 8
Sweet jest. Most sweet jests! most incony vulgar wit! *L. L. Lost* iv 1 144
Wink each at other; hold the sweet jest up *M. N. Dream* iii 2 239
Sweet Jew. Most beautiful pagan, most sweet Jew! *Mer. of Venice* ii 3 11
Sweet Jude. And so adieu, sweet Jude! nay, why dost thou stay? *L. L. Lost* v 2 629
Sweet Julia. Passionate Proteus, To the sweet Julia *T. G. of Ver.* i 2 125
Sweet Juliet, Thy beauty hath made me effeminate *Rom. and Jul.* iii 1 118
Sweet Kate. Nay, good sweet Kate, be merry *T. of Shrew* iv 1 146
Will you give thanks, sweet Kate; or else shall I? iv 1 162
I am sure, sweet Kate, this kindness merits thanks iv 3 41
Tell me, sweet Kate, and tell me truly too iv 5 28
Sweet Kate, embrace her for her beauty's sake iv 5 34
Come, my sweet Kate: Better once than never, for never too late v 1 154
Sweet Katharine. Marry, so I mean, sweet Katharine ii 1 269
Sweet king! the bishop hath a kindly gird 1 *Hen. VI.* iii 1 131
Sweet king-killer. O thou sweet king-killer [gold]! *T. of Athens* iv 3 382
Sweet knaves. That there should be small love 'mongst these sweet knaves, And all this courtesy! i 1 258
Sweet knight, I kiss thy neif 2 *Hen. IV.* ii 4 200
Sweet knight, thou art now one of the greatest men in this realm v 3 91
Sweet lady. Who is that, servant?—Yourself, sweet lady *T. G. of Ver.* ii 4 37
Sweet lady, entertain him To be my fellow-servant ii 4 104
Too low a mistress for so high a servant.—Not so, sweet lady ii 4 107
My love is buried.—Sweet lady, let me rake it from the earth iv 2 116
She's an excellent sweet lady *Much Ado* ii 3 165
If this sweet lady lie not guiltless here Under some biting error iv 1 171
You have killed a sweet lady, and her death shall fall heavy on you v 1 150
She is a most sweet lady.—Not unlike, sir, that may be *L. L. Lost* ii 1 207
She, sweet lady, dotes, Devoutly dotes, dotes in idolatry *M. N. Dream* i 1 108
What should I say, sweet lady? I was enforced to send it *Mer. of Venice* v 1 215
Some mollification for your giant, sweet lady *T. Night* i 5 219
What is your text?—Most sweet lady,— A comfortable doctrine i 5 238
How now, Malvolio!—Sweet lady, ho, ho iii 4 18
And witch sweet ladies with my words and looks 3 *Hen. VI.* iii 2 150
Thine eyes, sweet lady, have infected mine *Richard III.* i 2 150
Sweet ladies, will it please you sit? *Hen. VIII.* i 4 19
Sweet ladies: If I chance to talk a little wild, forgive me i 4 25
She's a good creature, and, sweet lady, does Deserve our better wishes v 1 25
To make a sweet lady sad is a sour offence *Troi. and Cres.* iii 1 79
What too curious dreg espies my sweet lady in the fountain of our love? iii 2 71
Most dearly welcome to the Greeks, sweet lady iv 5 18
May I, sweet lady, beg a kiss of you?—You may iv 5 47
Fare you well, then. Come, good sweet lady *Coriolanus* i 3 119
And live you yet? O my sweet lady, pardon ii 1 197
Alas, sweet lady, what imports this song? *Hamlet* iv 5 27
Good night, ladies; good night, sweet ladies; good night, good night iv 5 73
Who is thy lord?—He that is yours, sweet lady *Othello* iv 2 101
I'll leave you, my sweet lady, for a while *Pericles* iv 1 48
Sweet lamb. No sheep, sweet lamb, unless we feed on your lips *L. L. L.* ii 1 220
Sweet lass. Lay my arms before the legs of this sweet lass of France v 2 558
Sweet leaves. I'll drop the paper: Sweet leaves, shade folly iv 3 44
Ere he can spread his sweet leaves to the air *Rom. and Jul.* i 1 158
Sweet life. Sweet love! sweet lines! sweet life! *T. G. of Ver.* i 3 45
Sweet friend: Thy love ne'er alter till thy sweet life end! *M. N. Dream* ii 2 61
Kneeling before this ruin of sweet life *K. John* iv 3 65
I loved him, and will weep My date of life out for his sweet life's loss iv 3 106
How long fairly shall her sweet life last? *Richard. III.* iv 4 352
Sweet lines. Sweet love! sweet lines! sweet life! *T. G. of Ver.* i 3 45
Sweet look. I did never, no, nor never can, Deserve a sweet look *M. N. D.* ii 2 127
Sweet lord, you play me false *Tempest* v 1 172
Marry, that did I.—Sweet lord, and why? *L. L. Lost* i 1 127
Sweet lords, sweet lovers, O, let us embrace! iv 3 214
Sweet Lord Longaville, rein thy tongue v 2 662
O my sweet lord, that you will stay behind us! *All's Well* ii 1 24
I'll none of you.—Why, my sweet lord?—You'll kiss me hard *W. Tale* ii 1 4
Sweet lord, what is't that takes from thee Thy stomach, pleasure, and thy golden sleep? 1 *Hen. IV.* ii 3 43
Away, away! Once more, sweet lords, farewell 3 *Hen. VI.* ii 3 48
Farewell, sweet lords: let's meet at Coventry iv 8 32
By my troth, sweet lord, thou hast a fine forehead *Troi. and Cres.* iii 1 117
Sweet lord, who's a-field to-day? iii 1 142
Shall I, sweet lord, be bound to you so much? iv 5 284
Sweet Lord Menelaus.—Sweet draught: 'sweet' quoth 'a! v 1 81
Sweet lords, entreat her hear me but a word *T. Andron.* ii 3 138
What ho! Horatio!—Here, sweet lord, at your service *Hamlet* iii 2 58
A courtier; which could say 'Good morrow, sweet lord!' v 1 91
Sweet lord, if your lordship were at leisure, I should impart a thing v 2 91
Farewell, sweet lord, and sister *Lear* iii 7 21
Sweet lord, You know the goodness I intend upon you v 1 6
Sweet lout. Hang nothing but a calf's-skin, most sweet lout *K. John* iii 1 220
Sweet love! sweet lines! sweet life! Here is her hand *T. G. of Ver.* i 3 45
I grant, sweet love, that I did love a lady; But she is dead iv 2 105
As good to wink, sweet love, as look on night *Com. of Errors* iii 2 58
To hold the plough for her sweet love three years *L. L. Lost* v 2 893
What change is this? Sweet love,— Thy love! out, tawny Tartar! *M. N. Dream* iii 2 263
Wilt thou hear some music, my sweet love? iv 1 30
Say, sweet love, what thou desirest to eat iv 1 33
Sweet love, I see, changing his property, Turns to the sourest and most deadly hate *Richard II.* iii 2 135
Sweet love is food for fortune's tooth *Troi. and Cres.* iv 5 293
My words would bandy her to my sweet love, And his to me *R. and J.* ii 5 14
To live an unstain'd wife to my sweet love iv 1 88
I' faith, sweet love, I was coming to your house *Othello* iii 4 171
Sweet lovers. Sweet lords, sweet lovers, O, let us embrace! *L. L. Lost* iv 3 214
Hey ding a ding, ding: Sweet lovers love the spring *A. Y. Like It* v 3 22
Sweet lullaby. With melody Sing in our sweet lullaby *M. N. Dream* ii 2 14
Sweet madam. All hail, sweet madam, and fair time of day! *L. L. Lost* v 2 339
Teach us, sweet madam, for our rude transgression Some fair excuse v 2 431
My little body is aweary of this great world.—You would be, sweet madam, if your miseries were in the same abundance as your good fortunes are *Mer. of Venice* i 2 3
Sweet madam, give me hearing in a cause 1 *Hen. VI.* v 3 106
Farewell, sweet madam: but hark you, Margaret v 3 175
My ladies both, good day to you.—Sweet madam *Coriolanus* i 3 52
Sweet maid, we marry A gentler scion to the wildest stock *W. Tale* iv 4 92
I thought thy bride-bed to have deck'd, sweet maid *Hamlet* v 1 268
Sweet majesty, vouchsafe me,— Was not that Hector? *L. L. Lost* v 2 888
So your sweet majesty, Looking awry upon your lord's departure *Rich. II.* ii 2 20
With cheerful semblance and sweet majesty *Hen. V.* iv Prol. 40
Sweet manner. The pretty and sweet manner of it forced Those waters from me which I would have stopp'd iv 6 28
Sweet Maria. O sweet Maria, empress of my love! *L. L. Lost* iv 3 56
Sweet-marjoram. She was the sweet-marjoram of the salad *All's Well* iv 5 17
Give the word.—Sweet marjoram.—Pass *Lear* iv 6 94
Sweet marriage. 'Twas a sweet marriage, and we prosper well *Tempest* ii 1 72
Sweet masters, be patient: for your father's remembrance *As Y. Like It* i 1 66
O my gentle master! O my sweet master! ii 3 2
Farewell, sweet masters both; I must be gone *T. of Shrew* iii 1 85
Sweet May. She came adorned hither like sweet May *Richard II.* v 1 79
Sweet melody. My tongue should catch your tongue's sweet melody *M. N. Dream* i 1 189
Sweet men, come to him *Hen. V.* ii 1 125
Sweet mercy is nobility's true badge *T. Andron.* i 1 119
Sweet mermaid. O, train me not, sweet mermaid, with thy note *Com. of Errors* iii 2 45
Sweet milk. Adversity's sweet milk, philosophy *Rom. and Jul.* iii 3 55
Had I power, I should Pour the sweet milk of concord into hell *Macbeth* iv 3 98
Sweet misprision. Why, then incision Would let her out in saucers: sweet misprision! *L. L. Lost* iv 3 98
Sweet mistress. My sweet mistress Weeps when she sees me work *Temp.* iii 1 11
I give thee this For thy sweet mistress' sake *T. G. of Ver.* iv 4 182
Sweet mistress,—what your name is else, I know not *Com. of Errors* iii 2 29
Sweet Mistress Margaret, deserve well at my hands by helping me *M. Ado* v 2 1
Sweet Desdemona! O sweet mistress, speak! *Othello* v 2 121
Sweet Monsieur Parolles!—Noble heroes *All's Well* ii 1 39
Sweet Montague, be true. Stay but a little, I will come again *R. and J.* ii 2 137
Sweet Moon, I thank thee for thy sunny beams *M. N. Dream* v 1 277
Sweet Moor. Ah, my sweet Moor, sweeter to me than life! *T. Andron.* ii 3 51
Sweet mouth. She hath a sweet mouth.—That makes amends for her sour breath *T. G. of Ver.* iii 1 330
Sweet music. Hark!—Marvellous sweet music! *Tempest* iii 3 19
He makes sweet music with the enamell'd stones *T. G. of Ver.* ii 7 28
I am never merry when I hear sweet music *Mer. of Venice* v 1 69
How sour sweet music is, When time is broke! *Richard II.* v 5 42
Thou sing'st sweet music *Richard III.* iv 2 79
In sweet music is such art, Killing care and grief of heart *Hen. VIII.* iii 1 12
Stop my mouth.—And shall, albeit sweet music issues thence *T. and C.* iii 2 142
I am beholding to you For your sweet music this last night *Pericles* ii 5 26
Sweet musk-roses. With sweet musk-roses and with eglantine *M. N. D.* ii 1 252
Sweet Mutius. There lie thy bones, Sweet Mutius, with thy friends *T. Andron.* i 1 387
Sweet my child, let them be men of good repute *L. L. Lost* i 2 71
Sweet my coz. I pray thee, Rosalind, sweet my coz, be merry *As Y. L. It* i 2 1
Sweet my lord. Ay, sweet my lord; and so I take my leave *L. L. Lost* v 2 882
Then, sweet my lord, I'll call mine uncle down *Troi. and Cres.* iv 2 2
Sweet my mother, cast me not away! *Rom. and Jul.* iii 5 200
Sweet Nan. Therefore no more turn me to him, sweet Nan *Mer. Wives* iii 4 99
Once to-night Give my sweet Nan this ring iii 4 104
'Twixt twelve and one, Must my sweet Nan present the Fairy Queen iv 6 20
Sweet Ned,—to sweeten which name of Ned, I give thee this pennyworth of sugar 1 *Hen. IV.* ii 4 23
O Ned, sweet Ned! speak to thy mother, boy! 3 *Hen. VI.* v 5 51
Sweet Nell. O Nell, sweet Nell, if thou dost love thy lord 2 *Hen. VI.* i 2 17
Sweet Nell, ill can thy noble mind abrook The abject people gazing ii 4 10
Sweet news. Thou shamest the music of sweet news By playing it to me with so sour a face *Rom. and Jul.* ii 5 23
Sweet niece. Good niece, do, sweet niece Cressida *Troi. and Cres.* i 2 194
Sit down, sweet niece: brother, sit down by me *T. Andron.* iv 1 65
Sweet notice. At the least of thy sweet notice *L. L. Lost* i 1 278
Sweet nurse,—O Lord, why look'st thou sad? *Rom. and Jul.* ii 5 21
Sweet, sweet, sweet nurse, tell me, what says my love? ii 5 55
Sweet Octavia, You shall hear from me still *Ant. and Cleo.* iii 2 59
Sweet Oliver. O sweet Oliver, O brave Oliver *As Y. Like It* iii 3 101
Sweet one. Pardon me, sweet one, even for the vows We made each other but so late ago *T. Night* v 1 221
Sweet Ophelia. Dear maid, kind sister, sweet Ophelia! *Hamlet* iv 5 158
Sweet ornament that decks a thing divine! *T. G. of Ver.* ii 1 4
Those sweet ornaments, Whose circling shadows kings have sought to sleep in, And might not gain so great a happiness *T. Andron.* ii 4 18
Sweet Othello. I am glad to see you mad.—Why, sweet Othello *Othello* iv 1 250
Sweet of the night. Now comes in the sweet o' the night 2 *Hen. IV.* v 3 53
Sweet of the year. Then comes in the sweet o' the year *W. Tale* iv 3 3
Sweet ounce. My sweet ounce of man's flesh! *L. L. Lost* iii 1 136
Sweet Oxford, and my loving Montague 3 *Hen. VI.* iv 8 30
Thanks, gentle Somerset; sweet Oxford, thanks v 4 58
Sweet Pandarus,— Pray you, speak no more to me *Troi. and Cres.* i 1 89
Sweet pangs. If ever thou shalt love, In the sweet pangs of it remember me *T. Night* ii 4 16
Sweet partner, I must not yet forsake you *Hen. VIII.* i 4 103
Sweet passage. And give sweet passage to my sinful soul! 3 *Hen. VI.* ii 3 41
Sweet Patroclus. Go call Thersites hither, sweet Patroclus *Troi. and Cres.* iii 3 234
Sweet Patroclus, I am thwarted quite From my great purpose v 1 42
Sweet Paulina, Make me to think so twenty years together! *W. Tale* v 3 70
Sweet peace. Each several chamber bless, Through this palace, with sweet peace *M. N. Dream* v 1 425
Sweet peace conduct his sweet soul to the bosom Of good old Abraham! *Richard II.* iv 1 103
Sweet perfections. And fill'd Her sweet perfections with one self king *T. Night* i 1 39
Sweet Phebe, do not scorn me; do not, Phebe *As Y. Like It* iii 5 1
Sweet Phebe,— Ha, what say'st thou, Silvius?—Sweet Phebe, pity me iii 5 84
Sweet philosophy. To suck the sweets of sweet philosophy *T. of Shrew* i 1 28
Sweet Pistol. We'll ride all night. O sweet Pistol! Away! 2 *Hen. IV.* v 3 138
Sweet playfellow: pray thou for us *M. N. Dream* i 1 220
Sweet pleasure. At your sweet pleasure *L. L. Lost* v 1 90
It is the king's most sweet pleasure and affection v 1 92
I dedicate myself to your sweet pleasure *Cymbeline* i 6 136
Sweet poetry. Read to thee Sweet poetry and Tully's Orator *T. Andron.* iv 1 14
Sweet poison. Sweet, sweet, sweet poison for the age's tooth *K. John* i 1 213
Sweet Portia. I bid my very friends and countrymen, Sweet Portia, welcome.—So do I *Mer. of Venice* iii 2 227
Sweet Portia, Here are a few of the unpleasant'st words iii 2 253
Sweet Portia, If you did know to whom I gave the ring v 1 192

Sweet power. Their savage eyes turn'd to a modest gaze By the sweet power of music . . . . *Mer. of Venice* v 1 79
Amen to that, sweet powers! . . . . *Othello* ii 1 197
Sweet practiser, thy physic I will try . . . . *All's Well* ii 1 188
Sweet prince. Justice, sweet prince, against that woman! *Com. of Errors* v 1 197
Sweet prince, you learn me noble thankfulness . . . *Much Ado* iv 1 31
Sweet prince, why speak not you?—What should I speak? . . . iv 1 64
Sweet prince, let me go no farther to mine answer . . . v 1 236
Sweet prince, speak low; The king your father is disposed to sleep 2 *Hen. IV.* iv 5 16
Sweet princes, what I did, I did in honour . . . . v 2 35
Sweet prince, An if your grace mark every circumstance, You have great reason to do Richard right . . . . . 1 *Hen. VI.* iii 1 152
I dare presume, sweet prince, he thought no harm . . . . iv 1 179
That cropp'd the golden prime of this sweet prince . *Richard III.* i 2 248
Welcome, sweet prince, to London, to your chamber . . . iii 1 1
Sweet prince, the untainted virtue of your years . . . iii 1 7
Good night, sweet prince; And flights of angels sing thee to thy rest! *Hamlet* v 2 370
Sweet Proteus, no; now let us take our leave . . *T. G. of Ver.* i 1 56
Sweet Proteus, my direction-giver, Let us into the city presently . iii 2 90
Sweet Puck. Those that Hobgoblin call you and sweet Puck *M. N. D.* ii 1 40
Sweet Pyramus. And left sweet Pyramus translated there . . iii 2 32
Sweet queen. Weep not, sweet queen; for trickling tears are vain 1 *Hen. IV.* ii 4 431
You speak your fair pleasure, sweet queen . . *Troi. and Cres.* iii 1 51
Well, sweet queen, you are pleasant with me . . . . iii 1 67
Sweet queen, sweet queen! that's a sweet queen, i' faith . . iii 1 77
What says my sweet queen, my very very sweet queen? . . . iii 1 87
My niece is horribly in love with a thing you have, sweet queen . iii 1 107
How now, sweet queen!—One woe doth tread upon another's heel *Ham.* iv 7 163
Most sweet queen,— Nay, pray you, seek no colour for your going *A. and C.* i 3 31
One word, sweet queen: Of Cæsar seek your honour, with your safety . iv 15 45
O your sweet queen! That the strict fates had pleased you had brought her hither, To have bless'd mine eyes with her! . *Pericles* iii 3 7
Sweet recreation barr'd, what doth ensue? . . . *Com. of Errors* v 1 78
Sweet rehearsal. With sweet rehearsal of my morning's dream 2 *Hen. VI.* i 2 24
Sweet religion makes A rhapsody of words . . . *Hamlet* iii 4 47
Sweet remembrancer! Now, good digestion wait on appetite! *Macbeth* iii 4 37
Sweet repose. As sweet repose and rest Come to thy heart as that within my breast! . . . . *Rom. and Jul.* ii 2 123
Sweet retire. That their souls May make a peaceful and a sweet retire From off these fields . . . . . . *Hen. V.* iv 3 86
Sweet Revenge. O sweet Revenge, now do I come to thee *T. Andron.* v 2 67
I know thou dost; and, sweet Revenge, farewell . . . v 2 148
Then murder's out of tune, And sweet revenge grows harsh . *Othello* v 2 116
Sweet reversion. Where now remains a sweet reversion . 1 *Hen. IV.* iv 1 53
Sweet Richard. Save bidding farewell to so sweet a guest As my sweet Richard . . . . *Richard II.* ii 2 9
Sweet robe. Is not a buff jerkin a most sweet robe of durance? 1 *Hen. IV.* i 2 49
Sweet Robin. For bonny sweet Robin is all my joy . *Hamlet* iv 5 187
Sweet Rosalind. Two o'clock is your hour?—Ay, sweet Rosalind *As Y. Like It* iv 1 191
Sweet rose. Blow like sweet roses in this summer air . *L. L. Lost* v 2 293
Therefore, my sweet Rose, my dear Rose, be merry . *As Y. Like It* i 2 24
Sweet royalty, bestow on me the sense of hearing . *L. L. Lost* v 2 669
Sweet Rutland. These tears are my sweet Rutland's obsequies 3 *Hen. VI.* i 4 147
Sweet sacrifice. Make of your prayers one sweet sacrifice *Hen. VIII.* ii 1 77
Sweet safety. To seek sweet safety out In vaults and prisons *K. John* v 2 142
Sweet saint, for charity, be not so curst . . *Richard III.* i 2 49
Sweet sake. And run through fire I will for thy sweet sake *M. N. Dream* ii 2 103
Sweet savour. I hear, I speak; I smell sweet savours . *T. of Shrew* Ind. 2 73
Sweet-savoured. That never meat sweet-savour'd in thy taste, Unless I spake . . . . *Com. of Errors* ii 2 119
Sweet scrolls to fly about the streets of Rome! . . *T. Andron.* iv 4 16
Sweet self. The curate and your sweet self are good at such eruptions *L. L. Lost* v 1 120
You should be as your mother was When your sweet self was got *All's W.* iv 2 10
Happily may your sweet self put on The lineal state! . *K. John* v 7 101
Sweet sewer. 'Sweet' quoth 'a! sweet sink, sweet sewer *Troi. and Cres.* v 1 83
Sweet shade. Under the sweet shade of your government *Hen. V.* ii 2 28
Under their sweet shade, Aaron, let us sit . . *T. Andron.* ii 3 16
Sweet shortness. A second night of such sweet shortness . *Cymbeline* ii 4 44
Sweet sight. See'st thou this sweet sight? . . *M. N. Dream* iv 1 51
Sweet sink. 'Sweet' quoth 'a! sweet sink, sweet sewer . *Troi. and Cres.* v 1 82
Sweet sir. O this blessed hour!—O sweet Sir John! . *Mer. Wives* iii 3 49
Are you sure of your husband now?—He's a-birding, sweet Sir John . iv 2 8
Sweet Sir Andrew!—Bless you, fair shrew . . . *T. Night* i 3 49
Sweet Sir Toby, be patient for to-night . . . . . ii 3 142
By a horseman, or a footman?—A footman, sweet sir . *W. Tale* iv 3 68
How do you now?—Sweet sir, much better than I was . . . iv 3 119
'At your service, sir:' 'No, sir,' says question, 'I, sweet sir, at yours' *K. John* i 1 199
What's the news?—O, my sweet sir, news fitting to the night . v 6 19
Sweet sir, sit; I'll be with you anon; most sweet sir, sit . 2 *Hen. IV.* v 3 28
I'll keep you company.—Sweet sir, you honour me. . *Troi. and Cres.* v 1 93
Sweet sister, let me live . . . . . *Meas. for Meas.* iii 1 133
Meantime, sweet sister, We will not part from hence . . *T. Night* v 1 393
Sweet sleep. Foes to my rest and my sweet sleep's disturbers *Rich. III.* iv 2 74
Nor all the drowsy syrups of the world, Shall ever medicine thee to that sweet sleep Which thou owedst yesterday . . . . *Othello* iii 3 332
Sweet smell. With whose sweet smell the air shall be perfumed 2 *Hen. VI.* iii 1 255
Sweet smoke of rhetoric! He reputes me a cannon . . *L. L. Lost* iii 1 64
Sweet society. They are a sweet society of fair ones . . *Hen. VIII.* i 4 14
Sweet soil. England's ground, farewell; sweet soil, adieu *Richard II.* i 3 306
Sweet Somerset. No more, good York; sweet Somerset, be still 2 *Hen. VI.* iii 1 304
Sweet son. Pardon, sweet father.—Lives my sweet son? *T. of Shrew* v 1 115
Pardon me, Margaret; pardon me, sweet son . . 3 *Hen. VI.* i 1 228
When holy Harry died, and my sweet son . . *Richard III.* iv 4 25
My damned son, which thy two sweet sons smother'd . . . iv 4 134
Come, come, we'll prompt you.—I prithee now, sweet son *Coriolanus* iii 2 107
So should I rob my sweet sons of their fee . . *T. Andron.* ii 3 179
Sweet sorrow. Parting is such sweet sorrow, That I shall say good night till it be morrow . . . . *Rom. and Jul.* ii 2 185
Sweet soul. By my sweet soul, I mean setting thee at liberty *L. L. Lost* iii 1 124
Sweet soul, let's in, and there expect their coming *Mer. of Venice* v 1 49
Sweet peace conduct his sweet soul to the bosom Of good old Abraham! *Richard II.* iv 1 103
My soul shall thine keep company to heaven; Tarry, sweet soul, for mine . . . . *Hen. V.* iv 6 17
Sweet soul, take heed, Take heed of perjury . . . . . *Othello* v 2 50
Sweet sound. Nor is not moved with concord of sweet sounds *M. of Ven.* v 1 84
Like the sweet sound, That breathes upon a bank of violets . *T. Night* i 1 5
Silver hath a sweet sound . . . . *Rom. and Jul.* iv 5 134
Sweet sovereign, Leave us to ourselves . . . . *Cymbeline* i 1 154
Sweet sprites, the burthen bear . . . . *Tempest* i 2 381
Sweet stem from York's great stock . . . . . 1 *Hen. VI.* ii 5 41
Sweet Suffolk. Enough, sweet Suffolk; thou torment'st thyself 2 *Hen. VI.* iii 2 329
To France, sweet Suffolk: let me hear from thee . . . iii 2 405
Sweet-suggesting Love, if thou hast sinn'd . . *T. G. of Ver.* ii 6 7
Sweet summer. An odorous chaplet of sweet summer buds *M. N. Dream* ii 1 110
Sweet sway. If your sweet sway Allow obedience . . . . *Lear* ii 4 193
Sweet tale. That melted at the sweet tale of the sun's . 1 *Hen. IV.* ii 4 135
Sweet thoughts. These sweet thoughts do even refresh my labours *Temp.* iii 1 14
Sweet tidings. Did ever raven sing so like a lark, That gives sweet tidings of the sun's uprise? . . . . . . *T. Andron.* iii 1 159
Sweet Timandra. Pardon him, sweet Timandra; for his wits Are drown'd and lost . . . . *T. of Athens* iv 3 88
Sweet tongue. A blister on his sweet tongue, with my heart! *L. L. Lost* v 2 335
Had he heard the heavenly harmony Which that sweet tongue hath made . . . . *T. Andron.* ii 4 49
Sweet touch. A sweet touch, a quick venue of wit! . . *L. L. Lost* v 1 62
Sweet Troilus. No soul so near me As the sweet Troilus *Troi. and Cres.* iv 2 105
Sweet Tully. A Roman sworder and banditto slave Murder'd sweet Tully 2 *Hen. VI.* iv 1 136
Sweet uncle. Tell me, sweet uncle, what's the matter? *Troi. and Cres.* iv 2 84
Sweet uncleanness. To redeem him, Give up your body to such sweet uncleanness As she that he hath stain'd . . . *Meas. for Meas.* ii 4 54
Sweet understanding. A female; or, for thy more sweet understanding, a woman . . . . *L. L. Lost* i 1 267
Sweet use. But, O strange men! That can such sweet use make of what they hate . . . . *All's Well* iv 4 22
Sweet Valentine, adieu! Think on thy Proteus . *T. G. of Ver.* i 1 11
Sweet verbal. She told me, In a sweet verbal brief . . *All's Well* v 3 137
Sweet view. A pudency so rosy the sweet view on't Might well have warm'd old Saturn . . . . *Cymbeline* ii 5 11
Sweet villain! Most dear'st! my collop! . . . . *W. Tale* i 2 136
Sweet virgin. Employ thee then, sweet virgin, for our good 1 *Hen. VI.* iii 3 16
Sweet virtue. A sweet virtue in a maid with clean hands *T. G. of Ver.* iii 1 277
Sweet voice. He is a very paramour for a sweet voice . *M. N. Dream* iv 2 12
Most sweet voices! Better it is to die . . . . *Coriolanus* ii 3 119
I thank you for your voices: thank you: Your most sweet voices . ii 3 180
Sweet wag. I prithee, sweet wag, when thou art king? . 1 *Hen. IV.* i 2 17; 26
Sweet wag, shall there be gallows standing in England when thou art king? . . . . i 2 66
Sweet war-man. The sweet war-man is dead and rotten . *L. L. Lost* v 2 666
Sweet Warwick. Assist me, then, sweet Warwick . . . 3 *Hen. VI.* i 1 28
Even as thou wilt, sweet Warwick, let it be . . . . . ii 6 99
Sweet water. Call for sweet water, wash thy hands . *T. Andron.* ii 4 6
Which with sweet water nightly I will dew . . . *Rom. and Jul.* v 3 14
Sweet way. Beshrew thee, cousin, which didst lead me forth Of that sweet way I was in to despair! . . . . . . *Richard II.* iii 2 205
Sweet welkin, I must sigh in thy face . . . . *L. L. Lost* iii 1 68
Sweet wench. Fear not, sweet wench, they shall not touch thee *T. of S.* iii 2 240
Is not my hostess of the tavern a most sweet wench? . . 1 *Hen. IV.* i 2 45
Bear thou my hand, sweet wench, between thy teeth . *T. Andron.* iii 1 283
Sweet widow, by my state I swear to thee I speak no more than what my soul intends . . . . 3 *Hen. VI.* iii 2 93
Sweet wife. Alas, sweet wife, my honour is at pawn . 2 *Hen. IV.* ii 3 7
Come, my sweet wife, my dearest mother, and My friends *Coriolanus* iv 1 48
Sweet wind. When the sweet wind did gently kiss the trees *M. of Ven.* v 1 2
Sweet wit. I thank your pretty sweet wit for it . . 2 *Hen. VI.* i 2 231
Sweet woman. The sweet woman leads an ill life with him *Mer. Wives* ii 2 92
A fine woman! a fair woman! a sweet woman! . . . *Othello* iv 1 189
Sweet wood. Burn sweet wood to make the lodging sweet *T. of Shrew* Ind. 1 49
Sweet word. White-handed mistress, one sweet word with thee *L. L. Lost* v 2 230
Sweet words, Low-crooked court'sies, and base spaniel-fawning *J. Cæsar* iii 1 42
'Tis strange he [death] hides him in fresh cups, soft beds, Sweet words *Cymbeline* v 3 72
Sweet work. The most replenished sweet work of nature *Richard III.* iv 3 18
Sweet world. Bitter shame hath spoil'd the sweet world's taste *K. John* iii 4 110
Sweet York, sweet husband, be not of that mind *Richard II.* v 2 107
Sweet York, be patient. Hear me, gentle liege . . . . v 3 91
I long to hear it at full.—Sweet York, begin . . 2 *Hen. VI.* ii 2 7
Sweet youth. Forswear not thyself, sweet youth . *T. G. of Ver.* ii 5 3
That's as much as to say, the sweet youth's in love . *Much Ado* iii 2 52
Anon comes Pyramus, sweet youth and tall . . . *M. N. Dream.* v 1 145
Sweet youth, I pray you, chide a year together . *As Y. Like It* iii 5 64
Sweeten. There's not a grain of it the face to sweeten Of the whole dungy earth . . . . *W. Tale* ii 1 156
To sweeten which name of Ned, I give thee this pennyworth of sugar 1 *Hen. IV.* ii 4 24
Sweeten the bitter mock you sent his majesty . . *Hen. V.* ii 4 122
I cannot sing, Nor heel the high lavolt, nor sweeten talk *Troi. and Cres.* iv 4 88
Then sweeten with thy breath This neighbour air . *Rom. and Jul.* ii 6 26
All the perfumes of Arabia will not sweeten this little hand *Macbeth* v 1 57
Give me an ounce of civet, good apothecary, to sweeten my imagination *Lear* iv 6 133
With fairest flowers Whilst summer lasts and I live here, Fidele, I'll sweeten thy sad grave . . . . *Cymbeline* iv 2 220
Sweetened with the hope to have The present benefit . *Richard II.* ii 3 13
Sweeter. Aiming at Silvia as a sweeter friend . . *T. G. of Ver.* ii 6 30
Either death or life Shall thereby be the sweeter . *Meas. for Meas.* iii 1 6
Sweet clown, sweeter fool, sweetest lady! . . . *L. L. Lost* iv 3 17
It sounds much sweeter than by day . . . . *Mer. of Venice* v 1 100
We'll have thee to a couch Softer and sweeter . . *T. of Shrew* Ind. 2 40
She is sweeter than perfume itself To whom they go to . . . . i 2 153
As brown in hue As hazel nuts and sweeter than the kernels . . . ii 1 257
Violets dim, But sweeter than the lids of Juno's eyes . *W. Tale* iv 4 121
Gives not the hawthorn-bush a sweeter shade? . . 3 *Hen. VI.* ii 5 42
A sweeter and a lovelier gentleman . . . . *Richard III.* i 2 243
Ah, my sweet Moor, sweeter to me than life! . . *T. Andron.* ii 3 51
Our Romeo hath not been in bed to-night.—That last is true; the sweeter rest was mine . . . . *Rom. and Jul.* ii 3 43
To make society The sweeter welcome, we will keep ourself Till supper-time alone: while then, God be with you! . . . . *Macbeth* iii 1 43
O, the world hath not a sweeter creature . . . . *Othello* iv 1 194
Haply this life is best, If quiet life be best; sweeter to you That have a sharper known . . . . *Cymbeline* iii 3 30
Sweetest. As in the sweetest bud The eating canker dwells *T. G. of Ver.* i 1 42
In mine eye she is the sweetest lady that ever I looked on . *Much Ado* i 1 189

Sweetest. Sweet clown, sweeter fool, sweetest lady! . . . *L. L. Lost* iv 3 17
As a surfeit of the sweetest things The deepest loathing to the stomach brings, . . . So thou, my surfeit *M. N. Dream* ii 2 137
With sweetest touches pierce your mistress' ear . *Mer. of Venice* v 1 67
Sweetest nut hath sourest rind, Such a nut is Rosalind . *As Y. Like It* iii 2 115
He that sweetest rose will find Must find love's prick and Rosalind . iii 2 117
The queen, the queen, The sweet'st, dear'st creature's dead *W. Tale* iii 2 202
The sweet'st companion that e'er man Bred his hopes out of . . v 1 11
As the last taste of sweets, is sweetest last . *Richard II.* ii 1 13
Now comes in the sweetest morsel of the night . 2 *Hen. IV.* ii 4 396
And lull'd with sound of sweetest melody . . . iii 1 14
Their sweetest shade a grove of cypress trees! . . 2 *Hen. VI.* iii 2 323
The sweetest sleep, and fairest-boding dreams . *Richard III.* v 3 227
Thou hast the sweetest face I ever look'd on . *Hen. VIII.* iv 1 43
My mistress is the sweetest lady—Lord, Lord! . . *Rom. and Jul.* ii 4 211
The sweetest honey Is loathsome in his own deliciousness . . ii 6 11
Death lies on her like an untimely frost Upon the sweetest flower of all the field iv 5 29
Thou hast kill'd the sweetest innocent That e'er did lift up eye *Othello* v 2 199
Touch you the sourest points with sweetest terms . *Ant. and Cleo.* ii 2 24
Sweetest, fairest, As I my poor self did exchange for you . *Cymbeline* i 1 118
O sweetest, fairest lily! . . . . iv 2 201
And I must lose Two of the sweet'st companions in the world . v 5 349
Who though they feed On sweetest flowers, yet they poison breed *Pericles* i 1 133
The fairest, sweet'st, and best lies here, Who wither'd in her spring of year . . . . iv 4 34
Sweeting. What, sweeting, all amort? . . . *T. of Shrew* iv 3 36
Trip no further, pretty sweeting; Journeys end in lovers meeting *T. N.* ii 3 43
Ay, marry, sweeting, if we could do that . . 1 *Hen. VI.* iii 3 21
Thy wit is a very bitter sweeting; it is a most sharp sauce *Rom. and Jul.* ii 4 83
What's the matter?—All's well now, sweeting; come away to bed *Othello* ii 3 252
Sweetly. The air breathes upon us here most sweetly . *Tempest* ii 1 46
Smelling so sweetly, all musk, and so rushling . *Mer. Wives* ii 2 67
Take, O, take those lips away, That so sweetly were forsworn *M. for M.* iv 1 2
How sweetly you do minister to love! . . . *Much Ado* i 1 314
Look sweetly and say nothing, I am yours for the walk . . ii 1 91
The idea of her life shall sweetly creep Into his study of imagination iv 1 226
When tongues speak sweetly, then they name her name . *L. L. Lost* iii 1 167
And how most sweetly a' will swear! . . . . iv 1 148
The epithets are sweetly varied, like a scholar at the least . iv 2 9
The crow doth sing as sweetly as the lark When neither is attended *Mer. of Venice* v 1 102
I do not shame To tell you what I was, since my conversion So sweetly tastes, being the thing I am . . . *As Y. Like It* iv 3 138
I'll tell her plain She sings as sweetly as a nightingale . *T. of Shrew* ii 1 172
But riddle-like lives sweetly where she dies . . *All's Well* i 3 223
Speak sweetly, man, although thy looks be sour . *Richard II.* iii 2 193
The even mead, that erst brought sweetly forth The freckled cowslip *Hen. V.* v 2 48
Words sweetly placed and modestly directed . . 1 *Hen. VI.* v 3 179
All which secure and sweetly he enjoys . . . 3 *Hen. VI.* ii 5 50
The root From whence that tender spray did sweetly spring . . ii 6 50
Sweetly in force unto her fair life's end . . . *Richard III.* iv 4 351
And sweetly In all the rest show'd a most noble patience *Hen. VIII.* ii 1 35
Sin from my lips? O trespass sweetly urged! . . *Rom. and Jul.* i 5 111
He and myself Have travail'd in the great shower of your gifts, And sweetly felt it . . . . *T. of Athens* v 1 74
Is there no voice more worthy than my own, To sound more sweetly? *J. Cæsar* iii 1 50
The air Nimbly and sweetly recommends itself . . *Macbeth* i 6 2
It smells most sweetly in my sense.—A delicate odour . *Pericles* iii 2 60
Sweetmeats. Nosegays, sweetmeats, messengers Of strong prevailment in unharden'd youth . . . . . . *M. N. Dream* i 1 34
Their breaths with sweetmeats tainted are . . *Rom. and Jul.* i 4 76
Sweetness. To remit Their saucy sweetness that do coin heaven's image In stamps that are forbid . . . . *Meas. for Meas.* ii 4 45
And began To loathe the taste of sweetness . . 1 *Hen. IV.* iii 2 72
O, how hast thou with jealousy infected The sweetness of affiance! *Hen. V.* ii 2 127
Too subtle-potent, tuned too sharp in sweetness . *Troi. and Cres.* iii 2 25
O, our lives' sweetness! That we the pain of death would hourly die Rather than die at once! . . . . . . *Lear* v 3 184
O'erbear the shores of my mortality, And drown me with their sweetness . . . . *Pericles* v 1 196
Swell. Their understanding Begins to swell . . . *Tempest* v 1 80
For the water swells a man . . . . . *Mer. Wives* iii 5 16
Do but behold the tears that swell in me . . *L. L. Lost* iv 3 37
On the buds Was wont to swell like round and orient pearls *M. N. Dream* iv 1 59
Where great additions swell's, and virtue none, It is a dropsied honour *All's Well* ii 3 134
'Tis Polixenes Has made thee swell thus . . . *W. Tale* ii 1 62
So high above his limits swells the rage Of Bolingbroke . *Richard II.* iii 2 109
Shadows to the unseen grief That swells with silence in the tortured soul . . . . iv 1 298
Or swell my thoughts to any strain of pride . . 2 *Hen. IV.* iv 5 171
My sea shall suck them dry, And swell so much the higher by their ebb 3 *Hen. VI.* iv 8 56
As, by proof, we see The waters swell before a boisterous storm *Richard III.* ii 3 44
To stubborn spirits They swell, and grow as terrible as storms *Hen. VIII.* iii 1 164
Unless it swell past hiding, and then it's past watching *Troi. and Cres.* i 2 294
Here lurks no treason, here no envy swells . . *T. Andron.* ii 1 153
The ocean swells not so as Aaron storms . . . iv 2 139
And, not to swell our spirit, He shall be executed presently *T. of Athens* iii 5 102
Thy verse swells with stuff so fine and smooth That thou art even natural . . . . v 1 87
I have seen The ambitious ocean swell and rage and foam *J. Cæsar* i 3 7
Why, now, blow wind, swell billow, and swim bark! . . v 1 67
So from that spring whence comfort seem'd to come Discomfort swells *Macbeth* i 2 28
O, how this mother swells up toward my heart! . *Lear* ii 4 56
Blow the earth into the sea, Or swell the curled waters 'bove the main iii 1 6
Othello guard, And swell his sail with thine own powerful breath! *Oth.* ii 1 78
Swell, bosom, with thy fraught, For 'tis of aspics' tongues! . iii 3 449
The silken tackle Swell with the touches of those flower-soft hands *Ant. and Cleo.* ii 2 215
The higher Nilus swells, The more it promises . . . ii 7 23
The swan's down-feather, That stands upon the swell at full of tide . iii 2 49
Swelled. What a thing should I have been when I had been swelled! *Mer. Wives* iii 5 18
'Tis with my mind As with the tide swell'd up unto his height 2 *Hen. IV.* ii 3 63
And Cydnus swell'd above the banks . . . *Cymbeline* ii 4 71

Swelled. Cæsar's ambition, Which swell'd so much that it did almost stretch The sides o' the world . . . . *Cymbeline* iii 1 50
For beauty that made barren the swell'd boast Of him that best could speak . . . . v 5 162
Swell'st thou, proud heart? I'll give thee scope to beat . *Richard II.* iii 3 140
Swelling. Something showing a more swelling port . *Mer. of Venice* i 1 124
And in my heart the strong and swelling evil Of my conception *M. for M.* ii 4 6
Were she as rough As are the swelling Adriatic seas . *T. of Shrew* i 2 74
Did never float upon the swelling tide . . . *K. John* ii 1 74
There shall your swords and lances arbitrate The swelling difference *Richard II.* i 1 201
That pretty Welsh Which thou pour'st down from these swelling heavens I am too perfect in . . . . 1 *Hen. IV.* iii 1 202
Princes to act And monarchs to behold the swelling scene! . *Hen. V.* Prol. 4
Here he comes, swelling like a turkey-cock.—'Tis no matter for his swellings nor his turkey-cocks . . . . v 1 15
Is not quite exempt From envious malice of thy swelling heart 1 *Hen. VI.* iii 1 26
My mildness hath allay'd their swelling griefs . . 3 *Hen. VI.* iv 8 42
Between these swelling wrong-incensed peers . . *Richard III.* ii 1 51
Flowing and swelling o'er with arts and exercise . *Troi. and Cres.* iv 4 80
Ten thousand swelling toads, as many urchins . . *T. Andron.* ii 3 101
That my tongue may utter forth The venomous malice of my swelling heart! . . . . v 3 13
Two truths are told, As happy prologues to the swelling act . *Macbeth* i 3 128
Three lads of Cyprus, noble swelling spirits . . *Othello* ii 3 57
If they had swallow'd poison, 'twould appear By external swelling *Ant. and Cleo.* v 2 349
Swelter'd venom sleeping got, Boil thou first i' the charmed pot *Macbeth* iv 1 8
Sweno, the Norways' king, craves composition . . . . . i 2 59
Swept. The house trimmed, rushes strewed, cobwebs swept *T. of Shrew* iv 1 49
Thus have we swept suspicion from our seat . . 3 *Hen. VI.* v 7 13
Swerve not from the smallest article of it . . *Meas. for Meas.* iv 2 107
Were I the fairest youth That ever made eye swerve . *W. Tale* iv 4 385
Prophet may you be! If I be false, or swerve a hair from truth *T. and C.* iii 2 191
But, alas, I swerve: Many dream not to find, neither deserve *Cymbeline* v 4 129
Swerving. Constant in spirit, not swerving with the blood . *Hen. V.* ii 2 133
I have offended reputation, A most unnoble swerving . *Ant. and Cleo.* iii 11 50
Swift. This swift business I must uneasy make . . *Tempest* i 2 450
Perfected by the swift course of time . . . *T. G. of Ver.* i 3 23
Love, lend me wings to make my purpose swift! . . . ii 6 42
Having affairs to heaven, Intends you for his swift ambassador *Meas. for Meas.* iii 1 58
Convenient is it. Make a swift return . . . . iv 3 107
The swift celerity of his death, Which I did think with slower foot came on . . . . v 1 399
Having so swift and excellent a wit . . . . *Much Ado* iii 1 89
Away!—As swift as lead, sir . . . . . *L. L. Lost* iii 1 58
I say lead is slow.—You are too swift, sir, to say so . . iii 1 62
Courses as swift as thought in every power . . . iv 3 330
Swift as a shadow, short as any dream . . . *M. N. Dream* i 1 144
For night's swift dragons cut the clouds full fast . . . iii 2 379
My eyes, my lord, can look as swift as yours . *Mer. of Venice* iii 2 199
Stood on the extremest verge of the swift brook . *As Y. Like It* ii 1 42
And why not the swift foot of Time? had not that been as proper? . iii 2 324
He is very swift and sententious . . . . . . v 4 65
Thy greyhounds are as swift As breathed stags . . *T. of Shrew* Ind. 2 49
A good swift simile, but something currish . . . . v 2 54
Wishing clocks more swift? Hours, minutes? noon, midnight? *W. Tale* i 2 289
The good mind of Camillo tardied My swift command . . iii 2 164
Impute it not a crime To me or my swift passage . . . iv 1 5
Whose labour'd spirits, Forwearied in this action of swift speed *K. John* ii 1 233
Be swift like lightning in the execution . . *Richard II.* i 3 79
With all swift speed you must away to France . . . v 1 54
Three times did they drink, Upon agreement, of swift Severn's flood 1 *Hen. IV.* i 3 103
Whose swift wrath beat down The never-daunted Percy to the earth 2 *Hen. IV.* i 1 109
With all swift dispatch, To line and new repair our towns . *Hen. V.* ii 4 6
Our swift scene flies In motion of no less celerity Than that of thought iii Prol. 1
And teach lavoltas high and swift corantos . . . . iii 5 33
As swift as stones Enforced from the old Assyrian slings . . iv 7 64
So swift a pace hath thought . . . . v Prol. 15
One would have lingering wars with little cost; Another would fly swift, but wanteth wings . . . . . . 1 *Hen. VI.* i 1 75
Take all the swift advantage of the hours . . . *Richard III.* iv 1 49
True hope is swift, and flies with swallow's wings . . . v 2 23
Are you bound thither?—In all swift haste . . *Troi. and Cres.* i 1 119
His evasion, wing'd thus swift with scorn, Cannot outfly our apprehensions . . . . ii 3 123
Light boats sail swift, though greater hulks draw deep . . ii 3 277
Be thou my Charon, And give me swift transportance . . . iii 2 12
Like a wicked conscience still, That mouldeth goblins swift as frenzy's thoughts . . . . v 10 29
She how swift she comes . . . . . . *T. Andron.* iv 1 3
Now to the Goths, as swift as swallow flies . . . . iv 2 172
Two proper palfreys, black as jet, To hale thy vengeful waggon swift away . . . . v 2 51
Had she affections and warm youthful blood, She would be as swift in motion as a ball . . . . *Rom. and Jul.* ii 5 13
Too swift arrives as tardy as too slow . . . . . ii 6 15
O mischief, thou art swift To enter in the thoughts of desperate men! . v 1 35
It requires swift foot . . . . *T. of Athens* v 1 231
Beauteous and swift, the minions of their race . . *Macbeth* ii 4 15
I wish your horses swift and sure of foot . . . . iii 1 38
The valued file Distinguishes the swift, the slow, the subtle . iii 1 96
That a swift blessing May soon return to this our suffering country . iii 6 47
With wings as swift As meditation or the thoughts of love . *Hamlet* i 5 29
Swift as quicksilver it courses through The natural gates and alleys . i 5 66
Our posts shall be swift and intelligent betwixt us . . *Lear* iii 7 12
He, swift of foot, Outran my purpose . . . . *Othello* ii 3 232
To furnish me with some swift means of death For the fair devil . iii 3 477
Your ships are not well mann'd; Your mariners are muleters, reapers, people Ingross'd by swift impress . . . *Ant. and Cleo.* iii 7 37
This blows my heart: If swift thought break it not, a swifter mean Shall outstrike thought . . . . iv 6 35
Could best express how slow his soul sail'd on, How swift his ship *Cymb.* i 3 14
Swift, swift, you dragons of the night, that dawning May bare the raven's eye! . . . . ii 2 48
Make swift the pangs Of my queen's travails! . . . *Pericles* iii 1 13

Swifter. Fleeter than arrows, bullets, wind, thought, swifter things *L. L. Lost* v 2 261
I do wander every where, Swifter than the moon's sphere *M. N. Dream* ii 1 7
About the wood go swifter than the wind . . . . . iii 2 94
Swifter than arrow from the Tartar's bow . . . . iii 2 101
We the globe can compass soon, Swifter than the wandering moon . iv 1 103
The swifter speed the better *W. Tale* iv 4 683
With swifter spleen than powder can enforce *K. John* ii 1 448
Arrows fled not swifter toward their aim Than did our soldiers *2 Hen. IV.* i 1 123
Come off and on swifter than he that gibbets on the brewer's bucket . iii 2 282
A mind That doth renew swifter than blood decays . *Troi. and Cres.* iii 2 170
That it was which caused Our swifter composition . *Coriolanus* iii 1 3
Swifter than his tongue, His agile arm beats down their fatal points *Rom. and Jul.* iii 1 170
This blows my heart: If swift thought break it not, a swifter mean Shall outstrike thought . . *Ant. and Cleo.* iv 6 35
Swiftest. If thou linger in my territories Longer than swiftest expedition Will give thee time to leave . . *T. G. of Ver.* iii 1 164
Ay, madam, with the swiftest wing of speed . . *All's Well* iii 2 76
Dear boy, mount on my swiftest horse . . *1 Hen. VI.* iv 5 9
That swiftest wing of recompense is slow To overtake thee *Macbeth* i 4 17
The swiftest harts have posted you by land . *Cymbeline* iii 4 27
Swiftly. You That are of suppler joints, follow them swiftly . *Tempest* iii 3 107
Your praise is come too swiftly home before you . *As Y. Like It* ii 3 9
Softly and swiftly, sir; for the priest is ready . *T. of Shrew* v 1 1
Mark my counsel, Which must be even as swiftly follow'd . *W. Tale* i 2 409
How swiftly will this Feeble the woman's tailor run off! *2 Hen. IV.* iii 2 287
Both came swiftly running, Like to a pair of loving turtle-doves *1 Hen. VI.* ii 2 29
Tidings, as swiftly as the posts could run, Were brought me *3 Hen. VI.* ii 1 109
Swiftness. Even with the swiftness of putting on . . *T. Night* ii 5 187
May with reasonable swiftness add More feathers to our wings *Hen. V.* i 2 306
We may outrun, By violent swiftness, that which we run at . *Hen. VIII.* i 1 142
Tiger-footed rage, when it shall find The harm of unscann'd swiftness, will too late Tie leaden pounds to's heels . . *Coriolanus* iii 1 313
Swift-winged with desire to get a grave . . *1 Hen. VI.* ii 5 15
Be brief, That our swift-winged souls may catch the king's *Richard III.* ii 2 44
Swills your warm blood like wash, and makes his trough . . . v 2 9
Swill'd with the wild and wasteful ocean . . *Hen. V.* iii 1 14
Swim. To swim, to dive into the fire, to ride On the curl'd clouds *Tempest* i 2 191
'Tis as impossible that he's undrown'd As he that sleeps here swims . ii 1 238
Swum ashore, man, like a duck: I can swim like a duck . . ii 2 134
Though thou canst swim like a duck, thou art made like a goose . ii 2 136
Be thou here again Ere the leviathan can swim a league . *M. N. Dream* ii 1 174
If he fall in, good night! or sink or swim . . . *1 Hen. IV.* i 3 194
Which swims against your stream of quality . . *2 Hen. IV.* v 2 34
As I have seen a swan With bootless labour swim against the tide *3 Hen. VI.* i 4 20
Say you can swim; alas, 'tis but a while! . . . . v 4 29
I have ventured, Like little wanton boys that swim on bladders *Hen. VIII.* iii 2 359
Shouldst thou take the river Styx, I would swim after . *Troi. and Cres.* v 4 21
He that depends Upon your favours swims with fins of lead . *Coriolanus* i 1 184
Leap in with me into this angry flood, And swim to yonder point *J. Cæsar* i 2 104
Blow wind, swell billow, and swim bark! The storm is up . . v 1 67
'Tis a naughty night to swim in. . . . . . . *Lear* iii 4 116
Swimmer. Leander the good swimmer . . . . *Much Ado* v 2 31
As two spent swimmers, that do cling together And choke their art *Macb.* i 2 8
Swimming. With pretty and with swimming gait . *M. N. Dream* ii 1 130
That eats the swimming frog, the toad, the tadpole, the wall-newt *Lear* iii 4 134
Swine. 'Tis old, but true, Still swine eats all the draff *Mer. Wives* iv 2 109
Fire enough for a flint, pearl enough for a swine . *L. L. Lost* iv 2 91
O monstrous beast! how like a swine he lies! . . *T. of Shrew* Ind. 1 34
To lie like pawns lock'd up in chests and trunks, To hug with swine *K. John* v 2 142
This foul swine Lies now even in the centre of this isle . *Richard III.* v 2 10
What a god's gold, That he is worshipp'd in a baser temple Than where swine feed! . . . . *T. of Athens* v 1 52
Where hast thou been, sister?—Killing swine . . *Macbeth* i 3 2
And wast thou fain, poor father, To hovel thee with swine? . *Lear* iv 7 39
Swine-drunk. He will be swine-drunk . . . *All's Well* iv 3 286
Swine-herds. Three neat-herds, three swine-herds . *W. Tale* iv 4 332
Swine-keeping. Prodigals lately come from swine-keeping . *1 Hen. IV.* iv 2 38
Swing. So that the ram that batters down the wall, For the great swing and rudeness of his poise, They place before his hand that made the engine . . . . . . *Troi. and Cres.* i 3 207
Swinge. If they deny to come, Swinge me them soundly forth *T. of Shrew* v 2 104
Swinge-bucklers. You had not four such swinge-bucklers in all the inns court again . . . . . . *2 Hen. IV.* iii 2 24
Swinged. I was in love with my bed: I thank you, you swinged me for my love . . . . *T. G. of Ver.* ii 1 88
Now will he be swinged for reading my letter . . . . iii 1 392
I would have swinged him, or he should have swinged me *Mer. Wives* v 5 197
I had swinged him soundly . . . . *Meas. for Meas.* v 1 130
Saint George, that swinged the dragon . . *K. John* ii 1 288
I will have you as soundly swinged for this,—you blue-bottle rogue *2 Hen. IV.* v 4 21
If you be not swinged, I'll forswear half-kirtles . . . v 4 23
Swinish. When in swinish sleep Their drenched natures lie *Macbeth* i 7 67
They clepe us drunkards, and with swinish phrase Soil our addition *Ham.* i 4 19
Swinstead. Toward Swinstead, to the abbey there . *K. John* v 3 8
Set on toward Swinstead: to my litter straight . . . v 3 16
Switch. Fetch me a dozen crab-tree staves, and strong ones: these are but switches to 'em . . . . . . *Hen. VIII.* v 4 9
Switch and spurs; or I'll cry a match . . *Rom. and Jul.* ii 4 73
S. Withold footed thrice the old . . . . *Lear* iii 4 125
Switzers. Where are my Switzers? Let them guard the door *Hamlet* iv 5 97
Swollen. That swollen parcel of dropsies . *1 Hen. IV.* ii 4 496
Swoln. And breasted The surge most swoln that met him *Tempest* ii 1 117
The big year, swoln with some other grief, Is thought with child *2 Hen. IV.* Ind. 13
Imagined worth Holds in his blood such swoln and hot discourse *T. and C.* ii 3 183
Strangely-visited people, All swoln and ulcerous, pitiful to the eye *Macb.* iv 3 151
Swoon. So play the foolish throngs with one that swoons *Meas. for Meas.* ii 4 24
Help, hold his brows! he'll swoon! . . . *L. L. Lost* v 2 392
Speak, of all loves! I swoon almost with fear . *M. N. Dream* ii 2 154
Now counterfeit to swoon; why now fall down . *As Y. Like It* iii 5 17
Many will swoon when they do look on blood . . . iv 3 159
Did your brother tell you how I counterfeited to swoon? . . v 2 29
I am no woman, I'll not swoon at it . . . . *K. John* v 6 22
Swoon. Doth any name particular belong Unto the lodging where I first did swoon?—'Tis call'd Jerusalem . . *2 Hen. IV.* iv 5 234
Doth she swoon? use means for her recovery . . . *3 Hen. VI.* v 5 45
I swoon With this dead-killing news . . . *Richard III.* iv 1 35
Behold now presently, and swoon for what's to come upon thee *Coriol.* v 2 72
What cause, do you think, I have to swoon? . . . . v 2 107
He sleeps.—Swoons rather . . . . *Ant. and Cleo.* iv 9 27
Swooned. Some swooned, all sorrowed . . . *W. Tale* v 2 99
She swooned almost at my pleasing tale . . *T. Andron.* v 1 119
Swooning destruction, or some joy too fine . *Troi. and Cres.* iii 2 24
Swoop. All my pretty chickens and their dam At one fell swoop? *Macb.* iv 3 219
Swoopstake. Is't writ in your revenge, That, swoopstake, you will draw both friend and foe, Winner and loser? . . . . *Hamlet* iv 5 142
Sword. Put thy sword up, traitor; Who makest a show but darest not strike . . . . *Tempest* i 2 469
Sword, pike, knife, gun, or need of any engine, Would I not have . ii 1 161
Draw thy sword: one stroke Shall free thee . . . . ii 1 292
The elements, Of whom your swords are temper'd . . . iii 3 62
If you could hurt, Your swords are now too massy for your strengths . iii 3 67
If I were young again, the sword should end it.—It is petter that friends is the sword, and end it . . . . . *Mer. Wives* i 1 41
I bruised my shin th' other day with playing at sword and dagger . i 1 295
I have a sword and it shall bite upon my necessity . . . ii 1 135
With my long sword I would have made you four tall fellows skip like rats . . . . ii 1 236
The world's mine oyster, Which I with sword will open . . ii 2 3
If I see a sword out, my finger itches to make one . . . ii 3 47
What, the sword and the word! do you study them both, master parson? iii 1 44
Come, lay their swords to pawn. Follow me, lads of peace . iii 1 112
Not the king's crown, nor the deputed sword . *Meas. for Meas.* ii 2 60
He who the sword of heaven will bear Should be as holy as severe . iii 2 275
They are loose again.—And come with naked swords . *Com. of Errors* iv 4 148
I see these witches are afraid of swords . . . . iv 4 151
He is mad. Some get within him, take his sword away . . v 1 34
With drawn swords, Met us again and madly bent on us . . v 1 151
And thereupon I drew my sword on you; And then you fled . . v 1 262
Nor ever didst thou draw thy sword on me: I never saw the chain . v 1 266
By my sword, Beatrice, thou lovest me.—Do not swear, and eat it *Much Ado* iv 1 276
Never lay thy hand upon thy sword; I fear thee not . . . v 1 54
In faith, my hand meant nothing to my sword . . . . v 1 57
Give us the swords; we have bucklers of our own . . . v 2 18
If drawing my sword against the humour of affection would deliver me from the reprobate thought of it . . . . *L. L. Lost* i 2 62
Dumain was at my service, and his sword . . . . v 2 276
There's an eye Wounds like a leaden sword . . . . v 2 481
I'll slash; I'll do it by the sword . . . . . . v 2 701
I woo'd thee with my sword, And won thy love . *M. N. Dream* i 1 16
How fit a word Is that vile name to perish on my sword! . . ii 2 107
Pyramus must draw a sword to kill himself; which the ladies cannot abide . . . . iii 1 11
Let the prologue seem to say, we will do no harm with our swords . iii 1 19
He is defiled That draws a sword on thee . . . . . iii 2 411
Out, sword, and wound The pap of Pyramus . . . . v 1 301
Come, trusty sword; Come, blade, my breast imbrue . . . v 1 350
With a base and boisterous sword enforce A thievish living *As Y. Like It* ii 3 32
When I was in love I broke my sword upon a stone . . . ii 4 47
In the which hope I blush, and hide my sword . . . . ii 7 119
And so we measured swords and parted . . . . . v 4 91
Purposely to take His brother here and put him to the sword . v 4 164
An old rusty sword ta'en out of the town-armoury . *T. of Shrew* iii 2 47
And no sword worn But one to dance with! . . . *All's Well* ii 1 32
Noble heroes, my sword and yours are kin . . . . ii 1 40
On his sinister cheek; it was this very sword entrenched it . . ii 1 45
Go thou toward home; where I will never come Whilst I can shake my sword . . . . ii 5 96
Tell him that his sword can never win The honour that he loses . iii 2 96
Or the breaking of my Spanish sword.—We cannot afford you so . iv 1 52
I will never trust a man again for keeping his sword clean . iv 3 166
Would thou mightst never draw sword again . . *T. Night* i 3 68
I would I might never draw sword again . . . . . i 3 68
Therefore, on, or strip your sword stark naked . . . iii 4 274
Pray, sir, put your sword up, if you please.—Marry, will I, sir . iii 4 354
Cuff him soundly, but never draw thy sword . . . . iii 4 429
If thou darest tempt me further, draw thy sword . . . iv 1 45
I never hurt you: You drew your sword upon me without cause . v 1 191
Slander, Whose sting is sharper than the sword's . . *W. Tale* ii 3 86
Swear by this sword Thou wilt perform my bidding . . . ii 3 168
You here shall swear upon this sword of justice . . . iii 2 125
Lay aside the sword Which sways usurpingly these several titles *K. John* i 1 12
The peace of heaven is theirs that lift their swords In such a just and charitable war.—Well then, to work . . . . . . ii 1 35
Stay for an answer to your embassy, Lest unadvised you stain your swords with blood . . . . ii 1 45
With unhack'd swords and helmets all unbruised . . . . ii 1 254
Now doth Death line his dead chaps with steel; The swords of soldiers are his teeth, his fangs . . . . ii 1 353
Your sword is bright, sir; put it up again . . . . iv 3 79
Stand back, I say; By heaven, I think my sword's as sharp as yours . iv 3 82
Put up thy sword betime; Or I'll so maul you and your toasting-iron . iv 3 98
What my tongue speaks my right drawn sword may prove *Richard II.* i 1 46
By that sword I swear, Which gently laid my knighthood on my shoulder i 1 78
There shall your swords and lances arbitrate The swelling difference . i 1 200
Civil wounds plough'd up with neighbours' sword . . . . i 3 128
Lay on our royal sword your banish'd hands . . . . i 3 179
Let's fight with gentle words Till time lend friends and friends their helpful swords . . . . iii 3 132
Being all too base To stain the temper of my knightly sword . iv 1 29
Dishonourable boy! That lie shall lie so heavy on my sword, That it shall render vengeance and revenge . . . . iv 1 66
Breathless and faint, leaning upon my sword . . *1 Hen. IV.* i 3 32
My sword hacked like a hand-saw—ecce signum! . . . . ii 4 186
To hack thy sword as thou hast done, and then say it was in fight! . ii 4 288
Tell me now in earnest, how came Falstaff's sword so hacked? . ii 4 335
Thou hadst fire and sword on thy side, and yet thou rannest away . ii 4 348
A sword, whose temper I intend to stain With the best blood that I can meet . . . . v 2 94
This sword hath ended him: so shall it thee, Unless thou yield . v 3 9
Now, by my sword, I will kill all his coats; I'll murder all his wardrobe v 3 26
What, stand'st thou idle here? lend me thy sword . . . . v 3 41

Sword. If Percy be alive, thou get'st not my sword; but take my pistol 1 *Hen. IV.* v 3 52
They wound my thoughts worse than thy sword my flesh v 4 80
Full bravely hast thou flesh'd Thy maiden sword v 4 134
If the man were alive and would deny it, 'zounds, I would make him eat a piece of my sword v 4 157
Harry Monmouth fell Under the wrath of noble Hotspur's sword 2 *Hen. IV.* Ind. 30
Whose well-labouring sword Had three times slain the appearance of the king i 1 127
Give me my sword and cloak. Falstaff, good night ii 4 395
I will maintain the word with my sword to be a soldier-like word iii 2 83
Their lives That by indictment and by dint of sword Have since miscarried iv 1 128
To the place of difference call the swords Which must decide it iv 1 181
Turning the word to sword and life to death iv 2 10
And draw no swords but what are sanctified iv 4 4
There is not now a rebel's sword unsheathed iv 4 86
And blunt the sword That guards the peace and safety of your person v 2 87
You weigh this well; Therefore still bear the balance and the sword v 2 103
I do commit into your hand The unstained sword that you have used to bear v 2 114
We bear our civil swords and native fire As far as France v 5 112
Should famine, sword, and fire Crouch for employment *Hen. V.* Prol. 7
Take heed how you impawn our person, How you awake our sleeping sword i 2 22
Whose wrongs give edge unto the swords That make such waste in brief mortality i 2 27
Follow, my dear liege, With blood and sword and fire to win your right i 2 131
Now sits Expectation in the air, And hides a sword from hilts unto the point ii Prol. 9
It will toast cheese, and it will endure cold as another man's sword will ii 1 10
Show thy valour, and put up your sword ii 1 46
By this sword, I will.—Sword is an oath, and oaths must have their course ii 1 104
Sheathed their swords for lack of argument iii 1 21
Sword and shield, In bloody field, Doth win immortal fame iii 2 9
He hath a killing tongue and a quiet sword iii 2 36
With spirit of honour edged More sharper than your swords iii 5 39
If it come to the arbitrement of swords iv 1 168
The sceptre and the ball, The sword, the mace, the crown imperial iv 1 278
Or mangled shalt thou be by this my sword iv 4 41
His lords desire him to have borne His bruised helmet and his bended sword Before him through the city v Prol. 18
From Ireland coming, Bringing rebellion broached on his sword v Prol. 32
That never war advance His bleeding sword 'twixt England and fair France v 2 383
Fortune made his sword; By which the world's best garden he achieved Epil. 6
His brandish'd sword did blind men with his beams 1 *Hen. VI.* i 1 10
Valiant Talbot above human thought Enacted wonders with his sword i 1 122
Here is my keen-edged sword, Deck'd with five flower-de-luces on each side i 2 98
Thou art an Amazon And fightest with the sword of Deborah i 2 105
And not to wear, handle, or use any sword, weapon, or dagger, henceforward i 3 78
His sword did ne'er leave striking in the field i 4 81
The cry of Talbot serves me for a sword ii 1 79
I gird thee with the valiant sword of York iii 1 171
O, turn thy edged sword another way; Strike those that hurt iii 3 52
Lets fall his sword before your highness' feet iii 4 9
A stouter champion never handled sword iii 4 19
The law of arms is such That whoso draws a sword, 'tis present death iii 4 39
And left us to the rage of France his sword iv 6 3
Till with thy warlike sword, despite of fate, To my determined time thou gavest new date iv 6 8
When from the Dauphin's crest thy sword struck fire iv 6 10
The sword of Orleans hath not made me smart iv 6 42
When he perceived me shrink and on my knee, His bloody sword he brandish'd over me iv 7 6
Did flesh his puny sword in Frenchmen's blood iv 7 36
Kneel down: We here create thee the first duke of Suffolk, And gird thee with the sword 2 *Hen. VI.* i 1 65
Were there hope to conquer them again, My sword should shed hot blood i 1 118
Let me be blessed for the peace I make, Against this proud protector, with my sword! ii 1 37
Come with thy two-hand sword ii 1 46
I am not your king Till I be crown'd and that my sword be stain'd ii 2 65
Rebels there are up And put the Englishmen unto the sword iii 1 284
But here's a vengeful sword, rusted with ease, That shall be scoured iii 2 198
I care not: Never yet did base dishonour blur our name, But with our sword we wiped away the blot iv 1 40
Broke be my sword, my arms torn and defaced, And I proclaim'd a coward! iv 1 42
The Nevils all, Whose dreadful swords were never drawn in vain iv 1 92
Come, and get thee a sword, though made of a lath iv 2 1
I fear neither sword nor fire.—He need not fear the sword iv 2 63
We will have the mayor's sword borne before us iv 3 16
For God forbid so many simple souls Should perish by the sword! iv 4 11
Hath my sword therefore broke through London gates, that you should leave me? iv 8 23
My sword make way for me, for here is no staying iv 8 61
Fie on myself, that have a sword, and yet am ready to famish! iv 10 2
I'll make thee eat iron like an ostrich, and swallow my sword iv 10 31
Let this my sword report what speech forbears iv 10 57
Sword, I will hallow thee for this thy deed, And hang thee o'er my tomb iv 10 72
As I thrust thy body in with my sword, So wish I, I might thrust thy soul to hell iv 10 84
I cannot give due action to my words, Except a sword or sceptre balance it v 1 9
They'll pawn their swords for my enfranchisement v 1 113
So let it help me now against thy sword v 2 24
Sword, hold thy temper; heart, be wrathful still: Priests pray for enemies, but princes kill v 2 70
Now, by my sword, well hast thou fought to-day v 3 15
Were by the swords of common soldiers slain 3 *Hen. VI.* i 1 9
Will you we show our title to the crown? If not, our swords shall plead it i 1 103
Therefore fortify your hold, my lord.—Ay, with my sword i 2 53
Kill me with thy sword, And not with such a cruel threatening look i 3 16

Sword. Unsheathe your sword, and dub him presently 3 *Hen. VI.* ii 2 59
Arise a knight; And learn this lesson, draw thy sword in right ii 2 62
Unsheathe your sword, good father; cry 'Saint George!' ii 2 80
Two of thy name . . . Have sold their lives unto the house of York; And thou shalt be the third, if this sword hold v 1 75
Dispatch me here; Here sheathe thy sword, I'll pardon thee my death v 5 70
See how my sword weeps for the poor king's death! v 6 63
To hear the piteous moan that Rutland made When black-faced Clifford shook his sword at him *Richard III.* i 2 159
If thy revengeful heart cannot forgive, Lo, here I lend thee this sharp-pointed sword i 2 175
Take up the sword again, or take up me i 2 184
Well, well, put up your sword.—Say, then, my peace is made i 2 197
Take him over the costard with the hilts of thy sword i 4 160
A greater gift! O, that's the sword to it iii 1 116
Is the chair empty? is the sword unsway'd? Is the king dead? iv 4 470
Every man's conscience is a thousand swords, To fight against that v 2 17
To-morrow in the battle think on me, And fall thy edgeless sword v 3 135; 163
If you do free your children from the sword, Your children's children quit it in your age v 3 261
Advance your standards, draw your willing swords v 3 264
Our strong arms be our conscience, swords our law v 3 311
I know his sword Hath a sharp edge: it's long *Hen. VIII.* i 1 109
Your long coat, priest, protects you; thou shouldst feel My sword i' the life-blood of thee else iii 2 277
It is too starved a subject for my sword *Troi. and Cres.* i 1 96
There be hacks!—Be those with swords?—Swords! any thing, he cares not i 2 226
How his sword is bloodied, and his helm more hacked than Hector's! i 2 253
And the great Hector's sword had lack'd a master i 3 76
But when they would seem soldiers, they have galls, Good arms, strong joints, true swords i 3 238
Limbs are his instruments, In no less working than are swords and bows Directive by the limbs i 3 355
Since the first sword was drawn about this question, Every tithe soul, 'mongst many thousand dismes, Hath been as dear as Helen ii 2 18
You know a sword employ'd is perilous, And reason flies the object of all harm: Who marvels then, when Helenus beholds A Grecian and his sword, if he do set The very wings of reason to his heels? ii 2 40
There's not the meanest spirit on our party Without a heart to dare or sword to draw When Helen is defended ii 2 157
A' should not bear it so, a' should eat swords first ii 3 228
Let Æneas live, If to my sword his fate be not the glory, A thousand complete courses of the sun! iv 1 26
If e'er thou stand at mercy of my sword, Name Cressid iv 4 116
Wherein my sword had not impressure made Of our rank feud iv 5 131
The just gods gainsay That any drop thou borrow'dst from thy mother, My sacred aunt, should by my mortal sword Be drain'd! iv 5 134
When thou hast hung thy advanced sword i' the air, Not letting it decline on the declined iv 5 188
Were it a casque composed by Vulcan's skill, My sword should bite it v 2 171
The almighty sun shall dizzy with more clamour Neptune's ear In his descent than shall my prompted sword Falling on Diomed v 2 175
Even in the fan and wind of your fair sword, You bid them rise v 3 41
The venom'd vengeance ride upon our swords, Spur them to ruthful work v 3 47
Nor you, my brother, with your true sword drawn, Opposed to hinder me, should stop my way, But by my ruin v 3 56
Rest, sword; thou hast thy fill of blood and death v 8 4
My half-supp'd sword, that frankly would have fed, Pleased with this dainty bait, thus goes to bed v 8 19
Would the nobility lay aside their ruth, And let me use my sword *Coriol.* i 1 202
Than Hector's forehead when it spit forth blood At Grecian sword, contemning i 3 46
He had rather see the swords, and hear a drum, than look upon his schoolmaster i 3 60
Make us quick in work, That we with smoking swords may march from hence! i 4 11
O noble fellow! Who sensibly outdares his senseless sword i 4 53
Her [Fortune's] great charms Misguide thy opposers' swords! i 5 23
Filling the air with swords advanced and darts, We prove this very hour i 6 61
O, me alone! make you a sword of me? i 6 76
But cannot make my heart consent to take A bribe to pay my sword i 9 38
I thought to crush him in an equal force, True sword to sword i 10 15
In the brunt of seventeen battles since He lurch'd all swords of the garland ii 2 105
His sword, death's stamp, Where it did mark, it took ii 2 111
How often he had met you, sword to sword iii 1 13
Down with that sword! Tribunes, withdraw awhile iii 1 226
He has been bred i' the wars Since he could draw a sword iii 1 321
I would my son Were in Arabia, and thy tribe before him, His good sword in his hand.—What then? iv 2 25
Here I clip The anvil of my sword iv 5 116
Fights dragon-like, and does achieve as soon As draw his sword iv 7 24
All the swords In Italy, and her confederate arms, Could not have made this peace v 3 207
Let him feel your sword, Which we will second v 6 56
O that I had him, With six Aufidiuses, or more, his tribe, To use my lawful sword!—Insolent villain! v 6 131
Masters all, be quiet; Put up your swords v 6 136
My loving followers, Plead my successive title with your swords *T. An.* i 1 4
He circumscribed with his sword, And brought to yoke, the enemies of Rome i 1 68
Here Goths have given me leave to sheathe my sword i 1 85
With our swords, upon a pile of wood, Let's hew his limbs i 1 128
Your fortunes are alike in all, That in your country's service drew your swords i 1 175
Draw your swords, and sheathe them not Till Saturninus be Rome's emperor i 1 204
I consecrate My sword, my chariot, and my prisoners; Presents well worthy i 1 249
Convey her hence away, And with my sword I'll keep this door safe i 1 288
Give that changing piece To him that flourish'd for her with his sword i 1 310
And that my sword upon thee shall approve, And plead my passions ii 1 35
Give me a sword, I'll chop off my hands too iii 1 72
My sword shall soon dispatch it.—Sooner this sword shall plough thy bowels up iv 2 86
Part, fools! Put up your swords; you know not what you do *R. and J.* i 1 72
Put up thy sword, Or manage it to part these men with me i 1 75
Give me my long sword, ho!—A crutch, a crutch! why call you for a sword? i 1 82

Sword. In the instant came The fiery Tybalt, with his sword prepared *Rom. and Jul.* i 1 116
There lies more peril in thine eye Than twenty of their swords ii 2 72
When he enters the confines of a tavern claps me his sword upon the table iii 1 7
Will you pluck your sword out of his pilcher by the ears? make haste, lest mine be about your ears ere it be out iii 1 83
What mean these masterless and gory swords To lie discolour'd? v 3 142
What heart, head, sword, force, means, but is Lord Timon's? *T. of A.* ii 2 176
Hath in her more destruction than thy sword, For all her cherubin look iv 3 62
When neighbour states, But for thy sword and fortune, trod upon them iv 3 95
Let not thy sword skip one: Pity not honour'd age for his white beard iv 3 110
Let not the virgin's cheek Make soft thy trenchant sword iv 3 115
And shakes his threatening sword Against the walls of Athens v 1 169
Thou rather shalt enforce it with thy smile Than hew to't with thy sword v 4 46
I will use the olive with my sword, Make war breed peace v 4 82
Besides—I ha' not since put up my sword *J. Cæsar* i 3 19
Here, as I point my sword, the sun arises ii 1 106
Let us bathe our hands in Cæsar's blood Up to the elbows, and besmear our swords iii 1 107
Nor no instrument Of half that worth as those your swords iii 1 155
For your part, To you our swords have leaden points iii 1 173
Look; I draw a sword against conspirators; When think you that the sword goes up again? Never v 1 51
Or till another Cæsar Have added slaughter to the sword of traitors v 1 55
I was not born to die on Brutus' sword v 1 58
With this good sword, That ran through Cæsar's bowels, search this bosom v 3 41
Guide thou the sword. Cæsar, thou art revenged, Even with the sword that kill'd thee v 3 45
Come, Cassius' sword, and find Titinius' heart v 3 90
Thy spirit walks abroad, and turns our swords In our own proper entrails v 3 95
Hold then my sword, and turn away thy face, While I do run upon it v 5 47
I held the sword, and he did run on it v 5 65
Hold, take my sword. There's husbandry in heaven *Macbeth* ii 1 4
Give me my sword. Who's there?—A friend ii 1 9
Be alive again, And dare me to the desert with thy sword iii 4 104
Seize upon Fife; give to the edge o' the sword His wife, his babes iv 1 151
Let us rather Hold fast the mortal sword iv 3 3
When I shall tread upon the tyrant's head, Or wear it on my sword iv 3 46
It [avarice] hath been The sword of our slain kings iv 3 87
Be this the whetstone of your sword: let grief Convert to anger iv 3 228
Within my sword's length set him; if he 'scape, Heaven forgive him too! iv 3 234
Thou liest, abhorred tyrant; with my sword I'll prove the lie thou speak'st v 7 10
But swords I smile at, weapons laugh to scorn, Brandish'd by man that's of a woman born v 7 12
Either thou, Macbeth, Or else my sword with an unbatter'd edge I sheathe again undeeded v 7 19
Why should I play the Roman fool, and die On mine own sword? v 8 2
I have no words: My voice is in my sword v 8 7
As easy mayst thou the intrenchant air With thy keen sword impress v 8 10
We have sworn, my lord, already.—Indeed, upon my sword *Hamlet* i 5 147
Never to speak of this that you have seen, Swear by my sword i 5 154
Come hither, gentlemen, And lay your hands again upon my sword i 5 158
Never to speak of this that you have heard, Swear by my sword i 5 160
His antique sword, Rebellious to his arm, lies where it falls ii 2 490
But with the whiff and wind of his fell sword, The unnerved father falls ii 2 495
His sword, Which was declining on the milky head Of reverend Priam, seem'd i' the air to stick ii 2 499
With less remorse than Pyrrhus' bleeding sword Now falls on Priam ii 2 513
Make malicious sport In mincing with his sword her husband's limbs ii 2 537
The courtier's, soldier's, scholar's, eye, tongue, sword iii 1 159
Up, sword; and know thou a more horrid hent iii 3 88
Since yet thy cicatrice looks raw and red After the Danish sword iv 3 63
No trophy, sword, nor hatchment o'er his bones, No noble rite iv 5 214
With ease, Or with a little shuffling, you may choose A sword unbated iv 7 139
For that purpose, I'll anoint my sword iv 7 141
Six Barbary horses against six French swords, their assigns v 2 168
In cunning I must draw my sword upon you: Draw; seem to defend yourself *Lear* ii 1 31
Here stood he in the dark, his sharp sword out, Mumbling of wicked charms ii 1 40
With his prepared sword, he charges home My unprovided body ii 1 53
That such a slave as this should wear a sword, Who wears no honesty ii 2 78
Stop her there! Arms, arms, sword, fire! Corruption in the place! iii 6 58
Give me thy sword. A peasant stand up thus! iii 7 80
Bending his sword To his great master iv 2 74
Briefly thyself remember: the sword is out That must destroy thee iv 6 233
To be tender-minded Does not become a sword v 3 32
Draw thy sword, That, if my speech offend a noble heart, Thy arm may do thee justice: here is mine v 3 126
Despite thy victor sword and fire-new fortune, Thy valour and thy heart v 3 132
This sword, this arm, and my best spirits, are bent To prove upon thy heart, whereto I speak, Thou liest v 3 139
This sword of mine shall give them instant way, Where they shall rest for ever v 3 149
Take my sword, Give it the captain.—Haste thee, for thy life v 3 250
Keep up your bright swords, for the dew will rust them *Othello* i 2 59
Swords out, and tilting one at other's breast, In opposition bloody ii 3 183
A fellow crying out for help; And Cassio following him with determined sword ii 3 227
I heard the clink and fall of swords, And Cassio high in oath ii 3 234
What was he that you followed with your sword? What had he done to you? ii 3 286
'Tis but a man gone. Forth, my sword: he dies v 1 10
Ah, balmy breath, that dost almost persuade Justice to break her sword! v 2 17
I care not for thy sword; I'll make thee known, Though I lost twenty lives v 2 165
Fie! Your sword upon a woman? v 2 224
I am not valiant neither, But every puny whipster gets my sword v 2 244
It is a sword of Spain, the ice-brook's temper v 2 253
With this little arm and this good sword, I have made my way v 2 262
Wrench his sword from him.—I bleed, sir; but not kill'd v 2 288
Our Italy Shines o'er with civil swords *Ant. and Cleo.* i 3 45
Now, by my sword,— And target. Still he mends; But this is not the best i 3 82
Upon your sword Sit laurel victory! i 3 99

Sword. They have entertained cause enough To draw their swords *Ant. and Cleo.* ii 1 47
Have my learning from some true reports, That drew their swords with you ii 2 48
I did not think to draw my sword 'gainst Pompey ii 2 156
She made great Cæsar lay his sword to bed ii 2 232
Then put my tires and mantles on him, whilst I wore his sword Philippan ii 5 23
Let us know If 'twill tie up thy discontented sword ii 6 6
Whilst yet with Parthian blood thy sword is warm, The fugitive Parthians follow iii 1 6
Without the which a soldier, and his sword, Grants scarce distinction iii 1 28
Do you misdoubt This sword and these my wounds? iii 7 64
He at Philippi kept His sword e'en like a dancer iii 11 36
My sword, made weak by my affection, would Obey it on all cause iii 11 67
And answer me declined, sword against sword iii 13 27
I and my sword will earn our chronicle: There's hope in't yet iii 13 175
When valour preys on reason, It eats the sword it fights with iii 13 200
O, thy vile lady! She has robb'd me of my sword iv 14 23
I, that with my sword Quarter'd the world iv 14 57
Draw that thy honest sword, which thou hast worn Most useful for thy country iv 14 79
My sword is drawn.—Then let it do at once The thing why thou hast drawn it iv 14 88
This sword but shown to Cæsar, with this tidings, Shall enter me with him iv 14 112
Draw thy sword, and give me Sufficing strokes for death iv 14 116
This is his sword; I robb'd his wound of it; behold it stain'd v 1 24
Who in the wars o' the time Died with their swords in hand *Cymbeline* i 1 36
To be put to the arbitrement of swords i 4 53
You shall answer me with your sword i 4 176
The foul opinion You had of her pure honour gains or loses Your sword or mine, or masterless leaves both ii 4 60
Cassibelan, who was once at point—O giglot fortune!—to master Cæsar's sword iii 1 31
My body's mark'd With Roman swords, and my report was once First with the best iii 3 57
What shall I need to draw my sword? the paper Hath cut her throat already iii 4 34
'Tis slander, Whose edge is sharper than the sword iii 4 36
I draw the sword myself: take it, and hit The innocent mansion of my love iii 4 69
If mine enemy But fear the sword like me, he'll scarcely look on't iii 6 25
My horse is tied up safe: out, sword, and to a sore purpose! iv 1 24
With his own sword, Which he did wave against my throat, I have ta'en His head from him iv 2 149
Had it gone with us, We should not, when the blood was cool, have threaten'd Our prisoners with the sword v 5 78
Came to me With his sword drawn; foam'd at the mouth v 5 276
I came unto your court for honour's cause, . . . And he that otherwise accounts of me, This sword shall prove he's honour's enemy *Pericles* ii 5 64

Sword-and-buckler. That same sword-and-buckler Prince of Wales *1 Hen. IV.* i 3 230

Sworder. A Roman sworder and banditto slave Murder'd sweet Tully *2 Hen. VI.* iv 1 135
Like enough, high-battled Cæsar will Unstate his happiness, and be staged to the show, Against a sworder! *Ant. and Cleo.* iii 13 31

Sword-hilts. Hold thou my sword-hilts, whilst I run on it *J. Cæsar* v 5 28

Sword-men. Like to prove most sinewy sword-men *All's Well* ii 1 62

Swore I was assured to her *Com. of Errors* iii 2 145
Then swore he that he was a stranger here.—And true he swore iv 2 9
He swore he would marry her to-night *Much Ado* ii 1 176
Swore he would meet her, as he was appointed, next morning iii 3 170
He swore he would never marry iii 4 88
He swore a thing to me on Monday night, which he forswore on Tuesday morning v 1 168
Do not you love me? . . . they swore you did v 4 76
They swore that you were almost sick for me.—They swore that you were well-nigh dead for me v 4 80
I only swore to study with your grace *L. L. Lost* i 1 51
You swore to that, Biron, and to the rest.—By yea and nay, sir, then I swore in jest i 1 53
Yet confident I'll keep what I have swore i 1 114
Fleer'd and swore A better speech was never spoke before v 2 109
He swore that he did hold me dear As precious eyesight v 2 444
I never swore this lady such an oath.—By heaven, you did v 2 451
I had no judgement when to her I swore *M. N. Dream* iii 2 134
What lady is the same To whom you swore a secret pilgrimage? *M. of V.* i 1 120
And swore he would pay him again when he was able i 2 87
You swore to me, when I did give it you, That you would wear it till your hour of death v 1 152
A certain knight that swore by his honour they were good pancakes and swore by his honour the mustard was naught *As Y. Like It* i 2 66
They shook hands and swore brothers v 4 107
Swore so loud, That, all-amazed, the priest let fall the book *T. of Shrew* iii 2 162
He stamp'd and swore, As if the vicar meant to cozen him iii 2 169
How he swore, how she prayed, that never prayed before iv 1 81
And so I take my leave, In resolution as I swore before iv 2 43
I swore I leaped from the window of the citadel *All's Well* iv 1 60
We swore to you Dear amity and everlasting love *K. John* v 4 19
Swore the devil his true liegeman upon the cross of a Welsh hook *1 Hen. IV.* ii 4 371
Swore little; diced not above seven times a week iii 3 18
In kind heart and pity moved, Swore him assistance and perform'd it too iv 3 65
You swore to us, And you did swear that oath at Doncaster v 1 41
To this we swore our aid. But in short space It rain'd down fortune v 1 46
Which he swore, as he was a soldier, he would wear if alive *Hen. V.* iv 7 134
He swore consent to your succession, His oath enrolled *3 Hen. VI.* ii 1 172
And swore, with sobs, That he would labour my delivery *Richard III.* i 4 252
Helen herself swore th' other day *Trio. and Cres.* i 2 100
The prince must think me tardy and remiss, That swore to ride before him iv 4 144
Sure as death I swore I would not part a bachelor from the priest *T. An.* i 1 487
Who swore they saw Men all in fire walk up and down the streets *J. Cæsar* i 3 24
Then I swore thee, saving of thy life, That whatsoever I did bid thee do, Thou shouldst attempt it v 3 38
The scrimers of their nation, He swore, had neither motion, guard, nor eye, If you opposed them *Hamlet* iv 7 102
Swore as many oaths as I spake words, and broke them *Lear* iii 4 90
She swore, in faith, 'twas strange, 'twas passing strange *Othello* i 3 160
Swore to Cymbeline I was confederate with the Romans *Cymbeline* iii 3 67

Swore. And swore With his own single hand he'ld take us in . *Cymbeline* iv 2 120
What have we to lose, But that he swore to take, our lives? . . . iv 2 125
Swore, If I discover'd not which way she was gone, It was my instant death . . . . v 5 276
And here the bracelet of the truest princess That ever swore her faith . v 5 417
He made a groan at it, and swore he would see her to-morrow *Pericles* iv 2 118
Sworest. This is that face, thou cruel Angelo, Which once thou sworest was worth the looking on . . . . *Meas. for Meas.* v 1 208
What since thou sworest is sworn against thyself . . *K. John* iii 1 268
When I did make thee free, sworest thou not then To do this? *A. and C.* iv 14 81
Sworn. I can swim like a duck, I'll be sworn . . . . *Tempest* ii 2 134
What does else want credit, come to me, And I'll be sworn 'tis true . iii 3 26
I'll be sworn, I have sat in the stocks for puddings he hath stolen *T. G. of Ver.* iv 4 33
I'll be sworn on a book, she loves you . . . . *Mer. Wives* i 4 156
I would have sworn his disposition would have gone to the truth of his words . . . . ii 1 60
I'll be sworn, As my mother was, the first hour I was born . . . ii 2 38
I am sworn of the peace . . . . ii 3 55
Have you been true to us?—Ay, I'll be sworn . . . . . iii 3 29
Were you sworn to the duke, or to the deputy? . . *Meas. for Meas.* iv 2 196
I will be sworn these ears of mine Heard you confess *Com. of Errors* v 1 259
I would scarce trust myself, though I had sworn the contrary *Much Ado* i 1 198
I'll be sworn, if he be so, his conceit is false . . . . . ii 1 308
I will not be sworn but love may transform me to an oyster . . ii 3 25
I would have thought her spirit had been invincible against all assaults of affection.—I would have sworn it had . . . . . . ii 3 121
I'll be sworn upon't that he loves her . . . . . . v 4 85
Have sworn for three years' term to live with me . . . *L. L. Lost* i 1 16
If you are arm'd to do as sworn to do, Subscribe to your deep oaths . i 1 22
I have already sworn, That is, to live and study here three years . . i 1 34
Having sworn too hard a keeping oath, Study to break it . . . i 1 65
No, my good lord; I have sworn to stay with you . . . . . i 1 111
Put in practice that Which each to other hath so strongly sworn . . i 1 309
Hear me, dear lady; I have sworn an oath . . . . . . ii 1 97
I hear your grace hath sworn out house-keeping . . . . . ii 1 104
My hand is sworn Ne'er to pluck thee from thy thorn . . . . iv 3 111
Then fools you were these women to forswear, Or keeping what is sworn, you will prove fools . . . . iv 3 356
But will you hear? the king is my love sworn . . . . . . v 2 282
Since when, I'll be sworn, he wore none but a dishclout . . . . v 2 720
I'll be sworn, if thou be Launcelot, thou art mine own flesh *Mer. of Ven.* ii 2 97
I have sworn an oath that I will have my bond . . . . . iii 3 5
By our holy Sabbath have I sworn To have the due and forfeit of my bond . . . . iv 1 36
I dare be sworn for him he would not leave it Nor pluck it from his finger . . . . v 1 172
The first inter'gatory That my Nerissa shall be sworn on . . . . v 1 301
No more was this knight, swearing by his honour, for he never had any; or if he had, he had sworn it away . . . . *As Y. Like It* i 2 84
Although before the solemn priest I have sworn, I will not bed her *All's Well* ii 3 286
I have wedded her, not bedded her; and sworn to make the 'not' eternal . . . . iii 2 24
How have I sworn!—'Tis not the many oaths that makes the truth . iv 2 20
He had sworn to marry me When his wife's dead . . . . . v 3 71
Sir Toby will be sworn that I am no fox . . . . *T. Night* i 5 86
'Yet my state is well: I am a gentleman.' I'll be sworn thou art . . i 5 310
And, having sworn truth, ever will be true . . . . . . iv 3 33
Condemn'd by the king's own mouth, thereon His execution sworn *W. T.* i 2 446
I'll be sworn you would believe my saying, Howe'er you lean to the nayward . . . . ii 1 63
I am innocent as you.—I dare be sworn . . . . . . ii 2 29
I should blush To see you so attired, sworn, I think, To show myself a glass . . . . iv 4 13
Celebration of that nuptial which We two have sworn shall come . . iv 4 51
Thou hast sworn my love to be.—Thou hast sworn it more to me . . iv 4 312
Hast thou not spoke like thunder on my side, Been sworn my soldier? *K. John* iii 1 125
As now again to snatch our palm from palm, Unswear faith sworn . . iii 1 245
What since thou sworest is sworn against thyself . . . . . iii 1 268
That which thou hast sworn to do amiss Is not amiss when it is truly done . . . . iii 1 270
It is religion that doth make vows kept; But thou hast sworn against religion . . . . iii 1 280
I have sworn to do it; And with hot irons must I burn them out . . iv 1 58
Yet am I sworn and I did purpose, boy, With this same very iron to burn them out . . . . iv 1 124
Thus hath he sworn And I with him, and many moe with me . . . v 4 16
The noble duke hath sworn his coming is But for his own; and for the right of that We all have strongly sworn to give him aid *Richard II.* ii 3 148
The caterpillars of the commonwealth, Which I have sworn to weed . ii 3 167
Comprising all that may be sworn or said. . . . . . . iii 3 111
I'll be sworn upon all the books in England . . . *1 Hen. IV.* ii 4 55
Bring him hither, And I'll be sworn I have power to shame him hence iii 1 61
My face does you no harm.—No, I'll be sworn . . . . . iii 3 33
I'll be sworn my pocket was picked . . . . iii 3 69
I am sure they never learned that of me.—No, I'll be sworn . . . iv 2 79
Violation of all faith and troth Sworn to us in your younger enterprise v 1 71
Old Mistress Ursula, whom I have weekly sworn to marry . *2 Hen. IV.* i 2 270
I'll be sworn a' ne'er saw him but once in the Tilt-yard . . . iii 2 346
And sworn unto the practices of France, To kill us here . . *Hen. V.* ii 2 90
This knight . . . hath likewise sworn. But, O, What shall I say to thee? ii 2 93
As two yoke-devils sworn to either's purpose . . . . . ii 2 106
I have sworn to take him a box o' th' ear . . . . . . iv 7 132
Remember, lords, your oaths to Henry sworn . . . . *1 Hen. VI.* i 1 162
A dreadful oath, sworn with a solemn tongue! . . *2 Hen. VI.* iii 2 158
Lord Say, Jack Cade hath sworn to have thy head . . . . . iv 4 19
Against thy oath and true allegiance sworn . . . . . . v 1 20
Hast thou not sworn allegiance unto me?—I have . . . . . v 1 179
We his subjects sworn in all allegiance Will apprehend you *3 Hen. VI.* iii 1 70
You were sworn true subjects unto me . . . . iii 1 78
I return his sworn and mortal foe . . . . iii 3 257
Whom thou wert sworn to cherish and defend . . . . *Richard III.* i 4 213
Thou art sworn as deeply to effect what we intend As closely to conceal iii 1 158
Under the confession's seal He solemnly had sworn . . *Hen. VIII.* i 2 165
I'll be sworn 'tis true; he will weep you, an 'twere a man born in April *Troi. and Cres.* i 2 188
I'll be sworn and sworn upon't she never shrouded any but lazars . . i 2 ...
Swear the oaths now to her that you have sworn to me . . . . iii 2 44

Sworn. Is he here, say you? 'tis more than I know, I'll be sworn *Troi. and Cres.* iv 2 54
You fillip me o' the head.—No, I'll be sworn . . . . . iv 5 45
Both taxing me and gaging me to keep An oath that I have sworn . . v 1 47
You have sworn patience.—Fear me not . . . . v 2 62
'Tis sworn between us we shall ever strike Till one can do no more *Cor.* i 2 35
True! pow, wow.—True! I'll be sworn they are true . . . . ii 1 158
What may be sworn by, both divine and human, Seal what I end withal! iii 1 141
Friends now fast sworn, Whose double bosoms seem to wear one heart . iv 4 12
I thought there was more in him than I could think.—So did I, I'll be sworn . . . . iv 5 168
Our general has sworn you out of reprieve and pardon . . . . v 2 53
I was moved withal.—I dare be sworn you were . . . . . v 3 194
Then she hath sworn that she will still live chaste?—She hath *R. and J.* i 1 223
Be but sworn my love, And I'll no longer be a Capulet . . . . ii 2 35
Thy dear love sworn but hollow perjury . . . . iii 3 128
I am sworn not to give regard to you . . . . *T. of Athens* i 2 251
Had I so sworn as you Have done to this . . . . . *Macbeth* i 7 58
Now to my word; It is 'Adieu, adieu! remember me.' I have sworn't *Hamlet* i 5 112
We have sworn, my lord, already.—Indeed, upon my sword, indeed . i 5 147
If she should break it now!—'Tis deeply sworn . . . . . iii 2 235
Nothing: I have sworn; I am firm . . . . *Lear* i 1 248
To both these sisters have I sworn my love; Each jealous of the other . v 1 55
I dare be sworn I think that he is honest.—I think so too . *Othello* iii 3 125
Thou art sworn, Eros, That, when the exigent should come, . . . Thou then wouldst kill me . . . . *Ant. and Cleo.* iv 14 62
Thereto sworn by your command, Which my love makes religion to obey v 2 198
Her attendants are All sworn and honourable . . . . *Cymbeline* ii 4 125
I'll be sworn— No swearing. If you will swear you have not done't, you lie . . . . ii 4 143
Thou hast sworn to do't: 'Tis but a blow, which never shall be known *Pericles* iv 1 1
I am sworn To do my work with haste . . . . iv 1 70
Save poor me, the weaker.—I am sworn, And will dispatch . . . iv 1 91
Sworn brother. He hath every month a new sworn brother . *Much Ado* i 1 73
And Trust, his sworn brother, a very simple gentleman! . *W. Tale* iv 4 607
I am sworn brother, sweet, To grim Necessity . . . *Richard II.* v 1 20
I am sworn brother to a leash of drawers . . . . *1 Hen. IV.* ii 4 7
Talks as familiarly of John a Gaunt as if he had been sworn brother to him . . . . *2 Hen. IV.* iii 2 345
We'll be all three sworn brothers to France . . . *Hen. V.* ii 1 13
Nym and Bardolph are sworn brothers in filching . . . . . iii 2 47
I will, sir, flatter my sworn brother, the people . . *Coriolanus* ii 3 102
Sworn counsel. What to your sworn counsel I have spoken Is so from word to word . . . . *All's Well* iii 7 9
Sworn duty. Neglected my sworn duty in that case . *Richard II.* i 1 134
Sworn enemy. Thy friend, as thou usest him, and thy sworn enemy *T. Night* iii 4 187
Sworn friend. Now my sworn friend and then mine enemy *W. Tale* i 2 167
Sworn rioter. He's a sworn rioter . . . . . *T. of Athens* iii 5 68
Sworn servant. Being my sworn servant, The duke retain'd him his *Hen. VIII.* i 2 191
Sworn spouse. Commit not with man's sworn spouse . . . *Lear* iii 4 84
Sworn subjects. To Bolingbroke are we sworn subjects now *Richard II.* v 2 39
Sworn twelve. The jury, passing on the prisoner's life, May in the sworn twelve have a thief or two Guiltier than him they try *Meas. for Meas.* ii 1 20
Swound. I swound to see thee.—Would thou wouldst burst! *T. of Athens* iv 3 373
But, soft, I pray you: what, did Cæsar swound? . . . *J. Cæsar* i 2 253
How does the queen?—She swounds to see them bleed . . *Hamlet* v 2 319
Swounded. All in gore-blood; I swounded at the sight . *Rom. and Jul.* iii 2 56
It had almost choked Cæsar; for he swounded and fell down at it *J. C.* i 2 249
'Swounds, I should take it . . . . *Hamlet* ii 2 604
'Swounds, show me what thou 'lt do . . . . v 1 297
Swum ashore, man, like a duck: I can swim like a duck . . *Tempest* ii 2 133
You are over boots in love, And yet you never swum the Hellespont *T. G. of Ver.* i 1 26
Swung. He swung about his head and cut the winds *Rom. and Jul.* i 1 118
Sycamore. Under the cool shade of a sycamore . . . *L. L. Lost* v 2 89
Underneath the grove of sycamore That westward rooteth *Rom. and Jul.* i 1 128
The poor soul sat sighing by a sycamore tree, Sing all a green willow *Othello* iv 3 41
Sycorax. Hast thou forgot The foul witch Sycorax, who with age and envy Was grown into a hoop? . . . . *Tempest* i 2 258
This damn'd witch Sycorax, For mischiefs manifold and sorceries terrible To enter human hearing, from Argier, Thou know'st, was banish'd . . . . i 2 263
A torment To lay upon the damn'd, which Sycorax Could not again undo . . . . i 2 290
This island's mine, by Sycorax my mother, Which thou takest from me i 2 331
All the charms Of Sycorax, toads, beetles, bats, light on you! . . i 2 340
I never saw a woman, But only Sycorax my dam and she; But she as far surpasseth Sycorax As great'st does least . . . . . . iii 2 109
Syenna. Under the conduct of bold Iachimo, Syenna's brother *Cymbeline* iv 2 341
Sylla. And, like ambitious Sylla, overgorged With gobbets of thy mother's bleeding heart . . . . *2 Hen. VI.* iv 1 84
Syllable. Exactly do All points of my command.—To the syllable *Tempest* i 2 500
Which you shall find By every syllable a faithful verity *Meas. for Meas.* iv 3 131
Even to the utmost syllable of your worthiness . . . *All's Well* iii 6 75
Wish he were Something mistaken in't.—No, not a syllable . *Hen. VIII.* i 1 195
And who dare speak One syllable against him? . . . . . . v 1 39
To make a recordation to my soul Of every syllable . *Troi. and Cres.* v 2 117
I find the ass in compound with the major part of your syllables *Coriolanus* ii 1 65
Though but bastards and syllables Of no allowance to your bosom's truth . . . . iii 2 56
And yell'd out Like syllable of dolour . . . . . *Macbeth* iv 3 8
From day to day To the last syllable of recorded time . . . . v 5 21
One whom I will beat into clamorous whining, if thou deniest the least syllable of thy addition . . . . *Lear* ii 2 25
I heard Each syllable that breath made up between them . *Othello* iv 2 5
Resolve your angry father, if my tongue Did e'er solicit, or my hand subscribe To any syllable that made love to you . . . *Pericles* ii 5 70
I will believe you by the syllable Of what you shall deliver . . . v 1 169
Syllogism. If that this simple syllogism will serve, so . . *T. Night* i 5 55
Symbol. For her To win the Moor—were't to renounce his baptism, All seals and symbols of redeemed sin . . . . *Othello* ii 3 350
Sympathize. The senseless brands will sympathize The heavy accent of thy moving tongue . . . . *Richard II.* v 1 46
A blustering day.—Then with the losers let it sympathise . *1 Hen. IV.* v 1 7

Sympathize. The men do sympathize with the mastiffs in robustious and rough coming on . . . . *Hen. V.* iii 7 158
The thing of courage As roused with rage with rage doth sympathize *Troi. and Cres.* i 3 52
We sympathise: Jove, let Æneas live! . . . . . . iv 1 25
Sympathized. By this sympathized one day's error . *Com. of Errors* v 1 397
A message well sympathized . . . . *L. L. Lost* iii 1 52
Sympathy. There's sympathy: you are merry, so am I; ha, ha! then there's more sympathy: you love sack, and so do I; would you desire better sympathy? . . . *Mer. Wives* ii 1 7
Or, if there were a sympathy in choice, War, death, or sickness did lay siege to it . . . . *M. N. Dream* i 1 141
If that thy valour stand on sympathy, There is my gage *Richard II.* iv 1 33
If sympathy of love unite our thoughts . . . . . *2 Hen. VI.* i 1 23
O, what a sympathy of woe is this! . . . *T. Andron.* iii 1 148
O, he is even in my mistress' case, Just in her case! O woful sympathy! *Rom. and Jul.* iii 3 85
Loveliness in favour, sympathy in years, manners, and beauties *Othello* ii 1 232
The action of my life is like it, which I'll keep, if but for sympathy *Cymbeline* v 4 151
Synagogue. Meet me at our synagogue . . . *Mer. of Venice* iii 1 135
Synod. It hath in solemn synods been decreed . *Com. of Errors* i 1 13
Thus Rosalind of many parts By heavenly synod was devised *As Y. L. It* iii 2 158
The glorious gods sit in hourly synod about thy particular prosperity! *Coriolanus* v 2 74
Out, out, thou strumpet, Fortune! All you gods, In general synod, take away her power! . . . . *Hamlet* ii 2 516

Synod. Gods and goddesses, All the whole synod of them! *Ant. and Cleo.* iii 10 5
Help; Or we poor ghosts will cry To the shining synod of the rest *Cymb.* v 4 89
Syracusa. Merchant of Syracusa, plead no more . . *Com. of Errors* i 1 3
In Syracusa was I born, and wed Unto a woman . . . . i 1 37
But seven years since, in Syracusa, boy, Thou know'st we parted . v 1 320
It is not so: I ne'er saw Syracusa in my life . . . . v 1 325
During which time he ne'er saw Syracusa . . . . . v 1 328
Syracuse. No, sir, not I; I came from Syracuse . . . . v 1 363
Syracusian. It hath in solemn synods been decreed, Both by the Syracusians and ourselves . . . . i 1 14
If any born at Ephesus be seen At any Syracusian marts and fairs; Again: if any Syracusian born Come to the bay of Ephesus, he dies i 1 18
Syracusian, say in brief the cause Why thou departed'st from thy native home . . . . i 1 29
This very day a Syracusian merchant Is apprehended for arrival here . i 2 3
A reverend Syracusian merchant, Who put unluckily into this bay . v 1 124
Speak freely, Syracusian, what thou wilt . . . . . v 1 285
I tell thee, Syracusian, twenty years Have I been patron to Antipholus v 1 326
Syria. His conquering banner shook from Syria To Lydia *Ant. and Cleo.* i 2 106
Sossius, One of my place in Syria, his lieutenant . . . iii 1 18
Made her Of lower Syria, Cyprus, Lydia, Absolute queen . . iii 6 10
To Ptolemy he assign'd Syria, Cilicia, and Phœnicia . . . iii 6 16
Cæsar through Syria Intends his journey . . . . . v 2 200
The fairest in all Syria, I tell you what mine authors say *Pericles* i Gower 19
Syrup. With wholesome syrups, drugs, and holy prayers *Com. of Errors* v 1 104
Not poppy, nor mandragora, Nor all the drowsy syrups . . *Othello* iii 3 331

T

T. This is my lady's hand: these be her very C's, her U's and her T's *T. Night* ii 5 96; ii 5 99
I had a wound here that was like a T, But now 'tis made an H *Ant. and Cleo.* iv 7 7
Ta. Thou wo't, wo't thou? thou wo't, wo't ta? do, do, thou rogue! *2 Hen. IV.* ii 1 63
Table. The table wherein all my thoughts Are visibly character'd *T. G. of Ver.* ii 7 3
Three or four gentlemanlike dogs, under the duke's table . . iv 4 20
The dinner is on the table; my father desires your worships' company *Mer. Wives* i 1 270
The sanctimonious pirate, that went to sea with the Ten Commandments, but scraped one out of the table . . *Meas. for Meas.* i 2 9
A table full of welcome makes scarce one dainty dish *Com. of Errors* iii 1 23
Please you to gratify the table with a grace . . *L. L. Lost* iv 2 161
When he plays at tables, chides the dice In honourable terms . v 2 326
If any man in Italy have a fairer table . . *Mer. of Venice* ii 2 167
Bid them cover the table, serve in the meat . . . . iii 5 64
For the table, sir, it shall be served in; for the meat, sir, it shall be covered . . . . iii 5 66
Sit down and feed, and welcome to our table . . *As Y. Like It* ii 7 105
And in his waning age Set foot under thy table . *T. of Shrew* ii 1 404
Though bride and bridegroom wants For to supply the places at the table . . . . iii 2 249
To see him every hour; to sit and draw His arched brows, his hawking eye, his curls, In our heart's table . . . *All's Well* i 1 106
Now here, At upper end o' the table, now i' the middle . . *W. Tale* iv 4 59
A father Is at the nuptial of his son a guest That best becomes the table . . . . iv 4 407
Infixed I beheld myself Drawn in the flattering table of her eye *K. John* ii 1 503
Sitting in my Dolphin-chamber, at the round table . *2 Hen. IV.* ii 1 95
Wait upon him at his table as drawers . . . . . ii 2 190
Lisping to his master's old tables, his note-book, his counsel-keeper . ii 4 289
Therefore will he wipe his tables clean And keep no tell-tale to his memory . . . . iv 1 201
I here divorce myself Both from thy table, Henry, and thy bed *3 Hen. VI.* i 1 248
The great King of kings Hath in the tables of his law commanded That thou shalt do no murder . . . . . *Richard III.* i 4 201
You may, worst Of all this table, say so . . . *Hen. VIII.* v 3 79
At Priam's royal table do I sit . . . . *Troi. and Cres.* i 1 29
Why hast thou not served thyself in to my table so many meals? . ii 3 45
And wide unclasp the tables of their thoughts To every ticklish reader! iv 5 60
A perfecter giber for the table than a necessary bencher . *Coriolanus* ii 1 91
Set at upper end o' the table; no question asked him . . . iv 5 205
By the entreaty and grant of the whole table . . . . iv 5 213
Your soldiers use him as the grace 'fore meat, Their talk at table . iv 7 4
Turn the tables up, And quench the fire . . *Rom. and Jul.* i 5 29
When he enters the confines of a tavern claps me his sword upon the table . . . . iii 1 7
Let him have a table by himself, for he does neither affect company, nor is he fit for't, indeed . . . . . *T. of Athens* i 2 30
Th' ear, Taste, touch, and smell, pleased from thy table rise . . i 2 132
There is not so much left, to furnish out A moderate table . . iii 4 117
If there sit twelve women at the table, let a dozen of them be—as they are . . . . iii 6 88
Anon we'll drink a measure The table round . . . *Macbeth* iii 4 12
The table's full.—Here is a place reserved, sir.—Where?—Here, my good lord . . . . iii 4 46
I drink to the general joy o' the whole table . . . . iii 4 89
We may again Give to our tables meat, sleep to our nights . . iii 6 34
The funeral baked meats Did coldly furnish forth the marriage tables *Hamlet* i 2 181
From the table of my memory I'll wipe away all trivial fond records . i 5 98
My tables,—meet it is I set it down, That one may smile, and smile, and be a villain . . . . i 5 107
Your fat king and your lean beggar is but variable service, two dishes, but to one table . . . . iv 3 26
God be at your table!—Conceit upon her father . . . . . iv 5 44
Flashes of merriment, that were wont to set the table on a roar . v 1 211
Set me the stoups of wine upon that table . . . . . v 2 278

Table. Though forfeiters you cast in prison, yet You clasp young Cupid's tables . . . . *Cymbeline* iii 2 39
Their tables were stored full, to glad the sight . . *Pericles* i 4 28
Table-book. Brooch, table-book, ballad, knife, tape, glove . *W. Tale* iv 4 610
If I had play'd the desk or table-book, Or given my heart a winking *Ham.* ii 2 136
Tabled. Though the catalogue of his endowments had been tabled *Cymb.* i 4 6
Table-sport. Let me for ever be your table-sport . . *Mer. Wives* iv 2 169
Tablet. This tablet lay upon his breast . . . *Cymbeline* v 4 109
Table-talk. Pray thee, let it serve for table-talk . *Mer. of Venice* iii 5 93
Tabor. Then I beat my tabor . . . . . . *Tempest* iv 1 175
And now had he rather hear the tabor and the pipe . . *Much Ado* ii 3 15
I will play On the tabor to the Worthies, and let them dance the hay *L. L. Lost* v 1 161
Dost thou live by thy tabor?—No, sir, I live by the church . *T. Night* iii 1 2
The church stands by thy tabor, if thy tabor stand by the church . iii 1 10
You would never dance again after a tabor and pipe . . *W. Tale* iv 4 183
The shepherd knows not thunder from a tabor More than I know the sound of Marcius' tongue From every meaner man . . *Coriolanus* i 6 25
Tabors and cymbals and the shouting Romans, Make the sun dance . v 4 53
Taborer. I would I could see this taborer; he lays it on . *Tempest* iii 2 160
Tabourine. Beat loud the tabourines, let the trumpets blow *Tr. and Cr.* iv 5 275
Make mingle with our rattling tabourines . . . *Ant. and Cleo.* iv 8 37
Taciturnity. The secrets of nature Have not more gift in taciturnity *Troi. and Cres.* iv 2 75
Tacked. The half shirt is two napkins tacked together . *1 Hen. IV.* iv 2 47
Tackle. A rotten carcass of a boat, not rigg'd, Nor tackle, sail, nor mast *Tempest* i 2 147
The tackle of my heart is crack'd and burn'd . . . *K. John* v 7 52
Behold Upon the hempen tackle ship-boys climbing . . *Hen. V.* iii Prol. 8
Montague our topmast; what of him? Our slaughter'd friends the tackles . . . . *3 Hen. VI.* v 4 15
Though thy tackle's torn, Thou show'st a noble vessel . *Coriolanus* iv 5 67
The silken tackle Swell with the touches of those flower-soft hands *Ant. and Cleo.* ii 2 214
Tackled. And bring thee cords made like a tackled stair *Rom. and Jul.* ii 4 201
Tackling. The friends of France our shrouds and tacklings *3 Hen. VI.* v 4 18
Like a poor bark, of sails and tackling reft, Rush all to pieces *Richard III.* iv 4 233
Tadpole. I'll broach the tadpole on my rapier's point . *T. Andron.* iv 2 85
That eats the swimming frog, the toad, the tadpole, the wall-newt *Lear* iii 4 135
Taffeta. Beauties no richer than rich taffeta . . . *L. L. Lost* v 2 159
Taffeta phrases, silken terms precise, Three-piled hyperboles . v 2 406
As your French crown for your taffeta punk . . . . *All's Well* ii 2 23
And the tailor make thy doublet of changeable taffeta . . *T. Night* ii 4 77
A fair hot wench in flame-coloured taffeta . . . . *1 Hen. IV.* i 2 11
Tag. Will you hence, Before the tag return? . . . *Coriolanus* iii 1 248
Tag-rag. If the tag-rag people did not clap him and hiss him *J. Cæsar* i 2 260
Tah. 'Rah, tah, tah,' would a' say; 'bounce,' would a' say *2 Hen. IV.* iii 2 303
Tail. He were a brave monster indeed, if they were set in his tail *Tempest* iii 2 13
Where should I lose my tongue?—In thy tale.—In thy tail! *T. G. of Ver.* ii 3 55
Ask my dog: if he say ay, it will; if he say, no, it will; if he shake his tail and say nothing, it will . . . . ii 5 37
Thou hast got more hair on thy chin than Dobbin my fill-horse has on his tail.—It should seem, then, that Dobbin's tail grows backward: I am sure he had more hair of his tail than I have of my face when I last saw him . . . . *Mer. of Venice* ii 2 101
Who knows not where a wasp does wear his sting? In his tail *T. of Shrew* ii 1 215
Whose tongue?—Yours, if you talk of tails: and so farewell.—What, with my tongue in your tail? . . . . ii 1 218
Which being spotted Is goads, thorns, nettles, tails of wasps *W. Tale* i 2 329
And like a peacock sweep along his tail . . . . *1 Hen. VI.* iii 3 6
Clapp'd his tail between his legs and cried . . . *2 Hen. VI.* v 1 154
Come, tie his body to my horse's tail . . . *Troi. and Cres.* v 8 21
He's dead; and at the murderer's horse's tail, In beastly sort, dragg'd . v 10 4
Being once subdued in armed tail, Sweet honey and sweet notes together fail . . . . v 10 44
With a tithe-pig's tail Tickling a parson's nose as a' lies asleep *R. and J.* i 4 79
And, like a rat without a tail, I'll do, I'll do, and I'll do *Macbeth* i 3 9
My father compounded with my mother under the dragon's tail . *Lear* i 2 140
Never was so frail To change the cod's head for the salmon's tail *Othello* ii 1 156
Thereby hangs a tail.—Whereby hangs a tale, sir? . . . . iii 1 8

Tail. We do fear this body hath a tail More perilous than the head *Cymb.* iv 2 144
Tailor. Yet a tailor might scratch her where'er she did itch *Tempest* ii 2 55
This secrecy of thine shall be a tailor to thee *Mer. Wives* iii 3 34
Even now a tailor call'd me in his shop And show'd me silks *C. of Er.* iv 3 7
Robin Starveling, the tailor.—Here, Peter Quince *M. N. Dream* i 2 60
Down topples she, And 'tailor' cries, and falls into a cough ii 1 54
I, for my part, knew the tailor that made the wings she flew withal *Mer. of Venice* iii 1 30
I have undone three tailors; I have had four quarrels *As Y. Like It* v 4 48
The tailor stays thy leisure, To deck thy body *T. of Shrew* iv 3 59
Come, tailor, let us see these ornaments; Lay forth the gown iv 3 61
Thy gown? why, ay: come, tailor, let us see't iv 3 86
Why, what, i' devil's name, tailor, call'st thou this? iv 3 92
Say thou wilt see the tailor paid iv 3 166
Tailor, I'll pay thee for thy gown to-morrow iv 3 168
Pray you, sir, who's his tailor? *All's Well* ii 5 18
He, sir, 's a good workman, a very good tailor ii 5 21
The tailor make thy doublet of changeable taffeta *T. Night* ii 4 76
With open mouth swallowing a tailor's news *K. John* iv 2 195
'Tis the next way to turn tailor, or be red-breast teacher 1 *Hen. IV.* iii 1 264
What trade art thou, Feeble?—A woman's tailor, sir 2 *Hen. IV.* iii 2 161
If he had been a man's tailor, he'ld ha' pricked you iii 2 164
Well said, good woman's tailor! well said! iii 2 169
And entertain some score or two of tailors *Richard III.* i 2 257
Gallants, That fill the court with quarrels, talk, and tailors *Hen. VIII.* i 3 20
This peace is nothing, but to rust iron, increase tailors *Coriolanus* iv 5 235
And the tailor with his last, the fisher with his pencil *Rom. and Jul.* i 2 40
Didst thou not fall out with a tailor for wearing his new doublet before Easter? iii 1 30
Here's an English tailor come hither, for stealing out of a French hose: come in, tailor; here you may roast your goose *Macbeth* ii 3 15
You cowardly rascal, nature disclaims in thee: a tailor made thee.—Thou art a strange fellow: a tailor make a man?—Ay, a tailor, sir *Lear* ii 2 60
When nobles are their tailors' tutors iii 2 83
He held them sixpence all too dear, With that he call'd the tailor lown *Othello* ii 3 95
When it pleaseth their deities to take the wife of a man from him, it shows to man the tailors of the earth *Ant. and Cleo.* i 2 170
A gentlewoman's son.—That's more Than some, whose tailors are as dear as yours, Can justly boast of *Cymbeline* ii 3 84
Why should his mistress, who was made by him that made the tailor, not be fit too? iv 1 4
Know'st me not by my clothes?—No, nor thy tailor iv 2 81
Thou precious varlet, My tailor made them not iv 2 84
Tailor's-yard. You tailor's-yard, you sheath, you bow-case 1 *Hen. IV.* ii 4 273
Taint. But wise men, folly-fall'n, quite taint their wit *T. Night* iii 1 75
Pursue him now, lest the device take air and taint iii 4 145
Or any taint of vice whose strong corruption Inhabits our frail blood iii 4 390
Let no quarrel . . . Taint the condition of this present hour v 1 365
A pure unspotted heart, Never yet taint with love 1 *Hen. VI.* v 3 183
We come not by the way of accusation To taint that honour every good tongue blesses *Hen. VIII.* iii 1 55
Which, since they are of you, and odious, I will not taint my mouth with iii 2 332
Commotions, uproars, with a general taint Of the whole state v 3 28
We did our main opinion crush In taint of our best man *Troi. and Cres.* i 3 374
Danger, like an ague, subtly taints Even then when we sit idly in the sun iii 3 232
Pride, Which out of daily fortune ever taints The happy man *Coriolanus* iv 7 38
Here abjure The taints and blames I laid upon myself *Macbeth* iv 3 124
Till Birnam wood remove to Dunsinane, I cannot taint with fear v 3 3
Taint not thy mind, nor let thy soul contrive Against thy mother *Hamlet* i 5 85
Breathe his faults so quaintly That they may seem the taints of liberty ii 1 32
Or your fore-vouch'd affection Fall'n into taint *Lear* i 1 224
That my disports corrupt and taint my business *Othello* i 3 272
His unkindness may defeat my life, But never taint my love iv 2 161
His taints and honours Waged equal with him *Ant. and Cleo.* v 1 30
To taint his nobler heart and brain With needless jealousy *Cymbeline* v 4 65
Tainted. Corrupt, corrupt, and tainted in desire! *Mer. Wives* v 5 94
That thou hast, whether thou art tainted or free *Meas. for Meas.* i 2 44
Pray heaven his wisdom be not tainted! iv 4 5
Bear a fair presence, though your heart be tainted *Com. of Errors* iii 2 13
In law, what plea so tainted and corrupt? *Mer. of Venice* iii 2 75
I am a tainted wether of the flock, Meetest for death iv 1 114
A very tainted fellow, and full of wickedness *All's Well* iii 2 89
For, sure, the man is tainted in's wits *T. Night* iii 4 14
My age was never tainted with such shame 1 *Hen. VI.* iv 5 46
Corrupt and tainted with a thousand vices v 4 45
Nero will be tainted with remorse, To hear and see her plaints 3 *Hen. VI.* iii 1 40
Brought him forward, As a man sorely tainted, to his answer *Hen. VIII.* iv 2 14
Their breaths with sweetmeats tainted are *Rom. and Jul.* i 4 76
Act for me, if thy faith be not tainted with the breach of hers *Cymbeline* iii 4 27
Tainting. Punish my life for tainting of my love! *T. Night* v 1 141
Anger Cassio, either by speaking too loud, or tainting his discipline *Oth.* ii 1 275
If you buy ladies' flesh at a million a dram, you cannot preserve it from tainting *Cymbeline* i 4 148
Tainture. See here the tainture of thy nest, And look thyself be faultless, thou wert best 2 *Hen. VI.* ii 1 188
Take. For one thing she did They would not take her life *Tempest* i 2 267
Go take this shape And hither come in't i 2 303
Which any print of goodness wilt not take, Being capable of all ill! i 2 352
Good Lord, how you take it! ii 1 80
We two, my lord, Will guard your person while you take your rest ii 1 197
Open-eyed conspiracy His time doth take ii 1 302
I will not take too much for him ii 2 80
That dare not offer What I desire to give, and much less take What I shall die to want iii 1 78
Give him blows And take his bottle from him iii 2 73
Didst thou not say he lied?—Thou liest.—Do I so? take thou that iii 2 84
A murrain on your monster, and the devil take your fingers iii 2 89
Show thyself in thy likeness; if thou beest a devil, take't as thou list iii 2 138
The next advantage Will we take throughly iii 3 14
Thine own acquisition Worthily purchased, take my daughter iv 1 14
If I should take a displeasure against you, look you iv 1 202
He's a bastard one—had plotted with them To take my life v 1 274
Go, sirrah, to my cell; Take with you your companions v 1 292
What a thrice-double ass Was I, to take this drunkard for a god! v 1 296
To my poor cell, where you shall take your rest v 1 301
To hear the story of your life, which must Take the ear strangely v 1 313
Now let us take our leave *T. G. of Ver.* i 1 56
Take it for your pains.—No, no; you shall have it i 1 124
What said she? nothing?—No, not so much as 'Take this for thy pains' i 1 151
Take. Take the paper: see it be return'd *T. G. of Ver.* i 2 46
Why didst thou stoop, then?—To take a paper up that I let fall i 2 73
If you respect them, best to take them up i 2 134
And by and by a cloud takes all away! i 3 87
To fast, like one that takes diet ii 1 25
Yet I care not; And yet take this again; and yet I thank you ii 1 124
But since unwillingly, take them again. Nay, take them ii 1 129
If it please you, take it for your labour ii 1 139
We'll make exchange: here, take you this ii 2 6
Take a note of what I stand in need of ii 7 84
I now am full resolved to take a wife And turn her out to who will take her in iii 1 76
Take no repulse, whatever she doth say iii 1 100
My daughter takes his going grievously iii 2 14
You take the sum and substance that I have iv 1 15
I take your offer and will live with you iv 1 70
To take a fault upon me that he did iv 4 15
Go presently and take this ring with thee iv 4 70
Come, shadow, come, and take this shadow up iv 4 202
Here she stands: Take but possession of her with a touch v 4 130
Take thou thy Silvia, for thou hast deserved her v 4 147
Take your vizaments in that *Mer. Wives* i 1 39
And by my side wear steel? then, Lucifer take all! i 3 84
I will run no base humour: here, take the humour-letter i 3 85
Come, take-a your rapier, and come after my heel to the court i 4 61
Hang the trifle, woman! take the honour ii 1 46
Do what she will, say what she will, take all, pay all ii 2 123
Take all, or half, for easing me of the carriage ii 2 179
Take your rapier, Jack; I vill tell you how I vill kill him ii 3 13
Well; I will take him, then torture my wife iii 2 41
If he take her, let him take her simply iii 2 77
Without any pause or staggering take this basket on your shoulders iii 3 12
In the house by your consent, to take an ill advantage of his absence iii 3 116
I will now take the lecher; he is at my house iii 5 146
Take the basket again on your shoulders: your master is hard at door iv 2 110
Come, take it up.—Pray heaven it be not full of knight again iv 2 114
Appoint a meeting with this old fat fellow, Where we may take him iv 4 16
There he blasts the tree and takes the cattle iv 4 32
The devil take one party and his dam the other! iv 5 108
Take her by the hand and bid her go iv 6 37
Take her by the hand, away with her to the deanery v 3 2
I will never take you for my love again v 5 121
Why, did you take her in green?—Ay, by gar, and 'tis a boy v 5 221
Take thy commission *Meas. for Meas.* i 1 48
Therefore take your honours i 1 53
The jewel that we find, we stoop and take't Because we see it ii 1 24
I do repent me, as it is an evil, And take the shame with joy ii 3 36
I'll take it as a peril to my soul, It is no sin at all ii 4 65
Is't not a kind of incest, to take life From thine own sister's shame? iii 1 139
Take my defiance! Die, perish! iii 1 143
What a merit were it in death to take this poor maid from the world! iii 1 240
We take him to be a thief too, sir iii 2 17
Take him to prison, officer: Correction and instruction must both work iii 2 32
If you take it not patiently, why, your mettle is the more iii 2 79
Take, O, take those lips away, That so sweetly were forsworn iv 1 1
Take, then, this your companion by the hand iv 1 55
She'll take the enterprise upon her, father, If you advise it iv 1 66
If you will take it on you to assist him, it shall redeem you iv 2 10
Take him hence; to the rack with him! v 1 313
Take her hence, and marry her instantly v 1 382
Sweet Isabel, take my part; Lend me your knees v 1 435
Her brother's ghost his paved bed would break, And take her hence in horror v 1 441
Take this mercy to provide For better times to come v 1 489
Take him to prison; And see our pleasure herein executed v 1 526
Gaoler, take him to thy custody *Com. of Errors* i 1 156
Many a man would take you at your word i 2 17
Wilt thou flout me thus unto my face, Being forbid? There, take you that i 2 92
Hold your hands! Nay, an you will not, sir, I'll take my heels i 2 94
Look, when I serve him so, he takes it ill ii 1 12
Take thou that, and that.—Hold, sir, for God's sake! ii 2 23
As easy mayst thou . . . take unmingled thence that drop again, Without addition or diminishing, As take from me thyself and not me too ii 2 129
Though my cates be mean, take them in good part iii 1 28
Spread o'er the silver waves thy golden hairs, And as a bed I'll take them iii 2 49
Take the stranger to my house And with you take the chain iv 1 36
He is mad. Some get within him, take his sword away v 1 34
Run, master, run; for God's sake, take a house! v 1 36
And take perforce my husband from the abbess v 1 117
And vows, if he can take you, To scorch your face v 1 182
There, take it; and much thanks for my good cheer v 1 392
Take the pains To go with us into the abbey v 1 393
When you depart from me, sorrow abides and happiness takes his leave *Much Ado* i 1 102
In what key shall a man take you, to go in the song? i 1 188
In her bosom I'll unclasp my heart And take her hearing prisoner i 1 326
He meant to take the present time by the top i 2 15
It is impossible you should take true root i 3 24
I will even take sixpence in earnest of the bear-ward ii 1 42
Take of me my daughter, and with her my fortunes ii 1 313
And I take him to be valiant.—As Hector, I assure you ii 3 195
Just so much as you may take upon a knife's point ii 3 263
Any pains that I take for you is as easy as thanks ii 3 270
She cannot love, Nor take no shape nor project of affection iii 1 55
Why, then, take no note of him, but let him go iii 3 29
The most peaceable way for you, if you do take a thief, is to let him show himself what he is iii 3 61
Take their examination yourself and bring it me iii 5 53
Take her back again: Give not this rotten orange to your friend iv 1 32
O Fate! take not away thy heavy hand. Death is the fairest cover iv 1 116
As I dare take a serpent by the tongue v 1 90
Take her hand Before this friar and swear to marry her v 4 56
I will have thee; but, by this light, I take thee for pity v 4 93
I would take Desire prisoner *L. L. Lost* i 2 64
You must suffer him to take no delight nor no penance i 2 134
It was well done of you to take him at his word ii 1 217
Take this key, give enlargement to the swain iii 1 5
Doth the inconsiderate take salve for l'envoy? iii 1 79
Here, good my glass, take this for telling true iv 1 18

Take. Hold, take thou this, my sweet, and give me thine, So shall Biron take me for Rosaline *L. L. Lost* v 2 132

Say you so? Fair lord,—Take that for your fair lady v 2 240

I'll not be your half: Take all, and wean it; it may prove an ox v 2 250

But that you take what doth to you belong, It were a fault to snatch words from my tongue v 2 381

And to confirm it plain, You gave me this: but take it, sir, again v 2 453

We will turn it finely off, sir; we will take some care v 2 511

The whole world again Cannot pick out five such, take each one in his vein v 2 548

Let me take you a button-hole lower v 2 706

Flute, you must take Thisby on you *M. N. Dream* i 2 46

Ere I take this charm from off her sight, As I can take it ii 1 183

Take thou some of it, and seek through this grove ii 1 259

Do it for thy true-love take, Love and languish for his sake ii 2 28

O, take the sense, sweet, of my innocence! Love takes the meaning in love's conference ii 2 45

When I did him at this advantage take iii 2 16

Dark night, that from the eye his function takes iii 2 177

She shall not, though you take her part iii 2 322

Let her alone: speak not of Helena; Take not her part iii 2 333

This virtuous property, To take from thence all error with his might iii 2 368

And the country proverb known, That every man should take his own iii 2 459

Take this transformed scalp From off the head of this Athenian swain iv 1 69

Go, bring them in: and take your places, ladies v 1 84

Our sport shall be to take what they mistake v 1 90

What poor duty cannot do, noble respect Takes it in might, not merit v 1 92

I trust to take of truest Thisby sight v 1 280

Tongue, lose thy light; Moon, take thy flight v 1 310

With this field-dew consecrate, Every fairy take his gait v 1 423

The four strangers seek for you, madam, to take their leave *Mer. of Ven.* i 2 136

I think I may take his bond.—Be assured you may i 3 28

For when did friendship take A breed for barren metal of his friend? i 3 134

Supply your present wants and take no doit Of usance for my moneys i 3 141

To buy his favour, I extend this friendship: If he will take it, so i 3 170

You must take your chance ii 1 38

Hold here, take this: tell gentle Jessica I will not fail her ii 4 20

She hath directed How I shall take her from her father's house ii 4 31

There, take it, prince; and if my form lie there, Then I am yours ii 7 61

Take what wife you will to bed, I will ever be your head ii 9 70

I am sure, if he forfeit, thou wilt not take his flesh iii 1 54

If he had The present money to discharge the Jew, He would not take it iii 2 277

Take this same letter, And use thou all the endeavour of a man In speed iii 4 47

You are welcome: take your place iv 1 170

It [mercy] is twice blest; It blesseth him that gives and him that takes iv 1 187

Be merciful: Take thrice thy money; bid me tear the bond iv 1 234

Take then thy bond, take thou thy pound of flesh iv 1 308

I take this offer, then; pay the bond thrice iv 1 318

Why doth the Jew pause? take thy forfeiture iv 1 335

Nay, take my life and all; pardon not that: You take my house when you do take the prop That doth sustain my house; you take my life When you do take the means whereby I live iv 1 374

Take some remembrance of us, as a tribute, Not as a fee iv 1 422

I'll take this ring from you: Do not draw back your hand; I'll take no more iv 1 427

Since you do take it, love, so much at heart v 1 145

And neither man nor master would take aught But the two rings v 1 183

Let not me take him, then; For if I do, I'll mar the young clerk's pen v 1 236

Besides this nothing that he so plentifully gives me, the something that nature gave me his countenance seems to take from me *As Y. Like It* i 1 19

The same tradition takes not away my blood i 1 51

Wert thou not my brother, I would not take this hand from thy throat i 1 63

I could have taught my love to take thy father for mine i 2 12

That all the beholders take his part with weeping i 2 140

You will take little delight in it, I can tell you i 2 168

Wrestle with thy affections.—O, they take the part of a better wrestler! i 3 22

Do not seek to take your change upon you, To bear your griefs yourself i 3 104

I have five hundred crowns, The thrifty hire I saved . . . : Take that ii 3 43

Take upon command what help we have ii 7 125

Take the cork out of thy mouth that I may drink thy tidings iii 2 213

Nay, but the devil take mocking: speak, sad brow and true maid iii 2 226

Take a taste of my finding him, and relish it with good observance iii 2 246

Which I take to be either a fool or a cipher iii 2 308

I will not take her on gift of any man iii 3 69

Cry the man mercy; love him; take his offer iii 5 61

So take her to thee, shepherd: fare you well iii 5 63

Am not I your Rosalind?—I take some joy to say you are iv 1 90

You must say 'I take thee, Rosalind, for wife.'—I take thee, Rosalind iv 1 135

But I do take thee, Orlando, for my husband iv 1 139

You shall never take her without her answer, unless you take her without her tongue iv 1 175

Take thou no scorn to wear the horn iv 2 14

The faithful offer take Of me and all that I can make iv 3 60

We'll lead you thither. I pray you, will you take him by the arm? iv 3 163

Take a good heart and counterfeit to be a man iv 3 174

Therefore take the present time, With a hey, and a ho v 3 31

A poor humour of mine, sir, to take that that no man else will v 4 61

Purposely to take His brother here and put him to the sword v 4 163

I take him for the better dog *T. of Shrew* Ind. 1 25

Take him up and manage well the jest Ind. 1 45

Take him up gently and to bed with him Ind. 1 72

Go, sirrah, take them to the buttery Ind. 1 102

Take a lodging fit to entertain Such friends as time in Padua shall beget i 1 44

As though, belike, I knew not what to take, and what to leave i 1 104

Would take her with all faults, and money enough i 1 133

I had as lief take her dowry with this condition, to be whipped i 1 135

Is it possible That love should of a sudden take such hold? i 1 152

At once Uncase thee; take my colour'd hat and cloak i 1 212

Take your paper too, And let me have them very well perfumed i 2 151

Take you the lute, and you the set of books; You shall go see your pupils ii 1 107

Therefore, Kate, Take this of me, Kate of my consolation ii 1 191

Shall a buzzard take thee?—Ay, for a turtle, as he takes a buzzard ii 1 208

Take you your instrument, play you the whiles iii 1 22

Take it not unkindly, pray, That I have been thus pleasant with you both iii 1 57

'B mi,' Bianca, take him for thy lord, 'C fa ut,' that loves iii 1 75

The priest let fall the book; And, as he stoop'd again to take it up, The mad-brain'd bridegroom took him such a cuff iii 2 164

'Now take them up,' quoth he, 'if any list' iii 2 167

Take. You'll prove a jolly surly groom, That take it on you at the first so roundly *T. of Shrew* iii 2 216

Supply the bridegroom's place; And let Bianca take her sister's room iii 2 252

What, no man at door To hold my stirrup nor to take my horse! iv 1 124

There, take it to you, trenchers, cups, and all iv 1 168

And here I take the like unfeigned oath iv 2 32

Take thou the bill, give me thy mete-yard, and spare not me iv 3 152

Go, take it up unto thy master's use.—Villain, not for thy life: take up my mistress' gown for thy master's use! iv 3 159

Take no unkindness of his hasty words iv 3 169

Take you assurance of her, 'cum privilegio ad imprimendum solum' iv 4 92

Take the priest, clerk, and some sufficient honest witnesses iv 4 94

The tyranny of her sorrows takes all livelihood from her cheek *All's Well* i 1 58

After them, and take a more dilated farewell ii 1 59

I dare not say I take you; but I give Me and my service ii 3 109

Why, then, young Bertram, take her; she's thy wife.—My wife, my liege! ii 3 112

Take her by the hand, And tell her she is thine . . . —I take her hand ii 3 180

Well, thou hast a son shall take this disgrace off me ii 3 249

What's his will else?—That you will take your instant leave ii 4 49

This drives me to entreat you That presently you take your way for home ii 5 69

I take my young lord to be a very melancholy man iii 2 3

Alas! and would you take the letter of her? iii 4 1

We'll take your offer kindly iii 5 104

Take this purse of gold, And let me buy your friendly help iii 7 14

What is not holy, that we swear not by, But take the High'st to witness iv 2 24

Here, take my ring: My house, mine honour, yea, my life, be thine iv 2 51

I'll order take my mother shall not hear iv 2 55

That he might take a measure of his own judgements iv 3 38

When he swears oaths, bid him drop gold, and take it iv 3 252

Match, and well make it; He ne'er pays after-debts, take it before iv 3 255

Which I take to be too little for pomp to enter iv 5 54

Let's take the instant by the forward top v 3 39

Howe'er it pleases you to take it so, The ring was never hers v 3 88

Take him away . . . Away with him! We'll sift this matter further v 3 120

Take her away; I do not like her now; To prison with her v 3 282

Take her away.—I'll put in bail, my liege v 3 286

Your gentle hands lend us, and take our hearts Epil. 340

To take the death of her brother thus *T. Night* i 3 2

Your cousin, my lady, takes great exceptions to your ill hours i 3 5

I hope to see a housewife take thee between her legs and spin it off i 3 109

God bless thee, lady!—Take the fool away i 5 42

I take these wise men, that crow so at these set kind of fools, no better than the fools' zanies i 5 94

Take those things for bird-bolts that you deem cannon-bullets i 5 99

I told him you were sick; he takes on him to understand so much i 5 149

Come to me again, To tell me how he takes it i 5 301

If I do not, never trust me, take it how you will ii 3 204

Let still the woman take An elder than herself; so wears she to him ii 4 30

And does not Toby take you a blow o' the lips then? ii 5 75

My lady will strike him: if she do, he'll smile and take't for a great favour iii 2 89

Hob, nob, is his word; give't or take't iii 4 263

I take the fault on me: If you offend him, I for him defy you iii 4 344

Take him away: he knows I know him well.—I must obey iii 4 365

Let your bounty take a nap v 1 52

But more of that anon. Take him aside v 1 103

Take thy fortunes up; Be that thou know'st thou art v 1 151

Take her; but direct thy feet Where thou and I henceforth may never meet v 1 171

When at Bohemia You take my lord, I'll give him my commission *W. T.* i 2 40

Will you take eggs for money? i 2 161

Your highness Will take again your queen as yours at first i 2 336

Please your highness To take the urgent hour. Come, sir, away i 2 465

Take the boy to you: he so troubles me, 'Tis past enduring ii 1 1

The office Becomes a woman best; I'll take't upon me ii 2 32

Let him be Until a time may serve: for present vengeance, Take it on her ii 3 23

Unless he take the course that you have done, Commit me ii 3 48

When she will take the rein I let her run; But she'll not stumble ii 3 51

Take her hence.—A most unworthy and unnatural lord Can do no more ii 3 112

Take it hence And see it instantly consumed with fire ii 3 133

Take it up straight: Within this hour bring me word 'tis done ii 3 135

Go, take it to the fire; For thou set'st on thy wife.—I did not ii 3 140

Take it up.—I swear to do this ii 3 183

Devised And play'd to take spectators iii 2 38

Take her hence: Her heart is but o'ercharged; she will recover iii 2 150

Take your patience to you, And I'll say nothing iii 2 232

I'll take it up for pity: yet I'll tarry till my son come iii 3 77

It is my father's will I should take on me The hostess-ship o' the day iv 4 71

And take The winds of March with beauty iv 4 119

Come, take your flowers iv 4 132

If I were not in love with Mopsa, thou shouldst take no money of me iv 4 234

Your heart is full of something that does take Your mind from feasting iv 4 357

I take thy hand, this hand, As soft as dove's down and as white as it iv 4 373

No hope to help you, But as you shake off one to take another iv 4 580

Indeed, I have had earnest; but I cannot with conscience take it iv 4 660

Take your sweetheart's hat And pluck it o'er your brows, muffle your face iv 4 664

Thou shouldst a husband take by my consent, As I by thine a wife v 3 136

Then take my king's defiance from my mouth *K. John* i 1 21

Brother, take you my land, I'll take my chance i 1 151

O, take his mother's thanks, a widow's thanks! ii 1 32

But, ass, I'll take that burthen from your back ii 1 145

Which heaven shall take in nature of a fee ii 1 170

With my vex'd spirits I cannot take a truce iii 1 17

It is the curse of kings to be attended By slaves that take their humours for a warrant iv 2 209

Heaven take my soul, and England keep my bones! iv 3 10

How easy dost thou take all England up! iv 3 142

Take again From this my hand, as holding of the pope v 1 2

Even at your door, To cudgel you and make you take the hatch v 2 138

He means to recompense the pains you take By cutting off your heads v 4 15

How did he take it? who did taste to him?—A monk, I tell you v 6 28

Nor let my kingdom's rivers take their course Through my burn'd bosom v 7 38

Such offers of our peace As we with honour and respect may take v 7 85

Take but my shame, And I resign my gage *Richard II.* i 1 175

Take honour from me, and my life is done i 1 183

My companion peers, Take from my mouth the wish of happy years i 3 94

Return again, and take an oath with thee i 3 178

Take Hereford's rights away, and take from Time His charters ii 1 195

Take. Bid her send me presently a thousand pound: Hold, take my ring *Richard II.* ii 2 92
Heaven will take our souls And plague injustice with the pains of hell iii 1 33
My kind commends; Take special care my greetings be deliver'd iii 1 39
Take not, good cousin, further than you should iii 3 15
O God! that e'er this tongue of mine, That laid the sentence of dread banishment On yon proud man, should take it off again With words of sooth! iii 3 135
Bagot, forbear; thou shalt not take it up iv 1 30
Wilt thou, pupil-like, Take thy correction mildly? v 1 32
Thus give I mine, and thus take I thy heart v 1 96
'Twere no good part To take on me to keep and kill thy heart v 1 98
Takes on the point of honour to support So dissolute a crew v 3 11
The devil take Henry of Lancaster and thee! Patience is stale v 5 103
The guilt of conscience take thou for thy labour v 6 41
Where shall we take a purse to-morrow, Jack? *1 Hen. IV.* i 2 110
O, the devil take such cozeners! God forgive me! i 3 255
They dare not meet each other; Each takes his fellow for an officer ii 2 114
'Tis dangerous to take a cold, to sleep ii 3 9
What is't that takes from thee thy stomach, pleasure, and thy golden sleep? ii 3 43
They take it already upon their salvation ii 4 9
I would your grace would take me with you: whom means your grace? ii 4 506
Gelding the opposed continent as much As on the other side it takes from you iii 1 111
Shall I not take mine ease in mine inn? iii 3 92
Let us take a muster speedily: Doomsday is near iv 1 133
An if it do, take it for thy labour; and if it make twenty, take them all iv 2 7
And now, forsooth, takes on him to reform Some certain edicts iv 3 78
I am content that he shall take the odds v 1 97
And, will they take the offer of our grace, Both he and they and you v 1 106
We offer fair; take it advisedly v 1 114
Thou get'st not my sword; but take my pistol, if thou wilt v 3 52
Adieu, and take thy praise with thee to heaven! v 4 99
I'll take it upon my death, I gave him this wound v 4 154
I will take it as a sweet disgrace *2 Hen. IV.* i 1 89
Men of all sorts take a pride to gird at me i 2 7
He would not take his band and yours; he liked not the security i 2 37
He that looks upon me will take me without weighing i 2 188
I take but two shirts out with me, and I mean not to sweat i 2 234
O earth, yield us that king again, And take thou this! i 3 107
You are to take soldiers up in counties as you go ii 1 199
And turn all to a merriment, if you take not the heat ii 4 324
The winds, Who take the ruffian billows by the top iii 1 22
I will take your counsel iii 1 106
I will take such order that thy friends shall ring for thee iii 2 198
I take not on me here as a physician iv 1 60
You overween to take it so; This offer comes from mercy iv 1 149
Then take, my Lord of Westmoreland, this schedule iv 1 168
I take your princely word for these redresses.—I give it you iv 2 66
They take their courses East, west, north, south iv 2 103
I pray you, take me up, and bear me hence Into some other chamber iv 4 131
O my son, God put it in thy mind to take it hence! iv 5 179
Ignorant carriage is caught, as men take diseases, one of another v 1 85
I would not take a knighthood for my fortune v 3 133
Let us take any man's horses v 3 142
Carry Sir John Falstaff to the Fleet: Take all his company along with him v 5 98
I cannot now speak: I will hear you soon. Take them away v 5 101
Divide your happy England into four; Whereof take you one quarter into France *Hen. V.* i 2 215
For I can take, and Pistol's cock is up, And flashing fire will follow ii 1 55
Which makes much against my manhood, if I should take from another's pocket to put into mine iii 2 53
Ere theise eyes of mine take themselves to slomber iii 2 123
Look you, if you take the matter otherwise than is meant iii 2 136
If you would take the pains but to examine the wars of Pompey the Great iv 1 69
By this hand, I will take thee a box on the ear iv 1 231
I will do it, though I take thee in the king's company iv 1 236
Take from them now The sense of reckoning iv 1 307
I will the banner from a trumpet take, And use it for my haste iv 2 61
I beg The leading of the vaward.—Take it, brave York iv 3 131
Tell him my fury shall abate, and I The crowns will take iv 4 51
The devil take order now! I'll to the throng iv 5 22
York, all haggled over, Comes to him, where in gore he lay insteep'd, And takes him by the beard iv 6 13
It is not well done, mark you now, to take the tales out of my mouth iv 7 45
Take a trumpet, herald; Ride thou unto the horsemen on yon hill iv 7 59
Not a man of them that we shall take Shall taste our mercy iv 7 67
Your majesty takes no scorn to wear the leek upon Saint Tavy's day iv 7 107
I have sworn to take him a box o' th' ear iv 7 133
I beseech you take it for your own fault and not mine iv 8 57
Take it, God, For it is none but thine! iv 8 116
Be it death proclaimed through our host To boast of this or take that praise from God Which is his only iv 8 120
Me a groat!—Yes, verily and in truth, you shall take it v 1 64
I take thy groat in earnest of revenge v 1 67
Take with you free power to ratify, Augment, or alter v 2 86
I speak to thee plain soldier: if thou canst love me for this, take me v 2 157
Dear Kate, take a fellow of plain and uncoined constancy v 2 160
If thou would have such a one, take me; and take me, take a soldier; take a soldier, take a king v 2 175
A boy, half French, half English, that shall go to Constantinople and take the Turk by the beard v 2 222
For my English moiety take the word of a king and a bachelor v 2 229
Take her, fair son, and from her blood raise up Issue to me v 2 376
We'll take your oath, And all the peers', for surety of our leagues v 2 399
For their sake, In your fair minds let this acceptance take Epil. 14
Reignier, Duke of Anjou, doth take his part *1 Hen. VI.* i 1 94
Ten thousand soldiers with me I will take i 1 155
Take you no care; I'll never trouble you, if I may spy them i 4 21
Sirs, take your places and be vigilant ii 1 1
In that thou laid'st a trap to take my life ii 1 22
Belike your lordship takes us then for fools ii 2 62
Now will we take some order in the town ii 2 126
Charles and the rest will take thee in their arms iii 3 77
And in our coronation take your place iii 4 27
As good a man as York.—Hark ye; not so: in witness, take ye that iii 4 37
Governor of Paris, take your oath, That you elect no other king but him iv 1 3

Take. Let me persuade you take a better course *1 Hen. VI.* iv 1 132
And take foul scorn to fawn on him by sending iv 4 35
Pause, and take thy breath iv 6 4
Go, take their bodies hence.—I'll bear them hence iv 7 91
Then take my soul, my body, soul and all v 3 22
Kneel down and take my blessing, good my girl. Wilt thou not stoop? v 4 25
Take her away; for she hath lived too long v 4 34
Take this compact of a truce, Although you break it when your pleasure serves v 4 163
Take, therefore, shipping; post, my lord, to France v 5 87
I will take the Nevils' parts And make a show of love *2 Hen. VI.* i 1 240
Here, Hume, take this reward; make merry, man i 2 85
If you take not heed, you shall go near To call them both i 2 102
Take this fellow in, and send for his master i 3 36
Strangers in court do take her for the queen i 3 82
By water shall he die, and take his end i 4 36; 68
You, madam, shall with us. Stafford, take her to thee i 4 55
Follow the knave; and take this drab away ii 1 156
Will, thou shalt have my hammer: and here, Tom, take all the money that I have ii 3 76
So please your grace, we'll take her from the sheriff ii 4 17
Stanley is appointed now To take her with him to the Isle of Man ii 4 78
Go, and take me hence; I care not whither, for I beg no favour ii 4 91
I would have him dead . . . Ere you can take due orders for a priest iii 1 274
Worse than nought? nay, then, a shame take all! iii 1 307
Take thou this task in hand.—I am content iii 1 318
You will give them me: I take it kindly iii 1 346
Lords, take your places; and, I pray you all, Proceed no straiter iii 2 19
Cease, gentle queen, these execrations And let thy Suffolk take his heavy leave iii 2 306
Embrace and kiss and take ten thousand leaves iii 2 354
I go.—And take my heart with thee iii 2 408
Be not so rash; take ransom, let him live iv 1 28
And such As would, but that they dare not, take our parts iv 2 197
Take him away, and behead him iv 7 101
Go, take him away, I say, and strike off his head presently iv 7 115
Conditionally, that here thou take an oath To cease this civil war *3 Hen. VI.* i 1 196
This oath I willingly take and will perform i 1 201
It is war's prize to take all vantages i 4 59
There, take the crown, and, with the crown, my curse i 4 164
Hard-hearted Clifford, take me from the world i 4 167
See how the morning opes her golden gates, And takes her farewell of the glorious sun! ii 1 22
So many hours must I take my rest; So many hours must I contemplate ii 5 32
I, that haply take them from him now, May yet ere night yield both ii 5 58
I'll away before.—Nay, take me with thee, good sweet Exeter ii 5 137
Whose soul is that which takes her heavy leave? ii 6 42
Say that King Edward take thee for his queen?—'Tis better said than done iii 2 89
And all the unlook'd for issue of their bodies, To take their rooms iii 2 132
Deceive more slily than Ulysses could, And, like a Sinon, take another Troy iii 2 190
Where I must take like seat unto my fortune iii 3 10
We may surprise and take him at our pleasure iv 2 17
Come on, my masters, each man take his stand iv 3 1
He hath made a solemn vow Never to lie and take his natural rest iv 3 5
Let us fly while we may fly: If Warwick take us we are sure to die iv 4 35
And take the great-grown traitor unawares iv 8 63
And, weakling, Warwick takes his gift again; And Henry is my king v 1 37
Take the time; kneel down, kneel down: Nay, when? strike now v 1 48
Sweet Oxford, thanks.—And take his thanks that yet hath nothing else v 4 59
I will shortly send thy soul to heaven, If heaven will take the present at our hands *Richard III.* i 1 120
Which done, God take King Edward to his mercy! i 1 151
Vouchsafe to wear this ring.—To take is not to give i 2 203
To take her in her heart's extremest hate, With curses in her mouth i 2 232
And take deep traitors for thy dearest friends! i 3 224
Seize on him, Furies, take him to your torments! i 4 57
Take the devil in thy mind, and believe him not i 4 151
Take him over the costard with the hilts of thy sword i 4 159
Take not the quarrel from his powerful arm i 4 223
Take thou the fee, and tell him what I say i 4 284
I do beseech your majesty To take our brother Clarence to your grace ii 1 76
God is much displeased That you take with unthankfulness his doing ii 2 90
I'll give my voice, Which, I presume, he'll take in gentle part iii 4 21
Now will I in, to take some privy order iii 5 106
Play the maid's part, still answer nay, and take it iii 7 51
Happy were England, would this gracious prince Take on himself the sovereignty iii 7 79
We heartily solicit Your gracious self to take on you the charge iii 7 131
Take to your royal self This proffer'd benefit of dignity iii 7 195
I do beseech you, take it not amiss; I cannot nor I will not yield to you iii 7 206
I'll bear thy blame And take thy office from thee, on my peril iv 1 26
Take all the swift advantage of the hours; You shall have letters from me iv 1 49
Therefore take with thee my most heavy curse iv 4 187
If I did take the kingdom from your sons, To make amends, I'll give it to your daughter iv 4 294
We must have knocks; ha! must we not?—We must both give and take v 3 6
I'll strive, with troubled thoughts, to take a nap v 3 104
And take it from a heart that wishes towards you Honour *Hen. VIII.* i 1 103
Repeat your will and take it.—Thank your majesty i 2 13
Why, we take From every tree lop, bark, and part o' the timber i 2 95
Take good heed You charge not in your spleen a noble person i 2 173
Place you that side; I'll take the charge of this: His grace is entering i 4 20
For which I pay 'em A thousand thanks, and pray 'em take their pleasures i 4 74
I were unmannerly, to take you out, And not to kiss you i 4 95
To put me off, And take your good grace from me ii 4 22
Take thy lute, wench: my soul grows sad with troubles iii 1 1
I would your grace Would leave your griefs, and take my counsel iii 1 92
I know A way, if it take right, in spite of fortune Will bring me off iii 2 219
Now, who'll take it?—The king, that gave it.—It must be himself, then iii 2 250
Take an inventory of all I have, To the last penny iii 2 451
You come to take your stand here, and behold The Lady Anne pass iv 1 2
And heartily entreats you take good comfort iv 2 119
It will ne'er be well, 'Twill not, Sir Thomas Lovell, take't of me v 1 30
You must take Your patience to you, and be well contented v 1 104
You take a precipice for no leap of danger, And woo your own destruction v 1 139

Take. By virtue of that ring, I take my cause Out of the gripes of cruel men *Hen. VIII.* v 3 99

Respect him; Take him, and use him well, he's worthy of it v 3 155

Ye rascals: do you take the court for Paris-garden? v 4 2

With this kiss take my blessing: God protect thee! v 5 11

Some come to take their ease, And sleep an act or two Epil. 2

There's laying on, take't off who will, as they say *Troi. and Cres.* i 2 224

Had I a sister were a grace, or a daughter a goddess, he should take his choice i 2 258

Take but degree away, untune that string, And, hark, what discord follows! i 3 109

He bade me take a trumpet, And to this purpose speak i 3 263

Whosoever you take him to be, he is Ajax ii 1 70

I take to-day a wife, and my election Is led on in the conduct of my will ii 2 61

If ye take not that little little less than little wit from them that they have! ii 3 14

Take the instant way; For honour travels in a strait so narrow iii 3 153

What think you of this man that takes me for the general? iii 3 263

Would he not, a naughty man, let it sleep? a bugbear take him! iv 2 34

The devil take Antenor! the young prince will go mad iv 2 77

That the bless'd gods, as angry with my fancy, . . . take thee from me iv 4 29

I'll take that winter from your lips, fair lady iv 5 24

I'll make my match to live, The kiss you take is better than you give iv 5 38

I have seen thee pause and take thy breath, When that a ring of Greeks have hemm'd thee in iv 5 192

Take and take again such preposterous discoveries! v 1 27

Any man may sing her, if he can take her cliff; she's noted v 2 11

Takes my glove, And gives memorial dainty kisses to it v 2 79

He that takes that doth take my heart withal v 2 82

'Twas one's that loved me better than you will. But, now you have it, take it v 2 90

Nothing else holds fashion: a burning devil take them! v 2 197

Give me leave To take that course by your consent v 3 74

Shouldst thou take the river Styx, I would swim after v 4 20

Take thou Troilus' horse; Present the fair steed to my lady Cressid v 5 1

Here, there, and every where, he leaves and takes v 5 26

Farewell, bastard.—The devil take thee, coward! v 7 24

Now is my day's work done; I'll take good breath v 8 3

Whose course will on The way it takes, cracking ten thousand curbs *Cor.* i 1 72

The Volsces have much corn; take these rats thither To gnaw their garners i 1 253

Take your commission; hie you to your bands i 2 26

He that retires, I'll take him for a Volsce, And he shall feel mine edge i 4 28

Valiant Titus, take Convenient numbers to make good the city i 5 12

Take your choice of those That best can aid your action i 6 65

But cannot make my heart consent to take A bribe to pay my sword i 9 37

I, that now Refused most princely gifts, am bound to beg Of my lord general.—Take't; 'tis yours. What is't? i 9 81

At the least, if you take it as a pleasure to you in being so ii 1 34

Take my cap, Jupiter, and I thank thee. Hoo! ii 1 115

Take to you, as your predecessors have, Your honour with your form ii 2 147

They have chose a consul that will from them take Their liberties ii 3 222

Confusion May enter 'twixt the gap of both and take The one by the other iii 1 111

Enough, with over-measure.—No, take more iii 1 140

Here's he that would take from you all your power iii 1 182

Do not take His rougher accents for malicious sounds iii 3 54

What is the matter That being pass'd for consul with full voice, I am so dishonour'd that the very hour You take it off again? iii 3 61

You have contrived to take From Rome all season'd office iii 3 63

Whither wilt thou go? Take good Cominius With thee awhile iv 1 34

Take my prayers with you iv 2 44

They are in a ripe aptness to take all power from the people iv 3 24

Most glad of your company.—You take my part from me, sir iv 3 55

Whose plots have broke their sleep To take the one the other iv 4 20

Come, go in, And take our friendly senators by the hands iv 5 138

Take The one half of my commission iv 5 143

But I take him to be the greater soldier iv 5 175

As is the osprey to the fish, who takes it By sovereignty of nature iv 7 34

Yet, for I loved thee, Take this along; I writ it for thy sake v 2 96

His own impatience Takes from Aufidius a great part of blame v 6 147

Take him up. Help, three o' the chiefest soldiers v 6 149

Lest, then, the people, and patricians too, . . . take Titus' part *T. An.* i 1 446

Take this of me: Lucrece was not more chaste Than this Lavinia ii 1 108

There speak, and strike, brave boys, and take your turns ii 1 129

Seest thou this letter? take it up, I pray thee, And give the king ii 3 46

'Tis pity they should take him for a stag ii 3 71

Who found this letter? Tamora, was it you?—Andronicus himself did take it up ii 3 294

Come, brother, take a head; And in this hand the other will I bear iii 1 280

Grief has so wrought on him, He takes false shadows for true substances iii 2 80

See that you take no longer days, But send the midwife presently to me iv 2 165

Sirs, take you to your tools iv 3 6

For now he firmly takes me for Revenge v 2 73

Now will I hence about thy business, And take my ministers along v 2 133

Know you these two?—The empress' sons, I take them v 2 154

Take you in this barbarous Moor, This ravenous tiger v 3 4

Please you, therefore, draw nigh, and take your places v 3 24

O, take this warm kiss on thy pale cold lips! v 3 153

A pair of star-cross'd lovers take their life *Rom. and Jul.* Prol. 6

Take it in what sense thou wilt.—They must take it in sense that feel it i 1 31

Let us take the law of our sides; let them begin i 1 44

I will frown as I pass by, and let them take it as they list i 1 47

Take thou some new infection to thy eye i 2 50

Take our good meaning i 4 46

Be brisk awhile, and the longer liver take all i 5 17

Then move not, while my prayer's effect I take i 5 108

Take all myself.—I take thee at thy word: Call me but love ii 2 49

I will take thy word: yet, if thou swear'st, Thou mayst prove false ii 2 91

I'll take him down, an a' were lustier than he is, and twenty such Jacks ii 4 159

Peter, take my fan, and go before, and apace ii 4 232

Give me occasion.—Could you not take some occasion without giving? iii 1 46

Now, Tybalt, take the villain back again, That late thou gavest me iii 1 130

When he shall die, Take him and cut him out in little stars iii 2 22

I'll to my wedding-bed; And death, not Romeo, take my maidenhead! iii 2 137

And bid him come to take his last farewell iii 2 143

Here comes your father; tell him so yourself, And see how he will take it iii 5 126

Soft! take me with you, take me with you, wife iii 5 142

Take thou this vial, being then in bed, And this distilled liquor drink iv 1 93

Hold, take these keys, and fetch more spices, nurse iv 4 1

Take. You take your pennyworths now; Sleep for a week *Rom. and Jul.* iv 5 4

Let the county take you in your bed; He'll fright you up iv 5 10

The world affords no law to make thee rich; Then be not poor, but break it, and take this v 1 74

Hold, take this letter; early in the morning See thou deliver it v 3 23

But chiefly to take thence from her dead finger A precious ring v 3 30

Take thou that: Live, and be prosperous: and farewell, good fellow v 3 41

Eyes, look your last! Arms, take your last embrace! v 3 113

To help to take her from her borrow'd grave v 3 248

At the prefixed hour . . . , Came I to take her from her kindred's vault v 3 254

So thou apprehendest it: take it for thy labour *T. of Athens* i 1 212

I give thee warning on't.—I take no heed of thee i 2 34

You take us even at the best i 2 157

You may take my word, my lord i 2 220

I take all and your several visitations So kind to heart i 2 224

Take the bonds along with you, And have the dates in compt ii 1 34

Takes no account How things go from him ii 2 3

He would embrace no counsel, take no warning by my coming iii 1 28

Must I take the cure upon me? Has much disgraced me in't iii 3 12

Takes virtuous copies to be wicked iii 3 32

Fawn upon his debts And take down the interest into their gluttonous maws iii 4 52

Take't of my soul, my lord leans wondrously to discontent iii 4 70

We cannot take this for answer, sir iii 4 78

Tear me, take me, and the gods fall upon you! iii 4 100

He has a sin that often Drowns him, and takes his valour prisoner iii 5 69

Yet, more to move you, Take my deserts to his, and join 'em both iii 5 79

What, dost thou go? Soft! take thy physic first—thou too—and thou iii 6 110

Thou detestable town! Take thou that too, with multiplying bans! iv 1 34

All gone! and not One friend to take his fortune by the arm! iv 2 7

Let each take some; Nay, put out all your hands iv 2 27

I'll take the gold thou givest me, Not all thy counsel iv 3 129

Down with the nose, Down with it flat; take the bridge quite away iv 3 158

Get thee away, and take Thy beagles with thee iv 3 174

Take wealth and lives together; Do villany, do, since you protest to do't iv 3 436

Here, take: the gods out of my misery Have sent thee treasure iv 3 531

Neither wish I You take much pains to mend v 1 92

Make it known to us.—You'll take it ill v 1 93

Take The captainship, thou shalt be met with thanks v 1 163

Sack fair Athens, And take our goodly aged men by the beards v 1 175

I cannot choose but tell him, that I care not, And let him take't at worst v 1 181

Whoso please To stop affliction, let him take his haste, Come hither v 1 213

What's on this tomb I cannot read; the character I'll take with wax v 3 6

Take thou the destined tenth v 4 33

For those that were, it is not square to take On those that are, revenges v 4 36

Take this paper, And look you lay it in the prætor's chair *J. Cæsar* i 3 142

I go to take my stand, To see him pass on to the Capitol ii 4 25

Mark Antony, here, take you Cæsar's body iii 1 244

There shall I try, In my oration, how the people take The cruel issue iii 1 293

He would not take the crown; Therefore 'tis certain he was not ambitious iii 2 117

Mischief, thou art afoot, Take thou what course thou wilt! iii 2 266

And having brought our treasure where we will, Then take we down his load iv 1 25

Within, a heart Dearer than Plutus' mine, richer than gold: If that thou be'st a Roman, take it forth iv 3 103

We must take the current when it serves, Or lose our ventures iv 3 223

If thou dost nod, thou break'st thy instrument; I'll take it from thee iv 3 272

Therefore our everlasting farewell take v 1 116

This ensign here of mine was turning back; I slew the coward, and did take it from him v 3 4

Come hither, sirrah: In Parthia did I take thee prisoner v 3 37

Here, take thou the hilts; And, when my face is cover'd, as 'tis now, Guide thou the sword v 3 43

Take this garland on thy brow; Thy Brutus bid me give it thee v 3 85

Then take him to follow thee, That did the latest service to my master v 5 66

Have we eaten on the insane root That takes the reason prisoner? *Macbeth* i 3 85

Come to my woman's breasts, And take my milk for gall! i 5 49

Hold, take my sword. There's husbandry in heaven; Their candles are all out. Take thee that too ii 1 4

And take the present horror from the time, Which now suits with it ii 1 59

It [drink] sets him on, and it takes him off ii 3 36

We'll take to-morrow. Is't far you ride? iii 1 23

I will put that business in your bosoms, Whose execution takes your enemy off iii 1 105

Take any shape but that, and my firm nerves Shall never tremble iii 4 102

The malevolence of fortune nothing Takes from his high respect iii 6 29

I'll make assurance double sure, And take a bond of fate iv 1 84

Be lion-mettled, proud; and take no care Who chafes, who frets iv 1 90

If you will take a homely man's advice, Be not found here iv 2 68

Did heaven look on, And would not take their part? iv 3 224

I have seen her rise from her bed, throw her night-gown upon her, unlock her closet, take forth paper, fold it, write upon't v 1 6

Take thy face hence v 3 19

No planets strike, No fairy takes, nor witch hath power to charm *Hamlet* i 1 163

Take thy fair hour, Laertes; time be thine! i 2 62

He was a man, take him for all in all, I shall not look upon his like again i 2 187

Take each man's censure, but reserve thy judgement i 3 69

These blazes, daughter, . . . You must not take for fire i 3 120

The king doth wake to-night and takes his rouse i 4 8

Indeed it takes From our achievements, though perform'd at height i 4 20

Take you, as 'twere, some distant knowledge of him ii 1 13

See you now; Your bait of falsehood takes this carp of truth ii 1 63

Take this from this, if this be otherwise ii 2 156

You cannot, sir, take from me any thing that I will more willingly part withal ii 2 219

The more merit is in your bounty. Take them in ii 2 558

Who does me this? Ha! 'Swounds, I should take it ii 2 604

The spurns That patient merit of the unworthy takes iii 1 74

Take these again; for to the noble mind Rich gifts wax poor when givers prove unkind iii 1 100

Still better, and worse.—So you must take your husbands iii 2 262

I'll take the ghost's word for a thousand pound iii 2 297

And am I then revenged, To take him in the purging of his soul? iii 3 85

Take thy fortune; Thou find'st to be too busy is some danger iii 4 32

Tell us where 'tis, that we may take it thence And bear it to the chapel iv 2 7

Take you me for a sponge, my lord? iv 2 15

The devil take thy soul!—Thou pray'st not well. I prithee, take thy fingers from my throat v 1 281

Take. In the verity of extolment, I take him to be a soul of great article *Hamlet* v 2 121
Or that you will take longer time v 2 207
Here, Hamlet, take my napkin, rub thy brows v 2 299
That lord whose hand must take my plight shall carry Half my love *Lear* i 1 103
Take thy reward. Five days we do allot thee i 1 175
The gods to their dear shelter take thee, maid! i 1 185
Stranger'd with our oath, Take her, or leave her i 1 208
Who, in the lusty stealth of nature, take More composition i 2 11
My pretty knave! how dost thou?—Sirrah, you were best take my coxcomb i 4 109
Be then desired By her, that else will take the thing she begs i 4 269
Nuncle Lear, nuncle Lear, tarry and take the fool with thee i 4 339
Take you some company, and away to horse i 4 359
To take't again perforce! Monster ingratitude! i 5 43
My father hath set guard to take my brother ii 1 18
And take vanity the puppet's part against the royalty of her father ii 2 39
He must speak truth! An they will take it, so; if not, he's plain ii 2 106
And am bethought To take the basest and most poorest shape ii 3 7
To take the indisposed and sickly fit For the sound man ii 4 112
Make it your cause; send down, and take my part! ii 4 195
Unbonneted he runs, And bids what will take all iii 1 15
Open this purse, and take What it contains iii 1 45
The tempest in my mind Doth from my senses take all feeling else iii 4 13
Good my lord, take his offer; go into the house iii 4 161
Good my lord, soothe him; let him take the fellow.—Take him you on iii 4 182
Here is better than the open air; take it thankfully iii 6 1
Thou robed man of justice, take thy place iii 6 38
For one blast of thy minikin mouth, Thy sheep shall take no harm iii 6 46
My tears begin to take his part so much, They'll mar my counterfeiting iii 6 63
I prithee, take him in thy arms; I have o'erheard a plot of death upon him iii 6 95
The revenges we are bound to take upon your traitorous father are not fit for your beholding iii 7 8
Nay, then, come on, and take the chance of anger iii 7 79
Here, take this purse, thou whom the heavens' plagues Have humbled to all strokes iv 1 67
Where was his son when they did take his eyes? iv 2 89
He that helps him take all my outward worth iv 4 10
Therefore I do advise you, take this note: My lord is dead iv 5 29
I would not take this from report; it is, And my heart breaks at it iv 6 144
Take that of me, my friend, who have the power To seal the accuser's lips iv 6 173
If thou wilt weep my fortunes, take my eyes iv 6 180
You ever-gentle gods, take my breath from me! iv 6 221
Hence; Lest that the infection of his fortune take Like hold on thee iv 6 237
Villain, take my purse: If ever thou wilt thrive, bury my body iv 6 252
You do me wrong to take me out o' the grave iv 7 45
Which of them shall I take? Both? one? or neither? v 1 57
To take the widow Exasperates, makes mad her sister Goneril v 1 59
Take the shadow of this tree For your good host v 2 1
Some officers take them away: good guard v 3 1
Take thou my soldiers, prisoners, patrimony; Dispose of them, of me v 3 75
Well thought on: take my sword, Give it the captain v 3 250
Never tell me; I take it much unkindly *Othello* i 1 1
What cannot be preserved when fortune takes Patience her injury a mockery makes i 3 206
Whereof I take this that you call love to be a sect or scion i 3 336
He takes her by the palm: ay, well said, whisper ii 1 168
Then take thine auld cloak about thee ii 3 99
To take the safest occasion by the front To bring you in again iii 1 52
If I have any grace or power to move you, His present reconciliation take iii 3 47
Take no notice, nor build yourself a trouble iii 3 150
Are you a man? have you a soul or sense? God be wi' you; take mine office iii 3 375
Take me this work out.—O Cassio, whence came this? iii 4 180
I'ld have it copied: Take it, and do't; and leave me for this time iii 4 191
I was a fine fool to take it. I must take out the work? iv 1 155
Take me from this world with treachery and devise engines for my life iv 2 220
You may take him at your pleasure: I will be near iv 2 243
Be bold, and take thy stand.—I have no great devotion to the deed v 1 7
Take you this weapon, Which I have here recover'd from the Moor v 2 239
Look, where they come: Take but good note *Ant. and Cleo.* i 1 11
When it pleaseth their deities to take the wife of a man from him i 2 168
I should take you For idleness itself i 3 92
I take no pleasure In aught an eunuch has i 5 9
You take things ill which are not so, Or being, concern you not ii 2 29
To knit your hearts With an unslipping knot, take Antony Octavia to his wife ii 2 129
Take no offence that I would not offend you ii 5 99
Take your time.—Thou canst not fear us, Pompey, with thy sails ii 6 23
Be pleased to tell us—For this is from the present—how you take The offers ii 6 30
I came before you here a man prepared To take this offer ii 6 42
No, Antony, take the lot ii 6 63
If our eyes had authority, here they might take two thieves kissing ii 6 100
I have a health for you.—I shall take it, sir ii 6 143
They take the flow o' the Nile By certain scales i' the pyramid ii 7 20
Who seeks, and will not take when once 'tis offer'd, Shall never find it more ii 7 89
You take from me a great part of myself; Use me well in't iii 2 24
Thou must not take my former sharpness ill: I will employ thee back again iii 3 38
Take from his heart, take from his brain, from's time, What should not then be spared iii 7 12
I have a ship Laden with gold; take that, divide it; fly iii 11 5
Be gone: My treasure's in the harbour, take it iii 11 11
So she From Egypt drive her all-disgraced friend, Or take his life there iii 12 23
Take him hence.—Mark Antony!—Tug him away iii 13 101
To let a fellow that will take rewards And say 'God quit you!' be familiar iii 13 123
Woo't thou fight well?—I'll strike, and cry 'Take all' iv 2 8
I look on you As one that takes his leave iv 2 29
Now the witch take me, if I meant it thus! iv 2 37
My hearty friends, You take me in too dolorous a sense iv 2 39
Let us score their backs, And snatch 'em up, as we take hares, behind iv 7 13
Let him take thee, And hoist thee up to the shouting plebeians iv 12 33
Bring me how he takes my death iv 13 10
Take me up: I have led you oft: carry me now, good friends iv 14 138
Let's do it after the high Roman fashion, And make death proud to take us iv 15 88
If thou please To take me to thee, as I was to him I'll be to Cæsar v 1 10
Come, come, and take a queen Worth many babes and beggars! v 2 47
For the queen, I'll take her to my guard v 2 67

Take. Take to you no hard thoughts *Ant. and Cleo.* v 2 117
Take thou no care; it shall be heeded v 2 269
Have you done? Come then, and take the last warmth of my lips v 2 294
As soft as air, as gentle,—O Antony!—Nay, I will take thee too v 2 316
The king he takes the babe To his protection *Cymbeline* i 1 40
Look here, love; This diamond was my mother's: take it, heart i 1 112
Your son's my father's friend; he takes his part i 1 165
Take your own way i 5 31
Thou takest up Thou know'st not what; but take it for thy labour i 5 61
I prithee, take it; It is an earnest of a further good That I mean to thee i 5 64
I have given him that Which, if he take, shall quite unpeople her Of liegers i 5 79
The very middle of my heart Is warm'd by the rest, and takes it thankfully i 6 28
All's well, sir: take my power i' the court for yours i 6 179
May it please you To take them in protection?—Willingly i 6 193
And then a whoreson jackanapes must take me up for swearing ii 1 4
Cannot take two from twenty, for his heart, And leave eighteen ii 1 60
Take not away the taper, leave it burning ii 2 5
He cannot choose but take this service I have done fatherly ii 3 39
Here, take this too; It is a basilisk unto mine eye ii 4 106
Have patience, sir, And take your ring again; 'tis not yet won ii 4 114
Take thy hire; and all the fiends of hell Divide themselves between you! ii 4 129
That opportunity Which then they had to take from's, to resume We have again iii 1 15
Your father's wrath, should he take me in his dominion, could not be so cruel iii 2 41
Myself, Belarius, that am Morgan call'd, They take for natural father iii 3 107
I draw the sword myself: take it, and hit The innocent mansion of my love iii 4 69
Mine ear, Therein false struck, can take no greater wound iii 4 117
We must take a short farewell, Lest, being miss'd, I be suspected iii 4 188
Who's here? If any thing that's civil, speak; if savage, Take or lend iii 6 24
Swore With his own single hand he'ld take us in, Displace our heads iv 2 121
What have we to lose, But that he swore to take, our lives? iv 2 125
As the rudest wind, That by the top doth take the mountain pine iv 2 175
Wilt take thy chance with me? I will not say Thou shalt be so well master'd iv 2 382
If you will bless me, sir, and give me leave, I'll take the better care iv 4 45
You married ones, If each of you should take this course! v 1 3
Great the slaughter is Here made by the Roman; great the answer be Britons must take v 3 80
Take No stricter render of me than my all v 4 16
You are more clement than vile men, Who of their broken debtors take a third v 4 19
For Imogen's dear life take mine; and though 'Tis not so dear, yet 'tis a life v 4 22
Though light, take pieces for the figure's sake: You rather mine v 4 25
If you will take this audit, take this life, And cancel these cold bonds v 4 27
Bind the offender, And take him from our presence v 5 301
Take him hence: The whole world shall not save him v 5 320
Take that life, beseech you, Which I so often owe v 5 414
Thou know'st I have power To take thy life from thee *Pericles* i 2 57
I'll take thy word for faith, not ask thine oath i 2 120
Why, do'e take it, and the gods give thee good on't! ii 1 152
Here take your place: Marshal the rest, as they deserve their grace ii 3 18
He may my proffer take for an offence, Since men take women's gifts for impudence ii 3 68
Take I your wish, I leap into the seas ii 4 43
Loath to bid farewell, we take our leaves ii 5 13
He, obedient to their dooms, Will take the crown iii Gower 33
Lychorida, her nurse, she takes, And so to sea iii Gower 43
Take in your arms this piece Of your dead queen iii 1 17
You, and your lady, Take from my heart all thankfulness! iii 3 4
A vestal livery will I take me to, And never more have joy iii 4 10
Come, Leonine, take her by the arm, walk with her iv 1 30
Wife, take her in; instruct her what she has to do iv 2 58
Take you the marks of her, the colour of her hair, complexion, height, age iv 2 61
Making, to take your imagination, From bourn to bourn iv 4 3
You must take some pains to work her to your manage iv 6 69
How's this? We must take another course with you iv 6 129
Take her away; use her at thy pleasure iv 6 150
To take from you the jewel you hold so dear iv 6 164
Can you teach all this you speak of?—Prove that I cannot, take me home again iv 6 200

Take advantage. Speed then, to take advantage of the field *K. John* ii 1 297
What pricks you on To take advantage of the absent time? *Richard II.* ii 3 79

Take air. Lest the device take air and taint *T. Night* iv 3 145

Take alive. No enemy Shall ever take alive the noble Brutus *J. Cæsar* v 4 22

Take and give back affairs and their dispatch *T. Night* iv 3 18
In kissing, do you render or receive?—Both take and give *Troi. and Cres.* iv 5 37

Take arms. Or to take arms against a sea of troubles *Hamlet* iii 1 59

Take away. To take away The edge of that day's celebration *Tempest* iv 1 28
Take away these chalices. Go brew me a pottle of sack *Mer. Wives* iii 5 29
'Tis all as easy Falsely to take away a life true made *Meas. for Meas.* ii 4 47
To take away the life of a man! iii 2 122
Take away this villain; shut him up *L. L. Lost* i 2 158
Take away the conqueror, take away Alisander v 2 575
Here, take away this dish.—I pray you, let it stand *T. of Shrew* iv 3 44
Do you not hear, fellows? Take away the lady *T. Night* i 5 43
The lady bade take away the fool; therefore, I say again, take her away i 5 58
Conspiring with Camillo to take away the life of our sovereign *W. Tale* iii 2 16
Or take away with thee the very services thou hast done iv 2 18
Canonized and worshipp'd as a saint, That takes away by any secret course Thy hateful life *K. John* iii 1 178
Can honour ... take away the grief of a wound? 1 *Hen. IV.* v 1 134
Or else a feast And takes away the stomach; such are the rich 2 *Hen. IV.* iv 4 107
But wherefore did he take away the crown? iv 5 89
We'll pull his plumes and take away his train 1 *Hen. VI.* iii 3 7
I confess, I confess treason.—Take away his weapon 2 *Hen. VI.* ii 3 98
Sirs, take away the duke, and guard him sure iii 1 188
As the butcher takes away the calf And binds the wretch and beats it iii 1 210
Take away this captive scold.—Nay, take away this scolding crook-back rather.—Peace, wilful boy 3 *Hen. VI.* v 5 29
Where's Potpan, that he helps not to take away? *Rom. and Jul.* i 5 2
Mend my company, take away thyself.—So I shall mend mine own *T. of Athens* iv 3 283
It [drink] provokes the desire, but it takes away the performance *Macb.* ii 3 33
All you gods, In general synod, take away her [Fortune's] power! *Ham.* ii 2 516
Let me still take away the harms I fear, Not fear still to be taken *Lear* i 4 352

Take away. The office I do hold of you, Not only take away, but let your sentence Even fall upon my life . *Othello* i 3 119
He goes into Mauritania and takes away with him the fair Desdemona . iv 2 230
Let thine own hands take away her life . *Cymbeline* iii 4 28
Who either by public war or private treason Will take away your life *Per.* i 2 105
Take care. Every man shift for all the rest, and let no man take care for himself; for all is but fortune . *Tempest* v 1 257
Beseech you, Of your own state take care . *W. Tale* iv 4 459
Take choice. Come, and take choice of all my library . *T. Andron.* iv 1 34
Take cold. A taller man than I will take cold . *T. of Shrew* iv 1 11
Take comfort: he no more shall see my face . *M. N. Dream* i 1 202
For the sake of it, Be manly, and take comfort . *Pericles* iii 1 22
Take corruption. Shall in the general censure take corruption From that particular fault . *Hamlet* i 4 35
Take delight. I marvel your ladyship takes delight in such a barren rascal . *T. Night* i 5 89
Who should study to prefer a peace, If holy churchmen take delight in broils? . 1 *Hen. VI.* iii 1 111
Those you were wont to take delight in, the tragedians of the city *Hamlet* ii 2 341
Take dust. Are they like to take dust, like Mistress Mall's picture? *T. N.* i 3 135
Take exceptions. Lest he should take exceptions to my love *T. G. of Ver.* i 3 81
And yet she takes exceptions at your person . v 2 3
But you will take exceptions to my boon . 3 *Hen. VI.* iii 2 46
Take fire. Come, will this wood take fire? . *Mer. Wives* v 5 92
Take hands. Come unto these yellow sands, And then take hands *Tempest* i 2 377
What, bear her in hand until they come to take hands . *Much Ado* iv 1 306
Take hands. We will not dance.—Why take we hands, then? *L. L. Lost* v 2 219
Come, my queen, take hands with me, And rock the ground *M. N. D.* iv 1 90
Here's eight that must take hands To join in Hymen's bands *As Y. L. It* v 4 134
Take hands, a bargain! And, friends unknown, you shall bear witness *W. Tale* iv 4 394
Let's all take hands, Till that the conquering wine hath steep'd our sense In soft and delicate Lethe . *Ant. and Cleo.* ii 7 112
All take hands. Make battery to our ears with the loud music . ii 7 114
Take head. This Commodity Makes it take head from all indifferency *K. John* ii 1 579
Take heart. Our lamp is spent, it's out! Good sirs, take heart *A. and C.* iv 15 85
Take heed, As Hymen's lamps shall light you . *Tempest* iv 1 22
Take heed, have open eye, for thieves do foot by night: Take heed, ere summer comes or cuckoo-birds do sing *Mer. Wives* ii 1 126
The warrant's for yourself; take heed to't . *Meas. for Meas.* v 1 83
Take heed the queen come not within his sight *M. N. Dream* ii 1 19
Take heed, honest Launcelot; take heed, honest Gobbo *Mer. of Venice* ii 2 7
'Hic steterat Priami, take heed he hear us not . *T. of Shrew* iii 1 43
Take heed, Signior Baptista, lest you be cony-catched . v 1 101
Those girls of Italy, take heed of them . *All's Well* ii 1 19
Take heed of this French earl: the honour of a maid is her name . iii 5 12
Take heed of the allurement of one Count Rousillon, a foolish idle boy iv 3 241
Take heed of him; he stabbed me in mine own house . 2 *Hen. IV.* ii 1 14
Therefore take heed what guests you receive . ii 4 100
Therefore let men take heed of their company . v 1 86
Therefore take heed how you impawn our person *Hen. V.* i 2 21
Take heed, be wary how you place your words 1 *Hen. VI.* iii 2 3
Who cannot steal a shape that means deceit? Take heed 2 *Hen. VI.* iii 1 80
Take heed, lest by your heat you burn yourselves . v 1 160
Take heed of yonder dog! Look, when he fawns, he bites *Richard III.* i 3 289
Take heed; for he holds vengeance in his hands . i 4 204
Take heed you dally not before your king . ii 1 12
I say, take heed; Yes, heartily beseech you *Hen. VIII.* i 2 175
I warn'd ye; Take heed, for heaven's sake, take heed . iii 1 110
Let them take heed of Troilus, I can tell them that too . *Troi. and Cres.* i 2 60
Take heed, the quarrel's most ominous to us . v 7 20
Take heed, take heed, for such die miserable *Rom. and Jul.* iii 3 145
Take heed of Cassius; come not near Casca *J. Cæsar* ii 3 1
None so rank As may dishonour him; take heed of that *Hamlet* ii 1 21
Take heed, sirrah; the whip.—Truth's a dog must to kennel . *Lear* i 4 123
Take heed o' the foul fiend: obey thy parents . iii 4 82
Take heed on't; Make it a darling like your precious eye *Othello* iii 4 65
Sweet soul, take heed, Take heed of perjury . v 2 50
Come, down into the boat.—Take heed you fall not *Ant. and Cleo.* ii 7 136
Take hence the rest, and give them burial here . *Richard II.* v 5 119
Take hence that traitor from our sight . 2 *Hen. VI.* ii 3 103
Take hence this Jack, and whip him . *Ant. and Cleo.* iii 13 93
Take hold. O God, I fear thy justice will take hold On me, and you, and mine, and yours for this! . *Richard III.* ii 1 131
Will not let belief take hold of him Touching this dreaded sight *Hamlet* i 1 24
Let this tyrannous night take hold upon you *Lear* iii 4 156
Nor doth the general care Take hold on me . *Othello* i 3 55
Take horse. In the very heat And pride of their contention did take horse . 1 *Hen. IV.* i 1 60
Linger not, my lord; away, take horse 2 *Hen. VI.* iv 4 54
He sends to know your lordship's pleasure, If presently you will take horse with him . *Richard III.* iii 2 16
Take in. Yare, yare! Take in the topsail . *Tempest* i 1 7
Take in your love, and then let me alone . *T. of Shrew* iv 2 71
I think affliction may subdue the cheek, But not take in the mind *W. T.* iv 4 588
We shall be shorten'd in our aim, which was To take in many towns *Cor.* i 2 24
This no more dishonours you at all Than to take in a town with gentle words . iii 2 59
Take in that kingdom, and enfranchise that; Perform't . *Ant. and Cleo.* i 1 23
He could so quickly cut the Ionian sea, And take in Toryne . iii 7 24
Such assaults As would take in some virtue . *Cymbeline* iii 2 9
Take interest. Did he take interest?—No, not take interest, not, as you would say, Directly interest . *Mer. of Venice* i 3 76
Take it. Who hath got, as I take it, an ague . *Tempest* ii 2 68
Sir Proteus, as I take it.—Sir Proteus, gentle lady . *T. G. of Ver.* iv 2 90
As I take it, it is almost day . *Meas. for Meas.* iv 2 109
Who, as I take it, have stolen his birds' nest . *Much Ado* ii 1 237
I take it, your own business calls on you . *Mer. of Venice* i 1 63
And here, I take it, is the doctor come . iv 1 168
Whither is he gone?—Marry, as I take it, to Rousillon . *All's Well* v 1 28
This business Will raise us all.—To laughter, as I take it *W. Tale* ii 1 198
This apoplexy is, as I take it, a kind of lethargy 2 *Hen. IV.* i 2 126
I take it there's but two ways . v 3 115
His father was called Philip of Macedon, as I take it *Hen. V.* iv 7 22
Which, as I take it, is a kind of puppy To the old dam . *Hen. VIII.* i 1 175
One would take it, That never saw 'em pace before, the spavin Or springhalt reign'd among 'em . i 3 11
There, I take it, They may, 'cum privilegio,' wear away . i 3 33
I take it, she that carries up the train Is that old noble lady . iv 1 51
Take it. It stands agreed, I take it, by all voices . *Hen. VIII.* v 3 88
Which, as I take it, is a gentlemanlike offer . *Rom. and Jul.* ii 4 190
At twelve.—I take't 'tis later, sir . *Macbeth* ii 1 3
And this, I take it, Is the main motive . *Hamlet* i 1 104
He has imponed, as I take it, six French rapiers . v 2 156
This is Othello's ancient, as I take it . *Othello* v 1 51
Being charged, we will be still by land, Which, as I take't, we shall *Ant. and Cleo* iv 11 2
Takes it at heart. An you speak ill of the devil, how he takes it at heart! . *T. Night* iii 4 112
Take it to heart. Why should we in our peevish opposition Take it to heart? . *Hamlet* i 2 101
Take joy. It should take joy To see her in your arms *W. Tale* v 1 80
Take leave. Let's all sink with the king.—Let's take leave of him *Temp.* i 1 68
Take leave of thy old master and inquire My lodging out *Mer. of Venice* ii 2 162
Give them way till he take leave, and presently after him . *T. Night* ii 4 217
Till youth take leave and leave you to the crutch . 3 *Hen. VI.* iii 2 35
Leave! an you take leave till to-morrow morning . *Troi. and Cres.* iii 2 149
Take mercy On the poor souls . *Hen. V.* ii 4 103
Then God take mercy on brave Talbot's soul! . 1 *Hen. VI.* iv 3 34
Take my death. I will take my death, I never meant him any ill 2 *Hen. VI.* ii 3 90
O, let me pray before I take my death! . 3 *Hen. VI.* i 3 35
Take my leave. I take my leave of you . *Meas. for Meas.* i 4 90
I'll take my leave, And leave you to the hearing of the cause . ii 1 140
So I take my leave.—No, madam; we will bring you on your way *L. L. L.* v 2 882
I'll take my leave of the Jew in the twinkling of an eye . *Mer. of Venice* ii 2 176
I wish you well, and so I take my leave . iv 1 420
And here take my leave, To go about my preparation . 1 *Hen. VI.* i 1 165
Then here I take my leave of thee, fair son . iv 5 52
I take my leave with many thousand thanks . 3 *Hen. VI.* iii 2 56
I must to him too, Before he go to bed. I'll take my leave *Hen. VIII.* v 1 9
For this time will I take my leave, my lord.—Your leave! *T. and C.* iii 2 147
I'll take my leave.—And may, through all the world: 'tis yours *A. and C.* v 2 133
Take my oath. I'll take my oath on it, till he have made an oyster of me, he shall never make me such a fool . *Much Ado* ii 3 26
I here take my oath before this honourable assembly . *Lear* iii 6 49
Take note. Now 'tis awake, Takes note of what is done . *Meas. for Meas.* ii 2 94
I wish you now, then; Pray you, take note of it . v 1 80
My love hath in't a bond, Whereof the world takes note *All's Well* i 3 195
Hurt him in eleven places: my neice shall take note of it . *T. Night* iii 2 38
Or to take note how many pair of silk stockings thou hast 2 *Hen. IV.* ii 2 17
Far from this country Pindarus shall run, Where never Roman shall take note of him . *J. Cæsar* v 3 50
For let the world take note, You are the most immediate to our throne *Hamlet* i 2 108
Take note, take note, O world, To be direct and honest is not safe *Othello* iii 3 377
Take notice. The state takes notice of the private difference *Hen. VIII.* i 1 101
Take notice, lords, he has a loyal breast . iii 2 200
Thou hast thy mistress still, to boot, my son, Who shall take notice of thee . *Cymbeline* i 5 70
Take notice that I am in Cambria, at Milford-Haven . iii 2 44
Take occasion. You might take occasion to kiss . *As Y. Like It* iv 1 75
When you take occasions to see leeks hereafter, I pray you, mock at 'em; that is all . *Hen. V.* v 1 57
Much less to take occasion from their mouths To raise a mutiny 1 *Hen. VI.* iv 1 130
Take off. Silence awhile. Robin, take off this head . *M. N. Dream* iv 1 85
That we with thee May spend our wonder too, or take off thine *All's W.* ii 1 92
To take off so much grief from you as he Will piece up in himself *W. Tale* v 3 55
It would cost you a groaning to take off my edge . *Hamlet* iii 2 259
Takes off the rose From the fair forehead of an innocent love . iii 4 42
Speak, man: thy tongue May take off some extremity . *Cymbeline* iii 4 17
The heaviness and guilt within my bosom Takes off my manhood . v 2 2
Since, Jupiter, our son is good, Take off his miseries . v 4 86
Marina's life Seeks to take off by treason's knife . *Pericles* iv Gower 14
Take offence. They'll take no offence at our abuse.—Suppose they take offence without a cause . 3 *Hen. VI.* iv 1 14
Say if you had, Who takes offence at that would make me glad? *Pericles* ii 5 72
Take on. She does so take on with her men . *Mer. Wives* iii 5 40
He so takes on yonder with my husband . iv 2 22
Take on as you would follow, But yet come not . *M. N. Dream* iii 2 258
How will my mother for a father's death Take on with me! 3 *Hen. VI.* ii 5 104
Take order. If your worship will take order for the drabs *Meas. for Meas.* ii 1 246
Sent him home, Whilst to take order for the wrongs I went *Com. of Errors* v 1 146
Whiles I take order for mine own affairs . 2 *Hen. VI.* iii 1 320
I will take order for her keeping close . *Richard III.* iv 2 53
Some one take order Buckingham be brought To Salisbury . iv 4 539
Take out. I must take out the work? . *Othello* iv 1 156; 159
Wheresoever you had it, I'll take out no work on't . iv 1 161
The glove which your majesty is take out of the helmet of Alençon *Hen. V.* iv 8 28
Take pains. I took no more pains for those thanks than you take pains to thank me . *Much Ado* ii 3 260
Take pains; be perfect: adieu . *M. N. Dream* i 2 111
Take pain To allay with some cold drops of modesty . *Mer. of Venice* ii 2 194
Hath she no husband That will take pains to blow a horn before her? *K. John* i 1 219
Take part. With my nobler reason 'gainst my fury Do I take part *Temp.* v 1 27
Take patience. I pray you, sir, take patience . *Lear* ii 4 140
Take peace. There cannot be those numberless offences 'Gainst me, that I cannot take peace with . *Hen. VIII.* ii 1 85
Take physic, pomp; Expose thyself to feel what wretches feel . *Lear* iii 4 33
Take pity. He, sir, that takes pity on decayed men . *Com. of Errors* iv 3 25
If I do not take pity of her, I am a villain . *Much Ado* ii 3 271
You men of Harfleur, Take pity of your town and of your people *Hen. V.* iii 3 28
Take place. These fix'd evils sit so fit in him, That they take place, when virtue's steely bones Look bleak i' the cold wind . *All's Well* i 1 114
Arise, and take place by us: half your suit Never name to us *Hen. VIII.* i 2 10
For if It did take place, 'I do,' quoth he, 'perceive My king is tangled' iii 2 34
Take pleasure. You take pleasure then in the message? . *Much Ado* ii 3 262
I take pleasure in singing, sir.—I'll pay thy pleasure then . *T. Night* ii 4 69
Take possession. And to-night, When I should take possession of the bride, End ere I do begin . *All's Well* ii 5 28
His words do take possession of my bosom . *K. John* iv 1 32
Be resolute; I mean to take possession of my right . 3 *Hen. VI.* i 1 44
Take pride. Wherein—let no man hear me—I take pride *Meas. for Meas.* ii 4 10
Take prisoner. With a hideous crash Takes prisoner Pyrrhus' ear *Hamlet* ii 2 499
Which Takes prisoner the wild motion of mine eye . *Cymbeline* i 6 103
Take purses. We that take purses go by the moon . 1 *Hen. IV.* i 2 15
Shall the son of England prove a thief and take purses? . ii 4 452

Take root. We should take root here where we sit *Hen. VIII.* i 2 87
Take ship. Must die . . . Ere he take ship *Hen. V.* ii Prol. 30
Take suggestion. They'll take suggestion as a cat laps milk *Tempest* ii 1 288
Takes survey. And time, that takes survey of all the world, Must have a stop 1 *Hen. IV.* v 4 82
Take that. Bid him take that for coming a-night to Jane Smile *As Y. Like It* ii 4 48
You pluck my foot awry: Take that *T. of Shrew* iv 1 151
Take that, thou likeness of this railer here.—Sprawl'st thou? take that, to end thy agony 3 *Hen. VI.* v 5 38
Take that, and that: if all this will not do, I'll drown you *Richard III.* i 4 276
Nothing but songs of death? Take that, until thou bring me better news iv 4 510
Take the hint Which my despair proclaims *Ant. and Cleo.* iii 11 18
Take the sacrament To bury mine intents *Richard II.* iv 1 328
I'll take the sacrament on't, how and which way you will *All's Well* iv 3 156
Take the start. Use your legs, take the start, run away *Mer. of Venice* ii 2 6
Take the wall. I will take the wall of any man or maid *Rom. and Jul.* i 1 15
Take thought. If he love Cæsar, all that he can do Is to himself, take thought and die for Cæsar *J. Cæsar* ii 1 187
Take time to pause *M. N. Dream* i 1 83
And, whilst we breathe, take time to do him dead 3 *Hen. VI.* i 4 108
Take to. Have you any thing to take to?—Nothing but my fortune *T. G. of Ver.* iv 1 42
Take truce. Could not take truce with the unruly spleen *Rom. and Jul.* iii 1 162
Take up. Go take up these clothes here quickly *Mer. Wives* iii 3 155
'Tis unreasonable! Will you take up your wife's clothes? iv 2 147
I knew when seven justices could not take up a quarrel *As Y. Like It* v 4 104
Take up my mistress' gown for thy master's use! *T. of Shrew* iv 3 160
I have his horse to take up the quarrel *T. Night* iii 4 320
Take up the bastard; Take't up, I say; give't to thy crone *W. Tale* ii 3 76
How it chafes, how it rages, how it takes up the shore! iii 3 90
Look thee here; take up, take up, boy; open't. So, let's see iii 3 120
If guilty dread have left thee so much strength As to take up mine honour's pawn, then stoop . . . —I take it up *Richard II.* i 1 74
Perforce a third Must take up us 2 *Hen. IV.* i 3 73
Good my sovereign, Take up the English short *Hen. V.* i 4 72
I will take up that with 'Give the devil his due' iii 7 126
They keep the walls And dare not take up arms like gentlemen 1 *Hen. VI.* iii 2 70
Shall we go to Cheapside and take up commodities upon our bills? 2 *Hen. VI.* iv 7 135
Take up the sword again, or take up me *Richard III.* i 2 184
Take up the corse.—Towards Chertsey, noble lord? i 2 226
I wonder That such a keech can with his very bulk Take up the rays o' the beneficial sun *Hen. VIII.* i 1 56
I could myself Take up a brace o' the best of them *Coriolanus* iii 1 244
And schoolboys' tears take up The glasses of my sight! iii 2 116
Take up some other station; here's no place for you iv 5 32
Take up this good old man, and cheer the heart *T. Andron.* i 1 457
To take up a matter of brawl iv 3 92
Take up those cords: poor ropes, you are beguiled, Both you and I *Rom. and Jul.* iii 2 132
Take up the body.—Go fetch fire.—Pluck down benches *J. Cæsar* iii 2 261
Take up the bodies: such a sight as this Becomes the field *Hamlet* v 2 412
Be it lawful I take up what's cast away *Lear* i 1 256
Take up thy master: If thou shouldst dally half an hour, his life, With thine, and all that offer to defend him, Stand in assured loss: take up, take up iii 6 99
Take up this mangled matter at the best *Othello* i 3 173
Take up her bed; And bear her women from the monument *A. and C.* v 2 359
Take upon. One that takes upon him to be a dog indeed *T. G. of Ver.* iv 4 13
This way will I take upon me to wash your liver *As Y. Like It* iii 2 442
Look that you take upon you as you should *T. of Shrew* iv 2 108
This is flat knavery, to take upon you another man's name v 1 37
Now take upon me, in the name of Time, To use my wings *W. Tale* iv 1 3
'How comes that?' says he, that takes upon him not to conceive 2 *Hen. IV.* ii 2 123
She takes upon her bravely at first dash 1 *Hen. VI.* i 2 71
And she takes upon her to spy a white hair on his chin *Troi. and Cres.* i 2 153
But fear not yet To take upon you what is yours *Macbeth* iv 3 70
We Shall take upon's what else remains to do v 6 5
And take upon's the mystery of things, As if we were God's spies *Lear* v 3 16
You must either be directed by some that take upon them to know, or to take upon yourself that which I am sure you do not know *Cymb.* v 4 187
Take vantage. God forbid that! for he'll take vantages 3 *Hen. VI.* iii 2 25
Take vantage, heavy eyes, not to behold This shameful lodging *Lear* ii 2 178
Take vengeance. They take vengeance of such kind of men *T. Andron.* v 2 63
Take wreak. And with revengeful war Take wreak on Rome iv 3 33
Taken. You have taken it wiselier than I meant you should *Tempest* ii 1 21
On whom my pains, Humanely taken, all, all lost, quite lost iv 1 190
Now you have taken the pains to set it together, take it *T. G. of Ver.* i 1 123
But Valentine, if he be ta'en, must die iii 1 232
It was Eve's legacy, and cannot be ta'en from her iii 1 343
I have seen Sackerson loose twenty times, and have taken him by the chain *Mer. Wives* i 1 308
I am glad, though you have ta'en a special stand to strike at me v 5 247
There will be pity taken on you *Meas. for Meas.* i 2 112
I have ta'en a due and wary note upon't iv 1 38
Might in the times to come have ta'en revenge iv 4 33
I thought to have ta'en you at the Porpentine *Com. of Errors* iii 2 172
I was ta'en for him, and he for me v 1 387
He hath ta'en you newly into his grace *Much Ado* i 3 23
He hath ta'en the infection: hold it up ii 3 126
Ha' ta'en a couple of as arrant knaves as any in Messina iii 5 34
Your brother John is ta'en in flight, And brought with armed men back v 4 127
The manner of it is, I was taken with the manner *L. L. Lost* i 1 204
And taken following her into the park i 1 209
It was proclaimed a year's imprisonment, to be taken with a wench.—I was taken with none, sir: I was taken with a damsel i 1 290
I was taken with a maid i 1 299
I was taken with Jaquenetta, and Jaquenetta is a true girl i 1 314
To be cut off and taken In what part of your body pleaseth me *M. of Ven.* i 3 151
A pound of man's flesh taken from a man Is not so estimable i 3 166
The Prince of Arragon hath ta'en his oath, And comes to his election ii 9 2
Your grace hath ta'en great pains to qualify His rigorous course iv 1 7
Thou shalt have nothing but the forfeiture, To be so taken at thy peril iv 1 344
And never leave thee till he hath ta'en thy life *As Y. Like It* i 1 158
This duke Hath ta'en displeasure 'gainst his gentle niece i 2 290
A poor sequester'd stag, That from the hunter's aim had ta'en a hurt ii 1 34
The thorny point Of bare distress hath ta'en from me the show Of smooth civility ii 7 95
Taken. Being taken with the cramp was drowned *As Y. Like It* iv 1 104
He hath ta'en his bow and arrows and is gone forth to sleep iv 3 4
No profit grows where is no pleasure ta'en *T. of Shrew* i 1 39
Therefore this order hath Baptista ta'en i 2 126
Well ta'en, and like a buzzard ii 1 207
Nay, I have ta'en you napping, gentle love iv 2 46
And such assurance ta'en As shall with either part's agreement stand iv 4 49
It is reported that he has taken their greatest commander *All's Well* iii 5 5
Whatsome'er he is, He's bravely taken here iii 5 55
Of whom he hath taken a solemn leave iv 3 90
His confession is taken, and it shall be read to his face iv 3 130
Yet who would have suspected an ambush where I was taken? iv 3 336
It is excellently well penned, I have taken great pains to con it *T. Night* i 5 185
You might have saved me my pains, to have taken it away yourself ii 2 6
Of such note indeed, That were I ta'en here it would scarce be answer'd iii 3 28
His very genius hath taken the infection of the device iii 4 142
O, prove true, That I, dear brother, be now ta'en for you! iii 4 410
Was this taken By any understanding pate but thine? *W. Tale* i 2 222
I would not be a stander-by to hear My sovereign mistress clouded so, without My present vengeance taken i 2 281
I am robbed, sir, and beaten; my money and apparel ta'en from me iv 3 65
Have taken The shapes of beasts upon them iv 4 26
Had like to have given us one, if you had not taken yourself with the manner iv 4 751
I might have look'd upon my queen's full eyes, Have taken treasure from her lips v 1 54
My mother is assailed in our tent, And ta'en, I fear *K. John* iii 2 7
Half my power this night, Passing these flats, are taken by the tide v 6 40
Grievous sick, my lord, Suddenly taken *Richard II.* i 4 55
And, madam, there is order ta'en for you v 1 53
A dozen of them here have ta'en the sacrament v 2 97
But whether they be ta'en or slain we hear not v 6 4
Was by the rude hands of that Welshman taken 1 *Hen. IV.* i 1 41
If I be ta'en, I'll peach for this ii 2 47
There be four of us here have ta'en a thousand pound this day morning ii 4 176
Where is it?—Where is it! taken from us it is ii 4 179
Wert taken with the manner, and ever since thou hast blushed extempore ii 4 346
Choler, my lord, if rightly taken.—No, if rightly taken, halter ii 4 356
Thy state is taken for a joined-stool, thy golden sceptre for a leaden dagger ii 4 418
Shall we divide our right According to our threefold order ta'en? iii 1 71
Discomfited great Douglas, ta'en him once, Enlarged him iii 2 114
His corruption being ta'en from us, We, as the spring of all, shall pay for all v 2 22
Keeping such vile company as thou art hath in reason taken from me all ostentation of sorrow 2 *Hen. IV.* ii 2 53
Have, in my pure and immaculate valour, taken Sir John Colevile iv 3 41
The prince hath ta'en it hence: go, seek him out. Is he so hasty? iv 5 60
Taken and impounded as a stray *Hen. V.* i 2 160
Your fathers taken by the silver beards iii 3 36
Nothing compelled from the villages, nothing taken but paid for iii 6 116
What prisoners of good sort are taken, uncle? iv 8 80
Talbot is taken, whom we wont to fear 1 *Hen. VI.* i 2 14
Ten thousand French have ta'en the sacrament iv 2 28
He is ta'en or slain; For fly he could not, if he would have fled iv 4 42
I come to know what prisoners thou hast ta'en iv 7 56
Be not offended, nature's miracle, Thou art allotted to be ta'en by me v 3 55
I think I have taken my last draught in this world 2 *Hen. VI.* ii 3 73
Say he be taken, rack'd, and tortured iii 1 376
If you be ta'en, we then should see the bottom Of all our fortunes v 2 78
Had he been ta'en, we should have heard the news 3 *Hen. VI.* ii 1 4
Your foe is taken, And brought your prisoner to your palace gate iii 2 118
Taken from Paul's to be interred there *Richard III.* i 2 30
The queen your mother, and your brother York, Have taken sanctuary iii 1 28
Be not ta'en tardy by unwise delay iv 1 52
The Duke of Buckingham is taken; That is the best news iv 4 533
You have ta'en a tardy sluggard here v 3 225
As we have ta'en the sacrament, We will unite the white rose and the red v 5 18
I am sorry To see you ta'en from liberty *Hen. VIII.* i 1 205
All That made me happy at one stroke has taken For ever from the world ii 1 117
And high note's Ta'en of your many virtues ii 3 60
Cardinal Campeius Is stol'n away to Rome; hath ta'en no leave iii 2 57
A worthy fellow, and hath ta'en much pain In the king's business iii 2 72
Out of pity, taken A load would sink a navy, too much honour iii 2 382
Never greater, Nor, I'll assure you, better taken, sir iv 1 12
I should have ta'en some pains to bring together Yourself and your accusers v 1 119
If Troy be not taken till these two undermine it, the walls will stand till they fall of themselves *Troi. and Cres.* ii 3 9
Since I have taken such pains to bring you together iii 2 207
Patroclus ta'en or slain, and Palamedes Sore hurt and bruised v 5 13
Ajax hath ta'en Æneas: shall it be? No, by the flame of yonder glorious heaven, He shall not carry him: I'll be ta'en too, Or bring him off v 6 22
Of all the horses, Whereof we have ta'en good and good store *Coriolanus* i 9 32
We render you the tenth, to be ta'en forth, Before the common distribution i 9 34
The town is ta'en!—'Twill be deliver'd back on good condition i 10 1
A part That I shall blush in acting, and might well Be taken from the people ii 2 150
So putting him to rage, You should have ta'en the advantage of his choler ii 3 206
He was not taken well; he had not dined v 1 50
Then be joyful, Because the law hath ta'en revenge on them *T. Andron.* iii 1 117
We gaze so long Till the fresh taste be taken from that clearness ii 1 128
O, the gibbet-maker! he says that he hath taken them down again iv 3 81
Who's there? Romeo, arise; Thou wilt be taken. Stay awhile! *Rom. and Jul.* iii 3 75
Let me be ta'en, let me be put to death; I am content iii 5 17
If I would not have taken him at a word *J. Cæsar* i 2 269
But there's no heed to be taken of them i 2 277
Which, taken at the flood, leads on to fortune iv 3 219
He's ta'en. And, hark! they shout for joy v 3 32
O, coward that I am, to live so long, To see my best friend ta'en before my face! v 3 35
Tell Antony, Brutus is ta'en.—I'll tell the news v 4 16
Brutus is ta'en, Brutus is ta'en, my lord.—Where is he?—Safe, Antony v 4 18

Taken. He came not back : he is or ta'en or slain *J. Cæsar* v 5 3
In equal scale weighing delight and dole,—Taken to wife *Hamlet* i 2 14
Think yourself a baby ; That you have ta'en these tenders for true pay i 3 106
A man that fortune's buffets and rewards Hast ta'en with equal thanks iii 2 73
Let me still take away the harms I fear, Not fear still to be taken *Lear* i 4 353
If he be taken, he shall never more Be fear'd of doing harm ii 1 112
The duke's to blame in this ; 'twill be ill taken ii 2 166
O, I have ta'en Too little care of this ! Take physic, pomp iii 4 33
Away ! King Lear hath lost, he and his daughter ta'en v 2 6
Of being taken by the insolent foe And sold to slavery *Othello* i 3 137
When I have spoke of you dispraisingly, Hath ta'en your part iii 3 73
Thou hast taken against me a most just exception iv 2 210
His mouth is stopp'd ; Honest Iago hath ta'en order for't v 2 72
No vessel can peep forth, but 'tis as soon Taken as seen *Ant. and Cleo.* i 4 54
Cæsar has taken Toryne.—Can he be there in person? iii 7 56
Dear my lord, pardon,—I dare not, Lest I be taken iv 15 23
O Cleopatra ! thou art taken, queen.—Quick, quick, good hands v 2 38
I have pick'd the lock and ta'en The treasure of her honour *Cymbeline* ii 2 41
Why hast thou gone so far, To be unbent when thou hast ta'en thy stand? iii 4 111
I have ta'en His head from him iv 2 150
Thou thy worldly task hast done, Home art gone, and ta'en thy wages iv 2 261
Gods ! if you Should have ta'en vengeance on my faults, I never Had lived to put on this v 1 8
Great Jupiter be praised ! Lucius is taken v 3 84
I'll give it ; Yea, though thou do demand a prisoner, The noblest ta'en v 5 100
Her bond of chastity quite crack'd, I having ta'en the forfeit v 5 208
A certain stuff, which, being ta'en, would cease The present power of life v 5 255
Have you ta'en of it?—Most like I did, for I was dead v 5 258
Blame both my lord and me, that we have taken No care *Pericles* iv 1 38
Not spoken To any one, nor taken sustenance But to prorogue his grief v 1 25
Taken away. What he hath taken away from thy father perforce, I will render thee again in affection *As Y. Like It* i 2 21
The jewel of life By some damn'd hand was robb'd and ta'en away *K. John* v 1 41
If Hamlet from himself be ta'en away, And when he's not himself does wrong Laertes, Then Hamlet does it not *Hamlet* v 2 245
That I have ta'en away this old man's daughter, It is most true *Othello* i 3 78
Taken heart. Now I have taken heart thou vanishest *J. Cæsar* iv 3 288
Taken labours. His taken labours bid him me forgive *All's Well* iii 4 12
Taken napping. But I should blush, I know, To be o'erheard and taken napping so *L. L. Lost* iv 3 130
Taken note. They have ta'en note of us : keep on your way *Coriolanus* iv 2 10
By the Lord, Horatio, these three years I have taken note of it *Hamlet* v 1 151
Taken off. Your power and your command is taken off *Othello* v 2 331
Whose life, But that her flight prevented it, she had Ta'en off by poison *Cymbeline* v 5 47
I must have your maidenhead taken off *Pericles* iv 6 136
Taken out. I'll have my brains ta'en out and buttered *Mer. Wives* iii 5 7
An old rusty sword ta'en out of the town-armoury *T. of Shrew* iii 2 47
All my friends, which thou must make thy friends, Have but their stings and teeth newly ta'en out 2 *Hen. IV.* iv 5 206
I'll have the work ta'en out, And give't Iago *Othello* iii 3 296
Taken prisoner. Is not Angiers lost? Arthur ta'en prisoner? *K. John* iii 4 7
Then was that noble Worcester Too soon ta'en prisoner 2 *Hen. IV.* i 1 126
Divers gentlemen beside Were there surprised and taken prisoners 1 *Hen. VI.* iv 1 26
Is my sovereign slain?—Ay, almost slain, for he is taken prisoner 3 *Hen. VI.* iv 4 7
Taken up. I was taken up for laying them down *T. G. of Ver.* i 2 135
They three were taken up By fishermen of Corinth *Com. of Errors* i 1 111
He and I And the twin Dromio all were taken up v 1 350
We are like to prove a goodly commodity, being taken up of these men's bills *Much Ado* iii 3 191
And how was that ta'en up?—Faith, we met *As Y. Like It* v 4 50
You have ta'en up, Under the counterfeited zeal of God 2 *Hen. IV.* iv 2 26
Taker. He is sooner caught than the pestilence, and the taker runs presently mad *Much Ado* i 1 88
That the life-weary taker may fall dead *Rom. and Jul.* v 1 62
Takest. This island's mine, by Sycorax my mother, Which thou takest from me *Tempest* i 2 332
He's a better woodman than thou takest him for *Meas. for Meas.* iv 3 171
When thou wakest, Thou takest True delight *M. N. Dream* iii 2 454
Or else a fool That seest a game play'd home, the rich stake drawn, And takest it all for jest *W. Tale* i 2 249
For ever Unvenerable be thy hands, if thou Takest up the princess by that forced baseness ! ii 3 78
Call it a travel that thou takest for pleasure *Richard II.* i 3 262
Even here thou takest, As from my death-bed, thy last living leave v 1 38
If thou takest leave, thou wert better be hanged 2 *Hen. IV.* i 2 101
Farewell, thou woful welcomer of glory !—Adieu, poor soul, that takest thy leave of it ! *Richard III.* iv 1 91
Whatsoe'er thou takest me for, I'm sure Thou hast a cruel nature *Hen. VIII.* v 3 128
Thou takest up Thou know'st not what ; but take it for thy labour *Cymbeline* i 5 60
Taketh. She taketh most delight In music, instruments *T. of Shrew* i 1 92
Taking. What a taking was he in when your husband asked who was in the basket ! *Mer. Wives* iii 3 191
You'll mar the light by taking it in snuff *L. L. Lost* v 2 22
I neither lend nor borrow By taking nor by giving of excess *Mer. of Ven.* i 3 63
Yet art thou good for nothing but taking up *All's Well* ii 3 218
He stole from Florence, taking no leave, and I follow him v 3 144
Unless it be to report your lord's taking of this *T. Night* ii 2 11
The heavens, taking angry note, Have left me issueless *W. Tale* v 1 173
Taking note of thy abhorr'd aspect, Finding thee fit *K. John* iv 2 224
To shorten you, For taking so the head, your whole head's length *Richard II.* iii 3 13
The manner of their taking may appear At large discoursed in this paper v 6 9
If a man is through with them in honest taking up 2 *Hen. IV.* i 2 46
For taking their names upon you before you have earned them ii 4 154
Imagine me taking your part And in your power soft silencing your son v 2 96
Taking him from thence that is not there, You break no privilege *Richard III.* iii 1 53
Who now are here, taking their leaves of me *Coriolanus* iv 5 139
The kind prince, Taking thy part, hath rush'd aside the law *R. and J.* iii 3 26
Taking the measure of an unmade grave iii 3 70
The worst is filthy ; and would not hold taking *T. of Athens* i 2 159
You have condemn'd and noted Lucius Pella For taking bribes *J. Cæsar* iv 3 3
For taking one's part that's out of favour *Lear* i 4 111
Taking. No place, That guard, and most unusual vigilance, Does not attend my taking *Lear* ii 3 5
Strike her young bones, You taking airs, with lameness ! ii 4 166
Bless thee from whirlwinds, star-blasting, and taking ! iii 4 61
A jewel Well worth a poor man's taking iv 6 29
When he hath mused of taking kingdoms in *Ant. and Cleo.* iii 13 83
By taking Antony's course, you shall bereave yourself Of my good purposes v 2 129
Should we be taking leave As long a term as yet we have to live, The loathness to depart would grow *Cymbeline* i 1 106
For taking a beggar without less quality i 4 23
I have adventured To try your taking of a false report i 6 173
Taking advantage of our misery *Pericles* i 4 66
Taking-off. Against The deep damnation of his taking-off *Macbeth* i 7 20
Let her who would be rid of him devise His speedy taking off *Lear* v 1 65
Talbot. Warwick and Talbot, Salisbury and Gloucester *Hen. V.* iv 3 54
A dismal fight Betwixt the stout Lord Talbot and the French.—What ! wherein Talbot overcame? is't so?—O, no ; wherein Lord Talbot was o'erthrown 1 *Hen. VI.* i 1 106
Valiant Talbot above human thought Enacted wonders with his sword and lance i 1 121
His soldiers spying his undaunted spirit A Talbot ! a Talbot ! cried out i 1 128
A base Walloon, to win the Dauphin's grace, Thrust Talbot with a spear into the back i 1 138
Is Talbot slain? then I will slay myself, For living idly here i 1 141
Why live we idly here? Talbot is taken, whom we wont to fear i 2 14
Talbot, my life, my joy, again return'd ! How wert thou handled? i 4 23
Hast thou any life? Speak unto Talbot : nay, look up to him i 4 89
Talbot, farewell ; thy hour is not yet come i 5 13
Ascend, brave Talbot ; we will follow thee.—Not all together ii 1 28
Here will Talbot mount, or make his grave. Now, Salisbury, for thee ii 1 34
I think this Talbot be a fiend of hell ii 1 46
The cry of Talbot serves me for a sword ii 1 79
Which of this princely train Call ye the warlike Talbot? ii 2 35
Here is the Talbot : who would speak with him? ii 2 37
As your ladyship desired, By message craved, so is Lord Talbot come ii 3 13
Is this the scourge of France? Is this the Talbot, so much fear'd abroad? ii 3 16
Stay, my Lord Talbot ; for my lady craves To know the cause of your abrupt departure.—Marry, for that she's in a wrong belief, I go to certify her Talbot's here ii 3 29
I laugh to see your ladyship so fond To think that you have aught but Talbot's shadow Whereon to practise ii 3 46
Are you now persuaded That Talbot is but shadow of himself? ii 3 62
Victorious Talbot ! pardon my abuse : I find thou art no less than fame hath bruited ii 3 67
Be not dismay'd, fair lady ; nor misconstrue The mind of Talbot ii 3 74
Thou shalt rue this treason with thy tears, If Talbot but survive iii 2 37
I'll have a bout with you again, Or else let Talbot perish with this shame iii 2 57
Hold thy peace ; If Talbot do but thunder, rain will follow iii 2 59
Let's get us from the walls ; For Talbot means no goodness by his looks iii 2 72
There will we be too, ere it be long, Or else reproach be Talbot's greatest fame ! iii 2 76
Lord Talbot, do not so dishonour me : Here will I sit before the walls of Rouen iii 2 90
Will you fly, and leave Lord Talbot?—Ay, All the Talbots in the world iii 2 107
Warlike and martial Talbot, Burgundy Enshrines thee in his heart iii 2 118
What wills Lord Talbot pleaseth Burgundy iii 2 130
Let frantic Talbot triumph for a while And like a peacock sweep along his tail iii 3 5
We will entice the Duke of Burgundy To leave the Talbot and to follow us iii 3 20
There goes the Talbot, with his colours spread iii 3 31
When Talbot hath set footing once in France iii 3 64
My forces and my power of men are yours : So farewell, Talbot iii 3 84
Is this the Lord Talbot, uncle Gloucester? iii 4 13
Lord Talbot there shall talk with him And give him chastisement iv 1 68
English John Talbot, captains, calls you forth iv 2 3
Ten thousand French have ta'en the sacrament To rive their dangerous artillery Upon no Christian soul but English Talbot iv 2 30
God and Saint George, Talbot and England's right, Prosper our colours ! iv 2 55
He is march'd to Bourdeaux with his power, To fight with Talbot iv 3 5
Renowned Talbot doth expect my aid iv 3 12
Spur to the rescue of the noble Talbot iv 3 19
To Bourdeaux, York ! Else, farewell Talbot, France, and England's honour iv 3 23
O God, that Somerset, who in proud heart Doth stop my cornets, were in Talbot's place ! iv 3 25
Then God take mercy on brave Talbot's soul ; And on his son young John ! iv 3 34
This seven years did not Talbot see his son ; And now they meet iv 3 37
What joy shall noble Talbot have To bid his young son welcome to his grave? iv 3 39
This expedition was by York and Talbot Too rashly plotted iv 4 2
The over-daring Talbot Hath sullied all his gloss of former honour iv 4 5
York set him on to fight and die in shame, That, Talbot dead, great York might bear the name iv 4 9
Whither were you sent?—Whither, my lord? from bought and sold Lord Talbot iv 4 13
And Talbot perisheth by your default iv 4 28
The fraud of England, not the force of France, Hath now entrapp'd the noble-minded Talbot iv 4 37
For fly he could not, if he would have fled ; And fly would Talbot never iv 4 44
If he be dead, brave Talbot, then adieu ! iv 4 45
O young John Talbot ! I did send for thee To tutor thee in stratagems of war, That Talbot's name might be in thee revived iv 5 1
Is my name Talbot? and am I your son? And shall I fly? iv 5 12
The world will say, he is not Talbot's blood, That basely fled when noble Talbot stood iv 5 16
Fight, soldiers, fight : The regent hath with Talbot broke his word iv 6 2
Where is John Talbot? Pause, and take thy breath iv 6 4
That pure blood of mine Which thou didst force from Talbot, my brave boy iv 6 24
Before young Talbot from old Talbot fly, The coward horse that bears me fall and die ! iv 6 46
By all the glory you have won, An if I fly, I am not Talbot's son iv 6 51
Talk no more of flight, it is no boot ; If son to Talbot, die at Talbot's foot iv 6 53
Where is my other life? mine own is gone ; O, where's young Talbot? iv 7 2
Triumphant death, smear'd with captivity, Young Talbot's valour makes me smile at thee iv 7 4

Talbot. Two Talbots, winged through the lither sky, In thy despite shall 'scape mortality . . . . 1 *Hen. VI.* iv 7 21
I have what I would have, Now my old arms are young John Talbot's grave . . . . iv 7 32
How the young whelp of Talbot's, raging-wood, Did flesh his puny sword in Frenchmen's blood! . . . . iv 7 35
Young Talbot was not born To be the pillage of a giglot wench . . iv 7 40
But where's the great Alcides of the field, Valiant Lord Talbot? . . iv 7 61
Lord Talbot of Goodrig and Urchinfield . . . . . . iv 7 64
Is Talbot slain, the Frenchmen's only scourge, Your kingdom's terror? iv 7 77
I think this upstart is old Talbot's ghost. . . . . . iv 7 87
All will be ours, now bloody Talbot's slain . . . . . iv 7 96
I trust the ghost of Talbot is not there: Now he is gone, my lord, you need not fear . . . . v 2 16
Sir Walter Herbert, a renowned soldier; Sir Gilbert Talbot *Rich. III.* iv 5 10
Talbotites. This is the happy wedding torch That joineth Rouen unto her countrymen, But burning fatal to the Talbotites! 1 *Hen. VI.* iii 2 28
Tale. Your tale, sir, would cure deafness . . . . . *Tempest* i 2 106
My tale provokes that question . . . . i 2 140
If you trouble him any more in's tale, by this hand, I will supplant some of your teeth . . . . iii 2 56
Now, forward with your tale . . . . iii 2 91
At this time I will tell no tales . . . . v 1 129
Where should I lose my tongue?—In thy tale . . . *T. G. of Ver.* ii 3 54
My tales of love were wont to weary you . . . . . . ii 4 126
Shall tell you another tale, if matters grow to your likings . *Mer. Wives* i 1 79
Peace-a your tongue. Speak-a your tale . . . . . . i 4 86
What of that?—Well, thereby hangs a tale . . . . . i 4 159
There is an old tale goes . . . . iv 4 28
And did deliver to our age This tale of Herne the hunter for a truth . iv 4 38
I can tell thee pretty tales of the duke . . . *Meas. for Meas.* iv 3 175
This gentleman told somewhat of my tale . . . . . . v 1 84
Rely upon it till my tale be heard, And hold no longer out . . . v 1 370
A mad tale he told to-day at dinner . . . . *Com. of Errors* iv 3 89
Like the old tale, my lord: 'it is not so, nor 'twas not so' . *Much Ado* i 1 218
With the force And strong encounter of my amorous tale . . . i 1 327
I had my good wit out of the 'Hundred Merry Tales' . . . . ii 1 135
That tells a heavy tale for him: conclude, conclude he is in love . iii 2 63
I will owe thee an answer for that: and now forward with thy tale . iii 3 109
Thou hast shifted out of thy tale into telling me of the fashion . . iii 3 151
I tell this tale vilely . . . . iii 3 157
'Fore God, they are both in a tale . . . . iv 2 33
That aged ears play truant at his tales . . . . *L. L. Lost* ii 1 74
Dead, for my life!—Even so; my tale is told . . . . . v 2 729
For aught that I could ever read, Could ever hear by tale or history, The course of true love never did run smooth . . . *M. N. Dream* i 1 133
The wisest aunt, telling the saddest tale . . . . . . ii 1 51
Put in two scales, Will even weigh, and both as light as tales . . iii 2 133
He hears merry tales and smiles not . . . . *Mer. of Venice* i 2 52
When the tale is told, bid her be judge Whether Bassanio had not once a love . . . . iv 1 276
I could match this beginning with an old tale . . . *As Y. Like It* i 2 128
And then, from hour to hour, we rot and rot; And thereby hangs a tale ii 7 28
Saving your tale, . . . Let us, that are poor petitioners, speak too *T. of S.* ii 1 71
And thereby hangs a tale.—Let's ha't . . . . . . iv 1 60
This is to feel a tale, not to hear a tale.—And therefore 'tis called a sensible tale . . . . iv 1 65
What's that to thee?—Why, a horse.—Tell thou the tale . . . iv 1 74
If he be credulous and trust my tale, I'll make him glad . . . iv 2 67
My widow says, thus she conceives her tale . . . . . v 2 24
Upon the least occasion more mine eyes will tell tales of me . *T. Night* ii 1 43
Pray you, sit by us, And tell's a tale.—Merry or sad shall't be? *W. Tale* ii 1 23
A sad tale's best for winter: I have one Of sprites and goblins . . ii 1 25
And make stale The glistering of this present, as my tale Now seems to it iv 1 13
This news which is called true is so like an old tale . . . . v 2 30
Like an old tale still, which will have matter to rehearse, though credit be asleep and not an ear open . . . . v 2 66
Were it but told you, should be hooted at Like an old tale . . . v 3 117
Your tale must be how he employ'd my mother . . . *K. John* i 1 98
Tell o'er thy tale again: It cannot be; thou dost but say 'tis so . . iii 1 5
Then speak again; not all thy former tale, But this one word, whether thy tale be true . . . . iii 1 25
Tell him this tale; and from the mouth of England Add thus much more iii 1 152
Life is as tedious as a twice-told tale Vexing the dull ear of a drowsy man iii 4 108
As an ancient tale new told, And in the last repeating troublesome . iv 2 18
Another lean unwash'd artificer Cuts off his tale and talks . . . iv 2 202
As bid me tell my tale in express words . . . . . . iv 2 234
My death's sad tale may yet undeaf his ear . . . *Richard II.* ii 1 16
Too well, too well thou tell'st a tale so ill . . . . . iii 2 121
My tongue hath but a heavier tale to say . . . . . . iii 2 197
We'll tell tales.—Of sorrow or of joy?—Of either, madam . . . iii 4 10
Let them tell thee tales Of woeful ages long ago betid . . . . v 1 41
To quit their griefs, Tell thou the lamentable tale of me . . . v 1 44
Turn the key, That no man enter till my tale be done . . . . v 3 37
Good uncle, tell your tale; I have done . . . . 1 *Hen. IV.* i 3 256
I by thee have watch'd, And heard thee murmur tales of iron wars . ii 3 51
That his tale to me may be nothing but 'Anon' . . . . . ii 4 35
Pitiful-hearted Titan, that melted at the sweet tale of the sun's! . . ii 4 135
Mark now, how a plain tale shall put you down . . . . . ii 4 281
Many tales devised, Which oft the ear of greatness needs must hear . iii 2 23
I thank him, that he cuts me from my tale, For I profess not talking . v 2 91
This is the strangest tale that ever I heard.—This is the strangest fellow v 4 158
It is not well done, mark you now, to take the tales out of my mouth *Hen. V.* iv 7 45
And death approach not ere my tale be done . . . 1 *Hen. VI.* ii 5 62
This superficial tale Is but a preface of her worthy praise . . . v 5 10
Had I first been put to speak my mind, I think I should have told your grace's tale . . . . 2 *Hen. VI.* iii 1 44
Short tale to make, we at Saint Alban's met . . . 3 *Hen. VI.* ii 1 120
Then he was urged to tell my tale again . . . . *Richard III.* iii 7 31
Prepare her ears to hear a wooer's tale . . . . . . iv 4 327
An honest tale speeds best being plainly told . . . . . iv 4 358
Then in plain terms tell her my loving tale . . . . . iv 4 359
Why dost thou run so many mile about, When thou mayst tell thy tale a nearer way? Once more, what news? . . . . iv 4 462
Every tongue brings in a several tale, And every tale condemns me . v 3 194
In seeking tales and informations Against this man . . *Hen. VIII.* v 3 110
You shall tell me another tale . . . . . . *Troi. and Cres.* i 2 91
To end a tale of length, Troy in our weakness stands, not in her strength i 3 136
I shall tell you A pretty tale: it may be you have heard it *Coriolanus* i 1 93

Tale. You must not think to fob off our disgrace with a tale *Coriolanus* i 1 98
After your way his tale pronounced shall bury His reasons with his body v 6 58
No sooner had they told this hellish tale . . . . *T. Andron.* ii 3 105
They will not intercept my tale . . . . iii 1 40
To bid Æneas tell the tale twice o'er . . . . iii 2 27
Make my aunt merry with some pleasing tale . . . . . iii 2 47
Shall I read? This is the tragic tale of Philomel . . . . . iv 1 47
Let him tell the tale; Your hearts will throb . . . . . v 3 94
And could tell A whispering tale in a fair lady's ear . *Rom. and Jul.* i 5 25
Stop there.—Thou desirest me to stop in my tale against the hair.—Thou wouldst else have made thy tale large.—O, thou art deceived; I would have made it short: for I was come to the whole depth of my tale . . . . ii 4 99
The excuse that thou dost make in this delay Is longer than the tale . ii 5 34
I will be brief, for my short date of breath Is not so long as is a tedious tale . . . . v 3 230
A tale Told by an idiot, full of sound and fury, Signifying nothing *Macb.* v 5 26
I could a tale unfold whose lightest word Would harrow up thy soul *Ham.* i 5 15
And he, repulsed—a short tale to make—Fell into a sadness . . . ii 2 146
One speech in it I chiefly loved: 'twas Æneas' tale to Dido . . . ii 2 468
Prithee, say on: he's for a jig or a tale of bawdry, or he sleeps: say on ii 2 522
Mar a curious tale in telling it, and deliver a plain message bluntly *Lear* i 4 35
Nor tell tales of thee to high-judging Jove . . . . . . ii 4 231
Pray, and sing, and tell old tales, and laugh At gilded butterflies . . v 3 12
List a brief tale; And when 'tis told, O, that my heart would burst! . v 3 181
Told the most piteous tale of Lear and him That ever ear received . v 3 214
I will a round unvarnish'd tale deliver Of my whole course of love *Othello* i 3 90
I think this tale would win my daughter too . . . . . i 3 171
Whereby hangs a tale, sir?—Marry, sir, by many a wind-instrument . iii 1 9
I will make him tell the tale anew, Where, how, how oft, how long ago iv 1 85
Come, mistress, you must tell's another tale . . . . . v 1 125
'Tis thus; Who tells me true, though in his tale lie death, I hear him as he flatter'd . . . . *Ant. and Cleo.* i 2 102
Truths would be tales, Where now half tales be truths . . . . ii 2 136
If thou wert honourable, Thou wouldst have told this tale for virtue *Cymb.* i 6 143
She hath been reading late The tale of Tereus . . . . . . ii 2 45
You may then revolve what tales I have told you Of courts, of princes iii 3 14
And am right glad he is not standing here To tell this tale of mine . v 5 297
Shall we rest us here, And by relating tales of others' griefs, See if 'twill teach us to forget our own? . . . . *Pericles* i 4 2
Talent. A rare talent!—If a talent be a claw, look how he claws him with a talent . . . . *L. L. Lost* iv 2 64
And those that are fools, let them use their talents . . . *T. Night* i 5 16
Five talents is his debt, His means most short . . . *T. of Athens* i 1 95
Three talents on the present; in future, all . . . . . . i 1 141
I do return those talents, Doubled with thanks and service . . . i 2 6
Let the request be fifty talents . . . . ii 2 202
Bid 'em send o' the instant A thousand talents to me . . . . ii 2 208
In scarcity of friends, I clear'd him with five talents . . . . ii 2 235
Some good necessity Touches his friend, which craves to be remember'd With those five talents . . . . ii 2 238
Having great and instant occasion to use fifty talents . . . . iii 1 19
To borrow so many talents, nay, urged extremely for't . . . . iii 2 13
I should ne'er have denied his occasion so many talents . . . . iii 2 26
His lordship is but merry with me; He cannot want fifty five hundred talents . . . . iii 2 43
Fifty talents.—Tell out my blood . . . . iii 4 94
In you, which I account his beyond all talents . . . . *Cymbeline* i 6 80
Tale-porter. One Mistress Tale-porter, and five or six honest wives *W. T.* iv 4 273
Talk. No more: thou dost talk nothing to me . . . . *Tempest* ii 1 170
He's in his fit now and does not talk after the wisest . . . . ii 2 76
Sit then and talk with her; she is thine own . . . . . . iv 1 32
What sad talk was that Wherewith my brother held you? *T. G. of Ver.* i 3 1
She doth talk in her sleep.—It's no matter for that, so she sleep not in her talk . . . . iii 1 333
This Sir Proteus that we talk on . . . . iv 2 73
How likes she my discourse?—Ill, when you talk of war . . . . v 2 16
We had an hour's talk of that wart . . . . . *Mer. Wives* i 4 162
Go in with us and see: we have an hour's talk with you . . . . ii 1 172
Break their talk, Mistress Quickly: my kinsman shall speak for himself iii 4 22
Why, does he talk of him?—Of none but him . . . . . . iv 2 30
In good sadness, is he; and talks of the basket too . . . . . iv 2 94
Talk not to me; my mind is heavy: I will give over all . . . . iv 6 1
I had rather give my body than my soul.—I talk not of your soul *M. for M.* ii 4 57
Love talks with better knowledge, and knowledge with dearer love . iii 2 159
I would the duke we talk of were returned again . . . . . iii 2 183
If bawdy talk offend you, we'll have very little of it . . . . iv 3 188
As strange unto your town as to your talk . . . *Com. of Errors* ii 2 151
O spite of spites! We talk with goblins, owls, and sprites . . . ii 2 192
Who talks within there? ho, open the door! . . . . . . iii 1 38
Wilt thou still talk?—How say you now? . . . . iv 4 47
God help, poor souls, how idly do they talk! . . . . . . iv 4 132
Talk not of her: you shall find her the infernal Ate in good apparel *M. Ado* ii 1 262
If they were but a week married, they would talk themselves mad . . ii 1 369
Let me woo no more.—Because you talk of wooing, I will sing . . ii 3 51
Now you talk of a sheet of paper, I remember a pretty jest . . . ii 3 140
Our talk must only be of Benedick . . . . iii 1 17
My talk to thee must be how Benedick Is sick in love with Beatrice . iii 1 20
For the watch to babble and to talk is most tolerable and not to be endured . . . . iii 3 37
We will rather sleep than talk: we know what belongs to a watch . . iii 3 39
Did see her, hear her, at that hour last night Talk with a ruffian . . iv 1 92
Talk with a man out at a window! A proper saying! . . . . . iv 1 311
The watch heard them talk of one Deformed . . . . . . v 1 317
We'll talk with Margaret, How her acquaintance grew with this lewd fellow . . . . v 1 340
If any man be seen to talk with a woman within the term of three years *L. L. Lost* i 1 130
But a merrier man, Within the limit of becoming mirth, I never spent an hour's talk withal . . . . ii 1 68
We will talk no more of this matter . . . . iii 1 119
You talk greasily; your lips grow foul . . . . iv 1 139
I'll prove her fair, or talk till doomsday here . . . . . . iv 3 274
With visages display'd, to talk and greet . . . . v 2 144
For Pyramus and Thisby, says the story, did talk through the chink of a wall . . . . *M. N. Dream* iii 1 65
He doth nothing but talk of his horse . . . . *Mer. of Venice* i 2 45
I will buy with you, sell with you, talk with you, walk with you . . i 3 37
Talk you of young Master Launcelot? . . . . ii 2 50
Put on a sober habit, Talk with respect and swear but now and then . ii 2 200

Talk. I would not have my father See me in talk with thee *Mer. of Venice* ii 3 9
It is true, without any slips of prolixity or crossing the plain highway of talk . . . . iii 1 13
What talk you of the posy or the value? . . . . v 1 151
Turning these jests out of service, let us talk in good earnest *As Y. L. It* i 3 26
Who comes here; a young man and an old in solemn talk . . iii 4 21
Never talk to me; I will weep.—Do, I prithee. . . . iii 4 1
But what talk we of fathers, when there is such a man as Orlando? . iii 4 41
Since that thou canst talk of love so well, Thy company, which erst was irksome to me, I will endure . . . . . iii 5 94
'Tis but a peevish boy; yet he talks well; But what care I for words? iii 5 110
And practise rhetoric in your common talk . . . . *T. of Shrew* i 1 35
Sirrah, be gone, or talk not, I advise you . . . . i 2 44
A word ere you go; Are you a suitor to the maid you talk of? . i 2 230
Talk not to me: I will go sit and weep . . . . . ii 1 35
They call me Katharine that do talk of me . . . . ii 1 185
Whose tongue?—Yours, if you talk of tails . . . . ii 1 218
Nor hast thou pleasure to be cross in talk . . . . ii 1 251
But what talk I of this? Call forth Nathaniel, Joseph . . . iv 1 91
Talk not, Signior Gremio: I say he shall go to prison . . . v 1 99
Here is a wonder, if you talk of a wonder.—And so it is . . . v 2 106
It much repairs me To talk of your good father . . . *All's Well* i 2 31
Get you gone, sir; I'll talk with you more anon . . . i 3 68
I long to talk with the young noble soldier . . . . iv 5 109
I had talk of you last night . . . . . . v 2 56
I heard my lady talk of it yesterday . . . . *T. Night* i 3 15
Here standing To prate and talk for life and honour . *W. Tale* iii 2 42
I have deserved All tongues to talk their bitterest . . . iii 2 217
A thing to talk on when thou art dead and rotten . . . iii 3 82
My father and the gentlemen are in sad talk . . . . iv 4 317
But what talk we of these traitorly rascals, whose miseries are to be smiled at? . . . . iv 4 821
I heard them talk of a fardel and I know not what . . . v 2 125
Talks as familiarly of roaring lions As maids of thirteen do of puppy-dogs! . . . . *K. John* ii 1 459
He talks to me that never had a son . . . . . iii 4 91
If I talk to him, with his innocent prate He will awake my mercy . iv 1 25
And when they talk of him, they shake their heads And whisper one another . . . . iv 2 188
Another lean unwash'd artificer Cuts off his tale and talks . . iv 2 202
Of comfort no man speak: Let's talk of graves, of worms and epitaphs *Richard II.* iii 2 145
Let's choose executors and talk of wills . . . . . iii 2 148
Well, well, I see I talk but idly, and you laugh at me . . . iii 3 171
My wretchedness unto a row of pins, They'll talk of state . . iii 4 27
Amongst much other talk, that very time, I heard you say . . iv 1 14
I do remember well The very time Aumerle and you did talk . . iv 1 61
Talk so like a waiting-gentlewoman Of guns and drums and wounds *1 Hen. IV.* i 3 55
I'll talk to you When you are better temper'd to attend . . . i 3 234
Than feed on cates and have him talk to me In any summer-house . iii 1 163
Talk not of dying: I am out of fear Of death or death's hand . . iv 1 135
For a silken point I'll give my barony: never talk of it . . *2 Hen. IV.* i 1 54
I talk not of his majesty . . . . i 2 120
How ill it follows, after you have laboured so hard, you should talk so idly! . . . . ii 2 32
I was once of Clement's Inn, where I think they will talk of mad Shallow yet . . . . iii 2 16
Talks as familiarly of John a Gaunt as if he had been sworn brother to him iii 2 344
Our argument Is all too heavy to admit much talk . . . . v 2 24
Think, when we talk of horses, that you see them . . . *Hen. V.* Prol. 26
You must not dare, for shame, to talk of mercy . . . . ii 2 81
We talk, and, be Chrish, do nothing: 'tis shame for us all . . iii 2 116
What ish my nation? Who talks of my nation? . . . . iii 2 134
My lord high constable, you talk of horse and armour? . . . iii 7 8
I am content; so the maiden cities you talk of may wait on her . v 2 354
In private will I talk with thee apart . . . . *1 Hen. VI.* i 2 69
My lord, methinks, is very long in talk . . . . . i 2 118
Speak, sirrah, when you should; Must your bold verdict enter talk with lords? . . . . iii 1 63
Be wary how you place your words; Talk like the vulgar sort of market men . . . . iii 2 4
Summon a parley; we will talk with him. . . . . . iii 3 35
Lord Talbot there shall talk with him And give him chastisement . iv 1 68
Then talk no more of flight, it is no boot . . . . . iv 6 52
He talks at random; sure, the man is mad . . . . . v 3 84
That's a wooden thing!—He talks of wood: it is some carpenter . v 3 90
Lady, wherefore talk you so?—I cry you mercy, 'tis but Quid for Quo v 3 108
I come to talk of commonwealth affairs . . . . *2 Hen. VI.* i 3 157
Bring him near the king; His highness' pleasure is to talk with him ii 1 73
The day is almost spent: Lord Suffolk, you and I must talk of that event . . . . iii 1 326
Sometime he talks as if Duke Humphrey's ghost Were by his side . iii 2 373
Hale him away, and let him talk no more . . . . . iv 1 131
Thou hast men about thee that usually talk of a noun and a verb . iv 7 43
Talk not of France, sith thou hast lost it all . . . *3 Hen. VI.* i 1 110
Men may talk of kings, and why not I?—Ay, but thou talk'st as if thou wert a king . . . . iii 1 58
With my talk and tears, Both full of truth . . . . . iii 3 158
My lords, forbear this talk; here comes the king . . . . iv 1 6
But wherefore stay we? 'tis no time to talk . . . . . iv 5 24
What talk you of debating? . . . . iv 7 53
Shew him our commission; talk no more. . . . *Richard III.* i 4 90
My Lord of York will still be cross in talk . . . . . iii 1 126
Break off your talk, And give us notice of his inclination . . iii 1 177
Wot you what, my lord? To-day the lords you talk of are beheaded . iii 2 93
Go on before; I'll talk with this good fellow . . . . iii 2 97
When I met this holy man, Those men you talk of came into my mind . iii 2 118
Gallants, That fill the court with quarrels, talk, and tailors *Hen. VIII.* i 3 20
By your leave, sweet ladies: If I chance to talk a little wild, forgive me i 4 26
Then we shall have 'em Talk us to silence . . . . . i 4 45
I told your grace they would talk anon . . . . . . i 4 49
A strong faith to conceal it.—Let me have it; I do not talk much . ii 1 146
How you do talk! . . . . ii 3 44
I would somebody had heard her talk yesterday, as I did *Troi. and Cres.* i 1 46
Good morrow, cousin Cressid: what do you talk of? . . . i 2 45
Nay, if we talk of reason, Let's shut our gates and sleep . . ii 2 46
To see great Hector in his weeds of peace, To talk with him . . iii 3 240
I cannot sing, Nor heel the high lavolt, nor sweeten talk . . iv 4 88
As we walk, To our own selves bend we our needful talk . . . iv 4 141

Talk. Be silent, boy; I profit not by thy talk . . . *Troi. and Cres.* v 1 17
Because you talk of pride now,—will you not be angry? . . *Coriolanus* ii 1 28
You talk of pride: O that you could turn your eyes toward the napes of your necks! . . . . ii 1 41
What do ye talk? Have we not had a taste of his obedience? . . iii 1 317
I talk of you: Why did you wish me milder? . . . . . iii 2 13
What do you prate of service?—I talk of that, that know it . . iii 3 84
Come, what talk you Of Marcius? . . . . iv 6 46
Your soldiers use him as the grace 'fore meat, Their talk at table . iv 7 4
If you have heard your general talk of Rome, And of his friends there, it is lots to blanks, My name hath touch'd your ears . . . v 2 9
Talks like a knell, and his hum is a battery . . . . . v 4 21
Away, and talk not; trouble us no more . . . . *T. Andron.* i 1 478
Come, Lucius, come; stay not to talk with them . . . . ii 3 306
Thou map of woe, that thus dost talk in signs! . . . . iii 2 12
O, handle not the theme, to talk of hands, Lest we remember still that we have none. Fie, fie, how franticly I square my talk! . . iii 2 29
Keep there: now talk at pleasure of your safety . . . . iv 2 134
'Twill vex thy soul to hear what I shall speak; For I must talk of murders . . . . v 1 63
I am come to talk with thee.—No, not a word . . . . . v 2 16
How can I grace my talk, Wanting a hand to give it action? . . v 2 17
If thou didst know me, thou wouldest talk with me . . . . v 2 20
What, drawn, and talk of peace! I hate the word . *Rom. and Jul.* i 1 77
Nurse, give leave awhile, We must talk in secret:—nurse, come back again . . . . i 3 8
Marry, that 'marry' is the very theme I came to talk of . . . i 3 64
True, I talk of dreams, Which are the children of an idle brain . . i 4 96
This wind, you talk of, blows us from ourselves . . . . i 4 104
A gentleman, nurse, that loves to hear himself talk . . . ii 4 156
We talk here in the public haunt of men . . . . . . iii 1 53
Talk no more.—O, then I see that madmen have no ears . . . iii 3 60
How is't, my soul? let's talk; it is not day.—It is, it is: hie hence! iii 5 25
Talk not to me, for I'll not speak a word: Do as thou wilt . . iii 5 204
Did I dream it so? Or am I mad, hearing him talk of Juliet? . . v 3 80
Go hence, to have more talk of these sad things . . . . v 3 307
No talk of Timon, nothing of him expect . . . *T. of Athens* v 2 14
It will not let you eat, nor talk, nor sleep . . . . *J. Cæsar* ii 1 252
To keep with you at meals, comfort your bed, And talk to you sometimes . . . . ii 1 285
I have an hour's talk in store for you; Remember that you call on me. ii 2 121
Stand fast together, lest some friend of Cæsar's Should chance— Talk not of standing . . . . iii 1 89
Do not talk of him, But as a property . . . . . . iv 1 39
The deep of night is crept upon our talk, And nature must obey necessity . . . . iv 3 226
Ill spirit, I would hold more talk with thee . . . . . iv 3 289
We must out and talk . . . . v 1 22
Skirr the country round; Hang those that talk of fear . . *Macbeth* v 3 36
I would not, in plain terms, from this time forth, Have you so slander any moment leisure, As to give words or talk with the Lord Hamlet *Hamlet* i 3 134
Didst perceive?—Very well, my lord.—Upon the talk of the poisoning? iii 2 300
I will talk further with you.—No, do not. . . . . *Lear* iii 1 43
Go you and maintain talk with the duke . . . . . iii 3 16
First let me talk with this philosopher. What is the cause of thunder? iii 4 159
I'll talk a word with this same learned Theban. What is your study? iii 4 162
Hear poor rogues Talk of court news; and we'll talk with them too . v 3 14
I'll watch him tame and talk him out of patience . . . *Othello* iii 3 23
She reserves it evermore about her To kiss and talk to . . . iii 3 296
The handkerchief!—I pray, talk me of Cassio.—The handkerchief! . iii 4 92
Do not talk to me, Emilia; I cannot weep . . . . . iv 2 102
Come, come, you talk. . . . . iv 3 25
Talk you of killing?—Ay, I do.—Then heaven Have mercy on me! . v 2 33
The honour is sacred which he talks on now, Supposing that I lack'd it *Ant. and Cleo.* ii 2 85
Your hostages I have, so have you mine; And we shall talk before we fight . . . . ii 6 2
Sir, I will eat no meat, I'll not drink, sir; If idle talk will once be necessary, I'll not sleep neither . . . . v 2 50
Never talk on't; She hath been colted by him . . . *Cymbeline* ii 4 132
Why should excuse be born or e'er begot? We'll talk of that hereafter iii 2 68
Hear me with patience.—Talk thy tongue weary; speak . . . iii 4 115
It is too late to talk of love . . . . . . *Pericles* ii 3 113

Talked. I think there are, sir; I heard them talked of . . *Mer. Wives* i 1 301
And to be talk'd with in sincerity, As with a saint . . *Meas. for Meas.* i 4 36
Such a fellow is not to be talked withal . . . . . . v 1 348
What man was he talk'd with you yesternight Out at your window? *Much Ado* iv 1 84
I talk'd with no man at that hour . . . . iv 1 87
Here they stay'd an hour, And talk'd apace . . . . *L. L. Lost* v 2 369
Yourself and all the world, That talk'd of her, have talk'd amiss of her *T. of Shrew* ii 1 293
He was mad for her, and talked of Satan and of Limbo . . *All's Well* v 3 261
Thou know'st He dies to me again when talk'd of . . . *W. Tale* v 1 120
He talked very wisely, but I regarded him not; and yet he talked wisely *1 Hen. IV.* i 2 97
And still he smiled and talk'd . . . . i 3 41
Thou hast talk'd Of sallies and retires, of trenches, tents, Of palisadoes ii 3 53
To-day might I, hanging on Hotspur's neck, Have talk'd of Monmouth's grave . . . . *2 Hen. IV.* ii 3 45
But then he was rheumatic, and talked of the whore of Babylon *Hen. V.* ii 3 40
I'll sort occasion, As index to the story we late talk'd of *Richard III.* ii 2 149
My uncle Rivers talk'd how I did grow More than my brother . . ii 4 11
Like to a lonely dragon, that his fen Makes fear'd and talk'd of *Coriol.* iv 1 31
Are you so brave? I'll have you talked with anon . . . . iv 5 19
I nursed her daughter, that you talk'd withal . . *Rom. and Jul.* i 5 117
And for a hand, and a foot, and a body, though they be not to be talked on, yet they are past compare . . . . ii 5 43
And therefore have I little talk'd of love . . . . . iv 1 7
When could they say till now, that talk'd of Rome, That her wide walls encompass'd but one man? . . . . . . *J. Cæsar* i 2 154
Good gentlemen, he hath much talk'd of you . . . . *Hamlet* ii 2 19
You have been talk'd of since your travel much . . . . iv 7 72
Edmund and I have talk'd; And more convenient is he for my hand *Lear* iv 5 30
Dispatch we The business we have talk'd of . . . *Ant. and Cleo.* ii 2 169

Talker. Farewell: I'll grow a talker for this gear . . *Mer. of Venice* i 1 110
We will not stand to prate: Talkers are no good doers . *Richard III.* i 3 352
My good lord, have great care I be not found a talker . . *Hen. VIII.* ii 2 79

Talkest. To suggest thee from thy master thou talkest of . . *All's Well* iv 5 48

Talkest. Talkest thou nothing but of ladies? . . . . *T. Night* iv 2 30
Thou talkest of an admirable conceited fellow . . . *W. Tale* iv 4 203
What talkest thou to me of the hangman? . . . . *1 Hen. IV.* ii 1 73
Say, what art thou that talk'st of kings and queens? *3 Hen. VI.* iii 1 55
Thou talk'st as if thou wert a king.—Why, so I am, in mind . iii 1 59
Peace, peace, Mercutio, peace! Thou talk'st of nothing . *Rom. and Jul.* i 4 96
Who, without those means thou talkest of, didst thou ever know beloved?—Myself.—I understand thee . . . *T. of Athens* iv 3 313
Poor prattler, how thou talk'st! . . . . . *Macbeth* iv 2 64
Talking. I have done: but yet,— He will be talking . . *Tempest* ii 1 27
We were talking that our garments seem now as fresh as when we were at Tunis . . . . ii 1 96
I prithee now, lead the way without any more talking . . . ii 2 178
To chide myself Even for this time I spend in talking to thee *T. G. of V.* iv 2 104
I wonder that you will still be talking . . . . *Much Ado* i 1 117
She has been too long a talking of . . . . . . iii 2 107
A good old man, sir; he will be talking . . . . . iii 5 36
Because I would be talking of her . . . . *As Y. Like It* iv 1 91
I will weary you then no longer with idle talking . . . v 2 57
Talking with the deceiving father of a deceitful son . *T. of Shrew* iv 4 82
He finds that now scarce to be worth talking of . . *T. Night* iii 4 328
Talking of the Alps and Apennines . . . . . *K. John* i 1 202
I profess not talking; only this—Let each man do his best . *1 Hen. IV.* v 2 92
Talking of hawking; nothing else, my lord . . *2 Hen. VI.* ii 1 50
What, talking with a priest, lord chamberlain? . . *Richard III.* iii 2 114
Your grace is noble: Let me have such a bowl may hold my thanks, And save me so much talking . . . . . *Hen. VIII.* i 4 40
All else This talking lord can lay upon my credit, I answer is most false iii 2 265
What were you talking of when I came? . . . *Troi. and Cres.* i 2 48
Hector was stirring early.—That were we talking of, and of his anger i 2 53
What, blushing still? have you not done talking yet? . . . iii 2 109
No more talking on't; let it be done . . . . *Coriolanus* i 1 12
The general and his wife are talking of it; And she speaks for you *Oth.* iii 1 46
I have been talking with a suitor here . . . . . iii 3 42
I was the other day talking on the sea-bank with certain Venetians . iv 1 137
Tall. How tall was she?—About my stature . . . *T. G. of Ver.* iv 4 162
As tall a man of his hands as any is between this and his head *M. Wives* i 4 26
I would have made you four tall fellows skip like rats . . . ii 1 237
You were good soldiers and tall fellows . . . . . ii 2 11
If tall, a lance ill-headed; If low, an agate very vilely cut . *Much Ado* iii 1 64
The cowslips tall her pensioners be . . . . *M. N. Dream* ii 1 10
With her personage, her tall personage, Her height, forsooth, she hath prevail'd with him . . . . iii 2 292
Anon comes Pyramus, sweet youth and tall . . . . . v 1 145
Where the carcases of many a tall ship lie buried . *Mer. of Venice* iii 1 6
I am more than common tall . . . . . *As Y. Like It* i 3 117
He is not very tall; yet for his years he's tall: His leg is but so so . iii 5 118
Thou'rt a tall fellow: hold thee that to drink . . *T. of Shrew* iv 4 17
He's as tall a man as any's in Illyria.—What's that to the purpose? *T. N.* i 3 20
I am not tall enough to become the function well . . . iv 2 7
I'll swear to the prince thou art a tall fellow of thy hands and that thou wilt not be drunk; but I know thou art no tall fellow *W. Tale* v 2 177
I would thou wouldst be a tall fellow of thy hands . . . . v 2 181
By any means prove a tall fellow . . . . v 2 183
If I do not wonder how thou darest venture to be drunk, not being a tall fellow, trust me not . . . . v 2 185
With eight tall ships, three thousand men of war . . *Richard II.* ii 1 286
Which many a good tall fellow had destroy'd So cowardly . *1 Hen. IV.* i 3 62
A tall gentleman, by heaven, and a most gallant leader . *2 Hen. IV.* iii 2 67
Welcome, my tall fellow . . . . v 1 65
For women are shrews, both short and tall . . . . . v 3 36
Give me thy fist, thy fore-foot to me give: Thy spirits are most tall *Hen. V.* ii 1 72
Spoke like a tall fellow that respects his reputation . *Richard III.* i 4 156
Tall stockings, Short blister'd breeches . . . *Hen. VIII.* i 3 30
A very good blade! a very tall man! a very good whore! *Rom. and Jul.* ii 4 31
And yond tall anchoring bark, Diminish'd to her cock . . *Lear* iv 6 18
That he may bless this bay with his tall ship . . *Othello* ii 1 79
Bring me word how tall she is . . . . *Ant. and Cleo.* ii 5 118
And carry back to Sicily much tall youth That else must perish here . iii 6 7
Is she as tall as me?—She is not, madam.—Didst hear her speak? . iii 3 14
Taller. Few taller are so young . . . . . *L. L. Lost* v 2 846
Considering the weather, a taller man than I will take cold *T. of Shrew* iv 1 11
Tallest. Which is the greatest lady, the highest?—The thickest and the tallest . . . . *L. L. Lost* iv 1 47
Tallow. Send me a cool rut-time, Jove, or who can blame me to piss my tallow? . . . . *M. Wives* v 5 16
Her rags and the tallow in them will burn a Poland winter *Com. of Er.* iii 2 100
Call in ribs, call in tallow . . . . . . *1 Hen. IV.* ii 4 125
A wassail candle, my lord, all tallow . . . *2 Hen. IV.* i 2 179
Unlustrous as the smoky light That's fed with stinking tallow *Cymbeline* i 6 110
Tallow-catch. Thou whoreson, obscene, greasy tallow-catch *1 Hen. IV.* ii 4 252
Tallow-face. Out, you green-sickness carrion! out, you baggage! You tallow-face! . . . . *Rom. and Jul.* iii 5 158
Tally. Whereas, before, our forefathers had no other books but the score and the tally . . . . *2 Hen. VI.* iv 7 39
Talon. I was not an eagle's talon in the waist . . *1 Hen. IV.* ii 4 363
Is Beaufort term'd a kite? Where are his talons? . *2 Hen. VI.* iii 2 196
So doves do peck the falcon's piercing talons . . . *3 Hen. VI.* i 4 41
Thou art like the harpy, Which, to betray, dost, with thine angel's face, Seize with thine eagle's talons . . . . . *Pericles* iv 3 48
Tam. The tevil and his tam! what phrase is this? . . . *Mer. Wives* i 1 151
Tame. If I can recover him and keep him tame . . *Tempest* ii 2 71; 80
Whose golden touch could soften steel and stones, Make tigers tame *T. G. of Ver.* iii 2 80
Yet to be what I would not shall not make me tame . *Mer. Wives* iii 5 153
You are too cold; if you should need a pin, You could not with more tame a tongue desire it . . . . . *Meas. for Meas.* ii 2 46
If justice cannot tame you, she shall ne'er weigh more reasons *Much Ado* v 1 210
You are a tame man, go! . . . . . . *M. N. Dream* iii 2 259
I see love hath made thee a tame snake . . . *As Y. Like It* iv 3 70
I am he am born to tame you, Kate . . . . *T. of Shrew* ii 1 278
'Tis a world to see, How tame, when men and women are alone . ii 1 314
Thou knowest, winter tames man, woman, and beast . . . iv 1 24
He that knows better how to tame a shrew, Now let him speak . iv 1 213
God give him joy!—Ay, and he'll tame her . . . . . iv 2 53
Teacheth tricks eleven and twenty long, To tame a shrew . . iv 2 58
I have kept of them tame, and know their natures . . . *All's Well* ii 5 50
Cram's with praise, and make's As fat as tame things . . *W. Tale* i 2 92
And make them tame to their obedience . . . . *K. John* iv 2 262
And tame the savage spirit of wild war . . . . . . v 2 74
Tame. Yet can I not of such tame patience boast As to be hush'd *Rich. II.* i 1 52
Lions make leopards tame.—Yea, but not change his spots . . i 1 174
Their courage with hard labour tame and dull . . *1 Hen. IV.* iv 3 23
Like the fox, Who, ne'er so tame, so cherish'd and lock'd up, Will have a wild trick of his ancestors . . . . v 2 10
A tame cheater, i' faith; you may stroke him as gently as a puppy *2 Hen. IV.* ii 4 105
Still use of grief makes wild grief tame . . . . *Richard III.* iv 4 229
Those that tame wild horses Pace 'em not in their hands . *Hen. VIII.* v 3 21
Two curs shall tame each other . . . . . *Troi. and Cres.* i 3 391
You must be watched ere you be made tame, must you? . . . iii 2 46
We vow to weep seas, live in fire, eat rocks, tame tigers . . iii 2 84
Custom and condition Made tame and most familiar to my nature . iii 3 10
His remedies are tame i' the present peace And quietness *Coriolanus* iv 6 2
Be not too tame neither, but let your own discretion be your tutor *Ham.* iii 2 18
Start not so wildly from my affair.—I am tame, sir: pronounce . iii 2 322
At your age The hey-day in the blood is tame, it's humble . . iii 4 69
If that the heavens do not their visible spirits Send quickly down to tame these vile offences, It will come . . . . . *Lear* iv 2 47
A most poor man, made tame to fortune's blows . . . . iv 6 225
I'll watch him tame and talk him out of patience . . . *Othello* iii 3 23
I'll tame you; I'll bring you in subjection . . . . *Pericles* ii 5 75
Tamed. Winter tames man, woman, and beast; for it hath tamed my old master and my new mistress and myself . . *T. of Shrew* iv 1 24
Thou hast tamed a curst shrew.—'Tis a wonder, by your leave, she will be tamed so . . . . v 2 188
Tamed the king, and made the dauphin stoop . . . *3 Hen. VI.* ii 2 151
Would drink up The lees and dregs of a flat tamed piece *Troi. and Cres.* iv 1 62
Tamely. Stoop tamely to the foot of majesty . . . *2 Hen. IV.* iv 2 42
If we live thus tamely, To be thus jaded by a piece of scarlet *Hen. VIII.* iii 2 279
Fool me not so much To bear it tamely; touch me with noble anger *Lear* ii 4 279
Tameness. Any madness I ever yet beheld seemed but tameness, civility, and patience, to this his distemper . . . . *Mer. Wives* iv 2 27
He's mad that trusts in the tameness of a wolf . . . *Lear* iii 6 19
Tamer than sleep, fonder than ignorance . . . *Troi. and Cres.* i 1 10
Taming my wild heart to thy loving hand . . . . *Much Ado* iii 1 112
Taming-school. The taming-school! what, is there such a place? *T. of S.* iv 2 55
Tamora, the Queen of Goths—When Goths were Goths and Tamora was queen . . . . *T. Andron.* i 1 139
Lovely Tamora, queen of Goths . . . . i 1 315
I choose thee, Tamora, for my bride, And will create thee empress of Rome . . . . i 1 319
If ever Tamora Were gracious in those princely eyes of thine, Then hear me i 1 428
At my lovely Tamora's entreats, I do remit these young men's heinous faults . . . . i 1 483
This day shall be a love day, Tamora . . . . . . i 1 491
Now climbeth Tamora Olympus' top, Safe out of fortune's shot . ii 1 1
So Tamora: Upon her wit doth earthly honour wait . . . ii 1 9
Hark, Tamora, the empress of my soul . . . . . . ii 3 40
Semiramis, nay, barbarous Tamora, For no name fits thy nature but thy own! . . . . ii 3 118
O Tamora! thou bear'st a woman's face . . . . . . ii 3 136
O Tamora, be call'd a gentle queen, And with thine own hands kill me! ii 3 168
Where is my lord the king?—Here, Tamora, though grieved with killing grief . . . . ii 3 260
O Tamora! was ever heard the like? This is the pit . . . ii 3 276
Who found this letter? Tamora, was it you? . . . . . ii 3 293
There's for thyself, and that's for Tamora . . . . . iii 2 74
What! the lustful sons of Tamora Performers of this heinous, bloody deed? . . . . iv 1 79
For this care of Tamora, Herself and hers are highly bound to thee . iv 2 170
Thus it shall become High-witted Tamora to gloze with all . . iv 4 35
He will not entreat his son for us.—If Tamora entreat him, then he will iv 4 95
We'll follow where thou lead'st, . . . And be avenged on cursed Tamora v 1 16
I know thee well For our proud empress, mighty Tamora . . v 2 26
Thou sad man, I am not Tamora; She is thy enemy, and I thy friend . v 2 28
Of this was Tamora delivered; The issue of an irreligious Moor . v 3 120
As for that heinous tiger, Tamora, No funeral rite . . . v 3 195
Tamworth. From Tamworth thither is but one day's march *Richard III.* v 2 13
Tang. For she had a tongue with a tang . . . . *Tempest* ii 2 52
Let thy tongue tang arguments of state . . . . *T. Night* ii 5 163
Let thy tongue tang with arguments of state . . . . . iii 4 78
Tangle. You must lay lime to tangle her desires . *T. G. of Ver.* iii 2 68
'Od's my little life, I think she means to tangle my eyes too! *As Y. L. It* iii 5 44
Well appointed, Stands with the snares of war to tangle thee *1 Hen. VI.* iv 2 22
Fly thou how thou canst, they'll tangle thee . . . *2 Hen. VI.* ii 4 55
Tangled. His speech was like a tangled chain . . . *M. N. Dream* v 1 125
My king is tangled in affection to A creature of the queen's *Hen. VIII.* iii 2 35
Tank. Me tank you for dat . . . . *Mer. Wives* ii 3 75
Tanlings. To be still hot summer's tanlings . . . *Cymbeline* iv 4 29
Tanned. His hide is so tanned with his trade, that he will keep out water a great while . . . . *Hamlet* v 1 186
Tanner. There's Best's son, the tanner of Wingham . *2 Hen. VI.* iv 2 24
A tanner will last you nine year . . . . . . *Hamlet* v 1 183
Tanquam. Novi hominem tanquam te . . . . *L. L. Lost* v 1 10
Tanta est erga te mentis integritas, regina serenissima . *Hen. VIII.* iii 1 40
Tantæne animis cœlestibus iræ? . . . . . *2 Hen. VI.* ii 1 24
Tap. He shall draw, he shall tap . . . . . *Mer. Wives* i 3 11
This is the right fencing grace, my lord; tap for tap . *2 Hen. IV.* ii 1 206
Tape. Will you buy any tape, Or lace for your cape? . *W. Tale* iv 4 322
Tape, glove, shoe-tie, bracelet, horn-ring . . . . . iv 4 610
Taper. Waxen tapers on their heads, And rattles in their hands *Mer. W.* iv 4 50
Pinch him sound And burn him with their tapers . . . . iv 4 62
Tapers they are, with your sweet breaths puff'd out . *L. L. Lost* v 2 267
My inch of taper will be burnt and done . . . . *Richard II.* i 3 223
When our nuptial day was done, And tapers burn'd to bedward *Coriolanus* i 6 32
Tapers burn so bright and every thing In readiness for Hymenæus *T. An.* i 1 324
A precious ring, . . . Which, like a taper in some monument, Doth shine ii 3 228
Now, by the burning tapers of the sky, That shone so brightly . iv 2 89
Get me a taper in my study, Lucius . . . . . *J. Cæsar* ii 1 7
The taper burneth in your closet, sir . . . . ii 1 35
Now sit we close about this taper here, And call in question our necessities . . . . iv 3 164
How ill this taper burns! . . . . iv 3 275
Strike on the tinder, ho! Give me a taper! call up all my people! *Othello* i 1 142
What said she to you? Get more tapers; Raise all my kindred . . i 1 167
Take not away the taper, leave it burning . . . . *Cymbeline* ii 2 5
The flame o' the taper Bows towards her, and would under-peep her lids ii 2 19
Taper-light. With taper-light To seek the beauteous eye of heaven to garnish, Is wasteful and ridiculous excess . . . . *K. John* iv 2 14

Taper-light. I life would wish, and that I might Waste it for you, like taper-light . . . . *Pericles* i Gower 16
Tapestry. In the desk That's cover'd o'er with Turkish tapestry *Com. of Errors* iv 1 104
Like the shaven Hercules in the smirched worm-eaten tapestry *M. Ado* iii 3 146
My hangings all of Tyrian tapestry . . . . *T. of Shrew* ii 1 351
Fain to pawn both my plate and the tapestry of my dining-chambers 2 *Hen. IV.* ii 1 154
These bed-hangings and these fly-bitten tapestries . . ii 1 159
It was hang'd With tapestry of silk and silver . . *Cymbeline* ii 4 69
Taphouse. For mine own part, I never come into any room in a taphouse, but I am drawn in . . . *Meas. for Meas.* ii 1 219
Tapped. That blood already, like the pelican, Hast thou tapp'd out *Richard II.* ii 1 127
Tapster. A tapster is a good trade: an old cloak makes a new jerkin; a withered serving-man a fresh tapster . . . . . *Mer. Wives* i 3 17
You need not change your trade; I'll be your tapster still *Meas. for Meas.* i 2 112
What's to do here, Thomas tapster? let's withdraw . . i 2 116
What are you, sir?—He, sir! a tapster, sir . . . ii 1 63
What trade are you of, sir?—A tapster; a poor widow's tapster . ii 1 207
I would not have you acquainted with tapsters: they will draw you, Master Froth . . . . ii 1 215
Come you hither to me, Master tapster. What's your name, Master tapster? . . . . ii 1 223
You are partly a bawd, Pompey, howsoever you colour it in being a tapster . . . . ii 1 232
I am ill at reckoning; it fitteth the spirit of a tapster . . *L. L. Lost* i 2 43
The oath of a lover is no stronger than the word of a tapster *As Y. L. It* iii 4 34
Revolted tapsters and ostlers trade-fallen . . . 1 *Hen. IV.* iv 2 31
Pregnancy is made a tapster . . . . 2 *Hen. IV.* i 2 193
He has not past three or four hairs on his chin,— Indeed, a tapster's arithmetic may soon bring his particulars therein to a total *Troi. and Cres.* i 2 123
Thou gavest thine ears like tapsters that bid welcome To knaves *T. of A.* iv 3 215
Tar. She loved not the savour of tar nor of pitch . . *Tempest* ii 2 54
Civet is of a baser birth than tar, the very uncleanly flux of a cat *As Y. Like It* iii 2 70
Tardied. The good mind of Camillo tardied My swift command *W. Tale* iii 2 163
Tardily. Those that could speak low and tardily Would turn their own perfection to abuse, To seem like him . . . 2 *Hen. IV.* ii 3 26
Tardiness. A tardiness in nature Which often leaves the history unspoke That it intends to do . . . . *Lear* i 1 238
Tardy. Is your tardy master now at hand? . . *Com. of Errors* ii 1 44
An you be so tardy, come no more in my sight . . *As Y. Like It* iv 1 51
Whose manners still our tardy apish nation Limps after. *Richard II.* ii 1 22
These tardy tricks of yours will, on my life, One time or other break some gallows' back . . . . 2 *Hen. IV.* iv 3 31
Some tardy cripple bore the countermand . . . *Richard III.* ii 1 89
Be not ta'en tardy by unwise delay . . . . . . iv 1 52
You have ta'en a tardy sluggard here . . . . . . v 3 225
O, my lord, you're tardy . . . . *Hen. VIII.* i 4 7
The prince must think me tardy and remiss . . *Troi. and Cres.* iv 4 143
Too swift arrives as tardy as too slow . . . *Rom. and Jul.* ii 6 15
So is he now in execution Of any bold or noble enterprise, However he puts on this tardy form . . . . *J. Cæsar* i 2 303
Now this overdone, or come tardy off, though it make the unskilful laugh, cannot but make the judicious grieve . . *Hamlet* iii 2 28
Do you not come your tardy son to chide? . . . . . iii 4 106
Tardy-gaited. And chide the cripple tardy-gaited night . *Hen. V.* iv Prol. 20
Tarentum. From Tarentum and Brundusium He could so quickly cut the Ionian sea . . . . *Ant. and Cleo.* iii 7 22
Targe. That oft in field, with targe and shield . . *L. L. Lost* v 2 556
To part with unhack'd edges, and bear back Our targes undinted *Ant. and Cleo.* ii 6 39
Whose naked breast Stepp'd before targes of proof . . *Cymbeline* v 5 5
Target. But took all their seven points in my target, thus 1 *Hen. IV.* ii 4 224
Henceforward will I bear Upon my target three fair-shining suns 3 *Hen. VI.* ii 1 40
They That come to hear a merry bawdy play, A noise of targets *Hen. VIII.* Prol. 15
I had purpose Once more to hew thy target from thy brawn *Coriolanus* iv 5 126
The adventurous knight shall use his foil and target . . *Hamlet* ii 2 334
Now, by my sword,— And target. Still he mends *Ant. and Cleo.* i 3 82
Make a jolly march; Bear our hack'd targets like the men that owe them iv 8 31
Poison and treason are the hands of sin, Ay, and the targets . *Pericles* i 1 140
It was sometime target to a king; I know it by this mark . ii 1 143
Tarpeian. Bear him to the rock Tarpeian, and from thence Into destruction cast him . . . . *Coriolanus* iii 1 213
He shall be thrown down the Tarpeian rock With rigorous hands . iii 1 266
Pile ten hills on the Tarpeian rock, That the precipitation might down stretch Below the beam of sight . . . . iii 2 3
Let them pronounce the steep Tarpeian death, Vagabond exile, flaying . iii 3 88
Banish him our city, In peril of precipitation From off the rock Tarpeian iii 3 103
Tarquin. He received in the repulse of Tarquin seven hurts i' the body . ii 1 166
When Tarquin made a head for Rome, he fought Beyond the mark of others . . . . ii 2 92
Tarquin's self he met, And struck him on his knee . . . ii 2 98
A merrier day did never yet greet Rome, No, not the expulsion of the Tarquins . . . . v 4 46
And make proud Saturnine and his empress Beg at the gates, like Tarquin and his queen . . . . *T. Andron.* iii 1 299
As Tarquin erst, That left the camp to sin in Lucrece' bed . iv 1 63
My ancestors did from the streets of Rome The Tarquin drive *J. Cæsar* ii 1 54
With his stealthy pace, With Tarquin's ravishing strides . *Macbeth* ii 1 55
Our Tarquin thus Did softly press the rushes, ere he waken'd The chastity he wounded . . . . *Cymbeline* ii 2 12
Tarre. And like a dog that is compell'd to fight, Snatch at his master that doth tarre him on . . . . *K. John* iv 1 117
Pride alone Must tarre the mastiffs on, as 'twere their bone . *Tr. and Cr.* i 3 392
And the nation holds it no sin to tarre them to controversy . *Hamlet* ii 2 370
Tarred over with the surgery of our sheep . . *As Y. Like It* iii 2 63
Tarriance. I am impatient of my tarriance . . . *T. G. of Ver.* ii 7 90
Tarried. Have I not tarried?—Ay, the grinding; but you must tarry the bolting.—Have I not tarried?—Ay, the bolting, but you must tarry the leavening.—Still have I tarried.—Ay, to the leavening *Troi. and Cres.* i 1 17
I might have still held off, And then you would have tarried . . iv 2 18
Tarry. You'll lose the tide, if you tarry any longer . . *T. G. of Ver.* ii 3 39
Tarry I here, I but attend on death . . . . . . iii 1 186
By my trot, I tarry too long . . . . *Mer. Wives* i 4 64
Tarry you a little-a while . . . . i 4 93
Tarry. You may be gone; it is not good you tarry here . . *Mer. Wives* i 4 117
A Bohemian-Tartar tarries the coming down of thy fat woman . iv 5 21
Fare ye well.—Nay, tarry; I'll go along with thee . . *Meas. for Meas.* iv 3 174
Hindered by the sergeant, to tarry for the hoy Delay . *Com. of Errors* iv 3 40
Tarry, sweet Beatrice.—I am gone, though I am here . . *Much Ado* iv 1 294
Tarry, good Beatrice. By this hand, I love thee . . . . iv 1 327
Tarry, rash wanton: am not I thy lord?—Then I must be thy lady *M. N. Dream* ii 1 63
And tarry for the comfort of the day . . . . . . ii 2 38
I pray you, tarry: pause a day or two Before you hazard *Mer. of Venice* iii 2 1
Tarry a little; there is something else . . . . . iv 1 305
Tarry, Jew: The law hath yet another hold on you . . . iv 1 346
Make haste: thou know'st where I will tarry . . . . iv 2 18
I'll tarry no longer with you: farewell . . . *As Y. Like It* iii 2 309
Ay, it stands so that I may hardly tarry so long . *T. of Shrew* Ind. 2 127
I will therefore tarry in despite of the flesh and the blood . . Ind. 2 129
Tarry, Petruchio, I must go with thee . . . . . . i 2 117
I chafe you, if I tarry: let me go.—No, not a whit . . . ii 1 243
I cannot tarry: I knew a wench married in an afternoon . . iv 4 99
Tarry, holy pilgrim, But till the troops come by . . *All's Well* iii 5 42
If you tarry longer, I shall give worse payment . . . *T. Night* iv 1 20
I'll tarry till my son come; he hallooed but even now . *W. Tale* iii 3 78
If you will not, tarry at home and be hanged . . . 1 *Hen. IV.* i 2 147
If I tarry at home and go not, I'll hang you for going . . i 2 149
Well, come what will, I'll tarry at home . . . . . i 2 162
I will go drink with you, but I cannot tarry dinner. . 2 *Hen. IV.* iii 2 204
Tarry, dear cousin Suffolk! My soul shall thine keep company to heaven; Tarry, sweet soul, for mine . . . . . *Hen. V.* iv 6 15
Leave me, or tarry, Edward will be king . . . 3 *Hen. VI.* iv 1 65
Wilt thou go along?—Better do so than tarry and be hang'd . iv 5 26
They vex me past my patience! Pray you, pass on: I will not tarry *Hen. VIII.* ii 4 131
He that will have a cake out of the wheat must needs tarry the grinding.—Have I not tarried?—Ay, the grinding; but you must tarry the bolting.—Have I not tarried?—Ay, the bolting, but you must tarry the leavening . . . . . . *Troi. and Cres.* i 1 16
Prithee, tarry: You men will never tarry . . . . . iv 2 15
Good night and welcome, both at once, to those That go or tarry . . v 1 85
Old Nestor tarries; and you too, Diomed, Keep Hector company . v 1 87
Tarry with him till I turn again . . . . . . *T. Andron.* v 2 141
Tarry for the mourners, and stay dinner . . . *Rom. and Jul.* iv 5 150
It is more worthy to leap in ourselves, Than tarry till they push us *J. C.* v 5 25
If you will measure your lubber's length again, tarry . . . *Lear* i 4 101
Nuncle Lear, nuncle Lear, tarry and take the fool with thee . . i 4 338
But I will tarry; the fool will stay, And let the wise man fly . ii 4 83
Tarrying. Thisby, tarrying in mulberry shade . . . *M. N. Dream* v 1 149
There is no tarrying here . . . *Troi. and Cres.* ii 3 269; *J. Cæsar* v 5 30
There is nor flying hence nor tarrying here . . . *Macbeth* v 5 48
Tarsus. I now look from thee then, and to Tarsus Intend my travel *Per.* i 2 115
This Tarsus, o'er which I have the government . . . . i 4 21
The misery of Tarsus may be theirs . . . . i 4 55
At Tarsus, where each man Thinks all is writ he speken can . . ii Gower 11
And that in Tarsus was not best Longer for him to make his rest . ii Gower 25
We are near Tarsus.—Thither, gentle mariner, After thy course for Tyre iii 1 74
O, make for Tarsus! There will I visit Cleon, for the babe Cannot hold out . . . . iii 1 78
Whom our fast-growing scene must find At Tarsus . . . . iv Gower 7
The petty wrens of Tarsus will fly hence, And open this to Pericles . iv 3 22
Well-sailing ships and bounteous winds have brought This king to Tarsus . . . . iv 4 18
Leaves Tarsus and again embarks. He swears Never to wash his face . iv 4 27
The king my father did in Tarsus leave me . . . . . v 1 172
Thou that wast born at sea, buried at Tarsus, And found at sea again! . v 1 198
She is not dead at Tarsus, as she should have been, By savage Cleon . v 1 217
My purpose was for Tarsus, there to strike The inhospitable Cleon . v 1 253
She at Tarsus Was nursed with Cleon . . . . v 3 7
Tart. Another way, The news is not so tart . . . . *Lear* iv 2 88
So tart a favour To trumpet such good tidings! . . *Ant. and Cleo.* ii 5 38
Tartar. He's in Tartar limbo, worse than hell . . *Com. of Errors* iv 2 32
Swifter than arrow from the Tartar's bow . . . *M. N. Dream* iii 2 101
Sweet love,— Thy love! out, tawny Tartar, out! . . . . iii 2 263
Stubborn Turks and Tartars, never train'd To offices of tender courtesy *Mer. of Venice* iv 1 32
Which gratitude Through flinty Tartar's bosom would peep forth *All's W.* iv 4 7
Follow me.—To the gates of Tartar, thou most excellent devil of wit! *T. Night* ii 5 226
He might return to vasty Tartar back . . . . . *Hen. V.* ii 2 123
Bearing a Tartar's painted bow of lath . . . *Rom. and Jul.* i 4 5
Sliver'd in the moon's eclipse, Nose of Turk and Tartar's lips *Macbeth* iv 1 29
Tartly. How tartly that gentleman looks! . . . . *Much Ado* ii 1 3
Tartness. They cannot be too sweet for the king's tartness . *All's Well* iv 3 96
The tartness of his face sours ripe grapes . . . . *Coriolanus* v 4 18
Task. To thy strong bidding task Ariel and all his quality . *Tempest* i 2 192
This my mean task Would be as heavy to me as odious . . . iii 1 4
A heavier task could not have been imposed . . . *Com. of Errors* i 1 32
That liked, but had a rougher task in hand . . . . *Much Ado* i 1 301
O, these are barren tasks, too hard to keep! . . . *L. L. Lost* i 1 47
But now to task the tasker . . . . ii 1 20
Your task shall be, With all the fierce endeavour of your wit To enforce the pained impotent to smile . . . . v 2 862
The heavy ploughman snores, All with weary task fordone *M. N. Dream* v 1 381
Then turn your forces from this paltry siege And stir them up against a mightier task . . . . *K. John* ii 1 55
What earthy name to interrogatories Can task the free breath of a sacred king? . . . . iii 1 148
The task he undertakes Is numbering sands and drinking oceans dry *Richard II.* ii 2 145
This ague fit of fear is over-blown; An easy task it is to win our own . iii 2 191
I task the earth to the like . . . . iv 1 52
Nay, task me to my word; approve me, lord . . . 1 *Hen. IV.* iv 1 9
Some things of weight That task our thoughts, concerning us *Hen. V.* i 2 6
Every man now task his thought, That this fair action may on foot be brought. . . . . i 2 309
To my task will I; Bonfires in France forthwith I am to make 1 *Hen. VI.* i 1 152
I have perform'd my task and was espoused . . . 2 *Hen. VI.* i 1 9
Take thou this task in hand.—I am content . . . . . iii 1 318
Sound the trumpets, and about our task . . . . 3 *Hen. VI.* ii 1 200
Shall I not hear my task?—An easy task; 'tis but to love a king . iii 2 53
Come, let us to our holy task again . . . . . *Richard III.* iii 7 246
Come, let me see what task I have to do. . . . . *T. Andron.* iii 1 276

Task. And day by day I'll do this heavy task *T. Andron.* v 2 58
Gentle people, give me aim awhile, For nature puts me to a heavy task v 3 150
Whose sore task Does not divide the Sunday from the week *Hamlet* i 1 75
And dare not task my weakness with any more *Othello* ii 3 43
She might lie by an emperor's side and command him tasks iv 1 196
Those that do teach young babes Do it with gentle means and easy tasks iv 2 112
The long day's task is done, And we must sleep *Ant. and Cleo.* iv 14 35
Thou thy worldly task hast done, Home art gone, and ta'en thy wages *Cymbeline* iv 2 260
You have at large received The danger of the task you undertake *Pericles* i 1 2
Tasked. The gallants shall be task'd; For, ladies, we will every one be mask'd *L. L. Lost* v 2 126
And in the neck of that, task'd the whole state *1 Hen. IV.* iv 3 92
Like to a harvest-man that's task'd to mow Or all or lose his hire *Coriol.* i 3 39
Tasker. But now to task the tasker *L. L. Lost* ii 1 20
Tasking. Shuffle her away, While other sports are tasking of their minds *Mer. Wives* iv 6 30
How show'd his tasking? seem'd it in contempt? *1 Hen. IV.* v 2 51
Tassel. Thou tassel of a prodigal's purse *Troi. and Cres.* v 1 36
Tassel-gentle. Hist! Romeo, hist! O, for a falconer's voice, To lure this tassel-gentle back again! *Rom. and Jul.* ii 2 160
Taste. He shall taste of my bottle: if he have never drunk wine *Tempest* ii 2 77
We have stomachs. Will't please you taste of what is here? iii 3 42
You do yet taste Some subtilties o' the isle v 1 123
That never meat sweet-savour'd in thy taste, Unless I spake *Com. of Er.* ii 2 119
That we thankful should be, Which we of taste and feeling are *L. L. Lost* iv 2 30
Love's tongue proves dainty Bacchus gross in taste iv 3 339
Nor hath Love's mind of any judgement taste *M. N. Dream* i 1 236
Did I loathe this food; But, as in health, come to my natural taste iv 1 179
The ear of man hath not seen, man's hand is not able to taste iv 1 218
My father did something smack, something grow to, he had a kind of taste *Mer. of Venice* ii 2 19
And thou, a merry devil, Didst rob it of some taste of tediousness ii 3 3
Sans teeth, sans eyes, sans taste, sans every thing *As Y. Like It* ii 7 166
For a taste: If a hart do lack a hind, Let him seek out Rosalind iii 2 106
But take a taste of my finding him, and relish it with good observance iii 2 246
I do not shame To tell you what I was, since my conversion So sweetly tastes, being the thing I am iv 3 138
Will't please your honour taste of these conserves? *T. of Shrew* Ind. 2 3
Taste with a distempered appetite *T. Night* i 5 98
Taste your legs, sir; put them to motion.—My legs do better understand me, sir, than I understand what you mean by bidding me taste my legs iii 1 87
Men that put quarrels purposely on others, to taste their valour iii 4 267
I know not how it tastes; though it be dish'd For me to try how *W. T.* iii 2 73
Whose every word deserves To taste of thy most worst iii 2 180
This affliction has a taste as sweet As any cordial comfort v 3 76
And bitter shame hath spoil'd the sweet world's taste *K. John* iii 4 110
A holy vow, Never to taste the pleasures of the world iv 3 68
How did he take it? who did taste to him?—A monk, I tell you v 6 28
Things sweet to taste prove in digestion sour *Richard II.* i 3 236
The setting sun, and music at the close, As the last taste of sweets, is sweetest last ii 1 13
I live with bread like you, feel want, Taste grief, need friends iii 2 176
They might have lived to bear and he to taste Their fruits of duty iii 4 62
Will't please you to fall to?—Taste of it first, as thou art wont to do v 5 99
Wherein is he good, but to taste sack and drink it? *1 Hen. IV.* ii 4 501
Without the taste of danger and reproof iii 1 175
They surfeited with honey and began To loathe the taste of sweetness iii 2 72
Come, let me taste my horse, Who is to bear me like a thunderbolt iv 1 119
The armed commons Have of their puissance made a little taste *2 Hen. IV.* iii 3 52
Every idle, nice, and wanton reason Shall to the king taste of this action iv 1 192
But for you, rebels, look to taste the due Meet for rebellion iv 2 116
This bitter taste Yield his engrossments to the ending father iv 5 79
You show great mercy, if you give him life, After the taste of much correction *Hen. V.* ii 2 51
The taste whereof, God of his mercy give You patience to endure! ii 2 179
Not a man of them that we shall take Shall taste our mercy iv 7 68
That we may Taste of your wine and see what cates you have *1 Hen. VI.* ii 3 79
'Twas full of darnel; do you like the taste?—Scoff on, vile fiend! iii 2 44
Gall, worse than gall, the daintiest that they taste! *2 Hen. VI.* iii 2 322
Let them not live to taste this land's increase *Richard III.* v 5 38
This is strange to me.—How tastes it? is it bitter? *Hen. VIII.* iii 3 89
The Trojans taste our dear'st repute With their finest palate *Tr. and Cr.* i 3 337
I begin to relish thy advice; And I will give a taste of it forthwith i 3 389
When that the watery palate tastes indeed Love's thrice repured nectar iii 2 22
I do beseech you, as in way of taste, To give me now a little benefit iii 3 13
That defend her, Not palating the taste of her dishonour iv 1 59
Why tell you me of moderation? The grief is fine, full, perfect, that I taste iv 4 3
Why, my negation hath no taste of madness v 2 127
Both your voices blended, the great'st taste Most palates theirs *Coriol.* iii 1 103
Have we not had a taste of his obedience? iii 1 318
And in the fountain shall we gaze so long Till the fresh taste be taken from that clearness *T. Andron.* iii 1 128
When it did taste the wormwood on the nipple Of my dug *Rom. and Jul.* i 3 30
How much salt water thrown away in waste, To season love, that of it doth not taste! ii 3 72
The sweetest honey Is loathsome in his own deliciousness And in the taste confounds the appetite ii 6 13
Shall we in, And taste Lord Timon's bounty? *T. of Athens* i 1 285
Hail to thee, worthy Timon, and to all That of his bounties taste! i 2 129
Th' ear, Taste, touch, and smell, pleased from thy table rise i 2 132
Will the cold brook, Candied with ice, caudle thy morning taste? iv 3 226
The valiant never taste of death but once *J. Cæsar* ii 2 33
Good friends, go in, and taste some wine with me ii 2 126
And, in some taste, is Lepidus but so; He must be taught iv 1 34
I have almost forgot the taste of fears *Macbeth* v 5 9
Come, give us a taste of your quality *Hamlet* ii 2 452
He wrote this but as an essay or taste of my virtue *Lear* i 2 47
She will taste as like this as a crab does to a crab i 5 18
'Tis his own blame; hath put himself from rest, And must needs taste his folly ii 4 294
I'll prove it on thy heart, Ere I taste bread v 3 94
All friends shall taste The wages of their virtue v 3 302
Whose qualification shall come into no true taste again *Othello* ii 1 283
And which she after, Except she bend her humour, shall be assured To taste of too *Cymbeline* i 5 82
I'll now taste of thy drug iv 2 38
Taste. Let them be joyful too, For they shall taste our comfort *Cymb.* v 5 403
Inflamed desire in my breast To taste the fruit of yon celestial tree *Pericles* i 1 21
Those palates who, not yet two summers younger, Must have inventions to delight the taste i 4 40
Those cities that of plenty's cup And her prosperities so largely taste i 4 53
Yes, indeed shall you, and taste gentlemen of all fashions iv 2 83
Tasted. Never have you tasted our reward *1 Hen. VI.* iii 4 22
Praise us as we are tasted, allow us as we prove *Troi. and Cres.* iii 2 98
Being tasted, slays all senses with the heart *Rom. and Jul.* ii 3 26
For mine own part, I never tasted Timon in my life *T. of Athens* iii 2 84
Having often of your open bounty tasted v 1 61
I had been happy, if the general camp, Pioners and all, had tasted her sweet body, So I had nothing known *Othello* iii 3 346
If you can make't apparent That you have tasted her in bed *Cymbeline* ii 4 57
Tasting. But, tasting it, Their counsel turns to passion *Much Ado* v 1 22
Wilt thou undo the worth thou art unpaid for, By tasting of our wrath? *Cymbeline* v 5 308
Tattered. From this castle's tatter'd battlements Our fair appointments may be well perused *Richard II.* iii 3 52
You would think that I had a hundred and fifty tattered prodigals *1 Hen. IV.* iv 2 37
In tatter'd weeds, with overwhelming brows *Rom. and Jul.* v 1 39
Through tatter'd clothes small vices do appear *Lear* iv 6 168
Tattering. And wound our tattering colours clearly up *K. John* v 5 7
Tatters. O, it offends me to the soul to hear a robustious periwig-pated fellow tear a passion to tatters, to very rags *Hamlet* iii 2 11
Tattle. Then let the ladies tattle what they please *T. Andron.* iv 2 168
Tattling. She's a very tattling woman *Mer. Wives* iii 3 99
Peace your tattlings! iv 1 26
Too like my lady's eldest son, evermore tattling *Much Ado* ii 1 11
Taught thee each hour One thing or other *Tempest* i 2 354
You taught me language; and my profit on't Is, I know how to curse i 2 363
Will you troll the catch You taught me but while-ere? iii 2 127
How angerly I taught my brow to frown! *T. G. of Ver.* i 2 62
She hath taught her suitor, He being her pupil, to become her tutor ii 1 143
Herself hath taught her love himself to write unto her lover ii 1 174
I have taught him, even as one would say precisely, 'thus I would teach a dog' iv 4 5
I have purchased at an infinite rate, and that hath taught me to say this *Mer. Wives* ii 2 214
One that hath taught me more wit than ever I learned before in my life iv 5 61
I do love: and it hath taught me to rhyme and to be melancholy *L. L. Lost* iv 3 13
I see, sir, you are liberal in offers: You taught me first to beg *Mer. of Ven.* iv 1 439
They are taught their manage, and to that end riders dearly hired *As Y. Like It* i 1 13
I am not taught to make any thing i 1 32
I could have taught my love to take thy father for mine i 2 12
An old religious uncle of mine taught me to speak iii 2 362
He taught me how to know a man in love iii 2 388
More pleasant . . . Than hath been taught by any of my trade *T. of S.* iii 1 69
If she be froward, Then hast thou taught Hortensio to be untoward iv 5 79
I will show myself highly fed and lowly taught *All's Well* ii 2 4
Did you find me in yourself, sir? or were you taught to find me? ii 4 35
Taught him to face me out of his acquaintance *T. Night* v 1 91
Who taught you this?—I learnt it out of women's faces *W. Tale* ii 1 11
You taught me how to know the face of right *K. John* v 2 88
That taught me craft To counterfeit oppression of such grief *Richard II.* i 4 13
He that no more must say is listen'd more Than they whom youth and ease have taught to glose ii 1 10
I'll have a starling shall be taught to speak Nothing but 'Mortimer' *1 Hen. IV.* i 3 224
Hath taught us how to cherish such high deeds v 5 30
What foolish master taught you these manners, Sir John?—Master Gower, if they become me not, he was a fool that taught them me *2 Hen. IV.* ii 1 202
Jack Cade, the Duke of York hath taught you this *2 Hen. VI.* iv 2 162
Hath that poor monarch taught thee to insult? *3 Hen. VI.* i 4 124
A peevish fool was that of Crete, That taught his son the office of a fowl! v 6 19
Were you well served, you would be taught your duty *Richard III.* i 3 250
You are not to be taught That you have many enemies *Hen. VIII.* ii 4 157
Say, I taught thee, Say, Wolsey, that once trod the ways of glory iii 2 434
O, do not learn her wrath; she taught it thee *T. Andron.* ii 3 143
Yet rich conceit Taught thee to make vast Neptune weep for aye *T. of A.* v 4 78
He must be taught and train'd and bid go forth *J. Cæsar* iv 1 35
We but teach Bloody instructions, which, being taught, return To plague the inventor *Macbeth* i 7 9
Taught me to shift Into a madman's rags *Lear* v 3 186
It hath been taught us from the primal state, That he which is was wish'd until he were *Ant. and Cleo.* i 4 41
One of your great knowing Should learn, being taught, forbearance *Cymbeline* ii 3 103
My friends, The boy hath taught us manly duties iv 2 397
Where I was taught Of your chaste daughter the wide difference 'Twixt amorous and villanous v 5 193
I thank thee, who hath taught My frail mortality to know itself *Pericles* i 1 41
Taunt. Have I lived to stand at the taunt of one that makes fritters of English? *Mer. Wives* v 5 151
Did not her kitchen-maid rail, taunt, and scorn me? *Com. of Errors* iv 4 77
Taunt him with the license of ink *T. Night* iii 2 47
With scoffs and scorns and contumelious taunts *1 Hen. VI.* i 4 39
Becomes it thee to taunt his valiant age? iii 2 54
After many scorns, many foul taunts *3 Hen. VI.* ii 1 64
'Tis but his policy to counterfeit, Because he would avoid such bitter taunts ii 6 66
I will acquaint his majesty With those gross taunts *Richard III.* i 3 106
He prettily and aptly taunts himself iii 1 134
Incensed by his subtle mother To taunt and scorn you iii 1 153
Mark'd you his lip and eyes?—Nay, but his taunts *Coriolanus* i 1 259
Taunt my faults With such full license as both truth and malice Have power to utter *Ant. and Cleo.* i 2 111
With taunts Did gibe my missive out of audience ii 2 73
A good rebuke, Which might have well becomed the best of men, To taunt at slackness iii 7 28
Taunted. When I had at my pleasure taunted her *M. N. Dream* iv 1 62
To be thus taunted, scorn'd, and baited at *Richard III.* i 3 109
Taunting. I'll write to him a very taunting letter *As Y. Like It* iii 5 134
Tauntingly. It tauntingly replied To the discontented members *Coriol.* i 1 114
Taurus. That pure congealed white, high Taurus' snow *M. N. Dream* iii 2 141
Were we not born under Taurus? *T. Night* i 3 147

Taurus. See, see, thou hast shot off one of Taurus' horns *T. Andron.* iv 3 69
Who's his lieutenant, hear you?—They say, one Taurus *Ant. and Cleo.* iii 7 79
Taurus!—My lord?—Strike not by land; keep whole . iii 8 1
Tavern. Given to fornications, and to taverns . . . *Mer. Wives* v 5 167
Inquire at London, 'mongst the taverns there *Richard II.* v 3 5
And is not my hostess of the tavern a most sweet wench? *1 Hen. IV.* i 2 45
Why, what a pox have I to do with my hostess of the tavern? i 2 54
You lie, ye rogue; 'tis going to the king's tavern . ii 2 59
Walking with thee in the night betwixt tavern and tavern . iii 3 49
O, I could wish this tavern were my drum! . . iii 3 230
Knocking at the taverns, And asking every one for Sir John Falstaff *2 Hen. IV.* ii 4 388
And I will see what physic the tavern affords . *1 Hen. VI.* iii 1 148
One of those fellows that when he enters the confines of a tavern claps me his sword upon the table . . *Rom. and Jul.* iii 1 6
More like a tavern or a brothel Than a graced palace *Lear* i 4 266
Tavern-bills. The comfort is, you shall be called to no more payments, fear no more tavern-bills . . . . . *Cymbeline* v 4 161
Tavern-reckonings. If there were anything in thy pocket but tavern-reckonings, memorandums . . *1 Hen. IV.* iii 3 178
Tavy. Your majesty takes no scorn to wear the leek upon Saint Tavy's day . . . . . . *Hen. V.* iv 7 108
Tawdry-lace. You promised me a tawdry-lace . *W. Tale* iv 4 253
Tawny. The ground indeed is tawny.—With an eye of green in't *Tempest* ii 1 54
The worth of many a knight From tawny Spain . . *L. L. Lost* i 1 174
Sweet love,— Thy love! out, tawny Tartar, out! . *M. N. Dream* iii 2 263
We shall your tawny ground with your red blood Discolour *Hen. V.* iii 6 170
Peace, tawny slave, half me and half thy dam! . *T. Andron.* v 1 27
Turn The office and devotion of their view Upon a tawny front *A. and C.* i 1 6
Tawny-coat. Blue coats to tawny coats . . *1 Hen. VI.* i 3 47
Out, tawny coats! out, scarlet hypocrite! . . . i 3 56
Down with the tawny-coats! . . . . . iii 1 74
Tawny-finned. I will betray Tawny-finn'd fishes *Ant. and Cleo.* ii 5 12
Tax. Wisdom wishes to appear most bright When it doth tax itself *Meas. for Meas.* ii 4 79
To tax him with injustice?—Take him hence; to the rack with him! . v 1 312
You tax Signior Benedick too much; but he'll be meet with you *M. Ado* i 1 46
Tax not so bad a voice To slander music any more than once . . ii 3 46
Who cries out on pride, That can therein tax any private party? *As Y. Like It* ii 7 71
What darest thou venture?—Tax of impudence . *All's Well* ii 1 173
Shall tax my fears of little vanity, Having vainly fear'd too little v 3 122
The commons hath he pill'd with grievous taxes . *Richard II.* ii 1 246
Because I would not tax the needy commons . *2 Hen. VI.* iii 1 116
They tax our policy, and call it cowardice *Troi. and Cres.* i 3 197
I'll warrant she'll tax him home . . . *Hamlet* iii 3 29
I tax not you, you elements, with unkindness . *Lear* iii 2 16
Taxation. You'll be whipped for taxation one of these days *As Y. Like It* i 2 91
I bring no overture of war, no taxation of homage . *T. Night* i 5 225
He hath not money for these Irish wars, His burthenous taxations notwithstanding, But by the robbing of the banish'd duke *Richard II.* ii 1 260
Upon these taxations, The clothiers all, not able to maintain The many to them 'longing, have put off The spinsters, carders, fullers, weavers *Hen. VIII.* i 2 30
Taxation! Wherein? and what taxation? My lord cardinal, You that are blamed for it alike with us, Know you of this taxation? . i 2 37
Taxed. I am not a woman, to be touched with so many giddy offences as he hath generally taxed their whole sex withal . *As Y. Like It* iii 2 368
Be check'd for silence, But never tax'd for speech . *All's Well* i 1 77
A most perfidious slave, With all the spots o' the world tax'd and debosh'd . . . . v 3 206
Makes us traduced and tax'd of other nations . *Hamlet* i 4 18
Taxing. My taxing like a wild-goose flies, Unclaim'd of any man *As Y. Like It* ii 7 86
Taxing me and gaging me to keep An oath that I have sworn *Tr. and Cr.* v 1 46
Teach me how To name the bigger light, and how the less *Tempest* i 2 334
Well, I am standing water.—I'll teach you how to flow . ii 1 222
If thou hast sinn'd, Teach me, thy tempted subject, to excuse it! *T. G. of Ver.* ii 6 8
I have taught him, even as one would say precisely, 'thus I would teach a dog' . . . . iv 4 6
I will teach a scurvy jack-a-nape priest to meddle or make . *Mer. Wives* i 4 115
We'll teach him to know turtles from jays . . iii 3 44
You do ill to teach the child such words . . iv 1 67
He teaches him to hick and to hack, which they'll do fast enough of themselves . . . . . . iv 1 68
I will teach the children their behaviours . . . iv 4 66
I'll teach you how you shall arraign your conscience *Meas. for Meas.* ii 3 21
A sister desires access to you.—Teach her the way . ii 4 19
Teach sin the carriage of a holy saint; Be secret-false *Com. of Errors* iii 2 14
Teach me, dear creature, how to think and speak . iii 2 33
And teach your ears to list me with more heed . . iv 1 101
My love is thine to teach: teach it but how, And thou shalt see how apt it is to learn Any hard lesson . . . *Much Ado* i 1 293
I will but teach them to sing, and restore them to the owner . ii 1 239
I will teach you how to humour your cousin . . ii 1 395
I am too sudden-bold: To teach a teacher ill beseemeth me *L. L. Lost* ii 1 108
Who is the suitor?—Shall I teach you to know? . iv 1 110
Where is any author in the world Teaches such beauty as a woman's eye? iv 3 313
He teaches boys the horn-book . . . . . v 1 49
Action and accent did they teach him there . . v 2 99
Teach us, sweet madam, for our rude transgression Some fair excuse v 2 431
Then let us teach our trial patience . . *M. N. Dream* i 1 152
O, teach me how you look, and with what art You sway the motion of Demetrius' heart . . . . i 1 192
O that your frowns would teach my smiles such skill! . . i 1 195
I can easier teach twenty what were good to be done, than be one of the twenty to follow mine own teaching . . *Mer. of Venice* i 2 17
Whose own hard dealings teaches them suspect The thoughts of others i 3 163
That choose by show, Not learning more than the fond eye doth teach ii 9 27
The villany you teach me, I will execute . . . iii 1 74
I could teach you How to choose right, but I am then forsworn iii 2 10
O happy torment, when my torturer Doth teach me answers for deliverance! . . . . iii 2 38
That same prayer doth teach us all to render The deeds of mercy . iv 1 201
Now methinks You teach me how a beggar should be answer'd . iv 1 440
Nerissa teaches me what to believe . . . v 1 207
Unless you could teach me to forget a banished father . *As Y. Like It* i 2 5
If I can by any means light on a fit man to teach her *T. of Shrew* i 1 112
And bow'd her hand to teach her fingering . . ii 1 151

Teach. I must begin with rudiments of art; To teach you gamut in a briefer sort . . . . . . *T. of Shrew* iii 1 67
She seems a mistress To most that teach . . *W. Tale* iv 4 594
Teach us some fence! . . . . . . *K. John* ii 1 290
If thou teach me to believe this sorrow, Teach thou this sorrow how to make me die . . . . iii 1 29
Thou Fortune's champion that dost never fight But when her humorous ladyship is by To teach thee safety! . . . iii 1 120
My reasonable part produces reason How I may be deliver'd of these woes, And teaches me to kill or hang myself . . iii 4 56
The spirit of the time shall teach me speed . . iv 2 176
If thou but frown on me, or stir thy foot, Or teach thy hasty spleen to do me shame, I'll strike thee dead . . . iv 3 97
Teach thy necessity to reason thus . . *Richard II.* i 3 277
If I were thy nurse, thy tongue to teach, 'Pardon' should be the first word of thy speech . . . . . . v 3 113
Say 'pardon,' king; let pity teach thee how: The word is short . v 3 116
Dost thou teach pardon pardon to destroy? . . . v 3 120
I can teach you, cousin, to command The devil.—And I can teach thee, coz, to shame the devil By telling truth . *1 Hen. IV.* iii 1 56
If I had a thousand sons, the first humane principle I would teach them should be, to forswear thin potations . *2 Hen. IV.* iv 3 134
Creatures that by a rule in nature teach The act of order . *Hen. V.* i 2 188
It fits us then to be as provident As fear may teach us . . ii 4 12
Be copy now to men of grosser blood, And teach them how to war . iii 1 25
And teach lavoltas high and swift corantos . . iii 5 33
He let him outlive that day to see His greatness and to teach others how they should prepare . . . . iv 1 195
This story shall the good man teach his son . . iv 3 56
Let a Welsh correction teach you a good English condition . v 1 83
Vouchsafe to teach a soldier terms Such as will enter at a lady's ear v 2 99
My royal cousin, teach you our princess English? . . v 2 308
Then, good my lord, teach your cousin to consent winking.—I will wink on her to consent, my lord, if you will teach her to know my meaning . . . . v 2 331
And will not you maintain the thing you teach? . *1 Hen. VI.* iii 1 129
Your discretions better can persuade Than I am able to instruct or teach . . . . iv 1 159
Ah, Gloucester, teach me to forget myself! . *2 Hen. VI.* ii 4 27
Teach not thy lips such scorn, for they were made For kissing *Rich. III.* i 2 172
Since you teach me how to flatter you, Imagine I have said farewell i 2 224
Teach me to be your queen, and you my subjects: O, serve me well, and teach yourselves that duty! . . . . . . i 3 252
O thou well skill'd in curses, stay awhile, And teach me how to curse! iv 4 117
Revolving this will teach thee how to curse . . iv 4 123
You, that best should teach us, Have misdemean'd yourself *Hen. VIII.* v 3 13
This maxim out of love I teach: Achievement is command *Troi. and Cres.* i 2 318
Nature teaches beasts to know their friends . *Coriolanus* ii 1 6
And by my body's action teach my mind A most inherent baseness . iii 2 122
When did the tiger's young ones teach the dam? . *T. Andron.* ii 3 142
O, let me teach thee! for my father's sake, That gave thee life . ii 3 158
Teach her not thus to lay Such violent hands upon her tender life . iii 2 21
No, boy, not so; I'll teach thee another course . . iv 1 119
O, let me teach you how to knit again This scatter'd corn . v 3 70
O, teach me how I should forget to think . *Rom. and Jul.* i 1 232
Thou canst not teach me to forget.—I'll pay that doctrine, or else die in debt . . . . i 1 243
O, she doth teach the torches to burn bright! . . i 5 46
I'll teach them to prevent wild Alcibiades' wrath . *T. of Athens* v 1 206
It is a creature that I teach to fight, To wind, to stop, to run *J. Cæsar* iv 1 31
Herein I teach you How you shall bid God 'ild us for your pains *Macbeth* i 6 12
We but teach Bloody instructions, which, being taught, return To plague the inventor . . . . i 7 8
We'll teach you to drink deep ere you depart . *Hamlet* i 2 175
I do not know, my lord, what I should think.—Marry, I'll teach you . i 3 105
To what end, my lord?—That you must teach me . . ii 2 293
I loved your father, and we love ourself; And that, I hope, will teach you to imagine . . . . iv 7 35
And that should teach us There's a divinity that shapes our ends . v 2 9
Come, sir, arise, away! I'll teach you differences . *Lear* i 4 99
Sirrah, I'll teach thee a speech.—Do.—Mark it, nuncle . i 4 128
Dost thou know the difference, my boy, between a bitter fool and a sweet fool?—No, lad; teach me . . . . . i 4 153
Keep a schoolmaster that can teach thy fool to lie: I would fain learn to lie . . . . i 4 196
You reverend braggart, We'll teach you— Sir, I am too old to learn . ii 2 134
We'll set thee to school to an ant, to teach thee there's no labouring i' the winter . . . . ii 4 69
I should but teach him how to tell my story, And that would woo her *Oth.* i 3 165
For thy escape would teach me tyranny, To hang clogs on them . i 3 197
Let's teach ourselves that honourable stop, Not to outsport discretion ii 3 2
A knave teach me my duty! I'll beat the knave into a twiggen bottle . ii 3 151
Be as your fancies teach you; Whate'er you be, I am obedient . iii 3 88
Those that do teach young babes Do it with gentle means . iv 2 111
Teach me, Alcides, thou mine ancestor, thy rage . *Ant. and Cleo.* iv 12 43
Rest us here, And by relating tales of others' griefs, See if 'twill teach us to forget our own . . . . . . *Pericles* i 4 3
What I am, want teaches me to think on: A man throng'd up with cold . . . . ii 1 76
I believe you; Your honour and your goodness teach me to't . iii 3 26
I do beseech you To learn of me, who stand i' the gaps to teach you . iv 4 8
I can sing, weave, sew . . . ; And I will undertake all these to teach . iv 6 196
Can you teach all this you speak of?—Prove that I cannot . iv 6 199
Teacher. To teach a teacher ill beseemeth me . . *L. L. Lost* ii 1 108
'Tis the next way to turn tailor, or be red-breast teacher *1 Hen. IV.* iii 1 265
His training such, That he may furnish and instruct great teachers *Hen. VIII.* i 2 113
Thus may poor fools Believe false teachers . . *Cymbeline* iii 4 87
Teachest. Not only givest Me cause to wail but teachest me the way How to lament the cause . . . . . *Richard II.* iv 1 301
That hast such noble sense of thy friend's wrong! Thou teachest me *Oth.* v 1 33
Cross him in nothing.—Thou teachest like a fool *Ant. and Cleo.* i 3 10
Thou teachest me, O valiant Eros, what I should, and thou couldst not iv 14 96
Teacheth. The love Which teacheth thee that thou and I am one *As Y. Like It* i 3 99
Teacheth tricks eleven and twenty long, To tame a shrew *T. of Shrew* iv 2 57
Which my most inward true and duteous spirit Teacheth *2 Hen. IV.* iv 5 149
Teaching. I can easier teach twenty what were good to be done, than be one of the twenty to follow mine own teaching . *Mer. of Venice* i 2 19
I thank thee, Jew, for teaching me that word . . iv 1 341

Teaching. Teaching all that read to know The quintessence of every sprite — *As Y. Like It* iii 2 146
Be schoolmaster And undertake the teaching of the maid — *T. of Shrew* i 1 197
Stand by and mark the manner of his teaching — iv 2 5
Courage and hope both teaching him the practice — *T. Night* i 2 13
Teaching stern murder how to butcher thee — *Richard II.* i 2 32
This is his uncle's teaching — 1 *Hen. IV.* i 1 96
Such bold hostility, teaching his duteous land Audacious cruelty — iv 3 44
He master'd there a double spirit Of teaching and of learning instantly — v 2 65
Filling The whole realm by your teaching and your chaplains — *Hen. VIII.* v 3 16
That my teaching And the strong course of my authority Might go one way — v 3 34

Team. A team of horse shall not pluck that from me — *T. G. of Ver.* iii 1 265
We fairies, that do run By the triple Hecate's team — *M. N. Dream* v 1 391
He that ears my land spares my team — *All's Well* i 3 48
The heavenly-harness'd team Begins his golden progress in the east — 1 *Hen. IV.* iii 1 221
Drawn with a team of little atomies Athwart men's noses — *Rom. and Jul.* i 4 57

Tear. His tears run down his beard, like winter's drops From eaves — *Temp.* v 1 16
O hateful hands, to tear such loving words! Injurious wasps! — *T. G. of V.* i 2 105
That I'll tear away. And yet I will not, sith so prettily He couples it — i 2 125
The tide is now: nay, not thy tide of tears; That tide will stay me — ii 2 14
Yet did not this cruel-hearted cur shed one tear — ii 3 10
The dog all this while sheds not a tear nor speaks a word — ii 3 34
See how I lay the dust with my tears — ii 3 35
If the river were dry, I am able to fill it with my tears — ii 3 59
With penitential groans, With nightly tears, and daily heart-sore sighs — ii 4 132
A thousand oaths, an ocean of his tears, And instances of infinite of love — ii 7 69
His thoughts immaculate, His tears pure messengers sent from his heart — ii 7 77
A sea of melting pearl, which some call tears — iii 1 224
Nor silver-shedding tears Could penetrate her uncompassionate sire — iii 1 230
Say that upon the altar of her beauty You sacrifice your tears — iii 2 74
Write till your ink be dry, and with your tears Moist it again — iii 2 75
New-found oaths; which he will break As easily as I do tear his paper — iv 4 136
Which I so lively acted with my tears — iv 4 174
Left her in her tears, and dried not one of them with his comfort — *Meas. for Meas.* iii 1 234
He, a marble to her tears, is washed with them, but relents not — iii 1 239
Ah, do not tear away thyself from me! — *Com. of Errors* ii 2 126
And tear the stain'd skin off my harlot-brow — ii 2 138
O, train me not, sweet mermaid, with thy note, To drown me in thy sister's flood of tears — iii 2 46
And never rise until my tears and prayers Have won his grace — v 1 115
Did he break out into tears?—In great measure — *Much Ado* i 1 24
Weeps, sobs, beats her heart, tears her hair, prays, curses — ii 3 153
Who loved her so, that, speaking of her foulness, Wash'd it with tears — iv 1 156
If they speak but truth of her, These hands shall tear her — iv 1 193
Your over-kindness doth wring tears from me! — v 1 302
As doth thy face through tears of mine give light; Thou shinest in every tear that I do weep — *L. L. Lost* iv 3 32
Do but behold the tears that swell in me — iv 3 37
Do not love thyself; then thou wilt keep My tears for glasses — iv 3 40
Empress of my love! These numbers will I tear, and write in prose — iv 3 57
In your tears There is no certain princess that appears — iv 3 155
How now! what is in you? why dost thou tear it? — iv 3 200
A zealous laughter, so profound, That in this spleen ridiculous appears, To check their folly, passion's solemn tears — v 2 118
Raining the tears of lamentation For the remembrance of my father's death — v 2 819
Dreams and sighs, Wishes and tears, poor fancy's followers — *M. N. Dream* i 1 155
That will ask some tears in the true performing of it — i 2 27
I could play Ercles rarely, or a part to tear a cat in, to make all split — i 2 32
How came her eyes so bright? Not with salt tears — ii 2 92
Scorn and derision never come in tears — iii 2 123
A manly enterprise, To conjure tears up in a poor maid's eyes! — iii 2 158
Will you tear Impatient answers from my gentle tongue? — iii 2 286
Like tears that did their own disgrace bewail — iv 1 61
More merry tears The passion of loud laughter never shed — v 1 69
Come, tears, confound; Out, sword, and wound The pap of Pyramus — v 1 300
Adieu! tears exhibit my tongue. Most beautiful pagan! — *Mer. of Venice* ii 3 10
Even there, his eye being big with tears, Turning his face — ii 8 46
No sighs but of my breathing; no tears but of my shedding — iii 1 100
Be merciful: Take thrice thy money; bid me tear the bond — iv 1 234
Almost with tears I speak it — *As Y. Like It* i 1 160
I should have given him tears unto entreaties, Ere he should thus have ventured — i 2 250
The big round tears Coursed one another down his innocent nose — ii 1 38
Stood on the extremest verge of the swift brook, Augmenting it with tears — ii 1 43
Said with weeping tears 'Wear these for my sake' — ii 4 54
If ever from your eyelids wiped a tear — ii 7 116
Apish, shallow, inconstant, full of tears, full of smiles — iii 2 432
Have the grace to consider that tears do not become a man — iii 4 3
Betwixt us two Tears our recountments had most kindly bathed — iv 3 141
Tell this youth what 'tis to love.—It is to be all made of sighs and tears — v 2 90
Bid him shed tears, as being overjoy'd — *T. of Shrew* Ind. 1 120
If the boy have not a woman's gift To rain a shower of commanded tears, An onion will do well — Ind. 1 125
Shall sad Apollo weep, So workmanly the blood and tears are drawn — Ind. 2 62
Till the tears that she hath shed for thee Like envious floods o'er-run her lovely face, She was the fairest creature — Ind. 2 66
Your commendations, madam, get from her tears — *All's Well* i 1 54
These great tears grace his remembrance more Than those I shed for him — i 1 91
Now I see The mystery of your loneliness, and find Your salt tears' head — i 3 178
Grief would have tears, and sorrow bids me speak — iii 4 42
And how mightily some other times we drown our gain in tears! — iv 3 79
With adorations, fertile tears, With groans that thunder love — *T. Night* i 5 274
Never more Will I my master's tears to you deplore — iii 1 174
Him will I tear out of that cruel eye, Where he sits crowned — v 1 130
Were you a woman, as the rest goes even, I should my tears let fall upon your cheek — v 1 247
I have That honourable grief lodged here which burns Worse than tears drown — *W. Tale* ii 1 112
When you shall know your mistress Has deserved prison, then abound in tears — ii 1 120
Once a day I'll visit The chapel where they lie, and tears shed there Shall be my recreation — iii 2 240
From him, whose daughter His tears proclaim'd his, parting with her — v 1 160
They seemed almost, with staring on one another, to tear the cases of their eyes — v 2 14

Tear. It seemed sorrow wept to take leave of them, for their joy waded in tears — *W. Tale* v 2 50
I would fain say, bleed tears, for I am sure my heart wept blood — v 2 97
We wept, and there was the first gentleman-like tears that ever we shed — v 2 156
This day hath made Much work for tears in many an English mother — *K. John* ii 1 303
I am not mad: this hair I tear is mine — iii 4 45
I must be brief, lest resolution drop Out at mine eyes in tender womanish tears — iv 1 36
The iron of itself, though heat red-hot, Approaching near these eyes, would drink my tears — iv 1 62
The vilest stroke That ever wall-eyed wrath or staring rage Presented to the tears of soft remorse — iv 3 50
My heart hath melted at a lady's tears, Being an ordinary inundation — v 2 47
O that there were some virtue in my tears, That might relieve you! — v 7 44
That would give you thanks And knows not how to do it but with tears — v 7 109
My teeth shall tear The slavish motive of recanting fear — *Richard II.* i 1 192
O, let no noble eye profane a tear For me — i 3 59
What store of parting tears were shed? — i 4 5
And so by chance Did grace our hollow parting with a tear — i 4 9
Sorrow's eye, glazed with blinding tears, Divides one thing entire to many — ii 2 16
Little office The hateful commons will perform for us, Except like curs to tear us all to pieces — ii 2 139
And stain'd the beauty of a fair queen's cheeks With tears — iii 1 15
As a long-parted mother with her child Plays fondly with her tears and smiles in meeting — iii 2 9
The silver rivers drown their shores, As if the world were all dissolved to tears — iii 2 108
When their thundering shock At meeting tears the cloudy cheeks of heaven — iii 3 57
We'll make foul weather with despised tears — iii 3 161
And make some pretty match with shedding tears — iii 3 165
Nay, dry your eyes; Tears show their love, but want their remedies — iii 3 203
I could sing, would weeping do me good, And never borrow any tear of thee — iii 4 23
Here did she fall a tear; here in this place I'll set a bank of rue — iii 4 104
Full of tears am I, Drinking my griefs — iv 1 188
With mine own tears I wash away my balm — iv 1 207
Mine eyes are full of tears, I cannot see — iv 1 244
I see your brows are full of discontent, Your hearts of sorrow and your eyes of tears — iv 1 332
Behold, That you in pity may dissolve to dew, And wash him fresh again with true-love tears — v 1 10
His face still combating with tears and smiles — v 2 32
Look upon his face; His eyes do drop no tears, his prayers are in jest — v 3 101
These vain weak nails May tear a passage through the flinty ribs Of this hard world — v 5 20
Mine eyes, the outward watch, Whereto my finger, like a dial's point, Is pointing still, in cleansing them from tears — v 5 54
So sighs and tears and groans Show minutes, times, and hours — v 5 57
Weep not, sweet queen; for trickling tears are vain — 1 *Hen. IV.* ii 4 431
For tears do stop the flood-gates of her eyes — ii 4 435
I do not speak to thee in drink but in tears, not in pleasure but in passion — ii 4 458
Or I will tear the reckoning from his heart — iii 2 152
With tears of innocency and terms of zeal — iv 3 63
I could tear her: I'll be revenged of her — 2 *Hen. IV.* ii 4 167
With his eye brimful of tears, Then check'd and rated — iii 1 67
He hath a tear for pity and a hand Open as day for melting charity — iv 4 31
Thy due from me Is tears and heavy sorrows of the blood — iv 5 38
Washing with kindly tears his gentle cheeks — iv 5 84
Let all the tears that should bedew my hearse Be drops of balm to sanctify thy head: Only compound me with forgotten dust — iv 5 114
But for my tears, The moist impediments unto my speech — iv 5 139
That shall convert those tears By number into hours of happiness — v 2 60
Playing the mouse in absence of the cat, To tear and havoc more than she can eat — *Hen. V.* i 2 173
And on your head Turning the widows' tears, the orphans' cries — ii 4 106
Bestow'd more contrite tears Than from it issued forced drops of blood — iv 1 313
Will you have them weep our horses' blood? How shall we, then, behold their natural tears? — iv 2 13
And all my mother came into mine eyes And gave me up to tears — iv 6 32
Our isle be made a nourish of salt tears — 1 *Hen. VI.* i 1 50
Were our tears wanting to this funeral, These tidings would call forth their flowing tides — i 1 82
Rather with their teeth The walls they'll tear down than forsake the siege — i 2 40
Either renew the fight, Or tear the lions out of England's coat — i 5 28
Can you . . . behold My sighs and tears and will not once relent? — iii 1 108
France, thou shalt rue this treason with thy tears — iii 2 36
With a flood of tears . . . wash away thy country's stained spots — iii 3 56
I vow'd, base knight, when I did meet thee next, To tear the garter from thy craven's leg — iv 1 15
Thou art a collop of my flesh; And for thy sake have I shed many a tear — v 4 19
My sword should shed hot blood, mine eyes no tears — 2 *Hen. VI.* i 1 118
Mine eyes are full of tears, my heart of grief — ii 3 17
Follow'd with a rabble that rejoice To see my tears — ii 4 33
What, gone, my lord, and bid me not farewell!—Witness my tears, I cannot stay to speak — ii 4 86
For I should melt at an offender's tears — iii 1 126
With sad unhelpful tears, and with dimm'd eyes Look after him — iii 1 218
Might liquid tears or heart-offending groans . . . recall his life — iii 2 60
Thou wouldst have me drown'd on shore, With tears as salt as sea — iii 2 96
And to drain Upon his face an ocean of salt tears — iii 2 143
They will by violence tear him from your palace — iii 2 246
Give me thy hand, That I may dew it with my mournful tears — iii 2 340
And with the southern clouds contend in tears — iii 2 384
Prayers and tears have moved me, gifts could never — iv 7 73
Tears virginal Shall be to me even as the dew to fire — v 2 52
Father, tear the crown from the usurper's head — 3 *Hen. VI.* i 1 114
Hath thy fiery heart so parch'd thine entrails That not a tear can fall? — i 4 88
These tears are my sweet Rutland's obsequies — i 4 147
His passion moves me so That hardly can I check my eyes from tears — i 4 151
See, ruthless queen, a hapless father's tears: This cloth thou dip'dst in blood of my sweet boy, And I with tears do wash the blood away — i 4 156
The hearers will shed tears; Yea even my foes will shed fast-falling tears — i 4 161
What, weeping-ripe . . . ? Think but upon the wrong he did us all, And that will quickly dry thy melting tears — i 4 174
And burns me up with flames that tears would quench — ii 1 84
Tears then for babes; blows and revenge for me! — ii 1 86
Ten days ago I drown'd these news in tears — ii 1 104

Tear. My tears shall wipe away these bloody marks . . . 3 *Hen. VI.* ii 5 71
Weep, wretched man, I'll aid thee tear for tear; And let our hearts and eyes, like civil war, Be blind with tears . . . ii 5 76
How will my wife for slaughter of my son Shed seas of tears! . . . ii 5 106
Her tears will pierce into a marble heart; The tiger will be mild whiles she doth mourn; And Nero will be tainted with remorse, To hear and see her plaints, her brinish tears . . . iii 1 38
Wet my cheeks with artificial tears, And frame my face to all occasions iii 2 184
Such a cause as fills mine eyes with tears And stops my tongue . iii 3 13
With my talk and tears, Both full of truth . . . iii 3 158
For this I draw in many a tear And stop the rising of blood-sucking sighs, Lest with my sighs or tears I blast or drown King Edward's fruit . . . iv 4 21
Thy tears would wash this cold congealed blood That glues my lips . v 2 37
What I should say My tears gainsay . . . v 4 74
O, may such purple tears be alway shed From those that wish the downfall of our house! . . . v 6 64
Those eyes of thine from mine have drawn salt tears . *Richard III.* i 2 154
These eyes, which never shed remorseful tear . . . i 2 156
In that sad time My manly eyes did scorn an humble tear . . i 2 165
And wet his grave with my repentant tears . . . i 2 216
In her heart's extremest hate, With curses in her mouth, tears in her eyes i 2 233
Your eyes drop millstones, when fools' eyes drop tears . . i 3 354
You wept not for our father's death; How can we aid you with our kindred tears? . . . ii 2 63
May send forth plenteous tears to drown the world! . . ii 2 70
Alas, you three, on me, threefold distress'd, Pour all your tears! . . ii 2 87
The liquid drops of tears that you have shed Shall come again, transform'd to orient pearl . . . iv 4 321
I myself have many tears to wash Hereafter time . . . iv 4 389
I would these dewy tears were from the ground . . . v 3 284
Let fall a tear; The subject will deserve it . . *Hen. VIII.* Prol. 6
My drops of tears I'll turn to sparks of fire . . . ii 4 72
That his bones . . . May have a tomb of orphans' tears wept on 'em! . iii 2 399
I did not think to shed a tear In all my miseries . . . iii 2 428
Full of repentance, Continual meditations, tears, and sorrows . . iv 2 28
He has strangled His language in his tears . . . v 1 157
Good man, those joyful tears show thy true heart . . . v 3 175
I am weaker than a woman's tear, Tamer than sleep . *Troi. and Cres.* i 1 9
I'll spring up in his tears, an 'twere a nettle against May . . i 2 190
Words, vows, gifts, tears, and love's full sacrifice, He offers in another's enterprise . . . i 2 308
Lend me ten thousand eyes, And I will fill them with prophetic tears . ii 2 102
Cry, Trojans, cry! practise your eyes with tears! . . . ii 2 108
Tear my bright hair and scratch my praised cheeks . . . iv 2 113
With a single famish'd kiss, Distasted with the salt of broken tears . iv 4 50
Where are my tears? rain, to lay this wind, or my heart will be blown up by the root . . . iv 4 55
Their eyes o'ergalled with recourse of tears . . . v 3 55
He did so set his teeth and tear it . . . *Coriolanus* i 3 70
I'll report it Where senators shall mingle tears with smiles . . i 9 3
Before him he carries noise, and behind him he leaves tears . . ii 1 176
And schoolboys' tears take up The glasses of my sight! . . . iii 2 116
Come, leave your tears: a brief farewell . . . iv 1 1
Thy tears are salter than a younger man's, And venomous to thine eyes iv 1 22
To tear with thunder the wide cheeks o' the air . . . v 3 151
Their base throats tear With giving him glory . . . v 6 53
At his nurse's tears He whined and roar'd away your victory . . v 6 97
Hear'st thou, Mars?—Name not the god, thou boy of tears! . . v 6 101
Tear him to pieces. Do it presently . . . v 6 121
To re-salute his country with his tears, Tears of true joy . *T. Andron.* i 1 75
Rue the tears I shed, A mother's tears in passion for her son . . i 1 105
Lo, at this tomb my tributary tears I render, for my brethren's obsequies; And at thy feet I kneel, with tears of joy, Shed on the earth, for thy return . . . i 1 159
No man shed tears for noble Mutius; He lives in fame . . . i 1 389
Let it be your glory To see her tears . . . ii 3 140
Remember, boys, I pour'd forth tears in vain, To save your brother . ii 3 163
Upon my feeble knee I beg this boon, with tears not lightly shed . . ii 3 289
One hour's storm will drown the fragrant meads; What will whole months of tears thy father's eyes? . . . ii 4 55
Bitter tears, which now you see Filling the aged wrinkles in my cheeks iii 1 6
In the dust I write My heart's deep languor and my soul's sad tears: Let my tears stanch the earth's dry appetite . . . iii 1 13
In winter with warm tears I'll melt the snow . . . iii 1 20
Let me say, that never wept before, My tears are now prevailing orators iii 1 26
They humbly at my feet Receive my tears and seem to weep with me . iii 1 42
Thou hast no hands, to wipe away thy tears; Nor tongue, to tell me . iii 1 106
When I did name her brothers, then fresh tears Stood on her cheeks . iii 1 111
And made a brine-pit with our bitter tears . . . iii 1 129
Sweet father, cease your tears; for, at your grief, See how my wretched sister sobs . . . iii 1 136
Thy napkin cannot drink a tear of mine, For thou, poor man, hast drown'd it with thine own . . . iii 1 140
His napkin, with his true tears all bewet, Can do no service on her sorrowful cheeks . . . iii 1 146
If any power pities wretched tears, To that I call! . . . iii 1 209
Then must my earth with her continual tears Become a deluge . . iii 1 229
Why, I have not another tear to shed . . . iii 1 267
This sorrow is an enemy, And would usurp upon my watery eyes, And make them blind with tributary tears . . . iii 1 270
Against thy heart make thou a hole; That all the tears that thy poor eyes let fall May run into that sink, and soaking in Drown the lamenting fool in sea-salt tears . . . iii 2 18
She says she drinks no other drink but tears, Brew'd with her sorrow . iii 2 37
Thou art made of tears, And tears will quickly melt thy life away . iii 2 51
Beheld his tears, and laugh'd so heartily, That both mine eyes were rainy like to his . . . v 1 116
Set fire on barns and hay-stacks in the night, And bid the owners quench them with their tears . . . v 1 134
Stab them, or tear them on thy chariot-wheels . . . v 2 47
Kill'd her, for whom my tears have made me blind . . . v 3 49
Floods of tears will drown my oratory, And break my utterance . . v 3 90
Our brothers were beheaded; Our father's tears despised . . . v 3 101
Who drown'd their enmity in my true tears . . . v 3 107
Draw you near, To shed obsequious tears upon this trunk . . . v 3 152
Tear for tear, and loving kiss for kiss . . . v 3 156
My tears will choke me, if I ope my mouth . . . v 3 175
With tears augmenting the fresh morning's dew . *Rom. and Jul.* i 1 138
Being vex'd, a sea nourish'd with lovers' tears . . . i 1 198
Tear. When the devout religion of mine eye Maintains such falsehood, then turn tears to fires! . . . *Rom. and Jul.* i 2 94
My name, dear saint, is hateful to myself, Because it is an enemy to thee; Had I it written, I would tear the word . . . ii 2 57
Bondage is hoarse, and may not speak aloud; Else would I tear the cave where Echo lies . . . ii 2 162
Upon thy cheek the stain doth sit Of an old tear that is not wash'd off yet ii 3 76
Nor tears nor prayers shall purchase out abuses: Therefore use none . iii 1 198
Back, foolish tears, back to your native spring; Your tributary drops belong to woe, Which you, mistaking, offer up to joy . . . iii 2 102
Wash they his wounds with tears: mine shall be spent, When theirs are dry . . . iii 2 130
Then mightst thou speak, then mightst thou tear thy hair . . iii 3 68
There on the ground, with his own tears made drunk . . . iii 3 83
Art thou a man? thy form cries out thou art: Thy tears are womanish iii 3 110
What, wilt thou wash him from his grave with tears? . . . iii 5 71
How now! a conduit, girl? what, still in tears? Evermore showering? iii 5 130
Thy eyes, which I may call the sea, Do ebb and flow with tears . iii 5 134
The winds, thy sighs; Who, raging with thy tears, and they with them, Without a sudden calm, will overset Thy tempest-tossed body . iii 5 136
Have I little talk'd of love; For Venus smiles not in a house of tears iv 1 8
In his wisdom hastes our marriage, To stop the inundation of her tears iv 1 12
Poor soul, thy face is much abused with tears.—The tears have got small victory by that; For it was bad enough before their spite.—Thou wrong'st it, more than tears, with that report . . . iv 1 29
Dry up you tears, and stick your rosemary On this fair corse . iv 5 79
Fond nature bids us all lament, Yet nature's tears are reason's merriment iv 5 83
Which with sweet water nightly I will dew, Or, wanting that with tears distill'd by moans . . . v 3 15
I will tear thee joint by joint And strew this hungry churchyard with thy limbs . . . v 3 35
Tear me, take me, and the gods fall upon you! . *T. of Athens* iii 4 100
The sea's a thief, whose liquid surge resolves The moon into salt tears . iv 3 443
You witch me in it; Surprise me to the very brink of tears . . v 1 159
Draw them to Tiber banks, and weep your tears Into the channel *J. Cæsar* i 1 63
There is tears for his love; joy for his fortune; honour for his valour . iii 2 29
If you have tears, prepare to shed them now . . . iii 2 173
Tear him to pieces; he's a conspirator . . . iii 3 30
I am Cinna the poet.—Tear him for his bad verses . . . iii 3 34
Friends, I owe more tears To this dead man than you shall see me pay v 3 101
Shall blow the horrid deed in every eye, That tears shall drown the wind *Macbeth* i 7 25
Let's away; Our tears are not yet brew'd . . . ii 3 130
Cancel and tear to pieces that great bond Which keeps me pale! . . iii 2 49
Did he not straight In pious rage the two delinquents tear? . . iii 6 12
She follow'd my poor father's body, Like Niobe, all tears . *Hamlet* i 2 149
Ere yet the salt of most unrighteous tears Had left the flushing in her galled eyes, She married . . . i 2 154
Look, whether he has not turned his colour and has tears in's eyes . ii 2 543
All his visage wann'd, Tears in his eyes, distraction in's aspect . . ii 2 581
He would drown the stage with tears And cleave the general ear . . ii 2 588
To hear a robustious periwig-pated fellow tear a passion to tatters . iii 2 11
Then what I have to do Will want true colour; tears perchance for blood iii 4 130
Tears seven times salt, Burn out the sense and virtue of mine eye! . iv 5 154
And in his grave rain'd many a tear:—Fare you well, my dove! . . iv 5 166
Too much of water hast thou, poor Ophelia, And therefore I forbid my tears . . . iv 7 187
Woo't weep? woo't fight? woo't fast? woo't tear thyself? Woo't drink up eisel? . . . v 1 298
With cadent tears fret channels in her cheeks . . . *Lear* i 4 307
I am ashamed . . . That these hot tears, which break from me perforce, Should make thee worth them . . . i 4 320
Tears his white hair, Which the impetuous blasts, with eyeless rage, Catch in their fury, and make nothing of . . . iii 1 7
Is it not as this mouth should tear this hand For lifting food to't? . iii 4 15
My tears begin to take his part so much, They'll mar my counterfeiting iii 6 63
Apt enough to dislocate and tear Thy flesh and bones . . . iv 2 65
And now and then an ample tear trill'd down Her delicate cheek . . iv 3 14
Her smiles and tears Were like a better way . . . iv 3 20
All you unpublish'd virtues of the earth, Spring with my tears! . . iv 4 17
Therefore great France My mourning and important tears hath pitied iv 4 26
Mine own tears Do scald like molten lead . . . iv 7 47
Be your tears wet? yes, 'faith. I pray, weep not . . . iv 7 71
I did consent, And often did beguile her of her tears . *Othello* i 3 156
I'll tear her all to pieces.—Nay, but be wise: yet we see nothing done iii 3 431
If that the earth could teem with woman's tears, Each drop she falls would prove a crocodile . . . iv 1 256
As you say, obedient, Very obedient. Proceed you in your tears . . iv 1 267
Why do you weep? Am I the motive of these tears, my lord? . . iv 2 43
Her salt tears fell from her, and soften'd the stones . . . iv 3 47
I must weep, But they are cruel tears: this sorrow's heavenly . . v 2 21
Drop tears as fast as the Arabian trees Their medicinal gum . . v 2 350
We cannot call her winds and waters sighs and tears *Ant. and Cleo.* i 2 153
The tears live in an onion that should water this sorrow . . i 2 176
Then bid adieu to me, and say the tears Belong to Egypt . . . i 3 77
'Tis a strange serpent.—'Tis so. And the tears of it are wet . . ii 7 55
Fall not a tear, I say; one of them rates All that is won and lost . iii 11 69
Whilst they with joyful tears Wash the congealment from your wounds iv 8 9
Let me lament, With tears as sovereign as the blood of hearts . . v 1 41
O, that I had her here, to tear her limb-meal! . . *Cymbeline* ii 4 147
Sinon's weeping Did scandal many a holy tear . . . iii 4 62
My tears that fall Prove holy water on thee! . . . v 5 268
And wanting breath to speak help me with tears . . *Pericles* i 4 19
O, let those cities that of plenty's cup And her prosperities so largely taste, With their superfluous riots, hear these tears! . . . i 4 54
Nor come we to add sorrow to your tears, But to relieve them . . i 4 90
O, no tears, Lychorida, no tears: Look to your little mistress . . iii 3 38
With sighs shot through, and biggest tears o'ershower'd . . . iv 4 26
He bears A tempest, which his mortal vessel tears, And yet he rides it out . . . iv 4 30
When we with tears parted Pentapolis, The king my father gave you such a ring . . . v 3 38
Tear-falling pity dwells not in this eye . . . *Richard III.* iv 2 66
Tearful. With tearful eyes add water to the sea . . . 3 *Hen. VI.* v 4 8
Tearing. The tipsy Bacchanals, Tearing the Thracian singer *M. N. Dream* v 1 49
For what? for tearing a poor whore's ruff? . . . 2 *Hen. IV.* ii 4 156
Tearing His country's bowels out . . . *Coriolanus* v 3 102
Read thine own evil: No tearing, lady; I perceive you know it . *Lear* v 3 157
Then in the midst, a tearing groan did break The name of Antony *Ant. and Cleo.* iv 14 31

Tearsheet. Will you have Doll Tearsheet meet you at supper? 2 *Hen. IV.* ii 1 176
Mistress Tearsheet would fain hear some music . . . . . ii 4 13
Bid Mistress Tearsheet come to my master.—O, run, Doll, run . . ii 4 418
The lazar kite of Cressid's kind, Doll Tearsheet she by name . *Hen. V.* ii 1 81
Tear-stained. She comes; and I'll prepare My tear-stain'd eyes to see her miseries . . . . 2 *Hen. VI.* ii 4 16
Teat. Even at thy teat thou hadst thy tyranny . . . *T. Andron.* ii 3 145
An honour! were not I thine only nurse, I would say thou hadst suck'd wisdom from thy teat . . . . *Rom. and Jul.* i 3 68
Te Deum. Let there be sung 'Non nobis' and 'Te Deum' . *Hen. V.* iv 8 128
The choir, With all the choicest music of the kingdom, Together sung 'Te Deum' . . . . *Hen. VIII.* iv 1 92
Tedious. Twenty watchful, weary, tedious nights . . *T. G. of Ver.* i 1 31
You are a tedious fool: to the purpose . . *Meas. for Meas.* ii 1 119
Like a good thing, being often read, Grown fear'd and tedious . . ii 4 9
Neighbours, you are tedious . . . . *Much Ado* iii 5 20
If I were as tedious as a king, I could find it in my heart to bestow it all iii 5 23
I do repent The tedious minutes I with her have spent . *M. N. Dream* ii 2 112
O weary night, O long and tedious night, Abate thy hours! . . . iii 2 431
A tedious brief scene of young Pyramus And his love Thisbe . . v 1 56
Merry and tragical! tedious and brief! That is, hot ice . . . v 1 58
But by ten words, my lord, it is too long, Which makes it tedious . v 1 64
Where is the horse that doth untread again His tedious measures with the unbated fire That he did pace them first? . . *Mer. of Venice* ii 6 11
I have too grieved a heart To take a tedious leave . . . . ii 7 77
In respect it is not in the court, it is tedious . . . *As Y. Like It* iii 2 19
What tedious homily of love have you wearied your parishioners withal! iii 2 163
Knowing no burden of heavy tedious penury . . . . . . iii 2 342
Tedious it were to tell, and harsh to hear . . . *T. of Shrew* iii 2 107
'Tis very strange, that is the brief and the tedious of it . . *All's Well* ii 3 34
Life is as tedious as a twice-told tale . . . . . *K. John* iii 4 108
Every tedious stride I make Will but remember me . . *Richard II.* i 3 268
Within me grief hath kept a tedious fast . . . . ii 1 75
In winter's tedious nights sit by the fire With good old folks . . . v 1 40
Thinking his prattle to be tedious . . . . v 2 26
If all the year were playing holidays, To sport would be as tedious as to work; But when they seldom come, they wish'd for come 1 *Hen. IV.* i 2 229
Bring him out that . . . Can trace me in the tedious ways of art . . iii 1 48
He is as tedious As a tired horse, a railing wife . . . . iii 1 159
From heaven Ordained is to raise this tedious siege . . 1 *Hen. VI.* i 2 53
The Turk, that two and fifty kingdoms hath, Writes not so tedious a style iv 7 74
I would remove these tedious stumbling-blocks . . . 2 *Hen. VI.* i 2 64
My brain more busy than the labouring spider Weaves tedious snares iii 1 340
And, for the time shall not seem tedious, I'll tell thee . 3 *Hen. VI.* iii 1 9
It is better to be brief than tedious . . . . *Richard III.* i 4 90
Our crosses on the way Have made it tedious, wearisome, and heavy . iii 1 5
Cannot thy master sleep these tedious nights?—So it should seem . iii 2 6
Brief abstract and record of tedious days . . . . . . iv 4 28
Fair Philomela, she but lost her tongue, And in a tedious sampler sew'd her mind . . . . *T. Andron.* ii 4 39
So tedious is this day As is the night before some festival To an impatient child that hath new robes And may not wear them *R. and J.* iii 2 28
For my short date of breath Is not so long as is a tedious tale . . v 3 230
Away, Thou tedious rogue! . . . . *T. of Athens* iv 3 374
Should I wade no more, Returning were as tedious as go o'er. *Macbeth* iii 4 138
These tedious old fools! . . . . *Hamlet* ii 2 223
Fain I would beguile The tedious day with sleep . . . . . iii 2 237
It were a tedious difficulty, I think, To bring them to that prospect *Oth.* iii 3 397
And lovers' absent hours, More tedious than the dial eight score times iii 4 175
I see a man's life is a tedious one . . . . . *Cymbeline* iii 6 1
Pray; but be not tedious, For the gods are quick of ear . . *Pericles* iv 1 69
Upon what ground is his distemperature?—'Twould be too tedious to repeat . . . . v 1 28
Tediously. The cripple tardy-gaited night Who, like a foul and ugly witch, doth limp So tediously away . . . . . . *Hen. V.* iv Prol. 22
Beshrew the witch! with venomous wights she stays As tediously as hell . . . . *Troi. and Cres.* iv 2 13
Tediousness. All thy tediousness on me, ah? . . . . . *Much Ado* iii 5 26
Thou, a merry devil, Didst rob it of some taste of tediousness *Mer. of Ven.* ii 3 3
Very much beguiled The tediousness and process of my travel *Richard II.* ii 3 12
Brevity is the soul of wit, And tediousness the limbs . . *Hamlet* ii 2 91
Teem. Nothing teems But hateful docks, rough thistles . . *Hen. V.* v 2 51
Common mother, thou, Whose womb unmeasurable, and infinite breast, Teems, and feeds all . . . . *T. of Athens* iv 3 179
Go great with tigers, dragons, wolves, and bears; Teem with new monsters! . . . . iv 3 190
Each minute teems a new one [grief] . . . . . . *Macbeth* iv 3 176
If she must teem, Create her child of spleen! . . . . *Lear* i 4 303
If that the earth could teem with woman's tears, Each drop she falls would prove a crocodile . . . . *Othello* iv 1 256
Teeming. As those that feed grow full, as blossoming time That from the seedness the bare fallow brings To teeming foison *Meas. for Meas.* i 4 43
This England, This nurse, this teeming womb of royal kings *Richard II.* ii 1 51
Is not my teeming date drunk up with time? . . . . . . v 2 91
Oft the teeming earth Is with a kind of colic pinch'd . . 1 *Hen. IV.* iii 1 28
Teen. My heart bleeds To think o' the teen that I have turn'd you to *Temp.* i 2 64
O, what a scene of foolery have I seen, Of sighs, of groans, of sorrow, and of teen! . . . . *L. L. Lost* iv 3 164
And each hour's joy wreck'd with a week of teen . . *Richard III.* iv 1 97
I'll lay fourteen of my teeth,—And yet, to my teen be it spoken, I have but four,—She is not fourteen . . . . *Rom. and Jul.* i 3 13
Teeth. By this hand, I will supplant some of your teeth . . *Tempest* iii 2 57
She hath no teeth.—I care not for that neither, because I love crusts *T. G. of Ver.* iii 1 344
She is curst.—Well, the best is, she hath no teeth to bite . . . iii 1 348
In despite of the teeth of all rhyme and reason . . . *Mer. Wives* v 5 133
'Tis a secret must be locked within the teeth and the lips *Meas. for Meas.* iii 2 143
Dost thou jeer and flout me in the teeth? . . . *Com. of Errors* ii 2 22
Till, gnawing with my teeth my bonds in sunder, I gain'd my freedom v 1 249
Our two noses snapped off with two old men without teeth *Much Ado* v 1 116
Smiles on every one, To show his teeth as white as whale's bone *L. L. L.* v 2 332
They'll not show their teeth in way of smile . . *Mer. of Venice* i 1 55
Most true, I have lost my teeth in your service . . . *As Y. L. It* i 1 87
Sans teeth, sans eyes, sans taste, sans every thing . . . . ii 7 166
My very lips might freeze to my teeth . . . . *T. of Shrew* iv 1 7
Ask questions and sing; pick his teeth and sing . . . *All's Well* iii 2 8
A great man, I'll warrant; I know by the picking on's teeth *W. Tale* iv 4 780
When my knightly stomach is sufficed, Why then I suck my teeth *K. John* i 1 192
Now doth Death line his dead chaps with steel; The swords of soldiers are his teeth, his fangs . . . . ii 1 353
Teeth. To tug and scamble and to part by the teeth . . *K. John* iv 3 146
My teeth shall tear The slavish motive of recanting fear . . *Richard II.* i 1 192
You have engaol'd my tongue, Doubly portcullis'd with my teeth and lips i 3 167
That would set my teeth nothing on edge, Nothing so much 1 *Hen. IV.* iii 1 133
I have thrown A brave defiance in King Henry's teeth . . . . v 2 43
My friends, which thou must make thy friends, Have but their stings and teeth newly ta'en out . . . . 2 *Hen. IV.* iv 5 206
Puff! Puff in thy teeth, most recreant coward base! . . . . v 3 96
The 'solus' in thy teeth, and in thy throat! . . . . *Hen. V.* ii 1 51
Now set the teeth and stretch the nostril wide, Hold hard the breath iii 1 15
Rather with their teeth The walls they'll tear down . . 1 *Hen. VI.* i 2 39
If we be forbidden stones, we'll fall to it with our teeth . . . iii 1 90
Deliver'd strongly through my fixed teeth . . . . 2 *Hen. VI.* iii 2 313
We are like to have biting statutes, unless his teeth be pulled out . iv 7 19
What valour were it, when a cur doth grin, For one to thrust his hand between his teeth? . . . . 3 *Hen. VI.* i 4 57
Teeth hadst thou in thy head when thou wast born . . . . v 6 53
And the women cried 'O, Jesus bless us, he is born with teeth!' . . v 6 75
That dog, that had his teeth before his eyes, To worry lambs *Rich. III.* iv 4 49
In desperate manner Daring the event to the teeth . . *Hen. VIII.* i 2 36
He did so set his teeth and tear it . . . . . . *Coriolanus* i 3 70
Bid them wash their faces And keep their teeth clean . . . ii 3 67
What are your offices? You being their mouths, why rule you not their teeth? . . . . iii 1 36
Rend off thy silver hair, thy other hand Gnawing with thy teeth *T. An.* iii 1 262
Bear thou my hand, sweet wench, between thy teeth . . . . iii 1 283
Or get some little knife between thy teeth . . . . . . iii 2 16
I'll lay fourteen of my teeth,—And yet, to my teen be it spoken, I have but four,—She is not fourteen . . . . . . *Rom. and Jul.* i 3 12
Laments that virtue cannot live Out of the teeth of emulation *J. Cæsar* ii 3 14
Set in a note-book, learn'd, and conn'd by rote, To cast into my teeth . iv 3 99
You show'd your teeth like apes, and fawn'd like hounds . . . v 1 41
Defiance, traitors, hurl we in your teeth . . . . . . v 1 64
The worm that's fled Hath nature that in time will venom breed, No teeth for the present . . . . *Macbeth* iii 4 31
Even to the teeth and forehead of our faults, To give in evidence *Hamlet* iii 3 63
I shall live and tell him to his teeth, 'Thus didest thou' . . . iv 7 57
Chill pick your teeth, zir: come; no matter vor your foins . . *Lear* iv 6 250
Throw your vile guesses in the devil's teeth, From whence you have them *Othello* iii 4 184
By Isis, I will give thee bloody teeth . . . . *Ant. and Cleo.* i 5 70
When the best hint was given him, he not took't, Or did it from his teeth iii 4 10
Now I'll set my teeth, And send to darkness all that stop me . . iii 13 181
With thy sharp teeth this knot intrinsicate Of life at once untie . v 2 307
So sharp are hunger's teeth, that man and wife Draw lots who first shall die to lengthen life . . . . *Pericles* i 4 45
Teipsum. Medice, teipsum—Protector, see to't well, protect yourself 2 *Hen. VI.* ii 1 52
Telamon. He is more mad Than Telamon for his shield *Ant. and Cleo.* iv 13 2
Telamonius. Now, like Ajax Telamonius, On sheep or oxen could I spend my fury . . . . 2 *Hen. VI.* v 1 26
Tell your piteous heart There's no harm done . . . . *Tempest* i 2 14
You have often Begun to tell me what I am . . . . . . i 2 34
Of any thing the image tell me that Hath kept with thy remembrance . i 2 43
Then tell me If this might be a brother . . . . i 2 117
Where was she born? speak; tell me . . . . i 2 260
They'll tell the clock to any business that We say befits the hour . ii 1 289
This will shake your shaking, I can tell you, and that soundly: you cannot tell who's your friend . . . . ii 2 88
Tell not me; when the butt is out, we will drink water . . . . iii 2 1
Wilt thou tell a monstrous lie, being but half a fish? . . . . iii 2 32
This will I tell my master . . . . iii 2 124
At this time I will tell no tales . . . . v 1 129
If I did think, sir, I were well awake, I'ld strive to tell you . . v 1 230
But tell me, dost thou know my lady Silvia? . . *T. G. of Ver.* ii 1 44
Now, tell me, how do all from whence you came? . . . . ii 4 122
I tell thee, my master is become a hot lover.—Why, I tell thee, I care not ii 5 53
To lesson me and tell me some good mean . . . . . . ii 7 5
Tell me, good my lord, What compass will you wear your farthingale? . ii 7 50
But tell me, wench, how will the world repute me? . . . . ii 7 59
Now, tell me, Proteus, what's your will with me? . . . . iii 1 3
'Tis a woman, but what woman, I will not tell myself . . . . iii 1 267
Why, then will I tell thee—that thy master stays for thee . . . iii 1 381
Why didst not tell me sooner? pox of your love-letters! . . . iii 1 390
Tell us this: have you any thing to take to?—Nothing but my fortune iv 1 42
I tell you what Launce, his man, told me: he loved her out of all nick iv 2 75
And tells you currish thanks is good enough for such a present iv 4 53
Tell my lady I claim the promise for her heavenly picture . . iv 4 91
Bring my picture there. Go give your master this: tell him from me . iv 4 123
I'll tell you as we pass along, That you will wonder what hath fortuned v 4 168
Shall I tell you a lie? I do despise a liar . . . *Mer. Wives* i 1 69
That peradventures shall tell you another tale . . . . . . i 1 78
I will tell you what I am about.—Two yards, and more . . . . i 3 42
Notwithstanding,—to tell you in your ear; I would have no words of it i 4 109
It is no matter-a ver dat: do not you tell-a me dat? . . . . i 4 122
One that is your friend, I can tell you that by the way . . . . i 4 150
I will tell your worship more of the wart the next time . . . . i 4 171
Tell him, cavaleiro-justice; tell him, bully-rook . . . . . ii 1 206
Hark, I will tell you what our sport shall be . . . . . . ii 1 218
Tell him my name is Brook; only for a jest . . . . . . ii 1 224
Let me tell you in your ear, she's as fartuous a civil modest wife . . ii 2 100
One, I tell you, that will not miss you morning nor evening prayer . ii 2 101
She bade me tell your worship that her husband is seldom from home . ii 2 104
I will tell you, sir, if you will give me the hearing . . . . ii 2 182
I shall be with her, I may tell you, by her own appointment . . ii 2 272
I vill tell you how I vill kill him . . . . ii 3 13
I had as lief you would tell me of a mess of porridge . . . . iii 1 63
I cannot tell what the dickens his name is my husband had him of . iii 2 19
De maid is love-a me: my nursh-a Quickly tell me so mush . . . iii 2 66
And hath threatened to put me into everlasting liberty if I tell you of it iii 3 31
Go tell thy master I am alone . . . . iii 3 37
I'll deserve it.—Nay, I must tell you, so you do . . . . . iii 3 90
I come before to tell you . . . . iii 3 123
Gentlemen, I have dreamed to-night; I'll tell you my dream . . . iii 3 171
Tells me 'tis a thing impossible I should love thee but as a property.—May be he tells you true . . . . iii 4 9
I had a father, Mistress Anne; my uncle can tell you good jests of him iii 4 39
Tell Mistress Anne the jest, how my father stole two geese . . . iii 4 40
They can tell you how things go better than I can . . . . iii 4 68
I will visit her: tell her so; and bid her think what a man is . . iii 5 50

Tell. Shall we tell our husbands how we have served him? *Mer. Wives* iv 2 228
There is a friend of mine come to town, tells me there is three cozen-germans that has cozened all the hosts of Readins . . . . iv 5 78
I tell you for good will, look you: you are wise and full of gibes . iv 5 81
I cannot tell vat is dat: but it is tell-a me dat you make grand preparation iv 5 87
I will tell you: he beat me grievously, in the shape of a woman . v 1 21
I am in haste; go along with me: I'll tell you all . . . v 1 26
Follow me: I'll tell you strange things of this knave . . v 1 29
Tell her Master Slender hath married her daughter . . . v 5 182
You took the wrong.—What need you tell me that? . . . v 5 202
Did not I tell you how you should know my daughter? . . . v 5 207
But rather tell me, When I, that censure him, do so offend *Meas. for Meas.* ii 1 28
There are pretty orders beginning, I can tell you . . . ii 1 250
He's hearing of a cause; he will come straight: I'll tell him of you . ii 2 2
Did not I tell thee yea? hadst thou not order? . . . . ii 2 8
I would tell what 'twere to be a judge, And what a prisoner . . ii 2 69
My brother did love Juliet, And you tell me that he shall die for it . ii 4 143
I'll tell the world aloud What man thou art . . . . ii 4 153
Did I tell this, Who would believe me? . . . . . ii 4 171
I'll tell him yet of Angelo's request, And fit his mind to death . ii 4 186
What news, friar, of the duke?—I know none. Can you tell me of any? iii 2 92
Canst thou tell if Claudio die to-morrow or no? . . . . iii 2 180
So severe, that he hath forced me to tell him he is indeed Justice . . iii 2 268
Tell him he must awake, and that quickly too. . . . . iv 3 32
I can tell thee pretty tales of the duke.—You have told me too many . iv 3 175
Call at Flavius' house, And tell him where I stay . . . . iv 5 7
He tells me that, if peradventure He speak against me on the adverse side, I should not think it strange . . . . iv 6 5
Is this the man that you did tell us of? . . . . . . v 1 327
To tell sad stories of my own mishaps . . . . *Com. of Errors* i 1 121
Tell me, and dally not, where is the money? . . . . . i 2 59
What means this jest? I pray you, master, tell me . . . . ii 2 21
Shall I tell you why?—Ay, sir, and wherefore . . . . ii 2 43
Your own handwriting would tell you what I think . . . . iii 1 14
Right, sir; I'll tell you when, an you'll tell me wherefore . . . iii 1 39
He comes too late; And so tell your master . . . . . iii 1 50
Have at you with another; that's—When? can you tell? . . . iii 1 52
Thou baggage, let me in.—Can you tell for whose sake? . . . iii 1 57
What I should think of this, I cannot tell . . . . . iii 2 184
Tell her, in the desk That's cover'd o'er with Turkish tapestry There is a purse of ducats . . . . iv 1 103
Tell her I am arrested in the street And that shall bail me . . iv 1 106
What, is he arrested? Tell me at whose suit.—I know not at whose suit iv 2 43
And tell his wife that, being lunatic, He rush'd into my house . . iv 3 94
I tell you, 'twill sound harshly in her ears . . . . . iv 4 7
In company I often glanced it; Still did I tell him it was vile and bad . v 1 67
I tell you true; I have not breathed almost since I did see it . . v 1 180
She tells to your highness simple truth . . . . . . v 1 211
But tell me yet, dost thou not know my voice? . . . . . v 1 300
All these old witnesses—I cannot err—Tell me thou art my son . . v 1 318
What then became of them I cannot tell . . . . . . v 1 354
He hath indeed better bettered expectation than you must expect of me to tell you how . . . . *Much Ado* i 1 17
I tell him we shall stay here at the least a month . . . . i 1 149
Tell me truly how thou likest her . . . . i 1 180
Do you play the flouting Jack, to tell us Cupid is a good hare-finder? . i 1 186
I would your grace would constrain me to tell. . . . . . i 1 209
Tell him I will not fail him at supper . . . . . . i 1 279
I will assume thy part in some disguise And tell fair Hero I am Claudio i 1 324
I can tell you strange news that you yet dreamt not of . . . i 2 4
Go you and tell her of it . . . . i 2 25
If the prince be too important, tell him there is measure in every thing ii 1 74
To tell you true, I counterfeit him . . . . ii 1 121
Will you not tell me who told you so? . . . . . . ii 1 130
Nor will you not tell me who you are?—Not now . . . . ii 1 132
When I know the gentleman, I'll tell him what you say . . . ii 1 150
My cousin tells him in his ear that he is in her heart . . . ii 1 328
She cannot endure to hear tell of a husband . . . . . ii 1 362
Go in with me, and I will tell you my drift . . . . . ii 1 403
Spare not to tell him that he hath wronged his honour . . . ii 2 23
Tell them that you know that Hero loves me . . . . . ii 2 34
May I be so converted and see with these eyes? I cannot tell; I think not ii 3 24
I cannot tell what to think of it but that she loves him . . . ii 3 104
She will sit you, you heard my daughter tell you how . . . ii 3 116
My daughter tells us all . . . . ii 3 138
I pray you, tell Benedick of it, and hear what a' will say . . ii 3 177
Shall we go seek Benedick, and tell him of her love?—Never tell him, my lord . . . . ii 3 205
Whisper her ear and tell her, I and Ursula Walk in the orchard . . iii 1 4
And did they bid you tell her of it, madam?—They did entreat me . iii 1 39
But who dare tell her so? If I should speak, She would mock me into air iii 1 74
Yet tell her of it: hear what she will say . . . . . . iii 1 81
Indeed, that tells a heavy tale for him: conclude, conclude he is in love iii 2 63
What's the matter?—I came hither to tell you . . . . . iii 2 105
I tell this tale vilely:—I should first tell thee . . . . . iii 3 157
He is now as valiant as Hercules that only tells a lie and swears it . iv 1 324
My soul doth tell me Hero is belied . . . . v 1 42
I'll tell thee how Beatrice praised thy wit the other day . . . v 1 160
But I must tell thee plainly, Claudio undergoes my challenge . . v 2 56
Tell me for which of my bad parts didst thou first fall in love with me? v 2 60
Now tell me, how doth your cousin?—Very ill . . . . . v 2 90
Did I not tell you she was innocent? . . . . v 4 1
After that the holy rites are ended, I'll tell you largely of fair Hero's death . . . . v 4 69
This letter will tell you more . . . . . . *L. L. Lost* i 1 189
In two words, the dancing horse will tell you . . . . . i 2 57
Tell me precisely of what complexion.—Of the sea-water green . . i 2 85
Lord, how wise you are!—I will tell thee wonders . . . . i 2 144
I am less proud to hear you tell my worth Than you much willing to be counted wise In spending your wit . . . . ii 1 17
Tell him, the daughter of the King of France, On serious business, craving quick dispatch, Importunes personal conference . . . . ii 1 30
I will tell you sensibly.—Thou hast no feeling of it . . . . iii 1 114
Can you tell me by your wit What was a month old at Cain's birth? . iv 2 35
As a certain father saith,— Sir, tell not me of the father . . . iv 2 155
No thought can think, nor tongue of mortal tell . . . . . iv 3 42
Where lies thy grief, O, tell me, good Dumain? . . . . . iv 3 171
O, dismiss this audience, and I shall tell you more . . . . iv 3 210
To tell you plain, I'll find a fairer face not wash'd to-day . . . iv 3 272
But let that pass: for I must tell thee, it will please his grace . . v 1 107

Tell. Shall I tell you a thing?—We attend . . . . . *L. L. Lost* v 1 152
The princess bids you tell How many inches doth fill up one mile.—Tell her, we measure them by weary steps . . . . v 2 192
I will go tell him of fair Hermia's flight . . . . *M. N. Dream* i 1 246
Do I not in plainest truth Tell you, I do not, nor I cannot love you? . ii 1 201
For the more better assurance, tell them that I Pyramus am not Pyramus iii 1 21
Another prologue must tell he is not a lion . . . . . . iii 1 35
There indeed let him name his name, and tell them plainly . . . iii 1 47
O, once tell true, tell true, even for my sake! . . . . . iii 2 68
Nor is he dead, for aught that I can tell.—I pray thee, tell me then that he is well . . . . iii 2 76
Did not you tell me I should know the man By the Athenian garments? iii 2 348
Tell me how it came this night That I sleeping here was found . . iv 1 105
Methought I was—there is no man can tell what . . . . . iv 1 214
But ask me not what; for if I tell you, I am no true Athenian. I will tell you every thing, right as it fell out . . . . iv 2 30
All that I will tell you is, that the duke hath dined . . . . iv 2 34
All that I have to say, is, to tell you that the lanthorn is the moon . v 1 261
Tell not me; I know, Antonio Is sad to think upon his merchandise *Mer. of Venice* i 1 39
I'll tell thee more of this another time: But fish not, with this melancholy bait . . . . i 1 100
Tell me now what lady is the same To whom you swore a secret pilgrimage, That you to-day promised to tell me of? . . . . . i 1 119
Is your gold and silver ewes and rams?—I cannot tell . . . . i 3 97
I tell thee, lady, this aspect of mine Hath fear'd the valiant . . ii 1 8
Can you tell me whether one Launcelot, that dwells with him, dwell with him? . . . . ii 2 48
I will tell you news of your son: give me your blessing . . . . ii 2 82
You may tell every finger I have with my ribs . . . . . ii 2 114
Tell gentle Jessica I will not fail her . . . . ii 4 20
Was not that letter from fair Jessica?—I must needs tell thee all . ii 4 30
Who are you? Tell me, for more certainty . . . . . . ii 6 26
You were best to tell Antonio what you hear . . . . . . ii 8 33
Tell me once more what title thou dost bear . . . . . . ii 9 35
But tell us, do you hear whether Antonio have had any loss at sea or no? iii 1 44
There's something tells me, but it is not love, I would not lose you . iii 2 4
Tell me where is fancy bred, Or in the heart or in the head? . . . iii 2 63
I pray you, tell me how my good friend doth . . . . . . iii 2 236
Gaoler, look to him: tell not me of mercy . . . . . . iii 3 1
And tell quaint lies, How honourable ladies sought my love . . . iii 4 69
And twenty of these puny lies I'll tell . . . . iii 4 74
I'll tell thee all my whole device When I am in my coach . . . iii 4 81
I'll tell my husband, Launcelot, what you say . . . . . iii 5 29
He tells me flatly, there is no mercy for me in heaven . . . . iii 5 34
Commend me to your honourable wife: Tell her the process . . . iv 1 274
His ring I do accept most thankfully: And so, I pray you, tell him . iv 2 10
Tell him there's a post come from my master, with his horn full of good news . . . . v 1 46
Can you tell if Rosalind, the duke's daughter, be banished? *As Y. Like It* i 1 110
I'll tell thee, Charles: it is the stubbornest young fellow . . . i 1 148
Tell us the manner of the wrestling.—I will tell you the beginning . i 2 118
You will take little delight in it, I can tell you . . . . . i 2 169
If I had a thunderbolt in mine eye, I can tell who should down . . i 2 227
I can tell you that of late this duke Hath ta'en displeasure . . . i 2 289
Tell me whereon the likelihood depends . . . . i 3 59
Go, seek him: tell him I would speak with him . . . . . ii 7 7
Fie on thee! I can tell what thou wouldst do . . . . . . ii 7 62
The residue of your fortune, Go to my cave and tell me . . . . ii 7 197
I prithee now with most petitionary vehemence, tell me who it is . . iii 2 200
I prithee, tell me who is it quickly, and speak apace . . . . iii 2 208
I'll tell you who Time ambles withal, who Time trots withal . . . iii 2 327
I pray you, tell me your remedy . . . . iii 2 386
Tell me where it is.—Go with me to it and I'll show it you . . . iii 2 449
You shall tell me where in the forest you live . . . . . . iii 2 452
Have a good priest that can tell you what marriage is . . . . iii 3 87
I must tell you friendly in your ear, Sell when you can . . . . iii 5 59
Now tell me how long you would have her after you have possessed her iv 1 143
I'll tell thee, Aliena, I cannot be out of the sight of Orlando . . . iv 1 221
I do not shame To tell you what I was . . . . iv 3 137
He sent me hither, stranger as I am, To tell this story . . . . iv 3 154
I pray you, tell your brother how well I counterfeited. Heigh-ho! . iv 3 168
Did your brother tell you how I counterfeited to swoon? . . . . v 2 28
Tell this youth what 'tis to love.—It is to be all made of sighs and tears v 2 89
Another tell him of his hounds and horse . . . . *T. of Shrew* Ind. 1 61
For I tell you, sirs, If you should smile he grows impatient . . Ind. 1 98
Tell him from me, as he will win my love . . . . . . Ind. 1 109
Tell me thy mind; for I have Pisa left And am to Padua come . . i 1 21
Tell me, is it possible That love should of a sudden take such hold? . i 1 151
Both our inventions meet and jump in one.—Tell me thine first . . i 1 196
Tell me now, sweet friend, what happy gale Blows you to Padua? . . i 2 48
He tells you flatly what his mind is . . . . i 2 77
Tell me her father's name and 'tis enough . . . . . . i 2 94
I'll tell you news indifferent good for either . . . . . . i 2 181
And do you tell me of a woman's tongue? . . . . i 2 208
If I may be bold, Tell me, I beseech you, which is the readiest way? . i 2 220
Here I charge thee, tell Whom thou lovest best . . . . . ii 1 8
Tell them both, These are their tutors: bid them use them well . . ii 1 110
Then tell me, if I get your daughter's love, What dowry shall I have? . ii 1 120
I did but tell her she mistook her frets, And bow'd her hand . . . ii 1 150
Why then I'll tell her plain She sings as sweetly as a nightingale . . ii 1 171
I tell you, 'tis incredible to believe How much she loves me . . . ii 1 308
Tell us, what occasion of import Hath all so long detain'd you? . . iii 2 104
Tedious it were to tell, and harsh to hear . . . . . . iii 2 107
Tell me, how goes the world?—A cold world . . . . . . iv 1 35
Tell thou the tale: but hadst thou not crossed me, thou shouldst have heard . . . . iv 1 74
I tell thee, Kate, 'twas burnt and dried away . . . . . . iv 1 173
I tell you, sir, she bears me fair in hand . . . . . . iv 2 3
Now, tell me, I pray, You that durst swear . . . . . . iv 2 11
I tell thee, Licio, this is wonderful.—Mistake no more: I am not Licio iv 2 15
This I will advise you: First, tell me, have you ever been at Pisa? . iv 2 93
I cannot tell; I fear 'tis choleric . . . . iv 3 22
My tongue will tell the anger of my heart, Or else my heart concealing it will break . . . . iv 3 77
I tell thee, I, that thou hast marr'd her gown . . . . . . iv 3 115
Make her ready straight; And, if you will, tell what hath happened . iv 4 64
And what of all this?—I cannot tell . . . . iv 4 91
Tell me, sweet Kate, and tell me truly too . . . . . . iv 5 28
O, my son, my son! Tell me, thou villain, where is my son? . . . v 1 92

Tell. Why, tell me, is not this my Cambio?—Cambio is changed into Lucentio . . . . *T. of Shrew* v 1 125
I pray you, tell me what you meant by that . . . . v 2 27
Tell these headstrong women What duty they do owe their lords and husbands . . . . v 2 130
Tell me thy reason why thou wilt marry . . . . *All's Well* i 3 29
Tell my gentlewoman I would speak with her; Helen, I mean . i 3 72
I charge thee, As heaven shall work in me for thine avail, To tell me truly . . . . i 3 191
Take her by the hand, And tell her she is thine . . . . . ii 3 181
I must tell thee, sirrah, I write man; to which title age cannot bring thee . . . . ii 3 208
I would not tell you what I would, my lord: Faith, yes . . . . ii 5 89
Here they come will tell you more . . . . iii 2 45
Tell him that his sword can never win The honour that he loses . iii 2 96
Tell me what a sprat you shall find him . . . . iii 6 113
Tell the Count Rousillon, and my brother, We have caught the woodcock iv 1 99
I will tell you a thing, but you shall let it dwell darkly with you . iv 3 13
I tell thee so before, because I would not fall out with thee . . iv 5 60
I like him well; 'tis not amiss. And I was about to tell you . . iv 5 73
Unless thou tell'st me where thou hadst this ring, Thou diest within this hour.—I'll never tell you . . . . v 3 285
Tell them, there thy fixed foot shall grow . . . . *T. Night* i 4 17
Tell me where thou hast been, or I will not open my lips . . . i 5 1
I can tell thee where that saying was born, of 'I fear no colours' . i 5 9
Tell him he shall not speak with me.—He has been told so . . . i 5 155
Tell me if this be the lady of the house, for I never saw her . . i 5 182
Sweet lady. Tell me your mind: I am a messenger . . . . i 5 219
Unless, perchance, you come to me again, To tell me how he takes it . i 5 301
He left this ring behind him, Would I or not: tell him I'll none of it . i 5 321
I must be round with you. My lady bade me tell you . . . ii 3 103
Possess us; tell us something of him . . . . ii 3 149
Tell her, my love, more noble than the world, Prizes not quantity of dirty lands; The parts that fortune hath bestow'd upon her, Tell her, I hold as giddily as fortune . . . . ii 4 84
You cannot love her; You tell her so; must she not then be answer'd? ii 4 95
By my troth, I'll tell thee, I am almost sick . . . . . . iii 1 52
Stay; I prithee, tell me what thou think'st of me . . . . . iii 1 150
How hollow the fiend speaks within him! did not I tell you? . . iii 4 102
A little thing would make me tell them how much I lack of a man . iii 4 332
Ungird thy strangeness and tell me what I shall vent to my lady . iv 1 16
This will I tell my lady straight: I would not be in some of your coats . iv 1 32
Hey, Robin, jolly Robin, Tell me how thy lady does . . . . iv 2 79
I tell thee, I am as well in my wits as any man in Illyria . . iv 2 114
Now my foes tell me plainly I am an ass . . . . . . v 1 20
Grant it then And tell me, in the modesty of honour . . . . v 1 343
Why have you suffer'd me to be imprison'd . . . ? tell me why . v 1 352
Tell him, you are sure All in Bohemia's well . . . . *W. Tale* i 2 30
To tell, he longs to see his son, were strong . . . . . . i 2 34
What! have I twice said well? when was't before? I prithee tell me . i 2 91
Sir, I will tell you; Since I am charged in honour . . . . i 2 406
Tell's a tale.—Merry or sad shall't be?—As merry as you will . . ii 1 23
I will tell it softly; Yond crickets shall not hear it . . . . ii 1 30
Tell her, Emilia, I'll use that tongue I have . . . . . ii 2 51
Tell me what blessings I have here alive, That I should fear to die? . iii 2 108
I tell you 'Tis rigour and not law . . . . iii 2 114
I cannot tell, good sir, for which of his virtues it was . . . iv 3 93
He tells her something That makes her blood look out . . . . iv 4 159
He sings several tunes faster than you'll tell money . . . . iv 4 185
Scarce a maid westward but she sings it; 'tis in request, I can tell you iv 4 297
It becomes thy oath full well, Thou to me thy secrets tell . . iv 4 307
'Tis time to part them. He's simple and tells much . . . iv 4 355
Once or twice I was about to speak and tell him plainly . . . iv 4 454
What I do next, shall be to tell the king Of this escape . . . iv 4 676
There is no other way but to tell the king she's a changeling . . iv 4 703
I will tell the king all, every word, yea, and his son's pranks too . iv 4 717
Tell me, for you seem to be honest plain men, what you have to the king . . . . iv 4 823
Mark Her eye, and tell me for what dull part in't You chose her . v 1 64
Tells us 'Tis not a visitation framed, but forced By need and accident . v 1 90
Tell me, mine own, Where hast thou been preserved? . . . . v 3 123
James, There's toys abroad: anon I'll tell thee more . . *K. John* i 1 232
Then tell us, shall your city call us lord? . . . . . . ii 1 263
Gracing the scroll that tells of this war's loss . . . . . . ii 1 348
Where is she and her son? tell me, who knows . . . . . ii 1 543
Be well advised, tell o'er thy tale again . . . . iii 1 5
Tell him this tale; and from the mouth of England Add thus much more iii 1 152
So tell the pope, all reverence set apart To him . . . . . iii 1 159
He tells us Arthur is deceased to-night . . . . iv 2 85
As bid me tell my tale in express words . . . . iv 2 234
Return and tell him so: we know the worst . . . . . . iv 3 27
There tell the king he may inquire us out . . . . . . iv 3 115
And come ye now to tell me John hath made His peace with Rome? . v 2 91
How goes the day with us? O, tell me, Hubert.—Badly, I fear . . v 3 1
Send him word by me which way you go.—Tell him, toward Swinstead v 3 8
Who did taste to him?—A monk, I tell you . . . . . . v 6 29
Tell me, moreover, hast thou sounded him? . . . . *Richard II.* i 1 8
Farewell: What will ensue hereof, there's none can tell . . . ii 1 212
I had forgot to tell your lordship, To-day, as I came by, I called there . ii 2 93
Let me tell you this: I have had feeling of my cousin's wrongs . . ii 3 140
Fairly let her be entreated: Tell her I send to her my kind commends . iii 1 38
Both young and old rebel, And all goes worse than I have power to tell iii 2 120
Let us sit upon the ground And tell sad stories of the death of kings . iii 2 156
Tell Bolingbroke—for yond methinks he stands . . . . . iii 3 91
Letters came last night . . . That tell black tidings . . . . iii 4 71
And let them tell thee tales Of woeful ages long ago betid . . . v 1 41
To quit their griefs, Tell thou the lamentable tale of me . . . . v 1 44
My lord, you told me you would tell the rest, When weeping made you break the story off . . . . v 2 1
Can no man tell me of my unthrifty son? . . . . v 3 1
Tell us how near is danger, That we may arm us to encounter it . . v 3 47
The sound that tells what hour it is Are clamorous groans . . . v 5 55
Rode he on Barbary? Tell me, gentle friend, How went he under him? v 5 81
Bootless 'tis to tell you we will go . . . . . *1 Hen. IV.* i 1 29
The incomprehensible lies that this same fat rogue will tell us . . i 2 211
I tell thee, He durst as well have met the devil alone . . . . i 3 115
I will not send them: I will after straight And tell him so . . . i 3 127
Tell your tale; I have done.—Nay, if you have not, to it again . . i 3 256
I pray thee, lend me thine.—Ay, when? canst tell? . . . . ii 1 43
I heard him tell it to one of his company last night at supper . . ii 1 62

Tell. Hang him! let him tell the king: we are prepared . . *1 Hen. IV.* ii 3 37
Tell me, sweet lord, what is't that takes from thee Thy stomach? . ii 3 43
I'll break thy little finger, Harry, An if thou wilt not tell me all things true . . . . ii 3 91
Do you not love me? Nay, tell me if you speak in jest or no . . . ii 3 102
And tell me flatly I am no proud Jack, like Falstaff . . . . ii 4 12
I tell thee, Ned, thou hast lost much honour, that thou wert not with me . . . . ii 4 21
If I tell thee a lie, spit in my face, call me horse . . . . . ii 4 214
Come, tell us your reason: what sayest thou to this? . . . . ii 4 258
I would not tell you on compulsion . . . . ii 4 263
'Faith, tell me now in earnest . . . . ii 4 334
But tell me, Hal, art not thou horrible afeard? . . . . . . ii 4 402
Give me leave To tell you once again . . . . iii 1 37
O, while you live, tell truth and shame the devil! . . . . . iii 1 62
Shall I tell you, cousin? He holds your temper in a high respect . . iii 1 169
Good father, tell her that she and my aunt Percy Shall follow . . iii 1 196
Tell me else, Could such inordinate and low desires . . . Accompany the greatness of thy blood? . . . . iii 2 11
That men would tell their children 'This is he' . . . . . iii 2 48
But wherefore do I tell these news to thee? Why, Harry, do I tell thee of my foes? . . . . iii 2 121
In the closing of some glorious day Be bold to tell you that I am your son . . . . iii 2 134
I have heard the prince tell him, I know not how oft . . . . iii 3 96
Tell me, doth he keep his bed?—He did, my lord, four days ere I set forth . . . . iv 1 21
The king, I can tell you, looks for us all: we must away all night . iv 2 62
But tell me, Jack, whose fellows are these that come after? . . . iv 2 67
Tell your nephew, The Prince of Wales doth join with all the world . v 1 85
So tell your cousin, and bring me word What he will do . . . . v 1 109
Go you and tell him so.—Marry, and shall, and very willingly . . v 2 33
Tell me, tell me, How show'd his tasking? seem'd it in contempt? . v 2 50
Let me tell the world, If he outlive the envy of this day . . . v 2 66
I do haunt thee in the battle thus Because some tell me that thou art a king.—They tell thee true . . . . v 3 5
Why didst thou tell me that thou wert a king? . . . . . . v 3 24
Nay, you shall find no boy's play here, I can tell you . . . . v 4 76
Did you not tell me this fat man was dead? . . . . . . v 4 135
Tell thou the earl that the Lord Bardolph doth attend him here *2 Hen. IV.* i 1 2
The whiteness in thy cheek Is apter than thy tongue to tell thy errand i 1 69
Tell thou an earl his divination lies, And I will take it as a sweet disgrace . . . . i 1 88
Tells them he doth bestride a bleeding land, Gasping for life . . . i 1 207
Boy, tell him I am deaf.—You must speak louder . . . . . i 2 77
Worse than the name of rebellion can tell how to make it . . . i 2 90
Give me leave to tell you, you lie in your throat, if you say I am any other than an honest man.—I give thee leave to tell me so! . . . i 2 97
What tell you me of it? be it as it is . . . . i 2 129
Yet, in some respects, I grant, I cannot go: I cannot tell . . . i 2 190
The rest the paper tells . . . . ii 1 147
Tell me, how many good young princes would do so? . . . . ii 2 32
Shall I tell thee one thing, Poins?—Yes, faith . . . . . . ii 2 35
Albeit I could tell to thee, as to one it pleases me . . . . . ii 2 44
I tell thee, my heart bleeds inwardly . . . . ii 2 51
It is mine ancient.—Tilly-fally, Sir John, ne'er tell me . . . . ii 4 90
Said he, 'you are in an ill name:' now a' said so, I can tell whereupon . ii 4 98
Will you tell me, Master Shallow, how to choose a man? . . . iii 2 275
To tell you from his grace That he will give you audience . . . iv 1 142
There is a thing within my bosom tells me . . . . iv 1 183
And how accompanied? canst thou tell that? . . . . . . iv 4 52
May they fall As those that I am come to tell you of! . . . . iv 4 96
Heard he the good news yet? Tell it him . . . . iv 5 12
And any pretty little tiny kickshaws, tell William cook . . . . v 1 29
I'll to the king my master that is dead, And tell him who hath sent me v 2 41
My lord, I'll tell you; that self bill is urged . . . *Hen. V.* i 1 1
With frank and with uncurbed plainness Tell us the Dauphin's mind . i 2 245
Tell him he hath made a match with such a wrangler . . . . i 2 264
But tell the Dauphin I will keep my state, Be like a king . . . i 2 273
I cannot tell: things must be as they may . . . . ii 1 22
He might return to vasty Tartar back, And tell the legions 'I can never win' . . . . ii 2 124
Tells Harry that the king doth offer him Katharine his daughter . iii Prol. 29
Tell you the duke, it is not so good to come to the mines . . . iii 2 61
I will be so bold as to tell you I know the disciplines of war . . iii 2 152
If I find a hole in his coat, I will tell him my mind . . . . iii 6 89
I can tell your majesty, the duke is a prave man . . . . . iii 6 100
Tell him we could have rebuked him at Harfleur . . . . . iii 6 128
Tell him, for conclusion, he hath betrayed his followers . . . . iii 6 142
Turn thee back, And tell thy king I do not seek him now . . . iii 6 149
I tell thee, constable, my mistress wears his own hair . . . . iii 7 64
Tell him, I'll knock his leek about his pate Upon Saint Davy's day . iv 1 54
We have French quarrels enow, if you could tell how to reckon . . iv 1 241
Tell the constable We are but warriors for the working-day . . . iv 3 108
My poor soldiers tell me, yet ere night They'll be in fresher robes . iv 3 116
Tell him my fury shall abate, and I The crowns will take . . . iv 4 50
I'll tell you there is good men porn at Monmouth . . . . . iv 7 55
Not a man of them that we shall take Shall taste our mercy. Go and tell them so . . . . iv 7 68
I tell thee truly, herald, I know not if the day be ours or no . . iv 7 86
All the water in Wye cannot wash your majesty's Welsh plood out of your pody, I can tell you that . . . . iv 7 113
I can tell you, it will serve you to mend your shoes . . . . iv 8 73
This note doth tell me of ten thousand French That in the field lie slain iv 8 85
Is it not lawful, an please your majesty, to tell how many is killed? . iv 8 123
I will tell you, asse my friend . . . . v 1 4
And then I will tell him a little piece of my desires . . . . v 1 13
I cannot tell vat is dat.—No, Kate? I will tell thee in French . . v 2 187
Canst thou love me?—I cannot tell.—Can any of your neighbours tell? . v 2 207
I have a saving faith within me tells me thou shalt . . . . . v 2 217
Therefore tell me, most fair Katharine, will you have me? . . . v 2 252
I will tell thee aloud 'England is thine, Ireland is thine, France is thine' v 2 257
The circumstance I'll tell you more at large . . . . *1 Hen. VI.* i 1 109
Tell her I return great thanks, And in submission will attend on her . ii 2 51
But tell me, keeper, will my nephew come? . . . . ii 5 17
O, tell me when my lips do touch his cheeks, That I may kindly give one fainting kiss . . . . ii 5 39
Lean thine aged back against mine arm; And, in that ease, I'll tell thee ii 5 44
My tender years can tell Civil dissension is a viperous worm . . . iii 1 71
We came but to tell you That we are here . . . . iii 2 73

Tell. Hell our prison is. But tell me whom thou seek'st . 1 *Hen. VI.* iv 7 59
How canst thou tell she will deny thy suit, Before thou make a trial? . v 3 75
First, let me tell you whom you have condemn'd . . . . . v 4 36
I cannot tell; but this I am assured . . . . v 5 83
What dream'd my lord? tell me, and I'll requite it . . . 2 *Hen. VI.* i 2 23
I'll tell thee, Suffolk, why I am unmeet . . . . . . i 3 168
Tell me what fate awaits the Duke of Suffolk? . . . . . i 4 67
A miracle! a miracle!—Come to the king and tell him what miracle . ii 1 62
Tell us here the circumstance, That we for thee may glorify the Lord . ii 1 74
Tell me, sirrah, what's my name?—Alas, master, I know not . . ii 1 117
My conscience tells me you are innocent . . . . . . iii 1 141
To tell my love unto his dumb deaf trunk . . . . . iii 2 144
Tell them all from me, I thank them for their tender loving care . iii 2 279
I am sent to tell his majesty That even now he cries aloud for him . iii 2 377
Go tell this heavy message to the king . . . . . . iii 2 379
Tell the king from me, that . . . I am content he shall reign . . iv 2 164
I tell you that that Lord Say hath gelded the commonwealth . . iv 2 173
Tell me wherein have I offended most? . . . . . . iv 7 103
As free as heart can wish or tongue can tell . . . . . iv 7 133
Tell Kent from me, she hath lost her best man . . . . iv 10 78
Tell me, my friend, art thou the man that slew him? . . . . v 1 71
Foul stigmatic, that's more than thou canst tell . . . . v 1 215
Speak thou for me and tell them what I did . . . . 3 *Hen. VI.* i 1 16
My title's weak. Tell me, may not a king adopt an heir? . . . i 1 135
My conscience tells me he is lawful king . . . . . . i 1 150
Come, cousin, let us tell the queen these news . . . . . i 1 182
And tell him privily of our intent . . . . i 2 39
To tell thee whence thou camest, of whom derived, Were shame enough i 4 119
To add more measure to your woes, I come to tell you things sith then befall'n . . . . ii 1 106
Shall we on the helmets of our foes Tell our devotion with revengeful arms? . . . . ii 1 164
Tell me, didst thou never hear That things ill-got had ever bad success? ii 2 45
I'll tell thee what befel me on a day In this self-place . . . . iii 1 10
Whiles Warwick tells his title, smooths the wrong . . . . . iii 1 48
Tell me, then, have you not broke your oaths?—No . . . . iii 1 79
How many children hast thou, widow? tell me . . . . . iii 2 26
Tell me, madam, do you love your children?—Ay, full as dearly as I love myself . . . . iii 2 36
I'll tell you how these lands are to be got . . . . . . iii 2 42
To tell thee plain, I aim to lie with thee.—To tell you plain, I had rather lie in prison . . . . iii 2 69
I can tell you both Her suit is granted for her husband's lands . . iii 2 116
Be plain, Queen Margaret, and tell thy grief . . . . . iii 3 19
And with my tongue To tell the passion of my sovereign's heart . . iii 3 62
You tell a pedigree Of threescore and two years . . . . . iii 3 92
Tell me, even upon thy conscience . . . . iii 3 113
Tell me for truth the measure of his love . . . . . . iii 3 120
As my letters tell me, He's very likely now to fall from him . . . iii 3 208
Then, England's messenger, return in post, And tell false Edward . iii 3 223
Tell him, in hope he'll prove a widower shortly, I'll wear the willow garland . . . . iii 3 227; iv 1 99
Tell him, my mourning weeds are laid aside . . . . iii 3 229; iv 1 104
Tell him from me that he hath done me wrong . . . iii 3 231; iv 1 110
Tell me, brother Clarence, what think you Of this new marriage? . . iv 1 1
I mind to tell him plainly what I think . . . . . . iv 1 8
Setting your scorns and your mislike aside, Tell me some reason why . iv 1 25
In brief, Tell me their words as near as thou canst guess them . . iv 1 90
Tell me if you love Warwick more than me? If it be so, then both depart iv 1 137
Tell what answer Lewis and the Lady Bona send to him . . . iv 3 55
Come to me, friend or foe, And tell me who is victor, York or Warwick? v 2 6
I tell ye all I am your better, traitors as ye are . . . . . v 5 35
I tell thee, fellow, He that doth naught with her, excepting one, Were best he do it secretly, alone . . . . *Richard III.* i 1 98
If I thought that, I tell thee, homicide, These nails should rend that beauty from my cheeks . . . . i 2 125
I cannot tell: the world is grown so bad . . . . . . i 3 70
Threat you me with telling of the king? Tell him, and spare not . . i 3 114
With a piece of scripture, Tell them that God bids us do good for evil . i 3 335
What was your dream? I long to hear you tell it . . . . . i 4 8
I promise you, I am afraid to hear you tell it . . . . . i 4 65
Back to the Duke of Gloucester, tell him so.—I pray thee, stay a while i 4 119
'Twas wont to hold me but while one would tell twenty . . . i 4 122
You scarcely have the hearts to tell me so . . . . . . i 4 180
Take thou the fee, and tell him what I say . . . . . . i 4 284
Tell me, good grandam, is our father dead? . . . . . . ii 2 1
If 'twere not she, I cannot tell who told me . . . . . ii 4 34
What a slug is Hastings, that he comes not To tell us whether they will come or no! . . . . iii 1 23
Tell him his fears are shallow, wanting instance . . . . . iii 2 25
I'll tell him what you say . . . . iii 2 34; iii 7 70
I tell thee, man, 'tis better with me now Than when I met thee last . iii 2 100
But now, I tell thee—keep it to thyself . . . . . . iii 2 104
I pray you all, tell me what they deserve That do conspire my death? . iii 4 61
By great preservation, We live to tell it you . . . . . . iii 5 37
Tell them how Edward put to death a citizen . . . . . . iii 5 76
Then he was urged to tell my tale again . . . . iii 7 31
I come in perfect love to him; And so once more return and tell his grace . . . . iii 7 91
And thou shalt tell the process of their death . . . . . . iv 3 32
Tell o'er your woes again by viewing mine . . . . . . iv 4 39
Tell me, thou villain slave, where are my children? . . . . iv 4 144
Tell me . . . what honour, Canst thou demise to any child of mine? . iv 4 246
Tell her thou madest away her uncle Clarence, Her uncle Rivers . . iv 4 281
In plain terms tell her my loving tale.—Plain and not honest is too harsh iv 4 359
Why dost thou run so many mile about, When thou mayst tell thy tale a nearer way? Once more, what news? . . . . iv 4 462
Tell me, what doth he upon the sea?—Unless for that, my liege, I cannot guess . . . . iv 4 474
The news I have to tell your majesty Is, that by sudden floods . . iv 4 511
Sir Christopher, tell Richmond this from me . . . . . . iv 5 1
But, tell me, where is princely Richmond now?—At Pembroke . . iv 5 7
Tell him the queen hath heartily consented He shall espouse Elizabeth iv 5 17
Tell me, how fares our loving mother? . . . . v 3 82
Tell the clock there. Give me a calendar . . . . . . v 3 276
But, tell me, is young George Stanley living?—He is, my lord . . v 5 9
I cannot tell What heaven hath given him,—let some graver eye Pierce into that . . . . *Hen. VIII.* i 1 66
And front but in that file Where others tell steps with me . . . i 2 43
Neither the king nor's heirs, Tell you the duke, shall prosper . . i 2 169

Tell. Because they speak no English, thus they pray'd To tell your grace *Hen. VIII.* i 4 66
Pray, tell'em thus much from me . . . . i 4 77
But, pray, how pass'd it?—I'll tell you in a little . . . . . ii 1 11
Pray, tell him You met him half in heaven . . . . . . ii 1 87
May he live Longer than I have time to tell his years! . . . . ii 1 91
I must tell you, You tender more your person's honour . . . . ii 4 115
He tells you rightly.—Ye tell me what ye wish for both,—my ruin . iii 1 97
Tell me, If what I now pronounce you have found true . . . . iii 2 162
If I loved many words, lord, I should tell you You have as little honesty as honour . . . . iii 2 270
How goes her business?—That I can tell you too . . . . . iv 1 24
Something I can command. As I walk thither, I'll tell ye more . . iv 1 117
Didst thou not tell me, Griffith, as thou led'st me? . . . . . iv 2 5
Tell me how he died: If well, he stepp'd before me, happily . . . iv 2 9
Tell him, in death I bless'd him, For so I will . . . . . . iv 2 163
And, let me tell you, it will ne'er be well, 'Twill not . . . . v 1 29
This day, Sir, I may tell it you, I think I have Incensed the lords . v 1 42
I have news to tell you: come, come, give me your hand . . . v 1 94
And hither am I come . . . To tell you, fair beholders *Troi. and Cres.* Prol. 26
I was about to tell thee:—when my heart, As wedged with a sigh . i 1 34
O Pandarus! I tell thee, Pandarus,—When I do tell thee . . . . i 1 48
I tell thee I am mad In Cressid's love . . . . i 1 51
Let her to the Greeks; and so I'll tell her the next time I see her . i 1 84
Tell me, Apollo, for thy Daphne's love, What Cressid is, what Pandar? i 1 101
He'll lay about him to-day, I can tell them that . . . . . i 2 58
You shall tell me another tale . . . . i 2 90
I'll tell you them all by their names as they pass by . . . . i 2 198
Is not that a brave man? he's one of the flowers of Troy, I can tell you i 2 203
He has a shrewd wit, I can tell you; and he's a man good enough . i 2 207
Good boy, tell him I come. I doubt he be hurt . . . . . i 2 301
That thou shalt know, Trojan, he is awake, He tells thee so himself . i 3 256
Tell him of Nestor, one that was a man When Hector's grandsire suck'd i 3 291
Tell him from me I'll hide my silver beard in a gold beaver . . . i 3 295
Tell him that my lady Was fairer than his grandam and as chaste . . i 3 298
I will begin at thy heel, and tell what thou art by inches . . . ii 1 53
I'll tell you what I say of him.—What? . . . . ii 1 80
Because your speech hath none that tells him so . . . . . ii 2 36
Tell me, Patroclus, what's Achilles?—Thy lord, Thersites: then tell me, I pray thee, what's thyself? . . . . ii 3 47
Tell me, Patroclus, what art thou?—Thou mayst tell that knowest.—O, tell, tell . . . . ii 3 51
Go and tell him, We come to speak with him . . . . . . ii 3 130
They are burs, I can tell you; they'll stick where they are thrown . iii 2 120
Tell him I humbly desire the valiant Ajax to invite the most valorous Hector to come unarmed to my tent . . . . iii 3 274
Did not I tell you? Would he were knock'd i' the head! . . . . iv 2 35
Where's my lord? gone! Tell me, sweet uncle, what's the matter? . iv 2 84
Tell you the lady what she is to do, And haste her to the purpose . iv 3 4
Be moderate.—Why tell you me of moderation? . . . . . iv 4 2
But I can tell that in each grace of these There lurks a still and dumb-discoursive devil That tempts . . . . iv 4 91
I tell thee, lord of Greece, She is as far high-soaring o'er thy praises iv 4 125
I'll tell thee, Diomed, This brave shall oft make thee to hide thy head iv 4 138
The worthiest of them tell me name by name . . . . . . iv 5 160
Tell me, you heavens, in which part of his body Shall I destroy him? . iv 5 242
I tell thee, yea.—Wert thou an oracle to tell me so, I'ld not believe thee iv 5 252
As gentle tell me, of what honour was This Cressida in Troy? . . iv 5 287
I'll tell you what,— Foh, foh! come, tell a pin . . . . . v 2 21
Come, tell me whose it was.— . . . I will not tell you whose . . v 2 88
But if I tell how these two did co-act, Shall I not lie in publishing a truth? . . . . v 2 118
Like a prophet suddenly enrapt To tell thee that this day is ominous . v 3 66
Do deeds worth praise and tell you them at night . . . . . v 3 93
Unless a man were cursed, I cannot tell what to think on't . . . v 3 107
Tell her I have chastised the amorous Trojan, And am her knight by proof . . . . v 5 4
You understand me not that tell me so . . . . v 10 11
Hector is gone: Who shall tell Priam so, or Hecuba? . . . . v 10 15
I tell you, friends, most charitable care Have the patricians of you *Coriol.* i 1 67
I shall tell you A pretty tale: it may be you have heard it . . . i 1 92
What answer made the belly?—Sir, I shall tell you . . . . . i 1 111
I will tell you; If you'll bestow a small—of what you have little—Patience awhile . . . . i 1 128
I tell thee, daughter, I sprang not more in joy at first hearing he was a man-child than now in first seeing he had proved himself a man . i 3 16
Tell Valeria, We are fit to bid her welcome . . . . . . i 3 46
Go with me; and I'll tell you excellent news of your husband . . i 3 100
Will the time serve to tell? I do not think . . . . . . i 6 46
If I should tell thee o'er this thy day's work, Thou'ldst not believe thy deeds . . . . i 9 1
The augurer tells me we shall have news to-night . . . . . ii 1 1
Tell me one thing that I shall ask you . . . . ii 1 15
Yet they lie deadly that tell you you have good faces . . . . ii 1 67
If he show us his wounds and tell us his deeds . . . . . . ii 3 6
If he tell us his noble deeds, we must also tell him our noble acceptance ii 3 8
Tell us what hath brought you to't.—Mine own desert . . . . ii 3 69
Tell those friends, They have chose a consul that will from them take Their liberties . . . . ii 3 221
Tell me of corn! This was my speech, and I will speak 't again . . iii 1 61
Tell me, In peace what each of them by the other lose . . . . iii 2 43
Tell these sad women 'Tis fond to wail inevitable strokes . . . iv 1 25
This lies glowing, I can tell you, and is almost mature . . . . iv 3 26
I shall, between this and supper, tell you most strange things . . iv 3 43
Tell my master what a strange guest he has here.—And I shall . . iv 5 38
Why, thou Mars! I tell thee, We have a power on foot . . . . iv 5 124
He had, sir, a kind of face, methought,—I cannot tell how to term it . iv 5 164
Faith, look you, one cannot tell how to say that . . . . . iv 5 177
O slaves, I can tell you news,—news, you rascals! . . . . . iv 5 181
Tell not me: I know this cannot be.—Not possible . . . . . iv 6 55
I tell you, he does sit in gold, his eye Red as 'twould burn Rome . . v 1 63
I tell thee, fellow, Thy general is my lover . . . . . . v 2 13
Has he dined, canst thou tell? . . . . v 2 36
Tell me not Wherein I seem unnatural . . . . v 3 83
This boy, that cannot tell what he would have, But kneels and holds up hands . . . . v 3 174
Go tell the lords o' the city I am here: Deliver them this paper . . v 6 1
Sir, I cannot tell: We must proceed as we do find the people . . . v 6 15
Tell the traitor, in the high'st degree He hath abused your powers . v 6 85
Proud and ambitious tribune, canst thou tell? . . . . *T. Andron.* i 1 202

Tell. Tell me, Andronicus, doth this motion please thee?—It doth *T. An.* i 1 243
But I know it is: Whether by device or no, the heavens can tell . i 1 395
I tell you, lords, you do but plot your deaths By this device . ii 1 78
And one thing more That womanhood denies my tongue to tell . ii 3 174
O, tell me how it is; for ne'er till now Was I a child to fear I know not what . . . . ii 3 220
So, now go tell, an if thy tongue can speak . . . ii 4 1
Therefore I tell my sorrows to the stones . . . . iii 1 37
Thou hast no hands, to wipe away thy tears; Nor tongue, to tell me . iii 1 107
Tell him it was a hand that warded him From thousand dangers . iii 1 195
To bid Æneas tell the tale twice o'er, How Troy was burnt . . iii 2 27
Tell me, did you see Aaron the Moor?—Well, more or less . . iv 2 52
Tell the empress from me, I am of age To keep mine own . . iv 2 104
Two may keep counsel when the third's away: Go to the empress, tell her this . . . . iv 2 145
Give the mother gold, And tell them both the circumstance of all . iv 2 156
Deliver him this petition; Tell him, it is for justice and for aid . iv 3 15
Knock at my door, and tell me what he says . . . . iv 3 119
Tell on thy mind; I say thy child shall live . . . v 1 69
Tell him Revenge is come to join with him . . . . v 2 7
I will find them out; And in their ears tell them my dreadful name . v 2 39
Tell him the emperor and the empress too Feast at my house . . v 2 127
Will you bide with him, Whiles I go tell my lord the emperor? . . v 2 138
Tell us, old man, how shall we be employ'd? . . . . v 2 149
Tell us what Sinon hath bewitch'd our ears . . . . v 3 85
Let him tell the tale; Your hearts will throb and weep to hear him speak . . . . v 3 94
Yet tell me not, for I have heard it all *Rom. and Jul.* i 1 180
Tell me in sadness, who is that you love.—What, shall I groan and tell thee?—Groan! why, no; But sadly tell me who . . . i 1 205
In that vow Do I live dead that live to tell it now . . . i 1 230
I should have ask'd you that before.—Now I'll tell you without asking . . . . i 2 83
Faith, I can tell her age unto an hour.—She's not fourteen . . i 3 11
Tell me, daughter Juliet, How stands your disposition to be married? . i 3 64
I have worn a visor and could tell A whispering tale in a fair lady's ear i 5 24
His son is thirty.—Will you tell me that? . . . . . i 5 41
I tell you, he that can lay hold of her Shall have the chinks . . i 5 118
By a name I know not how to tell thee who I am . . . ii 2 54
How camest thou hither, tell me, and wherefore? . . . . ii 2 62
Hence will I to my ghostly father's cell, His help to crave, and my dear hap to tell . . . . ii 2 190
Where hast thou been, then?—I'll tell thee, ere thou ask it me again . ii 3 48
How We met, we woo'd and made exchange of vow, I'll tell thee . ii 3 63
Can any of you tell me where I may find the young Romeo?—I can tell you . . . . ii 4 125
Let me tell ye, if ye should lead her into a fool's paradise . . ii 4 175
I will tell her as much: Lord, Lord, she will be a joyful woman.—What wilt thou tell her, nurse? thou dost not mark me.—I will tell her, sir, that you do protest . . . . ii 4 184
I anger her sometimes and tell her that Paris is the properer man . ii 4 216
Though news be sad, yet tell them merrily . . . . . ii 5 22
Sweet, sweet, sweet nurse, tell me, what says my love? . . . ii 5 55
O, tell me, holy friar, Where is my lady's lord? . . . . iii 3 81
I'll tell my lady you will come.—Do so . . . . . iii 3 161
O' Thursday, tell her, She shall be married . . . . iii 4 20
But now I'll tell thee joyful tidings, girl . . . . . iii 5 105
Tell my lord and father, madam, I will not marry yet . . . iii 5 121
Tell him so yourself, And see how he will take it at your hands . iii 5 125
Tell my lady I am gone, Having displeased my father . . . iii 5 231
Tell me not, friar, that thou hear'st of this, Unless thou tell me how I may prevent it . . . . iv 1 50
Give me, give me! O, tell not me of fear! . . . . . iv 1 121
Go tell him of this: I'll have this knot knit up to-morrow morning . iv 2 23
And presently took post to tell it you . . . . . . v 1 21
Tell me, good my friend, What torch is yond, that vainly lends his light? v 3 124
There is no crossing him in's humour; Else I should tell him *T. of A.* i 2 167
I weigh my friend's affection with mine own; I'll tell you true . i 2 223
Tell him, My uses cry to me, I must serve my turn Out of mine own . ii 1 19
I can tell you one thing, my lord, and which I hear from common rumours . . . . iii 2 4
I tell you, denied, my lord.—What a strange case was that! . . iii 2 17
Tell him this from me, I count it one of my greatest afflictions . iii 2 61
I need not tell him that; he knows you are too diligent . . . iii 4 39
Tell out my blood.—Five thousand crowns, my lord.—Five thousand drops pay that . . . . iii 4 95
I'll tell you more anon. Here's a noble feast toward . . . iii 6 67
If thou wilt, Tell them there I have gold . . . . . iv 3 289
Tell him of an intent that's coming toward him . . . . v 1 22
Tell him Timon speaks it, In pity of our aged and our youth, I cannot choose but tell him, that I care not . . . . v 1 178
Commend me to them, And tell them that, to ease them of their griefs v 1 201
Tell my friends, Tell Athens, in the sequence of degree From high to low v 1 210
Tell me, good Brutus, can you see your face? . . . *J. Cæsar* i 2 51
I cannot tell what you and other men Think of this life . . . i 2 93
He will, after his sour fashion, tell you What hath proceeded . . i 2 180
Casca will tell us what the matter is . . . . . . i 2 189
I rather tell thee what is to be fear'd Than what I fear . . . i 2 211
Tell me truly what thou think'st of him . . . . . i 2 214
Tell us what hath chanced to-day, That Cæsar looks so sad . . i 2 216
Tell us the manner of it, gentle Casca.—I can as well be hanged as tell the manner of it: it was mere foolery . . . . . . i 2 234
Nay, an I tell you that, I'll ne'er look you i' the face again . . i 2 284
I could tell you more news too . . . . i 2 288
Am I not stay'd for? tell me.—Yes, you are . . . . . i 3 140
When I tell him he hates flatterers, He says he does, being then most flattered . . . . ii 1 207
Tell me, Brutus, Is it excepted I should know no secrets? . . . ii 1 280
Tell me your counsels, I will not disclose 'em . . . . ii 1 298
I will stay at home. Here's Decius Brutus, he shall tell them so . ii 2 57
Tell them that I will not come to-day: Cannot, is false . . . ii 2 62
Afeard to tell graybeards the truth? Decius, go tell them Cæsar will not come . . . . ii 2 67
Let me know some cause, Lest I be laugh'd at when I tell them so . ii 2 70
My dear dear love To your proceeding bids me tell you this . . ii 2 103
I would have had thee there, and here again, Ere I can tell thee what thou shouldst do there . . . . ii 4 5
Tell him, so please him come unto this place, He shall be satisfied . iii 1 140
Post back with speed, and tell him what hath chanced . . . iii 1 287
Will you stay awhile? I have o'ershot myself to tell you of it . . iii 2 155

Tell. I only speak right on; I tell you that which you yourselves do know . . . . *J. Cæsar* iii 2 228
Alas, you know not: I must tell you, then . . . . . iii 2 242
Let me tell you, Cassius, you yourself Are much condemn'd . . iv 3 9
Why comest thou?—To tell thee thou shalt see me at Philippi . . iv 3 284
Tell me what thou notest about the field . . . . . v 3 22
Tell Antony, Brutus is ta'en.—I'll tell the news . . . . v 4 16
I cannot tell. But I am faint, my gashes cry for help . . *Macbeth* i 2 41
Stay, you imperfect speakers, tell me more . . . . . i 3 70
Oftentimes, to win us to our harm, The instruments of darkness tell us truths . . . . i 3 124
Macduff lives in disgrace: sir, can you tell Where he bestows himself? iii 6 23
Tell me, thou unknown power, —He knows thy thought: Hear his speech, but say thou nought . . . . iv 1 69
That I may tell pale-hearted fear it lies, And sleep in spite of thunder . iv 1 85
Yet my heart Throbs to know one thing: tell me, if your art Can tell so much . . . . iv 1 101
Look not so pale.—I tell you yet again, Banquo's buried . . . v 1 69
Let the angel whom thou still hast served Tell thee . . . . v 8 15
Accursed be that tongue that tells me so! . . . . . . v 8 17
Good now, sit down, and tell me, he that knows . . . *Hamlet* i 1 70
The great cannon to the clouds shall tell . . . . . . i 2 126
Stay'd it long?—While one with moderate haste might tell a hundred . i 2 238
I must tell you, You do not understand yourself so clearly . . . i 3 95
Tell Why thy canonized bones, hearsed in death, Have burst their cerements . . . . i 4 46
But that I am forbid To tell the secrets of my prison-house . . . i 5 14
Good my lord, tell it.—No; you'll reveal it . . . . . i 5 118
There needs no ghost, my lord, come from the grave To tell us this . i 5 126
It is an honest ghost, that let me tell you . . . . . i 5 138
He tells me, my dear Gertrude, he hath found The head and source of all your son's distemper . . . . ii 2 54
As I perceived it, I must tell you that, Before my daughter told me . ii 2 133
I will tell you why; so shall my anticipation prevent your discovery . ii 2 304
Which, I tell you, must show fairly outward . . . . . ii 2 391
I will prophesy he comes to tell me of the players . . . . ii 2 405
My lord, I have news to tell you.—My lord, I have news to tell you . ii 2 408
How now, Ophelia! You need not tell us what Lord Hamlet said . iii 1 187
The players cannot keep counsel; they'll tell all.—Will he tell us what this show meant? . . . . iii 2 152
Be not you ashamed to show, he'll not shame to tell you what it means iii 2 156
I'll call upon you ere you go to bed, And tell you what I know . . iii 3 35
Tell him his pranks have been too broad to bear with . . . iii 4 2
Tell us where 'tis, that we may take it thence . . . . iv 2 7
My lord, you must tell us where the body is . . . . . iv 2 27
Tell him that, by his license, Fortinbras Craves the conveyance of a promised march Over his kingdom . . . . iv 4 2
Tell me, Laertes, Why thou art thus incensed . . . . . iv 5 125
Of them I have much to tell thee . . . . iv 6 30
Tell me Why you proceeded not against these feats . . . . iv 7 5
That I shall live and tell him to his teeth, 'Thus didest thou' . . iv 7 57
Is she to be buried in Christian burial . . ?—I tell thee she is . . v 1 3
And will not tell him of his action of battery . . . . . v 1 111
How long is that since?—Cannot you tell that? every fool can tell that v 1 160
Tell her, let her paint an inch thick, to this favour she must come . v 1 213
Tell me one thing.—What's that, my lord? . . . . . v 1 215
I tell thee, churlish priest, A ministering angel shall my sister be . v 1 263
It is very sultry,—as 'twere,—I cannot tell how . . . . v 2 104
O, I could tell you—But let it be . . . . v 2 348
And in this harsh world draw thy breath in pain, To tell my story . v 2 360
So tell him, with the occurrents, more and less, Which have solicited . v 2 368
Tell him his commandment is fulfill'd . . . . . . v 2 381
Tell me, my daughters,—Since now we will divest us . . . *Lear* i 1 49
Whilst I can vent clamour from my throat, I'll tell thee thou dost evil i 1 169
Leave her, sir; for, by the power that made me, I tell you all her wealth i 1 211
Go you, and tell my daughter I would speak with her . . . i 4 82
Tell him, so much the rent of his land comes to . . . . i 4 147
Ha! waking? 'tis not so. Who is it that can tell me who I am? . i 4 250
What's the matter, sir?—I'll tell thee: Life and death! . . . i 4 318
How far your eyes may pierce I cannot tell . . . . . i 4 368
Yet I can tell what I can tell.—Why, what canst thou tell? . . i 5 16
Thou canst tell why one's nose stands i' the middle on's face? . . i 5 19
Canst tell how an oyster makes his shell?—No.—Nor I neither . . i 5 26
I can tell why a snail has a house.—Why?—Why, to put his head in . i 5 29
If thou lovest me, tell me.—I love thee not . . . . . ii 2 6
Thou shalt have as many dolours for thy daughters as thou canst tell in a year . . . . ii 4 55
Tell the hot duke that—No, but not yet . . . . . . ii 4 105
Go tell the duke and's wife I'ld speak with them, Now, presently . ii 4 117
She will tell you who your fellow is That yet you do not know . . iii 1 48
When usurers tell their gold i' the field . . . . . . iii 2 89
I'll tell thee, friend, I am almost mad myself . . . . . iii 4 170
Truth to tell thee, The grief hath crazed my wits. What a night's this! iii 4 174
Frateretto calls me; and tells me Nero is an angler in the lake of darkness . . . . iii 6 7
Tell me whether a madman be a gentleman or a yeoman? . . . iii 6 10
Tell me what more thou know'st . . . . iv 2 98
For him 'tis well That of thy death and business I can tell . . iv 6 285
Tell me—but truly—but then speak the truth . . . . . v 1 8
So we'll live, And pray, and sing, and tell old tales . . . . v 3 12
Who are you? Mine eyes are not o' the best: I'll tell you straight . v 3 279
He's a good fellow, I can tell you that; He'll strike, and quickly to . v 3 284
Tush! never tell me; I take it much unkindly . . . *Othello* i 1 1
I am one, sir, that comes to tell you . . . . i 1 116
If you know not this, my manners tell me We have your wrong rebuke . i 1 130
I ran it through, even from my boyish days, To the very moment that he bade me tell it . . . . i 3 133
I should but teach him how to tell my story, And that would woo her . i 3 165
What tidings can you tell me of my lord? . . . . . . ii 1 88
First, I must tell thee this—Desdemona is directly in love with him . ii 1 220
I will ask him for my place again; he shall tell me I am a drunkard! . ii 3 307
I'll tell you what you shall do . . . . ii 3 319
Tell her there's one Cassio entreats her a little favour of speech . iii 1 27
When shall he come? Tell me, Othello . . . . . . iii 3 68
But, O, what damned minutes tells he o'er Who dotes, yet doubts! . iii 3 169
Tell me but this, Have you not sometimes seen a handkerchief Spotted with strawberries in your wife's hand? . . . . iii 3 433
To tell you where he lodges, is to tell you where I lie . . . iii 4 8
Tell him I have moved my lord on his behalf . . . . . iii 4 18
I will make him tell the tale anew, Where, how, how oft, how long ago iv 1 85

Tell. Now he importunes him To tell it o'er: go to; well said *Othello* iv 1 117
Now he tells how she plucked him to my chamber . iv 1 145
What is your pleasure, madam? How is't with you?—I cannot tell . iv 2 111
Very well.—I tell you 'tis not very well . iv 2 199
Dost thou in conscience think,—tell me, Emilia,—That there be women do abuse their husbands In such gross kind? . iv 3 61
Come, mistress, you must tell's another tale . v 1 125
Run you to the citadel, And tell my lord and lady what hath happ'd . v 1 127
But did you ever tell him she was false?—I did . v 2 178
Behold and see.—If it be love indeed, tell me how much *Ant. and Cleo.* i 1 14
Prithee, tell her but a worky-day fortune . i 2 55
He was not merry, Which seem'd to tell them his remembrance lay In Egypt with his joy . i 5 57
Let ill tidings tell Themselves when they be felt . ii 5 87
Be pleased to tell us—For this is from the present—how you take The offers we have sent you . ii 6 29
Go hang, sir, hang! Tell me of that? away! . ii 7 59
And— What, Octavia?—I'll tell you in your ear . iii 2 46
An army for an usher, and The neighs of horse to tell of her approach . iii 6 45
Tell him he wears the rose Of youth upon him . iii 13 20
Tell him, I am prompt To lay my crown at's feet, and there to kneel . iii 13 75
Tell him, from his all-obeying breath I hear The doom of Egypt . iii 13 77
Mock not, Enobarbus. I tell you true . iv 6 26
Clip your wives, your friends, Tell them your feats . iv 8 9
The augurers Say they know not, they cannot tell . iv 12 5
Go tell him I have slain myself; Say, that the last I spoke was 'Antony' . iv 13 7
She which by her death our Cæsar tells 'I am conqueror of myself' . iv 14 61
To tell them that this world did equal theirs Till they had stol'n our jewel . iv 15 77
Hear me, good friends,—But I will tell you at some meeter season . v 1 49
Antony Did tell me of you, bade me trust you . v 2 13
Tell him, That majesty, to keep decorum, must No less beg than a kingdom . v 2 16
Tell him I am his fortune's vassal, and I send him The greatness he has got . v 2 28
You have heard of me?—I cannot tell.—Assuredly you know me . v 2 72
You laugh when boys or women tell their dreams . v 2 74
I am loath to tell you what I would you knew . v 2 107
By your command, Which my love makes religion to obey, I tell you this v 2 200
Her physician tells me She hath pursued conclusions infinite Of easy ways to die . v 2 357
Ere I could tell him How I would think on him at certain hours . *Cymb.* i 3 26
I'll tell thee on the instant thou art then As great as is thy master . i 5 50
Tell thy mistress how The case stands with her; do't as from thyself . i 5 66
I kiss'd it: I hope it be not gone to tell my lord That I kiss aught but he ii 3 152
He is at Milford-Haven: read, and tell me How far 'tis thither . iii 2 51
Tell me how Wales was made so happy as To inherit such a haven . iii 2 62
When on my three-foot stool I sit and tell The warlike feats I have done iii 3 89
Present yourself, desire his service, tell him Wherein you're happy . iii 4 176
Yes; no wonder, When rich ones scarce tell true . iii 6 12
You did mistake him, sure.—I cannot tell: long is it since I saw him . iv 2 103
Let it to the sea, And tell the fishes he's the queen's son, Cloten . iv 2 153
A leg of Rome shall not return to tell What crows have peck'd them here v 3 92
And how you shall speed in your journey's end, I think you'll never return to tell one.—I tell thee, fellow, there are none want eyes to direct them the way I am going . v 4 191
I'll tell you, sir, in private, if you please To give me hearing . v 5 115
And am right glad he is not standing here To tell this tale of mine . v 5 297
I tell you what mine authors say *Pericles* i Gower 20
Tell thee, with speechless tongues and semblance pale . i 1 36
Death remember'd should be like a mirror, Who tells us life's but breath i 1 46
But I must tell you, now my thoughts revolt . i 1 78
Few love to hear the sins they love to act; 'Twould braid yourself too near for me to tell it . i 1 93
The blind mole casts Copp'd hills towards heaven, to tell the earth is throng'd By man's oppression . i 1 101
Nor tell the world Antiochus doth sin In such a loathed manner . i 1 146
Go tell their general we attend him here, To know for what he comes . i 4 79
From the finny subject of the sea These fishers tell the infirmities of men . ii 1 53
Do you know where ye are?—Not well.—Why, I'll tell you . ii 1 103
I'll tell you, he hath a fair daughter, and to-morrow is her birth-day . ii 1 113
Like to my father's picture, Which tells me in that glory once he was . ii 3 38
And furthermore tell him, we desire to know of him, Of whence he is . ii 3 73
Now to my daughter's letter: She tells me here, she'll wed the stranger knight . ii 5 16
Give this to the 'pothecary, And tell me how it works . iii 2 10
Prithee, tell me one thing first.—Come now, your one thing . iv 6 166
If I should tell my history, it would seem Like lies disdain'd in the reporting . v 1 119
Tell thy story; If thine consider'd prove the thousandth part Of my endurance, thou art a man . v 1 135
Tell me, if thou canst, What this maid is, or what is like to be? . v 1 185
She would never tell Her parentage . v 1 189
Tell me but that, For truth can never be confirm'd enough . v 1 202
But tell me now My drown'd queen's name . v 1 206
She shall tell thee all; When thou shalt kneel . v 1 218
Tell Helicanus, my Marina, tell him O'er, point by point, for yet he seems to doubt . v 1 226
Awake, and tell thy dream . v 1 250
Toward Ephesus Turn our blown sails; eftsoons I'll tell thee why . v 1 256

Tell me that. When would you use it? pray, sir, tell me that *T. G. of V.* iii 1 123
On what compulsion must I? tell me that . *Mer. of Venice* iv 1 183
Tell me that, and unyoke.—Marry, now I can tell . *Hamlet* v 1 59

Tell me this. I will try thee. Tell me this: who begot thee? *T. G. of V.* iii 1 293
Tell me this: has Ford's wife and Page's wife acquainted each other? *Mer. Wives* ii 2 113
Stop in your wind, sir: tell me this, I pray . *Com. of Errors* i 2 53
Pray you, tell me this; If he should break his day . *Mer. of Venice* i 3 164
I thank you, sir: and, pray you, tell me this . *As Y. Like It* i 2 280

Tell me true. But tell me true, will't be a match?—Ask my dog *T. G. of Ver.* ii 5 35
Come, tell me true: it shall be the better for you . *Meas. for Meas.* ii 1 232
Therefore tell me true; But tell me then, 'tis so . *All's Well* i 3 181
Tell me, sirrah, but tell me true, I charge you, Not fearing the displeasure . v 3 234
Tell me true, are you not mad indeed? or do you but counterfeit?—Believe me, I am not; I tell thee true . *T. Night* iv 2 121
And tell me, noble Diomed, faith, tell me true . *Troi. and Cres.* iv 1 51

Tell me true. How quickly were it gone!—You tell me true *T. of Athens* ii 2 163
But tell me true—For I must ever doubt, though ne'er so sure . iv 3 513
Now, as you are a Roman, tell me true.—Then like a Roman bear the truth I tell . *J. Cæsar* iv 3 187
'Tis thus; Who tells me true, though in his tale lie death, I hear him as he flatter'd . *Ant. and Cleo.* i 2 102

Tell tales. Upon the least occasion more mine eyes will tell tales of me *T. Night* ii 1 43
We'll tell tales.—Of sorrow or of joy?—Of either *Richard II.* iii 4 10
Nor tell tales of thee to high-judging Jove . *Lear* ii 4 231

Tell the truth. O wonderful, when devils tell the truth! *Richard III.* i 2 73
And till he tell the truth, Let the supposed fairies pinch him sound *Mer. Wives* iv 4 60

Tell thee what. I'll tell thee what, prince: a college of wit-crackers cannot flout me out of my humour . *Much Ado* v 4 101
I tell thee what, Antonio—I love thee . *Mer. of Venice* i 1 86
I'll tell thee what, my friend, He is a very serpent . *K. John* iii 3 60
Ha! I'll tell thee what; Thou'rt damn'd as black . iv 3 120
I tell thee what, Hal, if I tell thee a lie, spit in my face . *1 Hen. IV.* ii 4 213
I tell thee what, Corporal Bardolph, I could tear her . *2 Hen. IV.* ii 4 166
I'll tell thee what, thou damned tripe-visaged rascal . v 4 9
I'll tell thee what; yet go: Nay, but thou shalt stay too *Coriolanus* iv 2 22
I tell thee what: get thee to church o' Thursday . *Rom. and Jul.* iii 5 162

Tell you what. I'll tell you what, sir, an she stand him . *T. of Shrew* i 2 113
I tell you what; He held me last night at least nine hours *1 Hen. IV.* iii 1 155
I'll tell you what, you thin man in a censer . *2 Hen. IV.* v 4 20
I tell you what, Captain Gower; I do perceive he is not the man *Hen. V.* iii 6 86
I'll tell you what; I think it is our way *Richard III.* i 1 78
I'll tell you what, my cousin Buckingham,— What, my gracious lord? iii 1 89
I'll tell you what,— Foh, foh! come, tell a pin *Troi. and Cres.* v 2 21

Teller. The nature of bad news infects the teller . *Ant. and Cleo.* i 2 99

Tellest. What tellest thou me of black and blue? . *Mer. Wives* iv 5 117
What tell'st thou me of supping? . *Com. of Errors* iv 3 66
Thou tell'st me there is murder in mine eye *As Y. Like It* iii 5 10
Unless thou tell'st me where thou hadst this ring, Thou diest *All's Well* v 3 284
Too well, too well thou tell'st a tale so ill . *Richard II.* iii 2 121
Yet tell'st thou not how thou wert entertain'd . *1 Hen. VI.* i 4 38
Go boast of this: And if thou tell'st the heavy story right, Upon my soul, the hearers will shed tears . *3 Hen. VI.* i 4 160
Tellest thou me of 'ifs'? Thou art a traitor *Richard III.* iii 4 77
This thou tell'st me, As true thou tell'st me . *Troi. and Cres.* i 1 59
What tell'st thou me of robbing? . *Othello* i 1 105
Thou tell'st the world It is not worth leave-taking . *Ant. and Cleo.* v 2 300
The service that you three have done is more Unlike than this thou tell'st . *Cymbeline* v 5 354

Telling. Who having into truth, by telling of it, Made such a sinner of his memory, To credit his own lie *Tempest* i 2 100
Being so hard to me that brought your mind, I fear she'll prove as hard to you in telling your mind . *T. G. of Ver.* i 1 148
I telling you then, if you be remembered . *Meas. for Meas.* ii 1 113
Thou hast shifted out of thy tale into telling me of the fashion *M. Ado* iii 3 151
If he say it is so, he is, in telling true, but so . *L. L. Lost* i 1 227
Here, good my glass, take this for telling true . iv 1 18
The wisest aunt, telling the saddest tale . *M. N. Dream* ii 1 51
Bragging to the stars, Telling the bushes that thou look'st for wars . iii 2 408
We will have no telling.—Come on, I say . *T. of Shrew* v 2 132
Telling them I know my place as I would they should do theirs *T. Night* ii 5 59
Gardener, for telling me these news of woe, Pray God the plants thou graft'st may never grow *Richard II.* iii 4 100
Telling me the sovereign'st thing on earth Was parmaceti . *1 Hen. IV.* i 3 57
Sometime he angers me With telling me of the moldwarp and the ant . iii 1 149
Telling us she had a good dish of prawns . *2 Hen. IV.* ii 1 103
And breeds no bate with telling of discreet stories . ii 4 272
Are you so choleric With Eleanor, for telling but her dream? . *2 Hen. VI.* i 2 52
What! threat you me with telling of the king? *Richard III.* i 3 113
Be brief, lest that the process of thy kindness Last longer telling than thy kindness' date . iv 4 254
I can watch you for telling how I took the blow *Troi. and Cres.* i 2 294
I am one that, telling true under him, must say, you cannot pass *Coriol.* v 2 33
I can keep honest counsel, ride, run, mar a curious tale in telling it *Lear* i 4 35
Mark me with what violence she first loved the Moor, but for bragging and telling her fantastical lies *Othello* ii 1 225
Though I lose The praise of it by telling, you must know *Ant. and Cleo.* ii 6 44
The thanks I give Is telling you that I am poor of thanks . *Cymbeline* ii 3 94
Let your breath cool yourself, telling your haste . *Pericles* i 1 161

Tell-tale. Shall these papers lie like tell-tales here? . *T. G. of Ver.* i 2 133
I warrant you, no tell-tale nor no breed-bate . *Mer. Wives* i 4 12
We are no tell-tales, madam; fear you not *Mer. of Venice* v 1 123
Therefore will he wipe his tables clean And keep no tell-tale to his memory *2 Hen. IV.* iv 1 202
Let not the heavens hear these tell-tale women Rail *Richard III.* iv 4 149
You speak to Casca, and to such a man That is no fleering tell-tale *J. C.* i 3 117

Tellus. Hic ibat Simois; hic est Sigeia tellus *T. of Shrew* iii 1 28
'Sigeia tellus,' disguised thus to get your love . iii 1 33
Full thirty times hath Phœbus' cart gone round Neptune's salt wash and Tellus' orbed ground *Hamlet* iii 2 166
I will rob Tellus of her weed, To strew thy green with flowers *Pericles* iv 1 14

Temper. You may temper her by your persuasion *T. G. of Ver.* iii 2 64
Never could the strumpet, With all her double vigour, art, and nature, Once stir my temper . *Meas. for Meas.* ii 2 185
The poison of that lies in you to temper . *Much Ado* ii 2 21
A hot temper leaps o'er a cold decree *Mer. of Venice* i 2 20
My lord, You know your father's temper . *W. Tale* iv 4 478
A noble temper dost thou show in this . *K. John* v 2 40
Being all too base To stain the temper of my knightly sword *Richard II.* iv 1 29
He holds your temper in a high respect And curbs himself *1 Hen. IV.* iii 1 170
Here draw I A sword, whose temper I intend to stain . v 2 94
What man of good temper would endure this tempest of exclamation? *2 Hen. IV.* ii 1 87
His temper, therefore, must be well observed . iv 4 36
O that the living Harry had the temper Of him, the worst of these three! v 2 15
If thou canst love a fellow of this temper, Kate *Hen. V.* v 2 153
Between two blades, which bears the better temper . *1 Hen. VI.* ii 4 13
And temper clay with blood of Englishmen *2 Hen. VI.* iii 1 311
Sword, hold thy temper; heart, be wrathful still . v 2 70
For few men rightly temper with the stars *3 Hen. VI.* iv 6 29
'Tis she That tempers him to this extremity *Richard III.* i 1 65
Hearts of most hard temper Melt and lament for her *Hen. VIII.* ii 3 11
I know you have a gentle, noble temper, A soul as even as a calm . iii 1 165
In whom the tempers and the minds of all Should be shut up *T. and C.* i 3 57

Temper. You keep a constant temper . . . . . *Coriolanus* v 2 100
And temper him with all the art I have . . . . *T. Andron.* iv 4 109
Grind their bones to powder small And with this hateful liquor temper it v 2 200
Made me effeminate And in my temper soften'd valour's steel *R. and J.* iii 1 120
If you could find out but a man To bear a poison, I would temper it iii 5 98
His comfortable temper has forsook him ; he's much out of health, and keeps his chamber . . . . *T. of Athens* iii 4 71
Ye gods, it doth amaze me A man of such a feeble temper should So get the start of the majestic world . . . . . . *J. Cæsar* i 2 129
Our hearts Of brothers' temper do receive you in With all kind love . iii 1 175
To that dauntless temper of his mind, He hath a wisdom . *Macbeth* iii 1 52
And cast you, with the waters that you lose, To temper clay . *Lear* i 4 326
Keep me in temper : I would not be mad ! . . . . . . i 5 51
It is a sword of Spain, the ice-brook's temper . . . . *Othello* v 2 253
His captain's heart . . . reneges all temper . . . . *Ant. and Cleo.* i 1 8
But not every man patient after the noble temper of your lordship *Cymb.* ii 3 6
Very oft importuned me To temper poisons for her . . . . v 5 250
Temperality. Now you are in an excellent good temperality . 2 *Hen. IV.* ii 4 25
Temperance. It must needs be of subtle, tender and delicate temperance.—Temperance was a delicate wench . . . . *Tempest* ii 1 42
A gentleman of all temperance . . . . . . *Meas. for Meas.* iii 2 251
What, are you chafed? Ask God for temperance . . . *Hen. VIII.* i 1 124
Being once chafed, he cannot Be rein'd again to temperance *Coriolanus* iii 3 28
The king-becoming graces, As justice, verity, temperance, stableness, Bounty, perseverance, mercy, lowliness . . . . *Macbeth* iv 3 92
Acquire and beget a temperance that may give it smoothness *Hamlet* iii 2 8
Be by, good madam, when we do awake him ; I doubt not of his temperance . . . . *Lear* iv 7 24
For, I am sure, Though you can guess what temperance should be, You know not what it is . . . . *Ant. and Cleo.* iii 13 121
O, temperance, lady !—Sir, I will eat no meat, I'll not drink . . v 2 48
Temperate. Come, temperate nymphs, and help to celebrate . *Tempest* iv 1 132
She is not hot, but temperate as the morn . . . *T. of Shrew* ii 1 296
Peace, lady ! pause, or be more temperate . . . . *K. John* ii 1 195
Such temperate order in so fierce a cause Doth want example . . iii 4 12
My blood hath been too cold and temperate, Unapt to stir . 1 *Hen. IV.* i 3 1
Whiles yet the cool and temperate wind of grace O'erblows . *Hen. V.* iii 3 30
But there was more temperate fire under the pot of her eyes *Troi. and Cres.* i 2 160
Who can be wise, amazed, temperate and furious, Loyal and neutral, in a moment? No man . . . . *Macbeth* ii 3 114
Temperately. He cannot temperately transport his honours *Coriolanus* ii 1 240
Temperately proceed to what you would Thus violently redress . . iii 1 219
Nay, temperately ; your promise . . . . iii 3 67
My pulse, as yours, doth temperately keep time . . *Hamlet* iii 4 140
Tempered. The elements, Of whom your swords are temper'd *Tempest* iii 3 62
In the heat of blood, And lack of temper'd judgement . *Meas. for Meas.* v 1 478
Until his ink were temper'd with Love's sighs . . . *L. L. Lost* iv 3 347
So wouldst thou, if the truth of thy love to me were so righteously tempered as mine is to thee . . . . . . *As Y. Like It* i 2 14
I'll talk to you When you are better temper'd to attend . 1 *Hen. IV.* i 3 235
But he that temper'd thee bade thee stand up . . . *Hen. V.* ii 2 118
Were your days As green as Ajax' and your brain so temper'd *T. and C.* ii 3 265
So much ungently temper'd, To stop his ears against admonishment . v 3 1
By my holy order, I thought thy disposition better temper'd *R. and J.* iii 3 115
He is justly served ; It is a poison temper'd by himself . . *Hamlet* v 2 339
Tempering. I have him already tempering between my finger and my thumb, and shortly will I seal with him . . . 2 *Hen. IV.* iv 3 140
Tempering extremities with extreme sweet . . *Rom. and Jul.* ii Prol. 14
Tempest. Hast thou, spirit, Perform'd to point the tempest that I bade thee?—To every article . . . . *Tempest* i 2 194
I did say so, When first I raised the tempest . . . . . v 1 6
When did you lose your daughter?—In this last tempest . . . v 1 153
What tempest, I trow, threw this whale, with so many tuns of oil in his belly, ashore at Windsor? . . . . . . *Mer. Wives* ii 1 64
Let there come a tempest of provocation, I will shelter me here . . v 5 23
Which I could well Between them from the tempest of my eyes *M. N. D.* i 1 131
O, if it prove, Tempests are kind and salt waves fresh in love *T. Night* iii 4 419
By a roaring tempest on the flood, A whole armado of convicted sail Is scatter'd and disjoin'd . . . . *K. John* iii 4 1
Now happy he whose cloak and cincture can Hold out this tempest . iv 3 156
It was my breath that blew this tempest up . . . . . . v 1 17
This shower, blown up by tempest of the soul, Startles mine eyes . v 2 50
Nor reconcile This louring tempest of your home-bred hate *Richard II.* i 3 187
We hear this fearful tempest sing, Yet seek no shelter to avoid the storm ii 1 263
Such crimson tempest should bedrench The fresh green lap . . iii 3 46
Hollow whistling in the leaves Foretells a tempest . . . 1 *Hen. IV.* v 1 6
What man of good temper would endure this tempest of exclamation? 2 *Hen. IV.* ii 1 87
When tempest of commotion, like the south Borne with black vapour ii 4 392
In fierce tempest is he coming, In thunder and in earthquake *Hen. V.* ii 4 99
And this fell tempest shall not cease to rage . 2 *Hen. VI.* iii 1 351
When from thy shore the tempest beat us back, I stood upon the hatches iii 2 102
Rough and rugged, Like to the summer's corn by tempest lodged . . iii 2 176
Like to a ship that, having 'scaped a tempest, Is straightway calm'd . iv 9 32
Go to bed and dream again, To keep thee from the tempest of the field v 1 197
See, see what showers arise, Blown with the windy tempest of my heart, Upon thy wounds ! . . . . 3 *Hen. VI.* ii 5 86
Dogs howl'd, and hideous tempest shook down trees . . . v 6 46
After life ; O, then began the tempest to my soul . . *Richard III.* i 4 44
The Breton navy is dispersed by tempest . . . . . iv 4 523
This tempest, Dashing the garment of this peace . . *Hen. VIII.* i 1 92
Such a noise arose As the shrouds make at sea in a stiff tempest . . iv 1 72
In the wind and tempest of her frown . . . *Troi. and Cres.* i 3 26
Cheer the heart that dies in tempest of thy angry frown . *T. Andron.* i 1 458
To calm this tempest whirling in the court . . . . . iv 2 160
I have seen tempests, when the scolding winds Have rived the knotty oaks, . . . But never till to-night, never till now, Did I go through a tempest dropping fire . . . . *J. Cæsar* i 3 5
In the very torrent, tempest, and, as I may say, the whirlwind of passion, you must acquire and beget a temperance . *Hamlet* iii 2 7
Here is a hovel ; Some friendship will it lend you 'gainst the tempest *Lear* iii 2 62
The tempest in my mind Doth from my senses take all feeling else . iii 4 12
This tempest will not give me leave to ponder On things would hurt me more . . . . iii 4 24
The desperate tempest hath so bang'd the Turks . . . *Othello* ii 1 21
They were parted With foul and violent tempest . . . . ii 1 34
Tempests themselves, high seas and howling winds, The gutter'd rocks ii 1 68
If after every tempest comes such calms, May the winds blow ! . . ii 1 187
They are greater storms and tempests than almanacs can report *A. and C.* i 2 154
With thousand doubts How I might stop this tempest ere it came *Pericles* i 2 98
Tempest. The grisled north Disgorges such a tempest forth *Pericles* iii Gower 48
Ay me ! poor maid, Born in a tempest, when my mother died . . iv 1 19
He bears A tempest, which his mortal vessel tears, And yet he rides it out . . . . iv 4 30
Did you not name a tempest, A birth, and death? . . . . . v 3 33
Tempest-tossed. Will overset Thy tempest-tossed body . *Rom. and Jul.* iii 5 138
Tempest-tost. Though his bark cannot be lost, Yet it shall be tempest-tost . . . . *Macbeth* i 3 25
Tempestuous. Like as rigour of tempestuous gusts Provokes the mightiest hulk against the tide . . . . . . 1 *Hen. VI.* v 5 5
Scatter'd by winds and high tempestuous gusts . . *T. Andron.* v 3 69
Temple. There's nothing ill can dwell in such a temple . . *Tempest* i 2 457
The gorgeous palaces, The solemn temples, the great globe itself . . iv 1 153
Swore he would meet her, as he was appointed, next morning at the temple . . . . *Much Ado* iii 3 172
In the temple, in the town, the field, You do me mischief *M. N. Dream* ii 1 238
For she his hairy temples then had rounded With coronet of . . . flowers iv 1 56
In the temple, by and by, with us These couples shall eternally be knit iv 1 185
And he did bid us follow to the temple.—Why, then, we are awake . iv 1 202
The duke is coming from the temple, and there is two or three lords . iv 2 16
Her sunny locks Hang on her temples like a golden fleece *Mer. of Venice* i 1 170
First, forward to the temple : after dinner Your hazard shall be made ii 1 44
Here we have no temple but the wood . . . *As Y. Like It* iii 3 50
I have dispatch'd in post To sacred Delphos, to Apollo's temple *W. Tale* ii 1 183
The temple much surpassing The common praise it bears . . . iii 1 2
When living blood doth in these temples beat . . . . *K. John* iii 1 108
Within the hollow crown That rounds the mortal temples of a king Keeps Death his court and there the antic sits . *Richard II.* iii 2 161
Within their chiefest temple I'll erect A tomb. . . . 1 *Hen. VI.* ii 2 12
We sent unto the Temple, unto his chamber . . . . . ii 5 19
Adorn his temples with a coronet . . . . v 4 134
And will you pale your head in Henry's glory, And rob his temples of the diadem, Now in his life? . . . . 3 *Hen. VI.* i 4 104
The imperial metal, circling now thy brow, Had graced the tender temples of my child . . . . *Richard III.* iv 4 383
This long-usurped royalty From the dead temples of this bloody wretch Have I pluck'd off . . . . v 5 5
Looks upon the ground, Then lays his finger on his temple *Hen. VIII.* iii 2 115
Throng our large temples with the shows of peace ! *Coriolanus* iii 3 36
What's the news?—Your temples burned in their cement . . iv 6 85
Chaste as the icicle That's curdied by the frost from purest snow And hangs on Dian's temple . . . . v 3 67
Ladies, you deserve To have a temple built you . . . . v 3 207
Had I the power that some say Dian had, Thy temples should be planted presently With horns, as was Actæon's . . *T. Andron.* ii 3 62
What a god's gold, That he is worshipp'd in a baser temple Than where swine feed ! . . . . *T. of Athens* v 1 51
Sacrilegious murder hath broke ope The Lord's anointed temple *Macbeth* ii 3 73
But, as this temple waxes, The inward service of the mind and soul Grows wide withal . . . . *Hamlet* i 3 12
Rub him about the temples . . . . *Othello* iv 1 53
Keep unshaked That temple, thy fair mind ! . . . . *Cymbeline* ii 1 69
The smile mocking the sigh, that it would fly From so divine a temple iv 2 55
Our Jovial star reign'd at his birth, and in Our temple was he married v 4 106
The temple Of virtue was she ; yea, and she herself . . . . v 5 220
Let's quit this ground, And smoke the temple with our sacrifices . . v 5 398
In the temple of great Jupiter Our peace we'll ratify . . . . v 5 482
Diana's temple is not distant far, Where you may abide . . *Pericles* iii 4 13
My temple stands in Ephesus : hie thee thither . . . . . v 1 241
At Ephesus, the temple see, Our king and all his company . . . v 2 282
And placed her Here in Diana's temple . . . . . . v 3 25
How she came placed here in the temple . . . . . . v 3 67
Temple-garden. Grown to this faction in the Temple-garden 1 *Hen. VI.* ii 4 125
Temple-hall. Meet me to-morrow in the Temple-hall . 1 *Hen. IV.* iii 3 223
Within the Temple-hall we were too loud . . . 1 *Hen. VI.* ii 4 3
Temple-haunting. The temple-haunting martlet . . . . *Macbeth* i 6 4
Temporal. Of temporal royalties He thinks me now incapable *Tempest* i 2 110
Fasting maids whose minds are dedicate To nothing temporal *M. for M.* ii 2 155
His sceptre shows the force of temporal power . *Mer. of Venice* iv 1 190
For all the temporal lands which men devout By testament have given to the church Would they strip from us . . . . *Hen. V.* i 1 9
Is this an hour for temporal affairs? . . . . . *Hen. VIII.* ii 2 73
Much better She ne'er had known pomp : though't be temporal . . ii 3 13
So children temporal fathers do appease ; Gods are more full of mercy *Cymbeline* v 4 12
Temporary. Not scurvy, nor a temporary meddler . . *Meas. for Meas.* v 1 145
Temporize. Well, you will temporize with the hours . . *Much Ado* i 1 276
Too wilful-opposite, And will not temporize with my entreaties *K. John* v 2 125
If I could temporise with my affection . . . *Troi. and Cres.* iv 4 6
Temporized. All's well ; and might have been much better, if He could have temporized . . . . *Coriolanus* iv 6 17
Temporizer. A mindless slave, Or else a hovering temporizer . *W. Tale* i 2 302
Temps. Par la grace de Dieu, et en peu de temps . . . *Hen. V.* iii 4 44
Tempt. Who sins most? Ha ! Not she ; nor doth she tempt *M. for M.* ii 2 165
Ah, Luciana, did he tempt thee so? . . . . . *Com. of Errors* iv 2 1
With what persuasion did he tempt thy love? . . . . . . iv 2 13
Satan, avoid ! I charge thee, tempt me not . . . . . . iv 3 48
Devils soonest tempt, resembling spirits of light . . . *L. L. Lost* iv 3 257
Tempt not too much the hatred of my spirit . . . *M. N. Dream* ii 1 211
The fiend is at mine elbow and tempts me . . . *Mer. of Venice* ii 2 3
Do not tempt my misery . . . . *T. Night* iii 4 383
If thou darest tempt me further, draw thy sword . . . . . iv 1 45
But durst not tempt a minister of honour, Lest she should be denied *W. Tale* ii 2 50
You tempt him over-much . . . . v 1 73
The devil tempts thee here In likeness of a new untrimmed bride *K. John* iii 1 208
Nor tempt the danger of my true defence . . . . iv 3 84
Tempt us not to bear above our power ! . . . . v 6 38
You tempt the fury of my three attendants . . . 1 *Hen. VI.* iv 2 10
Know'st thou not any whom corrupting gold Would tempt? *Rich. III.* iv 2 35
Gold were as good as twenty orators, And will, no doubt, tempt him iv 2 39
Shall I be tempted of the devil thus?—Ay, if the devil tempt thee to do good . . . . iv 4 419
There lurks a still and dumb-discoursive devil That tempts most cunningly . . . . *Troi. and Cres.* iv 4 93
We are devils to ourselves, When we will tempt the frailty of our powers . . . . iv 4 98
Sweet honey Greek, tempt me no more to folly . . . . . v 2 18
Tempt not yet the brushes of the war. Unarm thee, go. . . . . v 3 34
He tempts judgement. . . . . v 7 22

Tempt. Good gentle youth, tempt not a desperate man . *Rom. and Jul.* v 3 59
But wherefore did you so much tempt the heavens? . *J. Cæsar* i 3 53
And tempt the rheumy and unpurged air To add unto his sickness . ii 1 266
Have mind upon your health, tempt me no farther . . . . iv 3 36
What, durst not tempt him!—For your life you durst not . iv 3 62
What if it tempt you toward the flood, my lord? . *Hamlet* i 4 69
Let the bloat king tempt you again to bed; Pinch wanton on your cheek; call you his mouse . . . . . iii 4 182
Tempt him with speed aboard; Delay it not; I'll have him hence to-night . . . . iv 3 56
Let not my worser spirit tempt me again To die before you please! *Lear* iv 6 222
The devil their virtue tempts, and they tempt heaven . *Othello* iv 1 8
Tempt him not so too far; I wish, forbear . *Ant. and Cleo.* i 3 11

Temptation. Amen: For I am that way going to temptation, Where prayers cross . . . . *Meas. for Meas.* ii 2 158
Most dangerous Is that temptation that doth goad us on To sin in loving virtue . . . . ii 2 182
Set a deep glass of rhenish wine on the contrary casket, for if the devil be within and that temptation without, I know he will choose it *Mer. of Venice* i 2 106
Temptations have since then been born to's . *W. Tale* i 2 77

Tempted. Teach me, thy tempted subject, to excuse it! . *T. G. of Ver.* ii 6 8
'Tis one thing to be tempted, Escalus, Another thing to fall *M. for M.* ii 1 17
Is this her fault or mine? The tempter or the tempted, who sins most? ii 2 163
I never tempted her with word too large . . . *Much Ado* iv 1 53
Yet was Samson so tempted, and he had an excellent strength *L. L. Lost* i 2 179
Had he been Adam, he had tempted Eve . . . . v 2 322
That man is not alive Might so have tempted him as you have *1 Hen. IV.* iii 1 174
How often have I tempted Suffolk's tongue! . *2 Hen. VI.* iii 2 114
Mine ear hath tempted judgment to desire . . *3 Hen. VI.* iii 3 133
Who from my cabin tempted me to walk Upon the hatches *Richard III.* i 4 12
Shall I be tempted of the devil thus?—Ay, if the devil tempt thee to do good . . . . iv 4 418
There lurks a still and dumb-discoursive devil That tempts most cunningly: but be not tempted . . . *Troi. and Cres.* iv 4 93
Shall I be tempted to infringe my vow In the same time 'tis made? *Cor.* v 3 20
You durst not so have tempted him.—I durst not!—No . *J. Cæsar* iv 3 59

Tempter. The tempter or the tempted, who sins most? *Meas. for Meas.* ii 2 163
These women are shrewd tempters with their tongues . *1 Hen. VI.* i 2 123
From fairies and the tempters of the night Guard me, beseech ye *Cymb.* ii 2 9

Tempting. Thy lips, those kissing cherries, tempting grow! *M. N. Dream* iii 2 140
With kind embracements, tempting kisses . *T. of Shrew* Ind. 1 118
I am much too venturous In tempting of your patience . *Hen. VIII.* i 2 55

Ten. When they will not give a doit to relieve a lame beggar, they will lay out ten to see a dead Indian . . . . *Tempest* ii 2 34
I see a passenger.—If there be ten, shrink not . . *T. G. of Ver.* iv 1 2
A dog as big as ten of yours . . . . . . iv 4 62
Her husband will be absence from his house between ten and eleven *Mer. Wives* ii 2 86
Between nine and ten, sayest thou?—Eight and nine, sir . . iii 5 54
For a fine, quaint . . . fashion, yours is worth ten on't . *Much Ado* iii 4 23
Two god-fathers: Had I been judge, thou shouldst have had ten more *Mer. of Venice* iv 1 399
Yet I have faced it with a card of ten . . *T. of Shrew* ii 1 407
Within ten year it will make itself ten, which is a goodly increase *All's Well* i 1 160
Among nine bad if one be good, There's yet one good in ten . . i 3 83
But grief makes one hour ten . . . . . *Richard II.* i 3 261
How many be there of them?—Some eight or ten . *1 Hen. IV.* ii 2 67
By ten We shall have each a hundred Englishmen . . *Hen. V.* iii 7 168
One to ten! Lean raw-boned rascals! . . . *1 Hen. VI.* i 2 34
What's o'clock?—Ten, my lord.—Ten is the hour that was appointed *2 Hen. VI.* ii 4 5
But, whiles he thought to steal the single ten, The king was slily finger'd from the deck! . . . . . *3 Hen. VI.* v 1 43
But what's o'clock?—Upon the stroke of ten.—Well, let it strike *Rich. III.* iv 2 115
Had it our name, the value of one ten . *Troi. and Cres.* ii 2 23
Vowing more than the perfection of ten and discharging less than the tenth part of one . . . . iii 2 94
Threescore and ten I can remember well . . *Macbeth* ii 4 1
And thou shalt have more Than two tens to a score . *Lear* i 4 140
What need you five and twenty, ten, or five? . . . ii 4 264
Not this hour, lieutenant; 'tis not yet ten o' the clock . *Othello* ii 3 14
In every ten [women] that they make, the devils mar five *Ant. and Cleo.* v 2 278
Ten, chased by one, Are now each one the slaughter-man of twenty *Cymbeline* v 3 48

Ten bones. By these ten bones, my lords, he did speak them to me *2 Hen. VI.* i 3 193

Ten Commandments. Went to sea with the Ten Commandments, but scraped one out of the table . . *Meas. for Meas.* i 2 8
With my nails, I'll set my ten commandments in your face . *2 Hen. VI.* i 3 145

Ten days. Within these ten days if that thou be'st found So near our public court as twenty miles, Thou diest for it . . *As Y. Like It* i 3 45
We have stay'd ten days, And hardly kept our countrymen together *Richard II.* ii 4 1
Ten days ago I drown'd these news in tears . . . *3 Hen. VI.* iii 1 104
That would be ten days' wonder at the least . . . iii 2 113

Ten fathom. O' my conscience, Wish him ten fathom deep *Hen. VIII.* i 1 51

Ten-fold. Cannot passionate our tenfold grief With folded arms *T. An.* iii 2 6
I will reward thee Once for thy spritely comfort, and ten-fold For thy good valour. Come thee on . . . *Ant. and Cleo.* iv 7 15

Ten groats. As fit as ten groats is for the hand of an attorney *All's Well* ii 2 22
The cheapest of us is ten groats too dear . . *Richard II.* v 5 68

Ten hills. Or pile ten hills on the Tarpeian rock . . *Coriolanus* iii 2 3

Ten hoops. The three-hooped pot shall have ten hoops . *2 Hen. VI.* iv 2 72

Ten leagues. She that dwells Ten leagues beyond man's life . *Tempest* ii 1 247

Ten masts at each make not the altitude . . . *Lear* iv 6 53

Ten meals. Give me but the ten meals I have lost . *2 Hen. VI.* iv 10 66

Ten mile. He would have walked ten mile a-foot to see a good armour *Much Ado* ii 3 16
Eight yards of uneven ground is threescore and ten miles afoot with me *1 Hen. IV.* ii 2 27
Not to come near our person by ten mile . . . *2 Hen. IV.* v 5 69

Ten nights. I am for you, though it cost me ten nights' watchings *M. Ado* ii 1 387
Now will he lie ten nights awake, carving the fashion of a new doublet ii 3 18

Ten o'clock. It hath struck ten o'clock.—The night is dark *Mer. Wives* v 2 11
It is ten o'clock: 'Thus we may see,' quoth he, 'how the world wags' *As Y. Like It* ii 7 22
Ten o'clock: within these three hours 'twill be time enough to go home *All's Well* iv 1 27

Ten pound. I sit at ten pounds a week . . . . . *Mer. Wives* i 3 8
Let it be ten pound, if thou canst . . . . *2 Hen. IV.* ii 1 160
A score of good ewes may be worth ten pounds . . . iii 2 57

Ten proofs. We have ten proofs to one that blood hath the victory *M. Ado* ii 3 171

Ten shares. A' would have ten shares . . . *Troi. and Cres.* ii 3 230

Ten shillings. If thou darest not stand for ten shillings . *1 Hen. IV.* i 2 157
Here's four Harry ten shillings in French crowns . *2 Hen. IV.* iii 2 236

Ten thousand times More rich . . . . *Mer. of Venice* iii 2 155
What if my house be troubled with a rat And I be pleased to give ten thousand ducats To have it baned? . . . . . . iv 1 45
A thousand knees Ten thousand years together, naked, fasting, Upon a barren mountain . . . . *W. Tale* iii 2 212
Even to that drop ten thousand wiry friends Do glue themselves *K. John* iii 4 64
They would be as a call To train ten thousand English to their side . iii 4 175
Ten thousand bloody crowns of mothers' sons . . *Richard II.* iii 3 96
That every day under his household roof Did keep ten thousand men . iv 1 283
Ten thousand bold Scots, two and twenty knights . *1 Hen. IV.* i 1 68
A day Wherein the fortune of ten thousand men Must bide the touch iv 4 9
O that we now had here But one ten thousand of those men in England That do no work to-day! . . . . . *Hen. V.* iv 3 17
This note doth tell me of ten thousand French That in the field lie slain iv 8 85
In these ten thousand they have lost, There are but sixteen hundred mercenaries . . . . iv 8 92
Ten thousand soldiers with me I will take . . *1 Hen. VI.* i 1 155
Ten thousand French have ta'en the sacrament . . . iv 2 28
I will stir up in England some black storm Shall blow ten thousand souls to heaven or hell . . . . . *2 Hen. VI.* iii 1 350
Quitting thee thereby of ten thousand shames . . . . iii 2 218
Embrace and kiss and take ten thousand leaves . . . iii 2 354
Better ten thousand base-born Cades miscarry Than you should stoop unto a Frenchman's mercy . . . . iv 8 49
Let ten thousand devils come against me . . . . . iv 10 65
These words will cost ten thousand lives this day . *3 Hen. VI.* ii 2 177
I and ten thousand in this luckless realm Had left no mourning widows ii 6 18
Than can the substance of ten thousand soldiers Armed in proof *Rich. III.* v 3 218
Lend me ten thousand eyes, And I will fill them with prophetic tears *Troi. and Cres.* ii 2 101
Cracking ten thousand curbs Of more strong link asunder . *Coriolanus* i 1 72
A thousand hissing snakes, Ten thousand swelling toads *T. Andron.* ii 3 101
Nothing grieves me heartily indeed But that I cannot do ten thousand more . . . . v 1 144
Ten thousand worse than ever yet I did Would I perform, if I might . v 3 187
That one word 'banished' Hath slain ten thousand Tybalts . *R. and J.* iii 2 114
He disbursed at Saint Colme's inch Ten thousand dollars . *Macbeth* i 2 62
Old Siward, with ten thousand warlike men, Already at a point . iv 3 134
Gracious England hath Lent us good Siward and ten thousand men . iv 3 190
There is ten thousand— Geese, villain?—Soldiers, sir . . v 3 13
To be honest, as this world goes, is to be one man picked out of ten thousand.—That's very true . . . . . *Hamlet* ii 2 179
To whose huge spokes ten thousand lesser things Are mortised . . iii 3 19
Ten thousand harms, more than the ills I know, My idleness doth hatch *Ant. and Cleo.* i 2 133
I will lay you ten thousand ducats to your ring . . *Cymbeline* i 4 138
My ten thousand ducats are yours . . . . . i 4 162
Above ten thousand meaner moveables Would testify . . . ii 2 29

Ten tides. Would thou mightst lie drowning The washing of ten tides! *Tempest* i 1 61

Ten times. She is Ten times more gentle than her father's crabbed . iii 1 8
These black masks Proclaim an enshield beauty ten times louder Than beauty could, display'd . . . . *Meas. for Meas.* ii 4 80
Nay, call us ten times frail; For we are soft as our complexions are . ii 4 128
Is it not strange and strange?—Nay, it is ten times strange . . v 1 42
This is all as true as it is strange: Nay, it is ten times true . . v 1 45
O, ten times faster Venus' pigeons fly! . . *Mer. of Venice* ii 6 5
In silver she's immured, Being ten times undervalued to tried gold . ii 7 53
If that will not suffice, I will be bound to pay it ten times o'er . iv 1 211
I love her ten times more than e'er I did . . *T. of Shrew* ii 1 162
Virginity by being once lost may be ten times found *All's Well* i 1 142
Ten times more dishonourable ragged than an old faced ancient *1 Hen. IV.* iv 2 33
Ten times better than the Nine Worthies . . *2 Hen. IV.* ii 4 238
Had ten times more valour than this roaring devil i' the old play *Hen. V.* iv 4 74
Thus is poor Suffolk ten times banished . . . *2 Hen. VI.* iii 2 357
He shall be beheaded for it ten times . . . . . iv 7 26
More inexorable, O, ten times more, than tigers of Hyrcania *3 Hen. VI.* i 4 155
Much is your sorrow; mine ten times so much . . . . ii 5 112
Ten times more beloved Than if thou never hadst deserved our hate . v 1 103
With interest Of ten times double gain of happiness . *Richard III.* iv 4 324
My heart is ten times lighter than my looks . . . . v 3 3
Ten times more ugly Than ever they were fair . . *Hen. VIII.* i 2 117
Thoughts, Which ten times faster glide than the sun's beams *R. and J.* ii 5 5
We shall obey, were she ten times our mother . . . *Hamlet* iii 2 345
O, treble woe Fall ten times treble on that cursed head! . . . v 1 270
Nine or ten times I had thought to have yerk'd him here under the ribs *Othello* i 2 4
Being barber'd ten times o'er, goes to the feast . *Ant. and Cleo.* ii 2 229
You have well deserved ten times as much As I have said you did . ii 6 79

Ten-times-barred-up. A jewel in a ten-times-barr'd-up chest Is a bold spirit in a loyal breast . . . . . . *Richard II.* i 1 180

Ten to one. 'Tis ten to one it maim'd you two outright . *T. of Shrew* v 2 62
That if we wrought out life 'twas ten to one . . *2 Hen. IV.* i 1 182
The French were almost ten to one . . . *1 Hen. VI.* iv 1 21
If once it be neglected, ten to one We shall not find like opportunity . v 4 157
Ten to one, old Joan had not gone out . . . *2 Hen. VI.* ii 1 4
Many a battle have I won in France, When as the enemy hath been ten to one: Why should I not now? . . . . *3 Hen. VI.* i 2 75
It is war's prize to take all vantages; And ten to one is no impeach of valour . . . . i 4 60
Ten to one, you'll meet him in the Tower . . . . . v 1 46
'Tis ten to one this play can never please All that are here *Hen. VIII.* Epil. 1

Ten voices. Some ten voices cried 'God save King Richard!' *Rich. III.* iii 7 36

Ten words. Some ten words long, Which is as brief as I have known a play; But by ten words, my lord, it is too long *M. N. Dream* v 1 61

Ten year. Hang all that offend that way but for ten year together, you'll be glad to give out a commission for more heads *M. for M.* ii 1 252
If this law hold in Vienna ten year, I'll rent the fairest house in it after three-pence a bay . . . . ii 1 254
Within ten year it will make itself ten, which is a goodly increase *All's W.* i 1 159
'Tis not ten years gone Since Richard and Northumberland, great friends, Did feast together . . . . . *2 Hen. IV.* iii 1 57
Ten years are spent since first he undertook This cause of Rome *T. An.* i 1 31

Tenable. Let it be tenable in your silence still . . . *Hamlet* i 2 248
Tenant. Your tenants, friends, and neighbouring gentlemen 1 *Hen. IV.* iii 1 90
Where are thy tenants and thy followers? . . . *Richard III.* iv 4 481
And lost your office On the complaint o' the tenants . . *Hen. VIII.* i 2 173
The gallows-maker; for that frame outlives a thousand tenants *Hamlet* v 1 50
I have been your tenant, and your father's tenant, these fourscore years
Lear iv 1 14
Tenantius. Had his titles by Tenantius whom He served with glory
Cymbeline i 1 31
Our fealty and Tenantius' right With honour to maintain . . . . v 4 73
Tenantless. Leave not the mansion so long tenantless! . *T. G. of Ver.* v 4 8
The graves stood tenantless and the sheeted dead Did squeak *Hamlet* i 1 115
Tench. I am stung like a tench . . . . 1 *Hen. IV.* ii 1 17
Tend to the master's whistle . . . . *Tempest* i 1 8
Sleep when I am drowsy and tend on no man's business . *Much Ado* i 3 17
The summer still doth tend upon my state . . . *M. N. Dream* iii 1 158
Lysander, whereto tends all this?—Away, you Ethiope! . . . iii 2 256
She deserves a lord That twenty such rude boys might tend upon *All's W.* iii 2 84
Where doing tends to ill, The truth is then most done not doing it *K. John* iii 1 272
Who didst thou leave to tend his majesty?—Why, know you not? . v 6 32
Tends that thou wouldst speak to the Duke of Hereford? *Richard II.* ii 1 232
They tend the crown, yet still with me they stay . . . . iv 1 199
Is not able to invent any thing that tends to laughter . . 2 *Hen. IV.* i 2 9
I shall be well content with any choice Tends to God's glory 1 *Hen. VI.* v 1 27
And, as we may, cherish Duke Humphrey's deeds, While they do tend
the profit of the land . . . . 2 *Hen. VI.* i 1 204
Threefold vengeance tend upon your steps! . . . . . iii 2 304
So many hours must I tend my flock . . . . 3 *Hen. VI.* ii 5 31
Worthier than himself Here tend the savage strangeness he puts on
Troi. and Cres. ii 3 135
Let us address to tend on Hector's heels . . . . . . iv 4 148
Ajax commands the guard to tend on you.—Thanks and good night . v 1 79
If it were so that our request did tend To save the Romans *Coriolanus* v 3 132
Come, you spirits That tend on mortal thoughts, unsex me here! *Macb.* i 5 42
The time invites you; go; your servants tend . . . *Hamlet* i 3 83
Love! his affections do not that way tend . . . . . iii 1 170
Hitherto doth love on fortune tend . . . . . . iii 2 216
The associates tend, and every thing is bent For England . . iv 3 47
The riotous knights That tend upon my father . . . *Lear* ii 1 97
Where twice so many Have a command to tend you . . . ii 4 266
Whereto we see in all things nature tends . . . *Othello* iii 3 231
Tend me to-night; May be it is the period of your duty *Ant. and Cleo.* iv 2 24
Tend me to-night two hours, I ask no more, And the gods yield you
for't! . . . . iv 2 32
In all obey her, Save when command to your dismission tends *Cymb.* ii 3 57
No motion That tends to vice in man, but I affirm It is the woman's part ii 5 21
Tendance. Which perforce I, her frail son, amongst my brethren mortal,
Must give my tendance to . . . . . . *Hen. VIII.* iii 2 149
Subdues and properties to his love and tendance All sorts of hearts
T. of Athens i 1 57
His lobbies fill with tendance, Rain sacrificial whisperings in his ear . i 1 80
She purposed, By watching, weeping, tendance, kissing, to O'ercome you
Cymbeline v 5 53
Tended. Had I not Four or five women once that tended me? *Tempest* i 2 47
From whence thou camest, how tended on . . . *All's Well* ii 1 210
Three months this youth hath tended upon me . . . *T. Night* v 1 102
Like the Nereides, So many mermaids, tended her i' the eyes *A. and C.* ii 2 212
Tender. Of subtle, tender, and delicate temperance . . *Tempest* ii 1 41
How does your content Tender your own good fortune? . . . ii 1 270
Who once again I tender to thy hand . . . . . . iv 1 5
If you now beheld them, your affections Would become tender . v 1 19
I thank you, madam, that you tender her . . *T. G. of Ver.* iv 4 145
Whose life's as tender to me as my soul . . . . . v 4 37
If hearty sorrow Be a sufficient ransom for offence, I tender't here . v 4 76
There is, as 'twere, a tender, a kind of tender, made afar off *Mer. Wives* i 1 215
That, had he twenty heads to tender down On twenty bloody blocks,
he'ld yield them up . . . . . *Meas. for Meas.* ii 4 180
Some tender money to me; some invite me . . *Com. of Errors* iv 3 4
He shall not die; so much we tender him . . . . . v 1 132
Wisdom and blood combating in so tender a body, we have ten proofs
to one that blood hath the victory . . . . *Much Ado* ii 3 171
If she should make tender of her love, 'tis very possible he'll scorn it . ii 3 186
Appertaining to thy young days, which we may nominate tender *L. L. L.* i 2 16
Receive such welcome at my hand As honour without breach of honour
may Make tender of to thy true worthiness . . . . ii 1 171
It will pay, If for his tender here I make some stay . *M. N. Dream* iii 2 87
And tender me, forsooth, affection . . . . . . iii 2 230
For never any thing can be amiss, When simpleness and duty tender it v 1 83
Here I tender it for him in the court . . . *Mer. of Venice* iv 1 209
Your brother is but young and tender . . . . *As Y. Like It* i 1 135
By my life, I do; which I tender dearly . . . . . v 2 77
I charge thee, tender well my hounds . . . *T. of Shrew* Ind. 1 16
You have show'd a tender fatherly regard . . . . . ii 1 288
If you should tender your supposed aid, He would receive it *All's Well* i 3 242
I come to tender it and my appliance With all bound humbleness . ii 1 116
The many will be too chill and tender, and they'll be for the flowery way iv 5 56
Who hath for four or five removes come short To tender it herself . v 3 132
Whom, by heaven I swear, I tender dearly . . . . *T. Night* v 1 129
You, that are thus so tender o'er his follies, Will never do him good
W. Tale ii 3 128
Away with't! Even thou, that hast A heart so tender o'er it . . ii 3 133
Honourable thoughts, Thoughts high for one so tender . . . iii 2 197
I will devise a death as cruel for thee As thou art tender to't . . iv 4 452
Tender your persons to his presence, whisper him in your behalfs . iv 4 826
She was as tender As infancy and grace . . . . . . v 3 26
Lest resolution drop Out at mine eyes in tender womanish tears *K. John* iv 1 36
The like tender of our love we make, To rest without a spot for evermore v 7 106
I tender you my service, Such as it is, being tender, raw, and young
Richard II. ii 3 41
And show'd thou makest some tender of my life . . 1 *Hen IV.* v 4 49
But we our kingdom's safety must so tender . . . *Hen. V.* ii 2 175
When death doth close his tender dying eyes . . 1 *Hen. VI.* iii 3 48
I tender so the safety of my liege . . . . 2 *Hen. VI.* iii 1 277
I thank them for their tender loving care. . . . . . iii 2 280
And so betide to me As well I tender you and all of yours! *Richard III.* ii 4 72
I tender not thy beauteous princely daughter . . . . . iv 4 405
To your highness' hand I tender my commission . . . *Hen. VIII.* ii 2 104
I do not know What kind of my obedience I should tender . . . ii 3 66
You tender more your person's honour than Your high profession
spiritual . . . . ii 4 116

Tender. A respect more tender, More holy and profound, than mine own
life . . . . *Coriolanus* iii 3 112
Loving kiss for kiss Thy brother Marcus tenders on thy lips *T. Andron.* v 3 157
Which name I tender As dearly as my own . . . *Rom. and Jul.* iii 1 74
I will make a desperate tender Of my child's love: I think she will be
ruled . . . . iii 4 12
A whining mammet, in her fortune's tender, To answer 'I'll not wed' . iii 5 186
Tender down Their services to Lord Timon . . *T. of Athens* i 1 54
'Tis not amiss we tender our loves to him, in this supposed distress of his v 1 14
And know How tender 'tis to love the babe that milks me . *Macbeth* i 7 55
He hath, my lord, of late made many tenders Of his affection to me *Ham.* i 3 99
Do you believe his tenders, as you call them?—I do not know . . i 3 103
You have ta'en these tenders for true pay, Which are not sterling . . i 3 106
Tender yourself more dearly; Or—not to crack the wind of the poor
phrase, Running it thus—you'll tender me a fool . . . i 3 107
This deed, for thine especial safety,—Which we do tender . . iv 3 43
Most royal majesty, I crave no more than what your highness offer'd,
Nor will you tender less . . . . *Lear* i 1 198
In the tender of a wholesome weal, Might in their working do you that
offence . . . . i 4 230
A maid so tender, fair, and happy, So opposite to marriage . *Othello* i 2 66
Let me my service tender on your lips . . . . *Cymbeline* i 6 140
Which is material To the tender of our present . . . . i 6 208
As if You were inspired to do those duties which You tender to her . ii 3 56
So tender of rebukes that words are strokes And strokes death to her . iii 5 40
Be but duteous, and true preferment shall tender itself to thee . . iii 5 160
Why should we be tender To let an arrogant piece of flesh threat us? . iv 2 126
So duteous, diligent, So tender over his occasions, true, So feat . v 5 87
Tender air. Embraced by a piece of tender air . . . v 4 140; v 5 437
Tender arm. Whom Fortune's tender arm With favour never clasp'd
T. of Athens iv 3 250
Tender ass. I am such a tender ass, if my hair do but tickle me, I must
scratch . . . . *M. N. Dream* iv 1 27
Tender babes. Pity, you ancient stones, those tender babes Whom envy
hath immured within your walls! . . . . *Richard III.* iv 1 99
Ah, my tender babes! My unblown flowers, new-appearing sweets! . iv 4 9
Tender-bodied. When yet he was but tender-bodied . *Coriolanus* i 3 6
Tender boy. Alas, the tender boy, in passion moved, Doth weep *T. An.* iii 2 48
Tender breeding. So far beneath your soft and tender breeding *T. Night* v 1 331
Tender brother. Thou didst kill our tender brother . 3 *Hen. VI.* ii 2 115
Tender care. What youth is that, Of whom you seem to have so tender
care? . . . . iv 6 66
Tender courtesy. Never train'd To offices of tender courtesy *M. of Ven.* iv 1 33
Tender days. Were't not affection chains thy tender days *T. G. of Ver.* i 1 3
Tender duty. How long Shall tender duty make me suffer wrong?
Richard II. ii 1 164
Tender eye. Scarf up the tender eye of pitiful day! . . *Macbeth* iii 2 47
Tender-feeling. Uneath may she endure the flinty streets, To tread them
with her tender-feeling feet. . . . . . . 2 *Hen. VI.* ii 4 9
Tender feet. The ruthless flint doth cut my tender feet . . . ii 4 34
Tender flattery. No visor does become black villany So well as soft and
tender flattery . . . . *Pericles* iv 4 45
Tender fork. Thou dost fear the soft and tender fork Of a poor worm
Meas. for Meas. iii 1 16
Tender George. Lest, being seen, thy brother, tender George, Be
executed in his father's sight . . . . . *Richard III.* v 3 95
Tender heart. Whose hand soever lanced their tender hearts, Thy head,
all indirectly, gave direction . . . . iv 4 224
Put in her tender heart the aspiring flame Of golden sovereignty . . iv 4 328
Tender-hefted. Thy tender-hefted nature shall not give Thee o'er to
harshness: her eyes are fierce . . . . . . *Lear* ii 4 174
Tender honour. Corrupt the tender honour of a maid . *All's Well* iii 5 75
Tender horns. Love's feeling is more soft and sensible Than are the
tender horns of cockled snails . . . . . *L. L. Lost* iv 3 338
Tender infancy. A virgin from her tender infancy . . 1 *Hen. VI.* v 4 50
Tender Juliet. That fair for which love groan'd for and would die, With
tender Juliet match'd, is now not fair *Rom. and Jul.* ii Prol. 4
Tender juvenal. How canst thou part sadness and melancholy, my
tender juvenal? . . . . *L. L. Lost* i 2 8
Why tender juvenal? why tender juvenal?—I spoke it, tender juvenal,
as a congruent epitheton appertaining to thy young days . . . i 2 12
Tender kinsman. To mew up Your tender kinsman . *K. John* iv 2 58
Tender kiss. To smooth that rough touch with a tender kiss . *R. and J.* i 5 98
Tender lady. On her frights and griefs, Which never tender lady hath
borne greater . . . . *W. Tale* ii 2 24
Tender lambkin. Thy tender lambkin now is king . . 2 *Hen. IV.* v 3 122
Tender lambs. Whilst I waited on my tender lambs . 1 *Hen. VI.* i 2 76
Tender leaves. To-day he puts forth The tender leaves of hopes; to-
morrow blossoms . . . . *Hen. VIII.* iii 2 353
Tender life. Teach her not thus to lay Such violent hands upon her
tender life . . . . *T. Andron.* iii 2 22
Tender limbs. Is't I That chase thee from thy country and expose Those
tender limbs of thine? . . . . *All's Well* iii 2 107
Tender love. The tender love I bear your grace, my lord, Makes me
most forward . . . . *Richard III.* iii 4 65
Tender-minded. To be tender-minded Does not become a sword . *Lear* v 3 31
Tender objects. For Hector in his blaze of wrath subscribes To tender
objects . . . . *Troi. and Cres.* iv 5 106
Tender ones. In protection of their tender ones . . 3 *Hen. VI.* ii 2 28
Tender patience. And prick my tender patience to those thoughts
Which honour and allegiance cannot think . . *Richard II.* ii 1 207
Tender playfellows. Two tender playfellows for dust . *Richard III.* iv 4 385
Tender preservation. In their dear care And tender preservation of our
person . . . . *Hen. V.* ii 2 59
Tender prince. Led by a delicate and tender prince . . *Hamlet* iv 4 48
The tender prince Would fain have come with me to meet your grace
Richard III. iii 1 28
On pure heart's love to greet the tender princes . . . . iv 1 4
Rude ragged nurse, old sullen playfellow For tender princes! . . iv 1 103
Tender sapling. Peace, tender sapling; thou art made of tears *T. An.* iii 2 50
Tender shame. But that her tender shame Will not proclaim against
her maiden loss, How might she tongue me! . *Meas. for Meas.* iv 4 26
Tender side. I kiss these fingers for eternal peace, And lay them gently
on thy tender side . . . . 1 *Hen. VI.* v 3 49
Tender-smelling. Most tender-smelling knight . . *L. L. Lost* v 2 569
Tender spray. From whence that tender spray did sweetly spring
3 *Hen. VI.* ii 6 50
Tender spring. Shed yet some small drops from thy tender spring *T. An.* v 3 167
Tender temples. The imperial metal, circling now thy brow, Had graced
the tender temples of my child . . . . . *Richard III.* iv 4 383

Tender thing. Too great oppression for a tender thing.—Is love a tender thing? it is too rough *Rom. and Jul.* i 4 24
Tender wit. By love the young and tender wit Is turn'd to folly *T. G. of V.* i 1 47
Tender years. My tender years can tell Civil dissension is a viperous worm 1 *Hen. VI.* iii 1 71
O, think upon the conquest of my father, My tender years! iv 1 149
Can make seem pleasing to her tender years *Richard III.* iv 4 342
Tender youth. Knowing that tender youth is soon suggested *T. G. of V.* iii 1 34
For that My tender youth was never yet attaint With any passion of inflaming love 1 *Hen. VI.* v 5 81
Tendered. Those at her father's churlish feet she tender'd *T. G. of Ver.* iii 1 225
My soul the faithfull'st offerings hath breathed out That e'er devotion tender'd! What shall I do? *T. Night* v 1 118
Nor to us hath tender'd The duty of the day *Cymbeline* iii 5 31
Tenderest. Why tender'st thou that paper to me, with A look untender? iii 4 11
Tendering their own worth from where they were glass'd *L. L. Lost* ii 1 244
A subject's love, Tendering the precious safety of my prince *Richard II.* i 1 32
Stood alone, Tendering my ruin and assail'd of none 1 *Hen. VI.* iv 7 10
His majesty, Tendering my person's safety, hath appointed *Richard III.* i 1 44
Tendering our sister's honour and our own *T. Andron.* i 1 476
Tenderly. You that have been so tenderly officious *W. Tale* ii 3 159
Tenderly apply to her Some remedies for life iii 2 153
O, good sir, tenderly, O!—Alas, poor soul!—O, good sir, softly, good sir! iv 3 74
My stooping duty tenderly shall show *Richard II.* iii 3 48
To his father, that so tenderly and entirely loves him *Lear* i 2 104
And will as tenderly be led by the nose As asses are *Othello* i 3 407
Tenderness. Think you I can a resolution fetch From flowery tenderness? *Meas. for Meas.* iii 1 83
Go, tenderness of years *L. L. Lost* iii 1 4
The tenderness of her nature became as a prey to her grief *All's Well* iv 3 60
How sometimes nature will betray its folly, Its tenderness! *W. Tale* i 2 152
Make blind itself with foolish tenderness 1 *Hen. IV.* iii 2 91
I'll thank myself For doing these fair rites of tenderness v 4 98
Filial tenderness, Shall, O dear father, pay thee plenteously 2 *Hen. IV.* iv 5 39
Well we know your tenderness of heart *Richard III.* iii 7 210
Melting with tenderness and kind compassion iv 3 7
My conscience first received a tenderness, Scruple, and prick *Hen. VIII.* ii 4 170
Not of a woman's tenderness to be, Requires nor child nor woman's face to see. I have sat too long *Coriolanus* v 3 129
Her delicate tenderness will find itself abused *Othello* ii 1 235
Weep no more, lest I give cause To be suspected of more tenderness Than doth become a man *Cymbeline* i 1 94
Tending. Thoughts tending to ambition, they do plot Unlikely wonders *Richard II.* v 5 18
Thoughts tending to content flatter themselves That they are not the first of fortune's slaves v 5 23
All tending to the good of their adversaries *Coriolanus* iv 3 44
Writings all tending to the great opinion That Rome holds of his name *J. Cæsar* i 2 322
And grace his speech Tending to Cæsar's glories iii 2 63
Give him tending; He brings great news *Macbeth* i 5 38
Tenedos. To Tenedos they come *Troi. and Cres.* Prol. 11
Tenement. Like to a tenement or pelting farm *Richard II.* ii 1 60
All your goods, lands, tenements, Chattels, and whatsoever *Hen. VIII.* iii 2 342
Tennis. Renouncing clean The faith they have in tennis, and tall stockings i 3 30
There o'ertook in's rouse; There falling out at tennis *Hamlet* ii 1 59
Tennis-balls. The old ornament of his cheek hath already stuffed tennis-balls *Much Ado* iii 2 47
What treasure, uncle?—Tennis-balls, my liege *Hen. V.* i 2 258
Tennis-court. A man whom both the waters and the wind, In that vast tennis-court, have made the ball *Pericles* ii 1 64
Tennis-court-keeper. The tennis-court-keeper knows better than I 2 *Hen. IV.* ii 2 21
Tenour. The tenour of them doth but signify My health *T. G. of Ver.* iii 1 56
He this very day receives letters of strange tenour *Meas. for Meas.* iv 2 216
Which with experimental seal doth warrant The tenour of my book *Much Ado* iv 1 169
Bid me tear the bond.—When it is paid according to the tenour *M. of V.* iv 1 235
It bears an angry tenour *As Y. Like It* iv 3 11
Is't not the tenour of his oracle? *W. Tale* v 1 38
I guess their tenour.—Like enough you do 1 *Hen. IV.* iv 4 7
Misuse the tenour of thy kinsman's trust? v 5 5
Their cold intent, tenour, and substance, thus 2 *Hen. IV.* iv 1 9
Be it your charge, my lord, To see perform'd the tenour of our word v 5 75
Whose tenours and particular effects You have enscheduled *Hen. V.* v 2 72
Whose tenour Was,—were he evil used, he would outgo His father *Hen. VIII.* i 2 206
Go learn me the tenour of the proclamation *Troi. and Cres.* ii 1 100
Myself have letters of the selfsame tenour *J. Cæsar* iv 3 171
Here are letters for you.—Their tenour good, I trust *Cymbeline* iii 4 36
This is the tenour of the emperor's writ iii 7 1
By the tenour of our strict edict, Your exposition misinterpreting, We might proceed to cancel of your days *Pericles* i 1 111
To the court of King Simonides Are letters brought, the tenour these iii Gower 24
Tent. I shall beat you to your tent, and prove a shrewd Cæsar to you *Meas. for Meas.* ii 1 263
Let us devise Some entertainment for them in their tents *L. L. Lost* iv 3 373
Their rough carriage so ridiculous Should be presented at our tent to us v 2 307
Whip to our tents, as roes run o'er land v 2 309
God save you! Where's the princess?—Gone to her tent v 2 311
In such a night Troilus methinks mounted the Troyan walls And sigh'd his soul toward the Grecian tents *Mer. of Venice* v 1 5
Costly apparel, tents, and canopies, Fine linen *T. of Shrew* ii 1 354
He shall suppose no other but that he is carried into the leaguer of the adversaries, when we bring him to our own tents *All's Well* iii 6 29
It is upon a file with the duke's other letters in my tent iv 3 232
She is sad and passionate at your highness' tent *K. John* ii 1 544
My mother is assailed in our tent, And ta'en, I fear iii 2 6
Thou hast talk'd Of sallies and retires, of trenches, tents 1 *Hen. IV.* ii 3 54
Lead him to his tent.—Come, my lord, I'll lead you to your tent.—Lead me? v 4 8
At my tent The Douglas is v 5 22
The armour that I saw in your tent to-night, are those stars or suns? *Hen. V.* iii 7 74
The English lie within fifteen hundred paces of your tents iii 7 136
And from the tents The armourers, accomplishing the knights iv Prol. 11
Walking from watch to watch, from tent to tent iv Prol. 30
Good old knight, Collect them all together at my tent iv 1 304
Tent. They have burned and carried away all that was in the king's tent *Hen. V.* iv 7 8
Go seek him, and bring him to my tent iv 7 176
Convey me Salisbury into his tent 1 *Hen. VI.* i 4 110
Herald, conduct me to the Dauphin's tent iv 7 51
We twain will go into his highness' tent 2 *Hen. VI.* v 1 55
With sleight and manhood stole to Rhesus' tents 3 *Hen. VI.* iv 2 20
What nobleman is that That with the king here resteth in his tent? iv 3 10
Wherefore else guard we his royal tent, But to defend his person? iv 3 21
This is his tent; and see where stand his guard iv 3 23
Here pitch our tents, even here in Bosworth field *Richard III.* v 3 1
Up with my tent there! here will I lie to-night; But where to-morrow? v 3 7
Give me some ink and paper in my tent v 3 23
By the second hour in the morning Desire the earl to see me in my tent v 3 32
In to our tent; the air is raw and cold v 3 46
Is my beaver easier than it was? And all my armour laid into my tent? v 3 51
About the mid of night come to my tent And help to arm me v 3 77
Under our tents I'll play the eaves-dropper, To see if any mean to shrink from me v 3 221
Methought their souls, whose bodies Richard murder'd, Came to my tent v 3 231
This found I on my tent this morning v 3 303
Look, how many Grecian tents do stand Hollow upon this plain *Troi. and Cres.* i 3 79
In his tent Lies mocking our designs i 3 145
Keeps his tent like him; Makes factious feasts i 3 190
What would you 'fore our tent?—Is this great Agamemnon's tent? i 3 215
Trumpet, blow loud, Send thy brass voice through all these lazy tents i 3 257
With his trumpet call Midway between your tents and walls of Troy i 3 278
So shall each lord of Greece, from tent to tent i 3 307
I will see you hanged, like clotpoles, ere I come any more to your tents ii 1 129
'Twixt our tents and Troy To-morrow morning call some knight to arms ii 1 135
The beacon of the wise, the tent that searches To the bottom of the worst ii 2 16
Where is Achilles?—Within his tent; but ill disposed ii 3 84
We saw him at the opening of his tent: He is not sick ii 3 91
Go you and greet him in his tent: 'Tis said he holds you well ii 3 189
Achilles stands i' the entrance of his tent iii 3 38
Entomb thyself alive And case thy reputation in thy tent iii 3 187
Invite the most valorous Hector to come unarmed to my tent iii 3 276
Who most humbly desires you to invite Hector to his tent iii 3 286
I would desire My famous cousin to our Grecian tents iv 5 151
Worthy warrior, welcome to our tents iv 5 200
I beseech you next To feast with me and see me at my tent iv 5 229
First, all you peers of Greece, go to my tent; There in the full convive we iv 5 271
In what place of the field doth Calchas keep?—At Menelaus' tent iv 5 279
After we part from Agamemnon's tent, To bring me thither iv 5 285
Who keeps the tent now?—The surgeon's box, or the patient's wound v 1 11
Thersites, help to trim my tent: This night in banqueting must all be spent v 1 50
Follow his torch; he goes to Calchas' tent v 1 92
They say he keeps a Trojan drab, and uses the traitor Calchas' tent v 1 105
Let one be sent To pray Achilles see us at our tent v 9 8
You vile abominable tents, Thus proudly pight upon our Phrygian plains v 10 23
Well might they fester 'gainst ingratitude, And tent themselves with death *Coriolanus* i 9 31
So, to our tent; Where, ere we do repose us, we will write To Rome i 9 73
Go we to our tent: The blood upon your visage dries i 9 92
'Tis a sore upon us, You cannot tent yourself iii 1 236
The smiles of knaves Tent in my cheeks! iii 2 116
A mile before his tent fall down, and knee The way into his mercy v 1 5
'Twas on a summer's evening, in his tent *J. Cæsar* iii 2 176
In my tent, Cassius, enlarge your griefs, And I will give you audience iv 2 46
Let no man Come to our tent till we have done our conference iv 2 51
Where is thy instrument?—Here in the tent iv 3 240
I'll have them sleep on cushions in my tent iv 3 243
Lie in my tent and sleep; It may be I shall raise you by and by iv 3 246
Fly further off; Mark Antony is in your tents v 3 10
Are those my tents where I perceive the fire? v 3 13
Bring us word unto Octavius' tent How every thing is chanced v 4 31
Within my tent his bones to-night shall lie, Most like a soldier v 5 78
I'll observe his looks; I'll tent him to the quick *Hamlet* ii 2 626
I shall attend you presently at your tent *Lear* v 1 33
She is not well; convey her to my tent v 3 106
And at thy tent is now Unloading of his mules *Ant. and Cleo.* iv 6 23
Go with me to my tent; where you shall see How hardly I was drawn into this war v 1 73
And mine ear, Therein false struck, can take no greater wound, Nor tent to bottom that *Cymbeline* iii 4 118
Tented. They have used Their dearest action in the tented field *Othello* i 3 85
Tenth. Should all despair That have revolted wives, the tenth of mankind Would hang themselves *W. Tale* i 2 199
The tenth of August last this dreadful lord, Retiring from the siege of Orleans, Having full scarce six thousand 1 *Hen. VI.* i 1 110
For your expenses . . . , Among the people gather up a tenth v 5 93
We have lost so many tenths of ours, To guard a thing not ours *T. and C.* ii 2 21
Vowing more than the perfection of ten and discharging less than the tenth part of one iii 2 95
Of all The treasure . . . , We render you the tenth *Coriolanus* i 9 34
If thy revenges hunger for that food Which nature loathes—take thou the destined tenth *T. of Athens* v 4 33
If, on the tenth day following, Thy banish'd trunk be found *Lear* i 1 179
Who of their broken debtors take a third, A sixth, a tenth *Cymbeline* v 4 20
Tent-royal. Which pillage they with merry march bring home To the tent-royal of their emperor *Hen. V.* i 2 196
Tenure. A lawyer? Where be his quiddities now, his quillets, his cases, his tenures, and his tricks? *Hamlet* v 1 108
Tercel. The falcon as the tercel, for all the ducks i' the river *Tr. and Cr.* iii 2 56
Tereus. But, sure, some Tereus hath deflowered thee *T. Andron.* ii 4 26
A craftier Tereus, cousin, hast thou met ii 4 41
This is the tragic tale of Philomel, And treats of Tereus' treason iv 1 48
She hath been reading late The tale of Tereus *Cymbeline* ii 2 45
Term. It is as much as I can do to keep the terms of my honour precise *Mer. Wives* ii 2 22
In such alligant terms; and in such wine and sugar ii 2 69
But stand under the adoption of abominable terms ii 2 309
Terms! names! Amaimon sounds well; Lucifer, well ii 2 310
The terms For common justice, you're as pregnant in *Meas. for Meas.* i 1 11
That is, were I under the terms of death ii 4 100
Hear Margaret term me Claudio *Much Ado* ii 2 44

Term. I was not born under a rhyming planet, nor I cannot woo in festival terms *Much Ado* v 2 41
Have sworn for three years' term to live with me *L. L. Lost* i 1 16
There are other strict observances; As, not to see a woman in that term i 1 37
If any man be seen to talk with a woman within the term of three years i 1 131
When he plays at tables, chides the dice In honourable terms v 2 327
Taffeta phrases, silken terms precise, Three-piled hyperboles v 2 406
You shall this twelvemonth term from day to day Visit the speechless sick v 2 860
She in mild terms begg'd my patience *M. N. Dream* iv 1 63
I like not fair terms and a villain's mind *Mer. of Venice* i 3 181
In terms of choice I am not solely led By nice direction of a maiden's eyes ii 1 13
Is indeed deceased, or, as you would say in plain terms, gone to heaven ii 2 68
Which, to term in gross, Is an unlesson'd girl, unschool'd, unpractised iii 2 160
If you had pleased to have defended it With any terms of zeal v 1 205
And rail'd on Lady Fortune in good terms, In good set terms *As Y. L. It* ii 7 16
With lawyers in the vacation; for they sleep between term and term iii 2 350
Twenty such vile terms, As had she studied to misuse me so *T. of Shrew* ii 1 159
Setting all this chat aside, Thus in plain terms ii 1 271
In the name of justice, Without all terms of pity *All's Well* ii 3 173
Methought it did relieve my passion much, More than light airs and recollected terms *T. Night* ii 4 5
Thou dishonest Satan! I call thee by the most modest terms iv 2 36
Whom thou, in terms so bloody and so dear, Hast made thine enemies v 1 74
The celestial habits, Methinks I so should term them *W. Tale* iii 1 5
Until it had return'd These terms of treason doubled down his throat *Richard II.* i 1 57
Shall I so much dishonour my fair stars, On equal terms to give him chastisement? iv 1 22
With many holiday and lady terms He question'd me 1 *Hen. IV.* i 3 46
Speak terms of manage to thy bounding steed; Cry 'Courage! to the field!' ii 3 52
There is not such a word Spoke of in Scotland as this term of fear iv 1 85
With tears of innocency and terms of zeal iv 3 63
'Tis not well That you and I should meet upon such terms As now we meet v 1 10
If a lie may do thee grace, I'll gild it with the happiest terms I have v 4 162
Did not we send grace, Pardon, and terms of love to all of you? v 5 3
If we can make our peace Upon such large terms and so absolute 2 *Hen. IV.* iv 1 186
So, like gross terms, The prince will in the perfectness of time Cast off his followers; and their memory Shall as a pattern or a measure live iv 4 73
The wearing out of six fashions, which is four terms, or two actions v 1 90
Call'st thou me host? Now, by this hand, I swear, I scorn the term *Hen. V.* ii 1 32
I will scour you with my rapier, as I may, in fair terms ii 1 60
I will cut thy throat, one time or other, in fair terms ii 1 74
What terms the enemy stood on iii 6 78
Thou hast given me most bitter terms iv 8 44
Terms Such as will enter at a lady's ear And plead his love-suit v 2 99
We have consented to all terms of reason v 2 357
Thou hast astonish'd me with thy high terms 1 *Hen. VI.* i 2 93
But what's that Pucelle whom they term so pure? ii 1 20
Among which terms he used his lavish tongue And did upbraid me ii 5 47
With other vile and ignominious terms iv 1 97
Makes me the bolder to salute my king With ruder terms 2 *Hen. VI.* i 1 30
Till term of eighteen months Be full expired i 1 67
I would invent as bitter-searching terms, As curst, as harsh, and horrible iii 2 311
To remove from thee The Duke of Somerset, whom he terms a traitor iv 9 30
In any case, be not too rough in terms iv 9 44
But thou wilt brave me with these saucy terms? iv 10 38
I could hew up rocks and fight with flint, I am so angry at these abject terms v 1 25
Poor queen! how love to me and to her son Hath made her break out into terms of rage! 3 *Hen. VI.* i 1 265
Proud insulting boy! Becomes it thee to be thus bold in terms? ii 2 85
His master's son, as worshipful he terms it, Shall lose the royalty *Richard III.* iii 4 41
Then in plain terms tell her my loving tale iv 4 359
She is my kinswoman; I would not, as they term it, praise her *T. and C.* i 1 44
And when he speaks, 'Tis like a chime a-mending; with terms unsquared i 3 159
Now to deliver her possession up On terms of base compulsion! ii 2 153
Let us depart, I pray you, Lest your displeasure should enlarge itself To wrathful terms v 2 38
A kind of face, methought,—I cannot tell how to term it *Coriolanus* iv 5 164
Durst not, look you, sir, show themselves, as we term it, his friends iv 5 221
All the bitterest terms That ever ear did hear to such effect *T. Andron.* ii 3 110
She will not stay the siege of loving terms *Rom. and Jul.* i 1 218
And expire the term Of a despised life closed in my breast i 4 109
The hate I bear thee can afford No better term than this,—thou art a villain iii 1 64
It would become me better than to close In terms of friendship with thine enemies *J. Cæsar* iii 1 203
Thou bloodier villain Than terms can give thee out! *Macbeth* v 8 8
To recover of us, by strong hand And terms compulsatory *Hamlet* i 1 103
Bound In filial obligation for some term To do obsequious sorrow i 2 91
I would not, in plain terms, from this time forth, Have you so slander any moment leisure i 3 132
I am thy father's spirit, Doom'd for a certain term to walk the night i 5 10
The terms of our estate may not endure Hazard so near us iii 3 5
A noble father lost; A sister driven into desperate terms iv 7 26
But in my terms of honour I stand aloof v 2 257
Parted you in good terms? *Lear* i 2 171
All's not offence that indiscretion finds And dotage terms so ii 4 200
Be judge yourself, Whether I in any just term am affined To love the Moor *Othello* i 1 39
He prated, And spoke such scurvy and provoking terms Against your honour i 2 7
In quarter, and in terms like bride and groom Devesting them for bed ii 3 180
Thrown such despite and heavy terms upon her, As true hearts cannot bear iv 2 116
A beggar in his drink Could not have laid such terms upon his callat iv 2 121
Touch you the sourest points with sweetest terms *Ant. and Cleo.* ii 2 24
When perforce he could not But pay me terms of honour, cold and sickly He vented them iii 4 7
Should we be taking leave As long a term as yet we have to live, The loathness to depart would grow *Cymbeline* i 1 107
If, in the holding or loss of that, you term her frail i 4 106

Term. If you seek us afterwards in other terms, you shall find us in our salt-water girdle *Cymbeline* iii 1 80
And 'mollis aer' We term it 'mulier' v 5 448
The sore terms we stand upon with the gods will be strong with us *Per.* iv 2 37

Termagant. 'Twas time to counterfeit, or that hot termagant Scot had paid me scot and lot too 1 *Hen. IV.* v 4 114
I would have such a fellow whipped for o'erdoing Termagant *Hamlet* iii 2 15

Termed. Him that you term'd, sir, 'The good old lord, Gonzalo' *Tempest* v 1 15
We may pity, though not pardon thee.—O, had the gods done so, I had not now Worthily term'd them merciless to us! *Com. of Errors* i 1 100
Is Beaufort term'd a kite? Where are his talons? 2 *Hen. VI.* iii 2 196
We John Cade, so termed of our supposed father iv 2 33
Kent, in the Commentaries Cæsar writ, Is term'd the civil'st place of all this isle; Sweet is the country iv 7 66
Meaning indeed his house, Which, by the sign thereof, was termed so *Richard III.* iii 5 79

Termination. If her breath were as terrible as her terminations, there were no living near her *Much Ado* ii 1 256

Terra. Falleth like a crab on the face of terra, the soil, the land *L. L. L.* iv 2 7
What say you of Kent?—Nothing but this; 'tis 'bona terra, mala gens' 2 *Hen. VI.* iv 7 61

Terram. In terram Salicam mulieres ne succedant *Hen. V.* i 2 38

Terras Astræa reliquit: Be you remember'd, Marcus, she's gone, she's fled *T. Andron.* iv 3 4

Terre. Via! les eaux et la terre.—Rien puis? l'air et le feu *Hen. V.* iv 2 4

Terrene. Alack, our terrene moon Is now eclipsed! *Ant. and Cleo.* iii 13 153

Terrestrial. Give me thy hand, terrestrial; so. Give me thy hand, celestial; so. *Mer. Wives* iii 1 108
When from under this terrestrial ball He fires the proud tops of the eastern pines And darts his light *Richard II.* iii 2 41

Terrible. Sorceries terrible To enter human hearing *Tempest* i 2 264
Every word stabs: if her breath were as terrible as her terminations, there were no living near her *Much Ado* ii 1 256
And the misery is, example, that so terrible shows in the wreck *All's W.* iii 5 23
When you sally upon him, speak what terrible language you will iv 1 3
A terrible oath, with a swaggering accent sharply twanged off *T. Night* iii 4 197
Terrible hell make war Upon their spotted souls for this offence! *Richard II.* iii 2 133
I would to God my name were not so terrible to the enemy as it is 2 *Hen. IV.* i 2 244
And withal How terrible in constant resolution *Hen. V.* ii 4 35
Then lend the eye a terrible aspect iii 1 9
Unto a feast of death, A terrible and unavoided danger 1 *Hen. VI.* iv 5 8
Ah, what a sign it is of evil life, Where death's approach is seen so terrible! 2 *Hen. VI.* iii 3 6
Such terrible impression made the dream *Richard III.* i 4 63
To stubborn spirits They swell, and grow as terrible as storms *Hen. VIII.* iii 1 164
Thou wast a soldier Even to Cato's wish, not fierce and terrible Only in strokes *Coriolanus* i 4 57
Sound to this coward and lascivious town Our terrible approach *T. of A.* v 4 2
Like the work we have in hand, Most bloody, fiery, and most terrible *J. C.* i 3 130
We are two lions litter'd in one day, And I the elder and more terrible ii 2 47
Norway himself, With terrible numbers *Macbeth* i 2 51
I am settled, and bend up Each corporal agent to this terrible feat i 7 80
Prophesying with accents terrible Of dire combustion and confused events ii 3 62
In the affliction of these terrible dreams That shake us nightly iii 2 18
Murders have been perform'd Too terrible for the ear iii 4 78
What needed, then, that terrible dispatch of it into your pocket? *Lear* i 2 32
In the most terrible and nimble stroke Of quick, cross lightning iv 7 34
What is the reason of this terrible summons? *Othello* i 1 82
All strange and terrible events are welcome *Ant. and Cleo.* iv 15 3
On our terrible seas, Like egg-shells moved upon their surges *Cymbeline* iii 1 27
A terrible childbed hast thou had, my dear; No light, no fire *Pericles* iii 1 57

Terribly. It struck mine ear most terribly *Tempest* ii 1 313
An you should do it too terribly, you would fright the duchess *M. N. D.* i 2 76
You'll swear, terribly swear Into strong shudders *T. of Athens* iv 3 136

Territory. If thou linger in my territories Longer than swiftest expedition Will give thee time to leave *T. G. of Ver.* iii 1 163
Turn thou no more To seek a living in our territory *As Y. Like It* iii 1 8
Lays most lawful claim To this fair island and the territories *K. John* i 1 10
Is well prepared To whip this dwarfish war, these pigmy arms, From out the circle of his territories v 2 136
Therefore, we banish you our territories *Richard II.* i 3 139
Welcome, brave earl, into our territories 1 *Hen. VI.* v 3 146
I am possess'd With more than half the Gallian territories v 4 139
All your interest in those territories Is utterly bereft you 2 *Hen. VI.* iii 1 84
Unless Lord Suffolk straight be done to death, Or banished fair England's territories, They will by violence tear him iii 2 245
Who am prepared against your territories, Though not for Rome itself *Coriolanus* iv 5 140
The Volsces with two several powers Are enter'd in the Roman territories iv 6 40
Caius Marcius Associated with Aufidius rages Upon our territories iv 6 77
Now we will divest us, both of rule, Interest of territory *Lear* i 1 51

Terror. There should be terrors in him that he should not come *M. Wives* iv 4 23
Lent him our terror, dress'd him with our love *Meas. for Meas.* i 1 20
Only to stick it in their children's sight For terror, not to use i 3 26
Let it keep one shape, till custom make it Their perch and not their terror ii 1 4
Now, to our perjury to add more terror, We are again forsworn *L. L. L.* v 2 470
Hence is it that we make trifles of terrors *All's Well* ii 3 4
This letter, being so excellently ignorant, will breed no terror *T. Night* iii 4 207
I, that please some, try all, both joy and terror Of good and bad *W. Tale* iv 1 1
Beating and hanging are terrors to me iv 3 30
O amiable lovely death! . . . Thou hate and terror to prosperity *K. John* iii 4 28
With no less terror than the elements Of fire and water *Richard II.* iii 3 55
I would thou wert the man That would divorce this terror from my heart v 4 9
As the poorest vassal is That doth with awe and terror kneel to it 2 *Hen. IV.* iv 5 177
The terror of the French, The scarecrow that affrights our children so 1 *Hen. VI.* i 4 42
And what a terror he had been to France ii 2 17
It cannot be this weak and writhled shrimp Should strike such terror ii 3 24
Our nation's terror and their bloody scourge! iv 2 16
Your kingdom's terror and black Nemesis iv 7 78
All the foul terrors in dark-seated hell— Enough 2 *Hen. VI.* iii 2 328
So full of dismal terror was the time! *Richard III.* i 4 7
As if thou wert distraught and mad with terror iii 5 4
In the battle think on Buckingham, And die in terror of thy guiltiness! v 3 170

Terror. Shadows to-night Have struck more terror to the soul of Richard
Than can the substance of ten thousand soldiers *Richard III.* v 3 217
I am fearful: wherefore frowns he thus? 'Tis his aspect of terror
Hen. VIII. v 1 88
Peace, plenty, love, truth, terror, That were the servants to this chosen
infant v 5 48
By his rare example made the coward Turn terror into sport. *Coriolanus* ii 2 109
With his sons, a terror to our foes, Hath yoked a nation strong *T. An.* i 1 29
Whose name was once our terror, now our comfort v 1 10
For exile hath more terror in his look, Much more than death *R. and J.* iii 3 13
The horrible conceit of death and night, Together with the terror of the
place iv 3 38
These apparent prodigies, The unaccustom'd terror of this night *J. Cæsar* ii 1 199
There is no terror, Cassius, in your threats iv 3 66
I will do such things,—What they are, yet I know not; but they shall
be The terrors of the earth *Lear* ii 4 285
It is the cowish terror of his spirit, That dares not undertake iv 2 12
He had not apprehension Of roaring terrors *Cymbeline* iv 2 111
Tertian. He is so shaked of a burning quotidian tertian *Hen. V.* ii 1 124
Tertio. Primo, secundo, tertio, is a good play *T. Night* v 1 39
Test. Thou Hast strangely stood the test *Tempest* iv 1 7
Let there be some more test made of my metal *Meas. for Meas.* i 1 49
Bring me to the test, And I the matter will re-word *Hamlet* iii 4 142
To vouch this, is no proof, Without more wider and more overt test
Othello i 3 107
Testament. The poor allottery my father left me by testament *As Y. L. It* i 1 77
'Poor deer,' quoth he, 'thou makest a testament As worldlings do' ii 1 47
That gem, Conferr'd by testament to the sequent issue *All's Well* v 3 197
He is come to open The purple testament of bleeding war *Richard II.* iii 3 94
Lands which men devout By testament have given to the church *Hen. V.* i 1 10
With blood he seal'd A testament of noble-ending love iv 6 27
Help Salisbury to make his testament *1 Hen. VI.* i 5 17
Performance is a kind of will or testament *T. of Athens* v 1 30
'Tis his will: Let but the commons hear this testament—Which,
pardon me, I do not mean to read *J. Cæsar* iii 2 135
The will! the testament!—They were villains, murderers: the will! iii 2 158
'Faith, they listened to me as they would have hearkened to their
father's testament *Pericles* iv 2 107
Tested. Not with fond shekels of the tested gold *Meas. for Meas.* ii 2 149
Tester I'll have in pouch when thou shalt lack *Mer. Wives* i 3 96
Hold, there's a tester for thee *2 Hen. IV.* iii 2 296
Testerned. I thank you, you have testerned me *T. G. of Ver.* i 1 153
Testify. To testify your bounty, I thank you, you have testerned me i 1 152
Here is the note of the fashion to testify *T. of Shrew* iv 3 131
Her mother liveth yet, can testify *1 Hen. VI.* v 4 12
And the bricks are alive at this day to testify it *2 Hen. VI.* iv 2 158
No warmth, no breath, shall testify thou livest *Rom. and Jul.* iv 1 98
Above ten thousand meaner moveables Would testify *Cymbeline* ii 2 30
So for her many a wight did die, As yon grim looks do testify *Pericles* i Gower 40
Testimonied in his own bringings-forth *Meas. for Meas.* iii 2 153
Testimony. And from this testimony of your own sex ii 4 131
Were testimonies against his worth and credit v 1 244
For testimony whereof, one in the prison . . . I have reserved alive v 1 470
Princes and counties! Surely, a princely testimony! *Much Ado* iv 1 318
Done in the testimony of a good conscience *L. L. Lost* iv 2 2
There is too great testimony in your complexion *As Y. Like It* iv 3 171
And by other warranted testimony *All's Well* ii 5 5
The ceremony of this compact Seal'd in my function, by my testimony
T. Night v 1 164
Bring me word 'tis done, And by good testimony *W. Tale* ii 3 136
The testimony on my part no other But what comes from myself iii 2 25
I hope your majesty is pear me testimony and witness *Hen. V.* iv 8 38
For testimony of her foul proceedings *T. Andron.* v 3 8
Suspend your indignation against my brother till you can derive from
him better testimony of his intent *Lear* i 2 88
If I bring you no sufficient testimony *Cymbeline* i 4 161
The testimonies whereof lie bleeding in me iii 4 22
Testiness. My mother, having power of his testiness, shall turn all into
my commendations iv 1 23
Testril. There's a testril of me too *T. Night* ii 3 34
Testy. Like a testy babe, will scratch the nurse *T. G. of Ver.* i 2 58
Lead these testy rivals so astray *M. N. Dream* iii 2 358
And finds the testy gentleman so hot, As he will lose his head ere give
consent *Richard III.* iii 4 39
A brace of unmeriting, proud, violent, testy magistrates, alias fools *Coriol.* ii 1 47
Must I stand and crouch Under your testy humour? *J. Cæsar* iv 3 46
And testy wrath Could never be her mild companion *Pericles* i 1 17
Tetchy and wayward was thy infancy; Thy school-days frightful *Rich. III.* iv 4 168
He's as tetchy to be woo'd to woo, As she is stubborn-chaste
Troi. and Cres. i 1 99
Pretty fool, To see it tetchy and fall out with the dug! *Rom. and Jul.* i 3 32
Tether. With a larger tether may he walk Than may be given you *Hamlet* i 3 125
Tetter. The rivelled fee-simple of the tetter *Troi. and Cres.* v 1 27
So shall my lungs Coin words till their decay against those measles,
Which we disdain should tetter us *Coriolanus* iii 1 79
A most instant tetter bark'd about, Most lazar-like *Hamlet* i 5 71
Tevil. The tevil and his tam! what phrase is this? *Mer. Wives* i 1 151
Tewksbury. His wit's as thick as Tewksbury mustard *2 Hen. IV.* ii 4 262
They do hold their course toward Tewksbury *3 Hen. VI.* v 3 19
Edward, her lord, whom I, some three months since, Stabb'd in my
angry mood at Tewksbury *Richard III.* i 2 242
Thou slewest my husband Henry in the Tower, And Edward, my poor
son, at Tewksbury i 3 120
False, fleeting, perjured Clarence, That stabb'd me in the field by
Tewksbury i 4 56
In the field by Tewksbury, When Oxford had me down ii 1 111
Think, how thou stab'dst me in my prime of youth At Tewksbury v 3 120
Text. And text underneath, 'Here dwells Benedick the married man'
Much Ado v 1 185
For society, saith the text, is the happiness of life *L. L. Lost* iv 2 168
And, certes, the text most infallibly concludes it iv 3 162
Beauteous as ink; a good conclusion.—Fair as a text B in a copy-book v 2 42
In religion, What damned error, but some sober brow Will bless it and
approve it with a text? *Mer. of Venice* iii 2 79
Where lies your text?—In Orsino's bosom *T. Night* i 5 240
You are now out of your text i 5 251
To hear with reverence Your exposition on the holy text *2 Hen. IV.* iv 2 7
What must be shall be.—That's a certain text *Rom. and Jul.* iv 1 21
No more; the text is foolish *Lear* iv 2 37
What shall be next, Pardon old Gower,—this longs the text *Pericles* ii Gower 40

Thaisa. Note it not you, Thaisa?—What is it To me, my father? *Pericles* ii 3 57
Is it no more to be your daughter than To say my mother's name was
Thaisa? Thaisa was my mother, who did end The minute I began v 1 212
Did wed At Pentapolis the fair Thaisa v 3 4
Look, Thaisa is Recovered.—O, let me look! v 3 27
The voice of dead Thaisa!—That Thaisa am I v 3 34
Flesh of thy flesh, Thaisa; Thy burden at the sea, and call'd Marina v 3 46
Still confirmation: Embrace him, dear Thaisa v 3 55
Thaisa, This prince, the fair-betrothed of your daughter, Shall marry her v 3 70
Thaliard, You are of our chamber, and our mind partakes Her private
actions to your secrecy i 1 151
Lord Thaliard from Antiochus is welcome i 3 31
How Thaliard came full bent with sin And had intent to murder him ii Gower 23
Thames. Empty it in the muddy ditch close by the Thames side *Mer. W.* iii 3 16
Like a barrow of butcher's offal, and to be thrown in the Thames iii 5 6
Let me pour in some sack to the Thames water iii 5 23
To be thrown into the Thames, and cooled, glowing hot, in that surge iii 5 122
I will be thrown into Etna, as I have been into Thames, ere I will leave her iii 5 129
As cold a night as 'tis, he could wish himself in Thames up to the neck
Hen. V. iv 1 120
Kill and knock down! throw them into Thames! *2 Hen. VI.* iv 8 3
Than. None that I more love than myself *Tempest* i 1 22
We are made to be no stronger Than faults may shake our frames
Meas. for Meas. ii 4 133
Hath amazed me more Than I dare blame my weakness *All's Well* ii 1 88
I had rather glib myself than they Should not produce fair issue *W. Tale* ii 1 149
Than my Lord Hastings no man might be bolder *Richard III.* iii 4 30
Thane. Who comes here?—The worthy thane of Ross *Macbeth* i 2 45
Whence camest thou, worthy thane?—From Fife, great king i 2 48
Assisted by that most disloyal traitor, The thane of Cawdor i 2 53
No more that thane of Cawdor shall deceive Our bosom interest i 2 63
All hail, Macbeth! hail to thee, thane of Glamis! i 3 48
All hail, Macbeth! hail to thee, thane of Cawdor! i 3 49
I know I am thane of Glamis; But how of Cawdor? the thane of Cawdor
lives i 3 71
You shall be king.—And thane of Cawdor too: went it not so? i 3 87
He bade me, from him, call thee thane of Cawdor: In which addition,
hail, most worthy thane! i 3 105
The thane of Cawdor lives: why do you dress me In borrow'd robes? i 3 108
Who was the thane lives yet; But under heavy judgement bears that life i 3 109
Glamis, and thane of Cawdor! The greatest is behind i 3 116
Those that gave the thane of Cawdor to me Promised no less to them i 3 119
Might yet enkindle you unto the crown, Besides the thane of Cawdor i 3 122
I am thane of Cawdor: If good, why do I yield to that suggestion? i 3 133
Sons, kinsmen, thanes, And you whose places are the nearest, know i 4 35
"Thane of Cawdor;" by which title, before, these weird sisters saluted me i 5 7
So please you, it is true: our thane is coming i 5 35
Your face, my thane, is as a book where men May read strange matters i 5 63
Where's the thane of Cawdor? We coursed him at the heels i 6 20
Why, worthy thane, You do unbend your noble strength, to think So
brainsickly ii 2 44
Is the king stirring, worthy thane?—Not yet ii 3 50
The thane of Fife had a wife: where is she now? v 1 47
Then fly, false thanes, And mingle with the English epicures v 3 7
Seyton, send out. Doctor, the thanes fly from me. Come, sir, dispatch v 3 49
The tyrant's people on both sides do fight; The noble thanes do bravely v 7 26
My thanes and kinsmen, Henceforth be earls, the first that ever Scotland
In such an honour named v 8 62
Thank. Give thanks you have lived so long, and make yourself ready
Tempest i 1 26
Heavens thank you for't! i 2 175
He shall not suffer indignity.—I thank my noble lord iii 2 43
I thank thee for that jest; here's a garment for't iv 1 241
To testify your bounty, I thank you, you have testerned me *T. G. of Ver.* i 1 152
I was in love with my bed: I thank you, you swinged me for my love i 1 88
I thank you, gentle servant: 'tis very clerkly done ii 1 114
And yet I care not; And yet take this again; and yet I thank you ii 1 124
We thank the giver.—Who is that, servant?—Yourself, sweet lady ii 4 33
I thank thee for thine honest care; Which to requite, command me iii 1 22
Thank me for this more than for all the favours Which all too much I
have bestow'd on thee iii 1 161
For your sake.—I thank you for your own iv 2 24
Good even to your ladyship.—I thank you for your music, gentlemen iv 2 86
She says your dog was a cur, and tells you currish thanks is good enough iv 4 53
She thanks you.—What say'st thou?—I thank you, madam, that you
tender her iv 4 143
And she shall thank you for 't, if e'er you know her iv 4 184
I thank your grace; the gift hath made me happy v 4 148
I am glad to see your worships well. I thank you for my venison *M. W.* i 1 81
I thank you always with my heart, la! with my heart.—Sir, I thank
you.—Sir, I thank you; by yea and no, I do i 1 85
Will't please your worship to come in, sir?—No, I thank you, forsooth i 1 277
The dinner attends you, sir.—I am not a-hungry, I thank you, forsooth i 1 280
I'll eat nothing; I thank you as much as though I did i 1 290
I pray you, sir, walk in.—I had rather walk here, I thank you i 1 293
I'll eat nothing, I thank you, sir.—By cock and pie, you shall not
choose, sir! i 1 315
Then did the sun on dunghill shine.—I thank thee for that humour i 3 71
She hath received your letter, for the which she thanks you a thousand
times ii 2 84
Marry, I thank you for it; I thank you for that good comfort iii 4 53
This is my doing.—I thank thee iii 4 103
I thank your worship: I shall make my master glad with these tidings iv 5 56
She determines Herself the glory of a creditor, Both thanks and use
Meas. for Meas. i 1 41
If myself might be his judge, He should receive his punishment in thanks i 4 28
I'll visit you again.—Most holy sir, I thank you iii 1 47
I thank you for this comfort. Fare you well, good father iii 1 280
If any thing fall to you upon this, more than thanks and good fortune iv 2 191
Our soul Cannot but yield you forth to public thanks v 1 7
Thanks, good friend Escalus, for thy much goodness v 1 534
Thanks, provost, for thy care and secrecy v 1 536
My errand, due unto my tongue, I thank him, I bare home *Com. of Er.* ii 1 73
Well, sir, I thank you.—Thank me, sir! for what? ii 2 50
Walk with me down to his house, I will discharge my bond and thank
you too iv 1 13
Some invite me; Some other give me thanks for kindnesses iv 3 5
But he, I thank him, gnaw'd in two my cords v 1 289
Much thanks for my good cheer v 1 392
I thank you: I am not of many words, but I thank you *Much Ado* i 1 158

Thank. That a woman conceived me, I thank her; that she brought me up, I likewise give her most humble thanks *Much Ado* i 1 240
I thank it, poor fool, it keeps on the windy side of care ii 1 326
I took no more pains for those thanks than you took pains to thank me ii 3 268
Any pains that I take for you is as easy as thanks ii 3 271
Give God thanks, and make no boast of it iii 3 20
I thank him; he hath bid me to a calf's head and a capon v 1 155
For your many courtesies I thank you: I must discontinue your company v 1 191
I thank thee for thy care and honest pains v 1 323
I discharge thee of thy prisoner, and I thank thee v 1 329
Thanks to you all, and leave us: fare you well v 3 28
I thank my beauty, I am fair that shoot *L. L. Lost* iv 1 11
I beseech your society.—And thank you too iv 2 167
Nay, I have verses too, I thank Biron v 2 34
And Lord Biron, I thank him, is my dear v 2 457
If your ladyship would say, 'Thanks, Pompey,' I had done.—Great thanks v 2 559
I thank you, gracious lords, For all your fair endeavours v 2 739
Excuse me so, coming too short of thanks For my great suit v 2 748
O, shall I say, I thank you, gentle wife?—Not so, my lord v 2 836
For this intelligence If I have thanks, it is a dear expense *M. N. Dream* i 1 249
Mine ear, I thank it, brought me to thy sound iii 2 182
The kinder we, to give them thanks for nothing v 1 89
Thanks, courteous wall: Jove shield thee well for this! v 1 179
Sweet Moon, I thank thee for thy sunny beams; I thank thee, Moon, for shining now so bright v 1 277
I thank my fortune for it, My ventures are not in one bottom *M. of Ven.* i 1 41
I'll grow a talker for this gear.—Thanks, i' faith i 1 111
Even for that I thank you i 3 22
I thank thee, good Tubal: good news, good news! ha, ha! where? iii 1 111
Get a wife.—I thank your lordship, you have got me one iii 2 198
I thank you for your wish, and am well pleased To wish it back on you iii 4 43
Your wife would give you little thanks for that, If she were by iv 1 288
A second Daniel! I thank thee, Jew, for teaching me that word iv 1 341
You are welcome home, my lord.—I thank you, madam v 1 133
I thank thee for thy love to me *As Y. Like It* i 1 143
Gentle cousin, Let us go thank him and encourage him i 2 252
Can I not say, I thank you? My better parts Are all thrown down i 2 261
It will make you melancholy, Monsieur Jaques.—I thank it ii 5 12
If ever I thank any man, I'll thank you ii 5 25
When a man thanks me heartily, methinks I have given him a penny and he renders me the beggarly thanks ii 5 27
I give heaven thanks and make no boast of them ii 5 38
I thank ye; and be blest for your good comfort! ii 7 135
I thank you most for him.—So had you need: I scarce can speak to thank you for myself ii 7 169
I thank you for your company; but, good faith, I had as lief have been myself alone iii 2 268
For fashion sake, I thank you too for your society iii 2 272
I am not a slut, though I thank the gods I am foul iii 3 38
Now, fellows, you are welcome.—We thank your honour *T. of Shrew* Ind. 1 80
I thank thee: thou shalt not lose by it Ind. 2 101
Thou'ldst thank me but a little for my counsel i 2 61
Pray, accept his service.—A thousand thanks ii 1 85
If she do bid me pack, I'll give her thanks, As though she bid me stay ii 1 178
And so, I take my leave, and thank you both ii 1 400
Honest company, I thank you all, That have beheld me give away myself iii 2 195
Will you give thanks, sweet Kate; or else shall I? iv 1 162
I am sure, sweet Kate, this kindness merits thanks iv 3 41
The poorest service is repaid with thanks; And so shall mine iv 3 45
I thank my good father, I am able to maintain it v 1 78
Tranio hits you now.—I thank thee for that gird v 2 58
Show what we alone must think, which never Returns us thanks *All's W.* i 1 200
My thanks and duty are your majesty's i 2 23
Stall this in your bosom; and I thank you for your honest care i 3 132
We thank you, maiden; But may not be so credulous of cure ii 1 117
Such thanks I give As one near death to those that wish him live ii 1 133
Proffers not took reap thanks for their reward ii 1 150
Thanks, sir; all the rest is mute ii 3 83
Thanks be given, she's very well and wants nothing i' the world ii 4 4
I thank you, and will stay upon your leisure iii 5 48
For which live long to thank both heaven and me! iv 2 67
I con him no thanks for't, in the nature he delivers it iv 3 174
What shall be done to him?—Nothing, but let him have thanks iv 3 195
Which gratitude Through flinty Tartar's bosom would peep forth, And answer, thanks iv 4 8
I have made a bold charter; but I thank my God it holds yet iv 5 98
But rather make you thank your pains for it v 1 33
Lend me a handkercher: so, I thank thee v 3 323
Jove, I thank thee: I will smile *T. Night* ii 5 194
I can no other answer make but thanks, And thanks iii 3 14
Time as long again Would be fill'd up, my brother, with our thanks *W. T.* i 2 4
Like a cipher, Yet standing in rich place, I multiply With one 'We thank you' many thousands moe That go before it i 2 8
Stay your thanks a while; And pay them when you part i 2 9
So you shall pay your fees When you depart, and save your thanks i 2 54
For this I'll blush you thanks iv 4 595
Now he thanks the old shepherd, which stands by v 2 59
On my knee I give heaven thanks I was not like to thee! *K. John* i 1 83
My mother, With all my heart I thank thee for my father! i 1 270
O, take his mother's thanks, a widow's thanks! ii 1 32
O heaven! I thank you, Hubert.—Silence; no more iv 1 132
I have a kind soul that would give you thanks And knows not how to do it but with tears v 7 108
We thank you both: yet one but flatters us *Richard II.* i 1 25
I thank my liege, that in regard of me He shortens four years of my son's exile i 3 216
Thanks, my countrymen, my loving friends i 4 34
I thank thee, gentle Percy; and be sure I count myself in nothing else so happy ii 3 45
All my treasury Is yet but unfelt thanks ii 3 61
Evermore thanks, the exchequer of the poor ii 3 65
There lies the substance: and I thank thee, king, For thy great bounty iv 1 299
Bespake them thus: 'I thank you, countrymen' v 2 20
Thanks, noble peer; The cheapest of us is ten groats too dear v 5 67
I thank thee not; for thou hast wrought A deed of slander v 6 34
What letters hast thou there?—I can but thank you *1 Hen. IV.* iv 1 13
I thank him, that he cuts me from my tale, For I profess not talking v 2 91
You may thank the unquiet time for your quiet o'er-posting that action *2 Hen. IV.* i 2 170

Thank. I thank your pretty sweet wit for it *2 Hen. IV.* i 2 231
And thy father is to give me thanks for it. No abuse, Hal: none. ii 4 350
Thou, like a kind fellow, gavest thyself away gratis; and I thank thee for thee iv 3 76
I am glad to see your worship.—I thank thee with all my heart v 1 64
By God's liggens, I thank thee v 3 69
Sure, we thank you. My learned lord, we pray you to proceed *Hen. V.* i 2 8
So tell your master.—I shall deliver so. Thanks to your highness iii 6 176
He gives you, upon his knees, a thousand thanks iv 4 64
Thanks, good my countryman.—By Jeshu, I am your majesty's countryman iv 7 115
You may, some of you, thank love for my blindness v 2 344
I return great thanks, And in submission will attend on her *1 Hen. VI.* ii 2 51
Thanks, gentle sir. Come, let us four to dinner ii 4 132
Never have you tasted our reward, Or been reguerdon'd with so much as thanks iii 4 23
I give thee kingly thanks, Because this is in traffic of a king v 3 163
Long live Queen Margaret, England's happiness!—We thank you all *2 Hen. VI.* i 1 38
We thank you all for this great favour done, In entertainment i 1 71
Long live our sovereign Richard, England's king!—We thank you, lords ii 2 64
I thank you all: drink, and pray for me, I pray you ii 3 72
I thank thee, Meg; these words content me much iii 2 26
God save your majesty!—I thank you, good people iv 2 78
Then, heaven, set ope thy everlasting gates, To entertain my vows of thanks! iv 9 14
And so, with thanks and pardon to you all, I do dismiss you iv 9 20
We'll all assist you; he that flies shall die.—Thanks *3 Hen. VI.* i 1 31
I take my leave with many thousand thanks iii 2 56
My love till death, my humble thanks, my prayers iii 2 62
Let me give humble thanks for all at once iii 3 221
I agree, and thank you for your motion iii 3 244
Take his thanks that yet hath nothing else v 4 59
Discharge the common sort With pay and thanks, and let's away v 5 88
I shall live, my lord, to give them thanks That were the cause of my imprisonment.—No doubt, no doubt *Richard III.* i 1 127
Let him thank me, that holp to send him thither i 2 107
I thank my God for my humility ii 1 72
Health and happy days!—I thank you, good my lord; and thank you all iii 1 19
How fares our cousin, noble Lord of York?—I thank you, gentle uncle iii 1 102
Have my weapon, little lord?—I would, that I might thank you as you call me iii 1 123
I thank his grace, I know he loves me well iii 4 15
Definitively thus I answer you. Your love deserves my thanks iii 7 154
O upright, just, and true-disposing God, How do I thank thee! iv 4 56
Didst thou love her brothers; And from my heart's love I do thank thee for it iv 4 260
How have ye done . . ?—I thank your grace, Healthful *Hen. VIII.* i 1 2
My life itself, and the best heart of it, Thanks you for this great care: I stood i' the level Of a full-charged confederacy, and give thanks To you that choked it i 2 2
Repeat your will and take it.—Thank your majesty i 2 13
Let me have such a bowl may hold my thanks, And save me so much talking i 4 39
I pay 'em A thousand thanks, and pray 'em take their pleasures i 4 74
I bid him welcome, And thank the holy conclave for their loves ii 2 100
Vouchsafe to speak my thanks and my obedience ii 3 71
But with thanks to God for such A royal lady ii 4 152
Here are some will thank you, If you speak truth iii 1 46
My lords, I thank you both for your good wills; Ye speak like honest men iii 1 68
Poor undeserver, I Can nothing render but allegiant thanks iii 2 176
The king shall know it, and, no doubt, shall thank you iii 2 348
The king has cured me, I humbly thank his grace iii 2 381
You may read the rest.—I thank you, sir iv 1 20
I sent your message; who return'd her thanks In the great'st humbleness v 1 64
I thank you; You are always my good friend v 3 58
How much are we bound to heaven In daily thanks v 3 115
Ye have been too prodigal: I thank ye heartily; so shall this lady v 5 14
Ye must all see the queen, and she must thank ye, She will be sick else v 5 74
Gone between and between, but small thanks for my labour *T. and C.* i 1 72
Thank the heavens, lord, thou art of sweet composure ii 3 251
What folly I commit, I dedicate to you.—I thank you for that iii 2 112
Oft have you—often have you thanks therefore iii 3 20
I said 'Good morrow, Ajax;' and he replies 'Thanks, Agamemnon' iii 3 262
So please you, save the thanks this prince expects iv 4 119
I thank thee, Hector: Thou art too gentle and too free a man iv 5 138
By Mars his gauntlet, thanks! Mock not, that I affect the untraded oath iv 5 177
Thanks and good night to the Greeks' general.—Good night, my lord v 1 80
Accept distracted thanks v 2 189
How does your little son?—I thank your ladyship; well *Coriolanus* i 3 58
A certain number, Though thanks to all, must I select from all i 6 81
We thank the gods Our Rome hath such a soldier i 9 8
I thank you, general; But cannot make my heart consent to take A bribe i 9 36
You shall perceive Whether I blush or no; howbeit, I thank you i 9 70
Take my cap, Jupiter, and I thank thee. Hoo! Marcius coming home! ii 1 115
O, he is wounded; I thank the gods for't ii 1 133
Whom We met here both to thank and to remember With honours like himself ii 2 51
Here was 'I thank you for your voices: thank you: Your most sweet voices' ii 3 179
Your soldiers use him as the grace 'fore meat, Their talk at table, and their thanks at end iv 7 4
Yet your good will Must have that thanks from Rome v 1 46
We have all Great cause to give great thanks v 4 63
Friends, that have been thus forward in my right, I thank you all *T. An.* i 1 57
Thanks to men Of noble minds is honourable meed i 1 215
I give thee thanks in part of thy deserts, And will with deeds requite i 1 236
Thanks, gentle Romans: may I govern so, To heal Rome's harms! v 3 147
I thank you all; I thank you, honest gentlemen; good night *R. and J.* i 5 125
Romeo shall thank thee, daughter, for us both.—As much to him, else is his thanks too much ii 6 22
Have you deliver'd to her our decree?—Ay, sir; but she will none, she gives you thanks iii 5 140
How! will she none? doth she not give us thanks? Is she not proud? iii 5 143
What is this? 'Proud,' and 'I thank you,' and 'I thank you not' iii 5 151
Thank me no thankings, nor proud me no prouds iii 5 153
I do return those talents, Doubled with thanks and service *T. of Athens* i 2 7
Feasts are too proud to give thanks to the gods i 2 62
And entertain'd me with mine own device; I am to thank you for't i 2 156
A trifle of our love.—With more than common thanks I will receive it i 2 214

Thank. He's ever sending: how shall I thank him, thinkest thou? . *T. of Athens* iii 2 37
The gods require our thanks . . . . . . iii 6 78
O, a root,—dear thanks!—Dry up thy marrows, vines, and plough-torn leas . . . . iv 3 192
Yet thanks I must you con That you are thieves profess'd . iv 3 428
I thank them; and would send them back the plague, Could I but catch it for them . . . . . . v 1 140
Thou shalt be met with thanks, Allow'd with absolute power . v 1 164
I thank thee, Brutus, That thou hast proved Lucilius' saying true *J. C.* v 5 58
We are sent To give thee from our royal master thanks . *Macbeth* i 3 101
Thanks for your pains . . . . i 3 117
That the proportion both of thanks and payment Might have been mine! i 4 19
Herein I teach you How you shall bid God 'ild us for your pains, And thank us for your trouble . . . . . . i 6 14
Good repose the while!—Thanks, sir: the like to you! . . . ii 1 30
At first And last the hearty welcome.—Thanks to your majesty . iii 4 2
See, they encounter thee with their hearts' thanks . . . iii 4 9
Thanks for that: There the grown serpent lies . . . . iii 4 28
Whate'er thou art, for thy good caution, thanks . . . iv 1 73
So, thanks to all at once and to each one, Whom we invite to see us . v 8 74
For this relief much thanks: 'tis bitter cold . . *Hamlet* i 1 8
For all, our thanks. Now follows, that you know . . . i 2 16
Your visitation shall receive such thanks As fits a king's remembrance ii 2 25
Meantime we thank you for your well-took labour: Go to your rest . ii 2 83
Beggar that I am, I am even poor in thanks; but I thank you: and sure, dear friends, my thanks are too dear a halfpenny . . ii 2 281
How does your honour for this many a day?—I humbly thank you; well, well . . . . iii 1 92
A man that fortune's buffets and rewards Hast ta'en with equal thanks iii 2 73
My brother shall know of it: and so I thank you for your good counsel iv 5 71
Put your bonnet to his right use; 'tis for the head.—I thank your lordship . . . . v 2 97
Where should we have our thanks?—Not from his mouth, Had it the ability of life to thank you . . . . . . v 2 383
I thank thee, fellow; thou servest me, and I'll love thee . . *Lear* i 4 97
My friendly knave, I thank thee: there's earnest of thy service . i 4 103
Proclaim it, That he which finds him shall deserve our thanks . ii 1 63
For him I thank your grace . . . . . . ii 1 119
You shall find Some that will thank you . . . . iii 1 37
I live To thank thee for the love thou show'dst the king . . iv 2 96
I thank you, sir: that's all . . . . . . iv 6 218
Hearty thanks: The bounty and the benison of heaven To boot, and boot! iv 6 227
Pray you, undo this button: thank you, sir. Do you see this? . v 3 309
Thanks, you the valiant of this warlike isle! . . *Othello* ii 1 43
I thank you, valiant Cassio. What tidings can you tell me of my lord? ii 1 87
Thank me, love me, and reward me, For making him egregiously an ass ii 1 317
He's never any thing but your true servant.—I know't; I thank you . iii 3 10
I thank you for this profit; and from hence I'll love no friend . iii 3 379
I greet thy love, Not with vain thanks, but with acceptance bounteous iii 3 470
I must thank him only, Lest my remembrance suffer ill report *A. and C.* ii 2 158
Make yourself my guest Whilst you abide here.—Humbly, sir, I thank you ii 2 250
And am well studied for a liberal thanks Which I do owe you . ii 6 48
Thanks to you, That call'd me timelier than my purpose hither . ii 6 51
So your desires are yours.—Thanks to my lord . . . iii 4 28
A halter'd neck which does the hangman thank For being yare about him iii 13 130
I thank you all; For doughty-handed are you . . . . iv 8 4
To this great fairy I'll commend thy acts, Make her thanks bless thee . iv 8 13
I have led you oft: carry me now, good friends, And have my thanks for all . . . . iv 14 140
He gives me so much of mine own, as I Will kneel to him with thanks v 2 21
A grief that smites My very heart at root.—I thank you, sir . . v 2 105
Adieu, good queen; I must attend on Cæsar.—Farewell, and thanks . v 2 207
This worthy signior, I thank him, makes no stranger of me . *Cymbeline* i 4 111
Leonatus is in safety And greets your highness dearly.—Thanks, good sir i 6 13
Are you well?—Thanks, madam; well . . . . . i 6 52
Take my power i' the court for yours.—My humble thanks . . i 6 180
The thanks I give Is telling you that I am poor of thanks . . ii 3 93
Sir—I thank her—that: She stripp'd it from her arm; I see her yet . ii 4 100
Look For fury not to be resisted. Thus defied, I thank thee for myself iii 1 69
You shall have better cheer Ere you depart; and thanks to stay and eat it . . . . iii 6 68
My tailor made them not.—Hence, then, and thank The man that gave them thee . . . . iv 2 84
He'ld take us in, Displace our heads where—thank the gods!—they grow . . . . iv 2 122
Ne'er thank thy master; live: And ask of Cymbeline what boon thou wilt . . . . v 5 96
I thank thee, who hath taught My frail mortality to know itself *Pericles* i 1 41
Thanks, fortune, yet, that, after all my crosses, Thou givest me somewhat to repair myself . . . . ii 1 127
The king my father, sir, has drunk to you.—I thank him . . ii 3 76
He thanks your grace; names himself Pericles, A gentleman of Tyre . ii 3 86
Thanks, gentlemen, to all; all have done well, But you the best . ii 3 108
Madam, my thanks and prayers . . . . . . iii 3 34
My recompense is thanks, that's all; Yet my good will is great . iii 4 17
What! I must have a care of you.—My thanks, sweet madam . iv 1 50
Down on thy knees, thank the holy gods as loud As thunder threatens us v 1 200
And who to thank, Besides the gods, for this great miracle . . v 3 57
Thank you for your pains *Much Ado* ii 3; *T. of Shrew* iii 2; *T. Night* i 5; *Richard II.* v 6; *Hen. V.* i 2; *J. Cæsar* ii 2; *Cymbeline* i 6

Thank God. I thank God and my cold blood, I am of your humour for that . . . . *Much Ado* i 1 131
Call the rest of the watch together and thank God you are rid of a knave iii 3 31
I thank God I am as honest as any man living that is an old man . iii 5 15
I thank God I have as little patience as another man . *L. L. Lost* i 2 170
I thank God, I thank God. Is't true, is't true? *Mer. of Venice* iii 1 107
I thank God I am not a woman . . . . *As Y. Like It* iii 2 366
Wast born i' the forest here?—Ay, sir, I thank God.—'Thank God;' a good answer . . . . v 1 26
What thing! why, a thing to thank God on.—I am no thing to thank God on . . . . 1 *Hen. IV.* iii 3 133
Thou see'st not well.—Yes, master, clear as day, I thank God 2 *Hen. VI.* ii 1 108
Fellow, thank God, and the good wine in thy master's way . . ii 3 98
I thank God, I have been so well brought up that I can write my name iv 2 112
I thank God and thee; He was the author, thou the instrument 3 *Hen. VI.* iv 6 17
Art thou my son?—Ay, I thank God, my father, and yourself *Rich. III.* iv 4 155

Thank heaven. Nor can do more than I do with her, I thank heaven *Mer. Wives* i 4 128

Thank heaven. I ne'er made my will yet, I thank heaven; I am not such a sickly creature. . . . . . . *Mer. Wives* iii 4 60
Thy wife?—Ay, sir; whom, I thank heaven, is an honest woman *Meas. for Meas.* ii 1 72
Down on your knees, And thank heaven, fasting, for a good man's love *As Y. Like It* iii 5 58
We understand it, and thank heaven for you . . *All's Well* ii 3 71

Thank myself. Even in thy behalf, I'll thank myself For doing these fair rites of tenderness . . . . . 1 *Hen. IV.* v 4 97

Thank my stars I am happy . . . . . *T. Night* ii 5 185

Thank yourself. You may thank yourself for this great loss . *Tempest* ii 1 123
Flatterers! Now, Brutus, thank yourself . . . *J. Cæsar* v 1 45

Thanked. Their blades, which, God be thanked, hurt not . *Much Ado* v 1 190
An honest exceeding poor man and, God be thanked, well to live *Mer. of Venice* ii 2 55
Now Lord be thanked for my good amends! . . *T. of Shrew* Ind. 2 99
You shall find yourself to be well thank'd, Whate'er falls more *All's W.* v 1 36
Jove, not I, is the doer of this, and he is to be thanked . *T. Night* ii 4 92
But, heaven be thank'd, it is but voluntary . . . *K. John* v 1 29
Well, God be thanked for these rebels . . . 1 *Hen. IV.* iii 3 214
But God be thanked for prevention . . . . *Hen. V.* ii 2 158
But, God be thanked, there's no need of me . . . *Richard III.* iii 7 165
Go not you hence Till I have thank'd you . . . *T. of Athens* i 1 254
She thank'd me, And bade me, if I had a friend that loved her, I should but teach him how to tell my story . . . . *Othello* i 3 163

Thankful. I will be thankful To any happy messenger *T. G. of Ver.* ii 4 52
Speaks like a most thankful and reverend youth . . *Much Ado* v 1 324
That we thankful should be, Which we of taste and feeling are *L. L. Lost* iv 2 29
The gift is good in those in whom it is acute, and I am thankful for it iv 2 74
God will send more, if the man will be thankful *As Y. Like It* iii 2 221
She's apt to learn and thankful for good turns . *T. of Shrew* ii 1 166
As to be—generally thankful . . . . . *All's Well* ii 3 44
Yet am I thankful: if my heart were great, 'Twould burst at this . iv 3 366
For the which I shall continue thankful . . . . . v 1 17
It is Jove's doing, and Jove make me thankful! . . *T. Night* iii 4 83
As I am a gentleman, I will live to be thankful to thee for't . . i 2 89
To be more thankful to thee shall be my study . . *W. Tale* iv 2 20
Sir, I am thankful to you . . . . . *Hen. VIII.* i 1 150
I have received much honour by your presence, And ye shall find me thankful . . . . v 5 73
With smiling fronts encountering, May give you thankful sacrifice *Coriol.* i 6 9
My faction if thou strengthen with thy friends, I will most thankful be *T. Andron.* i 1 215
Not proud, you have; but thankful, that you have: Proud can I never be of what I hate; But thankful even for hate, that is meant love *Rom. and Jul.* iii 5 147
Give the gods a thankful sacrifice . . . *Ant. and Cleo.* i 2 167
That he can hither come so soon, Is by your fancy's thankful doom *Per.* v 2 285

Thankfully. And thankfully rest debtor for the first . *Mer. of Venice* i 1 152
His ring I do accept most thankfully . . . . . . iv 2 9
Please you to dispose yourselves.—Most thankfully . *T. of Athens* i 2 162
You'll take it ill.—Most thankfully, my lord . . . . ii 1 94
Here is better than the open air; take it thankfully . . *Lear* iii 6 2
My heart Is warm'd by the rest, and takes it thankfully . *Cymbeline* i 6 28
But yet heaven's bounty towards him might Be used more thankfully . i 6 79
What he will do graciously, I will thankfully receive . *Pericles* iv 6 65

Thankfulness. Sweet prince, you learn me noble thankfulness *Much Ado* iv 1 31
We therefore have great cause of thankfulness . . . *Hen. V.* ii 2 32
O Lord, that lends me life, Lend me a heart replete with thankfulness! 2 *Hen. VI.* i 1 20
The gods bless you for your tidings; next, Accept my thankfulness *Coriolanus* v 4 62
Sprinkle our society with thankfulness . . . *T. of Athens* iii 6 80
Take from my heart all thankfulness! The gods Make up the rest! *Per.* iii 3 4

Thanking. Many and hearty thankings to you both . *Meas. for Meas.* v 1 4
Eat with us to-night, the charge and thanking Shall be for me *All's Well* iii 5 101
Thank me no thankings, nor proud me no prouds . *Rom. and Jul.* iii 5 153
He would have well becomed this place, and graced The thankings of a king . . . . *Cymbeline* v 5 407

Thankless. The drops of blood Shed for my thankless country *Coriol.* iv 5 76
Your friends fall'n off, Whose thankless natures—O abhorred spirits! *T. of Athens* v 1 63
How sharper than a serpent's tooth it is To have a thankless child! *Lear* i 4 311

Thanksgiving. In the thanksgiving before meat . *Meas. for Meas.* i 2 15
I cannot stay thanksgiving . . . . . *L. L. Lost* ii 1 193

Tharborough. I am his grace's tharborough . . . . . i 1 185

Thasos. Come, therefore, and to Thasos send his body . *J. Cæsar* v 3 104

That. None that I more love than myself . . . . *Tempest* i 1 22
The sky, it seems, would pour down stinking pitch, But that the sea, mounting to the welkin's cheek, Dashes the fire out . . . i 2 4
How is it That this lives in thy mind? . . . . . i 2 49
If thou remember'st aught ere thou camest here, How thou camest here thou mayst.—But that I do not . . . . i 2 52
I pray thee, mark me—that a brother should Be so perfidious! . . i 2 67
At that time Through all the signories it was the first . . . i 2 70
With that which . . . in my false brother Awaked an evil nature . . i 2 91
It is a hint That wrings mine eyes to't . . . . . i 2 135
Wherefore did they not That hour destroy us? . . . . i 2 139
That's my noble master! What shall I do? say what; what shall I do? i 2 299
I am all the subjects that you have, Which first was mine own king . i 2 341
Nothing of him that doth fade But doth suffer a sea-change . . i 2 399
'Widow Dido' said you? you make me study of that . . . ii 1 82
O, out of that 'no hope' What great hope have you! no hope that way is Another way so high a hope that even Ambition cannot pierce a wink beyond . . . . ii 1 239
If he were that which now he's like, that's dead . . . ii 1 282
I heard a humming, And that a strange one too, which did awake me . ii 1 318
He shall pay for him that hath him, and that soundly . . . ii 2 81
Open your mouth; here is that which will give language to you . ii 2 86
This will shake your shaking, I can tell you, and that soundly . ii 2 88
That a monster should be such a natural! . . . . iii 2 36
And that most deeply to consider is The beauty of his daughter . . iii 2 106
A witch, and one so strong That could control the moon . . v 1 270
Trim it handsomely.—Ay, that I will; and I'll be wise hereafter . v 1 294
Some love of yours hath writ to you in rhyme.—That I might sing it, madam, to a tune . . . . *T. G. of Ver.* i 2 80
Seem you that you are not?—Haply I do . . . . . ii 4 10
That I love—That I did love, for now my love is thaw'd . . ii 4 199
Cease to lament for that thou canst not help, And study help for that which thou lament'st . . . . iii 1 241

That. And more faults than hairs.—That's monstrous: O, that that were out! *T. G. of Ver.* iii 1 374
These are the villains That all the travellers do fear so much . iv 1 6
What is she, That all our swains commend her? . iv 2 40
I thank you for your music, gentlemen. Who is that that spake? iv 2 87
I have need of such a youth That can with some discretion do my business . iv 4 70
What would you with her, if that I be she? . iv 4 115
O miserable, unhappy that I am! . v 4 28
O time most accurst, 'Mongst all foes that a friend should be the worst! v 4 72
I doubt he be not well, that he comes not home . *Mer. Wives* i 4 43
O, that my husband saw this letter! . ii 1 103
May be the knave bragged of that he could not compass . iii 3 212
I will confess thy father's wealth Was the first motive that I woo'd thee iii 4 14
Was there a wise woman with thee?—Ay, that there was . iv 5 60
Over and above that you have suffered . v 5 177
Peace be in this place!—Who's that which calls? . *Meas. for Meas.* i 4 6
Had time cohered with place or place with wishing, Or that the resolute acting of your blood Could have attain'd the effect . ii 1 12
Be that you are, That is, a woman; if you be more, you're none . ii 4 135
'Tis no sin, Sith that the justice of your title to him Doth flourish the deceit . iv 1 74
I conjure thee . . . That thou neglect me not, with that opinion That I am touch'd with madness! Make not impossible That which but seems unlike . v 1 50
Charges she more than me?—Not that I know . v 1 200
My brother had but justice, In that he did the thing for which he died v 1 454
We discovered Two ships from far making amain to us, Of Corinth that, of Epidaurus this . *Com. of Errors* i 1 94
O, let me say no more! Gather the sequel by that went before . i 1 96
Lest that your goods too soon be confiscate . i 2 2
Think'st thou I jest? Hold, take thou that, and that . ii 2 23
I think the meat wants that I have.—In good time, sir; what's that? ii 2 57
Who is that at the door that keeps all this noise? . iii 1 61
There is something in the wind, that we cannot get in . iii 1 69
That supposed by the common rout Against your yet ungalled estimation That may with foul intrusion enter in . iii 1 101
She would have me as a beast: not that, I being a beast, she would have me; but that she, being a very beastly creature, lays claim to me . iii 2 87
Consent to pay thee that I never had! . iv 1 74
The reason that I gather he is mad, . . Is a mad tale he told . iv 3 87
Have you that I sent you for?—Here's that, I warrant you, will pay them all . iv 4 9
In the meantime let me be that I am and seek not to alter me *Much Ado* i 3 38
If you dare not trust that you see, confess not that you know . iii 2 122
Here's that shall drive some of them to a noncome . iii 5 67
Now thy image doth appear In the rare semblance that I loved it first . v 1 260
Fare you well now: and yet, ere I go, let me go with that I came . v 2 47
For barbarism spoke more Than for that angel knowledge you can say *L. L. Lost* i 1 113
What will Biron say when that he shall hear Faith so infringed? . iv 3 145
That sport best pleases that doth least know how . v 2 519
Through Athens I am thought as fair as she. But what of that? *M. N. Dream* i 1 228
Because that she as her attendant hath A lovely boy . ii 1 21
That fallen am I in dark uneven way, And here will rest me . iii 2 417
'Tis strange, my Theseus, that these lovers speak of . v 1 1
That you should think, we come not to offend, But with good will . v 1 109
Who riseth from a feast With that keen appetite that he sits down? *Mer. of Venice* ii 6 9
And fair she is, if that mine eyes be true, And true she is . ii 6 54
Since that the trade and profit of the city Consisteth of all nations . iii 3 30
They shall think we are accomplished With that we lack . iii 4 62
What prodigal portion have I spent, that I should come to such penury? *As Y. Like It* i 1 42
The courtesy of nations allows you my better, in that you are the first-born . i 1 50
The duke Hath banish'd me, his daughter.—That he hath not . i 3 97
O that I were a fool! I am ambitious for a motley coat . ii 7 42
Provided that you weed your better judgements Of all opinion that grows rank in them That I am wise . ii 7 47
Flow as hugely as the sea, Till that the weary very means do ebb . ii 7 73
I earn that I eat, get that I wear, owe no man hate . iii 2 77
That is another simple sin in you, to bring the ewes and the rams together . iii 2 82
I speak not this that you should bear a good opinion of my knowledge . v 2 59
Hearing how that every day Men of great worth resorted to this forest v 4 160
I will continue that I broach'd in jest . *T. of Shrew* i 2 84
What, master, read you? first resolve me that.—I read that I profess . iv 2 8
I love thee well, in that thou likest it not . iv 3 83
Whose state is such that cannot choose But lend and give *All's Well* i 3 220
Which is the Frenchman?—He; That with the plume . iii 5 81
Is it possible he should know what he is, and be that he is? . iv 1 49
Had you that craft, to reave her Of what should stead her most? . v 3 86
Sith wives are monsters to you, And that you fly them . v 3 156
She that hath a heart of that fine frame To pay this debt of love *T. Night* i 1 33
I swear, I am not that I play . i 5 196
That's it that always makes a good voyage of nothing . ii 4 80
That defence thou hast, betake thee to't . iii 4 240
Do not tempt my misery, Lest that it make me so unsound a man . iii 4 384
'That that is is;' . . . for, what is 'that' but 'that,' and 'is' but 'is?' iv 2 17
Then thou art As great as that thou fear'st . v 1 153
When that I was and a little tiny boy, With hey, ho . v 1 398
Thou dost, And that beyond commission, and I find it, And that to the infection of my brains . *W. Tale* i 2 145
Such allow'd infirmities that honesty Is never free of . i 2 263
He who shall speak for her is afar off guilty But that he speaks . ii 1 105
The heavens with that we have in hand are angry And frown upon's . iii 3 5
There is that in this fardel will make him scratch his beard . iv 4 727
When that my father lived, Your brother did employ my father much *K. John* i 1 95
What means that hand upon that breast of thine? . iii 1 21
Lest that their hopes prodigiously be cross'd . iii 1 91
Lest that France repent, And by disjoining hands, hell lose a soul . iii 1 196
Though that my death were adjunct to my act, By heaven, I would do it . iii 3 57
Now that their souls are topfull of offence . iii 4 180
Do you almost think, although you see, That you do see? . iv 3 44
Must I back Because that John hath made his peace with Rome? . v 2 96

That. I beg cold comfort; and you are so strait And so ingrateful, you deny me that.—O that there were some virtue in my tears, That might relieve you! . *K. John* v 7 43
Poor queen! so that thy state might be no worse, I would my skill were subject to thy curse . *Richard II.* iii 4 102
Whilst that my wretchedness doth bait myself . iv 1 238
Think I am dead and that even here thou takest, As from my death-bed, thy last living leave . v 1 38
Flatter themselves That they are not the first of fortune's slaves . v 5 24
Which now doth that I would not have it do . *1 Hen. IV.* iii 2 90
Well, I'll repent, and that suddenly, while I am in some liking . iii 3 5
When that this body did contain a spirit, A kingdom for it was too small v 4 89
Then was that noble Worcester Too soon ta'en prisoner . *2 Hen. IV.* i 1 125
That he now doth lack The very instruments of chastisement . iv 1 216
A little time before That our great-grandsire, Edward, sick'd and died . iv 4 128
O God, that right should thus overcome might! . iv 4 27
If that you will France win, Then with Scotland first begin *Hen. V.* i 2 167
Dispatch us with all speed, lest that our king Come here himself . ii 4 141
Since that my penitence comes after all, Imploring pardon . iv 1 321
Where that his lords desire him to have borne His bruised helmet v Prol. 17
We'll burst them open, if that you come not quickly . *1 Hen. VI.* i 3 28
Like to a pair of loving turtle-doves That could not live asunder . ii 2 32
Meditating that Shall dye your white rose in a bloody red . ii 4 60
It is not that offends; It is not that that hath incensed the duke . iii 1 36
To try if that our own be ours or no . iii 2 63
I gave a noble to the priest The morn that I was wedded . v 4 24
Answer that I shall ask; For, till thou speak, thou shalt not pass from hence.—Ask what thou wilt. That I had said and done! *2 Hen. VI.* i 4 29
Entreat her not the worse in that I pray You use her well . ii 4 81
Ah, that my fear were false! ah, that it were! . iii 1 193
Let him die, in that he is a fox, By nature proved an enemy to the flock iii 1 257
Be that thou hopest to be, or what thou art Resign to death . iii 1 333
That she, poor wretch, for grief can speak no more . *3 Hen. VI.* iii 1 47
How like you our choice, That you stand pensive, as half malcontent? iv 1 10
Scarce half made up, And that so lamely and unfashionable *Richard III.* i 1 22
In that you brook it ill, it makes him worse . i 3 3
He, poor soul, by your first order died, And that a winged Mercury did bear . ii 1 88
Mark'd you not How that the guilty kindred of the queen Look'd pale? ii 1 135
Oh, that deceit should steal such gentle shapes! . ii 2 27
Good news or bad, that thou comest in so bluntly? . iv 3 45
That their very labour Was to them as a painting . *Hen. VIII.* i 1 25
Which ever has and ever shall be growing, Till death, that winter, kill it . ii 2 179
Surrey durst better Have burnt that tongue than said so . iii 2 254
Mark but my fall, and that that ruin'd me . iii 2 439
'Tis very true: but that time offer'd sorrow; This, general joy . iv 1 6
Who's that that bears the sceptre? . iv 1 38
You saw The ceremony?—That I did . iv 1 60
That he is, For so I know he is, they know he is . v 1 43
But the fool will not: he there: that he: look you there *Troi. and Cres.* ii 1 91
Shall he be worshipp'd Of that we hold an idol more than he? . ii 3 199
Sweet queen, sweet queen! that's a sweet queen, i' faith . iii 1 77
The shaft confounds, Not that it wounds, But tickles still the sore . iii 1 129
Would he were knock'd i' the head! Who's that at door . iv 2 36
Why force you this?—Because that now it lies you on to speak *Coriol.* iii 2 52
Like a great sea-mark, standing every flaw, And saving those that eye thee! . v 3 75
Meanwhile I am possess'd of that is mine . *T. Andron.* i 1 408
That's my boy! thy father hath full oft . . . done the like . iv 1 110
Whilst that Lavinia 'tween her stumps doth hold The basin . v 2 183
And when that they are dead, Let me go grind their bones to powder . v 2 198
Tell me in sadness, who is that you love . *Rom. and Jul.* i 1 205
Only poor, That when she dies with beauty dies her store . i 1 222
I was your mother much upon these years That you are now a maid . i 3 73
That kind of fruit As maids call medlars, when they laugh alone . ii 1 35
That's my good son: but where hast thou been, then? . ii 3 47
You love your child so ill, That you run mad, seeing that she is well . iv 5 76
That nature, being sick of man's unkindness, Should yet be hungry! *T. of Athens* iv 3 176
That the whole life of Athens were in this! Thus would I eat it . iv 3 281
Where liest o' nights, Timon?—Under that's above me . iv 3 292
That you would have me seek into myself For that which is not in me *J. Cæsar* i 2 65
Thy honourable metal may be wrought From that it is disposed . i 2 314
You speak to Casca, and to such a man That is no fleering tell-tale . i 3 117
Crown him?—that;—And then, I grant, we put a sting in him . ii 1 15
Not that I loved Cæsar less, but that I loved Rome more . iii 2 22
When that the poor have cried, Cæsar hath wept . iii 2 96
My lord, I do not know that I did cry.—Yes, that thou didst . iv 3 298
Not that we love words better, as you do . v 1 28
That now Sweno, the Norways' king, craves composition . *Macbeth* i 2 58
They have made themselves, and that their fitness now Does unmake you . i 7 53
One did laugh in's sleep, and one cried 'Murder!' That they did wake each other . ii 2 24
Who did this more than bloody deed?—Those that Macbeth hath slain . ii 4 23
I will put that business in your bosoms, Whose execution takes your enemy off . iii 1 104
There cannot be That vulture in you, to devour so many . iv 3 74
Which was to my belief witness'd the rather, For that I saw . iv 3 185
I cannot but remember such things were, That were most precious to me iv 3 223
Naught that I am, Not for their own demerits, but for mine . iv 3 225
Now follows, that you know . *Hamlet* i 2 17
That it should come to this! But two months dead: nay, not so much i 2 137
As so 'tis put on me, And that in way of caution . i 3 95
Hath there been such a time—I'd fain know that—That I have positively said 'Tis so,' When it proved otherwise?—Not that I know . ii 2 153
Happy, in that we are not over-happy . ii 2 232
With this special observance, that you o'erstep not the modesty of nature iii 2 21
Players that I have seen play, and heard others praise, and that highly iii 2 33
If that his majesty would aught with us, We shall express our duty . iv 4 5
You have been talk'd of since your travel much, And that in Hamlet's hearing . iv 7 73
That we would do, We should do when we would . iv 7 119
As if it were Cain's jaw-bone, that did the first murder! . v 1 85
Since that respects of fortune are his love, I shall not be his wife . *Lear* i 1 251
Sith that both charge and danger Speak 'gainst so great a number . ii 4 242
Milk-liver'd man! That bear'st a check for blows, a head for wrongs . iv 2 51
Though that the queen on special cause is here, Her army is moved on iv 6 219

That. Hence; Lest that the infection of his fortune take Like hold on thee . . . *Lear* iv 6 237
Who's that which rings the bell?—Diablo, ho! The town will rise *Othello* ii 3 161
If you think fit, or that it may be done, Give me advantage . . iii 1 54
Though that her jesses were my dear heart-strings, I'ld whistle her off iii 3 261
If it be that, or any that was hers, It speaks against her with the other proofs . . . . iii 3 440
Till that a capable and wide revenge Swallow them up . . iii 3 459
You shall close prisoner rest, Till that the nature of your fault be known . . . . v 2 336
Sir, you and I must part, but that's not it . . *Ant. and Cleo.* i 3 87
I have not kept my square; but that to come Shall all be done by the rule . . . . ii 3 6
Thy demon, that's thy spirit which keeps thee, is Noble, courageous . ii 3 19
Till that the conquering wine hath steep'd our sense In soft and delicate Lethe . . . . ii 7 113
And threats the throat of that his officer That murder'd Pompey . iii 5 19
I follow'd that I blush to look upon: My very hairs do mutiny . . iii 11 12
Draw that thy honest sword, which thou hast worn Most useful for thy country . . . . iv 14 79
Let me rail so high, That the false housewife Fortune break her wheel iv 15 44
His voice was propertied As all the tuned spheres, and that to friends . v 2 84
You are too sure an augurer; That you did fear is done . . v 2 338
That such a crafty devil as is his mother Should yield the world this ass! a woman that Bears all down with her brain . *Cymbeline* ii 1 58
Thatch. Let us not hang like roping icicles Upon our houses' thatch *Hen. V.* iii 5 24
And thatch your poor thin roofs With burthens of the dead *T. of Athens* iv 3 144
Thatched. And flat meads thatch'd with stover . . *Tempest* iv 1 63
Why, then, your visor should be thatched . . . *Much Ado* ii 1 102
Worse than Jove in a thatched house! . . . *As Y. L. It* iii 3 11
Thaw. A man of continual dissolution and thaw . . *Mer. Wives* iii 5 119
I was duller than a great thaw . . . . . *Much Ado* ii 1 252
Where Phœbus' fire scarce thaws the icicles . . *Mer. of Venice* ii 1 5
Ere I should come by a fire to thaw me . . . *T. of Shrew* iv 1 9
Whose blush doth thaw the consecrated snow That lies on Dian's lap *T. of Athens* iv 3 386
O, that this too too solid flesh would melt, Thaw! . . . *Hamlet* i 2 130
Thawed. That I love—That I did love, for now my love is thaw'd *T. G. of Ver.* ii 4 200
That will be thaw'd from the true quality With that which melteth fools . . . . *J. Cæsar* iii 1 41
Thawing. His liberal eye doth give to every one, Thawing cold fear *Hen. V.* iv Prol 45
The. Be cunning in the working this . . . *Much Ado* ii 2 53
You need not fear, lady, the having any of these lords . *Mer. of Venice* i 2 109
And how, Audrey? am I the man yet? . . . *As Y. Like It* iii 3 3
God send you, sir, a speedy infirmity, for the better increasing your folly! . . . . *T. Night* i 5 85
O, the father, how he holds his countenance! . . . *1 Hen. IV.* ii 4 432
Such attribution should the Douglas have . . . . iv 1 3
Whose state so many had the managing, That they lost France *Hen. V.* Epil 11
Here is the Talbot: who would speak with him? . . *1 Hen. VI.* ii 2 37
There goes the Talbot, with his colours spread . . . iii 3 31
Who craves a parley with the Burgundy? . . . . iii 3 37
Brother, she is not worth what she doth cost The holding *Troi. and Cres.* ii 2 52
All is the fear and nothing is the love . . . *Macbeth* iv 2 12
Did these bones cost no more the breeding, but to play at loggats with 'em? . . . . *Hamlet* v 1 100
What can man's wisdom In the restoring his bereaved sense? *Lear* iv 4 9
And therefore I will attempt the doing it . . . *Othello* iii 4 22
The seeing these effects will be Both noisome and infectious *Cymbeline* i 5 25
Theatre. This wide and universal theatre Presents more woeful pageants than the scene Wherein we play in . . . *As Y. Like It* ii 7 137
Stand securely on their battlements, As in a theatre . *K. John* ii 1 375
As in a theatre, the eyes of men, After a well-graced actor leaves the stage, Are idly bent on him that enters next . *Richard II.* v 2 23
Clap him and hiss him, according as he pleased and displeased them, as they use to do the players in the theatre . . *J. Cæsar* i 2 263
That done, repair to Pompey's theatre . . . . . i 3 152
The censure of the which one must in your allowance o'erweigh a whole theatre of others . . . . . . *Hamlet* iii 2 31
Theban. I'll talk a word with this same learned Theban . *Lear* iii 4 162
Thebes. It was play'd When I from Thebes came last a conqueror *M. N. Dream* v 1 51
Thee. I have done thee worthy service; Told thee no lies, made thee no mistakings . . . . *Tempest* i 2 248
Thou wilt never get thee a husband, if thou be so shrewd *Much Ado* ii 1 20
This is thy office; Bear thee well in it and leave us alone . iii 1 13
I'll devise thee brave punishments for him . . . v 4 130
Thou'rt a tall fellow: hold thee that to drink . *T. of Shrew* iv 4 17
That defence thou hast, betake thee to't . . . *T. Night* iii 4 240
How agrees the devil and thee about thy soul, that thou soldest him? *1 Hen. IV.* i 2 127
There's nothing hid from me: In private will I talk with thee apart *1 Hen. VI.* i 2 69
Fear not, man, We are alone; here's none but thee and I . *2 Hen. VI.* i 2 69
Come, and get thee a sword, though made of a lath . . iv 2 1
Do not chafe thee, cousin . . . . . . *Troi. and Cres* iv 5 260
By thee beguiled, By cruel cruel thee quite overthrown! *Rom. and Jul.* iv 5 57
Art thou proud yet?—Ay, that I am not thee . . *T. of Athens* iv 3 277
I would not be thee, nuncle; thou hast pared thy wit o' both sides *Lear* i 4 204
Theft. His thefts were too open . . . . . *Mer. Wives* i 3 28
If Time be in debt and theft, and a sergeant in the way, Hath he not reason to turn back an hour in a day? . . *Com. of Errors* iv 2 61
When the suspicious head of theft is stopp'd . . *L. L. Lost* iv 3 336
I'll steal away.—There's honour in the theft . . *All's Well* ii 1 34
To steal cream indeed, for thy theft hath already made thee butter *1 Hen. IV.* iv 2 67
Am not I a prelate of the church?—Yes, as an outlaw in a castle keeps And useth it to patronage his theft . . . *1 Hen. VI.* iii 1 48
O, theft most base, That we have stol'n what we do fear to keep! *Troi. and Cres.* ii 2 92
We would give much, to use violent thefts, And rob in the behalf of charity . . . . v 3 21
'Twere a concealment Worse than a theft . . . *Coriolanus* i 9 22
There is boundless theft In limited professions . . *T. of Athens* iv 3 430
The laws, your curb and whip, in their rough power Have uncheck'd theft . . . . iv 3 447
There's warrant in that theft Which steals itself . . *Macbeth* ii 3 151
Theft. If he steal aught the whilst this play is playing, And 'scape detecting, I will pay the theft . . . . *Hamlet* iii 2 94
And yet I know not how conceit may rob The treasury of life, when life itself Yields to the theft . . . . . *Lear* iv 6 44
Euriphile, Whom for the theft I wedded, stole these children *Cymbeline* v 5 341
Their. Let's assist them, For our case is as theirs . . *Tempest* i 1 58
This love of theirs myself have often seen . . . *T. G. of Ver.* iii 1 24
When they weep and kneel, All their petitions are as freely theirs As they themselves would owe them . . . *Meas. for Meas.* i 4 82
God send every one their heart's desire! . . . . *Much Ado* iii 4 61
What is your intent?—The effect of my intent is to cross theirs *L. L. Lost* v 2 138
The peace of heaven is theirs that lift their swords In such a just and charitable war.—Well then, to work . . . *K. John* ii 1 35
But theirs is sweetened with the hope to have The present benefit *Richard II.* ii 3 13
Tears show their love, but want their remedies . . . iii 3 203
We have supplies to second our attempt: If they miscarry, theirs shall second them . . . . *2 Hen. IV.* iv 2 46
Contend in tears, Theirs for the earth's increase, mine for my sorrows *2 Hen. VI.* iii 2 385
Picardy Hath slain their governors . . . . . iv 1 89
I had rather be their servant in my way Than sway with them in theirs . . . . *Coriolanus* ii 1 220
Upon the part o' the people, in whose power We were elected theirs . iii 1 211
Where I, Even in theirs and in the commons' ears, Will vouch the truth of it . . . . v 6 4
As shall to thee blot out what wrongs were theirs And write in thee the figures of their love . . . . . *T. of Athens* v 1 156
Your servants ever Have theirs, themselves, and what is theirs, in compt, To make their audit at your highness' pleasure . *Macbeth* i 6 26
Them. I am the best of them that speak this speech . *Tempest* i 2 429
Your friends are well and have them much commended . *T. G. of Ver.* ii 4 123
Call at all the ale-houses, and bid those that are drunk get them to bed *Much Ado* iii 3 46
All their elves for fear Creep into acorn-cups and hide them there *M. N. Dream* ii 1 31
And they are coming after to warm them . . . *T. of Shrew* iv 1 5
For the which myself and them Bend their best studies . . *K. John* iv 2 50
They do prank them in authority, Against all noble sufferance *Coriolanus* iii 1 23
No, not with such friends That thought them sure of you . . v 3 8
Two such opposed kings encamp them still In man as well as herbs *Rom. and Jul.* ii 3 27
And all things change them to the contrary . . . . iv 5 90
But they did say their prayers, and address'd them Again to sleep *Macb.* ii 2 25
In quarter, and in terms like bride and groom Devesting them for bed *Othello* ii 3 181
Here's them in our country of Greece gets more with begging than we can do with working . . . . *Pericles* ii 1 68
Theme. Every day some sailor's wife, The masters of some merchant, and the merchant, Have just our theme of woe . . *Tempest* ii 1 6
Well, I am your theme: you have the start of me . . *Mer. Wives* v 5 170
To me she speaks; she moves me for her theme . *Com. of Errors* ii 2 183
At board he fed not for my urging it; Alone, it was the subject of my theme . . . . v 1 65
This weak and idle theme, No more yielding but a dream *M. N. Dream* v 1 434
Shall I to this lady?—Ay, that's the theme . . *T. Night* i 4 125
Part of his theme, but nothing Of his ill-ta'en suspicion . . *W. Tale* i 2 459
Your writing now Is colder than that theme . . . v 1 100
So blest a son, A son who is the theme of honour's tongue *1 Hen. IV.* i 1 81
In a theme so bloody-faced as this . . . *2 Hen. IV.* i 3 22
It is a theme as fluent as the sea . . . . *Hen. V.* iii 7 36
With your theme, I could O'ermount the lark . . *Hen. VIII.* ii 3 93
She is a theme of honour and renown . . . *Troi. and Cres.* ii 2 199
O deadly gall, and theme of all our scorns! . . . iv 5 30
Name her not now, sir; she's a deadly theme . . . iv 5 181
Do not give advantage To stubborn critics, apt, without a theme . v 2 131
And throw forth greater themes For insurrection's arguing *Coriolanus* i 1 224
Have hearts Inclinable to honour and advance The theme of our assembly ii 2 61
O, handle not the theme, to talk of hands . . *T. Andron.* iii 2 29
Here he comes, and I must ply my theme . . . v 2 80
Marry, that 'marry' is the very theme I came to talk of *Rom. and Jul.* i 3 63
As happy prologues to the swelling act Of the imperial theme *Macbeth* i 3 129
Whose common theme Is death of fathers . . . *Hamlet* i 2 103
I will fight with him upon this theme Until my eyelids will no longer wag.—O my son, what theme? . . . . . v 1 289
Their contestation Was theme for you, you were the word of war *A. and C.* ii 2 44
His gentle lady, Big of this gentleman our theme, deceased *Cymbeline* i 1 39
And will to ears and tongues Be theme and hearing ever . . iii 1 4
When a soldier was the theme, my name Was not far off . iii 3 59
Themselves. So soon asleep! I wish mine eyes Would, with themselves, shut up my thoughts . . . . . . *Tempest* ii 1 192
My charms I'll break, their senses I'll restore, And they shall be themselves . . . . v 1 32
My desires had instance and argument to commend themselves *M. Wives* ii 2 257
He teaches him to hick and to hack, which they'll do fast enough of themselves . . . . iv 1 69
Heaven doth with us as we with torches do, Not light them for themselves *Meas. for Meas.* i 1 34
So our decrees, Dead to infliction, to themselves are dead . i 3 28
All their petitions are as freely theirs As they themselves would owe them . . . . i 4 83
Thieves for their robbery have authority When judges steal themselves ii 2 177
Women are frail too.—Ay, as the glasses where they view themselves ii 4 125
If they were but a week married, they would talk themselves mad *M. Ado* ii 1 369
O heavens themselves!—Come, sir, I pray you, go . . *T. Night* iii 4 391
Valour and pride excel themselves in Hector . . *Troi. and Cres.* iv 5 79
Then thou wast not Out three years old . . . *Tempest* i 2 40
Then tell me If this might be a brother . . . . i 2 117
I, not remembering how I cried out then, Will cry it o'er again . i 2 133
Come unto these yellow sands, And then take hands . . i 2 377
Thou shalt be as free As mountain winds: but then exactly do All points of my command . . . . i 2 499
Who then? his spirit?—Neither.—What then?—Nothing *T. G. of Ver.* iii 1 195
You will not bail me, then, sir?—Then, Pompey, nor now *Meas. for Meas.* iii 2 85
First he did praise my beauty, then my speech . *Com. of Errors* ii 2 15
He is then a giant to an ape; but then is an ape a doctor to such a man *Much Ado* v 1 205
Well then, it now appears you need my help: Go to, then *Mer. of Venice* i 3 115
Talk with respect and swear but now and then . . . ii 2 200
There then; how then? what then? Let me see wherein *As Y. Like It* ii 7 83

Then. Then entertain him, then forswear him; now weep for him, then spit at him . . . . *As Y. Like It* iii 2 436
Loose now and then A scatter'd smile, and that I'll live upon . iii 5 103
Then call me husband: but in such a 'then' I write a 'never' *All's W.* iii 2 62
And more, more strong, then lesser is my fear, I shall indue you with *K. John* iv 2 42
A fool, a rogue, that now and then goes to the wars . . *Hen. V.* iii 6 71
Sometime the flood prevails, and then the wind; Now one the better, then another best . . . . 3 *Hen. VI.* ii 5 9
First, to do greetings to thy royal person; And then to crave a league of amity; And lastly, to confirm that amity . . . . iii 3 53
And then?—And then he sends you word . . . *Richard III.* iii 2 9
Our then dictator, Whom with all praise I point at, saw him fight *Coriol.* ii 2 93
And now and then an ample tear trill'd down Her delicate cheek *Lear* iv 3 14
But if I give my wife a handkerchief,— What then?—Why, then, 'tis hers . . . . *Othello* iv 1 11
Then does he say, he lent me Some shipping unrestored *Ant. and Cleo.* iii 6 26
Thence. By foul play, as thou say'st, were we heaved thence . *Tempest* i 2 62
The ministers for the purpose hurried thence Me and thy crying self . i 2 131
Thence I have follow'd it, Or it hath drawn me rather . . i 2 393
I will be thankful To my happy messenger from thence . *T. G. of Ver.* ii 4 53
Did not I in rage depart from thence?—In verity you did *Com. of Errors* iv 4 79
Come to the Centaur; fetch our stuff from thence . . . iv 4 153
Rushing in their houses, bearing thence Rings, jewels, any thing . v 1 143
We met him thitherward; for thence we came . . *All's Well* iii 2 55
Thence it came That she . . . was in mine eye The dust that did offend it v 3 52
By law and process of great nature thence Freed and enfranchised *W. T.* ii 2 60
Who would be thence that has the benefit of access? . . . . v 2 118
From hence to prison back again; From thence unto the place of execution . . . . 2 *Hen. VI.* ii 3 6
'Tis not the land I care for, wert thou thence . . . . iii 2 359
Swearing both They prosper best of all when I am thence . 3 *Hen. VI.* ii 5 18
And chides the sea that sunders him from thence, Saying, he'll lade it dry . . . . iii 2 138
When she comes! When is she thence? . . . . *Troi. and Cres.* i 1 31
In the great hand of God I stand; and thence Against the undivulged pretence I fight Of treasonous malice . . . *Macbeth* ii 3 136
Thence it is, That I to your assistance do make love . . iii 1 123
To feed were best at home; From thence the sauce to meat is ceremony iii 4 36
Theoric. Had the whole theoric of war in the knot of his scarf *All's Well* iv 3 162
The art and practic part of life Must be the mistress to this theoric *Hen. V.* i 1 52
Unless the bookish theoric, Wherein the toged consuls can propose *Othello* i 1 24
There. Foot it featly here and there . . . . . *Tempest* i 2 380
The rarest that e'er came there.—Bate, I beseech you, widow Dido . ii 1 99
What a blow was there given! . . . . ii 1 180
There, take the paper: see it be return'd . . *T. G. of Ver.* i 2 46
How now! what letter are you reading there? . . . . i 3 51
For what I will, I will, and there an end . . . . . i 3 65
That letter hath she deliver'd, and there an end . . . ii 1 168
I know Anne's mind,—that's neither here nor there . . *Mer. Wives* i 4 112
Let there be some more test made of my metal . . *Meas. for Meas.* i 1 49
Ay, touch him; there's the vein . . . . . . ii 2 70
There spake my brother; there my father's grave Did utter forth a voice iii 1 86
For, in conclusion, he did beat me there . . *Com. of Errors* ii 1 74
There is something in the wind, that we cannot get in . . iii 1 69
That goldsmith there, were he not pack'd with her, Could witness it . v 1 219
And in a dark and dankish vault at home There left me . . . v 1 248
If he be not in love with some woman, there is no believing old signs *Much Ado* iii 2 41
There will I leave you too, for here comes one in haste . . . v 2 95
There's an eye Wounds like a leaden sword . . . *L. L. Lost* v 2 480
Ghosts, wandering here and there, Troop home to churchyards *M. N. D.* iii 2 381
Why, there, there, there, there! a diamond gone! . *Mer. of Venice* iii 1 87
Thou art thy father's daughter; there's enough . *As Y. Like It* i 3 60
There, there, Hortensio, will you any wife? . . *T. of Shrew* i 1 56
The fouler fortune mine, and there an end . . . . . v 2 98
Why, there's a wench! Come on, and kiss me . . . . v 2 180
Why, there 'tis; so say I too.—Not to be helped . . *All's Well* ii 3 17
Well, I must be patient; there is no fettering of authority . . ii 3 251
There's for you.—Why, there's for thee, and there, and there *T. Night* iv 1 27
How now there!—This news is mortal . . . . *W. Tale* iii 2 148
There's a good grandam.—Good my mother, peace! . . *K. John* ii 1 163
My guilt be on my head, and there an end . . . *Richard II.* v 1 69
You cannot live long.—Why, there is it . . . 1 *Hen. IV.* iii 3 15
There is no quailing now, Because the king is certainly possess'd Of all iv 1 39
Let time shape, and there an end . . . . 2 *Hen. IV.* iii 2 358
There is my hand. You shall be as a father to my youth . . v 2 117
There all is marr'd; there lies a cooling card . . 1 *Hen. VI.* v 3 83
Where are you there? Sir John! nay, fear not, man . 2 *Hen. VI.* i 2 68
There's an army gathered together in Smithfield . . . iv 6 13
I had rather kill two enemies.—Why, there thou hast it *Richard III.* iv 2 73
I am glad they are going, For, sure, there's no converting of 'em *Hen. VIII.* i 3 43
There was the weight that pull'd me down . . . . iii 2 407
I will leave all as I found it, and there an end . . *Troi. and Cres.* i 1 91
Look how he looks! there's a countenance! . . . . . i 2 217
Look you there: there's no jesting; there's laying on, take't off who will, as they say: there be hacks! . . . . . . i 2 223
The fool will not: he there: that he: look you there . . ii 1 91
Guard thee well; For I'll not kill thee there, nor there, nor there . iv 5 254
Here, there, and every where, he leaves and takes . . . v 5 26
There was it: For which my sinews shall be stretch'd upon him *Coriol.* v 6 44
We cannot be here and there too . . . *Rom. and Jul.* i 5 15
Thy Juliet is alive . . . ; There art thou happy . . . . iii 3 137
We'll have some half a dozen friends, And there an end . . . iii 4 28
So that my speed to Mantua there was stay'd . . . . . v 2 12
I would have had thee there, and here again, Ere I can tell thee what thou shouldst do there . . . . *J. Cæsar* ii 4 4
We cut him off, If at Philippi we do face him there . . . iv 3 211
When the brains were out, The man would die, And there an end *Macb.* iii 4 80
Come in, without there!—What's your grace's will? . . . iv 1 135
Who's there?—Nay, answer me: stand, and unfold yourself . *Hamlet* i 1 1
Here and there Shark'd up a list of lawless resolutes . . . . i 1 97
You are stay'd for. There; my blessing with thee! . . . i 3 57
There put on him What forgeries you please . . . . ii 1 19
Why, there thou say'st: and the more pity . . . . . v 1 29
It was not brought me, my lord; there's the cunning of it . *Lear* i 2 63
There could I have him now,—and there,—and there again, and there . iii 4 62
There she shook The holy water from her heavenly eyes . . . iv 3 31
There I found 'em, there I smelt 'em out . . . . . . iv 6 104
There. O, ho, are you there with me? No eyes in your head? . . *Lear* iv 6 148
Please you, draw near. Louder the music there! . . . . iv 7 25
Mine eyes do itch; Doth that bode weeping?—'Tis neither here nor there . . . . *Othello* iv 3 59
There stand I in much peril: No, he must die . . . . . v 1 21
Speak there!—The man from Sicyon,—is there such an one? *Ant. and Cleo.* i 2 117
There's a great spirit gone! . . . . i 2 126
You and I have loved, but there's not it; That you know well . . i 3 88
The gods confound thee! dost thou hold there still?—Should I lie? . ii 5 92
Some wine, within there, and our viands! . . . . . . iii 11 73
There's all I'll do for you . . . . . . *Cymbeline* i 5 87
To the mountains; there secure us. To the king's party there's no going iv 4 9
There's the end. Has hurt me, and there's the end on't . *T. Night* v 1 202
There's the point. With him, we may.—Yea, marry, there's the point 2 *Hen. IV.* i 3 18
There's the point.—Which do not be entreated to . . *Ant. and Cleo.* ii 6 31
There's the question. That's false.—Ay, there's the question 2 *Hen. VI.* iv 2 149
How that might change his nature, there's the question . *J. Cæsar* ii 1 13
There then; how then? what then? Let me see . . *As Y. Like It* ii 7 83
Why, there then: thus I do escape the sorrow Of Antony's death *Ant. and Cleo.* iv 14 94
Thereabout. Five or six thousand horse, . . . or thereabouts *All's Well* iv 3 171
Do you know, and dare not? Be intelligent to me: 'tis thereabouts *W. Tale* i 2 378
O for a fine thief, of the age of two and twenty or thereabouts! 1 *Hen. IV.* iii 3 212
Thereabout of it especially, where he speaks of Priam's slaughter *Hamlet* ii 2 468
Ay, are you thereabouts? Why, then, good night indeed *Ant. and Cleo.* iii 10 29
Thereafter. How a score of ewes now?—Thereafter as they be 2 *Hen. IV.* iii 2 56
Thereat. Not for Bohemia, nor the pomp that may Be thereat glean'd *W. Tale* iv 4 500
Ah, that this sight should make so deep a wound, And yet detested life not shrink thereat! . . . . *T. Andron.* iii 1 248
Who, thereat enraged, Flew on him . . . . . . *Lear* iv 2 75
Thereby. I gave him gentle looks, thereby to find That which thyself hast now disclosed to me . . . . . . *T. G. of Ver.* iii 1 31
Thereby hangs a tale *Mer. Wives* i 4; *As Y. Like It* ii 7; *T. of Shrew* iv 1
Be absolute for death; either death or life Shall thereby be the sweeter *Meas. for Meas.* iii 1 6
Are we not all in love?—Nothing so sure; and thereby all forsworn *L. L. Lost* iv 3 283
Meaning thereby that grapes were made to eat and lips to open *As Y. Like It* v 1 38
That thou thereby Mayst smile at this . . . . *T. Night* iv 1 60
And thereby for sealing The injury of tongues in courts and kingdoms *W. Tale* i 2 337
The better act of purposes mistook Is to mistake again; though indirect, Yet indirection thereby grows direct . . . *K. John* iii 1 276
In regard of me He shortens four years of my son's exile: But little vantage shall I reap thereby . . . . . *Richard II.* i 3 218
To counterfeit dying, when a man thereby liveth, is to be no counterfeit 1 *Hen. IV.* v 4 119
It shall be with such strict and severe covenants As little shall the Frenchmen gain thereby . . . . . . 1 *Hen. VI.* v 4 115
O God, what mischiefs work the wicked ones, Heaping confusion on their own heads thereby! . . . . . . 2 *Hen. VI.* ii 1 187
Quitting thee thereby of ten thousand shames . . . . . iii 2 218
For thereby is England mained, and fain to go with a staff . . iv 2 171
To carve out dials quaintly, point by point, Thereby to see the minutes how they run . . . . 3 *Hen. VI.* ii 5 25
Thereby he may gather The ground of your ill-will, and so remove it *Richard III.* i 3 68
To save the Romans, thereby to destroy The Volsces . . *Coriolanus* v 3 133
That he thereby may give a likely guess . . . *T. Andron.* iii 3 207
The eagle suffers little birds to sing, And is not careful what they mean thereby . . . . iv 4 84
Thereby shall we shadow The numbers of our host . . . *Macbeth* v 4 5
Thereby hangs a tail.—Whereby hangs a tale, sir? . . *Othello* iii 1 8
Therefore wast thou Deservedly confined into this rock . . *Tempest* i 2 360
Therefore my son i' the ooze is bedded . . . . . iii 3 100
Therefore take heed, As Hymen's lamps shall light you . . iv 1 22
He is in haste; therefore, I pray you, go . . *T. G. of Ver.* i 3 89
Now therefore would I have thee to my tutor . . . . iii 1 84
A horse cannot fetch, but only carry; therefore is she better than a jade iii 1 276
Therefore it must with circumstance be spoken . . . . iii 2 36
An if I could, what should I get therefore? . . . *M. N. Dream* iii 2 78
Bootless 'tis to tell you we will go: Therefore we meet not now 1 *Hen. IV.* i 1 30
I know not your breeding.—Why then, lament therefore . 2 *Hen. IV.* v 3 113
We are therefore provided: will her ladyship behold? 2 *Hen. VI.* i 4 3
Hath my sword therefore broke through London gates, that you should leave me? . . . . iv 8 24
Therefore mistrust me not.—Where is thy power, then? . *Richard III.* iv 4 479
Oft have you—often have you thanks therefore . . *Troi. and Cres.* iii 3 20
Dogs that are as often beat for barking As therefore kept to do so *Coriolanus* ii 3 225
Therein. I prattle Something too wildly and my father's precepts I therein do forget . . . . *Tempest* iii 1 59
Since thou lovest, love still and thrive therein . *T. G. of Ver.* i 1 9
Have you the tongues?—My youthful travel therein made me happy . iv 1 34
You are therein in the right: but to the point. . *Meas. for Meas.* ii 1 100
Therein do men from children nothing differ . . . *Much Ado* v 1 33
Which therein works a miracle in nature . . . *Mer. of Venice* iii 2 90
I, delivering you, am satisfied And therein do account myself well paid iv 1 417
Who cries out on pride, That can therein tax any private party? *As Y. Like It* ii 7 71
I am a simple maid, and therein wealthiest . . . *All's Well* ii 3 72
Nor are you therein, by my life, deceived . . . . *T. Night* v 1 269
A servant grafted in my serious trust And therein negligent . *W. Tale* i 2 247
And therein fasting, hast thou made me gaunt . . . *Richard II.* ii 1 81
And, therein laid,—there lies Two kinsmen digg'd their graves with weeping eyes . . . . iii 3 168
Work, work your thoughts, and therein see a siege . . *Hen. V.* iii Prol. 25
Take some order in the town, Placing therein some expert officers 1 *Hen. VI.* iii 2 127
And then deny her aiding hand therein . . . . *Richard III.* i 3 96
He is my son; yea, and therein my shame . . . . . ii 2 29
Nor he deliver'd His gracious pleasure any way therein . . . iii 4 18
An ill husband, and am glad To have you therein my companion *Hen. VIII.* iii 2 143
Nothing doubting your present assistance therein . . *T. of Athens* iii 1 21

Therein. Therein, ye gods, you make the weak most strong; Therein, ye gods, you tyrants do defeat . . . . *J. Cæsar* i 3 91
On such regards of safety and allowance As therein are set down *Hamlet* ii 2 80
Comforting therein, that when old robes are worn out, there are members to make new . . . . *Ant. and Cleo.* i 2 170
You shall not find, Though you be therein curious, the least cause . iii 2 35
Thereof. Only, in lieu thereof, dispatch me hence . *T. G. of Ver.* ii 7 88
She brews good ale.—And thereof comes the proverb . . iii 1 305
Bid my wife Disburse the sum on the receipt thereof . *Com. of Errors* iv 1 38
And thereof comes that the wenches say 'God damn me' . iv 3 53
And thereof came it that the man was mad . . . . . v 1 68
Thereof the raging fire of fever bred . . . . v 1 75
The contempts thereof are as touching me . . . *L. L. Lost* i 1 191
And, in lieu thereof, impose on thee nothing but this . . iii 1 130
All the power thereof it doth apply To prove, by wit, worth in simplicity . . . . v 2 77
If you know aught which does behove my knowledge Thereof to be inform'd, imprison't not . . . . . . *W. Tale* i 2 396
Were I crown'd the most imperial monarch, Thereof most worthy . iv 4 384
What is thy news? Let King Cophetua know the truth thereof *2 Hen. IV.* v 3 106
The hope thereof makes Clifford mourn in steel . . . *3 Hen. VI.* i 1 58
Lest in revenge thereof, sith God is just, He be as miserably slain as I . i 3 41
But, God he knows, thy share thereof [of beauty] is small . . i 4 129
The bruit thereof will bring you many friends . . . . . . iv 7 64
As little joy may you suppose in me, That I enjoy, being the queen thereof.—A little joy enjoys the queen thereof . . *Richard III.* i 3 154
And I repent My part thereof that I have done to her . . iv 4 308
Meaning indeed his house, Which, by the sign thereof, was termed so . iii 5 79
The respects thereof are nice and trivial, All circumstances well considered . . . . iii 7 175
God he knows, and you may partly see, How far I am from the desire thereof . . . . iii 7 236
The gain of my attempt The least of you shall share his part thereof . v 3 268
Thereon. Of promise-breach Thereon dependent . . *Meas. for Meas.* v 1 411
In that each of you have forsworn his book, Can you still dream and pore and thereon look? . . . . *L. L. Lost* iv 3 298
Condemn'd by the king's own mouth, thereon His execution sworn *W. T.* i 2 445
Thereon I pawn my credit and mine honour . . . *3 Hen. VI.* iii 3 116
A pair of bleeding hearts; thereon engrave Edward and York *Rich. III.* iv 4 272
If he love her not And be not from his reason fall'n thereon . *Hamlet* ii 2 165
Which I'll guard them from, If thereon you rely . . *Ant. and Cleo.* v 2 133
Thereto. My heart accords thereto, And yet a thousand times it answers 'no' . . . . *T. G. of Ver.* i 3 90
Adding thereto moreover That he would wed me, or else die my lover *L. L. Lost* v 2 446
I undertook it, Vanquish'd thereto by the fair grace and speech *All's W.* v 3 133
His life I gave him and did thereto add My love . . *T. Night* v 1 83
You are certainly a gentleman, thereto Clerk-like experienced *W. Tale* i 2 391
The justice of your hearts will thereto add ''Tis pity she's not honest' ii 1 67
If my reason Will thereto be obedient, I have reason . . . iv 4 494
Any thing in or out of our demands, And we'll consign thereto *Hen. V.* v 2 90
Whom I with pain have woo'd and won thereto . . *1 Hen. VI.* v 3 138
I think 'twill serve, if he Can thereto frame his spirit *Coriolanus* iii 2 97
Great hurt and mischief; thereto witness may My surname . . iv 5 73
Add thereto a tiger's chaudron, For the ingredients . . *Macbeth* iv 1 33
Thereto prick'd on by a most emulate pride . . . . *Hamlet* i 1 83
And thereto add such reasons of your own As may compact it more *Lear* i 4 361
If she be black, and thereto have a wit, She'll find a white *Othello* ii 1 133
As thereto sworn by your command, . . . I tell you this *Ant. and Cleo.* v 2 198
Yourself So out of thought, and thereto so o'ergrown . *Cymbeline* iv 4 33
Thereunto. With all their honourable points of ignorance Pertaining thereunto . . . . *Hen. VIII.* i 3 27
I shall, first asking your pardon thereunto, recount the occasion *Hamlet* iv 7 46
There's none so foul and foolish thereunto, But does foul pranks *Othello* ii 1 142
Thereupon. And thereupon I drew my sword on you . *Com. of Errors* v 1 262
I was ta'en for him, and he for me, And thereupon these ERRORS are arose . . . . v 1 388
Only foul words; and thereupon I will kiss thee . . . *Much Ado* v 2 50
I am fair that shoot, And thereupon thou speak'st the fairest shoot *L. L. L.* iv 1 12
And thereupon I drink unto your grace . . . *2 Hen. IV.* v 2 68
And thereupon give me your daughter.—Take her, fair son . *Hen. V.* v 2 375
And thereupon he sends you this good news . . . *Richard III.* iii 2 48
I dare thereupon pawn the moiety of my estate to your ring *Cymbeline* i 4 118
Therewith angry, when it next came there, Took it in snuff *1 Hen. IV.* i 3 40
And bid her dry her weeping eyes therewith . . . *Richard III.* iv 4 278
What if I do obey? How may the duke be therewith satisfied? *Othello* i 2 88
Therewithal. Give her that ring and therewithal This letter *T. G. of Ver.* iv 4 90
My poor mistress, moved therewithal, Wept bitterly . . . iv 4 175
Thy slanders I forgive; and therewithal Remit thy other forfeits *Meas. for Meas.* v 1 525
And therewithal took measure of my body . . *Com. of Errors* iv 3 9
And therewithal to win me, if you please, Without the which I am not to be won . . . . *L. L. Lost* v 2 858
And therewithal Came to this vault to die, and lie with Juliet *R. and J.* v 3 289
But of that to-morrow, When therewithal we shall have cause of state *Macbeth* iii 1 34
To receive from his age, not alone the imperfections of long-engraffed condition, but therewithal the unruly waywardness . . *Lear* i 1 301
The fairest that I have look'd upon.—And therewithal the best *Cymbeline* ii 4 33
Thersites. When rank Thersites opes his mastic jaws, We shall hear music, wit, and oracle . . . . *Troi. and Cres.* i 3 73
And sets Thersites, A slave . . . , To match us in comparisons with dirt i 3 192
Mistress Thersites!—Thou shouldst strike him . . . ii 1 39
Who's there? Thersites! Good Thersites, come in and rail . . ii 3 25
Thersites is a fool to serve such a fool, and Patroclus is a fool positive . ii 3 69
Achilles hath inveigled his fool from him.—Who, Thersites?—He . ii 3 101
Ask me not what I would be, if I were not Thersites . . . v 1 71
Thersites' body is as good as Ajax', When neither are alive . *Cymbeline* iv 2 252
These. If any be Trinculo's legs, these are they . . . *Tempest* ii 2 109
These be fine things, an if they be not sprites . . . . ii 2 120
If these be true spies which I wear in my head, here's a goodly sight . v 1 259
Where have you been these two days loitering? . *T. G. of Ver.* iv 4 48
With these nails I'll pluck out these false eyes . *Com. of Errors* iv 4 107
These be the stops that hinder study quite . . . *L. L. Lost* i 1 70
These betray nice wenches, that would be betrayed without these . iii 1 23
For men's sake, the authors of these women . . . . . iv 3 359
What fools these mortals be! . . . . . . *M. N. Dream* iii 2 115
Where are these lads? where are these hearts? . . . . iv 2 25
Nor the lady's, which is nice, nor the lover's, which is all these *As Y. Like It* iv 1 15
For these two hours, Rosalind, I will leave thee *As Y. Like It* iv 1 180
These set kind of fools . . . . *T. Night* i 5 95
Speed thee well! There lie, and there thy character: there these *W. T.* iii 3 47
There shall not at your father's house these seven years Be born another such . . . . iv 4 589
I must leave you within these two hours . . . . . *1 Hen. IV.* ii 3 39
These fellows of infinite tongue . . . . *Hen. V.* v 2 163
Within these forty hours Surrey durst better Have burnt that tongue *Hen. VIII.* iii 2 253
These are the whole contents . . . . iv 2 154
Under these hard conditions as this time Is like to lay upon us *J. Cæsar* i 2 174
What he is, augmented, Would run to these and these extremities . ii 1 31
These many, then, shall die; their names are prick'd . . iv 1 1
These indeed seem, For they are actions that a man might play *Hamlet* i 2 83
These tedious old fools! . . . . ii 2 223
These kind of knaves I know, which in this plainness Harbour more craft . . . . *Lear* ii 2 107
Where virtue is, these are more virtuous . . . . . *Othello* iii 3 186
Are letters brought, the tenour these . . . . *Pericles* iii Gower 24
Theseus. 'Twas Ariadne passioning For Theseus' perjury *T. G. of Ver.* iv 4 173
Happy be Theseus, our renowned duke! . . . . *M. N. Dream* i 1 20
Your buskin'd mistress and your warrior love To Theseus must be wedded ii 1 72
Knowing I know thy love to Theseus . . . . . . ii 1 76
Intend you stay?—Perchance till after Theseus' wedding-day . ii 1 139
A play Intended for great Theseus' nuptial-day . . . . iii 2 12
To-morrow midnight solemnly Dance in Duke Theseus' house triumphantly . . . . iv 1 94
There shall the pairs of faithful lovers be Wedded with Theseus . . iv 1 97
'Tis strange, my Theseus, that these lovers speak of . . . v 1 1
Thessalian. Crook-knee'd, and dew-lapp'd like Thessalian bulls . iv 1 127
Thessaly. In Crete, in Sparta, nor in Thessaly . . . . iv 1 131
The boar of Thessaly Was never so emboss'd . . *Ant. and Cleo.* iv 13 2
Thetis. But let the ruffian Boreas once enrage The gentle Thetis *T. and C.* i 3 39
Let this be granted, and Achilles' horse Makes many Thetis' sons . i 3 212
How now, Ulysses!—Now, great Thetis' son!—What are you reading? . iii 3 94
We'll to our ship: Away, my Thetis! . . . *Ant. and Cleo.* iii 7 61
At her birth, Thetis, being proud, swallow'd some part o' the earth: Therefore the earth, fearing to be o'erflowed, Hath Thetis' birth-child on the heavens bestow'd . . . . *Pericles* iv 4 41
Thews. Care I for the limb, the thewes, the stature, bulk, and big assemblance of a man! Give me the spirit . . . *2 Hen. IV.* iii 2 276
For Romans now Have thews and limbs like to their ancestors *J. Cæsar* i 3 81
For nature, crescent, does not grow alone In thews and bulk *Hamlet* i 3 12
They do not love that do not show their love . . *T. G. of Ver.* i 2 31
They say that Love hath not an eye at all . . . . . ii 4 96
They can be meek that have no other cause . . *Com. of Errors* ii 1 33
Happy are they that hear their detractions and can put them to mending . . . . *Much Ado* ii 3 237
For to strange sores strangely they strain the cure . . . iv 1 254
They of those marches, gracious sovereign, Shall be a wall sufficient *Hen. V.* i 2 140
What stays had I but they? and they are gone . *Richard III.* ii 2 76
They say, The city is well stored.—Hang 'em! They say! *Coriolanus* i 1 194
They of Rome are enter'd in our counsels And know how we proceed . i 2 2
Which, thou dost confess, Were fit for thee to use as they to claim . i 2 83
Poor birds they are not set for . . . . . . *Macbeth* iv 2 36
And they in France of the best rank and station . . . *Hamlet* i 3 73
Thick. Thou shalt be pinch'd As thick as honeycomb . . *Tempest* i 2 329
Look how the floor of heaven Is thick inlaid with patines of bright gold *Mer. of Venice* v 1 59
Like a fountain troubled, Muddy, ill-seeming, thick . *T. of Shrew* v 2 143
O Lord, sir! Thick, thick, spare not me . . . . *All's Well* ii 2 47
Thoughts that would thick my blood . . . . . *W. Tale* i 2 171
Speaking thick, which nature made his blemish . . *2 Hen. IV.* ii 3 24
His wit's as thick as Tewksbury mustard . . . . . ii 4 262
So forlorn, that his dimensions to any thick sight were invincible . iii 2 336
Let it shine, then.—Thine's too thick to shine . . . . iv 3 64
This shoulder was ordain'd so thick to heave . . *3 Hen. VI.* v 7 23
Though perils did Abound, as thick as thought could make 'em *Hen. VIII.* iii 2 195
To-morrow blossoms, And bears his blushing honours thick upon him . iii 2 354
The dews of heaven fall thick in blessings on her! . . . iv 2 133
I'll about, And drive away the vulgar from the streets: So do you too, where you perceive them thick . . . . . . *J. Cæsar* i 1 76
Get higher on that hill; My sight was ever thick . . . . v 3 21
As thick as hail Came post with post . . . . . *Macbeth* i 3 97
Make thick my blood; Stop up the access and passage to remorse! . i 5 44
Come, thick night, And pall thee in the dunnest smoke of hell . i 5 51
Make the gruel thick and slab: Add thereto a tiger's chaudron . iv 1 32
Their eyes purging thick amber and plum-tree gum . . *Hamlet* ii 2 200
The people muddied, Thick and unwholesome in their thoughts . iv 5 82
Let her paint an inch thick, to this favour she must come . . v 1 214
All-shaking thunder, Smite flat the thick rotundity o' the world! *Lear* iii 2 7
Twenty several messengers: Why do you send so thick? *Ant. and Cleo.* i 5 63
In their thick breaths, Rank of gross diet, shall we be enclouded . v 2 211
Dissolve, thick cloud, and rain; that I may say, The gods themselves do weep! . . . . v 2 302
He furnaces The thick sighs from him . . . . *Cymbeline* i 6 67
Say, and speak thick; Love's counseller should fill the bores of hearing iii 2 58
Then began A stop i' the chaser, a retire, anon A rout, confusion thick . v 3 41
It nips me unto listening, and thick slumber Hangs upon mine eyes *Per.* v 1 235
Thick-coming fancies, That keep her from her rest . . *Macbeth* v 3 38
Thicken. Light thickens; and the crow Makes wing to the rooky wood iii 2 50
This may help to thicken other proofs That do demonstrate thinly *Oth.* iii 3 430
Thy lustre thickens, When he shines by . . . *Ant. and Cleo.* ii 3 27
Thicker. Your eyeglass Is thicker than a cuckold's horn . . *W. Tale* i 2 269
My heart beats thicker than a feverous pulse . . *Troi. and Cres.* iii 2 38
What if this cursed hand Were thicker than itself with brother's blood? *Hamlet* iii 3 44
Thickest. Which is the greatest lady, the highest?—The thickest and the tallest.—The thickest and the tallest! it is so . *L. L. Lost* iv 1 47
Are not you the chief woman? you are the thickest here . . iv 1 51
He bore him in the thickest troop As doth a lion in a herd of neat *3 Hen. VI.* ii 1 13
Thicket. The thicket is beset; he cannot 'scape . *T. G. of Ver.* v 3 11
The dogs did yell: put L to sore, then sorel jumps from thicket *L. L. L.* iv 2 60
Warily I stole into a neighbour thicket by, And overheard . . v 2 94
Leave off to wonder why I drew you hither, Into this chiefest thicket *3 Hen. VI.* iv 5 3
The hart Achilles Keeps thicket . . . . . *Troi. and Cres.* ii 3 270
Thick-eyed. To thick-eyed musing and cursed melancholy *1 Hen. IV.* ii 3 49

Thick-grown. Under this thick-grown brake we'll shroud ourselves 3 *Hen. VI.* iii 1 1
Thick-lipped. Come on, you thick-lipp'd slave . . . . *T. Andron.* iv 2 175
Thick-lips. What a full fortune does the thick-lips owe! . . . *Othello* i 1 66
Thick-pleached. Walking in a thick-pleached alley in mine orchard *M. Ado* i 2 10
Thick-ribbed. To reside In thrilling region of thick-ribbed ice *M. for M.* iii 1 123
Thick-skin. What wouldst thou have, boor? what, thick-skin? *M. W.* iv 5 2
The shallowest thick-skin of that barren sort . . . . *M. N. Dream* iii 2 13
Thief. I will rather trust . . . a thief to walk my ambling gelding *M. W.* ii 2 319
The jury, passing on the prisoner's life, May in the sworn twelve have a thief or two Guiltier than him they try . . . . *Meas. for Meas.* ii 1 20
He hath offended the law: and, sir, we take him to be a thief too, sir . iii 2 17
Every true man's apparel fits your thief: if it be too little for your thief, your true man thinks it big enough; if it be too big for your thief, your thief thinks it little enough . . . . iv 2 47
That Angelo is an adulterous thief, An hypocrite . . . . . v 1 40
What simple thief brags of his own attaint? . . . *Com. of Errors* iii 2 16
Nay, he's a thief too: have you not heard men say, That Time comes stealing on? . . . . iv 2 59
If you meet a thief, you may suspect him, by virtue of your office *Much Ado* iii 3 53
If we know him to be a thief, shall we not lay hands on him? . . iii 3 57
The most peaceable way for you, if you do take a thief, is to let him show himself what he is and steal out of your company . . . iii 3 62
But seest thou not what a deformed thief this fashion is? . . iii 3 131; 140
Has been a vile thief this seven year; a' goes up and down like a gentleman . . . . iii 3 134
Whither away so fast? A true man or a thief that gallops so? *L. L. Lost* iv 3 187
You juggler! you canker-blossom! You thief of love! . *M. N. Dream* iii 2 283
The thief gone with so much, and so much to find the thief *Mer. of Ven.* iii 1 97
Who doth he [Time] gallop withal?—With a thief to the gallows *As Y. Like It* iii 2 345
Nor dare I say 'tis mine, and yet it is; But, like a timorous thief, most fain would steal What law does vouch mine own . . *All's Well* ii 5 86
Come, night; end, day! For with the dark, poor thief, I'll steal away . iii 2 132
Notable pirate! thou salt-water thief! . . . . . *T. Night* v 1 72
Antonio never yet was thief or pirate . . . . v 1 77
Like to the Egyptian thief at point of death, Kill what I love . . v 1 121
This thief, this traitor, Bolingbroke . . . . *Richard II.* iii 2 47
Do not thou, when thou art king, hang a thief. . . . 1 *Hen. IV.* i 2 70
Nay, rather let me have it, as you are a false thief . . . . . ii 1 103
I am accursed to rob in that thief's company . . . . . . ii 2 10
Shall the son of England prove a thief and take purses? . . . . ii 4 452
Lie still, ye thief, and hear the lady sing in Welsh . . . . iii 1 238
O for a fine thief, of the age of two and twenty or thereabouts! . . iii 3 212
Welcome, my little tiny thief, and welcome indeed too . 2 *Hen. IV.* v 3 60
Foul felonious thief that fleeced poor passengers . . 2 *Hen. VI.* iii 1 129
And, like a thief, to come to rob my grounds . . . . . iv 10 36
The thief doth fear each bush an officer . . . . 3 *Hen. VI.* v 6 12
A very little thief of occasion will rob you of a great deal of patience *Coriolanus* ii 1 32
As good a trick as ever hangman served thief . . . *T. of Athens* ii 2 100
Thou'lt go, strong thief [gold], When gouty keepers of thee cannot stand iv 3 45
The sun's a thief, and with his great attraction Robs the vast sea . iv 3 439
The moon's an arrant thief, And her pale fire she snatches from the sun iv 3 440
The sea's a thief, whose liquid surge resolves The moon into salt tears . iv 3 442
The earth's a thief, That feeds and breeds by a composture stolen From general excrement: each thing's a thief . . . . iv 3 443
Like a giant's robe Upon a dwarfish thief . . . . *Macbeth* v 2 22
Pinion him like a thief, bring him before us . . . . *Lear* iii 7 23
Look with thine ears: see how yond justice rails upon yond simple thief iv 6 156
Change places; and, handy-dandy, which is the justice, which is the thief? . . . . iv 6 158
Down with him, thief! . . . . *Othello* i 2 57
O thou foul thief, where hast thou stow'd my daughter? . . . . i 2 62
The robb'd that smiles steals something from the thief . . . . i 3 208
You have been a great thief by sea.—And you by land . *Ant. and Cleo.* ii 6 96
A cunning thief, or a that way accomplished courtier, would hazard the winning . . . . *Cymbeline* i 4 100
'Tis gold Which makes the true man kill'd and saves the thief; Nay, sometime hangs both thief and true man . . . . ii 3 76
Thou art a robber, A law-breaker, a villain: yield thee, thief. . . iv 2 75
Thou injurious thief, Hear but my name, and tremble . . . . iv 2 86
Ay me, most credulous fool, Egregious murderer, thief, any thing! . v 5 211
That caused a lesser villain than myself, A sacrilegious thief, to do't . v 5 220
A curse upon him, die he like a thief, That robs thee of thy goodness! *Pericles* iv 6 121
Thief-stolen. Had I been thief-stol'n, As my two brothers, happy! *Cymb.* i 6 5
Thievery. It's an honourable kind of thievery . . . *T. G. of Ver.* iv 1 40
Injurious time now with a robber's haste Crams his rich thievery up, he knows not how . . . . *Troi. and Cres.* iv 4 45
I'll example you with thievery: The sun's a thief . *T. of Athens* iv 3 438
Thieves. The trumpery in my house, go bring it hither, For stale to catch these thieves . . . . *Tempest* iv 1 187
Take heed, have open eye, for thieves do foot by night . *Mer. Wives* ii 1 126
What know the laws That thieves do pass on thieves? . *Meas. for Meas.* ii 1 23
Thieves for their robbery have authority When judges steal themselves ii 2 176
When you shall please to play the thieves for wives, I'll watch as long for you then . . . . *Mer. of Venice* ii 6 23
Beauty provoketh thieves sooner than gold . . . *As Y. Like It* i 3 112
We are beset with thieves; Rescue thy mistress . . *T. of Shrew* iii 2 238
'Gainst knaves and thieves men shut their gate . . *T. Night* v 1 404
Then thieves and robbers range abroad unseen . . *Richard II.* iii 2 39
Thieves are not judged but they are by to hear . . . . . iv 1 123
Let not us that are squires of the night's body be called thieves of the day's beauty . . . . 1 *Hen. IV.* i 2 28
Thou shalt have the hanging of the thieves and so become a rare hangman . . . . i 2 75
A plague upon it when thieves cannot be true one to another! . . ii 2 29
The thieves have bound the true men. Now could thou and I rob the thieves . . . . ii 2 98
The thieves are all scatter'd and possess'd with fear . . . . ii 2 112
Falstaff and the rest of the thieves are at the door: shall we be merry? ii 4 99
Do you think I keep thieves in my house? . . . . . . iii 3 63
And pretty traps to catch the petty thieves . . . . *Hen. V.* i 2 177
So desperate thieves, all hopeless of their lives, Breathe out invectives 'gainst the officers . . . . 3 *Hen. VI.* i 4 42
So triumph thieves upon their conquer'd booty . . . . . i 4 63
But, thieves, unworthy of a thing so stol'n, That in their country did them that disgrace, We fear to warrant in our native place! *T. and C.* ii 2 94
Thieves. Place thieves And give them title, knee, and approbation With senators on the bench . . . . *T. of Athens* iv 3 35
Now, thieves.—Soldiers, not thieves.—Both too; and women's sons . iv 3 415
We are not thieves, but men that much do want . . . . . iv 3 418
Yet thanks I must you con That you are thieves profess'd, that you work not In holier shapes . . . . iv 3 429
Rascal thieves, Here's gold. Go, suck the subtle blood o' the grape . iv 3 431
Cut throats: All that you meet are thieves . . . . . . iv 3 449
Nothing can you steal, But thieves do lose it . . . . . . iv 3 451
I leave you To the protection of the prosperous gods, As thieves to keepers . . . . v 1 187
They have dealt with me like thieves of mercy . . . *Hamlet* iv 6 21
Knaves, thieves, and treachers, by spherical predominance . . *Lear* i 2 133
Thieves! thieves! Look to your house, your daughter, and your bags! *Othello* i 1 79
Kill men i' the dark!—Where be these bloody thieves?—How silent is this town! . . . . v 1 63
If our eyes had authority, here they might take two thieves kissing *Ant. and Cleo.* ii 6 100
I do nothing doubt you have store of thieves . . . *Cymbeline* i 4 107
These roguing thieves serve the great pirate Valdes . . *Pericles* iv 1 97
Thievish. Enforce A thievish living on the common road . *As Y. Like It* ii 3 33
The pilot's glass Hath told the thievish minutes how they pass *All's Well* ii 1 169
Or walk in thievish ways; or bid me lurk Where serpents are *Rom. and Jul.* iv 1 79
Thigh. Steal from the humble-bees, And for night-tapers crop their waxen thighs . . . . *M. N. Dream* iii 1 172
A gallant curtle-axe upon my thigh, A boar-spear in my hand *As Y. L. It* i 3 119
Taurus! That's sides and heart.—No, sir; it is legs and thighs *T. Night* i 3 149
I saw young Harry, with his beaver on, His cuisses on his thighs 1 *Hen. IV.* iv 1 105
With a new wound in your thigh, come you along with me . . . v 4 131
I'll take it upon my death, I gave him this wound in the thigh . . v 4 155
Our thighs pack'd with wax, our mouths with honey . 2 *Hen. IV.* iv 5 77
His thighs with darts Were almost like a sharp-quill'd porpentine 2 *Hen. VI.* iii 1 362
Seven hurts i' the body.—One i' the neck, and two i' the thigh *Coriolanus* ii 1 167
By her fine foot, straight leg, and quivering thigh . *Rom. and Jul.* ii 1 19
Giving myself a voluntary wound Here, in the thigh . . . *J. Cæsar* ii 1 301
Then laid his leg Over my thigh, and sigh'd, and kiss'd . . . *Othello* iii 3 425
I have a weapon; A better never did itself sustain Upon a soldier's thigh . . . . v 2 261
This is his hand; His foot Mercurial; his Martial thigh . . *Cymbeline* iv 2 310
Thimble. Thou thread, thou thimble, Thou yard! . . . *T. of Shrew* iv 3 108
That I'll prove upon thee, though thy little finger be armed in a thimble . . . . iv 3 149
Their thimbles into armed gauntlets change, Their needles to lances *K. John* v 2 156
Thin. Were all spirits and Are melted into air, into thin air . *Tempest* iv 1 150
You would say so, master, if your garments were thin . *Com. of Errors* iii 1 70
If frosts and fasts, hard lodging and thin weeds, Nip not the gaudy blossoms of your love . . . . *L. L. Lost* v 2 811
Having no other reason But that his beard grew thin and hungerly *T. of Shrew* iii 2 177
At so slender warning, You are like to have a thin and slender pittance iv 4 61
My face so thin That in mine ear I durst not stick a rose . *K. John* i 1 141
We will not line his thin bestained cloak With our pure honours . iv 3 24
White-beards have arm'd their thin and hairless scalps Against thy majesty . . . . *Richard II.* iii 2 112
For thin drink doth so over-cool their blood . . 2 *Hen. IV.* iv 3 98
The first humane principle I would teach them should be, to forswear thin potations . . . . iv 3 134
So thin that life looks through and will break out . . . . iv 4 120
You thin man in a censer, I will have you as soundly swinged for this . v 4 20
Come, you thin thing; come, you rascal . . . . v 4 34
His cold thin drink out of his leather bottle . . . 3 *Hen. VI.* ii 5 48
And gave himself, All thin and naked, to the numb cold night *Rich. III.* ii 1 117
They are too thin and bare to hide offences . . . . *Hen. VIII.* v 3 125
Vain fantasy, Which is as thin of substance as the air . *Rom. and Jul.* i 4 99
Thatch your poor thin roofs With burthens of the dead . *T. of Athens* iv 3 144
It doth posset And curd, like eager droppings into milk, The thin and wholesome blood . . . . *Hamlet* i 5 70
To watch—poor perdu!—With this thin helm . . . . *Lear* iv 7 36
Without more wider and more overt test Than these thin habits . *Othello* i 3 108
Thin-belly. Your arms crossed on your thin-belly doublet . *L. L. Lost* iii 1 19
Thin-faced. A coxcomb and a knave, a thin-faced knave! . . *T. Night* v 1 213
Thine. Wipe thou thine eyes; have comfort . . . . *Tempest* i 2 25
The very minute bids thee ope thine ear; Obey and be attentive . . i 2 37
The setting of thine eye and cheek proclaim A matter from thee . . ii 1 229
Sit then and talk with her; she is thine own . . . . . . iv 1 32
Do that good mischief which may make this island Thine own for ever iv 1 217
Mine eyes, even sociable to the show of thine, Fall fellowly drops . v 1 63
I claim her not, and therefore she is thine . . . *T. G. of Ver.* v 4 135
Grant one boon that I shall ask of you.—I grant it, for thine own. . v 4 151
Thine own true knight, By day or night . . . . *Mer. Wives* ii 1 15
It is thine host, thine Ephesian calls.—How now, mine host! . . iv 5 19
Thyself and thy belongings Are not thine own so proper as to waste *Meas. for Meas.* i 1 31
I am pale at mine heart to see thine eyes so red . . . . . iv 3 158
That never words were music to thine ear . . . *Com. of Errors* ii 2 116
Come, I will fasten on this sleeve of thine . . . . . . ii 2 175
Here, sweet, put up this: 'twill be thine another day . *L. L. Lost* iv 1 109
I am not yet so low But that my nails can reach unto thine eyes *M. N. Dream* iii 2 298
What means that hand upon that breast of thine? . . . *K. John* iii 1 21
Contaminated, base And misbegotten blood I spill of thine . 1 *Hen. VI.* iv 6 22
I cry thee mercy: There is my purse to cure that blow of thine *Richard III.* iv 4 516
So I love and honour thee and thine . . . . . . *T. Andron.* i 1 49
Full well, Andronicus, Agree these deeds with that proud brag of thine i 1 306
Thrice to thine and thrice to mine And thrice again . . . *Macbeth* i 3 35
Death of thy soul! those linen cheeks of thine Are counsellors to fear . v 3 16
Thine evermore, most dear lady, whilst this machine is to him *Hamlet* ii 2 123
To thee and thine hereditary ever Remain this ample third . . . *Lear* i 1 81
Thing. An acre of barren ground, long heath, brown furze, any thing *Tempest* i 1 71
Of any thing the image tell me that Hath kept with thy remembrance . i 2 43
Thou liest, malignant thing! . . . . i 2 257
For one thing she did They would not take her life. . . . . . i 2 266
Dull thing, I say so . . . . i 2 285

Thing. Took pains to make thee speak, taught thee each hour One thing or other *Tempest* i 2 355
Wouldst gabble like A thing most brutish i 2 357
I might call him A thing divine, for nothing natural I ever saw so noble i 2 418
What wert thou, if the King of Naples heard thee?—A single thing, as I am now i 2 432
If the ill spirit have so fair a house, Good things will strive to dwell with't i 2 459
Here is every thing advantageous to life.—True; save means to live ii 1 49
I' the commonwealth I would by contraries Execute all things ii 1 148
All things in common nature should produce Without sweat or endeavour ii 1 159
These be fine things, an if they be not sprites ii 2 121
I know thou darest, But this thing dare not iii 2 63
Some subtilties o' the isle, that will not let you Believe things certain v 1 125
I will requite you with as good a thing v 1 169
Till when, be cheerful And think of each thing well v 1 251
What things are these, my lord Antonio? Will money buy 'em? v 1 264
This is a strange thing as e'er I look'd on v 1 289
You may say what sights you see; I see things too. *T. G. of Ver.* i 2 139
Sweet ornament that decks a thing divine! ii 1 4
Are all these things perceived in me?—They are all perceived without ye ii 1 34
Should I have wish'd a thing, it had been he ii 4 82
Like a waxen image 'gainst a fire, Bears no impression of the thing it was ii 4 202
Love is like a child, That longs for every thing that he can come by iii 1 125
For good things should be praised iii 1 353
Of another thing she may, and that cannot I help iii 1 359
Falsehood, cowardice, and poor descent, Three things that women highly hold in hate iii 2 33
Have you any thing to take to?—Nothing but my fortune iv 1 42
She excels each mortal thing Upon the dull earth dwelling iv 2 51
You would have them always play but one thing?—I would always have one play but one thing iv 2 71
'Tis a foul thing when a cur cannot keep himself in all companies iv 4 11
To be a dog indeed, to be, as it were, a dog at all things iv 4 14
'Twas I did the thing you wot of iv 4 30
I will do a greater thing than that, upon your request *Mer. Wives* i 1 248
They are very ill-favoured rough things i 1 312
The boy never need to understand any thing ii 2 133
I shall discover a thing to you ii 2 190
Believe me, there's no such thing in me iii 3 72
Shall it be so?—Any thing iii 3 249
And tells me 'tis a thing impossible I should love thee but as a property iii 4 9
What a thing should I have been when I had been swelled! iii 5 17
Polecats! there are fairer things than polecats, sure iv 1 29
Come, to the forge with it then; shape it: I would not have things cool iv 2 240
I had other things to have spoken with her too iv 5 41
Follow me: I'll tell you strange things of this knave v 1 29
Follow. Strange things in hand, Master Brook! v 1 32
But so sound as things that are hollow *Meas. for Meas.* i 2 56
I hold you as a thing ensky'd and sainted i 4 34
'Tis one thing to be tempted, Escalus, Another thing to fall ii 1 17
Were past cure of the thing you wot of, unless they kept very good diet ii 1 115
His face is the worst thing about him ii 1 163
Your bum is the greatest thing about you ii 1 229
Dost thou desire her foully for those things That make her good? ii 2 174
Like a good thing, being often read, Grown fear'd and tedious ii 4 8
For I can speak Against the thing I say ii 4 60
I something do excuse the thing I hate, For his advantage ii 4 119
If I do lose thee, I do lose a thing That none but fools would keep iii 1 7
Death is a fearful thing.—And shamed life a hateful iii 1 116
I have spirit to do any thing that appears not foul in the truth of my spirit iii 1 213
What a ruthless thing is this in him! iii 2 121
Rather rejoicing to see another merry, than merry at any thing iii 2 250
To draw with idle spiders' strings Most ponderous and substantial things! iii 2 290
If any thing fall to you upon this, more than thanks and good fortune iv 2 190
This is a thing that Angelo knows not iv 2 214
Put not yourself into amazement how these things should be iv 2 220
If you have any thing to say to me, come to my ward iv 3 65
I would commune with you of such things That want no ear but yours iv 3 108
Did you such a thing?—Yes, marry, did I iv 3 181
Such a dependency of thing on thing, As e'er I heard in madness v 1 62
My brother had but justice, In that he did the thing for which he died v 1 454
I commend you to your own content.—He that commends me to mine own content Commends me to the thing I cannot get *Com. of Errors* i 2 34
Learn to jest in good time: there's a time for all things ii 2 66
Sure ones then.—Nay, not sure, in a thing falsing.—Certain ones then ii 2 95
Not on a band, but on a stronger thing; A chain, a chain! iv 2 50
Bearing thence Rings, jewels, any thing his rage did like v 1 144
Tell him there is measure in every thing *Much Ado* ii 1 75
We must follow the leaders.—In every good thing ii 1 158
Friendship is constant in all other things Save in the office and affairs of love ii 1 182
Will you look to those things I told you of? ii 1 351
A time too brief, too, to have all things answer my mind ii 1 376
Only to despite them, I will endeavour any thing ii 2 32
One foot in sea and one on shore, To one thing constant never ii 3 67
She is exceeding wise.—In every thing but in loving Benedick ii 3 168
If I see any thing to-night why I should not marry her to-morrow iii 2 126
Lay it to your heart: it is the only thing for a qualm iii 4 75
Are these things spoken, or do I but dream?—Sir, they are spoken, and these things are true iv 1 67
These things, come thus to light, Smother her spirits up iv 1 112
Why, doth not every earthly thing Cry shame upon her? iv 1 122
Is not that strange?—As strange as the thing I know not iv 1 271
Come, bid me do any thing for thee.—Kill Claudio iv 1 290
One that hath two gowns and every thing handsome about him iv 2 88
He swore a thing to me on Monday night, which he forswore on Tuesday v 1 168
What a pretty thing man is when he goes in his doublet and hose and leaves off his wit! v 1 202
They have verified unjust things v 1 223
Just and virtuous In any thing that I do know by her v 1 312
Well, I am glad that all things sort so well v 4 7
For man is a giddy thing, and this is my conclusion v 4 109
Things hid and barr'd, you mean, from common sense? *L. L. Lost* i 1 57
I will swear to study so, To know the thing I am forbid to know i 1 60
But like of each thing that in season grows i 1 107

Thing. To have what it would It doth forget to do the thing it should, And when it hath the thing it hunteth most, 'Tis won as towns with fire, so won, so lost *L. L. Lost* i 1 145
Sadness is one and the self-same thing, dear imp i 2 5
Do one thing for me that I shall entreat iii 1 154
You'll not be perjured, 'tis a hateful thing iv 3 157
When shall you see me write a thing in rhyme? Or groan for love? iv 3 181
To things of sale a seller's praise belongs, She passes praise iv 3 240
O, 'tis the sun that maketh all things shine iv 3 246
Shall I tell you a thing?—We attend v 1 152
He hath drawn my picture in his letter!—Any thing like? v 2 39
Fleeter than arrows, bullets, wind, thought, swifter things v 2 261
Fair gentle sweet, Your wit makes wise things foolish v 2 374
To your huge store Wise things seem foolish and rich things but poor v 2 378
When great things labouring perish in their birth v 2 521
So quick bright things come to confusion *M. N. Dream* i 1 149
Things base and vile, holding no quantity, Love can transpose i 1 232
The next thing then she waking looks upon, Be it on lion, bear, or wolf ii 1 179
Anoint his eyes; But do it when the next thing he espies May be the lady ii 1 262
Wake when some vile thing is near ii 2 34
Things growing are not ripe until their season ii 2 117
A surfeit of the sweetest things The deepest loathing to the stomach brings ii 2 137
There are things in this comedy of Pyramus and Thisby that will never please iii 1 9
To bring in—God shield us!—a lion among ladies, is a most dreadful thing iii 1 32
I am no such thing; I am a man as other men are iii 1 45
There is two hard things; that is, to bring the moonlight into a chamber iii 1 49
Then, there is another thing: we must have a wall iii 1 63
Their fears thus strong, Made senseless things begin to do them wrong iii 2 28
Some sleeves, some hats, from yielders all things catch iii 2 30
Those things do best please me That befal preposterously iii 2 120
How can these things in me seem scorn to you? iii 2 126
Vile thing, let loose, Or I will shake thee from me like a serpent! iii 2 260
And all things shall be peace iii 2 377
How came these things to pass? O, how mine eyes do loathe his visage now! iv 1 83
These things seem small and undistinguishable, Like far-off mountains iv 1 192
I see these things with parted eye, When every thing seems double iv 1 194
A paramour is, God bless us, a thing of naught iv 2 14
I will tell you every thing, right as it fell out iv 2 31
As imagination bodies forth The forms of things unknown v 1 15
Never anything can be amiss, When simpleness and duty tender it v 1 82
Gentle sweet, you shall see no such thing v 1 87
Wonder on, till truth make all things plain v 1 129
Such a thing bechanced would make me sad *Mer. of Venice* i 1 38
Is that any thing now? i 1 112
I will do any thing, Nerissa, ere I'll be married to a sponge i 2 107
A thing not in his power to bring to pass i 3 93
These things being bought and orderly bestow'd, Return in haste ii 2 179
All things that are, Are with more spirit chased than enjoy'd ii 6 12
I am enjoin'd by oath to observe three things ii 9 9
Therefore no more of it: hear other things iii 4 23
Howsoe'er thou speak'st, 'mong other things I shall digest it iii 5 94
Do all men kill the things they do not love?—Hates any man the thing he would not kill? iv 1 66
You may as well do any thing most hard, As seek to soften that iv 1 78
You, merchant, have you any thing to say?—But little iv 1 263
Two things provided more, that, for this favour, He presently become a Christian; The other, that he do record a gift iv 1 386
Grant me two things, I pray you, Not to deny me, and to pardon me iv 1 423
How many things by season season'd are To their right praise! v 1 107
A thing stuck on with oaths upon your finger v 1 168
Wanted the modesty To urge the thing held as a ceremony v 1 206
I'll not deny him any thing I have v 1 227
We will answer all things faithfully v 1 299
I'll fear no other thing So sore as keeping safe Nerissa's ring v 1 306
What make you here?—Nothing: I am not taught to make any thing *As Y. Like It* i 1 33
It is a thing of his own search and altogether against my will i 1 141
I confess me much guilty, to deny so fair and excellent ladies any thing i 2 197
Books in the running brooks, Sermons in stones, and good in every thing ii 1 17
That little cares for buying any thing ii 4 90
Assuredly the thing is to be sold ii 4 96
If this uncouth forest yield any thing savage, I will either be food for it or bring it for food to thee ii 6 7
Thou shalt not die for lack of a dinner, if there live any thing in this desert ii 6 18
I thought that all things had been savage here ii 7 107
Sans teeth, sans eyes, sans taste, sans every thing ii 7 166
All things that thou dost call thine Worth seizure do we seize iii 1 9
And every thing about you demonstrating a careless desolation iii 2 399
For every passion something and for no passion truly any thing iii 2 433
What 'poetical' is: is it honest in deed and word? is it a true thing? iii 3 18
Eyes, that are the frail'st and softest things iii 5 12
He'll make a proper man: the best thing in him Is his complexion iii 5 115
Can one desire too much of a good thing? iv 1 124
The horn, the horn, the lusty horn Is not a thing to laugh to scorn iv 2 19
Since my conversion So sweetly tastes, being the thing I am iv 3 138
There was never any thing so sudden but the fight of two rams v 2 33
How bitter a thing it is to look into happiness through another man's eyes! v 2 48
Believe then, if you please, that I can do strange things v 2 65
Though to have her and death were both one thing v 4 17
An ill-favoured thing, sir, but mine own v 4 60
Is not this a rare fellow, my lord? he's as good at any thing and yet a fool v 4 110
Then is there mirth in heaven, When earthly things made even Atone together v 4 115
That reason wonder may diminish, How thus we met, and these things finish v 4 146
I smell sweet savours and I feel soft things *T. of Shrew* Ind. 2 73
To labour and effect one thing specially i 1 120
One thing more rests, that thyself execute i 1 250
Supposing it a thing impossible i 2 123
O this learning, what a thing it is!—O this woodcock, what an ass it is! i 2 160
Ay, when the special thing is well obtain'd, That is, her love ii 1 129
And where two raging fires meet together They do consume the thing that feeds their fury ii 1 134

Thing. Sunday comes apace: We will have rings and things and fine array . . . . *T. of Shrew* ii 1 325
Pewter and brass and all things that belong To house or housekeeping . ii 1 357
And all things answerable to this portion . . . . . . ii 1 361
My field, my barn, My horse, my ox, my ass, my any thing . iii 2 234
The carpets laid, and every thing in order?—All ready . . iv 1 53
With many things of worthy memory, which now shall die in oblivion . iv 1 84
Now, my spruce companions, is all ready, and all things neat? . . iv 1 117
Then both, or one, or any thing thou wilt . . . . . iv 3 29
Caps and golden rings, With ruffs and cuffs and fardingales and things . iv 3 56
Thou hast faced many things.—I have.—Face not me . . . iv 3 123
So bedazzled with the sun That every thing I look on seemeth green . iv 5 47
'Tis [virginity] a withered pear: will you any thing with it? . *All's Well* i 1 178
To join like likes and kiss like native things . . . . i 1 238
Whose apprehensive senses All but new things disdain . . . i 2 61
It is not so with Him that all things knows As 'tis with us . . . ii 1 152
I see things may serve long, but not serve ever . . . . ii 2 60
To make modern and familiar, things supernatural and causeless . . ii 3 3
From lowest place when virtuous things proceed, The place is dignified ii 3 132
Truly, she's very well indeed, but for two things.—What two things? . ii 4 9
In every thing I wait upon his will . . . . ii 4 55
These things shall be done, sir . . . . ii 5 16
All these engines of lust are not the things they go under . . . iii 5 21
Never trust my judgement in any thing . . . . . . iii 6 35
I will tell you a thing, but you shall let it dwell darkly with you . . iv 3 13
As we are ourselves, what things are we!—Merely our own traitors . iv 3 24
Nor believe he can have every thing in him by wearing his apparel neatly . . . . iv 3 167
I could endure any thing before but a cat, and now he's a cat to me . iv 3 266
He has every thing that an honest man should not have . . . iv 3 290
Simply the thing I am Shall make me live . . . . . iv 3 369
Our rash faults Make trivial price of serious things we have . . . v 3 61
Am I or that or this for what he'll utter, That will speak any thing? . v 3 209
Things which would derive me ill will to speak of . . . . v 3 265
'Tis but the shadow of a wife you see, The name and not the thing . v 3 309
Wherefore are these things hid? . . . . *T. Night* i 3 133
Any thing that's mended is but patched . . . . . . i 5 52
Take those things for bird-bolts that you deem cannon-bullets . . i 5 100
And one thing more, that you be never so hardy to come again in his affairs . . . . ii 2 9
If you prized my lady's favour at any thing more than contempt . . ii 3 131
The devil a puritan that he is, or any thing constantly, but a time-pleaser . . . . ii 3 160
Their business might be every thing and their intent every where . . ii 4 79
I will smile; I will do every thing that thou wilt have me . . . ii 5 195
By the roses of the spring, By maidhood, honour, truth, and every thing iii 1 162
You have not seen such a thing as 'tis. I can hardly forbear hurling things at him . . . . iii 2 86
Let us satisfy our eyes With the memorials and the things of fame . iii 3 23
Why, every thing adheres together . . . . iii 4 86
You are idle shallow things: I am not of your element . . . . iii 4 137
A little thing would make me tell them how much I lack of a man . iii 4 332
Grant me another request.—Any thing . . . . . . v 1 5
And grew a twenty years removed thing While one would wink . . v 1 92
These things further thought on . . . . v 1 324
A foolish thing was but a toy, For the rain it raineth every day . . v 1 400
Cram's with praise, and make's As fat as tame things . . *W. Tale* i 2 92
Almost as like as eggs; women say so, That will say any thing . . i 2 131
Thou dost make possible things not so held . . . . . i 2 139
I have trusted thee, Camillo, With all the nearest things to my heart . i 2 236
If ever fearful To do a thing, where I the issue doubted . . . i 2 259
He has discover'd my design, and I Remain a pinch'd thing . . . ii 1 51
O thou thing! Which I'll not call a creature of thy place . . . ii 1 82
Any thing, my lord, That my ability may undergo . . . : any thing possible . . . . ii 3 163
Poor thing, condemn'd to loss! . . . . ii 3 192
Do not repent these things, for they are heavier Than all thy woes can stir . . . . iii 2 209
If such thing be, thy mother Appear'd to me last night . . . . iii 3 17
They were warmer that got this than the poor thing is here . . . iii 3 77
If thou'lt see a thing to talk on when thou art dead and rotten, come hither . . . . iii 3 82
Thou mettest with things dying, I with things new-born . . . . iii 3 117
So shall I do To the freshest things now reigning . . . . . iv 1 13
'Tis a sickness denying thee any thing . . . . iv 2 3
My money and apparel ta'en from me, and these detestable things put upon me . . . . iv 3 66
I shall there have money, or any thing I want . . . . . . iv 3 87
For I cannot be Mine own, nor any thing to any, if I be not thine . . iv 4 44
Strangle such thoughts as these with any thing That you behold . . iv 4 47
Her face o' fire With labour and the thing she took to quench it . . iv 4 61
So she does any thing; though I report it, That should be silent . . iv 4 177
A very pleasant thing indeed and sung lamentably . . . . . iv 4 190
Let's first see moe ballads; we'll buy the other things anon . . . iv 4 278
Things known betwixt us three, I'll write you down . . . . . iv 4 571
The gods do this year connive at us, and we may do any thing extempore . . . . iv 4 692
Show those things you found about her, those secret things . . . iv 4 713
Any thing that is fitting to be known, discover . . . . . iv 4 741
You might have spoken a thousand things that would Have done the time more benefit and graced Your kindness better . . . . . v 1 21
What might I have been, Might I a son and daughter now have look'd on, Such goodly things as you! . . . . v 1 178
At your request My father will grant precious things as trifles . . v 1 222
That any thing he sees, which moves his liking, I can with ease translate it to my will . . . . *K. John* ii 1 512
Having no external thing to lose But the word 'maid' . . . . ii 1 571
This day, all things begun come to ill end! . . . . . . iii 1 94
But thou hast sworn against religion, By what thou swear'st against the thing thou swear'st . . . . iii 1 281
I had a thing to say, But I will fit it with some better time . . . iii 3 25
Feeling what small things are boisterous there . . . . . iv 1 95
All things sweet to that you should use to do me wrong Deny their office . iv 1 118
Things sweet to taste prove in digestion sour . . . . *Richard II.* i 3 236
Writ in remembrance more than things long past . . . . . ii 1 14
Sorrow's eye, glazed with blinding tears, Divides one thing entire to many objects . . . . ii 2 17
With false sorrow's eye, Which for things true weeps things imaginary . ii 2 27
All is uneven, And every thing is left at six and seven . . . . ii 2 122
Things past redress are now with me past care . . . . . ii 3 171
Thing. Darest thou, thou little better thing than earth, Divine his downfal? . . . . *Richard II.* iii 4 78
Our scene is alter'd from a serious thing . . . . v 3 79
The better sort, As thoughts of things divine, are intermix'd With scruples . . . . v 5 12
Provide us all things necessary and meet me to-morrow night 1 *Hen. IV.* i 2 216
The sovereign'st thing on earth Was parmaceti for an inward bruise . i 3 57
I'll break thy little finger, Harry, An if thou wilt not tell me all things true . . . . ii 3 91
I would I were a weaver; I could sing psalms or any thing . . ii 4 146
There is a thing, Harry, which thou hast often heard of and it is known to many in our own land by the name of pitch . . . . . . ii 4 453
Wherein villanous, but in all things? wherein worthy, but in nothing? ii 4 505
To answer thee, or any man, For any thing he shall be charged withal . ii 4 566
I may, for some things true, wherein my youth Hath faulty wander'd . iii 2 26
Go, you thing, go.—Say, what thing? what thing?—What thing! why, a thing to thank God on.—I am no thing to thank God on, I would thou shouldst know it . . . . iii 3 131
I am good friends with my father and may do any thing.—Rob me the exchequer the first thing thou doest . . . . iii 3 204
These things indeed you have articulate . . . . v 1 72
He that but fears the thing he would not know Hath by instinct knowledge from others' eyes That what he fear'd is chanced . 2 *Hen. IV.* i 1 85
As the thing that's heavy in itself Upon enforcement flies with greatest speed . . . . i 1 119
Is not able to invent any thing that tends to laughter . . . . i 2 9
My master is deaf.—I am sure he is, to the hearing of any thing good . i 2 81
If it be a hot day, and I brandish any thing but a bottle, I would I might never spit white again . . . . i 2 236
It was alway yet the trick of our English nation, if they have a good thing, to make it too common . . . . i 2 241
A good wit will make use of any thing: I will turn diseases to commodity . . . . i 2 277
Past and to come seems best; things present worst . . . . i 3 108
I warrant you, he's an infinitive thing upon my score . . . . ii 1 26
Shall I tell thee one thing, Poins?—Yes, faith; and let it be an excellent good thing . . . . ii 2 37
And those two things, I confess, I cannot help . . . . . ii 2 73
For in every thing the purpose must weigh with the folly . . . ii 2 195
A man may prophesy, With a near aim, of the main chance of things . iii 1 83
Such things become the hatch and brood of time . . . . . iii 1 86
Are these things then necessities? Then let us meet them like necessities . . . . iii 1 92
I was called any thing; and I would have done any thing indeed too . iii 2 19
To be accommodated; which is an excellent thing . . . . . iii 2 88
Things that are mouldy lack use . . . . iii 2 119
She has nobody to do any thing about her when I am gone . . . iii 2 246
What thing, in honour, had my father lost, That need to be revived and breathed in me? . . . . iv 1 113
Every thing set off That might so much as think you enemies . . . iv 1 145
There is a thing within my bosom tells me . . . . . . iv 1 183
Sudden sorrow Serves to say thus, 'some good thing comes to-morrow' iv 2 84
When every thing is ended, then you come . . . . . . iv 3 30
Every thing lies level to our wish: Only, we want a little personal strength . . . . iv 4 7
See, sons, what things you are! How quickly nature falls into revolt! iv 5 65
It is a wonderful thing to see the semblable coherence of his men's spirits . . . . v 1 72
May be As things acquainted and familiar to us . . . . . v 2 139
Welcome: if thou wantest any thing, and wilt not call, beshrew thy heart . . . . v 3 59
Dead?—As nail in door: the things I speak are just . . . . v 3 127
Thou atomy, thou!—Come, you thin thing; come, you rascal . . v 4 34
Presume not that I am the thing I was . . . . v 5 60
Where, for any thing I know, Falstaff shall die of a sweat . . . Epil. 31
Therefore we must needs admit the means How things are perfected *Hen. V.* i 1 69
Some things of weight That task our thoughts . . . . . . i 2 5
Many things, having full reference To one consent, may work contrariously . . . . i 2 205
All things thought upon That may with reasonable swiftness add More feathers to our wings . . . . i 2 305
I cannot tell: things must be as they may . . . . . . ii 1 22
Any thing that may not misbecome The mighty sender . . . . ii 4 118
They will steal any thing, and call it purchase . . . . . iii 2 45
It is not a thing to rejoice at . . . . iii 6 55
Thou makest use of any thing . . . . iii 7 70
Yet sit and see, Minding true things by what their mockeries be . iv Prol. 53
There is some soul of goodness in things evil . . . . . iv 1 4
How can they charitably dispose of any thing, when blood is their argument? . . . . iv 1 149
The day, my friends, and all things stay for me . . . . . iv 1 325
Such outward things dwell not in my desires . . . . . . iv 3 27
All things are ready, if our minds be so . . . . iv 3 71
So would this be, if he durst steal any thing adventurously . . . iv 4 78
For there is figures in all things . . . . iv 7 35
Admit the excuse Of time, of numbers, and due course of things . v Prol. 4
There is occasions and causes why and wherefore in all things . . v 1 4
If I owe you any thing, I will pay you in cudgels . . . . . v 1 68
Defused attire And every thing that seems unnatural . . . . v 2 62
Any thing in or out of our demands, And we'll consign thereto . . v 2 89
That never looks in his glass for love of any thing he sees there . . v 2 155
After that things are set in order here, We'll follow them . 1 *Hen. VI.* ii 2 32
The plot is laid: if all things fall out right . . . . . . ii 3 4
And will not you maintain the thing you teach? . . . . . iii 1 129
Care is no cure, but rather corrosive, For things that are not to be remedied . . . . iii 3 4
For a toy, a thing of no regard . . . . iv 1 145
Tush, that's a wooden thing! . . . . v 3 89
You judge it straight a thing impossible To compass wonders . . . v 4 47
We'll see these things effected to the full . . . . . 2 *Hen. VI.* i 2 84
How now, fellow! wouldst any thing with me? . . . . . . i 3 11
Have you not beadles in your town, and things called whips? . . ii 1 136
O' God's name, see the lists and all things fit . . . . . . ii 3 54
Things are often spoke and seldom meant . . . . iii 1 268
Have you dispatch'd this thing?—Ay, my good lord, he's dead . . iii 2 6
Is all things well, According as I gave directions? . . . . . iii 2 11
O Thou that judgest all things, stay my thoughts! . . . . . iii 2 136
A jewel, lock'd into the wofull'st cask That ever did contain a thing of worth . . . . iii 2 410

Thing. Small things make base men proud . . . *2 Hen. VI.* iv 1 106
The first thing we do, let's kill all the lawyers . . . iv 2 83
Is not this a lamentable thing, that of the skin of an innocent lamb should be made parchment? . . . iv 2 86
I did but seal once to a thing, and I was never mine own man since . iv 2 90
And henceforward all things shall be in common . . . iv 7 20
And doubt not so to deal As all things shall redound unto your good . iv 9 47
You shall have pay and every thing you wish . . . v 1 47
Any thing I have, Is his to use . . . v 1 52
Do but think How sweet a thing it is to wear a crown . *3 Hen. VI.* i 2 29
To add more measure to your woes, I come to tell you things sith then befall'n . . . ii 1 106
Didst thou never hear That things ill-got had ever bad success? . . ii 2 46
If that be right which Warwick says is right, There is no wrong, but every thing is right . . . ii 2 132
Never will I undertake the thing Wherein thy counsel and consent is wanting . . . ii 6 101
I see the lady hath a thing to grant, Before the king will grant her humble suit . . . iii 2 12
Why, 'tis a happy thing To be the father unto many sons . . iii 2 104
That's the first thing that we have to do . . . iv 3 62
Yet in this one thing let me blame your grace, For choosing me . iv 6 30
He's sudden, if a thing comes in his head . . . v 5 86
You may partake of any thing we say . . . *Richard III.* i 1 89
Adders, spiders, toads, Or any creeping venom'd thing that lives! . i 2 20
I have done those things, Which now bear evidence against my soul . i 4 66
I'll not meddle with it [conscience]: it is a dangerous thing: . . . it is turned out of all towns and cities for a dangerous thing . . i 4 138
In common worldly things, 'tis call'd ungrateful, With dull unwillingness to repay a debt . . . ii 2 91
He was the wretched'st thing when he was young, So long a-growing . ii 4 18
You will part but with light gifts; In weightier things you'll say a beggar nay . . . iii 1 119
'Tis a vile thing to die, my gracious lord, When men are unprepared . iii 2 64
When is the royal day?—Are all things fitting for that royal time? . iii 4 4
Gold were as good as twenty orators, And will, no doubt, tempt him to any thing . . . iv 2 39
If to have done the thing you gave in charge Beget your happiness, be happy . . . iv 3 25
Yet one thing more, good Blunt, before thou go'st . . . v 3 33
All things are in readiness . . . v 3 52
A thing devised by the enemy . . . v 3 306
Things now, That bear a weighty and a serious brow . *Hen. VIII.* Prol. 1
The tract of every thing Would by a good discourser lose some life . i 1 40
Order gave each thing view; the office did Distinctly his full function i 1 44
Every man, After the hideous storm that follow'd, was A thing inspired i 1 91
The will of heaven Be done in this and all things! . . . i 1 210
You know no more than others; but you frame Things that are known alike . . . i 2 45
Things done well, And with a care, exempt themselves from fear; Things done without example, in their issue Are to be fear'd . . i 2 88
Things to strike honour sad . . . i 2 126
Pledge it, madam, For 'tis to such a thing,— You cannot show me . i 4 48
Every thing that heard him play, Even the billows of the sea, Hung their heads, and then lay by . . . iii 1 9
If ye be any thing but churchmen's habits . . . iii 1 117
Never attempt Any thing on him; for he hath a witchcraft . . iii 2 18
How sleek and wanton Ye appear in every thing may bring my ruin! . iii 2 242
All those things you have done of late, By your power legatine . . iii 2 338
Such things have been done. You are potently opposed . . . v 1 133
Never, before This happy child, did I get any thing . . . v 5 66
He hath the joints of every thing, but every thing so out of joint that he is a gouty Briareus . . . *Troi. and Cres.* i 2 29
I told you a thing yesterday; think on 't . . . i 2 185
Any thing, he cares not; an the devil come to him, it's all one . . i 2 227
Women are angels, wooing: Things won are done; joy's soul lies in the doing . . . i 2 313
Men prize the thing ungain'd more than it is . . . i 2 315
Then the thing of courage As roused with rage with rage doth sympathize i 3 51
What discord follows! each thing meets In mere oppugnancy . . i 3 110
Every thing includes itself in power, Power into will, will into appetite i 3 119
The baby figure of the giant mass Of things to come at large . . i 3 346
And tell what thou art by inches, thou thing of no bowels, thou! . . ii 1 54
We have lost so many tenths of ours, To guard a thing not ours . . ii 2 22
But, thieves, unworthy of a thing so stol'n . . . ii 2 94
Jove forbid there should be done amongst us Such things as might offend the weakest spleen! . . . ii 2 128
If any thing more than your sport and pleasure Did move your greatness ii 3 117
Things small as nothing, for request's sake only, He makes important . ii 3 179
My niece is horribly in love with a thing you have, sweet queen . . iii 1 106
In this rapture I shall surely speak The thing I shall repent . . iii 2 139
Through the sight I bear in things to love, I have abandon'd Troy . iii 3 4
Expressly proves That no man is the lord of any thing . . . iii 3 115
Nature, what things there are Most abject in regard and dear in use! What things again most dear in the esteem And poor in worth! . . iii 3 127
O, let not virtue seek Remuneration for the thing it was . . . iii 3 170
Praise new-born gawds, Though they are made and moulded of things past iii 3 177
Since things in motion sooner catch the eye Than what not stirs . . iii 3 183
No man alive can love in such a sort The thing he means to kill more excellently . . . iv 1 24
You do as chapmen do, Dispraise the thing that you desire to buy . iv 1 76
You are deceived, I think of no such thing . . . iv 2 40
Is as the very centre of the earth, Drawing all things to it . . . iv 2 111
Do not hold me to mine oath; Bid me do any thing but that . . . v 2 27
That a thing inseparate Divides more wider than the sky and earth . v 2 148
Patroclus will give me any thing for the intelligence . . . v 2 192
And what one thing, what another, that I shall leave you one o' these days v 3 103
Bastard in valour, in every thing illegitimate . . . v 7 18
Examine Their counsels and their cares, digest things rightly *Coriolanus* i 1 154
And were I any thing but what I am, I would wish me only he . . i 1 235
You two are old men: tell me one thing that I shall ask you . . ii 1 15
You know neither me, yourselves, nor any thing . . . ii 1 76
In troth, there's wondrous things spoke of him . . . ii 1 152
There's one thing wanting, which I doubt not but Our Rome will cast upon thee . . . ii 1 217
He was a thing of blood, whose every motion Was timed with dying cries ii 2 113
Look'd upon things precious as they were The common muck of the world . . . ii 2 129
You must think, if we give you any thing, we hope to gain by you . ii 3 78
What custom wills, in all things should we do't . . . ii 3 125

Thing. For your voices have Done many things, some less, some more *Coriolanus* ii 3 137
That of all things upon the earth he hated Your person most . . iii 1 14
It is a purposed thing, and grows by plot . . . iii 1 38
Hence, rotten thing! or I shall shake thy bones Out of thy garments . iii 1 179
Woollen vassals, things created To buy and sell with groats . . iii 2 9
The main blaze of it is past, but a small thing would make it flame again iv 3 21
I shall, between this and supper, tell you most strange things from Rome iv 3 44
If Jupiter Should from yond cloud speak divine things . . . iv 5 110
That I see thee here, Thou noble thing! more dances my rapt heart . iv 5 122
And vows revenge as spacious as between The young'st and oldest thing iv 6 68
He leads them like a thing Made by some other deity than nature . iv 6 90
Ye're goodly things, you voices! . . . iv 6 147
And is no less apparent To the vulgar eye, that he bears all things fairly iv 7 21
Or whether nature, Not to be other than one thing . . . iv 7 42
For such things as you, I can scarce think there's any, ye're so slight . v 2 109
The thing I have forsworn to grant may never Be held by you denials . v 3 80
No more! You have said you will not grant us any thing . . . v 3 87
It is no little thing to make Mine eyes to sweat compassion . . . v 3 195
He has wings; he's more than a creeping thing . . . v 4 14
He sits in his state, as a thing made for Alexander . . . v 4 23
And tapers burn so bright and every thing In readiness . *T. Andron.* i 1 324
Wherefore look'st thou sad, When every thing doth make a gleeful boast? ii 3 11
And one thing more That womanhood denies my tongue to tell . . ii 3 173
My compassionate heart Will not permit mine eyes once to behold The thing whereat it trembles by surmise . . . ii 3 219
O wondrous thing! How easily murder is discovered! . . . ii 3 286
Now, what a thing it is to be an ass! . . . iv 2 25
I'll show thee wondrous things, That highly may advantage thee to hear v 1 55
I know thou art religious And hast a thing within thee called conscience v 1 75
I have done a thousand dreadful things As willingly as one would kill a fly v 1 141
O any thing, of nothing first create! O heavy lightness! *Rom. and Jul.* i 1 183
Can you read any thing you see? . . . i 2 62
The nurse cursed in the pantry, and every thing in extremity . . i 3 102
Too great oppression for a tender thing.—Is love a tender thing? . . i 4 24
Dreamers often lie.—In bed asleep, while they do dream things true . i 4 52
And they unwashed too, 'tis a foul thing . . . i 5 6
And yet I wish but for the thing I have . . . ii 2 132
Is not this a lamentable thing, grandsire, that we should be thus afflicted? ii 4 33
Thou wast never with me for any thing when thou was not there for the goose . . . ii 4 79
An a' speak any thing against me, I'll take him down . . . ii 4 158
Truly it were an ill thing to be offered to any gentlewoman . . ii 4 179
And every cat and dog And little mouse, every unworthy thing . . iii 3 31
Things have fall'n out, sir, so unluckily, That we have had no time . iii 4 1
Thou wilt undertake A thing like death to chide away this shame . iv 1 74
Things that, to hear them told, have made me tremble . . . iv 1 86
Tush, I will stir about, And all things shall be well, I warrant thee . iv 2 40
What's there?—Things for the cook, sir; but I know not what . . iv 4 15
One poor and loving child, But one thing to rejoice and solace in . . iv 5 47
All things that we ordained festival, Turn from their office to black funeral . . . iv 5 84
Our bridal flowers serve for a buried corse, And all things change them to the contrary . . . iv 5 90
Leave me, and do the thing I bid thee do . . . v 1 30
Put this in any liquid thing you will, And drink it off . . . v 1 77
Fear comes upon me: O, much I fear some ill unlucky thing . . v 3 136
Go hence, to have more talk of these sad things . . . v 3 307
A thing slipp'd idly from me. Our poesy is as a gum . *T. of Athens* i 1 20
That few things loves better Than to abhor himself . . . i 1 59
Things of like value differing in the owners Are prized by their masters i 1 170
Takes no account How things go from him, nor resumes no care . . ii 2 4
I can tell you one thing, my lord, and which I hear from common rumours . . . iii 2 5
I am sick of that grief too, as I understand how all things go . . iii 6 20
Believe't, that we'll do any thing for gold . . . iv 3 150
What things in the world canst thou nearest compare to thy flatterers? —Women nearest; but men, men are the things themselves . . iv 3 318
Moe things like men! Eat, Timon, and abhor them . . . iv 3 398
Each thing's a thief . . . iv 3 445
What viler thing upon the earth than friends Who can bring noblest minds to basest ends! . . . iv 3 470
My long sickness Of health and living now begins to mend, And nothing brings me all things . . . v 1 191
You blocks, you stones, you worse than senseless things . *J. Cæsar* i 1 40
The eye sees not itself, But by reflection, by some other things . . i 2 53
I had as lief not be as live to be In awe of such a thing as I myself . i 2 96
And find a time Both meet to hear and answer such high things . . i 2 170
Scorn'd his spirit That could be moved to smile at any thing . . . i 2 207
If he had done or said any thing amiss, he desired their worships to think it was his infirmity . . . i 2 273
Did Cicero say any thing?—Ay, he spoke Greek . . . i 2 281
Are not you moved, when all the sway of earth Shakes like a thing unfirm? i 3 4
Saw you any thing more wonderful? . . . i 3 14
They are portentous things Unto the climate that they point upon . i 3 31
Men may construe things after their fashion, Clean from the purpose of the things themselves . . . i 3 35
Why all these things change from their ordinance Their natures . . i 3 66
When it serves For the base matter to illuminate So vile a thing as Cæsar! i 3 111
Since the quarrel Will bear no colour for the thing he is . . . ii 1 29
Between the acting of a dreadful thing And the first motion . . . ii 1 63
For he will never follow any thing That other men begin . . . ii 1 151
I will strive with things impossible; Yea, get the better of them . . ii 1 325
The things that threaten'd me Ne'er look'd but on my back . . . ii 2 10
There is one within, Besides the things that we have heard and seen, Recounts most horrid sights . . . ii 2 15
These things are beyond all use, And I do fear them . . . ii 2 25
Ay me, how weak a thing The heart of woman is! . . . ii 4 39
Thou shalt discourse To young Octavius of the state of things . . iii 1 296
Pluck down forms, windows, any thing . . . iii 2 264
Fortune is merry, And in this mood will give us any thing . . . iii 2 272
Things unluckily charge my fantasy: I have no will to wander forth of doors . . . iii 3 2
And now, Octavius, Listen great things . . . iv 1 41
Hath given me some worthy cause to wish Things done, undone . . iv 2 9
Every thing is well.—Good night, my lord . . . iv 3 236
Art thou any thing? Art thou some god, some angel, or some devil? . iv 3 278
Didst thou see any thing?—Nothing, my lord . . . iv 3 298
Now I change my mind, And partly credit things that do presage . . v 1 79
Why dost thou show to the apt thoughts of men The things that are not? v 3 69

Thing. Alas, thou hast misconstrued every thing! But, hold thee, take this garland *J. Cæsar* v 3 84
Bring us word unto Octavius' tent How every thing is chanced v 4 32
So should he look That seems to speak things strange *Macbeth* i 2 47
Why do you start; and seem to fear Things that do sound so fair? i 3 52
Would they had stay'd!—Were such things here as we do speak about? i 3 83
My dull brain was wrought With things forgotten i 3 150
To throw away the dearest thing he owed, As 'twere a careless trifle i 4 10
By doing every thing Safe toward your love and honour i 4 26
There's no such thing: It is the bloody business which informs Thus to mine eyes ii 1 47
You do unbend your noble strength, to think So brainsickly of things ii 2 46
Drink, sir, is a great provoker of three things.—What three things? ii 3 28
I have seen Hours dreadful and things strange ii 4 3
A thing most strange and certain ii 4 14
Well, may you see things well done there: adieu! ii 4 37
And all things else that might To half a soul and to a notion crazed iii 1 82
Things without all remedy Should be without regard: what's done is done iii 2 11
But let the frame of things disjoint, both the worlds suffer iii 2 16
Good things of day begin to droop and drowse iii 2 52
Things bad begun make strong themselves by ill iii 2 55
A thing of custom: 'tis no other; Only it spoils the pleasure of the time iii 4 97
Can such things be, And overcome us like a summer's cloud? iii 4 110
Strange things I have in head, that will to hand iii 4 139
Your vessels and your spells provide, Your charms and every thing beside iii 5 19
Only, I say, Things have been strangely borne iii 6 3
He has borne all things well iii 6 17
Yet my heart Throbs to know one thing iv 1 101
Things at the worst will cease, or else climb upward iv 2 24
Though all things foul would wear the brows of grace, Yet grace must still look so iv 3 23
Such welcome and unwelcome things at once 'Tis hard to reconcile iv 3 138
I cannot but remember such things were, That were most precious to me iv 3 222
None serve with him but constrained things Whose hearts are absent v 4 13
What, has this thing appear'd again to-night? *Hamlet* i 1 21
If there be any good thing to be done, That may to thee do ease i 1 130
And then it started like a guilty thing Upon a fearful summons i 1 148
In that and all things will we show our duty i 2 40
As common As any the most vulgar thing to sense i 2 99
Things rank and gross in nature Possess it merely i 2 136
Both in time, Form of the thing, each word made true and good i 2 210
And for my soul, what can it do to that, Being a thing immortal as itself? i 4 67
There are more things in heaven and earth, Horatio, Than are dreamt of in your philosophy i 5 166
As 'twere a thing a little soil'd i' the working ii 1 40
You cannot, sir, take from me any thing that I will more willingly part withal: except my life ii 2 220
What should we say, my lord?—Why, any thing, but to the purpose ii 2 287
No other thing to me than a foul and pestilent congregation of vapours ii 2 314
We'll e'en to't like French falconers, fly at any thing we see ii 2 450
Unless things mortal move them not at all ii 2 539
The play's the thing Wherein I'll catch the conscience of the king ii 2 633
The harlot's cheek, beautied with plastering art, Is not more ugly to the thing that helps it iii 1 52
Words of so sweet breath composed As made the things more rich iii 1 99
I could accuse me of such things that it were better my mother had not borne me iii 1 125
For any thing so overdone is from the purpose of playing iii 2 22
Look you now, how unworthy a thing you make of me! iii 2 380
To whose huge spokes ten thousand lesser things Are mortised iii 3 19
The king is a thing— A thing, my lord!—Of nothing iv 2 30
Every thing is bent For England iv 3 47
Every thing is seal'd and done That else leans on the affair iv 3 58
This thing's to do; Sith I have cause and will and strength and means iv 4 44
Speaks things in doubt, That carry but half sense iv 5 6
It sends some precious instance of itself After the thing it loves iv 5 163
As by your safety, wisdom, all things else, You mainly were stirr'd up iv 7 8
Or is it some abuse, and no such thing? iv 7 51
Can save the thing from death That is but scratch'd withal iv 7 146
Prithee, Horatio, tell me one thing.—What's that, my lord? v 1 216
If your lordship were at leisure, I should impart a thing to you v 2 92
If your mind dislike any thing, obey it v 2 227
What a wounded name, Things standing thus unknown, shall live behind me! v 2 356
Let me speak to the yet unknowing world How these things came about v 2 391
Should in this trice of time Commit a thing so monstrous *Lear* i 1 220
How old art thou?—Not so young, sir, to love a woman for singing, nor so old to dote on her for any thing i 4 41
I had rather be any kind o' thing than a fool i 4 203
Be then desired By her, that else will take the thing she begs i 4 269
Acquaint my daughter no further with any thing you know i 5 3
Unless things be cut shorter i 5 56
And I have one thing, of a queasy question, Which I must act ii 1 19
Our basest beggars Are in the poorest thing superfluous ii 4 268
I will do such things,—What they are, yet I know not; but they shall be The terrors of the earth ii 4 283
Or swell the curled waters 'bove the main, That things might change or cease iii 1 7
And dare, upon the warrant of my note, Commend a dear thing to you iii 1 19
Things that love night Love not such nights as these iii 2 42
The art of our necessities is strange, That can make vile things precious iii 2 71
There is some strange thing toward iii 3 20
This tempest will not give me leave to ponder On things would hurt me more iii 4 25
Thou art the thing itself: unaccommodated man is no more iii 4 111
Suffers most i' the mind, Leaving free things and happy shows behind iii 6 112
His roguish madness Allows itself to any thing iii 7 105
The lowest and most dejected thing of fortune Stands still in esperance iv 1 3
Thou changed and self-cover'd thing, for shame, Be-monster not thy feature iv 2 62
These things sting His mind so venomously iv 3 47
That thing you speak of, I took it for a man iv 6 77
To say 'ay' and 'no' to every thing that I said! iv 6 100
Go to, they are not men o' their words: they told me I was every thing iv 6 107
And, like a scurvy politician, seem To see the things thou dost not iv 6 176
And take upon's the mystery of things, As if we were God's spies v 3 16
Great thing of us forgot! v 3 236

Thing. Her voice was ever soft, Gentle, and low, an excellent thing in woman *Lear* v 3 273
Sir, I will answer any thing *Othello* i 1 121
Have you not read, Roderigo, Of some such thing? i 1 175
I'll refer me to all things of sense, If she in chains of magic were not bound i 2 64
Run from her guardage to the sooty bosom Of such a thing as thou i 2 71
In spite of nature, Of years, of country, credit, every thing i 3 97
With such things else of quality and respect As doth import you i 3 283
I am not merry; but I do beguile The thing I am, by seeming otherwise ii 1 124
Which thing to do, If this poor trash of Venice ... stand the putting on ii 1 311
I hold him to be unworthy of his place that does those things ii 3 105
I remember a mass of things, but nothing distinctly ii 3 289
Though other things grow fair against the sun, Yet fruits that blossom first will first be ripe ii 3 382
Two things are to be done ii 3 388
Whatever shall become of Michael Cassio, He's never any thing but your true servant.—I know't iii 3 9
I'll intermingle every thing he does With Cassio's suit iii 3 25
Such things in a false disloyal knave Are tricks of custom iii 3 121
As where's that palace whereinto foul things Sometimes intrude not? iii 3 137
Complexion, and degree, Whereto we see in all things nature tends iii 3 231
I would I might entreat your honour To scan this thing no further iii 3 245
Than keep a corner in the thing I love For others' uses iii 2 272
I have a thing for you.—A thing for me? it is a common thing iii 3 301
Can any thing be made of this? iii 4 10
Men's natures wrangle with inferior things, Though great ones are their object iii 4 144
But they must blab— Hath he said any thing?—He hath, my lord iv 1 29
Go in, and weep not; all things shall be well iv 2 171
She had a song of 'willow;' An old thing 'twas, but it express'd her fortune iv 3 29
The world's a huge thing: it is a great price For a small vice iv 3 69
I would not do such a thing for a joint-ring iv 3 73
What shall be said to thee?—Why, any thing: An honourable murderer, if you will v 2 293
Whom every thing becomes, to chide, to laugh, To weep *Ant. and Cleo.* i 1 49
Sweet Alexas, most any thing Alexas, almost most absolute Alexas i 2 2
Is this the man? Is't you, sir, that know things? i 2 8
Things that are past are done with me i 2 101
In each thing give him way, cross him in nothing i 3 9
His composure must be rare indeed Whom these things cannot blemish i 4 23
Last thing he did, dear queen, He kiss'd,—the last of many doubled kisses,—This orient pearl i 5 39
Whiles we are suitors to their throne, decays The thing we sue for ii 1 5
I learn, you take things ill which are not so, Or being, concern you not ii 2 29
For vilest things Become themselves in her ii 2 243
I have heard the Ptolemies' pyramises are very goodly things ii 7 40
What manner o' thing is your crocodile?—It is shaped, sir, like itself ii 7 46
Why, methinks, by him, This creature's no such thing.—Nothing, madam iii 3 44
I have one thing more to ask him yet, good Charmian: But 'tis no matter iii 3 48
Let determined things to destiny Hold unbewail'd their way iii 6 84
Things outward Do draw the inward quality after them, To suffer all alike iii 13 32
Let's hear him, for the things he speaks May concern Cæsar iv 9 25
My sword is drawn.—Then let it do at once The thing why thou hast drawn it iv 14 89
The breaking of so great a thing should make A greater crack v 1 14
It is great To do that thing that ends all other deeds v 2 5
Though written in our flesh, we shall remember As things but done by chance v 2 120
'Tis exactly valued; Not petty things admitted v 2 140
Toys, things of such dignity As we greet modern friends withal v 2 166
We, the greatest, are misthought For things that others do v 2 177
Cæsar's no merchant, to make prize with you Of things that merchants sold v 2 184
Hath a heart that is not Glad at the thing they scowl at *Cymbeline* i 1 15
It is a thing Too bad for bad report i 1 16
Thou basest thing, avoid! hence, from my sight! i 1 125
Disloyal thing, That shouldst repair my youth, thou heap'st A year's age on me i 1 131
Thou foolish thing! i 1 150
I did not take my leave of him, but had Most pretty things to say i 3 26
Those things I bid you do, get them dispatch'd i 3 39
The other is not a thing for sale, and only the gift of the gods i 4 92
We will have these things set down by lawful counsel i 4 178
What shalt thou expect, To be depender on a thing that leans? i 5 58
It is a thing I made, which hath the king Five times redeem'd from death i 5 62
Since doubting things go ill often hurts more Than to be sure they do i 6 95
I am not vexed more at any thing in the earth: a pox on't! ii 1 19
First, a very excellent good-conceited thing; after, a wonderful sweet air, with admirable rich words to it ii 3 18
With every thing that pretty is, My lady sweet, arise: Arise, arise ii 3 28
This is a thing Which you might from relation likewise reap ii 4 85
To apprehend thus, Draws us a profit from all things we see iii 3 18
And nature prompts them In simple and low things to prince it much iii 3 85
Would be interpreted a thing perplex'd Beyond self-explication iii 4 7
You shall find me, wretched man, a thing The most disdain'd of fortune iii 4 19
'Tis empty of all things but grief: Thy master is not there iii 4 71
She looks us like A thing more made of malice than of duty iii 5 33
He hath a drug of mine; I pray his absence Proceed by swallowing that, for he believes It is a thing most precious iii 5 59
I forgot to ask him one thing; I'll remember't anon iii 5 134
That is the second thing that I have commanded thee iii 5 157
Ho! who's here! If any thing that's civil, speak; if savage, Take or lend iii 6 23
Yet this imperceiverant thing loves him in my despite iv 1 15
Cowards father cowards and base things sire base iv 2 26
A thing More slavish did I ne'er than answering A slave without a knock iv 2 72
Was nothing but mutation, ay, and that From one bad thing to worse iv 2 134
All solemn things Should answer solemn accidents iv 2 191
Thou blessed thing! Jove knows what man thou mightst have made iv 2 206
What thing is it that I never Did see man die! scarce ever look'd on blood! iv 4 35
You are made Rather to wonder at the things your hear Than to work any v 3 54
Came crying 'mongst his foes, A thing of pity! v 4 47
Iachimo, Slight thing of Italy v 4 64

Thing. I never saw Such noble fury in so poor a thing *Cymbeline* v 5 8
This one thing only I will entreat; my boy, a Briton born, Let him be ransom'd v 5 83
There's other work in hand: I see a thing Bitter to me as death v 5 103
What think you?—The same dead thing alive v 5 123
Egregious murderer, thief, any thing That's due to all the villains past! v 5 211
It is I That all the abhorred things o' the earth amend By being worse v 5 216
If That box I gave you was not thought by me A precious thing v 5 242
O gods! I left out one thing which the queen confess'd v 5 244
The thing the which is flatter'd, but a spark *Pericles* i 2 40
O, sir, things must be as they may ii 1 119
Let me ask you one thing: What do you think of my daughter, sir? ii 5 32
Who dream'd, who thought of such a thing? iii Gower 38
Here is a thing too young for such a place iii 1 15
Thou canst not do a thing in the world so soon, To yield thee so much iv 1 3
Such a maidenhead were no cheap thing, if men were as they have been iv 2 65
But to have divinity preached there! did you ever dream of such a thing? iv 5 5
I'll do any thing now that is virtuous iv 5 8
Prithee, tell me one thing first.—Come now, your one thing iv 6 166
Do any thing but this thou doest. Empty Old receptacles iv 6 185
Some such thing I said, and said no more but what my thoughts Did warrant me was likely v 1 133
No needful thing omitted v 3 68
Things go. They can tell you how things go better than I can *Mer. Wives* iii 4 69
You shall hear how things go; and, I warrant, to your content iv 5 126
Besides, if things go well, Opinion that so sticks on Marcius shall Of his demerits rob Cominius *Coriolanus* i 1 274
Think. Canst thou remember . . . ? I do not think thou canst *Tempest* i 2 40
O, my heart bleeds To think o' the teen that I have turn'd you to! i 2 64
Of temporal royalties He thinks me now incapable i 2 111
I should sin To think but nobly of my grandmother i 2 119
I think he will carry this island home in his pocket ii 1 90
I am in my condition A prince, Miranda; I do think, a king iii 1 60
I shall think, or Phœbus' steeds are founder'd, Or Night kept chain'd below iv 1 30
May I be bold To think these spirits? iv 1 120
Your affections Would become tender.—Dost thou think so? v 1 19
I rather think You have not sought her help v 1 141
They devour their reason and scarce think Their eyes do offices of truth v 1 155
If I did think, sir, I were well awake, I'ld strive to tell you v 1 229
Till when, be cheerful And think of each thing well v 1 251
Truly, sir, I think you'll hardly win her *T. G. of Ver.* i 1 141
Of many good I think him best.—Your reason?—I have no other but a woman's reason; I think him so because I think him so i 2 21
Yet he, of all the rest, I think, best loves ye i 2 28
When I look on you, I can hardly think you my master ii 1 33
Perchance you think too much of so much pains?—No, madam ii 1 118
I think Crab my dog be the sourest-natured dog that lives ii 3 5
You have an exchequer of words, and, I think, no other treasure ii 4 44
I think 'tis no unwelcome news to you ii 4 81
I think she holds them prisoners still ii 4 92
If you think so, then stay at home and go not ii 7 62
And think my patience, more than thy desert, Is privilege iii 1 159
What joy is joy, if Silvia be not by? Unless it be to think that she is by iii 1 176
I have the wit to think my master is a kind of a knave iii 1 262
So I believe; but Thurio thinks not so iii 2 16
I think thou art not ignorant How she opposes her against my will iii 2 25
But she'll think that it is spoke in hate iii 2 34
She bids me think how I have been forsworn iv 2 10
Trust me, I think 'tis almost day iv 2 139
Thou art a gentleman—Think not I flatter, for I swear I do not iv 3 12
Think upon my grief, a lady's grief, And on the justice of my flying hence iv 3 28
I think verily he had been hanged for't iv 4 16
She is dead, belike?—Not so; I think she lives iv 4 80
To think upon her woes I do protest That I have wept iv 4 149
Belike she thinks that Proteus hath forsook her.—I think she doth iv 4 151
When she did think my master loved her well, She, in my judgement, was as fair as you iv 4 155
Alas, poor lady, desolate and left! I weep myself to think upon thy words iv 4 180
I think, If I had such a tire, this face of mine Were full as lovely iv 4 189
And think thee worthy of an empress' love v 4 141
What think you of this page, my lord?—I think the boy hath grace in him v 4 164
I think my cousin meant well *Mer. Wives* i 1 265
Be there bears i' the town?—I think there are, sir i 1 300
I shall think the worse of fat men, as long as I have an eye ii 1 56
I think the best way were to entertain him with hope ii 1 67
What doth he think of us?—Nay, I know not ii 1 85
Do you think there is truth in them?—Hang 'em, slaves! I do not think the knight would offer it ii 1 178
Surely I think you have charms, la; yes, in truth ii 2 107
I think myself in better plight for a lender than you are ii 2 172
And what they think in their hearts they may effect, they will break their hearts but they will effect ii 2 322
What is he?—I think you know him iii 1 60
I think, if your husbands were dead, you two would marry iii 2 14
I think I shall drink in pipe-wine first with him; I'll make him dance iii 2 90
I think my husband hath some special suspicion of Falstaff's being here iii 3 199
Bid her think what a man is: let her consider his frailty iii 5 51
Think of that,—a man of my kidney,—think of that iii 5 116
Think of that,—hissing hot,—think of that, Master Brook iii 5 123
Are you not ashamed? I think you have killed the poor woman iv 2 197
Hang her, witch!—By yea and no, I think the 'oman is a witch indeed iv 2 202
He will never, I think, in the way of waste, attempt us again iv 2 226
Methinks his flesh is punished, he shall have no desires.—So think I too iv 4 25
I am here a Windsor stag; and the fattest, I think, i' the forest v 5 14
I think the devil will not have me damned v 5 38
But those as sleep and think not on their sins, Pinch them, arms, legs v 5 57
I think we have watch'd you now v 5 107
Do you think . . . that ever the devil could have made you our delight? v 5 154
I think to repay that money will be a biting affliction v 5 177
If I did not think it had been Anne Page, would I might never stir! v 5 198
You took the wrong.— . . . I think so, when I took a boy for a girl v 5 202
What figure of us think you he will bear? *Meas. for Meas.* i 1 17
Nor do I think the man of safe discretion That does affect it i 1 72
I think thou never wast where grace was said i 2 19
Think. Do I speak feelingly now?—I think thou dost *Meas. for Meas.* i 2 37
I think I have done myself wrong, have I not? i 2 41
What we do not see We tread upon, and never think of it ii 1 26
She professes a hot-house, which, I think, is a very ill house too ii 1 66
Hoping you'll find good cause to whip them all.—I think no less ii 1 143
Let not your worship think me the poor duke's officer ii 1 186
What's o'clock, think you?—Eleven, sir.—I pray you home to dinner with me ii 1 290
I do think that you might pardon him, And neither heaven nor man grieve ii 2 49
Hail to you, provost! so I think you are ii 3 1
When must he die?—As I do think, to-morrow ii 3 16
When I would pray and think, I think and pray To several subjects ii 4 1
Think you I can a resolution fetch From flowery tenderness? iii 1 82
What should I think? Heaven shield my mother play'd my mother fair! iii 1 140
What think you of it?—The image of it gives me content already iii 1 269
But think What 'tis to cram a maw or clothe a back From such a filthy vice iii 2 22
If it be too little for your thief, your true man thinks it big enough; if it be too big for your thief, your thief thinks it little enough iv 2 48
You will think you have made no offence iv 2 199
One would think it were Mistress Overdone's own house iv 3 2
Here comes your ghostly father: do we jest now, think you? iv 3 52
Who thinks he knows that he ne'er knew my body, But knows he thinks that he knows Isabel's v 1 203
I think, if you handled her privately, she would sooner confess v 1 276
I should be guiltier than my guiltiness, To think I can be undiscernible v 1 373
The swift celerity of his death, Which I did think with slower foot came on v 1 400
I partly think A due sincerity govern'd his deeds v 1 450
I think the meat wants that I have *Com. of Errors* ii 2 57
Was I married to her in my dream? Or sleep I now and think I hear all this? ii 2 185
I am transformed, master, am I not?—I think thou art in mind ii 2 198
Your own handwriting would tell you what I think iii 1 14
Teach me, dear creature, how to think and speak iii 2 33
In that glorious supposition think He gains by death iii 2 50
If every one knows us and we know none, 'Tis time, I think, to trudge iii 2 158
What I should think of this, I cannot tell: But this I think, there's no man is so vain That would refuse so fair an offer'd chain iii 2 184
Ah, but I think him better than I say iv 2 25
One that thinks a man always going to bed and says 'God give you good rest!' iv 3 32
Here comes my man; I think he brings the money. How now, sir! iv 4 8
Speak softly: yonder, as I think, he walks v 1 9
This chain you had of me; can you deny it?—I think I had v 1 23
From whence, I think, you are come by miracle v 1 264
What an intricate impeach is this! I think you all have drunk of Circe's cup v 1 270
That is the chain, sir, which you had of me.—I think it be, sir v 1 379
I think this is your daughter.—Her mother hath many times told me so *Much Ado* i 1 104
I can be secret as a dumb man; I would have you think so i 1 212
Do you think I do not know you by your excellent wit? ii 1 126
But did you think the prince would have served you thus? ii 1 202
I told him, and I think I told him true ii 1 222
I' faith, lady, I think your blazon to be true ii 1 307
Show me briefly how.—I think I told your lordship a year since ii 2 12
May I be so converted and see with these eyes? I cannot tell; I think not ii 3 24
Since many a wooer doth commence his suit To her he thinks not worthy ii 3 53
I did never think that lady would have loved any man ii 3 96
I cannot tell what to think of it but that she loves him ii 3 105
I should think this a gull, but that the white-bearded fellow speaks it ii 3 123
Tell Benedick of it, and hear what a' will say.—Were it good, think you? ii 3 179
I did never think to marry: I must not seem proud ii 3 236
When I said I would die a bachelor, I did not think I should live till I were married ii 3 252
She cannot love, . . . She is so self-endeared.—Sure, I think so iii 1 56
His tongue is the clapper, for what his heart thinks his tongue speaks iii 2 14
You may think I love you not: let that appear hereafter iii 2 98
For my brother, I think he holds you well, and in dearness of heart iii 2 101
Think you of a worse title, and I will fit her to it iii 2 114
May this be so?—I will not think it iii 2 121
Who think you the most desartless man to be constable? iii 3 9
But I think they that touch pitch will be defiled iii 3 60
Nay, by'r lady, that I think a' cannot.—Five shillings to one on't iii 3 82
It is an offence to stay a man against his will.—By'r lady, I think it be so iii 3 89
Troth, I think your other rabato were better iii 4 6
I think you would have me say, 'saving your reverence, a husband' iii 4 32
You may think perchance that I think you are in love: nay, by'r lady, I am not such a fool to think what I list, nor I list not to think what I can, nor indeed I cannot think, if I would think my heart out of thinking, that you are in love iii 4 81
For, did I think thou wouldst not quickly die iv 1 126
Think you in your soul the Count Claudio hath wronged Hero? iv 1 331
As you hear of me, so think of me iv 1 338
I think he be angry indeed.—If he be, he knows how to turn his girdle v 1 141
Well, I will call Beatrice to you, who I think hath legs v 2 24
I love thee against my will.—In spite of your heart, I think v 2 69
How long is that, think you?—Question: why, an hour in clamour v 2 83
The sight whereof I think you had from me v 4 25
I think he thinks upon the savage bull. Tush; fear not, man v 4 43
Dost thou think I care for a satire or an epigram? v 4 103
I will think nothing to any purpose that the world can say against it v 4 106
For thy part, Claudio, I did think to have beaten thee v 4 111
Think not on him till to-morrow: I'll devise thee brave punishments for him v 4 129
When I was wont to think no harm all night *L. L. Lost* i 1 44
The world was very guilty of such a ballad some three ages since: but I think now 'tis not to be found i 2 117
Do the wise think them other? iii 1 81
I know not; but I think it was not he iv 1 3
How far dost thou excel, No thought can think, nor tongue of mortal tell iv 3 42
The letter is too long by half a mile.—I think no less v 2 55
Will they not, think you, hang themselves to-night? v 2 270
But this I think, When they are thirsty, fools would fain have drink v 2 371
Why look you pale? Sea-sick, I think, coming from Muscovy v 2 393
Art thou one of the Worthies?—It pleased them to think me worthy v 2 506
Is this Hector?—I think Hector was not so clean-timbered v 2 642
As fair as she. But what of that? Demetrius thinks not so *M. N. D.* i 1 228

Think. For that It is not night when I do see your face, Therefore I think I am not in the night *M. N. Dream* ii 1 222
If you think I come hither as a lion, it were pity of my life iii 1 43
Why should you think that I should woo in scorn? iii 2 122
You speak not as you think: it cannot be iii 2 191
You perhaps may think, Because she is something lower than myself, That I can match her iii 2 303
Think no more of this night's accidents But as the fierce vexation of a dream iv 1 73
As I think,—for truly would I speak, And now I do bethink me, so it is iv 1 154
Do not you think The duke was here, and bid us follow him? iv 1 199
That you should think, we come not to offend, But with good will v 1 109
By moonshine did these lovers think no scorn To meet at Ninus' tomb v 1 138
Such a wall, as I would have you think, That had in it a crannied hole v 1 158
My love thou art, my love I think.—Think what thou wilt v 1 196
If we shadows have offended, Think but this, and all is mended v 1 431
I should not see the sandy hour-glass run, But I should think of shallows and of flats *Mer. of Venice* i 1 26
I know, Antonio Is sad to think upon his merchandise i 1 40
I think he bought his doublet in Italy, his round hose in France i 2 79
What think you of the Scottish lord? i 2 83
I think the Frenchman became his surety and sealed under for another i 2 88
Yes, yes, it was Bassanio; as I think, he was so called i 2 127
I think I may take his bond.—Be assured you may i 3 27
I cannot think you are my son.—I know not what I shall think of that ii 2 92
'Twere damnation To think so base a thought ii 7 50
Or shall I think in silver she's immured? ii 7 52
I think he only loves the world for him ii 8 50
The Goodwins, I think they call the place iii 1 4
Like one of two contending in a prize, That thinks he hath done well in people's eyes iii 2 143
Which makes me think that this Antonio, Being the bosom lover of my lord, Must needs be like my lord iii 4 16
We'll see our husbands Before they think of us iii 4 59
That they shall think we are accomplished With that we lack iii 4 61
Be of good cheer, for truly I think you are damned iii 5 6
I think the best grace of wit will shortly turn into silence iii 5 49
The world thinks, and I think so too iv 1 17
I pray you, think you question with the Jew iv 1 70
Had you been there, I think you would have begg'd The ring v 1 221
The spirit of my father, which I think is within me, begins to mutiny *As Y. Like It* i 1 24
Let me see; what think you of falling in love?—Marry, I prithee, do i 2 27
Mistake me not so much To think my poverty is treacherous i 3 67
I think you have no money in your purse ii 4 13
As sure I think did never man love so ii 4 29
I think of as many matters as he, but I give heaven thanks and make no boast ii 5 37
I think he be transform'd into a beast; For I can no where find him like a man ii 7 1
Till thou canst quit thee by thy brother's mouth Of what we think against thee iii 1 12
Dost thou think, though I am caparisoned like a man, I have a doublet and hose in my disposition? iii 2 204
Do you not know I am a woman? when I think, I must speak iii 2 264
You have a nimble wit: I think 'twas made of Atalanta's heels iii 2 293
Though he go as softly as foot can fall, he thinks himself too soon there iii 2 346
Nay, certainly, there is no truth in him.—Do you think so?—Yes; I think he is not a pick-purse nor a horse-stealer, but for his verity in love, I do think him as concave as a covered goblet iii 4 23
Not true in love?—Yes, when he is in; but I think he is not in iii 4 29
'Od's my little life, I think she means to tangle my eyes too! iii 5 44
I shall think it a most plenteous crop To glean the broken ears iii 5 101
Think not I love him, though I ask for him; 'Tis but a peevish boy iii 5 109
I will scarce think you have swam in a gondola iv 1 37
A better jointure, I think, than you make a woman iv 1 56
I should think my honesty ranker than my wit iv 1 85
I will think you the most pathetical break-promise iv 1 196
I verily did think That her old gloves were on, but 'twas her hands iv 3 25
A body would think this was well counterfeited! iv 3 167
The fool doth think he is wise, but the wise man knows himself to be a fool v 1 34
I shall think my brother happy in having what he wishes for v 2 51
What think you, if he were convey'd to bed? *T. of Shrew* Ind. 1 37
Believe me, lord, I think he cannot choose Ind. 1 42
He shall think by our true diligence He is no less than what we say he is Ind. 1 70
'Be serviceable to my son,' quoth he, Although I think 'twas in another sense i 1 220
An she knew him as well as I do, she would think scolding would do little good upon him i 2 109
Think you a little din can daunt mine ears? i 2 200
You are passing welcome, And so I pray you all to think yourselves ii 1 114
I think she'll sooner prove a soldier: Iron may hold with her ii 1 146
A swearing Jack, That thinks with oaths to face the matter out ii 1 291
I thank you for your pains: I know you think to dine with me to-day iii 2 187
Think it not the worst of all your fortunes iv 2 104
Let's see; I think 'tis now some seven o'clock iv 3 189
Look, what I speak, or do, or think to do, You are still crossing it iv 3 194
What do you think is his name?—His name! as if I knew not his name v 1 83
He that is giddy thinks the world turns round v 2 20
I think thou hast the veriest shrew of all.—Well, I say no v 2 64
I think it would be the death of the king's disease *All's Well* i 1 25
I think not on my father; And these great tears grace his remembrance more Than those I shed for him i 1 90
'Twere all one That I should love a bright particular star And think to wed it i 1 98
And yet I know him a notorious liar, Think him a great way fool i 1 112
And show what we alone must think, which never Returns us thanks i 1 199
If I can remember thee, I will think of thee at court i 1 203
You were born under a charitable star.—Under Mars, I.—I especially think, under Mars.— . . . When he was predominant.—When he was retrograde, I think, rather.—Why think you so? i 1 207
I think I shall never have the blessing of God till I have issue o' my body i 3 26
I was very late more near her than I think she wished me i 3 111
Your son made me to think of this i 3 238
But think you, Helen, If you should tender your supposed aid, He would receive it? i 3 241
But know I think and think I know most sure ii 1 160
Think. I think, sir, you can eat none of this homely meat *All's Well* ii 2 48
You were lately whipped, sir, as I think.—O Lord, sir! spare not me ii 2 52
Is not this Helen?—'Fore God, I think so ii 3 51
Too good, To make yourself a son out of my blood.—Fair one, I think not so ii 3 104
I did think thee, for two ordinaries, to be a pretty wise fellow ii 3 211
I think thou wast created for men to breathe themselves upon thee ii 3 271
Strengthen'd with what apology you think May make it probable need ii 4 51
But I hope your lordship thinks not him a soldier ii 5 1
An idle lord, I swear.—I think so.—Why, do you not know him? ii 5 55
Therefore dare not Say what I think of it iii 1 14
My lord is gone, for ever gone.—Do not say so.—Think upon patience iii 2 50
I think I know your hostess As ample as myself iii 5 45
You came, I think, from France?—I did so iii 5 49
Think you it is so?—Ay, surely, mere the truth: I know his lady iii 5 57
Do you think I am so far deceived in him? iii 6 6
If you think your mystery in stratagem can bring this instrument iii 6 68
Why, do you think he will make no deed at all of this? iii 6 102
He must think us some band of strangers iv 1 16
In this disguise I think 't no sin To cozen him that would unjustly win iv 2 75
And thinks himself made in the unchaste composition iv 3 21
What think you he hath confessed?—Nothing of me, has a'? iv 3 128
Or whether he thinks it were not possible iv 3 203
I think I have his letter in my pocket.—Marry, we'll search iv 3 227
He will lie, sir, with such volubility, that you would think truth were a fool iv 3 284
Which he thinks is a patent for his sauciness iv 5 69
Lay a more noble thought upon mine honour Than for to think that I would sink it here v 3 181
Ask him upon his oath, if he does think He had not my virginity v 3 185
She hath that ring of yours.—I think she has v 3 210
I think thee now some common customer v 3 287
Perchance he is not drown'd: what think you, sailors? *T. Night* i 2 5
Fair lady, do you think you have fools in hand? i 3 69
What's your metaphor?—It's dry, sir.—Why, I think so i 3 78
When did I see thee so put down?—Never in your life, I think i 3 87
I think I have the back-trick simply as strong as any man in Illyria i 3 131
I did think, by the excellent constitution of thy leg, it was formed under the star of a galliard i 3 141
I think not so, my lord.—Dear lad, believe it i 4 29
Those wits, that think they have thee, do very oft prove fools i 5 36
What think you of this fool, Malvolio? doth he not mend? i 5 79
One would think his mother's milk were scarce out of him i 5 170
So they say; but I think it rather consists of eating and drinking ii 3 11
Dost thou think, because thou art virtuous, there shall be no more cakes? ii 3 123
Do not think I have wit enough to lie straight in my bed ii 3 147
The best persuaded of himself, so crammed, as he thinks, with excellencies ii 3 163
He shall think, by the letters . . . , that they come from my niece ii 3 178
I think I saw your wisdom there iii 1 46
For him, I think not on him: for his thoughts, Would they were blanks! iii 1 114
What might you think? Have you not set mine honour at the stake? iii 1 128
Baited it with all the unmuzzled thoughts That tyrannous heart can think iii 1 131
You do think you are not what you are.—If I think so, I think the same of you.—Then think you right iii 1 151
I think oxen and wainropes cannot hale them together iii 2 63
And your store, I think, is not for idle markets, sir iii 3 46
I think we do know the sweet Roman hand iii 4 30
Do not think I am mad: they have laid me here in hideous darkness iv 2 33
I think nobly of the soul, and no way approve his opinion iv 2 59
I would not have you to think that my desire of having is the sin of covetousness v 1 50
I think you set nothing by a bloody coxcomb v 1 194
Think of me as you please. I leave my duty a little unthought of and speak out of my injury v 1 317
To think me as well a sister as a wife v 1 325
I think there is not in the world either malice or matter to alter it *W. T.* i 1 36
That little thinks she has been sluiced in's absence i 2 194
'Tis powerful, think it, From east, west, north, and south i 2 202
Cogitation Resides not in that man that does not think,—My wife is slippery i 2 272
Dost think I am so muddy, so unsettled, To appoint myself? i 2 325
My son, Who I do think is mine and love as mine i 2 331
I am charged in honour and by him That I think honourable i 2 408
He thinks, nay, with all confidence he swears, As he had seen't i 2 414
Leave me, And think upon my bidding ii 3 207
Which not to have done I think had been in me Both disobedience and ingratitude iii 2 68
O, think what they have done And then run mad indeed, stark mad! iii 2 183
To whose feeling sorrows I might be some allay, or I o'erween to think so iv 2 9
I think it not uneasy to get the cause of my son's resort thither iv 2 56
I should blush To see you so attired, sworn, I think, To show myself a glass iv 4 13
I tremble To think your father, by some accident, Should pass this way iv 4 19
Flowers Of middle summer, and I think they are given To men of middle age iv 4 107
I think you have As little skill to fear as I have purpose To put you to't iv 4 151
He says he loves my daughter: I think so too iv 4 172
I think there is not half a kiss to choose Who loves another best iv 4 175
You would think a smock were a she-angel iv 4 210
More in them than you'ld think, sister.—Ay, good brother, or go about to think iv 4 218
Is it true, think you?—Very true, and but a month old iv 4 269
I cannot speak, nor think, Nor dare to know that which I know iv 4 462
I think, Camillo?—Even he, my lord iv 4 484
It does fulfil my vow; I needs must think it honesty iv 4 498
Sir, I think You have heard of my poor services iv 4 526
Please to think I love the king And through him what is nearest to him iv 4 532
I think affliction may subdue the cheek, But not take in the mind iv 4 587
I think you know my fortunes Do all lie there iv 4 601
Thou must think there's a necessity in't iv 4 648
And so still think of The wrong I did myself v 1 8
Say you see them not and think me still no gentleman born v 2 142
No longer shall you gaze on't, lest your fancy May think anon it moves v 3 61
He'll think anon it lives.—O sweet Paulina, Make me to think so twenty years together! v 3 70
You'll think—Which I protest against—I am assisted By wicked powers v 3 89
Those that think it is unlawful business I am about, let them depart v 3 96

Think. Of one mother, mighty king; That is well known; and, as I think, one father — *K. John* i 1 60
Till then, fair boy, Will I not think of home, but follow arms — ii 1 31
By my soul, I think His father never was so true begot — ii 1 129
Whether thy tale be true.—As true as I believe you think them false — iii 1 27
I love thee well; And, by my troth, I think thou lovest me well — iii 3 55
Come, grin on me, and I will think thou smilest And buss thee as thy wife — iii 4 34
I should forget my son, Or madly think a babe of clouts were he — iii 4 58
'Tis strange to think how much King John hath lost In this — iii 4 121
You may think my love was crafty love And call it cunning — iv 1 53
Some reasons . . . I have possess'd you with and think them strong — iv 2 41
Think you I bear the shears of destiny? — iv 2 91
Whate'er you think, good words, I think, were best — iv 3 28
What think you? have you beheld, Or have you read or heard? or could you think? Or do you almost think, although you see, That you do see? — iv 3 41
Stand back, I say; By heaven, I think my sword's as sharp as yours — iv 3 82
That you shall think the devil is come from hell — iv 3 100
I did not think the king so stored with friends — v 4 1
Where I may think the remnant of my thoughts In peace — v 4 46
I did not think to be so sad to-night As this hath made me — v 5 15
Hubert, I think?—Thou hast a perfect thought — v 6 6
Befriend me so much as to think I come one way of the Plantagenets — v 6 10
We think the eagle-winged pride . . . set on you To wake our peace — *Richard II.* i 3 129
Think not the king did banish thee, But thou the king — i 3 279
Those thoughts Which honour and allegiance cannot think — ii 1 208
Think what you will, we seize into our hands His plate — ii 1 209
So heavy sad As, though on thinking on no thought I think, Makes me with heavy nothing faint and shrink — ii 2 31
Though you think that all, as you have done, Have torn their souls — iii 3 82
We'll play at bowls.—'Twill make me think the world is full of rubs — iii 4 4
Think you then the king shall be deposed?—Depress'd he is already — iii 4 67
Although I be not he; And yet, amen, if heaven do think him me — iv 1 175
Learn, good soul, To think our former state a happy dream — v 1 18
Think I am dead and that even here thou takest, As from my death-bed, thy last living leave — v 1 38
Thou shalt think, Though he divide the realm and give thee half, It is too little — v 1 59
He shall think that thou, which know'st the way To plant unrightful kings, wilt know again . . . another way To pluck him headlong — v 1 62
Then am I king'd again: and by and by Think that I am unking'd — v 5 37
What think you, coz, Of this young Percy's pride? — *1 Hen. IV.* i 1 91
Redeeming time when men think least I will — i 2 241
I think his father loves him not And would be glad he met with some mischance — i 3 231
I speak not this in estimation, As what I think might be, but what I know — i 3 273
Bear ourselves as even as we can, The king will always think him in our debt, And think we think ourselves unsatisfied — i 3 286
I think this be the most villanous house in all London road for fleas — ii 1 15
I think you are more beholding to the night than to fern-seed — ii 1 97
I shall think the better of myself and thee during my life — ii 4 302
What think you they portend?—Hot livers and cold purses — ii 4 354
A most noble carriage; and, as I think, his age some fifty — ii 4 466
I think it is good morrow, is it not?—Indeed, my lord, I think it be two o'clock — ii 4 573
I think there's no man speaks better Welsh — iii 1 50
I'll sit and hear her sing: By that time will our book, I think, be drawn — iii 1 224
Do not think so; you shall not find it so — iii 2 129
I never see thy face but I think upon hell-fire and Dives — iii 3 35
If I did not think thou hadst been an ignis fatuus or a ball of wildfire — iii 3 44
What do you think, Sir John? do you think I keep thieves in my house? — iii 3 62
Dost thou think I'll fear thee as I fear thy father? — iii 3 170
Think how such an apprehension May turn the tide of fearful faction — iv 1 66
Men must think, If we without his help can make a head — iv 1 79
Yet all our joints are whole.—As heart can think — iv 1 84
You would think that I had a hundred and fifty tattered prodigals — iv 2 36
I am as vigilant as a cat to steal cream.—I think, to steal cream indeed — iv 2 66
I do not think a braver gentleman . . . is now alive — v 1 89
I think thou art enamoured On his follies — v 2 70
I did not think thee lord of such a spirit — v 4 18
Think not, Percy, To share with me in glory any more — v 4 63
I cannot think, my lord, your son is dead — *2 Hen. IV.* i 1 104
It is a kind of deafness.—I think you are fallen into the disease — i 2 135
I think we are a body strong enough, Even as we are — i 3 66
I think I am as like to ride the mare — ii 1 84
What wouldst thou think of me, if I should weep?—I would think thee a most princely hypocrite — ii 2 56
Thou art a blessed fellow to think as every man thinks — ii 2 61
What the good-year! do you think I would deny her? — ii 4 191
Not so; I did not think thou wast within hearing — ii 4 336
For the which I think thou wilt howl — ii 4 374
I was once of Clement's Inn, where I think they will talk of mad Shallow yet — iii 2 15
Every thing set off That might so much as think you enemies — iv 1 146
I think you are Sir John Falstaff, and in that thought yield me — iv 3 18
Do you think me a swallow, an arrow, or a bullet? — iv 3 35
Where is the prince your brother?—I think he's gone to hunt — iv 4 14
Thinking you dead, And dead almost, my liege, to think you were — iv 5 157
And hear, I think, the very latest counsel That ever I shall breathe — iv 5 183
I think the young king loves you not.—I know he doth not — v 2 9
This new and gorgeous garment, majesty, Sits not so easy on me as you think — v 2 45
You are, I think, assured I love you not.—I am assured — v 2 64
I did not think Master Silence had been a man of this mettle — v 3 40
Thou art now one of the greatest men in this realm.—By'r lady, I think a' be — v 3 93
Think, when we talk of horses, that you see them — *Hen. V.* Prol. 26
The hour, I think, is come To give him hearing: is it four o'clock? — i 1 92
Think you not that the powers we bear with us Will cut their passage? — ii 2 15
There's not, I think, a subject That sits in heart-grief and uneasiness — ii 2 26
I, to comfort him, bid him a' should not think of God — ii 3 21
But though we think it so, it is no matter — ii 4 42
Think we King Harry strong; And princes, look you strongly arm to meet him — ii 4 48
O, do but think You stand upon the rivage — iii Prol. 13
I think a' will plow up all, if there is not better directions — iii 2 67

Think. Peradventure I shall think you do not use me with that affability as in discretion you ought to use me — *Hen. V.* iii 2 138
I think in my very conscience he is as valiant a man as Mark Antony — iii 6 14
He longs to eat the English.—I think he will eat all he kills — iii 7 100
Is it meet, think you, that we should also, look you, be an ass and a fool? — iv 1 79
Is not that the morning which breaks yonder?—I think it be — iv 1 89
We see yonder the beginning of the day, but I think we shall never see the end of it — iv 1 92
I pray you, what thinks he of our estate?—Even as men wrecked — iv 1 98
Though I speak it to you, I think the king is but a man, as I am — iv 1 105
I think he would not wish himself any where but where he is — iv 1 124
It were not sin to think that, making God so free an offer, He let him outlive that day to see His greatness — iv 1 193
O Lord, O, not to-day, think not upon the fault My father made! — iv 1 310
And gentlemen in England now a-bed Shall think themselves accursed they were not here — iv 3 65
One, as he thinks, the most brave, valorous, and thrice-worthy — iv 4 65
I think it is in Macedon where Alexander is porn — iv 7 23
What think you, Captain Fluellen? is it fit this soldier keep his oath? — iv 7 137
How now, sir! you villain!—Do you think I'll be forsworn? — iv 8 13
Thou wouldst think I had sold my farm to buy my crown — v 2 128
Or shall we think the subtle-witted French Conjurers and sorcerers? — *1 Hen. VI.* i 1 25
A third thinks, . . . By guileful fair words peace may be obtain'd — i 1 76
I think, by some odd gimmors or device Their arms are set like clocks — i 2 41
When I have chased all thy foes from hence, Then will I think upon a recompense.—Meantime look gracious — i 2 116
I laugh to see your ladyship so fond To think that you have aught but Talbot's shadow Whereon to practise — ii 3 46
And think me honoured To feast so great a warrior in my house — ii 3 81
And say withal I think he held the right — ii 4 38
Think not, although in writing . . . , That therefore I have forged — iii 1 10
I think the Duke of Burgundy will fast Before he'll buy again at such a rate — iii 2 42
But where is Pucelle now? I think her old familiar is asleep — iii 2 122
O, think upon the conquest of my father, My tender years! — iv 1 148
Damsel of France, I think I have you fast: Unchain your spirits — v 3 30
Speaks Suffolk as he thinks?—Fair Margaret knows That Suffolk doth not flatter — v 3 141
I think she knows not well, There were so many, whom she may accuse — v 4 80
It is enough; I'll think upon the questions — *2 Hen. VI.* i 2 82
Beldam, I think we watch'd you at an inch. What, madam, are you there? — i 4 45
How think you by that? Were it not good your grace could fly to heaven? — ii 1 16
Would ye not think his cunning to be great, that could restore this cripple? — ii 1 132
This news, I think, hath turn'd your weapon's edge — ii 1 180
I think I have taken my last draught in this world — ii 3 73
I think she comes; and I'll prepare My tear-stain'd eyes to see her miseries — ii 4 15
Whilst I think I am thy married wife And thou a prince — ii 4 28
To think upon my pomp shall be my hell — ii 4 41
Had I first been put to speak my mind, I think I should have told — iii 1 44
Is it but thought so? what are they that think it? — iii 1 107
As the snake . . . doth sting a child That for the beauty thinks it excellent — iii 1 230
Say as you think, and speak it from your souls — iii 1 247
And thinks he that the chirping of a wren, By crying comfort from a hollow breast, Can chase away the first-conceived sound? — iii 2 42
And think it but a minute spent in sport — iii 2 338
That thou mightst think upon these by the seal — iii 2 344
What, think you much to pay two thousand crowns? — iv 1 18
I think he hath a very fair warning — iv 6 11
I think this word 'sallet' was born to do me good — iv 10 11
I do not mistake; But thou mistakest me much to think I do — v 1 130
But little thinks we shall be of her council — *3 Hen. VI.* i 1 36
Think you 'twere prejudicial to his crown? — i 1 144
For all the claim thou lay'st, Think not that Henry shall be so deposed — i 1 153
And, father, do but think How sweet a thing it is to wear a crown — i 2 28
Think but upon the wrong he did us all — i 4 173
The like yet never heard of. I think it cites us, brother, to the field — ii 1 34
But think you, lords, that Clifford fled with them?—No, 'tis impossible — ii 6 37
I think his understanding is bereft — ii 6 60
For, as we think, You are the king King Edward hath deposed — iii 1 68
I think he means to beg a child of her — iii 2 27
What think you Of this new marriage? — iv 1 1
I mind to tell him plainly what I think — iv 1 8
Speak freely what you think.—Then this is mine opinion — iv 1 28
I hear, yet say not much, but think the more — iv 1 83
Is Lewis so brave? belike he thinks me Henry — iv 1 96
Else might I think that Clarence, Edward's brother, Were but a feigned friend — iv 2 10
Had I not reason, think ye, to make haste — v 6 72
I'll tell you what; I think it is our way — *Richard III.* i 1 78
Fouler than heart can think thee, thou canst make No excuse current — i 2 83
Bear with her weakness, which, I think, proceeds From wayward sickness — i 3 28
Cannot a plain man live and think no harm? — i 3 51
Bid Gloucester think of this, and he will weep — i 4 245
Think you my uncle did dissemble, grandam?—Ay, boy.—I cannot think it — ii 2 31
The compact is firm and true in me.—And so in me; and so, I think, in all — ii 2 134
He thinks that you should bear me on your shoulders — iii 1 131
Think you, my lord, this little prating York Was not incensed by his subtle mother To taunt and scorn you? — iii 1 151
I'll send some packing that yet think not on it — iii 2 63
So 'twill do With some men else, who think themselves as safe As thou and I — iii 2 68
Think you, but that I know our state secure, I would be so triumphant? — iii 2 83
Your grace, we think, should soonest know his mind — iii 4 9
I think there's never a man in Christendom That can less hide his love — iii 4 53
What, think you we are Turks or infidels? — iii 5 41
I dance attendance here; I think the duke will not be spoke withal — iii 7 56
You might haply think Tongue-tied ambition, not replying, yielded — iii 7 144
Think now what I would say.—Say on — iv 2 10
But think how I may do thee good, And be inheritor of thy desire — iv 3 33

Think. Think that thy babes were fairer than they were, And he that slew them fouler than he is *Richard III.* iv 4 120
My daughter's mother thinks it with her soul.—What do you think? iv 4 256
What, thou?—I, even I: what think you of it, madam? iv 4 267
Think, how thou stab'dst me in my prime of youth At Tewksbury v 3 119
Think upon Grey, and let thy soul despair!—Think upon Vaughan v 3 141
Awake, and think our wrongs in Richard's bosom Will conquer him! v 3 144
I think there be six Richmonds in the field; Five have I slain to-day v 4 11
Think ye see The very persons of our noble story As they were living *Hen. VIII.* Prol. 25
Think you see them great, And follow'd with the general throng Prol. 27
Grievingly I think, The peace between the French and us not values The cost that did conclude it i 1 87
I would pray our monsieurs To think an English courtier may be wise, And never see the Louvre i 3 22
A running banquet ere they rested, I think would better please 'em i 4 13
I do not think he fears death.—Sure, he does not ii 1 37
Cardinal Campeius is arrived, and lately; As all think, for this business ii 1 161
I think you have hit the mark: but is't not cruel That she should feel the smart? ii 1 165
We are too open here to argue this; Let's think in private more ii 1 169
What think you of a duchess? have you limbs To bear that load of title? ii 3 38
It faints me, To think what follows ii 3 104
Do not deliver What here you've heard to her.—What do you think me? ii 3 107
I hold my most malicious foe, and think not At all a friend to truth ii 4 83
Can you think, lords, That any Englishman dare give me counsel? iii 1 83
Think us Those we profess, peace-makers, friends, and servants iii 1 166
Is he ready To come abroad?—I think, by this he is iii 2 83
If we did think His contemplation were above the earth, And fix'd on spiritual object, he should still Dwell in his musings iii 2 130
A time To think upon the part of business which I bear i' the state iii 2 145
And, when he thinks, good easy man, full surely His greatness is a-ripening, nips his root, And then he falls iii 2 356
Cromwell, I did not think to shed a tear In all my miseries iii 2 428
Hats, cloaks,—Doublets, I think,—flew up iv 1 74
I think your grace, Out of the pain you suffer'd, gave no ear to't iv 2 7
I may tell it you, I think I have Incensed the lords o' the council v 1 42
For I must think of that which company Would not be friendly to v 1 75
The strangest sight . . . I think your highness saw this many a day v 2 21
Do you think, my lords, The king will suffer but the little finger Of this man to be vex'd? v 3 105
You play the spaniel, And think with wagging of your tongue to win me v 3 127
He had better starve Than but once think this place becomes thee not v 3 133
The devil was amongst 'em, I think, surely v 4 62
The words I utter Let none think flattery, for they'll find 'em truth v 5 17
This day, no man think Has business at his house v 5 75
I swear to you, I think Helen loves him better than Paris *Troi. and Cres.* i 2 116
I think his smiling becomes him better than any man in all Phrygia i 2 134
I cannot choose but laugh, to think how she tickled his chin i 2 149
I think he went not forth to-day i 2 239
Doth think it rich To hear the wooden dialogue and sound i 3 154
And wake him to the answer, think you?—Yes, 'tis most meet i 3 332
Like merchants, show our foulest wares, And think, perchance, they'll sell i 3 360
I think, thy horse will sooner con an oration than thou learn a prayer ii 1 18
Dost thou think I have no sense, thou strikest me thus? ii 1 23
We may not think the justness of each act Such and no other than event doth form it ii 2 119
Lest perchance he think We dare not move the question ii 3 88
You shall not sin, If you do say we think him over-proud ii 3 132
What is he more than another?—No more than what he thinks he is.—Is he so much? Do you not think he thinks himself a better man than I am? ii 3 152
They think my little stomach to the war And your great love to me restrains you thus iii 3 220
What think you of this man that takes me for the general? iii 3 263
As black defiance As heart can think or courage execute iv 1 13
I constantly do think—Or rather, call my thought a certain knowledge iv 1 40
Come, you are deceived, I think of no such thing iv 2 40
And to his hand when I deliver her, Think it an altar iv 3 8
But be not tempted.—Do you think I will?—No iv 4 94
The prince must think me tardy and remiss, That swore to ride before him iv 4 143
What he has he gives, what thinks he shows iv 5 101
And modestly I think, The fall of every Phrygian stone will cost A drop of Grecian blood iv 5 222
Let it not be believed for womanhood! Think, we had mothers v 2 130
To square the general sex By Cressid's rule: rather think this not Cressid v 2 133
But they think we are too dear *Coriolanus* i 1 19
You must not think to fob off our disgrace with a tale i 1 97
What do you think, You, the great toe of this assembly? i 1 158
These are the words: I think I have the letter here i 2 7
Nor did you think it folly To keep your great pretences veil'd i 2 19
I think, you'll find They've not prepared for us i 2 29
She will but disease our better mirth.—In troth, I think she would i 3 118
How prevail'd you?—Will the time serve to tell? I do not think i 6 46
If any think brave death outweighs bad life i 6 71
What I think I utter, and spend my malice in my breath ii 1 58
Here's a letter from him: . . . and, I think, there's one at home for you ii 1 119
Think Rather our state's defective for requital Than we to stretch it out ii 2 53
I think if all our wits were to issue out of one skull, they would fly east, west, north, south ii 3 22
You must desire them To think upon you.—Think upon me! hang 'em! ii 3 62
You must think, if we give you any thing, we hope to gain by you ii 3 77
So his gracious nature Would think upon you for your voices ii 3 196
And do you think That his contempt shall not be bruising to you? ii 3 209
Think Upon the wounds his body bears iii 3 49
I know you well, sir, and you know me: your name, I think, is Adrian iv 3 2
Hath been! is it ended, then? Our state thinks not so iv 3 17
The man, I think, that shall set them in present action iv 3 52
What service is here! I think our fellows are asleep iv 5 2
Dost not Think me for the man I am iv 5 62
I thought there was more in him than I could think iv 5 167
He is simply the rarest man i' the world.—I think he is iv 5 170
Affecting one sole throne, Without assistance.—I think not so iv 6 33
Although it seems, And so he thinks, and is no less apparent iv 7 20
Think you he'll carry Rome?—All places yield to him ere he sits down iv 7 27
I think he'll be to Rome As is the osprey to the fish iv 7 33

Think. I'll undertake't: I think he'll hear me *Coriolanus* v 1 48
Can you . . . think to front his revenges with the easy groans of old women? v 2 44
Can you think to blow out the intended fire your city is ready to flame in? v 2 48
What cause, do you think, I have to swoon? v 2 106
For such things as you, I can scarce think there's any, ye're so slight v 2 110
The sorrow that delivers us thus changed Makes you think so v 3 40
Think with thyself How more unfortunate than all living women Are we v 3 96
Dost thou think I'll grace thee with that robbery? v 6 88
If thy sons were ever dear to thee, O, think my son to be as dear to me! *T. Andron.* i 1 108
Think you not how dangerous It is to jet upon a prince's right? ii 1 63
He that had wit would think that I had none ii 3 1
Let him that thinks of me so abjectly Know that this gold must coin a stratagem ii 3 4
Have I not reason, think you, to look pale? ii 3 91
That woe is me to think upon thy woes iii 1 240
If you love me, as I think you do, Let's kiss and part iii 1 287
I think we are not brought so low, But that between us we can kill a fly iii 2 76
I blush to think upon this ignomy iv 2 115
She is so employ'd, He thinks, with Jove in heaven iv 3 40
Brought him hither, To use as you think needful of the man v 1 39
And calls herself Revenge, and thinks me mad v 2 186
Forget to think of her.—O, teach me how I should forget to think *Rom. and Jul.* i 1 231
'Tis not hard, I think, For men so old as we to keep the peace i 2 2
Let two more summers wither in their pride, Ere we may think her ripe to be a bride i 2 11
And I will make thee think thy swan a crow i 2 92
To think it should leave crying and say 'Ay' i 3 51
It is an honour that I dream not of.— . . . Well, think of marriage now i 3 69
That birds would sing and think it were not night ii 2 22
I am too fond, And therefore thou mayst think my 'haviour light ii 2 99
Till strange love, grown bold, Think true love acted simple modesty iii 2 16
Doth she not think me an old murderer? iii 3 94
I think she will be ruled In all respects by me iii 4 13
I think you are happy in this second match, For it excels your first iii 5 224
I dreamt my lady came and found me dead—Strange dream, that gives a dead man leave to think! v 1 7
Fly hence, and leave me: think upon these gone; Let them affright thee v 3 60
Am I mad, hearing him talk of Juliet, To think it was so? v 3 81
What dost thou think 'tis worth?—Not worth my thinking *T. of Athens* i 1 218
We should think ourselves for ever perfect i 2 89
O you gods, think I, what need we have any friends? i 2 98
I laugh to think that babe a bastard i 2 117
I think no usurer but has a fool to his servant ii 2 103
Canst thou the conscience lack, To think I shall lack friends? ii 2 185
Ne'er speak, or think, That Timon's fortunes 'mong his friends can sink.—I would I could not think it ii 2 239
That thought is bounty's foe; Being free itself, it thinks all others so ii 2 242
Does he think so backwardly of me now, That I'll requite it last? iii 3 18
I cannot think but, in the end, the villanies of man will set him clear iii 3 30
I think One business does command us all; for mine Is money iii 4 3
What do you think the hour?—Labouring for nine iii 4 8
I cannot think but your age has forgot me iii 5 93
It should not be, by the persuasion of his new feasting.—I should think so iii 6 10
Think not on't, sir.—If you had sent but two hours before iii 6 49
Spare not the babe, Whose dimpled smiles from fools exhaust their mercy; Think it a bastard iv 3 120
Think, thy slave man rebels, and by thy virtue Set them into confounding odds! iv 3 391
Do you fear it? Then must I think you would not have it so *J. Cæsar* i 2 81
I cannot tell what you and other men Think of this life i 2 94
He thinks too much: such men are dangerous i 2 195
He desired their worships to think it was his infirmity i 2 272
Till then, think of the world i 2 311
Therefore think him as a serpent's egg ii 1 32
I think we are too bold upon your rest: Good morrow, Brutus ii 1 86
To think that or our cause or our performance Did need an oath ii 1 135
Shall we sound him? I think he will stand very strong with us ii 1 142
I think it is not meet, Mark Antony, so well beloved of Cæsar, Should outlive Cæsar ii 1 155
For Mark Antony, think not of him; For he can do no more than Cæsar's arm When Cæsar's head is off ii 1 181
Think you I am no stronger than my sex, Being so father'd? ii 1 296
Think you to walk forth? You shall not stir out of your house to-day ii 2 8
That every like is not the same, O Cæsar, The heart of Brutus yearns to think upon! ii 2 129
Be not fond, To think that Cæsar bears such rebel blood iii 1 40
He'll think your mother chides, and leave you so iv 3 123
I did not think you could have been so angry iv 3 143
What do you think Of marching to Philippi presently?—I do not think it good iv 3 196
Is not the leaf turn'd down Where I left reading? Here it is, I think iv 3 274
I think it is the weakness of mine eyes That shapes this monstrous apparition iv 3 276
He thinks he still is at his instrument iv 3 293
When think you that the sword goes up again? Never v 1 52
Think not, thou noble Roman, That ever Brutus will go bound to Rome v 1 111
Think upon what hath chanced, and, at more time, The interim having weigh'd it, let us speak Our free hearts each to other *Macbeth* i 3 153
To you they have show'd some truth.—I think not of them ii 1 21
You do unbend your noble strength, to think So brainsickly of things ii 2 45
I am afraid to think what I have done; Look on't again I dare not ii 2 51
Think of this, good peers, But as a thing of custom: 'tis no other iii 4 96
You make me strange Even to the disposition that I owe, When now I think you can behold such sights iii 4 114
And I do think That had he Duncan's sons under his key . . . , they should find What 'twere to kill a father iii 6 17
You may be rightly just, Whatever I shall think iv 3 31
I think our country sinks beneath the yoke; It weeps, it bleeds iv 3 39
My mind she has mated, and amazed my sight. I think, but dare not speak v 1 87
Bid them make haste.—I think I hear them. Stand, ho! *Hamlet* i 1 14
Is not this something more than fantasy? What think you on't? i 1 55
I think it be no other but e'en so i 1 108
Throw to earth This unprevailing woe, and think of us As of a father i 2 107

Think. Do not mock me, fellow-student; I think it was to see my mother's wedding *Hamlet* i 2 178
I think I saw him yesternight.—Saw? who?—My lord, the king your father i 2 189
And we did think it writ down in our duty To let you know of it i 2 222
No more.—No more but so?—Think it no more i 3 10
I do not know, my lord, what I should think.—Marry, I'll teach you: think yourself a baby i 3 104
What hour now?—I think it lacks of twelve.—No, it is struck i 4 3
Which might deprive your sovereignty of reason And draw you into madness? think of it i 4 74
How say you, then; would heart of man once think it? But you'll be secret? i 5 121
I do think . . . that I have found The very cause of Hamlet's lunacy ii 2 46
At our more consider'd time we'll read, Answer, and think upon this business ii 2 82
What do you think of me?—As of a man faithful and honourable ii 2 129
What might you think, When I had seen this hot love on the wing . . . what might you, Or my dear majesty your queen here, think, If I had play'd the desk or table-book? ii 2 131
Do you think 'tis this?—It may be, very likely ii 2 151
We think not so, my lord.—Why, then, 'tis none to you ii 2 254
To think, my lord, if you delight not in man, what lenten entertainment the players shall receive from you ii 2 328
I think their inhibition comes by the means of the late innovation ii 2 346
As I think, they have already order This night to play before him iii 1 20
What think you on't?—It shall do well iii 1 183
Confine him where Your wisdom best shall think iii 1 195
Nay, do not think I flatter; For what advancement may I hope from thee? iii 2 61
Do you think I meant country matters?—I think nothing, my lord iii 2 124
You think what now you speak; But what we do determine oft we break iii 2 196
So think thou wilt no second husband wed iii 2 224
'Sblood, do you think I am easier to be played on than a pipe? iii 2 386
Indeed would make one think there might be thought, Though nothing sure, yet much unhappily iv 5 12
I cannot choose but weep, to think they should lay him i' the cold ground iv 5 69
You must not think That we are made of stuff so flat and dull That we can let our beard be shook with danger And think it pastime iv 7 30
Why ask you this?—Not that I think you did not love your father iv 7 111
Let's further think of this iv 7 149
I think it be thine, indeed; for thou liest in't v 1 131
A whoreson mad fellow's it was: whose do you think it was? v 1 194
Dost thou think Alexander looked o' this fashion i' the earth? v 1 218
Does it not, thinks't thee, stand me now upon . . . To quit him with this arm? v 2 63
You will lose this wager, my lord.—I do not think so v 2 220
But thou wouldst not think how ill all's here about my heart v 2 222
My lord, I'll hit him now.—I do not think't v 2 306
I think our father will hence to-night.—That's most certain *Lear* i 1 287
In respect of that, I would fain think it were not.—It is his i 2 70
My duty cannot be silent when I think your highness wronged i 4 71
I'll resume the shape which thou dost think I have cast off for ever i 4 331
I am glad to see your highness.—Regan, I think you are; I know what reason I have to think so ii 4 131
I cannot think my sister in the least Would fail her obligation ii 4 143
Those that mingle reason with your passion Must be content to think you old ii 4 238
You think I'll weep; No, I'll not weep: I have full cause of weeping ii 4 285
When we our betters see bearing our woes, We scarcely think our miseries our foes iii 6 110
He that will think to live till he be old, Give me some help! iii 7 69
I such a fellow saw; Which made me think a man a worm iv 1 35
Think that the clearest gods, who make them honours Of men's impossibilities, have preserved thee iv 6 73
For, as I am a man, I think this lady To be my child Cordelia iv 7 69
Ay, so I think.—He knows not what he says v 3 292
We come to do you service and you think we are ruffians *Othello* i 1 110
Are they married, think you?—Truly, I think they are i 1 168
I think I can discover him, if you please To get good guard i 1 179
Is it they?—By Janus, I think no i 2 33
What is the matter, think you?—Something from Cyprus, as I may divine i 2 38
We must not think the Turk is so unskilful To leave that latest i 3 27
I think this tale would win my daughter too i 3 171
Heaven defend your good souls, that you think I will your serious and great business scant For she is with me i 3 267
With what else needful your good grace shall think To be sent after me i 3 287
Of a free and open nature, That thinks men honest that but seem to be so i 3 406
She that could think and ne'er disclose her mind ii 1 157
Will she love him still for prating? let not thy discreet heart think it ii 1 227
I dare think he'll prove to Desdemona A most dear husband ii 1 299
Do not think, gentlemen, I am drunk: this is my ancient ii 3 117
Very well then; you must not think then that I am drunk ii 3 122
I think you think I love you.—I have well approved it, sir ii 3 315
I protest, in the sincerity of love and honest kindness.—I think it freely ii 3 335
I think the issue will be, I shall have so much experience for my pains ii 3 372
I cannot think it, That he would steal away so guilty-like iii 3 38
I did not think he had been acquainted with her iii 3 99
What dost thou think?—Think, my lord!—Think, my lord! By heaven, he echoes me iii 3 105
My lord, you know I love you.—I think thou dost iii 3 117
I dare be sworn I think that he is honest.—I think so too iii 3 125
Men should be what they seem.—Why, then, I think Cassio's an honest man iii 3 129
I do not think but Desdemona's honest.—Long live she so! and long live you to think so! iii 3 225
I think my wife be honest and think she is not; I think that thou art just and think thou art not iii 3 384
It were a tedious difficulty, I think, To bring them to that prospect iii 3 397
I think the sun where he was born Drew all such humours from him iii 4 30
Nay, we must think men are not gods, Nor of them look for such observances iii 4 148
Pray heaven it be state-matters, as you think iii 4 155
And think it no addition, nor my wish, To have him see me woman'd iii 4 194
Will you think so?—Think so, Iago!—What, To kiss in private? iv 1 1
Think every bearded fellow that's but yoked May draw with you iv 1 67
Alas, poor rogue! I think, i' faith, she loves me iv 1 112
Bear some charity to my wit; do not think it so unwholesome iv 1 123
May be the letter moved him; For, as I think, they do command him home iv 1 247
If you think other, Remove your thought; it doth abuse your bosom iv 2 13

Think. Nay, I think it is scurvy, and begin to find myself fopped in it *Othello* iv 2 196
You shall think yourself bound to put it on him iv 2 248
Dost thou in conscience think,—tell me, Emilia,—That there be women do abuse their husbands In such gross kind? iv 3 61
In troth, I think thou wouldst not.—In troth, I think I should iv 3 70
I do not think there is any such woman.—Yes, a dozen iv 3 84
But I do think it is their husbands' faults If wives do fall iv 3 87
Is it sport? I think it is: and doth affection breed it? I think it doth iv 3 99
Let's think't unsafe To come in to the cry without more help v 1 43
I think that one of them is hereabout, And cannot make away v 1 57
Villany, villany! I think upon't, I think: I smell't: O villany! v 2 191
So come my soul to bliss, as I speak true; So speaking as I think, I die v 2 251
You shall understand what hath befall'n, Which, as I think, you know not v 2 308
You think none but your sheets are privy to your wishes *Ant. and Cleo.* i 2 41
I do think there is mettle in death, which commits some loving act upon her i 2 147
Why should I think you can be mine and true? i 3 27
Hardly gave audience, or Vouchsafed to think he had partners i 4 8
I must not think there are Evils enow to darken all his goodness i 4 10
You think of him too much.—O, 'tis treason! i 5 6
Yet have I fierce affections, and think What Venus did with Mars i 5 17
I did not think This amorous surfeiter would have donn'd his helm ii 1 32
His brother warr'd upon him; although, I think, Not moved by Antony ii 1 41
I did not think to draw my sword 'gainst Pompey ii 2 156
As I draw them up, I'll think them every one an Antony ii 5 14
Let me have your hand: I did not think, sir, to have met you here ii 6 50
You and I have known, sir.—At sea, I think.—We have, sir ii 6 87
I think the policy of that purpose made more in the marriage than the love of the parties.—I think so too ii 6 126
Though thou think me poor, I am the man Will give thee all the world ii 7 70
Cannot Think, speak, cast, write, sing, number, ho! iii 2 17
Like her! O Isis! 'tis impossible.—I think so iii 3 19
By Hercules, I think I am i' the right.—Soldier, thou art iii 7 68
What shall we do, Enobarbus?—Think, and die iii 13 1
Cæsar must think, When one so great begins to rage, he's hunted Even to falling iv 1 6
He thinks, being twenty times of better fortune, He is twenty men to one iv 2 3
Think you there was, or might be, such a man As this I dream'd of? v 2 93
You must think this, look you, that the worm will do his kind v 2 263
You must not think I am so simple but I know the devil himself will not eat a woman v 2 273
I think the king Be touch'd at very heart.—None but the king? *Cymbeline* i 1 9
I do not think So fair an outward and such stuff within Endows a man but he i 1 22
Whom in constancy you think stands so safe i 4 137
Will this hold, think you?—Signior Iachimo will not from it i 4 183
She doth think she has Strange lingering poisons i 5 33
Dost thou think in time She will not quench and let instructions enter? i 5 46
Think what a chance thou changest on, but think Thou hast thy mistress still i 5 68
To think that man . . . will his free hours languish for Assured bondage i 6 69
This secret Will force him think I have pick'd the lock ii 2 41
Or to report of you What I shall think is good ii 3 90
I do think I saw't this morning: confident I am Last night 'twas on mine arm ii 3 149
These boys know little they are sons to the king; Nor Cymbeline dreams that they are alive. They think they are mine iii 3 82
And I grieve myself To think, when thou shalt be disedged by her iii 4 96
Prithee, think There's livers out of Britain iii 4 142
I am most glad You think of other place iii 4 144
Sirrah, is this letter true?—Sir, as I think iii 5 107
To perform it directly and truly, I would think thee an honest man iii 5 114
O Jove! I think Foundations fly the wretched iii 6 6
But that it eats our victuals, I should think Here were a fairy iii 6 41
Think us no churls, nor measure our good minds By this rude place we live in iii 6 65
How you shall speed in your journey's end, I think you'll never return to tell v 4 190
So think of your estate.—Consider, sir, the chance of war v 5 74
Think more and more What's best to ask v 5 109
What think you?—The same dead thing alive v 5 122
That he could not But think her bond of chastity quite crack'd v 5 207
Think that you are upon a rock v 5 262
These two young gentlemen, that call me father And think they are my sons, are none of mine v 5 329
Think death no hazard in this enterprise *Pericles* i 1 5
Will think me speaking, though I swear to silence i 2 19
Antiochus you fear, And justly too, I think, you fear the tyrant i 2 103
And these our ships, you happily may think Are like the Trojan horse i 4 92
Where each man Thinks all is writ he speken can ii Gower 12
Let me ask you one thing: What do you think of my daughter, sir? ii 5 33
My daughter thinks very well of you; Ay, so well, that you must be her master ii 5 37
I am unworthy for her schoolmaster.—She thinks not so ii 5 41
May be, nor can I think the contrary, As great in blood as I myself ii 5 79
I think I shall have something to do with you iv 2 91
I think You'll turn a child again iv 3 3
Be one of those that think The petty wrens of Tarsus will fly hence iv 3 21
To think of what a noble strain you are, And of how coward a spirit iv 3 24
Think his pilot thought; So with his steerage shall your thoughts grow on iv 4 18
Patience, then, And think you now are all in Mytilene iv 4 51
I did not think Thou couldst have spoke so well; ne'er dream'd thou couldst iv 6 109
Think this his bark: Where what is done in action, more, if might, Shall be discover'd v Gower 22
I'ld wish no better choice, and think me rarely wed v 1 69
I think thou said'st Thou hadst been toss'd from wrong to injury v 1 130
It may be, You think me an imposter: no, good faith v 1 179

Think fit. Help me sort such needful ornaments As you think fit *Rom. and Jul.* iv 2 35
If you think fit, or that it may be done, Give me advantage of some brief discourse *Othello* iii 1 54

Think for. The conceit is deeper than you think for *T. of Shrew* iv 3 163

Think it best. Since the case so stands as now it doth, I think it best you married *Rom. and Jul.* iii 5 219

Think it fit. If he think it fit to shore them again *W. Tale* iv 4 869
If he shall think it fit, A saucy stranger in his court to mart As in a Romish stew, . . . he hath a court He little cares for *Cymbeline* i 6 150

Think it good. We'll rest us, Hermia, If you think it good *M. N. Dream* ii 2 37
What do you think Of marching . . . ?—I do not think it good *J. Cæsar* iv 3 198
Think it meet. If you think it meet, compound with him *Meas. for Meas.* iv 2 24
Nor did he think it meet To lay so dangerous and dear a trust On any soul removed *1 Hen. IV.* iv 1 33
Think it strange. I should not think it strange; for 'tis a physic That's bitter to sweet end *Meas. for Meas.* iv 6 7
You'ld think it strange if I should marry her *3 Hen. VI.* iii 2 111
Think it well. I think it well: And from this testimony of your own sex *Meas. for Meas.* ii 4 130
Sooner lost and worn Than women's are.—I think it well *T. Night* ii 4 36
Those that can pity, here May, if they think it well, let fall a tear *Hen. VIII.* Prol. 6
Think meet. If you think meet, this afternoon will post *K. John* v 7 94
I perchance hereafter shall think meet To put an antic disposition on *Ham.* i 5 171
My boon I make it, that you know me not Till time and I think meet *Lear* iv 7 11
She must overboard straight.—As you think meet *Pericles* iii 1 55
Think of. The most convenient place that I can think of *Hen. VIII.* ii 2 138
Something fears me to think of *Lear* iii 5 5
Think on. Sweet Valentine, adieu! Think on thy Proteus *T. G. of Ver.* i 1 12
Think on't, Jove; a foul fault! *Mer. Wives* v 5 12
Think on that; And mercy then will breathe within your lips *M. for M.* ii 2 77
Shall I have the thought To think on this? *Mer. of Venice* i 1 37
I pray thee, good Leonardo, think on this ii 2 178
Or I shall so be-mete thee with thy yard As thou shalt think on prating whilst thou livest! *T. of Shrew* iv 3 114
She uses me with a more exalted respect than any one else that follows her. What should I think on't? *T. Night* ii 5 32
And not a thought but thinks on dignity *2 Hen. VI.* iii 1 338
O, let me think on Hastings, and be gone! *Richard III.* iv 2 125
Think on the Tower and me: despair, and die! v 3 126
To-morrow in the battle think on me, And fall thy edgeless sword v 3 134
Think on Lord Hastings: despair, and die! v 3 148
In the battle think on Buckingham, And die in terror of thy guiltiness! v 3 169
I do not like their coming. Now I think on't, They should be good men *Hen. VIII.* iii 1 21
Well, cousin, I told you a thing yesterday; think on't.—So I do *T. and C.* i 2 186
Unless a man were cursed, I cannot tell what to think on't v 3 107
You shall not house with me: Look to't, think on't *Rom. and Jul.* iii 5 191
Thoughts which should indeed have died With them they think on *Macb.* iii 2 11
We with wisest sorrow think on him *Hamlet* i 2 6
And yet, within a month—Let me not think on't! i 2 146
Did these bones cost no more the breeding, but to play at loggats with 'em? mine ache to think on't v 1 101
We shall further think on't.—We must do something *Lear* i 1 311
It makes us, or it mars us; think on that *Othello* v 1 4
Think on thy sins.—They are loves I bear to you v 2 40
The borders maritime Lack blood to think on't *Ant. and Cleo.* i 4 52
Think on me, That am with Phœbus' amorous pinches black, And wrinkled deep? i 5 27
Ere I could tell him How I would think on him at certain hours *Cymbeline* i 3 27
Think on my words.—And shall do i 5 85
What is it to be false? To lie in watch there and to think on him? iii 4 43
Now I think on thee, My hunger's gone iii 6 15
Augustus lives to think on't: and so much For my peculiar care v 5 83
Left me breath Nothing to think on but ensuing death *Pericles* ii 1 7
But what I am, want teaches me to think on ii 1 76
Think scorn. I think scorn to sigh: methinks I should outswear Cupid *L. L. Lost* i 2 66
The nobility think scorn to go in leather aprons *2 Hen. VI.* iv 2 13
Their blood thinks scorn, Till it fly out and show them princes born *Cymb.* iv 4 53
Think well. If you think well to carry this as you may *Meas. for Meas.* iii 1 267
Think'st it much to tread the ooze Of the salt deep *Tempest* i 2 252
Thou think'st there is no more such shapes as he i 2 478
What think'st thou of the fair Sir Eglamour? *T. G. of Ver.* i 2 9
What think'st thou of the rich Mercatio?—Well of his wealth i 2 12
Let me have What thou thinkest meet and is most mannerly ii 7 58
Think'st thou I am so shallow, so conceitless? iv 2 96
Thou thinkest not of this now. Nay, I remember the trick you served me iv 4 37
Shall I do any good, thinkest thou? *Mer. Wives* i 4 152
Thinkest thou I'll endanger my soul gratis? ii 2 15
Is he at Master Ford's already, think'st thou? iv 1 2
Think'st thou thy oaths . . . Were testimonies against his worth? *Meas. for Meas.* v 1 242
Dost thou jeer and flout me in the teeth? Think'st thou I jest? *Com. of Er.* ii 2 23
Thou thinkest I am in sport *Much Ado* i 1 179
What thinkest thou? Had we fought, I doubt we should have been too young v 1 118
Thinkest thou, Hortensio, though her father be very rich, any man is so very a fool to be married to hell? *T. of Shrew* i 1 127
I prithee, tell me what thou think'st of me *T. Night* i 1 150
What thinkest thou of his opinion? iv 2 58
Thinkest thou, for that I insinuate, or toaze from thee thy business, I am therefore no courtier? *W. Tale* iv 4 759
O, thou think'st To serve me last *Richard II.* iii 4 94
Thou thinkest me as far in the devil's book as thou *2 Hen. IV.* ii 2 48
O hound of Crete, think'st thou my spouse to get? *Hen. V.* ii 1 77
Think'st thou the fiery fever will go out With titles blown from adulation? iv 1 270
Is't thou that thinkest to beguile me? *1 Hen. VI.* i 2 65
If thou think'st on heaven's bliss, Hold up thy hand *2 Hen. VI.* iii 3 27
Think'st thou that I will leave my kingly throne? *3 Hen. VI.* i 1 124
What! think'st thou that we fear them? i 2 53
If so thou think'st, vex him with eager words ii 6 68
What love, think'st thou, I sue so much to get? iii 2 61
Think'st thou I am an executioner?—A persecutor, I am sure v 6 30
What think'st thou? is it not an easy matter? *Richard III.* iii 1 161
What think'st thou, then, of Stanley? what will he? iii 1 167
What thinkest thou, will our friends prove all true?—No doubt v 3 213
What think'st thou, Norfolk?—A good direction, warlike sovereign v 3 301
Think'st thou to catch my life so pleasantly? *Troi. and Cres.* iv 5 249
Think'st thou it honourable for a noble man Still to remember wrongs? *Coriolanus* v 3 154
If thou think'st I am too quickly won, I'll frown *Rom. and Jul.* ii 2 95
O, think'st thou we shall ever meet again?—I doubt it not iii 5 51
How shall I thank him, thinkest thou? *T. of Athens* iii 2 37
What, think'st That the bleak air, thy boisterous chamberlain, Will put thy shirt on warm? iv 3 221
And tell me truly what thou think'st of him *J. Cæsar* i 2 214
I would not be the villain that thou think'st *Macbeth* iv 3 35
Thinkest. Think'st thou that duty shall have dread to speak, When power to flattery bows? *Lear* i 1 149
That justly think'st, and hast most rightly said i 1 186
Thou think'st 'tis much that this contentious storm Invades us to the skin iii 4 6
What will I do, thinkest thou?—Why, go to bed, and sleep *Othello* i 3 304
If thou but think'st him wrong'd and makest his ear A stranger to thy thoughts iii 3 143
Think'st thou I'ld make a life of jealousy? iii 3 177
Where think'st thou he is now? Stands he, or sits he? *Ant. and Cleo.* i 5 19
What thou think'st his very action speaks In every power that moves iii 12 35
Now, Iras, what think'st thou? Thou, an Egyptian puppet, shalt be shown v 2 207
Having thus far proceeded,—Unless thou think'st me devilish *Cymbeline* i 5 16
Thinking. 'Tis pity love should be so contrary; And thinking on it makes me cry 'alas!' *T. G. of Ver.* iv 4 89
Hath he any eyes? hath he any thinking? *Mer. Wives* iii 2 31
Belike thinking me remiss in mine office *Meas. for Meas.* iv 2 118
She told me, not thinking I had been myself *Much Ado* ii 1 250
An bad thinking do not wrest true speaking, I'll offend nobody iii 4 33
Indeed I cannot think, if I would think my heart out of thinking iii 4 85
Says his bravery is not on my cost, Thinking that I mean him *As Y. Like It* ii 7 81
I can live no longer by thinking v 2 55
I was thinking with what manners I might safely be admitted *All's W.* iv 5 93
I am wrapp'd in dismal thinkings v 3 128
Thinking his voice an armed Englishman *K. John* v 2 145
Who can hold a fire in his hand By thinking on the frosty Caucasus? . . . Or wallow naked in December snow By thinking on fantastic summer's heat? *Richard II.* i 3 295
Though on thinking on no thought I think, Makes me with heavy nothing faint and shrink ii 2 31
Thinking his prattle to be tedious v 2 26
Coming to look on you, thinking you dead, And dead almost *2 Hen. IV.* iv 5 156
Thinking of nothing else, putting all affairs else in oblivion v 5 26
I heard a bird so sing, Whose music, to my thinking, pleased the king v 5 114
Beshrew my father's ambition! he was thinking of civil wars when he got me *Hen. V.* v 2 242
As one that surfeits thinking on a want *2 Hen. VI.* iii 2 348
I was too hot to do somebody good, That is too cold in thinking of it now *Richard III.* i 3 312
With a heavy heart, Thinking on them, go I unto the Tower iii 1 150
Thinking that We are a queen, or long have dream'd so *Hen. VIII.* ii 4 70
I am afraid His thinkings are below the moon iii 2 134
Thinking it harder for our mistress to devise imposition enough than for us to undergo any difficulty imposed *Troi. and Cres.* iii 2 85
Thy master now lies thinking in his bed Of thee and me v 2 78
Thinking upon his services, took from you The apprehension *Coriolanus* ii 3 231
O'ercome with pride, ambitious past all thinking, Self-loving iv 6 31
Still blush, as thinking their own kisses sin *Rom. and Jul.* iii 3 39
What dost thou think 'tis worth?—Not worth my thinking *T. of Athens* i 1 219
I am thinking what I shall say I have provided for him v 1 34
For all that, to my thinking, he would fain have had it *J. Cæsar* i 2 240
To my thinking, he was very loath to lay his fingers off it i 2 242
Thinking by this face To fasten in our thoughts that they have courage v 1 10
Thinking by our late dear brother's death Our state to be disjoint *Hamlet* i 2 19
There is nothing either good or bad, but thinking makes it so ii 2 256
He must build churches, then; or else shall he suffer not thinking on iii 2 143
Or some craven scruple Of thinking too precisely on the event iv 4 41
I am thinking, brother, of a prediction I read this other day *Lear* i 2 152
'Tis probable and palpable to thinking *Othello* i 2 76
She puts her tongue a little in her heart, And chides with thinking ii 1 108
This advice is free I give and honest, Probal to thinking ii 3 344
Speak to me as to thy thinkings, As thou dost ruminate iii 3 131
It were enough To put him to ill thinking iii 4 29
The time shall not Out-go my thinking on you *Ant. and Cleo.* iii 2 61
My mistress exceeds in goodness the hugeness of your unworthy thinking *Cymbeline* i 4 157
I stole these babes; Thinking to bar thee of succession iii 3 102
I am thinking of the poor men that were cast away before us even now *Pericles* ii 1 18
Thinly. Cakes of roses Were thinly scatter'd, to make up a show *R. and J.* v 1 48
This may help to thicken other proofs That do demonstrate thinly *Oth.* iii 3 431
Third. This Is the third man that e'er I saw *Tempest* i 2 445
Every third thought shall be my grave v 1 311
'What cur is that?' says another: 'Whip him out,' says the third *T. G. of Ver.* iv 4 24
This is the third time; I hope good luck lies in odd numbers *Mer. Wives* v 1 2
Here stand a pair of honourable men; A third is fled *Much Ado* v 1 277
The third of the five vowels, if you repeat them; or the fifth, if I *L. L. L.* v 1 56
The third he caper'd, and cried, 'All goes well' v 2 113
Then, for the third part of a minute, hence *M. N. Dream* ii 2 2
He hath a third at Mexico, a fourth for England *Mer. of Venice* i 3 20
This Jacob from our holy Abram was . . . The third possessor i 3 75
This third, dull lead, with warning all as blunt ii 7 8
She wept for the death of a third husband iii 1 11
A third cannot be matched, unless the devil himself turn Jew iii 1 81
So he served the second, and so the third. Yonder they lie *As Y. Like It* i 2 137
The third, the Reply Churlish; the fourth, the Reproof Valiant v 4 98
Third, or fourth, or fifth borough, I'll answer him by law *T. of Shrew* Ind. 1 13
Another bear the ewer, the third a diaper Ind. 1 57
One that lies three thirds *All's Well* ii 5 32
One draught above heat makes him a fool; the second mads him; and a third drowns him *T. Night* i 5 141
He's in the third degree of drink, he's drowned i 5 143
I will plant you two, and let the fool make a third ii 3 189
And the old saying is, the third pays for all v 1 40
I have three daughters; the eldest is eleven; The second and the third, nine, and some five *W. Tale* ii 1 145
My third comfort, Starr'd most unluckily, is from my breast, The innocent milk in it most innocent mouth, Haled out to murder iii 2 99
For the third, if he fight longer than he sees reason, I'll forswear arms *1 Hen. IV.* i 2 208
Perforce a third Must take up us *2 Hen. IV.* i 3 72
And every third word a lie iii 2 330
The third, Sir Thomas Grey, knight, of Northumberland *Hen. V.* ii Prol. 24
The clocks do toll, And the third hour of drowsy morning name iv Prol. 16
A third thinks, without expense at all, By guileful fair words peace may be obtain'd *1 Hen. VI.* i 1 76
Duke of Clarence, Third son to the third Edward King of England ii 4 84
The lawful heir Of Edward king, the third of that descent ii 5 66

Third. Henry doth claim the crown from John of Gaunt, The fourth son; York claims it from the third . . . . 2 *Hen. VI.* ii 2 55
There's two of you; the devil make a third! . . . . . iii 2 303
Both Dukes of Somerset, Have sold their lives unto the house of York; And thou shalt be the third . . . . 3 *Hen. VI.* v 1 75
Now, by my George, my garter, and my crown,— Profaned, dishonour'd, and the third usurp'd . . . . *Richard III.* iv 4 367
The third day comes a frost, a killing frost . . . *Hen. VIII.* iii 2 355
He comes the third time home with the oaken garland . *Coriolanus* ii 1 138
Do more than counterpoise a full third part The charges of the action v 6 78
Two may keep counsel when the third's away . . . *T. Andron.* iv 2 144
Rests me his minim rest, one, two, and the third in your bosom *Rom. and Jul.* ii 4 23
Then he offered it the third time; he put it the third time by *J. Cæsar* i 2 244
And thy hair, Thou other gold-bound brow, is like the first. A third is like the former . . . . *Macbeth* iv 1 115
And I with them the third night kept the watch . . . *Hamlet* i 2 208
If Hamlet give the first or second hit, Or quit in answer of the third exchange, Let all the battlements their ordnance fire . . . . v 2 280
Come, for the third, Laertes: you but dally . . . . . v 2 308
To thee and thine hereditary ever Remain this ample third of our fair kingdom . . . . *Lear* i 1 82
What can you say to draw A third more opulent than your sisters? . i 1 88
Cornwall and Albany, With my two daughters' dowers digest this third i 1 130
This fellow has banished two on's daughters, and did the third a blessing . . . . i 4 115
Let him appear by the third sound of the trumpet . . . . v 3 113
The third o' the world is yours; which with a snaffle You may pace easy *Ant. and Cleo.* ii 2 63
A' bears the third part of the world, man; see'st not?—The third part, then, is drunk . . . . ii 7 96
Seizes him: so the poor third is up, till death enlarge his confine . . iii 5 12
That is the second thing that I have commanded thee: the third is, that thou wilt be a voluntary mute to my design . . *Cymbeline* iii 5 158
Who of their broken debtors take a third, A sixth, a tenth . . . v 4 19
And what's the third?—The third of Antioch . . . . *Pericles* ii 2 28
Third-borough. I must go fetch the third-borough . . *T. of Shrew* Ind. 1 12
Thirdly, they have verified unjust things . . . . *Much Ado* v 1 222
Thirdly, I ask thee what's their offence . . . . . . v 1 226
Thirst. With satiety seeks to quench his thirst . . . *T. of Shrew* i 1 24
Whose great decision hath much blood let forth And more thirsts after *All's Well* iii 1 4
That unhappy king, my master, whom I so much thirst to see *W. Tale* iv 4 524
Dost thou thirst, base Trojan, to have me fold up Parca's fatal web? *Hen. V.* v 1 20
Then be at peace, except ye thirst for blood . . 1 *Hen. VI.* iii 1 117
Whose unstanched thirst York and young Rutland could not satisfy 3 *Hen. VI.* ii 6 83
I speak this in hunger for bread, not in thirst for revenge . *Coriolanus* i 1 25
To all, and him, we thirst, And all to all . . . . *Macbeth* iii 4 91
Thirsting. The rascal people, thirsting after prey . 2 *Hen. VI.* iv 4 51
Thirsty. Like rats that ravin down their proper bane, A thirsty evil *Meas. for Meas.* i 2 134
This I think, When they are thirsty, fools would fain have drink *L. L. L.* v 2 372
None so dry or thirsty Will deign to sip or touch one drop of it *T. of S.* v 2 144
No more the thirsty entrance of this soil Shall daub her lips with her own children's blood . . . . 1 *Hen. IV.* i 1 5
Thy brother's blood the thirsty earth hath drunk . . 3 *Hen. VI.* ii 3 15
My heart is thirsty for that noble pledge . . . . *J. Cæsar* iv 3 160
Doth give me A more content in course of true delight Than to be thirsty after tottering honour . . . . *Pericles* iii 2 40
Thirteen. From her birth Had number'd thirteen years . . . *T. Night* v 1 252
That day that made my sister thirteen years . . . . . v 1 255
Here's a large mouth, indeed, . . . Talks as familiarly of roaring lions As maids of thirteen do of puppy-dogs! . . . . *K. John* ii 1 460
In thirteen battles Salisbury o'ercame . . . . 1 *Hen. VI.* i 4 78
In all shapes that man goes up and down in from fourscore to thirteen *T. of Athens* ii 2 120
Thirties. Thirty dozen moons with borrow'd sheen About the world have times twelve thirties been . . . . *Hamlet* iii 2 168
Thirtieth. Ere the thirtieth of May next ensuing . . . 2 *Hen. VI.* i 1 49
Thirty. Five and thirty leagues off and on . . . . *Tempest* iii 2 17
Some fifteen year or more.—Ay, and the time seems thirty unto me *T. of Shrew* Ind. 2 116
Being perhaps, for aught I see, two and thirty, a pip out . . i 2 33
How deep?—Thirty fathom . . . . *All's Well* iv 1 63
Of as able body as when he numbered thirty . . . . . . iv 5 86
Full thirty thousand marks of English coin . . . . *K. John* ii 1 530
How thirty, at least, he fought with . . . . . 1 *Hen. IV.* ii 2 211
Any time this two and thirty years . . . . iii 3 54
I have thirty miles to ride yet ere dinner time . . . . . iii 3 221
Thirty thousand.—Forty let it be . . . . iv 1 130
Didst thou not kiss me and bid me fetch thee thirty shillings? 2 *Hen. IV.* ii 1 111
Pamper'd jades of Asia, Which cannot go but thirty mile a-day . . ii 4 179
I judge their number Upon or near the rate of thirty thousand . . iv 1 22
Their power, I think, is thirty thousand strong . . 3 *Hen. VI.* ii 1 177
With a band of thirty thousand men Comes Warwick . . . . ii 1 68
Whom thou obeyed'st thirty and six years . . . . . . iii 3 96
The queen is valued thirty thousand strong . . . . . v 3 14
Thirty years.—What, man! 'tis not so much . . *Rom. and Jul.* i 5 35
His son is thirty.—Will you tell me that? . . . . . . i 5 41
Never, till Cæsar's three and thirty wounds Be well avenged . *J. Cæsar* v 1 53
Full thirty times hath Phœbus' cart gone round . . . *Hamlet* iii 2 165
Thirty dozen moons with borrow'd sheen About the world have times twelve thirties been . . . . iii 2 167
I have been sexton here, man and boy, thirty years . . . . v 1 177
Some five or six and thirty of his knights, Hot questrists after him *Lear* iii 7 16
How many, as you guess?—Of thirty sail . . . . . *Othello* i 3 37
I do think she's thirty.—Bear'st thou her face in mind? *Ant. and Cleo.* iii 3 31
Thirty one. Toad, that under cold stone Days and nights has thirty one Swelter'd venom sleeping got . . . . *Macbeth* iv 1 7
Thirty-three years have I but gone in travail Of you, my sons *Com. of Er.* v 1 400
This. But how is it That this lives in thy mind? . . . *Tempest* i 2 49
Why, this it is: my heart accords thereto . . . *T. G. of Ver.* i 3 90
Alas! this parting strikes poor lovers dumb . . . . . . ii 2 21
Nay, 'twill be this hour ere I have done weeping . . . . . ii 3 1
To this her mother's plot She seemingly obedient . . *Mer. Wives* iv 6 32
This is a strange abuse. Let's see thy face . . *Meas. for Meas.* v 1 205
Of Corinth that, of Epidaurus this . . . . . *Com. of Errors* i 1 94
Stop in your wind, sir: tell me this, I pray . . . . . . i 2 53
This. What shall become of this? what will this do? . . . *Much Ado* iv 1 211
Hymen now with luckier issue speed's Than this for whom we render'd up this woe . . . . v 3 33
I thank you, sir: and, pray you, tell me this . . . . *As Y. Like It* i 2 280
This I must do, or know not what to do: Yet this I will not do . . iii 3 34
Why, this's a heavy chance 'twixt him and you . . . *T. of Shrew* i 2 46
A poor officer of mine; and writ to me this other day . . *All's Well* iv 3 226
Do me this courteous office, as to know of the knight . . . *T. Night* iii 4 278
You denied to fight with me this other day . . . . *W. Tale* v 2 140
Further I will not flatter you, my lord, That all I see in you is worthy love, Than this . . . . *K. John* ii 1 518
Let me tell you this: I have had feeling of my cousin's wrongs *Rich. II.* ii 3 140
This and much more, much more than twice all this . . . . iii 1 28
I have forsworn his company hourly any time this two and twenty years 1 *Hen. IV.* ii 2 17
Out of this nettle, danger, we pluck this flower, safety . . . . ii 3 10
And said this other day you ought him a thousand pound . . . iii 3 152
They are both hanged; and so would this be . . . . *Hen. V.* iv 4 78
Why, this it is, when men are ruled by women . . . *Richard III.* i 1 62
Why, this it is; see, see! . . . . *Hen. VIII.* ii 3 81
What was his cause of anger?—The noise goes, this . *Troi. and Cres.* i 2 12
Hector's opinion Is this in way of truth . . . . ii 2 189
How far off lie these armies?—Within this mile and half . *Coriolanus* i 4 8
I shall, between this and supper, tell you most strange things . . iv 3 43
Within this three hours will fair Juliet wake . . . *Rom. and Jul.* v 2 24
Thus much of this [gold] will make black white, foul fair, Wrong right, base noble, old young, coward valiant. Ha, you gods! why this? what this, you gods? Why, this Will lug your priests and servants from your sides . . . . *T. of Athens* iv 3 28
This [gold] is it That makes the wappen'd widow wed again . . . iv 3 37
As far, my lord, as will fill up the time 'Twixt this and supper *Macbeth* iii 1 26
What, is this so?—Ay, sir, all this is so . . . . iv 1 124
This above all: to thine own self be true . . . . . *Hamlet* i 3 78
Say, why is this? wherefore? what should we do? . . . . . i 4 57
Take this from this, if this be otherwise . . . . ii 2 156
Good my lord, How does your honour for this many a day? . . . iii 1 91
Look here, upon this picture, and on this . . . . iii 4 53
And what judgement Would step from this to this? . . . . . iii 4 71
Heaven hath pleased it so, To punish me with this and this with me . iii 4 174
Now, out of this,— What out of this, my lord? . . . . . . iv 7 107
As a stranger to my heart and me Hold thee, from this, for ever . *Lear* i 1 118
Where's my fool? I have not seen him this two days . . . . i 4 77
This' a good block; It were a delicate stratagem . . . . . iv 6 187
This to hear Would Desdemona seriously incline . . . . *Othello* i 3 145
And this, and this, the greatest discords be That e'er our hearts shall make! . . . . ii 1 200
Why, this it is to have a name in great men's fellowship *Ant. and Cleo.* ii 7 12
To let him breathe between the heavens and earth, A private man in Athens: this for him . . . . iii 12 15
O Antony! I have follow'd thee to this . . . . v 1 36
That our stars, Unreconciliable, should divide Our equalness to this . v 1 48
Thisbe. Anon his Thisbe must be answered . . . *M. N. Dream* iii 2 18
A tedious brief scene of young Pyramus And his love Thisbe . . v 1 57
But, silence! here comes Thisbe . . . . v 1 267
Well run, Thisbe.—Well shone, Moon . . . . v 1 271
How chance Moonshine is gone before Thisbe comes back and finds her lover? . . . . v 1 319
A mote will turn the balance, which Pyramus, which Thisbe, is the better . . . . v 1 325
And hanged himself in Thisbe's garter . . . . v 1 366
In such a night Did Thisbe fearfully o'ertrip the dew . *Mer. of Venice* v 1 7
Thisbe a grey eye or so, but not to the purpose . . *Rom. and Jul.* ii 4 45
Thisby. Most cruel death of Pyramus and Thisby . . *M. N. Dream* i 2 13
You must take Thisby on you.—What is Thisby? a wandering knight? . i 2 46
Let me play Thisby too, I'll speak in a monstrous little voice . . i 2 54
Ah Pyramus, my lover dear! thy Thisby dear, and lady dear! . . i 2 56
No; you must play Pyramus: and, Flute, you Thisby . . . . i 2 58
Robin Starveling, you must play Thisby's mother . . . . . i 2 62
You, Pyramus' father: myself, Thisby's father . . . . . i 2 65
There are things in this comedy of Pyramus and Thisby that will never please . . . . iii 1 10
You know, Pyramus and Thisby meet by moonlight . . . . . iii 1 50
Pyramus and Thisby, says the story, did talk through the chink of a wall . . . . iii 1 65
Through that cranny shall Pyramus and Thisby whisper . . . . iii 1 73
Thisby, stand forth.—Thisby, the flowers of odious savours sweet . iii 1 83
Savours sweet: So hath thy breath, my dearest Thisby dear . . . iii 1 87
If I were fair, Thisby, I were only thine . . . . . . iii 1 106
In any case, let Thisby have clean linen . . . . iv 2 40
This beauteous lady Thisby is certain . . . . v 1 131
The trusty Thisby, coming first by night, Did scare away . . . v 1 141
And finds his trusty Thisby's mantle slain . . . . . . v 1 146
And Thisby, tarrying in mulberry shade, His dagger drew, and died . v 1 149
Through which the lovers, Pyramus and Thisby, Did whisper often . v 1 160
Alack, alack, I fear my Thisby's promise is forgot! . . . . v 1 174
But what see I? No Thisby do I see. O wicked wall! . . . . v 1 180
'Deceiving me' is Thisby's cue . . . . v 1 186
Now will I to the chink, To spy an I can hear my Thisby's face. Thisby! v 1 195
I trust to take of truest Thisby sight . . . . v 1 280
Thus Thisby ends: Adieu, adieu, adieu . . . . v 1 353
Thisne. I'll speak in a monstrous little voice, 'Thisne, Thisne' . . i 2 55
Thistle. There thou prickest her with a thistle . . . . *Much Ado* iii 4 76
Kill me a red-hipped humble-bee on the top of a thistle *M. N. Dream* iv 1 12
Nothing teems But hateful docks, rough thistles, kecksies, burs *Hen. V.* v 2 52
Thither. And thither will I bring thee . . . . . *T. G. of Ver.* i 1 55
'Twere good, I think, your lordship sent him thither . . . . i 3 29
I will go to her alone: How shall I best convey the ladder thither? . iii 1 128
Thither provoked and instigated by his distemper . . . *Mer. Wives* iii 5 77
When you have brought him thither, What shall be done with him? . iv 4 44
Thither I must, although against my will . . . . *Com. of Errors* iv 1 112
Our dinner done, and he not coming thither, I went to seek him . . v 1 224
Come, let us thither: this may prove food to my displeasure *Much Ado* i 3 67
I'll bring you thither, my lord, if you'll vouchsafe me . . . . iii 2 3
Please it your majesty Command me any service to her thither? *L. L. L.* v 2 312
Herein mean I to enrich my pain, To have his sight thither *M. N. Dream* i 1 251
Come, you and I will thither presently . . . . *Mer. of Venice* iv 1 455
Nothing remains but that I kindle the boy thither . . *As Y. Like It* i 1 179
I would I were at home.—We'll lead you thither . . . . . iv 3 162
Let your wedding be to-morrow: thither will I invite the duke . . v 2 16
There will we mount, and thither walk on foot . . . *T. of Shrew* iv 3 188

Thither. I fear, the angle that plucks our son thither . . *W. Tale* iv 2 52
I think it not uneasy to get the cause of my son's resort thither . iv 2 57
Till so much blood thither come again, Have I not reason to look pale? *Richard II.* iii 2 78
Whither I go, thither shall you go too; To-day will I set forth 1 *Hen. IV.* ii 3 118
Rome shall remedy this.—Roam thither, then . . 1 *Hen. VI.* iii 1 51
Thither go these news, as fast as horse can carry them . . 2 *Hen. VI.* i 4 78
We will commit thee thither, Until his army be dismiss'd . . iv 9 39
Will thither straight, for willingness rids way . . 3 *Hen. VI.* v 3 21
Down, down to hell; and say I sent thee thither . . . v 6 67
Let him thank me, that holp to send him thither . . *Richard III.* i 2 107
And thither bear your treasure and your goods . . . ii 4 69
It reaches far, and where 'twill not extend, Thither he darts it *Hen. VIII.* i 1 112
You are transported by calamity Thither where more attends you *Coriol.* i 1 78
Thitherward. We met him thitherward; for thence we came *All's Well* iii 2 55
Thoas. Amphimachus and Thoas deadly hurt . . . *Troi. and Cres.* v 5 12
Thomas. What's to do here, Thomas tapster? . . *Meas. for Meas.* i 2 115
Thomas of Norfolk, what say'st thou to this? . . . . *Richard II.* i 1 110
But Thomas, my dear lord, my life, my Gloucester . . . . i 2 16
Is not his brother, Thomas of Clarence, with him? . . 2 *Hen. IV.* iv 4 16
The prince thy brother? He loves thee, and thou dost neglect him, Thomas . . . iv 4 21
Learn this, Thomas, And thou shalt prove a shelter to thy friends . iv 4 41
Why art thou not at Windsor with him, Thomas?—He is not there to-day iv 4 50
The sixth was Thomas of Woodstock, Duke of Gloucester 2 *Hen. VI.* ii 2 16
Sir James Blunt, And Rice ap Thomas, with a valiant crew *Richard III.* iv 5 12
Thomas the Earl of Surrey . . . Went through the army, cheering up the soldiers . . . . v 3 69
Sir Thomas, Whither were you a-going?—To the cardinal's *Hen. VIII.* i 3 49
Come, good Sir Thomas, We shall be late else; which I would not be . i 3 64
Good hour of night, Sir Thomas! Whither so late? . . . v 1 5
Hear me, Sir Thomas: you're a gentleman Of mine own way . . v 1 27
Thorn. Tooth'd briers, sharp furzes, pricking goss, and thorns *Tempest* iv 1 180
Alack, my hand is sworn Ne'er to pluck thee from thy thorn *L. L. Lost* iv 3 112
Withering on the virgin thorn . . . . . . *M. N. Dream* i 1 77
One must come in with a bush of thorns and a lanthorn . . . iii 1 61
Briers and thorns at their apparel snatch . . . . . iii 2 29
This man, with lanthorn, dog, and bush of thorn, Presenteth Moonshine v 1 136
This thorn Doth to our rose of youth rightly belong . *All's Well* i 3 135
When you have our roses, You barely leave our thorns to prick ourselves iv 2 19
When briers shall have leaves as well as thorns, And be as sweet as sharp iv 4 32
Which being spotted Is goads, thorns, nettles, tails of wasps *W. Tale* i 2 329
But O, the thorns we stand upon! . . . . iv 4 596
And lose my way Among the thorns and dangers of this world *K. John* iv 3 141
Children yet unborn Shall feel this day as sharp to them as thorn *Richard II.* iv 1 323
And plant this thorn, this canker, Bolingbroke . . . 1 *Hen. IV.* i 3 176
Pluck a red rose from off this thorn with me . . . 1 *Hen. VI.* ii 4 33
Hath not thy rose a thorn, Plantagenet? . . . . . . ii 4 69
To mow down thorns that would annoy our foot, Is worthy praise 2 *Hen. VI.* iii 1 67
And I,—like one lost in a thorny wood, That rends the thorns and is rent with the thorns . . . . . . 3 *Hen. VI.* iii 2 175
What! can so young a thorn begin to prick? . . . . . v 5 13
Is love a tender thing? it is too rough, Too rude, too boisterous, and it pricks like thorn . . . . . *Rom. and Jul.* i 4 26
Leave her to heaven And to those thorns that in her bosom lodge *Hamlet* i 5 87
Thorn-bush. The lanthorn is the moon; I, the man in the moon; this thorn-bush, my thorn-bush . . . . . *M. N. Dream* v 1 263
Thornier. If she were a thornier piece of ground than she is . *Pericles* iv 6 153
Thorny hedgehogs, be not seen . . . . . *M. N. Dream* ii 2 10
The thorny point Of bare distress hath ta'en from me the show Of smooth civility . . . . *As Y. Like It* ii 7 94
Or Daphne roaming through a thorny wood . . *T. of Shrew* Ind. 2 59
Like one lost in a thorny wood, That rends the thorns and is rent 3 *Hen. VI.* iii 2 174
Brave followers, yonder stands the thorny wood . . . . . v 4 67
The sharp thorny points Of my alleged reasons drive this forward *Hen. VIII.* ii 4 224
Good my brother, Do not, as some ungracious pastors do, Show me the steep and thorny way to heaven . . . . *Hamlet* i 3 48
Thorough. Seeing her go thorough the streets . . *Mer. Wives* iv 5 32
Did make their retire To the court of his eye, peeping thorough desire *L. L. Lost* ii 1 235
Thorough bush, thorough brier, Over park, over pale, Thorough flood, thorough fire, I do wander every where . . . *M. N. Dream* ii 1 3
And thorough this distemperature we see The seasons alter . . . ii 1 106
How he glisters Thorough my rust! . . . . . . *W. Tale* iii 2 172
With Cain go wander thorough shades of night . . *Richard II.* v 6 43
The false revolting Normans thorough thee Disdain to call us lord 2 *Hen. VI.* iv 1 87
As a foreign recreant, be led With manacles thorough our streets *Coriolanus* v 3 115
Whose eyes do never give But thorough lust and laughter *T. of Athens* iv 3 492
These words become your lips as they pass thorough them . . v 1 198
You are contented to be led in triumph Thorough the streets *J. Cæsar* v 1 110
It pierced me thorough . . . . *Pericles* iv 3 35
Thoroughly woo her, wed her, and bed her, and rid the house of her! *T. of Shrew* i 1 149
Look into this business thoroughly . . . . 2 *Hen. VI.* ii 1 202
We shall heat you thoroughly anon . . . . v 1 159
These are almost thoroughly persuaded . . . . *Coriolanus* i 1 205
Those. O, I have suffer'd With those that I saw suffer . *Tempest* i 2 6
Those being all my study, The government I cast upon my brother . i 2 74
Of his bones are coral made; Those are pearls that were his eyes . . i 2 398
Is that paper nothing?—Nothing concerning me.—Then let it lie for those that it concerns . . . . *T. G. of Ver.* i 2 76
But those as sleep and think not on their sins, Pinch them *Mer. Wives* v 5 57
And bid those that are drunk get them to bed . . *Much Ado* iii 3 45
O, how ripe in show Thy lips, those kissing cherries, tempting grow! *M. N. Dream* iii 2 140
She hath spied him already with those sweet eyes . . . . v 1 328
'Nearest his heart:' those are the very words.—It is so *Mer. of Venice* iv 1 254
When you and those poor number saved with you Hung on our driving boat, I saw your brother . . . . *T. Night* i 2 10
Bind up those tresses. O, what love I note In the fair multitude of those her hairs! . . . . *K. John* iii 4 61
The names of those their nobles that lie dead . . . *Hen. V.* iv 8 96
God punish me With hate in those where I expect most love! *Richard III.* ii 1 35
Pray, think us Those we profess, peace-makers, friends . *Hen. VIII.* iii 1 167

Those. Take your choice of those That best can aid your action.—Those are they That most are willing . . . . . *Coriolanus* i 6 65
For those of old, And the late dignities heap'd up to them, We rest your hermits . . . . *Macbeth* i 6 18
O, by whom?—Those of his chamber, as it seem'd, had done't . . ii 3 106
I have known those which have walked in their sleep . . . v 1 66
Those he commands move only in command, Nothing in love . . . v 2 19
Those wicked creatures yet do look well-favour'd, When others are more wicked . . . . *Lear* ii 4 259
With those hands, that grasp'd the heaviest club, Subdue my worthiest self . . . . *Ant. and Cleo.* iv 12 46
Those arts they have as I Could put into them . . . *Cymbeline* v 5 338
Thou. Why, thou deboshed fish, thou . . . . . *Tempest* iii 2 29
Therefore know thou, for this I entertain thee . . *T. G. of Ver.* iv 4 75
Hast thou or word, or wit, or impudence, That yet can do thee office? *Meas. for Meas.* v 1 368
Thou drone, thou snail, thou slug, thou sot! . . . *Com. of Errors* ii 2 196
Thou drunkard, thou, what didst thou mean by this? . . . iii 1 10
What present hast thou there?—Some certain treason . *L. L. Lost* iv 3 189
Why, thou loss upon loss! the thief gone with so much . *Mer. of Venice* iii 1 96
Shed thou no blood, nor cut thou less nor more But just a pound of flesh . . . . iv 1 325
Dost thou believe't?—Ay, madam, knowingly . . . . *All's Well* i 3 257
If thou thou'st him some thrice, it shall not be amiss . . *T. Night* iii 2 48
O thou thing! Which I'll not call a creature of thy place . *W. Tale* ii 1 82
Thou dearest Perdita, . . . I prithee, darken not The mirth o' the feast iv 4 40
Thou wo't, wo't thou? thou wo't, wo't ta? do, do, thou rogue! do, thou hemp-seed!—Away, you scullion! . . . . . 2 *Hen. IV.* ii 1 63
Thou wouldst be gone to join with Richmond: I will not trust you *Richard III.* iv 4 491
I'm sure Thou hast a cruel nature and a bloody . . . *Hen. VIII.* v 3 129
Thou thing of no bowels, thou!—You dog! . . . . *Troi. and Cres.* ii 1 54
I shall forestall thee, Lord Ulysses, thou! . . . . . . iv 5 230
Thou damnable box of envy, thou, what meanest thou? . . . . v 1 29
Good thou, save me a piece of marchpane . . . . *Rom. and Jul.* i 5 9
Let molten coin be thy damnation, Thou disease of a friend! *T. of Athens* iii 1 56
I do not know that I did cry.—Yes, that thou didst . *J. Cæsar* iv 3 298
Thou canst not say I did it: never shake Thy gory locks at me *Macbeth* iii 4 50
Thouest. If thou thou'st him some thrice, it shall not be amiss *T. Night* iii 2 48
Though. We all were sea-swallow'd, though some cast again . *Tempest* ii 1 251
Though thou canst swim like a duck, thou art made like a goose . ii 2 134
Though the seas threaten, they are merciful . . . . . . v 1 178
I care not though he burn himself in love . . . *T. G. of Ver.* ii 5 55
Thy letters may be here, though thou art hence . . . . iii 1 248
He's a justice of peace in his country, simple though I stand here *M. W.* i 1 226
But what though? yet I live like a poor gentleman born . . . i 1 286
I'll eat nothing; I thank you as much as though I did . . . i 1 291
Patience unmoved! no marvel though she pause . *Com. of Errors* ii 1 32
Never any did so, though very many have been beside their wit *M. Ado* iv 1 127
What though care killed a cat, thou hast mettle enough in thee to kill care . . . . v 1 132
What though he love your Hermia? Lord, what though? *M. N. Dream* ii 2 109
What though I be not so in grace as you, So hung upon with love? . iii 2 232
My legs are longer though, to run away . . . . . . iii 2 343
What though you have no beauty,— . . . Must you be therefore proud? *As Y. Like It* iii 5 37
As though, belike, I knew not what to take . . . *T. of Shrew* i 1 104
I'll give her thanks, As though she bid me stay by her a week . . ii 1 179
Methinks he looks as though he were in love . . . . . iii 1 88
Would Katharine had never seen him though! . . . . . iii 2 26
Though that nature with a beauteous wall Doth oft close in pollution *T. Night* i 2 48
By chance but not by truth; what though? . . . . *K. John* i 1 169
Though that my death were adjunct to my act, By heaven, I would do it iii 3 57
I will wink and hold out mine iron: it is a simple one; but what though? . . . . *Hen. V.* ii 1 9
Though patience be a tired mare, yet she will plod . . . . ii 1 25
What though the mast be now blown overboard? . . 3 *Hen. VI.* v 4 3
What though I kill'd her husband and her father? . . *Richard III.* i 1 154
No marvel, my lord, though it affrighted you . . . . . i 4 64
I would not be so sick though for his place . . . *Hen. VIII.* ii 2 83
What we can do to him, though now the time Gives way to us, I much fear . . . . iii 2 15
What though I know her virtuous And well deserving? . . . . iii 2 97
I reck not though I end my life to-day . . . *Troi. and Cres.* v 6 26
No marvel, then, though he were ill affected . . . . *Lear* ii 1 100
Though that the queen on special cause is here, Her army is moved on iv 6 219
Though that his joy be joy, Yet throw such changes of vexation on't *Oth.* i 1 71
What though you fled From that great face of war? *Ant. and Cleo.* iii 13 4
Thought. More to know Did never meddle with my thoughts *Tempest* i 2 22
I wish mine eyes Would, with themselves, shut up my thoughts . . ii 1 192
These sweet thoughts do even refresh my labours . . . . iii 1 14
Thought is free . . . . iii 2 132; *T. Night* i 3 73
Here thought they to have done Some wanton charm . . *Tempest* iv 1 94
Come with a thought. I thank thee, Ariel: come.—Thy thoughts I cleave to . . . . iv 1 164
I thought to have told thee of it, but I fear'd Lest I might anger thee . iv 1 168
Give me thy hand. I do begin to have bloody thoughts . . . iv 1 220
I could not ask my father For his advice, nor thought I had one . . v 1 191
Every third thought shall be my grave . . . . . . v 1 311
Made wit with musing weak, heart sick with thought . *T. G. of Ver.* i 1 69
If you thought your love not cast away . . . . . . i 2 26
For contemning Love, Whose high imperious thoughts have punish'd me ii 4 130
The table wherein all my thoughts Are visibly character'd . . . ii 7 3
His oaths are oracles, His love sincere, his thoughts immaculate . . ii 7 76
Where I thought the remnant of mine age Should have been cherish'd . iii 1 74
My thoughts do harbour with my Silvia nightly . . . . iii 1 140
My herald thoughts in thy pure bosom rest them . . . . iii 1 144
Hope is a lover's staff; walk hence with that And manage it against despairing thoughts . . . . iii 1 247
A little time will melt her frozen thoughts . . . . . . iii 2 9
One Julia, that his changing thoughts forget, Would better fit his chamber . . . . iv 4 124
Would I might be dead If I in thought felt not her very sorrow! . . iv 4 177
Would any man have thought this? . . . . . *Mer. Wives* ii 2 304
Heaven make you better than your thoughts! . . . . . iii 3 219
How many numbers is in nouns?—Two.—Truly, I thought there had been one number more, because they say, 'Od's nouns' . . . iv 1 24
He is a better scholar than I thought he was . . . . . iv 1 83
That likewise have we thought upon . . . . iv 4 46

Thought. Whose flames aspire As thoughts do blow them, higher and higher *Mer. Wives* v 5 102
I was three or four times in the thought they were not fairies v 5 129
No, holy father; throw away that thought *Meas. for Meas.* i 3 1
I thought, by your readiness in the office, you had continued in it some time ii 1 275
Let it not sound a thought upon your tongue ii 2 140
Of those that lawless and incertain thought Imagine howling iii 1 127
With a thought that more depends on it than we must yet deliver iv 2 127
Consenting to the safeguard of your honour, I thought your marriage fit v 1 425
Thoughts are no subjects; Intents but merely thoughts v 1 458
I thought it was a fault, but knew it not v 1 468
Obedient to the stream, Was carried towards Corinth, as we thought *Com. of Errors* i 1 88
They three were taken up By fishermen of Corinth, as we thought i 1 112
I thought to have ask'd you.—And you said no iii 1 55
Here is the chain. I thought to have ta'en you at the Porpentine iii 2 172
Belike you thought our love would last too long, If it were chain'd together iv 1 25
And now he's there, past thought of human reason v 1 189
By my troth, I speak my thought *Much Ado* i 1 226
She loves him with an enraged affection; it is past the infinite of thought ii 3 106
I would have thought her spirit had been invincible against all assaults ii 3 119
You are thought here to be the most senseless and fit man for the constable iii 3 22
My elbow itched; I thought there would a scab follow iii 3 106
And thought they Margaret was Hero?—Two of them did iii 3 162
I like the new tire within excellently, if the hair were a thought browner iii 4 14
If half thy outward graces had been placed About thy thoughts iv 1 103
To turn all beauty into thoughts of harm iv 1 108
Thought I thy spirits were stronger than thy shames iv 1 127
Though he thought his accusation true iv 1 235
Sure as I have a thought or a soul iv 1 333
It will go near to be thought so shortly iv 2 24
I say to you, it is thought you are false knaves iv 2 30
Would deliver me from the reprobate thought of it *L. L. Lost* i 2 64
Most maculate thoughts, master, are masked under such colours i 2 97
Your own good thoughts excuse me, and farewell ii 1 176
By virtue, thou enforcest laughter; thy silly thought my spleen iii 1 77
Those thoughts to me were oaks, to thee like osiers bow'd iv 2 112
No thought can think, nor tongue of mortal tell iv 3 42
With the motion of all elements, Courses as swift as thought iv 3 330
I thought to close mine eyes some half an hour v 2 90
Fleeter than arrows, bullets, wind, thought, swifter things v 2 261
In such a presence here to plead my thoughts *M. N. Dream* i 1 61
I have heard so much, And with Demetrius thought to have spoke thereof i 1 112
It is a customary cross, As due to love as thoughts and dreams and sighs i 1 154
Through Athens I am thought as fair as she. But what of that? i 1 227
I must confess I thought you lord of more true gentleness ii 2 132
When I thought What harm a wind too great at sea might do *M. of Ven.* i 1 23
Shall I have the thought To think on this, and shall I lack the thought That such a thing bechanced would make me sad? i 1 36
Whose own hard dealings teaches them suspect The thoughts of others i 3 164
I would not change this hue, Except to steal your thoughts ii 1 12
Heaven and thy thoughts are witness ii 6 32
'Twere damnation To think so base a thought ii 7 50
O sinful thought! Never so rich a gem Was set in worse than gold ii 7 54
I thought upon Antonio when he told me ii 8 31
Be merry, and employ your chiefest thoughts To courtship ii 8 43
And yet a maiden hath no tongue but thought iii 2 8
Doubtful thoughts, and rash-embraced despair, And shuddering fear iii 2 109
Fair thoughts and happy hours attend on you! iii 4 41
And then 'tis thought Thou'lt show thy mercy and remorse iv 1 19
When every goose is cackling, would be thought No better a musician than the wren v 1 105
I beseech you, punish me not with your hard thoughts *As Y. Like It* i 2 196
Never so much as in a thought unborn Did I offend i 3 53
I thought that all things had been savage here ii 7 107
These trees shall be my books And in their barks my thoughts I'll character iii 2 6
There was no thought of pleasing you when she was christened iii 2 283
Certainly a woman's thought runs before her actions.—So do all thoughts iv 1 141
My friends told me as much, and I thought no less iv 1 188
That was begot of thought, conceived of spleen, and born of madness iv 1 217
I thought thy heart had been wounded with the claws of a lion v 2 25
One of them thought but of an If, as, 'If you said so, then I said so' v 4 105
Call home thy ancient thoughts from banishment *T. of Shrew* Ind. 2 33
Till I found it to be true, I never thought it possible or likely i 1 154
If you love the maid, Bend thoughts and wits to achieve her i 1 184
More Than words can witness, or your thoughts can guess ii 1 338
If thy thoughts, Bianca, be so humble To cast thy wandering eyes on every stale iii 1 89
'Tis thought your deer does hold you at a bay v 2 56
Lest it be rather thought you affect a sorrow than have it *All's Well* i 1 60
The best wishes that can be forged in your thoughts be servants to you! i 1 85
His good remembrance, sir, Lies richer in your thoughts than on his tomb i 2 49
She thought, I dare vow for her, they touched not any stranger sense i 3 113
Such were our faults, or then we thought them none i 3 141
Had from the conversation of my thoughts Haply been absent i 3 240
If seriously I may convey my thoughts In this my light deliverance ii 1 84
Humbly entreating from your royal thoughts A modest one ii 1 130
She, which late Was in my nobler thoughts most base ii 3 178
Your son will not be killed so soon as I thought he would iii 2 40
Make me but like my thoughts, and I shall prove A lover of thy drum iii 3 10
A friend whose thoughts more truly labour To recompense your love iv 4 17
When saucy trusting of the cozen'd thoughts Defiles the pitchy night iv 4 23
Noble she was, and thought I stood engaged v 3 95
The heavens have thought well on thee, Lafeu, To bring forth this discovery v 3 150
Lay a more noble thought upon mine honour v 3 180
Sir, for my thoughts, you have them ill to friend Till your deeds gain them v 3 182
Fairer prove your honour Than in my thought it lies v 3 184
'Tis thought among the prudent he would quickly have the gift of a grave *T. Night* i 3 33
An I thought that, I'ld forswear it i 3 93
He is a kind of puritan.—O, if I thought that, I'ld beat him like a dog! ii 3 153
She pined in thought, And with a green and yellow melancholy She sat ii 4 115
For his thoughts, Would they were blanks, rather than fill'd with me! iii 1 114
I come to whet your gentle thoughts On his behalf iii 1 116
Baited it with all the unmuzzled thoughts That tyrannous heart can think iii 1 130

Thought. An I thought he had been valiant and so cunning in fence I'ld have seen him damned ere I'ld have challenged him *T. Night* iii 4 311
Nor lean enough to be thought a good student iv 2 9
Come, boy, with me; my thoughts are ripe in mischief v 1 132
I had thought, sir, to have held my peace *W. Tale* i 2 28
Two lads that thought there was no more behind But such a day to-morrow i 2 63
His varying childness cures in me Thoughts that would thick my blood i 2 171
Or thought,—for cogitation Resides not in that man that does not think i 2 271
Or else be impudently negative, To have nor eyes nor ears nor thought i 2 275
With thoughts so qualified as your charities Shall best instruct you ii 1 113
No thought of him: The very thought of my revenges that way Recoil upon me ii 3 18
Being transported by my jealousies To bloody thoughts iii 2 160
Honourable thoughts, Thoughts high for one so tender iii 2 196
I did in time collect myself and thought This was so and no slumber iii 3 38
More than can be thought to begin from such a cottage iv 2 49
Lay aside the thoughts of Sicilia.—I willingly obey iv 2 58
For the life to come, I sleep out the thought of it iv 3 31
With these forced thoughts, I prithee, darken not The mirth o' the feast iv 4 41
Strangle such thoughts as these with any thing That you behold the while iv 4 47
It was thought she was a woman and was turned into a cold fish iv 4 282
By the pattern of mine own thoughts I cut out The purity of his iv 4 393
You have undone a man of fourscore three, That thought to fill his grave in quiet iv 4 465
And bids the other grow Faster than thought or time iv 4 565
If I thought it were a piece of honesty to acquaint the king withal, I would not do't iv 4 694
It is as bitter Upon thy tongue as in my thought v 1 19
With thought of such affections, Step forth mine advocate v 1 220
I thought of her, Even in these looks I made v 1 227
I thought she had some great matter there in hand v 2 113
If I had thought the sight of my poor image Would thus have wrought you,—for the stone is mine—I'ld not have show'd it v 3 57
I saw her, As I thought, dead v 3 140
From that supernal judge, that stirs good thoughts *K. John* ii 1 112
Though churlish thoughts themselves should be your judge ii 1 519
I would into thy bosom pour my thoughts iii 3 53
It makes the course of thoughts to fetch about iv 2 24
And fly like thought from them to me again iv 2 175
Within this bosom never enter'd yet The dreadful motion of a murderous thought iv 2 255
Could thought without this object, Form such another? iv 3 44
If I in act, consent, or sin of thought, Be guilty iv 3 135
Be great in act, as you have been in thought v 1 45
Where I may think the remnant of my thoughts In peace v 4 46
Hubert, I think?—Thou hast a perfect thought v 6 6
What doth our cousin lay to Mowbray's charge? It must be great that can inherit us So much as of a thought of ill in him *Richard II.* i 1 86
The eagle-winged pride Of sky-aspiring and ambitious thoughts i 3 130
He is gone; and with him go these thoughts i 4 37
Those thoughts Which honour and allegiance cannot think ii 1 207
Let us share thy thoughts, as thou dost ours ii 1 273
Speaking so, Thy words are but as thoughts; therefore, be bold ii 1 276
Though on thinking on no thought I think ii 2 31
Speak comfortable words.—Should I do so, I should belie my thoughts ii 2 77
I had thought, my lord, to have learn'd his health of you ii 3 24
'Tis thought the king is dead; we will not stay ii 4 7
Are we not high? High be our thoughts iii 2 89
Long have we stood To watch the fearful bending of thy knee, Because we thought ourself thy lawful king iii 3 74
What sport shall we devise here in this garden, To drive away the heavy thought of care? iii 4 2
Why am I sent for to a king, Before I have shook off the regal thoughts Wherewith I reign'd? iv 1 163
I thought you had been willing to resign.—My crown I am iv 1 190
You would have thought the very windows spake v 2 12
A generation of still-breeding thoughts, And these same thoughts people this little world v 5 8
No thought is contented. The better sort, As thoughts of things divine, are intermix'd With scruples v 5 11
Thoughts tending to ambition, they do plot Unlikely wonders v 5 18
Thoughts tending to content flatter themselves That they are not the first of fortune's slaves v 5 23
In this thought they find a kind of ease, Bearing their own misfortunes v 5 28
Now hath time made me his numbering clock: My thoughts are minutes v 5 51
But let him from my thoughts *1 Hen. IV.* i 1 91
Restore yourselves Into the good thoughts of the world again i 3 182
With a thought seven of the eleven I paid.—O monstrous! ii 4 242
Make my eyes look red, that it may be thought I have wept ii 4 424
And God forgive them that so much have sway'd Your majesty's good thoughts away from me! iii 2 131
If speaking truth In this fine age were not thought flattery iv 1 2
It will be thought By some, that know not why he is away iv 1 62
I thought your honour had already been at Shrewsbury iv 2 58
They wound my thoughts worse than thy sword my flesh v 4 80
But thought's the slave of life, and life time's fool v 4 81
Whiles the big year, swoln with some other grief, Is thought with child by the stern tyrant war *2 Hen. IV.* Ind. 14
Supposed sincere and holy in his thoughts, He's followed i 1 202
But if without him we be thought too feeble, My judgement is, we should not step too far i 3 19
Much smaller than the smallest of his thoughts i 3 30
O thoughts of men accursed! Past and to come seems best i 3 107
I had thought weariness durst not have attached one of so high blood ii 2 2
It would be every man's thought; and thou art a blessed fellow to think as every man thinks ii 2 60
Never a man's thought in the world keeps the road-way better than thine ii 2 62
And what accites your most worshipful thought to think so? ii 2 65
When a man is, being, whereby a' may be thought to be accommodated iii 2 87
All too confident To give admittance to a thought of fear iv 1 153
I think you are Sir John Falstaff, and in that thought yield me iv 3 19
Have I, in my poor and old motion, the expedition of thought? iv 3 37
Have broke their sleep with thoughts, their brains with care iv 5 69
I never thought to hear you speak again iv 5 92
Thy wish was father, Harry, to that thought iv 5 93
Thou hidest a thousand daggers in thy thoughts iv 5 107
If it did infect my blood with joy, Or swell my thoughts to any strain of pride iv 5 171
Question your royal thoughts, make the case yours v 2 91

Thought. Thy Doll, and Helen of thy noble thoughts, Is in base durance *2 Hen. IV.* v 5 35
Piece out our imperfections with your thoughts . . . *Hen. V.* Prol. 23
'Tis your thoughts that now must deck our kings . . . . . Prol. 28
Some things of weight That task our thoughts . . . . i 2 6
We have now no thought in us but France, Save those to God . . i 2 302
Let our proportions . . . Be soon collected and all things thought upon i 2 305
Every man now task his thought, That this fair action may on foot be brought . . . . i 2 309
And honour's thought Reigns solely in the breast of every man . ii Prol. 3
It will be thought we keep a bawdy house . . . . ii 1 37
And you, my gentle knight, give me your thoughts . . . . ii 2 14
I hoped there was no need to trouble himself with any such thoughts yet ii 3 23
In motion of no less celerity Than that of thought . . . iii Prol. 3
Work, work your thoughts, and therein see a siege . . iii Prol. 25
He scorns to say his prayers, lest a' should be thought a coward . iii 2 40
I am a soldier, A name that in my thoughts becomes me best . iii 3 6
But that we thought not good to bruise an injury till it were full ripe . iii 6 129
I thought upon one pair of English legs Did march three Frenchmen . iii 6 158
He hath not told his thought to the king?—No; nor it is not meet . iv 1 102
We are enow yet living in the field To smother up the English in our throngs, If any order might be thought upon . . . . . iv 5 21
Heave him away upon your winged thoughts Athwart the sea . v Prol. 8
So swift a pace hath thought . . . . v Prol. 15
In the quick forge and working-house of thought . . . . v Prol. 23
Your eyes advance, After your thoughts, straight back again . v Prol. 45
You thought, because he could not speak English in the native garb, he could not therefore handle an English cudgel . . . . v 1 79
Put off your maiden blushes; avouch the thoughts of your heart . . v 2 254
An army have I muster'd in my thoughts . . . . *1 Hen. VI.* i 1 101
Valiant Talbot above human thought Enacted wonders with his sword i 1 121
My thoughts are whirled like a potter's wheel; I know not where I am i 5 19
'Tis thought . . . They did amongst the troops of armed men Leap o'er the walls for refuge in the field . . . . ii 2 22
I thought I should have seen some Hercules . . . . . ii 3 19
In dumb significants proclaim your thoughts . . . . . ii 4 26
If thy thoughts were sifted, The king, thy sovereign, is not quite exempt From envious malice of thy swelling heart . . . iii 1 24
So perish they That grudge one thought against your majesty! . iii 1 176
Blame him not; I dare presume, sweet prince, he thought no harm . iv 1 179
I always thought It was both impious and unnatural . . . v 1 11
A virgin from her tender infancy, Chaste and immaculate in very thought . . . . v 4 51
I am sick with working of my thoughts . . . . . . v 5 86
If sympathy of love unite our thoughts . . . . *2 Hen. VI.* i 1 23
Banish the canker of ambitious thoughts . . . . . . i 2 18
May that thought, when I imagine ill Against my king and nephew, virtuous Henry, Be my last breathing in this mortal world! . . . i 2 19
Above the reach or compass of thy thought . . . . . i 2 46
I thought King Henry had resembled thee In courage, courtship . i 3 56
I never said nor thought any such matter: God is my witness . . i 3 191
Their master loves to be aloft And bears his thoughts above his falcon's pitch . . . . ii 1 12
Thine eyes and thoughts Beat on a crown, the treasure of thy heart . ii 1 19
This poor fellow, Which he had thought to have murder'd wrongfully . ii 3 107
'Tis thought, my lord, that you took bribes of France . . . —Is it but thought so? what are they that think it? . . . . . iii 1 104
Steel thy fearful thoughts, And change misdoubt to resolution . iii 1 331
Faster than spring-time showers comes thought on thought, And not a thought but thinks on dignity . . . . iii 1 337
O Thou that judgest all things, stay my thoughts, My thoughts, that labour to persuade my soul! . . . . iii 2 136
As being thought to contradict your liking, Makes them thus forward . iii 2 252
My thoughts do hourly prophesy Mischance . . . . . iii 2 283
And thought thee happy when I shook my head . . . . iv 1 55
I have thought upon it, it shall be so . . . . . . iv 7 15
These hands are free from guiltless blood-shedding, This breast from harbouring foul deceitful thoughts . . . . iv 7 109
I thought ye would never have given out . . . . . . iv 8 26
More like a king, more kingly in my thoughts . . . . . v 1 29
Unloose thy long-imprison'd thoughts, And let thy tongue be equal with thy heart . . . . v 1 88
Far be the thought of this from Henry's heart! . . *3 Hen. VI.* i 1 70
Bethink thee once again, And in thy thought o'er-run my former time . i 4 45
As I thought, March'd toward Saint Alban's to intercept the queen . ii 1 113
Why, then you mean not as I thought you did . . . . iii 2 65
Witch sweet ladies with my words and looks. O miserable thought! . iii 2 151
A man to be beloved? O monstrous fault, to harbour such a thought! iii 2 164
Those gracious words revive my drooping thoughts . . . . iii 3 21
My thoughts aim at a further matter . . . . . . iv 1 125
Such a pleasure as incaged birds Conceive when after many moody thoughts . . . . iv 6 13
If secret powers Suggest but truth to my divining thoughts . . iv 6 69
I thought, at least, he would have said the king . . . . v 1 29
But, whiles he thought to steal the single ten, The king was slily finger'd from the deck! . . . . v 1 43
I thought no less: it is his policy . . . . . . v 4 62
If you had, The thought of them would have stirr'd up remorse . v 5 64
What, will the aspiring blood of Lancaster Sink in the ground? I thought it would have mounted . . . . v 6 62
Dive, thoughts, down to my soul . . . . . *Richard III.* i 1 41
For my name of George begins with G, It follows in his thought that I am he . . . . i 1 59
'Tis very grievous to be thought upon. What, is he in his bed? . . i 1 141
If I thought that, I tell thee, homicide, These nails should rend that beauty from my cheeks . . . . i 2 125
Far be it from my heart, the thought of it! . . . . . i 3 150
And come to have the warrant, That we may be admitted where he is. —Well thought upon . . . . i 3 344
In falling, Struck me, that thought to stay him, overboard . . i 4 19
I thought thou hadst been resolute.—So I am, to let him live . . i 4 115
He little thought of this divided friendship . . . . . i 4 244
Less noble and less loyal, Nearer in bloody thoughts, but not in blood. ii 1 92
His fault was thought, And yet his punishment was cruel death . . ii 1 104
Welcome, dear cousin, my thoughts' sovereign . . . . . iii 1 2
I thought my mother, and my brother York, Would long ere this have met us . . . . iii 1 20
Then where you please, and shall be thought most fit . . . iii 1 66
Wherein my soul recorded The history of all her secret thoughts . . iii 5 28
All will come to nought, When such bad dealing must be seen in thought iii 6 14

Thought. In the mildness of your sleepy thoughts, Which here we waken to our country's good . . . . *Richard III.* iii 7 123
Seduced the pitch and height of all his thoughts To base declension . iii 7 188
Go thou to sanctuary, and good thoughts possess thee! . . . . iv 1 94
Having no more but thought of what thou wert, To torture thee the more iv 4 107
With pure heart's love, Immaculate devotion, holy thoughts . . . iv 4 404
'Tis thought that Richmond is their admiral . . . . . iv 4 437
I'll strive, with troubled thoughts, to take a nap . . . . v 3 104
They did perform Beyond thought's compass . . . . *Hen. VIII.* i 1 36
'If,' quoth he, 'I for this had been committed, As, to the Tower, I thought' . . . . i 2 194
The very thought of this fair company Clapp'd wings to me . . . i 4 8
Had the cardinal But half my lay thoughts in him, some of these Should find a running banquet . . . . i 4 11
I left him private, Full of sad thoughts and troubles . . . . ii 2 16
These sad thoughts, that work too much upon him. . . . . ii 2 58
In him It lies to cure me: and the cure is, to Remove these thoughts from you . . . . ii 4 102
Hence I took a thought, This was a judgement on me . . . . ii 4 193
Holy men I thought ye, Upon my soul, two reverend cardinal virtues . iii 1 102
She now begs, That little thought, when she set footing here, She should have bought her dignities so dear . . . . iii 1 183
Though perils did Abound, as thick as thought could make 'em . . iii 2 195
I had thought They had parted so much honesty among 'em . . v 2 27
I had thought I had had men of some understanding And wisdom . v 3 135
Truth shall nurse her, Holy and heavenly thoughts still counsel her . v 5 30
When fair Cressid comes into my thoughts,—So, traitor! 'When she comes!' When is she thence? . . . . . . *Troi. and Cres.* i 1 30
And that unbodied figure of the thought That gave't surmised shape . i 3 16
Would they but fat their thoughts With this cramm'd reason . . ii 2 48
Young men, whom Aristotle thought Unfit to hear moral philosophy . ii 2 166
Will you subscribe his thought, and say he is? . . . . . ii 3 156
And never suffers matter of the world Enter his thoughts . . . ii 3 197
Fair thoughts be your fair pillow! . . . . iii 1 49
Hot blood begets hot thoughts, and hot thoughts beget hot deeds . iii 1 142
Sweet, above thought I love thee . . . . iii 1 172
My thoughts were like unbridled children, grown Too headstrong. . iii 2 130
And fell so roundly to a large confession, To angle for your thoughts . iii 2 162
O that I thought it could be in a woman! . . . . . . iii 2 165
Keeps place with thought and almost, like the gods, Does thoughts unveil in their dumb cradles . . . . iii 3 200
I constantly do think—Or rather, call my thought a certain knowledge iv 1 41
Who, in your thoughts, merits fair Helen best? . . . . . iv 1 53
Give as soft attachment to thy senses As infants' empty of all thought! iv 2 6
With wings more momentary-swift than thought . . . . . iv 2 14
Wide unclasp the tables of their thoughts To every ticklish reader! . iv 5 60
Nor dignifies an impair thought with breath . . . . . iv 5 103
Could promise to himself A thought of added honour torn from Hector iv 5 145
Thou art thought to be Achilles' male varlet . . . . . v 1 17
I'll haunt thee like a wicked conscience still, That mouldeth goblins swift as frenzy's thoughts . . . . v 10 29
They do disdain us much beyond our thoughts . . . *Coriolanus* i 4 26
Where I thought to crush him in an equal force . . . . . i 10 14
'Tis thought That Marcius shall be consul . . . . . . ii 1 276
'Tis thought of every one Coriolanus will carry it . . . . ii 2 3
I had thought to have strucken him with a cudgel . . . . iv 5 155
I thought there was more in him than I could think . . . . iv 5 166
He bears himself more proudlier, Even to my person, than I thought he would . . . . iv 7 9
With such friends That thought them sure of you . . . . v 3 8
To grace him only That thought he could do more . . . . v 3 16
The god of soldiers . . . inform Thy thoughts with nobleness! . . v 3 72
How fair the tribune speaks to calm my thoughts! . . . *T. Andron.* i 1 46
Her to whom my thoughts are humbled all . . . . . . i 1 51
Arm thy heart, and fit thy thoughts, To mount aloft . . . . ii 1 12
Away with slavish weeds and servile thoughts! . . . . . ii 1 18
'Tis thought you have a goodly gift in horning . . . . . ii 3 67
Whose souls are not corrupted as 'tis thought . . . . . iii 1 9
That delightful engine of her thoughts, That blabb'd them with such pleasing eloquence . . . . iii 1 82
If I shall be thought thy son, Let me redeem my brothers both from death . . . . iii 1 180
O, how this villany Doth fat me with the very thoughts of it! . . . iii 1 204
Speechless complainer, I will learn thy thought . . . . . iii 2 39
Stir a mutiny in the mildest thoughts And arm the minds of infants . iv 1 85
Lord of my life, commander of my thoughts . . . . . . iv 4 28
King, be thy thoughts imperious, like thy name . . . . . iv 4 81
Being credulous in this mad thought . . . . v 2 74
Love's heralds should be thoughts, Which ten times faster glide than the sun's beams . . . . *Rom. and Jul.* ii 5 4
I thought all for the best . . . . iii 1 109
I thought thy disposition better temper'd . . . . . . iii 3 115
It may be thought we held him carelessly, . . . if we revel much . . iii 4 25
Wife, we scarce thought us blest That God had lent us but this only child . . . . iii 5 165
Proportion'd as one's thought would wish a man . . . . . iii 5 184
Have I thought long to see this morning's face, And doth it give me such a sight as this? . . . . iv 5 41
An unaccustom'd spirit Lifts me above the ground with cheerful thoughts . . . . v 1 5
O mischief, thou art swift To enter in the thoughts of desperate men! . v 1 36
O, this same thought did but forerun my need . . . . . v 1 53
Assurance bless your thoughts! . . . . . . *T. of Athens* ii 2 189
That thought is bounty's foe; Being free itself, it thinks all others so . ii 2 241
And 'mongst lords I be thought a fool . . . . iii 3 21
Upon that were my thoughts tiring, when we encountered . . . iii 6 4
What's to be thought of him? does the rumour hold for true? . . v 1 3
This breast of mine hath buried Thoughts of great value . *J. Cæsar* i 2 50
How I have thought of this and of these times, I shall recount hereafter i 2 169
All that he can do Is to himself, take thought and die for Cæsar . . ii 1 187
I wonder none of you have thought of him . . . . . . ii 1 217
Thy master is a wise and valiant Roman; I never thought him worse . iii 1 139
Do receive you in With all kind love, good thoughts, and reverence . iii 1 176
Is it fit, The three-fold world divided, he should stand One of the three to share it?—So you thought him . . . . iv 1 15
Thinking by this face To fasten in our thoughts that they have courage v 1 11
I will be here again, even with a thought . . . . . . v 3 19
Why dost thou show to the apt thoughts of men The things that are not? v 3 69
In a general honest thought And common good to all, made one of them v 5 71
My thought, whose murder yet is but fantastical . . . . *Macbeth* i 3 139

Thought. Come, you spirits That tend on mortal thoughts, unsex me here! *Macbeth* i 5 42
Restrain in me the cursed thoughts that nature Gives way to in repose! ii 1 8
This is a sorry sight.—A foolish thought, to say a sorry sight ii 2 22
These deeds must not be thought After these ways; so, it will make us mad ii 2 33
Be not lost So poorly in your thoughts ii 2 72
I had thought to have let in some of all professions ii 3 20
Which you thought had been Our innocent self iii 1 78
Always thought That I require a clearness iii 1 132
Those thoughts which should indeed have died With them they think on iii 2 10
The fit is momentary; upon a thought He will again be well iii 4 55
My former speeches have but hit your thoughts, Which can interpret further iii 6 1
Who cannot want the thought how monstrous It was? iii 6 8
He knows thy thought: Hear his speech, but say thou nought iv 1 69
Even now, To crown my thoughts with acts, be it thought and done iv 1 149
This tyrant, whose sole name blisters our tongues, Was once thought honest iv 3 13
That which you are my thoughts cannot transpose iv 3 21
Reconciled my thoughts To thy good truth and honour iv 3 116
Who would have thought the old man to have had so much blood in him? v 1 44
Thoughts speculative their unsure hopes relate v 4 19
Direness, familiar to my slaughterous thoughts, Cannot once start me v 5 14
Who, as 'tis thought, by self and violent hands Took off her life v 8 70
In what particular thought to work I know not *Hamlet* i 1 67
That duty done, My thoughts and wishes bend again toward France i 2 55
Give thy thoughts no tongue, Nor any unproportion'd thought his act i 3 59
With thoughts beyond the reaches of our souls i 4 56
With wings as swift As meditation or the thoughts of love i 5 30
There was no such stuff in my thoughts ii 2 325
Thus the native hue of resolution Is sicklied o'er with the pale cast of thought iii 1 85
With more offences at my beck than I have thoughts to put them in iii 1 128
That I have thought some of nature's journeymen had made men iii 2 37
That's a fair thought to lie between maids' legs iii 2 125
Our thoughts are ours, their ends none of our own iii 2 223
No second husband wed; But die thy thoughts when thy first lord is dead iii 2 225
Thoughts black, hands apt, drugs fit, and time agreeing iii 2 266
But in our circumstance and course of thought, 'Tis heavy with him iii 3 83
My words fly up, my thoughts remain below: Words without thoughts never to heaven go iii 3 97
A thought which, quarter'd, hath but one part wisdom And ever three parts coward iv 4 42
From this time forth, My thoughts be bloody, or be nothing worth! iv 4 66
They aim at it, And botch the words up fit to their own thoughts iv 5 10
Would make one think there might be thought, Though nothing sure, yet much unhappily iv 5 12
The people muddied, Thick and unwholesome in their thoughts iv 5 82
And there is pansies, that's for thoughts iv 5 177
A document in madness, thoughts and remembrance fitted iv 5 178
Thought and affliction, passion, hell itself, She turns to favour iv 5 188
So far he topp'd my thought, That I, in forgery of shapes and tricks, Come short of what he did iv 7 89
I thought thy bride-bed to have deck'd, sweet maid v 1 268
Sir, in this audience, Let my disclaiming from a purposed evil Free me so far in your most generous thoughts v 2 253
I thought the king had more affected the Duke of Albany than Cornwall *Lear* i 1 1
I loved her most, and thought to set my rest On her kind nursery i 1 125
Thought the profits of my death Were very pregnant and potential spurs ii 1 77
When false opinion, whose wrong thought defiles thee, In thy just proof, repeals and reconciles thee iii 6 119
Had he been where he thought, By this, had thought been past iv 6 44
Bear free and patient thoughts iv 6 80
The main descry Stands on the hourly thought iv 6 218
Better I were distract: So should my thoughts be sever'd from my griefs iv 6 289
That thought abuses you v 1 11
No farther, sir; a man may rot even here.—What, in ill thoughts again? v 2 9
O, she deceives me Past thought! *Othello* i 1 167
Nine or ten times I had thought to have yerk'd him here under the ribs i 2 5
If we make thought of this, We must not think the Turk is so unskilful i 3 26
Have there injointed them with an after fleet.—Ay, so I thought i 3 36
To put my father in impatient thoughts By being in his eye i 3 243
It is thought abroad, that 'twixt my sheets He has done my office i 3 393
Whose footing here anticipates our thoughts A se'nnight's speed ii 1 76
An index and obscure prologue to the history of lust and foul thoughts ii 1 265
Their breaths embraced together. Villanous thoughts, Roderigo! ii 1 267
The thought whereof Doth, like a poisonous mineral, gnaw my inwards ii 1 305
I thought you had received some bodily wound ii 3 266
Why dost thou ask?—But for a satisfaction of my thought; No further harm.—Why of thy thought, Iago? iii 3 97
He echoes me, As if there were some monster in his thought iii 3 107
If thou dost love me, Show me thy thought iii 3 116
Give thy worst of thoughts The worst of words iii 3 132
Utter my thoughts? Why, say they are vile and false? iii 3 136
Thou dost conspire against thy friend, Iago, If thou but think'st him wrong'd and makest his ear A stranger to thy thoughts iii 3 144
It were not for your quiet nor your good, Nor for my manhood, honesty, or wisdom, To let you know my thoughts iii 3 154
I'll know thy thoughts.—You cannot, if my heart were in your hand iii 3 162
He thought 'twas witchcraft—but I am much to blame iii 3 211
My speech should fall into such vile success As my thoughts aim not at iii 3 223
One may smell in such a will most rank, Foul disproportion, thoughts unnatural iii 3 233
In the mean time, Let me be thought too busy in my fears iii 3 253
I saw't not, thought it not, it harm'd not me iii 3 339
My bloody thoughts, with violent pace, Shall ne'er look back iii 3 457
She was a charmer, and could almost read The thoughts of people iii 4 58
I have this while with leaden thoughts been press'd iii 4 177
If you think other, Remove your thought; it doth abuse your bosom iv 2 14
If e'er my will did trespass 'gainst his love, Either in discourse of thought or actual deed iv 2 153
And makest me call what I intend to do A murder, which I thought a sacrifice v 2 65
I told him what I thought, and told no more Than what he found himself v 2 176
I think: I smell't: O villany!—I thought so then v 2 192
Thought. This did I fear, but thought he had no weapon *Othello* v 2 360
Our worser thoughts heavens mend! *Ant. and Cleo.* i 2 64
But on the sudden A Roman thought hath struck him i 2 87
She hath such a celerity in dying.—She is cunning past man's thought i 2 150
Being unseminar'd, thy freer thoughts May not fly forth of Egypt i 5 11
I know you could not lack, I am certain on't, Very necessity of this thought ii 2 58
'Tis a studied, not a present thought, By duty ruminated ii 2 140
Prove such a wife As my thoughts make thee iii 2 26
Queasy with his insolence Already, will their good thoughts call from him iii 6 21
You are abused Beyond the mark of thought iii 6 87
My lord, Forgive my fearful sails! I little thought You would have follow'd iii 11 55
It is my birth-day: I had thought to have held it poor iii 13 186
If swift thought break it not, a swifter mean Shall outstrike thought: but thought will do't, I feel iv 6 35
Being dried with grief, will break to powder, And finish all foul thoughts iv 9 18
That which is now a horse, even with a thought The rack dislimns iv 14 9
Whose heart I thought I had, for she had mine iv 14 16
But please your thoughts In feeding them with those my former fortunes iv 15 52
The arm of mine own body, and the heart Where mine his thoughts did kindle v 1 46
You do extend These thoughts of horror further than you shall Find cause v 2 63
My lord I must obey.—Take to you no hard thoughts v 2 117
Therefore be cheer'd; Make not your thoughts your prisons v 2 185
Thy thoughts Touch their effects in this v 2 332
Ere I could tell him How I would think on him at certain hours Such thoughts and such *Cymbeline* i 3 28
There's an Italian come; and, 'tis thought, one of Leonatus' friends ii 1 41
I thought her As chaste as unsunn'd snow ii 5 12
Be it lying, note it, The woman's; flattering, hers; deceiving, hers; Lust and rank thoughts, hers, hers ii 5 24
Though train'd up thus meanly I' the cave wherein they bow, their thoughts do hit The roofs of palaces iii 3 83
All good seeming, By thy revolt, O husband, shall be thought Put on for villany iii 4 57
True honest men being heard, like false Æneas, Were in his time thought false iii 4 61
I thought you would not back again.—Most like iii 4 119
I call'd; and thought To have begg'd or bought what I have took iii 6 47
I thought he slept, and put My clouted brogues from off my feet iv 2 213
I thought I was a cave-keeper, And cook to honest creatures iv 2 298
Yourself So out of thought, and thereto so o'ergrown, Cannot be question'd iv 4 33
'Tis thought the old man and his sons were angels v 3 85
My heart, That thought her like her seeming v 5 65
If That box I gave you was not thought by me A precious thing v 5 241
That headless man I thought had been my lord v 5 300
And at first meeting loved; Continued so, until we thought he died v 5 380
For many years thought dead, are now revived v 5 456
Her thoughts the king Of every virtue gives renown to men! *Pericles* i 1 13
Nor ask advice of any other thought But faithfulness and courage i 1 62
But I must tell you, now my thoughts revolt i 1 78
This change of thoughts, The sad companion, dull-eyed melancholy i 2 1
And subjects punish'd that ne'er thought offence i 2 27
I thought it princely charity to grieve them i 2 100
Those mothers who, to nousle up their babes, Thought nought too curious i 4 43
Which when any shall not gratify, Or pay you with unthankfulness in thought i 4 102
By Jove, I wonder, that is king of thoughts, These cates resist me, she but thought upon ii 3 28
Never did thought of mine levy offence ii 5 52
My actions are as noble as my thoughts ii 5 59
Who dream'd, who thought of such a thing? iii Gower 38
The sooner her vile thoughts to stead iv Gower 41
Which never could I so convey, Unless your thoughts went on my way iv Gower 50
Think his pilot thought; So with his steerage shall your thoughts grow on iv 4 18
Make the judgement good That thought you worthy of it iv 6 101
To her father turn our thoughts again, Where we left him v Gower 12
I said, and said no more but what my thoughts Did warrant me was likely v 1 134
Thought as much. I thought as much; he would be above the clouds *2 Hen. VI.* ii 1 15
I thought as much. One sorrow never comes but brings an heir *Pericles* i 4 62
Thought fit. Here is the scroll of every man's name, which is thought fit *M. N. Dream* i 2 5
Thought good. This have I thought good to deliver thee *Macbeth* i 5 11
Thought it fit. Which I least thought it fit To answer *Lear* ii 1 125
I thought it fit To send the old and miserable king To some retention v 3 45
Thought it good. They thought it good you hear a play *T. of Shrew* Ind. 2 136
We thought it good From our free person she should be confined *W. Tale* ii 1 193
Thought it meet. We thought it meet to hide our love *Meas. for Meas.* i 2 156
Thought meet. It was thought meet Paris should do some vengeance on the Greeks *Troi. and Cres.* ii 2 72
Thought of. To make us no better thought of, a little help will serve *Coriolanus* ii 3 15
Which since his coming forth is thought of *Lear* iv 3 4
Thought on. Trust me, I thought on her: she'll fit it *Mer. Wives* ii 1 166
These things further thought on, To think me as well a sister as a wife, One day shall crown the alliance on't *T. Night* v 1 324
Not little of his care To have them recompensed as thought on *W. Tale* iv 4 531
Have you thought on A place whereto you'll go? iv 4 547
That it is a shame to be thought on *2 Hen. IV.* ii 1 39
You are an honest woman, and well thought on iv 4 100
But how, my lord, shall we resist it now?—It must be thought on *Hen. V.* i 1 7
Is wonderful to be thought on iii 6 83
What ever have been thought on in this state, That could be brought to bodily act ere Rome Had circumvention? *Coriolanus* i 2 4
Who have thought On special dignities, which vacant lie *T. of Athens* v 1 144
As my master follow'd, As my great patron thought on in my prayers *Lear* i 1 144
Well thought on: take my sword, Give it the captain v 3 250
Your grace, that fed my country with your corn, For which the people's prayers still fall upon you, Must in your child be thought on *Per.* iii 3 20
Thoughten. Be you thoughten That I came with no ill intent iv 6 115

Thoughtest. Thou thought'st to help me; and such thanks I give As one near death *All's Well* ii 1 133
Thou thought'st thy griefs might equal mine, If both were open'd *Pericles* v 1 132
Thought-executing. You sulphurous and thought-executing fires *Lear* iii 2 4
Thoughtful. For this they have been thoughtful to invest Their sons with arts and martial exercises *2 Hen. IV.* iv 5 73
Thought-sick. With tristful visage, as against the doom, Is thought-sick at the act *Hamlet* iii 4 51
Thousand. I must remove Some thousands of these logs *Tempest* iii 1 10
Sometimes a thousand twangling instruments Will hum about mine ears iii 2 146
With twenty thousand soul-confirming oaths *T. G. of Ver.* ii 6 16
A thousand more mischances than this one Have learn'd me how to brook this v 3 3
I warrant he hath a thousand of these letters *Mer. Wives* ii 1 76
A word or two?—Two thousand, fair woman ii 2 43
Her reputation, her marriage-vow, and a thousand other her defences ii 2 259
And a thousand fragrant posies iii 1 20
As honest a 'omans as I will desires among five thousand iii 3 237
Shall have her, Though twenty thousand worthier come to crave her iv 4 90
Therein she doth evitate and shun A thousand irreligious cursed hours v 5 242
Was worth five thousand of you all *Meas. for Meas.* i 2 61
He would have paid for the nursing a thousand iii 2 126
And shrive you of a thousand idle pranks *Com. of Errors* ii 2 210
I have mark'd A thousand blushing apparitions To start into her face, a thousand innocent shames In angel whiteness beat away those blushes *Much Ado* iv 1 161
Yet there remains unpaid A hundred thousand more *L. L. Lost* ii 1 135
What, no more? Pay him six thousand, and deface the bond; Double six thousand, and then treble that *Mer. of Venice* iii 2 301
I have within my mind A thousand raw tricks of these bragging Jacks iii 4 77
Into a thousand that I have forgotten *As Y. Like It* ii 4 32
And, to be noted for a merry man, He'll woo a thousand *T. of Shrew* iii 2 15
Five or six thousand; but very weak and unserviceable *All's Well* iv 3 151
I will not give my part of this sport for a pension of thousands *T. Night* ii 5 197
I multiply With one 'We thank you' many thousands moe *W. Tale* i 2 8
One good deed dying tongueless Slaughters a thousand waiting upon that i 2 93
Many thousand on's Have the disease, and feel't not i 2 206
If I could find example Of thousands that had struck anointed kings i 2 358
I have look'd on thousands, who have sped the better By my regard i 2 389
Even to that drop ten thousand wiry friends Do glue themselves *K. John* iii 4 64
Told of a many thousand warlike French That were embattailed iv 2 199
Whose office is this day To feast upon whole thousands of the French v 2 178
You lose a thousand well-disposed hearts *Richard II.* ii 1 206
Where one on his side fights, thousands will fly ii 2 147
Bid time return, And thou shalt have twelve thousand fighting men! iii 2 70
Ten thousand bloody crowns of mothers' sons iii 3 96
But he, in twelve, Found truth in all but one; I, in twelve thousand, none iv 1 171
A thousand of his people butchered *1 Hen. IV.* i 1 42
Ten thousand bold Scots, two and twenty knights i 1 68
Thirty thousand.—Forty let it be iv 1 130
Whether our present five and twenty thousand May hold up head *2 Hen. IV.* i 3 16
The German hunting in water-work is worth a thousand of these bed-hangings ii 1 158
How many thousand of my poorest subjects Are at this hour asleep! iii 1 4
I cannot put him to a private soldier that is the leader of so many thousands iii 2 178
I judge their number Upon or near the rate of thirty thousand iv 1 22
Let me have five hundred of my thousand v 5 89
Six thousand and two hundred good esquires *Hen. V.* i 1 14
His jest will savour but of shallow wit, When thousands weep more than did laugh at it i 2 296
Of fighting men they have full three score thousand iv 3 3
O that we now had here But one ten thousand of those men in England! iv 3 17
Of knights, esquires, and gallant gentlemen, Eight thousand and four hundred iv 8 90
In these ten thousand they have lost, There are but sixteen hundred mercenaries iv 8 92
Having full scarce six thousand in his troop, By three and twenty thousand of the French Was round encompassed and set upon *1 Hen. VI.* i 1 112
Thousands more, that yet suspect no peril *2 Hen. VI.* iii 1 152
Better ten thousand base-born Cades miscarry Than you should stoop iv 8 49
With all the friends . . . , Will but amount to five and twenty thousand *3 Hen. VI.* ii 1 181
I and ten thousand in this luckless realm Had left no mourning widows ii 6 18
Many a thousand, Which now mistrust no parcel of my fear v 6 37
And cited up a thousand fearful times *Richard III.* i 4 14
Methought I saw a thousand fearful wrecks i 4 24
Six or seven thousand is their utmost power v 3 10
My conscience hath a thousand several tongues v 3 193
By my life, That promises moe thousands *Hen. VIII.* ii 3 97
On my Christian conscience, this one christening will beget a thousand v 4 38
A thousand complete courses of the sun *Troi. and Cres.* iv 1 27
I'ld make a quarry With thousands of these quarter'd slaves *Coriolanus* i 1 203
That's thousand to one good one ii 2 83
This morning for ten thousand of your throats I'ld not have given a doit v 4 59
A thousand hissing snakes, Ten thousand swelling toads *T. Andron.* ii 3 100
I would we had a thousand Roman dames At such a bay iv 2 41
To say amen.—And that would she for twenty thousand more iv 2 45
Art thou not sorry for these heinous deeds?—Ay, that I had not done a thousand more v 1 124
I have done a thousand dreadful things As willingly as one would kill a fly, And nothing grieves me heartily indeed But that I cannot do ten thousand more v 1 141
Show me a thousand that have done thee wrong, And I will be revenged on them v 2 96
Ten thousand worse than ever yet I did Would I perform, if I might v 3 187
A thousand moral paintings I can show *T. of Athens* i 1 90
Why have you that charitable title from thousands? i 2 95
And late, five thousand: to Varro and to Isidore He owes nine thousand ii 1 2
And here from gracious England have I offer Of goodly thousands *Macb.* iv 3 44
Ten thousand warlike men, Already at a point iv 3 134
There is ten thousand— Geese, villain?—Soldiers, sir v 3 13
To be honest, as this world goes, is to be one man picked out of ten thousand.—That's very true *Hamlet* ii 2 179
The heart-ache and the thousand natural shocks That flesh is heir to iii 1 62
To whose huge spokes ten thousand lesser things Are mortised iii 3 19
To have a thousand with red burning spits Come hissing in upon 'em *Lear* iii 6 16

Thousand. 'Twas mine, 'tis his, and has been slave to thousands *Othello* iii 3 158
That were excusable, that, and thousands more Of semblable import *Ant. and Cleo.* iii 4 2
A thousand, sir, Early though't be, have on their riveted trim iv 4 21
Above ten thousand meaner moveables Would testify *Cymbeline* ii 2 29
These three, Three thousand confident, in act as many v 3 29
O, the charity of a penny cord! it sums up thousands in a trice v 4 170
Thousand actions. So may a thousand actions, once afoot, End in one purpose *Hen. V.* i 2 211
Thousand beams. Whose bright faces Cast thousand beams upon me *Hen. VIII.* iv 2 89
Thousand blessings. Now promises Upon this land a thousand thousand blessings v 5 20
Thousand blue-caps. Mordake, and a thousand blue-caps more *1 Hen. IV.* ii 4 391
Thousand brothers. Forty thousand brothers Could not, with all their quantity of love, Make up my sum *Hamlet* v 1 292
Thousand businesses. A thousand businesses are brief in hand *K. John* iv 3 158
Thousand cares. I rest perplexed with a thousand cares *1 Hen. VI.* v 5 95
Thousand causes. For a thousand causes I would prolong awhile the traitor's life *3 Hen. VI.* i 4 51
Thousand chequins. Three or four thousand chequins were as pretty a proportion to live quietly *Pericles* iv 2 28
Thousand crowns. The payment of a hundred thousand crowns *L. L. L.* ii 1 130
He doth demand to have repaid A hundred thousand crowns; and not demands, On payment of a hundred thousand crowns, To have his title live ii 1 144
Bequeathed me by will but poor a thousand crowns *As Y. Like It* i 1 2
I will physic your rankness, and yet give no thousand crowns neither i 1 92
One half of my lands, And in possession twenty thousand crowns *T. of S.* ii 1 123
I will add Unto their losses twenty thousand crowns v 2 113
I'll add three thousand crowns To what is past already *All's Well* iii 7 35
You had rather refuse The offer of an hundred thousand crowns *Rich. II.* iv 1 16
A thousand crowns, or else lay down your head *2 Hen. VI.* iv 1 16
What, think you much to pay two thousand crowns, And bear the name and port of gentlemen? iv 1 18
He that brings his head unto the king Shall have a thousand crowns iv 8 70
Thou wilt betray me, and get a thousand crowns of the king iv 10 29
A wisp of straw were worth a thousand crowns *3 Hen. VI.* ii 2 144
Mine's three thousand crowns: what's yours?—Five thousand *T. of A.* iii 4 28
Five thousand crowns, my lord.—Five thousand drops pays that iii 4 96
Gives him three thousand crowns in annual fee *Hamlet* ii 2 73
Thousand curbs. Cracking ten thousand curbs Of more strong link asunder than can ever Appear in your impediment *Coriolanus* i 1 72
Thousand daggers. Thou hidest a thousand daggers in thy thoughts *2 Hen. IV.* iv 5 107
Thousand dangers. You pluck a thousand dangers on your head *Richard II.* ii 1 205
Tell him it was a hand that warded him From thousand dangers *T. An.* iii 1 196
Thousand deaths. Yet in this life Lie hid moe thousand deaths *Meas. for Meas.* iii 1 40
Willingly, To do you rest, a thousand deaths would die *T. Night* v 1 136
And I will die a hundred thousand deaths *1 Hen. IV.* iii 2 158
Within thine eyes sat twenty thousand deaths *Coriolanus* iii 3 70
A thousand deaths Would I propose to achieve her whom I love *T. An.* ii 1 79
Thousand devils. Let ten thousand devils come against me, and give me but the ten meals I have lost, and I'ld defy them all *2 Hen. VI.* iv 10 65
Thousand dismes. Every tithe soul, 'mongst many thousand dismes, Hath been as dear *Troi. and Cres.* ii 2 19
Thousand dollars. Ten thousand dollars to our general use *Macbeth* i 2 62
Thousand dolours. To three thousand dolours a year *Meas. for Meas.* i 2 50
Thousand doubts. With thousand doubts How I might stop this tempest ere it came *Pericles* i 2 97
Thousand drops. Five thousand drops pays that *T. of Athens* iii 4 97
Thousand ducats. Thy fee is a thousand ducats *Much Ado* ii 2 54
I have earned of Don John a thousand ducats iii 3 116
He had received a thousand ducats of Don John for accusing the Lady Hero iv 2 50
Three thousand ducats; 'tis a good round sum *Mer. of Venice* i 3 104
Is it possible A cur can lend three thousand ducats? i 3 123
A diamond gone, cost me two thousand ducats! iii 1 88
Two thousand ducats in that; and other precious, precious jewels iii 1 90
We'll play with them the first boy for a thousand ducats iii 2 217
What sum owes he the Jew?—For me three thousand ducats iii 2 300
You'll ask me, why I rather choose to have A weight of carrion flesh than to receive three thousand ducats iv 1 42
What if my house be troubled with a rat And I be pleased to give ten thousand ducats To have it baned? iv 1 45
For thy three thousand ducats here is six.—If every ducat in six thousand ducats Were in six parts and every part a ducat, I would not draw them iv 1 84
Three thousand ducats, due unto the Jew, We freely cope your courteous pains withal iv 1 411
A civil doctor, Which did refuse three thousand ducats of me v 1 211
Besides two thousand ducats by the year Of fruitful land *T. of Shrew* ii 1 371
Two thousand ducats by the year of land! My land amounts not to so much in all ii 1 374
He has three thousand ducats a year *T. Night* i 3 22
Twenty thousand ducats Will not debate the question of this straw *Ham.* iv 4 25
I will lay you ten thousand ducats to your ring *Cymbeline* i 4 138
My ten thousand ducats are yours; so is your diamond too i 4 162
Thousand English. They would be as a call To train ten thousand English to their side *K. John* iii 4 175
Thousand escapes of wit Make thee the father of their idle dreams *Meas. for Meas.* iv 1 63
Thousand eyes. Lend me ten thousand eyes, And I will fill them with prophetic tears *Troi. and Cres.* ii 2 101
Thousand fairs. I am compared to twenty thousand fairs *L. L. Lost* v 2 37
Thousand fathom. Forty thousand fathom above water. *W. Tale* iv 4 281
Thousand fiends. A thousand fiends, a thousand hissing snakes, Ten thousand swelling toads *T. Andron.* ii 3 100
Thousand flatterers. A thousand flatterers sit within thy crown *Richard II.* ii 1 100
Thousand flaws. This heart Shall break into a hundred thousand flaws, Or ere I'll weep *Lear* ii 4 288
Thousand-fold. Brings a thousand-fold more care to keep Than in possession any jot of pleasure *3 Hen. VI.* ii 2 52
O, yes, it doth; a thousand-fold it doth ii 5 46
Majesty and pomp, the which To leave a thousand-fold more bitter than 'Tis sweet at first to acquire *Hen. VIII.* ii 3 8
But more in Troilus thousand fold I see *Troi. and Cres.* i 2 310

Thousand French. From forth the ranks of many thousand French *Richard II.* ii 3 102
This note doth tell me of ten thousand French That in the field lie slain *Hen. V.* iv 8 85
Ten thousand French have ta'en the sacrament . . . 1 *Hen. VI.* iv 2 28
Thousand friends. Throng and sweat Of thousand friends *Hen. VIII.* Prol. 29
Thousand furlongs. Now would I give a thousand furlongs of sea for an acre of barren ground . . . . *Tempest* i 1 69
You may ride's With one soft kiss a thousand furlongs ere With spur we heat an acre . . . . *W. Tale* i 2 95
Thousand good-morrows. Mistress, a thousand good-morrows *T. G. of V.* ii 1 102
Thousand grains. Thou exist'st on many a thousand grains That issue out of dust . . . . *Meas. for Meas.* iii 1 20
Thousand halfpence. She tore the letter into a thousand halfpence *Much Ado* ii 3 146
Thousand harms. And frame your mind to mirth and merriment, Which bars a thousand harms . . . . . *T. of Shrew* Ind. 2 138
Ten thousand harms, more than the ills I know, My idleness doth hatch *Ant. and Cleo.* i 2 133
Thousand hearts. As it should pierce a hundred thousand hearts *M. N. Dream* ii 1 160
I bring you witnesses, Twice fifteen thousand hearts of England's breed *K. John* ii 1 275
A thousand hearts are great within my bosom . . . *Richard III.* v 3 347
Thousand Hectors. There is a thousand Hectors in the field *Tr. and Cr.* v 5 19
Thousand horse. Five or six thousand horse, I said . . *All's Well* iv 3 170
Canidius, Our nineteen legions thou shalt hold by land, And our twelve thousand horse . . . . *Ant. and Cleo.* iii 7 60
Thousand kisses. Fain would I go to chafe his paly lips With twenty thousand kisses . . . . 2 *Hen. VI.* iii 2 142
Of many thousand kisses the poor last I lay upon thy lips *Ant. and Cleo.* iv 15 20
Thousand knees. A thousand knees Ten thousand years together *W. T.* iii 2 211
Thousand leagues. Those musicians that shall play to you Hang in the air a thousand leagues from hence . . . . 1 *Hen. IV.* iii 1 227
Thousand leaves. Embrace and kiss and take ten thousand leaves 2 *Hen. VI.* iii 2 354
Thousand lives. It dies, an if it had a thousand lives . . 1 *Hen. VI.* v 4 75
These words will cost ten thousand lives this day . 3 *Hen. VI.* ii 2 177
If you contend, a thousand lives must wither . . . . ii 5 102
O, that the slave had forty thousand lives! One is too poor . *Othello* iii 3 442
Thousand loves. There shall your master have a thousand loves *All's W.* i 1 180
Thousand marks. Unless a thousand marks be levied *Com. of Errors* i 1 22
Where is the thousand marks thou hadst of me?—I have some marks of yours upon my pate, Some of my mistress' marks upon my shoulders, But not a thousand marks between you both . . . . i 2 81
He ask'd me for a thousand marks in gold . . . . ii 1 61
That I beat him And charged him with a thousand marks in gold . iii 1 8
Full thirty thousand marks of English coin . *K. John* ii 1 530
Thou hast saved me a thousand marks in links and torches 1 *Hen. IV.* iii 3 48
He that will caper with me for a thousand marks, let him lend me the money, and have at him! . . . . . . 2 *Hen. IV.* i 2 216
We give thee for reward a thousand marks . . 2 *Hen. VI.* v 1 79
Thousand men. Eight tall ships, three thousand men of war *Richard II.* ii 1 286
But now the blood of twenty thousand men Did triumph in my face . iii 2 76
That every day under his household roof Did keep ten thousand men . iv 1 283
A day Wherein the fortune of ten thousand men Must bide the touch 1 *Hen. IV.* iv 4 9
Five and twenty thousand men of choice . . . 2 *Hen. IV.* i 3 11
Why, now thou hast unwish'd five thousand men . *Hen. V.* iv 3 76
She is hard by with twenty thousand men . . 3 *Hen. VI.* i 2 51
We'll meet her in the field.—What, with five thousand men? . i 2 67
With a band of thirty thousand men Comes Warwick . . ii 2 68
A thousand men have broke their fasts to-day, That ne'er shall dine . ii 2 127
With five thousand men, Shall cross the seas, and bid false Edward battle . . . . iii 3 234
England hath Lent us good Siward and ten thousand men . *Macbeth* iv 3 190
To my shame, I see The imminent death of twenty thousand men *Hamlet* iv 4 60
Thousand nobles. Mowbray hath received eight thousand nobles *Rich. II.* i 1 88
Thousand noses. He had a thousand noses . . . *Lear* iv 6 70
Thousand nothings. Uses a known truth to pass a thousand nothings with . . . . *All's Well* ii 5 32
Thousand oaths. A thousand oaths, an ocean of his tears *T. G. of Ver.* ii 7 69
Thou didst then rend thy faith Into a thousand oaths . . v 4 48
I would break a thousand oaths to reign one year . 3 *Hen. VI.* i 2 17
Thousand parts. He that will divide a minute into a thousand parts *As Y. Like It* iv 1 45
Into a thousand parts divide one man . . . *Hen. V.* Prol. 24
Thousand pieces. What would he have borrowed of you?—A thousand pieces.—A thousand piece! . . . . . *T. of Athens* iii 6 23
I cannot be bated one doit of a thousand pieces . *Pericles* iv 2 55
Thousand poll. Amounts not to fifteen thousand poll . *All's Well* iv 3 190
Thousand pound. I had rather than a thousand pound he were out of the house . . . . *Mer. Wives* iii 3 131
I buy a thousand pound a year: I buy a rope . *Com. of Errors* iv 1 21
It will cost him a thousand pound ere a' be cured . . *Much Ado* i 1 90
Yea, an 'twere a thousand pound more than 'tis . . . iii 5 27
Bid her send me presently a thousand pound . . *Richard II.* ii 2 91
I will give thee for it a thousand pound . . 1 *Hen. IV.* iii 3 68
I would give a thousand pound I could run as fast as thou canst . ii 4 162
Four of us here have ta'en a thousand pound this day morning . ii 4 176
And said this other day you ought him a thousand pound.—Sirrah, do I owe you a thousand pound?—A thousand pound, Hal! a million iii 3 152
Will your lordship lend me a thousand pound to furnish me forth? 2 *Hen. IV.* i 2 250
I would have bestowed the thousand pound I borrowed of you . . v 5 12
Master Shallow, I owe you a thousand pound . . . v 5 77
Beside, A thousand pounds by the year: thus runs the bill . *Hen. V.* i 1 19
I'll give a thousand pound to look upon him . . 2 *Hen. VI.* iii 3 13
To which title A thousand pound a year, annual support *Hen. VIII.* ii 3 64
A thousand pounds a year for pure respect! No other obligation . ii 3 95
I'll take the ghost's word for a thousand pound . . . *Hamlet* iii 2 298
Granted Rome a tribute, Yearly three thousand pounds . *Cymbeline* iii 1 9
Thousand prayers. I'll pray a thousand prayers for thy death, No word to save thee . . . . . . *Meas. for Meas.* iii 1 146
Thousand proofs. This is his wife; That ring's a thousand proofs *All's Well* v 3 199
Thousand reasons. Many thousand reasons hold me back 2 *Hen. IV.* ii 3 66
Thousand rebels. A hundred thousand rebels die in this 1 *Hen. IV.* iii 2 160
Thousand salads. We may pick a thousand salads ere we light on such another herb . . . . *All's Well* iv 5 15

Thousand shames. Quitting thee thereby of ten thousand shames 2 *Hen. VI.* iii 2 218
Thousand shifts. I'll find a thousand shifts to get away . *K. John* iv 3 7
Thousand ships. She is a pearl, Whose price hath launch'd above a thousand ships . . . . *Troi. and Cres.* ii 2 82
Thousand sighs. A thousand thousand sighs to save . . *T. Night* ii 4 64
Through whom a thousand sighs are breathed for thee . 2 *Hen. VI.* iii 2 345
We two, that with so many thousand sighs Did buy each other *T. and C.* iv 4 41
Thousand similes. Did he not moralize this spectacle?—O, yes, into a thousand similes . . . . *As Y. Like It* ii 1 45
Thousand soldiers. Ten thousand soldiers with me I will take 1 *Hen. VI.* i 1 155
Than can the substance of ten thousand soldiers Armed in proof *Rich. III.* v 3 218
Thousand sons. If I had a thousand sons, the first humane principle I would teach them should be, to forswear thin potations 2 *Hen. IV.* iv 3 133
For emulation hath a thousand sons That one by one pursue *Tr. and Cr.* iii 3 156
Thousand souls. Shall send between the red rose and the white A thousand souls to death and deadly night . . . . 1 *Hen. VI.* ii 4 127
I will stir up in England some black storm Shall blow ten thousand souls to heaven or hell . . . . . . 2 *Hen. VI.* iii 1 350
Two thousand souls and twenty thousand ducats Will not debate the question of this straw . . . . *Hamlet* iv 4 25
Thousand spirits. I have a thousand spirits in one breast, To answer twenty thousand such as you . . . . *Richard II.* iv 1 58
Thousand strong. I have been dear to him, lad, some two thousand strong, or so . . . . *T. Night* iii 2 59
Westmoreland, seven thousand strong, Is marching hitherwards 1 *Hen. IV.* iv 1 88
The bishop and Northumberland Are fifty thousand strong 2 *Hen. IV.* iii 1 96
When but in all I was six thousand strong . . 1 *Hen. VI.* iv 1 20
Their power, I think, is thirty thousand strong . . 3 *Hen. VI.* ii 1 177
The queen is valued thirty thousand strong . . . . . v 3 14
Thousand swords. Every man's conscience is a thousand swords *Richard III.* v 2 17
Thousand talents. Send o' the instant A thousand talents to me *T. of Athens* ii 2 208
Thousand tenants. The gallows-maker; for that frame outlives a thousand tenants . . . . *Hamlet* v 1 50
Thousand thanks. A thousand thanks, Signior Gremio . *T. of Shrew* ii 1 85
He gives you, upon his knees, a thousand thanks . . *Hen. V.* iv 4 63
I take my leave with many thousand thanks . 3 *Hen. VI.* iii 2 56
For which I pay 'em A thousand thanks . . . *Hen. VIII.* i 4 74
Thousand things. You might have spoken a thousand things that would Have done the time more benefit . . . *W. Tale* v 1 21
Thousand Thousand. Farewell Till half an hour hence.—A thousand thousand! . . . . *Tempest* iii 1 91
A thousand thousand sighs to save . . . . *T. Night* ii 4 65
Promises Upon this land a thousand thousand blessings . *Hen. VIII.* v 5 20
She's the worse for all this.—O, a thousand thousand times . *Othello* iv 1 203
Thousand times. My heart accords thereto, And yet a thousand times it answers 'no' . . . . *T. G. of Ver.* i 3 91
I will write, Please you command, a thousand times as much . . ii 1 120
A thousand times good morrow.—As many, worthy lady, to yourself . iv 3 6
I have heard him say a thousand times His Julia gave it him . . iv 4 139
For the which she thanks you a thousand times . . *Mer. Wives* ii 2 84
Bids me a thousand times good night . . . . *Much Ado* iii 3 157
The vile encounters they have had A thousand times in secret . . iv 1 95
Forsworn Three thousand times within this three years' space *L. L. Lost* i 1 151
A thousand times more fair, ten thousand times More rich *Mer. of Ven.* iii 2 155
You are a thousand times a properer man Than she a woman *As Y. L. It* iii 5 51
Thou hast said to me a thousand times Thou never shouldst love woman like to me . . . . *T. Night* v 1 274
Though Suffolk dare him twenty thousand times . 2 *Hen. VI.* iii 2 206
Have a thousand times more cause than he To do this outrage *T. Andron.* v 3 51
A thousand times good night! . . . . . *Rom. and Jul.* ii 2 155
Commend me to thy lady.—Ay, a thousand times . . . ii 4 229
And call thee back With twenty hundred thousand times more joy Than thou went'st forth in lamentation . . . . . iii 3 153
Which she hath praised him with above compare So many thousand times . . . . iii 5 239
He hath borne me on his back a thousand times . . *Hamlet* v 1 205
She's the worse for all this.—O, a thousand thousand times . *Othello* iv 1 203
She with Cassio hath the act of shame A thousand times committed . v 2 212
Thousand Tybalts. That 'banished,' that one word 'banished,' Hath slain ten thousand Tybalts . . . . . *Rom. and Jul.* iii 2 114
Thousand verses. Some thousand verses of a faithful lover . *L. L. Lost* v 2 50
Thousand vices. Corrupt and tainted with a thousand vices 1 *Hen. VI.* v 4 45
Thousand watches. At all these wards I lie, at a thousand watches *Troi. and Cres.* i 2 288
Thousand welcomes. For one shot of five pence, thou shalt have five thousand welcomes . . . . *T. G. of Ver.* ii 5 10
Ye're welcome all.—A hundred thousand welcomes . *Coriolanus* ii 1 200
A thousand welcomes! And more a friend than e'er an enemy . . iv 5 151
Thousand widows. Many a thousand widows Shall this his mock mock out of their dear husbands . . . . *Hen. V.* i 2 284
Thousand wooers. Fair Leda's daughter had a thousand wooers *T. of S.* i 2 244
Thousand wrongs. And thou possessed with a thousand wrongs *K. John* ii 3 41
Thousand years. He hath been five thousand years a boy . *L. L. Lost* v 2 11
The poor world is almost six thousand years old . *As Y. Like It* iv 1 95
A thousand knees Ten thousand years together . . *W. Tale* iii 2 212
Now am I so hungry that if I might have a lease of my life for a thousand years I could stay no longer . . 2 *Hen. VI.* iv 10 6
An I should live a thousand years, I never should forget it *Rom. and Jul.* i 3 46
Live a thousand years, I shall not find myself so apt to die *J. Cæsar* iii 1 159
Thousand Yorks. For thousand Yorks he shall not hide his head 2 *Hen. VI.* v 1 85

Thousandth. And break but a part of the thousandth part of a minute in the affairs of love . . . . *As Y. Like It* iv 1 46
Tell thy story; If thine consider'd prove the thousandth part Of my endurance, thou art a man, and I Have suffer'd like a girl *Pericles* v 1 136
Thracian. The tipsy Bacchanals, Tearing the Thracian singer *M. N. D.* v 1 49
Stole to Rhesus' tents, And brought from thence the Thracian fatal steeds . . . . 3 *Hen. VI.* iv 2 21
With opportunity of sharp revenge Upon the Thracian tyrant *T. Andron.* i 1 138
And fell asleep, As Cerberus at the Thracian poet's feet . . . ii 4 51
The Thracian king, Adallas; King Malchus of Arabia . *Ant. and Cleo.* iii 6 71
Thraldom. From this world's thraldom to the joys of heaven *Richard III.* i 4 255
Thrall. Meantime look gracious on thy prostrate thrall . . 1 *Hen. VI.* i 2 117
Long time thy shadow hath been thrall to me . . . . ii 3 36
And make me die the thrall of Margaret's curse . . *Richard III.* iv 1 46
That were the slaves of drink and thralls of sleep . . . *Macbeth* iii 6 13

Thralled. Whose sudden sight hath thrall'd my wounded eye *T. of Shrew* i 1 225
Nor sense to ecstasy was ne'er so thrall'd But it reserved some quantity of choice, To serve in such a difference . . . *Hamlet* iii 4 74
Thrash. Thou art here but to thrash Trojans . . . *Troi. and Cres.* ii 1 50
First thrash the corn, then after burn the straw . *T. Andron.* ii 3 123
Thrasonical. His general behaviour vain, ridiculous, and thrasonical *L. L. Lost* v 1 14
Cæsar's thrasonical brag of 'I came, saw, and overcame' *As Y. Like It* v 2 34
Thread. Fetter strong madness in a silken thread . . *Much Ado* v 1 25
He draweth out the thread of his verbosity finer than the staple of his argument . . . . *L. L. Lost* v 1 18
O Fates, come, come, Cut thread and thrum . *M. N. Dream* v 1 291
Lay them in gore, Since you have shore With shears his thread of silk . v 1 348
Thou liest, thou thread, thou thimble, Thou yard ! . . *T. of Shrew* iv 3 108
Braved in mine own house with a skein of thread? . . . . iv 3 111
How did you desire it should be made?—Marry, sir, with needle and thread . . . . iv 3 121
Beat me to death with a bottom of brown thread . . . . iv 3 138
And the free maids that weave their thread with bones . *T. Night* ii 4 46
Any silk, any thread, Any toys for your head? . . *W. Tale* iv 4 325
If thou want'st a cord, the smallest thread That ever spider twisted from her womb Will serve to strangle thee . . *K. John* iv 3 127
All the shrouds wherewith my life should sail Are turned to one thread v 7 54
As for a camel To thread the postern of a small needle's eye *Richard II.* v 5 17
Let not Bardolph's vital thread be cut With edge of penny cord *Hen. V.* iii 6 49
Had not churchmen pray'd, His thread of life had not so soon decay'd *1 Hen. VI.* i 1 34
Argo, their thread of life is spun . . . . *2 Hen. VI.* iv 2 31
Being press'd to the war, Even when the navel of the state was touch'd, They would not thread the gates . . . . *Coriolanus* iii 1 124
And with a silk thread plucks it back again, So loving-jealous *R. and J.* ii 2 181
Pure grief Shore his old thread in twain . . . *Othello* v 2 206
Till the Destinies do cut his thread of life . . . *Pericles* i 2 108
Threadbare. A threadbare juggler and a fortune-teller *Com. of Errors* v 1 239
Set a new nap upon it.—So he had need, for 'tis threadbare *2 Hen. VI.* iv 2 8
Threaden. Behold the threaden sails . . . *Hen. V.* iii Prol. 10
Threading. Thus out of season, threading dark-eyed night . *Lear* ii 1 121
Threat. The wreck of all my friends, nor this man's threats *Tempest* i 2 488
He commanded her, With many bitter threats . . *T. G. of Ver.* iii 1 236
Thy threats have no more strength than her weak prayers *M. N. Dream* iii 2 250
With her head nimble in threats approach'd The opening *As Y. Like It* iv 3 110
Spare your threats: The bug which you would fright me with I seek *W. Tale* iii 2 92
Thou art in jeopardy.—No more than he that threats . *K. John* iii 1 347
And threat the glory of my precious crown . . . *Richard II.* iii 3 90
Frowns, words, and threats Shall be the war that Henry means to use *3 Hen. VI.* i 1 72
How I scorn his worthless threats ! . . . . i 1 101
Threat you me with telling of the king? Tell him . *Richard III.* i 3 113
Every one did threat To-morrow's vengeance on the head of Richard . v 3 205
Let these threats alone, Till accident or purpose bring you to't *T. and C.* iv 5 261
Are you so desperate grown, to threat your friends? . *T. Andron.* ii 1 40
These two heads do seem to speak to me, And threat me . . iii 1 273
Who threats, in course of this revenge, to do As much as ever Coriolanus did . . . . iv 4 67
Why do fond men expose themselves to battle, And not endure all threats? . . . . *T. of Athens* iii 5 43
And we, poor mates, stand on the dying deck, Hearing the surges threat iv 2 21
There is no terror, Cassius, in your threats . . . *J. Cæsar* iv 3 66
You have stol'n their buzzing, Antony, And very wisely threat before you sting . . . . v 1 38
Whiles I threat, he lives . . . . *Macbeth* ii 1 60
His liberty is full of threats to all; To you yourself, to us *Hamlet* iv 1 14
With plumed helm thy state begins to threat . . . *Lear* iv 2 57
Threats the throat of that his officer That murder'd Pompey *A. and C.* iii 5 19
Why should we be tender To let an arrogant piece of flesh threat us? *Cymb.* iv 2 127
Threaten. Though the seas threaten, they are merciful . . *Tempest* v 1 178
For lead? hazard for lead? This casket threatens . *Mer. of Venice* ii 7 18
They are limed with the twigs that threaten them . . *All's Well* iii 5 26
I with death and with Reward did threaten and encourage him *W. Tale* iii 2 165
The skies look grimly And threaten present blusters . . . iii 3 4
Threatens them With divers deaths in death . . . . . v 1 201
Threaten the threatener and outface the brow Of bragging horror *K. John* v 1 49
It is the Prince of Wales that threatens thee . . . *1 Hen. IV.* v 4 42
For coward dogs Most spend their mouths when what they seem to threaten Runs far before them . . . . . . *Hen. V.* ii 4 70
Steed threatens steed, in high and boastful neighs . . . iv Prol. 10
Threatens more Than Bargulus the strong Illyrian pirate *2 Hen. VI.* iv 1 107
Shelves and rocks that threaten us with wreck . . *3 Hen. VI.* v 4 23
To threaten me with death is most unlawful . . . *Richard III.* i 4 193
The heavens, as troubled with man's act, Threaten his bloody stage *Macb.* ii 4 6
An eye like Mars, to threaten and command . . . *Hamlet* iii 4 57
Such as have not thrived Upon the present state, whose numbers threaten . . . . *Ant. and Cleo.* i 3 52
The shipman's toil, With whom each minute threatens life or death *Pericles* i 3 25
Thank the holy gods as loud As thunder threatens us . . . v 1 201
Threatened to put me into everlasting liberty if I tell you of it *M. Wives* iii 3 30
Forbade her my house and hath threatened to beat her . . . iv 2 89
Threaten'd me To strike me, spurn me, nay, to kill me too *M. N. Dream* iii 2 312
To save unscratch'd your city's threatened cheeks . . *K. John* ii 1 225
Why answer not the double majesties This friendly treaty of our threaten'd town? . . . . ii 1 481
The law that threaten'd death becomes thy friend . . *Rom. and Jul.* iii 3 139
And threaten'd me with death . . . . v 3 276
The things that threaten'd me Ne'er look'd but on my back . *J. Cæsar* ii 2 10
With curst speech I threaten'd to discover him . . . *Lear* ii 1 68
Though I die for it, as no less is threatened me . . . . iii 3 19
Had it gone with us, We should not, when the blood was cool, have threaten'd Our prisoners with the sword . . . *Cymbeline* v 5 77
Threatener. Be fire with fire; Threaten the threatener . . *K. John* v 1 49
Threatenest. Thou meagre lead, Which rather threatenest than dost promise aught . . . . *Mer. of Venice* iii 2 105
Threatening. The threatening twigs of birch . . . *Meas. for Meas.* i 3 24
Excludes all pity from our threatening looks . . *Com. of Errors* i 1 10
Unknit that threatening unkind brow . . . . *T of Shrew* v 2 136
When Fortune means to men most good, She looks upon them with a threatening eye . . . . *K. John* iii 4 120
Therefore thy threatening colours now wind up . . . . v 2 73
Let's march without the noise of threatening drum . *Richard II.* iii 3 51
This is his claim, his threatening, and my message . . *Hen. V.* ii 4 110

Threatening. Kill me with thy sword, And not with such a cruel threatening look . . . . *3 Hen. VI.* i 3 17
Now death shall stop his dismal threatening sound . . . ii 6 58
I spy a black, suspicious, threatening cloud . . . . . v 3 4
Ransoming him, or pitying, threatening the other . . *Coriolanus* i 6 36
And we survive To tremble under Titus' threatening looks . *T. Andron.* i 1 134
Advanced above pale envy's threatening reach . . . . . ii 1 4
Doth not the sea wax mad, Threatening the welkin with his big-swoln face? . . . . iii 1 224
Not Enceladus, With all his threatening band of Typhon's brood, Nor great Alcides, nor the god of war, Shall seize this prey . . iv 2 94
Shakes his threatening sword Against the walls of Athens *T. of Athens* v 1 169
I have seen The ambitious ocean swell and rage and foam, To be exalted with the threatening clouds . . . . . *J. Cæsar* i 3 8
Threatening the flames With bisson rheum . . . . *Hamlet* ii 2 528
Our sever'd navy too Have knit again, and fleet, threatening most sealike . . . . *Ant. and Cleo.* iii 13 171
Threateningly. The honour, sir, that flames in your fair eyes, Before I speak, too threateningly replies . . . . . . *All's Well* ii 3 87
Threatest. Injurious duke, that threatest where's no cause . *2 Hen. VI.* i 4 51
Three. There's but five upon this isle: we are three of them . *Tempest* iii 2 7
You three From Milan did supplant good Prospero . . . . iii 3 69
I'll be thy second.—All three of them are desperate . . . iii 3 104
These three have robb'd me; and this demi-devil—For he's a bastard one—had plotted with them To take my life . . . . . v 1 272
We three, to hear it and end it between them . . *Mer. Wives* i 1 144
Vat be all you, one, two, tree, four, come for? . . . . . ii 3 22
I will do what I can for them all three; for so I have promised . . iii 4 111
I suffered the pangs of three several deaths . . . . . iii 5 110
Three of Master Ford's brothers watch the door with pistols . . iv 2 52
Let me bail these gentle three . . . . . *Meas. for Meas.* v 1 362
They three were taken up By fishermen of Corinth . . *Com. of Errors* i 1 111
If you three will but minister such assistance . . . *Much Ado* ii 1 385
In manner and form following, sir; all those three . . *L. L. Lost* i 1 208
To one more than two.—Which the base vulgar do call three . . i 2 51
Now here is three studied, ere ye'll thrice wink: and how easy it is to put 'years' to the word 'three,' and study three years in two words i 2 54
Of what complexion?—Of all the four, or the three, or the two . i 2 83
All those three I will prove.—What wilt thou prove? . . . iii 1 39
I am all these three.—And three times as much more . . . iii 1 47
The fox, the ape, the humble-bee, Were still at odds, being but three . iii 1 91
And, among three, to love the worst of all . . . . . iii 1 197
He came, saw, and overcame: he came, one; saw, two; overcame, three iv 1 71
I would not care a pin, if the other three were in . . . . iv 3 19
Are you not ashamed? nay, are you not, All three of you? . . iv 3 160
The king your mote did see; But I a beam do find in each of three iv 3 162
I will play three myself.—Thrice-worthy gentleman! . . . v 1 150
One sweet word with thee.—Honey, and milk, and sugar; there is three v 2 231
Write, 'Lord have mercy on us' on those three; They are infected . v 2 419
Are there but three?—No, sir; but it is vara fine, For every one pursents three . . . . v 2 487
I always took three threes for nine . . . . v 2 495
A beard, fair health, and honesty; With three-fold love I wish you all these three . . . . v 2 835
They have conjoined all three To fashion this false sport *M. N. Dream* iii 2 193
Yet but three? Come one more; Two of both kinds makes up four . iii 2 437
O Sisters Three, Come, come to me, With hands as pale as milk . v 1 343
So shall all the couples three Ever true in loving be . . . v 1 414
The Sisters Three and such branches of learning . *Mer. of Venice* ii 2 66
One of these three contains her heavenly picture . . . . ii 7 48
There you shall find three of your argosies Are richly come to harbour. v 1 276
Three proper young men, of excellent growth and presence *As Y. Like It* i 2 129
The eldest of the three wrestled with Charles, the duke's wrestler . i 2 133
Broke three of his ribs, that there is little hope of life in him . i 2 135
We three are married, but you two are sped . . . *T. of Shrew* v 2 185
And clap upon you two or three probable lies . . . *All's Well* iii 6 106
Did you never see the picture of 'we three?' . . . *T. Night* ii 3 17
Get ye all three into the box-tree . . . . ii 5 18
'Odours,' 'pregnant' and 'vouchsafed:' I'll get 'em all three all ready iii 1 102
He is a devil in private brawl: souls and bodies hath he divorced three iii 4 260
The bells of Saint Bennet, sir, may put you in mind; one, two, three . v 1 43
Three crabbed months had sour'd themselves to death . *W. Tale* i 2 102
And will by twos and threes at several posterns Clear them o' the city i 2 438
Let's see these four threes of herdsmen.—One three of them, by their own report, sir, hath danced before the king; and not the worst of the three but jumps twelve foot and a half by the squier . . iv 4 344
O sir! You have undone a man of fourscore three . . . . iv 4 464
Things known betwixt us three, I'll write you down . . . iv 4 571
We three are but thyself; and, speaking so, Thy words are but as thoughts . . . . *Richard II.* ii 1 275
We three here part that ne'er shall meet again . . . . . ii 2 143
If there were not two or three and fifty upon poor old Jack . *1 Hen. IV.* ii 4 206
Three misbegotten knaves in Kendal green came at my back . . ii 4 245
There's not three of my hundred and fifty left alive . . . v 3 38
I was born about three of the clock in the afternoon . . *2 Hen. IV.* i 2 210
So is the unfirm king In three divided . . . . . . i 3 74
Let grievous, ghastly, gaping wounds Untwine the Sisters Three! . ii 4 213
Three corrupted men, One, Richard Earl of Cambridge . *Hen. V.* ii Prol. 22
We'll be all three sworn brothers to France: let it be so . . . ii 1 13
I am boy to them all three: but all they three, though they would serve me, could not be man to me; for indeed three such antics do not amount to a man . . . . iii 2 30
So say I.—And I: and now we three have spoke it, It skills not greatly who impugns our doom . . . . *2 Hen. VI.* iii 1 280
How many children hast thou, widow? tell me.— . . . . Three *3 Hen. VI.* iii 2 29
Alas, you three, on me, threefold distress'd, Pour all your tears! *Richard III.* ii 2 86
Three at the least, that have By this so sicken'd their estates *Hen. VIII.* i 1 81
Falling in, after falling out, may make them three . *Troi. and Cres.* iii 1 113
I'll give you boot, I'll give you three for one . . . . . iv 5 40
These three lead on this preparation Whither 'tis bent . . *Coriolanus* i 2 15
You are three That Rome should dote on . . . . . . ii 1 203
How many stand for consulships?—Three, they say . . . . ii 2 3
Come by him where he stands, by ones, by twos, and by threes . ii 3 47
Take him up. Help, three o' the chiefest soldiers; I'll be one . v 6 150
As from a conduit with three issuing spouts . . . *T. Andron.* ii 4 30
Since birth, and heaven, and earth, all three do meet In thee at once *Rom. and Jul.* iii 3 120
Three? hum! It shows but little love or judgement in him *T. of Athens* iii 3 9
There's two or three of us have seen strange sights . . *J. Cæsar* i 3 138

Three. Count the clock.—The clock hath stricken three . *J. Cæsar* ii 1 192
Is it fit, The three-fold world divided, he should stand One of the three to share it? . iv 1 15
When shall we three meet again In thunder, lightning, or in rain? *Macb.* i 1 1
Who was't came by?—'Tis two or three, my lord, that bring you word iv 1 141
Three of the carriages, in faith, are very dear to fancy . *Hamlet* v 2 158
Six French swords, their assigns, and three liberal-conceited carriages v 2 169
Know that we have divided In three our kingdom . *Lear* i 1 39
Here's three on's are sophisticated! . iii 4 110
I was contracted to them both: all three Now marry in an instant v 3 228
The senate hath sent about three several guests To search you out *Oth.* i 2 46
Two or three groan: it is a heavy night . v 1 42
To you all three, The senators alone of this great world . *Ant. and Cleo.* ii 6 8
They have dispatch'd with Pompey, he is gone; The other three are sealing . iii 2 3
Three in Egypt Cannot make better note.—He's very knowing . iii 3 25
One, two, three: time, time! . *Cymbeline* ii 2 51
These three, Three thousand confident, in act as many . v 3 29
Thou shalt die for't.—We will die all three . v 5 310
The service that you three have done is more Unlike than this thou tell'st . v 5 353
Am I A mother to the birth of three? Ne'er mother Rejoiced deliverance more . v 5 369
I am, sir, The soldier that did company these three In poor beseeming v 5 408
We have but poor three, and they can do no more than they can do *Per.* iv 2 7
Three ages. The world was very guilty of such a ballad some three ages since . *L. L. Lost* i 2 117
Three and thirty. Never, till Cæsar's three and thirty wounds Be well avenged . *J. Cæsar* v 1 53
Three and three, We'll hold a feast in great solemnity . *M. N. Dream* iv 1 189
Three and twenty. I would there were no age between sixteen and three-and-twenty . *W. Tale* iii 3 60
By three and twenty thousand of the French Was round encompassed *1 Hen. VI.* i 1 113
O admirable youth! he ne'er saw three and twenty . *Troi. and Cres.* i 2 255
This skull has lain in the earth three and twenty years . *Hamlet* v 1 190
Three attendants, Lean famine, quartering steel, and climbing fire *1 Hen. VI.* iv 2 10
Three branches. An act hath three branches; it is, to act, to do, and to perform . *Hamlet* v 1 12
Three carters, three shepherds, three neat-herds, three swine-herds *W. T.* iv 4 331
Three chests. These three chests of gold, silver, and lead *Mer. of Venice* i 2 33
Three civil brawls, bred of an airy word . *Rom. and Jul.* i 1 96
Three corners. Come the three corners of the world in arms, And we shall shock them . *K. John* v 7 116
Three cozen-germans that has cozened all the hosts of Readins *M. W.* iv 5 79
Three daughters. I have three daughters; the eldest is eleven *W. Tale* ii 1 144
Upon my target three fair-shining suns.—Nay, bear three daughters *3 Hen. VI.* ii 1 41
Three days. Within these three days his head to be chopped off *Meas. for Meas.* i 2 69
No penance; but a' must fast three days a week . *L. L. Lost* i 2 135
I will be married to a wealthy widow, Ere three days pass *T. of Shrew* iv 2 38
He hath known you but three days, and already you are no stranger *T. Night* i 4 3
Sir, it is three days since I saw the prince . *W. Tale* iv 2 33
The Lady Constance in a frenzy died Three days before . *K. John* iv 2 123
And even these three days have I watch'd If I could see them *1 Hen. VI.* i 4 16
He shall not breathe infection in this air But three days longer *2 Hen. VI.* iii 2 288
If, after three days' space, thou here be'st found On any ground that I am ruler of, The world shall not be ransom for thy life . iii 2 295
And there they are like to dance these three days . *Hen. VIII.* v 4 68
I prithee, name the time, but let it not Exceed three days *Othello* iii 3 63
Within these three days let me hear thee say That Cassio's not alive . iii 3 472
Within three days You with your children will he send before *A. and C.* v 2 201
Three Doctor Faustuses. Away, like three German devils, three Doctor Faustuses . *Mer. Wives* iv 5 71
Three drops. I'll prove this truth with my three drops of blood *Troi. and Cres.* i 3 301
Three Dukes of Somerset, threefold renown'd *3 Hen. VI.* v 7 5
Three ears. Had I three ears, I'ld hear thee . *Macbeth* iv 1 78
Three examples of the like have been Within my age *Coriolanus* iv 6 50
Three farthings. Remuneration! O, that's the Latin word for three farthings: three farthings—remuneration . *L. L. Lost* iii 1 139
Three-farthing worth of silk . iii 1 150
Lest men should say 'Look, where three-farthings goes!' *K. John* i 1 143
Three fields. That won three fields of Sultan Solyman . *Mer. of Venice* ii 1 26
Three fingers. Unless you call three fingers on the ribs bare *1 Hen. IV.* iv 2 80
It had been better you had not kissed your three fingers so oft *Othello* ii 1 174
Threefold too little for carrying a letter to your lover *T. G. of Ver.* i 1 116
That power which gave me first my oath Provokes me to this threefold perjury . ii 6 5
With three-fold love I wish you all these three . *L. L. Lost* v 2 835
Shall we divide our right According to our threefold order ta'en? *1 Hen. IV.* iii 1 71
Threefold vengeance tend upon your steps! *2 Hen. VI.* iii 2 304
Or else you famish; that's a threefold death . *3 Hen. VI.* v 4 32
Threefold renown'd For hardy and undoubted champions . v 7 5
Alas, you three, on me, threefold distress'd, Pour all your tears! *Rich. III.* ii 2 86
Is it fit, The three-fold world divided, he should stand One of the three to share it? . *J. Cæsar* iv 1 14
Three fools. You three fools lack'd me fool to make up the mess *L. L. Lost* iv 3 207
Three-foot. Sometime for three-foot stool mistaketh me . *M. N. Dream* ii 1 52
When on my three-foot stool I sit and tell The warlike feats I have done *Cymbeline* iii 3 89
Three Frenchmen. I thought upon one pair of English legs Did march three Frenchmen . *Hen. V.* iii 6 159
Three gentlemen. O that the living Harry had the temper Of him, the worst of these three gentlemen! . *2 Hen. IV.* v 2 16
Three German devils. Away, like three German devils, three Doctor Faustuses *Mer. Wives* iv 5 70
Three glasses. Our ship—Which, but three glasses since, we gave out split . *Tempest* v 1 223
Three good friends. He that wants money, means, and content is without three good friends . *As Y. Like It* iii 2 26
Three good men. There live not three good men unhanged in England *1 Hen. IV.* ii 4 144
Three great argosies. My father hath no less Than three great argosies *T. of Shrew* ii 1 380
Three great oaths would scarce make that be believed . *All's Well* iv 1 64
Three great ones. In the which three great ones suffer . *W. Tale* ii 1 128
Three great ones of the city, In personal suit to make me his lieutenant, Off-capp'd to him . *Othello* i 1 8
Three half-pence. Bardolph stole a lute-case, bore it twelve leagues, and sold it for three half-pence . *Hen. V.* iii 2 46
Three-headed. Cerberus, that three-headed canis . *L. L. Lost* v 2 593
Three heads. His divisions . . . Are in three heads . *2 Hen. IV.* i 3 71
Three hits. The king, sir, hath laid, that in a dozen passes between yourself and him, he shall not exceed you three hits *Hamlet* v 2 174
Three-hooped. The three-hooped pot shall have ten hoops *2 Hen. VI.* iv 2 72
Three hours. Rest yourself; He's safe for these three hours . *Tempest* iii 1 21
Who three hours since Were wreck'd upon this shore . v 1 136
Your eld'st acquaintance cannot be three hours . v 1 186
I will about it; better three hours too soon than a minute too late *M. W.* ii 2 327
Me have stay six or seven, two, tree hours for him . ii 3 37
To sleep but three hours in the night . *L. L. Lost* i 1 42
What dances shall we have, To wear away this long age of three hours? *M. N. Dream* v 1 33
Within these three hours 'twill be time enough to go home *All's Well* iv 1 27
I was bred and born Not three hours' travel from this very place *T. N.* i 2 23
More than three hours the fight continued . *1 Hen. VI.* i 1 120
Within these three hours, Tullus, Alone I fought in your Corioli walls *Cor.* i 8 7
Ah, poor my lord, what tongue shall smooth thy name, When I, thy three-hours wife, have mangled it? . *Rom. and Jul.* iii 2 99
Within this three hours will fair Juliet wake . v 2 25
Almost midnight, madam.—I have read three hours then . *Cymbeline* ii 2 3
Three hundred. And have done any time these three hundred years *M. W.* i 1 13
O, what a world of vile ill-favour'd faults Looks handsome in three hundred pounds a-year! . iii 4 33
Mann'd with three hundred men, as I have heard *Richard II.* ii 3 54
A franklin in the wild of Kent hath brought three hundred marks *1 Hen. IV.* ii 1 60
There are two gentlemen Have in this robbery lost three hundred marks ii 4 569
I have got, in exchange of a hundred and fifty soldiers, three hundred and odd pounds . iv 2 15
Three-inch. Whom I, with this obedient steel, three inches of it, Can lay to bed for ever . *Tempest* ii 1 283
Away, you three-inch fool! I am no beast *T. of Shrew* iv 1 27
Am I but three inches? why, thy horn is a foot . iv 1 29
Three Judases, each one thrice worse than Judas! *Richard II.* iii 2 132
Three kings. Let me be married to three kings in a forenoon . *A. and C.* i 2 26
Then Three kings I had newly feasted . ii 2 76
Three knights upon our party slain to-day . *1 Hen. IV.* v 5 6
Three lads of Cyprus, noble swelling spirits . *Othello* ii 3 57
Three leagues. The forest is not three leagues off . *T. G. of Ver.* v 1 11
He was not three leagues off when I left him . *Much Ado* i 1 4
Three-legged Doubt not her care should be To comb your noddle with a three-legg'd stool . *T. of Shrew* i 1 64
Three limits. Divided it Into three limits very equally . *1 Hen. IV.* iii 1 73
Three long hours. From nine till twelve Is three long hours *R. and J.* ii 5 11
Three lords. There is two or three lords and ladies more married *M. N. D.* iv 2 16
The loss of those three lords torments my heart *3 Hen. VI.* i 1 270
Three-man. If I do, fillip me with a three-man beetle . *2 Hen. IV.* i 2 255
Three-man-song-men all, and very good ones . *W. Tale* iv 3 44
Three market-days. I have seen him whipped three market-days together *2 Hen. VI.* iv 2 62
Three men. You are three men of sin . *Tempest* iii 3 53
I keep but three men and a boy yet, till my mother be dead . *Mer. Wives* i 1 284
Three merry men be we . *T. Night* ii 3 81
Three mile. Within this three mile may you see it coming . *Macbeth* v 5 37
Three months. Three thousand ducats; well.—Ay, sir, for three months. —For three months; well . *Mer. of Venice* i 3 2
Three thousand ducats for three months and Antonio bound . i 3 9
And for three months.—I had forgot; three months; you told me so . i 3 67
Three months from twelve; then, let me see; the rate . i 3 105
Having been three months married to her, sitting in my state *T. Night* ii 5 49
For three months before, No interim, not a minute's vacancy v 1 97
Three months this youth hath tended upon me . v 1 102
Can no man tell me of my unthrifty son? 'Tis full three months since I did see him last . *Richard II.* v 3 2
Whom I, some three months since, Stabb'd in my angry mood *Richard III.* i 2 241
A man who for this three months hath not spoken To any one *Pericles* v 1 24
Three motives. Your three motives to the battle, with I know not how much more, should be demanded . *Cymbeline* v 5 388
Three Muses. The thrice three Muses mourning for the death Of Learning, late deceased . *M. N. Dream* v 1 52
Three nights. Wreck'd three nights ago on Goodwin Sands *K. John* v 3 11
Three nights after this, About the hour of eight *Hen. VIII.* iv 2 25
Three-nooked. Prove this a prosperous day, the three-nook'd world Shall bear the olive freely . *Ant. and Cleo.* iv 6 6
Three o'clock. The curfew-bell hath rung, 'tis three o'clock *Rom. and Jul.* iv 4 4
'Tis three o'clock; and, Romans, yet ere night We shall try fortune in a second fight . *J. Cæsar* v 3 109
Three odd ducats more Than I stand debted to this gentleman *C. of Er.* iv 1 30
Three opposers. I' the consul's view Slew three opposers *Coriolanus* ii 2 98
Three or four of his blind brothers and sisters went to it *T. G. of Ver.* iv 4 4
He thrusts me himself into the company of three or four gentlemanlike dogs . iv 4 19
My little son And three or four more of their growth *Mer. Wives* iv 4 48
I was three or four times in the thought they were not fairies v 5 128
Some three or four of you Go give him courteous conduct *Mer. of Venice* iv 1 147
Speaks three or four languages word for word without book *T. Night* i 3 27
Three or four loggerheads amongst three or four score hogsheads *1 Hen. IV.* ii 4 4
Paid money that I borrowed, three or four times . iii 3 21
Three or four bonds of forty pound a-piece, and a seal-ring . iii 3 116
So a' cried out 'God, God, God!' three or four times . *Hen. V.* ii 3 20
Towards three or four o'clock Look for the news . *Richard III.* iii 5 101
I was forced to wheel Three or four miles about . *Coriolanus* i 6 20
Three or four wenches, where I stood, cried 'Alas, good soul!' *J. Cæsar* i 2 274
Three or four thousand chequins were as pretty a proportion to live quietly . *Pericles* iv 2 28
Three parts. My lessons make no music in three parts . *T. of Shrew* iii 1 60
'Tis in three parts.—We had the tune on 't a month ago . *W. Tale* iv 4 299
Three parts of that receipt I had for Calais Disbursed I duly *Richard II.* i 1 126
Being three parts melted away with rotten dews . *Coriolanus* ii 3 35
Three parts of him Is ours already . *J. Cæsar* i 3 154
One part wisdom And ever three parts coward . *Hamlet* iv 4 43
Three party. The three party is, lastly and finally, mine host *Mer. Wives* i 1 142
Three-pence. A fruit-dish, a dish of some three-pence *Meas. for Meas.* ii 1 95
I could not give you three-pence again.—No, indeed . ii 1 107

Three-pence. I'll rent the fairest house in it after three-pence a bay *Meas. for Meas.* ii 1 255
A three-pence bow'd would hire me . . . . . *Hen. VIII.* ii 3 36
Rejourn the controversy of three pence to a second day of audience *Cor.* ii 1 80
Three performers are the file when all The rest do nothing . *Cymbeline* v 3 30
Three-pile. At the suit of Master Three-pile the mercer *Meas. for Meas.* iv 3 11
I have served Prince Florizel and in my time wore three-pile *W. Tale* iv 3 14
Three-piled. Thou'rt a three-piled piece, I warrant thee *Meas. for Meas.* i 2 33
Three-piled hyperboles, spruce affectation, Figures pedantical *L. L. Lost* v 2 407
Three pound of sugar, five pound of currants . . . . *W. Tale* iv 3 40
I have three pound to free Mouldy and Bullcalf . . 2 *Hen. IV.* iii 2 260
And yet will he, within three pound, lift as much as his brother *T. and C.* i 2 126
Three quarters. What's her name?—Nell, sir; but her name and three quarters, that's an ell and three quarters, will not measure her from hip to hip . . . . *Com. of Errors* iii 2 111
Thou yard, three-quarters, half-yard, quarter, nail! . *T. of Shrew* iv 3 109
Then stand till he be three quarters and a dram dead . *W. Tale* iv 4 814
Three reprieves. I have grated upon my good friends for three reprieves for you . . . . *Mer. Wives* ii 2 6
Threescore. Shall I never see a bachelor of threescore again? *Much Ado* i 1 201
Eight yards of uneven ground is threescore and ten miles afoot with me 1 *Hen. IV.* ii 2 27
As I think, his age some fifty, or, by'r lady, inclining to three score . ii 4 467
Of fighting men they have full three score thousand . . *Hen. V.* iv 3 3
You tell a pedigree Of threescore and two years . . 3 *Hen. VI.* iii 3 93
Threescore and ten I can remember well . . . . *Macbeth* ii 4 1
Three skirts. There is but three skirts for yourself. . *Mer. Wives* i 1 29
Three solidares. Here's three solidares for thee . *T. of Athens* iii 1 46
Three sons. There comes an old man and his three sons . *As Y. Like It* i 2 126
When that our princely father York Bless'd his three sons *Richard III.* i 4 242
Three souls. A catch that will draw three souls out of one weaver *T. N.* ii 3 61
Three-suited, hundred-pound, filthy, worsted-stocking knave . . *Lear* ii 2 16
Three suits. Hath had three suits to his back, six shirts to his body . iii 4 141
Three suns. Dazzle mine eyes, or do I see three suns?—Three glorious suns, each one a perfect sun . . . . . . 3 *Hen. VI.* ii 1 25
Henceforward will I bear Upon my target three fair-shining suns . . ii 1 40
Three swashers. I have observed these three swashers . *Hen. V.* iii 2 30
Three tailors. I have undone three tailors . . . *As Y. Like It* v 4 48
Three talents on the present; in future, all . . . *T. of Athens* i 1 141
Three things that women highly hold in hate . . *T. G. of Ver.* iii 2 33
I am enjoin'd by oath to observe three things . . *Mer. of Venice* ii 9 9
Drink, sir, is a great provoker of three things.—What three things? *Macb.* ii 3 28
Three thirds. One that lies three thirds . . . . . *All's Well* ii 5 31
Three thousand dolours a year.—Ay, and more . *Meas. for Meas.* i 2 50
Forsworn Three thousand times within this three years' space *L. L. Lost* i 1 151
Three thousand ducats; well.—Ay, sir, for three months *Mer. of Venice* i 3 1; 66
Three thousand ducats for three months and Antonio bound . . i 3 9
What sum owes he the Jew?—For me three thousand ducats . iii 2 300
For thy three thousand ducats here is six . . . . . iv 1 84
A civil doctor, Which did refuse three thousand ducats of me . v 1 211
I'll add three thousand crowns To what is past already . . *All's Well* iii 7 35
Why, he has three thousand ducats a year . . . *T. Night* i 3 22
With eight tall ships, three thousand men of war . *Richard II.* ii 1 286
Mine's three thousand crowns: what's yours? . . *T. of Athens* iii 4 28
Three thousand crowns in annual fee . . . . . *Hamlet* ii 2 73
These three, Three thousand confident, in act as many . *Cymbeline* v 3 29
Three threes. I always took three threes for nine . . *L. L. Lost* v 2 495
Three times. I am all these three.—And three times as much more . iii 1 48
And three times thrice is nine.—Not so, sir; under correction, sir . v 2 488
We know what we know: I hope, sir, three times thrice, sir,— Is not nine . . . . v 2 491
I do expect return Of thrice three times the value of this bond *M. of Ven.* i 3 161
Three times they breathed and three times did they drink 1 *Hen. IV.* i 3 102
Three times hath Henry Bolingbroke made head Against my power . iii 1 64
Had three times slain the appearance of the king . 2 *Hen. IV.* i 1 128
Ten times banished; Once by the king, and three times thrice by thee 2 *Hen. VI.* iii 2 357
Three times to-day I holp him to his horse, Three times bestrid him . v 3 8
Three times did Richard make a lane to me . . . 3 *Hen. VI.* i 4 9
Three times to-day my foot-cloth horse did stumble, And startled, when he look'd upon the Tower . . . . *Richard III.* iii 4 86
That fire-drake did I hit three times on the head, and three times was his nose discharged against me . . . . . *Hen. VIII.* v 4 46
Three umpires. There is three umpires in this matter . *Mer. Wives* i 1 139
Three usurers. You three serve three usurers?—Ay . *T. of Athens* ii 2 97
Are you three usurers' men?—Ay, fool . . . . . ii 2 101
Three veneys for a dish of stewed prunes . . . . *Mer. Wives* i 1 295
Three weird sisters. I dreamt last night of the three weird sisters *Macb.* ii 1 20
Three words. Rather than hold three words' conference with this harpy *Much Ado* ii 1 278
Three words, dear Romeo, and good night indeed . . *Rom. and Jul.* ii 2 142
Three world-sharers. These three world-sharers, these competitors, Are in thy vessel . . . . *Ant. and Cleo.* ii 7 76
Three Worthies. They would know Whether the three Worthies shall come in or no . . . . *L. L. Lost* v 2 486
Three years. For then thou wast not Out three years old . *Tempest* i 2 41
Have sworn for three years' term to live with me . . *L. L. Lost* i 1 16
I am resolved; 'tis but a three years' fast . . . . i 1 24
I have already sworn, That is, to live and study here three years . i 1 35
To study with your grace And stay here in your court for three years' space . . . . i 1 52
I'll keep what I have swore And bide the penance of each three years' day i 1 115
Item, If any man be seen to talk with a woman within the term of three years . . . . i 1 131
Forsworn Three thousand times within this three years' space . i 1 151
And so to study, three years is but short . . . . i 1 181
I have promised to study three years with the duke . . i 2 37
Put 'years' to the word 'three,' and study three years in two words . i 2 56
Till painful study shall outwear three years, No woman may approach ii 1 23
I have vowed to Jaquenetta to hold the plough for her sweet love three years . . . . v 2 893
I have, since I was three year old, conversed with a magician *As Y. L. It* v 2 66
I have brought him up ever since he was three years old *T. of Shrew* v 1 85
By the Lord, Horatio, these three years I have taken note of it *Hamlet* v 1 150
The eldest of them at three years old, I' the swathing-clothes the other *Cymbeline* i 1 58
At three and two years old, I stole these babes . . . iii 3 101
Thresher. Or like an idle thresher with a flail . . . 3 *Hen. VI.* ii 1 131
Threshold. Fell over the threshold, and broke my shin . *L. L. Lost* iii 1 118
And foot me as you spurn a stranger cur Over your threshold *M. of Ven.* i 3 120
Threshold. For many men that stumble at the threshold Are well foretold that danger lurks within . . . . . 3 *Hen. VI.* iv 7 11
I'll not over the threshold till my lord return. . . . *Coriolanus* i 3 82
More dances my rapt heart Than when I first my wedded mistress saw Bestride my threshold . . . . iv 5 124
Threw her sun-expelling mask away . . . . . *T. G. of Ver.* iv 4 158
What tempest, I trow, threw this whale, with so many tuns of oil in his belly, ashore at Windsor? . . . . . . *Mer. Wives* ii 1 65
They threw me off from behind one of them, in a slough of mire . iv 5 68
They threw on him Great pails of puddled mire . *Com. of Errors* v 1 172
Threw him and broke three of his ribs . . . . *As Y. Like It* i 2 135
He threw his eye aside, And mark what object did present itself . iv 3 103
And threw the sops all in the sexton's face . . . *T. of Shrew* iii 2 175
Wrapp'd in a paper, which contain'd the name Of her that threw it *All's Well* v 3 95
The story then goes false, you threw it him Out of a casement . v 3 229
You peevishly threw it to her . . . . . . *T. Night* ii 2 14
Threw off his spirit, his appetite, his sleep . . . *W. Tale* ii 3 16
Rude misgovern'd hands from windows' tops Threw dust and rubbish on King Richard's head . . . . *Richard II.* v 2 6
My heart's dear Harry, Threw many a northward look . 2 *Hen. IV.* ii 3 13
His own life hung upon the staff he threw; Then threw he down himself iv 1 126
And over Suffolk's neck He threw his wounded arm . . *Hen. V.* iv 6 25
A heart it was, bound in with diamonds, And threw it towards thy land 2 *Hen. VI.* iii 2 108
They threw their caps As they would hang them on the horns o' the moon . . . . *Coriolanus* i 1 216
As many coxcombs As you threw caps up will he tumble down . iv 6 135
Ah, Rome! Well, well; I made thee miserable What time I threw the people's suffrages On him . . . . . . *T. Andron.* iv 3 19
Clapped their chopped hands and threw up their sweaty night-caps *J. Cæsar* i 2 246
Bellow'd out As he'ld burst heaven; threw him on my father . *Lear* v 3 213
Like the base Indian, threw a pearl away Richer than all his tribe *Othello* v 2 347
Till fortune, tired with doing bad, Threw him ashore . *Pericles* ii Gower 38
They were too rough That threw her in the sea . . . iii 2 80
I threw her overboard with these very arms . . . . v 3 19
Threwest. Thou, that threw'st dust upon his goodly head 2 *Hen. IV.* i 3 103
Thrice. Twice or thrice was 'Proteus' written down *T. G. of Ver.* i 2 117
She was mine, and not mine, twice or thrice in that last article . iii 1 365
Why, he hath not been thrice in my company! . . *Mer. Wives* ii 1 26
Find a maid That, ere she sleep, has thrice her prayers said . . v 5 54
He hath twice or thrice cut Cupid's bow-string . . . *Much Ado* iii 2 11
How many is one thrice told?—I am ill at reckoning . *L. L. Lost* i 2 41
Now here is three studied, ere ye'll thrice wink . . i 2 54
And three times thrice is nine.—Not so, sir; under correction . v 2 488
We know what we know: I hope, sir, three times thrice, sir,— Is not nine . . . . v 2 491
The thrice three Muses mourning for the death Of Learning *M. N. Dream* v 1 32
I do expect return Of thrice three times the value of this bond *Mer. of Venice* i 3 161
Then to 'scape drowning thrice, and to be in peril of my life with the edge of a feather-bed . . . . ii 2 173
Shylock, there's thrice thy money offer'd thee . . . . iv 1 227
Take thrice thy money; bid me tear the bond . . . . iv 1 234
I take this offer, then; pay the bond thrice And let the Christian go . iv 1 318
He is thrice a villain that says such a father begot villains *As Y. Like It* i 1 61
A pair of old breeches thrice turned . . . *T. of Shrew* iii 2 44
Should be once heard and thrice beaten . . . *All's Well* ii 5 33
If thou thou'st him some thrice, it shall not be amiss . *T. Night* iii 2 48
Thrice bow'd before me, And gasping to begin some speech *W. Tale* iii 3 24
She hath privately twice or thrice a day, ever since the death of Hermione, visited that removed house . . . . v 2 115
Three Judases, each one thrice worse than Judas! . . *Richard II.* iii 2 132
Thrice from the banks of Wye And sandy-bottom'd Severn have I sent him Bootless home . . . . 1 *Hen. IV.* iii 1 65
I'll give thrice so much land To any well-deserving friend . . iii 1 137
Thrice hath this Hotspur . . . Discomfited great Douglas . . iii 2 112
Being now enraged with grief, Are thrice themselves . 2 *Hen. IV.* i 1 145
The river hath thrice flow'd, no ebb between . . . . iv 4 125
The grave doth gape For thee thrice wider than for other men . v 5 58
If we, with thrice such powers left at home, Cannot defend our own doors . . . . *Hen. V.* i 2 217
Thrice within this hour I saw him down; thrice up again . . iv 6 4
I have seen you gleeking and galling at this gentleman twice or thrice . v 1 79
Thrice is he armed that hath his quarrel just . . 2 *Hen. VI.* iii 2 233
Ten times banished; Once by the king, and three times thrice by thee iii 2 358
Thrice I led him off, Persuaded him from any further act . . v 3 9
And thrice cried 'Courage, father! fight it out!' . . 3 *Hen. VI.* i 4 10
Battles thrice six I have seen and heard of . . . *Coriolanus* ii 3 135
Have thrice disturb'd the quiet of our streets . . . *Rom. and Jul.* i 1 98
I'ld rather than the worth of thrice the sum, Had sent to me first, but for my mind's sake . . . . *T. of Athens* iii 3 22
They shouted thrice: what was the last cry for? . . . *J. Cæsar* i 2 226
Was the crown offered him thrice?—Ay, marry, was't, and he put it by thrice, every time gentler than other . . . . i 2 228
Thrice hath Calpurnia in her sleep cried out . . . . . ii 2 2
I thrice presented him a kingly crown, Which he did thrice refuse . iii 2 101
Thrice to thine and thrice to mine And thrice again, to make up nine *Macbeth* i 3 35
Thrice the brinded cat hath mew'd.—Thrice and once the hedge-pig whined . . . . iv 1 1
Thrice he walk'd By their oppress'd and fear-surprised eyes . *Hamlet* i 2 202
Thrice his head thus waving up and down, He raised a sigh so piteous . ii 1 93
With Hecate's ban thrice blasted, thrice infected . . . iii 2 269
S. Withold footed thrice the old . . . . . . *Lear* iii 4 125
Thrice-blessed they that master so their blood . . . *M. N. Dream* i 1 74
Thrice-crowned queen of night, survey With thy chaste eye *As Y. Like It* iii 2 2
Thrice-double. What a thrice-double ass Was I! . . . *Tempest* v 1 295
Thrice-driven. Hath made the flinty and steel couch of war My thrice-driven bed of down . . . . *Othello* i 3 232
Thrice-fair. So, thrice-fair lady, stand I, even so . *Mer. of Venice* iii 2 147
Thrice-famed. I do believe that violent hands were laid Upon the life of this thrice-famed duke . . . . 2 *Hen. VI.* iii 2 157
Thy parts of nature Thrice famed, beyond all erudition . *Troi. and Cres.* ii 3 254
Thrice-gentle Cassio! My advocation is not now in tune . *Othello* iii 4 122
Thrice-gorgeous ceremony, Not all these, laid in bed majestical, Can sleep so soundly as the wretched slave . . . . *Hen. V.* iv 1 283
Thrice-gracious queen, More than your lord's departure weep not *Rich. II.* ii 2 24
I shall hereafter, my thrice gracious lord, Be more myself 1 *Hen. IV.* iii 2 92

Thrice-noble lord, let me entreat of you To pardon me . *T. of Shrew* Ind. 2 120
Thy thrice noble cousin Harry Bolingbroke doth humbly kiss thy hand *Richard II.* iii 3 103
Thrice-noble Suffolk, 'tis resolutely spoke . . . *2 Hen. VI.* iii 1 266
Thrice noble Titus, spare my first-born son . . . *T. Andron.* i 1 120
Thrice-nobler than myself! Thou teachest me . . *Ant. and Cleo.* iv 14 95
Thrice-puissant. My thrice-puissant liege Is in the very May-morn of his youth . . . . *Hen. V.* i 2 119
Thrice renowned. My thrice renowned liege . . . *Richard III.* iv 2 13
Thrice-repured. Love's thrice repured nectar . . . *Troi. and Cres.* iii 2 23
Thrice-valiant. Well have we done, thrice valiant countrymen *Hen. V.* iv 6 1
Send for Lucius, thy thrice-valiant son . . . *T. Andron.* v 2 112
Thrice-victorious. The thrice-victorious Lord of Falconbridge *1 Hen. VI.* iv 7 67
Thrice-welcome, drowned Viola! . . . . . . *T. Night* v 1 248
Thrice welcome to us.—Methinks your looks are sad . . *1 Hen. VI.* i 2 47
Thrice wider. Know the grave doth gape For thee thrice wider than for other men . . . . *2 Hen. IV.* v 5 58
Thrice-worthy. I will play three myself.—Thrice-worthy gentleman! *L. L. Lost* v 1 151
Valorous, and thrice-worthy signieur of England . . . *Hen. V.* iv 4 66
This thrice worthy and right valiant lord . . . *Troi. and Cres.* ii 3 200
Thrid. I Have given you here a thrid of mine own life . . *Tempest* iv 1 3
Thrift. I am now about no waste; I am about thrift . . *Mer. Wives* i 3 47
French thrift, you rogues; myself and skirted page . . . i 3 93
I have a mind presages me such thrift . . . . *Mer. of Venice* i 1 175
My bargains and my well-won thrift, Which he calls interest . . i 3 51
Thrift is blessing, if men steal it not . . . . . . i 3 91
Their profits, Their own particular thrifts . . . . *W. Tale* i 2 311
How, i' the name of thrift, Does he rake this together! . . *Hen. VIII.* iii 2 109
I am a man That from my first have been inclined to thrift *T. of Athens* i 1 118
Thrift, thrift, Horatio! the funeral baked meats Did coldly furnish forth the marriage tables . . . . *Hamlet* i 2 180
Crook the pregnant hinges of the knee Where thrift may follow fawning iii 2 67
The instances that second marriage move Are base respects of thrift . iii 2 193
You some permit To second ills with ills, each elder worse, And make them dread it, to the doers' thrift . . . . *Cymbeline* v 1 15
Thriftless. What thriftless sighs shall poor Olivia breathe! . *T. Night* ii 2 40
As thriftless sons their scraping fathers' gold . . . *Richard. II.* v 3 69
Thriftless ambition, that wilt ravin up Thine own life's means! *Macbeth* ii 4 28
Thrifty. Like a thrifty goddess, she determines Herself the glory of a creditor, Both thanks and use . . . . . *Meas. for Meas.* i 1 39
Fast bind, fast find; A proverb never stale in thrifty mind *Mer. of Ven.* ii 5 55
The thrifty hire I saved under your father . . . *As Y. Like It* ii 3 39
They are thrifty honest men . . . . . . *2 Hen. VI.* iv 2 196
A thrifty shoeing-horn in a chain . . . . . *Troi. and Cres.* v 1 61
Thrill and shake Even at the crying of your nation's crow . *K. John* v 2 143
Art thou not horribly afraid? doth not thy blood thrill at it? *1 Hen. IV.* ii 4 407
I have a faint cold fear thrills through my veins . . *Rom. and Jul.* iv 3 15
Thrilled. A servant that he bred, thrill'd with remorse . . *Lear* iv 2 73
Thrilling. To reside In thrilling region of thick-ribbed ice . *M. for M.* iii 1 123
Thrive. Since thou lovest, love still and thrive therein . *T. G. of Ver.* i 1 9
How does your lady? and how thrives your love? . . . . ii 4 125
It is a life that I have desired: I will thrive . . . *Mer. Wives* i 3 22
We will thrive, lads, we will thrive . . . . . . i 3 81
If these four Worthies in their first show thrive . . . *L. L. Lost* v 2 541
This was a way to thrive, and he was blest . . . *Mer. of Venice* i 3 90
Here do I choose, and thrive I as I may . . . . . ii 7 60
Haply to wive and thrive as best I may . . . . *T. of Shrew* i 2 56
Honours thrive, When rather from our acts we them derive . *All's Well* ii 3 142
What angel shall Bless this unworthy husband? he cannot thrive . . iii 4 26
Live Safest in shame! being fool'd, by foolery thrive! . . . iv 3 374
A good lady and would not have knaves thrive long under her . . v 2 34
By swaggering could I never thrive . . . . . . *T. Night* v 1 408
I see this is the time that the unjust man doth thrive . . *W. Tale* iv 4 689
Grandam, I will not wish thy wishes thrive . . . . *K. John* iii 1 334
So thrive it in your game! and so, farewell . . . . . iv 2 95
Mine innocency and Saint George to thrive! . . . *Richard II.* i 3 84
That's as York thrives to beat back Bolingbroke . . . . ii 2 144
I intend to thrive in this new world . . . . . . iv 1 78
Ill mayst thou thrive, if thou grant any grace! . . . . v 3 99
Farewell, good brother: we shall thrive, I trust . . *1 Hen. IV.* iii 3 300
If Lord Percy thrive not, ere the king Dismiss his power, he means to visit us . . . . iv 4 36
And wholesome berries thrive and ripen best Neighbour'd by fruit of baser quality . . . . *Hen. V.* i 1 61
Silken dalliance in the wardrobe lies: Now thrive the armourers . ii Prol. 3
And so thrive Richard as thy foes may fall! . . . *1 Hen. VI.* iii 1 174
Say that he thrive, as 'tis great like he will . . . *2 Hen. VI.* iii 1 379
If we mean to thrive and do good, break open the gaols . . . iv 3 17
As I intend, Clifford, to thrive to-day, It grieves my soul to leave thee unassail'd . . . . v 2 17
If we thrive, promise them such rewards As victors wear . *3 Hen. VI.* ii 3 52
So thrive I, as I truly swear the like! . . . . *Richard III.* ii 1 11
I will never more remember Our former hatred, so thrive I and mine! . ii 1 24
If you thrive well, bring them to Baynard's Castle . . . . iii 5 98
So thrive I in my enterprise And dangerous success of bloody wars! . iv 4 235
As I intend to prosper and repent, So thrive I in my dangerous attempt! iv 4 398
But if I thrive, the gain of my attempt The least of you shall share his part thereof . . . . v 3 267
And presume to know What's done i' the Capitol; who's like to rise, Who thrives, and who declines . . . . . *Coriolanus* i 1 197
Live, and thrive!—Farewell, kind neighbours . . . . . iv 6 23
So thrive my soul— A thousand times good night! . *Rom. and Jul.* ii 2 154
Why should it thrive and turn to nutriment, When he is turn'd to poison? *T. of Athens* iii 1 61
His friends, like physicians, Thrive, give him over: must I take the cure? iii 3 12
If I thrive well, I'll visit thee again . . . . . . iv 3 170
Seek to thrive By that which has undone thee . . . . . iv 3 210
He thus advises us; not to have us thrive in our mystery . . . iv 3 457
I wish your enterprise to-day may thrive . . . *J. Cæsar* iii 1 13
What said Popilius Lena?—He wish'd to-day our enterprise might thrive iii 1 16
If this letter speed, And my invention thrive . . . . *Lear* i 2 20
Let copulation thrive . . . . iv 6 116
If ever thou wilt thrive, bury my body . . . . . . iv 6 253
Pray that the right may thrive . . . . v 2 2
Either say thou'lt do't, Or thrive by other means . . . . v 3 34
Throwing but shows of service on their lords, Do well thrive by them *Othello* i 1 53
Justly to your grave ears I'll present How I did thrive in this fair lady's love . . . . i 3 125
Thrive. Pompey Thrives in our idleness . . . . . *Ant. and Cleo.* i 4 76
If to-morrow Our navy thrive, I have an absolute hope Our landmen will stand up . . . . iv 3 10
Well, well; We shall thrive now . . . . iv 4 9
Of their broken debtors take a third, A sixth, a tenth, letting them thrive again On their abatement . . . . . *Cymbeline* v 4 20
His comforts thrive, his trials well are spent . . . . . v 4 104
I hope, sir, if you thrive, you'll remember from whence you had it *Per.* ii 1 157
Thrived. Such as have not thrived Upon the present state *Ant. and Cleo.* i 3 51
So he thrived, That he is promised to be wived . . . *Pericles* v 2 274
Thriving. Your free undertaking cannot miss A thriving issue *W. Tale* ii 2 45
To her I go, a jolly thriving wooer . . . . *Richard III.* iv 3 43
Throat. A pox o' your throat, you bawling, blasphemous, incharitable dog! . . . . *Tempest* i 1 43
Dew-lapp'd like bulls, whose throats had hanging at 'em Wallets of flesh iii 3 45
With an outstretch'd throat I'll tell the world aloud *Meas. for Meas.* ii 4 153
A pox o' your throats! Who makes that noise there? . . . . iv 3 26
Sigh a note and sing a note, sometime through the throat . *L. L. Lost* iii 1 15
I do nothing in the world but lie, and lie in my throat . . . iv 3 13
To move wild laughter in the throat of death? It cannot be . . v 2 865
Wert thou not my brother, I would not take this hand from thy throat till this other had pulled out thy tongue for saying so *As Y. Like It* i 1 63
And turn his merry note Unto the sweet bird's throat . . . . ii 5 4
The note lies in's throat, if he say I said so . . . *T. of Shrew* iv 3 133
I'll drink to her as long as there is a passage in my throat . *T. Night* i 3 42
Thou liest in thy throat; that is not the matter I challenge thee for . iii 4 172
With a foul traitor's name stuff I thy throat . . . . *Richard II.* i 1 44
Return'd These terms of treason doubled down his throat . . . i 1 57
Through the false passage of thy throat, thou liest . . . . i 1 125
Strike; down with them; cut the villains' throat: ah! . *1 Hen. IV.* ii 2 88
I had lied in my throat, if I had said so . . . *2 Hen. IV.* i 2 94
Men may sleep, and they may have their throats about them *Hen. V.* ii 1 24
The 'solus' in thy teeth, and in thy throat, And in thy hateful lungs! . ii 1 51
I will cut thy throat, one time or other, in fair terms . . . ii 1 73
Why the devil should we keep knives to cut one another's throats? . ii 1 96
There is throats to be cut, and works to be done . . . . iii 2 119
I will fetch thy rim out at thy throat In drops of crimson blood . . iv 4 15
Bid him prepare; for I will cut his throat . . . . . iv 4 34
Caused every soldier to cut his prisoner's throat . . . . iv 7 10
We'll cut the throats of those we have . . . . . . iv 7 66
I am no traitor.—That's a lie in thy throat . . . . . iv 8 17
We will not fly, but to our enemies' throats . . . *1 Hen. VI.* i 1 98
I'll turn my part thereof into thy throat . . . . . ii 4 79
Cut both the villains' throats; for die you shall . . *2 Hen. VI.* iv 1 20
Then is sin struck down like an ox, and iniquity's throat cut like a calf iv 2 29
So first the harmless sheep doth yield his fleece And next his throat unto the butcher's knife . . . . *3 Hen. VI.* v 6 9
In thy foul throat thou liest . . . . . . *Richard III.* i 2 93
Were you snarling all before I came, Ready to catch each other by the throat? . . . . i 3 189
All on foot he fights, Seeking for Richmond in the throat of death . v 4 5
Through the great bulk Achilles be thy guard, I'll cut thy throat *Troi. and Cres.* iv 4 131
My throat of war be turn'd, Which quired with my drum, into a pipe Small as an eunuch! . . . . *Coriolanus* iii 2 112
I also am Longer to live most weary, and present My throat to thee . iv 5 102
Unbuckling helms, fisting each other's throat . . . . . iv 5 131
Our throats are sentenced and stay upon execution . . . . v 4 8
This morning for ten thousand of your throats I'ld not have given a doit v 4 59
He came unto my hearth; Presented to my knife his throat . . . v 6 31
Their base throats tear With giving him glory . . . . . v 6 53
And withal Thrust these reproachful speeches down his throat *T. An.* ii 1 55
Till all these mischiefs be return'd again Even in their throats that have committed them . . . . iii 1 275
This one hand yet is left to cut your throats . . . . . v 2 82
I will be revenged: And now prepare your throats . . . . v 2 197
Sometime she driveth o'er a soldier's neck, And then dreams he of cutting foreign throats . . . . *Rom. and Jul.* i 4 83
Great men should drink with harness on their throats . *T. of Athens* i 2 53
And let the foes quietly cut their throats, Without repugnancy . . iii 5 44
Bankrupts, hold fast; Rather than render back, out with your knives, And cut your trusters' throats! . . . . iv 1 10
Whom the oracle Hath doubtfully pronounced thy throat shall cut . iv 3 121
Cut throats: All that you meet are thieves . . . . . iv 3 448
Their knives care not, While you have throats to answer . . . v 1 182
There's not a whittle in the unruly camp But I do prize it at my love before The reverend'st throat in Athens . . . . v 1 185
He plucked me ope his doublet and offered them his throat to cut *J. C.* i 2 268
I had most need of blessing, and 'Amen' Stuck in my throat *Macbeth* ii 2 33
I' the very throat on me: but I requited him for his lie . . . ii 3 43
His throat is cut; that I did for him.—Thou art the best o' the cut-throats . . . . iii 4 16
The cock, that is the trumpet to the morn, Doth with his lofty and shrill sounding throat Awake the god of day . . . . *Hamlet* i 1 151
Tweaks me by the nose? gives me the lie i' the throat, As deep as to the lungs? . . . . ii 2 601
To cut his throat i' the church.—No place, indeed, should murder sanctuarize . . . . iv 7 127
I prithee, take thy fingers from my throat . . . . . v 1 283
Whilst I can vent clamour from my throat, I'll tell thee thou dost evil *Lear* i 1 168
Whose rude throats The immortal Jove's dread clamours counterfeit *Oth.* iii 3 355
For me to devise a lodging and say he lies here or he lies there, were to lie in mine own throat . . . . iii 4 13
I took by the throat the circumcised dog, And smote him, thus . v 2 355
Bring it to that, The gold I give thee will I melt and pour Down thy ill-uttering throat . . . . *Ant. and Cleo.* ii 5 35
A health for you.—I shall take it, sir: we have used our throats in Egypt . . . . ii 6 [illegible]
Let me cut the cable; And, when we are put off, fall to their throats . ii 7 78
And threats the throat of that his officer That murder'd Pompey . . iii 5 19
What shall I need to draw my sword? the paper Hath cut her throat *Cymbeline* iii 4 35
With his own sword, Which he did wave against my throat, I have ta'en His head from him . . . . iv 2 150
Even in his throat—unless it be the king—That calls me traitor, I return the lie . . . . *Pericles* ii 5 56
Throb. Your hearts will throb and weep to hear him speak *T. Andron.* v 3 95
Yet my heart Throbs to know one thing . . . . *Macbeth* iv 1 101
Throbbing. Here may his head lie on my throbbing breast *2 Hen. VI.* iv 4 5
Throca movousus, cargo, cargo, cargo . . . . . *All's Well* iv 1 70

Throe. And a birth indeed Which throes thee much to yield . *Tempest* ii 1 231
That gave to me Many a groaning throe . . . . *Hen. VIII.* ii 4 199
Other incident throes That nature's fragile vessel doth sustain *T. of A.* v 1 203
With news the time's with labour, and throes forth, Each minute, some *Ant. and Cleo.* iii 7 81
Lucina lent not me her aid, But took me in my throes . *Cymbeline* v 4 44
Throne. In Arabia There is one tree, the phœnix' throne . *Tempest* iii 3 23
Let the devil Be sometime honour'd for his burning throne! *M. for M.* v 1 295
'Fore whose throne 'tis needful, Ere I can perfect mine intents, to kneel *All's Well* iv 4 3
Liver, brain, and heart, These sovereign thrones . . . *T. Night* i 1 38
We have left our throne Without a burthen . . . *W. Tale* i 2 2
Which owe A moiety of the throne, a great king's daughter . . iii 2 40
Draw our throne into a sheep-cote! . . . . iv 4 808
The lands and waters 'twixt your throne and his Measured to look upon you . . . . v 1 144
Here I and sorrows sit; Here is my throne . . . . *K. John* iii 1 74
Out of the path which shall directly lead Thy foot to England's throne iii 4 130
True to King Richard's throne, A loyal, just, and upright gentleman *Richard II.* i 3 86
This royal throne of kings, this scepter'd isle, This earth of majesty . ii 1 40
Shall see us rising in our throne, the east . . . . . iii 2 50
Ascend his throne, descending now from him . . . . . iv 1 111
In God's name, I'll ascend the regal throne.—Marry, God forbid! . iv 1 113
Thou ladder wherewithal The mounting Bolingbroke ascends my throne v 1 56
Another way To pluck him headlong from the usurped throne . v 1 65
That roan shall be my throne. Well, I will back him straight 1 *Hen. IV.* ii 3 73
And shake the peace and safety of our throne . . . . iii 2 117
God and his angels guard your sacred throne And make you long become it! . . . . *Hen. V.* i 2 7
That owe yourselves, your lives, and services To this imperial throne . i 2 35
Renew their feats: You are their heir; you sit upon their throne . i 2 117
Show my sail of greatness When I do rouse me in my throne of France i 2 275
The farced title running 'fore the king, The throne he sits on . iv 1 281
I'll hale the Dauphin headlong from his throne 1 *Hen. VI.* i 1 149
Finding his usurpation most unjust, Endeavour'd my advancement to the throne . . . . ii 5 69
What are you, I pray, But one imperious in another's throne? . iii 1 44
When I am dead and gone, May honourable peace attend thy throne! 2 *Hen. VI.* ii 3 38
Was ever king that joy'd an earthly throne, And could command no more content than I? . . . . iv 9 1
In that throne Which now the house of Lancaster usurps . 3 *Hen. VI.* i 1 22
Thou factious Duke of York, descend my throne, And kneel for grace . i 1 74
And shall I stand, and thou sit in my throne?—It must and shall be so i 1 84
Think'st thou that I will leave my kingly throne, Wherein my grandsire and my father sat? . . . . i 1 124
For chair and dukedom, throne and kingdom say; Either that is thine, or else thou wert not his . . . . ii 1 93
The next degree is England's royal throne . . . . . ii 1 193
To free King Henry from imprisonment And see him seated in the regal throne . . . . iv 3 64
Himself Likely in time to bless a regal throne . . . . . iv 6 74
Once more we sit in England's royal throne . . . . . v 7 1
And plant your joys in living Edward's throne . . *Richard III.* ii 2 100
Insulting tyranny begins to jet Upon the innocent and aweless throne . ii 4 52
Ere give consent His master's son, as worshipful he terms it, Shall lose the royalty of England's throne . . . . iii 4 42
We will plant some other in the throne, To the disgrace and downfall of your house . . . . iii 7 216
Sit, gods, upon your thrones, and smile at Troy! . . *Troi. and Cres.* v 10 7
Self-loving,— And affecting one sole throne, Without assistance *Coriol.* iv 6 32
He wants nothing of a god but eternity and a heaven to throne in . v 4 26
Your are but newly planted in your throne . . . *T. Andron.* i 1 444
Upon his brow shame is ashamed to sit; For 'tis a throne where honour may be crown'd Sole monarch of the universal earth *Rom. and Jul.* iii 2 93
My bosom's lord sits lightly in his throne . . . . v 1 3
This throne, this Fortune, and this hill . . . *T. of Athens* i 1 73
Our duties Are to your throne and state children and servants *Macbeth* i 4 25
It hath been The untimely emptying of the happy throne . . iv 3 68
The truest issue of thy throne By his own interdiction stands accursed iv 3 106
Sundry blessings hang about his throne, That speak him full of grace . iv 3 158
The head is not more native to the heart . . . Than is the throne of Denmark to thy father . . . . . . *Hamlet* i 2 49
Let the world take note, You are the most immediate to our throne . i 2 109
I could as well be brought To knee his throne . . . *Lear* ii 4 217
Yield up, O love, thy crown and hearted throne To tyrannous hate! *Oth.* iii 3 448
I will piece Her opulent throne with kingdoms . *Ant. and Cleo.* i 5 46
Whiles we are suitors to their throne, decays The thing we sue for . ii 1 4
The barge she sat in, like a burnish'd throne, Burn'd on the water . ii 2 196
Wouldst have made my throne A seat for baseness . . *Cymbeline* i 1 141
I will pursue her Even to Augustus' throne . . . . iii 5 101
Stand by my side, you whom the gods have made Preservers of my throne v 5 2
Had princes sit, like stars, about his throne, And he the sun *Pericles* ii 3 39
Throned. A certain aim he took At a fair vestal throned by the west *M. N. Dream* ii 1 158
It [mercy] becomes The throned monarch better than his crown *M. of V.* iv 1 189
It gives a very echo to the seat Where Love is throned . *T. Night* ii 4 22
What four throned ones could have weigh'd Such a compounded one? *Hen. VIII.* i 1 11
I have upon a high and pleasant hill Feign'd Fortune to be throned *T. of Athens* i 1 64
As who have not, that their great stars Throned and set high? *Lear* iii 1 23
Though you in swearing shake the throned gods . *Ant. and Cleo.* i 3 28
Throng. I am no gibbet for you. Go. A short knife and a throng! *M. W.* ii 2 18
So play the foolish throngs with one that swoons . *Meas. for Meas.* ii 4 24
Be quiet, people. Wherefore throng you hither? . *Com. of Errors* v 1 38
They throng who should buy first . . . . . *W. Tale* iv 4 612
In their throng and press to that last hold, Confound themselves *K. John* v 7 19
It is not a confident brow, nor the throng of words . 2 *Hen. IV.* ii 1 122
Nor do I as an enemy to peace Troop in the throngs of military men . iv 1 62
We are enow yet living in the field To smother up the English in our throngs . . . . *Hen. V.* iv 5 20
The devil take order now! I'll to the throng . . . . iv 5 22
To the shore Throng many doubtful hollow-hearted friends *Richard III.* iv 4 435
All several sins, all used in each degree, Throng to the bar . . v 3 199
Follow'd with the general throng and sweat Of thousand friends *Hen. VIII.* Prol. 28
Many mazed considerings did throng And press'd in with this caution ii 4 185
Seld-shown flamens Do press among the popular throngs *Coriolanus* ii 1 230
I have seen the dumb men throng to see him and The blind to hear him speak . . . . *Coriolanus* ii 1 278
Throng our large temples with the shows of peace, And not our streets with war! . . . . iii 3 36
Therefore, be abhorr'd All feasts, societies, and throngs of men! *T. of A.* iv 3 21
Fellow, come from the throng; look upon Cæsar . . *J. Cæsar* i 2 21
The throng that follows Cæsar at the heels, Of senators, of prætors ii 4 34
When slanders do not live in tongues; Nor cutpurses come not to throngs . . . . *Lear* iii 2 88
Thronged. Thou wilt be throng'd to shortly.—Throng'd to! *T. of Athens* iv 3 395
The earth is throng'd By man's oppression . . . *Pericles* i 1 101
What I am, want teaches me to think on: A man throng'd up with cold ii 1 77
Thronging. Come thronging soft and delicate desires . *Much Ado* i 1 305
Where be the thronging troops that follow'd thee? . *Richard III.* iv 4 96
Throstle. The throstle with his note so true . . *M. N. Dream* iii 1 130
If a throstle sing, he falls straight a capering . *Mer. of Venice* i 2 65
Throttle their practised accent in their fears . . *M. N. Dream* v 1 97
Through. These follies are within you and shine through you *T. G. of V.* ii 1 40
I do it for some piece of money, and go through with all *Meas. for Meas.* ii 1 285
Roaming clean through the bounds of Asia . . *Com. of Errors* i 1 134
Through Athens I am thought as fair as she . . *M. N. Dream* i 1 227
O sweet and lovely wall, Show me thy chink, to blink through with mine eyne! . . . . v 1 178
A merchant of great traffic through the world . . . *T. of Shrew* i 1 12
Thy casement I need not open, for I look through thee . . *All's Well* ii 3 226
I love the king And through him what is nearest to him *W. Tale* iv 4 533
O, I am press'd to death through want of speaking! . *Richard II.* iii 4 72
If a man is through with them in honest taking up, then they must stand upon security . . . . 2 *Hen. IV.* i 2 45
Who, half through, Gives o'er and leaves his part-created cost . i 3 59
The happiest youth, viewing his progress through, What perils past . iii 1 54
So thin that life looks through and will break out . . . iv 4 120
Then every soldier kill his prisoners; Give the word through *Hen. V.* iv 6 38
Through whom a thousand sighs are breathed for thee . 2 *Hen. VI.* iii 2 345
He's not yet through warm . . . . . *Troi. and Cres.* ii 3 232
I am half through; The one part suffer'd, the other will I do *Coriolanus* ii 3 130
Look, in this place ran Cassius' dagger through: . . . Through this the well-beloved Brutus stabb'd . . . . . *J. Cæsar* iii 2 178
I am young; but something You may deserve of him through me *Macb.* iv 3 15
My good intent May carry through itself to that full issue . . *Lear* i 4 3
Through tatter'd clothes small vices do appear . . . . iv 6 168
I ran it through, even from my boyish days . . . *Othello* i 3 132
When Antony is gone Through whom I might command it *Ant. and Cleo.* iii 3 6
I would revenges, That possible strength might meet, would seek us through And put us to our answer . . . *Cymbeline* iv 2 160
O rare instinct! When shall I hear all through? . . . v 5 382
I have gone through for this piece, you see . . . *Pericles* iv 2 47
With sighs shot through, and biggest tears o'ershower'd . . iv 4 26
Through and through. Thy slander hath gone through and through her heart . . . . *Much Ado* v 1 68
Through and through Cleanse the foul body of the infected world *As Y. Like It* ii 7 59
So lean, that blasts of January Would blow you through and through *W. Tale* iv 4 112
My buckler cut through and through . . . . 1 *Hen. IV.* ii 4 186
I'll through and through you! . . . . *Troi. and Cres.* v 10 26
Carries them through and through the most fond and winnowed opinions *Hamlet* v 2 200
Throughfare. The Hyrcanian deserts and the vasty wilds Of wide Arabia are as throughfares now . . . . *Mer. of Venice* ii 7 42
His body's a passable carcass, if he be not hurt: it is a throughfare for steel, if it be not hurt . . . . . . *Cymbeline* i 2 11
Throughly. The next advantage Will we take throughly . . *Tempest* iii 3 14
My bosom as a bed Shall lodge thee till thy wound be throughly heal'd *T. G. of Ver.* i 2 115
If he had been throughly moved, you should have heard him *Mer. Wives* i 4 95
My lord, we'll do it throughly . . . . *Meas. for Meas.* v 1 260
To quit me of them throughly . . . . . . *Much Ado* iv 1 202
I am informed throughly of the cause . . . *Mer. of Venice* iv 1 173
Now do your duty throughly, I advise you . . *T. of Shrew* iv 4 11
You scarce can right me throughly then to say You did mistake *W. Tale* ii 1 99
Right glad to catch this good occasion Most throughly to be winnow'd *Hen. VIII.* v 1 110
I'll be revenged Most throughly for my father . . . *Hamlet* iv 5 136
My point and period will be throughly wrought, Or well or ill . *Lear* iv 7 97
Will do's commission throughly . . . . . *Cymbeline* ii 4 12
I am throughly weary . . . . iii 6 36
Throughout. A man well known throughout all Italy . . *T. of Shrew* ii 1 69
Any sovereign state throughout the world . . . *K. John* v 2 82
And ne'er throughout the year to church thou go'st . 1 *Hen. VI.* i 1 42
Why ring not out the bells aloud throughout the town? . . . i 6 11
Throughout every town Proclaim them traitors . . 2 *Hen. VI.* iv 2 186
And follow thee my lord throughout the world . . *Rom. and Jul.* ii 2 148
In the sequence of degree From high to low throughout . *T. of Athens* v 1 212
Throw. I throw thy name against the bruising stones . *T. G. of Ver.* i 2 111
Throw it thence into the raging sea! . . . . i 2 122
Throw us that you have about ye: If not, we'll make you sit and rifle you . . . . iv 1 3
Throw cold water on thy choler . . . . . *Mer. Wives* ii 3 89
Throw foul linen upon him, as if it were going to bucking . . iii 3 139
Throw away that thought . . . . . . *Meas. for Meas.* i 3 1
O, were it but my life, I'ld throw it down for your deliverance . iii 1 105
He throws upon the gross world's baser slaves . . . *L. L. Lost* i 1 30
Abate throw at novum, and the whole world again Cannot pick out five such . . . . v 2 547
Throw away that spirit, And I shall find you empty of that fault . v 2 877
There the snake throws her enamell'd skin . . *M. N. Dream* ii 1 255
Upon thy eyes I throw All the power this charm doth owe . . ii 2 78
The greater throw May turn by fortune from the weaker hand *M. of V.* ii 1 33
How far that little candle throws his beams! . . . . . v 1 90
Not a word?—Not one to throw at a dog.—No, thy words are too precious to be cast away upon curs; throw some of them at me *As Y. Like It* i 3 3
He will throw a figure in her face and so disfigure her . *T. of Shrew* i 2 114
Off with that bauble, throw it under-foot . . . . . v 2 122
These warlike principles Do not throw from you . . *All's Well* ii 1 1
I had rather be in this choice than throw ames-ace for my life . . ii 3 84
I will throw thee from my care for ever . . . . . ii 3 169
Give me my veil: come, throw it o'er my face . . . *T. Night* i 5 175
Hold, sir, or I'll throw your dagger o'er the house . . . . iv 1 30

Throw. You can fool no more money out of me at this throw *T. Night* v 1 45
You throw a strange regard upon me v 1 219
Throw thine eye On yon young boy *K. John* iii 3 59
To paint the lily, To throw a perfume on the violet iv 2 12
Haste thee to the peers, Throw this report on their incensed rage iv 2 261
Pale trembling coward, there I throw my gage *Richard II.* i 1 69
Throw down, my son, the Duke of Norfolk's gage.—And, Norfolk, throw down his i 1 161
Myself I throw, dread sovereign, at thy foot i 1 165
Cousin, throw up your gage; do you begin i 1 186
And throw the rider headlong in the lists i 2 52
What reverence he did throw away on slaves i 4 27
With a mortal touch Throw death upon thy sovereign's enemies iii 2 22
Throw away respect, Tradition, form, and ceremonious duty iii 2 172
There I throw my gage, To prove it on thee to the extremest point iv 1 46
Who sets me else? by heaven, I'll throw at all iv 1 57
Here do I throw down this, If he may be repeal'd iv 1 84
This loose behaviour I throw off And pay the debt I never promised *1 Hen. IV.* i 2 232
Throw the quean in the channel.—Throw me in the channel! I'll throw thee in the channel. Wilt thou? wilt thou? *2 Hen. IV.* ii 1 51
When the king did throw his warder down, His own life hung upon the staff iv 1 125
Throw none away; the skin is good for your broken coxcomb *Hen. V.* v 1 56
Point, And nod their heads, and throw their eyes on thee! *2 Hen. VI.* ii 4 22
Madam, your penance done, throw off this sheet ii 4 105
Thus King Henry throws away his crutch Before his legs be firm iii 1 189
Kill and knock down! throw them into Thames! iv 8 2
Throw in the frozen bosoms of our part Hot coals of vengeance! v 2 35
In that hope I throw mine eyes to heaven *3 Hen. VI.* i 4 37
Shall we go throw away our coats of steel? ii 1 160
And he that throws not up his cap for joy Shall for the fault make forfeit of his head ii 1 196
I throw my hands, mine eyes, my heart to thee ii 3 36
Throw up thine eye! see, see what showers arise! ii 5 85
Look here, I throw my infamy at thee v 1 82
I'll throw thy body in another room v 6 92
Wilt thou, O God, fly from such gentle lambs, And throw them in the entrails of the wolf? *Richard III.* iv 4 23
Throw over her the veil of infamy iv 4 208
That am, have, and will be—Though all the world should crack their duty to you, And throw it from their soul *Hen. VIII.* iii 2 194
The remainder viands We do not throw in unrespective sieve *T. and C.* ii 2 71
An act that very chance doth throw upon him iii 3 131
Better would it fit Achilles much To throw down Hector than Polyxena iii 3 208
I will throw my glove to Death himself, That there's no maculation in thy heart iv 4 65
It will in time Win upon power and throw forth greater themes *Coriol.* i 1 224
Be said it must be meet, And throw their power i' the dust iii 1 171
Meal and bran together He throws without distinction iii 1 323
They to dust should grind it And throw't against the wind iii 2 104
Like to a bowl upon a subtle ground, I have tumbled past the throw v 2 21
Which made me down to throw my books, and fly *T. Andron.* iv 1 25
Throw her forth to beasts and birds of prey v 3 198
Throw your mistemper'd weapons to the ground *Rom. and Jul.* i 1 94
At many times I brought in my accounts, Laid them before you; you would throw them off *T. of Athens* ii 2 143
I perceive our masters may throw their caps at their money iii 4 101
Were I like thee, I'ld throw away myself iv 3 219
Throw thy glove, Or any token of thine honour else v 4 49
In at his windows throw, As if they came from several citizens, Writings all tending to the great opinion That Rome holds of his name *J. Cæsar* i 2 320
Throw this In at his window; set this up with wax Upon old Brutus' statue i 3 144
Metellus Cimber throws before thy seat An humble heart iii 1 34
To throw away the dearest thing he owed, As 'twere a careless trifle *Macbeth* i 4 10
Round about the cauldron go; In the poison'd entrails throw iv 1 5
Grease that's sweaten From the murderer's gibbet throw Into the flame iv 1 66
I have seen her rise from her bed, throw her night-gown upon her v 1 5
Throw physic to the dogs; I'll none of it v 3 47
Your leavy screens throw down, And show like those you are v 6 1
Before my body I throw my warlike shield v 8 33
Throw to earth This unprevailing woe, and think of us As of a father *Hamlet* i 2 106
Thou hast cleft my heart in twain.—O, throw away the worser part of it iii 4 157
And either . . . the devil, or throw him out With wondrous potency iii 4 169
If thou prate of mountains, let them throw Millions of acres on us! v 1 303
And in the cup an union shall he throw v 2 283
Tom will throw his head at them. Avaunt, you curs! *Lear* iii 6 67
Turn out that eyeless villain; throw this slave Upon the dunghill iii 7 96
Upon such sacrifices, my Cordelia, The gods themselves throw incense v 3 21
Though that his joy be joy, Yet throw such changes of vexation on't *Oth.* i 1 72
Yet opinion, a sovereign mistress of effects, throws a more safer voice on you i 3 226
Let's to the seaside, . . . to throw out our eyes for brave Othello ii 1 38
Throw your vile guesses in the devil's teeth, From whence you have them iii 4 184
I see that nose of yours, but not that dog I shall throw it to iv 1 144
Our slippery people . . . begin to throw Pompey the Great and all his dignities Upon his son *Ant. and Cleo.* i 2 194
Throw between them all the food thou hast, They'll grind the one the other iii 5 15
You therein throw away The absolute soldiership you have by land iii 7 42
Throw my heart Against the flint and hardness of my fault iv 9 15
It were for me To throw my sceptre at the injurious gods iv 15 76
I'll throw't into the creek Behind our rock *Cymbeline* iv 2 151
Spit, and throw stones, cast mire upon me v 5 222
The gods throw stones of sulphur on me v 5 240
Why did you throw your wedded lady from you? Think that you are upon a rock; and now Throw me again v 5 261
And she, like harmless lightning, throws her eye On him, her brothers v 5 394
Throws down one mountain to cast up a higher *Pericles* i 4 6
Now, the good gods Throw their best eyes upon't! iii 1 37
Thrower-out. The thrower-out Of my poor babe *W. Tale* iii 3 29
Throwest. Learn more than thou trowest, Set less than thou throwest *Lear* i 4 136
Throwing him into the water will do him a benefit *Mer. Wives* iii 3 194
Excuse his throwing into the water; and give him another hope iii 3 206
He is very courageous mad about his throwing into the water iv 1 5

Throwing. Dishonour not your eye By throwing it on any other object *Meas. for Meas.* v 1 23
Throwing it aside And stemming it with hearts of controversy *J. Cæsar* i 2 108
There has been much throwing about of brains.—Do the boys carry it away? *Hamlet* ii 2 375
With throwing thus my head, Dogs leap the hatch, and all are fled *Lear* iii 6 75
Throwing but shows of service on their lords, Do well thrive by them *Othello* i 1 52
Break out in peevish jealousies, Throwing restraint upon us iv 3 91
Throwing favours on The low Posthumus slanders so her judgement *Cymbeline* iii 5 75
Thrown. Like a barrow of butcher's offal, and to be thrown in the Thames? *Mer. Wives* iii 5 6
I have had ford enough; I was thrown into the ford iii 5 37
To be thrown into the Thames, and cooled, glowing hot iii 5 122
I will be thrown into Etna, as I have been into Thames, ere I will leave her iii 5 128
You say he has been thrown in the rivers iv 4 21
The wrong That she this day hath shameless thrown on me *Com. of Er.* v 1 202
My better parts Are all thrown down *As Y. Like It* i 2 262
They are but burs, cousin, thrown upon thee in holiday foolery i 3 13
And unregarded age in corners thrown ii 3 42
Put on a religious life And thrown into neglect the pompous court v 4 188
In Florence was it from a casement thrown me, Wrapp'd in a paper *All's W.* v 3 93
Not a friend greet My poor corpse, where my bones shall be thrown *T. N.* ii 4 63
Some have greatness thrown upon them v 1 379
The king hath thrown his warder down *Richard II.* i 3 118
Which waste of idle hours hath quite thrown down iii 4 66
But dust was thrown upon his sacred head v 2 30
Thrown over the shoulders like an herald's coat without sleeves *1 Hen. IV.* iv 2 48
I have thrown A brave defiance in King Henry's teeth v 2 42
They are burs, I can tell you; they'll stick where they are thrown *Troi. and Cres.* iii 2 120
He shall be thrown down the Tarpeian rock With rigorous hands *Coriol.* iii 1 266
That noble hand of thine, That hath thrown down so many enemies *T. Andron.* iii 1 164
How much salt water thrown away in waste, To season love! *R. and J.* ii 3 71
As we do turn our backs From our companion thrown into his grave *T. of Athens* iv 2 9
Shards, flints, and pebbles should be thrown on her *Hamlet* v 1 254
Thrown out his angle for my proper life v 2 66
Thy dowerless daughter, king, thrown to my chance, Is queen of us, of ours *Lear* i 1 259
I found it thrown in at the casement i 2 64
Thrown such despite and heavy terms upon her, As true hearts cannot bear *Othello* iv 2 116
Wherefore was he mock'd, To be exiled, and thrown From Leonati seat? *Cymbeline* v 4 59
Having thrown him from your watery grave, Here to have death *Pericles* ii 1 10
I'll swear she's dead, And thrown into the sea. But I'll see further iv 1 100
That these pirates, Not enough barbarous, had not o'erboard thrown me! iv 2 70
Early in blustering morn this lady was Thrown upon this shore v 3 23
Thrum. O Fates, come, come, Cut thread and thrum *M. N. Dream* v 1 291
Thrummed. There's her thrummed hat and her muffler too *Mer. Wives* iv 2 80
Thrush. The thrush and the jay Are summer songs for me and my aunts *W. Tale* iv 3 10
Thrust. That very duke Which was thrust forth of Milan *Tempest* v 1 160
Was Milan thrust from Milan, that his issue Should become kings of Naples? v 1 205
An unmannerly slave, that will thrust himself into secrets! *T. G. of V.* iii 1 393
Such as the fury of ungovern'd youth Thrust from the company of awful men iv 1 46
He thrusts me himself into the company of three or four gentlemanlike dogs iv 4 18
Though we would have thrust virtue out of our hearts *Mer. Wives* v 5 155
An thou wilt needs thrust thy neck into a yoke *Much Ado* i 1 203
Thrust thy sharp wit quite through my ignorance *L. L. Lost* v 2 398
Nor thrust your head into the public street *Mer. of Venice* ii 5 32
I have thrust myself into this maze, Haply to wive and thrive *T. of Shrew* i 2 55
And understand what advice shall thrust upon thee *All's Well* i 1 225
And some have greatness thrust upon 'em *T. Night* ii 5 158; iii 4 49
Betwixt the firmament and it you cannot thrust a bodkin's point *W. T.* iii 3 87
As you'ld thrust a cork into a hogshead iii 3 95
Thrust but these men away, and I'll forgive you *K. John* iv 1 83
Go, And thrust thyself into their companies iv 2 167
Slippers, which his nimble haste Had falsely thrust upon contrary feet iv 2 198
Thou shalt thrust thy hand as deep Into the purse of rich prosperity v 2 60
Yea, thrust this enterprise into my heart v 2 90
None of you will bid the winter come To thrust his icy fingers in my maw v 7 37
Where doth the world thrust forth a vanity—So it be new? *Richard II.* ii 1 24
If I know how or which way to order these affairs Thus thrust disorderly into my hands, Never believe me ii 2 110
I am eight times thrust through the doublet, four through the hose *1 Hen. IV.* ii 4 184
These four came all a-front, and mainly thrust at me ii 4 223
There is not a dangerous action can peep out his head but I am thrust upon it: well, I cannot last ever *2 Hen. IV.* i 2 239
If I can close with him, I care not for his thrust ii 1 21
Can thrust me from a level consideration ii 1 124
I'll thrust my knife in your mouldy chaps ii 4 138
Thrust him down stairs! I cannot endure such a fustian rascal ii 4 202
Thrust him down stairs! know we not Galloway nags? ii 4 203
Methought a' made a shrewd thrust at your belly ii 4 228
You might have thrust him and all his apparel into an eel-skin iii 2 350
He that makes the first thrust, I'll kill him *Hen. V.* ii 1 105
Thrust in between the paction of these kingdoms, To make divorce v 2 393
A base Walloon . . . Thrust Talbot with a spear into the back *1 Hen. VI.* i 1 138
Henry will be lord And thou be thrust out like a fugitive i 3 67
Thrust from the crown By shameful murder of a guiltless king *2 Hen. VI.* iv 1 94
He was thrust in the mouth with a spear, and 'tis not whole yet iv 7 10
And as I thrust thy body in with my sword, So wish I, I might thrust thy soul to hell iv 10 84
Offer him no violence, Unless he seek to thrust you out perforce *3 Hen. VI.* i 1 34
What valour were it, when a cur doth grin, For one to thrust his hand between his teeth, When he might spurn him with his foot away? i 4 57
How dare you thrust yourselves Into my private meditations? *Hen. VIII.* ii 2 65
If the time thrust forth A cause for thy repeal *Coriolanus* iv 1 40
Thrusts forth his horns again into the world; Which were inshell'd iv 6 44
Shall join To thrust the lie unto him iv 6 110
And withal Thrust these reproachful speeches down his throat *T. Andron.* ii 1 55

Thrust. Women, being the weaker vessels, are ever thrust to the wall: therefore I will push Montague's men from the wall, and thrust his maids to the wall . . . *Rom. and Jul.* i 1 20
While we were interchanging thrusts and blows, Came more and more . i 1 120
An envious thrust from Tybalt hit the life Of stout Mercutio . iii 1 173
You are welcome.—No; You shall not make me welcome: I come to have thee thrust me out of doors . . . *T. of Athens* i 2 25
Every minute of his being thrusts Against my near'st of life *Macbeth* iii 1 117
Go thrust him out at gates, and let him smell His way to Dover *Lear* iii 7 93
I found them close together, At blow and thrust . . . *Othello* ii 3 238
That thrust had been mine enemy indeed, But that my coat is better than thou know'st . . . v 1 24
Thrusteth. The lion dying thrusteth forth his paw . *Richard II.* v 1 29
Thrusting. By thrusting out a torch from yonder tower . *1 Hen. VI.* iii 2 23
Thrusting this report Into his ears; I may say, thrusting it . *J. Cæsar* v 3 74
All that we are evil in, by a divine thrusting on . . *Lear* i 2 137
Thumb. He is not quantity enough for that Worthy's thumb . *L. L. Lost* v 1 138
With his finger and his thumb, Cried, 'Via! we will do't' . v 2 111
And 'twixt his finger and his thumb he held A pouncet-box . *1 Hen. IV.* i 3 37
I have him already tempering between my finger and my thumb, and shortly will I seal with him *2 Hen. IV.* iv 3 141
He turned me about with his finger and his thumb . *Coriolanus* iv 5 160
I will bite my thumb at them; which is a disgrace to them, if they bear it.—Do you bite your thumb at us, sir?—I do bite my thumb, sir *Rom. and Jul.* i 1 49
I do not bite my thumb at you, sir, but I bite my thumb, sir . i 1 57
Here I have a pilot's thumb, Wreck'd as homeward he did come *Macbeth* i 3 28
By the pricking of my thumbs, Something wicked this way comes . iv 1 44
Govern these ventages with your fingers and thumb, give it breath *Ham.* iii 2 373
Thumb-ring. I could have crept into any alderman's thumb-ring *1 Hen. IV.* ii 4 365
Thump. I shoot thee at the swain.—Thump then and I flee . *L. L. Lost* iii 1 66
Dildos and fadings, 'jump her and thump her' *W. Tale* iv 4 196
Peter! what more?—Thump.—Thump! then see thou thump thy master well . *2 Hen. VI.* ii 3 84
When my heart, all mad with misery, Beats in this hollow prison of my flesh, Then thus I thump it down *T. Andron.* iii 2 11
Thumped. Thou hast thumped him with thy bird-bolt . *L. L. Lost* iv 3 23
These bastard Bretons; whom our fathers Have in their own land beaten, bobb'd, and thump'd . . . *Richard III.* v 3 334
Thunder. If it should thunder as it did before, I know not where to hide my head . . . *Tempest* ii 2 22
The thunder, That deep and dreadful organ-pipe iii 3 97
The dread rattling thunder v 1 44
Let it thunder to the tune of Green Sleeves, hail kissing-comfits *M. Wives* v 5 21
Could great men thunder As Jove himself does, Jove would ne'er be quiet, For every pelting, petty officer Would use his heaven for thunder; Nothing but thunder! . . . *Meas. for Meas.* ii 2 110
Thy eye Jove's lightning bears, thy voice his dreadful thunder *L. L. Lost* iv 2 119
I never heard so musical a discord, such sweet thunder *M. N. Dream* iv 1 123
As loud As thunder when the clouds in autumn crack . *T. of Shrew* i 2 96
And heaven's artillery thunder in the skies i 2 205
With adorations, fertile tears, With groans that thunder love *T. Night* i 5 275
And the ear-deafening voice o' the oracle, Kin to Jove's thunder *W. Tale* iii 1 10
The thunder of my cannon shall be heard *K. John* i 1 26
Our thunder from the south Shall rain their drift of bullets on this town ii 1 411
Hast thou not spoke like thunder on my side? iii 1 124
O, that my tongue were in the thunder's mouth! iii 4 38
Rattle the welkin's ear And mock the deep-mouth'd thunder . v 2 173
Let thy blows, doubly redoubled, Fall like amazing thunder *Richard II.* i 3 81
In fierce tempest is he coming, In thunder and in earthquake, like a Jove . . . *Hen. V.* ii 4 100
That engenders thunder in his breast And makes him roar *1 Hen. VI.* iii 1 39
If Talbot do but thunder, rain will follow iii 2 59
O that I were a god, to shoot forth thunder! . *2 Hen. VI.* iv 1 104
Who thunders to his captives blood and death *3 Hen. VI.* ii 1 127
Thy voice is thunder, but thy looks are humble *Richard III.* i 4 173
These are the youths that thunder at a playhouse . *Hen. VIII.* v 4 63
Jupiter forbid, And say in thunder 'Achilles go to him' *Troi. and Cres.* ii 3 209
By him that thunders, thou hast lusty arms iv 5 136
The shepherd knows not thunder from a tabor More than I know the sound of Marcius' tongue From every meaner man *Coriolanus* i 6 25
The commons made A shower and thunder with their caps and shouts ii 1 283
He would not flatter Neptune for his trident, Or Jove for's power to thunder iii 1 257
To tear with thunder the wide cheeks o' the air v 3 151
And sits aloft, Secure of thunder's crack or lightning flash *T. Andron.* ii 1 3
This dreadful night, That thunders, lightens, opens graves, and roars As doth the lion in the Capitol *J. Cæsar* i 3 74
When shall we three meet again In thunder, lightning, or in rain? *Macb.* i 1 2
Shipwrecking storms and direful thunders break i 2 26
I may tell pale-hearted fear it lies, And sleep in spite of thunder . iv 1 86
The great cannon to the clouds shall tell, And the king's rouse the heavens shall bruit again, Re-speaking earthly thunder *Hamlet* i 2 128
Anon the dreadful thunder Doth rend the region ii 2 508
Ay me, what act, That roars so loud, and thunders in the index? iii 4 52
The revenging gods 'Gainst parricides did all their thunders bend *Lear* ii 1 48
All-shaking thunder, Smite flat the thick rotundity o' the world! . iii 2 6
Nor rain, wind, thunder, fire, are my daughters: I tax not you, you elements, with unkindness . iii 2 15
Such sheets of fire, such bursts of horrid thunder . iii 2 46
First let me talk with this philosopher. What is the cause of thunder? iii 4 160
When the thunder would not peace at my bidding . iv 6 103
To stand against the deep dread-bolted thunder iv 7 33
Are there no stones in heaven But what serve for the thunder? *Othello* v 2 235
Favours, by Jove that thunders! What art thou, fellow? *Ant. and Cleo.* iii 13 85
But when he meant to quail and shake the orb, He was as rattling thunder v 2 86
He came in thunder; his celestial breath Was sulphurous to smell *Cymb.* v 4 114
For now the wind begins to blow; Thunder above and deeps below *Pericles* ii Gower 30
Wind, rain, and thunder, remember, earthly man Is but a substance that must yield to you ii 1 2
O, still Thy deafening, dreadful thunders; gently quench Thy nimble, sulphurous flashes! iii 1 5
Thunder shall not so awake the beds of eels iv 2 154
Down on thy knees, thank the holy gods as loud As thunder threatens us v 1 201
Thunder-bearer. I do not bid the thunder-bearer shoot . *Lear* ii 4 230
Thunderbolt. That hath lately suffered by a thunderbolt . *Tempest* ii 2 38
If I had a thunderbolt in mine eye, I can tell who should down *As Y. L. It* i 2 226
Let me taste my horse, Who is to bear me like a thunderbolt *1 Hen. IV.* iv 1 120
Thunderbolt. Be ready, gods, with all your thunderbolts; Dash him to pieces! *J. Cæsar* iv 3 81
Vaunt-couriers to oak-cleaving thunderbolts *Lear* iii 2 5
Some innocents 'scape not the thunderbolt *Ant. and Cleo.* ii 5 77
Thunder-claps. The precursors O' the dreadful thunder-claps *Tempest* i 2 202
Thunder-darter. O thou great thunder-darter of Olympus! *Troi. and Cres.* ii 3 11
Thunderer. The thunderer, whose bolt, you know, Sky-planted batters all rebelling coasts *Cymbeline* v 4 95
Thunderest. Foul-spoken coward, that thunder'st with thy tongue, And with thy weapon nothing darest perform! *T. Andron.* ii 1 58
Thundering. With no less terror than the elements Of fire and water, when their thundering shock At meeting tears the cloudy cheeks of heaven *Richard II.* iii 3 56
Thunder-like. With thy grim looks and The thunder-like percussion of thy sounds, Thou madest thine enemies shake . *Coriolanus* i 4 59
Thunder-master. No more, thou thunder-master, show Thy spite on mortal flies *Cymbeline* v 4 30
Thunder-stone. Have bared my bosom to the thunder-stone . *J. Cæsar* i 3 49
Fear no more the lightning-flash,— Nor the all-dreaded thunder-stone *Cymbeline* iv 2 271
Thunder-stroke. They dropp'd, as by a thunder-stroke . *Tempest* ii 1 204
I took him to be killed with a thunder-stroke ii 2 112
Thurio. Sir Thurio frowns on you.—Ay, boy, it's for love.—Not of you *T. G. of Ver.* ii 4 3
What, angry, Sir Thurio! do you change colour?—Give him leave, madam ii 4 23
Sir Thurio borrows his wit from your ladyship's looks ii 4 38
I speak to you, and you, sir Thurio; For Valentine, I need not cite him ii 4 84
To see such lovers, Thurio, as yourself: Upon a homely object Love can wink ii 4 97
For Thurio, he intends, shall wed his daughter ii 6 39
I'll quickly cross By some sly trick blunt Thurio's dull proceeding ii 6 41
I know you have determined to bestow her On Thurio iii 1 14
I have sought To match my friend Sir Thurio to my daughter iii 1 62
Sir Thurio, fear not but that she will love you, Now Valentine is banish'd iii 2 1
What might we do to make the girl forget The love of Valentine and love Sir Thurio? iii 2 30
Weed her love from Valentine, It follows not that she will love Sir Thurio iii 2 50
But you, Sir Thurio, are not sharp enough; You must lay lime iii 2 67
Already have I been false to Valentine And now I must be as unjust to Thurio iv 2 2
My father would enforce me marry Vain Thurio, whom my very soul abhors iv 3 17
Silvia's mine.—Thurio, give back, or else embrace thy death . v 4 126
Thursday. To-morrow, Francis; or Francis, o' Thursday *1 Hen. IV.* ii 4 74
On Thursday we ourselves will march iii 2 174
I shall receive money o' Thursday *2 Hen. IV.* ii 4 298
Well, Wednesday is too soon, O' Thursday let it be: o' Thursday, tell her, She shall be married *Rom. and Jul.* iii 4 20
But what say you to Thursday?—My lord, I would that Thursday were to-morrow.—Well, get you gone: o' Thursday be it, then iii 4 28
What day is that?—Marry, my child, early next Thursday morn iii 5 113
Proud me no prouds, But fettle your fine joints 'gainst Thursday next. iii 5 154
Get thee to church o' Thursday, Or never after look me in the face iii 5 162
I do not use to jest. Thursday is near; lay hand on heart, advise iii 5 192
On Thursday, sir? the time is very short. iv 1 1
When I may be a wife.—That may be must be, love, on Thursday next iv 1 20
Juliet, on Thursday early will I rouse ye: Till then, adieu iv 1 42
I hear thou must, and nothing may prorogue it, On Thursday next be married. iv 1 49
To-morrow?—No, not till Thursday; there is time enough iv 2 36
Thus. I am thus early come to know *T. G. of Ver.* iv 3 9
If study's gain be thus and this be so *L. L. Lost* i 1 67
'Thus must thou speak,' and 'thus thy body bear' v 2 100
Setting all this chat aside, Thus in plain terms *T. of Shrew* ii 1 271
My liege! my lord! but now a king, now thus *K. John* v 7 66
I have Before-time seen him thus *Coriolanus* i 6 24
The sorrow that delivers us thus changed Makes you think so v 3 39
After that, he came, thus sad, away?—Ay *J. Cæsar* i 2 279
Thus, Brutus, did my master bid me kneel iii 1 123
Thus thou must do, if thou have it *Macbeth* i 5 24
To be thus is nothing: But to be safely thus iii 1 49
Sit, worthy friends: my lord is often thus, And hath been from his youth iii 4 53
How long hath she been thus? *Hamlet* iv 5 67
Though the wisdom of nature can reason it thus and thus *Lear* i 2 114
I should e'en die with pity, To see another thus iv 7 54
'Tis in ourselves that we are thus or thus *Othello* i 3 323
Wear your eye thus, not jealous nor secure iii 3 198
The nobleness of life Is to do thus *Ant. and Cleo.* i 1 37
Wounding his belief in her renown With tokens thus, and thus *Cymbeline* v 5 203
Thus far. Know thus far forth *Tempest* i 2 177
Thus far I witness with him, That he dined not at home *Com. of Errors* v 1 254
Thus far can I praise him; he is of a noble strain *Much Ado* ii 1 393
Since we are stepp'd thus far in, I will continue *T. of Shrew* i 2 83
Take this purse of gold, And let me buy your friendly help thus far *All's Well* iii 7 15
Yet thus far I will boldly publish her *T. Night* ii 1 29
Thus far, with rough and all-unable pen *Hen. V.* Epil. 1
Yet thus far fortune maketh us amends *3 Hen. VI.* iv 7 2
Thus far our fortune keeps an upward course v 3 1
Nay, for a need, thus far come near my person *Richard III.* iii 5 85
Thus far into the bowels of the land Have we march'd on v 2 3
All good people, You that thus far have come to pity me *Hen. VIII.* ii 1 56
Yet thus far we are one in fortunes ii 1 121
I speak my good lord cardinal to this point, And thus far clear him ii 4 167
And thus far hear me, Cromwell iii 2 431
Yet thus far, Griffith, give me leave to speak him iv 2 32
Thus far . . . may it like your grace To let my tongue excuse all v 3 147
And thus far I confirm you *T. of Athens* i 2 98
Having thus far proceeded,—Unless thou think'st me devilish *Cymbeline* i 5 15
Since your kindness We have stretch'd thus far *Pericles* v 1 55
Thus high. Your heart is up, I know, Thus high at least *Richard II.* iii 3 195
When a' was a crack not thus high *2 Hen. IV.* iii 2 34
Thus high, by thy advice And thy assistance, is King Richard seated *Richard III.* iv 2 3
Thus long have we stood To watch *Richard II.* iii 3 72
Have I lived thus long . . . a wife, a true one? *Hen. VIII.* iii 1 125
His evasions have ears thus long *Troi. and Cres.* ii 1 75

Thus much. Were thus much overheard by a man *Much Ado* i 2 10
Thus much I have learnt *L. L. Lost* ii 1 84
Are you not [ashamed], All three of you, to be thus much o'ershot? iv 3 160
You would not do me thus much injury *M. N. Dream* iii 2 148
For these courtesies I'll lend you thus much moneys *Mer. of Venice* i 3 130
I have spoke thus much To mitigate the justice of thy plea iv 1 202
Thus much for greeting *T. of Shrew* iv 1 115
At least thus much: I'll pawn the little blood which I have left *W. Tale* ii 3 165
And from the mouth of England Add thus much more *K. John* iii 1 153
Dost thou understand thus much English, canst thou love me? *Hen. V.* v 2 205
Pray, tell 'em thus much from me *Hen. VIII.* i 4 77
But, thus much, they are foul ones iii 2 300
I will say thus much for him v 3 156
Only thus much I give your grace to know *T. Andron.* i 1 413
Thus much of this [gold] will make black white, foul fair *T. of Athens* iv 3 28
I am glad that my weak words Have struck but thus much show of fire *J. Cæsar* i 2 177
So much for him. Now for ourself and for this time of meeting: Thus much the business is *Hamlet* i 2 27
When your mistress hears thus much from you *Lear* iv 5 34
Thwack. We'll thwack him hence with distaffs *W. Tale* i 2 37
Why, here's he that was wont to thwack our general, Caius Marcius.—Why do you say 'thwack our general'?—I do not say 'thwack our general;' but he was always good enough for him *Coriolanus* iv 5 189
Thwart. Abetting him to thwart me in my mood *Com. of Errors* ii 2 172
Trial did draw Bias and thwart, not answering the aim *Troi. and Cres.* i 3 15
That it may live, And be a thwart disnatured torment to her! *Lear* i 4 305
Thwarted. If crooked fortune had not thwarted me *T. G. of Ver.* iv 1 22
Mocked at my gains, scorned my nation, thwarted my bargains *M. of V.* iii 1 59
I am thwarted quite From my great purpose *Troi. and Cres.* v 1 42
A greater power than we can contradict Hath thwarted our intents *Rom. and Jul.* v 3 154
Thwarting. O mischief strangely thwarting! *Much Ado* iii 2 135
That the people of this blessed land May not be punish'd with my thwarting stars *3 Hen. VI.* iv 6 22
Lesser had been The thwartings of your dispositions, if You had not show'd them how ye were disposed *Coriolanus* iii 2 21
Pericles Is now again thwarting the wayward seas *Pericles* iv 4 10
Thy eyes are almost set in thy head.—Where should they be set? *Tempest* iii 2 10
Thy slanders I forgive; and therewithal Remit thy other forfeits *Meas. for Meas.* v 1 526
Be not thy tongue thy own shame's orator *Com. of Errors* iii 2 10
In thy eye that shall appear When thou wakest, it is thy dear *M. N. D.* ii 2 32
Shall it not grieve thee dearer than thy death, To see thy Antony making his peace, Shaking the bloody fingers of thy foes? *J. Cæsar* iii 1 196
Thyme. I know a bank where the wild thyme blows *M. N. Dream* ii 1 249
Plant nettles, or sow lettuce, set hyssop, and weed up thyme *Othello* i 3 326
Thyreus. Try thy cunning, Thyreus; Make thine own edict for thy pains, which we Will answer as a law *Ant. and Cleo.* iii 12 31
What's your name?—My name is Thyreus.—Most kind messenger iii 13 73
Thyself. He whom next thyself Of all the world I loved *Tempest* i 2 68
Thyself hast loved; and I have heard thee say *T. G. of Ver.* iv 3 18
Alas, how then?—Why, thou must be thyself *Mer. Wives* iii 4 3
Thyself and thy belongings Are not thine own so proper as to waste Thyself upon thy virtues, they on thee *Meas. for Meas.* i 1 30
Thou art not thyself; For thou exist'st on many a thousand grains That issue out of dust iii 1 19
O, how comes it, That thou art thus estranged from thyself? *Com. of Er.* ii 2 122
Then, by myself— Thyself thyself misusest *Richard III.* iv 4 376
Holp'st to make me great, In hope thyself should govern Rome and me *T. Andron.* iv 4 60
Tib. As Tib's rush for Tom's forefinger *All's Well* ii 2 24
The damned doorkeeper to every Coistrel that comes inquiring for his Tib *Pericles* iv 6 176
Tiber. And one that loves a cup of hot wine with not a drop of allaying Tiber in't *Coriolanus* ii 1 53
I would they were a-bed!—I would they were in Tiber! iii 1 262
An universal shout, That Tiber trembled underneath her banks *J. Cæsar* i 1 50
Draw them to Tiber banks, and weep your tears Into the channel i 1 63
The troubled Tiber chafing with her shores i 2 101
So from the waves of Tiber Did I the tired Cæsar i 2 114
He hath left you all his walks, His private arbours, and new-planted orchards, On this side Tiber iii 2 254
Let Rome in Tiber melt, and the wide arch Of the ranged empire fall! *Ant. and Cleo.* i 1 33
Tiberio. The son and heir of old Tiberio *Rom. and Jul.* i 5 131
'Ticed. These two have 'ticed me hither to this place *T. Andron.* ii 3 92
Tick. I had rather be a tick in a sheep *Troi. and Cres.* iii 3 315
Tickle. Thy head stands so tickle on thy shoulders *Meas. for Meas.* i 2 177
If my hair do but tickle me, I must scratch *M. N. Dream* iv 1 28
If you tickle us, do we not laugh? if you poison us, do we not die? *Mer. of Venice* iii 1 68
To tickle our noses with spear-grass to make them bleed *1 Hen. IV.* ii 4 340
Nay, I'll tickle ye for a young prince, i' faith ii 4 489
You rampallian! you fustilarian! I'll tickle your catastrophe *2 Hen. IV.* ii 1 66
Paris is lost; the state of Normandy Stands on a tickle point *2 Hen. VI.* i 1 216
The shaft confounds, Not that it wounds, But tickles still the sore *Troi. and Cres.* iii 1 130
How the devil Luxury, with his fat rump and potato-finger, tickles these together! v 2 56
He'll tickle it for his concupy v 2 177
A torch for me: let wantons light of heart Tickle the senseless rushes with their heels *Rom. and Jul.* i 4 36
The clown shall make those laugh whose lungs are tickle o' the sere *Ham.* ii 2 337
How fine this tyrant Can tickle where she wounds! *Cymbeline* i 1 85
Tickle-brain. Peace, good pint-pot; peace, good tickle-brain *1 Hen. IV.* ii 4 438
Tickled. He would have tickled you othergates than he did *T. Night* v 1 198
She's tickled now; her fume needs no spurs *2 Hen. VI.* i 3 153
I cannot choose but laugh, to think how she tickled his chin *Tr. and Cr.* i 2 150
Tickled with good success, disdains the shadow Which he treads on *Cor.* i 1 264
Thus smiling, as some fly had tickled slumber, Not as death's dart *Cymb.* iv 2 210
Tickling. Die with mocks, Which is as bad as die with tickling *M. Ado* iii 1 80
Here comes the trout that must be caught with tickling *T. Night* ii 5 26
That smooth-faced gentleman, tickling Commodity *K. John* ii 1 573
Runs tickling up and down the veins iii 3 44
Expectation, tickling skittish spirits, On one and other side *Tr. and Cr.* Prol. 20
Tickling a parson's nose as a' lies asleep *Rom. and Jul.* i 4 80
Ticklish. And wide unclasp the tables of their thoughts To every ticklish reader! *Troi. and Cres.* iv 5 61
Tick-tack. Foolishly lost at a game of tick-tack *Meas. for Meas.* i 2 196

Tiddle taddle. There is no tiddle taddle nor pibble pabble in Pompey's camp *Hen. V.* iv 1 71
Tide. Would thou mightst lie drowning The washing of ten tides! *Temp.* i 1 61
The approaching tide Will shortly fill the reasonable shore v 1 80
Answer not; The tide is now: nay, not thy tide of tears; That tide will stay me longer than I should *T. G. of Ver.* ii 2 14
Away, ass! you'll lose the tide, if you tarry any longer ii 3 39
What's the unkindest tide?—Why, he that's tied here, Crab, my dog ii 3 43
Lose the tide, and the voyage, and the master, and the service, and the tied! ii 3 56
Both wind and tide stays for this gentleman *Com. of Errors* iv 1 46
'Tide life, 'tide death, I come without delay *M. N. Dream* v 1 205
Whose foot spurns back the ocean's roaring tides *K. John* ii 1 24
Float upon the swelling tide ii 1 74
It in golden letters should be set Among the high tides in the calendar iii 1 86
I was amazed Under the tide: but now I breathe again Aloft the flood iv 2 138
Half my power this night, Passing these flats, are taken by the tide v 6 40
What a tide of woes Comes rushing on this woeful land at once! *Rich. II.* ii 2 98
Such an apprehension May turn the tide of fearful faction *1 Hen. IV.* iv 1 67
'Tis with my mind As with the tide swell'd up unto his height *2 Hen. IV.* ii 3 63
The tide of blood in me Hath proudly flow'd in vanity till now v 2 129
Pouring, like the tide into a breach, With ample and brim fulness *Hen. V.* i 2 149
A' parted even just between twelve and one, even at the turning o' the tide ii 3 14
As men wrecked upon a sand, that look to be washed off the next tide iv 1 101
Nor the tide of pomp That beats upon the high shore of this world iv 1 281
Were our tears wanting to this funeral, These tidings would call forth their flowing tides *1 Hen. VI.* i 1 83
As rigour of tempestuous gusts Provokes the mightiest hulk against the tide v 5 6
As I have seen a swan With bootless labour swim against the tide *3 Hen. VI.* i 4 20
Like a mighty sea Forced by the tide to combat with the wind ii 5 6
Now begins a second storm to rise; For this is he that moves both wind and tide iii 3 48
That men must needs abide; It boots not to resist both wind and tide iv 3 59
Sail how thou canst, have wind and tide thy friend v 1 53
Bestride the rock; the tide will wash you off, Or else you famish v 4 31
How got they in, and be hang'd?—Alas, I know not; how gets the tide in? *Hen. VIII.* v 4 18
As if The passage and whole carriage of this action Rode on his tide *Troi. and Cres.* ii 3 141
Like to an enter'd tide, they all rush by And leave you hindmost iii 3 159
I have important business, The tide whereof is now v 1 90
Ne'er through an arch so hurried the blown tide *Coriolanus* v 4 50
Who marks the waxing tide grow wave by wave *T. Andron.* iii 1 95
Day, night, hour, tide, time, work, play, Alone, in company, still my care hath been To have her match'd *Rom. and Jul.* iii 5 178
A brave fellow! he keeps his tides well *T. of Athens* i 2 57
I charge thee, invite them all: let in the tide Of knaves once more iii 4 118
The ruins of the noblest man That ever lived in the tide of times *J. C.* iii 1 257
There is a tide in the affairs of men, Which, taken at the flood, leads on to fortune iv 3 218
Goes to and back, lackeying the varying tide *Ant. and Cleo.* i 4 46
The swan's down-feather, That stands upon the swell at full of tide iii 2 49
Tidings. I shall make my master glad with these tidings *Mer. Wives* iv 5 57
Take the cork out of thy mouth that I may drink thy tidings *As Y. L. It* iii 2 214
I am the second son of old Sir Rowland, That bring these tidings v 4 159
Pardon, my lord, for me and for my tidings *All's Well* ii 1 63
The tidings comes that they are all arrived *K. John* iv 2 115
Thou hast made me giddy With these ill tidings iv 2 132
I dare not say How near the tidings of our comfort is *Richard II.* ii 1 272
And yet we hear no tidings from the king ii 4 3
Is so arm'd To bear the tidings of calamity iii 2 105
Letters came last night . . . That tell black tidings iii 4 71
Where, when, and how, Camest thou by this ill tidings? iii 4 80
The tidings of this broil Brake off our business *1 Hen. IV.* i 1 47
That's the worst tidings that I hear of yet iv 1 127
What good tidings comes with you? *2 Hen. IV.* i 1 33
Turn'd me back With joyful tidings i 1 35
Good tidings, my Lord Hastings; for the which I do arrest thee iv 2 106
Tidings do I bring and lucky joys And golden times and happy news v 3 99
Sad tidings bring I to you out of France, Of loss, of slaughter *1 Hen. VI.* i 1 58
Were our tears wanting to this funeral, These tidings would call forth their flowing tides i 1 83
What tidings send our scouts? I prithee, speak v 2 10
What tidings with our cousin Buckingham? *2 Hen. VI.* ii 1 165
Health and glad tidings to your majesty! iv 9 7
Had he 'scaped, methinks we should have heard The happy tidings *3 Hen. VI.* ii 1 7
Tidings, as swiftly as the posts could run, Were brought me ii 1 109
My brother Gloucester, Who shall reward you better for my life Than Edward will for tidings of my death *Richard III.* i 4 237
Despiteful tidings! O unpleasing news! iv 1 37
I left them both, To bring this tidings to the bloody king iv 3 22
Colder tidings, yet they must be told iv 4 536
The tidings that I bring Will make my boldness manners *Hen VIII.* v 1 158
The gods bless you for your tidings *Coriolanus* v 4 61
Like a lark, That gives sweet tidings of the sun's uprise *T. Andron.* iii 1 159
Sirrah, what tidings? have you any letters? iv 3 78
These tidings nip me, and I hang the head As flowers with frost iv 4 70
And for my tidings gave me twenty kisses v 1 120
I bring thee tidings of the prince's doom *Rom. and Jul.* iii 3 8
But now I'll tell thee joyful tidings, girl.—And joy comes well iii 5 105
This letter doth make good the friar's words, Their course of love, the tidings of her death v 3 287
With her death That tidings came;—with this she fell distract *J. Cæsar* iv 3 155
These tidings will well comfort Cassius.—Where did you leave him? v 3 54
Piercing steel and darts envenomed Shall be as welcome to the ears of Brutus As tidings of this sight v 3 78
What is your tidings?—The king comes here to-night *Macbeth* i 5 31
When I came hither to transport the tidings, Which I have heavily borne iv 3 181
What tidings can you tell me of my lord? *Othello* ii 1 88
Upon certain tidings now arrived ii 2 2
Ram thou thy fruitful tidings in mine ears *Ant. and Cleo.* ii 5 24
So tart a favour To trumpet such good tidings! ii 5 39
But let ill tidings tell Themselves when they be felt ii 5 87
This sword but shown to Cæsar, with this tidings, Shall enter me with him iv 14 112
The gods rebuke me, but it is tidings To wash the eyes of kings v 1 27

Tidings. You shall hear The legions now in Gallia sooner landed In our not-fearing Britain than have tidings Of any penny tribute paid *Cymbeline* ii 4 19
My mistress, who did promise To yield me often tidings . iv 3 39
No tidings of him?—He hath been search'd among the dead and living . v 5 10
Tidings to the contrary Are brought your eyes; what need speak I? *Pericles* ii Gower 15
Tidy. Thou whoreson little tidy Bartholomew boar-pig . 2 *Hen. IV.* ii 4 250
Tie. Wrench awe from fools and tie the wiser souls To thy false seeming! *Meas. for Meas.* ii 4 14
What king so strong Can tie the gall up in the slanderous tongue? iii 2 199
Shave the head, and tie the beard iv 2 187
Tie up my love's tongue, bring him silently . *M. N. Dream* iii 1 206
Only sin And hellish obstinacy tie thy tongue . *All's Well* i 3 186
For by this knot thou shalt so surely tie Thy now unsured assurance to the crown *K. John* ii 1 470
There is my bond of faith, To tie thee to my strong correction *Richard II.* iv 1 77
Our horses they shall not see; I'll tie them in the wood . 1 *Hen. IV.* i 2 200
This moral ties me over to time and a hot summer *Hen. V.* v 2 339
Come, tie his body to my horse's tail; Along the field I will the Trojan trail . *Troi. and Cres.* v 8 21
He loves your people; But tie him not to be their bedfellow . *Coriolanus* ii 2 69
Will too late Tie leaden pounds to's heels . iii 1 314
Death, that hath ta'en her hence to make me wail, Ties up my tongue, and will not let me speak *Rom. and Jul.* iv 5 32
To the which my duties Are with a most indissoluble tie For ever knit *Macbeth* iii 1 17
He'll not feel wrongs Which tie him to an answer . *Lear* iv 2 14
Tie up the libertine in a field of feasts . *Ant. and Cleo.* ii 1 23
Let us know If 'twill tie up thy discontented sword . ii 6 6
The band that seems to tie their friendship together will be the very strangler of their amity . ii 6 129
To flatter Cæsar, would you mingle eyes With one that ties his points? iii 13 157
The words of your commission Will tie you to the numbers and the time Of their dispatch . *Cymbeline* iii 7 15
Or tie my treasure up in silken bags, To please the fool and death *Per.* iii 2 41
Tied. It is no matter if the tied were lost; for it is the unkindest tied that ever any man tied.—What's the unkindest tide?—Why, he that's tied here, Crab, my dog . *T. G. of Ver.* ii 3 41
Lose the tide, and the voyage, and the master, and the service, and the tied! . ii 3 57
Sith it your pleasure is, And I am tied to be obedient . *T. of Shrew* i 1 217
I'll not be tied to hours nor 'pointed times . iii 1 19
You have broken from his liking Where you were tied in duty *W. Tale* v 1 213
I would allow him odds, And meet him, were I tied to run afoot *Rich. II.* i 1 63
The rascal hath removed my horse, and tied him I know not where 1 *Hen. IV.* ii 2 12
And have their provender tied to their mouths . 1 *Hen. VI.* i 2 11
Edward will be king, And not be tied unto his brother's will 3 *Hen. VI.* iv 1 66
The Spaniard, tied by blood and favour to her, Must now confess *Hen. VIII.* ii 2 90
To confirm his goodness, Tied it by letters-patents . iii 2 250
One that, by suggestion, Tied all the kingdom . iv 2 36
Cressid is mine, tied with the bonds of heaven . *Troi. and Cres.* v 2 154
Fetter'd in amorous chains And faster bound to Aaron's charming eyes Than is Prometheus tied to Caucasus . *T. Andron.* ii 1 17
They have tied me to a stake; I cannot fly . *Macbeth* v 7 1
Horses are tied by the heads, dogs and bears by the neck, monkeys by the loins, and men by the legs . *Lear* ii 4 8
She hath tied Sharp-tooth'd unkindness, like a vulture, here . ii 4 136
I am tied to the stake, and I must stand the course . iii 7 54
Thou knew'st too well My heart was to thy rudder tied by the strings, And thou shouldst tow me after . *Ant. and Cleo.* iii 11 57
To whose kindnesses I am most infinitely tied . *Cymbeline* i 6 23
My horse is tied up safe: out, sword, and to a sore purpose! . v 1 24
She hath so strictly tied Her to her chamber, that 'tis impossible *Per.* ii 5 8
Tied-up. It rested in your grace To unloose this tied-up justice when you pleased *Meas. for Meas.* i 3 32
Tiger. Make tigers tame and huge leviathans Forsake unsounded deeps to dance on sands . *T. G. of Ver.* iii 2 80
Depart in patience, And let us to the Tiger all to dinner *Com. of Errors* iii 1 95
The mild hind Makes speed to catch the tiger . *M. N. Dream* ii 1 233
This is he that did the Tiger board . *T. Night* v 1 65
Thou mayst hold . . . A fasting tiger safer by the tooth . *K. John* iii 1 260
When the blast of war blows in our ears, Then imitate the action of the tiger; Stiffen the sinews . *Hen. V.* iii 1 6
O tiger's heart wrapt in a woman's hide! . 3 *Hen. VI.* i 4 137
More inexorable, O, ten times more, than tigers of Hyrcania . i 4 155
The tiger will be mild whiles she doth mourn . iii 1 39
The tiger now hath seized the gentle hind . *Richard III.* ii 4 50
The herd hath more annoyance by the breese Than by the tiger *T. and C.* i 3 49
When we vow to weep seas, live in fire, eat rocks, tame tigers iii 2 85
There is no more mercy in him than there is milk in a male tiger *Coriol.* v 4 31
When did the tiger's young ones teach the dam? . *T. Andron.* ii 3 142
Rome is but a wilderness of tigers? Tigers must prey . iii 1 54
This ravenous tiger, this accursed devil; Let him receive no sustenance v 3 5
That heinous tiger, Tamora, . . . No mournful bell shall ring her burial v 3 195
More fierce and more inexorable far Than empty tigers . *Rom. and Jul.* v 3 39
Go great with tigers, dragons, wolves, and bears . *T. of Athens* iv 3 189
Her husband's to Aleppo gone, master o' the Tiger . *Macbeth* i 3 7
Approach thou like the rugged Russian bear, The arm'd rhinoceros, or the Hyrcan tiger . iii 4 101
Add thereto a tiger's chaudron, For the ingredients of our cauldron . iv 1 33
Tigers, not daughters, what have you perform'd? . *Lear* iv 2 40
Tiger-footed. This tiger-footed rage, when it shall find The harm of unscann'd swiftness, will too late Tie leaden pounds to's heels *Cor.* iii 1 312
Tight. Two galliases, And twelve tight galleys . *T. of Shrew* ii 1 381
My queen's a squire More tight at this than thou . *Ant. and Cleo.* iv 4 15
Tightly. Bear you these letters tightly; Sail like my pinnace *Mer. Wives* i 3 88
He will clapper-claw thee tightly, bully.—Clapper-de-claw! vat is dat? ii 3 67
Tike. Base tike, call'st thou me host? . *Hen. V.* ii 1 31
Hound or spaniel, brach or lym, Or bobtail tike or trundle-tail *Lear* iii 6 73
Tile. I know his brains are forfeit to the next tile that falls . *All's Well* iv 3 217
Till. Blow, till thou burst thy wind, if room enough! . *Tempest* i 1 8
And now farewell Till half an hour hence . i 2 91
We'll wait upon your grace till after supper . *T. G. of Ver.* iii 2 96
I have seen corruption boil and bubble Till it o'er-run the stew *Meas. for Meas.* v 1 321
I never saw her till this time.—Villain, thou liest . *Com. of Errors* ii 2 164
Wonder not till further warrant: go but with me to-night *Much Ado* iii 2 115
In the common course of all treasons, we still see them reveal themselves, till they attain to their abhorred ends . *All's Well* iv 3 27
For, till thou speak, thou shalt not pass from hence . 2 *Hen. VI.* i 4 30
I long till Edward fall by war's mischance . 3 *Hen. VI.* iii 3 254
What shall be done? he will not hear, till feel. . *T. of Athens* ii 2 7
Be patient till the last . *J. Cæsar* iii 2 12
From the first corse till he that died to-day . *Hamlet* i 2 105
Prorogue his honour Even till a Lethe'd dulness! . *Ant. and Cleo.* ii 1 27
Till now. I did but smile till now . *Meas. for Meas.* v 1 233
Dilate at full What hath befall'n of them and thee till now *Com. of Errors* i 1 124
The curse never fell upon our nation till now; I never felt it till now *Mer. of Venice* iii 1 90
Till soon. Farewell till soon . *Richard III.* iv 3 35
Till that. Within this hour it will be dinner-time: Till that, I'll view the manners of the town . *Com. of Errors* i 2 12
Till that his passions, like a whale on ground, Confound themselves with working . 2 *Hen. IV.* iv 4 40
Fought so long, till that his thighs with darts Were almost like a sharp-quill'd porpentine . 2 *Hen. VI.* iii 1 362
Till that her garments, heavy with their drink, Pull'd the poor wretch from her melodious lay To muddy death . *Hamlet* iv 7 182
Till that a capable and wide revenge Swallow them up . *Othello* iii 3 459
Till then. My present business calls me from you now.—Farewell till then . *Com. of Errors* i 2 30
We'll draw cuts for the senior: till then lead thou first . v 1 422
Affliction may one day smile again; and till then, sit thee down, sorrow! . *L. L. Lost* i 1 317
Till the king come forth, and not till then . *Hen. V.* ii Prol. 41
Till when, be cheerful And think of each thing well . *Tempest* v 1 250
Tilled. Husbanded and tilled with excellent endeavour . 2 *Hen. IV.* iv 3 130
Tilly-fally, Sir John, ne'er tell me . ii 4 90
Tillyvally. Am I not of her blood? Tillyvally. Lady! . *T. Night* ii 3 83
Tilt. There shall he practise tilts and tournaments . *T. G. of Ver.* i 3 30
This is no world To play with mammets and to tilt with lips 1 *Hen. IV.* ii 3 95
Break a lance, And run a tilt at death within a chair 1 *Hen. VI.* iii 2 51
When in the city Tours Thou ran'st a tilt in honour of my love 2 *Hen. VI.* i 3 54
He tilts With piercing steel at bold Mercutio's breast . *Rom. and Jul.* iii 1 163
Tilter. Master Forthlight the tilter . *Meas. for Meas.* iv 3 17
As a puisny tilter, that spurs his horse but on one side *As Y. Like It* iii 4 46
Tilth. Bourn, bound of land, tilth, vineyard, none . *Tempest* ii 1 152
Expresseth his full tilth and husbandry *Meas. for Meas.* i 4 44
Tilting. Of his heart's meteors tilting in his face . *Com. of Errors* iv 2 6
Lo, he is tilting straight! . *L. L. Lost* v 2 483
Swords out, and tilting one at other's breast, In opposition bloody *Othello* ii 3 183
Tilt-yard. I'll be sworn a' ne'er saw him but once in the Tilt-yard 2 *Hen. IV.* iii 2 347
His study is his tilt-yard, and his loves Are brazen images . 2 *Hen. VI.* i 3 62
Timandra. Art thou Timandra?—Yes.—Be a whore still *T. of Athens* iv 3 81
Pardon him, sweet Timandra; for his wits Are drown'd . iv 3 88
Alcibiades reports it; Phrynia and Timandra had gold of him . v 1 6
Timber. And, like green timber, warp, warp *As Y. Like It* iii 3 90
We take From every tree lop, bark, and part o' the timber *Hen. VIII.* i 2 96
Timbered. My arrows, Too slightly timber'd for so loud a wind *Hamlet* iv 7 22
Is he well shipp'd?—His bark is stoutly timber'd . *Othello* ii 1 48
Time. 'Tis time I should inform thee farther . *Tempest* i 2 22
Canst thou remember A time before we came unto this cell? . i 2 39
What seest thou else In the dark backward and abysm of time? . i 2 50
At that time Through all the signories it was the first . i 2 70
More profit Than other princesses can that have more time For vainer hours . i 2 173
What is the time o' the day?—Past the mid season . i 2 239
The time 'twixt six and now Must by us both be spent most preciously i 2 240
What is't thou canst demand?—My liberty.—Before the time be out? i 2 246
Not since widow Dido's time.—Widow! a pox o' that! . ii 1 76
The truth you speak doth lack some gentleness And time to speak it in ii 1 138
Open-eyed conspiracy His time doth take . ii 1 302
I was the man i' the moon when time was . ii 2 142
She is Ten times more gentle than her father's crabbed . iii 1 8
Many a time The harmony of their tongues hath into bondage Brought my too diligent ear . iii 1 40
As you like this, give me the lie another time . iii 2 85
Beat him enough: after a little time I'll beat him too . iii 2 93
But one fiend at a time, I'll fight their legions o'er . iii 3 102
Their great guilt, Like poison given to work a great time after, Now 'gins to bite the spirits . iii 3 105
We shall lose our time, And all be turn'd to barnacles . iv 1 248
Time Goes upright with his carriage . v 1 2
At which time, my lord, You said our work should cease . v 1 4
At this time I will tell no tales . v 1 128
But wherefore waste I time to counsel thee? . *T. G. of Ver.* i 1 51
Thou hast metamorphosed me, Made me neglect my studies, lose my time . i 1 67
Did request me to importune you To let him spend his time no more at home . i 3 14
I have consider'd well his loss of time And how he cannot be a perfect man . i 3 19
Experience is by industry achieved And perfected by the swift course of time . i 3 23
And, in good time! now will we break with him . i 3 44
I am resolved that thou shalt spend some time . i 3 66
My heart accords thereto, And yet a thousand times it answers 'no' i 3 91
I will write, Please you command, a thousand times as much . ii 1 120
She, in modesty, Or else for want of idle time, could not again reply ii 1 172
You have said, sir.—Ay, sir, and done too, for this time . ii 4 30
An idle truant, Omitting the sweet benefit of time . ii 4 65
Here he means to spend his time awhile: I think 'tis no unwelcome news to you . ii 4 80
Pity the dearth that I have pined in, By longing for that food so long a time . ii 7 17
To be fantastic may become a youth Of greater time than I shall show to be . ii 7 48
Besides, the fashion of the time is changed . iii 1 86
Longer than swiftest expedition Will give thee time to leave . iii 1 165
Time is the nurse and breeder of all good . iii 1 243
The time now serves not to expostulate . iii 1 251
A little time will melt her frozen thoughts . iii 2 9
A little time, my lord, will kill that grief . iii 2 15
Intend to chide myself Even for this time I spend in talking to thee . iv 2 104
A thousand times good morrow . iv 3 6
I have heard him say a thousand times . iv 4 139

Time. I do protest That I have wept a hundred several times *T. G. of V.* iv 4 150
At that time I made her weep agood iv 4 170
Lovers break not hours, Unless it be to come before their time v 1 5
O time most accurst, 'Mongst all foes that a friend should be the worst! v 4 71
And have done any time these three hundred years *Mer. Wives* i 1 12
I have seen Sackerson loose twenty times, and have taken him by the chain i 1 307
His filching was like an unskilful singer; he kept not time i 3 29
I will tell your worship more of the wart the next time we have confidence i 4 172
In these times you stand on distance, your passes, stoccadoes ii 1 233
I have seen the time, with my long sword I would have made you four tall fellows skip like rats ii 1 236
For the which she thanks you a thousand times ii 2 84
Her husband is seldom from home; but she hopes there will come a time ii 2 106
Only give me so much of your time in exchange of it ii 2 242
At that time the jealous rascally knave her husband will be forth ii 2 275
Pray you, use your patience: in good time iii 1 84
He was carried out, the last time he searched for him, in a basket. iv 2 32
To meet him at the door with it, as they did last time iv 2 98
Help to search my house this one time iv 2 168
In that time Shall Master Slender steal my Nan away iv 4 73
When Slender sees his time To take her by the hand iv 6 36
This is the third time; I hope good luck lies in odd numbers v 1 2
Time wears: hold up your head, and mince v 1 8
When you see your time, take her by the hand v 3 2
And, as you trip, still pinch him to your time v 5 96
I was three or four times in the thought they were not fairies v 5 129
'Tis time I were choked with a piece of toasted cheese v 5 147
We shall write to you, As time and our concernings shall importune *Meas. for Meas.* i 1 57
I think thou never wast where grace was said.—No? a dozen times at least i 2 21
We thought it meet to hide our love Till time had made them for us i 2 157
For terror, not to use, in time the rod Becomes more mock'd than fear'd i 3 26
As blossoming time That from the seedness the bare fallow brings To teeming foison i 4 41
Had time cohered with place or place with wishing ii 1 11
Which at that very distant time stood, as it were, in a fruit-dish ii 1 94
The time is yet to come that she was ever respected with man, woman, or child ii 1 176
I shall have you whipt: so, for this time, Pompey, fare you well ii 1 265
I thought, by your readiness in the office, you had continued in it some time ii 1 276
Shall I attend your lordship?—At any time 'fore noon ii 2 160
Ten times louder Than beauty could, display'd ii 4 80
Call us ten times frail; For we are soft as our complexions are ii 4 128
This night's the time That I should do what I abhor to name iii 1 101
Between which time of the contract and limit of the solemnity, her brother Frederick was wrecked at sea iii 1 223
That the time may have all shadow and silence in it iii 1 257
Mistress Kate Keepdown was with child by him in the duke's time iii 2 212
Of this country, though my chance is now To use it for my time iii 2 231
How may likeness made in crimes, Making practice on the times, To draw with idle spiders' strings Most ponderous and substantial things! iii 2 288
Much upon this time have I promised here to meet iv 1 17
The time is come even now iv 1 21
You shall have your full time of imprisonment iv 2 12
Neither in time, matter, or other circumstance iv 2 108
Drunk many times a day, if not many days entirely drunk iv 2 157
I will have more time to prepare me, or they shall beat out my brains iv 3 57
These letters at fit time deliver me: The provost knows our purpose iv 5 1
A forted residence 'gainst the tooth of time And razure of oblivion v 1 12
Now is your time: speak loud and kneel before him v 1 19
Is it not strange and strange?—Nay, it is ten times strange v 1 42
Nay, it is ten times true; for truth is truth v 1 45
It may be right; but you are i' the wrong To speak before your time v 1 87
With ripen'd time Unfold the evil which is here wrapt up v 1 116
He in time may come to clear himself v 1 150
With such a time When I'll depose I had him in mine arms v 1 197
Since which time of five years I never spake with her v 1 222
In very good time: speak not you to him till we call upon you v 1 286
He is my brother too: but fitter time for that v 1 498
Time is their master, and when they see time They'll go or come *Com. of Errors* ii 1 8
And then, wherefore,—For urging it the second time to me ii 2 47
I think the meat wants that I have.—In good time, sir; what's that ii 2 58
Learn to jest in good time: there's a time for all things ii 2 65
A rule as plain as the plain bald pate of father Time himself ii 2 71
There's no time for a man to recover his hair that grows bald by nature ii 2 73
Why is Time such a niggard of hair, being, as it is, so plentiful an excrement? ii 2 78
You would all this time have proved there is no time for all things ii 2 101
But your reason was not substantial, why there is no time to recover ii 2 106
Time himself is bald and therefore to the world's end will have bald followers ii 2 107
The time was once when thou unurged wouldst vow ii 2 115
The porter for this time, sir, and my name is Dromio iii 1 43
She will well excuse Why at this time the doors are made against you iii 1 93
'Tis time, I think, to trudge, pack, and be gone iii 2 158
'Tis high time that I were hence iii 2 162
I bespoke it not.—Not once, nor twice, but twenty times you have iii 2 177
'Tis time that I were gone: It was two ere I left him iv 2 53
As if Time were in debt! how fondly dost thou reason!—Time is a very bankrupt and owes more than he's worth to season iv 2 57
Have you not heard men say, That Time comes stealing on by night and day? iv 2 60
If Time be in debt and theft, and a sergeant in the way, Hath he not reason to turn back an hour in a day? iv 2 61
Where would you had remain'd until this time, Free from these slanders! iv 4 69
His word might bear my wealth at any time v 1 8
And careful hours with time's deformed hand Have written strange defeatures in my face v 1 298
O time's extremity, Hast thou so crack'd and splitted my poor tongue? v 1 307
Twenty years . . . , During which time he ne'er saw Syracusa v 1 328
This is your daughter.—Her mother hath many times told me so *Much Ado* i 1 105
Well, as time shall try: 'In time the savage bull doth bear the yoke' i 1 262

Time. He meant to take the present time by the top and instantly break with you *Much Ado* i 2 15
I will use your skill. Good cousin, have a care this busy time i 2 29
The fault will be in the music, cousin, if you be not wooed in good time ii 1 73
Time goes on crutches till love have all his rites ii 1 372
A time too brief, too, to have all things answer my mind ii 1 375
The time shall not go dully by us ii 1 379
She'll be up twenty times a night, and there will she sit in her smock ii 3 136
At her mistress' chamber-window, bids me a thousand times good night iii 3 157
'Tis almost five o'clock, cousin; 'tis time you were ready iii 4 53
Brief, I pray you; for you see it is a busy time with me iii 5 6
The vile encounters they have had A thousand times in secret iv 1 95
Time hath not yet so dried this blood of mine iv 1 195
By this time our sexton hath reformed Signior Leonato of the matter v 1 262
Do not forget to specify, when time and place shall serve v 1 264
An old instance, Beatrice, that lived in the time of good neighbours v 2 79
Spite of cormorant devouring Time *L. L. Lost* i 1 4
Fit in his place and time.—In reason nothing.—Something then in rhyme i 1 98
All forsworn Three thousand times within this three years' space i 1 151
The time when. About the sixth hour; when beasts most graze, birds best peck i 1 237
So much for the time when. Now for the ground which i 1 241
An appertinent title to your old time, which we may name tough i 2 18
Another of these students at that time Was there with him ii 1 64
I am all these three.—And three times as much more iii 1 48
Or groan for love? or spend a minute's time In pruning me? iv 3 182
And since her time are colliers counted bright iv 3 267
We will with some strange pastime solace them, Such as the shortness of the time can shape iv 3 378
No time shall be omitted That will betime, and may by us be fitted iv 3 381
Some entertainment of time, some show in the posterior of this day v 1 126
Make him fawn and beg and seek And wait the season and observe the times v 2 63
And three times thrice is nine.—Not so, sir v 2 488
I hope, sir, three times thrice, sir,— Is not nine v 2 491
The extreme parts of time extremely forms All causes to the purpose v 2 750
For your fair sakes have we neglected time, Play'd foul play with our oaths v 2 765
Pleasant jest and courtesy, As bombast and as lining to the time v 2 791
A time, methinks, too short To make a world-without-end bargain in v 2 798
I'll stay with patience; but the time is long v 2 845
Four nights will quickly dream away the time *M. N. Dream* i 1 9
My soul consents not to give sovereignty.—Take time to pause i 1 83
Before the time I did Lysander see, Seem'd Athens as a paradise to me i 1 204
A time that lovers' flights doth still conceal i 1 212
That very time I saw, but thou couldst not ii 1 155
When we have chid the hasty-footed time For parting us iii 2 200
How shall we beguile The lazy time, if not with some delight? v 1 41
In courtesy, in all reason, we must stay the time v 1 259
Lovers, to bed; 'tis almost fairy time v 1 371
Nature hath framed strange fellows in her time *Mer. of Venice* i 1 51
I'll tell thee more of this another time i 1 100
Wherein my time something too prodigal Hath left me gaged i 1 129
And herein spend but time To wind about my love with circumstance i 1 153
Do you not remember, lady, in your father's time, a Venetian? i 2 124
Who then conceiving did in eaning time Fall parti-colour'd lambs i 3 88
Many a time and oft In the Rialto you have rated me i 3 107
You spurn'd me such a day; another time You call'd me dog i 3 128
I do expect return Of thrice three times the value of this bond i 3 161
O, ten times faster Venus' pigeons fly To seal love's bonds new-made! ii 6 5
Away! Our masquing mates by this time for us stay ii 6 59
Being ten times undervalued to tried gold ii 7 53
But stay the very riping of the time ii 8 40
Pick'd from the chaff and ruin of the times To be new-varnish'd ii 9 48
The fire seven times tried this: Seven times tried that judgement is, That did never choose amiss ii 9 63
Still more fool I shall appear By the time I linger here ii 9 74
O, these naughty times Put bars between the owners and their rights! iii 2 18
I speak too long; but 'tis to peize the time, To eke it and to draw it out iii 2 22
The seeming truth which cunning times put on To entrap the wisest iii 2 100
For you I would be trebled twenty times myself; A thousand times more fair, ten thousand times More rich iii 2 154
It is now our time, That have stood by and seen our wishes prosper, To cry, good joy iii 2 188
I do beseech you, Even at that time I may be married too iii 2 196
He would rather have Antonio's flesh Than twenty times the value iii 2 289
You shall have gold To pay the petty debt twenty times over iii 2 309
I oft deliver'd from his forfeitures Many that have at times made moan iii 3 23
Companions That do converse and waste the time together iii 4 12
Waste no time in words, But get thee gone iii 4 54
If that will not suffice, I will be bound to pay it ten times o'er iv 1 211
We trifle time: I pray thee, pursue sentence iv 1 298
Since nought so stockish, hard, and full of rage, But music for the time doth change his nature v 1 82
Fleet the time carelessly, as they did in the golden world *As Y. Like It* i 1 124
It is the first time that ever I heard breaking of ribs was sport for ladies i 2 146
You will try in time, in despite of a fall i 3 25
I was too young that time to value her i 3 73
If you outstay the time, upon mine honour, . . . you die i 3 90
Devise the fittest time and safest way To hide us from pursuit i 3 137
The fashion of these times, Where none will sweat but for promotion ii 3 59
I like this place, And willingly could waste my time in it ii 4 95
When I did hear The motley fool thus moral on the time ii 7 29
Lose and neglect the creeping hours of time ii 7 112
One man in his time plays many parts, His acts being seven ages ii 7 142
I was never so berhymed since Pythagoras' time iii 2 187
Groaning every hour would detect the lazy foot of Time as well as a clock.—And why not the swift foot of Time? iii 2 322
Time travels in divers paces with divers persons. I'll tell you who Time ambles withal, who Time trots withal, who Time gallops withal, and who he stands still withal iii 2 326
Time's pace is so hard that it seems the length of seven year iii 2 334
Who ambles Time withal?—With a priest that lacks Latin iii 2 336
Then they perceive not how Time moves iii 2 351
At which time would I, being but a moonish youth, grieve iii 2 429
Till that time Come not thou near me: and when that time comes, Afflict me with thy mocks, pity me not; As till that time I shall not pity thee iii 5 31
You are a thousand times a properer man Than she a woman iii 5 51
The time was that I hated thee, And yet it is not that I bear thee love iii 5 92

Time. In all this time there was not any man died in his own person *As Y. Like It* iv 1 96
Time is the old justice that examines all such offenders, and let Time try iv 1 203
We shall find a time, Audrey; patience, gentle Audrey . . . v 1 1
In the spring time, the only pretty ring time, When birds do sing . v 3 20
Therefore take the present time, With a hey, and a ho, and a hey nonino v 3 31
You are deceived, sir: we kept time, we lost not our time . . v 3 39
I count it but time lost to hear such a foolish song . . . v 3 41
The first time that I ever saw him Methought he was a brother . v 4 28
Upon a lie seven times removed . . . . . . v 4 71
You are come to me in happy time *T. of Shrew* Ind. 1 90
A goodly nap. But did I never speak of all that time? . . Ind. 2 84
Above some fifteen year or more.—Ay, and the time seems thirty unto me, Being all this time abandon'd from your bed Ind. 2 116
For the time I study, Virtue and that part of philosophy Will I apply . i 1 17
Take a lodging fit to entertain Such friends as time in Padua shall beget i 1 45
It is no time to chide you now; Affection is not rated from the heart . i 1 164
'Tis time to stir him from his trance . . . . . i 1 182
'Tis no time to jest, And therefore frame your manners to the time . i 1 232
'Tis now no time to vent our love: Listen to me . . . i 2 179
Have I not in my time heard lions roar? . . . . . i 2 201
It is a lusty wench; I love her ten times more than e'er I did . ii 1 162
Myself am moved to woo thee for my wife.—Moved! in good time . ii 1 196
I'll not be tied to hours nor 'pointed times, But learn my lessons as I please . . . . iii 1 19
I'll watch you better yet.—In time I may believe, yet I mistrust . iii 1 51
One girth six times pieced and a woman's crupper of velure . . iii 2 61
The morning wears, 'tis time we were at church . . . iii 2 113
I'll have no bigger: this doth fit the time, And gentlewomen wear such caps as these . . . . iv 3 69
You bid me make it orderly and well, According to the fashion and the time.—Marry, and did; but if you be remember'd, I did not bid you mar it to the time . . . . iv 3 95
Time it is, when raging war is done, To smile at scapes and perils overblown . . . . v 2 2
I'll venture so much of my hawk or hound, But twenty times so much upon my wife . . . . v 2 73
He that so generally is at all times good . . . *All's Well* i 1 9
Under whose practices he hath persecuted time with hope, and finds no other advantage in the process but only the losing of hope by time . . . . i 1 17
Virginity by being once lost may be ten times found . . i 1 142
He did look far Into the service of the time and was Discipled of the bravest . . . . i 2 27
At this time His tongue obey'd his hand . . . . . i 2 40
Such a man Might be a copy to these younger times . . . i 2 46
They wear themselves in the cap of the time . . . . ii 1 55
Four and twenty times the pilot's glass Hath told the thievish minutes ii 1 168
If I break time, or flinch in property Of what I spoke . . ii 1 190
So make the choice of thy own time . . . . . . ii 1 206
I play the noble housewife with the time, To entertain't so merrily with a fool . . . . ii 2 62
'Tis the rarest argument of wonder that hath shot out in our latter times . . . . ii 3 8
A second time receive The confirmation of my promised gift . . ii 3 55
Love make your fortunes twenty times above Her that so wishes! . ii 3 88
The great prerogative and rite of love, Which, as your due, time claims ii 4 43
Strew'd with sweets, Which they distil now in the curbed time . ii 4 46
You must not marvel, Helen, at my course, Which holds not colour with the time . . . . ii 5 64
In fine, delivers me to fill the time, Herself most chastely absent . iii 7 33
That time and place with this deceit so lawful May prove coherent . iii 7 38
That what in time proceeds May token to the future our past deeds . iv 2 62
How mightily some other times we drown our gain in tears! . . iv 3 79
From the time of his remembrance to this very instant disaster . iv 3 126
Time was, I did him a desired office, Dear almost as his life . . iv 4 5
Time will bring on summer, When briers shall have leaves as well as thorns . . . . iv 4 31
We must away; Our waggon is prepared, and time revives us . . iv 4 34
In happy time; This man may help me . . . . . . v 1 6
Though time seem so adverse and means unfit . . . . . v 1 26
My revenges were high bent upon him, And watch'd the time to shoot. v 3 11
So stand thou forth; The time is fair again . . . . . v 3 36
All is whole; Not one word more of the consumed time . . . v 3 38
The inaudible and noiseless foot of Time . . . . . v 3 41
I was in that credit with them at that time that I knew of their going . v 3 263
And at that time he got his wife with child . . . . v 3 302
What else may hap to time I will commit . . . . *T. Night* i 2 60
I would I had bestowed that time in the tongues that I have in fencing i 3 97
O time! thou must untangle this, not I; It is too hard a knot for me to untie! . . . . ii 2 41
'Tis not the first time I have constrained one to call me knave . ii 3 71
Is there no respect of place, persons, nor time in you?—We did keep time . . . . ii 3 99
Light airs and recollected terms Of these most brisk and giddy-paced times . . . . ii 4 6
Truly, sir, and pleasure will be paid, one time or another . . ii 4 73
You waste the treasure of your time . . . . . . ii 5 86
He must observe their mood on whom he jests, The quality of persons, and the time . . . . iii 1 70
Why, then, methinks 'tis time to smile again . . . . iii 1 137
The clock upbraids me with the waste of time . . . . iii 1 141
The double gilt of this opportunity you let time wash off . . iii 2 27
The quality of the time and quarrel Might well have given us bloody argument . . . . iii 3 31
I will bespeak our diet, Whiles you beguile the time . . . iii 3 41
At which time we will bring the device to the bar . . . iii 4 153
What's that to us? The time goes by: away! . . . . iii 4 398
What time we will our celebration keep According to my birth . iv 3 30
What wilt thou be When time hath sow'd a grizzle on thy case? . v 1 168
Do not embrace me till each circumstance Of place, time, fortune, do cohere . . . . v 1 259
Said to me a thousand times Thou never shouldst love woman like to me v 1 274
You shall from this time be Your master's mistress . . . v 1 333
Thus the whirligig of time brings in his revenges . . . v 1 385
When that is known and golden time convents, A solemn combination shall be made Of our dear souls . . . . v 1 391
Time as long again Would be fill'd up, my brother, with our thanks *W. T.* i 2 3
We'll part the time between's then; and in that I'll no gainsaying . i 2 18
She is spread of late Into a goodly bulk: good time encounter her! . ii 1 20

Time. She is something before her time deliver'd.—A boy?—A daughter *W. Tale* ii 2 25
Let him be Until a time may serve: for present vengeance, Take it on her . . . . ii 3 22
Thy lewd-tongued wife, Whom for this time we pardon . . . ii 3 173
As it hath been to us rare, pleasant, speedy, The time is worth the use. iii 1 14
We have landed in ill time: the skies look grimly . . . iii 3 3
I did in time collect myself and thought This was so and no slumber . iii 3 38
Now take upon me, in the name of Time, To use my wings . . iv 1 3
I witness to The times that brought them in . . . . iv 1 12
But let Time's news Be known when 'tis brought forth . . . iv 1 26
And what to her adheres, which follows after, Is the argument of Time iv 1 29
Of this allow, If ever you have spent time worse ere now; If never, yet that Time himself doth say He wishes earnestly you never may . iv 1 31
I have served Prince Florizel and in my time wore three-pile . iv 3 13
I bless the time When my good falcon made her flight across Thy father's ground . . . . iv 4 14
Now, in good time!—Not a word, a word; we stand upon our manners iv 4 163
Is it not too far gone? 'Tis time to part them . . . . iv 4 354
For this time, Though full of our displeasure, yet we free thee . iv 4 443
At this time He will allow no speech, which I do guess You do not purpose iv 4 478
One He chides to hell and bids the other grow Faster than thought or time . . . . iv 4 565
In this time of lethargy . . . . iv 4 626
This is the time that the unjust man doth thrive . . . iv 4 688
Those that are germane to him, though removed fifty times, shall all come iv 4 802
You might have spoken a thousand things that would Have done the time more benefit . . . . v 1 22
Every present time doth boast itself Above a better gone . . v 1 96
Infirmity Which waits upon worn times . . . . . . v 1 142
Remember since you owed no more to time Than I do now . . v 1 219
He at that time, over-fond of the shepherd's daughter . . v 2 126
Have been so any time these four hours . . . . . v 2 147
'Tis time; descend; be stone no more . . . . . v 3 99
In this wide gap of time since first We were dissever'd . . v 3 154
To treat of high affairs touching that time . . . *K. John* i 1 101
He came into the world Full fourteen weeks before the course of time . i 1 113
He is but a bastard to the time That doth not smack of observation . i 1 207
The adverse winds, Whose leisure I have stay'd, have given him time To land . . . . ii 1 58
And the hand of time Shall draw this brief into as huge a volume . ii 1 102
Their ordinance By this time from their fixed beds of lime Had been dishabited . . . . ii 1 219
Till that time Have we ramm'd up our gates against the world . ii 1 271
That name, Which till this time my tongue did ne'er pronounce . iii 1 307
Old Time the clock-setter, that bald sexton Time . . . iii 1 324
I had a thing to say, But I will fit it with some better time . . iii 3 26
Creep time ne'er so slow, Yet it shall come for me to do thee good . iii 3 31
John lays you plots; the times conspire with you . . . iii 4 146
Still and anon cheer'd up the heavy time, Saying, 'What lack you?' . iv 1 47
In the last repeating troublesome, Being urged at a time unseasonable iv 2 20
That the time's enemies may not have this To grace occasions . . iv 2 61
The spirit of the time shall teach me speed . . . . iv 2 176
We must embrace This gentle offer of the perilous time . . iv 3 13
Shall give a holiness, a purity, To the yet unbegotten sin of times . iv 3 54
The present time's so sick, That present medicine must be minister'd . v 1 14
Be stirring as the time; be fire with fire . . . . v 1 48
Have thou the ordering of this present time . . . . v 1 77
I am not glad that such a sore of time Should seek a plaster . . v 2 12
But such is the infection of the time . . . . . v 2 20
We hold our time too precious to be spent With such a brabbler . v 2 161
That you might The better arm you to the sudden time . . v 6 26
Let us pay the time but needful woe . . . . . v 7 110
The purest treasure mortal times afford Is spotless reputation *Rich. II.* i 1 177
By this time, had the king permitted us, One of our souls had wander'd in the air . . . . i 3 194
How long a time lies in one little word! . . . . . i 3 213
Ere the six years that he hath to spend Can change their moons and bring their times about . . . . i 3 220
Thou canst help time to furrow me with age, But stop no wrinkle . i 3 229
Thy grief is but thy absence for a time.—Joy absent, grief is present for that time . . . . i 3 258
When time shall call him home from banishment . . . . i 4 21
For sleeping England long time have I watch'd . . . . ii 1 77
His time is spent, our pilgrimage must be . . . . . ii 1 154
Take from Time His charters and his customary rights . . . ii 1 195
To-morrow next We will for Ireland; and 'tis time, I trow . . ii 1 218
I should to Plashy too; But time will not permit . . . ii 2 121
To know what pricks you on To take advantage of the absent time . ii 3 79
Thou art a banish'd man, and here art come Before the expiration of thy time . . . . ii 3 111
O, call back yesterday, bid time return! . . . . . iii 2 69
For time hath set a blot upon my pride . . . . . iii 2 81
The time hath been, Would you have been so brief with him . . iii 3 10
Let's fight with gentle words Till time lend friends . . . iii 3 132
In that dead time when Gloucester's death was plotted . . . iv 1 10
That very time, I heard you say . . . . . . iv 1 14
If thou deny'st it twenty times, thou liest . . . . . iv 1 38
I do remember well The very time Aumerle and you did talk . . iv 1 61
Many a time hath banish'd Norfolk fought For Jesu Christ . . iv 1 92
The time shall not be many hours of age More than it is . . v 1 57
Bear you well in this new spring of time, Lest you be cropp'd . v 2 50
Is not my teeming date drunk up with time? . . . . . v 2 91
Were he twenty times my son, I would appeach him . . . v 2 101
How sour sweet music is, When time is broke and no proportion kept! . v 5 43
Here have I the daintiness of ear To check time broke in a disorder'd string; But for the concord of my state and time Had not an ear to hear my true time broke . . . . v 5 46
I wasted time, and now doth time waste me; For now hath time made me his numbering clock: My thoughts are minutes . . . . v 5 49
So sighs and tears and groans Show minutes, times, and hours . v 5 58
My time Runs posting on in Bolingbroke's proud joy, While I stand fooling here . . . . v 5 58
If thou love me, 'tis time thou wert away . . . . . v 5 96
Find we a time for frighted peace to pant . . . *1 Hen. IV.* i 1 2
Thou hast called her to a reckoning many a time and oft . . i 2 56
The poor abuses of the time want countenance . . . . i 2 175
Redeeming time when men think least I will . . . . i 2 241
Said To such a person and in such a place, At such a time . . i 3 73
Three times they breathed and three times did they drink . . i 3 102

Time. Yet time serves wherein you may redeem Your banish'd honours 1 *Hen. IV.* i 3 180
In Richard's time,—what do you call the place?—A plague upon it i 3 242
And think we think ourselves unsatisfied, Till he hath found a time to pay i 3 288
When time is ripe, which will be suddenly i 3 294
What time do you mean to come to London? ii 1 46
I have forsworn his company hourly any time this two and twenty years ii 2 17
The friends you have named uncertain; the time itself unsorted ii 3 13
To drive away the time till Falstaff come ii 4 31
I am eight times thrust through the doublet, four through the hose ii 4 184
I do not only marvel where thou spendest thy time, but also how thou art accompanied ii 4 440
For I myself at this time have employ'd him ii 4 562
Three times hath Henry Bolingbroke made head Against my power iii 1 64
A shorter time shall send me to you iii 1 91
I'll sit and hear her sing: By that time will our book, I think, be drawn iii 1 224
The hope and expectation of thy time Is ruin'd iii 2 36
The time will come, That I shall make this northern youth exchange His glorious deeds for my indignities iii 2 144
He shall render every glory up, Yea, even the slightest worship of his time iii 2 151
Diced not above seven times a week iii 3 18
Paid money that I borrowed, three or four times iii 3 21
Any time this two and thirty years iii 3 54
How has he the leisure to be sick In such a justling time? iv 1 18
At the time of my departure thence He was much fear'd by his physicians iv 1 23
I would the state of time had first been whole Ere he by sickness had been visited iv 1 25
Ten times more dishonourable ragged than an old faced ancient iv 2 33
Faith, Sir John, 'tis more than time that I were there, and you too iv 2 60
Well we know the king Knows at what time to promise, when to pay iv 3 53
In short time after, he deposed the king iv 3 90
A prodigy of fear and a portent Of broached mischief to the unborn times v 1 21
For you my staff of office did I break In Richard's time v 1 35
And boldly did outdare The dangers of the time v 1 41
What with the injuries of a wanton time v 1 50
Moody beggars, starving for a time Of pellmell havoc and confusion v 1 81
He will suspect us still and find a time To punish this offence in other faults v 2 6
Some of us never shall A second time do such a courtesy v 2 101
What, is it a time to jest and dally now? v 3 57
But thought's the slave of life, and life time's fool; And time, that takes survey of all the world, Must have a stop v 4 81
'Twas time to counterfeit, or that hot termagant Scot had paid me scot and lot too v 4 114
The times are wild; contention, like a horse Full of high feeding, madly hath broke loose And bears down all before him 2 *Hen. IV.* i 1 9
Came not till now to dignify the times, Since Cæsar's fortunes i 1 22
Had three times slain the appearance of the king i 1 128
And approach The ragged'st hour that time and spite dare bring! i 1 151
We will all put forth, body and goods.—'Tis more than time i 1 187
Hath yet some smack of age in you, some relish of the saltness of time i 2 112
You may thank the unquiet time for your quiet o'erposting that action i 2 170
Virtue is of so little regard in these costermonger times i 2 191
His divisions, as the times do brawl, Are in three heads i 3 70
What trust is in these times? i 3 100
We are time's subjects, and time bids be gone i 3 110
Doth this become your place, your time, and business? ii 1 72
How many good young princes would do so, their fathers being so sick as yours at this time is? ii 2 34
Repent at idle times as thou mayest; and so, farewell ii 2 140
Thus we play the fools with the time ii 2 155
Put not you on the visage of the times ii 3 3
The time was, father, that you broke your word ii 3 10
There am I, Till time and vantage crave my company ii 3 68
Ten times better than the Nine Worthies ii 4 238
I feel me much to blame, So idly to profane the precious time ii 4 391
O God! that one might read the book of fate, And see the revolution of the times! iii 1 46
Other times, to see The beachy girdle of the ocean Too wide for Neptune's hips iii 1 49
'The time shall come,' thus did he follow it, 'The time will come, that foul sin, gathering head, Shall break into corruption' iii 1 75
Foretelling this same time's condition And the division of our amity iii 1 78
There is a history in all men's lives, Figuring the nature of the times deceased iii 1 81
Such things become the hatch and brood of time iii 1 86
Is thy name Mouldy?—Yea, an't please you.—'Tis the more time thou wert used iii 2 117
Mouldy, it is time you were spent iii 2 128
Let time shape, and there an end iii 2 358
We see which way the stream of time doth run iv 1 70
And have the summary of all our griefs, When time shall serve, to show iv 1 74
And to us all That feel the bruises of the days before, And suffer the condition of these times iv 1 101
Construe the times to their necessities, And you shall say indeed, it is the time, And not the king, that doth you injuries iv 1 105
The time misorder'd doth, in common sense, Crowd us iv 2 33
Will, on my life, One time or other break some gallows' back iv 3 32
The unguided days And rotten times that you shall look upon iv 4 60
The prince will in the perfectness of time Cast off his followers iv 4 74
The old folk, time's doting chronicles, Say it did so a little time before iv 4 126
For now a time is come to mock at form iv 5 119
And do arm myself To welcome the condition of the time v 2 11
Tidings do I bring and lucky joys And golden times and happy news of price v 3 100
O, if I had had time to have made new liveries v 5 11
Jumping o'er times, Turning the accomplishment of many years Into an hour-glass *Hen. V.* Prol. 29
The scambling and unquiet time Did push it out of farther question i 1 4
To give a greater sum Than ever at one time the clergy yet Did i 1 80
Such a mighty sum As never did the clergy at one time Bring in i 2 134
I say little; but when time shall serve, there shall be smiles ii 1 6
Men may sleep, and they may have their throats about them at that time ii 1 24
I will cut thy throat, one time or other, in fair terms ii 1 73
So a' cried out 'God, God, God!' three or four times ii 3 20
Honours that pertain By custom and the ordinance of times Unto the crown ii 4 83
Now he weighs time Even to the utmost grain ii 4 137
It is no time to discourse, so Chrish save me: the day is hot iii 2 112

Time. What he has spoke to me, that is well, I warrant you, when time is serve *Hen. V.* iii 6 69
'Tis not the first time you were overshot iii 7 134
Now is it time to arm: come, shall we about it? iii 7 167
Now entertain conjecture of a time iv Prol. 1
The time was blessedly lost wherein such preparation was gained iv 1 191
I should be angry with you, if the time were convenient iv 1 217
Time hath worn us into slovenry: But, by the mass, our hearts are in the trim iv 3 114
Ten times more valour than this roaring devil i' the old play iv 4 75
I humbly pray them to admit the excuse Of time, of numbers v Prol. 4
As in good time he may, from Ireland coming v Prol. 31
Have lost, or do not learn for want of time, The sciences v 2 57
This moral ties me over to time and a hot summer v 2 339
Small time, but in that small most greatly lived This star of England Epil. 5
Comets, importing change of times and states 1 *Hen. VI.* i 1 2
England ne'er had a king until his time i 1 8
During the time Edward the Third did reign i 2 31
Since your ladyship is not at leisure, I'll sort some other time to visit you ii 3 27
Were growing time once ripen'd to my will ii 4 99
In the time of Henry named the Fifth iii 1 196
Doth wish His days may finish ere that hapless time iii 1 201
Defer no time, delays have dangerous ends iii 2 33
Your grace may starve perhaps before that time iii 2 48
To my determined time thou gavest new date iv 6 9
Now the time is come That France must vail her lofty-plumed crest v 3 24
Now cursed be the time Of thy nativity! v 4 26
Be still awhile, till time do serve 2 *Hen. VI.* i 1 248
Next time I'll keep my dreams unto myself i 2 53
Look to't in time; She'll hamper thee, and dandle thee like a baby i 3 147
Last time, I danced attendance on his will i 3 174
Wizards know their times: Deep night, dark night, the silent of the night i 4 18
The time when screech-owls cry and ban-dogs howl And spirits walk i 4 21
That time best fits the work we have in hand i 4 23
Being call'd A hundred times and oftener, in my sleep ii 1 90
Many time and oft Myself have heard a voice to call him so ii 1 93
Had I twenty times so many foes, And each of them had twenty times their power, All these could not procure me any scathe ii 4 60
We know the time since he was mild and affable iii 1 9
These are petty faults to faults unknown, Which time will bring to light iii 1 65
Though Suffolk dare him twenty thousand times iii 2 206
Your loving uncle, twenty times his worth iii 2 268
Loather a hundred times to part than die iii 2 355
Ten times banished; Once by the king, and three times thrice by thee iii 2 357
Henry the Fifth, in whose time boys went to span-counter for French crowns iv 2 165
He shall be beheaded for it ten times iv 7 27
Many a time, but for a sallet, my brain-pan had been cleft with a brown bill iv 10 12
Many a time . . . it hath served me instead of a quart pot to drink in iv 10 14
Of one or both of us the time is come v 2 13
Who in rage forgets Aged contusions and all brush of time v 3 3
Three times to-day I holp him to his horse, Three times bestrid him v 3 8
Three times to-day You have defended me from imminent death v 3 18
'Tis not enough our foes are this time fled v 3 21
Make thy sepulchre And creep into it far before thy time 3 *Hen. VI.* i 1 237
Three times did Richard make a lane to me i 4 9
Bethink thee once again, And in thy thought o'er-run my former time i 4 45
And, whilst we breathe, take time to do him dead i 4 108
More inexorable, O, ten times more, than tigers of Hyrcania i 4 155
But in this troublous time what's to be done? ii 1 159
What time the shepherd, blowing of his nails, Can neither call it perfect day nor night ii 5 3
Then to divide the times: So many hours must I tend my flock ii 5 30
O heavy times, begetting such events! ii 5 63
O piteous spectacle! O bloody times! ii 5 73
Much is your sorrow; mine ten times so much ii 5 112
And, for the time shall not seem tedious, I'll tell thee what befel me iii 1 9
We will consider of your suit; And come some other time to know our mind iii 2 17
To cross me from the golden time I look for! iii 2 127
Yet heavens are just, and time suppresseth wrongs iii 3 77
Threescore and two years; a silly time To make prescription for a kingdom's worth iii 3 93
The time and case requireth haste iv 5 18
Wherefore stay we? 'tis no time to talk iv 5 24
Himself Likely in time to bless a regal throne iv 6 74
Take the time; kneel down, kneel down: Nay, when? v 1 48
Ten times more beloved Than if thou never hadst deserved our hate v 1 103
If she have time to breathe, be well assured Her faction will be full as strong as ours v 3 16
The night-crow cried, aboding luckless time v 6 45
And now what rests but that we spend the time With stately triumphs? v 7 42
Sent before my time Into this breathing world *Richard III.* i 1 20
Have no delight to pass away the time i 1 25
And twenty times made pause to sob and weep i 2 162
In that sad time My manly eyes did scorn an humble tear i 2 164
'Tis time to speak; my pains are quite forgot i 3 117
In all which time you and your husband Grey Were factious i 3 127
So full of dismal terror was the time! i 4 7
And cited up a thousand fearful times, During the wars i 4 14
And, in good time, here comes the noble duke ii 1 45
Now, in good time, here comes the Duke of York iii 1 95
Are all things fitting for that royal time?—It is iii 4 4
You, my noble lords, may name the time iii 4 19
Three times to-day my foot-cloth horse did stumble iii 4 86
Miserable England! I prophesy the fearfull'st time to thee That ever wretched age hath look'd upon iii 4 106
Both are ready in their offices, At any time, to grace my stratagems iii 5 11
At your meet'st advantage of the time iii 5 74
By just computation of the time iii 5 89
That no manner of person At any time have recourse unto the princes iii 5 109
Mellow'd by the stealing hours of time iii 7 168
From the corruption of abusing times iii 7 199
And, in good time, here the lieutenant comes iv 1 12
How chance the prophet could not at that time Have told me? iv 2 103
Thou didst prophesy the time would come That I should wish for thee iv 4 79
The course of justice wheel'd about, And left thee but a prey to time iv 4 106

Time. All the ruins of distressful times Repair'd with double riches of content . . . *Richard III.* iv 4 318
Advantaging their loan with interest Of ten times double gain of happiness . . . iv 4 324
I myself have many tears to wash Hereafter time, for time past wrong'd by thee . . . iv 4 390
Urge the necessity and state of times, And be not peevish-fond . . . iv 4 416
Where and what time your majesty shall please . . . iv 4 490
This is the day that, in King Edward's time, I wish'd might fall on me . v 1 13
My heart is ten times lighter than my looks . . . v 3 3
Much about cock-shut time . . . v 3 70
That which I would I cannot,—With best advantage will deceive the time . . . v 3 92
The leisure and the fearful time Cuts off the ceremonious vows of love . v 3 97
Why, then 'tis time to arm and give direction . . . v 3 236
The leisure and enforcement of the time Forbids to dwell upon . . v 3 238
All the whole time I was my chamber's prisoner . . *Hen. VIII.* i 1 12
Till this time pomp was single, but now married To one above itself . i 1 15
Ten times more ugly Than ever they were fair . . . i 2 117
To this point hast thou heard him At any time speak aught? . . i 2 146
I remember Of such a time . . . i 2 191
'Tis time to give 'em physic, their diseases Are grown so catching . . i 3 36
An honest country lord, as I am, beaten A long time out of play . . i 3 45
May he live Longer than I have time to tell his years! . . . And when old time shall lead him to his end, Goodness and he fill up one monument! . . . ii 1 91
A most unfit time to disturb him . . . ii 2 61
I'll make ye know your times of business . . . ii 2 72
By this time I know your back will bear a duchess . . . ii 3 98
You may, then, spare that time . . . ii 4 5
A true and humble wife, At all times to your will conformable . . ii 4 24
If, in the course And process of this time, you can report . . ii 4 38
I will be bold with time and your attention . . . ii 4 168
Let me have time and counsel for my cause . . . iii 1 79
If you omit The offer of this time, I cannot promise But that you shall sustain moe new disgraces . . . iii 2 4
What we can do to him, though now the time Gives way to us, I much fear . . . iii 2 15
You have scarce time To steal from spiritual leisure a brief span . . iii 2 139
For holy offices I have a time; a time To think . . . iii 2 144
Nature does require Her times of preservation . . . iii 2 147
No doubt, In time will find their fit rewards . . . iii 2 245
That time offer'd sorrow; This, general joy . . . iv 1 6
The times and titles now are alter'd strangely With me since first you knew me . . . iv 2 112
That gentle physic, given in time, had cured me . . . iv 2 122
Times to repair our nature With comforting repose, and not for us To waste these times . . . v 1 3
The fruit she goes with I pray for heartily, that it may find Good time . v 1 22
In the gap and trade of moe preferments, With which the time will load him . . . v 1 37
Come, lords, we trifle time away . . . v 3 179
That fire-drake did I hit three times on the head, and three times was his nose discharged against me . . . v 4 46
A thousand thousand blessings, Which time shall bring to ripeness . . v 5 21
All the expected good we're like to hear For this play at this time . Epil. 9
So I'll tell her the next time I see her . . *Troi. and Cres.* i 1 84
Well, the gods are above; time must friend or end . . . i 2 84
I have a young conception in my brain; Be you my time to bring it to some shape . . . i 3 313
All damage else—As honour, loss of time, travail, expense . . . ii 2 4
Instructed by the antiquary times, He must, he is, he cannot but be wise . . . ii 3 262
For this time will I take my leave . . . iii 2 147
When time is old and hath forgot itself . . . iii 2 192
The advantage of the time prompts me aloud To call for recompense . iii 3 2
That time, acquaintance, custom, and condition Made tame and most familiar . . . iii 3 9
Time hath, my lord, a wallet at his back, Wherein he puts alms for oblivion . . . iii 3 145
For time is like a fashionable host That slightly shakes his parting guest by the hand . . . iii 3 165
Love, friendship, charity, are subjects all To envious and calumniating time . . . iii 3 174
There is no help; The bitter disposition of the time Will have it so . . iv 1 48
Time, force, and death, Do to this body what extremes you can . . iv 2 107
Injurious time now with a robber's haste Crams his rich thievery up . iv 4 44
Fresh and fair, Anticipating time with starting courage . . . iv 5 2
That hast so long walk'd hand in hand with time . . . iv 5 203
I'ld fight with thee to-morrow. Well, welcome, welcome!—I have seen the time . . . iv 5 210
That old common arbitrator, Time, Will one day end it . . . iv 5 225
I will the second time, As I would buy thee, view thee limb by limb . iv 5 237
This place is dangerous; The time right deadly . . . v 2 39
When many times the captive Grecian falls, Even in the fan and wind of your fair sword, You bid them rise, and live . . . v 3 40
And at that time bequeathe you my diseases . . . v 10 57
There was a time when all the body's members Rebell'd against the belly . . . *Coriolanus* i 1 99
It will in time Win upon power . . . i 1 223
Will the time serve to tell? I do not think . . . i 6 46
And from this time, For what he did before Corioli, call him . . i 9 62
I mean to stride your steed, and at all times To undercrest your good addition . . . i 9 71
'Tis time It should be look'd to . . . i 9 93
Five times, Marcius, I have fought with thee . . . i 10 7
The prayers of priests nor times of sacrifice, Embarquements all of fury i 10 21
In which time I will make a lip at the physician . . . ii 1 126
He comes the third time home with the oaken garland . . . ii 1 138
Aufidius got off.—And 'twas time for him too, I'll warrant him that . ii 1 142
Suggested At some time when his soaring insolence Shall touch the people—which time shall not want . . . ii 1 270
Carry with us ears and eyes for the time, But hearts for the event . ii 1 285
And is content To spend the time to end it . . . ii 2 133
The dust on antique time would lie unswept . . . ii 3 126
Ready, when time shall prompt them, to make road Upon's again . . iii 1 5
Which will in time Break ope the locks o' the senate . . . iii 1 137
Put not your worthy rage into your tongue; One time will owe another . . . iii 1 242
The which shall turn you to no further harm Than so much loss of time iii 1 285

Time. The violent fit o' the time craves it as physic For the whole state . . . *Coriolanus* iii 2 33
And when such time they have begun to cry, Let them not cease . . iii 3 19
If the time thrust forth A cause for thy repeal . . . iv 1 40
The fittest time to corrupt a man's wife is when she's fallen out with her husband . . . iv 3 33
My grained ash an hundred times hath broke, And scarr'd the moon . iv 5 114
Thou hast beat me out Twelve several times . . . iv 5 128
We stood to't in good time . . . iv 6 10
This is a happier and more comely time . . . iv 6 27
So our virtues Lie in the interpretation of the time . . . iv 7 50
Yet one time he did call me by my name . . . v 1 9
Shall I be tempted to infringe my vow In the same time 'tis made? . . v 3 21
By the interpretation of full time May show like all yourself . . . v 3 69
That brought you forth this boy, to keep your name Living to time . v 3 127
Is't possible that so short a time can alter the condition of a man? . v 4 9
'Tis the first time that ever I was forced to scold . . . v 6 105
Five times he hath return'd Bleeding to Rome . . *T. Andron.* i 1 33
At dead time of the night . . . ii 3 99
Now is a time to storm; why art thou still? . . . iii 1 264
I made thee miserable What time I threw the people's suffrages On him iv 3 19
Till time beget some careful remedy . . . iv 3 30
Or somewhere else, So that perforce you must needs stay a time . . iv 3 41
And have a thousand times more cause than he . . . v 3 51
And break my utterance, even in the time When it should move you . v 3 91
Many a time he danced thee on his knee, Sung thee asleep . . . v 3 162
For this time, all the rest depart away . . *Rom. and Jul.* i 1 105
I must to the learned.—In good time . . . i 2 45
Since that time it is eleven years . . . i 3 35
Take our good meaning, for our judgement sits Five times in that ere once in our five wits . . . i 4 47
You must contrary me! marry, tis time. Well said, my hearts! . . i 5 87
Passion lends them power, time means, to meet . . . ii Prol. 13
A thousand times good night!—A thousand times the worse, to want thy light . . . ii 2 155
He fights as you sing prick-song, keeps time, distance, and proportion ii 4 21
Commend me to thy lady.—Ay, a thousand times . . . ii 4 229
Thoughts, Which ten times faster glide than the sun's beams . . ii 5 5
Till we can find a time To blaze your marriage, reconcile your friends iii 3 150
And call thee back With twenty hundred thousand times more joy Than thou went'st forth in lamentation . . . iii 3 153
Things have fall'n out, sir, so unluckily, That we have had no time to move our daughter . . . iii 4 2
These times of woe afford no time to woo . . . iii 4 8
And joy comes well in such a needy time . . . iii 5 106
Madam, in happy time, what day is that? . . . iii 5 112
Day, night, hour, tide, time, work, play, Alone, in company . . iii 5 178
To dispraise my lord with that same tongue Which she hath praised him with above compare So many thousand times . . . iii 5 239
On Thursday, sir? the time is very short . . . iv 1 1
My lord, we must entreat the time alone . . . iv 1 40
Out of thy long-experienced time, Give me some present counsel . . iv 1 60
We shall be much unfurnish'd for this time . . . iv 2 10
How if, when I am laid into the tomb, I wake before the time? . . iv 3 31
Ay, you have been a mouse-hunt in your time . . . iv 4 11
O lamentable day!—O woful time! . . . iv 5 30
Unhappy, wretched, hateful day! Most miserable hour that e'er time saw! . . . iv 5 44
Uncomfortable time, why camest thou now? . . . iv 5 60
'Tis no time to play now . . . iv 5 109
The time and my intents are savage-wild . . . v 3 37
Suspected, as the time and place Doth make against me . . . v 3 224
Being the time the potion's force should cease . . . v 3 249
Some minute ere the time Of her awaking . . . v 3 257
Let my old life Be sacrificed, some hour before his time . . . v 3 268
We'll share a bounteous time In different pleasures . . *T. of Athens* i 1 263
What time o' day is't, Apemantus?—Time to be honest.—That time serves still . . . i 1 265
Another time I'll hear thee . . . i 2 184
I must serve my turn Out of mine own; his days and times are past . ii 1 21
Please you, gentlemen, The time is unagreeable to this business . . ii 2 41
Wherefore ere this time Had you not fully laid my state before me? . ii 2 133
At many times I brought in my accounts, Laid them before you . . ii 2 142
Though you hear now, too late—yet now's a time . . . ii 2 152
My occasions have found time to use 'em toward a supply of money . ii 2 200
Many a time and often I ha' dined with him . . . iii 1 25
And canst use the time well, if the time use thee well . . . iii 1 39
This is no time to lend money, especially upon bare friendship . . iii 1 44
What a wicked beast was I to disfurnish myself against such a good time! . . . iii 2 50
It pleases time and fortune to lie heavy Upon a friend of mine . . iii 5 10
His right arm might purchase his own time And be in debt to none . iii 5 77
Will't hold? will't hold?—It does: but time will—and so . . . iii 6 71
You fools of fortune, trencher-friends, time's flies! . . . iii 6 106
Then was a blessed time.—As thine is now . . . iv 3 78
Thy nature did commence in sufferance, time Hath made thee hard in't iv 3 268
There is no time so miserable but a man may be true . . . iv 3 462
How rarely does it meet with this time's guise, When man was wish'd to love his enemies! . . . iv 3 472
Pity's sleeping: Strange times, that weep with laughing, not with weeping! . . . iv 3 493
You should have fear'd false times when you did feast . . . iv 3 520
Nothing at this time but my visitation . . . v 1 20
Promising is the very air o' the time: it opens the eyes of expectation . v 1 25
At all times alike Men are not still the same . . . v 1 124
'Twas time and griefs That framed him thus: time, with his fairer hand, Offering the fortunes of his former days, The former man may make him . . . v 1 126
You have gone on and fill'd the time With all licentious measure . . v 4 3
Now the time is flush, When crouching marrow in the bearer strong Cries of itself 'No more' . . . v 4 8
Many a time and oft Have you climb'd up to walls and battlements . . . *J. Cæsar* i 1 42
Men at some time are masters of their fates . . . i 2 139
How I have thought of this and of these times, I shall recount hereafter i 2 164
Find a time Both meet to hear and answer such high things . . i 2 169
Under these hard conditions as this time Is like to lay upon us . . i 2 174
He put it by thrice, every time gentler than other . . . i 2 230
Then he offered it the third time; he put it the third time by . . i 2 244
For this time I will leave you . . . i

Time. It is a strange-disposed time: But men may construe things after their fashion *J. Cæsar* i 3 33
The sufferance of our souls, the time's abuse,—If these be motives weak ii 1 115
The clock hath stricken three.—'Tis time to part ii 1 193
O, what a time have you chose out, brave Caius, To wear a kerchief! ii 1 314
Cowards die many times before their deaths ii 2 32
And you are come in very happy time, To bear my greeting ii 2 60
Break up the senate till another time, When Cæsar's wife shall meet with better dreams ii 2 98
Trebonius knows his time; for, look you, Brutus, He draws Mark Antony out of the way iii 1 25
'Tis but the time And drawing days out, that men stand upon iii 1 99
So are we Cæsar's friends, that have abridged His time of fearing death iii 1 105
How many times shall Cæsar bleed in sport! iii 1 114
Thou art the ruins of the noblest man That ever lived in the tide of times iii 1 257
You all do know this mantle: I remember the first time ever Cæsar put it on iii 2 175
In such a time as this it is not meet That every nice offence should bear his comment iv 3 7
I'll know his humour, when he knows his time iv 3 136
If we do lose this battle, then is this The very last time we shall speak together v 1 99
Time is come round, And where I did begin, there shall I end v 3 23
I shall find time, Cassius, I shall find time v 3 103
The ghost of Cæsar hath appear'd to me Two several times by night v 5 18
Fellow, wilt thou bestow thy time with me? v 5 61
Weary se'nnights nine times nine Shall he dwindle *Macbeth* i 3 22
If you can look into the seeds of time, And say which grain will grow i 3 58
Come what come may, Time and the hour runs through the roughest day i 3 147
At more time, The interim having weigh'd it, let us speak i 3 153
And referred me to the coming on of time i 5 10
To beguile the time, Look like the time; bear welcome in your eye i 5 64
But here, upon this bank and shoal of time, We'ld jump the life to come i 7 6
From this time Such I account thy love i 7 38
Nor time nor place Did then adhere, and yet you would make both i 7 51
Away, and mock the time with fairest show i 7 81
We would spend it in some words upon that business, If you would grant the time ii 1 24
And take the present horror from the time, Which now suits with it ii 1 59
Come in time; have napkins enow about you ii 3 6
Dire combustion and confused events New hatch'd to the woeful time ii 3 64
Had I but died an hour before this chance, I had lived a blessed time ii 3 97
Within the volume of which time I have seen Hours dreadful ii 4 2
As far, my lord, as will fill up the time 'Twixt this and supper iii 1 25
Goes Fleance with you?—Ay, my good lord: our time does call upon's iii 1 37
Let every man be master of his time Till seven at night iii 1 41
It was he in the times past which held you So under fortune iii 1 77
Acquaint you with the perfect spy o' the time, The moment on't iii 1 130
Our hostess keeps her state, but in best time We will require her welcome iii 4 5
The worm that's fled Hath nature that in time will venom breed iii 4 30
I' the olden time, Ere humane statute purged the gentle weal iii 4 75
The time has been, That, when the brains were out, the man would die iii 4 78
A thing of custom: 'tis no other; Only it spoils the pleasure of the time iii 4 98
You'll rue the time That clogs me with this answer iii 6 42
Harpier cries 'Tis time, 'tis time iv 1 3
Shall live the lease of nature, pay his breath To time and mortal custom iv 1 100
Time, thou anticipatest my dread exploits iv 1 144
Cruel are the times, when we are traitors And do not know ourselves iv 2 18
And what I can redress, As I shall find the time to friend, I will iv 3 10
The time you may so hoodwink iv 3 72
At no time broke my faith, would not betray The devil to his fellow iv 3 128
What, at any time, have you heard her say? v 1 14
Out, damned spot! out, I say!—One: two: why, then 'tis time to do't v 1 40
The time approaches That will with due decision make us know v 4 16
The time has been, my senses would have cool'd To hear a night-shriek v 5 10
She should have died hereafter; There would have been a time for such a word v 5 18
To-morrow, and to-morrow, Creeps in this petty pace from day to day To the last syllable of recorded time v 5 21
Yield thee, coward, And live to be the show and gaze o' the time v 8 24
Behold, where stands The usurper's cursed head: the time is free v 8 55
We shall not spend a large expense of time v 8 60
What's more to do, Which would be planted newly with the time v 8 65
By the grace of Grace, We will perform in measure, time, and place v 8 73
No fairy takes, nor witch hath power to charm, So hallow'd and so gracious is the time *Hamlet* i 1 164
Time be thine, And thy best graces spend it at thy will! i 2 62
Both in time, Form of the thing, each word made true and good i 2 209
Most humbly do I take my leave, my lord.—The time invites you; go i 3 83
'Tis told me, he hath very oft of late Given private time to you i 3 92
From this time Be somewhat scanter of your maiden presence i 3 120
That you, at such times seeing me, never shall, With arms encumber'd thus i 5 173
The time is out of joint: O cursed spite, That ever I was born to set it right! i 5 189
Vouchsafe your rest here in our court Some little time ii 2 14
Show us so much gentry and good will As to expend your time with us awhile ii 2 23
At our more consider'd time we'll read, Answer, and think upon this business ii 2 81
To expostulate . . . Why day is day, night night, and time is time, Were nothing but to waste night, day, and time ii 2 88
And more above, hath his solicitings, As they fell out by time, by means and place, All given to mine ear ii 2 127
Hath there been such a time—I'd fain know that—That I have positively said 'Tis so,' When it proved otherwise? ii 2 153
At such a time I'll loose my daughter to him ii 2 162
Happily he's the second time come to them ii 2 402
They are the abstract and brief chronicles of the time ii 2 549
Who would bear the whips and scorns of time, The oppressor's wrong? iii 1 70
This was sometime a paradox, but now the time gives it proof iii 1 115
With more offences at my beck than I have thoughts to put them in, imagination to give them shape, or time to act them in iii 1 129
The very age and body of the time his form and pressure iii 2 27
Full thirty times hath Phœbus' cart gone round Neptune's salt wash iii 2 165
Thirty dozen moons with borrow'd sheen About the world have times twelve thirties been iii 2 168
A second time I kill my husband dead, When second husband kisses me in bed iii 2 194

Time. Thoughts black, hands apt, drugs fit, and time agreeing *Hamlet* iii 2 266
We shall obey, were she ten times our mother iii 2 345
That, lapsed in time and passion, lets go by The important acting iii 4 107
My pulse, as yours, doth temperately keep time, And makes as healthful music iii 4 140
In the fatness of these pursy times Virtue itself of vice must pardon beg iii 4 153
What is a man, If his chief good and market of his time Be but to sleep and feed? a beast, no more iv 4 34
Tears seven times salt, Burn out the sense and virtue of mine eye! iv 5 154
That I know love is begun by time; And that I see, in passages of proof, Time qualifies the spark and fire of it iv 7 112
Weigh what convenience both of time and means May fit us to our shape iv 7 150
Which time she chanted snatches of old tunes iv 7 178
To contract, O, the time, for, ah, my behove, O, methought, there was nothing meet v 1 71
This fellow might be in's time a great buyer of land v 1 112
He hath borne me on his back a thousand times v 1 205
O, treble woe Fall ten times treble on that cursed head! v 1 270
Only got the tune of the time and outward habit of encounter v 2 198
He sends to know if your pleasure hold to play with Laertes, or that you will take longer time v 2 207
The king and queen and all are coming down.—In happy time v 2 214
Till that time, I do receive your offer'd love like love v 2 261
Had I but time—as this fell sergeant, death, Is strict in his arrest v 2 347
Should in this trice of time Commit a thing so monstrous *Lear* i 1 219
Time shall unfold what plaited cunning hides i 1 283
The best and soundest of his time hath been but rash i 1 298
This policy and reverence of age makes the world bitter to the best of our times i 2 50
We have seen the best of our time: machinations, hollowness, treachery i 2 122
Forbear his presence till some little time hath qualified the heat of his displeasure i 2 176
I'ld have thee beaten for being old before thy time i 5 46
You may do, then, in time ii 1 14
I have seen better faces in my time Than stands on any shoulder that I see ii 2 99
Some time I shall sleep out, the rest I'll whistle ii 2 163
And shall find time From this enormous state, seeking to give Losses their remedies ii 2 175
O, are you free? Some other time for that ii 4 135
I gave you all— And in good time you gave it ii 4 253
Then comes the time, who lives to see't, That going shall be used with feet iii 2 93
This prophecy Merlin shall make; for I live before his time iii 2 95
If wolves had at thy gate howl'd that stern time, Thou shouldst have said 'Good porter, turn the key' iii 7 63
'Tis the times' plague, when madmen lead the blind iv 1 48
The first time that we smell the air, We wawl and cry iv 6 183
If your will want not, time and place will be fruitfully offered iv 6 269
In the mature time With this ungracious paper strike the sight iv 6 282
My boon I make it, that you know me not Till time and I think meet iv 7 11
Yet it is danger To make him even o'er the time he has lost iv 7 80
Report is changeable. 'Tis time to look about iv 7 92
When time shall serve, let but the herald cry, And I'll appear v 1 48
Your haste Is now urged on you.—We will greet the time v 1 54
Know thou this, that men Are as the time is v 3 31
At this time We sweat and bleed: the friend hath lost his friend v 3 54
Time will bring it out v 3 163
The time will not allow the compliment Which very manners urges v 3 233
Nay, send in time.—Run, run, O, run! v 3 247
The weight of this sad time we must obey; Speak what we feel v 3 323
This counter-caster, He, in good time, must his lieutenant be *Othello* i 1 32
Wears out his time, much like his master's ass, For nought but provender i 1 47
And what's to come of my despised time Is nought but bitterness i 1 162
Nine or ten times I had thought to have yerk'd him here under the ribs i 2 4
Till fit time Of law and course of direct session Call thee to answer i 2 85
How! the duke in council! In this time of the night! i 2 94
We must obey the time i 3 301
I have looked upon the world for four times seven years i 3 313
There are many events in the womb of time which will be delivered i 3 377
If I would time expend with such a snipe, But for my sport and profit i 3 391
After some time, to abuse Othello's ear That he is too familiar with his wife i 3 401
What other course you please, which the time shall more favourably minister ii 1 277
On some odd time of his infirmity ii 3 132
As the time, the place, and the condition of this country stands, I could heartily wish this had not befallen ii 3 302
You or any man living may be drunk at a time, man ii 3 319
We work by wit, and not by witchcraft; And wit depends on dilatory time ii 3 379
In happy time, Iago.—You have not been a-bed, then? iii 1 32
I will bestow you where you shall have time To speak your bosom freely iii 1 57
Some other time.—But shall't be shortly?—The sooner, sweet, for you iii 3 55
I prithee, name the time, but let it not Exceed three days iii 3 62
Many a time, When I have spoke of you dispraisingly, Hath ta'en your part iii 3 71
Entreat your honour To scan this thing no further; leave it to time iii 3 245
My wayward husband hath a hundred times Woo'd me to steal it iii 3 292
A man that all his time Hath founded his good fortunes on your love iii 4 93
And lovers' absent hours, More tedious than the dial eight score times iii 4 175
I shall, in a more continuate time, Strike off this score of absence iii 4 178
Take it, and do't; and leave me for this time iii 4 191
That's not amiss; But yet keep time in all iv 1 93
She's the worse for all this.—O, a thousand thousand times! iv 1 203
Who keeps her company? What place? what time? what form? what likelihood? iv 2 138
That she with Cassio hath the act of shame A thousand times committed v 2 212
I have made my way through more impediments Than twenty times your stop v 2 264
To you, lord governor, Remains the censure of this hellish villain; The time, the place, the torture v 2 369
For the love of Love and her soft hours, Let's not confound the time with conference harsh *Ant. and Cleo.* i 1 45
But soon that war had end, and the time's state Made friends of them i 2 95
I have seen her die twenty times upon far poorer moment i 2 146
In time we hate that which we often fear i 3 12
When you sued staying, Then was the time for words i 3 34
The strong necessity of time commands Our services awhile i 3 42
But to confound such time, That drums him from his sport i 4 28
'Tis time we twain Did show ourselves i' the field i 4 73

Time. I shall be furnish'd to inform you rightly Both what by sea and land I can be able To front this present time *Ant. and Cleo.* i 4 79
That I might sleep out this great gap of time i 5 5
That am with Phœbus' amorous pinches black, And wrinkled deep in time i 5 29
Like to the time o' the year between the extremes Of hot and cold i 5 51
'Tis not a time For private stomaching ii 2 8
Every time Serves for the matter that is then born in't ii 2 9
You shall have time to wrangle in when you have nothing else to do ii 2 106
Time calls upon's: Of us must Pompey presently be sought ii 2 160
Being barber'd ten times o'er, goes to the feast ii 2 229
All which time Before the gods my knee shall bow my prayers To them for you ii 3 2
That time,—O times!—I laugh'd him out of patience ii 5 18
Ram thou thy fruitful tidings in mine ears, That long time have been barren ii 5 25
In praising Antony, I have dispraised Cæsar.—Many times, madam ii 5 108
Take your time.—Thou canst not fear us, Pompey, with thy sails ii 6 23
I ha' praised ye, When you have well deserved ten times as much ii 6 79
Be a child o' the time.—Possess it, I'll make answer ii 7 106
You shall hear from me still; the time shall not Out-go my thinking on you iii 2 60
Cheer your heart: Be you not troubled with the time iii 6 82
Take from his brain, from's time, What should not then be spared iii 7 12
With news the time's with labour, and throes forth, Each minute, some iii 7 81
To try thy eloquence, now tis time: dispatch iii 12 26
He makes me angry; And at this time most easy 'tis to do't iii 13 144
It portends alone The fall of Antony!—I must stay his time iii 13 155
The next time I do fight, I'll make death love me iii 13 192
He thinks, being twenty times of better fortune, He is twenty men to one iv 2 3
The time of universal peace is near iv 6 5
That, on my command, Thou then wouldst kill me: do't; the time is come iv 14 67
The star is fall'n.—And time is at his period iv 14 107
I remember now How he's employ'd: he shall in time be ready v 1 72
Who in the wars o' the time Died with their swords in hand *Cymbeline* i 1 35
Puts to him all the learnings that his time Could make him the receiver of i 1 43
You shall at least Go see my lord aboard: for this time leave me i 1 178
This gentleman at that time vouching—and upon warrant i 4 63
With five times so much conversation, I should get ground i 4 113
Doctor, your service for this time is ended; Take your own way i 5 30
There is No danger in what show of death it makes, More than the locking-up the spirits a time i 5 41
Dost thou think in time She will not quench and let instructions enter? i 5 46
It is a thing I made, which hath the king Five times redeem'd from death i 5 63
It were fit That all the plagues of hell should at one time Encounter such revolt i 6 111
Greet your lord with writing, do't to-night: I have outstood my time i 6 207
One, two, three: time, time! ii 2 51
Some more time Must wear the print of his remembrance out ii 3 47
Not any, but abide the change of time ii 4 4
My mother seem'd The Dian of that time: so doth my wife The nonpareil of this ii 5 7
Our kingdom is stronger than it was at that time iii 1 36
And for the gap That we shall make in time, from our hence-going And our return, to excuse iii 2 65
Nay, many times, Doth ill deserve by doing well iii 3 53
Paid More pious debts to heaven than in all The fore-end of my time iii 3 73
Like false Æneas, Were in his time thought false iii 4 61
The time inviting thee iii 4 108
But to win time To lose so bad employment iii 4 112
There's more to be consider'd; but we'll even All that good time will give us iii 4 185
The cure whereof, my lord, 'Tis time must do iii 5 38
She said upon a time—the bitterness of it I now belch from my heart iii 5 137
The words of your commission Will tie you to the numbers and the time Of their dispatch iii 7 15
Not beneath him in fortunes, beyond him in the advantage of the time iv 1 12
We'll leave you for this time: go in and rest.—We'll not be long away iv 2 43
But time hath nothing blurr'd those lines of favour Which then he wore iv 2 104
I wish my brother make good time with him, You say he is so fell iv 2 108
And in time May make some stronger head iv 2 138
My queen Upon a desperate bed, and in a time When fearful wars point at me iv 3 6
The time is troublesome. We'll slip you for a season iv 3 21
Let's withdraw; And meet the time as it seeks us iv 3 33
All other doubts, by time let them be clear'd iv 3 45
A doubt In such a time nothing becoming you, Nor satisfying us iv 4 15
They will waste their time upon our note, To know from whence we are iv 4 20
The time seems long; their blood thinks scorn, Till it fly out iv 4 53
'Tis now the time To ask of whence you are. Report it v 5 15
In which time she purposed . . . to O'ercome you with her show, and in time, When she had fitted you with her craft, to work Her son v 5 52
Since she is living, let the time run on To good or bad v 5 128
Upon a time,—unhappy was the clock That struck the hour! v 5 153
But in short time All offices of nature should again Do their due functions v 5 256
Nor the time nor place Will serve our long inter'gatories v 5 391
You, born in these latter times, When wit's more ripe *Pericles* i Gower 11
Being play'd upon before your time, Hell only danceth at so harsh a chime i 1 84
Your time's expired: Either expound now, or receive your sentence i 1 89
But thou know'st this, 'Tis time to fear when tyrants seem to kiss i 2 79
So round and safe, That time of both this truth shall ne'er convince i 2 123
Time's the king of men, He's both their parent, and he is their grave ii 3 45
We sit too long on trifles, And waste the time, which looks for other revels ii 3 93
If in which time expired, he not return, I shall with aged patience bear your yoke ii 4 47
And time that is so briefly spent With your fine fancies quaintly eche iii Gower 12
Nor have I time To give thee hallow'd to thy grave iii 1 59
Such strong renown as time shall ne'er decay iii 2 48
That I was shipp'd at sea, I well remember, Even on my eaning time iii 4 6
Only I carry winged time Post on the lame feet of my rhyme iv Gower 47
Thus time we waste, and longest leagues make short iv 4 1
Advanced in time to great and high estate iv 4 14
But time hath rooted out my parentage v 1 93
O, come, be buried A second time within these arms v 3 44
Time-bewasted. My oil-dried lamp and time-bewasted light Shall be extinct with age and endless night *Richard II.* i 3 221

Time enough. Bear it with you, lest I come not time enough *C. of Er.* iv 1 41
Within these three hours 'twill be time enough to go home *All's Well* iv 1 28
There's time enough for that *W. Tale* v 3 128
Time enough to go to bed with a candle, I warrant thee *1 Hen. IV.* ii 1 48
For this I shall have time enough to mourn *2 Hen. IV.* i 1 136
Save that there was not time enough to hear *Hen. V.* i 1 84
To-morrow?—No, not till Thursday; there is time enough *Rom. and Jul.* iv 2 36
Time forth. I would not, in plain terms, from this time forth, Have you so slander any moment leisure *Hamlet* i 3 132
O, from this time forth, My thoughts be bloody, or be nothing worth! iv 4 65
From this time forth I never will speak word *Othello* v 2 304
From this time forth I wear it as your enemy *Cymbeline* iii 5 13
Time-honoured. Old John of Gaunt, time-honour'd Lancaster *Richard II.* i 1 1
Time of action. An effeminate man In time of action *Troi. and Cres.* iii 3 219
Time of day. What time o' day?—The hour that fools should ask *L. L. L.* ii 1 122
All hail, sweet madam, and fair time of day! v 2 339
What is't o' clock?—You should ask me what time o' day *As Y. Like It* iii 2 318
I would I had some flowers o' the spring that might Become your time of day *W. Tale* iv 4 114
Now, Hal, what time of day is it, lad?— . . . What a devil hast thou to do with the time of the day? . . . I see no reason why thou shouldst be so superfluous to demand the time of the day *1 Hen. IV.* i 2 1
God give your lordship good time of day *2 Hen. IV.* i 2 107
Health and fair time of day; joy and good wishes! *Hen. V.* v 2 3
In the morn, When every one will give the time of day, He knits his brow *2 Hen. VI.* iii 1 14
Good time of day unto my gracious lord! *Richard III.* i 1 122
Good time of day unto your royal grace! i 3 18
Princely peers, a happy time of day! ii 1 47
God give your graces both A happy and a joyful time of day! iv 1 6
What time o' day is't, Apemantus?—Time to be honest *T. of Athens* i 1 265
The good time of day to you, sir.—I also wish it to you iii 6 1
'Tis the breathing time of day with me *Hamlet* v 2 181
Was blurted at and held a malkin Not worth the time of day *Pericles* iv 3 35
Time of death. He would avoid such bitter taunts Which in the time of death he gave our father *3 Hen. VI.* ii 6 67
Had you such leisure in the time of death To gaze! *Richard III.* i 4 34
Time of help. Now is the time of help; your eye in Scotland Would create soldiers *Macbeth* iv 3 186
Time of life. The time of life is short! To spend that shortness basely were too long *1 Hen. IV.* v 2 82
I do find it cowardly and vile, For fear of what might fall, so to prevent The time of life *J. Cæsar* v 1 106
Time of meeting. So much for him. Now for ourself and for this time of meeting *Hamlet* i 2 26
Time of moon. 'Tis not that time of moon with me to make one in so skipping a dialogue *T. Night* i 5 213
Time of night. Now it is the time of night That the graves all gaping wide, Every one lets forth his sprite *M. N. Dream* v 1 386
Have you no wit . . . , but to gabble like tinkers at this time of night? *T. Night* ii 3 95
The time of night when Troy was set on fire *2 Hen. VI.* i 4 20
What art thou that usurp'st this time of night? *Hamlet* i 1 46
'Tis now the very witching time of night, When churchyards yawn iii 2 406
Times of old. Sad stories chanced in the times of old *T. Andron.* iii 2 83
Time of pause. Justles roughly by All time of pause *Troi. and Cres.* iv 4 37
Time of peace. I, in this weak piping time of peace, Have no delight to pass away the time *Richard III.* i 1 24
Time of request. Answer the time of request *All's Well* i 1 168
Time of rest. I know young bloods look for a time of rest *J. Cæsar* iv 3 262
Time of scorn. A fixed figure for the time of scorn To point his slow unmoving finger at! *Othello* iv 2 54
Time of stay. Be merry, for our time of stay is short *Richard II.* ii 1 223
Time of storm. To help King Edward in his time of storm *3 Hen. VI.* iv 7 43
Time of trial. Until your further time of trial *2 Hen. VI.* iii 1 138
Time of war. These gates must not be shut But in the night or in the time of war *3 Hen. VI.* iv 7 36
Like rams In the old time of war *Hen. VIII.* iv 1 78
Time of year. We at time of year Do wound the bark, the skin of our fruit-trees *Richard II.* iii 4 57
Time out of mind. I have been an unlawful bawd time out of mind *Meas. for Meas.* iv 2 17
Old grub, Time out o' mind the fairies' coachmakers *Rom. and Jul.* i 4 69
Time-pleaser. Or any thing constantly, but a time-pleaser *T. Night* ii 3 160
Call'd them Time-pleasers, flatterers, foes to nobleness *Coriolanus* iii 1 45
Time to come. Heaven so speed me in my time to come! *Mer. Wives* iii 4 12
With dangerous sense, Might in the times to come have ta'en revenge *Meas. for Meas.* iv 4 33
Take this mercy to provide For better times to come v 1 490
Let myself and fortune Tug for the time to come *W. Tale* iv 4 508
Or fill up chronicles in time to come *1 Hen. IV.* i 3 171
Over whom, in time to come, I hope to reign *2 Hen. VI.* iv 2 138
What canst thou swear by now?—The time to come.—That thou hast wronged in the time o'erpast *Richard III.* iv 4 387
Swear not by time to come; for that thou hast Misused ere used, by time misused o'erpast iv 4 395
God, if thy will be so, Enrich the time to come with smooth-faced peace! v 5 33
And fame in time to come canonize us *Troi. and Cres.* ii 2 202
To make us wonder'd at in time to come *T. Andron.* iii 1 135
All these woes shall serve For sweet discourses in our time to come *Rom. and Jul.* iii 5 53
Time to time. From time to time I have acquainted you With the dear love I bear *Mer. Wives* iv 6 8
Men have died from time to time and worms have eaten them *As Y. L. It* iv 1 107
From time to time Envied against the people *Coriolanus* iii 3 94
He shall signify from time to time Every good hap to you *Rom. and Jul.* iii 3 170
Timed. He was a thing of blood, whose every motion Was timed with dying cries *Coriolanus* ii 2 114
Timeless. A pack of sorrows which would press you down, Being unprevented, to your timeless grave *T. G. of Ver.* iii 1 21
Who perform'd The bloody office of his timeless end *Richard II.* iv 1 5
Must I behold thy timeless cruel death? *1 Hen. VI.* v 4 5
Then you, belike, suspect these noblemen As guilty of Duke Humphrey's timeless death *2 Hen. VI.* iii 2 187
And orphans for their parents' timeless death—Shall rue the hour that ever thou wast born *3 Hen. VI.* v 6 42
The causer of the timeless deaths Of these Plantagenets *Richard III.* i 2 117
This fatal writ, The complot of this timeless tragedy *T. Andron.* ii 3 265
Poison, I see, hath been his timeless end *Rom. and Jul.* v 3 162

Timelier. That call'd me timelier than my purpose hither *Ant. and Cleo.* ii 6 52
Timely. And happy were I in my timely death *Com. of Errors* i 1 139
He did command me to call timely on him *Macbeth* ii 3 51
Now spurs the lated traveller apace To gain the timely inn . . iii 3 7
For certainties Either are past remedies, or, timely knowing, The remedy then born . . . . *Cymbeline* i 6 97
Timely-parted. Oft have I seen a timely-parted ghost, Of ashy semblance, meagre, pale, and bloodless . *2 Hen. VI.* iii 2 161
Timon. And critic Timon laugh at idle toys! . . . *L. L. Lost* iv 3 170
I have a jewel here— O, pray, let's see't: for the Lord Timon, sir? *T. of Athens* i 1 13
Tender down Their services to Lord Timon . . . . i 1 55
And returns in peace Most rich in Timon's nod . . . i 1 62
One do I personate of Lord Timon's frame . . . . i 1 69
To show Lord Timon that mean eyes have seen The foot above the head i 1 93
Most noble Timon, call the man before thee . . . . i 1 113
Stay thou for thy good morrow; When thou art Timon's dog . i 1 180
Thou art proud, Apemantus.—Of nothing so much as that I am not like Timon . . . . i 1 190
Thou art going to Lord Timon's feast?—Ay, to see meat fill knaves i 1 269
Shall we in, And taste Lord Timon's bounty? . . . . i 1 285
O you gods, what a number of men eat Timon, and he sees 'em not! i 2 40
Those healths will make thee and thy state look ill, Timon . i 2 58
Hail to thee, worthy Timon, and to all That of his bounties taste! i 2 128
Timon, I fear me thou wilt give away thyself in paper shortly i 2 247
If I want gold, steal but a beggar's dog, And give it Timon . ii 1 6
If I would sell my horse, and buy twenty more Better than he, why, give my horse to Timon . . . . ii 1 8
Haste you to Lord Timon; Importune him for my moneys . ii 1 15
When every feather sticks in his own wing, Lord Timon will be left a naked gull, Which flashes now a phœnix . . . . . ii 1 31
Aside, aside; here comes Lord Timon . . . . . ii 2 127
Who is not Timon's? What heart, head, sword, force, means, but is Lord Timon's? Great Timon, noble, worthy, royal Timon! . ii 2 175
Ne'er speak, or think, That Timon's fortunes 'mong his friends can sink ii 2 240
One of Lord Timon's men? a gift, I warrant . . . iii 1 4
The Lord Timon? he is my very good friend, and an honourable gentleman . . . . iii 2 1
Lord Timon's happy hours are done and past, and his estate shrinks from him . . . . iii 2 6
I was sending to use Lord Timon myself . . . . . iii 2 56
Timon is shrunk indeed; And he that's once denied will hardly speed . . . . iii 2 68
Timon has been this lord's father, And kept his credit with his purse iii 2 74
Timon's money Has paid his men their wages: he ne'er drinks, But Timon's silver treads upon his lip . . . . . . iii 2 76
I never tasted Timon in my life, Nor came any of his bounties over me iii 2 84
I fear 'tis deepest winter in Lord Timon's purse . . . iii 4 14
He wears jewels now of Timon's gift, For which I wait for money . iii 4 19
Mark, how strange it shows, Timon in this should pay more than he owes . . . . iii 4 22
I know my lord hath spent of Timon's wealth, And now ingratitude makes it worse than stealth . . . . iii 4 26
This is Timon's last; Who, stuck and spangled with your flatteries, Washes it off . . . . iii 6 100
Henceforth hated be Of Timon man and all humanity! . . iii 6 115
Know you the quality of Lord Timon's fury? . . . . iii 6 118
Lord Timon's mad.—I feel't upon my bones . . . . iii 6 129
Timon will to the woods; where he shall find The unkindest beast more kinder than mankind . . . . iv 1 35
Grant, as Timon grows, his hate may grow To the whole race of mankind! . . . . iv 1 39
Yet do our hearts wear Timon's livery; That see I by our faces iv 2 17
Wherever we shall meet, for Timon's sake, Let's yet be fellows . iv 2 24
His semblable, yea, himself, Timon disdains: Destruction fang mankind! . . . . iv 3 22
How came the noble Timon to this change?—As the moon does, by wanting light . . . . iv 3 66
Noble Timon, What friendship may I do thee?—None . . iv 3 69
I have but little gold of late, brave Timon . . . . iv 3 90
Give us some gold, good Timon: hast thou more? . . . iv 3 132
More counsel with more money, bounteous Timon . . . iv 3 167
Farewell, Timon: If I thrive well, I'll visit thee again . . iv 3 169
Hug their diseased perfumes, and have forgot That ever Timon was iv 3 208
Where liest o' nights, Timon?—Under that's above me . . iv 3 292
Then, Timon, presently prepare thy grave; Lie where the light foam of the sea may beat Thy grave-stone daily . . . . . iv 3 378
Moe things like men! Eat, Timon, and abhor them . . . iv 3 398
Save thee, Timon.—Now, thieves?—Soldiers, not thieves . . iv 3 414
Hail, worthy Timon!—Our late noble master! . . . . v 1 58
It is in vain that you would speak with Timon . . . . v 1 119
It is our part and promise to the Athenians To speak with Timon . v 1 124
Lord Timon! Timon! Look out, and speak to friends . . . v 1 130
Worthy Timon,— Of none but such as you, and you of Timon . v 1 137
Feeling in itself A lack of Timon's aid, hath sense withal Of it own fail, restraining aid to Timon . . . . v 1 150
Therefore, Timon,— Well, sir, I will; therefore, I will, sir; thus: If Alcibiades kill my countrymen, Let Alcibiades know this of Timon, That Timon cares not . . . . v 1 170
Tell him Timon speaks it, In pity of our aged and our youth, I cannot choose but tell him, that I care not . . . . . v 1 178
Say to Athens, Timon hath made his everlasting mansion Upon the beached verge of the salt flood . . . . v 1 218
Graves only be men's works and death their gain! Sun, hide thy beams! Timon hath done his reign . . . . v 1 226
We stand much hazard, if they bring not Timon . . . . v 2 5
This man was riding From Alcibiades to Timon's cave . . v 2 10
No talk of Timon, nothing of him expect . . . . . v 2 14
Timon is dead, who hath outstretch'd his span: Some beast rear'd this v 3 3
So did we woo Transformed Timon to our city's love By humble message v 4 19
Those enemies of Timon's and mine own Whom you yourselves shall set out for reproof Fall and no more . . . . v 4 56
Timon is dead; Entomb'd upon the very hem o' the sea . . v 4 65
Here lie I, Timon; who, alive, All living men did hate . . v 4 72
Dead Is noble Timon: of whose memory Hereafter more . . v 4 80
Timor. Gelidus timor occupat artus it is thee I fear . *2 Hen. VI.* iv 1 117
Timorous. Like a timorous thief, most fain would steal What law does vouch mine own . . . . *All's Well* ii 5 86
A warning bell, Sings heavy music to thy timorous soul . *1 Hen. VI.* iv 2 40
A little herd of England's timorous deer . . . . . iv 2 46
Timorous. Ah, timorous wretch! Thou hast undone thyself, thy son, and me . . . . *3 Hen. VI.* i 1 231
Never yet one hour in his bed Have I enjoy'd the golden dew of sleep, But have been waked by his timorous dreams . *Richard III.* iv 1 85
With like timorous accent and dire yell As when, by night and negligence, the fire Is spied in populous cities . . . *Othello* i 1 75
Timorously. We would have had you heard The traitor speak, and timorously confess . . . . *Richard III.* iii 5 57
Tinct. Plutus himself, That knows the tinct and multiplying medicine, Hath not in nature's mystery more science . . *All's Well* v 3 102
I see such black and grained spots As will not leave their tinct *Hamlet* iii 4 91
That great medicine hath With his tinct gilded thee . *Ant. and Cleo.* i 5 37
White and azure laced With blue of heaven's own tinct . *Cymbeline* ii 2 23
Tincture. If you can bring Tincture or lustre in her lip, her eye *W. Tale* iii 2 206
Great men shall press For tinctures, stains, relics . . *J. Cæsar* ii 2 89
Tinder. Strike on the tinder, ho! Give me a taper! . . *Othello* i 1 141
Tinder-box. I am glad I am so acquit of this tinder-box . *Mer. Wives* i 3 27
Tinder-like. Hasty and tinder-like upon too trivial motion . *Coriolanus* ii 1 55
Tingling. A kind of sleeping in the blood, a whoreson tingling *2 Hen. IV.* i 2 128
Tinker. Tom Snout, the tinker.—Here, Peter Quince . *M. N. Dream* i 2 63
Flute, the bellows-mender! Snout, the tinker! . . . . . iv 1 208
And now by present profession a tinker . . . *T. of Shrew* Ind. 2 22
I am a lord indeed And not a tinker nor Christophero Sly . . Ind. 2 75
To gabble like tinkers at this time of night . . . *T. Night* ii 3 95
If tinkers may have leave to live, And bear the sow-skin budget *W. T.* iv 3 19
Married a tinker's wife within a mile where my land and living lies iv 3 103
I can drink with any tinker in his own language during my life *1 Hen. IV.* ii 4 20
He was the lord ambassador Sent from a sort of tinkers to the king *2 Hen. VI.* iii 2 277
Tinsel. Round underborne with a bluish tinsel . . . *Much Ado* iii 4 22
Tiny. When that I was and a little tiny boy . . . *T. Night* v 1 398
A joint of mutton, and any pretty little tiny kickshaws . *2 Hen. IV.* v 1 29
Welcome, my little tiny thief, and welcome indeed too . . . v 3 60
He that has and a little tiny wit . . . . . . *Lear* iii 2 74
Tip. Tush, fear not, man; we'll tip thy horns with gold . *Much Ado* v 4 44
In love, i' faith, to the very tip of the nose . . *Troi. and Cres.* iii 1 138
By yonder blessed moon I swear That tips with silver all these fruit-tree tops— O, swear not by the moon . . *Rom. and Jul.* ii 2 108
Tipped. There is no staff more reverend than one tipped with horn *M. Ado* v 4 126
Tippling. To sit And keep the turn of tippling with a slave *Ant. and Cleo.* i 4 19
Tipsy. The riot of the tipsy Bacchanals . . . *M. N. Dream* v 1 48
Tiptoe. Will stand a tiptoe when this day is named . . *Hen. V.* iv 3 42
Jocund day Stands tiptoe on the misty mountain tops . *Rom. and Jul.* iii 5 10
Tire. If I had such a tire, this face of mine Were full as lovely as is this of hers . . . . *T. G. of Ver.* iv 4 190
The ship-tire, the tire-valiant, or any tire of Venetian admittance *M. W.* iii 3 61
And tire the hearer with a book of words . . . . . *Much Ado* i 1 309
I like the new tire within excellently, if the hair were a thought browner iii 4 13
Your wit's too hot, it speeds too fast, 'twill tire . . *L. L. Lost* ii 1 120
Long-during action tires The sinewy vigour of the traveller . . iv 3 307
As true as truest horse that yet would never tire . . *M. N. Dream* iii 1 98; 104
I have stay'd To tire your royalty . . . . . . *W. Tale* i 2 15
A merry heart goes all the day, Your sad tires in a mile-a . . iv 3 135
He tires betimes that spurs too fast betimes . . . *Richard II.* ii 1 36
Like an empty eagle Tire on the flesh of me and of my son! *3 Hen. VI.* i 1 269
Tire thee more Than all the complete armour that thou wear'st! *Rich. III.* iv 4 188
Like A full-hot horse, who being allow'd his way, Self-mettle tires him *Hen. VIII.* i 1 134
He hath faults, with surplus, to tire in repetition . . *Coriolanus* i 1 47
One that excels the quirks of blazoning pens, And in the essential vesture of creation Does tire the ingener . . . . . *Othello* ii 1 65
Then put my tires and mantles on him, whilst I wore his sword *A. and C.* ii 5 22
I much marvel that your lordship, having Rich tire about you *Pericles* iii 2 22
Tired. When gentlemen are tired, gives them a sob and 'rests them *Com. of Errors* iv 3 24
Imitari is nothing: so doth the hound his master, the ape his keeper, the tired horse his rider . . . . *L. L. Lost* iv 2 131
Fie, fie on all tired jades, on all mad masters! . . . *T. of Shrew* iv 1 1
First, know, my horse is tired; my master and mistress fallen out . iv 1 56
Till our very pastime, tired out of breath, prompt us to have mercy *T. Night* iii 4 152
To do that office of thine own good will Which tired majesty did make thee offer, The resignation of thy state . . . *Richard II.* iv 1 178
Spurr'd, gall'd, and tired by jauncing Bolingbroke . . . . v 5 94
When thou hast tired thyself in base comparisons, hear me . *1 Hen. IV.* ii 4 276
O, he is as tedious As a tired horse, a railing wife . . . iii 1 160
Though patience be a tired mare, yet she will plod . . *Hen. V.* ii 1 26
Truth tired with iteration . . . . . . *Troi. and Cres.* iii 2 183
I am weary; yea, my memory is tired. Have we no wine here? *Coriol.* i 9 91
If so be Thou darest not this and that to prove more fortunes Thou'rt tired . . . . iv 5 100
Then should not we be tired with this ado . . . *T. Andron.* ii 1 98
So from the waves of Tiber Did I the tired Cæsar . . . *J. Cæsar* i 2 115
Within a dull, stale, tired bed . . . . *Lear* i 2 13
I see a man's life is a tedious one: I have tired myself . *Cymbeline* iii 6 2
Till fortune, tired with doing bad, Threw him ashore *Pericles* ii Gower 37
Tirest. When thou shalt be disedged by her That now thou tirest on, how thy memory Will then be pang'd by me . . . *Cymbeline* iii 4 97
Tire-valiant. The tire-valiant, or any tire of Venetian admittance *M. W.* iii 3 60
Tiring. The one, to save the money that he spends in tiring *Com. of Er.* ii 2 99
The posts come tiring on . . . . . . *2 Hen. IV.* Ind. 37
Witness the tiring day and heavy night; Witness all sorrow *T. Andron.* v 2 24
Upon that were my thoughts tiring, when we encountered *T. of Athens* iii 6 5
Tiring-house. This green plot shall be our stage, this hawthorn-brake our tiring-house . . . . *M. N. Dream* iii 1 4
Tirra-lyra. The lark, that tirra-lyra chants . . . *W. Tale* iv 3 9
Tirrits. Here's a goodly tumult! I'll forswear keeping house, afore I'll be in these tirrits and frights . . . . . *2 Hen. IV.* ii 4 220
Tisick. I was before Master Tisick, the debuty, t'other day . . ii 4 92
A whoreson rascally tisick so troubles me . . *Troi. and Cres.* v 3 102
Tissue. Her pavilion—cloth-of-gold of tissue . . *Ant. and Cleo.* ii 2 204
Titan. Didst thou never see Titan kiss a dish of butter? pitiful-hearted Titan, that melted at the sweet tale of the sun's! . *1 Hen. IV.* ii 4 133
Let Titan rise as early as he dare. I'll through and through you! *Troi. and Cres.* v 10 25
Will, I hope, Reflect on Rome as Titan's rays on earth . *T. Andron.* i 1 226
Thy cheeks look red as Titan's face Blushing to be encounter'd with a cloud . . . . ii 4 31
And flecked darkness like a drunkard reels From forth day's path and Titan's fiery wheels . . . . *Rom. and Jul.* ii 3 4

Titan. Exposing it . . . to the greedy touch Of common-kissing Titan *Cymbeline* iii 4 166
Titania. Ill met by moonlight, proud Titania *M. N. Dream* ii 1 60
How canst thou thus for shame, Titania, Glance at my credit? ii 1 74
Why should Titania cross her Oberon? ii 1 119
I'll watch Titania when she is asleep ii 1 177
There sleeps Titania sometime of the night, Lull'd in these flowers ii 1 253
I wonder if Titania be awaked iii 2 1
So it came to pass, Titania waked and straightway loved an ass iii 2 34
Now, my Titania; wake you, my sweet queen iv 1 80
Tithe. Our corn's to reap, for yet our tithe's to sow *Meas. for Meas.* iv 1 76
No Italian priest Shall tithe or toll in our dominions *K. John* iii 1 154
The tithe of a hair was never lost in my house before 1 *Hen. IV.* iii 3 66
Every tithe soul, 'mongst many thousand dismes, Hath been as dear as Helen *Troi. and Cres.* ii 2 19
A slave that is not twentieth part the tithe Of your precedent lord *Hamlet* iii 4 97
Tithed. By decimation, and a tithed death *T. of Athens* v 4 31
Tithe-pig. With a tithe-pig's tail Tickling a parson's nose *Rom. and Jul.* i 4 79
Tithe-woman. We'ld find no fault with the tithe-woman *All's Well* i 3 89
Tithing. Whipped from tithing to tithing, and stock-punished *Lear* iii 4 140
Titinius. Alas, it cried 'Give me some drink, Titinius' *J. Cæsar* i 2 127
Let Lucius and Titinius guard our door iv 2 52
Stand fast, Titinius: we must out and talk v 1 22
O, look, Titinius, look, the villains fly! v 3 1
Look, look, Titinius; Are those my tents where I perceive the fire? v 3 12
Titinius, if thou lovest me, Mount thou my horse, and hide thy spurs in him v 3 14
Regard Titinius, And tell me what thou notest about the field v 3 21
Titinius is enclosed round about With horsemen, that make to him on the spur; Yet he spurs on. Now they are almost on him. Now, Titinius! v 3 28
It is but change, Titinius; for Octavius Is overthrown by noble Brutus' power, As Cassius' legions are by Antony v 3 51
Seek him, Titinius, whilst I go to meet The noble Brutus v 3 73
Come, Cassius' sword, and find Titinius' heart v 3 90
Where, Messala, doth his body lie?—Lo, yonder, and Titinius mourning it.—Titinius' face is upward v 3 92
Brave Titinius! Look, whether he have not crown'd dead Cassius! v 3 96
Why, now thou diest as bravely as Titinius v 4 10
Title. And this deceit loses the name of craft, Of disobedience, or unduteous title *Mer. Wives* v 5 240
The justice of your title to him Doth flourish the deceit *Meas. for Meas.* iv 1 74
So may Angelo, In all his dressings, characts, titles, forms, Be an arch-villain v 1 56
It may be I go under that title because I am merry *Much Ado* ii 1 212
Think you of a worse title, and I will fit her to it iii 2 114
An appertinent title to your old time, which we may name tough *L. L. L.* i 2 18
On payment of a hundred thousand crowns, To have his title live ii 1 146
What shalt thou exchange for rags? robes; for tittles? titles iv 1 85
What is Dictynna?—A title to Phœbe, to Luna, to the moon iv 2 39
Yield Thy crazed title to my certain right *M. N. Dream* i 1 92
Tell me once more what title thou dost bear *Mer. of Venice* ii 9 35
O that I had a title good enough to keep his name company! iii 1 15
The curst! A title for a maid of all titles the worst *T. of Shrew* i 2 130
And seal the title with a lovely kiss iii 2 125
May lawfully make title to as much love as she finds *All's Well* i 3 107
'Tis only title thou disdain'st in her, the which I can build up ii 3 124
The property by what it is should go, Not by the title ii 3 138
I write man; to which title age cannot bring thee ii 3 209
To know nothing, and to have nothing, is to be a great part of your title ii 4 27
Even as bad as those That vulgars give bold'st titles *W. Tale* ii 1 94
I am proof against that title and what shame else belongs to't iv 4 872
Lay aside the sword Which sways usurpingly these several titles *K. John* ii 1 13
I can produce A will that bars the title of thy son ii 1 192
Let us hear them speak Whose title they admit, Arthur's or John's ii 1 200
To verify our title with their lives ii 1 277
Shall gild her bridal bed and make her rich In titles, honours ii 1 492
John, to stop Arthur's title in the whole, Hath willingly departed with a part ii 1 562
As little prince, having so great a title To be more prince, as may be iv 1 10
To guard a title that was rich before, To gild refined gold iv 2 10
Until the heavens . . . Add an immortal title to your crown! *Rich. II.* i 1 24
Now his son is duke.—Barely in title, not in revenue ii 1 226
I must find that title in your tongue, Before I make reply ii 3 72
'Tis not my meaning To raze one title of your honour out ii 3 75
Only to be brief, Left I his title out iii 3 10
I have no name, no title, No, not that name was given me at the font iv 1 255
And therefore lost that title of respect Which the proud soul ne'er pays but to the proud 1 *Hen. IV.* i 3 8
I fear my brother Mortimer doth stir About his title ii 3 85
Gallants, lads, boys, hearts of gold, all the titles of good fellowship ii 4 307
Holds from all soldiers chief majority And military title capital iii 2 110
To pry Into his title, the which we find Too indirect for long continuance iv 3 104
A borrow'd title hast thou bought too dear v 3 23
I better brook the loss of brittle life Than those proud titles v 4 79
Unhidden passages Of his true titles to some certain dukedoms *Hen. V.* i 1 87
Or nicely charge your understanding soul With opening titles miscreate i 2 16
Make claim and title to the crown of France i 2 68
To find his title with some shows of truth i 2 72
All appear To hold in right and title of the female i 2 89
Rather choose to hide them in a net Than amply to imbar their crooked titles i 2 94
Think'st thou the fiery fever will go out With titles blown from adulation? iv 1 271
The farced title running 'fore the king, The throne he sits on iv 1 280
Thus the Mortimers, In whom the title rested, were suppress'd 1 *Hen. VI.* ii 5 92
For ever should they be expulsed from France And not have title of an earldom here iii 3 26
Him that thou magnifiest with all these titles Stinking and fly-blown lies here at our feet iv 7 75
Accept the title thou usurp'st v 4 151
Her father is no better than an earl, Although in glorious titles he excel v 5 38
Deliver up my title in the queen 2 *Hen. VI.* i 1 12
By the grace of God, and Hume's advice, Your grace's title shall be multiplied i 2 73
Am I a queen in title and in style, And must be made a subject to a duke? i 3 51
In this close walk to satisfy myself, In craving your opinion of my title ii 2 4
I will remedy this gear ere long, Or sell my title for a glorious grave iii 1 92
Title. To make commotion, as full well he can, Under the title of John Mortimer 2 *Hen. VI.* iii 1 359
I have consider'd with myself The title of this most renowned duke v 1 176
Will you we show our title to the crown? If not, our swords shall plead it in the field.—What title hast thou, traitor, to the crown? 3 *Hen. VI.* i 1 102
My title's good, and better far than his.—Prove it i 1 130
I know not what to say; my title's weak i 1 134
Be thy title right or wrong, Lord Clifford vows to fight in thy defence i 1 159
Write up his title with usurping blood i 1 169
Bears the title of a king,—As if a channel should be call'd the sea ii 2 140
Hadst thou been meek, our title still had slept ii 2 160
Whiles Warwick tells his title, smooths the wrong, Inferreth arguments iii 1 48
Between my soul's desire and me—The lustful Edward's title buried iii 2 129
Mischance hath trod my title down, And with dishonour laid me on the ground iii 3 8
Proud ambitious Edward Duke of York Usurps the regal title iii 3 28
If your title to the crown be weak, As may appear iii 3 145
It pleased his majesty To raise my state to title of a queen iv 1 68
This title honours me and mine iv 1 72
But we now forget Our title to the crown and only claim Our dukedom iv 7 46
Why shall we fight, if you pretend no title? iv 7 57
Princes have but their titles for their glories, An outward honour for an inward toil; . . . So that, betwixt their titles and low names, There's nothing differs but the outward fame *Richard III.* i 4 78
Ah, so much interest have I in thy sorrow As I had title in thy noble husband! ii 2 48
Too late he died that might have kept that title iii 1 99
Then I salute you with this kingly title iii 7 239
I mean the lord protector.—The Lord protect him from that kingly title! iv 1 20
A grandam's name is little less in love Than is the doting title of a mother iv 4 300
Under what title shall I woo for thee? iv 4 340
She shall be a high and mighty queen.—To wail the title, as her mother doth iv 4 348
I will love her everlastingly.—But how long shall that title 'ever' last? iv 4 350
A proper title of a peace; and purchased At a superfluous rate! *Hen. VIII.* i 1 98
How grounded he his title to the crown, Upon our fail? i 2 144
What think you of a duchess? have you limbs To bear that load of title? ii 3 39
To which title A thousand pound a year, annual support ii 3 63
I dare not make myself so guilty, To give up willingly that noble title iii 1 140
You must no more call it York-place, that's past; For, since the cardinal fell, that title's lost iv 1 96
The times and titles now are alter'd strangely With me iv 2 112
This good man,—few of you deserve that title,—This honest man v 3 138
Honour and lordship are my titles *Troi. and Cres.* iii 1 17
Where gentry, title, wisdom, Cannot conclude but by the yea and no Of general ignorance *Coriolanus* iii 1 144
My loving followers, Plead my successive title with your swords *T. An.* i 1 4
Be, as your titles witness, Imperious and impatient of your wrongs v 1 5
So Romeo would, were he not Romeo call'd, Retain that dear perfection which he owes Without that title *Rom. and Jul.* ii 2 47
Why have you that charitable title from thousands? *T. of Athens* i 2 94
Place thieves And give them title, knee, and approbation With senators iv 3 36
Crack the lawyer's voice, That he may never more false title plead iv 3 154
Pronounce his present death, And with his former title greet Macbeth *Macbeth* i 2 65
"Thane of Cawdor;" by which title, before, these weird sisters saluted me i 5 8
Wisdom! to leave his wife, to leave his babes, His mansion, and his titles in a place From whence himself does fly? iv 2 7
Goodness dare not check thee: wear thou thy wrongs; The title is affeer'd! iv 3 34
Now does he feel his title Hang loose about him v 2 20
The devil himself could not pronounce a title More hateful to mine ear v 7 8
All thy other titles thou hast given away; that thou wast born with *Lear* i 4 163
Whose age has charms in it, whose title more, To pluck the common bosom on his side v 3 48
Let the drum strike, and prove my title thine v 3 81
My title and my perfect soul Shall manifest me rightly *Othello* i 2 31
Husband, I come: Now to that name my courage prove my title! *A. and C.* v 2 291
Had his titles by Tenantius whom He served with glory *Cymbeline* i 1 31
You may wear her in title yours: but, you know, strange fowl light upon neighbouring ponds i 4 96
Knighthoods and honours, borne As I wear mine, are titles but of scorn v 2 7
What is your title?—I am Pericles of Tyre *Pericles* v 1 205
Titled goddess; And worth it, with addition! *All's Well* iv 2 2
Assubjugate his merit, As amply titled as Achilles is *Troi. and Cres.* ii 3 203
Title-leaf. This man's brow, like to a title-leaf, Foretells the nature of a tragic volume 2 *Hen. IV.* i 1 60
Titleless, Till he had forged himself a name *Coriolanus* v 1 13
Title-page. To place upon the volume of your deeds, As in a title-page, your worth in arms *Pericles* ii 3 4
Tittles. What shalt thou exchange for rags? robes; for tittles? titles *L. L. Lost* iv 1 85
Tittle-tattling. You must be tittle-tattling before all our guests *W. T.* iv 4 248
Titus. When your young nephew Titus lost his leg *T. Night* v 1 66
Advance, brave Titus: They do disdain us much beyond our thoughts *Coriolanus* i 4 25
Then, valiant Titus, take Convenient numbers to make good the city i 5 12
He should Be free as is the wind. Deliver him, Titus i 9 89
Renowned Titus, flourishing in arms *T. Andron.* i 1 38
So I love and honour thee and thine, Thy noble brother Titus and his sons i 1 50
Titus, unkind and careless of thine own i 1 86
Victorious Titus, rue the tears I shed, A mother's tears in passion for her son i 1 105
Thrice noble Titus, spare my first-born son.—Patient yourself, madam i 1 120
We survive To tremble under Titus' threatening looks i 1 134
In peace and honour live Lord Titus long; My noble lord and father! i 1 157
Lord Titus, my beloved brother, Gracious triumpher in the eyes of Rome! i 1 169
Titus, thou shalt obtain and ask the empery i 1 201
Proud Saturnine, interrupter of the good That noble-minded Titus means to thee! i 1 209
And, for an onset, Titus, to advance Thy name and honourable family i 1 238
Thanks, noble Titus, father of my life! How proud I am of thee i 1 253
Lord Titus, by your leave, this maid is mine i 1 276
Are you in earnest then, my lord?—Ay, noble Titus i 1 278
No, Titus, no; the emperor needs her not, Nor her, nor thee i 1 299
Titus, when wert thou wont to walk alone, Dishonour'd thus? i 1 339
O Titus, see, O, see what thou hast done! i 1 341

Titus. Renowned Titus, more than half my soul,— Dear father, soul and substance of us all *T. Andron.* i 1 373
This noble gentleman, Lord Titus here, Is in opinion and in honour wrong'd i 1 415
On mine honour dare I undertake For good Lord Titus' innocence in all i 1 437
Lest, then, the people, and patricians too, Upon a just survey, take Titus' part i 1 446
Rise, Titus, rise; my empress hath prevail'd i 1 459
Titus, I am incorporate in Rome, A Roman now adopted happily i 1 462
We'll give your grace bonjour.—Be it so, Titus, and gramercy too i 1 495
Titus, prepare thy aged eyes to weep; Or, if not so, thy noble heart to break iii 1 59
Patience, dear niece. Good Titus, dry thine eyes iii 1 138
If thou love thy sons, Let Marcus, Lucius, or thyself, old Titus, Or any one of you, chop off your hand iii 1 152
A deed of death done on the innocent Becomes not Titus' brother iii 2 57
Commander of my thoughts, Calm thee, and bear the faults of Titus' age iv 4 29
But, Titus, I have touch'd thee to the quick, Thy life-blood out iv 4 36
Titus, I am come to talk with thee.—No, not a word v 2 16
Marcus, my brother! 'tis sad Titus calls v 2 121
The feast is ready, which the careful Titus Hath ordain'd v 3 21
The villain is alive in Titus' house v 3 123
Now judge what cause had Titus to revenge These wrongs v 3 125
Go, go into old Titus' sorrowful house v 3 142
Well met; good morrow, Titus and Hortensius.—The like to you *T. of Athens* iii 4 1
Put in now, Titus.—My lord, here is my bill iii 4 85
To. My heart bleeds To think o' the teen that I have turn'd you to *Temp.* i 2 64
Tunis was never graced before with such a paragon to their queen ii 1 75
I'll to my book iii 1 94
I will stand to and feed, Although my last iii 3 49
My lord the duke, Stand to and do as we iii 3 52
Thy thoughts I cleave to iv 1 165
To Milan let me hear from thee by letters *T. G. of Ver.* i 1 57
Spirits are not finely touch'd But to fine issues *Meas. for Meas.* i 1 37
Or that his appetite Is more to bread than stone i 3 53
You must lay down the treasures of your body To this supposed, or else to let him suffer ii 4 97
Pardon it; The phrase is to the matter v 1 90
A heavier task could not have been imposed Than I to speak my griefs *Com. of Errors* i 1 33
Who heard me to deny it or forswear it? v 1 25
My wind cooling my broth Would blow me to an ague *Mer. of Venice* i 1 23
My father did something smack, something grow to ii 2 18
Fall to: I will not trouble you As yet, to question you *As Y. Like It* ii 7 171
Heaven would that she these gifts should have, And I to live and die her slave iii 2 162
I must and will have Katharine to my wife *T. of Shrew* ii 1 282
There, take it to you, trenchers, cups, and all iv 1 168
I am sure no man hath any quarrel to me *T. Night* iii 4 248
As rank as any flax-wench that puts to Before her troth-plight *W. Tale* i 2 277
Tell me, for you seem to be honest plain men, what you have to the king iv 4 824
Where these two Christian armies might combine The blood of malice in a vein of league, And not to spend it so unneighbourly! *K. John* v 2 39
Bid him repair to us to Ely House *Richard II.* ii 1 216
My lord, will't please you to fall to? v 5 98
Hostess, clap to the doors: watch to-night, pray to-morrow. 1 *Hen. IV.* ii 4 305
Can honour set to a leg? no: or an arm? no v 1 133
Fall to: if you can mock a leek, you can eat a leek *Hen. V.* v 1 38
Now, sir, to you, that were so hot at sea 1 *Hen. VI.* iii 4 28
May be, he hears the king Does whet his anger to him *Hen. VIII.* iii 2 92
Speak to the business, master secretary v 3 1
At length they came to the broom-staff to me v 4 57
The Greeks are strong and skilful to their strength *Troi. and Cres.* i 1 7
Good sooth: to, Achilles! to, Ajax! to! ii 1 119
To her own worth She shall be prized iv 4 135
A wager they have met.—My horse to yours, no *Coriolanus* i 4 2
And hark, what noise the general makes! To him! i 5 10
To's power he would Have made them mules ii 1 262
As soon moody to be moved.—And what to? *Rom. and Jul.* iii 1 15
What wouldst thou have to Athens?—Thee thither *T. of Athens* iv 3 287
This gentle and unforced accord of Hamlet Sits smiling to my heart *Ham.* i 2 124
To hell, allegiance! vows, to the blackest devil! iv 5 131
To whose young love The vines of France and milk of Burgundy Strive to be interess'd *Lear* i 1 85
A yeoman that has a gentleman to his son iii 6 14
I am hurt to danger *Othello* ii 3 197
I am not bound to that all slaves are free to iii 3 135
You must either be directed . . . , or to take upon yourself that *Cymb.* v 4 187
To and back. Goes to and back, lackeying the varying tide *Ant. and Cleo.* i 4 46
To and fro. I was employ'd in passing to and fro 1 *Hen. VI.* ii 1 69
Early and late, debating to and fro 2 *Hen. VI.* i 1 91
Was ever feather so lightly blown to and fro as this multitude? iv 8 57
To-and-fro-conflicting. To out-scorn The to-and-fro-conflicting wind and rain *Lear* iii 1 11
To be thus is nothing; But to be safely thus *Macbeth* iii 1 48
To be, or not to be: that is the question *Hamlet* iii 1 56
To-be-pitied. Such to-be-pitied and o'er-wrested seeming He acts thy greatness in *Troi. and Cres.* i 3 157
To bless. Now, the gods to bless your honour! *Pericles* iv 6 23
To day. Or go to bed now, being two hours to day *Mer. of Venice* v 1 303
To heart. Why should we in our peevish opposition Take it to heart? *Hamlet* i 2 101
To it. Fall to't, yarely, or we run ourselves aground *Tempest* i 1 3
I should do it With much more ease; for my good will is to it iii 1 30
To it presently! I am impatient of my tarriance *T. G. of Ver.* ii 7 89
Truly, sir, in my poor opinion, they will to't then *Meas. for Meas.* ii 1 246
Lord Angelo dukes it well in his absence; he puts transgression to't iii 2 101
It would unclog my heart Of what lies heavy to't *Coriolanus* iv 2 48
And to't they go like lightning *Rom. and Jul.* iii 1 177
You have my voice to it; the fault's Bloody *T. of Athens* iii 5 1
Thou rather shalt enforce it with thy smile Than hew to't with thy sword v 4 46
We'll e'en to't like French falconers, fly at any thing we see *Hamlet* ii 2 449
Toward Peloponnesus are they fled.—'Tis easy to't *Ant. and Cleo.* iii 10 32
A wonderful sweet air, with admirable rich words to it *Cymbeline* ii 3 20
To my knowledge. I never did her any, to my knowledge *Richard III.* i 3 309
To my thinking. Whose mind, to my thinking, pleased the king 2 *Hen. IV.* v 5 114
To my thinking, he would fain have had it *J. Cæsar* i 2 240
To night. I am not weary, and 'tis long to night *T. Night* iii 3 21
O setting sun, As in thy red rays thou dost sink to night *J. Cæsar* v 3 61
To sea. Set her two courses off to sea again *Tempest* i 1 53
I shall no more to sea, to sea, Here shall I die ashore ii 2 44
To wife. Will you, Orlando, have to wife this Rosalind? *As Y. Like It* iv 1 130
What dowry shall I have with her to wife? *T. of Shrew* ii 1 121
To crave the French king's sister To wife for Edward 3 *Hen. VI.* iii 1 31
But withal A woman that Lord Brutus took to wife *J. Cæsar* ii 1 293
In equal scale weighing delight and dole,—Taken to wife *Hamlet* i 2 14
To you. If she and I be pleased, what's that to you? *T. of Shrew* ii 1 305
Why, what's that to you? *Othello* iii 3 315
My being in Egypt, Cæsar, What was't to you?—No more than my residing here at Rome Might be to you *Ant. and Cleo.* ii 2 36
Toad. All the charms Of Sycorax, toads, beetles, bats, light on you! *Temp.* i 2 340
Which, like the toad, ugly and venomous, Wears yet a precious jewel in his head *As Y. Like It* ii 1 13
How she longed to eat adders' heads and toads carbonadoed *W. Tale* iv 4 268
Heavy-gaited toads lie in their way, Doing annoyance *Richard II.* iii 2 15
To be avoided, As venom toads, or lizards' dreadful stings 3 *Hen. VI.* ii 2 138
Adders, spiders, toads, Or any creeping venom'd thing *Richard III.* i 2 19
Never hung poison on a fouler toad i 2 148
The time will come when thou shalt wish for me To help thee curse that poisonous bunch-back'd toad i 3 246
Help me curse That bottled spider, that foul bunch-back'd toad! iv 4 81
Thou toad, thou toad, where is thy brother Clarence? iv 4 145
I do hate a proud man, as I hate the engendering of toads *Troi. and Cres.* ii 3 170
To be a dog, a mule, a cat, a fitchew, a toad, a lizard v 1 67
Ten thousand swelling toads, as many urchins *T. Andron.* ii 3 101
Here is the babe, as loathsome as a toad Amongst the fairest breeders iv 2 67
She, good soul, had as lief see a toad, a very toad, as see him *R. and J.* ii 4 215
Some say the lark and loathed toad change eyes iii 5 31
Engenders the black toad and adder blue *T. of Athens* iv 3 181
Slave!—Toad!—Rogue, rogue, rogue! I am sick of this false world iv 3 375
Toad, that under cold stone Days and nights has thirty-one Swelter'd venom sleeping got *Macbeth* iv 1 6
Poor Tom; that eats the swimming frog, the toad, the tadpole, the wall-newt, and the water *Lear* iii 4 135
I had rather be a toad, And live upon the vapour of a dungeon *Othello* iii 3 270
Keep it as a cistern for foul toads To knot and gender in! iv 2 61
Were it [thy name] Toad, or Adder, Spider, 'Twould move me sooner *Cymbeline* iv 2 90
Toad-spotted. A most toad-spotted traitor *Lear* v 3 138
Toadstool, learn me the proclamation *Troi. and Cres.* ii 1 22
Toast. Go fetch me a quart of sack; put a toast in't *Mer. Wives* iii 5 3
You are both, i' good truth, as rheumatic as two dry toasts 2 *Hen. IV.* ii 4 63
It will toast cheese, and it will endure cold as another man's sword *Hen. V.* ii 1 9
Either to harbour fled, Or made a toast for Neptune *Troi. and Cres.* i 3 45
Toasts-and-butter. None but such toasts-and-butter, with hearts in their bellies no bigger than pins' heads 1 *Hen. IV.* iv 2 22
Toasted. 'Tis time I were choked with a piece of toasted cheese *M. Wives* v 5 147
His breath stinks with eating toasted cheese 2 *Hen. VI.* iv 7 13
This piece of toasted cheese will do't *Lear* iv 6 90
Toasting-iron. I'll so maul you and your toasting-iron *K. John* iv 3 99
Toaze. Thinkest thou, for that I insinuate, or toaze from thee thy business, I am therefore no courtier? *W. Tale* iv 4 760
Toby. Sir Toby, you must come in earlier o' nights *T. Night* i 3 4
If Sir Toby would leave drinking, thou wert as witty a piece i 5 29
Sir Toby will be sworn that I am no fox i 5 85
Sweet Sir Toby, be patient for to-night ii 3 142
Toby approaches; courtesies there to me,— Shall this fellow live? ii 5 67
And does not Toby take you a blow o' the lips then? ii 5 75
I will read politic authors, I will baffle Sir Toby ii 5 176
No worse man than Sir Toby to look to me! iii 4 72
Hold, Toby; on thy life I charge thee, hold! iv 1 49
For the love of God, a surgeon! Send one presently to Sir Toby v 1 176
He has broke my head across and has given Sir Toby a bloody coxcomb too v 1 179
I was set on to do't by Sir Toby v 1 189
To put on yellow stockings and to frown Upon Sir Toby v 1 347
I confess, myself and Toby Set this device v 1 367
Maria writ The letter at Sir Toby's great importance v 1 371
Tod. Every 'leven wether tods; every tod yields pound and odd shilling *W. Tale* iv 3 33
To-day. Was there ever man a coward that hath drunk so much sack as I to-day? *Tempest* iii 2 31
What halloing and what stir is this to-day? *T. G. of Ver.* v 4 13
Well, I shall see her to-day *Mer. Wives* i 4 166
How now, Sir Hugh! no school to-day? iv 1 10
Hath any body inquired for me here to-day? *Meas. for Meas.* iv 1 17
I swear I will not die to-day for any man's persuasion iv 3 62
Come to my ward; for thence will not I to-day iv 3 67
We that know what 'tis to fast and pray Are penitent for your default to-day.—Stop in your wind, sir *Com. of Errors* i 2 52
Husband, I'll dine above with you to-day ii 2 209
I have not dined to-day.—Nor to-day here you must not iii 1 40
If thou hadst been Dromio to-day in my place, Thou wouldst have changed thy face for a name iii 1 46
Is that the chain you promised me to-day? iv 3 47
A mad tale he told to-day at dinner iv 3 89
My wife is in a wayward mood to-day iv 4 4
Wherefore didst thou lock me forth to-day? iv 4 98
Your husband all in rage to-day Came to my house iv 4 140
But for staying on our controversy, Had hoisted sail and put to sea to-day v 1 21
Myself, he, and my sister To-day did dine together v 1 208
Which of you two did dine with me to-day? v 1 369
That kitchen'd me for you to-day at dinner v 1 415
What was it you told me of to-day? *Much Ado* ii 3 93
A Dutchman to-day, a Frenchman to-morrow iii 2 33
Are you yet determined To-day to marry? v 4 37
To-day we shall have our dispatch *L. L. Lost* iv 1 5
I do dine to-day at the father's of a certain pupil of mine iv 2 159
I'll find a fairer face not wash'd to-day iv 3 273
That you to-day promised to tell me of *Mer. of Venice* i 1 121
Haste away, For we must measure twenty miles to-day iii 4 84
I may dismiss this court, Unless Bellario, a learned doctor, Whom I have sent for to determine this, Come here to-day iv 1 107
To-day my Lord of Amiens and myself Did steal behind him *As Y. Like It* ii 1 29
And twice to-day pick'd out the dullest scent *T. of Shrew* Ind. 1 24
What raiment will your honour wear to-day? Ind. 2 4
I know you think to dine with me to-day iii 2 187
I must away to-day, before night come iii 2 192

To-day. I will not go to-day; No, nor to-morrow, not till I please myself *T. of Shrew* iii 2 210
She eat no meat to-day, nor none shall eat . . . iv 1 200
I will not go to-day; and ere I do, It shall be what o'clock I say it is . iv 3 196
He had the wit which I can well observe To-day in our young lords *All's Well* i 2 33
I saw the man to-day, if man he be.—Find him, and bring him hither . v 3 203
Since the youth of the count's was to-day with my lady *T. Night* ii 3 143
When came he to this town?—To-day, my lord . . . . . v 1 97
A letter to you; I should have given't you to-day morning . . . v 1 294
Two lads that thought there was no more behind But such a day to-morrow as to-day, And to be boy eternal . . . . *W. Tale* i 2 64
Who but to-day hammer'd of this design . . . . . . ii 2 49
Are you sick, Hubert? you look pale to-day . . . . *K. John* iv 1 28
Once more to-day well met, distemper'd lords! . . . . iv 3 21
Farewell, my blood; which if to-day thou shed, Lament we may *Rich. II.* i 3 57
Let not to-morrow then ensue to-day . . . . . . ii 1 197
To-day, as I came by, I called there . . . . . . ii 2 94
To-day, to-day, unhappy day, too late, O'erthrows thy joys, friends, fortune, and thy state . . . . iii 2 71
To-day will I set forth, to-morrow you . . . . . *1 Hen. IV.* ii 3 119
'O my sweet Harry,' says she, 'how many hast thou killed to-day?' . ii 4 119
I am a rogue, if I drunk to-day . . . . ii 4 169
The Earl of Westmoreland set forth to-day; With him my son . iii 2 170
Your uncle Worcester's horse came but to-day . . . . iv 3 21
That no man might draw short breath to-day But I and Harry Monmouth! v 2 49
The Lord of Stafford dear to-day hath bought Thy likeness . . . v 3 7
Death hath not struck so fat a deer to-day, Though many dearer . v 4 107
If thou embowel me to-day, I'll give you leave to powder me and eat me too to-morrow . . . . v 4 112
Three knights upon our party slain to-day . . . . . v 5 6
His valour shown upon our crests to-day Hath taught us . . v 5 29
To-day might I, hanging on Hotspur's neck, Have talk'd of Monmouth's grave . . . . *2 Hen. IV.* ii 3 44
God, and not we, hath safely fought to-day . . . . . iv 2 121
He is not there to-day; he dines in London . . . . . iv 4 51
Your highness bade me ask for it to-day . . . . *Hen. V.* ii 2 63
Not to-day, O Lord, O, not to-day, think not upon the fault My father made! . . . . iv 1 310
That our French gallants shall to-day draw out . . . . iv 2 22
Farewell, kind lord; fight valiantly to-day . . . . . iv 3 12
O that we now had here But one ten thousand of those men in England That do no work to-day! . . . . iv 3 18
For he to-day that sheds his blood with me Shall be my brother . . iv 3 61
Why wear you your leek to-day? . . . . v 1 2
I will make you to-day a squire of low degree . . . . v 1 37
This brawl to-day, Grown to this faction in the Temple-garden *1 Hen. VI.* ii 4 124
If I to-day die not with Frenchmen's rage, To-morrow I shall die with mickle age . . . . iv 6 34
Had death been French, then death had died to-day . . . . iv 7 28
Duke Humphrey has done a miracle to-day . . . . *2 Hen. VI.* ii 1 161
We intend to try his grace to-day, If he be guilty, as 'tis published . iii 2 16
I am resolved to bear a greater storm Than any thou canst conjure up to-day . . . . v 1 199
As I intend, Clifford, to thrive to-day, It grieves my soul to leave thee v 2 17
Three times to-day I holp him to his horse . . . . . v 3 8
Now, by my sword, well hast thou fought to-day . . . . v 3 15
Three times to-day You have defended me from imminent death . . v 3 18
A thousand men have broke their fasts to-day, That ne'er shall dine unless thou yield the crown . . . . . *3 Hen. VI.* ii 2 127
Saw you the king to-day, my Lord of Derby? . . . *Richard III.* i 3 30
Why looks your grace so heavily to-day? . . . . . . i 4 1
Who slew to-day a riotous gentleman . . . . . . ii 1 100
To-day the lords you talk of are beheaded . . . . . iii 2 93
To-day shalt thou behold a subject die For truth . . . . iii 3 3
What of his heart perceive you in his face By any likelihood he show'd to-day? . . . . iii 4 57
Three times to-day my foot-cloth horse did stumble . . . . iii 4 86
I am not in the giving vein to-day . . . . iv 2 119
Who saw the sun to-day?—Not I, my lord . . . . . v 3 277
The sun will not be seen to-day; The sky doth frown . . . v 3 282
Not shine to-day! Why, what is that to me More than to Richmond? . v 3 285
I think there be six Richmonds in the field; Five have I slain to-day . v 4 12
To-day the French, All clinquant, all in gold, like heathen gods *Hen. VIII.* i 1 18
To-day he puts forth The tender leaves of hopes . . . . iii 2 352
What news, Æneas, from the field to-day? . . . *Troi. and Cres.* i 1 111
What good sport is out of town to-day! . . . . . . i 1 116
Hector, whose patience Is, as a virtue, fix'd, to-day was moved . . i 2 5
He'll lay about him to-day, I can tell them that . . . . i 2 58
Who said he came hurt home to-day? he's not hurt . . . . i 2 233
I think he went not forth to-day . . . . i 2 239
I take to-day a wife, and my election Is led on in the conduct of my will ii 2 61
Sweet lord, who's a-field to-day? . . . . iii 1 147
I would fain have armed to-day, but my Nell would not have it so . iii 1 150
I long to hear how they sped to-day . . . . . . iii 1 155
Unarm, unarm, and do not fight to-day . . . . . . v 3 3
How now, young man! mean'st thou to fight to-day? . . . . v 3 29
I am to-day i' the vein of chivalry . . . . . . v 3 32
I'll stand to-day for thee and me and Troy . . . . . v 3 36
Troilus, I would not have you fight to-day . . . . . v 3 50
Now is the cur Ajax prouder than the cur Achilles, and will not arm to-day . . . . v 4 17
Who hath done to-day Mad and fantastic execution . . . . v 5 37
I reck not though I end my life to-day . . . . . . v 6 26
When goes this forward?—To-morrow; to-day; presently *Coriolanus* iv 5 229
You have pray'd well to-day . . . . v 4 58
Be chosen with proclamations to-day, To-morrow yield up rule *T. Andron.* i 1 190
His Philomel must lose her tongue to-day . . . . . . ii 3 43
Jove shield your husband from his hounds to-day! . . . . ii 3 70
O, where is Romeo? saw you him to-day? . . . *Rom. and Jul.* i 1 123
Have you got leave to go to shrift to-day?—I have . . . . ii 5 68
I hunted with his honour to-day . . . . . *T. of Athens* ii 2 198
But wherefore art not in thy shop to-day? . . . . *J. Cæsar* i 1 31
He will, after his sour fashion, tell you What hath proceeded worthy note to-day . . . . i 2 181
Tell us what hath chanced to-day, That Cæsar looks so sad . . . i 2 216
It is doubtful yet, Whether Cæsar will come forth to-day, or no . ii 1 194
The persuasion of his augurers May hold him from the Capitol to-day . ii 1 201
You shall not stir out of your house to-day . . . . . . ii 2 9

To-day. What say the augurers?—They would not have you to stir forth to-day . . . . *J. Cæsar* ii 2 38
Cæsar should be a beast without a heart, If he should stay at home to-day for fear . . . . ii 2 43
Do not go forth to-day: call it my fear That keeps you in the house . ii 2 50
We'll send Mark Antony to the senate-house; And he shall say you are not well to-day . . . . ii 2 53
Tell them that I will not come to-day . . . . . . ii 2 62
I will not come to-day: tell them so, Decius . . . . . ii 2 64
And on her knee Hath begg'd that I will stay at home to-day . . ii 2 82
Remember that you call on me to-day . . . . . . ii 2 122
I wish your enterprise to-day may thrive . . . . . . iii 1 13
This tongue had not offended so to-day, If Cassius might have ruled . v 1 46
If you dare fight to-day, come to the field . . . . . v 1 65
Most noble Brutus, The gods to-day stand friendly! . . . . v 1 94
Goes the king hence to-day?—He does . . . . *Macbeth* ii 3 58
Who still hath cried, From the first corse till he that died to-day *Hamlet* i 2 105
In grace whereof, No jocund health that Denmark drinks to-day, But the great cannon to the clouds shall tell . . . . . . i 2 125
You have shown to-day your valiant strain . . . . *Lear* v 3 40
Such a handkerchief—I am sure it was your wife's—did I to-day See Cassio wipe his beard with . . . . *Othello* iii 3 438
Were I the wearer of Antonius' beard, I would not shave't to-day *Ant. and Cleo.* ii 2 8
If fortune be not ours to-day, it is Because we brave her . . . iv 4 4
O love, That thou couldst see my wars to-day! . . . . iv 4 16
Before the sun shall see's, we'll spill the blood That has to-day escaped iv 8 4
He hath fought to-day As if a god, in hate of mankind, had Destroy'd in such a shape . . . . iv 8 24
Their preparation is to-day by sea . . . . iv 10 1
Please your highness, I will from hence to-day . . . *Cymbeline* i 1 80
What I have lost to-day at bowls I'll win to-night of him . . ii 1 54
We'll hunt no more to-day, nor seek for danger Where there's no profit iv 2 162
To-day how many would have given their honours To have saved their carcases! . . . . v 3 66

Toe. Each one, tripping on his toe, Will be here with mop and mow *Tempest* iv 1 46
If he awake, From toe to crown he'll fill our skins with pinches . iv 1 233
Turn'd on the toe, and down he fell . . . . *L. L. Lost* v 2 114
Such shoes as my toes look through the over-leather . *T. of Shrew* Ind. 2 12
Till his brains turn o' the toe like a parish-top . . . *T. Night* i 3 44
Plays the rogue with my great toe . . . . . *2 Hen. IV.* i 2 274
He is all the mother's, from the top to toe . . . *Richard III.* iii 1 156
Was mouldy ere your grandsires had nails on their toes . *Troi. and Cres.* ii 1 116
He rises on the toe: that spirit of his In aspiration lifts him from the earth . . . . iv 5 15
What do you think, You, the great toe of this assembly? . *Coriolanus* i 1 160
Ladies that have their toes Unplagued with corns . . *Rom. and Jul.* i 5 18
Fill me from the crown to the toe top-full Of direst cruelty! . *Macbeth* i 5 43
Eye of newt and toe of frog, Wool of bat and tongue of dog . . iv 1 14
Arm'd, my lord.—From top to toe?—My lord, from head to foot *Hamlet* i 2 228
The toe of the peasant comes so near the heel of the courtier, he galls his kibe . . . . v 1 152
The man that makes his toe What he his heart should make Shall of a corn cry woe . . . . *Lear* iii 2 31

Tofore. It is an epilogue or discourse, to make plain Some obscure precedence that hath tofore been sain . . . . . *L. L. Lost* iii 1 83
My noble sister; O, would thou wert as thou tofore hast been! *T. Andron.* iii 1 294

Toge. Why in this woolvish toge should I stand here, To beg? *Coriolanus* ii 3 122

Toged. Unless the bookish theoric, Wherein the toged consuls can propose As masterly as he . . . . *Othello* i 1 25

Together. I'll manacle thy neck and feet together . . . *Tempest* i 2 461
They fell together all, as by consent . . . . . . ii 1 203
Draw together; And when I rear my hand, do you the like . . ii 1 294
Confined together In the same fashion as you gave in charge . . v 1 7
Is she the goddess that hath sever'd us, And brought us thus together? v 1 188
Now you have taken the pains to set it together, take it . *T. G. of Ver.* i 1 124
We have conversed and spent our hours together . . . . ii 4 63
They do no more adhere and keep place together than the Hundredth Psalm to the tune of 'Green Sleeves' . . . . *Mer. Wives* ii 1 63
Let's consult together against this greasy knight . . . . ii 1 111
I would be loath to turn them together . . . . . . ii 1 193
As idle as she may hang together, for want of company . . . iii 2 13
Our revolted wives share damnation together . . . . . iii 2 40
We'll a-birding together; I have a fine hawk . . . . . iii 3 247
Good hearts, what ado here is to bring you together! . . . iv 5 129
We two must go together . . . . v 3 5
'Tis so with me. Let us withdraw together . . . *Meas. for Meas.* i 1 82
If you head and hang all that offend that way but for ten year together ii 1 252
You say, seven years together?—And a half, sir . . . . ii 1 277
To bring you thus together, 'tis no sin . . . . . . iv 1 73
We'll pluck a crow together . . . . . *Com. of Errors* iii 1 83
You thought our love would last too long, If it were chain'd together . iv 1 26
Myself, he, and my sister To-day did dine together . . . . v 1 208
Then all together They fell upon me . . . . v 1 245
These are the parents to these children, Which accidentally are met together . . . . v 1 361
Thus did she, an hour together, trans-shape thy particular virtues *M. Ado* v 1 172
The treason and you go in peace away together . . . *L. L. Lost* iv 3 192
Reason and love keep little company together now-a-days *M. N. Dream* iii 1 147
Were met together to rehearse a play . . . . . . iii 2 11
So we grew together, Like to a double cherry, seeming parted . . iii 2 208
I wonder of their being here together . . . . . . iv 1 136
Get your apparel together, good strings to your beards . . . iv 2 36
And they have conspired together . . . . . *Mer. of Venice* ii 5 22
Where every something, being blent together, Turns to a wild of nothing iii 2 183
Companions That do converse and waste the time together . . . iii 4 12
We turned o'er many books together . . . . iv 1 157
I'll rhyme you so eight years together . . . . *As Y. Like It* iii 2 101
This fellow will but join you together as they join wainscot . . iii 3 88
Sweet youth, I pray you, chide a year together . . . . iii 5 64
They are in the very wrath of love and they will together . . . v 2 44
And where two raging fires meet together They do consume the thing that feeds their fury . . . . *T. of Shrew* ii 1 133
We have 'greed so well together, That upon Sunday is the wedding-day ii 1 299
Remain with me till they meet together . . . . *All's Well* iv 5 92
They have seemed to be together, though absent . . . *W. Tale* i 1 32
As well as one so great and so forlorn May hold together . . . ii 2 23
A thousand knees Ten thousand years together . . . . . iii 2 212

Together. Let nature crush the sides o' the earth together And mar the seeds within! *W. Tale* iv 4 489
Make me to think so twenty years together! v 3 71
He was not so resolved when last we spake together *Richard II.* ii 3 29
He spake it twice, And urged it twice together v 4 5
If I were not at half-sword with a dozen of them two hours together 1 *Hen. IV.* ii 4 183
When means and lavish manners meet together 2 *Hen. IV.* iv 4 64
All those legs and arms and heads, chopped off in a battle, shall join together at the latter day *Hen. V.* iv 1 143
Join we together, for the public good, In what we can 2 *Hen. VI.* i 1 199
I have seen him whipped three market-days together iv 2 62
Should notwithstanding join our lights together 3 *Hen. VI.* ii 1 37
God forbid that I should wish them sever'd Whom God hath join'd together iv 1 22
But lately splinter'd, knit, and join'd together *Richard III.* ii 2 118
I looked upon him o' Wednesday half an hour together *Coriolanus* i 3 64
What, do we meet together? *T. of Athens* iii 4 3
Put on manly readiness, And meet i' the hall together *Macbeth* ii 3 140
Two nights together had these gentlemen . . . Been thus encounter'd *Hamlet* i 2 196
Sometimes he walks four hours together ii 2 160
Spake you with him?—Ay, two hours together *Lear* i 2 170
They met so near with their lips that their breaths embraced together *Othello* ii 1 266
I found them close together, At blow and thrust ii 3 237
I cannot hope Cæsar and Antony shall well greet together *Ant. and Cleo.* ii 1 39
Would we had spoke together! ii 2 167
Wisdom and fortune combating together iii 13 79
The king Hath charged you should not speak together *Cymbeline* i 1 83
Her beauty and her brain go not together i 2 32
Sir, we have known together in Orleans i 4 36
And for two nights together Have made the ground my bed iii 6 2
Grief and patience, rooted in him both, Mingle their spurs together iv 2 58
The four opposing coigns Which the world together joins *Pericles* iii Gower 18
When my maiden priests are met together, Before the people all v 1 243

Toil. Is there more toil? *Tempest* i 2 242
Whose spirits toil in frame of villanies *Much Ado* iv 1 191
They have pitched a toil; I am toiling in a pitch *L. L. Lost* iv 3 2
Finding barren practisers, Scarce show a harvest of their heavy toil iv 3 326
Unapt to toil and trouble in the world *T. of Shrew* v 2 166
This toil of ours should be a work of thine *K. John* ii 1 93
After such bloody toil, we bid good night v 5 6
When I was dry with rage and extreme toil 1 *Hen. IV.* i 3 31
Indigent faint souls past corporal toil *Hen. V.* i 1 16
So service shall with steeled sinews toil ii 2 36
Winding up days with toil and nights with sleep iv 1 296
Your faithful service and your toil in war 1 *Hen. VI.* iii 4 21
And did my brother Bedford toil his wits, To keep by policy what Henry got? 2 *Hen. VI.* i 1 83
Forspent with toil, as runners with a race, I lay me down 3 *Hen. VI.* ii 3 1
Princes have but their titles for their glories, An outward honour for an inward toil *Richard III.* i 4 79
The madams too, Not used to toil, did almost sweat to bear The pride upon them *Hen. VIII.* i 1 24
And know by measure Of their observant toil the enemies' weight *Troi. and Cres.* i 3 203
The which if you with patient ears attend, What here shall miss, our toil shall strive to mend *Rom. and Jul.* Prol. 14
I am the drudge and toil in your delight ii 5 77
Stop thy unhallow'd toil, vile Montague! v 3 54
Unicorns may be betray'd with trees, And bears with glasses, elephants with holes, Lions with toils *J. Cæsar* ii 1 206
Double, double toil and trouble; Fire burn and cauldron bubble *Macbeth* iv 1 20
Why this same strict and most observant watch So nightly toils *Hamlet* i 1 72
You go about to recover the wind of me, as if you would drive me into a toil iii 2 362
But she looks like sleep, As she would catch another Antony In her strong toil of grace *Ant. and Cleo.* v 2 351
The toil o' the war, A pain that only seems to seek out danger I' the name of fame and honour *Cymbeline* iii 3 49
I am weak with toil, yet strong in appetite iii 6 37
The shipman's toil, With whom each minute threatens life or death *Per.* i 3 24

Toiled. Have toil'd their unbreathed memories *M. N. Dream* v 1 74
And toil'd with works of war, retired himself To Italy *Richard II.* iv 1 96
Who like a brother toil'd in my affairs 2 *Hen. IV.* iii 1 62

Toiling. They have pitched a toil; I am toiling in a pitch *L. L. Lost* iv 3 3
Straying from the way; Not knowing how to find the open air, But toiling desperately to find it out 3 *Hen. VI.* iii 2 178

Token. Give her no token but stones; for she's as hard as steel *T. G. of V.* i 1 148
It seems you loved not her, to leave her token iv 4 79
On that token, The maid hath given consent to go with him *Mer. Wives* iv 6 44
Are there no other tokens Between you 'greed? *Meas. for Meas.* iv 1 41
Say, by this token, I desire his company iv 3 144
Either send the chain or send me by some token *Com. of Errors* iv 1 56
You are not free, For the Lord's tokens on you do I see.—No, they are free that gave these tokens to us *L. L. Lost* v 2 424
Expound the meaning or moral of his signs and tokens *T. of Shrew* iv 4 80
In token of which duty, if he please, My hand is ready v 2 178
I follow him not By any token of presumptuous suit *All's Well* i 3 204
Their promises, enticements, oaths, tokens, and all these engines of lust iii 5 20
I sent to her . . . Tokens and letters which she did re-send iii 6 123
That what in time proceeds May token to the future our past deeds iv 2 63
Send forth your amorous token for fair Maudlin v 3 68
I bade her, if her fortunes ever stood Necessitied to help, that by this token I would relieve her v 3 85
Do you not read some tokens of my son In the large composition? *K. John* i 1 87
Embrace, That all their eyes may bear those tokens home 2 *Hen. IV.* iv 2 64
This token serveth for a flag of truce 1 *Hen. VI.* iii 1 138
I must trouble you again; No loving token to his majesty? v 3 181
I will not so presume To send such peevish tokens to a king v 3 186
Go, by this token: rise, and lend thine ear *Richard III.* iv 2 80
Ay, a token from Troilus.—By the same token, you are a bawd *Troi. and Cres.* i 2 306
Here is a letter from Queen Hecuba, A token from her daughter v 1 45
Give me some token for the surety of it v 2 60
In token of the which, My noble steed, known to the camp, I give him *Coriolanus* i 9 60
See, how with signs and tokens she can scrowl *T. Andron.* ii 4 5
Throw thy glove, Or any token of thine honour else *T. of Athens* v 4 50

Token. It is the part of men to fear and tremble, When the most mighty gods by tokens send Such dreadful heralds *J. Cæsar* i 3 55
Admit no messengers, receive no tokens *Hamlet* ii 2 144
Send Thy token of reprieve.—Well thought on: take my sword *Lear* v 3 249
But she so loves the token, For he conjured her she should ever keep it *Othello* iii 3 293
O Cassio, whence came this? This is some token from a newer friend iii 4 181
This is some minx's token, and I must take out the work? iv 1 159
I never gave him token.—By heaven, I saw my handkerchief in 's hand v 2 61
It was a handkerchief, an antique token My father gave my mother v 2 216
Some nobler token I have kept apart For Livia and Octavia *A. and C.* v 2 168
Wounding his belief in her renown With tokens thus, and thus *Cymb.* v 5 203

Tokened. How appears the fight?—On our side like the token'd pestilence, Where death is sure *Ant. and Cleo.* iii 10 9

Told thee no lies, made thee no mistakings *Tempest* i 2 248
As I told thee before, I am subject to a tyrant, a sorcerer iii 2 48
Why, as I told thee, 'tis a custom with him iii 2 95
Methought the billows spoke and told me of it; The winds did sing it iii 3 96
I thought to have told thee of it, but I fear'd Lest I might anger thee iv 1 168
I told you, sir, they were red-hot with drinking iv 1 171
This is the gentleman I told your ladyship Had come *T. G. of Ver.* ii 4 87
I'll tell you what Launce, his man, told me: he loved her out of all nick iv 2 75
You heard what this knave told me, did you not?—Yes: and you heard what the other told me? *Mer. Wives* ii 1 174
I could have told you more ii 1 232
When I have told you that, I have told you all ii 2 229
I ha' told them over and over; they lack no direction iii 3 18
I told you, sir, my daughter is disposed of iii 4 74
Went you not to her yesterday, sir, as you told me you had appointed? v 1 15
Now, sir, what news?—I told you *Meas. for Meas.* iv 2 118
I can tell thee pretty tales of the duke.—You have told me too many of him already iv 3 176
This gentleman told somewhat of my tale v 1 84
There was a friar told me of this man v 1 484
He told his mind upon mine ear: Beshrew his hand *Com. of Errors* ii 1 48
Swore I was assured to her; told me what privy marks I had about me iii 2 146
I sent thee for a rope And told thee to what purpose and what end iv 1 97
A mad tale he told to-day at dinner, Of his own doors being shut iv 3 89
What I told you then, I hope I shall have leisure to make good v 1 374
Hath the fellow any wit that told you this? *Much Ado* i 2 17
Daughter, remember what I told you ii 1 69
I told him, and I think I told him true ii 1 223
The gentleman that danced with her told her she is much wronged by you ii 1 244
She told me, not thinking I had been myself, that I was the prince's jester ii 1 249
Show me briefly how.—I think I told your lordship a year since ii 2 12
The old man's daughter told us all v 1 179
I was told you were in a consumption v 4 96
How many is one thrice told?—I am ill at reckoning *L. L. Lost* i 2 41
Who gave thee this letter?—I told you; my lord iv 1 103
If they have measured many, The measure then of one is easily told v 2 190
Some carry-tale, some please-man, . . . Told our intents before v 2 467
The king your father— Dead, for my life!—Even so; my tale is told v 2 729
I told him of your stealth unto this wood. He follow'd you *M. N. D.* iii 2 310
Fair Helen told me of their stealth, Of this their purpose iv 1 165
All the story of the night told over, And all their minds transfigured v 1 23
That have I told my love, In glory of my kinsman Hercules v 1 46
You shall see, it will fall pat as I told you v 1 188
The iron tongue of midnight hath told twelve: Lovers, to bed v 1 370
To yield myself His wife who wins me by that means I told you *M. of V.* ii 1 19
All that glisters is not gold; Often have you heard that told ii 7 66
I reason'd with a Frenchman yesterday, Who told me ii 8 28
I thought upon Antonio when he told me ii 8 31
I freely told you, all the wealth I had Ran in my veins, I was a gentleman; And then I told you true iii 2 257
When I told you My state was nothing, I should then have told you That I was worse than nothing iii 2 261
Speak me fair in death: And, when the tale is told, bid her be judge iv 1 276
I would have told you of good wrestling *As Y. Like It* i 2 116
Thou art a gallant youth: I would thou hadst told me of another father i 2 243
You told me you salute not at the court, but you kiss your hands iii 2 49
He asked me of what parentage I was; I told him, of as good as he iii 4 40
My friends told me as much, and I thought no less iv 1 187
Have you told him all her faults? *T. of Shrew* i 2 187
'Twas told me you were rough and coy and sullen ii 1 245
I told you, I, he was a frantic fool, Hiding his bitter jests iii 2 12
Nay, I told you your son was well beloved v 1 26
The pilot's glass Hath told the thievish minutes how they pass *All's Well* ii 1 169
I have told my neighbour how you have been solicited iii 5 15
They told me that your name was Fontibell iv 2 1
My mother told me just how he would woo, As if she sat in 's heart iv 2 69
I have told your lordship already, the stocks carry him iv 3 121
And say a soldier, Dian, told thee this, Men are to mell with iv 3 256
She told me, In a sweet verbal brief v 3 136
I told him you were sick; he takes on him to understand so much *T. N.* i 5 148
I told him you were asleep; he seems to have a foreknowledge of that i 5 150
She never told her love, But let concealment, like a worm i' the bud, Feed on her damask cheek ii 4 113
Maria once told me she did affect me ii 5 28
Since when, my watch hath told me, toward my grave I have travell'd but two hours v 1 165
And now I do bethink me, it was she First told me thou wast mad v 1 357
Entreat him to a peace: He hath not told us of the captain yet v 1 390
I told her so, my lord, On your displeasure's peril *W. Tale* ii 3 44
It was told me I should be rich by the fairies iii 3 121
Have I not told thee how I was cozened by the way and lost all my money? iv 4 254
Will't please you, sir, be gone? I told you what would come of this iv 4 458
How often have I told you 'twould be thus! iv 4 485
Told him I heard them talk of a fardel and I know not what v 2 125
Were it but told you, should be hooted at Like an old tale v 3 116
An if an angel should have come to me And told me Hubert should put out mine eyes, I would not have believed him *K. John* iv 1 69
This act is as an ancient tale new told, And in the last repeating troublesome iv 2 18
For when you should be told they do prepare, The tidings comes that they are all arrived iv 2 114
Told of a many thousand warlike French That were embattailed iv 2 199
That villain Hubert told me he did live.—So, on my soul, he did v 1 42
Bid his ears a little while be deaf, Till I have told this slander *Richard II.* i 1 113
My lord, you told me you would tell the rest v 2 1

Told. I saw the prince, And told him of those triumphs held at Oxford *Richard II.* v 3 14
For now the devil, that told me I did well, Says that this deed is chronicled in hell . . . v 5 116
As by discharge of their artillery . . . the news was told . 1 *Hen. IV.* i 1 58
It holds current that I told you yesternight . . . ii 1 59
What, four? thou saidst but two even now.—Four, Hal; I told thee four . . . ii 4 220
So I told him, my lord; and I said I heard your grace say so . . iii 3 120
A mad fellow met me on the way and told me I had unloaded all the gibbets and pressed the dead bodies . . . iv 2 39
I told him gently of our grievances, Of his oath-breaking . . v 2 37
He told me that rebellion had bad luck . . . 2 *Hen. IV.* i 1 41
And would have told him half his Troy was burnt . . . i 1 73
Whereby I told thee they were ill for a green wound . . ii 1 105
And told him there were five more Sir Johns . . . ii 4 6
I saw it, and told John a Gaunt he beat his own name . . iii 2 348
I was told that by one that knows him better than you . *Hen. V.* iii 7 113
He hath not told his thought to the king?—No; nor it is not meet . iv 1 102
Especially for those occasions At Eltham Place I told your majesty 1 *Hen. VI.* iii 1 156
Hadst thou been his mother, thou couldst have better told . 2 *Hen. VI.* ii 1 81
Had I first been put to speak my mind, I think I should have told . iii 1 44
A cunning man did calculate my birth And told me that by water I should die . . . iv 1 35
And at each word's deliverance Stab poniards in our flesh till all were told, The words would add more anguish than the wounds 3 *Hen. VI.* ii 1 98
How haps it, in this smooth discourse, You told not? . . . iii 3 89
Dare he presume to scorn us in this manner?—I told your majesty as much . . . iii 3 179
A wizard told him that by G His issue disinherited should be *Richard III.* i 1 56
Like a child, Told the sad story of my father's death . . i 2 161
Who told me how the poor soul did forsake The mighty Warwick? . ii 1 109
Who told me, in the field by Tewksbury, . . . he rescued me? . . ii 1 111
Pretty York, who told thee this?—Grandam, his nurse . . . ii 4 31
If 'twere not she, I cannot tell who told me . . . ii 4 34
My grandam told me he was murder'd there . . . iii 1 145
I now repent I told the pursuivant, As 'twere triumphing . . iii 4 90
How chance the prophet could not at that time Have told me? . iv 2 104
A bard of Ireland told me once, I should not live long after I saw Richmond . . . iv 2 109
An honest tale speeds best being plainly told . . . iv 4 358
Your highness told me I should post before.—My mind is changed . iv 4 455
Colder tidings, yet they must be told . . . iv 4 536
I told my lord the duke, . . . The monk might be deceived . *Hen. VIII.* i 2 178
I told your grace they would talk anon . . . i 4 49
I have told him What and how true thou art: he will advance thee . iii 2 415
I told ye all, When we first put this dangerous stone a-rolling, 'Twould fall upon ourselves . . . v 3 103
I have told you enough of this: for my part, I'll not meddle *Tr. and Cr.* i 1 13
Well, cousin, I told you a thing yesterday; think on't . . . i 2 185
This shall be told our lovers . . . i 3 284
I have told you how Diomed, a whole week by days, Did haunt you . iv 1 9
'Tis true that you have lately told us; The Volsces are in arms *Coriol.* i 1 231
Where is that slave Which told me they had beat you to your trenches? i 6 40
Could you not have told him As you were lesson'd? . . . ii 3 184
You have told them home; And, by my troth, you have cause . . iv 2 48
If you had told as many lies in his behalf as you have uttered words . v 2 24
They told me, here, at dead time of the night . . *T. Andron.* ii 3 99
No sooner had they told this hellish tale, But straight they told me they would bind me here . . . ii 3 105
She laugh'd, and told the Moor he should not choose But give them . iv 3 74
And when I told the empress of this sport, She swooned almost . . v 1 118
Many a matter hath he told to thee, Meet and agreeing with thine infancy . . . v 3 164
Things that, to hear them told, have made me tremble . *Rom. and Jul.* iv 1 86
I think He told me Paris should have married Juliet . . v 3 78
I have told more of you to myself than you can with modesty speak in your own behalf; and thus far I confirm you . . *T. of Athens* i 2 96
I have told my lord of you; he is coming down to you . . . iii 1 1
Many a time and often I ha' dined with him, and told him on't . . iii 1 25
I ha' told him on't, but I could ne'er get him from't . . iii 1 30
While they have told their money and let out Their coin upon large interest . . . iii 5 107
Thou wast told thus; Thou gavest thine ears like tapsters . . iv 3 214
Two truths are told, As happy prologues to the swelling act . *Macbeth* i 3 127
It is a tale Told by an idiot, full of sound and fury . . . v 5 27
What's the news with you? You told us of some suit . . *Hamlet* i 2 43
'Tis told me, he hath very oft of late Given private time to you . i 3 91
I perceived it, I must tell you that, Before my daughter told me . ii 2 134
Certain players We o'er-raught on the way: of these we told him . iii 1 17
One scene of it comes near the circumstance Which I have told thee . iii 2 82
I have told you what I have seen and heard; but faintly, nothing like the image and horror of it . . . *Lear* i 2 190
I told him, the revenging gods 'Gainst parricides did all their thunders bend . . . ii 1 47
I told him of the army that was landed; He smiled at it . . iv 2 5
I told him you were coming; His answer was 'The worse' . . iv 2 6
He call'd me sot, And told me I had turn'd the wrong side out . . iv 2 9
Told me I had white hairs in my beard ere the black ones were there . iv 6 98
They told me I was every thing; 'tis a lie, I am not ague-proof . iv 6 106
List a brief tale; And when 'tis told, O, that my heart would burst! . v 3 182
I ask'd his blessing, and from first to last Told him my pilgrimage . v 3 196
Told the most piteous tale of Lear and him That ever ear received . v 3 214
I have told thee often, and I re-tell thee again and again . *Othello* i 3 372
From this present hour of five till the bell have told eleven . . ii 2 11
When I told thee he was of my counsel In my whole course of wooing, thou criedst 'Indeed!' . . . iii 3 111
She told her, while she kept it, 'Twould make her amiable . . iii 4 58
The jewels you have had from me to deliver to Desdemona would half have corrupted a votarist: you have told me she hath received them iv 2 190
My husband!—Ay, 'twas he that told me first: An honest man he is . v 2 147
I told him what I thought, and told no more Than what he found himself . . . v 2 176
You told a lie; an odious, damned lie . . . v 2 180
Our ills told us Is as our earing . . . *Ant. and Cleo.* i 2 114
So Fulvia told me. I prithee, turn aside and weep for her . . i 3 75
Next day I told him of myself; which was as much As to have ask'd him pardon . . . ii 2 78
My news I might have told hereafter.—'Twill be naught . . iii 5 23

Told. I have told him, Lepidus was grown too cruel . *Ant. and Cleo.* iii 6 32
As I told you always, her beauty and her brain go not together *Cymbeline* i 2 31
If thou wert honourable, Thou wouldst have told this tale for virtue . i 6 143
Who told you of this stranger?—One of your lordship's pages . . ii 1 43
Revolve what tales I have told you Of courts, of princes, of the tricks in war . . . iii 3 14
My fault being nothing—as I have told you oft . . . iii 3 65
Two beggars told me I could not miss my way: will poor folks lie? . iii 6 8
Whoso ask'd her for his wife, His riddle told not, lost his life *Per.* i Gower 38
Action may Conveniently the rest convey; Which might not what by me is told . . . iii Gower 57
If you have told Diana's altar true, This is your wife . . . v 3 17
As I told you *Mer. Wives* iii 3; *Meas. for Meas.* ii 1; *Mer. of Venice* i 3; *T. of Shrew* iii 1; *Rom. and Jul.* ii 4; *J. Cæsar* i 2
Told me of. What was it you told me of to-day, that your niece Beatrice was in love? . . . *Much Ado* ii 3 92
Indeed, 'tis true that Henry told me of . . . 3 *Hen. VI.* v 6 69
Told me so. Say the woman told me so.—May I be bold to say so? *Mer. Wives* iv 5 53
This is your daughter.—Her mother hath many times told me so *M. Ado* i 1 105
I had forgot; three months; you told me so . . . *Mer. of Venice* i 3 68
He told me so himself; and he said he cared not who knew it *Hen. V.* iii 7 116
And when my uncle told me so, he wept, And hugg'd me *Richard III.* ii 2 23
Told on. There the villain stopp'd; Whilst Dighton thus told on . . iv 3 17
Told on it. He must be told on't, and he shall . . . *W. Tale* ii 2 31
Told so. I have been told so of many . . . *As Y. Like It* iii 2 361
Tell him he shall not speak with me.—Has been told so . . *T. Night* i 5 156
Let him be told so; lest perchance he think We dare not *Troi. and Cres.* ii 3 88
Told the truth. The duke hath told the truth . . 2 *Hen. VI.* ii 1 28
Told thee of. These nine in buckram that I told thee of . . 1 *Hen. IV.* ii 4 236
Told us of. A pretty jest your daughter told us of . . . *Much Ado* ii 3 141
Told you of. Niece, will you look to those things I told you of? . . ii 1 352
This is the gentleman I told you of . . . *T. of Shrew* iv 4 20
You have forgot the will I told you of . . . *J. Cæsar* iii 2 243
Told you so. If you live to see this come to pass, say Pompey told you so . . . *Meas. for Meas.* ii 1 256
Will you not tell me who told you so? . . . *Much Ado* ii 1 130
That eye that told you so look'd but a-squint . . . *Lear* v 3 72
Toldest. And told'st me of a mistress and a dinner . *Com. of Errors* ii 2 18
Thou told'st me they were stolen unto this wood . . *M. N. Dream* ii 1 191
Thou told'st me thou didst hold him in thy hate . . . *Othello* i 1 7
He says thou told'st him that his wife was false: I know thou didst not v 2 173
Thou told'st me, when we came from horse, the place Was near *Cymbeline* iii 4 1
Toledo. The archbishopric of Toledo . . . *Hen. VIII.* ii 1 164
Tolerable. Thou didst make tolerable vent of thy travel . . *All's Well* ii 3 212
To babble and to talk is most tolerable and not to be endured *Much Ado* iii 3 37
Toll. I will buy me a son-in-law in a fair, and toll for this . *All's Well* v 3 149
No Italian priest Shall tithe or toll in our dominions . . *K. John* iii 1 154
The country cocks do crow, the clocks do toll . . *Hen. V.* iv Prol. 15
Tolling. Sounds ever after as a sullen bell, Remember'd tolling a departing friend . . . 2 *Hen. IV.* i 1 103
Tom. And Tom bears logs into the hall . . . *L. L. Lost* v 2 924
Tom Snout, the tinker.—Here, Peter Quince . . . *M. N. Dream* i 2 63
As Tib's rush for Tom's forefinger . . . *All's Well* ii 2 24
Good Tom Drum, lend me a handkercher . . . v 3 322
I prithee, Tom, beat Cut's saddle, put a few flocks in the point 1 *Hen. IV.* ii 1 6
Call them all by their christen names, as Tom, Dick, and Francis . ii 4 9
Here, Tom, take all the money that I have . . 2 *Hen. VI.* ii 3 76
My cue is villanous melancholy, with a sigh like Tom o' Bedlam . *Lear* i 2 148
Poor Turlygod! poor Tom! That's something yet: Edgar I nothing am ii 3 20
Fathom and half, fathom and half! Poor Tom! . . . iii 4 38
A spirit, a spirit: he says his name's poor Tom . . . iii 4 43
Who gives any thing to poor Tom? . . . iii 4 51
Bless thy five wits! Tom's a-cold,—O, do de, do de, do de . . iii 4 59
Do poor Tom some charity, whom the foul fiend vexes . . . iii 4 61
Set not thy sweet heart on proud array. Tom's a-cold . . . iii 4 85
Poor Tom; that eats the swimming frog, the toad, the tadpole . . iii 4 134
Mice and rats, and such small deer, Have been Tom's food for seven long year . . . iii 4 145
Poor Tom's a-cold.—Go in with me . . . iii 4 152
The foul fiend haunts poor Tom in the voice of a nightingale . . iii 6 31
Hopdance cries in Tom's belly for two white herring . . . iii 6 32
Tom will throw his head at them.—Avaunt, you curs! . . . iii 6 67
Or bobtail tike or trundle-tail, Tom will make them weep and wail . iii 6 74
Come, march to wakes and fairs and market-towns. Poor Tom, thy horn is dry . . . iii 6 78
Tom, away! Mark the high noises . . . iii 6 117
'Tis poor mad Tom.—And worse I may be yet . . . iv 1 28
Poor Tom's a-cold. I cannot daub it further . . . iv 1 54
Poor Tom hath been scared out of his good wits . . . iv 1 59
Five fiends have been in poor Tom at once . . . iv 1 62
Give me thy arm: Poor Tom shall lead thee . . . iv 1 82
Tomb. In a tomb where never scandal slept, Save this of hers *Much Ado* v 1 70
Hang her an epitaph upon her tomb And sing it to her bones . . v 1 293
If a man do not erect in this age his own tomb ere he dies . . v 2 80
Hang thou there upon the tomb, Praising her when I am dumb . . v 3 9
With songs of woe, Round about her tomb they go . . . v 3 15
Let fame, that all hunt after in their lives, Live register'd upon our brazen tombs . . . *L. L. Lost* i 1 2
I'll meet thee, Pyramus, at Ninny's tomb . . . *M. N. Dream* iii 1 99
To meet at Ninus' tomb, there, there to woo . . . v 1 139
Wilt thou at Ninny's tomb meet me straightway? . . . v 1 204
This is old Ninny's tomb. Where is my love? . . . v 1 268
A tomb Must cover thy sweet eyes . . . v 1 335
Gilded tombs do worms infold . . . *Mer. of Venice* ii 7 69
His good remembrance, sir, Lies richer in your thoughts than on his tomb . . . *All's Well* i 2 49
The mere word's a slave Debosh'd on every tomb . . . ii 3 145
Where dust and damn'd oblivion is the tomb Of honour'd bones indeed ii 3 147
So went he suited to his watery tomb . . . *T. Night* v 1 241
By the honourable tomb he swears . . . *Richard II.* iii 3 105
Thou King Richard's tomb, And not King Richard . . . v 1 12
In his tomb lie my affections . . . 2 *Hen. IV.* v 2 124
Go, my dread lord, to your great-grandsire's tomb . . *Hen. V.* i 2 103
Within their chiefest temple I'll erect A tomb . . . 1 *Hen. VI.* ii 2 13
Shall all thy mother's hopes lie in one tomb? . . . iv 5 34
Is all thy comfort shut in Gloucester's tomb? . . 2 *Hen. VI.* iii 2 78
Sword, I will hallow thee for this thy deed, And hang thee o'er my tomb . . . iv 10 73
And cried 'A crown, or else a glorious tomb!' . . . 3 *Hen. VI.* i 4 15

Tomb. That his bones, When he has run his course and sleeps in blessings, May have a tomb of orphans' tears wept on 'em! *Hen. VIII.* iii 2 399
And power, unto itself most commendable, Hath not a tomb so evident as a chair To extol what it hath done *Coriolanus* iv 7 52
Andronicus, stain not thy tomb with blood *T. Andron.* i 1 116
Lo, at this tomb my tributary tears I render, for my brethren's obsequies i 1 159
Away! he rests not in this tomb i 1 349
Till we with trophies do adorn thy tomb i 1 388
By my father's reverend tomb, I vow ii 3 296
The earth that's nature's mother is her tomb *Rom. and Jul.* ii 3 9
Methinks I see thee, now thou art below, As one dead in the bottom of a tomb iii 5 56
How if, when I am laid into the tomb, I wake before the time? iv 3 30
Poor living corse, closed in a dead man's tomb! v 2 30
If thou be merciful, Open the tomb, lay me with Juliet v 3 73
With instruments upon them, fit to open These dead men's tombs v 3 201
But then a noise did scare me from the tomb v 3 262
Anon comes one with light to ope the tomb v 3 283
What's on this tomb I cannot read; the character I'll take with wax *T. of Athens* v 3 5
Which is not tomb enough and continent To hide the slain *Hamlet* iv 4 64
If thou shouldst not be glad, I would divorce me from thy mother's tomb *Lear* ii 4 133
With female fairies will his tomb be haunted *Cymbeline* iv 2 217
Peaceful night, The tomb where grief should sleep *Pericles* i 2 5
Tombé. Je m'estime heureux que je suis tombé entre les mains d'un chevalier *Hen. V.* iv 4 59
Tombless. Lay these bones in an unworthy urn, Tombless i 2 229
Tomboys. To be partner'd With tomboys hired with that self exhibition Which your own coffers yield! *Cymbeline* i 6 122
To-morrow, may it please you *T. G. of Ver.* i 3 39
To-morrow be in readiness to go: Excuse it not i 3 70
Which to-morrow, by his master's command, he must carry iv 2 78
Let him be sent for to-morrow, eight o'clock, to have amends *Mer. W.* iii 3 210
I pray you now, remembrance to-morrow on the lousy knave iii 3 255
The duke himself will be to-morrow at court iv 3 2
Is it your will Claudio shall die to-morrow? *Meas. for Meas.* ii 2 7
He must die to-morrow.—To-morrow! O, that's sudden! Spare him, spare him! ii 2 82
Be satisfied; Your brother dies to-morrow ii 2 105
I will bethink me: come again to-morrow ii 2 144
At what hour to-morrow Shall I attend your lordship? ii 2 159
When must he die?—As I do think, to-morrow ii 3 16
Your partner, as I hear, must die to-morrow . . . —Must die to-morrow! ii 3 37
Answer me to-morrow, Or, by the affection that now guides me most, I'll prove a tyrant to him ii 4 167
Your best appointment make with speed; To-morrow you set on iii 1 61
This night's the time That I should do what I abhor to name, Or else thou diest to-morrow iii 1 103
Be ready, Claudio, for your death to-morrow iii 1 107
To-morrow you must die; go to your knees and make ready iii 1 171
Canst thou tell if Claudio die to-morrow or no?—Why should he die? iii 2 180
Claudio must die to-morrow: let him be furnished with divines iii 2 220
Here's a fellow will help you to-morrow in your execution iv 2 24
Provide your block and your axe to-morrow four o'clock iv 2 56
By eight to-morrow Thou must be made immortal iv 2 67
Have you no countermand for Claudio yet, But he must die to-morrow? iv 2 96
The duke comes home to-morrow; nay, dry your eyes iv 3 132
They say the duke will be here to-morrow iv 3 162
And that to-morrow you will bring it home *Com. of Errors* iii 1 5
When mean you to go to church?—To-morrow, my lord *Much Ado* ii 1 372
When are you married, madam?—Why, every day, to-morrow iii 1 101
Have thy counsel Which is the best to furnish me to-morrow iii 1 103
A Dutchman to-day, a Frenchman to-morrow iii 2 34
Means your lordship to be married to-morrow?—You know he does iii 2 92
If you love her then, to-morrow wed her iii 2 118
If I see any thing to-night why I should not marry her to-morrow iii 2 127
The wedding being there to-morrow, there is a great coil to-night iii 3 99
To-morrow then I will expect your coming v 1 305
We look for you to-morrow.—We will not fail v 1 338
Think not on him till to-morrow v 4 129
To-morrow you shall have a sight of them.—It shall suffice me *L. L. Lost* ii 1 166
Excuse me, and farewell: To-morrow shall we visit you again ii 1 177
To-morrow truly will I meet with thee *M. N. Dream* i 1 178
Will to-morrow midnight solemnly Dance iv 1 93
I shall hardly spare a pound of flesh To-morrow *Mer. of Venice* iii 3 34
To-morrow the wrestling is *As Y. Like It* i 1 99
What, you wrestle to-morrow before the new duke? i 1 126
To-morrow, sir, I wrestle for my credit i 1 132
If he come to-morrow, I'll give him his payment i 1 166
You have my consent. Let your wedding be to-morrow v 2 16
Clubs cannot part them.—They shall be married to-morrow v 2 46
By so much the more shall I to-morrow be at the height of heart-heaviness v 2 50
Why then, to-morrow I cannot serve your turn? v 2 53
To set her before your eyes to-morrow human as she is v 2 74
If you will be married to-morrow, you shall v 2 80
To-morrow meet me all together v 2 121
I will marry you, if ever I marry woman, and I'll be married to-morrow v 2 123
I will satisfy you, if ever I satisfied man, and you shall be married to-morrow v 2 125
To-morrow is the joyful day, Audrey; to-morrow will we be married v 3 1
To-morrow I intend to hunt again *T. of Shrew* Ind. 1 29
If I die to-morrow, this is hers, If whilst I live she will be only mine ii 1 363
You know to-morrow is the wedding-day iii 1 84
I will not go to-day; No, nor to-morrow, not till I please myself iii 2 211
To-morrow't shall be mended, And, for this night, we'll fast for company iv 1 179
I'll pay thee for thy gown to-morrow iv 3 168
Be gone to-morrow; and be sure of this, What I can help thee to thou shalt not miss *All's Well* i 3 261
To-morrow I'll to the wars, she to her single sorrow ii 3 312
To-morrow to the field iii 1 23
He will be here to-morrow, or I am deceived by him iv 5 87
I'll ride home to-morrow *T. Night* i 3 94
If that the youth will come this way to-morrow, I'll give him reasons for't i 5 324
Shall we go see the reliques of this town?—To-morrow, sir iii 3 20
I beseech you come again to-morrow iii 4 230
Pay them when you part.—Sir, that's to-morrow *W. Tale* i 2 10
No longer stay.—One seven-night longer.—Very sooth, to-morrow i 2 17
To-morrow. Two lads that thought there was no more behind But such a day to-morrow as to-day, And to be boy eternal *W. Tale* i 2 64
The day shall not be up so soon as I, To try the fair adventure of to-morrow *K. John* v 5 22
Let not to-morrow then ensue to-day *Richard II.* ii 1 197
To-morrow next We will for Ireland; and 'tis time, I trow ii 1 217
To-morrow must we part; Be merry, for our time of stay is short ii 1 222
Where shall we take a purse to-morrow? *1 Hen. IV.* i 2 110
Now, my good sweet honey lord, ride with us to-morrow i 2 180
To-day will I set forth, to-morrow you ii 3 119
To-morrow, Francis; or Francis, o' Thursday ii 4 73
Clap to the doors: watch to-night, pray to-morrow ii 4 306
Thou wilt be horribly chid to-morrow when thou comest to thy father ii 4 410
I will, by to-morrow dinner-time, Send him to answer thee ii 4 564
To-morrow, cousin Percy, you and I And my good Lord of Worcester will set forth iii 1 83
Meet me to-morrow in the temple hall at two o'clock in the afternoon iii 3 223
Let it be seen to-morrow in the battle Which of us fears iv 3 13
To-morrow, good Sir Michael, is a day Wherein the fortune of ten thousand men Must bide the touch iv 4 8
I'll give you leave to powder me and eat me too to-morrow v 4 113
What a disgrace is it to me to remember thy name! or to know thy face to-morrow! *2 Hen. IV.* ii 2 16
I shall receive money o' Thursday: shalt have a cap to-morrow ii 4 298
Sudden sorrow Serves to say thus, 'some good thing comes to-morrow' iv 2 84
To-morrow shall you bear our full intent Back to our brother England *Hen. V.* ii 4 114
To-morrow shall you know our mind at full ii 4 140
To-morrow for the march are we addrest iii 3 58
And on to-morrow bid them march away iii 6 181
Some of them will fall to-morrow, I hope iii 7 77
I will trot to-morrow a mile, and my way shall be paved with English faces iii 7 86
He never did harm, that I heard of.—Nor will do none to-morrow iii 7 110
Then shall we find to-morrow they have only stomachs to eat and none to fight iii 7 165
If ever thou come to me and say, after to-morrow, 'This is my glove' iv 1 230
To-morrow the king himself will be a clipper iv 1 245
Feast his neighbours, And say 'To-morrow is Saint Crispian' iv 3 46
To-morrow I shall die with mickle age *1 Hen. VI.* iv 6 35
To-morrow toward London back again *2 Hen. VI.* ii 1 201
Meet me to-morrow in Saint George's field, You shall have pay v 1 46
To-morrow then belike shall be the day *3 Hen. VI.* iv 3 7
To-morrow, or next day, they will be here *Richard III.* ii 4 3
Summon him to-morrow to the Tower iii 1 172
For we to-morrow hold divided councils iii 1 179
His ancient knot of dangerous adversaries To-morrow are let blood iii 1 183
To-morrow, then, I judge a happy day iii 4 6
To-morrow, in mine opinion, is too sudden iii 4 45
He doth entreat your grace To visit him to-morrow or next day iii 7 60
To-morrow will it please you to be crown'd?—Even when you please, since you will have it so.—To-morrow, then iii 7 242
Here will I lie to-night; But where to-morrow? Well, all's one for that v 3 8
Make no delay; For, lords, to-morrow is a busy day v 3 18
Gives signal of a goodly day to-morrow v 3 21
Come, gentlemen, Let us consult upon to-morrow's business v 3 45
Stir with the lark to-morrow, gentle Norfolk v 3 56
Saddle white Surrey for the field to-morrow v 3 64
Let me sit heavy on thy soul to-morrow! v 3 118; 131; 139
To-morrow in the battle think on me, And fall thy edgeless sword v 3 134
And every one did threat To-morrow's vengeance on the head of Richard v 3 206
And, to-morrow, they Made Britain India *Hen. VIII.* i 1 20
To-day he puts forth The tender leaves of hopes; to-morrow blossoms iii 2 353
And will to-morrow with his trumpet call *Troi. and Cres.* i 3 277
Achilles will not to the field to-morrow ii 3 172
To-morrow We must with all our main of power stand fast ii 3 272
Bring word if Hector will to-morrow Be answer'd in his challenge iii 3 34
Now shall we see to-morrow—An act that very chance doth throw upon him iii 3 130
He must fight singly to-morrow with Hector iii 3 247
If to-morrow be a fair day, by eleven o'clock it will go one way or other iii 3 296
Let him die, With every joint a wound, and that to-morrow! iv 1 29
By this white beard, I'ld fight with thee to-morrow iv 5 209
To-morrow do I meet thee, fell as death; To-night all friends iv 5 269
I'll heat his blood with Greekish wine to-night, Which with my scimitar I'll cool to-morrow v 1 2
I am thwarted quite From my great purpose in to-morrow's battle v 1 43
To-morrow will I wear it on my helm v 2 93
When goes this forward?—To-morrow; to-day; presently *Coriolanus* iv 5 229
We will before the walls of Rome to-morrow Set down our host v 3 1
Be chosen with proclamations to-day, To-morrow yield up rule *T. Andron.* i 1 191
To-morrow, an it please your majesty To hunt the panther i 1 492
If that thy bent of love be honourable, Thy purpose marriage, send me word to-morrow *Rom. and Jul.* ii 2 144
Leave me to my grief: To-morrow will I send ii 2 154
At what o'clock to-morrow Shall I send to thee? ii 2 168
Ask for me to-morrow, and you shall find me a grave man iii 1 101
I will, and know her mind early to-morrow iii 4 10
What say you to Thursday?—My lord, I would that Thursday were to-morrow iii 4 29
Wednesday is to-morrow: To-morrow night look that thou lie alone iv 1 90
Sort such needful ornaments As you think fit to furnish me to-morrow iv 2 35
Go, nurse, go with her: we'll to church to-morrow iv 2 37
To prepare him up Against to-morrow iv 2 46
Such necessaries As are behoveful for our state to-morrow iv 3 8
You'll be sick to-morrow For this night's watching iv 4 7
Lord Lucullus entreats your company to-morrow to hunt with him *T. of A.* i 2 194
I was writing of my epitaph; It will be seen to-morrow v 1 189
Will you dine with me to-morrow?—Ay, if I be alive *J. Cæsar* i 2 294
To-morrow, if you please to speak with me, I will come home to you i 2 308
He did bid Antonius Send word to you he would be there to-morrow i 3 38
The senators to-morrow Mean to establish Cæsar as a king i 3 85
Is not to-morrow, boy, the ides of March? ii 1 40
Good-night: Early to-morrow will we rise, and hence iv 3 230
Duncan comes here to-night.—And when goes hence?—To-morrow *Macb.* i 5 61
Desired your good advice, which still hath been both grave and prosperous, In this day's council; but we'll take to-morrow iii 1 23
But of that to-morrow, When therewithal we shall have cause of state iii 1 33
Get thee gone: to-morrow We'll hear, ourselves, again iii 4 31
I will to-morrow, And betimes I will, to the weird sisters iii 4 132

To-morrow. To-morrow, and to-morrow, and to-morrow, Creeps in this petty pace from day to day To the last syllable of recorded time *Macbeth* v 5 19
Follow him, friends: we'll hear a play to-morrow *Hamlet* ii 2 561
To-morrow is Saint Valentine's day, All in the morning betime iv 5 48
To-morrow shall I beg leave to see your kingly eyes iv 7 44
Our troops set forth to-morrow: stay with us *Lear* iv 5 16
And they are ready To-morrow, or at further space, to appear v 3 53
We will have more of this to-morrow *Othello* i 3 379
To-morrow with your earliest Let me have speech with you ii 3 7
Shall't be to-night at supper?—No, not to-night.—To-morrow dinner, then? iii 3 58
Kill me to-morrow: let me live to-night!—Nay, if you strive v 2 80
I will hope Of better deeds to-morrow *Ant. and Cleo.* i 1 62
To-morrow, Cæsar, I shall be furnish'd to inform you rightly i 4 76
Know, that to-morrow the last of many battles We mean to fight iv 1 11
To-morrow, soldier, By sea and land I'll fight iv 2 4
Perchance to-morrow You'll serve another master iv 2 27
Know, my hearts, I hope well of to-morrow iv 2 42
To-morrow is the day.—It will determine one way iv 3 1
If to-morrow Our navy thrive, I have an absolute hope Our landmen will stand up iv 3 9
To-morrow, Before the sun shall see's, we'll spill the blood That has to-day escaped iv 8 2
Only for this night; I must aboard to-morrow *Cymbeline* i 6 199
I thank you for your pains: But not away to-morrow!—O, I must i 6 204
Lucius the Roman comes to Milford-Haven To-morrow iii 4 146
He hath a fair daughter, and to-morrow is her birth-day *Pericles* ii 1 113
To-morrow all for speeding do their best ii 3 116
We shall have him here to-morrow with his best ruff on iv 2 110
And swore he would see her to-morrow iv 2 118
To-morrow morning. I do invite you to-morrow morning to my house to breakfast *Mer. Wives* iii 3 245
See that Claudio Be executed by nine to-morrow morning *Meas. for Meas.* ii 1 34
To-morrow morning are to die Claudio and Barnardine iv 2 7
To-morrow morning come you to my house *Much Ado* v 1 295
Until to-morrow morning, lords, farewell v 1 337
I will come to your worship to-morrow morning *L. L. Lost* iii 1 161
It shall be done to-morrow morning, if I live *T. Night* iii 4 115
To-morrow morning let us meet him then *K. John* iv 3 18
To-morrow morning, by four o'clock, early at Gadshill! 1 *Hen. IV.* i 2 138
Hath commanded To-morrow morning to the council-board He be convented *Hen. VIII.* v 1 51
To-morrow morning call some knight to arms *Troi. and Cres.* ii 1 136
Leave! an you take leave till to-morrow morning iii 2 149
I'll have this knot knit up to-morrow morning *Rom. and Jul.* iv 2 24
Shall I be married then to-morrow morning? No, no: this shall forbid it iv 3 22
To-morrow night. Get us some excellent music; for to-morrow night *Much Ado* ii 3 88
Steal forth thy father's house to-morrow night *M. N. Dream* i 1 164
To-morrow night, when Phœbe doth behold Her silver visage in the watery glass i 1 209
Then to the wood will he to-morrow night Pursue her i 1 247
Request you and desire you, to con them by to-morrow night i 2 103
I have bespoke supper to-morrow night in Eastcheap 1 *Hen. IV.* i 2 144
Provide us all things necessary and meet me to-morrow night i 2 216
Sup with me to-morrow night 2 *Hen. VI.* i 4 84
I will not meet with you to-morrow night *Troi. and Cres.* v 2 73
Wednesday is to-morrow: To-morrow night look that thou lie alone *Rom. and Jul.* iv 1 90
We'll ha't to-morrow night *Hamlet* ii 2 565
Why, then, to-morrow night; or Tuesday morn; On Tuesday noon *Oth.* iii 3 60
Tomyris. I shall as famous be by this exploit As Scythian Tomyris by Cyrus' death 1 *Hen. VI.* ii 3 6
Ton. O pardonnez moi!—Say'st thou me so? is that a ton of moys? *Hen. V.* iv 4 23
Tongs. Let's have the tongs and the bones *M. N. Dream* iv 1 32
Tongue. What a spendthrift is he of his tongue! *Tempest* ii 1 23
Who with cloven tongues Do hiss me into madness ii 2 13
For she had a tongue with a tang, Would cry to a sailor, Go hang! ii 2 52
The harmony of their tongues hath into bondage Brought my too diligent ear iii 1 41
My man-monster hath drown'd his tongue in sack iii 2 14
Keep a good tongue in thy head iii 2 39; 120
Although they want the use of tongue, a kind Of excellent dumb discourse iii 3 38
No tongue! all eyes! be silent iv 1 59
Why dost thou stop my mouth?—For fear thou shouldst lose thy tongue.—Where should I lose my tongue?—In thy tale *T. G. of Ver.* ii 3 52
Fie, fie, unreverend tongue! to call her bad ii 6 14
That man that hath a tongue, I say, is no man, If with his tongue he cannot win a woman iii 1 105
She is too liberal.—Of her tongue she cannot iii 1 356
Have you the tongues?—My youthful travel therein made me happy iv 1 33
Peace-a your tongue. Speak-a your tale *Mer. Wives* i 4 85
Mock-water, in our English tongue, is valour, bully ii 3 62
Mortality and mercy in Vienna Live in thy tongue and heart *M. for M.* i 1 46
To jest, Tongue far from heart i 4 33
If you should need a pin, You could not with more tame a tongue desire it ii 2 46
Let it not sound a thought upon your tongue ii 2 140
Whilst my invention, hearing not my tongue, Anchors on Isabel ii 4 3
I have no tongue but one ii 4 139
O perilous mouths, That bear in them one and the self-same tongue, Either of condemnation or approof! ii 4 173
What king so strong Can tie the gall up in the slanderous tongue? iii 2 199
Peace, ho, be here!—The tongue of Isabel iv 3 111
How might she tongue me! Yet reason dares her no iv 4 28
The law cries out Most audible, even from his proper tongue v 1 413
So that my errand, due unto my tongue, I thank him, I bare home upon my shoulders *Com. of Errors* ii 1 72
Be not thy tongue thy own shame's orator; Look sweet, speak fair iii 2 10
My tongue, though not my heart, shall have his will iv 2 18
My heart prays for him, though my tongue do curse iv 2 28
Good now, hold thy tongue.—Nay, rather persuade him to hold his hands iv 4 22
O time's extremity, Hast thou so crack'd and splitted my poor tongue? v 1 308
A bird of my tongue is better than a beast of yours *Much Ado* i 1 140
I would my horse had the speed of your tongue, and so good a continuer i 1 143
Then half Signior Benedick's tongue in Count John's mouth ii 1 12
Tongue. Thou wilt never get thee a husband, if thou be so shrewd of thy tongue *Much Ado* ii 1 21
Therefore all hearts in love use their own tongues ii 1 184
Here's a dish I love not: I cannot endure my Lady Tongue ii 1 284
He hath a heart as sound as a bell and his tongue is the clapper iii 2 13
What his heart thinks his tongue speaks iii 2 14
What pace is this that thy tongue keeps?—Not a false gallop iii 4 93
Out of all eyes, tongues, minds, and injuries iv 1 245
And men are only turned into tongue, and trim ones too iv 1 323
As I dare take a serpent by the tongue v 1 90
'Nay,' said I, 'he hath the tongues:' 'That I believe,' said she v 1 167
There's a double tongue; there's two tongues v 1 170
Done to death by slanderous tongues Was the Hero that here lies v 3 3
On pain of losing her tongue *L. L. Lost* i 1 124
One whom the music of his own vain tongue Doth ravish i 1 167
My father's wit and my mother's tongue, assist me! i 2 101
Beauty is bought by judgement of the eye, Not utter'd by base sale of chapmen's tongues ii 1 16
Which his fair tongue, conceit's expositor, Delivers in such apt and gracious words That aged ears play truant at his tales ii 1 72
His tongue, all impatient to speak and not see, Did stumble with haste ii 1 238
I only have made a mouth of his eye, By adding a tongue ii 1 252
To jig off a tune at the tongue's end, canary to it with your feet iii 1 12
When tongues speak sweetly, then they name her name iii 1 167
Well learned is that tongue that well can thee commend iv 2 116
That sings heaven's praise with such an earthly tongue iv 2 122
How far dost thou excel, No thought can think, nor tongue of mortal tell iv 3 42
Lend me the flourish of all gentle tongues,—Fie, painted rhetoric! iv 3 238
Love's tongue proves dainty Bacchus gross in taste iv 3 339
His tongue filed, his eye ambitious, his gait majestical v 1 11
What, was your vizard made without a tongue? v 2 242
You have a double tongue within your mask v 2 245
The tongues of mocking wenches are as keen As is the razor's edge invisible v 2 256
A blister on his sweet tongue, with my heart! v 2 335
It were a fault to snatch words from my tongue v 2 382
Never will I trust to speeches penn'd, Nor to the motion of a schoolboy's tongue v 2 403
Sweet Lord Longaville, rein thy tongue v 2 662
The news I bring Is heavy in my tongue v 2 727
A heavy heart bears not a nimble tongue v 2 747
The world's large tongue Proclaims you for a man replete with mocks v 2 852
A jest's prosperity lies in the ear Of him that hears it, never in the tongue Of him that makes it v 2 872
Your eyes are lode-stars; and your tongue's sweet air More tuneable than lark to shepherd's ear *M. N. Dream* i 1 183
My tongue should catch your tongue's sweet melody i 1 189
You spotted snakes with double tongue, Thorny hedgehogs, be not seen ii 2 9
Tie up my love's tongue, bring him silently iii 1 206
With doubler tongue Than thine, thou serpent, never adder stung iii 2 72
Will you tear Impatient answers from my gentle tongue? iii 2 287
Like to Lysander sometime frame thy tongue iii 2 360
Man's hand is not able to taste, his tongue to conceive iv 1 218
In the modesty of fearful duty I read as much as from the rattling tongue Of saucy and audacious eloquence v 1 102
Tongue, lose thy light; Moon, take thy flight v 1 309
Tongue, not a word: Come, trusty sword v 1 349
The iron tongue of midnight hath told twelve v 1 370
If we have unearned luck Now to 'scape the serpent's tongue v 1 440
Well, keep me company but two years moe, Thou shalt not know the sound of thine own tongue *Mer. of Venice* i 1 109
Silence is only commendable In a neat's tongue dried and a maid not vendible i 1 112
I cannot get a service, no; I have ne'er a tongue in my head ii 2 166
Adieu! tears exhibit my tongue ii 3 10
Tell me, for more certainty, Albeit I'll swear that I do know your tongue ii 6 27
And yet a maiden hath no tongue but thought iii 2 8
There is no power in the tongue of man To alter me iv 1 241
Wert thou not my brother, I would not take this hand from thy throat till this other had pulled out thy tongue for saying so *As Y. Like It* i 1 64
What passion hangs these weights upon my tongue? i 2 269
Finds tongues in trees, books in the running brooks, Sermons in stones ii 1 16
Come, sing; and you that will not, hold your tongues ii 5 31
Let me see wherein My tongue hath wrong'd him ii 7 84
Tongues I'll hang on every tree, That shall civil sayings show iii 2 135
Cry 'holla' to thy tongue, I prithee; it curvets unseasonably iii 2 257
Faster than his tongue Did make offence his eye did heal it up iii 5 116
You shall never take her without her answer, unless you take her without her tongue iv 1 176
That flattering tongue of yours won me iv 1 189
If that an eye may profit by a tongue, Then should I know you by description iv 3 84
A pair of very strange beasts, which in all tongues are called fools v 4 38
With soft low tongue and lowly courtesy *T. of Shrew* Ind. 1 114
Make her bear the penance of her tongue i 1 89
I will charm him first to keep his tongue.—So had you need i 1 214
Renown'd in Padua for her scolding tongue i 2 100
Do you tell me of a woman's tongue, That gives not half so great a blow to hear As will a chestnut in a farmer's fire? i 2 208
One as famous for a scolding tongue As is the other for beauteous modesty i 2 254
In his tail.—In his tongue.—Whose tongue?—Yours, if you talk of tails: and so farewell.—What, with my tongue in your tail? ii 1 216
My very lips might freeze to my teeth, my tongue to the roof of my mouth iv 1 7
To tame a shrew and charm her chattering tongue iv 2 58
Best you stop your ears. My tongue will tell the anger of my heart, Or else my heart concealing it will break iv 3 77
At this time His tongue obey'd his hand *All's Well* i 2 41
Only sin And hellish obstinacy tie thy tongue i 3 186
Many a man's tongue shakes out his master's undoing ii 4 24
My tongue is too foolhardy; but my heart hath the fear of Mars before it and of his creatures, not daring the reports of my tongue iv 1 32
This is the first truth that e'er thine own tongue was guilty of iv 1 36
Tongue, I must put you into a butter-woman's mouth and buy myself another of Bajazet's mule iv 1 44
I understand thee, and can speak thy tongue iv 1 82
Ere my heart Durst make too bold a herald of my tongue v 3 46
When my tongue blabs, then let mine eyes not see *T. Night* i 2 63

Tongue. Would I had bestowed that time in the tongues that I have in fencing . . . . *T. Night* i 3 97
Thy tongue, thy face, thy limbs, actions, and spirit, Do give thee five-fold blazon . . . . i 5 311
Methought her eyes had lost her tongue, For she did speak in starts . ii 2 21
Let thy tongue tang arguments of state . . . . ii 5 163
Let thy tongue tang with arguments of state . . . . . . iii 4 77
A reverend carriage, a slow tongue, in the habit of some sir of note . iii 4 81
'Tis my picture; Refuse it not; it hath no tongue to vex you . . iii 4 229
That very envy and the tongue of loss Cried fame and honour on him . v 1 61
There is no tongue that moves, none, none i' the world, So soon as yours could win me . . . . *W. Tale* i 2 20
For sealing The injury of tongues in courts and kingdoms . . . i 2 338
If I prove honey-mouth'd, let my tongue blister . . . . . ii 2 33
Tell her, Emilia, I'll use that tongue I have . . . . . ii 2 52
A callat Of boundless tongue, who late hath beat her husband! . . ii 3 91
Thou art worthy to be hang'd, That wilt not stay her tongue . . . ii 3 110
I have deserved All tongues to talk their bitterest . . . . . iii 2 217
'Tis well they are whispering: clamour your tongues, and not a word more . . . . iv 4 250
It is as bitter Upon thy tongue as in my thought . . . . . v 1 19
When she has obtain'd your eye, Will have your tongue too . . . v 1 106
The accent of his tongue affecteth him . . . . . *K. John* i 1 86
He gives the bastinado with his tongue: Our ears are cudgell'd . . ii 1 463
Without my wrong There is no tongue hath power to curse him right . iii 1 183
Since law itself is perfect wrong, How can the law forbid my tongue to curse? . . . . iii 1 190
France, thou mayst hold a serpent by the tongue . . . . . iii 1 258
And like a civil war set'st oath to oath, Thy tongue against thy tongue iii 1 265
That name, Which till this time my tongue did ne'er pronounce . . iii 1 307
The midnight bell Did, with his iron tongue and brazen mouth, Sound on iii 3 38
Hear me without thine ears, and make reply Without a tongue . . iii 3 50
O, that my tongue were in the thunder's mouth! . . . . . iii 4 38
Prodigies and signs, Abortives, presages, and tongues of heaven . . iii 4 158
I would not have believed him,—no tongue but Hubert's . . . iv 1 70
Hold your tongue.—Hubert, the utterance of a brace of tongues Must needs want pleading for a pair of eyes: Let me not hold my tongue, let me not, Hubert; Or, Hubert, if you will, cut out my tongue, So I may keep mine eyes . . . . iv 1 97
One that am the tongue of these To sound the purposes of all their hearts . . . . iv 2 47
But this from rumour's tongue I idly heard; if true or false I know not iv 2 123
Can give audience To any tongue, speak it of what it will . . . iv 2 140
The deed, which both our tongues held vile to name . . . . iv 2 241
Whose tongue soe'er speaks false, Not truly speaks . . . . iv 3 91
My tongue shall hush again this storm of war . . . . . v 1 20
I do know the scope And warrant limited unto my tongue . . . v 2 123
Let the tongue of war Plead for our interest and our being here . . v 2 164
Thou art my friend, that know'st my tongue so well. Who art thou? . v 6 8
Pardon me, That any accent breaking from thy tongue Should 'scape the true acquaintance of mine ear . . . . v 6 14
What my tongue speaks my right drawn sword may prove *Richard II.* i 1 46
The trial of a woman's war, The bitter clamour of two eager tongues . i 1 49
Ere my tongue Shall wound my honour with such feeble wrong . . i 1 190
Now my tongue's use is to me no more Than an unstringed viol . . i 3 161
Within my mouth you have engaol'd my tongue, Doubly portcullis'd . i 3 166
Speechless death, Which robs my tongue from breathing native breath . i 3 173
Upon good advice, Whereto thy tongue a party-verdict gave . . . i 3 234
You gave leave to my unwilling tongue Against my will. . . . i 3 245
When the tongue's office should be prodigal To breathe the abundant dolour of the heart . . . . i 3 256
My heart disdained that my tongue Should so profane the word . . i 4 12
The tongues of dying men Enforce attention like deep harmony . . ii 1 5
This tongue that runs so roundly in thy head Should run thy head from thy unreverent shoulders . . . . ii 1 122
His tongue is now a stringless instrument . . . . . . ii 1 149
It must break with silence, Ere't be disburden'd with a liberal tongue . ii 1 229
I must find that title in your tongue, Before I make reply . . . ii 3 72
Whose double tongue may with a mortal touch Throw death . . . iii 2 21
Discomfort guides my tongue And bids me speak of nothing but despair iii 2 65
More health and happiness betide my liege Than can my care-tuned tongue deliver him! . . . . iii 2 92
My tongue hath but a heavier tale to say . . . . . . iii 2 197
He does me double wrong That wounds me with the flatteries of his tongue . . . . iii 2 216
O God! that e'er this tongue of mine, That laid the sentence of dread banishment On yon proud man, should take it off again! . . . iii 3 133
How dares thy harsh rude tongue sound this unpleasing news? . . iii 4 74
I know your daring tongue Scorns to unsay what once it hath deliver'd iv 1 8
With mine own tongue deny my sacred state . . . . . . iv 1 209
The senseless brands will sympathize The heavy accent of thy moving tongue . . . . v 1 47
Whilst all tongues cried 'God save thee!' . . . . . . v 2 11
No joyful tongue gave him his welcome home . . . . . . v 2 29
My tongue cleave to my roof within my mouth . . . . . v 3 31
If I were thy nurse, thy tongue to teach, 'Pardon' should be the first word . . . . v 3 113
Thine eye begins to speak; set thy tongue there . . . . . v 3 125
What my tongue dares not, that my heart shall say . . . . v 5 97
So blest a son, A son who is the theme of honour's tongue . *1 Hen. IV.* i 1 81
Minutes capons and clocks the tongues of bawds . . . . . i 2 9
I shall never hold that man my friend Whose tongue shall ask me for one penny . . . . i 3 91
To prove that true Needs no more but one tongue for all those wounds, Those mouthed wounds . . . . i 3 96
Forbad my tongue to speak of Mortimer . . . . i 3 220
This woman's mood, Tying thine ear to no tongue but thine own! . . i 3 238
Gave the tongue a helpful ornament, A virtue that was never seen in you iii 1 125
Thy tongue Makes Welsh as sweet as ditties highly penn'd . . . iii 1 208
I cannot flatter; I do defy The tongues of soothers . . . . iv 1 7
Trimm'd up your praises with a princely tongue . . . . . v 2 57
I, that have not well the gift of tongue . . . . . . v 2 78
The earthy and cold hand of death Lies on my tongue . . . . v 4 85
Upon my [Rumour's] tongues continual slanders ride . *2 Hen. IV.* Ind. 6
From Rumour's tongues They bring smooth comforts false . . . Ind. 39
The whiteness in thy cheek Is apter than thy tongue to tell thy errand i 1 69
But Priam found the fire ere he his tongue . . . . . . i 1 74
See what a ready tongue suspicion hath! . . . . . . i 1 84
If he be slain, say so; The tongue offends not that reports his death . i 1 97
His tongue Sounds ever after as a sullen bell . . . . . i 1 101

Tongue. Pray God his tongue be hotter! . . . . . . *2 Hen. IV.* i 2 40
There's for your silence.—I have no tongue, sir . . . . . ii 2 179
The harsh and boisterous tongue of war . . . . iv 1 49
Turning . . . your tongue divine To a loud trumpet and a point of war iv 1 51
I have a whole school of tongues in this belly of mine, and not a tongue of them all speaks any other word but my name . . . . . iv 3 20
Which [sherris], delivered o'er to the voice, the tongue, which is the birth, becomes excellent wit . . . . iv 3 109
Studies his companions Like a strange tongue . . . . . . iv 4 69
If my tongue cannot entreat you to acquit me, will you command me to use my legs? . . . . Epil. 18
My tongue is weary; when my legs are too, I will bid you good night . Epil. 34
He hath a killing tongue and a quiet sword . . . . *Hen. V.* iii 2 36
Turn the sands into eloquent tongues, and my horse is argument for them all . . . . iii 7 37
I will be glad to hear you confess it brokenly with your English tongue v 2 107
That the tongues of men are full of deceits?—Oui, dat de tongues of de mans is be full of deceits . . . . v 2 121
Fellows of infinite tongue, that can rhyme themselves into ladies' favours . . . . v 2 164
I will tell thee in French; which I am sure will hang upon my tongue like a new-married wife about her husband's neck . . . . v 2 189
Thy speaking of my tongue, and I thine, most truly-falsely . . v 2 203
Your lips, Kate: there is more eloquence in a sugar touch of them than in the tongues of the French council . . . . v 2 303
Our tongue is rough, coz, and my condition is not smooth . . . v 2 313
These women are shrewd tempters with their tongues . *1 Hen. VI.* i 2 123
And yet thy tongue will not confess thy error . . . . . . ii 4 67
Among which terms he used his lavish tongue And did upbraid me . ii 5 47
Which obloquy set bars before my tongue . . . . . . ii 5 49
Plantagenet, I see, must hold his tongue . . . . . . iii 1 61
The envious barking of your saucy tongue . . . . . . iii 4 33
This fellow here, with envious carping tongue, Upbraided me . . iv 1 90
Fell banning hag, enchantress, hold thy tongue! . . . . . v 3 42
Hast not a tongue? is she not here? . . . . v 3 68
Beauty's princely majesty is such, Confounds the tongue . . . v 3 71
So York must sit and fret and bite his tongue . . *2 Hen. VI.* i 1 230
This knave's tongue begins to double . . . . i 3 94
Unburthens with his tongue The envious load that lies upon his heart . ii 1 156
My heart accordeth with my tongue, Seeing the deed is meritorious . iii 1 269
So shall my name with slander's tongue be wounded . . . . iii 2 68
How often have I tempted Suffolk's tongue! . . . . . . iii 2 114
A dreadful oath, sworn with a solemn tongue! . . . . . iii 2 158
Were there a serpent seen, with forked tongue . . . . . iii 2 259
My tongue should stumble in mine earnest words . . . . . iii 2 316
This hand of mine hath writ in thy behalf And therefore shall it charm thy riotous tongue . . . . iv 1 64
Suffolk's imperial tongue is stern and rough, Used to command . . iv 1 121
Can he that speaks with the tongue of an enemy be a good counsellor, or no? . . . . iv 2 181
This tongue hath parley'd unto foreign kings For your behoof . . iv 7 82
He has a familiar under his tongue; he speaks not o' God's name . . iv 7 114
Be as free as heart can wish or tongue can tell . . . . . iv 7 133
Then, York, unloose thy long-imprison'd thoughts, And let thy tongue be equal with thy heart . . . . v 1 89
View this face, And bite thy tongue, that slanders him with cowardice *3 Hen. VI.* i 4 47
Whose tongue more poisons than the adder's tooth! . . . . . i 4 112
Whose heavy looks foretell Some dreadful story hanging on thy tongue ii 1 44
Nor can my tongue unload my heart's great burthen . . . . ii 1 81
Give no limits to my tongue: I am a king, and privileged to speak . ii 2 119
I am resolved That Clifford's manhood lies upon his tongue . . . ii 2 125
Well I wot, thou hast thy mother's tongue . . . . . . ii 2 134
Shamest thou not . . . To let thy tongue detect thy base-born heart? . ii 2 143
His ill-boding tongue no more shall speak . . . . . . ii 6 59
Such a cause as fills mine eyes with tears And stops my tongue . . iii 3 14
And with my tongue To tell the passion of my sovereign's heart . . iii 3 61
Peace, wilful boy, or I will charm your tongue . . . . . v 5 31
A cherry lip, a bonny eye, a passing pleasing tongue *Richard III.* i 1 94
Fairer than tongue can name thee, let me have Some patient leisure . i 2 81
I was provoked by her slanderous tongue . . . . i 2 97
My tongue could never learn sweet smoothing words . . . . i 2 169
My proud heart sues and prompts my tongue to speak . . . . i 2 171
I would I knew thy heart.—'Tis figured in my tongue . . . . i 2 194
Be assured We come to use our hands and not our tongues . . . i 3 353
Have I a tongue to doom my brother's death, And shall the same give pardon to a slave? . . . . ii 1 102
For reverence to some alive, I give a sparing limit to my tongue . . iii 7 194
My woe-wearied tongue is mute and dumb . . . . iv 4 18
My tongue should to thy ears not name my boys Till that my nails were anchor'd in thine eyes . . . . iv 4 230
My conscience hath a thousand several tongues, And every tongue brings in a several tale, And every tale condemns me . . . . v 3 193
And no discerner Durst wag his tongue in censure . . *Hen. VIII.* i 1 33
The tract of every thing Would by a good discourser lose some life, Which action's self was tongue to . . . . i 1 42
This makes bold mouths: Tongues spit their duties out . . . . i 2 61
Traduced by ignorant tongues, which neither know My faculties nor person . . . . i 2 72
Give 'em welcome; you can speak the French tongue . . . . i 4 57
Stop the rumour, and allay those tongues That durst disperse it . . ii 1 152
These news are every where; every tongue speaks em . . . . ii 2 39
Hath sent One general tongue unto us, this good man . . . . ii 2 96
So good a lady that no tongue could ever Pronounce dishonour of her . ii 3 3
I am happy Above a number, if my actions Were tried by every tongue . iii 1 35
A strange tongue makes my cause more strange, suspicious . . . iii 1 45
We come not . . . To taint that honour every good tongue blesses . . iii 1 55
He hath a witchcraft Over the king in's tongue . . . . . iii 2 19
Durst better Have burnt that tongue than said so . . . . . iii 2 254
Still in thy right hand carry gentle peace, To silence envious tongues . iii 2 446
The archbishop Is the king's hand and tongue . . . . . . v 1 38
There's none stands under more calumnious tongues Than I myself . . v 1 112
You play the spaniel, And think with wagging of your tongue to win me . . . . v 3 127
May it like your grace To let my tongue excuse all . . . . . v 3 149
I had as lief Helen's golden tongue had commended Troilus for a copper nose . . . . *Troi. and Cres.* i 2 114
Knit all the Greekish ears To his experienced tongue . . . . i 3 68
Which, from the tongue of roaring Typhon dropp'd, Would seem hyperboles . . . . i 3 160

Tongue. I shall cut out your tongue.—'Tis no matter; I shall speak as much as thou afterwards . . . *Troi. and Cres.* ii 1 121
Sweet, bid me hold my tongue, For in this rapture I shall surely speak The thing I shall repent . . . iii 2 137
Speaking is for beggars; he wears his tongue in's arms . . . iii 3 271
O, these encounterers, so glib of tongue! . . . iv 5 58
Matchless, firm of word, Speaking in deeds and deedless in his tongue . iv 5 98
The arm our soldier, Our steed the leg, the tongue our trumpeter *Coriol.* i 1 121
I know the sound of Marcius' tongue From every meaner man . . i 6 26
All tongues speak of him, and the bleared sights Are spectacled to see him . . . ii 1 221
For their tongues to be silent, and not confess so much, were a kind of ingrateful injury . . . ii 2 34
We are to put our tongues into those wounds and speak for them . . ii 3 7
A single honour, in giving him our own voices with our own tongues . ii 3 50
Plague upon't! I cannot bring My tongue to such a pace . . . ii 3 57
Or had you tongues to cry Against the rectorship of judgement? . . ii 3 212
Of him that did not ask, but mock, bestow Your sued-for tongues . ii 3 216
The tribunes of the people, The tongues o' the common mouth . . iii 1 22
Are these your herd? Must these have voices, that can yield them now And straight disclaim their tongues? . . . iii 1 35
At once pluck out The multitudinous tongue . . . iii 1 156
Put not your worthy rage into your tongue; One time will owe another iii 1 241
His heart's his mouth: What his breast forges, that his tongue must vent . . . iii 1 258
But with such words that are but roted in Your tongue . . . iii 2 56
Must I with base tongue give my noble heart A lie that it must bear? . iii 2 100
A beggar's tongue Make motion through my lips! . . . iii 2 117
Never trust to what my tongue can do I' the way of flattery further . iii 2 136
Within thine eyes sat twenty thousand deaths, In thy hands clutch'd as many millions, in Thy lying tongue both numbers . . . iii 3 72
Your favour is well approved by your tongue . . . iv 3 10
Your good tongue, More than the instant army we can make, Might stop our countryman.—No, I'll not meddle . . . v 1 36
Foul-spoken coward, that thunder'st with thy tongue, And with thy weapon nothing darest perform! . . . *T. Andron.* ii 1 58
The palace full of tongues, of eyes, and ears . . . ii 1 127
This is the day of doom for Bassianus: His Philomel must lose her tongue . . . ii 3 43
And one thing more That womanhood denies my tongue to tell . . ii 3 174
Now go tell, an if thy tongue can speak, Who 'twas that cut thy tongue ii 4 1
She hath no tongue to call, nor hands to wash; And so let's leave her ii 4 7
And, lest thou shouldst detect him, cut thy tongue . . . ii 4 27
Philomela, she but lost her tongue, And in a tedious sampler sew'd her mind . . . ii 4 38
Had he heard the heavenly harmony Which that sweet tongue hath made, he would have dropp'd his knife . . . ii 4 49
And tribunes with their tongues doom men to death . . . iii 1 47
Thou hast no hands, to wipe away thy tears; Nor tongue, to tell me who hath martyr'd thee . . . iii 1 107
Or shall we bite our tongues, and in dumb shows Pass the remainder of our hateful days? . . . iii 1 131
Let us, that have our tongues, Plot some device of further misery . iii 1 133
Had she a tongue to speak, now would she say That to her brother . iii 1 144
For losers will have leave To ease their stomachs with their bitter tongues . . . iii 1 234
That, were his heart Almost impregnable, his old ears deaf, Yet should both ear and heart obey my tongue . . . iv 4 99
They cut thy sister's tongue and ravish'd her . . . v 1 92
Would I were a devil, . . . So I might have your company in hell, But to torment you with my bitter tongue! . . . v 1 150
Her tongue, and that more dear Than hands or tongue, her spotless chastity . . . v 2 176
That my tongue may utter forth The venomous malice of my swelling heart! . . . v 3 12
They ravish'd her, and cut away her tongue . . . v 3 57
With his solemn tongue he did discourse To love-sick Dido's sad attending ear . . . v 3 81
My ears have not yet drunk a hundred words Of that tongue's utterance, yet I know the sound . . . *Rom. and Jul.* ii 2 59
Else would I tear the cave where Echo lies, And make her airy tongue more hoarse than mine . . . ii 2 163
How silver-sweet sound lovers' tongues by night, Like softest music! . ii 2 166
What early tongue so sweet saluteth me? . . . ii 3 32
Let rich music's tongue Unfold the imagined happiness . . . ii 6 27
Swifter than his tongue, His agile arm beats down their fatal points . iii 1 170
Every tongue that speaks But Romeo's name speaks heavenly eloquence iii 2 32
Blister'd be thy tongue For such a wish! . . . iii 2 90
Ah, poor my lord, what tongue shall smooth thy name? . . . iii 2 98
Hold your tongue, Good prudence; smatter with your gossips, go . iii 5 171
To dispraise my lord with that same tongue Which she hath praised him with above compare . . . iii 5 237
Death, that hath ta'en her hence to make me wail, Ties up my tongue . iv 5 32
He speaks the common tongue, Which all men speak with him *T. of A.* i 1 174
Who had the world as my confectionary, The mouths, the tongues, the eyes, and hearts of men At duty . . . iv 3 261
But I should infect my hands.—I would my tongue could rot them off! iv 3 370
That speak'st with every tongue, To every purpose! O thou touch of hearts [gold]! . . . iv 3 389
For each true word, a blister! and each false Be as a cauterizing to the root o' the tongue, Consuming it with speaking! . . . v 1 136
I hear a tongue, shriller than all the music . . . *J. Cæsar* i 2 16
That tongue of his that bade the Romans Mark him and write his speeches i 2 125
Vouchsafe good morrow from a feeble tongue . . . ii 1 313
Set a huge mountain 'tween my heart and tongue! . . . ii 4 7
To beg the voice and utterance of my tongue . . . iii 1 261
Put a tongue In every wound of Cæsar that should move The stones . iii 2 232
This tongue had not offended so to-day, If Cassius might have ruled . v 1 46
Brutus' tongue Hath almost ended his life's history . . . v 5 39
And chastise with the valour of my tongue All that impedes thee *Macb.* i 5 28
Bear welcome in your eye, Your hand, your tongue . . . i 5 66
Horror, horror! Tongue nor heart Cannot conceive nor name thee! . ii 3 69
Why do we hold our tongues, That most may claim this argument for ours? . . . ii 3 125
Present him eminence, both with eye and tongue . . . iii 2 31
Eye of newt and toe of frog, Wool of bat and tongue of dog . . iv 1 15
This tyrant, whose sole name blisters our tongues . . . iv 3 12
Let not your ears despise my tongue for ever . . . iv 3 201
O, I could play the woman with mine eyes And braggart with my tongue! iv 3 231
Thou comest to use thy tongue; thy story quickly . . . v 5 29

Tongue. Accursed be that tongue that tells me so, For it hath cow'd my better part of man! . . . *Macbeth* v 8 17
But break, my heart; for I must hold my tongue . . . *Hamlet* i 2 159
Whatsoever else shall hap to-night, Give it an understanding, but no tongue . . . i 2 250
Give thy thoughts no tongue, Nor any unproportion'd thought his act . i 3 59
When the blood burns, how prodigal the soul Lends the tongue vows . i 3 117
Who this had seen, with tongue in venom steep'd, 'Gainst Fortune's state would treason have pronounced . . . ii 2 533
Murder, though it have no tongue, will speak With most miraculous organ . . . ii 2 622
The courtier's, soldier's, scholar's, eye, tongue, sword . . . iii 1 159
Speak the speech, I pray you, as I pronounced it to you, trippingly on the tongue: but if you mouth it . . . iii 2 2
Let the candied tongue lick absurd pomp . . . iii 2 65
I will speak daggers to her, but use none; My tongue and soul in this be hypocrites . . . iii 2 415
Come, come, you answer with an idle tongue.—Go, go, you question with a wicked tongue . . . iii 4 11
What have I done, that thou darest wag thy tongue In noise so rude against me? . . . iii 4 39
Caps, hands, and tongues, applaud it to the clouds . . . iv 5 107
Delays as many As there are tongues, are hands, are accidents . . iv 7 122
That skull had a tongue in it, and could sing once . . . v 1 83
Is't not possible to understand in another tongue? . . . v 2 132
He does well to commend it himself; there are no tongues else for's turn v 2 191
I am sure, My love's More richer than my tongue . . . *Lear* i 1 80
A still-soliciting eye, and such a tongue As I am glad I have not . . i 1 234
I will hold my tongue; so your face bids me, though you say nothing . i 4 214
Struck me with her tongue, Most serpent-like, upon the very heart . ii 4 162
When slanders do not live in tongues; Nor cutpurses come not to throngs iii 2 87
Thy tongue some say of breeding breathes . . . v 3 143
Had I your tongues and eyes, I'ld use them so That heaven's vault should crack . . . v 3 258
Would she give you so much of her lips As of her tongue she oft bestows on me, You'ld have enough. . . . *Othello* ii 1 102
She puts her tongue a little in her heart, And chides with thinking . ii 1 107
Had tongue at will and yet was never loud . . . ii 1 150
I had rather have this tongue cut from my mouth Than it should do offence . . . ii 3 221
Swell, bosom, with thy fraught, For 'tis of aspics' tongues! . . . iii 3 450
Nay, guiltiness will speak, Though tongues were out of use . . v 1 110
Go to, charm your tongue.—I will not charm my tongue; I am bound to speak . . . v 2 183
Speak to me home, mince not the general tongue . . . *Ant. and Cleo.* i 2 109
You have broken The article of your oath; which you shall never Have tongue to charge me with . . . ii 2 83
Your reason?—I see it in My motion, have it not in my tongue . . ii 3 14
Give to a gracious message An host of tongues; but let ill tidings tell Themselves when they be felt . . . ii 5 87
Repent that e'er thy tongue Hath so betray'd thine act . . . ii 7 83
Mine own tongue Splits what it speaks . . . ii 7 130
Ho! hearts, tongues, figures, scribes, bards, poets, cannot Think, speak, cast, write, sing, number, ho! . . . iii 2 16
Her tongue will not obey her heart, nor can Her heart inform her tongue iii 2 47
Dull of tongue, and dwarfish! What majesty is in her gait? . . . iii 3 19
Sink Rome, and their tongues rot That speak against us! . . . iii 7 16
This is but a custom in your tongue; you bear a graver purpose *Cymb.* i 4 150
'Tis your graces That from my mutest conscience to my tongue Charms this report out . . . i 6 116
If you can penetrate her with your fingering, so; we'll try with tongue too ii 3 16
And will to ears and tongues Be theme and hearing ever . . . iii 1 3
Speak, man: thy tongue May take off some extremity, which to read Would be even mortal to me . . . iii 4 16
Slander, . . . whose tongue Outvenoms all the worms of Nile . . iii 4 36
Hear me with patience.—Talk thy tongue weary; speak . . . iii 4 115
The enemy full-hearted, Lolling the tongue with slaughtering . . v 3 8
'Tis still a dream, or else such stuff as madmen Tongue and brain not . v 4 147
His mistress' picture; which by his tongue being made, And then a mind put in't . . . v 5 175
By thine own tongue thou art condemn'd, and must Endure our law . v 5 298
Tell thee, with speechless tongues and semblance pale . . . *Pericles* i 1 36
All love the womb that their first being bred, Then give my tongue like leave to love my head . . . i 1 108
Peace, peace, and give experience tongue . . . i 2 37
How durst thy tongue move anger to our face? . . . i 2 54
Our tongues and sorrows do sound deep Our woes into the air . . i 4 13
Our eyes do weep, Till tongues fetch breath that may proclaim them louder . . . i 4 15
My veins are chill, And have no more of life than may suffice To give my tongue that heat to ask your help . . . ii 1 79
Resolve your angry father, if my tongue Did e'er solicit, or my hand subscribe To any syllable that made love to you . . . ii 5 68
Tongueless. One good deed dying tongueless Slaughters a thousand waiting upon that . . . *W. Tale* i 2 92
Which blood, like sacrificing Abel's, cries, Even from the tongueless caverns of the earth . . . *Richard II.* i 1 105
Or else our grave, Like Turkish mute, shall have a tongueless mouth *Hen. V.* i 2 232
What tongueless blocks were they! would they not speak? *Richard III.* iii 7 42
Tongue-tied. Love, therefore, and tongue-tied simplicity In least speak most . . . *M. N. Dream* v 1 104
Tongue-tied our queen? speak you . . . *W. Tale* i 2 27
Since you are tongue-tied and so loath to speak . . . 1 *Hen. VI.* ii 4 25
Give my tongue-tied sorrows leave to speak . . . 3 *Hen. VI.* iii 3 22
You might haply think Tongue-tied ambition, not replying, yielded *Richard III.* iii 7 145
Yet do they ease the heart.—If so, then be not tongue-tied . . iv 4 132
Cupid grant all tongue-tied maidens here Bed, chamber, Pandar! *Troi. and Cres.* iii 2 219
They vanish tongue-tied in their guiltiness . . . *J. Cæsar* i 1 67
To-night. For this, be sure, to-night thou shalt have cramps . *Tempest* i 2 325
Let it be to-night; For, now they are oppress'd with travel . . . iii 3 14
I say, to-night: no more . . . iii 3 17
I have dreamed to-night; I'll tell you my dream . . . *Mer. Wives* iii 3 171
I pray thee, once to-night Give my sweet Nan this ring . . . iii 4 103
To-night at Herne's oak, just 'twixt twelve and one . . . iv 6 19
The matter will be known to-night, or never . . . v 1 11
On whom to-night I will be revenged . . . v 1 30
Thou shalt eat a posset to-night at my house . . . v 5 180

To-night. For he to-night shall lie with Mistress Ford *Mer. Wives* v 5 259
With Angelo to-night shall lie His old betrothed *Meas. for Meas.* iii 2 292
I desire his company At Mariana's house to-night iv 3 145
I will not harbour in this town to-night *Com. of Errors* iii 2 154
Is there any ship puts forth to-night? iv 3 35
I will not stay to-night for all the town iv 4 161
I know we shall have revelling to-night *Much Ado* i 1 322
He swore he would marry her to-night ii 1 177
Go but with me to-night, you shall see her chamber-window entered iii 2 116
If I see any thing to-night why I should not marry her to-morrow iii 2 126
The wedding being there to-morrow, there is a great coil to-night iii 3 100
But know that I have to-night wooed Margaret iii 3 154
Our watch to-night . . . ha' ta'en a couple of as arrant knaves iii 5 33
Sing it to her bones, sing it to-night v 1 294
To-morrow then I will expect your coming; To-night I take my leave v 1 306
To-night I'll mourn with Hero v 1 339
Will they not, think you, hang themselves to-night? *L. L. Lost* v 2 270
Prepare; I will away to-night.—Madam, not so; I do beseech you, stay v 2 737
The king doth keep his revels here to-night *M. N. Dream* ii 1 18
The prince his master will be here to-night *Mer. of Venice* i 2 139
I do feast to-night My best-esteem'd acquaintance ii 2 180
I bar to-night: you shall not gauge me By what we do to-night ii 2 208
To sup to-night with my new master the Christian ii 4 18
Will you prepare you for this masque to-night? ii 4 23
I did dream of money-bags to-night ii 5 18
I have no mind of feasting forth to-night ii 5 37
No masque to-night: the wind is come about ii 6 64
I desire no more delight Than to be under sail and gone to-night ii 6 68
We'll away to-night And be a day before our husbands home iv 2 2
Do you intend to stay with me to-night? *T. of Shrew* Ind. 1 81
There is a lord will hear you play to-night Ind. 1 93
Is't possible you will away to-night?—I must away to-day iii 2 191
Last night she slept not, nor to-night she shall not iv 1 201
This contract; whose ceremony Shall seem expedient on the now-born brief, And be perform'd to-night *All's Well* ii 3 187
Madam, my lord will go away to-night ii 4 40
Will she away to-night?—As you'll have her ii 5 24
To-night, When I should take possession of the bride, End ere I do begin ii 5 27
Eat with us to-night, the charge and thanking Shall be for me iii 5 101
You shall see his fall to-night iii 6 108
Why then to-night Let us assay our plot iii 7 43
We shall not then have his company to-night?—Not till after midnight iv 3 33
I have to-night dispatched sixteen businesses, a month's length a-piece iv 3 98
I have letters that my son will be here to-night iv 5 91
Sweet Sir Toby, be patient for to-night *T. Night* ii 3 142
Away to-night! Your followers I will whisper to the business *W. Tale* i 2 436
He took good rest to-night; 'Tis hoped his sickness is discharged ii 3 10
He hath not slept to-night; commanded None should come at him ii 3 31
He tells us Arthur is deceased to-night *K. John* iv 2 85
Of Arthur, whom they say is kill'd to-night On your suggestion iv 2 165
They say five moons were seen to-night iv 2 182
I did not think to be so sad to-night As this hath made me v 5 15
Keep good quarter and good care to-night v 5 20
Gadshill lies to-night in Rochester *1 Hen. IV.* i 2 143
I will set forward to-night. How now, Kate! I must leave you ii 3 38
Watch to-night, pray to-morrow ii 4 306
Worcester is stolen away to-night ii 4 392
Our soldiers shall march through; we'll to Sutton Co'fil' to-night iv 2 3
We'll fight with him to-night.—It may not be iv 3 1
Be advised; stir not to-night.—Do not, my lord iv 3 5
Yea, or to-night.—Content.—To-night, say I iv 3 14
How might we see Falstaff bestow himself to-night in his true colours, and not ourselves be seen? *2 Hen. IV.* ii 2 187
I must a dozen mile to-night iii 2 311
I trust, lords, we shall lie to-night together iv 2 97
By cock and pie, sir, you shall not away to-night v 1 2
We will aboard to-night. Why, how now, gentlemen! *Hen. V.* ii 2 71
To-night in Harfleur will we be your guest; To-morrow for the march iii 3 57
The armour that I saw in your tent to-night, are those stars or suns upon it? iii 7 74
Being captain of the watch to-night *1 Hen. VI.* ii 1 61
There hath at least five Frenchmen died to-night ii 2 9
I did dream to-night The duke was dumb and could not speak a word *2 Hen. VI.* iii 2 31
For you shall sup with Jesu Christ to-night v 1 214
More than the infant that is born to-night *Richard III.* ii 1 71
At Stony-Stratford will they be to-night ii 4 2
He dreamt to-night the boar had razed his helm iii 2 11
Here will I lie to-night; But where to-morrow? Well, all's one for that v 3 7
And so, God give you quiet rest to-night! v 3 43
It's supper-time, my lord; It's nine o'clock.—I will not sup to-night v 3 48
Shadows to-night Have struck more terror to the soul of Richard v 3 216
I will play no more to-night; My mind's not on't *Hen. VIII.* v 1 56
What exploit's in hand? where sups he to-night? *Troi. and Cres.* iii 1 90
My brother Troilus lodges there to-night: Rouse him iv 1 42
Hast not slept to-night? would he not, a naughty man, let it sleep? iv 2 33
To-morrow do I meet thee, fell as death; To-night all friends iv 5 270
There Diomed doth feast with him to-night iv 5 280
I'll heat his blood with Greekish wine to-night v 1 1
The augurer tells me we shall have news to-night *Coriolanus* ii 1 2
I will make my very house reel to-night ii 1 121
Therefore it is decreed He dies to-night iii 1 290
I dream'd a dream to-night.—And so did I *Rom. and Jul.* i 4 50
For that which thou hast heard me speak to-night ii 2 87
Although I joy in thee, I have no joy of this contract to-night ii 2 117
What satisfaction canst thou have to-night? ii 2 126
Our Romeo hath not been in bed to-night ii 3 42
Came he not home to-night?—Not to his father's ii 4 2
'Tis very late, she'll not come down to-night iii 4 5
To-night she is mew'd up to her heaviness iii 4 11
I'll not to bed to-night; let me alone iv 2 42
I pray thee, leave me to myself to-night iv 3 2
Hire post-horses; I will hence to-night v 1 26
Well, Juliet, I will lie with thee to-night. Let's see for means v 1 34
What cursed foot wanders this way to-night? v 3 19
How oft to-night Have my old feet stumbled at graves! v 3 121
Alas, my liege, my wife is dead to-night v 3 210
I dreamt of a silver basin and ewer to-night *T. of Athens* iii 1 6
Will you sup with me to-night, Casca?—No *J. Cæsar* i 2 292

To-night. Never till to-night, never till now, Did I go through a tempest dropping fire *J. Cæsar* i 3 9
Why you are heavy, and what men to-night Have had resort to you ii 1 275
Nor heaven nor earth have been at peace to-night ii 2 1
She dreamt to-night she saw my statua ii 2 76
Is thy master coming?—He lies to-night within seven leagues of Rome iii 1 286
I dreamt to-night that I did feast with Cæsar iii 3 1
Bid the commanders Prepare to lodge their companies to-night iv 3 140
Within my tent his bones to-night shall lie, Most like a soldier v 5 78
The king comes here to-night.—Thou'rt mad to say it *Macbeth* i 5 32
Duncan comes here to-night.—And when goes hence?—To-morrow i 5 60
Fair and noble hostess, We are your guest to-night i 6 25
To-night we hold a solemn supper, sir, And I'll request your presence iii 1 14
'T must be done to-night, And something from the palace iii 1 131
Thy soul's flight, If it find heaven, must find it out to-night iii 1 142
Is Banquo gone from court?—Ay, madam, but returns again to-night iii 2 2
Be bright and jovial among your guests to-night iii 2 28
It will be rain to-night.—Let it come down iii 3 16
Do we but find the tyrant's power to-night, Let us be beaten, if we cannot fight v 6 7
What, has this thing appear'd again to-night? *Hamlet* i 1 21
Let us impart what we have seen to-night Unto young Hamlet i 1 169
Hold you the watch to-night?—We do, my lord i 2 225
I will watch to-night; Perchance 'twill walk again i 2 242
Whatsoever else shall hap to-night, Give it an understanding, but no tongue i 2 249
The king doth wake to-night and takes his rouse i 4 8
Never make known what you have seen to-night i 5 144
There is a play to-night before the king iii 2 80
Refrain to-night, And that shall lend a kind of easiness To the next abstinence iii 4 165
Ah, mine own lord, what have I seen to-night! iv 1 5
Delay it not; I'll have him hence to-night: Away! iv 3 57
I think our father will hence to-night.—That's most certain *Lear* i 1 288
The king gone to-night! subscribed his power! i 2 24
The duke be here to-night? The better! best! ii 1 16
My master, My worthy arch and patron, comes to-night ii 1 61
What will hap more to-night, safe 'scape the king! iii 6 121
He to-night hath boarded a land carack *Othello* i 2 50
We lack'd your counsel and your help to-night.—So did I yours i 3 51
You must away to-night.—With all my heart i 3 279
The lieutenant to-night watches on the court of guard ii 1 219
Watch you to-night; for the command, I'll lay't upon you ii 1 271
Good Michael, look you to the guard to-night ii 3 1
Not to-night, good Iago: I have very poor and unhappy brains for drinking ii 3 34
I have drunk but one cup to-night, and that was craftily qualified too ii 3 40
If I can fasten but one cup upon him, With that which he hath drunk to-night already ii 3 51
To Desdemona hath to-night caroused Potations pottle-deep ii 3 55
Three lads of Cyprus . . . Have I to-night fluster'd with flowing cups ii 3 60
And Cassio high in oath; which till to-night I ne'er might say before ii 3 235
I have been to-night exceedingly well cudgelled ii 3 371
Shall't be to-night at supper?—No, not to-night.—To-morrow dinner, then? iii 3 57
An you'll come to supper to-night, you may iv 1 166
Let her rot, and perish, and be damned to-night iv 1 192
To-night, I do entreat that we may sup together iv 1 272
To-night Lay on my bed my wedding sheets iv 2 104
He sups to-night with a harlotry, and thither will I go to him iv 2 239
That song to-night Will not go from my mind iv 3 30
Go know of Cassio where he supp'd to-night v 1 117
Have you pray'd to-night, Desdemona? v 2 25
Kill me to-morrow: let me live to-night!—Nay, if you strive v 2 80
What sport to-night?—Hear the ambassadors *Ant. and Cleo.* i 1 47
To-night we'll wander through the streets and note The qualities of people i 1 53
Mine, and most of our fortunes, to-night, shall be—drunk to bed i 2 45
To-night I'll force The wine peep through their scars iii 13 190
Let's to-night Be bounteous at our meal iv 2 9
Well, my good fellows, wait on me to-night iv 2 20
Tend me to-night; May be it is the period of your duty iv 2 24
Tend me to-night two hours, I ask no more iv 2 32
If you please To greet your lord with writing, do't to-night *Cymbeline* i 6 206
Did you hear of a stranger that's come to court to-night? ii 1 36
What I have lost to-day at bowls I'll win to-night of him ii 1 54
This chanced to-night.—Most likely, sir.—Nay, certainly to-night *Per.* iii 2 77
We shall have him here to-morrow with his best ruff on.—To-night, to-night iv 2 112
I'll bring home some to-night iv 2 157

Too. Lest too light winning Make the prize light *Tempest* i 2 451
I am more serious than my custom: you Must be so too ii 1 220
I heard a humming, And that a strange one too ii 1 318
What thou sayest?—Ay, and what I do too *T. G. of Ver.* ii 5 30
As take from me thyself and not me too *Com. of Errors* ii 2 131
Pretty and witty, wild and yet, too, gentle iii 1 110
What a multitude are here! They grow still too *Hen. VIII.* v 4 72
You scratch'd your head, And too impatiently stamp'd with your foot *J. Cæsar* ii 1 244

Too much. O, but I love his lady too too much *T. G. of Ver.* ii 4 205
He is of too high a region; he knows too much *Mer. Wives* iii 2 74
You have too much respect upon the world *Mer. of Venice* i 1 74
Can one desire too much of a good thing? *As Y. Like It* iv 1 123
Alas, your too much love and care of me Are heavy orisons 'gainst this poor wretch! *Hen. V.* ii 2 52
Doth add more grief to too much of mine own *Rom. and Jul.* i 1 195
I beseech you instantly to visit My too much changed son *Hamlet* ii 2 36
Something too much of this iii 2 79
For goodness, growing to a plurisy, Dies in his own too much iv 7 119
To amplify too much, would make much more *Lear* v 3 206

Too thin. They are too thin and bare to hide offences *Hen. VIII.* v 3 125

Too too. Her defences, which now are too too strongly embattled against me *Mer. Wives* ii 2 260
Exceeding fantastical; too too vain, too too vain *L. L. Lost* v 2 532
They in themselves, good sooth, are too too light *Mer. of Venice* ii 6 42
O, 'tis a fault too too unpardonable! *3 Hen. VI.* i 4 106
O, that this too too solid flesh would melt! *Hamlet* i 2 129

Took. I took him to be killed with a thunder-stroke *Tempest* ii 2 112
I remember the trick you served me when I took my leave *T. G. of Ver.* iv 4 38
Be thou ashamed that I have took upon me Such an immodest raiment v 4 105
I took't upon mine honour thou hadst it not *Mer. Wives* ii 2 12

Took. They took me on their shoulders . . . . *Mer. Wives* iii 5 101
You took the wrong.— . . . I think so, when I took a boy for a girl . v 5 200
If he took you a box o' the ear, you might have your action of slander
Meas. for Meas. ii 1 189
He that might the vantage best have took Found out the remedy . . ii 2 74
Which had you rather, that the most just law Now took your brother's
life ; or, to redeem him, Give up your body? . . . . ii 4 53
Hath homely age the alluring beauty took From my poor cheek? *C. of Er.* ii 1 89
And therewithal took measure of my body . . . . iv 3 9
He rush'd into my house and took perforce My ring away . . . iv 3 95
He took this place for sanctuary, And it shall privilege him . . v 1 94
A most outrageous fit of madness took him . . . . . v 1 139
I bestrid thee in the wars and took Deep scars to save thy life . . v 1 192
This pernicious slave, Forsooth, took on him as a conjurer . . v 1 242
Rude fishermen of Corinth By force took Dromio and my son from them v 1 352
You may say they are not the men you took them for . . *Much Ado* iii 3 51
I do love that country girl that I took in the park . . *L. L. Lost* i 2 123
You took the moon at full, but now she's changed . . . . v 2 214
I always took three threes for nine . . . . . . v 2 495
A certain aim he took At a fair vestal throned by the west *M. N. Dream* ii 1 157
I took him sleeping,—that is finish'd too . . . . . iii 2 38
She is indeed more than I took her for . . . *Mer. of Venice* iii 5 46
The boy, his clerk, That took some pains in writing . . . v 1 182
So was I when your highness took his dukedom . . *As Y. Like It* i 3 61
I remember the wooing of a peascod instead of her, from whom I took
two cods . . . . ii 4 52
He took some care To get her cunning schoolmasters . . *T. of Shrew* i 1 191
Took him such a cuff That down fell priest and book and book and priest iii 2 165
He took the bride about the neck And kiss'd her lips . . . iii 2 179
Proffers not took reap thanks for their reward . . . *All's Well* ii 1 150
I took this lark for a bunting . . . . ii 5 6
And shall do so ever, though I took him at's prayers . . . . ii 5 45
Such a ring as this, The last that e'er I took her leave at court, I saw
upon her finger . . . . v 3 79
I took great pains to study it, and 'tis poetical . . . *T. Night* i 5 206
I cannot love him ; He might have took his answer long ago . . . i 5 282
Some hour before you took me from the breach of the sea . . . ii 1 23
She took the ring of me : I'll none of it . . . . . . ii 2 13
A fool that the lady Olivia's father took much delight in . . . ii 4 12
It might have since been answer'd in repaying What we took from them iii 3 34
This is that Antonio That took the Phœnix . . . . . . v 1 64
We took him for a coward, but he's the very devil incardinate . . v 1 184
He took good rest to-night ; 'Tis hoped his sickness is discharged *W. T.* ii 3 10
He straight declined, droop'd, took it deeply . . . . . ii 3 14
Her face o' fire With labour and the thing she took to quench it . iv 4 61
Or from the all that are took something good, To make a perfect woman v 1 14
The shepherd's daughter, so he then took her to be . . . . v 2 127
The king's son took me by the hand, and called me brother . . . v 2 151
From thy admiring daughter took the spirits . . . . . v 3 41
Fair fall the bones that took the pains for me! . . . *K. John* i 1 78
The advantage of his absence took the king . . . . . i 1 102
And took it on his death That this my mother's son was none of his . i 1 110
We, perusing o'er these notes, May know wherefore we took the
sacrament . . . . v 2 6
Hotspur took Mordake the Earl of Fife . . . . *1 Hen. IV.* i 1 70
A pouncet-box, which ever and anon He gave his nose and took't away
again ; Who therewith angry, when it next came there, Took it in
snuff . . . . i 3 39
All those wounds, Those mouthed wounds, which valiantly he took . . i 3 97
I made me no more ado but took all their seven points in my target . ii 4 223
Falling from a hill, he was so bruised That the pursuers took him . v 5 22
Being bruited once, took fire and heat away . . . *2 Hen. IV.* i 1 114
In his flight, Stumbling in fear, was took . . . . . i 1 131
He gave it like a rude prince, and you took it like a sensible lord . . i 2 219
A famous rebel art thou, Colevile.—And a famous true subject took him iv 3 70
Where is the crown? who took it from my pillow? . . . . iv 5 58
Had you been as I took you for, I made no offence . . *Hen. V.* iv 8 58
Most of the rest slaughter'd or took likewise . . . *1 Hen. VI.* i 1 147
I pray, my lord, pardon me ; I took ye for my lord protector *2 Hen. VI.* i 3 14
'Tis thought, my lord, that you took bribes of France . . . iii 1 104
I took a costly jewel from my neck, A heart it was . . . . iii 2 106
That dread King that took our state upon him . . . . . iii 2 154
Thy mother took into her blameful bed Some stern untutor'd churl . iii 2 212
Suddenly a grievous sickness took him . . . . . . iii 2 370
We took him setting of boys' copies.—Here's a villain! . . . . iv 2 95
An oath is of no moment, being not took Before a true and lawful
magistrate, That hath authority . . . . . *3 Hen. VI.* i 2 22
Now looks he like a king! Ay, this is he that took King Henry's chair i 4 97
They took his head, and on the gates of York They set the same . . ii 1 65
When he took a beggar to his bed . . . . ii 2 154
And go we, brothers, to the man that took him . . . . . iii 2 121
I took him for the plainest harmless creature That breathed *Richard III.* iii 5 25
Thus I took the vantage of those few, 'Thanks, gentle citizens' . . iii 7 37
Took he upon him, Without the privity o' the king, to appoint Who
should attend on him? . . . . *Hen. VIII.* i 1 73
By commission and main power, took 'em from me . . . . . ii 2 7
Hence I took a thought, This was a judgement on me . . . . ii 4 193
I can watch you for telling how I took the blow . . *Troi. and Cres.* i 2 294
The seas and winds, old wranglers, took a truce . . . . ii 2 75
You have a Trojan prisoner, call'd Antenor, Yesterday took . . . iii 3 19
A murrain on't! I took this for silver . . . . *Coriolanus* i 5 3
His sword, death's stamp, Where it did mark, it took . . . . ii 2 112
Your loves, Thinking upon his services, took from you The apprehension ii 3 231
Consumed with fire, and took What lay before them . . . . iv 6 78
I took him ; Made him joint-servant with me . . . . . v 6 31
I took some pride To do myself this wrong . . . . . v 6 37
And from her bosom took the enemy's point . . . *T. Andron.* v 3 111
Then have my lips the sin that they have took . . *Rom. and Jul.* i 5 110
Very well took, i' faith ; wisely, wisely . . . . . . ii 4 131
And presently took post to tell it you . . . . . . v 1 21
We took this mattock and this spade from him . . . . . v 3 185
Perchance some single vantages you took . . . *T. of Athens* ii 2 138
Your words have took such pains as if they labour'd . . . . iii 5 26
Such instigations have been often dropp'd Where I have took them up
J. Cæsar ii 1 50
Therefore I took your hands, but was, indeed, Sway'd from the point . iii 1 218
And took his voice who should be prick'd to die, In our black sentence iv 1 16
Who, having some advantage on Octavius, Took it too eagerly . . v 3 7
He took me by the wrist and held me hard . . . . *Hamlet* ii 1 87
Which done, she took the fruits of my advice . . . . . ii 2 145
Took. He took my father grossly, full of bread ; With all his crimes
broad blown, as flush as May . . . . . . *Hamlet* iii 3 80
Thou wretched, rash, intruding fool, farewell! I took thee for thy better iii 4 32
The hot-blooded France, that dowerless took Our youngest born . *Lear* ii 4 215
They took from me the use of mine own house . . . . . iii 3 3
Cry you mercy, I took you for a joint-stool . . . . . iii 6 54
She took them, read them in my presence . . . . . . iv 3 13
That thing you speak of, I took it for a man . . . . . iv 6 78
All levied in my name, have in my name Took their discharge . . v 3 105
Which I observing, Took once a pliant hour, and found good means *Oth.* i 3 151
She let it drop by negligence, And, to the advantage, I, being here,
took't up . . . . iii 3 312
I took you for that cunning whore of Venice That married with Othello iv 2 89
I took by the throat the circumcised dog, And smote him, thus . . v 2 355
When the best hint was given him, he not took't . . *Ant. and Cleo.* iii 4 9
She levell'd at our purposes, and, being royal, Took her own way . . v 2 340
Took such sorrow That he quit being . . . . . *Cymbeline* i 1 37
Which he took, As we do air, fast as 'twas minister'd . . . . i 1 44
Thou wast their nurse ; they took thee for their mother . . . iii 3 104
Took pity From most true wretchedness . . . . . . iii 4 62
And thought To have begg'd or bought what I have took . . . iii 6 48
Though you took his life, as being our foe, Yet bury him as a prince . iv 2 250
Lucina lent not me her aid, But took me in my throes . . . . v 4 44
Which, being took, Should by the minute feed on life . . . . v 5 50
Like a noble lord in love and one That had a royal lover, took his hint v 5 172
This king unto him took a fere, Who died and left a female heir *Per.* i Gower 21
With whom the father liking took, And her to incest did provoke . i Gower 25
On what cause I know not—Took some displeasure at him . . . i 3 21
The rough seas, that spare not any man, Took it in rage . . . ii 1 138
Took alive. Our will is Antony be took alive . . . *Ant. and Cleo.* iv 6 2
Took an oath. I took an oath that he should quietly reign . *3 Hen. VI.* i 2 15
Took away. The body That took away the match from Isabel *M. for M.* v 1 211
All in rage to-day Came to my house and took away my ring *Com. of Er.* iv 4 141
Took captive. Whose words all ears took captive . . . *All's Well* v 3 17
Took effect. Which so took effect As I intended . . . *Rom. and Jul.* v 3 244
Took exceptions. He first took exceptions at this badge *1 Hen. VI.* iv 1 105
Took heel to do't, And yet died too! . . . . . . *Cymbeline* v 3 67
Took horse. They summon'd up their meiny, straight took horse *Lear* ii 4 35
Took leave. The same suit he wore when he took leave . *Cymbeline* iii 5 128
Took note. As I took note of the place, it cannot be far . *T. of Athens* v 1 1
Took occasion. You took occasion to be quickly woo'd . *1 Hen. IV.* v 1 56
Took odds to combat a poor famish'd man . . . *2 Hen. VI.* iv 10 47
Took off. By self and violent hands Took off her life . . *Macbeth* v 8 71
Took pains. I pitied thee, Took pains to make thee speak . *Tempest* i 2 354
I took no more pains for those thanks than you took pains to thank me
Much Ado ii 3 269
My brother, Who, as you say, took pains to get this son . *K. John* i 1 121
Took prisoner. O no, he lives ; but is took prisoner . *1 Hen. VI.* i 1 145
Took stand. Though we upon this mountain's basis by Took stand
for idle speculation . . . . *Hen. V.* iv 2 31
Took to wife. A woman that Lord Brutus took to wife . *J. Cæsar* ii 1 293
Took up. What is't that you took up so gingerly? . . *T. G. of Ver.* i 2 70
Why had I not with charitable hand Took up a beggar's issue? *M. Ado* iv 1 134
Took up the child: 'Yea,' quoth he, 'dost thou fall upon thy face?'
Rom. and Jul. i 3 40
He took up my legs sometime, yet I made a shift to cast him *Macbeth* ii 3 45
Tookest. Wondering how thou took'st it . . . . *All's Well* ii 1 93
Thou took'st a beggar ; wouldst have made my throne A seat for
baseness . . . . *Cymbeline* i 1 141
Tool. Some strange Indian with the great tool . . . *Hen. VIII.* v 4 35
Sirs, take you to your tools . . . . . . *T. Andron.* iv 3 6
Draw thy tool; here comes two of the house of the Montagues *R. and J.* i 1 37
Some coiner with his tools Made me a counterfeit . . . *Cymbeline* ii 5 5
Having work More plentiful than tools to do't . . . . . v 3 9
Tooth. A forted residence 'gainst the tooth of time . *Meas. for Meas.* v 1 12
A jealous woman Poisons more deadly than a mad dog's tooth *C. of Er.* v 1 70
Thy tooth is not so keen, Because thou art not seen *As Y. Like It* ii 7 177
An old trot with ne'er a tooth in her head . . . *T. of Shrew* i 2 80
I'll like a maid the better, whilst I have a tooth in my head *All's Well* ii 3 48
Doth set my pugging tooth on edge . . . . . . *W. Tale* iv 3 7
As soft as dove's down and as white as it, Or Ethiopian's tooth . . iv 4 375
Sweet, sweet, sweet poison for the age's tooth . . . *K. John* i 1 213
Thou mayst hold . . . A fasting tiger safer by the tooth . . . iii 1 260
Fell sorrow's tooth doth never rankle more Than when he bites, but
lanceth not the sore . . . . *Richard II.* i 3 302
I am the veriest varlet that ever chewed with a tooth . *1 Hen. IV.* ii 2 26
And the wild dog Shall flesh his tooth on every innocent *2 Hen. IV.* iv 5 133
Whose tongue more poisons than the adder's tooth! . *3 Hen. VI.* i 4 112
And when he bites, His venom tooth will rankle to the death *Rich. III.* i 3 291
'Twas full two years ere I could get a tooth . . . . . ii 4 29
Your colt's tooth is not cast yet . . . . . *Hen. VIII.* i 3 48
But still sweet love is food for fortune's tooth . *Troi. and Cres.* iv 5 293
Whilst our poor malice Remains in danger of her former tooth *Macbeth* iii 2 15
Scale of dragon, tooth of wolf, Witches' mummy, maw and gulf . . iv 1 22
How sharper than a serpent's tooth it is To have a thankless child! *Lear* i 4 310
Be thy mouth or black or white, Tooth that poisons if it bite . . iii 6 70
My name is lost ; By treason's tooth bare-gnawn and canker-bit . . v 3 122
Being troubled with a raging tooth, I could not sleep . . *Othello* iii 3 414
Toothache. I have the toothache.—Draw it!—Hang it! . . *Much Ado* iii 2 21
What! sigh for the toothache?—Where is but a humour or a worm . iii 2 26
Yet is this no charm for the toothache . . . . . . iii 2 72
There was never yet philosopher That could endure the toothache
patiently . . . . v 1 36
Indeed, sir, he that sleeps feels not the tooth-ache . . *Cymbeline* v 4 178
Tooth-drawer. Worn in the cap of a tooth-drawer . . *L. L. Lost* v 2 622
Toothed. Through Tooth'd briers, sharp furzes, pricking goss *Tempest* iv 1 180
Tooth-pick. Unsuitable ; just like the brooch and the tooth-pick, which
wear not now . . . . *All's Well* i 1 171
Now your traveller, He and his toothpick at my worship's mess *K. John* i 1 190
Toothpicker. I will fetch you a toothpicker now from the furthest inch
of Asia . . . . *Much Ado* ii 1 274
Top. The top of admiration! worth What's dearest to the world! *Tempest* iii 1 38
Since I plucked geese, played truant, and whipped top . *Mer. Wives* v 1 27
How would you be, If He, which is the top of judgement, should But
judge you as you are? . . . . *Meas. for Meas.* ii 2 76
Hath yet a kind of medicine in itself, That skins the vice o' the top . ii 2 136
He meant to take the present time by the top . . . *Much Ado* i 2 16
Do you not educate youth at the charge-house on the top of the
mountain? . . . . *L. L. Lost* v 1 87
Kill me a red-hipped humble-bee on the top of a thistle *M. N. Dream* iv 1 12

Top. We will, fair queen, up to the mountain's top — *M. N. Dream* iv 1 114
As well forbid the mountain pines To wag their high tops *Mer. of Venice* iv 1 76
Moss'd with age And high top bald with dry antiquity — *As Y. Like It* iv 3 106
And bow'd his eminent top to their low ranks — *All's Well* i 2 43
Let's take the instant by the forward top — v 3 39
The centre is not big enough to bear A school-boy's top — *W. Tale* ii 1 103
This is the very top, The height, the crest, or crest unto the crest *K. John* iv 3 45
The vaulty top of heaven Figured quite o'er with burning meteors — v 2 52
He fires the proud tops of the eastern pines — *Richard II.* iii 2 42
Where rude misgovern'd hands from windows' tops Threw dust and rubbish on King Richard's head — v 2 5
He is walked up to the top of the hill: I'll go seek him — *1 Hen. IV.* ii 2 8
The winds, Who take the ruffian billows by the top — *2 Hen. IV.* iii 1 22
I will have it in a particular ballad else, with mine own picture on the top — iv 3 53
Discourse, I prithee, on this turret's top — *1 Hen. VI.* i 4 26
From top of honour to disgrace's feet — *2 Hen. VI.* i 2 49
Naked on a mountain top, Where biting cold would never let grass grow iii 2 336
Emmanuel.—They use to write it on the top of letters — iv 2 107
As on a mountain top the cedar shows — v 1 205
The raven rook'd her on the chimney's top — *3 Hen. VI.* v 6 47
Like to autumn's corn, Have we mow'd down in tops of all their pride! v 7 4
Our aery buildeth in the cedar's top, And dallies with the wind *Rich. III.* i 3 264
Forward, capable: He is all the mother's, from the top to toe — iii 1 156
Orpheus with his lute made trees, And the mountain tops that freeze, Bow themselves when he did sing — *Hen. VIII.* iii 1 4
Yond towers, whose wanton tops do buss the clouds, Must kiss their own feet.—I must not believe you — *Troi. and Cres.* iv 5 220
To the spire and top of praises vouch'd, Would seem but modest *Coriol.* i 9 24
He turned me about with his finger and his thumb, as one would set up a top — iv 5 161
Now climbeth Tamora Olympus' top — *T. Andron.* ii 1 1
I have dogs, my lord, Will . . . climb the highest promontory top — ii 2 22
That tips with silver all these fruit-tree tops — *Rom. and Jul.* ii 2 108
Jocund day Stands tiptoe on the misty mountain tops — iii 5 10
Fortune . . . Spurns down her late beloved, all his dependants Which labour'd after him to the mountain's top — *T. of Athens* i 1 86
Wears upon his baby-brow the round And top of sovereignty *Macbeth* iv 1 89
Not in the legions Of horrid hell can come a devil more damn'd In evils to top Macbeth — iv 3 57
Arm'd, my lord.—From top to toe?—My lord, from head to foot *Hamlet* i 2 228
An aery of children, little eyases, that cry out on the top of question — ii 2 355
Whose judgements in such matters cried in the top of mine — ii 2 459
Ilium, Seeming to feel this blow, with flaming top Stoops to his base — ii 2 497
You would sound me from my lowest note to the top of my compass — iii 2 383
They fool me to the top of my bent — iii 2 401
Unpeg the basket on the house's top, Let the birds fly — iii 4 193
Edmund the base Shall top the legitimate — *Lear* i 2 21
All the stored vengeances of heaven fall On her ingrateful top! — ii 4 165
When shall we come to the top of that same hill? — iv 6 1
To amplify too much, would make much more, And top extremity — v 3 207
My brother, my competitor In top of all design — *Ant. and Cleo.* v 1 43
Whose top to climb Is certain falling — *Cymbeline* iii 3 47
As the rudest wind, That by the top doth take the mountain pine — iv 2 175
Soft, ho! what trunk is here Without his top? — iv 2 354
As the tops of trees, Which fence the roots they grow by — *Pericles* i 2 29
A wither'd branch, that's only green at top; The motto, 'In hac spe vivo' — ii 2 43
Know that our griefs are risen to the top, And now at length they overflow — ii 4 23

Topas. Make him believe thou art Sir Topas the curate — *T. Night* iv 2 2
Sayest thou that house is dark?—As hell, Sir Topas — iv 2 39
Sir Topas!—My most exquisite Sir Topas! — iv 2 66
I was one, sir, in this interlude; one Sir Topas, sir; but that's all one. v 1 381

Top-branch. Whose top-branch overpeer'd Jove's spreading tree *3 Hen. VI.* v 2 14

Topfull. Now that their souls are topfull of offence — *K. John* iii 4 180
Fill me from the crown to the toe top-full Of direst cruelty! — *Macbeth* i 5 43

Top-gallant. Which to the high top-gallant of my joy Must be my convoy in the secret night — *Rom. and Jul.* ii 4 202

Topless. Thy topless deputation he puts on — *Troi. and Cres.* i 3 152

Topmast. Down with the topmast! yare! lower, lower! — *Tempest* i 1 37
On the topmast, The yards, and bowsprit, would I flame distinctly — i 2 199
Say Warwick was our anchor; what of that? And Montague our topmast; what of him? — *3 Hen. VI.* v 4 14
With sands that will not bear your enemies' boats, But suck them up to the topmast — *Cymbeline* iii 1 22

Topped. So far he topp'd my thought — *Hamlet* iv 7 89
Like to groves, being topp'd, they higher rise — *Pericles* i 4 9

Topping. And topping all others in boasting — *Coriolanus* ii 1 23

Topple. Down topples she, And 'tailor' cries — *M. N. Dream* ii 1 53
Topples down Steeples and moss-grown towers — *1 Hen. IV.* iii 1 32
Though castles topple on their warders' heads — *Macbeth* iv 1 56
I'll look no more; Lest my brain turn, and the deficient sight Topple down headlong — *Lear* iv 6 24
The very principals did seem to rend, And all-to topple — *Pericles* iii 2 17

Top-proud. This top-proud fellow, Whom from the flow of gall I name not but From sincere motions — *Hen. VIII.* i 1 151

Topsail. Take in the topsail. Tend to the master's whistle — *Tempest* i 1 7

Topsy-turvy. With his help We shall o'erturn it topsy-turvy down *1 Hen. IV.* iv 1 82

Torch. No bed-right shall be paid Till Hymen's torch be lighted *Tempest* iv 1 97
Heaven doth with us as we with torches do — *Meas. for Meas.* i 1 33
Put your torches out: The wolves have prey'd — *Much Ado* v 3 24
Thou hast saved me a thousand marks in links and torches *1 Hen. IV.* iii 3 48
Here dies the dusky torch of Mortimer, Choked with ambition *1 Hen. VI.* ii 5 122
How will she specify Where is the best and safest passage in?—By thrusting out a torch from yonder tower — iii 2 23
Behold, this is the happy wedding torch! — iii 2 26
The burning torch in yonder turret stands — iii 2 30
Follow his torch; he goes to Calchas' tent — *Troi. and Cres.* v 1 92
Stand where the torch may not discover us — v 2 5
Give me a torch: I am not for this ambling — *Rom. and Jul.* i 4 11
A torch for me: let wantons light of heart Tickle the senseless rushes with their heels — i 4 35
O, she doth teach the torches to burn bright! — i 5 46
Good night. More torches here! Come on then, let's to bed — i 5 127
Give me thy torch, boy: hence, and stand aloof — v 3 1
What, with a torch! muffle me, night, awhile — v 3 21
What torch is yond, that vainly lends his light To grubs and eyeless skulls? — v 3 125

Torch. This is the place; there, where the torch doth burn *Rom. and Jul.* v 3 171
A common slave—you know him well by sight—Held up his left hand, which did flame and burn Like twenty torches join'd — *J. Cæsar* i 3 17
Light, ho, here! Fly, brother. Torches, torches! — *Lear* ii 1 34
Did desire you To burn this night with torches — *Ant. and Cleo.* i 2 41
Since the torch is out, Lie down, and stray no farther — iv 14 46
What is the fourth?—A burning torch that's turned upside down; The word, 'Quod me alit, me extinguit' — *Pericles* ii 2 32

Torch-bearer. We have not spoke us yet of torch-bearers *Mer. of Venice* ii 4 5
I am provided of a torch-bearer — ii 4 24
Fair Jessica shall be my torch-bearer — ii 4 40
Descend, for you must be my torch-bearer — ii 6 40
It is some meteor that the sun exhales, To be to thee this night a torch-bearer, And light thee on thy way — *Rom. and Jul.* iii 5 14

Torcher. Ere twice the horses of the sun shall bring Their fiery torcher his diurnal ring — *All's Well* ii 1 165

Torch-light. Statilius show'd the torch-light, but, my lord, He came not back — *J. Cæsar* v 5 2

Torch-staves. The horsemen sit like fixed candlesticks, With torch-staves in their hand — *Hen. V.* iv 2 46

Tore. She tore the letter into a thousand halfpence — *Much Ado* ii 3 146
To see how the bear tore out his shoulder-bone — *W. Tale* iii 3 97
I tore them from their bonds and cried aloud — *K. John* iii 4 70
I tore it from the traitor's bosom — *Richard II.* v 3 55

Torment. Dost thou forget From what a torment I did free thee? *Tempest* i 2 251
Thou best know'st What torment I did find thee in — i 2 287
It was a torment To lay upon the damn'd — i 2 289
Here comes a spirit of his, and to torment me For bringing wood in slowly — ii 2 15
Do not torment me: Oh!—What's the matter? — ii 2 58
The spirit torments me; Oh! — ii 2 66
Do not torment me, prithee; I'll bring my wood home faster — ii 2 74
All torment, trouble, wonder, and amazement Inhabits here — v 1 104
Some foul mischance Torment me for my love's forgetfulness! *T. G. of V.* ii 2 12
And why not death rather than living torment? — iii 1 170
That which now torments me to rehearse: I kill'd a man — iv 1 26
And swears she never will: that's her torment — *Much Ado* ii 3 130
He would make but a sport of it and torment the poor lady worse — ii 3 163
A world of torments though I should endure, I would not yield *L. L. Lost* v 2 353
Thou shalt not from this grove Till I torment thee for this injury *M. N. Dream* ii 1 147
O happy torment, when my torturer Doth teach me answers for deliverance! But let me to my fortune — *Mer. of Venice* iii 2 37
What studied torments, tyrant, hast for me? — *W. Tale* iii 2 176
I'll forgive you, Whatever torment you do put me to — *K. John* iv 1 84
I grieve to hear what torments you endured — *1 Hen. VI.* i 4 57
The loss of those three lords torments my heart — *3 Hen. VI.* i 1 270
Is as a fury to torment my soul — i 3 31
Torment myself to catch the English crown: And from that torment I will free myself — iii 2 180
Seize on him, Furies, take him to your torments! — *Richard III.* i 4 57
Who shall hinder me to wail and weep, To chide my fortune, and torment myself? — ii 2 35
By hell and all hell's torments, I will not speak a word! *Troi. and Cres.* v 2 43
To torment you with my bitter tongue — *T. Andron.* v 1 150
Art thou sent to me, To be a torment to mine enemies? — v 2 42
That same pale hard-hearted wench, that Rosaline, Torments him so, that he will sure run mad — *Rom. and Jul.* ii 4 5
What devil art thou, that dost torment me thus? — iii 2 43
If thou wert the ass, thy dulness would torment thee — *T. of Athens* iv 3 335
If she must teem, Create her child of spleen; that it may live, And be a thwart disnatured torment to her! — *Lear* i 4 305
It is silliness to live when to live is torment — *Othello* i 3 309
I never will speak word.—What, not to pray?—Torments will ope your lips — v 2 305
If there be any cunning cruelty That can torment him much and hold him long, It shall be his — v 2 334
There shall she see my valour, which will then be a torment to her contempt — *Cymbeline* iii 5 143
I am glad to be constrain'd to utter that Which torments me to conceal v 5 142

Tormenta. Si fortuna me tormenta, spero contenta — *2 Hen. IV.* v 5 102

Tormente. Si fortune me tormente, sperato me contento — ii 4 195

Tormented. Shut up in prison, kept without my food, Whipp'd and tormented and—God-den, good fellow — *Rom. and Jul.* i 2 57

Tormentest. Fiend, thou torment'st me ere I come to hell! *Richard II.* iv 1 270
Enough, sweet Suffolk; thou torment'st thyself — *2 Hen. VI.* iii 2 329

Tormenting. Whilst some tormenting dream Affrights thee *Richard III.* i 3 226
When I to sulphurous and tormenting flames Must render up myself *Ham.* i 5 3

Tormentor. These words hereafter thy tormentors be! *Richard II.* ii 1 136

Torn. Now prove Our loving lawful, and our faith not torn *L. L. Lost* iv 3 285
Bedabbled with the dew and torn with briers — *M. N. Dream* iii 2 443
Upon his arm The lionness had torn some flesh away *As Y. Like It* iv 3 148
He was torn to pieces with a bear — *W. Tale* v 2 68
From my own windows torn my household coat — *Richard II.* iii 1 24
Have torn their souls by turning them from us — iii 3 83
France should have torn and rent my very heart, Before I would have yielded to this league — *2 Hen. VI.* i 1 126
Broke be my sword, my arms torn and defaced, And I proclaim'd a coward through the world! — iv 1 42
What so many may do, Not being torn a-pieces, we have done *Hen. VIII.* v 4 80
A thought of added honour torn from Hector — *Troi. and Cres.* iv 5 145
Though thy tackle's torn, Thou show'st a noble vessel — *Coriolanus* iv 5 67
Torn from forth that pretty hollow cage — *T. Andron.* iii 1 84
And shrieks like mandrakes' torn out of the earth — *Rom. and Jul.* iv 3 47

Torrent. And are enforced from our most quiet there By the rough torrent of occasion — *2 Hen. IV.* iv 1 72
The torrent roar'd, and we did buffet it With lusty sinews — *J. Cæsar* i 2 107
In the very torrent, tempest, and, as I may say, the whirlwind of passion *Hamlet* iii 2 6

Tortive. As knots, by the conflux of meeting sap, Infect the sound pine and divert his grain Tortive and errant from his course of growth *Troi. and Cres.* i 3 9

Tortoise. There's other business for thee: Come, thou tortoise! *Tempest* i 2 316
In his needy shop a tortoise hung, An alligator stuff'd — *Rom. and Jul.* v 1 42

Torture. Well; I will take him, then torture my wife — *Mer. Wives* iii 2 41
Refuse me, hate me, torture me to death! — *Much Ado* iv 1 186
That same Biron I'll torture ere I go — *L. L. Lost* v 2 60
I'll plague him; I'll torture him: I am glad of it — *Mer. of Venice* iii 1 122
Extended With vilest torture let my life be ended — *All's Well* ii 1 177
He calls for the tortures: what will you say without 'em? — iv 3 137

Torture. Charge thee, On thy soul's peril and thy body's torture *W. Tale* ii 3 181
What old or newer torture Must I receive? . . . . . . iii 2 178
The curses he shall have, the tortures he shall feel . . . iv 4 796
How now, foolish rheum! Turning dispiteous torture out of door! *K. John* iv 1 34
Let hell want pains enough to torture me . . . . . iv 3 138
To the infernal deep, with Erebus and tortures vile also . *2 Hen. IV.* ii 4 171
Let there be enow: Place barrels of pitch upon the fatal stake, That so her torture may be shortened . . . . . . *1 Hen. VI.* v 4 58
You go about to torture me in vain . . . . . . *2 Hen. VI.* ii 1 146
You did devise Strange tortures for offenders never heard of . . . iii 1 122
Torture him with grievous lingering death . . . . . iii 2 247
From thee to die were torture more than death . . . . iii 2 401
O, torture me no more! I will confess . . . . . iii 3 11
While we devise fell tortures for thy faults . . . *3 Hen. VI.* ii 6 72
Having no more but thought of what thou wert, To torture thee *Richard III.* iv 4 108
On pain of torture, from those bloody hands Throw your mistemper'd weapons to the ground. . . . . . *Rom. and Jul.* i 1 93
This torture should be roar'd in dismal hell . . . . . iii 2 44
There is no world without Verona walls, But purgatory, torture, hell itself . . . . iii 3 18
This is dear mercy, and thou seest it not.—'Tis torture, and not mercy . iii 3 29
Than on the torture of the mind to lie In restless ecstasy . *Macbeth* iii 2 21
If thou dost slander her and torture me, Never pray more . *Othello* iii 3 368
To you, lord governor, Remains the censure of this hellish villain; The time, the place, the torture . . . . v 2 369
My enfranched bondman, whom He may at pleasure whip, or hang, or torture, As he shall like . . . . . *Ant. and Cleo.* iii 13 150
So it must be, for now All length is torture: since the torch is out, Lie down . . . . iv 14 46
We'll enforce it from thee By a sharp torture . . . *Cymbeline* iv 3 12
Whose answer would be death Drawn on with torture . . . . iv 4 14
Bitter torture shall Winnow the truth from falsehood . . . . v 5 133
Thou 'lt torture me to leave unspoken that Which, to be spoke, would torture thee . . . . v 5 139
Tortured. I grow to you, and our parting is a tortured body *All's Well* ii 1 36
How have the hours rack'd and tortured me, Since I have lost thee! *T. Night* v 1 226
The unseen grief That swells with silence in the tortured soul *Rich. II.* iv 1 298
Murder indeed, that bloody sin, I tortured Above the felon *2 Hen. VI.* iii 1 131
Say he be taken, rack'd, and tortured . . . . . . iii 1 376
Torturer. O happy torment, when my torturer Doth teach me answers for deliverance! . . . . *Mer. of Venice* iii 2 37
I play the torturer, by small and small To lengthen out the worst *Richard II.* iii 2 198
Send out For torturers ingenious . . . . . . *Cymbeline* v 5 215
Torturest. Thou torturest me, Tubal: it was my turquoise *Mer. of Ven.* iii 1 125
Torturing. To ease the anguish of a torturing hour . *M. N. Dream* v 1 37
We have devised Some never-heard-of torturing pain for them *T. An.* ii 3 285
Toryne. Is it not strange, . . . He could so quickly cut the Ionian sea, And take in Toryne? . . . . . . *Ant. and Cleo.* iii 7 24
Cæsar has taken Toryne.—Can he be there in person? . . . iii 7 56
Toss. Such pitiful rascals.—Tut, tut; good enough to toss *1 Hen. IV.* iv 2 71
A rascally slave! I will toss the rogue in a blanket . . *2 Hen. IV.* ii 4 240
On which I'll toss the flower-de-luce of France . . *2 Hen. VI.* v 1 11
Back do I toss these treasons to thy head . . . . . *Lear* v 3 146
Even now Did the sea toss upon our shore this chest . . *Pericles* iii 2 50
Tossed. A weasel hath not such a deal of spleen As you are toss'd with *1 Hen. IV.* ii 3 82
The soldiers should have toss'd me on their pikes Before I would have granted to that act . . . . *3 Hen. VI.* i 1 244
And often up and down my sons were toss'd . . . *Richard III.* ii 4 58
My relief Must not be toss'd and turn'd to me in words . *T. of Athens* ii 1 26
I never saw so huge a billow, sir, As toss'd it upon shore . *Pericles* iii 2 59
I think thou said'st Thou hadst been toss'd from wrong to injury . v 1 131
Tosseth. What book is that she tosseth so? . . . *T. Andron.* iv 1 41
Tossing. Your mind is tossing on the ocean . . . *Mer. of Venice* i 1 8
How brooks your grace the air, After your late tossing on the breaking seas?—Needs must I like it well. . . . . . . *Richard II.* iii 2 3
Toss-pots. With toss-pots still had drunken heads . . . *T. Night* v 1 412
Tost. Having all lost, By waves from coast to coast is tost *Pericles* ii Gower 34
Total. Indeed, a tapster's arithmetic may soon bring his particulars therein to a total . . . . *Troi. and Cres.* i 2 124
Head to foot Now is he total gules . . . . . *Hamlet* ii 2 479
Totally. He doth but mistake the truth totally . . *Tempest* ii 1 57
Tottering. Which hung so tottering in the balance . . *All's Well* i 3 129
What news, what news, in this our tottering state? . *Richard III.* iii 2 37
Doth give me A more content in course of true delight Than to be thirsty after tottering honour . . . . *Pericles* iii 2 40
Totters. If th' other two be brained like us, the state totters . *Tempest* iii 2 8
Touch me and speak to me . . . . ii 2 105
Hast thou, which art but air, a touch, a feeling Of their afflictions? . v 1 21
O, touch me not; I am not Stephano, but a cramp . . . . v 1 286
Didst thou but know the inly touch of love . . *T. G. of Ver.* ii 7 18
I am to break with thee of some affairs That touch me near . . . iii 1 60
Whose golden touch could soften steel and stones, Make tigers tame . iii 2 79
Let go that rude uncivil touch, Thou friend of an ill fashion! . . v 4 60
Take but possession of her with a touch: I dare thee . . . . v 4 130
With trial-fire touch me his finger-end . . . *Mer. Wives* v 5 88
Ay, touch him; there's the vein . . . . *Meas. for Meas.* ii 2 70
No loss shall touch her by my company . . . . . . iii 1 181
From their abominable and beastly touches I drink, I eat, array myself iii 2 25
That no particular scandal once can touch But it confounds the breather iv 4 30
Who is as free from touch or soil with her As she from one ungot . v 1 141
Yet the gold bides still, That others touch . . . *Com. of Errors* ii 1 111
That never object pleasing in thine eye, That never touch well welcome to thy hand . . . . ii 2 118
How dearly would it touch thee to the quick, Shouldst thou but hear . ii 2 132
This touches me in reputation . . . . iv 1 71
I think they that touch pitch will be defiled . . . *Much Ado* iii 3 60
And one day in a week to touch no food . . . . *L. L. Lost* i 1 39
Never durst poet touch a pen to write Until his ink were temper'd with Love's sighs . . . . iv 3 346
A sweet touch, a quick venue of wit! snip, snap, quick, and home! . v 1 62
O brave touch! Could not a worm, an adder, do so much? *M. N. Dream* iii 2 70
Have you no modesty, no maiden shame, No touch of bashfulness? . iii 2 286
Not one vessel 'scape the dreadful touch Of merchant-marring rocks? *Mer. of Venice* iii 2 273
Soft stillness and the night Become the touches of sweet harmony . v 1 57

Touch. With sweetest touches pierce your mistress' ear And draw her home with music . . . . . . *Mer. of Venice* v 1 67
Any air of music touch their ears, You shall perceive them make a mutual stand . . . . v 1 76
Forbear, I say: He dies that touches any of this fruit . *As Y. Like It* ii 7 98
Till he be first sufficed, . . . I will not touch a bit . . . . ii 7 133
To have the touches dearest prized . . . . iii 2 160
His kissing is as full of sanctity as the touch of holy bread . . iii 4 15
Some lively touches of my daughter's favour . . . . . v 4 27
Before you touch the instrument, To learn the order of my fingering, I must begin with rudiments of art . . . . *T. of Shrew* iii 1 64
Here she stands, touch her whoever dare . . . . . iii 2 235
Fear not, sweet wench, they shall not touch thee . . . . iii 2 240
And not presume to touch a hair of my master's horse-tail . . iv 1 96
And I expressly am forbid to touch it, For it engenders choler . iv 1 174
The poorest service is repaid with thanks; And so shall mine, before you touch the meat.—I thank you, sir . . . . iv 3 46
None so dry or thirsty Will deign to sip or touch one drop of it . v 2 145
This she delivered in the most bitter touch of sorrow . . *All's Well* i 3 122
Whose simple touch Is powerful to araise King Pepin . . . . ii 1 78
Do not touch my lord. Whoever shoots at him, I set him there . . iii 2 114
I perceive in you so excellent a touch of modesty . . . *T. Night* ii 1 13
Not worthy to touch Fortune's fingers . . . . . . ii 5 171
One of the prettiest touches of all . . . . . . *W. Tale* v 2 89
May be he will not touch young Arthur's life . . . *K. John* iii 4 160
I will not touch thine eye For all the treasure that thine uncle owes . iv 1 122
No person be so bold Or daring-hardy as to touch the lists *Richard II.* i 3 43
Put into his hands That knows no touch to tune the harmony . . i 3 165
And shortly mean to touch our northern shore . . . . . ii 1 288
Why have those banish'd and forbidden legs Dared once to touch a dust of England's ground? . . . . ii 3 91
Whose double tongue may with a mortal touch Throw death . . . iii 2 21
Where fathom-line could never touch the ground . . *1 Hen. IV.* i 3 204
The lion will not touch the true prince . . . . . . ii 4 300
You ran away upon instinct, you will not touch the true prince . . ii 4 332
A day Wherein the fortune of ten thousand men Must bide the touch . iv 4 10
Thus do the hopes we have in him touch ground . *2 Hen. IV.* i 1 17
Touch her soft mouth, and march . . . . . *Hen. V.* ii 3 61
The nimble gunner With linstock now the devilish cannon touches iii Prol. 33
The earth sings when he touches it . . . . iii 7 17
Behold, as may unworthiness define, A little touch of Harry in the night iv Prol. 47
Your lips, Kate: there is more eloquence in a sugar touch of them . v 2 303
O, tell me when my lips do touch his cheeks . . . *1 Hen. VI.* ii 5 39
Do not fear nor fly! For I will touch thee but with reverent hands . v 3 47
Ready to starve and dare not touch his own . . . *2 Hen. VI.* i 1 229
Their touch affrights me as a serpent's sting . . . . . iii 2 47
Their softest touch as smart as lizards' stings! . . . . . iii 2 325
This deep disgrace . . . Touches me deeper than you can imagine *Rich. III.* i 1 112
No beast so fierce but knows some touch of pity . . . . i 2 71
Who shall be nearest, Will touch us all too near, if God prevent not . ii 3 26
To touch his growth nearer than he touch'd mine . . . . iii 4 25
But touch this sparingly, as 'twere far off . . . . . . iii 5 93
Now do I play the touch, To try if thou be current gold indeed . iv 2 8
I have a touch of your condition, Which cannot brook the accent of reproof . . . . iv 4 157
His curses and his blessings Touch me alike . . . *Hen. VIII.* ii 2 54
To the prejudice of her present state, Or touch of her good person . ii 4 155
Give your friend Some touch of your late business . . . . v 1 13
Let me touch your hand; To our pavilion shall I lead you *Troi. and Cres.* i 3 304
Do not these high strains Of divination in our sister work Some touches of remorse? . . . . ii 2 115
One touch of nature makes the whole world kin . . . . . iii 3 175
I know no touch of consanguinity; No kin, no love, no blood . . iv 2 103
If the drink you give me touch my palate adversely, I make a crooked face at it . . . . *Coriolanus* ii 1 61
At some time when his soaring insolence Shall touch the people . . ii 1 271
My friends of noble touch, when I am forth, Bid me farewell, and smile iv 1 49
He dies upon my scimitar's sharp point That touches this my first-born son and heir! . . . . *T. Andron.* iv 2 92
Touch not the boy; he is of royal blood . . . . . . v 1 49
Ready stand To smooth that rough touch with a tender kiss . *R. and J.* i 5 98
For saints have hands that pilgrims' hands do touch . . . . i 5 101
O, that I were a glove upon that hand, That I might touch that cheek! ii 2 25
For the Lord Timon, sir?—If he will touch the estimate *T. of Athens* i 1 14
Here is a touch; is't good?—I will say of it, It tutors nature: artificial strife Lives in these touches, livelier than life . . . i 1 36
Th' ear, Taste, touch, and smell, pleased from thy table rise . . i 2 132
Bid him suppose some good necessity Touches his friend . . . ii 2 237
Touch them with several fortunes . . . . iv 3 5
O thou touch of hearts [gold]! Think, thy slave man rebels . . iv 3 390
Forget not, in your speed, Antonius, To touch Calpurnia . *J. Cæsar* i 2 7
Mine's a suit That touches Cæsar nearer: read it, great Cæsar.—What touches us ourself shall be last served . . . . iii 1 7
Touch thy instrument a strain or two . . . . . . iv 3 257
Malice domestic, foreign levy, nothing, Can touch him further *Macbeth* iii 2 26
He loves us not; He wants the natural touch . . . . . iv 2 9
But at his touch—Such sanctity hath heaven given his hand—They presently amend . . . . iv 3 143
Come you more nearer Than your particular demands will touch it *Ham.* ii 1 12
Your majesty and we that have free souls, it touches us not . . iii 2 252
Believe me, I cannot.—I do beseech you.—I know no touch of it, my lord iii 2 371
The sun no sooner shall the mountains touch, But we will ship him hence iv 1 29
I'll touch my point With this contagion, that, if I gall him slightly, It may be death . . . . iv 7 147
Another hit; what say you?—A touch, a touch, I do confess . . v 2 297
Fool me not so much To bear it tamely; touch me with noble anger *Lear* ii 4 279
Might I but live to see thee in my touch, I'ld say I had eyes again! . iv 1 25
They cannot touch me for coining; I am the king himself . . . iv 6 83
This judgement of the heavens, that makes us tremble, Touches us not with pity . . . . v 3 232
Rough quarries, rocks, and hills whose heads touch heaven . *Othello* i 3 141
Thou art no soldier.—Touch me not so near . . . . . ii 3 220
When I have a suit Wherein I mean to touch your love indeed, It shall be full of poise and difficult weight . . . . iii 3 81
If it touch not you, it comes near nobody . . . . . . iv 1 209
If to preserve this vessel for my lord From any other foul unlawful touch Be not to be a strumpet, I am none . . . . . . iv 2 84
Would have walked barefoot to Palestine for a touch of his nether lip . iv 3 39
With more urgent touches, Do strongly speak to us . *Ant. and Cleo.* i 2 187

Touch. Touch you the sourest points with sweetest terms *Ant. and Cleo.* ii 2 24
The silken tackle Swell with the touches of those flower-soft hands . ii 2 215
I would not be the party that should desire you to touch him . v 2 246
Thy thoughts Touch their effects in this . v 2 333
A touch more rare Subdues all pangs, all fears *Cymbeline* i 1 135
This hand, whose touch, Whose every touch, would force the feeler's soul To the oath of loyalty . i 6 101
That I might touch! But kiss; one kiss! Rubies unparagon'd! . ii 2 16
Exposing it . . . to the greedy touch Of common-kissing Titan . iii 4 165
Heavens, How deeply you at once do touch me! . iv 3 4
But yield me to the veriest hind that shall Once touch my shoulder . v 3 78
He's no man on whom perfections wait That, knowing sin within, will touch the gate *Pericles* i 1 80
Touch not, upon thy life, For that's an article within our law . i 1 87
Touched. Which touch'd The very virtue of compassion in thee *Tempest* i 2 26
Never till this day Saw I him touch'd with anger so distemper'd . iv 1 145
Spirits are not finely touch'd But to fine issues *Meas. for Meas.* i 1 36
If so your heart were touch'd with that remorse As mine is . ii 2 54
Hath he borne himself penitently in prison? how seems he to be touched? iv 2 148
Neglect me not, with that opinion That I am touch'd with madness! . v 1 51
Give me the scope of justice; My patience here is touch'd . v 1 235
Unless I spake, or look'd, or touch'd, or carved to thee . *Com. of Errors* ii 2 120
There's no true drop of blood in him, to be truly touched with love *Much Ado* iii 2 19
Touch'd with human gentleness and love . *Mer. of Venice* iv 1 25
You touch'd my vein at first *As Y. Like It* ii 7 94
I thank God I am not a woman, to be touched with so many giddy offences . iii 2 366
If love have touch'd you, nought remains but so . *T. of Shrew* i 1 166
I dare vow for her, they touched not any stranger sense . *All's Well* i 3 114
Hearing your high majesty is touch'd With that malignant cause . ii 1 113
That you have touch'd his queen Forbiddenly . *W. Tale* i 2 416
Their familiarity, Which was as gross as ever touch'd conjecture . ii 1 176
He is touch'd To the noble heart . iii 2 222
Our ship hath touch'd upon The deserts of Bohemia . iii 3 1
By his command Have I here touch'd Sicilia . v 1 139
Which, being touch'd and tried, Proves valueless . *K. John* iii 1 100
The life of all his blood Is touch'd corruptibly . v 7 2
Whose beard the silver hand of peace hath touch'd . *2 Hen. IV.* iv 1 43
Touch'd with choler, hot as gunpowder . *Hen. V.* iv 7 188
When his holy state is touch'd so near . *1 Hen. VI.* iii 1 58
That face of his the hungry cannibals Would not have touch'd *3 Hen. VI.* i 4 153
To touch his growth nearer than he touch'd mine . *Richard III.* iv 4 25
Touch'd you the bastardy of Edward's children? . iii 7 4
The fairest hand I ever touch'd! . *Hen. VIII.* i 4 75
I have touch'd the highest point of all my greatness . iii 2 223
He touch'd the ports desired . *Troi. and Cres.* ii 2 76
For my private part, I am no more touch'd than all Priam's sons . ii 2 126
There you touch'd the life of our design . ii 2 194
His stubborn buckles, With these your white enchanting fingers touch'd iii 1 164
Thus to have said, As you were fore-advised, had touch'd his spirit *Cor.* ii 3 199
Even when the navel of the state was touch'd, They would not thread the gates . iii 1 123
It is lots to blanks, My name hath touch'd your ears . v 2 11
He would not then have touch'd them for his life . *T. Andron.* ii 4 47
I have touch'd thee to the quick, Thy life-blood out . iv 4 36
They have all been touch'd and found base metal . *T. of Athens* iii 3 6
Seeing his reputation touch'd to death, He did oppose his foe . iii 5 19
Our elders say, The barren, touched in this holy chase, Shake off their sterile curse . *J. Cæsar* i 2 8
Shall no man else be touch'd but only Cæsar? . ii 1 154
What villain touch'd his body, that did stab, And not for justice? . iv 3 20
You have loved him well: He hath not touch'd you yet . *Macbeth* iv 3 14
If by direct or by collateral hand They find us touch'd . *Hamlet* iv 5 207
Will Cæsar speak?—Not till he hears how Antony is touch'd *A. and C.* ii 2 142
Cæsar is touch'd . v 1 33
I think the king Be touch'd at very heart . *Cymbeline* i 1 10
With shame—The first that ever touch'd him . iii 1 25
Struck down Some mortally, some slightly touch'd . v 3 10
With golden fruit, but dangerous to be touch'd . *Pericles* i 1 28
What this fourteen years no razor touch'd . v 3 75
Toucheth. Know now, upon advice, it toucheth us both . *T. of Shrew* i 1 118
The quarrel toucheth none but us alone . *1 Hen. VI.* iv 1 118
It toucheth you, my lord, as much as me . *Richard III.* i 3 262
Nothing can proceed that toucheth us Whereof I shall not have intelligence . iii 2 23
As far as toucheth my particular . *Troi. and Cres.* ii 2 9
For this business, It toucheth us, as France invades our land *Lear* v 1 25
Touching. We may soon our satisfaction have Touching that point *Meas. for Meas.* i 1 84
Often touching will Wear gold . *Com. of Errors* ii 1 111
The contempts thereof are as touching me . *L. L. Lost* i 1 191
When King Pepin of France was a little boy, as touching the hit it . iv 1 123
When Queen Guinover of Britain was a little wench, as touching the hit it . iv 1 126
Touching now the point of human skill . *M. N. Dream* ii 2 119
Dangerous rocks, Which touching but my gentle vessel's side, Would scatter all her spices on the stream . *Mer. of Venice* i 1 32
To treat of high affairs touching that time . *K. John* i 1 101
Which I have open'd to his grace at large, As touching France *Hen. V.* i 1 79
Touching our person seek we no revenge . ii 2 174
As partly touching or concerning the disciplines of the war . iii 2 102
As touching the direction of the military discipline . iii 2 107
Thou art reverent Touching thy spiritual function, not thy life *1 Hen. VI.* iii 1 50
Touching the Duke of York, I will take my death, I never meant him any ill, nor the king, nor the queen . *2 Hen. VI.* ii 3 89
Our late decree in parliament Touching King Henry's oath . *3 Hen. VI.* ii 1 119
Forthwith shall articles be drawn Touching the jointure . iii 3 136
What said Northumberland as touching Richmond? . *Richard III.* v 3 271
Digest things rightly Touching the weal o' the common . *Coriolanus* i 1 155
And, touching hers, make blessed my rude hand . *Rom. and Jul.* i 5 53
O insupportable and touching loss! Upon what sickness? . *J. Cæsar* iv 3 151
Will not let belief take hold of him Touching this dreaded sight *Hamlet* i 1 25
So please you, something touching the Lord Hamlet . i 3 89
Touching this vision here, It is an honest ghost, that let me tell you . i 5 137
Though he speak of comfort Touching the Turkish loss . *Othello* ii 1 32
This paper is the history of my knowledge Touching her flight *Cymbeline* iii 5 100
That on the touching of her lips I may Melt and no more be seen *Pericles* v 3 42
Touchstone. Travellers must be content.—Ay, be so, good Touchstone *As Y. Like It* ii 4 19
Touchstone. How like you this shepherd's life, Master Touchstone? *As Y. Like It* iii 2 12
Thou art in a parlous state, shepherd.—Not a whit, Touchstone . iii 2 46
Holding out gold that's by the touchstone tried . *Pericles* ii 2 37
Tough. My tough senior.—Why tough senior? . *L. L. Lost* i 2 10
An appertinent title to your old time, which we may name tough . i 2 18
My love and fear glued many friends to thee; And, now I fall, thy tough commixture melts . *3 Hen. VI.* ii 6 6
O sides, you are too tough; Will you yet hold? . *Lear* ii 4 200
That would upon the rack of this tough world Stretch him out longer . v 3 314
Tougher. We are tougher, brother, Than you can put us to't . *W. Tale* i 2 15
Toughness. I confess me knit to thy deserving with cables of perdurable toughness . *Othello* i 3 343
Touraine. Ireland, Poictiers, Anjou, Touraine, Maine . *K. John* i 1 11
Anjou, Touraine, Maine, In right of Arthur do I claim of thee . ii 1 152
For Anjou and fair Touraine, Maine, Poictiers . ii 1 487
Then do I give Volquessen, Touraine, Maine, Poictiers, and Anjou . ii 1 527
The which at Touraine, in Saint Katharine's churchyard, Out of a great deal of old iron I chose forth . *1 Hen. VI.* i 2 100
Tournaments. There shall he practise tilts and tournaments *T. G. of Ver.* i 3 30
Tourney. There are princes and knights come from all parts of the world to just and tourney for her love . *Pericles* ii 1 116
Wilt thou tourney for the lady?—I'll show the virtue I have borne in arms . ii 1 150
Tours. Maine, Blois, Poictiers, and Tours, are won away . *1 Hen. VI.* iv 3 45
In the famous ancient city Tours . *2 Hen. VI.* i 1 5
When in the city Tours Thou ran'st a tilt in honour of my love . i 3 53
Touse. We'll touse you Joint by joint, but we will know *Meas. for Meas.* v 1 313
Tow. Thou knew'st too well My heart was to thy rudder tied by the strings, And thou shouldst tow me after . *Ant. and Cleo.* iii 11 58
Toward. I will be thy adversary toward Anne Page . *Mer. Wives* ii 3 99
Thou labour'st by thy flight to shun And yet runn'st toward him still *Meas. for Meas.* iii 1 13
In his love toward her ever most kind and natural . iii 1 229
What, a play toward! I'll be an auditor; An actor too perhaps *M. N. Dream* iii 1 81
There is some ill a-brewing towards my rest . *Mer. of Venice* ii 5 17
I have toward heaven breathed a secret vow To live in prayer . iii 4 27
And sigh'd his soul toward the Grecian tents, Where Cressid lay . v 1 5
His big manly voice, Turning again toward childish treble *As Y. Like It* ii 7 162
There is, sure, another flood toward, and these couples are coming to the ark . v 4 35
Here's some good pastime toward . *T. of Shrew* i 1 68
Toward the education of your daughters, I here bestow a simple instrument . ii 1 99
Come on, i' God's name; once more toward our father's . iv 5 1
This is Lucentio's house: My father's bears more toward the market-place . v 1 10
By all likelihood, some cheer is toward.—They're busy within . v 1 14
'Tis a good hearing when children are toward . v 2 182
Seek to eke out that Wherein toward me my homely stars have fail'd *All's Well* ii 5 80
Go thou toward home; where I will never come Whilst I can shake my sword . ii 5 95
This was a great argument of love in her toward you . *T. Night* iii 2 13
The clearstores toward the south north are as lustrous as ebony . iv 2 41
Since when, . . . toward my grave I have travell'd but two hours . v 1 165
What incidency thou dost guess of harm Is creeping toward me *W. Tale* i 2 404
Upon which errand I now go toward him; therefore follow me . v 1 232
It draws toward supper in conclusion so . *K. John* i 1 204
Arrows fled not swifter toward their aim . *2 Hen. IV.* i 1 123
Here's goodly stuff toward! . ii 4 214
And now dispatch we toward the court, my lords . iv 3 82
March to the bridge; it now draws toward night . *Hen. V.* iii 6 179
They are all in order and march toward us . *2 Hen. VI.* iv 2 198
Why, that is spoken like a toward prince . *3 Hen. VI.* ii 2 66
We look'd toward England, And cited up a thousand fearful times *Richard III.* i 4 13
Towards three or four o'clock Look for the news . iii 5 101
But oft have hinder'd, oft, The passages made toward it *Hen. VIII.* ii 4 165
We have a trifling foolish banquet towards . *Rom. and Jul.* i 5 124
Here's a noble feast toward . *T. of Athens* iii 6 68
I must serve him so too, tell him of an intent that's coming toward him v 1 23
They confess Toward thee forgetfulness too general, gross . v 1 147
By doing every thing Safe toward your love and honour. *Macbeth* i 4 27
We love him highly, And shall continue our graces towards him . i 6 30
With Tarquin's ravishing strides, towards his design Moves like a ghost ii 1 55
What might be toward, that this sweaty haste Doth make the night joint-labourer with the day? . *Hamlet* i 1 77
O proud death, What feast is toward in thine eternal cell? . v 2 376
Have you heard of no likely wars toward? . *Lear* ii 1 11
There is some strange thing toward, Edmund; pray you, be careful . iii 3 21
Do you hear aught, sir, of a battle toward?—Most sure and vulgar . iv 6 213
I perceive, Four feasts are toward . *Ant. and Cleo.* ii 6 75
Not know me yet?—Cold-hearted toward me? . iii 13 158
Apply yourself to our intents, Which towards you are most gentle . v 2 127
The flame o' the taper Bows toward her . *Cymbeline* ii 2 20
Towardly. I have observed thee always for a towardly prompt spirit—give thee thy due . *T. of Athens* iii 1 37
Tower. The cloud-capp'd towers, the gorgeous palaces . *Tempest* iv 1 152
I nightly lodge her in an upper tower . *T. G. of Ver.* iii 1 35
Would serve to scale another Hero's tower . iii 1 119
Heralds, from off our towers we might behold, From first to last *K. John* ii 1 325
How high thy glory towers, When the rich blood of kings is set on fire! ii 1 350
Like an eagle o'er his aery towers, To souse annoyance that comes near v 2 149
Strong as a tower in hope, I cry amen . *Richard II.* i 3 102
Go, some of you convey him to the Tower. . iv 1 316
This is the way To Julius Cæsar's ill-erected tower . v 1 2
You must to Pomfret, not unto the Tower . v 1 52
Topples down Steeples and moss-grown towers . *1 Hen. IV.* iii 1 33
I'll to the Tower with all the haste I can, To view the artillery *1 Hen. VI.* i 1 167
I am come to survey the Tower this day . i 3 1
Here's Beaufort, that regards nor God nor king, Hath here distrain'd the Tower to his use . i 3 61
He is protector of the realm, And would have armour here out of the Tower . i 3 67
Through a secret grate of iron bars In yonder tower to overpeer the city . i 4 11
Accursed tower! accursed fatal hand That hath contrived this woful tragedy! . i 4 76

Tower. Thou laid'st a trap to take my life, As well at London bridge as at the Tower . . . . 1 *Hen. VI.* iii 1 23
By thrusting out a torch from yonder tower . . . . iii 2 23
Even with the earth Shall lay your stately and air-braving towers . iv 2 13
No marvel . . . My lord protector's hawks do tower so well . 2 *Hen. VI.* ii 1 10
The lord mayor craves aid of your honour from the Tower . . . iv 5 5
The rebels have assay'd to win the Tower . . . . . . iv 5 9
If you can, burn down the Tower too . . . . iv 6 17
Tell him I'll send Duke Edmund to the Tower . . . . . iv 9 38
The Duke of Somerset is in the Tower.—Upon thine honour? . . . v 1 41
Let him to the Tower, And chop away that factious pate of his . v 1 134
See that he be convey'd unto the Tower . . . . 3 *Hen. VI.* iii 2 120
Hence with him to the Tower; let him not speak . . . . . iv 8 57
And, ten to one, you'll meet him in the Tower . . . . . v 1 46
Be sure to hear some news.—What? what?—The Tower, the Tower . v 5 50
As I guess, To make a bloody supper in the Tower . . . . . v 5 85
Hath appointed This conduct to convey me to the Tower *Richard III.* i 1 45
His majesty hath some intent That you shall be new-christen'd in the Tower . . . . i 1 50
'Tis not the king that sends you to the Tower . . . . . i 1 63
Her brother there, That made him send Lord Hastings to the Tower . i 1 68
I dare adventure to be sent to the Tower. 'Tis time to speak . . i 3 116
Thou slewest my husband Henry in the Tower, And Edward, my poor son . . . . i 3 119
Methoughts that I had broken from the Tower . . . . . . i 4 9
Some day or two Your highness shall repose you at the Tower . . iii 1 65
I do not like the Tower, of any place. Did Julius Cæsar build that place? . . . . iii 1 68
Entreat of her To meet you at the Tower and welcome you . . . iii 1 139
What, will you go unto the Tower, my lord? . . . . . . iii 1 140
I shall not sleep in quiet at the Tower . . . . iii 1 142
With a heavy heart, Thinking on them, go I unto the Tower . . iii 1 150
Summon him to-morrow to the Tower, To sit about the coronation . iii 1 172
Come to me; And we will both together to the Tower . . . . iii 2 32
What, shall we toward the Tower? the day is spent . . . . iii 2 91
Then was I going prisoner to the Tower . . . . iii 2 102
Go you toward the Tower?—I do, my lord; but long I shall not stay . iii 2 119
My foot-cloth horse did stumble, And startled, when he look'd upon the Tower . . . . iii 4 87
She's wandering to the Tower, On pure heart's love . . . . iv 1 3
Whither away?—No farther than the Tower . . . . . . iv 1 8
Stay, yet look back with me unto the Tower. Pity, you ancient stones! iv 1 98
Tyrrel, I mean those bastards in the Tower . . . . . . iv 2 76
The chaplain of the Tower hath buried them . . . . . . iv 3 29
Besides, the king's name is a tower of strength . . . . . v 3 12
Think on the Tower and me: despair, and die! . . . . . . v 3 126
Dream on thy cousins smother'd in the Tower. . . . . . . v 3 151
'Tis his highness' pleasure You shall to the Tower . . *Hen. VIII.* i 1 207
To the Tower, till you know How he determines further . . . . i 1 213
'If,' quoth he, 'I for this had been committed, As, to the Tower, I thought, I would have play'd The part my father meant to act . i 2 194
Be well contented To make your house our Tower . . . . . v 1 106
For better trial of you, From hence you be committed to the Tower . v 3 54
I take it, by all voices, that forthwith You be convey'd to the Tower . v 3 89
Is there no other way of mercy, But I must needs to the Tower, my lords? . . . . v 3 93
Receive him, And see him safe i' the Tower . . . . . . v 3 97
The eastern tower, Whose height commands as subject all the vale *Troi. and Cres.* i 2 2
Yond towers, whose wanton tops do buss the clouds, Must kiss their own feet . . . . iv 5 220
O, bid me leap, rather than marry Paris, From off the battlements of yonder tower . . . . *Rom. and Jul.* iv 1 78
Nor are they such That these great towers, trophies, and schools should fall For private faults in them . . . . . *T. of Athens* v 4 25
To towers and windows, yea, to chimney-tops, Your infants in your arms . . . . *J. Cæsar* i 1 44
Nor stony tower, nor walls of beaten brass, Nor airless dungeon . . i 3 93
Child Rowland to the dark tower came . . . . . . *Lear* iii 4 187
Whose towers bore heads so high they kiss'd the clouds . . *Pericles* i 4 24

Towered. A tower'd citadel, a pendent rock . . . *Ant. and Cleo.* iv 14 4

Tower-hill. No audience, but the tribulation of Tower-hill *Hen. VIII.* v 4 65

Towering. A falcon, towering in her pride of place . . . *Macbeth* ii 4 12
The bravery of his grief did put me Into a towering passion . *Hamlet* v 2 80

Town. Unfrequented woods I better brook than flourishing peopled towns . . . . *T. G. of Ver.* v 4 3
Why do your dogs bark so? be there bears i' the town? . . *Mer. Wives* i 1 299
Which of you know Ford of this town?—I ken the wight . . . . i 3 39
Though the priest o' the town commended him for a true man . . ii 1 149
There is a gentlewoman in this town; her husband's name is Ford . ii 2 198
Go you through the town to Frogmore . . . . iii 3 78
There is a friend of mine come to town . . . . . . iv 5 78
Do not these fair yokes Become the forest better than the town? . . v 5 112
Admit no traffic to our adverse towns . . . . . . *Com. of Errors* i 1 15
According to the statute of the town . . . . i 2 6
I'll view the manners of the town, Peruse the traders . . . . . i 2 12
Will you walk with me about the town? . . . . i 2 22
They say this town is full of cozenage . . . . i 2 97
In Ephesus I am but two hours old, As strange unto your town as to your talk . . . . ii 2 151
What needs all that, and a pair of stocks in the town? . . . . iii 1 60
Your town is troubled with unruly boys . . . . iii 1 62
I will not harbour in this town to-night . . . . iii 2 154
Besides, I have some business in the town . . . . . . iv 1 35
I will not stay to-night for all the town; Therefore away . . . iv 4 161
Put unluckily into this bay Against the laws and statutes of this town v 1 126
Brought to this town by that most famous warrior, Duke Menaphon . v 1 367
All the gallants of the town are come to fetch you to church *Much Ado* iii 4 97
'Tis won as towns with fire, so won, so lost . . . . *L. L. Lost* i 1 147
In the wood, a league without the town . . . . . *M. N. Dream* i 1 165
Meet me in the palace wood, a mile without the town . . . . i 2 104
In the temple, in the town, the field, You do me mischief . . . ii 1 238
I am fear'd in field and town . . . . iii 2 398
As a walled town is more worthier than a village . . *As Y. Like It* iii 3 59
'Tis Hymen peoples every town . . . . v 4 149
Honour, high honour and renown, To Hymen, god of every town! . . v 4 152
Some show to welcome us to town . . . . . . *T. of Shrew* i 1 47
Hearing thy mildness praised in every town, Thy virtues spoke of . ii 1 192
While he did bear my countenance in the town . . . . . . v 1 129
Shall we go see the reliques of this town? . . . . . *T. Night* iii 3 19
Town. Beguile the time and feed your knowledge With viewing of the town . . . . *T. Night* iii 3 42
There I found this credit, That he did range the town to seek me out . iv 3 7
I expose myself, pure for his love, Into the danger of this adverse town v 1 87
When came he to this town?—To-day, my lord . . . . . . v 1 96
Which to confirm, I'll bring you to a captain in this town . . . v 1 261
Our cannon shall be bent Against the brows of this resisting town *K. John* ii 1 38
We'll lay before this town our royal bones . . . . . . ii 1 41
His marches are expedient to this town, His forces strong . . . ii 1 60
Advanced here Before the eye and prospect of your town . . . ii 1 208
We tread In warlike march these greens before your town . . . ii 1 242
We will bear home that lusty blood again Which here we came to spout against your town . . . . ii 1 256
For him, and in his right, we hold this town . . . . . . ii 1 268
While they weigh so even, We hold our town for neither, yet for both . ii 1 333
Both conjointly bend Your sharpest deeds of malice on this town. . . ii 1 380
Being wrong'd as we are by this peevish town . . . . . . ii 1 402
Our thunder from the south Shall rain their drift of bullets on this town ii 1 412
This friendly treaty of our threaten'd town . . . . . . ii 1 481
This rich fair town We make him lord of . . . . ii 1 552
Let me have no subject enemies, When adverse foreigners affright my towns! . . . . iv 2 172
These islanders shout out 'Vive le roi!' as I have bank'd their towns . v 2 104
The rebels have consumed with fire Our town of Cicester *Richard II.* v 6 3
This have I rumour'd through the peasant towns . . 2 *Hen. IV.* Ind. 33
She says up and down the town that her eldest son is like you . ii 1 114
He heard of your grace's coming to town: there's a letter for you . ii 2 108
No word to your master that I am yet come to town . . . . ii 2 177
Is old Double of your town living yet?—Dead, sir.—Jesu, Jesu, dead! . iii 2 46
Girding with grievous siege castles and towns. . . . . *Hen. V.* i 2 152
As many ways meet in one town; As many fresh streams meet in one salt sea . . . . i 2 208
To line and new repair our towns of war . . . . ii 4 7
I would have blowed up the town, so Chrish save me, la! . . . iii 2 97
The town is beseeched, and the trumpet call us to the breach . . iii 2 115
The town sounds a parley . . . . iii 2 149
How yet resolves the governor of the town? . . . . . . iii 3 1
Take pity of your town and of your people . . . . . . iii 3 28
We yield our town and lives to thy soft mercy . . . . . . iii 3 48
What call you the town's name where Alexander the Pig was born? . iv 7 13
The loss of those great towns Will make him burst his lead 1 *Hen. VI.* i 1 63
France is revolted from the English quite, Except some petty towns . i 1 91
What towns of any moment but we have? . . . . i 2 5
Let's leave this town; for they are hare-brain'd slaves . . . i 2 37
Chief master-gunner am I of this town . . . . i 4 6
And like thee, Nero, Play on the lute, beholding the towns burn . . i 4 96
Recover'd is the town of Orleans . . . . i 6 9
Why ring not out the bells aloud throughout the town? . . . . i 6 11
In the market-place, The middle centre of this cursed town . . . ii 2 6
Razeth your cities and subverts your towns . . . . . . iii 3 65
Either to get the town again or die . . . . iii 2 79
In this late-betrayed town Great Cœur-de-lion's heart was buried . . iii 2 82
Now will we take some order in the town . . . . . . iii 2 126
See the cities and the towns defaced By wasting ruin of the cruel foe . iii 3 45
Hath reclaim'd . . . Twelve cities and seven walled towns of strength iii 4 7
Have we not lost most part of all the towns, By treason, falsehood? . v 4 108
You claim no interest In any of our towns of garrison . . . . v 4 168
Thy sale of offices and towns in France . . . . 2 *Hen. VI.* i 3 138
Have you not beadles in your town, and things called whips? . . ii 1 136
You made in a day, my lord, whole towns to fly . . . . . iii 1 164
By means whereof the towns each day revolted . . . . . iii 1 63
Throughout every town Proclaim them traitors that are up with Cade . iv 2 186
Here's the Lord Say, which sold the towns in France . . . . iv 7 23
Lest they consult about the giving up of some more towns in France . iv 7 141
And seized upon their towns and provinces . . . . . 3 *Hen. VI.* i 1 109
Set it on York gates; So York may overlook the town of York . . i 4 180
Welcome, my lord, to this brave town of York . . . . . . ii 2 1
And in the towns, as they do march along, Proclaims him king . . ii 2 70
His soldiers lurking in the towns about . . . . iv 2 15
But why commands the king That his chief followers lodge in towns about him? . . . . iv 3 13
Edward will defend the town and thee, And all those friends . . iv 7 38
Wilt thou leave the town and fight? Or shall we beat the stones about thine ears? . . . . v 1 107
It [conscience] is turned out of all towns and cities for a dangerous thing *Richard III.* i 4 146
In the centre of this isle, Near to the town of Leicester . . . . v 2 12
And safe in Leicester town . . . . v 5 10
As you are known The first and happiest hearers of the town *Hen. VIII.* Prol. 24
Hark, what good sport is out of town to-day! . . . *Troi. and Cres.* i 1 116
Yonder walls, that pertly front your town . . . . iv 5 219
Go in and cheer the town: we'll forth and fight, Do deeds worth praise v 3 92
We shall be shorten'd in our aim, which was To take in many towns *Coriolanus* i 2 24
Summon the town.—How far off lie these armies? . . . . . i 4 7
Call thither all the officers o' the town, Where they shall know our mind i 5 28
If we lose the field, We cannot keep the town . . . . . . i 7 5
The town is ta'en!—'Twill be deliver'd back on good condition . . i 10 1
Did curse Against the Volsces, for they had so vilely Yielded the town iii 1 11
This no more dishonours you at all Than to take in a town with gentle words . . . . iii 2 59
My birth-place hate I, and my love's upon This enemy town. . . . iv 4 24
For the defence of a town, our general is excellent . . . . . iv 5 178
Your native town you enter'd like a post, And had no welcomes home . v 6 50
I would not for the wealth of all the town Here in my house do him disparagement . . . . *Rom. and Jul.* i 5 71
There is a nobleman in town, one Paris, that would fain lay knife aboard ii 4 213
Unless philosophy can make a Juliet, Displant a town . . . . iii 3 59
The searchers of the town, Suspecting that we both were in a house . v 2 8
Nothing I'll bear from thee, But nakedness, thou detestable town! *T. of Athens* iv 1 33
Sound to this coward and lascivious town Our terrible approach . . v 4 1
All thy powers Shall make their harbour in our town . . . . . v 4 53
The poor distressed Lear's i' the town . . . . *Lear* iv 3 40
Is not he in town?—He's now in Florence . . . . . . *Othello* i 3 44
The town is empty; on the brow o' the sea Stand ranks of people. . . ii 1 53
Who's that which rings the bell?—Diablo, ho! The town will rise . . ii 3 162
In a town of war, Yet wild, the people's hearts brimful of fear, To manage private and domestic quarrel! . . . . ii 3 213
Lest by his clamour—as it so fell out—The town might fall in fright . ii 3 232

Town. Look with care about the town, And silence those whom this vile brawl distracted . . . . *Othello* ii 3 255
How silent is this town!—Ho! murder! murder!—What may you be? v 1 64
His steel was in debt; it went o' the backside the town . *Cymbeline* i 2 14
Made Lud's town with rejoicing fires bright And Britons strut with courage . . . iii 1 32
Your grace is welcome to our town and us *Pericles* i 4 106
Spend thou that in the town: report what a sojourner we have . iv 2 148
Town-armoury. An old rusty sword ta'en out of the town-armoury *T. of Shrew* iii 2 47
Town bull. Even such kin as the parish heifers are to the town bull *2 Hen. IV.* ii 2 172
Town-crier. I had as lief the town-crier spoke my lines . *Hamlet* iii 2 4
Town-gates. He carried the town-gates on his back like a porter *L. L. L.* i 2 75
Town's end. Bid my lieutenant Peto meet me at town's end *1 Hen. IV.* iv 2 10
And they are for the town's end, to beg during life . . . v 3 39
Township. I am but a poor petitioner of our whole township *2 Hen. VI.* i 3 27
Townsmen. Whose party do the townsmen yet admit? . . *K. John* ii 1 361
Here comes the townsmen on procession . . . *2 Hen. VI.* ii 1 68
Town way. Old Windsor way, and every way but the town way *M. W.* iii 1 7
Toy. Give me a note: your ladyship can set.—As little by such toys as may be possible . . . . *T. G. of Ver.* i 2 82
I do not like des toys . . . . *Mer. Wives* i 4 46
Elves, list your names: silence, you airy toys . . . . v 5 46
And critic Timon laugh at idle toys! . . . . *L. L. Lost* iv 3 170
A toy, my liege, a toy: your grace needs not fear it . . . iv 3 201
I never may believe These antique fables, nor these fairy toys *M. N. D.* v 1 3
I am very glad to see you: even a toy in hand here, sir . *As Y. Like It* iii 3 77
Tut, a toy! An old Italian fox is not so kind, my boy *T. of Shrew* ii 1 404
A knack, a toy, a trick, a baby's cap: Away with it! . . . iv 3 67
Haply your eye shall light upon some toy You have desire to purchase *T. Night* iii 3 44
A foolish thing was but a toy, For the rain it raineth every day . . v 1 400
Dreams are toys: Yet for this once, yea, superstitiously, I will be squared by this . . . . *W. Tale* iii 3 39
Any toys for your head, Of the new'st and finest, finest wear-a? . . iv 4 326
There's toys abroad: anon I'll tell thee more . . . *K. John* i 1 232
Let the welkin roar. Shall we fall foul for toys? . *2 Hen. IV.* ii 4 183
For a toy, a thing of no regard, . . . Destroy'd themselves *1 Hen. VI.* iv 1 145
Such like toys as these Have moved his highness . *Richard III.* i 1 60
Being but a toy, which is no grief to give . . . . iii 1 114
If no inconstant toy, nor womanish fear, Abate thy valour *Rom. and Jul.* iv 1 119
All is but toys: renown and grace is dead; The wine of life is drawn, and the mere lees Is left . . . . . *Macbeth* ii 3 99
Hold it a fashion and a toy in blood . . . . *Hamlet* i 3 6
The very place puts toys of desperation, Without more motive, into every brain . . . . i 4 75
As sin's true nature is, Each toy seems prologue to some great amiss . iv 5 18
Light-wing'd toys Of feather'd Cupid seel with wanton dullness *Othello* i 3 269
Pray heaven it be state-matters, as you think, And no conception nor no jealous toy Concerning you . . . . . . iii 4 156
I some lady trifles have reserved, Immoment toys . *Ant. and Cleo.* v 2 166
Triumphs for nothing and lamenting toys Is jollity for apes . *Cymbeline* iv 2 193
Trace. As we do trace this alley up and down . . *Much Ado* iii 1 16
Knight of his train, to trace the forests wild . . *M. N. Dream* ii 1 25
Can trace me in the tedious ways of art . . *1 Hen. IV.* iii 1 47
Now, all my joy Trace the conjunction! . . . *Hen. VIII.* iii 2 45
The traces of the smallest spider's web . . *Rom. and Jul.* i 4 61
Give to the edge o' the sword His wife, his babes, and all unfortunate souls That trace him in his line . . . . *Macbeth* iv 1 153
Why may not imagination trace the noble dust of Alexander? *Hamlet* v 1 224
And who else would trace him, his umbrage, nothing more . . v 2 125
The search so slow, That could not trace them! . . *Cymbeline* i 1 65
He hath been search'd among the dead and living, But no trace of him v 5 12
Track. To stain the track Of his bright passage to the occident *Rich. II.* iii 3 66
The weary sun hath made a golden set, And, by the bright track of his fiery car, Gives signal of a goodly day to-morrow *Richard III.* v 3 20
Tract. The tract of every thing Would by a good discourser lose some life, Which action's self was tongue to . . . *Hen. VIII.* i 1 40
Flies an eagle flight, bold and forth on, Leaving no tract behind *T. of A.* i 1 50
Tractable. Thou shalt find me tractable to any honest reason *1 Hen. IV.* iii 3 194
If thou dost find him tractable to us, Encourage him *Richard III.* iii 1 174
This tractable obedience is a slave To each incensed will . *Hen. VIII.* i 2 64
Much more gentle, and altogether more tractable . . *Troi. and Cres.* ii 3 160
That you will be more mild and tractable. . . . *T. Andron.* ii 1 470
I doubt not but I shall find them tractable enough . . *Pericles* iv 6 211
Trade. A tapster is a good trade . . . . . *Mer. Wives* i 3 18
They shall be my East and West Indies, and I will trade to them both . i 3 79
Though you change your place, you need not change your trade *Meas. for Meas.* i 2 111
What trade are you of, sir?—A tapster . . . . . ii 1 206
What do you think of the trade, Pompey? is it a lawful trade? . . ii 1 237
The valiant heart's not whipt out of his trade . . . . ii 1 270
Thy sin's not accidental, but a trade . . . . . . iii 1 149
Your hangman is a more penitent trade than your bawd . . . iv 2 53
I will instruct thee in my trade; follow . . . . . . iv 2 58
All great doers in our trade, and are now 'for the Lord's sake' . iv 3 20
The trade and profit of the city Consisteth of all nations *Mer. of Venice* iii 3 30
Unto the tranect, to the common ferry Which trades to Venice . . iii 4 54
In a briefer sort, More pleasant, pithy, and effectual, Than hath been taught by any of my trade . . . . . . *T. of Shrew* iii 1 69
My niece is desirous you should enter, if your trade be to her *T. Night* iii 1 83
In the king's highway, Some way of common trade . *Richard II.* iii 3 156
His forward spirit Would lift him where most trade of danger ranged *2 Hen. IV.* i 1 174
What trade art thou, Feeble?—A woman's tailor, sir . . . iii 2 160
Others, like merchants, venture trade abroad . . . *Hen. V.* i 2 192
Stands in the gap and trade of moe preferments . . *Hen. VIII.* v 1 36
Brethren and sisters of the hold-door trade . . *Troi. and Cres.* v 10 52
And come home beloved Of all the trades in Rome . . *Coriolanus* iii 2 134
Now the red pestilence strike all trades in Rome! . . . . iv 1 13
Instruction, manners, mysteries, and trades . . *T. of Athens* iv 1 18
Enough to make a whore forswear her trade . . . . iv 3 133
I'll believe him as an enemy, and give over my trade . . . iv 3 460
Speak, what trade art thou?—Why, sir, a carpenter . *J. Cæsar* i 1 5
A trade, sir, that, I hope, I may use with a safe conscience . . i 1 13
There, the murderers, Steep'd in the colours of their trade . *Macbeth* ii 3 121
How did you dare To trade and traffic with Macbeth In riddles and affairs of death? . . . . iii 5 4
Have you any further trade with us? . . . . . *Hamlet* iii 2 346
Trade. His hide is so tanned with his trade, that he will keep out water a great while *Hamlet* v 1 187
A stone-cutter or a painter could not have made him so ill, though he had been but two hours at the trade . . . . . *Lear* ii 2 65
Bad is the trade that must play fool to sorrow, Angering itself and others iv 1 40
Half way down Hangs one that gathers samphire, dreadful trade! . iv 6 15
Though in the trade of war I have slain men . . . *Othello* i 2 1
Music, moody food Of us that trade in love . . *Ant. and Cleo.* ii 5 2
If there be not a conscience to be used in every trade, we shall never prosper . . . . *Pericles* iv 2 12
Neither is our profession any trade; it's no calling . . . iv 2 42
How long have you been at this trade?—What trade, sir?—Why, I cannot name't but I shall offend.—I cannot be offended with my trade iv 6 73
Traded. And he, long traded in it, makes it seem Like rivers of remorse and innocency . . . . *K. John* iv 3 109
Two traded pilots 'twixt the dangerous shores Of will and judgement *Troi. and Cres.* ii 2 64
Trade-fallen. Revolted tapsters and ostlers trade-fallen . *1 Hen. IV.* iv 2 32
Trader. Peruse the traders, gaze upon the buildings . *Com. of Errors* i 2 13
Marking the embarked traders on the flood . . *M. N. Dream* ii 1 127
And traders riding to London with fat purses . . *1 Hen. IV.* i 2 141
Good traders in the flesh, set this in your painted cloths *Troi. and Cres.* v 10 46
Tradesman. Let me have no lying: it becomes none but tradesmen *W. T.* iv 4 745
Our tradesmen singing in their shops . . . . *Coriolanus* iv 6 8
I meddle with no tradesman's matters . . . . . *J. Cæsar* i 1 25
Trading. It is like we shall have good trading that way . *1 Hen. IV.* ii 4 401
Tradition. The same tradition takes not away my blood . *As Y. Like It* i 1 51
Throw away respect, Tradition, form, and ceremonious duty *Richard II.* iii 2 173
Will you mock at an ancient tradition? . . . . *Hen. V.* v 1 74
Traditional. Too ceremonious and traditional . . *Richard III.* iii 1 45
Traduced. A divulged shame Traduced by odious ballads . *All's Well* ii 1 175
I am Traduced by ignorant tongues . . . . *Hen. VIII.* i 2 72
Makes us traduced and tax'd of other nations . . . *Hamlet* i 4 18
A turban'd Turk Beat a Venetian and traduced the state . *Othello* v 2 354
He is already Traduced for levity . . . . *Ant. and Cleo.* iii 7 14
Traducement. Worse than a theft, no less than a traducement *Coriolanus* i 9 22
Traffic. No kind of traffic Would I admit; no name of magistrate *Tempest* ii 1 148
To admit no traffic to our adverse towns . . . *Com. of Errors* i 1 15
A merchant of great traffic through the world . . . . *T. of Shrew* i 1 12
Which, for traffic's sake, Most of our city did . . . *T. Night* iii 3 34
My traffic is sheets; when the kite builds, look to lesser linen *W. Tale* iv 3 23
I give thee kingly thanks, Because this is in traffic of a king *1 Hen. VI.* v 3 164
Is now the two hours' traffic of our stage . . . *Rom. and Jul.* Prol. 12
Painting is almost the natural man; For since dishonour traffics with man's nature, He is but outside . . . . . *T. of Athens* i 1 158
Traffic confound thee, if the gods will not!—If traffic do it, the gods do it.—Traffic's thy god; and thy god confound thee! . . . . i 1 244
How did you dare To trade and traffic with Macbeth In riddles and affairs of death? . . . . *Macbeth* iii 5 4
Trafficker. Do overpeer the petty traffickers . . *Mer. of Venice* i 1 12
Tragedian. Has led the drum before the English tragedians . *All's Well* iv 3 299
I can counterfeit the deep tragedian; Speak and look back *Richard III.* iii 5 5
Those you were wont to take delight in, the tragedians of the city *Ham.* ii 2 342
Tragedy. It would have been a fine tragedy: and so it is *M. N. Dream* v 1 367
Who on the French ground play'd a tragedy . . . *Hen. V.* i 2 106
Accursed fatal hand That hath contrived this woful tragedy! *1 Hen. VI.* i 4 77
Will not conclude their plotted tragedy . . . . . *2 Hen. VI.* iii 1 153
Even so suspicious is this tragedy . . . . iii 2 194
As if the tragedy Were play'd in jest by counterfeiting actors *3 Hen. VI.* ii 3 27
I live to look upon their tragedy . . . . . . *Richard III.* iii 2 59
Too late I bring this fatal writ, The complot of this timeless tragedy *T. Andron.* ii 3 265
O, why should nature build so foul a den, Unless the gods delight in tragedies? . . . . iv 1 60
The best actors in the world, either for tragedy, comedy, history *Hamlet* ii 2 416
I'll mark the play.—For us, and for our tragedy . . . . iii 2 159
Tragic. Before the always wind-obeying deep Gave any tragic instance of our harm . . . . *Com. of Errors* i 1 65
This man's brow, like to a title-leaf, Foretells the nature of a tragic volume . . . . *2 Hen. IV.* i 1 61
Loud-howling wolves arouse the jades That drag the tragic melancholy night . . . . *2 Hen. VI.* iv 1 4
My breast can better brook thy dagger's point Than can my ears that tragic history . . . . *3 Hen. VI.* v 6 28
To make an act of tragic violence . . . . . *Richard III.* ii 2 39
And the beholders of this tragic play . . . . . . iv 4 68
This is the tragic tale of Philomel . . . . . *T. Andron.* iv 1 47
Look on the tragic loading of this bed; This is thy work . *Othello* v 2 363
Tragical. 'Very tragical mirth.' Merry and tragical! . *M. N. Dream* v 1 57
And tragical, my noble lord, it is . . . . v 1 66
Why look you still so stern and tragical? . . . *1 Hen. VI.* iii 1 125
Hoping the consequence Will prove as bitter, black, and tragical *Richard III.* iv 4 7
Tragical-historical, tragical-comical-historical-pastoral . *Hamlet* ii 2 417
Trail. If I cry out thus upon no trail, never trust me . *Mer. Wives* iv 2 208
Tie his body to my horse's tail; Along the field I will the Trojan trail *Troi. and Cres.* v 8 22
Beat thou the drum, that it speak mournfully: Trail your steel pikes *Coriolanus* v 6 152
I do think, or else this brain of mine Hunts not the trail of policy so sure As it hath used to do . . . . *Hamlet* ii 2 47
How cheerfully on the false trail they cry! . . . . . iv 5 109
This is an aspic's trail . . . . *Ant. and Cleo.* v 2 354
Trail'st thou the puissant pike?—Even so . . . . *Hen. V.* iv 1 40
Train. I invite your highness and your train To my poor cell . *Tempest* v 1 300
Dignified with this high honour—To bear my lady's train *T. G. of Ver.* ii 4 159
O, train me not, sweet mermaid, with thy note . *Com. of Errors* iii 2 45
That hinder study quite And train our intellects to vain delight *L. L. Lost* i 1 71
In her train there is a gentle lady . . . . . . iii 1 166
Knight of his train, to trace the forests wild . . . *M. N. Dream* ii 1 25
Was he met there? his train? Camillo with him . . . *W. Tale* ii 1 33
What train?—But few, And those but mean . . . . . v 1 92
My best train I have from your Sicilian shores dismiss'd . . . v 1 163
They would be as a call To train ten thousand English to their side *K. John* iii 4 175
We did train him on . . . . *1 Hen. V.* v 2 21
Let our trains March by us, that we may peruse the men *2 Hen. IV.* iv 2 93
Which of this princely train Call ye the warlike Talbot? . *1 Hen. VI.* ii 2 34
We'll pull his plumes and take away his train . . . . . iii 3 7
Here at hand the Dauphin and his train Approacheth . . . . v 4 100

Train. She vaunted . . . , The very train of her worst wearing gown Was better worth than all my father's lands — *2 Hen. VI.* i 3 88
Me seemeth good, that, with some little train, Forthwith from Ludlow the young prince be fetch'd Hither to London, to be crown'd our king . . . —Why with some little train? — *Richard III.* ii 2 120
Honour's train Is longer than his foreskirt — *Hen. VIII.* ii 3 97
A royal train, believe me — iv 1 37
She that carries up the train Is that old noble lady, Duchess of Norfolk iv 1 51
You train me to offend you — *Troi. and Cres.* v 3 4
Why are you sequester'd from all your train? — *T. Andron.* ii 3 75
And all the rest look like a chidden train — *J. Cæsar* i 2 184
By many of these trains hath sought to win me Into his power *Macbeth* iv 3 118
Stars with trains of fire and dews of blood, Disasters in the sun *Hamlet* i 1 117
Be then desired By her . . . A little to disquantity your train *Lear* i 4 270
My train are men of choice and rarest parts, That all particulars of duty know — i 4 285
How chance the king comes with so small a train? — ii 4 64
She hath abated me of half my train — ii 4 161
'Tis not in thee To grudge my pleasures, to cut off my train — ii 4 177
Return and sojourn with my sister, Dismissing half your train — ii 4 207
Shut up your doors: He is attended with a desperate train — ii 4 308
Trained. Never train'd To offices of tender courtesy — *Mer. of Venice* iv 1 32
You have trained me like a peasant — *As Y. Like It* i 1 71
They were trained together in their childhoods — *W. Tale* i 1 24
I was train'd up in the English court — *1 Hen. IV.* iii 1 122
Henry the Fifth he first train'd to the wars — *1 Hen. VI.* i 4 79
For that cause I train'd thee to my house — ii 3 35
He was never trained up in arms — *Richard III.* v 3 272
Hath yoked a nation strong, train'd up in arms — *T. Andron.* i 1 30
I train'd thy brethern to that guileful hole — v 1 104
Nobly train'd, Stuff'd, as they say, with honourable parts *Rom. and Jul.* iii 5 182
He must be taught and train'd and bid go forth — *J. Cæsar* iv 1 35
Though train'd up thus meanly I' the cave wherein they bow, their thoughts do hit The roofs of palaces — *Cymbeline* iii 3 82
These gentle princes . . . these twenty years Have I train'd up — v 5 338
By Cleon train'd In music, letters — *Pericles* iv Gower 7
Training. His training such, That he may furnish and instruct great teachers, And never seek for aid out of himself — *Hen. VIII.* i 2 112
Give her princely training, that she may be Manner'd as she is born — *Pericles* iii 3 16
Thou art a piece of virtue, and I doubt not but thy training hath been noble — iv 6 119
Traitor. Speak not you for him; he's a traitor — *Tempest* i 2 460
Put thy sword up, traitor; Who makest a show but darest not strike . i 2 469
I here could pluck his highness' frown upon you And justify you traitors — v 1 128
But cannot be true servant to my master, Unless I prove false traitor to myself — *T. G. of Ver.* iv 4 110
Thou art a traitor to say so: thou wouldst make an absolute courtier — *Mer. Wives* iii 3 65
Our doubts are traitors And make us lose the good we oft might win By fearing to attempt — *Meas. for Meas.* i 4 77
Hath almost made me traitor to myself — *Com. of Errors* iii 2 167
Walk aside the true folk, and let the traitors stay — *L. L. Lost* iv 3 213
Judas Maccabæus clipt is plain Judas.—A kissing traitor — v 2 604
Thus do all traitors: If their purgation did consist in words, They are as innocent as grace itself — *As Y. Like It* i 3 54
I trust thee not.—Yet your mistrust cannot make me a traitor — i 3 58
What's that to me? my father was no traitor — i 3 65
If she be a traitor, Why so am I; we still have slept together — i 3 74
Your virtues, gentle master, Are sanctified and holy traitors — ii 3 13
A foul contending rebel And graceless traitor to her loving lord *T. of S.* v 2 160
There commendations go with pity; they are virtues and traitors too — *All's Well* i 1 50
A traitor you do look like; but such traitors His majesty seldom fears ii 1 99
As we are ourselves, what things are we!—Merely our own traitors . iv 3 25
She's a traitor and Camillo is A federary with her — *W. Tale* ii 1 89
Traitors! Will you not push her out? — ii 3 72
A nest of traitors!—I am none, by this good light — ii 3 81
Thou, traitor, hast set on thy wife to this — ii 3 131
Thou old traitor, I am sorry that by hanging thee I can But shorten thy life one week — iv 4 431
He doth espy Himself love's traitor — *K. John* ii 1 507
Thou art a traitor and a miscreant, Too good to be so — *Richard II.* i 1 39
With a foul traitor's name stuff I thy throat — i 1 44
And when I mount, alive may I not light, If I be traitor! — i 1 83
Like a false traitor and injurious villain — i 1 91
Like a traitor coward, Sluiced out his innocent soul through streams of blood — i 1 102
A villain, A recreant and most degenerate traitor — i 1 144
Interchangeably hurl down my gage Upon this overweening traitor's foot i 1 147
A traitor to my God, my king, and me — i 3 24
He is a traitor, foul and dangerous, To God of heaven, King Richard, and to me — i 3 39
Thomas Mowbray, A traitor to his God, his king, and him — i 3 108
If ever I were traitor, My name be blotted from the book of life! — i 3 201
And all the rest revolted faction traitors — ii 2 57
What was his reason? . . . —Because your lordship was proclaimed traitor — ii 3 30
I wot your love pursues A banish'd traitor — ii 3 60
Uncle me no uncle: I am no traitor's uncle — ii 3 88
This thief, this traitor, Bolingbroke — iii 2 47
Send Defiance to the traitor, and so die — iii 3 130
Where kings grow base, To come at traitors' calls and do them grace iii 3 181
Whom you call king, Is a foul traitor to proud Hereford's king — iv 1 135
Salt water blinds them not so much But they can see a sort of traitors here — iv 1 246
If I turn mine eyes upon myself, I find myself a traitor with the rest iv 1 248
Treason! foul treason! Villain! traitor! slave! — v 2 72
Look to thyself; Thou hast a traitor in thy presence there — v 3 40
I tore it from the traitor's bosom, king — v 3 55
The traitor lives, the true man's put to death — v 3 73
Shall thy old dugs once more a traitor rear? — v 3 90
Help to order several powers To Oxford, or where'er these traitors are . v 3 141
Two of the dangerous consorted traitors — v 6 15
I'll be a traitor then, when thou art king.—I care not — *1 Hen. IV.* i 2 164
Shall our coffers, then, Be emptied to redeem a traitor home? — i 3 86
He calls us rebels, traitors; and will scourge With haughty arms this hateful name in us — v 2 40
I do arrest thee, traitor, of high treason — *2 Hen. IV.* iv 2 107
Traitor. Some guard these traitors to the block of death, Treason's true bed — *2 Hen. IV.* iv 2 122
Colevile shall be still your name, a traitor your degree — iv 3 7
The sum is paid; the traitors are agreed — *Hen. V.* ii Prol. 33
'Fore God, his grace is bold, to trust these traitors — ii 2 1
Why thou shouldst do treason, Unless to dub thee with the name of traitor — ii 2 120
An arrant traitor as any is in the universal world, or in France, or in England! — iv 8 10
I am no traitor.—That's a lie in thy throat — iv 8 16
What's the matter?—My liege, here is a villain and a traitor — iv 8 26
What noise is this? what traitors have we here? — *1 Hen. VI.* i 3 15
With witches and the help of hell!—Traitors have never other company ii 1 19
Condemn'd to die for treason, but no traitor — ii 4 97
And I am lowted by a traitor villain — iv 3 13
So should we save a valiant gentleman By forfeiting a traitor — iv 3 27
Wrathful fury makes me weep, That thus we die, while remiss traitors sleep — iv 3 29
We lose, they daily get; All 'long of this vile traitor Somerset — iv 3 33
A fouler fact Did never traitor in the land commit — *2 Hen. VI.* i 3 177
Doth any one accuse York for a traitor?—What mean'st thou? — i 3 182
I'll have thy head for this thy traitor's speech — i 3 197
Lay hands upon these traitors and their trash — i 4 44
Go, take hence that traitor from our sight — ii 3 103
To keep your royal person From treason's secret knife and traitors' rage iii 1 174
'Twixt each groan Say 'Who's a traitor? Gloucester he is none' . iii 1 222
Away with him! he's a villain and a traitor — iv 2 115
More than that, he can speak French; and therefore he is a traitor — iv 2 177
Throughout every town Proclaim them traitors that are up with Cade . iv 2 187
Lord Say, the traitors hate thee; Therefore away with us — iv 4 43
The rascal people, thirsting after prey, Join with the traitor — iv 4 52
Is the traitor Cade surprised? Or is he but retired to make him strong? iv 9 8
To remove from thee The Duke of Somerset, whom he terms a traitor . iv 9 30
Is't Cade that I have slain, that monstrous traitor? — iv 10 71
To heave the traitor Somerset from hence — v 1 61
Lo, I present your grace a traitor's head — v 1 66
Which darest not, no, nor canst not rule a traitor — v 1 95
O monstrous traitor! I arrest thee, York, Of capital treason — v 1 106
Obey, audacious traitor; kneel for grace — v 1 108
The bastard boys of York Shall be the surety for their traitor father v 1 116
He is a traitor; let him to the Tower — v 1 134
Why, what a brood of traitors have we here! — v 1 141
I am thy king, and thou a false-heart traitor — v 1 143
A subtle traitor needs no sophister — v 1 191
Thy father was a traitor to the crown.—Exeter, thou art a traitor to the crown — *3 Hen. VI.* i 1 79
What title hast thou, traitor, to the crown? — i 1 104
For a thousand causes I would prolong awhile the traitor's life — i 4 52
Off with the traitor's head, And rear it in the place your father's stands ii 6 85
Ha! durst the traitor breathe out so proud words? — iv 1 112
It is more than needful Forthwith that Edward be pronounced a traitor iv 6 54
Take the great-grown traitor unawares — iv 8 63
The city being but of small defence, We'll quickly rouse the traitors v 1 65
O passing traitor, perjured and unjust! — v 1 106
Which, traitor, thou wouldst have me answer to — v 5 21
I tell ye all I am your better, traitors as ye are — v 5 36
O traitors! murderers! They that stabb'd Cæsar shed no blood at all v 5 52
Thy friends suspect for traitors while thou livest, And take deep traitors for thy dearest friends! — *Richard III.* i 3 223
And, like a traitor to the name of God, Didst break that vow — i 4 210
Thou art a traitor: Off with his head! — iii 4 77
Here is the head of that ignoble traitor — iii 5 22
He was the covert'st shelter'd traitor That ever lived — iii 5 33
The subtle traitor This day had plotted, in the council-house To murder me — iii 5 37
Both have well proceeded, To warn false traitors from the like attempts iii 5 49
We would have had you heard The traitor speak — iii 5 57
My counsel is my shield; We must be brief when traitors brave the field — iv 3 57
Reward to him that brings the traitor in — iv 4 518
What traitor hears me, and says not amen? — v 5 22
Abate the edge of traitors, gracious Lord! — v 5 35
Would Have put his knife into him.—A giant traitor! — *Hen. VIII.* i 2 199
By day and night, He's traitor to the height — i 2 214
I have this day received a traitor's judgement, And by that name must die — ii 1 58
Thou art a proud traitor, priest.—Proud lord, thou liest — iii 2 252
Must I go like a traitor thither? — v 3 96
When fair Cressid comes into my thoughts,—So, traitor! *Troi. and Cres.* i 1 31
Left my possession, Incurr'd a traitor's name — iii 3 6
He keeps a Trojan drab, and uses the traitor Calchas' tent — v 1 105
O traitor Diomed! turn thy false face, thou traitor, And pay thy life! . v 6 6
O traitors and bawds, how earnestly are you set a-work! — v 10 37
Has spoken like a traitor, and shall answer As traitors do — *Coriolanus* iii 1 162
We are peremptory to dispatch This viperous traitor — iii 1 287
For which you are a traitor to the people.—How! traitor! — iii 3 66
Call me their traitor! Thou injurious tribune! — iii 3 69
Tell the traitor, in the high'st degree He hath abused your powers.— Traitor! how now!—Ay, traitor, Marcius! — v 6 85
Traitors, avaunt! Where is the emperor's guard? — *T. Andron.* i 1 283
Traitor, restore Lavinia to the emperor.—Dead, if you will — i 1 296
Traitor, if Rome have law or we have power, Thou and thy faction shall repent this rape — i 1 403
Print thy sorrows plain, That we may know the traitors and the truth! iv 1 76
Take wreak on Rome for this ingratitude, And vengeance on the traitor iv 3 34
Her spotless chastity, Inhuman traitors, you constrain'd and forced . v 2 178
That is, because the traitor murderer lives — *Rom. and Jul.* iii 5 85
But set them down horrible traitors — *T. of Athens* iv 3 118
If thou read this, O Cæsar, thou mayst live; If not, the Fates with traitors do contrive — *J. Cæsar* ii 3 16
They were traitors: honourable men!—The will! the testament! — iii 2 157
Ingratitude, more strong than traitors' arms, Quite vanquish'd him . iii 2 189
Look you here, Here is himself, marr'd, as you see, with traitors — iii 2 201
O woful day!—O traitors, villains!—O most bloody sight! — iii 2 205
Revenge! About! Seek! Burn! Fire! Kill! Slay! Let not a traitor live! — iii 2 209
We'll burn his body in the holy place, And with the brands fire the traitors' houses — iii 2 260
Or till another Cæsar Have added slaughter to the sword of traitors — v 1 55
Cæsar, thou canst not die by traitors' hands, Unless thou bring'st them v 1 56

Traitor. Defiance, traitors, hurl we in your teeth: If you dare fight to-day, come . . . . *J. Cæsar* v 1 64
Assisted by that most disloyal traitor The thane of Cawdor . *Macbeth* i 2 52
When our actions do not, Our fears do make us traitors . . . iv 2 4
Cruel are the times, when we are traitors And do not know ourselves . iv 2 18
Was my father a traitor, mother?—Ay, that he was . . . iv 2 44
What is a traitor?—Why, one that swears and lies.—And be all traitors that do so?—Every one that does so is a traitor . . . iv 2 46
He's a traitor.—Thou liest, thou shag-hair'd villain! . . . . iv 2 82
To course his own shadow for a traitor . . . . . *Lear* iii 4 58
He hath no daughters, sir.—Death, traitor! . . . . . iii 4 72
Who s there? the traitor?—Ingrateful fox! 'tis he . . . . iii 7 27
O filthy traitor!—Unmerciful lady as you are, I'm none . . . iii 7 32
So white, and such a traitor! . . . . iii 7 37
What confederacy have you with the traitors Late footed in the kingdom? . . . . iii 7 44
If you do chance to hear of that blind traitor, Preferment falls on him that cuts him off . . . . iv 5 37
Thou old unhappy traitor, Briefly thyself remember . . . . iv 6 232
Wherefore, bold peasant, Darest thou support a publish'd traitor? . iv 6 236
What in the world he is That names me traitor, villain-like he lies . v 3 98
Thou art a traitor; False to thy gods, thy brother, and thy father . v 3 133
From the extremest upward of thy head To the descent and dust below thy foot, A most toad-spotted traitor . . . . v 3 138
A plague upon you, murderers, traitors all! I might have saved her . v 3 269
Gutter'd rocks and congregated sands,—Traitors ensteep'd . *Othello* ii 1 70
O, Men's vows are women's traitors! . . . . . *Cymbeline* iii 4 56
Those that are betray'd Do feel the treason sharply, yet the traitor Stands in worse case of woe . . . . iii 4 88
Who call'd me traitor, mountaineer, and swore . . . he'ld take us in . iv 2 120
What of him? he is A banish'd traitor . . . . . . v 5 318
Indeed a banish'd man; I know not how a traitor . . . . v 5 320
Traitor, thou liest.—Traitor!—Ay, traitor.—Even in his throat—unless it be the king—That calls me traitor, I return the lie . *Pericles* ii 5 55
Traitorly. But what talk we of these traitorly rascals? . *W. Tale* iv 4 821
Traitorous. With Charles, Alençon, and that traitorous rout 1 *Hen. VI.* iv 1 173
The traitorous Warwick with the men of Bury Set all upon me 2 *Hen. VI.* iii 2 240
A traitorous innovator, A foe to the public weal . . *Coriolanus* iii 1 175
Thy traitorous haughty sons, Confederates all . . . *T. Andron.* i 1 302
The cruel father and his traitorous sons . . . . . i 1 452
Mortal revenge upon these traitorous Goths . . . . . iv 1 93
His traitorous sons, That died by law for murder of our brother . iv 4 53
With witchcraft of his wit, with traitorous gifts . . *Hamlet* i 5 43
The revenges we are bound to take upon your traitorous father . *Lear* iii 7 8
Traitorously discovered the secrets of your army . *All's Well* iv 3 339
As all you know, Harmless Richard was murder'd traitorously 2 *Hen. VI.* ii 2 27
Good Duke Humphrey traitorously is murder'd . . . . iii 2 123
Thou hast most traitorously corrupted the youth of the realm in erecting a grammar school . . . . iv 7 35
Traitress. A counsellor, a traitress, and a dear . . *All's Well* i 1 184
Trammel. If the assassination Could trammel up the consequence *Macb.* i 7 3
Trample. Doing annoyance to the treacherous feet Which with usurping steps do trample thee . . . . *Richard II.* iii 2 17
Where subjects' feet May hourly trample on their sovereign's head . iii 3 157
Trampled. Lie there for pavement to the abject rear, O'er-run and trampled on . . . . *Troi. and Cres.* iii 3 163
Trampling contemptuously on thy disdain . . . *T. G. of Ver.* i 2 112
Trance. Nay, then, 'tis time to stir him from his trance . *T. of Shrew* i 1 182
Tranced. The trumpets sounded, And there I left him tranced *Lear* v 3 218
Tranect. With imagined speed Unto the tranect, to the common ferry Which trades to Venice . . . . . *Mer. of Venice* iii 4 53
Tranio. Gramercies, Tranio, well dost thou advise . . *T. of Shrew* i 1 41
Peace, Tranio!—Well said, master; mum! and gaze your fill . . i 1 72
O Tranio, till I found it to be true, I never thought it possible or likely i 1 153
Tranio, I burn, I pine, I perish, Tranio, If I achieve not this young modest girl. Counsel me, Tranio, for I know thou canst; Assist me, Tranio, for I know thou wilt . . . . i 1 160
It follows thus; Thou shalt be master, Tranio, in my stead . . i 1 207
Tranio, at once Uncase thee; take my colour'd hat and cloak . . i 1 211
Has my fellow Tranio stolen your clothes? Or you stolen his? . . i 1 228
Tranio here, to save my life, Puts my apparel and my countenance on . i 1 233
And not a jot of Tranio in your mouth: Tranio is changed into Lucentio i 1 241
When I am alone, why, then I am Tranio . . . . . i 1 248
That Lucentio that comes a-wooing, 'Priami,' is my man Tranio . . iii 1 35
Tranio, you jest: but have you both forsworn me? . . . . iv 2 48
I have brought him up ever since he was three years old, and his name is Tranio . . . . v 1 86
Where is that damned villain Tranio, That faced and braved me? . . v 1 123
Bianca's love Made me exchange my state with Tranio . . . v 1 128
Tranio hits you now.—I thank thee for that gird, good Tranio . . v 2 57
Tranquil. Farewell the tranquil mind! farewell content! *Othello* iii 3 348
Tranquillity. With nobility and tranquillity, burgomasters and great oneyers . . . . 1 *Hen. IV.* ii 1 84
Transcend. That praise, sole pure, transcends . . *Troi. and Cres.* i 3 244
Transcendence. In a most weak—and debile minister, great power, great transcendence . . . . *All's Well* ii 3 40
Transfigured. All their minds transfigured so together . *M. N. Dream* v 1 24
Transform. Lest he transform me to a piece of cheese! . *Mer. Wives* v 5 86
Transform me then, and to your power I'll yield . . *Com. of Errors* iii 2 40
I will not be sworn but love may transform me to an oyster . *Much Ado* ii 3 25
The power of beauty will sooner transform honesty from what it is *Ham.* iii 1 112
Put away These dispositions, that of late transform you . . *Lear* i 4 242
That we should, with joy, pleasance, revel, and applause, transform ourselves into beasts! . . . . *Othello* ii 3 293
I, an ass, am onion-eyed: for shame, Transform us not to women *Ant. and Cleo.* iv 2 36
Transformation. How I have been transformed and how my transformation hath been washed and cudgelled . . . . . *Mer. Wives* iv 5 98
Their transformations Were never for a piece of beauty rarer . *W. Tale* iv 4 31
Such beastly shameless transformation . . . . . 1 *Hen. IV.* i 1 44
From a prince to a prentice? a low transformation! . . 2 *Hen. IV.* ii 2 194
The goodly transformation of Jupiter there, his brother, the bull *Troi. and Cres.* v 1 59
What a beast art thou already, that seest not thy loss in transformation! *T. of Athens* iv 3 349
Something have you heard Of Hamlet's transformation . . *Hamlet* ii 2 5
Transformed. If it should come to the ear of the court, how I have been transformed . . . . *Mer. Wives* iv 5 98
I am transformed, master, am I not? . . . . *Com. of Errors* ii 2 197
She had transform'd me to a curtal dog and made me turn i' the wheel . iii 2 151
Transformed. Dumain transform'd! four woodcocks in a dish! *L. L. L.* iv 3 82
With what strict patience have I sat, To see a king transformed to a gnat! . . . . iv 3 166
Take this transformed scalp From off the head of this Athenian swain *M. N. Dream* iv 1 69
Cupid himself would blush To see me thus transformed to a boy *Mer. of Venice* ii 6 39
I think he be transform'd into a beast . . . . *As Y. Like It* ii 7 1
Is my Richard both in shape and mind Transform'd and weaken'd? *Richard II.* v 1 27
Look, if the fat villain have not transformed him ape . 2 *Hen. IV.* ii 2 77
The liquid drops of tears that you have shed Shall come again, transform'd to orient pearl . . . . *Richard III.* iv 4 322
So did we woo Transformed Timon to our city's love . *T. of Athens* v 4 19
A hundred ghastly women, Transformed with their fear . . *J. Cæsar* i 3 24
The triple pillar of the world transform'd Into a strumpet's fool *A. and C.* i 1 12
Transgressed. I would not marry her, though she were endowed with all that Adam had left him before he transgressed . . *Much Ado* ii 1 260
I have then sinned against his experience and transgressed against his valour . . . . *All's Well* ii 5 11
Transgresses. Virtue that transgresses is but patched with sin *T. Night* i 5 53
Transgressing. Come, you transgressing slave; away! . . *L. L. Lost* i 2 159
Until thou bid me joy, By pardoning Rutland, my transgressing boy *Richard II.* v 3 96
Transgression. My false transgression, That makes me reasonless to reason thus . . . . *T. G. of Ver.* ii 4 197
He puts transgression to't . . . . . . *Meas. for Meas.* iii 2 101
The flat transgression of a school-boy . . . . . *Much Ado* ii 1 229
Wilt thou make a trust a transgression? The transgression is in the stealer . . . . ii 1 232
Teach us, sweet madam, for our rude transgression, Some fair excuse *L. L. Lost* v 2 431
Heaven lay not my transgression to my charge! . . . *K. John* i 1 256
At thy good heart's oppression.—Why, such is love's transgression *Rom. and Jul.* i 1 191
Translate. Happy is your grace, That can translate the stubbornness of fortune Into so quiet and so sweet a style . . . *As Y. Like It* ii 1 19
Translate thy life into death, thy liberty into bondage . . . v 1 58
I can with ease translate it to my will . . . . . *K. John* ii 1 513
Wherefore do you so ill translate yourself? . . . . 2 *Hen. IV.* iv 1 47
With private soul Did in great Ilion thus translate him to me *T. and C.* iv 5 112
And Translate his malice towards you into love . . . *Coriolanus* ii 3 197
Whose present grace to present slaves and servants Translates his rivals *T. of Athens* i 1 72
Than the force of honesty can translate beauty into his likeness *Hamlet* iii 1 113
You must translate: 'tis fit we understand them . . . . iv 1 2
Translated her will, out of honesty into English . . . *Mer. Wives* i 3 54
Were the world mine, Demetrius being bated, The rest I'ld give to be to you translated . . . . *M. N. Dream* i 1 191
Bless thee, Bottom! bless thee! thou art translated . . . . iii 1 122
And left sweet Pyramus translated there . . . . iii 2 32
Translation. A huge translation of hypocrisy, Vilely compiled *L. L. Lost* v 2 51
Transmigrate. It lives by that which nourisheth it; and the elements once out of it, it transmigrates . . . . . *Ant. and Cleo.* ii 7 51
Transmutation. By education a card-maker, by transmutation a bear-herd *T. of Shrew* Ind. 2 21
Transparent. Through the transparent bosom of the deep . *L. L. Lost* iv 3 31
Run through fire I will for thy sweet sake. Transparent Helena! *M. N. Dream* ii 2 104
It hath bay windows transparent as barricadoes . . . *T. Night* iv 2 40
Like to the glorious sun's transparent beams . . . 2 *Hen. VI.* iii 1 353
Transparent heretics, be burnt for liars! . . . . *Rom. and Jul.* i 2 96
Transport. To transport him in the mind he is Were damnable *M. for M.* iv 3 72
I shall not need transport my words by you . . . *Richard II.* iii 3 81
He cannot temperately transport his honours . . . . *Coriolanus* ii 1 240
I came hither to transport the tidings, Which I have heavily borne *Macb.* iv 3 181
As level as the cannon to his blank, Transports his poison'd shot *Hamlet* iv 1 43
Might not you Transport her purposes by word? . . . . *Lear* iv 5 20
Transportance. And give me swift transportance to those fields Where I may wallow in the lily-beds . . . . . . *Troi. and Cres.* iii 2 12
Transported. Being transported And rapt in secret studies . *Tempest* i 2 76
He cannot be heard of. Out of doubt he is transported . *M. N. Dream* iv 2 4
Being transported by my jealousies To bloody thoughts . . *W. Tale* iii 2 159
My lord's almost so far transported that He'll think anon it lives . v 3 69
The scene Is now transported, gentles, to Southampton . . *Hen. V.* ii Prol. 35
Her ashes . . . Transported shall be at high festivals . . 1 *Hen. VI.* i 6 26
My Lord of Winchester we mean Shall be transported presently to France . . . . v 1 40
You are transported by calamity Thither where more attends you *Coriol.* i 1 77
Thy letters have transported me beyond This ignorant present *Macbeth* i 5 57
Transported, with no worse nor better guard But with a knave of common hire, a gondolier . . . . *Othello* i 1 125
Transporting. If a servant, under his master's command transporting a sum of money, be assailed by robbers . . . . . *Hen. V.* iv 1 159
That Suffolk should demand a whole fifteenth For costs and charges in transporting her! . . . . 2 *Hen. VI.* i 1 134
Transpose. Things base and vile, holding no quantity, Love can transpose to form and dignity . . . . *M. N. Dream* i 1 233
That which you are my thoughts cannot transpose . . . *Macbeth* iv 3 21
Trans-shape. Thus did she, an hour together, trans-shape thy particular virtues . . . . *Much Ado* v 1 172
Transylvanian. The poor Transylvanian is dead . . . *Pericles* iv 2 23
Trap. I will say 'marry trap' with you, if you run the nuthook's humour on me . . . . *Mer. Wives* i 1 170
Some Cupid kills with arrows, some with traps . . . *Much Ado* iii 1 106
Pretty traps to catch the petty thieves . . . . . *Hen. V.* i 2 177
Thou laid'st a trap to take my life . . . . . 1 *Hen. VI.* iii 1 22
My brain more busy than the labouring spider Weaves tedious snares to trap mine enemies . . . . 2 *Hen. VI.* iii 1 340
Protect mine innocence, or I fall into The trap is laid for me! *Hen. VIII.* v 1 142
Trapped. Wilt thou ride? thy horses shall be trapp'd . *T. of Shrew* Ind. 2 43
Four milk-white horses, trapp'd in silver . . . . *T. of Athens* i 2 189
Trapping. We are some of her trappings . . . . . *T. Night* v 1 10
These but the trappings and the suits of woe . . . . *Hamlet* i 2 86
Trash. Who to advance and who To trash for over-topping . *Tempest* i 2 81
Let it alone, thou fool; it is but trash . . . . . . iv 1 223
Lay hands upon these traitors and their trash . . . . 2 *Hen. VI.* i 4 44
And such a one that dare Maintain—I know not what: 'tis trash *T. and C.* ii 1 138
What trash is Rome, What rubbish, and what offal, when it serves For the base matter to illuminate So vile a thing as Cæsar! . *J. Cæsar* i 3 108

Trash. Sell the mighty space of our large honours For so much trash as may be grasped thus . . . . *J. Cæsar* iv 3 26
To wring From the hard hands of peasants their vile trash . . iv 3 74
This poor trash of Venice, whom I trash For his quick hunting *Othello* ii 1 312
Who steals my purse steals trash ; 'tis something, nothing . . iii 3 157
I do suspect this trash To be a party in this injury . . . v 1 85
Travail. Thirty-three years have I but gone in travail Of you, my sons *Com. of Errors* v 1 400
But on this travail look for greater birth . . . . *Much Ado* iv 1 215
Obey our will, which travails in thy good . . . . *All's Well* ii 3 165
Is all our travail turn'd to this effect? . . . . . 1 *Hen. VI.* v 4 102
God safely quit her of her burthen, and With gentle travail ! . *Hen. VIII.* v 1 71
I have had my labour for my travail . . . . . . *Troi. and Cres.* i 1 70
As honour, loss of time, travail, expense, Wounds . . . . ii 2 4
Is very likely to load our purposes with what they travail for *T. of A.* v 1 17
The lady shrieks, and well-a-near Does fall in travail with her fear *Pericles* iii Gower 52
Make swift the pangs Of my queen's travails ! . . . . . iii 1 14
Travailed. He and myself Have travail'd in the great shower of your gifts, And sweetly felt it . . . . . . *T. of Athens* v 1 73
Travel. For, now they are oppress'd with travel . . . *Tempest* iii 3 15
When thou haply seest Some rare note-worthy object in thy travel *T. G. of Ver.* i 1 13
Great impeachment to his age, In having known no travel in his youth i 3 16
Whither travel you?—To Verona . . . . iv 1 16
My youthful travel therein made me happy . . . . . iv 1 34
And happy were I in my timely death, Could all my travels warrant me they live . . . . *Com. of Errors* i 1 140
With long travel I am stiff and weary . . . . i 2 15
A soldier, a man of travel, that hath seen the world . . *L. L. Lost* v 1 114
How many weary steps, Of many weary miles you have o'ergone, Are number'd in the travel of one mile? . . . . v 2 197
What danger will it be to us, Maids as we are, to travel forth so far ! *As Y. Like It* i 3 111
Would he not be a comfort to our travel? . . . . . . i 3 133
Here's a young maid with travel much oppress'd And faints for succour ii 4 74
Time travels in divers paces with divers persons . . . . iii 2 326
Contemplation of my travels, in which my often rumination wraps me . iv 1 18
And to travel for it too ! . . . . iv 1 29
Travel you far on, or are you at the farthest ? . . . *T. of Shrew* iv 2 73
Thou didst make tolerable vent of thy travel . . . . *All's Well* ii 3 213
Will he travel higher, or return again into France? . . . . iv 3 50
I was bred and born Not three hours' travel from this very place *T. Night* i 2 23
After a demure travel of regard . . . . ii 5 59
But jealousy what might befall your travel, Being skilless in these parts iii 3 8
Call it a travel that thou takest for pleasure . . . . *Richard II.* i 3 262
Hath very much beguiled The tediousness and process of my travel . ii 3 12
If I travel but four foot by the squier further afoot, I shall break my wind . . . . 1 *Hen. IV.* ii 2 12
To stand stained with travel, and sweating with desire to see him 2 *Hen. IV.* v 5 25
Who two hours since I met in travel toward his warlike father 1 *Hen. VI.* iv 3 36
But now of late, not able to travel with her furred pack . 2 *Hen. VI.* iv 2 51
Tall stockings, Short blister'd breeches, and those types of travel *Hen. VIII.* i 3 31
Honour travels in a strait so narrow, Where one but goes abreast *Troi. and Cres.* iii 3 154
How chances it they travel? their residence, both in reputation and profit, was better both ways . . . . *Hamlet* ii 2 343
You have been talk'd of since your travel much . . . . iv 7 72
Of my redemption thence And portance in my travels' history . *Othello* i 3 139
Which not to have been blest withal would have discredited your travel *Ant. and Cleo.* i 2 161
Mark Antony is every hour in Rome Expected : since he went from Egypt 'tis A space for further travel . . . . ii 1 31
What he learns by this May prove his travel, not her danger . *Cymbeline* iii 5 103
Go travel for a while, Till that his rage and anger be forgot . *Pericles* i 2 106
Tyre, I now look from thee then, and to Tarsus Intend my travel . . i 2 116
His seal'd commission, left in trust with me, Doth speak sufficiently he's gone to travel . . . . i 3 14
I have understood Your lord has betook himself to unknown travels . i 3 35
We with our travels will endeavour us . . . . ii 4 56
Travelled. And he supposes me travell'd to Poland . . *Meas. for Meas.* i 3 14
Since when, . . . toward my grave I have travell'd but two hours *T. N.* v 1 166
As I travell'd hither through the land, I find the people strangely fantasied ; Possess'd with rumours . . . . *K. John* iv 2 143
What is't for ?—The reformation of our travell'd gallants . *Hen. VIII.* i 3 19
For speculation turns not to itself, Till it hath travell'd and is mirror'd there Where it may see itself . . . . . . *Troi. and Cres.* iii 3 110
I have watched and travell'd hard ; Some time I shall sleep out . *Lear* ii 2 162
Deny to speak with me? They are sick? they are weary? They have travell'd all the night? . . . . ii 4 90
Travellers ne'er did lie, Though fools at home condemn 'em . *Tempest* iii 3 26
These are the villains That all the travellers do fear so much *T. G. of Ver.* iv 1 6
As fast lock'd up in sleep as guiltless labour When it lies starkly in the traveller's bones . . . . *Meas. for Meas.* iv 2 70
Brave Master Shooty the great traveller . . . . iv 3 18
Our court, you know, is haunted With a refined traveller of Spain *L. L. L.* i 1 164
I may speak of thee as the traveller doth of Venice . . . . . iv 2 97
Motion and long-during action tires The sinewy vigour of the traveller . iv 3 308
But travellers must be content . . . . *As Y. Like It* ii 4 18
A traveller ! By my faith, you have great reason to be sad . . . iv 1 21
Farewell, Monsieur Traveller : look you lisp and wear strange suits . iv 1 33
Or is it else your pleasure, Like pleasant travellers, to break a jest Upon the company you overtake? . . . . *T. of Shrew* iv 5 72
You are a vagabond and no true traveller . . . . . *All's Well* ii 3 277
A good traveller is something at the latter end of a dinner . . . ii 5 30
Now your traveller, He and his toothpick at my worship's mess *K. John* i 1 189
List if thou canst hear the tread of travellers . . . 1 *Hen. IV.* ii 2 35
Now spurs the lated traveller apace To gain the timely inn . *Macbeth* iii 3 6
The undiscover'd country from whose bourn No traveller returns *Hamlet* iii 1 80
By your pardon, sir, I was then a young traveller . . . *Cymbeline* i 4 47
If we had of every nation a traveller, we should lodge them with this sign *Pericles* iv 2 123
Travellest. Withal make known Which way thou travellest *T. of Shrew* iv 5 51
Travelling along this coast, I here am come by chance . *L. L. Lost* v 2 557
That means, Travelling some journey, to repose him here *T. of Shrew* Ind. 1 76
Travelling towards York, With much ado . . . . . . *Richard II.* v 5 73
'Tis day, And yet dark night strangles the travelling lamp . *Macbeth* ii 4 7
Unto us it is A cell of ignorance ; travelling a-bed . . *Cymbeline* iii 3 33
Travel-tainted. Here, travel-tainted as I am . . . 2 *Hen. IV.* iv 3 40

Travers. Here comes my servant Travers . . . . . 2 *Hen. IV.* i 1 28
Now, Travers, what good tidings comes with you? . . . . . . i 1 33
Why should that gentleman that rode by Travers Give then such instances of loss? . . . . i 1 55
Traverse. To see thee fight, to see thee foin, to see thee traverse *M. W.* ii 3 25
Quite traverse, athwart the heart of his lover . . . *As Y. Like It* iii 4 45
Hold, Wart, traverse ; thus, thus, thus . . . . . 2 *Hen. IV.* iii 2 291
Traverse ! go, provide thy money . . . . *Othello* i 3 378
Traversed. Have wander'd with our traversed arms and breathed Our sufferance vainly . . . . *T. of Athens* v 4 7
Tray, Blanch, and Sweet-heart, see, they bark at me . . . . *Lear* iii 6 66
Tray-trip. Shall I play my freedom at tray-trip? . . . . *T. Night* ii 5 208
Treachers. Knaves, thieves, and treachers, by spherical predominance *Lear* i 2 133
Treacherous. A treacherous army levied, one midnight . . . *Tempest* i 2 128
Treacherous man ! Thou hast beguiled my hopes . . . *T. G. of Ver.* v 4 63
And greedily devour the treacherous bait . . . . . *Much Ado* iii 1 28
He will . . . entrap thee by some treacherous device . *As Y. Like It* i 1 157
Mistake me not so much To think my poverty is treacherous . . . i 3 67
Paying the fine of rated treachery Even with a treacherous fine of all your lives . . . . *K. John* v 4 38
The treacherous feet Which with usurping steps do trample thee *Richard II.* iii 2 16
With full as many lies As may be holloa'd in thy treacherous ear . . iv 1 54
O loyal father of a treacherous son ! . . . . v 3 60
And saved the treacherous labour of your son . . . . 1 *Hen. IV.* v 4 57
A nest of hollow bosoms, which he fills With treacherous crowns *Hen. V.* ii Prol. 22
But, O ! the treacherous Fastolfe wounds my heart . . 1 *Hen. VI.* i 4 35
Sheep run not half so treacherous from the wolf . . . . . i 5 30
The treacherous manner of his mournful death . . . . . . ii 2 16
Like a dastard and a treacherous coward . . . . . 3 *Hen. VI.* ii 2 114
As true and just As I am subtle, false, and treacherous . *Richard III.* i 1 37
And with thy treacherous blade Unrip'dst the bowels of thy sovereign's son . . . . i 4 211
Deep, hollow, treacherous, and full of guile, Be he unto me ! . . . ii 1 38
Thy age confirm'd, proud, subtle, bloody, treacherous . . . iv 4 171
Fie, treacherous hue, that will betray with blushing The close enacts and counsels of the heart ! . . . . *T. Andron.* iv 2 117
Or my true heart with treacherous revolt Turn to another *Rom. and Jul.* iv 1 58
I am not treacherous.—But Macbeth is . . . . . . *Macbeth* iv 3 18
Remorseless, treacherous, lecherous, kindless villain ! . . *Hamlet* ii 2 609
The treacherous instrument is in thy hand, Unbated and envenom'd . v 2 327
Out, treacherous villain ! Thou call'st on him that hates thee . *Lear* iii 7 87
O treacherous villains ! What are you there? come in . . *Othello* v 1 58
To write and read Be henceforth treacherous ! . . . . *Cymbeline* iv 2 317
Treacherously hast thou vanquish'd him . . . . . 3 *Hen. VI.* i 1 72
Treachery. I cannot now prove constant to myself, Without some treachery used to Valentine . . . . *T. G. of Ver.* ii 6 32
I slew him manfully in fight, Without false vantage or base treachery iv 1 29
Those that betray them do no treachery . . . . . *Mer. Wives* v 3 24
He is composed and framed of treachery . . . . . *Much Ado* v 1 257
She should be confined, Lest that the treachery of the two fled hence Be left her to perform . . . . *W. Tale* ii 1 195
Your breathing shall expire, Paying the fine of rated treachery *K. John* v 4 37
On some known ground of treachery in him . . . . *Richard II.* i 1 11
God for his mercy, what treachery is here ! . . . . v 2 75
So sell His sovereign's life to death and treachery . . . *Hen. V.* ii 2 11
What treachery was used ?—No treachery ; but want of men and money 1 *Hen. VI.* i 1 68
And for thy treachery, what's more manifest? . . . . . . iii 1 21
If Talbot but survive thy treachery . . . . iii 2 37
O monstrous treachery ! can this be so? . . . . iv 1 61
Lost most part of all the towns, By treason, falsehood, and by treachery iv 4 109
And wilt thou still be hammering treachery? . . . . . 2 *Hen. VI.* i 2 47
To kings that fear their subjects' treachery . . . . 3 *Hen. VI.* ii 5 45
O, treachery ! Fly, good Fleance, fly, fly, fly ! Thou mayst revenge *Macbeth* iii 3 17
Thou shag-hair'd villain !—What, you egg ! Young fry of treachery ! . iv 2 84
I am justly kill'd with mine own treachery . . . . . *Hamlet* v 2 318
O villany ! Ho ! let the door be lock'd : Treachery ! Seek it out . . v 2 323
We have seen the best of our time : machinations, hollowness, treachery *Lear* i 2 123
Of Gloucester's treachery, And of the loyal service of his son . . iv 2 6
Take me from this world with treachery and devise engines for my life *Oth.* iv 2 221
Tread. And think'st it much to tread the ooze Of the salt deep *Tempest* i 2 252
Tread softly, that the blind mole may not Hear a foot fall . . . iv 1 194
Ask him why, that hour of fairy revel, In their so sacred paths he dares to tread In shape profane . . . . *Mer. Wives* iv 4 59
What we do not see We tread upon, and never think of it *Meas. for Meas.* ii 1 26
The poor beetle, that we tread upon, In corporal sufferance finds a pang as great As when a giant dies . . . . iii 1 79
I do affect the very ground, which is base, where her shoe, which is baser, guided by her foot, which is basest, doth tread *L. L. Lost* i 2 174
O, if the streets were paved with thine eyes, Her feet were much too dainty for such tread ! . . . . iv 3 279
Measured many a mile To tread a measure with you on this grass . . v 2 187
The ladies call him sweet ; The stairs, as he treads on them, kiss his feet v 2 330
When turtles tread, and rooks, and daws . . . . v 2 915
And the quaint mazes in the wanton green For lack of tread are undistinguishable . . . . *M. N. Dream* ii 1 100
And, like a forester, the groves may tread . . . . . . iii 2 390
A kinder gentleman treads not the earth . . . . *Mer. of Venice* ii 8 35
France is a dog-hole, and it no more merits The tread of a man's foot *All's Well* ii 3 292
For this down-trodden equity, we tread In warlike march these greens *K. John* ii 1 241
To tread down fair respect of sovereignty . . . . . . iii 1 58
O then, tread down my need, and faith mounts up ! . . . . iii 1 215
Wheresoe'er this foot of mine doth tread, He lies before me . . iii 3 62
But tread the stranger paths of banishment . . . . *Richard II.* i 3 143
On my heart they tread now whilst I live . . . . . . iii 3 158
For accordingly You tread upon my patience . . . . 1 *Hen. IV.* i 3 4
List if thou canst hear the tread of travellers . . . . . . ii 2 35
An if we live, we live to tread on kings . . . . v 2 86
By this heavenly ground I tread on . . . . . . 2 *Hen. IV.* ii 1 152
I will not change my horse with any that treads but on four pasterns *Hen. V.* iii 7 12
Swear by her foot, that she may tread out the oath . . . . iii 7 103
Uneath may she endure the flinty streets, To tread them with her tender-feeling feet . . . . 2 *Hen. VI.* ii 4 9

Tread. The envious people laugh And bid me be advised how I tread *2 Hen. VI.* ii 4 36
I'll rend thy bear And tread it under foot with all contempt . v 1 209
Like one that stands upon a promontory, And spies a far-off shore where he would tread *3 Hen. VI.* iii 2 136
Tread on the sand; why, there you quickly sink . v 4 30
Go, tread the path that thou shalt ne'er return *Richard III.* i 1 117
Such a nature, Tickled with good success, disdains the shadow Which he treads on at noon *Coriolanus* i 1 265
He'll beat Aufidius' head below his knee And tread upon his neck . i 3 50
Or else Triumphantly tread on thy country's ruin . v 3 116
Thou shalt no sooner March to assault thy country than to tread— Trust to't, thou shalt not—on thy mother's womb . v 3 123
A' shall not tread on me; I'll run away till I am bigger . v 3 127
Tread not upon him. Masters all, be quiet; Put up your swords . v 6 135
Well-apparell'd April on the heel Of limping winter treads *Rom. and Jul.* i 2 28
So shall no foot upon the churchyard tread . . . But thou shalt hear it v 3 5
He ne'er drinks, But Timon's silver treads upon his lip *T. of Athens* iii 2 78
I shall tread upon the tyrant's head, Or wear it on my sword *Macbeth* iv 3 45
Himself the primrose path of dalliance treads *Hamlet* i 3 50
One woe doth tread upon another's heel, So fast they follow . iv 7 164
If you will give me leave, I will tread this unbolted villain into mortar *Lear* ii 2 71
The land bids me tread no more upon't; It is ashamed to bear me! *Ant. and Cleo.* iii 11 1
Up to yond hill; Your legs are young; I'll tread these flats . *Cymbeline* iii 3 11
You should tread a course Pretty and full of view . iii 4 149
Whose delightful steps Shall make the gazer joy to see him tread . *Per.* ii 1 165

Treadest. The grass whereon thou tread'st the presence strew'd *Rich. II.* i 3 289

Treading. With many hundreds treading on his heels *K. John* iv 2 149
He moves like an engine, and the ground shrinks before his treading *Cor.* v 4 20

Treason, felony, Sword, pike, knife, gun, or need of any engine, Would I not have *Tempest* ii 1 160
Some treason, masters: yet stand close . *Much Ado* iii 3 113
Some certain treason.—What makes treason here? . *L. L. Lost* iv 3 190
Treason and you go in peace away together . iv 3 192
Our parson misdoubts it; 'twas treason, he said . iv 3 194
To see no woman; Flat treason 'gainst the kingly state of youth . iv 3 293
Confess What treason there is mingled with your love.—None but that ugly treason of mistrust . *Mer. of Venice* iii 2 27
As well be amity and life 'Tween snow and fire, as treason and my love iii 2 31
Is fit for treasons, stratagems, and spoils . v 1 85
Treason is not inherited, my lord *As Y. Like It* i 3 63
In the common course of all treasons, we still see them reveal themselves . *All's Well* iv 3 26
Thou art here accused and arraigned of high treason . *W. Tale* iii 2 14
To appeal each other of high treason . *Richard II.* i 1 27
Until it had return'd These terms of treason doubled down his throat . i 1 57
All the treasons for these eighteen years Complotted and contrived i 1 95
Confess thy treasons ere thou fly the realm . i 3 198
In condition of the worst degree, In gross rebellion and detested treason ii 3 109
Murders, treasons, and detested sins . iii 2 44
His treasons will sit blushing in his face . iii 2 51
Every stride he makes upon my land Is dangerous treason . iii 3 93
For your pains, Of capital treason we arrest you here . iv 1 151
Treason! foul treason! Villain! traitor! slave! . v 2 72
Fool-hardy king: Shall I for love speak treason to thy face? . v 3 44
Thou shalt know The treason that my haste forbids me show . v 3 50
Then treasons make me wish myself a beggar, And so I am . v 5 33
Shall we buy treason? and indent with fears? . *1 Hen. IV.* i 3 87
For treason is but trusted like the fox . v 2 9
For the which I do arrest thee, traitor, of high treason . *2 Hen. IV.* iv 2 107
Of capital treason I attach you both.—Is this proceeding just? iv 2 109
The block of death, Treason's true bed and yielder up of breath . iv 2 123
This grace of kings must die, If hell and treason hold their promises *Hen. V.* ii Prol. 29
Treason and murder ever kept together, As two yoke-devils . ii 2 105
But thou, 'gainst all proportion, didst bring in Wonder to wait on treason ii 2 110
All other devils that suggest by treasons Do botch and bungle up damnation . ii 2 114
But he that temper'd thee bade thee stand up, Gave thee no instance why thou shouldst do treason . ii 2 119
I arrest thee of high treason, by the name of Richard Earl of Cambridge ii 2 145
I arrest thee of high treason, by the name of Henry Lord Scroop of Masham . ii 2 147
I arrest thee of high treason, by the name of Thomas Grey, knight . ii 2 149
Never did faithful subject more rejoice At the discovery of most dangerous treason Than I do at this hour joy o'er myself . ii 2 162
Since God so graciously hath brought to light This dangerous treason . ii 2 186
It is no English treason to cut French crowns . iv 1 245
I will give treason his payment into plows, I warrant you . iv 8 15
A most contagious treason come to light . iv 8 22
For treason executed in our late king's days . *1 Hen. VI.* ii 4 91
By his treason, stand'st not thou attainted? . ii 4 92
Condemn'd to die for treason, but no traitor . ii 4 97
France, thou shalt rue this treason with thy tears . iii 2 36
O, let no words, but deeds, revenge this treason! . iii 2 49
Let him perceive how ill we brook his treason . iv 1 74
There Minotaurs and ugly treasons lurk . v 3 189
Have we not lost most part of all the towns, By treason, falsehood? . v 4 109
Here is a man accused of treason . *2 Hen. VI.* i 3 180
This is the man That doth accuse his master of high treason . i 3 185
Hold! I confess, I confess treason . ii 3 97
And in his simple show he harbours treason . iii 1 54
As innocent From meaning treason to our royal person As is the sucking lamb . iii 1 70
I do arrest thee of high treason here . iii 1 97
The purest spring is not so free from mud As I am clear from treason . iii 1 102
I shall not want false witness to condemn me, Nor store of treasons iii 1 169
To keep your royal person From treason's secret knife and traitors' rage iii 1 174
It shall be treason for any that calls me other than Lord Mortimer iv 6 6
My followers' base and ignominious treasons makes me betake me to my heels . iv 8 66
I arrest thee, York, Of capital treason 'gainst the king and crown . v 1 107
Nor should thy prowess want praise and esteem, But that 'tis shown ignobly and in treason . v 2 23
Neither by treason nor hostility To seek to put me down . *3 Hen. VI.* i 1 199
When care, mistrust, and treason waits on him . ii 5 54
And not bewray thy treason with a blush . iii 3 97
Both shall buy this treason Even with the dearest blood your bodies bear v 1 68

Treason. Piercing as the mid-day sun, To search the secret treasons of the world . *3 Hen. VI.* v 2 18
You may partake of any thing we say: We speak no treason *Richard III.* i 1 90
We would have had you heard The traitor speak, and timorously confess The manner and the purpose of his treason . iii 5 58
Let them not live to taste this land's increase That would with treason wound this fair land's peace! . v 5 39
Which, as I take it, is a kind of puppy To the old dam, treason *Hen. VIII.* i 1 176
I Arrest thee of high treason, in the name Of our most sovereign king . i 1 201
And point by point the treasons of his master He shall again relate . i 2 7
His peers, upon this evidence, Have found him guilty of high treason . ii 1 27
What treason were it to the ransack'd queen! . *Troi. and Cres.* ii 2 150
Throw their power i' the dust.—Manifest treason! . *Coriolanus* iii 1 172
Here lurks no treason, here no envy swells . *T. Andron.* i 1 153
Treason, my lord! Lavinia is surprised! . i 1 284
This is the tragic tale of Philomel, And treats of Tereus' treason . iv 1 48
Pallas, Jove, or Mercury, Inspire me, that I may this treason find! . iv 1 67
Abominable deeds, Complots of mischief, treason, villanies . v 1 65
I speak no treason.—O, God ye god-den . *Rom. and Jul.* iii 5 173
All of us fell down, Whilst bloody treason flourish'd over us . *J. Cæsar* iii 2 196
But treasons capital, confess'd and proved, Have overthrown him *Macb.* i 3 115
Very frankly he confess'd his treasons, Implored your highness' pardon i 4 5
Committed treason enough for God's sake, yet could not equivocate to heaven . ii 3 11
Awake, awake! Ring the alarum-bell. Murder and treason! . ii 3 79
After life's fitful fever he sleeps well; Treason has done his worst . iii 2 24
'Gainst Fortune's state would treason have pronounced . *Hamlet* ii 2 534
Such love must needs be treason in my breast . iii 2 188
Such divinity doth hedge a king, That treason can but peep to what it would . iv 5 124
Then, venom, to thy work.—Treason! treason! . v 2 334
In cities, mutinies; in countries, discord; in palaces, treason . *Lear* i 2 117
O heavens! that this treason were not, or not I the detector! . iii 5 13
It was he That made the overture of thy treasons to us . iii 7 89
Stay yet; hear reason. Edmund, I arrest thee On capital treason . v 3 83
To prove upon thy head Thy heinous, manifest, and many treasons . v 3 92
My name is lost; By treason's tooth bare-gnawn and canker-bit . v 3 122
Back do I toss these treasons to thy head . v 3 146
How got she out? O treason of the blood! . *Othello* i 1 170
O, never was there queen So mightily betray'd! yet at the first I saw the treasons planted . *Ant. and Cleo.* i 3 26
You think of him too much.—O, 'tis treason! . i 5 7
Those that are betray'd Do feel the treason sharply, yet the traitor Stands in worse case of woe . *Cymbeline* iii 4 88
Your pleasure was my mere offence, my punishment Itself, and all my treason . v 5 335
Beaten for loyalty Excited me to treason . v 5 345
Poison and treason are the hands of sin, Ay, and the targets . *Pericles* i 1 139
Who either by public war or private treason Will take away your life . i 2 104
Marina's life Seeks to take off by treason's knife . iv Gower 14

Treasonable. Hark, how the villain would close now, after his treasonable abuses! . *Meas. for Meas.* v 1 347

Treasonous. I do know To be corrupt and treasonous.—Say not 'treasonous'. *Hen. VIII.* i 1 156
Against the undivulged pretence I fight Of treasonous malice *Macbeth* ii 3 138

Treasure. You have an exchequer of words, and, I think, no other treasure to give your followers . *T. G. of Ver.* ii 4 44
We'll bring thee to our crews, And show thee all the treasure we have got iv 1 75
Either You must lay down the treasures of your body To this supposed, or else to let him suffer . *Meas. for Meas.* ii 4 96
If so, our copper buys no better treasure . *L. L. Lost* iv 3 386
In Baptista's keep my treasure is: He hath the jewel of my life *T. of S.* i 2 118
Nay, now I see She is your treasure, she must have a husband . ii 1 32
The tailor stays thy leisure, To deck thy body with his ruffling treasure iv 3 60
I have writ my letters, casketed my treasure . *All's Well* ii 5 26
You waste the treasure of your time . *T. Night* ii 5 85
Have taken treasure from her lips— And left them More rich *W. Tale* v 1 54
I will not touch thine eye For all the treasure that thine uncle owes *K. John* iv 1 123
The purest treasure mortal times afford Is spotless reputation *Richard II.* i 1 177
And given my treasures and my rights of thee To thick-eyed musing *1 Hen. IV.* ii 3 48
He therefore sends you, meeter for your spirit, This tun of treasure *Hen. V.* i 2 255
What treasure, uncle?—Tennis-balls, my liege . i 2 258
Thine eyes and thoughts Beat on a crown, the treasure of thy heart *2 Hen. VI.* ii 1 20
Omitting Suffolk's exile, my soul's treasure . iii 2 382
If thou be'st death, I'll give thee England's treasure, Enough to purchase such another island, So thou wilt let me live . iii 3 2
Will I dam up this thy yawning mouth For swallowing the treasure of the realm . iv 1 74
Our people and our peers are both misled, Our treasure seized *3 Hen. VI.* iii 3 36
His subjects slain, His statutes cancell'd, and his treasure spent . v 4 79
Go; And thither bear your treasure and your goods . *Richard III.* ii 4 69
This last costly treaty, the interview, That swallow'd so much treasure *Hen. VIII.* i 1 166
His treasure, Rich stuffs, and ornaments of household . iii 2 125
Of all The treasure in this field achieved and city, We render you the tenth, to be ta'en forth . *Coriolanus* i 9 33
My dear wife's estimate, her womb's increase, And treasure of my loins iii 3 115
There to dispose this treasure in mine arms . *T. Andron.* iv 2 173
He that is strucken blind cannot forget The precious treasure of his eyesight lost . *Rom. and Jul.* i 1 239
They answer, . . . That now they are at fall, want treasure *T. of Athens* ii 2 214
It is noised he hath a mass of treasure . iv 3 404
Here, take: the gods out of my misery Have sent thee treasure . iv 3 532
And having brought our treasure where we will, Then take we down his load, and turn him off . *J. Cæsar* iv 1 24
Though the treasure Of nature's germens tumble all together *Macbeth* iv 1 58
Or if thou hast uphoarded in thy life Extorted treasure . *Hamlet* i 1 137
Or your chaste treasure open To his unmaster'd importunity . i 3 31
O Jephthah, judge of Israel, what a treasure hadst thou! . ii 2 423
They slack their duties, And pour our treasures into foreign laps *Othello* iv 3 89
The firm Roman to great Egypt sends This treasure of an oyster *Ant. and Cleo.* i 5 44
Be gone: My treasure's in the harbour, take it . iii 11 11
To the sea-side straightway: I will possess you of that ship and treasure iii 11 21
His chests and treasure He has not with him.—Is he gone? . iv 5 10
Send his treasure after; do it; Detain no jot, I charge thee . iv 5 12
Antony Hath after thee sent all thy treasure, with His bounty overplus iv 6 21

Treasure. This secret Will force him think I have pick'd the lock and ta'en The treasure of her honour . . . . . *Cymbeline* ii 2 42
You must Forget that rarest treasure of your cheek, Exposing it . . iii 4 163
Tie my treasure up in silken bags, To please the fool and death *Pericles* iii 2 41
Besides this treasure for a fee, The gods requite his charity! . . ii 1 74
Treasure-house. Why, then to thee, thou silver treasure-house *M. of V.* ii 9 34
Treasurer. This is my treasurer: let him speak, my lord *Ant. and Cleo.* v 2 142
Treasury. I would have ransack'd The pedlar's silken treasury *W. Tale* iv 4 361
All my treasury Is yet but unfelt thanks . . . *Richard II.* ii 3 60
As rich with praise As is the ooze and bottom of the sea With sunken wreck and sumless treasuries . . . . *Hen. V.* i 2 165
Thy wife's attire Have cost a mass of public treasury . . 2 *Hen. VI.* i 3 134
Could fly to heaven?—The treasury of everlasting joy . . . ii 1 18
And revel in Lavinia's treasury . . . . . . *T. Andron.* ii 1 131
I know not how conceit may rob The treasury of life . . . *Lear* iv 6 43
Treat. Say what the play treats on, then read the names *M. N. Dream* i 2 9
That part of philosophy Will I apply That treats of happiness *T. of Shrew* i 1 19
To treat of high affairs touching that time . . . *K. John* i 1 101
This is the tragic tale of Philomel, And treats of Tereus' treason *T. An.* iv 1 48
Treatise. I would have salved it with a longer treatise . . *Much Ado* i 1 317
My fell of hair Would at a dismal treatise rouse and stir . *Macbeth* v 5 12
Treaty. This friendly treaty of our threaten'd town . . *K. John* ii 1 481
This last costly treaty, the interview, That swallow'd so much treasure *Hen. VIII.* i 1 165
What good condition can a treaty find I' the part that is at mercy? *Cor.* i 10 6
We are convented Upon a pleasing treaty . . . . . . ii 2 59
Making a treaty where There was a yielding . . . . . v 6 68
Thy father, Pompey, would ne'er have made this treaty . *Ant. and Cleo.* ii 6 85
Now I must To the young man send humble treaties . . . iii 11 62
Treble. Which to do Trebles thee o'er . . . . . *Tempest* ii 1 221
Double and treble admonition, and still forfeit in the same kind! *Meas. for Meas.* iii 2 205
Twice treble shame on Angelo, To weed my vice and let his grow! . iii 2 283
Double six thousand, and then treble that . . . *Mer. of Venice* iii 2 302
His big manly voice, Turning again toward childish treble *As Y. Like It* ii 7 162
My instrument's in tune.—Let's hear. O fie! the treble jars *T. of Shrew* iii 1 39
The case of a treble hautboy was a mansion for him, a court 2 *Hen. IV.* iii 2 351
England shall double gild his treble guilt . . . . . iv 5 129
Our battalion trebles that account . . . . . *Richard III.* v 3 11
Let him make treble satisfaction . . . . . . *T. Andron.* v 1 8
And some I see That two-fold balls and treble sceptres carry *Macbeth* iv 1 121
O, treble woe Fall ten times treble on that cursed head! . . *Hamlet* v 1 270
The boatswain whistles, and The master calls, and trebles their confusion *Pericles* iv 1 65
Trebled. For you I would be trebled twenty times myself *Mer. of Venice* iii 2 154
Treble-sinewed. I will be treble-sinew'd, hearted, breathed, And fight maliciously . . . . *Ant. and Cleo.* iii 13 178
Trebonius. Is Decius Brutus and Trebonius there? . . . *J. Cæsar* i 3 148
This is Trebonius.—He is welcome hither.—This, Decius Brutus . . ii 1 94
What, Trebonius! I have an hour's talk in store for you . . . ii 2 120
Have an eye to Cinna; trust not Trebonius; mark well Metellus Cimber ii 3 3
Trebonius doth desire you to o'er-read, At your best leisure, this his humble suit . . . . iii 1 4
Trebonius knows his time; for, look you, Brutus, He draws Mark Antony out of the way . . . . iii 1 25
Though last, not least in love, yours, good Trebonius . . . iii 1 189
Tree. By this bottle! which I made of the bark of a tree . *Tempest* ii 2 128
If you prove a mutineer,—the next tree! . . . . . . iii 2 41
That in Arabia There is one tree, the phœnix' throne . . . iii 3 23
Vat be all you, one, two, tree, four, come for? . . *Mer. Wives* ii 3 22
Me have stay six or seven, two, three hours for him, and he is no come ii 3 37
And there he blasts the tree and takes the cattle . . . . iv 4 32
Glow-worms shall our lanterns be, To guide our measure round about the tree . . . . v 5 83
Is not Love a Hercules, Still climbing trees in the Hesperides? *L. L. Lost* iv 3 341
Mine, as sure as bark on tree . . . . v 2 285
The cuckoo then, on every tree, Mocks married men . . . . v 2 908
When the sweet wind did gently kiss the trees . . *Mer. of Venice* v 1 2
Therefore the poet Did feign that Orpheus drew trees, stones, and floods v 1 80
Finds tongues in trees, books in the running brooks . *As Y. Like It* ii 1 16
Thou prunest a rotten tree, That cannot so much as a blossom yield . ii 3 63
Under the greenwood tree Who loves to lie with me . . . . ii 5 1
Cover the while; the duke will drink under this tree . . . ii 5 33
These trees shall be my books And in their barks my thoughts I'll character . . . . iii 2 5
Carve on every tree The fair, the chaste, and unexpressive she . . iii 2 9
I found them on a tree.—Truly, the tree yields bad fruit . . . iii 2 122
Tongues I'll hang on every tree, That shall civil sayings show . . iii 2 135
Wondering how thy name should be hanged and carved upon these trees iii 2 183
I found him under a tree, like a dropped acorn.—It may well be called Jove's tree, when it drops forth such fruit . . . . . . iii 2 248
Mar no more trees with writing love-songs in their barks . . . iii 2 276
Are you he that hangs the verses on the trees? . . . . . iii 2 411
Will you dispatch us here under this tree, or shall we go with you? . iii 3 66
There stands the castle, by yon tuft of trees . . *Richard II.* ii 3 53
Let's step into the shadow of these trees . . . . . . iii 4 25
If then the tree may be known by the fruit, as the fruit by the tree; then, peremptorily I speak it . . . . 1 *Hen. IV.* ii 4 471
He upon whose side The fewest roses are cropp'd from the tree 1 *Hen. VI.* ii 4 41
How camest thou so?—A fall off of a tree . . . . 2 *Hen. VI.* ii 1 96
O, born so, master.—What, and wouldst climb a tree? . . . ii 1 98
Their sweetest shade a grove of cypress trees! . . . . . iii 2 323
His wonted sleep under a fresh tree's shade . . . . 3 *Hen. VI.* ii 5 49
Whose top-branch overpeer'd Jove's spreading tree . . . . v 2 14
Dogs howl'd, and hideous tempest shook down trees . . . . v 6 46
An indigested and deformed lump, Not like the fruit of such a goodly tree . . . . v 6 52
And, that I love the tree from whence thou sprang'st, Witness the loving kiss I give the fruit . . . . v 7 31
The standers-by had wet their cheeks, Like trees bedash'd with rain *Richard III.* i 2 164
The royal tree hath left us royal fruit . . . . iii 7 167
We take From every tree lop, bark, and part o' the timber *Hen. VIII.* i 2 96
Orpheus with his lute made trees, And the mountain tops that freeze, Bow themselves when he did sing . . . . iii 1 3
He that had wit would think that I had none, To bury so much gold under a tree, And never after to inherit it . . . *T. Andron.* ii 3 2
The trees, though summer, yet forlorn and lean, O'ercome with moss . ii 3 94
A halter, soldiers! hang him on this tree . . . . . . v 1 47
And on their skins, as on the bark of trees, Have with my knife carved v 1 138

Tree. Come, he hath hid himself among these trees . . *Rom. and Jul.* ii 1 30
Sit under a medlar tree, And wish his mistress were that kind of fruit ii 1 34
These moss'd trees, That have outlived the eagle . . *T. of Athens* iv 3 223
I have a tree, which grows here in my close, That mine own use invites me to cut down . . . . v 1 208
Whoso please To stop affliction, let him take his haste, Come hither, ere my tree hath felt the axe, And hang himself . . . . . v 1 214
He loves to hear That unicorns may be betray'd with trees . *J. Cæsar* ii 1 204
Stones have been known to move and trees to speak . . *Macbeth* iii 4 123
Though bladed corn be lodged and trees blown down . . . iv 1 55
Who can impress the forest, bid the tree Unfix his earth-bound root? . iv 1 95
If thou speak'st false, Upon the next tree shalt thou hang alive . v 5 39
Like fruit unripe, sticks on the tree . . . . . . *Hamlet* iii 2 200
And by the happy hollow of a tree Escaped the hunt . . . *Lear* ii 3 2
Here, father, take the shadow of this tree For your good host . . v 2 1
The poor soul sat sighing by a sycamore tree . . . . *Othello* iv 3 41
When I have pluck'd the rose, I cannot give it vital growth again, It must needs wither: I'll smell it on the tree . . . . . . v 2 15
Drop tears as fast as the Arabian trees Their medicinal gum . . . v 2 350
Yea, like the stag, when snow the pasture sheets, The barks of trees thou browsed'st . . . . *Ant. and Cleo.* i 4 66
The trees by the way Should have borne men . . . . . . iii 6 46
Blue promontory With trees upon't, that nod unto the world . . iv 14 6
Then was I as a tree Whose boughs did bend with fruit . *Cymbeline* iii 3 60
Hang there like fruit, my soul, Till the tree die! . . . . . v 5 264
Inflamed desire in my breast To taste the fruit of yon celestial tree *Per.* i 1 21
Hope, succeeding from so fair a tree As your fair self, doth tune us otherwise . . . . i 1 114
Who am no more but as the tops of trees, Which fence the roots they grow by . . . . i 2 29
Tremble. The most mighty Neptune Seem to besiege and make his bold waves tremble . . . . *Tempest* i 2 205
Make thee roar That beasts shall tremble at thy din . . . . i 2 371
Mark how he trembles in his ecstasy! . . . . *Com. of Errors* iv 4 54
Hector trembles.—Pompey is moved . . . . . *L. L. Lost* v 2 693
I would entreat you,—not to fear, not to tremble . *M. N. Dream* iii 1 43
Quake and tremble here, When lion rough in wildest rage doth roar . v 1 224
I will kill thee a hundred and fifty ways: therefore tremble *As Y. L. It* v 1 63
Innocence shall make False accusation blush and tyranny Tremble *W. Tale* iii 2 33
I tremble To think your father, by some accident, Should pass this way iv 4 18
O, tremble, for you hear the lion roar . . . . . *K. John* ii 1 294
With my vex'd spirits I cannot take a truce, But they will quake and tremble . . . . iii 1 18
Shall they seek the lion in his den, And fright him there? and make him tremble there? O, let it not be said . . . . v 1 58
My inward soul With nothing trembles . . . . *Richard II.* ii 2 12
Self-affrighted tremble at his sin . . . . iii 2 53
The heavens were all on fire, the earth did tremble . . 1 *Hen. IV.* iii 1 24
Such as my heart doth tremble to unfold . . . . 2 *Hen. VI.* ii 1 166
Small curs are not regarded when they grin; But great men tremble when the lion roars . . . . iii 1 19
So looks the pent-up lion o'er the wretch That trembles under his devouring paws; And so he walks . . . . . 3 *Hen. VI.* i 3 13
And made the forest tremble when they roar'd . . . . . v 7 12
What, do you tremble? are you all afraid? Alas, I blame you not *Richard III.* i 2 43
Which of you trembles not that looks on me? . . . . . . i 3 160
Tremble and start at wagging of a straw, Intending deep suspicion . iii 5 7
And made to tremble The region of my breast . . . . *Hen. VIII.* ii 4 183
As if the world Were feverous and did tremble . . . . *Coriolanus* i 4 61
We survive To tremble under Titus' threatening looks . . *T. Andron.* i 1 134
And virtue stoops and trembles at her frown . . . . . . ii 1 11
My compassionate heart Will not permit mine eyes once to behold The thing whereat it trembles by surmise . . . . ii 3 219
Those lily hands Tremble, like aspen-leaves, upon a lute . . . ii 4 45
Patience perforce with wilful choler meeting Makes my flesh tremble in their different greeting . . . . *Rom. and Jul.* i 5 92
Things that, to hear them told, have made me tremble . . . . iv 1 86
Here is a friar, that trembles, sighs, and weeps . . . . . v 3 184
It is the part of men to fear and tremble, When the most mighty gods by tokens send Such dreadful heralds . . . . . *J. Cæsar* i 3 54
Go show your slaves how choleric you are, And make your bondmen tremble . . . . iv 3 44
Take any shape but that, and my firm nerves Shall never tremble *Macb.* iii 4 103
You tremble and look pale: Is not this something more than fantasy? *Hamlet* i 1 53
You that look pale and tremble at this chance . . . . . v 2 345
Tremble, thou wretch, Thou hast within thee undivulged crimes *Lear* iii 2 51
This judgement of the heavens, that makes us tremble, Touches us not with pity . . . . v 3 231
First, to be hanged, and then to confess.—I tremble at it . *Othello* iv 1 40
Thou injurious thief, Hear but my name, and tremble . . *Cymbeline* iv 2 87
I cannot tremble at it: were it Toad, or Adder, Spider, 'Twould move me sooner . . . . iv 2 90
Good faith, I tremble still with fear . . . . iv 2 303
Minister'st a potion unto me That thou wouldst tremble to receive thyself . . . . *Pericles* i 2 69
Trembled and shook; for why, he stamp'd and swore . *T. of Shrew* iii 2 169
Shook and trembled at the ill neighbourhood . . . . . *Hen. V.* i 2 154
That Tiber trembled underneath her banks . . . . . *J. Cæsar* i 1 50
A hand that kings Have lipp'd, and trembled kissing . *Ant. and Cleo.* ii 5 30
Tremblest. Thou tremblest; and the whiteness in thy cheek Is apter than thy tongue to tell thy errand . . . . . 2 *Hen. IV.* i 1 68
By the eternal God, whose name and power Thou tremblest at, answer that I shall ask . . . . 2 *Hen. VI.* i 4 29
How now! why look'st thou pale? why tremblest thou? . . . . iii 2 27
Trembling. I know it by thy trembling . . . . . *Tempest* ii 2 83
He ought to enter into a quarrel with fear and trembling . *Much Ado* ii 3 203
Not yet on summer's death, nor on the birth Of trembling winter *W. T.* iv 4 81
Pale trembling coward, there I throw my gage . . . *Richard II.* i 1 69
Stand bare and naked, trembling at themselves . . . . . iii 2 46
Who then, affrighted with their bloody looks, Ran fearfully among the trembling reeds . . . . 1 *Hen. IV.* i 3 105
He turn'd an eye of death, Trembling even at the name of Mortimer . i 3 144
Rouse up fear and trembling, and do observance to my mercy 2 *Hen. IV.* iv 3 16
Shakes his head and trembling stands aloof . . . . 2 *Hen. VI.* i 1 227
Such safety finds The trembling lamb environed with wolves 3 *Hen. VI.* i 1 242
The bird that hath been limed in a bush, With trembling wings misdoubteth every bush . . . . v 6 14

Trembling. With the very noise I trembling waked . *Richard III.* i 4 61
Cold fearful drops stand on my trembling flesh . . v 3 181
Sixth part of each? A trembling contribution! . *Hen. VIII.* i 2 95
You have brought A trembling upon Rome, such as was never So in-capable of help . . . . . . *Coriolanus* iv 6 119
A chilling sweat o'er-runs my trembling joints . *T. Andron.* ii 3 212
If trembling I inhabit then, protest me The baby of a girl . *Macbeth* iii 4 105
Tremblingly she stood And on the sudden dropp'd . *Ant. and Cleo.* v 2 346
Tremor cordis. I have tremor cordis on me: my heart dances *W. Tale* i 2 110
Trempling. How full of chollors I am, and trempling of mind! *Mer. W.* iii 1 12
Trench. Thou hast talk'd Of sallies and retires, of trenches, tents, Of palisadoes, frontiers, parapets . . . 1 *Hen. IV.* ii 3 54
Yea, but a little charge will trench him here . . . iii 1 112
It will not be: retire into your trenches . . 1 *Hen. VI.* i 5 33
We'll beat them to their wives, As they us to our trenches followed *Coriolanus* i 4 42
I saw our party to their trenches driven, And then I came away . i 6 12
Where is that slave Which told me they had beat you to your trenches? i 6 40
Witness these trenches made by grief and care . . *T. Andron.* v 2 23
Trenchant. Let not the virgin's cheek Make soft thy trenchant sword *T. of Athens* iv 3 115
Trenched. This weak impress of love is as a figure Trenched in ice, which with an hour's heat Dissolves . . *T. G. of Ver.* iii 2 7
Safe in a ditch he bides, With twenty trenched gashes on his head *Macb.* iii 4 27
Trencher. Nor scrape trencher, nor wash dish . . . *Tempest* ii 2 187
He steps me to her trencher and steals her capon's leg . *T. G. of Ver.* iv 4 10
Holding a trencher, jesting merrily . . . . *L. L. Lost* v 2 477
There, take it to you, trenchers, cups, and all . . *T. of Shrew* iv 1 168
How often hast thou waited at my cup, Fed from my trencher? 2 *Hen VI.* iv 1 57
Thou pratest, and pratest; serve with thy trencher, hence! *Coriolanus* iv 5 54
Where's Potpan, that he helps not to take away? He shift a trencher? he scrape a trencher! . . . . *Rom. and Jul.* i 5 2
My estate deserves an heir more raised Than one which holds a trencher *T. of Athens* i 1 120
I found you as a morsel cold upon Dead Cæsar's trencher *Ant. and Cleo.* iii 13 117
Trencher-friends, time's flies, Cap and knee slaves . *T. of Athens* iii 6 106
Trencher-knight. Some mumble-news, some trencher-knight . *L. L. Lost* v 2 464
Trencher-man. He is a very valiant trencher-man . . *Much Ado* i 1 51
Trenching. No more shall trenching war channel her fields . 1 *Hen. IV.* i 1 7
Trent. England, from Trent and Severn hitherto . . . . . iii 1 74
To you The remnant northward, lying off from Trent . . . iii 1 79
And here the smug and silver Trent shall run In a new channel . iii 1 102
Come, you shall have Trent turn'd.—I do not care . . . iii 1 136
Trespass. And the thunder . . . : it did bass my trespass . *Tempest* iii 3 99
Be plainer with me; let me know my trespass By its own visage *W. Tale* i 2 265
Nor guilty of, If any be, the trespass of the queen . . . ii 2 63
Poor trespasses, More monstrous standing by . . . . iii 2 190
Indeed, paid down More penitence than done trespass . . . v 1 4
A trespass that doth vex my grieved soul . . . *Richard II.* i 1 138
Wilt thou not hide the trespass of thine own? . . . . v 2 89
My nephew's trespass may be well forgot . . . 1 *Hen. IV.* v 2 16
That caves and womby vaultages of France Shall chide your trespass *Hen. V.* ii 4 125
His trespass yet lives guilty in thy blood . . . 1 *Hen. VI.* ii 4 94
Murder indeed, that bloody sin, I tortured Above the felon or what trespass else . . . . 2 *Hen. VI.* iii 1 132
I am so sorry for my trespass made . . . . . 3 *Hen. VI.* v 1 92
Sin from my lips? O trespass sweetly urged! Give me my sin again *Rom. and Jul.* i 5 111
Lay not that flattering unction to your soul, That not your trespass, but my madness speaks . . . . . . *Hamlet* iii 4 146
Such as basest and contemned'st wretches For pilferings and most common trespasses Are punish'd with . . . . *Lear* ii 2 151
Your son and daughter found this trespass worth The shame which here it suffers . . . . ii 4 44
His trespass, in our common reason—Save that, they say, the wars must make examples Out of their best—is not almost a fault To incur a private check . . . . *Othello* iii 3 64
If e'er my will did trespass 'gainst his love, Either in discourse of thought or actual deed . . . . iv 2 152
His wife that's dead did trespasses to Cæsar . *Ant. and Cleo.* ii 1 40
Très-Puissant. Excusez-moi, je vous supplie, mon très-puissant seigneur *Hen. V.* v 2 277
Tressel and Berkeley, go along with me . . . . *Richard III.* i 2 222
Tresses. Bind up those tresses. O, what love I note In the fair multi-tude of those her hairs! . . . . . . *K. John* iii 4 61
Comets, importing change of times and states, Brandish your crystal tresses in the sky! . . . . 1 *Hen. VI.* i 1 3
Treys. There is three.—Nay then, two treys . . *L. L. Lost* v 2 232
Trial. Make not too rash a trial of him, for He's gentle . *Tempest* i 2 467
All thy vexations Were but my trials of thy love . . . . iv 1 6
A trial, come.—Come, will this wood take fire? . . *Mer. Wives* v 5 92
He made trial of you only . . . . . *Meas. for Meas.* iii 1 202
Put your trial in the villain's mouth Which here you come to accuse . v 1 304
Let my trial be mine own confession . . . . . . v 1 377
They will scarcely believe this without trial . . . *Much Ado* ii 2 41
With grey hairs and bruise of many days, Do challenge thee to trial of a man . . . . v 1 66
At the least of thy sweet notice, bring her to trial . . *L. L. Lost* i 1 279
It frosts and fasts, hard lodging and thin weeds Nip not the gaudy blossoms of your love, But that it bear this trial and last love . v 2 813
Let us teach our trial patience, Because it is a customary cross *M. N. D.* i 1 152
Whose trial shall better publish his commendation . *Mer. of Venice* iv 1 165
Let your fair eyes and gentle wishes go with me to my trial *As Y. Like It* i 2 199
All patience and impatience, All purity, all trial, all observance . v 2 104
Do not plunge thyself too far in anger, lest thou hasten thy trial *All's W.* ii 3 223
Make the trial of it in any constant question . . *T. Night* iv 2 52
For, as she hath Been publicly accused, so shall she have A just and open trial . . . . *W. Tale* iii 3 205
O that he were alive, and here beholding His daughter's trial! . . iii 2 122
In dreadful trial of our kingdom's king . . . . *K. John* ii 1 286
Thou hast not saved one drop of blood, In this hot trial, more than we ii 1 342
The trial of a woman's war, The bitter clamour of two eager tongues *Richard II.* i 1 48
I'll answer thee in any fair degree, Or chivalrous design of knighty trial i 1 81
Order the trial, marshal, and begin . . . . . . i 3 99
There is my honour's pawn; Engage it to the trial, if thou darest . iv 1 56
When he's return'd, Against Aumerle we will enforce his trial . . iv 1 90
All rest under gage Till we assign you to your days of trial . . iv 1 106
Be it your charge To keep him safely till his day of trial . . iv 1 153

Trial. I fear the power of Percy is too weak To wage an instant trial 1 *Hen. IV.* iv 4 20
Many a soul Shall pay full dearly for this encounter, If once they join in trial . . . . v 1 85
How canst thou tell she will deny thy suit, Before thou make a trial of her love? . . . . 1 *Hen. VI.* v 3 76
To keep, until your further time of trial . . . 2 *Hen. VI.* iii 1 138
Bring me unto my trial when you will . . . . . . iii 3 8
By this one bloody trial of sharp war . . . . *Richard III.* v 2 16
He is attach'd; Call him to present trial . . . *Hen. VIII.* i 2 211
By that wretch betray'd, And without trial fell . . . . ii 1 111
I had my trial, And, must needs say, a noble one . . . ii 1 118
Must now confess, if they have any goodness, The trial just and noble . ii 2 92
If the trial of the law o'ertake ye, You'll part away disgraced . . iii 2 96
At our last encounter, The Duke of Buckingham came from his trial . iv 1 5
Till further trial in those charges Which will require your answer . v 1 103
'Tis his highness' pleasure, And our consent, for better trial of you . v 3 53
Meant for his trial, And fair purgation to the world . . . v 3 151
Trial did draw Bias and thwart, not answering the aim . *Troi. and Cres.* i 3 14
Which are indeed nought else But the protractive trials of great Jove . i 3 20
A sportful combat, Yet in the trial much opinion dwells . . i 3 336
He hath resisted law, And therefore law shall scorn him further trial *Coriolanus* iii 1 268
Only make trial what your love can do For Rome . . . . v 1 40
I hope it is not so low with him as he made it seem in the trial of his several friends . . . . *T. of Athens* iii 6 6
They fall their crests, and, like deceitful jades, Sink in the trial *J. Cæsar* iv 2 27
It would come to immediate trial, if your lordship would vouchsafe the answer.—How if I answer 'no'?—I mean, my lord, the opposition of your person in trial . . . . *Hamlet* v 2 175
Do but blow them to their trial, the bubbles are out . . . v 2 202
Look, where he stands and glares! Wantest thou eyes at trial? . *Lear* iii 6 26
I'll see their trial first. Bring in the evidence . . . . iii 6 37
Give true evidence to his love, which stands An honourable trial *Ant. and Cleo.* i 3 75
Will poor folks lie, That have afflictions on them, knowing 'tis A punishment or trial? Yes; no wonder . . . . *Cymbeline* iii 6 11
His comforts thrive, his trials well are spent . . . . . v 4 104
Trial-day. I pray Your highness to assign our trial day . *Richard II.* i 1 151
Be brought against me at my trial-day . . . . 2 *Hen. VI.* iii 1 114
Trial-fire. With trial-fire touch me his finger-end . *Mer. Wives* v 5 88
Trib, trib, fairies; come; and remember your parts . . . v 5 1
Tribe. Cursed be my tribe, If I forgive him! . . *Mer. of Venice* i 3 52
Tubal, a wealthy Hebrew of my tribe, Will furnish me . . . i 3 58
Sufferance is the badge of all our tribe . . . . . . i 3 111
Here comes another of the tribe: a third cannot be matched . . iii 1 80
Have you collected them by tribes?—I have . . . *Coriolanus* iii 3 11
I would my son Were in Arabia, and thy tribe before him . . iv 2 24
Call all your tribes together, praise the gods, And make triumphant fires . . . . v 5 2
O that I had him, With six Aufidiuses, or more, his tribe, To use my lawful sword! . . . . v 6 130
A whole tribe of fops, Got 'tween asleep and wake . . . *Lear* i 2 14
If sanctimony . . . be not too hard for my wits and all the tribe of hell *Othello* i 3 364
Good heaven, the souls of all my tribe defend From jealousy! . . iii 3 175
Like the base Indian, threw a pearl away Richer than all his tribe . v 2 348
Tribulation. No audience, but the tribulation of Tower-hill *Hen. VIII.* v 4 65
Tribunal. I am going with my pigeons to the tribunal plebs *T. Andron.* iv 3 92
On a tribunal silver'd, Cleopatra and himself in chairs of gold Were publicly enthroned . . . . *Ant. and Cleo.* iii 6 3
Tribune. What is granted them?—Five tribunes . . . *Coriolanus* i 1 219
When we were chosen tribunes for the people,— Mark'd you his lip? . i 1 258
The common file—a plague! tribunes for them! . . . . i 6 43
Where the dull tribunes, That, with the fusty plebeians, hate thine honours . . . . i 9 6
We recommend to you, tribunes of the people, Our purpose to them . ii 2 155
The tribunes Endue you with the people's voice . . . . ii 3 146
Lay A fault on us, your tribunes . . . . ii 3 235
These are the tribunes of the people, The tongues o' the common mouth iii 1 21
Tribunes, give way; he shall to the market-place . . . . iii 1 31
Let me deserve so ill as you, and make me Your fellow tribune . . iii 1 52
Never be so noble as a consul, Nor yoke with him for tribune . . iii 1 57
What should the people do with these bald tribunes? . . . . iii 1 165
Tribunes! Patricians! Citizens! What, ho! . . . . . iii 1 186
You, tribunes To the people! Coriolanus, patience! . . . . iii 1 190
Hear me, people; peace!—Let's hear our tribune . . . . iii 1 193
Beseech you, tribunes, hear me but a word . . . . . iii 1 216
Down with that sword! Tribunes, withdraw awhile . . . . iii 1 226
I could myself Take up a brace o' the best of them; yea, the two tribunes . . . . iii 1 244
The noble tribunes are the people's mouths, And we their hands . . iii 1 271
If, by the tribunes' leave, and yours, good people, I may be heard . iii 1 282
Noble tribunes, It is the humane way . . . . . . iii 1 326
What must I do?—Return to the tribunes.—Well, what then? . . iii 2 36
The tribunes do attend you: arm yourself To answer mildly . . iii 2 138
List to your tribunes. Audience! peace, I say! . . . . iii 3 40
Call me their traitor! Thou injurious tribune! . . . . . iii 3 69
In the name o' the people And in the power of us the tribunes . . iii 3 100
The gods preserve our noble tribunes! . . . . . . iii 3 143
To take all power from the people and to pluck from them their tribunes . . . . iv 3 25
Who shall ask it? The tribunes cannot do't for shame . . . iv 6 109
The tribunes are no soldiers . . . . iv 7 31
A pair of tribunes that have rack'd for Rome, To make coals cheap . v 1 16
Is worth of consuls, senators, patricians, A city full; of tribunes, such as you, A sea and land full . . . . v 4 57
How fair the tribune speaks to calm my thoughts! . . *T. Andron.* i 1 46
Thanks, gentle tribune, noble brother . . . . . . i 1 171
Send thee by me, their tribune and their trust, This palliament . . i 1 181
Proud and ambitious tribune, canst thou tell? . . . . . i 1 202
People of Rome, and people's tribunes here, I ask your voices . . i 1 217
The people will accept whom he admits.—Tribunes, I thank you . . i 1 223
No, foolish tribune, no; no son of mine . . . . . . i 1 343
The tribune and his nephews kneel for grace . . . . . i 1 480
Hear me, grave fathers! noble tribunes, stay! For pity of mine age . iii 1 1
O reverend tribunes! O gentle, aged men! . . . . . . iii 1 23
You lament in vain: The tribunes hear you not . . . . iii 1 28
Grave tribunes, once more I entreat of you,— My gracious lord, no tribune hears you speak . . . . iii 1 32

Tribune. Yet in some sort they [the stones] are better than the tribunes *T. Andron.* iii 1 39
Were they but attired in grave weeds, Rome could afford no tribune like to these. A stone is soft as wax,—tribunes more hard than stones; A stone is silent, and offendeth not, And tribunes with their tongues doom men to death . . . . iii 1 44
It did me good, before the palace gate To brave the tribune . . . iv 2 36
To you the tribunes . . . he commends His absolute commission *Cymb.* iii 7 8
Tributary. Lo, at this tomb my tributary tears I render *T. Andron.* i 1 159
And make them blind with tributary tears . . . . . . iii 1 270
Back, foolish tears, . . . Your tributary drops belong to woe *R. and J.* iii 2 103
What tributaries follow him to Rome? *J. Cæsar* i 1 38
As England was his faithful tributary . . . . . *Hamlet* v 2 39
Whip him. Were't twenty of the greatest tributaries That do acknowledge Cæsar . . . . *Ant. and Cleo.* iii 13 96
The imperious seas breed monsters, for the dish Poor tributary rivers as sweet fish . . . . *Cymbeline* iv 2 36
Tribute. To give him annual tribute, do him homage *Tempest* i 2 113
In lieu o' the premises Of homage and I know not how much tribute . i 2 124
Draw thy sword: one stroke Shall free thee from the tribute which thou payest . . . . ii 1 293
The virgin tribute paid by howling Troy To the sea-monster . *M. of V.* iii 2 56
Take some remembrance of us, as a tribute, Not as a fee . . . iv 1 422
Craves no other tribute at thy hands But love, fair looks *T. of Shrew* v 2 152
Subjected tribute to commanding love . . . . *K John* i 1 264
And had the tribute of his supple knee . . . . *Richard II.* i 4 33
Duer paid to the hearer than the Turk's tribute . 2 *Hen. IV.* iii 2 331
Upon condition thou wilt swear To pay him tribute . 1 *Hen. VI.* v 4 130
The proudest peer in the realm shall not wear a head on his shoulders, unless he pay me tribute . . . . . 2 *Hen. VI.* iv 7 128
Receive them then, the tribute that I owe, Mine honour's ensigns humbled at thy feet . . . . *T. Andron.* i 1 251
His majesty shall have tribute of me . . . . . . *Hamlet* ii 2 333
He shall with speed to England, For the demand of our neglected tribute iii 1 178
I think He'll grant the tribute, send the arrearages . *Cymbeline* ii 4 13
You shall hear The legions now in Gallia sooner landed . . . than have tidings Of any penny tribute paid . . . . ii 4 20
For him And his succession granted Rome a tribute . . . . iii 1 8
There's no more tribute to be paid: our kingdom is stronger than it was iii 1 34
Why tribute? why should we pay tribute? If Cæsar can hide the sun from us with a blanket, or put the moon in his pocket, we will pay him tribute for light; else, sir, no more tribute . . . . . iii 1 42
Till the injurious Romans did extort This tribute from us, we were free iii 1 49
Thou comest not, Caius, now for tribute; that The Britons have razed out . . . . v 5 69
Promising To pay our wonted tribute, from the which We were dissuaded . . . . v 5 462
Trice. On a trice, so please you, Even in a dream, were we divided *Temp.* v 1 238
In a trice, Like to the old Vice . . . . . . *T. Night* iv 2 133
Should in this trice of time Commit a thing so monstrous *Lear* i 1 219
O, the charity of a penny cord! it sums up thousands in a trice *Cymb.* v 4 171
Trick. Felt a fever of the mad and play'd Some tricks of desperation *Temp.* i 2 210
Do you put tricks upon's with savages and men of Ind? . . . ii 2 60
I must use you In such another trick . . . . . . iv 1 37
I'll quickly cross By some sly trick blunt Thurio's dull proceeding *T. G. of Ver.* ii 6 41
Nay, I remember the trick you served me when I took my leave . iv 4 38
Didst thou ever see me do such a trick? . . . . . . iv 4 43
I'll ne'er be drunk whilst I live again, but in honest, civil, godly company, for this trick . . . . . . *Mer. Wives* i 1 188
We will yet have more tricks with Falstaff . . . . . iii 3 203
If I be served such another trick, I'll have my brains ta'en out and buttered . . . . iii 5 7
Like an angry ape, Plays such fantastic tricks before high heaven As make the angels weep . . . . . *Meas. for Meas.* ii 2 121
Why would he for the momentary trick Be perdurably fined? . . iii 1 114
Is it sad, and few words? or how? The trick of it? . . . iii 2 54
It was a mad fantastical trick of him to steal from the state . . iii 2 98
I spoke it but according to the trick . . . . . . v 1 510
I shall break that merry sconce of yours That stands on tricks when I am undisposed . . . . *Com. of Errors* i 2 80
You always end with a jade's trick: I know you of old . *Much Ado* i 1 145
This can be no trick: the conference was sadly borne . . . ii 3 229
Some tricks, some quillets, how to cheat the devil . . *L. L. Lost* iv 3 288
Yet I have a trick Of the old rage: bear with me, I am sick . . v 2 416
I see the trick on't: here was a consent, Knowing aforehand of our merriment . . . . v 2 460
That smiles his cheek in years and knows the trick To make my lady laugh . . . . v 2 465
Such tricks hath strong imagination . . . . . *M. N. Dream* v 1 18
I have within my mind A thousand raw tricks of these bragging Jacks, Which I will practise . . . . . . *Mer. of Venice* iii 4 77
An you serve me such another trick, never come in my sight more *As Y. Like It* iv 1 40
That teacheth tricks eleven and twenty long, To tame a shrew *T. of S.* iv 2 57
'Tis a cockle or a walnut-shell, A knack, a toy, a trick, a baby's cap iv 3 67
Heart too capable Of every line and trick of his sweet favour *All's Well* i 1 107
A man that had this trick of melancholy sold a goodly manor for a song iii 2 9
Go thy ways: let my horses be well looked to, without any tricks.—If I put any tricks upon 'em, sir, they shall be jades' tricks . . iv 5 62
Tricks he hath had in him, which gentlemen have . . . . v 3 239
Put thyself into the trick of singularity: she thus advises thee *T. Night* ii 5 164; iii 4 79
I'll question you Of my lord's tricks and yours when you were boys *W. T.* i 2 61
And I Remain a pinch'd thing; yea, a very trick For them to play at will . . . . ii 1 51
Copy of the father, eye, nose, lip, The trick of's frown . . . ii 3 100
Are you in earnest, sir? I smell the trick on't . . . . iv 4 657
He hath a trick of Cœur-de-lion's face . . . . *K. John* i 1 85
I know a trick worth two of that, i' faith . . . . 1 *Hen. IV.* ii 1 41
What trick, what device, what starting-hole, canst thou now find? . ii 4 290
Come, let's hear, Jack; what trick hast thou now? . . . . ii 4 293
A villanous trick of thine eye and a foolish hanging of thy nether lip . ii 4 446
So cherish'd and lock'd up, Will have a wild trick of his ancestors . v 2 11
It was alway yet the trick of our English nation, if they have a good thing, to make it too common . . . . . 2 *Hen. IV.* i 2 240
These tardy tricks of yours will, on my life, One time or other break some gallows' back . . . . iv 3 31
Which they trick up with new-tuned oaths . . . . *Hen. V.* iii 6 80
I, that am not shaped for sportive tricks . . . . *Richard III.* i 1 14
Trick. At this instant He bores me with some trick . . . *Hen. VIII.* i 1 128
The sly whoresons Have got a speeding trick to lay down ladies . . i 3 40
That trick of state Was a deep envious one . . . . . . ii 1 44
I abhor This dilatory sloth and tricks of Rome . . . . . ii 4 237
All his tricks founder, and he brings his physic After his patient's death iii 2 40
Thou canst strike, canst thou? a red murrain o' thy jade's tricks! *Troi. and Cres.* ii 1 21
Well said, adversity! and what need these tricks? . . . . . v 1 15
What would you have me do?—A juggling trick,—to be secretly open . v 2 24
You are never without your tricks: you may, you may . *Coriolanus* ii 3 38
By some chance, Some trick not worth an egg, shall grow dear friends . iv 4 21
The very trick on't . . . . iv 6 70
With twenty popish tricks and ceremonies . . . . *T. Andron.* v 1 76
Is it your trick to make me ope the door, That so my sad decrees may fly away? . . . . v 2 10
This trick may chance to scathe you, I know what . . *Rom. and Jul.* i 5 86
As good a trick as ever hangman served thief . . . *T. of Athens* ii 2 99
There are no tricks in plain and simple faith . . . . *J. Cæsar* iv 2 22
That, for a fantasy and trick of fame, Go to their graves like beds *Ham.* iv 4 61
Says she hears There's tricks i' the world; and hems, and beats her heart . . . . iv 5 5
That I, in forgery of shapes and tricks, Come short of what he did . iv 7 90
And therefore I forbid my tears: but yet It is our trick . . . iv 7 188
Here's fine revolution, an we had the trick to see't . . . . v 1 99
Where be his quiddities now, his quillets, his cases, his tenures, and his tricks? . . . . v 1 109
Good sir, no more; these are unsightly tricks . . . . . *Lear* ii 4 159
The trick of that voice I do well remember: Is't not the king? . iv 6 108
If such tricks as these strip you out of your lieutenantry, it had been better you had not kissed your three fingers so oft . . . *Othello* ii 1 172
Such things in a false disloyal knave Are tricks of custom . . . iii 3 122
This is a trick to put me from my suit: Pray you, let Cassio be received again . . . . iii 4 87
Beshrew him for't! How comes this trick upon him? . . . . iv 2 129
'Tis one of those odd tricks which sorrow shoots Out of the mind *Ant. and Cleo.* iv 2 14
You laugh when boys or women tell their dreams; Is't not your trick? v 2 75
You may then revolve what tales I have told you Of courts, of princes, of the tricks in war . . . . *Cymbeline* iii 3 15
Nature prompts them In simple and low things to prince it much Beyond the trick of others . . . . iii 3 86
Tricked. Horridly trick'd With blood of fathers, mothers, daughters *Hamlet* ii 2 479
Tricking. Go get us properties And tricking for our fairies *Mer. Wives* iv 4 79
Trickling. Weep not, sweet queen; for trickling tears are vain 1 *Hen. IV.* ii 4 431
Tricksy. My tricksy spirit! . . . . *Tempest* v 1 226
That for a tricksy word Defy the matter . . . *Mer. of Venice* iii 5 74
Trident. Make his bold waves tremble, Yea, his dread trident shake *Tempest* i 2 206
He would not flatter Neptune for his trident . . *Coriolanus* iii 1 256
Tried. He cannot be a perfect man, Not being tried and tutor'd in the world . . . . *T. G. of Ver.* i 3 21
I have tried: I can find out no rhyme to 'lady' but 'baby' *Much Ado* v 2 36
Being ten times undervalued to tried gold . . . *Mer. of Venice* ii 7 53
The fire seven times tried this: Seven times tried that judgement is . ii 9 63
I would I had that corporal soundness now, As when thy father and myself in friendship First tried our soldiership! . . . *All's Well* i 2 26
I wish, my liege, You had only in your silent judgement tried it *W. Tale* ii 1 171
The party tried The daughter of a king, our wife . . . . iii 2 2
Which, being touch'd and tried, Proves valueless . . . *K. John* iii 1 100
Let this dissension first be tried by fight . . . . 1 *Hen. VI.* iv 1 116
Therefore Left I the court, to see this quarrel tried . 2 *Hen. VI.* ii 3 53
Stubborn to justice, apt to accuse it, and Disdainful to be tried by't *Hen. VIII.* ii 4 123
If my actions Were tried by every tongue, every eye saw 'em . . iii 1 35
Touch'd his spirit And tried his inclination . . . *Coriolanus* ii 3 200
For he hath still been tried a holy man . . . . *Rom. and Jul.* iv 3 29
He might have tried Lord Lucius or Lucullus . . . *T. of Athens* iii 3 2
You may do your will; But he's a tried and valiant soldier *J. Cæsar* iv 1 28
We have tried the utmost of our friends, Our legions are brim-full iv 3 214
Those friends thou hast, and their adoption tried, Grapple them to thy soul with hoops of steel . . . . *Hamlet* i 3 62
Holding out gold that's by the touchstone tried . . . *Pericles* ii 2 37
Trier. You were used To say extremity was the trier of spirits *Coriolanus* iv 1 4
Trifle. For every trifle are they set upon me . . . . . *Tempest* ii 2 8
Whether thou be'st he or no, Or some enchanted trifle to abuse me . v 1 112
Alas, how love can trifle with itself! . . . . *T. G. of Ver.* iv 4 188
Hang the trifle, woman! take the honour. What is it? dispense with trifles . . . . *Mer. Wives* ii 1 46
Trifles, nosegays, sweetmeats, messengers Of strong prevailment in unharden'd youth . . . . *M. N. Dream* i 1 34
Sail upon the land, To fetch me trifles . . . . ii 1 133
Here's a small trifle of wives: alas, fifteen wives is nothing! *Mer. of Venice* ii 2 170
We trifle time: I pray thee, pursue sentence . . . . . . iv 1 298
Alas, it is a trifle! I will not shame myself to give you this . . iv 1 430
But a trifle neither, in good faith, if the learned should speak truth of it: here it is . . . . *All's Well* ii 2 36
We make trifles of terrors, ensconcing ourselves into seeming knowledge ii 3 4
Let him that makes but trifles of his eyes First hand me *W. Tale* ii 3 62
Was likewise a snapper-up of unconsidered trifles . . . . . iv 3 26
Old sir, I know She prizes not such trifles as these are . . . iv 4 368
At your request My father will grant precious things as trifles . . v 1 222
I'ld beg your precious mistress, Which he counts but a trifle . . v 1 224
Answers 'Some fourteen,' an hour after; 'a trifle, a trifle' 1 *Hen. IV.* ii 4 121
A trifle, some eight-penny matter . . . . iii 3 119
Let us not forego That for a trifle that was bought with blood! 1 *Hen. VI.* iv 1 150
His tyranny for trifles . . . . *Richard III.* i 7 9
I may perceive These cardinals trifle with me . . . . *Hen. VIII.* ii 4 236
Come, lords, we trifle time away . . . . v 3 179
Here, my lord, a trifle of our love . . . . . *T. of Athens* i 2 213
I have received some small kindnesses from him, as money, plate, jewels, and such-like trifles . . . . iii 2 24
Win us with honest trifles, to betray's In deepest consequence *Macbeth* i 3 125
To throw away the dearest thing he owed, As 'twere a careless trifle . i 4 11
I fear'd he did but trifle, And meant to wreck thee . . . . *Hamlet* ii 1 112
His knights grow riotous, and himself upbraids us On every trifle *Lear* i 3 7
Why I do trifle thus with his despair Is done to cure it . . . . iv 6 33
That's but a trifle here . . . . v 3 295

Trifle. Do not believe That, from the sense of all civility, I thus would play and trifle with your reverence . . . . . . *Othello* i 1 133
Trifles light as air Are to the jealous confirmations strong As proofs of holy writ . . . . iii 3 322
With a solemn earnestness, More than indeed belong'd to such a trifle . v 2 228
I some lady trifles have reserved, Immoment toys . . *Ant. and Cleo.* v 2 165
As I my poor self did exchange for you, To your so infinite loss, so in our trifles I still win of you . . . . . *Cymbeline* i 1 120
Either your unparagoned mistress is dead, or she's outprized by a trifle i 4 88
Come, gentlemen, we sit too long on trifles, And waste the time *Pericles* iii 3 92
Trifled. But this sore night Hath trifled former knowings *Macbeth* ii 4 4
Trifler. Away, you trifler! Love! I love thee not . . . 1 *Hen. IV.* ii 3 93
Trifling. But this is trifling; And all the more it seeks to hide itself, The bigger bulk it shows . . . . . *Tempest* iii 1 79
If it were not for one trifling respect, I could come to such honour! *Mer. Wives* ii 1 45
Prepare not to be gone; We have a trifling foolish banquet towards *Rom. and Jul.* i 5 124
When, for some trifling present, you have bid me Return so much, I have shook my head and wept . . . . *T. of Athens* ii 2 145
For Hamlet and the trifling of his favour, Hold it a fashion and a toy *Hamlet* i 3 5
Trigon. Look, whether the fiery Trigon, his man, be not lisping to his master's old tables . . . . . . 2 *Hen. IV.* ii 4 288
Trilled. Now and then an ample tear trill'd down Her delicate cheek *Lear* iv 3 14
Trim. In all her trim, freshly beheld Our royal, good, and gallant ship *Tempest* v 1 236
As you look To have my pardon, trim it handsomely . . . . v 1 293
The ship is in her trim; the merry wind Blows fair from land *Com. of Errors* iv 1 90
Men are only turned into tongue, and trim ones too . . *Much Ado* iv 1 323
Trim gallants, full of courtship and of state . . . . *L. L. Lost* v 2 363
A trim exploit, a manly enterprise! . . . . . *M. N. Dream* iii 2 157
They come like sacrifices in their trim . . . . 1 *Hen. IV.* iv 1 113
What is in that word honour? what is that honour? air. A trim reckoning! . . . . v 1 137
By the mass, our hearts are in the trim . . . . *Hen. V.* iv 3 115
What a loss our ladies Will have of these trim vanities! . . *Hen. VIII.* i 3 38
There's a trim rabble let in . . . . v 4 75
O, this is trim! . . . . *Troi. and Cres.* iv 5 33
Come, come, Thersites, help to trim my tent . . . . . v 1 50
My noble steed . . . I give him, With all his trim belonging . *Coriolanus* i 9 62
'Twas Trim sport for them that had the doing of it . . . *T. Andron.* v 1 96
Young Adam Cupid, he that shot so trim, When King Cophetua loved the beggar-maid! . . . . *Rom. and Jul.* ii 1 13
Go waken Juliet, go and trim her up; I'll go and chat with Paris . . iv 4 24
A thousand, sir, Early though't be, have on their riveted trim *Ant. and Cleo.* iv 4 22
Dainty trims, wherein You made great Juno angry . . *Cymbeline* iii 4 167
Like one another's glass to trim them by . . . . *Pericles* i 4 27
Trimly. Neat and trimly dress'd, Fresh as a bridegroom . 1 *Hen. IV.* i 3 33
Trimmed. I was trimm'd in Madam Julia's gown . . *T. G. of Ver.* iv 4 166
Sweeter than the lustful bed On purpose trimm'd up for Semiramis *T. of Shrew* Ind. 2 41
Is supper ready, the house trimmed, rushes strewed, cobwebs swept? . iv 1 48
O, what pity is it That he had not so trimm'd and dress'd his land As we this garden! . . . . *Richard II.* iii 4 56
Trimm'd up your praises with a princely tongue . . . 1 *Hen. IV.* v 2 57
Being now trimm'd in thine own desires . . . . 2 *Hen. IV.* i 3 94
Trimm'd like a younker prancing to his love! . . . 3 *Hen. VI.* ii 1 24
Cut her hands and trimm'd her as thou saw'st . . . *T. Andron.* v 1 93
She was wash'd and cut and trimm'd . . . . v 1 95
Trimm'd in forms and visages of duty . . . . . *Othello* i 1 50
His banners sable, trimm'd with rich expense . . . *Pericles* v Gower 19
Trimming. O detestable villain! call'st thou that trimming? *T. Andron.* v 1 94
I found her trimming up the diadem On her dead mistress . *A. and C.* v 2 345
Trinculo. I am Trinculo—be not afeard—thy good frien ' Trinculo *Temp.* ii 2 105
If thou beest Trinculo, come forth: I'll pull thee by the lesser legs . ii 2 107
If any be Trinculo's legs, these are they. Thou art very Trinculo indeed! . . . . ii 2 108
How camest thou to be the siege of this moon-calf? can he vent Trinculos? . . . . ii 2 111
Trinculo, the king and all our company else being drowned, we will inherit here: here; bear my bottle: fellow Trinculo, we'll fill him by and by again . . . . ii 2 178
Trinculo, keep a good tongue in your head . . . . . iii 2 40
I will stand, and so shall Trinculo . . . . iii 2 47
Trinculo, run into no further danger . . . . iii 2 76
Trinculo and thyself shall be viceroys. Dost thou like the plot, Trinculo? . . . . iii 2 116
Put off that gown, Trinculo; by this hand, I'll have that gown . iv 1 227
And Trinculo is reeling ripe . . . . v 1 279
Trinkets. As if my trinkets had been hallowed and brought a benediction to the buyer . . . . *W. Tale* iv 4 613
We'll see your trinkets here all forthcoming . . . 2 *Hen. VI.* i 4 56
Trip. And, as you trip, still pinch him to your time. . *Mer. Wives* v 5 96
Trip and go, my sweet; deliver this paper . . . *L. L. Lost* iv 2 144
In silence sad, Trip we after night's shade . . . *M. N. Dream* iv 1 101
Trip away; make no stay; Meet me all by break of day . . . . v 1 428
Trip, Audrey! trip, Audrey! I attend, I attend . . *As Y. Like It* v 1 68
Trip no further, pretty sweeting; Journeys end in lovers meeting *T. N.* ii 3 43
Thy craft so quickly grow, That thine own trip shall be thine overthrow v 1 170
To trip the course of law and blunt the sword . 2 *Hen. IV.* v 2 87
Then trip him, that his heels may kick at heaven . . *Hamlet* iii 3 93
These her women Can trip me, if I err . . . . *Cymbeline* v 5 35
I have heard, you knights of Tyre Are excellent in making ladies trip *Pericles* ii 3 103
Tripartite. Our indentures tripartite are drawn . . 1 *Hen. IV.* iii 1 80
Tripe. How say you to a fat tripe finely broil'd? . *T. of Shrew* iv 3 20
Tripe-visaged. Thou damned tripe-visaged rascal . . 2 *Hen. IV.* v 4 9
Triple. We fairies, that do run By the triple Hecate's team *M. N. Dream* v 1 391
He bade me store up, as a triple eye, Safer than mine own two *All's Well* ii 1 111
Carry him to Rome, And set the triple crown upon his head 2 *Hen VI.* i 3 66
You shall see in him The triple pillar of the world . . *Ant. and Cleo.* i 1 12
Triple-turn'd whore! 'tis thou Hast sold me to this novice . . iv 12 13
Triplex. The triplex, sir, is a good tripping measure . . *T. Night* v 1 41
Tripoli. As far as Rome; And so to Tripoli, if God lend me life *T. of S.* iv 2 76
Tripolis. He hath an argosy bound to Tripolis . . *Mer. of Venice* i 3 18
Hath an argosy cast away, coming from Tripolis . . . . . iii 1 106
What, not one hit? From Tripolis, from Mexico, and England? . . iii 2 271

Tripped up the wrestler's heels and your heart . . . *As Y. Like It* iii 2 224
By this we gather You have tripp'd since . . . . . *W. Tale* i 2 76
I'll not be struck, my lord. Nor tripped neither . . . . *Lear* i 4 95
Is it two days ago since I tripped up thy heels, and beat thee? . . ii 2 32
And flattering his displeasure, Tripp'd me behind . . . . . ii 2 126
Tripping. Each one, tripping on his toe, Will be here with mop and mow *Tempest* iv 1 46
The triplex, sir, is a good tripping measure . . . . *T. Night* v 1 41
Pale-visaged maids Like Amazons come tripping after drums *K. John* v 2 155
And all the Greekish girls shall tripping sing . . *Troi. and Cres.* iii 3 211
Trippingly. This ditty, after me, Sing, and dance it trippingly *M. N. D.* v 1 403
As I pronounced it to you, trippingly on the tongue . . *Hamlet* iii 2 2
Tristful. For God's sake, lords, convey my tristful queen . 1 *Hen. IV.* ii 4 434
This solidity and compound mass, With tristful visage, as against the doom, Is thought-sick at the act . . . . . *Hamlet* iii 4 50
Triton. Hear you this Triton of the minnows? . . . *Coriolanus* iii 1 89
Triumph. We will include all jars With triumphs, mirth . *T. G. of Ver.* v 4 161
What, at the wheels of Cæsar? art thou led in triumph? *Meas. for Meas.* iii 2 46
Air, would I might triumph so! . . . . . *L. L. Lost* iv 3 110
How will he spend his wit! How will he triumph, leap, and laugh at it! . . . . iv 3 148
With pomp, with triumph, and with revelling . . . *M. N. Dream* i 1 19
Sorrow on thee and all the pack of you, That triumph thus upon my misery! Go, get thee gone . . . . . . *T. of Shrew* iv 3 34
But now the blood of twenty thousand men Did triumph in my face *Richard II.* iii 2 77
What, was I born to this, that my sad look Should grace the triumph of great Bolingbroke? . . . . iii 4 99
When triumph is become an alehouse guest . . . . . v 1 15
What news from Oxford? hold those justs and triumphs? . . . v 2 52
For gay apparel 'gainst the triumph day . . . . . . v 2 66
I saw the prince, And told him of those triumphs held at Oxford . v 3 14
Thou art a perpetual triumph, an everlasting bonfire-light! 1 *Hen. IV.* iii 3 46
Nobility lies trodden on, And rebels' arms triumph in massacres! . . v 4 14
France, triumph in thy glorious prophetess! . . . 1 *Hen. VI.* i 6 8
Let frantic Talbot triumph for a while And like a peacock sweep along his tail . . . . iii 3 5
Or one that, at a triumph having vow'd To try his strength . . . v 5 31
When thou didst ride in triumph through the streets . 2 *Hen. VI.* ii 4 14
Which I will bear in triumph to the king . . . . . iv 10 89
So triumph thieves upon their conquer'd booty . . 3 *Hen. VI.* i 4 63
How ill-beseeming is it in thy sex To triumph, like an Amazonian trull! i 4 114
And here's the heart that triumphs in their death . . . i 4 8
Let thy dauntless mind Still ride in triumph over all mischance . iii 3 18
I'll throw thy body in another room And triumph, Henry, in thy day of doom . . . . v 6 93
And now what rests but that we spend the time With stately triumphs? v 7 43
We have not yet set down this day of triumph . . *Richard III.* iii 4 44
Triumph not in my woes! God witness with me, I have wept for thine iv 4 59
I, with mine enemies, Will triumph o'er my person . . *Hen. VIII.* v 1 124
Wouldst thou have laugh'd had I come coffin'd home, That weep'st to see me triumph? . . . . *Coriolanus* ii 1 194
To beautify thy triumphs and return, Captive to thee . . *T. Andron.* i 1 110
But safer triumph is this funeral pomp, That hath aspired to Solon's happiness And triumphs over chance in honour's bed . . . i 1 176
Whom thou in triumph long Hast prisoner held, fetter'd in amorous chains . . . . ii 1 14
Violent delights have violent ends And in their triumph die . *R. and J.* ii 6 10
Alive, in triumph! and Mercutio slain! Away to heaven, respective lenity! . . . . iii 1 127
We make holiday, to see Cæsar and to rejoice in his triumph . *J. Cæsar* i 1 36
And do you now strew flowers in his way That comes in triumph over Pompey's blood? Be gone! . . . . i 1 56
Are all thy conquests, glories, triumphs, spoils, Shrunk to this little measure? . . . . iii 1 149
Bring him with triumph home unto his house . . . . . iii 2 54
Then, if we lose this battle, You are contented to be led in triumph? . v 1 109
The kettle-drum and trumpet thus bray out The triumph of his pledge *Hamlet* i 4 12
Every man put himself into triumph . . . . . *Othello* ii 2 4
Do you triumph, Roman? do you triumph? . . . . . . iv 1 121
Be thou sorry To follow Cæsar in his triumph, since Thou hast been whipp'd for following him . . . . . *Ant. and Cleo.* iii 13 136
Vanish, or I shall give thee thy deserving, And blemish Cæsar's triumph iv 12 33
And false-play'd my glory Unto an enemy's triumph . . . . iv 14 20
Her life in Rome Would be eternal in our triumph . . . . v 1 66
He'll lead me, then, in triumph?—Madam, he will . . . . v 2 109
Triumphs for nothing and lamenting toys Is jollity for apes . *Cymbeline* iv 2 193
Are the knights ready to begin the triumph? . . . . *Pericles* ii 2 1
Our daughter, In honour of whose birth these triumphs are . . ii 2 5
He comes To an honour'd triumph strangely furnished . . . ii 2 53
Being on shore, honouring of Neptune's triumphs . . . . v 1 17
Triumphant. Of colour like the red rose on triumphant brier *M. N. D.* iii 1 96
England, bound in with the triumphant sea . . . *Richard II.* ii 1 61
And spent not that Which his triumphant father's hand had won . . ii 1 181
Like captives bound to a triumphant car . . . . 1 *Hen. VI.* i 1 22
Triumphant death, smear'd with captivity . . . . . iv 7 3
And now to London with triumphant march . . . 3 *Hen. VI.* ii 6 87
Think you, but that I know our state secure, I would be so triumphant as I am? . . . . *Richard III.* iii 2 84
Bound with triumphant garlands will I come . . . . . iv 4 333
Praise the gods, And make triumphant fires . . . . *Coriolanus* v 5 3
I'll bury thee in a triumphant grave . . . . *Rom. and Jul.* v 3 83
She's a most triumphant lady, if report be square to her *Ant. and Cleo.* ii 2 189
So thy grand captain Antony Shall set thee on triumphant chariots . iii 1 10
Triumphantly. Dance in Duke Theseus' house triumphantly *M. N. Dream* iv 1 94
The dancing banners of the French, . . . triumphantly display'd *K. John* ii 1 309
Or else Triumphantly tread on thy country's ruin . . *Coriolanus* v 3 116
Triumphed. O Douglas, hadst thou fought at Holmedon thus, I never had triumph'd upon a Scot . . . . 1 *Hen. IV.* v 3 15
Not Cæsar's valour hath o'erthrown Antony, But Antony's hath triumph'd on itself.—So it should be . . . *Ant. and Cleo.* iv 15 15
Triumpher. Gracious triumpher in the eyes of Rome! . . *T. Andron.* i 1 170
Enter in our ears like great triumphers In their applauding gates *T. of A.* v 1 199
Triumphing. So ridest thou triumphing in my woe . . *L. L. Lost* iv 3 36
As 'twere triumphing at mine enemies . . . . *Richard III.* iii 4 91
And there Ride on the pants triumphing! . . . *Ant. and Cleo.* iv 8 16
Triumvirate. He frets That Lepidus of the triumvirate Should be deposed iii 6 28
Triumviry. Thou makest the triumviry, the corner-cap of society *L. L. Lost* iv 3 53

Trivial. Our rash faults Make trivial price of serious things . *All's Well* v 3 61
And yet we have but trivial argument, More than mistrust 2 *Hen. VI.* iii 1 241
The respects thereof are nice and trivial . *Richard III.* iii 7 175
Hasty and tinder-like upon too trivial motion . *Coriolanus* ii 1 55
From the table of my memory I'll wipe away all trivial fond records *Ham.* i 5 99
When we debate Our trivial difference loud, we do commit Murder in healing wounds . *Ant. and Cleo.* ii 2 21
Upon importance of so slight and trivial a nature . *Cymbeline* i 4 45
Troat. It is a shallenge : I will cut his troat in de park . *Mer. Wives* i 4 115
Trod. He trod the water, Whose enmity he flung aside *Tempest* ii 1 115
He's a present for any emperor that ever trod on neat's-leather . ii 2 73
Here's a maze trod indeed Through forth-rights and meanders ! . iii 3 2
This is as strange a maze as e'er men trod . v 1 242
I have trod a measure ; I have flattered a lady . *As Y. Like It* v 4 45
Had you first died, and he been thus trod down *Richard II.* ii 3 126
As ever his black shoe trod upon God's ground and his earth . *Hen. V.* iv 7 149
But now mischance hath trod my title down . 3 *Hen. VI.* iii 3 8
Would I had never trod this English earth ! . *Hen. VIII.* iii 1 143
Wolsey, that once trod the ways of glory . iii 2 435
Forgetting thy great deeds, when neighbour states, But for thy sword and fortune, trod upon them . *T. of Athens* iv 3 95
As proper men as ever trod upon neat's leather have gone upon my handiwork . *J. Cæsar* i 1 29
I trod upon a worm against my will, But I wept for it . *Pericles* iv 1 79
Trodden. If we walk not in the trodden paths . *As Y. Like It* i 3 15
O then, tread down my need, and faith mounts up ; Keep my need up, and faith is trodden down ! . *K. John* iii 1 216
The camomile, the more it is trodden on the faster it grows . 1 *Hen. IV.* ii 4 442
Where stain'd nobility lies trodden on . v 4 13
The smallest worm will turn being trodden on . 3 *Hen. VI.* ii 2 17
A little fire is quickly trodden out . iv 8 7
Troien. Priam's six-gated city, Dardan, and Tymbria, Helias, Chetas, Troien, And Antenorides . *Troi. and Cres.* Prol. 16
Troilus the first employer of pandars . *Much Ado* v 2 31
In such a night Troilus methinks mounted the Troyan walls *M. of Ven.* v 1 4
Troilus had his brains dashed out with a Grecian club . *As Y. Like It* iv 1 97
Where's my spaniel Troilus? . *T. of Shrew* iv 1 153
I would play Lord Pandarus of Phrygia, sir, to bring a Cressida to this Troilus . *T. Night* iii 1 59
Each Trojan that is master of his heart, Let him to field ; Troilus, alas ! hath none . *Troi. and Cres.* i 1 5
How now, Prince Troilus ! wherefore not afield?—Because not there . i 1 108
Troilus will not come far behind him ; let them take heed of Troilus . i 2 59
Troilus is the better man of the two.—O Jupiter ! there's no comparison. —What, not between Troilus and Hector? . i 2 63
I say Troilus is Troilus.—Then you say as I say ; for, I am sure, he is not Hector.—No, nor Hector is not Troilus . i 2 70
He is himself.—Himself ! Alas, poor Troilus, I would he were . i 2 77
No, Hector is not a better man than Troilus.—Excuse me.—He is elder i 2 86
I had as lief Helen's golden tongue had commended Troilus for a copper nose . i 2 115
But to prove to you that Helen loves Troilus,— Troilus will stand to the proof, if you'll prove it so.—Troilus ! why, he esteems her no more than I esteem an addle egg . i 2 141
At what was all this laughing?—Marry, at the white hair that Helen spied on Troilus' chin . i 2 165
I'll tell you them all by their names as they pass by ; but mark Troilus i 2 200
When comes Troilus? I'll show you Troilus anon : if he see me, you shall see him nod at me . i 2 210
Would I could see Troilus now ! You shall see Troilus anon . i 2 235
'Tis Troilus ! there's a man, niece ! Hem ! Brave Troilus ! the prince of chivalry ! . i 2 248
O brave Troilus ! Look well upon him, niece : look you how his sword is bloodied . i 2 251
I could live and die i' the eyes of Troilus . i 2 264
I had rather be such a man as Troilus than Agamemnon and all Greece i 2 266
There is among the Greeks Achilles, a better man than Troilus . i 2 269
To bring, uncle?—Ay, a token from Troilus . i 2 306
More in Troilus thousand fold I see Than in the glass of Pandar's praise may be . i 2 310
Paris and Troilus, you have both said well . ii 2 163
I come to speak with Paris from the Prince Troilus . iii 1 41
How chance my brother Troilus went not?—He hangs the lip at something . iii 1 151
Troilus shall be such to Cressid as what envy can say worst shall be a mock for his truth, and what truth can speak truest not truer than Troilus . iii 2 103
Prince Troilus, I have loved you night and day For many weary months iii 2 122
True swains in love shall in the world to come Approve their truths by Troilus . iii 2 181
'As true as Troilus' shall crown up the verse, And sanctify the numbers iii 2 189
Let all constant men be Troiluses, all false women Cressids ! . iii 2 210
Call my thought a certain knowledge—My brother Troilus lodges there iv 1 42
Troilus had rather Troy were borne to Greece Than Cressid borne from Troy . iv 1 46
Is not Prince Troilus here?—Here ! what should he do here? . iv 2 49
Thou must to thy father, and be gone from Troilus : 'twill be his death iv 2 97
No kin, no love, no blood, no soul so near me As the sweet Troilus . iv 2 105
Make Cressid's name the very crown of falsehood, If ever she leave Troilus ! . iv 2 107
Crack my clear voice with sobs and break my heart With sounding Troilus iv 2 115
Good my brother Troilus, Tell you the lady what she is to do . iv 3 3
An altar, and thy brother Troilus A priest there offering to it his own heart . iv 3 8
O Troilus ! Troilus !—What a pair of spectacles is here ! . iv 4 13
A hateful truth.—What, and from Troilus too?—From Troy and Troilus iv 4 33
Be not moved, Prince Troilus : Let me be privileged by my place and message, To be a speaker free . iv 4 131
The prince must think me tardy and remiss . —'Tis Troilus' fault . iv 4 145
They call him Troilus, and on him erect A second hope, as fairly built as Hector . iv 5 108
Call my brother Troilus to me, And signify this loving interview . iv 5 154
Troilus, farewell ! one eye yet looks on thee . v 2 107
May worthy Troilus be half attach'd With that which here his passion doth express? . v 2 161
Call my father to persuade.—No, faith, young Troilus ; doff thy harness v 3 31
What vice is that, good Troilus? chide me for it . v 3 39
Troilus, I would not have you fight to-day.—Who should withhold me? v 3 50
Take thou Troilus' horse ; Present the fair steed to my lady Cressid . v 5 1
He is arm'd and at it, Roaring for Troilus . v 5 37
Troilus, thou coward Troilus, show thy head !—Troilus, I say ! where's Troilus? . *Troi. and Cres.* v 6 1
Yea, Troilus? O, well fought, my youngest brother ! . v 6 12
Trojan. There are other Trojans that thou dreamest not of . 1 *Hen. IV.* ii 1 77
Compare with Cæsars, and with Cannibals, And Trojan Greeks 2 *Hen. IV.* ii 4 181
Dost thou thirst, base Trojan, To have me fold up Parca's fatal web? *Hen. V.* v 1 20
Base Trojan, thou shalt die.—You say very true . v 1 32
With hope to find the like event in love, But prosper better than the Trojan did . 1 *Hen. VI.* v 5 106
On one and other side, Trojan and Greek, Sets all on hazard *T. and C.* Prol. 21
Each Trojan that is master of his heart, Let him to field . i 1 4
There is among the Greeks A lord of Trojan blood, nephew to Hector . i 2 13
This Trojan scorns us ; or the men of Troy Are ceremonious courtiers . i 3 233
But peace, Æneas, Peace, Trojan ; lay thy finger on thy lips ! . i 3 240
That thou shalt know, Trojan, he is awake, He tells thee so himself . i 3 255
Hector, in view of Trojans and of Greeks, Shall make it good . i 3 273
Here the Trojans taste our dear'st repute With their finest palate . i 3 337
Thou scurvy-valiant ass ! thou art here but to thrash Trojans . ii 1 50
Cry, Trojans, cry ! lend me ten thousand eyes, And I will fill them . ii 2 101
Cry, Trojans, cry ! practise your eyes with tears ! . ii 2 108
Cry, Trojans, cry ! a Helen and a woe : Cry, cry ! . ii 2 111
I would not wish a drop of Trojan blood Spent more in her defence . ii 2 197
A whoreson dog, that shall palter thus with us ! Would he were a Trojan ! ii 3 245
What wouldst thou of us, Trojan? make demand.—You have a Trojan prisoner . iii 3 17
For every scruple Of her contaminated carrion weight, A Trojan hath been slain . iv 1 72
Since she could speak, She hath not given so many good words breath As for her Greeks and Trojans suffer'd death . iv 1 74
The Trojans' trumpet.—Yonder comes the troop . iv 5 64
Half Hector comes to seek This blended knight, half Trojan and half Greek . iv 5 86
What Trojan is that same that looks so heavy?—The youngest son of Priam . iv 5 95
Were thy commixtion Greek and Trojan so That thou couldst say 'This hand is Grecian all, And this is Trojan' . iv 5 124
Signify this loving interview To the expecters of our Trojan part . iv 5 156
I have, thou gallant Trojan, seen thee oft Labouring for destiny . iv 5 183
Ah, sir, there's many a Greek and Trojan dead, Since first I saw yourself iv 5 214
They say he keeps a Trojan drab, and uses the traitor Calchas' tent . v 1 104
Was Cressid here?—I cannot conjure, Trojan . v 2 125
That same young Trojan ass, that loves the whore there . v 4 6
Tell her I have chastised the amorous Trojan, And am her knight by proof v 5 4
Pause, if thou wilt.—I do disdain thy courtesy, proud Trojan . v 6 15
Hark ! a retire upon our Grecian part.—The Trojan trumpets sound the like . v 8 16
Tie his body to my horse's tail ; Along the field I will the Trojan trail . v 8 22
Like the Trojan horse was stuff'd within With bloody veins *Pericles* i 4 93
Troll. Will you troll the catch You taught me but while-ere? *Tempest* iii 2 126
Troll-my-dames. A fellow, sir, that I have known to go about with troll-my-dames . *W. Tale* iv 3 92
Tromperies. Les langues des hommes sont pleines de tromperies *Hen. V.* v 2 119
Troop. In troops I have dispersed them 'bout the isle . *Tempest* i 2 220
I second thee ; troop on . *Mer. Wives* i 3 114
Where is Nan now and her troop of fairies? . v 3 12
A huge infectious troop Of pale distemperatures . *Com. of Errors* v 1 81
Ghosts, wandering here and there, Troop home to churchyards *M. N. D.* iii 2 382
Tarry, holy pilgrim, But till the troops come by *All's Well* iii 5 43
The troop is past. Come, pilgrim . iii 5 96
I, with a troop of Florentines, will suddenly surprise him . iii 6 23
The troops are all scattered, and the commanders very poor rogues iv 3 152
Like a jolly troop of huntsmen, come Our lusty English . *K. John* ii 1 321
Is not the Lady Constance in this troop? I know she is not . ii 1 540
This unhair'd sauciness and boyish troops The king doth smile at . v 2 133
Would it not shame thee in so fair a troop To read a lecture? *Richard II.* iv 1 231
Hath beaten down young Hotspur and his troops 2 *Hen. IV.* Ind. 25
Took fire and heat away From the best-temper'd courage in his troops . i 1 115
Nor do I as an enemy to peace Troop in the throngs of military men iv 1 62
Having full scarce six thousand in his troop . 1 *Hen. VI.* i 1 112
Our English troops retire, I cannot stay them . i 5 2
A witch, by fear, not force, like Hannibal, Drives back our troops . i 5 22
They did amongst the troops of armed men Leap o'er the walls for refuge ii 2 24
With his colours spread, And all the troops of English after him . iii 3 32
Unite Your troops of horsemen with his bands of foot . iv 1 165
As he march'd along, By your espials were discovered Two mightier troops than that the Dauphin led . iv 3 7
She sweeps it through the court with troops of ladies 2 *Hen. VI.* i 3 80
Have I seen this stubborn Cade Oppose himself against a troop of kerns iii 1 361
The city favours them, And they have troops of soldiers at their beck 3 *Hen. VI.* i 1 68
He bore him in the thickest troop As doth a lion in a herd of neat . ii 1 13
Let us all together to our troops, And give them leave to fly that will not stay . ii 3 49
Some troops pursue the bloody-minded queen . ii 6 33
With his troops doth march amain to London . iv 8 4
At Daintry, with a puissant troop . v 1 6
He wonders to what end you have assembled Such troops of citizens to speak with him . *Richard III.* iii 7 85
Where be the thronging troops that follow'd thee? . iv 4 96
From troop to troop Went through the army, cheering up the soldiers . v 3 70
What is't?—A noble troop of strangers ; For so they seem . *Hen. VIII.* i 4 53
No sun shall ever usher forth mine honours, Or gild again the noble troops iii 2 411
Saw you not, even now, a blessed troop Invite me to a banquet? . iv 2 87
Break among the press, and find a way out To let the troop pass fairly v 4 89
The Trojans' trumpet.—Yonder comes the troop . *Troi. and Cres.* iv 5 64
What says the other troop?—They are dissolved : hang 'em ! *Coriolanus* i 1 208
There will the lovely Roman ladies troop . *T. Andron.* ii 1 113
Rome's royal empress, Unfurnish'd of her well-beseeming troop . ii 3 56
From our troops I stray'd To gaze upon a ruinous monastery . v 1 20
I'll cheer up My discontented troops, and lay for hearts *T. of Athens* iii 5 115
Hide thy spurs in him, Till he have brought thee up to yonder troops, And here again ; that I may rest assured Whether yond troops are friend or enemy . *J. Cæsar* v 3 18
Honour, love, obedience, troops of friends, I must not look to have *Macb.* v 3 25
All the large effects That troop with majesty . *Lear* i 1 134
Our troops set forth to-morrow : stay with us ; The ways are dangerous iv 5 16
It were a delicate stratagem, to shoe A troop of horse with felt . iv 6 189
Here comes another troop to seek for you . *Othello* i 2 54
Farewell the plumed troop, and the big wars, That make ambition virtue ! iii 3 349

Troop. Nay, the dust Should have ascended to the roof of heaven, Raised by your populous troops . . . *Ant. and Cleo.* iii 6 50
Dido and her Æneas shall want troops, And all the haunt be ours . iv 14 53
Away, boy, from the troops, and save thyself . . . *Cymbeline* v 2 14
Trooping. So shows a snowy dove trooping with crows *Rom. and Jul.* i 5 50
Trophy. The mere word's a slave Debosh'd on every tomb, on every grave A lying trophy . . . . *All's Well* ii 3 146
Giving full trophy, signal, and ostent Quite from himself to God *Hen. V.* v Prol. 21
Worn as a memorable trophy of predeceased valour . . . v 1 76
No blood !—Away, you fool ! it more becomes a man Than gilt his trophy *Coriolanus* i 3 43
Till we with trophies do adorn thy tomb . . . *T. Andron.* i 1 388
Nor are they such That these great towers, trophies, and schools should fall For private faults in them . . *T. of Athens* v 4 25
Let no images Be hung with Cæsar's trophies . . *J. Cæsar* i 1 74
No trophy, sword, nor hatchment o'er his bones, No noble rite *Hamlet* iv 5 214
Down her weedy trophies and herself Fell in the weeping brook . iv 7 175
Tropically. What do you call the play?—The Mouse-trap. Marry, how? Tropically . . . . iii 2 247
Trot. Cashier : let them wag ; trot, trot *Mer. Wives* i 3 7
By my trot, I tarry too long. Od's me ! . . . . i 4 64
By my trot, dere is no duke dat the court is know to come . iv 5 89
What sayest thou, Trot? Is the world as it was, man? *Meas. for Meas.* iii 2 52
I'll tell you who Time ambles withal, who Time trots withal *As Y. Like It* iii 2 328
Who doth he trot withal?—Marry, he trots hard with a young maid between the contract of her marriage and the day it is solemnized . iii 2 330
An old trot with ne'er a tooth in her head . . . *T. of Shrew* i 2 80
He trots the air ; the earth sings when he touches it . *Hen. V.* iii 7 16
Even as your horse bears your praises ; who would trot as well, were some of your brags dismounted . . . . . . iii 7 83
I will trot to-morrow a mile, and my way shall be paved with English faces . . . . iii 7 86
I will dismount, and by the waggon-wheel Trot, like a servile footman *T. Andron.* v 2 55
Dolphin my boy, my boy, sessa ! let him trot by . *Lear* iii 4 104
Troth. His fins like arms ! Warm o' my troth ! *Tempest* ii 2 36
And, by my two faiths and troths, my lord, I spoke mine *Much Ado* i 1 228
Or, having sworn too hard a keeping oath, Study to break it and not break my troth . . . . . . *L. L. Lost* i 1 66
O' my troth, most sweet jests ! . . . . . . iv 1 144
You would for paradise break faith and troth . . . iv 3 143
For virtue's office never breaks men's troth . . . v 2 350
To speak troth, I have forgot our way . . *M. N. Dream* ii 2 36
One heart, one bed, two bosoms, and one troth . . . ii 2 42
Two bosoms and a single troth . . . . . . ii 2 50
Good troth, you do me wrong, good sooth, you do . . . ii 2 129
Then fate o'er-rules, that, one man holding troth, A million fail . iii 2 92
Dangerous countenance, And violation of all faith and troth *1 Hen. IV.* v 1 70
Nay, good troth.—Yes, troth, and troth ; you would not be a queen? *Hen. VIII.* ii 3 34
Faith and troth, Strain'd purely from all hollow bias-drawing *Troi. and Cres.* iv 5 168
He was too hard for him directly, to say the troth on't . *Coriolanus* iv 5 198
Bid her alight, And her troth plight, And, aroint thee, witch ! *Lear* iii 4 128
I will remain The loyal'st husband that did e'er plight troth *Cymbeline* i 1 96
Good troth, I have stol'n nought, nor would not . . . iii 6 48
My lord, Now fear is from me, I'll speak troth . . . v 5 274
By my troth *Mer. Wives* i 1 ; *Meas. for Meas.* iv 3 ; *Com. of Errors* iii 1 ; *Much Ado* i 1
Troth-plight. Deserves a name As rank as any flax-wench that puts to Before her troth-plight *W. Tale* i 2 278
Who, heavens directing, Is troth-plight to your daughter . v 3 151
She did you wrong ; for you were troth-plight to her . *Hen. V.* ii 1 21
Trotting. Sole imperator and great general Of trotting 'paritors *L. L. L.* iii 1 188
Trotting-horse. Made him proud of heart, to ride on a bay trotting-horse over four-inched bridges . . . . . *Lear* iii 4 57
Trouble. To cabin : silence ! trouble us not *Tempest* i 1 19
Alack, what trouble Was I then to you ! . . . . i 2 151
If you trouble him any more in's tale, by this hand, I will supplant some of your teeth . . . . iii 2 55
All torment, trouble, wonder, and amazement Inhabits here . . v 1 104
This babble shall not henceforth trouble me . . *T. G. of Ver.* i 2 98
And yet I thank you, Meaning henceforth to trouble you no more . ii 1 125
I have a bag of money here troubles me : if you will help to bear it *Mer. Wives* ii 2 178
Come, trouble not yourself . . . . iii 4 92
Not this, but troubles of the marriage-bed . *Com. of Errors* ii 1 27
I'll be gone, sir, and not trouble you . . . . iv 3 71
I wonder much That you would put me to this shame and trouble . v 1 14
You are come to meet your trouble . . . . . *Much Ado* i 1 97
Never came trouble to my house in the likeness of your grace . i 1 99
For trouble being gone, comfort should remain . . . i 1 100
And to trouble you with no more suit . . . *Mer. of Venice* i 2 112
Is it your dear friend that is thus in trouble?—The dearest friend to me iii 2 293
I will not trouble you As yet, to question you . *As Y. Like It* ii 7 171
Unapt to toil and trouble in the world . . *T. of Shrew* v 2 166
O good Antonio, forgive me your trouble . . . *T. Night* ii 1 35
Prompted by your present trouble, Out of my lean and low ability I'll lend you something . . . . iii 4 377
My stay To you a charge and trouble : to save both, Farewell *W. Tale* i 2 26
Take the boy to you : he so troubles me, 'Tis past enduring . . ii 1 1
My father and the gentlemen are in sad talk, and we'll not trouble them iv 4 317
We honour you with trouble . . . . v 3 9
Lest they desire upon this push to trouble Your joys with like relation v 3 129
I'll beg one boon, And then be gone and trouble you no more *Rich. II.* iv 1 303
I prithee, trouble me no more with vanity . . *1 Hen. IV.* i 2 91
Be happy, he will trouble you no more . . *2 Hen. IV.* iv 5 128
I hoped there was no need to trouble himself with any such thoughts yet . . . . *Hen. V.* ii 3 22
Fell jealousy, Which troubles oft the bed of blessed marriage . v 2 392
Take you no care ; I'll never trouble you . . *1 Hen. VI.* i 4 22
Madam, I have been bold to trouble you . . . . ii 3 25
I would his troubles likewise were expired, That so he might recover ii 5 31
Away, my masters ! trouble us no more ; But join in friendship . iii 1 144
Are you not ashamed With this immodest clamorous outrage To trouble and disturb the king and us? . . . . iv 1 127
But, madam, I must trouble you again . . . . . v 3 180
'Tis not my speeches that you do mislike, But 'tis my presence that doth trouble ye. Rancour will out . . . *2 Hen. VI.* i 1 141
She will light to listen to the lays, And never mount to trouble you again . . . . *2 Hen. VI.* i 3 94
I will deal with him That henceforth he shall trouble us no more . iii 1 324
Whose filth and dirt Troubles the silver spring where England drinks . iv 1 72
O, let me view his visage, being dead, That living wrought me such exceeding trouble . . . . v 1 70
I'll not trouble thee with words.—Nor I, but stoop with patience *3 Hen. VI.* v 5 5
And all the trouble thou hast turn'd me to . . . . v 5 16
Foul devil, for God's sake, hence, and trouble us not *Richard III.* i 2 50
But you must trouble him with lewd complaints . . . i 3 61
Ely with Richmond troubles me more near Than Buckingham . iv 3 49
I left him private, Full of sad thoughts and troubles *Hen. VIII.* ii 2 16
My soul grows sad with troubles ; Sing, and disperse 'em, if thou canst . . . . iii 1 1
Patience, be near me still ; and set me lower : I have not long to trouble thee . . . . iv 2 77
His long trouble now is passing Out of this world . . iv 2 162
Dear, trouble not yourself : the morn is cold . *Troi. and Cres.* iv 2 1
Trouble him not ; To bed, to bed : sleep kill those pretty eyes ! . iv 2 3
I trouble you.—No, not a whit . . . . . . v 1 75
A whoreson rascally tisick so troubles me . . . . v 3 102
'Twas never my desire yet to trouble the poor with begging *Coriolanus* ii 3 76
I will make much of your voices, and so trouble you no further . ii 3 117
Stand, Aufidius, And trouble not the peace . . . v 6 129
What should I don this robe, and trouble you? . *T. Andron.* i 1 189
So, trouble me no more, but get you gone . . . . i 1 367
Away, and talk not ; trouble us no more . . . . i 1 478
I have a head, sir, that will find out logs, And never trouble Peter *Rom. and Jul.* iv 4 18
I will be gone, sir, and not trouble you.—So shalt thou show me friendship . . . . v 3 40
Must he needs trouble me in't,—hum !—'bove all others? *T. of Athens* iii 3 1
I returned you an empty messenger.—O, sir, let it not trouble you . iii 6 42
How dost thou pity him whom thou dost trouble? I had rather be alone . . . . iv 3 98
Trouble him no further ; thus you still shall find him . . v 1 216
I turn the trouble of my countenance Merely upon myself . *J. Cæsar* i 2 38
We are too bold upon your rest : Good morrow, Brutus ; do we trouble you? . . . . ii 1 87
I trouble thee too much, but thou art willing.—It is my duty, sir iv 3 259
The love that follows us sometime is our trouble *Macbeth* i 6 11
Bid God 'ild us for your pains, And thank us for your trouble . i 6 14
I know this is a joyful trouble to you ; But yet 'tis one . . ii 3 53
Double, double toil and trouble ; Fire burn and cauldron bubble . iv 1 10
For a charm of powerful trouble, Like a hell-broth boil and bubble . iv 1 18
Unnatural deeds Do breed unnatural troubles . . . . v 1 80
Raze out the written troubles of the brain . . . . v 3 42
A mote it is to trouble the mind's eye . . . *Hamlet* i 1 112
Indeed, indeed, sirs, but this troubles me. Hold you the watch to-night? i 2 224
Or to take arms against a sea of troubles, And by opposing end them . iii 1 59
It is such a kind of gain-giving, as would perhaps trouble a woman . v 2 226
I'll not trouble thee : Yet have I left a daughter . . *Lear* i 4 275
I prithee, daughter, do not make me mad : I will not trouble thee, my child . . . . ii 4 222
Trouble him not, his wits are gone . . . . . iii 6 94
Trouble him no more Till further settling . . . . iv 7 81
Nor build yourself a trouble Out of his scattering and unsure observance . . . . *Othello* iii 3 150
Trouble yourself no further.—O, pardon me ; 'twill do me good to walk iv 3 1
Trouble yourselves no further : pray you, hasten Your generals after *Ant. and Cleo.* iv 4 1
You lay out too much pains For purchasing but trouble . *Cymbeline* ii 3 93
I'll show you those in troubles reign . . . . *Pericles* ii Gower 7
I leap into the seas, Where's hourly trouble for a minute's ease . ii 4 44
That is the cause we trouble you so early ; 'Tis not our husbandry . iii 2 19
Troubled. Bear with my weakness ; my old brain is troubled *Tempest* iv 1 159
By my troth, your town is troubled with unruly boys *Com. of Errors* iii 1 62
They would else have been troubled with a pernicious suitor *Much Ado* i 1 130
What if my house be troubled with a rat? . . *Mer. of Venice* iv 1 44
Well, sir, get you in : I will not long be troubled with you *As Y. Like It* i 1 81
With pure love and troubled brain . . . . . . iv 3 3
Troubled with the lampass, infected with the fashions . *T. of Shrew* iii 2 52
Your husband, being troubled with a shrew, Measures my husband's sorrow by his woe . . . . v 2 28
A woman moved is like a fountain troubled, Muddy, ill-seeming, thick v 2 142
I would not by my will have troubled you . . . *T. Night* iii 3 1
Fresh expectation troubled not the land With any long'd-for change *K. John* iv 2 7
That close aspect of his Does show the mood of a much troubled breast iv 2 73
This fever, that hath troubled me so long, Lies heavy on me . . v 3 3
Like the meteors of a troubled heaven, All of one nature . *1 Hen. IV.* i 1 10
We will not now be troubled with reply : We offer fair ; take it advisedly . . . . v 1 113
It is the disease of not listening . . . that I am troubled withal *2 Hen. IV.* i 2 139
But I am troubled here with them myself . . *2 Hen. VI.* iv 5 8
My mind was troubled with deep melancholy . . . . v 1 34
And better 'twere you troubled him than France . *3 Hen. VI.* iii 3 155
I'll strive, with troubled thoughts, to take a nap . . *Richard III.* v 3 104
My mind is troubled, like a fountain stirr'd . . *Troi. and Cres.* iii 3 311
I have been troubled in my sleep this night, But dawning day new comfort hath inspired . . . . *T. Andron.* ii 2 9
Was ever seen An emperor in Rome thus overborne, Troubled, confronted thus? . . . . iv 4 3
A troubled mind drave me to walk abroad . . . *Rom. and Jul.* i 1 127
Upon a raw and gusty day, The troubled Tiber chafing with her shores *J. Cæsar* i 2 101
The heavens, as troubled with man's act, Threaten his bloody stage *Macb.* ii 4 5
She is troubled with thick-coming fancies, That keep her from her rest . v 3 38
Being troubled with a raging tooth, I could not sleep . *Othello* iii 3 414
Lepidus . . . is troubled With the green sickness . . *Ant. and Cleo.* iii 2 5
That year, indeed, he was troubled with a rheum . . . . iii 2 57
Cheer your heart : Be you not troubled with the time . . . iii 6 82
Troubler. Hurl down their indignation On thee, the troubler of the poor world's peace ! . . . . *Richard III.* i 3 221
But, not to be a troubler of your peace, I will end here . . *Pericles* v 1 153
Troublesome. I'll rather be unmannerly than troublesome . *Mer. Wives* i 1 325
This act is as an ancient tale new told, And in the last repeating troublesome . . . . *K. John* iv 2 19
And be like them to Percy troublesome . . . . . *2 Hen. IV.* ii 3 4

Troublesome. Why doth the crown lie there upon his pillow, Being so troublesome a bedfellow? *2 Hen. IV.* iv 5 22
I myself know well How troublesome it sat upon my head . iv 5 187
What other Would you expect? you are strangely troublesome *Hen. VIII.* v 3 94
Away! get you away.—Now thou'rt troublesome *Coriolanus* iv 5 17
The time is troublesome . *Cymbeline* iv 3 21
Troublest. Thou troublest me; I am not in the vein *Richard III.* iv 2 122
Troublous. My troublous dream this night doth make me sad *2 Hen. VI.* i 2 22
But in this troublous time what's to be done? . *3 Hen. VI.* ii 1 159
So part we sadly in this troublous world, To meet with joy in sweet Jerusalem . . . v 5 7
I fear, I fear 'twill prove a troublous world *Richard III.* ii 3 5
Trough. And makes his trough In your embowell'd bosoms . v 2 9
Trout. Groping for trouts in a peculiar river . *Meas. for Meas.* i 2 91
Here comes the trout that must be caught with tickling *T. Night* ii 5 25
Trovato. Con tutto il cuore, ben trovato . *T. of Shrew* i 2 24
Trow. Who's within there? ho!—Who's there, I trow! . *Mer. Wives* i 4 140
What tempest, I trow, threw this whale . . . ashore at Windsor? . ii 1 64
What means the fool, trow?—Nothing I . *Much Ado* iii 4 59
And trow you what he call'd me?—Qualm, perhaps *L. L. Lost* v 2 279
Trow you who hath done this?—Is it a man? . *As Y. Like It* iii 2 189
I trow this is his house . *T. of Shrew* i 2 4
Trow you whither I am going? . i 2 165
We will for Ireland; and 'tis time, I trow *Richard II.* ii 1 218
'Twas time, I trow, to wake and leave our beds *1 Hen. VI.* ii 1 41
Winchester will not submit, I trow, Or be inferior to the proudest peer v 1 56
And, as I trow,—Which I do well; for I am sure . *Hen. VIII.* i 1 184
'Twas no need, I trow, To bid me trudge . *Rom. and Jul.* i 3 33
Are you so hot? marry, come up, I trow . ii 5 64
What is the matter, trow? . *Cymbeline* i 6 47
Trowel. Well said: that was laid on with a trowel . *As Y. Like It* i 2 112
Trow'st thou that e'er I'll look upon the world? . *2 Hen. VI.* ii 4 38
Why, trow'st thou, Warwick, That Clarence is so harsh? *3 Hen. VI.* v 1 85
Learn more than thou trowest, Set less than thou throwest . *Lear* i 4 135
Troy. Shall I Sir Pandarus of Troy become, And by my side wear steel? *Mer. Wives* i 3 83
He presents Hector of Troy . *L. L. Lost* v 2 537
Was not that Hector?—The worthy knight of Troy . v 2 890
The virgin tribute paid by howling Troy To the sea-monster *M. of Ven.* iii 2 56
Was this fair face the cause, quoth she, Why the Grecians sacked Troy? *All's Well* i 3 75
Ah, thou, the model where old Troy did stand . *Richard II.* v 1 11
And would have told him half his Troy was burnt . *2 Hen. IV.* i 1 73
Thou art as valorous as Hector of Troy, worth five of Agamemnon ii 4 237
The time of night when Troy was set on fire . *2 Hen. VI.* i 4 20
When he to madding Dido would unfold His father's acts commenced in burning Troy . iii 2 118
And stood against them, as the hope of Troy Against the Greeks that would have enter'd Troy . *3 Hen. VI.* ii 1 51
I'll play the orator as well as Nestor, Deceive more slily than Ulysses could, And, like a Sinon, take another Troy . iii 2 190
Farewell, my Hector, and my Troy's true hope . iv 8 25
In Troy, there lies the scene . *Troi. and Cres.* Prol. 1
Their vow is made To ransack Troy . Prol. 8
With massy staples And corresponsive and fulfilling bolts, Sperr up the sons of Troy . Prol. 19
Why should I war without the walls of Troy, That find such cruel battle here within? . i 1 2
Is not that a brave man? he's one of the flowers of Troy, I can tell you i 2 203
He's one o' the soundest judgements in Troy, whosoever, and a proper man of person . i 2 208
After seven years' siege yet Troy walls stand . i 3 12
Troy, yet upon his basis, had been down, . . . But for these instances i 3 75
'Tis this fever that keeps Troy on foot, Not her own sinews . i 3 135
Troy in our weakness stands, not in her strength . i 3 137
This Trojan scorns us; or the men of Troy Are ceremonious courtiers i 3 233
Sir, you of Troy, call you yourself Æneas?—Ay, Greek, that is my name i 3 245
He hears nought privately that comes from Troy.—Nor I from Troy come not to whisper him . i 3 249
Let him know, What Troy means fairly shall be spoke aloud . i 3 259
We have, great Agamemnon, here in Troy A prince call'd Hector . i 3 260
With his trumpet call Midway between your tents and walls of Troy i 3 278
'Twixt our tents and Troy To-morrow morning call some knight to arms ii 1 135
Troy must not be, nor goodly Ilion stand; Our firebrand brother, Paris, burns us all . ii 2 109
A Helen and a woe: Cry, cry! Troy burns, or else let Helen go ii 2 112
If Troy be not taken till these two undermine it, the walls will stand till they fall of themselves . ii 3 8
Fresh kings are come to Troy . ii 3 272
Hector, Deiphobus, Helenus, Antenor, and all the gallantry of Troy iii 1 149
When waterdrops have worn the stones of Troy . iii 2 193
Through the sight I bear in things to love, I have abandon'd Troy iii 3 5
A Trojan prisoner, call'd Antenor, Yesterday took: Troy holds him very dear . iii 3 19
Often have you thanks therefore—Desired my Cressid in right great exchange, Whom Troy hath still denied . iii 3 22
You know my mind, I'll fight no more 'gainst Troy . iii 3 56
As if his foot were on brave Hector's breast And great Troy shrieking iii 3 141
All the commerce that you have had with Troy As perfectly is ours as yours . iii 3 205
In humane gentleness, Welcome to Troy! . iv 1 21
Troilus had rather Troy were borne to Greece Than Cressid borne from Troy . iv 1 46
Pray you, come in: I would not for half Troy have you seen here . iv 2 42
Is it so concluded?—By Priam and the general state of Troy . iv 2 69
I will not go from Troy . iv 2 115
And is it true that I must go from Troy?—A hateful truth . iv 4 32
The glory of our Troy doth this day lie On his fair worth . iv 4 149
Give with thy trumpet a loud note to Troy, Thou dreadful Ajax . iv 5 3
And this is Trojan; the sinews of this leg All Greek, and this all Troy iv 5 127
My well-famed lord of Troy, no less to you . iv 5 173
As gentle tell me, of what honour was This Cressida in Troy? . iv 5 288
From whence, fragment?—Why, thou full dish of fool, from Troy . v 1 10
Hector, by this, is arming him in Troy . v 2 183
Doubt thou not, brave boy, I'll stand to-day for thee and me and Troy v 3 36
Now if thou lose thy stay, Thou on him leaning, and all Troy on thee, Fall all together . v 3 61
Look, how thy wounds do bleed at many vents! Hark, how Troy roars! . v 3 83
Hector, I take my leave: Thou dost thyself and all our Troy deceive . v 3 90
Troy. Diomed has got that same scurvy doting foolish young knave's sleeve of Troy . *Troi. and Cres.* v 4 5
So, Ilion, fall thou next! now, Troy, sink down! Here lies thy heart . v 8 11
Great Troy is ours, and our sharp wars are ended . v 9 10
Sit, gods, upon your thrones, and smile at Troy! . v 10 7
Let him that will a screech-owl aye be call'd, Go in to Troy, and say there, Hector's dead . v 10 17
In a word, Scare Troy out of itself . v 10 21
Strike a free march to Troy! with comfort go: Hope of revenge shall hide our inward woe . v 10 30
The self-same gods that arm'd the Queen of Troy With opportunity of sharp revenge . *T. Andron.* i 1 136
What fool hath added water to the sea, Or brought a faggot to bright-burning Troy? . iii 1 69
To bid Æneas tell the tale twice o'er, How Troy was burnt . iii 2 28
And I have read that Hecuba of Troy Ran mad for sorrow . iv 1 20
That baleful burning night When subtle Greeks surprised King Priam's Troy . v 3 84
Or who hath brought the fatal engine in That gives our Troy, our Rome, the civil wound . v 3 87
As Æneas, our great ancestor, Did from the flames of Troy upon his shoulder The old Anchises bear . *J. Cæsar* i 2 113
Troyan. Hector was but a Troyan in respect of this *L. L. Lost* v 2 639
Unless you play the honest Troyan, the poor wench is cast away v 2 681
When the false Troyan under sail was seen *M. N. Dream* i 1 174
In such a night Troilus methinks mounted the Troyan walls *Mer. of Ven.* v 1 4
Truant. An idle truant, Omitting the sweet benefit of time *T. G. of Ver.* ii 4 64
Since I plucked geese, played truant, and whipped top *Mer. Wives* v 1 27
'Tis double wrong, to truant with your bed And let her read it in thy looks at board . *Com. of Errors* iii 2 17
Hang him, truant! there's no true drop of blood in him *Much Ado* iii 2 18
That aged ears play truant at his tales . *L. L. Lost* ii 1 74
I will never be a truant, love, Till I have learn'd thy language *1 Hen. IV.* iii 1 207
I may speak it to my shame, I have a truant been to chivalry v 1 94
And chid his truant youth with such a grace . v 2 63
I have been a truant in the law . *1 Hen. VI.* ii 4 7
No Latin; I am not such a truant since my coming, As not to know the language I have lived in . *Hen. VIII.* iii 1 43
With truant vows to her own lips he loves *Troi. and Cres.* i 3 270
But what, in faith, make you from Wittenberg?—A truant disposition, good my lord . *Hamlet* i 2 169
I know you are no truant. But what is your affair in Elsinore? . i 2 173
Truce. Keep then fair league and truce with thy true bed *Com. of Errors* ii 2 147
With my vex'd spirits I cannot take a truce *K. John* iii 1 17
And even before this truce, but new before . iii 1 233
Make compromise, Insinuation, parley, and base truce To arms invasive v 1 68
Call'd for the truce of Winchester and Gloucester . *1 Hen. VI.* ii 4 118
Loving countrymen, This token serveth for a flag of truce . iii 1 138
I have awhile given truce unto my wars, To do my duty . iii 4 3
It is thus agreed That peaceful truce shall be proclaim'd in France v 4 117
Take this compact of a truce, Although you break it when your pleasure serves . v 4 163
Excitements to the field, or speech for truce *Troi. and Cres.* i 3 182
Who in this dull and long-continued truce Is rusty grown . i 3 262
The seas and winds, old wranglers, took a truce And did him service ii 2 75
Health to you, valiant sir, During all question of the gentle truce iv 1 11
Could not take truce with the unruly spleen Of Tybalt *Rom. and Jul.* iii 1 162
Truckle-bed. There's his chamber, his house, his castle, his standing-bed and truckle-bed . *Mer. Wives* iv 5 7
I'll to my truckle-bed; This field-bed is too cold for me to sleep *R. and J.* ii 1 39
Trudge, plod away o' the hoof; seek shelter, pack! . *Mer. Wives* i 3 91
Take this basket on your shoulders: that done, trudge with it in all haste . iii 3 13
'Tis time, I think, to trudge, pack, and be gone . *Com. of Errors* iii 2 158
That trudge betwixt the king and Mistress Shore *Richard III.* i 1 73
Trudge about Through fair Verona; find those persons out *Rom. and Jul.* i 2 34
'Shake' quoth the dove-house: 'twas no need, I trow, To bid me trudge i 3 34
True. They would not take her life. Is not this true? *Tempest* i 2 267
Here is every thing advantageous to life.—True; save means to live ii 1 50
And crown what I profess with kind event If I speak true! . iii 1 70
What does else want credit, come to me, And I'll be sworn 'tis true iii 3 26
Look thou be true; do not give dalliance Too much the rein . iv 1 51
Mark but the badges of these men, my lords, Then say if they be true . v 1 268
But tell me true, will't be a match?—Ask my dog . *T. G. of Ver.* ii 5 35
Too fair, too true, too holy, To be corrupted with my worthless gifts . iv 2 5
That you are well derived.—True; from a gentleman to a fool . v 2 24
I do despise a liar as I do despise one that is false, or as I despise one that is not true . *Mer. Wives* i 1 71
Is this true, Pistol?—No; it is false, if it is a pick-purse . i 1 162
And this is true; I like not the humour of lying . i 1 132
My name is Corporal Nym; I speak and I avouch; 'tis true . i 1 138
Your worship says very true: I pray your worship, come a little nearer ii 2 49
Have you been true to us?—Ay, I'll be sworn . iii 3 28
May be he tells you true.—No, heaven so speed me in my time to come! iii 4 11
'Tis old, but true, Still swine eats all the draff . iv 2 109
But if it prove true, Master Page, have you any way then to unfool me again? . iv 2 119
My intelligence is true; my jealousy is reasonable . iv 2 155
All this is true.—Why, very well, then . *Meas. for Meas.* ii 1 117
Come, tell me true: it shall be the better for you . ii 1 233
Say what you can, my false o'erweighs your true . ii 4 170
I know this to be true; therefore prepare yourself to death . iii 1 169
When he makes water his urine is congealed ice; that I know to be true iii 2 118
Too many . . . if they be true; if not true, none were enough . iv 3 177
This is all as true as it is strange: Nay, it is ten times true . v 1 44
Let your reason serve To make the truth appear where it seems hid, And hide the false seems true . v 1 67
This is most likely!—O, that it were as like as it is true! . v 1 104
To speak, as from his mouth, what he doth know Is true and false . v 1 156
As this is true, Let me in safety raise me from my knees! . v 1 230
'Tis true; she rides me and I long for grass . *Com. of Errors* ii 2 202
And true he swore, though yet forsworn he were . iv 2 10
Upon my life, I tell you true; I have not breathed almost since I did see it . v 1 180
That she may be the better prepared for an answer, if peradventure this be true . *Much Ado* i 2 24
To tell you true, I counterfeit him.—You could never do him so ill-well ii 1 121
I told him, and I think I told him true . ii 1 223
I think your blazon to be true . ii 1 308
What fire is in mine ears? Can this be true? . iii 1 107

True. Are you good men and true?—Yea, or else it were pity *Much Ado* iii 3 1
Are these things spoken, or do I but dream?—Sir, they are spoken, and these things are true . . . —True! O God! . . iv 1 68
And wish he had not so accused her, No, though he thought his accusation true . . . . iv 1 235
She was charged with nothing But what was true and very full of proof v 1 105
I said, thou hadst a fine wit: 'True,' said she, 'a fine little one' . v 1 162
That eye my daughter lent her: 'tis most true . . . . v 4 23
It may be so: but if he say it is so, he is, in telling true, but so *L. L. Lost* i 1 227
True it is, I was taken with Jaquenetta, and Jaquenetta is a true girl i 1 313
Here, good my glass, take this for telling true. . . . . iv 1 18
True, that thou art beauteous; truth itself, that thou art lovely . iv 1 61
Now the number is even.—True, true; we are four. . . iv 3 211
As true we are as flesh and blood can be . . . . . iv 3 215
The numbers true; and, were the numbering too, I were the fairest goddess . . . . v 2 35
Madam, speak true. It is not so, my lord . . . . . v 2 364
For how can this be true, That you stand forfeit, being those that sue? . . . . v 2 426
I was the world's commander,— Most true, 'tis right . . v 2 572
We to ourselves prove false, By being once false for ever to be true . v 2 783
I'll serve thee true and faithfully . . . . . . v 2 841
True, he hath my love, And what is mine my love shall render him *M. N. Dream* i 1 95
My heart Is true as steel . . . . ii 1 197
As true as truest horse that yet would never tire, I'll meet thee . iii 1 98
The throstle with his note so true, The wren with little quill . . iii 1 130
The sun was not so true unto the day As he to me . . . . iii 2 50
O! once tell true, tell true, even for my sake!. . . . iii 2 68
Bearing the badge of faith, to prove them true . . . . iii 2 127
Now I do wish it, love it, long for it, And will for evermore be true to it iv 1 181
More strange than true . . . . v 1 2
A good moral, my lord: it is not enough to speak, but to speak true . v 1 121
Not Shafalus to Procrus was so true. . . . . . . v 1 200
So shall all the couples three Ever true in loving be . . . v 1 415
Fair she is, if that mine eyes be true, And true she is, as she hath proved herself, And therefore, like herself, wise, fair, and true, Shall she be placed in my constant soul *Mer. of Venice* ii 6 54
It is true, without any slips of prolixity or crossing the plain highway of talk . . . . iii 1 12
I thank God, I thank God. Is't true, is't true? . . . . iii 1 107
Antonio is certainly undone.—Nay, that's true, that's very true . . iii 1 130
You that choose not by the view, Chance as fair and choose as true! . iii 2 133
As doubtful whether what I see be true, Until confirm'd, sign'd, ratified by you . . . . iii 2 148
Is this true, Nerissa?—Madam, it is, so you stand pleased withal . iii 2 210
I freely told you, . . . I was a gentleman; And then I told you true . iii 2 259
How true a gentleman you send relief . . . . . . iii 4 6
'Tis very true: O wise and upright judge! . . . . . iv 1 250
Most true, I have lost my teeth in your service *As Y. Like It* i 1 86
As true a lover As ever sigh'd upon a midnight pillow . . . ii 4 26
True is it that we have seen better days . . . . . ii 7 120
Not true in love?—Yes, when he is in; but I think he is not in . iii 4 28
He would answer, I spake not true: this is called the Reproof Valiant v 4 82
If sight and shape be true, Why then, my love adieu! . . . v 4 126
This to be true, I do engage my life . . . . . . v 4 171
If it be true that good wine needs no bush, 'tis true that a good play needs no epilogue . . . . Epil. 3
'Tis very true: thou didst it excellent *T. of Shrew* Ind. 1 89
Till I found it to be true, I never thought it possible or likely . i 1 153
Why, thou say'st true; it is a paltry cap, A custard-coffin . . iv 3 81
This is true that I say: an I had thee in place where, thou shouldst know it . . . . iv 3 150
Right true it is, your son Lucentio here Doth love my daughter . iv 4 40
But is this true? or is it else your pleasure? . . . . . iv 5 71
Padua affords nothing but what is kind.—For both our sakes, I would that word were true . . . . v 2 15
For I the ballad will repeat, Which men full true shall find . *All's Well* i 3 65
Therefore tell me true; But tell me then, 'tis so . . . . i 3 181
If yourself, Whose aged honour cities a virtuous youth, Did ever in so true a flame of liking Wish chastely and love dearly . . . . i 3 217
Wherefore? tell true.—I will tell truth; by grace itself I swear . i 3 225
Then my dial goes not true: I took this lark for a bunting . . ii 5 6
The merit of service is seldom attributed to the true and exact performer iii 6 64
'Tis not the many oaths that makes the truth But the plain single vow that is vow'd true . . . . iv 2 22
By her own letters, which makes her story true . . . . iv 3 66
I will say true,—or thereabouts, set down, for I'll speak truth . iv 3 171
By my troth, sir, if I were to live this present hour, I will tell true iv 3 183
Tell me, sirrah, but tell me true, I charge you . . . . v 3 234
My part of death, no one so true Did share it . . . *T. Night* ii 4 58
Nay, but say true; does it work upon him? . . . . . ii 5 214
Prove true, imagination, O, prove true! . . . . . . iii 4 409
But tell me true, are you not mad indeed? or do you but counterfeit?— Believe me, I am not; I tell thee true . . . . . . iv 2 121
And, having sworn truth, ever will be true . . . . . iv 3 33
If this be so, as yet the glass seems true . . . . . v 1 272
And all those swearings keep as true in soul . . . . . v 1 277
Yet were it true To say this boy were like me . . . *W. Tale* i 2 134
Which to reiterate were sin As deep as that, though true . . . i 2 284
'Tis most dangerous.—Say it be, 'tis true . . . . . i 2 298
If I Had servants true about me, that bare eyes . . . . i 2 309
All's true that is mistrusted . . . . ii 1 48
If this prove true, they'll pay for't . . . . . . ii 1 146
More it would content me To have her honour true than your suspicion ii 1 160
I Do come with words as medicinal as true, Honest as either . . ii 3 37
My past life Hath been as continent, as chaste, as true, As I am now unhappy . . . . iii 2 35
Very true, sir; he, sir, he; that's the rogue that put me into this apparel iv 3 110
I love a ballad in print o' life, for then we are sure they are true . iv 4 264
Is it true, think you?—Very true, and but a month old . . . iv 4 269
The ballad is very pitiful and as true.—Is it true too, think you? . iv 4 286
One of these is true: I think affliction may subdue the cheek . . iv 4 586
True, too true, my lord . . . . v 1 12
Your mother was most true to wedlock . . . . . . v 1 124
How goes it now, sir? this news which is called true is so like an old tale . . . . v 2 30
Most true, if ever truth were pregnant by circumstance . . . v 2 33
My bed was ever to thy son as true As thine was to thy husband *K. John* ii 1 124

True. Speak again; not all thy former tale, But this one word, whether thy tale be true.—As true as I believe you think them false That give you cause to prove my saying true . . . . . *K. John* iii 1 26
Like true, inseparable, faithful loves, Sticking together in calamity . iii 4 66
If that be true, I shall see my boy again . . . . . iii 4 78
This from rumour's tongue I idly heard; if true or false I know not . iv 2 124
May this be possible? may this be true? . . . . . . v 4 21
Why should I then be false, since it is true That I must die here and live hence by truth? . . . . v 4 28
Whoever spoke it, it is true, my lord . . . . . . v 5 19
Nought shall make us rue, If England to itself do rest but true . v 7 118
Look, what I speak, my life shall prove it true *Richard II.* i 1 87
True to King Richard's throne, A loyal, just, and upright gentleman . i 3 86
Was not Gaunt just, and is not Harry true? . . . . . ii 1 192
Now, afore God—God forbid I say true! . . . . . . ii 1 200
'Tis with false sorrow's eye, Which for things true weeps things imaginary ii 2 27
Now God in heaven forbid!—Ah, madam, 'tis too true . . . ii 2 52
Little joy have I To breathe this news; yet what I say is true . . iii 4 82
His honour is as true In this appeal as thou art all unjust . . iv 1 44
'Tis very true: you were in presence then; And you can witness with me this is true.—As false, by heaven, as heaven itself is true . . iv 1 62
Your mother well hath pray'd, and prove you true . . . . v 3 145
By the lord, thou sayest true, lad . . . . . . *1 Hen. IV.* i 2 44
To prove that true Needs no more but one tongue for all those wounds i 3 95
A plague upon it when thieves cannot be true one to another! . . ii 2 30
A good plot as ever was laid; our friends true and constant . . ii 3 19
I'll break thy little finger, Harry, An if thou wilt not tell me all things true . . . . ii 3 91
Thou sayest true; it is like we shall have good trading . . . ii 4 400
I may, for some things true, wherein my youth Hath faulty wander'd and irregular, Find pardon on my true submission . . . . iii 2 26
Thou sayest true, hostess; and he slanders thee most grossly . . iii 3 149
Some tell me that thou art a king.—They tell thee true . . . v 3 6
No counterfeit, but the true and perfect image of life indeed . . v 4 120
But what mean I To speak so true at first? . . . *2 Hen. IV.* Ind. 28
That freely render'd me these news for true . . . . . i 1 27
You are too great to be by me gainsaid: Your spirit is too true . i 1 92
I am a gentleman; thou art a drawer.—Very true, sir . . . ii 4 313
If damn'd commotion so appear'd, In his true, native, and most proper shape . . . . iv 1 37
Acquitted by a true substantial form And present execution of our wills iv 1 173
I am passing light in spirit.—So much the worse, if your own rule be true . . . . iv 2 86
Which my most inward true and duteous spirit Teacheth . . . iv 5 148
There's a saying very old and true . . . . . *Hen. V.* i 2 166
I could make as true a boast as that, if I had a sow to my mistress . iii 7 66
'Tis true that we are in great danger; The greater therefore should our courage be . . . . iv 1 1
It is the greatest admiration in the universal world, when the true and aunchient prerogatifes and laws of the wars is not kept . . . iv 1 67
The saying is true, 'The empty vessel makes the greatest sound' . . iv 4 73
Your majesty says very true . . . . iv 7 101
Thou shalt die.—You say very true, scauld knave, when God's will is . v 1 33
To say to thee that I shall die, is true . . . . . . v 2 158
And if thou vanquishest, thy words are true . . . *1 Hen. VI.* i 2 96
That shall maintain what I have said is true . . . . . ii 4 73
If Richard will be true, not that alone But all the whole inheritance I give . . . . iii 1 163
'Tis true, I gave a noble to the priest The morn that I was wedded . v 4 23
So long as I am loyal, true, and crimeless . . . . *2 Hen. VI.* ii 4 63
That he is dead, good Warwick, 'tis too true . . . . . iii 2 130
Deny it, if you can.—Nay, 'tis too true . . . . . . iv 2 155
May Iden live to merit such a bounty, And never live but true unto his liege! . . . . v 1 82
I am resolved for death or dignity.—The first I warrant thee, if dreams prove true . . . . v 1 195
I cleft his beaver with a downright blow: That this is true, father, behold his blood . . . . *3 Hen. VI.* i 1 13
An oath is of no moment, being not took Before a true and lawful magistrate . . . . i 2 23
If this news be true, Poor queen and son, your labour is but lost . . iii 1 31
He knows the game: how true he keeps the wind! . . . . iii 2 14
Knows not Montague that of itself England is safe, if true within itself? iv 1 40
So God help Montague as he proves true! . . . . . . iv 1 143
If the rest be true which I have heard, Thou camest— I'll hear no more v 6 55
Indeed, 'tis true that Henry told me of . . . . . . v 6 69
As true and just As I am subtle, false, and treacherous . *Richard III.* i 1 36
I would I knew thy heart.—'Tis figured in my tongue.—I fear me both are false.—Then never man was true . . . . i 2 196
The compact is firm and true in me.—And so in me . . . . ii 2 133
Ay, sir, it is too true; God help the while! . . . . . ii 3 8
If this rule were true, he should be gracious.—Why, madam, so, no doubt, he is . . . . ii 4 20
So deal with him as I prove true to you . . . . . . iv 4 499
What thinkest thou, will our friends prove all true?—No doubt . . v 3 213
To make that only true we now intend . . . . . *Hen. VIII.* Prol. 21
They are set here for examples.—True, they are so. . . . . i 3 62
'Tis most true These news are every where; every tongue speaks 'em . ii 2 38
Heaven witness, I have been to you a true and humble wife . . . ii 4 23
I pray you, tell me, If what I now pronounce you have found true . iii 2 163
I have told him What and how true thou art: he will advance thee . iii 2 416
Must I needs forego So good, so noble, and so true a master? . . iii 2 423
This thou tell'st me, As true thou tell'st me, when I say I love her *Troi. and Cres.* i 1 60
Was he angry?—So he says here.—True, he was so: I know the cause too i 2 57
To say truth, brown and not brown.—To say the truth, true and not true i 2 106
This is her question.—That's true; make no question of that . . i 2 174
I told you a thing yesterday; think on't.—So I do.—I'll be sworn 'tis true . . . . i 2 188
With his trumpet call . . ., To rouse a Grecian that is true in love . i 3 279
Be true to my lord: if he flinch, chide me for it . . . . iii 2 113
Who shall be true to us, When we are so unsecret to ourselves? . . iii 2 132
I am as true as truth's simplicity And simpler than the infancy of truth iii 2 176
As true as steel, as plantage to the moon, As sun to day . . . iii 2 184
As true as Troilus' shall crown up the verse, And sanctify the numbers iii 2 189
Tell me true, Even in the soul of sound good-fellowship. . . . iv 1 51
You'll be so true to him, to be false to him . . . . . iv 2 58
And is it true that I must go from Troy?—A hateful truth . . . iv 4 32
Hear me, my love: be thou but true of heart,— I true! how now! . iv 4 60
I speak not 'be thou true,' as fearing thee . . . . . . iv 4 64

True. But 'be thou true,' say I, to fashion in My sequent protestation; be thou true, And I will see thee . . . *Troi. and Cres.* iv 4 68
O, you shall be exposed, my lord, to dangers As infinite as imminent! but I'll be true . . . . iv 4 71
But yet be true.—O heavens! 'be true' again! . . . iv 4 76
Will you be true?—Who, I? alas, it is my vice, my fault . . iv 4 103
The moral of my wit Is 'plain and true;' there's all the reach of it . iv 4 110
You know 'tis true, That you are odd, and he is even with you . iv 5 43
'True is it, my incorporate friends,' quoth he . . . . *Coriolanus* i 1 134
In earnest, it's true; I heard a senator speak it . . . . i 3 106
This is true, on mine honour; and so, I pray, go with us . . i 3 112
The gods grant them true!—True! pow, wow.—True! I'll be sworn they are true . . . . ii 1 156
Answer to us.—Say, then: 'tis true, I ought so . . . iii 3 62
If Jupiter Should from yond cloud speak divine things, And say 'Tis true,' I'ld not believe them more Than thee . . . iv 5 111
But is this true, sir?—Ay; and you'll look pale Before you find it other iv 6 101
A side that would be glad to have This true which they so seem to fear iv 6 152
I am one that, telling true under him, must say, you cannot pass . v 2 33
Friend, Art thou certain this is true? is it most certain? . . v 4 47
False hound! If you have writ your annals true, 'tis there . v 6 114
As true a dog as ever fought at head . . . . . *T. Andron.* v 1 102
The villain is alive in Titus' house, And as he is, to witness this is true v 3 124
But he, his own affections' counsellor, Is to himself—I will not say how true—But to himself so secret . . . . *Rom. and Jul.* i 1 154
Dreamers often lie.—In bed asleep, while they do dream things true . i 4 52
True, I talk of dreams, Which are the children of an idle brain . i 4 96
I'll prove more true Than those that have more cunning to be strange . ii 2 100
Sweet Montague, be true. Stay but a little, I will come again . . ii 2 137
Our Romeo hath not been in bed to-night.—That last is true . . ii 3 43
I warrant thee, my man's as true as steel . . . . . ii 4 210
Prince, as thou art true, For blood of ours, shed blood of Montague . iii 1 153
Affection makes him false; he speaks not true . . . . iii 1 182
There shall no figure at such rate be set As that of true and faithful Juliet . . . . v 3 302
I weigh my friend's affection with mine own; I'll tell you true *T. of Athens* i 2 223
Were it all yours to give it in a breath, How quickly were it gone!—You tell me true . . . . ii 2 163
I am here No richer in return.—Is't true? can't be? . . . ii 2 212
Thou art true and honest; ingeniously I speak, No blame belongs to thee ii 2 230
Upon my soul, 'tis true, sir . . . . iii 2 48
True, as you said, Timon is shrunk indeed . . . . iii 2 68
Your lord sends now for money.—Most true, he does . . . iii 4 18
Nothing emboldens sin so much as mercy.—Most true . . . iii 5 4
There is no time so miserable but a man may be true . . iv 3 463
Had I a steward So true, so just, and now so comfortable? . . iv 3 498
But tell me true—For I must ever doubt, though ne'er so sure . iv 3 513
Does the rumour hold for true, that he's so full of gold? . . v 1 4
'Tis true, this god did shake: His coward lips did from their colour fly *J. Cæsar* i 2 121
You are my true and honourable wife . . . . . . ii 1 288
If this were true, then should I know this secret . . . ii 1 291
That I did love thee, Cæsar, O, 'tis true . . . . . iii 1 194
You have forgot the will I told you of.—Most true . . . iii 2 244
Make your vaunting true, And it shall please me well . . iv 3 52
Now, as you are a Roman, tell me true.—Then like a Roman bear the truth I tell . . . . iv 3 187
If we do meet again, we'll smile indeed; If not, 'tis true this parting was well made . . . . v 1 122
In all my life I found no man but he was true to me . . . v 5 35
I thank thee, Brutus, That thou hast proved Lucilius' saying true . v 5 59
What, can the devil speak true? . . . . . *Macbeth* i 3 107
So please you, it is true: our thane is coming . . . . i 5 35
Both of you Know Banquo was your enemy.—True, my lord . . iii 1 115
Now, I see, 'tis true; For the blood-bolter'd Banquo smiles upon me . iv 1 122
O, relation Too nice, and yet too true! . . . . . iv 3 174
Both in time, Form of the thing, each word made true and good *Hamlet* i 2 210
'Tis very strange.—As I do live, my honour'd lord, 'tis true . i 2 221
To thine own self be true, And it must follow, as the night the day, Thou canst not then be false to any man . . . . . i 3 78
That he is mad, 'tis true: 'tis true 'tis pity; And pity 'tis 'tis true . ii 2 97
To be honest, as this world goes, is to be one man picked out of ten thousand.—That's very true, my lord . . . . . ii 2 180
In the secret parts of fortune? O, most true; she is a strumpet . ii 2 240
The world's grown honest.—Then is doomsday near: but your news is not true . . . . ii 2 244
'Tis too true! How smart a lash that speech doth give my conscience! iii 1 49
So young, and so untender?—So young, my lord, and true . . *Lear* i 1 109
My mind as generous, and my shape as true, As honest madam's issue . i 2 8
They'll have me whipped for speaking true, thou'lt have me whipped for lying . . . . i 4 201
If it be true, all vengeance comes too short Which can pursue the offender . . . . ii 1 90
But, true it is, from France there comes a power . . . iii 1 30
True or false, it hath made thee earl of Gloucester . . . . iii 5 18
Holds it true, sir, that the Duke of Cornwall was so slain? . . iv 7 85
Ripeness is all: come on.—And that's true too . . . . v 2 11
Thou hast spoken right, 'tis true; The wheel is come full circle . v 3 173
I kill'd the slave that was a-hanging thee.—'Tis true, my lords, he did . v 3 275
It is too true an evil: gone she is . . . . . . *Othello* i 1 161
'Tis true, most worthy signior; The duke's in council . . . i 2 91
That I have ta'en away this old man's daughter, It is most true; true, I have married her . . . . i 3 79
I know not if't be true; But I, for mere suspicion in that kind, Will do as if for surety . . . . i 3 394
It is true, or else I am a Turk: You rise to play and go to bed to work ii 1 115
I will gyve thee in thine own courtship. You say true; 'tis so, indeed ii 1 172
Or his good nature Prizes the virtue that appears in Cassio, And looks not on his evils: is not this true? . . . . . . ii 3 140
I see 'tis true. Look here, Iago; All my fond love thus do I blow to heaven . . . . iii 3 444
Is't possible?—'Tis true: there's magic in the web of it . . . iii 4 69
Indeed! is't true?—Most veritable; therefore look to't well . . iii 4 75
Say true.—I am a very villain else.—Have you scored me? Well . . iv 1 128
If she be not honest, chaste, and true, There's no man happy . . iv 2 17
Why, what art thou?—Your wife, my lord; your true And loyal wife iv 2 34
Is that true? why, then Othello and Desdemona return again to Venice iv 2 227
Thou art rash as fire, to say That she was false: O, she was heavenly true! . . . . v 2 135
True. I told him what I thought, and told no more Than what he found himself was apt and true . . . . *Othello* v 2 177
So come my soul to bliss, as I speak true; So speaking as I think, I die v 2 250
'Tis thus; Who tells me true, though in his tale lie death, I hear him as he flatter'd . . . . *Ant. and Cleo.* i 2 102
Why should I think you can be mine and true, Though you in swearing shake the throned gods, Who have been false? . . . . i 3 27
Eight wild-boars roasted whole at a breakfast, and but twelve persons there; is this true? . . . . ii 2 185
Be it art or hap, He hath spoken true . . . . . . ii 3 33
All men's faces are true, whatsome'er their hands are . . . ii 6 102
Cæsar's sister is called Octavia.—True, sir . . . . . ii 6 117
The news is true, my lord; he is descried . . . . . iii 7 55
I tell you true: best you safed the bringer Out of the host . iv 6 26
The negligence may well be laugh'd at, Yet is it true, sir . *Cymbeline* i 1 67
If this be true,—As I have such a heart that both mine ears Must not in haste abuse—if it be true, How should I be revenged? . . . i 6 129
She writes so to you, doth she?—O, no, no, no! 'tis true . . ii 4 106
By Jupiter he swears. 'Tis true:—nay, keep the ring—'tis true . ii 4 123
True honest men being heard, like false Æneas, Were in his time thought false . . . . iii 4 60
Sirrah, is this letter true?—Sir, as I think . . . . . iii 5 106
Be true.—Thou bid'st me to my loss: for true to thee Were to prove false, which I will never be, To him that is most true . . iii 5 162
Will poor folks lie . . .? Yes; no wonder, When rich ones scarce tell true . . . . iii 6 12
I dare be bound he's true and shall perform All parts of his subjection iv 3 18
Wherein I am false I am honest; not true, to be true . . . iv 3 42
Further to boast were neither true nor modest, Unless I add, we are honest . . . . v 5 18
So tender over his occasions, true, So feat, so nurse-like . . . v 5 87
Why cloud they not their sights perpetually, If this be true? *Pericles* i 1 75
If it be true that I interpret false, Then were it certain you were not so bad . . . . i 1 124
O, 'tis too true.—But see what heaven can do! . . . . i 4 32
Is not this true?—Our cheeks and hollow eyes do witness it . . . i 4 50
Thou sayest true; they're too unwholesome . . . . . ii 2 22
If you have told Diana's altar true, This is your wife . . . v 3 17
True acquaintance. 'Scape the true acquaintance of mine ear *K. John* v 6 15
True advantage. Has an eye can stamp and counterfeit advantages, though true advantage never present itself . . . *Othello* ii 1 248
True affections. More after our commandment than as guided By your own true affections . . . . *Coriolanus* ii 3 239
True allegiance. Against thy oath and true allegiance sworn 2 *Hen. VI.* v 1 20
True-anointed. England's true-anointed lawful king . 3 *Hen. VI.* iii 3 29
True apothecary. O true apothecary! Thy drugs are quick . *R. and J.* v 3 119
True appeal. Aumerle is guilty of my true appeal . . *Richard II.* iv 1 79
True applause. You have deserved High commendation, true applause, and love . . . . *As Y. Like It* i 2 275
'True as I live,' and 'as God shall mend me,' and 'as sure as day' 1 *Hen. IV.* iii 1 254
True Athenian. If I tell you, I am no true Athenian . *M. N. Dream* iv 2 30
True avouch. I might not this believe Without the sensible and true avouch Of mine own eyes . . . . *Hamlet* i 1 57
True badge. Sweet mercy is nobility's true badge . . . *T. Andron.* i 1 119
True beauty. For virtue and true beauty of the soul . *Hen. VIII.* iv 2 144
I ne'er saw true beauty till this night . . . *Rom. and Jul.* i 5 55
True bed. Keep then fair league and truce with thy true bed *Com. of Er.* ii 2 147
The block of death, Treason's true bed and yielder up of breath 2 *Hen. IV.* iv 2 123
True beginning. That is the true beginning of our end . *M. N. Dream* v 1 111
True begot. Whether I be as true begot or no, That still I lay upon my mother's head . . . . *K. John* i 1 75
I think His father never was so true begot . . . . . i 1 130
True-begotten. This is my true-begotten father! . . *Mer. of Venice* ii 2 36
True behalf. In right and true behalf Of thy deceased brother *K. John* i 1 7
True bent. I can give his humour the true bent . . *J. Cæsar* ii 1 210
True-betrothed. My true-betrothed love and now my wife . *T. Andron.* i 1 406
True birth. Revolts from true birth, stumbling on abuse *Rom. and Jul.* ii 3 20
True blank. Let me still remain The true blank of thine eye . *Lear* i 1 161
True blood. Your youth, And the true blood which peepeth fairly through't . . . . *W. Tale* iv 4 148
For he that steeps his safety in true blood Shall find but bloody safety and untrue . . . . *K. John* iii 4 147
Be satisfied, dear God, with our true blood *Richard III.* iii 3 21
True-born. Though banish'd yet a trueborn Englishman . . *Richard II.* i 3 309
A true-born gentleman And stands upon the honour of his birth 1 *Hen. VI.* ii 4 27
True bosom. Which if thou please to hide in this true bosom *Richard III.* i 2 176
True-bred. She's a beagle, true-bred, and one that adores me *T. Night* ii 3 195
I know them to be as true-bred cowards as ever turned back 1 *Hen. IV.* i 2 206
The knave will stick by thee, I can assure thee that. A' will not out; he is true bred . . . . 2 *Hen. IV.* v 3 71
I'll lean upon one crutch and fight with t'other, Ere stay behind this business.—O, true-bred! . . . . *Coriolanus* i 1 247
True cause. Wrenching the true cause the false way . . 2 *Hen. IV.* ii 1 121
If you would consider the true cause Why all these fires . . *J. Cæsar* i 3 62
True challenger. Your crown and kingdom, indirectly held From him the native and true challenger . . . . *Hen. V.* ii 4 95
True chivalry. For Christian service and true chivalry . *Richard II.* ii 1 54
True colour. How might we see Falstaff bestow himself to-night in his true colours? . . . . 2 *Hen. IV.* ii 2 187
Then what I have to do Will want true colour . . . . *Hamlet* iii 4 130
True complaint. Till you have heard me in my true complaint *Meas. for Meas.* v 1 24
True conceit. You have a noble and a true conceit Of god-like amity *Mer. of Venice* iii 4 2
True condition. I am solicited, not by a few, And those of true condition *Hen. VIII.* i 2 19
True-confirmed. I am my master's true-confirmed love . *T. G. of Ver.* iv 4 108
True constancy. Here is my hand for my true constancy . . ii 2 8
True contents. If truth holds true contents . . . *As Y. Like It* v 4 136
True contract. Thus stands it with me: upon a true contract *M. for M.* i 2 149
True course. As it appears In the true course of all the question *M. Ado* v 4 6
True cuckold. There is no true cuckold but calamity . . *T. Night* i 5 56
True date. Here comes the almanac of my true date . *Com. of Errors* i 2 41
True debitor. You have no true debitor and creditor but it . *Cymbeline* v 4 171
True decision. Ears more deaf than adders to the voice Of any true decision . . . . *Troi. and Cres.* ii 2 173
True defence. Nor tempt the danger of my true defence . *K. John* iv 3 84

True delight. Thou takest True delight In the sight . *M. N. Dream* iii 2 455
We will begin these rites, As we do trust they'll end, in true delights *As Y. Like It* v 4 204
Which doth give me A more content in course of true delight *Pericles* iii 2 39
True-derived. Unto a lineal true-derived course . *Richard III.* iii 7 200
True descent. To bar my master's heirs in true descent . iii 2 54
Till we can clear these ambiguities, And know their spring, their head, their true descent . *Rom. and Jul.* v 3 218
True-devoted. A true-devoted pilgrim is not weary To measure kingdoms with his feeble steps . . . . . . *T. G. of Ver.* ii 7 9
True diction. To make true diction of him, his semblable is his mirror *Hamlet* v 2 123
True diligence. As he shall think by our true diligence He is no less than what we say he is . . . . *T. of Shrew* Ind. 1 70
True disciplines. He has no more directions in the true disciplines of the wars . . . . *Hen. V.* iii 2 76
True-disposing. O upright, just, and true-disposing God! *Richard III.* iv 4 55
True-divining. Thou hast a true-divining heart . *T. Andron.* ii 3 214
True drop. There's no true drop of blood in him . *Much Ado* iii 2 18
True drunkard. I will, like a true drunkard, utter all to thee . iii 3 111
True duty. Attend on you With all true duty . . . . *K. John* iii 3 73
Put meekness in thy mind, Love, charity, obedience, and true duty! *Richard III.* ii 2 108
The last true duties of thy noble son! . *T. Andron.* v 3 155
True election. If it be a sin to make a true election, she is damned *Cymb.* i 2 30
True English. By mine honour, in true English, I love thee . *Hen. V.* v 2 237
True enough; Though 'tis a saying, sir, not due to me . *W. Tale* iii 2 58
True event. Let our just censures Attend the true event . *Macbeth* v 4 15
True evidence. From true evidence of good esteem . 2 *Hen. VI.* iii 2 21
Give true evidence to his love, which stands An honourable trial *Ant. and Cleo.* i 3 74
True experience. Grave witnesses of true experience . *T. Andron.* v 3 78
True face. Now, my masters, for a true face and good conscience 1 *Hen. IV.* ii 4 550
There is never a fair woman has a true face.—No slander *Ant. and Cleo.* ii 6 105
True faith. You to a love that your true faith doth merit *As Y. Like It* v 4 194
Sends allegiance and true faith of heart To his most royal person *Richard II.* iii 3 37
Thorough the hazards of this untrod state With all true faith *J. Cæsar* iii 1 137
True fear. In true fear They gave us our demands . *Coriolanus* iii 1 134
O, these flaws and starts, Impostors to true fear . *Macbeth* iii 4 64
True fellow. As honest a true fellow as any is in Bohemia . *W. Tale* v 2 169
True-fixed. Of whose true-fix'd and resting quality There is no fellow in the firmament . . . . . *J. Cæsar* iii 1 61
True folk. Walk aside the true folk, and let the traitors stay . *L. L. Lost* iv 3 213
True followers. You may not live to wear All your true followers out *Ant. and Cleo.* iv 14 134
True friar. Instruct me How I may formally in person bear me Like a true friar . . . . *Meas. for Meas.* i 3 48
True friend. Thou counterfeit to thy true friend! . *T. G. of Ver.* v 4 53
Bring your true friend along . . . . . . *Mer. of Venice* iii 2 310
True friendship. Where there is true friendship, there needs none *T. of Athens* i 2 18
True gait. There do muster true gait, eat, speak, and move *All's Well* ii 1 55
True gentleman. If it be ne'er so false, a true gentleman may swear it in the behalf of his friend . . . . *W. Tale* v 2 175
Why, now you speak Like a good child and a true gentleman *Hamlet* iv 5 148
True gentleness. I thought you lord of more true gentleness *M. N. D.* ii 2 132
True girl. Jaquenetta is a true girl . . . . *L. L. Lost* i 1 315
True ground. The true ground of all these piteous woes We cannot without circumstance descry . . . *Rom. and Jul.* v 3 180
True Guiderius. Whom I call Polydore, Most worthy prince, as yours, is true Guiderius . . . . . . *Cymbeline* v 5 358
True hand. That true hand that fought Rome's quarrel out *T. Andron.* v 3 102
True hate. Yet 'tis greater skill In a true hate, to pray they have their will . . . . *Cymbeline* ii 5 34
True heart. With my hand I seal my true heart's love . *Richard III.* ii 1 10
Every tongue speaks 'em, And every true heart weeps for't *Hen. VIII.* ii 2 40
With a true heart And brother-love I do it . . . . v 3 172
Good man, those joyful tears show thy true heart . . . v 3 175
Or my true heart with treacherous revolt Turn to another *Rom. and Jul.* iv 1 58
In my true heart I find she names my very deed of love . *Lear* i 1 72
Thrown such despite and heavy terms upon her As true hearts cannot bear . . . . *Othello* iv 2 117
True hearted. I have true-hearted friends, Not mutinous in peace 3 *Hen. VI.* iv 8 9
I swear he is true-hearted; and a soul None better in my kingdom *Hen. VIII.* v 1 154
The noble and true-hearted Kent banished! his offence, honesty! *Lear* i 2 126
True heir. King Edward's fruit, true heir to the English crown 3 *Hen. VI.* iv 4 24
True honour. Could to no issue of true honour bring *Rom. and Jul.* iv 1 65
True hope. Farewell, my Hector, and my Troy's true hope 3 *Hen. VI.* iv 8 25
True hope is swift, and flies with swallow's wings *Richard III.* v 2 23
True humour. That is my true humour . . . *Mer. Wives* i 3 112
True indeed. That's her torment.—'Tis true, indeed . *Much Ado* ii 3 131
The allusion holds in the exchange.—'Tis true indeed . *L. L. Lost* iv 2 43
Care for us! True, indeed! They ne'er cared for us yet *Coriolanus* i 1 81
It is true, indeed.—'Tis a strange truth . . . *Othello* v 2 188
True industrious. Here is a dear, a true industrious friend 1 *Hen. IV.* i 1 62
True inheritance. To conquer France, his true inheritance 2 *Hen. VI.* i 1 82
True inheritor. The quarrel of a true inheritor . 2 *Hen. IV.* iv 5 169
True intelligence. If like a Christian thou hadst truly borne Betwixt our armies true intelligence . . . . 1 *Hen. IV.* v 5 10
True intent. We do not come as minding to content you, Our true intent is . . . . *M. N. Dream* v 1 114
True Jack Falstaff, valiant Jack Falstaff . . . 1 *Hen. IV.* ii 4 523
True joints. Against them both my true joints bended be *Richard II.* v 3 98
True joy. Tears of true joy for his return to Rome . *T. Andron.* i 1 76
True judgement. Do you question me, as an honest man should do, for my simple true judgement? . . . . *Much Ado* i 1 168
She cannot be so much without true judgement . . iii 1 88
Your dishonour Mangles true judgement and bereaves the state *Coriol.* iii 1 158
True king. That rise thus nimbly by a true king's fall . *Richard II.* iv 1 318
If this rebellious earth Have any resting for her true king's queen v 1 6
Tell me, even upon thy conscience, Is Edward your true king? 3 *Hen. VI.* iii 3 114
But Henry now shall wear the English crown, And be true king indeed iv 3 50
True knight. Thine own true knight, By day or night . *Mer. Wives* ii 1 15
A mellifluous voice, as I am true knight . . . *T. Night* ii 3 54
Speak like a true knight, so defend thee heaven! . *Richard II.* i 3 34

True knight. A' should have sent me two and twenty yards of satin, as I am a true knight . . . . . . 2 *Hen. IV.* i 2 50
A true knight, Not yet mature, yet matchless, firm of word *Tr. and Cr.* iv 5 96
Give this ring to my true knight, And bid him come . *Rom. and Jul.* iii 2 142
He, true knight, No lesser of her honour confident . *Cymbeline* v 5 186
True knowledge he has in their disposition . *Coriolanus* ii 2 15
True labourer. I am a true labourer: I earn that I eat *As Y. Like It* iii 2 77
True liegeman. And swore the devil his true liegeman . 1 *Hen. IV.* ii 4 372
You shall become true liegemen to his crown . 1 *Hen. VI.* v 4 128
True life. Which I wonder'd Could be so rarely and exactly wrought, Since the true life on't was— This is true *Cymbeline* ii 4 76
True likeness. If conjure up love in her in his true likeness, he must appear naked and blind . . . . . . *Hen. V.* v 2 321
True line. Of the true line and stock of Charles the Great . i 2 71
True lip. That kiss I carried from thee, dear; and my true lip Hath virgin'd it e'er since . . . . . *Coriolanus* v 3 47
True love. A contract of true love to celebrate . *Tempest* iv 1 84
Come, temperate nymphs, and help to celebrate A contract of true love iv 1 133
What, gone without a word? Ay, so true love should do *T. G. of Ver.* ii 2 17
With twenty odd-conceited true-love knots . . . ii 7 46
I am but a shadow; And to your shadow will I make true love . iv 2 126
No grief did ever come so near thy heart As when thy lady and thy true love died . . . . iv 3 20
How can that be true love which is falsely attempted? . *L. L. Lost* i 2 176
That shall express my true love's fasting pain . . . iv 3 122
The course of true love never did run smooth . *M. N. Dream* i 1 134
Do it for thy true-love take, Love and languish for his sake . ii 2 28
Thou hast mistaken quite And laid the love-juice on some true-love's sight . . . . iii 2 89
Some true love turn'd and not a false turn'd true . . iii 2 91
Between the pale complexion of true love And the red glow of scorn *As Y. Like It* iii 4 56
Your true love's coming, That can sing both high and low . *T. Night* ii 3 41
Nothing but this; your true love for my master . . iii 4 233
True love Between our kingdoms and our royal selves . *K. John* iii 1 231
It shall be still thy true love's recompense . *Richard II.* ii 3 49
And wash him fresh again with true-love tears . . . v 1 10
Bear her my true love's kiss; and so, farewell. *Richard III.* iv 4 430
Thou overheard'st, ere I was ware, My true love's passion *Rom. and Jul.* ii 2 104
My true love is grown to such excess I cannot sum up sum of half my wealth . . . . ii 6 33
Till strange love, grown bold, Think true love acted simple modesty . iii 2 16
What cursed foot wanders this way to-night, To cross my obsequies and true love's rite? . . . . v 3 20
What's here? a cup, closed in my true love's hand? . v 3 161
How should I your true love know From another one? . *Hamlet* iv 5 23
Which bewept to the grave did go With true-love showers . iv 5 39
True lover. If then true lovers have been ever cross'd, It stands as an edict in destiny . . . . . . *M. N. Dream* i 1 150
We that are true lovers run into strange capers . *As Y. Like It* ii 4 55
Then there is no true lover in the forest . . . . . iii 2 320
If you be a true lover, hence, and not a word . . . iv 3 74
For such as I am all true lovers are . . . . *T. Night* ii 4 17
Lay me, O, where Sad true lover never find my grave, To weep there! . ii 4 66
Full of grace and fair regard.—And a true lover of the holy church *Hen. V.* i 1 23
True loyalty. When I protest true loyalty to her, She twits me with my falsehood . . . . *T. G. of Ver.* iv 2 7
True made. 'Tis all as easy Falsely to take away a life true made As to put metal in restrained means To make a false one . *Meas. for Meas.* ii 4 47
True madness. To define true madness, What is't but to be nothing else but mad? . . . . *Hamlet* ii 2 93
True maid. Speak, sad brow and true maid . *As Y. Like It* iii 2 227
True man. Though the priest o' the town commended him for a true man . . . . *Mer. Wives* ii 1 149
Every true man's apparel fits your thief: if it be too little for your thief, your true man thinks it big enough . . *Meas. for Meas.* iv 2 46
If you meet a thief, you may suspect him, by virtue of your office, to be no true man . . . . *Much Ado* iii 3 54
Whither away so fast? A true man or a thief that gallops so? *L. L. Lost* iv 3 187
The traitor lives, the true man's put to death . *Richard II.* v 3 73
The most omnipotent villain that ever cried 'Stand' to a true man 1 *Hen. IV.* i 2 122
Thou shalt have a share in our purchase, as I am a true man . . ii 1 101
To turn true man and to leave these rogues . . . ii 2 24
The thieves have bound the true men . . . . . ii 2 98
And swear it was the blood of true men . . . . ii 4 343
So true men yield, with robbers so o'ermatch'd . . 3 *Hen. VI.* i 4 64
'Tis gold Which makes the true man kill'd and saves the thief; Nay, sometime hangs both thief and true man . . *Cymbeline* ii 3 76
True-meant. His givings-out were of an infinite distance From his true-meant design . . . . *Meas. for Meas.* i 4 55
True melancholy. O sovereign mistress of true melancholy *Ant. and Cleo.* iv 9 12
True Menenius. Thou old and true Menenius . *Coriolanus* iv 1 21
True minute. Knew the true minute when Exception bid him speak *All's Well* i 2 39
True mother. Between the chaste unsmirched brow Of my true mother *Hamlet* iv 5 120
True moving. Mars his true moving, even as in the heavens So in the earth, to this day is not known . . . . 1 *Hen. VI.* i 2 1
True nature. There the action lies In his true nature . *Hamlet* iii 3 62
As sin's true nature is, Each toy seems prologue to some great amiss . iv 5 17
True need. But, for true need,—You heavens, give me that patience, patience I need! . . . . *Lear* ii 4 273
True nobility is exempt from fear . . 2 *Hen. VI.* iv 1 129
And, like her true nobility, she has Carried herself towards me *Hen. VIII.* ii 4 142
Sith true nobility Warrants these words in princely courtesy *T. Andron.* i 1 271
True noblesse would Learn him forbearance . *Richard II.* iv 1 119
True obedience. Love, fair looks, and true obedience . *T. of Shrew* v 2 153
With grant of our most just and right desires, And true obedience 2 *Hen. IV.* iv 2 41
But if you mind to hold your true obedience, Give me assurance 3 *Hen. VI.* iv 1 140
True observance. And ever shall With true observance seek *All's Well* ii 5 79
True of heart. They [women] are as true of heart as we . *T. Night* ii 4 109
Hear me, my love: be thou but true of heart,— I true! how now! *Troi. and Cres.* iv 4 60
True of mind and made of no such baseness As jealous creatures are *Oth.* iii 4 27
True old woe. This borrow'd passion stands for true old woe *Pericles* iv 4 24
True one. Stealing her soul with many vows of faith And ne'er a true one *Mer. of Venice* v 1 20

True one. Let me speak myself, Since virtue finds no friends—a wife a true one . . . . *Hen. VIII.* iii 1 126
True opinion. How blest am I In my just censure, in my true opinion! *W. Tale* ii 1 37
True order. The manner and true order of the fight . 2 *Hen. IV.* iv 4 100
True ornaments to know a holy man . . . . *Richard III.* iii 7 99
True Paulina, We shall not marry till thou bid'st us . *W. Tale* v 1 81
True pay. That you have ta'en these tenders for true pay, Which are not sterling . . . . *Hamlet* i 3 106
True peace. And grant it may with thee in true peace live! 2 *Hen. IV.* iv 5 220
First, madam, I entreat true peace of you, Which I will purchase *Rich. III.* ii 1 62
Truepenny. Say'st thou so? art thou there, truepenny? . *Hamlet* i 5 150
True perfection. Her true perfection, or my false transgression *T. G. of V.* ii 4 197
How many things by season season'd are To their right praise and true perfection! . . . . . *Mer. of Venice* v 1 108
True performing. That will ask some tears in the true performing of it *M. N. Dream* i 2 27
True piece of gold. Never call a true piece of gold a counterfeit 1 *Hen. IV.* ii 4 539
True Pisanio,—Who long'st, like me, to see thy lord . *Cymbeline* iii 2 54
True place. That screws me from my true place in your favour *T. Night* v 1 126
True Plantagenet. In honour of a true Plantagenet . 1 *Hen. VI.* ii 5 52
Rise, Richard, like a true Plantagenet . . . . iii 1 172
True prayer. With true prayers That shall be up at heaven and enter there Ere sun-rise . . . . *Meas. for Meas.* ii 2 151
Let them have That mercy which true prayer ought to have *Richard II.* v 3 110
True preferment. Be but duteous, and true preferment shall tender itself to thee . . . . . *Cymbeline* iii 5 159
True preserver. My true preserver, and a loyal sir . . *Tempest* v 1 69
True prince. The true prince may, for recreation sake, prove a false thief 1 *Hen. IV.* i 2 173
Was it for me to kill the heir-apparent? should I turn upon the true prince? . . . . ii 4 298
The lion will not touch the true prince . . . . ii 4 300
I for a valiant lion, and thou for a true prince . . . . ii 4 303
You ran away upon instinct, you will not touch the true prince . ii 4 332
Thou show'dst a subject's shine, I a true prince . . *Pericles* i 2 124
True Promethean. The academes From whence doth spring the true Promethean fire . . . . . *L. L. Lost* iv 3 304
True proof. In the reproof of chance Lies the true proof of men *T. and C.* i 3 34
True purchasing. Not without his true purchasing . *Coriolanus* ii 1 155
True quality. O, mickle is the powerful grace that lies In herbs, plants, stones, and their true qualities . . . *Rom. and Jul.* ii 3 16
Such rebel blood That will be thaw'd from the true quality *J. Cæsar* iii 1 41
True redress. I defy all counsel, all redress, But that which ends all counsel, true redress, Death . . . . *K. John* iii 4 24
True repentance. God of his mercy give You patience to endure, and true repentance Of all your dear offences! . . *Hen. V.* ii 2 180
True report. If she be accused in true report, Bear with her weakness *Richard III.* i 3 27
If it be a just and true report that goes of his having . *T. of Athens* v 1 18
I did inquire it; And have my learning from some true reports *A. and C.* ii 2 47
True right. As I in justice and true right express it . 2 *Hen. VI.* v 2 25
True rites. Cæsar shall Have all true rites . . *J. Cæsar* iii 1 241
True Romans. Remember What you have said, and show yourselves true Romans . . . . ii 1 223
True Romeo. The noble Paris and true Romeo dead *Rom. and Jul.* v 3 259
True root. Where it is impossible you should take true root but by the fair weather that you make yourself . . . *Much Ado* i 3 25
True rule. I am not so nice, To change true rules for old inventions *T. of Shrew* iii 1 81
So long as out of limit and true rule You stand . 1 *Hen. IV.* iv 3 39
True seed. How much low peasantry would then be glean'd From the true seed of honour! . . . . *Mer. of Venice* ii 9 47
True sense. Establish him in his true sense again . *Com. of Errors* iv 4 51
But a sickly part of one true sense Could not so mope . *Hamlet* iii 4 80
True servant. But cannot be true servant to my master, Unless I prove false traitor to myself . . . . *T. G. of Ver.* iv 4 109
He's never any thing but your true servant.—I know't; I thank you *Othello* iii 3 9
True service. As my true service shall deserve your love *Richard II.* iii 3 199
If thou wouldst not be a villain, but do me true service . *Cymbeline* iii 5 110
True servitor. Henceforth I am thy true servitor . 3 *Hen. VI.* iii 3 196
True shrift. I would thou wert so happy by thy stay, To hear true shrift *Rom. and Jul.* i 1 165
True sincerity. Make a riot on the gentle brow Of true sincerity *K. John* iii 1 248
True sonnet. It is with me as the very true sonnet is . *T. Night* iii 4 24
True sorrow. Impatience waiteth on true sorrow . 3 *Hen. VI.* iii 3 42
True sovereign. Thy constant friend, And their true sovereign . iv 1 78
True speaking. An bad thinking do not wrest true speaking, I'll offend nobody . . . . *Much Ado* iii 4 34
True spies. If these be true spies which I wear in my head, here's a goodly sight . . . . *Tempest* v 1 259
True spirit. As I am a true spirit, welcome! . *Mer. Wives* v 5 33
True state. Bring him on to some confession Of his true state *Hamlet* iii 1 10
True strength. Here is the guess of their true strength and forces *Lear* v 1 52
True subject. I'll swear upon that bottle to be thy true subject *Tempest* ii 2 130
As the flourish when true subjects bow To a new-crowned monarch *Mer. of Venice* iii 2 49
Contrary to the faith and allegiance of a true subject . *W. Tale* iii 2 20
Camillo a true subject; Leontes a jealous tyrant . . . iii 2 134
I have done the part of a careful friend and a true subject . 2 *Hen. IV.* ii 4 349
A famous rebel art thou, Colevile.—And a famous true subject took him iv 3 70
Like true subjects, sons of your progenitors, Go cheerfully together 1 *Hen. VI.* iv 1 166
And you were sworn true subjects unto me . . 3 *Hen. VI.* iii 1 78
We are true subjects to the king, King Edward . . . iii 1 94
True subjection. I do bequeath my faithful services And true subjection everlastingly . . . . *K. John* v 7 105
True submission. Find pardon on my true submission 1 *Hen. IV.* iii 2 28
True substances. Grief has so wrought on him, He takes false shadows for true substances . . . . *T. Andron.* iii 2 80
True succeeders. The true succeeders of each royal house *Richard III.* v 5 30
True swains in love shall in the world to come Approve their truths by Troilus . . . . *Troi. and Cres.* iii 2 180
True sword. They have galls, Good arms, strong joints, true swords i 3 238
Nor you, my brother, with your true sword drawn, Opposed to hinder me, should stop my way . . . . . . v 3 56
I thought to crush him in an equal force, True sword to sword *Coriolanus* i 10 15
True taste. Whose qualification shall come into no true taste again but by the displanting of Cassio . . . . *Othello* ii 1 283

True tears. His napkin, with his true tears all bewet . *T. Andron.* iii 1 146
Who drown'd their enmity in my true tears . . . v 3 107
True thing. Is it honest in deed and word? is it a true thing? *As Y. L. It* iii 3 18
Yet sit and see, Minding true things by what their mockeries be *Hen. V.* iv Prol. 53
True time. Had not an ear to hear my true time broke . *Richard II.* v 5 48
True titles. The . . . unhidden passages Of his true titles . *Hen. V.* i 1 87
True traveller. You are a vagabond and no true traveller *All's Well* ii 3 277
True use. Like a usurer, abound'st in all, And usest none in that true use indeed . . . . *Rom. and Jul.* iii 3 124
True valour. In a false quarrel there is no true valour . *Much Ado* v 1 120
True valour is turned bear-herd: pregnancy is made a tapster 2 *Hen. IV.* i 2 192
True wars. Though I cannot make true wars, I'll frame convenient peace *Coriolanus* v 3 190
True wit. It rejoiceth my intellect: true wit! . . *L. L. Lost* v 1 64
True woman. Now, as I am a true woman, holland of eight shillings an ell . . . . 1 *Hen. IV.* iii 3 82
True word. Speak, and be hang'd: For each true word, a blister! *T. of A.* v 1 135
True worthiness. As honour without breach of honour may Make tender of to thy true worthiness . . . . *L. L. Lost* ii 1 171
True wretchedness. Took pity From most true wretchedness *Cymbeline* iii 4 63
True wrongs. They bring smooth comforts false, worse than true wrongs 2 *Hen. IV.* Ind. 40
True zeal. His prayers are full of false hypocrisy; Ours of true zeal and deep integrity . . . . *Richard II.* v 3 108
Truer. You have spoken truer than you purposed . . *Tempest* ii 1 20
But truer stars did govern Proteus' birth . . . *T. G. of Ver.* ii 7 74
It is not truer he is Angelo Than this is all as true as it is strange *Meas. for Meas.* v 1 43
There are no faces truer than those that are so washed . *Much Ado* i 1 27
More fairer than fair, beautiful than beauteous, truer than truth itself *L. L. Lost* iv 1 63
Be out of hope, of question, of doubt; Be certain, nothing truer *M. N. D.* iii 2 280
Is there no exorcist Beguiles the truer office of mine eyes? *All's Well* v 3 306
Far truer spoke than meant . . . . 2 *Hen. VI.* iii 1 183
That hand, which, for thy love, did kill thy love, Shall, for thy love, kill a far truer love . . . . . *Richard III.* i 2 191
He hath a lady, wiser, fairer, truer, Than ever Greek did compass in his arms . . . . *Troi. and Cres.* i 3 275
And what truth can speak truest not truer than Troilus. . iii 2 106
There was never a truer rhyme . . . . . . iv 4 22
Never man Sigh'd truer breath . . . . *Coriolanus* iv 5 121
Ne'er did poor steward wear a truer grief For his undone lord *T. of Athens* iv 3 487
And I the truer, So to be false with her . . . *Cymbeline* i 5 43
Truer-hearted. But an honester and truer-hearted man . 2 *Hen. IV.* ii 4 414
Truest. As true as truest horse that yet would never tire *M. N. Dream* iii 1 98
By thy . . . glittering gleams, I trust to take of truest Thisby sight v 1 280
The truest poetry is the most feigning . . . *As Y. Like It* iii 3 19
And what truth can speak truest not truer than Troilus *Troi. and Cres.* iii 2 705
Here is no use for gold.—The best and truest; For here it sleeps, and does no hired harm . . . . . . *T. of Athens* iv 3 290
The truest issue of thy throne By his own interdiction stands accursed *Macbeth* iv 3 106
He is one The truest manner'd . . . . . *Cymbeline* i 6 166
O, never say hereafter But I am truest speaker . . . v 5 376
The bracelet of the truest princess That ever swore her faith . v 5 416
Truie. Le chien est retourné à son propre vomissement, et la truie lavée au bourbier . . . . *Hen. V.* iii 7 69
Trull. Am sure I scared the Dauphin and his trull . 1 *Hen. VI.* ii 2 28
How ill-beseeming is it in thy sex To triumph, like an Amazonian trull, Upon their woes! . . . . . 3 *Hen. VI.* i 4 114
And let my spleenful sons this trull deflour . *T. Andron.* ii 3 191
Gives his potent regiment to a trull, That noises it against us *A. and C.* iii 6 95
Truly, sir, I think you'll hardly win her . *T. G. of Ver.* i 1 141
I do as truly suffer As e'er I did commit . . . . v 4 76
If I read it not truly, my ancient skill beguiles me . *Meas. for Meas.* iv 2 164
Most strange, but yet most truly, will I speak . . . v 1 37
I pray thee tell me truly how thou likest her . . *Much Ado* i 1 180
There's no true drop of blood in him, to be truly touched with love . iii 2 19
Bid her answer truly.—I charge thee do so, as thou art my child . iv 1 76
To make you answer truly to your name . . . . iv 1 80
They were never so truly turned over and over as my poor self in love . v 2 34
To-morrow truly will I meet with thee . . . *M. N. Dream* i 1 178
I swear, I cannot truly say how I came here; But, as I think,—for truly would I speak, And now I do bethink me, so it is . . iv 1 154
Truly, the moon shines with a good grace . . . . v 1 272
It would have been a fine tragedy: and so it is, truly . . v 1 367
As mine eye doth his effigies witness Most truly limn'd *As Y. Like It* ii 7 195
Truly, thou art damned like an ill-roasted egg, all on one side . iii 2 38
For every passion something and for no passion truly any thing . iii 2 434
If you will see a pageant truly play'd . . . . iii 4 55
Tell me, sweet Kate, and tell me truly too . *T. of Shrew* iv 5 28
Howe'er, I charge thee, As heaven shall work in me for thine avail, To tell me truly . . . . *All's Well* i 3 191
Had you not lately an intent,—speak truly,—To go to Paris? . i 3 224
I may truly say, it is a novelty to the world . . . ii 3 22
And truly, as I hope to live . . . . . . iv 3 147
A friend whose thoughts more truly labour To recompense your love . iv 4 17
'Tis beauty truly blent, whose red and white Nature's own sweet and cunning hand laid on . . . . *T. Night* i 5 257
To make us say 'This is put forth too truly' . . . *W. Tale* i 2 14
Give us better credit: We have always truly served you . . ii 3 148
His innocent babe truly begotten . . . . . . iii 2 135
Be pleased then To pay that duty which you truly owe . . *K. John* ii 1 247
That which thou hast sworn to do amiss Is not amiss when it is truly done . . . . iii 1 271
Whose tongue soe'er speaks false, Not truly speaks; who speaks not truly, lies . . . . iv 3 92
Speak truly, on thy knighthood and thy oath . . *Richard II.* i 3 14
And as I truly fight, defend me heaven! . . . . . i 3 25
Thou hast forgotten to demand that truly which thou wouldst truly know . . . . 1 *Hen. IV.* i 2 5
Now am I, if a man should speak truly, little better than one of the wicked . . . . i 2 106
As truly as a man of falsehood may . . . . . ii 1 71
As I am truly given to understand . . . . . iv 4 11
If like a Christian thou hadst truly borne Betwixt our armies true intelligence . . . . v 5 9
I have served your worship truly, sir, this eight years . 2 *Hen. IV.* v 1 52
The service that I truly did his life Hath left me open to all injuries v 2 7

Truly. This most memorable line, In every branch truly demonstrative *Hen. V.* ii 4 89
As duly, but not as truly, As bird doth sing on bough . . . iii 2 19
I tell thee truly, herald, I know not if the day be ours or no . . iv 7 86
The moon ; for it shines bright and never changes, but keeps his course truly . . . . v 2 173
More truly now may this be verified . . . . . 1 *Hen. VI.* i 2 32
I'll ship them all for Ireland.—I'll see it truly done . 2 *Hen. VI.* iii 1 330
He that is truly dedicate to war Hath no self-love . . . v 2 37
So thrive I, as I truly swear the like ! . . . . *Richard III.* ii 1 11
Truly pitying My father's loss, like a most royal prince . *Hen. VIII.* ii 1 112
As you are truly noble, As you respect the common good . . iii 2 289
Never so truly happy, my good Cromwell. I know myself now . . iii 2 377
God shall be truly known . . . . v 5 37
Fears make devils of cherubins ; they never see truly *Troi. and Cres.* iii 2 75
Too modest are you ; More cruel to your good report than grateful To us that give you truly . . . . . . *Coriolanus* i 9 55
Be that you seem, truly your country's friend . . . . . iii 1 218
Yes, mercy, if you report him truly.—I paint him in the character . v 4 27
So soon forsaken ? young men's love then lies Not truly in their hearts, but in their eyes . . . . . . *Rom. and Jul.* ii 3 68
There's none Can truly say he gives, if he receives . *T. of Athens* i 2 11
He's truly valiant that can wisely suffer The worst that man can breathe . . . . iii 5 31
Answer every man directly.—Ay, and briefly.—Ay, and wisely.—Ay, and truly, you were best . . . . . *J. Cæsar* iii 3 13
Answer every man directly and briefly, wisely and truly . . iii 3 17
Your name, sir, truly.—Truly, my name is Cinna . . . iii 3 29
What I am truly, Is thine and my poor country's to command *Macbeth* iv 3 131
Well, march we on, To give obedience where 'tis truly owed . . v 2 26
With all forms, moods, shapes of grief, That can denote me truly *Hamlet* i 2 83
Truly to speak, and with no addition, We go to gain a little patch of ground . . . . iv 4 17
All this can I Truly deliver.—Let us haste to hear it . . . v 2 397
To serve him truly that will put me in trust . . . . *Lear* i 4 15
I shall serve you, sir, Truly, however else . . . . . ii 1 119
Tell me—but truly—but then speak the truth . . . . . v 1 8
We cannot all be masters, nor all masters Cannot be truly follow'd *Oth.* i 1 44
As truly as to heaven I do confess the vices of my blood . . . i 3 122
If he be not one that truly loves you, That errs in ignorance and not in cunning, I have no judgement in an honest face . . . . iii 3 48
Swear thou art honest.—Heaven doth truly know it.—Heaven truly knows that thou art false as hell . . . . . . iv 2 38
By her election may be truly read What kind of man he is *Cymbeline* i 1 53
It shall safe be kept, And truly yielded you . . . . . i 6 210
Report should render him hourly to your ear As truly as he moves . iii 4 154
The handmaids of all women, or, more truly, Woman it pretty self . iii 4 159
What villany soe'er I bid thee do, to perform it directly and truly, I would think thee an honest man . . . . iii 5 113
I am near to the place where they should meet, if Pisanio have mapped it truly . . . . iv 1 2
Try many, all good, serve truly, never Find such another master . . iv 2 373
No lesser of her honour confident Than I did truly find her . . v 5 188

Truly-falsely. But thy speaking of my tongue, and I thine, most truly-falsely, must needs be granted to be much at one . *Hen. V.* v 2 203

Trump. Whilst any trump did sound, or drum struck up, His sword did ne'er leave striking in the field . . . . . . 1 *Hen. VI.* i 4 80
When fame shall in our islands sound her trump . *Troi. and Cres.* iii 3 210
Proclaim our honours, lords, with trump and drum . *T. Andron.* i 1 275
What means that trump? How now? . . . . *T. of Athens* i 2 120
Farewell the neighing steed, and the shrill trump ! . . . *Othello* iii 3 351

Trumpery. The trumpery in my house, go bring it hither . *Tempest* iv 1 186
I have sold all my trumpery . . . . *W. Tale* iv 4 608

Trumpet. Bid them bring the trumpets to the gate . *Meas. for Meas.* iv 5 9
Twice have the trumpets sounded ; The generous and gravest citizens Have hent the gates, and very near upon The duke is entering . iv 6 12
To be the trumpet of his own virtues . . . . . *Much Ado* v 2 87
The trumpet sounds : be mask'd ; the maskers come . *L. L. Lost* v 2 157
If they but hear perchance a trumpet sound, Or any air of music touch their ears . . . . *Mer. of Venice* v 1 75
Your husband is at hand ; I hear his trumpet . . . . . v 1 122
Sirrah, go see what trumpet 'tis that sounds . *T. of Shrew* Ind. 1 74
Loud 'larums, neighing steeds, and trumpets' clang . . . . i 2 207
Hark ! you may know by their trumpets . . . . *All's Well* iii 5 9
The king's coming ; I know by his trumpets . . . . . v 2 55
If I prove honey-mouth'd, let my tongue blister And never to my red-look'd anger be The trumpet any more . . . . *W. Tale* ii 2 35
So hence ! Be thou the trumpet of our wrath . . . *K. John* i 1 27
Some trumpet summon hither to the walls These men of Angiers . . ii 1 198
Our trumpet call'd you to this gentle parle . . . . . ii 1 205
Braying trumpets and loud churlish drums, Clamours of hell . . iii 1 303
What lusty trumpet thus doth summon us? . . . . . . v 2 117
The Duke of Norfolk, sprightfully and bold, Stays but the summons of the appellant's trumpet . . . . . . *Richard II.* i 3 4
Sound, trumpets ; and set forward, combatants . . . . . i 3 117
With harsh-resounding trumpets' dreadful bray . . . . . i 3 135
Through brazen trumpet send the breath of parley Into his ruin'd ears iii 3 33
The southern wind Doth play the trumpet to his purposes 1 *Hen. IV.* v 1 4
The trumpet sounds retreat ; the day is ours . . . . . v 4 163
Your pens to lances and your tongue divine To a loud trumpet 2 *Hen. IV.* iv 1 52
Their eyes of fire sparkling through sights of steel And the loud trumpet blowing them together . . . . iv 1 122
More rushes, more rushes.—The trumpets have sounded twice . . v 5 2
The work ish give over, the trompet sound the retreat . *Hen. V.* iii 2 94
The town is beseeched, and the trumpet call us to the breach . . iii 2 116
Then let the trumpets sound The tucket sonance and the note to mount iv 2 34
I will the banner from a trumpet take, And use it for my haste . iv 2 61
Take a trumpet, herald ; Ride thou unto the horsemen on yon hill . iv 7 59
Sound, trumpets, alarum to the combatants ! . . . 2 *Hen. VI.* ii 3 95
The angry trumpet sounds alarum And dead men's cries do fill the empty air . . . . v 2 3
Now let the general trumpet blow his blast ! . . . . . . v 2 43
Sound drums and trumpets, and to London all . . . . . v 3 32
Sound drums and trumpets, and the king will fly . . . 3 *Hen. VI.* i 1 118
But sound the trumpets, and about our task . . . . . ii 1 200
Sound trumpets ! let our bloody colours wave ! . . . . . ii 2 173
Sound trumpet ; Edward shall be here proclaim'd . . . . iv 7 69
Go, trumpet, to the walls, and sound a parle . . . . . v 1 16
Two braver men Ne'er spurr'd their coursers at the trumpet's sound . v 7 9
Sound drums and trumpets ! farewell sour annoy ! . . . . v 7 45
Trumpet. A flourish, trumpets ! strike alarum, drums ! *Richard III.* iv 4 148
Sound drums and trumpets boldly and cheerfully ; God and Saint George ! . . . . v 3 269
The trumpets sound : stand close, the queen is coming . *Hen. VIII.* iv 1 36
Hark ! the trumpets sound ; They're come already from the christening v 4 86
But those, we fear, We have frighted with our trumpets . . . . Epil. 4
What trumpet? look, Menelaus.—From Troy . *Troi. and Cres.* i 3 213
I bring a trumpet to awake his ear, To set his sense on the attentive bent . . . . i 3 251
Trumpet, blow loud, Send thy brass voice through all these lazy tents i 3 256
He bade me take a trumpet, And to this purpose speak . . . i 3 263
And will to-morrow with his trumpet call Midway between your tents i 3 277
With a trumpet 'twixt our tents and Troy To-morrow morning call . ii 1 135
Pride is his own glass, his own trumpet, his own chronicle . . ii 3 166
Give with thy trumpet a loud note to Troy, Thou dreadful Ajax . . iv 5 3
Thou, trumpet, there's my purse. Now crack thy lungs . . . iv 5 6
No trumpet answers.—'Tis but early days . . . . . . iv 5 12
Let the trumpets blow, That this great soldier may his welcome know iv 5 275
Ho ! bid my trumpet sound.—No notes of sally . . . . . v 3 13
Hark ! a retire upon our Grecian part.—The Trojan trumpets sound the like . . . . v 8 16
Go sound thy trumpet in the market-place . . . . *Coriolanus* i 5 27
When drums and trumpets shall I' the field prove flatterers . . . i 9 42
Hark ! the trumpets.—These are the ushers of Marcius . . . ii 1 173
The trumpets, sackbuts, psalteries, and fifes, Tabors and cymbals and the shouting Romans, Make the sun dance . . . . . . v 4 52
Why do the emperor's trumpets flourish thus? . . . *T. Andron.* iv 2 49
The trumpets show the emperor is at hand . . . . . . v 3 16
Then, dreadful trumpet, sound the general doom ! . *Rom. and Jul.* iii 2 67
What trumpet's that?—'Tis Alcibiades, and some twenty horse *T. of A.* i 1 249
Feast your ears with the music awhile, if they will fare so harshly o' the trumpet's sound . . . . iii 6 37
What's the business, That such a hideous trumpet calls to parley? *Macbeth* ii 3 87
Make all our trumpets speak ; give them all breath, Those clamorous harbingers . . . . v 6 9
The cock, that is the trumpet to the morn . . . . . *Hamlet* i 1 150
The kettle-drum and trumpet thus bray out The triumph of his pledge i 4 11
She should in ground unsanctified have lodged Till the last trumpet . v 1 253
Let the kettle to the trumpet speak, The trumpet to the cannoneer without . . . . v 2 287
Hark, the duke's trumpets ! I know not why he comes . . *Lear* ii 1 81
What trumpet's that?—I know't, my sister's . . . . . ii 4 185
If you have victory, let the trumpet sound For him that brought it . v 1 41
Call by thy trumpet : he that dares approach, On him, on you, who not? v 3 99
Let the trumpet sound,—And read out this.—Sound, trumpet ! . . v 3 107
Let him appear by the third sound of the trumpet . . . . v 3 114
Ask him his purposes, why he appears Upon this call o' the trumpet . v 3 119
Where they shall rest for ever. Trumpets, speak ! . . . . v 3 150
Twice then the trumpets sounded, And there I left him tranced . . v 3 217
My downright violence and storm of fortunes May trumpet to the world *Othello* i 3 251
The Moor ! I know his trumpet . . . . ii 1 180
What trumpet is that same?—Something from Venice, sure . . iv 1 226
So tart a favour To trumpet such good tidings ! . . *Ant. and Cleo.* ii 5 39
These drums ! these trumpets, flutes ! what ! . . . . . ii 7 138
He must not live to trumpet forth my infamy . . . . *Pericles* i 1 145

Trumpet-clangor. There roar'd the sea, and trumpet-clangor sounds 2 *Hen. IV.* v 5 42

Trumpeter. Is it not meant damnable in us, to be trumpeters of our unlawful intents? . . . . *All's Well* iv 3 32
Trumpeter : Summon their general unto the wall . . 1 *Hen. VI.* iv 2 1
The arm our soldier, Our steed the leg, the tongue our trumpeter *Coriol.* i 1 121
Trumpeters, With brazen din blast you the city's ear . *Ant. and Cleo.* iv 8 35

Trumpet-tongued. His virtues Will plead like angels, trumpet-tongued, against The deep damnation of his taking-off . . . *Macbeth* i 7 19

Truncheon. The marshal's truncheon, nor the judge's robe *Meas. for Meas.* ii 2 61
An captains were of my mind they would truncheon you out 2 *Hen. IV.* ii 4 154
Thy leg a stick compared with this truncheon . . . 2 *Hen. VI.* iv 10 52
Who should withhold me? Not fate, obedience, nor the hand of Mars Beckoning with fiery truncheon my retire . . . *Troi. and Cres.* v 3 53
Thrice he walk'd By their oppress'd and fear-surprised eyes, Within his truncheon's length . . . . *Hamlet* i 2 204

Truncheoners. When I might see from far some forty truncheoners draw to her succour . . . . *Hen. VIII.* v 4 54

Trundle-tail. Brach or lym, Or bobtail tike or trundle-tail . . *Lear* iii 6 73

Trunk. He was The ivy which had hid my princely trunk . . *Tempest* i 2 86
Neither press, coffer, chest, trunk, well, vault, but he hath an abstract *Mer. Wives* iv 2 62
You consenting to't, Would bark your honour from that trunk you bear *Meas. for Meas.* iii 1 72
That souls of animals infuse themselves Into the trunks of men *M. of V.* iv 1 133
The beauteous evil Are empty trunks o'erflourish'd by the devil *T. N.* iii 4 404
If therefore you dare trust my honesty, That lies enclosed in this trunk which you Shall bear along impawn'd, away to-night . . *W. Tale* i 2 435
To lie like pawns lock'd up in chests and trunks, To hug with swine *K. John* v 2 141
Why dost thou converse with that trunk of humours? . 1 *Hen. IV.* ii 4 495
But health, alack, with youthful wings is flown From this bare wither'd trunk . . . . 2 *Hen. IV.* iv 5 230
Here I am ; My ransom is this frail and worthless trunk . *Hen. V.* iii 6 163
To tell my love unto his dumb deaf trunk . . . . 2 *Hen. VI.* iii 2 144
Leaving thy trunk for crows to feed upon . . . . . . iv 10 90
Until my mis-shaped trunk that bears this head Be round impaled with a glorious crown . . . . 3 *Hen. VI.* iii 2 170
The honour'd mould Wherein this trunk was framed . . *Coriolanus* v 3 23
Drag hence her husband to some secret hole, And make his dead trunk pillow to our lust . . . . *T. Andron.* ii 3 130
Draw you near, To shed obsequious tears upon this trunk . . . v 3 152
And that the trunk may be discharged of breath . . *Rom. and Jul.* v 1 63
Whose bare unhoused trunks, To the conflicting elements exposed, Answer mere nature . . . . *T. of Athens* iv 3 229
If, on the tenth day following, Thy banish'd trunk be found in our dominions, The moment is thy death . . . . *Lear* i 1 180
They are in a trunk, Attended by my men . . . . *Cymbeline* i 6 196
Send your trunk to me ; it shall safe be kept, And truly yielded you . i 6 209
I have enough : To the trunk again, and shut the spring of it . . ii 2 47
Soft, ho ! what trunk is here Without his top? . . . . . iv 2 353

Trunk sleeve. 'With a trunk sleeve :'—I confess two sleeves *T. of Shrew* iv 3 142

Trunk-work. Some trunk-work, some behind-door-work . . . *W. Tale* iii 3 75

Trust. My trust, Like a good parent, did beget of him A falsehood in its contrary as great As my trust was . . . . *Tempest* i 2 93
We dare trust you in this kind, Because we know . *T. G. of Ver.* iii 2 56
I am sorry I must never trust thee more . . . . v 4 69
A secure ass: he will trust his wife; he will not be jealous. I will rather trust a Fleming with my butter *Mer. Wives* ii 2 315
If I cry out thus upon no trail, never trust me when I open again . . iv 2 209
I trust it will grow to a most prosperous perfection *Meas. for Meas.* iii 1 271
Trust not my holy order, If I pervert your course . . . . iv 3 152
On my trust, a man that never yet Did, as he vouches, misreport your grace . . . . v 1 147
How darest thou trust So great a charge from thine own custody? *Com. of Errors* i 2 60
A man is well holp up that trusts to you . . . . . . iv 1 22
My wife is in a wayward mood to-day, And will not lightly trust the messenger . . . . iv 4 5
I would scarce trust myself, though I had sworn the contrary *Much Ado* i 1 197
Because I will not do them the wrong to mistrust any, I will do myself the right to trust none . . . . i 1 246
I trust you will be ruled by your father . . . . . . ii 1 53
Let every eye negotiate for itself And trust no agent . . . . ii 1 186
Wilt thou make a trust a transgression? . . . . . . ii 1 232
If he do not dote on her upon this, I will never trust my expectation . ii 3 220
If you dare not trust that you see, confess not that you know . . iii 2 122
Call me a fool; Trust not my reading nor my observations . . . iv 1 167
Trust not my age, My reverence, calling, nor divinity . . . . iv 1 169
O, never will I trust to speeches penn'd! . . . . . *L. L. Lost* v 2 402
Your oath I will not trust; but go with speed . . . . . v 2 804
To trust the opportunity of night And the ill counsel . *M. N. Dream* ii 1 217
I perceive A weak bond holds you: I'll not trust your word . . . iii 2 268
I will not trust you, I, Nor longer stay in your curst company . . iii 2 340
By thy . . . glittering gleams, I trust to take of truest Thisby sight . v 1 280
I no question make To have it of my trust or for my sake *Mer. of Venice* i 1 185
If I do not put on a sober habit, . . . never trust me more . . . ii 2 206
If that I do not dream or be not frantic,—As I do trust I am not *As Y. Like It* i 3 52
Let it suffice thee that I trust thee not . . . . . . i 3 57
We will begin these rites, As we do trust they'll end, in true delights . v 4 204
I trust I may go too, may I not? . . . . . *T. of Shrew* i 1 102
'Hic est Sigeia tellus,' I trust you not . . . . iii 1 43
Thus I'll visit her.—But thus, I trust, you will not marry her . . iii 2 117
If he be credulous and trust my tale, I'll make him glad . . . iv 2 67
Why, sir, I trust I may have leave to speak; And speak I will . . iv 3 73
Then never trust me, if I be afeard . . . . v 2 17
Love all, trust a few, Do wrong to none . . . . . *All's Well* i 1 73
Though more to know could not be more to trust . . . . . ii 1 209
Trust him not in matter of heavy consequence . . . . . ii 5 49
Never trust my judgement in any thing . . . . iii 6 34
Give me trust, the count he is my husband, And what to your sworn counsel I have spoken Is so from word to word . . . . . iii 7 8
I will never trust a man again for keeping his sword clean . . . iv 3 165
You never had a servant to whose trust Your business was more welcome iv 4 15
If my lady have not called up her steward Malvolio and bid him turn you out of doors, never trust me . . . . . . *T. Night* ii 3 79
If I do not, never trust me, take it how you will . . . . . ii 3 204
But you'll not deliver't?—Never trust me, then . . . . . iii 2 62
I am ready to distrust mine eyes And wrangle with my reason that persuades me To any other trust but that I am mad . . . . . iv 3 15
A servant grafted in my serious trust And therein negligent . *W. Tale* i 2 246
If therefore you dare trust my honesty, That lies enclosed in this trunk i 2 434
I never wish'd to see you sorry; now I trust I shall . . . . ii 1 124
Than when I feel and see her no farther trust her . . . . . ii 1 136
If she dares trust me with her little babe, I'll show't the king . . ii 2 37
Trust it, He shall not rule me.—La you now, you hear . . . . ii 3 49
That I may call thee something more than man And after that trust to thee . . . . iv 4 547
What a fool Honesty is! and Trust, his sworn brother, a very simple gentleman! . . . . iv 4 607
I will trust you. Walk before toward the sea-side . . . . . iv 4 855
If I do not wonder how thou darest venture to be drunk, not being a tall fellow trust me not . . . . v 2 185
Which trust accordingly, kind citizens . . . . . *K. John* ii 1 231
I trust we shall, If not fill up the measure of her will, Yet in some measure satisfy her . . . . ii 1 555
It cannot be; thou dost but say 'tis so: I trust I may not trust thee . iii 1 7
Trust not those cunning waters of his eyes . . . . . . iv 3 107
Some honest Christian trust me with a gage, That Norfolk lies *Rich. II.* iv 1 83
Farewell, good brother: we shall thrive, I trust . . . *1 Hen. IV.* i 3 300
Thou wilt not utter what thou dost not know; And so far will I trust thee ii 3 115
Thou shalt have charge and sovereign trust herein . . . . . iii 2 161
Nor did he think it meet To lay so dangerous and dear a trust On any soul iv 1 34
You have deceived our trust, And made us doff our easy robes of peace v 1 11
Speak; we will not trust our eyes Without our ears . . . . v 4 139
Wouldst thou turn our offers contrary? Misuse the tenour of thy kinsman's trust? . . . . v 5 5
What trust is in these times? . . . . . . *2 Hen. IV.* i 3 100
I trust, lords, we shall lie to-night together . . . . . . ii 2 97
'Fore God, his grace is bold, to trust these traitors . . . *Hen. V.* ii 2 1
Let senses rule; the word is 'Pitch and Pay:' Trust none . . . ii 3 52
If I live to see it, I will never trust his word after . . . . iv 1 207
Upon the which, I trust, Shall witness live in brass of this day's work . iv 3 96
No prophet will, I trust, if she prove false . . . . *1 Hen. VI.* i 2 150
You may not, my lord, despise her gentle suit.—Ne'er trust me then . ii 2 48
I trust ere long to choke thee with thine own . . . . . . iii 2 46
What is the trust or strength of foolish man? . . . . . . iii 2 112
That will not trust thee but for profit's sake . . . . . . iii 3 63
So farewell, Talbot; I'll no longer trust thee . . . . . . iii 3 84
You, his false hopes, the trust of England's honour, Keep off aloof . iv 4 20
I trust the ghost of Talbot is not there . . . . iv 4 26
Trust nobody, for fear you be betray'd . . . . . *2 Hen. VI.* iv 4 58
The trust I have is in mine innocence, And therefore am I bold . . iv 4 59
In them I trust; for they are soldiers, Witty, courteous, liberal *3 Hen. VI.* i 2 42
And trust not simple Henry nor his oaths . . . . i 2 59
Trust not him that hath once broken faith . . . . iv 4 30
His minority Is put unto the trust of Richard Gloucester *Richard III.* i 3 12
Every man that means to live well endeavours to trust to himself . . i 4 148
I wonder he is so fond To trust the mockery of unquiet slumbers . . iii 2 27
I will not trust you, sir . . . . iv 4 492
You shall hear—This was his gentleman in trust—of him . *Hen. VIII.* i 2 125
They that my trust must grow to, live not here . . . . . iii 1 80

Trust. If you please To trust us in your business, we are ready *Hen. VIII.* iii 1 173
Trust to me, Ulysses, Our imputation shall be oddly poised *Troi. and Cres.* i 3 338
I will no more trust him when he leers than I will a serpent when he hisses . . . . v 1 96
But will you, then?—In faith, I will, la; never trust me else . . v 2 59
He that trusts to you, Where he should find you lions, finds you hares *Coriolanus* i 1 174
Hang ye! Trust ye? With every minute you do change a mind . . i 1 185
Know you on which side They have placed their men of trust? . . . i 6 52
Their bands i' the vaward are the Antiates, Of their best trust . . i 6 54
Or never trust to what my tongue can do I' the way of flattery further iii 2 136
Thou shalt no sooner March to assault thy country than to tread—Trust to't, thou shalt not—on thy mother's womb . . . . . v 3 124
Send thee by me, their tribune and their trust, This palliament *T. An.* i 1 181
I'll trust, by leisure, him that mocks me once . . . . . . i 1 301
I see thou wilt not trust the air With secrets . . . . . . iv 2 169
There's no trust, No faith, no honesty in men . . . *Rom. and Jul.* iii 2 85
Trust to't, bethink you; I'll not be forsworn . . . . . . iii 5 197
If I may trust the flattering truth of sleep, My dreams presage some joyful news at hand . . . . v 1 1
I wonder men dare trust themselves with men . . . *T. of Athens* i 2 44
Grant I may never prove so fond, To trust man on his oath or bond . i 2 66
Spare your oaths, I'll trust to your conditions . . . . . . iv 3 139
Trust not the physician; His antidotes are poison . . . . . iv 3 434
There's never a one of you but trusts a knave, That mightily deceives you v 1 96
Trust not Trebonius; mark well Metellus Cimber . . . . *J. Cæsar* ii 3 3
Compell'd these skipping kerns to trust their heels . . . *Macbeth* i 2 30
He was a gentleman on whom I built An absolute trust . . . . . i 4 14
He's here in double trust; First, as I am his kinsman . . . . i 7 12
And damn'd all those that trust them! . . . . iv 1 139
To desperation turn my trust and hope! . . . . . . *Hamlet* iii 2 228
My two schoolfellows, Whom I will trust as I will adders fang'd . . iii 4 203
To serve him truly that will put me in trust . . . . . . *Lear* i 4 15
Well, you may fear too far.—Safer than trust too far . . . . i 4 351
If I would stand against thee, would the reposal Of any trust, virtue, or worth in thee, Make thy words faith'd? . . . . ii 1 71
Natures of such deep trust we shall much need . . . . . . ii 1 117
I will lay trust upon thee; and thou shalt find a dearer father in my love iii 5 25
He's mad that trusts in the tameness of a wolf, a horse's health, a boy's love . . . . iii 6 19
Sick, O, sick!—If not, I'll ne'er trust medicine . . . . . v 3 96
Trust to thy single virtue . . . . v 3 103
Trust not your daughters' minds By what you see them act . *Othello* i 1 171
The trust, the office I do hold of you, Not only take away, but let your sentence Even fall upon my life . . . . i 3 118
A man he is of honesty and trust . . . . i 3 285
I fear the trust Othello puts him in . . . . ii 3 131
O, 'tis treason!—Madam, I trust, not so . . . . *Ant. and Cleo.* i 5 7
O noble emperor, do not fight by sea; Trust not to rotten planks . . iii 7 63
The rest That fell away have entertainment, but No honourable trust . iv 6 18
None about Cæsar trust but Proculeius.—My resolution and my hands I'll trust; None about Cæsar . . . . iv 15 49
Antony Did tell me of you, bade me trust you; but I do not greatly care to be deceived, That have no use for trusting . . . . . v 2 13
O slave, of no more trust Than love that's hired! What, goest thou back? v 2 154
No harm, I trust, is done?—There might have been . . *Cymbeline* i 1 161
And leave her in such honour as you have trust in . . . . . i 4 165
I do know her spirit, And will not trust one of her malice . . . i 5 35
Reflect upon him accordingly, as you value your trust . . . . . i 6 25
The credit that thy lady hath of thee Deserves thy trust . . . . i 6 158
Here are letters for you.—Their tenour good, I trust . . . . ii 4 36
Pray you, trust me here: I'll rob none but myself . . . . . iv 2 14
For death remember'd should be like a mirror, Who tells us life's but breath, to trust it error . . . . *Pericles* i 1 46
His seal'd commission, left in trust with me, Doth speak sufficiently . i 3 13

Trust me. Now, trust me, 'tis an office of great worth . *T. G. of Ver.* i 2 44
Now trust me, madam, it came hardly off . . . . ii 1 115
Trust me, I think 'tis almost day.—Not so . . . . . . iv 2 138
Trust me, I was going to your house.—And, trust me, I was coming to you *Mer. Wives* ii 1 33
Trust me, a mad host . . . . iii 1 115
Trust me, a good knot: I have good cheer at home . . . . . iii 2 52
Let's go in, gentlemen; but, trust me, we'll mock him . . . . iii 3 244
Trust me, he beat him most pitifully . . . . iv 2 212
Trust me, were it not against our laws, . . . My soul should sue *C. of Er.* i 1 143
Trust me, sweet, Out of this silence yet I pick'd a welcome *M. N. Dream* v 1 99
Trust me, I take him for the better dog . . . . *T. of Shrew* Ind. 1 25
Trust me, my lord, all hitherto goes well . . . . *3 Hen. VI.* iv 2 1
A goodly lady, trust me; of the hue That I would choose *T. Andron.* i 1 261
But trust me, gentleman, I'll prove more true . . *Rom. and Jul.* ii 2 100
Thou look'st pale.—And trust me, love, in my eye so do you . . . iii 5 58
Trust me, I could do much,—Prithee, no more . . . . *Othello* iii 3 74

Trusted. Who should be trusted, when one's own right hand Is perjured to the bosom? . . . . *T. G. of Ver.* v 4 67
I am trusted with a muzzle and enfranchised with a clog . *Much Ado* i 3 34
My ventures are not in one bottom trusted, Nor to one place *M. of V.* i 1 42
And his affections dark as Erebus: Let no such man be trusted . . v 1 88
I have trusted thee, Camillo, With all the nearest things to my heart *W. Tale* i 2 235
For treason is but trusted like the fox . . . . . . *1 Hen. IV.* v 2 9
I wish'd to fall By the false faith of him I trusted most . *Richard III.* v 1 17
Let him in nought be trusted, For speaking false in that *Hen. VIII.* ii 4 135
That trusted home Might yet enkindle you unto the crown . *Macbeth* i 3 120
They stared, and were distracted; no man's life Was to be trusted with them . . . . ii 3 111
The worm is not to be trusted but in the keeping of wise people *A. and C.* v 2 267

Truster. Bankrupts, hold fast; Rather than render back, out with your knives, And cut your trusters' throats . . . . *T. of Athens* iv 1 10
Nor shall you do mine ear that violence, To make it truster of your own report Against yourself . . . . *Hamlet* i 2 172

Trusting. 'Tis no trusting to yond foolish lout . . . *T. G. of Ver.* iv 4 71
Saucy trusting of the cozen'd thoughts Defiles the pitchy night *All's W.* iv 4 23
Not trusting to this halting legate here . . . . . . *K. John* v 2 174
And but in purged judgement trusting neither . . . . *Hen. V.* ii 2 136
'Tis better using France than trusting France . . . *3 Hen. VI.* iv 1 42
I do not greatly care to be deceived, That have no use for trusting *Ant. and Cleo.* v 2 15

Trusty. A trusty villain, sir, that very oft, When I am dull with care and melancholy, Lightens my humour . . . . *Com. of Errors* i 2 19

Trusty. Which Lion hight by name, The trusty Thisby, coming first by night, Did scare away *M. N. Dream* v 1 141

Anon comes Pyramus, And finds his trusty Thisby's mantle slain v 1 146

I am thy lover's grace; And, like Limander, am I trusty still v 1 198

Come, trusty sword; Come, blade, my breast imbrue v 1 350

My trusty servant, well approved in all *T. of Shrew* i 1 7

Your ancient, trusty, pleasant servant Grumio i 2 47

He might at some great and trusty business in a main danger fail you *All's Well* iii 6 16

Stay yet another day, thou trusty Welshman *Richard II.* ii 4 5

Our trusty brother-in-law and the abbot, With all the rest of that consorted crew v 3 137

Like to a trusty squire did run away *1 Hen. VI.* iv 1 23

Our trusty friend, unless I be deceived *3 Hen. VI.* iv 7 41

Use careful watch, choose trusty sentinels *Richard III.* v 3 54

For I must bear thee to a trusty Goth *T. Andron.* v 1 34

Farewell; be trusty, and I'll quit thy pains: Farewell *Rom. and Jul.* ii 4 204

This trusty servant Shall pass between us *Lear* iv 2 18

Your trusty and most valiant servitor *Othello* i 3 40

Truth. Who having into truth, by telling of it, Made such a sinner of his memory, To credit his own lie *Tempest* i 2 100

He doth but mistake the truth totally ii 1 57

The truth you speak doth lack some gentleness And time to speak it in ii 1 137

They devour their reason and scarce think Their eyes do offices of truth v 1 156

Truth hath better deeds than words to grace it *T. G. of Ver.* ii 2 18

Speak the truth by her; if not divine, Yet let her be a principality ii 4 151

Do him not that wrong To bear a hard opinion of his truth ii 7 81

If you knew his pure heart's truth, You would quickly learn to know him by his voice iv 2 88

If my augury deceive me not, Witness good bringing up, fortune, and truth iv 4 74

Hear the truth of it: he came of an errand to me *Mer. Wives* i 4 80

In truth, sir, and she is pretty, and honest, and gentle i 4 148

I would have sworn his disposition would have gone to the truth of his words ii 1 61

Do you think there is truth in them?—Hang 'em, slaves! ii 1 178

Surely I think you have charms, la; yes, in truth ii 2 108

And did deliver to our age This tale of Herne the hunter for a truth iv 4 38

And till he tell the truth, Let the supposed fairies pinch him sound iv 4 60

The truth being known, We'll all present ourselves iv 4 62

You do amaze her: hear the truth of it v 5 233

Away! let's go learn the truth of it *Meas. for Meas.* i 2 82

To say the truth, I had as lief have the foppery of freedom i 2 137

Do not believe it. Fewness and truth, 'tis thus i 4 39

Why, very well; I hope here be truths ii 1 131

She, having the truth of honour in her iii 1 166

I have spirit to do any thing that appears not foul in the truth of my spirit iii 1 214

There is scarce truth enough alive to make societies secure iii 2 240

To speak so indirectly I am loath: I would say the truth iv 6 2

For truth is truth To the end of reckoning v 1 45

Let your reason serve To make the truth appear where it seems hid v 1 66

Confess the truth, and say by whose advice Thou camest here to complain v 1 113

As there is sense in truth and truth in virtue v 1 226

Against my soul's pure truth why labour you? *Com. of Errors* iii 2 37

I long to know the truth hereof at large iv 4 146

But she tells to your highness simple truth! v 1 211

My lord, in truth, thus far I witness with him v 1 254

There shall appear such seeming truth of Hero's disloyalty *Much Ado* ii 2 49

They have the truth of this from Hero ii 3 230

They say the lady is fair; 'tis a truth, I can bear them witness ii 3 239

It were not good She knew his love . . . —Why, you speak truth iii 1 59

Never gives to truth and virtue that Which simpleness and merit purchaseth iii 1 69

This it is, sir.—Yes, in truth it is, sir.—What is it, my good friends? iii 5 8

O, what authority and show of truth Can cunning sin cover itself withal! iv 1 36

To burn the errors that these princes hold Against her maiden truth iv 1 166

If they speak but truth of her, These hands shall tear her iv 1 192

In most comely truth, thou deservest it v 2 8

Truth it is, good signior, Your niece regards me with an eye of favour v 4 21

As, painfully to pore upon a book To seek the light of truth; while truth the while Doth falsely blind the eyesight of his look *L. L. Lost* i 1 75

I suffer for the truth, sir i 1 313

At that time Was there with him, if I have heard a truth ii 1 65

It is so; truth is truth iv 1 48

True, that thou art beauteous: truth itself, that thou art lovely iv 1 62

More fairer than fair, beautiful than beauteous, truer than truth itself. iv 1 64

The naked truth of it is, I have no shirt v 2 716

In plainest truth Tell you, I do not, nor I cannot love you *M. N. Dream* ii 1 200

To say the truth, reason and love keep little company together now-a-days iii 1 146

Vows so born, In their nativity all truth appears iii 2 125

When truth kills truth, O devilish-holy fray! iii 2 129

Wonder on, till truth make all things plain v 1 129

The truth is so: And this the cranny is, right and sinister v 1 163

In truth, I know it is a sin to be a mocker *Mer. of Venice* i 2 61

Truth will come to light; murder cannot be hid long; a man's son may, but at the length truth will out ii 2 83

Promise me life, and I'll confess the truth iii 2 34

The seeming truth which cunning times put on To entrap the wisest iii 2 100

If this will not suffice, it must appear That malice bears down truth iv 1 214

Even so void is your false heart of truth v 1 189

So wouldst thou, if the truth of thy love to me were so righteously tempered as mine is to thee *As Y. Like It* i 2 13

I will follow thee, To the last gasp, with truth and loyalty ii 3 70

Nay, certainly, there is no truth in him iii 4 22

If there be truth in sight, you are my daughter.—If there be truth in sight, you are my Rosalind v 4 124

To join in Hymen's bands, If truth holds true contents v 4 136

Come, go along, and see the truth hereof *T. of Shrew* iv 5 75

A prophet I, madam; and I speak the truth the next way *All's Well* i 3 63

It is the show and seal of nature's truth i 3 138

Sin And hellish obstinacy tie thy tongue, That truth should be suspected i 3 187

Tell true.—I will tell truth; by grace itself I swear i 3 226

A trifle neither, in good faith, if the learned should speak truth of it ii 2 37

Before me thou'rt a knave: this had been truth, sir ii 4 31

Uses a known truth to pass a thousand nothings with ii 5 32

Think you it is so?—Ay, surely, mere the truth iii 5 58

This is the first truth that e'er thine own tongue was guilty of iv 1 35

'Tis not the many oaths that makes the truth, But the plain single vow iv 2 21

Truth. Now will I charge you in the band of truth *All's Well* iv 2 56

I'll speak truth.—He's very near the truth in this iv 3 172

A truth's a truth, the rogues are marvellous poor iv 3 178

He will lie, sir, with such volubility, that you would think truth were a fool iv 3 285

Whose nature sickens but to speak a truth v 3 207

I have spoke the truth v 3 230

This story know, To make the even truth in pleasure flow v 3 326

By maidhood, honour, truth, and every thing *T. Night* iii 1 162

I have one heart, one bosom, and one truth, And that no woman has iii 1 170

And, having sworn truth, ever will be true iv 3 33

I Have utter'd truth: which if you seek to prove, I dare not stand by *W. Tale* i 2 443

Cannot or will not Relish a truth ii 1 167

Such as he Whose ignorant credulity will not Come up to the truth ii 1 193

If the good truth were known ii 1 200

The great Apollo suddenly will have The truth of this appear ii 3 201

As you were past all shame,—Those of your fact are so—so past all truth iii 2 86

Hast thou read truth?—Ay, my lord; even so As it is here set down.—There is no truth at all i' the oracle iii 2 139

Whom I proclaim a man of truth, of mercy iii 2 158

Thou didst speak but well When most the truth iii 2 234

Dismantle you, and, as you can, disliken The truth of your own seeming iv 4 667

Thou speak'st truth. No more such wives; therefore, no wife v 1 55

Most true, if ever truth were pregnant by circumstance v 2 33

But for the certain knowledge of that truth I put you o'er to heaven *K. John* i 1 61

I shame to speak, But truth is truth i 1 105

I am thy grandam, Richard; call me so.—Madam, by chance but not by truth i 1 169

Where doing tends to ill, The truth is then most done not doing it iii 1 273

And makest an oath the surety for thy truth Against an oath iii 1 282

The truth thou art unsure To swear, swears only not to be forsworn iii 1 283

Makes sound opinion sick and truth suspected iv 2 26

Under whose conduct came those powers of France That thou for truth givest out are landed here? iv 2 130

Wherefore didst thou so?—Foreknowing that the truth will fall out so iv 2 154

The life, the right, and truth of all this realm Is fled to heaven iv 3 144

Since it is true That I must die here and live hence by truth v 4 29

Both to defend my loyalty and truth To God, my king *Richard II.* i 3 19

As jocund as to jest Go I to fight: truth hath a quiet breast i 3 96

You never shall, so help you truth and God! i 3 183

They breathe truth that breathe their words in pain ii 1 8

Yet best beseeming me to speak the truth iv 1 116

But he, in twelve, Found truth in all but one iv 1 171

The truth of what we are Shows us but this v 1 19

I am in parliament pledge for his truth And lasting fealty v 2 44

If they speak more or less than truth, they are villains *1 Hen. IV.* ii 4 190

Art thou mad? is not the truth the truth? ii 4 255

Said he would swear truth out of England but he would make you believe it ii 4 337

And I can teach thee, coz, to shame the devil By telling truth iii 1 59

O, while you live, tell truth and shame the devil! iii 1 62

There's neither faith, truth, nor womanhood in me else iii 3 125

No more truth in thee than in a drawn fox iii 3 128

There's no room for faith, truth, nor honesty in this bosom of thine iii 3 174

If speaking truth In this fine age were not thought flattery iv 1 1

And the shirt, to say the truth, stolen from my host at Saint Alban's iv 2 50

Thou shakest thy head and hold'st it fear or sin To speak a truth *2 Hen. IV.* i 1 96

I hear for certain, and do speak the truth i 1 188

But, to speak truth, This present grief had wiped it from my mind i 1 210

All tallow: if I did say of wax, my growth would approve the truth i 2 181

I warrant you, is as red as any rose, in good truth, la! ii 4 28

In very truth, sir, I had as lief be hanged, sir, as go iii 2 237

If truth and upright innocency fail me, I'll to the king v 2 39

Let King Cophetua know the truth thereof v 3 106

I speak the truth: When Pistol lies, do this v 3 123

Pistol speaks nought but truth v 5 40

Whose right Suits not in native colours with the truth *Hen. V.* i 2 17

With some shows of truth, Though, in pure truth, it was corrupt and naught i 2 72

Though the truth of it stands off as gross As black and white ii 2 103

In good truth, the poet makes a most excellent description of it [Fortune] iii 6 39

Thou art framed of the firm truth of valour iv 3 14

Yes, verily and in truth, you shall take it v 1 64

What means this silence? Dare no man answer in a case of truth? *1 Hen. VI.* ii 4 2

Then say at once if I maintain'd the truth ii 4 5

The truth appears so naked on my side That any purblind eye may find it out ii 4 20

If he suppose that I have pleaded truth ii 4 29

No coward nor no flatterer, But dare maintain the party of the truth ii 4 32

Then for the truth and plainness of the case, I pluck this ii 4 46

Pale they look with fear, as witnessing The truth on our side ii 4 64

Long since we were resolved of your truth, Your faithful service iii 4 20

To say the truth, this fact was infamous And ill beseeming iv 1 30

Stubbornly he did repugn the truth About a certain question in the law iv 1 94

To say the truth, it is your policy To save your subjects from such massacre v 4 159

Father, the duke hath told the truth *2 Hen. VI.* ii 2 28

God in justice hath reveal'd to us The truth and innocence of this poor fellow ii 3 106

I say no more than truth, so help me God! iii 1 120

In thy face I see The map of honour, truth, and loyalty iii 1 203

And, to speak truth, thou deservest no less iv 3 11

To conclude with truth, Their weapons like to lightning came and went *3 Hen. VI.* ii 1 128

All dissembling set aside, Tell me for truth the measure of his love iii 3 120

With my talk and tears, Both full of truth iii 3 159

If secret powers Suggest but truth to my divining thoughts iv 6 69

In sign of truth, I kiss your highness' hand iv 8 26

And thus I seal my truth, and bid adieu iv 8 29

To say the truth, so Judas kiss'd his master, And cried 'all hail!' v 7 33

O wonderful, when devils tell the truth! *Richard III.* i 2 73

Cannot a plain man live and think no harm, But thus his simple truth must be abused? i 3 52

Truth should live from age to age, As 'twere retail'd to all posterity iii 1 76

They, for their truth, might better wear their heads Than some that have accused them wear their hats iii 2 94

Truth. To-day shalt thou behold a subject die For truth, for duty, and for loyalty . . . . *Richard III.* iii 3 4
We see it, and will say it.—In saying so, you shall but say the truth . iii 7 238
He said the truth : and what said Surrey then? . . . . . v 3 273
Such as give Their money out of hope they may believe, May here find truth too . . . . *Hen. VIII.* Prol. 9
To rank our chosen truth with such a show As fool and fight is . . Prol. 18
On my soul, I'll speak but truth . . . . i 2 177
I am richer than my base accusers, That never knew what truth meant ii 1 105
But that slander, sir, Is found a truth now . . . . . ii 1 154
Have you limbs To bear that load of title?—No, in truth . . ii 3 39
I hold my most malicious foe, and think not At all a friend to truth . ii 4 84
How may he wound, And worthily, my falsehood ! yea, as much As you have done my truth . . . . ii 4 98
Out with it boldly : truth loves open dealing . . . . iii 1 39
Here are some will thank you, If you speak truth . . . iii 1 47
Forgetting, like a good man, your late censure Both of his truth and him iii 1 65
But how to make ye suddenly an answer, . . . In truth, I know not . iii 1 74
In the way of loyalty and truth . . . . iii 2 272
And spotless shall mine innocence arise, When the king knows my truth iii 2 302
And do justice For truth's sake and his conscience . . . . iii 2 397
Thou hast forced me, Out of thy honest truth, to play the woman . iii 2 430
Let all the ends thou aim'st at be thy country's, Thy God's, and truth's iii 2 448
Whom I most hated living, thou hast made me, With thy religious truth and modesty, Now in his ashes honour . . . . . iv 2 74
Thy truth and thy integrity is rooted In us, thy friend . . . v 1 114
The good I stand on is my truth and honesty . . . . . v 1 122
Not ever The justice and the truth o' the question carries The due o' the verdict with it . . . . v 1 130
You are a sectary, That's the plain truth . . . . . . v 3 71
The words I utter Let none think flattery, for they'll find 'em truth . v 5 17
Truth shall nurse her, Holy and heavenly thoughts still counsel her . v 5 29
Peace, plenty, love, truth, terror, That were the servants to this chosen infant . . . . v 5 48
I speak no more than truth.—Thou dost not speak so much *Tr. and Cr.* i 1 64
To say truth, brown and not brown.—To say the truth, true and not true i 2 104
I'll prove this truth with my three drops of blood . . . . i 3 301
Hector's opinion Is this in way of truth . . . . . . ii 2 189
That shall not serve your turn ; that shall it not, in truth, la . iii 1 82
What envy can say worst shall be a mock for his truth, and what truth can speak truest not truer than Troilus . . . . . iii 2 105
That my integrity and truth to you Might be affronted with the match and weight Of such a winnow'd purity in love . . . . iii 2 172
I am as true as truth's simplicity And simpler than the infancy of truth iii 2 177
True swains in love shall in the world to come Approve their truths by Troilus . . . . iii 2 181
Truth tired with iteration, As true as steel, as plantage to the moon . iii 2 183
After all comparisons of truth, As truth's authentic author to be cited iii 2 187
If I be false, or swerve a hair from truth, When time is old . . iii 2 191
Is it true that I must go from Troy?—A hateful truth . . . iv 4 33
Whiles others fish with craft for great opinion, I with great truth catch mere simplicity ; Whilst some with cunning gild their copper crowns, With truth and plainness I do wear mine bare . . . iv 4 106
Fear not my truth : the moral of my wit Is 'plain and true' . . iv 4 109
You part in anger.—Doth that grieve thee? O wither'd truth ! . v 2 46
But if I tell how these two did co-act, Shall I not lie in publishing a truth? . . . . v 2 119
In truth, la, go with me ; and I'll tell you excellent news . *Coriolanus* i 3 100
Though thou speak'st truth, Methinks thou speak'st not well . . i 6 13
Let him alone ; He did inform the truth . . . . . . i 6 42
And mountainous error be too highly heapt For truth to o'er-peer . ii 3 128
Though but bastards and syllables Of no allowance to your bosom's truth iii 2 57
I will not do't, Lest I surcease to honour mine own truth . . iii 2 121
Insisting on the old prerogative And power i' the truth o' the cause . iii 3 18
And so did I ; and, to say the truth, so did very many of us . . iv 6 143
I, Even in theirs and in the commons' ears, Will vouch the truth of it . v 6 5
I raised him, and I pawn'd Mine honour for his truth . . . v 6 22
That we may know the traitors and the truth ! . . . *T. Andron.* iv 1 76
My scars can witness . . . That my report is just and full of truth . v 3 115
Now you have heard the truth, what say you, Romans? . . . v 3 128
To say truth, Verona brags of him . . . . . *Rom. and Jul.* i 5 69
In truth, fair Montague, I am too fond . . . . . . ii 2 98
This is the truth, or let Benvolio die . . . . . . iii 1 180
That is no slander, sir, which is a truth . . . . . . iv 1 33
If I may trust the flattering truth of sleep, My dreams presage some joyful news at hand . . . . v 1 1
Peace, justice, truth, Domestic awe, night-rest . . *T. of Athens* iv 1 16
Ye've heard that I have gold ; I am sure you have : speak truth . v 1 80
To speak truth of Cæsar, I have not known when his affections sway'd More than his reason . . . . *J. Cæsar* ii 1 19
To be afeard to tell graybeards the truth . . . . . ii 2 67
Now, as you are a Roman, tell me true.—Then like a Roman bear the truth iv 3 188
I' the name of truth, Are ye fantastical? . . . . . . *Macbeth* i 3 52
Oftentimes, to win us to our harm, The instruments of darkness tell us truths . . . . i 3 124
Two truths are told, As happy prologues to the swelling act . . i 3 127
Why hath it given me earnest of success, Commencing in a truth? . i 3 133
I dreamt last night of the three weird sisters: To you they have show'd some truth . . . . ii 1 21
If there come truth from them—As upon thee, Macbeth, their speeches shine . . . . iii 1 6
Reconciled my thoughts To thy good truth and honour . . . iv 3 117
And delight No less in truth than life . . . . . . iv 3 130
I have two nights watched with you, but can perceive no truth in your report . . . . v 1 2
To doubt the equivocation of the fiend That lies like truth . . v 5 44
And of the truth herein This present object made probation *Hamlet* i 1 155
What is between you? give me up the truth . . . . . i 3 98
Your bait of falsehood takes this carp of truth . . . . ii 1 63
Doubt truth to be a liar ; But never doubt I love . . . . ii 2 118
If circumstances lead me, I will find Where truth is hid . . ii 2 158
Will you ha' the truth on't? . . . . v 1 26
Let it be so ; thy truth, then, be thy dower . . . . *Lear* i 1 110
Truth's a dog must to kennel ; he must be whipped out . . . i 4 124
He cannot flatter, he, An honest mind and plain, he must speak truth ! ii 2 105
Be simple answerer, for we know the truth . . . . . iii 7 43
All my reports go with the modest truth ; Nor more nor clipp'd, but so iv 7 5
Tell me—but truly—but then speak the truth . . . . . v 1 8
I will maintain My truth and honour firmly . . . . . v 3 101
Go forth, And give us truth who 'tis that is arrived . . *Othello* ii 1 58
Truth. If partially affined, or leagued in office, Thou dost deliver more or less than truth, Thou art no soldier . . . . *Othello* ii 3 219
Yet, I persuade myself, to speak the truth Shall nothing wrong him . ii 3 223
Strong circumstances, Which lead directly to the door of truth . . iii 3 407
You charge me most unjustly.—With nought but truth . . . iv 2 187
Send for him hither ; Let him confess a truth . . . . . v 2 68
She said so : I must needs report the truth . . . . . v 2 128
Nay, stare not, masters : it is true, indeed.—'Tis a strange truth . v 2 188
Such full license as both truth and malice Have power to utter *A. and C.* i 2 112
Speak no more.—That truth should be silent I had almost forgot . ii 2 109
Truths would be tales, Where now half tales be truths . . . ii 2 136
She sent you word she was dead ; But, fearing since how it might work, hath sent Me to proclaim the truth . . . . . . iv 14 126
Speak the truth, Seleucus.—Madam, I had rather seal my lips . v 2 144
Do here pronounce, By the very truth of it, I care not for you *Cymbeline* ii 3 113
My circumstances, Being so near the truth as I will make them, Must first induce you to believe . . . . ii 4 62
Let there be no honour Where there is beauty ; truth, where semblance ; love, Where there's another man . . . . . . ii 4 109
Disloyal ! No : She's punish'd for her truth . . . . . iii 2 7
How ! that I should murder her? Upon the love and truth and vows which I Have made to thy command? . . . . . . iii 2 12
Briefly die their joys That place them on the truth of girls and boys . v 5 107
Bitter torture shall Winnow the truth from falsehood . . . v 5 134
Time of both this truth shall ne'er convince . . . *Pericles* i 2 123
Thou seem'st a palace For the crown'd Truth to dwell in . . . v 1 123
For truth can never be confirm'd enough, Though doubts did ever sleep v 1 203
A figure of truth, of faith, of loyalty . . . . . v 3 Gower 92
Truth is. The truth is, she and I, long since contracted, Are now so sure *Mer. Wives* v 5 236
The very truth is that the Jew, having done me wrong, doth cause me, as my father, being, I hope, an old man, shall frutify unto you *Mer. of Venice* ii 2 140
Well, the truth is, Sir John, you live in great infamy . 2 *Hen. IV.* i 2 155
The truth is, I am only old in judgement and understanding . . i 2 214
The truth is, poverty hath distracted her . . . . . . ii 1 116
Truth is, that Fulvia, To have me out of Egypt, made wars here *A. and C.* ii 2 94
Try. Bring her to try with main-course . . . . . . *Tempest* i 1 38
Some to the wars, to try their fortune there ; Some to discover islands *T. G. of Ver.* i 3 8
I will try thee. Tell me this : who begot thee? . . . . iii 1 293
This proves that thou canst not read.—Come, fool, come ; try me in thy paper . . . . iii 1 299
I will lay a plot to try that . . . . *Mer. Wives* iii 3 202
We'll try that ; for I'll appoint my men to carry the basket again . iv 2 96
The jury, passing on the prisoner's life, May in the sworn twelve have a thief or two Guiltier than him they try . . . *Meas. for Meas.* ii 1 21
I'll teach you how you shall arraign your conscience, And try your penitence . . . . ii 3 22
And desired her To try her gracious fortune . . . . . v 1 76
Try all the friends thou hast in Ephesus . . . *Com. of Errors* i 1 153
Well, I will marry one day, but to try . . . . . . ii 1 42
That's a question : how shall we try it?—We'll draw cuts . . v 1 421
As time shall try : 'In time the savage bull doth bear the yoke' *Much Ado* i 1 262
To try whose right, Of thine or mine, is most in Helena *M. N. Dream* iii 2 336
Follow my voice : we'll try nc manhood here . . . . . iii 2 412
Go forth ; Try what my credit can in Venice do . . *Mer. of Venice* i 1 180
I pray you, lead me to the caskets To try my fortune . . . ii 1 24
I will try confusions with him . . . . ii 2 39
Hath a disposition to come in disguised against me to try a fall *As Y. L. It* i 1 132
I come but in, as others do, to try with him the strength of my youth . i 2 181
You shall try but one fall . . . . i 2 216
Hem them away.—I would try, if I could cry 'hem' and have him . i 3 19
You will try in time, in despite of a fall . . . . . . i 3 24
Time is the old justice that examines all such offenders, and let Time try iv 1 204
I'll try how you can sol, fa, and sing it . . . . *T. of Shrew* i 2 17
I am a gentleman.—That I'll try . . . . ii 1 220
If he were living, I would try him yet . . . . *All's Well* i 2 72
Would your honour But give me leave to try success . . . i 3 253
What I can do can do no hurt to try . . . . . . ii 1 137
Thy physic I will try, That ministers thine own death if I die . . ii 1 188
I would I knew in what particular action to try him . . . iii 6 19
I know not how it tastes ; though it be dish'd For me to try how *W. Tale* iii 2 74
I, that please some, try all, both joy and terror Of good and bad . iv 1 1
Give me the lie, do, and try whether I am not now a gentleman born . v 2 144
The day shall not be up so soon as I, To try the fair adventure of to-morrow . . . . *K. John* v 5 22
Mine honour let me try ; In that I live and for that will I die *Richard II.* i 1 184
Now shall he try his friends that flatter'd him . . . . . ii 2 85
Here do I throw down this, If he may be repeal'd, to try his honour . iv 1 85
Try fortune with him in a single fight . . . . 1 *Hen. IV.* v 1 100
Let the end try the man . . . . 2 *Hen. IV.* ii 2 50
But, for all our loves, First let them try themselves . . . . ii 3 56
You knew I was at your back, and spoke it on purpose to try my patience . . . . ii 4 334
We ready are to try our fortunes To the last man . . . . iv 2 43
I put it on my head, To try with it, as with an enemy . . . iv 5 167
If it come to the arbitrement of swords, can try it out . . *Hen. V.* iv 1 169
To try her skill, Reignier, stand thou as Dauphin in my place 1 *Hen. VI.* i 2 60
My courage try by combat, if thou darest . . . . . . i 2 89
Presently we'll try : come, let's away . . . . . . i 2 149
We'll try what these dastard Frenchmen dare . . . . . i 4 111
Your lordship takes us then for fools, To try if that our own be ours or no . . . . iii 2 63
Unchain your spirits now with spelling charms And try if they can gain your liberty . . . . v 3 32
Or one that, at a triumph having vow'd To try his strength . . . v 5 32
My Lord of York, try what your fortune is . . . 2 *Hen. VI.* iii 1 309
Try your hap against the Irishmen . . . . iii 1 314
Say we intend to try his grace to-day, If he be guilty, as 'tis published . iii 2 16
Give us leave : I'll try this widow's wit . . . 3 *Hen. VI.* iii 2 33
Now do I play the touch, To try if thou be current gold indeed *Rich. III.* iv 2 9
I gave ye Power as he was a counsellor to try him, Not as a groom *Hen. VIII.* v 3 143
There's some of ye, I see, More out of malice than integrity, Would try him to the utmost, had ye mean. . . . . v 3 146
You cannot shun Yourself.—Let me go and try . . . *Troi. and Cres.* iii 2 154
Come, try upon yourselves what you have seen me . . . *Coriolanus* iii 1 225
I'll try whether my old wit be in request With those that have but little ii 1 251
Defying Those whose great power must try him . . . . . iii 3 80

Try. Your Moor and you Are singled forth to try experiments *T. Andron.* ii 3 69
I'll try if they can lick their fingers.—How canst thou try them so? *Rom. and Jul.* iv 2 4
And try the argument of hearts by borrowing . *T. of Athens* ii 2 187
I account them blessings; for by these Shall I try friends . . ii 2 192
I think this honourable lord did but try us this other day . . iii 6 3
This breaking of his has been but a try for his friends . . v 1 11
There shall I try, In my oration, how the people take The cruel issue of these bloody men . . . . . . *J. Cæsar* iii 1 292
And, Romans, yet ere night We shall try fortune in a second fight . v 3 110
And thou opposed, being of no woman born, Yet I will try the last *Macb.* v 8 32
How may we try it further? . . . . . . *Hamlet* ii 2 159
We will try it.—But, look, where sadly the poor wretch comes reading ii 2 167
Who in want a hollow friend doth try, Directly seasons him his enemy iii 2 218
What then? what rests? Try what repentance can: what can it not? . iii 3 65
And, like the famous ape, To try conclusions, in the basket creep . iii 4 195
Fight for a plot Whereon the numbers cannot try the cause . . iv 4 63
Ise try whether your costard or my ballow be the harder . . *Lear* iv 6 246
Had it pleased heaven To try me with affliction . . . *Othello* iv 2 48
And what may follow, To try a larger fortune . . . *Ant. and Cleo.* ii 6 34
I'll try you on the shore.—And shall, sir: give's your hand . . ii 7 133
To try thy eloquence, now 'tis time: dispatch; From Antony win Cleopatra . . . . iii 12 26
Try thy cunning, Thyreus; Make thine own edict for thy pains . . iii 12 31
I will try the forces Of these thy compounds . . . *Cymbeline* i 5 18
To try the vigour of them and apply Allayments to their act . . i 5 21
I have adventured To try your taking of a false report . . . i 6 173
If you can penetrate her with your fingering, so; we'll try with tongue ii 3 16
Try many, all good, serve truly, never Find such another master . iv 2 373
Tub. She hath eaten up all her beef, and she is herself in the tub *Meas. for Meas.* iii 2 59
Make use of thy salt hours: season the slaves For tubs and baths *T. of A.* iv 3 86
That satiate yet unsatisfied desire, that tub Both fill'd and running *Cymb.* i 6 48
Tubal, a wealthy Hebrew of my tribe, Will furnish me . *Mer. of Venice* i 3 58
How now, Tubal! what news from Genoa? . . . . . iii 1 83
I thank thee, good Tubal: good news, good news! ha, ha! where? in Genoa? . . . . iii 1 111
Thou torturest me, Tubal: it was my turquoise . . . . iii 1 126
Go, Tubal, fee me an officer; bespeak him a fortnight before . . iii 1 131
Go, go, Tubal, and meet me at our synagogue; go, good Tubal; at our synagogue, Tubal . . . . iii 1 134
I have heard him swear To Tubal and to Chus, his countrymen . . iii 2 287
Tub-fast. Bring down rose-cheeked youth To the tub-fast *T. of Athens* iv 3 87
Tuck. Dismount thy tuck, be yare in thy preparation . *T. Night* iii 4 244
Tucket. Let the trumpets sound The tucket sonance . . *Hen. V.* iv 2 35
Tuesday. But Tuesday night last gone in's garden-house He knew me as a wife . . . . *Meas. for Meas.* v 1 229
He swore a thing to me on Monday night, which he forswore on Tuesday morning . . . . *Much Ado* v 1 170
As a pancake for Shrove Tuesday, a morris for May-day . . *All's Well* ii 2 25
A purse of gold most resolutely snatched on Monday night and most dissolutely spent on Tuesday morning . . . *1 Hen. IV.* i 2 40
Whom I sent On Tuesday last to listen after news . . . *2 Hen. IV.* i 1 29
On Tuesday last, A falcon, towering in her pride of place, Was by a mousing owl hawk'd at and kill'd . . . . *Macbeth* ii 4 11
Why, then, to-morrow night; or Tuesday morn; On Tuesday noon *Oth.* iii 3 60
Tuft. Write In emerald tufts, flowers purple, blue, and white *Mer. Wives* v 5 74
If you will know my house, 'Tis at the tuft of olives here *As Y. Like It* iii 5 75
Behind the tuft of pines I met them . . . . *W. Tale* ii 1 34
There stands the castle, by yon tuft of trees . . *Richard II.* ii 3 53
Tug. Let myself and fortune Tug for the time to come . *W. Tale* iv 4 508
And England now is left To tug and scamble . . . *K. John* iv 3 146
Beware your beard; I mean to tug it and to cuff you soundly *1 Hen. VI.* i 3 48
Tug him away: being whipp'd, Bring him again . *Ant. and Cleo.* iii 13 102
Tugged. As one that grasp'd And tugg'd for life . . *2 Hen. VI.* iii 2 173
So weary with disasters, tugg'd with fortune . . . *Macbeth* iii 1 112
Tugging. Both tugging to be victors, breast to breast . *3 Hen. VI.* ii 5 11
Tuition. So I commit you— To the tuition of God . . . *Much Ado* i 1 283
Tullus. Thou Shalt see me once more strike at Tullus' face *Coriolanus* i 1 244
Within these three hours, Tullus, Alone I fought in your Corioli walls, And made what work I pleased . . . . i 8 7
If, Tullus, Not yet thou knowest me, and, seeing me, dost not Think me for the man I am, necessity Commands me name myself . . iv 5 60
O Tullus,— Thou hast done a deed whereat valour will weep . . v 6 133
Tully. A Roman sworder and banditto slave Murder'd sweet Tully *2 Hen. VI.* iv 1 136
Cornelia never with more care Read to her sons than she hath read to thee Sweet poetry and Tully's Orator . . . *T. Andron.* iv 1 14
Tumble. With that, they all did tumble on the ground . *L. L. Lost* v 2 115
Hammering treachery, To tumble down thy husband and thyself *2 Hen. VI.* i 2 48
Like a drunken sailor on a mast, Ready, with every nod, to tumble down Into the fatal bowels of the deep . . . *Richard III.* iii 4 102
As many coxcombs As you threw caps up will he tumble down *Coriol.* iv 6 135
Tumble me into some loathsome pit . . . . *T. Andron.* ii 3 176
Though the treasure Of nature's germens tumble all together *Macbeth* iv 1 59
Let us grant, it is not Amiss to tumble on the bed of Ptolemy *A. and C.* i 4 17
As to a whale; a' plays and tumbles, driving the poor fry before him *Pericles* ii 1 34
Tumbled. As a little snow, tumbled about, Anon becomes a mountain *K. John* iii 4 176
Now Phaëthon hath tumbled from his car, And made an evening at the noontide prick . . . . *3 Hen. VI.* i 4 33
Like to a bowl upon a subtle ground, I have tumbled past the throw *Coriolanus* v 2 21
Quoth she, before you tumbled me, You promised me to wed *Hamlet* iv 5 63
Said not I as much when I saw the porpus how he bounced and tumbled? . . . . *Pericles* ii 1 27
Tumbler. And wear his colours like a tumbler's hoop! . *L. L. Lost* iii 1 190
Tumbling. Like hedgehogs which Lie tumbling in my barefoot way *Tempest* ii 2 11
While we lie tumbling in the hay . . . . *W. Tale* iv 3 12
Overboard, Into the tumbling billows of the main . . *Richard III.* i 4 20
Tumbling-trick. Let them play it. Is not a comonty a Christmas gambold or a tumbling-trick? . . . . . *T. of Shrew* Ind. 2 140
Tumult. Hostility and civil tumult reigns Between my conscience and my cousin's death . . . . *K. John* iv 2 247
Here's a goodly tumult! I'll forswear keeping house . *2 Hen. IV.* ii 4 219
What stir is this? what tumult's in the heavens? . . *1 Hen. VI.* i 4 98
What tumult's this?—An uproar, I dare warrant . . . iii 1 74
For what hath broach'd this tumult but thy pride? . . *3 Hen. VI.* ii 2 159
Tumultuous wars Shall kin with kin and kind with kind confound *Richard II.* iv 1 140
Nought rests for me in this tumultuous strife . . . *1 Hen. VI.* i 3 70
Why, what tumultuous clamour have we here? . . *2 Hen. VI.* iii 2 239
Now here a period of tumultuous broils . . . . *3 Hen. VI.* v 5 1
Tun. This whale, with so many tuns of oil in his belly . *Mer. Wives* ii 1 65
An old fat man; a tun of man is thy companion . . *1 Hen. IV.* ii 4 493
He therefore sends you, meeter for your spirit, This tun of treasure *Hen. V.* i 2 255
Drawn tuns of blood out of thy country's breast . . *Coriolanus* iv 5 105
Tun-dish. For filling a bottle with a tun-dish . . *Meas. for Meas.* iii 2 182
Tune. Set all hearts i' the state To what tune pleased his ear . *Tempest* i 2 85
This is a very scurvy tune to sing at a man's funeral . . . ii 2 46
This is a scurvy tune too: but here's my comfort . . . . ii 2 57
That's not the tune.—What is this same?—This is the tune of our catch, played by the picture of Nobody . . . . . iii 2 133
Some love of yours hath writ to you in rhyme.—That I might sing it, madam, to a tune . . . . *T. G. of Ver.* i 2 80
Sing it to the tune of 'Light o' love.'—It is too heavy for so light a tune i 2 83
Keep tune there still, so you will sing it out: And yet methinks I do not like this tune . . . . i 2 90
To their instruments Tune a deploring dump . . . . iii 2 85
Now, gentlemen, Let's tune, and to it lustily awhile . . . iv 2 25
He plays false, father.—How? out of tune on the strings? . . . iv 2 60
And to the nightingale's complaining notes Tune my distresses . . v 4 6
No more adhere and keep place together than the Hundredth Psalm to the tune of 'Green Sleeves' . . . . . *Mer. Wives* ii 1 64
Let it thunder to the tune of Green Sleeves, hail kissing-comfits . v 5 21
What sayest thou to this tune, matter, and method? *Meas. for Meas.* iii 2 50
Do you speak in the sick tune?—I am out of all other tune *Much Ado* iii 4 42
It would neither serve for the writing nor the tune . . *L. L. Lost* i 2 119
To jig off a tune at the tongue's end, canary to it with your feet . iii 1 12
Keep not too long in one tune, but a snip and away . . . iii 1 22
And profound Solomon to tune a jig, And Nestor play at push-pin . iv 3 168
I would sing my song without a burden: thou bringest me out of tune *As Y. Like It* iii 2 262
'Tis no matter how it be in tune, so it make noise enough . . . iv 2 9
Both in a tune, like two gipsies on a horse . . . . . v 3 16
You'll leave his lecture when I am in tune?—That will be never: tune your instrument . . . . *T. of Shrew* iii 1 24
My instrument's in tune.—Let's hear. O fie! the treble jars . . iii 1 38
Madam, 'tis now in tune.—All but the base.—The base is right . . iii 1 46
You dare not.—Out o' tune, sir: ye lie . . . . *T. Night* ii 3 122
Seek him out, and play the tune the while . . . . . ii 4 14
How dost thou like this tune?—It gives a very echo to the seat Where Love is throned . . . . ii 4 20
If it be aught to the old tune, my lord . . . . . . v 1 111
He sings several tunes faster than you'll tell money . . *W. Tale* iv 4 184
He utters them as he had eaten ballads and all men's ears grew to his tunes . . . . iv 4 186
Forewarn him that he use no scurrilous words in's tunes . . . iv 4 216
Here's one to a very doleful tune . . . . iv 4 265
This is a passing merry one and goes to the tune of 'Two maids wooing a man' . . . . iv 4 295
'Tis in three parts.—We had the tune on't a month ago . . . iv 4 300
He would not stir his pettitoes till he had both tune and words . iv 4 619
That knows no touch to tune the harmony . . . *Richard II.* i 3 165
An I have not ballads made on you all and sung to filthy tunes *1 Hen. IV.* ii 2 49
And sung those tunes to the over-scutched huswives that he heard the carmen whistle . . . . *2 Hen. IV.* iii 2 340
A raven's note, Whose dismal tune bereft my vital powers *2 Hen. VI.* iii 2 41
Such a noise arose As the shrouds make at sea in a stiff tempest, As loud, and to as many tunes . . . . . . *Hen. VIII.* iv 1 73
But he is not in this tune, is he?—No, but he's out o' tune thus *Troi. and Cres.* iii 3 301
If it may stand with the tune of your voices that I may be consul *Coriol.* ii 3 92
It is the lark that sings so out of tune, Straining harsh discords *Rom. and Jul.* iii 5 27
This is a sleepy tune. O murderous slumber! . . . *J. Cæsar* iv 3 267
Went it not so?—To the selfsame tune and words . . . *Macbeth* i 3 88
This tune goes manly. Come, go we to the king; our power is ready . iv 3 235
Now see that noble and most sovereign reason, Like sweet bells jangled, out of tune and harsh . . . . . . *Hamlet* iii 1 166
She chanted snatches of old tunes; As one incapable of her own distress . . . . iv 7 178
Only got the tune of the time and outward habit of encounter . . v 2 198
Who sometime, in his better tune, remembers . . . *Lear* iv 3 41
My advocation is not now in tune . . . . . *Othello* iii 4 123
Then murder's out of tune, And sweet revenge grows harsh . . v 2 115
The oars were silver, Which to the tune of flutes kept stroke *A. and C.* ii 2 200
And scald rhymers Ballad us out o' tune . . . . . v 2 216
Come on; tune: if you can penetrate her with your fingering, so *Cymb.* ii 3 15
For notes of sorrow out of tune are worse Than priests and fanes that lie iv 2 241
Breathe not where princes are.—The tune of Imogen! . . . v 5 238
The fingers of the powers above do tune The harmony of this peace . v 5 466
Yet hope, succeeding from so fair a tree As your fair self, doth tune us otherwise . . . . *Pericles* i 1 115
Tuneable. More tuneable than lark to shepherd's ear . *M. N. Dream* i 1 184
A cry more tuneable Was never holla'd to, nor cheer'd with horn . iv 1 129
Who had even tuned his bounty to sing happiness to him *All's Well* iv 3 12
With an accent tuned in selfsame key Retorts to chiding fortune *Troi. and Cres.* i 3 53
Some joy too fine, Too subtle-potent, tuned too sharp in sweetness . iii 2 25
O, you are well tuned now! But I'll set down the pegs that make this music, As honest as I am . . . . . . *Othello* ii 1 201
Tuned. His lecture will be done ere you have tuned . *T. of Shrew* iii 1 23
His voice was propertied As all the tuned spheres . *Ant. and Cleo.* v 2 84
Tuners. The pox of such antic, lisping, affecting fantasticoes; these new tuners of accents! . . . . . . *Rom. and Jul.* ii 4 30
Tunis. In Afric, at the marriage of the king's fair daughter Claribel to the King of Tunis . . . . *Tempest* ii 1 71
Tunis was never graced before with such a paragon to their queen . ii 1 74
She was of Carthage, not of Tunis.—This Tunis, sir, was Carthage . ii 1 82
Our garments seem now as fresh as when we were at Tunis at the marriage ii 1 97
Claribel.—She that is queen of Tunis; she that dwells Ten leagues beyond man's life . . . . ii 1 246
Tis true, my brother's daughter's queen of Tunis; So is she heir of Naples . . . . ii 1 255
How shall that Claribel Measure us back to Naples? Keep in Tunis . ii 1 259

Tunis. In one voyage Did Claribel her husband find at Tunis . *Tempest* v 1 209
Tupping. An old black ram Is tupping your white ewe . . *Othello* i 1 89
Turban. The gates of monarchs Are arch'd so high that giants may jet through And keep their impious turbans on . . . *Cymbeline* iii 3 6
Turbaned. A malignant and a turban'd Turk Beat a Venetian *Othello* v 2 353
Turbulence. I have dream'd Of bloody turbulence . *Troi. and Cres.* v 3 11
Turbulent. Who once a day with his embossed froth The turbulent surge shall cover . . . *T. of Athens* v 1 221
With turbulent and dangerous lunacy . . . *Hamlet* iii 1 4
'T has been a turbulent and stormy night . . . *Pericles* iii 2 4
Turd. If dere be one or two, I shall make-a the turd . *Mer. Wives* iii 3 253
Turf. A good lustre of conceit in a turf of earth . . *L. L. Lost* iv 2 90
One turf shall serve as pillow for us both . . . *M. N. Dream* ii 2 41
Who you saw sitting by me on the turf . . . *As Y. Like It* iii 4 52
A good soft pillow for that good white head Were better than a churlish turf of France.—Not so, my liege . . . *Hen. V.* iv 1 15
At his head a grass-green turf, At his heels a stone . . *Hamlet* iv 5 31
Close by the battle, ditch'd, and wall'd with turf . . *Cymbeline* v 3 14
Turfy mountains, where live nibbling sheep . . . *Tempest* iv 1 62
Turk. Tester I'll have in pouch when thou shalt lack, Base Phrygian Turk! . . . *Mer. Wives* i 3 97
An you be not turned Turk, there's no more sailing by the star *M. Ado* iii 4 57
Turks and Tartars, never train'd To offices of tender courtesy *M. of V.* iv 1 32
She defies me, Like Turk to Christian . . *As Y. Like It* iv 3 33
I would send them to the Turk, to make eunuchs of . . *All's Well* ii 3 94
Streaming the ensign of the Christian cross Against black pagans, Turks, and Saracens . . . *Richard II.* iv 1 95
Peace shall go sleep with Turks and infidels . . . iv 1 139
Turk Gregory never did such deeds in arms as I have done this day *1 Hen. IV.* v 3 46
Duer paid to the hearer than the Turk's tribute . *2 Hen. IV.* iii 2 331
That shall go to Constantinople and take the Turk by the beard *Hen. V.* v 2 222
Here is a silly stately style indeed! The Turk, that two and fifty kingdoms hath, Writes not so tedious a style as this . *1 Hen. VI.* iv 7 73
What, think you we are Turks or infidels? . . *Richard III.* iii 5 41
Nose of Turk and Tartar's lips, Finger of birth-strangled babe *Macbeth* iv 1 29
If the rest of my fortunes turn Turk with me . . . *Hamlet* iii 2 287
In woman out-paramoured the Turk . . . *Lear* iii 4 94
When we consider The importancy of Cyprus to the Turk, And let ourselves again but understand, That as it more concerns the Turk than Rhodes, So may he with more facile question bear it . *Othello* i 3 20
We must not think the Turk is so unskilful To leave that latest which concerns him first . . . i 3 27
Let the Turk of Cyprus us beguile; We lose it not, so long as we can smile . . . i 3 210
The Turk with a most mighty preparation makes for Cyprus . i 3 221
The desperate tempest hath so bang'd the Turks, That their designment halts . . . ii 1 21
Nay, it is true, or else I am a Turk . . . ii 1 115
Our wars are done, the Turks are drown'd . . . ii 1 204
Are we turn'd Turks, and to ourselves do that Which heaven hath forbid the Ottomites? . . . ii 3 170
In Aleppo once, Where a malignant and a turban'd Turk Beat a Venetian v 2 353
Turkey. Fine linen, Turkey cushions boss'd with pearl . *T. of Shrew* ii 1 355
The turkeys in my pannier are quite starved . *1 Hen. IV.* ii 1 29
Turkey-cock. Contemplation makes a rare turkey-cock of him *T. Night* ii 5 36
Here he comes, swelling like a turkey-cock.—'Tis no matter for his swellings nor his turkey-cocks . . . *Hen. V.* v 1 16
Turkish. Cover'd o'er with Turkish tapestry . . *Com. of Errors* iv 1 104
This is the English, not the Turkish court . . *2 Hen. IV.* v 2 47
Else our grave, Like Turkish mute, shall have a tongueless mouth *Hen. V.* i 2 232
They all confirm A Turkish fleet, and bearing up to Cyprus . *Othello* i 3 8
What's the business?—The Turkish preparation makes for Rhodes . i 3 14
If that the Turkish fleet Be not enshelter'd and embay'd, they are drown'd . . . ii 1 17
Though he speak of comfort Touching the Turkish loss, yet he looks sadly, And prays the Moor be safe . . . ii 1 32
Importing the mere perdition of the Turkish fleet . . . ii 2 4
Turlygod. Poor Turlygod! poor Tom! That's something yet . *Lear* ii 3 20
Turmoil. And there I'll rest, as after much turmoil A blessed soul doth in Elysium . . . *T. G. of Ver.* ii 7 37
Turmoiled. Who would live turmoiled in the court, And may enjoy such quiet walks as these? . . . *2 Hen. VI.* iv 10 18
Turn. Do not turn me about; my stomach is not constant . *Tempest* ii 2 119
I'll turn my mercy out o' doors and make a stock-fish of thee . . iii 2 78
A turn or two I'll walk, To still my beating mind . . . iv 1 162
I'll turn you out of my kingdom . . . iv 1 253
If you turn not, you will return the sooner . *T. G. of Ver.* ii 2 4
I now am full resolved to take a wife And turn her out to who will take her in . . . iii 1 77
A cloak as long as thine will serve the turn?—Ay, my good lord . iii 1 131
Why, any cloak will serve the turn, my lord . . . iii 1 134
Thou hast stayed so long that going will scarce serve the turn . iii 1 389
I have a sonnet that will serve the turn To give the onset . . iii 2 93
A slave, that still an end turns me to shame! . . . iv 4 67
I must turn away some of my followers . . . *Mer. Wives* i 3 4
I shall turn your head out of my door . . . i 4 131
If he should intend this voyage towards my wife, I would turn her loose to him . . . ii 1 189
I do not misdoubt my wife; but I would be loath to turn them together ii 1 193
As you have one eye upon my follies, as you hear them unfolded, turn another into the register of your own . . . ii 2 193
For he swears he'll turn me away . . . iii 3 32
I see I cannot get thy father's love; Therefore no more turn me to him iii 4 2
If he be chaste, the flame will back descend And turn him to no pain . v 5 90
Pinch him, and burn him, and turn him about . . . v 5 105
Will none but Herne the hunter serve your turn? . . . v 5 108
So every scope by the immoderate use Turns to restraint *Meas. for Meas.* i 2 132
Turn you the key, and know his business of him . . . i 4 8
Gentle my lord, turn back.—I will bethink me . . . ii 2 143
Hark how I'll bribe you: good my lord, turn back . . . ii 2 145
You will turn good husband now . . . iii 2 73
You weigh equally; a feather will turn the scale . . . iv 2 32
If you have occasion to use me for your own turn, you shall find me yare iv 2 60
For your kindness I owe you a good turn . . . iv 2 62
We in your motion turn and you may move us . *Com. of Errors* iii 2 24
She had transform'd me to a curtal dog and made me turn i' the wheel . iii 2 151
If any hour meet a sergeant, a' turns back for very fear . . iv 2 56
Hath he [Time] not reason to turn back an hour in a day? . . iv 2 62
I could find in my heart to stay here still and turn witch . . iv 4 160
Turn. I hope you have no intent to turn husband, have you? . *Much Ado* i 1 196
So turns she every man the wrong side out . . . iii 1 68
How giddily a' [fortune] turns about all the hot bloods . . iii 3 140
To turn all beauty into thoughts of harm . . . iv 1 108
But, tasting it, Their counsel turns to passion . . . v 1 23
I think he be angry indeed.—If he be, he knows how to turn his girdle v 1 142
This maid will not serve your turn, sir.—This maid will serve my turn *L. L. Lost* i 1 300
The first and second cause will not serve my turn . . . i 2 184
Assist me, some extemporal god of rhyme, for I am sure I shall turn sonnet . . . i 2 190
Every object that the one doth catch The other turns to a mirth-moving jest . . . ii 1 71
O, but for my love, day would turn to night! . . . iv 3 233
Her favour turns the fashion of the days . . . iv 3 262
Nor to their penn'd speech render we no grace, But while 'tis spoke each turn away her face . . . v 2 148
Let us confess and turn it to a jest . . . v 2 390
We will turn it finely off, sir; we will take some care . . v 2 511
Even that falsehood, in itself a sin, Thus purifies itself and turns to grace v 2 786
Turn melancholy forth to funerals . . . *M. N. Dream* i 1 15
And thence from Athens turn away our eyes, To seek new friends . i 1 218
And roar, and burn, Like horse, hound, hog, bear, fire, at every turn . iii 1 114
I have enough to serve mine own turn . . . iii 1 154
High Taurus' snow, Fann'd with the eastern wind, turns to a crow . iii 2 142
Counterfeit sad looks, Make mouths upon me when I turn my back . iii 2 238
Turns into yellow gold his salt green streams . . . iii 2 393
The poet's pen Turns them to shapes and gives to airy nothing A local habitation and a name . . . v 1 16
A mote will turn the balance . . . v 1 324
The Hebrew will turn Christian: he grows kind . *Mer. of Venice* i 3 180
The greater throw May turn by fortune from the weaker hand . ii 1 34
Turn up on your right hand at the next turning, but, at the next turning of all, on your left; marry, at the very next turning, turn of no hand, but turn down indirectly to the Jew's house . . . ii 2 42
A third cannot be match'd, unless the devil himself turn Jew . . iii 1 82
Turn you where your lady is And claim her with a loving kiss . iii 2 138
Where every something, being blent together, Turns to a wild of nothing iii 2 184
Nothing in the world Could turn so much the constitution Of any constant man . . . iii 2 249
And turn two mincing steps Into a manly stride . . . iii 4 67
Why, shall we turn to men?—Fie, what a question's that! . . iii 4 78
I think the best grace of wit will shortly turn into silence . . iii 5 49
If the scale do turn But in the estimation of a hair, Thou diest . iv 1 330
When I break that oath, let me turn monster . . *As Y. Like It* i 2 23
And turn his merry note Unto the sweet bird's throat . . ii 5 3
If it do come to pass That any man turn ass . . . ii 5 53
Turn thou no more To seek a living in our territory . . . iii 1 7
Do this expediently and turn him going . . . iii 1 18
Twice did he turn his back and purposed so . . . iv 3 128
Why then, to-morrow I cannot serve your turn for Rosalind? . . v 2 54
Fit for her turn, well read in poetry . . . *T. of Shrew* i 2 170
This I know, She is not for your turn, the more my grief . . ii 1 63
She's apt to learn and thankful for good turns . . . ii 1 166
Now, Kate, I am a husband for your turn . . . ii 1 274
Whate'er he be, It skills not much, we'll fit him to our turn . . iii 2 134
I spied An ancient angel coming down the hill, Will serve the turn . iv 2 62
He that is giddy thinks the world turns round . . . v 2 20
This young maid might do her A shrewd turn, if she pleased *All's Well* iii 5 71
I would the cutting of my garments would serve the turn . . iv 1 51
And writ to me this other day to turn him out o' the band . . iv 3 227
Love that comes too late . . . To the great sender turns a sour offence v 3 59
Till his brains turn o' the toe like a parish-top . . *T. Night* i 3 44
And bid him turn you out of doors . . . i 5 78
It cannot but turn him into a notable contempt . . . ii 5 224
Oft good turns Are shuffled off with such uncurrent pay . . iii 3 15
O, then my best blood turn To an infected jelly! . . *W. Tale* i 2 417
Turn then my freshest reputation to A savour that may strike the dullest nostril! . . . i 2 420
Great Apollo Turn all to the best! . . . iii 1 15
I turn my glass and give my scene such growing As you had slept between iv 1 16
Would sing her song and dance her turn . . . iv 4 58
Now were I happy, if His going I could frame to serve my turn . . iv 4 520
Who knows how that may turn back to my advancement? . . iv 4 867
Turn, good lady; Our Perdita is found . . . v 3 120
Then turn your forces from this paltry siege . . . *K. John* ii 1 54
Turn face to face and bloody point to point . . . ii 1 390
Turn thou the mouth of thy artillery, As we will ours, against these saucy walls . . . ii 1 403
Nay, rather turn this day out of the week, This day of shame . . iii 1 87
Thou shalt turn To ashes, ere our blood shall quench that fire . . iii 1 344
There end thy brave, and turn thy face in peace . . . v 2 159
I turn to thee, And mark my greeting well . . . *Richard II.* i 1 35
Let my sovereign turn away his face And bid his ears a little while be deaf i 1 111
I turn me from my country's light To dwell in solemn shades of endless night . . . i 3 176
I know my uncle York Hath power enough to serve our turn . . iii 2 90
Sweet love, I see, changing his property, Turns to the sourest and most deadly hate . . . iii 2 136
I will turn thy falsehood to thy heart, Where it was forged . . iv 1 39
If I turn mine eyes upon myself, I find myself a traitor with the rest . iv 1 247
The love of wicked men converts to fear; That fear to hate, and hate turns one or both To worthy danger . . . v 1 67
Give me leave that I may turn the key, That no man enter . . v 3 36
As good a deed as drink, to turn true man and to leave these rogues *1 Hen. IV.* ii 2 24
Was it for me to kill the heir-apparent? should I turn upon the true prince? . . . ii 4 297
'Tis the next way to turn tailor, or be red-breast teacher . . iii 1 264
Turns head against the lion's armed jaws . . . iii 2 102
Think how such an apprehension May turn the tide of fearful faction . iv 1 67
To turn and wind a fiery Pegasus And witch the world with noble horsemanship . . . iv 1 109
It pleased your majesty to turn your looks Of favour from myself . v 1 30
And wouldst thou turn our offers contrary? . . . v 5 4
But now the bishop Turns insurrection to religion . . *2 Hen. IV.* i 1 201
A good wit will make use of any thing: I will turn diseases to commodity i 2 278
Would turn their own perfection to abuse, To seem like him . . ii 3 27
He'll not swagger with a Barbary hen, if her feathers turn back in any show of resistance . . . ii 4 108

Turn. The weight of a hair will turn the scales between their avoirdupois 2 *Hen. IV.* ii 4 276
He will drive you out of your revenge and turn all to a merriment . ii 4 324
Now doth it turn and ebb back to the sea . . . . v 2 131
Turn him to any cause of policy, The Gordian knot of it he will unloose *Hen. V.* i 1 45
Your own reasons turn into your bosoms, As dogs upon their masters . ii 2 82
You see this chase is hotly follow'd, friends.—Turn head, and stop pursuit . . . . ii 4 69
Turn thee back, And tell thy king I do not seek him now . . iii 6 148
Turn the sands into eloquent tongues, and my horse is argument for them all . . . . iii 7 36
You may as well go about to turn the sun to ice with fanning in his face iv 1 212
They will pluck The gay new coats o'er the French soldiers' heads And turn them out of service . . . . iv 3 119
So did he turn and over Suffolk's neck He threw his wounded arm . iv 6 24
Well, bawd I'll turn, And something lean to cutpurse of quick hand . v 1 90
A black beard will turn white; a curled pate will grow bald . v 2 168
I see our wars Will turn unto a peaceful comic sport . . 1 *Hen. VI.* ii 2 45
Laughest thou, wretch? thy mirth shall turn to moan . . ii 3 44
Peevish boy.—Turn not thy scorns this way . . . ii 4 77
I'll turn my part thereof into thy throat . . . . ii 4 79
O, turn thy edged sword another way; Strike those that hurt . iii 3 52
Done like a Frenchman: turn, and turn again! . . . iii 3 85
No way canst thou turn thee for redress, But death doth front thee iv 2 25
Turn on the bloody hounds with heads of steel . . . iv 2 51
The stout Parisians do revolt And turn again unto the warlike French . v 2 3
Peace be amongst them, if they turn to us! . . . v 2 6
Will nothing turn your unrelenting hearts? . . . v 4 59
Dost thou turn away and hide thy face? I am no loathsome leper 2 *Hen. VI.* iii 2 74
Or turn our stern upon a dreadful rock . . . . iii 2 91
Like an overcharged gun, recoil, And turn the force of them upon thyself . . . . iii 2 332
With thy lips to stop my mouth; So shouldst thou either turn my flying soul, Or I should breathe it so into thy body . . iii 2 397
To dress the commonwealth, and turn it, and set a new nap upon it iv 2 6
Steel, if thou turn the edge, or cut not out the burly-boned clown . iv 10 59
All will revolt from me, and turn to him . . 3 *Hen. VI.* i 1 151
Turn this way, Henry, and regard them not . . . i 1 189
My followers to the eager foe Turn back and fly, like ships before the wind . . . . i 4 4
Once again cry 'Charge upon our foes!' But never once again turn back and fly . . . . ii 1 185
The smallest worm will turn being trodden on . . . ii 2 17
Then 'twas my turn to fly, and now 'tis thine.—You said so much before ii 2 105
Then none but I shall turn his jest to sorrow . . . iii 3 261
I defy thee, And to my brother turn my blushing cheeks . . v 1 99
Thy turn is next, and then the rest, Counting myself but bad till I be best . . . . v 6 90
First I'll turn yon fellow in his grave; And then return *Richard III.* i 2 261
O gentle villain, do not turn away! . . . . i 3 163
And turn you all your hatred now on me? . . . . i 3 190
Dallies with the wind and scorns the sun.—And turns the sun to shade i 3 266
Whenever Buckingham doth turn his hate On you or yours . . ii 1 32
Thou wilt die, by God's just ordinance, Ere from this war thou turn a conqueror . . . . iv 4 184
Thus doth he force the swords of wicked men To turn their own points on their masters' bosoms . . . . v 1 24
The mind growing once corrupt, They turn to vicious forms . *Hen. VIII.* i 2 117
That blind priest, like the eldest son of fortune, Turns what he list . ii 2 22
In God's name, Turn me away . . . . . ii 4 42
My drops of tears I'll turn to sparks of fire . . . ii 4 73
You turn the good we offer into envy.—Ye turn me into nothing . iii 1 113
Come, you and I must walk a turn together; I have news to tell you . v 1 93
By some that hate me—God turn their hearts! I never sought their malice . . . . v 2 15
Do my Lord of Canterbury A shrewd turn, and he is your friend for ever . . . . v 3 178
But sorrow, that is couch'd in seeming gladness, Is like that mirth fate turns to sudden sadness . . *Troi. and Cres.* i 1 40
We turn not back the silks upon the merchant, When we have soil'd them . . . . ii 2 69
Nay, that shall not serve your turn; that shall it not, in truth, la . iii 1 81
Yet that which seems the wound to kill, Doth turn oh! oh! to ha! ha! he! . . . . iii 1 133
Speculation turns not to itself, Till it hath travell'd and is mirror'd there Where it may see itself . . . . iii 3 109
To what form but that he is, should wit larded with malice and malice forced with wit turn him to? . . . . v 1 64
Look, how thy eye turns pale! Look, how thy wounds do bleed at many vents! . . . . v 3 81
Go, wind, to wind, there turn and change together . . . v 3 110
Turn thy false face, thou traitor, And pay thy life thou owest me! . v 6 6
Turn, slave, and fight.—What art thou? . . . . v 7 13
Hector's dead: There is a word will Priam turn to stone . . v 10 18
Turn thy solemness out o' door, and go along with us . *Coriolanus* i 3 120
O that you could turn your eyes toward the napes of your necks! . ii 1 42
I know not where to turn: O, welcome home: And welcome, general . ii 1 198
And by his rare example made the coward Turn terror into sport . ii 2 109
Wants not spirit To say he'll turn your current in a ditch . . iii 1 96
The which shall turn you to no further harm Than so much loss of time . . . . iii 1 284
Thus I turn my back: There is a world elsewhere . . . iii 3 134
O world, thy slippery turns! . . . . . iv 4 12
Speed thee straight, And make my misery serve thy turn . . iv 5 94
And turns up the white o' the eye to his discourse . . . iv 5 208
Some news is come That turns their countenances . . . iv 6 59
Assuage thy wrath, and turn the dregs of it upon this varlet here . v 2 83
He turns away: Down, ladies; let us shame him with our knees . v 3 168
Is she not then beholding to the man That brought her for this high good turn so far? . . . *T. Andron.* i 1 397
Why, then, it seems, some certain snatch or so Would serve your turns.—Ay, so the turn were served . . . . ii 1 96
There speak, and strike, brave boys, and take your turns . . ii 1 129
The milk thou suck'dst from her did turn to marble . . . ii 3 144
My hand will serve the turn: My youth can better spare my blood than you . . . . iii 1 165
Circle me about, That I may turn me to each one of you . . iii 1 278
See how busily she turns the leaves! What would she find? . . iv 1 45

Turn. I would we had a thousand Roman dames At such a bay, by turn to serve our lust . . . *T. Andron.* iv 2 42
All the water in the ocean Can never turn the swan's black legs to white . . . . iv 2 102
Speak him fair, And tarry with him till I turn again . . . v 2 141
Now is my turn to speak . . . . . v 3 119
I will back thee.—How! turn thy back and run? . . *Rom. and Jul.* i 1 41
Turn thee, Benvolio, look upon thy death . . . . i 1 74
Turn giddy, and be holp by backward turning . . . . i 2 48
When the devout religion of mine eye Maintains such falsehood, then turn tears to fires! . . . . i 2 94
More light, you knaves; and turn the tables up, And quench the fire . i 5 29
Let lips do what hands do; They pray, grant thou, lest faith turn to despair . . . . i 5 106
Turn back, dull earth, and find thy centre out . . . ii 1 2
Virtue itself turns vice, being misapplied . . . . ii 3 21
This alliance may so happy prove, To turn your households' rancour to pure love . . . . ii 3 92
Therefore turn and draw.—I do protest, I never injured thee. . . iii 1 70
Who, all as hot, turns deadly point to point . . . iii 1 165
Was stout Tybalt slain, And, as he fell, did Romeo turn and fly . . iii 1 179
The law that threaten'd death becomes thy friend And turns it to exile iii 3 140
Or my true heart with treacherous revolt Turn to another . . iv 1 59
All things that we ordained festival, Turn from their office to black funeral . . . . iv 5 85
My uses cry to me, I must serve my turn Out of mine own *T. of Athens* ii 1 20
Has friendship such a faint and milky heart, It turns in less than two nights? . . . . iii 1 58
Why should it thrive and turn to nutriment, When he is turn'd to poison? . . . . iii 1 61
I'll look you out a good turn . . . . . iii 2 67
Matrons, turn incontinent! Obedience fail in children! . . . iv 1 3
As we do turn our backs From our companion thrown into his grave . iv 2 8
'Tis most just That thou turn rascal . . . . iv 3 217
It almost turns my dangerous nature mild . . . . iv 3 499
I'll meet you at the turn . . . . . v 1 50
I turn the trouble of my countenance Merely upon myself . *J. Cæsar* i 2 38
You have no such mirrors as will turn Your hidden worthiness into your eye . . . . i 2 56
Lowliness is young ambition's ladder, Whereto the climber-upward turns his face; But when he once attains the upmost round, He then unto the ladder turns his back . . . . ii 1 23
If this be known, Cassius or Cæsar never shall turn back . . iii 1 21
And turn pre-ordinance and first decree Into the law of children . iii 1 38
Pluck but his name out of his heart, and turn him going . . iii 3 38
Turn him off, Like to the empty ass, to shake his ears, And graze in commons . . . . iv 1 25
If arguing make us sweat, The proof of it will turn to redder drops . v 1 49
Thy spirit walks abroad, and turns our swords In our own proper entrails . . . . v 3 95
Hold then my sword, and turn away thy face, While I do run upon it . v 5 47
Your pains Are register'd where every day I turn The leaf to read them *Macbeth* i 3 151
With an absolute 'Sir, not I,' The cloudy messenger turns me his back iii 6 41
Turn, hell-hound, turn!—Of all men else I have avoided thee . v 8 3
With this regard their currents turn awry . . . *Hamlet* iii 1 87
To desperation turn my trust and hope! . . . . iii 2 228
If the rest of my fortunes turn Turk with me . . . iii 2 287
But, O, what form of prayer Can serve my turn? . . . iii 3 52
Thy madness shall be paid with weight, Till our scale turn the beam . iv 5 157
Affliction, passion, hell itself, She turns to favour and to prettiness . iv 5 189
But they knew what they did; I am to do a good turn for them . iv 6 22
He does well to commend it himself; there are no tongues else for's turn . . . . v 2 192
Shall our abode Make with you by due turns . . . . *Lear* i 1 137
To turn thy hated back Upon our kingdom . . . . i 1 178
Turn all her mother's pains and benefits To laughter and contempt . i 4 308
I'ld turn it all To thy suggestion, plot, and damned practice . . ii 1 74
And turn their halcyon beaks With every gale and vary of their masters ii 2 84
Fortune, good night: smile once more; turn thy wheel! . . ii 2 180
Fortune, that arrant whore, Ne'er turns the key to the poor . . ii 4 53
Let the wise man fly: The knave turns fool that runs away . . ii 4 85
Shall of a corn cry woe, And turn his sleep to wake . . iii 2 34
My wits begin to turn. Come on, my boy: how dost, my boy? art cold? . . . . iii 2 67
This cold night will turn us all to fools and madmen . . iii 4 80
If wolves had at thy gate howl'd that stern time, Thou shouldst have said 'Good porter, turn the key . . . . iii 7 64
Turn out that eyeless villain; throw this slave Upon the dunghill . iii 7 96
If she live long, And in the end meet the old course of death, Women will all turn monsters . . . . iii 7 102
I'll look no more; Lest my brain turn . . . . iv 6 23
And turn our impress'd lances in our eyes Which do command them . v 3 50
I follow him to serve my turn upon him; We cannot all be masters *Oth.* i 1 42
So will I turn her virtue into pitch . . . . ii 3 366
Exchange me for a goat, When I shall turn the business of my soul To such exsufflicate and blown surmises . . . . iii 3 181
She can turn, and turn, and yet go on, And turn again . . iv 1 264
Turn thy complexion there, Patience, thou young and rose-lipp'd cherubin . . . . iv 2 62
There's money for your pains: I pray you, turn the key and keep our counsel . . . . iv 2 94
Did he live now, This sight would make him do a desperate turn . v 2 207
Turn The office and devotion of their view Upon a tawny front *Ant. and Cleo.* i 1 4
I prithee, turn aside and weep for her; Then bid adieu to me . . i 3 76
To sit And keep the turn of tippling with a slave . . . i 4 19
For what good turn?—For the best turn i' the bed . . . ii 5 58
Melt Egypt into Nile! and kindly creatures Turn all to serpents! . ii 5 79
When it appears to you where this begins, Turn your displeasure that way . . . . iii 4 34
Antony, most large In his abominations, turns you off . . . iii 6 94
The Egyptian admiral, With all their sixty, fly and turn the rudder . iii 10 3
I turn you not away; but, like a master Married to your good service, stay till death . . . . iv 2 30
Turn from me, then, that noble countenance, Wherein the worship of the whole world lies . . . . iv 14 85
I'll fetch a turn about the garden . . . . *Cymbeline* i 1 81
Spare your arithmetic: never count the turns; Once, and a million! . ii 4 142
Money, youth?—All gold and silver rather turn to dirt! . . . iii 6 54

Turn. My mother, having power of his testiness, shall turn all into my commendations . . . . *Cymbeline* iv 1 23
Then I'll turn craver too, and so I shall 'scape whipping *Pericles* ii 1 92
I never spake bad word, nor did ill turn To any living creature . iv 1 76
When nature framed this piece, she meant thee a good turn . . . iv 2 151
I think You'll turn a child again . . . . iv 3 4
Here we her place; And to her father turn our thoughts again . v Gower 12
Turn your eyes upon me. You are like something that— What country-woman? . . . . v 1 102
Toward Ephesus Turn our blown sails . . . . v 1 256
To rage the city turn, That him and his they in his palace burn v 3 Gower 96
Turnbull Street. The feats he hath done about Turnbull Street *2 Hen. IV.* iii 2 329
Turncoat. Then is courtesy a turncoat . . . . *Much Ado* i 1 125
Let your close fire predominate his smoke, And be no turncoats *T. of A.* iv 3 143
Turned. My heart bleeds To think o' the teen that I have turn'd you to *Tempest* i 2 64
We shall lose our time, And all be turn'd to barnacles, or to apes . iv 1 249
Even so by love the young and tender wit Is turn'd to folly *T. G. of Ver.* i 1 48
I have turned away my other guests . . . . *Mer. Wives* iv 3 12
I knew of your purpose; turned my daughter into green . . . v 5 214
She would have made Hercules have turned spit . . . *Much Ado* ii 1 261
And now is he turned orthography; his words are a very fantastical banquet . . . . ii 3 21
O day untowardly turned!—O mischief strangely thwarting! . . . iii 2 134
An you be not turned Turk, there's no more sailing by the star . . iii 4 57
And men are only turned into tongue, and trim ones too . . . iv 1 323
Never so truly turned over and over as my poor self in love . . v 2 35
None are so surely caught, when they are catch'd, As wit turn'd fool *L. L. Lost* v 2 70
The fourth turn'd on the toe, and down he fell . . . . . . v 2 114
The fairest dames, That ever turn'd their—backs—to mortal views!—Their eyes, villain, their eyes.—That ever turn'd their eyes to mortal views! . . . . v 2 161
With cunning hast thou filch'd my daughter's heart, Turn'd her obedience *M. N. Dream* i 1 37
What graces in my love do dwell, That he hath turn'd a heaven unto a hell! . . . . i 1 207
Must perforce ensue Some true love turn'd and not a false turn'd true . iii 2 91
Like far-off mountains turned into clouds . . . . . . iv 1 193
The ewes, being rank, In the end of autumn turned to the rams *M. of V.* i 3 82
We turned o'er many books together: he is furnished with my opinion iv 1 156
Their savage eyes turn'd to a modest gaze By the sweet power of music v 1 78
Leander, he would have lived many a fair year, though Hero had turned nun . . . . *As Y. Like It* iv 1 101
You are a fool And turn'd into the extremity of love . . . iv 3 23
Art thou god to shepherd turn'd, That a maiden's heart hath burn'd? . iv 3 40
An old jerkin, a pair of old breeches thrice turned . . *T. of Shrew* iii 2 45
You, that have turn'd off a first so noble wife, May justly diet me *All's Well* v 3 220
That instant was I turn'd into a hart . . . . . *T. Night* i 1 21
Or, to be turned away, is not that as good as a hanging to you? . i 5 18
How quickly the wrong side may be turned outward! . . . . iii 1 14
Yond gull Malvolio is turned heathen, a very renegado . . . iii 2 74
It was thought she was a woman and was turned into a cold fish *W. T.* iv 4 284
Which we, God knows, have turn'd another way, To our own vantage *K. John* ii 1 549
Or turn'd an eye of doubt upon my face . . . . . . iv 2 233
All the shrouds wherewith my life should sail Are turned to one thread v 7 54
I know them to be as true-bred cowards as ever turned back . *1 Hen. IV.* i 2 206
Then his cheek look'd pale, And on my face he turn'd an eye of death . i 3 143
This house is turned upside down . . . . ii 1 11
Thy father's beard is turned white with the news . . . . . ii 4 393
I had rather hear a brazen canstick turn'd, Or a dry wheel grate . iii 1 131
You shall have Trent turn'd.—I do not care . . . . . iii 1 136
This house is turned bawdy-house; they pick pockets . . . iii 3 114
When he saw The fortune of the day quite turn'd from him . . v 5 18
Sir John Umfrevile turn'd me back With joyful tidings . *2 Hen. IV.* i 1 34
All the rest Turn'd on themselves, like dull and heavy lead . . i 1 118
'Gan vail his stomach and did grace the shame Of those that turn'd their backs . . . . i 1 130
That true valour is turned bear-herd . . . . i 2 192
Have you turned him out o' doors?—Yea, sir. The rascal's drunk . ii 4 229
He, by conversing with them, is turned into a justice-like serving-man v 1 76
So shall the world perceive, That I have turn'd away my former self . v 5 62
This mock of his Hath turn'd his balls to gun-stones . . *Hen. V.* i 2 282
Turned away the fat knight with the great-belly doublet . . iv 7 50
You see them perspectively, the cities turned into a maid . . v 2 348
O, were mine eye-balls into bullets turn'd, That I in rage might shoot them at your faces! . . . . *1 Hen. VI.* iv 7 79
Is all our travail turn'd to this effect? . . . . . . v 4 102
This news, I think, hath turn'd your weapon's edge . *2 Hen. VI.* ii 1 180
I beseech God on my knees thou mayst be turned to hobnails . . iv 10 62
Even at this sight My heart is turn'd to stone . . . . . v 2 50
These words have turn'd my hate to love . . . *3 Hen. VI.* iii 3 199
And turn'd my captive state to liberty, My fear to hope . . . iv 6 3
And all the trouble thou hast turn'd me to . . . . . . v 5 16
It [conscience] is turned out of all towns and cities for a dangerous thing *Richard III.* i 4 145
That high All-Seer that I dallied with Hath turn'd my feigned prayer on my head . . . . v 1 21
She is a pearl, Whose price hath launch'd above a thousand ships, And turn'd crown'd kings to merchants . . . . *Troi. and Cres.* ii 2 83
Unless she said 'My mind is now turn'd whore' . . . . . v 2 114
My throat of war be turn'd . . . into a pipe Small as an eunuch! *Cor.* iii 2 112
He turned me about with his finger and his thumb, as one would set up a top . . . . iv 5 159
Unkindly banished, The gates shut on me, and turn'd weeping out *T. An.* v 3 105
And turn'd that black word death to banishment . . *Rom. and Jul.* iii 3 27
Immediate are my needs, and my relief Must not be toss'd and turn'd to me in words, But find supply immediate . . . *T. of Athens* ii 1 26
Why should it thrive and turn to nutriment, When he is turn'd to poison? iii 1 62
Speak; Cæsar is turn'd to hear.—Beware the ides of March . *J. Cæsar* i 2 17
Let me see; is not the leaf turn'd down Where I left reading? . . iv 3 273
Myself have to mine own turn'd enemy . . . . . . v 3 2
Turn'd wild in nature, broke their stalls, flung out . . . *Macbeth* ii 4 16
And, with his head over his shoulder turn'd, He seem'd to find his way without his eyes . . . . *Hamlet* ii 1 97
Look, whether he has not turned his colour and has tears in's eyes . ii 2 542
Cæsar, dead and turn'd to clay, Might stop a hole to keep the wind away v 1 236
Turned. The foul practice Hath turn'd itself on me; lo, here I lie, Never to rise . . . . *Hamlet* v 2 329
Then he call'd me sot, And told me I had turn'd the wrong side out *Lear* iv 2 9
Stripp'd her from his benediction, turn'd her To foreign casualties . iv 3 45
Whom love hath turn'd almost the wrong side out . . . *Othello* ii 3 54
Are we turn'd Turks, and to ourselves do that Which heaven hath forbid the Ottomites? . . . . ii 3 170
My heart is turned to stone; I strike it, and it hurts my hand . iv 1 193
Some such squire he was That turn'd your wit the seamy side without . iv 2 146
She turn'd to folly, and she was a whore.—Thou dost belie her . . v 2 132
Thou, the greatest soldier of the world, Art turn'd the greatest liar *Ant. and Cleo.* i 3 39
For my part, I am sorry it is turned to a drinking . . . . . ii 6 108
Follow'd him, till he had melted from The smallness of a gnat to air, and then Have turn'd mine eye and wept . . . *Cymbeline* i 3 22
She hath been reading late The tale of Tereus; here the leaf's turn'd down ii 2 45
The most patient man in loss, the most coldest that ever turned up ace ii 3 2
What is here? The scriptures of the loyal Leonatus, All turn'd to heresy? iii 4 84
I had rather Have skipp'd from sixteen years of age to sixty, To have turn'd my leaping-time into a crutch . . . . iv 2 200
It is a day turn'd strangely: or betimes Let's re-inforce, or fly . v 2 17
Their own nobleness, which could have turn'd A distaff to a lance . v 3 33
Some, turn'd coward But by example—O, a sin in war! . . . v 3 35
Why hast thou thus adjourn'd The graces for his merits due, Being all to dolours turn'd? . . . . v 4 80
'Tis come at last, and 'tis turned to a rusty armour . . *Pericles* ii 1 125
A burning torch that's turned upside down . . . . . . ii 2 32
Turned forth. I am the turned forth, be it known to you *T. Andron.* v 3 109
Turnest. Ah, now thou turn'st away thy face for shame! . . ii 4 28
Speak no more: Thou turn'st mine eyes into my very soul . *Hamlet* iii 4 89
Turneth. Like the spring that turneth wood to stone . . . iv 7 20
Turning. If they lead to any ill, I will leave them at the next turning *Much Ado* ii 1 160
Humour it with turning up your eyelids, sigh a note . *L. L. Lost* iii 1 13
And deny himself for Jove, Turning mortal for thy love . . iv 3 120
Turn up on your right hand at the next turning, but, at the next turning of all, on your left; marry, at the very next turning, turn of no hand . . . . *Mer. of Venice* ii 2 43
Turning his face, he put his hand behind him . . . . . ii 8 47
Turning these jests out of service, let us talk in good earnest *As Y. L. It* i 3 25
Turning again toward childish treble, pipes And whistles in his sound . ii 7 162
And, for turning away, let summer bear it out . . . *T. Night* i 5 21
Turning with splendour of his precious eye The meagre cloddy earth to glittering gold . . . . *K. John* iii 1 79
How now, foolish rheum! Turning dispiteous torture out of door! . iv 1 34
Have torn their souls by turning them from us . . *Richard II.* iii 3 83
From the one side to the other turning, Bareheaded . . . v 2 18
Turning your books to graves, your ink to blood . . *2 Hen. IV.* iv 1 50
Turning the word to sword and life to death . . . . . iv 2 10
Turning past evils to advantages . . . . iv 4 78
Turning the accomplishment of many years Into an hour-glass *Hen. V.* Prol. 30
A' parted even just between twelve and one, even at the turning o' the tide ii 3 13
And on your head Turning the widows' tears, the orphans' cries . ii 4 106
She [Fortune] is turning, and inconstant, and mutability, and variation iii 6 36
Turn giddy, and be holp by backward turning . . *Rom. and Jul.* i 2 48
Puffs away from thence, Turning his face to the dew-dropping south . i 4 103
This ensign here of mine was turning back; I slew the coward *J. Cæsar* v 3 3
If a man were porter of hell-gate, he should have old turning the key *Macbeth* ii 3 2
Which secret art, By turning o'er authorities, I have, Together with my practice, made familiar . . . . *Pericles* iii 2 33
Turnips. Alas, I had rather be set quick i' the earth And bowl'd to death with turnips! . . . . *Mer. Wives* iii 4 91
Turph. Old John Naps of Greece And Peter Turph . . *T. of Shrew* Ind. 2 96
Turpitude. Minds sway'd by eyes are full of turpitude *Troi. and Cres.* v 2 112
How wouldst thou have paid My better service, when my turpitude Thou dost so crown with gold! . . . . . . *Ant. and Cleo.* iv 6 33
Turquoise. It was my turquoise; I had it of Leah when I was a bachelor *Mer. of Venice* iii 1 126
Turret. Discourse, I prithee, on this turret's top . . *1 Hen. VI.* i 4 26
The burning torch in yonder turret stands . . . . . . iii 2 30
Turtle. I will find you twenty lascivious turtles ere one chaste man *Mer. Wives* ii 1 83
We'll teach him to know turtles from jays . . . . . . iii 3 44
Will these turtles be gone? . . . . *L. L. Lost* iv 3 212
When turtles tread, and rooks, and daws . . . . v 2 915
O slow-wing'd turtle! shall a buzzard take thee?—Ay, for a turtle *T. of S.* ii 1 208
So turtles pair, That never mean to part . . . . *W. Tale* iv 4 154
I, an old turtle, Will wing me to some wither'd bough . . . v 3 132
As true as steel, as plantage to the moon, As sun to day, as turtle to her mate, As iron to adamant . . . . . *Troi. and Cres.* iii 2 185
Turtle-doves. Like to a pair of loving turtle-doves That could not live asunder day or night . . . . *1 Hen. VI.* ii 2 30
Tuscan. Gentlemen that mean to see The Tuscan service . *All's Well* i 2 14
They have married me! I'll to the Tuscan wars . . . . . ii 3 290
Tush! I may as well say the fool's the fool . . . . *Much Ado* iii 3 130
Tush, tush! fear boys with bugs . . . . . *T. of Shrew* i 2 211
Tut, tut! Grace me no grace, nor uncle me no uncle . *Richard II.* ii 3 86
Tut, tut; good enough to toss; food for powder . . *1 Hen. IV.* iv 2 71
Tut, tut, here is a mannerly forbearance . . . . *1 Hen. VI.* i 4 19
Tut, that's a foolish observation . . . . . . *3 Hen. VI.* ii 6 108
Tut, were it farther off, I'll pluck it down . . . . . . iii 2 195
Tut, tut, Thou troublest me; I am not in the vein . *Richard III.* iv 2 121
Tutor. More time For vainer hours and tutors not so careful . *Tempest* i 2 174
What? I say, My foot my tutor? Put thy sword up . . . . i 2 469
She hath taught her suitor, He being her pupil, to become her tutor *T. G. of Ver.* ii 1 144
Therefore would I have thee to my tutor—For long agone I have forgot to court . . . . iii 1 84
Such fiery numbers as the prompting eyes Of beauty's tutors *L. L. Lost* iv 3 323
To my daughters; and tell them both, These are their tutors *T. of Shrew* ii 1 111
Give sorrow leave awhile to tutor me To this submission *Richard II.* iv 1 166
Thou shalt be as thou wast, The tutor and the feeder of my riots *2 Hen. IV.* v 5 66
I did send for thee To tutor thee in stratagems of war . *1 Hen. VI.* iv 5 2
Ah, tutor, look where bloody Clifford comes! . . . *3 Hen. VI.* i 3 2
An assinego may tutor thee: thou scurvy-valiant ass! . *Troi. and Cres.* ii 1 49
Heaven bless thee from a tutor, and discipline come not near thee! . iii 3 32
Famed be thy tutor, and thy parts of nature Thrice famed . . . ii 3 253
Villains, like thyself!—Indeed, I was their tutor to instruct them *T. An.* v 1 98

Tutor. And yet thou wilt tutor me from quarrelling! *Rom. and Jul.* iii 1 32
I will say of it, It tutors nature *T. of Athens* i 1 37
Be not too tame neither, but let your own discretion be your tutor *Hamlet* iii 2 19
When nobles are their tailors' tutors; No heretics burn'd *Lear* iii 2 83
Tutored. He cannot be a perfect man, Not being tried and tutor'd in the world *T. G. of Ver.* i 3 21
Their sons are well tutored by you, and their daughters profit *L. L. L.* iv 2 77
Hath been tutor'd in the rudiments Of many desperate studies *As Y. L. It* v 4 31
Whose learning and good letters peace hath tutor'd *2 Hen. IV.* iv 1 44
Then gave I her, so tutor'd by my art, A sleeping potion *Rom. and Jul.* v 3 243
Tu-whit; Tu-who, a merry note, While greasy Joan doth keel the pot *L. L. Lost* v 2 928
Twain. The Duke of Milan And his brave son being twain *Tempest* i 2 438
Go with me To bless this twain, that they may prosperous be iv 1 104
Such remedy as, to save a head, To cleave a heart in twain *M. for M.* iii 1 63
This glove.—Did he not send you twain? *L. L. Lost* v 2 48
Neither of either; I remit both twain v 2 459
Let Lion, Moonshine, Wall, and lovers twain At large discourse *M. N. D.* v 1 151
Till I come again, No bed shall e'er be guilty of my stay, No rest be interposer 'twixt us twain *Mer. of Venice* iii 2 329
What's that to you? 'Tis bargain'd 'twixt us twain *T. of Shrew* ii 1 306
O Perdita, what have we twain forgot! *W. Tale* iv 4 674
'Tis not the trial of a woman's war, The bitter clamour of two eager tongues, Can arbitrate this cause betwixt us twain *Richard II.* i 1 50
Twice saying 'pardon' doth not pardon twain, But makes one pardon strong v 3 134
No more can I be sever'd from your side, Than can yourself yourself in twain divide *1 Hen. VI.* iv 5 49
Methought this staff, mine office-badge in court, Was broke in twain *2 Hen. VI.* i 2 26
We twain will go into his highness' tent v 1 55
You twain, of all the rest, Are near to Warwick by blood *3 Hen. VI.* iv 1 135
When my heart, As wedged with a sigh, would rive in twain *T. and C.* i 1 35
In the imitation of these twain i 3 185
Let Mars divide eternity in twain, And give him half iii 3 256
They two are twain.—Falling in, after falling out, may make them three iii 1 111
The obligation of our blood forbids A gory emulation 'twixt us twain iv 5 123
Go, counsellor; Thou and my bosom henceforth shall be twain *R. and J.* iii 5 240
With that hand that cut thy youth in twain To sunder his v 3 99
I must become a borrower of the night For a dark hour or twain *Macb.* iii 1 28
Sleep rock thy brain; And never come mischance between us twain! *Hamlet* iii 2 238
O Hamlet, thou hast cleft my heart in twain iii 4 156
Thou wilt o'ertake us, hence a mile or twain *Lear* iv 1 44
Thou hast one daughter, Who redeems nature from the general curse Which twain have brought her to iv 6 211
Friends of my soul, you twain Rule in this realm v 3 319
Pure grief Shore his old thread in twain *Othello* v 2 206
The nobleness of life Is to do thus; when such a mutual pair And such a twain can do't *Ant. and Cleo.* i 1 38
'Tis time we twain Did show ourselves i' the field i 4 73
His soldiership Is twice the other twain ii 1 35
Wars 'twixt you twain would be As if the world should cleave iii 4 30
Great men . . . Could not out-peer these twain *Cymbeline* iii 6 87
For this from stiller seats we came, Our parents and us twain v 4 70
Twanged. With a swaggering accent sharply twanged off *T. Night* iii 4 198
Twangling. Sometimes a thousand twangling instruments Will hum about mine ears *Tempest* iii 2 146
While she did call me rascal fiddler And twangling Jack *T. of Shrew* ii 1 159
Tway. I wad full fain hear some question 'tween you tway *Hen. V.* iii 2 128
Tweaks. Plucks off my beard, and blows it in my face? Tweaks me by the nose? *Hamlet* ii 2 601
Twelfth. O, the twelfth day of December *T. Night* ii 3 90
Twelve year since, Miranda, twelve year since *Tempest* i 2 53
I will rend an oak And peg thee in his knotty entrails till Thou hast howl'd away twelve winters i 2 296
To-night at Herne's oak, just 'twixt twelve and one *Mer. Wives* iv 6 19
Procure the vicar To stay for me at church 'twixt twelve and one. iv 6 49
The Windsor bell hath struck twelve; the minute draws on v 5 1
The jury, passing on the prisoner's life, May in the sworn twelve have a thief or two Guiltier than him they try *Meas. for Meas.* ii 1 20
The clock hath strucken twelve upon the bell *Com. of Errors* i 2 45
What man was he talk'd with you yesternight Out at your window betwixt twelve and one? *Much Ado* iv 1 85
Until the twelve celestial signs Have brought about the annual reckoning *L. L. Lost* v 2 807
The iron tongue of midnight hath told twelve *M. N. Dream* v 1 370
Three months from twelve; then, let me see; the rate *Mer. of Venice* i 3 105
Let her go by.—Yea, leave that labour to great Hercules; And let it be more than Alcides' twelve *T. of Shrew* i 2 258
Besides two galliases, And twelve tight galleys ii 1 381
Jumps twelve foot and a half by the squier *W. Tale* iv 4 347
Thou shalt have twelve thousand fighting men *Richard II.* iii 2 70
But he, in twelve, Found truth in all but one; I, in twelve thousand, none iv 1 170
Since the old days of goodman Adam to the pupil age of this present twelve o'clock at midnight *1 Hen. IV.* ii 4 107
Some twelve days hence Our general forces at Bridgenorth shall meet iii 2 177
A' parted even just between twelve and one, even at the turning o' the tide *Hen. V.* ii 3 13
Bardolph stole a lutecase, bore it twelve leagues, and sold it iii 2 46
There is twelve pence for you; and I pray you to serve God iv 8 67
Twelve cities and seven walled towns of strength *1 Hen. VI.* iii 4 7
In which assault we lost twelve hundred men iv 1 24
Seven earls, twelve barons, and twenty reverend bishops *2 Hen. VI.* i 1 8
Thou hast beat me out Twelve several times *Coriolanus* iv 5 128
We would muster all From twelve to seventy iv 5 135
At twelve year old, I bade her come. What, lamb! what, lady-bird! *Rom. and Jul.* i 3 2
From nine till twelve Is three long hours, yet she is not come ii 5 10
If there sit twelve women at the table, let a dozen of them be—as they are *T. of Athens* iii 6 87
How goes the night, boy?—The moon is down; I have not heard the clock.—And she goes down at twelve *Macbeth* ii 1 3
You come most carefully upon your hour.—'Tis now struck twelve *Ham.* i 1 7
Upon the platform, 'twixt eleven and twelve, I'll visit you i 2 252
What hour now?—I think it lacks of twelve.—No, it is struck i 4 3
And thirty dozen moons with borrow'd sheen About the world have times twelve thirties been iii 2 168
Twelve. The king, sir, hath laid, that in a dozen passes between yourself and him, he shall not exceed you three hits: he hath laid on twelve for nine *Hamlet* v 2 174
I am some twelve or fourteen moonshines Lag of a brother *Lear* i 2 5
If you will watch his going thence, which I will fashion to fall out between twelve and one, you may take him *Othello* iv 2 243
Eight wild-boars roasted whole at a breakfast, and but twelve persons there; is this true? *Ant. and Cleo.* ii 2 184
Our nineteen legions thou shalt hold by land And our twelve thousand horse iii 7 60
One twelve moons more she'll wear Diana's livery *Pericles* ii 5 10
I must needs be gone; My twelve months are expired iii 3 2
Twelvemonth. I have this twelvemonth been her bedfellow *Much Ado* iv 1 151
A twelvemonth shall you spend, and never rest, But seek the weary beds of people sick *L. L. Lost* v 2 831
A twelvemonth and a day I'll mark no words that smooth-faced wooers say v 2 837
At the twelvemonth's end I'll change my black gown for a faithful friend v 2 843
You shall this twelvemonth term from day to day Visit the speechless sick v 2 860
Befall what will befall, I'll jest a twelvemonth in an hospital v 2 881
It wants a twelvemonth and a day, And then 'twill end v 2 887
Twenty of these puny lies I'll tell, That men shall swear I have discontinued school Above a twelvemonth *Mer. of Venice* iii 4 76
Bring him dead or living Within this twelvemonth *As Y. Like It* iii 1 7
To betray a she-lamb of a twelvemonth to a crooked-pated, old, cuckoldly ram iii 2 86
The daughter of a count That died some twelvemonth since *T. Night* i 2 37
But this our purpose now is twelve month old *1 Hen. IV.* i 1 28
I shall laugh at this a twelve-month hence *Richard III.* iii 2 57
A twelvemonth longer, let me entreat you to Forbear *Pericles* ii 4 45
For this twelvemonth she'll not undertake A married life ii 5 3
Twelve score. As easy as a cannon will shoot point-blank twelve score *Mer. Wives* iii 2 34
I know his death will be a march of twelve-score *1 Hen. IV.* ii 4 598
Dead! a' would have clapped i' the clout at twelve score *2 Hen. IV.* iii 2 52
Twentieth. The twentieth part Of one poor scruple *Mer. of Venice* iv 1 329
A slave that is not twentieth part the tithe Of your precedent lord *Ham.* iii 4 98
Twenty. With twenty watchful, weary, tedious nights *T. G. of Ver.* i 1 31
I'll knit it up in silken strings With twenty odd-conceited true-love knots ii 7 46
I will find you twenty lascivious turtles ere one chaste man *Mer. Wives* ii 1 82
Good even and twenty, good Master Page! ii 1 203
Not one wise man among twenty that will praise himself *Much Ado* v 2 76
I can easier teach twenty what were good to be done, than be one of the twenty to follow mine own teaching *Mer. of Venice* i 2 17
I have sent twenty out to seek for you ii 6 66
And twenty of these puny lies I'll tell iii 4 74
How old are you, friend?—Five and twenty, sir *As Y. Like It* v 1 21
Apollo plays And twenty caged nightingales do sing *T. of Shrew* Ind. 2 38
Twenty more such names and men as these Which never were Ind. 2 97
With twenty such vile terms, As had she studied to misuse me so ii 1 159
Petruchio is the master; That teacheth tricks eleven and twenty long iv 2 57
She deserves a lord That twenty such rude boys might tend upon *All's Well* iii 2 84
Come kiss me, sweet and twenty, Youth's a stuff will not endure *T. N.* ii 3 52
O for a fine thief, of the age of two and twenty or thereabouts! *1 Hen. IV.* iii 3 212
This bottle makes an angel.—An if it do, take it for thy labour; and if it make twenty, take them all iv 2 8
When he was not six and twenty strong, Sick in the world's regard iv 3 56
That's to make him eat twenty of his words *2 Hen. IV.* ii 2 149
There are twenty weak and wearied posts Come from the north ii 4 385
The French may lay twenty French crowns to one, they will beat us *Hen. V.* iv 1 242
None else of name; and of all other men But five and twenty iv 8 111
Seven earls, twelve barons, and twenty reverend bishops *2 Hen. VI.* i 1 8
Five men to twenty! though the odds be great, I doubt not, uncle, of our victory *3 Hen. VI.* i 2 72
More unlikely Than to accomplish twenty golden crowns! iii 2 152
I hope my holy humour will change; 'twas wont to hold me but while one would tell twenty *Richard III.* i 4 122
He would kiss you twenty with a breath *Hen. VIII.* i 4 30
O' my conscience, twenty of the dog-days now reign in's nose v 4 43
O admirable youth! he ne'er saw three and twenty *Troi. and Cres.* i 2 256
Of five and twenty valiant sons, Half of the number that King Priam had, Behold the poor remains! *T. Andron.* i 1 79
And buried one and twenty valiant sons, Knighted in field i 1 195
There lies more peril in thine eye Than twenty of their swords *R. and J.* ii 2 72
Some twenty of them fought in this black strife, And all those twenty could but kill one life iii 1 184
Go hire me twenty cunning cooks iv 2 2
He owes nine thousand; besides my former sum, Which makes it five and twenty *T. of Athens* ii 1 3
If I would sell my horse, and buy twenty more Better than he, why, give my horse to Timon ii 1 7
Let no assembly of twenty be without a score of villains iii 6 86
As rich men deal gifts, Expecting in return twenty for one iv 3 517
With twenty trenched gashes on his head; The least a death to nature *Macbeth* iii 4 27
Now they rise again, With twenty mortal murders on their crowns iii 4 81
How will you do for a husband?—Why, I can buy me twenty at any market iv 2 40
Give twenty, forty, fifty, an hundred ducats a-piece for his picture *Ham.* ii 2 382
Harbour more craft . . . Than twenty silly ducking observants *Lear* ii 2 109
There's not a nose among twenty but can smell him that's stinking ii 4 72
Bring but five and twenty: to no more Will I give place or notice ii 4 251
What, must I come to you With five and twenty, Regan? said you so? ii 4 257
What need you five and twenty, ten, or five, To follow in a house where twice so many Have a command to tend you? ii 4 264
Twenty several messengers: Why do you send so thick? *Ant. and Cleo.* i 5 62
Whip him. Were't twenty of the greatest tributaries That do acknowledge Cæsar iii 13 96
Cannot take two from twenty, for his heart, And leave eighteen *Cymb.* ii 1 60
Ten, chased by one, Are now each one the slaughter-man of twenty v 3 49
Twenty adieus, my frozen Muscovits *L. L. Lost* v 2 265
Twenty angels. I had myself twenty angels given me this morning *Mer. Wives* ii 2 73
Twenty brothers. The same tradition takes not away my blood, were there twenty brothers betwixt us *As Y. Like It* i 1 52
Twenty consciences, That stand 'twixt me and Milan *Tempest* ii 1 278

Twenty crowns. What is the wager?—Twenty crowns . *T. of Shrew* v 2 70
Twenty fifteens. He that made us pay one and twenty fifteens 2 *Hen. VI.* iv 7 24
Twenty-five. He had, before this last expedition, twenty-five wounds upon him.—Now it's twenty-seven . . . . . *Coriolanus* ii 1 170
Twenty glow-worms shall our lanterns be . . . *Mer. Wives* v 5 82
Twenty heads. That, had he twenty heads to tender down On twenty bloody blocks, he'ld yield them up . . . . . *Meas. for Meas.* ii 4 180
Twenty horse. 'Tis Alcibiades, and some twenty horse . *T. of Athens* i 1 250
Twenty hundred thousand times more joy . . *Rom. and Jul.* iii 3 153
Twenty husbands. If I should marry him, I should marry twenty husbands . . . . *Mer. of Venice* i 2 67
Twenty kisses. And for my tidings gave me twenty kisses *T. Andron.* v 1 120
Twenty knights. Ten thousand bold Scots, two and twenty knights 1 *Hen. IV.* i 1 68
Twenty lives. I'll make thee known, Though I lost twenty lives *Othello* v 2 166
Twenty men. If you had the strength Of twenty men, it would dispatch you straight . . . . *Rom. and Jul.* v 1 79
He thinks, being twenty times of better fortune, He is twenty men to one . . . . *Ant. and Cleo.* iv 2 4
Twenty merchants . . . have all persuaded with him . *Mer. of Venice* iii 2 281
Twenty mile. This boy will carry a letter twenty mile, as easy as a cannon will shoot point-blank twelve score . . *Mer. Wives* iii 2 33
Haste away, For we must measure twenty miles to-day *Mer. of Venice* iii 4 84
Within these ten days if that thou be'st found So near our public court as twenty miles, Thou diest for it . . . *As Y. Like It* i 3 46
Twenty money-bags. A usurer's wife was brought to bed of twenty money-bags . . . . *W. Tale* iv 4 266
Twenty nine. I have known thee these twenty nine years . 2 *Hen. IV.* ii 4 413
Twenty nobles. Pray thee, Sir John, let it be but twenty nobles . . ii 1 166
Twenty nosegays. She hath made me four and twenty nosegays for the shearers . . . . *W. Tale* iv 3 44
Twenty one. Were I but twenty one, . . . I should call you brother . v 1 126
Twenty orators. Gold were as good as twenty orators . *Richard III.* iv 2 38
Twenty pair. Why, lady, Love hath twenty pair of eyes *T. G. of Ver.* ii 4 95
Twenty pieces. What a head have I! It beats as it would fall in twenty pieces . . . . *Rom. and Jul.* ii 5 50
Twenty popish tricks and ceremonies . . . *T. Andron.* v 1 76
Twenty pounds of money, which must be paid to Master Brook *Mer. W.* v 5 117
I would not lose the dog for twenty pound . . . *T. of Shrew* Ind. 1 21
And money lent you, four and twenty pound . 1 *Hen. IV.* iii 3 85
Twenty prisoners. Who will go to hazard with me for twenty prisoners? *Hen. V.* iii 7 94
Twenty seas. I as rich in having such a jewel As twenty seas, if all their sand were pearl . . . . . . *T. G. of Ver.* ii 4 170
Twenty shadows. Each substance of a grief hath twenty shadows *Richard II.* ii 2 14
Twenty Sir John Falstaffs. If he were twenty Sir John Falstaffs, he shall not abuse Robert Shallow, esquire . . . . *Mer. Wives* i 1 3
Twenty-six. Within the year of our redemption Four hundred twenty-six *Hen. V.* i 2 61
There lie dead One hundred twenty six . . . . iv 8 88
Twenty sons. For two and twenty sons I never wept . *T. Andron.* iii 1 10
Twenty such. Wilt thou have me?—Ay, and twenty such *As Y. Like It* iv 1 119
An a' speak any thing against me, I'll take him down, an a' were lustier than he is, and twenty such Jacks . . . *Rom. and Jul.* ii 4 160
Twenty thousand soul-confirming oaths . . *T. G. of Ver.* ii 6 16
He, none but he, shall have her, Though twenty thousand worthier come to crave her . . . . *Mer. Wives* iv 4 90
I am compared to twenty thousand fairs . . . . *L. L. Lost* v 2 37
And in possession twenty thousand crowns . . . *T. of Shrew* ii 1 123
And I will add Unto their losses twenty thousand crowns . . v 2 113
But now the blood of twenty thousand men Did triumph in my face *Richard II.* iii 2 76
Is not the king's name twenty thousand names? Arm, arm, my name! iii 2 85
I have a thousand spirits in one breast, To answer twenty thousand such as you . . . . iv 1 59
Five and twenty thousand men of choice . . . . . 2 *Hen. IV.* i 3 11
Whether our present five and twenty thousand May hold up head . i 3 16
By three and twenty thousand of the French Was round encompassed 1 *Hen. VI.* i 1 113
Fain would I go to chafe his paly lips With twenty thousand kisses 2 *Hen. VI.* iii 2 142
Though Suffolk dare him twenty thousand times . . . iii 2 206
She is hard by with twenty thousand men; And therefore fortify 3 *Hen. VI.* i 2 51
All the friends . . . Will but amount to five and twenty thousand . ii 1 181
Within thine eyes sat twenty thousand deaths . *Coriolanus* iii 3 70
To say amen.—And that would she for twenty thousand more *T. An.* iv 2 45
Two thousand souls and twenty thousand ducats Will not debate the question of this straw . . . . *Hamlet* iv 4 25
While, to my shame, I see The imminent death of twenty thousand men iv 4 60
Twenty-three. Methoughts I did recoil Twenty-three years, and saw myself unbreech'd *W. Tale* i 2 155
Twenty three days They have been absent: 'tis good speed . . . ii 3 198
Twenty times. I have seen Sackerson loose twenty times . *Mer. Wives* i 1 307
Not once, nor twice, but twenty times you have . *Com. of Errors* iii 2 177
She'll be up twenty times a night . . . . . . *Much Ado* ii 3 136
Yet, for you I would be trebled twenty times myself . *Mer. of Venice* iii 2 154
He would rather have Antonio's flesh Than twenty times the value of the sum . . . . iii 2 289
You shall have gold To pay the petty debt twenty times over . . iii 2 309
I'll venture so much of my hawk or hound, But twenty times so much upon my wife . . . . *T. of Shrew* v 2 73
Four and twenty times the pilot's glass Hath told the thievish minutes how they pass . . . . *All's Well* ii 1 168
Love make your fortunes twenty times above Her that so wishes! . ii 3 88
If thou deny'st it twenty times, thou liest . . . *Richard II.* iv 1 38
Were he twenty times my son, I would appeach him . . . v 2 101
Had I twenty times so many foes, And each of them had twenty times their power, All these could not procure me any scathe . 2 *Hen. VI.* ii 4 60
Your loving uncle, twenty times his worth, They say, is shamefully bereft of life . . . . ii 2 268
And twenty times made pause to sob and weep . *Richard III.* i 2 162
I have made my way through more impediments Than twenty times your stop . . . . *Othello* v 2 264
I have seen her die twenty times upon far poorer moment *Ant. and Cleo.* i 2 146
He thinks, being twenty times of better fortune, He is twenty men to one . . . . iv 2 3
Twenty to one then he is shipp'd already . . . . *T. G. of Ver.* i 1 72
Twenty torches. Which did flame and burn Like twenty torches *J. Cæsar* i 3 17
Twenty yards. Sent me two and twenty yards of satin . . 2 *Hen. IV.* i 2 50

Twenty years Have I been patron to Antipholus . . *Com. of Errors* v 1 326
Near twenty years ago, in Genoa, Where we were lodgers *T. of Shrew* iv 4 4
And grew a twenty years removed thing While one would wink *T. Night* v 1 92
Make me to think so twenty years together! . . . . *W. Tale* v 3 71
Shall I draw the curtain?—No, not these twenty years . . v 3 84
I have forsworn his company hourly any time this two and twenty years 1 *Hen. IV.* ii 2 17
Four hundred one and twenty years After defunction of King Pharamond . . . . *Hen. V.* i 2 57
The patterns that by God and by French fathers Had twenty years been made . . . . ii 4 62
That, like a jewel, has hung twenty years About his neck *Hen. VIII.* ii 2 32
I have been your wife, in this obedience, Upward of twenty years . ii 4 36
'Tis since the nuptial of Lucentio, Come pentecost as quickly as it will, Some five and twenty years . . . . *Rom. and Jul.* i 5 39
At what o'clock to-morrow Shall I send to thee?—At the hour of nine.—I will not fail: 'tis twenty years till then . . . . ii 2 170
Why, he that cuts off twenty years of life Cuts off so many years of fearing death . . . . *J. Cæsar* iii 1 101
This skull has lain in the earth three and twenty years . . *Hamlet* v 1 190
How long is this ago?—Some twenty years . . . *Cymbeline* i 1 62
This twenty years This rock and these demesnes have been my world iii 3 69
These gentle princes . . . these twenty years Have I train'd up . v 5 337
Twice. Before you can say 'come' and 'go,' And breathe twice *Tempest* iv 1 45
I drink the air before me, and return Or ere your pulse twice beat . v 1 103
If this prove A vision of the Island, one dear son Shall I twice lose v 1 177
But twice or thrice was 'Proteus' written down . . *T. G. of Ver.* i 2 117
Lo, here in one line is his name twice writ, 'Poor forlorn Proteus' . i 2 123
She was mine, and not mine, twice or thrice in that last article . iii 1 365
Who asked them once or twice what they had in their basket *Mer. Wives* iii 5 103
Twice treble shame on Angelo, To weed my vice and let his grow! *Meas. for Meas.* iii 2 283
In action all of precept, he did show me The way twice o'er . . iv 1 41
Ere twice the sun hath made his journal greeting To the under generation iv 3 92
Twice have the trumpets sounded; The generous and gravest citizens Have hent the gates, and very near upon The duke is entering . iv 6 12
Ere the ships could meet by twice five leagues . *Com. of Errors* i 1 101
I bespoke it not.—Not once, nor twice, but twenty times you have . iii 2 177
A victory is twice itself when the achiever brings home full numbers *Much Ado* i 1 8
He hath twice or thrice cut Cupid's bow-string . . . . iii 2 10
As his your case is such; You chide at him, offending twice as much *L. L. Lost* iv 3 132
And so, adieu; Twice to your visor, and half once to you . . v 2 227
What, wouldst thou have a serpent sting thee twice? . *Mer. of Venice* iv 1 69
It [mercy] is twice blest; It blesseth him that gives and him that takes iv 1 186
Yes, here I tender it for him in the court; Yea, twice the sum . iv 1 210
Twice did he turn his back and purposed so . . . *As Y. Like It* iv 3 128
And twice to-day pick'd out the dullest scent . . *T. of Shrew* Ind. 1 24
These I will assure her, And twice as much, whate'er thou offer'st next ii 1 382
Ere twice the horses of the sun shall bring Their fiery torcher his diurnal ring, Ere twice in murk and occidental damp Moist Hesperus hath quench'd his sleepy lamp . . . . *All's Well* ii 1 164
What! have I twice said well? when was't before? *W. Tale* i 2 90
Why, lo you now, I have spoke to the purpose twice . . . . i 2 106
Or the fann'd snow that's bolted By the northern blasts twice o'er . iv 4 376
Once or twice I was about to speak and tell him plainly . . iv 4 453
She hath privately twice or thrice a day . . . visited that removed house v 2 114
Twice fifteen thousand hearts of England's breed . . *K. John* ii 1 275
Till twice five summers have enrich'd our fields . *Richard II.* i 3 141
This and much more, much more than twice all this, Condemns you . iii 1 28
Twice for one step I'll groan, the way being short . . . v 1 91
Twice saying 'pardon' doth not pardon twain, But makes one pardon strong . . . . v 3 134
He spake it twice, And urged it twice together . . . . . v 4 4
Contracted bachelors, such as had been asked twice on the banns 1 *Hen. IV.* iv 2 18
If I cannot once or twice in a quarter bear out a knave against an honest man, I have but a very little credit . . . . . 2 *Hen. IV.* v 1 53
I have been merry twice and once ere now . . . . . v 3 42
The trumpets have sounded twice.—'Twill be two o'clock ere they come v 5 2
Who twice a-day their wither'd hands hold up Toward heaven *Hen. V.* iv 1 316
Their wounded steeds . . . Yerk out their armed heels at their dead masters, Killing them twice . . . . iv 7 84
I have seen you gleeking and galling at this gentleman twice or thrice v 1 79
O, twice my father, twice am I thy son! . . . . 1 *Hen. VI.* iv 6 6
Twice by awkward wind from England's bank Drove back again 2 *Hen. VI.* iii 2 83
I will not bandy with thee word for word, But buckle with thee blows, twice two for one . . . . 3 *Hen. VI.* i 4 50
The early village-cock Hath twice done salutation to the morn *Rich. III.* v 3 210
I'll have five hundred voices of that sound.—I twice five hundred *Coriolanus* ii 3 220
[Censorinus,] nobly named so, Twice being [by the people chosen] censor ii 3 252
To bid Æneas tell the tale twice o'er, How Troy was burnt *T. Andron.* iii 2 27
Thou art a fool to bid me farewell twice . . . . *T. of Athens* i 1 273
All our service In every point twice done and then done double *Macbeth* i 6 15
This dreaded sight, twice seen of us . . . . . . *Hamlet* i 1 25
Twice before, and jump at this dead hour, With martial stalk hath he gone by . . . . i 1 65
For they say an old man is twice a child . . . . ii 2 403
And my father died within these two hours.—Nay, 'tis twice two months iii 2 136
Thy fifty yet doth double five-and-twenty, And thou art twice her love *Lear* ii 4 263
What need you five and twenty, ten, or five, To follow in a house where twice so many Have a command to tend you? . . . . . ii 4 265
Once or twice she heaved the name of 'father' Pantingly forth . . iv 3 27
Twice then the trumpets sounded, And there I left him tranced . v 3 217
His soldiership Is twice the other twain . . . . *Ant. and Cleo.* i 1 35
What say'st thou?—Wilt thou be lord of the whole world? That's twice ii 7 68
I'll make a journey twice as far, to enjoy A second night . *Cymbeline* ii 4 43
He [Cæsar] was carried From off our coast, twice beaten . . iii 1 26
And on it said a century of prayers, Such as I can, twice o'er . . iv 2 392
Two boys, an old man twice a boy, a lane, Preserved the Britons . v 3 57
If King Pericles Come not home in twice six moons . *Pericles* iii Gower 31
The diamonds of a most praised water Do appear, to make the world twice rich . . . . iii 2 103
I had rather than twice the worth of her she had ne'er come here . . iv 6 1
Twice-sod simplicity, bis coctus! O thou monster Ignorance! *L. L. Lost* iv 2 23
Twice-told. Life is as tedious as a twice-told tale . . . *K. John* iii 4 108

Twig. As fond fathers, Having bound up the threatening twigs of birch, Only to stick it in their children's sight *Meas. for Meas.* i 3 24
They are limed with the twigs that threaten them *All's Well* iii 5 26
I must go look my twigs: he shall be caught iii 6 115
Give some supportance to the bending twigs *Richard II.* iii 4 32
Her hedges even-pleach'd, Like prisoners wildly overgrown with hair, Put forth disorder'd twigs *Hen. V.* v 2 44
Twiggen. I'll beat the knave into a twiggen bottle *Othello* ii 3 152
Twilled. Banks with pioned and twilled brims *Tempest* iv 1 64
Twin. A meaner woman was delivered Of such a burden, male twins, both alike *Com. of Errors* i 1 56
To him one of the other twins was bound, Whilst I had been like heedful of the other i 1 82
By men of Epidamnum he and I And the twin Dromio all were taken up v 1 350
An apple, cleft in two, is not more twin Than these two creatures *T. N.* v 1 230
Ever witness for him Those twins of learning that he raised in you, Ipswich and Oxford! *Hen. VIII.* iv 2 58
Who twin, as 'twere, in love Unseparable *Coriolanus* iv 4 15
When vantage like a pair of twins appear'd, Both as the same *A. and C.* iii 10 12
Her inkle, silk, twin with the rubied cherry *Pericles* v Gower 8
Twin-born. O hard condition, Twin-born with greatness *Hen. V.* iv 1 251
Twin-brother. Here's the twin-brother of thy letter *Mer. Wives* ii 1 74
Twine. Being that I flow in grief, The smallest twine may lead me *M. Ado* iv 1 252
Let me twine Mine arms about that body *Coriolanus* iv 5 112
Twink. Ay, with a twink.—Before you can say 'come' and 'go' *Tempest* iv 1 43
That in a twink she won me to her love *T. of Shrew* ii 1 312
Twinkle. Having some business, do entreat her eyes To twinkle in their spheres till they return *Rom. and Jul.* ii 2 17
Twinkled. I should have been that I am, had the maidenliest star in the firmament twinkled on my bastardizing *Lear* i 2 144
Twinkling. At first I did adore a twinkling star *T. G. of Ver.* ii 6 9
I'll take my leave of the Jew in the twinkling of an eye *Mer. of Venice* ii 2 177
As plays the sun upon the glassy streams, Twinkling another counterfeited beam, So seems this gorgeous beauty 1 *Hen. VI.* v 3 63
Twinned. We were as twinn'd lambs that did frisk i' the sun *W. Tale* i 2 67
Twinn'd brothers of one womb, Whose procreation, residence, and birth, Scarce is dividant *T. of Athens* iv 3 3
Though he had twinn'd with me, both at a birth, Shall lose me *Othello* ii 3 212
And the twinn'd stones Upon the number'd beach *Cymbeline* i 6 35
Twist. Was't not to this end That thou began'st to twist so fine a story? *Much Ado* i 1 313
Breaking his oath and resolution like A twist of rotten silk *Coriolanus* v 6 96
Twisted. The smallest thread That ever spider twisted from her womb Will serve to strangle thee *K. John* iv 3 128
Like a poor prisoner in his twisted gyves *Rom. and Jul* ii 2 180
Twit. She twits me with my falsehood to my friend *T. G. of Ver.* iv 2 8
Becomes it thee to taunt his valiant age And twit with cowardice a man half dead? 1 *Hen. VI.* iii 2 55
Hath he not twit our sovereign lady here With ignominious words? 2 *Hen. VI.* iii 1 178
Twitting. There's for twitting me with perjury 3 *Hen. VI.* v 5 40
Two. We two, my lord, Will guard your person while you take your rest *Tempest* ii 1 196
Fair encounter Of two most rare affections! iii 1 75
If th' other two be brained like us, the state totters iii 2 7
A turn or two I'll walk, To still my beating mind iv 1 162
Two of these fellows you Must know and own v 1 274
'Tis a word or two Of commendations *T. G. of Ver.* i 3 52
I cannot be so soon provided: Please you, deliberate a day or two i 3 73
Thou hast no faith left now, unless thou'dst two; And that's far worse than none v 4 50
He cares not what he puts into the press, when he would put us two *Mer. Wives* ii 1 80
Shall I vouchsafe your worship a word or two?—Two thousand ii 2 42
Vat be all you, one, two, tree, four, come for? ii 3 22
Bear vitness that me have stay six or seven, two, tree hours for him ii 3 37
I think, if your husbands were dead, you two would marry iii 2 15
If there is one, I shall make two in the company.—If dere be one or two, I shall make-a the turd iii 3 250
How many numbers is in nouns?—Two iv 1 23
We two will still be the ministers iv 2 234
Let us two devise to bring him thither iv 4 27
Upon their sight, We two in great amazedness will fly iv 4 55
Go before into the Park: we two must go together v 3 4
May in the sworn twelve have a thief or two Guiltier than him *M. for M.* ii 1 20
Longing, saving your honour's reverence, for stewed prunes; sir, we had but two in the house ii 1 93
Longing, as I said, for prunes; and having but two in the dish, as I said ii 1 103
My business is a word or two with Claudio iii 1 48
For what reason?—For two; and sound ones too *Com. of Errors* ii 2 92
For if we two be one and thou play false, I do digest the poison of thy flesh ii 2 144
It was two ere I left him, and now the clock strikes one iv 2 54
I was his bondman, sir, But he, I thank him, gnaw'd in two my cords v 1 289
Which of you two did dine with me to-day? v 1 369
He'll but break a comparison or two on me *Much Ado* ii 1 153
Let us go sit here upon the church-bench till two, and then all to bed iii 3 95
Thought they Margaret was Hero?—Two of them did iii 3 164
Two of them have the very bent of honour iv 1 188
If thou kill'st me, boy, thou shalt kill a man.—He shall kill two of us v 1 80
How now? two of my brother's men bound! v 1 214
One more than two.—Which the base vulgar do call three *L. L. Lost* i 2 50
Of what complexion?—Of all the four, or the three, or the two, or one of the four i 2 84
He came, saw, and overcame: he came, one; saw, two; overcame, three iv 1 71
You two are book-men iv 2 35
Am I the first that have been perjured so?—I could put thee in comfort. Not by two that I know iv 3 52
I will repeat them,—a, e, i,— The sheep: the other two concludes it,—o, u v 1 59
It shall be written in eight and six.—No, make it two more *M. N. Dream* iii 1 26
Then will two at once woo one; That must needs be sport alone iii 2 118
All the counsel that we two have shared, The sisters' vows iii 2 198
With two seeming bodies, but one heart; Two of the first iii 2 213
Yet but three? Come one more; Two of both kinds makes up four iii 2 438
I had rather have a handful or two of dried peas iv 1 41
I know you two are rival enemies iv 1 147
Hear a Bergomask dance between two of our company? v 1 361
Since you have found Antonio, We two will leave you *Mer. of Venice* i 1 70
God defend me from these two! i 2 57

Two. With one fool's head I came to woo, But I go away with two *Mer. of Venice* ii 9 76
I pray you, tarry: pause a day or two Before you hazard iii 2 1
I would detain you here some month or two Before you venture for me iii 2 9
Like one of two contending in a prize iii 2 142
I'll hold thee any wager, When we are both accoutred like young men, I'll prove the prettier fellow of the two iii 4 64
Which of the two was daughter of the duke? *As Y. Like It* i 2 281
And we two will rail against our mistress the world and all our misery iii 2 295
Betwixt us two Tears our recountments had most kindly bathed iv 3 140
Here come two of the banished duke's pages v 3 5
Let me have audience for a word or two v 4 157
Let me entreat of you To pardon me yet for a night or two *T. of Shrew* Ind. 2 121
Did you yet ever see Baptista's daughter?—No, sir; but hear I do that he hath two i 2 253
Are you at the farthest?—Sir, at the farthest for a week or two iv 2 74
'Tis almost two; And 'twill be supper-time ere you come there iv 3 191
What if a man bring him a hundred pound or two, to make merry withal? v 1 23
Since you have begun, Have at you for a bitter jest or two! v 2 45
As the jest did glance away from me, 'Tis ten to one it maim'd you two outright v 2 62
We three are married, but you two are sped v 2 185
I am Cressid's uncle, That dare leave two together *All's Well* ii 1 101
He bade me store up, as a triple eye, Safer than mine own two ii 1 112
I will plant you two, and let the fool make a third *T. Night* ii 3 188
We'll whisper o'er a couplet or two of most sage saws iii 4 412
Nay, then I must have an ounce or two of this malapert blood from you iv 1 47
The bells of Saint Bennet, sir, may put you in mind; one, two, three v 1 43
An apple, cleft in two, is not more twin Than these two creatures v 1 230
Was not my lord The verier wag o' the two? *W. Tale* i 2 66
We two will walk, my lord, And leave you to your graver steps i 2 172
And will by twos and threes at several posterns Clear them o' the city. i 2 438
Lest that the treachery of the two fled hence Be left her to perform ii 1 195
They have scared away two of my best sheep iii 3 66
Nutmegs, seven; a race or two of ginger iv 3 50
One of these two must be necessities, Which then will speak iv 4 38
That nuptial which We two have sworn shall come iv 4 51
An hour or two before The stumbling night did part our weary powers *K. John* v 5 17
Thou, Aumerle, didst send two of thy men To execute the noble duke *Richard II.* iv 1 81
So two, together weeping, make one woe v 1 86
And these two beget A generation of still-breeding thoughts v 5 7
Two of the dangerous consorted traitors v 6 15
For two of them, I know them to be as true-bred cowards as ever turned back 1 *Hen. IV.* i 2 205
Soft; I know a trick worth two of that ii 1 41
'Twas a pennyworth, was't not?—O Lord, I would it had been two! ii 4 67
I have peppered two of them; two I am sure I have paid, two rogues ii 4 212
What, four? thou saidst but two even now.—Four, Hal; I told thee four ii 4 218
These nine in buckram that I told thee of— So, two more already ii 4 237
O monstrous! eleven buckram men grown out of two! ii 4 244
We two saw you four set on four and bound them ii 4 279
Then did we two set on you four; and, with a word, out-faced you ii 4 282
A rescue! a rescue!—Good people, bring a rescue or two 2 *Hen. IV.* ii 1 62
They will put on two of our jerkins and aprons ii 4 18
You two never meet but you fall to some discord ii 4 61
What's a joint of mutton or two in a whole Lent? ii 4 376
Here come two of Sir John Falstaff's men, as I think iii 2 59
Here is two more called than your number iii 2 200
To end one doubt by death Revives two greater in the heirs of life iv 1 200
There hath been a man or two lately killed about her v 4 7
Come, shall I make you two friends? We must to France together *Hen. V.* ii 1 94
As man and wife, being two, are one in love v 2 389
There's two of you; the devil make a third! 2 *Hen. VI.* iii 2 303
I will not bandy with thee word for word, But buckle with thee blows, twice two for one 3 *Hen. VI.* i 4 50
He means to beg a child of her.—Nay, whip me then: he'll rather give her two iii 2 28
Brothers, you muse what chat we two have had iii 2 109
Two of thy name, both Dukes of Somerset Have sold their lives v 1 73
And entertain some score or two of tailors *Richard III.* i 2 257
For God's sake, let not us two be behind ii 2 147
Some day or two Your highness shall repose you at the Tower iii 1 64
Those that come to see Only a show or two *Hen. VIII.* Prol. 10
All the good our English Have got by the late voyage is but merely A fit or two o' the face i 3 7
O, that your lordship were but now confessor To one or two of these! i 4 16
I thought ye, Upon my soul, two reverend cardinal virtues iii 1 103
Now, sir, you speak of two The most remark'd i' the kingdom v 1 32
Some come to take their ease, And sleep an act or two Epil. 3
Troilus is the better man of the two.—O Jupiter! there's no comparison *Troi. and Cres.* i 2 64
What is or is not, serves As stuff for these two to make paradoxes i 3 184
If Troy be not taken till these two undermine it, the walls will stand ii 3 9
He! no, she'll none of him; they two are twain iii 1 110
We two, that with so many thousand sighs Did buy each other iv 4 41
With too much blood and too little brain, these two may run mad v 1 54
And you too, Diomed, Keep Hector company an hour or two v 1 88
If I tell how these two did co-act, Shall I not lie in publishing a truth? v 2 118
You two are old men: tell me one thing that I shall ask you *Coriolanus* ii 1 15
In what enormity is Marcius poor in, that you two have not in abundance? ii 1 19
Do you two know how you are censured here in the city? ii 1 24
Seven hurts i' the body.—One i' the neck, and two i' the thigh ii 1 167
Come by him where he stands, by ones, by twos, and by threes ii 3 47
If, by the tribunes' leave, and yours, good people, I may be heard, I would crave a word or two iii 1 283
He said 'twas folly, For one poor grain or two, to leave unburnt v 1 27
For one poor grain or two! I am one of those; his mother, wife, his child v 1 28
'Tis not the difference of a year or two Makes me less gracious *T. An.* ii 1 31
These two have 'ticed me hither to this place: A barren detested vale ii 3 92
Two of thy whelps, fell curs of bloody kind ii 3 281
Two may keep counsel when the third's away iv 2 144
Know you these two?—The empress' sons, I take them v 2 153
For that vile fault Two of her brothers were condemn'd to death v 2 174
Here comes two of the house of the Montagues *Rom. and Jul.* i 1 38
Being thus frighted swears a prayer or two And sleeps again i 4 87

Two. Two of the fairest stars in all the heaven, Having some business *Rom. and Jul.* ii 2 15
Rests me his minim rest, one, two, and the third in your bosom . ii 4 23
A sail, a sail!—Two, two; a shirt and a smock . . . . . ii 4 109
Did you ne'er hear say, Two may keep counsel, putting one away? . ii 4 209
Sound the general doom! For who is living, if those two are gone? . iii 2 68
Do you like this haste? We'll keep no great ado,—a friend or two . iii 4 23
You that way and you this, but two in company . *T. of Athens* v 1 109
The Athenians, By two of their most reverend senate, greet thee . v 1 132
Touch thy instrument a strain or two . . . . . . *J. Cæsar* iv 3 257
Thou know'st that we two went to school together . . . . v 5 26
When we have mark'd with blood those sleepy two Of his own chamber *Macbeth* i 7 75
There are two lodged together.—One cried 'God bless us!' and 'Amen' the other . . . . ii 2 26
One: two: why, then 'tis time to do't.—Hell is murky! . . . v 1 40
Bid the players make haste. Will you two help to hasten them? *Hamlet* iii 2 55
What's his weapon?—Rapier and dagger.—That's two of his weapons . v 2 153
This fellow has banished two on's daughters . . . . . . *Lear* i 4 114
Let's away to prison: We two alone will sing like birds i' the cage . v 3 9
If fortune brag of two she loved and hated, One of them we behold . v 3 280
'Tis not a year or two shows us a man: They are all but stomachs *Othello* iii 4 103
How is't, brother!—My leg is cut in two.—Marry, heaven forbid! . v 1 72
A word or two before you go.—I have done the state some service . v 2 338
Such two that would by all likelihood have confounded one the other *Cymbeline* i 4 53
Her son Cannot take two from twenty, for his heart, And leave eighteen ii 1 60
One, two, three: time, time! . . . . ii 2 51
Make pastime with us a day or two, or longer . . . . . . iii 1 79
Let what is here contain'd relish of love, Of my lord's health, of his content, yet not That we two are asunder . . . . . . iii 2 32
He that strikes The venison first shall be the lord o' the feast; To him the other two shall minister . . . . iii 3 76
I will prove that two on's are as good As I have given out him . . v 5 311
And I must lose Two of the sweet'st companions in the world . . v 5 349
How they may be, and yet in two, As you will live, resolve it you *Pericles* i 1 70
I saw you lately, When you caught hurt in parting two that fought . iv 1 88
Two actions. The wearing out of six fashions, which is four terms, or two actions . . . . 2 *Hen. IV.* v 1 90
Two affirmatives. Conclusions to be as kisses, if your four negatives make your two affirmatives . . . . *T. Night* v 1 24
Two ancient urns. I will befriend thee more with rain, That shall distil from these two ancient urns . . . . . . *T. Andron.* iii 1 17
Two and fifty. Though she have as many diseases as two and fifty horses *T. of Shrew* i 2 81
The Turk, that two and fifty kingdoms hath . . . 1 *Hen. VI.* iv 7 73
Here's but two and fifty hairs on your chin . . *Troi. and Cres.* i 2 171
'Two and fifty hairs,' quoth he, 'and one white' . . . . . i 2 175
Two and forty. Thou shalt continue two and forty hours *Rom. and Jul.* iv 1 105
Two and thirty. Was it fit for a servant to use his master so, being perhaps, for aught I see, two and thirty, a pip out? . . *T. of Shrew* i 2 33
I have maintained that salamander of yours with fire any time this two and thirty years . . . . 1 *Hen. IV.* iii 3 54
Two and twenty. Would any but these boiled brains of nineteen and two-and-twenty hunt this weather? . . . . . . *W. Tale* iii 3 65
Two and twenty knights, Balk'd in their own blood . 1 *Hen. IV.* i 1 68
I have forsworn his company hourly any time this two and twenty years ii 2 17
O for a fine thief, of the age of two and twenty or thereabouts! . iii 3 212
A' should have sent me two and twenty yards of satin . 2 *Hen. IV.* i 2 49
For two and twenty sons I never wept . . . . . *T. Andron.* iii 1 10
Two and two. Must we all march?—Yea, two and two, Newgate fashion 1 *Hen. IV.* iii 3 104
Two Antipholuses. These two Antipholuses, these two so like *Com. of Errors* v 1 357
Two arrant cowards. An the Prince and Poins be not two arrant cowards, there's no equity stirring . . . . . 1 *Hen. IV.* ii 2 106
Two artificial gods. Like two artificial gods, Have with our needles created both one flower . . . . *M. N. Dream* iii 2 203
Two aspicious persons. Our watch, sir, have indeed comprehended two aspicious persons . . . . *Much Ado* iii 5 50
Two authorities. When two authorities are up, Neither supreme, how soon confusion May enter . . . . *Coriolanus* iii 1 109
Two backs. Are now making the beast with two backs . . . *Othello* i 1 118
Two bad ways. One of two bad ways you must conceit me, Either a coward or a flatterer . . . . *J. Cæsar* iii 1 192
Two beadles. The running banquet of two beadles . . *Hen. VIII.* v 4 69
Two bears. Then the two bears will not bite one another *Much Ado* iii 2 80
Two beggars told me I could not miss my way . . *Cymbeline* iii 6 8
Two blades. Between two blades, which bears the better temper 1 *Hen. VI.* ii 4 13
Two blushing pilgrims. My lips, two blushing pilgrims *Rom. and Jul.* i 5 97
Two bosoms. One heart, one bed, two bosoms, and one troth *M. N. Dream* ii 2 42
Two bosoms interchained with an oath; So then two bosoms and a single troth . . . . ii 2 49
Two boys. I have two boys Seek Percy and thyself about the field 1 *Hen. IV.* v 4 31
This was strange chance: A narrow lane, an old man, and two boys *Cymbeline* v 3 52
Two boys, an old man twice a boy, a lane, Preserved the Britons . v 3 57
Two brace. Has sent your honour two brace of greyhounds *T. of Athens* i 2 195
Two branches. Made thy body bare Of her two branches *T. Andron.* ii 4 18
Two brave bears. Call hither to the stake my two brave bears 2 *Hen. VI.* v 1 144
The two brave bears, Warwick and Montague . . . 3 *Hen. VI.* v 7 10
Two braver men Ne'er spurr'd their coursers . . . . . . v 7 8
Two brides. If the emperor's court can feast two brides, You are my guest, Lavinia . . . . *T. Andron.* i 1 489
Two broken points. Chapeless; with two broken points *T. of Shrew* iii 2 48
Two brothers. To rescue my two brothers from their death *T. Andron.* iii 1 49
The counterfeit presentment of two brothers . . . . *Hamlet* iii 4 54
Had I been thief-stol'n, As my two brothers, happy! . . *Cymbeline* i 6 6
Sleep, . . . thou hast created A mother and two brothers . . . v 4 125
Two buckets. Like a deep well That owes two buckets *Richard II.* iv 1 185
Two bullets. I will discharge upon her, Sir John, with two bullets 2 *Hen. IV.* ii 4 124
Two bushels. His reasons are as two grains of wheat hid in two bushels of chaff . . . . *Mer. of Venice* i 1 115
Two chamberlains. His two chamberlains Will I with wine and wassail so convince . . . . *Macbeth* i 7 63
Two chantries. I have built Two chantries . . . *Hen. V.* iv 1 318
Two charming words. That parting kiss which I had set Betwixt two charming words . . . . *Cymbeline* i 3 35
Two children. By her he had two children at one birth . 2 *Hen. VI.* iv 2 147
Wept like two children in their deaths' sad stories . *Richard III.* iv 3 8
Two Christian armies. Where these two Christian armies might combine . . . . *K. John* v 2 37
Two churchmen. Stand betwixt two churchmen, good my lord *Rich. III.* iii 7 48
Two clergymen. See, where he stands between two clergymen! . . iii 7 95
Two Cliffords, as the father and the son, And two Northumberlands 3 *Hen. VI.* v 7 7
Two cods. I remember the wooing of a peascod instead of her, from whom I took two cods . . . . *As Y. Like It* ii 4 52
Two commands. How, in one house, Should many people, under two commands, Hold amity? . . . . *Lear* ii 4 244
Two councils. He says there are two councils held . *Richard III.* iii 2 12
Two counties. Those two counties I will undertake Your grace shall well and quietly enjoy . . . . 1 *Hen. VI.* v 3 158
Two countries. To be a Dutchman to-day, a Frenchman to-morrow, or in the shape of two countries at once . . . . *Much Ado* iii 2 34
Two courses. Set her two courses off to sea again . . . *Tempest* i 1 52
Two cousins. Then there were two cousins laid up . *As Y. Like It* i 3 7
Of our two cousins coming into London . . . . *Richard II.* v 2 3
Two coxcombs. Would I had two coxcombs and two daughters! *Lear* i 4 118
Two crafts. O, 'tis most sweet, When in one line two crafts directly meet . . . . *Hamlet* iii 4 210
Two creatures. An apple, cleft in two, is not more twin Than these two creatures . . . . *T. Night* v 1 231
What do you pity, sir?—Two creatures heartily . . *Cymbeline* i 6 83
Two crowns. I'll give thee two crowns.—What two crowns shall they be?—Why, after I have cut the egg i' the middle, and eat up the meat, the two crowns of the egg . . . . *Lear* i 4 170
Two crutches. Pluck'd two crutches from my feeble limbs *Richard III.* ii 2 58
Two curs shall tame each other . . . . . *Troi. and Cres.* i 3 391
Two daughters. With my two daughters' dowers digest this third *Lear* i 1 130
Would I had two coxcombs and two daughters! . . . . . i 4 118
Hast thou given all to thy two daughters? And art thou come to this? iii 4 49
Two days. After two days I will discharge thee . . . *Tempest* i 2 298
Spirit, fine spirit! I'll free thee Within two days for this . . . i 2 421
Where have you been these two days loitering? . . *T. G. of Ver.* iv 4 48
You shall find, within these two days he will be here *Meas. for Meas.* iv 2 213
'Twill be two days ere I shall see you, so I leave you . *All's Well* ii 5 75
My people did expect my hence departure Two days ago . *W. Tale* i 2 451
My lord, some two days since I saw the prince . . *Richard II.* v 3 13
They have been up these two days.—They have the more need to sleep now . . . . 2 *Hen. VI.* iv 2 2
That scarce, some two days since, were worth a noble . *Richard III.* i 3 82
And Juliet bleeding, warm, and newly dead, Who here hath lain these two days buried . . . . *Rom. and Jul.* v 3 176
If, after two days' shine, Athens contain thee . . . *T. of Athens* iii 5 101
Ere we were two days old at sea . . . . *Hamlet* iv 6 15
But where's my fool? I have not seen him this two days . . *Lear* i 4 78
Is it two days ago since I tripped up thy heels, and beat thee? . ii 2 31
Your way is shorter; My purposes do draw me much about: You'll win two days upon me . . . . *Ant. and Cleo.* ii 4 9
Her old servant I have not seen these two days . . . *Cymbeline* iii 5 55
Two deep divines. Meditating with two deep divines *Richard III.* iii 7 75
Two deep enemies, Foes to my rest . . . . iv 2 73
Two delinquents. Did he not straight In pious rage the two delinquents tear? . . . . *Macbeth* iii 6 12
Two desperate men. As doth the fury of two desperate men *K. John* iii 1 32
Two dishes, but to one table . . . . *Hamlet* iv 3 26
Two dog-apes. Like the encounter of two dog-apes . *As Y. Like It* ii 5 27
Two dogs. Between two dogs, which hath the deeper mouth 1 *Hen. VI.* ii 4 12
Two domestic powers. Equality of two domestic powers Breed scrupulous faction . . . . *Ant. and Cleo.* i 3 47
Two dozen odd. For your voices bear Of wounds two dozen odd *Coriol.* ii 3 135
Two dreadful battles. Like heralds 'twixt two dreadful battles set *K. John* iv 2 78
Two Dromios. These two Dromios, one in semblance . *Com. of Errors* v 1 358
Two dry toasts. As rheumatic as two dry toasts . . . 2 *Hen. IV.* ii 4 62
Two dukedoms. Henry was well pleased To change two dukedoms for a duke's fair daughter . . . . 2 *Hen. VI.* i 1 219
Till Suffolk gave two dukedoms for his daughter . . . . . . i 3 90
Two eager tongues. The bitter clamour of two eager tongues *Rich. II.* i 1 49
Two ears. And that my two ears can witness . . . *Com. of Errors* ii 1 46
Two earthly women. If two gods should play some heavenly match And on the wager lay two earthly women . . . . *Mer. of Venice* iii 5 85
Two Edward shovel-boards, that cost me two shilling and two pence a-piece . . . . *Mer. Wives* i 1 159
Two enemies. Darest thou resolve to kill a friend of mine?—Ay, my lord; But I had rather kill two enemies . . . *Richard III.* iv 2 72
Two equal men. The queen shall be acquainted Forthwith *Hen. VIII.* ii 2 108
Two estates. Fortune, she said, was no goddess, that had put such difference betwixt their two estates . . . . *All's Well* i 3 117
Two extremes. His flaw'd heart, . . . 'Twixt two extremes of passion, joy and grief, Burst smilingly . . . . *Lear* v 3 198
Two eyes. But for her eye, I would not love her; yes, for her two eyes *L. L. Lost* iv 3 11
What stars do spangle heaven with such beauty, As those two eyes become that heavenly face? . . . . *T. of Shrew* iv 5 32
Make thy two eyes, like stars, start from their spheres . . *Hamlet* i 5 17
Two fair daughters. He that has the two fair daughters . *T. of Shrew* i 2 222
Two fair queens. Reverend looker on of two fair queens *Richard III.* iv 1 31
Two fair sons. That bore thee at a burden two fair sons *Com. of Errors* v 1 343
Two faiths. By my two faiths and troths, my lord . . *Much Ado* i 1 228
Two faults, madonna, that drink and good counsel will amend *T. Night* i 5 47
Two foes. From forth the fatal loins of these two foes A pair of star-cross'd lovers take their life . . . . . . *Rom. and Jul.* Prol. 5
Twofold. Doth with a twofold vigour lift me up . . *Richard II.* i 3 71
Doubly divorced! Bad men, you violate A twofold marriage . . . v 1 72
A good sherris-sack hath a two-fold operation in it. . 2 *Hen. IV.* iv 3 104
And some I see That two-fold balls and treble sceptres carry *Macbeth* iv 1 121
And what's in prayer but this two-fold force, To be forestalled ere we come to fall, Or pardon'd being down? . . . . *Hamlet* iii 3 48
Two friends. Even thus two friends condemn'd Embrace and kiss and take ten thousand leaves . . . . 2 *Hen. VI.* iii 2 353
Set deadly enmity between two friends . . . . *T. Andron.* v 1 131
Ay me, most wretched, That have my heart parted betwixt two friends! *Ant. and Cleo.* iii 6 77
Two full moons. Methought his eyes Were two full moons . . *Lear* iv 6 70
Two galliases, And twelve tight galleys . . . . *T. of Shrew* ii 1 380
Two gallons. Item, Sack, two gallons, 5s. 8d. . . . 1 *Hen. IV.* ii 4 587
Two geese. My father stole two geese out of a pen . . *Mer. Wives* iii 4 41

Two gentlemen Have in this robbery lost three hundred marks 1 *Hen. IV.* ii 4 568
Two gipsies. Both in a tune, like two gipsies on a horse *As Y. Like It* v 3 16
Two girls. Between two girls, which hath the merriest eye 1 *Hen. VI.* ii 4 15
Two glasses. What is the time o' the day?—Past the mid season.—At least two glasses . . . . *Tempest* i 2 240
Two godfathers. In christening shalt thou have two godfathers *M. of V.* iv 1 398
Two gods. If two gods should play some heavenly match And on the wager lay two earthly women . . . . iii 5 84
Two goodly sons. A joyful mother of two goodly sons *Com. of Errors* i 1 51
Two gowns. One that hath two gowns and every thing handsome about him . . . . *Much Ado* iv 2 88
Two grains. His reasons are as two grains of wheat hid in two bushels of chaff . . . . *Mer. of Venice* i 1 115
Two great cardinals. The two great cardinals Wait in the presence *Hen. VIII.* iii 1 16
Two grey eyes, with lids to them . . . . . . *T. Night* i 5 266
Two-hand. Come with thy two-hand sword . . . 2 *Hen. VI.* ii 1 46
Two hands. Is your tardy master now at hand?—Nay, he's at two hands with me, and that my two ears can witness *Com. of Errors* ii 1 45
Till Cranmer, Cromwell, her two hands, and she, Sleep in their graves *Hen. VIII.* v 1 31
Two hard things. There is two hard things; that is, to bring the moonlight into a chamber . . . . *M. N. Dream* iii 1 48
Two hates. No space of earth shall sunder our two hates *Troi. and Cres.* v 10 27
Two hawks. Between two hawks, which flies the higher pitch 1 *Hen. VI.* ii 4 11
Two-headed. Now, by two-headed Janus, Nature hath framed strange fellows in her time . . . . *Mer. of Venice* i 1 50
Two heads. These two heads do seem to speak to me, And threat me *T. Andron.* iii 1 272
Two helps. I, with your two helps, will so practise on Benedick *M. Ado* ii 1 397
Two holes. I spied his eyes, and methought he had made two holes in the ale-wife's new petticoat . . . . . . 2 *Hen. IV.* ii 2 88
Two honest men. Had I once lived to see two honest men? *T. of Athens* v 1 59
Two honours. There were two honours lost, yours and your son's 2 *Hen. IV.* ii 3 16
Two horses. Between two horses, which doth bear him best 1 *Hen. VI.* ii 4 14
Two hours. He promised to meet me two hours since . *Meas. for Meas.* i 2 76
I know you not: In Ephesus I am but two hours old *Com. of Errors* ii 2 150
'Tis now but four o'clock: we have two hours To furnish us *Mer. of Ven.* ii 4 8
Whether till the next night she had rather stay, Or go to bed now, being two hours to day . . . . v 1 303
For these two hours, Rosalind, I will leave thee.—Alas! dear love, I cannot lack thee two hours . . . . . *As Y. Like It* iv 1 180
If I were but two hours younger, I'ld beat thee . *All's Well* ii 3 268
Here he comes, to beguile two hours in a sleep . . . iv 1 25
My watch hath told me, toward my grave I have travell'd but two hours *T. Night* v 1 166
How now, Kate! I must leave you within these two hours 1 *Hen. IV.* ii 3 39
I am a rogue, if I were not at half-sword with a dozen of them two hours together . . . . ii 4 183
An the indentures be drawn, I'l away within these two hours . iii 1 266
Who two hours since I met in travel toward his warlike father 1 *Hen. VI.* iv 3 35
If this right hand would buy two hours' life . . 3 *Hen. VI.* ii 6 80
And do expect him here some two hours hence . . . . v 1 10
My uncle grew so fast That he could gnaw a crust at two hours old *Richard III.* ii 4 28
I have been broad awake two hours and more . . *T. Andron.* ii 2 17
Is now the two hours' traffic of our stage . . . *Rom. and Jul.* Prol. 12
If you had sent but two hours before . . . *T. of Athens* iii 6 50
My father died within these two hours.—Nay, 'tis twice two months *Hamlet* iii 2 135
Spake you with him?—Ay, two hours together . . . *Lear* i 2 170
A stone-cutter or a painter could not have made him so ill, though he had been but two hours at the trade . . . . . *Lear* ii 2 65
Tend me to-night two hours, I ask no more . . *Ant. and Cleo.* iv 2 32
Two households, both alike in dignity, In fair Verona . *Rom. and Jul.* Prol. 1
Two houses. Ignomy in ransom and free pardon Are of two houses *Meas. for Meas.* ii 4 112
Two hundred ducats.—Say, how grows it due? . . *Com. of Errors* iv 4 137
Vaumond, Bentii, two hundred and fifty each . . . *All's Well* iv 3 188
Six thousand and two hundred good esquires . . . *Hen. V.* iv 8 83
For his ransom he will give you two hundred crowns . . . iv 4 49
And mine, a hundred and forty.—And mine, two hundred . *Othello* i 3 4
A sibyl, that had number'd in the world The sun to course two hundred compasses . . . . iii 4 71
Two husbands. I see two husbands, or mine eyes deceive me *Com. of Er.* v 1 331
Two in one. You shall not stay alone Till holy church incorporate two in one . . . . *Rom. and Jul.* ii 6 37
Two kingdoms must With fearful bloody issue arbitrate . . *K. John* i 1 37
Two kings. Did you see the meeting of the two kings? . . *W. Tale* v 2 44
Then the two kings called my father brother . . . . v 2 152
The two kings, Equal in lustre, were now best, now worst . *Hen. VIII.* i 1 28
Two kinsmen digg'd their graves with weeping eyes . . *Richard II.* iii 3 169
Two ladies. Never two ladies loved as they do . . *As Y. Like It* i 1 117
Two lads that thought there was no more behind But such a day to-morrow as to-day . . . . *W. Tale* i 2 63
Two latter. Careless heirs May the two latter darken . *Pericles* iii 2 29
Two learned men. That the two learned men have compiled *L. L. Lost* v 2 895
Two leathern jerkins. Put on two leathern jerkins and aprons 2 *Hen. IV.* ii 2 189
Two-legged. Then am I no two-legged creature . . 1 *Hen. IV.* ii 4 207
Two legs. I would fain see the man, that has but two legs *Hen. V.* iv 7 169
Two letters for her name fairly set down in studs . *T. of Shrew* iii 2 62
Two lights. Those suns of glory, those two lights of men *Hen. VIII.* i 1 6
Two lions. We are two lions litter'd in one day . . *J. Cæsar* ii 2 46
Two lips, indifferent red; item, two grey eyes, with lids to them *T. Night* i 5 265
Two long days. 'Twill be Two long days' journey . . *K. John* iv 3 20
Two lovely berries moulded on one stem . . . *M. N. Dream* iii 2 211
Two maids. To the tune of 'Two maids wooing a man' . *W. Tale* iv 4 295
Two meanings. I moralize two meanings in one word . *Richard III.* iii 1 83
Two men. Send him by your two men to Datchet-mead . *Mer. Wives* iii 3 141
An two men ride of a horse, one must ride behind . . *Much Ado* iii 5 40
Like two men That vow a long and weary pilgrimage . . *Richard II.* i 3 48
When good manners shall lie all in one or two men's hands *Rom. and Jul.* i 5 5
Sure I am two men there are not living To whom he more adheres *Ham.* ii 2 20
Two mightier troops than that the Dauphin led . . 1 *Hen. VI.* iv 3 7
Two mighty eagles. On our former ensign Two mighty eagles fell *J. C.* v 1 81
Two mighty monarchies. Are now confined two mighty monarchies *Hen. V.* Prol. 20
Two miles. There is a monastery two miles off . . *Mer. of Venice* iii 4 31
Two mincing steps. Turn two mincing steps Into a manly stride . . iii 4 67

Two mirrors of his princely semblance Are crack'd in pieces *Richard III.* ii 2 51
Two mistresses. I must of another errand to Sir John Falstaff from my two mistresses . . . . *Mer. Wives* iii 4 114
Two moist elements. Bounding between the two moist elements *Troi. and Cres.* i 3 41
Two moles. I will bring these two moles, these blind ones, aboard him *W. Tale* iv 4 868
Two months. She is gone; she is two months on her way . *L. L. Lost* v 2 679
Within these two months, that's a month before This bond expires *Mer. of Venice* i 3 159
Thy loving voyage Is but for two months victuall'd . *As Y. Like It* v 4 198
His wife some two months since fled from his house . *All's Well* iv 3 56
I'll find A Marshalsea shall hold ye play these two months *Hen. VIII.* v 4 90
Some two months hence my will shall here be made . *Troi. and Cres.* v 10 53
Some two months hence up higher toward the north . *J. Cæsar* ii 1 109
That it should come to this! But two months dead: nay, not so much, not two . . . . *Hamlet* i 2 138
My father died within these two hours.—Nay, 'tis twice two months . iii 2 136
O heavens! die two months ago, and not forgotten yet? . . . iii 2 139
Two months since, Here was a gentleman of Normandy . . . iv 7 82
Two more summers. Let two more summers wither in their pride *Rom. and Jul.* i 2 10
Two napkins. There's but a shirt and a half in all my company; and the half shirt is two napkins tacked together . 1 *Hen. IV.* iv 2 47
Two Neapolitans. O Stephano, two Neapolitans 'scaped! . *Tempest* ii 2 118
Two neighbours. Now is the mural down between the two neighbours *M. N. Dream* v 1 208
Two nephews. To ransom my two nephews from their death *T. Andron.* iii 1 173
Two nights. Has friendship such a faint and milky heart, It turns in less than two nights? . . . . *T. of Athens* iii 1 58
I have two nights watched with you, but can perceive no truth in your report . . . . *Macbeth* v 1 1
Are so fortified against our story What we have two nights seen *Hamlet* i 1 33
Two nights together had these gentlemen . . . Been thus encounter'd . i 2 196
For two nights together Have made the ground my bed . *Cymbeline* iii 6 2
Two noble beasts. Here come two noble beasts in, a man and a lion *M. N. Dream* v 1 220
Two noble partners. You shall have two noble partners *Hen. VIII.* v 3 168
Two noble sons. Here are the heads of thy two noble sons *T. Andron.* iii 1 237
Two noses. We had like to have had our two noses snapped off with two old men without teeth . . . . *Much Ado* v 1 115
Two notes. 'D sol re,' one clef, two notes have I . *T. of Shrew* iii 1 77
Two notorious benefactors.—Benefactors? Well; what benefactors? *Meas. for Meas.* ii 1 50
Two o'clock. Sure, Luciana, it is two o'clock . . . *Com. of Errors* ii 1 3
By two o'clock I will be with thee again.—Ay, go your ways *As Y. L. It* iv 1 185
Two o'clock is your hour—Ay, sweet Rosalind? . . . . . iv 1 190
How say you now? Is it not past two o'clock? and here much Orlando! iv 3 1
What's o'clock?—I think it be two o'clock . . . 1 *Hen. IV.* ii 1 37
It is good morrow, is it not?—Indeed, my lord, I think it be two o'clock ii 4 574
Meet me to-morrow in the temple hall at two o'clock in the afternoon . iii 3 224
'Twill be two o'clock ere they come from the coronation . 2 *Hen. IV.* v 5 3
Now is it time to arm: come, shall we about it?—It is now two o'clock *Hen. V.* iii 7 168
Two old men without teeth. . . . . *Much Ado* v 1 116
Two ordinaries. I did think thee, for two ordinaries, to be a pretty wise fellow . . . . *All's Well* ii 3 211
Two or three lords and ladies more married . . *M. N. Dream* iv 2 16
And clap upon you two or three probable lies . . . *All's Well* iii 6 106
If there were not two or three and fifty upon poor old Jack . 1 *Hen. IV.* ii 4 206
There's two or three of us have seen strange sights . . *J. Cæsar* i 3 138
Who was't came by?—'Tis two or three, my lord . . . *Macbeth* iv 1 141
Two or three groan: it is a heavy night: These may be counterfeits *Oth.* v 1 42
Two other husbands. I think, if your husbands were dead, you two would marry.—Be sure of that,—two other husbands *Mer. Wives* iii 2 16
Two other sons, who in the wars o' the time Died . . *Cymbeline* i 1 35
Two paces. Now two paces of the vilest earth Is room enough 1 *Hen. IV.* v 4 91
Two parties. Whence come you?—From the two parties *Mer. Wives* iv 5 107
The English army, that divided was Into two parties, is now conjoin'd in one, And means to give you battle . . . 1 *Hen. VI.* v 2 12
Two pasties. And make two pasties of your shameful heads *T. Andron.* v 2 190
Two pence. What money is in my purse?—Seven groats and two pence 2 *Hen. IV.* i 2 263
If you do not all show like gilt two-pences to me . . . iv 3 55
Two pernicious daughters. That have with two pernicious daughters join'd . . . . *Lear* iii 2 22
Two persons. One face, one voice, one habit, and two persons *T. Night* v 1 223
Two pile. 'Tis a goodly patch of velvet: his left cheek is a cheek of two pile and a half . . . . *All's Well* iv 5 103
Two pitch-balls stuck in her face for eyes . . *L. L. Lost* iii 1 199
Two points. But I am resolved on two points . . . *T. Night* i 5 24
God's light, with two points on your shoulder? much! . . 2 *Hen. IV.* ii 4 142
Two poles. Bring them both upon two poles hither. . 2 *Hen. VI.* iv 7 119
Two princely boys! They are as gentle As zephyrs . . *Cymbeline* iv 2 171
Two princes. Would the two princes lie? . . . . *Much Ado* iv 1 154
Two proper palfreys, black as jet . . . . . *T. Andron.* v 2 50
Two props of virtue for a Christian prince . . . *Richard III.* iii 7 96
Two Provincial roses on my razed shoes . . . . *Hamlet* iii 2 288
Two pulls at once; His lady banish'd, and a limb lopp'd off . 2 *Hen. VI.* ii 3 41
Two raging fires. Where two raging fires meet together . *T. of Shrew* ii 1 133
Two rams. There was never any thing so sudden but the fight of two rams *As Y. Like It* v 2 31
Two razes. I have a gammon of bacon and two razes of ginger 1 *Hen. IV.* ii 1 26
Two reverend bishops. What two reverend bishops Were those that went on each side of the queen? . . . . . *Hen. VIII.* iv 1 99
Two right reverend fathers, Divinely bent to meditation *Richard III.* iii 7 61
Two rings. And neither man nor master would take aught But the two rings . . . . *Mer. of Venice* v 1 184
Two rogues. Two I am sure I have paid, two rogues in buckram suits 1 *Hen. IV.* ii 4 213
Two Romans. Are yet two Romans living such as these? . *J. Cæsar* v 3 98
Two scales. Put in two scales, Will even weigh . . *M. N. Dream* iii 2 132
Two schoolfellows, Whom I will trust as I will adders . *Hamlet* iii 4 202
Two sealed bags of ducats, Of double ducats . . . *Mer. of Venice* ii 8 18
Two seeming bodies, but one heart . . . . *M. N. Dream* iii 2 212
Two several powers Are enter'd in the Roman territories . *Coriolanus* iv 6 39
Two several times. The ghost of Cæsar hath appear'd to me Two several times by night . . . . *J. Cæsar* v 5 18
Two ships. We discovered Two ships from far making amain to us *Com. of Errors* i 1 93

Two shirts. I take but two shirts out with me, and I mean not to sweat extraordinarily . . . . 2 *Hen. IV.* i 2 234
Two short hours. I'll undertake may see away their shilling Richly in two short hours . . . . *Hen. VIII.* Prol. 13
Two sisters. Let this kiss Repair those violent harms that my two sisters Have in thy reverence made! . . . . . *Lear* iv 7 28
Two sleeves. 'With a trunk sleeve:'—I confess two sleeves *T. of Shrew* iv 3 143
Two soldiers. Yonder is heavy news within between two soldiers and my young lady! . . . . *All's Well* iii 2 36
Two sons. See, thy two sons' heads, Thy warlike hand . *T. Andron.* iii 1 255
'Twas her two sons that murder'd Bassianus . . . . . . v 1 91
Confederate with the queen and her two sons . . . . . v 1 108
When, for his hand, he had his two sons' heads . . . . v 1 115
The king's two sons Are stol'n away and fled . . . *Macbeth* ii 4 25
Is she sole child to the king?—His only child. He had two sons . *Cymb.* i 1 57
Thy lopp'd branches point Thy two sons forth . . . . . v 5 455
Two special reasons; Which may to you, perhaps, seem much unsinew'd *Hamlet* iv 7 9
Two spent swimmers, that do cling together And choke their art *Macbeth* i 2 8
Two spouts. Gasping to begin some speech, her eyes Became two spouts *W. Tale* iii 3 26
Two stars keep not their motion in one sphere . . . . 1 *Hen. IV.* v 4 65
Two stock-fishes. He was begot between two stock-fishes *Meas. for Meas.* iii 2 116
Two stones, two rich and precious stones, Stolen! . . *Mer. of Venice* ii 8 20
I will make him a philosopher's two stones to me . . 2 *Hen. IV.* iii 2 355
Like a philosopher, with two stones moe than's artificial one *T. of A.* ii 2 117
Two strange followers. Dogg'd with two strange followers *Tr. and Cr.* i 3 365
Two striplings—lads more like to run The country base . *Cymbeline* v 3 19
Two such. 'Twere pity two such friends should be long foes *T. G. of Ver.* v 4 118
My wife, not meanly proud of two such boys . . . *Com. of Errors* i 1 59
I have seen two such sights, by sea and by land! . . . *W. Tale* iii 3 84
If my legs were two such riding-rods, My arms such eel-skins *K. John* i 1 140
Two such silver currents, when they join, Do glorify the banks . . ii 1 441
Two such shores to two such streams made one, Two such controlling bounds shall you be . . . . ii 1 443
Never two such kingdoms did contend Without much fall of blood *Hen. V.* i 2 24
O, what a scandal is it to our crown, That two such noble peers as ye should jar! . . . . 1 *Hen. VI.* iii 1 70
If two such murderers as yourselves came to you . . *Richard III.* i 4 268
Meeting two such wealsmen as you are . . . . . . *Coriolanus* ii 1 59
Two such opposed kings encamp them still In man as well as herbs, grace, and rude will . . . . *Rom. and Jul.* ii 3 27
An there were two such, we should have none shortly . . . . iii 1 16
Love, and be friends, as two such men should be . . . *J. Cæsar* iv 3 131
Apes and monkeys 'Twixt two such shes would chatter this way *Cymb.* i 6 40
Two summers. Not yet two summers younger . . . . . *Pericles* i 4 39
Two sweet babes. A mother only mock'd with two sweet babes *Richard III.* iv 4 87
Two sweet sons. My damned son, which thy two sweet sons smother'd iv 4 134
Two Talbots, winged through the lither sky . . . 1 *Hen. VI.* iv 7 21
Two tender playfellows for dust . . . . . . *Richard III.* iv 4 385
Two tens. And thou shalt have more Than two tens to a score . *Lear* i 4 140
Two thieves. If our eyes had authority, here they might take two thieves kissing . . . . *Ant. and Cleo.* ii 6 100
Two things provided more . . . . *Mer. of Venice* iv 1 386
Grant me two things, I pray you, Not to deny me, and to pardon me . iv 1 423
She's very well indeed, but for two things.—What two things? *All's W.* ii 4 9
And those two things, I confess, I cannot help . . . 2 *Hen. IV.* ii 2 73
Two things are to be done . . . . *Othello* ii 3 388
Two thousand. A thousand good-morrows.— . . . To you two thousand *T. G. of Ver.* ii 1 106
Shall I vouchsafe your worship a word or two?—Two thousand *M. Wives* ii 2 43
A diamond gone, cost me two thousand ducats! . . *Mer. of Venice* iii 1 88
Two thousand ducats in that; and other precious, precious jewels . iii 1 90
Two thousand ducats by the year Of fruitful land . *T. of Shrew* ii 1 371; 374
I have been dear to him, lad, some two thousand strong, or so *T. Night* iii 2 59
What, think you much to pay two thousand crowns? 2 *Hen. VI.* iv 1 18
Two thousand souls and twenty thousand ducats Will not debate the question of this straw . . . . *Hamlet* iv 4 25
Two tongues. There's a double tongue; there's two tongues . *Much Ado* v 1 171
Two traded pilots 'twixt the dangerous shores Of will and judgement *Troi. and Cres.* ii 2 64
Two treys. There is three.—Nay then, two treys . . . *L. L. Lost* v 2 232
Two tribunes. I could myself Take up a brace o' the best of them; yea, the two tribunes . . . . *Coriolanus* iii 1 244
Two truths are told, As happy prologues to the swelling act . *Macbeth* i 3 127
Two usuries. 'Twas never merry world since, of two usuries, the merriest was put down . . . . *Meas. for Meas.* iii 2 6
Two villains. If where thou art two villains shall not be, Come not near him . . . . *T. of Athens* v 1 112
Two villains, whose false oaths prevail'd Before my perfect honour *Cymbeline* iii 3 66
Two voices. Four legs and two voices: a most delicate monster! *Tempest* ii 2 93
Two wagers. I will fetch my gold and have our two wagers recorded *Cymbeline* i 4 181
Two ways. I take it there's but two ways, either to utter them, or to conceal them . . . . 2 *Hen. IV.* v 3 116
Two weak evils. Oppress'd with two weak evils, age and hunger *As Y. Like It* ii 7 132
Two white herring. Hopdance cries in Tom's belly for two white herring . . . . *Lear* iii 6 33
Two winking Cupids Of silver, each on one foot standing . *Cymbeline* ii 4 89
Two women placed together makes cold weather . . *Hen. VIII.* i 4 22
Two words. How easy it is to put 'years' to the word 'three,' and study three years in two words . . . . *L. L. Lost* i 2 56
Two worlds. Thou hast lost by this a kingdom.—No, my lord; I have got two worlds by't . . . . *Cymbeline* v 5 374
Two worthy voices. There's in all two worthy voices begged *Coriolanus* ii 3 86
Two yards. I will tell you what I am about.—Two yards, and more *Mer. Wives* i 3 44
Indeed, I am in the waist two yards about . . . . . . i 3 46
Two years. Keep me company but two years moe, Thou shalt not know the sound of thine own tongue . . . . *Mer. of Venice* i 1 108
Did feast together, and in two years after Were they at wars 2 *Hen. IV.* iii 1 59
You tell a pedigree Of threescore and two years . . 3 *Hen. VI.* iii 3 93
'Twas full two years ere I could get a tooth . . *Richard III.* ii 4 29
His son was but a ward two years ago . . . *Rom. and Jul.* i 5 42
Whereon, At three and two years old, I stole these babes . *Cymbeline* iii 3 101
Two yoke-devils. Treason and murder ever kept together, As two yoke-devils . . . . *Hen. V.* ii 2 106

Two young gentlemen. These two young gentlemen, that call me father And think they are my sons, are none of mine *Cymbeline* v 5 328
Tybalt. Came The fiery Tybalt, with his sword prepared *Rom. and Jul.* i 1 116
Livia; Signior Valentio and his cousin Tybalt; Lucio . . . . i 2 73
Tybalt, the kinsman of old Capulet, Hath sent a letter to his father's house . . . . ii 4 6
Is he a man to encounter Tybalt?—Why, what is Tybalt?—More than prince of cats . . . . ii 4 17
Tybalt, the reason that I have to love thee Doth much excuse the appertaining rage To such a greeting . . . . iii 1 65
Tybalt, you rat-catcher, will you walk?—What wouldst thou have with me? . . . . iii 1 78
Tybalt, Mercutio, the prince expressly hath Forbidden bandying . . iii 1 91
My reputation stain'd With Tybalt's slander,—Tybalt, that an hour Hath been my kinsman! . . . . iii 1 117
Here comes the furious Tybalt back again.—Alive, in triumph! and Mercutio slain! . . . . iii 1 126
Now, Tybalt, take the villain back again, That late thou gavest me iii 1 130
Romeo, away, be gone! The citizens are up, and Tybalt slain . iii 1 138
Tybalt, that murderer, which way ran he?—There lies that Tybalt . iii 1 143
Tybalt, my cousin! O my brother's child! O prince! O cousin! husband! . . . . iii 1 151
Who began this bloody fray?—Tybalt, here slain, whom Romeo's hand did slay . . . . iii 1 157
Could not take truce with the unruly spleen Of Tybalt deaf to peace . iii 1 163
With one hand beats Cold death aside, and with the other sends It back to Tybalt, whose dexterity Retorts it . . . . . . iii 1 168
Tybalt hit the life Of stout Mercutio, and then Tybalt fled . . iii 1 173
Ere I Could draw to part them, was stout Tybalt slain . . . iii 1 178
Romeo slew Tybalt, Romeo must not live . . . . . . iii 1 186
His fault concludes but what the law should end, The life of Tybalt . iii 1 191
O Tybalt, Tybalt, the best friend I had! O courteous Tybalt! . . iii 2 61
Is Romeo slaughter'd, and is Tybalt dead? My dear-loved cousin? . iii 2 65
Tybalt is gone, and Romeo banished; Romeo that kill'd him, he is banished.—O God! did Romeo's hand shed Tybalt's blood? . . iii 2 69
My husband lives, that Tybalt would have slain; And Tybalt's dead, that would have slain my husband . . . . iii 2 105
Wherefore weep I then? Some word there was, worser than Tybalt's death . . . . iii 2 108
'Tybalt is dead, and Romeo—banished;' That 'banished,' that one word 'banished,' Hath slain ten thousand Tybalts. Tybalt's death Was woe enough, if it had ended there . . . . iii 2 112
Why follow'd not, when she said 'Tybalt's dead,' Thy father, or thy mother? . . . . iii 2 118
But with a rearward following Tybalt's death, 'Romeo is banished,' to speak that word, Is father, mother, Tybalt, Romeo, Juliet, All slain, all dead . . . . iii 2 121
Where is my father, and my mother, nurse?—Weeping and wailing over Tybalt's corse . . . . iii 2 128
An hour but married, Tybalt murdered, Doting like me and like me banished . . . . iii 3 66
Then starts up, And Tybalt calls; and then on Romeo cries . . iii 3 101
Hast thou slain Tybalt? wilt thou slay thyself? And slay thy lady too? iii 3 116
Tybalt would kill thee, But thou slew'st Tybalt; there art thou happy too . . . . iii 3 137
Look you, she loved her kinsman Tybalt dearly, And so did I . . iii 4 3
Tybalt being slain so late, It may be thought we held him carelessly . iii 4 24
Give him such an unaccustom'd dram, That he shall soon keep Tybalt company . . . . iii 5 92
Make the bridal bed In that dim monument where Tybalt lies . . iii 5 203
Immoderately she weeps for Tybalt's death . . . . . . iv 1 6
Where bloody Tybalt, yet but green in earth, Lies festering in his shroud . . . . iv 3 42
And pluck the mangled Tybalt from his shroud . . . . . iv 3 52
Stay, Tybalt, stay! Romeo, I come! this do I drink to thee . . iv 3 57
Tybalt, liest thou there in thy bloody sheet? . . . . . v 3 97
Their stol'n marriage-day Was Tybalt's dooms-day . . . . v 3 234
For whom, and not for Tybalt, Juliet pined . . . . . . v 3 236
Tyburn. The shape of Love's Tyburn that hangs up simplicity *L. L. Lost* iv 3 54
Tying thine ear to no tongue but thine own! . . . . 1 *Hen. IV.* i 3 238
Which easily endures not article Tying him to aught . *Coriolanus* ii 3 205
For tying his new shoes with old riband . . . . *Rom. and Jul.* iii 1 31
Tying her duty, beauty, wit, and fortunes In an extravagant and wheeling stranger Of here and every where . . . . *Othello* i 1 136
Tymbria. Priam's six-gated city, Dardan, and Tymbria, Helias, Chetas, Troien, And Antenorides . . . . . *Troi. and Cres.* Prol. 16
Type. Thy father bears the type of King of Naples, Of both the Sicils and Jerusalem . . . . 3 *Hen. VI.* i 4 121
The high imperial type of this earth's glory . . *Richard III.* iv 4 244
Tall stockings, Short blister'd breeches, and those types of travel *Hen. VIII.* i 3 31
Typhon. With terms unsquared, Which, from the tongue of roaring Typhon dropp'd, Would seem hyperboles . . . *Troi. and Cres.* i 3 160
Not Enceladus, With all his threatening band of Typhon's brood *T. An.* iv 2 94
Tyrannical. In this point charge him home, that he affects Tyrannical power . . . . *Coriolanus* iii 3 2
That you have contrived . . . to wind Yourself into a power tyrannical iii 3 65
Tyrannically. Little eyases, that cry out on the top of question, and are most tyrannically clapped for't . . . . . . *Hamlet* ii 2 356
Tyrannize. Is as a fiend confined to tyrannize On unreprievable condemned blood . . . . *K. John* v 7 47
This poor right hand of mine Is left to tyrannize upon my breast *T. An.* iii 2 8
I threw the people's suffrages On him that thus doth tyrannize o'er me iv 3 20
Tyrannous. But it is tyrannous To use it like a giant *Meas. for Meas.* ii 2 108
Were he meal'd with that Which he corrects, then were he tyrannous . iv 2 87
With all the unmuzzled thoughts That tyrannous heart can think *T. Night* iii 1 131
Fear you his tyrannous passion more, alas, Than the queen's life? *W. Tale* ii 3 28
Let us be clear'd Of being tyrannous, since we so openly Proceed in justice iii 2 5
The tyrannous and bloody deed is done . . . . . *Richard III.* iv 3 1
Alas, that love, so gentle in his view, Should be so tyrannous and rough in proof! . . . . *Rom. and Jul.* i 1 176
Baked and impasted with the parching streets, That lend a tyrannous and damned light To their lord's murder . . . . . *Hamlet* ii 2 482
And let this tyrannous night take hold upon you . . . *Lear* iii 4 156
Yield up, O Love, thy crown and hearted throne To tyrannous hate! *Oth.* iii 3 449
Like the tyrannous breathing of the north . . . . *Cymbeline* i 3 36
I knew him tyrannous; and tyrants' fears Decrease not . . *Pericles* i 2 84
Tyranny. Whether the tyranny be in his place, Or in his eminence that fills it up, I stagger in . . . . *Meas. for Meas.* i 2 167

Tyranny. Sith 'twas my fault to give the people scope, 'Twould be my tyranny to strike and gall them . . . . *Meas. for Meas.* i 3 36
I do oppose My patience to his fury, and am arm'd To suffer, with a quietness of spirit, The very tyranny and rage of his *Mer. of Venice* iv 1 13
The tyranny of her sorrows takes all livelihood from her cheek *All's Well* i 1 57
Something savours Of tyranny and will ignoble make you *W. Tale* ii 3 120
Innocence shall make False accusation blush and tyranny Tremble iii 2 32
Thy tyranny Together working with thy jealousies . . . . iii 2 180
A naked subject to the weeping clouds And waste for churlish winter's tyranny . . . . *2 Hen. IV.* i 3 62
That tyranny, which never quaff'd but blood, Would, by beholding him, have wash'd his knife With gentle eye-drops . . . iv 5 86
That hast by tyranny these many years Wasted our country *1 Hen. VI.* ii 3 40
My father's execution Was nothing less than bloody tyranny . . ii 5 100
The period of thy tyranny approacheth . . . . iv 2 17
Anon, from thy insulting tyranny, Coupled in bonds of perpetuity iv 7 19
That England was defamed by tyranny *2 Hen. VI.* iii 1 123
If my death might make this island happy And prove the period of their tyranny, I would expend it with all willingness . iii 1 149
Upon thy eyeballs murderous tyranny Sits in grim majesty . . iii 2 49
By shameful murder . . . And lofty proud encroaching tyranny . iv 1 96
Insulting tyranny begins to jet Upon the innocent . *Richard III.* ii 4 51
His enforcement of the city wives; His tyranny for trifles . . iii 7 9
Bruised underneath the yoke of tyranny . . . . v 2 2
The first was I that help'd thee to the crown; The last was I that felt thy tyranny . . . . . . v 3 168
Best of my flesh, Forgive my tyranny . . . *Coriolanus* v 3 43
Even at thy teat thou hadst thy tyranny . . *T. Andron.* ii 3 145
And wonder greatly that man's face can fold In pleasing smiles such murderous tyranny . . . . . ii 3 267
Mine eyes are cloy'd with view of tyranny . . . iii 2 55
That part of tyranny that I do bear I can shake off at pleasure *J. Cæsar* i 3 99
So let high-sighted tyranny range on, Till each man drop by lottery . ii 1 118
Liberty! Freedom! Tyranny is dead! . . . . iii 1 78
Great tyranny! lay thou thy basis sure, For goodness dare not check thee . . . . . *Macbeth* iv 3 32
Boundless intemperance In nature is a tyranny . . . iv 3 67
Our exiled friends abroad That fled the snares of watchful tyranny . v 8 67
Find an idle and fond bondage in the oppression of aged tyranny . *Lear* i 2 52
The tyranny of the open night's too rough For nature to endure . iii 4 2
For thy escape would teach me tyranny, To hang clogs on them *Othello* i 3 197
Tyrant. A plague upon the tyrant that I serve! *Tempest* ii 2 166
As I told thee before, I am subject to a tyrant, a sorcerer . . iii 2 49
There it goes, Silver!—Fury, Fury! there, Tyrant, there! hark! . iv 1 258
You seem'd of late to make the law a tyrant . *Meas. for Meas.* ii 4 114
Or, by the affection that now guides me most, I'll prove a tyrant to him ii 4 169
This would make mercy swear and play the tyrant . . . iii 2 207
Being a professed tyrant to their sex . . . *Much Ado* i 1 170
His lines would ravish savage ears And plant in tyrants mild humility *L. L. Lost* iv 3 349
What is Pyramus? a lover, or a tyrant?—A lover, that kills himself *M. N. Dream* i 2 24
My chief humour is for a tyrant: I could play Ercles rarely . . i 2 31
This is Ercles' vein, a tyrant's vein; a lover is more condoling . i 2 42
Thus must I from the smoke into the smother; From tyrant duke unto a tyrant brother . . . . *As Y. Like It* i 2 300
Swearing that we Are mere usurpers, tyrants, and what's worse . ii 1 61
That eyes . . . Should be call'd tyrants, butchers, murderers! . . iii 5 14
She Phebes me: mark how the tyrant writes . . . iv 3 39
Live you the marble-breasted tyrant still *T. Night* v 1 127
I'll not call you tyrant; But this most cruel usage of your queen . . . something savours Of tyranny . . . . *W. Tale* ii 3 116
Were I a tyrant, Where were her life? she durst not call me so, If she did know me one . . . . . . ii 3 122
Leontes a jealous tyrant; his innocent babe truly begotten . . iii 2 135
What studied torments, tyrant, hast for me? What wheels? racks? fires? iii 2 176
But, O thou tyrant! Do not repent these things, for they are heavier Than all thy woes can stir . . . . . iii 2 208
Ay me! this tyrant fever burns me up *K. John* v 3 14
Whiles the big year, swoln with some other grief, Is thought with child by the stern tyrant war *2 Hen. IV.* Ind. 14
We are no tyrant, but a Christian king *Hen. V.* i 2 241
Beauty that the tyrant oft reclaims . . *2 Hen. VI.* v 2 54
For how can tyrants safely govern home, Unless abroad they purchase great alliance? To prove him tyrant this reason may suffice *3 Hen. VI.* iii 3 69
And force the tyrant from his seat by war . . . iii 3 206
To prevent the tyrant's violence, . . . I'll hence forthwith . . iv 4 29
Tyrants themselves wept when it was reported *Richard III.* i 3 185
Defacer of God's handiwork, That excellent grand tyrant of the earth . iv 4 52
A bloody tyrant and a homicide; One raised in blood . . . v 3 246
If you do sweat to put a tyrant down, You sleep in peace, the tyrant being slain . . . . v 3 255
If I confess much, you will play the tyrant . *Troi. and Cres.* iii 2 127
With opportunity of sharp revenge Upon the Thracian tyrant *T. Andron.* i 1 138

Tyrant. 'Tis all one, I will show myself a tyrant . . *Rom. and Jul.* i 1 26
Beautiful tyrant! fiend angelical! Dove-feather'd raven! . . . iii 2 75
Pity is the virtue of the law, And none but tyrants use it cruelly *T. of Athens* iii 6 9
Therein, ye gods, you tyrants do defeat . . . *J. Cæsar* i 3 92
And why should Cæsar be a tyrant then? Poor man! . . . i 3 103
This Cæsar was a tyrant.—Nay, that's certain. . . . iii 2 74
I am the son of Marcus Cato, ho! A foe to tyrants . . . v 4 5
From broad words and 'cause he fail'd His presence at the tyrant's feast, I hear Macduff lives in disgrace . . *Macbeth* iii 6 22
The son of Duncan, From whom this tyrant holds the due of birth . iii 6 25
This tyrant, whose sole name blisters our tongues, Was once thought honest . . . . iv 3 12
For the whole space that's in the tyrant's grasp, And the rich East to boot iv 3 36
When I shall tread upon the tyrant's head, Or wear it on my sword . iv 3 45
O nation miserable, With an untitled tyrant bloody-scepter'd! . . iv 3 104
The tyrant has not batter'd at their peace?—No; they were well at peace iv 3 178
To my belief witness'd the rather, For that I saw the tyrant's power a-foot . . . . iv 3 185
What does the tyrant?—Great Dunsinane he strongly fortifies . . v 2 11
We learn no other but the confident tyrant Keeps still in Dunsinane . v 4 8
Do we but find the tyrant's power to-night, Let us be beaten, if we cannot fight . . . . v 6 7
Thou liest, abhorred tyrant; with my sword I'll prove the lie thou speak'st . . . . v 7 10
Tyrant, show thy face! If thou be'st slain and with no stroke of mine, My wife and children's ghosts will haunt me still . . . v 7 14
The tyrant's people on both sides do fight; The noble thanes do bravely v 7 25
And underwrit, 'Here may you see the tyrant' . . . v 8 27
So, as a painted tyrant, Pyrrhus stood . . . *Hamlet* ii 2 502
'Twas yet some comfort, When misery could beguile the tyrant's rage *Lear* iv 6 63
The tyrant custom, most grave senators . . . *Othello* i 3 230
How fine this tyrant Can tickle where she wounds! . *Cymbeline* i 1 84
Fear no more the frown o' the great; Thou art past the tyrant's stroke iv 2 265
But thou know'st this, 'Tis time to fear when tyrants seem to kiss *Pericles* i 2 79
And tyrants' fears Decrease not, but grow faster than the years . i 2 84
Antiochus you fear, And justly too, I think, you fear the tyrant . . i 2 103
Tyre. Young prince of Tyre, you have at large received The danger of the task you undertake . . . . i 1 1
Young prince of Tyre, . . . We might proceed to cancel of your days . i 1 110
We hate the prince of Tyre, and thou must kill him . . . i 1 156
Tyre, I now look from thee then, and to Tarsus Intend my travel . . i 2 115
So, this is Tyre, and this the court. Here must I kill King Pericles . i 3 1
Hush! here come the lords of Tyre . . . . . i 3 10
You shall not need, my fellow peers of Tyre, Further to question . . i 3 11
This we desire, As friends to Antioch, we may feast in Tyre . . i 3 40
We have heard your miseries as far as Tyre . . . . i 4 88
And to fulfil his prince' desire, Sends word of all that haps in Tyre ii Gower 22
A gentleman of Tyre; my name, Pericles; My education been in arts and arms . . . . ii 3 81
A gentleman of Tyre, Who only by misfortune of the seas Bereft of ships ii 3 87
I have heard, you knights of Tyre Are excellent in making ladies trip . ii 3 102
That she loves the knight of Tyre! 'Tis the king's subtilty to have my life . . . . ii 5 43
From Tyre, Fame answering the most strange inquire, To the court of King Simonides, Are letters brought . . . iii Gower 21
The men of Tyrus on the head Of Helicanus would set on The crown of Tyre . . . . iii Gower 28
He must hence depart to Tyre: His queen with child makes her desire iii Gower 39
We are near Tarsus.—Thither, gentle mariner, Alter thy course for Tyre iii 1 76
Imagine Pericles arrived at Tyre, Welcomed and settled . . iv Gower 1
Sir, Our vessel is of Tyre, in it the king . . . . v 1 23
I pray, What is your title?—I am Pericles of Tyre . . . v 1 206
To perform thy just command, I here confess myself the king of Tyre . v 3 2
When I did fly from Tyre, I left behind an ancient substitute . . v 3 50
Tyrian. My hangings all of Tyrian tapestry . . *T. of Shrew* ii 1 351
From whence Lysimachus our Tyrian ship espies *Pericles* v Gower 18
Tyrrel. His name, my lord, is Tyrrel.—I partly know the man *Richard III.* iv 2 40
Is thy name Tyrrel?—James Tyrrel, and your most obedient subject . iv 2 67
Tyrrel, I mean those bastards in the Tower . . . iv 2 76
Come hither, Tyrrel: Go, by this token: rise, and lend thine ear . iv 2 79
Shall we hear from thee, Tyrrel, ere we sleep?—Ye shall, my lord iv 2 84
Kind Tyrrel, am I happy in thy news? . . . . iv 3 24
Didst thou see them dead?—I did, my lord.—And buried, gentle Tyrrel? iv 3 28
Come to me, Tyrrel, soon at after supper, And thou shalt tell the process iv 3 31
Tyrus. The men of Tyrus on the head Of Helicanus would set on The crown of Tyre . . . . . *Pericles* iii Gower 26
O, make for Tarsus! There will I visit Cleon, for the babe Cannot hold out to Tyrus . . . . iii 1 80
My twelve months are expired, and Tyrus stands In a litigious peace . iii 3 2
She was of Tyrus the king's daughter, On whom foul death hath made this slaughter . . . . iv 4 36
Our son and daughter shall in Tyrus reign . . . . v 3 82

U

U. A, e, i,— The sheep: the other two concludes it,—o, u . *L. L. Lost* v 1 60
This is my lady's hand: these be her very C's, her U's, and her T's *T. Night* ii 5 96
Ubique. Hic et ubique? then we'll shift our ground *Hamlet* i 5 155
Udders. A lioness, with udders all drawn dry, Lay couching *As Y. Like It* iv 3 115
Udge. So Got udge me, that is a virtuous mind . *Mer. Wives* i 1 191
Uglier. As with age his body uglier grows, So his mind cankers *Tempest* iv 1 191
The more fair and crystal is the sky, The uglier seem the clouds *Rich. II.* i 1 42
Ugliest. Where hateful death put on his ugliest mask . *2 Hen. IV.* i 1 66
Ugly. I am as ugly as a bear . . . *M. N. Dream* ii 2 94
That ugly treason of mistrust, Which makes me fear *Mer. of Venice* iii 2 28
The toad, ugly and venomous, Wears yet a precious jewel in his head *As Y. Like It* ii 1 13

Ugly. I cannot brook thy sight: This news hath made thee a most ugly man . . . . *K. John* iii 1 37
Ugly and slanderous to thy mother's womb, Full of unpleasing blots . iii 1 44
There is not yet so ugly a fiend of hell As thou shalt be . . iv 3 123
Breaking through the foul and ugly mists Of vapours . *1 Hen. IV.* i 2 226
To dress the ugly form Of base and bloody insurrection . *2 Hen. IV.* iv 1 39
The cripple tardy-gaited night Who, like a foul and ugly witch, doth limp So tediously away . . . . *Hen. V.* iv Prol. 21
See, how the ugly witch doth bend her brows! . . *1 Hen. VI.* v 3 34
Stay; Thou mayst not wander in that labyrinth; There Minotaurs and ugly treasons lurk . . . . v 3 189
Whose ugly and unnatural aspect May fright the hopeful mother *Rich. III.* i 2 23
Whilst some tormenting dream Affrights thee with a hell of ugly devils! i 3 227

Ugly. O, I have pass'd a miserable night, So full of ugly sights, of ghastly dreams! *Richard III.* i 4 3
What ugly sights of death within mine eyes! i 4 23
Ten times more ugly Than ever they were fair *Hen. VIII.* i 2 117
Look, Hector, how the sun begins to set; How ugly night comes breathing at his heels *Troi. and Cres.* v 8 6
You undergo too strict a paradox, Striving to make an ugly deed look fair *T. of Athens* iii 5 25
Banish me! Banish your dotage; banish usury, That makes the senate ugly iii 5 100
The harlot's cheek, beautied with plastering art, Is not more ugly *Ham.* iii 1 52
O most small fault, How ugly didst thou in Cordelia show! *Lear* i 4 289
He hath a daily beauty in his life That makes me ugly *Othello* v 1 20
Go, get thee hence: Hadst thou Narcissus in thy face, to me Thou wouldst appear most ugly *Ant. and Cleo.* ii 5 97
Being an ugly monster, 'Tis strange he [death] hides him in fresh cups *Cymbeline* v 3 70
Ulcer. Pour'st in the open ulcer of my heart Her eyes, her hair *T. and C.* i 1 53
But, to the quick o' the ulcer:—Hamlet comes back *Hamlet* iv 7 124
Ulcerous. She, whom the spital-house and ulcerous sores Would cast the gorge at *T. of Athens* iv 3 39
Strangely-visited people, All swoln and ulcerous, pitiful to the eye *Macb.* iv 3 151
It will but skin and film the ulcerous place *Hamlet* iii 4 147
Ulysses. Deceive more slily than Ulysses could 3 *Hen. VI.* iii 2 189
As Ulysses and stout Diomede With sleight and manhood stole to Rhesus' tents iv 2 19
Let it please both, Thou great, and wise, to hear Ulysses speak *T. and C.* i 3 69
Most wisely hath Ulysses here discover'd The fever whereof all our power is sick i 3 138
The nature of the sickness found, Ulysses, What is the remedy? i 3 140
Who, as Ulysses says, opinion crowns With an imperial voice i 3 186
What says Ulysses?—I have a young conception in my brain i 3 311
Ulysses, Our imputation shall be oddly poised In this wild action i 3 338
Ulysses, Now I begin to relish thy advice i 3 387
There's Ulysses and old Nestor, whose wit was mouldy ere your grandsires had nails on their toes ii 1 114
Here is Ulysses: I'll interrupt his reading. How now, Ulysses! iii 3 92
They retort that heat again To the first giver.—This is not strange, Ulysses iii 3 102
I know your favour, Lord Ulysses, well iv 5 213
I shall forestall thee, Lord Ulysses, thou! iv 5 230
That same dog-fox, Ulysses, is not proved worth a blackberry v 4 12
You would be another Penelope: yet, they say, all the yarn she spun in Ulysses' absence did but fill Ithaca full of moths *Coriolanus* i 3 93
Umber. With a kind of umber smirch my face *As Y. Like It* i 3 114
Umbered. Each battle sees the other's umber'd face *Hen. V.* iv Prol. 9
Umbra. Fauste, precor gelida quando pecus omne sub umbra Ruminat *L. L. Lost* iv 2 96
Umbrage. Who else would trace him, his umbrage, nothing more *Hamlet* v 2 125
Umfrevile. Sir John Umfrevile turn'd me back With joyful tidings 2 *Hen. IV.* i 1 34
Umpire. There is three umpires in this matter, as I understand *M. Wives* i 1 139
Whom right and wrong Have chose as umpire *L. L. Lost* i 1 170
Just death, kind umpire of men's miseries 1 *Hen. VI.* ii 5 29
Let me be umpire in this doubtful strife iv 1 151
'Twixt my extremes and me this bloody knife Shall play the umpire *Rom. and Jul.* iv 1 63
Unable. Why does my blood thus muster to my heart, Making both it unable for itself, And dispossessing all my other parts? *M. for M.* ii 4 21
Come, come, you froward and unable worms! *T. of Shrew* v 2 169
Thus far, with rough and all-unable pen, Our bending author hath pursued the story *Hen. V.* Epil. 1
Yet are these feet, whose strengthless stay is numb, Unable to support this lump of clay 1 *Hen. VI.* ii 5 14
Sapless age and weak unable limbs iv 5 4
A love that makes breath poor, and speech unable *Lear* i 1 61
Welcome is peace, if he on peace consist; If wars, we are unable to resist *Pericles* i 4 84
Unaccommodated man is no more but such a poor, bare, forked animal as thou art *Lear* iii 4 111
Unaccompanied. Which honour must Not unaccompanied invest him only *Macbeth* i 4 40
Unaccustomed. Set this unaccustom'd fight aside 1 *Hen. VI.* iii 1 93
What unaccustom'd cause procures her hither? *Rom. and Jul.* iii 5 68
Shall give him such an unaccustom'd dram iii 5 91
An unaccustom'd spirit Lifts me above the ground with cheerful thoughts v 1 4
These apparent prodigies, The unaccustom'd terror of this night *J. Cæsar* ii 1 199
Unaching. Show them the unaching scars which I should hide *Coriol.* ii 2 152
Unacquainted. The hearts Of all his people shall revolt from him And kiss the lips of unacquainted change *K. John* iii 4 166
To grace the gentry of a land remote, And follow unacquainted colours here v 2 32
Am become As new into the world, strange, unacquainted *Tr. and Cr.* iii 3 12
Unactive. Idle and unactive, Still cupboarding the viand *Coriolanus* i 1 102
Unadvised. Pardon me, madam; I have unadvised Deliver'd you a paper that I should not *T. G. of Ver.* iv 4 127
Stay for an answer to your embassy, Lest unadvised you stain your swords with blood *K. John* ii 1 45
Thou unadvised scold, I can produce A will that bars the title of thy son ii 1 191
This harness'd masque and unadvised revel, This unhair'd sauciness v 2 132
Although our mother, unadvised, Gave you a dancing-rapier *T. Andron.* ii 1 38
Although I joy in thee, I have no joy of this contract to-night: It is too rash, too unadvised, too sudden *Rom. and Jul.* ii 2 118
Unadvisedly. Men shall deal unadvisedly sometimes *Richard III.* iv 4 292
Unagreeable. The time is unagreeable to this business *T. of Athens* ii 2 41
Unaneled. Unhousel'd, disappointed, unaneled, No reckoning made *Ham.* i 5 77
Unanswered. But your petition Is yet unanswer'd *W. Tale* v 1 229
Unappeased. That so the shadows be not unappeased *T. Andron.* i 1 100
Unapt. Our bodies soft and weak and smooth, Unapt to toil *T. of Shrew* v 2 166
Too cold and temperate, Unapt to stir at these indignities 1 *Hen. IV.* i 3 2
I am a soldier and unapt to weep 1 *Hen. VI.* v 3 133
We pout upon the morning, are unapt To give or to forgive *Coriolanus* v 1 52
Unaptness. And that unaptness made your minister *T. of Athens* ii 2 140
Unarm. I'll unarm again: Why should I war? *Troi. and Cres.* i 1 1
Where?—At your own house; there he unarms him i 2 300
Sweet Helen, I must woo you To help unarm our Hector iii 1 163
Unarm, unarm, and do not fight to-day v 3 3
But vows to every purpose must not hold: Unarm, sweet Hector v 3 25
Unarm. Unarm thee, go, and doubt thou not, brave boy, I'll stand to-day for thee *Troi. and Cres.* v 3 35
Unarm, Eros; the long day's task is done, And we must sleep *A. and C.* iv 14 35
Unarmed. If he should do so, He leaves his back unarm'd 2 *Hen. IV.* i 3 79
Begin to melt And drop upon our bare unarmed heads ii 4 394
Hollow-hearted friends, Unarm'd, and unresolved to beat them back *Richard III.* iv 4 436
Courtiers as free, as debonair, unarm'd, As bending angels *Troi. and Cres.* i 3 235
Invite the Trojan lords after the combat To see us here unarm'd iii 3 237
Desire the valiant Ajax to invite the most valorous Hector to come unarmed iii 3 276
And great Achilles Doth long to see unarm'd the valiant Hector iv 5 153
I am unarm'd; forego this vantage, Greek.—Strike, fellows, strike v 8 9
Unassailable holds on his rank, Unshaked of motion *J. Cæsar* iii 1 69
Unassailed. It grieves my soul to leave thee unassail'd 2 *Hen. VI.* v 2 18
Unattainted. Go thither; and, with unattainted eye, Compare her face with some that I shall show *Rom. and Jul.* i 2 90
Unattempted. But for my hand, as unattempted yet, Like a poor beggar, raileth on the rich *K. John* ii 1 591
Unattended. Your constancy Hath left you unattended *Macbeth* ii 2 69
Unauspicious. To whose ingrate and unauspicious altars My soul the faithfull'st offerings hath breathed out *T. Night* v 1 116
Unauthorized. What, To kiss in private?—An unauthorized kiss *Othello* iv 1 2
Unavoided is the danger now, For suffering so the causes *Richard II.* ii 1 268
Thou art come unto a feast of death, A terrible and unavoided danger 1 *Hen. VI.* iv 5 8
A cockatrice hast thou hatch'd to the world, Whose unavoided eye is murderous *Richard III.* iv 1 56
All unavoided is the doom of destiny iv 4 217
Unawares. Hath wrought this hellish mischief unawares 1 *Hen. VI.* iii 2 39
So we, well cover'd with the night's black mantle, At unawares may beat down Edward's guard 3 *Hen. VI.* iv 2 23
Either betray'd by falsehood of his guard Or by his foe surprised at unawares iv 4 9
Away betimes, . . . And take the great-grown traitor unawares iv 8 63
And all my powers do their bestowing lose, Like vassalage at unawares encountering The eye of majesty *Troi. and Cres.* iii 2 40
Unbacked. Like unback'd colts, they prick'd their ears *Tempest* iv 1 176
Unbaked. Whose villanous saffron would have made all the unbaked and doughy youth of a nation in his colour *All's Well* iv 5 3
Unbanded. Your bonnet unbanded, your sleeve unbuttoned *As Y. L. It* iii 2 398
Unbar. Death, who is the key To unbar these locks *Cymbeline* v 4 8
Unbarbed. Must I go show them my unbarbed sconce? *Coriolanus* iii 2 99
Unbashful. Nor did not with unbashful forehead woo The means of weakness and debility *As Y. Like It* ii 3 50
Unbated. Where is the horse that doth untread again His tedious measures with the unbated fire That he did pace them first? *M. of V.* ii 6 11
With a little shuffling, you may choose A sword unbated *Hamlet* iv 7 139
The treacherous instrument is in thy hand, Unbated and envenom'd v 2 328
Unbattered. Or else my sword with an unbatter'd edge I sheathe again undeeded *Macbeth* v 7 19
Unbecoming. A gap in our great feast, And all-thing unbecoming iii 1 13
Unbefitting. As love is full of unbefitting strains *L. L. Lost* v 2 770
Unbegot. They shall strike Your children yet unborn and unbegot *Richard II.* iii 3 88
Unbegotten. Shall give a holiness, a purity, To the yet unbegotten sin of times *K. John* iv 3 54
Unbelieved. As I, thus wrong'd, hence unbelieved go! *Meas. for Meas.* v 1 119
Unbend. Why, worthy thane, You do unbend your noble strength *Macb.* ii 2 45
Unbent. Why hast thou gone so far, To be unbent when thou hast ta'en thy stand, The elected deer before thee? *Cymbeline* iii 4 111
Unbewailed. But let determined things to destiny Hold unbewail'd their way *Ant. and Cleo.* iii 6 85
Unbid. O unbid spite! is sportful Edward come? 3 *Hen. VI.* v 1 18
Unbidden guests Are often welcomest when they are gone 1 *Hen. VI.* ii 2 55
Unbind my hands, I'll pull them off myself *T. of Shrew* ii 1 4
O gentle, aged men! Unbind my sons, reverse the doom of death *T. An.* iii 1 24
Unbitted. We have reason to cool our raging motions, our carnal stings, our unbitted lusts *Othello* i 3 335
Unblessed. Every inordinate cup is unblessed and the ingredient is a devil ii 3 311
Unblest. Minion, your dear lies dead, And your unblest fate hies v 1 34
Unbloodied. Although the kite soar with unbloodied beak 2 *Hen. VI.* iii 2 193
Unblown. Ah, my tender babes! My unblown flowers! *Richard III.* iv 4 10
Unbodied. And that unbodied figure of the thought That gave't surmised shape *Troi. and Cres.* i 3 16
Unbolt. I'll call mine uncle down; He shall unbolt the gates iv 2 3
How shall I understand you?—I will unbolt to you *T. of Athens* i 1 51
Unbolted. I will tread this unbolted villain into mortar *Lear* ii 2 71
Unbonneted he runs, And bids what will take all iii 1 14
My demerits May speak unbonneted to as proud a fortune As this *Othello* i 2 23
Unbookish. His unbookish jealousy must construe Poor Cassio's smiles, gestures, and light behaviour, Quite in the wrong iv 1 102
Unborn. Never so much as in a thought unborn Did I offend *As Y. Like It* i 3 53
Some unborn sorrow, ripe in fortune's womb, Is coming towards me *Richard II.* ii 2 10
And they shall strike Your children yet unborn and unbegot iii 3 88
The children yet unborn Shall feel this day as sharp to them as thorn iv 1 322
A portent Of broached mischief to the unborn times 1 *Hen. IV.* v 1 21
Some are yet ungotten and unborn That shall have cause to curse *Hen. V.* i 2 287
All cause unborn, could never be the motive Of our so frank donation *Coriolanus* iii 1 129
Acted over In states unborn and accents yet unknown *J. Cæsar* iii 1 113
The unborn event I do commend to your content *Pericles* iv Gower 45
Unbosom. Their several counsels they unbosom shall To loves mistook *L. L. Lost* v 2 141
Unbound. But he, I thank him, gnaw'd in two my cords: Now am I Dromio and his man unbound *Com. of Errors* v 1 290
Fresh men set upon us— And unbound the rest 1 *Hen. IV.* ii 4 201
This unbound lover, To beautify him, only lacks a cover *Rom. and Jul.* i 3 87
Unbounded. He was a man Of an unbounded stomach *Hen. VIII.* iv 2 34
Unbowed. Subject his coronet to his crown and bend The dukedom yet unbow'd *Tempest* i 2 115
And passeth by with stiff unbowed knee, Disdaining duty 2 *Hen. VI.* iii 1 16
Unbraced. Thus unbraced, Casca, as you see, Have bared my bosom to the thunder-stone *J. Cæsar* i 3 48
Is Brutus sick? and is it physical To walk unbraced? ii 1 262
With his doublet all unbraced; No hat upon his head *Hamlet* ii 1 78
Unbraided. Has he any unbraided wares? *W. Tale* iv 4 204
Unbreathed. Now have toiled their unbreathed memories *M. N. Dream* v 1 74

Unbreeched. Methoughts I did recoil Twenty-three years, and saw myself unbreech'd *W. Tale* i 2 155
Unbridled. This is not well, rash and unbridled boy *All's Well* iii 2 30
My thoughts were like unbridled children *Troi. and Cres.* iii 2 130
Unbroke. God keep all vows unbroke that swear to thee! *Richard II.* iv 1 215
Unbruised. Live unbruised and love my cousin *Much Ado* v 4 112
With unhack'd swords and helmets all unbruised *K. John* ii 1 254
On Dardan plains The fresh and yet unbruised Greeks do pitch Their brave pavilions *Troi. and Cres.* Prol. 14
Thou hast years upon thee; and thou art too full Of the wars' surfeits, to go rove with one That's yet unbruised *Coriolanus* iv 1 47
Where unbruised youth with unstuff'd brain Doth couch his limbs *Rom. and Jul.* ii 3 37
Unbuckle. I cannot with conscience take it.—Unbuckle, unbuckle *W. T.* iv 4 661
He that unbuckles this, till we do please To daff 't for our repose, shall hear a storm *Ant. and Cleo.* iv 4 12
Unbuckling helms, fisting each other's throat *Coriolanus* iv 5 131
Unbuild. To unbuild the city and to lay all flat.—What is the city? iii 1 198
Unburden. And from your love I have a warranty To unburden all my plots and purposes *Mer. of Venice* i 1 133
Unburthens with his tongue The envious load that lies upon his heart *2 Hen. VI.* iii 1 156
Unburied. Whose loves I prize As the dead carcasses of unburied men That do corrupt my air *Coriolanus* iii 3 122
Careless of thine own, Why suffer'st thou thy sons, unburied yet, To hover on the dreadful shore of Styx? *T. Andron.* i 1 87
Unburnt. 'Twas folly, For one poor grain or two, to leave unburnt, And still to nose the offence *Coriolanus* v 1 27
Unburthened. Conferring them on younger strengths, while we Unburthen'd crawl toward death *Lear* i 1 42
Unbutton. Off, off, you lendings! come, unbutton here iii 4 114
Unbuttoned. Your bonnet unbanded, your sleeve unbuttoned *As Y. L. It* iii 2 399
Unbuttoning thee after supper and sleeping upon benches *1 Hen. IV.* i 2 3
Uncapable of pity, void and empty From any dram of mercy *M. of Ven.* iv 1 5
How do you mean, removing of him?—Why, by making him uncapable of Othello's place; knocking out his brains *Othello* iv 2 235
Uncape. Let me stop this way first. So, now uncape *Mer. Wives* iii 3 176
Uncase thee; take my colour'd hat and cloak *T. of Shrew* i 1 212
Uncasing. Do you not see Pompey is uncasing for the combat? *L. L. Lost* v 2 707
Uncaught. Not in this land shall he remain uncaught *Lear* ii 1 59
Comest thou smiling from The world's great snare uncaught? *A. and C.* iv 8 18
Uncertain. O, how this spring of love resembleth The uncertain glory of an April day *T. G. of Ver.* i 3 85
As 'twere, a man assured of a— Uncertain life, and sure death *All's Well* ii 3 20
Be not uncertain; For, by the honour of my parents, I Have utter'd truth *W. Tale* i 2 441
Did take horse, Uncertain of the issue any way *1 Hen. IV.* i 1 61
The purpose you undertake is dangerous; the friends you have named uncertain ii 3 12
Murder her brothers, and then marry her! Uncertain way of gain! *Richard III.* iv 2 64
Thou know'st, great son, The end of war's uncertain *Coriolanus* v 3 141
The people will remain uncertain whilst 'Twixt you there's difference v 6 17
In life's uncertain voyage, I will some kindness do them! *T. of Athens* v 1 205
And left me bare to weather.—Uncertain favour! *Cymbeline* iii 3 64
Uncertainty. Until I know this sure uncertainty, I'll entertain the offer'd fallacy *Com. of Errors* ii 2 187
Shall happily meet, To bear our fortunes in our own strong arms, Which now we hold at much uncertainty *1 Hen. IV.* i 3 299
And here remain with your uncertainty! Let every feeble rumour shake your hearts! *Coriolanus* iii 3 124
Unchain your spirits now with spelling charms And try if they can gain your liberty *1 Hen. VI.* v 3 31
Unchanging. Thy face is, visard-like, unchanging *3 Hen. VI.* i 4 116
Uncharge. But even his mother shall uncharge the practice And call it accident *Hamlet* iv 7 68
Uncharged. Descend, and open your uncharged ports *T. of Athens* v 4 55
Uncharitably with me have you dealt *Richard III.* i 3 275
Unchary. And laid mine honour too unchary out *T. Night* iii 4 222
Unchaste. Lust is but a bloody fire, Kindled with unchaste desire *Mer. Wives* v 5 100
And thinks himself made in the unchaste composition *All's Well* iv 3 22
It is no vicious blot, murder, or foulness, No unchaste action *Lear* i 1 231
Away he posts With unchaste purpose and with oath *Cymbeline* v 5 284
Unchecked. It lives there unchecked that Antonio hath a ship of rich lading wrecked on the narrow seas *Mer. of Venice* iii 1 2
Each thing's a thief: The laws, your curb and whip, in their rough power Have uncheck'd theft *T. of Athens* iv 3 447
Unchilded. He Hath widow'd and unchilded many a one *Coriolanus* v 6 153
Uncivil. I have much to do To keep them from uncivil outrages *T. G. of V.* v 4 17
Let go that rude uncivil touch, Thou friend of an ill fashion! v 4 60
If you prized my lady's favour at any thing more than contempt, you would not give means for this uncivil rule *T. Night* ii 3 132
This is as uncivil as strange iii 4 277
Let thy fair wisdom, not thy passion, sway In this uncivil and unjust extent Against thy peace iv 1 57
Still so constant, lord.—What, to perverseness? you uncivil lady! v 1 115
The king of heaven forbid our lord the king Should so with civil and uncivil arms Be rush'd upon! *Richard II.* iii 3 102
The uncivil kerns of Ireland are in arms *2 Hen. VI.* iii 1 310
Unclaimed. If he be free, Why then my taxing like a wild-goose flies, Unclaim'd of any man *As Y. Like It* ii 7 87
Unclasp. In her bosom I'll unclasp my heart *Much Ado* i 1 325
And now I will unclasp a secret book *1 Hen. IV.* i 3 188
Wide unclasp the tables of their thoughts To every ticklish reader! *Troi. and Cres.* iv 5 60
Unclasp, unclasp: Thanks, gentlemen, to all; all have done well *Per.* ii 3 107
Unclasp'd To thee the book even of my secret soul *T. Night* i 4 13
To my kingly guest Unclasp'd my practice *W. Tale* iii 2 168
Uncle. My brother and thy uncle, call'd Antonio *Tempest* i 2 66
Thy false uncle—Dost thou attend me?—Sir, most heedfully i 2 77
Pray you, uncle, tell Mistress Anne the jest, how my father stole two geese out of a pen, good uncle *Mer. Wives* iii 4 39
Your father and my uncle hath made motions: if it be my luck, so iii 4 66
Duke Menaphon, your most renowned uncle *Com. of Errors* v 1 368
He hath an uncle here in Messina will be very much glad of it *Much Ado* i 1 18
My uncle's fool, reading the challenge, subscribed for Cupid i 1 40
Niece, will you look to those things I told you of?—I cry you mercy, uncle i 2 353
I am sorry for her, as I have just cause, being her uncle and her guardian ii 3 173
Uncle. Madam, you must come to your uncle. Yonder's old coil at home *Much Ado* v 2 97
And moreover I will go with thee to thy uncle's v 2 106
Why, then your uncle and the prince and Claudio Have been deceived v 4 75
When Jacob grazed his uncle Laban's sheep *Mer. of Venice* i 3 72
And no less beloved of her uncle than his own daughter *As Y. Like It* i 1 116
If my uncle, thy banished father, had banished thy uncle, the duke my father i 2 9
Daughter to the banish'd duke, And here detain'd by her usurping uncle i 2 286
Get you from our court.—Me, uncle?—You, cousin i 3 44
Then, dear uncle, Never so much as in a thought unborn Did I offend i 3 52
Whither shall we go?—To seek my uncle in the forest of Arden i 3 109
An old religious uncle of mine taught me to speak iii 2 362
There is none of my uncle's marks upon you iii 2 387
Tutor'd in the rudiments Of many desperate studies by his uncle v 4 32
I am Cressid's uncle, That dare leave two together *All's Well* ii 1 100
Thy unnatural uncle, English John *K. John* ii 1 10
My uncle's will in this respect is mine ii 1 510
But Fortune, O, . . . She adulterates hourly with thine uncle John iii 1 56
Upon my knee I beg, go not to arms Against mine uncle iii 1 309
And thy uncle will As dear be to thee as thy father was iii 3 3
I doubt My uncle practises more harm to me iv 1 20
I will not touch thine eye For all the treasure that thine uncle owes iv 1 123
O me! my uncle's spirit is in these stones iv 3 9
Good uncle, let this end where it begun *Richard II.* i 1 158
Uncle, even in the glasses of thine eyes I see thy grieved heart i 3 208
Why, uncle, thou hast many years to live i 3 225
How fares our noble uncle, Lancaster?—What comfort, man? ii 1 71
We do seize to us The plate, coin, revenues, and moveables, Whereof our uncle Gaunt did stand possess'd ii 1 162
We create, in absence of ourself, Our uncle York lord governor of England ii 1 220
Uncle, for God's sake, speak comfortable words ii 2 76
How fares your uncle?—I had thought, my lord, to have learn'd his health of you ii 3 23
Here comes his grace in person.—My noble uncle! ii 3 82
My gracious uncle— Tut, tut! Grace me no grace, nor uncle me no uncle: I am no traitor's uncle ii 3 85
My gracious uncle, let me know my fault: On what condition stands it? ii 3 106
There repose you for this night.—An offer, uncle, that we will accept ii 3 162
Uncle, you say the queen is at your house iii 1 36
Where lies our uncle with his power? Speak sweetly, man iii 2 192
Mistake not, uncle, further than you should iii 3 14
Uncle, give me your hands: nay, dry your eyes iii 3 202
Is not my arm of length, That reacheth from the restful English court As far as Calais, to mine uncle's head? iv 1 13
What is the matter, uncle? speak; Recover breath v 3 46
Good uncle, help to order several powers To Oxford v 3 140
Uncle, farewell: and, cousin too, adieu: Your mother well hath pray'd v 3 144
This is his uncle's teaching: this is Worcester, Malevolent to you *1 Hen. IV.* i 1 96
'Twas where the madcap duke his uncle kept, His uncle York i 3 244
God forgive me! Good uncle, tell your tale; I have done i 3 256
Is there not my father, my uncle, and myself? ii 3 26
Your uncle Worcester's horse came but to-day iv 3 21
My father and my uncle and myself Did give him that same royalty iv 3 54
In the morning early shall my uncle Bring him our purposes iv 3 110
What treasure, uncle?—Tennis-balls, my liege *Hen. V.* i 2 258
Noble uncle, thus ignobly used, Your nephew . . . comes *1 Hen. VI.* ii 5 35
Now thy uncle is removing hence; As princes do their courts ii 5 104
O, uncle, would some part of my young years Might but redeem the passage of your age! ii 5 107
Uncles of Gloucester and of Winchester, The special watchmen of our English weal iii 1 65
Fie, uncle Beaufort! I have heard you preach iii 1 127
O loving uncle, kind Duke of Gloucester, How joyful am I made by this! iii 1 142
And you, good uncle, banish all offence v 5 96
Uncle, how now!—Pardon me, gracious lord; Some sudden qualm hath struck me at the heart *2 Hen. VI.* i 1 53
Mine uncle Beaufort and myself, With all the learned council of the realm i 1 88
We will keep it still.—Ay, uncle, we will keep it, if we can i 1 107
Uncle, what shall we say to this in law? i 3 207
Good uncle, hide such malice; With such holiness can you do it? ii 1 25
Faith, holy uncle, would 'twere come to that! ii 1 38
Call our uncle to our presence straight; Say we intend to try his grace iii 2 15
Why look'st thou pale? why tremblest thou? Where is our uncle? iii 2 28
Your loving uncle, twenty times his worth, They say, is shamefully bereft of life iii 2 268
Mine uncles, You are come to Sandal in a happy hour *3 Hen. VI.* i 2 62
Though the odds be great, I doubt not, uncle, of our victory i 2 73
My uncles both are slain in rescuing me i 4 2
Thine uncles and myself Have in our armours watch'd the winter's night v 7 16
The king my uncle is to blame for this: God will revenge it *Richard III.* ii 2 13
When my uncle told me so, he wept, And hugg'd me in his arm ii 2 23
Think you my uncle did dissemble, grandam?—Ay, boy ii 2 31
The king Had virtuous uncles to protect his grace ii 3 21
I could have given my uncle's grace a flout ii 4 24
My uncle grew so fast That he could gnaw a crust at two hours old ii 4 27
I want more uncles here to welcome me iii 1 6
Those uncles which you want were dangerous iii 1 12
What say you, uncle?—I say, without characters, fame lives long iii 1 80
Uncle, give me this dagger.—My dagger, little cousin? with all my heart iii 1 110
A beggar, brother?—Of my kind uncle, that I know will give iii 1 113
To mitigate the scorn he gives his uncle, He prettily and aptly taunts himself iii 1 133
I fear no uncles dead.—Nor none that live, I hope iii 1 146
And by their uncle cozen'd Of comfort, kingdom, kindred, freedom, life iv 4 222
Tell her thou madest away her uncle Clarence, Her uncle Rivers iv 4 281
Shall I say, her uncle? Or, he that slew her brothers and her uncles? iv 4 338
When were you at Ilium?—This morning, uncle *Troi. and Cres.* i 2 47
Well, uncle, what folly I commit, I dedicate to you iii 2 110
You know now your hostages; your uncle's word and my firm faith iii 2 116
I'll call mine uncle down; He shall unbolt the gates iv 2 2
It is your uncle.—A pestilence on him! now will he be mocking iv 2 20
Go hang yourself, you naughty mocking uncle! iv 2 26
Who's that at door? good uncle, go and see iv 2 36

Uncle. Tell me, sweet uncle, what's the matter? . *Troi. and Cres.* iv 2 84
Shall thy good uncle, and thy brother Lucius, And thou, and I, sit round about some fountain? . . . . *T. Andron.* iii 1 122
Is not this a heavy case, To see thy noble uncle thus distract? . . iv 3 26
A matter of brawl betwixt my uncle and one of the emperial's men . iv 3 93
Good uncle, take you in this barbarous Moor . . . . v 3 4
Inhuman dog! unhallow'd slave! Sirs, help our uncle to convey him in v 3 15
Uncle, draw you near, To shed obsequious tears upon this trunk . v 3 151
Uncle, do you know the cause?—I neither know it nor can learn *R. and J.* i 1 149
Why, uncle, 'tis a shame.—Go to, go to; You are a saucy boy . . i 5 84
You, worthy uncle, Shall, with my cousin, your right-noble son, Lead our first battle . . . . *Macbeth* v 6 2
We have here writ To Norway, uncle of young Fortinbras . *Hamlet* i 2 28
Married with my uncle, My father's brother . . . . i 2 151
O my prophetic soul! My uncle! . . . . . . i 5 41
Upon my secure hour thy uncle stole, With juice of cursed hebenon . i 5 61
So, uncle, there you are. Now to my word . . . . i 5 110
Makes vow before his uncle never more To give the assay of arms . . ii 2 70
It is not very strange; for mine uncle is king of Denmark . . ii 2 380
I'll have these players Play something like the murder of my father Before mine uncle . . . . ii 2 625
Even with the very comment of thy soul Observe mine uncle . . iii 2 85
Go not to mine uncle's bed; Assume a virtue, if you have it not . iii 4 159
I scarce did know you, uncle: there lies your niece . *Othello* v 2 201
Uncle, I must come forth.—If thou attempt it, it will cost thee dear . v 2 254
Cassibelan, thine uncle,—Famous in Cæsar's praises . *Cymbeline* iii 1 5
Unclean. And, fairy-like, to pinch the unclean knight . *Mer. Wives* iv 4 57
To cast away honesty upon a foul slut were to put good meat into an unclean dish . . . . *As Y. Like It* iii 3 36
For where an unclean mind carries virtuous qualities, there commendations go with pity . . . . . . *All's Well* i 1 48
That has fallen into the unclean fishpond of her displeasure . . v 2 22
Where civil blood makes civil hands unclean . *Rom. and Jul.* Prol. 4
Uncleanliness. Might have been accused in fornication, adultery, and all uncleanliness . . . . . . *Meas. for Meas.* ii 1 82
Uncleanly. You kiss your hands: that courtesy would be uncleanly, if courtiers were shepherds . . . . *As Y. Like It* iii 2 51
Civet is of a baser birth than tar, the very uncleanly flux of a cat . iii 2 70
Uncleanly scruples! fear not you: look to't . . *K. John* iv 1 7
All you whose souls abhor The uncleanly savours of a slaughter-house . iv 3 112
Who has a breast so pure, But some uncleanly apprehensions Keep leets and law-days? . . . . *Othello* iii 3 139
Uncleanness. Or, to redeem him, Give up your body to such sweet uncleanness As she that he hath stain'd . *Meas. for Meas.* ii 4 54
Uncle-father. My uncle-father and aunt-mother are deceived *Hamlet* ii 2 393
Unclew. If I should pay you for't as 'tis extoll'd, It would unclew me quite . . . . *T. of Athens* i 1 168
Unclog. Could I meet 'em But once a-day, it would unclog my heart *Coriolanus* iv 2 47
Uncoined. A fellow of plain and uncoined constancy . *Hen. V.* v 2 161
Uncolted. Thou liest; thou art not colted, thou art uncolted 1 *Hen. IV.* ii 2 42
Uncomeliness. And gave such orderly and well-behaved reproof to all uncomeliness . . . . *Mer. Wives* ii 1 60
Uncomfortable time, why camest thou now To murder, murder our solemnity? O child! O child! . . . *Rom. and Jul.* iv 5 60
Uncompassionate. Nor silver-shedding tears Could penetrate her uncompassionate sire . . . . . . *T. G. of Ver.* iii 1 231
Uncomprehensive. Finds bottom in the uncomprehensive deeps *Troi. and Cres.* iii 3 198
Unconfinable. Why, thou unconfinable baseness, it is as much as I can do to keep the terms of my honour precise . *Mer. Wives* ii 2 21
Unconfirmed. That shows thou art unconfirmed . . . *Much Ado* iii 3 124
Untrained, or rather, unlettered, or ratherest, unconfirmed *L. L. Lost* iv 2 19
Unconquered. Of an invincible unconquer'd spirit! . 1 *Hen. VI.* iv 2 32
The unconquered soul of Cade is fled . . . 2 *Hen. VI.* iv 10 69
Unconsidered. A snapper-up of unconsidered trifles . *W. Tale* iv 3 26
Love yourself, and in that love Not unconsider'd leave your honour *Hen. VIII.* i 2 15
Unconstant. O despiteful love! unconstant womankind! *T. of Shrew* iv 2 14
So jest with heaven, Make such unconstant children of ourselves *K. John* iii 1 243
I will henceforth be no more unconstant . . 3 *Hen. VI.* v 1 102
Such unconstant starts are we like to have from him . . *Lear* i 1 304
Unconstrained. Will you with free and unconstrained soul Give me this maid? . . . . *Much Ado* iv 1 25
Suppose, my lords, he did it unconstrain'd . . 3 *Hen. VI.* i 1 143
Uncontemned. Which of the peers Have uncontemn'd gone by him, or at least Strangely neglected? . . . . *Hen. VIII.* iii 2 10
Uncontrolled. Embrace His golden Uncontroll'd enfranchisement *Richard II.* i 3 90
Uncorrected. Green clover, Wanting the scythe, all uncorrected, rank, Conceives by idleness . . . . . . *Hen. V.* v 2 50
Uncounted. The blunt monster with uncounted heads 2 *Hen. IV.* Ind. 18
Uncouple in the western valley; let them go: Dispatch, I say *M. N. Dream* iv 1 112
Uncouple here and let us make a bay . . *T. Andron.* ii 2 3
Uncourteous. Upon some stubborn and uncourteous parts We had conceived against him . . . . . . *T. Night* v 1 369
Uncouth. If this uncouth forest yield any thing savage *As Y. Like It* ii 6 6
I am surprised with an uncouth fear . . . *T. Andron.* ii 3 211
Uncover, dogs, and lap.—What does his lordship mean? . *T. of Athens* iii 6 95
Uncovered slander, unmitigated rancour . . . *Much Ado* iv 1 307
And sooner dance upon a bloody pole Than stand uncover'd to the vulgar groom . . . . 2 *Hen. VI.* iv 1 128
In thy best robes uncover'd on the bier Thou shalt be borne *R. and J.* iv 1 110
Thou wert better in thy grave than to answer with thy uncovered body this extremity of the skies . . . . . . *Lear* iii 4 106
Uncropped. If thou be'st yet a fresh uncropped flower, Choose thou thy husband . . . . *All's Well* v 3 327
Uncrossed. Such gain the cap of him that makes 'em fine, Yet keeps his book uncross'd: no life to ours . . . *Cymbeline* iii 3 26
Uncrown. Therefore I'll uncrown him ere't be long . 3 *Hen. VI.* iii 3 232
Unction. Lay not that flattering unction to your soul . *Hamlet* iii 4 145
I'll anoint my sword. I bought an unction of a mountebank . iv 7 142
Unctuous. With liquorish draughts And morsels unctuous, greases his pure mind . . . . *T. of Athens* iv 3 195
Uncuckolded. It is a deadly sorrow to behold a foul knave uncuckolded *Ant. and Cleo.* i 2 76
Uncurable. Send succours, lords, and stop the rage betime, Before the wound do grow uncurable . . . 2 *Hen. VI.* iii 1 286
Uncurable discomfit Reigns in the hearts of all our present parts . . v 2 86
Uncurbable. So much uncurbable, her garboils, Cæsar, Made out of her impatience . . . . *Ant. and Cleo.* ii 2 67
Uncurbed. With frank and with uncurbed plainness Tell us *Hen. V.* i 2 244
Uncurls. My fleece of woolly hair that now uncurls Even as an adder when she doth unroll To do some fatal execution *T. Andron.* ii 3 34
Uncurrent. Oft good turns Are shuffled off with such uncurrent pay *T. Night* iii 3 16
With what encounter so uncurrent I Have strain'd to appear thus *W. T.* iii 2 50
Pray God, your voice, like a piece of uncurrent gold, be not cracked *Hamlet* ii 2 448
Uncurse. Again uncurse their souls; their peace is made *Richard II.* iii 2 137
Undaunted. His soldiers spying his undaunted spirit . 1 *Hen. VI.* i 1 127
Undaunted spirit in a dying breast! . . . . . . iii 2 99
Her valiant courage and undaunted spirit, More than in women commonly is seen . . . . v 5 70
Thy undaunted mettle should compose Nothing but males *Macbeth* i 7 73
Undeaf. My death's sad tale may yet undeaf his ear . *Richard II.* ii 1 16
Undeck. I have given here my soul's consent To undeck the pompous body of a king . . . . iv 1 250
Undeeded. Either thou, Macbeth, Or else my sword with an unbatter'd edge I sheathe again undeeded . . . . *Macbeth* v 7 20
Under. The mariners all under hatches stow'd . . *Tempest* i 2 230
I saw him beat the surges under him, And ride upon their backs . ii 1 114
Now is the jerkin under the line . . . . iv 1 236
Merrily, merrily shall I live now Under the blossom that hangs on the bough . . . . v 1 94
My staff understands me.—It stands under thee, indeed *T. G. of Ver.* ii 5 32
'Tis a great charge to come under one body's hand . *Mer. Wives* i 4 105
That I will, come cut and long-tail, under the degree of a squire . iii 4 48
Lest I might be too rash: Under your good correction . *Meas. for Meas.* ii 2 10
Fainting under The pleasing punishment that women bear *Com. of Errors* i 1 46
There's nothing situate under heaven's eye But hath his bound . ii 1 16
As under privilege of age to brag What I have done being young *M. Ado* v 1 60
Moreover, sir, which indeed is not under white and black, this plaintiff here, the offender, did call me ass . . . . . . v 1 313
Their daughters profit very greatly under you . . . *L. L. Lost* iv 2 78
Not so, sir; under correction, sir; I hope it is not so . . v 2 489
When the false Troyan under sail was seen . *M. N. Dream* i 1 174
Slow in pursuit, but match'd in mouth like bells, Each under each . iv 1 129
The Frenchman became his surety and sealed under for another *M. of V.* i 2 89
Under the greenwood tree Who loves to lie with me *As Y. Like It* ii 5 1
Under the shade of melancholy boughs . . . . . ii 7 111
He does it under name of perfect love . . . *T. of Shrew* iv 3 12
Keep thy friend Under thy own life's key . . . *All's Well* i 1 76
You were born under a charitable star.—Under Mars, I.—I especially think, under Mars.—Why under Mars?—The wars have so kept you under that you must needs be born under Mars . . . i 1 204
All these engines of lust are not the things they go under . iii 5 22
Were we not born under Taurus?—Taurus! That's sides and heart *T. N.* i 3 147
Under your hard construction must I sit . . . . . iii 1 126
I have eyes under my service which look upon his removedness *W. Tale* iv 2 40
But as we, under heaven, are supreme head, So under Him that great supremacy, Where we do reign, we will alone uphold *K. John* iii 1 155
I am, sir, under the king, in some authority.—Under which king? 2 *Hen. IV.* v 3 117
Substitutes Under the lordly monarch of the north . 1 *Hen. VI.* v 3 6
Ye familiar spirits, that are cull'd Out of the powerful regions under earth . . . . v 3 11
The net has fall'n upon me! I shall perish Under device and practice *Hen. VIII.* i 1 204
But am bolden'd Under your promised pardon . . . . i 2 56
There's none stands under more calumnious tongues Than I myself . v 1 112
Yet go we under our opinion still That we have better men *Troi. and Cres.* i 3 383
The noble senate, who, Under the gods, keep you in awe *Coriolanus* i 1 191
Under your patience, gentle empress, 'Tis thought you have a goodly gift in horning . . . . *T. Andron.* ii 3 66
Sir, your jewel Hath suffer'd under praise . . *T. of Athens* i 1 165
Under favour, pardon me, If I speak like a captain . . . iii 5 40
Here, under leave of Brutus and the rest . . . *J. Cæsar* iii 2 86
Bear them as the ass bears gold, To groan and sweat under the business iv 1 22
And, under him, My Genius is rebuked . . . *Macbeth* iii 1 55
It was he in the times past which held you So under fortune . . iii 1 78
Had he Duncan's sons under his key—As, an't please heaven, he shall not . . . . iii 6 18
My device, Under the which he shall not choose but fall . *Hamlet* iv 7 66
In sincere verity, Under the allowance of your great aspect . *Lear* ii 2 112
In our sports my better cunning faints Under his chance *Ant. and Cleo.* ii 3 35
Whose ministers would prevail Under the service of a child as soon . iii 13 24
Thy Cæsar knighted me; my youth I spent Much under him *Cymbeline* iii 1 71
Under-bear. Get thee gone And leave those woes alone which I alone Am bound to under-bear . . . . . . *K. John* iii 1 65
Underbearing. Wooing poor craftsmen with the craft of smiles And patient underbearing of his fortune . . . . *Richard II.* i 4 29
Underborne. Skirts, round underborne with a bluish tinsel . *Much Ado* iii 4 21
Undercrest your good addition To the fairness of my power . *Coriolanus* i 9 72
Under fiends. I will fight Against my canker'd country with the spleen Of all the under fiends . . . . iv 5 98
Under-foot. Off with that bauble, throw it under-foot . *T. of Shrew* v 2 122
Under generation. Ere twice the sun hath made his journal greeting To the under generation . . . . . *Meas. for Meas.* iv 3 93
Under globe. Approach, thou beacon to this under globe! . . *Lear* ii 2 170
Undergo. I had rather crack my sinews, break my back, Than you should such dishonour undergo . . . . . *Tempest* iii 1 27
What dangerous action, stood it next to death, Would I not undergo for one calm look! . . . . *T. G. of Ver.* v 4 42
If any in Vienna be of worth To undergo such ample grace and honour, It is Lord Angelo . . . . . . *Meas. for Meas.* i 1 24
But I must tell thee plainly, Claudio undergoes my challenge *Much Ado* v 2 57
Thrice-blessed they that master so their blood, To undergo such maiden pilgrimage . . . . *M. N. Dream* i 1 75
Any thing, my lord, That my ability may undergo . . *W. Tale* ii 3 164
If you will not change your purpose But undergo this flight, make for Sicilia . . . . iv 4 554
Go closely in with me: Much danger do I undergo for thee . *K. John* iv 1 134
Is't not I That undergo this charge? who else but I? . . . v 2 100
Shall it be, That you a world of curses undergo? . . 1 *Hen. IV.* i 3 164
Know our own estate, How able such a work to undergo . 2 *Hen. IV.* i 3 54
I will not undergo this sneap without reply . . . . . ii 1 133
Thinking it harder for our mistress to devise imposition enough than for us to undergo any difficulty imposed . . . *Troi. and Cres.* iii 2 86

Undergo. You undergo too strict a paradox, Striving to make an ugly deed look fair . . . . *T. of Athens* iii 5 24
I have moved already Some certain of the noblest-minded Romans To undergo with me an enterprise . . . . *J. Cæsar* i 3 123
Be they as pure as grace, As infinite as man may undergo . *Hamlet* i 4 34
I am the master of my speeches, and would undergo what's spoken *Cymb.* i 4 153
Undergoes, More goddess-like than wife-like, such assaults . . iii 2 7
Undergo those employments wherein I should have cause to use thee . iii 5 110
Undergoing. Raised in me An undergoing stomach, to bear up *Tempest* i 2 157
Undergone. Some kinds of baseness Are nobly undergone . . iii 1 3
Under-ground. A spirit raised from depth of under-ground . 2 *Hen. VI.* i 2 79
Underhand. By underhand means laboured to dissuade him *As Y. Like It* i 1 146
All that have miscarried By underhand corrupted foul injustice *Rich. III.* v 1 6
Under-hangman. Styled The under-hangman of his kingdom . *Cymbeline* ii 3 135
Under-honest. We think him over-proud And under-honest . *Tr. and Cr.* ii 3 133
Underlings. The fault, dear Brutus, is not in our stars, But in ourselves, that we are underlings . . . . *J. Cæsar* i 2 141
Undermine. Man, sitting down before you, will undermine you *All's Well* i 1 130
They . . . Have hired me to undermine the duchess . . 2 *Hen. VI.* i 2 98
If Troy be not taken till these two undermine it, the walls will stand till they fall of themselves . . . . *Troi. and Cres.* ii 3 9
Underminers. Bless our poor virginity from underminers! *All's Well* i 1 131
Underneath. Yea, and text underneath, 'Here dwells Benedick' *M. Ado* v 1 185
Before him, And underneath that consecrated roof . . *T. Night* iv 3 25
Till these rebels, now afoot, Come underneath the yoke of government 2 *Hen. IV.* iv 4 10
The strawberry grows underneath the nettle . . . *Hen. V.* i 1 60
Pray God she prove not masculine ere long, If underneath the standard of the French She carry armour as she hath begun . 1 *Hen. VI.* i 2 23
So doth the swan her downy cygnets save, Keeping them prisoner underneath her wings . . . . v 3 57
Underneath an alehouse' paltry sign . . . . 2 *Hen. VI.* v 2 67
So, underneath the belly of their steeds, That stain'd their fetlocks in his smoking blood, The noble gentleman gave up the ghost 3 *Hen. VI.* ii 3 20
My most loving friends, Bruised underneath the yoke of tyranny *Richard III.* v 2 2
Suddenly I heard a child cry underneath a wall . *T. Andron.* v 1 24
Underneath the grove of sycamore . . . , So early walking *Rom. and Jul.* i 1 128
Underneath whose arm An envious thrust from Tybalt hit the life Of stout Mercutio, and then Tybalt fled . . . . . iii 1 172
An universal shout, That Tiber trembled underneath her banks *J. Cæsar* i 1 50
Groaning underneath this age's yoke . . . . . i 2 61
Under-peep. The flame o' the taper Bows toward her, and would under-peep her lids . . . . *Cymbeline* ii 2 20
Underprizing. Yet look, how far The substance of my praise doth wrong this shadow In underprizing it . . . *Mer. of Venice* iii 2 129
Underprop. What munition sent, To underprop this action? . *K. John* v 2 99
Here am I left to underprop his land, Who, weak with age, cannot support myself: Now comes the sick hour . *Richard II.* ii 2 82
Under-skinker. This pennyworth of sugar, clapped even now into my hand by an under-skinker . . . . 1 *Hen. IV.* ii 4 26
Understand. Do you understand me?—Methinks I do . *Tempest* ii 1 268
I understand thee not.—What a block art thou, that thou canst not! My staff understands me . . . . *T. G. of Ver.* ii 5 25
I'll but lean, and my staff understands me.—It stands under thee, indeed.—Why, stand-under and under-stand is all one . . ii 5 31
Peace, I pray you. Now let us understand. There is three umpires in this matter, as I understand . . . . . *Mer. Wives* i 1 140
Do you understand me?—Ay, sir, you shall find me reasonable . i 1 216
I shall do that that is reason.—Nay, but understand me. . . . i 1 219
And the boy never need to understand any thing . . . ii 2 133
I must let you understand I think myself in better plight for a lender . ii 2 171
O, understand my drift . . . . ii 2 251
This I can let you understand, the greater file of the subject held the duke to be wise . . . . . *Meas. for Meas.* iii 2 144
I am made to understand that you have lent him visitation . iii 2 255
To make you understand this in a manifested effect, I crave but four days' respite . . . . iv 2 169
Beshrew his hand, I scarce could understand it *Com. of Errors* ii 1 49
So doubtfully that I could scarce understand them. . . ii 1 54
Who, every word by all my wit being scann'd, Want wit in all one word to understand . . . . ii 2 153
I understand thee not.—No? why, 'tis a plain case . . iv 3 21
I understand you not: my griefs are double . . . *L. L. Lost* v 2 762
And by these badges understand the king . . . . v 2 764
You must understand he goes but to see a noise that he heard *M. N. D.* iii 1 93
I understand not what you mean by this . . . . iii 2 236
I say nothing to him, for he understands not me, nor I him *Mer. of Ven.* i 2 74
My meaning in saying he is a good man is to have you understand me that he is sufficient . . . . i 3 16
I understand, moreover, upon the Rialto, he hath a third at Mexico . i 3 19
But there the duke was given to understand . . . ii 8 7
Lest you should not understand me well,—And yet a maiden hath no tongue but thought,—I would detain you here some month or two iii 2 7
I pray thee, understand a plain man in his plain meaning . . iii 5 62
Understand that at the receipt of your letter I am very sick . iv 1 150
I am given, sir, secretly to understand . . *As Y. Like It* i 1 130
Give me your hand, And let me all your fortunes understand . ii 7 200
What must we understand by this?—Some of my shame . . iv 3 95
You understand me?—I, sir! ne'er a whit . . *T. of Shrew* i 1 240
And see you read no other lectures to her: You understand me . i 2 149
Sir, understand you this of me in sooth . . . . i 2 259
Look that you take upon you as you should; You understand me, sir . iv 2 109
This, by the way, I let you understand; My father is here look'd for every day . . . . iv 2 115
I desire your holy wishes.—How understand we that? . *All's Well* i 1 69
Understand what advice shall thrust upon thee; else thou diest . i 1 224
Not much employment for you: you understand me?—Most fruitfully. ii 2 72
We understand it, and thank heaven for you . . . . ii 3 71
Though you understand it not yourselves, no matter; for we must not seem to understand him . . . . iv 1 4
Boskos vauvado: I understand thee, and can speak thy tongue . iv 1 81
My suit, as I do understand, you know . . . . v 3 160
I told him you were sick; he takes on him to understand so much *T. N.* i 5 149
In your denial I would find no sense; I would not understand it . . i 5 286
I understand you, sir; 'tis well begged . . . . iii 1 60
My legs do better understand me, sir, than I understand what you mean iii 1 89
Business, my lord! I think most understand Bohemia stays here longer *W. Tale* i 2 229
Sir, You speak a language that I understand not . . . iii 2 81
Understand. I understand the business, I hear it . . *W. Tale* iv 4 684
Dost thou understand me? Thou art his keeper . *K. John* iii 3 63
On the winking of authority To understand a law . . . iv 2 212
Thou didst understand me by my signs And didst in signs again parley with sin . . . . iv 2 237
The chopping French we do not understand . . *Richard II.* v 3 124
Let me not understand you, then; speak it in Welsh . 1 *Hen. IV.* iii 1 119
I understand thy looks . . . . iii 1 201
I understand thy kisses and thou mine, And that's a feeling disputation iii 1 205
I perceive the devil understands Welsh; And 'tis no marvel he is so humorous . . . . iii 1 233
At Shrewsbury, As I am truly given to understand . . . iv 4 11
We understand him well, How he comes o'er us with our wilder days *Hen. V.* i 2 266
I do partly understand your meaning.—Why then, rejoice therefore . iii 6 52
How say you, lady?—Sauf votre honneur, me understand vell . v 2 135
But, Kate, dost thou understand thus much English, canst thou love me? v 2 205
As more at large your grace shall understand . . 2 *Hen. VI.* ii 1 177
And, as I further have to understand, Is new committed 3 *Hen. VI.* iv 4 10
To let you understand, If case some one of you would fly from us . v 4 33
Write to me very shortly, And you shall understand from me her mind *Richard III.* iv 4 429
And understand again like honest men . . . *Hen. VIII.* i 3 32
The king Shall understand it presently . . . . . v 2 10
Your painted gloss discovers, To men that understand you, words and weakness . . . . v 3 72
Friend, we understand not one another: I am too courtly and thou art too cunning . . . . *Troi. and Cres.* iii 1 29
Understand more clear, What's past and what's to come is strew'd with husks . . . . iv 5 165
You do discomfort all the host.—You understand me not that tell me so v 10 11
I understand thee well . . . . *Coriolanus* iv 7 17
Mark, Marcus, mark! I understand her signs . *T. Andron.* iii 1 143
And, for he understands you are in arms, He craves a parley . v 1 158
How shall I understand you?—I will unbolt to you . *T. of Athens* i 1 51
Cease till after dinner, That I may make his lordship understand . ii 2 43
I am sick of that grief too, as I understand how all things go . iii 6 20
I understand thee; thou hadst some means to keep a dog . iv 3 316
You seem to understand me, By each at once her choppy finger laying Upon her skinny lips . . . . *Macbeth* i 3 43
You do not understand yourself so clearly As it behoves my daughter *Hamlet* i 3 96
My love is too unmannerly.—I do not well understand that . . iii 2 365
These profound heaves: You must translate: 'tis fit we understand them iv 1 2
So much was our love, We would not understand what was most fit iv 1 20
I understand you not, my lord.—I am glad of it . . . iv 2 24
What, art a heathen? How dost thou understand the Scripture?. . v 1 41
Is't not possible to understand in another tongue? . . . v 2 131
The contents, as in part I understand them, are to blame . *Lear* i 2 43
I do beseech you To understand my purposes aright . . . i 4 260
I have inform'd them so.—Inform'd them! Dost thou understand me, man? . . . . ii 4 100
He's made for ever.—I do not understand.—He's married *Othello* i 2 52
Let ourselves again but understand, That as it more concerns the Turk i 3 21
I understand a fury in your words, But not the words . . . iv 2 32
I say thy husband: dost understand the word? My friend, thy husband v 2 153
Sir, you shall understand what hath befall'n, Which, as I think, you know not . . . . v 2 307
Is't not your trick?—I understand not, madam . . *Ant. and Cleo.* v 2 75
And give me directly to understand you have prevailed . *Cymbeline* i 4 171
I will make One of her women lawyer to me, for I yet not understand the case myself . . . . ii 3 80
Here I give to understand, If e'er this coffin drive a-land *Pericles* iii 2 68
I understand you not.—O, take her home, mistress, take her home . iv 2 133
Understandest. There's more in me than thou understand'st *T. and C.* iv 5 240
Understandeth. Who understandeth thee not, loves thee not *L. L. Lost* iv 2 101
Understanding. Their understanding Begins to swell . *Tempest* v 1 79
Art thou lunatics? hast thou no understandings for thy cases? *Mer. W.* iv 1 72
Fortune hath conveyed to my understanding . . *Meas. for Meas.* iii 1 190
A female; or, for thy more sweet understanding, a woman . *L. L. Lost* i 1 267
Understanding that the curate and your sweet self are good at such eruptions . . . . v 1 119
A man's good wit seconded with the forward child Understanding *As Y. Like It* iii 3 14
Thou perishest; or, to thy better-understanding, diest . . v 1 57
I speak as my understanding instructs me . . . *W. Tale* i 1 20
Was this taken By any understanding pate but thine? . . i 2 223
I am only old in judgement and understanding . . 2 *Hen. IV.* i 2 215
Nicely charge your understanding soul With opening titles miscreate *Hen. V.* i 2 15
I' faith, Kate, my wooing is fit for thy understanding . . . v 2 126
I think his understanding is bereft . . . . 3 *Hen. VI.* ii 6 60
Will leave us never an understanding friend . . *Hen. VIII.* Prol. 22
I had thought I had had men of some understanding And wisdom of my council . . . . v 3 135
A mind impatient, An understanding simple and unschool'd . *Hamlet* i 2 97
Whatsoever else shall hap to-night, Give it an understanding, but no tongue . . . . i 2 250
That thus hath put him So much from the understanding of himself . ii 2 9
I speak in understanding . . . . *Lear* iv 5 28
Understood. This learned constable is too cunning to be understood *Much Ado* v 1 234
Thou hast spoken no word all this while.—Nor understood none neither *L. L. Lost* v 1 158
How blow? how blow? speak to be understood . . . v 2 294
When a man's verses cannot be understood . . *As Y. Like It* iii 3 12
Is it not a language I speak?—A most harsh one, and not to be understood without bloody succeeding . . . . . *All's Well* iii 3 198
But to answer you as you would be understood . . . iv 3 123
There's none can tell; But by bad courses may be understood That their events can never fall out good . . . *Richard II.* ii 1 213
These oracles are hardly attain'd, And hardly understood . 2 *Hen. VI.* i 4 75
You are well understood to be a perfecter giber for the table than a necessary bencher in the Capitol . . . *Coriolanus* ii 1 90
Those that understood him smiled at one another . . *J. Cæsar* i 2 285
Augurs and understood relations have By magot-pies and choughs and rooks brought forth The secret'st man of blood . . *Macbeth* iii 4 124
I have understood Your lord has betook himself to unknown travels *Per.* i 3 34
Undertake. I may undertake A journey to my loving Proteus *T. G. of V.* ii 7 6
Then you must undertake to slander him . . . . . iii 2 38

Undertake. My suit then is desperate; you'll undertake her no more? *Mer. Wives* iii 5 127
I will in the interim undertake one of Hercules' labours . *Much Ado* ii 1 380
Either he avoids them with great discretion, or undertakes them with a most Christian-like fear . . . . ii 3 199
I will, on my privilege I have with the parents of the foresaid child or pupil, undertake your ben venuto *L. L. Lost* iv 2 163
You must needs play Pyramus.—Well, I will undertake it *M. N. Dream* i 2 92
You will be schoolmaster And undertake the teaching of the maid *T. of S.* i 1 197
Here is a gentleman . . . Will undertake to woo curst Katharine . . i 2 184
His name and credit shall you undertake . . . . . iv 2 106
Which you hear him so confidently undertake to do . . *All's Well* iii 6 22
By the hand of a soldier, I will undertake it . . . . iii 6 76
Is not this a strange fellow, my lord, that so confidently seems to undertake this business? . . . . iii 6 94
What the devil should move me to undertake the recovery of this drum? iv 1 37
If your life be saved, will you undertake to betray the Florentine? iv 3 326
By my troth, I would not undertake her in this company *T. Night* i 3 61
Would you undertake another suit, I had rather hear you to solicit that Than music from the spheres . . . . iii 1 119
Back you shall not to the house, unless you undertake that with me . iii 4 272
I'll show't the king and undertake to be Her advocate to the loud'st *W. Tale* ii 2 38
Please you, sir, to undertake the business for us, here is that gold I have iv 4 836
What you bid me undertake, Though that my death were adjunct to my act, By heaven, I would do it . . . . *K. John* iii 3 56
The task he undertakes Is numbering sands and drinking oceans dry *Richard II.* ii 2 145
'The purpose you undertake is dangerous;'—why, that's certain *1 Hen. IV.* ii 3 7
I'll undertake to make thee Henry's queen . *1 Hen. VI.* v 3 117
Those two counties I will undertake Your grace shall well and quietly enjoy . . . . v 3 158
Will they undertake to do me good?—This they have promised *2 Hen. VI.* i 2 77
And never will I undertake the thing Wherein thy counsel and consent is wanting . . . . *3 Hen. VI.* ii 6 101
I'll undertake to land them on our coast . . . . . iii 3 205
Your beauty was the cause of that effect; Your beauty, which did haunt me in my sleep To undertake the death of all the world *Richard III.* i 2 123
Lay no hands on me: The deed you undertake is damnable . . . i 4 197
Upon my life, my lord, I'll undertake it . . . . . v 3 42
I'll undertake may see away their shilling Richly . *Hen. VIII.* Prol. 12
Sir Nicholas Vaux, Who undertakes you to your end . . . ii 1 97
This shall I undertake; and 'tis a burden Which I am proud to bear *Troi. and Cres.* iii 3 36
I'll go to him, and undertake to bring him Where he shall answer *Cor.* iii 1 324
I'll undertake't: I think he'll hear me . . . . . . v 1 47
On mine honour dare I undertake For good Lord Titus' innocence *T. An.* i 1 436
Thou wilt undertake A thing like death to chide away this shame *Rom. and Jul.* iv 1 73
If he be now return'd, As checking at his voyage, and that he means No more to undertake it, I will work him To an exploit *Hamlet* iv 7 64
What would you undertake, To show yourself your father's son in deed? iv 7 125
It is the cowish terror of his spirit, That dares not undertake *Lear* iv 2 13
I do agnize A natural and prompt alacrity I find in hardness, and do undertake These present wars . . . . . . *Othello* i 3 234
In the morning I will beseech the virtuous Desdemona to undertake for me . . . . ii 3 337
It is not fit your lordship should undertake every companion that you give offence to . . . . *Cymbeline* ii 1 29
Wherefore then Didst undertake it? . . . . . . iii 4 105
The legions now in Gallia are Full weak to undertake our wars . iii 7 5
You have at large received The danger of the task you undertake *Pericles* i 1 2
For this twelvemonth she'll not undertake A married life . . . ii 5 3
And I will undertake all these to teach . . . . . iv 6 196
Undertaken. You know What you have underta'en to do in's absence *W. Tale* iii 2 79
Undertaker. Nay, if you be an undertaker, I am for you *T. Night* iii 4 349
For Cassio, let me be his undertaker: you shall hear more by midnight *Othello* iv 1 224
Undertaking. How will the world repute me For undertaking so unstaid a journey? . . . . *T. G. of Ver.* ii 7 60
It is virtuous to be constant in any undertaking . *Meas. for Meas.* iii 2 239
Which holy undertaking with most austere sanctimony she accomplished *All's Well* iv 3 59
Your free undertaking cannot miss A thriving issue . *W. Tale* ii 2 44
Else might the world convince of levity As well my undertakings as your counsels . . . . *Troi. and Cres.* ii 2 131
Nor nothing monstrous neither?—Nothing, but our undertakings . iii 2 83
Fordoes itself And leads the will to desperate undertakings . *Hamlet* ii 1 104
Either he so undertaking, Or they so suffering . . *Cymbeline* iv 2 142
Undertook. And better in my mind not undertook . *Mer. of Venice* ii 4 7
I undertook it, Vanquish'd thereto by the fair grace and speech Of the poor suppliant . . . . *All's Well* v 3 132
We left the prince my brother here, my liege, Who undertook to sit and watch by you . . . . *2 Hen. IV.* iv 5 53
Ten years are spent since first he undertook This cause of Rome *T. An.* i 1 31
One of them imports The death of Cassio to be undertook By Roderigo *Othello* v 2 311
Undervalued. Her name is Portia, nothing undervalued To Cato's daughter, Brutus' Portia . . . . . . *Mer. of Venice* i 1 165
In silver she's immured, Being ten times undervalued to tried gold . ii 7 53
Underwent. You are fool'd, discarded, and shook off By him for whom these shames ye underwent . . . . . *1 Hen. IV.* i 3 179
Underwrit. And underwrit, 'Here may you see the tyrant' . *Macbeth* v 8 26
Underwrite in an observing kind His humorous predominance *Tr. and Cr.* ii 3 137
Under-wrought. Thou hast under-wrought his lawful king . *K. John* ii 1 95
Undescried. To shipboard Get undescried . . . . *W. Tale* iv 4 669
Undeserved. Let none presume To wear an undeserved dignity *M. of V.* ii 9 40
Some undeserved fault I'll find about the making of the bed *T. of Shrew* iv 1 202
This is hard and undeserved measure, my lord . . *All's Well* ii 3 273
The fire is dead with grief, Being create for comfort, to be used In undeserved extremes . . . . *K. John* iv 1 108
Undeserver. Men of merit are sought after: the undeserver may sleep, when the man of action is called on . . . . *2 Hen. IV.* ii 4 406
Poor undeserver, I Can nothing render but allegiant thanks *Hen. VIII.* iii 2 175
To sell and mart your offices for gold To undeservers . . *J. Cæsar* iv 3 12
Undeserving as I am, My duty pricks me on . *T. G. of Ver.* iii 1 7
To the manner of the days, In courtesy gives undeserving praise *L. L. L.* v 2 366
Undetermined. In undetermined differences of kings . . *K. John* ii 1 355

Undid. If you would put me to verses or to dance for your sake, Kate, why you undid me . . . . *Hen. V.* v 2 138
Whose wind did seem To glow the delicate cheeks which they did cool, And what they undid did . . . . . . *Ant. and Cleo.* ii 2 210
Undinted. To part with unhack'd edges, and bear back Our targes undinted . . . . ii 6 39
Undiscernible. I should be guiltier than my guiltiness, To think I can be undiscernible . . . . *Meas. for Meas.* v 1 373
Undiscovered. This mystery remained undiscovered *W. Tale* v 2 130
Full often, like a shag-hair'd crafty kern, Hath he conversed with the enemy, And undiscover'd come to me again . . *2 Hen. VI.* iii 1 369
The undiscover'd country from whose bourn No traveller returns *Hamlet* iii 1 79
Undishonoured. I live unstain'd, thou undishonoured *Com. of Errors* ii 2 148
Undisposed. I shall break that merry sconce of yours That stands on tricks when I am undisposed . . . . i 2 80
Undistinguishable. And the quaint mazes in the wanton green For lack of tread are undistinguishable . . . . *M. N. Dream* ii 1 100
These things seem small and undistinguishable . . . . iv 1 192
Undistinguished. O undistinguish'd space of woman's will! . *Lear* iv 6 278
Undividable, incorporate, Am better than thy dear self's better part *Com. of Errors* ii 2 124
Undivulged. Against the undivulged pretence I fight Of treasonous malice *Macbeth* ii 3 137
Hast within thee undivulged crimes, Unwhipp'd of justice . *Lear* iii 2 52
Undo. It was a torment To lay upon the damn'd, which Sycorax Could not again undo . . . . *Tempest* i 2 291
Proof enough to misuse the prince, to vex Claudio, to undo Hero *M. Ado* ii 2 29
To do what, signior?—To bind me, or undo me; one of them . . v 4 20
Our states are forfeit: seek not to undo us . . *L. L. Lost* v 2 425
I will undo This hateful imperfection of her eyes . *M. N. Dream* iv 1 67
I'll Discover that which shall undo the Florentine . . *All's Well* iv 1 80
That quaffing and drinking will undo you . . . *T. Night* i 3 14
If you will not undo what you have done, that is, kill him . . ii 1 38
They would do that Which should undo more doing . *W. Tale* i 2 312
Which lames report to follow it and undoes description to do it . v 2 63
Now mark me, how I will undo myself . . . *Richard II.* iv 1 203
My womb, my womb, my womb, undoes me . . . *2 Hen. IV.* iv 3 25
If you look for a good speech now, you undo me . . . . Epil. 5
What to your wisdoms seemeth best, Do or undo . . *2 Hen. VI.* iii 1 196
That parchment, being scribbled o'er, should undo a man . . iv 2 88
Warwick, as ourself, Shall do and undo as him pleaseth best *3 Hen. VI.* ii 6 105
Have, out of malice To the good queen, possess'd him with a scruple That will undo her . . . . *Hen. VIII.* ii 1 159
This love will undo us all. O Cupid, Cupid, Cupid! . *Troi. and Cres.* iii 1 120
My good friends, mine honest neighbours, Will you undo yourselves? *Coriolanus* i 1 65
This petty brabble will undo us all . . . . . *T. Andron.* ii 1 62
Villain, what hast thou done?—That which thou canst not undo . iv 2 71
How unluckily it happened, that I should purchase the day before for a little part, and undo a great deal of honour! . . *T. of Athens* iii 2 53
We must speak by the card, or equivocation will undo us . *Hamlet* v 1 149
So distribution should undo excess, And each man have enough . *Lear* iv 1 73
Pray you, undo this button: thank you, sir. Do you see this? . v 3 309
By how much she strives to do him good, She shall undo her credit *Oth.* ii 3 365
Thou wouldst not.—In troth, I think I should; and undo't when I had done . . . . iv 3 71
Undo that prayer, by crying out as loud, 'O, bless my brother!' *Ant. and Cleo.* iii 4 17
What Can it [gold] not do and undo? . . . . . *Cymbeline* ii 3 78
Wilt thou undo the worth thou art unpaid for, By tasting of our wrath? v 5 307
Were I chief lord of all this spacious world, I'ld give it to undo the deed *Pericles* iv 3 6
She's able to freeze the god Priapus, and undo a whole generation . iv 6 4
If your peevish chastity . . . shall undo a whole household . . iv 6 132
She's born to undo us . . . . iv 6 158
Undoing. Many a man's tongue shakes out his master's undoing *All's W.* ii 4 24
Undoing all, as all had never been! . . . . . *2 Hen. VI.* i 1 103
To the mere undoing Of all the kingdom . . . *Hen. VIII.* iii 2 329
I see your end; 'Tis my undoing . . . . v 3 62
Do not abuse my master's bounty by The undoing of yourself *A. and C.* v 2 44
Undone. A man is never undone till he be hanged . *T. G. of Ver.* ii 5 5
We are undone; these are the villains That all the travellers do fear so much . . . . iv 1 5
You're shamed, you're overthrown, you're undone for ever! *Mer. Wives* iii 3 103
You are undone.—'Tis not so, I hope.—Pray heaven it be not so! . iii 3 117
He will be here anon.—I am undone! The knight is here . . iv 2 42
I am undone! Fly, run, hue and cry, villain! I am undone! . iv 5 93
She is wronged, she is slandered, she is undone . . *Much Ado* iv 1 315
But Antonio is certainly undone.—Nay, that's true . *Mer. of Venice* iii 1 129
I have undone three tailors; I have had four quarrels . *As Y. Like It* v 4 47
Now we are undone and brought to nothing . . . *T. of Shrew* v 1 44
O, I am undone! I am undone! . . . . v 1 70
Yonder he is: deny him, forswear him, or else we are all undone . v 1 114
I am undone: there is no living, none, If Bertram be away . *All's Well* i 1 95
Undone, and forfeited to cares for ever! . . . . . . ii 3 284
She hath recovered the king, and undone me . . . . . iii 2 22
You are undone, captain, all but your scarf; that has a knot on't yet . iv 3 358
Otherwise a seducer flourishes, and a poor maid is undone . . v 3 147
Even here undone! I was not much afeard . . . *W. Tale* iv 4 452
O sir! You have undone a man of fourscore three . . . . iv 4 464
Undone! undone! If I might die within this hour, I have lived To die when I desire . . . . iv 4 471
O, we are undone, both we and ours for ever!—Hang ye, gorbellied knaves, are ye undone? No, ye fat chuffs . . *1 Hen. IV.* ii 2 91
Then are we all undone. It is not possible, it cannot be . . v 2 3
I am undone by his going; I warrant you, he's an infinitive thing upon my score . . . . *2 Hen. IV.* ii 1 25
My old dame will be undone now for one to do her husbandry . . iii 2 124
Ah, timorous wretch! Thou hast undone thyself, thy son, and me *3 Hen. VI.* i 1 232
This paper has undone me: 'tis the account Of all that world of wealth I have drawn together For mine own ends . . *Hen. VIII.* iii 2 210
The man's undone for ever . . . . . . *Troi. and Cres.* iii 3 258
Will you undo yourselves?—We cannot, sir, we are undone already *Cor.* i 1 66
Leaves nothing undone that may fully discover him their opposite . ii 2 22
We are all undone, unless The noble man have mercy . . . iv 6 107
He hath left undone That which shall break his neck or hazard mine . iv 7 24
We are all undone! Now help, or woe betide thee evermore! *T. An.* iv 2 55
Thou hast undone our mother.—Villain, I have done thy mother.—And therein, hellish dog, thou hast undone. Woe to her chance! . iv 2 75

Undone. He's dead, he's dead! We are undone, lady, we are undone! *Rom. and Jul.* iii 2 38
Where's our master? Are we undone? cast off? nothing remaining? *T. of Athens* iv 2 2
Poor honest lord, brought low by his own heart, Undone by goodness! iv 2 38
Be thou a flatterer now, and seek to thrive By that which has undone thee! . . . . iv 3 211
Ne'er did poor steward wear a truer grief For his undone lord . iv 3 488
Hath given me some worthy cause to wish Things done, undone *J. Cæsar* iv 2 9
That which rather thou dost fear to do Than wishest should be undone *Macbeth* i 5 26
What's done cannot be undone.—To bed, to bed, to bed! . . . . v 1 75
I gin to be aweary of the sun, And wish the estate o' the world were now undone . . . . v 5 50
Do you smell a fault?—I cannot wish the fault undone . . . *Lear* i 1 17
Their best conscience Is not to leave't undone, but keep't unknown *Oth.* iii 3 204
O, I am spoil'd, undone by villains! Give me some help . . v 1 54
Alas! he is betray'd and I undone . . . . v 2 76
Lie they upon thy hand, And be undone by 'em! . . *Ant. and Cleo.* ii 5 106
Better to leave undone, than by our deed Acquire too high a fame when him we serve's away . . . . iii 1 14
We are all undone.—Why, worthy father, what have we to lose? *Cymb.* iv 2 123
If by which time our secret be undone, This mercy shows we'll joy in such a son . . . . *Pericles* i 1 117
Why, are you foolish? Can it be undone? . . . . . . iv 3 1
Undoubted. Rest Unquestion'd welcome and undoubted blest *All's Well* ii 1 211
And till it be undoubted, we do lock Our former scruple . *K. John* ii 1 369
Brave Burgundy, undoubted hope of France! . . . 1 *Hen. VI.* iii 3 41
Threefold renown'd For hardy and undoubted champions . 3 *Hen. VI.* v 7 6
Undoubtedly Was fashion'd to much honour from his cradle *Hen. VIII.* iv 2 49
Undoubtful. Came not to an undoubtful proof . . *Meas. for Meas.* iv 2 142
Undreamed. To unpath'd waters, undream'd shores . *W. Tale* iv 4 578
Undress. Madam, undress you and come now to bed . *T. of Shrew* Ind. 2 119
Undressed, unpolished, uneducated, unpruned . . *L. L. Lost* iv 2 17
Undrowned. 'Tis as impossible that he's undrown'd As he that sleeps here swims.—I have no hope That he's undrown'd . *Tempest* ii 1 237
Unduteous. And this deceit loses the name of craft, Of disobedience, or unduteous title . . . . *Mer. Wives* v 5 240
Undutiful. I know my duty; you are all undutiful . . 3 *Hen. VI.* v 5 33
Unearned. If we have unearned luck Now to 'scape the serpent's tongue, We will make amends ere long . . *M. N. Dream* v 1 439
Unearthly. How ceremonious, solemn, and unearthly It was! *W. Tale* iii 1 7
Uneasiness. There's not, I think, a subject That sits in heart-grief and uneasiness . . . . *Hen. V.* ii 2 27
Uneasy. This swift business I must uneasy make, lest too light winning Make the prize light . . . . *Tempest* i 2 451
From whose simplicity I think it not uneasy to get the cause *W. Tale* iv 2 56
Why rather, sleep, liest thou in smoky cribs, Upon uneasy pallets? 2 *Hen. IV.* iii 1 10
Then happy low, lie down! Uneasy lies the head that wears a crown . iii 1 31
Uneath may she endure the flinty streets, To tread them . 2 *Hen. VI.* ii 4 8
Uneducated. Unpolished, uneducated, unpruned, untrained *L. L. Lost* iv 2 17
Uneffectual. And 'gins to pale his uneffectual fire . . . *Hamlet* i 5 90
Unelected. You should have ta'en the advantage of his choler And pass'd him unelected . . . . *Coriolanus* ii 3 207
Unequal. To lay a heavy and unequal hand Upon our honours 2 *Hen. IV.* iv 1 102
A poor earl's daughter is unequal odds . . . 1 *Hen. VI.* v 5 34
To shape my legs of an unequal size; To disproportion . 3 *Hen. VI.* iii 2 159
Unequal match'd, Pyrrhus at Priam drives; in rage strikes wide *Hamlet* ii 2 493
To punish me for what you make me do Seems much unequal *A. and C.* ii 5 101
Uneven. In most uneven and distracted manner . *Meas. for Meas.* iv 4 3
Fallen am I in dark uneven way . . . . . *M. N. Dream* iii 2 417
All is uneven, And every thing is left at six and seven . *Richard II.* ii 2 121
These high wild hills and rough uneven ways Draws out our miles ii 3 4
More uneven and unwelcome news Came from the north . 1 *Hen. IV.* i 1 50
Eight yards of uneven ground is threescore and ten miles afoot with me ii 2 26
Uneven is the course, I like it not . . . *Rom. and Jul.* iv 1 5
Unexamined. Untainted, unexamined, free, at liberty *Richard III.* iii 6 9
Unexecuted. Leave unexecuted Your own renowned knowledge *A. and C.* iii 7 45
Unexpected. By how much unexpected, by so much We must awake endeavour for defence . . . . *K. John* ii 1 80
All unwarily Devoured by the unexpected flood . . . . v 7 64
Unexperienced. And thou return unexperienced to thy grave *T. of S.* iv 1 86
Unexpressive. The fair, the chaste, and unexpressive she *As Y. Like It* iii 2 10
Unfaithful. Chosen out of the gross band of the unfaithful . . iv 1 199
Unfallible. Believe my words, For they are certain and unfallible 1 *Hen. VI.* i 2 59
Unfamed. Nor none so noble Whose life were ill bestow'd or death unfamed Where Helen is the subject . . . . *Troi. and Cres.* ii 2 159
Unfashionable. Scarce half made up, And that so lamely and unfashionable That dogs bark at me . . . . *Richard III.* i 1 22
Unfasten. That, plucking to unfix an enemy, He doth unfasten so and shake a friend . . . . 2 *Hen. IV.* iv 1 209
Unfather'd heirs and loathly births of nature . . . iv 4 122
Unfed. Your houseless heads and unfed sides . . . *Lear* iii 4 30
Unfee'd. 'Tis like the breath of an unfee'd lawyer; you gave me nothing for't . . . . i 4 142
Unfeeling fools can with such wrongs dispense . . . *Com. of Errors* ii 1 103
This is no answer, thou unfeeling man . . *Mer. of Venice* iv 1 63
And dull unfeeling barren ignorance Is made my gaoler . *Richard II.* i 3 168
And with my fingers feel his hand unfeeling . . 2 *Hen. VI.* iii 2 145
Unfeigned. And here I take the like unfeigned oath . *T. of Shrew* iv 2 32
I come, in kindness and unfeigned love, First, to do greetings 3 *Hen. VI.* iii 3 51
So much his friend, ay, his unfeigned friend . . . . iii 3 202
Unfeignedly. I most unfeignedly beseech your lordship to make some reservation of your wrongs . . . . . . *All's Well* ii 3 259
Ask me if I can refrain from love; For I do love her most unfeignedly . . . . *K. John* ii 1 526
Let him kiss your hand; And what you do, do it unfeignedly *Rich. III.* ii 1 22
Unfellowed. In his meed he's unfellowed . . . . *Hamlet* v 2 150
Unfelt. All my treasury Is yet but unfelt thanks . *Richard II.* ii 3 61
For unfelt imagination, They often feel a world of restless cares *Rich. III.* i 4 80
To show an unfelt sorrow is an office Which the false man does easy *Macbeth* ii 3 142
Unfenced. Even till unfenced desolation Leave them as naked as the vulgar air . . . . *K. John* ii 1 386
Unfilial. You offer him, if this be so, a wrong Something unfilial *W. Tale* iv 4 417
Unfilled. I hate it as an unfilled can . . . . *T. Night* ii 3 7
The veins unfill'd, our blood is cold, and then We pout upon the morning . . . . *Coriolanus* v 1 51

Unfinished. The chain unfinish'd made me stay thus long *Com. of Errors* iii 2 173
Deform'd, unfinish'd, sent before my time Into this breathing world, scarce half made up . . . . *Richard III.* i 1 20
Though unfinish'd, yet so famous, So excellent in art *Hen. VIII.* iv 2 61
Unfirm. Our [men's] fancies are more giddy and unfirm . *T. Night* ii 4 34
So is the unfirm king In three divided . . . 2 *Hen. IV.* i 3 73
So shall no foot upon the churchyard tread, Being loose, unfirm, with digging up of graves, But thou shalt hear it . . *Rom. and Jul.* v 3 6
When all the sway of earth Shakes like a thing unfirm . . *J. Cæsar* i 3 4
Unfit. You 'mongst men Being most unfit to live . . *Tempest* iii 3 58
Unfit to live or die: O gravel heart! . . . *Meas. for Meas.* iv 3 68
Though time seem so adverse and means unfit . *All's Well* v 1 26
I am a subject fit to jest withal, But far unfit to be a sovereign 3 *Hen. VI.* iii 2 92
And thou unfit for any place but hell.—Yes, one place else *Richard III.* i 2 109
Why would you heap these cares on me? I am unfit for state and majesty . . . . iii 7 205
Unfit for other life, compell'd by hunger And lack of other means *Hen. VIII.* i 2 34
Besides, You'll find a most unfit time to disturb him . . ii 2 61
Young men, whom Aristotle thought Unfit to hear moral philosophy *Troi. and Cres.* ii 2 167
I am very ill at ease, Unfit for mine own purposes . . *Othello* iii 3 33
Unfitness. If she sustain him and his hundred knights, When I have show'd the unfitness . . . . *Lear* i 4 356
Unfix. That, plucking to unfix an enemy, He doth unfasten so and shake a friend . . . . 2 *Hen. IV.* iv 1 208
That suggestion Whose horrid image doth unfix my hair . *Macbeth* i 3 135
Who can impress the forest, bid the tree Unfix his earth-bound root? . iv 1 96
Unfledged. In those unfledged days was my wife a girl . . *W. Tale* i 2 78
But do not dull thy palm with entertainment Of each new-hatch'd, unfledged comrade . . . . *Hamlet* i 3 65
We, poor unfledged, Have never wing'd from view o' the nest *Cymbeline* iii 3 27
Unfold. And I to Ford shall eke unfold . . . *Mer. Wives* i 3 105
Of government the properties to unfold, Would seem in me to affect speech and discourse . . . . *Meas. for Meas.* i 1 3
There is a kind of character in thy life, That to the observer doth thy history Fully unfold . . . . i 1 30
Unfold the evil which is here wrapt up In countenance! . . . v 1 117
Brief as the lightning in the collied night, That, in a spleen, unfolds both heaven and earth . . . . . *M. N. Dream* i 1 146
To you our minds we will unfold . . . . i 1 208
Never to unfold to any one Which casket 'twas I chose *Mer. of Venice* ii 9 10
Unfold to us some warlike resistance . . . . *All's Well* i 1 127
O, then unfold the passion of my love . . . . *T. Night* i 4 24
I charge thee, by thy reverence, Here to unfold . . . what thou dost know . . . . v 1 155
Both joy and terror Of good and bad, that makes and unfolds error *W. Tale* iv 1 2
Here in the view of men I will unfold some causes of your deaths *Richard II.* iii 1 7
The worst is worldly loss thou canst unfold. Say, is my kingdom lost? iii 2 94
Still unfold The acts commenced on this ball of earth . 2 *Hen. IV.* Ind. 4
When we are wrong'd and would unfold our griefs, We are denied access iv 1 77
We pray you to proceed And justly and religiously unfold . *Hen. V.* i 2 10
What shall I know of thee?—My master's mind.—Unfold it . . . iii 6 124
What tidings . . . ?—Such as my heart doth tremble to unfold 2 *Hen. VI.* ii 1 166
As Ascanius did When he to madding Dido would unfold His father's acts iii 2 117
What news?—Such news, my lord, as grieves me to unfold *Richard III.* ii 4 39
Let rich music's tongue Unfold the imagined happiness *Rom. and Jul.* ii 6 28
Unfold to me, yourself, your half, Why you are heavy . *J. Cæsar* ii 1 274
I shall unfold to thee, as we are going . . . . . ii 1 330
Some holy angel Fly to the court of England and unfold His message! *Macbeth* iii 6 46
Who's there?—Nay, answer me: stand, and unfold yourself . *Hamlet* i 1 2
Pity me not, but lend thy serious hearing To what I shall unfold . i 5 6
I could a tale unfold whose lightest word Would harrow up thy soul . i 5 15
Time shall unfold what plaited cunning hides . . . *Lear* i 1 283
Doubtless sees and knows more, much more, than he unfolds *Othello* iii 3 243
O heaven, that such companions thou'ldst unfold! . . . iv 2 141
The Moor May unfold me to him; there stand I in much peril . v 1 21
Crush him together rather than unfold His measure duly . *Cymbeline* i 1 26
'Faith, I shall unfold equal discourtesy To your best kindness . ii 3 101
I must, For mine own part, unfold a dangerous speech . . v 5 313
Unfolded. As you have one eye upon my follies, as you hear them unfolded, turn another into the register of your own *Mer. Wives* ii 2 193
To what purpose have you unfolded this to me? . . . ii 2 227
In the divorce his contrary proceedings Are all unfolded *Hen. VIII.* iii 2 27
Must I be unfolded With one that I have bred? *Ant. and Cleo.* v 2 170
Unfoldeth. Mine own escape unfoldeth to my hope . *T. Night* i 2 19
Unfolding. Look, the unfolding star calls up the shepherd *Meas. for Meas.* iv 2 218
To my unfolding lend your prosperous ear . . *Othello* i 3 245
Unfool. Have you any way then to unfool me again? *Mer. Wives* iv 2 120
Unforced. This gentle and unforced accord of Hamlet Sits smiling to my heart . . . . *Hamlet* i 2 123
It is a most pregnant and unforced position . . . *Othello* ii 1 239
Unforfeited. They are wont To keep obliged faith unforfeited *M. of Ven.* ii 6 7
Unfortified. A heart unfortified, a mind impatient . . *Hamlet* i 2 96
Unfortunate. I am that he, that unfortunate he . *As Y. Like It* iii 2 414
My duty to you. Your unfortunate son . . . *All's Well* iii 2 28
Oft have shot at them, Howe'er unfortunate I miss'd my aim 1 *Hen. VI.* i 4 4
But is he gracious in the people's eye?—The more that Henry was unfortunate . . . . 3 *Hen. VI.* iii 3 118
How more unfortunate than all living women Are we come hither *Coriol.* v 3 97
I am e'en sick of shame, that, when your lordship this other day sent to me, I was so unfortunate a beggar . . *T. of Athens* iii 6 47
Give to the edge o' the sword His wife, his babes, and all unfortunate souls That trace him in his line . . . . . *Macbeth* iv 1 152
What thing was that Which parted from you?—A poor unfortunate beggar . . . . *Lear* iv 6 68
I am unfortunate in the infirmity, and dare not task my weakness *Oth.* ii 3 42
Where is this rash and most unfortunate man?—That's he that was Othello . . . . v 2 283
He said he was gentle, but unfortunate; Dishonestly afflicted *Cymbeline* iv 2 39
Unfought. Mort de ma vie! if they march along Unfought withal *Hen. V.* iii 5 12
Unfrequented woods I better brook than flourishing peopled towns *T. G. of Ver.* v 4 2
Many unfrequented plots there are Fitted by kind for rape *T. Andron.* ii 1 115
Unfriended. A stranger, Unguided and unfriended . . . *T. Night* iii 3 10
Unfriended, new-adopted to our hate, Dower'd with our curse . *Lear* i 1 206

Unfriendly. The unfriendly elements Forgot thee utterly *Pericles* iii 1 58
Unfurnish. Thy speeches Will bring me to consider that which may Unfurnish me of reason *W. Tale* v 1 123
Unfurnished. Having made one, Methinks it should have power to steal both his And leave itself unfurnish'd *Mer. of Venice* iii 2 126
But empty lodgings and unfurnish'd walls *Richard II.* i 2 68
The Scot on his unfurnish'd kingdom Came pouring, like the tide *Hen. V.* i 2 148
Rome's royal empress, Unfurnish'd of her well-beseeming troop *T. An.* ii 3 56
We shall be much unfurnish'd for this time *Rom. and Jul.* iv 2 10
Ungained. Men prize the thing ungain'd more than it is *Troi. and Cres.* i 2 315
Achievement is command; ungain'd, beseech i 2 319
Ungalled. And that supposed by the common rout Against your yet ungalled estimation *Com. of Errors* iii 1 102
Why, let the stricken deer go weep, The hart ungalled play *Hamlet* iii 2 283
Ungartered. When you chid at Sir Proteus for going ungartered *T. G. of V.* ii 1 79
Your hose should be ungartered, your bonnet unbanded *As Y. Like It* iii 2 398
His stockings foul'd, Ungarter'd, and down-gyved to his ancle *Hamlet* ii 1 80
Ungenitured. This ungenitured agent will unpeople the province with continency *Meas. for Meas.* iii 2 184
Ungentle. Vicious, ungentle, foolish, blunt, unkind *Com. of Errors* iv 2 21
It is my study To seem despiteful and ungentle to you *As Y. Like It* v 2 86
For this ungentle business, Put on thee by my lord *W. Tale* iii 3 34
To the fearful usage, At least ungentle, of the dreadful Neptune v 1 154
To crush our old limbs in ungentle steel *1 Hen. IV.* v 1 13
As that ungentle gull, the cuckoo's bird, Useth the sparrow v 1 60
Ungentle queen, to call him gentle Suffolk! No more, I say *2 Hen. VI.* iii 2 290
Smile, gentle heaven! or strike, ungentle death! *3 Hen. VI.* ii 3 6
What stern ungentle hands Have lopp'd and hew'd and made thy body bare Of her two branches? *T. Andron.* ii 4 16
When I ask'd you what the matter was, You stared upon me with ungentle looks; I urged you further *J. Cæsar* ii 1 242
Cæsar cannot live To be ungentle *Ant. and Cleo.* v 1 60
Though most ungentle fortune Have placed me in this sty *Pericles* iv 6 103
Ungentleness. You have done me much ungentleness *As Y. Like It* v 2 83
Ungently. Why speaks my father so ungently? *Tempest* i 2 444
When was my lord so much ungently temper'd? *Troi. and Cres.* v 3 1
You've ungently, Brutus, Stole from my bed *J. Cæsar* ii 1 237
Ungird thy strangeness and tell me what I shall vent to my lady *T. Night* iv 1 16
Ungodly. Be husband to me, heavens! Let not the hours of this ungodly day Wear out the day in peace *K. John* iii 1 109
Ungored. I have a voice and precedent of peace, To keep my name ungored *Hamlet* v 2 261
Ungot. As free from touch or soil with her As she from one ungot *Meas. for Meas.* v 1 142
Ungotten. And some are yet ungotten and unborn That shall have cause to curse *Hen. V.* i 2 287
Ungoverned. Such as the fury of ungovern'd youth Thrust from the company of awful men *T. G. of Ver.* iv 1 45
The estate is green and yet ungovern'd *Richard III.* ii 2 127
Which pleaseth God above, And all good men of this ungovern'd isle iii 7 110
The children live, whose parents thou hast slaughter'd, Ungovern'd youth iv 4 392
Seek for him; Lest his ungovern'd rage dissolve the life That wants the means to lead it *Lear* iv 4 19
Ungracious wretch, Fit for the mountains and the barbarous caves *T. N.* iv 1 51
That word 'grace' In an ungracious mouth is but profane *Richard II.* ii 3 89
Swearest thou, ungracious boy? henceforth ne'er look on me *1 Hen. IV.* ii 4 490
And there cut off thy most ungracious head; Which I will bear *2 Hen. VI.* iv 10 88
Nor I, ungracious, speak unto myself For him, poor soul *Richard III.* ii 1 127
Peace, you ungracious clamours! peace, rude sounds! *Troi. and Cres.* i 1 92
Do not, as some ungracious pastors do, Show me the steep and thorny way to heaven *Hamlet* i 3 47
With this ungracious paper strike the sight Of the death-practised duke *Lear* iv 6 283
Ungrateful. Injurious Hermia! most ungrateful maid! *M. N. Dream* iii 2 195
In common worldly things, 'tis call'd ungrateful *Richard III.* ii 2 91
Pouring war Into the bowels of ungrateful Rome *Coriolanus* iv 5 136
Thy father hath full oft For his ungrateful country done the like *T. An.* iv 1 111
It comes from old Andronicus, Shaken with sorrows in ungrateful Rome iv 3 17
O, see the monstrousness of man When he looks out in an ungrateful shape! *T. of Athens* iii 2 80
Ungravely. Which most gibingly, ungravely, he did fashion *Coriolanus* ii 3 233
Ungrown. With lustier maintenance than I did look for Of such an ungrown warrior *1 Hen. IV.* v 4 23
Unguarded. To her unguarded nest the weasel Scot Comes sneaking and so sucks her princely eggs *Hen. V.* i 2 170
What cannot you and I perform upon The unguarded Duncan? *Macbeth* i 7 70
Having found the back-door open Of the unguarded hearts *Cymbeline* v 3 46
Unguem. O, I smell false Latin; dunghill for unguem *L. L. Lost* v 1 84
Unguided. A stranger, Unguided and unfriended *T. Night* iii 3 10
The unguided days And rotten times that you shall look upon *2 Hen. IV.* iv 4 59
Unhacked. With unhack'd swords and helmets all unbruised *K. John* ii 1 254
To part with unhack'd edges, and bear back Our targes undinted *Ant. and Cleo.* ii 6 38
Unhair. I'll spurn thine eyes Like balls before me; I'll unhair thy head ii 5 64
Unhaired. This unhair'd sauciness and boyish troops *K. John* v 2 133
Unhallowed. Thou unreverend and unhallow'd friar *Meas. for Meas.* v 1 307
Whilst thou lay'st in thy unhallow'd dam, Infused itself in thee *M. of V.* iv 1 136
State holy or unhallow'd, what of that? *1 Hen. VI.* iii 1 59
Let never day nor night unhallow'd pass, But still remember what the Lord hath done *2 Hen. VI.* ii 1 85
Help me out From this unhallow'd and blood-stained hole *T. Andron.* ii 3 210
And bid that strumpet, your unhallow'd dam, Like to the earth swallow her own increase v 2 191
Away, inhuman dog! unhallow'd slave! v 3 14
Stop thy unhallow'd toil, vile Montague! *Rom. and Jul.* v 3 54
O, that the gods Would set me free from this unhallow'd place! *Pericles* iv 6 107
Unhand me, gentlemen. By heaven, I'll make a ghost of him that lets me! *Hamlet* i 4 84
Unhandled colts, Fetching mad bounds, bellowing and neighing *M. of V.* v 1 72
Hath ta'en no leave; Has left the cause o' the king unhandled *Hen. VIII.* iii 2 58
Unhandsome. Were she other than she is, she were unhandsome *M. Ado* i 1 177
It is no more unhandsome than to see the lord the prologue *As Y. L. It* Epil. 2
A slovenly unhandsome corse *1 Hen. IV.* i 3 44
I was, unhandsome warrior as I am, Arraigning his unkindness *Othello* iii 4 151
Unhanged. There live not three good men unhanged in England *1 Hen. IV.* ii 4 144
Unhappied. By you unhappied and disfigured clean *Richard II.* iii 1 10
Unhappily. With child, perhaps?—Unhappily, even so *Meas. for Meas.* i 2 160
I'll tell you, cardinal, I should judge now unhappily *Hen. VIII.* i 4 89
There might be thought, Though nothing sure, yet much unhappily *Ham.* iv 5 13
I promise you, the effects he writes of succeed unhappily *Lear* i 2 157
Unhappiness. She hath often dreamed of unhappiness and waked herself with laughing *Much Ado* ii 1 361
And that be heir to his unhappiness! *Richard III.* i 2 25
Unhappy messenger, To plead for that which I would not obtain *T. G. of V.* iv 4 104
My mates . . . Have some unhappy passenger in chase v 4 15
O miserable, unhappy that I am!—Unhappy were you, madam, ere I came v 4 28
By thy approach thou makest me most unhappy v 4 31
The fair sister To her unhappy brother Claudio?—Why 'her unhappy brother'? let me ask *Meas. for Meas.* i 4 20
Unhappy Claudio! wretched Isabel! Injurious world! iv 3 126
So I, to find a mother and a brother, In quest of them, unhappy, lose myself *Com. of Errors* i 2 40
O most unhappy day!—O most unhappy strumpet! iv 4 126
And a shrewd unhappy gallows too *L. L. Lost* v 2 12
I am the unhappy subject of these quarrels *Mer. of Venice* v 1 238
O unhappy youth! Come not within these doors *As Y. Like It* ii 3 16
Thou seest we are not all alone unhappy ii 7 136
Happy be thy speed! But be thou arm'd for some unhappy words *T. of Shrew* ii 1 140
A shrewd knave and an unhappy.—So he is *All's Well* iv 5 66
My past life Hath been as continent, as chaste, as true, As I am now unhappy; which is more Than history can pattern *W. Tale* iii 2 36
Kings are no less unhappy, their issue not being gracious iv 2 30
That unhappy king, my master, whom I so much thirst to see iv 4 523
To-day, to-day, unhappy day, too late, O'erthrows thy joys *Richard II.* iii 2 71
Then it was when the unhappy king,—Whose wrongs in us God pardon!—did set forth *1 Hen. IV.* i 3 148
Ay me, unhappy! To be a queen, and crown'd with infamy! *2 Hen. VI.* iii 2 70
Why do you wring your hands, and beat your breast, And cry 'O Clarence, my unhappy son!' *Richard III.* ii 2 4
Live, and beget a happy race of kings! Edward's unhappy sons do bid thee flourish v 3 158
I am the most unhappy woman living *Hen. VIII.* iii 1 147
The unhappy son of old Andronicus *T. Andron.* ii 3 250
Accursed, unhappy, wretched, hateful day! *Rom. and Jul.* iv 5 43
Unhappy fortune! by my brotherhood, The letter was not nice v 2 17
Unhappy that I am, I cannot heave My heart into my mouth *Lear* i 1 93
Thou old unhappy traitor, Briefly thyself remember iv 6 232
Where didst thou see her? O unhappy girl! With the Moor? *Othello* i 1 164
I have very poor and unhappy brains for drinking ii 3 35
There's some wonder in this handkerchief: I am most unhappy in the loss of it iii 4 102
Is there division 'twixt my lord and Cassio?—A most unhappy one iv 1 243
A more unhappy lady, If this division chance, ne'er stood between, Praying for both parts *Ant. and Cleo.* iii 4 12
Upon a time,—unhappy was the clock That struck the hour! *Cymbeline* v 5 153
And make a conquest of unhappy me, Whereas no glory's got *Pericles* i 4 69
Unhardened. Nosegays, sweetmeats, messengers Of strong prevailment in unharden'd youth *M. N. Dream* i 1 35
Unharmed. From love's weak childish bow she lives unharm'd *R. and J.* i 1 217
Unhatched. He is knight, dubbed with unhatched rapier *T. Night* iii 4 257
Some unhatch'd practice Made demonstrable here in Cyprus to him Hath puddled his clear spirit *Othello* iii 4 141
Unheard. If you be afeard to hear the worst, Then let the worst unheard fall on your head *K. John* iv 2 136
Return me, as Cominius is return'd, Unheard; what then? *Coriolanus* v 1 43
This if she perform, She shall not sue unheard *Ant. and Cleo.* iii 12 24
The seaman's whistle Is as a whisper in the ears of death, Unheard *Per.* iii 1 10
Unhearts. To bite his lip And hum at good Cominius, much unhearts me *Coriolanus* v 1 49
Unheedful vows may heedfully be broken *T. G. of Ver.* ii 6 11
Unheedfully. Wouldst thou then counsel me to fall in love?—Ay, madam, so you stumble not unheedfully i 2 3
Unheedy. Wings and no eyes figure unheedy haste *M. N. Dream* i 1 237
Unhelpful. With sad unhelpful tears, and with dimm'd eyes *2 Hen. VI.* iii 1 218
Unhidden. The severals and unhidden passages Of his true titles *Hen. V.* i 1 86
Unholy. To keep me from a most unholy match *T. G. of Ver.* iv 3 30
Will you be put in mind of his blind fortune, Which was your shame, by this unholy braggart? *Coriolanus* v 6 119
Mere implorators of unholy suits *Hamlet* i 3 129
His daughter's woe and heavy well-a-day In her unholy service *Pericles* iv 4 50
Unhoped. Such as fill my heart with unhoped joys *3 Hen. VI.* iii 3 172
Unhopefullest. Not the unhopefullest husband that I know *Much Ado* ii 1 392
Unhorse. He would unhorse the lustiest challenger *Richard II.* v 3 19
Unhospitable. Which to a stranger, Unguided and unfriended, often prove Rough and unhospitable *T. Night* iii 3 11
Unhoused. Whose bare unhoused trunks, To the conflicting elements exposed, Answer mere nature *T. of Athens* iv 3 229
I would not my unhoused free condition Put into circumscription *Othello* i 2 26
Unhousel'd, disappointed, unaneled, No reckoning made *Hamlet* i 5 77
Unhurtful. You imagine me too unhurtful an opposite *Meas. for Meas.* iii 2 175
Unicorn. Now I will believe That there are unicorns *Tempest* iii 3 22
Wert thou the unicorn, pride and wrath would confound thee *T. of A.* iv 3 339
He loves to hear That unicorns may be betray'd with trees *J. Cæsar* ii 1 204
Unimproved. Of unimproved mettle hot and full *Hamlet* i 1 96
Uninhabitable and almost inaccessible *Tempest* ii 1 37
Unintelligent. That your senses, unintelligent of our insufficience, may, though they cannot praise us, as little accuse us *W. Tale* i 1 16
Union. Disdain and discord shall bestrew The union of your bed *Tempest* iv 1 21
Seeming parted, But yet an union in partition *M. N. Dream* iii 2 210
This union shall do more than battery can To our fast-closed gates *K. John* ii 1 446
And in the cup an union shall he throw *Hamlet* v 2 283
Is thy union here? Follow my mother v 2 337
Unite Your troops of horsemen with his bands of foot *1 Hen. VI.* iii 1 164
In this beauteous face A world of earthly blessings to my soul, If sympathy of love unite our thoughts *2 Hen. VI.* i 1 23
We will unite the white rose and the red *Richard III.* v 5 19
Unite in your complaints, And force them with a constancy *Hen. VIII.* iii 2 1
Since love our hearts and Hymen did our hands Unite commutual in most sacred bands *Hamlet* iii 2 170
Cæsar should again unite His favour with the radiant Cymbeline *Cymb.* v 5 474
United. And, in the lawful name of marrying, To give our hearts united ceremony *Mer. Wives* iv 6 51
Dissever your united strengths, And part your mingled colours *K. John* ii 1 388
Like a broken limb united, Grow stronger for the breaking *2 Hen. IV.* iv 1 222
The united vessel of their blood, Mingled with venom of suggestion iv 4 44
You peers, continue this united league *Richard III.* ii 1 2
Unity. That which you hear you'll swear you see, there is such unity in the proofs *W. Tale* v 2 35

Unity. Make me happy in your unity . . . . *Richard III.* ii 1 31
If thou hadst fear'd to break an oath by Him, The unity the king thy brother made Had not been broken . . . . . iv 4 379
Rend and deracinate The unity and married calm of states *Troi. and Cres.* i 3 100
If there be rule in unity itself, This is not she . . . . . v 2 141
Uproar the universal peace, confound All unity on earth . *Macbeth* iv 3 100
If I were bound to divine of this unity, I would not prophesy so *A. and C.* ii 6 124
Universal plodding poisons up The nimble spirits in the arteries *L. L. L.* iv 3 305
Hearing applause and universal shout, Giddy in spirit . *Mer. of Venice* iii 2 144
This wide and universal theatre Presents more woeful pageants *As Y. L. It* ii 7 137
If all the world could have seen't, the woe had been universal *W. Tale* v 2 100
A largess universal like the sun His liberal eye doth give *Hen. V.* iv Prol. 43
It is the greatest admiration in the universal world . . . . iv 1 66
An arrant traitor as any is in the universal world, or in France, or in England! . . . . iv 8 11
And appetite, an universal wolf, So doubly seconded with will and power, Must make perforce an universal prey . *Troi. and Cres.* i 3 121
Where honour may be crown'd Sole monarch of the universal earth *Rom. and Jul.* iii 2 94
Have you not made an universal shout, That Tiber trembled? *J. Cæsar* i 1 49
Uproar the universal peace, confound All unity on earth . *Macbeth* iv 3 99
And put yourself under his shrowd, The universal landlord *A. and C.* iii 13 72
The time of universal peace is near: Prove this a prosperous day . . iv 6 5
Universe. When creeping murmur and the poring dark Fills the wide vessel of the universe . . . . *Hen. V.* iv Prol. 3
University. Some to the studious universities . . . *T. G. of Ver.* i 3 10
While I play the good husband at home, my son and my servant spend all at the university . . . . *T. of Shrew* v 1 72
My lord, you played once i' the university, you say? . *Hamlet* iii 2 104
Unjointed. This bald unjointed chat of his, my lord, I answer'd indirectly, as I said . . . . . . *1 Hen. IV.* i 3 65
Unjust. And now I must be as unjust to Thurio . . *T. G. of Ver.* iv 2 2
'Twas Ariadne passioning For Theseus' perjury and unjust flight . . iv 4 173
His unjust unkindness, that in all reason should have quenched her love, hath . . . made it more violent . . . . *Meas. for Meas.* iii 1 249
The duke's unjust, Thus to retort your manifest appeal . . . . v 1 302
We'll touse you Joint by joint, but we will know his purpose. What, 'unjust!' . . . . v 1 315
In this unjust divorce of us, Fortune had left to both of us alike What to delight in . . . . . *Com. of Errors* i 1 105
They have verified unjust things . . . . . *Much Ado* v 1 223
Oft our displeasures, to ourselves unjust, Destroy our friends *All's Well* v 3 63
In this uncivil and unjust extent Against thy peace . *T. Night* iv 1 57
This is the time that the unjust man doth thrive . . *W. Tale* iv 4 688
His honour is as true In this appeal as thou art all unjust *Richard II.* iv 1 45
That men of your nobility and power Did gage them both in an unjust behalf . . . . *1 Hen. IV.* i 3 173
A man knows not where to have her.—Thou art an unjust man in saying so . . . . iii 3 146
Such as indeed were never soldiers, but discarded unjust serving-men . iv 2 30
Finding his usurpation most unjust, Endeavour'd my advancement *1 Hen. VI.* ii 5 68
O passing traitor, perjured and unjust! . . . . *3 Hen. VI.* v 1 106
A false-hearted rogue, a most unjust knave . . *Troi. and Cres.* v 1 96
Say my request's unjust, And spurn me back . . *Coriolanus* v 3 164
My lord, you are unjust, and, more than so . . *T. Andron.* i 1 292
I should forge Quarrels unjust against the good and loyal *Macbeth* iv 3 83
Unjustly. I think't no sin To cozen him that would unjustly win *All's W.* iv 2 76
Alive may I not light, If I be traitor or unjustly fight! . *Richard II.* i 1 83
Which Salique land the French unjustly glose To be the realm of France *Hen. V.* i 2 40
And I, unjustly too, must grant it you . . *Richard III.* ii 1 125
Be satisfied, dear God, with our true blood, Which, as thou know'st, unjustly must be spilt . . . . iii 3 22
You charge me most unjustly.—With nought but truth . *Othello* iv 2 186
Heaven and my conscience knows Thou didst unjustly banish me *Cymb.* iii 3 100
Unkennel. I'll warrant we'll unkennel the fox *Mer. Wives* iii 3 174
If his occulted guilt Do not itself unkennel in one speech *Hamlet* iii 2 86
Unkept. Stays me here at home unkept . . *As Y. Like It* i 1 9
Unkind. Look, here is writ 'kind Julia.' Unkind Julia! *T. G. of Ver.* i 2 109
So thou, that hast no unkind mate to grieve thee, With urging helpless patience wouldst relieve me . . . *Com. of Errors* ii 1 38
Foolish, blunt, unkind, Stigmatical in making, worse in mind . iv 2 21
You are unkind, Demetrius; be not so . . *M. N. Dream* iii 2 162
You give your wife too unkind a cause of grief *Mer. of Venice* v 1 175
Blow, blow, thou winter wind, Thou art not so unkind As man's ingratitude . . . . *As Y. Like It* ii 7 175
Fie, fie! unknit that threatening unkind brow . . *T. of Shrew* v 2 136
None can be called deform'd but the unkind . . *T. Night* iii 4 402
'My lady is unkind, perdy.'—Fool!—'Alas, why is she so?' . . iv 2 81
Unkind remembrance! thou and eyeless night Have done me shame *K. John* v 6 12
As you yourself have forged against yourself By unkind usage *1 Hen. IV.* v 1 69
'Tis much when sceptres are in children's hands; But more when envy breeds unkind division . . . . . *1 Hen. VI.* iv 1 193
Seek not a scorpion's nest, Nor set no footing on this unkind shore *2 Hen. VI.* iii 2 87
Henry, though he be infortunate, Assure yourselves, will never be unkind . . . . iv 9 19
I have a kind of self resides with you; But an unkind self, that itself will leave, To be another's fool . . . . *Troi. and Cres.* iii 2 156
Titus, unkind and careless of thine own . . . *T. Andron.* i 1 86
What hast thou done, unnatural and unkind?—Kill'd her . . . v 3 48
Ah, what an unkind hour Is guilty of this lamentable chance! *R. and J.* v 3 145
We were not all unkind, nor all deserve The common stroke of war *T. of Athens* v 4 21
To the noble mind Rich gifts wax poor when givers prove unkind *Ham.* iii 1 101
Bid them farewell, Cordelia, though unkind . . . *Lear* i 1 263
Nothing could have subdued nature To such a lowness but his unkind daughters . . . . iii 4 73
There's fall'n between him and my lord An unkind breach . *Othello* iv 1 237
Unkindest. It is the unkindest tied that ever any man tied.—What's the unkindest tide? . . . . . . *T. G. of Ver.* ii 3 42
He shall find The unkindest beast more kinder than mankind *T. of Athens* iv 1 36
This was the most unkindest cut of all . . . *J. Cæsar* iii 2 187
Unkindly. But why unkindly didst thou leave me so? . *M. N. Dream* iii 2 183
Take it not unkindly, pray, That I have been thus pleasant *T. of Shrew* iii 1 57
Myself unkindly banished, The gates shut on me . . *T. Andron.* v 3 104
I hope it remains not unkindly with your lordship that I returned you an empty messenger . . . . . *T. of Athens* iii 6 39
Unkindly. Rushing out of doors, to be resolved If Brutus so unkindly knock'd. . . . . *J. Cæsar* iii 2 184
Tush! never tell me; I take it much unkindly . . . . *Othello* i 1 1
Unkindness. I hope we shall drink down all unkindness . *Mer. Wives* i 1 204
Thy unkindness shall his death draw out To lingering sufferance *Meas. for Meas.* ii 4 166
His unjust unkindness, that in all reason should have quenched her love iii 1 250
Unkindness blunts it more than marble hard . . *Com. of Errors* ii 1 93
Take no unkindness of his hasty words . . . *T. of Shrew* iv 3 169
Is there any unkindness between my lord and you, monsieur? *All's W.* ii 5 35
O'er and o'er divides him 'Twixt his unkindness and his kindness *W. T.* iv 4 563
And thy unkindness be like crooked age . . . . *Richard II.* ii 1 133
Thou wouldst have me drown'd on shore, With tears as salt as sea, through thy unkindness . . . . . *2 Hen. VI.* iii 2 96
As a discontented friend, grief-shot With his unkindness *Coriolanus* v 1 45
That nature, being sick of man's unkindness, Should yet be hungry! *T. of Athens* iv 3 176
Give me a bowl of wine. In this I bury all unkindness . . *J. Cæsar* iv 3 159
Who may I rather challenge for unkindness Than pity for mischance! *Macbeth* iii 4 42
Which I have rather blamed as mine own jealous curiosity than as a very pretence and purpose of unkindness . . . . . *Lear* i 4 76
She hath tied Sharp-tooth'd unkindness, like a vulture, here . . . ii 4 137
I tax not you, you elements, with unkindness . . . . iii 2 16
His own unkindness, That stripp'd her from his benediction . . . iv 3 44
I was, unhandsome warrior as I am, Arraigning his unkindness *Othello* iii 4 152
Unkindness may do much; And his unkindness may defeat my life . iv 2 159
We see how mortal an unkindness is to them [women] *Ant. and Cleo.* i 2 138
Unkinged. God save King Harry, unking'd Richard says! *Richard II.* iv 1 220
Then crushing penury Persuades me I was better when a king; Then am I king'd again: and by and by Think that I am unking'd by Bolingbroke . . . . v 5 37
Unkinglike. For ourself To show less sovereignty than they, must needs Appear unkinglike . . . . *Cymbeline* iii 5 7
Unkiss. Let me unkiss the oath 'twixt thee and me . *Richard II.* v 1 74
Unkissed. Foul breath is noisome; therefore I will depart unkissed *Much Ado* v 2 54
Unknit that threatening unkind brow . . . . *T. of Shrew* v 2 136
Will you again unknit This churlish knot of all-abhorred war? *1 Hen. IV.* v 1 15
I would he had continued to his country As he began, and not unknit himself The noble knot he made . . . . . *Coriolanus* iv 2 31
Unknit that sorrow-wreathen knot . . . . *T. Andron.* iii 2 4
Unknowing. Let me speak to the yet unknowing world How these things came about . . . . *Hamlet* v 2 390
Unknown. 'Tis not unknown to thee that I have sought To match my friend . . . . *T. G. of Ver.* iii 1 61
O, give me pardon, That I, your vassal, have employ'd and pain'd Your unknown sovereignty! . . . . . *Meas. for Meas.* v 1 392
Her sober virtue, years, and modesty, Plead on her part some cause to you unknown . . . . *Com. of Errors* iii 1 91
Against my soul's pure truth why labour you To make it wander in an unknown field? . . . . iii 2 38
This I wonder at, That he, unknown to me, should be in debt . . iv 2 48
No part of it is mine; This shame derives itself from unknown loins *Much Ado* iv 1 137
As imagination bodies forth The forms of things unknown *M. N. Dream* v 1 15
'Tis not unknown to you, Antonio, How much I have disabled mine estate . . . . *Mer. of Venice* i 1 122
My affection hath an unknown bottom, like the bay of Portugal *As Y. Like It* iv 1 212
A noble gentleman, To whom my father is not all unknown *T. of Shrew* i 2 241
Nor is your firm resolve unknown to me . . . . . . ii 1 93
'Tis not unknown to you, madam, I am a poor fellow . *All's Well* i 3 14
When we should submit ourselves to an unknown fear . . . . ii 3 6
To the unknown beloved, this, and my good wishes . *T. Night* ii 5 101
What his happier affairs may be, are to me unknown . *W. Tale* iv 2 35
Pray you, bid These unknown friends to's welcome . . . . iv 4 65
A bargain! And, friends unknown, you shall bear witness to't . iv 4 395
For all the sun sees . . . or the profound seas hide In unknown fathoms iv 4 502
And for the world, familiar to us and unknown . . . *Hen. V.* ii 7 40
My worth unknown, no loss is known in me . . . *1 Hen. VI.* iv 5 23
Petty faults to faults unknown, Which time will bring to light *2 Hen. VI.* iii 1 64
For divers unknown reasons, I beseech you, Grant me this boon *Richard III.* i 2 218
For what these nobles were committed Is all unknown to me . . ii 4 48
The unknown Ajax. Heavens, what a man is there! a very horse *Troi. and Cres.* iii 3 125
Our business is not unknown to the senate . . . *Coriolanus* i 1 58
The end of it Unknown to the beginning . . . . . . iii 1 329
Too early seen unknown, and known too late! . . *Rom. and Jul.* i 5 141
How many ages hence Shall this our lofty scene be acted over In states unborn and accents yet unknown! . . . . . *J. Cæsar* iii 1 113
The posture of your blows are yet unknown . . . . . v 1 33
Tell me, thou unknown power,— He knows thy thought *Macbeth* iv 1 69
I am yet Unknown to woman, never was forsworn . . . . iv 3 126
You may glean, Whether aught, to us unknown, afflicts him thus *Hamlet* ii 2 17
What a wounded name, Things standing thus unknown, shall live behind me! . . . . v 2 356
By the law of arms thou wast not bound to answer An unknown opposite *Lear* v 3 153
Not another comfort like to this Succeeds in unknown fate *Othello* ii 1 195
Their best conscience Is not to leave't undone, but keep't unknown . iii 3 204
Being done unknown, I should have found it afterwards well done *Ant. and Cleo.* ii 7 84
I am ashamed To look upon the holy sun, to have The benefit of his blest beams, remaining So long a poor unknown . . . *Cymbeline* iv 4 43
Unknown, Pitied nor hated, to the face of peril Myself I'll dedicate . v 1 27
When as a lion's whelp shall, to himself unknown, without seeking find v 4 139; v 5 436
Unknown to you, unsought, were clipp'd about With this most tender air . . . . v 5 451
I have understood Your lord has betook himself to unknown travels *Per.* i 3 35
Unlace. What's the matter, That you unlace your reputation thus? *Oth.* ii 3 194
Unlaid. Ghost unlaid forbear thee!—Nothing ill come near thee! *Cymb.* iv 2 278
Princes' bloods were shed, To keep his bed of blackness unlaid ope *Pericles* i 2 89
Unlawful. I have been an unlawful bawd time out of my mind *Meas. for Meas.* iv 2 16
Hath not else his eye Stray'd his affection in unlawful love? *Com. of Er.* v 1 51
May be the amorous count solicits her In the unlawful purpose *All's W.* iii 5 73
Is it not meant damnable in us, to be trumpeters of our unlawful intents? iv 3 32

Unlawful. Those that think it is unlawful business I am about, let them depart . . . *W. Tale* v 3 96
As doth a ruler with unlawful oaths . . . *1 Hen. VI.* v 5 30
To threaten me with death is most unlawful . . . *Richard III.* i 4 193
By her, in his unlawful bed, he got This Edward . . . iii 7 190
If to preserve this vessel for my lord From any other foul unlawful touch Be not to be a strumpet, I am none . . . *Othello* iv 2 84
I will give over my suit and repent my unlawful solicitation . . . iv 2 202
And all the unlawful issue that their lust Since then hath made *Ant. and Cleo.* iii 6 7
Unlawfully. I had rather my brother die by the law than my son should be unlawfully born . . . *Meas. for Meas.* iii 1 196
Unlawfully made drunk with innocents' blood! . . . *Richard III.* iv 4 30
That he hath used thee.—How? unlawfully?—Ay.—He will not say so *Othello* v 2 70
Unlearned. I will prove those verses to be very unlearned . *L. L. Lost* iv 2 165
How shall they credit A poor unlearned virgin? . . . *All's Well* i 3 246
I know thee well; But in thy fortunes am unlearn'd and strange *T. of Athens* iv 3 56
Royalty unlearn'd, honour untaught, Civility not seen from other *Cymb.* iv 2 178
Unless. From Naples Can have no note, unless the sun were post *Tempest* ii 1 248
And my ending is despair, Unless I be relieved by prayer . . . Epil. 16
A round hose, madam, now's not worth a pin, Unless you have a cod-piece to stick pins on . . . *T. G. of Ver.* ii 7 56
What joy is joy, if Silvia be not by? Unless it be to think that she is by iii 1 176
Unless I look on Silvia in the day, There is no day for me . . . iii 1 180
No more; unless the next word that thou speak'st Have some malignant power . . . iii 1 237
Cannot be true servant to my master Unless I prove false traitor to myself . . . iv 4 110
The painter flatter'd her a little, Unless I flatter with myself too much iv 4 193
Lovers break not hours, Unless it be to come before their time . v 1 5
Unless he know some strain in me, that I know not myself *Mer. Wives* ii 1 90
Unless experience be a jewel that I have purchased at an infinite rate ii 2 212
You die, Sir John. Unless you go out disguised . . . iv 2 68
All hope is gone, Unless you have the grace by your fair prayer *M. for M.* i 4 69
His goods confiscate . . . , Unless a thousand marks be levied *Com. of Er.* i 1 22
That never meat sweet-savour'd in thy taste, Unless I spake . . ii 2 120
Unless the fear of death doth make me dote, I see my son . . v 1 195
You could never do him so ill-well, unless you were the very man *M. Ado* ii 1 122
Will you have me, lady?—No, my lord, unless I might have another for working-days . . . ii 1 340
There is no appearance of fancy in him, unless it be a fancy that he hath to strange disguises . . . iii 2 32
And what have I to give you back, whose worth May counterpoise this rich and precious gift?—Nothing, unless you render her again . iv 1 30
Unless you play the honest Troyan, the poor wench is cast away *L. L. L.* v 2 681
Unless you can find sport in their intents . . . *M. N. Dream* v 1 79
I will die as chaste as Diana, unless I be obtained by the manner of my father's will . . . *Mer. of Venice* i 2 117
'Tis vile, unless it may be quaintly order'd . . . ii 4 6
A third cannot be matched, unless the devil himself turn Jew . iii 1 81
Not sick, my lord, unless it be in mind; Nor well, unless in mind . iii 2 237
The clerk that never means to do it, Unless he live until he be a man . v 1 283
Would you not have me honest?—No, truly, unless thou wert hard-favoured . . . *As Y. Like It* iii 3 29
You shall never take her without her answer, unless you take her without her tongue . . . iv 1 176
With more successful words Than you, unless you were a scholar *T. of S.* i 2 159
He cannot thrive, Unless her prayers . . . reprieve him *All's Well* iii 4 27
We must not seem to understand him, unless some one among us whom we must produce for an interpreter . . . iv 1 5
Thou hast spoken all already, unless thou canst say they are married . v 3 268
For ever may my knees grow to the earth, My tongue cleave to my roof within my mouth, Unless a pardon ere I rise or speak *Richard II.* v 3 32
Unless a brother should a brother dare To gentle exercise . *1 Hen. IV.* v 2 54
Unless my study and my books be false, The argument you held was wrong in you . . . *1 Hen. VI.* ii 4 56
Thou art come too soon, Unless thou wert more loyal *2 Hen. VI.* iii 1 96
Unless I find him guilty, he shall not die . . . iv 2 103
Unless you be possess'd with devilish spirits, You cannot but forbear . iv 7 80
Nor knows he how to live but by the spoil, Unless by robbing . iv 8 42
It boots thee not, proud queen, Unless the adage must be verified, That beggars mounted run their horse to death . . . *3 Hen. VI.* i 4 126
A thousand men have broke their fasts to-day, That ne'er shall dine unless thou yield the crown . . . ii 2 128
Why, I, in this weak piping time of peace, Have no delight to pass away the time, Unless to spy my shadow in the sun . *Richard III.* i 1 26
Unless it be whilst some tormenting dream Affrights thee with a hell . i 3 226
What doth he upon the sea?—Unless for that, my liege, I cannot guess. —Unless for that he comes to be your liege, You cannot guess . iv 4 475
Unless, by not so doing, our good city Cleave in the midst *Coriolanus* iii 2 27
We are all undone, unless The noble man have mercy . . . iv 6 107
All hope is vain, Unless his noble mother, and his wife . . . v 1 71
Here nothing breeds, Unless the nightly owl or fatal raven *T. Andron.* ii 3 97
Unless the bookish theoric, Wherein the toged consuls can propose *Oth.* i 1 24
Unless thou think'st me devilish . . . *Cymbeline* i 5 16
Here's nothing to be got now-a-days, unless thou canst fish for't *Pericles* ii 1 73
Unlessoned. An unlesson'd girl, unschool'd, unpractised *Mer. of Venice* iii 2 161
Unlettered. That unlettered small-knowing soul . . . *L. L. Lost* i 1 253
Uneducated, unpruned, untrained, or rather, unlettered . . . iv 2 18
His addiction was to courses vain, His companies unletter'd. *Hen. V.* i 1 55
Unlicensed. Why, as it were unlicensed of your loves, He would depart, I'll give some light unto you . . . *Pericles* i 3 17
Unlicked. Like to a chaos, or an unlick'd bear-whelp . *3 Hen. VI.* iii 2 161
Unlike. Make not impossible That which but seems unlike *Meas. for Meas.* v 1 52
She is a most sweet lady.—Not unlike, sir, that may be . *L. L. Lost* ii 1 208
How much unlike art thou to Portia! How much unlike my hopes! *Mer. of Venice* ii 9 57
What occasion of import Hath all so long detain'd you from your wife, And sent you hither so unlike yourself? . *T. of Shrew* iii 2 106
Demean himself Unlike the ruler of a commonweal. . *2 Hen. VI.* i 1 189
How proud, how peremptory, and unlike himself . . . iii 1 8
Not much Unlike young men, whom Aristotle thought Unfit to hear moral philosophy . . . *Troi. and Cres.* ii 2 166
You are like to do such business.—Not unlike, Each way, to better yours *Coriolanus* iii 1 48
This accident is not unlike my dream: Belief of it oppresses me *Othello* i 1 143
How much unlike art thou Mark Antony! . . . *Ant. and Cleo.* i 5 35
The gods made you, Unlike all others, chaffless . . . *Cymbeline* i 6 178
Unlike. Let thy effects So follow, to be most unlike our courtiers, As good as promise . . . *Cymbeline* v 4 136
The service that you three have done is more Unlike than this thou tell'st . . . v 5 354
Unlikely. Thoughts tending to ambition, they do plot Unlikely wonders *Richard II.* v 5 19
And more unlikely Than to accomplish twenty golden crowns! *3 Hen. VI.* iii 2 151
This is unlikely: He and Aufidius can no more atone Than violentest contrariety . . . *Coriolanus* iv 6 71
Unlimited. Scene individable, or poem unlimited . . . *Hamlet* ii 2 419
Unlineal. Thence to be wrench'd with an unlineal hand . *Macbeth* iii 1 63
Unlinked. It unlink'd itself, And with indented glides did slip away Into a bush . . . *As Y. Like It* iv 3 112
Unload. Thou bear'st thy heavy riches but a journey, And death unloads thee . . . *Meas. for Meas.* iii 1 28
To you Duke Humphrey must unload his grief . . *2 Hen. VI.* i 1 76
Nor can my tongue unload my heart's great burthen . *3 Hen. VI.* ii 1 81
Unloaded all the gibbets and pressed the dead bodies . *1 Hen. IV.* iv 2 40
Unloading. At thy tent is now Unloading of his mules . *Ant. and Cleo.* iv 6 24
Unlock. Climb o'er the house to unlock the little gate . *L. L. Lost* i 1 109
Give me a key for this, And instantly unlock my fortunes here *M. of V.* ii 9 52
I like thy armour well; I'll frush it and unlock the rivets all, But I'll be master of it . . . *Troi. and Cres.* v 6 29
I have seen her rise from her bed, . . . unlock her closet . *Macbeth* v 1 6
Unlocked. My purse, my person, my extremest means, Lie all unlock'd to your occasions . . . *Mer. of Venice* i 1 139
Unlooked. But by some unlook'd accident cut off . . *Richard III.* i 3 214
Unlooked for. How much unlook'd for is this expedition! . *K. John* ii 1 79
Go we, as well as haste will suffer us, To this unlook'd for, unprepared pomp . . . ii 1 560
A heavy sentence, my most sovereign liege, And all unlook'd for *Rich. II.* i 3 155
Honour comes unlooked for, and there's an end . *1 Hen. IV.* v 3 64
And all the unlook'd for issue of their bodies . *3 Hen. VI.* iii 2 131
Who should that be? belike, unlook'd-for friends . . . v 1 14
Ah, sirrah, this unlook'd-for sport comes well . *Rom. and Jul.* i 5 31
Unloose. It rested in your grace To unloose this tied-up justice *M. for M.* i 3 32
The Gordian knot of it he will unloose, Familiar as his garter *Hen. V.* i 1 46
Unloose thy long-imprison'd thoughts . . . *2 Hen. VI.* v 1 88
Wanton Cupid Shall from your neck unloose his amorous fold *T. and C.* iii 3 223
Like rats, oft bite the holy cords a-twain Which are too intrinse t' unloose . . . *Lear* ii 2 81
Unloosed. Where I am robb'd and bound, There must I be unloosed *Hen. VIII.* ii 4 147
Unloved. But miserable most, to love unloved . . *M. N. Dream* iii 2 234
Love, which, left unshown, Is often left unloved . *Ant. and Cleo.* iii 6 53
Unloving. Which argued thee a most unloving father . *3 Hen. VI.* ii 2 25
Unluckily. A reverend Syracusian merchant, Who put unluckily into this bay . . . *Com. of Errors* v 1 125
Thus the bowl should run, And not unluckily against the bias *T. of S.* iv 5 25
My third comfort, Starr'd most unluckily, is from my breast, . . . Haled out to murder . . . *W. Tale* iii 2 100
Which, if like an ill venture it come unluckily home, I break *2 Hen. IV.* Epil. 13
Things have fall'n out, sir, so unluckily, That we have had no time to move our daughter . . . *Rom. and Jul.* iii 4 1
How unluckily it happened! . . . *T. of Athens* iii 2 51
And things unluckily charge my fantasy . . . *J. Cæsar* iii 3 2
Unlucky. The contrarious winds that held the king So long in his unlucky Irish wars . . . *1 Hen. IV.* v 1 53
Brought hither in a most unlucky hour . . *T. Andron.* ii 3 251
I can discover all The unlucky manage of this fatal brawl *Rom. and Jul.* iii 1 148
Fear comes upon me: O, much I fear some ill unlucky thing . v 3 136
When you shall these unlucky deeds relate, Speak of me as I am *Othello* v 2 341
Unlustrous as the smoky light That's fed with stinking tallow *Cymbeline* i 6 109
Unmade. Taking the measure of an unmade grave . *Rom. and Jul.* iii 3 70
Unmake. They have made themselves, and that their fitness now Does unmake you . . . *Macbeth* i 7 54
She may make, unmake, do what she list . . . *Othello* ii 3 352
Unmanly. And die in bands for this unmanly deed! . *3 Hen. VI.* i 1 186
New customs, Though they be never so ridiculous, Nay, let 'em be unmanly, yet are follow'd . . . *Hen. VIII.* i 3 4
A poor unmanly melancholy sprung From change of fortune *T. of Athens* iv 3 203
'Tis unmanly grief; It shows a will most incorrect to heaven *Hamlet* i 2 94
Unmanned. Hood my unmann'd blood, bating in my cheeks *R. and J.* iii 2 14
What, quite unmann'd in folly?—If I stand here, I saw him . *Macbeth* iii 4 73
Unmannered. You heedless joltheads and unmanner'd slaves! *T. of S.* iv 1 169
Unmanner'd dog! stand thou, when I command . *Richard III.* i 2 39
Unmannerly slave, that will thrust himself into secrets! *T. G. of Ver.* iii 1 393
I'll rather be unmannerly than troublesome . . *Mer. Wives* ii 1 325
Being so full of unmannerly sadness in his youth . *Mer. of Venice* i 2 54
This apish and unmannerly approach . . . The king doth smile at *K. John* v 2 131
He smiled and talk'd, And as the soldiers bore dead bodies by, He call'd them untaught knaves, unmannerly . . . *1 Hen. IV.* i 3 43
Even he escapes not Language unmannerly . . . *Hen. VIII.* i 2 27
I were unmannerly to take you out, And not to kiss you . . i 4 95
Forgive me, If I have used myself unmannerly . . . iii 1 176
My haste made me unmannerly . . . iv 2 105
Unmannerly intruder as thou art! . . . *T. Andron.* ii 3 65
Their daggers Unmannerly breech'd with gore . . *Macbeth* ii 3 122
If my duty be too bold, my love is too unmannerly . . *Hamlet* iii 2 364
Be Kent unmannerly, When Lear is mad . . . *Lear* i 1 147
Unmarried. Pale primroses, That die unmarried . . *W. Tale* iv 4 123
Unmask. My husband bids me; now I will unmask. *Meas. for Meas.* v 1 206
The chariest maid is prodigal enough, If she unmask her beauty to the moon . . . *Hamlet* i 3 37
Unmastered. Or your chaste treasure open To his unmaster'd importunity i 3 32
Unmatchable. Most radiant, exquisite, and unmatchable beauty *T. N.* i 5 181
This, so sole and so unmatchable, Shall give a holiness . *K. John* iv 3 52
Their mastiffs are of unmatchable courage . . . *Hen. V.* iii 7 151
Thy demon, that's thy spirit which keeps thee, is Noble, courageous, high, unmatchable, Where Cæsar's is not . . *Ant. and Cleo.* ii 3 20
Unmatched. Against whose fury and unmatched force The aweless lion could not wage the fight . . . *K. John* i 1 265
Of an excellent And unmatch'd wit and judgement. . *Hen. VIII.* ii 4 47
Is merely love, Duty, and zeal to your unmatched mind *T. of Athens* iv 3 523
That unmatch'd form and feature of blown youth Blasted with ecstasy *Hamlet* iii 1 167
Unmeasurable. That I hope is an unmeasurable distance *Mer. Wives* ii 1 109
Whose womb unmeasurable, and infinite breast, Teems, and feeds all *T. of Athens* iv 3 178
Unmeet. A creature unprepared, unmeet for death . *Meas. for Meas.* iv 3 71

Unmeet. Prove you that any man with me conversed At hours unmeet *Much Ado* iv 1 184

Vow, alack, for youth unmeet, Youth so apt to pluck a sweet! *L. L. Lost* iv 3 113

York is most unmeet of any man.—I'll tell thee, Suffolk, why I am unmeet: First, for I cannot flatter thee. *2 Hen. VI.* i 3 167

Unmellowed. His head unmellow'd, but his judgement ripe *T. G. of Ver.* ii 4 70

Unmerciful. O filthy traitor!—Unmerciful lady as you are, I'm none *Lear* iii 7 33

Unmeritable. My desert Unmeritable shuns your high request *Rich. III.* iii 7 155

This is a slight unmeritable man, Meet to be sent on errands. *J. Cæsar* iv 1 12

Unmeriting, proud, violent, testy magistrates, alias fools. *Coriolanus* ii 1 47

Unminded. A poor unminded outlaw sneaking home *1 Hen. IV.* iv 3 58

Unmindful. Dull, unmindful villain, Why stand'st thou still? *Rich. III.* iv 4 444

Unmingled. As easy mayst thou fall A drop of water in the breaking gulf And take unmingled thence that drop again *Com. of Errors* ii 2 129

What hath mass or matter, by itself Lies rich in virtue and unmingled *Troi. and Cres.* i 3 30

Unmitigable. In her most unmitigable rage *Tempest* i 2 276

Unmitigated. Uncovered slander, unmitigated rancour *Much Ado* iv 1 308

Unmixed. All alone shall live . . . , Unmix'd with baser matter *Hamlet* i 5 104

Unmoaned. Our fatherless distress was left unmoan'd *Richard III.* ii 2 64

Unmoved. Patience unmoved! no marvel though she pause *Com. of Errors* ii 1 32

Unmoving. Alas, to make me A fixed figure for the time of scorn To point his slow unmoving finger at! *Othello* iv 2 55

Unmusical. A name unmusical to the Volscians' ears *Coriolanus* iv 5 64

Unmuzzle. Now unmuzzle your wisdom *As Y. Like It* i 2 74

Unmuzzled. Baited it with all the unmuzzled thoughts That tyrannous heart can think *T. Night* iii 1 130

Unnatural. I do forgive thee, Unnatural though thou art *Tempest* v 1 79

He did render him the most unnatural That lived amongst men.—And well he might so do, For well I know he was unnatural *As Y. Like It* iv 3 123

A most unworthy and unnatural lord Can do no more *W. Tale* ii 3 113

And to rebuke the usurpation Of thy unnatural uncle *K. John* ii 1 10

Defused attire And every thing that seems unnatural *Hen. V.* v 2 62

Behold the wounds, the most unnatural wounds, Which thou thyself hast given her woful breast. *1 Hen. VI.* iii 3 50

I always thought It was both impious and unnatural v 1 12

Seeing thou hast proved so unnatural a father *3 Hen. VI.* i 1 218

How fell, how butcherly, Erroneous, mutinous, and unnatural! ii 5 90

Why, trow'st thou, Warwick, That Clarence is so harsh, so blunt, unnatural? v 1 86

Whose ugly and unnatural aspect May fright the hopeful mother *Richard III.* i 2 23

Thy deed, inhuman and unnatural, Provokes this deluge most unnatural i 2 60

It is a quarrel most unnatural, To be revenged on him that loveth you. i 2 134

A most unnatural and faithless service! *Hen. VIII.* ii 1 123

Like an unnatural dam Should now eat up her own! *Coriolanus* iii 1 293

Tell me not Wherein I seem unnatural v 3 84

The gods look down, and this unnatural scene They laugh at v 3 184

What hast thou done, unnatural and unkind?—Kill'd her *T. Andron.* v 3 48

Lady, come from that nest Of death, contagion, and unnatural sleep *Rom. and Jul.* v 3 152

'Tis unnatural, Even like the deed that's done *Macbeth* ii 4 10

Foul whisperings are abroad: unnatural deeds Do breed unnatural troubles v 1 80

Revenge his foul and most unnatural murder.—Murder!—Murder most foul, as in the best it is; But this most foul, strange, and unnatural *Hamlet* i 5 25

Let me be cruel, not unnatural: I will speak daggers to her iii 2 413

So shall you hear Of carnal, bloody, and unnatural acts v 2 392

Her offence Must be of such unnatural degree, That monsters it *Lear* i 1 222

Abhorred villain! Unnatural, detested, brutish villain! worse than brutish! i 2 81

Seeing how loathly opposite I stood To his unnatural purpose ii 1 52

You unnatural hags, I will have such revenges on you both ii 4 281

Of how unnatural and bemadding sorrow The king hath cause to plain. iii 1 38

Alack, alack, Edmund, I like not this unnatural dealing iii 3 2

Most savage and unnatural!—Go to; say you nothing iii 3 7

Foh! one may smell in such a will most rank, Foul disproportion, thoughts unnatural. But pardon me *Othello* iii 3 233

That death's unnatural that kills for loving v 2 42

Slay us, or receive us For barbarous and unnatural revolts *Cymbeline* iv 4 6

You call my course unnatural, You not your child well loving *Pericles* iv 3 36

Unnaturally. My son, Whom I unnaturally shall disinherit *3 Hen. VI.* i 1 193

Unnaturalness. Of unnaturalness between the child and the parent *Lear* i 2 157

Unnecessarily. Lords that can prate As amply and unnecessarily *Tempest* ii 1 264

Unnecessary. Who in unnecessary action swarm About our squares of battle *Hen. V.* iv 2 27

Thou whoreson zed! thou unnecessary letter! *Lear* ii 2 69

I confess that I am old; Age is unnecessary ii 4 157

Unneighbourly. Might combine The blood of malice in a vein of league, And not to spend it so unneighbourly! *K. John* v 2 39

Unnerved. Strikes wide; But with the whiff and wind of his fell sword The unnerved father falls *Hamlet* ii 2 496

Unnoble. I have offended reputation, A most unnoble swerving *A. and C.* iii 11 50

Unnoted. They may jest Till their own scorn return to them unnoted *All's Well* i 2 34

With such sober and unnoted passion He did behave his anger *T. of A.* iii 5 21

Unnumbered. The skies are painted with unnumber'd sparks *J. Cæsar* iii 1 63

The murmuring surge, That on the unnumber'd idle pebbles chafes *Lear* iv 6 21

Unowed. The unowed interest of proud-swelling state *K. John* iv 3 147

Unpack my heart with words, And fall a-cursing, like a very drab *Hamlet* ii 2 614

Unpaid. Yet there remains unpaid A hundred thousand *L. L. Lost* ii 1 134

That duty leave unpaid to you, Which daily she was bound to proffer *Cymbeline* iii 5 48

Unpaid-for. Prouder than rustling in unpaid-for silk iii 3 24

Wilt thou undo the worth thou art unpaid for, By tasting of our wrath? v 5 307

Unparagoned. Either your unparagoned mistress is dead, or she's outprized by a trifle i 4 87

But kiss; one kiss! Rubies unparagon'd, How dearly they do't. ii 2 17

Unparalleled. If, one by one, you wedded all the world, Or from the all that are took something good, To make a perfect woman, she you kill'd Would be unparallel'd *W. Tale* v 1 16

Whence men have read His fame unparallel'd *Coriolanus* v 2 16

Now boast thee, death, in thy possession lies A lass unparallel'd *Ant. and Cleo.* v 2 319

Unpardonable. O, 'tis a fault too too unpardonable! *3 Hen. VI.* i 4 106

Unpartial. In the unpartial judging of this business *Hen. VIII.* ii 2 107

Unpathed. To unpath'd waters, undream'd shores *W. Tale* iv 4 578

Unpaved. Which horse-hairs and calves'-guts, nor the voice of unpaved eunuch to boot, can never amend *Cymbeline* ii 3 34

Unpay. Pay her the debt you owe her, and unpay the villany you have done her *2 Hen. IV.* ii 1 130

Unpeaceable. Away, unpeaceable dog, or I'll spurn thee hence! *T. of A.* i 1 280

Unpeg the basket on the house's top, Let the birds fly *Hamlet* iii 4 193

Unpeople. This ungenitured agent will unpeople the province with continency *Meas. for Meas.* iii 2 184

First shall war unpeople this my realm *3 Hen. VI.* i 1 126

He shall have every day a several greeting, Or I'll unpeople Egypt *Ant. and Cleo.* i 5 78

Which, if he take, shall quite unpeople her Of liegers for her sweet *Cymb.* i 5 79

Unpeopled. To let you enter his unpeopled house *L. L. Lost* ii 1 88

Why should this a desert be? For it is unpeopled? No *As Y. Like It* iii 2 134

Unfurnish'd walls, Unpeopled offices, untrodden stones. *Richard II.* i 2 69

Unperfectness. One unperfectness shows me another *Othello* ii 3 298

Unpicked. Now comes in the sweetest morsel of the night, and we must hence and leave it unpicked *2 Hen. IV.* ii 4 397

Unpin. Even his stubbornness, his checks, his frowns,—Prithee, unpin me,—have grace and favour in them *Othello* iv 3 21

Shall I go fetch your night-gown?—No, unpin me here iv 3 34

Unpinked. And Gabriel's pumps were all unpink'd i' the heel *T. of Shrew* iv 1 136

Unpitied. And your deliverance with an unpitied whipping *M. for M.* iv 2 13

Unpitied let me die, And well deserved *All's Well* ii 1 191

But at hand, at hand, Ensues his piteous and unpitied end *Richard III.* iv 4 74

Be deaf to my unpitied folly, And all the gods go with you! *A. and C.* i 3 98

Unpitifully. He beat him most unpitifully, methought *Mer. Wives* iv 2 215

Unplagued. Ladies that have their toes Unplagued with corns will have a bout with you *Rom. and Jul.* i 5 19

Unplausive. 'Tis like he'll question me Why such unplausive eyes are bent on him *Troi. and Cres.* iii 3 43

Unpleasantest. Here are a few of the unpleasant'st words That ever blotted paper! *Mer. of Venice* iii 2 254

Unpleased. Me rather had my heart might feel your love Than my unpleased eye see your courtesy *Richard II.* iii 3 193

Unpleasing. O word of fear, Unpleasing to a married ear! *L. L. Lost* v 2 912

Full of unpleasing blots and sightless stains *K. John* iii 1 45

How dares thy harsh rude tongue sound this unpleasing news? *Rich. II.* iii 4 74

Despiteful tidings! O unpleasing news!—Be of good cheer *Richard III.* iv 1 37

Straining harsh discords and unpleasing sharps *Rom. and Jul.* iii 5 28

Unpolicied. O, couldst thou speak, That I might hear thee call great Cæsar ass Unpolicied! *Ant. and Cleo.* v 2 311

Unpolished, uneducated, unpruned, untrained *L. L. Lost* iv 2 17

You logger-headed and unpolish'd grooms! *T. of Shrew* iv 1 128

'Tis like the commons, rude unpolish'd hinds *2 Hen. VI.* iii 2 271

Unpolluted. From her fair and unpolluted flesh May violets spring! *Ham.* v 1 262

Unpossessed. Is the king dead? the empire unpossess'd? *Richard III.* iv 4 471

Unpossessing. He replied, 'Thou unpossessing bastard!' *Lear* ii 1 69

Unpossible. For us to levy power Proportionable to the enemy Is all unpossible *Richard II.* ii 2 126

Unpractised. An unlesson'd girl, unschool'd, unpractised *Mer. of Venice* iii 2 161

And skilless as unpractised infancy *Troi and Cres.* i 1 12

Unpregnant. Makes me unpregnant And dull to all proceedings *M. for M.* iv 4 23

Peak, Like John-a-dreams, unpregnant of my cause, And can say nothing *Hamlet* ii 2 595

Unpremeditated. Ask me what question thou canst possible, And I will answer unpremeditated *1 Hen. VI.* i 2 88

Unprepared. A creature unprepared, unmeet for death *Meas. for Meas.* iv 3 71

Go we . . . To this unlook'd for, unprepared pomp *K. John* ii 1 560

'Tis a vile thing to die, my gracious lord, When men are unprepared *Richard III.* iii 2 65

Being unprepared, Our will became the servant to defect *Macbeth* ii 1 17

I would not kill thy unprepared spirit; No; heaven forfend! *Othello* v 2 31

Unpressed. Have I my pillow left unpress'd in Rome? *Ant. and Cleo.* iii 13 106

Unprevailing. We pray you, throw to earth This unprevailing woe *Ham.* i 2 107

Unprevented. A pack of sorrows which would press you down, Being unprevented *T. G. of Ver* iii 1 21

Unprizable. A bawbling vessel was he captain of, For shallow draught and bulk unprizable *T. Night* v 1 58

Your ring may be stolen too: so your brace of unprizable estimations *Cymbeline* i 4 99

Unprized. Not all the dukes of waterish Burgundy Can buy this unprized precious maid of me *Lear* i 1 262

Unprofitable. Your suit's unprofitable; stand up, I say *Meas. for Meas.* v 1 460

Come, come, no more of this unprofitable chat *1 Hen IV.* iii 1 63

And with her, to dowry, Some petty and unprofitable dukedoms *Hen. V.* iii Prol. 31

How weary, stale, flat, and unprofitable, Seem to me all the uses of this world! Fie on't! ah fie! *Hamlet* i 2 133

How your favour's changed With this unprofitable woe! *Pericles* iv 1 26

Unprofited. Be clamorous and leap all civil bounds Rather than make unprofited return *T. Night* i 4 22

Unproper. There's millions now alive That nightly lie in those unproper beds Which they dare swear peculiar *Othello* iv 1 69

Unproperly Show duty, as mistaken all this while Between the child and parent *Coriolanus* v 3 54

Unproportioned. Give thy thoughts no tongue, Nor any unproportion'd thought his act *Hamlet* i 3 60

Unprovide. I'll not expostulate with her, lest her body and beauty unprovide my mind again *Othello* iv 1 218

Unprovided. First were we sad, fearing you would not come; Now sadder, that you come so unprovided *T. of Shrew* iii 2 101

I am heinously unprovided *1 Hen. IV.* iii 3 213

If they die unprovided, no more is the king guilty of their damnation than he was before guilty of those impieties for the which they are now visited *Hen. V.* iv 1 183

It is his policy To haste thus fast, to find us unprovided *3 Hen. VI.* v 4 63

Where is your boar-spear, man? Fear you the boar, and go so unprovided? *Richard III.* iii 2 75

With his prepared sword, he charges home My unprovided body *Lear* ii 1 54

Only, my friend, I yet am unprovided Of a pair of bases *Pericles* ii 1 166

Unprovokes. Lechery, sir, it [drink] provokes, and unprovokes; it provokes the desire, but it takes away the performance *Macbeth* ii 3 32

Unpruned, untrained, or rather, unlettered *L. L. Lost* iv 2 18

Her fruit-trees all unpruned, her hedges ruin'd *Richard II.* iii 4 45

Her vine, the merry cheerer of the heart, Unpruned dies *Hen. V.* v 2 42

Unpublished. All blest secrets, All you unpublish'd virtues of the earth, Spring with my tears! *Lear* iv 4 16

Unpurged. To dare the vile contagion of the night And tempt the rheumy and unpurged air To add unto his sickness *J. Cæsar* ii 1 266

Unpurposed. Do it at once; Or thy precedent services are all But accidents unpurposed *Ant. and Cleo.* iv 14 84

Unqualitied. Speak to him: He is unqualitied with very shame *A. and C.* iii 11 44
Unqueened. Although unqueen'd, yet like A queen, and daughter to a king, inter me . . . . *Hen. VIII.* iv 2 171
Unquestionable. An unquestionable spirit, which you have not *As Y. Like It* iii 2 393
Unquestioned. Leaves unquestion'd Matters of needful value *M. for M.* i 1 55
But rest Unquestion'd welcome and undoubted blest . *All's Well* ii 1 211
Unquiet meals make ill digestions . . . . . *Com. of Errors* v 1 74
Never shall you lie by Portia's side With an unquiet soul *Mer. of Venice* iii 2 308
'Tis well you offer it behind her back; The wish would make else an unquiet house . . . . iv 1 294
Thank the unquiet time for your quiet o'er-posting that action 2 *Hen. IV.* i 2 170
The scambling and unquiet time Did push it out of farther question *Hen. V.* i 1 4
Unquiet wrangling days, How many of you have mine eyes beheld! *Richard III.* ii 4 55
I wonder he is so fond To trust the mockery of unquiet slumbers . iii 2 27
Thunder above and deeps below Make such unquiet . *Pericles* ii Gower 31
Unquietly. One minded like the weather, most unquietly . . *Lear* iii 1 2
Unquietness. A fool that betroths himself to unquietness . *Much Ado* i 3 50
He went hence but now, And certainly in strange unquietness *Othello* iii 4 133
Unraised. But pardon, gentles all, The flat unraised spirits . *Hen. V.* Prol. 9
Unraked. Where fires thou find'st unraked and hearths unswept *M. Wives* v 5 48
Unread. The wise and fool, the artist and unread, The hard and soft, seem all affined and kin . . . . . . *Troi. and Cres.* i 3 24
Unready. What, all unready so?—Unready! ay, and glad we 'scaped so well . . . . 1 *Hen. VI.* ii 1 39
Unreal. With what's unreal thou coactive art . . . . *W. Tale* i 2 141
Hence, horrible shadow! Unreal mockery, hence! . . *Macbeth* iii 4 107
Unreasonable. 'Tis unreasonable! Will you take up your wife's clothes? *Mer. Wives* iv 2 147
What man is there so much unreasonable? . . . *Mer. of Venice* v 1 203
Unreasonable creatures feed their young . . . . . 3 *Hen. VI.* ii 2 26
Thy wild acts denote The unreasonable fury of a beast . *Rom. and Jul.* iii 3 111
Unreasonably. Fie, you confine yourself most unreasonably . *Coriolanus* i 3 84
Unreclaimed. A savageness in unreclaimed blood . . . *Hamlet* ii 1 34
Unreconciled. If you bethink yourself of any crime Unreconciled as yet to heaven . . . . *Othello* v 2 27
Unreconciliable. That our stars, Unreconciliable, should divide Our equalness to this . . . . *Ant. and Cleo.* v 1 47
Unrecounted. And may be left To some ears unrecounted *Hen. VIII.* iii 2 48
Unrecuring. Seeking to hide herself, as doth the deer That hath received some unrecuring wound . . . . . . *T. Andron.* iii 1 90
Unregarded. And unregarded age in corners thrown . *As Y. Like It* ii 3 42
Unregistered. Besides what hotter hours, Unregister'd in vulgar fame, you have Luxuriously pick'd out . . . . *Ant. and Cleo.* iii 13 119
Unrelenting. Will nothing turn your unrelenting hearts? . 1 *Hen. VI.* v 4 59
Slaughter'd by the ireful arm Of unrelenting Clifford . 3 *Hen. VI.* ii 1 58
But be your heart to them As unrelenting flint to drops of rain *T. An.* ii 3 141
Unremoveable. How unremoveable and fix'd he is In his own course *Lear* ii 4 94
Unremoveably. His discontents are unremoveably Coupled to nature.—Our hope in him is dead . . . . . . *T. of Athens* v 1 227
Unreprievable. A fiend confined to tyrannize On unreprievable condemned blood . . . . *K. John* v 7 48
Unresolved. Unarm'd, and unresolved to beat them back *Richard III.* iv 4 436
Unrespective. I will converse with iron-witted fools And unrespective boys . . . . iv 2 29
The remainder viands We do not throw in unrespective sieve *Tr. and Cr.* ii 2 71
Unrest. Thy sun sets weeping in the lowly west, Witnessing storms to come, woe, and unrest . . . . *Richard II.* ii 4 22
Rest thy unrest on England's lawful earth! . . . *Richard III.* iv 4 29
You sleeping safe, they bring to you unrest . . . . v 3 320
And so repose, sweet gold, for their unrest . . *T. Andron.* ii 3 8
But let her rest in her unrest awhile . . . . . iv 2 31
The sport is at the best.—Ay, so I fear; the more is my unrest *R. and J.* i 5 122
Unrestored. Then does he say, he lent me Some shipping unrestored: lastly, he frets . . . . *Ant. and Cleo.* iii 6 27
Unrestrained. With unrestrained loose companions . *Richard II.* v 3 7
Unrevenged. Whose deaths are yet unrevenged . . 1 *Hen. IV.* v 3 44
She shall not strike Dame Eleanor unrevenged . . 2 *Hen. VI.* i 3 150
Unreverend. Fie, fie, unreverend tongue! to call her bad *T. G. of Ver.* ii 6 14
Thou unreverend and unhallow'd friar . . . *Meas. for Meas.* v 1 307
Ay, thou unreverend boy, Sir Robert's son . . . *K. John* i 1 227
Unreverent. See not your bride in these unreverent robes *T. of Shrew* iii 2 114
This tongue that runs so roundly in thy head Should run thy head from thy unreverent shoulders . . . . . . *Richard II.* ii 1 123
Unreverent Gloster!—Thou art reverent Touching thy spiritual function, not thy life . . . . 1 *Hen. VI.* iii 1 49
Unreversed. The doom—Which, unreversed, stands in effectual force *T. G. of Ver.* iii 1 223
Unrewarded. Wit shall not go unrewarded while I am king . *Tempest* iv 1 242
Unrighteous. Ere yet the salt of most unrighteous tears Had left the flushing in her galled eyes . . . . *Hamlet* i 2 154
Unrightful. Thou, which know'st the way To plant unrightful kings *Richard II.* v 1 63
Unripe. Like fruit unripe, sticks on the tree . . . . *Hamlet* iii 2 200
Unrip'dst the bowels of thy sovereign's son . . *Richard III.* i 4 212
Unrivalled. Plead a new state in thy unrival'd merit . *T. G. of Ver.* v 4 144
Unroll. That now uncurls Even as an adder when she doth unroll *T. An.* ii 3 35
Unrolled. Let me be unrolled and my name put in the book of virtue! *W. Tale* iv 3 130
Unroofed. The rabble should have first unroof'd the city, Ere so prevail'd with me . . . . *Coriolanus* i 1 222
Unroosted. Thou art woman-tired, unroosted By thy dame Partlet *W. Tale* ii 3 74
Unroot. You do so grow in my requital As nothing can unroot you *All's Well* v 1 6
Unrough youths that even now Protest their first of manhood . *Macbeth* v 2 10
Unruly. The mean is drown'd with your unruly bass . *T. G. of Ver.* i 2 96
Like an impediment in the current, made it more violent and unruly *Meas. for Meas.* iii 1 252
But, too unruly deer, he breaks the pale And feeds from home *Com. of Er.* ii 1 100
Your town is troubled with unruly boys . . . . . . iii 1 62
A sceptre snatch'd with an unruly hand Must be as boisterously maintain'd as gain'd . . . . *K. John* iii 4 135
Like glistering Phaëthon, Wanting the manage of unruly jades *Rich. II.* iii 3 179
Like unruly children, make their sire Stoop with oppression . . . iii 4 30
And yet I love him.—Make way, unruly woman! . . . . v 2 110
Pinch'd and vex'd By the imprisoning of unruly wind . 1 *Hen. IV.* iii 1 30
Could not take truce with the unruly spleen Of Tybalt deaf to peace *Rom. and Jul.* iii 1 162
There's not a whittle in the unruly camp But I do prize it *T. of Athens* v 1 183
Unruly. The night has been unruly . . . . . . *Macbeth* ii 3 59
The unruly waywardness that infirm and choleric years bring with them . . . . *Lear* i 1 301
Unsafe. No obstacle, no incredulous or unsafe circumstance . *T. Night* iii 4 88
These dangerous unsafe lunes i' the king, beshrew them! . *W. Tale* ii 2 30
Unsafe the while, that we Must lave our honours in these flattering streams . . . . *Macbeth* iii 2 32
Let's think 't unsafe To come in to the cry without more help *Othello* v 1 43
Unsaluted. I prate, And the most noble mother of the world Leave unsaluted: sink, my knee, i' the earth . . . . *Coriolanus* v 3 50
Unsanctified. Where is your husband?—I hope, in no place so unsanctified Where such as thou mayst find him . . . . *Macbeth* iv 2 81
She should in ground unsanctified have lodged Till the last trumpet *Ham.* v 1 252
The post unsanctified Of murderous lechers . . . . *Lear* iv 6 281
Unsatiate. When that my mother went with child Of that unsatiate Edward . . . . *Richard III.* iii 5 87
Unsatisfied. Restore But that one half which is unsatisfied . *L. L. Lost* ii 1 139
The king will always . . . think we think ourselves unsatisfied 1 *Hen. IV.* i 3 287
Though he were unsatisfied in getting, Which was a sin . *Hen. VIII.* iv 2 55
O, wilt thou leave me so unsatisfied?—What satisfaction canst thou have to-night? . . . . *Rom. and Jul.* ii 2 125
Report me and my cause aright To the unsatisfied . . . *Hamlet* v 2 351
The cloyed will, That satiate yet unsatisfied desire . . . *Cymbeline* i 6 48
Unsavoury. Thou hast the most unsavoury similes . . . 1 *Hen. IV.* i 2 89
Unsavoury news! but how made he escape? . . . 3 *Hen. VI.* iv 6 80
Come, bitter conduct, come, unsavoury guide! . . *Rom. and Jul.* v 3 116
All viands that I eat do seem unsavoury, Wishing him my meat *Pericles* ii 3 31
Unsay. Call you me fair? that fair again unsay . . *M. N. Dream* i 1 181
Your daring tongue Scorns to unsay what once it hath deliver'd *Rich. II.* iv 1 9
Never rise To do him wrong or any way impeach What then he said, so he unsay it now . . . . 1 *Hen. IV.* i 3 76
Said I for this, the girl was like to him? I will have more, or else unsay't; and now, While it is hot . . . . *Hen. VIII.* v 1 175
Unscaleable. Paled in With rocks unscaleable and roaring waters *Cymb.* iii 1 20
Unscanned. This tiger-footed rage, when it shall find The harm of unscann'd swiftness, will too late Tie leaden pounds to's heels *Coriol.* iii 1 313
Unscarred. So she may live unscarr'd of bleeding slaughter *Richard III.* iv 4 209
Let the unscarr'd braggarts of the war Derive some pain from you *T. of Athens* iv 3 161
Unschooled. An unlesson'd girl, unschool'd, unpractised *Mer. of Venice* iii 2 161
An understanding simple and unschool'd . . . . . *Hamlet* i 2 97
Unscissar'd shall this hair of mine remain, Though I show ill in't *Pericles* iii 3 29
Unscorched. Yet his hand, Not sensible of fire, remain'd unscorch'd *J. C.* i 3 18
Unscoured. Like unscour'd armour, hung by the wall . *Meas. for Meas.* i 2 171
Unscratched. To save unscratch'd your city's threatened cheeks *K. John* ii 1 225
Unseal. I have better news in store for you Than you expect: unseal this letter soon . . . . *Mer. of Venice* v 1 275
Look'd he o' the inside of the paper?—Presently He did unseal them *Hen. VIII.* iii 2 79
Making so bold, My fears forgetting manners, to unseal Their grand commission . . . . *Hamlet* v 2 17
I know not what: I'll love thee much, Let me unseal the letter . *Lear* iv 5 22
Unsealed. Your oaths Are words and poor conditions, but unseal'd *All's Well* iv 2 30
Unseamed. He unseam'd him from the nave to the chaps . *Macbeth* i 2 22
Unsearched. And leave you not a man-of-war unsearch'd *T. Andron.* iv 3 22
Unseasonable. At any unseasonable instant of the night . *Much Ado* ii 2 16
Troublesome, Being urged at a time unseasonable . . *K. John* iv 2 20
Like an unseasonable stormy day . . . . . *Richard II.* iii 2 106
Unseasonably. Cry 'holla' to thy tongue, I prithee; it curvets unseasonably . . . . *As Y. Like It* iii 2 258
Unseasoned. Emboldened me to this unseasoned intrusion *Mer. Wives* ii 2 174
'Tis an unseason'd courtier; good my lord, Advise him . *All's Well* i 1 80
These unseason'd hours perforce must add Unto your sickness 2 *Hen. IV.* iii 1 105
Unseconded. Him did you leave, Second to none, unseconded by you ii 3 34
Unsecret. Why have I blabb'd? who shall be true to us, When we are so unsecret to ourselves? . . . . *Troi. and Cres.* iii 2 133
Unseduced. If she remain unseduced, . . . you shall answer me . *Cymb.* i 4 173
Unseeing. I should have scratch'd out your unseeing eyes *T. G. of Ver.* iv 4 209
Unseeming. And wrong the reputation of your name, In so unseeming to confess receipt . . . . *L. L. Lost* ii 1 156
Unseemly woman in a seeming man! . . . . . *Rom. and Jul.* iii 3 112
Unseen, inscrutable, invisible, As a nose on a man's face! . *T. G. Ver.* ii 1 141
Here can I sit alone, unseen of any . . . . v 4 4
Who, falling there to find his fellow forth, Unseen, inquisitive, confounds himself . . . . *Com. of Errors* i 2 38
Through the velvet leaves the wind, All unseen, can passage find *L. L. L.* iv 3 106
O, you have lived in desolation here, Unseen, unvisited . . . v 2 358
He wears his honour in a box unseen . . . . . *All's Well* ii 3 296
And all eyes Blind with the pin and web but theirs, theirs only, That would unseen be wicked? . . . . *W. Tale* i 2 292
Then thieves and robbers range abroad unseen . . *Richard II.* iii 2 39
The emptier ever dancing in the air, The other down, unseen, and full of water . . . . iv 1 187
These external manners of laments Are merely shadows to the unseen grief . . . . iv 1 297
Grew like the summer grass, fastest by night, Unseen, yet crescive *Hen. V.* i 1 66
And Romeo Leap to these arms, untalk'd of and unseen *Rom. and Jul.* iii 2 7
Seeing, unseen, We may of their encounter frankly judge *Hamlet* iii 1 33
Whiles rank corruption, mining all within, Infects unseen . . . iii 4 149
In this brainish apprehension, kills The unseen good old man . . iv 1 12
O, sir, you had then left unseen a wonderful piece of work *Ant. and Cleo.* i 2 159
Unseminared. 'Tis well for thee, That, being unseminar'd, thy freer thoughts May not fly forth of Egypt . . . . i 5 11
Unseparable. Who twin, as 'twere, in love Unseparable . *Coriolanus* iv 4 16
Unserviceable. Very weak and unserviceable . . . *All's Well* iv 3 152
Unsettle. His wits begin to unsettle.—Canst thou blame him? . *Lear* iii 4 167
Unsettled. The best comforter To an unsettled fancy . . *Tempest* v 1 59
Prepared I was not For such a business; therefore am I found So much unsettled . . . . *All's Well* ii 5 68
He something seems unsettled.—How, my lord! . . . *W. Tale* i 2 147
Dost think I am so muddy, so unsettled, To appoint myself in this vexation? . . . . i 2 325
All the unsettled humours of the land . . . . . *K. John* ii 1 66
As well For your own quiet, as to rectify What is unsettled in the king *Hen. VIII.* ii 4 64
Unsevered. I have heard you say, Honour and policy, like unsever'd friends, I' the war do grow together . . . . *Coriolanus* iii 2 42
Unsex. You spirits That tend on mortal thoughts, unsex me here! *Macb.* i 5 42

Unshaked. I do know but one That unassailable holds on his rank, Unshaked of motion . . . . J. Cæsar iii 1 70
The heavens hold firm The walls of thy dear honour, keep unshaked That temple, thy fair mind! . . . . Cymbeline ii 1 68
Unshaken. And stand unshaken yours.—'Tis nobly spoken Hen. VIII. iii 2 199
Which now, like fruit unripe, sticks on the tree; But fall, unshaken, when they mellow be . . . . Hamlet iii 2 201
Unshaped. Her speech is nothing, Yet the unshaped use of it doth move The hearers to collection . . . . Hamlet iv 5 8
Unshapen. On me, that halt and am unshapen thus? . Richard III. i 2 251
Unshapes. Good night. This deed unshapes me quite . Meas. for Meas. iv 4 23
Unsheathe your sword, and dub him presently . . . . 3 Hen. VI. ii 2 59
Unsheathe your sword, good father; cry 'Saint George!' . . ii 2 80
Therefore be still.—Then, executioner, unsheathe thy sword . . . ii 2 123
Unsheathed. There is not now a rebel's sword unsheathed 2 Hen. IV. iv 4 86
Unshout the noise that banish'd Marcius, Repeal him . Coriolanus v 5 4
Unshown. Prevented The ostentation of our love, which, left unshown, Is often left unloved . . . . Ant. and Cleo. iii 6 52
Unshrinking. In the unshrinking station where he fought Macbeth v 8 42
Unshrubbed. My bosky acres and my unshrubb'd down . . Tempest iv 1 81
Unshunnable. 'Tis destiny unshunnable, like death . . Othello iii 3 275
Unshunned. An unshunned consequence; it must be so Meas. for Meas. iii 2 62
Unsifted. Affection! pooh! you speak like a green girl, Unsifted in such perilous circumstance . . . . Hamlet i 3 102
Unsightly. Good sir, no more; these are unsightly tricks . Lear ii 4 159
Unsinewed. For two special reasons; Which may to you, perhaps, seem much unsinew'd, But yet to me they are strong . . . Hamlet iv 7 10
Unsisting. That spirit's possess'd with haste That wounds the unsisting postern with these strokes . . . . Meas. for Meas. iv 2 92
Unskilful. His filching was like an unskilful singer . . . Mer. Wives i 3 29
And, though unskilful, why not Ned and I For once allow'd the skilful pilot's charge? We will not from the helm . . . 3 Hen. VI. v 4 19
Though it make the unskilful laugh, cannot but make the judicious grieve . . . . Hamlet iii 2 29
We must not think the Turk is so unskilful To leave that latest which concerns him first . . . . Othello i 3 27
Unskilfully. You speak unskilfully; or if your knowledge be more it is much darkened in your malice . . . . Meas. for Meas. iii 2 156
Unslipping. To knit your hearts With an unslipping knot Ant. and Cleo. ii 2 129
Unsmirched. The chaste unsmirched brow Of my true mother Hamlet iv 5 119
Unsoiled. My unsoil'd name, the austereness of my life . Meas. for Meas. ii 4 155
Unsolicited I left no reverend person in this court . . Hen. VIII. ii 4 219
There's not a god left unsolicited . . . . . . T. Andron. iv 3 60
Unsorted. The time itself unsorted; and your whole plot too light for the counterpoise of so great an opposition . . . 1 Hen. IV. ii 3 13
Unsought. Hopeless to find, yet loath to leave unsought . Com. of Errors i 1 136
Love sought is good, but given unsought is better . . . T. Night iii 1 168
Answering the letter of the oracle, Unknown to you, unsought Cymbeline v 5 451
Unsound. Do not tempt my misery, Lest that it make me so unsound a man As to upbraid you . . . . T. Night iii 4 384
Unsounded. Huge leviathans Forsake unsounded deeps . T. G. of Ver. iii 2 81
Gloucester is a man Unsounded yet and full of deep deceit 2 Hen. VI. iii 1 57
Unspeak. Even now I put myself to thy direction, and Unspeak mine own detraction . . . . Macbeth iv 3 123
Unspeakable. To speak my griefs unspeakable . . Com. of Errors i 1 33
You have an unspeakable comfort of your young prince . . W. Tale i 1 37
From very nothing . . . is grown into an unspeakable estate . iv 2 46
When I do forget The least of these unspeakable deserts . T. Andron. i 1 256
These wrongs, unspeakable, past patience, Or more than any living man could bear . . . . v 3 126
Unspeaking. His description Proved us unspeaking sots . Cymbeline v 5 178
Unsphere. Though you would seek to unsphere the stars with oaths W. T. i 2 48
Unspoke. A tardiness in nature Which often leaves the history unspoke That it intends to do . . . . Lear i 1 239
Unspoken. Thou'lt torture me to leave unspoken that Which, to be spoke, would torture thee . . . . Cymbeline v 5 139
Unspotted. No king . . . can try it out with all unspotted soldiers Hen. V. iv 1 169
A pure unspotted heart, Never yet taint with love . . . 1 Hen. VI. v 3 182
A heart unspotted is not easily daunted . . . . 2 Hen. VI. iii 1 100
A most unspotted lily shall she pass To the ground . . Hen. VIII. v 5 62
My riches to the earth from whence they came; But my unspotted fire of love to you . . . . Pericles i 1 53
Unsquared. And when he speaks, 'Tis like a chime a-mending; with terms unsquared . . . . Troi. and Cres. i 3 159
Unstable. And give way the while To unstable slightness Coriolanus iii 1 148
Unstaid. How will the world repute me For undertaking so unstaid a journey? . . . . T. G. of Ver. ii 7 60
For such as I am all true lovers are, Unstaid and skittish . T. Night ii 4 18
Will the king come, that I may breathe my last In wholesome counsel to his unstaid youth? . . . . Richard II. ii 1 2
Unstained. Do plainly give you out an unstain'd shepherd . W. Tale iv 4 149
With a heart full of unstained love . . . . . . K. John ii 1 16
The unstain'd sword that you have used to bear . . 2 Hen. IV. v 2 114
I will do it without fear or doubt, To live an unstain'd wife Rom. and Jul. iv 1 88
Unstanched. As leaky as an unstanched wench . . . Tempest i 1 51
Whose unstanched thirst York and young Rutland could not satisfy 3 Hen. VI. ii 6 83
Unstate. I would unstate myself, to be in a due resolution . . Lear i 2 108
Like enough, high-battled Cæsar will Unstate his happiness! Ant. and Cleo. iii 13 30
Unsteadfast. To o'er-walk a current roaring loud On the unsteadfast footing of a spear . . . . 1 Hen. IV. i 3 193
Unstooping. The unstooping firmness of my upright soul . Richard II. i 1 121
Unstringed. Now my tongue's use is to me no more Than an unstringed viol or a harp . . . . i 3 162
Unstuffed. Where unbruised youth with unstuff'd brain Doth couch his limbs, there golden sleep doth reign . . . . Rom. and Jul. ii 3 37
Unsubstantial. Shall I believe That unsubstantial death is amorous? . v 3 103
Welcome, then, Thou unsubstantial air that I embrace! . . . Lear iv 1 7
Unsuitable. Out of fashion: richly suited, but unsuitable . All's Well i 1 170
So unsuitable to her disposition, being addicted to a melancholy T. N. ii 5 222
Unsuiting. A passion most unsuiting such a man . . . Othello iv 1 78
Unsullied. As pure As the unsullied lily . . . . . L. L. Lost v 2 352
Unsunned. I thought her As chaste as unsunn'd snow . . Cymbeline ii 5 13
Unsure. What's to come is still unsure . . . . . T. Night ii 3 50
The truth thou art unsure To swear, swears only not to be forsworn K. John iii 1 283
An habitation giddy and unsure Hath he that buildeth on the vulgar heart. O thou fond many! . . . . 2 Hen. IV. i 3 89
Thoughts speculative their unsure hopes relate . . . Macbeth v 4 19

Unsure. Exposing what is mortal and unsure To all that fortune, death, and danger dare, Even for an egg-shell . . . . . Hamlet iv 4 51
Take no notice, nor build yourself a trouble Out of his scattering and unsure observance . . . . Othello iii 3 151
Unsured. By this knot thou shalt so surely tie Thy now unsured assurance to the crown . . . . K. John ii 1 471
Unsuspected. That so I may, by this device, at least Have leave and leisure to make love to her And unsuspected court her T. of Shrew i 2 137
That ignoble traitor, The dangerous and unsuspected Hastings Rich. III. iii 5 23
Unswayable. To this end, He bow'd his nature, never known before But to be rough, unswayable, and free . . . . Coriolanus v 6 26
Unswayed. Is the chair empty? is the sword unsway'd? Richard III. iv 4 470
Unswear. To snatch our palm from palm, Unswear faith sworn K. John iii 1 245
Hath he said any thing?—He hath, my lord; but be you well assured, No more than he'll unswear . . . . Othello iv 1 31
Unswept. Where fires thou find'st unraked and hearths unswept Mer. W. v 5 48
What custom wills, in all things should we do't, The dust on antique time would lie unswept . . . . Coriolanus ii 3 126
Unsworn. You are yet unsworn. When you have vow'd, you must not speak with men . . . . Meas. for Meas. i 4 9
Untainted. Your brother saved, your honour untainted . . . . iii 1 264
What stronger breastplate than a heart untainted! . . 2 Hen. VI. iii 2 232
Sweet prince, the untainted virtue of your years Hath not yet dived into the world's deceit . . . . Richard III. iii 1 7
Untainted, unexamined, free, at liberty . . . . iii 6 9
Untalked of. Leap to these arms, untalk'd of and unseen Rom. and Jul. iii 2 7
Untangle. O time! thou must entangle this, not I . . . T. Night ii 2 41
Untangled. And bakes the elf-locks in foul sluttish hairs, Which once untangled much misfortune bodes . . . . Rom. and Jul. i 4 91
Untasted. Like fair fruit in an unwholesome dish, Are like to rot untasted . . . . Troi. and Cres. ii 3 130
Untaught. Their untaught love Must needs appear offence Meas. for Meas. ii 4 29
As the soldiers bore dead bodies by, He call'd them untaught knaves 1 Hen. IV. i 3 43
Stern and rough, Used to command, untaught to plead for favour 2 Hen. VI. iv 1 122
O thou untaught! what manners is in this? . . . . Rom. and Jul. v 3 214
To royalty unlearn'd, honour untaught . . . . . Cymbeline iv 2 178
Untempering. Notwithstanding the poor and untempering effect of my visage . . . . Hen. V. v 2 241
Untender. So young, and so untender?—So young, my lord, and true Lear i 1 108
Why tender'st thou that paper to me, with A look untender? Cymbel. iii 4 12
Untendered. Which by thee lately Is left untender'd.—And, to kill the marvel, Shall be so ever . . . . iii 1 10
Untent. Why will he not upon our fair request Untent his person and share the air with us? . . . . Troi. and Cres. ii 3 178
Untented. The untented woundings of a father's curse Pierce every sense about thee! . . . . Lear i 4 322
Unthankful. I will lift the down-trod Mortimer As high in the air as this unthankful king . . . . 1 Hen. IV. i 3 136
Unthankfulness. Else thou diest in thine unthankfulness All's Well i 1 226
God is much displeased That you take with unthankfulness his doing Richard III. ii 2 90
O deadly sin! O rude unthankfulness! . . . . . Rom. and Jul. iii 3 24
When any shall not gratify, Or pay you with unthankfulness in thought Pericles i 4 102
Unthink. To unthink your speaking And to say so no more Hen. VIII. ii 4 104
Unthought of. I leave my duty a little unthought of and speak out of my injury . . . . T. Night v 1 318
This all-praised knight, And your unthought-of Harry . 1 Hen. IV. iii 2 141
Unthought-on. As the unthought-on accident is guilty To what we wildly do . . . . W. Tale iv 4 549
Unthread the rude eye of rebellion . . . . . . K. John v 4 11
Unthrift. With an unthrift love did run from Venice Mer. of Venice v 1 16
And given away To upstart unthrifts . . . . . . Richard II. ii 3 122
What man didst thou ever know unthrift that was beloved after his means? . . . . T. of Athens iv 3 311
Unthrifty. Left in the fearful guard Of an unthrifty knave Mer. of Venice i 3 177
Our absence makes us unthrifty to our knowledge . . . W. Tale v 2 121
Can no man tell me of my unthrifty son? . . . . Richard II. v 3 1
Untie. Set Caliban and his companions free; Untie the spell . Tempest v 1 253
I prithee, sister Kate, untie my hands . . . . . T. of Shrew ii 1 21
It is too hard a knot for me to untie! . . . . . . T. Night ii 2 42
The amity that wisdom knits not, folly may easily untie Troi. and Cres. ii 3 111
Though you untie the winds and let them fight Against the churches Macbeth iv 1 52
With thy sharp teeth this knot intrinsicate Of life at once untie Ant. and Cleo. v 2 308
Or senseless speaking or a speaking such As sense cannot untie Cymb. v 4 149
Untied.—Your sleeve unbuttoned, your shoe untied . As Y. Like It iii 2 399
If fires be hot, knives sharp, or waters deep, Untied I still my virgin knot will keep . . . . Pericles iv 2 160
Until. I will not show my face Until my husband bid me Meas. for Meas. v 1 170
Until I know this sure uncertainty, I'll entertain the offer'd fallacy Com. of Errors ii 2 187
At home; Where would you had remain'd until this time! . . . iv 4 69
Until last night, I have this twelvemonth been her bedfellow Much Ado iv 1 150
Things growing are not ripe until their season . . . M. N. Dream ii 2 117
Now, until the break of day, Through this house each fairy stray . v 1 408
As doubtful whether what I see be true, Until confirm'd Mer. of Venice iii 2 149
I will ne'er come in your bed Until I see the ring . . . . . v 1 191
Let him be Until a time may serve . . . . W. Tale ii 3 22
I was not angry since I came to France Until this instant . Hen. V. iv 7 59
England ne'er had a king until his time . . . . . 1 Hen. VI. i 1 8
Had slipp'd our claim until another age . . . . 3 Hen. VI. ii 2 162
I am hush'd until our city be afire, And then I'll speak . Coriolanus v 3 181
Stir not until the signal . . . . J. Cæsar v 1 26
Untimbered. Where's then the saucy boat Whose weak untimber'd sides but even now Co-rivall'd greatness? . . . . . Troi. and Cres. i 3 43
Untimely. Weeping after this untimely bier . . . . Richard II. v 6 52
By the house of York My father came untimely to his death 3 Hen. VI. iii 3 187
How sweet a plant have you untimely cropp'd! You have no children, butchers! . . . . v 5 62
Whilst I . . . lament The untimely fall of virtuous Lancaster Rich. III. i 2 4
Abortive be it, Prodigious, and untimely brought to light! . . . i 2 22
Die in his youth by like untimely violence! . . . . i 3 201
Untimely storms make men expect a dearth . . . . . . ii 3 35
Untimely smother'd in their dusky graves . . . . . . iv 4 70
An untimely ague Stay'd me a prisoner in my chamber . . Hen. VIII. i 1 4
By some vile forfeit of untimely death . . . . . Rom. and Jul. i 4 111

Untimely. That gallant spirit hath aspired the clouds, Which too untimely here did scorn the earth *Rom. and Jul.* iii 1 123
Death lies on her like an untimely frost Upon the sweetest flower iv 5 28
Tybalt's dooms-day, whose untimely death Banish'd the new-made bridegroom v 3 234
Here untimely lay The noble Paris and true Romeo dead v 3 258
It hath been The untimely emptying of the happy throne *Macbeth* iv 3 68
Macduff was from his mother's womb Untimely ripp'd v 8 16
Let them know, both what we mean to do, And what's untimely done *Hamlet* iv 1 40
I bleed apace: Untimely comes this hurt: give me your arm *Lear* iii 7 98
O, untimely death! iv 6 256
Untirable. To an untirable and continuate goodness *T. of Athens* i 1 11
Untired. Hath he so long held out with me untired, And stops he now for breath? *Richard III.* iv 2 44
Bear it as our Roman actors do, With untired spirits *J. Cæsar* ii 1 227
Untitled. O nation miserable, With an untitled tyrant! *Macbeth* iv 3 104
Unto. Canst thou remember A time before we came unto this cell? *Temp.* i 2 39
Come unto these yellow sands, And then take hands i 2 376
I must unto the road, to disembark Some necessaries *T. G. of Ver.* ii 4 187
As strange unto your town as to your talk *Com. of Errors* ii 2 151
My inwardness and love Is very much unto the prince *Much Ado* iv 1 248
Now, unto thy bones good night! Yearly will I do this rite v 3 22
He hath turn'd a heaven unto a hell! *M. N. Dream* i 1 207
The sun was not so true unto the day As he to me iii 2 50
I am not yet so low But that my nails can reach unto thine eyes iii 2 298
I told him of your stealth unto this wood. He follow'd you iii 2 310
Say to me what I should do That in your knowledge may by me be done, And I am prest unto it *Mer. of Venice* i 1 160
Which humbleness may drive unto a fine iv 1 372
I should have given him tears unto entreaties *As Y. Like It* i 2 250
I will unto Venice, To buy apparel 'gainst the wedding-day *T. of Shrew* ii 1 316
Madam, I'll follow you unto the death *K. John* i 1 154
Like a shifted wind unto a sail, It makes the course of thoughts to fetch about iv 2 23
Unto my mother's prayers I bend my knee *Richard II.* v 3 97
I see our wars Will turn unto a peaceful comic sport *1 Hen. VI.* ii 2 45
Faith, I can tell her age unto an hour.—She's not fourteen *Rom. and Jul.* i 3 11
This slave, Unto his honour, has my lord's meat in him *T. of Athens* iii 1 60
The power of Cæsar, and His power unto Octavia *Ant. and Cleo.* ii 2 146
Unto thy value I will mount myself Upon a courser *Pericles* ii 1 163
Untold. We do our longing stay To hear the rest untold v 3 84
Untouched. Left nothing fitting for the purpose Untouch'd, or slightly handled, in discourse *Richard III.* iii 7 19
He shall be satisfied; and, by my honour, Depart untouch'd *J. Cæsar* iii 1 142
Untoward. If she be froward, Then hast thou taught Hortensio to be untoward *T. of Shrew* iv 5 79
What means this scorn, thou most untoward knave? *K. John* i 1 243
Untowardly. O day untowardly turned! *Much Ado* iii 2 134
Untraded. Mock not, that I affect the untraded oath *Troi. and Cres.* iv 5 178
Untrained. Unpolished, uneducated, unpruned, untrained *L. L. Lost* iv 2 18
A shepherd's daughter, My wit untrain'd in any kind of art *1 Hen. VI.* i 2 73
Untread. Where is the horse that doth untread again His tedious measures with the unbated fire That he did pace them first? *Mer. of Venice* ii 6 10
By the which We will untread the steps of damned flight *K. John* v 4 52
Untreasured. They found the bed untreasured of their mistress *As Y. Like It* ii 2 7
Untried. I slide O'er sixteen years and leave the growth untried *W. Tale* iv 1 6
Untrimmed. The devil tempts thee here In likeness of a new untrimmed bride *K. John* iii 1 209
Untrod. Thorough the hazards of this untrod state *J. Cæsar* iii 1 136
Untrodden. Unpeopled offices, untrodden stones *Richard II.* i 2 69
Untroubled. Quiet untroubled soul, awake, awake! *Richard III.* v 3 149
Untrue. Might not you Forestall our sport, to make us thus untrue? *L. L. Lost* v 2 473
If it appear not plain and prove untrue, Deadly divorce step between me and you! *All's Well* v 3 318
For he that steeps his safety in true blood Shall find but bloody safety and untrue *K. John* iii 4 148
When to my good lord I prove untrue, I'll choke myself *Cymbeline* i 5 86
Untrussing. This Claudio is condemned for untrussing *Meas. for Meas.* iii 2 190
Untruth. Moreover, they have spoken untruths *Much Ado* v 1 220
I would to God, So my untruth had not provoked him to it *Richard II.* ii 2 101
He would say untruths; and be ever double *Hen. VIII.* iv 2 38
False, false, false! Let all untruths stand by thy stained name, And they'll seem glorious *Troi. and Cres.* v 2 179
Untune that string, And, hark, what discord follows! i 3 109
Untuneable. They are harsh, untuneable, and bad *T. G. of Ver.* iii 1 208
No great matter in the ditty, yet the note was very untuneable *As Y. L. It* v 3 37
Untuned. My only son Knows not my feeble key of untuned cares *Com. of Errors* v 1 310
Roused up with boisterous untuned drums *Richard II.* i 3 134
The untuned and jarring senses, O, wind up Of this child-changed father! *Lear* iv 7 16
Untutored. Thy mother took into her blameful bed Some stern untutor'd churl *2 Hen. VI.* iii 2 213
Untutor'd lad, thou art too malapert.—I know my duty *3 Hen. VI.* v 5 32
Thou speak'st like him's untutor'd to repeat *Pericles* i 4 74
Untwine. Let grievous, ghastly, gaping wounds Untwine the Sisters Three! *2 Hen. IV.* ii 4 213
Grow, patience! And let the stinking elder, grief, untwine His perishing root with the increasing vine! *Cymbeline* iv 2 59
Unurged. The time was once when thou unurged wouldst vow *Com. of Errors* ii 2 115
We swear A voluntary zeal and an unurged faith *K. John* v 2 10
Unused. Gave us not That capability and god-like reason To fust in us unused *Hamlet* iv 4 39
Albeit unused to the melting mood, Drop tears *Othello* v 2 349
Unusual. How came it Claudio was beheaded At an unusual hour? *Meas. for Meas.* v 1 463
As if they saw . . . Some comet or unusual prodigy *T. of Shrew* iii 2 98
These your unusual weeds to each part of you Do give a life *W. Tale* iv 4 1
Strange, unusual blood, When man's worst sin is, he does too much good! *T. of Athens* iv 2 38
The king's a-bed: He hath been in unusual pleasure *Macbeth* ii 1 13
No place, That guard, and most unusual vigilance Does not attend my taking *Lear* ii 3 4
Unvalued jewels, All scatter'd in the bottom of the sea *Richard III.* i 4 27
He may not, as unvalued persons do, Carve for himself *Hamlet* i 3 19
Unvanquished. Shall I, for lucre of the rest unvanquish'd, Detract so much? *1 Hen. VI.* v 4 141
Unvarnished. I will a round unvarnish'd tale deliver *Othello* i 3 90
Unveil. Does thoughts unveil in their dumb cradles *Troi. and Cres.* iii 3 200
Unvenerable. For ever Unvenerable be thy hands! *W. Tale* ii 3 77
Unvexed. With a blessed and unvex'd retire *K. John* ii 1 253
Unviolated. The unviolated honour of your wife *Com. of Errors* iii 1 88
Unvirtuous. The poor unvirtuous fat knight *Mer. Wives* iv 2 232
Unvisited. You have lived in desolation here, Unseen, unvisited *L. L. L.* v 2 358
Unvulnerable. That thou mayst prove To shame unvulnerable *Coriolanus* v 3 73
Unwares. O God! it is my father's face, Whom in this conflict I unwares have kill'd *3 Hen. VI.* ii 5 62
Unwarily Devoured by the unexpected flood *K. John* v 7 63
Unwashed. Another lean unwash'd artificer Cuts off his tale iv 2 201
Rob me the exchequer the first thing thou doest, and do it with unwashed hands too *1 Hen. IV.* iii 3 206
When good manners shall lie all in one or two men's hands and they unwashed too, 'tis a foul thing *Rom. and Jul.* i 5 5
Unwatched. Madness in great ones must not unwatch'd go *Hamlet* iii 1 196
Unwearied. The kindest man, The best-condition'd and unwearied spirit In doing courtesies *Mer. of Venice* iii 2 295
Unwed. This servitude makes you to keep unwed *Com. of Errors* ii 1 26
Unwedgeable and gnarled oak *Meas. for Meas.* ii 2 116
Unweeded. 'Tis an unweeded garden, That grows to seed *Hamlet* i 2 135
Unweighed. What an unweighed behaviour hath this Flemish drunkard picked—with the devil's name!—out of my conversation? *Mer. Wives* ii 1 23
Unweighing. A very superficial, ignorant, unweighing fellow *M. for M.* iii 2 147
Unwelcome. I think 'tis no unwelcome news to you *T. G. of Ver.* ii 4 81
More uneven and unwelcome news Came from the north *1 Hen. IV.* i 1 50
The first bringer of unwelcome news Hath but a losing office *2 Hen. IV.* i 1 100
I fear We shall be much unwelcome.—That I assure you *Troi. and Cres.* iv 1 45
Such welcome and unwelcome things at once 'Tis hard to reconcile *Macb.* iv 3 138
Unwept. Our fatherless distress was left unmoan'd; Your widow-dolour likewise be unwept! *Richard III.* ii 2 65
Unwhipped. Undivulged crimes, Unwhipp'd of justice *Lear* iii 2 53
Unwholesome. Wicked dew as e'er my mother brush'd With raven's feather from unwholesome fen Drop on you! *Tempest* i 2 322
We'll use this unwholesome humidity, this gross watery pumpion *M. W.* iii 3 42
The very blood to suck!—And that's but unwholesome food, they say *Hen. V.* ii 3 59
Like fair fruit in an unwholesome dish, Are like to rot untasted *T. and C.* ii 3 129
You are they That made the air unwholesome, when you cast Your stinking greasy caps in hooting at Coriolanus' exile *Coriolanus* iv 6 130
The people muddied, Thick and unwholesome in their thoughts *Hamlet* iv 5 82
Bear some charity to my wit; do not think it so unwholesome *Othello* iv 1 124
They're too unwholesome, o' conscience *Pericles* iv 2 22
Unwieldy. And clap their female joints In stiff unwieldy arms *Rich. II.* iii 2 115
I give this heavy weight from off my head And this unwieldy sceptre from my hand iv 1 205
But old folks, many feign as they were dead; Unwieldy, slow *R. and J.* ii 5 17
Unwilling. Which I was much unwilling to proceed in *T. G. of Ver.* ii 1 112
Unwilling I agreed; alas! too soon We came aboard *Com. of Errors* i 1 61
Patience, I pray you; 'twas a fault unwilling *T. of Shrew* iv 1 159
But you gave leave to my unwilling tongue Against my will to do myself this wrong *Richard II.* i 3 245
I do not care; but rather, because I am unwilling *2 Hen. IV.* iii 2 240
If he be leaden, icy-cold, unwilling, Be thou so too *Richard III.* iii 1 176
One of which fell with him, Unwilling to outlive the good that did it *Hen. VIII.* iv 2 60
Unwillingly. If thou neglect'st or dost unwillingly What I command, I'll rack thee with old cramps *Tempest* i 2 368
Very quaintly writ; But since unwillingly, take them again *T. G. of Ver.* ii 1 129
If you did know . . . how unwillingly I left the ring *Mer. of Venice* v 1 196
Creeping like snail Unwillingly to school *As Y. Like It* ii 7 147
More straining on for plucking back, not following My leash unwillingly *W. Tale* iv 4 477
I have, and most unwillingly, of late Heard many grievous, I do say, my lord, Grievous complaints of you *Hen. VIII.* v 1 97
Unwillingness. Which I with some unwillingness pronounce *Richard II.* i 3 149
'Tis call'd ungrateful, With dull unwillingness to repay a debt *Richard III.* ii 2 92
I in all haste was sent.—And I in all unwillingness will go iv 1 58
Unwind. As you unwind her love from him, Lest it should ravel and be good to none, You must provide to bottom it on me *T. G. of Ver.* iii 2 51
Stand for your own; unwind your bloody flag *Hen. V.* i 2 101
Unwiped. Their daggers, which unwiped we found Upon their pillows *Macbeth* ii 3 108
Unwise. Be not ta'en tardy by unwise delay *Richard III.* iv 1 52
O good but most unwise patricians! *Coriolanus* iii 1 91
Never mind Was to be so unwise, to be so kind *T. of Athens* ii 2 6
Unwisely, not ignobly, have I given ii 2 183
Unwished. Unto his lordship, whose unwished yoke My soul consents not to give sovereignty *M. N. Dream* i 1 81
Now thou hast unwish'd five thousand men *Hen. V.* iv 3 76
Unwitted. As if some planet had unwitted men *Othello* ii 3 182
Unwittingly. If I unwittingly, or in my rage, Have aught committed that is hardly borne *Richard III.* ii 1 56
Wot you what I found There,—on my conscience, put unwittingly? *Hen. VIII.* iii 2 123
Unwonted. This is unwonted Which now came from him *Tempest* i 2 497
Awakens me with this unwonted putting-on *Meas. for Meas.* iv 2 120
Unworthier. Miss that which one unworthier may attain *Mer. of Venice* ii 1 37
Unworthiest. Degree being vizarded, The unworthiest shows as fairly in the mask *Troi. and Cres.* i 3 84
If I profane with my unworthiest hand This holy shrine *Rom. and Jul.* i 5 95
And that, in my regard, Of the unworthiest siege *Hamlet* iv 7 77
Unworthily. And so unworthily disgrace the man *T. G. of Ver.* iii 1 29
Unworthily Thou wast installed in that high degree *1 Hen. VI.* iii 1 16
Unworthiness. Wherefore weep you?—At mine unworthiness *Tempest* iii 1 77
Every night he comes With musics of all sorts and songs composed To her unworthiness *All's Well* iii 7 41
Mean and gentle all Behold, as may unworthiness define *Hen. V.* iv Prol. 46
Hence, from my sight! If after this command thou fraught the court With thy unworthiness, thou diest *Cymbeline* i 1 127
Unworthy. 'Tis a passing shame That I, unworthy body as I am, Should censure thus on lovely gentlemen *T. G. of Ver.* i 2 18
Examine himself, to see how much he is unworthy so good a lady *M. Ado* ii 3 217
Only give me leave, Unworthy as I am, to follow you *M. N. Dream* ii 1 207
That which God made, a poor unworthy brother of yours *As Y. Like It* i 1 36
The city-woman bears The cost of princes on unworthy shoulders ii 7 76
The most hollow lover and the most unworthy iv 1 197

Unworthy. Forswear her, As one unworthy all the former favours *T. of Shrew* iv 2 30
Take her hand, Proud scornful boy, unworthy this good gift *All's Well* ii 3 158
What angel shall Bless this unworthy husband? . . . iii 4 26
Write, Rinaldo, To this unworthy husband of his wife . . . iii 4 30
A most unworthy and unnatural lord Can do no more *W. Tale* ii 3 113
That makes himself, but for our honour therein, Unworthy thee . iv 4 448
Thou canst not, cardinal, devise a name So slight, unworthy *K. John* iii 1 150
On this unworthy scaffold to bring forth So great an object *Hen. V.* Prol. 10
Lay these bones in an unworthy urn, Tombless . . . i 2 228
He left me proudly, as unworthy fight *1 Hen. VI.* iv 7 43
I am unworthy to be Henry's wife.—No, gentle madam; I unworthy am
To woo so fair a dame to be his wife . . . . . v 3 122
If Somerset be unworthy of the place, Let York be regent *2 Hen. VI.* i 3 108
Unworthy though thou art, I'll cope with thee And do some service . iii 2 230
By His majesty I swear, Whose far unworthy deputy I am . . iii 2 286
Could it not enforce them to relent, That were unworthy to behold the
same? . . . . iv 4 18
For doing worthy vengeance on thyself, Which didst unworthy
slaughter upon others . . . . . . *Richard III.* i 2 88
I am a poor fall'n man, unworthy now To be thy lord and master
Hen. VIII. iii 2 413
But, thieves, unworthy of a thing so stol'n . . *Troi. and Cres.* ii 2 94
She is as far high-soaring o'er thy praises As thou unworthy to be call'd
her servant . . . . iv 4 127
To my poor unworthy notice, He mock'd us . . . . *Coriolanus* ii 3 166
Unworthy brother, and unworthy sons! . . . *T. Andron.* i 1 346
Every cat and dog And little mouse, every unworthy thing *R. and J.* iii 3 31
Doth she not count her blest, Unworthy as she is? . . . iii 5 145
The spurns That patient merit of the unworthy takes . *Hamlet* iii 1 74
Look you now, how unworthy a thing you make of me! . . . iii 2 379
I hold him to be unworthy of his place that does those things *Othello* ii 3 104
Bestow'd his lips on that unworthy place, As it rain'd kisses *A. and C.* iii 13 84
My mistress exceeds in goodness the hugeness of your unworthy
thinking . . . . *Cymbeline* i 4 157
I am unworthy for her schoolmaster.—She thinks not so *Pericles* ii 5 40
Unwrung. Let the galled jade wince, our withers are unwrung *Hamlet* iii 2 253
Unyoke this seizure and this kind regreet . . . . *K. John* iii 1 241
Ay, tell me that, and unyoke . . . . . . *Hamlet* v 1 59
Unyoked. Uphold The unyoked humour of your idleness . *1 Hen. IV.* i 2 220
Like youthful steers unyoked, they take their courses . *2 Hen. IV.* iv 2 103
Up. I wish mine eyes Would, with themselves, shut up my thoughts
Tempest ii 1 192
All the infections that the sun sucks up From bogs, fens, flats . . ii 2 1
What is't that you took up so gingerly?—Nothing *T. G. of Ver.* i 2 70
With true prayers That shall be up at heaven and enter there *M. for M.* ii 2 152
She'll be up twenty times a night, and there will she sit *Much Ado* ii 3 136
Up to the mountain's top And mark the musical confusion Of hounds
and echo in conjunction . . . . . . *M. N. Dream* iv 1 114
And what's worse, To fright the animals and to kill them up *As Y. L. It* ii 1 62
Pluck up thy spirits; look cheerfully upon me . *T. of Shrew* iv 3 38
Not to be a-bed after midnight is to be up betimes . . *T. Night* ii 3 2
To be up after midnight and to go to bed then, is early . . . ii 3 7
So long as nature Will bear up with this exercise . . *W. Tale* iii 2 242
Your discontenting father strive to qualify And bring him up to liking iv 4 544
And he that stands upon a slippery place Makes nice of no vile hold to
stay him up . . . . *K. John* iii 4 138
It was my breath that blew this tempest up . . . . . v 1 17
The day shall not be up so soon as I . . . . . . v 5 21
Up, cousin, up; your heart is up, I know, Thus high at least *Rich. II.* iii 3 194
Mount, mount, my soul! thy seat is up on high . . . . v 5 112
They are up already, and call for eggs . . . . *1 Hen. IV.* ii 1 64
That runs o' horseback up a hill perpendicular . . . . ii 4 378
Douglas, Mortimer, Capitulate against us and are up . . . iii 2 120
Up, and away! Our soldiers stand full fairly for the day . . v 3 28
Which is almost to pluck a kingdom down And set another up *2 Hen. IV.* i 3 50
Threw many a northward look to see his father Bring up his powers . ii 3 14
Engross'd and piled up The canker'd heaps of strange-achieved gold iv 5 71
Harry the Fifth is crown'd: up, vanity! Down, royal state! . . iv 5 120
Winding up days with toil and nights with sleep . . *Hen. V.* iv 1 296
I come amain, To signify that rebels there are up *2 Hen. VI.* iii 1 283
They have been up these two days.—They have the more need to sleep
now . . . . iv 2 2
It was never merry world in England since gentlemen came up . iv 2 10
Up Fish Street! down Saint Magnus' Corner! . . . . . iv 8 1
How many days will finish up the year . . . . *3 Hen. VI.* ii 5 28
Up with my tent there! here will I lie to-night *Richard III.* v 3 7
You great fellow, Stand close up, or I'll make your head ache *Hen. VIII.* v 4 92
All princely graces, That mould up such a mighty piece as this is . v 5 27
Helen was not up, was she? . . . . . *Troi. and Cres.* i 2 50
And over and over he comes, and up again; catched it again *Coriolanus* i 3 68
When two authorities are up, Neither supreme, how soon confusion
May enter . . . . iii 1 109
When they shall see, sir, his crest up again, and the man in blood . iv 5 225
The hunt is up, the morn is bright and grey . . *T. Andron.* ii 2 1
Whither should they come?—Up.—Whither?—To supper *Rom. and Jul.* i 2 76
Away, be gone! The citizens are up, and Tybalt slain . . . iii 1 138
Is she not down so late, or up so early? . . . . . . iii 5 67
Go thou to Juliet, help to deck up her . . . . . . iv 2 41
Prepare him up Against to-morrow . . . . iv 2 45
What misadventure is so early up, That calls our person? . . v 3 188
I have been up this hour, awake all night . . . *J. Cæsar* ii 1 88
Antony, that revels long o' nights, Is notwithstanding up . . ii 2 117
Marching along by them, By them shall make a fuller number up . iv 3 208
When think you that the sword goes up again? . . . . v 1 52
The storm is up, and all is on the hazard . . . . . . v 1 68
For those of old, And the late dignities heap'd up to them . *Macbeth* i 6 19
If the assassination Could trammel up the consequence . . . i 7 3
Shut up In measureless content . . . . ii 1 16
Up, up, and see The great doom's image! Malcolm! Banquo! . . ii 3 82
Saw you not his face?—O, yes, my lord; he wore his beaver up *Hamlet* i 2 230
And you, my sinews, grow not instant old, But bear me stiffly up . i 5 95
Up, sword; and know thou a more horrid hent . . . . iii 3 88
You shall nose him as you go up the stairs into the lobby . . iv 3 39
Up from my cabin, My sea-gown scarf'd about me . . . . v 2 12
But the great one that goes up the hill, let him draw thee after *Lear* ii 4 75
When shall we come to the top of that same hill?—You do climb up
it now . . . . iv 6 2
There's my gauntlet; I'll prove it on a giant. Bring up the brown
bills . . . . iv 6 91

Up. Here, in the sands, Thee I'll rake up . . . . . *Lear* iv 6 281
Upon his own appeal, seizes him: so the poor third is up *Ant. and Cleo.* iii 5 13
I am glad I was up so late; for that's the reason I was up so early *Cymb.* ii 3 38
If she be up, I'll speak with her; if not, Let her lie still and dream . ii 3 69
The game is up . . . . iii 3 107
Up and down. Here's my mother's breath up and down *T. G. of Ver.* ii 3 32
And wander up and down to view the city . *Com. of Errors* i 2 31
Here's his dry hand up and down: you are he, you are he *Much Ado* ii 1 124
As we do trace this alley up and down . . . . . iii 1 16
A' goes up and down like a gentleman: I remember his name . iii 3 135
We have been up and down to seek thee . . . . . . v 1 122
I will walk up and down here, and I will sing . . *M. N. Dream* iii 1 126
Up and down, up and down, I will lead them up and down . . . iii 2 396
Goblin, lead them up and down . . . . iii 2 399
We have been up and down to seek him . . . *Mer. of Venice* iv 1 79
What, up and down, carved like an apple-tart? . *T. of Shrew* iv 3 89
Where is he, That holds in chase mine honour up and down? *K. John* i 1 223
Runs tickling up and down the veins, Making that idiot, laughter . iii 3 44
And wild amazement hurries up and down . . . . . v 1 35
You follow the young prince up and down, like his ill angel *2 Hen. IV.* i 2 185
She says up and down the town that her eldest son is like you . ii 1 114
Here by the cheeks I'll drag thee up and down . . . *1 Hen. VI.* i 3 51
As the dam runs lowing up and down . . . . *2 Hen. VI.* iii 1 214
Like an angry hive of bees That want their leader, scatter up and down iii 2 126
The plebeians have got your fellow-tribune And hale him up and down
Coriolanus v 4 40
For up and down she doth resemble thee . . . *T. Andron.* v 2 107
Sending me about, To catch my death with jaunting up and down!
Rom. and Jul. ii 5 53
In all shapes that man goes up and down in from fourscore to thirteen
T. of Athens ii 2 119
Who swore they saw Men all in fire walk up and down the streets *J. C.* i 3 25
Thrice his head thus waving up and down, He raised a sigh *Hamlet* ii 1 93
Run barefoot up and down, threatening the flames . . . ii 2 528
I must go up and down like a cock that nobody can match . *Cymbeline* ii 1 23
Up early. And to be up early and down late . . *Mer. Wives* i 4 108
Up higher to the plain; where we'll set forth In best appointment *K. John* ii 1 295
Some two months hence up higher toward the north . . *J. Cæsar* ii 1 109
She'll prove on cats and dogs, Then afterward up higher . *Cymbeline* i 5 39
Up late. I know, to be up late is to be up late . . . *T. Night* ii 3 5
Up to the chins. There dancing up to the chins . . . *Tempest* iv 1 183
Up to the ears. The mailed Mars shall on his altar sit Up to the ears
in blood . . . . *1 Hen. IV.* iv 1 117
Up to the elbows. Let us bathe our hands in Cæsar's blood Up to the
elbows . . . . *J. Cæsar* iii 1 107
Up to the neck. He could wish himself in Thames up to the neck
Hen. V. iv 1 120
Upbraid. This Sir Prudence, who Should not upbraid our course *Temp.* ii 1 287
I did upbraid her and fall out with her . . . *M. N. Dream* iv 1 55
The clock upbraids me with the waste of time . . . *T. Night* iii 1 141
Lest that it make me so unsound a man As to upbraid you . . . iii 4 385
And I had many living to upbraid My gain . . . *2 Hen. IV.* iv 5 193
He used his lavish tongue And did upbraid me with my father's death
1 Hen. VI. ii 5 48
As well they may upbraid me with my crown, Because, forsooth, the
king of Scots is crown'd . . . . iv 1 156
Yet let memory, From false to false, among false maids in love, Upbraid
my falsehood! . . . . *Troi. and Cres.* iii 2 198
If you refuse your aid In this so never-needed help, yet do not Up-
braid's with our distress . . . . . . *Coriolanus* v 1 35
Now minutely revolts upbraid his faith-breach . . . *Macbeth* v 2 18
His knights grow riotous, and himself upbraids us On every trifle *Lear* i 3 6
There is besides in Roderigo's letter, How he upbraids Iago *Othello* v 2 325
Upbraided. Without desert—Hath oftentimes upbraided me withal
Com. of Errors iii 1 113
I spake unto this crown as having sense, And thus upbraided it *2 Hen. IV.* iv 5 159
None of the French upbraided or abused in disdainful language *Hen. V.* iii 6 117
Thus upbraided, chid, and rated at . . . . . . *2 Hen. VI.* iii 1 175
Upbraiding. Thou say'st his meat was sauced with thy upbraidings
Com. of Errors v 1 73
I have too long borne Your blunt upbraidings . . *Richard III.* i 3 104
Up-cast. Was there ever man had such luck! when I kissed the jack,
upon an up-cast to be hit away! . . . . . *Cymbeline* ii 1 2
Up-fill this osier cage of ours With baleful weeds . *Rom. and Jul.* ii 3 7
Uphoarded. If thou hast uphoarded in thy life Extorted treasure *Ham.* i 1 136
Uphold. The noble lord Most honourably doth uphold his word *L. L. L.* v 2 449
Even he that did uphold the very life Of my dear friend *Mer. of Venice* v 1 214
We will alone uphold, Without the assistance of a mortal hand *K. John* iii 1 157
That which upholdeth him that thee upholds, His honour . . . iii 1 315
Faulconbridge, In spite of spite, alone upholds the day . . . v 4 5
And will awhile uphold The unyoked humour of your idleness *1 Hen. IV.* i 2 219
While life upholds this arm, This arm upholds the house of Lancaster
3 Hen. VI. iii 3 106
Whate'er I forge to feed his brain-sick fits, Do you uphold *T. Andron.* v 2 72
Upholdeth. That which upholdeth him that thee upholds, His honour
K. John iii 1 315
Upholding the nice fashion of your country . . . . *Hen. V.* v 2 299
Uplift. Mechanic slaves With greasy aprons, rules, and hammers, shall
Uplift us to the view . . . . *Ant. and Cleo.* v 2 211
Your low-laid son our godhead will uplift: His comforts thrive *Cymb.* v 4 103
Uplifted. Your swords are now too massy for your strengths And will
not be uplifted . . . . *Tempest* iii 3 68
And with uplifted arms is safe arrived At Ravenspurgh *Richard II.* ii 2 50
How were I then uplifted! but, alas! I am as true as truth's simplicity
Troi. and Cres. iii 2 175
I think withal There would be hands uplifted in my right . *Macbeth* iv 3 42
Upmost. But when he once attains the upmost round, He then unto
the ladder turns his back . . . . *J. Cæsar* ii 1 24
Upon. Methinks he hath no drowning mark upon him . . *Tempest* i 1 31
This music crept by me upon the waters . . . . . . i 2 391
Mercy upon us!—Art thou afeard? . . . . iii 2 141
Upon some book I love I'll pray for thee . . . *T. G. of Ver.* i 1 20
Upon a homely object Love can wink . . . . . . ii 4 98
Unless I look on Silvia in the day, There is no day for me to look upon iii 1 181
She excels each mortal thing Upon the dull earth dwelling . . . iv 2 52
As one should say, one that takes upon him to be a dog indeed . iv 4 13
Much upon this riddle runs the wisdom of the world *Meas. for Meas.* iii 2 242
Much upon this time have I promised here to meet . . . . iv 1 17
I made my promise Upon the heavy middle of the night To call upon him iv 1 36
I have ta'en a due and wary note upon't . . . . . . iv 1 38

Upon. If any thing fall to you upon this, more than thanks and good fortune *Meas. for Meas.* iv 2 190
Very near upon The duke is entering iv 6 14
Out upon thee, hind!—Here's too much 'out upon thee!' *Com. of Er.* iii 1 77
Or else it stood upon the choice of friends *M. N. Dream* i 1 139
And make a heaven of hell, To die upon the hand I love so well ii 1 244
He may prove More fond on her than she upon her love ii 1 266
Nor is my whole estate Upon the fortune of this present year *M. of Ven.* i 1 44
You have too much respect upon the world i 1 74
The figure of an angel Stamped in gold, but that's insculp'd upon ii 7 57
As I remember, Adam, it was upon this fashion *As Y. Like It* i 1 1
Is it even so? begin you to grow upon me? i 1 90
This shepherd's passion Is much upon my fashion ii 4 62
Barefoot plod I the cold ground upon *All's Well* iii 4 6
I am yours Upon your will to suffer iv 4 30
Approach; Strike all that look upon with marvel *W. Tale* v 3 100
Perchance it frowns More upon humour than advised respect *K. John* iv 2 214
I will upon all hazards well believe Thou art my friend v 6 7
It stands your grace upon to do him right *Richard II.* ii 3 138
Nay, all of you that stand and look upon iv 1 237
Thou hast done much harm upon me, Hal 1 *Hen. IV.* i 2 103
Examine me upon the particulars of my life ii 4 414
One that no persuasion can do good upon iii 1 200
We may boldly spend upon the hope of what Is to come in iv 1 54
Every loop from whence The eye of reason may pry in upon us iv 1 72
I judge their number Upon or near the rate of thirty thousand 2 *Hen. IV.* iv 1 22
'Tis good for men to love their present pains Upon example *Hen. V.* iv 1 19
Upon condition I may quietly Enjoy mine own 1 *Hen. VI.* v 3 153
And look upon, as if the tragedy Were play'd in jest 3 *Hen. VI.* ii 3 27
It stands me much upon, To stop all hopes *Richard III.* iv 2 59
My sweet sleep's disturbers Are they that I would have thee deal upon iv 2 75
Nor ever more Upon this business my appearance make *Hen. VIII.* ii 4 132
The hour prefix'd Of her delivery . . . Comes fast upon *Troi. and Cres.* iv 3 3
He is my prize; I will not look upon v 6 10
My birth-place hate I, and my love's upon This enemy town *Coriolanus* iv 4 23
I was your mother much upon these years That you are now a maid *Rom. and Jul.* i 3 72
Fear comes upon me: O, much I fear some ill unlucky thing v 3 135
He comes upon a wish *J. Cæsar* iii 2 271
The deep of night is crept upon our talk iv 3 226
It comes upon me. Art thou any thing? Art thou some god? iv 3 278
New honours come upon him, Like our strange garments *Macbeth* i 3 144
Think upon what hath chanced i 3 153
When we can entreat an hour to serve, We would spend it in some words upon that business ii 1 23
Our tears are not yet brew'd.—Nor our strong sorrow Upon the foot of motion ii 3 131
Let your highness Command upon me iii 1 16
These evils thou repeat'st upon thyself Have banish'd me from Scotland iv 3 112
My first false speaking Was this upon myself iv 3 131
To see my mother's wedding.—Indeed, my lord, it follow'd hard upon *Ham.* i 2 179
My life upon her faith! *Othello* i 3 295
Let her not say 'tis I that keep you here: I have no power upon you *Ant. and Cleo.* i 3 23
My purposes do draw me much about: You'll win two days upon me ii 4 9
Since I saw you last, There is a change upon you ii 6 54
To him again: tell him he wears the rose Of youth upon him iii 13 21
My queen and Eros Have by their brave instruction got upon me A nobleness in record iv 14 98
Is he dead?—His death's upon him, but not dead iv 15 7
Whiles he is vaulting variable ramps, In your despite, upon your purse *Cymbeline* i 6 135
You shall not now be stol'n, you have locks upon you v 4 1
Upon mine honour, sir, I heard a humming *Tempest* ii 1 317
Upon mine honour, he shall never know *T. G. of Ver.* iii 1 48
Upon mine honour, thou shalt marry her *Meas. for Meas.* v 1 524
Upon thine honour, is he prisoner?—Upon mine honour, he is prisoner 2 *Hen. VI.* v 1 43
Upon my faith. Nor heard from her, Upon my faith and honour *M. for M.* v 1 224
Upon my life, then, you took the wrong *Mer. Wives* v 5 200
Upon my life, by some device or other The villain is o'er-raught *C. of Er.* i 2 95
Mistress, upon my life, I tell you true v 1 180
Upon my life, Petruchio means but well, Whatever fortune stays him *T. of Shrew* iii 2 22
Upon my life, This spirit, dumb to us, will speak to him *Hamlet* i 1 170
Upon my soul. An odious, damned lie; Upon my soul, a lie *Othello* v 2 181
Upper. I nightly lodge her in an upper tower *T. G. of Ver.* iii 1 35
Now here, At upper end o' the table, now i' the middle *W. Tale* iv 4 59
Let my woes frown on the upper hand *Richard III.* iv 4 37
Our neighbours, The upper Germany, can dearly witness *Hen. VIII.* v 3 30
Set at upper end o' the table; no question asked him *Coriolanus* iv 5 205
You said the enemy would not come down, But keep the hills and upper regions: It proves not so *J. Cæsar* v 1 3
Upreared. And hangs resolved correction in the arm That was uprear'd to execution 2 *Hen. IV.* iv 1 214
Two mighty monarchies, Whose high upreared and abutting fronts The perilous narrow ocean parts asunder *Hen. V.* Prol. 21
His hair uprear'd, his nostrils stretched with struggling 2 *Hen. VI.* iii 2 171
Upright. And time Goes upright with his carriage *Tempest* v 1 3
As upright as the cedar *L. L. Lost* iv 3 89
It is very meet The Lord Bassanio live an upright life *Mer. of Venice* iii 5 79
O wise and upright judge! How much more elder art thou than thy looks! iv 1 250
O upright judge! Mark, Jew: O learned judge! iv 1 313; 323
Nor partialize The unstooping firmness of my upright soul *Richard II.* i 1 121
True to King Richard's throne, A loyal, just, and upright gentleman i 3 87
Would God that any in this noble presence Were enough noble to be upright judge Of noble Richard! iv 1 118
Away, you whoreson upright rabbit, away! 2 *Hen. IV.* ii 2 91
If truth and upright innocency fail me, I'll to the king my master v 2 39
We know your grace to be a man Just and upright 1 *Hen. VI.* iii 1 95
I have seen Him caper upright like a wild Morisco 2 *Hen. VI.* iii 1 365
Comb down his hair; look, look! it stands upright, Like lime-twigs iii 3 15
With whom an upright zeal to right prevails 3 *Hen. VI.* v 1 78
It is a reeling world, indeed, my lord; And I believe 'twill never stand upright Till Richard wear the garland *Richard III.* iii 2 39
O upright, just, and true-disposing God, How do I thank thee! iv 4 55
Give me a staff of honour for mine age, But not a sceptre to control the world: Upright he held it, lords, that held it last *T. Andron.* i 1 200
Upright. Oft have I digg'd up dead men from their graves, And set them upright at their dear friends' doors *T. Andron.* v 1 136
Who dares, who dares, In purity of manhood stand upright? *T. of Athens* iv 3 14
For all beneath the moon Would I not leap upright *Lear* iv 6 27
O, give me cord, or knife, or poison, Some upright justicer! *Cymbeline* v 5 214
Uprighteously. You may most uprighteously do a poor wronged lady a merited benefit *Meas. for Meas.* iii 1 205
Uprightness. So I do affy In thy uprightness and integrity *T. Andron.* i 1 48
Uprise. Like a lark, That gives sweet tidings of the sun's uprise iii 1 159
O sun, thy uprise shall I see no more: Fortune and Antony part here *Ant. and Cleo.* iv 12 18
Uprising. Against the steep uprising of the hill *L. L. Lost* iv 1 2
Uproar. What tumult's this?—An uproar, I dare warrant 1 *Hen. VI.* iii 1 74
Are all in uproar, And danger serves among them *Hen. VIII.* i 2 36
Commotions, uproars, with a general taint Of the whole state v 3 28
By uproar sever'd, like a flight of fowl Scatter'd by winds *T. Andron.* v 3 68
Uproar the universal peace, confound All unity on earth *Macbeth* iv 3 99
Up-roused. Thy earliness doth me assure Thou art up-roused by some distemperature *Rom. and Jul.* ii 3 40
Upshoot. Then will she get the upshoot by cleaving the pin *L. L. Lost* iv 1 138
Upshot. I cannot pursue with any safety this sport to the upshot *T. N.* iv 2 76
And, in this upshot, purposes mistook Fall'n on the inventors' heads *Hamlet* v 2 395
Upside down. This house is turned upside down 1 *Hen. IV.* ii 1 11
A burning torch that's turned upside down *Pericles* ii 2 32
Up-spring. Keeps wassail, and the swaggering up-spring reels *Hamlet* i 4 9
Up-stairs. His industry is up-stairs and down-stairs 1 *Hen. IV.* ii 4 112
Up-staring. The king's son Ferdinand, With hair up-staring *Tempest* i 2 213
Upstart. My rights and royalties Pluck'd from my arms perforce and given away To upstart unthrifts *Richard II.* ii 3 122
I think this upstart is old Talbot's ghost 1 *Hen. VI.* iv 7 87
Up-swarmed. And both against the peace of heaven and him Have here up-swarm'd them 2 *Hen. IV.* iv 2 30
Upward. I have lived fourscore years and upward *Mer. Wives* iii 1 56
A Spaniard from the hip upward, no doublet *Much Ado* iii 2 36
She shall be buried with her face upwards iii 2 71
What upward lies The street should see as she walk'd overhead *L. L. L.* iv 3 280
And so upward and upward, and all was as cold as any stone *Hen. V.* ii 3 27
Thus far our fortune keeps an upward course 3 *Hen. VI.* v 3 1
I have been your wife, in this obedience, Upward of twenty years *Hen. VIII.* ii 4 36
Teem with new monsters, whom thy upward face Hath to the marbled mansion all above Never presented! *T. of Athens* iv 3 190
Titinius' face is upward.—He is slain *J. Cæsar* v 3 93
Things at the worst will cease, or else climb upward To what they were before *Macbeth* iv 2 24
I am a very foolish fond old man, Fourscore and upward *Lear* iv 7 61
From the extremest upward of thy head To the descent and dust below thy foot v 3 136
Urchins Shall, for that vast of night that they may work, All exercise on thee *Tempest* i 2 326
We'll dress Like urchins, ouphes, and fairies, green and white *Mer. W.* iv 4 49
Ten thousand swelling toads, as many urchins *T. Andron.* ii 3 101
Urchinfield. Lord Talbot of Goodrig and Urchinfield 1 *Hen. VI.* iv 7 64
Urchin-shows. Fright me with urchin-shows *Tempest* ii 2 5
Urge not my father's anger, Eglamour, But think upon my grief *T. G. of V.* iv 3 27
I urge this childhood proof, Because what follows is pure innocence *Mer. of Venice* i 1 144
Wanted the modesty To urge the thing held as a ceremony v 1 206
Give Helen this, And urge her to a present answer back *All's Well* ii 2 67
From England bring That right in peace which here we urge in war *K. John* ii 1 47
Urge them while their souls Are capable of this ambition ii 1 475
Murder, as hating what himself hath done, Doth lay it open to urge on revenge iv 3 38
To horse, to horse! urge doubts to them that fear *Richard II.* ii 1 299
Urge it no more, my Lord Northumberland iv 1 271
To say 'I love you:' then if you urge me farther than to say 'do you in faith?' I wear out my suit *Hen. V.* v 2 131
Urge it no more 3 *Hen. VI.* i 1 98
I'll in, to urge his hatred more to Clarence, With lies well steel'd *Richard III.* i 1 147
In those busy days Which here you urge to prove us enemies i 3 146
Urge neither charity nor shame to me i 3 274
How canst thou urge God's dreadful law to us? i 4 214
They did urge it still unto the king! God will revenge it ii 1 137
Moreover, urge his hateful luxury, And bestial appetite iii 5 80
Urge the necessity and state of times, And be not peevish-fond iv 4 416
Urge the king To do me this last right.—By heaven, I will *Hen. VIII.* iv 2 157
My accusers, Be what they will, may stand forth face to face, And freely urge against me v 3 48
He knows not What I can urge against him *Coriolanus* iv 7 19
Ah, wherefore dost thou urge the name of hands? *T. Andron.* iii 2 26
Therefore I urge thy oath v 1 78
To that I'll urge him v 1 81
If his occasion were not virtuous, I should not urge it half so faithfully *T. of Athens* iii 2 46
Urge it no more, On height of our displeasure iii 5 86
An earnest inviting, which many my near occasions did urge me to put off iii 6 12
What, urge you your petitions in the street? Come to the Capitol *J. C.* iii 1 11
Urge me no more, I shall forget myself iv 3 35
It is my duty, sir.—I should not urge thy duty past thy might iv 3 261
The time will not allow the compliment Which very manners urges *Lear* v 3 234
My brother never Did urge me in his act: I did inquire it *Ant. and Cleo.* ii 2 46
He may at pleasure whip, or hang, or torture, As he shall like, to quit me: urge it thou iii 13 151
Urged. She hath made compare Between our statures; she hath urged her height *M. N. Dream* iii 2 291
I cannot speak to her, yet she urged conference *As Y. Like It* i 2 270
Patience once more, whiles our compact is urged v 4 5
Thou art the issue of my dear offence, Which was so strongly urged past my defence *K. John* i 1 258
Troublesome, Being urged at a time unseasonable iv 2 20
You urged me as a judge; but I had rather You would have bid me argue like a father *Richard II.* i 3 237
Wilt know again, Being ne'er so little urged, another way v 1 64
He spake it twice, And urged it twice together, did he not? v 4 5
When I urged the ransom once again Of my wife's brother, then his cheek look'd pale 1 *Hen. IV.* i 3 141
I never in my life Did hear a challenge urged more modestly v 2 53

Urged. What I have done my safety urged me to — *1 Hen. IV.* v 5 11
My lord, I'll tell you; that self bill is urged — *Hen. V.* i 1 1
How now for mitigation of this bill Urged by the commons? — i 1 71
Well then the peace, Which you before so urged, lies in his answer — v 2 76
A woman's voice may do some good, When articles too nicely urged be stood on — v 2 94
Oaths, which I never use till urged, nor never break for urging — v 2 151
Well urged, my Lord of Warwick — *1 Hen. VI.* iii 1 152
It should be put To no apparent likelihood of breach, Which haply by much company might be urged — *Richard III.* ii 2 137
Thou know'st our reasons urged upon the way; What think'st thou? — iii 1 160
Then he was urged to tell my tale again — iii 7 31
The king's attorney on the contrary Urged on the examinations *Hen. VIII.* ii 1 16
I urged our old acquaintance, and the drops That we have bled together — *Coriolanus* v 1 10
Bid a sick man in sadness make his will: Ah, word ill urged! *R. and J.* i 1 209
Sin from my lips? O trespass sweetly urged! Give me my sin again i 5 111
Bethink How nice the quarrel was, and urged withal Your high displeasure — iii 1 159
Urged extremely for't and showed what necessity belonged to't *T. of A.* iii 2 14
Shall no man else be touch'd but only Cæsar?—Decius, well urged *J. C.* ii 1 155
I urged you further; then you scratch'd your head — ii 1 243
Your haste Is now urged on you.—We will greet the time — *Lear* v 1 54

Urgent. Please your highness To take the urgent hour — *W. Tale* i 2 465
For not alone The death of Fulvia, with more urgent touches, Do strongly speak to us — *Ant. and Cleo.* i 2 187

Urgest. As thou urgest justice, be assured Thou shalt have justice, more than thou desirest — *Mer. of Venice* iv 1 315
Why urgest thou so oft young Arthur's death? — *K. John* iv 2 204

Urging. With urging helpless patience wouldst relieve me *Com. of Errors* ii 1 39
And then, wherefore,—For urging it the second time to me — ii 2 47
In bed he slept not for my urging it; At board he fed not for my urging it — v 1 63
Besides her urging of her wreck at sea — v 1 359
I will not vex your souls . . . With too much urging — *Richard II.* iii 1 4
Oaths, which I never use till urged, nor never break for urging *Hen. V.* v 2 152
The urging of that word 'judgement' hath bred a kind of remorse in me — *Richard III.* i 4 109
Put not another sin upon my head, By urging me to fury *Rom. and Jul.* v 3 63

Urinal. These follies are within you and shine through you like the water in an urinal — *T. G. of Ver.* ii 1 41
I will knog his urinals about his knave's costard — *Mer. Wives* iii 1 14
I will knog your urinals about your knave's cogscomb — iii 1 91

Urine. When he makes water his urine is congealed ice . *Meas. for Meas.* iii 2 118
Others, when the bagpipe sings i' the nose, Cannot contain their urine — *Mer. of Venice* iv 1 50
What three things does drink especially provoke?—Marry, sir, nose-painting, sleep, and urine — *Macbeth* ii 3 32

Urn. Lay these bones in an unworthy urn, Tombless — *Hen. V.* i 2 228
In an urn more precious Than the rich-jewel'd coffer of Darius *1 Hen. VI.* i 6 24
The most noble corse that ever herald Did follow to his urn . *Coriolanus* v 6 146
O earth, I will befriend thee more with rain, That shall distil from these two ancient urns — *T. Andron.* iii 1 17

Ursa major. My nativity was under Ursa major — *Lear* i 2 141

Ursula, bring my picture there. Go give your master this *T. G. of Ver.* iv 4 122
Whisper her ear and tell her, I and Ursula Walk in the orchard *M. Ado* iii 1 4
No, truly, Ursula, she is too disdainful — iii 1 34
Good Ursula, wake my cousin Beatrice, and desire her to rise — iii 4 1
Help to dress me, good coz, good Meg, good Ursula — iii 4 99
Why, then my cousin, Margaret, and Ursula Are much deceived — v 4 78
And this to old Mistress Ursula, whom I have weekly sworn to marry — *2 Hen. IV.* i 2 269

Us. Let's assist them, For our case is as theirs — *Tempest* i 1 57
Let's all sink with the king.—Let's take leave of him — i 1 67
And Hymen now with luckier issue speed's — *Much Ado* v 3 32
We'll rest us, Hermia, if you think it good — *M. N. Dream* ii 2 37
Disguise us at my lodging and return, All in an hour . *Mer. of Venice* ii 4 2
We have not spoke us yet of torch-bearers — ii 4 5
Let us prepare Some welcome for the mistress of the house — v 1 37
Come, shall we go and kill us venison? — *As Y. Like It* ii 1 21
How mightily sometimes we make us comforts of our losses! *All's Well* iv 3 77
We are tougher, brother, Than you can put us to't — *W. Tale* ii 2 16
Cram's with praise, and make's As fat as tame things — i 2 91
We are yours i' the garden: shall's attend you there? — i 2 178
It fits us then to be as provident As fear may teach us . *Hen. V.* ii 4 12
Away, captains! let's get us from the walls — *1 Hen. VI.* iii 2 71
If he covetously reserve it, how shall's get it? — *T. of Athens* iv 3 408
Let's make us medicines of our great revenge — *Macbeth* iv 3 214
Since now we will divest us, both of rule, Interest of territory — *Lear* i 1 50
She looks us like A thing more made of malice than of duty *Cymbeline* iii 5 32
Say, where shall's lay him?—By good Euriphile, our mother — iv 2 233
From stiller seats we came, Our parents and us twain — v 4 70
Shall's have a play of this? Thou scornful page, There lie thy part — v 5 228
Shall's go hear the vestals sing? — *Pericles* iv 5 7

Usage. I am very comptible, even to the least sinister usage . *T. Night* i 5 188
This most cruel usage of your queen . . . something savours Of tyranny — *W. Tale* ii 3 117
To the fearful usage, At least ungentle, of the dreadful Neptune — v 1 153
It was my breath that blew this tempest up, Upon your stubborn usage of the pope — *K. John* v 1 18
As you yourself have forged against yourself By unkind usage *1 Hen. IV.* v 1 69
Yet, if this servile usage once offend, Go and be free again *1 Hen. VI.* v 3 58
He hath good usage and great liberty — *3 Hen. VI.* iv 5 6
The lustre in your eye, heaven in your cheek, Pleads your fair usage — *Troi. and Cres.* iv 4 121
Princely shall be thy usage every way — *T. Andron.* i 1 266
Resolve me, with all modest haste, which way Thou mightst deserve, or they impose, this usage — *Lear* ii 4 26
Who may haply be a little angry for my so rough usage . *Cymbeline* iv 1 22

Usance. In low simplicity He lends out money gratis and brings down The rate of usance — *Mer. of Venice* i 3 46
You have rated me About my moneys and my usances — i 3 109
Supply your present wants and take no doit Of usance for my moneys . i 3 142

Use. We will not hand a rope more; use your authority — *Tempest* i 1 25
All corners else o' the earth Let liberty make use of — i 2 492
Letters should not be known; riches, poverty, And use of service, none ii 1 151
No use of metal, corn, or wine, or oil; No occupation — ii 1 153
Of such sensible and nimble lungs that they always use to laugh at nothing — ii 1 175
They Will not, nor cannot, use such vigilance As when they are fresh . iii 3 16

Use. They want the use of tongue, a kind Of excellent dumb discourse — *Tempest* iii 3 38
I must use you In such another trick — iv 1 36
Most cruelly Didst thou, Alonso, use me and my daughter — v 1 72
Made use and fair advantage of his days — *T. G. of Ver.* ii 4 68
I must unto the road, to disembark Some necessaries that I needs must use ii 4 188
If I can check my erring love, I will; If not, to compass her I'll use my skill — ii 4 214
Base men, that use them to so base effect! — ii 7 73
Advise me where I may have such a ladder.—When would you use it? . iii 1 123
I'll use thee kindly for thy mistress' sake, That used me so . iv 4 207
He bears an honourable mind, And will not use a woman lawlessly . v 3 14
How use doth breed a habit in a man! — v 4 1
Though Love use Reason for his physician, he admits him not for his counsellor — *Mer. Wives* ii 1 5
Use your art of wooing; win her to consent to you — ii 2 244
I will use her as the key of the cuckoldly rogue's coffer — ii 2 285
Pray you, use your patience: in good time — iii 1 83
Hath he any eyes? hath he any thinking? Sure, they sleep; he hath no use of them — iii 2 32
We'll use this unwholesome humidity, this gross watery pumpion . iii 3 42
You use me well, Master Ford, do you?—Ay, I do so — iii 3 215
Into the chimney.—There they always use to discharge their birding-pieces — iv 2 58
Devise but how you'll use him when he comes — iv 4 26
Fairies use flowers for their charactery — v 5 77
Ignorance itself is a plummet o'er me: use me as you will . v 5 173
Determines Herself the glory of a creditor, Both thanks and use *M. for M.* i 1 41
So every scope by the immoderate use Turns to restraint — i 2 131
Only to stick it in their children's sight For terror, not to use . i 3 26
To give fear to use and liberty, Which have for long run by the hideous law i 4 62
That do nothing but use their abuses in common houses — ii 1 42
O, it is excellent To have a giant's strength; but it is tyrannous To use it like a giant — ii 2 109
For every pelting, petty officer Would use his heaven for thunder . ii 2 113
His use was to put a ducat in her clack-dish — iii 2 134
Not of this country, though my chance is now To use it for my time . iii 2 231
Let him abide here with you; if not, use him for the present and dismiss him — iv 2 26
If you have occasion to use me for your own turn, you shall find me yare iv 2 60
I familiarly sometimes Do use you for my fool and chat with you — *Com. of Errors* ii 2 27
An you use these blows long, I must get a sconce for my head . ii 2 37
How the world is changed with you! When were you wont to use my sister thus? — ii 2 155
If you did wed my sister for her wealth, Then for her wealth's sake use her with more kindness — iii 2 6
I know not what use to put her to but to make a lamp of her . iii 2 97
You use this dalliance to excuse Your breach of promise — iv 1 48
Thy jealous fits Have scared thy husband from the use of wits . v 1 86
My dull deaf ears a little use to hear — v 1 316
I cry you mercy, friend; go you with me, and I will use your skill *M. Ado* i 2 28
Can you make no use of your discontent?—I make all use of it, for I use it only — i 3 40
Therefore all hearts in love use their own tongues — ii 1 184
I gave him use for it, a double heart for his single one — ii 1 288
By this hand, I love thee.—Use it for my love some other way . iv 1 329
Wilt thou use thy wit?—It is in my scabbard: shall I draw it? . v 1 124
If you use them, Margaret, you must put in the pikes with a vice . v 2 20
I love to hear him lie And I will use him for my minstrelsy . *L. L. Lost* i 1 177
Not looking on a woman's face, You have in that forsworn the use of eyes iv 3 310
Use me but as your spaniel, spurn me, strike me . *M. N. Dream* ii 1 205
What worser place can I beg in your love,—And yet a place of high respect with me,—Than to be used as you use your dog? — ii 1 210
But I should use thee worse, For thou, I fear, hast given me cause to curse — iii 2 45
If you were men, as men you are in show, You would not use a gentle lady so — iii 2 152
Her passion ends the play.—Methinks she should not use a long one . v 1 322
You neither lend nor borrow Upon advantage.—I do never use it *M. of V.* i 3 71
And all for use of that which is mine own — i 3 114
Use your legs, take the start, run away — ii 2 5
Use all the observance of civility, Like one well studied in a sad ostent ii 2 204
Use your pleasure: if your love do not persuade you to come, let not my letter — iii 2 323
And use thou all the endeavour of a man In speed — iii 4 48
You may as well use question with the wolf Why he hath made the ewe bleat — iv 1 73
I do beseech you, Make no more offers, use no farther means . iv 1 81
Like your asses and your dogs and mules, You use in abject and in slavish parts — iv 1 92
Herein Fortune shows herself more kind Than is her custom: it is still her use To let the wretched man outlive his wealth — iv 1 268
I am content; so he will let me have The other half in use . iv 1 383
Use thy discretion; I had as lief thou didst break his neck as his finger — *As Y. Like It* i 1 152
Sweet are the uses of adversity, Which, like the toad, ugly and venomous ii 1 12
This night he means To burn the lodging where you use to lie . ii 3 23
I guess By the stern brow and waspish action Which she did use . iv 3 10
He uses his folly like a stalking-horse — v 4 111
To good wine they do use good bushes — Epil. 5
Music and poesy use to quicken you — *T. of Shrew* i 1 36
And paint your face and use you like a fool — i 1 65
I advise You use your manners discreetly in all kind of companies . i 1 247
Was it fit for a servant to use his master so? — i 2 32
Tell them both, These are their tutors: bid them use them well . ii 1 111
'Tis for my mistress.—Go, take it up unto thy master's use . iv 3 159
Take up my mistress' gown to his master's use! O, fie, fie, fie! . iv 3 164
Be able for thine enemy Rather in power than use . *All's Well* i 1 75
Get thee a good husband, and use him as he uses thee — i 1 229
Use a more spacious ceremony to the noble lords — ii 1 51
Which should, indeed, give us a further use to be made . ii 3 41
O'er whom both sovereign power and father's voice I have to use . ii 3 61
In such a business give me leave to use The help of mine own eyes . ii 3 114
And uses a known truth to pass a thousand nothings with . ii 5 32
Can serve the world for no honest use; therefore you must die . iv 3 341
O strange men! That can such sweet use make of what they hate . iv 4 22
I put you to The use of your own virtues — v 1 16
He hence removed last night and with more haste Than is his use . v 1 24
Use the carp as you may; for he looks like a poor, . . . rascally knave v 2 23

Use. And those that are fools, let them use their talents *T. Night* i 5 15
The free maids that weave their thread with bones Do use to chant it ii 4 47
She uses me with a more exalted respect than any one else that follows her ii 5 31
And the impressure her Lucrece, with which she uses to seal ii 5 104
Would not a pair of these have bred, sir?—Yes, being kept together and put to use iii 1 57
In my sight she uses thee kindly: but thou liest in thy throat iii 4 171
I am one of those gentle ones that will use the devil himself with courtesy iv 2 37
Denied me mine own purse, Which I had recommended to his use v 1 94
The shrug, the hum or ha, these petty brands That calumny doth use *W. T.* ii 1 72
Lest barbarism . . . Should a like language use to all degrees ii 1 85
Tell her, Emilia, I'll use that tongue I have ii 2 52
As it hath been to us rare, pleasant, speedy, The time is worth the use on't iii 1 14
So long as nature Will bear up with this exercise, so long I daily vow to use it iii 2 243
Now take upon me, in the name of Time, To use my wings iv 1 4
Forewarn him that he use no scurrilous words in's tunes iv 4 215
And what I saw, to my good use I remembered iv 4 616
Use our commission in his utmost force *K. John* iii 3 11
If heaven be pleased that you must use me ill, Why then you must iv 1 55
O, spare mine eyes, Though to no use but still to look on you! iv 1 103
All things that you should use to do me wrong Deny their office iv 1 118
Fierce fire and iron . . . , Creatures of note for mercy-lacking uses iv 1 121
Deliver him to safety; and return, For I must use thee iv 2 159
Use all your power To stop their marches 'fore we are inflamed v 1 6
What in the world should make me now deceive, Since I must lose the use of all deceit? v 4 27
My fair name, Despite of death that lives upon my grave, To dark dishonour's use thou shalt not have *Richard II.* i 1 169
And now my tongue's use is to me no more Than an unstringed viol i 3 161
If not, I'll use the advantage of my power iii 3 42
The prisoners . . . To his own use he keeps *1 Hen. IV.* i 1 94
When we need Your use and counsel, we shall send for you i 3 21
Do not use it oft, let me entreat you iii 1 176
Render'd such aspect As cloudy men use to their adversaries iii 2 83
I make as good use of it as many a man doth of a Death's-head iii 3 33
You strain too far. I rather of his absence make this use iv 1 76
A good wit will make use of any thing *2 Hen. IV.* i 2 277
And made her serve your uses both in purse and in person ii 1 127
The inventory of thy shirts, as, one for superfluity, and another for use ii 2 21
But do you use me thus, Ned? must I marry your sister? ii 2 150
Most excellent, i' faith! things that are mouldy lack use iii 2 119
I will not use many words with you. Fare you well iii 2 309
Our men more perfect in the use of arms, Our armour all as strong iv 1 155
And learning a mere hoard of gold kept by a devil, till sack commences it and sets it in act and use iv 3 126
Comes to no further use But to be known and hated iv 4 72
I will use him well: a friend i' the court is better than a penny in purse v 1 33
I then did use the person of your father v 2 73
With this remembrance, that you use the same With the like bold, just, and impartial spirit v 2 115
This Davy serves you for good uses; he is your serving-man v 3 11
If my tongue cannot entreat you to acquit me, will you command me to use my legs? Epil. 19
How he comes o'er us with our wilder days, Not measuring what use we made of them *Hen. V.* i 2 268
Wouldst thou have practised on me for thy use! ii 2 99
Good bawcock, bate thy rage; use lenity, sweet chuck! iii 2 26
You do not use me with that affability as in discretion you ought to use me iii 2 138
Fortify it strongly 'gainst the French: Use mercy to them all iii 3 54
I would desire the duke to use his good pleasure, and put him to execution iii 6 57
Thou makest use of any thing.—Yet do I not use my horse for my mistress iii 7 70
I will the banner from a trumpet take, And use it for my haste iv 2 62
Downright oaths, which I never use till urged, nor never break for urging v 2 151
As a child's bearing-cloth I'll use to carry thee out of this place *1 Hen. VI.* i 3 43
Here's Beaufort, . . . Hath here distrain'd the Tower to his use i 3 61
And not to wear, handle, or use any sword, weapon, or dagger i 3 78
Thy words condemn thy brat and thee: Use no entreaty v 4 85
Entreat her not the worse in that I pray You use her well *2 Hen. VI.* ii 4 82
Or any groat I hoarded to my use iii 1 113
Thy name?—Emmanuel.—They use to write it on the top of letters iv 2 107
Dost thou use to write thy name? or hast thou a mark to thyself? iv 2 109
Lands, goods, horse, armour, any thing I have, Is his to use v 1 53
Words and threats Shall be the war that Henry means to use *3 Hen. VI.* i 1 73
Thy face is, visard-like, unchanging, Made impudent with use of evil deeds i 4 117
I'll draw it [my sword] as apparent to the crown, And in that quarrel use it to the death ii 2 65
Use her honourably.—Ay, Edward will use women honourably iii 2 123
Stand aside, While I use further conference with Warwick iii 3 111
How should you govern any kingdom, That know not how to use ambassadors, . . . Nor how to use your brothers brotherly? iv 3 36
If we use delay, Cold biting winter mars our hoped-for hay iv 8 60
What, doth she swoon? use means for her recovery v 5 45
Be assured We come to use our hands and not our tongues *Richard III.* i 3 353
To the Tower, Where, he shall see, the boar will use us kindly iii 2 33
Old sullen playfellow For tender princes, use my babies well! iv 1 103
But that still use of grief makes wild grief tame iv 4 229
Hie thee to thy charge; Use careful watch, choose trusty sentinels v 3 54
Conscience is but a word that cowards use v 3 309
You're welcome . . . into our kingdom: Use us and it *Hen. VIII.* ii 2 78
We are ready To use our utmost studies in your service iii 1 174
I am glad your grace has made that right use of it iii 2 386
Make use now, and provide For thine own future safety iii 2 420
You are to blame . . . To use so rude behaviour; go to, kneel iv 2 103
The best persuasions to the contrary Fail not to use v 1 148
Respect him; Take him, and use him well, he's worthy of it v 3 155
He is a gouty Briareus, many hands and no use *Troi. and Cres.* i 2 30
If thou use to beat me, I will begin at thy heel, and tell what thou art ii 1 52
I have derision medicinable, To use between your strangeness and his pride iii 3 45
Nature, what things there are Most abject in regard and dear in use! iii 3 128
We must use expostulation kindly, For it is parting from us iv 4 62
Thou dost not use me courteously, To shame the zeal of my petition to thee iv 4 123
I charge thee use her well, even for my charge iv 4 128
They say he keeps a Trojan drab, and uses the traitor Calchas' tent v 1 104

Use. We would give much, to use violent thefts, And rob in the behalf of charity *Troi. and Cres.* v 3 21
Be happy that my arms are out of use v 6 16
Would the nobility lay aside their ruth, And let me use my sword *Coriol.* i 1 202
You see how he intends to use the people.—May they perceive's intent! ii 2 159
But yet a brain that leads my use of anger To better vantage iii 2 30
Hast not the soft way which, thou dost confess, Were fit for thee to use iii 2 83
So use it That my revengeful services may prove As benefits to thee iv 5 94
Your soldiers use him as the grace 'fore meat iv 7 3
If thy captain knew I were here, he would use me with estimation v 2 56
O that I had him, With six Aufidiuses, . . . To use my lawful sword! v 6 131
To him that, for your honour and your state, Will use you nobly *T. An.* i 1 260
Use her as you will, The worse to her, the better loved of me ii 3 166
In bootless prayer have they been held up, And they have served me to effectless use iii 1 76
Then I'll go fetch an axe.—But I will use the axe iii 1 186
Did you not use his daughter very friendly? iv 2 40
Surprised him suddenly, and brought him hither, To use as you think needful of the man v 1 39
Beauty too rich for use, for earth too dear! *Rom. and Jul.* i 5 49
Have not saints lips, and holy palmers too?—Ay, pilgrim, lips that they must use in prayer i 5 104
He may not have access To breathe such vows as lovers use to swear ii Prol. 10
Nor aught so good but strain'd from that fair use Revolts from true birth ii 3 19
And thou must stand by too, and suffer every knave to use me at his pleasure?—I saw no man use you at his pleasure ii 4 164
And, as you shall use me hereafter, dry-beat the rest iii 1 82
Nor tears nor prayers shall purchase out abuses: Therefore use none iii 1 199
'Banished?' O friar, the damned use that word in hell iii 3 47
Like a usurer, abound'st in all, And usest none in that true use iii 3 124
Look to't, think on't, I do not use to jest iii 5 191
Is dead; or 'twere as good he were, As living here and you no use of him iii 5 227
Cordial and not poison, go with me To Juliet's grave; for there must I use thee v 1 86
But breeds the giver a return exceeding All use of quittance *T. of Athens* i 1 291
Might we but have that happiness, my lord, that you would once use our hearts i 2 87
The most needless creatures living, should we ne'er have use for 'em i 2 101
Tell him, My uses cry to me, I must serve my turn Out of mine own ii 1 20
Men and men's fortunes could I frankly use As I can bid thee speak ii 2 188
My occasions have found time to use 'em toward a supply of money ii 2 200
I have been bold . . . To them to use your signet and your name ii 2 210
Having great and instant occasion to use fifty talents iii 1 19
And canst use the time well, if the time use thee well iii 1 39
Requesting your lordship to supply his instant use with so many talents iii 2 41
I was sending to use Lord Timon myself, these gentlemen can witness iii 2 56
Will you befriend me so far, as to use mine own words to him? iii 2 65
Had his necessity made use of me, I would have put my wealth into donation iii 2 89
Pity is the virtue of the law, And none but tyrants use it cruelly iii 5 9
They love thee not that use thee; Give them diseases iv 3 83
Make use of thy salt hours: season the slaves For tubs and baths iv 3 85
Men report Thou dost affect my manners, and dost use them iv 3 199
Here is no use for gold.—The best and truest; For here it sleeps, and does no hired harm iv 3 290
In the plainer and simpler kind of people, the deed of saying is quite out of use v 1 28
Special dignities, which vacant lie For thy best use and wearing v 1 146
I have a tree, which grows here in my close, That mine own use invites me to cut down v 1 209
That thou wilt use the wars as thy redress And not as our confusion v 4 51
Bring me into your city, And I will use the olive with my sword v 4 82
A trade, sir, that, I hope, I may use with a safe conscience *J. Cæsar* i 1 14
Were I a common laugher, or did use To stale with ordinary oaths my love To every new protester i 2 72
If the tag-rag people did not clap him and hiss him, . . . as they use to do the players in the theatre, I am no true man i 2 262
Those sparks of life That should be in a Roman you do want, Or else you use not. You look pale and gaze i 3 59
These things are beyond all use, And I do fear them ii 2 25
Blood and destruction shall be so in use And dreadful objects so familiar iii 1 265
Which, out of use and staled by other men, Begin his fashion iv 1 38
I'll use you for my mirth, yea, for my laughter, When you are waspish iv 3 49
Of your philosophy you make no use, If you give place to accidental evils iv 3 145
According to his virtue let us use him, With all respect v 5 76
Ten thousand dollars to our general use *Macbeth* i 2 62
And make my seated heart knock at my ribs, Against the use of nature i 3 137
New honours come upon him, Like our strange garments, cleave not to their mould But with the aid of use i 3 146
And such an instrument I was to use ii 1 43
My strange and self-abuse Is the initiate fear that wants hard use iii 4 143
Thou comest to use thy tongue; thy story quickly v 5 29
Stay, illusion! If thou hast any sound, or use of voice, Speak to me *Ham.* i 1 128
How weary, stale, flat, and unprofitable, Seem to me all the uses of this world! i 2 134
The need we have to use you did provoke Our hasty sending ii 2 3
More matter, with less art.—Madam, I swear I use no art at all ii 2 96
A foolish figure; But farewell it, for I will use no art ii 2 99
The adventurous knight shall use his foil and target ii 2 334
My lord, I will use them according to their desert.—God's bodykins, man, much better: use every man after his desert, and who should 'scape whipping? Use them after your own honour and dignity ii 2 552
Do not saw the air too much with your hand, thus, but use all gently iii 2 6
Shows a most pitiful ambition in the fool that uses it iii 2 50
I will speak daggers to her, but use none iii 2 414
To the use of actions fair and good He likewise gives a frock or livery iii 4 163
For use almost can change the stamp of nature iii 4 168
Her speech is nothing, Yet the unshaped use of it doth move iv 5 8
To what base uses we may return, Horatio! v 1 223
What is the reason that you use me thus? I loved you ever v 1 312
Put your bonnet to his right use; 'tis for the head v 2 95
The queen desires you to use some gentle entertainment to Laertes v 2 215
Use well our father: To your professed bosoms I commit him *Lear* i 1 274
Can you make no use of nothing, nuncle?—Why, no, boy i 4 144
I would you would make use of that good wisdom, Whereof I know you are fraught i 4 240
Shalt see thy other daughter will use thee kindly i 5 14

Use. Occasions, noble Gloucester, of some poise, Wherein we must have use of your advice . . . . *Lear* ii 1 123

Bestow Your needful counsel to our business, Which craves the instant use . . . . ii 1 130

Why dost thou use me thus? I know thee not . . . . ii 2 11

Why, madam, if I were your father's dog, You should not use me so . ii 2 144

When I desired their leave that I might pity him, they took from me the use of mine own house . . . . . . iii 3 3

She that herself will sliver and disbranch From her material sap, perforce must wither And come to deadly use . . . . iv 2 36

Thou hotly lust'st to use her in that kind For which thou whipp'st her iv 6 166

Use me well; You shall have ransom . . . . . iv 6 195

This would make a man a man of salt, To use his eyes for garden water-pots . . . . iv 6 200

Now then we'll use His countenance for the battle . . . . v 1 62

So to use them As we shall find their merits and our safety May equally determine . . . . v 3 43

I'ld use them so That heaven's vault should crack . . . v 3 258

Men do their broken weapons rather use Than their bare hands . *Othello* i 3 174

Adieu, brave Moor; use Desdemona well . . . . . i 3 292

Fairness and wit, The one's for use, the other useth it . . . ii 1 131

Than keep a corner in the thing I love For others' uses . . . iii 3 273

Be not acknown on't; I have use for it . . . . . iii 3 319

Is it his use? Or did the letters work upon his blood? . . . iv 1 285

Then let them use us well: else let them know, The ills we do, their ills instruct us so . . . . iv 3 103

Heaven me such uses send, Not to pick bad from bad, but by bad mend! . . . . iv 3 105

Nay, guiltiness will speak, Though tongues were out of use . . v 1 110

My full heart Remains in use with you . . . *Ant. and Cleo.* i 3 44

It only stands Our lives upon to use our strongest hands . . ii 1 51

But, sirrah, mark, we use To say the dead are well . . . ii 5 32

Antony will use his affection where it is: he married but his occasion here . . . . ii 6 139

You take from me a great part of myself; Use me well in't . . iii 2 25

Cæsar, having made use of him in the wars 'gainst Pompey . . iii 5 7

I do not greatly care to be deceived, That have no use for trusting . v 2 15

Make your best use of this: I have perform'd Your pleasure and my promise . . . . v 2 203

That Mulmutius which Ordain'd our laws, whose use the sword of Cæsar Hath too much mangled . . . . *Cymbeline* iii 1 56

Hail, thou fair heaven! We house i' the rock, yet use thee not so hardly As prouder livers do . . . . iii 3 8

Gone she is To death or to dishonour; and my end Can make good use of either . . . . iii 5 64

Undergo those employments wherein I should have cause to use thee . iii 5 111

Sing him to the ground, As once our mother; use like note and words . iv 2 237

Slay us, or receive us For barbarous and unnatural revolts During their use, and slay us after . . . . iv 4 7

There are none want eyes to direct them the way I am going, but such as wink and will not use them . . . . v 4 194

What an infinite mock is this, that a man should have the best use of eyes to see the way of blindness! . . . . . . v 4 196

But custom what they did begin Was with long use account no sin *Pericles* i Gower 30

As houses are defiled for want of use, They are now starved for want of exercise . . . . i 4 37

We commit no crime To use one language in each several clime . . iv 4 6

Without any more virginal fencing, will you use him kindly? . . iv 6 63

Take her away; use her at thy pleasure . . . . . iv 6 150

I will use My utmost skill in his recovery . . . . . v 1 75

Used. I have used thee, Filth as thou art, with human care *Tempest* i 2 345

I cannot now prove constant to myself, Without some treachery used to Valentine . . . . *T. G. of Ver.* ii 6 32

I'll use thee kindly for thy mistress' sake, That used me so . . iv 4 208

Awakens me with this unwonted putting-on; methinks strangely, for he hath not used it before . . . . *Meas. for Meas.* iv 2 121

I will not let him stir Till I have used the approved means *Com. of Errors* v 1 103

Borrows money in God's name, the which he hath used so long and never paid . . . . *Much Ado* v 1 320

This civil war of wits were much better used On Navarre . *L. L. Lost* ii 1 226

What worser place can I beg in your love . . . Than to be used as you use your dog? . . . . *M. N. Dream* ii 1 210

A beggar, that was used to come so smug upon the mart *Mer. of Venice* iii 1 48

Who were below him He used as creatures of another place *All's Well* i 2 42

Thy pains not used must by thyself be paid: Proffers not took reap thanks for their reward . . . . ii 1 149

Gently: the fiend is rough, and will not be roughly used *T. Night* iii 4 124

Your greatness Hath not been used to fear . . . *W. Tale* iv 4 18

No wife: one worse, And better used, would make her sainted spirit Again possess her corpse . . . . v 1 57

The fire is dead with grief, Being create for comfort, to be used In undeserved extremes . . . . *K. John* iv 1 107

Whom he hath used rather for sport than need . . . . v 2 175

Where it would not, I have used my credit.—Yea, and so used it 1 *Hen. IV.* i 2 63

Our house . . . little deserves The scourge of greatness to be used on it i 3 11

And being fed by us you used us so As that ungentle gull, the cuckoo's bird, Useth the sparrow . . . . v 1 59

Is thy name Mouldy?—Yea, an't please you.—'Tis the more time thou wert used.—Ha, ha, ha! . . . . . 2 *Hen. IV.* iii 2 117

I do commit into your hand The unstained sword that you have used to bear . . . . v 2 114

And put him to execution; for discipline ought to be used . *Hen. V.* iii 6 59

His eyes are humbler than they used to be . . . . . iv 7 70

How were they lost? what treachery was used?—No treachery 1 *Hen. VI.* i 1 68

Is he come?—Ay, noble uncle, thus ignobly used . . . ii 5 35

He used his lavish tongue And did upbraid me with my father's death . ii 5 47

Hast thou by secret means Used intercession to obtain a league? . v 4 148

To the Isle of Man; There to be used according to your state 2 *Hen. VI.* ii 4 95

And shall I then be used reproachfully?—Like to a duchess, and Duke Humphrey's lady; According to that state you shall be used . . ii 4 97

Suffolk's imperial tongue is stern and rough, Used to command . iv 1 122

Thou hast caused printing to be used . . . . . . iv 7 39

Even with those wings Which sometime they have used with fearful flight, Make war . . . . 3 *Hen. VI.* ii 2 30

Now the battle's ended, If friend or foe, let him be gently used . ii 6 45

Swear not by time to come; for that thou hast Misused ere used *Richard III.* iv 4 396

All several sins, all used in each degree, Throng to the bar . . v 3 198

Used. The madams too, Not used to toil, did almost sweat to bear The pride upon them . . . . *Hen. VIII.* i 1 24

Whose tenour Was,—were he evil used, he would outgo His father . i 2 207

Pray, forgive me, If I have used myself unmannerly . . . iii 1 176

Let me be used with honour: strew me over With maiden flowers . iv 2 168

They were used to bend, To send their smiles before them to Achilles; To come as humbly as they used to creep To holy altars *T. and C.* iii 3 71

I sometime lay here in Corioli At a poor man's house; he used me kindly *Coriolanus* i 9 83

Not one amongst us, save yourself, but says He used us scornfully . ii 3 171

Whoever gave that counsel, to give forth The corn o' the storehouse gratis, as 'twas used Sometime in Greece . . . . . iii 1 114

Whose rage doth rend Like interrupted waters and o'erbear What they are used to bear . . . . iii 1 250

Put him to choler straight: he hath been used Ever to conquer . . iii 3 25

You were used To say extremity was the trier of spirits . . . iv 1 3

You were used to load me With precepts . . . . . iv 1 9

And, for the extent Of egal justice, used in such contempt *T. Andron.* iv 4 4

For worse than Philomel you used my daughter . . . . v 2 195

Nor with such free and friendly conference As he hath used of old *J. C.* iv 2 18

The rest is labour, which is not used for you . . . *Macbeth* i 4 44

And used their very daggers . . . . i 7 76

Hunts not the trail of policy so sure As it hath used to do . *Hamlet* ii 2 48

Old fools are babes again; and must be used With checks as flatteries *Lear* i 3 19

I have used it, nuncle, ever since thou madest thy daughters thy mother i 4 187

Then comes the time, who lives to see't, That going shall be used with feet . . . . iii 2 94

They have used Their dearest action in the tented field . *Othello* i 3 84

This only is the witchcraft I have used: Here comes the lady . i 3 169

Knavery's plain face is never seen till used . . . . ii 1 321

Good wine is a good familiar creature, if it be well used . . . ii 3 314

'Tis meet I should be used so, very meet . . . . . iv 2 107

He hath confess'd.—What, my lord?—That he hath used thee . v 2 70

I have a health for you.—I shall take it, sir: we have used our throats in Egypt . . . . *Ant. and Cleo.* ii 6 143

We Have used to conquer, standing on the earth, And fighting . . iii 7 66

Yet heaven's bounty towards him might Be used more thankfully *Cymb.* i 6 79

Why should this change of thoughts . . . Be my so used a guest? *Per.* i 2 3

He asks of you, that never used to beg . . . . . . ii 1 66

If there be not a conscience to be used in every trade, we shall never prosper . . . . iv 2 12

Useful. To be a secondary at control, Or useful serving-man . *K. John* v 2 81

Thy honest sword, which thou hast worn Most useful for thy country *Ant. and Cleo.* iv 14 80

Useless. Thy brains, Now useless, boil'd within thy skull! . *Tempest* v 1 60

User. Ce sont mots de son mauvais, corruptible, gros, et impudique, et non pour les dames d'honneur d'user . . . . *Hen. V.* iii 4 58

Usest. Thy friend, as thou usest him, and thy sworn enemy . *T. Night* iii 4 186

Thine, by yea and no, which is as much as to say, as thou usest him 2 *Hen. IV.* ii 2 143

Ay, but thou usest to forswear thyself: 'Twas sin before 3 *Hen. VI.* v 5 75

Like a usurer, abound'st in all, And usest none in that true use *R. and J.* iii 3 124

Useth. As that ungentle gull, the cuckoo's bird, Useth the sparrow 1 *Hen. IV.* v 1 61

As an outlaw in a castle keeps And useth it to patronage his theft 1 *Hen. VI.* iii 1 48

When love begins to sicken and decay, It useth an enforced ceremony *J. C.* iv 2 21

Fairness and wit, The one's for use, the other useth it . . *Othello* ii 1 131

Usher. No sun shall ever usher forth mine honours . *Hen. VIII.* iii 2 410

Hark! the trumpets.—These are the ushers of Marcius . *Coriolanus* ii 1 174

The wife of Antony Should have an army for an usher . *Ant. and Cleo.* iii 6 44

Ushering. In ushering Mend him who can . . . *L. L. Lost* v 2 328

Using painting, do prove my occupation a mystery . *Meas. for Meas.* iv 2 40

And make reply Without a tongue, using conceit alone . *K. John* iii 3 50

Using the names of men instead of men . . . 2 *Hen. IV.* i 3 57

I have loaden me with many spoils, Using no other weapon but his name . . . . 1 *Hen. VI.* ii 1 81

'Tis better using France than trusting France . . 3 *Hen. VI.* iv 1 42

Crave pardon of your majesty.—For what, lieutenant? for well using me? . . . . iv 6 9

Unless, by using means, I lame the foot Of our design *Coriolanus* iv 7 7

Using those thoughts which should indeed have died With them they think on . . . . *Macbeth* iii 2 10

Usual. Where is our usual manager of mirth? . . . *M. N. Dream* v 1 35

You may as well go stand upon the beach And bid the main flood bate his usual height . . . . *Mer. of Venice* iv 1 72

Was it [music] not to refresh the mind of man After his studies or his usual pain? . . . . *T. of Shrew* iii 1 12

If . . . he make this way Under the colour of his usual game 3 *Hen. VI.* iv 5 11

It was usual with him, every day It would infect his speech *Hen. VIII.* i 2 132

Such wanton, wild, and usual slips As are companions noted and most known To youth and liberty . . . . *Hamlet* ii 1 22

Usually. Men about thee that usually talk of a noun and a verb 2 *Hen. VI.* iv 7 43

He does usually, So all men do, from hence to the palace gate Make it their walk . . . . *Macbeth* iii 3 12

Usurer. About your neck, like an usurer's chain . . . *Much Ado* ii 1 197

He was wont to call me usurer; let him look to his bond *Mer. of Venice* iii 1 50

How a usurer's wife was brought to bed of twenty money-bags *W. Tale* iv 4 266

Bless me from marrying a usurer! . . . . iv 4 271

Thou art a most pernicious usurer, Froward by nature . 1 *Hen. VI.* iii 1 17

Make edicts for usury, to support usurers . . . *Coriolanus* i 1 84

Like a usurer, abound'st in all, And usest none in that true use *R. and J.* iii 3 123

Poor rogues, and usurers' men! bawds between gold and want! *T. of A.* ii 2 61

You three serve three usurers?—Ay; would they served us! . . ii 2 97

I think no usurer but has a fool to his servant . . . . ii 2 103

Pity not honour'd age for his white beard; He is an usurer . . iv 3 112

When usurers tell their gold i' the field . . . . . *Lear* iii 2 89

The usurer hangs the cozener . . . . iv 6 167

Usuring. Is this the balsam that the usuring senate Pours into captains' wounds? . . . . *T. of Athens* iii 5 110

Is not thy kindness subtle, covetous, If not a usuring kindness? . iv 3 516

Usurp. Thou dost here usurp The name thou owest not . . *Tempest* i 2 453

Usurp the beggary he was never born to . . *Meas. for Meas.* iii 2 99

In that kind, swears you do more usurp Than doth your brother *As Y. Like It* ii 1 27

I know the boy will well usurp the grace, Voice, gait, and action of a gentlewoman . . . . *T. of Shrew* Ind. 1 131

Are you the lady of the house?—If I do not usurp myself, I am *T. Night* i 5 198

If you are she, you do usurp yourself; for what is yours to bestow is not yours to reserve . . . . i 5 200

Usurp. Thou dost usurp authority.—Excuse; it is to beat usurping down *K. John* ii 1 118
Call not me slanderer; thou and thine usurp The dominations . ii 1 175
No hand of blood and bone Can gripe the sacred handle of our sceptre, Unless he do profane, steal, or usurp. *Richard II.* iii 3 81
Would he not fall down, Since pride must have a fall, and break the neck Of that proud man that did usurp his back? . v 5 89
Doth but usurp the sacred name of knight *1 Hen. VI.* iv 1 40
Nor shall proud Lancaster usurp my right, Nor hold the sceptre in his childish fist . *2 Hen. VI.* i 1 244
In that throne Which now the house of Lancaster usurps *3 Hen. VI.* i 1 23
Henry had none, but did usurp the place . i 2 25
To whom do lions cast their gentle looks? Not to the beast that would usurp their den . ii 2 12
Proud ambitious Edward Duke of York Usurps the regal title . iii 3 28
And why not queen?—Because thy father Henry did usurp . iii 3 79
'Tis my right, And Henry but usurps the diadem . iv 7 66
The sorrow that I have, by right is yours, And all the pleasures you usurp are mine . *Richard III.* i 3 173
Thou didst usurp my place, and dost thou not Usurp the just proportion of my sorrow? . iv 4 109
This sorrow is an enemy, And would usurp upon my watery eyes *T. An.* iii 1 269
On wholesome life usurp immediately *Hamlet* iii 2 271
To thee a woman's services are due: My fool usurps my body *Lear* iv 2 28
Death may usurp on nature many hours, And yet the fire of life kindle again The o'erpress'd spirits . *Pericles* iii 2 82
Usurpation. To rebuke the usurpation Of thy unnatural uncle *K. John* ii 1 9
So looks the strand whereon the imperious flood Hath left a witness'd usurpation . *2 Hen. IV.* i 1 63
The Percies of the north, Finding his usurpation most unjust *1 Hen. VI.* ii 5 68
Usurped. If nothing lets to make us happy both But this my masculine usurp'd attire . *T. Night* v 1 257
All reverence set apart To him and his usurp'd authority *K. John* iii 1 160
No, not that name was given me at the font, But 'tis usurp'd *Rich. II.* iv 1 257
Another way To pluck him headlong from the usurped throne . v 1 65
Hugh Capet also, who usurp'd the crown Of Charles *Hen. V.* i 2 69
Their crooked titles Usurp'd from you and your progenitors . i 2 95
His state usurp'd, His realm a slaughter-house, his subjects slain, His statutes cancell'd . *3 Hen. VI.* v 4 77
Had I not reason, think ye, to make haste, And seek their ruin that usurp'd our right? . v 6 73
Woe's scene, world's shame, grave's due by life usurp'd! *Richard III.* iv 4 27
Now, by my George, my garter, and my crown,— Profaned, dishonour'd, and the third usurp'd . iv 4 367
The crown, usurp'd, disgraced his kingly glory . iv 4 371
The wonder is, he hath endured so long: He but usurp'd his life *Lear* v 3 317
Defeat thy favour with an usurped beard . *Othello* i 3 346
Usurper. Swearing that we Are mere usurpers, tyrants . *As Y. Like It* ii 1 61
Who is it thou dost call usurper, France? . *K. John* ii 1 120
Lewis the Tenth, Who was sole heir to the usurper Capet *Hen. V.* i 2 78
And that your majesty was an usurper . *2 Hen. VI.* i 3 188
Calls your grace usurper openly And vows to crown himself . iv 4 30
Father, tear the crown from the usurper's head . *3 Hen. VI.* i 1 114
Though usurpers sway the rule awhile, Yet heavens are just . iii 3 76
I would have play'd The part my father meant to act upon The usurper Richard . *Hen. VIII.* i 2 196
Behold, where stands The usurper's cursed head . *Macbeth* v 8 55
Usurpest. Accept the title thou usurp'st . *1 Hen. VI.* v 4 151
Thou usurp'st my father's right and mine . *3 Hen. VI.* v 5 37
What art thou that usurp'st this time of night? *Hamlet* i 1 46
Usurping. It is dross, Usurping ivy, brier, or idle moss . *Com. of Errors* ii 2 180
It mourns that painting and usurping hair Should ravish doters *L. L. L.* iv 3 259
Detain'd by her usurping uncle, To keep his daughter company *As Y. L. It* i 2 286
His heels have deserved it, in usurping his spurs so long *All's Well* iv 3 119
Thou dost usurp authority.—Excuse; it is to beat usurping down *K. John* ii 1 119
Who is it thou dost call usurper, France?—Let me make answer; thy usurping son . ii 1 121
That strumpet Fortune, that usurping John! . iii 1 61
The treacherous feet Which with usurping steps do trample thee *Rich. II.* iii 2 17
Thou most usurping proditor, And not protector . *1 Hen. VI.* i 3 31
Thou art a traitor to the crown In following this usurping Henry *3 Hen. VI.* i 1 81
And over the chair of state, where now he sits Write up his title with usurping blood . i 1 169
We set the axe to thy usurping root . ii 2 165
The wretched, bloody, and usurping boar *Richard III.* v 2 7
Crush down with a heavy fall The usurping helmets of our adversaries! v 3 112
Buckingham, Who first raised head against usurping Richard *Hen. VIII.* ii 1 108
Usurpingly. Desiring thee to lay aside the sword Which sways usurpingly these several titles *K. John* i 1 13
Usury. 'Twas never merry world since, of two usuries, the merriest was put down . *Meas. for Meas.* iii 2 7
Make edicts for usury, to support usurers *Coriolanus* i 1 84
Banish your dotage; banish usury, That makes the senate ugly *T. of A.* iii 5 99
Did you but know the city's usuries And felt them knowingly *Cymb.* iii 3 45
Ut, re, sol, la, mi, fa . *L. L. Lost* iv 2 102
Take him for thy lord, 'C fa ut,' that loves with all affection *T. of Shrew* iii 1 76
Utensil. He has brave utensils,—for so he calls them,—Which, when he has a house, he'll deck withal . *Tempest* iii 2 104
Every particle and utensil labelled to my will . *T. Night* i 5 264
Utility. Losing both beauty and utility . *Hen. V.* v 2 53
Utis. By the mass, here will be old Utis . *2 Hen. IV.* ii 4 22
Utmost. Let him be prepared; For that's the utmost of his pilgrimage *Meas. for Meas.* ii 1 36
Here's the note How much your chain weighs to the utmost carat *Com. of Errors* iv 1 28
I know them, yea, And what they weigh, even to the utmost scruple *Much Ado* v 1 93
Even to the utmost syllable of your worthiness . *All's Well* iii 6 74
Even till that utmost corner of the west Salute thee for her king *K. John* ii 1 29
Use our commission in his utmost force . iii 3 11
The very list, the very utmost bound Of all our fortunes *1 Hen. IV.* iv 1 51
That we now possess'd The utmost man of expectation . *2 Hen. IV.* i 3 65
Six or seven thousand is their utmost power . *Richard III.* v 3 10
We are ready To use our utmost studies in your service . *Hen. VIII.* iii 1 174
More out of malice than integrity, Would try him to the utmost . v 3 146
The general's fault, though he perform To the utmost of a man *Coriolanus* i 1 272
Where he shall answer, by a lawful form, In peace, to his utmost peril . iii 1 326
Back,—that's the utmost of your having . v 2 61

Utmost. We have tried the utmost of our friends . *J. Cæsar* iv 3 214
Given to captivity me and my utmost hopes . *Othello* ii 2 51
Here is my butt, And very sea-mark of my utmost sail . v 2 268
I will use My utmost skill in his recovery . *Pericles* v 1 76
Utter. His backward voice is to utter foul speeches . *Tempest* ii 2 95
My duty pricks me on to utter that Which else no worldly good should draw from me . *T. G. of Ver.* iii 1 8
There my father's grave Did utter forth a voice *Meas. for Meas.* iii 1 87
The vile conclusion I now begin with grief and shame to utter . v 1 96
I'll utter what my sorrow gives me leave . *Com. of Errors* i 1 36
I will, like a true drunkard, utter all to thee . *Much Ado* iii 3 112
I charge you, on your souls, to utter it . iv 1 14
There is not chastity enough in language Without offence to utter them iv 1 99
This fellow pecks up wit as pigeons pease, And utters it again *L. L. Lost* v 2 316
I implore so much expense of thy royal sweet breath as will utter a brace of words . v 2 524
Eat no onions nor garlic, for we are to utter sweet breath *M. N. Dream* iv 2 44
I never heard a passion so confused, So strange, outrageous, and so variable, As the dog Jew did utter . *Mer. of Venice* ii 8 14
Am I or that or this for what he'll utter, That will speak any thing? *All's Well* v 3 208
That cons state without book and utters it by great swarths . *T. Night* ii 3 161
Then didst thou utter 'I am yours for ever' . *W. Tale* i 2 104
Mark my counsel, Which must be even as swiftly follow'd as I mean to utter it . i 2 410
He utters them as he had eaten ballads and all men's ears grew to his tunes . iv 4 185
Money's a medler, That doth utter all men's ware-a . iv 4 330
Lady, you utter madness, and not sorrow . *K. John* iii 4 43
I well believe Thou wilt not utter what thou dost not know . *1 Hen. IV.* ii 3 114
You stock-fish! O for breath to utter what is like thee! . ii 4 272
But for the light in thy face, the son of utter darkness . iii 3 42
There's but two ways, either to utter them, or to conceal them *2 Hen. IV.* v 3 116
Utter more to me; and withal devise something to do thyself good . v 3 139
I foresee with grief The utter loss of all the realm of France *1 Hen. VI.* v 4 112
Had I sufficient skill to utter them, Would make a volume of enticing lines . v 5 13
To thy foul disgrace And utter ruin of the house of York . *3 Hen. VI.* i 1 254
These very words I've heard him utter to his son-in-law . *Hen. VIII.* i 2 136
That what he spoke My chaplain to no creature living, but To me, should utter . i 2 167
And the words I utter Let none think flattery, for they'll find 'em truth v 5 16
Lo, lo, lo, lo, what modicums of wit he utters! . *Troi. and Cres.* ii 1 75
What I think I utter, and spend my malice in my breath *Coriolanus* ii 1 58
Let them not speak to me; But let them hear what fearful words I utter *T. Andron.* v 2 169
That my tongue may utter forth The venomous malice of my swelling heart! . v 3 12
Nor can I utter all our bitter grief, But floods of tears will drown my oratory . v 3 89
Utter your gravity o'er a gossip's bowl; For here we need it not *Rom. and Jul.* iii 5 175
Such mortal drugs I have; but Mantua's law Is death to any he that utters them . v 1 67
Know you how much the people may be moved By that which he will utter? . *J. Cæsar* iii 1 235
This must be known; which, being kept close, might move More grief to hide than hate to utter love *Hamlet* ii 1 119
Utter my thoughts? Why, say they are vile and false? . *Othello* iii 3 136
Such full license as both truth and malice Have power to utter *Ant. and Cleo.* i 2 113
Whose virtue and whose general graces speak That which none else can utter . ii 2 133
I am glad to be constrain'd to utter that Which torments me to conceal *Cymbeline* v 5 141
Utterance. As mine honesty puts it to utterance . *W. Tale* i 1 22
Hubert, the utterance of a brace of tongues Must needs want pleading for a pair of eyes . *K. John* iv 1 98
With all the gracious utterance thou hast Speak to his gentle hearing *Richard II.* iii 3 125
But he has a merit, To choke it in the utterance . *Coriolanus* iv 7 49
Floods of tears will drown my oratory, And break my utterance *T. Andron.* v 3 91
My ears have not yet drunk a hundred words Of that tongue's utterance, yet I know the sound . *Rom. and Jul.* ii 2 59
To beg the voice and utterance of my tongue . *J. Cæsar* iii 1 261
Action, nor utterance, nor the power of speech, To stir men's blood . iii 2 226
Come fate into the list, And champion me to the utterance! . *Macbeth* iii 1 72
These cannot I command to any utterance of harmony *Hamlet* iii 2 378
Which he to seek of me again, perforce, Behoves me keep at utterance *Cymbeline* iii 1 73
Uttered. If this were so, so were it uttered . *Much Ado* i 1 217
I have drunk poison whiles he utter'd it . v 1 253
Graves, yawn and yield your dead, Till death be uttered, Heavily, heavily . v 3 20
Beauty is bought by judgement of the eye, Not utter'd by base sale of chapmen's tongues . *L. L. Lost* ii 1 16
By the honour of my parents, I Have utter'd truth . *W. Tale* i 2 443
My heart hath one poor string to stay it by, Which holds but till thy news be uttered . *K. John* v 7 56
More is to be said and to be done Than out of anger can be uttered *1 Hen. IV.* i 1 107
I'll assure you, a' uttered as prave words at the pridge as you shall see in a summer's day . *Hen. V.* iii 6 66
These were her words, utter'd with mild disdain *3 Hen. VI.* iv 1 98
My conscience first received a tenderness, Scruple, and prick, on certain speeches utter'd . *Hen. VIII.* ii 4 171
I shall lack voice: the deeds of Coriolanus Should not be utter'd feebly *Coriolanus* ii 2 87
If you had told as many lies in his behalf as you have uttered words in your own, you should not pass here . v 2 25
All this uttered With gentle breath, calm look, knees humbly bow'd *Rom. and Jul.* iii 1 160
And uttered such a deal of stinking breath . *J. Cæsar* i 2 247
It is not madness That I have utter'd: bring me to the test . *Hamlet* iii 4 142
I know his heart. What he hath utter'd I have writ my sister . *Lear* i 4 354
Uttereth. I'll commend her volubility, And say she uttereth piercing eloquence . *T. of Shrew* ii 1 177
Uttering such dulcet and harmonious breath . *M. N. Dream* ii 1 151
Utterly. The knight is here.—Why then you are utterly shamed *M. W.* iv 2 43

Utterly. That he is, saving your reverence, a whoremaster, that I utterly deny . . . . 1 *Hen. IV.* ii 4 516
My lungs are wasted so That strength of speech is utterly denied me 2 *Hen. IV.* iv 5 218
Either to quell the Dauphin utterly, Or bring him in obedience 1 *Hen. VI.* i 1 163
All your interest in those territories Is utterly bereft you 2 *Hen. VI.* iii 1 85
I say again, I utterly abhor, yea, from my soul Refuse you *Hen. VIII.* ii 4 81
You may hurt yourself, ay, utterly Grow from the king's acquaintance iii 1 160
Now Antony must leave her utterly.—Never ; he will not *Ant. and Cleo.* ii 2 238
No light, no fire : the unfriendly elements Forgot thee utterly *Pericles* iii 1 59

Uttermost. Out of doubt you do me now more wrong In making question of my uttermost . . . . *Mer. of Venice* i 1 156
That shall be rack'd, even to the uttermost, To furnish thee . . . i 1 181
I will be free Even to the uttermost, as I please, in words *T. of Shrew* iv 3 80
A man that I love and honour with my soul, . . . and my uttermost power . . . . *Hen. V.* iii 6 9
So be it ; either to the uttermost, Or else a breath . *Troi. and Cres.* iv 5 91
By the eighth hour : is that the uttermost?—Be that the uttermost *J. Cæsar* ii 1 213
I'll move your suit And seek to effect it to my uttermost . *Othello* iii 4 167

V

Vacancy. No interim, not a minute's vacancy, Both day and night did we keep company . . . . *T. Night* v 1 98
How is't with you, That you do bend your eye on vacancy? . *Hamlet* iii 4 117
If he fill'd His vacancy with his voluptuousness . *Ant. and Cleo.* i 4 26
The air ; which, but for vacancy, Had gone to gaze on Cleopatra too . ii 2 221
Vacant. War-thoughts Have left their places vacant, in their rooms Come thronging soft and delicate desires . . *Much Ado* i 1 304
Repeats his words, Remembers me of all his gracious parts, Stuffs out his vacant garments with his form . *K. John* iii 4 97
Who with a body fill'd and vacant mind Gets him to rest . *Hen. V.* iv 1 286
My person ; which I weigh not, Being of those virtues vacant *Hen. VIII.* v 1 125
Special dignities, which vacant lie For thy best use . *T. of Athens* v 1 145
Vacation. Who stays it [Time] still withal?—With lawyers in the vacation *As Y. Like It* iii 2 349
Vagabond. You are a vagabond and no true traveller . *All's Well* ii 3 277
That I shall stand condemn'd A wandering vagabond . *Richard II.* ii 3 120
A sort of vagabonds, rascals, and runaways, A scum of Bretons *Rich. III.* v 3 316
Let them pronounce the steep Tarpeian death, Vagabond exile *Coriolanus* iii 3 89
Like to a vagabond flag upon the stream, Goes to and back *Ant. and Cleo.* i 4 45
Vagrom. You shall comprehend all vagrom men *Much Ado* iii 3 26
Vail your regard Upon a wrong'd, I would fain have said, a maid! *M. for M.* v 1 20
Then vail your stomachs, for it is no boot, And place your hands below your husband's foot . . . . . *T. of Shrew* v 2 176
'Gan vail his stomach and did grace the shame Of those that turn'd their backs . . . . 2 *Hen. IV.* i 1 129
The time is come That France must vail her lofty-plumed crest 1 *Hen. VI.* v 3 25
Even with the vail and darking of the sun, To close the day up *T. and C.* v 8 7
If he have power, Then vail your ignorance *Coriolanus* iii 1 98
There are certain condolements, certain vails . . . *Pericles* ii 1 157
Like lesser lights, Did vail their crowns to his supremacy . ii 3 42
Or when She would with rich and constant pen Vail to her mistress Dian . . . . iv Gower 29
Vailed. Do not for ever with thy vailed lids Seek for thy noble father in the dust . . . . *Hamlet* i 2 70
Vailing. Are angels vailing clouds, or roses blown . *L. L. Lost* v 2 297
Vailing her high-top lower than her ribs To kiss her burial *Mer. of Venice* i 1 28
Vaillant. Le plus brave, vaillant, et très distingué seigneur . *Hen. V.* iv 4 60
Vain. But in vain ; Mars's hot minion is return'd again . *Tempest* iv 1 97
Be gone! I will not hear thy vain excuse . *T. G. of Ver.* iii 1 168
My father would enforce me marry Vain Thurio . . iv 3 17
As school-maids change their names By vain though apt affection *Meas. for Meas.* i 4 48
Change for an idle plume, Which the air beats for vain . ii 4 12
I will open my lips in vain, or discover his government . iii 1 199
Seals of love, but seal'd in vain, seal'd in vain . . iv 1 6
'Tis holy sport to be a little vain, When the sweet breath of flattery conquers strife . . . . . *Com. of Errors* iii 2 27
There's no man is so vain That would refuse so fair an offer'd chain iii 2 185
These be the stops that hinder study quite And train our intellects to vain delight . . . . *L. L. Lost* i 1 71
All delights are vain ; but that most vain, Which with pain purchased doth inherit pain . . . . i 1 72
This article is made in vain, Or vainly comes the admired princess hither . . . . i 1 140
One whom the music of his own vain tongue Doth ravish . . i 1 167
It would ill become me to be vain, indiscreet, or a fool . . iv 2 31
His eye ambitious, his gait majestical, and his general behaviour vain . v 1 13
O vain petitioner! beg a greater matter . . . . v 2 207
Exceeding fantastical ; too too vain, too too vain . . v 2 532
Love is full of unbefitting strains, All wanton as a child, skipping and vain . . . . v 2 771
The winds, piping to us in vain, As in revenge . . *M. N. Dream* ii 1 88
The ox hath therefore stretch'd his yoke in vain . . ii 1 93
I know I love in vain, strive against hope . . *All's Well* i 3 207
Yet she writes, Pursuit would be but vain . . . iii 4 25
Brings in the champion Honour on my part, Against your vain assault iv 2 51
Endeavour thyself to sleep, and leave thy vain bibble babble . *T. Night* iv 2 105
The want of which vain dew Perchance shall dry your pities . *W. Tale* ii 1 109
I saw her, As I thought, dead, and have in vain said many A prayer upon her grave . . . . v 3 140
Thy word Is but the vain breath of a common man . *K. John* iii 1 8
All in vain comes counsel to his ear . *Richard II.* ii 1 4
Where words are scarce, they are seldom spent in vain . . ii 1 7
If heart's presages be not vain, We three here part that ne'er shall meet again . . . . iii 2 142
Infusing him with self and vain conceit . . . iii 2 166
Let no man speak again To alter this, for counsel is but vain . iii 2 214
These vain weak nails May tear a passage through the flinty ribs Of this hard world . . . . v 5 19
Weep not, sweet queen ; for trickling tears are vain . 1 *Hen. IV.* ii 4 431
And stand the push Of every beardless vain comparative . iii 2 67
But he did long in vain . . . . 2 *Hen. IV.* ii 3 14
If any rebel or vain spirit of mine Did . . . Give entertainment . iv 5 172
My lord chief-justice, speak to that vain man . . v 5 48
His addiction was to courses vain, His companies unletter'd . *Hen. V.* i 1 54
Borne By a vain, giddy, shallow, humorous youth . . ii 4 28
We may as bootless spend our vain command Upon the enraged soldiers iii 3 24

Vain. Use no entreaty, for it is in vain.—Then lead me hence 1 *Hen. VI.* v 4 85
I am not able to stand alone : You go about to torture me in vain 2 *Hen. VI.* ii 1 146
But all in vain are these mean obsequies . . . iii 2 146
Against the senseless winds shalt grin in vain . . . iv 1 77
Whose dreadful swords were never drawn in vain . . iv 1 92
Your oath, my lord, is vain and frivolous. Therefore, to arms! 3 *Hen. VI.* i 2 27
Let me live.—In vain thou speak'st, poor boy . . . i 3 21
But all in vain ; they had no heart to fight . . . ii 1 135
Poor painted queen, vain flourish of my fortune! . *Richard III.* i 3 241
I call'd thee then vain flourish of my fortune . . iv 4 82
He was brought to this By a vain prophecy . . *Hen. VIII.* i 2 147
Vain pomp and glory of this world, I hate ye : I feel my heart new open'd . . . . iii 2 365
All hope is vain, Unless his noble mother, and his wife ; Who, as I hear, mean to solicit him For mercy to his country . . *Coriolanus* v 1 70
Lose not so noble a friend on vain suppose . *T. Andron.* i 1 440
Make them know what 'tis to let a queen Kneel in the streets and beg for grace in vain . . . . i 1 455
Remember, boys, I pour'd forth tears in vain, To save your brother . ii 3 163
You lament in vain : The tribunes hear you not ; no man is by . iii 1 27
I'll chop off my hands too ; For they have fought for Rome, and all in vain . . . . iii 1 73
For hands, to do Rome service, are but vain . . . iii 1 80
In delay We waste our lights in vain, like lamps by day *Rom. and Jul.* i 4 45
The children of an idle brain, Begot of nothing but vain fantasy . i 4 98
'Tis in vain To seek him here that means not to be found . ii 1 41
Forbid him her resort ; Myself have spoke in vain . . *T. of Athens* i 1 128
You breathe in vain.—In vain! . . . . . iii 5 59
It is in vain that you would speak with Timon . . . v 1 119
Stay not, all's in vain.—Why, I was writing of my epitaph . . v 1 187
We speak in vain.—But yet I love my country . . . v 1 193
It is, as the air, invulnerable, And our vain blows malicious mockery *Hamlet* i 1 146
Now, by Apollo, king, Thou swear'st thy gods in vain . . *Lear* i 1 163
O vain fool!—Thou changed and self-cover'd thing, for shame . iv 2 61
He knows not what he says : and vain it is That we present us to him . v 3 293
Not with vain thanks, but with acceptance bounteous . . *Othello* iii 3 470
But, O vain boast! Who can control his fate? 'tis not so now . v 2 264
Hail, royal sir!—It is in vain ; he will not speak to you . *Pericles* v 1 41
Vainer. More time For vainer hours and tutors not so careful *Tempest* i 2 174
Vain-glory. A woman, I dare say without vain-glory *Hen. VIII.* iii 1 127
For if Hector break not his neck i' the combat, he'll break't himself in vain-glory . . . . *Troi. and Cres.* iii 3 260
What need these feasts, pomps, and vain-glories? . . *T. of Athens* i 2 249
I dare speak it to myself—for it is not vain-glory for a man and his glass to confer in his own chamber . . . *Cymbeline* iv 1 8
Vainly comes the admired princess hither . . . *L. L. Lost* i 1 141
Having vainly fear'd too little . . . . . *All's Well* v 3 123
Our cannons' malice vainly shall be spent Against the invulnerable clouds of heaven . . . . *K. John* ii 1 251
Jerusalem ; Which vainly I supposed the Holy Land . 2 *Hen. IV.* iv 5 239
But benefit no further Than vainly longing . . *Hen. VIII.* i 2 81
That vainly lends his light To grubs and eyeless skulls *Rom. and Jul.* v 3 125
And breathed Our sufferance vainly . . . *T. of Athens* v 4 8
Vainness. I hate ingratitude more in a man Than lying, vainness, babbling, drunkenness . . . . *T. Night* iii 4 389
Being free from vainness and self-glorious pride . . *Hen. V.* v Prol. 20
Vais. Je m'en vais à la cour—la grande affaire . . *Mer. Wives* i 4 54
Valance of Venice gold in needlework . . . . *T. of Shrew* ii 1 356
Valanced. Thy face is valanced since I saw thee last . *Hamlet* ii 2 442
Valdes. These roguing thieves serve the great pirate Valdes . *Pericles* iv 1 97
Vale. This way to the melancholy vale, The place of death *Com. of Errors* v 1 120
Great is his comfort in this earthly vale . . . 2 *Hen. VI.* ii 1 70
Those two lights of men Met in the vale of Andren . . *Hen. VIII.* i 1 7
The eastern tower, Whose height commands as subject all the vale *Troi. and Cres.* i 2 3
A barren detested vale, you see it is . . . . *T. Andron.* ii 3 93
Not a hollow cave or lurking-place, No vast obscurity or misty vale . v 2 36
I am declined Into the vale of years . . . . *Othello* iii 3 266
To the vales, And hold our best advantage . . *Ant. and Cleo.* iv 11 3
As the rudest wind, That by the top doth take the mountain pine, And make him stoop to the vale . . . . . . *Cymbeline* iv 2 176
Valence. Great Earl of Washford, Waterford, and Valence 1 *Hen. VI.* iv 7 63
Valentine. Sweet Valentine, adieu! Think on thy Proteus *T. G. of Ver.* i 1 11
Commend thy grievance to my holy prayers, For I will be thy beadsman, Valentine . . . . i 1 18
And thither will I bring thee, Valentine.—Sweet Proteus, no . i 1 55
His companion, youthful Valentine, Attends the emperor in his royal court . . . . i 3 26
'Tis a word or two Of commendations sent from Valentine . . i 3 53
Here's a million of manners.—Sir Valentine and servant, to you two thousand . . . . ii 1 106
For Valentine, I need not cite him to it : I will send him hither to you ii 4 85
Is it mine, or Valentine's praise? . . . . . ii 4 196
Methinks my zeal to Valentine is cold, And that I love him not as I was wont . . . . ii 4 203

Valentine. Julia I lose and Valentine I lose: If I keep them, I needs must lose myself; If I lose them, thus find I by their loss For Valentine myself, for Julia Silvia . . . *T. G. of Ver.* ii 6 19
Valentine I'll hold an enemy, Aiming at Silvia as a sweeter friend . ii 6 29
I cannot now prove constant to myself, Without some treachery used to Valentine . . . . ii 6 32
I'll give her father notice . . .; Who, all enraged, will banish Valentine ii 6 38
But, Valentine being gone, I'll quickly cross By some sly trick blunt Thurio's dull proceeding . . . . ii 6 40
Sir Valentine, my friend, This night intends to steal away your daughter iii 1 10
And oftentimes have purposed to forbid Sir Valentine her company . iii 1 27
Sir Valentine is coming.—Sir Valentine, whither away so fast? . iii 1 50
There's not a hair on's head but 'tis a Valentine.—Valentine?—No . iii 1 192
Friend Valentine, a word.—My ears are stopt and cannot hear good news . . . . iii 1 204
Is Silvia dead?—No, Valentine.—No Valentine, indeed, for sacred Silvia iii 1 210
Hath she forsworn me?—No, Valentine.—No Valentine, if Silvia have forsworn me . . . . iii 1 213
But Valentine, if he be ta'en, must die . . . . . iii 1 232
Come, Valentine.—O my dear Silvia! Hapless Valentine! . . iii 1 259
Fear not but that she will love you, Now Valentine is banish'd . iii 2 2
She opposes her against my will.—She did, my lord, when Valentine was here . . . . iii 2 27
What might we do to make the girl forget The love of Valentine and love Sir Thurio?—The best way is to slander Valentine . . . . iii 2 30
Weed her love from Valentine, It follows not that she will love Sir Thurio . . . . iii 2 49
By praising me as much As you in worth dispraise Sir Valentine . . iii 2 55
On Valentine's report, You are already Love's firm votary . . . iii 2 57
Temper her by your persuasion To hate young Valentine and love my friend . . . . iii 2 65
Already have I been false to Valentine And now I must be as unjust to Thurio . . . . iv 2 1
Valentine thy friend Survives; to whom, thyself art witness, I am betroth'd . . . . iv 2 109
I likewise hear that Valentine is dead.—And so suppose am I . iv 2 113
Thou art not ignorant what dear good will I bear unto the banish'd Valentine . . . . iv 3 15
I would to Valentine, To Mantua, where I hear he makes abode . . iv 3 22
Why then, She's fled unto that peasant Valentine . . . . . v 2 35
O Valentine, this I endure for thee! . . . . v 3 15
Withdraw thee, Valentine: who's this comes here? . . . . . v 4 18
O, Heaven be judge how I love Valentine! . . . . . . v 4 36
Let go that rude uncivil touch, Thou friend of an ill fashion!—Valentine! v 4 61
My shame and guilt confounds me. Forgive me, Valentine . . . v 4 74
Your grace is welcome to a man disgraced, Banished Valentine . . v 4 124
I do applaud thy spirit, Valentine, And think thee worthy of an empress' love . . . . v 4 140
Sir Valentine, Thou art a gentleman and well derived; Take thou thy Silvia . . . . v 4 145
Saint Valentine is past: Begin these wood-birds but to couple now? *M. N. Dream* iv 1 144
Publius, come hither, Caius, and Valentine! . . . . *T. Andron.* v 2 151
Mercutio and his brother Valentine . . . . *Rom. and Jul.* i 2 70
To-morrow is Saint Valentine's day, All in the morning betime, And I a maid at your window, To be your Valentine . . . *Hamlet* iv 5 48

Valentinus. Thou shalt spend some time With Valentinus *T. G. of Ver.* i 3 67
Give the like notice To Valentinus, Rowland, and to Crassus *M. for M.* iv 5 8

Valentio. Signior Valentio and his cousin Tybalt . . *Rom. and Jul.* i 2 72

Valeria. Madam, the Lady Valeria is come to visit you . . *Coriolanus* i 3 29
Tell Valeria, We are fit to bid her welcome . . . . . . i 3 46
The noble sister of Publicola, . . . dear Valeria! . . . . . v 3 67

Valerius. He hath outrun us, But Moyses and Valerius follow him *T. G. of Ver.* v 3 8

Valiant. Let me lick thy shoe. I'll not serve him; he is not valiant *Temp.* iii 2 27
I would my valiant master would destroy thee! . . . . . iii 2 53
Valiant, wise, remorseful, well accomplish'd . . . *T. G. of Ver.* iv 3 13
The valiant heart's not whipt out of his trade . . *Meas. for Meas.* ii 1 270
Thou'rt by no means valiant; For thou dost fear the soft and tender fork Of a poor worm . . . . iii 1 15
He is a very valiant trencher-man; he hath an excellent stomach *M. Ado* i 1 51
Would it not grieve a woman to be overmastered with a piece of valiant dust? . . . . ii 1 64
I take him to be valiant.—As Hector, I assure you . . . . ii 3 195
He is now as valiant as Hercules that only tells a lie and swears it . iv 1 324
This aspect of mine Hath fear'd the valiant . . *Mer. of Venice* ii 1 9
And wherefore are you gentle, strong, and valiant? . *As Y. Like It* ii 3 6
He would answer, I spake not true: this is called the Reproof Valiant v 4 83
The fourth, the Reproof Valiant; the fifth, the Countercheck Quarrelsome . . . . v 4 99
Our virginity, though valiant, in the defence yet is weak . *All's Well* i 1 127
And of very valiant approof.—You have it from his own deliverance . ii 5 3
He is very great in knowledge and accordingly valiant . . . . ii 5 9
I know thou'rt valiant; and, to the possibility of thy soldiership, will subscribe for thee. . . . . iii 6 88
In voices well divulged, free, learn'd, and valiant . . . *T. Night* i 5 279
Whatsoever thou art, thou art but a scurvy fellow.—Good, and valiant iii 4 164
An I thought he had been valiant and so cunning in fence . . iii 4 312
Thou coward! Thou little valiant, great in villany! . . *K. John* iii 1 116
Your valiant kinsman, Faulconbridge, Desires your majesty to leave the field . . . . v 3 5
Rouse up thy youthful blood, be valiant and live . . . *Richard II.* i 3 83
The hollow bank Bloodstained with these valiant combatants *1 Hen. IV.* i 3 107
Darest thou be so valiant as to play the coward with thy indenture? . ii 4 52
Thou knowest I am as valiant as Hercules . . . . . . ii 4 299
I for a valiant lion, and thou for a true prince . . . . . ii 4 303
Valiant Jack Falstaff, and therefore more valiant, being, as he is, old . ii 4 523
Valiant as a lion And wondrous affable and as bountiful As mines of India iii 1 167
My name is Harry Percy.—Why, then I see A very valiant rebel of the name . . . . v 4 62
And speaking thick, which nature made his blemish, Became the accents of the valiant . . . . *2 Hen. IV.* ii 3 25
Ah, you whoreson little valiant villain, you! . . . . . . ii 4 225
Valiant as the wrathful dove or most magnanimous mouse . . . iii 2 170
Was reputed then In England the most valiant gentleman . . . iv 1 132
Hereof [of sherris] comes it that Prince Harry is valiant . . . iv 3 127
Of drinking . . . fertile sherris, that he is become very hot and valiant iv 3 132
Awake remembrance of these valiant dead . . . . *Hen. V.* i 2 115
An Irishman, a very valiant gentleman, i' faith . . . . . iii 2 71
Can sodden water . . . Decoct their cold blood to such valiant heat? . iii 5 20

Valiant. In my very conscience he is as valiant a man as Mark Antony *Hen. V.* iii 6 15
I know him to be valiant.—I was told that by one that knows him . iii 7 112
A valiant and most expert gentleman . . . . iii 7 139
That island of England breeds very valiant creatures . . . . iii 7 151
That's a valiant flea that dare eat his breakfast on the lip of a lion . iii 7 156
A lad of life, an imp of fame; Of parents good, of fist most valiant . iv 1 46
Those that leave their valiant bones in France, Dying like men . iv 3 98
I do know Fluellen valiant And, touch'd with choler, hot as gunpowder iv 7 187
Where valiant Talbot above human thought Enacted wonders *1 Hen. VI.* i 1 121
I gird thee with the valiant sword of York . . . . i 1 171
Becomes it thee to taunt his valiant age? . . . . . . iii 2 54
Regard this dying prince, The valiant Duke of Bedford . . . . iii 2 87
Rouen hangs her head for grief That such a valiant company are fled . iii 2 125
Of noble birth, Valiant and virtuous, full of haughty courage . . iv 1 35
A breathing valiant man, Of an invincible unconquer'd spirit! . . iv 2 31
So should we save a valiant gentleman By forfeiting a traitor . . iv 3 26
O, where's young Talbot? where is valiant John? . . . . . iv 7 2
The great Alcides of the field, Valiant Lord Talbot, Earl of Shrewsbury iv 7 61
Success unto our valiant general, And happiness to his accomplices! . v 2 8
Her valiant courage and undaunted spirit, More than in women commonly v 5 70
But wherefore weeps Warwick, my valiant son? . . . *2 Hen. VI.* i 1 115
Valiant I am.—A' must needs; for beggary is valiant . . . . iv 2 57
The people liberal, valiant, active, wealthy . . . . . . iv 7 68
Buckle with thee blows, twice two for one.—Hold, valiant Clifford! *3 Hen. VI.* i 4 51
Where's that valiant crook-back prodigy, Dicky your boy? . . . . i 4 75
The blood That valiant Clifford, with his rapier's point, Made issue . i 4 80
I cannot joy, until I be resolved Where our right valiant father is become . . . . ii 1 10
His name that valiant duke hath left with thee . . . . . . ii 1 89
O valiant lord, the Duke of York is slain! . . . . . . ii 1 100
'Twas odds, belike, when valiant Warwick fled . . . . . ii 1 148
King Edward, valiant Richard, Montague, Stay we no longer . . ii 1 198
As Priam was for all his valiant sons . . . . ii 5 120
Where is the post that came from valiant Oxford? . . . . . v 1 1
Commend me to my valiant brother . . . . v 2 42
Methinks a woman of this valiant spirit Should . . . Infuse his breast v 4 39
In God's name, lords, Be valiant and give signal to the fight . . v 4 82
What valiant foemen, like to autumn's corn, Have we mow'd down! . v 7 3
Framed in the prodigality of nature, Young, valiant, wise *Richard III.* i 2 245
Sir James Blunt, And Rice ap Thomas, with a valiant crew . . iv 5 12
Valiant gentlemen, Let us survey the vantage of the field . . . v 3 14
Once more, adieu: be valiant, and speed well! . . . . . v 3 102
Fierce to their skill and to their fierceness valiant . *Troi. and Cres.* i 1 8
Less valiant than the virgin in the night . . . . i 1 11
He is as valiant as the lion, churlish as the bear, slow as the elephant . i 2 21
So to be valiant is no praise at all . . . . ii 2 145
She is . . . A spur to valiant and magnanimous deeds . . . . ii 2 200
I am yours, You valiant offspring of great Priamus . . . . ii 2 207
You are as strong, as valiant, as wise, no less noble, much more gentle ii 3 159
He is not emulous, as Achilles is.—Know the whole world, he is as valiant . . . . ii 3 243
I humbly desire the valiant Ajax to invite the most valorous Hector . iii 3 275
I had rather be a tick in a sheep than such a valiant ignorance . . iii 3 315
A valiant Greek, Æneas,—take his hand . . . . iv 1 7
Health to you, valiant sir, During all question of the gentle truce . iv 1 10
The hour prefix'd Of her delivery to this valiant Greek Comes fast upon iv 3 2
Great Achilles Doth long to see unarm'd the valiant Hector . . iv 5 153
Most gentle and most valiant Hector, welcome . . . . . iv 5 227
The present wars devour him: he is grown Too proud to be so valiant *Coriolanus* i 1 263
Titus Lartius, a most valiant Roman . . . . i 2 14
Valiant Titus, take Convenient numbers to make good the city . . i 5 12
Officious, and not valiant, you have shamed me In your condemned seconds . . . . i 8 14
And who resist Are mock'd for valiant ignorance . . . . . iv 6 104
Bearing his valiant sons In coffins from the field . . . *T. Andron.* i 1 34
Must my sons be slaughter'd in the streets, For valiant doings? . . i 1 113
Buried one and twenty valiant sons, Knighted in field . . . . i 1 195
A valiant son-in-law thou shalt enjoy . . . . i 1 311
Bear the faults of Titus' age, The effects of sorrow for his valiant sons . iv 4 30
To move is to stir; and to be valiant is to stand . . *Rom. and Jul.* i 1 11
Thus then in brief: The valiant Paris seeks you for his love . . i 3 74
He's truly valiant that can wisely suffer The worst that man can breathe, and make his wrongs His outsides . . . . *T. of Athens* iii 5 31
Why then, women are more valiant That stay at home . . . . iii 5 47
If by this crime he owes the law his life, Why, let the war receive't in valiant gore . . . . iii 5 84
Thus much of this [gold] will make black white, foul fair, Wrong right, base noble, old young, coward valiant . . . . iv 3 29
Thou valiant Mars [gold]! Thou ever young, fresh, loved, and delicate wooer! . . . . iv 3 384
The valiant never taste of death but once . . . . . *J. Cæsar* ii 2 33
Brutus is noble, wise, valiant, and honest . . . . iii 1 126
Thy master is a wise and valiant Roman; I never thought him worse . iii 1 138
Yours, Cinna; and, my valiant Casca, yours . . . . . . iii 1 188
As he was valiant, I honour him: but, as he was ambitious, I slew him iii 2 27
You may do your will; But he's a tried and valiant soldier . . . iv 1 28
O valiant cousin! worthy gentleman! . . . . . . *Macbeth* i 2 24
He is full so valiant, And in his commendations I am fed . . . i 4 54
Some say he's mad; others that lesser hate him Do call it valiant fury v 2 14
Our valiant Hamlet—For so this side of our known world esteem'd him *Hamlet* i 1 84
Lost by his father, with all bonds of law, To our most valiant brother . i 2 25
Where I could not be honest, I never yet was valiant . . . *Lear* v 1 24
Sir, you have shown to-day your valiant strain, And fortune led you well . . . . v 3 40
Your trusty and most valiant servitor . . . . *Othello* i 3 40
Valiant Othello, we must straight employ you Against the general enemy i 3 48
To his honours and his valiant parts Did I my soul and fortunes consecrate . . . . i 3 254
Thanks, you the valiant of this warlike isle! . . . . . . ii 1 43
If thou be'st valiant,—as, they say, base men being in love have then a nobility in their natures more than is native to them . . . ii 1 216
It is Othello's pleasure, our noble and valiant general . . . . ii 2 2
I am not valiant neither, But every puny whipster gets my sword . v 2 244
Say, the brave Antony.—The valiant Cæsar! . . *Ant. and Cleo.* i 5 69
Antony Is valiant, and dejected . . . . iv 12 7
Thou teachest me, O valiant Eros, what I should, and thou couldst not iv 14 96

Valiant. Do his bidding ; strike : Thou mayst be valiant in a better cause *Cymbeline* iii 4 74
'Tis all the better ; Your valiant Britons have their wishes in it . . iii 5 20
Yet famine, Ere clean it o'erthrow nature, makes it valiant . . . iii 6 20
This was my master, A very valiant Briton and a good . . . iv 2 369
No longer exercise Upon a valiant race thy harsh And potent injuries . v 4 83
Prithee, valiant youth, Deny't again.—I have spoke it, and I did it . v 5 289
Valiantly. Those mouthed wounds, which valiantly he took 1 *Hen. IV.* i 3 97
But keeps the bridge most valiantly, with excellent discipline *Hen. V.* iii 6 12
Fight valiantly to-day : And yet I do thee wrong to mind thee of it . iv 3 12
O, he smiles valiantly.—Does he not? . . *Troi. and Cres.* i 2 137
A Roman by a Roman Valiantly vanquish'd . . *Ant. and Cleo.* iv 15 58
Valiantness. Thy valiantness was mine, thou suck'dst it from me, But owe thy pride thyself . . . *Coriolanus* iii 2 129
Valiant-young. More active-valiant or more valiant-young . 1 *Hen. IV.* v 1 90
Validity. Behold this ring, Whose high respect and rich validity Did lack a parallel . . . . . *All's Well* v 3 192
Nought enters there, Of what validity and pitch soe'er . *T. Night* i 1 12
More validity, More honourable state, more courtship lives In carrion-flies than Romeo . . . . *Rom. and Jul.* iii 3 33
Purpose is but the slave to memory, Of violent birth, but poor validity *Hamlet* iii 2 199
No less in space, validity, and pleasure, Than that conferr'd on Goneril *Lear* i 1 83
Valley. Uncouple in the western valley ; let them go . *M. N. Dream* iv 1 112
Nay, the valley, The pretty dimples of his chin and cheek . *W. Tale* ii 3 100
The stars, I see, will kiss the valleys first : The odds for high and low's alike . . . . v 1 206
Rush on his host, as doth the melted snow Upon the valleys *Hen. V.* iii 5 51
This valley fits the purpose passing well . . . . *T. Andron.* ii 3 84
I'll meet you in the valleys . . . . . *Cymbeline* iii 3 78
Valorous. Thou art as valorous as Hector of Troy . 2 *Hen. IV.* ii 4 236
A most furious knight and valorous enemy . . . . . iv 3 43
The most brave, valorous, and thrice-worthy signieur of England *Hen. V.* iv 4 66
Desire the valiant Ajax to invite the most valorous Hector *Troi. and Cres.* iii 3 275
Valorously. And ay'll pay't as valorously as I may . . *Hen. V.* iii 2 125
Valour. And even with such-like valour men hang and drown Their proper selves . . . . *Tempest* iii 3 59
So full of valour that they smote the air For breathing in their faces . iv 1 172
What says she to my valour?—O, sir, she makes no doubt of that *T. G. of Ver.* v 2 19
Mock-water, in our English tongue, is valour, bully . *Mer. Wives* ii 3 63
He is of a noble strain, of approved valour, and confirmed honesty *Much Ado* ii 1 395
For shape, for bearing, argument, and valour, Goes foremost in report . iii 1 96
Manhood is melted into courtesies, valour into compliment . . . iv 1 322
In a false quarrel there is no true valour . . . . . . v 1 120
Adieu, valour ! rust, rapier ! be still, drum ! . . . *L. L. Lost* i 2 187
Most rude melancholy, valour gives thee place . . . . . iii 1 69
For valour, is not Love a Hercules, Still climbing trees in the Hesperides? iv 3 340
Bootless speed, When cowardice pursues and valour flies *M. N. Dream* ii 1 234
This lion is a very fox for his valour.—True ; and a goose for his discretion . . . . v 1 234
His valour cannot carry his discretion . . . . v 1 236
His discretion, I am sure, cannot carry his valour . . . . . v 1 240
These assume but valour's excrement To render them redoubted ! *Mer. of Venice* iii 2 87
The composition that your valour and fear makes in you is a virtue of a good wing . . . . *All's Well* i 1 217
I have then sinned against his experience, and transgressed against his valour . . . . ii 5 11
The great dignity that his valour hath here acquired for him shall at home be encountered with a shame as ample . . . . iv 3 80
You shall demand . . . what his valour, honesty, and expertness in wars iv 3 201
You have answered to his reputation with the duke and to his valour . iv 3 278
To awake Your dormouse valour, to put fire in your heart . *T. Night* iii 2 21
Redeem it by some laudable attempt either of valour or policy.—An't be any way, it must be with valour ; for policy I hate . . . iii 2 31
Why, then, build me thy fortunes upon the basis of valour . . . iii 2 36
There is no love-broker in the world can more prevail in man's commendation with woman than report of valour . . . . . . iii 2 41
Set upon Aguecheek a notable report of valour . . . . . iii 4 210
Men that put quarrels purposely on others, to taste their valour . . iii 4 267
As you are like to find him in the proof of his valour . . . iii 4 292
Whose valour plucks dead lions by the beard . . . *K. John* ii 1 138
As so defend thee heaven and thy valour ! . . . . *Richard II.* i 3 15
To prove, by God's grace and my body's valour . . . . . i 3 37
Securely I espy Virtue with valour couched in thine eye . . . i 3 98
If that thy valour stand on sympathy, There is my gage . . . iv 1 33
As full of valour as of royal blood : Both have I spill'd . . . v 5 114
There's no more valour in that Poins than in a wild-duck . 1 *Hen. IV.* ii 2 107
The better part of valour is discretion . . . . v 4 121
Let them that should reward valour bear the sin upon their own heads v 4 153
His valour shown upon our crests to-day Hath taught us how to cherish such high deeds . . . . v 5 29
True valour is turned bear-herd. . . . . . 2 *Hen. IV.* i 2 192
I never knew yet but rebuke and check was the reward of valour . . iv 3 35
Have, in my pure and immaculate valour, taken Sir John Colevile . . iv 3 41
Doth any deed of courage ; and this valour comes of sherris . . . iv 3 122
Show thy valour, and put up your sword . . . *Hen. V.* ii 1 45
A soldier, firm and sound of heart, And of buxom valour . . . iii 6 28
'Tis a hooded valour ; and when it appears, it will bate . . . . iii 7 121
There is much care and valour in this Welshman . . . . . iv 1 86
Let us but blow on them, The vapour of our valour will o'erturn them . iv 2 24
Thou art framed of the firm truth of valour . . . . . . iv 3 14
He is as full of valour as of kindness ; Princely in both . . . . iv 3 15
Mark then abounding valour in our English . . . . . . iv 3 104
Bardolph and Nym had ten times more valour than this roaring devil . iv 4 75
Worn as a memorable trophy of predeceased valour . . . . . v 1 76
Only this proof I'll of thy valour make . . . . . 1 *Hen. VI.* i 2 94
Where is my strength, my valour, and my force? . . . . . i 5 1
And there erects Thy noble deeds as valour's monuments . . . . iii 2 120
Triumphant death, . . . Young Talbot's valour makes me smile at thee iv 7 4
Spend his youth, His valour, coin, and people, in the wars 2 *Hen. VI.* i 1 79
By my valour, the most complete champion that ever I heard ! . iv 10 58
I, that never feared any, am vanquished by famine, not by valour . iv 10 81
He that loves himself Hath not essentially but by circumstance The name of valour . . . . v 2 40
What valour were it, when a cur doth grin, For one to thrust his hand between his teeth? . . . . 3 *Hen. VI.* i 4 56
Valour. It is war's prize to take all vantages ; And ten to one is no impeach of valour . . . . 3 *Hen. VI.* i 4 60
'Twas not your valour, Clifford, drove me thence.—No, nor your manhood that durst make you stay . . . . ii 2 107
That Julius Cæsar was a famous man ; With what his valour did enrich his wit, His wit set down to make his valour live . *Richard III.* iii 1 86
A man into whom nature hath so crowded humours that his valour is crushed into folly . . . . . . *Troi. and Cres.* i 2 23
Even so Doth valour's show and valour's worth divide In storms of fortune . . . . i 3 46
And at this sport Sir Valour dies ; cries 'O, enough, Patroclus !' . . i 3 176
That knows his valour, and knows not his fear . . . . . . i 3 268
What propugnation is in one man's valour, To stand the push and enmity? . . . . ii 2 136
Valour and pride excel themselves in Hector . . . . . . iv 5 79
I do stand engaged to many Greeks, Even in the faith of valour . . v 3 69
Bastard in mind, bastard in valour, in every thing illegitimate . . v 7 18
Worshipful mutiners, Your valour puts well forth . . . *Coriolanus* i 1 255
My valour's poison'd With only suffering stain by him . . . . i 10 17
It is held That valour is the chiefest virtue . . . . . . ii 2 88
Their mutinies and revolts, wherein they show'd Most valour . . . iii 1 127
And do contest As hotly and as nobly with thy love As ever in ambitious strength I did Contend against thy valour . . . . iv 5 119
Thou hast done a deed whereat valour will weep . . . . . v 6 134
O sweet Juliet, Thy beauty hath made me effeminate And in my temper soften'd valour's steel ! . . . . . . *Rom. and Jul.* iii 1 120
Thy noble shape is but a form of wax, Digressing from the valour of a man . . . . iii 3 127
If no inconstant toy, nor womanish fear, Abate thy valour in the acting it iv 1 120
To bring manslaughter into form and set quarrelling Upon the head of valour ; which indeed Is valour misbegot . . . *T. of Athens* iii 5 28
To revenge is no valour, but to bear . . . . iii 5 39
If there be Such valour in the bearing, what make we Abroad? . . iii 5 46
How full of valour did he bear himself In the last conflict ! . . . iii 5 65
He has a sin that often Drowns him, and takes his valour prisoner . iii 5 69
And to steel with valour The melting spirits of women . . . *J. Cæsar* ii 1 121
There is tears for his love ; joy for his fortune ; honour for his valour . iii 2 30
Like valour's minion carved out his passage . . . . *Macbeth* i 2 19
No sooner justice had with valour arm'd Compell'd these skipping kerns to trust their heels . . . . i 2 29
And chastise with the valour of my tongue All that impedes thee . . i 5 28
Art thou afeard To be the same in thine own act and valour As thou art in desire? . . . . i 7 40
He hath a wisdom that doth guide his valour To act in safety . . iii 1 53
Finding ourselves too slow of sail, we put on a compelled valour *Hamlet* iv 6 17
What is your difference? speak.—I am scarce in breath, my lord.—No marvel, you have so bestirred your valour . . . . *Lear* ii 2 59
Despite thy victor sword and fire-new fortune, Thy valour, and thy heart v 3 133
I mean purpose, courage, and valour . . . . . *Othello* iv 2 219
When valour preys on reason, It eats the sword it fights with *A. and C.* iii 13 199
I will reward thee Once for thy spritely comfort, and ten-fold For thy good valour . . . . iv 7 16
Not Cæsar's valour hath o'erthrown Antony, But Antony's hath triumph'd on itself.—So it should be . . . . iv 15 14
Our valour is to chase what flies . . . . . *Cymbeline* iii 3 42
There shall she see my valour, which will then be a torment to her contempt . . . . iii 5 143
Though valour Becomes thee well enough . . . . iv 2 155
Valour That wildly grows in them, but yields a crop As if it had been sow'd . . . . iv 2 179
Let me make men know More valour in me than my habits show . . v 1 30
Valuation. Our valuation shall be such That every slight and false-derived cause . . . Shall to the king taste of this action 2 *Hen. IV.* iv 1 189
No reason I, since of your lives you set So slight a valuation *Cymbeline* iv 4 49
Value. I found thee of more value Than stamps in gold . *Mer. Wives* iii 4 15
Leaves unquestion'd Matters of needful value . . . . *Meas. for Meas.* i 1 56
Stones whose rates are either rich or poor As fancy values them . . ii 2 151
Her wit Values itself so highly that to her All matter else seems weak : she cannot love . . . . *M. Ado* iii 1 53
But being lack'd and lost, Why, then we rack the value . . . . iv 1 222
He swore that he did hold me dear As precious eyesight, and did value me Above this world . . . . *L. L. Lost* v 2 445
I do expect return Of thrice three times the value of this bond *M. of Ven.* i 3 161
Weigh thy value with an even hand . . . . ii 7 25
Besides commends and courteous breath, Gifts of rich value . . . ii 9 91
He would rather have Antonio's flesh Than twenty times the value of the sum . . . . iii 2 289
Thy wealth being forfeit to the state, Thou hast not left the value of a cord . . . . iv 1 366
There's more depends on this than on the value . . . . . iv 1 434
What talk you of the posy or the value? . . . . v 1 151
I was too young that time to value her ; But now I know her *As Y. L. It* i 3 73
Of much less value is my company Than your good words *Richard II.* ii 3 19
The lady's virtuous gifts, Her beauty, and the value of her dower 1 *Hen. VI.* v 1 44
The peace between the French and us not values The cost . *Hen. VIII.* i 1 88
It values not your asking : Our mistress' sorrows we were pitying . ii 3 52
How much more is his life in value with him? . . . . . . v 3 108
Had it our name, the value of one ten . . . . *Troi. and Cres.* ii 2 23
But value dwells not in particular will . . . . ii 2 53
Rome must know The value of her own . . . . . *Coriolanus* i 9 21
We shall be blest to do, if he remember A kinder value of the people . ii 2 63
Which were his fellows but of late, Some better than his value *T. of A.* i 1 79
Things of like value differing in the owners Are prized by their masters i 1 170
This breast of mine hath buried Thoughts of great value . . *J. Cæsar* i 2 50
It appears not which of the dukes he values most . . . . *Lear* i 1 5
You less know how to value her desert Than she to scant her duty . ii 4 141
He must be weighed rather by her value than his own . . *Cymbeline* i 4 16
Reflect upon him accordingly, as you value your trust . . . . i 6 24
Jewels Of rich and exquisite form ; their values great . . . . i 6 190
So bravely done, so rich, that it did strive In workmanship and value . ii 4 74
Unto thy value I will mount myself Upon a courser . . . *Pericles* ii 1 163
He was seated in a chariot Of an inestimable value . . . . . ii 4 8
Valued. Thy substance, valued at the highest rate, Cannot amount unto a hundred marks . . . . *Com. of Errors* i 1 24
Although not valued to the money's worth . . . . *L. L. Lost* ii 1 137
Let his deservings and my love withal Be valued 'gainst your wife's commandment . . . . *Mer. of Venice* iv 1 451
Our business valued, some twelve days hence Our general forces at Bridgenorth shall meet . . . . 1 *Hen. IV.* iii 2 177

Valued. Making you ever better than his praise By still dispraising praise valued with you — 1 *Hen. IV.* v 2 60
All the temporal lands which men devout By testament have given to the church Would they strip from us; being valued thus — *Hen. V.* i 1 11
We never valued this poor seat of England — i 2 269
The queen is valued thirty thousand strong — 3 *Hen. VI.* v 3 14
What is aught, but as 'tis valued? — *Troi. and Cres.* ii 2 52
The valued file Distinguishes the swift, the slow, the subtle — *Macbeth* iii 1 95
Beyond what can be valued, rich or rare — *Lear* i 1 58
The king must take it ill, That he's so slightly valued in his messenger ii 2 153
'Tis exactly valued; Not petty things admitted — *Ant. and Cleo.* v 2 139
Valueless. Which, being touch'd and tried, Proves valueless — *K. John* iii 1 101
Valuing. Mine that I was proud on, mine so much That I myself was to myself not mine, Valuing of her — *Much Ado* iv 1 141
Van. Plant those that have revolted in the van — *Ant. and Cleo.* iv 6 9
Vane. If speaking, why, a vane blown with all winds — *Much Ado* iii 1 66
Didst thou not hear somebody?—No; 'twas the vane on the house — iii 3 138
What vane? what weathercock? did you ever hear better? — *L. L. Lost* iv 1 97
Vanish like hailstones, go; Trudge, plod away o' the hoof! — *Mer. Wives* i 3 90
Keep some state in thy exit, and vanish — *L. L. Lost* v 2 598
Ah, would the scandal vanish with my life! — *Richard II.* ii 1 67
They vanish tongue-tied in their guiltiness — *J. Cæsar* i 1 67
Put up your pipes in your bag, for I'll away: go; vanish into air *Othello* iii 1 21
Vanish, or I shall give thee thy deserving — *Ant. and Cleo.* iv 12 32
Vanished. They vanish'd strangely.—No matter, since They have left their viands behind — *Tempest* iii 3 40
There is a proclamation that you are vanished — *T. G. of Ver.* iii 1 216
Well moused, Lion.—And so the lion vanished — *M. N. Dream* v 1 275
And so he vanish'd: then came wandering by A shadow like an angel — *Richard III.* i 4 52
A gentler judgement vanish'd from his lips — *Rom. and Jul.* iii 3 10
The things that threaten'd me Ne'er look'd but on my back; when they shall see The face of Cæsar, they are vanished — *J. Cæsar* ii 2 12
Whither are they vanish'd?—Into the air — *Macbeth* i 3 80
They made themselves air, into which they vanished — i 5 5
The morning cock crew loud, And at the sound it shrunk in haste away, And vanish'd from our sight — *Hamlet* i 2 220
Wing'd From the spongy south to this part of the west, There vanish'd in the sunbeams — *Cymbeline* iv 2 350
Lessen'd herself, and in the beams o' the sun So vanish'd — v 5 473
Vanishest. Now I have taken heart thou vanishest — *J. Cæsar* iv 3 288
Dost thou lie still? If thus thou vanishest, thou tell'st the world It is not worth leave-taking — *Ant. and Cleo.* v 2 300
Vanity. I must Bestow upon the eyes of this young couple Some vanity of mine art — *Tempest* iv 1 41
O heaven, the vanity of wretched fools! — *Meas. for Meas.* v 1 164
For your writing and reading, let that appear when there is no need of such vanity — *Much Ado* iii 3 22
Shall tax my fears of little vanity, Having vainly fear'd too little *All's W.* v 3 122
O vanity of sickness! fierce extremes In their continuance will not feel themselves — *K. John* v 7 13
Where doth the world thrust forth a vanity—So it be new . . . That is not quickly buzz'd into his ears? — *Richard II.* ii 1 24
Light vanity, insatiate cormorant, Consuming means, soon preys upon itself — ii 1 38
And some few vanities that make him light — iii 4 86
I prithee, trouble me no more with vanity — 1 *Hen. IV.* i 2 92
That grey iniquity, that father ruffian, that vanity in years — ii 4 500
Sir Walter Blunt: there's honour for you! here's no vanity! — v 3 33
I can no longer brook thy vanities — v 4 74
I should have a heavy miss of thee, If I were much in love with vanity! v 4 106
Harry the Fifth is crown'd: up, vanity! Down, royal state! 2 *Hen. IV.* iv 5 120
The tide of blood in me Hath proudly flow'd in vanity till now — v 2 130
His vanities forespent Were but the outside of the Roman Brutus *Hen. V.* ii 4 36
To that end, As matching to his youth and vanity, I did present him with the Paris balls — ii 4 130
He stands between two clergymen!—Two props of virtue for a Christian prince, To stay him from the fall of vanity — *Richard III.* iii 7 97
What had he To do in these fierce vanities? — *Hen. VIII.* i 1 54
What did this vanity But minister communication of A most poor issue? i 1 85
What a loss our ladies Will have of these trim vanities! — i 3 38
My prayers Are not words duly hallow'd, nor my wishes More worth than empty vanities — ii 3 69
O heavy lightness! serious vanity! Mis-shapen chaos! — *Rom. and Jul.* i 1 184
A lover may bestride the gossamer That idles in the wanton summer air, And yet not fall; so light is vanity — ii 6 20
Hoy-day, what a sweep of vanity comes this way! — *T. of Athens* i 2 137
And take vanity the puppet's part against the royalty of her father *Lear* ii 2 39
To do the act that might the addition earn Not the world's mass of vanity could make me — *Othello* iv 2 164
Vanquish. Were't not a shame, that whilst you live at jar, The fearful French, whom you late vanquished, Should make a start o'er seas and vanquish you? — 2 *Hen. VI.* iv 8 45
Ere wildness Vanquish my staider senses — *Cymbeline* iii 4 10
Vanquished. However, but a folly bought with wit, Or else a wit by folly vanquished — *T. G. of Ver.* i 1 35
If you, in your own proof, Have vanquish'd the resistance of her youth, And made defeat of her virginity — *Much Ado* iv 1 47
I undertook it, Vanquish'd thereto by the fair grace and speech Of the poor suppliant — *All's Well* v 3 133
That stout Pendragon in his litter sick Came to the field and vanquished his foes — 1 *Hen. VI.* iii 2 96
I am vanquish'd; these haughty words of hers Have batter'd me like roaring cannon-shot — iii 3 78
And thus I said: 'Thou maiden youth, be vanquish'd by a maid' — iv 7 38
Sorrow and grief have vanquish'd all my powers; And, vanquish'd as I am, I yield to thee — 2 *Hen. VI.* ii 1 183
The fearful French, whom you late vanquished — iv 8 44
I, that never feared any, am vanquished by famine, not by valour — iv 10 80
And treacherously hast thou vanquish'd him, For hand to hand he would have vanquish'd thee — 3 *Hen. VI.* ii 1 72
Ingratitude, more strong than traitors' arms, Quite vanquish'd him *J. C.* iii 2 190
Macbeth shall never vanquish'd be until Great Birnam wood to high Dunsinane hill Shall come against him — *Macbeth* iv 1 92
Thou art not vanquish'd, But cozen'd and beguiled — *Lear* v 3 153
Not cowardly put off my helmet to My countryman,—a Roman by a Roman Valiantly vanquish'd — *Ant. and Cleo.* iv 15 58
Our men be vanquish'd ere they do resist — *Pericles* i 2 26
Vanquisher. He would pawn his fortunes To hopeless restitution, so he might Be call'd your vanquisher — *Coriolanus* iii 1 17
Vanquisher. A moiety competent Was gaged by our king; which had return'd To the inheritance of Fortinbras, Had he been vanquisher — *Hamlet* i 1 93
Vanquishest. If thou vanquishest, thy words are true; Otherwise I renounce all confidence — 1 *Hen. VI.* i 2 96
Vantage. With the vantage of mine own excuse Hath he excepted most against my love — *T. G. of Ver.* i 3 82
I slew him manfully in fight, Without false vantage or base treachery iv 1 29
And when the doctor spies his vantage ripe, To pinch her by the hand, and, on that token, The maid hath given consent to go *Mer. Wives* iv 6 43
He that might the vantage best have took Found out the remedy *M. for M.* ii 2 74
Where you may have such vantage on the duke, He shall not pass you iv 6 11
Thy fault's thus manifested; Which, though thou wouldst deny, denies thee vantage — v 1 418
My fortunes every way as fairly rank'd, If not with vantage — *M. N. D.* i 1 102
And be my vantage to exclaim on you — *Mer. of Venice* iii 2 176
We mean to look into, And watch our vantage in this business *T. of S.* iii 2 146
Which we, God knows, have turn'd another way, To our own vantage — *K. John* ii 1 550
But little vantage shall I reap thereby — *Richard II.* i 3 218
O happy vantage of a kneeling knee! Yet am I sick for fear — v 3 132
I am as like to ride the mare, if I have any vantage of ground to get up — 2 *Hen. IV.* ii 1 85
If they get ground and vantage of the king, Then join you with them ii 3 53
There am I, Till time and vantage crave my company — ii 3 68
'Tis no wisdom to confess so much Unto an enemy of craft and vantage — *Hen. V.* iii 6 153
Such a wretch, Winding up days with toil and nights with sleep, Had the fore-hand and vantage of a king — iv 1 297
You fled for vantage, every one will swear; But, if I bow, they'll say it was for fear — 1 *Hen. VI.* iv 5 28
Gives away his own, To match with her that brings no vantages 2 *Hen. VI.* i 1 131
It is war's prize to take all vantages — 3 *Hen. VI.* i 4 59
Unless she chance to fall.—God forbid that! for he'll take vantages iii 2 25
But you have all the vantage of her wrong — *Richard III.* i 3 310
And thus I took the vantage of those few — iii 7 37
Which in his greatest need will shrink from him.—All for our vantage v 2 22
Let us survey the vantage of the field — v 3 15
I am unarm'd; forego this vantage, Greek.—Strike, fellows, strike — *Troi. and Cres.* v 8 9
Thou go'st foremost: Thou rascal, that art worst in blood to run, Lead'st first to win some vantage — *Coriolanus* i 1 164
Both observe and answer The vantage of his anger — ii 3 268
But yet a brain that leads my use of anger To better vantage — iii 2 31
At your vantage, . . . let him feel your sword, Which we will second v 6 54
Perchance some single vantages you took — *T. of Athens* ii 2 138
The Norweyan lord surveying vantage . . . Began a fresh assault *Macb.* i 2 31
Did line the rebel With hidden help and vantage — i 3 113
No jutty, frieze, Buttress, nor coign of vantage — i 6 7
'Tis meet that some more audience than a mother, Since nature makes them partial, should o'erhear The speech, of vantage — *Hamlet* iii 3 33
I have some rights of memory in this kingdom, Which now to claim my vantage doth invite me — v 2 401
Take vantage, heavy eyes, not to behold This shameful lodging — *Lear* ii 2 178
As many to the vantage as would store the world they played for *Oth.* iv 3 86
These offers, Which serve not for his vantage, he shakes off *Ant. and Cleo.* iii 7 34
When vantage like a pair of twins appear'd, Both as the same — iii 10 12
When shall we hear from him?—Be assured, madam, With his next vantage — *Cymbeline* i 3 24
Who lets go by no vantages that may Prefer you to his daughter — ii 3 50
Mine Italian brain 'Gan in your duller Britain operate Most vilely; for my vantage, excellent — v 5 198
Vantbrace. And in my vantbrace put this wither'd brawn *Troi. and Cres.* i 3 297
Vapians. Of the Vapians passing the equinoctial of Queubus — *T. Night* ii 3 24
Vaporous. Make haste; The vaporous night approaches *Meas. for Meas.* iv 1 58
Upon the corner of the moon There hangs a vaporous drop profound — *Macbeth* iii 5 24
Vapour. The sun, gazing upon the earth, Dispersed those vapours *C. of Er.* i 1 90
Vows are but breath, and breath a vapour is — *L. L. Lost* iv 3 68
Breaking through the foul and ugly mists Of vapours — 1 *Hen. IV.* i 2 227
Like the south Borne with black vapour, doth begin to melt 2 *Hen. IV.* ii 4 393
It [sherris] ascends me into the brain; dries me there all the foolish and dull and crudy vapours — iv 3 106
Let us but blow on them, The vapour of our valour will o'erturn them — *Hen. V.* iv 2 24
As far as I could well discern For smoke and dusky vapours 1 *Hen. VI.* ii 2 27
The very beams will dry those vapours up — 3 *Hen. VI.* v 3 12
And in the vapour of my glory smother'd — *Richard III.* iii 7 164
Time's flies, Cap and knee slaves, vapours, and minute-jacks! *T. of A.* iii 6 107
A foul and pestilent congregation of vapours — *Hamlet* ii 2 315
I had rather be a toad, And live upon the vapour of a dungeon *Othello* iii 3 271
A vapour sometime like a bear or lion, A tower'd citadel *Ant. and Cleo.* iv 14 3
In their thick breaths, Rank of gross diet, shall we be enclouded, And forced to drink their vapour — v 2 213
Vara. But it is vara fine, For every one pursents three — *L. L. Lost* v 2 487
Variable. I never heard a passion so confused, So strange, outrageous, and so variable — *Mer. of Venice* ii 8 13
Leads fill'd, and ridges horsed With variable complexions *Coriolanus* ii 1 228
O, swear not by the moon, the inconstant moon, That monthly changes in her circled orb, Lest that thy love prove likewise variable *R. and J.* ii 2 111
Haply the seas and countries different With variable objects shall expel This something-settled matter in his heart — *Hamlet* iii 1 180
Your fat king and your lean beggar is but variable service — iv 3 25
Whiles he is vaulting variable ramps, In your despite — *Cymbeline* i 6 134
Variance. That which is the strength of their amity shall prove the immediate author of their variance — *Ant. and Cleo.* ii 6 138
Variation. Stain'd with the variation of each soil Betwixt that Holmedon and this seat of ours — 1 *Hen. IV.* i 1 64
She [Fortune] is turning, and inconstant, and mutability, and variation — *Hen. V.* iii 6 36
Are all one reckonings, save the phrase is a little variations — iv 7 19
Varied. No damsel neither, sir; she was a virgin.—It is so varied too *L. L. L.* i 1 296
The epithets are sweetly varied, like a scholar at the least — iv 2 9
Varying in subjects as the eye doth roll To every varied object — v 2 775
Like a sweet melodious bird, it sung Sweet varied notes — *T. Andron.* iii 1 86
Varies. But fortune's mood Varies again — *Pericles* iii Gower 47
Variest. Thou variest no more from picking of purses than giving direction doth from labouring — 1 *Hen. IV.* ii 1 55
Variety. Age cannot wither her, nor custom stale Her infinite variety: other women cloy The appetites they feed — *Ant. and Cleo.* ii 2 241

Varld. Dat I vill not for the varld I shall leave behind *Mer. Wives* i 4 66
Varlet. Say again, where didst thou leave these varlets? *Tempest* iv 1 170
How Falstaff, varlet vile, His dove will prove, his gold will hold *M. W.* i 3 106
Hang him, dishonest varlet! we cannot misuse him enough iv 2 104
Varlet, thou liest; thou liest, wicked varlet! *Meas. for Meas.* ii 1 174
O thou caitiff! O thou varlet! O thou wicked Hannibal! ii 1 182
Thou seest, thou wicked varlet, now, what's come upon thee: thou art to continue now, thou varlet ii 1 199
Thou naughty varlet!—Away! you are an ass, you are an ass *Much Ado* iv 2 74
I am the veriest varlet that ever chewed with a tooth *1 Hen. IV.* ii 2 25
Thou naughty varlet, tell me, where hast thou been this month? ii 4 474
Away, varlets! Draw, Bardolph: cut me off the villain's head *2 Hen. IV.* ii 1 50
A good varlet, a good varlet, a very good varlet, Sir John v 3 13
Montez à cheval! My horse! varlet! laquais! ha! *Hen. V.* iv 2 2
Call here my varlet; I'll unarm again *Troi. and Cres.* i 1 1
Thou art thought to be Achilles' male varlet.—Male varlet, you rogue! what's that? v 1 18
Nothing but lechery! all incontinent varlets! v 1 106
That dissembling abominable varlet v 4 3
The good gods assuage thy wrath, and turn the dregs of it upon this varlet here *Coriolanus* v 2 84
What a brazen-faced varlet art thou! *Lear* ii 2 30
Out, varlet, from my sight!—What means your grace? ii 4 190
Thou precious varlet, My tailor made them not *Cymbeline* iv 2 83
Varletry. Shall they hoist me up And show me to the shouting varletry Of censuring Rome? *Ant. and Cleo.* v 2 56
Varletto. Where be my horses? speak well of them, varletto *Mer. Wives* iv 5 66
Varnish. They are both the varnish of a complete man *L. L. Lost* i 2 46
Beauty doth varnish age, as if new-born iv 3 244
Set a double varnish on the fame The Frenchman gave you *Hamlet* iv 7 133
Varnished. To gaze on Christian fools with varnish'd faces *Mer. of Venice* ii 5 33
To have his pomp and all what state compounds But only painted, like his varnish'd friends? *T. of Athens* iv 2 36
Varrius. I thank thee, Varrius; thou hast made good haste *M. for M.* iv 5 11
There's other of our friends Will greet us here anon, my gentle Varrius iv 5 13
How now, Varrius!—This is most certain that I shall deliver *A. and C.* ii 1 27
Varro. To Varro and to Isidore He owes nine thousand *T. of Athens* ii 1 1
Good even, Varro: what, You come for money? ii 2 9
One Varro's servant, my good lord ii 2 27
Good morrow, Titus and Hortensius.—The like to you, kind Varro iii 4 2
I'll have them sleep on cushions in my tent.—Varro and Claudius! *J. Cæsar* iv 3 244
Boy, Lucius! Varro! Claudius! Sirs, awake! Claudius! iv 3 290
Vary. Once more I'll mark how love can vary wit *L. L. Lost* iv 3 100
Vary deserved praise on my palfrey *Hen. V.* iii 7 35
Turn their halcyon beaks With every gale and vary of their masters *Lear* ii 2 85
Varying in subjects as the eye doth roll To every varied object *L. L. Lost* v 2 774
And with his varying childness cures in me Thoughts that would thick my blood *W. Tale* i 2 170
Goes to and back, lackeying the varying tide *Ant. and Cleo.* i 4 46
O sun, Burn the great sphere thou movest in! darkling stand The varying shore o' the world iv 15 11
Vassal. His art is of such power, It would control my dam's god, Setebos, And make a vassal of him *Tempest* i 2 374
O, give me pardon, That I, your vassal, have employ'd and pain'd Your unknown sovereignty! *Meas. for Meas.* v 1 391
Me?—'that shallow vassal,'— Still me? *L. L. Lost* i 1 256
Have commiseration on thy heroical vassal! iv 1 65
Bows not his vassal head and strucken blind Kisses the base ground iv 3 224
My dear lord he is; and I His servant live, and will his vassal die *All's W.* i 3 165
Such a one, thy vassal, whom I know Is free for me to ask, thee to bestow ii 1 202
That lift your vassal hands against my head *Richard II.* iii 3 89
Through vassal fear, Base inclination, and the start of spleen *1 Hen. IV.* iii 2 124
Keep it from my head And make me as the poorest vassal is *2 Hen. IV.* iv 5 176
For humours do abound: Knocks go and come; God's vassals drop and die *Hen. V.* iii 2 8
Whose low vassal seat The Alps doth spit and void his rheum upon iii 5 51
Perish ye, with your audacious prate! Presumptuous vassals *1 Hen. VI.* iv 1 125
It is impossible that I should die By such a lowly vassal *2 Hen. VI.* iv 1 111
And he that hath commanded is the king.—Erroneous vassal! *Rich. III.* i 4 200
Woollen vassals, things created To buy and sell with groats *Coriolanus* iii 2 9
Thou swear'st thy gods in vain.—O, vassal! miscreant! *Lear* i 1 163
In my bosom shall she never come, To make my heart her vassal *A. and C.* ii 6 57
Tell him I am his fortune's vassal, and I send him The greatness he has got v 2 29
No more kin to me Than I to your highness; who, being born your vassal, Am something nearer *Cymbeline* v 5 113
Vassalage. All my powers do their bestowing lose, Like vassalage at unawares encountering The eye of majesty *Troi. and Cres.* iii 2 40
Vast. Urchins Shall, for that vast of night that they may work, All exercise on thee *Tempest* i 2 327
One sees more devils than vast hell can hold *M. N. Dream* v 1 9
Though absent, shook hands, as over a vast, and embraced *W. Tale* i 1 33
And vast confusion waits, As doth a raven on a sick-fall'n beast *K. John* iv 3 152
To seek the empty, vast, and wandering air *Richard III.* i 4 39
We shall not send O'er the vast world to seek a single man *Coriolanus* iv 1 42
As Philomela was, Forced in the ruthless, vast, and gloomy woods *T. Andron.* iv 1 53
No vast obscurity or misty vale v 2 36
Wert thou as far As that vast shore wash'd with the farthest sea *R. and J.* ii 2 83
The sun's a thief, and with his great attraction Robs the vast sea *T. of A.* iv 3 440
Yet rich conceit Taught thee to make vast Neptune weep for aye v 4 78
In the dead vast and middle of the night, Been thus encounter'd *Hamlet* i 2 118
Antres vast and deserts idle, Rough quarries, rocks, and hills *Othello* i 3 140
A man whom both the waters and the wind, In that vast tennis-court, have made the ball For them to play upon *Pericles* ii 1 64
Thou god of this great vast, rebuke these surges! iii 1 1
Vastidity. A restraint, Though all the world's vastidity you had *Meas. for Meas.* iii 1 69
Vasty. The vasty wilds Of wide Arabia are as throughfares now *M. of V.* ii 7 41
I can call spirits from the vasty deep.—Why, so can I *1 Hen. IV.* iii 1 52
Can this cockpit hold The vasty fields of France? *Hen. V.* Prol. 12
He might return to vasty Tartar back, And tell the legions ii 2 123
The poor souls for whom this hungry war Opens his vasty jaws ii 4 105
Vaudemont, Beaumont, Grandpré, Roussi, and Fauconberg iii 5 43
Fauconberg and Foix, Beaumont and Marle, Vaudemont and Lestrale iv 8 105
Vaughan. Whet me To be revenged on Rivers, Vaughan, Grey *Rich. III.* i 3 333
Lord Rivers and Lord Grey are sent to Pomfret, With them Sir Thomas Vaughan ii 4 43
Vaughan. And so falls it out With Rivers, Vaughan, Grey *Richard III.* iii 2 67
Come, Grey, come, Vaughan, let us all embrace: And take our leave iii 3 24
Rivers, Vaughan, Grey, Untimely smother'd in their dusky graves iv 4 69
Vaughan, and all that have miscarried By underhand corrupted foul injustice v 1 5
Think upon Vaughan, and, with guilty fear, Let fall thy lance v 3 142
Vault. 'Twixt the green sea and the azured vault Set roaring war *Tempest* v 1 43
Neither press, coffer, chest, trunk, well, vault, but he hath an abstract *Mer. Wives* iv 2 62
And in a dark and dankish vault at home There left me *Com. of Errors* v 1 247
To hug with swine, to seek sweet safety out In vaults and prisons *K. John* v 2 143
It stuck upon him as the sun, In the grey vault of heaven *2 Hen. IV.* ii 3 19
And more he spoke, Which sounded like a clamour in a vault *3 Hen. VI.* v 2 44
That same ancient vault Where all the kindred of the Capulets lie *Rom. and Jul.* iv 1 111
There's a fearful point! Shall I not, then, be stifled in the vault? iv 3 33
As in a vault, an ancient receptacle, Where, for these many hundred years, the bones Of all my buried ancestors are pack'd iv 3 39
I saw her laid low in her kindred's vault v 1 20
Her beauty makes This vault a feasting presence full of light v 3 86
Go with me to the vault.—I dare not, sir v 3 131
Then all alone Came I to take her from her kindred's vault v 3 254
And threaten'd me with death, going in the vault, If I departed not v 3 276
And therewithal Came to this vault to die, and lie with Juliet v 3 290
When our vaults have wept With drunken spilth of wine *T. of Athens* ii 2 168
The wine of life is drawn, and the mere lees Is left this vault to brag of *Macbeth* ii 3 101
O, you are men of stones: Had I your tongues and eyes, I'ld use them so That heaven's vault should crack *Lear* v 3 259
Vaultage. That caves and womby vaultages of France Shall chide your trespass *Hen. V.* ii 4 124
Vaulted. And vaulted with such ease into his seat *1 Hen. IV.* iv 1 107
Hath nature given them eyes To see this vaulted arch? *Cymbeline* i 6 33
Vaulting. If I could win a lady at leap-frog, or by vaulting into my saddle with my armour on my back, under the correction of bragging be it spoken, I should quickly leap into a wife *Hen. V.* v 2 142
Vaulting ambition, which o'erleaps itself And falls on the other *Macbeth* i 7 27
Whiles he is vaulting variable ramps, In your despite *Cymbeline* i 6 134
Vaulty. And put my eyeballs in thy vaulty brows *K. John* iii 4 30
The vaulty top of heaven Figured quite o'er with burning meteors v 2 52
That is not the lark, whose notes do beat The vaulty heaven *R. and J.* iii 5 22
Vaumond. Mine own company, Chitopher, Vaumond, Bentii *All's Well* iv 3 187
Vaunt. And such high vaunts of his nobility *2 Hen. VI.* iii 1 50
Arm, arm, my lord; the foe vaunts in the field.—Come, bustle *Rich. III* v 3 288
Our play Leaps o'er the vaunt and firstlings of those broils *Tr. and Cr.* Prol. 27
Vaunt-couriers to oak-cleaving thunderbolts *Lear* iii 2 5
Vaunted. She vaunted 'mongst her minions t'other day, The very train of her worst wearing gown Was better worth than all my father's lands *2 Hen. VI.* i 3 87
Vaunter. You know I am no vaunter, I; My scars can witness *T. An.* v 3 113
Vaunting. Many a nobleman lies stark and stiff Under the hoofs of vaunting enemies *1 Hen. IV.* v 3 43
Rouse thy vaunting veins: Boy, bristle thy courage up *Hen. V.* ii 3 4
Make your vaunting true, And it shall please me well *J. Cæsar* iv 3 52
Vauntingly. I heard thee say, and vauntingly thou spakest it *Richard II.* iv 1 36
Vaux. Whither goes Vaux so fast? what news, I prithee? *2 Hen. VI.* iii 2 367
Then give my charge up to Sir Nicholas Vaux *Hen. VIII.* ii 1 96
Vaward. Since we have the vaward of the day *M. N. Dream* iv 1 110
We that are in the vaward of our youth, I must confess, are wags *2 Hen. IV.* i 2 199
My lord, most humbly on my knee I beg The leading of the vaward *Hen. V.* iv 3 130
He, being in the vaward, placed behind With purpose to relieve *1 Hen. VI.* i 1 132
Their bands i' the vaward are the Antiates, Of their best trust *Coriolanus* i 6 53
Veal, quoth the Dutchman. Is not 'veal' a calf? *L. L. Lost* v 2 247
Vede. Venetia, Venetia, Chi non ti vede non ti pretia iv 2 100
Vegetives. The blest infusions That dwell in vegetives, in metals *Pericles* iii 2 36
Vehemence. I prithee now with most petitionary vehemence *As Y. L. It* iii 2 200
Vehemency. Would it apply well to the vehemency of your affection, that I should win what you would enjoy? *Mer. Wives* ii 2 247
With such vehemency he should pursue Faults proper to himself *Meas. for Meas.* v 1 109
And with what vehemency The occasion shall instruct you *Hen. VIII.* v 1 148
Vehement. Loud applause and Aves vehement *Meas. for Meas.* i 1 71
Yet for your vehement oaths, You should have been respective *M. of V.* v 1 155
By long and vehement suit I was seduced *K. John* i 1 254
And by their vehement instigation, In this just suit come I *Richard III.* iii 7 139
Note, if your lady strain his entertainment With any strong or vehement importunity *Othello* iii 3 251
Vehor. Till I find the stream To cool this heat, a charm to calm these fits, Per Styga, per manes vehor *T. Andron.* ii 1 135
Veil. Pluck the borrowed veil of modesty *Mer. Wives* iii 2 42
I am advised to do it; He says, to veil full purpose *Meas. for Meas.* iv 6 4
Give me my veil: come, throw it o'er my face *T. Night* i 5 175
Obscured his contemplation Under the veil of wildness *Hen. V.* i 1 64
These eyes, that now are dimm'd with death's black veil *3 Hen. VI.* v 2 16
Throw over her the veil of infamy *Richard III.* iv 4 208
Veiled. Like a cloistress, she will veiled walk *T. Night* i 1 28
Keep your great pretences veil'd till when They needs must show *Coriol.* i 2 20
Our veil'd dames Commit the war of white and damask in Their nicely-gawded cheeks to the wanton spoil Of Phœbus' burning kisses ii 1 231
Be not deceived: if I have veil'd my look, I turn the trouble of my countenance Merely upon myself *J. Cæsar* i 2 37
Veiling. The beauteous scarf Veiling an Indian beauty *Mer. of Venice* iii 2 99
Vein. To do me business in the veins o' the earth *Tempest* i 2 255
Ay, touch him; there's the vein *Meas. for Meas.* ii 2 70
I am glad to see you in this merry vein *Com. of Errors* ii 2 20
The fellow finds his vein And yielding to him humours well his frenzy iv 4 83
The whole world again Cannot pick out five such, take each one in his vein *L. L. Lost* v 2 548
This is Ercles' vein, a tyrant's vein; a lover is more condoling *M. N. D.* i 2 42
There is no following her in this fierce vein iii 2 82
Only my blood speaks to you in my veins *Mer. of Venice* iii 2 178
I freely told you, all the wealth I had Ran in my veins, I was a gentleman iii 2 258
You touch'd my vein at first *As Y. Like It* ii 7 94
See, my lord, Would you not deem it breathed? and that those veins Did verily bear blood? *W. Tale* v 3 64
Whose veins bound richer blood than Lady Blanch? *K. John* ii 1 431

Vein. As fire cools fire Within the scorched veins of one new-burn'd *K. John* iii 1 278
Runs tickling up and down the veins, Making that idiot, laughter . iii 3 44
Whiles warm life plays in that infant's veins . . . . . iii 4 132
Might combine The blood of malice in a vein of league . . . v 2 38
On his part I'll empty all these veins, And shed my dear blood 1 *Hen. IV.* i 3 133
I must speak in passion, and I will do it in King Cambyses' vein . ii 4 426
Purge the obstructions which begin to stop Our very veins of life 2 *Hen. IV.* iv 1 66
The blood and courage that renowned them Runs in your veins *Hen. V.* i 2 119
Nym, rouse thy vaunting veins: Boy, bristle thy courage up . ii 3 4
Scarce blood enough in all their sickly veins To give each naked curtle-axe a stain . . . . iv 2 20
And now to Paris, in this conquering vein: All will be ours 1 *Hen. VI.* iv 7 95
I'll have more lives Than drops of blood were in my father's veins 3 *Hen. VI.* i 1 97
'Tis thy presence that exhales this blood From cold and empty veins *Richard III.* i 2 59
I am not in the giving vein to-day . . . . . . iv 2 119
Thou troublest me; I am not in the vein . . . . . iv 2 122
Checks and disasters Grow in the veins of actions highest rear'd *T. and C.* i 3 6
O, this is well; he rubs the vein of him . . . . . ii 3 210
For every false drop in her bawdy veins A Grecian's life hath sunk iv 1 69
Doff thy harness, youth; I am to-day i' the vein of chivalry . v 3 32
The strongest nerves and small inferior veins From me receive *Coriolanus* i 1 142
The veins unfill'd, our blood is cold, and then We pout upon the morning . . . . v 1 51
That quench the fire of your pernicious rage With purple fountains issuing from your veins . . . . *Rom. and Jul.* i 1 92
When presently through all thy veins shall run A cold and drowsy humour . . . . iv 1 95
I have a faint cold fear thrills through my veins . . . iv 3 15
Let me have A dram of poison, such soon-speeding gear As will disperse itself through all the veins . . . . . v 1 61
There is gold, and here My bluest veins to kiss . *Ant. and Cleo.* ii 5 29
Thou shalt not lack The flower that's like thy face, pale primrose, nor The azured harebell, like thy veins . . *Cymbeline* iv 2 222
Like the Trojan horse was stuff'd within With bloody veins *Pericles* i 4 94
My veins are chill, And have no more of life than may suffice To give my tongue that heat to ask your help . . . . ii 1 77

Velure. A woman's crupper of velure . . *T. of Shrew* iii 2 62

Velutus. Junius Brutus, Sicinius Velutus, and I know not—'Sdeath! *Cor.* i 1 221

Velvet. But a pair of shears between us.—I grant; as there may between the lists and the velvet . . *Meas. for Meas.* i 2 31
Thou art the list.—And thou the velvet: thou art good velvet . i 2 32
I had as lief be a list of an English kersey as be piled, as thou art piled, for a French velvet . . . . . . i 2 36
A velvet brow, With two pitch-balls stuck in her face for eyes *L. L. Lost* iii 1 198
Through the velvet leaves the wind, All unseen, can passage find . iv 3 105
Being there alone, Left and abandon'd of his velvet friends *As Y. Like It* ii 1 50
Why, this was moulded on a porringer; A velvet dish . *T. of Shrew* iv 3 65
A silken doublet! a velvet hose! a scarlet cloak! and a copatain hat! v 1 69
With a patch of velvet on's face: whether there be a scar under't or no, the velvet knows; but 'tis a goodly patch of velvet *All's Well* iv 5 100
Calling my officers about me, in my branched velvet gown . *T. Night* ii 5 54
And saw myself unbreech'd, In my green velvet coat . *W. Tale* i 2 156
He frets like a gummed velvet . . . . . . 1 *Hen. IV.* ii 2 2
Armed in their stings, Make boot upon the summer's velvet buds *Hen. V.* i 2 196

Velvet-guards. And leave 'in sooth,' And such protest of pepper-ginger-bread, To velvet-guards and Sunday-citizens . 1 *Hen. IV.* iii 1 261

Vendible. For silence is only commendable In a neat's tongue dried and a maid not vendible . . . . . *Mer. of Venice* i 1 112
The longer kept, the less worth: off with't while 'tis vendible *All's Well* i 1 168

Venerable. Set down your venerable burden And let him feed *As Y. L. It* ii 7 167
His image, which methought did promise Most venerable worth *T. N.* iii 4 397
And such again As venerable Nestor . . *Troi. and Cres.* i 3 65
That most venerable man which I Did call my father *Cymbeline* ii 5 3

Venereal. No, madam, these are no venereal signs . *T. Andron.* ii 3 37

Venetia, Venetia, Chi non ti vede non ti pretia . *L. L. Lost* iv 2 99

Venetian. The tire-valiant, or any tire of Venetian admittance *M. Wives* iii 3 61
A Venetian, a scholar, and a soldier . . *Mer. of Venice* i 2 124
There is alighted at your gate A young Venetian . . . ii 9 87
Lorenzo and his infidel? What, and my old Venetian friend Salerio? iii 2 222
The Venetian law Cannot impugn you as you do proceed . . iv 1 178
A frail vow betwixt an erring barbarian and a supersubtle Venetian *Oth.* i 3 363
I was the other day talking on the sea-bank with certain Venetians . iv 1 138
Cassio, my lord, hath kill'd a young Venetian Call'd Roderigo . v 2 112
You shall close prisoner rest, Till that the nature of your fault be known To the Venetian state . . . . . . v 2 337
In Aleppo once, Where a malignant and a turban'd Turk Beat a Venetian v 2 354

Veneys. Three veneys for a dish of stewed prunes . *Mer. Wives* i 1 296

Venge my Gloucester's death.—God's is the quarrel . *Richard II.* i 2 36
Tell you the Dauphin I am coming on, To venge me as I may *Hen. V.* i 2 292
And crave I may have liberty to venge this wrong . 1 *Hen. VI.* iii 4 42
I'll venge thy death, Or die renowned by attempting it . 3 *Hen. VI.* ii 1 87
Would none but I might venge my cousin's death! *Rom. and Jul.* iii 5 87
This shows you are above, You justicers, that these our nether crimes So speedily can venge! . . . . . . *Lear* iv 2 80
It is an office of the gods to venge it, Not mine to speak on 't *Cymbeline* i 6 92

Vengeance. The rarer action is In virtue than in vengeance *Tempest* v 1 28
A vengeance on't! there 'tis . . . . *T. G. of Ver.* ii 3 21
Genitive case!—Ay.—Genitive,—horum, harum, horum.—Vengeance of Jenny's case! fie on her! . . . . *Mer. Wives* iv 1 64
Whiles the eye of man did woo me, That could do no vengeance to me *As Y. Like It* iv 3 48
A vengeance on your crafty wither'd hide! . *T of Shrew* ii 1 406
I would not be a stander-by to hear My sovereign mistress clouded so, without My present vengeance taken . . . *W. Tale* i 2 281
Let him be Until a time may serve: for present vengeance, Take it on her ii 3 22
The sweet'st, dear'st creature's dead, and vengeance for't Not dropp'd down yet . . . . iii 2 202
Not he alone shall suffer what wit can make heavy and vengeance bitter iv 4 801
Tongues of heaven, Plainly denouncing vengeance upon John *K. John* iii 4 159
[Heaven] Will rain hot vengeance on offenders' heads . *Richard II.* i 2 8
That lie shall lie so heavy on my sword, That it shall render vengeance iv 1 67
A plague of all cowards, I say, and a vengeance too! . 1 *Hen. IV.* ii 4 128
Thou art only mark'd For the hot vengeance and the rod of heaven . iii 2 10
And his soul Shall stand sore charged for the wasteful vengeance *Hen. V.* i 2 283
War is his beadle, war is his vengeance . . . . . iv 1 178
Will cry for vengeance at the gates of heaven . . 1 *Hen. VI.* v 4 53
Vengeance. Threefold vengeance tend upon your steps! . . 2 *Hen. VI.* iii 2 304
Throw in the frozen bosoms of our part Hot coals of vengeance! . v 2 36
And every drop cries vengeance for his death, 'Gainst thee . 3 *Hen. VI.* i 4 148
Away! for vengeance comes along with them . . . . ii 5 134
Yet will I keep thee safe, And they shall feel the vengeance of my wrath iv 1 82
Shouldst thou stand excused; For doing worthy vengeance on thyself *Richard III.* i 2 87
He holds vengeance in his hands, To hurl upon their heads that break his law.—And that same vengeance doth he hurl on thee, For false forswearing . . . . i 4 204
And every one did threat To-morrow's vengeance on the head of Richard . . . . v 3 206
It was thought meet Paris should do some vengeance on the Greeks *Troi. and Cres.* ii 2 73
After this, the vengeance on the whole camp! or rather, the bone-ache! ii 3 19
The venom'd vengeance ride upon our swords . . . . v 3 47
Great Achilles Is arming, weeping, cursing, vowing vengeance . v 5 31
He's vengeance proud, and loves not the common people *Coriolanus* ii 2 6
What the vengeance! Could he not speak 'em fair? . . . iii 1 262
With her sacred wit To villany and vengeance consecrate *T. Andron.* ii 1 121
Vengeance is in my heart, death in my hand . . . . ii 3 38
Had you not by wondrous fortune come, This vengeance on me had they executed . . . . ii 3 113
Take wreak on Rome for this ingratitude, And vengeance on the traitor iv 3 34
Befall what may befall, I'll speak no more but 'Vengeance rot you all!' v 1 58
To ease the gnawing vulture of thy mind, By working wreakful vengeance . . . . v 2 32
Rapine and Murder; therefore called so, Cause they take vengeance of such kind of men . . . . v 2 63
We will have vengeance for it, fear thou not: Then weep no more *R. and J.* iii 5 88
Can vengeance be pursued further than death? . . . . v 3 55
Aroused vengeance sets him new a-work . . . . *Hamlet* ii 2 510
O, vengeance! Why, what an ass am I! . . . . . ii 2 610
All vengeance comes too short Which can pursue the offender *Lear* ii 1 90
Vengeance! plague! death! confusion! Fiery? what quality? . ii 4 96
All the stored vengeances of heaven fall On her ingrateful top! . ii 4 164
I shall see The winged vengeance overtake such children . . iii 7 66
If you see vengeance,— Hold your hand, my lord . . . iii 7 72
Arise, black vengeance, from thy hollow cell! . . *Othello* iii 3 447
O, vengeance, vengeance! Me of my lawful pleasure she restrain'd *Cymb.* ii 5 8
Gods! if you Should have ta'en vengeance on my faults, I never Had lived to put on this: so had you saved The noble Imogen to repent, and struck Me, wretch more worth your vengeance . . . v 1 8
The most high gods not minding longer To withhold the vengeance *Per.* ii 4 4

Vengeful. Here's a vengeful sword, rusted with ease, That shall be scoured in his rancorous heart . . . 2 *Hen. VI.* iii 2 198
Provide thee two proper palfreys, black as jet, To hale thy vengeful waggon swift away . . . . . . *T. Andron.* v 2 51

Veni, vidi, vici; which to annothanize in the vulgar,—O base and obscure vulgar!—videlicet, He came, saw, and overcame . *L. L. Lost* iv 1 68

Venial. So they do nothing, 'tis a venial slip . *Othello* iv 1 9

Venice. If Cupid have not spent all his quiver in Venice . *Much Ado* i 1 274
I may speak of thee as the traveller doth of Venice . *L. L. Lost* iv 2 98
Gratiano speaks an infinite deal of nothing, more than any man in all Venice . . . . *Mer. of Venice* i 1 115
Therefore go forth; Try what my credit can in Venice do . . i 1 180
And brings down The rate of usance here with us in Venice . i 3 46
All the boys in Venice follow him, Crying, his stones, his daughter, and his ducats . . . . ii 8 23
There came divers of Antonio's creditors in my company to Venice iii 1 119
Were he out of Venice, I can make what merchandise I will . . iii 1 133
What's the news from Venice? How doth that royal merchant, good Antonio? . . . . iii 2 241
First go with me to church and call me wife, And then away to Venice. iii 2 306
The commodity that strangers have With us in Venice . . . iii 3 28
Unto the tranect, to the common ferry Which trades to Venice . . iii 4 54
Fie upon your law! There is no force in the decrees of Venice . iv 1 102
This strict court of Venice Must needs give sentence 'gainst the merchant . . . . iv 1 204
There is no power in Venice Can alter a decree established . iv 1 218
Shall I lay perjury upon my soul? No, not for Venice . . iv 1 230
Thy lands and goods Are, by the laws of Venice, confiscate Unto the state of Venice . . . . iv 1 311
It is enacted in the laws of Venice . . . . . . iv 1 348
The dearest ring in Venice will I give you, And find it out by proclamation iv 1 435
With an unthrift love did run from Venice As far as Belmont . v 1 16
I will unto Venice, To buy apparel 'gainst the wedding-day *T. of Shrew* ii 1 316
Father, and wife, and gentlemen, adieu; I will to Venice . . ii 1 324
Turkey cushions boss'd with pearl, Valance of Venice gold in needlework ii 1 356
Know you not the cause? Your ships are stay'd at Venice . . iv 2 83
I told him that your father was at Venice, And that you look'd for him iv 4 15
And there at Venice gave His body to that pleasant country's earth *Richard II.* iv 1 97
Tell'st thou me of robbing? this is Venice; My house is not a grange *Oth.* i 1 105
A noble ship of Venice Hath seen a grievous wreck and sufferance . ii 1 22
But, sir, be you ruled by me: I have brought you from Venice . ii 1 271
If this poor trash of Venice . . . stand the putting on . . ii 1 312
With no money at all and a little more wit, return again to Venice . ii 3 375
In Venice they do let heaven see the pranks They dare not show their husbands . . . . iii 3 202
Something, sure, of state, Either from Venice, or some unhatch'd practice . . . . iii 4 141
What trumpet is that same?—Something from Venice, sure . . iv 1 227
The duke and senators of Venice greet you . . . . iv 1 230
This would not be believed in Venice, Though I should swear I saw't . iv 1 253
Sir, I obey the mandate, And will return to Venice . . . iv 1 271
I took you for that cunning whore of Venice That married with Othello iv 2 89
The messengers of Venice stay the meat: Go in, and weep not . iv 2 170
There is especial commission come from Venice . . . . iv 2 226
Why, then Othello and Desdemona return again to Venice . . iv 2 228
I know a lady in Venice would have walked barefoot to Palestine for a touch of his nether lip . . . . iv 3 38
Roderigo.—What, of Venice?—Even he, sir: did you know him? . v 1 91

Venison. I thank you for my venison, Master Shallow . *Mer. Wives* i 1 81
I wished your venison better; it was ill killed . . . . i 1 84
We have a hot venison pasty to dinner: come, gentlemen . . i 1 202
Come, shall we go and kill us venison? . . *As Y. Like It* ii 1 21
He that strikes The venison first shall be the lord o' the feast *Cymbeline* iii 3 75
Scarce ever look'd on blood, But that of coward hares, hot goats, and venison! . . . . iv 4 37

Venit. Videsne quis venit?—Video, et gaudeo . *L. L. Lost* v 1 33
Venom. The venom clamours of a jealous woman . . *Com. of Errors* v 1 69
Thy reason, dear venom, give thy reason . . *T. Night* iii 2 2
There may be in the cup A spider steep'd, and one may drink, depart, And yet partake no venom . . . *W. Tale* ii 1 41
To whose venom sound The open ear of youth doth always listen *Richard II.* ii 1 19
Which live like venom where no venom else But only they have privilege to live . . . . ii 1 157
Spiders, that suck up thy venom, And heavy-gaited toads lie in their way . . . . iii 2 14
The united vessel of their blood, Mingled with venom of suggestion *2 Hen. IV.* iv 4 45
The venom of such looks, we fairly hope, Have lost their quality *Hen. V.* v 2 18
To be avoided, As venom toads, or lizards' dreadful stings . *3 Hen. VI.* ii 2 138
When he bites, His venom tooth will rankle to the death *Richard III.* i 3 291
Anointed let me be with deadly venom . . . . iv 1 62
You shall digest the venom of your spleen, Though it do split you *J. C.* iv 3 47
The worm that's fled Hath nature that in time will venom breed *Macb.* iii 4 30
Toad, that under cold stone Days and nights has thirty one Swelter'd venom sleeping got . . . . iv 1 8
Who this had seen, with tongue in venom steep'd, 'Gainst Fortune's state would treason have pronounced . . . *Hamlet* ii 2 533
The point envenom'd too! Then, venom, to thy work . . v 2 333
Venomed. Pierced to the soul with slander's venom'd spear *Richard II.* i 1 171
Adders, spiders, toads, Or any creeping venom'd thing that lives *Richard III.* i 2 20
The venom'd vengeance ride upon our swords . *Troi. and Cres.* v 3 47
The gilded newt and eyeless venom'd worm . . *T. of Athens* iv 3 182
If he by chance escape your venom'd stuck, Our purpose may hold there *Hamlet* iv 7 162
Venom-mouthed. This butcher's cur is venom-mouth'd, and I Have not the power to muzzle him . . . *Hen. VIII.* i 1 120
Venomous. Like the toad, ugly and venomous . . *As Y. Like It* ii 1 13
With venomous wights she stays As tediously as hell . *Troi. and Cres.* iv 2 12
Thy tears are salter than a younger man's, And venomous to thine eyes *Coriolanus* iv 1 23
And prompt me, that my tongue may utter forth The venomous malice of my swelling heart! . . . . *T. Andron.* v 3 13
Poor venomous fool, Be angry, and dispatch . *Ant. and Cleo.* v 2 308
Venomously. These things sting His mind so venomously . *Lear* iv 3 48
Thou stormest venomously; Wilt thou spit all thyself? . *Pericles* iii 1 7
Vent. Thou didst vent thy groans As fast as mill-wheels strike *Tempest* i 2 280
How camest thou to be the siege of this moon-calf? can he vent Trinculos? . . . . ii 2 111
The which he vents In mangled forms . . *As Y. Like It* ii 7 41
'Tis now no time to vent our love: Listen to me . . *T. of Shrew* i 2 179
Thou didst make tolerable vent of thy travel . . *All's Well* ii 3 213
Vent thy folly somewhere else: Thou know'st not me.—Vent my folly! *T. Night* iv 1 12
Tell me what I shall vent to my lady: shall I vent to her that thou art coming? . . . . iv 1 17
Which of you will stop The vent of hearing when loud Rumour speaks? *2 Hen. IV.* Ind. 2
They vent reproaches Most bitterly on you . . . *Hen. VIII.* i 2 23
Look, how thy wounds do bleed at many vents! . *Troi. and Cres.* v 3 82
Then we shall ha' means to vent Our musty superfluity . . *Coriolanus* i 1 229
What his breast forges, that his tongue must vent . . iii 1 258
Let me have war, say I; it exceeds peace as far as day does night; it's spritely, waking, audible, and full of vent . . . iv 5 238
Whilst I can vent clamour from my throat, I'll tell thee thou dost evil *Lear* i 1 168
Here, on her breast, There is a vent of blood and something blown *Ant. and Cleo.* v 2 352
Air comes in: there's none abroad so wholesome as that you vent *Cymb.* i 2 5
Will you rhyme upon't, And vent it for a mockery? . . v 3 56
Ventages. Govern these ventages with your fingers and thumb *Hamlet* iii 2 373
Vented. With these shreds They vented their complainings . *Coriolanus* i 1 213
When perforce he could not But pay me terms of honour, cold and sickly He vented them . . . *Ant. and Cleo.* iii 4 8
Ventidius. Noble Ventidius! Well; I am not of that feather to shake off My friend when he must need me . . . *T. of Athens* i 1 99
By no means, Honest Ventidius; you mistake my love: I gave it freely ever . . . . i 2 9
Ventidius lately Buried his father; by whose death he's stepp'd Into a great estate . . . . ii 2 231
And now Ventidius is wealthy too, Whom he redeem'd from prison . iii 3 3
Has Ventidius and Lucullus denied him? And does he send to me? . iii 3 8
If we compose well here, to Parthia: Hark, Ventidius . *Ant. and Cleo.* ii 2 16
Get thee gone: Say to Ventidius I would speak with him . . ii 3 31
O, come, Ventidius, You must to Parthia: your commission's ready . ii 3 40
Noble Ventidius, Whilst yet with Parthian blood thy sword is warm, The fugitive Parthians follow . . . . iii 1 5
Thou hast, Ventidius, that Without the which a soldier, and his sword, Grants scarce distinction . . . . iii 1 27
Ventricle. Begot in the ventricle of memory . . *L. L. Lost* iv 2 70
Venture. That I may venture to depart alone . . *T. G. of Ver.* iv 3 36
Had I such venture forth, The better part of my affections would Be with my hopes abroad . . . . *Mer. of Venice* i 1 15
Misfortune to my ventures out of doubt Would make me sad . . i 1 21
My ventures are not in one bottom trusted, Nor to one place . . i 1 42
Other ventures he hath squandered abroad . . . . . i 3 21
This was a venture, sir, that Jacob served for . . . . i 3 92
I would detain you here some month or two Before you venture for me iii 2 10
Have all his ventures fail'd? What, not one hit? . . . . iii 2 270
I play a merchant's part, And venture madly on a desperate mart *T. of Shrew* ii 1 329
Twenty crowns! I'll venture so much of my hawk or hound, But twenty times so much upon my wife . . . . . . v 2 72
I'ld venture The well-lost life of mine on his grace's cure *All's Well* i 3 253
Upon thy certainty and confidence What darest thou venture? . ii 1 173
If I do not wonder how thou darest venture to be drunk *W. Tale* v 2 184
I am afraid; and yet I'll venture it . . . . *K. John* iv 3 5
We venture thee, Albeit considerations infinite Do make against it *1 Hen. IV.* v 1 101
And, upon my life, Spoke at a venture . . *2 Hen. IV.* i 1 59
And since we are o'erset, venture again . . . . . i 1 185
To venture upon the charged chambers bravely . . . . ii 4 56
There's a whole merchant's venture of Bourdeaux stuff in him . ii 4 69
But to the purpose, and so to the venture . . . . . Epil. 8
Venture. If like an ill venture it come unluckily home, I break *2 Hen. IV.* Epil. 12
Others, like merchants, venture trade abroad . . . *Hen. V.* i 2 192
Thou lovedst plums well, that wouldst venture so . *2 Hen. VI.* ii 1 101
To desperate ventures and assured destruction . *Richard III.* v 3 319
And held for certain The king will venture at it . . *Hen. VIII.* ii 1 156
But this cannot continue.—If it do, I'll venture one have-at-him . ii 2 85
Beshrew me, I would, And venture maidenhead for't . . ii 3 25
In faith, for little England You'ld venture an emballing . . ii 3 47
Since it serves my purpose, I will venture To stale't a little more *Coriol.* i 1 94
He had rather venture all his limbs for honour Than one on's ears to hear it . . . . ii 2 84
We must take the current when it serves, Or lose our ventures *J. Cæsar* iv 3 224
When he reads Thy personal venture in the rebels' fight, His wonders and his praises do contend . . . . . *Macbeth* i 3 91
Ere long you are like to hear, If you dare venture in your own behalf *Lear* iv 2 20
I should venture purgatory for't . . . . . *Othello* iv 3 77
With diseased ventures That play with all infirmities for gold *Cymbeline* i 6 123
Ventured. I should have given him tears unto entreaties, Ere he should thus have ventured . . . . . *As Y. Like It* i 2 251
'Twas ten to one; And yet we ventured, for the gain proposed *2 Hen. IV.* i 1 183
I have ventured, Like little wanton boys that swim on bladders, This many summers in a sea of glory . . . . *Hen. VIII.* iii 2 358
There are that dare; and I myself have ventured To speak my mind of him . . . . v 1 40
Yet have I ventured to come seek you out . . . *Lear* iii 4 157
Venturing. I'll make a shaft or a bolt on't: 'slid, 'tis but venturing *Mer. Wives* iii 4 25
Venturous. I have a venturous fairy that shall seek The squirrel's hoard *M. N. Dream* iv 1 39
Ne'er heard I of a warlike enterprise More venturous or desperate than this . . . . *1 Hen. VI.* ii 1 45
Get you to my house; I will reward you for this venturous deed *2 Hen. VI.* iii 2 9
Thy prime of manhood daring, bold, and venturous . *Richard III.* iv 4 170
I am much too venturous In tempting of your patience . *Hen. VIII.* i 2 54
Venue. A sweet touch, a quick venue of wit! . *L. L. Lost* v 1 62
Venus. Tell me, heavenly bow, If Venus or her son, as thou dost know, Do now attend the queen? . . . . *Tempest* iv 1 87
You are more intemperate in your blood Than Venus . *Much Ado* iv 1 61
Then was Venus like her mother, for her father is but grim *L. L. Lost* iv 1 255
By the simplicity of Venus' doves, By that which knitteth souls *M. N. D.* i 1 171
As bright, as clear, As yonder Venus in her glimmering sphere . iii 2 61
Let her shine as gloriously As the Venus of the sky . . iii 2 107
Ten times faster Venus' pigeons fly To seal love's bonds . *Mer. of Venice* ii 6 5
That same wicked bastard of Venus that was begot of thought *As Y. Like It* iv 1 216
Saturn and Venus this year in conjunction! . . *2 Hen. IV.* ii 4 286
Bright star of Venus fall'n down on the earth . . *1 Hen. VI.* i 2 144
The mortal Venus, the heart-blood of beauty, love's invisible soul *Troi. and Cres.* iii 1 34
By Venus' hand I swear, No man alive can love in such a sort . iv 1 22
Beg, then.—Why then for Venus' sake, give me a kiss . . iv 5 49
Your quondam wife swears still by Venus' glove . . . iv 5 179
In characters as red as Mars his heart Inflamed with Venus . . v 2 165
Though Venus govern your desires, Saturn is dominator over mine *T. Andron.* ii 3 30
Speak to my gossip Venus one fair word, One nick-name for her purblind son and heir, Young Adam Cupid . . *Rom. and Jul.* ii 1 11
I little talk'd of love; For Venus smiles not in a house of tears . iv 1 8
Yet have I fierce affections, and think What Venus did with Mars *Ant. and Cleo.* i 5 18
O'er-picturing that Venus where we see The fancy outwork nature . ii 2 205
For feature, laming The shrine of Venus, or straight-pight Minerva *Cymbeline* v 5 164
Venuto. I will . . . undertake your ben venuto . *L. L. Lost* iv 2 164
Alla nostra casa ben venuto, molto honorato signor . *T. of Shrew* i 2 25
Be it so, Petruchio, I shall be your ben venuto . . . . i 2 282
Ver. This side is Hiems, Winter, this Ver, the Spring . *L. L. Lost* v 2 901
Ver, begin.—When daisies pied and violets blue . . . v 2 903
Verb. Thou hast men about thee that usually talk of a noun and a verb *2 Hen. VI.* iv 7 43
Verba. Pauca verba, Sir John; goot worts.—Good worts! good cabbage *Mer. Wives* i 1 123
You shall not say me nay: pauca verba . . *L. L. Lost* iv 2 171
Verbal. She told me, In a sweet verbal brief . . *All's Well* v 3 137
Made she no verbal question? . . . . . . *Lear* iv 3 26
You put me to forget a lady's manners, By being so verbal *Cymbeline* ii 3 111
Verbatim. I have forged, or am not able Verbatim to rehearse the method of my pen . . . . *1 Hen. VI.* iii 1 13
Verbosity. He draweth out the thread of his verbosity finer than the staple of his argument . . . . . . *L. L. Lost* v 1 18
Verdict. Giving my verdict on the white rose side . . *1 Hen. VI.* ii 4 48
Speak, sirrah, when you should; Must your bold verdict enter talk with lords? . . . . iii 1 63
What lawful quest have given their verdict up Unto the frowning judge *Richard III.* i 4 189
And not ever The justice and the truth o' the question carries The due o' the verdict with it . . . . . . *Hen. VIII.* v 1 131
Let us kill him, and we'll have corn at our own price. Is't a verdict? *Coriolanus* i 1 11
Verdun. Lord Verdun of Alton, Lord Cromwell of Wingfield *1 Hen. VI.* iv 7 65
Verdure. He was The ivy which had hid my princely trunk, And suck'd my verdure out on't . . . . *Tempest* i 2 87
Blasting in the bud, Losing his verdure even in the prime *T. G. of Ver.* i 1 49
Vere. The Lord Aubrey Vere, Was done to death . *3 Hen. VI.* iii 3 102
Verge. Stood on the extremest verge of the swift brook . *As Y. Like It* ii 1 42
To the furthest verge That ever was survey'd by English eye *Richard II.* ii 1 93
Yet, incaged in so small a verge, The waste is no whit lesser than thy land . . . . ii 1 102
Whom we raise, We will make fast within a hallow'd verge . *2 Hen. VI.* i 4 25
I would to God that the inclusive verge Of golden metal that must round my brow Were red-hot steel! . . . . *Richard III.* iv 1 59
Timon hath made his everlasting mansion Upon the beached verge of the salt flood . . . . *T. of Athens* v 1 219
You are old; Nature in you stands on the very verge Of her confine *Lear* ii 4 149
You are now within a foot Of the extreme verge . . . iv 6 26
Verges. Goodman Verges, sir, speaks a little off the matter *Much Ado* iii 5 10
Comparisons are odorous: palabras, neighbour Verges . . . iii 5 19
Well said, i' faith, neighbour Verges: well, God's a good man . iii 5 39

Verier. Was not my lord The verier wag o' the two? . . *W. Tale* i 2 66
There are verier knaves desire to live, for all he be a Roman . *Cymbeline* v 4 209
Veriest. Were he the veriest antic in the world . *T. of Shrew* Ind. 1 101
I think thou hast the veriest shrew of all.—Well, I say no . . v 2 64
I am the veriest varlet that ever chewed with a tooth . . 1 *Hen. IV.* ii 2 25
Fight I will no more, But yield me to the veriest hind . . *Cymbeline* v 3 77
Verified. They have verified unjust things . . *Much Ado* v 1 222
More truly now may this be verified . . . . 1 *Hen. VI.* i 2 32
I perceive that will be verified Henry the Fifth did sometime prophesy v 1 30
It boots thee not, proud queen, Unless the adage must be verified, That
beggars mounted run their horse to death . . . . 3 *Hen. VI.* i 4 126
The common voice, I see, is verified Of thee, which says thus *Hen. VIII.* v 3 176
For I have ever verified my friends, Of whom he's chief, with all the size
that verity Would without lapsing suffer . . . *Coriolanus* v 2 17
Verify. To verify our title with their lives . . *K. John* ii 1 277
He is an ass, as in the world: I will verify as much in his beard *Hen. V.* iii 2 75
Verily. I saw their weapons drawn: there was a noise, That's verily
Tempest ii 1 321
I think verily he had been hanged for't . . . . *T. G. of Ver.* iv 4 16
I verily did think That her old gloves were on . . *As Y. Like It* iv 3 25
Verily, I speak it in the freedom of my knowledge . *W. Tale* i 1 12
Nay, but you will?—I may not, verily.—Verily! . . . . i 2 45
Verily, You shall not go: a lady's 'Verily' 's As potent as a lord's . . i 2 49
My prisoner? or my guest? by your dread 'Verily,' One of them you
shall be . . . . i 2 55
Would you not deem it breathed? and that those veins Did verily bear
blood? . . . . v 3 65
Yes, verily and in truth, you shall take it . . . *Hen. V.* v 1 64
Verily, I swear, 'tis better to be lowly born . . *Hen. VIII.* ii 3 18
Verily, I do not jest with you . . . . . *Coriolanus* i 3 103
Veritable. Indeed! is't true?—Most veritable . . . *Othello* iii 4 76
Vérité. En vérité, vous prononcez les mots aussi droit que les natifs
Hen. V. iii 4 40
Verity. You shall find By every syllable a faithful verity *Meas. for Meas.* iv 3 131
Did not I in rage depart from thence?—In verity you did *Com. of Errors* iv 4 80
But for his verity in love, I do think him as concave as a covered goblet
or a worm-eaten nut . . . . . . *As Y. Like It* iii 4 25
Point from point, to the full arming of the verity . . *All's Well* iv 3 73
So like an old tale, that the verity of it is in strong suspicion *W. Tale* v 2 31
And that he doubted 'Twould prove the verity of certain words *Hen. VIII.* i 2 159
With all the size that verity Would without lapsing suffer *Coriolanus* v 2 18
Why, by the verities on thee made good, May they not be my oracles as
well? . . . . *Macbeth* iii 1 8
The king-becoming graces, As justice, verity, temperance . . iv 3 92
In the verity of extolment, I take him to be a soul of great article *Ham.* v 2 122
In sincere verity, Under the allowance of your great aspect . *Lear* ii 2 111
Vermin. What is your study?—How to prevent the fiend, and to kill
vermin . . . . iii 4 164
Vernon. My cousin Vernon! welcome, by my soul . 1 *Hen. IV.* iv 1 86
Certain horse Of my cousin Vernon's are not yet come up . . iv 3 20
But there is Mordake, Vernon, Lord Harry Percy . . . iv 4 24
Bear Worcester to the death and Vernon too . . . . v 5 14
Good Master Vernon, it is well objected . . . 1 *Hen. VI.* ii 4 43
Good Master Vernon, I am bound to you . . . . . ii 4 128
Veroles. Do you know the French knight that cowers i' the hams?—Who,
Monsieur Veroles? . . . . *Pericles* iv 2 115
Verona. There is a lady in Verona here Whom I affect . *T. G. of Ver.* iii 1 81
Whither travel you?—To Verona.—Whence came you?—From Milan . iv 1 17
Myself was from Verona banished For practising to steal away a lady . iv 1 47
Do not name Silvia thine; if once again, Verona shall not hold thee . v 4 129
Verona, for a while I take my leave, To see my friends in Padua *T. of Shrew* i 2 1
And my good friend Petruchio! How do you all at Verona? . . i 2 22
What happy gale Blows you to Padua here from old Verona? . . i 2 49
Born in Verona, old Antonio's son: My father dead, my fortune lives
for me . . . . i 2 191
Give me leave. I am a gentleman of Verona, sir . . . ii 1 47
Two households, both alike in dignity, In fair Verona *Rom. and Jul.* Prol. 2
Made Verona's ancient citizens Cast by their grave beseeming ornaments i 1 99
Trudge about Through fair Verona; find those persons out . . i 2 35
Fair Rosaline whom thou so lovest, With all the admired beauties of
Verona . . . . i 2 89
Younger than you, Here in Verona, ladies of esteem, Are made already
mothers . . . . i 3 70
Verona's summer hath not such a flower . . . . . i 3 77
Verona brags of him To be a virtuous and well-govern'd youth . . i 5 69
The prince expressly hath Forbidden bandying in Verona streets . iii 1 92
Hence from Verona art thou banished: Be patient, for the world is
broad and wide.—There is no world without Verona walls . iii 3 15
News from Verona!—How now, Balthasar! Dost thou not bring me
letters? . . . . v 1 12
While Verona by that name is known, There shall no figure at such rate
be set As that of true and faithful Juliet . . . . v 3 300
Veronesa. The ship is here put in, A Veronesa . . . *Othello* ii 1 26
Versal. She looks as pale as any clout in the versal world *Rom. and Jul.* ii 4 219
Verse. He writes verses, he speaks holiday . . *Mer. Wives* iii 2 69
Whose names yet run smoothly in the even road of a blank verse *M. Ado* v 2 34
Or rather, as Horace says in his—What, my soul, verses? . *L. L. Lost* iv 2 105
Let me hear a staff, a stanze, a verse; lege, domine . . . iv 2 107
But to return to the verses: did they please you, Sir Nathaniel? . . iv 2 156
I will prove those verses to be very unlearned . . . . iv 2 164
Nay, I have verses too, I thank Biron: The numbers true . . v 2 34
Some thousand verses of a faithful lover, A huge translation of hypocrisy v 2 50
Sung With feigning voice verses of feigning love . . *M. N. Dream* i 1 31
I'll give you a verse to this note that I made yesterday . *As Y. Like It* ii 5 48
Hang there, my verse, in witness of my love . . . . iii 2 1
This is the very false gallop of verses . . . . . iii 2 119
Didst thou hear these verses?—O, yes, I heard them all, and more too . iii 2 172
Some of them had in them more feet than the verses would bear . . iii 2 175
The feet might bear the verses.—Ay, but the feet were lame and could
not bear themselves without the verse and therefore stood lamely
in the verse . . . . iii 2 177
Mar no moe of my verses with reading them ill-favouredly . . iii 2 278
Are you he that hangs the verses on the trees? . . . . iii 2 411
When a man's verses cannot be understood . . . . . iii 3 12
That's a brave man! he writes brave verses, speaks brave words . . iii 4 44
Nay, then, God be wi' you, an you talk in blank verse . . . iv 1 32
Thus your verse Flow'd with her beauty once . . . *W. Tale* v 1 101
Marry, if you would put me to verses or to dance for your sake, Kate,
why you undid me . . . . *Hen. V.* v 2 137
By magic verses have contrived his end . . . . 1 *Hen. VI.* i 1 27

Verse. 'As true as Troilus' shall crown up the verse . *Troi. and Cres.* iii 2 189
We may live to have need of such a verse . . . . . iv 4 24
What verse for it? what instance for it? Let me see . . . . v 10 40
O, 'tis a verse in Horace; I know it well: I read it in the grammar long
ago.—Ay, just; a verse in Horace . . . . *T. Andron.* iv 2 22
When we for recompense have praised the vile, It stains the glory in
that happy verse Which aptly sings the good . . *T. of Athens* i 1 16
Thy verse swells with stuff so fine and smooth That thou art even natural v 1 87
I am Cinna the poet.—Tear him for his bad verses . . *J. Cæsar* iii 3 34
The lady shall say her mind freely, or the blank verse shall halt for't
Hamlet ii 2 339
Versing. Playing on pipes of corn and versing love . . *M. N. Dream* ii 1 67
Vert. Vetch me in my closet un boitier vert, a box, a green-a box *M. W.* i 4 47
Very. O, the cry did knock Against my very heart . . *Tempest* i 2 9
The wreck, which touch'd The very virtue of compassion in thee . . i 2 27
The hour's now come; The very minute bids thee ope thine ear . . i 2 37
The very rats Instinctively have quit it . . . . . i 2 147
Ay, or very falsely pocket up his report . . . . . ii 1 67
Will you laugh me asleep, for I am very heavy? . . . . ii 1 189
Thou art very Trinculo indeed! . . . . ii 2 109
The very instant that I saw you, did My heart fly to your service . . iii 1 64
Here on this grass-plot, in this very place . . . . . iv 1 73
Spring come to you at the farthest In the very end of harvest! . . iv 1 115
And that very duke Which was thrust forth of Milan . . . v 1 159
Indeed, a sheep doth very often stray . . . . *T. G. of Ver.* i 1 74
I thank you, gentle servant: 'tis very clerkly done . . . ii 1 114
All the kind of the Launces have this very fault . . . . ii 3 3
He is a stone, a very pebble stone, and has no more pity in him than a
dog . . . . ii 3 11
Dine, sup, and sleep, Upon the very naked name of love . . . ii 4 142
This very night; for Love is like a child, That longs for every thing . iii 1 124
'Tis an ill office for a gentleman, Especially against his very friend . iii 2 41
So false that he grieves my very heart-strings . . . . iv 2 62
I am very loath to be your idol, sir . . . . . . iv 2 129
My father would enforce me marry Vain Thurio, whom my very soul
abhors . . . . iv 3 17
Why do I pity him That with his very heart despiseth me? . . . iv 4 99
Would I might be dead If I in thought felt not her very sorrow! . . iv 4 177
And now it is about the very hour . . . . . . v 1 2
By my troth, you are very well met . . . . . *Mer. Wives* i 1 199
There's the point, sir.—Marry, is it; the very point of it . . i 1 230
And the very yea and the no is . . . . i 4 98
This is the very same; the very hand, the very words . . . ii 1 84
Very rogues, now they be out of service . . . . . ii 1 182
I must very much lay open mine own imperfection . . . . ii 2 191
Methinks you prescribe to yourself very preposterously . . . ii 2 249
'Tis the very riches of thyself That now I aim at . . . . iii 4 17
You are a very simplicity 'oman . . . . iv 1 31
At the very instant of Falstaff's and our meeting . . . . iv 3 16
The duke is very strangely gone from hence . . *Meas. for Meas.* i 4 50
But we do learn By those that know the very nerves of state . . i 4 53
A man whose blood Is very snow-broth . . . . . . i 4 58
'Tis very pregnant, The jewel that we find, we stoop and take't . . ii 1 23
Which at that very distant time stood, as it were, in a fruit-dish . . ii 1 94
This very man, having eaten the rest, as I said . . . . ii 1 104
Mine were the very cipher of a function, To fine the faults . . ii 2 39
Respites me a life, whose very comfort Is still a dying horror! . . ii 3 41
A very superficial, ignorant, unweighing fellow . . . . iii 2 147
The very debt of your calling . . . . iii 2 264
Upon the very siege of justice . . . . iv 2 101
He this very day receives letters of strange tenour . . . . iv 2 215
Is the axe upon the block, sirrah?—Very ready, sir . . . iv 3 40
The very mercy of the law cries out Most audible . . . . v 1 412
The very block Where Claudio stoop'd to death . . . . v 1 419
That very hour and in the self-same inn . . . *Com. of Errors* i 1 54
This very day a Syracusian merchant Is apprehended . . . . i 2 3
Even her very words Didst thou deliver to me . . . . . ii 2 165
If any hour meet a sergeant, a' turns back for very fear . . . iv 2 56
Time is a very bankrupt and owes more than he's worth to season . iv 2 58
You could never do him so ill-well, unless you were the very man *M. Ado* ii 1 123
My very visor began to assume life and scold with her . . . ii 1 248
The very night before the intended wedding . . . . . iii 2 45
Two of them have the very bent of honour . . . . . iv 1 188
In this very manner refused, and upon the grief of this suddenly died . v 2 65
I have deceived even your very eyes . . . . . . v 1 238
I do affect the very ground, which is base . . . *L. L. Lost* i 2 172
A very beadle to a humorous sigh . . . . iii 1 177
There is the very remuneration I had of thy master . . . . v 1 76
The very all of all is,—but, sweet heart, I do implore secrecy . . v 1 115
In very likeness of a roasted crab . . . . . *M. N. Dream* ii 1 48
That very time I saw, but thou couldst not . . . . . ii 1 155
He is a very paramour for a sweet voice . . . . . . iv 2 12
The very best at a beast, my lord, that e'er I saw . . . . v 1 232
Not one among them but I dote on his very absence *Mer. of Venice* i 2 120
The Jew is the very devil incarnal . . . . ii 2 28
The boy was the very staff of my age, my very prop . . . ii 2 70
My master's a very Jew: give him a present! give him a halter . . ii 2 112
In very brief, the suit is impertinent to myself . . . . ii 2 146
But stay the very riping of the time . . . . . . ii 8 40
'Confess' and 'love' Had been the very sum of my confession . . iii 2 36
And swearing till my very roof was dry With oaths of love . . iii 2 206
I bid my very friends and countrymen, Sweet Portia, welcome . . iii 2 226
To suffer, with a quietness of spirit, The very tyranny and rage of his . iv 1 13
'Nearest his heart:' those are the very words . . . . iv 1 254
Thou hast contrived against the very life Of the defendant . . . iv 1 360
Even he that did uphold the very life Of my dear friend . . . v 1 214
Our very petticoats will catch them . . . . *As Y. Like It* i 3 15
Till that the weary very means do ebb . . . . . . ii 7 73
This is the very false gallop of verses . . . . . . iii 2 119
What would you say to me now, an I were your very very Rosalind? . iv 1 71
They are in the very wrath of love and they will together . . . v 2 44
Any man is so very a fool to be married to hell . . *T. of Shrew* i 1 129
And now I find report a very liar . . . . ii 1 246
Such an injury would vex a very saint . . . . . . iii 2 28
A very monster in apparel, and not like a Christian footboy . . iii 2 71
And I seeing this came thence for very shame . . . . . iii 2 182
That feed'st me with the very name of meat . . . . . iv 3 32
Consumes itself to the very paring . . . . . *All's Well* i 1 155
It was this very sword entrenched it . . . . . . ii 1 45
That's it; I would have said the very same . . . . . ii 3 29

Very. Very weak and unserviceable *All's Well* iv 3 151
An I were not a very coward, I'ld compel it of you iv 3 356
I was bred and born Not three hours' travel from this very place *T. N.* i 2 23
He's a very fool and a prodigal.—Fie, that you'll say so! i 3 25
Whose fair flower Being once display'd, doth fall that very hour ii 4 40
Thy mind is a very opal ii 4 77
I will be point-devise the very man ii 5 178
Words are very rascals since bonds disgraced them iii 1 24
That very envy and the tongue of loss Cried fame and honour on him v 1 61
One seven-night longer.—Very sooth, to-morrow *W. Tale* i 2 17
In pure white robes, Like very sanctity iii 3 23
Whose very naming punishes me with the remembrance iv 2 24
I did purpose, boy, With this same very iron to burn them out *K. John* iv 1 125
You shall see now in very sincerity of fear and cold heart 1 *Hen. IV.* ii 3 32
So many of his shadows thou hast met And not the very king v 4 31
In very truth, sir, I had as lief be hanged, sir, as go 2 *Hen. IV.* iii 2 237
A full commission, In very ample virtue of his father iv 1 163
The very casques That did affright the air at Agincourt *Hen. V.* Prol. 13
As very infants prattle of thy pride 1 *Hen. VI.* iii 1 16
The very parings of our nails Shall pitch a field when we are dead iii 1 102
All our general force Might with a sally of the very town Be buckled with iv 4 4
A virgin from her tender infancy, Chaste and immaculate in very thought v 4 51
Should have torn and rent my very heart, Before I would have yielded 2 *Hen. VI.* i 1 126
The very train of her worst wearing gown Was better worth i 3 88
With the very shaking of their chains They may astonish these fell-lurking curs v 1 145
To see this sight, it irks my very soul 3 *Hen. VI.* ii 2 6
In the very pangs of death he cried, Like to a dismal clangor ii 3 17
With fiery eyes sparkling for very wrath ii 5 131
At my depart, these were his very words iv 1 92
The very beams will dry those vapours up v 3 12
When he shall split thy very heart with sorrow *Richard III.* i 3 300
Such hideous cries, that with the very noise I trembling waked i 4 60
This same very day your enemies, The kindred of the queen, must die iii 2 49
Even of your mettle, of your very blood iv 4 302
The very thought of this fair company Clapp'd wings to me *Hen. VIII.* i 4 8
They say he is a very man per se, And stands alone *Troi. and Cres.* i 2 15
As if that luck, in very spite of cunning, Bade him win all v 5 41
A curse begin at very root on's heart, That is not glad to see thee! *Coriolanus* ii 1 202
The very trick on't iv 6 70
A very little I have yielded to v 3 16
Steel to the very back, Yet wrung with wrongs *T. Andron.* iv 3 47
And used their very daggers *Macbeth* i 7 76
I have found The very cause of Hamlet's lunacy *Hamlet* ii 2 49
This is the very coinage of your brain: This bodiless creation ecstasy Is very cunning in iii 4 137
A very riband in the cap of youth, Yet needful too iv 7 78
The very conveyances of his lands will hardly lie in this box v 1 119
I'll write straight to my sister, To hold my very course *Lear* i 3 26
Than as a very pretence and purpose of unkindness i 4 75
Vain it is That we present us to him.—Very bootless v 3 294
Even now, now, very now *Othello* i 1 88
Yet do I hold it very stuff o' the conscience To do no contrived murder i 2 2
Very nature will instruct her in it and compel her to some second choice ii 1 237
I should make very forges of my cheeks iv 2 74
I know you could not lack . . . Very necessity of this thought *A. and C.* ii 2 58
Yea, very force entangles Itself with strength iv 14 48
Though I think the king Be touch'd at very heart *Cymbeline* i 1 10
I am absolute 'Twas very Cloten iv 2 107
Thou dost approve thyself the very same: Thy name well fits thy faith iv 2 380
To me The very doors and windows savour vilely *Pericles* iv 6 117
And justify in knowledge She is thy very princess v 1 220
Vesper. These signs; They are black vesper's pageants *Ant. and Cleo.* iv 14 8
Vessel. A brave vessel, Who had, no doubt, some noble creature in her, Dash'd all to pieces *Tempest* i 2 6
Not so much perdition as an hair Betid to any creature in the vessel i 2 31
All but mariners Plunged in the foaming brine and quit the vessel i 2 211
Wrecked at sea, having in that perished vessel the dowry of his sister *Meas. for Meas.* iii 1 225
Jaquenetta,—so is the weaker vessel called *L. L. Lost* i 1 276
I keep her as a vessel of thy law's fury i 1 277
Rocks, Which touching but my gentle vessel's side, Would scatter all her spices on the stream *Mer. of Venice* i 1 32
There miscarried A vessel of our country richly fraught ii 8 30
And not one vessel 'scape the dreadful touch Of merchant-marring rocks? iii 2 273
I must comfort the weaker vessel, as doublet and hose ought to *As Y. Like It* ii 4 6
Believing thee a vessel of too great a burthen *All's Well* ii 3 215
A bawbling vessel was he captain of *T. Night* v 1 57
I never saw a vessel of like sorrow, So fill'd and so becoming *W. Tale* iii 3 21
And most opportune to our need I have A vessel rides fast by iv 4 512
You are the weaker vessel, as they say, the emptier vessel 2 *Hen. IV.* ii 4 66
That the united vessel of their blood . . . Shall never leak iv 4 44
The poring dark Fills the wide vessel of the universe *Hen. V.* iv Prol. 3
The saying is true, 'The empty vessel makes the greatest sound' iv 4 73
As ravenous fishes, do a vessel follow That is new-trimm'd *Hen. VIII.* i 2 79
As weeds before A vessel under sail, so men obey'd *Coriolanus* ii 2 110
Though thy tackle's torn, Thou show'st a noble vessel iv 5 68
Women, being the weaker vessels, are ever thrust to the wall *R. and J.* i 1 20
If I would broach the vessels of my love, And try the argument of hearts by borrowing *T. of Athens* ii 2 186
Other incident throes That nature's fragile vessel doth sustain v 1 204
Now is that noble vessel full of grief, That it runs over *J. Cæsar* v 5 13
Put rancours in the vessel of my peace *Macbeth* iii 1 67
Your vessels and your spells provide, Your charms and every thing beside iii 5 18
Let's to the seaside, ho! As well to see the vessel that's come in *Othello* ii 1 37
If to preserve this vessel for my lord From any other foul unlawful touch Be not to be a strumpet, I am none iv 2 83
No vessel can peep forth, but 'tis as soon Taken as seen *Ant. and Cleo.* i 4 53
These three world-sharers, these competitors, Are in thy vessel ii 7 77
Strike the vessels, ho! Here is to Cæsar! ii 7 103
Winds of all the corners kiss'd your sails, To make your vessel nimble *Cymbeline* ii 4 29
From this most bravest vessel of the world Struck the main-top! iv 2 319
Vessel. Hath stuff'd these hollow vessels with their power, To beat us down *Pericles* i 4 67
Their vessel shakes On Neptune's billow iii Gower 44
He bears A tempest, which his mortal vessel tears, And yet he rides it out iv 4 30
Seeing this goodly vessel ride before us, I made to it v 1 18
Our vessel is of Tyre, in it the king v 1 23
Vestal. A certain aim he took At a fair vestal throned by the west *M. N. Dream* ii 1 158
She is envious; Her vestal livery is but sick and green *Rom. and Jul.* ii 2 8
Who, even in pure and vestal modesty, Still blush, as thinking their own kisses sin iii 3 38
Women are not In their best fortunes strong; but want will perjure The ne'er-touch'd vestal *Ant. and Cleo.* iii 12 31
A vestal livery will I take me to, And never more have joy *Pericles* iii 4 10
Shall's go hear the vestals sing?—I'll do any thing now that is virtuous iv 5 7
Vestment. Do their gay vestments his affections bait? *Com. of Errors* ii 1 94
Nor sight of priests in holy vestments bleeding, Shall pierce *T. of Athens* iv 3 125
Vesture. To bear my lady's train, lest the base earth Should from her vesture chance to steal a kiss *T. G. of Ver.* ii 4 160
Whilst this muddy vesture of decay Doth grossly close it in *Mer. of Ven.* v 1 64
Nor on him put The napless vesture of humility *Coriolanus* ii 1 250
What, weep you when you but behold Our Cæsar's vesture wounded? *J. Cæsar* iii 2 200
In the essential vesture of creation Does tire the ingener *Othello* ii 1 64
Vetch. Go and vetch me in my closet un boitier vert, a box *Mer. Wives* i 4 46
Vetches. Thy rich leas Of wheat, rye, barley, vetches, oats, and pease *Tempest* iv 1 61
Vex. Away, I say! stay'st thou to vex me here? *T. G. of Ver.* iv 4 66
Proof enough to misuse the prince, to vex Claudio *Much Ado* ii 2 29
Such an injury would vex a very saint, Much more a shrew *T. of Shrew* iii 2 28
'Tis my picture; Refuse it not; it hath no tongue to vex you *T. Night* iii 4 229
A trespass that doth vex my grieved soul *Richard II.* i 1 138
Vex not yourself, nor strive not with your breath ii 1 3
I will not vex your souls—Since presently your souls must part your bodies iii 1 2
Discover how with most advantage They may vex us 1 *Hen. VI.* i 4 13
Not all these lords do vex me half so much As that proud dame 2 *Hen. VI.* i 3 78
If so thou think'st, vex him with eager words 3 *Hen. VI.* ii 6 68
Now, the Lord help, They vex me past my patience! *Hen. VIII.* ii 4 130
A sight to vex the father's soul withal *T. Andron.* v 1 52
'Twill vex thy soul to hear what I shall speak v 1 62
Why dost thou seek me out?—To vex thee.—Always a villain's office or a fool's *T. of Athens* iv 3 236
Do poor Tom some charity, whom the foul fiend vexes *Lear* iii 4 62
Vex not his ghost: O, let him pass! v 3 313
Vex not his prescience; be attentive *Ant. and Cleo.* i 2 20
Which, as I say, to vex her I will execute *Cymbeline* iii 5 147
Vexation. All thy vexations Were but my trials of thy love *Tempest* iv 1 5
It would be much vexation to your age *T. G. of Ver.* iii 1 16
Full of vexation come I, with complaint *M. N. Dream* i 1 22
Think no more of this night's accidents But as the fierce vexation of a dream iv 1 74
You do me most insupportable vexation.—I would it were hell-pains *All's Well* ii 3 244
Dost think I am so muddy, so unsettled, To appoint myself in this vexation? *W. Tale* i 2 326
Vexation almost stops my breath, That sunder'd friends greet in the hour of death 1 *Hen. VI.* iv 3 41
Your children were vexation to your youth *Richard III.* iv 4 305
Follow him . . . with all despite; Give him deserved vexation *Coriol.* iii 3 140
Though that his joy be joy, Yet throw such changes of vexation on't, As it may lose some colour *Othello* i 1 72
Harm not yourself with your vexation: I am senseless of your wrath *Cymbeline* i 1 134
O, that husband! My supreme crown of grief! and those repeated Vexations of it! i 6 5
Vexed. I am vex'd; Bear with my weakness *Tempest* iv 1 158
He's shrewdly vexed at something: look, he has spied us *All's Well* iii 5 92
Whose passage, vex'd with thy impediment, Shall leave his native channel *K. John* ii 1 336
With my vex'd spirits I cannot take a truce iii 1 17
Oft the teeming earth Is with a kind of colic pinch'd and vex'd 1 *Hen. IV.* iii 1 29
He is vex'd at something *Hen. VIII.* iii 2 104
Do you think, my lords, The king will suffer but the little finger Of this man to be vex'd? v 3 107
The nobility are vex'd, whom we see have sided In his behalf *Coriolanus* iv 2 2
Being vex'd, a sea nourish'd with lovers' tears *Rom. and Jul.* i 1 198
I am so vexed, that every part about me quivers ii 4 170
Is my poor heart so for a kinsman vex'd iii 5 96
Vexed I am Of late with passions of some difference *J. Cæsar* i 2 39
He was met even now As mad as the vex'd sea *Lear* iv 4 2
I am not vexed more at any thing in the earth *Cymbeline* ii 1 19
Vexest. How vexest thou this man! talkest thou nothing but of ladies? *T. Night* iv 2 29
Vexeth. When grief, and blood ill-temper'd, vexeth him *J. Cæsar* iv 3 115
Vexing. Life is as tedious as a twice-told tale Vexing the dull ear of a drowsy man *K. John* iii 4 109
Via. Mistress Page have I encompassed you? go to; via! *Mer. Wives* ii 2 159
In via, in way, of explication *L. L. Lost* iv 2 14
Via, goodman Dull! thou hast spoken no word all this while v 1 156
Another, with his finger and his thumb, Cried, 'Via! we will do't' v 2 112
'Via!' says the fiend; 'away!' says the fiend *Mer. of Venice* ii 2 11
Via! les eaux et la terre.—Rien puis? l'air et le feu *Hen. V.* iv 2 4
Why, Via! to London will we march amain 3 *Hen. VI.* ii 1 182
Vial. You gods, look down And from your sacred vials pour your graces Upon my daughter's head! *W. Tale* v 3 122
Edward's seven sons . . . Were as seven vials of his sacred blood *Rich. II.* i 2 12
Take thou this vial, being then in bed, And this distilled liquor drink thou off *Rom. and Jul.* iv 1 93
Come, vial. What if this mixture do not work at all iv 3 20
With juice of cursed hebenon in a vial *Hamlet* i 5 62
Where be the sacred vials thou shouldst fill With sorrowful water? *Ant. and Cleo.* i 3 63
Viand. No matter, since They have left their viands behind *Tempest* iii 3 41
Let their beds Be made as soft as yours and let their palates Be season'd with such viands *Mer. of Venice* iv 1 97
His viands sparkling in a golden cup 3 *Hen. VI.* ii 5 52
The remainder viands We do not throw in unrespective sieve *Troi. and Cres.* ii 2 70
Idle and unactive, Still cupboarding the viand *Coriolanus* i 1 103

Viand. Love, I am full of lead. Some wine, within there, and our viands! *Ant. and Cleo.* iii 11 73
'Twas at a feast,—O, would Our viands had been poison'd! *Cymbeline* v 5 156
All viands that I eat do seem unsavoury, Wishing him my meat *Pericles* ii 3 31

Vicar. Procure the vicar To stay for me at church 'twixt twelve and one *Mer. Wives* iv 6 48
I'll to the vicar: Bring you the maid, you shall not lack a priest . iv 6 52
I have been with Sir Oliver Martext, the vicar . . . *As Y. Like It* iii 3 43
He stamp'd and swore, As if the vicar meant to cozen him *T. of Shrew* iii 2 170

Vice. Well, your old vice still; mistake the word *T. G. of Ver.* iii 1 283
Here follow her vices.—Close at the heels of her virtues . . . . . iii 1 324
She is slow in words.—O villain, that set this down among her vices! . iii 1 338
All sects, all ages smack of this vice . *Meas. for Meas.* ii 2 5
There is a vice that most I do abhor . . . . ii 2 29
Hath yet a kind of medicine in itself, That skins the vice o' the top . ii 2 136
Ha! fie, these filthy vices! . . . . ii 4 42
And rather proved the sliding of your brother A merriment than a vice ii 4 116
O dishonest wretch! Wilt thou be made a man out of my vice? . . iii 1 138
But think What 'tis to cram a maw or clothe a back From such a filthy vice iii 2 24
It [lechery] is too general a vice, and severity must cure it . . . iii 2 106
The vice is of a great kindred; it is well allied . . . . . iii 2 108
Twice treble shame on Angelo, To weed my vice and let his grow! . . iii 2 284
Craft against vice I must apply . . . . iii 2 291
When vice makes mercy, mercy's so extended . . . . . . iv 2 115
Apparel vice like virtue's harbinger; Bear a fair presence *Com. of Errors* iii 2 12
You must put in the pikes with a vice . . . . *Much Ado* v 2 21
You nickname virtue; vice you should have spoke . *L. L. Lost* v 2 349
There is no vice so simple but assumes Some mark of virtue *Mer. of Ven.* iii 2 81
On that vice in him will my revenge find notable cause to work *T. Night* ii 3 165
Or any taint of vice whose strong corruption Inhabits our frail blood . iii 4 390
I'll be with you again, In a trice, Like to the old Vice . . . . iv 2 134
As he had seen't or been an instrument To vice you to't *W. Tale* i 2 416
I ne'er heard yet That any of these bolder vices wanted Less impudence to gainsay what they did Than to perform it first . . . . . . iii 2 56
I cannot tell, good sir, for which of his virtues it was, but he was certainly whipped out of the court.—His vices, you would say . . . iv 3 96
Being rich, my virtue then shall be To say there is no vice but beggary *K. John* ii 1 596
So shall my virtue be his vice's bawd . . . . *Richard II.* v 3 67
That reverend vice, that grey iniquity, that father ruffian . *1 Hen. IV.* ii 4 499
An I but fist him once; an a' come but within my vice . *2 Hen. IV.* ii 1 24
How subject we old men are to this vice of lying! . . . . . iii 2 326
And now is this Vice's dagger become a squire . . . . . iii 2 343
This your air of France Hath blown that vice in me . . *Hen. V.* iii 6 161
Corrupt and tainted with a thousand vices . . . . *1 Hen. VI.* v 4 45
Like the formal vice, Iniquity, I moralize two meanings in one word *Richard III.* iii 1 82
So smooth he daub'd his vice with show of virtue . . . . . iii 5 29
What a vice were it in Ajax now,— If he were proud . *Troi. and Cres.* ii 3 246
Will you be true?—Who, I? alas, it is my vice, my fault . . . iv 4 104
Brother, you have a vice of mercy in you, Which better fits a lion than a man.—What vice is that? . . . . v 3 37
What he cannot help in his nature, you account a vice in him *Coriolanus* i 1 43
Virtue itself turns vice, being misapplied; And vice sometimes by action dignified . . . . *Rom. and Jul.* ii 3 22
My poor country Shall have more vices than it had before . *Macbeth* iv 3 47
In whom I know All the particulars of vice so grafted . . . iv 3 51
A vice of kings; A cutpurse of the empire and the rule . *Hamlet* iii 4 98
In the fatness of these pursy times Virtue itself of vice must pardon beg iii 4 154
Thy state is the more gracious; for 'tis a vice to know him . . v 2 87
Through tatter'd clothes small vices do appear . . . *Lear* iv 6 168
As duteous to the vices of thy mistress As badness would desire . iv 6 258
The gods are just, and of our pleasant vices Make instruments to plague us v 3 170
As truly as to heaven I do confess the vices of my blood . *Othello* i 3 123
Do but see his vice; 'Tis to his virtue a just equinox . . . ii 3 128
Unless self-charity be sometimes a vice, And to defend ourselves it be a sin . . . . ii 3 202
She holds it a vice in her goodness not to do more than she is requested ii 3 326
O wretched fool, That livest to make thine honesty a vice! . . . iii 3 376
Did you perceive how he laughed at his vice? . . . . . iv 1 181
The world's a huge thing: it is a great price For a small vice . iv 3 70
It is not Cæsar's natural vice to hate Our great competitor *Ant. and Cleo.* i 4 2
It is a vice in her ears . . . . *Cymbeline* ii 3 33
No motion That tends to vice in man, but I affirm It is the woman's part ii 5 21
Even to vice They are not constant, but are changing still One vice, but of a minute old, for one Not half so old as that . . . . . ii 5 29
For vice repeated is like the wandering wind, Blows dust in others' eyes, to spread itself . . . . *Pericles* i 1 96
Kings are earth's gods; in vice their law's their will . . . . i 1 103

Vicegerent. Great deputy, the welkin's vicegerent . . *L. L. Lost* i 1 222

Viceroy. Trinculo and thyself shall be viceroys . . *Tempest* iii 2 116
Submit thyself, Thou shalt be placed as viceroy under him . *1 Hen. VI.* v 4 131
Shall I, for lucre of the rest unvanquish'd, Detract so much from that prerogative, As to be call'd but viceroy? . . . . . . v 4 143

Vici. He it was that might rightly say, Veni, vidi, vici . . *L. L. Lost* iv 1 68

Vicious, ungentle, foolish, blunt, unkind . . . . *Com. of Errors* iv 2 21
She hath lived too long, To fill the world with vicious qualities *1 Hen. VI.* v 4 35
The mind growing once corrupt, They turn to vicious forms *Hen. VIII.* i 2 117
Praise his most vicious strain, And call it excellent . *T. of Athens* iv 3 213
For some vicious mole of nature in them . . . . *Hamlet* i 4 24
It is no vicious blot, murder, or foulness, No unchaste action . *Lear* i 1 230
The dark and vicious place where thee he got Cost him his eyes . v 3 172
Though I perchance am vicious in my guess . . . *Othello* iii 3 145
It had been vicious To have mistrusted her . . . *Cymbeline* v 5 65

Viciousness. When we in our viciousness grow hard—O misery on't!—the wise gods seel our eyes . . . . . *Ant. and Cleo.* iii 13 111

Victor. Open your gates and give the victors way . *K. John* ii 1 324
We shall see Justice design the victor's chivalry . *Richard II.* i 1 203
But if your father had been victor there, He ne'er had borne it out of Coventry . . . . *2 Hen. IV.* iv 1 134
Late did he shine upon the English side; Now we are victors *1 Hen. VI.* i 2 4
Such rewards As victors wear at the Olympian games . *3 Hen. VI.* ii 3 53
Both tugging to be victors, breast to breast, Yet neither conqueror . ii 5 11
Come to me, friend or foe, And tell me who is victor? . . . . v 2 6
Do you purpose A victor shall be known? . . *Troi. and Cres.* iv 5 67
Despite thy victor sword and fire-new fortune . . . *Lear* v 3 132
Forthwith they fly . . . slaves, The strides they victors made *Cymbeline* v 3 43
And, Caius Lucius, Although the victor, we submit to Cæsar . . v 5 460

Victorious. Shall that victorious hand be feebled here? . *K. John* v 2 146
This is a stem Of that victorious stock . . . *Hen. V.* ii 4 63
Victorious Talbot! pardon my abuse . . . *1 Hen. VI.* ii 3 67
Welcome, brave captain and victorious lord! . . . . . iii 4 16
Salisbury, and victorious Warwick, Received deep scars in France *2 Hen. VI.* i 1 86
And so to arms, victorious father, To quell the rebels and their complices v 1 211
Now are our brows bound with victorious wreaths . *Richard III.* i 1 5
Our princely father York Bless'd his three sons with his victorious arm i 4 242
God and your arms be praised, victorious friends; The day is ours v 5 1
Hail, Rome, victorious in thy mourning weeds! . *T. Andron.* i 1 70
Gracious conqueror, Victorious Titus, rue the tears I shed . . . i 1 105
O, bless me here with thy victorious hand! . . . . . i 1 163
Where rather I'll expect victorious life Than death and honour *Ant. and Cleo.* iv 2 43

Victory. A victory is twice itself when the achiever brings home full numbers . . . . *Much Ado* i 1 8
We have ten proofs to one that blood hath the victory . . . ii 3 172
The conclusion is victory: on whose side? the king's . *L. L. Lost* iv 1 75
Set the deer's horns upon his head, for a branch of victory *As Y. L. It* iv 2 6
Victory, with little loss, doth play Upon the dancing banners of the French . . . . *K. John* ii 1 307
She shall give the day, And kiss him with a glorious victory . . ii 1 394
Lift me up To reach at victory above my head . . . *Richard II.* i 3 72
Disgraced me in my happy victories . . . . . *1 Hen. IV.* iv 3 97
Why is Rumour here? I run before King Harry's victory *2 Hen. IV.* Ind. 23
Hark, how they shout!—This had been cheerful after victory . iv 2 88
Death's dishonourable victory We with our stately presence glorify *1 Hen. VI.* i 1 20
Let us banquet royally, After this golden day of victory . . . i 6 31
Yet heavens have glory for this victory! . . . . . . iii 2 117
I hope ere long To be presented, by your victories, With Charles . iv 1 172
Saint George and victory! fight, soldiers, fight . . . . iv 6 1
It warm'd thy father's heart with proud desire Of bold-faced victory . iv 6 12
This monument of the victory will I bear . . . *2 Hen. VI.* iv 3 12
You are strong and manly; God on our side, doubt not of victory . iv 8 54
Iden, farewell, and be proud of thy victory . . . . . iv 10 78
When I return with victory from the field I'll see your grace *3 Hen. VI.* i 1 261
Though the odds be great, I doubt not, uncle, of our victory . . i 2 73
Let our bloody colours wave! And either victory, or else a grave . ii 2 174
Plant courage in their quailing breasts; For yet is hope of life and victory ii 3 55
To whom God will, there be the victory! . . . . . . ii 5 15
Why, so! then am I sure of victory. Now therefore let us hence . iv 1 147
The harder match'd, the greater victory . . . . . v 1 70
Lords, to the field; Saint George and victory! . . . . v 1 113
We are graced with wreaths of victory . . . . . . v 3 2
Laid open all your victories in Scotland, Your discipline in war *Rich. III.* iii 7 15
There the little souls of Edward's children Whisper the spirits of thine enemies And promise them success and victory . . . . . iv 4 193
Fortune and victory sit on thy helm! . . . . v 3 79
Peise me down to-morrow, When I should mount with wings of victory v 3 106
Make us thy ministers of chastisement, That we may praise thee in the victory! . . . . v 3 114
Sleep thou a quiet sleep; Dream of success and happy victory! . v 3 165
Methought their souls, whose bodies Richard murder'd, Came to my tent, and cried on victory . . . . v 3 231
Boldly and cheerfully; God and Saint George! Richmond and victory! v 3 270
Upon them! Victory sits on our helms . . . . . . v 3 351
What shall be done To him that victory commands? . *Troi. and Cres.* iv 5 66
Brings a' victory in his pocket? the wounds become him . *Coriolanus* ii 1 135
Alas, how can we for our country pray, Whereto we are bound, together with thy victory, Whereto we are bound? . . . . . . v 3 108
O my mother, mother! O! You have won a happy victory to Rome . v 3 186
But at his nurse's tears He whined and roar'd away your victory . v 6 98
Thy face is much abused with tears.—The tears have got small victory by that; For it was bad enough before . . . *Rom. and Jul.* iv 1 30
I'll pawn my victories, all My honours to you . . . *T. of Athens* iii 5 81
Put on my brows this wreath of victory, And bid me give it thee *J. C.* v 3 85
To conclude, The victory fell on us.—Great happiness! . *Macbeth* i 2 58
If you have victory, let the trumpet sound For him that brought it *Lear* v 1 41
All the gods go with you! upon your sword Sit laurel victory! *A. and C.* i 3 100
They are beaten, sir; and our advantage serves For a fair victory . iv 7 12
Why so sadly Greet you our victory? . . . . . *Cymbeline* v 5 24
To whom this wreath of victory I give, And crown you king *Pericles* ii 3 10

Victress. She shall be sole victress, Cæsar's Cæsar . *Richard III.* iv 4 336

Victual. I am one that am nourished by my victuals . *T. G. of Ver.* ii 1 180
You had musty victual, and he hath holp to eat it . . *Much Ado* i 1 50
I will desire you to live in the mean time, and eat your victuals *Hen. V.* v 1 35
I must go victual Orleans forthwith . . . . . *1 Hen. VI.* i 5 14
But that it eats our victuals, I should think Here were a fairy *Cymbeline* iii 6 41

Victualled. Thy loving voyage Is but for two months victuall'd *As Y. L. It* v 4 198

Victuallers. All victuallers do so: what's a joint of mutton or two in a whole Lent? . . . . *2 Hen. IV.* ii 4 375

Videlicet, He came, saw, and overcame . . . *L. L. Lost* iv 1 70
And thus she means, videlicet . . . . . *M. N. Dream* v 1 330
Not any man died in his own person, videlicet, in a love-cause *As Y. L. It* iv 1 97
I saw him enter such a house of sale, Videlicet, a brothel . *Hamlet* ii 1 61

Video. Videsne quis venit?—Video, et gaudeo . . *L. L. Lost* v 1 34

Vides. Magni Dominator poli, Tam lentus audis scelera? tam lentus vides? . . . . *T. Andron.* iv 1 82

Videsne quis venit?—Video, et gaudeo . . . *L. L. Lost* v 1 33

Vidi. He it was that might rightly say, Veni, vidi, vici . . . iv 1 68

Vie. Mort de ma vie! if they march along Unfought withal *Hen. V.* iii 5 11
Gardez ma vie, et je vous donnerai deux cents écus . . . . iv 4 44
Mort de ma vie! all is confounded, all! . . . . . . iv 5 3
Nature wants stuff To vie strange forms with fancy . *Ant. and Cleo.* v 2 98
With the dove of Paphos might the crow Vie feathers white *Per.* iv Gower 33

Vied. And kiss on kiss She vied so fast, protesting oath on oath, That in a twink she won me to her love . . . . . . *T. of Shrew* ii 1 311

Vienna. If any in Vienna be of worth To undergo such ample grace and honour, It is Lord Angelo . . . . *Meas. for Meas.* i 1 23
Mortality and mercy in Vienna Live in thy tongue and heart . . . i 1 45
All houses in the suburbs of Vienna must be plucked down . . . i 2 98
I have deliver'd to Lord Angelo, A man of stricture and firm abstinence, My absolute power and place here in Vienna . . . . . i 3 13
Where were you born, friend?—Here in Vienna, sir . . . . ii 1 203
The law will not allow it, Pompey; nor it shall not be allowed in Vienna ii 1 241
If this law hold in Vienna ten year, I'll rent the fairest house in it after three-pence a bay . . . . ii 1 254
We shall find this friar a notable fellow.—As any in Vienna . . . v 1 269
My business in this state Made me a looker on here in Vienna . . v 1 319
This play is the image of a murder done in Vienna . . . *Hamlet* iii 2 249

View. What a fool is she, that knows I am a maid, And would not force the letter to my view! . . . *T. G. of Ver.* i 2 54
Sometimes the beam of her view gilded my foot . . *Mer. Wives* i 3 69
Women are frail too.—Ay, as the glasses where they view themselves *Meas. for Meas.* ii 4 125
Under penalty, to deliver his head in the view of Angelo . . iv 2 177
I'll view the manners of the town, Peruse the traders *Com. of Errors* i 2 12
I will go lose myself And wander up and down to view the city . i 2 31
The fairest dames, That ever turn'd their—backs—to mortal views! *L. L. Lost* v 2 161
Thy fair virtue's force perforce doth move me On the first view to say, to swear, I love thee . . . . *M. N. Dream* iii 1 144
And then I will her charmed eye release From monster's view . . iii 2 377
Throughfares now For princes to come view fair Portia *Mer. of Venice* ii 7 43
With bleared visages, come forth to view The issue of the exploit . iii 2 59
With much much more dismay I view the fight than thou that makest the fray . . . . iii 2 62
You that choose not by the view, Chance as fair and choose as true! . iii 2 132
To view with hollow eye and wrinkled brow An age of poverty . . iv 1 270
A need Greater than shows itself at the first view . . *All's Well* ii 5 73
We are reconciled, and the first view shall kill All repetition . . v 3 21
Return this answer: The element itself, till seven years' heat, Shall not behold her face at ample view . . . . *T. Night* i 1 27
Fortune forbid my outside have not charm'd her! She made good view of me . . . . ii 2 20
Wrecked the same instant of their master's death and in the view of the shepherd . . . . *W. Tale* v 2 76
May this be true?—Have I not hideous death within my view? *K. John* v 4 22
Here in the view of men I will unfold some causes of your deaths *Rich. II.* iii 1 6
Fetch hither Richard, that in common view He may surrender . . iv 1 155
'Tis meet we all go forth To view the sick and feeble parts of France *Hen. V.* ii 4 22
The king himself is rode to view their battle . . . . . iv 3 2
Give us leave, great king, To view the field in safety . . . iv 7 85
I demand, before this royal view, What rub or what impediment there is v 2 32
Lords, view these letters full of bad mischance . . 1 *Hen. VI.* i 1 89
I'll to the Tower with all the haste I can, To view the artillery . . i 1 168
I count each one And view the Frenchmen how they fortify . . i 4 61
My lord protector, view the letter Sent from our uncle Duke of Burgundy iv 1 48
When the dusky sky began to rob My earnest-gaping sight of thy land's view, I took a costly jewel from my neck . . 2 *Hen. VI.* iii 2 105
And even with this I lost fair England's view . . . . iii 2 110
View his breathless corpse, And comment then upon his sudden death iii 2 132
Come hither, gracious sovereign, view this body . . . iii 2 149
O, let me view his visage, being dead, That living wrought me such exceeding trouble . . . . v 1 69
Even to affright thee with the view thereof . . . . . v 1 207
Richard, in the view of many lords, Resign'd the crown . 3 *Hen. VI.* i 1 138
And, if thou canst for blushing, view this face, And bite thy tongue . i 4 46
Untimely brought to light, Whose ugly and unnatural aspect May fright the hopeful mother at the view . . . . . *Richard III.* i 2 24
If thou delight to view thy heinous deeds, Behold this pattern . . i 2 53
Then you lost The view of earthly glory . . . . *Hen. VIII.* i 1 14
Order gave each thing view; the office did Distinctly his full function . i 1 44
And, under your fair conduct, Crave leave to view these ladies . . i 4 71
Which when the people Had the full view of, such a noise arose . . iv 1 71
Hector, in view of Trojans and of Greeks, Shall make it good *T. and C.* i 3 273
To talk with him and to behold his visage, Even to my full of view . iii 3 241
I have fed mine eyes on thee; I have with exact view perused thee . iv 5 232
I will the second time, As I would buy thee, view thee limb by limb . iv 5 238
Gives all gaze and bent of amorous view On the fair Cressid . . iv 5 282
Has our general met the enemy?—They lie in view . *Coriolanus* i 4 4
But then Aufidius was within my view, And wrath o'erwhelm'd my pity i 9 85
And i' the consul's view Slew three opposers . . . . . ii 2 97
Mine eyes are cloy'd with view of tyranny . . *T. Andron.* iii 2 55
Alas, that love, so gentle in his view, Should be so tyrannous and rough in proof!—Alas, that love, whose view is muffled still, Should, without eyes, see pathways to his will! . . . *Rom. and Jul.* i 1 175
Which on more view, of many mine being one May stand in number . i 2 32
Who else would soar above the view of men . . *J. Cæsar* i 1 79
On the view and knowing of these contents, Without debatement *Hamlet* v 2 44
Give order that these bodies High on a stage be placed to the view . v 2 389
The enemy's in view; draw up your powers . . . *Lear* v 1 51
I never did like molestation view On the enchafed flood . . *Othello* ii 1 16
His goodly eyes . . . now bend, now turn, The office and devotion of their view Upon a tawny front . . . . *Ant. and Cleo.* i 1 5
And do invite you to my sister's view, Whither straight I'll lead you . ii 2 170
Mine eyes did sicken at the sight, and could not Endure a further view iii 10 18
Mechanic slaves With greasy aprons . . . shall Uplift us to the view . v 2 211
With A pudency so rosy the sweet view on't Might well have warm'd old Saturn . . . . *Cymbeline* ii 5 11
We, poor unfledged, Have never wing'd from view o' the nest . . iii 3 28
You should tread a course Pretty and full of view . . . . iii 4 150
Her face, like heaven, enticeth thee to view Her countless glory *Pericles* i 1 30
O you powers That give heaven countless eyes to view men's acts! . i 1 73
She'll wed the stranger knight, Or never more to view nor day nor light ii 5 17
Viewed. The saddest spectacle that e'er I view'd . 3 *Hen. VI.* ii 1 67
And the first he view'd, He did it with a serious mind . *Hen. VIII.* iii 2 79
Lady Anne . . . This day was view'd in open as his queen . . iii 2 404
Viewest. Here thou viewest, beholdest, surveyest, or seest . *L. L. Lost* i 1 246
Vieweth. The sun with one eye vieweth all the world . 1 *Hen. VI.* i 4 84
Viewing. And feed your knowledge With viewing of the town *T. Night* iii 3 42
The happiest youth, viewing his progress through, What perils past 2 *Hen. IV.* iii 1 54
Tell o'er your woes again by viewing mine . . *Richard. III.* iv 4 39
In viewing o'er the rest o' the selfsame day, He finds thee in the stout Norweyan ranks . . . . *Macbeth* i 3 94
Viewless. To be imprison'd in the viewless winds . *Meas. for Meas.* iii 1 124
Vigil. Will yearly on the vigil feast his neighbours . . *Hen. V.* iv 3 45
Vigilance. They Will not, nor cannot, use such vigilance As when they are fresh . . . . *Tempest* iii 3 16
Shall Henry's conquest, Bedford's vigilance, Your deeds of war, and all our counsel die? . . . . 2 *Hen. VI.* i 1 96
No port is free; no place, That guard, and most unusual vigilance, Does not attend my taking . . . . *Lear* ii 3 4
Vigilant. I am as vigilant as a cat to steal cream . 1 *Hen. IV.* iv 2 64
Sirs, take your places and be vigilant . . . 1 *Hen. VI.* ii 1 1
The kingly-crowned head, the vigilant eye, The counsellor heart *Coriolanus* i 1 119
Vigitant. Adieu: be vigitant, I beseech you . . . . *Much Ado* iii 3 100

Vigour. Thy nerves are in their infancy again And have no vigour in them . . . . *Tempest* i 2 485
Never could the strumpet, With all her double vigour, art, and nature, Once stir my temper . . . . . *Meas. for Meas.* ii 2 184
My bones bear witness, That since have felt the vigour of his rage *Com. of Errors* iv 4 81
Long-during action tires The sinewy vigour of the traveller *L. L. Lost* iv 3 308
The grappling vigour and rough frown of war Is cold in amity *K. John* iii 1 104
Doth with a twofold vigour lift me up To reach at victory *Richard II.* i 3 71
And, for thy vigour, Bull-bearing Milo his addition yield To sinewy Ajax *Troi. and Cres.* ii 3 257
For beauty, wit, High birth, vigour of bone, desert in service . . iii 3 172
This myself, The vigour and the picture of my youth . *T. Andron.* iv 2 108
With a sudden vigour it doth posset And curd . . . . *Hamlet* i 5 68
To try the vigour of them and apply Allayments to their act . *Cymbeline* i 5 21
Vile. We detest such vile base practices . . . . *T. G. of Ver.* iv 1 73
How Falstaff, varlet vile, His dove will prove, his gold will hold *M. Wives* i 3 106
O, what a world of vile ill-favour'd faults Looks handsome in three hundred pounds a-year! . . . . iii 4 32
I often glanced it; Still did I tell him it was vile and bad *Com. of Errors* v 1 67
Her feet were much too dainty for such tread!—O vile! . *L. L. Lost* iv 3 280
Things base and vile, holding no quantity, Love can transpose *M. N. D.* i 1 232
Her mantle she did fall, Which Lion vile with bloody mouth did stain . v 1 144
Since lion vile hath here deflower'd my dear . . . . v 1 297
'Tis vile, unless it may be quaintly order'd . . . *Mer. of Venice* ii 4 6
O vile, Intolerable, not to be endured! . . . . *T. of Shrew* v 2 93
But O how vile an idol proves this god! . . . . *T. Night* iii 4 399
In such a love so vile a lout as he . . . . . *K. John* ii 1 509
The deed, which both our tongues held vile to name . . . iv 2 241
So it be new, there's no respect how vile . . . . *Richard II.* ii 1 25
To the infernal deep, with Erebus and tortures vile also . 2 *Hen. IV.* ii 4 171
O thou dull god [sleep], why liest thou with the vile In loathsome beds? iii 1 15
Let vultures vile seize on his lungs also! . . . . . v 3 146
I would have you solus.—'Solus,' egregious dog? O viper vile! *Hen. V.* ii 1 49
O braggart vile and damned furious wight! . . . . . ii 1 64
Self-love, my liege, is not so vile a sin As self-neglecting . . ii 4 74
We shall much disgrace With four or five most vile and ragged foils iv Prol. 50
Be he ne'er so vile, This day shall gentle his condition . . . iv 3 62
In writing I preferr'd The manner of thy vile outrageous crimes 1 *Hen. VI.* iii 1 11
With other vile and ignominious terms . . . . . . iv 1 97
To be a queen in bondage is more vile Than is a slave in base servility . v 3 112
This argues what her kind of life hath been, Wicked and vile . . v 4 16
You vile abominable tents, Thus proudly pight . *Troi. and Cres.* v 10 23
Call him noble that was now your hate, Him vile that was your garland *Coriolanus* i 1 188
For nought so vile that on the earth doth live But to the earth some special good doth give . . . . *Rom. and Jul.* ii 3 17
When we for recompense have praised the vile, It stains the glory in that happy verse Which aptly sings the good . . . *T. of Athens* i 1 15
To illuminate So vile a thing as Cæsar! . . . . *J. Cæsar* i 3 111
Who is here so vile that will not love his country? . . . . iii 2 35
I do find it cowardly and vile, For fear of what might fall, so to prevent The time of life . . . . v 1 104
Bark'd about, Most lazar-like, with vile and loathsome crust . *Hamlet* i 5 72
Our flesh and blood is grown so vile, my lord, That it doth hate what gets it . . . . *Lear* iii 4 150
Wisdom and goodness to the vile seem vile: Filths savour but themselves . . . . iv 2 38
Utter my thoughts? Why, say they are vile and false? . . *Othello* iii 3 136
In killing creatures vile, as cats and dogs, Of no esteem . . *Cymbeline* v 5 252
If neglection Should therein make me vile, the common body, By you relieved, would force me to my duty . . . . . *Pericles* iii 3 21
Vile apparel. Neither in gold nor silver, but in vile apparel . 2 *Hen. IV.* i 2 20
Vile beginners. Where are the vile beginners of this fray? *Rom. and Jul.* iii 1 146
Vile bezonians. Great men oft die by vile bezonians . 2 *Hen. VI.* iv 1 134
Vile blows. Whom the vile blows and buffets of the world Have so incensed that I am reckless what I do . . . . . *Macbeth* iii 1 109
Vile brawl. Silence those whom this vile brawl distracted . *Othello* ii 3 256
Vile company. Keeping such vile company as thou art hath in reason taken from me all ostentation of sorrow . . 2 *Hen. IV.* ii 2 52
Vile-concluded. A most base and vile-concluded peace . . *K. John* ii 1 586
Vile conclusion. The vile conclusion I now begin with grief and shame to utter . . . . *Meas. for Meas.* v 1 95
Vile confederates. And a rabble more Of vile confederates *Com. of Errors* v 1 236
Vile conquest. More than Octavius and Mark Antony By this vile conquest shall attain unto . . . . *J. Cæsar* v 5 38
Vile contagion. To dare the vile contagion of the night . . . ii 1 265
Vile daggers. When your vile daggers Hack'd one another in the sides of Cæsar . . . . v 1 39
Vile deed. This vile deed We must, with all our majesty and skill, Both countenance and excuse . . . . *Hamlet* iv 1 30
Vile-drawing. This vile-drawing bias, This sway of motion . *K. John* ii 1 577
Vile earth, to earth resign; end motion here! . *Rom. and Jul.* iii 2 59
Vile encounters. Confess'd the vile encounters they have had *Much Ado* iv 1 94
Vile-esteemed. And craved death Rather than I would be so vile-esteem'd 1 *Hen. VI.* i 4 33
Vile fault. For that vile fault Two of her brothers were condemn'd to death . . . . *T. Andron.* v 2 173
Vile fiend. Scoff on, vile fiend and shameless courtezan! 1 *Hen. VI.* iii 2 45
Vile forfeit. By some vile forfeit of untimely death . *Rom. and Jul.* i 4 111
Vile gold. By the merit of vile gold, dross, dust . . *K. John* iii 1 165
Vile guesses. Throw your vile guesses in the devil's teeth . *Othello* iii 4 184
Vile guns. And but for these vile guns, He would himself have been a soldier . . . . 1 *Hen. IV.* i 3 63
Vile heads. And in that paste let their vile heads be baked *T. Andron.* v 2 201
Vile hold. He that stands upon a slippery place Makes nice of no vile hold to stay him up . . . . *K. John* iii 4 138
Vile instrument! Thou shalt not damn my hand . . *Cymbeline* iii 4 75
Vile intent. Your vile intent must needs seem horrible . *K. John* iv 1 96
Vile jelly. Out, vile jelly! Where is thy lustre now? . . *Lear* iii 7 83
Vile king. O thou vile king, Give me my father! . . *Hamlet* iv 5 115
Vile lady. O, thy vile lady! She has robb'd me of my sword *Ant. and Cleo.* iv 14 22
Vile life. I like it very well; but in respect that it is private, it is a very vile life . . . . *As Y. Like It* iii 2 17
Vile Martext. A most wicked Sir Oliver, Audrey, a most vile Martext v 1 6
Vile matter. Was ever book containing such vile matter So fairly bound? *Rom. and Jul.* iii 2 83
Vile means. For I can raise no money by vile means . *J. Cæsar* iv 3 71
Vile men. I know you are more clement than vile men . . *Cymbeline* v 4 18

Vile misprision. In vile misprision shackle up My love . *All's Well* ii 3 159
Vile Montague. Stop thy unhallow'd toil, vile Montague! *Rom. and Jul.* v 3 54
Vile name. O, how fit a word Is that vile name to perish on my sword! *M. N. Dream* ii 2 107
Vile offence. My end Was wrought by nature, not by vile offence *C. of Er.* i 1 35
If that the heavens do not their visible spirits Send quickly down to tame these vile offences, It will come . *Lear* iv 2 47
Vile one. I rather added A lustre to it.—O thou vile one! *Cymbeline* i 1 143
Vile owl. I bade the vile owl go learn me the tenour of the proclamation *Troi. and Cres.* ii 1 99
Vile part. Tell me, In what vile part of this anatomy Doth my name lodge? *Rom. and Jul.* iii 3 106
Vile participation. Thou hast lost thy princely privilege With vile participation 1 *Hen. IV.* iii 2 87
Vile phrase. A vile phrase; 'beautified' is a vile phrase *Hamlet* ii 2 111
Vile politician. This vile politician, Bolingbroke 1 *Hen. IV.* i 3 241
Vile principal. One that knows What she should shame to know herself But with her most vile principal *W. Tale* ii 1 92
Vile prison. In the vile prison of afflicted breath *K. John* iii 4 19
Vile race. Thy vile race, Though thou didst learn, had that in't which good natures Could not abide to be with *Tempest* i 2 358
Vile rascal. Were I his lady, I would poison that vile rascal *All's Well* iii 5 87
Vile reproach. Let not Bardolph's vital thread be cut With edge of penny cord and vile reproach *Hen. V.* iii 6 50
Vile Scot. Hold up thy head, vile Scot, or thou art like Never to hold it up again! 1 *Hen. IV.* v 4 39
Vile sense. How stiff is my vile sense, That I stand up! *Lear* iv 6 286
Vile sort. How many nobles then should hold their places, That must strike sail to spirits of vile sort! 2 *Hen. IV.* v 2 18
Vile squealing. The vile squealing of the wry-neck'd fife *Mer. of Venice* ii 5 30
Vile stuff. I never knew man hold vile stuff so dear *L. L. Lost* iv 3 276
Vile submission. O calm, dishonourable, vile submission! *Rom. and Jul.* iii 1 76
Vile success. My speech should fall into such vile success *Othello* iii 3 222
Vile suspects. You do me shameful injury, Falsely to draw me in these vile suspects *Richard III.* i 3 89
Vile terms. With twenty such vile terms *T. of Shrew* iii 1 159
Vile thief. A' has been a vile thief this seven year *Much Ado* iii 3 134
Vile thing. Wake when some vile thing is near *M. N. Dream* ii 2 34
Hang off, thou cat, thou burr! vile thing, let loose! iii 2 260
'Tis a vile thing to die, my gracious lord, When men are unprepared *Richard III.* iii 2 64
The art of our necessities is strange, That can make vile things precious *Lear* iii 2 71
Vile thoughts. The sooner her vile thoughts to stead *Pericles* iv Gower 41
Vile traitor. All 'long of this vile traitor Somerset 1 *Hen. VI.* iv 3 33
Vile trash. Than to wring From the hard hands of peasants their vile trash *J. Cæsar* iv 3 74
Vile wall. That vile Wall which did these lovers sunder *M. N. Dream* v 1 133
O, kiss me through the hole of this vile wall! v 1 202
Vile world. O, let the vile world end! 2 *Hen. VI.* v 2 40
Vile worm, thou wast o'erlook'd even in thy birth *Mer. Wives* v 5 87
Vilely. Let me be vilely painted *Much Ado* i 1 267
If tall, a lance ill-headed; If low, an agate very vilely cut iii 1 65
I tell this tale vilely iii 3 157
A huge translation of hypocrisy, Vilely compiled *L. L. Lost* v 2 52
And to what end Their shallow shows and prologue vilely penn'd v 2 305
Very vilely in the morning, when he is sober, and most vilely in the afternoon, when he is drunk *Mer. of Venice* i 2 92
How would he look, to see his work so noble Vilely bound up? *W. Tale* iv 4 22
Am I not fallen away vilely since this last action? 1 *Hen. IV.* iii 3 1
He speaks most vilely of you, like a foul-mouthed man as he is iii 3 122
Doth it not show vilely in me to desire small beer? 2 *Hen. IV.* ii 2 7
How vilely did you speak of me even now before this honest, virtuous, civil gentlewoman! ii 4 327
He came to me; and did curse Against the Volsces, for they had so vilely Yielded the town *Coriolanus* iii 1 10
Ha, ha! how vilely doth this cynic rhyme! *J. Cæsar* iv 3 133
Mine Italian brain 'Gan in your duller Britain operate Most vilely *Cymb.* v 5 198
To me The very doors and windows savour vilely *Pericles* iv 6 117
Vileness. Good alone Is good without a name. Vileness is so *All's Well* ii 3 136
Viler. What viler thing upon the earth than friends Who can bring noblest minds to basest ends! *T. of Athens* iv 3 470
Vilest. With vilest torture let my life be ended *All's Well* ii 1 177
The bloodiest shame, The wildest savagery, the vilest stroke *K. John* iv 3 48
But now two paces of the vilest earth Is room enough 1 *Hen. IV.* v 4 91
For vilest things Become themselves in her *Ant. and Cleo.* ii 2 243
Vill. I tell you for good vill *Mer. Wives* iv 5 90
Village. Sir Oliver Martext, the vicar of the next village *As Y. Like It* iii 3 44
As a walled town is more worthier than a village iii 3 60
Frighting her pale-faced villages with war *Richard II.* ii 3 94
Met him in boroughs, cities, villages, Attended him on bridges 1 *Hen. IV.* iv 3 69
Give express charge, that in our marches through the country, there be nothing compelled from the villages *Hen. V.* iii 6 116
Come, go we in procession to the village iv 8 118
I love France so well that I will not part with a village of it v 2 184
Low farms, Poor pelting villages, sheep-cotes, and mills *Lear* ii 3 18
Village-cock. The early village-cock Hath twice done salutation to the morn *Richard III.* v 3 209
Village-curs. Like to village-curs, Bark when their fellows do *Hen. VIII.* ii 4 159
Villager. Brutus had rather be a villager Than to repute himself a son of Rome Under these hard conditions *J. Cæsar* i 2 172
Villagery. Are not you he That frights the maidens of the villagery? *M. N. Dream* ii 1 35
Villain. A villain, sir, I do not love to look on *Tempest* i 2 309
Villain, forbear.—Why, sir, I'll strike nothing *T. G. of Ver.* iii 1 202
She is slow in words.—O villain, that set this down among her vices! iii 1 337
These are the villains That all the travellers do fear so much iv 1 5
It's an honourable kind of thievery.—Peace, villain! iv 1 41
O diable, diable! vat is in my closet? Villain! larron! *Mer. Wives* i 4 71
Set down the basket, villain! Somebody call my wife iv 2 121
Hue and cry, villain, go! Assist me, knight. I am undone! iv 5 92
Thou thyself art a wicked villain, despite of all grace *Meas. for Meas.* i 2 27
Precise villains they are, that I am sure of ii 1 54
And put your trial in the villain's mouth Which here you come to accuse v 1 304
And in the witness of his proper ear, To call him villain v 1 311
How the villain would close now, after his treasonable abuses! v 1 346
A trusty villain, sir, that very oft . . . Lightens my humour *Com. of Er.* i 2 19
By some device or other The villain is o'er-raught of all my money i 2 96
Sure my master is horn-mad.—Horn-mad, thou villain! ii 1 58
Villain. Where is the thousand marks I gave thee, villain? *Com. of Er.* ii 1 65
Villain, thou didst deny the gold's receipt ii 2 17
I never saw her till this time.—Villain, thou liest ii 2 165
Here's a villain that would face me down iii 1 6
O villain! thou hast stolen both mine office and my name iii 1 44
To Adriana, villain, hie thee straight: Give her this key iv 1 102
Five hundred ducats, villain, for a rope? iv 4 13
Thou whoreson, senseless villain!—I would I were senseless iv 4 25
Dined at home! Thou villain, what sayest thou? iv 4 71
Dissembling villain, thou speak'st false iv 4 103
Out on thee, villain! wherefore dost thou mad me? iv 4 129
Thou art a villain to impeach me thus: I'll prove mine honour v 1 29
If thou darest stand.—I dare, and do defy thee for a villain v 1 32
A hungry lean-faced villain, A mere anatomy, a mountebank v 1 237
It must not be denied but I am a plain-dealing villain *Much Ado* i 3 34
If I do not take pity of her, I am a villain; if I do not love her, I am a Jew ii 3 272
For when rich villains have need of poor ones, poor ones may make what price they will iii 3 121
Who hath indeed, most like a liberal villain, Confess'd the vile encounters iv 1 93
Is he not approved in the height a villain? iv 1 303
For God defend but God should go before such villains! iv 2 22
The prince's brother was a villain.—Write down Prince John a villain iv 2 42
This is flat perjury, to call a prince's brother villain iv 2 44
O villain! thou wilt be condemned into everlasting redemption for this iv 2 58
No, thou villain, thou art full of piety, as shall be proved upon thee iv 2 81
She is dead, slander'd to death by villains v 1 88
You are a villain; I jest not: I will make it good how you dare v 1 146
I desire nothing but the reward of a villain v 1 251
Which is the villain? let me see his eyes v 1 269
Even I alone.—No, not so, villain; thou beliest thyself v 1 275
Villain, thou shalt fast for thy offences ere thou be pardoned *L. L. Lost* i 2 151
Take away this villain; shut him up.—Come, you transgressing slave i 2 158
I shall know, sir, when I have done it.—Why, villain, thou must know first iii 1 160
That ever turn'd their—backs—to mortal views!—Their eyes, villain v 2 162
Speak thou now.—Here, villain; drawn and ready. Where art thou? *M. N. Dream* iii 2 402
The villain is much lighter-heel'd than I: I follow'd fast iii 2 415
An evil soul producing holy witness Is like a villain with a smiling cheek, A goodly apple rotten at the heart *Mer. of Venice* i 3 101
He grows kind.—I like not fair terms and a villain's mind i 3 180
The villain Jew with outcries raised the duke ii 8 4
Wilt thou lay hands on me, villain?—I am no villain *As Y. Like It* i 1 58
He is thrice a villain that says such a father begot villains i 1 61
Some villains of my court Are of consent and sufferance in this ii 2 2
I never loved my brother in my life.—More villain thou iii 1 15
Villain, I say, knock me here soundly.—Knock you here, sir! *T. of Shrew* i 2 8
A senseless villain! Good Hortensio, I bade the rascal knock i 2 36
Off with my boots, you rogues! you villains, when? iv 1 147
You whoreson villain! will you let it fall? iv 1 158
How durst you, villains, bring it from the dresser, And serve it thus? iv 1 166
Go, take it up unto thy master's use.—Villain, not for thy life iv 3 160
Lay hands on the villain: I believe a' means to cozen somebody v 1 39
What, you notorious villain, didst thou never see thy master's father? v 1 54
O fine villain! A silken doublet! a velvet hose! a scarlet cloak! v 1 68
Thy father! O villain! he is a sail-maker in Bergamo v 1 80
O, my son, my son! Tell me, thou villain, where is my son? v 1 93
Thus strangers may be haled and abused: O monstrous villain! v 1 112
I'll slit the villain's nose, that would have sent me to the gaol v 1 134
Here comes the little villain. How now, my metal of India! *T. Night* ii 5 16
Thou killest me like a rogue and a villain iii 4 180
Look on me with your welkin eye: sweet villain! *W. Tale* i 2 136
That false villain Whom I employ'd was pre-employ'd by him ii 1 48
Should a villain say so, The most replenish'd villain in the world, He were as much more villain ii 1 78
Would I knew the villain, I would land-damn him ii 1 142
Thou darest not say so, villain, for thy life *K. John* iii 1 132
Avaunt, thou hateful villain, get thee gone!—I am no villain iv 3 77
What wilt thou do, renowned Faulconbridge? Second a villain and a murderer? iv 3 102
It shall be as all the ocean, Enough to stifle such a villain up iv 3 133
That villain Hubert told me he did live v 1 42
A monk, I tell you; a resolved villain, Whose bowels suddenly burst out v 6 29
I spit at him; Call him a slanderous coward and a villain *Richard II.* i 1 61
Like a false traitor and injurious villain i 1 91
It issues from the rancour of a villain i 1 143
O villains, vipers, damn'd without redemption! iii 2 129
Treason! foul treason! Villain! traitor! slave! v 2 72
By mine honour, by my life, by my troth, I will appeach the villain v 2 79
Hence, villain! never more come in my sight v 2 86
Villain, I'll make thee safe.—Stay thy revengeful hand v 3 41
My heart is not confederate with my hand.—It was, villain v 3 54
Villain, thy own hand yields thy death's instrument v 5 107
I will give it over: by the Lord, an I do not, I am a villain 1 *Hen. IV.* i 2 108
I'll make one; an I do not, call me villain and baffle me i 2 113
This is the most omnipotent villain that ever cried 'Stand' to a true man i 2 121
An 'twere not as good deed as drink, to break the pate on thee, I am a very villain ii 1 34
The stony-hearted villains know it well enough ii 2 28
Strike; down with them; cut the villains' throats ii 2 87
Your money!—Villains!—Got with much ease ii 2 110
O villain! thy lips are scarce wiped since thou drunkest last ii 4 170
If they speak more or less than truth, they are villains ii 4 191
Four, in buckram suits.—Seven, by these hilts, or I am a villain else ii 4 229
O villain, thou stolest a cup of sack eighteen years ago ii 4 345
If thy pocket were enriched with any other injuries but these, I am a villain iii 3 182
The villains march wide betwixt the legs, as if they had gyves on iv 2 43
Cut me off the villain's head: throw the quean in the channel 2 *Hen. IV.* ii 1 51
Ah, thou honey-suckle villain! wilt thou kill God's officers and the king's? ii 1 56
And look, if the fat villain have not transformed him ape ii 2 77
These villains will make the word as odious as the word 'occupy' ii 4 160
Ah, you whoreson little valiant villain, you! ii 4 225
Ah, villain!—A rascally slave! I will toss the rogue in a blanket ii 4 239
Thou wert better thou hadst struck thy mother, thou paper-faced villain v 4 12

Villain. What ish my nation? Ish a villain, and a bastard, and a knave . . . *Hen. V.* iii 2 133
Is it fit this soldier keep his oath?—He is a craven and a villain else . iv 7 139
His reputation is as arrant a villain and a Jacksauce . . . iv 7 148
How now, sir! you villain?—Do you think I'll be forsworn? . . . iv 8 12
What's the matter?—My liege, here is a villain and a traitor. . . iv 8 26
You may not be let in.—Villains, answer you so? . . . 1 *Hen. VI.* i 3 8
Villain, thou know'st the law of arms is such That whoso draws a sword, 'tis present death . . . iii 4 38
A plague upon that villain Somerset, That thus delays! . . . iv 3 9
Talbot doth expect my aid, And I am lowted by a traitor villain . . iv 3 13
God is my witness, I am falsely accused by the villain . . 2 *Hen. VI.* i 3 192
Base dunghill villain and mechanical, I'll have thy head for this . . i 3 196
Do not cast away an honest man for a villain's accusation . . . i 3 206
It made me laugh to see the villain run . . . ii 1 155
Cut both the villains' throats; for die you shall . . . iv 1 20
This villain here, Being captain of a pinnace, threatens . . . iv 1 106
Here's a villain!—Has a book in his pocket with red letters in't . iv 2 96
He's a villain and a traitor.—Away with him, I say! hang him . iv 2 115
Stand, villain, stand, or I'll fell thee down . . . iv 2 123
Villain, thy father was a plasterer; And thou thyself a shearman . iv 2 140
Ah, barbarous villains! . . . could it not enforce them to relent? . iv 4 15
Ah, villain, thou wilt betray me, and get a thousand crowns . . iv 10 28
And with the issuing blood Stifle the villain . . . 3 *Hen. VI.* ii 6 83
Butchers and villains! bloody cannibals! . . . v 5 61
Since I cannot prove a lover, To entertain these fair well-spoken days, I am determined to prove a villain . . . *Richard III.* i 1 30
Villains, set down the corse; or, by Saint Paul, I'll make a corse of him that disobeys . . . i 2 36
Villain, thou know'st no law of God nor man: No beast so fierce . i 2 70
A murderous villain, and so still thou art . . . i 3 134
O gentle villain, do not turn away! . . . i 3 163
Against the form of law, Proceed thus rashly to the villain's death . iii 5 43
Although they were flesh'd villains, bloody dogs, Melting with tenderness iv 3 6
'Almost changed my mind; But O! the devil'—there the villain stopp'd iv 3 16
Tell me, thou villain slave, where are my children? . . . iv 4 144
Dull, unmindful villain, Why stand'st thou still? . . . iv 4 444
I am a villain: yet I lie, I am not. Fool, of thyself speak well . v 3 191
Every tongue brings in a several tale, And every tale condemns me for a villain . . . v 3 195
It is the prettiest villain: she fetches her breath as short as a new-ta'en sparrow . . . *Troi. and Cres.* iii 2 35
O heavens! you love me not.—Die I a villain, then! . . . iv 4 85
Blow, villain, till thy sphered bias cheek Outswell the colic of puff'd Aquilon . . . iv 5 8
Send that Greekish whore-masterly villain, with the sleeve, back . v 4 8
Insolent villain!—Kill, kill, kill, kill, kill him! . . *Coriolanus* v 6 131
What, villain boy! Barr'st me my way in Rome? . . *T. Andron.* i 1 290
'And shall!' what villain was it spake that word? . . . i 1 359
You are both decipher'd, that's the news, For villains mark'd with rape iv 2 9
And so I leave you both: like bloody villains . . . iv 2 17
Villain, what hast thou done?—That which thou canst not undo.—Thou hast undone our mother.—Villain, I have done thy mother . . iv 2 73
Stay, murderous villains! will you kill your brother? . . . iv 2 88
And who should find them but the empress' villain? . . . iv 3 73
Villain, art not thou the carrier?—Ay, of my pigeons, sir; nothing else iv 3 86
Drag the villain hither by the hair; Nor age nor honour shall shape privilege . . . iv 4 56
Villain, thou mightst have been an emperor . . . v 1 30
'Peace, villain, peace!'—even thus he rates the babe . . . v 1 33
O detestable villain! call'st thou that trimming? . . . v 1 94
O barbarous, beastly villains, like thyself!—Indeed, I was their tutor . v 1 97
Show me a villain that hath done a rape, And I am sent to be revenged v 2 94
Villains, forbear! we are the empress' sons . . . v 2 163
Villains, for shame you could not beg for grace. Hark, wretches! . v 2 180
The villain is alive in Titus' house, And as he is, to witness this is true v 3 123
Thou villain Capulet,—Hold me not, let me go . . *Rom. and Jul.* i 1 86
A villain that is hither come in spite, To scorn at our solemnity . i 5 64
Young Romeo is it?—'Tis he, that villain Romeo . . . i 5 66
It fits, when such a villain is a guest: I'll not endure him . . i 5 77
The hate I bear thee can afford No better term than this,—thou art a villain . . . iii 1 64
Villain am I none; Therefore farewell; I see thou know'st me not . iii 1 67
Where is my page? Go, villain, fetch a surgeon . . . iii 1 97
A braggart, a rogue, a villain, that fights by the book of arithmetic! . iii 1 105
Now, Tybalt, take the villain back again, That late thou gavest me . iii 1 130
A damned saint, an honourable villain! . . . iii 2 79
But, wherefore, villain, didst thou kill my cousin? That villain cousin would have kill'd my husband . . . iii 2 100
Thou weep'st not so much for his death, As that the villain lives which slaughter'd him.—What villain, madam?—That same villain, Romeo iii 5 80
Villain and he be many miles asunder . . . iii 5 82
Condemned villain, I do apprehend thee: Obey, and go with me . v 3 56
Your lordship's a goodly villain. The devil knew not what he did when he made man politic . . . *T. of Athens* iii 3 28
Let no assembly of twenty be without a score of villains . . iii 6 87
Henceforth be no feast, Whereat a villain's not a welcome guest . iii 6 113
That, by killing of villains, Thou wast born to conquer my country . iv 3 105
Why dost thou seek me out?—To vex thee.—Always a villain's office or a fool's . . . iv 3 237
All villains that do stand by thee are pure . . . iv 3 366
I never had honest man about me, I; all I kept were knaves, to serve in meat to villains . . . iv 3 485
Must thou needs stand for a villain in thine own work? . . . v 1 40
Yet remain assured That he's a made-up villain . . . v 1 101
I'll give you gold, Rid me these villains from your companies . . v 1 104
If where thou art two villains shall not be, Come not near him . v 1 112
If thou wouldst not reside But where one villain is, then him abandon v 1 114
They were villains, murderers: the will! read the will . . *J. Cæsar* iii 2 159
O woful day!—O traitors, villains!—O most bloody sight! . . iii 2 205
What villain touch'd his body, that did stab, And not for justice? . iv 3 20
Villains, you did not so, when your vile daggers Hack'd one another in the sides of Cæsar . . . v 1 39
Look, the villains fly! Myself have to mine own turn'd enemy . . v 3 1
He's a traitor.—Thou liest, thou shag-hair'd villain! . . *Macbeth* iv 2 83
I would not be the villain that thou think'st . . . iv 3 35
There is ten thousand— Geese, villain?—Soldiers, sir . . . v 3 13
Thou bloodier villain Than terms can give thee out! . . . v 8 7
O villain, villain, smiling, damned villain! My tables,—meet it is I set it down, That one may smile, and smile, and be a villain . *Hamlet* i 5 106

Villain. There's ne'er a villain dwelling in all Denmark But he's an arrant knave . . . *Hamlet* i 5 123
Am I a coward? Who calls me villain? breaks my pate across? . . ii 2 599
Bloody, bawdy, villain! Remorseless, treacherous, lecherous, kindless villain! . . . ii 2 609
That would be scann'd: A villain kills my father; and for that, I, his sole son, do this same villain send To heaven . . . iii 3 76
A murderer and a villain; A slave that is not twentieth part the tithe Of your precedent lord . . . iii 4 96
O villain, villain! His very opinion in the letter! Abhorred villain! Unnatural, detested, brutish villain! worse than brutish! Go, sirrah, seek him; I'll apprehend him: abominable villain! . *Lear* i 2 80
This villain of mine comes under the prediction; there's son against father . . . i 2 119
Find out this villain, Edmund; it shall lose thee nothing; do it carefully i 2 124
As if we were villains by necessity; fools by heavenly compulsion . i 2 132
Some villain hath done me wrong.—That's my fear . . . i 2 180
Where's the villain?—Here stood he in the dark . . . ii 1 39
Where is the villain, Edmund?—Fled this way, sir. . . . ii 1 43
Strong and fasten'd villain! Would he deny his letter? . . . ii 1 79
All ports I'll bar; the villain shall not 'scape . . . ii 1 82
If you will give me leave, I will tread this unbolted villain into mortar ii 2 71
Seek out the villain Gloucester.—Hang him instantly.—Pluck out his eyes . . . iii 7 3
Villain, thou shalt find— By the kind gods, 'tis most ignobly done . iii 7 34
What do you mean?—My villain!—Nay, then, come on . . . iii 7 78
Out, treacherous villain! Thou call'st on him that hates thee . iii 7 87
Turn out that eyeless villain; throw this slave Upon the dunghill . iii 7 96
Fools do those villains pity who are punish'd Ere they have done their mischief . . . iv 2 54
Villain, take my purse: If ever thou wilt thrive, bury my body . iv 6 252
I know thee well: a serviceable villain . . . iv 6 257
Thou art a villain.—You are—a senator . . . *Othello* i 1 119
And what's he then that says I play the villain? . . . ii 3 342
How am I then a villain To counsel Cassio to this parallel course? . ii 3 354
Villain, be sure thou prove my love a whore, Be sure of it . . iii 3 359
Prithee, say true.—I am a very villain else . . . iv 1 129
Some eternal villain, Some busy and insinuating rogue . . . iv 2 130
I know his gait, 'tis he.—Villain, thou diest! . . . v 1 23
O, villain that I am!—It is even so . . . v 1 29
O, help!—Hark!—O wretched villain.—Two or three groan . . v 1 41
O, I am spoil'd, undone by villains! Give me some help . . v 1 54
O treacherous villains! What are you there? come in, and give some help . . . v 1 58
O murderous slave! O villain!—O damn'd Iago! O inhuman dog! . v 1 61
Here's Cassio hurt by villains.—Cassio! . . . v 1 69
Disprove this villain, if thou be'st a man: He says thou told'st him that his wife was false: I know thou didst not, thou'rt not such a villain . . . v 2 172
Are there no stones in heaven But what serve for the thunder?—Precious villain! . . . v 2 235
He's gone, but his wife's kill'd.—'Tis a notorious villain . . v 2 239
I'll after that same villain, For 'tis a damned slave. . . . v 2 242
Where is that viper? bring the villain forth . . . v 2 285
O villain!—Most heathenish and most gross! . . . v 2 313
And this, it seems, Roderigo meant to have sent this damned villain . v 2 316
To you, lord governor, Remains the censure of this hellish villain . v 2 368
If thou say so, villain, Thou kill'st thy mistress . . *Ant. and Cleo.* ii 5 26
Hence, Horrible villain! or I'll spurn thine eyes Like balls before me . ii 5 63
I am alone the villain of the earth, And feel I am so most . . iv 6 30
Slave, soulless villain, dog! O rarely base! . . . v 2 157
The villain would not stand me.—No; but he fled forward still *Cymbeline* i 2 15
Two villains, whose false oaths prevail'd Before my perfect honour . iii 3 66
Thou then look'dst like a villain; now methinks Thy favour's good enough . . . iii 4 50
Some villain, ay, and singular in his art, Hath done you both this cursed injury . . . iii 4 124
You precious pandar! Villain, Where is thy lady? . . . iii 5 81
Close villain, I'll have this secret from thy heart, or rip Thy heart to find it . . . iii 5 85
O, my all-worthy lord!—All-worthy villain! Discover where thy mistress is . . . iii 5 94
If thou wouldst not be a villain, but do me true service, undergo those employments wherein I should have cause to use thee . . . iii 5 109
Even there, thou villain Posthumus, will I kill thee . . . iii 5 135
I cannot find those runagates; that villain Hath mock'd me . . iv 2 62
What are you That fly me thus? some villain mountaineers? . . iv 2 71
Thou art a robber, A law-breaker, a villain: yield thee, thief . . iv 2 75
Thou villain base, Know'st me not by my clothes?—No, nor thy tailor, rascal . . . iv 2 80
What's thy name?—Cloten, thou villain.—Cloten, thou double villain, be thy name . . . iv 2 88
Thief, any thing That's due to all the villains past, in being, To come! v 5 212
That caused a lesser villain than myself, A sacrilegious thief, to do't . v 5 219
Every villain Be call'd Posthumus Leonatus; and Be villany less than 'twas! . . . v 5 223
For if a king bid a man be a villain, he's bound by the indenture of his oath to be one . . . *Pericles* i 3 9
Thou hast bewitch'd my daughter, and thou art A villain . . . ii 5 50
I am sworn, And will dispatch.—Hold, villain! . . . iv 1 93
O villain Leonine! Whom thou hast poison'd too . . . iv 3 9
Did seek to murder me: and having woo'd A villain to attempt it . v 1 175

Villain-like. What in the world he is That names me traitor, villain-like he lies . . . *Lear* v 3 98
I am Posthumus, That kill'd thy daughter:—villain-like, I lie *Cymbeline* v 5 218

Villanous. With foreheads villanous low . . . *Tempest* iv 1 250
And I shall not only receive this villanous wrong . . *Mer. Wives* ii 2 308
The rankest compound of villanous smell that ever offended nostril . iii 5 93
More than the villanous inconstancy of man's disposition is able to bear iv 5 111
One that hath spoke most villanous speeches . . *Meas. for Meas.* v 1 265
A secret and villanous contriver against me his natural brother *As Y. L. It* i 1 151
There is not one so young and so villanous this day living . . i 1 161
Whose villanous saffron would have made all the unbaked and doughy youth of a nation in his colour . . . *All's Well* iv 5 2
Great pity, so it was, This villanous salt-petre should be digg'd Out of the bowels of the harmless earth . . . 1 *Hen. IV.* i 3 60
I think this be the most villanous house in all London road for fleas . ii 1 15
There is nothing but roguery to be found in villanous man . . ii 4 138
A villanous coward! Go thy ways, old Jack; die when thou wilt . ii 4 140
There's villanous news abroad . . . ii 4 366

Villanous. But chiefly a villanous trick of thine eye . . . 1 *Hen. IV.* ii 4 445
Wherein villanous, but in all things? wherein worthy, but in nothing? ii 4 504
That villanous abominable misleader of youth . . . ii 4 508
Company, villanous company, hath been the spoil of me . . . iii 3 11
Here is come to do some villanous shame To the dead bodies *R. and J.* v 3 52
No villanous bounty yet hath pass'd my heart *T. of Athens* ii 2 182
Villanous, and shows a most pitiful ambition in the fool that uses it *Hamlet* iii 2 48
My cue is villanous melancholy, with a sigh like Tom o' Bedlam *Lear* i 2 147
Then have we a prescription to die when death is our physician.—O villanous! . . . *Othello* i 3 312
Villanous thoughts, Roderigo! when these mutualities so marshal the way . . . ii 1 266
A closet lock and key of villanous secrets: And yet she'll kneel and pray . . . iv 2 22
The Moor's abused by some most villanous knave . . . iv 2 139
He begg'd of me to steal it.—Villanous whore! . . . v 2 229
Where I was taught Of your chaste daughter the wide difference 'Twixt amorous and villanous *Cymbeline* v 5 195
Villanously. Never yet Did, as he vouches, misreport your grace.—My lord, most villanously . . . *Meas. for Meas.* v 1 149
And cross-gartered?—Most villanously . . . *T. Night* iii 2 80
Villany. I will consent to act any villany against him *Mer. Wives* ii 1 102
I cannot fence.—Villany, take your rapier . . . ii 3 16
Pinch him, fairies, mutually; Pinch him for his villany . . . v 5 104
The commendation is not in his wit, but in his villany . *Much Ado* ii 1 146
Is it possible that any villany should be so dear?—Thou shouldst rather ask if it were possible any villany should be so rich . . . iii 3 117
Partly by the dark night, which did deceive them, but chiefly by my villany . . . iii 3 168
Whose spirits toil in frame of villanies . . . iv 1 191
O, in a tomb where never scandal slept, Save this of hers, framed by thy villany!—My villany?—Thine . . . v 1 71
My villany they have upon record . . . v 1 246
And fled he is upon this villany . . . v 1 258
There's villany abroad: this letter will tell you more . *L. L. Lost* i 1 189
The villany you teach me, I will execute . . . *Mer. of Venice* iii 1 74
Ay, there's the villany.—Error i' the bill, sir; error i' the bill *T. of S.* iv 3 145
Go to: but I will in, to be revenged for this villany . . . v 1 140
He hath out-villained villany so far, that the rarity redeems him *All's W.* iv 3 305
Let villany itself forswear't . . . *W. Tale* i 2 361
Thou wretch, thou coward! Thou little valiant, great in villany! *K. John* iii 1 116
Fit for bloody villany, Apt, liable to be employ'd in danger . . . iv 2 225
Trust not those cunning waters of his eyes, For villany is not without such rheum . . . iv 3 108
Wherein crafty, but in villany? wherein villanous, but in all things? 1 *Hen. IV.* ii 4 504
And what should poor Jack Falstaff do in the days of villany? . iii 3 187
Pay her the debt you owe her, and unpay the villany you have done her 2 *Hen. IV.* ii 1 130
Their villany goes against my weak stomach . . . *Hen. V.* iii 2 56
Contagious clouds Of heady murder, spoil, and villany . . . iii 3 32
Come to me again And given me notice of their villanies . 2 *Hen. VI.* iii 1 370
Thus I clothe my naked villany With old odd ends . . . *Richard III.* i 3 336
Unfrequented plots there are Fitted by kind for rape and villany *T. An.* ii 1 116
With her sacred wit To villany and vengeance consecrate . . . ii 1 121
Cunningly effected, will beget A very excellent piece of villany . . ii 3 7
How this villany Doth fat me with the very thoughts of it! . . iii 1 203
Intolerable wrongs! Shall I endure this monstrous villany? . . iv 4 51
Villanies Ruthful to hear, yet piteously perform'd . . . v 1 65
In the end, the villanies of man will set him clear . *T. of Athens* iii 3 30
Washes it off, and sprinkles in your faces Your reeking villany . . iii 6 103
There's nothing level in our cursed natures, But direct villany . . iv 3 20
Do villany, do, since you protest to do't, Like workmen . . . iv 3 437
The multiplying villanies of nature Do swarm upon him *Macbeth* i 2 11
Being thus be-netted round with villanies . . . *Hamlet* v 2 29
O villany! Ho! let the door be lock'd: Treachery! Seek it out . v 2 322
O mistress, villany hath made mocks with love! . . . *Othello* v 2 151
Villany, villany, villany! I think upon't, I think: I smell't: O villany!—I thought so then:—I'll kill myself for grief:—O villany, villany! . . . v 2 190
This wretch hath part confess'd his villany: Did you and he consent? . v 2 296
In me 'tis villany; In thee 't had been good service *Ant. and Cleo.* ii 7 80
All good seeming, By thy revolt, O husband, shall be thought Put on for villany; not born where't grows . . . *Cymbeline* iii 4 58
That is, what villany soe'er I bid thee do, to perform it directly and truly . . . iii 5 112
Nothing routs us but The villany of our fears . . . v 2 13
To become the geck and scorn O' th' other's villany . . . v 4 68
By villany I got this ring: 'twas Leonatus' jewel . . . v 5 142
Every villain Be call'd Posthumus Leonatus; and Be villany less than 'twas! . . . v 5 225
No visor does become black villany So well as soft and tender flattery *Pericles* iv 4 44
Villiago. I see them lording it in London streets, Crying 'Villiago!' unto all they meet . . . 2 *Hen. VI.* iv 8 48
Vinaigre. Mort du vinaigre! is not this Helen? . . . *All's Well* ii 3 50
Vincentio, come of the Bentivolii. Vincentio's son brought up in Florence *T. of Shrew* i 1 13
Who shall bear your part, And be in Padua here Vincentio's son? . . i 1 200
Son to Vincentio.—A mighty man of Pisa . . . ii 1 104
Supposed Lucentio Must get a father, call'd 'supposed Vincentio' . ii 1 410
I am Lucentio, 'hic est,' son unto Vincentio of Pisa . . . iii 1 32
We'll fit him to our turn,—And he shall be Vincentio of Pisa . iii 2 135
If he be credulous and trust my tale, I'll make him glad to seem Vincentio, And give assurance to Baptista Minola, As if he were the right Vincentio . . . iv 2 68
Among them know you one Vincentio?—I know him not . . iv 2 96
Think it not the worst of all your fortunes That you are like to Sir Vincentio . . . iv 2 105
Imagine 'twere the right Vincentio.—Tut, fear not me . . . iv 4 12
My name is call'd Vincentio; my dwelling Pisa; And bound I am to Padua . . . iv 5 55
Let me embrace with old Vincentio, And wander we to see thy honest son . . . iv 5 68
But who is here? mine old master Vincentio! . . . v 1 44
Notorious villain, didst thou never see thy master's father, Vincentio? . v 1 55
He is mine only son, and heir to the lands of me, Signior Vincentio v 1 89
I dare swear this is the right Vincentio.—Swear, if thou darest . . v 1 103
Vincere. Aio te, Æacida, Romanos vincere posse . . . 2 *Hen. VI.* i 4 65

Vindicative. He in heat of action Is more vindicative than jealous love *Troi. and Cres.* iv 5 107
Vine. Vines with clustering bunches growing . . . *Tempest* iv 1 112
Thou art an elm, my husband, I a vine . . . *Com. of Errors* ii 2 176
Her vine, the merry cheerer of the heart, Unpruned dies . *Hen. V.* v 2 41
Like to a wither'd vine That droops his sapless branches . 1 *Hen. VI.* ii 5 11
That spoil'd your summer fields and fruitful vines . *Richard III.* v 2 8
Every man shall eat in safety, Under his own vine . . *Hen. VIII.* v 5 35
Peace, plenty, love . . . Shall then be his, and like a vine grow to him v 5 50
Dry up thy marrows, vines, and plough-torn leas . *T. of Athens* iv 3 193
To whose young love The vines of France and milk of Burgundy Strive to be interess'd . . . *Lear* i 1 86
Thou monarch of the vine, Plumpy Bacchus with pink eyne! *A. and C.* ii 7 120
Grow, patience! And let the stinking elder, grief, untwine His perishing root with the increasing vine! . . . *Cymbeline* iv 2 60
Vinegar. Of such vinegar aspect That they'll not show their teeth in way of smile, Though Nestor swear the jest be laughable *Mer. of Venice* i 1 54
I warrant there's vinegar and pepper in't . . . *T. Night* iii 4 158
Coming in to borrow a mess of vinegar . . . 2 *Hen. IV.* ii 1 103
Vinewedst. Speak then, thou vinewedst leaven, speak . *Troi. and Cres.* ii 1 15
Vineyard. Bourn, bound of land, tilth, vineyard, none . *Tempest* ii 1 152
Thy pole-clipt vineyard; And thy sea-marge, sterile and rocky-hard iv 1 68
With a vineyard back'd; And to that vineyard is a planched gate *Meas. for Meas.* iv 1 29
A little door Which from the vineyard to the garden leads . . iv 1 33
Let us quit all And give our vineyards to a barbarous people *Hen. V.* iii 5 4
Our vineyards, fallows, meads, and hedges, Defective in their natures, grow to wildness . . . v 2 54
Viol. My tongue's use is to me no more Than an unstringed viol *Rich. II.* i 3 162
You are a fair viol, and your sense the strings . . *Pericles* i 1 81
The viol once more: how thou stirr'st, thou block! The music there! iii 2 90
Viola. And say 'Thrice-welcome, drowned Viola!' . . *T. Night* v 1 248
And died that day when Viola from her birth Had number'd thirteen years . . . v 1 251
I am Viola: which to confirm, I'll bring you to a captain in this town . v 1 260
Violate. Thou didst seek to violate The honour of my child . *Tempest* i 2 347
That his own hand may strike his honour down That violates the smallest branch herein . . . *L. L. Lost* i 1 21
By my oath—Which God defend a knight should violate! . *Richard II.* i 3 18
Bad men, you violate A twofold marriage . . . v 1 71
Experience, manhood, honour, ne'er before Did violate so itself *A. and C.* iii 10 24
With unchaste purpose and with oath to violate My lady's honour *Cymb.* v 5 284
Violated vows 'Twixt the souls of friend and friend . *As Y. Like It* iii 2 141
Violation Of sacred chastity and of promise-breach . *Meas. for Meas.* v 1 409
It cannot fail but by The violation of my faith . . *W. Tale* iv 4 488
Dangerous countenance, And violation of all faith and troth . 1 *Hen. IV.* v 1 70
What is't to me, when you yourselves are cause, If your pure maidens fall into the hand Of hot and forcing violation? . . *Hen. V.* iii 3 21
Viol-de-gamboys. He plays o' the viol-de-gamboys . . *T. Night* i 3 27
Violence. Blown with restless violence round about . *Meas. for Meas.* iii 1 125
Be certain what you do, sir, lest your justice Prove violence . *W. Tale* ii 1 128
They will by violence tear him from your palace And torture him 2 *Hen. VI.* iii 2 246
Offer him no violence, Unless he seek to thrust you out perforce 3 *Hen. VI.* i 1 33
To prevent the tyrant's violence,—For trust not him that hath once broken faith,—I'll hence forthwith unto the sanctuary . . iv 4 29
Die in his youth by like untimely violence! . . *Richard III.* i 3 201
What means this scene of rude impatience?—To make an act of tragic violence . . . ii 2 39
That seal, You ask with such a violence, the king, Mine and your master, with his own hand gave me . . . *Hen. VIII.* iii 2 246
Would not go with me, But, as it seems, did violence on herself *R. and J.* v 3 264
We do it wrong, being so majestical, To offer it the show of violence *Ham.* i 1 144
I would not hear your enemy say so, Nor shall you do mine ear that violence . . . i 2 171
The violence of either grief or joy Their own enactures with themselves destroy . . . iii 2 206
You but dally; I pray you, pass with your best violence . . v 2 309
My downright violence and storm of fortunes May trumpet to the world *Othello* i 3 250
Mark me with what violence she first loved the Moor, but for bragging ii 1 224
Unless self-charity be sometimes a vice, And to defend ourselves it be a sin When violence assails us . . . ii 3 204
Be'st thou sad or merry, The violence of either thee becomes *A. and C.* i 5 60
The violence of action hath made you reek as a sacrifice . . *Cymbeline* i 2 2
If you did know my parentage, You would not do me violence *Pericles* v 1 101
Violent. To these violent proceedings all my neighbours shall cry aim *Mer. Wives* iii 2 44
Like an impediment in the current, made it more violent *Meas. for Meas.* iii 1 252
You leaden messengers, That ride upon the violent speed of fire *All's W.* iii 2 112
This jealousy Is for a precious creature: as she's rare, Must it be great, and as his person's mighty, Must it be violent . . *W. Tale* i 2 454
He cracks his gorge, his sides, With violent hefts . . . ii 1 45
The violent carriage of it Will clear or end the business . . . iii 1 17
O, I am scalded with my violent motion, And spleen of speed! *K. John* v 7 49
For violent fires soon burn out themselves . . *Richard II.* ii 1 34
Murder not then the fruit within my womb, Although ye hale me to a violent death . . . 1 *Hen. VI.* v 4 64
The duke yet lives that Henry shall depose; But him outlive, and die a violent death . . . 2 *Hen. VI.* i 4 34; 63
Persuade my soul Some violent hands were laid on Humphrey's life . iii 2 138
Violent hands were laid Upon the life of this thrice-famed duke . . iii 2 156
We may outrun, By violent swiftness, that which we run at *Hen. VIII.* i 1 142
To use violent thefts, And rob in the behalf of charity *Troi. and Cres.* v 3 21
Worthy sir, thou bleed'st; Thy exercise hath been too violent *Coriolanus* i 5 16
Unmeriting, proud, violent, testy magistrates, alias fools . . ii 1 47
Those cold ways . . . are very poisonous Where the disease is violent . iii 1 222
The violent fit o' the time craves it as physic For the whole state . iii 2 33
And is almost mature for the violent breaking out . . . iv 3 27
In a violent popular ignorance, given your enemy your shield . . v 2 43
Teach her not thus to lay Such violent hands upon her tender life *T. An.* iii 2 22
What violent hands can she lay on her life? . . . iii 2 25
Do on them some violent death; They have been violent to me and mine v 2 108
These violent delights have violent ends . . . *Rom. and Jul.* ii 6 9
The expedition of my violent love Outrun the pauser, reason *Macbeth* ii 3 116
But float upon a wild and violent sea Each way and move . . iv 2 21
Where violent sorrow seems A modern ecstasy . . . iv 3 169
Who, as 'tis thought, by self and violent hands Took off her life . v 8 70
The very ecstasy of love, Whose violent property fordoes itself *Hamlet* ii 1 103
Purpose is but the slave to memory, Of violent birth, but poor validity iii 2 199

Violent. And he most violent author Of his own just remove *Hamlet* iv 5 80
You are hot and dry—As make your bouts more violent to that end iv 7 159
'Tis worse than murder, To do upon respect such violent outrage *Lear* ii 4 24
Let this kiss Repair those violent harms . . . . . . iv 7 28
It was a violent commencement, and thou shalt see an answerable sequestration . . . *Othello* i 3 350
They were parted With foul and violent tempest . . . . ii 1 34
Even so my bloody thoughts, with violent pace, Shall ne'er look back . iii 3 457
When I was born: Never was waves nor wind more violent *Pericles* iv 1 60
Violentest. Can no more atone Than violentest contrariety *Coriolanus* iv 6 73
Violenteth in a sense as strong As that which causeth it *Troi. and Cres.* iv 4 4
Violently. A mighty rock; Which being violently borne upon, Our helpful ship was splitted . . . *Com. of Errors* i 1 103
Thou art violently carried away from grace . . . 1 *Hen. IV.* ii 4 491
Temperately proceed to what you would Thus violently redress *Coriol.* iii 1 220
As violently as hasty powder fired Doth hurry *Rom. and Jul.* v 1 64
If you violently proceed against him, mistaking his purpose, it would make a great gap in your own honour . . . *Lear* i 2 89
Violet. Lying by the violet in the sun, Do as the carrion does *M. for M.* ii 2 166
Daisies pied and violets blue And lady-smocks all silver-white *L. L. L.* v 2 904
Where oxlips and the nodding violet grows *M. N. Dream* ii 1 250
Like the sweet sound, That breathes upon a bank of violets . *T. Night* i 1 6
Violets dim, But sweeter than the lids of Juno's eyes *W. Tale* iv 4 120
To paint the lily, To throw a perfume on the violet . . *K. John* iv 2 12
Welcome, my son: who are the violets now That strew the green lap of the new come spring? *Richard II.* v 2 46
The violet smells to him as it doth to me . *Hen. V.* iv 1 106
A violet in the youth of primy nature, Forward, not permanent *Hamlet* i 3 7
There's a daisy: I would give you some violets, but they withered iv 5 184
From her fair and unpolluted flesh May violets spring! . . . v 1 263
The violets, cowslips, and the primroses, Bear to my closet . *Cymbeline* i 5 83
They are as gentle As zephyrs blowing below the violet . . iv 2 172
Purple violets, and marigolds, Shall as a carpet hang upon thy grave *Pericles* iv 1 16
Viper. O villains, vipers, damn'd without redemption! . *Richard II.* iii 2 129
I would have you solus.—'Solus,' egregious dog? O viper vile! *Hen. V.* ii 1 49
Why, they are vipers: is love a generation of vipers? *Troi. and Cres.* iii 1 146
Where is this viper That would depopulate the city? *Coriolanus* iii 1 263
Where is that viper? bring the villain forth *Othello* v 2 285
I am no viper, yet I feed On mother's flesh which did me breed *Pericles* i 1 64
Viperous. Civil dissension is a viperous worm . . . . 1 *Hen. VI.* iii 1 72
We are peremptory to dispatch This viperous traitor *Coriolanus* iii 1 287
Nay, the secrets of the grave This viperous slander enters . *Cymbeline* iii 4 41
Vir sapit qui pauca loquitur; a soul feminine saluteth us . *L. L. Lost* iv 2 82
Virgilia, turn thy solemness out o' door, and go along with us *Coriolanus* i 3 120
Virgin. O, if a virgin, And your affection not gone forth, I'll make you The queen of Naples *Tempest* i 2 447
The white cold virgin snow upon my heart Abates the ardour of my liver . . . . . . iv 1 55
Hail, virgin, if you be, as those cheek-roses Proclaim you are! *Meas. for Meas.* i 4 16
I would not . . . play with all virgins so i 4 33
Pardon, goddess of the night, Those that slew thy virgin knight *M. Ado* v 3 13
This was no damsel neither, sir; she was a virgin.—It is so varied too; for it was proclaimed 'virgin' *L. L. Lost* i 1 295
But, damosella virgin, was this directed to you? . . . . iv 2 132
By this virgin palm now kissing thine, I will be thine . v 2 816
Withering on the virgin thorn Grows, lives, and dies in single blessedness.—So will I grow, so live, so die, my lord, Ere I will yield my virgin patent up *M. N. Dream* i 1 77
None of noble sort Would so offend a virgin . . iii 2 160
The best-regarded virgins of our clime Have loved it too *Mer. of Venice* ii 1 10
What says the silver with her virgin hue? ii 7 22
The virgin tribute paid by howling Troy To the sea-monster . iii 2 56
A poor virgin, sir, an ill-favoured thing, sir, but mine own *As Y. Like It* v 4 60
Young budding virgin, fair and fresh and sweet *T. of Shrew* iv 5 37
Is there no military policy, how virgins might blow up men? *All's Well* i 1 133
There was never virgin got till virginity was first lost. That you were made of is metal to make virgins . . . . i 1 140
I will stand for't a little, though therefore I die a virgin . . i 1 146
He that hangs himself is a virgin: virginity murders itself . i 1 151
Dian no queen of virgins, that would suffer her poor knight surprised . i 3 119
In the most bitter touch of sorrow that e'er I heard virgin exclaim in . i 3 123
How shall they credit A poor unlearned virgin? . . . i 3 246
I will bestow some precepts of this virgin Worthy the note . iii 5 103
That wear upon your virgin branches yet Your maidenheads growing *W. Tale* iv 4 115
Your fresh-fair virgins and your flowering infants *Hen. V.* iii 3 14
Beguiling virgins with the broken seals of perjury . . iv 1 172
A maid yet rosed over with the virgin crimson of modesty v 2 323
Employ thee then, sweet virgin, for our good 1 *Hen. VI.* iii 3 16
Such commendations as becomes a maid, A virgin, and his servant v 3 178
A virgin from her tender infancy, Chaste and immaculate in very thought v 4 50
She hath been liberal and free.—And yet, forsooth, she is a virgin pure v 4 83
To force a spotless virgin's chastity, To reave the orphan 2 *Hen. VI.* v 1 186
Yet a virgin, A most unspotted lily shall she pass To the ground *Hen. VIII.* v 5 61
Less valiant than the virgin in the night . . . . *Troi. and Cres.* i 1 11
Virgins and boys, mid-age and wrinkled eld, Soft infancy . ii 2 104
Into a pipe Small as an eunuch, or the virgin voice That babies lulls asleep *Coriolanus* iii 2 114
Let not the virgin's cheek Make soft thy trenchant sword *T. of Athens* iv 3 114
Giving our holy virgins to the stain Of contumelious, beastly, mad-brain'd war v 1 176
Yet here she is allow'd her virgin crants, Her maiden strewments *Ham.* v 1 255
She'll wear Diana's livery; This by the eye of Cynthia hath she vow'd, And on her virgin honour will not break it *Pericles* ii 5 12
My masters, you say she's a virgin?—O, sir, we doubt it not . iv 2 45
If fires be hot, knives sharp, or waters deep, Untied I still my virgin knot will keep iv 2 160
Your house, but for this virgin that doth prop it, Would sink and overwhelm you . . . . . . iv 6 127
Thy name, my most kind virgin? Recount, I do beseech thee . v 1 141
Virginal. Tears virginal Shall be to me even as the dew to fire 2 *Hen. VI.* v 2 52
The easy groans of old women, the virginal palms of your daughters *Coriolanus* v 2 45
Without any more virginal fencing, will you use him kindly? *Pericles* iv 6 62
Virginalling. Still virginalling Upon his palm! *W. Tale* i 2 125
Virgined. That kiss I carried from thee, dear; and my true lip Hath virgin'd it e'er since . . . *Coriolanus* v 3 48

Virginity. There is Anne Page, which is daughter to Master Thomas Page, which is pretty virginity . . . *Mer. Wives* i 1 47
If I would yield him my virginity, Thou mightst be freed *M. for M.* iii 1 98
Vanquish'd the resistance of her youth, And made defeat of her virginity . . . *Much Ado* iv 1 48
I deny her virginity: I was taken with a maid *L. L. Lost* i 1 298
With the rich worth of your virginity *M. N. Dream* ii 1 219
Are you meditating on virginity? . . . *All's Well* i 1 121
Man is enemy to virginity; how may we barricado it against him? . i 1 124
Our virginity, though valiant, in the defence yet is weak . i 1 126
Bless our poor virginity from underminers and blowers up! . i 1 131
Virginity being blown down, man will quicklier be blown up i 1 134
It is not politic in the commonwealth of nature to preserve virginity i 1 138
Loss of virginity is rational increase and there was never virgin got till virginity was first lost . . . . . . i 1 139
Virginity by being once lost may be ten times found . . . i 1 142
To speak on the part of virginity, is to accuse your mothers . i 1 148
Virginity murders itself; and should be buried in highways . i 1 151
Virginity breeds mites, much like a cheese; consumes itself to the very paring . . . . . i 1 153
Virginity is peevish, proud, idle, made of self-love . i 1 156
[Virginity] the longer kept, the less worth: off with't while 'tis vendible i 1 167
Virginity, like an old courtier, wears her cap out of fashion . i 1 169
Your virginity, your old virginity, is like one of our French withered pears, it looks ill, it eats drily . . . i 1 174
Will you any thing with it?—Not my virginity yet . . i 1 179
Who is a whale to virginity and devours up all the fry it finds . iv 3 249
Ask him upon his oath, if he does think He had not my virginity . v 3 186
To general filths Convert o' the instant, green virginity! *T. of Athens* iv 1 7
Take you the marks of her, . . . with warrant of her virginity *Pericles* iv 2 63
How now! How a dozen of virginities? . . . iv 6 22
Crack the glass of her virginity, and make the rest malleable . iv 6 151
Virginius. Was it well done of rash Virginius To slay his daughter with his own right hand? . . . *T. Andron.* v 3 36
I am as woful as Virginius was, And have a thousand times more cause v 3 50
Virgin-knot. If thou dost break her virgin-knot before All sanctimonious ceremonies . . . *Tempest* iv 1 15
Virgin-like. Senseless bauble, Art thou a feodary for this act, and look'st So virgin-like without? . . *Cymbeline* iii 2 22
Virgin-violator. An hypocrite, a virgin-violator *Meas. for Meas.* v 1 41
Virgo. Now, masters, draw. O, well said, Lucius! Good boy, in Virgo's lap; give it Pallas *T. Andron.* iv 3 64
Virtue. Which touch'd The very virtue of compassion in thee . *Tempest* i 2 27
Thy mother was a piece of virtue . . . i 2 56
For several virtues Have I liked several women . . iii 1 42
The rarer action is In virtue than in vengeance . . v 1 28
The gentleman Is full of virtue, bounty, worth, and qualities *T. G. of V.* iii 1 65
She can milk; look you, a sweet virtue in a maid with clean hands . iii 1 278
She can wash and scour.—A special virtue; for then she need not be washed and scoured . . . . . . iii 1 314
She hath many nameless virtues.—That's as much as to say, bastard virtues . . . . . . iii 1 320
Here follow her vices.—Close at the heels of her virtues . iii 1 325
To be slow in words is a woman's only virtue . . iii 1 339
To make a virtue of necessity . . . iv 1 62
Thrust virtue out of our hearts by the head and shoulders *Mer. Wives* v 5 155
As to waste Thyself upon thy virtues, they on thee *Meas. for Meas.* i 1 32
If our virtues Did not go forth of us, 'twere all alike As if we had them not i 1 34
Whom I believe to be most strait in virtue . . ii 1 9
Some rise by sin, and some by virtue fall . . ii 1 38
From thee, even from thy virtue! What's this? . . ii 2 161
Most dangerous Is that temptation that doth goad us on To sin in loving virtue . . . . . . ii 2 183
Your virtue hath a license in't, Which seems a little fouler than it is . ii 4 145
Nature dispenses with the deed so far That it becomes a virtue . iii 1 136
He hath made an assay of her virtue to practise his judgement . iii 1 164
Virtue is bold, and goodness never fearful . . iii 1 215
Back-wounding calumny The whitest virtue strikes . . iii 2 198
Pattern in himself to know, Grace to stand, and virtue go . iii 2 278
As there is sense in truth and truth in virtue . . v 1 226
I have confess'd her and I know her virtue . . v 1 533
Her sober virtue, years, and modesty, Plead on her part *Com. of Errors* iii 1 90
Apparel vice like virtue's harbinger; Bear a fair presence . iii 2 12
Stuffed with all honourable virtues . . . *Much Ado* i 1 57
Can virtue hide itself? Go to, mum, you are he: graces will appear . ii 1 127
Never gives to truth and virtue that Which simpleness and merit purchaseth . . . . . . iii 1 69
You may suspect him, by virtue of your office, to be no true man . iii 3 54
Comes not that blood as modest evidence To witness simple virtue? iv 1 39
Hero itself can blot out Hero's virtue . . . iv 1 83
Then we find The virtue that possession would not show us . iv 1 223
But no man's virtue nor sufficiency To be so moral when he shall endure The like himself . . . . . . v 1 29
Thus did she, an hour together, trans-shape thy particular virtues . v 1 172
To be the trumpet of his own virtues . . . v 2 88
The only soil of his fair virtue's gloss, If virtue's gloss will stain with any soil, Is a sharp wit . . . *L. L. Lost* ii 1 47
A well-accomplish'd youth, Of all that virtue love for virtue loved ii 1 57
By virtue, thou enforcest laughter; thy silly thought my spleen . iii 1 76
The virtue of your eye must break my oath.—You nickname virtue; vice you should have spoke; For virtue's office never breaks men's troth . . . . . . v 2 348
Your virtue is my privilege . . . *M. N. Dream* ii 1 220
Thy fair virtue's force perforce doth move me On the first view . iii 1 143
The virtue of my heart, The object and the pleasure of mine eye, Is only Helena . . . . . . iv 1 174
She is fair and, fairer than that word, Of wondrous virtues *Mer. of Ven.* i 1 163
There is no vice so simple but assumes Some mark of virtue . iii 2 82
I might in virtues, beauties, livings, friends, Exceed account . iii 2 158
Silence bestows that virtue on it, madam . . . v 1 101
If you had known the virtue of the ring, . . . You would not then have parted with the ring . . . . . . v 1 199
The people praise her for her virtues And pity her . *As Y. Like It* i 2 292
Your virtues, gentle master, Are sanctified and holy traitors to you ii 3 12
Every eye which in this forest looks Shall see thy virtue witness'd every where . . . . . . iii 2 8
You'll be rotten ere you be half ripe, and that's the right virtue of the medlar . . . . . . iii 2 127
The worst fault you have is to be in love.—'Tis a fault I will not change for your best virtue . . . iii 2 302

Virtue. Virtue is no horn-maker . . . *As Y. Like It* iv 1 63
Your If is the only peace-maker; much virtue in If . . . v 4 108
Your patience and your virtue well deserves it . . . v 4 193
For the time I study, Virtue and that part of philosophy Will I apply that treats of happiness By virtue specially to be achieved *T. of S.* i 1 18
We do admire This virtue and this moral discipline . . . i 1 30
Thy virtues spoke of, and thy beauty sounded . . . ii 1 193
Show more sign of her obedience, Her new-built virtue and obedience . v 2 118
He that so generally is at all times good must of necessity hold his virtue to you . . . *All's Well* i 1 10
They are virtues and traitors too . . . i 1 50
Thy blood and virtue Contend for empire in thee! . . . i 1 71
When virtue's steely bones Look bleak i' the cold wind . . . i 1 114
The composition that your valour and fear makes in you is a virtue of a good wing . . . i 1 218
Thou dislikest Of virtue for the name: but do not so . . . ii 3 131
Where great additions swell 's, and virtue none, It is a dropsied honour ii 3 134
Virtue and she Is her own dower; honour and wealth from me . ii 3 150
More saucy with lords and honourable personages than the commission of your birth and virtue gives you heraldry . . . ii 3 279
It were fit you knew him; lest, reposing too far in his virtue, which he hath not, he might at some great and trusty business in a main danger fail you . . . iii 6 15
Our virtues would be proud, if our faults whipped them not . iv 3 84
Our crimes would despair, if they were not cherished by our virtues . iv 3 87
Drunkenness is his best virtue, for he will be swine-drunk . iv 3 285
I put you to The use of your own virtues . . . v 1 16
I pray you yet; Since you lack virtue, I will lose a husband . . v 3 222
Is it a world to hide virtues in? . . . *T. Night* i 3 140
Virtue that transgresses is but patched with sin; and sin that amends is but patched with virtue . . . i 5 52
Good my mouse of virtue, answer me . . . i 5 69
Virtue is beauty, but the beauteous evil Are empty trunks o'erflourish'd by the devil . . . iii 4 403
For calumny will sear Virtue itself . . . *W. Tale* ii 1 74
Kings are no less unhappy, their issue not being gracious, than they are in losing them when they have approved their virtues . . iv 2 32
I cannot tell, good sir, for which of his virtues it was, but he was certainly whipped out of the court . . . iv 3 94
There's no virtue whipped out of the court: they cherish it to make it stay there . . . iv 3 97
Let me be unrolled and my name put in the book of virtue! . . iv 3 131
O, that must be I' the virtue of your daughter . . . iv 4 398
Whilst I remember Her and her virtues, I cannot forget My blemishes in them . . . v 1 7
And done a rape Upon the maiden virtue of the crown . *K. John* ii 1 98
If zealous love should go in search of virtue, Where should he find it purer? . . . ii 1 428
Such as she is, in beauty, virtue, birth, Is the young Dauphin . ii 1 432
Being rich, my virtue then shall be To say there is no vice but beggary ii 1 595
O that there were some virtue in my tears, That might relieve you! . v 7 44
Securely I espy Virtue with valour couched in thine eye . *Richard II.* i 3 98
Teach thy necessity to reason thus; There is no virtue like necessity . i 3 278
So shall my virtue be his vice's bawd . . . v 3 67
The virtue of this jest will be, the incomprehensible lies that this same fat rogue will tell us . . . *1 Hen. IV.* i 2 208
Is there no virtue extant? . . . ii 4 132
For, Harry, I see virtue in his looks . . . ii 4 470
Then, peremptorily I speak it, there is virtue in that Falstaff . ii 4 473
Gave the tongue a helpful ornament, A virtue that was never seen in you iii 1 126
If thou wert any way given to virtue, I would swear by thy face . . iii 3 38
Virtue is of so little regard in these costermonger times . . *2 Hen. IV.* i 2 190
We catch of you; grant that, my poor virtue, grant that . . ii 4 51
A full commission, In very ample virtue of his father . . . iv 1 163
It is no hidden virtue in him.—By my faith, sir, but it is . *Hen. V.* iii 7 118
Virtue he had, deserving to command . . . *1 Hen. VI.* i 1 9
Bethink thee on her virtues that surmount, And natural graces . v 3 191
Her virtues graced with external gifts Do breed love's settled passions . v 5 3
Noble she is, but if she have forgot Honour and virtue . . *2 Hen. VI.* ii 1 195
Virtue is choked with foul ambition And charity chased hence . . iii 1 143
O miserable age! virtue is not regarded in handicrafts-men . . iv 2 11
'Tis virtue that doth make them [women] most admired; The contrary doth make thee wonder'd at . . . *3 Hen. VI.* i 4 130
That love which virtue begs and virtue grants . . . iii 2 63
Where fame, late entering at his heedful ears, Hath placed thy beauty's image and thy virtue . . . iii 3 64
His love was an eternal plant, Whereof the root was fix'd in virtue's ground . . . iii 3 125
Sweet prince, the untainted virtue of your years Hath not yet dived into the world's deceit . . . *Richard III.* iii 1 7
So smooth he daub'd his vice with show of virtue . . . iii 5 29
Your discipline in war, wisdom in peace, Your bounty, virtue, fair humility . . . iii 7 17
Between two clergymen!—Two props of virtue for a Christian prince . iii 7 96
The garter, blemish'd, pawn'd his knightly virtue . . . iv 4 370
The rough brake That virtue must go through . . . *Hen. VIII.* i 2 76
By whose virtue, The court of Rome commanding, you, my lord Cardinal of York, are join'd with me . . . ii 2 104
I speak sincerely, and high note's Ta'en of your many virtues . . ii 3 60
Holy men I thought ye, Upon my soul, two reverend cardinal virtues . iii 1 103
Let me speak myself, Since virtue finds no friends . . . iii 1 126
You wrong your virtues With these weak women's fears . . . iii 1 168
Press not a falling man too far! 'tis virtue: His faults lie open to the laws iii 2 333
Men's evil manners live in brass; their virtues We write in water . iv 2 45
Still so rising, That Christendom shall ever speak his virtue . . iv 2 63
For virtue and true beauty of the soul, For honesty and decent carriage iv 2 144
My person; which I weigh not, Being of those virtues vacant . . v 1 125
You are a counsellor, And, by that virtue, no man dare accuse you . v 3 50
By virtue of that ring, I take my cause Out of the gripes of cruel men . v 3 99
Saba was never More covetous of wisdom and fair virtue Than this pure soul shall be . . . v 5 28
All the virtues that attend the good Shall still be doubled on her . . v 5 28
Hector, whose patience Is, as a virtue, fix'd, to-day was moved *T. and C.* i 2 5
There is no man hath a virtue that he hath not a glimpse of . . i 2 25
Gentleness, virtue, youth, . . . the spice and salt that season a man . i 2 276
And what hath mass or matter, by itself Lies rich in virtue and unmingled . . . i 3 30
A man distill'd Out of our virtues . . . i 3 351
Yet all his virtues, Not virtuously on his own part beheld, Do in our eyes begin to lose their gloss . . . ii 3 126

Virtue. Your mind is the clearer, Ajax, and your virtues the fairer *Troi. and Cres.* ii 3 164
His virtues shining upon others Heat them and they retort that heat again . . . iii 3 100
Let not virtue seek Remuneration for the thing it was . . . iii 3 169
We in silence hold this virtue well, We'll but commend what we intend to sell . . . iv 1 77
Fair virtues all, To which the Grecians are most prompt and pregnant . iv 4 89
To be partly proud; which he is, even to the altitude of his virtue *Cor.* i 1 41
Your virtue is To make him worthy whose offence subdues him . . i 1 178
It is held That valour is the chiefest virtue, and Most dignifies the haver ii 2 88
I would they would forget me, like the virtues Which our divines lose by 'em . . . ii 3 63
Who lack not virtue, no, nor power, but that Which they have given to beggars . . . iii 1 73
So our virtues Lie in the interpretation of the time . . . iv 7 49
The virtue of your name Is not here passable . . . v 2 12
The imperial seat, to virtue consecrate, To justice, continence *T. Andron.* i 1 14
Patron of virtue, Rome's best champion, Successful in the battles . . i 1 65
O sacred receptacle of my joys, Sweet cell of virtue and nobility! . . i 1 93
Outlive thy father's days, And fame's eternal date, for virtue's praise! . i 1 168
Whose virtues will, I hope, Reflect on Rome as Titan's rays on earth . i 1 225
Inter His noble nephew here in virtue's nest, That died in honour . i 1 376
He lives in fame that died in virtue's cause . . . i 1 390
And virtue stoops and trembles at her frown . . . ii 1 11
Many for many virtues excellent, None but for some . *Rom. and Jul.* ii 3 13
Virtue itself turns vice, being misapplied . . . ii 3 21
In grateful virtue I am bound To your free heart . . *T. of Athens* i 2 5
His right noble mind, illustrious virtue, And honourable carriage . . iii 2 87
I am an humble suitor to your virtues; For pity is the virtue of the law iii 5 7
He is a man, setting his fate aside, Of comely virtues . . . iii 5 15
That 'gainst the stream of virtue they may strive, And drown themselves in riot! . . . iv 1 27
Think, thy slave man rebels, and by thy virtue Set them into confounding odds . . . iv 3 391
I know that virtue to be in you, Brutus, As well as I do know your outward favour . . . *J. Cæsar* i 2 90
His countenance, like richest alchemy, Will change to virtue . . . i 3 160
Do not stain The even virtue of our enterprise . . . ii 1 133
By the right and virtue of my place, I ought to know . . . ii 1 269
My heart laments that virtue cannot live Out of the teeth of emulation ii 3 13
According to his virtue let us use him, With all respect . . . v 5 76
That his virtues Will plead like angels, trumpet-tongued . *Macbeth* i 7 18
With this strange virtue, He hath a heavenly gift of prophecy . iv 3 156
And now no soil nor cautel doth besmirch The virtue of his will *Hamlet* i 3 16
Virtue itself 'scapes not calumnious strokes . . . i 3 38
Their virtues else . . . Shall in the general censure take corruption From that particular fault . . . i 4 33
Virtue, as it never will be moved, Though lewdness court it in a shape of heaven . . . i 5 53
So shall I hope your virtues Will bring him to his wonted way again . iii 1 40
For virtue cannot so inoculate our old stock but we shall relish of it . iii 1 119
To show virtue her own feature, scorn her own image . . . iii 2 25
That blurs the grace and blush of modesty, Calls virtue hypocrite . iii 4 42
To flaming youth let virtue be as wax, And melt in her own fire . iii 4 84
Forgive me this my virtue; For in the fatness of these pursy times Virtue itself of vice must pardon beg . . . iii 4 152
Assume a virtue, if you have it not . . . iii 4 160
Tears seven times salt, Burn out the sense and virtue of mine eye! . iv 5 155
My virtue or my plague, be it either which—She's so conjunctive to my life . . . iv 7 13
Collected from all simples that have virtue Under the moon . . . iv 7 145
Thee and thy virtues here I seize upon . . . *Lear* i 1 255
He wrote this but as an essay or taste of my virtue . . . i 2 47
Would the reposal Of any trust, virtue, or worth in thee Make thy words faith'd? . . . ii 1 71
Whose virtue and obedience doth this instant So much commend itself . ii 1 115
Thou perjured, and thou simular man of virtue That art incestuous . iii 2 54
All you unpublish'd virtues of the earth, Spring with my tears! . . iv 4 16
That minces virtue, and does shake the head To hear of pleasure's name iv 6 122
Trust to thy single virtue . . . v 3 103
All friends shall taste The wages of their virtue . . . v 3 303
If virtue no delighted beauty lack . . . *Othello* i 3 290
I confess it is my shame to be so fond; but it is not in my virtue to amend it.—Virtue! a fig! 'tis in ourselves that we are thus or thus i 3 320
Do but see his vice; 'Tis to his virtue a just equinox . . . ii 3 128
Prizes the virtue that appears in Cassio, And looks not on his evils . ii 3 139
I turn her virtue into pitch, And out of her own goodness make the net ii 3 366
Sings, plays, and dances well; Where virtue is, these are more virtuous iii 3 186
Farewell the plumed troop, and the big wars, That make ambition virtue! . . . iii 3 350
They that mean virtuously, and yet do so, The devil their virtue tempts iv 1 8
Whose solid virtue The shot of accident, nor dart of chance, Could neither graze nor pierce . . . iv 1 277
Whose virtue and whose general graces speak That which none else can utter . . . *Ant. and Cleo.* ii 2 132
And ambition, The soldier's virtue, rather makes choice of loss . . iii 1 23
The piece of virtue, which is set Betwixt us as the cement of our love . iii 2 28
O infinite virtue, comest thou smiling from The world's great snare uncaught? . . . iv 8 17
Her own price Proclaims how she esteem'd him and his virtue *Cymbeline* i 1 52
She holds her virtue still and I my mind . . . i 4 69
Apply Allayments to their act, and by them gather Their several virtues i 5 23
If thou wert honourable, Thou wouldst have told this tale for virtue . i 6 143
Thou wert dignified enough, Even to the point of envy, if 'twere made Comparative for your virtues . . . ii 3 134
The vows of women Of no more bondage be, to where they are made, Than they are to their virtues . . . ii 4 112
Undergoes, More goddess-like than wife-like, such assaults As would take in some virtue . . . iii 2 9
And had the virtue Which their own conscience seal'd them . . . iii 6 84
Let his virtue join With my request . . . v 5 88
Not dispraising whom we praised,—therein He was as calm as virtue . v 5 174
The temple Of virtue was she; yea, and she herself . . . v 5 221
And her thoughts the king Of every virtue gives renown to men! *Pericles* i 1 14
I'll show the virtue I have borne in arms . . . ii 1 151
Virtue and cunning were endowments greater Than nobleness and riches iii 2 27
O lady, Much less in blood than virtue, yet a princess! . . . iv 3 7
Thou art a piece of virtue, and I doubt not but thy training hath been noble . . . iv 6 118

Virtue. I can sing, weave, sew, and dance, With other virtues, which I'll keep from boast . . . . *Pericles* iv 6 195
Virtue preserved from fell destruction's blast, Led on by heaven v 3 Gower 89
Virtuous. A virtuous gentlewoman, mild and beautiful! *T. G. of Ver.* iv 4 185
So God udge me, that is a virtuous mind . . *Mer. Wives* i 1 191
The honest woman, the modest wife, the virtuous creature! . . . iv 2 136
A very virtuous maid, And to be shortly of a sisterhood *Meas. for Meas.* ii 2 20
Do as the carrion does, not as the flower, Corrupt with virtuous season ii 2 168
But this virtuous maid Subdues me quite . . . . ii 2 185
It is virtuous to be constant in any undertaking . . . . iii 2 239
She is a virtuous and a reverend lady . . *Com. of Errors* v 1 134
One woman is fair, yet I am well; another is wise, yet I am well; another virtuous, yet I am well . . . . . . *Much Ado* ii 3 29
Rich she shall be, that's certain; wise, or I'll none; virtuous, or I'll never cheapen her . . . . ii 3 33
She's an excellent sweet lady; and, out of all suspicion, she is virtuous ii 3 166
They say the lady is fair; 'tis a truth, I can bear them witness; and virtuous; 'tis so, I cannot reprove it . . . . ii 3 240
Always hath been just and virtuous In any thing that I do know by her v 1 311
My loving lords, That are vow-fellows with this virtuous duke *L. L. Lost* ii 1 38
Such separation as may well be said Becomes a virtuous bachelor and a maid, So far be distant . . . . *M. N. Dream* ii 2 59
This herb . . .; Whose liquor hath this virtuous property . . iii 2 367
Your father was ever virtuous; and holy men at their death have good inspirations . . . . *Mer. of Venice* i 2 30
She robs thee of thy name; And thou wilt show more bright and seem more virtuous When she is gone . . . . *As Y. Like It* i 3 83
Why are you virtuous? why do people love you? . . . ii 3 5
My Rosalind is virtuous.—And I am your Rosalind . . . iv 1 64
To deck his fortune with his virtuous deeds . . *T. of Shrew* i 1 16
Have you not a daughter Call'd Katharina, fair and virtuous? . ii 1 43
Make myself a suitor to your daughter, Unto Bianca, fair and virtuous ii 1 92
Give away myself To this most patient, sweet, and virtuous wife . iii 2 196
For where an unclean mind carries virtuous qualities, there commendations go with pity . . . . *All's Well* i 1 48
Whose aged honour cites a virtuous youth . . . . . i 3 216
To each of you one fair and virtuous mistress Fall, when Love please! . ii 3 63
If she be All that is virtuous, save what thou dislikest . . . ii 3 129
From lowest place when virtuous things proceed, The place is dignified by the doer's deed . . . . ii 3 132
By the misprising of a maid too virtuous For the contempt of empire . iii 2 33
The most virtuous gentlewoman that ever nature had praise for creating iv 5 9
What's she?—A virtuous maid, the daughter of a count *T. Night* i 2 36
I suppose him virtuous, know him noble, Of great estate . . . i 5 277
Dost thou think, because thou art virtuous, there shall be no more cakes and ale? . . . . ii 3 124
Virtuous Dauphin, alter not the doom Forethought by heaven! *K. John* iii 1 311
There is a virtuous man whom I have often noted in thy company 1 *Hen. IV.* ii 4 460
I was as virtuously given as a gentleman need to be; virtuous enough iii 3 17
Well, God be thanked for these rebels, they offend none but the virtuous iii 3 215
If a man will make courtesy and say nothing, he is virtuous 2 *Hen. IV.* ii 1 136
You virtuous ass, you bashful fool, must you be blushing? . . ii 2 80
This honest, virtuous, civil gentlewoman! . . . . . ii 4 328
Whether pure fear and entire cowardice doth not make thee wrong this virtuous gentlewoman . . . . ii 4 353
Like the bee, culling from every flower The virtuous sweets . . . iv 5 76
His new-come champion, virtuous Joan of Arc . . . 1 *Hen. VI.* ii 2 20
The virtuous lady, Countess of Auvergne . . . . . . ii 2 38
O, my good lords, and virtuous Henry, Pity the city of London! . . iii 1 76
Valiant and virtuous, full of haughty courage . . . . . iv 1 35
As liking of the lady's virtuous gifts, Her beauty . . . . v 1 43
Virtuous and holy; chosen from above, By inspiration of celestial grace v 4 39
She is content to be at your command; Command, I mean, of virtuous chaste intents . . . . v 5 20
When I imagine ill Against my king and nephew, virtuous Henry, Be my last breathing in this mortal world! . . 2 *Hen. VI.* i 2 20
The shepherd of the flock, That virtuous prince, the good Duke Humphrey . . . . ii 2 74
The duke is virtuous, mild, and too well given To dream on evil . . iii 1 72
Let my sovereign, virtuous Henry, Command my eldest son . . . v 1 48
I'll leave my son my virtuous deeds behind . . . 3 *Hen. VI.* i 2 49
That virtuous Lady Bona, thy fair sister . . . . . . iii 3 56
Sir Edward, she is fair and virtuous, Therefore delay not . . . iii 3 245
Your grace hath still been famed for virtuous; And now may seem as wise as virtuous . . . . iv 6 27
We speak no treason, man: we say the king Is wise and virtuous *Richard III.* i 1 91
Obsequiously lament The untimely fall of virtuous Lancaster . . i 2 4
O, he was gentle, mild, and virtuous!—The fitter for the King of heaven i 2 104
A virtuous and a Christian-like conclusion . . . . . i 3 316
Oh, that deceit should steal such gentle shapes, And with a virtuous vizard hide foul guile! . . . . ii 2 28
Then the king Had virtuous uncles to protect his grace . . . ii 3 21
Virtuous and fair, royal and gracious.—And must she die for this? . iv 4 204
Virtuous and holy, be thou conqueror! . . . . v 3 128
Fearing he would rise, he was so virtuous, Kept him a foreign man *Hen. VIII.* ii 2 128
He was a fool; For he would needs be virtuous . . . . ii 2 133
What though I know her virtuous And well deserving? yet I know her for A spleeny Lutheran . . . . iii 2 97
No great good lover of the archbishop's, The virtuous Cranmer . . iv 1 105
Beseeching him to give her virtuous breeding,—She is young . . iv 2 134
O virtuous fight, When right with right wars who shall be most right! *Troi. and Cres.* iii 2 178
A kind of godly jealousy—Which, I beseech you, call a virtuous sin . iv 4 83
Account me the more virtuous that I have not been common in my love . . . . *Coriolanus* ii 3 100
No, though it were as virtuous to lie as to live chastely . . . v 2 27
All bond and privilege of nature, break! Let it be virtuous to be obstinate . . . . v 3 26
In a bad quarrel slain a virtuous son . . . . *T. Andron.* i 1 342
Verona brags of him To be a virtuous and well-govern'd youth *R. and J.* i 5 70
The lady of the house, And a good lady, and a wise and virtuous . i 5 116
An honest gentleman, and a courteous, and a kind, and a handsome, and, I warrant, a virtuous . . . . ii 5 58
Commend me to thy honourable virtuous lord . . *T. of Athens* iii 2 31
If his occasion were not virtuous, I should not urge it half so faithfully iii 2 45
Strives to appear foul! takes virtuous copies to be wicked . . . iii 3 32
A good and virtuous nature may recoil In an imperial charge *Macbeth* iv 3 19
Virtuous. A plot upon her virtuous husband's life . . . . *Lear* iv 6 279
I will beseech the virtuous Desdemona to undertake for me . *Othello* ii 3 336
That she will to virtuous Desdemona Procure me some access . . iii 1 37
Sings, plays, and dances well; Where virtue is, these are more virtuous iii 3 186
I do beseech you That by your virtuous means I may again Exist . iii 4 111
Vouching . . . his to be more fair, virtuous, wise, chaste . *Cymbeline* i 4 64
The piece of tender air, thy virtuous daughter, Which we call 'mollis aer' . . . . v 5 446
What do you think of my daughter, sir?—A most virtuous princess *Per.* ii 5 34
Then, as you are as virtuous as fair, Resolve your angry father . ii 5 67
Shall's go hear the vestals sing?—I'll do any thing now that is virtuous iv 5 8
Virtuously. I pity much your grievances; Which since I know they virtuously are placed, I give consent to go along with you *T. G. of Ver.* iv 3 38
I was as virtuously given as a gentleman need to be . 1 *Hen. IV.* iii 3 16
Yet all his virtues, Not virtuously on his own part beheld, Do in our eyes begin to lose their gloss . . . . . *Troi. and Cres.* iii 3 127
We are so virtuously bound— And so am I to you . *T. of Athens* i 2 232
They that mean virtuously, and yet do so, The devil their virtue tempts *Othello* iv 1 7
Visage. This outward-sainted deputy, Whose settled visage and deliberate word Nips youth i' the head . . . *Meas. for Meas.* iii 1 90
Satisfy the deputy with the visage Of Ragozine, more like to Claudio . iv 3 79
Show your knave's visage, with a pox to you! . . . . . v 1 358
We meet, With visages display'd, to talk and greet . . *L. L. Lost* v 2 144
When Phœbe doth behold Her silver visage in the watery glass *M. N. D.* i 1 210
O, how mine eyes do loathe his visage now! . . . . . iv 1 84
Men whose visages Do cream and mantle like a standing pond *M. of Ven.* i 1 88
The rest aloof are the Dardanian wives, With bleared visages . . iii 2 59
Her business looks in her With an importing visage . *All's Well* v 3 136
The youth bears in his visage no great presage of cruelty *T. Night* iii 2 69
Be plainer with me; let me know my trespass By its own visage *W. Tale* i 2 266
The selfsame sun that shines upon his court Hides not his visage from our cottage but Looks on alike . . . . iv 4 456
Through casements darted their desiring eyes Upon his visage *Rich. II.* v 2 15
Put not you on the visage of the times . . . 2 *Hen. IV.* ii 3 3
Why . . . Peace . . . Should not . . . put up her lovely visage? *Hen. V.* v 2 37
Notwithstanding the poor and untempering effect of my visage . . v 2 241
O, let me view his visage, being dead, That living wrought me such exceeding trouble . . . . 2 *Hen. VI.* v 1 69
There's more in 't than fair visage . . . . *Hen. VIII.* iii 2 88
To talk with him and to behold his visage, Even to my full of view *Troi. and Cres.* iii 3 240
The blood upon your visage dries; 'tis time It should be look'd to *Coriol.* i 9 93
Give me a case to put my visage in: A visor for a visor! *Rom. and Jul.* i 4 29
Put on a most importunate aspect, A visage of demand . *T. of Athens* ii 1 29
O, then by day Where wilt thou find a cavern dark enough To mask thy monstrous visage? . . . . *J. Cæsar* ii 1 81
Nor the dejected 'haviour of the visage . . . . . *Hamlet* i 2 81
All his visage wann'd, Tears in his eyes, distraction in's aspect . . ii 2 580
With devotion's visage And pious action we do sugar o'er The devil himself . . . . iii 1 47
Whereto serves mercy But to confront the visage of offence? . . . iii 3 47
With tristful visage, as against the doom, Is thought-sick at the act . iii 4 50
With her nails She'll flay thy wolvish visage . . . . *Lear* i 4 330
A plague upon your epileptic visage! Smile you my speeches? . . ii 2 87
Trimm'd in forms and visages of duty . . . . . *Othello* i 1 50
I saw Othello's visage in his mind . . . . i 3 253
Her name, that was as fresh As Dian's visage, is now begrimed and black iii 3 387
Let Patient Octavia plough thy visage up With her prepared nails *Ant. and Cleo.* iv 12 38
Visard-like. Thy face is, visard-like, unchanging, Made impudent with use of evil deeds . . . . 3 *Hen. VI.* i 4 116
Visible. Though Fortune, visible an enemy, Should chase us . *W. Tale* v 1 216
Thou visible god [gold], That solder'st close impossibilities! *T. of Athens* iv 3 387
If that the heavens do not their visible spirits Send quickly down to tame these vile offences, It will come . . . . . *Lear* iv 2 46
Here I am Antony; Yet cannot hold this visible shape *Ant. and Cleo.* iv 14 14
Though his actions were not visible, yet Report should render him hourly to your ear As truly as he moves . . . *Cymbeline* iii 4 152
Visibly. The table wherein all my thoughts Are visibly character'd *T. G. of Ver.* ii 7 4
Vision. This is a most majestic vision, and Harmonious charmingly *Temp.* iv 1 118
Like the baseless fabric of this vision . . . . . . iv 1 151
If this prove A vision of the Island, one dear son Shall I twice lose . v 1 176
Hum! ha! is this a vision? is this a dream? do I sleep? *Mer. Wives* iii 5 141
All this derision Shall seem a dream and fruitless vision *M. N. Dream* iii 2 371
What visions have I seen! Methought I was enamour'd of an ass . iv 1 81
I have had a most rare vision . . . . iv 1 210
You have but slumber'd here While these visions did appear . . v 1 433
To a vision so apparent rumour Cannot be mute . . . *W. Tale* i 2 270
A holy maid hither with me I bring, Which by a vision sent to her from heaven Ordained is to raise this tedious siege . . 1 *Hen. VI.* i 2 52
God's mother deigned to appear to me And in a vision full of majesty . i 2 79
Thy ife hath dream'd; thy mother hath had visions *Troi. and Cres.* v 3 63
This dream is all amiss interpreted; It was a vision fair and fortunate *J. Cæsar* ii 2 84
Art thou not, fatal vision, sensible To feeling as to sight? *Macbeth* ii 1 36
Touching this vision here, It is an honest ghost, that let me tell you *Ham.* i 5 137
Last night the very gods show'd me a vision . . *Cymbeline* iv 2 346
The vision Which I made known to Lucius . . . Is full accomplish'd v 5 467
Pure Dian, bless thee for thy vision! . . . . . *Pericles* v 3 69
Visit. We'll visit Caliban my slave, who never Yields us kind answer *Tempest* i 2 308
Do not omit the heavy offer of it [sleep]: It seldom visits sorrow . . ii 1 195
In these fits I leave them, while I visit Young Ferdinand . . . iii 3 91
And I likewise will visit thee with mine [my letters] *T. G. of Ver.* i 1 60
Visit by night your lady's chamber-window With some sweet concert iii 2 83
I will visit her: tell her so; and bid her think what a man is *M. Wives* ii 5 50
I will, as 'twere a brother of your order, Visit both prince and people *Meas. for Meas.* i 3 45
I come to visit the afflicted spirits Here in the prison . . . ii 3 4
Dear sir, ere long I'll visit you again.—Most holy sir, I thank you . iii 1 46
I am going to visit the prisoner. Fare you well . . . . . iii 2 272
Soon at supper-time I'll visit you And then receive my money *C. of Er.* iii 2 179
The prince and Claudio promised by this hour To visit me . *Much Ado* v 4 14
I will visit thee at the lodge.—That's hereby . . . *L. L. Lost* i 2 140
Excuse me, and farewell: To-morrow shall we visit you again . . ii 1 177
But what, but what, come they to visit us? . . . . . . v 2 119
We came to visit you, and purpose now To lead you to our court . . v 2 343

Visit. From day to day Visit the speechless sick *L. L. Lost* v 2 861
We will visit you at supper-time *Mer. of Venice* ii 2 215
Welcome his friends, Visit his countrymen and banquet them *T. of Shrew* i 1 202
Thus I'll visit her.—But thus, I trust, you will not marry her iii 2 116
And bound I am to Padua; there to visit A son of mine iv 5 56
Sir Topas the curate, who comes to visit Malvolio the lunatic *T. Night* iv 2 25
If you shall chance, Camillo, to visit Bohemia *W. Tale* i 1 1
Please your ladyship To visit the next room ii 2 47
I told her so, my lord, On your displeasure's peril and on mine, She should not visit you ii 3 46
Once a day I'll visit The chapel where they lie iii 2 239
You have vouchsafed . . . my poor house to visit v 3 6
Bid him—ah, what?—With all good speed at Plashy visit me *Richard II.* i 2 66
All places that the eye of heaven visits Are to a wise man ports i 3 275
And hath sent post haste To entreat your majesty to visit him i 4 56
Let's all go visit him: Pray God we may make haste, and come too late! i 4 63
He means to visit us, For he hath heard of our confederacy *1 Hen. IV.* iv 4 37
At your return visit our house; let our old acquaintance be renewed *2 Hen. IV.* iii 2 314
I'll through Gloucestershire; and there will I visit Master Robert Shallow iv 3 139
Forth he goes and visits all his host, Bids them good morrow *Hen. V.* iv Prol. 32
Countess of Auvergne, . . . By me entreats, great lord, thou wouldst vouchsafe To visit her poor castle *1 Hen. VI.* ii 2 41
Since your ladyship is not at leisure, I'll sort some other time to visit you ii 3 27
He doth entreat your grace To visit him to-morrow or next day *Richard III.* iii 7 60
By your patience, I may not suffer you to visit them iv 1 16
First, mine own service to your grace; the next, The king's request that I would visit you *Hen. VIII.* iv 2 116
I prithee, Diomed, visit me no more.—Now she sharpens *Troi. and Cres.* v 2 74
Madam, the Lady Valeria is come to visit you *Coriolanus* i 3 29
Come, you must go visit the good lady that lies in.—I will wish her speedy strength, and visit her with my prayers; but I cannot go thither i 3 85
Whether to knock against the gates of Rome, Or rudely visit them in parts remote iv 5 148
Certain nobles of the senate Newly alighted, and come to visit you *T. of Athens* i 2 181
If I thrive well, I'll visit thee again.—If I hope well, I'll never see thee more iv 3 170
As dear to me as are the ruddy drops That visit my sad heart *J. Cæsar* ii 1 290
And thither will I straight to visit him: He comes upon a wish iii 2 270
They could be content To visit other places v 1 9
He might not beteem the winds of heaven Visit her face too roughly *Ham.* i 2 142
Upon the platform, 'twixt eleven and twelve, I'll visit you i 2 253
You shall do marvellous wisely, good Reynaldo, Before you visit him, to make inquire Of his behaviour ii 1 4
I beseech you instantly to visit My too much changed son ii 2 35
What make you at Elsinore?—To visit you, my lord; no other occasion ii 2 279
You know not why we came to visit you,— Thus out of season *Lear* ii 1 120
Vouchsafing here to visit me, Doing the honour *Ant. and Cleo.* v 2 160
When last I went to visit her, She pray'd me to excuse her keeping close *Cymbeline* iii 5 45
O, make for Tarsus! There will I visit Cleon *Pericles* iii 1 79
Visitation. Thou art infected! This visitation shows it *Tempest* iii 1 32
I am made to understand that you have lent him visitation *Meas. for Meas.* iii 2 255
What would they, say they?—Nothing but peace and gentle visitation *L. L. Lost* v 2 181
In loving visitation was with me a young doctor *Mer. of Venice* iv 1 153
Sicilia means to pay Bohemia the visitation which he justly owes him *W. Tale* i 1 7
What colour for my visitation shall I Hold up before him? iv 4 566
'Tis not a visitation framed, but forced By need and accident v 1 91
The visitation of the winds, Who take the ruffian billows by the top, Curling their monstrous heads *2 Hen. IV.* iii 1 21
Beseech you pardon me, Who, earnest in the service of my God, Neglect the visitation of my friends *Richard III.* iii 7 107
But he came To whisper Wolsey,—here makes visitation *Hen. VIII.* i 1 179
Your queen Desires your visitation, and to be Acquainted with this stranger v 1 167
I will corrupt the Grecian sentinels, To give thee nightly visitation *Troi. and Cres.* iv 4 75
I take all and your several visitations So kind to heart *T. of Athens* i 2 224
What have you now to present unto him?—Nothing at this time but my visitation v 1 20
Your visitation shall receive such thanks As fits a king's remembrance *Hamlet* ii 2 25
Is it your own inclining? Is it a free visitation? ii 2 284
This visitation Is but to whet thy almost blunted purpose iii 4 110
Visited. These lords are visited; you are not free *L. L. Lost* v 2 422
By day's approach look to be visited *M. N. Dream* iii 2 430
So the sins of my mother should be visited upon me *Mer. of Venice* iii 5 16
Imprison'd, Kept in a dark house, visited by the priest *T. Night* v 1 350
She hath privately twice or thrice a day, ever since the death of Hermione, visited that removed house *W. Tale* v 2 116
Thy sins are visited in this poor child *K. John* ii 1 179
I would the state of time had first been whole Ere he by sickness had been visited: His health was never better worth *1 Hen. IV.* iv 1 26
Guilty of those impieties for the which they are now visited *Hen. V.* iv 1 185
Your hand, and yours: Ere in our own house I do shade my head, The good patricians must be visited *Coriolanus* ii 1 212
Visiting. We have cross'd, To execute the charge my father gave me For visiting your highness *W. Tale* v 1 163
Buckingham and I Are come from visiting his majesty *Richard III.* i 3 32
And we lay by Our appertainments, visiting of him *Troi. and Cres.* ii 3 87
To associate me, Here in this city visiting the sick *Rom. and Jul.* v 2 7
That no compunctious visitings of nature Shake my fell purpose *Macbeth* i 5 46
There is nothing left remarkable Beneath the visiting moon *A. and C.* iv 15 68
Visitor. The visitor will not give him o'er so *Tempest* ii 1 11
To lock up honesty and honour from The access of gentle visitors! *W. T.* ii 2 11
You see this confluence, this great flood of visitors *T. of Athens* i 1 42
Visor. My visor is Philemon's roof; within the house is Jove.—Why, then, your visor should be thatched *Much Ado* ii 1 99
The ladies follow her and but one visor remains ii 1 164
My very visor began to assume life and scold with her ii 1 248
And so, adieu; Twice to your visor, and half once to you *L. L. Lost* v 2 227
I beseech you, sir, to countenance William Visor of Woncot *2 Hen. IV.* v 1 42

Visor. There is many complaints, Davy, against that Visor: that Visor is an arrant knave *2 Hen. IV.* v 1 45
Give me a case to put my visage in: A visor for a visor! *Rom. and Jul.* i 4 30
I have worn a visor and could tell A whispering tale in a fair lady's ear i 5 24
No visor does become black villany So well as soft and tender flattery *Pericles* iv 4 44
Vita. Lux tua vita mihi ii 2 21
Vitæ. Integer vitæ, scelerisque purus, Non eget Mauri jaculis *T. Andron.* iv 2 20
Vital. The vital commoners and inland petty spirits muster me all to their captain, the heart *2 Hen. IV.* iv 3 119
Let not Bardolph's vital thread be cut With edge of penny cord *Hen. V.* iii 6 49
Whose dismal tune bereft my vital powers *2 Hen. VI.* iii 2 41
When I have pluck'd the rose, I cannot give it vital growth again *Othello* v 2 14
Vitement. J'ai gagné deux mots d'Anglois vitement *Hen. V.* iii 4 14
Vitness. Bear vitness that me have stay six or seven . . . hours *M. W.* ii 3 36
Vitruvio. The lady widow of Vitruvio; Signior Placentio *Rom. and Jul.* i 2 69
Vivant. O Dieu vivant! *Hen. V.* iii 5 5
Vivâ voce. Divers witnesses; which the duke desired To have brought vivâ voce to his face *Hen. VIII.* ii 1 18
Vive. Have I not heard these islanders shout out 'Vive le roi!'? *K. John* v 2 104
Vivo. The motto, 'In hac spe vivo' *Pericles* ii 2 44
Vixen. She was a vixen when she went to school *M. N. Dream* iii 2 324
Viz. How many pair of silk stockings thou hast, viz. these, and those *2 Hen. IV.* ii 2 18
Vizaments. Take your vizaments in that *Mer. Wives* i 1 39
Vizard. I'll go buy them vizards iv 4 70
What, was your vizard made without a tongue? *L. L. Lost* v 2 242
You have a double tongue within your mask, And would afford my speechless vizard half v 2 246
Will they not, think you, hang themselves to-night? Or ever, but in vizards, show their faces? v 2 271
Which of the vizards was it that you wore?—Where? when? what vizard? v 2 385
That vizard; that superfluous case That hid the worse and show'd the better face v 2 387
Nor never come in vizard to my friend, Nor woo in rhyme v 2 404
I have vizards for you all; you have horses for yourselves *1 Hen. IV.* i 2 142
Our vizards we will change after we leave them i 2 199
On with your vizards: there's money of the king's coming down the hill ii 2 55
Oh, that deceit should steal such gentle shapes, And with a virtuous vizard hide foul guile! *Richard III.* ii 2 28
Make our faces vizards to our hearts, Disguising what they are *Macbeth* iii 2 34
Vizarded. They must all be mask'd and vizarded *Mer. Wives* iv 6 40
Degree being vizarded, The unworthiest shows as fairly in the mask *Troi. and Cres.* i 3 83
Vlouting-stock. You are wise and full of gibes and vlouting-stocks *Mer. Wives* iv 5 83
Vlouting-stog. He has made us his vlouting-stog iii 1 120
Vocation. Why, Hall, 'tis my vocation, Hal; 'tis no sin for a man to labour in his vocation *1 Hen. IV.* i 2 116
Will'd me to leave my base vocation And free my country *1 Hen. VI.* i 2 80
Yet it is said, labour in thy vocation *2 Hen. VI.* iv 2 18
Vocativo. What is the focative case, William?—O,—vocativo, O.—Remember, William; focative is caret *Mer. Wives* iv 1 54
Vocatur. Neighbour vocatur nebour; neigh abbreviated ne *L. L. Lost* v 1 25
Voice. I should know that voice: it should be—but he is drowned *Temp.* ii 2 90
Four legs and two voices: a most delicate monster! His forward voice now is to speak well of his friend; his backward voice is to utter foul speeches and to detract ii 2 93
Voices That, if I then had waked after long sleep, Will make me sleep again iii 2 147
You would quickly learn to know him by his voice *T. G. of Ver.* iv 2 89
The hardest voice of her behaviour, to be Englished rightly, is, 'I am Sir John Falstaff's' *Mer. Wives* i 3 51
There's money for thee; let me have thy voice in my behalf i 4 167
Implore her, in my voice, that she make friends *Meas. for Meas.* i 2 185
Who's that which calls?—It is a man's voice i 4 7
I, now the voice of the recorded law, Pronounce a sentence ii 4 61
There my father's grave Did utter forth a voice iii 1 87
I remember you, sir, by the sound of your voice v 1 331
But tell me yet, dost thou not know my voice? *Com. of Errors* v 1 300
Not know my voice! O time's extremity! v 1 307
Tax not so bad a voice To slander music any more than once *Much Ado* ii 3 46
I pray God his bad voice bode no mischief ii 3 83
Thy eye Jove's lightning bears, thy voice his dreadful thunder *L. L. Lost* iv 2 119
The voice of all the gods Make heaven drowsy with the harmony iv 3 344
Sung With feigning voice verses of feigning love *M. N. Dream* i 1 31
Wanting your father's voice, The other must be held the worthier i 1 54
My ear should catch your voice, my eye your eye i 1 188
I'll speak in a monstrous little voice i 2 54
I will aggravate my voice so that I will roar you as gently as any sucking dove i 2 84
But hark, a voice! stay thou but here awhile iii 1 88
As if our hands, our sides, voices, and minds, Had been incorporate iii 2 207
Follow my voice: we'll try no manhood here iii 2 412
He is a very paramour for a sweet voice.—You must say 'paragon' iv 2 12
I see a voice: now will I to the chink, To spy an I can hear my Thisby's face v 1 194
Thou art too wild, too rude and bold of voice *Mer. of Venice* ii 2 190
Being season'd with a gracious voice, Obscures the show of evil iii 2 76
Speak between the change of man and boy With a reed voice iii 4 67
The offender's life lies in the mercy Of the duke only, 'gainst all other voice iv 1 356
That is the voice, Or I am much deceived, of Portia v 1 110
He knows me as the blind man knows the cuckoo, By the bad voice v 1 113
In my voice most welcome shall you be *As Y. Like It* ii 4 87
My voice is ragged: I know I cannot please you ii 5 15
His big manly voice, Turning again toward childish treble ii 7 161
Spitting or saying we are hoarse, which are the only prologues to a bad voice v 3 14
God be wi' you; and God mend your voices! v 3 42
I know the boy will well usurp the grace, Voice, gait, and action of a gentlewoman *T. of Shrew* Ind. 1 132
O'er whom both sovereign power and father's voice I have to use *A. W.* ii 3 60
Art not acquainted with him? knows he not thy voice?—No, sir iv 1 11
In voices well divulged, free, learn'd, and valiant *T. Night* i 5 279
A mellifluous voice, as I am true knight.—A contagious breath ii 3 54
Without any mitigation or remorse of voice ii 3 98
My matter hath no voice, lady, but to your own most pregnant and vouchsafed ear iii 1 99

Voice. Nor know I you by voice or any feature . . . *T. Night* iii 4 387
To him in thine own voice, and bring me word how thou findest him iv 2 71
One face, one voice, one habit, and two persons, A natural perspective! v 1 223
The burst And the ear-deafening voice o' the oracle *W. Tale* iii 1 9
That fell anatomy Which cannot hear a lady's feeble voice . *K. John* iii 4 41
Thinking his voice an armed Englishman . . . . . . v 2 145
Boys, with women's voices, Strive to speak big . *Richard II.* iii 2 113
O, 'tis our setter: I know his voice . . . 1 *Hen. IV.* ii 2 53
Is not your voice broken? your wind short? your chin double? 2 *Hen. IV.* i 2 206
For my voice, I have lost it with halloing and singing of anthems . i 2 212
Rumour doth double, like the voice and echo, The numbers of the feard . . . . iii 1 97
For all the country in a general voice Cried hate upon him . iv 1 136
To us the speaker in his parliament; To us the imagined voice of God himself . . . . iv 2 19
Which, delivered o'er to the voice, the tongue, which is the birth, becomes excellent wit . . . . iv 3 109
My voice shall sound as you do prompt mine ear . . . v 2 119
Hath got the voice in hell for excellence . . . *Hen. V.* ii 2 113
Go speak: the duke will hear thy voice . . . . . iii 6 48
Now we speak upon our cue, and our voice is imperial . . iii 6 131
My brother Gloucester's voice? Ay; I know thy errand . . iv 1 323
I did never know so full a voice issue from so empty a heart . iv 4 72
I will go with them: Haply a woman's voice may do some good . v 2 93
In broken music; for thy voice is music and thy English broken . v 2 263
Having neither the voice nor the heart of flattery about me . v 2 315
Is it you whose voice I hear? Open the gates . . . 1 *Hen. VI.* i 3 16
Well didst thou, Richard, to suppress thy voice . . . iv 1 182
Boiling choler chokes The hollow passage of my poison'd voice . iv 4 121
Lords, with one cheerful voice welcome my love . . 2 *Hen. VI.* i 1 36
Clapping their hands, and crying with loud voice . . . i 1 160
Many time and oft Myself have heard a voice to call him so . ii 1 94
With his grumbling voice Was wont to cheer his dad in mutinies 3 *Hen. VI.* i 4 76
Thy voice is thunder, but thy looks are humble . . *Richard III.* i 4 173
My voice is now the king's, my looks mine own . . . i 4 174
But, that I'll give my voice on Richard's side, To bar my master's heirs in true descent, God knows I will not do it to the death . . iii 2 53
Name the time; And in the duke's behalf I'll give my voice . . iii 4 20
William Lord Hastings had pronounced your part,—I mean, your voice iii 4 29
And some ten voices cried 'God save King Richard!' . . iii 7 36
So many miseries have crazed my voice . . . . . iv 4 17
I have no further gone in this than by A single voice . *Hen. VIII.* i 2 70
What warlike voice, And to what end, is this? . . . i 4 50
In committing freely Your scruple to the voice of Christendom . ii 2 88
All the clerks . . . in Christian kingdoms Have their free voices . ii 2 94
And the voice is now Only about her coronation . . . iii 2 405
Tell me how he died . . . —Well, the voice goes, madam . . iv 2 11
It stands agreed, I take it, by all voices . . . . v 3 88
The common voice, I see, is verified Of thee . . . . v 3 176
Not in confidence Of author's pen or actor's voice . *Troi. and Cres.* Prol. 24
Pour'st in the open ulcer of my heart Her eyes, her hair, . . . her voice i 1 54
Who, as Ulysses says, opinion crowns With an imperial voice . i 3 187
All the Greekish heads, which with one voice Call Agamemnon head . i 3 221
Trumpet, blow loud, Send thy brass voice through all these lazy tents i 3 257
If the dull brainless Ajax come safe off, We'll dress him up in voices i 3 382
What shriek is this?—'Tis our mad sister, I do know her voice . ii 2 98
Have ears more deaf than adders to the voice Of any true decision . ii 2 172
In second voice we'll not be satisfied; We come to speak with him . ii 3 149
They that have the voice of lions and the act of hares, are they not monsters? . . . . iii 2 95
Who, like an arch, reverberates The voice again . . . iii 3 121
Crack my clear voice with sobs and break my heart . . iv 2 114
Will you the knights Shall to the edge of all extremity Pursue each other, or shall be divided By any voice or order of the field? . iv 5 70
Give me leave To take that course by your consent and voice . v 3 74
I shall lack voice: the deeds of Coriolanus Should not be utter'd feebly *Coriolanus* ii 2 86
The people Must have their voices; neither will they bate One jot of ceremony . . . . ii 2 144
Once, if he do require our voices, we ought not to deny him . . ii 3 1
Are you all resolved to give your voices? But that's no matter . ii 3 41
Every one of us has a single honour, in giving him our own voices with our own tongues . . . . ii 3 50
Your good voice, sir; what say you?—You shall ha't, worthy sir . ii 3 84
There's in all two worthy voices begged. I have your alms: adieu . ii 3 87
If it may stand with the tune of your voices that I may be consul, I have here the customary gown . . . . ii 3 92
We hope to find you our friend; and therefore give you our voices heartily ii 3 112
I will make much of your voices, and so trouble you no further . ii 3 116
Most sweet voices! Better it is to die, better to starve, Than crave the hire which first we do deserve . . . . ii 3 119
Here come moe voices. Your voices: for your voices I have fought; Watch'd for your voices; for your voices bear Of wounds two dozen odd . . . . ii 3 132
For your voices have Done many things, some less, some more: your voices . . . . ii 3 136
He has done nobly, and cannot go without any honest man's voice . ii 3 140
God save thee, noble consul!—Worthy voices! . . . . ii 3 145
You have stood your limitation; and the tribunes Endue you with the people's voice . . . . ii 3 147
Have you chose this man?—He has our voices, sir . . . ii 3 164
To my poor unworthy notice, He mock'd us when he begg'd our voices ii 3 167
'I would be consul,' says he: 'aged custom, But by your voices, will not so permit me; Your voices therefore' . . . . . ii 3 177
I thank you for your voices: thank you: Your most sweet voices: now you have left your voices, I have no further with you . . . ii 3 179
Of such childish friendliness To yield your voices . . . ii 3 184
If he should still malignantly remain Fast foe to the plebeii, your voices might Be curses to yourselves . . . . ii 3 192
So his gracious nature Would think upon you for your voices . . ii 3 196
We may deny him yet.—And will deny him: I'll have five hundred voices of that sound . . . . ii 3 219
Make them of no more voice Than dogs that are as often beat for barking As therefore kept to do so . . . . ii 3 223
Made you against the grain To voice him consul . . . ii 3 242
Have I had children's voices? . . . . iii 1 30
Must these have voices, that can yield them now And straight disclaim their tongues? . . . . iii 1 34
Both your voices blended, the great'st taste Most palates theirs . iii 1 103
Voice. Why, shall the people give One that speaks thus their voice?—I'll give my reasons, More worthier than their voices *Coriolanus* iii 1 119
A pipe Small as an eunuch, or the virgin voice That babies lulls asleep iii 2 114
Have you a catalogue Of all the voices that we have procured? . iii 3 9
I do demand, If you submit you to the people's voices? . . . iii 3 44
Being pass'd for consul with full voice . . . . . iii 3 59
With a voice as free As I do pray the gods . . . . iii 3 73
And suffer'd me by the voice of slaves to be Whoop'd out of Rome . iv 5 83
You that stood so much Upon the voice of occupation . . . iv 6 97
As many coxcombs As you threw caps up will he tumble down, And pay you for your voices . . . . iv 6 136
Ye're goodly things, you voices!—You have made Good work! . . iv 6 147
A special party, have, by common voice, In election for the Roman empery, Chosen Andronicus . . . . *T. Andron.* i 1 21
People of Rome, and people's tribunes here, I ask your voices . . i 1 218
With voices and applause of every sort, Patricians and plebeians . . i 1 230
For well I know The common voice do cry it shall be so . . v 3 140
An she agree, within her scope of choice Lies my consent and fair according voice . . . . *Rom. and Jul.* i 2 19
This, by his voice, should be a Montague. Fetch me my rapier, boy . i 5 56
O, for a falconer's voice, To lure this tassel-gentle back again! . . ii 2 159
The lark and loathed toad change eyes; O, now I would they had changed voices too! Since arm from arm that voice doth us affray iii 5 32
This same should be the voice of Friar John . . . . v 2 2
They answer, in a joint and corporate voice . . *T. of Athens* ii 2 213
You have my voice to it; the fault's Bloody; 'tis necessary he should die iii 5 1
Crack the lawyer's voice, That he may never more false title plead . iv 3 153
And buy men's voices to commend our deeds . . . *J. Cæsar* ii 1 146
Is there no voice more worthy than my own? . . . . iii 1 49
Your voice shall be as strong as any man's In the disposing of new dignities . . . . iii 1 177
To beg the voice and utterance of my tongue . . . . iii 1 261
With a monarch's voice Cry 'Havoc,' and let slip the dogs of war . iii 1 272
And took his voice who should be prick'd to die, In our black sentence iv 1 16
Methought I heard a voice cry 'Sleep no more!' . . *Macbeth* ii 2 35
I have no words: My voice is in my sword . . . . v 8 7
Whose voices I desire aloud with mine . . . . . v 8 58
If thou hast any sound, or use of voice, Speak to me . . *Hamlet* i 1 128
You cannot speak of reason to the Dane, And lose your voice . . i 2 45
Unto the voice and yielding of that body Whereof he is the head . i 3 23
Which is no further Than the main voice of Denmark goes withal . i 3 28
Give every man thy ear, but few thy voice; Take each man's censure . i 3 68
Pray God, your voice, like a piece of uncurrent gold, be not cracked ii 2 447
A broken voice, and his whole function suiting With forms to his conceit ii 2 582
You have the voice of the king himself for your succession . . iii 2 356
There is much music, excellent voice, in this little organ . . iii 2 385
I have a voice and precedent of peace, To keep my name ungored . v 2 260
He has my dying voice; So tell him, with the occurrents, more and less v 2 367
Of that I shall have also cause to speak, And from his mouth whose voice will draw on more . . . . v 2 403
With roaring voices, Strike in their numb'd and mortified bare arms Pins, wooden pricks, nails . . . . *Lear* ii 3 14
The foul fiend haunts poor Tom in the voice of a nightingale . . iii 6 32
Methinks thy voice is alter'd; and thou speak'st In better phrase and matter . . . . iv 6 7
I know that voice . . . . iv 6 96
The trick of that voice I do well remember . . . . iv 6 108
Her voice was ever soft, Gentle, and low, an excellent thing in woman v 3 272
Most reverend signior, do you know my voice?—Not I . . *Othello* i 1 93
The magnifico is much beloved, And hath in his effect a voice potential i 2 13
Opinion, a sovereign mistress of effects, throws a more safer voice on you i 3 226
Let me find a charter in your voice, To assist my simpleness . . i 3 246
Let her have your voices . . . . i 3 261
Murder! murder!—The voice of Cassio: Iago keeps his word . . v 1 28
Alas! that was my lady's voice. Help! help, ho! help! O lady, speak again! . . . . v 2 119
His voice was propertied As all the tuned spheres . *Ant. and Cleo.* v 2 83
Which horse-hairs and calves'-guts, nor the voice of unpaved eunuch to boot, can never amend . . . . . . *Cymbeline* ii 3 34
Neither want my means for thy relief nor my voice for thy preferment iii 5 115
The snatches in his voice, And burst of speaking, were as his . iv 2 105
Though now our voices Have got the mannish crack, sing him to the ground . . . . iv 2 235
I have drawn her picture with my voice . . . . *Pericles* iv 2 102
Voice and favour! You are, you are—O royal Pericles! . . . v 3 13
The voice of dead Thaisa!—That Thaisa am I, supposed dead And drown'd . . . . v 3 34
Voiced. Whom the world Voiced so regardfully . . *T. of Athens* iv 3 81
Void of all profanation in the world that good Christians ought to have *Meas. for Meas.* ii 1 55
You, that did void your rheum upon my beard And foot me *Mer. of Ven.* i 3 118
Uncapable of pity, void and empty From any dram of mercy . . iv 1 5
Even so void is your false heart of truth . . . . . v 1 189
Whose low vassal seat The Alps doth spit and void his rheum upon *Hen. V.* iii 5 52
If they will fight with us, bid them come down, Or void the field . iv 7 62
Which makes me hope you are not void of pity . . 2 *Hen. VI.* iv 7 69
It was thy device By this alliance to make void my suit 3 *Hen. VI.* iii 3 142
To drink those men Upon whose age we void it up again *T. of Athens* i 2 143
I'll get me to a place more void, and there Speak . . *J. Cæsar* ii 4 37
'Voided. If I had fear'd death, of all the men i' the world I would have 'voided thee . . . . *Coriolanus* iv 5 88
Voiding. In our voiding lobby hast thou stood And duly waited? 2 *Hen. VI.* iv 1 61
Volable. A most acute juvenal; volable and free of grace! . *L. L. Lost* iii 1 67
Volant. Le cheval volant, the Pegasus, chez les narines de feu! *Hen. V.* iii 7 14
Volk. Good gentleman, go your gait, and let poor volk pass . *Lear* iv 6 243
Volley. A fine volley of words, gentlemen, and quickly shot off *T. G. of V.* ii 4 33
With a volley of our needless shot, After such bloody toil . *K. John* v 5 5
To the ambassadors of England gives This warlike volley . *Hamlet* v 2 363
Every man shall bear as loud As his strong sides can volley *Ant. and Cleo.* ii 7 118
Volquessen. I give Volquessen, Touraine, Maine, Poictiers . *K. John* ii 1 527
Volsce. The news is, sir, the Volsces are in arms . *Coriolanus* i 1 228
The Volsces are in arms.—They have a leader, Tullus Aufidius . i 1 232
The Volsces have much corn; take these rats thither To gnaw their garners . . . . i 1 253
The Volsces shunning him: Methinks I see him stamp thus, and call thus . . . . i 3 34
Thus it is: the Volsces have an army forth . . . . . i 3 107
He that retires, I'll take him for a Volsce, And he shall feel mine edge i 4 28

Volsce. Spies of the Volsces Held me in chase . . . . *Coriolanus* i 6 18
If these shows be not outward, which of you But is four Volsces? . . i 6 78
I would I were a Roman; for I cannot, Being a Volsce, be that I am . i 10 5
Having determined of the Volsces and To send for Titus Lartius . ii 2 41
So then the Volsces stand but as at first, Ready, when time shall prompt them, to make road Upon's again . . . . iii 1 4
On safe-guard he came to me; and did curse Against the Volsces . iii 1 10
Who hath done To thee particularly and to all the Volsces Great hurt . iv 5 72
The Volsces with two several powers Are enter'd in the Roman territories . . . . iv 6 39
It cannot be The Volsces dare break with us.—Cannot be! . . iv 6 48
Let the Volsces Plough Rome, and harrow Italy . . . . . v 3 33
Aufidius, and you Volsces, mark; for we'll Hear nought from Rome in private . . . . v 3 92
Did tend To save the Romans, thereby to destroy The Volsces . . v 3 134
While the Volsces May say 'This mercy we have show'd;' the Romans, 'This we received' . . . . v 3 136
Volscian. I have a note from the Volscian state, to find you out there . iv 3 11
A name unmusical to the Volscians' ears, And harsh in sound to thine . iv 5 64
I hope to see Romans as cheap as Volscians. They are rising . . iv 5 249
If Marcius should be join'd with Volscians,— If! He is their god . iv 6 89
He bears all things fairly, And shows good husbandry for the Volscian state . . . . iv 7 22
Though I owe My revenge properly, my remission lies In Volscian breasts . . . . v 2 91
My partner in this action, You must report to the Volscian lords . v 3 3
This fellow had a Volscian to his mother; His wife is in Corioli . v 3 178
Good news; the ladies have prevail'd, The Volscians are dislodged . v 4 44
Like an eagle in a dove-cote, I Flutter'd your Volscians in Corioli . v 6 116
Voltimand. We here dispatch You, good Cornelius, and you, Voltimand, For bearers of this greeting to old Norway . . . *Hamlet* i 2 34
Welcome, my good friends! Say, Voltimand, what from our brother Norway? . . . . ii 2 59
Volubility. I'll commend her volubility, And say she uttereth piercing eloquence . . . . *T. of Shrew* ii 1 176
He will lie, sir, with such volubility, that you would think truth were a fool . . . . *All's Well* iv 3 284
Voluble. If voluble and sharp discourse be marr'd, Unkindness blunts it more than marble hard . . . . . . *Com. of Errors* ii 1 92
So sweet and voluble is his discourse . . . *L. L. Lost* ii 1 76
A knave very voluble . . . . *Othello* ii 1 242
Volume. With volumes that I prize above my dukedom . *Tempest* i 2 167
Volumes of report Run with these false and most contrarious quests *Meas. for Meas.* iv 1 61
Devise, wit; write, pen; for I am for whole volumes in folio *L. L. Lost* i 2 191
And the hand of time Shall draw this brief into as huge a volume *K. John* ii 1 103
He should have had a volume of farewells . . . *Richard II.* i 4 18
Like to a title-leaf, Fortells the nature of a tragic volume . *2 Hen. IV.* i 1 61
A volume of enticing lines, Able to ravish any dull conceit . *1 Hen. VI.* v 5 14
Such indexes, although small pricks To their subsequent volumes *Troi. and Cres.* i 3 344
That for the poorest piece Will bear the knave by the volume *Coriol.* iii 3 33
Read o'er the volume of young Paris' face And find delight writ there with beauty's pen; . . . And what obscured in this fair volume lies Find written in the margent of his eyes *Rom. and Jul.* i 3 81
Within the volume of which time I have seen Hours dreadful *Macbeth* ii 4 2
All alone shall live Within the book and volume of my brain *Hamlet* i 5 103
I' the world's volume Our Britain seems as of it, but not in't *Cymbeline* iii 4 140
To place upon the volume of your deeds, As in a title-page, your worth in arms, Were more than you expect . . . . . *Pericles* ii 3 3
Volumnia Is worth of consuls, senators, patricians, A city full *Coriolanus* v 4 55
Volumnius. Come hither, good Volumnius; list a word . . *J. Cæsar* v 5 15
Thou seest the world, Volumnius, how it goes; Our enemies have beat us v 5 22
Good Volumnius, Thou know'st that we two went to school together . v 5 25
Voluntary. Besides, the lottery of my destiny Bars me the right of voluntary choosing . . . . . . *Mer. of Venice* ii 1 16
Have put themselves into voluntary exile with him . *As Y. Like It* i 1 107
Rash, inconsiderate, fiery voluntaries . . . . *K. John* ii 1 67
Thy voluntary oath Lives in this bosom, dearly cherished . . iii 3 23
I did suppose it should be on constraint; But, heaven be thank'd, it is but voluntary . . . . v 1 29
Albeit we swear A voluntary zeal and an unurged faith . . . . v 2 10
I serve here voluntary.—Your last service was sufferance, 'twas not voluntary: no man is beaten voluntary: Ajax was here the voluntary, and you as under an impress . . *Troi. and Cres.* ii 1 103
Giving myself a voluntary wound Here, in the thigh . *J. Cæsar* ii 1 300
By their own importunate suit, Or voluntary dotage of some mistress *Othello* iv 1 27
That thou wilt be a voluntary mute to my design . . *Cymbeline* iii 5 158
Voluptuously. I had rather had eleven die nobly for their country than one voluptuously surfeit out of action . . . . *Coriolanus* i 3 27
Voluptuousness. There's no bottom, none, In my voluptuousness *Macb.* iv 3 61
If he fill'd His vacancy with his voluptuousness, Full surfeits, and the dryness of his bones, Call on him for't . . . *Ant. and Cleo.* i 4 26
Vomissement. Le chien est retourné à son propre vomissement *Hen. V.* iii 7 69
Vomit. And now thou wouldst eat thy dead vomit up . *2 Hen. IV.* i 3 99
Base lackey peasants, Whom their o'er-cloyed country vomits forth *Richard III.* v 3 318
My bowels cannot hide her woes, But like a drunkard must I vomit them . . . . *T. Andron.* iii 1 232
He gives your Hollander a vomit, ere the next pottle can be filled *Othello* ii 3 86
Sluttery to such neat excellence opposed Should make desire vomit emptiness, Not so allured to feed . . . . . *Cymbeline* i 6 45
Vorld. He is de coward Jack priest of de vorld . . *Mer. Wives* ii 3 33
Vortnight. 'Twould not ha' bin zo long as tis by a vortnight . *Lear* iv 6 245
Votaress. His mother was a votaress of my order . *M. N. Dream* ii 1 123
The imperial votaress passed on, In maiden meditation, fancy-free . ii 1 163
His woeful queen we leave at Ephesus, Unto Diana there a votaress *Pericles* iv Gower 4
Votarist. The sisterhood, the votarists of Saint Clare . *Meas. for Meas.* i 4 5
Gold? No, gods, I am no idle votarist: roots, you clear heavens! *T. of A.* iv 3 27
The jewels you have had from me to deliver to Desdemona would half have corrupted a votarist . . . . *Othello* iv 2 190
Votary. But wherefore waste I time to counsel thee That art a votary to fond desire? . . . . *T. G. of Ver.* i 1 52
You are already Love's firm votary And cannot soon revolt . . . iii 2 58
Who are the votaries, my loving lords? . . . *L. L. Lost* ii 1 37
This Biron is one of the votaries with the king . . . iv 2 141
I am a votary; I have vowed to Jaquenetta to hold the plough for her sweet love three years . . . . v 2 892

Vouch. The austereness of my life, My vouch against you *Meas. for Meas.* ii 4 156
A man that never yet Did, as he vouches, misreport your grace . . v 1 148
Away with him to prison!—What can you vouch against him? . . v 1 326
Most fain would steal What law does vouch mine own . . *All's Well* ii 5 87
And make my vouch as strong As shore of rock . . *Hen. VIII.* i 1 157
To beg of Hob and Dick, that do appear, Their needless vouches *Coriol.* ii 3 124
The blood he hath lost—Which, I dare vouch, is more than that he hath iii 1 300
I, Even in theirs and in the commons' ears, Will vouch the truth of it v 6 5
He that would vouch it in any place but here . . . *T. Andron.* i 1 360
Will his vouchers vouch him no more of his purchases? . . *Hamlet* v 1 117
I therefore vouch again That with some mixtures powerful o'er the blood . . . He wrought upon her.—To vouch this, is no proof *Othello* i 3 103
Vouch with me, heaven, I therefore beg it not . . . . . i 3 262
In the authority of her merit, did justly put on the vouch of very malice ii 1 147
Vouched. Almost beyond credit,— As many vouched rarities are *Tempest* ii 1 60
A certainty, vouch'd from our cousin Austria . . . *All's Well* i 2 5
Which, to the spire and top of praises vouch'd, Would seem but modest *Coriolanus* i 9 24
The feast is sold That is not often vouch'd, while 'tis a-making, 'Tis given with welcome . . . . *Macbeth* iii 4 34
Voucher. His recognizances, his fines, his double vouchers *Hamlet* v 1 114
Will his vouchers vouch him no more of his purchases, and double ones too? . . . . v 1 117
Here's a voucher, Stronger than ever law could make . *Cymbeline* ii 2 39
Vouching. This gentleman at that time vouching . . . . i 4 63
Vouchsafe my prayer May know if you remain upon this island *Tempest* i 2 422
Vouchsafe me yet your picture for my love . . *T. G. of Ver.* iv 2 121
Vouchsafe me, for my meed, but one fair look . . . . v 4 23
Shall I vouchsafe your worship a word or two?—Two thousand, fair woman: and I'll vouchsafe thee the hearing . . *Mer. Wives* ii 2 41
Vouchsafe a word, young sister, but one word . . *Meas. for Meas.* iii 1 152
Most mighty duke, vouchsafe me speak a word *Com. of Errors* v 1 282
Vouchsafe to take the pains To go with us . . . . . v 1 393
I'll bring you thither, my lord, if you'll vouchsafe me . . *Much Ado* iii 2 4
Vouchsafe to read the purpose of my coming . . . *L. L. Lost* ii 1 109
Out of your favours, heavenly spirits, vouchsafe Not to behold . . v 2 165
Vouchsafe to show the sunshine of your face . . . . . v 2 201
Vouchsafe, bright moon, and these thy stars, to shine . . . v 2 205
Then, in our measure do but vouchsafe one change. Thou bid'st me beg v 2 209
The music plays; vouchsafe some motion to it.—Our ears vouchsafe it v 2 216
Will you vouchsafe with me to change a word?—Name it . . . v 2 238
Command me any service to her thither?—That she vouchsafe me audience . . . . v 2 313
And purpose now To lead you to our court; vouchsafe it then . . v 2 344
That you vouchsafe In your rich wisdom to excuse or hide . . v 2 741
Behold, the French amazed vouchsafe a parle . . . *K. John* ii 1 226
Vouchsafe awhile to stay, And I shall show you peace and fair-faced league . . . . ii 1 416
She is bound in honour still to do What you in wisdom still vouchsafe to say . . . . ii 1 523
Upon which better part our prayers come in, If thou vouchsafe them . iii 1 294
I come with gracious offers from the king, If you vouchsafe me hearing *1 Hen. IV.* iv 3 31
Vouchsafe to those that have not read the story, That I may prompt them . . . . *Hen. V.* v Prol. 1
Will you vouchsafe to teach a soldier terms Such as will enter at a lady's ear? . . . . v 2 99
By me entreats, great lord, thou wouldst vouchsafe To visit her *1 Hen. VI.* ii 2 40
Vouchsafe To give me hearing what I shall reply . . . . . iii 1 27
Lady, vouchsafe to listen what I say . . . . v 3 103
Agree to any covenants, and procure That Lady Margaret do vouchsafe to come . . . . v 5 89
And never more abase our sight so low As to vouchsafe one glance unto the ground . . . . *2 Hen. VI.* i 2 16
If thou vouchsafe to grant That virtuous Lady Bona, thy fair sister *3 Hen. VI.* iii 3 55
Vouchsafe, at our request, to stand aside, While I use further conference iii 3 110
If King Lewis vouchsafe to furnish us With some few bands . . iv 3 203
Vouchsafe, divine perfection of a woman, Of these supposed evils *Rich. III.* i 2 75
Vouchsafe, defused infection of a man, For these known evils . . i 2 78
Vouchsafe to wear this ring.—To take is not to give . . . i 2 202
If your back Cannot vouchsafe this burthen, 'tis too weak Ever to get a boy.—How you do talk! . . . . . . *Hen. VIII.* ii 3 43
Vouchsafe to speak my thanks and my obedience . . . . ii 3 71
My lord, will you vouchsafe me a word? . . . *Troi. and Cres.* iii 1 64
Vouchsafe my labour, and long live your lordship! . . *T. of Athens* i 1 152
I beseech your honour, Vouchsafe me a word; it does concern you near i 2 183
Vouchsafe good morrow from a feeble tongue . . . *J. Cæsar* ii 1 313
If Brutus will vouchsafe that Antony May safely come to him . . iii 1 130
Vouchsafe your rest here in our court Some little time . . *Hamlet* ii 2 13
Good my lord, vouchsafe me a word with you . . . . . iii 2 307
If your lordship would vouchsafe the answer.—How if I answer 'no'? . v 2 176
On my knees I beg That you'll vouchsafe me raiment, bed, and food *Lear* ii 4 158
I have assailed her with music, but she vouchsafes no notice *Cymbeline* ii 3 45
Vouchsafed. To your own most pregnant and vouchsafed ear.—'Odours,' 'pregnant' and 'vouchsafed' . . . . *T. Night* iii 1 100
You have vouchsafed . . . my poor house to visit . . . *W. Tale* v 3 4
Hardly gave audience, or Vouchsafed to think he had partners *A. and C.* i 4 8
Vouchsafing here to visit me, Doing the honour of thy lordliness . v 2 160
Voutsafe me, look you, a few disputations with you . . . *Hen. V.* iii 2 101
Vow. Be more abstemious, Or else, good night your vow! . . *Tempest* iv 1 54
Whose vows are, that no bed-right shall be paid Till Hymen's torch be lighted . . . . iv 1 96
Unheedful vows may heedfully be broken . . . *T. G. of Ver.* ii 6 11
Whose composed rhymes Should be full-fraught with serviceable vows iii 2 70
When to her beauty I commend my vows, She bids me think how I have been forsworn . . . . iv 2 9
Thy flattery, That hast deceived so many with thy vows . . . iv 2 98
By Jove I vow, I should have scratch'd out your unseeing eyes . . iv 4 208
Swallowed his vows whole, pretending in her discoveries of dishonour *Meas. for Meas.* iii 1 235
By the vow of mine order I warrant you . . . . . . iv 2 180
I am combined by a sacred vow And shall be absent . . . . iv 3 149
As strongly As words could make up vows . . . . . . v 1 228
The time was once when thou unurged wouldst vow *Com. of Errors* ii 2 115
And from my false hand cut the wedding-ring And break it with a deep-divorcing vow . . . . ii 2 140
He cries for you and vows, if he can take you, To scorch your face . v 1 182
All-telling fame Doth noise abroad, Navarre hath made a vow *L. L. Lost* ii 1 22
Vows for thee broke deserve not punishment . . . . . . iv 3 63

Vow. Thou being a goddess, I forswore not thee: My vow was earthly, thou a heavenly love . . . *L. L. Lost* iv 3 66
Vows are but breath, and breath a vapour is . . . iv 3 68
Vow, alack, for youth unmeet, Youth so apt to pluck a sweet! . . . iv 3 113
I, that hold it sin To break the vow I am engaged in . . . iv 3 178
Forsworn the use of eyes And study too, the causer of your vow . . . iv 3 311
We have made a vow to study, lords, And in that vow we have forsworn our books . . . iv 3 318
So hold your vow: Nor God, nor I, delights in perjured men . . . v 2 345
Yields you up . . . To death, or to a vow of single life . . . *M. N. Dream* i 1 121
By all the vows that ever men have broke, In number more than ever women spoke . . . i 1 175
When I vow, I weep; and vows so born, In their nativity all truth appears iii 2 124
These vows are Hermia's: will you give her o'er? . . . iii 2 130
Your vows to her and me, put in two scales, Will even weigh . . . iii 2 132
To vow, and swear, and superpraise my parts, When I am sure you hate me iii 2 153
The sisters' vows, the hours that we have spent . . . iii 2 199
I have toward heaven breathed a secret vow To live in prayer *M. of V.* iii 4 27
She made me vow That I should neither sell nor give nor lose it . . . iv 1 442
Stealing her soul with many vows of faith And ne'er a true one . . . v 1 19
Of violated vows 'Twixt the souls of friend and friend . *As Y. Like It* iii 2 141
Do not fall in love with me, For I am falser than vows made in wine . iii 5 73
Here I firmly vow Never to woo her more, but do forswear her *T. of S.* iv 2 28
Call it a rush-candle, Henceforth I vow it shall be so for me . . . iv 5 15
She thought, I dare vow for her, they touched not any stranger sense *All's Well* i 3 113
Blessing upon your vows! and in your bed Find fairer fortune! . . . ii 3 97
Barefoot plod I the cold ground upon, With sainted vow . . . iii 4 7
I know not what the success will be, my lord; but the attempt I vow . iii 6 87
I prithee, do not strive against my vows: I was compell'd to her . iv 2 14
'Tis not the many oaths that makes the truth, But the plain single vow iv 2 22
His vows are forfeited to me, and my honour's paid to him . . . v 3 142
You give away heaven's vows, and those are mine . . . v 3 171
I by vow am so embodied yours, That she which marries you must marry me . . . v 3 173
For still we [men] prove Much in our vows, but little in our love *T. Night* ii 4 121
Therefore draw, for the supportance of his vow . . . iii 4 329
Pardon me, sweet one, even for the vows We made each other but so late ago. . . . v 1 221
I may not, verily.—Verily! You put me off with limber vows *W. Tale* i 2 47
So long as nature Will bear up with this exercise, so long I daily vow to use it . . . iii 2 243
This is desperate, sir.—So call it: but it does fulfil my vow . . . iv 4 497
This is a match, And made between's by vows . . . v 3 138
Link'd together With all religious strength of sacred vows *K. John* iii 1 229
O, let thy vow First made to heaven, first be to heaven perform'd! . iii 1 265
It is religion that doth make vows kept . . . iii 1 279
Thy later vows against thy first Is in thyself rebellion to thyself . iii 1 288
Breathing to his breathless excellence The incense of a vow, a holy vow iv 3 67
I make a vow, Such neighbour nearness to our sacred blood Should nothing privilege him . . . *Richard II.* i 1 118
Like two men That vow a long and weary pilgrimage . . . i 3 49
God keep all vows unbroke that swear to thee! . . . iv 1 215
And I will die a hundred thousand deaths Ere break the smallest parcel of this vow . . . *1 Hen. IV.* iii 2 159
He heard him swear and vow to God He came but to be Duke of Lancaster iv 3 60
He presently, as greatness knows itself, Steps me a little higher than his vow . . . iv 3 75
It is necessary, look your grace, that he keep his vow and his oath *Hen. V.* iv 7 146
Then keep thy vow, sirrah, when thou meetest the fellow . . . iv 7 151
Now have I paid my vow unto his soul . . . *1 Hen. VI.* ii 2 7
Thy humble servant vows obedience And humble service . . . iii 1 167
Vow, Burgundy, by honour of thy house, Prick'd on by public wrongs. iii 2 77
My vows are equal partners with thy vows . . . iii 2 85
He did vow upon his knees he would be even with me . *2 Hen. VI.* i 3 203
What instance gives Lord Warwick for his vow? . . . iii 2 159
Be brave, then; for your captain is brave, and vows reformation . iv 2 70
Calls your grace usurper openly And vows to crown himself . . . iv 4 31
Then, heaven, set ope thy everlasting gates, To entertain my vows! . iv 9 14
Who can be bound by any solemn vow To do a murderous deed? . . . v 1 184
Before I see thee seated in that throne Which now the house of Lancaster usurps, I vow by heaven these eyes shall never close . *3 Hen. VI.* i 1 24
Be thy title right or wrong, Lord Clifford vows to fight in thy defence . i 1 160
'Tis not my fault, Nor wittingly have I infringed my vow . . . ii 2 8
Here on my knee I vow to God above, I'll never pause again . . . ii 3 29
I do bend my knee with thine; And in this vow do chain my soul to thine! . . . ii 3 34
And here, to pledge my vow, I give my hand . . . iii 3 250
Give me assurance with some friendly vow, That I may never have you in suspect . . . iv 1 141
He hath made a solemn vow Never to lie and take his natural rest . iv 3 4
And, like a traitor to the name of God, Didst break that vow *Richard III.* i 4 211
A pleasing cordial . . . Is this thy vow unto my sickly heart . . . ii 1 42
Your mother lives a witness to that vow . . . iii 7 180
The leisure and the fearful time Cuts off the ceremonious vows of love. v 3 98
My vows and prayers Yet are the king's . . . *Hen. VIII.* ii 1 88
And their vow is made To ransack Troy . . . *Troi. and Cres.* Prol. 7
Words, vows, gifts, tears, and love's full sacrifice, He offers . . . i 2 308
With truant vows to her own lips he loves, And dare avow her beauty . i 3 270
When we vow to weep seas, live in fire, eat rocks, tame tigers . iii 2 84
Strangles our dear vows Even in the birth of our own labouring breath iv 4 39
My major vow lies here, this I'll obey . . . v 1 49
If souls guide vows, if vows be sanctimonies . . . v 2 139
The gods are deaf to hot and peevish vows: They are polluted offerings v 3 16
It is the purpose that makes strong the vow; But vows to every purpose must not hold . . . v 3 23
By the vows We have made to endure friends . . . *Coriolanus* i 6 57
Vows revenge as spacious as between The young'st and oldest thing . iv 6 67
Shall I be tempted to infringe my vow In the same time 'tis made? . v 3 20
We do, and vow to heaven and to his highness, That what we did was mildly as we might . . . *T. Andron.* i 1 474
This minion stood upon her chastity, Upon her nuptial vow . . . ii 3 125
By my father's reverend tomb, I vow They shall be ready . . . ii 3 296
And swear unto my soul to right your wrongs. The vow is made. . iii 1 280
Thou shalt vow By that same god, what god soe'er it be . . . v 1 81
She hath forsworn to love, and in that vow Do I live dead *Rom. and Jul.* i 1 229
He may not have access To breathe such vows as lovers use to swear ii Prol. 10
What satisfaction canst thou have to-night?—The exchange of thy love's faithful vow for mine . . . ii 2 127
When and where and how We met, we woo'd and made exchange of vow ii 3 62

Vow. His familiars to his buried fortunes Slink all away, leave their false vows with him, Like empty purses pick'd . *T. of Athens* iv 2 11
By all your vows of love and that great vow Which did incorporate and make us one . . . *J. Cæsar* ii 1 272
With almost all the holy vows of heaven . . . *Hamlet* i 3 114
When the blood burns, how prodigal the soul Lends the tongue vows . i 3 117
Do not believe his vows; for they are brokers . . . i 3 127
It went hand in hand even with the vow I made to her in marriage . i 5 49
Makes vow before his uncle never more To give the assay of arms . ii 2 70
Most deject and wretched, That suck'd the honey of his music vows . iii 1 164
I'll not be juggled with: To hell, allegiance! vows, to the blackest devil! . . . iv 5 131
Thou hast sought to make us break our vow, Which we durst never yet *Lear* i 1 171
Let our reciprocal vows be remembered . . . iv 6 267
A frail vow betwixt an erring barbarian and a supersubtle Venetian *Oth.* i 3 362
If I do vow a friendship, I'll perform it To the last article . . . iii 3 21
In the due reverence of a sacred vow I here engage my words . . . iii 3 461
Riotous madness, To be entangled with those mouth-made vows! *Ant. and Cleo.* i 3 30
The vows of women Of no more bondage be, to where they are made, Than they are to their virtues . . . *Cymbeline* ii 4 110
How! that I should murder her? Upon the love and truth and vows which I Have made to thy command? . . . iii 2 12
So he wishes you all happiness, that remains loyal to his vow . . . iii 2 47
O, Men's vows are women's traitors! . . . iii 4 56
I believe you; Your honour and your goodness teach me to't, Without your vows . . . *Pericles* iii 3 27
Vowed. When you have vow'd, you must not speak with men But in the presence of the prioress . . . *Meas. for Meas.* i 4 10
This is the hand which, with a vow'd contract, Was fast belock'd in thine v 1 209
Ah, never faith could hold, if not to beauty vow'd! . . . *L. L. Lost* iv 2 110
And where that you have vow'd to study, lords, In that each of you have forsworn his book, Can you still dream? . . . iv 3 296
I hate a breaking cause to be Of heavenly oaths, vow'd with integrity . v 2 356
I have vowed to Jaquenetta to hold the plough for her sweet love three years . . . v 2 892
'Tis not the many oaths that makes the truth, But the plain single vow that is vow'd true . . . *All's Well* iv 2 22
Thine, as he vowed to thee in thine ear . . . iv 3 260
Whose protection Is most divinely vow'd . . . *K. John* ii 1 237
I vow'd, base knight, when I did meet thee next, To tear the garter from thy craven's leg, Which I have done . . . *1 Hen. VI.* iv 1 14
At a triumph having vow'd To try his strength, forsaketh yet the lists v 5 31
So mighty are his vowed enemies . . . *2 Hen. VI.* iii 1 220
But both of you were vow'd Duke Humphrey's foes . . . iii 2 182
You both have vow'd revenge On him, his sons, his favourites *3 Hen. VI.* i 1 55
They join, embrace, and seem to kiss, As if they vow'd some league inviolable . . . ii 1 30
King of Albion, My lord and sovereign, and thy vowed friend . . . iii 3 50
Killing that love which thou hast vow'd to cherish . *Rom. and Jul.* iii 3 129
This by the eye of Cynthia hath she vow'd . . . *Pericles* ii 5 11
Vowedst. Upon whose grave thou vow'dst pure chastity *T. G. of Ver.* iv 3 21
Vowel. The third of the five vowels, if you repeat them . *L. L. Lost* v 1 56
Say thou but 'I,' And that bare vowel 'I' shall poison more Than the death-darting eye of cockatrice . . . *Rom. and Jul.* iii 2 46
Vow-fellows. Who are the votaries, my loving lords, That are vow-fellows with this virtuous duke? . . . *L. L. Lost* ii 1 38
Vowing more than the perfection of ten and discharging less than the tenth part of one . . . *Troi. and Cres.* iii 2 93
Great Achilles Is arming, weeping, cursing, vowing vengeance . v 5 31
Vox. An your ladyship will have it as it ought to be, you must allow Vox *T. Night* v 1 304
Voyage. In one voyage Did Claribel her husband find at Tunis *Tempest* v 1 208
Thou'lt lose the flood, and, in losing the flood, lose thy voyage, and, in losing thy voyage, lose thy master . . . *T. G. of Ver.* ii 3 47
Lose the tide, and the voyage, and the master, and the service, and the tied! . . . ii 3 56
If he should intend this voyage towards my wife, I would turn her loose to him . . . *Mer. Wives* ii 1 189
Our wealth increased By prosperous voyages I often made *Com. of Errors* i 1 41
I am bound To Persia and want guilders for my voyage . . . iv 1 4
Who is his companion? Is there no young squarer now that will make a voyage with him to the devil? . . . *Much Ado* i 1 83
And return again, As from a voyage, rich with merchandise *M. N. Dream* ii 1 134
As dry as the remainder biscuit After a voyage . . . *As Y. Like It* ii 7 40
Thy loving voyage Is but for two months victuall'd . . . v 4 197
My determinate voyage is mere extravagancy . . . *T. Night* ii 1 11
That's it that always makes a good voyage of nothing . . . ii 4 81
I am bound to your niece, sir; I mean, she is the list of my voyage . iii 1 86
So much As might have drawn one to a longer voyage . . . iii 3 7
I'll make a voyage to the Holy Land, To wash this blood off *Richard II.* v 6 49
All the good our English Have got by the late voyage is but merely A fit or two o' the face . . . *Hen. VIII.* i 3 6
With other incident throes That nature's fragile vessel doth sustain In life's uncertain voyage . . . *T. of Athens* v 1 205
All the voyage of their life Is bound in shallows and in miseries *J. Cæsar* iv 3 220
Arm you, I pray you, to this speedy voyage . . . *Hamlet* iii 3 24
If he be now return'd, As checking at his voyage . . . iv 7 63
If you make your voyage upon her and give me directly to understand you have prevail'd, I am no further your enemy . *Cymbeline* i 4 170
Like fragments in hard voyages, became The life o' the need . . . v 3 44
He will repent the breadth of his great voyage . . . *Pericles* iv 1 37
She would serve after a long voyage at sea . . . iv 6 49
Vraiment. Oui, vraiment, sauf votre grace, ainsi dit-il . *Hen. V.* v 2 114
It is not a fashion for the maids in France to kiss before they are married, would she say?—Oui, vraiment . . . v 2 292
Vulcan. Cupid is a good hare-finder and Vulcan a rare carpenter *Much Ado* i 1 187
It was besmear'd As black as Vulcan in the smoke of war . *T. Night* v 1 56
As like as Vulcan and his wife . . . *Troi. and Cres.* i 3 168
Were it a casque composed by Vulcan's skill, My sword should bite it v 2 170
Better than he have worn Vulcan's badge. . . . *T. Andron.* ii 1 89
And my imaginations are as foul As Vulcan's stithy . . . *Hamlet* iii 2 89
Vulgar. A vulgar comment will be made of it . . . *Com. of Errors* iii 1 100
One more than two.—Which the base vulgar do call three *L. L. Lost* i 2 51
Which to annothanize in the vulgar,—O base and obscure vulgar! . iv 1 70
O' my troth, most sweet jests! most incony vulgar wit! . . . iv 1 144
Therefore, you clown, abandon,—which is in the vulgar leave *As Y. L. It* v 1 53
'Tis a vulgar proof, That very oft we pity enemies . . . *T. Night* iii 1 135
Even as bad as those That vulgars give bold'st titles . . . *W. Tale* ii 1 94

Vulgar. I'ld play incessantly upon these jades, Even till unfenced desolation Leave them as naked as the vulgar air *K. John* ii 1 387
So common-hackney'd in the eyes of men, So stale and cheap to vulgar company *1 Hen. IV.* iii 2 41
An habitation giddy and unsure Hath he that buildeth on the vulgar heart. O thou fond many! *2 Hen. IV.* i 3 90
So do our vulgar drench their peasant limbs In blood of princes *Hen. V.* iv 7 80
Talk like the vulgar sort of market men *1 Hen. VI.* iii 2 4
And sooner dance upon a bloody pole Than stand uncover'd to the vulgar groom *2 Hen. VI.* iv 1 128
What is granted them?—Five tribunes to defend their vulgar wisdoms *Coriolanus* i 1 219
Do press among the popular throngs and puff To win a vulgar station ii 1 231
So he thinks, and is no less apparent To the vulgar eye iv 7 21
I'll about, And drive away the vulgar from the streets *J. Cæsar* i 1 75
Is as common As any the most vulgar thing to sense *Hamlet* i 2 99
Vulgar. Be thou familiar, but by no means vulgar *Hamlet* i 3 61
Most sure and vulgar: every one hears that *Lear* iv 6 214
Besides what hotter hours, Unregister'd in vulgar fame *Ant. and Cleo.* iii 13 119
Vulgarly. So vulgarly and personally accused *Meas. for Meas.* v 1 160
Vulgo. What, wench! Castiliano vulgo! *T. Night* i 3 45
Vulnerable. Let fall thy blade on vulnerable crests *Macbeth* v 8 11
Vulture. Let vultures gripe thy guts! *Mer. Wives* i 3 94
Let vultures vile seize on his lungs also! *2 Hen. IV.* v 3 146
While the vulture of sedition Feeds in the bosom of such great commanders, Sleeping neglection doth betray to loss *1 Hen. VI.* iv 3 47
I am Revenge; sent from the infernal kingdom, To ease the gnawing vulture of thy mind *T. Andron.* v 2 31
There cannot be That vulture in you, to devour so many *Macbeth* iv 3 74
O Regan, she hath tied Sharp-tooth'd unkindness, like a vulture, here *Lear* ii 4 137
Vurther. Chill not let go, zir, without vurther 'casion iv 6 239

W

Waddled. Then she could stand alone; nay, by the rood, She could have run and waddled all about *Rom. and Jul.* i 3 37
Wade to the market-place in Frenchmen's blood *K. John* ii 1 42
Fright fair peace And make us wade even in our kindred's blood *Rich. II.* i 3 138
Should I wade no more, Returning were as tedious as go o'er *Macbeth* iii 4 137
Waded. How she waded through the dirt *T. of Shrew* iv 1 80
Their joy waded in tears *W. Tale* v 2 50
Wafer-cakes. Oaths are straws, men's faiths are wafer-cakes *Hen. V.* ii 3 53
Waft. But, soft! who wafts us yonder? *Com. of Errors* ii 2 111
And waft her love To come again to Carthage *Mer. of Venice* v 1 11
A braver choice of dauntless spirits Than now the English bottoms have waft o'er Did never float *K. John* ii 1 73
I charge thee waft me safely cross the Channel *2 Hen. VI.* iv 1 114
Come, Suffolk, I must waft thee to thy death iv 1 116
Our high admiral Shall waft them over with our royal fleet *3 Hen. VI.* iii 3 253
Away with her, and waft her hence to France v 7 41
Whom Fortune with her ivory hand wafts to her *T. of Athens* i 1 70
Waftage. A ship you sent me to, to hire waftage *Com. of Errors* iv 1 95
I stalk about her door, Like a strange soul upon the Stygian banks Staying for waftage *Troi. and Cres.* iii 2 11
Wafting his eyes to the contrary and falling A lip *W. Tale* i 2 372
Wafture. You answer'd not, But, with an angry wafture of your hand, Gave sign for me to leave you *J. Cæsar* ii 1 246
Wag. Why, boy! why, wag! how now! what's the matter? Look up *T. G. of Ver.* v 4 86
Discard, bully Hercules; cashier: let them wag; trot, trot *Mer. Wives* i 3 7
Here, boys, here, here! shall we wag?—Have with you ii 1 238
And I will provoke him to't, or let him wag ii 3 74
'Tis good; vell said.—Let us wag, then ii 3 101
Bid sorrow wag, cry 'hem!' when he should groan *Much Ado* v 1 16
Making the bold wag by their praises bolder *L. L. Lost.* v 2 108
You may as well forbid the mountain pines To wag their high tops and to make no noise *Mer. of Venice* iv 1 76
'Thus we may see,' quoth he, 'how the world wags' *As Y. Like It* ii 7 23
Was not my lord The verier wag o' the two? *W. Tale* i 2 66
I prithee, sweet wag, when thou art king *1 Hen. IV.* i 2 18
Then, sweet wag, when thou art king, let not us ... be called thieves i 2 26
How now, mad wag! what, in thy quips and thy quiddities? i 2 50
How now, blown Jack! how now, quilt!—What, Hal! how now, mad wag! iv 2 55
We that are in the vaward of our youth, I must confess, are wags too *2 Hen. IV.* i 2 200
'Tis merry in hall when beards wag all, And welcome merry Shrove-tide v 3 37
And no discerner Durst wag his tongue in censure *Hen. VIII.* i 1 33
Let me see the proudest He, that dares most, but wag his finger at thee v 3 131
The empress never wags But in her company there is a Moor. *T. Andron.* v 2 87
What have I done, that thou darest wag thy tongue In noise so rude? *Hamlet* iii 4 39
I will fight with him upon this theme Until my eyelids will no longer wag v 1 290
Wage. The aweless lion could not wage the fight *K. John* i 1 266
Too weak To wage an instant trial *1 Hen. IV.* iv 4 20
My life I never held but as a pawn To wage against thy enemies *Lear* i 1 158
I abjure all roofs, and choose To wage against the enmity o' the air ii 4 212
To wake and wage a danger profitless *Othello* i 3 30
Dared him to single fight.—Ay, and to wage this battle *Ant. and Cleo.* iii 7 32
I will wage against your gold, gold to it *Cymbeline* i 4 144
The commodity wages not with the danger *Pericles* iv 2 34
Waged. He waged me with his countenance, as if I had been mercenary *Coriolanus* v 6 40
He hath waged New wars 'gainst Pompey; made his will *Ant. and Cleo.* iii 4 3
His taints and honours Waged equal with him v 1 31
Wager. For a good wager, first begins to crow *Tempest* ii 1 28
Done. The wager?—A laughter.—A match! ii 1 32
I'll hold thee any wager *Mer. of Venice* iii 4 62
And on the wager lay two earthly women, And Portia one iii 5 85
He whose wife is most obedient ... Shall win the wager ... —Content. What is the wager?—Twenty crowns *T. of Shrew* v 2 69
Now, fair befal thee, good Petruchio! The wager thou hast won v 2 112
Nay, I will win my wager better yet v 2 116
'Twas I won the wager, though you hit the white v 2 186
Yonder comes news. A wager they have met.—My horse to yours, no *Cor.* i 4 1
Bring you in fine together And wager on your heads *Hamlet* iv 7 135
We'll make a solemn wager on your cunnings iv 7 156
Bade me signify to you that he has laid a great wager on your head v 2 106
You will lose this wager, my lord.—I do not think so v 2 219
I embrace it freely; And will this brother's wager frankly play v 2 264
Cousin Hamlet, You know the wager?—Very well, my lord v 2 271
I durst, my lord, to wager she is honest, Lay down my soul at stake *Othello* iv 2 12
I make my wager rather against your confidence than her reputation *Cymbeline* i 4 120
Wager. I will fetch my gold and have our two wagers recorded *Cymb.* i 4 181
She is alone the Arabian bird, and I Have lost the wager i 6 18
The description Of what is in her chamber nothing saves The wager ii 4 95
I have heard of riding wagers, Where horses have been nimbler than the sands iii 2 73
We have a maid in Mytilene, I durst wager, Would win some words of him *Pericles* v 1 43
Wagered. The king, sir, hath wagered with him six Barbary horses *Ham.* v 2 154
'Twas merry when You wager'd on your angling *Ant. and Cleo.* ii 5 16
Wager'd with him Pieces of gold 'gainst this which then he wore *Cymb.* v 5 182
Wages. Thou for wages followest thy master; thy master for wages follows not thee *T. G. of Ver.* iii 1 94
'Tis a maid, for she is her master's maid, and serves for wages iii 1 270
And ere we have thy youthful wages spent, We'll light upon some settled low content *As Y. Like It* ii 3 67
We will mend thy wages ii 4 94
Our praises are our wages *W. Tale* i 2 94
Do you mean to stop any of William's wages, about the sack he lost? *2 Hen. IV.* v 1 25
Their wages duly paid 'em, And something over to remember me by *Hen. VIII.* iv 2 150
Timon's money Has paid his men their wages *T. of Athens* iii 2 77
All friends shall taste The wages of their virtue *Lear* v 3 303
Thou thy worldly task hast done, Home art gone, and ta'en thy wages *Cymbeline* iv 2 261
Wagging. Tremble and start at wagging of a straw *Richard III.* iii 5 7
And think with wagging of your tongue to win me *Hen. VIII.* v 3 127
It is not worth the wagging of your beards *Coriolanus* ii 1 96
As zephyrs blowing below the violet, Not wagging his sweet head *Cymbeline* iv 2 173
Waggish. As waggish boys in game themselves forswear *M. N. Dream* i 1 240
A waggish courage; Ready in gibes, quick-answer'd, saucy *Cymbeline* iii 4 160
Waggling. I know you by the waggling of your head *Much Ado* ii 1 119
Waggon. We must away; Our waggon is prepared *All's Well* iv 4 34
For the flowers now, that frighted thou let'st fall From Dis's waggon! *W. Tale* iv 4 118
Provide thee two proper palfreys, black as jet, To hale thy vengeful waggon swift away *T. Andron.* v 2 51
Waggoner. I'll come and be thy waggoner, And whirl along with thee v 2 48
Her waggoner a small grey-coated gnat *Rom. and Jul.* i 4 64
Such a waggoner As Phaëthon would whip you to the west iii 2 2
Waggon-spokes. Her waggon-spokes made of long spinners' legs i 4 59
Waggon-wheel. I will dismount, and by the waggon-wheel Trot *T. An.* v 2 54
Wagtail. Spare my gray beard, you wagtail? *Lear* ii 2 73
Wail. Since, to wail friends lost Is not by much so wholesome-profitable As to rejoice at friends but newly found *L. L. Lost* v 2 759
My lord, wise men ne'er sit and wail their woes, But presently prevent the ways to wail *Richard II.* iii 2 178
That not only givest Me cause to wail but teachest me the way How to lament the cause iv 1 301
And none but women left to wail the dead *1 Hen. VI.* i 1 51
And can do nought but wail her darling's loss *2 Hen. VI.* iii 1 216
Great lords, wise men ne'er sit and wail their loss, But cheerly seek how to redress their harms *3 Hen. VI.* v 4 1
Long mayst thou live to wail thy children's loss! *Richard III.* i 3 204
It were lost sorrow to wail one that's lost ii 2 11
Oh, who shall hinder me to wail and weep, To chide my fortune? ii 2 34
All of us have cause To wail the dimming of our shining star ii 2 102
The citizens, who haply may Misconstrue us in him and wail his death iii 5 61
For joyful mother, one that wails the name iv 4 99
She shall be a high and mighty queen.—To wail the title, as her mother doth iv 4 348
The children live, whose parents thou hast slaughter'd, Ungovern'd youth, to wail it in their age; The parents live, whose children thou hast butcher'd, Old wither'd plants, to wail it with their age iv 4 392
Had she no lover there That wails her absence? *Troi. and Cres.* iv 5 289
'Tis fond to wail inevitable strokes, As 'tis to laugh at 'em *Coriolanus* iv 1 26
Death, that hath ta'en her hence to make me wail *Rom. and Jul.* iv 5 31
But wail his fall Who I myself struck down *Macbeth* iii 1 122
What I believe I'll wail, What know believe iv 3 8
Tom will make them weep and wail *Lear* iii 6 74
Wailed. No evil lost is wail'd when it is gone *Com. of Errors* iv 2 24
What willingly he did confound he wail'd, Believe't *Ant. and Cleo.* iii 2 58
Wailful. Lay lime to tangle her desires By wailful sonnets *T. G. of Ver.* iii 2 69
Wailing. My mother weeping, my father wailing, my sister crying ii 3 7
I'll fight for France. Away with these disgraceful wailing robes! *1 Hen. VI.* i 1 86
Why stand we like soft-hearted women here, Wailing our losses? *3 Hen. VI.* ii 3 26
But none can cure their harms by wailing them *Richard III.* ii 2 103
Where is my father, and my mother, nurse?—Weeping and wailing over Tybalt's corse *Rom. and Jul.* iii 2 128

Wain. Charles' wain is over the new chimney . . . 1 *Hen. IV.* ii 1 2
Wainropes. Oxen and wainropes cannot hale them together . *T. Night* iii 2 64
Wainscot. This fellow will but join you together as they join wainscot;
then one of you will prove a shrunk panel *As Y. Like It* iii 3 88
Waist. Now on the beak, Now in the waist, the deck, in every cabin *Temp.* i 2 197
I am in the waist two yards about; but I am now about no waste *M. W.* i 3 46
His neck will come to your waist,—a cord, sir. *Meas. for Meas.* iii 2 42
A German from the waist downward, all slops . . . *Much Ado* iii 2 35
An your waist, mistress, were as slender as my wit, One o' these maids'
girdles for your waist should be fit *L. L. Lost* iv 1 49
When shall you hear that I Will praise . . . a brow, a breast, a waist? iv 3 185
Those sleeping stones, That as a waist doth girdle you about *K. John* ii 1 217
When I was about thy years, Hal, I was not an eagle's talon in the waist;
I could have crept into any alderman's thumb-ring . . 1 *Hen. IV.* ii 4 364
I would my means were greater, and my waist slenderer . 2 *Hen. IV.* i 2 162
Girdled with a waist of iron And hemm'd about with grim destruction
1 *Hen. VI.* iv 3 20
And buckle in a waist most fathomless With spans and inches *T. and C.* ii 2 30
Then you live about her [fortune's] waist, or in the middle of her
favours? . . . . *Hamlet* ii 2 236
Down from the waist they are Centaurs, Though women all above *Lear* iv 6 126
Wait. It sounds no more: and, sure, it waits upon Some god *Tempest* i 2 388
Your father would speak with you.—I wait upon his pleasure *T. G. of V.* ii 4 117
We'll wait upon your grace till after supper . . . . iii 2 96
As wretches have o'ernight That wait for execution in the morn . iv 2 134
Where have you been? I must wait on myself, must I? *Mer. Wives* i 1 208
My father desires your worships' company.—I will wait on him . i 1 272
For all you are my man, go wait upon my cousin . . . . i 1 282
The wealth I have waits on my consent, and my consent goes not that way iii 2 78
Let us withdraw . . . —I'll wait upon your honour *Meas. for Meas.* i 1 85
Eat when I have stomach and wait for no man s leisure . *Much Ado* i 3 16
Shall we go prove what's to be done?—We'll wait upon your lordship i 3 77
I'll wait upon them: I am ready . . . . . ii 5 61
How I would make him fawn and beg and seek And wait! . *L. L. Lost* v 2 63
Never more to dance, Nor never more in Russian habit wait . v 2 401
Come, wait upon him; lead him to my bower . *M. N. Dream* iii 1 202
More than to us Wait in your royal walks, your board, your bed! . v 1 31
Not I, but my affairs, have made you wait *Mer. of Venice* ii 6 22
He waits on thee; But I will charm him first to keep his tongue *T. of S.* i 1 213
Wait you on him, I charge you, as becomes . . . i 1 238
Are you so formal, sir? well, I must wait, And watch withal . iii 1 61
In every thing I wait upon his will.—I shall report it so *All's Well* ii 4 55
I thank thee: wait on me home, I'll make sport with thee . v 3 323
Infirmity Which waits upon worn times . . . *W. Tale* v 1 142
And vast confusion waits, As doth a raven on a sick-fall'n beast *K. John* iv 3 152
My soul shall wait on thee to heaven, As it on earth hath been thy
servant . . . . v 7 72
You, my noble prince, . . . Shall wait upon your father's funeral v 7 98
Thy friends are fled to wait upon thy foes *Richard II.* ii 4 23
If he will not yield, Rebuke and dread correction wait on us 1 *Hen. IV.* v 1 111
Thou art fitter to be worn in my cap than to wait at my heels 2 *Hen. IV.* i 2 18
Wait close; I will not see him . . . . . i 2 65
Shall I entreat you with me to dinner?—I must wait upon my good lord ii 1 196
Put on two leathern jerkins and aprons, and wait upon him . . ii 2 190
I'll wait upon you, and I long to hear it . . . *Hen. V.* i 1 98
Thou, 'gainst all proportion, didst bring in Wonder to wait on treason . ii 2 110
The maiden cities you talk of may wait on her . . . v 2 354
Heralds, wait on us: Instead of gold, we'll offer up our arms 1 *Hen. VI.* i 1 45
Where be these warders, that they wait not here? Open the gates . i 3 3
When care, mistrust, and treason waits on him . 3 *Hen. VI.* ii 5 54
What means this armed guard That waits upon your grace? *Richard III.* i 1 43
But come, let us in . . . —We wait upon your grace . . i 1 140
Come, will you go?—I'll wait upon your lordship . . . iii 2 125
The two great cardinals Wait in the presence . . *Hen. VIII.* ii 1 17
All fast? what means this? Ho! Who waits there? Sure, you know me? v 2 4
Your grace must wait till you be call'd for . . . . v 2 7
They would shame to make me Wait else at door, a fellow-counsellor v 2 17
To let . . . This honest man wait like a lousy footboy At chamber-door v 3 139
I purpose not to wait on fortune till These wars determine *Coriolanus* v 3 119
I am not bid to wait upon this bride . . . *T. Andron.* i 1 338
Upon her wit doth earthly honour wait . . . . ii 1 10
I will be bright, and shine in pearl and gold, To wait upon this new-
made empress. To wait, said I? to wanton with this queen . ii 1 20
I must hence to wait; I beseech you, follow straight.—We follow thee
Rom. and Jul. i 3 103
I like it: wait attendance Till you hear further from me *T. of Athens* i 1 161
I do beseech you, good my lords, keep on; I'll wait upon you instantly ii 2 36
He wears jewels now of Timon's gift, For which I wait for money . iii 4 20
What do ye ask of me, my friend?—We wait for certain money . iii 4 46
Or, if you will, Come home to me, and I will wait for you *J. Cæsar* i 2 310
You murdering ministers, Wherever in your sightless substances You
wait on nature's mischief! . . . . . *Macbeth* i 5 51
Letting 'I dare not' wait upon 'I would,' Like the poor cat i' the adage i 7 44
Now, good digestion wait on appetite, And health on both! . . iii 4 38
We'll wait upon you.—No such matter: I will not sort you with the rest
of my servants . . . . *Hamlet* ii 2 273
The hey-day in the blood is tame, it's humble, And waits upon the
judgement . . . . iii 4 70
Wait upon him. Strengthen your patience in our last night's speech . v 1 316
My good fellows, wait on me to-night: Scant not my cups *Ant. and Cleo.* iv 2 20
Know, sir, that I Will not wait pinion'd at your master's court . v 2 53
Thus ready for the way of life or death, I wait the sharpest blow *Pericles* i 1 55
For he's no man on whom perfections wait That, knowing sin within,
will touch the gate . . . . i 1 79
So, on your patience evermore attending, New joy wait on you! v 3 Gower 101
Waited. Whilst I waited on my tender lambs . 1 *Hen. VI.* i 2 76
How often hast thou waited at my cup, Fed from my trencher? 2 *Hen. VI.* iv 1 56
Stood And duly waited for my coming forth . . . iv 1 62
No sun shall ever usher forth mine honours, Or gild again the noble
troops that waited Upon my smiles . . . *Hen. VIII.* iii 2 411
Lucius and I'll go brave it at the court: Ay, marry, will we, sir; and
we'll be waited on . . . . . *T. Andron.* iv 1 122
Bid them prepare within: I am to blame to be thus waited for *J. Cæsar* ii 2 119
Waiteth. O, but impatience waiteth on true sorrow . 3 *Hen. VI.* iii 3 42
Waiting. Full oft we see Cold wisdom waiting on superfluous folly
All's Well i 1 116
One good deed dying tongueless Slaughters a thousand waiting upon
that . . . . *W. Tale* i 2 93
In some sort it jumps with my humour as well as waiting . 1 *Hen. IV.* i 2 78
If money were as certain as your waiting, 'Twere sure enough *T. of A.* iii 4 47

Waiting-gentlewoman. Dress him in my apparel and make him my
waiting-gentlewoman . . . . . . *Much Ado* ii 1 37
I am in the favour of Margaret, the waiting gentlewoman . . . ii 2 14
I am not bookish, yet I can read waiting-gentlewoman in the 'scape *W. T.* iii 3 74
Talk so like a waiting-gentlewoman Of guns and drums . 1 *Hen. IV.* i 3 55
Waiting-vassals. Your waiting-vassals Have done a drunken slaughter
Richard III. ii 1 121
Waiting-women. By all Diana's waiting-women yond . *Troi. and Cres.* v 2 91
Possesses chambermaids and waiting-women . . . *Lear* iv 1 65
Wake. Keep in Tunis, And let Sebastian wake. . . *Tempest* ii 1 260
Did't not wake you? It struck mine ear most terribly . . ii 1 312
My horns are his horns, whether I wake or sleep . *T. G. of Ver.* i 1 80
He will not wake.—Who can do good on him? . *Meas. for Meas.* iv 2 71
Depart in peace, and let the child wake her with crying *Much Ado* iii 3 74
Wake my cousin Beatrice, and desire her to rise . . . iii 4 1
Gentlemen both, we will not wake your patience . . . v 1 102
Retails his wares At wakes and wassails, meetings, markets, fairs
L. L. Lost v 2 318
What thou seest when thou dost wake, Do it for thy true-love take
M. N. Dream ii 2 27
When thou wakest, it is thy dear: Wake when some vile thing is near ii 2 34
What angel wakes me from my flowery bed? . . . . iii 1 132
When they next wake, all this derision Shall seem a dream . . iii 2 370
Now, my Titania; wake you, my sweet queen . . . iv 1 80
Go, bid the huntsmen wake them with their horns . . . iv 1 143
Sleep when he wakes and creep into the jaundice By being peevish
Mer. of Venice i 1 85
Wake Diana with a hymn: With sweetest touches pierce your
mistress' ear . . . . v 1 66
When he wakes, Would not the beggar then forget himself? *T. of S.* Ind. 1 40
Procure me music ready when he wakes . . . . Ind. 1 50
To bed with him; And each one to his office when he wakes . Ind. 1 73
He haunts wakes, fairs, and bear-baitings . . *W. Tale* iv 3 109
With rival-hating envy, set on you To wake our peace *Richard II.* i 3 132
Making such difference 'twixt wake and sleep As is the difference
betwixt day and night . . . . . 1 *Hen. IV.* iii 1 219
Since all is well, keep it so: wake not a sleeping wolf.—To wake a wolf
is as bad as to smell a fox . . . . 2 *Hen. IV.* i 2 174
'Twas time, I trow, to wake and leave our beds . 1 *Hen. VI.* ii 1 41
Watch thou and wake when others be asleep . . 2 *Hen. VI.* i 1 249
He will say 'twas done cowardly, when he wakes.—When he wakes!
why, fool, he shall never wake till the judgement-day *Richard III.* i 4 104
Richmond, sleep in peace, and wake in joy; Good angels guard thee! v 3 155
Therefore best Not wake him in his slumber . . *Hen. VIII.* i 1 122
She is asleep: good wench, let's sit down quiet, For fear we wake her iv 2 82
And wake him to the answer, think you? . . *Troi. and Cres.* i 3 332
This, I presume, will wake him . . . . . . ii 2 213
Uncouple here and let us make a bay And wake the emperor *T. Andron.* ii 2 4
If I do dream, would all my wealth would wake me! If I do wake,
some planet strike me down, That I may slumber in eternal sleep! ii 4 13
If you hunt these bear-whelps, then beware: The dam will wake . iv 1 97
And then anon Drums in his ear, at which he starts and wakes *R. and J.* i 4 86
How if, when I am laid into the tomb, I wake before the time that
Romeo Come? . . . . iv 3 31
O, if I wake, shall I not be distraught, Environed with all these
hideous fears? . . . . iv 3 49
How sound is she asleep! I must needs wake her . . . iv 5 9
What, dress'd! and in your clothes! and down again! I must needs
wake you . . . . iv 5 13
Within this three hours will fair Juliet wake . . . v 2 25
She wakes; and I entreated her come forth . . . v 3 260
I will not do thee so much wrong to wake thee . *J. Cæsar* iv 3 270
Hath it slept since? And wakes it now, to look so green and pale? *Macb.* i 7 37
One did laugh in's sleep, and one cried 'Murder!' That they did wake
each other . . . . ii 2 24
Wake Duncan with thy knocking! I would thou couldst! . . ii 2 74
Upon his aid To wake Northumberland and warlike Siward . . iii 6 31
The king doth wake to-night and takes his rouse, Keeps wassail *Hamlet* i 4 8
A whole tribe of fops, Got 'tween asleep and wake . . . *Lear* i 2 15
Shall of a corn cry woe, And turn his sleep to wake . . iii 2 34
Come, march to wakes and fairs and market-towns. Poor Tom, thy
horn is dry . . . . iii 6 77
So please your majesty That we may wake the king . . iv 7 18
He wakes; speak to him.—Madam, do you; 'tis fittest . . iv 7 42
Neglecting an attempt of ease and gain, To wake and wage a danger
profitless . . . . *Othello* i 3 30
She wakes.—Who's there? Othello?—Ay, Desdemona . . v 2 22
Hark! the drums Demurely wake the sleepers . *Ant. and Cleo.* iv 9 31
Where is the queen?—Speak softly, wake her not . . . v 2 323
Do't, and to bed then.—I'll wake mine eye-balls blind first *Cymbeline* iii 4 104
The dream's here still: even when I wake, it is Without me, as
within me . . . . iv 2 306
Poor wretches that depend On greatness' favour dream as I have done,
Wake and find nothing . . . . v 4 128
How come these staggers on me?—Wake, my mistress! . . v 5 233
Waked. Voices That, if I then had waked after long sleep, Will make
me sleep again . . . . *Tempest* iii 2 148
That, when I waked, I cried to dream again . . . . iii 2 151
Graves at my command Have waked their sleepers, oped, and let 'em
forth . . . . v 1 49
I am waked with it when I sleep; raised with it when I sit *Com. of Er.* iv 4 36
She hath often dreamed of unhappiness and waked herself with
laughing . . . . *Much Ado* ii 1 361
So it came to pass, Titania waked and straightway loved an ass
M. N. Dream iii 2 34
That, when he waked, of force she must be eyed . . . iii 2 40
It would seem strange unto him when he waked . *T. of Shrew* Ind. 1 43
You have been in a dream; Or when you waked, so waked as if you
slept . . . . Ind. 2 82
It were but necessary you were waked . . . 2 *Hen. VI.* iii 2 261
With the very noise I trembling waked . . . *Richard III.* i 4 61
But have been waked by his timorous dreams . . . . iv 1 85
The busy day, Waked by the lark, hath roused the ribald crows
Troi. and Cres. iv 2 9
And waked half dead with nothing . . . . *Coriolanus* iv 5 132
If our father would sleep till I waked him, you should enjoy half his
revenue for ever . . . . *Lear* i 2 55
Hum—conspiracy!—'Sleep till I waked him' . . . . i 2 58
One that slept in the contriving of lust, and waked to do it . . iii 4 93
'Tis the soldiers' life To have their balmy slumbers waked with strife *Oth.* ii 3 258

Waked. Thou hadst been better have been born a dog Than answer my waked wrath! . . . *Othello* iii 3 363
When I waked, I found This label on my bosom . . *Cymbeline* v 5 429
Wakefield. After the bloody fray at Wakefield fought . . 3 *Hen. VI.* ii 1 107
Waken. If Warwick knew in what estate he stands, 'Tis to be doubted he would waken him . . . . iv 3 19
Your sleepy thoughts, Which here we waken to our country's good *Richard III.* iii 7 124
I ask, that I might waken reverence . . . . *Troi. and Cres.* i 3 227
What, nurse, I say! Go waken Juliet, go and trim her up *Rom. and Jul.* iv 4 24
Wakened. Thou hast quarrelled with a man for coughing in the street, because he hath wakened thy dog . . . . . . iii 1 28
May the winds blow till they have waken'd death! . . . *Othello* ii 1 188
Our Tarquin thus Did softly press the rushes, ere he waken'd The chastity he wounded . . . . *Cymbeline* ii 2 13
Wakest. In thy eye that shall appear When thou wakest, it is thy dear: Wake when some vile thing is near . . . *M. N. Dream* ii 2 33
When thou wakest, let love forbid Sleep his seat on thy eyelid . . ii 2 80
When thou wakest, if she be by, Beg of her for remedy . . . iii 2 108
When thou wakest, Thou takest True delight In the sight . . . iii 2 453
Now, when thou wakest, with thine own fool's eyes peep . . iv 1 89
Sleepest or wakest thou, jolly shepherd? Thy sheep be in the corn *Lear* iii 6 43
Waking. What, art thou waking?—Do you not hear me speak? *Tempest* ii 1 209
Thou let'st thy fortune sleep—die, rather; wink'st Whiles thou art waking . . . . ii 1 217
Am I in earth, in heaven, or in hell? Sleeping or waking? *Com. of Errors* ii 2 215
The next thing then she waking looks upon, . . . She shall pursue it with the soul of love . . . . . . *M. N. Dream* ii 1 179
That every man should take his own, In your waking shall be shown . iii 2 460
I shall reply amazedly, Half sleep, half waking . . . iv 1 152
Giddy for lack of sleep, With oaths kept waking . . *T. of Shrew* iv 3 10
Our own love waking cries to see what's done, While shame full late sleeps out the afternoon . . . . . . *All's Well* v 3 65
For ne'er was dream So like a waking . . . . *W. Tale* iii 3 19
Sleeping or waking must I still prevail? . . . 1 *Hen. VI.* ii 1 56
By day, by night, waking and in my dreams, In courtly company or at my beads . . . . 2 *Hen. VI.* i 1 26
Sleeping or waking, 'tis no matter how, So he be dead . . . iii 1 263
Blood-sucker of sleeping men!—Thou shalt be waking while I shed thy blood . . . . iii 2 227
Sleeping and waking, O, defend me still! . . . *Richard III.* v 3 117
You are one will keep 'em waking; Pray, sit between these ladies *Hen. VIII.* i 4 23
Shame whereof hath ever since kept Hector fasting and waking *T. and C.* i 2 37
Let me have war, say I; . . . it's spritely, waking, audible *Coriolanus* iv 5 238
He and I Will watch thy waking . . . . *Rom. and Jul.* iv 1 116
Is it not like that I, So early waking, . . . shall I not be distraught? . iv 3 46
At the prefixed hour of her waking, Came I to take her from her kindred's vault . . . . v 3 253
Ha! waking? 'tis not so. Who is it that can tell me who I am? *Lear* i 4 249
Wales. I am the last of noble Edward's sons, Of whom thy father, Prince of Wales, was first . . . . . . *Richard II.* ii 1 172
When all athwart there came A post from Wales loaden with heavy news . . . . 1 *Hen. IV.* i 1 37
That same sword-and-buckler Prince of Wales . . . . i 3 230
Though I be but Prince of Wales, yet I am the king of courtesy . ii 4 11
You Prince of Wales!—Why, you whoreson round man, what's the matter? . . . . ii 4 154
And he of Wales, that gave Amamon the bastinado . . . ii 4 370
Clipp'd in with the sea That chides the banks of England, Scotland, Wales . . . . iii 1 45
All westward, Wales beyond the Severn shore, . . . To Owen Glendower iii 1 76
The Prince of Wales and I Must have some private conference . iii 2 1
The nimble-footed madcap Prince of Wales, And his comrades . iv 1 95
Bear me like a thunderbolt Against the bosom of the Prince of Wales . iv 1 121
Suffer'd his kinsman March . . . to be engaged in Wales . . iv 3 95
The Prince of Wales, Lord John of Lancaster, The noble Westmoreland iv 4 29
The Prince of Wales doth join with all the world In praise of Henry Percy . . . . v 1 86
And, Prince of Wales, so dare we venture thee . . . . v 1 101
The Prince of Wales stepp'd forth before the king . . . v 2 46
And God forbid a shallow scratch should drive The Prince of Wales from such a field as this! . . . . v 4 12
It is the Prince of Wales that threatens thee . . . . v 4 42
I am the Prince of Wales; and think not, Percy, To share with me in glory . . . . v 4 63
Nor can one England brook a double reign, Of Harry Percy and the Prince of Wales . . . . v 4 67
Myself and you, son Harry, will towards Wales, To fight with Glendower . . . . v 5 39
I hear his majesty is returned with some discomfort from Wales 2 *Hen. IV.* i 2 119
The king, my lord, and Harry Prince of Wales Are near at hand . ii 1 146
Comes the king back from Wales, my noble lord? . . . ii 1 189
To the son of the king, nearest his father, Harry Prince of Wales . ii 2 131
Lord bless that sweet face of thine! O Jesu, are you come from Wales? ii 4 318
The Prince of Wales! Where is he? let me see him: He is not here . iv 5 54
That black name, Edward, Black Prince of Wales . . *Hen. V.* ii 4 56
Your great-uncle Edward the Plack Prince of Wales . . . iv 7 97
The first, Edward the Black Prince, Prince of Wales . 2 *Hen. VI.* ii 2 11
Edward thy son, which now is Prince of Wales, For Edward my son, which was Prince of Wales . . . . . *Richard III.* i 3 199
At Pembroke, or at Ha'rford-west, in Wales . . . . iv 5 7
Tell me how Wales was made so happy as To inherit such a haven *Cymb.* iii 2 62
Walk. A turn or two I'll walk, To still my beating mind *Tempest* iv 1 162
To walk alone, like one that had the pestilence . *T. G. of Ver.* ii 1 21
When you walked, to walk like one of the lions . . . ii 1 29
Hope is a lover's staff; walk hence with that . . . iii 1 246
As we walk along, I dare be bold With our discourse to make your grace to smile . . . . v 4 162
I pray you, sir, walk in.—I had rather walk here . *Mer. Wives* i 1 292
I will rather trust . . . a thief to walk my ambling gelding . ii 2 319
Thou mightst as well say I love to walk by the Counter-gate . iii 3 85
Come, come, walk in the Park: I pray you, pardon me . . iii 3 240
Doth all the winter-time, at still midnight, Walk round about an oak . iv 4 31
There want not many that do fear In deep of night to walk by this Herne's oak . . . . iv 4 40
I will keep my sides to myself, my shoulders for the fellow of this walk v 5 29
The vaporous night approaches.—Will't please you walk aside? *Meas. for Meas.* iv 1 59
Thou hast made good haste: Come, we will walk . . . iv 5 12
Walk. You must walk by us on our other hand; And good supporters are you . . . . *Meas. for Meas.* v 1 17
Will you walk with me about the town? . . *Com. of Errors* i 2 22
Let him walk from whence he came, lest he catch cold on's feet . iii 1 37
Come to the mart, Where I will walk till thou return to me . . iii 2 156
Pleaseth you walk with me down to his house, I will discharge my bond iv 1 12
Speak softly: yonder, as I think, he walks . . . . v 1 9
'Tis pity that thou livest To walk where any honest men resort . v 1 28
Will you walk in to see their gossiping? . . . . . v 1 419
Lady, will you walk about with your friend? . . . *Much Ado* ii 1 89
So you walk softly and look sweetly and say nothing, I am yours for the walk; and especially when I walk away . . . . ii 1 91
My lord, will you walk? dinner is ready . . . . . ii 3 218
Whisper her ear and tell her, I and Ursula Walk in the orchard . iii 1 5
Walk aside with me: I have studied eight or nine wise words to speak to you . . . . iii 2 73
Than those that walk and wot not what they are . . *L. L. Lost* i 1 91
And, as I am a gentleman, betook myself to walk . . . . i 1 237
O, a most dainty man! To see him walk before a lady and to bear her fan! . . . . iv 1 147
Walk aside the true folk, and let the traitors stay . . . iv 3 213
I will walk up and down here, and I will sing, that they shall hear I am not afraid . . . . *M. N. Dream* iii 1 126
Hop in his walks and gambol in his eyes . . . . iii 1 168
More than to us Wait in your royal walks, your board, your bed! . v 1 31
I will buy with you, sell with you, talk with you, walk with you, and so following . . . . *Mer. of Venice* i 3 37
Where is your master?—Yonder, sir, he walks . . . . ii 2 183
We should hold day with the Antipodes, If you would walk in absence of the sun . . . . v 1 128
They are but burs, cousin . . . : if we walk not in the trodden paths, our very petticoats will catch them . . . *As Y. Like It* i 3 14
Say thou wilt walk; we will bestrew the ground . . *T. of Shrew* Ind. 2 42
You walk like a stranger: may I be so bold to know the cause of your coming? . . . . ii 1 87
We will go walk a little in the orchard, And then to dinner . . ii 1 112
O, let me see thee walk: thou dost not halt . . . . ii 1 258
You may go walk, and give me leave a while . . . . iii 1 59
There will we mount, and thither walk on foot . . . . iv 3 188
But, like a cloistress, she will veiled walk . . . *T. Night* i 1 28
My very walk should be a jig . . . . i 3 138
Get ye all three into the box-tree: Malvolio's coming down this walk ii 5 19
Foolery, sir, does walk about the orb like the sun, it shines every where iii 1 43
I do not without danger walk these streets . . . . iii 3 25
Do not then walk too open.—It doth not fit me . . . . iii 3 37
Will you walk towards him? I will make your peace with him if I can iii 4 295
Here comes the countess: now heaven walks on earth . . . v 1 100
We two will walk, my lord, And leave you to your graver steps *W. Tale* i 2 172
I have heard, but not believed, the spirits o' the dead May walk again . iii 3 17
Much better than I was; I can stand and walk . . . . iv 3 120
Walk before toward the sea-side; go on the right hand . . . iv 4 855
Who dares not stir by day must walk by night . . . *K. John* i 1 172
Walks up and down with me, Puts on his pretty looks, repeats his words iii 4 94
What! mother dead! How wildly then walks my estate in France! . iv 2 128
Nor attend the foot That leaves the print of blood where'er it walks . iv 3 26
Why, here walk I in the black brow of night, To find you out . v 6 17
For ever will I walk upon my knees . . . . *Richard II.* v 3 93
We have the receipt of fern-seed, we walk invisible . . 1 *Hen. IV.* ii 1 96
Front them in the narrow lane; Ned Poins and I will walk lower . ii 2 63
We'll walk afoot awhile, and ease our legs . . . . ii 2 83
Falstaff sweats to death, And lards the lean earth as he walks along . ii 2 116
Go, hide thee behind the arras: the rest walk up above . . ii 4 550
I do here walk before thee like a sow that hath overwhelmed all her litter but one . . . . 2 *Hen. IV.* i 2 12
If you would walk off, I would prick your guts a little . . *Hen. V.* ii 1 61
Should with his lion gait walk the whole world . . . . ii 2 122
Ban-dogs howl And spirits walk and ghosts break up their graves 2 *Hen. VI.* i 4 22
Give me leave In this close walk to satisfy myself, In craving your opinion . . . . ii 2 3
Who would live turmoiled in the court, And may enjoy such quiet walks as these? . . . . iv 10 19
And so he walks, insulting o'er his prey, And so he comes 3 *Hen. VI.* i 3 14
My parks, my walks, my manors that I had, Even now forsake me . v 2 24
Who from my cabin tempted me to walk Upon the hatches *Richard III.* i 4 12
As I walk thither, I'll tell ye more . . . . *Hen. VIII.* iv 1 116
Affairs that walk, As they say spirits do, at midnight . . . v 1 13
Come, you and I must walk a turn together; I have news to tell you . v 1 93
Give me thy hand, stand up: Prithee, let's walk . . . v 1 116
How now, how now!—Sirrah, walk off . . . *Troi. and Cres.* iii 2 7
Come in: I'll go get a fire.—Will you walk in, my lord? . . iii 2 64
Will you walk in, my lord?—What, blushing still? . . . iii 2 107
Walk into her house; I'll bring her to the Grecian presently . . iv 3 5
As we walk, To our own selves bend we our needful talk . . iv 4 140
Did see and hear, devise, instruct, walk, feel . . *Coriolanus* i 1 105
When he walks, he moves like an engine, and the ground shrinks . v 4 19
When wert thou wont to walk alone, Dishonour'd thus? . . *T. Andron.* i 1 339
The forest walks are wide and spacious . . . . . ii 1 114
And so let's leave her to her silent walks . . . . . ii 4 8
A troubled mind drave me to walk abroad . . *Rom. and Jul.* i 1 127
Tybalt, you rat-catcher, will you walk?—What wouldst thou have with me? . . . . iii 1 78
Or walk in thievish ways; or bid me lurk Where serpents are . . iv 1 79
I will walk myself To County Paris, to prepare him up . . . iv 2 44
In all shapes that man goes up and down in from fourscore to thirteen, this spirit walks in . . . . *T. of Athens* ii 2 121
Pray you, walk near: I'll speak with you anon . . . . ii 2 132
With his disease of all-shunn'd poverty, Walks, like contempt, alone . iv 2 15
Being mechanical, you ought not walk Upon a labouring day without the sign Of your profession . . . . *J. Cæsar* i 1 3
And we petty men Walk under his huge legs and peep about . . i 2 137
Who swore they saw Men all in fire walk up and down the streets . i 3 25
This disturbed sky Is not to walk in . . . . . . i 3 40
Is Brutus sick? and is it physical To walk unbraced? . . . ii 1 262
Think you to walk forth? You shall not stir out of your house to-day ii 2 8
Besmear our swords: Then walk we forth, even to the market-place . iii 1 108
He hath left you all his walks, His private arbours, and new-planted orchards, . . . common pleasures, To walk abroad, and recreate yourselves . . . . iii 2 252
O Julius Cæsar, thou art mighty yet! Thy spirit walks abroad . . v 3 95

Walk. Thou sure and firm-set earth, Hear not my steps, which way they walk . . . *Macbeth* ii 1 57
As from your graves rise up, and walk like sprites, To countenance this horror! . . . ii 3 84
So all men do, from hence to the palace gate Make it their walk . . iii 3 14
Men must not walk too late . . . iii 6 7
For which, they say, you spirits oft walk in death . . . *Hamlet* i 1 138
The morn, in russet mantle clad, Walks o'er the dew of yon high eastward hill . . . . . i 1 167
I will watch to-night; Perchance 'twill walk again . . . i 2 243
With a larger tether may he walk Than may be given you . . i 3 125
Then it draws near the season Wherein the spirit held his wont to walk i 4 6
I am thy father's spirit, Doom'd for a certain term to walk the night . i 5 10
You know, sometimes he walks four hours together Here in the lobby . ii 2 160
Have you a daughter?—I have, my lord.—Let her not walk i' the sun . ii 2 185
Will you walk out of the air, my lord?—Into my grave . . ii 2 208
Ophelia, walk you here. Gracious, so please you, We will bestow ourselves . . . . . iii 1 43
I will walk here in the hall: if it please his majesty . . v 2 180
This is not Lear: Doth Lear walk thus? speak thus? . . *Lear* i 4 247
He begins at curfew, and walks till the first cock . . . iii 4 121
The fishermen, that walk upon the beach, Appear like mice . iv 6 17
Will't please your highness walk?—You must bear with me . . iv 7 83
Walk hereabout: If I do find him fit, I'll move your suit *Othello* iii 4 165
Trouble yourself no further.—O, pardon me; 'twill do me good to walk iv 3 2
Will you walk, sir? O,—Desdemona,— My lord? . . . iv 3 4
Be brief; I will walk by: I would not kill thy unprepared spirit . . v 2 30
Stands he, or sits he? Or does he walk? or is he on his horse? *A. and C.* i 5 20
Walk; let's see if other watchmen Do hear what we do . . . iv 3 18
Yet I'll move him To walk this way . . . . . *Cymbeline* i 1 104
Walk awhile.—About some half-hour hence, I pray you, speak with me i 1 176
I'll be thy master: walk with me; speak freely . . . v 5 119
Not an hour, In the day's glorious walk, or peaceful night *Pericles* i 2 4
Walk with Leonine; the air is quick there . . . iv 1 28
Come, Leonine, take her by the arm, walk with her . . . iv 1 30
Go, I pray you, Walk, and be cheerful once again . . . iv 1 40
I know 'tis good for you. Walk half an hour, Leonine, at the least iv 1 46
Pray, walk softly, do not heat your blood . . . . iv 1 49

Walked. When you walked, to walk like one of the lions *T. G. of Ver.* ii 1 28
He would have walked ten mile a-foot to see a good armour *Much Ado* ii 3 16
Now for the ground which; which, I mean, I walked upon . *L. L. Lost* i 1 242
As she goes, what upward lies The street should see as she walk'd overhead . . . . . iv 3 281
It was the friar of orders grey, As he forth walked on his way *T. of S.* iv 1 149
Were I the ghost that walk'd, I'ld bid you mark Her eye *W. Tale* v 1 63
Walk'd your first queen's ghost, it should take joy To see her in your arms . . . . . v 1 80
In those holy fields Over whose acres walk'd those blessed feet 1 *Hen. IV.* i 1 25
Where's Poins, Hal?—He is walked up to the top of the hill . . ii 2 8
His lordship is walk'd forth into the orchard . . 2 *Hen. IV.* i 1 4
He walk'd o'er perils, on an edge, More likely to fall in than to get o'er i 1 170
He's walk'd the way of nature; And to our purposes he lives no more v 2 4
A guard of chosen shot I had That walked about me every minute while 1 *Hen. VI.* i 4 54
Good old chronicle, That hast so long walk'd hand in hand with time *Troi. and Cres.* iv 5 203
Myself hath often over-heard them say, When I have walked like a private man . . . *T. Andron.* iv 4 75
Walk'd about the streets, Submitting me unto the perilous night *J. C.* i 3 46
At supper, You suddenly arose, and walk'd about, Musing and sighing ii 1 239
And the right-valiant Banquo walk'd too late . . *Macbeth* iii 6 5
When was it she last walked? . . . . . . v 1 3
Yet I have known those which have walked in their sleep . . v 1 66
Thrice he walk'd By their oppress'd and fear-surprised eyes *Hamlet* i 2 202
I know a lady in Venice would have walked barefoot to Palestine for a touch of his nether lip . . . *Othello* iv 3 39
In his livery Walk'd crowns and crownets . . *Ant. and Cleo.* v 2 91

Walkest. As if thou never walk'st further than Finsbury 1 *Hen. IV.* iii 1 257

Walking in a thick-pleached alley in mine orchard . *Much Ado* i 2 9
I think you are more beholding to the night than to fern-seed for your walking invisible . . . 1 *Hen. IV.* ii 1 99
Walking with thee in the night betwixt tavern and tavern . iii 3 49
Walking from watch to watch, from tent to tent *Hen. V.* iv Prol. 30
My choler being over-blown With walking once about the quadrangle 2 *Hen. VI.* i 3 156
From the city's side, So early walking did I see your son *Rom. and Jul.* i 1 130
This fearful night, There is no stir or walking in the streets *J. Cæsar* i 3 127
It is the bright day that brings forth the adder; And that craves wary walking . . . . . . ii 1 15
Besides her walking and other actual performances *Macbeth* v 1 13
Out, out, brief candle! Life's but a walking shadow, a poor player v 5 24
I will be walking on the works; Repair there to me . *Othello* iii 2 3
Where's Antony?—He's walking in the garden—thus *Ant. and Cleo.* iii 5 17

Walking-staff. My sceptre for a palmer's walking-staff . *Richard II.* iii 3 151

Wall. He hath raised the wall and houses too . . *Tempest* ii 1 87
Like unscour'd armour, hung by the wall . *Meas. for Meas.* i 2 171
When icicles hang by the wall And Dick the shepherd blows his nail *L. L. Lost* v 2 922
We must have a wall in the great chamber; for Pyramus and Thisby, says the story, did talk through the chink of a wall.—You can never bring in a wall . . . *M. N. Dream* iii 1 64
Some man or other must present Wall: and let him have some plaster, or some loam, or some rough-cast about him, to signify wall . iii 1 69
This man, with lime and rough-cast, doth present Wall, that vile Wall v 1 133
And through Wall's chinks, poor souls, they are content To whisper v 1 134
Let Lion, Moonshine, Wall, and lovers twain At large discourse . v 1 151
It doth befall That I, one Snout by name, present a wall; And such a wall, as I would have you think, That had in it a crannied hole or chink . . . . . . v 1 157
This loam, this rough-cast, and this stone doth show That I am that same wall . . . . . . v 1 163
Pyramus draws near the wall: silence!—O grim-look'd night! . v 1 170
O wall, O sweet, O lovely wall, That stand'st between her father's ground and mine! Thou wall, O wall, O sweet and lovely wall, Show me thy chink! . . . . . v 1 175
Thanks, courteous wall: Jove shield thee well for this! . . v 1 179
O wicked wall, through whom I see no bliss! Cursed be thy stones for thus deceiving me!—The wall, methinks, being sensible, should curse again . . . . . . v 1 181
She is to enter now, and I am to spy her through the wall . v 1 187

Wall. O wall, full often hast thou heard my moans! *M. N. Dream* v 1 190
O, kiss me through the hole of this vile wall!—I kiss the wall's hole v 1 202
Thus have I, Wall, my part discharged so; And, being done, thus Wall away doth go.—Now is the mural down . . . v 1 206
No remedy, my lord, when walls are so wilful to hear without warning v 1 210
Moonshine and Lion are left to bury the dead.—Ay, and Wall too.—No, I assure you; the wall is down that parted their fathers . . v 1 357
Like the martlet, Builds in the weather on the outward wall *M. of Ven.* ii 9 29
In such a night Troilus methinks mounted the Troyan walls . v 1 4
I'll leave her houses three or four as good, Within rich Pisa walls *T. of S.* ii 1 369
Nature with a beauteous wall Doth oft close in pollution *T. Night* i 2 48
Some trumpet summon hither to the walls These men of Angiers *K. John* ii 1 198
Who is it that hath warn'd us to the walls?—'Tis France, for England . ii 1 201
Ready mounted are they to spit forth Their iron indignation 'gainst your walls . . . . . . ii 1 212
Bullets wrapp'd in fire, To make a shaking fever in your walls . ii 1 228
Crave harbourage within your city walls . . . ii 1 234
'Tis not the roundure of your old-faced walls Can hide you . ii 1 259
Turn thou the mouth of thy artillery, As we will ours, against these saucy walls . . . . . . ii 1 404
Within this wall of flesh There is a soul counts thee her creditor . iii 3 20
The wall is high, and yet will I leap down . . . iv 3 1
But empty lodgings and unfurnish'd walls . . *Richard II.* i 2 68
Set in the silver sea, Which serves it in the office of a wall . ii 1 47
As if this flesh which walls about our life Were brass impregnable . iii 2 167
And with a little pin Bores through his castle wall . . iii 2 170
All the walls With painted imagery had said at once 'Jesu preserve thee!' . . . . . . v 2 15
The flinty ribs Of this hard world, my ragged prison walls . v 5 21
For thy walls, a pretty slight drollery, or the story of the Prodigal 2 *Hen. IV.* ii 1 156
Within the girdle of these walls Are now confined two mighty monarchies . . . . . *Hen. V.* Prol. 19
They of those marches, gracious sovereign, Shall be a wall sufficient i 2 141
Or close the wall up with our English dead . . iii 1 2
And their most reverend heads dash'd to the walls . . iii 3 37
They are all girdled with maiden walls that war hath never enter'd v 2 349
Of old I know them; rather with their teeth The walls they'll tear down than forsake the siege . . . 1 *Hen. VI.* i 2 40
In iron walls they deem'd me not secure . . . i 4 49
Advance our waving colours on the walls . . . i 6 1
If any noise or soldier you perceive Near to the walls . . ii 1 3
They did amongst the troops of armed men Leap o'er the walls . ii 2 25
Like peasant foot-boys do they keep the walls . . iii 2 69
Let's get us from the walls; For Talbot means no goodness by his looks iii 2 71
I sit before the walls of Rouen And will be partner of your weal or woe iii 2 91
Trumpeter; Summon their general unto the wall . . iv 2 1
There are squadrons pitch'd, To wall thee from the liberty of flight iv 2 24
At your father's castle walls We'll crave a parley, to confer with him v 3 129
On a brick wall have I climbed into this garden 2 *Hen. VI.* iv 10 7
Climbing my walls in spite of me the owner . . . iv 10 37
Bound to revenge, Wert thou environ'd with a brazen wall 3 *Hen. VI.* ii 4 4
Go, trumpet, to the walls, and sound a parle . . v 1 16
See how the surly Warwick mans the wall!—O unbid spite! . . v 1 17
Within the guilty closure of thy walls Richard the Second here was hack'd to death . . . *Richard III.* iii 3 11
Hark! a drum.—Catesby, o'erlook the walls . . iii 5 17
Those tender babes Whom envy hath immured within your walls! . iv 1 100
I'll unarm again: Why should I war without the walls of Troy, That find such cruel battle here within? *Troi. and Cres.* i 1 2
That after seven years' siege yet Troy walls stand . . i 3 12
So that the ram that batters down the wall, For the great swing and rudeness of his poise, They place before his hand that made the engine . . . . i 3 206
With his trumpet call Midway between your tents and walls of Troy i 3 278
The walls will stand till they fall of themselves . . ii 3 10
Yonder walls, that pertly front your town . . . iv 5 219
Sigh'd forth proverbs, That hunger broke stone walls *Coriolanus* i 1 210
No better than picture-like to hang by the wall, if renown made it not stir i 3 12
Tullus Aufidius, is he within your walls? . . . i 4 13
We'll break our walls, Rather than they shall pound us up . i 4 16
Alone I fought in your Corioli walls, And made what work I pleased i 8 8
A braver warrior Lives not this day within the city walls *T. Andron.* i 1 26
Ye sanguine, shallow-hearted boys! Ye white-limed walls! . iv 2 98
Suddenly I heard a child cry underneath a wall . . v 1 24
I pry'd me through the crevice of a wall . . . v 1 114
I will take the wall of any man or maid . . *Rom. and Jul.* i 1 15
For the weakest goes to the wall . . . . . i 1 18
Women, being the weaker vessels, are ever thrust to the wall . i 1 20
I will push Montague's men from the wall, and thrust his maids to the wall . . . . i 1 21
Sitting in the sun under the dove-house wall . . . i 3 27
He ran this way, and leap'd this orchard wall . . ii 1 5
The orchard walls are high and hard to climb, And the place death ii 2 63
With love's light wings did I o'er-perch these walls . . ii 2 66
There is no world without Verona walls, But purgatory, torture, hell itself . . . . iii 3 17
O thou wall, That girdlest in those wolves, dive in the earth, And fence not Athens! . . . . . *T. of Athens* iv 1 1
The gods confound—hear me, you good gods all—The Athenians both within and out that wall! . . . . . iv 1 38
How has the ass broke the wall, that thou art out of the city? . iv 3 354
And shakes his threatening sword Against the walls of Athens . v 1 170
These walls of ours Were not erected by their hands from whom You have received your griefs . . . . . v 4 22
Many a time and oft Have you climb'd up to walls and battlements *J. C.* i 1 43
When could they say till now, that talk'd of Rome, That her wide walls encompass'd but one man? . . . . . i 2 155
Nor stony tower, nor walls of beaten brass, Nor airless dungeon . i 3 93
Hang out our banners on the outward walls . . *Macbeth* v 5 1
O, that that earth, which kept the world in awe, Should patch a wall to expel the winter's flaw! . . . . *Hamlet* v 1 239
I will tread this unbolted villain into mortar, and daub the walls of a jakes with him . . . . . . *Lear* ii 2 72
Prisoners, patrimony; Dispose of them, of me; the walls are thine . v 3 76
The heavens hold firm The walls of thy dear honour! . *Cymbeline* ii 1 68
Poor I am stale, a garment out of fashion; And, for I am richer than to hang by the walls, I must be ripp'd . . . . iii 4 54

Walled. A lady wall'd about with diamonds! . . *L. L. Lost* v 2 3
As a walled town is more worthier than a village . *As Y. Like It* iii 3 59

Walled. Twelve cities and seven walled towns of strength . 1 *Hen. VI.* iii 4 7
We'll wear out, In a wall'd prison, packs and sects of great ones *Lear* v 3 18
Ditch'd, and wall'd with turf . *Cymbeline* v 3 14
Wallet. Whose throats had hanging at 'em Wallets of flesh *Tempest* iii 3 46
Time hath, my lord, a wallet at his back . *Troi. and Cres.* iii 3 145
Wall-eyed. The vilest stroke That ever wall-eyed wrath or staring rage Presented . . . . . *K. John* iv 3 49
Wall-eyed slave, whither wouldst thou convey This growing image of thy fiend-like face? . . . . . *T. Andron.* v 1 44
Wall-newt. That eats the swimming frog, the toad, the tadpole, the wall-newt, and the water . . . . *Lear* iii 4 135
Wallon and Picardy are friends to us . . 1 *Hen. VI.* ii 1 10
Walloon. A base Walloon, to win the Dauphin's grace, Thrust Talbot with a spear into the back . . . . i 1 137
Wallow. Or wallow naked in December snow By thinking on fantastic summer's heat . . . *Richard II.* i 3 298
To those fields Where I may wallow in the lily-beds . *Troi. and Cres.* iii 2 13
Walnut. As jealous as Ford, that searched a hollow walnut for his wife's leman . . . . *Mer. Wives* iv 2 171
Walnut-shell. 'Tis a cockle or a walnut-shell, A knack, a toy *T. of Shrew* iv 3 66
Walter. Nicholas, Philip, Walter, Sugarsop, and the rest . iv 1 92
And Walter's dagger was not come from sheathing . . iv 1 138
A dear, a true industrious friend, Sir Walter Blunt . 1 *Hen. IV.* i 1 63
Two and twenty knights Balk'd in their own blood did Sir Walter see . i 1 69
Welcome, Sir Walter Blunt; and would to God You were of our determination! . . . . . iv 3 32
Who are you? Sir Walter Blunt: there's honour for you! here's no vanity! . . . . . v 3 32
I like not such grinning honour as Sir Walter hath . . v 3 63
Make boot of this; The other, Walter Whitmore, is thy share 2 *Hen. VI.* iv 1 14
My name is Walter Whitmore. How now! why start'st thou? . . iv 1 31
Gaultier or Walter, which it is, I care not . . . iv 1 38
Walter,— Come, Suffolk, I must waft thee to thy death . iv 1 115
Sir Walter Herbert, a renowned soldier . . *Richard III.* iv 5 9
Sir William Brandon, And you, Sir Walter Herbert, stay with me . v 3 28
Walter Lord Ferrers, Sir Robert Brakenbury, and Sir William Brandon v 5 13
Wan. Ay me, poor man, how pale and wan he looks! *Com. of Errors* iv 4 111
So shaken as we are, so wan with care . . 1 *Hen. IV.* i 1 1
Why doth your highness look so pale and wan? *T. Andron.* ii 3 90
Wand. She is as white as a lily and as small as a wand *T. G. of Ver.* ii 3 23
The skilful shepherd peel'd me certain wands . *Mer. of Venice* i 3 85
On the pieces of the broken wand Were placed the heads . 2 *Hen. VI.* i 2 28
Wander. And wander up and down to view the city *Com. of Errors* i 2 31
Against my soul's pure truth why labour you To make it wander in an unknown field? Are you a god? . . . . iii 2 38
And here we wander in illusions . . . . iv 3 43
How now, spirit! whither wander you?—Over hill, over dale *M. N. D.* ii 1 1
I do wander every where, Swifter than the moon's sphere . ii 1 6
Therefore he gives them good leave to wander. . *As Y. Like It* i 1 109
How now, wit! whither wander you? . . . . i 2 59
And wander we to see thy honest son . . *T. of Shrew* iv 5 69
And when I wander here and there, I then do most go right *W. Tale* iv 3 17
What a deal of world I wander from the jewels that I love *Richard II.* i 3 270
Where'er I wander, boast of this I can, Though banish'd, yet a trueborn Englishman . . . . . i 3 308
With Cain go wander thorough shades of night . . v 6 43
That we may wander o'er this bloody field To look our dead *Hen. V.* iv 7 75
Stay; Thou mayst not wander in that labyrinth . 1 *Hen. VI.* v 3 188
Madam, you wander from the good we aim at . *Hen. VIII.* iii 1 138
When the planets In evil mixture to disorder wander, What plagues and what portents! . . . *Troi. and Cres.* i 3 95
What cursed foot wanders this way to-night, To cross my obsequies? *Rom. and Jul.* v 3 19
I have no will to wander forth of doors, Yet something leads me *J. Cæsar* iii 3 3
And all alone To-night we'll wander through the streets and note The qualities of people . . . *Ant. and Cleo.* i 1 53
Safe mayst thou wander, safe return again . . *Cymbeline* iii 5 105
I may wander From east to occident, cry out for service . iv 2 371
Wandered. As he in penance wander'd through the forest *T. G. of Ver.* v 2 38
The heedful slave Is wander'd forth, in care to seek me out *Com. of Errors* ii 2 3
Had the king permitted us, One of our souls had wander'd in the air *Richard II.* i 3 195
Wherein my youth Hath faulty wander'd . . . 1 *Hen. IV.* iii 2 27
And he himself wander'd away alone, No man knows whither *Richard III.* iv 4 514
And wander'd hither to an obscure plot . . *T. Andron.* ii 3 77
Have wander'd with our traversed arms . . . *T. of Athens* v 4 7
Wanderer. I am that merry wanderer of the night . *M. N. Dream* ii 1 43
Hast thou the flower there? Welcome, wanderer.—Ay, there it is . ii 1 247
The wrathful skies Gallow the very wanderers of the dark . *Lear* iii 2 44
Wandering. What is Thisby? a wandering knight? . *M. N. Dream* i 2 47
Fair love, you faint with wandering in the wood . . ii 2 35
At whose approach, ghosts, wandering here and there, Troop home to churchyards . . . . . iii 2 381
We the globe can compass soon, Swifter than the wandering moon . iv 1 103
Be so humble To cast thy wandering eyes on every stale *T. of Shrew* iii 1 90
A gnat, a wandering hair, Any annoyance in that precious sense *K. John* iv 1 93
Will you permit that I shall stand condemn'd A wandering vagabond? *Richard II.* ii 3 120
Revell'd in the night Whilst we were wandering with the antipodes . iii 2 49
Phœbus, he, 'that wandering knight so fair' . 1 *Hen. IV.* i 2 16
Come, come, return; return, thou wandering lord . 1 *Hen. VI.* iii 3 76
Hath this lovely face Ruled, like a wandering planet, over me? 2 *Hen. VI.* iv 4 16
Would not let it forth To seek the empty, vast, and wandering air *Rich. III.* i 4 39
Then came wandering by A shadow like an angel . . i 4 52
She's wandering to the Tower, On pure heart's love . iv 1 3
Between our Ilium and where she resides, Let it be call'd the wild and wandering flood . . . *Troi. and Cres.* i 1 105
After conflict such as was supposed The wandering prince and Dido once enjoy'd . . . . *T. Andron.* ii 3 22
Whose phrase of sorrow Conjures the wandering stars . *Hamlet* v 1 279
For vice repeated is like the wandering wind . . *Pericles* i 1 96
Wanderingly. Your shafts of fortune, though they hurt you mortally, Yet glance full wanderingly on us . . . iii 3 7
Wand-like. Her stature to an inch; as wand-like straight . v 1 110
Wane. But, O, methinks, how slow This old moon wanes! *M. N. Dream* i 1 4
It appears, by his small light of discretion, that he is in the wane . v 1 258
Waned. I shall interchange My waned state for Henry's regal crown 3 *Hen. VI.* iv 7 4
But all the charms of love, Salt Cleopatra, soften thy waned lip! *Ant. and Cleo.* ii 1 21

Waning. Far more beautiful Than any woman in this waning age *T. of Shrew* Ind. 2 65
Your father were a fool To give thee all, and in his waning age Set foot under thy table . . . . . ii 1 403
I seek not to wax great by others' waning . 2 *Hen. VI.* iv 10 22
Slily have I lurk'd, To watch the waning of mine adversaries *Richard III.* iv 4 4
Wanion. Come away, or I'll fetch thee with a wanion . *Pericles* ii 1 17
Wanned. All his visage wann'd, Tears in his eyes, distraction in's aspect *Hamlet* ii 2 580
Want. What would I do?—'Scape being drunk for want of wine *Tempest* ii 1 146
That dare not offer What I desire to give, and much less take What I shall die to want . . . . . iii 1 79
And what does else want credit, come to me, And I'll be sworn 'tis true . . . . . iii 3 25
Although they want the use of tongue, a kind Of excellent dumb discourse . . . . . iii 3 38
Scarcity and want shall shun you; Ceres' blessing so is on you . iv 1 116
Now I want Spirits to enforce, art to enchant . . Epil. 13
When you looked sadly, it was for want of money . *T. G. of Ver.* ii 1 31
In modesty, Or else for want of idle time, could not again reply . ii 1 172
And duty never yet did want his meed . . . ii 4 112
He wants wit that wants resolved will . . . ii 6 12
Because myself do want my servants' fortune . . iii 1 147
A linguist and a man of such perfection As we do in our quality much want . . . . . iv 1 58
Want no money, Sir John; you shall want none.—Want no Mistress Ford, Master Brook; you shall want none *Mer. Wives* ii 2 268
As idle as she may hang together, for want of company . iii 2 14
There want not many that do fear In deep of night to walk by this Herne's oak . . . . . iv 4 39
Have I laid my brain in the sun and dried it, that it wants matter? . v 5 144
He wants advice.—He will hear none . . *Meas. for Meas.* iv 2 154
For I would commune with you of such things That want no ear but yours . . . . . iv 3 109
Is it dinner-time?—No, sir; I think the meat wants that I have *Com. of Errors* ii 2 57
By all my wit being scann'd, Want wit in all one word to understand . ii 2 153
Who, all for want of pruning, with intrusion Infect thy sap . ii 2 181
I am bound To Persia and want guilders for my voyage . iv 1 4
If he be sad, he wants money . . . *Much Ado* iii 2 20
If their sons be ingenuous, they shall want no instruction . *L. L. Lost* iv 2 81
Where nothing wants that want itself doth seek . . iv 3 237
It was enjoined him in Rome for want of linen . . v 2 719
It wants a twelvemonth and a day, And then 'twill end . v 2 887
How chance the roses there do fade so fast?—Belike for want of rain *M. N. Dream* i 1 130
I will draw a bill of properties, such as our play wants . i 2 108
The human mortals want their winter here . . ii 1 101
To supply the ripe wants of my friend, I'll break a custom *Mer. of Venice* i 3 64
Supply your present wants and take no doit Of usance for my moneys i 3 141
He that wants money, means, and content is without three good friends *As Y. Like It* iii 2 26
By how much defence is better than no skill, by so much is a horn more precious than to want . . . . . iii 3 64
Let them want nothing that my house affords . *T. of Shrew* Ind. 1 104
What mockery will it be, To want the bridegroom when the priest attends! . . . . . iii 2 5
Though bride and bridegroom wants For to supply the places at the table, You know there wants no junkets at the feast . iii 2 248
And that which spites me more than all these wants, He does it under name of perfect love . . . . . iv 3 11
He cannot want the best That shall attend his love. . *All's Well* i 1 81
She's very well and wants nothing i' the world; but yet she is not well ii 4 4
Whose want, and whose delay, is strew'd with sweets, Which they distil now . . . . . ii 4 45
And I shall lose my life for want of language . . iv 1 77
Well, sir, for want of other idleness, I'll bide your proof . *T. Night* i 5 70
The want of which vain dew Perchance shall dry your pities . *W. Tale* ii 1 109
Better not to have had thee than thus to want thee . iv 2 15
I shall there have money, or any thing I want . . iv 3 87
For instance, sir, That you may know you shall not want, one word . iv 4 605
My clown, who wants but something to be a reasonable man . iv 4 617
He is not she; And she again wants nothing, to name want, If want it be not that she is not he . . . *K. John* ii 1 435
Such temperate order in so fierce a cause Doth want example . iii 4 13
The utterance of a brace of tongues Must needs want pleading for a pair of eyes . . . . . iv 1 99
Let hell want pains enough to torture me . . . iv 3 138
And send them after to supply our wants . . *Richard II.* i 4 51
I live with bread like you, feel want, Taste grief, need friends . iii 2 175
It adds more sorrow to my want of joy: For what I have I need not to repeat; And what I want it boots not to complain . . iii 4 16
O, I am press'd to death through want of speaking! . . iii 4 72
The poor abuses of the time want countenance . 1 *Hen. IV.* i 2 175
And let my soul Want mercy, if I do not join with him . i 3 132
Fie upon this quiet life! I want work . . . ii 4 118
Defect of manners, want of government, Pride, haughtiness . iii 1 184
His present want Seems more than we shall find it . iv 1 44
Never yet did insurrection want Such water-colours to impaint his cause v 1 79
Only, we want a little personal strength . . 2 *Hen. IV.* iv 4 8
What you want in meat, we'll have in drink . . . v 3 30
And yet my sky shall not want.—That may be . *Hen. V.* iii 7 78
Ourselves and children Have lost, or do not learn for want of time . v 2 57
Whose want gives growth to the imperfections Which you have cited . v 2 69
What treachery was used?—No treachery; but want of men and money 1 *Hen. VI.* i 1 69
They want their porridge and their fat bull-beeves . . i 2 9
Heaven, be thou gracious to none alive, If Salisbury wants mercy! . i 4 86
Good morrow, gallants! want ye corn for bread? . . iii 2 41
Because you want the grace that others have . . v 4 46
They'll o'ergrow the garden And choke the herbs for want of husbandry 2 *Hen. VI.* iii 1 33
I shall not want false witness to condemn me . . iii 1 168
We want a colour for his death: 'Tis meet he be condemn'd by course of law . . . . . iii 1 236
Like an angry hive of bees That want their leader . . iii 2 126
As one that surfeits thinking on a want . . . iii 2 348
No want of resolution in me, but only my followers' base . . treasons iv 8 65
Nor should thy prowess want praise and esteem, But that 'tis shown ignobly . . . . . v 2 22

Want. 'Tis government that makes them [women] seem divine; The want thereof makes thee abominable . . . . . 3 *Hen. VI.* i 4 133
Ay, therein Clarence shall not want his part . . . iv 6 57
O, welcome, Oxford! for we want thy help . . . v 1 66
My want of strength, my sick heart shows, That I must yield my body to the earth . . . . v 2 8
I, that am rudely stamp'd, and want love's majesty To strut before a wanton ambling nymph . . . *Richard III.* i 1 16
I want more uncles here to welcome me . . . iii 1 6
Those uncles which you want were dangerous . . . iii 1 12
Are all things fitting for that royal time?—It is, and wants but nomination . . . . iii 4 5
O, now I want the priest that spake to me . . . iii 4 89
This noble isle doth want her proper limbs . . . iii 7 125
Besides, the king's name is a tower of strength, Which they upon the adverse party want . . . . . . v 3 13
Let's want no discipline, make no delay . . . v 3 17
For want of means, poor rats, had hang'd themselves . . v 3 331
What his high hatred would effect wants not A minister . *Hen. VIII.* i 1 107
If I blush, It is to see a nobleman want manners.—I had rather want those than my head . . . . . . iii 2 308
Out of which frailty And want of wisdom, you, that best should teach us, Have misdemean'd yourself . . . . v 3 13
A fair young maid that yet wants baptism, You must be godfather v 3 162
Want similes, truth tired with iteration, As true as steel *Troi. and Cres.* iii 2 183
For your wants, Your suffering in this dearth, you may as well Strike at the heaven with your staves . . . *Coriolanus* i 1 68
'Tis not to save labour, nor that I want love . . . i 3 90
When his soaring insolence Shall touch the people—which time shall not want . . . . ii 1 271
Wants not spirit To say he'll turn your current in a ditch . iii 1 95
The inheritance of their loves and safeguard Of what that want might ruin . . . . iii 2 69
Why stay we to be baited With one that wants her wits? . . iv 2 44
He wants nothing of a god but eternity and a heaven to throne in . v 4 24
Thy years want wit, thy wit wants edge, And manners . *T. Andron.* ii 1 26
Thy niece and I, poor creatures, want our hands . . . iii 2 5
Her life was beast-like, and devoid of pity; And, being so, shall have like want of pity . . . . v 3 200
Good night!—A thousand times the worse, to want thy light *R. and J.* ii 2 156
Much of grief shows still some want of wit . . . iii 5 74
If I want gold, steal but a beggar's dog, And give it Timon *T. of Athens* ii 1 5
If you did know, my lord, my master's wants . . . ii 2 29
Poor rogues, and usurers' men! bawds between gold and want! . ii 2 62
In some sort, these wants of mine are crown'd, That I account them blessings . . . . ii 2 190
Now they are at fall, want treasure, cannot Do what they would . ii 2 214
Fie, no, do not believe it; he cannot want for money . . iii 2 10
He cannot want fifty five hundred talents.—But in the mean time he wants less . . . . iii 2 43
It is the pasture lards the rother's sides, The want that makes him lean iv 3 13
The want whereof doth daily make revolt In my penurious band . iv 3 91
Want of gold, and the falling-from of his friends, drove him into this melancholy . . . . iv 3 401
We are not thieves, but men that much do want.—Your greatest want is, you want much of meat . . . . . . iv 3 418
Why should you want? Behold, the earth hath roots . . iv 3 420
Want! why want?—We cannot live on grass, on berries, water . iv 3 424
What an alteration of honour Has desperate want made! . . iv 3 469
Those sparks of life That should be in a Roman you do want . *J. Cæsar* i 3 58
My strange and self-abuse Is the initiate fear that wants hard use *Macb.* iii 4 143
Who cannot want the thought how monstrous It was? . . iii 6 8
He loves us not; He wants the natural touch . . . iv 2 9
A beast, that wants discourse of reason, Would have mourn'd longer *Ham.* i 2 150
Who in want a hollow friend doth try, Directly seasons him his enemy iii 2 218
Then what I have to do Will want true colour; tears perchance for blood iii 4 130
Keeps himself in clouds, And wants not buzzers to infect his ear . iv 5 90
If for I want that glib and oily art, To speak and purpose not . *Lear* i 1 227
But even for want of that for which I am richer . . . i 1 233
You have obedience scanted, And well are worth the want that you have wanted . . . . i 1 282
He that keeps nor crust nor crum, Weary of all, shall want some . i 4 218
You are much more attask'd for want of wisdom Than praised . i 4 366
You cannot see your way.—I have no way, and therefore want no eyes iv 1 20
Lest his ungovern'd rage dissolve the life That wants the means to lead it . . . . iv 4 20
If your will want not, time and place will be fruitfully offered . iv 6 269
For want of these required conveniences, her delicate tenderness will find itself abused . . . . . . *Othello* ii 1 234
How do you now, lieutenant?—The worser that you give me the addition Whose want even kills me . . . . . iv 1 106
I had newly feasted, and did want Of what I was i' the morning *Ant. and Cleo.* ii 2 76
I do not know Wherefore my father should revengers want, Having a son . . . . iii 6 11
Women are not In their best fortunes strong; but want will perjure The ne'er-touch'd vestal . . . . . . iii 12 30
Dido and her Æneas shall want troops, And all the haunt be ours. iv 14 53
Nature wants stuff To vie strange forms with fancy . . v 2 97
Thou shouldst neither want my means for thy relief nor my voice *Cymbeline* iii 5 115
There wants no diligence in seeking him, And will, no doubt, be found iv 3 20
The want is but to put those powers in motion That long to move iv 3 31
Who find in my exile the want of breeding, The certainty of this hard life . . . . iv 4 26
You come in faint for want of meat, depart reeling with too much drink . . . . v 4 163
There are none want eyes to direct them the way I am going. . v 4 192
Who wanteth food, and will not say he wants it? . . *Pericles* i 4 11
If heaven slumber while their creatures want, They may awake their helps . . . . i 4 16
As houses are defiled for want of use, They are now starved for want of exercise . . . . iv 6 37
What I have been I have forgot to know; But what I am, want teaches me to think on . . . . ii 1 76
Come, sir; Here is a lady that wants breathing too . . . ii 3 101
Wherein we are not destitute for want, But weary for the staleness . v 1 57
Wanted the modesty To urge the thing held as a ceremony *Mer. of Venice* v 1 205
Whose worthiness would stir it up where it wanted rather than lack it where there is such abundance . . . . . *All's Well* i 1 11

Wanted. I ne'er heard yet That any of these bolder vices wanted Less impudence . . . . *W. Tale* iii 2 56
Being wanted, he may be more wonder'd at . . 1 *Hen. IV.* i 2 225
He wanted pikes to set before his archers . . 1 *Hen. VI.* i 1 116
Shame that they wanted cunning, in excess Hath broke their hearts *T. of Athens* v 4 28
And well are worth the want that you have wanted . . . *Lear* i 1 282
Out of her impatience, which not wanted Shrewdness of policy too *Ant. and Cleo.* ii 2 68
Wantest. Look, what thou want'st shall be sent after thee *T. G. of Ver.* i 3 74
It seems thou want'st breaking: out upon thee, hind! . *Com. of Errors* iii 1 77
Thou want'st a rough pash and the shoots that I have . *W. Tale* i 2 128
If thou want'st a cord, the smallest thread That ever spider twisted from her womb Will serve to strangle thee . . . *K. John* iv 3 127
If thou wantest any thing, and wilt not call, beshrew thy heart 2 *Hen. IV.* v 3 59
Why art thou old, and want'st experience? . . . 2 *Hen. VI.* v 1 171
Before black-corner'd night, Find what thou want'st . *T. of Athens* v 1 48
Look, where he stands and glares! Wantest thou eyes at trial? *Lear* iii 6 26
Wanteth. There wanteth but a mean to fill your song . *T. G. of Ver.* i 2 95
Another would fly swift, but wanteth wings . . 1 *Hen. VI.* i 2 75
There wanteth now our brother Gloucester here, To make the perfect period of this peace . . . . . . *Richard III.* ii 1 43
Who wanteth food, and will not say he wants it? . . *Pericles* i 4 11
Wanting. Wanting guilders to redeem their lives . *Com. of Errors* i 1 8
Wanting your father's voice, The other must be held the worthier *M. N. Dream* i 1 54
And take upon command what help we have That to your wanting may be minister'd . . . . *As Y. Like It* ii 7 126
A weary way . . . , wanting your company . *Richard II.* ii 3 10
Like glistering Phaëthon, Wanting the manage of unruly jades . . iii 3 179
If of joy, being altogether wanting, It doth remember me the more of sorrow . . . . iii 4 13
The freckled cowslip, burnet, and green clover, Wanting the scythe *Hen. V.* v 2 50
Were our tears wanting to this funeral, These tidings would call forth their flowing tides . . . . . . 1 *Hen. VI.* i 1 82
Such a worthy leader, wanting aid, Unto his dastard foemen is betray'd i 1 143
Like lions wanting food, Do rush upon us as their hungry prey . i 2 27
In thy shoulder do I build my seat, And never will I undertake the thing Wherein thy counsel and consent is wanting . 3 *Hen. VI.* ii 6 102
Tell him his fears are shallow, wanting instance . *Richard III.* iii 2 25
Their negotiations all must slack, Wanting his manage *Troi. and Cres.* iii 3 25
Only There's one thing wanting, which I doubt not but Our Rome will cast upon thee . . . . *Coriolanus* ii 1 217
Wanting strength to do thee so much good . *T. Andron.* ii 3 238
How can I grace my talk, Wanting a hand to give it action? . . v 2 18
Let them find me here: My life were better ended by their hate, Than death prorogued, wanting of thy love . . *Rom. and Jul.* ii 2 78
Which with sweet water nightly I will dew, Or, wanting that, with tears . . . . v 3 15
How came the noble Timon to this change?—As the moon does, by wanting light to give . . . . . . *T. of Athens* iv 3 67
He that is robb'd, not wanting what is stol'n, Let him not know't, and he's not robb'd at all . . . . . . *Othello* iii 3 342
And wanting breath to speak help me with tears . . *Pericles* i 4 19
Wanton. Here thought they to have done Some wanton charm *Tempest* iv 1 95
Dare you presume to harbour wanton lines? . . *T. G. of Ver.* i 2 42
She says it is a fair one.—Nay then, the wanton lies . . v 2 10
Your worship's a wanton! Well, heaven forgive you and all of us! *Mer. Wives* ii 2 57
One who never feels The wanton stings and motions of the sense *Meas. for Meas.* i 4 59
Not to be married, Not to knit my soul to an approved wanton *M. Ado* iv 1 45
A wightly wanton with a velvet brow . . . *L. L. Lost* iii 1 198
O, rhymes are guards on wanton Cupid's hose . . . iv 3 58
Spied a blossom passing fair, Playing in the wanton air . . iv 3 104
Love is full of unbefitting strains, All wanton as a child, skipping and vain . . . . v 2 771
Tarry, rash wanton: am not I thy lord? . . *M. N. Dream* ii 1 63
The quaint mazes in the wanton green For lack of tread are undistinguishable . . . . ii 1 99
To see the sails conceive And grow big-bellied with the wanton wind ii 1 129
Golden locks Which make such wanton gambols with the wind *M. of V.* iii 2 93
A wild and wanton herd, Or race of youthful and unhandled colts . v 1 71
Carry him gently to my fairest chamber And hang it round with all my wanton pictures . . . . . . *T. of Shrew* Ind. 1 47
Cytherea all in sedges hid, Which seem to move and wanton with her breath . . . . Ind. 2 54
Lays down his wanton siege before her beauty . *All's Well* iii 7 18
I liked her, And boarded her i' the wanton way of youth . . v 3 211
They that dally nicely with words may quickly make them wanton *T. Night* iii 1 18
To dally with that word might make my sister wanton . . iii 1 23
How now, you wanton calf! Art thou my calf? . *W. Tale* i 2 126
And then you'ld wanton with us, If we would have you. . ii 1 18
The proud day . . . Is all too wanton and too full of gawds *K. John* iii 3 36
Shall a beardless boy, A cocker'd silken wanton, brave our fields? . v 1 70
Four lagging winters and four wanton springs End in a word *Richard II.* i 3 214
Or shall we play the wantons with our woes? . . . iii 3 164
We make woe wanton with this fond delay: Once more, adieu . v 1 101
Which he, young wanton and effeminate boy, Takes on the point of honour to support . . . . v 3 10
She bids you on the wanton rushes lay you down 1 *Hen. IV.* iii 1 214
Wanton as youthful goats, wild as young bulls . . . iv 1 103
What with the absent king, What with the injuries of a wanton time . v 1 50
Hence, thou sickly quoif! Thou art a guard too wanton for the head 2 *Hen. IV.* i 1 148
Surfeiting and wanton hours Have brought ourselves into a burning fever . . . . iv 1 55
Every slight and false-derived cause, Yea, every idle, nice, and wanton reason . . . . iv 1 191
Lascivious, wanton, more than well beseems A man of thy profession and degree . . . . 1 *Hen. VI.* iii 1 19
And fitter is my study and my books Than wanton dalliance . . v 1 23
The wanton Edward, and the lusty George . . 3 *Hen. VI.* i 4 74
Matching more for wanton lust than honour . . . iii 3 210
I, that am rudely stamp'd, and want love's majesty To strut before a wanton ambling nymph . . . . . *Richard III.* i 1 17
How sleek and wanton Ye appear in every thing may bring my ruin! *Hen. VIII.* iii 2 241

Wanton. I have ventured, Like little wanton boys that swim on bladders, This many summers in a sea of glory *Hen. VIII.* iii 2 359
The ravish'd Helen, Menelaus' queen, With wanton Paris sleeps *Troi. and Cres.* Prol. 10
The weak wanton Cupid Shall from your neck unloose his amorous fold iii 3 222
Her wanton spirits look out At every joint and motive of her body iv 5 56
Yond towers, whose wanton tops do buss the clouds, Must kiss their own feet iv 5 220
To the wanton spoil Of Phœbus' burning kisses *Coriolanus* ii 1 233
To wanton with this queen, This goddess, this Semiramis *T. Andron.* ii 1 21
A torch for me : let wantons light of heart Tickle the senseless rushes with their heels *Rom. and Jul.* i 4 35
I would have thee gone : And yet no further than a wanton's bird ii 2 178
Now comes the wanton blood up in your cheeks, They'll be in scarlet straight ii 5 72
A lover may bestride the gossamer That idles in the wanton summer air, And yet not fall ii 6 19
My plenteous joys, Wanton in fulness, seek to hide themselves In drops of sorrow *Macbeth* i 4 34
Such wanton, wild, and usual slips As are companions noted *Hamlet* ii 1 22
Pinch wanton on your cheek ; call you his mouse iii 4 183
I pray you, pass with your best violence; I am afeard you make a wanton of me v 2 310
She knapped 'em o' the coxcombs with a stick, and cried 'Down, wantons, down!' *Lear* ii 4 126
As flies to wanton boys, are we to the gods, They kill us for their sport iv 1 38
When light-wing'd toys Of feather'd Cupid seel with wanton dullness *Othello* i 3 270
He hath not yet made wanton the night with her; and she is sport for Jove ii 3 16
O, 'tis the spite of hell, the fiend's arch-mock, To lip a wanton in a secure couch, And to suppose her chaste! iv 1 72
So sick I am not, yet I am not well; But not so citizen a wanton as To seem to die ere sick *Cymbeline* iv 2 8
Wantonness. The spirit of wantonness is, sure, scared out of him *M. W.* iv 2 223
I rather will suspect the sun with cold Than thee with wantonness iv 4 8
The blood of youth burns not with such success As gravity's revolt to wantonness *L. L. Lost* v 2 74
Young gentlemen would be as sad as night, Only for wantonness *K. John* iv 1 16
England did never owe so sweet a hope, So much misconstrued in his wantonness 1 *Hen. IV.* v 2 69
How one man eats into another's pride, While pride is fasting in his wantonness! *Troi. and Cres.* iii 3 137
And make your wantonness your ignorance *Hamlet* iii 1 152
Want-wit. And such a want-wit sadness makes of me, That I have much ado to know myself *Mer. of Venice* i 1 6
Wappened. This is it [gold] That makes the wappen'd widow wed again *T. of Athens* iv 3 38
War. 'Twixt the green sea and the azured vault Set roaring war *Tempest* v 1 44
War with good counsel, set the world at nought *T. G. of Ver.* i 1 68
Some to the wars, to try their fortune there; Some to discover islands i 3 8
How likes she my discourse?—Ill, when you talk of war v 2 16
What with the war, what with the sweat, what with the gallows, and what with poverty, I am custom-shrunk *Meas. for Meas.* i 2 83
For which I must not plead, but that I am At war 'twixt will and will not ii 2 33
Herein you war against your reputation *Com. of Errors* iii 1 86
In her forehead; armed and reverted, making war against her heir iii 2 127
Long since thy husband served me in my wars v 1 161
When I bestrid thee in the wars and took Deep scars to save thy life v 1 192
Is Signior Mountanto returned from the wars? *Much Ado* i 1 31
I pray you, how many hath he killed and eaten in these wars? i 1 43
He hath done good service, lady, in these wars i 1 49
There is a kind of merry war betwixt Signior Benedick and her i 1 62
Saying, I liked her ere I went to wars i 1 307
Brave conquerors,—for so you are, That war against your own affections And the huge army of the world's desires *L. L. Lost* i 1 9
The one half of an entire sum Disbursed by my father in his wars ii 1 132
This civil war of wits were much better used ii 1 226
Or, if there were a sympathy in choice, War, death, or sickness did lay siege to it *M. N. Dream* i 1 142
Some war with rere-mice for their leathern wings ii 2 4
Art thou bragging to the stars, Telling the bushes that thou look'st for wars? iii 2 408
Such war of white and red within her cheeks! *T. of Shrew* iv 5 30
Time it is, when raging war is done, To smile at scapes and perils overblown v 2 2
I am ashamed that women are so simple To offer war where they should kneel for peace v 2 162
Why under Mars?—The wars have so kept you under that you must needs be born under Mars *All's Well* i 1 209
Have fought with equal fortune and continue A braving war i 2 3
O, 'tis brave wars!—Most admirable: I have seen those wars ii 1 25
His cicatrice, an emblem of war, here on his sinister cheek ii 1 44
I'll to the Tuscan wars, and never bed her ii 3 290
It no more merits The tread of a man's foot: to the wars! ii 3 292
To the wars, my boy, to the wars! ii 3 295
War is no strife To the dark house and the detested wife ii 3 308
Now have you heard The fundamental reasons of this war iii 1 2
Expose Those tender limbs of thine to the event Of the none-sparing war iii 2 108
Write, that from the bloody course of war . . . your dear son may hie iii 4 8
It was a disaster of war that Cæsar himself could not have prevented iii 6 55
In the mean time, what hear you of these wars? iv 3 45
That had the whole theoric of war in the knot of his scarf iv 3 163
What his valour, honesty, and expertness in wars iv 3 202
He's more and more a cat.—What say you to his expertness in war? iv 3 297
I can tell thee where that saying was born, of 'I fear no colours.'—Where, good Mistress Mary?—In the wars *T. Night* i 5 12
I bring no overture of war, no taxation of homage i 5 225
It was besmear'd As black as Vulcan in the smoke of war v 1 56
The proud control of fierce and bloody war, To enforce these rights *K. John* i 1 17
Here have we war for war and blood for blood, Controlment for controlment i 1 19
Richard, that robb'd the lion of his heart And fought the holy wars ii 1 4
Shadowing their right under your wings of war ii 1 14
The peace of heaven is theirs that lift their swords In such a just and charitable war ii 1 36
From England bring That right in peace which here we urge in war ii 1 47
Peace be to England, if that war return From France to England ii 1 89
War. 'Tis not the roundure of your old-faced walls Can hide you from our messengers of war *K. John* ii 1 260
Gracing the scroll that tells of this war's loss ii 1 348
From a resolved and honourable war, To a most base . . . peace ii 1 585
The grappling vigour and rough frown of war Is cold in amity iii 1 104
Peace!—War! war! no peace! peace is to me a war iii 1 113
And like a civil war set'st oath to oath, Thy tongue against thy tongue iii 1 264
Now for the bare-pick'd bone of majesty Doth dogged war bristle his angry crest And snarleth iv 3 149
My tongue shall hush again this storm of war And make fair weather v 1 20
Glister like the god of war, When he intendeth to become the field v 1 54
And tame the savage spirit of wild war v 2 74
Your breath first kindled the dead coal of wars v 2 83
Who else but I . . . Sweat in this business and maintain this war? v 2 102
Before I drew this gallant head of war, And cull'd these fiery spirits v 2 113
And is well prepared To whip this dwarfish war v 2 135
Let the tongue of war Plead for our interest and our being here v 2 164
With purpose presently to leave this war v 7 86
A woman's war, The bitter clamour of two eager tongues *Richard II.* i 1 48
Why he cometh hither Thus plated in habiliments of war i 3 28
We will ourself in person to this war i 4 42
His coffers shall make coats To deck our soldiers for these Irish wars i 4 62
This fortress built by Nature for herself Against infection and the hand of war ii 1 44
In war was never lion raged more fierce, In peace was never gentle lamb more mild ii 1 173
Wars have not wasted it, for warr'd he hath not ii 1 252
More hath he spent in peace than they in wars ii 1 255
He hath not money for these Irish wars ii 1 259
With eight tall ships, three thousand men of war ii 1 286
With signs of war about his aged neck ii 2 74
How shall we do for money for these wars? ii 2 104
And what stir Keeps good old York there with his men of war? ii 3 52
Frighting her pale-faced villages with war ii 3 94
The one in fear to lose what they enjoy, The other to enjoy by rage and war ii 4 14
Terrible hell make war Upon their spotted souls for this offence! iii 2 133
Some slain in war; Some haunted by the ghosts they have deposed iii 2 157
He is come to open The purple testament of bleeding war iii 3 94
And toil'd with works of war, retired himself To Italy iv 1 96
Tumultuous wars Shall kin with kin and kind with kind confound iv 1 140
No more shall trenching war channel her fields 1 *Hen. IV.* i 1 7
The edge of war, like an ill-sheathed knife, No more shall cut his master i 1 17
He never did fall off, my sovereign liege, But by the chance of war i 3 95
And heard thee murmur tales of iron wars ii 3 51
Thy spirit within thee hath been so at war And thus hath so bestirr'd thee ii 3 59
We must all to the wars, and thy place shall be honourable ii 4 596
She'll be a soldier too, she'll to the wars iii 1 195
To the fire-eyed maid of smoky war All hot and bleeding will we offer them iv 1 114
When he was personal in the Irish war iv 3 88
Will you again unknit This churlish knot of all-abhorred war? v 1 16
The contrarious winds that held the king So long in his unlucky Irish wars v 1 53
Sound all the lofty instruments of war, And by that music let us all embrace v 2 98
Whiles the big year, swoln with some other grief, Is thought with child by the stern tyrant war 2 *Hen. IV.* Ind. 14
You cast the event of war, my noble lord, And summ'd the account of chance i 1 166
A young knave, and begging! Is there not wars? is there not employment? i 2 85
I have the wars for my colour, and my pension shall seem the more reasonable i 2 275
If this present quality of war, Indeed the instant action i 3 36
O yet, for God's sake, go not to these wars! ii 3 9
To look upon the hideous god of war In disadvantage ii 3 35
Thou art going to the wars; and whether I shall ever see thee again or no, there is nobody cares ii 4 72
And in two years after Were they at wars iii 1 60
And were these inward wars once out of hand, We would, dear lords, unto the Holy Land iii 1 107
Thou shalt go to the wars in a gown; we will have away thy cold iii 2 196
Into the harsh and boisterous tongue of war iv 1 49
Turning your books to graves, your ink to blood, Your pens to lances, and your tongue divine To a loud trumpet and a point of war iv 1 52
Show awhile like fearful war, To diet rank minds sick of happiness iv 1 63
Whereon this Hydra son of war is born iv 2 38
Doth the man of war stay all night? v 1 31
That war, or peace, or both at once, may be As things . . . familiar to us v 2 138
List his discourse of war, and you shall hear A fearful battle render'd you in music *Hen. V.* i 1 43
Take heed . . . How you awake our sleeping sword of war i 2 22
Let our proportions for these wars Be soon collected i 2 304
We doubt not of a fair and lucky war ii 2 184
Cheerly to sea; the signs of war advance ii 2 192
To line and new repair our towns of war With men of courage ii 4 7
Though war nor no known quarrel were in question ii 4 17
Assembled and collected, As were a war in expectation ii 4 20
Take mercy On the poor souls for whom this hungry war Opens his vasty jaws ii 4 104
When the blast of war blows in our ears, Then imitate the action of the tiger iii 1 5
Be copy now to men of grosser blood, And teach them how to war iii 1 25
Look you, the mines is not according to the disciplines of the war iii 2 64
He has no more directions in the true disciplines of the wars, look you, of the Roman disciplines, than is a puppy-dog iii 2 76
Of great expedition and knowledge in th' aunchient wars iii 2 83
In the disciplines of the pristine wars of the Romans iii 2 87
As partly touching or concerning the disciplines of the war, the Roman wars iii 2 103
The day is hot, and the weather, and the wars, and the king, and the dukes iii 2 114
Impious war, Array'd in flames like to the prince of fiends iii 3 15
Now and then goes to the wars, to grace himself at his return into London under the form of a soldier iii 6 71
And this they con perfectly in the phrase of war iii 6 79
When the true and aunchient prerogatifes and laws of the wars is not kept iv 1 68
If you would take the pains but to examine the wars of Pompey the Great iv 1 69
You shall find the ceremonies of the wars, and the cares of it iv 1 73
Some, making the wars their bulwark, that have before gored the gentle bosom of peace with pillage and robbery iv 1 173

War. War is his beadle, war is his vengeance *Hen. V.* iv 1 178
Therefore should every soldier in the wars do as every sick man in his bed iv 1 188
And is good knowledge and literatured in the wars iv 7 157
And patches will I get unto these cudgell'd scars, And swear I got them in the Gallia wars v 1 94
Beshrew my father's ambition! he was thinking of civil wars when he got me v 2 243
They are all girdled with maiden walls that war hath never entered v 2 349
That never war advance His bleeding sword 'twixt England and fair France v 2 382
One would have lingering wars with little cost *1 Hen. VI.* i 1 74
Nor men nor money hath he to make war i 2 17
Halcyon days, Since I have entered into these wars i 2 132
A foe to citizens, One that still motions war and never peace i 3 63
Henry the Fifth he first train'd to the wars i 4 79
I see our wars Will turn unto a peaceful comic sport, When ladies crave to be encounter'd with ii 2 44
And prosperous be thy life in peace and war!—And peace, no war, befall thy parting soul! ii 5 114
I have awhile given truce unto my wars, To do my duty iii 4 3
We were resolved of your truth, Your faithful service, and your toil in war iii 4 21
The Dauphin, well appointed, Stands with the snares of war to tangle thee iv 2 22
If he miscarry, farewell wars in France iv 3 16
I did send for thee To tutor thee in stratagems of war iv 5 2
Great marshal to Henry the Sixth Of all his wars within the realm of France iv 7 71
Enjoy mine own, . . . Free from oppression or the stroke of war v 3 155
To ease your country of distressful war, And suffer you to breathe in fruitful peace v 4 126
Or we will plague thee with incessant wars v 4 154
What! did my brother Henry spend his youth, His valour, coin, and people, in the wars? *2 Hen. VI.* i 1 79
Shall Henry's conquest, Bedford's vigilance, Your deeds of war, and all our counsel die? i 1 97
I myself, Rather than bloody war shall cut them short, Will parley iv 4 12
Wilt thou go dig a grave to find out war, And shame thine honourable age with blood? v 1 169
Thus war hath given thee peace, for thou art still v 2 29
O war, thou son of hell, Whom angry heavens do make their minister! v 2 33
He that is truly dedicate to war Hath no self-love v 2 37
Frowns, words, and threats Shall be the war that Henry means to use *3 Hen. VI.* i 1 73
No: first shall war unpeople this my realm i 1 126
In dreadful war mayst thou be overcome, Or live in peace abandon'd! i 1 187
To cease this civil war, and, whilst I live, To honour me as thy king i 1 197
God forbid your grace should be forsworn.—I shall be, if I claim by open war i 2 19
It is war's prize to take all vantages i 4 59
He was lately sent . . . With aid of soldiers to this needful war ii 1 147
As famous and as bold in war As he is famed for mildness, peace, and prayer ii 1 155
Make war with him that climb'd unto their nest ii 2 31
Like to the morning's war, When dying clouds contend with growing light ii 5 1
So is the equal poise of this fell war ii 5 13
O bloody times! Whiles lions war and battle for their dens ii 5 74
Let our hearts and eyes, like civil war, Be blind with tears ii 5 77
Good fortune bids us pause, And smooth the frowns of war ii 6 32
And force the tyrant from his seat by war iii 3 206
I long till Edward fall by war's mischance, For mocking marriage with a dame of France iii 3 254
Matter of marriage was the charge he gave me, But dreadful war shall answer his demand iii 3 259
An olive branch and laurel crown, As likely to be blest in peace and war iv 6 35
We shall have more wars before't be long iv 6 91
These gates must not be shut But in the night or in the time of war iv 7 36
I have true-hearted friends, Not mutinous in peace, yet bold in war iv 8 10
So blunt, unnatural, To bend the fatal instruments of war Against his brother? v 1 87
Grim-visaged war hath smooth'd his wrinkled front *Richard III.* i 1 9
If not by war, by surfeit die your king, As ours by murder! i 3 197
A thousand fearful times, During the wars of York and Lancaster i 4 15
Art thou yet to thy own soul so blind, That thou wilt war with God? i 4 260
The conquerors Make war upon themselves; blood against blood ii 4 62
My princely father then had wars in France iii 5 88
Your discipline in war, wisdom in peace, Your bounty, virtue iii 7 16
Or with the clamorous report of war Thus will I drown your exclamations iv 4 152
Ere from this war thou turn a conqueror iv 4 184
So thrive I in my enterprise And dangerous success of bloody wars! iv 4 236
Infer fair England's peace by this alliance.—Which she shall purchase with still lasting war iv 4 344
To reap the harvest of perpetual peace By this one bloody trial of sharp war v 2 16
To the arbitrement Of bloody strokes and mortal-staring war v 3 90
The pretence for this Is named, your wars in France *Hen. VIII.* i 2 60
Nay, ladies, fear not; By all the laws of war you're privileged i 4 52
More pangs and fears than wars or women have iii 2 370
Like rams In the old time of war iv 1 78
Ships, Fraught with the ministers and instruments Of cruel war *Troi. and Cres.* Prol. 5
Do as your pleasures are: Now good or bad, 'tis but the chance of war Prol. 31
I'll unarm again: Why should I war without the walls of Troy, That find such cruel battle here within? i 1 2
As there were husbandry in war, Before the sun rose he was harness'd light i 2 7
Makes factious feasts; rails on our state of war, Bold as an oracle i 3 191
Count wisdom as no member of the war, Forestall prescience i 3 198
Yoke you like draught-oxen and make you plough up the wars ii 1 117
And what else dear that is consumed In hot digestion of this cormorant war ii 2 6
For that, methinks, is the curse dependant on those that war for a placket ii 3 22
Now, the dry serpigo on the subject! and war and lechery confound all! ii 3 81
Bring action hither, this cannot go to war ii 3 145
Please it our great general To call together all his state of war ii 3 271
In that I'll war with you.—O virtuous fight, When right with right wars who shall be most right! iii 2 178
They think my little stomach to the war And your great love to me restrains you thus iii 3 220
We have had pelting wars, since you refused The Grecians' cause iv 5 267

War. Still, wars and lechery; nothing else holds fashion *Troi. and Cres.* v 2 195
Let grow thy sinews till their knots be strong, And tempt not yet the brushes of the war v 3 34
Hector, then 'tis wars.—Troilus, I would not have you fight to-day v 3 49
Great Troy is ours, and our sharp wars are ended v 9 10
If the wars eat us not up, they will *Coriolanus* i 1 87
What would you have, you curs, That like nor peace nor war? i 1 173
Were half to half the world by the ears and he Upon my party, I'ld revolt, to make Only my wars with him i 1 239
Attend upon Cominius to these wars.—It is your former promise i 1 241
The present wars devour him: he is grown Too proud to be so valiant i 1 262
To a cruel war I sent him; from whence he returned, his brows bound with oak i 3 15
I'll not over the threshold till my lord return from the wars i 3 83
They nothing doubt prevailing and to make it brief wars i 3 112
By the fires of heaven, I'll leave the foe And make my wars on you i 4 40
When steel grows soft as the parasite's silk, Let him be made a coverture for the wars! i 9 46
Caius Marcius Wears this war's garland i 9 60
He gives my son the whole name of the war ii 1 149
The war of white and damask in Their nicely-gawded cheeks ii 1 232
Of no more soul nor fitness for the world Than camels in the war ii 1 267
When, by and by, the din of war gan pierce His ready sense ii 2 119
Being press'd to the war, Even when the navel of the state was touch'd iii 1 122
Being i' the war, Their mutinies and revolts, wherein they show'd Most valour, spoke not for them iii 1 125
He has been bred i' the wars Since he could draw a sword iii 1 320
When one but of my ordinance stood up To speak of peace or war iii 2 13
Honour and policy, like unsever'd friends, I' the war do grow together iii 2 43
If it be honour in your wars to seem The same you are not, which, for your best ends, You adopt your policy, how is it less or worse, That it shall hold companionship in peace With honour, as in war, since that to both It stands in like request? iii 2 46
My throat of war be turn'd, Which quired with my drum, into a pipe Small as an eunuch! iii 2 112
Throng our large temples with the shows of peace, And not our streets with war! iii 3 37
Thou art too full Of the wars' surfeits, to go rove with one That's yet unbruised iv 1 46
Your noble Tullus Aufidius will appear well in these wars iv 3 36
Many an heir Of these fair edifices 'fore my wars Have I heard groan iv 4 3
Pouring war Into the bowels of ungrateful Rome, Like a bold flood o'er-bear iv 5 135
Let me have war, say I; it exceeds peace as far as day does night iv 5 236
And as war, in some sort, may be said to be a ravisher, so it cannot be denied but peace is a great maker of cuckolds iv 5 242
The wars for my money. I hope to see Romans as cheap as Volscians iv 5 248
A worthy officer i' the war; but insolent, O'ercome with pride iv 6 30
With the deepest malice of the war Destroy what lies before 'em iv 6 41
Commanding peace Even with the same austerity and garb As he controll'd the war iv 7 45
And stick i' the wars Like a great sea-mark, standing every flaw v 3 73
For myself, son, I purpose not to wait on fortune till These wars determine v 3 120
Thou know'st, great son, The end of war's uncertain v 3 141
Has cluck'd thee to the wars and safely home, Loaden with honour v 3 163
Aufidius, though I cannot make true wars, I'll frame convenient peace v 3 190
With bloody passage led your wars even to The gates of Rome v 6 76
Breaking his oath and resolution like A twist of rotten silk, never admitting Counsel o' the war v 6 97
He by the senate is accited home From weary wars *T. Andron.* i 1 28
Sleep in peace, slain in your country's wars! i 1 91
Welcome, nephews, from successful wars, You that survive, and you that sleep! i 1 172
Though chance of war hath wrought this change of cheer i 1 264
For pity of mine age, whose youth was spent In dangerous wars iii 1 3
Nor the god of war Shall seize this prey out of his father's hands iv 2 95
With revengeful war Take wreak on Rome for this ingratitude iv 3 32
This to Mercury; This to Apollo; this to the god of war iv 4 15
He dies.—Hard fate! he might have died in war *T. of Athens* iii 5 75
If by this crime he owes the law his life, Why, let the war receive't in valiant gore; For law is strict, and war is nothing more iii 5 84
Religious canons, civil laws are cruel; Then what should war be? iv 3 61
Let the unscarr'd braggarts of the war Derive some pain from you iv 3 161
Giving our holy virgins to the stain Of contumelious, beastly, mad-brain'd war v 1 177
We were not all unkind, nor all deserve The common stroke of war v 4 22
That thou wilt use the wars as thy redress And not as our confusion v 4 51
Make war breed peace, make peace stint war, make each Prescribe to other v 4 83
Poor Brutus, with himself at war, Forgets the shows of love to other men *J. Cæsar* i 2 46
Fierce fiery warriors fought upon the clouds, In ranks and squadrons and right form of war ii 2 20
That mothers shall but smile when they behold Their infants quarter'd with the hands of war iii 1 268
Cry 'Havoc,' and let slip the dogs of war iii 1 273
What should the wars do with these jigging fools? Companion, hence iv 3 137
Contending 'gainst obedience, as they would make War with mankind *Macbeth* ii 4 18
Hath so exasperate the king that he Prepares for some attempt of war iii 6 39
But certain issue strokes must arbitrate: Towards which advance the war v 4 21
The noble thanes do bravely in the war v 7 26
Why such daily cast of brazen cannon, And foreign mart for implements of war; Why such impress of shipwrights? *Hamlet* i 1 74
So like the king That was and is the question of these wars i 1 111
You from the Polack wars, and you from England, Are here arrived v 2 387
The soldiers' music and the rites of war Speak loudly for him v 2 410
Have you heard of no likely wars toward? *Lear* ii 1 11
Let's then determine With the ancient of war on our proceedings v 1 32
I hold you but a subject of this war, Not as a brother v 3 60
With a bombast circumstance Horribly stuff'd with epithets of war *Othello* i 1 14
He's embark'd With such loud reason to the Cyprus wars i 1 151
Though in the trade of war I have slain men i 2 1
Hath made the flinty and steel couch of war My thrice-driven bed of down i 3 231
I do agnize A natural and prompt alacrity I find in hardness, and do undertake These present wars i 3 235
If I be left behind, A moth of peace, and he go to the war, The rites for which I love him are bereft me i 3 257

War. Put money in thy purse ; follow thou the wars *Othello* i 3 345
Our wars are done. The desperate tempest hath so bang'd the Turks ii 1 20
In a town of war, Yet wild, the people's hearts brimful of fear, To manage private and domestic quarrel ! ii 3 213
The wars must make examples Out of their best iii 3 65
Farewell the plumed troop, and the big wars, That make ambition virtue ! iii 3 349
All quality, Pride, pomp, and circumstance of glorious war ! iii 3 354
Those his goodly eyes, That o'er the files and musters of the war Have glow'd like plated Mars *Ant. and Cleo.* i 1 3
But soon that war had end, and the time's state Made friends of them i 2 95
Whose better issue in the war, from Italy, Upon the first encounter, drave them i 2 97
Pompey's name strikes more Than could his war resisted i 4 55
Mark Antony In Egypt sits at dinner, and will make No wars without doors ii 1 13
I did not think This amorous surfeiter would have donn'd his helm For such a petty war ii 1 34
Your wife and brother Made wars upon me ; and their contestation Was theme for you, you were the word of war ii 2 43
And make the wars alike against my stomach, Having alike your cause ii 2 50
Could not with graceful eyes attend those wars Which fronted mine own peace ii 2 60
Would we had all such wives, that the men might go to wars with the women ! ii 2 66
Truth is, that Fulvia, To have me out of Egypt, made wars here ii 2 95
It raises the greater war between him and his discretion ii 7 10
Who does i' the wars more than his captain can Becomes his captain's captain iii 1 21
Signify what in his name, That magical word of war, we have effected iii 1 31
He hath waged New wars 'gainst Pompey ; made his will, and read it iii 4 4
Lady, I'll raise the preparation of a war Shall stain your brother iii 4 26
Wars 'twixt you twain would be As if the world should cleave, and that slain men Should solder up the rift iii 4 30
Cæsar and Lepidus have made wars upon Pompey.—This is old : what is the success? iii 5 4
Cæsar, having made use of him in the wars 'gainst Pompey, presently denied him rivality iii 5 8
Mark Antony, Hearing that you prepared for war, acquainted My grieved ear iii 6 58
Who now are levying The kings o' the earth for war iii 6 68
Thou hast forspoke my being in these wars, And say'st it is not fit iii 7 3
'Tis said in Rome That Photinus an eunuch and your maids Manage this war iii 7 16
A charge we bear i' the war, And, as the president of my kingdom, will Appear there for a man iii 7 17
Dealt on lieutenantry, and no practice had In the brave squares of war iii 11 40
What though you fled From that great face of war, whose several ranges Frighted each other? why should he follow? iii 13 5
That thou couldst see my wars to-day, and knew'st The royal occupation ! iv 4 16
That he and Cæsar might Determine this great war in single fight ! iv 4 37
Thou Hast sold me to this novice ; and my heart Makes only wars on thee iv 12 15
This grave charm,—Whose eye beck'd forth my wars, and call'd them home iv 12 26
I made these wars for Egypt : and the queen,—Whose heart I thought I had iv 14 15
O, wither'd is the garland of the war, The soldier's pole is fall'n iv 15 64
My mate in empire, Friend and companion in the front of war v 1 44
You shall see How hardly I was drawn into this war v 1 74
Who in the wars o' the time Died with their swords in hand *Cymbeline* i 1 35
I do believe, Statist though I am none, nor like to be, That this will prove a war ii 4 17
War and confusion In Cæsar's name pronounce I 'gainst thee iii 1 66
Revolve what tales I have told you Of courts, of princes, of the tricks in war iii 3 15
The toil o' the war, A pain that only seems to seek out danger I' the name of fame and honour iii 3 49
From whence he moves His war for Britain iii 5 26
The legions now in Gallia are Full weak to undertake our wars iii 7 5
What have you dream'd of late of this war's purpose? iv 2 345
My queen Upon a desperate bed, and in a time When fearful wars point at me iv 3 7
These present wars shall find I love my country, Even to the note o' the king iv 3 43
If in your country wars you chance to die, That is my bed too, lads iv 4 51
For friends kill friends, and the disorder's such As war were hoodwink'd v 2 16
Turn'd coward But by example—O, a sin in war, Damn'd in the first beginners ! v 3 36
[Death] hath more ministers than we That draw his knives i' the war v 3 73
Consider, sir, the chance of war : the day Was yours by accident v 5 75
Never was a war did cease, Ere bloody hands were wash'd, with such a peace v 5 484
Here they stand martyrs, slain in Cupid's wars *Pericles* i 1 38
And with the ostent of war will look so huge, Amazement shall drive courage from the state i 2 25
When Signior Sooth here does proclaim a peace, He flatters you, makes war upon your life i 2 45
When all, for mine, if I may call offence, Must feel war's blow, who spares not innocence i 2 93
Who either by public war or private treason Will take away your life i 2 104
Welcome is peace, if he on peace consist ; If wars, we are unable to resist i 4 84
What would you have me do? go to the wars, would you? iv 6 181

Warble, child ; make passionate my sense of hearing *L. L. Lost* iii 1 1
Come, warble, come *As Y. Like It* ii 5 38

Warbling. Both warbling of one song, both in one key *M. N. Dream* iii 2 206
Rehearse your song by rote, To each word a warbling note v 1 405

Ward. Come from thy ward, For I can here disarm thee *Tempest* i 2 471
I could drive her then from the ward of her purity *Mer. Wives* ii 2 258
Are there not men in your ward sufficient to serve it? *Meas. for Meas.* ii 1 281
If you have any thing to say to me, come to my ward iv 3 66
I should wrong it, To lock it in the wards of covert bosom v 1 10
The best ward of mine honour is rewarding my dependents *L. L. Lost* iii 1 133
I must attend his majesty's command, to whom I am now in ward *All's Well* i 1 5
Say this to him, He's beat from his best ward *W. Tale* i 2 33
What wards, what blows, what extremities he endured 1 *Hen. IV.* i 2 212
Thou knowest my old ward ; here I lay, and thus I bore my point ii 4 215
Maid Marian may be the deputy's wife of the ward to thee iii 3 130

Ward. Ere they will have me go to ward, They'll pawn their swords 2 *Hen. VI.* v 1 112
Then, if you fight against God's enemy, God will in justice ward you as his soldiers *Richard III.* v 3 254
You are such a woman ! one knows not at what ward you lie *T. and C.* i 2 283
At all these wards I lie, at a thousand watches i 2 288
If I cannot ward what I would not have hit, I can watch you for telling how I took the blow i 2 292
His son is thirty.—Will you tell me that? His son was but a ward two years ago *Rom. and Jul.* i 5 42
Doors, that were ne'er acquainted with their wards Many a bounteous year, must be employ'd Now to guard sure their master *T. of Athens* iii 3 38
Many confines, wards, and dungeons, Denmark being one o' the worst *Ham.* ii 2 252
The father should be as ward to the son, and the son manage his revenue *Lear* i 2 79

Warded. It was a hand that warded him From thousand dangers *T. An.* iii 1 195

Warden. I must have saffron to colour the warden pies *W. Tale* iv 3 48

Warder. Stay, the king hath thrown his warder down *Richard II.* i 3 118
When the king did throw his warder down, His own life hung upon the staff he threw 2 *Hen. IV.* iv 1 125
Where be these warders, that they wait not here? 1 *Hen. VI.* i 3 3
That memory, the warder of the brain, Shall be a fume *Macbeth* i 7 65
Though castles topple on their warders' heads iv 1 56

Wardrobe. Look what a wardrobe here is for thee !—Let it alone, thou fool ; it is but trash *Tempest* iv 1 222
The lady of the Strachy married the yeoman of the wardrobe *T. Night* ii 5 45
Obtaining of suits, whereof the hangman hath no lean wardrobe 1 *Hen. IV.* i 2 82
I will kill all his coats ; I'll murder all his wardrobe v 3 27
Silken dalliance in the wardrobe lies *Hen. V.* ii Prol. 2

Ware. Retails his wares At wakes and wassails *L. L. Lost* v 2 317
Big enough for the bed of Ware in England *T. Night* iii 2 51
Has he any unbraided wares? *W. Tale* iv 4 204
Money's a medler, That doth utter all men's ware-a iv 4 330
Let us, like merchants, show our foulest wares, And think, perchance, they'll sell *Troi. and Cres.* i 3 359

'Ware pencils, ho ! let me not die your debtor *L. L. Lost* v 2 43
Thou speakest wiser than thou art ware of *As Y. Like It* ii 4 58
I shall ne'er be ware of mine own wit till I break my shins against it ii 4 59
Come, come, you'll do him wrong ere you're ware *Troi. and Cres.* iv 2 57
'Loo, Paris, 'loo ! The bull has the game : ware horns, ho! v 7 12
He was ware of me And stole into the covert of the wood *Rom. and Jul.* i 1 131
I should have been more strange, I must confess, But that thou overheard'st, ere I was ware ii 2 103

Warily I stole into a neighbour thicket by *L. L. Lost* v 2 93
They that ride so and ride not warily, fall into foul bogs *Hen. V.* ii 7 61

Warlike. Your many war-like, court-like, and learned preparations *M. W.* ii 2 237
Unfold to us some warlike resistance.—There is none *All's Well* i 1 128
These warlike principles Do not throw from you ii 1 1
Where the warlike Smalus, That noble honour'd lord, is fear'd and loved *W. Tale* v 1 157
We tread In warlike march these greens before your town *K. John* ii 1 242
Many thousand warlike French That were embattailed iv 2 199
And flesh his spirit in a warlike soil v 1 71
Warlike John ; and in his forehead sits A bare-ribb'd death v 2 176
By the buried hand of warlike Gaunt *Richard II.* iii 3 109
The noble Westmoreland and warlike Blunt 1 *Hen. IV.* iv 4 30
Then should the warlike Harry, like himself, Assume the port of Mars *Hen. V.* Prol. 5
Invoke his warlike spirit, And your great-uncle's, Edward the Black Prince i 2 104
Thou shalt be fortunate, If thou receive me for thy warlike mate 1 *Hen. VI.* i 2 92
Ne'er heard I of a warlike enterprise More venturous or desperate ii 1 44
Which of this princely train Call ye the warlike Talbot? ii 2 35
The reason moved these warlike lords to this ii 5 70
Warlike and martial Talbot, Burgundy Enshrines thee in his heart iii 2 118
To Bourdeaux, warlike duke ! to Bourdeaux, York ! iv 3 22
He dies, we lose ; I break my warlike word ; We mourn, France smiles iv 3 31
Young John, who two hours since I met in travel toward his warlike father iv 3 36
Till with thy warlike sword, despite of fate, To my determined time thou gavest new date iv 6 8
Leaden age, Quicken'd with youthful spleen and warlike rage iv 6 13
The stout Parisians do revolt And turn again unto the warlike French v 2 3
May he be suffocate, That dims the honour of this warlike isle ! 2 *Hen. VI.* i 1 125
Northumberland, Whose warlike ears could never brook retreat 3 *Hen. VI.* i 1 5
So fled his enemies my warlike father ii 1 19
The king, Who look'd full gently on his warlike queen ii 1 123
When thy warlike father, like a child, Told the sad story *Richard III.* i 2 160
When thou didst crown his warlike brows with paper i 3 175
What think'st thou, Norfolk?—A good direction, warlike sovereign v 3 302
What warlike voice, And to what end, is this? *Hen. VIII.* i 4 50
The deep-drawing barks do there disgorge Their warlike fraughtage *Troi. and Cres.* Prol. 13
You brace of warlike brothers, welcome hither iv 5 175
He says he is content: The warlike service he has done, consider *Cor.* iii 3 49
They are in a most warlike preparation iv 3 17
By the gods that warlike Goths adore *T. Andron.* ii 1 61
Thy two sons' heads, Thy warlike hand, thy mangled daughter here iii 1 256
Is warlike Lucius general of the Goths? iv 4 69
Thy thrice-valiant son, Who leads towards Rome a band of warlike Goths v 2 113
Welcome, dread queen ; Welcome, ye warlike Goths v 3 27
To wake Northumberland and warlike Siward *Macbeth* iii 6 31
Old Siward, with ten thousand warlike men iv 3 134
Before my body I throw my warlike shield v 8 33
Together with that fair and warlike form *Hamlet* i 1 47
Our queen, The imperial jointress to this warlike state i 2 9
A pirate of very warlike appointment gave us chase iv 6 15
What warlike noise is this?—Young Fortinbras . . . To the ambassadors of England gives This warlike volley v 2 360
Since thy outside looks so fair and warlike *Lear* v 3 142
For that it stands not in such warlike brace *Othello* i 3 24
Michael Cassio, Lieutenant to the warlike Moor Othello ii 1 27
Thanks, you the valiant of this warlike isle, That so approve the Moor ! ii 1 43
Noble swelling spirits, . . . The very elements of this warlike isle ii 3 59
Welcome : Thou look'st like him that knows a warlike charge *A. and C.* iv 4 19
Did put the yoke upon's ; which to shake off Becomes a warlike people *Cymbeline* iii 1 53
Subtle as the fox for prey, Like warlike as the wolf for what we eat iii 3 41
When on my three-foot stool I sit and tell The warlike feats I have done iii 3 90

Warm. Legged like a man! and his fins like arms! Warm o' my troth *Tempest* ii 2 35
This sensible warm motion to become A kneaded clod *Meas. for Meas.* iii 1 120
Allowed by order of law a furred gown to keep him warm . iii 2 9
Your cake there is warm within; you stand here in the cold *Com. of Er.* iii 1 71
When I am cold, he heats me with beating; when I am warm, he cools me with beating . . . . iv 4 35
If he have wit enough to keep himself warm, let him bear it *Much Ado* i 1 69
Why should a man, whose blood is warm within, Sit like his grandsire cut in alabaster? . . . . . . *Mer. of Venice* i 1 83
Go to thy cold bed, and warm thee . *T. of Shrew* Ind. 1 10; *Lear* iii 4 48
Balm his foul head in warm distilled waters *T. of Shrew* Ind. 1 48
Am I not wise?—Yes; keep you warm.—Marry, so I mean . . ii 1 268
I am sent before to make a fire, and they are coming after to warm them iv 1 5
But I, with blowing the fire, shall warm myself . . . iv 1 10
To watch the night in storms, the day in cold, Whilst thou liest warm at home . . . . v 2 151
O, thus she stood, Even with such life of majesty, warm life, As now it coldly stands! . . . . . . *W. Tale* v 3 35
Masterly done: The very life seems warm upon her lip . . v 3 66
O, she's warm! If this be magic, let it be an art Lawful as eating . v 3 109
Whiles warm life plays in that infant's veins . *K. John* iii 4 132
Full of warm blood, of mirth, of gossiping . . . . v 2 59
The sun that warms you here shall shine on me . *Richard II.* i 3 145
Such a commodity of warm slaves, as had as lieve hear the devil as a drum . . . . *1 Hen. IV.* iv 2 19
The sherris warms it and makes it course from the inwards *2 Hen. IV.* iv 3 115
Maids, well summered and warm kept, are like flies at Bartholomew-tide *Hen. V.* v 2 335
I fear me you but warm the starved snake . . *2 Hen. VI.* iii 1 343
Whiles thy head is warm and new cut off, Write in the dust this *3 Hen. VI.* v 1 55
Swills your warm blood like wash *Richard III.* v 2 9
He's not yet through warm: force him with praises: pour in *T. and C.* ii 3 232
I am not warm yet; let us fight again.—As Hector pleases . iv 5 118
By his looks methinks 'Tis warm at's heart . . *Coriolanus* ii 3 160
A crimson river of warm blood, Like to a bubbling fountain *T. Andron.* ii 4 22
In winter with warm tears I'll melt the snow . . . iii 1 20
O, take this warm kiss on thy pale cold lips! . . . . v 3 153
Had she affections and warm youthful blood She would be as swift in motion as a ball . . . . . *Rom. and Jul.* ii 5 12
Thy lips are warm . . . . v 3 167
And Juliet bleeding, warm, and newly dead . . . . v 3 175
Romeo dead; and Juliet, dead before, Warm and new kill'd . v 3 197
What, think'st That the bleak air, thy boisterous chamberlain, Will put thy shirt on warm? . . . . . *T. of Athens* iv 3 223
It warms the very sickness in my heart . . . *Hamlet* iv 7 56
Thou out of heaven's benediction comest To the warm sun! . *Lear* ii 2 169
If only to go warm were gorgeous, Why, nature needs not what thou gorgeous wear'st, Which scarcely keeps thee warm . . . ii 4 271
In, fellow, there, into the hovel: keep thee warm . . . iii 4 179
Wear your gloves, Or feed on nourishing dishes, or keep you warm *Oth.* iii 3 78
Whilst yet with Parthian blood thy sword is warm, The fugitive Parthians follow; spur through Media . . *Ant. and Cleo.* iii 1 6
It would warm his spirits, To hear from me you had left Antony . iii 13 69
I have a gown here; come, put it on; keep thee warm . *Pericles* ii 1 84
War-man. The sweet war-man is dead and rotten *L. L. Lost* v 2 666
War-marked. Distract your army, which doth most consist Of war-mark'd footmen . . . . *Ant. and Cleo.* iii 7 45
Warmed and cooled by the same winter and summer . *Mer. of Venice* iii 1 65
He breathes, my lord. Were he not warm'd with ale, This were a bed but cold to sleep so soundly . . . *T. of Shrew* Ind. 1 32
Snakes, in my heart-blood warm'd, that sting my heart! *Richard II.* iii 2 131
It warm'd thy father's heart with proud desire . *1 Hen. VI.* iv 6 11
My work hath yet not warm'd me . . . . *Coriolanus* i 5 18
So far I read aloud: But even the very middle of my heart Is warm'd by the rest . . . . *Cymbeline* i 6 28
A pudency so rosy the sweet view on't Might well have warm'd old Saturn . . . . ii 5 12
Warmer. Quake in the present winter's state and wish That warmer days would come . . . . ii 4 6
They were warmer that got this than the poor thing is here . *W. Tale* iii 3 76
Warming. The second property of your excellent sherris is, the warming of the blood . . . . *2 Hen. IV.* iv 3 111
Warming-pan. Bardolph, put thy face between his sheets, and do the office of a warming-pan . . . . . . *Hen. V.* ii 1 88
Warmth. But what warmth is there in your affection towards any of these princely suitors? . . . . . *Mer. of Venice* i 2 36
No warmth, no breath, shall testify thou livest . *Rom. and Jul.* iv 1 98
Their blood is caked, 'tis cold, it seldom flows; 'Tis lack of kindly warmth they are not kind . . . . *T. of Athens* ii 2 226
From the loathed warmth whereof deliver me . . . *Lear* iv 6 272
Have you done? Come then, and take the last warmth of my lips *A. and C.* v 2 294
Nature awakes; a warmth Breathes out of her . . *Pericles* iii 2 93
Warn. And for lovers lacking—God warn us!—matter, the cleanliest shift is to kiss . . . . . . *As Y. Like It* iv 1 77
And sent to warn them to his royal presence . . *Richard III.* i 3 39
What, dost thou scorn me for my gentle counsel? And soothe the devil that I warn thee from? . . . . i 3 298
Both have well proceeded, To warn false traitors from the like attempts iii 5 49
This sight of death is as a bell, That warns my old age to a sepulchre *Rom. and Jul.* v 3 207
Their battles are at hand; They mean to warn us at Philippi here *J. C.* v 1 5
Warned. Who is it that hath warn'd us to the walls? . *K. John* ii 1 201
You have good judgement in horsemanship.—Be warned by me, then: they that ride so and ride not warily, fall into foul bogs *Hen. V.* iii 7 60
Look to it well and say you are well warn'd . *1 Hen. VI.* ii 4 103
His grace not being warn'd thereof before . . *Richard III.* iii 7 86
But say, I warn'd ye; Take heed, for heaven's sake, take heed *Hen. VIII.* iii 1 109
Warning. He has given him warning . . . *Meas. for Meas.* iii 2 36
No remedy, my lord, when walls are so wilful to hear without warning *M. N. Dream* v 1 211
Dull lead, with warning all as blunt . . . *Mer. of Venice* ii 7 8
The worst is this, that, at so slender warning, You are like to have a thin and slender pittance . . . . . *T. of Shrew* iv 4 60
Our hearts receive your warnings . . . . *All's Well* ii 1 22
Which as a beacon gives warning . . . . *2 Hen. IV.* iv 3 117
The Dauphin's drum, a warning bell, Sings heavy music *1 Hen. VI.* iv 2 39
Somewhat too sudden, sirs, the warning is . . . . v 2 14
I think he hath a very fair warning . . . *2 Hen. VI.* iv 6 12
And to be on foot at an hour's warning . . . *Coriolanus* iv 3 50

Warning. The boy gives warning something doth approach *Rom. and Jul.* v 3 18
I come to observe; I give thee warning on't.—I take no heed of thee *T. of A.* i 2 33
He would embrace no counsel, take no warning by my coming . iii 1 28
Instruments of fear and warning Unto some monstrous state *J. Cæsar* i 3 70
These does she apply for warnings, and portents, And evils imminent . ii 2 80
At his warning, Whether in sea or fire, in earth or air, The extravagant and erring spirit hies To his confine . . . . . *Hamlet* i 1 152
Warp. There is our commission, From which we would not have you warp . . . . *Meas. for Meas.* i 1 15
Though thou the waters warp, Thy sting is not so sharp *As Y. Like It* ii 7 187
One of you will prove a shrunk panel and, like green timber, warp, warp iii 3 90
Methinks My favour here begins to warp . . . *W. Tale* i 2 365
Warped. Such a warped slip of wilderness Ne'er issued from his blood *Meas. for Meas.* iii 1 142
Contempt his scornful perspective did lend me, Which warp'd the line of every other favour . . . . *All's Well* v 3 49
Whose warp'd looks proclaim What store her heart is made on . *Lear* iii 6 56
War-proof. Whose blood is fet from fathers of war-proof . *Hen. V.* iii 1 18
Warrant. I'll warrant him for drowning . . . *Tempest* i 1 49
Rather like a dream than an assurance That my remembrance warrants i 2 46
She will become thy bed, I warrant. And bring thee forth brave brood iii 2 112
Each putter-out of five for one will bring us Good warrant of . iii 3 49
His worth is warrant for his welcome hither . . *T. G. of Ver.* ii 4 102
And instances of infinite of love Warrant me welcome to my Proteus . ii 7 71
Upon this warrant shall you have access Where you with Silvia may confer . . . . iii 2 60
Who writes himself 'Armigero,' in any bill, warrant, quittance *Mer. Wives* i 1 10
I warrant he hath a thousand of these letters . . . ii 1 76
I'll warrant we'll unkennel the fox . . . . . iii 3 174
With the warrant of womanhood and the witness of a good conscience . iv 2 220
I'll warrant they'll have him publicly shamed . . . . iv 2 235
I warrant they would whip me with their fine wits . . . iv 5 101
And have not they suffered? Yes, I warrant; speciously one of them . iv 5 114
You shall hear how things go; and, I warrant, to your content . iv 5 127
'Tis surely for a name.—I warrant it is . . *Meas. for Meas.* i 2 176
The provost hath A warrant for his execution . . . . i 4 74
I'll not warrant that; for I can speak Against the thing I say . ii 4 59
If you be one, as you are well express'd By all external warrants . ii 4 137
Look, here's the warrant, Claudio, for thy death . . . iv 2 66
We have very oft awaked him, as if to carry him to execution, and showed him a seeming warrant for it . . . . . . iv 2 160
Claudio, whom here you have warrant to execute, is no greater forfeit to the law than Angelo . . . . iv 2 167
By the vow of mine order I warrant you . . . . . iv 2 180
Clap into your prayers; for, look you, the warrant's come . iv 3 44
I warrant your honour.—The warrant's for yourself . . . v 1 83
His purpose surfeiting, he sends a warrant For my poor brother's head v 1 102
Had you a special warrant for the deed? . . . . . v 1 464
A doubtful warrant of immediate death . . *Com. of Errors* i 1 69
Happy were I in my timely death, Could all my travels warrant me they live . . . . i 1 140
I warrant, her rags and the tallow in them will burn a Poland winter . iii 2 99
I'll give thee, ere I leave thee, so much money, To warrant thee . iv 4 3
I know who loves him.— . . . I warrant, one that knows him not *M. Ado* iii 2 66
Wonder not till further warrant: go but with me to-night . . iii 2 115
Not so good; and I warrant your cousin will say so . . . iii 4 10
Trust not my reading nor my observations, Which with experimental seal doth warrant The tenour of my book . . . . . . iv 1 168
If I know more of any man alive Than that which maiden modesty doth warrant, Let all my sins lack mercy! . . . . iv 1 181
Folly, in wisdom hatch'd, Hath wisdom's warrant . . *L. L. Lost* v 2 71
He for a man, God warrant us; she for a woman, God bless us *M. N. D.* v 1 326
You shall try but one fall.—No, I warrant your grace, you shall not entreat him to a second . . . . *As Y. Like It* i 2 217
Which, I warrant, she is apter to do than to confess she does . iii 2 407
Your features! Lord warrant us! what features? . . . . iii 3 5
But I'll warrant him heart-whole . . . . iv 1 49
She's madly mated.—I warrant him, Petruchio is Kated *T. of Shrew* iii 2 247
I warrant thou art a merry fellow and carest for nothing *T. Night* iii 1 30
I warrant there's vinegar and pepper in't.—Is't so saucy?—Ay, is't, I warrant him . . . . iii 4 158
I know not what I shall incur to pass it, Having no warrant *W. Tale* ii 2 58
Which is enough, I'll warrant, As this world goes, to pass for honest . ii 3 71
I am false of heart that way; and that he knew, I warrant him . iv 3 117
Under whose warrant I impeach thy wrong . . . *K. John* ii 1 116
There's law and warrant, lady, for my curse.—And for mine too . iii 1 184
I hope your warrant will bear out the deed . . . . iv 1 6
I warrant I love you more than you do me . . . . iv 1 31
He show'd his warrant to a friend of mine . . . . iv 2 70
It is the curse of kings to be attended By slaves that take their humours for a warrant . . . . iv 2 209
The holy legate comes apace, To give us warrant from the hand of heaven v 2 66
As you answer, I do know the scope And warrant limited unto my tongue v 2 123
I warrant they have made peace with Bolingbroke . *Richard II.* iii 2 127
Cracking the strong warrant of an oath, Mark'd with a blot . iv 1 235
A foolish hanging of thy nether lip, that doth warrant me . *1 Hen. IV.* ii 4 447
Hope gives not so much warrant as despair . . *2 Hen. IV.* i 3 40
So; murder, I warrant now. Alas, alas! put up your naked weapons . ii 4 221
She shall have whipping-cheer enough, I warrant her . . . v 4 6
If you look in the maps of the 'orld, I warrant you sall find . *Hen. V.* iv 7 25
My fainting words do warrant death . . . . *1 Hen. VI.* ii 5 95
An uproar, I dare warrant, Begun through malice of the bishop's men iii 1 74
Upon thy princely warrant, I descend To give thee answer of thy just demand . . . . v 3 143
Beside, his wealth doth warrant a liberal dower . . . . v 5 46
See where they come: I'll warrant they'll make it good . *2 Hen. VI.* v 1 122
I am resolved for death or dignity.—The first I warrant thee . v 1 195
Then I'll warrant you all your lands . . . *3 Hen. VI.* iii 2 21
And come to have the warrant, That we may be admitted *Richard III.* i 3 342
Art thou afraid?—Not to kill him, having a warrant for it; but to be damned for killing him, from which no warrant can defend us . i 4 112
'Thus hath the duke inferr'd;' But nothing spake in warrant from himself . . . . iii 7 33
Here is a warrant from The king to attach Lord Montacute . *Hen. VIII.* i 1 216
Follow your envious courses, men of malice; You have Christian warrant for 'em . . . . iii 2 244
I warrant, Helen, to change, would give an eye to boot . *Troi. and Cres.* i 2 259
We fear to warrant in our native place . . . . . ii 2 96
O, I warrant, how he mammocked it! . . . . *Coriolanus* i 3 71
See, they have shut him in.—To the pot, I warrant him . . . i 4 47

Warrant. Aufidius got off.—And 'twas time for him too, I'll warrant him that . . . *Coriolanus* ii 1 142
On the sudden, I warrant him consul . . . ii 1 238
Do not cry havoc, where you should but hunt With modest warrant iii 1 276
A noble fellow, I warrant him . . . v 2 115
True nobility Warrants these words in princely courtesy *T. Andron.* i 1 272
A pattern, precedent, and lively warrant For me . . . v 3 44
I warrant, an I should live a thousand years, I never should forget it *Rom. and Jul.* i 3 46
I warrant, it had upon its brow A bump as big as a young cockerel's stone i 3 52
He is not the flower of courtesy, but, I'll warrant him, as gentle as a lamb ii 5 44
A courteous, and a kind, and a handsome, and, I warrant, a virtuous ii 5 58
I am peppered, I warrant, for this world . . . iii 1 102
Mistress! what, mistress! Juliet! fast, I warrant her, she iv 5 1
One of Lord Timon's men? a gift, I warrant . *T. of Athens* iii 1 5
There's warrant in that theft Which steals itself *Macbeth* ii 3 151
Perchance 'twill walk again.—I warrant it will . *Hamlet* i 2 243
It out-herods Herod: pray you, avoid it.—I warrant your honour . iii 2 17
I'll warrant she'll tax him home . . . iii 3 29
And dare, upon the warrant of my note, Commend a dear thing to you *Lear* iii 1 18
A practiser Of arts inhibited and out of warrant . . . *Othello* i 2 79
She's a most exquisite lady.—And, I'll warrant her, full of game ii 3 19
I warrant it grieves my husband, As if the case were his . iii 3 3
I give thee warrant of thy place: assure thee, If I do vow a friendship, I'll perform it To the last article . . . iii 3 20
If 'twere no other,— 'Tis but so, I warrant . . . iv 2 168
Vouching—and upon warrant of bloody affirmation . *Cymbeline* i 4 63
Which gave advantage to an ancient soldier, An honest one, I warrant . v 3 16
Her hair, complexion, height, age, with warrant of her virginity *Pericles* iv 2 63
Your bride goes to that with shame which is her way to go with warrant iv 2 139
Some such thing I said, and said no more but what my thoughts Did warrant me was likely . . . v 1 135
Warrant thee. I warrant thee, nobody hears; mine own people *M. W.* ii 2 51
Remember you your cue.—I warrant thee . . . iii 3 40
A three-piled piece, I warrant thee *Meas. for Meas.* i 2 33
I warrant thee, Claudio, the time shall not go dully by us *Much Ado* ii 1 378
Time enough to go to bed with a candle, I warrant thee . 1 *Hen. IV.* ii 1 49
Let out the prisoners.—Fear not that, I warrant thee . 2 *Hen. VI.* iv 3 19
I am strong-framed, he cannot prevail with me, I warrant thee *Rich. III.* i 4 155
I warrant thee, my man's as true as steel . *Rom. and Jul.* ii 4 210
I will stir about, And all things shall be well, I warrant thee iv 2 40
Thou shalt find That I'll resume the shape which thou dost think I have cast off for ever: thou shalt, I warrant thee *Lear* i 4 332
What, goest thou back? thou shalt Go back, I warrant thee . *A. and C.* v 2 156
Warrant you. My lord, be not angry.—No, I warrant you *Tempest* iv 1 187
I would it were no worse.—I'll warrant you, 'tis as well . *T. G. of Ver.* ii 1 170
I warrant you, my lord, more grace than boy . . v 4 166
I warrant you, the women have so cried and shrieked at it *Mer. Wives* i 1 308
I warrant you, no tell-tale nor no breed-bate . . i 4 12
Gentlemen, with their coaches, I warrant you, coach after coach ii 2 66
I warrant you, he's the man should fight with him . . iii 1 70
She'll make you amends, I warrant you . . . iii 5 49
'Hang-hog' is Latin for bacon, I warrant you . . . iv 1 50
Here's that, I warrant you, will pay them all *Com. of Errors* iv 4 10
I'll make her come, I warrant you, presently . *Much Ado* iii 1 14
She's limed, I warrant you: we have caught her, madam iii 1 104
We will spare for no wit, I warrant you . . iii 5 66
In most profound earnest; and, I'll warrant you, for the love of Beatrice v 1 199
I warrant you, with pure love and troubled brain *As Y. Like It* iv 3 3
My lord, I warrant you we will play our part . *T. of Shrew* Ind. 69
Well read in poetry And other books, good ones, I warrant ye . i 2 171
O Lord, sir! Nay, put me to't, I warrant you *All's Well* ii 2 50
Knows he not thy voice?—No, sir, I warrant you . . iv 1 12
O, 'twill be admirable!—Sport royal, I warrant you *T. Night* ii 3 187
'With a foolish knight,'— That's me, I warrant you . ii 5 87
My prayers, minx!—No, I warrant you, he will not hear of godliness iii 4 134
This being done, let the law go whistle: I warrant you . *W. Tale* iv 4 716
I warrant you, that man is not alive Might so have tempted him 1 *Hen. IV.* iii 1 173
I warrant you, he's an infinitive thing upon my score . 2 *Hen. IV.* ii 1 25
I warrant you, as common as the way between Saint Alban's and London ii 2 184
Your colour, I warrant you, is as red as any rose, in good truth, la! ii 4 27
Whether she be damned for that, I know not.—No, I warrant you ii 4 369
What he has spoke to me, that is well, I warrant you, when time is serve *Hen. V.* iii 6 69
You shall find, I warrant you, that there is no tiddle taddle nor pibble pabble . . . iv 1 70
I will give treason his payment into plows, I warrant you . iv 8 15
Tis a good silling, I warrant you, or I will change it . iv 8 76
Thou shalt find me at the governor's.—Father, I warrant you 1 *Hen. VI.* i 4 21
Stir with the lark to-morrow, gentle Norfolk.—I warrant you *Rich. III.* v 3 57
Will you set your wit to a fool's?—No, I warrant you . *Troi. and Cres.* ii 1 95
There's wondrous things spoke of him.—Wondrous! ay, I warrant you *Coriolanus* ii 1 154
I warrant you, madam, we will make that sure *T. Andron.* ii 3 133
See you do it bravely.—I warrant you, sir, let me alone . iv 3 114
All covered dishes!—Royal cheer, I warrant you.—Doubt not that *T. of Athens* iii 6 56
I'll warrant you, Fear me not . . . *Hamlet* iii 4 6
All may be well enough.—I warrant you, madam . *Ant. and Cleo.* iii 3 51
Remember what I have said.—I warrant you, madam *Pericles* iv 1 47
I threw her overboard with these very arms.—Upon this coast, I warrant you . . . v 3 20
Warranted. The business he hath helmed must upon a warranted need give him a better proclamation . . *Meas. for Meas.* iii 2 151
You have it from his own deliverance.—And by other warranted testimony . . . *All's Well* ii 5 5
Warranted By a commission from the consistory *Hen. VIII.* ii 4 91
And the chance of goodness Be like our warranted quarrel! *Macbeth* iv 3 137
Warranteth. Discover thine infirmity, That warranteth by law to be thy privilege . . 1 *Hen. VI.* v 4 61
Warrantize. Break up the gates, I'll be your warrantize . i 3 13
Warranty. From your love I have a warranty To unburden all my plots and purposes . . . *Mer. of Venice* i 1 132
Her obsequies have been as far enlarged As we have warranty *Hamlet* v 1 250
But with such general warranty of heaven As I might love . *Othello* v 2 60
Warred. Wars have not wasted it, for warr'd he hath not *Richard II.* ii 1 252
His wife that's dead did trespasses to Cæsar; His brother warr'd upon him . . . *Ant. and Cleo.* ii 1 41

Warren. I found him here as melancholy as a lodge in a warren *M. Ado* ii 1 222
Warrener. He hath fought with a warrener . . *Mer. Wives* i 4 28
Warrest. Why, thy godhead laid apart, Warr'st thou with a woman's heart? . . . *As Y. Like It* iv 3 45
Warr'st thou 'gainst Athens?—Ay, Timon, and have cause *T. of Athens* iv 3 102
Warring. Was this a face To be opposed against the warring winds? *Lear* iv 7 32
Warrior. That most famous warrior, Duke Menaphon *Com. of Errors* v 1 367
Your buskin'd mistress and your warrior love . . *M. N. Dream* ii 1 71
This infant warrior in his enterprizes Discomfited great Douglas 1 *Hen. IV.* iii 2 113
And there is my Lord of Worcester and a head Of gallant warriors . iv 4 26
With lustier maintenance than I did look for Of such an ungrown warrior . . . v 4 23
They will give Their bodies to the lust of English youth To new-store France with bastard warriors . . . *Hen. V.* iii 5 31
My good Lord Exeter, And my kind kinsman, warriors all, adieu! iv 3 10
Tell the constable We are but warriors for the working-day . iv 3 109
And think me honoured To feast so great a warrior in my house 1 *Hen. VI.* ii 3 82
If we could do that, France were no place for Henry's warriors . iii 3 22
'Tis a mere French word; We English warriors wot not what it means . iv 7 55
And when the hardiest warriors did retire, Richard cried 'Charge!' 3 *Hen. VI.* i 4 14
Brave warriors, Clifford and Northumberland, Come . i 4 66
Why then it sorts, brave warriors, let's away . . ii 1 209
Brave warriors, march amain towards Coventry . . iv 8 64
Women and children of so high a courage, And warriors faint! . v 4 51
Let us to Priam's hall, To greet the warriors . *Troi. and Cres.* iii 1 162
Let an old man embrace thee; And, worthy warrior, welcome to our tents . . . iv 5 200
Flower of warriors, How is't with Titus Lartius? . *Coriolanus* i 6 32
Yet welcome, warriors: We call a nettle but a nettle . ii 1 206
Thou art my warrior; I holp to frame thee . . v 3 62
A nobler man, a braver warrior, Lives not this day . *T. Andron.* i 1 25
And bring you up To be a warrior, and command a camp . iv 2 180
Approved warriors, and my faithful friends . . v 1 1
Fierce fiery warriors fought upon the clouds . *J. Cæsar* ii 2 19
O my fair warrior!—My dear Othello! . . *Othello* ii 1 184
I was, unhandsome warrior as I am, Arraigning his unkindness with my soul . . . iii 4 151
Commend unto his lips thy favouring hand: Kiss it, my warrior *Ant. and Cleo.* iv 8 24
Wart. Have not your worship a wart above your eye? . *Mer. Wives* i 4 157
We had an hour's talk of that wart . . . i 4 162
I will tell your worship more of the wart the next time . . i 4 171
The mole in my neck, the great wart on my left arm *Com. of Errors* iii 2 148
Thomas Wart!—Where's he?—Here, sir.—Is thy name Wart?—Yea, sir.—Thou art a very ragged wart . . 2 *Hen. IV.* iii 2 147
I would Wart might have gone, sir . . . iii 2 174
Here's Wart; you see what a ragged appearance it is . iii 2 279
Put me a caliver into Wart's hand, Bardolph.—Hold, Wart, traverse; thus . . . iii 2 290
Well said, i' faith, Wart; thou'rt a good scab: hold, there's a tester for thee . . . iii 2 295
Alas, poor chin! many a wart is richer . . *Troi. and Cres.* i 2 155
Make Ossa like a wart! . . . *Hamlet* v 1 306
War-thoughts Have left their places vacant . *Much Ado* i 1 303
War-wearied. Drops bloody sweat from his war-wearied limbs 1 *Hen. VI.* iv 4 18
Warwick. Go call the Earls of Surrey and of Warwick . 2 *Hen. IV.* iii 1 1
Warwick and Talbot, Salisbury and Gloucester . *Hen. V.* iv 3 54
My Lord of Warwick, and my brother Gloucester, Follow Fluellen closely . . . iv 7 178
Judge you, my Lord of Warwick, then, between us . 1 *Hen. VI.* ii 4 10
If thou be not then created York, I will not live to be accounted Warwick . . . ii 4 120
O, Warwick, Warwick! I forsee with grief The utter loss of all the realm . . . v 4 111
Brave York, Salisbury, and victorious Warwick . . 2 *Hen. VI.* i 1 86
But wherefore weeps Warwick, my valiant son? . . i 1 115
Warwick, my son, the comfort of my age . . . i 1 190
So God help Warwick, as he loves the land, And common profit of his country! . . . i 1 205
Maine is lost; That Maine which by main force Warwick did win . i 1 210
Salisbury and Warwick are no simple peers . . i 3 77
Ambitious Warwick, let thy betters speak.—The cardinal's not my better . . . i 3 112
All in this presence are thy betters, Warwick.—Warwick may live to be the best of all . . . i 3 114
Peace, headstrong Warwick!—Image of pride, why should I hold my peace? . . . i 3 178
Invite my Lords of Salisbury and Warwick To sup with me to-morrow . i 4 83
The Earl of Warwick Shall one day make the Duke of York a king ii 2 78
Richard shall live to make the Earl of Warwick The greatest man in England but the king . . . ii 2 81
What instance gives Lord Warwick for his vow? . . iii 2 159
What dares not Warwick, if false Suffolk dare him? . . iii 2 203
The traitorous Warwick, with the men of Bury Set all upon me . iii 2 240
Good Warwick, go with me; I have great matters to impart to thee iii 2 298
The princely Warwick, and the Nevils all, . . . are rising up in arms . iv 1 91
Bid Salisbury and Warwick come to me . . . v 1 147
And such a piece of service will you do, If you oppose yourselves to match Lord Warwick . . . v 1 156
Why, Warwick, hath thy knee forgot to bow? . . . v 1 161
Clifford of Cumberland, 'tis Warwick calls . . v 2 1
Clifford of Cumberland, Warwick is hoarse with calling thee to arms . v 2 7
Hold, Warwick, seek thee out some other chase . . v 2 14
What says Lord Warwick? shall we after them?—After them! nay, before them . . . v 3 27
Assist me, then, sweet Warwick, and I will . . 3 *Hen. VI.* i 1 28
Nor he that loves him best, The proudest he that holds up Lancaster, Dares stir a wing, if Warwick shake his bells . . i 1 47
Back'd by the power of Warwick, that false peer, To aspire unto the crown . . . i 1 52
Westmoreland shall maintain.—And Warwick shall disprove it . i 1 89
My Lord of Warwick, hear me but one word: Let me for this my life-time reign as king . . . i 1 170
Warwick and the duke enforced me.—Enforced thee! art thou king? . i 1 229
Warwick is chancellor and the lord of Calais . . i 1 238
Thou shalt to London presently, And whet on Warwick to this enterprise . . . i 2 37
Let noble Warwick, Cobham, and the rest, . . . strengthen themselves i 2 56

Warwick. O Warwick, Warwick! that Plantagenet . . . Is by the stern lord Clifford done to death . 3 *Hen. VI.* ii 1 101
'Twas odds, belike, when valiant Warwick fled . ii 1 148
Ay, now methinks I hear great Warwick speak: Ne'er may he live to see a sunshine day, That cries 'Retire,' if Warwick bid him stay . ii 1 186
Lord Warwick, on thy shoulder will I lean . ii 1 189
Why, how now, long-tongued Warwick! dare you speak? . ii 2 102
If that be right which Warwick says is right, There is no wrong . ii 2 131
Ah, Warwick, why hast thou withdrawn thyself? . ii 3 14
Warwick, revenge! brother, revenge my death! . ii 3 19
O Warwick, I do bend my knee with thine; And in this vow do chain my soul to thine! . ii 3 33
Gentle Warwick, Let me embrace thee in my weary arms . ii 3 44
Nay, Warwick, single out some other chase; For I myself will hunt this wolf to death . ii 4 12
My father, being the Earl of Warwick's man, Came on the part of York ii 5 65
Fly! for all your friends are fled, And Warwick rages like a chafed bull ii 5 126
Warwick and the rest; I stabb'd your fathers' bosoms, split my breast ii 6 29
Shall Warwick cut the sea to France, And ask the Lady Bona for thy queen . ii 6 89
Even as thou wilt, sweet Warwick, let it be . ii 6 99
Warwick, as ourself, Shall do and undo as him pleaseth best . ii 6 104
The great commanding Warwick Is thither gone, to crave the French king's sister . iii 1 29
Warwick is a subtle orator, And Lewis a prince soon won with moving words . iii 1 33
Ay, but she's come to beg, Warwick, to give . iii 1 42
Whiles Warwick tells his title, smooths the wrong, Inferreth arguments iii 1 48
Our Earl of Warwick, Edward's greatest friend.—Welcome, brave Warwick! . iii 3 45
King Lewis and Lady Bona, hear me speak, Before you answer Warwick iii 3 66
Then Warwick disannuls great John of Gaunt . iii 3 81
Why, Warwick, canst thou speak against thy liege, Whom thou obeyed'st thirty and six years? . iii 3 95
Stand aside, While I use further conference with Warwick.—Heavens grant that Warwick's words bewitch him not! . iii 3 111
Deceitful Warwick! it was thy device By this alliance to make void my suit . iii 3 141
Peace, impudent and shameless Warwick, peace, Proud setter up and puller down of kings! . iii 3 156
Warwick, this is some post to us or thee . iii 3 162
Our fair queen and mistress Smiles at her news, while Warwick frowns at his . iii 3 168
This proveth Edward's love and Warwick's honesty . iii 3 180
Warwick, these words have turn'd my hate to love . iii 3 199
Give thy hand to Warwick; And, with thy hand, thy faith irrevocable, That only Warwick's daughter shall be thine . iii 3 246
How could he stay till Warwick made return? . iv 1 5
How like you our choice, That you stand pensive, as half malcontent?—As well as Lewis of France, or the Earl of Warwick . iv 1 11
They are but Lewis and Warwick: I am Edward, Your king and Warwick's . iv 1 15
Warwick, doing what you gave in charge, Is now dishonoured by this new marriage.—What if both Lewis and Warwick be appeased? . iv 1 32
But what said Warwick to these injuries? . iv 1 107
But say, is Warwick friends with Margaret?—Ay, gracious sovereign; they are so link'd in friendship, That young Prince Edward marries Warwick's daughter . iv 1 115
Sit you fast, For I will hence to Warwick's other daughter . iv 1 120
You that love me and Warwick, follow me . iv 1 123
Clarence and Somerset both gone to Warwick! Yet am I arm'd against the worst can happen . iv 1 127
You twain, of all the rest, Are near to Warwick by blood and by alliance: Tell me if you love Warwick more than me? . iv 1 136
Lose no hour, Till we meet Warwick with his foreign power . iv 1 149
Then, gentle Clarence, welcome unto Warwick; And welcome, Somerset iv 2 6
For Warwick and his friends, God and Saint George! . iv 2 29
He hath made a solemn vow Never to lie and take his natural rest Till Warwick or himself be quite suppress'd . iv 3 6
To-morrow then belike shall be the day, If Warwick be so near . iv 3 8
If Warwick knew in what estate he stands, 'Tis to be doubted he would waken him . iv 3 18
The duke! Why, Warwick, when we parted, Thou call'dst me king . iv 3 30
What late misfortune is befall'n King Edward?—What! loss of some pitch'd battle against Warwick? . iv 4 4
The Bishop of York, Fell Warwick's brother and by that our foe . iv 4 12
Bear it as you may: Warwick may lose, that now hath won the day . iv 4 15
But, madam, where is Warwick then become? . iv 4 25
Let us fly while we may fly: If Warwick take us we are sure to die . iv 4 35
Shield thee from Warwick's frown; And pray that I may repossess the crown . iv 5 28
But, Warwick, after God, thou set'st me free, And chiefly therefore I thank God and thee . iv 6 16
Warwick, although my head still wear the crown, I here resign my government to thee . iv 6 23
No, Warwick, thou art worthy of the sway . iv 6 32
He consents, if Warwick yield consent; For on thy fortune I repose myself . iv 6 46
We'll forward towards Warwick and his mates . iv 7 82
Yet, as we may, we'll meet both thee and Warwick . iv 7 86
Towards Coventry bend we our course, Where peremptory Warwick now remains . iv 8 59
Here Southam lies: The drum your honour hears marcheth from Warwick . v 1 13
See how the surly Warwick mans the wall! . v 1 17
Now, Warwick, wilt thou ope the city gates, Speak gentle words? . v 1 21
Confess who set thee up and pluck'd thee down, Call Warwick patron v 1 27
'Twas I that gave the kingdom to thy brother.—Why then 'tis mine, if but by Warwick's gift . v 1 35
Warwick takes his gift again; And Henry is my king, Warwick his subject.—But Warwick's king is Edward's prisoner: And, gallant Warwick, do but answer this: What is the body when the head is off? . v 1 37
Alas, that Warwick had no more forecast! . v 1 42
Yet you are Warwick still.—Come, Warwick, take the time; kneel down v 1 47
Wind-changing Warwick now can change no more . v 1 57
Come; thou wilt, if Warwick call.—Father of Warwick, know you what this means? . v 1 80
Why, trow'st thou, Warwick, That Clarence is so harsh, so blunt, unnatural? . v 1 85
Warwick. And so, proud-hearted Warwick, I defy thee . 3 *Hen. VI.* v 1 98
What, Warwick, wilt thou leave the town and fight? . v 1 107
And bid thee battle, Edward, if thou darest.—Yes, Warwick, Edward dares, and leads the way . v 1 112
Warwick was a bug that fear'd us all . v 2 2
I seek for thee, That Warwick's bones may keep thine company . v 2 4
And tell me who is victor, York or Warwick? Why ask I that? . v 2 6
And who durst smile when Warwick bent his brow? . v 2 22
Ah, Warwick, Warwick! wert thou as we are, We might recover all our loss . v 2 29
Ah, Warwick! Montague hath breathed his last; And to the latest gasp cried out for Warwick . v 2 40
But at last I well might hear, deliver'd with a groan, 'O, farewell, Warwick!' . v 2 47
Save yourselves; For Warwick bids you all farewell, to meet in heaven v 2 49
Say Warwick was our anchor; what of that? And Montague our topmast; what of him? . v 4 13
The two brave bears, Warwick and Montague, That in their chains fetter'd the kingly lion . v 7 10
Then I'll marry Warwick's youngest daughter . *Richard III.* i 1 153
Poor Clarence did forsake his father, Warwick; Yea, and forswore himself . i 3 135
Renowned Warwick; Who cried aloud, 'What scourge for perjury Can this dark monarchy afford false Clarence?' . i 4 49
How the poor soul did forsake The mighty Warwick, and did fight for me . ii 1 110
He hates me for my father Warwick; And will, no doubt, shortly be rid of me . iv 1 86

Warwickshire. What a devil dost thou in Warwickshire? 1 *Hen. IV.* iv 2 56
Say, if thou darest, proud Lord of Warwickshire, That I am faulty in Duke Humphrey's death . 2 *Hen. VI.* iii 2 201
In Warwickshire I have true-hearted friends, Not mutinous in peace, yet bold in war . 3 *Hen. VI.* iv 8 9

War-worn. Their gesture sad Investing lank-lean cheeks and war-worn coats . *Hen. V.* iv Prol. 26

Wary. I have ta'en a due and wary note upon't *Meas. for Meas.* iv 1 38
There are cozeners abroad; therefore it behoves men to be wary *W. Tale* iv 4 257
But yet be wary in thy studious care . 1 *Hen. VI.* ii 5 97
Take heed, be wary how you place your words . ii 2 3
The day is broke; be wary, look about . *Rom. and Jul.* iii 5 40
It is the bright day that brings forth the adder; And that craves wary walking . *J. Cæsar* ii 1 15
Be wary then; best safety lies in fear . *Hamlet* i 3 43
Come, begin: And you, the judges, bear a wary eye . v 2 290
Noble swelling spirits, That hold their honours in a wary distance *Oth.* ii 3 58
Let us be wary, let us hide our loves . iii 3 420

Was. As I was then Advertising and holy to your business, . . . I am still Attorney'd at your service . *Meas. for Meas.* v 1 387
Tell me this; Which of the two was daughter of the duke That here was at the wrestling? . *As Y. Like It* i 2 282
You have heard him swear downright he was.—'Was' is not 'is' . iii 4 32
The time was that I hated thee, And yet it is not that I bear thee love iii 5 92
I do not shame To tell you what I was, since my conversion . iv 3 137
A body would think this was well counterfeited! . iv 3 167
The lords at Pomfret, when they rode from London, Were jocund, and supposed their state was sure . *Richard III.* iii 2 86
I gave ye Power as he was a counsellor to try him . *Hen. VIII.* v 3 143
You were used To say extremity was the trier of spirits . *Coriolanus* iv 1 4
Thy temples should be planted presently With horns, as was Actæon's *T. Andron.* ii 3 63
She means that there was more than one Confederate in the fact: ay, more there was . v 1 38
Was I with you there for the goose?—Thou wast never with me for any thing when thou wast not there for the goose . *Rom. and Jul.* ii 4 78

Wash. Nor scrape trencher, nor wash dish . *Tempest* ii 2 187
Item: She can wash and scour.—A special virtue . *T. G. of Ver.* iii 1 313
I wash, wring, brew, bake, scour, dress meat and drink . *Mer. Wives* i 4 101
Buck! I would I could wash myself of the buck! Buck, buck, buck! . iii 3 167
And when was he wont to wash his face? . *Much Ado* iii 2 56
The wide sea Hath drops too few to wash her clean again . iv 1 143
The moon, the governess of floods, Pale in her anger, washes all the air, That rheumatic diseases do abound . *M. N. Dream* ii 1 104
To wash your liver as clean as a sound sheep's heart *As Y. Like It* iii 2 442
He went but forth to wash him in the Hellespont and being taken with the cramp was drowned . iv 1 103
Will't please your mightiness to wash your hands? . *T. of Shrew* Ind. 2 78
Shall I have some water? Come, Kate, and wash . iv 1 157
He was my son; But I do wash his name out of my blood . *All's Well* iii 2 70
I will wash off gross acquaintance . *T. Night* ii 5 176
The double gilt of this opportunity you let time wash off . iii 2 27
How prettily the young swain seems to wash The hand was fair before! *W. Tale* iv 4 377
No longer than we well could wash our hands . *K. John* iii 1 234
These Lincoln Washes have devoured them . v 6 41
Were in the Washes all unwarily Devoured by the unexpected flood . v 7 63
To wash your blood From off my hands, here in the view of men I will unfold some causes of your death . *Richard II.* iii 1 5
Not all the water in the rough rude sea Can wash the balm off from an anointed king . iii 2 55
With mine own tears I wash away my balm . iv 1 207
Though some of you with Pilate wash your hands Showing an outward pity; yet . . . water cannot wash away your sin . iv 1 239
Dissolve to dew, And wash him fresh again with true-love tears . v 1 10
I'll make a voyage to the Holy Land, To wash this blood off from my guilty hand . v 6 50
Washes his hands, and says to his wife 'Fie upon this quiet life!' 1 *Hen. IV.* ii 4 116
Go, wash thy face, and draw the action . 2 *Hen. IV.* ii 1 162
Do as every sick man in his bed, wash every mote out of his conscience *Hen. V.* iv 1 189
All the water in Wye cannot wash your majesty's Welsh plood out of your pody . iv 7 111
Return thee therefore with a flood of tears, And wash away thy country's stained spots . 1 *Hen. VI.* iii 3 57
That I may dew it with my mournful tears; Nor let the rain of heaven wet this place, To wash away my woful monuments 2 *Hen. VI.* iii 2 342
Not able to travel with her furred pack, she washes bucks here at home iv 2 51
And I with tears do wash the blood away . 3 *Hen. VI.* i 4 158
Thy tears would wash this cold congealed blood . ii 2 37

Wash. Bestride the rock; the tide will wash you off, Or else you famish *3 Hen. VI.* v 4 31
How fain, like Pilate, would I wash my hands Of this most grievous guilty murder done! *Richard III.* i 4 279
I myself have many tears to wash Hereafter time iv 4 389
Swills your warm blood like wash, and makes his trough In your embowell'd bosoms, this foul swine v 2 9
I will go wash; And when my face is fair, you shall perceive Whether I blush or no *Coriolanus* i 9 68
Against the hospitable canon, would I Wash my fierce hand in's heart i 10 27
Bid them wash their faces And keep their teeth clean ii 3 66
Thy sons make pillage of her chastity And wash their hands in Bassianus' blood *T. Andron.* ii 3 45
Go home, call for sweet water, wash thy hands.—She hath no tongue to call, nor hands to wash; And so let's leave her ii 4 6
Wash they his wounds with tears *Rom. and Jul.* iii 2 130
What, wilt thou wash him from his grave with tears? v 3 71
Who, stuck and spangled with your flatteries, Washes it off *T. of Athens* iii 6 102
Let's all cry 'Peace, freedom, and liberty!'—Stoop, then, and wash *J. Cæsar* iii 1 111
Go get some water, And wash this filthy witness from your hand *Macbeth* ii 2 47
Will all great Neptune's ocean wash this blood Clean from my hand? ii 2 60
Wash your hands, put on your nightgown; look not so pale v 1 68
Full thirty times hath Phœbus' cart gone round Neptune's salt wash *Hamlet* iii 2 166
Is there not rain enough in the sweet heavens To wash it white as snow? iii 3 46
Roast me in sulphur! Wash me in steep-down gulfs of liquid fire! *Othello* v 2 280
It's monstrous labour, when I wash my brain, And it grows fouler *Ant. and Cleo.* ii 7 105
Whilst they with joyful tears Wash the congealment from your wounds iv 8 10
The gods rebuke me, but it is tidings To wash the eyes of kings v 1 28
Rebuke these surges, Which wash both heaven and hell *Pericles* iii 1 2
And from the ladder-tackle washes off A canvas-climber iv 1 61
He swears Never to wash his face, nor cut his hairs: He puts on sackcloth iv 4 28
Washed. Then she need not be washed and scoured *T. G. of Ver.* iii 1 315
How my transformation hath been washed and cudgelled *Mer. Wives* iv 5 99
He, a marble to her tears, is washed with them, but relents not *Meas. for Meas.* iii 1 239
There are no faces truer than those that are so washed *Much Ado* i 1 27
Who loved her so, that, speaking of her foulness, Wash'd it with tears iv 1 156
Your mistresses dare never come in rain, For fear their colours should be wash'd away *L. L. Lost* iv 3 271
To tell you plain, I'll find a fairer face not wash'd to-day iv 3 273
Not with salt tears: If so, my eyes are oftener wash'd than hers *M. N. Dream* ii 2 93
She looks as clear As morning roses newly wash'd with dew *T. of Shrew* ii 1 174
Which, wash'd away, shall scour my shame with it *1 Hen. IV.* iii 2 137
Would, by beholding him, have wash'd his knife With gentle eye-drops *2 Hen. IV.* iv 5 87
Was this easy? May this be wash'd in Lethe, and forgotten? v 2 72
Is in your conscience wash'd As pure as sin with baptism *Hen. V.* i 2 31
As men wrecked upon a sand, that look to be washed off the next tide iv 1 101
Even then that sunshine brew'd a shower for him, That wash'd his father's fortunes forth *3 Hen. VI.* ii 2 157
Thy place is fill'd, thy sceptre wrung from thee, Thy balm wash'd off iii 1 17
When scarce the blood was well wash'd from his hands Which issued from my other angel husband *Richard III.* iv 1 68
I, that was wash'd to death with fulsome wine, Poor Clarence! v 3 132
For that I have not wash'd My nose that bled *Coriolanus* i 9 47
Why, she was wash'd and cut and trimm'd *T. Andron.* v 1 95
Wert thou as far As that vast shore wash'd with the farthest sea, I would adventure for such merchandise *Rom. and Jul.* ii 2 83
What a deal of brine Hath wash'd thy sallow cheeks for Rosaline! ii 3 70
Upon thy cheek the stain doth sit Of an old tear that is not wash'd off yet ii 3 76
The jewels of our father, with wash'd eyes Cordelia leaves you *Lear* i 1 271
Never was a war did cease, Ere bloody hands were wash'd, with such a peace *Cymbeline* v 5 485
The sea hath cast me on the rocks, Wash'd me from shore to shore *Per.* ii 1 6
A plague on them, they ne'er come but I look to be washed ii 1 29
Washer. His cook, or his laundry, his washer, and his wringer *Mer. Wives* i 2 5
Washford. Great Earl of Washford, Waterford, and Valence *1 Hen. VI.* iv 7 63
Washing. Would thou mightst lie drowning The washing of ten tides! *Tempest* i 1 61
I am half afraid he will have need of washing *Mer. Wives* iii 3 194
Thou didst swear to me then, as I was washing thy wound, to marry me and make me my lady thy wife *2 Hen. IV.* ii 1 99
Washing with kindly tears his gentle cheeks iv 5 84
It is an accustomed action with her, to seem thus washing her hands *Macbeth* v 1 33
Wasp. Injurious wasps, to feed on such sweet honey! *T. G. of Ver.* i 2 106
Come, come, you wasp; i' faith, you are too angry *T. of Shrew* ii 1 210
Who knows not where a wasp does wear his sting? In his tail ii 1 214
Which being spotted Is goads, thorns, nettles, tails of wasps *W. Tale* i 2 329
'Nointed over with honey, set on the head of a wasp's nest iv 4 814
There be moe wasps that buzz about his nose *Hen. VIII.* iii 2 55
When ye have the honey ye desire, Let not this wasp outlive *T. Andron.* ii 3 132
Waspish. As I guess By the stern brow and waspish action *As Y. Like It* iv 3 9
If I be waspish, best beware my sting *T. of Shrew* ii 1 211
From this day forth, I'll use you for my mirth, yea, for my laughter, When you are waspish *J. Cæsar* iv 3 50
Waspish-headed. Her waspish-headed son has broke his arrows *Tempest* iv 1 99
Wasp-stung. What a wasp-stung and impatient fool Art thou! *1 Hen. IV.* i 3 236
Wassail. And retails his wares At wakes and wassails *L. L. Lost* v 2 318
A wassail candle, my lord, all tallow *2 Hen. IV.* i 2 179
His two chamberlains Will I with wine and wassail so convince *Macbeth* i 7 64
Takes his rouse, Keeps wassail, and the swaggering up-spring reels *Hamlet* i 4 9
Antony, Leave thy lascivious wassails *Ant. and Cleo.* i 4 56
Wast ever in court, shepherd?—No, truly.—Then thou art damned *As Y. Like It* iii 2 34
Thou wast never with me for any thing when thou was not there for the goose *Rom. and Jul.* ii 4 79
Waste. Which, part of it, I'll waste With such discourse *Tempest* v 1 302
But wherefore waste I time to counsel thee? *T. G. of Ver.* i 1 51
I am now about no waste; I am about thrift *Mer. Wives* i 3 47
He will never, I think, in the way of waste, attempt us again iv 2 226
Thyself and thy belongings Are not thine own so proper as to waste Thyself upon thy virtues, they on thee *Meas. for Meas.* i 1 31
You but waste your words ii 2 72
Waste. Having waste ground enough, Shall we desire to raze the sanctuary? *Meas. for Meas.* ii 2 170
Like cover'd fire, Consume away in sighs, waste inwardly *Much Ado* iii 1 78
Never did mockers waste more idle breath *M. N. Dream* iii 2 168
You do me now more wrong In making question of my uttermost Than if you had made waste of all I have *Mer. of Venice* i 1 157
Therefore I part with him, and part with him To one that I would have him help to waste His borrow'd purse ii 5 50
Companions That do converse and waste the time together iii 4 12
Waste no time in words, But get thee gone: I shall be there before thee iii 4 54
I like this place, And willingly could waste my time in it *As Y. Like It* ii 4 95
Go find him out, And we will nothing waste till you return ii 7 134
You waste the treasure of your time *T. Night* iii 5 85
The clock upbraids me with the waste of time iii 1 141
The waste is no whit lesser than thy land *Richard II.* ii 1 103
Which waste of idle hours hath quite thrown down iii 4 66
I wasted time, and now doth time waste me v 5 49
Your means are very slender, and your waste is great *2 Hen. IV.* i 2 160
A naked subject to the weeping clouds And waste for churlish winter's tyranny i 3 62
That action, hence borne out, May waste the memory of the former days iv 5 216
Give edge unto the swords That make such waste in brief mortality *Hen. V.* i 2 28
All fell feats Enlink'd to waste and desolation iii 3 18
Know you not, The fire that mounts the liquor till't run o'er, In seeming to augment it wastes it? *Hen. VIII.* i 1 145
Times to repair our nature With comforting repose, and not for us To waste v 1 5
Then she hath sworn that she will still live chaste?—She hath, and in that sparing makes huge waste *Rom. and Jul.* i 1 224
In delay We waste our lights in vain, like lamps by day i 4 45
How much salt water thrown away in waste, To season love! ii 3 71
Still in motion Of raging waste? It cannot hold; it will not *T. of Athens* ii 1 4
So shall he waste his means, weary his soldiers *J. Cæsar* iv 3 200
Were nothing but to waste night, day, and time *Hamlet* ii 2 89
To have the expense and waste of his revenues *Lear* ii 1 102
It is now high supper-time, and the night grows to waste: about it *Oth.* iv 2 250
He fishes, drinks, and wastes The lamps of night in revel *Ant. and Cleo.* i 4 4
Feast the army; we have store to do't, And they have earn'd the waste iv 1 16
It is not likely . . . That they will waste their time upon our note *Cymbeline* iv 4 20
Should by the minute feed on life and lingering By inches waste you v 5 52
I life would wish, and that I might Waste it for you, like taper-light *Pericles* i Gower 16
Come, gentlemen, we sit too long on trifles, And waste the time ii 3 93
Thus time we waste, and longest leagues make short iv 4 1
Wasted. Hath homely age the alluring beauty took From my poor cheek? then he hath wasted it *Com. of Errors* ii 1 90
Neeze and swear A merrier hour was never wasted there *M. N. Dream* ii 1 57
Now the wasted brands do glow, Whilst the screech-owl, screeching loud v 1 382
Wars have not wasted it, for warr'd he hath not *Richard II.* ii 1 252
I wasted time, and now doth time waste me v 5 49
Yet youth, the more it is wasted the sooner it wears *1 Hen. IV.* ii 4 443
Hath his quick wit wasted in giving reckonings *2 Hen. IV.* i 2 193
The king hath wasted all his rods On late offenders iv 1 215
My lungs are wasted so That strength of speech is utterly denied me iv 5 217
That hast by tyranny these many years Wasted our country *1 Hen. VI.* ii 3 41
Would he were wasted, marrow, bones, and all! *3 Hen. VI.* iii 2 125
As I earnestly did fix mine eye Upon the wasted building *T. Andron.* v 1 23
March is wasted fourteen days.—'Tis good *J. Cæsar* ii 1 59
Since these arms of mine had seven years' pith, Till now some nine moons wasted *Othello* i 3 84
I have wasted myself out of my means iv 2 187
Wasteful. Lacking the burden of lean and wasteful learning *As Y. L. It* iii 2 341
To seek the beauteous eye of heaven to garnish, Is wasteful *K. John* iv 2 16
And Bolingbroke Hath seized the wasteful king *Richard II.* iii 4 55
His soul Shall stand sore charged for the wasteful vengeance *Hen. V.* i 2 283
Swill'd with the wild and wasteful ocean iii 1 14
I have retired me to a wasteful cock, And set mine eyes at flow *T. of A.* ii 2 171
And his gash'd stabs look'd like a breach in nature For ruin's wasteful entrance *Macbeth* ii 3 120
Wasting. My wasting lamps some fading glimmer left *Com. of Errors* v 1 315
These eyes, like lamps whose wasting oil is spent, Wax dim *1 Hen. VI.* ii 5 8
And see the cities and the towns defaced By wasting ruin iii 3 46
Watch. He's winding up the watch of his wit *Tempest* ii 1 12
Will guard your person while you take your rest, And watch your safety ii 1 198
To watch, like one that fears robbing *T. G. of Ver.* ii 1 25
I'll go watch.—Go; and we'll have a posset for't soon at night *M. Wives* i 4 7
Three of Master Ford's brothers watch the door with pistols iv 2 53
Being chosen for the prince's watch *Much Ado* iii 3 6
The most senseless and fit man for the constable of the watch iii 3 24
Call the rest of the watch together and thank God you are rid of a knave iii 3 30
For the watch to babble and to talk is most tolerable and not to be endured iii 3 36
We will rather sleep than talk: we know what belongs to a watch iii 3 40
Indeed, the watch ought to offend no man iii 3 87
I pray you, watch about Signior Leonato's door iii 3 98
Our watch to-night, excepting your worship's presence, ha' ta'en a couple of as arrant knaves as any in Messina iii 5 33
Our watch, sir, have indeed comprehended two aspicious persons iii 5 49
You must call forth the watch that are their accusers.—Yea, marry, that's the eftest way. Let the watch come forth iv 2 36
And also, the watch heard them talk of one Deformed v 1 316
Being a watch, But being watch'd that it may still go right! *L. L. Lost* iii 1 194
And I to sigh for her! to watch for her! To pray for her! iii 1 202
Having once this juice, I'll watch Titania when she is asleep *M. N. D.* ii 1 177
I shot his fellow of the self-same flight The self-same way with more advised watch, To find the other forth *Mer. of Venice* i 1 142
I do not doubt, As I will watch the aim i 1 150
When you shall please to play the thieves for wives, I'll watch as long for you ii 6 24
Lie not a night from home; watch me like Argus v 1 230
Lay couching, head on ground, with catlike watch *As Y. Like It* iv 3 116
I'll watch you better yet.—In time I may believe *T. of Shrew* iii 1 50
Are you so formal, sir? well, I must wait, And watch withal iii 1 62
My fellow-schoolmaster Doth watch Bianca's steps so narrowly iii 2 141
That by degrees we mean to look into, And watch our vantage iii 2 146
Watch her, as we watch these kites That bate and beat iv 1 198
She shall watch all night: And if she chance to nod I'll rail and brawl iv 1 208
To painful labour both by sea and land, To watch the night in storms v 2 150

Watch. Perchance wind up my watch, or play with my—some rich jewel *T. Night* ii 5 66
Since when, my watch hath told me, toward my grave I have travell'd but two hours v 1 165
Be heedful: hence, and watch *K. John* iv 1 5
I would you were a little sick, That I might sit all night and watch with you iv 1 30
Thus long have we stood To watch the fearful bending of thy knee *Richard II.* iii 3 73
Such, they say, as stand in narrow lanes, And beat our watch v 3 9
My thoughts are minutes; and with sighs they jar Their watches on unto mine eyes, the outward watch v 5 52
Clap to the doors: watch to-night, pray to-morrow 1 *Hen. IV.* ii 4 306
The sheriff with a most monstrous watch is at the door ii 4 530
I will sit and watch here by the king 2 *Hen. IV.* iv 5 20
As he whose brow with homely biggen bound Snores out the watch of night iv 5 28
My brother here, my liege, Who undertook to sit and watch by you iv 5 53
The hum of either army stilly sounds, That the fix'd sentinels almost receive The secret whispers of each other's watch *Hen. V.* iv Prol. 7
Walking from watch to watch, from tent to tent iv Prol. 30
But in gross brain little wots What watch the king keeps to maintain the peace iv 1 300
Since they, so few, watch such a multitude 1 *Hen. VI.* i 1 161
Now do thou watch, for I can stay no longer i 4 18
Constrain'd to watch in darkness, rain, and cold ii 1 7
Had your watch been good, This sudden mischief never could have fall'n ii 1 58
That, being captain of the watch to-night, Did look no better to that weighty charge ii 1 61
If we have entrance, as I hope we shall, And that we find the slothful watch but weak iii 2 7
And then do execution on the watch iii 2 35
Yet let us watch the haughty cardinal 2 *Hen. VI.* i 1 174
Watch thou and wake when others be asleep i 1 249
Ten is the hour that was appointed me To watch i 4 7
Slily have I lurk'd, To watch the waning of mine adversaries *Rich. III.* iv 4 4
Hie thee to thy charge; Use careful watch, choose trusty sentinels v 3 54
Give me a watch. Saddle white Surrey for the field to-morrow v 3 63
Bid my guard watch; leave me v 3 76
At all these wards I lie, at a thousand watches.—Say one of your watches.—Nay, I'll watch you for that *Troi. and Cres.* i 2 289
If I cannot ward what I would not have hit, I can watch you for telling how I took the blow i 2 293
Yea, watch His pettish lunes, his ebbs, his flows ii 3 138
I'll watch him Till he be dieted to my request *Coriolanus* v 1 56
The measure done, I'll watch her place of stand *Rom. and Jul.* i 5 52
Care keeps his watch in every old man's eye ii 3 35
Stay not till the watch be set, For then thou canst not pass to Mantua iii 3 148
Either be gone before the watch be set, Or by the break of day iii 3 167
And he and I Will watch thy waking iv 1 116
But I will watch you from such watching now iv 4 12
O Lord, they fight! I will go call the watch v 3 71
Stay not to question, for the watch is coming v 3 158
Where is the county's page, that raised the watch? v 3 279
My master drew on him; And then I ran away to call the watch v 3 285
There is one within, Besides the things that we have heard and seen, Recounts most horrid sights seen by the watch *J. Cæsar* ii 2 16
So please you, we will stand and watch your pleasure iv 3 249
Alarum'd by his sentinel, the wolf, Whose howl's his watch *Macbeth* ii 1 54
And near approaches The subject of our watch iii 3 8
As I did stand my watch upon the hill, I look'd toward Birnam v 5 33
If you do meet Horatio and Marcellus, The rivals of my watch *Hamlet* i 1 13
I have entreated him along With us to watch the minutes of this night i 1 27
Jump at this dead hour, With martial stalk hath he gone by our watch i 1 65
Tell me, he that knows, Why this same strict and most observant watch So nightly toils? i 1 71
Is the main motive of our preparations, The source of this our watch i 1 106
Well may it sort that this portentous figure Comes armed through our watch i 1 110
Break we our watch up; and by my advice, Let us impart what we have seen i 1 168
On their watch, In the dead vast and middle of the night i 2 197
And I with them the third night kept the watch i 2 208
Hold you the watch to-night?—We do, my lord i 2 225
I will watch to-night; Perchance 'twill walk again i 2 242
Fell into a sadness, then into a fast, Thence to a watch ii 2 148
For some must watch, while some must sleep: So runs the world away iii 2 284
Follow her close; give her good watch, I pray you iv 5 75
Good Gertrude, set some watch over your son v 1 319
Brother, I say! My father watches: O sir, fly this place *Lear* ii 1 22
To watch—poor perdu!—With this thin helm? iv 7 35
At this odd-even and dull watch o' the night *Othello* i 1 124
The lieutenant to-night watches on the court of guard ii 1 219
Watch you to-night; for the command, I'll lay't upon you ii 1 271
We must to the watch.—Not this hour, lieutenant ii 3 12
And he's to watch: Three lads of Cyprus . . . watch too ii 3 56
To the platform, masters; come, let's set the watch ii 3 125
He'll watch the horologe a double set, If drink rock not his cradle ii 3 135
Help, masters!—Here's a goodly watch indeed! ii 3 160
Good night, lieutenant; I must to the watch ii 3 340
I'll watch him tame and talk him out of patience iii 3 23
If you will watch his going thence, which I will fashion to fall out between twelve and one, you may take him at your pleasure iv 2 241
What, ho! no watch? no passage? murder! murder! v 1 37
How he upbraids Iago, that he made him Brave me upon the watch v 2 326
Soldiers, have careful watch.—And you. Good night *Ant. and Cleo.* iv 3 7
What is it to be false? To lie in watch there and to think on him? To weep 'twixt clock and clock? *Cymbeline* iii 4 43
Watch-case. And leavest the kingly couch A watch-case or a common 'larum-bell 2 *Hen. IV.* iii 1 17
Watch-dog. Hark, hark! Bow-wow. The watch-dogs bark *Tempest* i 2 383
Watched. It hath been the longest night That e'er I watch'd *T. G. of V.* iv 2 141
Do not fly; I think we have watch'd you now *Mer. Wives* v 5 107
Being a watch, But being watch'd that it may still go right! *L. L. Lost* iii 1 195
I have watch'd so long That I am dog-weary *T. of Shrew* iv 2 59
My revenges were high bent upon him, And watch'd the time to shoot *All's Well* v 3 11
For sleeping England long time have I watch'd *Richard II.* ii 1 77
In thy faint slumbers I by thee have watch'd 1 *Hen. IV.* ii 3 50
Watched. Even these three days have I watch'd, If I could see them 1 *Hen. VI.* i 4 16
Beldam, I think we watch'd you at an inch 2 *Hen. VI.* i 4 45
You watch'd her well: A pretty plot, well chosen to build upon! i 4 58
I have watch'd the night, Ay, night by night, in studying good iii 1 110
And watch'd him how he singled Clifford forth 3 *Hen. VI.* ii 1 12
Thine uncles and myself Have in our armours watch'd the winter's night v 7 17
You must be watched ere you be made tame, must you? *Troi. and Cres.* iii 2 45
For your voices I have fought; Watch'd for your voices *Coriolanus* ii 3 134
For all the frosty nights that I have watch'd *T. Andron.* iii 1 5
I have watch'd ere now All night for lesser cause *Rom. and Jul.* iv 4 9
I have two nights watched with you, but can perceive no truth in your report. When was it she last walked? *Macbeth* v 1 1
Where was this?—My lord, upon the platform where we watch'd *Hamlet* i 2 213
I have watched and travell'd hard; Some time I shall sleep out *Lear* ii 2 162
Watcher. Love hath chased sleep from my enthralled eyes And made them watchers of mine own heart's sorrow *T. G. of Ver.* ii 4 135
Hark! more knocking. Get on your nightgown, lest occasion call us, And show us to be watchers *Macbeth* ii 2 71
Watchful. With twenty watchful, weary, tedious nights *T. G. of Ver.* i 1 31
Despite of brooded watchful day, I would into thy bosom pour my thoughts: But, ah, I will not! *K. John* iii 3 52
And like the watchful minutes to the hour, Still and anon cheer'd up the heavy time iv 1 46
Keep'st the ports of slumber open wide To many a watchful night! 2 *Hen. IV.* iv 5 25
By their watchful fires Sit patiently and inly ruminate *Hen. V.* iv Prol. 23
Not sleeping, to engross his idle body, But praying, to enrich his watchful soul *Richard III.* iii 7 77
To thee I do commend my watchful soul, Ere I let fall the windows of mine eyes v 3 115
Cry mercy, lords and watchful gentlemen v 3 224
The providence that's in a watchful state Knows almost every grain of Plutus' gold *Troi. and Cres.* iii 3 196
What watchful cares do interpose themselves Betwixt your eyes and night? *J. Cæsar* ii 1 98
That fled the snares of watchful tyranny *Macbeth* v 8 67
Watching. Though it cost me ten nights' watchings *Much Ado* ii 1 387
Watching breeds leanness, leanness is all gaunt *Richard II.* ii 1 78
These cheeks are pale for watching for your good 2 *Hen. VI.* iv 7 90
Unless it swell past hiding, and then it's past watching *Troi. and Cres.* i 2 295
You'll be sick to-morrow For this night's watching *Rom. and Jul.* iv 4 8
But I will watch you from such watching now iv 4 12
A great perturbation in nature, to receive at once the benefit of sleep, and do the effects of watching! *Macbeth* v 1 12
I have a pain upon my forehead here.—'Faith, that's with watching *Othello* iii 3 285
I slept not, but profess Had that was well worth watching *Cymbeline* ii 4 68
She purposed, By watching, weeping, tendance, kissing, to O'ercome you v 5 53
Watchman. You speak like an ancient and most quiet watchman *M. Ado* iii 3 42
The special watchmen of our English weal 1 *Hen. VI.* iii 1 66
I shall the effect of this good lesson keep, As watchman to my heart *Hamlet* i 3 46
Let's see if other watchmen Do hear what we do *Ant. and Cleo.* iv 3 18
Watchword. When I give the watch-'ords, do as I pid you *Mer. Wives* v 4 3
Our watchword was 'Hem boys!' 2 *Hen. IV.* iii 2 231
Water. He'll be hang'd yet, Though every drop of water swear against it And gape at widest to glut him *Tempest* i 1 62
If by your art, my dearest father, you have Put the wild waters in this roar, allay them i 2 2
Some food we had and some fresh water i 2 160
Madest much of me, wouldst give me Water with berries in't i 2 334
This music crept by me upon the waters i 2 391
Being rather new-dyed than stained with salt water ii 1 64
He trod the water, Whose enmity he flung aside ii 1 115
I am standing water.—I'll teach you how to flow ii 1 221
When the butt is out, we will drink water; not a drop before iii 2 2
Or with bemock'd-at stabs Kill the still-closing waters iii 3 64
These follies are within you and shine through you like the water in an urinal *T. G. of Ver.* ii 1 41
If all their sand were pearl, The water nectar, and the rocks pure gold ii 4 171
Trenched in ice, which with an hour's heat Dissolves to water iii 2 8
When didst thou see me heave up my leg and make water against a gentlewoman's farthingale? iv 4 41
Sheathe thy impatience, throw cold water on thy choler *Mer. Wives* ii 3 89
Throwing him into the water will do him a benefit iii 3 194
Excuse his throwing into the water; and give him another hope iii 3 207
A woman would run through fire and water for such a kind heart iii 4 107
A death that I abhor; for the water swells a man iii 5 16
Come, let me pour in some sack to the Thames water iii 5 23
He is very courageous mad about his throwing into the water iv 1 5
When he makes water his urine is congealed ice *Meas. for Meas.* iii 2 117
Command these fretting waters from your eyes With a light heart iv 3 151
I am fain to dine and sup with water and bran iv 3 159
I to the world am like a drop of water That in the ocean seeks another drop *Com. of Errors* i 2 35
As easy mayst thou fall A drop of water in the breaking gulf ii 2 128
That's a fault that water will mend.—No, sir, 'tis in grain iii 2 107
Which falls into mine ears as profitless As water in a sieve *Much Ado* v 1 5
You shall fast a week with bran and water *L. L. Lost* i 1 303
Beg a greater matter; Thou now request'st but moonshine in the water v 2 208
I promise you your kindred hath made my eyes water ere now *M. N. D.* iii 1 200
Which, when I saw rehearsed, I must confess, Made mine eyes water v 1 69
Enrobe the roaring waters with my silks *Mer. of Venice* i 1 34
Then there is the peril of waters, winds, and rocks i 3 25
Mark me now; now will I raise the waters ii 2 52
Empties itself, as doth an inland brook Into the main of waters v 1 97
Though thou the waters warp, Thy sting is not so sharp *As Y. Like It* ii 7 187
Balm his foul head in warm distilled waters *T. of Shrew* Ind. 1 48
And therefore fire, fire; cast on no water iv 1 21
Where are my slippers? Shall I have some water? iv 1 156
Yet in this captious and intenible sieve I still pour in the waters of my love *All's Well* i 3 209
I love not many words.—No more than a fish loves water iii 6 92
Water once a day her chamber round With eye-offending brine *T. Night* i 1 29
I would not so much as make water but in a sink-a-pace i 3 139
'Tis with him in standing water, between boy and man i 5 168
She is drowned already, sir, with salt water ii 1 32
Carry his water to the wise woman.—Marry, and it shall be done iii 4 114

Water. My most exquisite Sir Topas!—Nay, I am for all waters *T. N.* iv 2 68
False As o'er-dyed blacks, as wind, as waters, false As dice . *W. Tale* i 2 132
Though a devil Would have shed water out of fire ere done't . . . ii 2 194
The men are not yet cold under water . . . . iii 3 108
Never gazed the moon Upon the water as he'll stand . . . . iv 4 173
On Wednesday the four-score of April, forty thousand fathom above water . . . . iv 4 281
A wild dedication of yourselves To unpath'd waters, undream'd shores iv 4 578
The lands and waters 'twixt your throne and his Measured to look upon you . . . . v 1 144
Caught the water, though not the fish . . . . v 2 91
Being as like As rain to water, or devil to his dam . . . *K. John* ii 1 128
Unless thou let his silver water keep A peaceful progress to the ocean . ii 1 339
Trust not those cunning waters of his eyes . . . . . . iv 3 107
Wouldst thou drown thyself, Put but a little water in a spoon . iv 3 131
Commend these waters to those baby eyes That never saw the giant world enraged . . . . v 2 56
Not all the water in the rough rude sea Can wash the balm off from an anointed king . . . . *Richard II.* iii 2 54
Should meet With no less terror than the elements Of fire and water . iii 3 56
Be he the fire, I'll be the yielding water: The rage be his, whilst on the earth I rain My waters . . . . iii 3 58
Two buckets, filling one another, The emptier ever dancing in the air, The other down, unseen, and full of water . . . . . iv 1 187
You Pilates Have here deliver'd me to my sour cross, And water cannot wash away your sin . . . . iv 1 242
Yet salt water blinds them not so much But they can see a sort of traitors . . . . iv 1 245
What, the commonwealth their boots? will she hold out water? 1 *Hen. IV.* ii 1 93
There will be a world of water shed Upon the parting of your wives and you . . . . iii 1 94
What says the doctor to my water?—He said, sir, the water itself was a good healthy water . . . . 2 *Hen. IV.* i 2 2
As fierce As waters to the sucking of a gulf . . . *Hen. V.* ii 4 10
Can sodden water . . . Decoct their cold blood to such valiant heat? . iii 5 18
The dull elements of earth and water never appear in him . . . iii 7 23
The pretty and sweet manner of it forced Those waters from me . . iv 6 29
All the water in Wye cannot wash your majesty's Welsh plood out of your pody . . . . iv 7 111
Glory is like a circle in the water, Which never ceaseth to enlarge itself Till by broad spreading it disperse to nought . . 1 *Hen. VI.* i 2 133
By water shall he die, and take his end . . . . 2 *Hen. VI.* i 4 36; 68
Smooth runs the water where the brook is deep . . . . . iii 1 53
A cunning man did calculate my birth And told me that by water I should die . . . . iv 1 35
And if thine eyes can water for his death, I give thee this to dry thy cheeks withal . . . . 3 *Hen. VI.* i 4 82
Is't meet that he Should leave the helm and like a fearful lad With tearful eyes add water to the sea? . . . . v 4 8
For every word I speak, Ye see, I drink the water of mine eyes . . v 4 75
What dreadful noise of waters in mine ears! . . . . *Richard III.* i 4 22
As, by proof, we see The waters swell before a boisterous storm . ii 3 44
By sudden floods and fall of waters, Buckingham's army is dispersed . iv 4 512
When they once perceive The least rub in your fortunes, fall away Like water from ye . . . . *Hen. VIII.* ii 1 130
Men's evil manners live in brass; their virtues We write in water . iv 2 46
The bounded waters Should lift their bosoms higher than the shores *Troi. and Cres.* i 3 111
More dregs than water, if my fears have eyes . . . . . . iii 2 72
As false As air, as water, wind, or sandy earth . . . . . iii 2 199
Would the fountain of your mind were clear again, that I might water an ass at it! . . . . iii 3 314
Of the same house Publius and Quintus were, That our best water brought by conduits hither . . . . . . *Coriolanus* ii 3 250
Whose rage doth rend Like interrupted waters . . . . . iii 1 249
My son! thou art preparing fire for us; look thee, here's water to quench it . . . . v 2 78
Sith priest and holy water are so near . . . . *T. Andron.* i 1 323
More water glideth by the mill Than wots the miller of . . . ii 1 85
Go home, call for sweet water, wash thy hands . . . . . ii 4 6
What fool hath added water to the sea? . . . . iii 1 68
That kiss is comfortless As frozen water to a starved snake . . iii 1 252
For all the water in the ocean Can never turn the swan's black legs to white . . . . iv 2 101
How much salt water thrown away in waste, To season love! *R. and J.* ii 3 71
Thy canopy is dust and stones;—Which with sweet water nightly I will dew . . . . v 3 14
'Tis a good form.—And rich: here is a water, look ye *T. of Athens* i 1 18
Here's that which is too weak to be a sinner, honest water . . . i 2 59
Mine eyes cannot hold out water, methinks . . . . . . i 2 111
She's e'en setting on water to scald such chickens as you are . . ii 2 71
Mouth-friends! smoke and luke-warm water Is your perfection . . iii 6 99
We cannot live on grass, on berries, water, As beasts and birds and fishes iv 3 425
How shall I requite you? Can you eat roots, and drink cold water? . v 1 77
Passion, I see, is catching; for mine eyes, Seeing those beads of sorrow stand in thine, Began to water . . . . . *J. Cæsar* iii 1 285
The earth hath bubbles, as the water has, And these are of them *Macb.* i 3 79
Go get some water, And wash this filthy witness from your hand . . ii 2 46
A little water clears us of this deed: How easy is it, then! . . . ii 2 67
If thou couldst, doctor, cast The water of my land, find her disease, And purge it to a sound and pristine health . . . . . v 3 51
Too much of water hast thou, poor Ophelia . . . . *Hamlet* iv 7 186
Here lies the water; good: here stands the man; good: if the man go to this water, and drown himself, it is, will he, nill he, he goes,—mark you that; but if the water come to him and drown him, he drowns not himself . . . . v 1 17
His hide is so tanned with his trade, that he will keep out water a great while . . . . v 1 187
Your water is a sore decayer of your whoreson dead body . . . v 1 188
Beweep this cause again, I'll pluck ye out, And cast you, with the waters that you lose, To temper clay . . . . *Lear* i 4 325
Blow the earth into the sea, Or swell the curled waters 'bove the main iii 1 6
When brewers mar their malt with water . . . . iii 2 82
Eats the swimming frog, the toad, the tadpole, the wall-newt, and the water . . . . iii 4 136
She shook The holy water from her heavenly eyes, And clamour moisten'd iv 3 32
The wind-shaked surge, with high and monstrous mane, Seems to cast water on the burning bear . . . . *Othello* ii 1 14
I cannot weep; nor answer have I none, But what should go by water iv 2 104
She was false as water.—Thou art rash as fire, to say That she was false v 2 134

Water. We cannot call her winds and waters sighs and tears *Ant. and Cleo.* i 2 153
Indeed the tears live in an onion that should water this sorrow . . i 2 177
Where be the sacred vials thou shouldst fill With sorrowful water? . i 3 64
The barge she sat in, like a burnish'd throne, Burn'd on the water . ii 2 197
The oars were silver, . . . and made The water which they beat to follow faster, As amorous of their strokes . . . . ii 2 201
You have done well by water.—And you by land . . . . . ii 6 89
It cannot be denied what I have done by land.—Nor what I have done by water . . . . ii 6 94
And makes it indistinct, As water is in water . . . . . . iv 14 11
His steeds to water at those springs On chaliced flowers that lies *Cymb.* ii 3 23
Ribb'd and paled in With rocks unscaleable and roaring waters . . iii 1 20
My tears that fall Prove holy water on thee! . . . . . . v 5 269
A man whom both the waters and the wind, In that vast tennis-court, have made the ball . . . . *Pericles* ii 1 63
'Twas we that made up this garment through the rough seams of the waters . . . . ii 1 156
As chiding a nativity As fire, air, water, earth, and heaven can make . iii 1 33
The belching whale And humming water must o'erwhelm thy corpse . iii 1 64
The diamonds of a most praised water Do appear . . . . . iii 2 102
If fires be hot, knives sharp, or waters deep, Untied I still my virgin knot will keep . . . . iv 2 159
Water-colours. Never yet did insurrection want Such water-colours to impaint his cause . . . . 1 *Hen. IV.* v 1 80
Water-drop. To melt myself away in water-drops! . . . *Richard II.* iv 1 262
When waterdrops have worn the stones of Troy . . *Troi. and Cres.* iii 2 193
Let not women's weapons, water-drops, Stain my man's cheeks! *Lear* ii 4 280
Watered. He water'd his new plants with dews of flattery . *Coriolanus* v 6 23
There was a Spaniard's mouth so watered, that he went to bed to her very description . . . . *Pericles* iv 2 108
Water-flowing. My mercy dried their water-flowing tears 3 *Hen. VI.* iv 8 43
Water-fly. How the poor world is pestered with such waterflies, diminutives of nature! . . . . *Troi. and Cres.* v 1 38
Dost know this water-fly?—No . . . . *Hamlet* v 2 84
And let the water-flies Blow me into abhorring! . . *Ant. and Cleo.* v 2 59
Waterford. Great Earl of Washford, Waterford, and Valence 1 *Hen. VI.* iv 7 63
Watering. When you breathe in your watering, they cry 'hem!' 1 *Hen. IV.* ii 4 17
Waterish. Not all the dukes of waterish Burgundy Can buy this unprized precious maid of me . . . . *Lear* i 1 261
Or feed upon such nice and waterish diet . . . . . *Othello* iii 3 15
Water-pots. This would make a man a man of salt, To use his eyes for garden water-pots . . . . *Lear* iv 6 200
Water-rats. There be land-rats and water-rats . . *Mer. of Venice* i 3 23
Water-rugs. Spaniels, curs, Shoughs, water-rugs, and demi-wolves are clept All by the name of dogs . . . . *Macbeth* iii 1 94
Water side. To the water side I must conduct your grace . *Hen. VIII.* ii 1 95
Water-spaniel. She hath more qualities than a water-spaniel *T. G. of Ver.* iii 1 271
Water-standing. Many an orphan's water-standing eye . 3 *Hen. VI.* v 6 40
Water-thieves. There be land-rats and water-rats, water-thieves and land-thieves, I mean pirates . . . . *Mer. of Venice* i 3 24
Waterton. Sir Robert Waterton and Francis Quoint . *Richard II.* ii 1 284
Water-walled. England, . . . That water-walled bulwark . *K. John* ii 1 27
Water-work. The story of the Prodigal, or the German hunting in water-work . . . . 2 *Hen. IV.* ii 1 158
Watery. The queen o' the sky, Whose watery arch and messenger am I *Tempest* iv 1 71
We'll use this unwholesome humidity, this gross watery pumpion *M. W.* iii 3 43
Lords of the wide world and wild watery seas . . *Com. of Errors* ii 1 21
To shine, Those clouds removed, upon our watery eyne . . *L. L. Lost* v 2 206
When Phœbe doth behold Her silver visage in the watery glass *M. N. D.* i 1 210
Quench'd in the chaste beams of the watery moon . . . . ii 1 162
The moon methinks looks with a watery eye . . . . . . iii 1 203
The watery kingdom, whose ambitious head Spits in the face of heaven, is no bar To stop the foreign spirits . . *Mer. of Venice* ii 7 44
My eye shall be the stream And watery death-bed for him . . . iii 2 47
An onion . . . Shall in despite enforce a watery eye . *T. of Shrew* Ind. 1 128
So went he suited to his watery tomb . . . . . . *T. Night* v 1 241
Nine changes of the watery star hath been The shepherd's note *W. Tale* i 2 1
Whose rocky shore beats back the envious siege Of watery Neptune *Richard II.* ii 1 63
That I, being govern'd by the watery moon, May send forth plenteous tears to drown the world! . . . . *Richard III.* ii 2 69
What will it be, When that the watery palate tastes indeed Love's thrice repured nectar? . . . . *Troi. and Cres.* iii 2 22
This sorrow is an enemy, And would usurp upon my watery eyes *T. An.* iii 1 269
The collars of the moonshine's watery beams . . . *Rom. and Jul.* i 4 62
Having thrown him from your watery grave, Here to have death *Pericles* ii 1 10
From their watery empire recollect All that may men approve or men detect! . . . . ii 1 54
Wave. The fire and cracks Of sulphurous roaring the most mighty Neptune Seem to besiege and make his bold waves tremble *Tempest* i 2 205
Courtsied when you have and kiss'd The wild waves whist . . . i 2 379
His bold head 'Bove the contentious waves he kept . . . . ii 1 118
Spread o'er the silver waves thy golden hairs . . *Com. of Errors* iii 2 48
Now, by the salt wave of the Mediterraneum, a sweet touch! *L. L. Lost* v 1 61
I saw him hold acquaintance with the waves So long as I could see *T. N.* i 2 16
O, if it prove, Tempests are kind and salt waves fresh in love . . iii 4 419
I had a sister, Whom the blind waves and surges have devour'd . . v 1 236
When you do dance, I wish you A wave o' the sea . . *W. Tale* iv 4 141
And spend her strength with over-matching waves . . 3 *Hen. VI.* i 4 21
Let our bloody colours wave! And either victory, or else a grave . . ii 2 173
As doth a sail, fill'd with a fretting gust, Command an argosy to stem the waves . . . . ii 6 36
As good to chide the waves as speak them fair . . . . . v 4 24
There's no hoped-for mercy with the brothers More than with ruthless waves . . . . v 4 36
So many so minded, Wave thus, to express his disposition . *Coriolanus* i 6 74
We shall hardly in our ages see Their banners wave again . . . iii 1 8
Who marks the waxing tide grow wave by wave . . *T. Andron.* iii 1 95
So from the waves of Tiber Did I the tired Cæsar [bear] . . *J. Cæsar* i 2 114
Though the yesty waves Confound and swallow navigation up *Macbeth* iv 1 53
With what courteous action It waves you to a more removed ground *Ham.* i 4 61
It waves me forth again: I'll follow it . . . . i 4 68
It waves me still. Go on; I'll follow thee.—You shall not go, my lord i 4 78
With his own sword, Which he did wave against my throat, I have ta'en His head from him . . . . *Cymbeline* iv 2 150
Some slain before; some dying; some their friends O'er-borne i' the former wave . . . . v 3 48
Let A Roman and a British ensign wave Friendly together . . . . v 5 480

Wave. Having all lost, By waves from coast to coast is tost . *Per.* ii Gower 34
When was this?—When I was born: Never was waves nor wind more violent . . . . iv 1 60
Waved. He waved indifferently 'twixt doing them neither good nor harm *Coriolanus* ii 2 19
He had a thousand noses, Horns whelk'd and waved like the enridged sea. . . . . *Lear* iv 6 71
Then waved his handkerchief?—And kiss'd it, madam . *Cymbeline* i 3 6
Waver. Thou almost makest me waver in my faith . *Mer. of Venice* iv 1 130
Waverer. But come, young waverer, come, go with me . *Rom. and Jul.* ii 3 89
Wavering. Our fancies are more giddy and unfirm, More longing, wavering, sooner lost and worn, Than women's are . *T. Night* ii 4 35
The wavering commons: for their love Lies in their purses *Richard II.* ii 2 129
The still-discordant wavering multitude . 2 *Hen. IV.* Ind. 19
Remember where we are; In France, amongst a fickle wavering nation 1 *Hen. VI.* iv 1 138
Wave-worn. To the shore, that o'er his wave-worn basis bow'd *Tempest* ii 1 120
Waving. Even as the waving sedges play with wind . *T. of Shrew* Ind. 2 55
Advance our waving colours on the walls. . 1 *Hen. VI.* i 6 1
Stands colossus-wise, waving his beam . *Troi. and Cres.* v 5 9
With his hat, thus waving it in scorn, 'I would be consul,' says he *Coriol.* ii 3 175
Waving thy head, Which often, thus, correcting thy stout heart . . iii 2 77
Waving our red weapons o'er our heads, Let's all cry 'Peace, freedom, and liberty!' . . . . *J. Cæsar* iii 1 109
Thrice his head thus waving up and down, He raised a sigh . *Hamlet* ii 1 93
He did keep The deck, with glove, or hat, or handkerchief, Still waving *Cymbeline* i 3 12
Wawl. The first time that we smell the air, We wawl and cry . *Lear* iv 6 184
Wax. Break the neck of the wax, and every one give ear . *L. L. Lost* iv 1 59
That was the way to make his godhead wax . . . . v 2 10
One To whom you are but as a form in wax . . . *M. N. Dream* i 1 49
Since I nor wax nor honey can bring home, I quickly were dissolved from my hive, To give some labourers room . . *All's Well* i 2 65
By your leave, wax. Soft! and the impressure her Lucrece . *T. Night* ii 5 103
Even as a form of wax Resolveth from his figure 'gainst the fire *K. John* v 4 24
A wassail candle, my lord, all tallow: if I did say of wax, my growth would approve the truth . . . . . . 2 *Hen. IV.* i 2 180
Our thighs pack'd with wax, our mouths with honey . . iv 5 77
Old I do wax; and from my weary limbs Honour is cudgelled *Hen. V.* v 1 89
A fair face will wither; a full eye will wax hollow . . v 2 170
The elder I wax, the better I shall appear . . . v 2 247
These eyes, like lamps whose wasting oil is spent, Wax dim . 1 *Hen. VI.* ii 5 9
Some say the bee stings: but I say, 'tis the bee's wax 2 *Hen. VI.* iv 2 89
I seek not to wax great by others' waning, Or gather wealth, I care not iv 10 22
Have wrought the easy-melting king like wax . 3 *Hen. VI.* ii 1 171
As red as fire! nay, then her wax must melt . . . iii 2 51
A stone is soft as wax,—tribunes more hard than stones *T. Andron.* iii 1 45
If the winds rage, doth not the sea wax mad, Threatening the welkin? iii 1 223
Lady, such a man As all the world—why, he's a man of wax *R. and J.* i 3 76
Come on then, let's to bed. Ah, sirrah, by my fay, it waxes late . i 5 128
Thy noble shape is but a form of wax, Digressing from the valour of a man . . . . iii 3 126
My free drift Halts not particularly, but moves itself In a wide sea of wax . . . . *T. of Athens* i 1 47
What's on this tomb I cannot read; the character I'll take with wax . v 3 6
And on his grave-stone this insculpture, which With wax I brought away . . . . v 4 68
Set this up with wax Upon old Brutus' statue . . *J. Cæsar* i 3 145
But, as this temple waxes, The inward service of the mind and soul Grows wide withal . . . . *Hamlet* i 3 12
He waxes desperate with imagination.—Let's follow . . i 4 87
To the noble mind Rich gifts wax poor when givers prove unkind. . iii 1 101
To flaming youth let virtue be as wax, And melt in her own fire . . iii 4 84
Let us see: Leave, gentle wax; and, manners, blame us not . *Lear* iv 6 264
Good wax, thy leave. Blest be You bees that make these locks of counsel! . . . . *Cymbeline* iii 2 35
Waxed. Wringing her hands, whose whiteness so became them As if but now they waxed pale for woe . *T. G. of Ver.* iii 1 228
By the benefit of his wished light, The seas wax'd calm . *Com. of Errors* i 1 92
His pupil age Man-enter'd thus, he waxed like a sea . *Coriolanus* ii 2 103
Ay, but the days are wax'd shorter with him . . *T. of Athens* iii 4 11
Waxen. Which, like a waxen image 'gainst a fire, Bears no impression of the thing it was . . . . *T. G. of Ver.* ii 4 201
With rounds of waxen tapers on their heads . . *Mer. Wives* iv 4 50
And waxen in their mirth and neeze and swear . . *M. N. Dream* ii 1 56
The honey-bags steal from the humble-bees, And for night-tapers crop their waxen thighs . . . . iii 1 172
How easy is it for the proper-false In women's waxen hearts to set their forms! . . . . *T. Night* ii 2 31
Steel my lance's point, That it may enter Mowbray's waxen coat *Rich. II.* i 3 75
Not worshipp'd with a waxen epitaph . . . *Hen. V.* i 2 233
What! art thou, like the adder, waxen deaf? Be poisonous too 2 *Hen. VI.* iii 2 76
Way. Out of our way, I say . . . . . . *Tempest* i 1 29
Thou art inclined to sleep; 'tis a good dulness, And give it way . . i 2 186
Pity move my father To be inclined my way! . . . . i 2 447
No hope that way is Another way so high a hope . . . ii 1 240
Nor lead me, like a firebrand, in the dark Out of my way . . ii 2 7
Then like hedgehogs which Lie tumbling in my barefoot way . . ii 2 11
The storm is come again! my best way is to creep under his gaberdine ii 2 39
Come on your ways; open your mouth . . . . . ii 2 85
I prithee now, lead the way without any more talking . . ii 2 177
Freedom, hey-day, freedom!—O brave monster! Lead the way . ii 2 192
Lingering perdition, worse than any death Can be at once, shall step by step attend You and your ways . . . . . . iii 3 79
It is you that have chalk'd forth the way Which brought us hither . v 1 203
He would have given it you; but I, being in the way, Did in your name receive it: pardon the fault . . . . *T. G. of Ver.* i 2 39
And, being blind, How could he see his way to seek out you? . ii 4 94
Alas, the way is wearisome and long! . . . . . ii 7 8
For which the youthful lover now is gone And this way comes he. . iii 1 42
How and which way I may bestow myself . . . . iii 1 87
The best way is to slander Valentine With falsehood . . iii 2 31
And, for the ways are dangerous to pass, I do desire thy worthy company . . . . iv 3 24
If the gentle spirit of moving words Can no way change you . . iv 4 56
Come, come.—Nay, pray you, lead the way . . *Mer. Wives* i 1 318
Go your ways, and ask of Doctor Caius' house which is the way . i 2 1
His worst fault is, that he is given to prayer; he is something peevish that way . . . . i 4 14
Way. Speak a good word to Mistress Anne Page for my master in the way of marriage . . . . *Mer. Wives* i 4 89
One that is your friend, I can tell you that by the way . . i 4 150
I think the best way were to entertain him with hope . . . ii 1 67
I pray, come a little nearer this ways . . . . ii 2 46; 50
I defy all angels, in any such sort, as they say, but in the way of honesty . . . . ii 2 75
Go thy ways; I'll make more of thy old body than I have done . ii 2 144
They say, if money go before, all ways do lie open . . ii 2 175
Which way have you looked for Master Caius . . . ?— . . . Every way; old Windsor way, and every way but the town way.—I most fehemently desire you you will also look that way . . . iii 1 3
Yonder he is coming, this way . . . . . . iii 1 27
I desire you in friendship, and I will one way or other make you amends iii 1 89
Nay, keep your way, little gallant . . . . . iii 2 1
The wealth I have waits on my consent, and my consent goes not that way . . . . iii 2 79
We'll unkennel the fox. Let me stop this way first . . . iii 3 175
Go your ways, and play; go . . . . . . iv 1 81
Have you any way then to unfool me again? . . . . iv 2 120
He will never, I think, in the way of waste, attempt us again . iv 2 226
There is no better way than that they spoke of . . . iv 4 17
If he be amazed, he will every way be mocked . . . v 3 20
Give leave, my lord, That we may bring you something on the way *Meas. for Meas.* i 1 62
If you head and hang all that offend that way but for ten year together ii 1 252
Amen: For I am that way going to temptation, Where prayers cross . ii 2 158
A sister desires access to you.—Teach her the way . . . ii 4 19
Admit no other way to save his life . . . . . ii 4 88
Then must your brother die.—And 'twere the cheaper way . . ii 4 105
Is the world as it was, man? Which is the way? Is it sad, and few words? . . . . iii 2 53
Come your ways, sir; come.—You will not bail me, then? . . iii 2 84
Something too crabbed that way . . . . . . iii 2 105
Angelo was not made by man and woman after this downright way of creation . . . . iii 2 112
He was not inclined that way.—O, sir, you are deceived . . iii 2 130
But shall you on your knowledge find this way? . . . iv 1 37
In action all of precept, he did show me The way twice o'er . . iv 1 41
Let me have way, my lord, To find this practice out . . . v 1 238
I will go darkly to work with her.—That's the way . . . v 1 280
And must be buried but as an intent That perish'd by the way . . v 1 458
Post to the road: An if the wind blow any way from shore, I will not harbour in this town to-night . . . *Com. of Errors* iii 2 153
If Time be in debt and theft, and a sergeant in the way, Hath he not reason to turn back an hour in a day? . . . . . . iv 2 61
His wife, acquainted with his fits, On purpose shut the doors against his way . . . . iv 3 92
The duke himself in person Comes this way . . . . v 1 120
By the way we met My wife, her sister, and a rabble more . . v 1 235
But keep your way, i' God's name; I have done . *Much Ado* i 1 144
A proper squire! And who, and who? which way looks he? . . i 3 55
If I can cross him any way, I bless myself every way . . . i 3 71
I shall lessen God's sending that way . . . . . ii 1 24
What fashion will you wear the garland of? about your neck . . . ? or under your arm . . . ? You must wear it one way . . . ii 1 198
The most peaceable way for you, if you do take a thief, is to let him show himself what he is . . . . iii 3 61
I have only been Silent so long and given way unto This course of fortune . . . . iv 1 158
Is there any way to show such friendship?—A very even way . . iv 1 265
Use it for my love some other way than swearing by it . . . iv 1 329
Master constable, you go not the way to examine . . . iv 2 35
Yea, marry, that's the eftest way . . . . . iv 2 38
Good morrow, masters: each his several way . . . . v 3 29
What then, do you see?—Ay, our way to be gone . *L. L. Lost* i 1 257
The way is but short: away!—As swift as lead, sir. . . . iii 1 57
A kind of insinuation, as it were, in via, in way, of explication . iv 2 14
Which accidentally, or by the way of progression, hath miscarried . iv 2 144
God amend us, God amend! we are much out o' the way . . iv 3 76
Masks and merry hours Forerun fair Love, strewing her way with flowers . . . . iv 3 380
That is the way to make an offence gracious, though few have the grace to do it . . . . v 1 147
That was the way to make his godhead wax . . . . v 2 10
She is gone; she is two months on her way . . . . v 2 679
Why, that's the way to choke a gibing spirit . . . . v 2 868
And so I take my leave.—No, madam; we will bring you on your way v 2 883
When blood is nipp'd and ways be foul, Then nightly sings the staring owl . . . . v 2 926
You that way: we this way . . . . v 2 941
My love is more than his; My fortunes every way as fairly rank'd *M. N. Dream* i 1 101
Go thy way: thou shalt not from this grove Till I torment thee . . ii 1 146
To speak troth, I have forgot our way: We'll rest us . . . ii 2 36
Puppet? why so? ay, that way goes the game. . . . iii 2 289
Lead these testy rivals so astray As one come not within another's way iii 2 359
Fallen am I in dark uneven way, And here will rest me . . . iii 2 417
Fairies, be gone, and be all ways away . . . . . iv 1 46
Let's follow him; And by the way let us recount our dreams . . iv 1 204
That they'll not show their teeth in way of smile . *Mer. of Venice* i 1 55
I shot his fellow of the self-same flight The self-same way . . i 1 142
If you please To shoot another arrow that self way . . . i 1 148
This was a way to thrive, and he was blest: And thrift is blessing . i 3 90
If you choose wrong Never to speak to lady afterward In way of marriage . . . . ii 1 42
I pray you, which is the way to master Jew's? . . . . ii 2 35
By God's sonties, 'twill be a hard way to hit . . . . ii 2 47
Never in my life To woo a maid in way of marriage. . . . ii 9 13
Meeting with Salerio by the way, He did entreat me, past all saying nay . . . . iii 2 231
You are gone both ways.—I shall be saved by my husband . . iii 5 20
Welcome to our house: It must appear in other ways than words. . v 1 140
Like the mending of highways In summer, where the ways are fair enough . . . . v 1 264
Fair ladies, you drop manna in the way Of starved people . . v 1 294
Call him in. 'Twill be a good way . . . *As Y. Like It* i 1 99
Come your ways.—Now Hercules be thy speed, young man! . . i 2 221
Devise the fittest time and safest way To hide us from pursuit . . i 3 137
But come thy ways; we'll go along together . . . . ii 3 66

Way. That is the way to make her scorn you still . . *As Y. Like It* ii 4 22
And little recks to find the way to heaven By doing deeds of hospitality ii 4 81
Why, sir, must they be so? The 'why' is plain as way to parish church . ii 7 52
This way will I take upon me to wash your liver . . . . iii 2 441
And by the way you shall tell me where in the forest you live . . iii 2 452
Go your ways, go your ways; I knew what you would prove . . iv 1 186
Go your way to her, for I see love hath made thee a tame snake . iv 3 70
I will kill thee a hundred and fifty ways . . . . . . v 1 63
My way is to conjure you; and I'll begin with the women . . Epil. 11
Never need to fear: I wis it is not half way to her heart . *T. of Shrew* i 1 62
While I make way from hence to save my life . . . . . . i 1 239
Tell me, I beseech you, which is the readiest way To the house? . i 2 220
She struck me on the head, And through the instrument my pate made way . . . . ii 1 155
There lies your way; You may be jogging whiles your boots are green . iii 2 212
I'll bring mine action on the proudest he That stops my way . . iii 2 237
Fie on all tired jades, on all mad masters, and all foul ways! . . iv 1 2
It was the friar of orders grey, As he forth walked on his way . iv 1 149
She, poor soul, Knows not which way to stand, to look, to speak . iv 1 188
Another way I have to man my haggard, To make her come . . iv 1 196
Here I'll fling the pillow, there the bolster, This way the coverlet . iv 1 205
This is a way to kill a wife with kindness . . . . . iv 1 211
This, by the way, I let you understand; My father is here look'd for . iv 2 115
Shall I lead the way? Welcome! one mess is like to be your cheer . iv 4 69
Go thy ways; the field is won.—Well, forward, forward! . . . iv 5 23
And withal make known Which way thou travellest . . . . iv 5 51
Well, go thy ways, old lad; for thou shalt ha't . . . . v 2 181
I know him a notorious liar, Think him a great way fool . *All's Well* i 1 112
A prophet I, madam; and I speak the truth the next way . . i 3 63
Nay, come your ways.—This haste hath wings indeed.—Nay, come your ways . . . . ii 1 96
What impossibility would slay In common sense, sense saves another way ii 1 181
My state that way is dangerous, since I cannot yet find in my heart to repent . . . . ii 5 12
This drives me to entreat you That presently you take your way for home ii 5 69
We have lost our labour; they are gone a contrary way . . . iii 5 8
Is this the way?—Ay, marry, is't. Hark you! they come this way . iii 5 40
Put him to't; let him have his way . . . . iii 6 2
He can come no other way but by this hedge-corner . . . . iv 1 1
I'll take the sacrament on't, how and which way you will . . iv 3 157
The flowery way that leads to the broad gate and the great fire . iv 5 57
Go thy ways, I begin to be aweary of thee . . . . . iv 5 59
Go thy ways: let my horses be well looked to, without any tricks . iv 5 61
But to the brightest beams Distracted clouds give way . . . v 3 35
I liked her, And boarded her i' the wanton way of youth . . v 3 211
If it were yours by none of all these ways, How could you give it him? v 3 276
Tell me where thou hast been, or I will not open my lips so wide as a bristle may enter in way of thy excuse . . . *T. Night* i 5 3
Apt, in good faith; very apt. Well, go thy way . . . . i 5 29
Will you hoist sail, sir? here lies your way . . . . . i 5 216
If that the youth will come this way to-morrow, I'll give him reasons for't i 5 324
I will drop in his way some obscure epistles of love . . . ii 3 168
If I cannot recover your niece, I am a foul way out . . . ii 3 201
Come thy ways, Signior Fabian.—Nay, I'll come . . . . ii 5 1
There lies your way, due west.—Then westward-ho! . . . . iii 1 145
An't be any way, it must be with valour; for policy I hate . . iii 2 32
There is no way but this . . . . iii 2 42
Which way is he, in the name of sanctity? . . . . . iii 4 93
Hold thy peace; this is not the way: do you not see you move him? . iii 4 121
No way but gentleness; gently, gently: the fiend is rough . . iii 4 123
Give them way till he take leave, and presently after him . . iii 4 217
Let him alone: I'll go another way to work with him . . . iv 1 36
I think nobly of the soul, and no way approve his opinion . . iv 2 59
Ever will be true.—Then lead the way, good father . . . iv 3 34
If thou inclinest that way, thou art a coward . . . . *W. Tale* i 2 243
Which way to be prevented, if to be; If not, how best to bear it . . i 2 405
Never Saw I men scour so on their way: I eyed them Even to their ships ii 1 35
The very thought of my revenges that way Recoil upon me . . . ii 3 19
If one jot beyond The bound of honour, or in act or will That way inclining . . . . iii 2 53
Could not move the gods To look that way thou wert . . . iii 2 215
Home, home, the next way. We are lucky, boy . . . . iii 3 129
Come, good boy, the next way home.—Go you the next way with your findings . . . . iii 3 131
I am no fighter: I am false of heart that way . . . . iv 3 116
Shall I bring thee on the way?—No, good-faced sir . . . . iv 3 122
Jog on, jog on, the foot-path way, And merrily hent the stile-a . iv 3 132
I tremble To think your father, by some accident, Should pass this way iv 4 20
Were never for a piece of beauty rarer, Nor in a way so chaste . iv 4 33
It is A way to make us better friends, more known . . . iv 4 66
You woo'd me the false way . . . . iv 4 151
Have I not told thee how I was cozened by the way and lost all my money? . . . . iv 4 255
There is no other way but to tell the king . . . . . iv 4 704
So must thy grave Give way to what's seen now! . . . . v 1 98
Meets he on the way The father of this seeming lady . . . v 1 190
Therefore follow me And mark what way I make . . . . v 1 233
Our country manners give our betters way . . . . *K. John* i 1 156
Good fortune come to thee! For thou wast got i' the way of honesty . i 1 181
Open your gates and give the victors way . . . . . ii 1 324
In beauty, virtue, birth, Is the young Dauphin every way complete . ii 1 433
Which we, God knows, have turn'd another way, To our own vantage . ii 1 549
I'll tell thee what, my friend, He is a very serpent in my way . iii 3 61
Thrust thyself into their companies: I have a way to win their loves again . . . . iv 2 168
And lose my way Among the thorns and dangers of this world . . iv 3 140
Send him word by me which way you go . . . . . . v 3 7
Befriend me so much as to think I come one way of the Plantagenets . v 6 11
What shall I say? to safeguard thine own life, The best way is to venge my Gloucester's death . . . . *Richard II.* i 2 36
Now no way can I stray; Save back to England, all the world's my way i 3 206
Look, what thy soul holds dear, imagine it To lie that way thou go'st . i 3 287
I'll bring thee on thy way: Had I thy youth and cause, I would not stay i 3 304
How far brought you high Hereford on his way? . . . . . i 4 2
Direct not him whose way himself will choose . . . . . ii 1 29
Why, so! go all which way it will! . . . . ii 2 87
If I know how or which way to order these affairs Thus thrust disorderly into my hands, Never believe me . . . . ii 2 109
These high wild hills and rough uneven ways Draws out our miles . ii 3 4
Your fair discourse hath been as sugar, Making the hard way sweet . ii 3 7

Way. But I bethink me what a weary way From Ravenspurgh to Cotswold . . . . *Richard II.* ii 3 8
In braving arms, Be his own carver and cut out his way . . . ii 3 144
And heavy-gaited toads lie in their way . . . . . . iii 2 15
Wise men ne'er sit and wail their woes, But presently prevent the ways to wail . . . . iii 2 179
Beshrew thee, cousin, which didst lead me forth Of that sweet way I was in to despair! . . . . iii 2 205
Or I'll be buried in the king's highway, Some way of common trade . iii 3 156
They well deserve to have, That know the strong'st and surest way to get iii 3 201
That not only givest Me cause to wail but teachest me the way How to lament the cause . . . . iv 1 301
This way the king will come; this is the way To Julius Cæsar's ill-erected tower . . . . v 1 1
He shall think that thou, which know'st the way To plant unrightful kings, wilt know again . . . another way To pluck him headlong . v 1 62
Go, count thy way with sighs; I mine with groans.—So longest way shall have the longest moans . . . . v 1 89
Twice for one step I'll groan, the way being short, And piece the way out with a heavy heart . . . . v 1 91
Make way, unruly woman! . . . . v 2 110
In mutual well-beseeming ranks, March all one way . . *1 Hen. IV.* i 1 15
Uncertain of the issue any way . . . . i 1 61
Never rise To do him wrong or any way impeach What then he said . i 3 75
Peas and beans are as dank here as a dog, and that is the next way to give poor jades the bots . . . . ii 1 10
What, the commonwealth their boots? will she hold out water in foul way? . . . . ii 1 93
Go thy ways, old Jack; die when thou wilt . . . . . ii 4 141
It is like we shall have good trading that way . . . . . ii 4 401
Can trace me in the tedious ways of art . . . . . . iii 1 48
In the way of bargain, mark ye me, I'll cavil on the ninth part of a hair iii 1 139
I will not sing.—'Tis the next way to turn tailor, or be red-breast teacher iii 1 264
A mad fellow met me on the way and told me I had unloaded all the gibbets . . . . iv 2 39
If that the king Have any way your good deserts forgot . . . iv 3 46
Rebellion lay in his way, and he found it . . . . . . v 1 28
And posted day and night To meet you on the way . . . . v 1 36
I'll pierce him. If he do come in my way, so . . . . . v 3 60
Our duty this way lies; for God's sake, come . . . . . v 4 16
I over-rode him on the way . . . . *2 Hen. IV.* i 1 30
He ask'd the way to Chester; and of him I did demand what news . i 1 39
He seem'd in running to devour the way, Staying no longer question . i 1 47
Counsel every man The aptest way for safety and revenge . . . i 1 213
You should have been well on your way to York . . . . ii 1 73
Your manner of wrenching the true cause the false way . . . ii 1 121
As common as the way between Saint Alban's and London . . . ii 2 184
Gentle daughter, Give even way unto my rough affairs . . . ii 3 2
'Tis with my mind As with the tide swell'd up unto his height, That makes a still-stand, running neither way . . . . ii 3 64
Let it go which way it will, he that dies this year is quit for the next . iii 2 254
We see which way the stream of time doth run . . . . . iv 1 70
He is not here.—This door is open; he is gone this way . . . iv 5 56
Rob, murder, and commit The oldest sins the newest kind of ways . iv 5 127
God knows, my son, By what by-paths and indirect crook'd ways I met this crown . . . . iv 5 185
He's walk'd the way of nature; And to our purposes he lives no more . v 2 4
I gave bold way to my authority And did commit you . . . . v 2 82
There's but two ways, either to utter them, or to conceal them . . v 3 116
As many arrows, loosed several ways, Come to one mark; as many ways meet in one town . . . . *Hen. V.* i 2 207
Hath brought to light This dangerous treason lurking in our way . ii 2 186
We doubt not now But every rub is smoothed on our way . . . ii 2 188
I knew there was but one way; for his nose was as sharp as a pen . ii 3 16
In the way of argument, look you, and friendly communication . . iii 2 104
We will come on, Though France himself and such another neighbour Stand in our way . . . . iii 6 167
And my way shall be paved with English faces . . . . . iii 7 87
I will not say so, for fear I should be faced out of my way . . iii 7 90
The deep-mouth'd sea, Which like a mighty whiffler 'fore the king Seems to prepare his way . . . . v Prol. 13
I know no ways to mince it in love, but directly to say 'I love you' . v 2 130
Who cannot see many a fair French city for one fair French maid that stands in my way . . . . v 2 346
So the maid that stood in the way for my wish shall show me the way to my will . . . . v 2 355
Better far, I guess, That we do make our entrance several ways *1 Hen. VI.* ii 1 30
Then how or which way should they first break in?—Question, my lords, no further of the case, How or which way . . . . ii 1 71
Turn not thy scorns this way, Plantagenet . . . . . . ii 4 77
Her meaning is, No way to that, for weakness . . . . . iii 2 25
O, turn thy edged sword another way; Strike those that hurt . . iii 3 52
And no way canst thou turn thee for redress . . . . . iv 2 25
He seems a knight, And will not any way dishonour me . . . v 3 102
And smooth my way upon their headless necks . . . *2 Hen. VI.* i 2 65
Let's stand close: my lord protector will come this way by and by . i 3 2
Fellow, thank God, and the good wine in thy master's way . . . ii 3 99
Go, lead the way; I long to see my prison . . . . . ii 4 110
As the dam runs lowing up and down, Looking the way her harmless young one went . . . . iii 1 215
As a splitted bark, so sunder we: This way fall I to death.—This way for me . . . . iii 2 412
My sword make way for me, for here is no staying . . . . iv 8 62
Now is it manhood, wisdom, and defence, To give the enemy way . . v 2 76
Turn this way, Henry, and regard them not . . . . *3 Hen. VI.* i 1 189
Now sways it this way, like a mighty sea Forced by the tide to combat with the wind; Now sways it that way, like the selfsame sea Forced to retire by fury of the wind . . . . ii 5 5
No way to fly, nor strength to hold out flight . . . . . ii 6 24
And chides the sea that sunders him from thence, Saying, he'll lade it dry to have his way . . . . iii 2 139
Seeking a way and straying from the way . . . . . . iii 2 176
From that torment I will free myself, Or hew my way out with a bloody axe . . . . iii 2 181
Why, then, let's on our way in silent sort . . . . . . iv 2 28
Often but attended with weak guard, Comes hunting this way . . iv 5 8
If about this hour he make this way Under the colour of his usual game, He shall here find his friends . . . . iv 5 10
This way, my lord; for this way lies the game.—Nay, this way, man . iv 5 14
Edward dares, and leads the way. Lords, to the field . . . . v 1 112

Way. We, having now the best at Barnet field, Will thither straight, for willingness rids way *3 Hen. VI.* v 3 21
Work thou the way,—and thou shalt execute v 7 25
I think it is our way, If we will keep in favour with the king, To be her men and wear her livery *Richard III.* i 1 78
The readiest way to make the wench amends Is to become her husband i 1 155
Why, then, give way, dull clouds, to my quick curses! i 3 196
By the way, I'll sort occasion, As index to the story we late talk'd of ii 2 148
The weary way hath made you melancholy iii 1 3
Our crosses on the way Have made it tedious, wearisome, and heavy iii 1 4
My brother York Would long ere this have met us on the way iii 1 21
Thou know'st our reasons urged upon the way; What think'st thou? iii 1 160
Nor he deliver'd His gracious pleasure any way therein iii 4 18
You shall have letters from me to my son To meet you on the way iv 1 51
Murder her brothers, and then marry her! Uncertain way of gain! iv 2 64
This is not the way To win your daughter.—There is no other way iv 4 284
Why dost thou run so many mile about, When thou mayst tell thy tale a nearer way? iv 4 462
Towards London they do bend their course, If by the way they be not fought withal iv 5 15
Not propp'd by ancestry, whose grace Chalks successors their way *Hen. VIII.* i 1 60
He gives us note, The force of his own merit makes his way i 1 64
Like A full-hot horse, who being allow'd his way, Self-mettle tires him i 1 133
When the way was made, And paved with gold i 1 187
Men of his way should be most liberal; They are set here for examples i 3 61
Our breach of duty this way Is business of estate ii 2 69
I would not be a young count in your way, For more than blushing comes to ii 3 41
Pray you, keep your way: When you are call'd, return ii 4 128
Go thy ways, Kate: That man i' the world who shall report he has A better wife, let him in nought be trusted ii 4 133
Or Laid any scruple in your way, which might Induce you to the question on't ii 4 150
Which forced such way, That many mazed considerings did throng ii 4 184
If your business Seek me out, and that way I am wife in, Out with it boldly iii 1 38
We come not by the way of accusation, To taint that honour every good tongue blesses, Nor to betray you any way to sorrow iii 1 54
Our places, The way of our profession is against it iii 1 157
What we can do to him, though now the time Gives way to us, I much fear iii 2 16
The king in this perceives him, how he coasts And hedges his own way iii 2 39
Is there no way to cure this? iii 2 216
I know A way, if it take right, in spite of fortune Will bring me off again iii 2 219
In the way of loyalty and truth iii 2 272
To furnish Rome, and to prepare the ways You have for dignities iii 2 328
Wolsey, that once trod the ways of glory, And sounded all the depths and shoals of honour, Found thee a way, out of his wreck, to rise in iii 2 435
Ye shall go my way, which Is to the court, and there ye shall be my guests iv 1 114
You're a gentleman Of mine own way v 1 28
Be of good cheer; They shall no more prevail than we give way to v 1 143
I am glad I came this way so happily v 2 9
My teaching And the strong course of my authority Might go one way v 3 36
Is there no other way of mercy, But I must needs to the Tower? v 3 92
Break among the press, and find a way out To let the troop pass fairly v 4 88
Make way there for the princess.—You great fellow, Stand close up v 4 91
And those about her From her shall read the perfect ways of honour v 5 38
Lead the way, lords: Ye must all see the queen v 5 73
There's a fellow! Go thy way, Hector! There's a brave man *T. and C.* i 2 216
He ne'er saw three and twenty. Go thy way, Troilus, go thy way! i 2 256
Making their way With those of nobler bulk! i 3 36
Hector's opinion Is this in way of truth ii 2 189
Come your ways; an you draw backward, we'll put you i' the fills iii 2 47
I do beseech you, as in way of taste, To give me now a little benefit iii 3 13
I will lead the way iii 3 54
Take the instant way; For honour travels in a strait so narrow iii 3 153
If you give way, Or hedge aside from the direct forthright iii 3 157
If to-morrow be a fair day, by eleven o'clock it will go one way or other iii 3 297
Here lies our way iv 1 79
I'll give her to thy hand; And by the way possess thee what she is iv 4 114
Which way would Hector have it?—He cares not; he'll obey conditions iv 5 71
I have, thou gallant Trojan, seen thee oft Labouring for destiny make cruel way Through ranks of Greekish youth iv 5 184
Nor you, my brother, . . . should stop my way, But by my ruin v 3 57
Mere words, no matter from the heart; The effect doth operate another way v 3 109
You must in no way say he is covetous *Coriolanus* i 1 43
Whose course will on The way it takes, cracking ten thousand curbs i 1 72
But it proceeds or comes from them to you And no way from yourselves i 1 158
When youth with comeliness plucked all gaze his way i 3 8
I'll potch at him some way Or wrath or craft may get him i 10 15
Give way there, and go on! ii 1 210
I had rather be their servant in my way, Than sway with them in theirs ii 1 219
Make way, they are coming ii 2 40
Their consent of one direct way should be at once to all the points o' the compass ii 3 25
Which way do you judge my wit would fly?— . . . 'Twould, sure, southward.—Why that way?—To lose itself in a fog ii 3 27
You are like to do such business.—Not unlike, Each way, to better yours iii 1 49
If you will pass To where you are bound, you must inquire your way iii 1 54
This so dishonour'd rub, laid falsely I' the plain way of his merit iii 1 61
Which we disdain should tetter us, yet sought The very way to catch them iii 1 80
Give way the while To unstable slightness iii 1 147
Fie, fie, fie! This is the way to kindle, not to quench iii 1 197
That is the way to lay the city flat; To bring the roof to the foundation iii 1 204
Those cold ways, That seem like prudent helps, are very poisonous Where the disease is violent iii 1 220
It is the humane way: the other course Will prove too bloody iii 1 327
We'll proceed In our first way iii 1 334
Thou art their soldier, and being bred in broils Hast not the soft way iii 2 82
Never trust to what my tongue can do I' the way of flattery further iii 2 137
A wild exposture to each chance That starts i' the way before thee iv 1 37
They have ta'en note of us: keep on your way iv 2 10
If he give me way, I'll do his country service iv 4 25
And set down—As best thou art experienced . . . —thine own ways iv 5 146
O'erborne their way, consumed with fire, and took What lay before them iv 6 78
Like beasts And cowardly nobles, gave way unto your clusters iv 6 122

Way. A mile before his tent fall down, and knee The way into his mercy *Coriolanus* v 1 6
You know the very road into his kindness, And cannot lose your way v 1 60
You know the way home again v 2 103
Made him joint-servant with me; gave him way In all his own desires v 6 32
After your way his tale pronounced shall bury His reasons with his body v 6 58
Romans, make way: the good Andronicus, Patron of virtue *T. Andron.* i 1 64
Make way to lay them by their brethren i 1 89
Princely shall be thy usage every way i 1 266
What, villain boy! Barr'st me my way in Rome? i 1 291
What reproachful words are these?—But go thy ways i 1 309
This way, or not at all, stand you in hope ii 1 119
I have horse will follow where the game Makes way ii 2 24
This way to death my wretched sons are gone iii 1 98
Then which way shall I find Revenge's cave? iii 1 271
Come, Marcus; come, kinsmen; this is the way iv 3 1
Ravish a maid, or plot the way to do it v 1 129
Examine other beauties.—'Tis the way To call hers exquisite *R. and J.* i 1 234
He ran this way, and leap'd this orchard wall ii 1 5
Go thy ways, wench; serve God. What, have you dined at home? ii 5 45
Hie you to church; I must another way ii 5 74
Mercutio's soul Is but a little way above our heads, Staying for thine iii 1 132
Which way ran he that kill'd Mercutio? Tybalt, that murderer, which way ran he? iii 1 142
To be to thee this night a torch-bearer, And light thee on thy way iii 5 15
Or walk in thievish ways; or bid me lurk Where serpents are iv 1 79
What cursed foot wanders this way to-night? v 3 19
Lead, boy: which way?—Yea, noise? then I'll be brief v 3 168
Let the health go round.—Let it flow this way, my good lord.—Flow this way! A brave fellow! *T. of Athens* i 2 55
What a sweep of vanity comes this way! They dance! they are mad women i 2 137
I have been bold—For that I knew it the most general way—To them to use your signet and your name ii 2 209
Methinks he should the sooner pay his debts, And make a clear way to the gods iii 4 77
I will fear to catch it and give way iv 3 358
You that way and you this, but two in company v 1 109
And do you now strew flowers in his way? *J. Cæsar* i 1 55
Go you down that way towards the Capitol; This way will I i 1 68
Stand you directly in Antonius' way, When he doth run his course i 2 3
The sun arises, Which is a great way growing on the south ii 1 107
This by Calpurnia's dream is signified.—And this way have you well expounded it ii 2 91
Look about you: security gives way to conspiracy ii 3 8
Which way hast thou been?—At mine own house ii 4 21
Look you, Brutus, He draws Mark Antony out of the way iii 1 26
I spurn thee like a cur out of my way iii 1 46
One of two bad ways you must conceit me, Either a coward or a flatterer iii 1 192
Either led or driven, as we point the way iv 1 23
Must I give way and room to your rash choler? iv 3 39
You wrong me every way; you wrong me, Brutus iv 3 55
Or why Upon this blasted heath you stop our way? *Macbeth* i 3 77
A step On which I must fall down, or else o'erleap, For in my way it lies i 4 50
It is too full o' the milk of human kindness To catch the nearest way i 5 19
Restrain in me the cursed thoughts that nature Gives way to in repose! ii 1 9
Thou marshall'st me the way that I was going ii 1 42
Thou sure and firm-set earth, Hear not my steps, which way they walk ii 1 57
These deeds must not be thought After these ways; so, it will make us mad ii 2 34
Some of all professions that go the primrose way to the everlasting bonfire ii 3 21
Our safest way Is to avoid the aim ii 3 148
Who did strike out the light?—Was't not the way? iii 3 19
Did you send to him, sir?—I hear it by the way iii 4 130
For mine own good, All causes shall give way iii 4 136
By the pricking of my thumbs, Something wicked this way comes iv 1 45
But float upon a wild and violent sea Each way and move iv 2 22
More suffer and more sundry ways than ever, By him that shall succeed iv 3 48
But abound In the division of each several crime, Acting it many ways iv 3 97
Near Birnam wood Shall we well meet them; that way are they coming v 2 6
My way of life Is fall'n into the sear, the yellow leaf v 3 22
And all our yesterdays have lighted fools The way to dusty death v 5 23
That way the noise is. Tyrant, show thy face! v 7 14
This way, my lord; the castle's gently render'd v 7 24
Do not, as some ungracious pastors do, Show me the steep and thorny way to heaven *Hamlet* i 3 48
In way of caution, I must tell you, You do not understand yourself i 3 95
Look to't, I charge you: come your ways.—I shall obey, my lord i 3 135
He seem'd to find his way without his eyes ii 1 98
But, in the beaten way of friendship, what make you at Elsinore? ii 2 277
We coted them on the way; and hither are they coming ii 2 330
Their residence, both in reputation and profit, was better both ways ii 2 345
It so fell out, that certain players We o'er-raught on the way iii 1 17
I hope your virtues Will bring him to his wonted way again iii 1 41
Believe none of us. Go thy ways to a nunnery iii 1 132
Love! his affections do not that way tend iii 1 170
They must sweep my way, And marshal me to knavery iii 4 204
Come, I will make you way for these your letters iv 6 32
Nothing, neither way.—Have at you now! v 2 312
Therefore beseech you To avert your liking a more worthier way *Lear* i 1 214
Where is the villain, Edmund?—Fled this way, sir ii 1 44
One that wouldst be a bawd, in way of good service ii 2 21
Draw, you rascal; come your ways.—Help, ho! murder! help! ii 2 42
Resolve me, with all modest haste, which way Thou mightst deserve ii 4 25
Winter's not gone yet, if the wild-geese fly that way ii 4 47
'Tis best to give him way; he leads himself ii 4 301
In which your pain That way, I'll this iii 1 54
Neither to speak of him, entreat for him, nor any way sustain him iii 3 6
O, that way madness lies; let me shun that; No more of that iii 4 21
This way, my lord.—With him; I will keep still with my philosopher iii 4 180
That nature thus gives way to loyalty, something fears me to think of iii 5 4
All the power of his wits have given way to his impatience iii 6 5
Go thrust him out at gates, and let him smell His way to Dover iii 7 94
You cannot see your way.—I have no way, and therefore want no eyes iv 1 19
Thou wilt o'ertake us, hence a mile or twain, I' the way toward Dover iv 1 45
Know'st thou the way to Dover?—Both stile and gate, horse-way and foot-path iv 1 57
I marvel our mild husband Not met us on the way iv 2 2

Way. Our wishes on the way May prove effects . . . . *Lear* iv 2 14
One way I like this well; . . . another way, The news is not so tart . iv 2 83
Her smiles and tears Were like a better way . . . . iv 3 21
Our troops set forth to-morrow: stay with us; The ways are dangerous iv 5 17
Half way down Hangs one that gathers samphire, dreadful trade! . iv 6 14
Have you never found my brother's way To the forfended place? . v 1 10
If thou dost As this instructs thee, thou dost make thy way To noble fortunes . . . . v 3 29
This sword of mine shall give them instant way, Where they shall rest for ever. . . . . v 3 149
Some one way, some another. Do you know Where we may apprehend her? . . . . *Othello* i 1 177
To mourn a mischief that is past and gone Is the next way to draw new mischief on . . . . i 3 205
If thou wilt needs damn thyself, do it a more delicate way than drowning . . . . i 3 360
A pox of drowning thyself! it is clean out of the way . . . i 3 366
When these mutualities so marshal the way, hard at hand comes the master and main exercise . . . . . . ii 1 268
And passion, having my best judgement collied, Assays to lead the way ii 3 207
What, man! there are ways to recover the general again . . ii 3 272
Ay, that's the way: Dull not device by coldness and delay . . ii 3 393
I'll devise a mean to draw the Moor Out of the way . . . iii 1 40
Is't lost? is't gone? speak, is it out o' the way? . . . iii 4 80
There is no other way; 'tis she must do't: And, lo, the happiness! . iii 4 107
I pray you, bring me on the way a little, And say if I shall see you soon at night.—'Tis but a little way that I can bring you . . . iii 4 197
Nay, that's not your way . . . . iv 1 197
Did they never whisper?—Never, my lord.—Nor send you out o' the way? . . . . iv 2 7
Whether he kill Cassio, Or Cassio him, or each do kill the other, Every way makes my gain . . . . v 1 14
I have made my way through more impediments Than twenty times your stop . . . . v 2 263
I kiss'd thee ere I kill'd thee; no way but this; Killing myself, to die upon a kiss . . . . v 2 358
In each thing give him way, cross him in nothing.—Thou teachest like a fool; the way to lose him . . . *Ant. and Cleo.* i 3 9
Yet must Antony No way excuse his soils . . . . . i 4 24
I know not, Menas, How lesser enmities may give way to greater . ii 1 43
Small to greater matters must give way.—Not if the small come first . ii 2 11
Your way is shorter; My purposes do draw me much about . . ii 4 7
Though he be painted one way like a Gorgon, The other way's a Mars . ii 5 116
Will you lead, lords?—Show us the way . . . . . ii 6 83
Thine, if thou wilt ha't.—Show me which way . . . . ii 7 75
That stands upon the swell at full of tide, And neither way inclines . iii 2 50
Let all the number of the stars give light To thy fair way! . . iii 2 66
When it appears to you where this begins, Turn your displeasure that way . . . . iii 4 34
The trees by the way Should have borne men . . . . iii 6 46
Let determined things to destiny Hold unbewail'd their way . . iii 6 85
Quite forego The way which promises assurance . . . . iii 7 47
Six kings already Show me the way of yielding . . . . iii 10 35
I am so lated in the world, that I Have lost my way for ever . . iii 11 4
You shall Have letters from me to some friends that will Sweep your way . . . . iii 11 17
I will seek Some way to leave him . . . . . . iii 13 201
Let the old ruffian know I have many other ways to die . . . iv 1 5
To-morrow is the day.—It will determine one way . . . . iv 3 2
So, so; come, give me that: this way; well said . . . . iv 4 28
That she preparedly may frame herself To the way she's forced to . v 1 56
Make way there: Cæsar! . . . . v 2 111
That's the way To fool their preparation . . . . . v 2 224
Something given to lie; as a woman should not do, but in the way of honesty . . . . v 2 253
She levell'd at our purposes, and, being royal, Took her own way . . v 2 340
She hath pursued conclusions infinite Of easy ways to die . . . v 2 359
To this hour no guess in knowledge Which way they went . *Cymbeline* i 1 61
I'll move him To walk this way . . . . i 1 104
Past hope, and in despair; that way, past grace . . . . i 1 137
Fie! you must give way . . . . i 1 158
A cunning thief, or a that way accomplished courtier, would hazard . i 4 101
Your service for this time is ended; Take your own way . . . i 5 31
Apes and monkeys 'Twixt two such shes would chatter this way . . i 6 40
Is there no way for men to be but women Must be half-workers? . . ii 5 1
By the way Tell me how Wales was made so happy as To inherit such a haven . . . . iii 2 61
There's no more to say; Accessible is none but Milford way . . . iii 2 84
Two beggars told me I could not miss my way: will poor folks lie? . iii 6 9
The boy Fidele's sickness Did make my way long forth . . . iv 2 149
To Milford-Haven; which is the way?—I thank you.—By yond bush? . iv 2 291
This way, the Romans Must or for Britons slay us, or receive us . . iv 4 4
Gan to look The way that they did, and to grin like lions . . . v 3 38
Forthwith they fly Chickens, the way which they stoop'd eagles . . v 3 42
Most welcome, bondage! for thou art a way, I think, to liberty . . v 4 3
You know not which way you shall go.—Yes, indeed do I, fellow . . v 4 181
There are none want eyes to direct them the way I am going . . v 4 193
What an infinite mock is this, that a man should have the best use of eyes to see the way of blindness! I am sure hanging's the way of winking . . . . v 4 197
Swore, If I discover'd not which way she was gone, It was my instant death . . . . v 5 277
Thus ready for the way of life or death, I wait the sharpest blow *Pericles* i 1 54
What need we fear? The ground's the lowest, and we are half way there i 4 78
What a drunken knave was the sea to cast thee in our way! . . ii 1 62
He had need mean better than his outward show Can any way speak . ii 2 49
Go thy ways, good mariner: I'll bring the body presently . . iii 1 81
Which never could I so convey, Unless your thoughts went on my way iv Gower 50
Come your ways. My masters, you say she's a virgin? . . . iv 2 44
Your bride goes to that with shame which is her way to go with warrant iv 2 139
There's no way to be rid on't but by the way to the pox . . iv 6 16
If the peevish baggage would but give way to customers . . . iv 6 20
Persever in that clear way thou goest, And the gods strengthen thee! . iv 6 113
Come your ways.—Whither would you have me? . . . iv 6 134; 138
Will you not go the way of women-kind? . . . . . iv 6 159
Come, mistress; come your ways with me.—Whither wilt thou have me? . . . . iv 6 161
Any of these ways are yet better than this . . . . . iv 6 188
Come, I'll do for thee what I can; come your ways . . . iv 6 212

Way. It is not good to cross him; give him way . . . *Pericles* v 1 232
We do our longing stay To hear the rest untold: sir, lead's the way . v 3 84
Waylaid. Peto and Gadshill shall rob those men that we have already waylaid . . . . *1 Hen. IV.* i 2 183
Waylay. I will waylay thee going home . . . *T. Night* iii 4 176
Wayward. Fie, fie, how wayward is this foolish love! . *T. G. of Ver.* i 2 57
My wife is in a wayward mood to-day . . . *Com. of Errors* iv 4 4
To make an account of her life to a clod of wayward marl . *Much Ado* ii 1 65
This wimpled, whining, purblind, wayward boy . . *L. L. Lost* iii 1 181
Impute his words To wayward sickliness and age in him *Richard II.* ii 1 142
Bear with her weakness, which, I think, proceeds From wayward sickness, and no grounded malice . . . . . *Richard III.* i 3 29
Tetchy and wayward was thy infancy; Thy school-days frightful . . iv 4 168
My heart is wondrous light, Since this same wayward girl is so reclaim'd *Rom. and Jul.* iv 2 47
All you have done Hath been but for a wayward son . *Macbeth* iii 5 11
My wayward husband hath a hundred times Woo'd me to steal it *Othello* iii 3 292
Pericles Is now again thwarting the wayward seas . . *Pericles* iv 4 10
Though wayward fortune did malign my state . . . . . v 1 90
Waywarder. The wiser, the waywarder . . . . *As Y. Like It* iv 1 162
Waywardness. The unruly waywardness that infirm and choleric years bring with them . . . . *Lear* i 1 302
We. Then go we near her, that her ear lose nothing . . *Much Ado* iii 1 32
Trip we after night's shade: We the globe can compass soon *M. N. D.* iv 1 101
Let us go and find him out . . .—Do we so . . *Mer. of Venice* ii 8 53
But go we in, I pray thee, Jessica, And ceremoniously let us prepare v 1 36
And, to cut off all strife, here sit we down . . . *T. of Shrew* iii 1 21
We, poising us in her defective scale, Shall weigh thee . . *All's Well* ii 3 161
Go we, as well as haste will suffer us . . . . *K. John* ii 1 559
Put we our quarrel to the will of heaven . . . . *Richard II.* i 2 6
Prepare we for our marriage . . . . *Hen. V.* v 2 398
Embrace we then this opportunity As fitting best . . . *1 Hen. VI.* ii 1 13
Join we together, for the public good . . . . . *2 Hen. VI.* i 1 199
Well, for this night we will repose us here . . . . . ii 1 200
My lord, break we off; we know your mind at full . . . . ii 2 77
Here stand we both, and aim we at the best . . . *3 Hen. VI.* iii 1 8
What heir of York is there alive but we? . . . *Richard III.* iv 4 472
I am about to weep; but, thinking that We are a queen . . *Hen. VIII.* ii 4 71
Go to my tent; There in the full convive we . . . *Troi. and Cres.* iv 5 272
Pursue we him on knees . . . . v 3 10
And to poor we Thine enmity's most capital . . . . *Coriolanus* v 3 103
Then sit we down, and let us all consult . . . . *T. Andron.* iv 2 132
Let no man abide this deed, But we the doers . . . . *J. Cæsar* iii 1 95
And we fools of nature So horridly to shake our disposition . . *Hamlet* i 4 54
A charge we bear i' the war . . . . . . *Ant. and Cleo.* iii 7 17
[Death] hath more ministers than we That draw his knives i' the war *Cymbeline* v 3 72
For this from stiller seats we came, Our parents and us twain . . v 4 69
Well; my peace we will begin . . . . v 5 459
We three. Did you never see the picture of 'we three'? . . *T. Night* ii 3 17
When shall we three meet again? . . . . *Macbeth* i 1 1
Weak. Made wit with musing weak, heart sick with thought *T. G. of Ver.* i 1 69
Smother'd in errors, feeble, shallow, weak . . *Com. of Errors* iii 2 35
Her wit Values itself so highly that to her All matter else seems weak *Much Ado* iii 1 54
Their sense thus weak, lost with their fears thus strong *M. N. Dream* iii 2 27
And this weak and idle theme, No more yielding but a dream . . v 1 434
Why are our bodies soft and weak and smooth, Unapt to toil? *T. of Shrew* v 2 165
Our lances are but straws, Our strength as weak, our weakness past compare . . . . v 2 174
Our virginity, though valiant, in the defence yet is weak . *All's Well* i 1 127
In thee some blessed spirit doth speak His powerful sound within an organ weak . . . . ii 1 179
In a most weak—and debile minister, great power . . . . ii 3 39
My heart is heavy and mine age is weak; Grief would have tears . . iii 4 41
Five or six thousand; but very weak and unserviceable . . . iv 3 151
Fancies too weak for boys, too green and idle For girls of nine *W. Tale* iii 2 182
Who, weak with age, cannot support myself . . . *Richard II.* ii 2 83
I cannot mend it, I must needs confess, Because my power is weak . ii 3 154
The power of Percy is too weak To wage an instant trial . *1 Hen. IV.* iv 4 19
A prince should not be so loosely studied as to remember so weak a composition . . . . *2 Hen. IV.* ii 2 10
Can a weak empty vessel bear such a huge full hogshead? . . . ii 4 67
There are twenty weak and wearied posts Come from the north . . ii 4 385
My cloud of dignity Is held from falling with so weak a wind That it will quickly drop . . . . iv 5 100
Which of a weak and niggardly projection Doth, like a miser, spoil his coat with scanting A little cloth . . . . . *Hen. V.* ii 4 46
Kneeling at our feet, but a weak and worthless satisfaction . . . iii 6 141
My army but a weak and sickly guard . . . . . . iii 6 164
Orleans is besieged; The English army is grown weak and faint *1 Hen. VI.* i 1 158
Christ's mother helps me, else I were too weak . . . . i 2 106
It cannot be this weak and writhled shrimp Should strike such terror . ii 3 23
Kind keepers of my weak decaying age . . . . . . ii 5 1
And that we find the slothful watch but weak, I'll by a sign give notice iii 2 7
When sapless age and weak unable limbs Should bring thy father to his drooping chair . . . . iv 5 4
My ancient incantations are too weak, And hell too strong . . . v 3 27
I must make fair weather yet a while, Till Henry be more weak *2 Hen. VI.* v 1 31
I know not what to say; my title's weak . . . . *3 Hen. VI.* i 1 134
And weak we are and cannot shun pursuit . . . . . ii 3 13
If your title to the crown be weak, . . . 'tis but reason that I be released iii 3 145
So weak of courage and in judgement That they'll take no offence . v 1 12
I, in this weak piping time of peace . . . . . *Richard III.* i 1 24
The king is sickly, weak, and melancholy, And his physicians fear him i 1 136
If your back Cannot vouchsafe this burthen, 'tis too weak Ever to get a boy.—How you do talk! . . . . *Hen. VIII.* ii 3 43
I am a simple woman, much too weak To oppose your cunning . . ii 4 106
Where's then the saucy boat Whose weak untimber'd sides but even now Co-rivall'd greatness? . . . . *Troi. and Cres.* i 3 43
The weak wanton Cupid Shall from your neck unloose his amorous fold iii 3 222
If I could temporise with my affection, Or brew it to a weak and colder palate . . . . iv 4 7
From love's weak childish bow she lives unharm'd . . *Rom. and Jul.* i 1 217
Here's that which is too weak to be a sinner, honest water *T. of Athens* i 2 59
Therein, ye gods, you make the weak most strong . . . *J. Cæsar* i 3 91
If these be motives weak, break off betimes . . . . . ii 1 116
Ay me, how weak a thing The heart of woman is! . . . . ii 4 39
But all's too weak: For brave Macbeth—well he deserves that name *Macb.* i 2 15
To offer up a weak poor innocent lamb To appease an angry god . . iv 3 16

Weak. I pray you, father, being weak, seem so *Lear* ii 4 204
Here I stand, your slave, A poor, infirm, weak, and despised old man . iii 2 20
His flaw'd heart, Alack, too weak the conflict to support! v 3 197
One [life] is too poor, too weak for my revenge *Othello* iii 3 443
The Jove of power make me most weak, most weak, Your reconciler! *Ant. and Cleo.* iii 4 29
My sword, made weak by my affection, would Obey it on all cause . iii 11 67
Mine eyes are weak : Fold down the leaf where I have left . *Cymbeline* ii 2 3
I am weak with toil, yet strong in appetite iii 6 37
The legions now in Gallia are Full weak to undertake our wars iii 7 5
Weak age. To relief of lazars and weak age *Hen. V.* i 1 15
Weak arm. Nor near nor farther off, my gracious lord, Than this weak arm *Richard II.* iii 2 65
Weak beginnings. Which in their seeds And weak beginnings lie intreasured *2 Hen. IV.* iii 1 85
Weak bond. I perceive A weak bond holds you *M. N. Dream* iii 2 268
Weak breath. With such weak breath as this? No, you are deceived *Cor.* v 2 50
Weak condition. It is not for your health thus to commit Your weak condition to the raw cold morning *J. Cæsar* ii 1 236
Weak dealing. It were an ill thing to be offered to any gentlewoman, and very weak dealing *Rom. and Jul.* ii 4 180
Weak disabling. To be afeard of my deserving Were but a weak disabling of myself *Mer. of Venice* ii 7 30
Weak door. To push destruction and perpetual shame Out of the weak door of our fainting land *K. John* v 7 78
Weak evils. Oppress'd with two weak evils, age and hunger *As Y. Like It* ii 7 132
Weak fear. I hold as little counsel with weak fear As you *1 Hen. IV.* iv 3 11
Weak function. Even as her appetite shall play the god With his weak function *Othello* ii 3 354
Weak guard. And, often but attended with weak guard . *3 Hen. VI.* iv 5 7
Weak hams. A plentiful lack of wit, together with most weak hams *Ham.* ii 2 202
Weak hand. Against self-slaughter There is a prohibition so divine That cravens my weak hand *Cymbeline* iii 4 80
Weak-hearted. To endure more miseries and greater far Than my weak-hearted enemies dare offer *Hen. VIII.* iii 2 390
Weak-hinged. Your own weak-hinged fancy *W. Tale* ii 3 119
Weak impress. This weak impress of love is as a figure Trenched in ice *T. G. of Ver.* iii 2 6
Weak legions. To beat assailing death from his weak legions *1 Hen. VI.* iv 4 16
Weak list. You and I cannot be confined within the weak list of a country's fashion *Hen. V.* v 2 295
Weak masters. By whose aid, Weak masters though ye be, I have bedimm'd The noontide sun *Tempest* v 1 41
Weak men. Then, if angels fight, Weak men must fall *Richard II.* iii 2 62
Weak merits. Nor from mine own weak merits will I draw The smallest fear or doubt *Othello* iii 3 187
Weak mind. Other gambol faculties a' has, that show a weak mind and an able body *2 Hen. IV.* ii 4 273
Weak monster. A very weak monster! The man i' the moon! *Tempest* ii 2 148
Weak nails. How these vain weak nails May tear a passage through the flinty ribs Of this hard world *Richard II.* v 5 19
Weak ones. What we oft do best, By sick interpreters, once weak ones, is Not ours, or not allow'd *Hen. VIII.* i 2 82
Weak oratory. If my weak oratory Can from his mother win the Duke of York, Anon expect him here *Richard III.* iii 1 37
Weak pia mater. One of thy kin has a most weak pia mater *T. Night* i 5 123
Weak prayers. Thy threats have no more strength than her weak prayers *M. N. Dream* iii 2 250
Weak remembrance. This lord of weak remembrance, this *Tempest* ii 1 232
Weak shoulders, overborne with burthening grief *1 Hen. VI.* ii 5 10
Weak slave. That shows thee a weak slave *Rom. and Jul.* i 1 17
Weak spirits. And our weak spirits ne'er been higher rear'd With stronger blood *W. Tale* i 2 72
Weak stomach. Their villany goes against my weak stomach *Hen. V.* iii 2 56
Weak straws. Those that with haste will make a mighty fire Begin it with weak straws *J. Cæsar* i 3 108
Weak supposal. Holding a weak supposal of our worth . *Hamlet* i 2 18
Weak surmises. I speak not out of weak surmises *Cymbeline* iii 4 24
Weak wind. 'Tis far too huge to be blown out With that same weak wind which enkindled it *K. John* v 2 87
Weak wit. With my weak wit, And to such men of gravity *Hen. VIII.* iii 1 72
Weak woman. What can be their business With me, a poor weak woman? iii 1 20
You wrong your virtues With these weak women's fears iii 1 169
Weak words. I am glad that my weak words Have struck but thus much show of fire from Brutus *J. Cæsar* i 2 176
Weaken. To weaken and discredit our exposure *Troi. and Cres.* i 3 195
Either his notion weakens, his discernings Are lethargied *Lear* i 4 248
Abused her delicate youth with drugs or minerals That weaken motion *Othello* i 2 75
Weakened. Is my Richard both in shape and mind Transform'd and weaken'd? *Richard II.* v 1 27
Even so my limbs, Weaken'd with grief, being now enraged with grief, Are thrice themselves *2 Hen. IV.* i 1 144
Weaker. Supportable To make the dear loss, have I means much weaker *Tempest* v 1 146
Jaquenetta,—so is the weaker vessel called *L. L. Lost* i 1 276
The greater throw May turn by fortune from the weaker hand *M. of Ven.* ii 1 34
Or Charles or something weaker masters thee *As Y. Like It* i 2 272
I must comfort the weaker vessel, as doublet and hose ought ii 4 6
You are the weaker vessel, as they say, the emptier vessel *2 Hen. IV.* ii 4 65
I am weaker than a woman's tear, Tamer than sleep *Troi. and Cres.* i 1 9
Raised only, that the weaker sort may wish Good Marcius home again *Coriolanus* iv 6 69
Women, being the weaker vessels, are ever thrust to the wall *R. and J.* i 1 20
Your grace hath laid the odds o' the weaker side *Hamlet* v 2 272
Strong Enobarb Is weaker than the wine *Ant. and Cleo.* ii 7 130
Come you between, And save poor me, the weaker *Pericles* iv 1 91
Weakest. The weakest kind of fruit Drops earliest *Mer. of Venice* iv 1 115
He that of greatest works is finisher Oft does them by the weakest minister *All's Well* ii 1 140
Such things as might offend the weakest spleen *Troi. and Cres.* ii 2 128
For the weakest goes to the wall *Rom. and Jul.* i 1 18
Conceit in weakest bodies strongest works *Hamlet* iii 4 114
Weakling. And, weakling, Warwick takes his gift again *3 Hen. VI.* v 1 37
Weakly. I will not adventure my discretion so weakly *Tempest* ii 1 188
'Tis sure they found some place But weakly guarded *1 Hen. VI.* ii 1 74
Then you are weakly made : pluck off a little *Hen. VIII.* ii 3 40
Weakness. My father's loss, the weakness which I feel *Tempest* i 2 487
I am vex'd; Bear with my weakness; my old brain is troubled iv 1 159
But only he Owe and succeed thy weakness *Meas. for Meas.* ii 4 123
Weakness. Whose weakness married to thy stronger state Makes me with thy strength to communicate *Com. of Errors* ii 2 177
Did not with unbashful forehead woo The means of weakness *As Y. L. It* ii 3 51
Our strength as weak, our weakness past compare *T. of Shrew* v 2 174
Hath amazed me more Than I dare blame my weakness *All's Well* ii 1 88
It is but weakness To bear the matter thus; mere weakness *W. Tale* ii 3 1
To my litter straight; Weakness possesseth me, and I am faint *K. John* v 3 17
To fear the foe, since fear oppresseth strength, Gives in your weakness strength unto your foe *Richard II.* iii 2 181
England shall repent his folly, see his weakness *Hen. V.* iii 6 132
Her meaning is, No way to that, for weakness *1 Hen. VI.* iii 2 25
What cannot be avoided 'Twere childish weakness to lament *3 Hen. VI.* v 4 38
Bear with her weakness, which, I think, proceeds From wayward sickness, and no grounded malice *Richard III.* i 3 29
Your painted gloss discovers, To men that understand you, words and weakness *Hen. VIII.* v 3 72
Troy in our weakness stands, not in her strength *Troi. and Cres.* i 3 137
Your silence, Cunning in dumbness, from my weakness draws My very soul of counsel! iii 2 140
Since thou know'st Thy country's strength and weakness *Coriolanus* iv 5 146
Ha! who comes here? I think it is the weakness of mine eyes That shapes this monstrous apparition *J. Cæsar* iv 3 276
Thence to a watch, thence into a weakness, Thence to a lightness *Hamlet* ii 2 148
Out of my weakness and my melancholy, . . . Abuses me to damn me ii 2 630
And dare not task my weakness with any more *Othello* ii 3 43
O noble weakness! If they had swallow'd poison, 'twould appear *Ant. and Cleo.* v 2 347
Weal. We do no further ask Than whereupon our weal, on you depending, Counts it your weal he have his liberty *K. John* iv 2 65
And sit at chiefest stern of public weal *1 Hen. VI.* i 1 177
The special watchmen of our English weal iii 1 66
I sit before the walls of Rouen And will be partner of your weal or woe iii 2 92
Content with any choice Tends to God's glory and my country's weal . v 1 27
Digest things rightly Touching the weal o' the common *Coriolanus* i 1 155
Your liberties and the charters that you bear I' the body of the weal . ii 3 189
A traitorous innovator, A foe to the public weal iii 1 176
Brief sounds determine of my weal or woe *Rom. and Jul.* iii 2 51
His particular to foresee, Smells from the general weal *T. of Athens* iv 3 160
I' the olden time, Ere humane statute purged the gentle weal *Macbeth* iii 4 76
Meet we the medicine of the sickly weal, And with him pour we in our country's purge Each drop of us v 2 27
That spirit upon whose weal depend and rest The lives of many *Hamlet* iii 3 14
In the tender of a wholesome weal, Might in their working do you that offence, Which else were shame *Lear* i 4 230
Wealsmen. Meeting two such wealsmen as you are—I cannot call you Lycurguses *Coriolanus* ii 1 59
Wealth. What think'st thou of the rich Mercatio?—Well of his wealth; but of himself, so so *T. G. of Ver.* i 2 13
More faults than hairs, and more wealth than faults iii 1 362
More wealth than faults.—Why, that word makes the faults gracious . iii 1 376
I have little wealth to lose: A man I am cross'd with adversity iv 1 11
Let him take her simply; the wealth I have waits on my consent *Mer. Wives* iii 2 78
I would not ha' your distemper in this kind for the wealth of Windsor Castle iii 3 232
My state being gall'd with my expense, I seek to heal it only by his wealth iii 4 6
I will confess thy father's wealth Was the first motive that I woo'd thee iii 4 13
Our wealth increased By prosperous voyages I often made *Com. of Errors* i 1 40
If you did wed my sister for her wealth, Then for her wealth's sake use her with more kindness iii 2 5
His word might bear my wealth at any time v 1 8
Hath he not lost much wealth by wreck of sea? Buried some dear friend? v 1 49
It is all the wealth that he hath left, to be known a reasonable creature *Much Ado* i 1 70
To love, to wealth, to pomp, I pine and die *L. L. Lost* i 1 31
For all the wealth that ever I did see, I would not have him know iv 3 149
I freely told you, all the wealth I had Ran in my veins *Mer. of Venice* iii 2 257
Wilt thou show the whole wealth of thy wit in an instant? iii 5 61
Let the wretched man outlive his wealth iv 1 269
Thy wealth being forfeit to the state, Thou hast not left the value of a cord iv 1 365
For half thy wealth, it is Antonio's iv 1 370
Nor pluck it from his finger, for the wealth That the world masters v 1 173
I once did lend my body for his wealth v 1 249
Let's away, And get our jewels and our wealth together *As Y. Like It* i 3 136
Leaving his wealth and ease, A stubborn will to please ii 5 54
As wealth is burden of my wooing dance *T. of Shrew* i 2 68
With wealth enough and young and beauteous i 2 86
A merchant of incomparable wealth iv 2 98
Virtue and she Is her own dower; honour and wealth from me *All's Well* ii 3 151
I am not worthy of the wealth I owe, Nor dare I say 'tis mine, and yet it is ii 5 84
For the wealth of all the world, Will not offend thee *K. John* iv 1 131
And bound them, and were masters of their wealth *1 Hen. IV.* ii 4 280
Were it good To set the exact wealth of all our states All at one cast? iv 1 46
Beside, his wealth doth warrant a liberal dower *1 Hen. VI.* v 5 46
So abject, base, and poor, To choose for wealth and not for perfect love v 5 50
A worthless king, Having neither subject, wealth, nor diadem *2 Hen. VI.* iv 1 82
Wherein have I offended most? Have I affected wealth or honour? iv 7 104
I seek not to wax great by others' waning, Or gather wealth, I care not iv 10 23
I have not been desirous of their wealth, Nor much oppress'd them *3 Hen. VI.* iv 8 44
A woman's heart; which ever yet Affected eminence, wealth *Hen. VIII.* ii 3 29
What piles of wealth hath he accumulated To his own portion! iii 2 107
'Tis the account Of all that world of wealth I have drawn together iii 2 211
That goodness Of gleaning all the land's wealth into one iii 2 284
With such a costly loss of wealth and friends *Troi. and Cres.* iv 1 60
Would half my wealth Would buy this for a lie! *Coriolanus* iv 6 160
If I do dream, would all my wealth would wake me! *T. Andron.* ii 4 13
I would not for the wealth of all the town Here in my house do him disparagement: Therefore be patient *Rom. and Jul.* i 5 71
My true love is grown to such excess I cannot sum up sum of half my wealth ii 6 34
Thus honest fools lay out their wealth on court'sies *T. of Athens* i 2 241
I would not, for the wealth of Athens, I had done't now iii 2 57
Had his necessity made use of me, I would have put my wealth into donation iii 2 90
Who cannot keep his wealth must keep his house iii 3 42

Wealth. I know my lord hath spent of Timon's wealth, And now ingratitude makes it worse than stealth . . . *T. of Athens* iii 4 26
Good fellows all, The latest of my wealth I'll share amongst you . iv 2 24
Who would not wish to be from wealth exempt, Since riches point to misery? . . . . iv 2 31
Hadst thou wealth again, Rascals should have't . . . iv 3 217
Were all the wealth I have shut up in thee, I'ld give thee leave to hang it . . . . iv 3 279
Take wealth and lives together; Do villany, do, since you protest to do't iv 3 436
And whilst this poor wealth lasts To entertain me as your steward . iv 3 495
I'ld exchange For this one wish, that you had power and wealth . iv 3 528
Such heaps and sums of love and wealth As shall to thee blot out what wrongs were theirs . . . . v 1 155
I should forge Quarrels unjust against the good and loyal, Destroying them for wealth . . . . *Macbeth* iv 3 84
This is the imposthume of much wealth and peace . . *Hamlet* iv 4 27
By the power that made me, I tell you all her wealth . . . *Lear* i 1 211
The one may be sold, or given, if there were wealth enough for the purchase, or merit for the gift . . . . . *Cymbeline* i 4 90
Wealthiest. I am a simple maid, and therein wealthiest . *All's Well* ii 3 72
Wealthily. I come to wive it wealthily in Padua; If wealthily, then happily in Padua . . . . *T. of Shrew* i 2 75
Wealthy. And see my wealthy Andrew dock'd in sand . *Mer. of Venice* i 1 27
Tubal, a wealthy Hebrew of my tribe, Will furnish me . . . . i 3 58
In such a night Did Jessica steal from the wealthy Jew . . . . v 1 15
I will be married to a wealthy widow, Ere three days pass *T. of Shrew* iv 2 37
She is of good esteem, Her dowry wealthy, and of worthy birth . . iv 5 65
Had Henry got an empire by his marriage, And all the wealthy kingdoms of the west . . . . *2 Hen. VI.* i 1 154
Sweet is the country, because full of riches; The people liberal, valiant, active, wealthy . . . . iv 7 68
Yet not so wealthy as an English yeoman . . . . *3 Hen. VI.* i 4 123
I am wealthy in my friends . . . . *T. of Athens* ii 2 193
And now Ventidius is wealthy too, Whom he redeem'd from prison . iii 3 3
She shunn'd The wealthy curled darlings of our nation . . *Othello* i 2 68
Wean. Take all, and wean it: it may prove an ox . . . *L. L. Lost* v 2 250
And I the rather wean me from despair . . . *3 Hen. VI.* iv 4 17
I will restore to thee The people's hearts, and wean them from themselves . . . . *T. Andron.* i 1 211
Weaned. 'Tis since the earthquake now eleven years; And she was wean'd . . . . *Rom. and Jul.* i 3 24
Weapon. Come from thy ward, For I can here disarm thee with this stick And make thy weapon drop . . . . . . *Tempest* i 2 473
I saw their weapons drawn: there was a noise, That's verily. . . ii 1 320
'Tis best we stand upon our guard . . .: let's draw our weapons . . ii 1 322
I have appointed mine host of de Jarteer to measure our weapon *Mer. W.* i 4 125
My merry host hath had the measuring of their weapons . . . ii 1 216
What weapons is he?—No weapons, sir . . . . iii 1 30
It appears so by his weapons. Keep them asunder. . . . . iii 1 73
Nay, good master parson, keep in your weapon . . . . iii 1 76
They are dangerous weapons for maids . . . . *Much Ado* v 2 22
Get you your weapons in your hand . . . . . *M. N. Dream* iv 1 11
Fed with the same food, hurt with the same weapons . *Mer. of Venice* iii 1 64
Draw forth thy weapon, we are beset with thieves . *T. of Shrew* iii 2 238
Their weapons only Seem'd on our side . . . . . *2 Hen. IV.* i 1 197
He cares not what mischief he does, if his weapon be out . . . ii 1 17
Alas, alas! put up your naked weapons, put up your naked weapons . ii 4 222
Skill in the weapon is nothing without sack . . . . . iv 3 123
By the means whereof a' breaks words, and keeps whole weapons *Hen. V.* iii 2 38
Not to wear, handle, or use any sword, weapon, or dagger . *1 Hen. VI.* i 3 78
Using no other weapon but his name . . . . ii 1 81
Forbidden late to carry any weapon, Have fill'd their pockets full of pebble stones . . . . iii 1 79
His weapons holy saws of sacred writ, His study is his tilt-yard *2 Hen. VI.* i 3 61
This news, I think, hath turn'd your weapon's edge . . . . ii 1 180
Take away his weapon. Fellow, thank God, and the good wine in thy master's way. . . . . ii 3 98
Be well assured You put sharp weapons in a madman's hands . . iii 1 347
How now, lords! your wrathful weapons drawn Here in our presence! iii 2 237
Lay your weapons down; Home to your cottages . . . . . iv 2 131
Who hateth him . . . , Shake he his weapon at us and pass by . . iv 8 18
If our words will serve.—And if words will not, then our weapons shall v 1 140
Thy son's blood cleaving to my blade Shall rust upon my weapon *3 Hen. VI.* i 3 51
Their weapons like to lightning came and went . . . . ii 1 129
Ah, kill me with thy weapon, not with words! . . . . . v 6 26
What, would you have my weapon, little lord? . . . *Richard III.* iii 1 122
Empale him with your weapons round about . . . *Troi. and Cres.* v 7 5
Down with him! down with him!—Weapons, weapons, weapons! *Coriol.* iii 1 185
Masters, lay down your weapons.—Go not home . . . . . iii 1 331
Foul-spoken coward, that thunder'st with thy tongue, And with thy weapon nothing darest perform! . . . . . *T. Andron.* ii 1 59
But wherefore stand'st thou with thy weapon drawn? . . . . iii 1 48
My grandsire . . . hath sent by me The goodliest weapons of his armoury iv 2 11
The old man hath found their guilt, And sends them weapons wrapp'd about with lines, That wound, beyond their feeling . . . . iv 2 27
With this, my weapon drawn, I rush'd upon him, Surprised him suddenly v 1 37
My naked weapon is out: quarrel, I will back thee . *Rom. and Jul.* i 1 39
From those bloody hands Throw your mistemper'd weapons to the ground . . . . i 1 94
I saw no man use you at his pleasure; if I had, my weapon should quickly have been out, I warrant you . . . . ii 4 166
Beat down their weapons. Gentlemen, for shame, forbear this outrage! iii 1 89
Waving our red weapons o'er our heads, Let's all cry 'Peace!' *J. Cæsar* iii 1 109
But swords I smile at, weapons laugh to scorn . . . *Macbeth* v 7 12
To know a man well, were to know himself.—I mean, sir, for his weapon *Hamlet* v 2 148
What's his weapon?—Rapier and dagger.—That's two of his weapons . v 2 151
Weapons! arms! What's the matter here? . . . . . *Lear* ii 2 50
Let not women's weapons, water-drops, Stain my man's cheeks! . . ii 4 280
Six shirts to his body, horse to ride, and weapon to wear . . . iii 4 142
Get weapons, ho! And raise some special officers of night . *Othello* i 1 182
You shall more command with years Than with your weapons . . i 2 61
Men do their broken weapons rather use Than their bare hands . i 3 174
Here's one comes in his shirt, with light and weapons . . . v 1 47
Take you this weapon, Which I have here recover'd from the Moor . v 2 239
I have another weapon in this chamber; It is a sword of Spain . v 2 252
It will cost thee dear: Thou hast no weapon, and perforce must suffer . v 2 256
I have a weapon; A better never did itself sustain Upon a soldier's thigh v 2 259
Weapon. This did I fear, but thought he had no weapon; For he was great of heart . . . . *Othello* v 2 360
Weaponed. Be not afraid, though you do see me weapon'd . . v 2 266
Wear. If these be true spies which I wear in my head . . *Tempest* v 1 259
What compass will you wear your farthingale? . . . *T. G. of Ver.* ii 7 51
How shall I fashion me to wear a cloak? . . . . . . iii 1 135
I'll wear a boot, to make it [my leg] somewhat rounder . . . . . v 2 6
Shall I Sir Pandarus of Troy become, And by my side wear steel? *M. W.* i 3 84
Does he not wear a great round beard, like a glover's paring-knife? . i 4 20
Away, I say; time wears: hold up your head, and mince . . . v 1 8
The impression of keen whips I'ld wear as rubies . *Meas. for Meas.* ii 4 101
Bestowed her on her own lamentation, which she yet wears for his sake iii 1 238
Your good worship will be my bail.—No, indeed, will I not, Pompey; it is not the wear . . . . iii 2 78
And often touching will Wear gold . . . . *Com. of Errors* ii 1 112
So to deny This chain which now you wear so openly . . . . v 1 17
He wears his faith but as the fashion of his hat; it ever changes *M. Ado* i 1 75
Hath not the world one man but he will wear his cap with suspicion? . i 1 200
An thou wilt needs thrust thy neck into a yoke, wear the print of it . i 1 203
What fashion will you wear the garland of? . . . You must wear it one way . . . . ii 1 196
Your grace is too costly to wear every day . . . . . . ii 1 342
Let her wear it out with good counsel.—Nay, that's impossible: she may wear her heart out first . . . . ii 3 207
As to show a child his new coat and forbid him to wear it . . . iii 2 7
One Deformed is one of them: I know him; a' wears a lock . . . iii 3 183
I'll wear this.—By my troth, 's not so good . . . . . . iii 4 8
My cousin's a fool, and thou art another: I'll wear none but this . iii 4 12
God give me joy to wear it! for my heart is exceeding heavy . . . iii 4 24
Doth not my wit become me rarely?—It is not seen enough, you should wear it in your cap . . . . iii 4 71
Let him kill one first; Win me and wear me; let him answer me . . v 1 82
Dost thou wear thy wit by thy side?—Never any did so . . . . v 1 126
They say he wears a key in his ear and a lock hanging by it . . v 1 318
If a man will be beaten with brains, a' shall wear nothing handsome about him . . . . v 4 105
And I to be a corporal of his field, And wear his colours! . *L. L. Lost* iii 1 190
This favour thou shalt wear, And then the king will court thee for his dear . . . . v 2 130
Come on, then; wear the favours most in sight . . . . . v 2 136
Pardon me, sir, this jewel did she wear . . . . v 2 456
And that a' wears next his heart for a favour . . . . . v 2 721
Who is here? Weeds of Athens he doth wear . . . *M. N. Dream* ii 2 71
What dances shall we have, To wear away this long age of three hours? v 1 33
Swear but now and then, Wear prayer-books in my pocket *Mer. of Venice* ii 2 201
Let none presume To wear an undeserved dignity . . . . . ii 9 40
How many cowards, whose hearts are all as false As stairs of sand, wear yet upon their chins The beards of Hercules! . . . . . . iii 2 84
Making them lightest that wear most of it . . . . . . iii 2 91
And wear my dagger with the braver grace . . . . . . iii 4 65
Give me your gloves, I'll wear them for your sake . . . . . iv 1 426
You swore to me . . . That you would wear it till your hour of death . v 1 153
God's my judge, The clerk will ne'er wear hair on's face that had it . v 1 158
Wear this for me, one out of suits with fortune . . *As Y. Like It* i 2 258
Sweet are the uses of adversity, Which, like the toad, ugly and venomous, Wears yet a precious jewel in his head . . . . ii 1 14
Said with weeping tears 'Wear these for my sake' . . . . . ii 4 54
O noble fool! A worthy fool! Motley's the only wear . . . . ii 7 34
I earn that I eat, get that I wear, owe no man hate, envy no man's happiness . . . . iii 2 78
Look you lisp and wear strange suits . . . . iv 1 34
What shall he have that kill'd the deer? His leather skin and horns to wear . . . . iv 2 12
Take thou no scorn to wear the horn; It was a crest ere thou wast born iv 2 14
How it grieves me to see thee wear thy heart in a scarf! . . . . v 2 23
Ask him what apparel he will wear . . . . . *T. of Shrew* Ind. 1 60
What raiment will your honour wear to-day? . . . . . Ind. 2 4
Ne'er ask me what raiment I'll wear; for I have no more doublets than backs . . . . Ind. 2 9
Who knows not where a wasp does wear his sting? In his tail . . ii 1 214
The morning wears, 'tis time we were at church . . . . . iii 2 113
Could I repair what she will wear in me, As I can change these . . iii 2 120
This doth fit the time, And gentlewomen wear such caps as these . . iv 3 70
Why, sir, what 'cerns it you if I wear pearl and gold? . . . . v 1 77
Virginity, like an old courtier, wears her cap out of fashion . *All's Well* i 1 169
Just like the brooch and the tooth-pick, which wear not now . . i 1 172
A virtue of a good wing, and I like the wear well . . . . . i 1 219
It will wear the surplice of humility over the black gown of a big heart i 3 98
They wear themselves in the cap of the time . . . . . . ii 1 54
He wears his honour in a box unseen, That hugs his kicky-wicky here at home . . . . ii 3 296
A ring the county wears, That downward hath succeeded in his house . iii 7 22
This exceeding posting day and night Must wear your spirits low . . v 1 2
Since you have made the days and nights as one, To wear your gentle limbs in my affairs . . . . v 1 4
I have seen her wear it; and she reckon'd it At her life's rate . . v 3 90
I am sure I saw her wear it.—You are deceived . . . . . v 3 91
That's as much to say as I wear not motley in my brain . *T. Night* i 5 63
So wears she to him, So sways she level in her husband's heart . . ii 4 31
Here, wear this jewel for me, 'tis my picture . . . . . . iii 4 228
Meddle you must, that's certain, or forswear to wear iron about you . iii 4 276
He that wears her like his medal, hanging About his neck . *W. Tale* i 2 307
With a countenance as clear As friendship wears at feasts . . . i 2 344
That wear upon your virgin branches yet Your maidenheads growing . iv 4 115
Is there no manners left among maids? will they wear their plackets where they should bear their faces? . . . . iv 4 245
Any toys for your head, Of the new'st and finest, finest wear-a? . . iv 4 327
His garments are rich, but he wears them not handsomely . . . iv 4 776
Thou wear a lion's hide! doff it for shame, And hang a calf's skin *K. John* iii 1 128
Pluck a glove, And wear it as a favour . . . . . *Richard II.* v 3 18
And for his sake wear the detested blot Of murderous subornation *1 Hen. IV.* i 3 162
He that doth redeem her thence might wear Without corrival all her dignities . . . . i 3 206
I'll never wear hair on my face more . . . . ii 4 153
Yet youth, the more it is wasted the sooner it wears . . . . ii 4 443
I will wear a garment all of blood And stain my favours in a bloody mask iii 2 135
My uncle and myself Did give him that same royalty he wears . . iv 3 55
I am the Douglas, fatal to all those That wear those colours . . . v 4 27
The whoreson smooth-pates do now wear nothing but high shoes *2 Hen. IV.* i 2 44
And wears his boots very smooth, like unto the sign of the leg . . ii 4 270

Wear. Then happy low, lie down! Uneasy lies the head that wears a crown . . . . 2 *Hen. IV.* iii 1 31
He that wears the crown immortally Long guard it yours! . . . iv 5 144
I will deeply put the fashion on And wear it in my heart . . . v 2 53
I tell thee, constable, my mistress wears his own hair . *Hen. V.* iii 7 64
If their heads had any intellectual armour, they could never wear such heavy head-pieces . . . . iii 7 148
Do not you wear your dagger in your cap that day . . . . iv 1 56
Give me any gage of thine, and I will wear it in my bonnet . . iv 1 224
This will I also wear in my cap . . . . iv 1 229
It yearns me not if men my garments wear . . . . . iv 3 26
Your majesty takes no scorn to wear the leek upon Saint Tavy's day.—I wear it for a memorable honour . . . . iv 7 107
Which he swore, as he was a soldier, he would wear if alive . . iv 7 135
Wear thou this favour for me and stick it in thy cap . . . iv 7 160
It is the soldier's; I by bargain should Wear it myself . . . iv 7 183
He that I gave it to in change promised to wear it in his cap . . iv 8 31
Keep it, fellow; And wear it for an honour in thy cap . . . iv 8 63
But why wear you your leek to-day? Saint Davy's day is past . . v 1 1
Thou shalt wear me, if thou wear me, better and better . . . v 2 250
Not to wear, handle, or use any sword, weapon, or dagger . 1 *Hen. VI.* i 3 78
Well, I'll find friends to wear my bleeding roses . . . . ii 4 72
For these my friends in spite of thee shall wear . . . . ii 4 106
This pale and angry rose . . . Will I for ever and my faction wear . ii 4 109
Will I upon thy party wear this rose . . . . ii 4 123
Pluck a flower.—In your behalf still will I wear the same . . ii 4 130
You, that were so hot at sea, Disgracing of these colours that I wear . iii 4 29
Or whether that such cowards ought to wear This ornament of knighthood . . . . iv 1 28
With envious carping tongue, Upbraided me about the rose I wear . iv 1 91
I see no reason, if I wear this rose, That any one should therefore be suspicious . . . . iv 1 152
But yet I like it not, In that he wears the badge of Somerset . . iv 1 177
Nor hold the sceptre in his childish fist, Nor wear the diadem 2 *Hen. VI.* i 1 246
Though in this place most master wear no breeches . . . . i 3 149
As thus to name the several colours we do wear . . . . ii 1 129
I wear no knife to slaughter sleeping men . . . . . iii 2 197
Thou oughtest not to let thy horse wear a cloak . . . . iv 7 55
The proudest peer in the realm shall not wear a head on his shoulders . iv 7 127
Thou shalt wear it as a herald's coat . . . . iv 10 75
I'll wear aloft my burgonet, As on a mountain top the cedar shows . v 1 204
And, father, do but think How sweet a thing it is to wear a crown 3 *Hen. VI.* i 2 29
I cannot rest Until the white rose that I wear be dyed Even in the lukewarm blood of Henry's heart . . . . i 2 33
York cannot speak, unless he wear a crown. A crown for York! . . i 4 93
As I hear, You, that are king, though he do wear the crown . . ii 2 90
Promise them such rewards As victors wear at the Olympian games . ii 3 53
He plies her hard; and much rain wears the marble . . . . iii 2 50
In hope he'll prove a widower shortly, I'll wear the willow-garland iii 3 228; iv 1 100
But Henry now shall wear the English crown, And be true king indeed iv 3 49
Although my head still wear the crown, I here resign my government iv 6 23
His head by nature framed to wear a crown, His hand to wield a sceptre iv 6 72
To be her men and wear her livery . . . . *Richard III.* i 1 80
Wear both of them, for both of them are thine . . . . . i 2 206
It is too heavy for your grace to wear.—I weigh it lightly, were it heavier iii 1 120
Till Richard wear the garland of the realm.—How! wear the garland! . iii 2 40
They, for their truth, might better wear their heads Than some that have accused them wear their hats . . . . iii 2 94
Shall we wear these honours for a day? Or shall they last? . . . iv 2 5
Wear it, enjoy it, and make much of it . . . . v 5 7
They may, 'cum privilegio,' wear away The lag end of their lewdness *Hen. VIII.* i 3 34
To be perk'd up in a glistering grief, And wear a golden sorrow . . ii 3 22
We are contented To wear our mortal state to come with her . . ii 4 228
Garlands, Griffith, which I feel I am not worthy yet to wear . . iv 2 92
Who wears his wit in his belly and his guts in his head *Troi. and Cres.* ii 1 79
A plague of opinion! a man may wear it on both sides . . . iii 3 266
Speaking is for beggars; he wears his tongue in's arms . . . iii 3 271
Wear this sleeve.—And you this glove . . . . iv 4 72
Whilst some with cunning gild their copper crowns, With truth and plainness I do wear mine bare . . . . iv 4 108
To-morrow will I wear it on my helm, And grieve his spirit . . v 2 93
Stand fast, and wear a castle on thy head! . . . . . . v 2 187
That Caius Marcius Wears this war's garland . . . *Coriolanus* i 9 60
Such eyes the widows in Corioli wear, And mothers that lack sons . ii 1 195
Friends now fast sworn, Whose double bosoms seem to wear one heart . iv 4 13
And his own notion—Who wears my stripes impress'd upon him . . v 6 108
Upon his bloody finger he doth wear A precious ring . *T. Andron.* ii 3 226
Her vestal livery is but sick and green And none but fools do wear it; cast it off . . . . *Rom. and Jul.* ii 2 9
Here comes my man.—But I'll be hang'd, sir, if he wear your livery . iii 1 60
So tedious is this day As is the night before some festival To an impatient child that hath new robes And may not wear them . . . iii 2 31
How goes the world?—It wears, sir, as it grows . . *T. of Athens* i 1 3
Honour me so much As to advance this jewel; accept it and wear it . i 2 176
He wears jewels now of Timon's gift, For which I wait for money . . iii 4 19
E'en as if your lord should wear rich jewels, And send for money for 'em iii 4 23
Make his wrongs His outsides, to wear them like his raiment, carelessly iii 5 33
Yet do our hearts wear Timon's livery; That see I by our faces . iv 2 17
Thy flatterers yet wear silk, drink wine, lie soft; Hug their diseased perfumes . . . . iv 3 206
Ne'er did poor steward wear a truer grief For his undone lord . . iv 3 487
He shall wear his crown by sea and land, In every place, save here *J. Cæsar* i 3 87
I know where I will wear this dagger then . . . . . . i 3 89
O, what a time have you chose out, brave Caius, To wear a kerchief! . ii 1 315
My hands are of your colour; but I shame To wear a heart so white *Macb.* ii 2 65
Who wear our health but sickly in his life, Which in his death were perfect iii 1 107
Wears upon his baby-brow the round And top of sovereignty . . iv 1 88
Though all things foul would wear the brows of grace, Yet grace must still look so . . . . iv 3 23
Wear thou thy wrongs; The title is affeer'd! . . . . . iv 3 33
When I shall tread upon the tyrant's head, Or wear it on my sword . iv 3 46
The serpent that did sting thy father's life Now wears his crown *Hamlet* i 5 40
And I will wear him In my heart's core, ay, in my heart of heart . iii 2 77
Nay then, let the devil wear black, for I'll have a suit of sables . iii 2 137
O, you must wear your rue with a difference . . . . . iv 5 183
Youth no less becomes The light and careless livery that it wears Than settled age his sables . . . . iv 7 80
Wear. As peace should still her wheaten garland wear . . *Hamlet* v 2 41
If thou follow him, thou must needs wear my coxcomb . . *Lear* i 4 116
They know not how their wits to wear, Their manners are so apish . i 4 183
Why art thou angry?—That such a slave as this should wear a sword, Who wears no honesty . . . . ii 2 78
Ha, ha! he wears cruel garters . . . . ii 4 7
When a man's over-lusty at legs, then he wears wooden nether-stocks . ii 4 10
Fathers that wear rags Do make their children blind . . . ii 4 48
Six shirts to his body, horse to ride, and weapon to wear . . iii 4 143
If you did wear a beard upon your chin, I'd shake it on this quarrel . iii 7 76
Wear this; spare speech; Decline your head . . . . . iv 2 21
But I will wear my heart upon my sleeve For daws to peck at *Othello* i 1 64
'Tis as I should entreat you wear your gloves, Or feed on nourishing dishes . . . . iii 3 77
Observe her well with Cassio; Wear your eye thus, not jealous nor secure iii 3 198
Wear thy good rapier bare, and put it home: Quick, quick . . . v 1 2
Tell him he wears the rose Of youth upon him . . *Ant. and Cleo.* iii 13 20
Woe, woe are we, sir, you may not live to wear All your true followers out iv 14 133
Quicken with kissing: had my lips that power, Thus would I wear them out . . . . iv 15 40
Although they wear their faces to the bent Of the king's looks *Cymbeline* i 1 13
For my sake wear this; It is a manacle of love . . . . . i 1 121
You may wear her in title yours: but, you know, strange fowl light upon neighbouring ponds . . . . i 4 96
Some more time Must wear the print of his remembrance out . . ii 3 48
If you could wear a mind Dark as your fortune is . . . . iii 4 146
Your hand, my lord.—Receive it friendly; but from this time forth I wear it as your enemy . . . . iii 5 14
Thy words, I grant, are bigger, for I wear not My dagger in my mouth iv 2 78
O sweetest, fairest lily! My brother wears thee not the one half so well As when thou grew'st thyself . . . . iv 2 202
Knighthoods and honours, borne As I wear mine, are titles but of scorn v 2 7
One twelve moons more she'll wear Diana's livery . . . *Pericles* ii 5 10
A maid-child call'd Marina; who, O goddess, Wears yet thy silver livery v 3 7
There well appears The worth that learned charity aye wears . v 3 Gower 94
Wear out. At home, Wear out thy youth with shapeless idleness *T. G. of Ver.* i 1 8
I see that the fashion wears out more apparel than the man *Much Ado* iii 3 149
Let not the hours of this ungodly day Wear out the day in peace *K. John* iii 1 110
If you urge me farther than to say 'do you in faith?' I wear out my suit . . . . *Hen. V.* v 2 132
You wear out a good wholesome forenoon in hearing a cause . *Coriolanus* ii 1 77
O, so light a foot Will ne'er wear out the everlasting flint *Rom. and Jul.* ii 6 17
Why dost thou lead these men about the streets?—Truly, sir, to wear out their shoes, to get myself into more work . . . *J. Cæsar* i 1 33
O ruin'd piece of nature! This great world Shall so wear out to nought *Lear* iv 6 138
And we'll wear out, In a wall'd prison, packs and sects of great ones . v 3 17
Wears out his time, much like his master's ass, For nought but provender . . . . *Othello* i 1 47
Wearer. That clear honour Were purchased by the merit of the wearer! *Mer. of Venice* ii 9 43
The celestial habits, . . . Methinks I so should term them, and the reverence Of the grave wearers . . . . . *W. Tale* iii 1 6
Were I the wearer of Antonius' beard, I would not shave't to-day *Ant. and Cleo.* ii 2 7
Wearest. So thou the garland wear'st successively . . 2 *Hen. IV.* iv 5 202
Soldier, why wearest thou that glove in thy cap? . . *Hen. V.* iv 7 125
Which, in the day of battle, tire thee more Than all the complete armour that thou wear'st! . . . . *Richard III.* iv 4 189
If only to go warm were gorgeous, Why, nature needs not what thou gorgeous wear'st, Which scarcely keeps thee warm . . . *Lear* ii 4 272
Wearied. When this burns, 'Twill weep for having wearied you *Tempest* iii 1 19
O most gentle pulpiter! what tedious homily of love have you wearied your parishioners withal! . . . . . . *As Y. Like It* iii 2 164
Rendering faint quittance, wearied and out-breathed . 2 *Hen. IV.* i 1 108
There are twenty weak and wearied posts Come from the north . . ii 4 385
Weariest. The weariest and most loathed worldly life *Meas. for Meas.* iii 1 129
Wearily. You look wearily . . . . *Tempest* iii 1 32
Weariness. I cannot blame thee, Who am myself attach'd with weariness iii 3 5
Is't come to that? I had thought weariness durst not have attached one of so high blood . . . . 2 *Hen. IV.* ii 2 3
Weariness Can snore upon the flint, when resty sloth Finds the down pillow hard . . . . *Cymbeline* iii 6 33
Wearing. He comes in like a perjure, wearing papers . *L. L. Lost* iv 3 48
Nor believe he can have every thing in him by wearing his apparel neatly . . . . *All's Well* iv 3 167
Your high self . . . you have obscured With a swain's wearing *W. Tale* iv 4 9
In continual laughter the wearing out of six fashions . 2 *Hen. IV.* v 1 89
Be you contented, wearing now the garland . . . . . . v 2 84
Could not keep quiet in his conscience, Wearing the crown . *Hen. V.* i 2 80
Wearing leeks in their Monmouth caps . . . . iv 7 104
The very train of her worst wearing gown Was better worth than all my father's lands . . . . 2 *Hen. VI.* i 3 88
That when the single sole of it is worn, the jest may remain after the wearing sole singular . . . . *Rom. and Jul.* ii 4 68
Didst thou not fall out with a tailor for wearing his new doublet before Easter? . . . . iii 1 30
You mend the jewel by the wearing it.—Well mock'd . *T. of Athens* i 1 172
Thought On special dignities, which vacant lie For thy best use and wearing . . . . v 1 146
Many wearing rapiers are afraid of goose-quills . . . *Hamlet* ii 2 359
Give me my nightly wearing, and adieu: We must not now displease him . . . . *Othello* iv 3 16
All is well yet. Sparkles this stone as it was wont? or is't not Too dull for your good wearing? . . . . *Cymbeline* ii 4 41
We will nothing pay For wearing our own noses . . . . iii 1 14
Wearisome. Alas, the way is wearisome and long! . . *T. G. of Ver.* ii 7 8
Rough uneven ways Draws out our miles, and makes them wearisome *Richard II.* ii 3 5
Our crosses on the way Have made it tedious, wearisome, and heavy *Richard III.* iii 1 5
Weary. You sunburnt sicklemen, of August weary . . . *Tempest* iv 1 134
With twenty watchful, weary, tedious nights . . *T. G. of Ver.* i 1 31
How thrives your love?—My tales of love were wont to weary you . ii 4 126
A true-devoted pilgrim is not weary To measure kingdoms . . ii 7 9
And make a pastime of each weary step . . . . . . ii 7 35
Not to be weary with you, he's in prison . . *Meas. for Meas.* i 4 25
Dies ere the weary sun set in the west . . *Com. of Errors* i 2 7
For with long travel I am stiff and weary . . . . . . i 2 15

Weary. Tell her, we measure them by weary steps . . . *L. L. Lost* v 2 194
How many weary steps, Of many weary miles you have o'ergone, Are number'd in the travel of one mile? . . . v 2 195
And never rest, But seek the weary beds of people sick . . . v 2 832
O weary night, O long and tedious night, Abate thy hours! *M. N. Dream* iii 2 431
Never so weary, never so in woe, Bedabbled with the dew . . . iii 2 442
Whilst the heavy ploughman snores, All with weary task fordone . v 1 381
In sooth, I know not why I am so sad: It wearies me; you say it wearies you . . . . *Mer. of Venice* i 1 2
O Jupiter, how weary are my spirits!—I care not for my spirits, if my legs were not weary . . . . . *As Y. Like It* ii 4 1
Flow as hugely as the sea, Till that the weary very means do ebb . ii 7 73
Who after me hath many a weary step Limp'd in pure love . . ii 7 130
'Tis a fault I will not change for your best virtue. I am weary of you . iii 2 302
I will weary you then no longer with idle talking . . . v 2 56
Was ever man so rayed? was ever man so weary? *T. of Shrew* iv 1 4
Go see your lodging.—I am not weary, and 'tis long to night . *T. Night* iii 3 21
We weary you.—You weary those that refresh us . *W. Tale* iv 4 342
The stumbling night did part our weary powers . . *K. John* v 5 18
Like two men That vow a long and weary pilgrimage . *Richard II.* i 3 49
The sullen passage of thy weary steps Esteem as foil . . . i 3 265
By this the weary lords Shall make their way seem short . . ii 3 16
His weary joints would gladly rise, I know . . . . v 3 105
Patience is stale, and I am weary of it . . . . v 5 104
But if you go,— So far afoot, I shall be weary, love . *1 Hen. IV.* ii 3 87
Before God, I am exceeding weary.—Is't come to that? . *2 Hen. IV.* ii 2 1
And the continent, Weary of solid firmness, melt itself Into the sea! . iii 1 48
The king is weary Of dainty and such picking grievances . . iv 1 197
Unless some dull and favourable hand Will whisper music to my weary spirit . . . . iv 5 3
I stay too long by thee, I weary thee . . . . iv 5 94
My tongue is weary; when my legs are too, I will bid you good night . Epil. 34
Unto the weary and all-watched night . . . *Hen. V.* iv Prol. 38
Old I do wax; and from my weary limbs Honour is cudgelled . v 1 89
He fighteth as one weary of his life . . . *1 Hen. VI.* i 2 26
Art thou not weary, John? how dost thou fare? . . . iv 6 27
Let me embrace thee in my weary arms . . . *3 Hen. VI.* ii 3 45
And still, as you are weary of the weight, Rest you *Richard III.* i 2 31
The weary way hath made you melancholy . . . . iii 1 3
My burthen'd yoke; From which even here I slip my weary neck . iv 4 112
The weary sun hath made a golden set . . . . v 3 19
These famish'd beggars, weary of their lives . . . . v 3 329
The last hour Of my long weary life is come upon me . *Hen. VIII.* ii 1 133
Now has left me, Weary and old with service . . . iii 2 363
O, father abbot, An old man, broken with the storms of state, Is come to lay his weary bones among ye . . . . . . iv 2 22
I have loved you night and day For many weary months *Troi. and Cres.* iii 2 123
I am weary; yea, my memory is tired. Have we no wine here? *Coriol.* i 9 91
In a word, I also am Longer to live most weary . . . iv 5 101
He by the senate is accited home From weary wars . *T. Andron.* i 1 28
Now at once run on The dashing rocks thy sea-sick weary bark! *R. and J.* v 3 118
Methinks, I could deal kingdoms to my friends, And ne'er be weary *T. of Athens* i 2 227
I'm weary of this charge, the gods can witness . . . iii 4 25
But life, being weary of these wordly bars, Never lacks power to dismiss itself . . . . *J. Cæsar* i 3 96
So shall he waste his means, weary his soldiers, Doing himself offence iv 3 200
Weary se'nnights nine times nine Shall he dwindle, peak, and pine *Macb.* i 3 22
And I another So weary with disasters, tugg'd with fortune . . iii 1 112
How weary, stale, flat, and unprofitable Seem to me all the uses of this world! Fie on't! ah fie! . . . . . . *Hamlet* i 2 133
Who would fardels bear, To grunt and sweat under a weary life? . iii 1 77
Put on what weary negligence you please, You and your fellows *Lear* i 3 12
He that keeps nor crust nor crum, Weary of all, shall want some . i 4 218
All weary and o'er-watch'd, Take vantage, heavy eyes, not to behold This shameful lodging . . . . ii 2 177
Deny to speak with me? They are sick? they are weary? . . ii 4 89
Eight score eight hours? and lovers' absent hours, More tedious than the dial eight score times? O weary reckoning! . *Othello* iii 4 176
Hear me with patience.—Talk thy tongue weary; speak *Cymbeline* iii 4 115
I am throughly weary.—I am weak with toil, yet strong in appetite . iii 6 36
Wherein we are not destitute for want, But weary for the staleness *Per.* v 1 58
Wearying thy hearer in thy mistress' praise . *As Y. Like It* ii 4 38
Weasel. I can suck melancholy out of a song, as a weasel sucks eggs . ii 5 13
A weasel hath not such a deal of spleen As you are toss'd with *1 Hen. IV.* ii 3 81
To her unguarded nest the weasel Scot Comes sneaking . *Hen. V.* i 2 170
Methinks it is like a weasel.—It is backed like a weasel . *Hamlet* iii 2 396
Quick-answer'd, saucy, and As quarrelous as the weasel . . *Cymbeline* iii 4 162
Weather. A plague upon this howling! they are louder than the weather . . . . *Tempest* i 1 40
It is foul weather in us all, good sir, When you are cloudy.—Foul weather? . . . . ii 1 141
Here's neither bush nor shrub, to bear off any weather at all . . ii 2 19
Where it is impossible you should take true root but by the fair weather that you make yourself . . . . . *Much Ado* i 3 25
And so, farewell.—Fair weather after you! . . *L. L. Lost* ii 2 149
Many can brook the weather that love not the wind . . . iv 2 34
Like the martlet, Builds in the weather on the outward wall *Mer. of Venice* ii 9 29
No enemy But winter and rough weather . . . *As Y. Like It* ii 5 47
You and you are sure together, As the winter to foul weather . . v 4 142
Considering the weather, a taller man than I will take cold *T. of Shrew* iv 1 11
'Tis in grain, sir; 'twill endure wind and weather . . *T. Night* i 5 256
'Tis like to be loud weather . . . . . . *W. Tale* iii 3 11
Would any but these boiled brains of nineteen and two-and-twenty hunt this weather? . . . . iii 3 65
Both roaring louder than the sea or weather . . . . iii 3 104
Whose honour and whose honesty till now Endured all weathers . v 1 195
Extremity of weather continuing, this mystery remained undiscovered v 2 129
So foul a sky clears not without a storm: Pour down thy weather *K. John* iv 2 109
And make fair weather in your blustering land . . . . v 1 21
We'll make foul weather with despised tears . . *Richard II.* iii 3 161
Home without boots, and in foul weather too! How 'scapes he agues? *1 Hen. IV.* iii 1 68
This is hot weather, gentlemen . . . . *2 Hen. IV.* iii 2 101
The day is hot, and the weather, and the wars, and the king, and the dukes . . . . *Hen. V.* iii 2 113
Is not amiss to cool a man's stomach this hot weather . *2 Hen. VI.* iv 10 10
But I must make fair weather yet a while . . . . v 1 30

Weather. Two women placed together makes cold weather . *Hen. VIII.* i 4 22
Mine honour keeps the weather of my fate . . *Troi. and Cres.* v 3 26
Who's there, besides foul weather?—One minded like the weather *Lear* iii 1 1
A storm or robbery, call it what you will, Shook down my mellow hangings, nay, my leaves, And left me bare to weather *Cymbeline* iii 3 64
Weather-beaten. I sent him Bootless home and weather-beaten back *1 Hen. IV.* iii 1 67
Weather-bitten. Like a weather-bitten conduit of many kings' reigns *W. Tale* v 2 60
Weathercock. Inscrutable, invisible, As a nose on a man's face, or a weathercock on a steeple! . . . . . *T. G. of Ver.* ii 1 142
Where had you this pretty weathercock? . . . *Mer. Wives* iii 2 18
What vane? what weathercock? did you ever hear better? *L. L. Lost* iv 1 97
Weather-fends. In the line-grove which weather-fends your cell *Tempest* v 1 10
Weave. The free maids that weave their thread with bones . *T. Night* ii 4 46
My brain more busy than the labouring spider Weaves tedious snares *2 Hen. VI.* iii 1 340
The better! best! This weaves itself perforce into my business *Lear* ii 1 17
I can sing, weave, sew, and dance, With other virtues . *Pericles* iv 6 194
Weaved. She weaved the sleided silk With fingers long, small, white as milk . . . . iv Gower 21
Weaved-up. And must I ravel out My weaved-up folly? . *Richard II.* iv 1 229
Weaver. I fear not Goliath with a weaver's beam . *Mer. Wives* v 1 24
Answer as I call you. Nick Bottom, the weaver.—Ready *M. N. Dream* i 2 19
I Pyramus am not Pyramus, but Bottom the weaver . . . iii 1 23
Shall we rouse the night-owl in a catch that will draw three souls out of one weaver? . . . . *T. Night* ii 3 61
I would I were a weaver; I could sing psalms or any thing *1 Hen. IV.* ii 4 146
And Dick the Butcher,— . . . And Smith the weaver . *2 Hen. VI.* iv 2 30
The spinsters, carders, fullers, weavers . . . *Hen. VIII.* i 2 33
Weaving spiders, come not here; Hence, you long-legg'd spinners! *M. N. Dream* ii 2 20
Web. The web of our life is of a mingled yarn, good and ill together *All's Well* iv 3 83
And all eyes Blind with the pin and web but theirs, theirs only *W. Tale* i 2 291
Dost thou thirst, base Trojan, To have me fold up Parca's fatal web? *Hen. V.* v 1 21
Why strew'st thou sugar on that bottled spider, Whose deadly web ensnareth thee about? Fool, fool! . . . *Richard III.* i 3 243
But, spider-like, Out of his self-drawing web, he gives us note *Hen. VIII.* i 1 63
It will not in circumvention deliver a fly from a spider, without drawing their massy irons and cutting the web *Troi. and Cres.* ii 3 19
The traces of the smallest spider's web . . . *Rom. and Jul.* i 4 61
He gives the web and the pin, squints the eye, and makes the hare-lip *Lear* iii 4 122
With as little a web as this will I ensnare as great a fly as Cassio *Othello* ii 1 169
There's magic in the web of it . . . . . . iii 4 69
Wed. For Thurio, he intends, shall wed his daughter . *T. G. of Ver.* ii 6 39
In Syracusa was I born, and wed Unto a woman . *Com. of Errors* i 1 37
If you did wed my sister for her wealth, Then for her wealth's sake use her with more kindness . . . . iii 2 5
If you love her then, to-morrow wed her . . . *Much Ado* iii 2 118
In the congregation, where I should wed, there will I shame her . iii 2 128
Adding thereto moreover That he would wed me . . *L. L. Lost* v 2 447
I will wed thee in another key, With pomp, with triumph *M. N. Dream* i 1 18
I beseech your grace that I may know The worst that may befall me in this case, If I refuse to wed Demetrius . . . . . i 1 64
Either prepare to die . . . , Or else to wed Demetrius . . i 1 88
Men are April when they woo, December when they wed *As Y. Like It* iv 1 148
That you'll marry me, Or else refusing me, to wed this shepherd . v 4 22
I'll have no husband, if you be not he: Nor ne'er wed woman, if you be not she . . . . v 4 130
Wed her and bed her and rid the house of her! . . *T. of Shrew* i 1 149
I would not wed her for a mine of gold . . . . . i 2 92
Will not promise her to any man Until the elder sister first be wed i 2 263
If she deny to wed, I'll crave the day When I shall ask the banns . ii 1 180
You have show'd a tender fatherly regard, To wish me wed to one half lunatic . . . . ii 1 289
Who woo'd in haste and means to wed at leisure . . . iii 2 11
Yet never means to wed where he hath woo'd . . . iii 2 17
'Twere all one That I should love a bright particular star And think to wed it, he is so above me . . . . . . *All's Well* i 1 98
See that you come Not to woo honour, but to wed it . . . ii 1 15
And in your bed Find fairer fortune, if you ever wed! . . ii 3 98
I dare not make myself so guilty, To give up willingly that noble title Your master wed me to . . . . . *Hen. VIII.* iii 1 141
I wonder at this haste; that I must wed Ere he, that should be husband, comes to woo . . . . . *Rom. and Jul.* iii 5 119
And then to have a wretched puling fool, A whining mammet, in her fortune's tender, to answer 'I'll not wed' . . . iii 5 187
This is it [gold] That makes the wappen'd widow wed again *T. of Athens* iv 3 38
In second husband let me be accurst! None wed the second but who kill'd the first . . . . *Hamlet* iii 2 190
So think thou wilt no second husband wed . . . . iii 2 224
Quoth she, before you tumbled me, You promised me to wed . . iv 5 64
When I shall wed, That lord whose hand must take my plight shall carry Half my love with him, half my care and duty *Lear* i 1 102
She tells me here, she'll wed the stranger knight, Or never more to view nor day nor light . . . . . . *Pericles* ii 5 16
If it please your majesty.—It pleaseth me so well, that I will see you wed . . . . ii 5 92
I'ld wish no better choice, and think me rarely wed . . v 1 69
Who, frighted from my country, did wed At Pentapolis the fair Thaisa v 3 3
Wedded. But, were you wedded, you would bear some sway *Com. of Er.* ii 1 28
Is she wedded or no?—To her will, sir, or so . . *L. L. Lost* ii 1 211
Your warrior love To Theseus must be wedded . . *M. N. Dream* ii 1 72
There shall the pairs of faithful lovers be Wedded . . . iv 1 97
I' faith, he'll have a lusty widow now, That shall be woo'd and wedded in a day . . . . *T. of Shrew* iv 2 51
I have wedded her, not bedded her; and sworn to make the 'not' eternal . . . . *All's Well* iii 2 23
If, one by one, you wedded all the world, . . . she you kill'd Would be unparallel'd . . . . *W. Tale* v 1 13
Give consent, Thy daughter shall be wedded to my king *1 Hen. VI.* v 3 137
I gave a noble to the priest The morn that I was wedded . . v 3 24
And wedded be thou to the hags of hell . . . *2 Hen. VI.* iv 1 79
More dances my rapt heart Than when I first my wedded mistress saw *Coriolanus* iv 5 123
Come forth, thou fearful man: Affliction is enamour'd of thy parts, And thou art wedded to calamity . . . *Rom. and Jul.* iii 3 3

Wedded. Death is my son-in-law, Death is my heir; My daughter he hath wedded . . . . . . *Rom. and Jul.* iv 5 39
She's wedded; Her husband banish'd; she imprison'd . *Cymbeline* i 1 7
A foolish suitor to a wedded lady, That hath her husband banish'd i 6 2
Why did you throw your wedded lady from you? . . . v 5 261
Euriphile, Whom for the theft I wedded, stole these children . v 5 341
Since King Pericles, My wedded lord, I ne'er shall see again, A vestal livery will I take me to . . . . *Pericles* iii 4 9
Weddest. And, when thou wed'st, let sorrow haunt thy bed! *Rich. III.* iv 1 74
Wedding. Wooing, wedding, and repenting, is as a Scotch jig *Much Ado* ii 1 76
The wedding, mannerly-modest, as a measure, full of state and ancientry ii 1 79
Bring them to see this the very night before the intended wedding ii 2 46
The wedding being there to-morrow, there is a great coil to-night . iii 3 99
Begone, I say, I will not to wedding with thee *As Y. Like It* iii 3 107
You have my consent. Let your wedding be to-morrow . v 2 15
Wedding is great Juno's crown: O blessed bond of board and bed! v 4 147
Thou offer'st fairly to thy brothers' wedding . . . v 4 173
And have prepared great store of wedding cheer . *T. of Shrew* iii 2 188
Come, come, in wooing sorrow let's be brief, Since, wedding it, there is such length in grief . . . *Richard II.* v 1 94
The happy wedding torch That joineth Rouen unto her countrymen 1 *Hen. VI.* iii 2 26
Our wedding cheer to a sad burial feast . . *Rom. and Jul.* iv 5 87
I think it was to see my mother's wedding . . *Hamlet* i 2 178
Prithee, to-night Lay on my bed my wedding sheets: remember *Othello* iv 2 105
Wedding-bed. If he be married, My grave is like to be my wedding bed . . . . *Rom. and Jul.* i 5 137
I'll to my wedding-bed; And death, not Romeo, take my maidenhead! . . . . . . iii 2 136
Wedding-day. Even the night before her wedding-day . *Much Ado* iii 2 117
This wedding-day Perhaps is but prolong'd . . . iv 1 255
On his wedding-day at night . . . . . *M. N. Dream* i 2 7
Perchance till after Theseus' wedding-day . . . ii 1 139
Come, away! For you shall hence upon your wedding-day *Mer. of Ven.* iii 2 313
She must have a husband; I must dance bare-foot on her wedding day *T. of Shrew* ii 1 33
Sunday is the wedding-day.—I'll see thee hang'd on Sunday first . ii 1 300
I will unto Venice, To buy apparel 'gainst the wedding-day . ii 1 317
You know to-morrow is the wedding-day . . . . iii 1 84
Why, sir, you know this is your wedding-day . . . iii 2 99
Father, to arms!—Upon thy wedding-day? . . *K. John* iii 1 300
Then, I'll say A man may weep upon his wedding-day *Hen. VIII.* Prol. 32
Ere you go to bed, Prepare her, wife, against this wedding-day *R. and J.* iii 4 32
The night before thy wedding-day Hath Death lain with thy wife. iv 5 35
Wedding-dower. Let her beauty be her wedding-dower *T. G. of Ver.* iii 1 78
Wedding-garment. And every officer his wedding-garment on *T. of S.* iv 1 51
Wedding-ring. And from my false hand cut the wedding-ring *C. of Er.* ii 2 139
Wedge. Wedges of gold, great anchors, heaps of pearl . *Richard III.* i 4 26
Blunt wedges rive hard knots . . . *Troi. and Cres.* i 3 316
Wedged. Where a finger Could not be wedged in more . *Hen. VIII.* iv 1 58
When my heart, As wedged with a sigh, would rive in twain *T. and C.* i 1 35
Your wit will not so soon out as another man's will; 'tis strongly wedged up in a blockhead . . . . *Coriolanus* ii 3 30
Wedlock. She kneels and prays For happy wedlock hours *Mer. of Venice* v 1 32
As pigeons bill, so wedlock would be nibbling . *As Y. Like It* iii 3 82
'Tis Hymen peoples every town; High wedlock then be honoured v 4 150
Your mother was most true to wedlock . . . *W. Tale* v 1 124
Your brother is legitimate; Your father's wife did after wedlock bear him . . . . . . *K. John* i 1 117
What is wedlock forced but a hell, An age of discord? . . 1 *Hen. VI.* v 5 62
I'll join mine eldest daughter and my joy To him forthwith in holy wedlock bands . . . . . . 3 *Hen. VI.* iii 3 243
And prove it too, against mine honour aught, My bond to wedlock *Hen. VIII.* ii 4 40
That she was false to wedlock?—Ay, with Cassio . *Othello* v 2 142
Wedlock-hymn. Whiles a wedlock-hymn we sing, Feed yourselves with questioning . . . . . *As Y. Like It* v 4 143
Wednesday. O,—sixpence, that I had o' Wednesday last *Com. of Errors* i 2 55
Fair sir, you spit on me on Wednesday last . *Mer. of Venice* i 3 127
A fish, that appeared upon the coast on Wednesday . *W. Tale* iv 4 280
On Wednesday next we solemnly set down Our coronation *Richard II.* iv 1 319
On Wednesday next our council we Will hold at Windsor . 1 *Hen. IV.* i 1 103
On Wednesday next, Harry, you shall set forward . . iii 2 173
Who hath it [honour]? he that died o' Wednesday. Doth he feel it? no v 1 138
By a sea-coal fire, upon Wednesday in Wheeson week . 2 *Hen. IV.* ii 1 96
As he said to me, 'twas no longer ago than Wednesday last . ii 4 94
I looked upon him o' Wednesday half an hour together . *Coriolanus* i 3 64
Mark you me, on Wednesday next—But, soft! what day is this? *Rom. and Jul.* iii 4 17
Well, Wednesday is too soon, O' Thursday let it be . . iii 4 19
Go home, be merry, give consent To marry Paris: Wednesday is to-morrow . . . . iv 1 90
Or Tuesday morn; On Tuesday noon, or night; on Wednesday morn *Othello* iii 3 61
Wee. He hath but a little wee face, with a little yellow beard *Mer. Wives* i 4 22
Weed. Shall bestrew The union of your bed with weeds so loathly *Temp.* iv 1 21
Such weeds As may beseem some well-reputed page *T. G. of Ver.* ii 7 42
But say this weed her love from Valentine, It follows not that she will love Sir Thurio . . . . iii 2 49
Most biting laws, The needful bits and curbs to headstrong weeds *Meas. for Meas.* i 3 20
Twice treble shame on Angelo, To weed my vice and let his grow! . iii 2 284
Come, let us hence, and put on other weeds . *Much Ado* v 3 30
He weeds the corn and still lets grow the weeding . *L. L. Lost* i 1 96
If frosts and fasts, hard lodging and thin weeds, Nip not the gaudy blossoms of your love . . . . . . v 2 811
Weed this wormwood from your fruitful brain . . . v 2 857
Weed wide enough to wrap a fairy in . . *M. N. Dream* ii 1 256
Who is here? Weeds of Athens he doth wear . . . ii 2 71
Weed your better judgements Of all opinion that grows rank in them That I am wise . . . . . *As Y. Like It* ii 7 45
I'll bring you to a captain in this town, Where lie my maiden weeds *T. Night* v 1 262
Give me thy hand; And let me see thee in thy woman's weeds . v 1 280
These your unusual weeds to each part of you Do give a life *W. Tale* iv 4 1
The caterpillars of the commonwealth, Which I have sworn to weed *Richard II.* ii 3 167
The noisome weeds, which without profit suck The soil's fertility . iii 4 38
The whole land Is full of weeds, her fairest flowers choked up . iii 4 44
The weeds which his broad-spreading leaves did shelter . . iii 4 50

Weed. Full well he knows He cannot so precisely weed this land 2 *Hen IV.* iv 1 205
Most subject is the fattest soil to weeds . . . . . iv 4 54
Thus may we gather honey from the weed . . . *Hen. V.* iv 1 11
So, one by one, we'll weed them all at last . . . 2 *Hen. VI.* i 3 102
Now 'tis the spring, and weeds are shallow-rooted . . . iii 1 31
For what doth cherish weeds but gentle air? . . . 3 *Hen. VI.* ii 6 21
Tell him, my mourning weeds are laid aside, And I am ready to put armour on . . . . iii 3 229; iv 1 104
Small herbs have grace, great weeds do grow apace *Richard III.* ii 4 13
I would not grow so fast, Because sweet flowers are slow and weeds make haste . . . . ii 4 15
You said that idle weeds are fast in growth . . . iii 1 103
He's a rank weed, Sir Thomas, And we must root him out *Hen. VIII.* v 1 52
To see great Hector in his weeds of peace, To talk with him *T. and C.* iii 3 239
As weeds before A vessel under sail, so men obey'd . *Coriolanus* ii 2 109
With a proud heart he wore his humble weeds . . . ii 3 161
Forget not With what contempt he wore the humble weed . ii 3 229
Hail, Rome, victorious in thy mourning weeds! . . *T. Andron.* i 1 70
Away with slavish weeds and servile thoughts! . . . ii 1 18
And, were they [the stones] but attired in grave weeds, Rome could afford no tribune like to these . . . . . . iii 1 43
No funeral rite, nor man in mourning weeds, No mournful bell shall ring v 3 196
I must up-fill this osier cage of ours With baleful weeds *Rom. and Jul.* ii 3 8
In tatter'd weeds, with overwhelming brows, Culling of simples . v 1 39
To dew the sovereign flower and drown the weeds . *Macbeth* v 2 30
Duller shouldst thou be than the fat weed That roots itself in ease on Lethe wharf, Wouldst thou not stir in this . . . *Hamlet* i 5 32
Thou mixture rank, of midnight weeds collected . . . iii 2 268
Do not spread the compost on the weeds, To make them ranker . iii 4 151
His sables and his weeds, Importing health and graveness . . iv 7 81
There, on the pendent boughs her coronet weeds Clambering to hang . iv 7 173
Darnel, and all the idle weeds that grow In our sustaining corn *Lear* iv 4 5
These weeds are memories of those worser hours: I prithee, put them off iv 7 7
If we will plant nettles, or sow lettuce, set hyssop, and weed up thyme *Othello* i 3 326
O thou weed, Who art so lovely fair and smell'st so sweet! . . iv 2 67
We bring forth weeds, When our quick minds lie still *Ant. and Cleo.* i 2 113
With wild wood-leaves and weeds I ha' strew'd his grave . *Cymbeline* iv 2 390
I'll disrobe me Of these Italian weeds and suit myself As does a Briton v 1 23
I will rob Tellus of her weed, To strew thy green with flowers *Pericles* iv 1 14
Weeded. Each word thou hast spoke hath weeded from my heart A root of ancient envy . . . . . . *Coriolanus* iv 5 108
Weeder-out. A weeder-out of his proud adversaries *Richard III.* i 3 123
Weeding. He weeds the corn and still lets grow the weeding *L. L. Lost* i 1 96
Weedy. Down her weedy trophies and herself Fell in the weeping brook *Hamlet* iv 7 175
Week. You would lift the moon out of her sphere, if she would continue in it five weeks without changing . . . . *Tempest* ii 1 184
I sit at ten pounds a week . . . . . *Mer. Wives* i 3 8
They have had my house a week at command . . . . iv 3 12
She'll burn a week longer than the whole world . *Com. of Errors* iii 2 101
This week he hath been heavy, sour, sad, And much different from the man he was . . . . v 1 45
If they were but a week married, they would talk themselves mad *M. Ado* ii 1 369
And one day in a week to touch no food . . . *L. L. Lost* i 1 39
You shall fast a week with bran and water . . . . i 1 303
But a' must fast three days a week . . . . . i 2 135
What was a month old at Cain's birth, that's not five weeks old as yet? iv 2 36
And raught not to five weeks when he came to five-score . iv 2 41
O that I knew he were but in by the week! . . . . v 2 61
At seventeen years many their fortunes seek; But at fourscore it is too late a week . . . . . *As Y. Like It* ii 3 74
I'll give her thanks, As though she bid me stay by her a week *T. of S.* ii 1 179
At the farthest for a week or two: But then up farther . . ii 2 74
And for a week escape a great deal of discoveries . *All's Well* iii 6 99
Of your royal presence I'll adventure The borrow of a week *W. Tale* i 2 39
I am sorry that by hanging thee I can But shorten thy life one week iv 4 433
He came into the world Full fourteen weeks before the course of time *K. John* i 1 113
Rather turn this day out of the week, This day of shame . . iii 1 87
It would be argument for a week, laughter for a month . 1 *Hen. IV.* ii 2 101
Virtuous enough; swore little; diced not above seven times a week . iii 3 18
So many weeks ere the poor fools will ean . . 3 *Hen. VI.* ii 5 36
Eighty odd years of sorrow have I seen, And each hour's joy wreck'd with a week of teen . . . . . *Richard III.* iv 1 97
Great-bellied women, That had not half a week to go . *Hen. VIII.* iv 1 77
Diomed, a whole week by days, Did haunt you in the field *T. and C.* iv 1 9
The man must not be hanged till the next week . *T. Andron.* iv 3 82
Cast me not away! Delay this marriage for a month, a week *R. and J.* iii 5 201
You take your pennyworths now; Sleep for a week . . . iv 5 5
'Twas due on forfeiture, my lord, six weeks And past *T. of Athens* ii 2 30
Whose sore task Does not divide the Sunday from the week . *Hamlet* i 1 76
What, keep a week away? seven days and nights? . . *Othello* iii 4 173
If one of mean affairs May plod it in a week, why may not I Glide thither in a day? . . . . *Cymbeline* iii 2 53
Weekly. Whom I have weekly sworn to marry since I perceived the first white hair on my chin . . . . . 2 *Hen. IV.* i 2 270
Ween you of better luck, I mean, in perjured witness, than your master? *Hen. VIII.* v 1 135
Weening to redeem And have install'd me in the diadem . . 1 *Hen. VI.* ii 5 88
Weep. He does hear me; And that he does I weep . . . *Tempest* i 2 434
My sweet mistress Weeps when she sees me work . . . iii 1 12
When this burns, 'Twill weep for having wearied you . . iii 1 19
I am a fool To weep at what I am glad of . . . . iii 1 74
Wherefore weep you?—At mine unworthiness . . . . iii 1 76
To weep, like a young wench that had buried her grandam *T. G. of Ver.* ii 1 23
Now should I kiss my father; well, he weeps on . . . ii 3 29
To that I'll speak, to that I'll sigh and weep . . . iv 2 123
At that time I made her weep agood, For I did play a lamentable part iv 4 170
I weep myself to think upon thy words . . . . . iv 4 180
When maidens sue, Men give like gods; but when they weep and kneel, All their petitions are as freely theirs . . *Meas. for Meas.* i 4 81
Plays such fantastic tricks before high heaven As make the angels weep ii 2 122
I'll weep what's left away, and weeping die . *Com. of Errors* ii 1 115
No longer will I be a fool, To put the finger in the eye and weep . ii 2 206
How much better is it to weep at joy than to joy at weeping! *Much Ado* i 1 28
Then down upon her knees she falls, weeps, sobs, beats her heart . ii 3 153
Lady Beatrice, have you wept all this while?—Yea, and I will weep a while longer . . . . iv 1 258

Weep. He shall live no longer in monument than the bell rings and the widow weeps . . . . *Much Ado* v 2 82
Thou shinest in every tear that I do weep . . . . *L. L. Lost* iv 3 33
Thou wilt keep My tears for glasses, and still make me weep . . iv 3 40
And when she weeps, weeps every little flower . . *M. N. Dream* iii 1 204
Look, when I vow, I weep; and vows so born, In their nativity all truth appears . . . . iii 2 124
Should I anatomize him to thee as he is, I must blush and weep *As Y. Like It* i 1 164
Then entertain him, then forswear him; now weep for him, then spit at him . . . . iii 2 437
Never talk to me; I will weep.—Do, I prithee . . . . iii 4 1
Have I not cause to weep?—As good cause as one would desire; therefore weep . . . . iii 4 4
I will weep for nothing, like Diana in the fountain . . . iv 1 154
And at that sight shall sad Apollo weep . . . *T. of Shrew* Ind. 2 61
Poor girl! she weeps. Go ply thy needle; meedle not with her . . ii 1 24
I will go sit and weep Till I can find occasion of revenge . . ii 1 35
I cannot blame thee now to weep; For such an injury would vex a very saint . . . . iii 2 27
And I in going, madam, weep o'er my father's death anew . *All's Well* i 1 3
He weeps like a wench that had shed her milk . . . . iv 3 123
Oft our displeasures, to ourselves unjust, Destroy our friends and after weep their dust . . . . v 3 64
Mine eyes smell onions; I shall weep anon . . . . . v 3 321
Lay me, O, where Sad true lover never find my grave, To weep there! *T. Night* ii 4 67
Weep I cannot, But my heart bleeds . . . . . *W. Tale* iii 3 51
I'll queen it no inch farther, But milk my ewes and weep . . . iv 4 461
His mother shames him so, poor boy, he weeps . . . *K. John* ii 1 166
I loved him, and will weep My date of life out for his sweet life's loss . iv 3 105
I must withdraw and weep Upon the spot of this enforced cause . . v 2 29
Thrice-gracious queen, More than your lord's departure weep not *Richard II.* ii 2 25
'Tis with false sorrow's eye, Which for things true weeps things imaginary . . . . ii 2 27
I weep for joy To stand upon my kingdom once again . . . iii 2 4
Thou shouldst please me better, wouldst thou weep.—I could weep, madam, would it do you good . . . . iii 4 20
And in compassion weep the fire out . . . . v 1 48
Weep thou for me in France, I for thee here . . . . . v 1 87
Weep not, sweet queen; for trickling tears are vain . *1 Hen. IV.* ii 4 431
My daughter weeps: she will not part with you . . . . iii 1 194
Cries out upon abuses, seems to weep Over his country's wrongs . . iv 3 81
What wouldst thou think of me, if I should weep?—I would think thee a most princely hypocrite . . . . . *2 Hen. IV.* ii 2 57
If I do sweat, they are the drops of thy lovers, and they weep for thy death . . . . iv 3 15
The blood weeps from my heart when I do shape In forms imaginary the unguided days And rotten times that you shall look upon . . iv 4 58
Let me but bear your love, I'll bear your cares: Yet weep that Harry's dead . . . . v 2 59
His jest will savour but of shallow wit, When thousands weep more than did laugh at it . . . . *Hen. V.* i 2 296
I will weep for thee; For this revolt of thine, methinks, is like Another fall of man . . . . ii 2 140
Will you have them weep our horses' blood? How shall we, then, behold their natural tears? . . . . iv 2 12
Wounds will I lend the French instead of eyes, To weep their intermissive miseries . . . . *1 Hen. VI.* i 1 88
Mad ire and wrathful fury makes me weep . . . . . iv 3 28
I am a soldier and unapt to weep Or to exclaim on fortune's fickleness . v 3 133
But wherefore weeps Warwick, my valiant son? . . *2 Hen. VI.* i 1 115
Weeps over them and wrings his hapless hands And shakes his head . i 1 226
His fortunes I will weep and 'twixt each groan Say 'Who's a traitor?' iii 1 221
Die, Margaret! For Henry weeps that thou dost live so long . . iii 2 121
Think therefore on revenge and cease to weep. But who can cease to weep and look on this? . . . . iv 4 3
Wouldst have me weep? why, now thou hast thy will . *3 Hen. VI.* i 4 144
I should not for my life but weep with him, To see how inly sorrow gripes his soul . . . . i 4 170
I cannot weep; for all my body's moisture Scarce serves to quench my furnace-burning heart . . . . ii 1 79
To weep is to make less the depth of grief: Tears then for babes . . ii 1 85
I, that did never weep, now melt with woe . . . . . ii 3 46
Weep, wretched man, I'll aid thee tear for tear . . . . ii 5 76
I'll bear thee hence, where I may weep my fill . . . . ii 5 113
She weeps, and says her Henry is deposed . . . . . iii 1 45
We will not from the helm to sit and weep, But keep our course . . v 4 21
See how my sword weeps for the poor king's death! . . . . v 6 63
And twenty times made pause to sob and weep . . *Richard III.* i 2 162
He will weep.—Ay, millstones; as he lesson'd us to weep . . . i 4 245
Oh, who shall hinder me to wail and weep, To chide my fortune? . . ii 2 34
She for an Edward weeps, and so do I; I for a Clarence weep, so doth not she: These babes for Clarence weep, and so do I; I for an Edward weep, so do not they . . . . ii 2 82
And often up and down my sons were toss'd, For me to joy and weep their gain and loss . . . . ii 4 59
So dear I loved the man, that I must weep . . . . . iii 5 24
Send to her, by the man that slew her brothers, A pair of bleeding hearts; thereon engrave Edward and York; then haply she will weep iv 4 273
And make poor England weep in streams of blood! . . . . v 5 37
And, if you can be merry then, I'll say A man may weep upon his wedding-day . . . . *Hen. VIII.* Prol. 32
And dare be bold to weep for Buckingham . . . . . ii 1 72
Every tongue speaks 'em, And every true heart weeps for't . . . ii 2 40
I am about to weep; but . . . my drops of tears I'll turn to sparks of fire . . . . ii 4 70
No friends, no hope; no kindred weep for me; Almost no grave allow'd me . . . . iii 1 150
My heart weeps to see him So little of his great self . . . . iii 2 335
Nay, an you weep, I am fall'n indeed . . . . . . iii 2 375
Look, the good man weeps! He's honest, on mine honour . . . v 1 152
Every flower Did, as a prophet, weep what it foresaw *Troi. and Cres.* i 2 10
He will weep you, an 'twere a man born in April . . . . i 2 188
When we vow to weep seas, live in fire, eat rocks, tame tigers . . iii 2 84
I'll go in and weep,— Do, do.—Tear my bright hair . . . . iv 2 111
Your eyes, half out, weep out at Pandar's fall; Or if you cannot weep, yet give some groans . . . . v 10 49
I could weep And I could laugh, I am light and heavy . *Coriolanus* ii 1 200
Weep. Come, let's not weep . . . . *Coriolanus* iv 1 54
Constrains them weep and shake with fear and sorrow . . . . v 3 100
Thou hast done a deed whereat valour will weep . . . . . v 6 134
When I do weep, they [the stones] humbly at my feet Receive my tears and seem to weep with me . . . . *T. Andron.* iii 1 41
Prepare thy aged eyes to weep; Or, if not so, thy noble heart to break iii 1 59
Perchance she weeps because they kill'd her husband . . . . iii 1 114
At your grief, See how my wretched sister sobs and weeps . . . iii 1 137
When heaven doth weep, doth not the earth o'erflow? . . . . iii 1 222
To weep with them that weep doth ease some deal . . . . iii 1 245
The tender boy, in passion moved, Doth weep to see his grandsire's heaviness . . . . iii 2 49
Your hearts will throb and weep to hear him speak . . . . v 3 95
Dost thou not laugh?—No, coz, I rather weep . . *Rom. and Jul.* i 1 189
All this is comfort; wherefore weep I then? . . . . . iii 2 107
O, she says nothing, sir, but weeps and weeps . . . . . iii 3 99
Yet let me weep for such a feeling loss.—So shall you feel the loss, but not the friend Which you weep for.—Feeling so the loss, I cannot choose but ever weep the friend . . . . iii 5 75
Immoderately she weeps for Tybalt's death, And therefore have I little talk'd of love . . . . iv 1 6
Come weep with me; past hope, past cure, past help! . . . iv 1 45
And weep ye now, seeing she is advanced Above the clouds? . . . iv 5 73
The obsequies that I for thee will keep Nightly shall be to strew thy grave and weep . . . . v 3 17
Here is a friar, that trembles, sighs, and weeps . . . . v 3 184
Why dost thou weep? Canst thou the conscience lack, To think I shall lack friends? Secure thy heart . . . *T. of Athens* ii 2 184
What, dost thou weep? Come nearer. Then I love thee, Because thou art a woman . . . . iv 3 489
Pity's sleeping: Strange times, that weep with laughing, not with weeping! . . . . iv 3 493
Taught thee to make vast Neptune weep for aye On thy low grave . v 4 78
Draw them to Tiber banks, and weep your tears Into the channel *J. Cæsar* i 1 63
Thy heart is big, get thee apart and weep. Passion, I see, is catching iii 1 282
As Cæsar loved me, I weep for him; as he was fortunate, I rejoice at it iii 2 26
O, now you weep; and, I perceive, you feel The dint of pity: these are gracious drops. Kind souls, what, weep you when you but behold Our Cæsar's vesture wounded? . . . . iii 2 197
O, I could weep My spirit from mine eyes! . . . . . iv 3 99
How wilt thou do for a father?—If he were dead, you'ld weep for him *Macbeth* iv 2 61
Let us seek out some desolate shade, and there Weep our sad bosoms empty . . . . iv 3 2
I think our country sinks beneath the yoke; It weeps, it bleeds . . iv 3 40
What's Hecuba to him, or he to Hecuba, That he should weep for her? *Hamlet* ii 2 586
Why, let the stricken deer go weep, The hart ungalled play . . iii 2 282
He weeps for what is done . . . . iv 1 27
I cannot choose but weep, to think they should lay him i' the cold ground . . . . iv 5 69
Woo't weep? woo't fight? woo't fast? woo't tear thyself? Woo't drink up eisel? . . . . v 1 298
Then they for sudden joy did weep, And I for sorrow sung . . *Lear* i 4 191
You think I'll weep; No, I'll not weep: I have full cause of weeping; but this heart Shall break into a hundred thousand flaws, Or ere I'll weep . . . . ii 4 285
But I will punish home: No, I will weep no more . . . . iii 4 17
Tom will make them weep and wail . . . . iii 6 74
If thou wilt weep my fortunes, take my eyes . . . . . iv 6 180
Be your tears wet? yes, 'faith. I pray, weep not: If you have poison for me, I will drink it . . . . iv 7 71
The good-years shall devour them, flesh and fell, Ere they shall make us weep . . . . v 3 25
Do deeds to make heaven weep, all earth amazed . . . *Othello* iii 3 371
So hangs, and lolls, and weeps upon me; so hales, and pulls me: ha, ha, ha! . . . . iv 1 143
Make her amends; she weeps.—O devil, devil! . . . . . iv 1 255
She can weep, sir, weep; And she's obedient, as you say, obedient . iv 1 265
Alas the heavy day! Why do you weep? Am I the motive of these tears? . . . . iv 2 42
I cannot weep; nor answer have I none, But what should go by water iv 2 103
Do not weep, do not weep. Alas the day! . . . . . . iv 2 124
To be call'd whore? would it not make one weep? . . . . iv 2 127
Go in, and weep not; all things shall be well . . . . . iv 2 171
I must weep, But they are cruel tears . . . . v 2 20
Whom every thing becomes, to chide, to laugh, To weep *Ant. and Cleo.* i 1 50
Weep for her; Then bid adieu to me, and say the tears Belong to Egypt i 3 76
Pompey doth this day laugh away his fortune.—If he do, sure, he cannot weep't back again . . . . ii 6 111
Octavia weeps To part from Rome; Cæsar is sad . . . . iii 2 3
Will Cæsar weep?—He has a cloud in's face . . . . . . iii 2 51
What does he mean?—To make his followers weep . . . . iv 2 24
Look, they weep, And I, an ass, am onion-eyed . . . . . iv 2 34
Nay, weep not, gentle Eros; there is left us Ourselves to end ourselves iv 14 21
I will o'ertake thee, Cleopatra, and Weep for my pardon . . iv 14 45
Dissolve, thick cloud, and rain; that I may say, The gods themselves do weep! . . . . v 2 303
O lady, weep no more, lest I give cause To be suspected of more tenderness Than doth become a man . . . . . *Cymbeline* i 1 93
The approbation of those that weep this lamentable divorce . . i 4 20
Weeps she still, say'st thou? Dost thou think in time She will not quench? . . . . i 5 46
What is it to be false? To lie in watch there and to think on him? To weep 'twixt clock and clock? . . . . iii 4 44
I cannot sing: I'll weep, and word it with thee . . . . iv 2 240
I'll weep and sigh; And leaving so his service, follow you . . iv 2 392
Our eyes do weep, Till tongues fetch breath that may proclaim them louder . . . . *Pericles* i 4 14
Live, And make us weep to hear your fate, fair creature . . . iii 2 104
To weep that you live as ye do makes pity in your lovers . . . iv 2 129
Why do you weep? It may be, You think me an imposter . . . v 1 178
Tell me, if thou canst, What this maid is, or what is like to be, That thus hath made me weep? . . . . v 1 187
She would never tell Her parentage; being demanded that, She would sit still and weep . . . . v 1 191
Weepest. What's the matter? why weepest thou, man? . *T. G. of Ver.* ii 3 38
Aumerle, thou weep'st, my tender-hearted cousin! . . . *Richard II.* iii 3 160
Wouldst thou have laugh'd had I come coffin'd home, That weep'st to see me triumph? . . . . *Coriolanus* ii 1 194

Weepest. Well, girl, thou weep'st not so much for his death, As that the villain lives which slaughter'd him . *Rom. and Jul.* iii 5 79
I drink to you.—Thou weepest to make them drink . *T. of Athens* i 2 113
Weep'st thou for him to my face? . . . . *Othello* v 2 77
Thou weep'st, and speak'st . . . . . . *Cymbeline* v 5 352
Weeping. Sitting on a bank, Weeping . . . *Tempest* i 2 390
Nay, 'twill be this hour ere I have done weeping . *T. G. of Ver.* ii 3 2
My mother weeping, my father wailing, my sister crying . ii 3 7
Now should not the shoe speak a word for weeping . ii 3 28
The incessant weepings of my wife, Weeping before for what she saw must come, . . . Forced me to seek delays . *Com. of Errors* i 1 71
I'll weep what's left away, and weeping die . . . ii 1 115
But if that I am I, then well I know Your weeping sister is no wife of mine . . . . iii 2 42
How much better is it to weep at joy than to joy at weeping! *Much Ado* i 1 29
I fear he will prove the weeping philosopher when he grows old *M. of V.* i 2 53
All the beholders take his part with weeping . *As Y. Like It* i 2 140
First, for his weeping into the needless stream . . ii 1 46
Weeping and commenting Upon the sobbing deer . . ii 1 65
Said with weeping tears 'Wear these for my sake' . ii 4 53
I am not prone to weeping, as our sex Commonly are . *W. Tale* ii 1 108
The marigold, that goes to bed wi' the sun And with him rises weeping iv 4 106
Methinks I see Leontes opening his free arms and weeping His welcomes forth . . . . iv 4 559
The last leave of thee takes my weeping eye . . . *Richard II.* i 2 74
Thy sun sets weeping in the lowly west . . . . ii 4 21
So, weeping, smiling, greet I thee, my earth . . . iii 2 10
There lies Two kinsmen digg'd their graves with weeping eyes . iii 3 169
I could sing, would weeping do me good . . . . iii 4 22
Rue, even for ruth, here shortly shall be seen, In the remembrance of a weeping queen . . . . iii 4 107
Tell thou the lamentable tale of me And send the hearers weeping to their beds . . . . v 1 45
So two, together weeping, make one woe . . . . v 1 86
You told me you would tell the rest, When weeping made you break the story off . . . . v 2 2
Grace my mournings here; In weeping after this untimely bier . v 6 52
A naked subject to the weeping clouds . . . . *2 Hen. IV.* i 3 61
Thou'lt set me a-weeping, an thou sayest so . . . ii 4 301
Makes me from wondering fall to weeping joys . . *2 Hen. VI.* i 1 34
I would be blind with weeping, sick with groans, Look pale as primrose iii 2 62
Made them blind with weeping . . . . . *Richard III.* i 2 167
That dead saint which then I weeping follow'd . . . iv 1 70
Grand tyrant of the earth, That reigns in galled eyes of weeping souls . iv 4 53
For my daughters, Richard, They shall be praying nuns, not weeping queens . . . . iv 4 201
And bid her dry her weeping eyes therewith . . . . iv 4 278
Great Achilles Is arming, weeping, cursing, vowing vengeance *T. and C.* v 5 31
If that I could for weeping, you should hear,—Nay, and you shall hear some . . . . *Coriolanus* iv 2 13
Daughter, speak you: He cares not for your weeping . . . v 3 156
And here my brother, weeping at my woes . . *T. Andron.* iii 1 100
She is the weeping welkin, I the earth . . . . . iii 1 227
The gates shut on me, and turn'd weeping out . . . . v 3 105
I cannot speak to him for weeping; My tears will choke me . . v 3 174
Where is my father, and my mother, nurse?—Weeping and wailing *Rom. and Jul.* iii 2 128
Even so lies she, Blubbering and weeping, weeping and blubbering . iii 3 87
Evermore weeping for your cousin's death? What, wilt thou wash him from his grave with tears? . . . . iii 5 70
To trust man on his oath or bond; Or a harlot, for her weeping *T. of A.* i 2 67
Pity's sleeping: Strange times, that weep with laughing, not with weeping! . . . . iv 3 493
Had I as many eyes as thou hast wounds, Weeping as fast as they stream forth thy blood . . . . . . *J. Cæsar* iii 1 201
Poor soul! his eyes are red as fire with weeping . . . iii 2 120
Down her weedy trophies and herself Fell in the weeping brook *Hamlet* iv 7 176
You think I'll weep; No, I'll not weep: I have full cause of weeping *Lear* ii 4 287
Mine eyes do itch; Doth that bode weeping?—'Tis neither here nor there . . . . *Othello* iv 3 59
Sinon's weeping Did scandal many a holy tear. . . . *Cymbeline* iii 4 61
She purposed, By watching, weeping, tendance, kissing, to O'ercome you . . . . v 5 53
Here stands a lord, and there a lady weeping . . . *Pericles* i 4 47
Here she comes weeping for her only mistress' death . . iv 1 11
I am great with woe, and shall deliver weeping . . . iv 1 107
I was born, As my good nurse Lychorida hath oft Deliver'd weeping . v 1 162
Weeping-ripe. The king was weeping-ripe for a good word . *L. L. Lost* v 2 274
What, weeping-ripe, my Lord Northumberland? . *3 Hen. VI.* i 4 172
Weet. In which I bind, On pain of punishment, the world to weet We stand up peerless . . . . *Ant. and Cleo.* i 1 39
Weigh. Then wisely, good sir, weigh Our sorrow with our comfort *Temp.* ii 1 8
We cannot weigh our brother with ourself . . . *Meas. for Meas.* ii 2 126
You weigh equally; a feather will turn the scale . . . iv 2 31
Here's the note How much your chain weighs to the utmost carat *Com. of Errors* iv 1 28
I know them, yea, And what they weigh, even to the utmost scruple *Much Ado* v 1 93
If justice cannot tame you, she shall ne'er weigh more reasons in her balance . . . . v 1 211
You are a light wench.—Indeed I weigh not you . . *L. L. Lost* v 2 26
You weigh me not? O, that's you care not for me . . . . v 2 27
Weigh oath with oath, and you will nothing weigh: Your vows to her and me, put in two scales, Will even weigh . . *M. N. Dream* iii 2 131
Weigh thy value with an even hand . . . *Mer. of Venice* ii 7 25
Are there balance here to weigh The flesh? . . . . iv 1 255
Impossible be strange attempts to those That weigh their pains in sense and do suppose What hath been cannot be . . . *All's Well* i 1 240
We, poising us in her defective scale, Shall weigh thee to the beam . ii 3 162
Let every word weigh heavy of her worth That he does weigh too light iii 4 31
I warrant, good creature, wheresoe'er she is, Her heart weighs sadly . v 3 70
For life, I prize it As I weigh grief, which I would spare . *W. Tale* iii 2 44
While they weigh so even, We hold our town for neither, yet for both *K. John* ii 1 332
Her dowry shall weigh equal with a queen . . . . . ii 1 486
With that odds he weighs King Richard down . . . *Richard II.* iii 4 89
How able such a work to undergo, To weigh against his opposite *2 Hen. IV.* i 3 55
In every thing the purpose must weigh with the folly . . . ii 2 196
How have I frighted thee, That thou no more wilt weigh my eyelids down? . . . . iii 1 7
Weigh. You are right, justice, and you weigh this well . . *2 Hen. IV.* v 2 102
'Tis best to weigh The enemy more mighty than he seems . *Hen. V.* ii 4 43
Now he weighs time Even to the utmost grain. . . . . ii 4 137
Weigh it but with the grossness of this age . . . *Richard III.* iii 1 46
I weigh it lightly, were it heavier . . . . iii 1 121
Let us be lead within thy bosom, Richard, And weigh thee down to ruin! . . . . v 3 153
My friends, They that must weigh out my afflictions, They that my trust must grow to, live not here . . . . *Hen. VIII.* iii 1 88
My person; which I weigh not, Being of those virtues vacant . . v 1 124
Weigh you the worth and honour of a king So great as our dread father in a scale Of common ounces? . . . *Troi. and Cres.* ii 2 26
Both merits poised, each weighs nor less nor more . . . iv 1 65
Weigh him well, And that which looks like pride is courtesy . . iv 5 81
But your people, I love them as they weigh . . *Coriolanus* ii 2 78
Give him thy daughter: What you bestow, in him I'll counterpoise, And make him weigh with her . . . . *T. of Athens* i 1 146
I weigh my friend's affection with mine own; I'll tell you true . i 2 222
But who is man that is not angry? Weigh but the crime with this . iii 5 58
A recompense more fruitful Than their offence can weigh down by the dram . . . . v 1 154
It doth become the mouth as well; Weigh them, it is as heavy *J. Cæsar* i 2 146
That perilous stuff Which weighs upon the heart . . . *Macbeth* v 3 45
Then weigh what loss your honour may sustain . . . *Hamlet* i 3 29
Weigh what convenience both of time and means May fit us to our shape . . . . iv 7 150
Which do not be entreated to, but weigh What it is worth embraced *Ant. and Cleo.* ii 6 32
How heavy weighs my lord! Our strength is all gone into heaviness iv 15 32
'Tween man and man they weigh not every stamp . . *Cymbeline* v 4 24
Weighed. The fair soul herself Weigh'd between loathness and obedience, at Which end o' the beam should bow . . . *Tempest* ii 1 130
If he had so offended, He would have weigh'd thy brother by himself *Meas. for Meas.* v 1 111
If that the injuries be justly weigh'd . . . . *T. Night* v 1 375
Their fortunes both are weigh'd: In your lord's scale is nothing but himself, And some few vanities . . . . . *Richard II.* iii 4 84
I have in equal balance justly weigh'd What wrongs our arms may do, what wrongs we suffer. . . . . . . *2 Hen. IV.* iv 1 67
What four throned ones could have weigh'd Such a compounded one? *Hen. VIII.* i 1 11
I weigh'd the danger which my realms stood in By this my issue's fail ii 4 197
With thee and all thy best parts bound together, Weigh'd not a hair of his. . . . . iii 2 259
Commit my cause in balance to be weigh'd . . . *T. Andron.* i 1 55
As the bark . . . Returns with precious lading to the bay From whence at first she weigh'd her anchorage . . . . . . i 1 73
In that crystal scales let there be weigh'd Your lady's love against some other maid That I will show you . . . *Rom. and Jul.* i 2 101
At more time, The interim having weigh'd it, let us speak . *Macbeth* i 3 154
All these are portable, With other graces weigh'd . . . iv 3 90
But you must fear, His greatness weigh'd, his will is not his own *Hamlet* i 3 17
Where 'tis so, the offender's scourge is weigh'd, But never the offence iv 3 6
Equalities are so weighed, that curiosity in neither can make choice of either's moiety . . . . *Lear* i 1 6
He must be weighed rather by her value than his own . *Cymbeline* i 4 15
Hath endured a grief Might equal yours, if both were justly weigh'd *Per.* v 1 89
Weigh'st thy words before thou givest them breath . . *Othello* iii 3 119
Weighing. More nor less to others paying Than by self-offences weighing *Meas. for Meas.* iii 2 280
It was my negligence, Not weighing well the end . . . *W. Tale* i 2 258
I hope he that looks upon me will take me without weighing *2 Hen. IV.* i 2 189
Growing on the south, Weighing the youthful season of the year . *J. C.* ii 1 108
In equal scale weighing delight and dole . . . . *Hamlet* i 2 13
Weight. Make us pay down for our offence by weight . *Meas. for Meas.* i 2 125
Burdened With lesser weight but not with lesser woe *Com. of Errors* i 1 109
But were we burden'd with like weight of pain, As much or more we should ourselves complain . . . . ii 1 36
An there be any matter of weight chances, call up me . . *Much Ado* iii 3 91
'Twill be heavier soon by the weight of a man . . . . iii 4 26
I would bend under any heavy weight That he'll enjoin me to . . v 1 287
The plea of no less weight Than Aquitaine, a dowry for a queen *L. L. L.* ii 1 7
Look on beauty, And you shall see 'tis purchased by the weight *M. of V.* iii 2 89
You'll ask me, why I rather choose to have A weight of carrion flesh iv 1 41
I see thou lovest me not with the full weight that I love thee *As Y. L. It* i 2 9
What passion hangs these weights upon my tongue? . . . . i 2 269
And yet as heavy as my weight should be.—Should be! *T. of Shrew* ii 1 206
Strange is it that our bloods, Of colour, weight, and heat, pour'd all together, Would quite confound distinction . . . *All's Well* ii 3 126
But in despair die under their black weight . . . *K. John* iii 1 297
Yet one word more: grief boundeth where it falls, Not with the empty hollowness, but weight . . . . *Richard II.* i 2 59
Make their sire Stoop with oppression of their prodigal weight . . iii 4 31
I will undo myself: I give this heavy weight from off my head . iv 1 204
God keep lead out of me! I need no more weight than mine own bowels *1 Hen. IV.* v 3 35
So did our men, heavy in Hotspur's loss, Lend to this weight such lightness with their fear . . . . *2 Hen. IV.* i 1 122
The weight of a hair will turn the scales between their avoirdupois . ii 4 276
We would be resolved, Before we hear him, of some things of weight *Hen. V.* i 2 5
Desert and merit According to the weight and worthiness . . . ii 2 35
Which in weight to re-answer, his pettiness would bow under . . iii 6 136
Supply his place; I mean, in bearing weight of government *3 Hen. VI.* iv 6 51
Thou art no Atlas for so great a weight . . . . . v 1 36
And heave it shall some weight, or break my back . . . . v 7 24
And still, as you are weary of the weight, Rest you . *Richard III.* i 2 31
In such a point of weight, so near mine honour . . *Hen. VIII.* iii 1 71
There was the weight that pull'd me down . . . . . iii 2 407
I shall clear myself, Lay all the weight ye can upon my patience . v 3 66
Know by measure Of their observant toil the enemies' weight *T. and C.* i 3 203
With the match and weight Of such a winnow'd purity in love . . iii 2 173
For every scruple Of her contaminated carrion weight, A Trojan hath been slain . . . . iv 1 71
As much as I do Cressid love, So much by weight hate I her Diomed . v 2 168
Thy madness shall be paid with weight, Till our scale turn the beam *Ham.* iv 5 156
The weight of this sad time we must obey; Speak what we feel . *Lear* v 3 323
Full of poise and difficult weight And fearful to be granted . *Othello* iii 3 82
Hear me this prayer, though thou deny me a matter of more weight *Ant. and Cleo.* i 2 71

Weight. No way excuse his soils, when we do bear So great weight in his lightness *Ant. and Cleo.* i 4 25
O happy horse, to bear the weight of Antony! Do bravely, horse! i 5 21
With what haste The weight we must convey with's will permit iii 1 36
How heavy weighs my lord! Our strength is all gone into heaviness, That makes the weight iv 15 34
Your loss is as yourself, great; and you bear it As answering to the weight v 2 102
From whose so many weights of baseness cannot A dram of worth be drawn *Cymbeline* iii 5 88
I love thee; I have spoke it: How much the quantity, the weight as much, As I do love my father iv 2 17
Weightier. I see, you will part but with light gifts; In weightier things you'll say a beggar nay *Richard III.* iii 1 119
Durst commend a secret to your ear Much weightier than this *Hen. VIII.* v 1 18
If, after two days' shine, Athens contain thee, Attend our weightier judgement *T. of Athens* iii 5 102
Weightless. There lies a downy feather which stirs not: Did he suspire, that light and weightless down Perforce must move *2 Hen. IV.* iv 5 33
Weighty. My reasons are both good and weighty *T. of Shrew* i 1 253
Made me acquainted with a weighty cause Of love iv 4 26
Did look no better to that weighty charge *1 Hen. VI.* ii 1 62
This weighty business will not brook delay *2 Hen. VI.* i 1 170
Make merry, man, With thy confederates in this weighty cause i 2 86
What counsel give you in this weighty cause? iii 1 289
With lies well steel'd with weighty arguments *Richard III.* i 1 148
Will you go To give your censures in this weighty business? ii 2 144
Things now, That bear a weighty and a serious brow *Hen. VIII.* Prol. 2
This secret is so weighty, 'twill require A strong faith to conceal it ii 1 144
There ye shall meet about this weighty business ii 2 140
To know How you stand minded in the weighty difference iii 1 58
Words cannot carry Authority so weighty iii 2 234
Weird. The weird sisters, hand in hand, Posters of the sea and land *Macb.* i 3 32
These weird sisters saluted me, and referred me to the coming on of time i 5 8
I dreamt last night of the three weird sisters ii 1 20
Thou hast it now: king, Cawdor, Glamis, all, As the weird women promised iii 1 2
I will to-morrow, And betimes I will, to the weird sisters iii 4 133
What's your grace's will?—Saw you the weird sisters? iv 1 136
Weke, weke! so cries a pig prepared to the spit *T. Andron.* iv 2 146
Welcome. To thee and thy company I bid A hearty welcome *Tempest* v 1 111
Welcome him then according to his worth *T. G. of Ver.* ii 4 83
I beseech you, Confirm his welcome with some special favour ii 4 101
You are welcome to a worthless mistress.—I'll die on him that says so but yourself.—That you are welcome? ii 4 113
Once more, new servant, welcome: I'll leave you to confer of home affairs ii 4 118
Welcome to Milan!—Forswear not thyself, sweet youth, for I am not welcome ii 5 1
A man is never undone till he be hanged, nor never welcome to a place till some certain shot be paid and the hostess say 'Welcome!' ii 5 6
For one shot of five pence, thou shalt have five thousand welcomes ii 5 11
Instances of infinite of love Warrant me welcome to my Proteus ii 7 71
Your grace is welcome to a man disgraced v 4 123
Wife, bid these gentlemen welcome *Mer. Wives* i 1 201
Such Brooks are welcome to me, that o'erflow such liquor ii 2 157
I make bold to press with so little preparation upon you.—You're welcome ii 2 164
As I am a true spirit, welcome! v 5 33
Your're welcome: what's your will? *Meas. for Meas.* ii 2 26
Grace and good company!—Who's there? come in: the wish deserves a welcome iii 1 45
My business is a word or two with Claudio.—And very welcome iii 1 49
Welcome, how agreed?—She'll take the enterprise upon her iv 1 65
Gave healthful welcome to their shipwreck'd guests *Com. of Errors* i 1 115
That never touch well welcome to thy hand ii 2 118
Our cheer May answer my good will and your good welcome iii 1 20
I hold your dainties cheap, sir, and your welcome dear iii 1 21
A table full of welcome makes scarce one dainty dish iii 1 23
Good meat, sir, is common; that every churl affords.—And welcome more common iii 1 25
Small cheer and great welcome makes a merry feast iii 1 26
Here is neither cheer, sir, nor welcome: we would fain have either iii 1 66
To that end am I returned.—And to that end, sir, I will welcome you iv 4 18
Let me bid you welcome, my lord *Much Ado* i 1 156
Welcome the sour cup of prosperity! *L. L. Lost* i 1 315
Fair princess, welcome to the court of Navarre.—'Fair' I give you back again; and 'welcome' I have not yet ii 1 90
And welcome to the wide fields too base to be mine ii 1 93
You shall be welcome, madam, to my court.—I will be welcome, then ii 1 95
Meantime receive such welcome at my hand ii 1 169
You are welcome, sir: adieu.—Farewell to me, sir, and welcome to you ii 1 213
Welcome, pure wit! thou partest a fair fray v 2 484
Welcome, Mercade; But that thou interrupt'st our merriment v 2 724
Hast thou the flower there? Welcome, wanderer *M. N. Dream* ii 1 247
Great clerks have purposed To greet me with premeditated welcomes v 1 94
And in conclusion dumbly have broke off, Not paying me a welcome v 1 99
Trust me, sweet, Out of this silence yet I pick'd a welcome v 1 100
If I could bid the fifth welcome with so good a heart as I can bid the other four farewell I should be glad *Mer. of Venice* i 2 140
Cold, indeed; and labour lost: Then, farewell, heat, and welcome, frost! ii 7 75
If that the youth of my new interest here Have power to bid you welcome iii 2 225
I bid my very friends and countrymen, Sweet Portia, welcome.—So do I, my lord: They are entirely welcome iii 2 227
Nerissa, cheer yon stranger; bid her welcome iii 2 240
Bid your friends welcome, show a merry cheer iii 2 314
You are welcome: take your place iv 1 170
Ceremoniously let us prepare Some welcome for the mistress of the house v 1 38
Give welcome to my friend. This is the man, this is Antonio v 1 133
You are very welcome to our house: It must appear in other ways than words v 1 139
Sir, grieve not you; you are welcome notwithstanding v 1 239
In my voice most welcome shall you be *As Y. Like It* ii 4 87
Sit down and feed, and welcome to our table ii 7 105
Good old man, Thou art right welcome as thy master is ii 7 198
Salutation and greeting to you all!—Good my lord, bid him welcome v 4 40

Welcome. My dear niece, welcome thou art to me! Even daughter, welcome, in no less degree *As Y. Like It* v 4 153
Welcome, young man; Thou offer'st fairly to thy brothers' wedding v 4 172
Bid them come near. Now, fellows, you are welcome *T. of Shrew* Ind. 1 79
Take them to the buttery, And give them friendly welcome every one Ind. 1 103
What company is this?—Master, some show to welcome us to town i 1 47
Welcome his friends, Visit his countrymen and banquet them i 1 201
You're welcome, sir; and he, for your good sake ii 1 61
I may have welcome 'mongst the rest that woo ii 1 97
You are passing welcome, And so I pray you all to think yourselves ii 1 113
You are welcome, sir.—And yet I come not well iii 2 90
Welcome, you;—how now, you;—what, you;—fellow, you iv 1 114
Come, Kate, and wash, and welcome heartily iv 1 157
God save you, sir!—And you, sir! you are welcome. Travel you far on? iv 2 72
Welcome! one mess is like to be your cheer iv 4 70
I think I shall command your welcome here v 1 13
Bid my father welcome, While I with self-same kindness welcome thine v 2 4
Feast with the best, and welcome to my house v 2 8
Welcome, count; My son's no dearer *All's Well* i 2 75
But rest Unquestion'd welcome and undoubted blest ii 1 211
Welcome shall they be; And all the honours that can fly from us Shall on them settle iii 1 19
My husband hies him home; where . . . We'll be before our welcome iv 4 14
You never had a servant to whose trust Your business was more welcome iv 4 16
If it end so meet, The bitter past, more welcome is the sweet v 3 334
Welcome, ass. Now let's have a catch *T. Night* ii 3 18
If you can separate yourself and your misdemeanours, you are welcome to the house ii 3 106
How thou lovest us, show in our brother's welcome *W. Tale* i 2 174
Pray you, bid These unknown friends to's welcome iv 4 65
Bid us welcome to your sheep-shearing, As your good flock shall prosper iv 4 69
Grace and remembrance be to you both, And welcome to our shearing! iv 4 77
If not, my senses, better pleased with madness, Do bid it welcome iv 4 496
Methinks I see Leontes opening his free arms and weeping His welcomes forth iv 4 560
Most dearly welcome! And your fair princess,—goddess! v 1 130
I give you welcome with a powerless hand *K. John* ii 1 15
Let them be welcome then; we are prepared ii 1 83
This tyrant fever burns me up, And will not let me welcome this good news v 3 15
And what hear there for welcome but my groans? *Richard II.* i 2 70
I know no cause Why I should welcome such a guest as grief ii 2 7
Nor friends nor foes, to me welcome you are ii 3 170
More welcome is the stroke of death to me iii 1 31
Welcome, my lord: how far off lies your power? iii 2 63
All the walls With painted imagery had said at once 'Jesu preserve thee! welcome, Bolingbroke!' v 2 17
Welcome, my son: who are the violets now? v 2 46
One that never spake other English in his life than 'Eight shillings and sixpence,' and 'You are welcome' *1 Hen. IV.* ii 4 28
Welcome, by my soul.—Pray God my news be worth a welcome iv 1 86
He shall be welcome too. Where is his son, The nimble-footed madcap? iv 1 94
My father gave him welcome to the shore iv 3 59
The Lord preserve thy good grace! by my troth, welcome to London *2 Hen. IV.* ii 4 316
By this light flesh and corrupt blood, thou art welcome ii 4 321
Did with the least affection of a welcome Give entertainment iv 5 173
Do arm myself To welcome the condition of the time v 2 11
'Tis merry in hall when beards wag all, And welcome merry Shrove-tide v 3 38
Welcome, my little tiny thief, and welcome indeed too v 3 60
Welcome these pleasant days! v 3 148
How many would the peaceful city quit, To welcome him! *Hen. V.* v Prol. 34
Thrice welcome to us.—Methinks your looks are sad *1 Hen. VI.* i 2 47
By message craved, so is Lord Talbot come.—And he is welcome ii 3 14
Welcome, high prince, the mighty Duke of York!—Perish, base prince! iii 1 177
What joy shall noble Talbot have To bid his young son welcome to his grave? iv 3 40
Welcome, brave earl, into our territories v 3 146
Lords, with one cheerful voice welcome my love *2 Hen. VI.* i 1 36
Welcome is banishment; welcome were my death ii 3 14
Welcome, my lord, to this brave town of York *3 Hen. VI.* ii 2 1
O, welcome, Oxford! for we want thy help v 1 66
Now welcome more, and ten times more beloved, Than if thou never hadst deserved our hate v 1 103
My good lord chamberlain! Well are you welcome to the open air *Richard III.* i 1 124
Welcome, destruction, death, and massacre! I see, as in a map, the end of all ii 4 53
Welcome, sweet prince, to London, to your chamber.—Welcome, dear cousin iii 1 1
I want more uncles here to welcome me iii 1 6
Entreat of her To meet you at the Tower and welcome you iii 1 139
To meet you on the way, and welcome you iv 1 51
There they hull, expecting but the aid Of Buckingham to welcome them ashore iv 4 439
Ladies, a general welcome from his grace Salutes ye all *Hen. VIII.* i 4 1
Good company, good wine, good welcome, Can make good people i 4 6
You're welcome, my fair guests i 4 35
This, to confirm my welcome; And to you all, good health i 4 37
Go, give 'em welcome; you can speak the French tongue i 4 57
And once more I shower a welcome on ye; welcome all i 4 63
You're welcome, Most learned reverend sir, into our kingdom ii 2 76
And once more in mine arms I bid him welcome ii 2 99
Cranmer is return'd with welcome, Install'd lord archbishop of Canterbury iii 2 400
Yourself shall feast with us before you go And find the welcome of a noble foe *Troi. and Cres.* i 3 309
Welcome ever smiles, And farewell goes out sighing iii 3 168
In humane gentleness, Welcome to Troy! now, by Anchises' life, Welcome, indeed! iv 1 21
Most dearly welcome to the Greeks, sweet lady iv 5 18
I'll take that winter from your lips, fair lady: Achilles bids you welcome iv 5 25
Encounterers, so glib of tongue, That give accosting welcome ere it comes iv 5 59
As welcome as to one That would be rid of such an enemy; But that's no welcome: understand more clear iv 5 163
From heart of very heart, great Hector, welcome iv 5 171
Let an old man embrace thee; And, worthy warrior, welcome to our tents iv 5 200
Well, welcome, welcome!—I have seen the time iv 5 210
Most gentle and most valiant Hector, welcome iv 5 227

Welcome. Let the trumpets blow, That this great soldier may his welcome know . . . *Troi. and Cres.* iv 5 276
Welcome, brave Hector; welcome, princes all . . . v 1 77
Good night and welcome, both at once, to those That go or tarry . . v 1 84
Tell Valeria, We are fit to bid her welcome . . . *Coriolanus* i 3 47
Welcome to Rome, renowned Coriolanus!—No more of this . ii 1 184
Ye're welcome all.—A hundred thousand welcomes . . . ii 1 199
You will be welcome with this intelligence . . . iv 3 30
A thousand welcomes! And more a friend than e'er an enemy . iv 5 151
Your hand: most welcome! . . . iv 5 153
Repeal him with the welcome of his mother; Cry 'Welcome, ladies, welcome!'—Welcome, ladies, Welcome! . . . v 5 5
And with loud 'larums welcome them to Rome . . . *T. Andron.* i 1 147
Welcome, nephews, from successful wars, You that survive! . . i 1 172
Come down, and welcome me to this world's light . . . v 2 33
Welcome, dread Fury, to my woful house: Rapine and Murder, you are welcome too . . . v 2 82
Welcome, all: although the cheer be poor, 'Twill fill your stomachs . v 3 28
And you, among the store, One more, most welcome . *Rom. and Jul.* i 2 23
To them say, My house and welcome on their pleasure stay . . . i 2 37
Come, death, and welcome! Juliet wills it so . . . iii 5 24
Welcome from Mantua: what says Romeo? . . . v 2 3
Painting is welcome. The painting is almost the natural man *T. of Athens* i 1 156
Right welcome, sir! Ere we depart, we'll share a bounteous time . i 1 262
Hollow welcomes, Recanting goodness, sorry ere 'tis shown . . i 2 16
More welcome are ye to my fortunes Than my fortunes to me . . i 2 19
You are welcome.—No; You shall not make me welcome: I come to have thee thrust me out of doors . . . i 2 23
I take no heed of thee; thou 'rt an Athenian, therefore welcome . . i 2 35
They're welcome all; let 'em have kind admittance: Music, make their welcome! . . . i 2 134
There are certain nobles of the senate Newly alighted, and come to visit you.—They are fairly welcome . . . i 2 182
None so welcome.—I take all and your several visitations So kind to heart i 2 223
You are very respectively welcome, sir . . . iii 1 7
In nothing bless them, and to nothing are they welcome . . . iii 6 94
Thou gavest thine ears like tapsters that bid welcome To knaves . iv 3 215
When there is nothing living but thee, thou shalt be welcome . . iv 3 361
Old feeble carrions and such suffering souls That welcome wrongs *J. C.* ii 1 131
Piercing steel and darts envenomed Shall be as welcome to the ears of Brutus As tidings of this sight . . . v 3 77
Let's after him, Whose care is gone before to bid us welcome *Macbeth* i 4 57
Bear welcome in your eye, Your hand, your tongue . . . i 5 65
To make society The sweeter welcome, we will keep ourself Till supper-time alone . . . iii 1 43
Sit down: at first And last the hearty welcome . . . iii 4 2
Our hostess keeps her state, but in best time We will require her welcome iii 4 6
My heart speaks they are welcome . . . iii 4 8
You do not give the cheer: the feast is sold That is not often vouch'd, while 'tis a-making, 'Tis given with welcome . . . iii 4 35
May kindly say, Our duties did his welcome pay . . . iv 1 132
Such welcome and unwelcome things at once 'Tis hard to reconcile . iv 3 138
This is wondrous strange!—And therefore as a stranger give it welcome *Hamlet* i 5 165
He that plays the king shall be welcome; his majesty shall have tribute of me . . . ii 2 332
There are the players.—Gentlemen, you are welcome to Elsinore . ii 2 387; 573
The appurtenance of welcome is fashion and ceremony . . . ii 2 389
You are welcome: but my uncle-father and aunt-mother are deceived . ii 2 393
You are welcome, masters: welcome, all. I am glad to see thee well . ii 2 440
You are welcome.—Nay, good my lord, this courtesy is not of the right breed . . . iii 2 325
Your lordship is right welcome back to Denmark . . . v 2 81
I serve you, madam: Your graces are right welcome . . . *Lear* ii 1 131
Meeting here the other messenger, Whose welcome, I perceived, had poison'd mine . . . ii 4 39
I look'd not for you yet, nor am provided For your fit welcome . . ii 4 236
Where thou shalt meet Both welcome and protection . . . iii 6 99
Welcome, then, Thou unsubstantial air that I embrace! . . . iv 1 6
My name is Roderigo.—The worser welcome . . . *Othello* i 1 95
Welcome, gentle signior; We lack'd your counsel and your help to-night i 3 50
Good ancient, you are welcome. Welcome, mistress . . . ii 1 97
You are welcome, sir, to Cyprus.—Goats and monkeys! . . . iv 1 274
Your honour is most welcome.—Will you walk, sir? O,—Desdemona . iv 3 4
Welcome to Rome.—Thank you.—Sit.—Sit, sir . . *Ant. and Cleo.* ii 2 28
Welcome from Egypt, sir.—Half the heart of Cæsar, worthy Mecænas! ii 2 174
Your mother came to Sicily and did find Her welcome friendly . . ii 6 47
Welcome to Rome; Nothing more dear to me . . . iii 6 85
Best of comfort; And ever welcome to us.—Welcome, lady . . . iii 6 90
Welcome, dear madam. Each heart in Rome does love and pity you . iii 6 91
Bid that welcome Which comes to punish us, and we punish it . . iv 14 136
All strange and terrible events are welcome, But comforts we despise . iv 15 3
Welcome, welcome! die where thou hast lived: Quicken with kissing . iv 15 38
Thanks, good sir: You're kindly welcome . . . *Cymbeline* i 6 14
You are as welcome, worthy sir, as I Have words to bid you . . . i 6 29
I was going, sir, To give him welcome . . . i 6 55
His majesty bids you welcome. Make pastime with us a day or two . iii 1 78
I know your master's pleasure and he mine: All the remain is 'Welcome!' iii 1 87
You shall have better cheer Ere you depart; . . . Boys, bid him welcome iii 6 69
And such a welcome as I'ld give to him After long absence, such is yours iii 6 73
Most welcome! Be sprightly, for you fall 'mongst friends . . . iii 6 74
The night to the owl and morn to the lark less welcome . . . iii 6 94
Most welcome, bondage! for thou art a way, I think, to liberty . . v 4 3
Welcome is peace, if he on peace consist; If wars, we are unable to resist *Pericles* i 4 83
Your grace is welcome to our town and us.—Which welcome we'll accept . . . i 4 106
Moreo'er puddings and flap-jacks, and thou shalt be welcome . . ii 1 87
To say you're welcome were superfluous . . . ii 3 2
Lord Helicane, a word.—With me? and welcome . . . ii 4 22
Thou art the rudeliest welcome to this world That ever was prince's child . . . iii 1 30
O, here is The lady that I sent for. Welcome, fair one! . . . v 1 65
Welcome guest. Henceforth be no feast, Whereat a villain's not a welcome guest . . . *T. of Athens* iii 6 113
Welcome hither. His worth is warrant for his welcome hither *T. G. of Ver.* ii 4 102
They stand at the door, master; bid them welcome hither *Com. of Errors* iii 1 68
Welcome hither; If that the youth of my new interest here Have power to bid you welcome . . . *Mer. of Venice* iii 2 223

Welcome hither. Be truly welcome hither: I am the duke That loved your father . . . *As Y. Like It* ii 7 195
Welcome hither, As is the spring to the earth . . . *W. Tale* v 1 151
Embrace him, love him, give him welcome hither . . . *K. John* ii 1 11
His noble cousin is right welcome hither . . . *Richard II.* iii 3 122
You brace of warlike brothers, welcome hither . *Troi. and Cres.* iv 5 175
This is Trebonius.—He is welcome hither.—This, Decius Brutus.—He is welcome too . . . *J. Cæsar* ii 1 94
Welcome hither: I have begun to plant thee . . . *Macbeth* i 4 27
My ever-gentle cousin, welcome hither . . . iv 3 161
You are welcome hither.—Nor no man else . . . *Lear* v 3 289
Welcome hither: Your letters did withhold our breaking forth *A. and C.* iii 6 78
Welcome home. Dear lady, welcome home . . . *Mer. of Venice* v 1 113
But God sort all! You are welcome home, my lord . . . v 1 132
And welcome home again discarded faith . . . *K. John* v 4 12
Six frozen winters spent, Return with welcome home from banishment *Richard II.* i 3 212
No joyful tongue gave him his welcome home . . . v 2 29
Your wives shall welcome home the conquerors . . *Richard III.* v 3 260
O, welcome home: And welcome, general: and ye're welcome all *Coriol.* ii 1 198
Your native town you enter'd like a post, And had no welcomes home . v 6 51
You are most welcome home.—I have not deserved it . . . v 6 61
Go to your rest; at night we'll feast together: Most welcome home! *Hamlet* ii 2 85
Welcome news. He hath brought us smooth and welcome news *1 Hen. IV.* i 1 66
Welcomed. Driven out of doors with it when I go from home; welcomed home with it when I return . . . *Com. of Errors* iv 4 38
The entertainment Her sister Katharine welcomed you withal *T. of S.* iii 1 3
Welcomed all, served all; Would sing her song and dance her turn *W. T.* iv 4 57
Welcomed and settled to his own desire . . . *Pericles* iv Gower 2
Welcomer. Farewell, thou woful welcomer of glory! *Richard III.* iv 1 90
Welcomest. I have heard it said, unbidden guests Are often welcomest when they are gone . . . *1 Hen. VI.* ii 2 56
Welfare. The welfare of us all Hangs on the cutting short that fraudful man . . . *2 Hen. VI.* iii 1 80
Nor how to study for the people's welfare . . . *3 Hen. VI.* iv 3 39
That have preserved her welfare in my blood . . . *T. Andron.* v 3 110
Welkin. The sea, mounting to the welkin's cheek, Dashes the fire out *Tempest* i 2 4
Wilt thou revenge?—By welkin and her star!—With wit or steel? *M. W.* i 3 101
Great deputy, the welkin's vicegerent and sole dominator *L. L. Lost* i 1 221
By thy favour, sweet welkin, I must sigh in thy face . . . iii 1 68
Like a jewel in the ear of caelo, the sky, the welkin, the heaven . iv 2 5
The starry welkin cover thou anon With drooping fog *M. N. Dream* iii 2 356
Wilt thou hunt? Thy hounds shall make the welkin answer them *T. of Shrew* Ind. 2 47
But shall we make the welkin dance indeed? . . . *T. Night* ii 3 59
Who you are and what you would are out of my welkin, I might say 'element' . . . iii 1 65
Look on me with your welkin eye . . . *W. Tale* i 2 136
And another shall As loud as thine rattle the welkin's ear *K. John* v 2 172
But stay'd and made the western welkin blush . . . v 5 2
Nay, rather damn them with King Cerberus; and let the welkin roar *2 Hen. IV.* ii 4 182
Amaze the welkin with your broken staves! . . . *Richard III.* v 3 341
With our sighs we'll breathe the welkin dim, And stain the sun *T. An.* iii 1 212
Doth not the sea wax mad, Threatening the welkin with his big-swoln face? . . . iii 1 224
Hark, how her sighs do blow! She is the weeping welkin, I the earth . iii 1 227
Well. Awake, dear heart, awake! thou hast slept well; Awake! *Tempest* i 2 305
Thou hast done well, fine Ariel! Follow me . . . i 2 494
'Twas a sweet marriage, and we prosper well in our return . . ii 1 73
Thou dost talk nothing to me.—I do well believe your highness . . ii 1 172
Do not approach Till thou dost hear me call.—Well, I conceive . iv 1 50
A silly answer and fitting well a sheep . . . *T. G. of Ver.* i 1 81
I would it were no worse.—I'll warrant you, 'tis as well . . ii 1 170
Your friends are well and have them much commended . . . ii 4 123
Where meet we?—At Saint Gregory's well . . . iv 2 84
I am glad to see your worships well . . . *Mer. Wives* i 1 80
No, I thank you, forsooth, heartily; I am very well . . . i 1 278
Will it do well?—We will do it . . . i 3 82
Neither press, coffer, chest, trunk, well, vault, but he hath an abstract iv 2 62
Though it do well, I do not relish well Their loud applause *M. for M.* i 1 70
I pray she may; as well for the encouragement of the like . . i 2 192
Give up your place, And you shall well be spared . . . ii 2 14
If you think well to carry this as you may . . . iii 1 267
I know not where; but wheresoever, I wish him well . . . iii 2 97
The count is neither sad, nor sick, nor merry, nor well . *Much Ado* ii 1 304
One woman is fair, yet I am well; another is wise, yet I am well; another virtuous, yet I am well . . . ii 3 28
Is my lord well, that he doth speak so wide? . . . iv 1 63
I wish your worship well; God restore you to health! . . . v 1 333
This is not so well as I looked for, but the best that ever I heard *L. L. L.* i 1 281
Nothing becomes him ill that he would well . . . ii 1 46
Hence, away! now all is well: One aloof stand sentinel . *M. N. Dream* ii 2 25
I have a device to make all well. Write me a prologue . . . iii 1 18
Tell them plainly he is Snug the joiner.—Well, it shall be so . . iii 1 48
Tell me then that he is well.—An if I could, what should I get therefore? iii 2 77
Fare ye well: We leave you now with better company . *Mer. of Venice* i 1 58
You look not well, Signior Antonio; You have too much respect upon the world . . . i 1 73
That thinks he hath done well in people's eyes, Hearing applause . iii 2 143
Not sick, my lord, unless it be in mind; Nor well, unless in mind . iii 2 238
You may as well go stand upon the beach And bid the main flood bate his usual height; You may as well use question with the wolf Why he hath made the ewe bleat for the lamb; You may as well forbid the mountain pines To wag their high tops . . .; You may as well do any thing most hard . . . iv 1 71
I pray you, give me leave to go from hence; I am not well . . iv 1 396
I wish you well, and so I take my leave . . . iv 1 420
He that escapes me without some broken limb shall acquit him well *As Y. Like It* i 1 134
Yet he talks well; But what care I for words? yet words do well . iii 5 110
For his years he's tall: His leg is but so so; and yet 'tis well . . iii 5 119
Your patience and your virtue well deserves it . . . v 4 193
An onion will do well for such a shift . . . *T. of Shrew* Ind. 1 126
The meat was well, if you were so contented . . . iv 1 172
You bid me make it orderly and well, According to the fashion . . iv 3 94
Now shall he—I know not what he shall. God send him well! *All's Well* i 1 190
He is one— What one, i' faith?—That I wish well . . . i 1 193

Well. What's pity?—That wishing well had not a body in't, Which might be felt *All's Well* i 1 195
Is she well?—She is not well; but yet she has her health: she's very merry; but yet she is not well: but thanks be given, she's very well and wants nothing i' the world; but yet she is not well ii 4 1
If she be very well, what does she ail, that she's not very well?—Truly, she's very well indeed, but for two things ii 4 6
It does indifferent well in a flame-coloured stock *T. Night* i 3 144
I am as well in my wits, fool, as thou art.—But as well? iv 2 95
I tell thee, I am as well in my wits as any man in Illyria iv 2 114
What! have I twice said well? when was't before? *W. Tale* i 2 90
With all the nearest things to my heart, as well My chamber-councils i 2 236
I cannot name the disease; and it is caught Of you that yet are well i 2 387
I cannot speak So well, nothing so well; no, nor mean better iv 4 392
What were more holy Than to rejoice the former queen is well? v 1 30
Behold, and say 'tis well. I like your silence v 3 20
Sir Robert could do well: marry, to confess, Could he get me? *K. John* i 1 236
All shall yet go well.—What can go well, when we have run so ill? iii 4 4
When workmen strive to do better than well, They do confound their skill iv 2 28
Meantime but ask What you would have reform'd that is not well iv 2 44
Who kill'd this prince?—'Tis not an hour since I left him well iv 3 104
I left him well.—Go, bear him in thine arms. I am amazed iv 3 139
To dive like buckets in concealed wells v 2 139
Would not this ill do well? Well, well, I see I talk but idly *Richard II.* iii 3 170
Like a deep well That owes two buckets, filling one another iv 1 184
Thou sayest well, and it holds well too *1 Hen. IV.* i 2 34
In some sort it jumps with my humour as well as waiting in the court i 2 78
These news, Having been well, that would have made me sick, Being sick, have in some measure made me well *2 Hen. IV.* i 1 138
Since all is well, keep it so: wake not a sleeping wolf i 2 173
You like well and bear your years very well iii 2 92
I am glad to see you well 2 *Hen. IV.* iii 2; *Hamlet* i 2; ii 2
Doth she hold her own well?—Old, old, Master Shallow *2 Hen. IV.* iii 2 218
These fellows will do well iii 2 307
What would my lord and father?—Nothing but well to thee iv 4 19
Stand from him, give him air; he'll straight be well iv 4 116
How doth the king?—Exceeding well; his cares are now all ended v 2 3
We understand him well, How he comes o'er us with our wilder days *Hen. V.* i 2 266
Ill will never said well iii 7 123
Look to it well and say you are well warn'd *1 Hen. VI.* ii 4 103
Yet hasty marriage seldom proveth well *3 Hen. VI.* iv 1 18
Would all were well! but that will never be *Richard III.* i 3 40
How fares the prince?—Well, madam, and in health ii 4 40
How fares our loving brother?—Well, my dread lord iii 1 97
Nor none so bad, but it may well be told iv 4 459
Things done well, And with a care, exempt themselves from fear *Hen. VIII.* i 2 88
You hold a fair assembly; you do well i 4 87
My conscience,—which I then did feel full sick, and yet not well ii 4 204
Yoke together, As I will lend you cause, my doing well With my well saying! iii 2 151
'Tis well said again; And 'tis a kind of good deed to say well iii 2 152
Let me tell you, it will ne'er be well, 'Twill not, Sir Thomas Lovell v 1 29
And the end Was ever, to do well v 3 37
'Tis said he holds you well, and will be led At your request *Tr. and Cr.* ii 3 190
We know each other well.—We do; and long to know each other worse iv 1 30
Make wells and Niobes of the maids and wives, Cold statues of the youth v 10 19
Though thou speak'st truth, Methinks thou speak'st not well *Coriolanus* i 6 14
Farewell, my wife, my mother: I'll do well yet iv 1 21
You say well.—Yea, is the worst well? very well took, i' faith *R. and J.* ii 4 130
'Tis not so deep as a well, nor so wide as a church-door; but 'tis enough iii 1 99
I am not well.—Evermore weeping for your cousin's death? iii 5 69
You love your child so ill, That you run mad, seeing that she is well iv 5 76
Is my father well? How fares my Juliet? that I ask again; For nothing can be ill, if she be well.—Then she is well, and nothing can be ill v 1 14
Good day, sir.—I am glad you're well *T. of Athens* i 1 1
His health is well, sir.—I am right glad that his health is well iii 1 12
And canst use the time well, if the time use thee well iii 1 39
How fare you?—Ever at the best, hearing well of your lordship iii 6 29
I never did thee harm.—Yes, thou spokest well of me iv 3 173
Our great need of him You have right well conceited *J. Cæsar* i 3 162
Ligarius doth bear Cæsar hard, Who rated him for speaking well of Pompey ii 1 216
Make me acquainted with your cause of grief.—I am not well in health ii 1 257
He shall say you are not well to-day: Let me, upon my knee, prevail in this.—Mark Antony shall say I am not well; And, for thy humour, I will stay at home ii 2 53
Yes, bring me word, boy, if thy lord look well, For he went sickly forth ii 4 13
Gentlemen, rise: his highness is not well.—Sit, worthy friends *Macbeth* iii 4 52
The fit is momentary; upon a thought He will again be well iii 4 56
How does my wife?—Why, well.—And all my children?—Well too iv 3 177
They were well at peace when I did leave 'em iv 3 179
They say he parted well, and paid his score: And so, God be with him! v 8 52
My father's spirit in arms! all is not well; I doubt some foul play *Ham.* i 2 255
How does my good Lord Hamlet?—Well, God-a-mercy ii 2 172
Well be with you, gentlemen! ii 2 398
How does your honour for this many a day?—I humbly thank you; well, well, well iii 1 92
What think you on't?—It shall do well iii 1 184
Each opposite that blanks the face of joy Meet what I would have well and it destroy! iii 2 231
I've seen myself, and served against, the French, And they can well on horseback iv 7 85
The gallows does well; but how does it well? it does well to those that do ill v 1 52
He says, my lord, your daughter is not well *Lear* i 4 55
Striving to better, oft we mar what's well i 4 369
May be he is not well: Infirmity doth still neglect all office ii 4 106
My point and period will be throughly wrought, Or well or ill, as this day's battle's fought iv 7 98
I am not well; else I should answer From a full-flowing stomach v 3 73
She is not well; convey her to my tent v 3 106
He bears the sentence well that nothing bears But the free comfort *Oth.* i 3 212
He holds me well; The better shall my purpose work on him i 3 396
Nor know I aught But that he's well and will be shortly here ii 1 90
I am sorry For your displeasure; but all will sure be well iii 1 45
Why do you speak so faintly? Are you not well? iii 3 283

Well. That was not so well; yet would I knew That stroke would prove the worst! *Othello* iv 1 284
Well; go to; very well.—Very well! go to! I cannot go to, man; nor 'tis not very well iv 2 194
Very well.—I tell you 'tis not very well iv 2 198
You have done well, That men must lay their murders on your neck v 2 169
Then must you speak Of one that loved not wisely but too well v 2 344
But let it be: I am quickly ill, and well, So Antony loves *Ant. and Cleo.* i 3 72
I shall do well: The people love me, and the sea is mine ii 1 8
First, madam, he is well.—Why, there's more gold. But, sirrah, mark, we use To say the dead are well ii 5 31
If not well, Thou shouldst come like a Fury crown'd with snakes ii 5 39
If thou say Antony lives, is well, . . . I'll set thee in a shower of gold ii 5 43
Madam, he's well.—Well said.—And friends with Cæsar ii 5 46
How farest thou, soldier?—Well; And well am like to do ii 6 73
I am not so well as I should be, but I'll ne'er out.—Not till you have slept ii 7 35
Since my lord Is Antony again, I will be Cleopatra.—We will yet do well iii 13 188
Know, my hearts, I hope well of to-morrow iv 2 42
'Tis well thou'rt gone, If it be well to live iv 12 39
Approach, ho! All's not well: Cæsar's beguiled v 2 326
What, dear sir, Thus raps you? Are you well?—Thanks, madam; well *Cymbeline* i 6 51
Continues well my lord? His health, beseech you?—Well, madam i 6 56
Nay, many times, Doth ill deserve by doing well iii 3 54
You are not well: remain here in the cave; We'll come to you after hunting iv 2 1
So sick I am not, yet I am not well iv 2 7
Well or ill, I am bound to you.—And shalt be ever iv 2 45
Howsoe'er, My brother hath done well iv 2 147
Thanks, gentlemen, to all; all have done well, But you the best *Pericles* ii 3 108
My daughter thinks very well of you; Ay, so well, that you must be her master ii 5 37
Well accompanied With reverend fathers *Richard III.* iii 5 99
Well accomplished. Valiant, wise, remorseful, well accomplish'd *T. G. of Ver.* iv 3 13
A well-accomplish'd youth, Of all that virtue love for virtue loved *L. L. Lost* ii 1 56
Well-acquainted. As if I were their well-acquainted friend *Com. of Errors* iv 3 2
Well-a-day. O well-a-day, Mistress Ford! *Mer. Wives* iii 3 106
I am as well in my wits as any man in Illyria.—Well-a-day that you were, sir! *T. Night* iv 2 116
O well a day, Lady, if he be not drawn now! *Hen. V.* ii 1 38
Ah, well-a-day! he's dead, he's dead, he's dead! *Rom. and Jul.* iii 2 37
Help, help! my lady's dead! O, well-a-day, that ever I was born! iv 5 15
When, well-a-day, we could scarce help ourselves *Pericles* ii 1 23
While our scene must play His daughter's woe and heavy well-a-day iv 4 49
Well-advised. Sleeping or waking? mad or well-advised? *Com. of Errors* ii 2 215
And were you well advised?—I was, fair madam *L. L. Lost* v 2 434
Be well advised, tell o'er thy tale again *K. John* iii 1 5
To pray for them that have done scathe to us.—So do I ever: being well advised *Richard III.* i 3 318
Hath any well-advised friend proclaim'd Reward? iv 4 517
My grandsire, well advised, hath sent by me *T. Andron.* iv 2 10
Well-a-near Does fall in travail with her fear *Pericles* iii Gower 51
Well-apparell'd April on the heel Of limping winter treads *Rom. and Jul.* i 2 27
Well-appointed. York is up With well-appointed powers *2 Hen. IV.* i 1 190
What well-appointed leader fronts us here? iv 1 25
Suppose that you have seen The well-appointed king *Hen. V.* iii Prol. 4
The Dauphin, well appointed, Stands with the snares of war *1 Hen. VI.* iv 2 21
Flocks of friends, And very well appointed, as I thought *3 Hen. VI.* ii 1 113
Well armed. In strong proof of chastity well arm'd *Rom. and Jul.* i 1 216
They boast To have well-armed friends *Lear* iii 7 20
Well-balanced. By cold gradation and well-balanced form, We shall proceed *Meas. for Meas.* iv 3 104
Well-behaved. Gave such orderly and well-behaved reproof *Mer. Wives* ii 1 59
Well-beloved. That same noble prelate, well beloved *1 Hen. IV.* i 3 267
My learn'd and well-beloved servant, Cranmer *Hen. VIII.* ii 4 238
Through this the well-beloved Brutus stabb'd *J. Cæsar* iii 2 180
Well-beseeming. In mutual well-beseeming ranks *1 Hen. IV.* i 1 14
Rome's royal empress, Unfurnish'd of her well-beseeming troop *T. An.* ii 3 56
Well-born. As many and as well-born bloods as those *K. John* ii 1 278
Well bred. A gentleman well bred and of good name *2 Hen. IV.* iv 1 26
Well-chosen. Here comes the king.—And his well-chosen bride *3 Hen. VI.* iv 1 7
The horses . . . I saw well chosen, ridden, and furnished *Hen. VIII.* ii 2 2
Well coloured. These eyes, that see thee now well coloured, Shall see thee wither'd *1 Hen. VI.* iv 2 37
Well come. Very well met, and well come *Meas. for Meas.* iv 1 26
Well-dealing. Merchants, our well-dealing countrymen *Com. of Errors* i 1 7
Well defended. Whose salt imagination yet hath wrong'd Your well defended honour *Meas. for Meas.* v 1 407
Not only well defended But taken and impounded as a stray *Hen. V.* i 2 159
Well demanded, wench: My tale provokes that question *Tempest* i 2 139
Well derived. What says she to my birth?—That you are well derived *T. G. of Ver.* v 2 23
Sir Valentine, Thou art a gentleman and well derived v 4 146
I am, my lord, as well derived as he, As well possess'd *M. N. Dream* i 1 99
My son corrupts a well-derived nature With his inducement *All's Well* iii 2 90
Well-deserved. You to a long and well-deserved bed *As Y. Like It* v 4 196
Well-deserving. Whereof you are a well-deserving pillar *Mer. of Venice* iv 1 239
Is not his heir a well-deserving son? *Richard II.* ii 1 194
I'll give thrice so much land To any well-deserving friend *1 Hen. IV.* iii 1 138
What though I know her virtuous And well deserving? *Hen. VIII.* iii 2 98
Well-disposed. You lose a thousand well-disposed hearts *Richard II.* ii 1 206
Well-divided. He was nor sad nor merry.—O well-divided disposition! *Ant. and Cleo.* i 5 53
Well done. Is't not well done?—Excellently done, if God did all *T. Night* i 5 253
Well, may you see things well done there: adieu! *Macbeth* ii 4 37
Is this well done?—It is well done, and fitting for a princess *A. and C.* v 2 328
Well-educated. Define, define, well-educated infant *L. L. Lost* i 2 99
Well enough. He does well enough if he be disposed *T. Night* ii 3 87
Fear not, neighbour, you shall do well enough *2 Hen. VI.* ii 3 61
Fear not thy sons; they shall do well enough *T. Andron.* ii 3 305
Why, but you are now well enough: how came you thus recovered? *Oth.* ii 3 295
All may be well enough.—I warrant you *Ant. and Cleo.* iii 3 50
Well entered. 'Tis our hope, sir, After well enter'd soldiers, to return *All's Well* ii 1 6
Well-experienced. A well-experienced archer hits the mark His eye doth level at *Pericles* i 1 164
Well-famed. My well-famed lord of Troy, no less to you *Troi. and Cres.* iv 5 173

Well-favoured. Not so fair, boy, as well-favoured . . . *T. G. of Ver.* ii 1 54
She is not so fair as, of you, well favoured . . . . ii 1 57
Masses of money; for the which his wife seems to me well-favoured *Mer. Wives* ii 2 285
To be a well-favoured man is the gift of fortune . . . *Much Ado* iii 3 15
He is very well-favoured and he speaks very shrewishly . . *T. Night* i 5 169
Those wicked creatures yet do look well-favour'd, When others are more wicked . . . . . . *Lear* ii 4 259
You are well favour'd, and your looks foreshow You have a gentle heart *Pericles* iv 1 86
Well fitted in arts, glorious in arms . . . . *L. L. Lost* ii 1 45
Well forewarning. What boded this, but well forewarning wind? *2 Hen. VI.* iii 2 85
Well fortified. We are well fortified And strong enough . *1 Hen. VI.* iv 2 19
Well-foughten. In this glorious and well-foughten field . . *Hen. V.* iv 6 18
Well-found. In what he did profess, well found . . . *All's Well* ii 1 105
And last general In our well-found successes . . . . *Coriolanus* ii 2 48
Well governed. A virtuous and well govern'd youth . *Rom. and Jul.* i 5 70
Well-graced. The eyes of men, After a well-graced actor leaves the stage, Are idly bent on him that enters next *Richard II.* v 2 24
Well-hallowed. And to put forth My rightful hand in a well-hallow'd cause . . . . . . *Hen. V.* i 2 293
Well-knit. O well-knit Samson! strong-jointed Samson! . *L. L. Lost* i 2 77
Well-known. But what need I thus My well-known body to anatomize Among my household? . . . . *2 Hen. IV.* Ind. 21
Well-labouring. Whose well-labouring sword Had three times slain the appearance of the king . . . . i 1 127
Well-learned. With reverend fathers and well-learned bishops *Rich. III.* iii 5 100
Well-liking wits they have; gross, gross; fat, fat . . *L. L. Lost* v 2 268
Well-lost. I'ld venture The well-lost life of mine on his grace's cure *All's Well* i 3 254
Well made. Half won is match well made; match, and well make it iv 3 254
Well married. He is not like to marry me well; and not being well married, it will be a good excuse for me hereafter to leave my wife *As Y. Like It* iii 3 94
She's not well married that lives married long . . *Rom. and Jul.* iv 5 77
Well-meaning. Plain well-meaning soul . . . *Richard II.* ii 1 128
Well-meant. Springs not from Edward's well-meant honest love, But from deceit bred by necessity . . . . *3 Hen. VI.* iii 3 67
Well met. Very well met, and well come . . . *Meas. for Meas.* iv 1 26
Well-minded Clarence, be thou fortunate! . . . *3 Hen. VI.* iv 8 27
Well mounted. Myself, well mounted, hardly have escaped . *K. John* v 6 42
Well-nigh. One that is well-nigh worn to pieces with age *Mer. Wives* ii 1 21
That swore that you were well-nigh dead for me . . *Much Ado* v 4 81
Well noted. In this the antique and well noted face Of plain old form is much disfigured . . . . *K. John* iv 2 21
Well o'erta'en. Fair sir, you are well o'erta'en . *Mer. of Venice* iv 2 5
Well-ordered. There is a law in each well-order'd nation *Troi. and Cres.* ii 2 180
Well-paid. With his banners and his well-paid ranks *Ant. and Cleo.* iii 1 32
Well-painted. O well-painted passion! . . . . *Othello* iv 1 268
Well penned. Besides that it is excellently well penned . *T. Night* i 5 185
Well placed. Give the devil his due.—Well placed . . *Hen. V.* iii 7 128
Well pleased To change two dukedoms for a duke's fair daughter *2 Hen. VI.* i 1 218
And sends the poor well pleased from my gate . . . . iv 10 25
Well possessed. I am, my lord, as well derived as he, As well possess'd; my love is more . . . . *M. N. Dream* i 1 100
Well-practised. I will stoop and humble my intents To your well-practised wise directions . . . . . *2 Hen. IV.* v 2 121
Well-proportioned. His well-proportion'd beard made rough and rugged, Like to the summer's corn by tempest lodged *2 Hen. VI.* iii 2 175
Well read in poetry And other books, good ones . . *T. of Shrew* i 2 170
He is a worthy gentleman, Exceedingly well read . *1 Hen. IV.* iii 1 166
Well remembered. Your noble and right well remember'd father's *2 Hen. IV.* iv 1 112
Well repaid. He is well repaid; He is frank'd up to fatting *Richard III.* i 3 313
Well-reputed. Fit me with such weeds As may beseem some well-reputed page . . . . *T. G. of Ver.* ii 7 43
I grant I am a woman; but withal A woman well-reputed *J. Cæsar* ii 1 295
Well-respected. If well-respected honour bid me on, I hold as little counsel with weak fear As you . . . . *1 Hen. IV.* iv 3 10
Well said, brazen-face! hold it out . . . . *Mer. Wives* iv 2 141
Well said, old mocker: I must needs be friends with thee *L. L. Lost* v 2 552
And well said too; for who shall go about To cozen fortune? *M. of Ven.* ii 9 37
Well said: that was laid on with a trowel . . *As Y. Like It* i 2 112
Well said! thou lookest cheerly . . . . ii 6 14
Well said, master; mum! and gaze your fill . . *T. of Shrew* i 1 73
Talkest thou nothing but of ladies?—Well said . . *T. Night* iv 2 31
Well then, once in my days I'll be a madcap.—Why, that's well said *1 Hen. IV.* i 2 161
Well said, my noble Scot . . . . iv 1 1
Well said, Hal! to it, Hal! Nay, you shall find no boy's play here v 4 75
It is well said, in faith, sir; and it is well said indeed too *2 Hen. IV.* iii 2 74
Well said, good woman's tailor! well said, courageous Feeble! . iii 2 169
Well said, i' faith, Wart; thou'rt a good scab . . . . iii 2 295
Spread, Davy: well said, Davy . . . . v 3 10
Well said, my masters; and welcome all . . . *2 Hen. VI.* i 4 16
'Tis well said again; And 'tis a kind of good deed to say well *Hen. VIII.* ii 4 152
Well said, my lord! well, you say so in fits . *Troi. and Cres.* iii 1 61
Well said, adversity! and what need these tricks? . . . . v 1 14
Now she sharpens: well said, whetstone! . . . . . v 2 75
Well said, noble woman! . . . . *Coriolanus* iii 2 31
Well said, my hearts! You are a princox . . *Rom. and Jul.* i 5 88
Mass, and well said; a merry whoreson, ha! . . . . . iv 4 19
Swear.—Well said, old mole! . . . . *Hamlet* i 5 162
My lord, I did intend it.—Marry, well said; very well said . ii 1 6
He takes her by the palm: ay, well said, whisper . . *Othello* ii 1 169
He, he, 'tis he. O, that's well said; the chair . . . . v 1 98
Madam, he's well.—Well said . . . . . *Ant. and Cleo.* ii 5 46
Well said, well said; the fire and cloths . . . *Pericles* iii 2 87
Well-sailing ships and bounteous winds have brought This king to Tarsus . . . . iv 4 17
Well saying. Yoke together, As I will lend you cause, my doing well With my well saying! . . . . . . *Hen. VIII.* iii 2 152
Well-seeming. Her combinate husband, this well-seeming Angelo *Meas. for Meas.* iii 1 232
Mis-shapen chaos of well-seeming forms! . . . *Rom. and Jul.* i 1 185
Well seen. A schoolmaster Well seen in music . . . *T. of Shrew* i 2 134
Well-spoken. A knight well-spoken, neat, and fine . *T. G. of Ver.* i 2 10
I cannot prove a lover, To entertain these fair well-spoken days *Rich. III.* i 1 29
Clarence is well-spoken, and perhaps May move your hearts to pity . i 3 348

Well summered. For maids, well summered and warm kept, are like flies at Bartholomew-tide . . . . *Hen. V.* v 2 335
Well to friend. I know that we shall have him well to friend *J. Cæsar* iii 1 143
Well to live. An honest exceeding poor man and, God be thanked, well to live . . . . *Mer. of Venice* ii 2 55
If the sins of your youth are forgiven you, you're well to live *W. Tale* iii 3 125
Well took, i' faith, wisely, wisely . . . . *Rom. and Jul.* ii 4 131
Meantime we thank you for your well-took labour . . *Hamlet* ii 2 83
Well-tuned. The babbling echo mocks the hounds, Replying shrilly to the well-tuned horns . . . . . . *T. Andron.* ii 3 18
You are well tuned now! But I'll set down the pegs that make this music . . . . *Othello* ii 1 202
Well warned. Look to it well and say you are well warn'd *1 Hen. VI.* ii 4 103
Well-warranted. And you, my noble and well-warranted cousin *M. for M.* v 1 254
Well-weighing. With well-weighing sums of gold, to corrupt him *A. W.* iv 3 203
Well welcome. That never touch well welcome to thy hand *Com. of Er.* ii 2 118
This deed will be well welcome to Lorenzo . . *Mer. of Venice* iv 2 4
Well-willers. I beseech you, be ruled by your well-willers *Mer. Wives* i 1 72
Well-wished. Even so The general, subject to a well-wish'd king *M. for M.* ii 4 27
Well-won. My well-won thrift, Which he calls interest *Mer. of Venice* i 3 51
Well worthy. The lady is very well worthy.—You speak this to fetch me in . . . . *Much Ado* i 1 224
Welsh. Sir Hugh the Welsh priest and Caius the French doctor *Mer. W.* ii 1 209
Gallia and Gaul, French and Welsh, soul-curer and body-curer! . . iii 1 100
Where is Nan now and her troop of fairies, and the Welsh devil Hugh? v 3 13
Defend me from that Welsh fairy, lest he transform me to a piece of cheese! . . . . v 5 85
Am I ridden with a Welsh goat too? shall I have a coxcomb of frize? . v 5 145
I am not able to answer the Welsh flannel . . . . . . v 5 172
Swore the devil his true liegeman upon the cross of a Welsh hook *1 Hen. IV.* ii 4 372
I think there's no man speaks better Welsh . . . . . iii 1 50
Speak it in Welsh.—I can speak English, lord, as well as you . iii 1 120
My wife can speak no English, I no Welsh . . . . . iii 1 193
That pretty Welsh Which thou pour'st down from these swelling heavens I am too perfect in . . . . iii 1 201
Thy tongue Makes Welsh as sweet as ditties highly penn'd . . iii 1 209
Now I perceive the devil understands Welsh . . . . . iii 1 233
Lie still, ye thief, and hear the lady sing in Welsh . . . iii 1 239
Now God help thee!—To the Welsh lady's bed . . . . iii 1 247
He leaves his back unarm'd, the French and Welsh Baying him at the heels . . . . *2 Hen. IV.* i 3 79
Against the Welsh, himself and Harry Monmouth . . . . i 3 83
I am Welsh, you know, good countryman.—All the water in Wye cannot wash your majesty's Welsh plood out of your pody *Hen. V.* iv 7 110
Henceforth let a Welsh correction teach you a good English condition v 1 82
Welshman. I will rather trust a Fleming with my butter, Parson Hugh the Welshman with my cheese . . . . . *Mer. Wives* ii 2 317
Thou trusty Welshman: The king reposeth all his confidence in thee *Richard II.* ii 4 5
All the Welshmen, hearing thou wert dead, Art gone to Bolingbroke . iii 2 73
By this intelligence we learn The Welshmen are dispersed . . . iii 3 2
Was by the rude hands of that Welshman taken . . *1 Hen. IV.* i 1 41
Art thou of Cornish crew?—No, I am a Welshman . . *Hen. V.* iv 1 51
There is much care and valour in this Welshman . . . . iv 1 86
The Welshmen did good service in a garden where leeks did grow . iv 7 102
With all the friends that thou, brave Earl of March, Amongst the loving Welshmen canst procure . . . . . . *3 Hen. VI.* ii 1 180
Buckingham, back'd with the hardy Welshmen, Is in the field *Richard III.* iv 3 47
You cannot guess wherefore the Welshman comes . . . . iv 4 477
Welshwomen. Such beastly shameless transformation By those Welshwomen done as may not be Without much shame retold or spoken of *1 Hen. IV.* i 1 45
Wen. I do allow this wen to be as familiar with me as my dog *2 Hen. IV.* i 2 115
Wench. As leaky as an unstanched wench . . . . . *Tempest* i 1 51
Well demanded, wench: My tale provokes that question . . . i 2 139
'Tis a spirit.—No, wench; it eats and sleeps . . . . . i 2 412
Foolish wench! To the most of men this is a Caliban . . . i 2 479
Temperance was a delicate wench.—Ay, and a subtle . . . ii 1 43
To weep, like a young wench that had buried her grandam *T. G. of V.* ii 1 24
But tell me, wench, how will the world repute me? . . . . ii 7 59
What need a man care for a stock with a wench, when she can knit him a stock? . . . . iii 1 312
O, to him, to him, wench! he will relent . . *Meas. for Meas.* ii 2 124
I was once before him for getting a wench with child . . . iv 3 180
Dost thou conjure for wenches, that thou call'st for such store? *C. of Er.* iii 1 34
I know a wench of excellent discourse, Pretty and witty . . . iii 1 109
Here she comes in the habit of a light wench: and thereof comes that the wenches say 'God damn me;' that's as much to say 'God make me a light wench' . . . . iv 3 53
Light is an effect of fire, and fire will burn; ergo, light wenches will burn iv 3 58
With a wench.—'with a child of our grandmother Eve' . . *L. L. Lost* i 1 265
Sirrah, what say you to this?—Sir, I confess the wench . . . i 1 285
It was proclaimed a year's imprisonment, to be taken with a wench . i 1 290
As it is base for a soldier to love, so am I in love with a base wench . i 2 62
And that's great marvel, loving a light wench . . . . . i 2 129
Do you hear, my mad wenches?—No.—What then, do you see? . ii 1 256
These are complements, these are humours; these betray nice wenches iii 1 24
When Queen Guinover of Britain was a little wench . . . iv 1 126
Light wenches may prove plagues to men forsworn . . . . iv 3 385
You are a light wench.—Indeed I weigh not you . . . . . v 2 25
Arm, wenches, arm! encounters mounted are Against your peace . . v 2 82
The tongues of mocking wenches are as keen As is the razor's edge . v 2 256
Farewell, mad wenches; you have simple wits . . . . . v 2 264
This gallant pins the wenches on his sleeve . . . . . v 2 321
And, to begin, wench,—so God help me, la!—My love to thee is sound v 2 414
The poor wench is cast away: she's quick . . . . . . v 2 682
If Fortune be a woman, she's a good wench for this gear *Mer. of Venice* ii 2 175
That wench is stark mad or wonderful froward . . . *T. of Shrew* i 1 69
It is a lusty wench; I love her ten times more than e'er I did . . ii 1 161
Thou canst not look askance, Nor bite the lip, as angry wenches will . ii 1 250
What said the wench when he rose again?—Trembled and shook . . iii 2 168
Fear not, sweet wench, they shall not touch thee, Kate . . . iii 2 240
I knew a wench married in an afternoon as she went to the garden for parsley . . . . iv 4 99
Why, there's a wench! Come on, and kiss me, Kate . . . . v 2 180
He weeps like a wench that had shed her milk . . . *All's Well* iv 3 123
She's a good wench.—She's a beagle, true-bred . . . *T. Night* ii 3 194
A fustian riddle!—Excellent wench, say I . . . . . . ii 5 120
I could marry this wench for this device.—So could I too . . . ii 5 199
There is nothing in the between but getting wenches with child *W. Tale* iii 3 62

Wench. Wenches, I'll buy for you both. Pedlar, let's have the first choice . . . . *W. Tale* iv 4 318
They have a dance which the wenches say is a gallimaufry of gambols . iv 4 335
Grew so in love with the wenches' song, that he would not stir . iv 4 618
And the blessed sun himself a fair hot wench . . . . 1 *Hen. IV.* i 2 11
And is not my hostess of the tavern a most sweet wench? . . . i 2 46
There's not a better wench in England . . . . 2 *Hen. IV.* ii 1 161
Must I marry your sister?—God send the wench no worse fortune! . ii 2 152
Farewell, good wenches: if I be not sent away post, I will see you again ii 4 407
When they marry, they get wenches: they are generally fools and cowards . . . . iv 3 101
Young Talbot was not born To be the pillage of a giglot wench 1 *Hen. VI.* iv 7 41
The readiest way to make the wench amends Is to become her husband and her father . . . . . . *Richard III.* i 1 155
Take thy lute, wench: my soul grows sad with troubles *Hen. VIII.* iii 1 1
Alas, poor wenches, where are now your fortunes! . . . . iii 1 148
When the brown wench Lay kissing in your arms . . . . iii 2 295
Good wench, let's sit down quiet, For fear we wake her . . . iv 2 81
Mark her eyes!—She is going, wench: pray, pray . . . . iv 2 99
When I am dead, good wench, Let me be used with honour . . . iv 2 167
Thou must be gone, wench, thou must be gone . . *Troi. and Cres.* iv 2 95
He loved me—O false wench! . . . . v 2 70
Bear thou my hand, sweet wench, between thy teeth *T. Andron.* iii 1 283
That same pale hard-hearted wench, that Rosaline, Torments him so, that he will sure run mad . . . . . *Rom. and Jul.* ii 4 4
He is already dead; stabbed with a white wench's black eye . . ii 4 14
Go thy ways, wench; serve God. What, have you dined at home? . ii 5 45
Like a misbehaved and sullen wench, Thou pout'st upon thy fortune . iii 3 143
Three or four wenches, where I stood, cried 'Alas, good soul!' *J. Cæsar* i 2 274
No heretics burn'd, but wenches' suitors . . . . *Lear* iii 2 84
Look, here it is.—A good wench; give it me . . *Othello* iii 3 313
O ill-starr'd wench! Pale as thy smock! . . . . . v 2 272
Prithee, how many boys and wenches must I have? . *Ant. and Cleo.* i 2 36
Royal wench! She made great Cæsar lay his sword to bed . . ii 2 231
One daughter, and a wench full grown, Even ripe for marriage-rite *Pericles* iv Gower 16

Wenching. What's become of the wenching rogues? *Troi. and Cres.* v 4 35

Wenchless. We lost too much money this mart by being too wenchless *Pericles* iv 2 5

Wench-like. Have done; And do not play in wench-like words with that Which is so serious . . . . . . *Cymbeline* iv 2 230

Wend you with this letter . . . . . *Meas. for Meas.* iv 3 150
Hopeless and helpless doth Ægeon wend, But to procrastinate his life-less end . . . . *Com. of Errors* i 1 158
And back to Athens shall the lovers wend . . *M. N. Dream* iii 2 372

Went. As proper a man as ever went on four legs . . *Tempest* ii 2 63
All this service Have I done since I went . . . . . v 1 226
Three or four of his blind brothers and sisters went to it *T. G. of Ver.* iv 4 5
Went you not to her yesterday, sir, as you told me? . *Mer. Wives* v 1 14
I went to her, Master Brook, as you see, like a poor old man . . v 1 16
I went to her in white, and cried 'mum,' and she cried 'budget' . v 5 209
Now, mistress, how chance you went not with Master Slender?—Why went you not with master doctor, maid? . . . . . v 5 230
Went to sea with the Ten Commandments, but scraped one out *M. for M.* i 2 8
There went but a pair of shears between us . . . . . i 2 28
I have heard of the lady, and good words went with her name . ii 1 220
I went To this pernicious caitiff deputy . . . . . v 1 87
Let me say no more! Gather the sequel by that went before *Com. of Er.* i 1 96
If you went in pain, master, this 'knave' would go sore . . . ii 1 65
He that went, like a bass-viol, in a case of leather . . . iv 3 23
Whilst to take order for the wrongs I went . . . . . v 1 146
Our dinner done, and he not coming thither, I went to seek him . v 1 225
In our last conflict four of his five wits went halting off . *Much Ado* i 1 66
When you went onward on this ended action . . . . . i 1 299
I liked her ere I went to wars.—Thou wilt be like a lover presently i 1 307
Away went Claudio enraged; swore he would meet her . . . iii 3 170
See, see; here comes the man we went to seek . . . . v 1 110
She was a vixen when she went to school . . *M. N. Dream* iii 2 324
The duke, Who went with him to search Bassanio's ship *Mer. of Venice* ii 8 5
Wheresoe'er we went, like Juno's swans, Still we went coupled *As Y. L. It* i 3 77
How looked he? Wherein went he? What makes he here? . . iii 2 234
He went but forth to wash him in the Hellespont . . . . iv 1 103
Went they not quickly, I should die with laughing . *T. of Shrew* iii 2 243
I knew a wench married in an afternoon as she went to the garden . iv 4 100
A month ago I went from hence, And then 'twas fresh in murmur *T. N.* i 2 31
And when she went away now, 'Let this fellow be looked to' . . iii 4 84
Such and so In favour was my brother, and he went Still in this fashion iii 4 416
So went he suited to his watery tomb . . . . . . v 1 241
They that went on crutches ere he was born desire yet their life to see him a man . . . . *W. Tale* i 1 44
I do feel it gone, But know not how it went . . . . . iii 2 97
Since last I went to France to fetch his queen . . *Richard II.* i 1 131
Rode he on Barbary? Tell me, gentle friend, How went he under him? v 5 82
Went to a bawdy-house not above once in a quarter—of an hour 1 *Hen. IV.* iii 3 19
So went on, Foretelling this same time's condition . . 2 *Hen. IV.* iii 1 77
Never went with his forces into France But that the Scot on his un-furnish'd kingdom Came pouring . . . . . . *Hen. V.* i 2 147
He's in Arthur's bosom, if ever man went to Arthur's bosom . . ii 3 10
A' made a finer end and went away an it had been any christom child . ii 3 11
Pride went before, ambition follows him . . . 2 *Hen. VI.* i 1 180
Up and down, Looking the way her harmless young one went . . iii 1 215
Jove sometime went disguised, and why not I? . . . . iv 1 48
In whose time boys went to span-counter for French crowns . . iv 2 166
Their weapons like to lightning came and went . . 3 *Hen. VI.* ii 1 129
Whose father for his hoarding went to hell . . . . . ii 2 48
Watch'd the winter's night, Went all afoot in summer's scalding heat v 7 18
When that my mother went with child Of that unsatiate Edward *Richard III.* iii 5 86
From troop to troop Went through the army, cheering up the soldiers v 3 71
Which went Beyond all man's endeavours . . *Hen. VIII.* iii 2 168
When you went Ambassador to the emperor . . . . . iii 2 317
What two reverend bishops Were those that went on each side of the queen? . . . . iv 1 100
So went to bed; where eagerly his sickness Pursued him still . iv 2 24
Who were those went by?—Queen Hecuba and Helen *Troi. and Cres.* i 2 1
That's Helenus. I think he went not forth to-day . . . . i 2 239
If you'll avouch 'twas wisdom Paris went—As you must needs . ii 2 84
How chance my brother Troilus went not?—He hangs the lip at some-thing . . . . iii 1 151

Went. The cry went once on thee, And still it might, and yet it may again *Troi. and Cres.* iii 3 184
Was that my father that went hence so fast? . . *Rom. and Jul.* i 1 168
Nor are they living Who were the motives that you first went out *T. of Athens* v 4 27
When went there by an age, since the great flood, But it was famed with more than with one man? . . . . . . *J. Cæsar* i 2 152
He was quick mettle when he went to school . . . . . i 2 300
Who glared upon me, and went surly by, Without annoying me . . i 3 21
And, I am sure, It did not lie there when I went to bed . . . ii 1 38
Bring me word, boy, if thy lord look well, For he went sickly forth . ii 4 14
Thou know'st that we two went to school together . . . . v 5 26
Thane of Cawdor too: went it not so?—To the selfsame tune *Macbeth* i 3 87
Was it so late, friend, ere you went to bed, That you do lie so late? . ii 3 24
You made it known to us.—I did so, and went further . . . iii 1 85
When was it she last walked?—Since his majesty went into the field . v 1 4
It went hand in hand even with the vow I made to her in marriage *Ham.* i 5 49
He seem'd to find his way without his eyes; For out o' doors he went without their helps . . . . ii 1 99
I went round to work, And my young mistress thus I did bespeak . ii 2 139
Unless the poet and the player went to cuffs in the question . . ii 2 373
Since he went into France, I have been in continual practice . . v 2 220
So, out went the candle, and we were left darkling . . *Lear* i 4 237
Never lack'd gold and yet went never gay . . . *Othello* ii 1 151
I prithee, call him back.—Went he hence now? . . . . iii 3 51
O, yes; and went between us very oft . . . . . . iii 3 100
He went hence but now, And certainly in strange unquietness . . iii 4 132
Since he went from Egypt 'tis A space for further travel *Ant. and Cleo.* ii 1 30
His power went out in such distractions as Beguiled all spies . iii 7 77
Alexas did revolt; and went to Jewry on Affairs of Antony . . iv 6 12
And to this hour no guess in knowledge Which way they went *Cymbeline* i 1 61
His steel was in debt; it went o' the backside the town . . . i 2 14
If she went before others I have seen, . . . I could not but believe she excelled many . . . . i 4 78
Is it fit I went to look upon him? is there no derogation in't? . ii 1 46
When last I went to visit her, She pray'd me to excuse her keeping close iii 5 45
How long is't since she went to Milford-Haven? . . . . iii 5 153
Is he at home?—He went hence even now . . . . . iv 2 189
Gone! they went hence so soon as they were born . . . . v 4 126
I went to Antioch, Where as thou know'st, against the face of death, I sought the purchase of a glorious beauty . . . . *Pericles* i 2 70
Unless your thoughts went on my way . . . . . iv Gower 50
He went to bed to her very description . . . . . . iv 2 109

Went'st not thou to her for a purse of ducats? . . *Com. of Errors* iv 4 90
And thou, poor soul, Art then forsaken, as thou went'st forlorn! 3 *Hen. VI.* iii 1 54
Call thee back With twenty hundred thousand times more joy Than thou went'st forth in lamentation . . . . . *Rom. and Jul.* iii 3 154

Wept. I have inly wept, Or should have spoke ere this . . *Tempest* v 1 200
A Jew would have wept to have seen our parting . *T. G. of Ver.* ii 3 12
My grandam, having no eyes, look you, wept herself blind at my parting ii 3 14
To think upon her woes I do protest That I have wept . . . iv 4 150
My poor mistress, moved therewithal, Wept bitterly . . . . iv 4 176
Have you wept all this while?—Yea, and I will weep a while longer *Much Ado* iv 1 257
For the which she wept heartily and said she cared not . . . v 1 175
Made her neighbours believe she wept for the death of a third husband *Mer. of Venice* iii 1 11
In such manner that it seemed sorrow wept to take leave of them *W. T.* v 2 49
I would fain say, bleed tears, for I am sure my heart wept blood . v 2 97
So we wept, and there was the first gentleman-like tears that ever we shed . . . . v 2 155
Give me a cup of sack to make my eyes look red, that it may be thought I have wept . . . . 1 *Hen. IV.* ii 4 424
And when with grief he wept, The ruthless queen gave him to dry his cheeks A napkin . . . . 3 *Hen. VI.* ii 1 60
My father York and Edward wept, To hear the piteous moan *Richard III.* i 2 157
Tyrants themselves wept when it was reported . . . . . i 3 185
Northumberland, then present, wept to see it . . . . . i 3 187
He wept, And hugg'd me in his arm, and kindly kiss'd my cheek . ii 2 23
Good aunt, you wept not for our father's death . . . . ii 2 62
Wept like two children in their deaths' sad stories . . . . iv 3 8
Triumph not in my woes! God witness with me, I have wept for thine iv 4 60
That his bones, When he has run his course and sleeps in blessings, May have a tomb of orphans' tears wept on 'em! . . *Hen. VIII.* iii 2 399
For two and twenty sons I never wept, Because they died in honour's lofty bed . . . . *T. Andron.* iii 1 10
Let me say, that never wept before, My tears are now prevailing orators iii 1 25
When, for some trifling present, you have bid me Return so much, I have shook my head and wept . . . . . *T. of Athens* ii 2 146
When our vaults have wept With drunken spilth of wine . . . ii 2 168
When that the poor have cried, Cæsar hath wept . . *J. Cæsar* iii 2 96
He wept when at Philippi he found Brutus slain *Ant. and Cleo.* iii 2 55
What willingly he did confound he wail'd, Believe't, till I wept too . iii 2 59
Follow'd him, till he had melted from The smallness of a gnat to air, and then Have turn'd mine eye and wept . . . . *Cymbeline* i 3 22
I trod upon a worm against my will, But I wept for it . *Pericles* iv 1 80
We wept after her hearse, And yet we mourn . . . . . iv 3 41

Were. If I did think, sir, I were well awake, I'ld strive to tell you *Temp.* v 1 229
Why, ne'er repent it, if it were done so. But were you banish'd? *T. G. of Ver.* iv 1 30
His givings-out were of an infinite distance From his true-meant design *Meas. for Meas.* i 4 54
Were he my kinsman, brother, or my son, It should be thus with him . ii 2 81
Were he meal'd with that Which he corrects, then were he tyrannous . iv 2 86
One would think it were Mistress Overdone's own house . . iv 3 3
How dearly would it touch thee to the quick, Shouldst thou but hear I were licentious! . . . . *Com. of Errors* ii 2 133
Were she other than she is, she were unhandsome . . *Much Ado* i 1 176
I could say she were worse: think you of a worse title . . . ii 2 113
If there were a sympathy in choice, War, death, or sickness *M. N. Dream* i 1 141
Thou told'st me they were stolen unto this wood . . . . ii 1 191
An 'twere to me, I should be mad at it . . . *Mer. of Venice* v 1 176
Why, I were best to cut my left hand off And swear I lost the ring . v 1 177
Which never were nor no man ever saw . . . *T. of Shrew* Ind. 2 98
Were it not that my fellow-schoolmaster Doth watch Bianca's steps so narrowly, 'Twere good, methinks, to steal our marriage . . . iii 2 140
I tell thee, I am as well in my wits as any man in Illyria.—Well-a-day that you were, sir! . . . . *T. Night* iv 2 116
Most true, if ever truth were pregnant by circumstance . . *W. Tale* v 2 33

Were. If ever I were traitor, My name be blotted from the book of life! *Richard II.* i 3 201
I am a rogue, if I were not at half-sword with a dozen of them *1 Hen. IV.* ii 4 182
I am the sorrier; would 'twere otherwise. . . . *2 Hen. IV.* v 2 32
If the deed were ill, Be you contented . . . . v 2 83
That one day bloom'd and fruitful were the next . . *1 Hen. VI.* i 6 7
If ever any grudge were lodged between us . *Richard III.* ii 1 65
If 'twere not she, I cannot tell who told me . . . ii 4 34
If we did think His contemplation were above the earth *Hen. VIII.* iii 2 131
As 'twere in love's particular, be more To me, your friend, than any . iii 2 189
You were used To say extremity was the trier of spirits . *Coriolanus* iv 1 3
If ever Bassianus, Cæsar's son, Were gracious in the eyes of royal Rome *T. Andron.* i 1 11
If to fight for king and commonweal Were piety in thine, it is in these . i 1 115
And they it were that ravished our sister . . . . v 3 99
All have not offended; For those that were, it is not square to take On those that are, revenges . . . . . *T. of Athens* v 4 36
If it were so, it was a grievous fault . . . *J. Cæsar* iii 2 84
A king of infinite space, were it not that I have bad dreams . *Hamlet* ii 2 262
It hath been taught us from the primal state, That he which is was wish'd until he were . . . . . . *Ant. and Cleo.* i 4 42
Were't not that we stand up against them all, 'Twere pregnant they should square between themselves . . . . . ii 1 44
But that it eats our victuals, I should think Here were a fairy *Cymb.* iii 6 42
This most constant wife; who, even now, . . . were clipp'd about With this most tender air . . . . v 5 451
Wert. Thou wert immured, restrained, captivated, bound . *L. L. Lost* iii 1 125
What wert thou Till this madman show'd thee? and what art thou now? v 2 337
Either thou art most ignorant by age, Or thou wert born a fool *W. Tale* ii 1 174
The Welshmen, hearing thou wert dead, Are gone to Bolingbroke *Richard II.* iii 2 73
Vauntingly thou spakest it, That thou wert cause of noble Gloucester's death . . . . iv 1 37
I was a poor groom of thy stable, king, When thou wert king . v 5 73
Thou hast lost much honour, that thou wert not with me . *1 Hen. IV.* ii 4 22
And wert taken with the manner, and ever since thou hast blushed . ii 4 346
Why didst thou tell me that thou wert a king? . . . v 3 24
I would thou wert a man's tailor . . . . *2 Hen. IV.* iii 2 175
How wert thou handled being prisoner? . . . *1 Hen. VI.* i 4 24
Yet tell'st thou not how thou wert entertain'd. . . . i 4 38
Why didst thou say, of late thou wert despised? . . . ii 5 42
Done in the heart of France, When thou wert regent . *2 Hen. VI.* i 1 197
Since thou wert king—as who is king but thou? . . . i 3 126
Where wert thou born?—At Berwick in the north . . . ii 1 82
No less beloved Than when thou wert protector to thy king . . ii 3 27
Whom thou wert sworn to cherish and defend . . *Richard III.* i 4 213
His nurse! why, she was dead ere thou wert born . . . ii 4 33
Thou wert not wont to be so dull: Shall I be plain? . . iv 2 17
A dream of what thou wert, a breath, a bubble, A sign of dignity . iv 4 88
When wert thou wont to walk alone, Dishonour'd thus? . *T. Andron.* i 1 339
O, would thou wert as thou tofore hast been! . . . iii 1 294
Wert thou thus surprised, sweet girl? . . . . . iv 1 51
O thou Othello, that wert once so good . . . . *Othello* v 2 291
West. Go thou with her to the west end of the wood . *T. G. of Ver.* v 3 9
Dies ere the weary sun set in the west . . *Com. of Errors* i 2 7
It standeth north-north-east and by east from the west corner *L. L. Lost* i 1 249
By east, west, north, and south, I spread my conquering might . v 2 566
A certain aim he took At a fair vestal throned by the west *M. N. Dream* ii 1 158
West of this place, down in the neighbour bottom . *As Y. Like It* iv 3 79
There lies your way, due west.—Then westward-ho! . *T. Night* iii 1 145
'Tis powerful, think it, From east, west, north, and south . *W. Tale* i 2 203
Even till that utmost corner of the west Salute thee for her king *K. John* ii 1 29
By east and west let France and England mount Their battering cannon ii 1 381
We from the west will send destruction Into this city's bosom . ii 1 409
Thy sun sets weeping in the lowly west, Witnessing storms to come *Richard II.* ii 4 21
Send danger from the east unto the west, So honour cross it from the north to south, And let them grapple . . *1 Hen. IV.* i 3 195
From the orient to the drooping west, Making the wind my post-horse *2 Hen. IV.* Ind. 3
West of this forest, scarcely off a mile, In goodly form comes on the enemy . . . . iv 1 19
Like youthful steers unyoked, they take their courses East, west, north, south . . . . iv 2 104
And all the wealthy kingdoms of the west . . *2 Hen. VI.* i 1 154
What do they in the north, When they should serve their sovereign in the west? . . . . *Richard III.* iv 4 486
Here's a lord,—come knights from east to west, And cull their flower, Ajax shall cope the best . . . *Troi. and Cres.* ii 3 274
They have press'd a power, but it is not known Whether for east or west *Coriolanus* i 2 10
They would fly east, west, north, south . . . . ii 3 24
Such a waggoner As Phaëthon would whip you to the west *Rom. and Jul.* iii 2 3
The west yet glimmers with some streaks of day . *Macbeth* iii 3 5
This heavy-headed revel east and west Makes us traduced . *Hamlet* i 4 17
Put in every honest hand a whip To lash the rascals naked through the world Even from the east to the west! . . . . *Othello* iv 2 144
Wing'd From the spongy south to this part of the west . . *Cymbeline* iv 2 349
The Roman eagle, From south to west on wing soaring aloft, Lessen'd herself . . . . v 5 471
The imperial Cæsar should again unite His favour with the radiant Cymbeline, Which shines here in the west. . . . . . v 5 476
West Indies. They shall be my East and West Indies . *Mer. Wives* i 3 79
Westerly. Is this wind westerly that blows?—South-west *Pericles* iv 1 51
Western. The sun begins to gild the western sky . *T. G. of Ver.* v 1 1
Whose western side is with a vineyard back'd . *Meas. for Meas.* iv 1 29
It fell upon a little western flower, Before milk-white . *M. N. Dream* ii 1 166
My love shall hear the music of my hounds. Uncouple in the western valley . . . . iv 1 112
From the east to western Ind, No jewel is like Rosalind. *As Y. Like It* iii 2 93
The sun of heaven methought was loath to set, But stay'd and made the western welkin blush . . . . . . *K. John* v 5 2
Our glorious sun, Ere he attain his easeful western bed . *3 Hen. VI.* v 3 6
My gracious sovereign, on the western coast Rideth a puissant navy *Richard III.* iv 4 433
Are they not now upon the western shore? . . . . iv 4 482
From the western isles Of kerns and gallowglasses is supplied *Macbeth* i 2 12
Westminster, be it your charge To keep him safely . *Richard II.* iv 1 152
The grand conspirator, Abbot of Westminster. . . . v 6 19
What news?—The king your father is at Westminster . *2 Hen. IV.* ii 4 384
Westminster. Methought I sat in seat of majesty In the cathedral church of Westminster . . . . *2 Hen. VI.* i 2 37
And vows to crown himself in Westminster . . . . iv 4 31
Come, madam, you must straight to Westminster . *Richard. III.* iv 1 32
Westmoreland. Let me hear Of you, my gentle cousin Westmoreland *1 Hen. IV.* i 1 31
The Earl of Westmoreland set forth to-day; With him my son . iii 2 170
The Earl of Westmoreland, seven thousand strong, Is marching hither-wards . . . . iv 1 88
The noble Westmoreland and warlike Blunt; And many moe corrivals . iv 4 30
Deliver up my Lord of Westmoreland . . . . . v 2 29
A brave defiance in King Henry's teeth, And Westmoreland, that was engaged, did bear it . . . . v 2 44
We breathe too long: come, cousin Westmoreland, Our duty this way lies . . . . v 4 15
My cousin Westmoreland Towards York shall bend you with your dearest speed . . . . v 5 35
Young Prince John And Westmoreland and Stafford fled the field *2 Hen. IV.* i 1 18
Under the conduct of young Lancaster And Westmoreland . . . i 1 135
Say on, my Lord of Westmoreland, in peace: What doth concern your coming? . . . . iv 1 29
O Westmoreland, thou art a summer bird . . . . iv 4 91
My Lord of Westmoreland, and uncle Exeter, We will aboard to-night *Hen. V.* ii 2 70
What's he that wishes so? My cousin Westmoreland? . . . iv 3 19
Rather proclaim it, Westmoreland, through my host . . . iv 3 34
I cannot brook it.—Be patient, gentle Earl of Westmoreland . *3 Hen. VI.* i 1 61
And that the Lord of Westmoreland shall maintain . . . i 1 88
Westward. There's scarce a maid westward but she sings it . *W. Tale* iv 4 296
All westward, Wales beyond the Severn shore . . *1 Hen. IV.* iii 1 76
The grove of sycamore That westward rooteth from the city's side *Rom. and Jul.* i 1 129
When yond same star that's westward from the pole Had made his course *Hamlet* i 1 36
Westward-ho. There lies your way, due west.—Then westward-ho! *T. N.* iii 1 146
Wet. She at least is banish'd from your eye, Who hath cause to wet the grief on't . . . . *Tempest* ii 1 127
That the property of rain is to wet and fire to burn . *As Y. Like It* iii 2 27
This distemper'd messenger of wet, The many-colour'd Iris . *All's Well* i 3 157
The ruddiness upon her lip is wet; You'll mar it if you kiss it *W. Tale* v 3 81
Canst thou, O partial sleep, give thy repose To the wet sea-boy? *2 Hen. IV.* iii 1 27
O, you shall see him laugh till his face be like a wet cloak ill laid up! v 1 95
Nor let the rain of heaven wet this place . . *2 Hen. VI.* iii 2 341
And wet my cheeks with artificial tears . . *3 Hen. VI.* iii 2 184
That all the standers-by had wet their cheeks . *Richard III.* i 2 163
And wet his grave with my repentant tears . . . . i 2 216
When the rain came to wet me once, and the wind to make me chatter *Lear* iv 6 102
Be your tears wet? yes, 'faith. I pray, weep not . . . iv 7 71
'Tis a strange serpent.—'Tis so. And the tears of it are wet *A. and C.* ii 7 55
Who with wet cheeks Were present when she finish'd . *Cymbeline* v 5 35
Wether. I am a tainted wether of the flock, Meetest for death *Mer. of Ven.* iv 1 114
Every 'leven wether tods; every tod yields pound and odd shilling *W. T.* iv 3 33
Wetting. That's more to me than my wetting . . . *Tempest* iv 1 211
Wezand. Paunch him with a stake, Or cut his wezand with thy knife iii 2 99
Whale. This whale, with so many tuns of oil in his belly *Mer. Wives* ii 1 65
Smiles on every one, To show his teeth as white as whale's bone *L. L. Lost* v 2 332
Who is a whale to virginity and devours up all the fry it finds *All's Well* iv 3 249
Till that his passions, like a whale on ground, Confound themselves with working . . . . *2 Hen. IV.* iv 4 40
They fly or die, like scaled sculls Before the belching whale *Tr. and Cr.* v 5 23
It is backed like a weasel.—Or like a whale?—Very like a whale *Hamlet* iii 2 398
I can compare our rich misers to nothing so fitly as to a whale *Pericles* ii 1 33
Such whales have I heard on o' the land, who never leave gaping . ii 1 36
The belching whale And humming water must o'erwhelm thy corpse . iii 1 63
Wharf. Duller shouldst thou be than the fat weed That roots itself in ease on Lethe wharf . . . . *Hamlet* i 5 33
From the barge A strange invisible perfume hits the sense Of the adjacent wharfs . . . . *Ant. and Cleo.* ii 2 218
What. Thee, my daughter, who Art ignorant of what thou art *Tempest* i 2 18
Wherefore this ghastly looking?—What's the matter? . . . ii 1 309
I do beseech you—Chiefly that I might set it in my prayers—What is your name? . . . . iii 1 36
What with the gallows and what with poverty, I am custom-shrunk *Meas. for Meas.* i 2 84
With an outstretch'd throat I'll tell the world aloud What man thou art ii 4 154
What's mine is yours and what is yours is mine . . . v 1 543
What, will you walk with me about the town? . *Com. of Errors* i 2 22
What now? how chance thou art return'd so soon? . . . i 2 42
What is he for a fool that betroths himself to unquietness? . *Much Ado* i 3 49
All this is so: but what of this, my lord? . . . . iv 1 73
What we have we prize not to the worth Whiles we enjoy it . . iv 1 220
But what, but what, come they to visit us? . . . *L. L. Lost* v 2 119
I am thought as fair as she. But what of that? . *M. N. Dream* i 1 228
What news on the Rialto? . . . . . . *Mer. of Venice* i 3 39
And what of him? did he take interest? . . . . i 3 76
O father Abram, what these Christians are! . . . . i 3 162
Nor no ill luck stirring but what lights on my shoulders . . iii 1 99
Call you 'em stanzos?—What you will, Monsieur Jaques . *As Y. Like It* ii 5 20
What! this gentleman will out-talk us all . . . *T. of Shrew* i 2 248
And, to be short, what not, that's sweet and happy? . . . v 2 110
But what of that? if it please the eye of one . . *T. Night* iii 4 23
I love thee not a jar o' the clock behind What lady-she her lord *W. Tale* i 2 44
What now, my son! have I not ever said? . . . *K. John* i 1 31
Look, what I speak, my life shall prove it true . *Richard II.* i 1 87
Well, come what will, I'll tarry at home . . . *1 Hen. IV.* i 2 162
What a plague mean ye to colt me thus? . . . . ii 2 39
I tell thee what, Hal, if I tell thee a lie, spit in my face . . ii 4 214
What tell you me of it? be it as it is . . . *2 Hen. IV.* i 2 129
What! canst thou not forbear me half an hour? . . . iv 5 110
Be what thou wilt, thou art my prisoner . . . *1 Hen. VI.* v 3 45
Is it but thought so? what are they that think it? . *2 Hen. VI.* iii 1 107
With promise of his sister, and what else . . *3 Hen. VI.* iii 1 51
Ay, what of that? it was my will and grant . . . . iv 1 49
Let me put in your minds, if you forget, What you have been ere now, and what you are; Withal, what I have been, and what I am *Rich. III.* i 3 132
What! were you snarling all before I came? . . . . i 3 188
What, shall we toward the Tower? the day is spent . . . iii 2 91
Having no more but thought of what thou wert . . . . iv 4 107

What. What! we have many goodly days to see . . *Richard III.* iv 4 320
What need you note it? pray you, keep your way . . *Hen. VIII.* ii 4 128
What is aught, but as 'tis valued? . . . *Troi. and Cres.* ii 2 52
And what one thing, what another, that I shall leave you . v 3 103
What says she there?—Words, words, mere words . . v 3 107
What ever have been thought on in this state? . . *Coriolanus* i 2 4
What must I do?—Return to the tribunes.—Well, what then? what then? iii 2 35
I'll tell thee what; yet go: Nay, but thou shalt stay too . iv 2 22
What then?—What then! He'd make an end of thy posterity . iv 2 25
What should I don this robe, and trouble you? . . . *T. Andron.* i 1 189
I made thee miserable What time I threw the people's suffrages On him iv 3 19
How canst thou believe an oath?—What if I do not? . . v 1 73
What boots it thee to call thyself a sun? . . . . v 3 18
What dares the slave Come hither, cover'd with an antic face? *R. and J.* i 5 57
This trick may chance to scathe you, I know what . . . i 5 86
What is her mother?—Marry, bachelor, Her mother is the lady of the house . . . . i 5 114
She speaks, yet she says nothing: what of that? . . . ii 2 12
What if her eyes were there, they in her head? . . . ii 2 18
What's in a name? that which we call a rose By any other name would smell as sweet . . . . ii 2 43
I tell thee what: get thee to church o' Thursday . . . iii 5 162
What if this mixture do not work at all? . . . . iv 3 21
To have his pomp and all what state compounds But only painted *T. of Athens* iv 2 35
What you would work me to, I have some aim . . . *J. Cæsar* i 2 163
What you have said I will consider; what you have to say I will with patience hear . . . . i 2 167
What night is this!—A very pleasing night to honest men . . i 3 42
What's to do?—A piece of work that will make sick men whole . ii 1 326
What it is, my Caius, I shall unfold to thee, as we are going . ii 1 329
What now, Lucilius! is Cassius near?—He is at hand . . iv 2 3
What thou wouldst highly, That wouldst thou holily . *Macbeth* i 5 21
What man dare, I dare: Approach thou like the rugged Russian bear . iii 4 99
What is the night?—Almost at odds with morning . . . iii 4 126
What you have spoke, it may be so perchance . . . . iv 3 11
Fear not yet To take upon you what is yours . . . . iv 3 70
What's he That was not born of woman? Such a one Am I to fear . v 7 2
What, is Horatio there?—A piece of him . . . . *Hamlet* i 1 19
So fortified against our story What we have two nights seen . . i 1 33
What a piece of work is a man! how noble in reason! . . ii 2 315
What will hap more to-night, safe 'scape the king! . . *Lear* iii 6 121
What in the world he is That names me traitor, villain-like he lies . v 3 97
Her length of sickness, with what else more serious Importeth thee *Ant. and Cleo.* i 2 124
What should I stay— In this vile world? . . . . v 2 316
What shall I need to draw my sword? . . . *Cymbeline* iii 4 34
What mortality is! . . . . iv 1 16
Jove knows what man thou mightst have made . . . iv 2 207
What thing is it that I never Did see man die! . . . iv 4 35
Be what it is, The action of my life is like it, which I'll keep . v 4 149
What though? yet I live like a poor gentleman born *Mer. Wives* i 1 286
What though care kill'd a cat, thou hast mettle enough in thee to kill care *Much Ado* v 1 132
What though he love your Hermia? Lord, what though? *M. N. Dream* ii 2 109
What though I be not so in grace as you? . . . . iii 2 232
But what though? Courage! . . . . . *As Y. Like It* iii 3 51
What though you have no beauty,— . . . Must you be therefore proud? iii 5 37
Call me so.—Madam, by chance but not by truth; what though? *K. John* i 1 169
It is a simple one; but what though? it will toast cheese . *Hen. V.* ii 1 9
What though I be enthrall'd? he seems a knight . . *1 Hen. VI.* v 3 101
What though the common people favour him? . . . *2 Hen. VI.* i 1 158
What though the mast be now blown overboard? . . *3 Hen. VI.* v 4 3
What though I know her virtuous And well-deserving? . *Hen. VIII.* iii 2 97
Whatever. Take no repulse, whatever she doth say . . *T. G. of Ver.* iii 1 100
I grant it, for thine own, whate'er it be . . . . v 4 151
Whate'er I read to her, I'll plead for you As for my patron *T. of Shrew* i 2 155
These I will assure her, And twice as much, whate'er thou offer'st next ii 1 382
Means but well, Whatever fortune stays him from his word . . iii 2 23
I am to get a man,—whate'er he be, It skills not much . . iii 2 133
Whate'er the course, the end is the renown . . *All's Well* iv 4 36
And you shall find yourself to be well thank'd, Whate'er falls more . v 1 37
I'll forgive you, Whatever torment you do put me to . . *K. John* iv 1 84
Whate'er you think, good words, I think, were best . . . iv 3 28
But also to effect Whatever I shall happen to devise . *Richard II.* iv 1 330
Whate'er I be, Nor I nor any man that but man is With nothing shall be pleased, till he be eased With being nothing . . . . v 5 38
Omit All the occurrences, whatever chanced . . . *Hen. V.* v Prol. 40
Whate'er we like, thou art protector . . . . *1 Hen. VI.* i 1 37
Whate'er occasion keeps him from us now . . . *2 Hen. VI.* iii 1 3
Scorning whate'er you can afflict me with . . . *3 Hen. VI.* i 4 38
Whate'er it bodes, henceforward will I bear Upon my target three fair-shining suns . . . . ii 1 39
Whate'er it be, be thou still like thyself . . . . iii 3 15
Whatever praises itself but in the deed, devours the deed *Troi. and Cres.* ii 3 166
If not Achilles, nothing.—Therefore Achilles: but, whate'er, know this iv 5 77
My sight is very dull, whate'er it bodes . . . *T. Andron.* ii 3 195
Whate'er I forge to feed his brain-sick fits, Do you uphold . . v 2 71
Whate'er thou hear'st or seest, stand all aloof . . *Rom. and Jul.* v 3 26
Whate'er thou art, for thy good caution, thanks . . *Macbeth* iv 1 73
You may be rightly just, Whatever I shall think . . . iv 3 31
Whatever shall become of Michael Cassio, He's never any thing but your true servant . . . . *Othello* iii 3 8
Be as your fancies teach you; Whate'er you be, I am obedient . . v 3 89
Whate'er the ocean pales, or sky inclips, Is thine . *Ant. and Cleo.* ii 7 74
Fare thee well, dame, whate'er becomes of me . . . iv 4 29
Would I could free't!—Or I, whate'er it be, What pain it cost *Cymbeline* iii 6 80
Whate'er it be, 'Tis wondrous heavy . . . . . *Pericles* iii 2 52
Let's have fresh ones, whate'er we pay for them . . . iv 2 10
Whatsoever I have merited, either in my mind or in my means, meed, I am sure, I have received none . . . . . *Mer. Wives* ii 2 210
Let me not find you before me again upon any complaint whatsoever *Meas. for Meas.* ii 1 261
Whatsoever you may hear to the contrary . . . . iv 2 123
Whatsoever a man denies, you are now bound to believe him *Com. of Er.* v 1 305
Whatsoever comes athwart his affection ranges evenly with mine *M. Ado* ii 2 6
And bear his charge of wooing, whatsoe'er . . *T. of Shrew* i 2 216
I'll assure her of Her widowhood, be it that she survive me, In all my lands and leases whatsoever . . . . ii 1 126
[Good] As any man in Illyria, whatsoever he be . . . *T. Night* i 3 124
Whatsoever. Whatsoever thou art, thou art but a scurvy fellow *T. Night* iii 4 162
Whatsoever cunning fiend it was That wrought upon thee . *Hen. V.* ii 2 111
Rude companion, whatsoe'er thou be, I know thee not . *2 Hen. VI.* iv 10 33
Whatsoever you will employ me in, . . . I will perform it *Richard III.* i 1 108
To doom the offenders, whatsoever they be . . . . iii 4 67
To forfeit all your goods, lands, tenements, Chattels, and whatsoever *Hen. VIII.* iii 2 343
Whatsoe'er thou takest me for, I'm sure Thou hast a cruel nature . v 3 128
As if that whatsoever god who leads him Were slily crept into his human powers And gave him graceful posture . . . . *Coriolanus* ii 1 235
That whatsoever I did bid thee do, Thou shouldst attempt it *J. Cæsar* v 3 39
Whatsoever else shall hap to-night, Give it an understanding, but no tongue . . . . *Hamlet* i 2 249
A banished rascal; and he's another, whatsoever he be . . *Cymbeline* ii 1 43
Whatsome'er he is, He's bravely taken here . . . *All's Well* iii 5 54
All men's faces are true, whatsome'er their hands are *Ant. and Cleo.* ii 6 102
What-ye-call't. God even, good Master What-ye-call't . *As Y. Like It* iii 3 74
Wheat. Thy rich leas Of wheat, rye, barley, vetches, oats, and pease *Tempest* iv 1 61
When wheat is green, when hawthorn buds appear . . *M. N. Dream* i 1 185
His reasons are as two grains of wheat hid in two bushels of chaff *Mer. of Venice* i 1 115
Shall we sow the headland with wheat?—With red wheat, Davy *2 Hen. IV.* v 1 16
He that will have a cake out of the wheat must needs tarry the grinding.—Have I not tarried? . . . . *Troi. and Cres.* i 1 15
Mildews the white wheat, and hurts the poor creature of earth *Lear* iii 4 123
I must Rid all the sea of pirates; then, to send Measures of wheat to Rome; this 'greed upon . . . . . . *Ant. and Cleo.* ii 6 37
Wheaten. As peace should still her wheaten garland wear *Hamlet* v 2 41
Wheel. Then may I set the world on wheels, when she can spin for her living . . . . *T. G. of Ver.* iii 1 317
What, at the wheels of Cæsar? art thou led in triumph? *Meas. for Meas.* iii 2 46
Transformed me to a curtal dog and made me turn i' the wheel *C. of Er.* iii 2 151
Before the wheels of Phœbus, round about Dapples the drowsy east *Much Ado* v 3 26
Let us sit and mock the good housewife Fortune from her wheel *As Y. Like It* i 2 35
What wheels? racks? fires? what flaying? boiling? In leads or oils? *W. Tale* iii 2 177
I had rather hear a brazen canstick turn'd, Or a dry wheel grate on the axle-tree . . . . *1 Hen. IV.* iii 1 132
Would not this nave of a wheel have his ears cut off? . *2 Hen. IV.* ii 4 278
By cruel fate, And giddy Fortune's furious fickle wheel . . *Hen. V.* iii 6 29
Fortune is blind; and she is painted also with a wheel . . iii 6 35
My thoughts are whirled like a potter's wheel . . . *1 Hen. VI.* i 5 19
Though fortune's malice overthrow my state, My mind exceeds the compass of her wheel . . . . *3 Hen. VI.* iv 3 47
Mark what I say. Attend me where I wheel . . *Troi. and Cres.* v 7 2
I was forced to wheel Three or four miles about . . *Coriolanus* i 6 19
Present me Death on the wheel or at wild horses' heels . . iii 2 2
And flecked darkness like a drunkard reels From forth day's path and Titan's fiery wheels . . . . *Rom. and Jul.* ii 3 4
Break all the spokes and fellies from her [Fortune's] wheel, And bowl the round nave down the hill of heaven . . . . *Hamlet* ii 2 517
It is a massy wheel, Fix'd on the summit of the highest mount . iii 3 17
O, how the wheel becomes it! It is the false steward . . iv 5 172
Fortune, good night: smile once more; turn thy wheel! . *Lear* ii 2 180
Let go thy hold when a great wheel runs down a hill . . ii 4 73
Thou art a soul in bliss; but I am bound Upon a wheel of fire . iv 7 47
The wheel is come full circle; I am here . . . . v 3 174
Would it were all, That it might go on wheels! . *Ant. and Cleo.* ii 7 99
Let me rail so high, That the false housewife Fortune break her wheel, Provoked by my offence . . . . iv 15 44
And would so, had it been a carbuncle Of Phœbus' wheel . *Cymbeline* v 5 190
Wheeled. Thus hath the course of justice wheel'd about . *Richard III.* iv 4 105
Whilst the wheel'd seat Of fortunate Cæsar, drawn before him, branded His baseness that ensued . . . . . *Ant. and Cleo.* iv 14 75
Wheeling. Tying her duty, beauty, wit, and fortunes In an extravagant and wheeling stranger . . . . *Othello* i 1 137
Wheeson. Upon Wednesday in Wheeson week . . . *2 Hen. IV.* ii 1 96
Wheezing. Raw eyes, dirt-rotten livers, wheezing lungs . *Troi. and Cres.* v 1 24
Whelk. His face is all bubukles, and whelks, and knobs . *Hen. V.* iii 6 108
Whelked. Horns whelk'd and waved like the enridged sea . *Lear* iv 6 71
Whelm. She is my prize, or ocean whelm them all! . *Mer. Wives* ii 2 143
Whelp. A freckled whelp hag-born—not honour'd with A human shape *Tempest* i 2 283
I fear thee as I fear the roaring of the lion's whelp . *1 Hen. IV.* iii 3 167
Stood smiling to behold his lion's whelp Forage in blood . *Hen. V.* i 2 109
They call'd us for our fierceness English dogs; Now, like to whelps, we crying run away . . . . *1 Hen. VI.* i 5 26
How the young whelp of Talbot's, raging-wood, Did flesh his puny sword in Frenchmen's blood! . . . . iv 7 35
Two of thy whelps, fell curs of bloody kind, Have here bereft my brother of his life . . . . *T. Andron.* ii 3 281
'Tis better playing with a lion's whelp Than with an old one dying *Ant. and Cleo.* iii 13 94
When as a lion's whelp shall, to himself unknown, without seeking find *Cymbeline* v 4 138; v 5 435
Thou, Leonatus, art the lion's whelp . . . . . v 5 443
Whelped. Thou wast whelped a dog, and thou shalt famish a dog's death *T. of Athens* ii 2 90
A lioness hath whelped in the streets . . . . *J. Cæsar* ii 2 17
When. Nay, good, be patient.—When the sea is . . . *Tempest* i 1 17
There's other business for thee: Come, thou tortoise! when? . . i 2 316
Courtsied when you have and kiss'd The wild waves whist . . i 2 378
You rub the sore, When you should bring the plaster . . . ii 1 139
When did you lose your daughter?—In this last tempest . . v 1 152
Till when, be cheerful And think of each thing well . . . v 1 250
What a thing should I have been when I had been swelled! *Mer. Wives* iii 5 17
I have seen, When, after execution, judgement hath Repented *M. for M.* ii 2 11
When spake I such a word?—Even now, even here . *Com. of Errors* ii 2 13
The time was once when thou unurged wouldst vow . . . ii 2 115
I'll tell you when, an you'll tell me wherefore . . . . ii 1 39
I may say so, when I please.—And when please you to say so? *Much Ado* ii 1 95
I have known when there was no music with him but the drum . ii 3 13
I have known when he would have walked ten mile a-foot . . ii 3 16
I know When thou hast stolen away from fairy land . *M. N. Dream* ii 1 65
Have to wife this Rosalind?—I will.—Ay, but when? . *As Y. Like It* iv 1 133
I knew when seven justices could not take up a quarrel . . v 4 103
When, Harry, when? Obedience bids I should not bid again *Richard II.* i 1 162

When. I pray thee, lend me thine.—Ay, when? canst tell? . 1 *Hen. IV.* ii 1 43
Since when, his oath is broke . . . . . 3 *Hen. VI.* ii 2 89
Thou anon shalt hear of me again ; Till when, go seek thy fortune *Troi. and Cres.* v 6 19
When and where and how We met, we woo'd, and made exchange of vow, I'll tell thee as we pass . . . *Rom and Jul.* ii 3 61
When, Lucius, when? awake, I say! what, Lucius! . *J. Cæsar* ii 1 5
When as your husband all in rage to-day Came to my house *Com. of Errors* iv 4 140
Many a battle have I won in France, When as the enemy hath been ten to one . . . . 3 *Hen. VI.* i 2 75
A woful looker-on When as the noble Duke of York was slain . ii 1 46
So Judas kiss'd his master, And cried 'all hail!' when as he meant all harm . . . . v 7 34
When as the one is wounded with the bait, The other rotted *T. Andron.* iv 4 92
When as a lion's whelp shall . . . without seeking find *Cymb.* v 4 138 ; v 5 435
Whence. Nought knowing Of whence I am . . *Tempest* i 2 19
Tell me, how do all from whence you came? . . *T. G. of Ver.* ii 4 122
Whither travel you?—To Verona.—Whence came you?—From Milan iv 1 18
Whence comes this restraint?—From too much liberty *Meas. for Meas.* i 2 128
Bliss and goodness on you!—Of whence are you? . . . iii 2 229
Lend him your kind pains To find out this abuse, whence 'tis derived v 1 247
Let him walk from whence he came, lest he catch cold on's feet *C. of Er.* iii 1 37
From whence, I think, you are come by miracle . . . v 1 264
The academes From whence doth spring the true Promethean fire *L. L. L.* iv 3 304
She's in earth, from whence God send her quickly! . *All's Well* ii 4 13
Whence honour but of danger wins a scar, As oft it loses all . iii 2 124
From whence, set forth in pomp, She came adorned hither *Richard II.* v 1 78
From whence he intercepted did return To be deposed . 1 *Hen. IV.* i 3 151
What tumult's in the heavens? Whence cometh this alarum? 1 *Hen. VI.* i 4 99
Disperse that cloud And blow it to the source from whence it came 3 *Hen. VI.* v 3 11
Whence men have read His fame unparallel'd . . *Coriolanus* v 2 15
Our poesy is as a gum, which oozes From whence 'tis nourish'd *T. of A.* i 1 22
As whence the sun 'gins his reflection Shipwrecking storms and direful thunders break, So from that spring whence comfort seem'd to come Discomfort swells . . . . *Macbeth* i 2 25
'Tis now the time To ask of whence you are . . *Cymbeline* v 5 16
Tell him, we desire to know of him, Of whence he is . *Pericles* ii 3 74
Whencesoever. It is my son, young Harry Percy, Sent from my brother Worcester, whencesoever . . . . *Richard II.* ii 3 22
Whenever. And that shall be the day, whene'er it lights 1 *Hen. IV.* iii 2 138
Whenever Buckingham doth turn his hate On you or yours *Rich. III.* ii 1 32
He hath left undone That which shall break his neck or hazard mine, Whene'er we come to our account . . *Coriolanus* iv 7 26
That, whenever you have need, You may be armed . *T. Andron.* iv 2 15
Whensoever. And all probation will make up full clear, Whensoever he's convented . . . . *Meas. for Meas.* v 1 158
Now or whensoever, provided I be so able as now . . *Hamlet* v 2 210
Where the bee sucks, there suck I : In a cowslip's bell I lie . *Tempest* v 1 88
To be in love, where scorn is bought with groans . *T. G. of Ver.* i 1 29
Where your good word cannot advantage him, Your slander never can endamage him . . . . iii 2 42
O, 'tis the curse in love, and still approved, When women cannot love where they're beloved! . . . . v 4 44
Look where he comes ; and my good man too . . *Mer. Wives* ii 1 106
Other some [say] he is in Rome : but where is he, think you?—I know not where ; but wheresoever, I wish him well . *Meas. for Meas.* iii 2 94
Where that you have vow'd to study, lords, In that each of you have forsworn his book, Can you still dream? . . . *L. L. Lost* iv 3 296
Where I have come, great clerks have purposed To greet me *M. N. Dream* v 1 93
Why, this is like the mending of highways In summer, where the ways are fair enough . . . . *Mer. of Venice* v 1 264
O, I know where you are : nay, 'tis true . . . *As Y. Like It* v 2 32
An I had thee in place where, thou shouldst know it . *T. of Shrew* iv 3 151
A savour that may strike the dullest nostril Where I arrive . *W. Tale* i 2 422
Get you hence, for I must go Where it fits not you to know . iv 4 304
You have broken from his liking Where you were tied in duty . v 1 213
Where fearing dying pays death servile breath . . *Richard II.* iii 2 185
Where, when, and how, Camest thou by this ill tidings? . . iii 4 79
Dieu de batailles! where have they this mettle? . . *Hen. V.* iii 5 15
Where that his lords desire him to have borne His bruised helmet v Prol. 17
Unto Saint Alban's, Where as the king and queen do mean to hawk 2 *Hen. VI.* i 2 58
Where thou art, there is the world itself . . . . . iii 2 362
But see where Somerset and Clarence comes! . . 3 *Hen. VI.* iv 2 3
He is in heaven, where thou shalt never come . . *Richard III.* i 2 106
Where is thy husband now? where be thy brothers? Where are thy children? . . . . iv 4 92
Where be the bending peers that flatter'd thee? Where be the thronging troops that follow'd thee? . . . . iv 4 95
In a strait so narrow, Where one but goes abreast . *Troi. and Cres.* iii 3 155
Here, there, and every where, he leaves and takes . . . v 5 26
Where against My grained ash an hundred times hath broke *Coriolanus* iv 5 113
I am not here ; This is not Romeo, he's some other where *Rom. and Jul.* i 1 204
When and where and how We met, we woo'd, and made exchange of vow ii 3 61
I have heard, Where many of the best respect . . . Have wish'd *J. Cæsar* i 2 59
As little is the wisdom, where the flight So runs against all reason *Macb.* iv 2 13
Where is your husband?—I hope, in no place so unsanctified Where such as thou mayst find him . . . . iv 2 82
But soft, behold! lo, where it comes again! . . . *Hamlet* i 1 126
Thou losest here, a better where to find . . . . . *Lear* i 1 264
Where he arrives he moves All hearts against us . . . iv 5 10
A mighty strength they carry.—Where have you this? 'tis false *Ant. and Cleo.* ii 1 18
Whereabout. I must not have you henceforth question me Whither I go, nor reason whereabout . . . . . 1 *Hen. IV.* ii 3 107
For fear Thy very stones prate of my whereabout . *Macbeth* ii 1 58
Whereas I was black and swart before . . . 1 *Hen. VI.* i 2 84
Whereas he From John of Gaunt doth bring his pedigree . ii 5 76
Whereas the contrary bringeth bliss . . . . . . v 5 64
Whereas, before, our forefathers had no other books but the score and the tally, thou hast caused printing to be used . 2 *Hen. VI.* iv 7 37
Whereas reproof, obedient and in order, Fits kings . . *Pericles* i 2 42
Whereas no glory's got to overcome . . . . . . i 4 70
Whereat, with blade, with bloody blameful blade, He bravely broach'd his boiling bloody breast . . . . . *M. N. Dream* v 1 147
Whereat the great Lord of Northumberland, Whose warlike ears could never brook retreat, Cheer'd up the drooping army . 3 *Hen. VI.* ii 1 4
Thou hast done a deed whereat valour will weep . *Coriolanus* v 6 134
To behold The thing whereat it trembles by surmise . *T. Andron.* ii 3 219
Whereat. Henceforth be no feast, Whereat a villain's not a welcome guest . . . . *T. of Athens* iii 6 113
Whereat grieved, That so his sickness, age, and impotence Was falsely borne in hand, sends out arrests . . . . . *Hamlet* ii 2 65
Whereat I, wretch, Made scruple of his praise . . *Cymbeline* v 5 181
Whereby. You take my life When you do take the means whereby I live *Mer. of Venice* iv 1 377
By this light, whereby I see thy beauty . . *T. of Shrew* ii 1 275
Whereby we stand opposed by such means As you yourself have forged 1 *Hen. IV.* v 1 67
Whereby thou didst desire to eat some ; whereby I told thee they were ill for a green wound . . . . . . 2 *Hen. IV.* ii 1 104
Or when a man is, being, whereby a' may be thought to be accommodated . . . . iii 2 86
Until that act . . . be repeal'd Whereby my son is disinherited 3 *Hen. VI.* i 1 250
Whereby his suit was granted Ere it was ask'd . . *Hen. VIII.* i 1 186
From me receive that natural competency Whereby they live *Coriolanus* i 1 144
Use our hearts, whereby we might express some part of our zeals *T. of A.* i 2 88
Whereby he does receive Particular addition . . . *Macbeth* iii 1 99
Thereby hangs a tail.—Whereby hangs a tale, sir? . . *Othello* iii 1 9
Whereby I see that Time's the king of men . . . *Pericles* ii 3 45
Wherefore did they not That hour destroy us? . . . *Tempest* i 2 138
Wherefore weep you?—At mine unworthiness . . . . iii 1 76
But wherefore waste I time to counsel thee? . . *T. G. of Ver.* i 1 51
I cannot choose But pity her.—Wherefore shouldst thou pity her? . iv 4 83
Wherefore ; for they say every why hath a wherefore *Com. of Errors* ii 2 44
Wherefore,—For urging it the second time to me . . . ii 2 46
When in the why and the wherefore is neither rhyme nor reason . ii 2 49
I'll tell you when, an you'll tell me wherefore . . . iii 1 39
Say, wherefore didst thou lock me forth to-day? . . . iv 4 98
And wherefore are you gentle, strong, and valiant? . *As Y. Like It* ii 3 6
Wherefore are these things hid? wherefore have these gifts a curtain before 'em? are they like to take dust? . . . *T. Night* i 3 133
But wherefore do you droop? why look you sad? . . *K. John* v 1 44
Wherefore was I born? . . . . . . *Richard II.* ii 3 122
Peace to this meeting, wherefore we are met! . . . *Hen. V.* v 2 1
Wherefore a guard of chosen shot I had . . . 1 *Hen. VI.* i 4 53
O Romeo, Romeo! wherefore art thou Romeo? Deny thy father *Rom. and Jul.* ii 2 33
Wherein all my thoughts Are visibly character'd . *T. G. of Ver.* ii 7 3
Wherein I must very much lay open mine own imperfection *Mer. Wives* ii 2 190
Yea, my gravity, Wherein—let no man hear me—I take pride *M. for M.* ii 4 10
Wherein have I so deserved of you, That you extol me thus? . . v 1 507
Wherein it doth impair the seeing sense, It pays the hearing double recompense . . . . *M. N. Dream* iii 2 179
Wherein my time something too prodigal Hath left me gaged *M. of Ven.* i 1 129
I swear to thee, even by thine own fair eyes, Wherein I see myself . v 1 243
Let me see wherein My tongue hath wrong'd him . *As Y. Like It* ii 7 83
What said he? How looked he? Wherein went he? What makes he here? . . . . iii 2 234
I have some sport in hand Wherein your cunning can assist me *T. of Shrew* Ind. 1 92
A fit man to teach her that wherein she delights . . . i 1 113
Wherein have you played the knave with fortune, that she should scratch you, who of herself is a good lady? . . . *All's Well* v 2 31
Thou art a wickedness, Wherein the pregnant enemy does much *T. Night* ii 2 29
Wherein our entertainment shall shame us we will be justified in our loves . . . . *W. Tale* i 1 9
Let me know my fault : On what condition stands it and wherein? *Richard II.* ii 3 107
Yet time serves wherein you may redeem Your banish'd honours 1 *Hen. IV.* i 3 180
Wherein crafty, but in villany? wherein villanous, but in all things? wherein worthy, but in nothing? . . . . ii 4 503
Wherein the fortune of ten thousand men Must bide the touch . iv 4 9
Wherein have you been galled by the king? . . 2 *Hen. IV.* iv 1 89
Wherein, my friends, have I offended you?—Offended us you have not *Richard III.* i 4 182
Councils, Wherein thyself shalt highly be employ'd . . . iii 1 180
Wherein my soul recorded The history of all her secret thoughts . iii 5 27
Taxation! Wherein? and what taxation? . . . *Hen. VIII.* i 2 38
By this declension, Into the madness wherein now he raves *Hamlet* ii 2 150
Wherein necessity, of matter beggar'd, Will nothing stick our person to arraign . . . . iv 5 92
Whereinto. Where's that palace whereinto foul things Sometimes intrude not? . . . . *Othello* iii 3 137
Whereof. To perform an act Whereof what's past is prologue . *Tempest* ii 1 253
What stuff 'tis made of, whereof it is born, I am to learn *Mer. of Venice* i 1 4
Whereof who chooses his meaning chooses you . . . i 2 34
I charge you by the law, Whereof you are a well-deserving pillar . iv 1 239
In sign whereof, Please ye we may contrive this afternoon . *T. of Shrew* i 2 275
In those sciences, Whereof I know she is not ignorant . . ii 1 58
My love hath in't a bond, Whereof the world takes note . . *All's Well* i 3 195
To cure the desperate languishings whereof The king is render'd lost . i 3 235
Whereof the execution did cry out Against the non-performance *W. Tale* i 2 260
In haste whereof, most heartily I pray Your highness to assign our trial day . . . . *Richard II.* i 1 150
The revenue whereof shall furnish us For our affairs in hand . . 4 46
Whereof a little More than a little is by much too much 1 *Hen. IV.* iii 2 72
The taste whereof, God of his mercy give You patience to endure! *Hen. V.* ii 2 179
The enterprise whereof Shall be to you, as us, like glorious . ii 2 182
By the means whereof a' breaks words, and keeps whole weapons . . iii 2 37
What is that wrong whereof you both complain? . . 1 *Hen. VI.* iv 1 87
By means whereof his highness hath lost France . 2 *Hen. VI.* i 1 106
Instead whereof let this supply the room . . . 3 *Hen. VI.* ii 6 54
Every action that hath gone before, Whereof we have record . *Tr. and Cr.* i 3 14
The breath is gone whereof this praise is made . . *T. of Athens* i 2 179
Whereof ingrateful man . . . greases his pure mind . . iv 3 194
Now, gods that we adore, whereof comes this? . . . *Lear* i 4 312
His bed my gaol ; from the loathed warmth whereof deliver me . iv 6 273
Whereon. To that Whereon this month I have been hammering *T. G. of V.* i 3 18
The state, whereon I studied, Is like a good thing . *Meas. for Meas.* ii 4 7
And rock the ground whereon these sleepers be . . *M. N. Dream* iv 1 91
Tell me whereon the likelihood depends . . . *As Y. Like It* i 3 59
On the like occasion whereon my services are now on foot . *W. Tale* i 1 2
Whereon this Hydra son of war is born . . . 2 *Hen. IV.* iv 2 38
Whereon, as an offender to your father, I gave bold way . . v 2 81
Your franchises, whereon you stood, confined Into an auger's bore *Cor.* iv 6 86
We see the ground whereon these woes do lie . . *Rom. and Jul.* v 3 179
Infected be the air whereon they ride! . . . . . *Macbeth* iv 1 138

Whereon. Whereon his brains still beating puts him thus From fashion of himself . . . . . . *Hamlet* iii 1 182
Whereon do you look?—On him, on him! Look you, how pale he glares! . . . . . . iii 4 124
Fight for a plot Whereon the numbers cannot try the cause . . . iv 4 63
A chalice for the nonce, whereon but sipping, If he by chance escape your venom'd stuck, Our purpose may hold there . . . iv 7 161
Whereon it came That I was cast . . . . *Othello* v 2 326
Whereout. And make distinct the very breach whereout Hector's great spirit flew . . . . . *Troi. and Cres.* iv 5 245
Wheresoever. I know not where; but wheresoever, I wish him well *Meas. for Meas.* iii 2 96
Happy is Hermia, wheresoe'er she lies . . . *M. N. Dream* ii 2 90
Wheresoe'er we went, like Juno's swans, Still we went coupled *As Y. L. It* i 3 77
Find out thy brother, wheresoe'er he is; Seek him with candle . iii 1 5
Good creature, wheresoe'er she is, Her heart weighs sadly *All's Well* iii 5 69
And wheresoe'er this foot of mine doth tread, He lies before me *K. John* iii 3 62
For wheresoe'er thou art in this world's globe, I'll have an Iris that shall find thee out. . . . . *2 Hen. VI.* iii 2 406
And wheresoe'er he is, he's surely dead . . . *3 Hen. VI.* ii 6 41
With resolution, wheresoe'er I meet thee, . . . To plague thee . v 1 95
Poor naked wretches, wheresoe'er you are, That bide the pelting of this pitiless storm . . . . . *Lear* iii 4 28
Wheresoever you had it, I'll take out no work on't. . *Othello* iv 1 160
Wheresomever. Would I were with him, wheresome'er he is! *Hen. V.* ii 3 7
Whereto if you'll a willing ear incline, What's mine is yours and what is yours is mine . . . . . *Meas. for Meas.* v 1 542
Whereto tends all this? . . . . . *M. N. Dream* iii 2 256
Whereto thy speech serves for authority . . . *T. Night* i 2 20
Have you thought on A place whereto you'll go . . *W. Tale* iv 4 548
Whereto thy tongue a party-verdict gave . . . *Richard II.* i 3 234
Whereto, when they shall know what men are rich, They shall subscribe them . . . . i 4 49
Whereto my finger, like a dial's point, Is pointing still . . v 5 53
How can we for our country pray, Whereto we are bound, together with thy victory, Whereto we are bound? . . *Coriolanus* v 3 108
An old accustom'd feast, Whereto I have invited many a guest *R. and J.* i 2 21
That lowliness is young ambition's ladder, Whereto the climber-upward turns his face . . . . . . *J. Cæsar* ii 1 23
And you shall speak In the same pulpit whereto I am going . iii 1 250
When Duncan is asleep—Whereto the rather shall his day's hard journey Soundly invite him . . . . . *Macbeth* i 7 62
Whereto serves mercy But to confront the visage of offence? *Hamlet* iii 3 46
And that his soul may be as damn'd and black As hell, whereto it goes iii 3 95
Compounded it with dust, whereto 'tis kin . . . iv 2 6
Why of that loam, whereto he was converted, might they not stop a beer-barrel? . . . . v 1 234
Infirmity doth still neglect all office Whereto our health is bound *Lear* ii 4 108
To prove upon thy heart, whereto I speak, Thou liest . . v 3 140
Whereto we see in all things nature tends . . *Othello* iii 3 231
Excuse her keeping close, Whereto constrain'd by her infirmity *Cymb.* iii 5 47
Whereuntil. We know whereuntil it doth amount . *L. L. Lost* v 2 493
The actors, sir, will show whereuntil it doth amount . . v 2 501
Whereunto I never Purpose return . . . *Cymbeline* iii 4 109
Whereunto your levy Must be supplyant . . . . . iii 7 13
Whereupon I command thee to open thy affair . . *W. Tale* iv 4 763
Whereupon, after a little amazedness, we were all commanded out . v 2 5
We do no further ask Than whereupon our weal, on you depending *K. John* iv 2 65
Whereupon the Earl of Worcester Hath broke his staff *Richard II.* ii 2 58
Hath sent to know The nature of your griefs, and whereupon You conjure from the breast of civil peace Such bold hostility *1 Hen. IV.* iv 3 42
The children are not in the fault; whereupon the world increases *2 Hen. IV.* ii 2 20
Now a' said so, I can tell whereupon . . . . ii 4 99
Whereupon He is retired, to ripe his growing fortunes . . iv 1 12
I did steer Toward this remedy, whereupon we are Now present *Hen. VIII.* ii 4 201
Whereupon I will show you a chamber with a bed . *Troi. and Cres.* iii 2 215
Whereupon the Grecians begin to proclaim barbarism . . v 4 17
Whereupon she grew round-wombed . . . . . *Lear* i 1 14
Whereupon—Methinks, I see him now— Ay, so thou dost *Cymbeline* v 5 208
Wherever. Yet a tailor might scratch her where'er she did itch *Tempest* ii 2 55
Wherever they are gone, That youth is surely in their company *As Y. L. It* ii 2 15
Wherever sorrow is, relief would be . . . . . iii 5 86
The foot That leaves the print of blood where'er it walks *K. John* iv 3 26
Where'er I wander, boast of this I can, Though banish'd, yet a trueborn Englishman . . . . *Richard II.* i 3 308
Order several powers To Oxford, or where'er these traitors are . v 3 141
Take leave until we meet again, Where'er it be, in heaven or in earth *3 Hen. VI.* ii 3 43
Wherever the bright sun of heaven shall shine . . *Hen. VIII.* v 5 51
Wherever we shall meet, for Timon's sake, Let's yet be fellows *T. of A.* iv 2 24
Wherever in your sightless substances You wait on nature's mischief *Macbeth* i 5 50
Wherewith. What sad talk was that Wherewith my brother held you? *T. G. of Ver.* i 3 2
Which with,—O, with—but with this I passion to say wherewith *L. L. L.* i 1 264
All the shrouds wherewith my life should sail Are turned to one thread *K. John* v 7 53
Before I have shook off the regal thoughts Wherewith I reign'd *Rich. II.* iv 1 164
Wherewith already France is overrun . . . *1 Hen. VI.* i 1 102
To add to your laments, Wherewith you now bedew King Henry's hearse i 1 104
Knowledge the wing wherewith we fly to heaven . *2 Hen. VI.* iv 7 79
Thy balm wash'd off wherewith thou wast annointed . *3 Hen. VI.* iii 1 17
Those honours deep and broad wherewith Your majesty loads our house *Macbeth* i 6 17
Wherewithal. Thou ladder wherewithal The mounting Bolingbroke ascends my throne . . . . *Richard II.* v 1 55
No doubt he's noble . —He may, my lord; has wherewithal *Hen. VIII.* i 3 59
Whet. Why dost thou whet thy knife so earnestly? . . *Mer. of Venice* iv 1 121
I come to whet your gentle thoughts On his behalf . *T. Night* iii 1 116
For England go: I will whet on the king. . . . *K. John* iii 4 181
Peace, good queen, And whet not on these furious peers . *2 Hen. VI.* ii 1 34
To London presently, And whet on Warwick to this enterprise *3 Hen. VI.* i 2 37
They believe it; and withal whet me To be revenged *Richard III.* i 3 332
May be, he hears the king Does whet his anger to him . *Hen. VIII.* iii 2 92
Since Cassius first did whet me against Cæsar, I have not slept *J. Cæsar* ii 1 61
This visitation Is but to whet thy almost blunted purpose *Hamlet* iii 4 111
Whether. I'll be your servant, Whether you will or no . . *Tempest* iii 1 86
Whether thou be'st he or no, Or some enchanted trifle . . . v 1 111
Whether this be Or be not, I'll not swear . . . . . v 1 122
Whether. Whether it be the fault and glimpse of newness, Or whether that the body public be A horse. . . . . *Meas. for Meas.* i 2 163
Whether the tyranny be in his place, Or in his eminence . . i 2 167
Good sir, say whether you'll answer me or no . . *Com. of Errors* iv 1 60
Thou shalt remain here, whether thou wilt or no . *M. N. Dream* iii 1 156
See me no more, whether he be dead or no . . . . iii 2 81
And now who knows But you, Lorenzo, whether I am yours? *M. of Ven.* ii 6 31
Move these eyes? Or whether, riding on the balls of mine, Seem they in motion? . . . . iii 2 117
In a doubt Whether those peals of praise be his or no . . iii 2 146
Whether wisely or no, let the forest judge . . *As Y. Like It* iii 2 129
Whether that thy youth and kind Will the faithful offer take . iv 3 59
Whether dost thou profess thyself, a knave or a fool? . *All's Well* iv 5 23
Give me the lie, do, and try whether I am not now a gentleman born *W. Tale* v 2 144
But whether I be as true begot or no, That still I lay upon my mother's head . . . . *K. John* i 1 75
Whether hadst thou rather be a Faulconbridge And like thy brother, to enjoy thy land, Or the reputed son of Cœur-de-lion? . . i 1 134
Not all thy former tale, But this one word, whether thy tale be true . iii 1 26
I know not whether God will have it so . . *1 Hen. IV.* iii 2 4
Look, whether the withered elder hath not his poll clawed *2 Hen. IV.* ii 4 281
Or whether that such cowards ought to wear This ornament of knighthood, yea or no . . . . *1 Hen. VI.* iv 1 28
Brave death by speaking, whether he will or no . . . iv 7 25
Whether your grace be worthy, yea or no, Dispute not that . *2 Hen. VI.* i 3 110
Where should he die? Can I make men live, whether they will or no? iii 3 10
He comes not To tell us whether they will come or no! *Richard III.* iii 1 23
I know not whether to depart in silence, Or bitterly to speak . . iii 7 141
Or whether his fall enraged him, or how 'twas . . *Coriolanus* i 3 69
I'll try whether my old wit be in request . . . . . iii 1 251
Whether 'twas pride . . . ; whether defect of judgement . . . ; or whether nature . . . . iv 7 37
But I know it is: Whether by device or no, the heavens can tell *T. An.* i 1 395
It is doubtful yet, Whether Cæsar will come forth to-day, or no *J. Cæsar* ii 1 194
And whether we shall meet again I know not . . . . v 1 115
Brave Titinius! Look, whether he have not crown'd dead Cassius! . v 3 97
You may glean, Whether aught, to us unknown, afflicts him thus *Ham.* ii 2 17
Whether I in any just term am affined To love the Moor. . *Othello* i 1 39
Whetstone. And hath sent this natural for our whetstone; for always the dulness of the fool is the whetstone of the wits *As Y. Like It* i 2 57
Now she sharpens: well said, whetstone! . . *Troi. and Cres.* v 2 75
Be this the whetstone of your sword: let grief Convert to anger *Macbeth* iv 3 228
Whetted. Which thou hast whetted on thy stony heart . *2 Hen. IV.* iv 5 108
The murderous knife was dull and blunt Till it was whetted on thy stone-hard heart . . . . *Richard III.* iv 4 227
Whettest. Fool, fool! thou whet'st a knife to kill thyself . i 3 244
Whew! A plague upon you all! Give me my horse, you rogues *1 Hen. IV.* ii 2 30
Whey. And feed on curds and whey, and suck the goat . *T. Andron.* iv 2 178
Whey-face. What soldiers, whey-face?—The English force, so please you *Macbeth* v 3 17
Which. I'll bring thee to the present business Which now's upon's; without the which this story Were most impertinent . *Tempest* i 2 137
I am all the subjects that you have, Which first was mine own king i 2 342
This gallant which thou seest Was in the wreck . . . . i 2 413
Which, of he or Adrian, for a good wager, first begins to crow? . ii 1 28
It is you that have chalk'd forth the way Which brought us hither . v 1 204
Yet there has been earls, nay, which is more, pensioners *Mer. Wives* ii 2 78
Masses of money; for the which his wife seems to me well-favoured . ii 2 284
Which means she to deceive, father or mother?—Both . . iv 6 46
Is the world as it was, man? Which is the way? . *Meas. for Meas.* iii 2 53
Purchased by such sin For which the pardoner himself is in . . iv 2 112
And, which was strange, the one so like the other As could not be distinguish'd but by names. . . . . *Com. of Errors* i 1 52
Which, God he knows, I saw not: for the which He did arrest me . v 1 229
Which is the natural man, And which the spirit? . . . v 1 333
I have many ill qualities.—Which is one? . . . *Much Ado* ii 1 107
I am a wise fellow, and, which is more, an officer, and, which is more, a householder, and, which is more, as pretty a piece of flesh as any is in Messina . . . . iv 2 83
For the which she wept heartily and said she cared not . . v 1 175
From my lord to my lady.—From which lord to which lady? *L. L. Lost* iv 1 105
We thankful should be, Which we of taste and feeling are . . iv 2 30
The contents Dies in the zeal of that which it presents . . . v 2 519
Therewithal to win me, if you please, Without the which I am not to be won . . . . v 2 859
Ten words long, Which is as brief as I have known a play *M. N. Dream* v 1 62
A mote will turn the balance, which Pyramus, which Thisbe, is the better . . . . v 1 324
If Hercules and Lichas play at dice Which is the better man *M. of Ven.* ii 1 33
The party 'gainst the which he doth contrive Shall seize one half . iv 1 352
A civil doctor, Which did refuse three thousand ducats of me . v 1 212
In the which hope I blush, and hide my sword . *As Y. Like It* ii 7 119
In the which, my instruction shall serve to naturalize thee *All's Well* i 1 222
Half of the which dare not shake the snow from off their cassocks . iv 3 191
I have your own letter that induced me to the semblance I put on; with the which I doubt not but to do myself much right *T. Night* v 1 316
In such forms which here were presupposed Upon thee in the letter . v 1 358
Such an affection, which cannot choose but branch now . *W. Tale* i 1 26
Which draught to me were cordial . . . . . . i 2 318
It is an heretic that makes the fire, Not she which burns in't . ii 3 116
More than mistress of Which comes to me in name of fault, I must not At all acknowledge . . . . iii 2 61
I cannot tell, good sir, for which of his virtues it was . . iv 3 94
What fair swain is this Which dances with your daughter? . iv 4 167
There lies such secrets in this fardel and box, which none must know but the king. . . . . iv 4 784
Slander's venom'd spear, The which no balm can cure but his heart-blood Which breathed this poison . . . . *Richard II.* i 1 172
The better part of valour is discretion; in the which better part I have saved my life . . . . *1 Hen. IV.* v 4 122
Upon the which, I trust, Shall witness live in brass of this day's work *Hen. V.* iv 3 96
And, which is more, she is not so divine, So full-replete. . *1 Hen. VI.* v 5 16
O God, which this blood madest, revenge his death! . *Richard III.* i 2 62
Which of you trembles not that looks on me? . . . . . i 3 160
Which of my damned son, which thy two sweet sons smother'd . . iv 4 134
You have put me now to such a part which never I shall discharge *Coriolanus* iii 2 105
According to the which, thou shalt discourse . . . *J. Cæsar* iii 1 295

Which. And, which is worse, all you have done Hath been but for a wayward son . . . . *Macbeth* iii 5 10
That he which hath your noble father slain Pursued my life . *Hamlet* iv 7 4
My virtue or my plague, be it either which . . . . iv 7 13
It appears not which of the dukes he values most . . *Lear* i 1 5
Our foster-nurse of nature is repose, The which he lacks . iv 4 13
The which immediacy may well stand up, And call itself your brother v 3 65
The rites for which I love him are bereft me . . *Othello* i 3 258
If by which time our secret be undone . . . . *Pericles* i 1 117
If in which time expired, he not return . . . . ii 4 47
Your bride goes to that with shame which is her way to go with warrant iv 2 139
Which is which. Stand apart; I know not which is which *Com. of Er.* v 1 364
The mazed world, By their increase, now knows not which is which *M. N. Dream* ii 1 114
I know not which is which.—Canst not read? . . . *T. of Athens* ii 2 82
What is the night?—Almost at odds with morning, which is which *Macbeth* iii 4 127
Which way. How and which way I may bestow myself *T. G. of Ver.* iii 1 87
Which way have you looked for Master Caius? . . *Mer. Wives* iii 1 3
A proper squire! And who, and who? which way looks he? *Much Ado* i 3 55
Withal make known Which way thou travellest . . *T. of Shrew* iv 5 51
I'll take the sacrament on't, how and which way you will *All's Well* iv 3 157
Which way is he, in the name of sanctity? . . *T. Night* iii 4 93
Which way to be prevented, if to be; If not, how best to bear it *W. T.* i 2 405
Send him word by me which way you go . . . *K. John* v 3 7
Why, so! go all which way it will! . . . . *Richard II.* ii 2 87
If I know how or which way to order these affairs . . ., Never believe me ii 2 109
Let it go which way it will, he that dies this year is quit for the next *2 Hen. IV.* iii 2 254
We see which way the stream of time doth run . . . iv 1 70
Then how or which way should they first break in? . . *1 Hen. VI.* ii 1 71
Which way would Hector have it?—He cares not . . *Troi. and Cres.* iv 5 71
Think you so? Which way do you judge my wit would fly? *Coriolanus* ii 3 27
Then which way shall I find Revenge's cave? . . . *T. Andron.* iii 1 271
Which way ran he that kill'd Mercutio? . . . *Rom. and Jul.* iii 1 142
Which way hast thou been?—At mine own house . . *J. Cæsar* ii 4 21
Sure and firm-set earth, Hear not my steps, which way they walk *Macb.* ii 1 57
Resolve me, with all modest haste, which way Thou mightst deserve *Lear* ii 4 25
Is thine, if thou wilt ha't.—Show me which way . . *Ant. and Cleo.* ii 7 75
To this hour no guess in knowledge Which way they went *Cymbeline* i 1 61
Look you, sir, you know not which way you shall go . . v 4 181
If I discover'd not which way she was gone, It was my instant death . v 5 277
Whiff. But with the whiff and wind of his fell sword The unnerved father falls . . . . *Hamlet* ii 2 495
Whiffler. The deep-mouth'd sea, Which like a mighty whiffler 'fore the king Seems to prepare his way . . . *Hen. V.* v Prol. 12
While. Will guard your person while you take your rest. *Tempest* ii 1 197
If you'll sit down, I'll bear your logs the while . . . iii 1 24
But, while thou livest, keep a good tongue in thy head . . iii 2 120
Wit shall not go unrewarded while I am king of this country . iv 1 242
Now the dog all this while sheds not a tear . . *T. G. of Ver.* ii 3 34
She shut the doors upon me, While she with harlots feasted *Com. of Er.* v 1 205
Have you wept all this while?—Yea, and I will weep a while longer *Much Ado* iv 1 257
While truth the while Doth falsely blind the eyesight of his look *L. L. L.* i 1 75
Where have you been all this while? You a lover! *As Y. Like It* iv 1 39
Let him go while the humour lasts . . . . *T. of Shrew* i 2 107
Now I well perceive You have but jested with me all this while . ii 1 20
I have spoke to the purpose twice: The one for ever earn'd a royal husband; The other for some while a friend . . *W. Tale* i 2 108
Woe the while! O, cut my lace, lest my heart, cracking it, Break too! iii 2 173
Bad world the while! This must not be thus borne . *K. John* iv 2 100
Let the trumpets sound While we return these dukes what we decree *Richard II.* i 3 122
You have but mistook me all this while: I live with bread like you . iii 2 174
God help the while! a bad world, I say . . . *1 Hen. IV.* ii 4 145
Wherefore a guard of chosen shot I had That walk'd about me every minute while . . . . *1 Hen. VI.* i 4 54
To see if I can eat grass, or pick a sallet another while . *2 Hen. VI.* iv 10 9
I must make fair weather yet a while, Till Henry be more weak . v 1 30
Say you can swim; alas, 'tis but a while! Tread on the sand *3 Hen. VI.* v 4 29
Unexamined, free, at liberty. Here's a good world the while! *Rich. III.* iii 6 10
I know, within a while All the best men are ours . *Hen. VIII.* Epil. 12
And give way the while To unstable slightness . . *Coriolanus* iii 1 147
But, woe the while! our fathers' minds are dead . . *J. Cæsar* i 3 82
Good repose the while!—Thanks, sir: the like to you! . *Macbeth* ii 1 29
We will keep ourself Till supper-time alone: while then, God be with you! . . . . iii 1 44
'While the grass grows,'—the proverb is something musty *Hamlet* iii 2 358
I have this while with leaden thoughts been press'd . *Othello* iii 4 177
What shall I do the while? where bide? how live? . *Cymbeline* iii 4 131
While ago. A great while ago the world begun . . *T. Night* v 1 414
While as the silly owner of the goods Weeps over them . *2 Hen. VI.* i 1 225
While-ere. Will you troll the catch You taught me but while-ere? *Temp.* iii 2 127
Whiles we stood here securing your repose . . . . ii 1 310
Whiles I Persuade this rude wretch willingly to die *Meas. for Meas.* iv 3 84
What we have we prize not to the worth Whiles we enjoy it *Much Ado* iv 1 221
Whiles we shut the gates upon one wooer, another knocks at the door *Mer. of Venice* i 2 147
Whiles, like a doe, I go to find my fawn . . *As Y. Like It* ii 7 128
Take you your instrument, play you the whiles . *T. of Shrew* iii 1 22
You may be jogging whiles your boots are green . . . iii 2 213
I will bespeak our diet, Whiles you beguile the time . *T. Night* iii 3 41
He shall conceal it Whiles you are willing it shall come to note . iv 3 29
Whiles I was protector, Pity was all the fault that was in me *2 Hen. VI.* iii 1 124
Whiles lions war and battle for their dens, Poor harmless lambs abide their enmity . . . . *3 Hen. VI.* ii 5 74
Never at heart's ease Whiles they behold a greater than themselves *J. C.* i 2 209
Whiles we are suitors to their throne, decays The thing we sue for *Ant. and Cleo.* ii 1 4
While that the armed hand doth fight abroad . . *Hen. V.* i 2 178
While that the coulter rusts That should deracinate such savagery . v 2 46
Whilst. I'll ne'er be drunk whilst I live again . . *Mer. Wives* i 1 186
Where I will never come Whilst I can shake my sword or hear the drum . . . . *All's Well* ii 5 96
I saw a smith stand with his hammer, thus, The whilst his iron did on the anvil cool . . . . *K. John* iv 2 194
Whilst you have fed upon my signories . . . *Richard II.* iii 1 22
Alack, poor Richard! where rode he the whilst? . . . v 2 22

Whilst. And, whilst we breathe, take time to do him dead . *3 Hen. VI.* i 4 108
Whilst I awhile obsequiously lament . . . . *Richard III.* i 2 3
If he steal aught the whilst this play is playing . *Hamlet* iii 2 93
Whilst I can vent clamour from my throat, I'll tell thee thou dost evil *Lear* i 1 168
If you'll go fetch him, We'll say our song the whilst . *Cymbeline* iv 2 254
Whine. Dost thou come here to whine? To outface me? . *Hamlet* v 1 300
Whip him, fellows, Till, like a boy, you see him cringe his face, And whine aloud for mercy . . . . *Ant. and Cleo.* iii 13 101
Whined. At his nurse's tears He whined and roar'd away your victory *Coriolanus* v 6 98
Thrice the brinded cat hath mew'd.—Thrice and once the hedge-pig whined . . . . *Macbeth* iv 1 2
Whining. This wimpled, whining, purblind, wayward boy *L. L. Lost* iii 1 181
Then the whining school-boy, with his satchel . *As Y. Like It* ii 7 145
A wretched puling fool, A whining mammet . . *Rom. and Jul.* iii 5 186
One whom I will beat into clamorous whining . . . *Lear* ii 2 25
Whip. 'What cur is that?' says another: 'Whip him out,' says the third *T. G. of Ver.* iv 4 23
And goes me to the fellow that whips the dogs: 'Friend,' quoth I, 'you mean to whip the dog?' . . . . iv 4 27
He makes me no more ado, but whips me out of the chamber . iv 4 31
I warrant they would whip me with their fine wits . *Mer. Wives* iv 5 101
Hoping you'll find good cause to whip them all . *Meas. for Meas.* ii 1 142
Whip me? No, no; let carman whip his jade: The valiant heart's not whipt out of his trade . . . . ii 1 269
The impression of keen whips I'ld wear as rubies . . . ii 4 101
I'll whip you from your foining fence . . . *Much Ado* v 1 84
I, that have been love's whip; A very beadle to a humorous sigh *L. L. L.* iii 1 176
Now step I forth to whip hypocrisy . . . . . iv 3 151
Thou disputest like an infant: go, whip thy gig . . . v 1 69
I will whip about your infamy circum circa,—a gig of a cuckold's horn v 1 72
Whip to our tents, as roes run o'er land . . . . v 2 309
Come, thou child; I'll whip thee with a rod . *M. N. Dream* iii 2 410
Deserves as well a dark house and a whip as madmen do *As Y. Like It* iii 2 421
His presence must be the whip of the other . . *All's Well* iv 3 42
Which to hinder Were in your love a whip to me . . *W. Tale* i 2 25
And is well prepared To whip this dwarfish war . . *K. John* v 2 135
Have you not beadles in your town, and things called whips? *2 Hen. VI.* ii 1 137
Sirrah beadle, whip him till he leap over that same stool . ii 1 148
He means to beg a child of her.—Nay, whip me then . *3 Hen. VI.* iii 2 28
Let's whip these stragglers o'er the seas again . *Richard III.* v 3 327
Wert thou the Hector That was the whip of your bragg'd progeny, Thou shouldst not 'scape me here . . . . *Coriolanus* i 8 12
Lest you shall chance to whip your information And beat the messenger who bids beware Of what is to be dreaded . . . . iv 6 53
Go whip him 'fore the people's eyes:—his raising; Nothing but his report iv 6 60
And not a hair upon a soldier's head Which will not prove a whip . iv 6 134
Her whip of cricket's bone, the lash of film . . *Rom. and Jul.* i 4 63
Such a waggoner As Phaëthon would whip you to the west . . iii 2 3
Each thing's a thief: The laws, your curb and whip, in their rough power Have uncheck'd theft . . . . . *T. of Athens* iv 3 446
Wilt thou whip thine own faults in other men? . . . v 1 40
Not all the whips of heaven are large enough . . . . v 1 64
For who would bear the whips and scorns of time? . . *Hamlet* iii 1 70
Behind the arras hearing something stir, Whips out his rapier, cries, 'A rat, a rat!' . . . . iv 1 10
Take heed, sirrah; the whip . . . . . . *Lear* i 4 123
Whip me such honest knaves . . . . . . *Othello* i 1 49
Put in every honest hand a whip To lash the rascals naked through the world . . . . iv 2 142
Whip me, ye devils, From the possession of this heavenly sight! . v 2 277
Take hence this Jack, and whip him . . . *Ant. and Cleo.* iii 13 93
Whip him. Were't twenty of the greatest tributaries That do acknowledge Cæsar . . . . iii 13 96
Whip him, fellows, Till, like a boy, you see him cringe his face, And whine aloud for mercy. . . . . iii 13 99
My enfranched bondman, whom He may at pleasure whip, or hang, or torture . . . . iii 13 150
Whip thee, gosling: I think I shall have something to do with you *Per.* iv 2 91
Whipped. Since I plucked geese, played truant, and whipped top *M. W.* v 1 27
Or to bind him up a rod, as being worthy to be whipped . *Much Ado* ii 1 227
She deserves well.—To be whipped . . . . *L. L. Lost* i 2 125
Then shall Hector be whipped for Jaquenetta that is quick by him . v 2 686
You'll be whipped for taxation one of these days . *As Y. Like It* i 2 91
With this condition, to be whipped at the high cross every morning *T. of Shrew* i 1 136
You were lately whipped, sir, as I think . . . *All's Well* ii 2 52
An they were sons of mine, I'd have them whipped . . . ii 3 93
Our virtues would be proud, if our faults whipped them not . . iv 3 85
From whence he was whipped for getting the shrieve's fool with child . iv 3 212
He shall be whipped through the army with this rhyme in's forehead . iv 3 261
I cannot tell, good sir, for which of his virtues it was, but he was certainly whipped out of the court . . . . . . *W. Tale* iv 3 95
There's no virtue whipped out of the court: they cherish it . . iv 3 97
I am whipp'd and scourged with rods, Nettled and stung . *1 Hen. IV.* i 3 239
Consideration, like an angel, came And whipp'd the offending Adam out of him . . . . *Hen. V.* i 1 29
Let them be whipped through every market-town . . *2 Hen. VI.* ii 1 158
I have seen him whipped three market-days together . . . iv 2 62
What talk you Of Marcius?—Go see this rumourer whipp'd *Coriolanus* iv 6 47
Shut up in prison, kept without my food, Whipp'd and tormented *Rom. and Jul.* i 2 57
I would have such a fellow whipped for o'erdoing Termagant *Hamlet* iii 2 15
Truth's a dog must to kennel; he must be whipped out . . *Lear* i 4 125
If I speak like myself in this, let him be whipped that first finds it so . i 4 180
An you lie, sirrah, we'll have you whipped . . . . i 4 198
They'll have me whipped for speaking true, thou'lt have me whipped for lying; and sometimes I am whipped for holding my peace . i 4 200
Whipped from tithing to tithing, and stock-punished . . . iii 4 139
Thou shalt be whipp'd with wire, and stew'd in brine . *Ant. and Cleo.* ii 5 65
You will be whipp'd.—Approach, there! Ah, you kite! . . iii 13 88
Tug him away: being whipp'd, Bring him again . . . . iii 13 102
Is he whipp'd?—Soundly, my lord.—Cried he? . . . . iii 13 131
And be thou sorry To follow Cæsar in his triumph, since Thou hast been whipp'd for following him . . . . iii 13 137
My messenger He hath whipp'd with rods: dares me to personal combat iv 1 3
Are all your beggars whipped, then?—O, not all, my friend, not all *Per.* ii 1 94
If all your beggars were whipped, I would wish no better office than to be beadle . . . . ii 1 96

Whippers. The lunacy is so ordinary that the whippers are in love too *As Y. Like It* iii 2 424
Whippest. Strip thine own back; Thou hotly lust'st to use her in that kind For which thou whipp'st her . . . . . *Lear* iv 6 167
Whipping. You shall have your full time of imprisonment and your deliverance with an unpitied whipping . . . *Meas. for Meas.* iv 2 14
Marrying a punk, my lord, is pressing to death, whipping, and hanging v 1 529
To see great Hercules whipping a gig . . . *L. L. Lost* iv 3 167
Indeed your 'O Lord, sir!' is very sequent to your whipping: you would answer very well to a whipping, if you were but bound to't *All's Well* ii 2 56
If you mean to save yourself from whipping, leap me over this stool *2 Hen. VI.* ii 1 144
Use every man after his desert, and who should 'scape whipping? *Hamlet* ii 2 556
I did but crave.—But crave! Then I'll turn craver too, and so I shall 'scape whipping . . . . . . *Pericles* ii 1 93
Whipping-cheer. She shall have whipping-cheer enough, I warrant her *2 Hen. IV.* v 4 5
Whipster. I am not valiant neither, But every puny whipster gets my sword . . . . . . *Othello* v 2 244
Whipstock. Malvolio's nose is no whipstock . *T. Night* ii 3 28
He appears To have practised more the whipstock than the lance *Pericles* ii 2 51
Whipt. In plain dealing, Pompey, I shall have you whipt *Meas. for Meas.* ii 1 264
The valiant heart's not whipt out of his trade . . ii 1 270
I had rather it would please you I might be whipt.—Whipt first, sir, and hanged after . . . . . . v 1 512
The nuptial finish'd, Let him be whipt and hang'd . . v 1 519
I whipt me behind the arras; and there heard it agreed *Much Ado* i 3 63
Whirl. And justice always whirls in equal measure . . *L. L. Lost* iv 3 384
I having hold of both, They whirl asunder and dismember me *K. John* iii 1 330
Five moons were seen to-night; Four fixed, and the fifth did whirl about . . . . . . iv 2 183
I am giddy; expectation whirls me round . *Troi. and Cres.* iii 2 19
And whirl along with thee about the globe . *T. Andron.* v 2 49
Whirled. My thoughts are whirled like a potter's wheel . *1 Hen. VI.* i 5 19
Whirligig. Thus the whirligig of time brings in his revenges *T. Night* v 1 385
Whirling. To calm this tempest whirling in the court *T. Andron.* iv 2 160
These are but wild and whirling words, my lord *Hamlet* i 5 133
Whirlipool. Through ford and whirlipool, o'er bog and quagmire *Lear* iii 4 53
Whirlwind. That some whirlwind bear Unto a ragged fearful-hanging rock And throw it thence! . . . *T. G. of Ver.* i 2 120
Confounds thy fame as whirlwinds shake fair buds . *T. of Shrew* v 2 140
What wouldst thou have to Athens?—Thee thither in a whirlwind *T. of Athens* iv 3 288
In the very torrent, tempest, and, as I may say, the whirlwind of passion *Hamlet* iii 2 7
Bless thee from whirlwinds, star-blasting, and taking! . *Lear* iii 4 60
Whirring. This world to me is like a lasting storm, Whirring me from my friends . . . . . . *Pericles* iv 1 21
Whisper. Sweet, now, silence! Juno and Ceres whisper seriously *Tempest* iv 1 125
To whisper and conspire against my youth? . *T. G. of Ver.* i 2 43
Whisper her ear and tell her, I and Ursula Walk in the orchard *M. Ado* iii 1 4
When you then were here, What did you whisper in your lady's ear? *L. L. Lost* v 2 436
Rosaline, What did the Russian whisper in your ear? . v 2 443
And through that cranny shall Pyramus and Thisby whisper *M. N. Dream* iii 1 73
And through Wall's chink, poor souls, they are content To whisper v 1 135
The lovers, Pyramus and Thisby, Did whisper often very secretly v 1 161
This the cranny is, right and sinister, Through which the fearful lovers are to whisper . . . . . . v 1 165
The blushes in my cheeks thus whisper me . *All's Well* ii 3 75
I'll whisper with the general, and know his pleasure . iv 3 329
We'll whisper o'er a couplet or two of most sage saws *T. Night* iii 4 412
Your followers I will whisper to the business *W. Tale* i 2 437
Tender your persons to his presence, whisper him in your behalfs iv 4 827
So much my conscience whispers in your ear . *K. John* i 1 42
How they whisper: urge them while their souls Are capable of this ambition . . . . . . ii 1 475
When they talk of him, they shake their heads And whisper one another iv 2 189
And lean-look'd prophets whisper fearful change *Richard II.* ii 4 11
Unless some dull and favourable hand Will whisper music to my weary spirit.—Call for the music . . *2 Hen. IV.* iv 5 3
The fix'd sentinels almost receive The secret whispers of each others' watch: Fire answers fire . . . *Hen. V.* iv Prol. 7
Whispers to his pillow as to him The secrets of his overcharged soul *2 Hen. VI.* iii 2 375
Why whisper you, my lords, and answer not? . *3 Hen. VI.* i 1 149
And there the little souls of Edward's children Whisper the spirits of thine enemies And promise them success . . *Richard III.* iv 4 192
'Twas indeed his colour, but he came To whisper Wolsey . *Hen. VIII.* i 1 179
Nor I from Troy come not to whisper him *Troi. and Cres.* i 3 250
Never admitted A private whisper, no, not with such friends *Coriolanus* v 3 7
Some devil whisper curses in mine ear, And prompt me! *T. Andron.* v 3 11
If Cæsar hide himself, shall they not whisper 'Lo, Cæsar is afraid?' *J. Cæsar* ii 2 100
The grief that does not speak Whispers the o'er-fraught heart *Macbeth* iv 3 210
At least, the whisper goes so . . . . *Hamlet* i 1 80
Whose whisper o'er the world's diameter, As level as the cannon to his blank, Transports his poison'd shot . . . . iv 1 41
The people muddied, Thick and unwholesome in their thoughts and whispers . . . . . . iv 5 82
He takes her by the palm: ay, well said, whisper . *Othello* ii 1 169
Did they never whisper?—Never, my lord.—Nor send you out o' the way?—Never . . . . . . iv 2 6
The seaman's whistle Is as a whisper in the ears of death, Unheard *Per.* iii 1 9
There is something glows upon my cheek, And whispers in mine ear 'Go not' . . . . . . v 1 97
Whispered. As you have whisper'd faithfully you were . *As Y. Like It* ii 7 192
I mean the whispered ones, for they are yet but ear-kissing arguments *Lear* ii 1 8
Whispering. With whispering and most guilty diligence *Meas. for Meas.* iv 1 39
With bated breath and whispering humbleness *Mer. of Venice* i 3 125
They're here with me already, whispering, rounding *W. Tale* i 2 217
Is whispering nothing? Is leaning cheek to cheek? . i 2 284
'Tis well they are whispering: clamour your tongues, and not a word more . . . . . . iv 4 250
And could tell A whispering tale in a fair lady's ear *Rom. and Jul.* i 5 25
Rain sacrificial whisperings in his ear . *T. of Athens* i 1 81
Foul whisperings are abroad . . . . *Macbeth* v 1 79
Whist. Courtsied when you have and kiss'd The wild waves whist *Tempest* i 2 379
Whistle. Take in the topsail. Tend to the master's whistle . *Tempest* i 1 8
His big manly voice, Turning again toward childish treble, pipes And whistles in his sound . . . *As Y. Like It* ii 7 163
Is there not milking-time, when you are going to bed, or kiln-hole, to whistle off these secrets? . . . *W. Tale* iv 4 248
Let the law go whistle . . . . . iv 4 715
And sung those tunes to the over-scutched huswives that he heard the carmen whistle . . . . *2 Hen. IV.* iii 2 342
Hear the shrill whistle which doth order give . *Hen. V.* iii Prol. 9
Whistle then to me, As signal that thou hear'st something approach *Rom. and Jul.* v 3 7
Some time I shall sleep out, the rest I'll whistle . . *Lear* ii 2 163
I have been worth the whistle . . . . iv 2 29
I'ld whistle her off and let her down the wind, To prey at fortune *Othello* iii 3 262
The seaman's whistle Is as a whisper in the ears of death, Unheard *Per.* iii 1 8
The boatswain whistles, and The master calls, and trebles their confusion iv 1 64
Whistling. To dance our ringlets to the whistling wind . *M. N. Dream* ii 1 86
Hollow whistling in the leaves Foretells a tempest . . *1 Hen. IV.* v 1 5
Did sit alone, Whistling to the air . . *Ant. and Cleo.* ii 2 221
Whit. You delight not in music.—Not a whit, when it jars so *T. G. of Ver.* iv 2 67
It is marring indeed, if he quarter it.—Not a whit . *Mer. Wives* i 1 27
We must leave the killing out, when all is done.—Not a whit *M. N. D.* iii 1 17
Thou art in a parlous state, shepherd.—Not a whit . *As Y. Like It* iii 2 46
You understand me?—I, sir! ne'er a whit . . *T. of Shrew* i 1 240
So shall I no whit be behind in duty . . . . i 2 175
I chafe you, if I tarry: let me go.—No, not a whit . . ii 1 244
The waste is no whit lesser than thy land . *Richard II.* ii 1 103
Doth not thy blood thrill at it?—Not a whit . *1 Hen. IV.* ii 4 408
You give him then advantage.—Not a whit . . iv 3 2
Woe, woe for England! not a whit for me . *Richard III.* iii 4 82
I trouble you.—No, not a whit . . . *Troi. and Cres.* v 1 76
Well, more or less, or ne'er a whit at all . *T. Andron.* iv 2 53
You'll be sick to-morrow For this night's watching.—No, not a whit *Rom. and Jul.* iv 4 9
Our youths and wildness shall no whit appear . *J. Cæsar* ii 1 148
Say you are not fit.—Not a whit . . . *Hamlet* v 2 230
The stone's too hard to come by.—Not a whit . . *Cymbeline* ii 4 46
Famous in Cæsar's praises, no whit less Than in his feats deserving it iii 1 6
White. The white cold virgin snow upon my heart Abates the ardour of my liver . . . . . . *Tempest* iv 1 55
She is as white as a lily and as small as a wand *T. G. of Ver.* ii 3 22
Fairies, green and white, With rounds of waxen tapers on their heads *Mer. Wives* iv 4 49
The queen of all the fairies, Finely attired in a robe of white . iv 4 72
Thus it rests: Her father means she shall be all in white . iv 6 35
I come to her in white, and cry 'mum;' she cries 'budget' . v 2 6
What needs either your 'mum' or her 'budget?' the white will decipher her well enough . . . . . v 2 10
Fairies, black, grey, green, and white, You moonshine revellers . v 5 41
Write In emerald tufts, flowers purple, blue, and white . . v 5 74
I went to her in white, and cried 'mum,' and she cried 'budget' v 5 209
Which indeed is not under white and black . *Much Ado* v 1 314
My love is most immaculate white and red . *L. L. Lost* i 2 95
If she be made of white and red, Her faults will ne'er be known i 2 104
What is she in the white?—A woman sometimes . . ii 1 197
Smiles on every one, To show his teeth as white as whale's bone . v 2 332
I here protest, By this white glove,—how white the hand, God knows! v 2 411
That pure congealed white, high Taurus' snow . *M. N. Dream* iii 2 141
O, let me kiss This princess of pure white, this seal of bliss! . iii 2 144
Who, inward search'd, have livers white as milk *Mer. of Venice* iii 2 86
Such war of white and red within her cheeks! . *T. of Shrew* iv 5 30
'Twas I won the wager, though you hit the white . . v 2 186
Whose red and white Nature's own sweet and cunning hand laid on *T. Night* i 5 257
My shroud of white, stuck all with yew, O, prepare it! . . ii 4 56
Lawn as white as driven snow; Cyprus black as e'er was crow *W. Tale* iv 4 220
I take thy hand, this hand, As soft as dove's down and as white as it iv 4 374
Thy father's beard is turned white with the news . *1 Hen. IV.* ii 4 393
If it be a hot day, and I brandish any thing but a bottle, I would I might never spit white again . . . *2 Hen. IV.* i 2 237
Left the liver white and pale, which is the badge of pusillanimity . iv 3 113
Though the truth of it stands off as gross As black and white *Hen. V.* ii 2 104
A black beard will turn white; a curled pate will grow bald . v 2 169
Shall send between the red rose and the white A thousand souls to death and deadly night . . . . . *1 Hen. VI.* ii 4 126
The red rose and the white are on his face . . *3 Hen. VI.* ii 5 97
Her hand, In whose comparison all whites are ink . *Troi. and Cres.* i 1 56
Here's but two and fifty hairs on your chin, and one of them is white . i 2 172
With these your white enchanting fingers touch'd . . iii 1 164
The war of white and damask in Their nicely-gawded cheeks . *Coriolanus* ii 1 232
Sanctifies himself with's hand and turns up the white o' the eye . iv 5 209
This palliament of white and spotless hue . . *T. Andron.* i 1 182
All the water in the ocean Can never turn the swan's black legs to white iv 2 102
Thus much of this [gold] will make black white, foul fair *T. of Athens* iv 3 28
My hands are of your colour; but I shame To wear a heart so white *Macbeth* ii 2 65
Is there not rain enough in the sweet heavens To wash it white as snow? . . . . *Hamlet* iii 3 46
White his shroud as the mountain snow . . . . iv 5 35
His beard was as white as snow, All flaxen was his poll . . iv 5 195
'Gainst a head So old and white as this . . . *Lear* iii 2 24
Be thy mouth or black or white, Tooth that poisons if it bite . iii 6 69
So white, and such a traitor!—Naughty lady . . . iii 7 37
I'll fetch some flax and whites of eggs To apply to his bleeding face . iii 7 106
She'll find a white that shall her blackness fit . . *Othello* ii 1 134
My very hairs do mutiny; for the white Reprove the brown for rashness, and they them For fear and doting . . *Ant. and Cleo.* iii 11 13
White and azure laced With blue of heaven's own tinct . *Cymbeline* ii 2 22
She weaved the sleided silk With fingers long, small, white as milk *Pericles* iv Gower 22
With the dove of Paphos might the crow Vie feathers white . . iv Gower 33
For flesh and blood, sir, white and red, you shall see a rose . iv 6 37
White bastard. We shall have all the world drink brown and white bastard . . . . . . *Meas. for Meas.* iii 2 4
White beard. By my white beard, You offer him, if this be so, a wrong Something unfilial . . . . . *W. Tale* iv 4 415
White-beards have arm'd their thin and hairless scalps . *Richard II.* iii 2 112
A white beard? a decreasing leg? an increasing belly? . *2 Hen. IV.* i 2 204
By this white beard, I'ld fight with thee to-morrow . *Troi. and Cres.* iv 5 209
Pity not honour'd age for his white beard; He is an usurer *T. of Athens* iv 3 111

White beard. Ha! Goneril, with a white beard! . . . . *Lear* iv 6 97
Who deserved So long a breeding as his white beard came to . *Cymbeline* v 3 17
White-bearded. I should think this a gull, but that the white-bearded fellow speaks it . . . . *Much Ado* ii 3 124
Falstaff, that old white-bearded Satan . . . . *1 Hen. IV.* ii 4 509
White bosom. In her excellent white bosom, these, &c. . . *Hamlet* ii 2 113
White canvas. Your white canvas doublet will sully . . *1 Hen. IV.* ii 4 83
White death. Let the white death sit on thy cheek for ever . *All's Well* ii 3 77
White ewe. An old black ram Is tupping your white ewe . . *Othello* i 1 89
White-faced. That pale, that white-faced shore, Whose foot spurns back the ocean's roaring tides . . . *K. John* ii 1 23
White flags. By the semblance Of their white flags display'd, they bring us peace . . . . *Pericles* i 4 72
White flakes. Had you not been their father, these white flakes Had challenged pity of them . . . . *Lear* iv 7 30
White-Friars. To White-Friars; there attend my coming *Richard III.* i 2 227
White glove. By this white glove,—how white the hand, God knows! *L. L. Lost* v 2 411
White hair. Superfluity comes sooner by white hairs, but competency lives longer . . . . *Mer. of Venice* i 2 9
That he is old, the more the pity, his white hairs do witness it *1 Hen. IV.* ii 4 514
Not a white hair on your face but should have his effect of gravity *2 Hen. IV.* i 2 182
Whom I have weekly sworn to marry since I perceived the first white hair on my chin . . . . i 2 271
How ill white hairs become a fool and jester! . . . v 5 52
Would bring white hairs unto a quiet grave . . *3 Hen. VI.* ii 5 40
And she takes upon her to spy a white hair on his chin *Troi. and Cres.* i 2 153
At what was all this laughing?—Marry, at the white hair that Helen spied on Troilus' chin . . . . i 2 164
That white hair is my father, and all the rest are his sons . i 2 176
Tears his white hair, Which the impetuous blasts, with eyeless rage, Catch in their fury . . . . *Lear* iii 1 7
And told me I had white hairs in my beard ere the black ones were there . . . . iv 6 99
White hand. To her white hand see thou do commend This . *L. L. Lost* iii 1 169
By the white hand of Rosalind, I am that he, that unfortunate he *As Y. Like It* iii 2 413
My lady has a white hand . . . . *T. Night* ii 3 28
Ere I could make thee open thy white hand And clap thyself my love *W. Tale* i 2 103
By the white hand of my lady, he's a gallant prince . *Hen. V.* iii 7 101
She came and puts me her white hand to his cloven chin *Troi. and Cres.* i 2 131
She has a marvellous white hand, I must needs confess . . i 2 151
Henceforth The white hand of a lady fever thee . *Ant. and Cleo.* iii 13 138
White-handed mistress, one sweet word with thee . . *L. L. Lost* v 2 230
White Hart. Leave me at the White Hart in Southwark *2 Hen. VI.* iv 8 25
White head. I was born about three of the clock in the afternoon, with a white head . . . . *2 Hen. IV.* i 2 211
A good soft pillow for that good white head Were better than a churlish turf of France . . . . *Hen. V.* iv 1 14
You sulphurous and thought-executing fires, Vaunt-couriers to oak-cleaving thunderbolts, Singe my white head! . . *Lear* iii 2 6
White herring. Hopdance cries in Tom's belly for two white herring . iii 6 33
White investments. Whose white investments figure innocence *2 Hen. IV.* iv 1 45
White-limed. Ye white-limed walls! ye alehouse painted signs! *T. An.* iv 2 98
White-livered. He is white-livered and red-faced . . *Hen. V.* iii 2 34
White-liver'd runagate, what doth he there? . *Richard III.* iv 4 465
White luces. They may give the dozen white luces in their coat.—It is an old coat.—The dozen white louses do become an old coat well *Mer. Wives* i 1 16
White robes. In pure white robes, Like very sanctity . *W. Tale* iii 3 22
White rose. From off this brier pluck a white rose with me *1 Hen. VI.* ii 4 30
I pluck this white rose with Plantagenet . . . . ii 4 36
Giving my verdict on the white rose side . . . . ii 4 48
Prick not your finger as you pluck it off, Lest bleeding you do paint the white rose red . . . . ii 4 50
Meditating that Shall dye your white rose in a bloody red . ii 4 61
I cannot rest Until the white rose that I wear be dyed Even in the lukewarm blood of Henry's heart . . *3 Hen. VI.* i 2 33
We will unite the white rose and the red . . *Richard III.* v 5 19
White sheet. The white sheet bleaching on the hedge . *W. Tale* iv 3 5
White spot. Is beaten black and blue, that you cannot see a white spot about her . . . . *Mer. Wives* iv 5 116
White stockings. The serving-men in their new fustian, their white stockings . . . . *T. of Shrew* iv 1 50
White Surrey. Saddle white Surrey for the field to-morrow *Richard III.* v 3 64
White upturned. Unto the white-upturned wondering eyes *R. and J.* ii 2 29
White wench. Stabbed with a white wench's black eye . . ii 4 14
White wheat. Makes the hare-lip; mildews the white wheat . *Lear* iii 4 123
White wonder. They may seize On the white wonder of dear Juliet's hand . . . . *Rom. and Jul.* iii 3 36
Whitehall. 'Tis now the king's, and call'd Whitehall . *Hen. VIII.* iv 1 97
Whiteness. Wringing her hands, whose whiteness so became them As if but now they waxed pale for woe . . *T. G. of Ver.* iii 1 227
I looked for the chalky cliffs, but I could find no whiteness in them *Com. of Errors* iii 2 130
A thousand innocent shames In angel whiteness beat away those blushes . . . . *Much Ado* iv 1 163
Sully The purity and whiteness of my sheets . . . *W. Tale* i 2 327
The whiteness in thy cheek Is apter than thy tongue to tell thy errand *2 Hen. IV.* i 1 68
Whiter than the paper it writ on Is the fair hand that writ *Mer. of Venice* ii 4 13
Upon the wings of night Whiter than new snow on a raven's back *Rom. and Jul.* iii 2 19
That whiter skin of hers than snow, And smooth as monumental alabaster . . . . *Othello* v 2 4
Cytherea, How bravely thou becomest thy bed, fresh lily, And whiter than the sheets! . . . . *Cymbeline* ii 2 16
Whitest. Back-wounding calumny The whitest virtue strikes *M. for M.* iii 2 198
That dye is on me Which makes my whitest part black . *Hen. VIII.* i 1 209
Whither. Then tell me, whither were I best to send him? *T. G. of Ver.* i 3 24
Whither travel you?—To Verona.—Whence came you? . . iv 1 16
How now, Meg!—Whither go you, George? . . *Mer. Wives* iii 1 153
Whither go you?—Truly, sir, to see your wife . . . iii 2 9
Whither bear you this?—To the laundress, forsooth . . iii 3 162
They fled Into this abbey, whither we pursued them *Com. of Errors* v 1 155
Come, will you go with me?—Whither?—Even to the next willow *M. Ado* ii 1 193
How now, spirit! whither wander you? . . . *M. N. Dream* ii 1 1
Whither. O my poor Rosalind, whither wilt thou go? *As Y. Like It* i 3 92
Why, whither, Adam, wouldst thou have me go?—No matter whither ii 3 29
A man that had a wife with such a wit, he might say 'Wit, whither wilt?' . . . . iv 1 168
I do beseech you, whither is he gone? . . . *All's Well* v 1 27
I must go Where it fits not you to know.—Whither?—O, whither? *W. T.* iv 3 305
Then whither he goes, thither let me go . . *Richard II.* v 1 85
I must not have you henceforth question me Whither I go, nor reason whereabout: Whither I must, I must . . *1 Hen. IV.* ii 3 107
Whither I go, thither shall you go too . . . . ii 3 118
A fool go with thy soul, whither it goes! . . . . v 3 22
O, whither shall we fly from this reproach?—We will not fly *1 Hen. VI.* i 1 97
Whither were you sent?—Whither, my lord? . . . iv 4 12
Go, and take me hence; I care not whither, for I beg no favour *2 Hen. VI.* ii 4 92
Whither goes Vaux so fast? what news, I prithee? . . iii 2 367
Ah, whither shall I fly to 'scape their hands? . . . *3 Hen. VI.* i 3 1
Not that I fear to stay, but love to go Whither the queen intends . ii 5 139
Whither shall we then?—To Lynn, my lord, And ship from thence . v 5 20
He himself wander'd away alone, No man knows whither *Richard III.* iv 4 515
These three lead on this preparation Whither 'tis bent . *Coriolanus* i 2 16
Whither should they come?—Up.—Whither?—To supper *Rom. and Jul.* i 2 75
But, good sir, Whither will you have me? . . . *Pericles* v 1 178
Whither away. Sir Valentine, whither away so fast? . *T. G. of Ver.* iii 1 51
Whither away so fast? A true man or a thief that gallops so? *L. L. L.* iv 3 186
God speed fair Helena! whither away? . . . *M. N. Dream* i 1 180
Young budding virgin, fair and fresh and sweet, Whither away? *T. of S.* iv 5 38
Whither away, Sir John Fastolfe, in such haste?—Whither away! to save myself . . . . *1 Hen. VI.* iii 2 104
Whither away so fast?—I promise you, I scarcely know myself *Rich. III.* ii 3 1
Whither away?—No farther than the Tower . . . iv 1 7
Whither away so fast?—O, God save ye! Even to the hall *Hen. VIII.* ii 1 1
Whiting-time. Or—it is whiting-time—send him by your two men to Datchet-mead . . . . *Mer. Wives* iii 3 140
Whitmore. The other, Walter Whitmore, is thy share . *2 Hen. VI.* iv 1 14
My name is Walter Whitmore. How now! why start'st thou? . iv 1 31
Stay, Whitmore; for thy prisoner is a prince . . . iv 1 44
Whitsters. Carry it among the whitsters in Datchet-mead *Mer. Wives* iii 3 14
Whitsun. Methinks I play as I have seen them do In Whitsun pastorals *W. Tale* iv 4 134
Busied with a Whitsun morris-dance . . . . *Hen. V.* ii 4 25
Whittle. There's not a whittle in the unruly camp But I do prize it at my love before The reverend'st throat in Athens *T. of Athens* v 1 183
Whizzing. The exhalations whizzing in the air Give so much light that I may read by them . . . . *J. Cæsar* ii 1 44
Who. A brave vessel, Who had, no doubt, some noble creature in her *Tempest* i 2 7
Who to advance and who To trash for over-topping . . . i 2 80
Banish'd from your eye, Who hath cause to wet the grief on't . ii 1 127
Who wouldst thou strike?—Nothing. . . . *T. G. of Ver.* iii 1 200
A gentleman, Who, in my mood, I stabb'd unto the heart . iv 1 51
Who by repentance is not satisfied Is nor of heaven nor earth . v 4 79
Like a drop of water . . . Who, falling there to find his fellow *C. of Er.* i 2 37
Who think you the most desartless man to be constable? *Much Ado* iii 3 9
Consider who the king your father sends, To whom he sends *L. L. Lost* ii 1 2
Ripe as the pomewater, who now hangeth like a jewel in the ear of caelo iv 2 4
And now who knows But you, Lorenzo, whether I am yours? *M. of Ven.* ii 6 30
The first, of gold, who this inscription bears . . . ii 7 4
I'll tell you who Time ambles withal, who Time trots withal *As Y. L. It* iii 2 327
Give thyself unto my sick desires, Who then recover . *All's Well* iv 2 36
Jove knows I love: But who? Lips, do not move; No man must know *T. Night* ii 5 108
Nothing so certain as your anchors, who Do their best office *W. Tale* iv 4 581
Make proselytes Of who she but bid follow . . . v 1 109
The world, who of itself is peised well . . . *K. John* ii 1 575
Rotten opinion, who hath writ me down After my seeming *2 Hen. IV.* v 2 128
Who join'st thou with but with a lordly nation? . *1 Hen. VI.* iii 3 62
Pray you, who does the wolf love?—The lamb . . *Coriolanus* ii 1 8
My arm'd knees, Who bow'd but in my stirrup . . . iii 2 119
Who should I swear by? thou believest no god . . *T. Andron.* v 1 71
Cut the winds, Who nothing hurt withal hiss'd him in scorn *R. and J.* i 1 119
Who once a day . . . The turbulent surge shall cover *T. of Athens* v 1 220
'Tis Cæsar that you mean; is it not, Cassius?—Let it be who it is *J. Cæsar* i 3 80
And I will set this foot of mine as far As who goes farthest . i 3 120
Who was the thane lives yet; But under heavy judgement bears that life . . . . *Macbeth* i 3 109
Who can be wise, amazed, temperate and furious, Loyal and neutral, in a moment? No man . . . . ii 3 114
But wail his fall Who I myself struck down . . . iii 1 123
Who may I rather challenge for unkindness Than pity for mischance! . iii 4 42
The dead man's knell Is there scarce ask'd for who . . iv 3 171
What is the matter, my lord?—Between who? . . *Hamlet* ii 2 196
Run, O, run!—To who, my lord? Who hath the office? . *Lear* v 3 248
Who let us not therefore blame . . . . *Othello* ii 3 15
Who steals my purse steals trash; 'tis something, nothing . iii 3 157
What's the matter with my lord?—With who? . . . iv 2 99
'Tis thus; Who tells me true, though in his tale lie death, I hear him as he flatter'd . . . . *Ant. and Cleo.* i 2 102
Who seeks, and will not take when once 'tis offer'd, Shall never find it more . . . . ii 7 89
Who does i' the wars more than his captain can Becomes his captain's captain . . . . iii 1 21
Yield thee, thief.—To who? to thee? What art thou? . *Cymbeline* iv 2 76
Who worse than a physician Would this report become? . . v 5 27
Whoa, ho! ho, father Page!—Son, how now! how now, son! *Mer. Wives* v 5 187
Whoa, ho, hoa!—Hilloa, loa!—What, art so near? . *W. Tale* iii 3 79
Whoever. As any is in Windsor, whoe'er be the other *Mer. Wives* ii 2 103
Whoever bound him, I will loose his bonds And gain a husband *C. of Er.* v 1 339
Whoe'er a' was, a' show'd a mounting mind . . *L. L. Lost* iv 1 4
And here she stands, touch her whoever dare . *T. of Shrew* iii 2 235
Whoever shoots at him, I set him there; Whoever charges on his forward breast, I am the caitiff that do hold him to't *All's Well* iii 2 115
'Twas mine, 'twas Helen's, Whoever gave it you . . . v 3 105
Whoe'er I woo, myself would be his wife . . . *T. Night* i 4 42
Whoever wins, on that side shall I lose . . . *K. John* iii 1 335
Whoever spoke it, it is true, my lord . . . . v 5 19
But mine I am sure thou art, whoe'er thou be . . *1 Hen. IV.* v 4 37
As good a man as he, sir, whoe'er I am . . *2 Hen. IV.* iv 3 12
Whoe'er helps thee, 'tis thou that must help me . *1 Hen. VI.* i 2 107
Whoe'er he be, you may not be let in . . . . i 3 7
Whoever got thee, there thy mother stands . . . *3 Hen. VI.* ii 2 133

Whoever. Whoever journeys to the prince, For God's sake, let not us two be behind . . . . *Richard III.* ii 2 146
Whoever the king favours, The cardinal instantly will find employment *Hen. VIII.* ii 1 47
Whoever gave that counsel, to give forth The corn *Coriolanus* iii 1 113
Go, some of you, whoe'er you find attach . . . . *Rom. and Jul.* v 3 173
Open, locks, Whoever knocks! . . . . *Macbeth* iv 1 47
Whoe'er he be that in this foul proceeding Hath thus beguiled your daughter of herself . . . . *Othello* i 3 65

Whole. Sure, it was the roar Of a whole herd of lions . . *Tempest* ii 1 316
Hast any more of this?—The whole butt, man . . . ii 2 137
Are they broken?—No, they are both as whole as a fish . *T. G. of Ver.* ii 5 20
Let them keep their limbs whole and hack our English . *Mer. Wives* iii 1 79
Your hearts are mighty, your skins are whole, and let burnt sack be the issue . . . . iii 1 111
Swallowed his vows whole, pretending in her discoveries of dishonour *Meas. for Meas.* iii 1 235
Who sent whole armadoes of caracks to be ballast at her nose *C. of Er.* iii 2 140
In our last conflict four of his five wits went halting off, and now is the whole man governed with one . . . . *Much Ado* i 1 67
I stood like a man at a mark, with a whole army shooting at me . ii 1 254
Our whole discourse Is all of her; say that thou overheard'st us . . iii 1 5
And there, before the whole congregation, shame her . . . iii 3 173
Is our whole dissembly appeared? . . . . iv 2 1
Did mean, upon his words, to disgrace Hero before the whole assembly iv 2 57
A whole bookful of these quondam carpet-mongers . . . v 2 32
Devise, wit; write, pen; for I am for whole volumes in folio *L. L. Lost* i 2 191
And then the whole quire hold their hips and laugh . *M. N. Dream* ii 1 55
I'll believe as soon This whole earth may be bored . . . iii 2 53
Nor is my whole estate Upon the fortune of this present year *M. of Ven.* i 1 43
I'll tell thee all my whole device When I am in my coach . . . iii 4 81
Wilt thou show the whole wealth of thy wit in an instant? . . . iii 5 61
I am not a woman, to be touched with so many giddy offences as he hath generally taxed their whole sex withal . . *As Y. Like It* iii 2 368
That had the whole theoric of war in the knot of his scarf . *All's Well* iv 3 162
All is whole; Not one word more of the consumed time. . . . v 3 37
I'll be revenged on the whole pack of you . . . *T. Night* v 1 386
There's not a grain of it the face to sweeten Of the whole dungy earth *W. Tale* ii 1 157
The whole matter And copy of the father, eye, nose, lip . . . ii 3 98
I had not left a purse alive in the whole army . . . . iv 4 631
This might have been prevented and made whole . . *K. John* i 1 35
John, to stop Arthur's title in the whole, Hath willingly departed with a part . . . . ii 1 562
A whole armado of convicted sail Is scatter'd . . . . iii 4 2
Death, whose office is this day To feast upon whole thousands of the French . . . . v 2 178
The whole land Is full of weeds, her fairest flowers choked up *Rich. II.* iii 4 43
That would, if matters should be looked into, for their own credit sake, make all whole . . . . 1 *Hen. IV.* ii 1 81
Your whole plot too light for the counterpoise of so great an opposition ii 3 13
I would the state of time had first been whole Ere he by sickness had been visited . . . . iv 1 25
Yet all goes well, yet all our joints are whole . . . . . iv 1 83
What may the king's whole battle reach unto? . . . . . iv 1 129
My whole charge consists of ancients, corporals, lieutenants . . . iv 2 25
And in the neck of that, task'd the whole state . . . . iv 3 92
There's a whole merchant's venture of Bourdeaux stuff in him 2 *Hen. IV.* ii 4 68
What's a joint of mutton or two in a whole Lent? . . . . ii 4 376
His apparel is built upon his back and the whole frame stands upon pins iii 2 155
I have a whole school of tongues in this belly of mine . . . iv 3 20
And put the world's whole strength Into one giant arm, it shall not force This lineal honour from me . . . . iv 5 44
And his whole kingdom into desolation . . . . *Hen. V.* ii 2 173
By the means whereof a' breaks words, and keeps whole weapons . . iii 2 37
All the whole army stood agazed on him . . . . 1 *Hen. VI.* i 1 126
Were the whole frame here, It is of such a spacious lofty pitch, Your roof were not sufficient to contain't . . . . . . ii 3 54
Not that alone But all the whole inheritance I give . . . iii 1 164
To be call'd but viceroy of the whole? No, lord ambassador. . . v 4 143
That Suffolk should demand a whole fifteenth For costs and charges! 2 *Hen. VI.* i 1 133
You made in a day, my lord, whole towns to fly . . . . iii 1 164
Men's flesh preserved so whole do seldom win . . . . . iii 1 301
He was thrust in the mouth with a spear, and 'tis not whole yet . . iv 7 11
All the whole time I was my chamber's prisoner . . *Hen. VIII.* i 1 12
A commission from the consistory, Yea, the whole consistory of Rome . ii 4 93
To bring my whole cause 'fore his holiness, And to be judged by him . ii 4 120
These are the whole contents . . . . iv 2 154
Misdemean'd yourself, . . . in filling The whole realm, by your teaching v 3 16
Commotions, uproars, with a general taint Of the whole state . . v 3 29
O, tell, tell.—I'll decline the whole question . . *Troi. and Cres.* ii 3 55
As if The passage and whole carriage of this action Rode on his tide . ii 3 140
You have broke it, cousin: and, by my life, you shall make it whole again . . . . iii 1 54
You told how Diomed, a whole week by days, Did haunt you in the field iv 1 9
Give him note of our approach, With the whole quality wherefore. . iv 1 44
This whole night Hath nothing been but shapes and forms of slaughter v 3 11
Unto the appetite and affection common Of the whole body *Coriolanus* i 1 108
I am the store-house and the shop Of the whole body . . . i 1 138
Wherein he gives my son the whole name of the war . . . ii 1 149
The violent fit o' the time craves it as physic For the whole state . iii 2 34
The other has half, by the entreaty and grant of the whole table . iv 5 213
What will whole months of tears thy father's eyes? . *T. Andron.* ii 4 55
Thou hast more of the wild-goose in one of thy wits than, I am sure, I have in my whole five . . . . . *Rom. and Jul.* ii 4 78
I would have made it short: for I was come to the whole depth of my tale . . . . ii 4 104
This reverend holy friar, All our whole city is much bound to him . iv 2 32
His hate may grow To the whole race of mankind, high and low! *T. of A.* iv 1 40
That the whole life of Athens were in this! Thus would I eat it . . iv 3 281
Whose star-like nobleness gave life and influence To their whole being! v 1 67
A piece of work that will make sick men whole.—But are not some whole that we must make sick? . . . . . *J. Cæsar* ii 1 327
Whole as the marble, founded as the rock . . . *Macbeth* iii 4 22
Fill full. I drink to the general joy o' the whole table . . . iii 4 89
For the whole space that's in the tyrant's grasp, And the rich East to boot . . . . iv 3 36
I would not have such a heart in my bosom for the dignity of the whole body . . . . v 1 62
Whole. It us befitted To bear our hearts in grief and our whole kingdom *Hamlet* i 2 3
On his choice depends The safety and health of this whole state . . i 3 21
So the whole ear of Denmark Is by a forged process of my death Rankly abused . . . . i 5 36
And his whole function suiting With forms to his conceit . . . ii 2 582
The censure of the which one must in your allowance o'erweigh a whole theatre of others . . . . iii 2 31
Half a share.—A whole one, I . . . . iii 2 291
Vouchsafe me a word with you.—Sir, a whole history . . . . iii 2 309
Go to the creating a whole tribe of fops . . . . *Lear* i 2 14
I will a round unvarnish'd tale deliver Of my whole course of love *Othello* i 3 91
I told thee he was of my counsel In my whole course of wooing . . iii 3 112
If you'll patch a quarrel, As matter whole you have not to make it with, It must not be with this . . . . . *Ant. and Cleo.* ii 2 53
Eight wild-boars roasted whole at a breakfast, and but twelve persons there . . . . ii 2 183
His whole action grows Not in the power on't . . . . . iii 7 69
You keep by land The legions and the horse whole, do you not? . . iii 7 72
Publicola, and Cælius, are for sea: But we keep whole by land . . iii 7 75
Strike not by land; keep whole: provoke not battle, Till we have done at sea . . . . iii 8 3
Gods and goddesses, All the whole synod of them! . . . . iii 10 5
Wash the congealment from your wounds, and kiss The honour'd gashes whole . . . . iv 8 11
Because thine eye Presumes to reach, all thy whole heap must die *Per.* i 1 33
Till they've swallowed the whole parish, church, steeple, bells, and all ii 1 38
She's able to freeze the god Priapus, and undo a whole generation . iv 6 4
Shall undo a whole household . . . . iv 6 132

Whole world. She'll burn a week longer than the whole world *C. of Er.* iii 2 102
The whole world again Cannot pick out five such . . *L. L. Lost* v 2 547
Should with his lion gait walk the whole world . . . *Hen. V.* ii 2 122
Know you not How your state stands i' the world, with the whole world? . . . . *Hen. VIII.* v 1 127
He is not emulous, as Achilles is.—Know the whole world, he is as valiant.—A whoreson dog! . . . . *Troi. and Cres.* ii 3 243
One touch of nature makes the whole world kin . . . . iii 3 175
For the whole world,—why, who would not make her husband a cuckold to make him a monarch? . . . . *Othello* iv 3 75
Beshrew me, if I would do such a wrong For the whole world . . iv 3 79
Wilt thou be lord of the whole world? . . . *Ant. and Cleo.* ii 7 68
That noble countenance, Wherein the worship of the whole world lies iv 14 86
We could not stall together In the whole world . . . . v 1 40
Take him hence: The whole world shall not save him . *Cymbeline* v 5 321

Wholesome. In state as wholesome as in state 'tis fit . *Mer. Wives* v 5 63
With wholesome syrups, drugs, and holy prayers *Com. of Errors* v 1 104
To the most wholesome physic of thy health-giving air *L. L. Lost* i 1 235
Is not the grease of a mutton as wholesome as the sweat of a man? *As Y. Like It* iii 2 58
Get me some repast; I care not what, so it be wholesome food *T. of S.* iv 3 16
If from me he have wholesome beverage, Account me not your servant *W. Tale* i 2 346
That I may breathe my last In wholesome counsel . *Richard II.* ii 1 2
Weeds, which without profit suck The soil's fertility from wholesome flowers . . . . iii 4 39
Her wholesome herbs Swarming with caterpillars . . . . iii 4 46
Wholesome berries thrive and ripen best Neighbour'd by fruit of baser quality . . . . *Hen. V.* i 1 61
Bosom up my counsel, You'll find it wholesome . . *Hen. VIII.* i 1 113
Which are not wholesome To those which would not know them, and yet must Perforce be their acquaintance . . . . . . i 2 45
And not wholesome to Our cause, that she should lie i' the bosom of Our hard-ruled king . . . . iii 2 99
If they would yield us but the superfluity, while it were wholesome *Cor.* i 1 18
Repeal daily any wholesome act established against the rich . . i 1 85
You wear out a good wholesome forenoon in hearing a cause . . ii 1 77
Speak to 'em, I pray you, In wholesome manner . . . . iii 3 66
What, is Brutus sick, And will he steal out of his wholesome bed? *J. C.* ii 1 264
When shalt thou see thy wholesome days again? . . *Macbeth* iv 3 105
The nights are wholesome; then no planets strike . . *Hamlet* i 1 162
And curd, like eager droppings into milk, The thin and wholesome blood i 5 70
As wholesome as sweet, and by very much more handsome than fine . ii 2 465
Thy natural magic and dire property On wholesome life usurp immediately . . . . iii 2 271
If it shall please you to make me a wholesome answer . . . iii 2 328
Sir, I cannot.—What, my lord?—Make you a wholesome answer . . iii 2 333
Here is your husband; like a mildew'd ear, Blasting his wholesome brother . . . . iii 4 65
In the tender of a wholesome weal, Might in their working do you that offence, Which else were shame . . . . . *Lear* i 4 230
'Tis on such ground, and to such wholesome end, As clears her from all blame . . . . ii 4 146
It seems not meet, nor wholesome to my place, To be produced *Othello* i 1 146
In wholesome wisdom He might not but refuse you . . . iii 1 49
Air comes in: there's none abroad so wholesome as that you vent *Cymb.* i 2 4
How now! wholesome iniquity have you that a man may deal withal? *Pericles* iv 6 28

Wholesome-profitable. To wail friends lost Is not by much so wholesome-profitable . . . . *L. L. Lost* v 2 760

Wholesomest. The best and wholesomest spirits of the night Envelope you! . . . . *Meas. for Meas.* iv 2 76

Wholly. I stand wholly for you: but my wife, master doctor, is for you altogether . . . . *Mer. Wives* iii 2 63
And shape his service wholly to my hests . . . *L. L. Lost* v 2 65
Know you the musicians?—Wholly, sir . . . *Troi. and Cres.* iii 1 22
You shall be mistress, and command him wholly . . . . iv 4 122
Which wholly depends on your abode . . . . *Ant. and Cleo.* i 2 182
Sleep hath seized me wholly. To your protection I commend me, gods *Cymbeline* ii 2 7

Whom. He whom next thyself Of all the world I loved . *Tempest* i 2 68
The elements, Of whom your swords are temper'd . . . . iii 3 62
Most wicked sir, whom to call brother Would even infect my mouth . v 1 130
On whom it will, it will; On whom it will not, so; yet still 'tis just *Meas. for Meas.* i 2 126
Thy wife?—Ay, sir; whom, I thank heaven, is an honest woman . . ii 1 72
My wife and I, Fixing our eyes on whom our care was fix'd *Com. of Errors* i 1 85
Than whom no mortal so magnificent! . . . . *L. L. Lost* iii 1 180
O wicked wall, through whom I see no bliss! . . *M. N. Dream* v 1 181
I may neither choose whom I would nor refuse whom I dislike *Mer. of Venice* i 2 25

Whom. Your mistress, from the whom, I see, There's no disjunction to be made . . . . *W. Tale* iv 4 539
Whom they say is kill'd to-night On your suggestion . *K. John* iv 2 165
Whom we raise, We will make fast within a hallow'd verge . 2 *Hen. VI.* i 4 24
Fame, at the which he aims, In whom already he's well graced *Coriol.* i 1 268
I shall unfold to thee, as we are going To whom it must be done *J. Cæsar* ii 1 331
Make choice of whom your wisest friends you will . *Hamlet* iv 5 204
Whom in constancy you think stands so safe . . *Cymbeline* i 4 137
Whoo-bub. Had not the old man come in with a whoo-bub *W. Tale* iv 4 629
Whoop, do me no harm, good man . . . . iv 4 199
Whoop, Jug! I love thee . . . . . . *Lear* i 4 245
Whooped. Suffer'd me by the voice of slaves to be Whoop'd out of Rome *Coriolanus* iv 5 84
Whore. Mo marrying 'mong his subjects?—None, man; all idle; whores and knaves . . . . *Tempest* ii 1 166
Fie on her! never name her, child, if she be a whore . *Mer. Wives* iv 1 65
Ever your fresh whore and your powdered bawd . *Meas. for Meas.* iii 2 61
Your whores, sir, being members of my occupation, using painting . iv 2 39
I beseech your highness, do not marry me to a whore . . v 1 521
For what? for tearing a poor whore's ruff in a bawdy-house? 2 *Hen. IV.* ii 4 157
Let's beat him before his whore . . . . . ii 4 280
And the whores called him mandrake . . . . iii 2 338
But then he was rheumatic, and talked of the whore of Babylon *Hen. V.* ii 3 41
Thou that givest whores indulgences to sin . 1 *Hen. VI.* i 3 35
All the argument is a cuckold and a whore . . *Troi. and Cres.* ii 3 79
Each weighs nor less nor more; But he as he, the heavier for a whore . iv 1 66
Male varlet, you rogue! what's that?—Why, his masculine whore . v 1 20
She could not publish more, Unless she said 'My mind is now turn'd whore' . . . . v 2 114
Patroclus will give me any thing for the intelligence of this whore . v 2 193
That same young Trojan ass, that loves the whore there . . v 4 7
Hold thy whore, Grecian!—now for thy whore, Trojan!—now the sleeve! v 4 25
If the son of a whore fight for a whore, he tempts judgement . v 7 22
'Zounds, ye whore! is black so base a hue? . . *T. Andron.* iv 2 71
A very good blade! a very tall man! a very good whore! *Rom. and Jul.* ii 4 32
Come, damned earth, Thou common whore of mankind, that put'st odds Among the rout of nations . . . . *T. of Athens* iv 3 42
This fell whore of thine Hath in her more destruction than thy sword . iv 3 61
Be a whore still: they love thee not that use thee . . . iv 3 83
Enough to make a whore forswear her trade, And to make whores, a bawd iv 3 133
Be whores still; And he whose pious breath seeks to convert you, Be strong in whore, allure him . . . . iv 3 139
More money, bounteous Timon.—More whore, more mischief first . iv 3 168
Fortune, on his damned quarrel smiling, Show'd like a rebel's whore *Macb.* i 2 15
Like a whore, unpack my heart with words, And fall a-cursing *Hamlet* ii 2 614
Leave thy drink and thy whore, And keep in-a-door . . *Lear* i 4 137
Fortune, that arrant whore, Ne'er turns the key to the poor . ii 4 52
And bawds and whores do churches build . . . . iii 2 90
He's mad that trusts in . . . a horse's health, a boy's love, or a whore's oath iii 6 21
Hold thy bloody hand! Why dost thou lash that whore? . . iv 6 165
Villain, be sure thou prove my love a whore, Be sure of it . *Othello* iii 3 359
She gave it him, and he hath given it his whore . . . iv 1 187
This is a subtle whore, A closet lock and key of villanous secrets . iv 2 21
Was this fair paper, this most goodly book, Made to write 'whore' upon? iv 2 72
What, not a whore?—No, as I shall be saved . . . iv 2 86
I took you for that cunning whore of Venice That married with Othello iv 2 89
He call'd her whore: a beggar in his drink Could not have laid such terms upon his callat . . . . iv 2 120
To be call'd whore? would it not make one weep? . . . iv 2 127
Why should he call her whore? who keeps her company? . . iv 2 137
I cannot say 'whore:' It doth abhor me now I speak the word . iv 2 161
She turn'd to folly, and she was a whore.—Thou dost belie her . v 2 132
He begg'd of me to steal it.—Villanous whore! . . . v 2 229
If it lay in their hands to make me a cuckold, they would make themselves whores, but they'ld do't! . . . *Ant. and Cleo.* i 2 82
He hath given his empire Up to a whore . . . . iii 6 67
Triple-turn'd whore! 'tis thou Hast sold me to this novice . iv 12 13
I shall see Some squeaking Cleopatra boy my greatness I' the posture of a whore . . . . v 2 221
She hath bought the name of whore thus dearly . *Cymbeline* ii 4 128
Whored. He that hath kill'd my king and whored my mother *Hamlet* v 2 64
Whoremaster. The deputy cannot abide a whoremaster *Meas. for Meas.* iii 2 37
That he is, saving your reverence, a whoremaster, that I utterly deny 1 *Hen. IV.* ii 4 516
We may account thee a whore-master and a knave . *T. of Athens* ii 2 111
What is a whoremaster, fool?—A fool in good clothes . . ii 2 113
An admirable evasion of whore-master man, to lay his goatish disposition to the charge of a star! . . . . . *Lear* i 2 137
Whoremasterly. That Greekish whoremasterly villain *Troi. and Cres.* v 4 7
Whoremonger. If he be a whoremonger, and comes before him, he were as good go a mile on his errand . . *Meas. for Meas.* iii 2 37
Whoreson. Hang, cur! hang, you whoreson, insolent noisemaker! *Temp.* i 1 46
Why, thou whoreson ass, thou mistakest me . . *T. G. of Ver.* ii 5 49
How now, you whoreson peasant! Where have you been? . . iv 4 47
Thou whoreson, senseless villain!—I would I were senseless *Com. of Er.* iv 4 25
You whoreson loggerhead! you were born to do me shame *L. L. Lost* iv 3 204
You peasant swain! you whoreson malt-horse drudge! . *T. of Shrew* iv 1 132
You whoreson villain! will you let it fall? . . . iv 1 158
A whoreson beetle-headed, flap-ear'd knave! . . . iv 1 160
Cut the villains' throats: ah! whoreson caterpillars! bacon-fed knaves! 1 *Hen. IV.* ii 2 88
Why, you whoreson round man, what's the matter? . . ii 4 155
Thou knotty-pated fool, thou whoreson, obscene, greasy tallow-catch . ii 4 252
Thou whoreson, impudent, embossed rascal . . . iii 3 177
Thou whoreson mandrake, thou art fitter to be worn in my cap 2 *Hen. IV.* i 2 16
A whoreson Achitophel! a rascally yea-forsooth knave! . . i 2 40
The whoreson smooth-pates do now wear nothing but high shoes . i 2 43
Moreover, his highness is fallen into this same whoreson apoplexy . i 2 123
A kind of sleeping in the blood, a whoreson tingling . . i 2 128
Away, you whoreson upright rabbit, away! . . . ii 2 91
Ah, you whoreson little valiant villain, you! . . . ii 4 225
Let me wipe thy face; come on, you whoreson chops . . ii 4 235
Thou whoreson little tidy Bartholomew boar-pig . . . ii 4 250
Thou whoreson mad compound of majesty . . . . ii 4 319
You whoreson candle-mine, you, how vilely did you speak of me! . ii 4 326
What disease hast thou?—A whoreson cold, sir, a cough . . iii 2 193
The sly whoresons Have got a speeding trick to lay down ladies *Hen. VIII.* i 3 39
You whoreson cur!—Do, do.—Thou stool for a witch! . *Troi. and Cres.* ii 1 44
A whoreson dog, that shall palter thus with us! . . . ii 3 244
You ruinous butt, you whoreson indistinguishable cur . . . v 1 32
Whoreson. A whoreson tisick, a whoreson rascally tisick so troubles me *Troi. and Cres.* v 3 101
Well said; a merry whoreson, ha! Thou shalt be logger-head *R. and J.* iv 4 19
Your water is a sore decayer of your whoreson dead body . *Hamlet* v 1 189
Whose was it?—A whoreson mad fellow's it was . . . v 1 193
There was good sport at his making, and the whoreson must be acknowledged . . . . *Lear* i 1 24
You whoreson dog! you slave! you cur!—I am none of these . i 4 89
A whoreson, glass-gazing, superserviceable, finical rogue . . ii 2 19
Draw, you whoreson cullionly, barber-monger, draw . . . ii 2 35
Thou whoreson zed! thou unnecessary letter! . . . ii 2 69
These same whoreson devils do the gods great harm in their women *Ant. and Cleo.* v 2 277
And then a whoreson jackanapes must take me up for swearing *Cymb.* ii 1 4
Whoreson dog! I give him satisfaction? Would he had been one of my rank! . . . . ii 1 16
Whoring. This is the fruit of whoring . . . . *Othello* v 1 116
Whorish. You, like a lecher, out of whorish loins Are pleased to breed out your inheritors . . . . . *Troi. and Cres.* iv 1 63
Whose. He trod the water, Whose enmity he flung aside *Tempest* ii 1 116
Whose high imperious thoughts have punish'd me . . *T. G. of Ver.* ii 4 130
To her whose worth makes other worthies nothing . . . ii 4 166
Orpheus' lute . . . , Whose golden touch could soften steel and stones iii 2 79
Whose was't?—It is no matter, now I have't again . *Troi. and Cres.* v 2 71
Tell me whose it was.—'Twas one's that loved me better than you will v 2 88
Whoso. Their love Lies in their purses, and whoso empties them By so much fills their hearts with deadly hate . . *Richard II.* ii 2 130
The law of arms is such That whoso draws a sword, 'tis present death 1 *Hen. VI.* iii 4 39
Whoso please To stop affliction, let him take his haste . *T. of Athens* v 1 212
Whoso ask'd her for his wife, His riddle told not, lost his life *Per.* i Gower 37
Whosoever. If thou do pardon, whosoever pray, More sins for this forgiveness prosper may . . . . . *Richard II.* v 3 83
Margaret my name, . . . whosoe'er thou art . . 1 *Hen. VI.* v 3 52
Whosoe'er gainsays King Edward's right, By this I challenge him 3 *Hen. VI.* iv 7 74
He's one o' the soundest judgements in Troy, whosoever *Troi. and Cres.* i 2 208
Whosoever you take him to be, he is Ajax . . . . ii 1 70
Why, that's my spirit! But was not this nigh shore? . . *Tempest* i 2 215
Why speaks my father so ungently? . . . . . . i 2 444
Why, how now? ho, awake! Why are you drawn? Wherefore this ghastly looking? . . . . ii 1 308
Why didst thou stoop, then?—To take a paper up . *T. G. of Ver.* i 2 72
Why, this it is: my heart accords thereto . . . . i 3 90
'Tis not to have you gone; For why, the fools are mad, if left alone . iii 1 99
Ask me no reason why I love you . . . *Mer. Wives* iii 1 4
Shall I tell you why?—Ay, sir, and wherefore; for they say every why hath a wherefore . . . . . . *Com. of Errors* ii 2 43
When in the why and the wherefore is neither rhyme nor reason . ii 2 49
Why, Jessica, I say!—Why, Jessica! . . . *Mer. of Venice* ii 5 6
The 'why' is plain as way to parish church . *As Y. Like It* ii 7 52
Trembled and shook; for why, he stamp'd and swore . *T. of Shrew* iii 2 169
It shall be what o'clock I say it is.—Why, so this gallant will command the sun . . . . iv 3 198
But then more 'why?' why have they dared to march? . *Richard II.* ii 3 92
For why the senseless brands will sympathize The heavy accent . v 1 46
There is occasions and causes why and wherefore in all things *Hen. V.* v 1 3
Then fly. What, from myself? Great reason why . *Richard III.* v 3 185
For why my bowels cannot hide her woes . . *T. Andron.* iii 1 231
Say, why is this? wherefore? what should we do? . . *Hamlet* i 4 57
She must not speak Why she dares not come over to thee . *Lear* iii 6 30
Why I do trifle thus with his despair Is done to cure it . . iv 6 33
Why, why is this? Think'st thou I'ld make a life of jealousy? *Othello* iii 3 176
Then let it do at once The thing why thou hast drawn it *Ant. and Cleo.* iv 14 89
Why so. Puppet? why so? ay, that way goes the game *M. N. Dream* iii 2 289
No news of them? Why, so: and I know not what's spent in the search *Mer. of Venice* iii 1 95
I love you better.—And why so, my lord? . . . *W. Tale* iii 1 7
Your son was gone before I came.—He was? Why, so! go all which way it will! . . . . *Richard II.* ii 2 87
Why, so: now have I done a good day's work . . *Richard III.* ii 1 1
Unreal mockery, hence! Why, so: being gone, I am a man again *Macb.* iii 4 107
Glad at the thing they scowl at.—And why so? . . *Cymbeline* i 1 15
Wick. There lives within the very flame of love A kind of wick or snuff that will abate it . . . . *Hamlet* iv 7 116
Wicked. Thou poisonous slave, got by the devil himself Upon thy wicked dam! . . . . *Tempest* i 2 320
As wicked dew as e'er my mother brush'd With raven's feather from unwholesome fen Drop on you both! . . . . . . i 2 321
You, most wicked sir, whom to call brother Would even infect my mouth . . . . v 1 130
What a Herod of Jewry is this! O wicked, wicked world! *Mer. Wives* ii 1 20
Till the wicked fire of lust have melted him in his own grease . ii 1 68
As poor as Job?—And as wicked as his wife? . . . v 5 165
Thou thyself art a wicked villain, despite of all grace *Meas. for Meas.* i 2 27
Varlet, thou liest; thou liest, wicked varlet! . . . ii 1 174
O thou caitiff! O thou varlet! O thou wicked Hannibal! . . ii 1 183
Prove this, thou wicked Hannibal, or I'll have mine action of battery on thee . . . . ii 1 187
What is't your worship's pleasure I shall do with this wicked caitiff? . ii 1 193
Thou seest, thou wicked varlet, now, what's come upon thee . ii 1 199
Fie, sirrah! a bawd, a wicked bawd! . . . . . iii 2 20
What wicked and dissembling glass of mine Made me compare with Hermia's sphery eyne? . . . . . . *M. N. Dream* ii 2 98
O wicked wall, through whom I see no bliss! . . . . v 1 181
If thou never sawest good manners, then thy manners must be wicked; and wickedness is sin . . . . . . *As Y. Like It* iii 2 44
That same wicked bastard of Venus that was begot of thought . iv 1 216
A most wicked Sir Oliver, Audrey, a most vile Martext . . v 1 5
A wicked creature, as you and all flesh and blood are . *All's Well* i 3 37
Which, if it speed, Is wicked meaning in a lawful deed . . iii 7 45
And all eyes Blind with the pin and web but theirs, theirs only, That would unseen be wicked? . . . . *W. Tale* i 2 292
But then you'll think . . . I am assisted By wicked powers . . v 3 91
A wicked will; A woman's will; a canker'd grandam's will! . *K. John* ii 1 193
A wicked day, and not a holy day! What hath this day deserved? . iii 1 83
The image of a wicked heinous fault Lives in his eye . . iv 2 71
The love of wicked men converts to fear . . . *Richard II.* v 1 66
Now am I, if a man should speak truly, little better than one of the wicked. I must give over this life . . . . 1 *Hen. IV.* i 2 106

Wicked. If sack and sugar be a fault, God help the wicked! *1 Hen. IV.* ii 4 517
I dispraised him before the wicked, that the wicked might not fall in love with him . . . *2 Hen. IV.* ii 4 346
Is she of the wicked? is thine hostess here of the wicked? or is thy boy of the wicked? or honest Bardolph, whose zeal burns in his nose, of the wicked? . . . . ii 4 355
This argues what her kind of life hath been, Wicked and vile *1 Hen. VI.* v 4 16
I never had to do with wicked spirits . . . . . v 4 42
Raising up wicked spirits from under ground . . *2 Hen. VI.* ii 1 174
O God, what mischiefs work the wicked ones! . . . . ii 1 186
By wicked means to frame our sovereign's fall . . . iii 1 52
God grant me too Thou mayst be damned for that wicked deed! *Rich. III.* i 2 103
Thus doth he force the swords of wicked men To turn their own points on their masters' bosoms . . . . v 1 23
I true! how now! what wicked deem is this? . *Troi. and Cres.* iv 4 61
I'll haunt thee like a wicked conscience still . . . . v 10 28
This wicked emperor may have shipp'd her hence . *T. Andron.* iv 3 23
Look round about the wicked streets of Rome . . . . v 2 98
Some direful slaughtering death, As punishment for his most wicked life v 3 145
Ancient damnation! O most wicked fiend! . . . *Rom. and Jul.* iii 5 235
What a wicked beast was I to disfurnish myself! . *T. of Athens* iii 2 49
How fairly this lord strives to appear foul! takes virtuous copies to be wicked . . . . iii 3 33
Seek not my name: a plague consume you wicked caitiffs left! . . v 4 71
Nature seems dead, and wicked dreams abuse The curtain'd sleep *Macb.* ii 1 50
By the pricking of my thumbs, Something wicked this way comes . iv 1 45
O, most wicked speed, to post With such dexterity to incestuous sheets! *Hamlet* i 2 156
Be thy intents wicked or charitable, . . . I will speak to thee . . i 4 42
O wicked wit and gifts, that have the power So to seduce! . . i 5 44
Oft 'tis seen the wicked prize itself Buys out the law . . . iii 3 59
You answer with an idle tongue.—Go, go, you question with a wicked tongue . . . . iii 4 12
Whose wicked deed thy most ingenious sense Deprived thee of . . v 1 271
Here stood he in the dark, his sharp sword out, Mumbling of wicked charms . . . . *Lear* ii 1 41
Those wicked creatures yet do look well-favour'd, When others are more wicked . . . . ii 4 259
An odious, damned lie; Upon my soul, a lie, a wicked lie . *Othello* v 2 181
From the which We were dissuaded by our wicked queen . *Cymbeline* v 5 463
The epitaph is for Marina writ By wicked Dionyza . . *Pericles* iv 4 33
Till cruel Cleon, with his wicked wife, Did seek to murder me . . v 1 173
For wicked Cleon and his wife, . . . him and his they in his palace burn v 3 Gower 95

Wickedest. The wicked'st caitiff on the ground May seem as shy, as grave, as just . . . . *Meas. for Meas.* v 1 53
Wickedness. 'Tis not good that children should know any wickedness *Mer. Wives* ii 2 134
The word is too good to paint out her wickedness . . *Much Ado* iii 2 113
Wickedness is sin, and sin is damnation . . . *As Y. Like It* iii 2 44
I do marry that I may repent.—Thy marriage, sooner than thy wickedness *All's Well* i 3 40
A very tainted fellow, and full of wickedness . . . . iii 2 89
Disguise, I see, thou art a wickedness . . . . *T. Night* ii 2 28
What rein can hold licentious wickedness When down the hill he holds his fierce career? . . . . *Hen. V.* iii 3 22
The imputation of his wickedness, by your rule, should be imposed upon his father . . . . iv 1 156
Such is thy audacious wickedness . . . . *1 Hen. VI.* iii 1 14
I'll never care what wickedness I do, If this man come to good . *Lear* iii 7 99
Knows he the wickedness?—Ay, my good lord . . . . iv 2 92
Wide. This is a strange repose, to be asleep With eyes wide open *Tempest* ii 1 214
I never heard a man of his place, gravity, and learning, so wide of his own respect.—What is he? . . . . . . *Mer. Wives* iii 1 58
Lords of the wide world and wild watery seas . *Com. of Errors* ii 1 21
Is my lord well, that he doth speak so wide? . . . *Much Ado* iv 1 63
The wide sea Hath drops too few to wash her clean again . . iv 1 142
Kill Claudio.—Ha! not for the wide world . . . . iv 1 292
And welcome to the wide fields too base to be mine . . *L. L. Lost* ii 1 93
Wide o' the bow hand! i' faith, your hand is out . . . iv 1 135
There the snake throws her enamell'd skin, Weed wide enough to wrap a fairy in . . . . *M. N. Dream* ii 1 256
That the graves all gaping wide, Every one lets forth his sprite . . v 1 387
Nor is the wide world ignorant of her worth . . *Mer. of Venice* i 1 167
The vasty wilds Of wide Arabia are as throughfares now . . . ii 7 42
He'll go along o'er the wide world with me . . *As Y. Like It* i 3 134
This wide and universal theatre Presents more woeful pageants . . ii 7 137
His youthful hose, well saved, a world too wide For his shrunk shank . ii 7 160
I will not open my lips so wide as a bristle may enter . *T. Night* i 5 2
I slide O'er sixteen years and leave the growth untried Of that wide gap *W. Tale* iv 1 7
Each one demand and answer to his part Perform'd in this wide gap of time v 3 154
And wide havoc made For bloody power to rush upon your peace *K. John* ii 1 220
You men of Angiers, open wide your gates . . . . ii 1 300
The mouth of passage shall we fling wide ope, And give you entrance . ii 1 449
We in the world's wide mouth Live scandalized . . *1 Hen. IV.* i 3 153
The villains march wide betwixt the legs, as if they had gyves on . . iv 2 43
The beachy girdle of the ocean Too wide for Neptune's hips *2 Hen. IV.* iii 1 51
Golden care! That keep'st the ports of slumber open wide . . iv 5 24
Now set the teeth and stretch the nostril wide, Hold hard the breath *Hen. V.* iii 1 15
In liberty of bloody hand shall range With conscience wide as hell . iii 3 13
The poring dark Fills the wide vessel of the universe . . iv Prol. 3
Or earth, gape open wide and eat him quick! . . . *Richard III.* i 2 65
Hector would not lose So rich advantage of a promised glory As smiles upon the forehead of this action For the wide world's revenue *Troi. and Cres.* ii 2 206
No such matter; you are wide: come, your disposer is sick . . iii 1 97
And wide unclasp the tables of their thoughts To every ticklish reader! iv 5 60
To tear with thunder the wide cheeks o' the air . . *Coriolanus* v 3 151
Commander of our commonweal, The wide world's emperor . *T. Andron.* i 1 248
The forest walks are wide and spacious . . . . . ii 1 114
Proves thee far and wide a broad goose . . . *Rom. and Jul.* ii 4 91
'Tis not so deep as a well, nor so wide as a church-door; but 'tis enough iii 1 100
Be patient, for the world is broad and wide . . . . iii 3 16
My free drift Halts not particularly, but moves itself In a wide sea of wax *T. of Athens* i 1 47
That talk'd of Rome, That her wide walls encompass'd but one man *J. C.* i 2 155
But, as this temple waxes, The inward service of the mind and soul Grows wide withal . . . . *Hamlet* i 3 14

Wide. Unequal match'd, Pyrrhus at Priam drives; in rage strikes wide *Hamlet* ii 2 494
To his good friends thus wide I'll ope my arms . . . . iv 5 145
Her clothes spread wide; And, mermaid-like, awhile they bore her up . iv 7 176
When did you die?—Still, still, far wide!—He's scarce awake . *Lear* iv 7 50
Till that a capable and wide revenge Swallow them up . . *Othello* iii 3 459
Let Rome in Tiber melt, and the wide arch Of the ranged empire fall! Here is my space . . . . *Ant. and Cleo.* i 1 33
Where I was taught Of your chaste daughter the wide difference 'Twixt amorous and villanous . . . . *Cymbeline* v 5 194
Wide-chapped. This wide-chapp'd rascal—would thou mightst lie drowning The washing of ten tides! . . . . *Tempest* i 1 60
Wide-enlarged. Nature charged That one body should be fill'd With all graces wide-enlarged . . . . *As Y. Like It* iii 2 151
Widens. For the followers fortune widens them, Not for the fliers *Coriol.* i 4 44
Wider. The grave doth gape For thee thrice wider than for other men *2 Hen. IV.* v 5 58
His arms spread wider than a dragon's wings . . . *1 Hen. VI.* i 1 11
That a thing inseparate Divides more wider than the sky and earth *Troi. and Cres.* v 2 149
To vouch this, is no proof, Without more wider and more overt test *Oth.* i 3 107
Wide-skirted. With plenteous rivers and wide-skirted meads . . *Lear* i 1 66
Widest. He'll be hang'd yet, Though every drop of water swear against it And gape at widest to glut him . . . . . . *Tempest* i 1 63
Wide-stretched. And all wide-stretched honours . . . *Hen. V.* ii 4 82
Widow. Not since widow Dido's time.—Widow! a pox o' that! How came that widow in? widow Dido! . . . . . . *Tempest* ii 1 76
'Widow Dido' said you? you make me study of that . . . . ii 1 81
Milan and Naples have Moe widows in them of this business' making Than we bring men to comfort them . . . . ii 1 133
What trade are you of, sir?—A tapster; a poor widow's tapster *M. for M.* ii 1 207
Are you a maid?—No, my lord.—A widow, then?—Neither, my lord.—Why, you are nothing then: neither maid, widow, nor wife? . . v 1 175
She may be a punk; for many of them are neither maid, widow, nor wife v 1 180
His possessions . . . We do instate and widow you withal . . . v 1 429
He shall live no longer in monument than the bell rings and the widow weeps.—And how long is that? . . . . . . *Much Ado* v 2 82
I have a widow aunt, a dowager Of great revenue . . . *M. N. Dream* i 1 157
Eleven widows and nine maids is a simple coming-in for one man *M. of V.* ii 2 171
My maid Nerissa and myself meantime Will live as maids and widows . iii 2 312
I will be married to a wealthy widow, Ere three days pass *T. of Shrew* iv 2 37
He'll have a lusty widow now, That shall be woo'd and wedded in a day iv 2 50
Have to my widow! and if she be froward, Then hast thou taught Hortensio to be untoward . . . . iv 5 78
With thy loving widow, Feast with the best, and welcome to my house v 2 7
Now, for my life, Hortensio fears his widow . . . . . v 2 16
My widow says, thus she conceives her tale . . . . . v 2 24
Very well mended. Kiss him for that, good widow . . . . v 2 25
To her, widow!—A hundred marks, my Kate does put her down . . v 2 34
O, take his mother's thanks, a widow's thanks! . . . *K. John* ii 1 32
Many a widow's husband grovelling lies, Coldly embracing the discolour'd earth . . . . ii 1 305
A widow, husbandless, subject to fears, A woman, naturally born to fears iii 1 14
A widow cries; be husband to me, heavens! . . . . . iii 1 108
To God, the widow's champion and defence . . . *Richard II.* i 2 43
I am a poor widow of Eastcheap . . . . . *2 Hen. IV.* ii 1 76
Are you not ashamed to enforce a poor widow to so rough a course? . ii 1 89
So came I a widow; And never shall have length of life enough To rain upon remembrance with mine eyes . . . . ii 3 57
And she a mourning widow of her nobles . . . . . *Hen. V.* i 2 158
Many a thousand widows Shall this his mock mock out of their dear husbands . . . . i 2 284
On your head Turning the widows' tears, the orphans' cries . . ii 4 106
To wring the widow from her custom'd right . . . *2 Hen. VI.* v 1 188
I and ten thousand in this luckless realm Had left no mourning widows for our death . . . . *3 Hen. VI.* ii 6 19
Widow, we will consider of your suit . . . . . . iii 2 16
And what your pleasure is, shall satisfy me.—Ay, widow? . . . iii 2 21
How many children hast thou, widow? tell me . . . . . iii 2 26
Lords, give us leave: I'll try this widow's wit . . . . . iii 2 33
The widow likes him not, she knits her brows . . . . . iii 2 82
Sweet widow, by my state I swear to thee I speak no more than what my soul intends . . . . iii 2 93
You cavil, widow: I did mean, my queen. . . . . . iii 2 99
Thou art a widow, and thou hast some children . . . . iii 2 102
The widow likes it not, for she looks very sad . . . . . iii 2 110
Widow, go you along. Lords, use her honourably . . . . iii 2 123
Many an old man's sigh and many a widow's, And many an orphan's . v 6 39
The jealous o'erworn widow and herself, Since that our brother dubb'd them gentlewomen, Are mighty gossips . . . . *Richard III.* i 1 81
Were it to call King Edward's widow sister, I will perform it . . i 1 109
And made her widow to a woful bed . . . . i 2 249
Thou art a widow; yet thou art a mother, And hast the comfort of thy children left thee . . . . ii 2 55
Was never widow had so dear a loss! . . . . ii 2 77
A beauty-waning and distressed widow, Even in the afternoon of her best days . . . . iii 7 185
'Be thou,' quoth I, 'accursed, For making me, so young, so old a widow!' iv 1 73
See what now thou art: For happy wife, a most distressed widow . iv 4 98
Princess dowager And widow to Prince Arthur . . . *Hen. VIII.* iii 2 71
Such eyes the widows in Corioli wear, And mothers that lack sons *Cor.* ii 1 195
A goodly city is this Antium. City, 'Tis I that made thy widows . iv 4 2
The lady widow of Vitruvio . . . . . . *Rom. and Jul.* i 2 69
This is it [gold] That makes the wappen'd widow wed again *T. of Athens* iv 3 38
Each new morn New widows howl, new orphans cry . . *Macbeth* iv 3 5
Both here and hence pursue me lasting strife, If, once a widow, ever I be wife!—If she should break it now! . . . . . *Hamlet* iii 2 233
But being widow, and my Gloucester with her, May all the building in my fancy pluck Upon my hateful life . . . . . *Lear* iv 2 85
To take the widow Exasperates, makes mad her sister Goneril . . v 1 59
Some excellent fortune! Let me be married to three kings in a forenoon, and widow them all . . . . *Ant. and Cleo.* i 2 27
Can from the lap of Egypt's widow pluck The ne'er-lust-wearied Antony ii 1 37
She was a widow,— Widow! Charmian, hark.—And I do think she's thirty . . . . iii 3 30
His wife's sole son—a widow That late he married . . *Cymbeline* i 1 5
Widow-comfort. My widow-comfort, and my sorrows' cure! . *K. John* iii 4 105
Widow-dolour. Our fatherless distress was left unmoan'd; Your widow-dolour likewise be unwept! . . . . . . *Richard III.* ii 2 65
Widowed. He Hath widow'd and unchilded many a one . . *Coriolanus* v 6 153

Widower. What if he had said 'widower Æneas' too? *Tempest* ii 1 79
Here we'll stay To see our widower's second marriage-day . *All's Well* v 3 70
A widower: his vows are forfeited to me, and my honour's paid to him v 3 142
Tell him, in hope he'll prove a widower shortly, I'll wear the willow garland for his sake . . . 3 *Hen. VI.* iii 3 227; iv 1 99
Great Mark Antony Is now a widower . *Ant. and Cleo.* ii 2 122
Widowhood. I'll assure her of Her widowhood, be it that she survive me, In all my lands . *T. of Shrew* ii 1 125
Widow lady. How may we content This widow lady? *K. John* ii 1 548
Widow-maker. O, it grieves my soul, That I must draw this metal from my side To be a widow-maker! v 2 17
Wield. O base Hungarian wight! wilt thou the spigot wield? *Mer. Wives* i 3 24
His head by nature framed to wear a crown, His hand to wield a sceptre 3 *Hen. VI.* iv 6 73
Ancient citizens Cast by their grave beseeming ornaments, To wield old partisans, in hands as old *Rom. and Jul.* i 1 101
I love you more than words can wield the matter *Lear* i 1 56
Wife. Farewell my wife and children!—Farewell, brother! *Tempest* i 1 65
Every day some sailor's wife, The masters of some merchant and the merchant Have just our theme of woe ii 1 4
I am your wife, if you will marry me; If not, I'll die your maid iii 1 83
Hail, many-colour'd messenger, that ne'er Dost disobey the wife of Jupiter iv 1 77
So rare a wonder'd father and a wife Makes this place Paradise iv 1 123
Ferdinand, her brother, found a wife Where he himself was lost v 1 210
Worth and qualities Beseeming such a wife as your fair daughter *T. G. of Ver.* iii 1 66
I now am full resolved to take a wife And turn her out iii 1 76
Wife, bid these gentlemen welcome *Mer. Wives* i 1 201
Briefly, I do mean to make love to Ford's wife: I spy entertainment in her i 3 48
Page's wife, who even now gave me good eyes too i 3 66
Sir John affects thy wife.—Why, sir, my wife is not young ii 1 115
Love my wife!—With liver burning hot ii 1 120
He loves your wife; there's the short and the long. ii 1 136
'Tis true: my name is Nym and Falstaff loves your wife. ii 1 139
If he should intend this voyage towards my wife, I would turn her loose to him ii 1 189
I do not misdoubt my wife; but I would be loath to turn them together ii 1 192
A secure fool, and stands so firmly on his wife's frailty ii 1 242
Good morrow, good wife.—Not so, an't please your worship ii 2 35
Let me tell you in your ear, she's as fartuous a civil modest wife ii 2 101
Has Ford's wife and Page's wife acquainted each other how they love me? ii 2 114
Never a wife in Windsor leads a better life than she does ii 2 122
The jealous wittolly knave hath masses of money; for the which his wife seems to me well-favoured ii 2 284
I will predominate over the peasant, and thou shalt lie with his wife ii 2 295
Who says this is improvident jealousy? my wife hath sent to him ii 2 303
Page is an ass, a secure ass: he will trust his wife ii 2 315
I will rather trust a Fleming with my butter . . . than my wife with herself ii 2 320
Whither go you?—Truly, sir, to see your wife iii 2 11
Is your wife at home indeed?—Indeed she is iii 2 26
He pieces out his wife's inclination; he gives her folly motion iii 2 35
And now she's going to my wife, and Falstaff's boy with her. iii 2 36
Well; I will take him, then torture my wife iii 2 41
I stand wholly for you: but my wife, master doctor, is for you altogether iii 2 63
Your wife is as honest a 'omans as I will desires among five thousand iii 3 236
Come, wife; come, Mistress Page. I pray you, pardon me iii 3 242
And, forsooth, to search his house for his wife's love iii 5 79
In her invention and Ford's wife's distraction, they conveyed me into a buck-basket iii 5 87
Set down the basket, villain! Somebody call my wife iv 2 122
Now shall the devil be shamed. What, wife, I say! Come, come forth! iv 2 125
Mistress Ford, the honest woman, the modest wife, the virtuous creature iv 2 136
'Tis unreasonable! Will you take up your wife's clothes? iv 2 148
As jealous as Ford, that searched a hollow walnut for his wife's leman. iv 2 171
Pardon me, wife. Henceforth do what thou wilt iv 4 6
I will be revenged, and I will deliver his wife into your hand v 1 31
I will never mistrust my wife again v 5 141
As poor as Job?—And as wicked as his wife? v 5 165
I will desire thee to laugh at my wife, that now laughs at thee v 5 181
If Anne Page be my daughter, she is, by this, Doctor Caius' wife v 5 186
She is fast my wife, Save that we do the denunciation lack *Meas. for Meas.* i 2 151
My wife, sir, whom I detest before heaven and your honour,— How? thy wife? ii 1 69
How dost thou know that, constable?—Marry, sir, by my wife ii 1 80
What was done to Elbow's wife, that he hath cause to complain of? ii 1 120
What was done to Elbow's wife, once more?—Once, sir? ii 1 145
I beseech you, sir, ask him what this man did to my wife ii 1 149
How could Master Froth do the constable's wife any harm? ii 1 165
His wife is a more respected person than any of us all ii 1 172
But if he be a married man, he's his wife's head iv 2 4
Why, you are nothing then: neither maid, widow, nor wife? v 1 178
She may be a punk; for many of them are neither maid, widow, nor wife v 1 180
I am affianced this man's wife as strongly As words could make up vows v 1 227
Tuesday night last gone in's garden-house He knew me as a wife v 1 230
Look that you love your wife; her worth worth yours v 1 502
My wife, not meanly proud of two such boys *Com. of Errors* i 1 59
The incessant weepings of my wife, Weeping before for what she saw must come i 1 71
My wife and I, Fixing our eyes on whom our care was fix'd i 1 84
What mistress, slave, hast thou?—Your worship's wife i 2 88
It seems he hath great care to please his wife ii 1 56
'I know,' quoth he, 'no house, no wife, no mistress' ii 1 71
Some other mistress hath thy sweet aspects; I am not Adriana nor thy wife ii 2 114
And in his blows Denied my house for his, me for his wife ii 2 161
You must excuse us all; My wife is shrewish when I keep not hours iii 1 2
And that I did deny my wife and house iii 1 9
Are you there, wife? you might have come before.—Your wife, sir knave! iii 1 63
Draw within the compass of suspect The unviolated honour of your wife iii 1 88
My wife—but, I protest, without desert—Hath oftentimes upbraided me iii 1 112
Be it for nothing but to spite my wife iii 1 118
Comfort my sister, cheer her, call her wife: 'Tis holy sport to be a little vain iii 2 26
Your weeping sister is no wife of mine, Nor to her bed no homage do I owe iii 2 42
Thou hast no husband yet nor I no wife. Give me thy hand. iii 2 68
Wife. As from a bear a man would run for life, So fly I from her that would be my wife *Com. of Errors* iii 2 160
She that doth call me husband, even my soul Doth for a wife abhor iii 2 164
Go home with it and please your wife withal iii 2 178
Buy a rope's end: that will I bestow Among my wife and her confederates iv 1 17
Take the chain and bid my wife Disburse the sum on the receipt thereof iv 1 37
The chain!—Why, give it to my wife and fetch your money iv 1 54
Belike his wife, acquainted with his fits, On purpose shut the doors iv 3 91
And tell his wife that, being lunatic, He rush'd into my house iv 3 94
My wife is in a wayward mood to-day iv 4 4
Come, go along; my wife is coming yonder iv 4 43
She that would be your wife now ran from you iv 4 152
Ill it doth beseem your holiness To separate the husband and the wife v 1 111
That woman there! She whom thou gavest to me to be my wife v 1 198
By the way we met My wife, her sister, and a rabble more v 1 235
If thou be'st the man That hadst a wife once call'd Æmilia v 1 342
She now shall be my sister, not my wife v 1 416
I would scarce trust myself, though I had sworn the contrary, if Hero would be my wife *Much Ado* i 1 198
She were an excellent wife for Benedick ii 1 366
An it be the right husband and the right wife iii 4 37
When I lived, I was your other wife: And when you loved, you were my other husband v 4 60
Thou art sad; get thee a wife, get thee a wife v 4 124
What, I! I love! I sue! I seek a wife! *L. L. Lost* iii 1 191
Is ebony like her? O wood divine! A wife of such wood were felicity iv 3 249
But what to me, my love? but what to me? A wife? v 2 834
Shall I say, I thank you, gentle wife?—Not so, my lord v 2 836
To have defeated you and me, You of your wife and me of my consent, Of my consent that she should be your wife *M. N. Dream* iv 1 163
Hedged me by his wit, to yield myself His wife who wins me *Mer. of Ven.* ii 1 19
And I am sure Margery your wife is my mother ii 2 95
I shall end this strife, Become a Christian and thy loving wife ii 3 21
Take what wife you will to bed, I will ever be your head ii 9 70
I may be married too.—With all my heart, so thou canst get a wife iii 2 197
First go with me to church and call me wife, And then away to Venice iii 2 305
I shall grow jealous of you shortly, Launcelot, if you thus get my wife into corners iii 5 32
Say thy opinion, How dost thou like the Lord Bassanio's wife? iii 5 77
Even such a husband Hast thou of me as she is for a wife iii 5 89
Commend me to your honourable wife iv 1 273
I am married to a wife Which is as dear to me as life itself; But life itself, my wife, and all the world, Are not with me esteem'd above thy life iv 1 282
Your wife would give you little thanks for that, If she were by iv 1 288
I have a wife, whom, I protest, I love: I would she were in heaven iv 1 290
Good sir, this ring was given me by my wife iv 1 441
If your wife be not a mad-woman, . . . She would not hold out enemy for ever. iv 1 445
Let his deservings Be valued 'gainst your wife's commandment iv 1 451
A light wife doth make a heavy husband v 1 130
You were to blame, I must be plain with you, To part so slightly with your wife's first gift v 1 167
You give your wife too unkind a cause of grief: An 'twere to me, I should be mad at it v 1 175
When I am absent, then lie with my wife v 1 285
That is the dowry of his wife; 'tis none of his own getting *As Y. Like It* iii 3 56
It will be a good excuse for me hereafter to leave my wife iii 3 95
But he comes armed in his fortune and prevents the slander of his wife iv 1 62
Will you, Orlando, have to wife this Rosalind? iv 1 130
I take thee, Rosalind, for wife.—I might ask you for your commission iv 1 137
A man that had a wife with such a wit, he might say 'Wit, whither wilt?' iv 1 167
You might keep that check for it till you met your wife's wit going to your neighbour's bed iv 1 170
Wherein your lady and your humble wife May show her duty *T. of S.* Ind. 1 116
Where is my wife?—Here, noble lord: what is thy will with her? Ind. 2 104
Are you my wife and will not call me husband? Ind. 2 106
My lord and husband; I am your wife in all obedience Ind. 2 109
Madam wife, they say that I have dream'd And slept above some fifteen year Ind. 2 114
Come, madam wife, sit by my side and let the world slip Ind. 2 145
Will you any wife?—I pray you, sir, is it your will To make a stale of me? i 1 56
Shall I then come roundly to thee And wish thee to a shrewd ill-favour'd wife? i 2 60
If thou know One rich enough to be Petruchio's wife i 2 67
I can, Petruchio, help thee to a wife With wealth enough i 2 85
Such a life, with such a wife, were strange! i 2 194
If I get your daughter's love, What dowry shall I have with her to wife? ii 1 121
Myself am moved to woo thee for my wife.—Moved! in good time ii 1 195
Your father hath consented That you shall be my wife ii 1 272
Never make denial; I must and will have Katharine to my wife ii 1 282
Father, and wife, and gentlemen, adieu; I will to Venice ii 1 323
If I may have your daughter to my wife, I'll leave her houses three or four ii 1 367
Lo, there is mad Petruchio's wife, If it would please him come and marry her! iii 2 19
What occasion of import Hath all so long detain'd you from your wife? iii 2 105
When the priest Should ask, if Katharine should be his wife, 'Ay, by gogs-wouns,' quoth he iii 2 161
Is my master and his wife coming? iv 1 18
This is a way to kill a wife with kindness. iv 1 211
She's like to be Lucentio's wife.—I pray the gods she may! iv 4 66
The sister to my wife, this gentlewoman, Thy son by this hath married iv 5 62
Let's each one send unto his wife; And he whose wife is most obedient . . . Shall win the wager which we will propose v 2 66
I'll venture so much of my hawk or hound, But twenty times so much upon my wife v 2 73
A kind one too: Pray God, sir, your wife send you not a worse v 2 84
Go and entreat my wife To come to me forthwith.—O, ho! entreat her! v 2 86
Where's my wife?—She says you have some goodly jest in hand v 2 90
Where is your sister, and Hortensio's wife? v 2 101
I hope to have friends for my wife's sake *All's Well* i 3 43
He that comforts my wife is the cherisher of my flesh and blood i 3 50
Ergo, he that kisses my wife is my friend i 3 53
Young Bertram, take her; she's thy wife.—My wife, my liege! ii 3 112
A poor physician's daughter my wife! Disdain Rather corrupt me ever! ii 3 122

Wife. War is no strife To the dark house and the detested wife *All's Well* ii 3 309
Till I have no wife, I have nothing in France iii 2 77
Nothing in France, until he have no wife! iii 2 81
Write, write, Rinaldo, To this unworthy husband of his wife iii 4 30
'Tis a hard bondage to become the wife Of a detesting lord iii 5 67
I would he loved his wife: if he were honester He were much goodlier iii 5 82
My mother did but duty; such, my lord, As you owe to your wife iv 2 13
You have won A wife of me, though there my hope be done iv 2 65
He had sworn to marry me When his wife's dead iv 2 72
He has much worthy blame laid upon him for shaking off so good a wife iv 3 8
His wife some two months since fled from his house iv 3 56
Buried a wife, mourned for her; writ to my lady mother iv 3 101
I would cozen the man of his wife and do his service iv 5 28
And I would give his wife my bauble, sir, to do her service iv 5 32
A wife Whose beauty did astonish the survey Of richest eyes v 3 15
Upon his many protestations to marry me when his wife was dead v 3 140
Why do you look so strange upon your wife?—She's none of mine v 3 168
This is his wife; That ring's a thousand proofs v 3 198
You, that have turn'd off a first so noble wife, May justly diet me v 3 220
This ring was mine; I gave it his first wife v 3 280
I am either maid, or else this old man's wife v 3 294
And at that time he got his wife with child v 3 302
'Tis but the shadow of a wife you see, The name and not the thing v 3 308
For I can guess that by thy honest aid Thou kept'st a wife herself v 3 330
A barful strife! Whoe'er I woo, myself would be his wife *T. Night* i 4 42
Your wife is like to reap a proper man iii 1 144
More than my life, More, by all mores, than e'er I shall love wife v 1 139
To think me as well a sister as a wife v 1 325
In those unfledged days was my wife a girl *W. Tale* i 2 78
And arms her with the boldness of a wife To her allowing husband! i 2 184
Now while I speak this, holds his wife by the arm i 2 193
My wife is slippery i 2 273
My wife's a hobby-horse, deserves a name As rank as any flax-wench i 2 276
The covering sky is nothing; Bohemia nothing; My wife is nothing i 2 295
Were my wife's liver Infected as her life, she would not live i 2 304
If it prove She's otherwise, I'll keep my stables where I lodge my wife ii 1 135
He dreads his wife.—So I would you did ii 3 79
Thou, traitor, hast set on thy wife to this ii 3 131
Thou set'st on thy wife.—I did not, sir ii 3 141
The daughter of a king, our wife, and one Of us too much beloved iii 2 3
Thou ne'er shalt see Thy wife Paulina more iii 3 36
He compassed a motion of the Prodigal Son, and married a tinker's wife iv 3 104
When my old wife lived, upon This day she was both pantler, butler, cook, Both dame and servant iv 4 55
How a usurer's wife was brought to bed of twenty money-bags at a burthen iv 4 266
Reason my son Should choose himself a wife iv 4 418
No more such wives; therefore, no wife v 1 56
Fear thou no wife; I'll have no wife, Paulina v 1 68
But my arrival and my wife's in safety Here where we are v 1 167
Is this the daughter of a king?—She is, When once she is my wife v 1 209
Thou shouldst a husband take by my consent, As I by thine a wife v 3 137
Your brother is legitimate; Your father's wife did after wedlock bear him *K. John* i 1 117
Philip, good old sir Robert's wife's eldest son i 1 159
What motive may Be stronger with thee than the name of wife? iii 1 314
Come, grin on me, and I will think thou smilest And buss thee as thy wife iii 4 35
I was Geffrey's wife; Young Arthur is my son, and he is lost iii 4 46
You, in the right of Lady Blanch your wife, May then make all the claim iii 4 142
Thy sometimes brother's wife With her companion grief must end her life *Richard II.* i 2 54
You violate A twofold marriage, 'twixt my crown and me, And then betwixt me and my married wife v 1 73
My wife to France: from whence, set forth in pomp, She came v 1 78
What doth he with a bond That he is bound to? Wife, thou art a fool v 2 68
And when I urged the ransom once again Of my wife's brother, then his cheek look'd pale *1 Hen. IV.* i 3 142
I know you wise, but yet no farther wise Than Harry Percy's wife ii 3 111
And says to his wife 'Fie upon this quiet life! I want work'. ii 4 117
And that damned brawn shall play Dame Mortimer his wife ii 4 124
O, he is as tedious As a tired horse, a railing wife iii 1 160
This is the deadly spite that angers me; My wife can speak no English iii 1 193
You swear like a comfit-maker's wife iii 1 253
And for womanhood, Maid Marian may be the deputy's wife of the ward iii 3 130
I would thou shouldst know it; I am an honest man's wife iii 3 137
He hath the horn of abundance, and the lightness of his wife shines through it: and yet cannot he see *2 Hen. IV.* i 2 53
An I could get me but a wife in the stews, I were manned, horsed, and wived i 2 60
Thou didst swear to me then, as I was washing thy wound, to marry me and make me my lady thy wife ii 1 100
Did not goodwife Keech, the butcher's wife, come in then? ii 1 102
Loving wife, and gentle daughter, Give even way unto my rough affairs ii 3 1
Alas, sweet wife, my honour is at pawn ii 3 7
May I ask how my lady his wife doth? iii 2 71
A soldier is better accommodated than with a wife iii 2 73
Like an offensive wife That hath enraged him on to offer strokes, As he is striking, holds his infant up iv 1 210
Be merry, be merry, my wife has all; For women are shrews, both short and tall v 3 35
Here comes Ancient Pistol and his wife *Hen. V.* ii 1 29
If I could win a lady at leap-frog, . . . I should quickly leap into a wife v 2 145
I will tell thee in French; which I am sure will hang upon my tongue like a new-married wife about her husband's neck v 2 190
Shall Kate be my wife?—So please you v 2 351
As man and wife, being two, are one in love v 2 389
Thy wife is proud; she holdeth thee in awe, More than God *1 Hen. VI.* i 1 39
Fond man, remember that thou hast a wife v 3 80
I am unworthy to be Henry's wife.—No, gentle madam; I unworthy am To woo so fair a dame to be his wife v 3 122
Art thou not second woman in the realm, And the protector's wife? *2 Hen. VI.* i 2 44
Keeping my house, and lands, and wife, and all, from me.—Thy wife too! i 3 20
Not all these lords do vex me half so much As that proud dame, the lord protector's wife i 3 79

Wife. More like an empress than Duke Humphrey's wife *2 Hen. VI.* i 3 81
Thy wife's attire Have cost a mass of public treasury i 3 133
What woman is this?—His wife, an't like your worship ii 1 80
My wife desired some damsons, And made me climb, with danger of my life ii 1 102
The protector's wife, The ringleader and head of all this rout ii 1 169
And, for my wife, I know not how it stands ii 1 192
Stand forth, Dame Eleanor Cobham, Gloucester's wife ii 3 1
Whilst I think I am thy married wife ii 4 28
Sometime I'll say, I am Duke Humphrey's wife, And he a prince ii 4 42
My wife descended of the Lacies,— She was, indeed, a pedler's daughter, and sold many laces iv 2 47
Come, wife, let's in, and learn to govern better iv 9 48
How will my wife for slaughter of my son Shed seas of tears! *3 Hen. VI.* ii 5 105
Warwick Is thither gone, to crave the French king's sister To wife for Edward iii 1 31
He, on his right, asking a wife for Edward iii 1 44
And be a witness That Bona shall be wife to the English king iii 3 139
Tell me some reason why the Lady Grey Should not become my wife iv 1 26
Bestow'd the heir Of the Lord Bonville on your new wife's son iv 1 57
Is it for a wife That thou art malcontent? I will provide thee iv 1 59
Know not how to use ambassadors, Nor how to be contented with one wife iv 3 37
My Lady Grey his wife, Clarence, 'tis she That tempers him *Richard III.* i 1 64
We say that Shore's wife hath a pretty foot, A cherry lip i 1 93
Hear the lamentations of poor Anne, Wife to thy Edward i 2 10
If ever he have wife, let her be made As miserable by the death of him As I am made! i 2 26
Notwithstanding she's your wife, And loves not me i 3 22
Die neither mother, wife, nor England's queen! i 3 209
Execute thy wrath in me alone, O, spare my guiltless wife and my poor children! i 4 72
He cannot lie with his neighbour's wife, but it [conscience] detects him i 4 141
Wife, love Lord Hastings, let him kiss your hand ii 1 21
Seal thou this league With thy embracements to my wife's allies ii 1 30
And this is Edward's wife, that monstrous witch iii 4 72
His apparent open guilt omitted, I mean, his conversation with Shore's wife iii 5 31
Edward is your brother's son: So say we too, but not by Edward's wife iii 7 178
And make me die . . . Nor mother, wife, nor England's counted queen iv 1 47
Be thy wife—if any be so mad—As miserable by the life of thee As thou hast made me by my dear lord's death! iv 1 75
Rumour it abroad That Anne, my wife, is sick and like to die iv 2 52
Stanley, he is your wife's son: well, look to it iv 2 90
Look to your wife: if she convey Letters to Richmond, you shall answer it iv 2 95
And Anne my wife hath bid the world good night iv 3 39
O Harry's wife, triumph not in my woes! iv 4 59
See what now thou art: For happy wife, a most distressed widow iv 4 98
Farewell, York's wife, and queen of sad mischance iv 4 114
The king, that calls your beauteous daughter wife, Familiarly shall call thy Dorset brother iv 4 315
When I was found False to his children or his wife's allies v 1 15
That wretched Anne thy wife, That never slept a quiet hour with thee v 3 159
Thy adversary's wife doth pray for thee v 3 166
What's the cause?—It seems the marriage with his brother's wife Has crept too near his conscience *Hen. VIII.* ii 2 17
Heaven witness, I have been to you a true and humble wife ii 4 23
I have been your wife, in this obedience, Upward of twenty years ii 4 35
Who shall report he has A better wife, let him in nought be trusted ii 4 135
Respecting this our marriage with the dowager, Sometimes our brother's wife ii 4 181
If your business Seek me out, and that way I am wife in, Out with it boldly iii 1 38
Let me speak myself, Since virtue finds no friends—a wife, a true one iii 1 126
No man living Could say 'This is my wife' there; all were woven So strangely in one piece iv 1 80
Strew me over With maiden flowers, that all the world may know I was a chaste wife to my grave iv 2 170
There was a haberdasher's wife of small wit near him v 4 49
As like as Vulcan and his wife *Troi. and Cres.* i 3 168
I take to-day a wife, and my election Is led on in the conduct of my will ii 2 61
How may I avoid, Although my will distaste what it elected, The wife I chose? ii 2 67
What nearer debt in all humanity Than wife is to the husband? ii 2 176
If Helen then be wife to Sparta's king, As it is known she is ii 2 183
Your quondam wife swears still by Venus' glove iv 5 179
Come, go back: Thy wife hath dream'd; thy mother hath had visions v 3 63
Here's a letter from him: the state hath another, his wife another *Cor.* ii 1 119
What is it?—Coriolanus must I call thee?—But, O, thy wife! ii 1 192
The fourth would return for conscience sake, to help to get thee a wife ii 3 37
I am in this, Your wife, your son, these senators, the nobles iii 2 65
Look, I am going: Commend me to my wife iii 2 135
More holy and profound than mine own life, My dear wife's estimate iii 3 114
If you had been the wife of Hercules, Six of his labours you'ld have done iv 1 17
Droop not; adieu. Farewell, my wife, my mother: I'll do well yet iv 1 20
Come, my sweet wife, my dearest mother, and My friends of noble touch iv 1 48
I have heard it said, the fittest time to corrupt a man's wife is when she's fallen out with her husband iv 3 34
Nay, I hear nothing: his mother and his wife Hear nothing from him iv 6 18
His mother, wife, his child, And this brave fellow too, we are the grains v 1 29
So that all hope is vain, Unless his noble mother, and his wife; Who, as I hear, mean to solicit him v 1 71
Wife, mother, child, I know not. My affairs Are servanted to others v 2 88
My wife comes foremost; then the honour'd mould Wherein this trunk was framed v 3 22
Even he, your wife, this lady, and myself, Are suitors to you v 3 77
Making the mother, wife, and child to see The son, the husband, and the father tearing His country's bowels out v 3 101
And bear the palm for having bravely shed Thy wife and children's blood v 3 118
His wife is in Corioli and his child Like him by chance v 3 179
Pray you, Stand to me in this cause. O mother! wife! v 3 199
And given up, For certain drops of salt, your city Rome, I say 'your city,' to his wife and mother v 6 94
Dead, if you will; but not to be his wife *T. Andron.* i 1 297
My true-betrothed love and now my wife i 1 406
His wife but yesternight was brought to bed iv 2 153
Signior Martino and his wife and daughters *Rom. and Jul.* i 2 67
Mine uncle Capulet, his wife, and daughters i 2 71

Wife. Hence to Friar Laurence' cell; There stays a husband to make you a wife . . . . . *Rom. and Jul.* ii 5 71
Ah, poor my lord, what tongue shall smooth thy name, When I, thy three-hours wife, have mangled it? . . . iii 2 99
Wife, go you to her ere you go to bed . . . . . . iii 4 15
Ere you go to bed, Prepare her, wife, against this wedding-day . iii 4 32
How now, wife! Have you deliver'd to her our decree? . . iii 5 138
Take me with you, wife. How! will she none? . . . iii 5 142
Wife, we scarce thought us blest That God had lent us but this only child iii 5 165
Happily met, my lady and my wife!—That may be, sir, when I may be a wife . . . . iv 1 18
I will do it without fear or doubt, To live an unstain'd wife to my sweet love . . . . iv 1 88
Tush, I will stir about, And all things shall be well, I warrant thee, wife iv 2 40
Nurse! Wife! What, ho! What, nurse, I say! Go waken Juliet . iv 4 23
O son! the night before thy wedding-day Hath Death lain with thy wife iv 5 36
O, how may I Call this a lightning? O my love! my wife! . . v 3 91
O heavens! O wife, look how our daughter bleeds! . . . v 3 202
My wife is dead to-night; Grief of my son's exile hath stopp'd her breath v 3 210
Romeo, there dead, was husband to that Juliet; And she, there dead, that Romeo's faithful wife . . . . v 3 232
If it be no more, Portia is Brutus' harlot, not his wife.—You are my true and honourable wife . . . . . . *J. Cæsar* ii 1 287
I grant I am a woman; but withal A woman that Lord Brutus took to wife . . . . ii 1 293
O ye gods, Render me worthy of this noble wife! . . . ii 1 303
My wife stays me at home: She dreamt to-night she saw my statua . ii 2 75
Break up the senate till another time, When Cæser's wife shall meet with better dreams . . . . ii 2 99
Had you your letters from your wife, my lord? . . . iv 3 181
A sailor's wife had chestnuts in her lap, And munch'd, and munch'd, and munch'd . . . . *Macbeth* i 3 4
And make joyful The hearing of my wife with your approach . i 4 46
This diamond he greets your wife withal, By the name of most kind hostess . . . . ii 1 15
O, full of scorpions is my mind, dear wife! . . . . iii 2 36
Seize upon Fife; give to the edge o' the sword His wife, his babes . iv 1 152
Wisdom! to leave his wife, to leave his babes, His mansion, and his titles in a place From whence himself does fly? . . . iv 2 6
Wife and child, Those precious motives, those strong knots of love . iv 3 26
How does my wife?—Why, well.—And all my children?—Well too . iv 3 176
Your castle is surprised; your wife and babes Savagely slaughter'd . iv 3 204
My children too?—Wife, children, servants, all That could be found . iv 3 211
And I must be from thence! My wife kill'd too?—I have said . iv 3 213
The thane of Fife had a wife: where is she now? . . . v 1 47
If thou be'st slain and with no stroke of mine, My wife and children's ghosts will haunt me still . . . . v 7 16
In equal scale weighing delight and dole,—Taken to wife . . *Hamlet* i 2 14
Both here and hence pursue me lasting strife, If, once a widow, ever I be wife!—If she should break it now! . . . . . iii 2 233
You shall see anon how the murderer gets the love of Gonzago's wife iii 2 275
You are the queen, your husband's brother's wife; And—would it were not so!— you are my mother . . . . iii 4 15
Father and mother is man and wife; man and wife is one flesh . iv 3 54
I hoped thou shouldst have been my Hamlet's wife . . . v 1 267
What says our second daughter, Our dearest Regan, wife to Cornwall? *Lear* i 1 69
Since that respects of fortune are his love, I shall not be his wife . i 1 252
Go tell the duke and's wife I'ld speak with them, Now, presently . ii 4 117
Your—wife, so I would say—Affectionate servant . . . iv 6 275
For your claim, fair sister, I bar it in the interest of my wife . v 3 85
He hath commission from thy wife and me To hang Cordelia . . v 3 253
A fellow almost damn'd in a fair wife . . . . . *Othello* i 1 21
I crave fit disposition for my wife, Due reference of place . . i 3 237
To his conveyance I assign my wife, With what else needful . . i 3 286
Let thy wife attend on her; And bring them after in the best advantage i 3 297
Abuse Othello's ear That he is too familiar with his wife . . i 3 402
Nothing can or shall content my soul Till I am even'd with him, wife for wife . . . . ii 1 308
I'll tell you what you shall do. Our general's wife is now the general ii 3 320
My wife must move for Cassio to her mistress; I'll set her on . ii 3 389
And bring him jump when he may Cassio find Soliciting his wife . ii 3 393
If the gentlewoman that attends the general's wife be stirring . iii 1 27
I have made bold, Iago, To send in to your wife . . . iii 1 36
The general and his wife are talking of it; And she speaks for you stoutly iii 1 46
Was not that Cassio parted from my wife?—Cassio, my lord! No, sure iii 3 37
I heard thee say even now, thou likedst not that, When Cassio left my wife . . . . iii 3 110
'Tis not to make me jealous To say my wife is fair, feeds well, loves company, Is free of speech . . . . iii 3 184
I speak not yet of proof. Look to your wife; observe her well with Cassio . . . . iii 3 197
If more thou dost perceive, let me know more; Set on thy wife to observe . . . . iii 3 240
A thing for me? it is a common thing— Ha!—To have a foolish wife . iii 3 304
I think my wife be honest and think she is not . . . iii 3 384
Have you not sometimes seen a handkerchief Spotted with strawberries in your wife's hand? . . . . iii 3 435
But such a handkerchief—I am sure it was your wife's—did I to-day See Cassio wipe his beard with . . . . iii 3 438
But if I give my wife a handkerchief,— What then?—Why, then, 'tis hers iv 1 10
How oft, how long ago, and when He hath, and is again to cope your wife iv 1 87
And to see how he prizes the foolish woman your wife! . . . iv 1 186
'Tis Lodovico Come from the duke: and, see, your wife is with him . iv 1 228
What, strike his wife!—'Faith, that was not so well; yet would I knew That stroke would prove the worst! . . . . . . iv 1 283
Why, what art thou?—Your wife, my lord; your true And loyal wife . iv 2 34
If she come in, she'll sure speak to my wife: My wife! my wife! what wife? I have no wife. O, insupportable! . . . . . v 2 96
He says thou told'st him that his wife was false: I know thou didst not v 2 173
The woman falls; sure, he hath kill'd his wife . . . . v 2 236
He's gone, but his wife's kill'd.—'Tis a notorious villain . . v 2 238
Fulvia thy wife first came into the field . . . *Ant. and Cleo.* i 2 92
Fulvia thy wife is dead.—Where died she?—In Sicyon . . . i 2 122
When it pleaseth their deities to take the wife of a man from him, it shows to man the tailors of the earth . . . . . . i 2 169
His wife that's dead did trespasses to Cæsar . . . . ii 1 40
Your wife and brother Made wars upon me . . . . . ii 2 42
As for my wife, I would you had her spirit in such another . . ii 2 61
The third o' the world is yours; which with a snaffle You may pace easy, but not such a wife . . . . ii 2 64

Wife. Take Antony Octavia to his wife; whose beauty claims No worse a husband . . . . *Ant. and Cleo.* ii 2 130
She was the wife of Caius Marcellus.—But she is now the wife of Marcus Antonius . . . . ii 6 117
Who would not have his wife so?—Not he that himself is not so . ii 6 132
Prove such a wife As my thoughts make thee . . . . iii 2 25
The wife of Antony Should have an army for an usher . . . iii 6 43
Your wife Octavia, with her modest eyes And still conclusion . iv 15 27
The heir of's kingdom, whom He purposed to his wife's sole son . *Cymb.* i 1 5
Keep it till you woo another wife, When Imogen is dead . . . i 1 113
My mother seem'd The Dian of that time: so doth my wife The nonpareil of this . . . . ii 5 7
Married your royalty, was wife to your place; Abhorr'd your person . v 5 39
My queen, my life, my wife! O Imogen, Imogen, Imogen! . . v 5 226
'Mollis aer' We term it 'mulier:' which 'mulier' I divine Is this most constant wife . . . . v 5 449
Whoso ask'd her for his wife, His riddle told not, lost his life *Pericles* i Gower 37
He's father, son, and husband mild; I mother, wife, and yet his child i 1 69
So sharp are hunger's teeth, that man and wife Draw lots who first shall die . . . . i 4 45
What a man cannot get, he may lawfully deal for—his wife's soul . ii 1 121
You, sir, hear you, Either be ruled by me, or I will make you—Man and wife . . . . ii 5 84
That Cleon's wife, with envy rare, A present murderer does prepare iv Gower 37
Wife, take her in; instruct her what she has to do . . . iv 2 58
The main grief springs from the loss Of a beloved daughter and a wife . v 1 30
My dearest wife was like this maid, and such a one My daughter might have been . . . . v 1 108
Cruel Cleon, with his wicked wife, Did seek to murder me . . v 1 173
Before the people all, Reveal how thou at sea didst lose thy wife . v 1 245
This is your wife.—Reverend appearer, no . . . . v 3 18
For wicked Cleon and his wife, . . . him and his they in his palace burn . . . . v 3 Gower 95

Wife-like. Thy meekness saint-like, wife-like government *Hen. VIII.* ii 4 138
Undergoes, More goddess-like than wife-like, such assaults *Cymbeline* iii 2 8

Wight. O base Hungarian wight! wilt thou the spigot wield? *Mer. Wives* i 3 23
I ken the wight: he is of substance good . . . . . i 3 40
A most illustrious wight, A man of fire-new words . . *L. L. Lost* i 1 178
O braggart vile and damned furious wight! . . . *Hen. V.* ii 1 64
With venomous wights she stays As tediously as hell . *Troi. and Cres.* iv 2 12
She was a wight, if ever such wight were,— To do what?—To suckle fools and chronicle small beer . . . . . *Othello* ii 1 159
He was a wight of high renown, And thou art but of low degree . ii 3 96
So for her many a wight did die, As yon grim looks do testify *Per.* i Gower 39

Wightly. A wightly wanton with a velvet brow . . *L. L. Lost* iii 1 198

Wild. If . . . you have Put the wild waters in this roar, allay them *Temp.* i 2 2
Courtsied when you have and kiss'd The wild waves whist . . i 2 379
He strays With willing sport to the wild ocean . . *T. G. of Ver.* ii 7 32
This fellow were a king for our wild faction! . . . . iv 1 37
He kept company with the wild prince and Poins . . *Mer. Wives* iii 2 74
Other bars he lays before me, My riots past, my wild societies . iii 4 8
Shooty the great traveller, and wild Half-can that stabbed Pots *Meas. for Meas.* iv 3 19
Lords of the wide world and wild watery seas . . *Com. of Errors* ii 1 21
Of excellent discourse, Petty and witty, wild and yet, too, gentle . iii 1 110
I know her spirits are as coy and wild As haggerds of the rock *M. Ado* iii 1 35
I will requite thee, Taming my wild heart to thy loving hand . iii 1 112
To move wild laughter in the throat of death? It cannot be *L. L. Lost* v 2 865
To trace the forests wild . . . . . . *M. N. Dream* ii 1 25
And leave thee to the mercy of wild beasts . . . . ii 1 228
I know a bank where the wild thyme blows . . . . ii 1 249
Thou art too wild, too rude and bold of voice . . *Mer. of Venice* ii 2 190
Lest through thy wild behaviour I be misconstrued . . . ii 2 196
The vasty wilds Of wide Arabia are as throughfares now . . ii 7 41
Turns to a wild of nothing, save of joy, Express'd and not express'd . iii 2 184
In such a night Stood Dido with a willow in her hand Upon the wild sea banks . . . . v 1 11
A wild and wanton herd, Or race of youthful and unhandled colts . v 1 71
And to the skirts of this wild wood he came . . *As Y. Like It* v 4 165
I am he am born to tame you Kate, And bring you from a wild Kate to a Kate Conformable as other household Kates . *T. of Shrew* ii 1 279
In an act of this importance 'twere Most piteous to be wild . *W. Tale* ii 1 182
More promising Than a wild dedication of yourselves To unpath'd waters iv 4 577
How like you this wild counsel, mighty states? . . *K. John* ii 1 395
And wild amazement hurries up and down . . . . . v 1 35
Thy threatening colours now wind up; And tame the savage spirit of wild war . . . . v 2 74
These high wild hills and rough uneven ways Draws out our miles *Richard II.* ii 3 4
To fight Against the irregular and wild Glendower . . *1 Hen. IV.* i 1 40
A franklin in the wild of Kent hath brought three hundred marks with him . . . . ii 1 60
Wanton as youthful goats, wild as young bulls . . . . iv 1 103
Who, ne'er so tame, . . . Will have a wild trick of his ancestors . v 2 11
Never did I hear Of any prince so wild a libertine . . . v 2 72
The times are wild; contention, like a horse Full of high feeding, madly hath broke loose And bears down all before him . *2 Hen. IV.* i 1 9
Now let not Nature's hand Keep the wild flood confined! let order die! i 1 154
And the wild dog Shall flesh his tooth on every innocent . . iv 5 132
My father is gone wild into his grave, For in his tomb lie my affections v 2 123
His confounded base, Swill'd with the wild and wasteful ocean *Hen. V.* iii 1 14
Our scions, put in wild and savage stock, Spirt up so suddenly . iii 5 7
Their wounded steeds Fret fetlock deep in gore and with wild rage Yerk out their armed heels . . . . iv 7 82
By this unheedful, desperate, wild adventure . . *1 Hen. VI.* iv 4 7
I have seen Him caper upright like a wild Morisco . *2 Hen. VI.* iii 1 365
Into as many gobbets will I cut it As wild Medea young Absyrtus did v 2 58
Thy school-days frightful, desperate, wild, and furious *Richard III.* iv 4 169
But that still use of grief makes wild grief tame . . . iv 4 229
If I chance to talk a little wild, forgive me . . *Hen. VIII.* i 4 26
Thus hulling in The wild sea of my conscience . . . . ii 4 200
Yet my duty, As doth a rock against the chiding flood, Should the approach of this wild river break . . . . . . iii 2 198
Those that tame wild horses Pace 'em not in their hands to make 'em gentle . . . . v 3 21
Between our Ilium and where she resides, Let it be call'd the wild and wandering flood . . . . *Troi. and Cres.* i 1 105
Our imputation shall be oddly poised In this wild action . . i 3 340
Present me Death on the wheel or at wild horses' heels . *Coriolanus* iii 2 2
Determine on some course, More than a wild exposture to each chance iv 1 36

Wild. The present peace And quietness of the people, which before Were in wild hurry . . . *Coriolanus* iv 6 4
Thy wild acts denote The unreasonable fury of a beast . *Rom. and Jul.* iii 3 110
Your looks are pale and wild, and do import Some misadventure . . v 1 28
With wild looks, bid me devise some mean To rid her from this second marriage . . . . v 3 240
So soon we shall drive back Of Alcibiades the approaches wild *T. of A.* v 1 167
I'll teach them to prevent wild Alcibiades' wrath . . . v 1 206
What are these So wither'd and so wild in their attire? . . *Macbeth* i 3 40
Turn'd wild in nature, broke their stalls, flung out . . . . ii 4 16
But float upon a wild and violent sea Each way and move . . iv 2 21
These are but wild and whirling words, my lord . . . *Hamlet* i 5 133
He's very wild; Addicted so and so . . . . ii 1 18
Wild and usual slips As are companions noted and most known To youth ii 1 22
Let this same be presently perform'd, Even while men's minds are wild v 2 405
Shut up your doors, my lord; 'tis a wild night . . . *Lear* ii 4 311
Now a little fire in a wild field were like an old lecher's heart . iii 4 117
He hath achieved a maid That paragons description and wild fame *Othello* ii 1 62
In a town of war, Yet wild, the people's hearts brimful of fear, To manage private and domestic quarrel . . . . ii 3 214
Go, you wild bedfellow, you cannot soothsay . . . *Ant. and Cleo.* i 2 51
The wild disguise hath almost Antick'd us all . . . . . ii 7 131
The ingratitude of this Seleucus does Even make me wild . . . v 2 154
This object, which Takes prisoner the wild motion of mine eye *Cymbeline* i 6 103
With wild wood-leaves and weeds I ha' strew'd his grave . . iv 2 390
I am wild in my beholding. O heavens bless my girl! . . *Pericles* v 1 224

Wild-boars. Eight wild-boars roasted whole at a breakfast, And but twelve persons there . . . . . *Ant. and Cleo.* ii 2 183

Wild-cat. He sleeps by day More than the wild-cat . . *Mer. of Venice* ii 5 48
But will you woo this wild-cat?—Will I live? . . . *T. of Shrew* i 2 197
Bells in your parlours, wild-cats in your kitchens . . *Othello* ii 1 111

Wild-duck. There's no more valour in that Poins than in a wild-duck 1 *Hen. IV.* ii 2 108
Fear the report of a caliver worse than a struck fowl or a hurt wild-duck iv 2 21

Wilder. How he comes o'er us with our wilder days, Not measuring what use we made of them . . . . . . *Hen. V.* i 2 267
Affairs, that walk, As they say spirits do, at midnight, have In them a wilder nature than the business That seeks dispatch by day *Hen. VIII.* v 1 15

Wilderness. To make a virtue of necessity And live, as we do, in this wilderness . . . . *T. G. of Ver.* iv 1 63
Such a warped slip of wilderness Ne'er issued from his blood *M. for M.* iii 1 142
I would not have given it for a wilderness of monkeys . *Mer. of Venice* iii 1 128
I dare meet Surrey in a wilderness, And spit upon him . *Richard II.* iv 1 74
O, thou wilt be a wilderness again, Peopled with wolves! 2 *Hen. IV.* iv 5 137
A wilderness is populous enough, So Suffolk had thy heavenly company 2 *Hen. VI.* iii 2 360
Dost thou not perceive That Rome is but a wilderness of tigers? *T. An.* iii 1 54
Now I stand as one upon a rock Environ'd with a wilderness of sea . iii 1 94

Wildest. The wildest hath not such a heart as you . . *M. N. Dream* ii 1 229
When lion rough in wildest rage doth roar . . . . . v 1 225
You see, sweet maid, we marry A gentler scion to the wildest stock *W. Tale* iv 4 93
This is the bloodiest shame, The wildest savagery . . . *K. John* iv 3 48

Wildfire. If I did not think thou hadst been an ignis fatuus or a ball of wildfire, there's no purchase in money . . . 1 *Hen. IV.* iii 3 45

Wild-fowl. There is not a more fearful wild-fowl than your lion living; and we ought to look to't . . . . . *M. N. Dream* iii 1 33
What is the opinion of Pythagoras concerning wild fowl? . *T. Night* iv 2 55

Wild-geese. As wild geese that the creeping fowler eye *M. N. Dream* iii 2 20
Drive all thy subjects afore thee like a flock of wild-geese 1 *Hen. IV.* ii 4 152
They flock together in consent, like so many wild-geese . 2 *Hen. IV.* v 1 79
Winter's not gone yet, if the wild-geese fly that way . . *Lear* ii 4 46

Wild-goose. Like a wild-goose flies, Unclaim'd of any man *As Y. Like It* ii 7 86
If thy wits run the wild-goose chase, I have done, for thou hast more of the wild-goose in one of thy wits than, I am sure, I have in my whole five . . . . *Rom. and Jul.* ii 4 75

Wildly. But I prattle Something too wildly . . . *Tempest* iii 1 58
Here's Mistress Page at the door, sweating and blowing and looking wildly . . . . *Mer. Wives* iii 3 94
When he demean'd himself rough, rude, and wildly *Com. of Errors* v 1 88
As the unthought-on accident is guilty To what we wildly do *W. Tale* iv 4 550
And speak of something wildly By us perform'd before . . . v 1 129
What! mother dead! How wildly then walks my estate in France! *K. John* iv 2 128
What means our cousin, that he stares and looks So wildly? *Richard II.* v 3 25
Her hedges even-pleach'd, Like prisoners wildly overgrown with hair *Hen. V.* v 2 43
Put your discourse into some frame and start not so wildly from my affair *Hamlet* iii 2 321
Forth at your eyes your spirits wildly peep . . . . iii 4 119
Valour That wildly grows in them, but yields a crop As if it had been sow'd . . . . *Cymbeline* iv 2 180

Wild-mare. Drinks off candles' ends for flap-dragons, and rides the wild-mare with the boys . . . . 2 *Hen. IV.* ii 4 268

Wildness. This same starved justice hath done nothing but prate to me of the wildness of his youth . . . . . . iii 2 328
If I do feign, O, let me in my present wildness die! . . . iv 5 153
The breath no sooner left his father's body, But that his wildness, mortified in him, Seem'd to die too . . . . *Hen. V.* i 1 26
Obscured his contemplation Under the veil of wildness . . . i 1 64
Meads and hedges, Defective in their natures, grow to wildness . . v 2 55
Our youths and wildness shall no whit appear. . . *J. Cæsar* ii 1 148
He is given To sports, to wildness, and much company . . ii 1 189
For your part, Ophelia, I do wish That your good beauties be the happy cause Of Hamlet's wildness . . . . . *Hamlet* iii 1 40
Put thyself Into a haviour of less fear, ere wildness Vanquish my staider senses. What's the matter? . . . . . *Cymbeline* iii 4 9

Wiles. Sure, these are but imaginary wiles . . *Com. of Errors* iv 3 10
At what ward you lie.— . . . Upon my wit, to defend my wiles *T. and C.* i 2 285

Wilful. Divulge Page himself for a secure and wilful Actæon *Mer. Wives* iii 2 44
No remedy, my lord, when walls are so wilful to hear without warning *M. N. Dream* v 1 211
And do a wilful stillness entertain, With purpose . *Mer. of Venice* i 1 90
I owe you much, and, like a wilful youth, That which I owe is lost . i 1 146
I shall drive you then to confess the wilful abuse . 2 *Hen. IV.* ii 4 339
We shall see wilful adultery and murder committed . *Hen. V.* ii 1 40
How will their grudging stomachs be provoked To wilful disobedience! 1 *Hen. VI.* iv 1 142
. . . . 3 *Hen. VI.* v 5 31
Peace, wilful boy, or I will charm your tongue . *Richard III.* iii 7 28
And ask'd the mayor what meant this wilful silence

Wilful. Nought hath pass'd, But even with law, against the wilful sons *T. Andron.* iv 4 8
Patience perforce with wilful choler meeting Makes my flesh tremble in their different greeting . . . . . . *Rom. and Jul.* i 5 91
To wilful men, The injuries that they themselves procure Must be their schoolmasters . . . . *Lear* ii 4 305

Wilful-blame. My lord, you are too wilful-blame . . 1 *Hen. IV.* iii 1 177

Wilfully. Still thou mistakest, Or else committ'st thy knaveries wilfully *M. N. Dream* iii 2 346
They wilfully themselves exile from light . . . . iii 2 386
Why thou against the church, our holy mother, So wilfully dost spurn *K. John* iii 1 142
Wilfully betray'd The lives of those that he did lead to fight 1 *Hen. IV.* i 3 81
Is she to be buried in Christian burial that wilfully seeks her own salvation?—I tell thee she is . . . . . . *Hamlet* v 1 2

Wilful-negligent. If ever I were wilful-negligent, It was my folly *W. T.* i 2 255

Wilfulness. Never Hydra-headed wilfulness So soon did lose his seat and all at once . . . . *Hen. V.* i 1 35

Wilful-opposite. The Dauphin is too wilful-opposite . *K. John* v 2 124

Will. The wills above be done! but I would fain die a dry death *Tempest* i 1 71
He needs will be Absolute Milan . . . . i 2 108
I should do it With much more ease; for my good will is to it . . iii 1 30
I am your wife, if you will marry me; If not, I'll die your maid . iii 1 83
But I'll be your servant, Whether you will or no . . . iii 1 86
To salute the emperor And to commend their service to his will *T. G. of V.* i 3 42
Relying on your lordship's will And not depending on his friendly wish.—My will is something sorted with his wish . . . . i 3 61
For what I will, I will, and there an end . . . . i 3 65
He wants wit that wants resolved will . . . . . ii 6 12
Then stay at home and go not.—Nay, that I will not . . ii 7 63
What's your will with me? . . . . iii 1 3
Thou art not ignorant How she opposes her against my will . . iii 2 26
What's your will?—That I may compass yours . . . iv 2 92
My will is even this: That presently you hie, you home to bed . iv 2 93
Thou art not ignorant what dear good will I bear . . . iv 3 14
This ring I gave him when he parted from me, To bind him to remember my good will . . . . iv 4 103
These are my mates, that make their wills their law . . v 4 14
Therefore, precisely, can you carry your good will to the maid? *Mer. W.* i 1 238
Od's plessed will! I will not be absence at the grace . . . i 1 273
He hath studied her will, and translated her will, out of honesty into English . . . . i 3 54
Do what she will, say what she will, take all, pay all, go to bed when she list, rise when she list, all is as she will . . . ii 2 123
Money is a good soldier, sir, and will on . . . . ii 2 176
I will about it; better three hours too soon than a minute too late ii 2 327
Got's will, and his passion of my heart! . . . . iii 1 62
I hope I have your good will, father Page . . . . iii 2 61
What is your will?—My will! 'od's heartlings, that's a pretty jest indeed! I ne'er made my will yet . . . . . . iii 4 58
Let me have your good will . . . . . . iii 4 86
I'll no pullet-sperm in my brewage . . . . . iii 5 32
He hath my good will, And none but he, to marry with Nan Page iv 4 84
I tell you for good will, look you . . . . . iv 5 82
Obedient to your grace's will, I come to know your pleasure *M. for M.* i 1 26
On whom it will, it will; On whom it will not, so; yet still 'tis just . i 2 126
He must die.—Be it as your wisdom will . . . . ii 1 32
Is it your will Claudio shall die to-morrow?—Did not I tell thee yea? . ii 2 7
What's your will?—I am a woeful suitor to your honour . . ii 2 26
For which I must not plead, but that I am At war 'twixt will and will not ii 2 33
But can you, if you would?—Look, what I will not, that I cannot do . ii 2 52
Redeem thy brother By yielding up thy body to my will . . ii 4 164
Bidding the law make court'sy to their will . . . . ii 4 175
O, know he is the bridle of your will.—There's none but asses will be bridled so . . . . *Com. of Errors* ii 1 13
Let your will attend on their accords . . . . . ii 1 25
Pray God our cheer May answer my good will and your good welcome . iii 1 20
Hold you still: I'll fetch my sister, to get her good will . . iii 2 70
What is your will that I shall do with this?—What please yourself . iii 2 174
Thither I must, although against my will . . . . iv 1 112
My tongue, though not my heart, shall have his will . . . iv 2 18
Never could maintain his part but in the force of his will *Much Ado* i 1 239
If it will not be, I'll leave you.—Alas, poor hurt fowl! now will he creep into sedges . . . . ii 1 208
I told him true, that your grace had got the good will of this young lady ii 1 224
I have broke with her father, and his good will obtained . . ii 1 311
Against my will I am sent to bid you come in to dinner . . ii 3 266
I would not hang a dog by my will, much more a man . . . iii 3 67
And it is an offence to stay a man against his will . . . iii 3 88
I do suffer love indeed, for I love thee against my will . . . v 2 68
Margaret was in some fault for this, Although against her will . . v 4 5
But, for my will, my will is your good will May stand with ours . v 4 28
Which is Beatrice?—I answer to that name. What is your will? . v 4 73
We attend, Like humble-visaged suitors, his high will . *L. L. Lost* ii 1 34
A sharp wit matched with too blunt a will; Whose edge hath power to cut, whose will still wills It should none spare . . . . ii 1 49
He'll be forsworn.—Not for the world, fair madam, by my will . . ii 1 99
Why, will shall break it: will and nothing else . . . . ii 1 100
Is she wedded or no?—To her will, sir, or so . . . . ii 1 212
What's your will, sir? what's your will?—I have a letter . . iv 1 52
'Tis our will That some plain man recount their purposes . . v 2 175
To add more terror, We are again forsworn, in will and error . . v 2 471
Prepare to die For disobedience to your father's will . *M. N. Dream* i 1 87
Look you arm yourself To fit your fancies to your father's will . i 1 118
The will of man is by his reason sway'd . . . . ii 2 115
Reason becomes the marshal to my will And leads me to your eyes . ii 2 120
With all good will, with all my heart, In Hermia's love I yield you . iii 2 164
I will overbear your will . . . . iv 1 184
If we offend, it is with our good will. That you should think, we come not to offend, But with good will . . . . v 1 108
So is the will of a living daughter curbed by the will of a dead father. Is it not hard? . . . . *Mer. of Venice* i 2 27
You should refuse to perform your father's will, if you should refuse to accept him . . . . i 2 101
I will die as chaste as Diana, unless I be obtained by the manner of my father's will . . . . i 2 118
What is your will?—I am bid forth to supper . . . . ii 5 10
Bassanio, lord Love, if thy will it be! . . . . . ii 9 101
Let me have judgement and the Jew his will . . . . iv 1 83
To do a great right, do a little wrong, And curb this cruel devil of his will iv 1 217

Will. Bequeathed me by will but poor a thousand crowns *As Y. Like It* i 1 2
My father charged you in his will to give me good education i 1 70
I will not long be troubled with you; you shall have some part of your will i 1 82
It is a thing of his own search and altogether against my will i 1 142
His will hath in it a more modest working i 2 214
Leaving his wealth and ease, A stubborn will to please ii 5 55
Why look you so upon me?—For no ill will I bear you iii 5 71
'Od's my will! Her love is not the hare that I do hunt iv 3 17
Here, noble lord: what is thy will with her?—Are you my wife and will not call me husband? *T. of Shrew* Ind. 2 105
Arm'd With his good will and thy good company i 1 6
Will you any wife?—I pray you, sir, is it your will? i 1 56
Sorry am I that our good will effects Bianca's grief i 1 86
Have you married my daughter without asking my good will? v 1 137
We will content you, go to: but I will in, to be revenged for this villany v 1 138
What is your will, sir, that you send for me? v 2 100
Peevish, sullen, sour, And not obedient to his honest will v 2 158
'Tis a withered pear: will you any thing with it? *All's Well* i 1 177
If I may have your ladyship's good will to go to the world i 3 19
I do beg your good will in this case i 3 23
Will you eat no grapes, my royal fox? Yes, but you will my noble grapes ii 1 73
Thy will by my performance shall be served ii 1 205
Check thy contempt: Obey our will, which travails in thy good ii 3 165
I hope, sir, I have your good will to have mine own good fortunes ii 4 15
What's his will else?—That you will take your instant leave ii 4 48
In every thing I wait upon his will.—I shall report it so ii 4 55
He desires Some private speech with you.—I shall obey his will ii 5 62
Yet in his idle fire, To buy his will, it would not seem too dear iii 7 27
And this night he fleshes his will in the spoil of her honour iv 3 19
I am yours Upon your will to suffer iv 4 30
And inform him So 'tis our will he should v 3 27
Things which would derive me ill will to speak of v 3 265
Wit, an't be thy will, put me into good fooling! *T. Night* i 5 35
I am sick, or not at home; what you will, to dismiss it i 5 117
Let him be the devil, an he will, I care not i 5 136
It shall be inventoried, and every particle and utensil labelled to my will i 5 265
You peevishly threw it to her; and her will is, it should be so returned ii 2 15
We men may say more, swear more: but indeed Our shows are more than will ii 4 120
I'll no more with thee. Hold, there's expenses for thee iii 1 48
I would not by my will have troubled you iii 3 1
Pray God, he keep his oath!—I do assure you, 'tis against my will iii 4 342
There's comfort in't Whiles other men have gates and those gates open'd, As mine, against their will *W. Tale* i 2 198
Yea, a very trick For them to play at will ii 1 52
And so The king's will be perform'd! ii 1 115
If one jot beyond The bound of honour, or in act or will That way iii 2 52
Their sacred wills be done! iii 3 7
Good luck, an't be thy will! what have we here? iii 3 70
It is my father's will I should take on me The hostess-ship o' the day iv 4 71
'Tis your counsel My lord should to the heavens be contrary, Oppose against their wills v 1 46
Here come those I have done good to against my will v 2 135
Upon his death-bed he by will bequeath'd His lands to me *K. John* i 1 109
Let me have what is mine, My father's land, as was my father's will i 1 115
Shall then my father's will be of no force . . . ?—Of no more force to dispossess me, sir, Than was his will to get me i 1 130
I can produce A will that bars the title of thy son.—Ay, who doubts that? a will! a wicked will; A woman's will; a canker'd grandam's will! ii 1 192
My uncle's will in this respect is mine ii 1 510
I can with ease translate it to my will; Or if you will, to speak more properly, I will enforce it ii 1 513
If not fill up the measure of her will, Yet in some measure satisfy her ii 1 556
Will't not be? Will not a calf's-skin stop that mouth of thine? iii 1 298
A grave unto a soul; Holding the eternal spirit, against her will iii 4 18
Since all and every part of what we would Doth make a stand at what your highness will iv 2 39
Although my will to give is living, The suit which you demand is gone and dead iv 2 83
Put we our quarrel to the will of heaven *Richard II.* i 2 6
Your will be done: this must my comfort be i 3 144
But you gave leave to my unwilling tongue Against my will i 3 246
Then all too late comes counsel to be heard, Where will doth mutiny with wit's regard ii 1 28
Let's choose executors and talk of wills: And yet not so iii 2 148
I know it, uncle, and oppose not myself Against their will iii 3 19
To do what service am I sent for hither?—To do that office of thine own good will iv 1 177
Whither?—Whither you will, so I were from your sights iv 1 315
But heaven hath a hand in these events, To whose high will we bound our calm contents v 2 38
Well, come what will, I'll tarry at home *1 Hen. IV.* i 2 162
Stand.—So I do, against my will ii 2 52
Now, master sheriff, what is your will with me? ii 4 555
I will sooner have a beard grow in the palm of my hand than he shall get one on his cheek *2 Hen. IV.* i 2 23
Francis Pickbone, and Will Squele, a Cotswold man iii 2 23
I will do my good will, sir: you can have no more iii 2 167
For your part, Bullcalf, grow till you come unto it: I will none of you iii 2 271
Our cause the best; Then reason will our hearts should be as good iv 1 157
Well, by my will we shall admit no parley iv 1 159
Acquitted by a true substantial form And present execution of our wills iv 1 174
Blunt not his love, . . . By seeming cold or careless of his will iv 4 29
But this lies all within the will of God, To whom I do appeal *Hen. V.* i 2 289
He wills you, in the name of God Almighty, That you divest yourself ii 4 77
If my father render fair return, It is against my will ii 4 128
Ill will never said well iii 7 123
God's will! I pray thee, wish not one man more iv 3 23
God's will! my liege, would you and I alone . . . could fight! iv 3 74
God's will and his pleasure, captain, I beseech you now, come apace iv 8 2
I will none of your money.—It is with a good will iv 8 72
Thou shalt die.—You say very true, scauld knave, when God's will is v 1 34
Grow like savages,—as soldiers will That nothing do but meditate on blood v 2 59
The maid that stood in the way for my wish shall show me the way to my will v 2 356
Who willed you? or whose will stands but mine? *1 Hen. VI.* i 3 11
He will be here, and yet he is not here: How can these contrarieties agree? ii 3 58

Will. I have been a truant in the law, And never yet could frame my will to it; And therefore frame the law unto my will *1 Hen. VI.* ii 4 8
You do paint the white rose red And fall on my side so, against your will ii 4 51
Now, by God's will, thou wrong'st him, Somerset ii 4 82
Were growing time once ripen'd to my will ii 4 99
As will the rest, so willeth Winchester.—If Richard will be true iii 1 162
What wills Lord Talbot pleaseth Burgundy iii 2 130
Doth this churlish superscription Pretend some alteration in good will? iv 1 54
I know it will excuse This sudden execution of my will v 5 99
Sweet aunt, be quiet; 'twas against her will.—Against her will! *2 Hen. VI.* i 3 146
Last time, I danced attendance on his will Till Paris was besieged i 3 174
If I die, I give thee my apron: and, Will, thou shalt have my hammer ii 3 75
Cold news, Lord Somerset: but God's will be done! iii 1 86
Bring me unto my trial when you will. Died he not in his bed? iii 3 8
To revenge it, shalt thou die; And so should these, if I might have my will iv 1 27
If he revenge it not, yet will his friends; So will the queen iv 1 145
Peace with his soul, heaven, if it be thy will! v 2 30
Like rich hangings in a homely house, So was his will in his old feeble body v 3 13
Wouldst have me weep? why, now thou hast thy will *3 Hen. VI.* i 4 144
Beseeching thee, if with thy will it stands ii 3 38
Would I were dead! if God's good will were so ii 5 19
Scotland hath will to help, but cannot help iii 3 34
I am Edward, Your king and Warwick's, and must have my will.—And shall have your will iv 1 16
It was my will and grant; And for this once my will shall stand for law iv 1 49
Edward will be king, And not be tied unto his brother's will iv 1 65
What answers Clarence to his sovereign's will?—That he consents iv 6 45
Or did he make the jest against his will? v 1 30
Shall I go win my daughter to thy will?—And be a happy mother *Richard III.* iv 4 426
And let their heirs, God, if thy will be so, Enrich the time to come! v 5 32
The will of heaven Be done in this and all things! *Hen. VIII.* i 1 209
The will of heaven be done, and the king's pleasure By me obey'd! i 1 215
This tractable obedience is a slave To each incensed will i 2 65
We must not rend our subjects from our laws, And stick them in our will i 2 94
His will is most malignant; and it stretches Beyond you, to your friends i 2 141
The cardinal Will have his will, and she must fall ii 1 167
O, God's will! much better She ne'er had known pomp ii 3 12
A true and humble wife, At all times to your will conformable ii 4 24
Your words, Domestics to you, serve your will as't please Yourself ii 4 114
I thank you both for your good wills; Ye speak like honest men iii 1 68
It's heaven's will: Some spirit put this paper in the packet iii 2 128
Who dare cross 'em, Bearing the king's will from his mouth expressly? iii 2 235
Till I find more than will or words to do it, . . . I dare and must deny it iii 2 236
To conclude, Without the king's will or the state's allowance, A league iii 2 322
If your will pass, I shall both find your lordship judge and juror v 3 59
Then every thing includes itself in power, Power into will, will into appetite; And appetite, an universal wolf, So doubly seconded with will and power *Troi. and Cres.* i 3 120
What is aught, but as 'tis valued?—But value dwells not in particular will ii 2 53
The will dotes that is attributive To what infectiously itself affects ii 2 58
My election Is led on in the conduct of my will; My will enkindled by mine eyes and ears, Two traded pilots 'twixt the dangerous shores Of will and judgement ii 2 62
How may I avoid, Although my will distaste what it elected, The wife I chose? ii 2 66
Were I alone to pass the difficulties And had as ample power as I have will ii 2 140
Great minds, of partial indulgence To their benumbed wills ii 2 179
Nor, by my will, assubjugate his merit, As amply titled as Achilles is ii 3 202
That the will is infinite and the execution confined iii 2 88
I have derision medicinable, To use between your strangeness and his pride, Which his own will shall have desire to drink iii 3 46
There is between my will and all offences A guard of patience v 2 53
What he will he does, and does so much That proof is call'd impossibility v 5 28
Some two months hence my will shall here be made v 10 53
Like a fawning greyhound in the leash, To let him slip at will *Coriolanus* i 6 39
He that has but effected his good will Hath overta'en mine act i 9 18
It shall be to him then as our good wills, A sure destruction ii 1 258
Your wit will not so soon out as another man's will ii 3 29
Custom calls me to't: What custom wills, in all things should we do't ii 3 125
It is a purposed thing, and grows by plot, To curb the will of the nobility iii 1 39
He must, and will. Prithee now, say you will, and go about it iii 2 97
Do your will.—Away! the tribunes do attend you iii 2 137
Direct me, if it be your will, Where great Aufidius lies iv 4 7
Though we willingly consented to his banishment, yet it was against our will iv 6 146
Your good will Must have that thanks from Rome, after the measure As you intended well v 1 45
Good faith, I'll prove him, Speed how it will v 1 61
He that hath a will to die by himself fears it not from another v 2 111
They shall be ready at your highness' will To answer their suspicion *T. An.* ii 3 297
It shall not die.—Aaron, it must; the mother wills it so iv 2 82
Ten thousand worse than ever yet I did Would I perform, if I might have my will v 3 188
Alas, that love, whose view is muffled still, Should, without eyes, see pathways to his will! *Rom. and Jul.* i 1 178
Bid a sick man in sadness make his will: Ah, word ill urged! i 1 208
Get her heart, My will to her consent is but a part i 2 17
What is your will?—This is the matter:—Nurse, give leave awhile i 3 6
It is my will, the which if thou respect, Show a fair presence i 5 74
Two such opposed kings encamp them still In man as well as herbs, grace, and rude will ii 3 28
Bear hence this body and attend our will iii 1 201
God's will, What simpleness is this! I come, I come! iii 3 76
What's your will?—Let me come in, and you shall know my errand iii 3 78
I have more care to stay than will to go iii 5 23
Come, death, and welcome! Juliet wills it so iii 5 24
Have you deliver'd to her our decree?—Ay, sir; but she will none iii 5 140
If . . . Thou hast the strength of will to slay thyself iv 1 72
He'll fright you up, i' faith. Will it not be? iv 5 11
The heavens do lour upon you for some ill; Move them no more by crossing their high will iv 5 95
My poverty, but not my will, consents.—I pay thy poverty, and not thy will v 1 75

Will. There are certain ladies most desirous of admittance.—Ladies! what are their wills? *T. of Athens* i 2 123
I'll ever serve his mind with my best will iv 2 49
Performance is a kind of will or testament v 1 30
Making your wills The scope of justice v 4 4
We put a sting in him, That at his will he may do danger with *J. Cæsar* ii 1 17
The cause is in my will: I will not come; That is enough ii 2 71
None that I know will be, much that I fear may chance ii 4 32
Here's a parchment with the seal of Cæsar; I found it in his closet, 'tis his will iii 2 134
Beg a hair of him for memory, And, dying, mention it within their wills iii 2 140
We'll hear the will: read it, Mark Antony.—The will, the will! we will hear Cæsar's will iii 2 143
Being men, hearing the will of Cæsar, It will inflame you iii 2 148
They were traitors: honourable men!—The will! the testament! iii 2 158
The will! read the will.—You will compel me, then, to read the will? Then make a ring about the corpse of Cæsar, And let me show you him that made the will iii 2 160
You have forgot the will I told you of.—Most true. The will! Let's stay and hear the will.—Here is the will iii 2 243
I have no will to wander forth of doors, Yet something leads me forth iii 3 3
Fetch the will hither, and we shall determine How to cut off some charge in legacies iv 1 8
You may do your will; But he's a tried and valiant soldier iv 1 27
Then, with your will, go on; We'll along ourselves, and meet them iv 3 224
Be thou my witness that against my will, As Pompey was, am I compell'd v 1 74
I am free; yet would not so have been, Durst I have done my will v 3 48
Cæsar, now be still: I kill'd not thee with half so good a will v 5 51
Being unprepared, Our will became the servant to defect *Macbeth* ii 1 18
Though I could With barefaced power sweep him from my sight And bid my will avouch it, yet I must not iii 1 120
I will to-morrow, And betimes I will, to the weird sisters iii 4 132
Strange things I have in head, that will to hand iii 4 139
Come in, without there!—What's your grace's will? iv 1 135
All continent impediments would o'erbear That did oppose my will iv 3 65
Scotland hath foisons to fill up your will, Of your mere own iv 3 88
And at last Upon his will I seal'd my hard consent *Hamlet* i 2 60
Time be thine, And thy best graces spend it at thy will! i 2 63
'Tis unmanly grief; It shows a will most incorrect to heaven i 2 95
No soil nor cautel doth besmirch The virtue of his will i 3 16
But you must fear, His greatness weigh'd, his will is not his own i 3 17
Won to his shameful lust The will of my most seeming virtuous queen i 5 46
And leads the will to desperate undertakings As oft as any passion ii 1 104
It will please you To show us so much gentry and good will As to expend your time with us awhile ii 2 21
And like a neutral to his will and matter, Did nothing ii 2 503
Puzzles the will And makes us rather bear those ills we have iii 1 80
Our wills and fates do so contrary run That our devices still are overthrown iii 2 221
Pray can I not, Though inclination be as sharp as will iii 3 39
Since frost itself as actively doth burn And reason pandars will iii 4 88
'This thing's to do;' Sith I have cause and will and strength and means iv 4 45
She is importunate, indeed distract: Her mood will needs be pitied iv 5 3
That treason can but peep to what it would, Acts little of his will iv 5 125
Who shall stay you?—My will, not all the world iv 5 137
Nature her custom holds, Let shame say what it will iv 7 189
In my terms of honour I stand aloof; and will no reconcilement v 2 258
We have this hour a constant will to publish Our daughters' several dowers, that future strife May be prevented *Lear* i 1 44
Banished two on's daughters, and did the third a blessing against his will i 4 116
Woe, that too late repents,—O, sir, are you come? Is it your will? i 4 280
I'll forbear; And am fall'n out with my more headier will ii 4 111
What will hap more to-night, safe 'scape the king! iii 6 121
O you mighty gods! . . . If I could bear it longer, and not fall To quarrel with your great opposeless wills iv 6 38
'Twas yet some comfort, When misery could beguile the tyrant's rage, And frustrate his proud will iv 6 64
If your will want not, time and place will be fruitfully offered iv 6 269
O undistinguish'd space of woman's will! iv 6 278
Be govern'd by your knowledge, and proceed I' the sway of your own will iv 7 20
The let-alone lies not in your good will.—Nor in thine, lord v 3 79
Our bodies are our gardens, to the which our wills are gardeners *Othello* i 3 324
The power and corrigible authority of this lies in our wills i 3 330
It [love] is merely a lust of the blood and a permission of the will i 3 340
These Moors are changeable in their wills i 3 353
To get his place and to plume up my will In double knavery i 3 399
Ever fair and never proud, Had tongue at will and yet was never loud ii 1 150
God's will, lieutenant, hold! You will be shamed for ever ii 3 162
One may smell in such a will most rank, Foul disproportion iii 3 232
Though I may fear Her will, recoiling to her better judgement iii 3 236
If e'er my will did trespass 'gainst his love iv 2 152
Soothsayer!—Your will?—Is this the man? *Ant. and Cleo.* i 2 7
He stays upon your will.—Let him appear i 2 119
When good will is show'd, though 't come too short, The actor may plead pardon ii 5 8
He hath waged New wars 'gainst Pompey; made his will, and read it To public ear iii 4 4
To come thus was I not constrain'd, but did On my free will iii 6 57
Is Antony or we in fault for this?—Antony only, that would make his will Lord of his reason iii 13 3
Cæsar's will?—Hear it apart.—None but friends: say boldly iii 13 46
Like boys unto a muss, kings would start forth, And cry 'Your will?' iii 13 92
Begin the fight: Our will is Antony be took alive; Make it so known iv 6 2
That life, a very rebel to my will, May hang no longer on me iv 9 14
Not being Fortune, he's but Fortune's knave, A minister of her will v 2 4
Courtesies, which I will be ever to pay and yet pay still *Cymbeline* i 4 39
Blest be those, How mean soe'er, that have their honest wills i 6 8
The cloyed will, That satiate yet unsatisfied desire i 6 47
Not the wronger Of her or you, having proceeded but By both your wills ii 4 56
'Tis greater skill In a true hate, to pray they have their will: The very devils cannot plague them better ii 5 34
The legions garrison'd in Gallia, After your will, have cross'd the sea iv 2 334
Sir, my life is yours; I humbly set it at your will iv 3 13
Do your best wills, And make me blest to obey! v 1 16
There be some of them too that die against their wills; so should I v 4 211
Be my helps, As I am son and servant to your will! *Pericles* i 1 23
I'll make my will then, and, as sick men do Who know the world, see heaven i 1 47

Will. Kings are earth's gods; in vice their law's their will *Pericles* i 1 103
I am too little to contend, Since he's so great can make his will his act i 2 18
But bring they what they will and what they can, What need we fear? i 4 76
My shipwreck now's no ill, Since I have here my father's gift in's will ii 1 140
Honour be but a goal to my will, This day I'll rise, or else add ill to ill ii 1 171
Beauty hath his power and will, Which can as well inflame as it can kill ii 2 34
Either frame Your will to mine,—and you, sir, hear you, Either be ruled by me, or I will make you—Man and wife ii 5 82
My recompense is thanks, that's all; Yet my good will is great iii 4 18
I trod upon a worm against my will, But I wept for it iv 1 79
What is your will?—That he have his v 1 5
Will he, nill he, he goes,—mark you that *Hamlet* v 1 19
Will you, nill you, I will marry you *T. of Shrew* ii 1 273
Willed. He will'd me In heedfull'st reservation to bestow them *All's W.* i 3 230
At Worcester must his body be interr'd; For so he will'd it *K. John* v 7 100
In a vision full of majesty Will'd me to leave my base vocation 1 *Hen. VI.* i 2 80
So we answer him: We do no otherwise than we are will'd.—Who willed you? i 3 10
Would they speak with me?—They will'd me say so, madam *Hen. VIII.* iii 1 18
In feather'd briefness sails are fill'd, And wishes fall out as they're will'd *Pericles* v 2 281
Willeth. As will the rest, so willeth Winchester 1 *Hen. VI.* iii 1 162
William. Come hither, William; hold up your head; come *Mer. Wives* iv 1 17
William, how many numbers is in nouns?—Two iv 1 21
What is 'lapis,' William?—A stone.—And what is 'a stone,' William? iv 1 32
That is a good William. What is he, William, that does lend articles? iv 1 39
What is the focative case, William?—O,—vocativo, O iv 1 53
Show me now, William, some declensions of your pronouns iv 1 76
Is thy name William?—William, sir.—A fair name *As Y. Like It* v 1 22
I dare say my cousin William is become a good scholar 2 *Hen. IV.* iii 2 11
Let me see: yea, marry, William cook, bid him come hither v 1 12
But for William cook: are there no young pigeons? v 1 17
Do you mean to stop any of William's wages, about the sack he lost? v 1 25
And any pretty little tiny kickshaws, tell William cook v 1 29
Edward the Third, my lords, had seven sons: . . . The second, William of Hatfield . . . ; William of Windsor was the seventh and last 2 *Hen. VI.* ii 2 12
An easy matter To make William Lord Hastings of our mind *Rich. III.* iii 1 162
William Lord Hastings had pronounced your part,—I mean, your voice iii 4 28
Willing. With a heart as willing As bondage e'er of freedom *Tempest* iii 1 88
He strays With willing sport to the wild ocean *T. G. of Ver.* ii 7 32
An honest, willing, kind fellow, as ever servant shall come in house withal, and, I warrant you, no tell-tale *Mer. Wives* i 4 10
Whereto if you'll a willing ear incline, What's mine is yours *M. for M.* v 1 542
He may stay him: marry, not without the prince be willing *Much Ado* iii 3 86
Than you much willing to be counted wise In spending your wit *L. L. L.* ii 1 18
Proud of employment, willingly I go.—All pride is willing pride ii 1 36
I was as willing to grapple as he was to board ii 1 218
If killed, but one dead that is willing to be so *As Y. Like It* i 2 201
You say, you'll marry me, if I be willing?—That will I v 4 11
Upon some agreement Me shall you find ready and willing *T. of Shrew* iv 4 34
You will not extort from me what I am willing to keep in *T. Night* ii 1 14
Take leave of her, she is very willing to bid you farewell ii 3 108
My willing love, The rather by these arguments of fear, Set forth in your pursuit iii 3 11
He shall conceal it Whiles you are willing it shall come to note iv 3 29
What you will have, I'll give, and willing too *Richard II.* iii 3 206
Who with willing soul Adopts thee heir iv 1 108
I thought you had been willing to resign.—My crown I am iv 1 190
Willing you overlook this pedigree *Hen. V.* ii 4 90
We send To know what willing ransom he will give iii 5 63
I do not seek him now; But could be willing to march on to Calais iii 6 150
I'll send them all as willing as I live: Lands, goods, horse, armour, any thing I have 2 *Hen. VI.* v 1 51
I defy thee; Not willing any longer conference 3 *Hen. VI.* ii 2 171
Advance your standards, draw your willing swords *Richard III.* v 3 264
If they be still and willing, I'll undertake may see away their shilling Richly in two short hours *Hen. VIII.* Prol. 11
My legs . . . bow to the earth, Willing to leave their burthen iv 2 3
Pray you to deliver This to my lord the king.—Most willing, madam iv 2 130
Take your choice of those That best can aid your action.—Those are they That most are willing *Coriolanus* i 6 67
He craves a parley . . . , Willing you to demand your hostages *T. An.* v 1 160
The swallow follows not summer more willing than we your lordship.—Nor more willingly leaves winter *T. of Athens* iii 6 32
Willing misery Outlives incertain pomp, is crown'd before iv 3 242
I perhaps speak this Before a willing bondman *J. Cæsar* i 3 113
I trouble thee too much, but thou art willing iv 3 259
We have willing dames enough *Macbeth* iv 3 73
And what so poor a man as Hamlet is May do, to express his love and friending to you, God willing, shall not lack *Hamlet* i 5 187
The gentleman willing, and the king hold his purpose, I will win for him v 2 183
Most willing spirits, That promise noble service *Cymbeline* iv 2 338
Willingest. The willing'st sin I ever yet committed May be absolved in English *Hen. VIII.* iii 1 49
Willingly. How churlishly I chid Lucetta hence, When willingly I would have had her here! *T. G. of Ver.* i 2 61
Thou know'st how willingly I would effect The match iii 2 22
Most willingly humbles himself to the determination of justice *M. for M.* iii 2 257
Whiles I Persuade this rude wretch willingly to die iv 3 85
I crave death more willingly than mercy; 'Tis my deserving v 1 481
You embrace your charge too willingly *Much Ado* i 1 103
Proud of employment, willingly I go *L. L. Lost* ii 1 35
I like this place, And willingly could waste my time in it *As Y. Like It* ii 4 95
As willingly as e'er I came from school *T. of Shrew* iii 2 152
And I, most jocund, apt, and willingly, To do you rest, a thousand deaths would die *T. Night* v 1 135
I willingly obey your command *W. Tale* iv 2 60
John, to stop Arthur's title in the whole, Hath willingly departed with a part *K. John* ii 1 563
Well shall you perceive how willingly I will both hear and grant you iv 2 45
Never could the noble Mortimer Receive so many, and all willingly 1 *Hen. IV.* i 3 111
Go you and tell him so.—Marry, and shall, and very willingly v 2 34
If he do come in my way, so: if he do not, if I come in his willingly, let him make a carbonado of me v 3 61
I accept the combat willingly 2 *Hen. VI.* i 3 216
As willingly do I the same resign As e'er thy father Henry made it mine; And even as willingly at thy feet I leave it ii 3 33
I'll yield myself to prison willingly, Or unto death, to do my country good iv 9 42

Willingly. This oath I willingly take and will perform . 3 *Hen. VI.* i 1 201
Unto my Lord Cobham, With whom the Kentishmen will willingly rise i 2 41
I dare not make myself so guilty, To give up willingly that noble title Your master wed me to *Hen. VIII.* iii 1 140
Please you To hear Cominius speak?—Most willingly . *Coriolanus* ii 2 66
Though we willingly consented to his banishment, yet it was against our will . . . . iv 6 144
I will most willingly attend your ladyship . . *T. Andron.* iv 1 28
I have done a thousand dreadful things As willingly as one would kill a fly . . . . v 1 142
Could we but learn from whence his sorrows grow, We would as willingly give cure as know . . . . *Rom. and Jul.* i 1 161
The swallow follows not summer more willing than we your lordship. —Nor more willingly leaves winter . . *T. of Athens* iii 6 33
From whence though willingly I came to Denmark . . *Hamlet* i 2 52
You cannot, sir, take from me any thing that I will more willingly part withal . . . . ii 2 220
What willingly he did confound he wail'd, Believe't . *Ant. and Cleo.* iii 2 58
May it please you To take them in protection?—Willingly . *Cymbeline* i 6 193
Poor sick Fidele! I'll willingly to him . . . . iv 2 167
You must seem to do that fearfully which you commit willingly *Pericles* iv 2 128
Willingness. I would expend it with all willingness 2 *Hen. VI.* iii 1 150
We, having now the best at Barnet field, Will thither straight, for willingness rids way . . . . . 3 *Hen VI.* v 3 21
Willoughby. Beaumond, and Willoughby, With all their powerful friends, are fled to him . . . . *Richard II.* ii 2 54
What a weary way From Ravenspurgh to Cotswold will be found In Ross and Willoughby, wanting your company . . . . ii 3 10
Here come the Lords of Ross and Willoughby, Bloody with spurring . ii 3 57
Willow. Will you go with me?—Whither?—Even to the next willow *Much Ado* ii 1 194
In such a night Stood Dido with a willow in her hand . *Mer. of Venice* v 1 10
Why, what would you?—Make me a willow cabin at your gate *T. Night* i 5 287
Tell him, in hope he'll prove a widower shortly, I'll wear the willow garland for his sake . . . . . 3 *Hen. VI.* iii 3 228; iv 1 100
There is a willow grows aslant a brook . . . *Hamlet* iv 7 167
She had a song of 'willow;' An old thing 'twas, but it express'd her fortune, And she died singing it. . . . *Othello* iv 3 28
The poor soul sat sighing by a sycamore tree, Sing all a green willow . iv 3 42
Her hand on her bosom, her head on her knee, Sing willow, willow, willow . . . . iv 3 44
The fresh streams ran by her, and murmur'd her moans; Sing willow, willow, willow . . . . iv 3 46
Her salt tears fell from her, and soften'd the stones;—Lay by these:— Sing willow, willow, willow . . . . . . iv 3 49
Sing all a green willow must be my garland . . . . iv 3 51
I will play the swan, And die in music. Willow, willow, willow . v 2 248
Willow-tree. I offered him my company to a willow-tree . *Much Ado* ii 1 225
Wilt. Abhorred slave, Which any print of goodness wilt not take! *Temp.* i 2 352
Wilt thou be gone? Sweet Valentine, adieu! . . . *T. G. of Ver.* i 1 11
So we be rid of them, do with 'em what thou wilt . . 1 *Hen. VI.* iv 7 94
Be what thou wilt, thou art my prisoner . . . . . v 3 45
Wilt break my heart?—I had rather break mine own . . *Lear* iii 4 4
Wiltshire. Go, Bushy, to the Earl of Wiltshire straight *Richard II.* i 4 53
The Earl of Wiltshire hath the realm in farm . . . . ii 1 256
Straight to Bristol castle: The Earl of Wiltshire is already there . . ii 2 136
Where is the Earl of Wiltshire? where is Bagot? What is become of Bushy? . . . . iii 2 122
The Earl of Wiltshire, Bushy, Green.—What, are they dead?—They are iii 4 53
Here's the Earl of Wiltshire's blood, Whom I encounter'd 3 *Hen. VI.* i 1 14
Wimpled. This wimpled, whining, purblind, wayward boy *L. L. Lost* iii 1 181
Win. Hast put thyself Upon this island as a spy, to win it . *Tempest* i 2 455
What said she?—Truly, sir, I think you'll hardly win her *T. G. of Ver.* i 1 141
Cannot your Grace win her to fancy him? . . . . iii 1 67
Win her with gifts, if she respect not words . . . . iii 1 89
That man that hath a tongue, I say, is no man, If with his tongue he cannot win a woman . . . . iii 1 105
Win her to consent to you: if any man may, you may as soon as any *Mer. Wives* ii 2 245
Would it apply well to the vehemency of your affection, that I should win what you would enjoy? . . . . ii 2 248
Make us lose the good we oft might win By fearing to attempt *M. for M.* i 4 78
He's coming; I perceive't.—Pray heaven she win him! . . . ii 2 125
Such a man would win any woman in the world . . *Much Ado* ii 1 17
Win me and wear me; let him answer me . . . . . v 1 82
He hath wit to make an ill shape good, And shape to win grace *L. L. Lost* ii 1 60
Master, will you win your love with a French brawl . . . iii 1 8
As thou wilt win my favour, good my knave, Do one thing for me . iii 1 153
What fool is not so wise To lose an oath to win a paradise? . . iv 3 73
Shall we resolve to woo these girls of France?—And win them too . iv 3 372
To weed this wormwood from your fruitful brain, And therewithal to win me . . . . v 2 858
To yield myself His wife who wins me by that means I told you *Mer. of Venice* ii 1 19
Yea, mock the lion when he roars for prey, To win thee, lady . . ii 1 31
He may win; And what is music then? . . . . . iii 2 47
No; we shall ne'er win at that sport, and stake down . . . iii 2 219
Tell him from me, as he will win my love, He bear himself with honourable action . . . . . . *T. of Shrew* Ind. 1 109
Provided that he win her.—I would I were as sure of a good dinner . i 2 217
I will compound this strife: 'Tis deeds must win the prize . . ii 1 344
Kindness in women, not their beauteous looks, Shall win my love . iv 2 42
He whose wife is most obedient To come at first when he doth send for her, Shall win the wager . . . . v 2 69
I will win my wager better yet . . . . v 2 116
Tell him that his sword can never win The honour that he loses *All's W.* iii 2 96
Whence honour but of danger wins a scar, As oft it loses all . . . iii 2 124
Only in this disguise I think't no sin To cozen him that would unjustly win . . . . iv 2 76
Which nothing, but to close Her eyes myself, could win me to believe . v 3 119
This wins him, liver and all . . . . . . *T. Night* ii 5 106
There is no tongue that moves, none, none i' the world, So soon as yours could win me . . . . *W. Tale* i 2 21
He that perforce robs lions of their hearts May easily win a woman's *K. John* i 1 269
I'll give thee more Than e'er the coward hand of France can win . . ii 1 158
Win you this city without stroke or wound . . . . ii 1 418
That daily break-vow, he that wins of all, Of kings, of beggars, old men ii 1 569
Husband, I cannot pray that thou mayst win . . . . . iii 1 331
Whoever wins, on that side shall I lose . . . . . iii 1 335

Win. Thrust thyself into their companies: I have a way to win their loves again . . . . *K. John* iv 2 168
Have I not here the best cards for the game, To win this easy match? . v 2 106
And to win renown Even in the jaws of danger and of death . . . v 2 115
I say again, if Lewis do win the day, He is forsworn . . . v 4 30
A treacherous fine of all your lives, If Lewis by your assistance win the day . . . . v 4 39
His noble hand Did win what he did spend and spent not that Which his triumphant father's hand had won . . . *Richard II.* ii 1 180
We must win your grace to go with us To Bristol castle . . . ii 3 163
This ague fit of fear is over-blown; An easy task it is to win our own . iii 2 191
Our holy lives must win a new world's crown . . . . v 1 24
How heinous e'er it be, To win thy after-love I pardon thee . . v 3 35
Trench him here And on this north side win this cape of land 1 *Hen. IV.* iii 1 113
By this face, This seeming brow of justice, did he win The hearts of all iv 3 83
With the losers let it sympathise, For nothing can seem foul to those that win . . . . v 1 8
But mine I am sure thou art, whoe'er thou be, And thus I win thee . v 4 38
That thou mightst win the more thy father's love, Pleading so wisely in excuse of it . . . . 2 *Hen. IV.* iv 5 180
With blood and sword and fire to win your right . . . *Hen. V.* i 2 131
If that you will France win, Then with Scotland first begin . . . i 2 167
I can never win A soul so easy as that Englishman's . . . ii 2 124
And sword and shield, In bloody field, Doth win immortal fame . . iii 2 11
These be good humours! your honour wins bad humours . . . iii 2 28
If I could win a lady at leap-frog, or by vaulting into my saddle . v 2 142
A base Walloon, to win the Dauphin's grace, Thrust Talbot with a spear into the back . . . . 1 *Hen. VI.* i 1 137
Henry born at Monmouth should win all And Henry born at Windsor lose all . . . . iii 1 198
I'll win this Lady Margaret. For whom? Why, for my king . v 3 88
Anjou and Maine! myself did win them both . . . 2 *Hen. VI.* i 1 119
Maine is lost; That Maine which by main force Warwick did win . i 1 210
I meant Maine, Which I will win from France, or else be slain . . i 1 213
Men's flesh preserved so whole do seldom win . . . . iii 1 301
The rebels have assay'd to win the Tower . . . . iv 5 9
By words or blows here let us win our right . . . 3 *Hen. VI.* i 1 37
I'll win them, fear it not: And thus most humbly I do take my leave . i 2 60
They had no heart to fight, And we in them no hope to win the day . ii 1 136
By this account then Margaret may win him . . . . iii 1 35
And in conclusion wins the king from her, With promise of his sister . iii 1 50
And yet to win her, all the world to nothing! . . . *Richard III.* i 2 238
If my weak oratory Can from his mother win the Duke of York, Anon expect him here . . . . iii 1 38
An if I live until I be a man, I'll win our ancient right in France again iii 1 92
But, sure, I fear, we shall ne'er win him to it . . . . iii 7 80
This is not the way To win your daughter.—There is no other way . iv 4 285
Shall I go win my daughter to thy will?—And be a happy mother by the deed . . . . iv 4 426
Our wrongs in Richard's bosom Will conquer him! awake, and win the day! . . . . v 3 145
Those whom we fight against Had rather have us win than him they follow . . . . v 3 244
How can man, then, The image of his Maker, hope to win by it? *Hen. VIII.* iii 2 442
Cherish those hearts that hate thee; Corruption wins not more than honesty . . . . iii 2 444
I did never win of you before.—But little, Charles; Nor shall not, when my fancy's on my play . . . . v 1 58
Win straying souls with modesty again, Cast none away . . v 3 64
You play the spaniel, And think with wagging of your tongue to win me v 3 127
I was fain to draw mine honour in, and let 'em win the work . . v 4 61
Why was my Cressid then so hard to win?—Hard to seem won *Troi. and Cres.* iii 2 124
Greekish girls shall tripping sing, 'Great Hector's sister did Achilles win' . . . . iii 3 212
Believe, I come to lose my arm, or win my sleeve . . . v 3 96
As if that luck, in very spite of cunning, Bade him win all . . v 5 42
Thou rascal, that art worst in blood to run, Lead'st first to win some vantage . . . . *Coriolanus* i 1 164
It will in time Win upon power and throw forth greater themes . . i 1 224
We have at disadvantage fought and did Retire to win our purpose . i 6 50
Do press among the popular throngs and puff To win a vulgar station . ii 1 231
An evident calamity, though we had Our wish, which side should win . v 3 113
O Cassius, if you could But win the noble Brutus to our party *J. Cæsar* i 3 141
Oftentimes, to win us to our harm, The instruments of darkness tell us truths, Win us with honest trifles, to betray's . . . *Macbeth* i 3 123
Wouldst not play false, And yet wouldst wrongly win . . . i 5 23
By many of these trains hath sought to win me Into his power . . iv 3 118
I will win for him an I can; if not, I will gain nothing . . *Hamlet* v 2 183
I have been in continual practice; I shall win at the odds . . v 2 222
Our son shall win.—He's fat, and scant of breath . . . v 2 298
I will not be, though I should win your displeasure to entreat me to't *Lear* ii 2 119
We'll talk with them too, Who loses and who wins; who's in, who's out . . . . v 3 15
I think this tale would win my daughter too . . . . *Othello* i 3 171
Probal to thinking and indeed the course To win the Moor again . ii 3 345
And then for her To win the Moor—were't to renounce his baptism . ii 3 349
So, so: they laugh that win . . . . iv 1 125
What shall I do to win my lord again? Good friend, go to him . . iv 2 149
His cocks do win the battle still of mine, When it is all to nought *Ant. and Cleo.* ii 3 36
My purposes do draw me much about: You'll win two days upon me . ii 4 9
Husband win, win brother, Prays, and destroys the prayer; no midway iii 4 18
To try thy eloquence, now 'tis time: dispatch; From Antony win Cleopatra . . . . iii 12 27
So soon as I can win the offended king, I will be known your advocate *Cymbeline* i 1 75
As I my poor self did exchange for you, To your so infinite loss, so in our trifles I still win of you . . . . i 1 121
What I have lost to-day at bowls I'll win to-night of him . . ii 1 54
You are most hot and furious when you win . . . . . ii 3 7
I would I were so sure To win the king as I am bold her honour Will remain hers . . . . ii 4 2
But to win time To lose so bad employment . . . . iii 4 112
To attain In suit the place of's bed and win this ring . . v 5 185
If I cannot win you to this love, Go search like nobles . . *Pericles* ii 4 49
Whom if you find, and win unto return, You shall like diamonds sit about his crown . . . . ii 4 52
We have a maid in Mytilene, I durst wager, Would win some words of him . . . . v 1 44

Wince. I will sit as quiet as a lamb; I will not stir, nor wince *K. John* iv 1 81
Let the galled jade wince, our withers are unwrung *Hamlet* iii 2 253
Winchester. I may not open; The Cardinal of Winchester forbids *1 Hen. VI.* i 3 19
Arrogant Winchester, that haughty prelate i 3 23
Winchester goose, I cry, a rope! a rope! Now beat them hence i 3 53
In the next parliament Call'd for the truce of Winchester and Gloucester ii 4 118
Else would I have a fling at Winchester.—Uncles of Gloucester and of Winchester, The special watchmen of our English weal iii 1 64
Can you, my Lord of Winchester, behold My sighs and tears and will not once relent? iii 1 107
Here, Winchester, I offer thee my hand.—Fie, uncle Beaufort! iii 1 126
My Lord of Winchester, relent! What, shall a child instruct you what to do? iii 1 132
Is my Lord of Winchester install'd, And call'd unto a cardinal's degree? v 1 28
Winchester will not submit, I trow, Or be inferior to the proudest peer v 1 56
Speak, Winchester; for boiling choler chokes The hollow passage of my poison'd voice v 4 120
I can read no further.—Uncle of Winchester, I pray, read on *2 Hen. VI.* i 1 56
Winchester, I know your mind; 'Tis not my speeches that you do mislike i 1 139
Confine yourself To Asher House, my Lord of Winchester's *Hen. VIII.* iii 2 231
The one of Winchester, Newly preferr'd from the king's secretary iv 1 101
He of Winchester Is held no great good lover of the archbishop's iv 1 103
My good Lord of Winchester, I thank you; You are always my good friend v 3 58
My Lord of Winchester, you are a little, By your good favour, too sharp v 3 73
You were ever good at sudden commendations, Bishop of Winchester v 3 123
My fear is this, Some galled goose of Winchester would hiss *Tr. and Cr.* v 10 55
Wincot. Ask Marian Hacket, the fat ale-wife of Wincot *T. of Shrew* Ind. 2 23
Wind. Blow, till thou burst thy wind, if room enough! *Tempest* i 1 9
To sigh To the winds whose pity, sighing back again, Did us but loving wrong i 2 150
To tread the ooze Of the salt deep, To run upon the sharp wind of the north i 2 254
Thou shalt be as free As mountain winds i 2 499
Another storm brewing; I hear it sing i' the wind ii 2 20
May as well Wound the loud winds iii 3 63
The billows spoke and told me of it; The winds did sing it to me iii 3 97
I have bedimm'd The noontide sun, call'd forth the mutinous winds v 1 42
Be calm, good wind, blow not a word away *T. G. of Ver.* i 2 118
If the wind were down, I could drive the boat with my sighs ii 3 59
A man may hear this shower sing in the wind *Mer. Wives* iii 2 38
If my wind were but long enough to say my prayers, I would repent iv 5 104
To be imprison'd in the viewless winds *Meas. for Meas.* iii 1 124
Was carried with more speed before the wind *Com. of Errors* i 1 110
Stop in your wind, sir: tell me this, I pray i 2 53
There is something in the wind, that we cannot get in iii 1 69
A man may break a word with you, sir, and words are but wind iii 1 75
If the wind blow any way from shore, I will not harbour in this town to-night iii 2 153
Both wind and tide stays for this gentleman iv 1 46
The ship is in her trim; the merry wind Blows fair from land iv 1 90
Sits the wind in that corner? *Much Ado* ii 3 102
If speaking, why, a vane blown with all winds; If silent, why, a block moved with none iii 1 66
Foul wind is but foul breath, and foul breath is noisome v 2 53
Many can brook the weather that love not the wind *L. L. Lost* iv 2 34
Through the velvet leaves the wind, All unseen, can passage find iv 3 105
Fleeter than arrows, bullets, wind, thought, swifter things v 2 261
When all aloud the wind doth blow And coughing drowns the parson's saw v 2 931
To dance our ringlets to the whistling wind *M. N. Dream* ii 1 86
The winds, piping to us in vain, As in revenge, have suck'd up from the sea Contagious fogs ii 1 88
See the sails conceive And grow big-bellied with the wanton wind ii 1 129
About the wood go swifter than the wind iii 2 94
High Taurus' snow, Fann'd with the eastern wind iii 2 142
Sleep thou, and I will wind thee in my arms iv 1 45
Plucking the grass, to know where sits the wind *Mer. of Venice* i 1 18
My wind cooling my broth Would blow me to an ague, when I thought What harm a wind too great at sea might do i 1 22
And herein spend but time To wind about my love with circumstance i 1 154
The four winds blow in from every coast Renowned suitors i 1 168
And then there is the peril of waters, winds, and rocks i 3 26
The scarfed bark puts from her native bay, Hugg'd and embraced by the strumpet wind! How like the prodigal doth she return, With over-weather'd ribs and ragged sails, Lean, rent, and beggar'd by the strumpet wind! ii 6 16
The wind is come about; Bassanio presently will go aboard ii 6 64
Golden locks Which make such wanton gambols with the wind iii 2 93
In such a night as this, When the sweet wind did gently kiss the trees v 1 2
The icy fang And churlish chiding of the winter's wind *As Y. Like It* ii 1 7
I must have liberty Withal, as large a charter as the wind ii 7 48
Blow, blow, thou winter wind, Thou art not so unkind As man's ingratitude ii 7 174
Her worth, being mounted on the wind, Through all the world bears Rosalind iii 2 95
Wind away, Begone, I say, I will not to wedding with thee iii 3 104
Like foggy south puffing with wind and rain iii 5 50
Even as the waving sedges play with wind *T. of Shrew* Ind. 2 55
Such wind as scatters young men through the world To seek their fortunes i 2 50
Have I not heard the sea puff'd up with winds Rage like an angry boar? i 2 202
Though little fire grows great with little wind, Yet extreme gusts will blow out fire and all ii 1 135
As mountains are for winds, That shake not, though they blow perpetually ii 1 141
When virtue's steely bones Look bleak i' the cold wind *All's Well* i 1 115
I sent to her, By this same coxcomb that we have i' the wind iii 6 122
Prithee, allow the wind.—Nay, you need not to stop your nose v 2 10
'Tis in grain, sir; 'twill endure wind and weather *T. Night* i 5 255
I frown the while; and perchance wind up my watch ii 5 66
When that I was and a little tiny boy, With hey, ho, the wind and the rain v 1 399
Embraced, as it were, from the ends of opposed winds *W. Tale* i 1 34
No sneaping winds at home, to make us say 'This is put forth too truly' i 2 13
False As o'er-dyed blacks, as wind, as waters, false As dice i 2 132
I am a feather for each wind that blows ii 3 154
And take The winds of March with beauty iv 4 120
To be the slaves of chance and flies Of every wind that blows iv 4 552
Wind. The adverse winds, Whose leisure I have stay'd, have given him time *K. John* ii 1 57
No distemper'd day, No common wind, no customed event iii 4 155
And, like a shifted wind unto a sail, It makes the course of thoughts to fetch about iv 2 23
Therefore thy threatening colours now wind up v 2 73
'Tis far too huge to be blown out With that same weak wind which enkindled it v 2 87
Nor entreat the north To make his bleak winds kiss my parched lips v 7 40
The north-east wind, Which then blew bitterly against our faces, Awaked the sleeping rheum *Richard II.* i 4 6
We see the wind sit sore upon our sails, And yet we strike not ii 1 265
The wind sits fair for news to go to Ireland, But none returns ii 2 123
Betwixt the wind and his nobility *1 Hen. IV.* i 3 45
If I travel but four foot by the squier further afoot, I shall break my wind ii 2 14
Oft the teeming earth Is with a kind of colic pinch'd and vex'd By the imprisoning of unruly wind Within her womb iii 1 30
It shall not wind with such a deep indent, To rob me of so rich a bottom here.—Not wind? it shall, it must iii 1 104
How now, lad! is the wind in that door, i' faith? iii 3 102
All plumed like estridges that with the wind Baited like eagles iv 1 98
As if an angel dropp'd down from the clouds, To turn and wind a fiery Pegasus iv 1 109
The southern wind Doth play the trumpet to his purposes v 1 3
And the contrarious winds that held the king So long v 1 52
From the orient to the drooping west, Making the wind my post-horse *2 Hen. IV.* Ind. 4
Is not your voice broken? your wind short? your chin double? i 2 206
In the visitation of the winds, Who take the ruffian billows by the top iii 1 21
We shall be winnow'd with so rough a wind That even our corn shall seem as light as chaff iv 1 194
My cloud of dignity Is held from falling with so weak a wind iv 5 100
What wind blew you hither, Pistol?—Not the ill wind which blows no man to good v 3 89
Now sits the wind fair, and we will aboard *Hen. V.* ii 2 12
Behold the threaden sails, Borne with the invisible and creeping wind iii Prol. 11
Whiles yet the cool and temperate wind of grace O'erblows iii 3 30
Yet, by your leave, the wind was very high *2 Hen. VI.* ii 1 3
The winds grow high; so do your stomachs, lords ii 1 55
Nay, then, this spark will prove a raging fire, If wind and fuel be brought to feed it with iii 1 303
And twice by awkward wind from England's bank Drove back again iii 2 83
What boded this, but well forewarning wind? iii 2 85
And thou . . . Against the senseless winds shalt grin in vain iv 1 77
Turn back and fly, like ships before the wind *3 Hen. VI.* i 4 4
For raging wind blows up incessant showers i 4 145
For selfsame wind that I should speak withal Is kindling coals that fires all my breast, And burns me up ii 1 82
Like a mighty sea Forced by the tide to combat with the wind ii 5 6
Like the selfsame sea Forced to retire by fury of the wind ii 5 8
Sometime the flood prevails, and then the wind; Now one the better ii 5 9
Ill blows the wind that profits nobody ii 5 55
Look, as I blow this feather from my face, And as the air blows it to me again, Obeying with my wind when I do blow, And yielding to another when it blows iii 1 86
He knows the game: how true he keeps the wind! iii 2 14
Now begins a second storm to rise; For this is he that moves both wind and tide iii 3 48
It boots not to resist both wind and tide iv 3 59
Sail how thou canst, have wind and tide thy friend v 1 53
And kept low shrubs for winter's powerful wind v 2 15
But keep our course, though the rough wind say no, From shelves and rocks v 4 22
Dallies with the wind and scorns the sun *Richard III.* i 3 265
O ill-dispersing wind of misery! iv 1 53
In the wind and tempest of her [fortune's] frown *Troi. and Cres.* i 3 26
When the splitting wind Makes flexible the knees of knotted oaks i 3 49
What raging of the sea! shaking of earth! Commotion in the winds! i 3 98
Speak frankly as the wind i 3 253
The seas and winds, old wranglers, took a truce And did him service ii 2 75
She does so blush, and fetches her wind so short iii 2 33
As false As air, as water, wind, or sandy earth, As fox to lamb iii 2 199
Where are my tears? rain, to lay this wind, or my heart will be blown up by the root iv 4 56
Even in the fan and wind of your fair sword, You bid them rise, and live v 3 41
Go, wind, to wind, there turn and change together v 3 110
And one infect another Against the wind a mile! *Coriolanus* i 4 34
Were he the butcher of my son, he should Be free as is the wind i 9 89
They to dust should grind it And throw't against the wind iii 2 104
To wind Yourself into a power tyrannical iii 3 64
Then let the mutinous winds Strike the proud cedars 'gainst the fiery sun v 3 59
The green leaves quiver with the cooling wind *T. Andron.* ii 3 14
Like to a bubbling fountain stirr'd with wind ii 4 23
If the winds rage, doth not the sea wax mad? iii 1 223
And, if she wind you once, She's with the lion deeply still in league iv 1 97
The angry northern wind Will blow these sands, like Sibyl's leaves, abroad iv 1 104
My son and I will have the wind of you iv 2 133
You were as good to shoot against the wind iv 3 57
Scatter'd by winds and high tempestuous gusts v 3 69
Which . . . He swung about his head and cut the winds *Rom. and Jul.* i 1 118
As thin of substance as the air And more inconstant than the wind i 4 100
This wind, you talk of, blows us from ourselves i 4 104
In one little body Thou counterfeit'st a bark, a sea, a wind iii 5 132
The bark thy body is, Sailing in this salt flood; the winds, thy sighs iii 5 135
Pursy insolence shall break his wind With fear and horrid flight *T. of A.* v 4 12
When the scolding winds Have rived the knotty oaks *J. Cæsar* i 3 5
Listen well; I heard a bustling rumour, like a fray, And the wind brings it from the Capitol ii 4 19
It is a creature that I teach to fight, To wind, to stop, to run directly on iv 1 32
They pass by me as the idle wind, Which I respect not iv 3 68
Blow wind, swell billow, and swim bark! The storm is up v 1 67
I'll give thee a wind.—Thou'rt kind.—And I another *Macbeth* i 3 11
And what seem'd corporal melted As breath into the wind i 3 82
Shall blow the horrid deed in every eye, That tears shall drown the wind i 7 25
Though you untie the winds and let them fight Against the churches iv 1 52
Blow, wind! come, wrack! At least we'll die with harness on our back v 5 51
He might not beteem the winds of heaven Visit her face too roughly *Ham.* i 2 141
As the winds give benefit And convoy is assistant, do not sleep i 3 2

Wind. The wind sits in the shoulder of your sail, And you are stay'd for *Hamlet* i 3 56
Not to crack the wind of the poor phrase, Running it thus . i 3 108
When the wind is southerly I know a hawk from a handsaw . . ii 2 397
But with the whiff and wind of his fell sword The unnerved father falls ii 2 495
The bold winds speechless and the orb below As hush as death . ii 2 507
Why do you go about to recover the wind of me? . . iii 2 362
Mad as the sea and wind, when both contend Which is the mightier . iv 1 7
Prepare thyself; The bark is ready, and the wind at help . . iv 3 46
My arrows, Too slightly timber'd for so loud a wind . . . iv 7 22
And for his death no wind of blame shall breathe . . . iv 7 67
Cæsar, dead and turn'd to clay, Might stop a hole to keep the wind away v 1 237
Believe me, 'tis very cold; the wind is northerly . . . v 2 98
Wind me into him, I pray you: frame the business after your own wisdom *Lear* i 2 106
An thou canst not smile as the wind sits, thou'lt catch cold shortly . i 4 112
With presented nakedness out-face The winds and persecutions of the sky ii 3 12
The night comes on, and the bleak winds Do sorely ruffle . . ii 4 303
Bids the wind blow the earth into the sea, Or swell the curled waters . iii 1 5
Strives in his little world of man to out-scorn The to-and-fro-conflicting wind and rain . . . . . . iii 1 11
Blow, winds, and crack your cheeks! rage! blow! . . . iii 2 1
Spit, fire! spout, rain! Nor rain, wind, thunder, fire, are my daughters iii 2 15
Such groans of roaring wind and rain, I never Remember to have heard iii 2 47
He that has and a little tiny wit,—With hey, ho, the wind and the rain iii 2 75
Through the sharp hawthorn blows the cold wind . . . iii 4 47
Still through the hawthorn blows the cold wind: Says suum, mun, ha, no, nonny . . . . . . iii 4 102
You are not worth the dust which the rude wind Blows in your face . iv 2 30
When the rain came to wet me once, and the wind to make me chatter iv 6 103
The untuned and jarring senses, O, wind up Of this child-changed father! iv 7 16
Was this a face To be opposed against the warring winds? . . iv 7 32
Methinks the wind hath spoke aloud at land . . *Othello* ii 1 5
High seas and howling winds, The gutter'd rocks and congregated sands ii 1 68
If after every tempest come such calms, May the winds blow till they have waken'd death! . . . . . . ii 1 188
My boat sails freely, both with wind and stream . . . ii 3 65
I'ld whistle her off and let her down the wind, To prey at fortune . iii 3 262
The bawdy wind that kisses all it meets Is hush'd . . . iv 2 78
Hark! who is't that knocks?—It's the wind . . . . iv 3 54
Blow me about in winds! roast me in sulphur! . . . v 2 279
We cannot call her winds and waters sighs and tears *Ant. and Cleo.* i 2 153
Purple the sails, and so perfumed that The winds were love-sick with them . . . . ii 2 199
Fans, whose wind did seem To glow the delicate cheeks which they did cool . . . . ii 2 208
The least wind i' the world will blow them down . . . ii 7 2
I have eyes upon him, And his affairs come to me on the wind . iii 6 63
Though my reason Sits in the wind against me . . . iii 10 37
Winds of all the corners kiss'd your sails, To make your vessel nimble *Cymbeline* ii 4 28
When we shall hear The rain and wind beat dark December . . iii 3 37
Rides on the posting winds and doth belie All corners of the world . iii 4 38
To commix With winds that sailors rail at . . . . iv 2 56
As the rudest wind, That by the top doth take the mountain pine . iv 2 174
When expect you them?—With the next benefit o' the wind . . iv 2 342
For vice repeated is like the wandering wind, Blows dust in others' eyes, to spread itself . . . . . *Pericles* i 1 96
For now the wind begins to blow; Thunder above and deeps below ii Gower 29
Wind, rain, and thunder, remember, earthly man Is but a substance that must yield to you . . . . . . ii 1 2
A man whom both the waters and the wind, In that vast tennis-court, have made the ball For them to play upon . . . . ii 1 63
And thou, that hast Upon the winds command, bind them in brass! . iii 1 3
The sea works high, the wind is loud, and will not lie till the ship be cleared of the dead . . . . . . iii 1 48
When canst thou reach it?—By break of day, if the wind cease . iii 1 77
Give you up to the mask'd Neptune and The gentlest winds of heaven . iii 3 37
Is this wind westerly that blows?—South-west . . . iv 1 51
When I was born, the wind was north.—Was't so? . . . iv 1 52
When I was born: Never was waves nor wind more violent . . iv 1 60
The stuff we have, a strong wind will blow it to pieces . . . iv 2 20
Bounteous winds have brought This king to Tarsus . . . iv 4 17
Driven before the winds, he is arrived Here where his daughter dwells v Gower 14
Wind-changing Warwick now can change no more . . *3 Hen. VI.* v 1 57
Winded. I will have a recheat winded in my forehead . *Much Ado* i 1 243
Windgalls. Full of windgalls, sped with spavins . *T. of Shrew* iii 2 53
Winding. Look, he's winding up the watch of his wit . *Tempest* ii 1 12
And so by many winding nooks he strays With willing sport to the wild ocean . . . . *T. G. of Ver.* ii 7 31
Winding up days with toil and nights with sleep . . *Hen. V.* iv 1 296
Winding-sheet. Their colours . . . Shall be my winding-sheet *3 Hen. VI.* i 1 129
These arms of mine shall be thy winding-sheet . . . ii 5 114
Wind-instruments. Are these, I pray you, wind-instruments?—Ay, marry, are they, sir.—O, thereby hangs a tail . . . *Othello* iii 1 6
Windlasses. With windlasses and with assays of bias, By indirections find directions out . . . . . *Hamlet* ii 1 65
Windmill. I had rather live With cheese and garlic in a windmill *1 Hen. IV.* iii 1 162
Sir John, do you remember since we lay all night in the windmill? *2 Hen. IV.* iii 2 207
Wind-obeying. Before the always wind-obeying deep *Com. of Errors* i 1 64
Window. How I must climb her window, The ladder made of cords *T. G. of Ver.* ii 4 181
What lets but one may enter at her window? . . . . iii 1 113
Now must we to her window, And give some evening music to her ear . iv 2 16
What man was he talk'd with you yesternight Out at your window? *Much Ado* iv 1 85
Talk with a man out at a window! A proper saying! . . . iv 1 311
Behold the window of my heart, mine eye . . *L. L. Lost* v 2 848
Thou hast by moonlight at her window sung . *M. N. Dream* i 1 30
Look out at window, for all this; There will come a Christian by *M. of V.* ii 5 41
His father is come from Padua and here looking out at the window *T. of S.* v 1 32
See where he looks out of the window . . . . . v 1 58
So, my good window of lattice, fare thee well . . *All's Well* ii 3 224
Though I swore I leaped from the window of the citadel—How deep? iv 1 60
It hath bay windows transparent as barricadoes . . *T. Night* iv 2 40
In at the window, or else o'er the hatch . . *K. John* i 1 171
Now my soul hath elbow-room; It would not out at windows nor at doors . . . . v 7 29
Window. From my own windows torn my household coat *Richard II.* iii 1 24
Where rude misgovern'd hands from windows' tops Threw dust and rubbish on King Richard's head . . . . . . v 2 5
You would have thought the very windows spake . . . . v 2 12
I could discern no part of his face from the window . *2 Hen. IV.* ii 2 87
Our windows are broke down in every street And we for fear compell'd to shut our shops . . . . . *1 Hen. VI.* iii 1 84
Lo, in these windows that let forth thy life, I pour the helpless balm of my poor eyes . . . . . . *Richard III.* i 2 12
Ere I let fall the windows of mine eyes . . . . . v 3 116
She came to him th' other day into the compassed window *Troi. and Cres.* i 2 120
Stalls, bulks, windows, Are smother'd up, leads fill'd . *Coriolanus* ii 1 226
An hour before the worshipp'd sun Peer'd forth the golden window of the east . . . . *Rom. and Jul.* i 1 126
In his chamber pens himself, Shuts up his windows, locks fair daylight out . . . . i 1 145
But, soft! what light through yonder window breaks? It is the east . ii 2 2
Then, window, let day in, and let life out . . . . iii 5 41
Thy eyes' windows fall, Like death, when he shuts up the day of life . iv 1 100
Climb'd up . . . To towers and windows, yea, to chimney-tops *J. Cæsar* i 1 44
I will this night, In several hands, in at his windows throw . . i 2 320
Throw this In at his window; set this up with wax . . . i 3 145
Searching the window for a flint, I found This paper, thus seal'd up . ii 1 36
Pluck down benches.—Pluck down forms, windows, any thing . iii 2 264
And I a maid at your window, To be your Valentine . . *Hamlet* iv 5 50
Downy windows, close; And golden Phœbus never be beheld Of eyes again so royal! . . . . . . *Ant. and Cleo.* v 2 319
Bows toward her, and would under-peep her lids, To see the enclosed lights, now canopied Under these windows . . . *Cymbeline* ii 2 22
I will write all down: Such and such pictures; there the window . ii 2 25
Thy crystal window ope; look out . . . . . . v 4 81
To me The very doors and windows savour vilely . . *Pericles* iv 6 117
Window-bars. Those milk-paps, That through the window-bars bore at men's eyes . . . . *T. of Athens* iv 3 116
Windowed. Your loop'd and window'd raggedness . . *Lear* iii 4 31
Wouldst thou be window'd in great Rome and see Thy master thus? *Ant. and Cleo.* iv 14 72
Windpipe. Let gallows gape for dog; let man go free And let not hemp his wind-pipe suffocate . . . . . *Hen. V.* iii 6 45
If I were a huge man, I should fear to drink at meals; Lest they should spy my windpipe's dangerous notes . . . *T. of Athens* i 2 52
Windring. You nymphs, call'd Naiads, of the windring brooks *Tempest* iv 1 128
Wind-shaked. The wind-shaked surge, with high and monstrous mane, Seems to cast water on the burning bear . . . *Othello* ii 1 13
Wind-shaken. He's the rock, the oak not to be wind-shaken *Coriolanus* v 2 117
Windsor. Never a woman in Windsor knows more of Anne's mind than I do . . . . *Mer. Wives* i 4 136
What tempest, I trow, threw this whale . . . ashore at Windsor? . ii 1 66
The best courtier of them all, when the court lay at Windsor . . ii 2 63
She's as fartuous a civil modest wife . . . as any is in Windsor . ii 2 103
Never a wife in Windsor leads a better life than she does . . ii 2 122
If there be a kind woman in Windsor, she is one . . . ii 2 126
Old Windsor way, and every way but the town way . . . iii 1 6
Your husband's coming hither, woman, with all the officers in Windsor iii 3 114
Your husband's coming, with half Windsor at his heels . . iii 3 121
I would not ha' your distemper in this kind for the wealth of Windsor Castle . . . . iii 3 232
Herne the hunter, Sometime a keeper here in Windsor forest . . iv 4 29
All present ourselves, dis-horn the spirit, And mock him home to Windsor . . . . iv 4 64
The Windsor bell hath struck twelve; the minute draws on . . v 5 1
I am here a Windsor stag; and the fattest, I think, i' the forest . v 5 14
Cricket, to Windsor chimneys shalt thou leap . . . . v 5 47
About, about; Search Windsor Castle, elves, within and out . . v 5 60
Now, good Sir John, how like you Windsor wives? . . . v 5 110
We'll bring you to Windsor, to one Master Brook . . . v 5 174
Ay, by gar, and 'tis a boy: by gar, I'll raise all Windsor . . v 5 223
On Wednesday next our council we Will hold at Windsor . *1 Hen. IV.* i 1 104
In Wheeson week, when the prince broke thy head for liking his father to a singing-man of Windsor . . . . *2 Hen. IV.* ii 1 98
I think he's gone to hunt, my lord, At Windsor . . . iv 4 14
Why art thou not at Windsor with him, Thomas? . . . iv 4 50
That Henry born at Monmouth should win all And Henry born at Windsor lose all . . . . . . *1 Hen. VI.* iii 1 199
Edward the Third, my lords, had seven sons: . . . William of Windsor was the seventh and last . . . . *2 Hen. VI.* ii 2 17
Wind-swift. Therefore hath the wind-swift Cupid wings *Rom. and Jul.* ii 5 8
Windy. Poor fool, it keeps on the windy side of care . *Much Ado* ii 1 327
Still you keep o' the windy side of the law . . *T. Night* iii 4 181
Melted by the windy breath Of soft petitions, pity, and remorse *K. John* ii 1 477
See what showers arise, Blown with the windy tempest of my heart! *3 Hen. VI.* ii 5 86
Full of words?—Windy attorneys to their client woes *Richard III.* iv 4 127
Suits of solemn black, Nor windy suspiration of forced breath *Hamlet* i 2 79
Wine. 'Scape being drunk for want of wine . . . *Tempest* ii 1 146
No use of metal, corn, or wine, or oil; No occupation . . ii 1 153
If he have never drunk wine afore, it will go near to remove his fit ii 2 78
If all the wine in my bottle will recover him, I will help his ague . ii 2 96
My cellar is in a rock by the sea-side where my wine is hid . . ii 2 138
Help to bear this away where my hogshead of wine is . . . iv 1 252
He is drunk now: where had he wine? . . . . . v 1 278
Daughter, carry the wine in; we'll drink within . . *Mer. Wives* i 1 195
And in such wine and sugar of the best and the fairest . . ii 2 70
Wine and metheglins, and to drinkings and swearings and starings . v 5 167
Neither disturbed with the effect of wine, Nor heady-rash *Com. of Errors* v 1 215
Drink some wine ere you go: fare you well . . *Much Ado* iii 5 57
And let my liver rather heat with wine Than my heart cool with mortifying groans . . . . . . *Mer. of Venice* i 1 81
I pray thee, set a deep glass of rhenish wine on the contrary casket . i 2 104
There is . . . more [difference] between your bloods than there is between red wine and rhenish . . . . iii 1 44
As wine comes out of a narrow-mouthed bottle . *As Y. Like It* iii 2 211
Do not fall in love with me, For I am falser than vows made in wine . iii 5 73
If it be true that good wine needs no bush . . . . Epil. 4
Yet to good wine they do use good bushes . . . . Epil. 5
But after many ceremonies done, He calls for wine . *T. of Shrew* iii 2 172
There's one grape yet; I am sure thy father drunk wine . *All's Well* ii 3 106
Let us therefore eat and drink. Marian, I say! a stoup of wine! *T. Night* ii 3 14
That's a marvellous searching wine . . . *2 Hen. IV.* ii 4 30
By this wine, I'll thrust my knife in your mouldy chaps . . ii 4 138

Wine. Nor a man cannot make him laugh; but that's no marvel, he drinks no wine . . . . 2 *Hen. IV.* iv 3 96
Give Master Bardolph some wine, Davy.—Sweet sir, sit . . v 3 26
A cup of wine, sir?—A cup of wine that's brisk and fine . . v 3 47
We consider It was excess of wine that set him on . . *Hen. V.* ii 2 42
Shall our quick blood, spirited with wine, Seem frosty? . . iii 5 21
That we may Taste of your wine and see what cates you have 1 *Hen. VI.* ii 3 79
Fellow, thank God, and the good wine in thy master's way 2 *Hen. VI.* ii 3 99
The pissing-conduit run nothing but claret wine this first year of our reign . . . . iv 6 4
Give me a cup of wine.—You shall have wine enough . *Richard III.* i 4 166
Fill me a bowl of wine. Give me a watch. Saddle white Surrey . . v 3 63
Give me a bowl of wine: I have not that alacrity of spirit, Nor cheer of mind, that I was wont to have . . . . . v 3 72
I, that was wash'd to death with fulsome wine, Poor Clarence! . . v 3 132
Good company, good wine, good welcome, Can make good people *Hen. VIII.* i 4 6
The red wine first must rise In their fair cheeks . . . . . i 4 43
I'll heat his blood with Greekish wine to-night, Which with my scimitar I'll cool to-morrow . . . . . *Troi. and Cres.* v 1 1
I am weary; yea, my memory is tired. Have we no wine here? *Coriol.* i 9 92
One that loves a cup of hot wine with not a drop of allaying Tiber in't ii 1 52
Wine, wine, wine! What service is here! I think our fellows are asleep iv 5 1
When we have stuff'd These pipes and these conveyances of our blood With wine and feeding . . . . v 1 55
I pray, come and crush a cup of wine. Rest you merry! *Rom. and Jul.* i 2 86
To see meat fill knaves and wine heat fools . . *T. of Athens* i 1 271
When our vaults have wept With drunken spilth of wine . . . ii 2 169
Fill me some wine . . . . iii 1 8
Please your lordship, here is the wine . . . . . . iii 1 32
Thy flatterers yet wear silk, drink wine, lie soft; Hug their diseased perfumes . . . . iv 3 206
Good friends, go in, and taste some wine with me . . *J. Cæsar* ii 2 126
Give me a bowl of wine. In this I bury all unkindness . . . iv 3 158
Fill, Lucius, till the wine o'erswell the cup; I cannot drink too much of Brutus' love . . . . iv 3 161
His two chamberlains Will I with wine and wassail so convince *Macbeth* i 7 64
The wine of life is drawn, and the mere lees Is left this vault to brag of ii 3 100
Give me some wine; fill full. I drink to the general joy o' the whole table . . . . iii 4 88
Set me the stoups of wine upon that table . . . *Hamlet* v 2 278
Wine loved I deeply, dice dearly . . . . . . *Lear* iii 4 93
The wine she drinks is made of grapes . . . . *Othello* ii 1 256
Come, lieutenant, I have a stoup of wine . . . . . ii 3 30
Some wine, ho! And let me the canakin clink, clink . . . ii 3 70
Why, then, let a soldier drink. Some wine, boys! . . . . ii 3 76
O thou invisible spirit of wine, if thou hast no name to be known by, let us call thee devil! . . . . ii 3 283
Good wine is a good familiar creature, if it be well used . . . ii 3 313
Wine enough Cleopatra's health to drink . . . *Ant. and Cleo.* i 2 11
Sit,—and some wine! A health to Lepidus! . . . . . ii 7 33
The conquering wine hath steep'd our sense In soft and delicate Lethe . ii 7 113
Strong Enobarb Is weaker than the wine . . . . . . ii 7 130
Love, I am full of lead. Some wine, within there, and our viands! . iii 11 73
To-night I'll force The wine peep through their scars . . . iii 13 191
I am dying, Egypt, dying: Give me some wine, and let me speak a little iv 15 42
Therefore to make his entrance more sweet, Here, say we drink this standing-bowl of wine to him . . . . . . *Pericles* ii 3 65

Wing. Who with thy saffron wings upon my flowers Diffusest honey-drops, refreshing showers . . . . *Tempest* iv 1 78
Love, lend me wings to make my purpose swift, As thou hast lent me wit to plot this drift! . . . . . . *T. G. of Ver.* ii 6 42
Much less shall she that hath Love's wings to fly . . . . ii 7 11
Which hath been on the wing of all occasions . . *Mer. Wives* ii 2 209
There's a partridge wing saved, for the fool will eat no supper *Much Ado* ii 1 155
Their conceits have wings Fleeter than arrows, bullets, wind *L. L. Lost* v 2 260
Wings and no eyes figure unheedy haste . . . *M. N. Dream* i 1 237
Some war with rere-mice for their leathern wings . . . . ii 2 4
Pluck the wings from painted butterflies To fan the moonbeams . . iii 1 175
Death-counterfeiting sleep With leaden legs and batty wings doth creep iii 2 365
Do them reverence, As they fly by them with their woven wings *Mer. of Venice* i 1 14
I, for my part, knew the tailor that made the wings she flew withal . iii 1 30
Is a virtue of a good wing, and I like the wear well. . *All's Well* i 1 218
This haste hath wings indeed . . . . ii 1 96
Return you thither?—Ay, madam, with the swiftest wing of speed . iii 2 76
Excellent command,—to charge in with our horse upon our own wings! iii 6 52
And with what wing the staniel checks at it! . . . *T. Night* ii 5 124
Now take upon me, in the name of Time, To use my wings . *W. Tale* iv 1 4
I, an old turtle, Will wing me to some wither'd bough . . . v 3 133
Shadowing their right under your wings of war . . *K. John* ii 1 14
Shake off our slavish yoke, Imp out our drooping country's broken wing . . . . *Richard II.* ii 1 292
Let me wonder, Harry, At thy affections, which do hold a wing Quite from the flight of all thy ancestors . . . 1 *Hen. IV.* iii 2 30
But with nimble wing We were enforced, for safety sake, to fly . . v 1 64
O, with what wings shall his affections fly Towards fronting peril and opposed decay! . . . . 2 *Hen. IV.* iv 4 65
Health, alack, with youthful wings is flown From this bare wither'd trunk . . . . iv 5 229
That may with reasonable swiftness add More feathers to our wings *Hen. V.* i 2 307
Thus with imagined wing our swift scene flies . . . . . iii Prol. 1
When they stoop, they stoop with the like wing . . . . . iv 1 112
Though they can outstrip men, they have no wings to fly from God . iv 1 177
His arms spread wider than a dragon's wings . . . 1 *Hen. VI.* i 1 11
One would have lingering wars with little cost; Another would fly swift, but wanteth wings . . . . i 1 75
I hear the enemy: Out, some light horsemen, and peruse their wings . iv 2 43
So doth the swan her downy cygnets save, Keeping them prisoner underneath her wings . . . . v 3 57
That love to be protected Under the wings of our protector's grace 2 *Hen. VI.* i 3 41
Have all limed bushes to betray thy wings, And, fly thou how thou canst, they'll tangle thee . . . . ii 4 54
Who, with their drowsy, slow, and flagging wings, Clip dead men's graves iv 1 5
Ignorance is the curse of God, Knowledge the wing wherewith we fly to heaven . . . . iv 7 79
Nor he that loves him best, The proudest he that holds up Lancaster, Dares stir a wing, if Warwick shake his bells . . . 3 *Hen. VI.* i 1 47
Wing. Even with those wings Which sometime they have used with fearful flight, Make war with him that climb'd unto their nest 3 *Hen. VI.* ii 2 29
They follow us with wings; And weak we are and cannot shun pursuit ii 3 12
The bird that hath been limed in a bush, With trembling wings misdoubteth every bush . . . . v 6 14
And yet, for all his wings, the fool was drown'd . . . . v 6 20
The sun that sear'd the wings of my sweet boy . . . . v 6 23
Then fiery expedition be my wing, Jove's Mercury! . *Richard III.* iv 3 54
If yet your gentle souls fly in the air And be not fix'd in doom perpetual, Hover about me with your airy wings! . . . . . . iv 4 13
True hope is swift, and flies with swallow's wings . . . . v 2 23
When I should mount with wings of victory . . . . . v 3 106
The very thought of this fair company Clapp'd wings to me . *Hen. VIII.* i 4 9
Now, good angels Fly o'er thy royal head, and shade thy person Under their blessed wings! . . . . v 1 161
If he do set The very wings of reason to his heels . . *Troi. and Cres.* ii 2 44
Your full consent Gave wings to my propension . . . . ii 2 133
From Cupid's shoulder pluck his painted wings, And fly with me . . iii 2 15
Men, like butterflies, Show not their mealy wings but to the summer . iii 3 79
With wings more momentary-swift than thought . . . . iv 2 14
The dragon wing of night o'erspreads the earth . . . . v 8 17
This Marcius is grown from man to dragon: he has wings . *Coriolanus* v 4 14
How would he hang his slender gilded wings, And buzz! . *T. Andron.* iii 2 61
With the shadow of his wings He can at pleasure stint their melody . iv 4 85
Borrow Cupid's wings, And soar with them above a common bound *Rom. and Jul.* i 4 17
The cover of the wings of grasshoppers, The traces of the smallest spider's web . . . . i 4 60
With love's light wings did I o'er-perch these walls. . . . ii 2 66
And therefore hath the wind-swift Cupid wings . . . . . ii 5 8
Upon the wings of night Whiter than new snow on a raven's back . iii 2 18
I do fear, When every feather sticks in his own wing, Lord Timon will be left a naked gull . . . . *T. of Athens* ii 1 30
These growing feathers pluck'd from Cæsar's wing Will make him fly an ordinary pitch, Who else would soar . . . . *J. Cæsar* i 1 77
I perceive But cold demeanour in Octavius' wing . . . . v 2 4
That swiftest wing of recompense is slow To overtake thee . *Macbeth* i 4 17
Light thickens; and the crow Makes wing to the rooky wood . . iii 2 51
Adder's fork and blind-worm's sting, Lizard's leg and howlet's wing . iv 1 17
With wings as swift As meditation or the thoughts of love . *Hamlet* i 5 29
But what might you think, When I had seen this hot love on the wing? ii 2 132
Save me, and hover o'er me with your wings, You heavenly guards! . iii 4 103
The crows and choughs that wing the midway air . . . *Lear* iv 6 13
'Tis his schoolmaster: An argument that he is pluck'd, when hither He sends so poor a pinion of his wing . . . *Ant. and Cleo.* iii 12 4
I'll catch thine eyes, Though they had wings: slave, soulless villain, dog! . . . . v 2 157
And your lord—The best feather of our wing . . . *Cymbeline* i 6 186
O, for a horse with wings! . . . . iii 2 50
My revenge is now at Milford: would I had wings to follow it! . . iii 5 161
The king himself Of his wings destitute, the army broken . . v 3 5
His royal bird Prunes the immortal wing and cloys his beak . . v 4 118
The Roman eagle, From south to west on wing soaring aloft . . v 5 471

Winged. The beasts, the fishes, and the winged fowls Are their males' subjects . . . . *Com. of Errors* ii 1 18
Therefore is wing'd Cupid painted blind . . . *M. N. Dream* i 1 235
So do all thoughts; they are winged . . . . *As Y. Like It* iv 1 142
Bear this sealed brief With winged haste to the lord marshal 1 *Hen. IV.* iv 4 2
With winged heels, as English Mercuries . . . . *Hen. V.* ii Prol. 7
Heave him away upon your winged thoughts Athwart the sea . v Prol. 8
Two Talbots, winged through the lither sky, In thy despite shall 'scape mortality . . . . 1 *Hen. VI.* iv 7 21
It stands upright, Like lime-twigs set to catch my winged soul 2 *Hen. VI.* iii 3 16
Whose haughty spirit, winged with desire, Will cost my crown 3 *Hen. VI.* i 1 267
But he, poor soul, by your first order died, And that a winged Mercury did bear; Some tardy cripple bore the countermand *Richard III.* ii 1 88
Whose puissance on either side Shall be well winged with our chiefest horse . . . . v 3 300
His evasion, wing'd thus swift with scorn, Cannot outfly our apprehensions . . . . *Troi. and Cres.* ii 3 123
Thou art As glorious to this night, being o'er my head, As is a winged messenger of heaven . . . . *Rom. and Jul.* ii 2 28
I shall see The winged vengeance overtake such children . . *Lear* iii 7 66
We, poor unfledged, Have never wing'd from view o' the nest *Cymbeline* iii 3 28
Haply, despair hath seized her, Or, wing'd with fervour of her love, she's flown . . . . iii 5 61
The Roman eagle, wing'd From the spongy south to this part of the west iv 2 348
Only I carry winged time Post on the lame feet of my rhyme *Per.* iv Gower 47

Wingfield. Lord Cromwell of Wingfield, Lord Furnival of Sheffield 1 *Hen. VI.* iv 7 66

Wingham. There's Best's son, the tanner of Wingham . 2 *Hen. VI.* iv 2 24

Wink. Even Ambition cannot pierce a wink beyond . . . *Tempest* ii 1 242
To the perpetual wink for aye might put This ancient morsel . . ii 1 285
I see things too, although you judge I wink . . . *T. G. of Ver.* i 2 139
Upon a homely object Love can wink . . . . . . ii 4 98
Such pearls as put out ladies' eyes; For I had rather wink than look on them . . . . v 2 14
He that speaks to them shall die: I'll wink and couch . *Mer. Wives* v 5 52
As good to wink, sweet love, as look on night . *Com. of Errors* iii 2 58
And then, to sleep but three hours in the night, And not be seen to wink of all the day . . . . *L. L. Lost* i 1 43
Now here is three studied, ere ye'll thrice wink . . . . i 2 54
Wink each at other; hold the sweet jest up . . *M. N. Dream* iii 2 239
You saw my master wink and laugh upon you? . . *T. of Shrew* iv 4 75
Grew a twenty years removed thing While one would wink . *T. Night* v 1 93
Mightst bespice a cup, To give mine enemy a lasting wink . *W. Tale* i 2 317
Every wink of an eye some new grace will be born . . . . v 2 119
Was this the face That, like the sun, did make beholders wink? *Rich. II.* iv 1 284
I dare not fight; but I will wink and hold out mine iron . *Hen. V.* ii 1 8
Yet they do wink and yield, as love is blind and enforces . . . v 2 327
I will wink on her to consent, my lord, if you will teach her to know my meaning . . . . v 2 333
Let me see thine eyes: wink now: now open them . . 2 *Hen. VI.* ii 1 105
Wink at the Duke of Suffolk's insolence, At Beaufort's pride . . ii 2 70
Thou shalt not sigh, nor hold thy stumps to heaven, Nor wink, nor nod *T. Andron.* iii 2 43
Spread thy close curtain, love-performing night, That runaways' eyes may wink, and Romeo Leap to these arms . . *Rom. and Jul.* iii 2 6
Good boy, wink at me, and say thou sawest me not . *T. of Athens* iii 1 47

Wink. Let not light see my black and deep desires : The eye wink at the hand . . . *Macbeth* i 4 52
As her winks, and nods, and gestures yield them . . . *Hamlet* iv 5 11
Heaven stops the nose at it and the moon winks . . . *Othello* iv 2 77
Since I received command to do this business I have not slept one wink. —Do't, and to bed then . . . *Cymbeline* iii 4 103
There are none want eyes to direct them the way I am going, but such as wink and will not use them . . . v 4 194
Winked. I have not winked since I saw these sights . *W. Tale* iii 3 106
If little faults, proceeding on distemper, Shall not be wink'd at *Hen. V.* ii 2 55
Winkest. Thou let'st thy fortune sleep—die, rather ; wink'st Whiles thou art waking . . . *Tempest* ii 1 216
Winking. Confronts your city's eyes, your winking gates . *K. John* ii 1 215
On the winking of authority To understand a law . . . iv 2 211
Led his powers to death And winking leap'd into destruction 2 *Hen. IV.* i 3 33
Foolish curs, that run winking into the mouth of a Russian bear! *Hen. V.* iii 7 153
Teach your cousin to consent winking.—I will wink on her to consent v 2 332
I for winking at your discords too Have lost a brace of kinsmen *R. and J.* v 3 294
If I had play'd the desk or table-book, Or given my heart a winking *Ham.* ii 2 137
And winking Mary-buds begin To ope their golden eyes . *Cymbeline* ii 3 26
Two winking Cupids Of silver, each on one foot standing . . ii 4 89
I am sure hanging's the way of winking . . . v 4 198
Winner. And, being a winner, God give you good night! *T. of Shrew* v 2 187
Go together, You precious winners all . . . *W. Tale* v 3 131
The gentler gamester is the soonest winner . . *Hen. V.* iii 6 120
Beshrew the winners, for they play'd me false! . . 2 *Hen. VI.* iii 1 184
You will draw both friend and foe, Winner and loser . *Hamlet* iv 5 143
I now Profess myself the winner of her honour, Together with your ring *Cymbeline* ii 4 53
The event Is yet to name the winner . . . iii 5 15
Winning. Lest too light winning Make the prize light . *Tempest* i 2 451
And learn me how to lose a winning match, Play'd for a pair of stainless maidenhoods . . . *Rom. and Jul.* iii 2 12
A cunning thief, or a that way accomplished courtier, would hazard the winning both of first and last . . . *Cymbeline* i 4 102
You are most hot and furious when you win.—Winning will put any man into courage . . . ii 3 8
Winnow. Distinction, with a broad and powerful fan, Puffing at all, winnows the light away . . . *Troi. and Cres.* i 3 28
Bitter torture shall Winnow the truth from falsehood *Cymbeline* v 5 134
Winnowed. We shall be winnow'd with so rough a wind That even our corn shall seem as light as chaff . . 2 *Hen. IV.* iv 1 194
Catch this good occasion Most throughly to be winnow'd *Hen. VIII.* v 1 110
Of such a winnow'd purity in love . . *Troi. and Cres.* iii 2 174
Through and through the most fond and winnowed opinions *Hamlet* v 2 201
Winter. I will rend an oak And peg thee in his knotty entrails till Thou hast howl'd away twelve winters . . *Tempest* i 2 296
His tears run down his beard, like winter's drops From eaves of reeds . v 1 16
And make rough winter everlastingly . . . *T. G. of Ver.* ii 4 163
Because it is an open room and good for winter *Meas. for Meas.* ii 1 136
Six or seven winters more respect Than a perpetual honour . . iii 1 76
Her rags and the tallow in them will burn a Poland winter *Com. of Er.* iii 2 100
Though now this grained face of mine be hid In sap-consuming winter's drizzled snow . . . v 1 312
A wither'd hermit, five-score winters worn, Might shake off fifty *L. L. L.* iv 3 242
This side is Hiems, Winter, this Ver, the Spring . . v 2 901
The human mortals want their winter here . *M. N. Dream* ii 1 101
The childing autumn, angry winter, change Their wonted liveries . . ii 1 112
Warmed and cooled by the same winter and summer as a Christian is *Mer. of Venice* iii 1 66
As the icy fang And churlish chiding of the winter's wind *As Y. Like It* ii 1 7
Therefore my age is as a lusty winter, Frosty, but kindly . . ii 3 52
Here shall he see No enemy But winter and rough weather . ii 5 47
Blow, blow, thou winter wind, Thou art not so unkind As man's ingratitude . . . ii 7 174
Winter garments must be lined, So must slender Rosalind . . iii 2 111
A nun of winter's sisterhood kisses not more religiously . . iii 4 17
You and you are sure together, As the winter to foul weather . v 4 142
Thou knowest winter tames man, woman, and beast . *T. of Shrew* iv 1 24
A sad tale's best for winter : I have one Of sprites and goblins *W. Tale* ii 1 25
Naked, fasting, Upon a barren mountain, and still winter In storm perpetual . . . iii 2 213
For the red blood reigns in the winter's pale . . . iv 3 4
These keep Seeming and savour all the winter long . . . iv 4 75
Well you fit our ages With flowers of winter . . . iv 4 79
Not yet on summer's death, nor on the birth Of trembling winter . iv 4 81
Which sixteen winters cannot blow away, So many summers dry . v 3 50
Dead, forsook, cast off : And none of you will bid the winter come To thrust his icy fingers in my maw . . . *K. John* v 7 36
Six frozen winters spent, Return with welcome home from banishment *Richard II.* i 3 211
Four lagging winters and four wanton springs End in a word . i 3 214
What is six winters? they are quickly gone.—To men in joy . . i 3 260
I have worn so many winters out, And know not now what name to call myself! . . . iv 1 258
In winter's tedious nights sit by the fire With good old folks . . v 1 40
Leaves his part-created cost A naked subject to the weeping clouds And waste for churlish winter's tyranny . . . 2 *Hen. IV.* i 3 62
As humorous as winter and as sudden As flaws congealed in the spring of day . . . iv 4 34
Thou art a summer bird, Which ever in the haunch of winter sings The lifting up of day . . . iv 4 92
The winter coming on and sickness growing . . . *Hen. V.* iii 3 55
In winter's cold and summer's parching heat . . 2 *Hen. VI.* i 1 81
After summer evermore succeeds Barren winter, with his wrathful nipping cold . . . ii 4 3
Well could I curse away a winter's night, Though standing naked on a mountain top . . . iii 2 335
That winter lion, who in rage forgets Aged contusions and all brush of time . . . v 3 2
Melt with woe That winter should cut off our spring-time so 3 *Hen. VI.* ii 3 47
If we use delay, Cold biting winter mars our hoped-for hay . . iv 8 61
And kept low shrubs from winter's powerful wind . . . v 2 15
Let Æsop fable in a winter's night ; His currish riddles sort not with this place . . . v 5 25
Thine uncles and myself Have in our armours watch'd the winter's night v 7 17
Now is the winter of our discontent Made glorious summer *Richard III.* i 1 1
When great leaves fall, the winter is at hand . . . ii 3 33
Ever shall be growing, Till death, that winter, kill it . *Hen. VIII.* iii 2 179
I'll take that winter from your lips, fair lady . . *Troi. and Cres.* iv 5 24
Winter. In winter with warm tears I'll melt the snow . *T. Andron.* iii 1 20
This goodly summer with your winter mix'd . . . v 2 172
Well-apparell'd April on the heel Of limping winter treads *Rom. and Jul.* i 2 28
One cloud of winter showers, These flies are couch'd . *T. of Athens* ii 2 180
I fear 'tis deepest winter in Lord Timon's purse ; That is, one may reach deep enough, and yet Find little . . . iii 4 14
Nor more willingly leaves winter ; such summer-birds are men . . iii 6 33
With one winter's brush Fell from their boughs and left me open, bare iv 3 264
We can both Endure the winter's cold as well as he . . *J. Cæsar* i 2 99
A woman's story at a winter's fire, Authorized by her grandam *Macbeth* iii 4 65
O, that that earth, which kept the world in awe, Should patch a wall to expel the winter's flaw! . . . *Hamlet* v 1 239
Winter's not gone yet, if the wild-geese fly that way . *Lear* ii 4 46
We'll set thee to school to an ant, to teach thee there's no labouring i' the winter . . . ii 4 69
Poor and content is rich and rich enough, But riches fineless is as poor as winter To him that ever fears he shall be poor . . *Othello* iii 3 173
For his bounty, There was no winter in't . . . *Ant. and Cleo.* v 2 87
Not any, but abide the change of time, Quake in the present winter's state and wish That warmer days would come . . . *Cymbeline* ii 4 5
Fear no more the heat o' the sun, Nor the furious winter's rages . iv 2 259
To be still hot summer's tanlings and The shrinking slaves of winter . iv 4 30
Superstitiously Doth swear to the gods that winter kills the flies *Pericles* iv 3 50
Winter-cricket. Thou flea, thou nit, thou winter-cricket thou! *T. of S.* iv 3 110
Winter-ground. Yea, and furr'd moss besides, when flowers are none, To winter-ground thy corse . . . *Cymbeline* iv 2 229
Winterly. If't be summer news, Smile to't before ; if winterly, thou need'st But keep that countenance still . . . iii 4 13
Winter-time. Doth all the winter-time, at still midnight, Walk round about an oak . . . *Mer. Wives* iv 4 30
Wipe thou thine eyes ; have comfort . . . *Tempest* i 2 25
Belike, boy then, you are in love ; for last morning you could not see to wipe my shoes . . . *T. G. of Ver.* ii 1 86
Ill, to example ill, Would from my forehead wipe a perjured note *L. L. L.* iv 3 125
Wipe not out the rest of thy services by leaving me now . *W. Tale* iv 2 11
Lift up thy looks : From my succession wipe me, father . . iv 4 491
Let me wipe off this honourable dew, That silverly doth progress on thy cheeks : My heart hath melted . . . *K. John* v 2 45
Wipe off the dust that hides our sceptre's gilt . . *Richard II.* ii 1 294
Alas, poor ape, how thou sweatest! come, let me wipe thy face 2 *Hen. IV.* ii 4 234
Therefore will he wipe his tables clean And keep no tell-tale to his memory . . . iv 1 201
Our obedience to the king wipes the crime of it out of us . *Hen. V.* iv 1 139
And this thy son's blood cleaving to my blade Shall rust upon my weapon, till thy blood, Congeal'd with this, do make me wipe off both . . . 3 *Hen. VI.* i 3 52
Drain the life-blood of the child, To bid the father wipe his eyes withal i 4 139
My tears shall wipe away these bloody marks . . . ii 5 71
'Tis, as it were, a parcel of their feast, and to be executed ere they wipe their lips . . . *Coriolanus* iv 5 232
Thou hast no hands, to wipe away thy tears . . *T. Andron.* iii 1 106
Ah, my Lavinia, I will wipe thy cheeks . . . iii 1 142
May I govern so, To heal Rome's harms, and wipe away her woe! . . v 3 148
To wipe out our ingratitude with loves Above their quantity *T. of Athens* v 4 17
From the table of my memory I'll wipe away all trivial fond records *Ham.* i 5 99
I dare not drink yet, madam ; by and by.—Come, let me wipe thy face v 2 305
O, let me kiss that hand!—Let me wipe it first ; it smells of mortality *Lear* iv 6 136
Wipe thine eyes ; The good-years shall devour them, flesh and fell . v 3 23
Such a handkerchief—I am sure it was your wife's—did I to-day See Cassio wipe his beard with . . . *Othello* iii 3 439
Let this fellow Be nothing of our strife ; if we contend, Out of our question wipe him . . . *Ant. and Cleo.* iii 2 81
Wipe thine eyes : Some falls are means the happier to arise *Cymbeline* iv 2 402
Wiped. If ever from your eyelids wiped a tear . . *As Y. Like It* ii 7 116
And sat at good men's feasts and wiped our eyes . . . ii 7 122
O villain! thy lips are scarce wiped since thou drunkest last 1 *Hen. IV.* ii 4 170
To speak truth, This present grief had wiped it from my mind 2 *Hen. IV.* i 1 211
This blot that they object against your house Shall be wiped out 1 *Hen. VI.* ii 4 117
Why, yet thy scandal were not wiped away, But I in danger 2 *Hen. VI.* ii 4 65
Never yet did base dishonour blur our name, But with our sword we wiped away the blot . . . iv 1 40
Ne'er shall this blood be wiped from thy point . . . iv 10 74
But I would have the soil of her fair rape Wiped off, in honourable keeping her . . . *Troi. and Cres.* ii 2 149
The man was noble, But with his last attempt he wiped it out *Coriol.* v 3 146
Macduff, this noble passion, Child of integrity, hath from my soul Wiped the black scruples . . . *Macbeth* iv 3 116
Wiping. His bloody brow With his mail'd hand then wiping . *Coriolanus* i 3 38
Wire. Thou shalt be whipp'd with wire, and stew'd in brine *A. and C.* ii 5 65
Wiry. To that drop ten thousand wiry friends Do glue themselves *K. John* iii 4 64
Wis. There be fools alive, I wis, Silver'd o'er . . *Mer. of Venice* ii 9 68
You shall never need to fear : I wis it is not half way to her heart *T. of Shrew* i 1 62
I wis your grandam had a worser match . . . *Richard III.* i 3 102
Here have you seen a mighty king His child, I wis, to incest bring *Pericles* ii Gower 2
Wisdom. He must die.—Be it as your wisdom will . *Meas. for Meas.* ii 1 32
Thus wisdom wishes to appear most bright When it doth tax itself . ii 4 78
Much upon this riddle runs the wisdom of the world . . . iii 2 242
Show your wisdom, daughter, In your close patience . . . iv 3 122
If you can, pace your wisdom In that good path that I would wish it go iv 3 137
Pray heaven his wisdom be not tainted! . . . iv 4 5
Your long experience of her wisdom, Her sober virtue *Com. of Errors* iii 1 89
Wisdom and blood combating in so tender a body, we have ten proofs to one that blood hath the victory . . . *Much Ado* ii 3 170
If their wisdoms be misled in this, The practice of it lives in John iv 1 189
'Tis not wisdom thus to second grief Against yourself . . . v 1 2
What your wisdoms could not discover, these shallow fools have brought to light . . . v 1 239
For wisdom's sake, a word that all men love . . . *L. L. Lost* iv 3 357
Folly, in wisdom hatch'd, Hath wisdom's warrant and the help of school v 2 70
Vouchsafe In your rich wisdom to excuse or hide The liberal opposition v 2 742
With purpose to be dress'd in an opinion Of wisdom, gravity *M. of Ven.* i 1 92
When they do choose, They have the wisdom by their wit to lose . . ii 9 81
I and my friend Have by your wisdom been this day acquitted . . iv 1 409
Now unmuzzle your wisdom . . . *As Y. Like It* i 2 74
The wisdom of your duty, fair Bianca, Hath cost me an hundred crowns *T. of Shrew* v 2 127
Full oft we see Cold wisdom waiting on superfluous folly . *All's Well* i 1 116
His love and wisdom . . . may plead For amplest credence . . . i 2 9

Wisdom. One that, in her sex, her years, profession, Wisdom, and constancy, hath amazed me . . . . *All's Well* ii 1 87
Youth, beauty, wisdom, courage, all That happiness and prime can happy call . . . . ii 1 184
'Twill be two days ere I shall see you, so I leave you to your wisdom . ii 5 76
Thus your own proper wisdom Brings in the champion Honour . . iv 2 49
God give them wisdom that have it; and those that are fools, let them use their talents . . . . *T. Night* i 5 14
I think I saw your wisdom there . . . . iii 1 47
Let thy fair wisdom, not thy passion, sway . . . . . . iv 1 56
What wisdom stirs amongst you? Come, sir, now I am for you again *W. Tale* ii 1 21
With wisdom I might fear, my Doricles, You woo'd me the false way . iv 4 150
What say you, my niece?—That she is bound in honour still to do What you in wisdom still vouchsafe to say . . . . . *K. John* ii 1 523
Wisdom cries out in the streets, and no man regards it . . 1 *Hen. IV.* i 2 99
Wisdom, loyalty, and mere dislike Of our proceedings kept the earl from hence . . . . iv 1 64
And 'tis but wisdom to make strong against him . . . . iv 4 39
Divorce not wisdom from your honour . . . . . 2 *Hen. IV.* i 1 162
I will speak no more: Do what you will; your wisdom be your guide . ii 3 6
'Tis no wisdom to confess so much Unto an enemy of craft *Hen. V.* iii 6 152
Augment, or alter, as your wisdoms best Shall see advantageable . . v 2 87
Her grace in speech, Her words y-clad with wisdom's majesty 2 *Hen. VI.* i 1 33
What to your wisdoms seemeth best, Do or undo . . . . iii 1 195
Now is it manhood, wisdom, and defence, To give the enemy way . . v 2 75
Whose wisdom was a mirror to the wisest . . . 3 *Hen. VI.* iii 3 84
Till then, 'tis wisdom to conceal our meaning . . . . . iv 7 60
Do so, it is a point of wisdom . . . . . . *Richard III.* i 4 99
Your discipline in war, wisdom in peace, Your bounty, virtue, fair humility . . . . iii 7 16
This general applause and loving shout Argues your wisdoms and your love . . . . iii 7 40
Abusing better men than they can be, Out of a foreign wisdom *Hen. VIII.* i 3 29
Your grace has given a precedent of wisdom Above all princes . . ii 2 86
Of disposition gentle, and of wisdom O'ertopping woman's power . . ii 4 87
Out of which frailty And want of wisdom, you, that best should teach us, Have misdemean'd yourself . . . . v 3 13
I had thought I had had men of some understanding And wisdom of my council . . . . v 3 136
Saba was never More covetous of wisdom and fair virtue Than this pure soul shall be . . . . v 5 25
Count wisdom as no member of the war, Forestall prescience *Tr. and Cr.* i 3 198
If you'll avouch 'twas wisdom Paris went—As you must needs . . ii 2 84
Why do you now The issue of your proper wisdoms rate? . . . ii 2 89
The amity that wisdom knits not, folly may easily untie . . . ii 3 110
I will not praise thy wisdom, Which, like a bourn, a pale, a shore, confines Thy spacious and dilated parts . . . . . . ii 3 259
What is granted them?—Five tribunes to defend their vulgar wisdoms *Coriolanus* i 1 219
Since the wisdom of their choice is rather to have my hat than my heart . . . . ii 3 104
Where gentry, title, wisdom, Cannot conclude but by the yea and no Of general ignorance . . . . iii 1 144
Whose wisdom hath her fortune conquered . . . . . *T. Andron.* i 1 336
Were not I thine only nurse, I would say thou hadst suck'd wisdom from thy teat . . . . *Rom. and Jul.* i 3 68
Why, my lady wisdom? hold your tongue, Good prudence . . . iii 5 171
And in his wisdom hastes our marriage . . . . iv 1 11
If, in thy wisdom, thou canst give no help, Do thou but call my resolution wise . . . . iv 1 52
The ass more captain than the lion, the felon Loaden with irons wiser than the judge, If wisdom be in suffering . . *T. of Athens* iii 5 51
Alas, my lord, Your wisdom is consumed in confidence . . *J. Cæsar* ii 2 49
Why I, that did love Cæsar when I struck him, Have thus proceeded.—I doubt not of your wisdom . . . . iii 1 183
Censure me in your wisdom, and awake your senses, that you may the better judge . . . . iii 2 17
He hath a wisdom that doth guide his valour To act in safety *Macbeth* iii 1 53
He shall spurn fate, scorn death, and bear His hopes 'bove wisdom, grace, and fear . . . . iii 5 31
Advise him to a caution, to hold what distance His wisdom can provide iii 6 45
You know not Whether it was his wisdom or his fear.—Wisdom! to leave his wife, to leave his babes, His mansion, and his titles in a place From whence himself does fly? . . . . iv 2 6
As little is the wisdom, where the flight So runs against all reason . iv 2 13
Wisdom To offer up a weak poor innocent lamb To appease an angry god iv 3 15
And modest wisdom plucks me From over-credulous haste . . . iv 3 119
Nor have we herein barr'd Your better wisdoms . . . *Hamlet* i 2 15
If he says he loves you, It fits your wisdom so far to believe it . . i 3 25
Thus do we of wisdom and of reach, With windlasses and with assays of bias, By indirections find directions out . . . . ii 1 64
Confine him where Your wisdom best shall think . . . . . iii 1 195
Your wisdom should show itself more richer to signify this to his doctor iii 2 316
Hath but one part wisdom And ever three parts coward . . . iv 4 42
As by your safety, wisdom, all things else, You mainly were stirr'd up . iv 7 8
Frame the business after your own wisdom . . . . . . *Lear* i 2 107
Though the wisdom of nature can reason it thus and thus . . . i 2 113
But away! go to; have you wisdom? so . . . . i 4 102
Make use of that good wisdom, Whereof I know you are fraught . . i 4 240
More attask'd for want of wisdom Than praised for harmful mildness . i 4 366
And what they may incense him to, being apt To have his ear abused, wisdom bids fear . . . . ii 4 310
Wisdom and goodness to the vile seem vile: Filths savour but themselves iv 2 38
What can man's wisdom In the restoring his bereaved sense? . . iv 4 8
I pray, desire her call her wisdom to her . . . . iv 5 35
In wisdom I should ask thy name . . . . v 3 141
She that in wisdom never was so frail To change the cod's head for the salmon's tail, She that could think . . . . . . *Othello* ii 1 155
In wholesome wisdom He might not but refuse you . . . . iii 1 49
That your wisdom yet, From one that so imperfectly conceits, Would take no notice . . . . iii 3 148
It were not for your quiet nor your good, Nor for my manhood, honesty, or wisdom, To let you know my thoughts . . . . . . iii 3 153
If beauty, wisdom, modesty, can settle The heart of Antony, Octavia is A blessed lottery to him . . . . . . *Ant. and Cleo.* ii 2 246
Wisdom and fortune combating together . . . . iii 13 79
Nay, blush not, Cleopatra; I approve Your wisdom in the deed . . v 2 150
'Twere good You lean'd unto his sentence with what patience Your wisdom may inform you . . . . *Cymbeline* i 1 79

Wisdom. For wisdom sees, those men Blush not in actions blacker than the night, Will shun no course to keep them from the light *Pericles* i 1 134
Fit counsellor and servant for a prince, Who by thy wisdom makest a prince thy servant . . . . i 2 64
The care I had and have of subjects' good On thee I lay, whose wisdom's strength can bear it . . . . i 2 119
To wisdom he's a fool that will not yield . . . . ii 4 54
Wise. I'll be wise hereafter And seek for grace. . . . . *Tempest* v 1 294
He [Love] masters you: And he that is so yoked by a fool, Methinks, should not be chronicled for wise . . . . . *T. G. of Ver.* i 1 41
What seem I that I am not?—Wise.—What instance of the contrary? . ii 4 15
Holy, fair, and wise is she; The heaven such grace did lend her . . iv 2 41
Valiant, wise, remorseful, well accomplish'd . . . . . . iv 3 13
'Convey,' the wise it call. 'Steal!' foh! a fico for the phrase! *M. Wives* i 3 32
He is wise, sir; he knew your worship would kill him, if he came . ii 3 10
Sir Hugh hath shown himself a wise and patient churchman . . . ii 3 57
You are wise and full of gibes and vlouting-stocks . . . . . iv 5 82
If it were damnable, he being so wise, Why would he for the momentary trick Be perdurably fined? . . . . . . *Meas. for Meas.* iii 1 113
The greater file of the subject held the duke to be wise.—Wise! . . iii 2 145
I am sorry, one so learned and so wise . . . Should slip so grossly . v 1 475
Be wise: an if you give it her, The devil will shake her chain *C. of Er.* iv 3 76
One woman is fair, yet I am well; another is wise . . . . *Much Ado* ii 3 29
Rich she shall be, that's certain; wise, or I'll none; virtuous . . ii 3 32
She is virtuous.—And she is exceeding wise . . . . . . ii 3 167
Very wise.—He doth indeed show some sparks that are like wit . . ii 3 192
In the managing of quarrels you may say he is wise . . . . ii 3 197
And virtuous; 'tis so, I cannot reprove it; and wise, but for loving me ii 3 241
How wise, how noble, young, how rarely featured . . . . . iii 1 60
'Nay, said I, 'the gentleman is wise:' 'Certain,' said she, 'a wise gentleman' . . . . v 1 166
Thou and I are too wise to woo peaceably . . . . v 2 73
Therefore is it most expedient for the wise . . . to be the trumpet of his own virtues . . . . v 2 86
Lord, how wise you are!—I will tell thee wonders . . . *L. L. Lost* i 2 143
Willing to be counted wise In spending your wit in the praise of mine . ii 1 18
His ignorance were wise, Where now his knowledge must prove ignorance ii 1 102
Doth the inconsiderate take salve for l'envoy, and the word l'envoy for a salve?—Do the wise think them other? . . . . iii 1 81
What fool is not so wise To lose an oath to win a paradise? . . . iv 3 72
Folly in fools bears not so strong a note As foolery in the wise . . v 2 76
This proves you wise and rich, for in my eye,— I am a fool . . . v 2 379
Thou art as wise as thou art beautiful . . . . . . *M. N. Dream* iii 1 151
Therefore only are reputed wise For saying nothing . . *Mer. of Venice* i 1 96
She is wise, if I can judge of her, And fair she is, if that mine eyes be true ii 6 53
Like herself, wise, fair, and true, Shall she be placed in my constant soul ii 6 56
Had you been as wise as bold, Young in limbs, in judgement old . . ii 7 70
Yea, a Daniel! O wise young judge, how I do honour thee! . . . iv 1 224
Provided that you weed your better judgments Of all opinion that grows rank in them That I am wise . . . . . . *As Y. Like It* ii 7 47
Learn of the wise, and perpend . . . . iii 2 69
But she is wise.—Or else she could not have the wit to do this . . iv 1 160
Art thou wise?—Ay, sir, I have a pretty wit . . . . . . v 1 31
The fool doth think he is wise . . . . v 1 35
A witty mother! witless else her son.—Am I not wise? . . *T. of Shrew* ii 1 267
Though he be blunt, I know him passing wise . . . . . . iii 2 24
She is young, wise, fair; In these to nature she's immediate heir *All's W.* ii 3 138
Infirmity, that decays the wise, doth ever make the better fool *T. Night* i 5 82
This fellow is wise enough to play the fool; And to do that well craves a kind of wit . . . . iii 1 67
Praises, of whose taste the wise are fond . . . . . *Richard II.* ii 1 18
I know you wise, but yet no farther wise Than Harry Percy's wife 1 *Hen. IV.* ii 3 110
The wise may make some dram of a scruple, or indeed a scruple itself 2 *Hen. IV.* i 2 148
Thus we play the fools with the time, and the spirits of the wise sit in the clouds and mock us . . . . ii 2 155
All are banish'd till their conversations Appear more wise and modest . v 5 107
Be wise and circumspect . . . . 2 *Hen. VI.* i 1 157
Were none more wise than I—And yet herein I judge mine own wit good iii 1 231
If this fellow be wise, he'll never call ye Jack Cade more . . . iv 6 10
Famed for virtuous; And now may seem as wise as virtuous 3 *Hen. VI.* iv 6 27
A wise stout captain, and soon persuaded! . . . . iv 7 30
We speak no treason, man: we say the king Is wise and virtuous *Richard III.* i 1 91
Framed in the prodigality of nature, Young, valiant, wise . . . . i 2 245
So wise so young, they say, do never live long. . . . . . . iii 1 79
To think an English courtier may be wise, And never see the Louvre *Hen. VIII.* i 3 22
A scholar, and a ripe and good one; Exceeding wise, fair-spoken . . iv 2 52
You're a gentleman Of mine own way; I know you wise, religious . v 1 28
Not only good and wise, but most religious . . . . v 3 116
The bold and coward, The wise and fool, the artist and unread, The hard and soft, seem all affined and kin . . . . *Troi. and Cres.* i 3 24
Yet let it please both, Thou great, and wise, to hear Ulysses speak . i 3 69
Modest doubt is call'd The beacon of the wise . . . . . . ii 2 16
As strong, as valiant, as wise, no less noble, much more gentle . . ii 3 159
Instructed by the antiquary times, He must, he is, he cannot but be wise ii 3 263
But you are wise, Or else you love not, for to be wise and love Exceeds man's might; that dwells with gods above . . . . iii 2 162
If Aaron now be wise, Then is all safe, the anchor's in the port *T. An.* iv 4 37
She is too fair, too wise, wisely too fair, To merit bliss by making me despair . . . . *Rom. and Jul.* i 1 227
And a good lady, and a wise and virtuous . . . . i 5 116
He is wise; And, on my life, hath stol'n him home to bed . . . ii 1 3
If, in thy wisdom, thou canst give no help, Do thou but call my resolution wise . . . . iv 1 53
I have noted thee always wise . . . . *T. of Athens* iii 1 34
Thou art wise; and thou knowest well enough . . . . . . iii 1 43
Methinks thou art more honest now than wise . . . . . . iv 3 509
Brutus is wise, and, were he not in health, He would embrace the means to come by it . . . . *J. Cæsar* ii 1 258
Thus he bade me say: Brutus is noble, wise, valiant, and honest . . iii 1 126
Thy master is a wise and valiant Roman; I never thought him worse . iii 1 138
They are wise and honourable, And will, no doubt, with reasons answer you . . . . iii 2 218
Who can be wise, amazed, temperate and furious, Loyal and neutral, in a moment? No man . . . . *Macbeth* ii 3 114
He is noble, wise, judicious, and best knows The fits o' the season . iv 2 16
A queen, fair, sober, wise . . . . *Hamlet* iii 4 189

Wise. To converse with him that is wise, and says little . . . *Lear* i 4 17
As you are old and reverend, you should be wise . . . i 4 261
Thou shouldst not have been old till thou hadst been wise . i 5 49
Wise in our negligence, have secret feet In some of our best ports . iii 1 32
If she be fair and wise, fairness and wit, The one's for use, the other useth it.—Well praised! . . . *Othello* ii 1 130
I should be wise, for honesty 's a fool And loses that it works for . iii 3 382
Nay, but be wise: yet we see nothing done; She may be honest yet . iii 3 432
O, thou art wise; 'tis certain . . . . . . iv 1 75
My lord?—Are you wise?—What, is he angry? . . . iv 1 245
Be wise, and get you home.—I will not . . . v 2 223
More fair, virtuous, wise, chaste, constant-qualified . *Cymbeline* i 4 64
But if I were as wise as honest, then My purpose would prove well . iii 4 121
Those that I reverence those I fear, the wise: At fools I laugh, not fear them . . . iv 2 95
Thou art a grave and noble counsellor, Most wise in general . *Pericles* v 1 185
But in no wise Till he had done his sacrifice . . . v 2 276
Wise bearing or ignorant carriage is caught . . *2 Hen. IV.* v 1 84
Wise burgher. They had gone down too, but that a wise burgher put in for them . . . . *Meas. for Meas.* i 2 103
Wise care. Full of wise care is this your counsel . *Richard III.* iv 1 48
Wise company. What do you in this wise company? *T. of Athens* ii 2 77
Wise consent. If't be your pleasure and most wise consent . . *Othello* i 1 122
Wise council. They had gather'd a wise council to them *Hen. VIII.* ii 4 51
Wise directions. I will stoop and humble my intents To your well-practised wise directions . . *2 Hen. IV.* v 2 121
Wise father. It is a wise father that knows his own child *Mer. of Venice* ii 2 80
Wise fellow. I am a wise fellow, and, which is more, an officer *Much Ado* iv 2 83
I did think thee, for two ordinaries, to be a pretty wise fellow *All's W.* ii 3 212
I perceive he was a wise fellow, and had good discretion . *Pericles* i 3 4
Wise gentleman. 'Certain,' said she, 'a wise gentleman' . *Much Ado* v 1 166
Wise girls. We are wise girls to mock our lovers so . *L. L. Lost* v 2 58
Wise gods. O misery on't!—the wise gods seel our eyes *Ant. and Cleo.* iii 13 112
Wise Laertes' son Did graciously plead for his funerals . *T. Andron.* i 1 380
Wise man. There's not one wise man among twenty that will praise himself . . . . *Much Ado* v 2 76
I must be one of these same dumb wise men . . *Mer. of Venice* i 1 106
Pity, that fools may not speak wisely what wise men do foolishly *As Y. Like It* i 2 93
The little foolery that wise men have makes a great show . i 2 96
The wise man's folly is anatomized Even by the squandering glances of the fool . . . . ii 7 56
The fool doth think he is wise, but the wise man knows himself to be a fool . . . v 1 35
And I, that am sure I lack thee, may pass for a wise man . *T. Night* i 5 38
I take these wise men, that crow so at these set kind of fools, no better than the fools' zanies . . . i 5 95
Journeys end in lovers meeting, Every wise man's son doth know . ii 3 45
This is a practise As full of labour as a wise man's art . . iii 1 73
Wise men, folly-fall'n, quite taint their wit . . . iii 1 75
These wise men that give fools money get themselves a good report . iv 1 23
All places that the eye of heaven visits Are to a wise man ports *Rich. II.* i 3 276
Wise men ne'er sit and wail their woes . . . iii 2 178
For though it [music] have holp madmen to their wits, In me it seems it will make wise men mad . . . v 5 63
Let me embrace thee, sour adversity, For wise men say it is the wisest course . . . *3 Hen. VI.* iii 1 25
Wise men ne'er sit and wail their loss, But cheerly seek how to redress their harms . . . v 4 1
When clouds appear, wise men put on their cloaks . . *Richard III.* ii 3 32
O, then I see that madmen have no ears.—How should they, when that wise men have no eyes? . . *Rom. and Jul.* iii 3 62
Thou art not altogether a fool.—Nor thou altogether a wise man *T. of Athens* ii 2 123
Wise men know well enough what monsters you make of them *Hamlet* iii 1 143
Fools had ne'er less wit in a year; For wise men are grown foppish *Lear* i 4 182
When a wise man gives thee better counsel, give me mine again . ii 4 76
The fool will stay, And let the wise man fly . . . ii 4 84
Here's a night pities neither wise man nor fool . . . iii 2 13
Here's grace and a cod-piece; that's a wise man and a fool . iii 2 41
Wise mother. This Jacob from our holy Abram was, As his wise mother wrought in his behalf, The third possessor *Mer. of Venice* i 3 74
Wise nature. It was wise nature's end in the donation . *Cymbeline* v 5 367
Wise officer. This comes off well; here's a wise officer . *Meas. for Meas.* ii 1 57
Wise ones. There's none so foul and foolish thereunto, But does foul pranks which fair and wise ones do . . *Othello* ii 1 143
Wise people. The worm is not to be trusted but in the keeping of wise people . . . . *Ant. and Cleo.* v 2 267
Wise physician. You have showed yourself a wise physician *Mer. Wives* ii 3 56
Wise powers. The wise powers Deny us for our good *Ant. and Cleo.* ii 1 6
Wise prince. That wise prince, Henry the Fifth . . *3 Hen. VI.* iii 3 85
Wise rebellion. Being one o' the lowest, basest, poorest, Of this most wise rebellion . . . *Coriolanus* i 1 162
Wise remedy. I will no longer endure it, though yet I know no wise remedy how to avoid it . . . *As Y. Like It* i 1 26
Wise saws. Full of wise saws and modern instances . . ii 7 156
Wise things. Your wit makes wise things foolish . . *L. L. Lost* v 2 374
To your huge store Wise things seem foolish and rich things but poor . v 2 378
Wise woman. Was't not the wise woman of Brentford? . *Mer. Wives* iv 5 27
Was there a wise woman with thee?—Ay, that there was . . iv 5 59
Carry his water to the wise woman . . . . *T. Night* iii 4 114
Wise words. I have studied eight or nine wise words to speak to you *Much Ado* iii 2 74
More noble blows than ever thou wise words . . *Coriolanus* iv 2 21
Wiselier. You have taken it wiselier than I meant you should *Tempest* ii 1 21
Wisely. Then wisely, good sir, weigh Our sorrow with our comfort . ii 1 8
What says my bully-rook? speak scholarly and wisely . . *Mer. Wives* i 3 3
If I could speak so wisely under an arrest, I would send for certain of my creditors . . . . *Meas. for Meas.* i 2 135
We must do it wisely.—We will spare for no wit, I warrant you *M. Ado* iii 5 65
My conscience, hanging about the neck of my heart, says very wisely to me 'My honest friend' . . *Mer. of Venice* ii 2 15
Pity, that fools may not speak wisely what wise men do foolishly *As Y. Like It* i 2 93
Looking on it with lack-lustre eye, Says very wisely, 'It is ten o'clock' ii 7 22
He that a fool doth very wisely hit Doth very foolishly . . ii 7 53
You have said; but whether wisely or no, let the forest judge . iii 2 129
Here comes my lady: make your excuse wisely, you were best *T. Night* i 5 33
For folly that he wisely shows is fit . . . . iii 1 74
By I know how much an ounce.—Very wisely, puppies! . *W. Tale* iv 4 726

Wisely. He talked very wisely, but I regarded him not; and yet he talked wisely, and in the street too . . . . *1 Hen. IV.* i 2 97
That thou mightst win the more thy father's love, Pleading so wisely in excuse of it . . . . *2 Hen. IV.* iv 5 181
Most wisely hath Ulysses here discover'd The fever whereof all our power is sick . . . *Troi. and Cres.* i 3 138
Well know they what they speak that speak so wisely . . . iii 2 159
She is too fair, too wise, wisely too fair, To merit bliss by making me despair . . . *Rom. and Jul.* i 1 227
Wisely and slow; they stumble that run fast . . . ii 3 94
Yea, is the worst well? very well took, i' faith; wisely, wisely . ii 4 132
Tell my lady I am gone . . . —Marry, I will; and this is wisely done . iii 5 234
He's truly valiant that can wisely suffer . . *T. of Athens* iii 5 31
Answer every man directly.—Ay, and briefly.—Ay, and wisely *J. Cæsar* iii 3 12
To answer every man directly and briefly, wisely and truly: wisely I say, I am a bachelor . . . iii 3 17
And very wisely threat before you sting . . . . v 1 38
Was not that nobly done? Ay, and wisely too . . . *Macbeth* iii 6 14
You shall do marvellous wisely, good Reynaldo . . *Hamlet* ii 1 3
And, as you said, and wisely was it said . . . iii 3 30
Then must you speak Of one that loved not wisely but too well *Othello* v 2 344
For idiots in this case of favour would Be wisely definite *Cymbeline* i 6 43
Wiseness. Yet have I something in me dangerous, Which let thy wiseness fear . . . . *Hamlet* v 1 286
Wiser. He is the wiser man, master doctor: he is a curer of souls *M. W.* ii 3 39
Which is the wiser here? Justice or Iniquity? . . *Meas. for Meas.* ii 1 180
Wrench awe from fools and tie the wiser souls To thy false seeming! . ii 4 14
Albeit my wrongs might make one wiser mad . *Com. of Errors* v 1 217
Thus men may grow wiser every day . . *As Y. Like It* i 2 145
Thou speakest wiser than thou art ware of . . . ii 4 58
She could not have the wit to do this: the wiser, the waywarder . iv 1 162
I will be a fool in question, hoping to be the wiser by your answer *All's Well* ii 2 41
I will not bate thee a scruple.—Well, I shall be wiser . . ii 3 235
Why, I say nothing.—Marry, you are the wiser man . . ii 4 23
When our throats are cut, he may be ransomed, and we ne'er the wiser *Hen. V.* iv 1 206
But in these nice sharp quillets of the law, Good faith, I am no wiser than a daw . . . *1 Hen. VI.* ii 4 18
He hath a lady, wiser, fairer, truer, Than ever Greek did compass in his arms . . . *Troi. and Cres.* i 3 275
The ass more captain than the lion, the felon Loaden with irons wiser than the judge, If wisdom be in suffering . *T. of Athens* iii 5 50
You are afraid, and therein the wiser . . . *Cymbeline* i 4 146
Wisest. He's in his fit now and does not talk after the wisest *Tempest* ii 2 77
The wisest aunt, telling the saddest tale . . . *M. N. Dream* ii 1 51
The seeming truth which cunning times put on To entrap the wisest *Mer. of Venice* iii 2 101
'Twas a fear Which oft infects the wisest . . . *W. Tale* i 2 262
The wisest beholder, that knew no more but seeing, could not say . v 2 18
Let me embrace thee, sour adversity, For wise men say it is the wisest course . . . . *3 Hen. VI.* iii 1 25
Whose wisdom was a mirror to the wisest . . . iii 3 84
The wisest prince that there had reign'd by many A year before *Hen. VIII.* ii 4 49
You wisest Grecians, pardon me this brag . *Troi. and Cres.* iv 5 257
We with wisest sorrow think on him . . . *Hamlet* i 2 6
We'll call up our wisest friends; And let them know, both what we mean to do, And what's untimely done . . . iv 1 38
Make choice of whom your wisest friends you will, And they shall hear iv 5 204
Your name is great In mouths of wisest censure . *Othello* ii 3 193
Wish. I wish mine eyes Would, with themselves, shut up my thoughts *Tempest* ii 1 191
I would not wish Any companion in the world but you . . iii 1 54
We wish your peace . . . . . . iv 1 163
I wish Myself were mudded in that oozy bed . . . v 1 150
Let grief and sorrow still embrace his heart That doth not wish you joy! . . . . . . v 1 215
Wish me partaker in thy happiness When thou dost meet good hap *T. G. of Ver.* i 1 14
And how stand you affected to his wish?—As one relying on your lordship's will And not depending on his friendly wish.—My will is something sorted with his wish . . . i 3 60
What's your will?—That I may compass yours.—You have your wish . iv 2 93
Recking as little what betideth me As much I wish all good befortune you . . . . . iv 3 41
Bear witness, Heaven, I have my wish for ever . . . v 4 119
Anne is a good girl, and I wish— Out, alas! here comes my master *M. W.* i 4 36
Now shall I sin in my wish: I would thy husband were dead . iii 3 52
Who mutually hath answer'd my affection, . . . Even to my wish . iv 6 12
Wisdom wishes to appear most bright When it doth tax itself *M. for M.* ii 4 78
Grace and good company!—Who's there? come in: the wish deserves a welcome . . . . . iii 1 45
I know not where; but wheresoever, I wish him well . . iii 2 97
And well could wish You had not found me here so musical . iv 1 10
If you can, pace your wisdom In that good path that I would wish it go iv 3 138
Nor wish'd to hold my peace.—I wish you now, then . . v 1 79
The prince hath got your Hero.—I wish him joy of her . *Much Ado* ii 1 200
I could wish he would modestly examine himself . . ii 3 213
I persuaded them, if they loved Benedick, To wish him wrestle with affection . . . . . iii 1 42
Then shall he mourn, . . . And wish he had not so accused her . iv 1 234
God keep your worship! I wish your worship well . . v 1 333
At Christmas I no more desire a rose Than wish a snow in May's new-fangled mirth; But like of each thing that in season grows *L. L. Lost* i 1 106
Thy own wish wish I thee in every place! . . . ii 1 179
More sacks to the mill! O heavens, I have my wish! . . iv 3 81
O that I had my wish!—And I had mine!—And I mine too! . . iv 3 92
That the lover, sick to death, Wish himself the heaven's breath . iv 3 108
Dost thou not wish in heart The chain were longer and the letter short? v 2 55
Construe my speeches better, if you may.—Then wish me better . v 2 342
And I will wish thee never more to dance . . . v 2 400
A beard, fair health, and honesty; With three-fold love I wish you all these three . . . . . v 2 835
As due to love as thoughts and dreams and sighs, Wishes and tears *M. N. Dream* i 1 155
Sleep give thee all his rest!—With half that wish the wisher's eyes be press'd! . . . . . ii 2 65
I would wish you,—or I would request you,—or I would entreat you . iii 1 41
Now I do wish it, love it, long for it, And will for evermore be true to it iv 1 180
So may you miss me; But if you do, you'll make me wish a sin *M. of V.* iii 2 13

Wish. For myself alone I would not be ambitious in my wish, To wish myself much better . . . . *Mer. of Venice* iii 2 152
It is now our time, That have stood by and seen our wishes prosper . iii 2 189
I wish you all the joy that you can wish; For I am sure you can wish none from me . . . . iii 2 192
I wish your ladyship all heart's content.—I thank you for your wish, and am well pleased To wish it back on you . . . . . iii 4 42
I'll repent, And wish, for all that, that I had not kill'd them . iii 4 73
'Tis well you offer it behind her back; The wish would make else an unquiet house . . . . iv 1 294
I wish you well, and so I take my leave . . . . . . iv 1 420
But were the day come, I should wish it dark . . . . . v 1 304
Let your fair eyes and gentle wishes go with me *As Y. Like It* i 2 198
O, a good wish upon you! you will try in time . . . . i 3 24
Wish, for her sake more than for mine own, My fortunes were more able ii 4 76
Do you wish then that the gods had made me poetical?—I do, truly iii 3 23
I shall think my brother happy in having what he wishes for . v 2 52
All made of passion and all made of wishes, All adoration, duty . v 2 101
I will wish him to her father . . . . . . *T. of Shrew* i 1 113
Would I were so too!—So could I, faith, boy, to have the next wish after i 1 244
Shall I then come roundly to thee And wish thee to a shrewd ill-favour'd wife? . . . . i 2 60
Thou 'rt too much my friend, And I 'll not wish thee to her . . . i 2 64
A tender fatherly regard, To wish me wed to one half lunatic . . ii 1 289
Not so well apparell'd As I wish you were . . . . . iii 2 92
I desire your holy wishes.—How understand we that? . . *All's Well* i 1 68
The best wishes that can be forged in your thoughts be servants to you! i 1 84
He is one— What one, i' faith?—That I wish well . . . i 1 193
We, the poorer born, Whose baser stars do shut us up in wishes . . i 1 197
This he wish'd: I after him do after him wish too . . . . i 2 64
I wish might be found in the calendar of my past endeavours . . i 3 4
Did ever in so true a flame of liking Wish chastely and love dearly . i 3 218
Such thanks I give As one near death to those that wish him live . ii 1 134
Love make your fortunes twenty times above Her that so wishes! . ii 3 89
My wish receive, Which great Love grant! . . . . . . ii 3 90
Would not put my reputation now In any staining act.—Nor would I wish you . . . . iii 7 7
And I wish it happily effected . . . . iv 5 84
To the unknown beloved, this, and my good wishes . . . *T. Night* ii 5 102
Would it be better, madam, than I am? I wish it might . . . iii 1 156
I wish, my liege, You had only in your silent judgement tried it *W. Tale* ii 1 170
If never, yet that Time himself doth say He wishes earnestly you never may . . . . iv 1 32
No more than were I painted I would wish This youth should say 'twere well . . . . iv 4 101
When you do dance, I wish you A wave o' the sea . . . . iv 4 140
Were I to get again, Madam, I would not wish a better father *K. John* i 1 260
Lo, upon thy wish, Our messenger Chatillon is arrived! . . . ii 1 50
Father, I may not wish the fortune thine; Grandam, I will not wish thy wishes thrive . . . . iii 1 333
I had a mighty cause To wish him dead, but thou hadst none to kill him iv 2 206
And wish, so please my sovereign, ere I move . . . *Richard II.* i 1 45
Take from my mouth the wish of happy years . . . . . i 3 94
Then treasons make me wish myself a beggar, And so I am . . . v 5 33
To thy sacred state wish I all happiness . . . . . . v 6 6
Though I did wish him dead, I hate the murderer, love him murdered . v 6 39
My breakfast, come! O, I could wish this tavern were my drum! *1 Hen. IV.* iii 3 230
Good, an God will!—As good as heart can wish . *2 Hen. IV.* i 1 13
Here doth he wish his person, with such powers As might hold sortance with his quality . . . . iv 1 10
You wish me health in very happy season . . . . . . iv 2 79
Every thing lies level to our wish: Only, we want a little personal strength . . . . iv 4 7
Thy wish was father, Harry, to that thought . . . . . iv 5 93
And I do wish your honours may increase . . . . . . v 2 104
With an inward wish You would desire the king were made a prelate *Hen. V.* i 1 39
Not one behind that doth not wish Success and conquest to attend on us ii 2 23
If wishes would prevail with me, My purpose should not fail with me iii 2 16
As cold a night as 'tis, he could wish himself in Thames up to the neck iv 1 120
I think he would not wish himself any where but where he is . . iv 1 124
I dare say you love him not so ill, to wish him here alone . . . iv 1 130
What's he that wishes so? My cousin Westmoreland? . . . iv 3 18
God's will! I pray thee, wish not one man more . . . . iv 3 23
No, faith, my coz, wish not a man from England . . . . iv 3 30
Thou dost not wish more help from England, coz? . . . . iv 3 73
Joy and good wishes To our most fair and princely cousin Katharine! . v 2 3
The maid that stood in the way for my wish shall show me the way to my will . . . . v 2 355
The rest I wish thee gather: But yet be wary in thy studious care *1 Hen. VI.* ii 5 96
Exeter doth wish His days may finish ere that hapless time . . . iii 1 200
Good wishes, praise, and prayers Shall Suffolk ever have of Margaret . v 3 173
I wish some ravenous wolf had eaten thee! . . . . . . v 4 31
Their wives be as free as heart can wish or tongue can tell *2 Hen. VI.* iv 7 133
Never subject long'd to be a king As I do long and wish to be a subject . . . . iv 9 6
And as I thrust thy body in with my sword, So wish I, I might thrust thy soul to hell . . . . iv 10 85
You shall have pay and every thing you wish . . . . . v 1 47
Bid'st thou me rage? why, now thou hast thy wish . . *3 Hen. VI.* i 4 143
So do I wish the crown, being so far off . . . . . . iii 2 140
God forbid that I should wish them sever'd Whom God hath join'd together . . . . iv 1 21
I rather wish you foes than hollow friends . . . . . iv 1 139
O, may such purple tears be alway shed From those that wish the downfall of our house! . . . . v 6 65
More direful hap betide that hated wretch . . . Than I can wish to adders, spiders, toads! . . . . *Richard III.* i 2 19
Though I wish thy death, I will not be the executioner . . . . i 2 185
His royal person,—Whom God preserve better than you would wish! . i 3 59
If heaven have any grievous plague in store Exceeding those that I can wish upon thee, O, let them keep it till thy sins be ripe! . . . i 3 218
The time will come when thou shalt wish for me . . . . i 3 245
This was my wish: 'Be thou,' quoth I, 'accursed, For making me, so young, so old a widow!' . . . . iv 1 72
I wish the bastards dead; And I would have it suddenly perform'd . iv 2 18
Thou didst prophesy the time would come That I should wish for thee iv 4 80
And take it from a heart that wishes towards you Honour *Hen. VIII.* i 1 103

Wish. I am sorry To hear this of him; and could wish he were Something mistaken . . . . *Hen. VIII.* i 1 195
Not friended by his wish, to your high person His will is most malignant i 2 140
Hate him perniciously, and, o' my conscience, Wish him ten fathom deep . . . . ii 1 51
Those that sought it I could wish more Christians . . . . ii 1 64
My prayers Are not words duly hallow'd, nor my wishes More worth than empty vanities; yet prayers and wishes Are all I can return . ii 3 68
Ye tell me what ye wish for both,—my ruin . . . . . iii 1 98
I will not wish ye half my miseries; I have more charity . . iii 1 108
Wherein he appears As I would wish mine enemy . . . . iii 2 28
May you be happy in your wish, my lord! For, I profess, you have it . iii 2 43
Speedily I wish To hear from Rome . . . . iii 2 89
After my death I wish no other herald, No other speaker of my living actions, To keep mine honour from corruption . . . . . iv 2 69
As you wish Christian peace to souls departed, Stand these poor people's friend . . . . iv 2 156
But for the stock, Sir Thomas, I wish it grubb'd up now . . . v 1 23
She's a good creature, and, sweet lady, does Deserve our better wishes v 1 26
I wish your highness A quiet night . . . . v 1 76
I would not wish a drop of Trojan blood Spent more in her defence *Troi. and Cres.* ii 2 197
Their fraction is more our wish than their faction . . . . ii 3 108
'Tis Agamemnon's wish, and great Achilles Doth long to see unarm'd the valiant Hector . . . . iv 5 152
Were I any thing but what I am, I would wish me only he *Coriolanus* i 1 236
I wish you much mirth.—Well then, farewell . . . . . i 3 123
A soldier Even to Cato's wish, not fierce and terrible Only in strokes i 4 57
Ye Roman gods! Lead their successes as we wish our own . . i 6 7
I could wish You were conducted to a gentle bath . . . . i 6 62
I have lived To see inherited my very wishes . . . . . ii 1 215
I wish no better Than have him hold that purpose and to put it In execution . . . . ii 1 255
And to our noble consul Wish we all joy and honour . . . ii 2 157
I wish I had a cause to seek him there, To oppose his hatred fully . iii 1 19
And wish To jump a body with a dangerous physic . . . . iii 1 153
Why did you wish me milder? would you have me False to my nature? iii 2 14
Plant love among's! . . . —Amen, amen.—A noble wish . . iii 3 38
Raised only, that the weaker sort may wish Good Marcius home again . iv 6 69
Yet I wish, sir,—I mean for your particular,— you had not Join'd . iv 7 12
An evident calamity, though we had Our wish, which side should win . v 3 113
I say no more, Nor wish no less; and so, I take my leave *T. Andron.* i 1 402
But to your wishes' height advance you both . . . . . ii 1 125
A charitable wish and full of love . . . . iv 2 43
Oft have you heard me wish for such an hour, And now I find it . v 2 160
Which I wish may prove More stern and bloody than the Centaurs' feast v 2 203
An I might live to see thee married once, I have my wish *Rom. and Jul.* i 3 62
Sit under a medlar tree, And wish his mistress were that kind of fruit ii 1 35
And yet I wish but for the thing I have . . . . . . ii 2 132
Blister'd be thy tongue For such a wish! . . . . . . iii 2 91
With honourable parts, Proportion'd as one's thought would wish a man iii 5 184
O most wicked fiend! Is it more sin to wish me thus forsworn? . iii 5 236
I could wish my best friend at such a feast . . *T. of Athens* i 2 81
Being of no power to make his wishes good . . . . . . i 2 202
The good time of day to you, sir.—I also wish it to you . . . iii 6 2
Who would not wish to be from wealth exempt, Since riches point to misery and contempt? . . . . iv 2 31
I do wish thou wert a dog, That I might love thee something . iv 3 54
The one is filling still, never complete; The other, at high wish . iv 3 245
For any benefit that points to me, Either in hope or present, I'ld exchange For this one wish . . . . iv 3 528
'Tis not monstrous in you, neither wish I You take much pains to mend v 1 91
Every one doth wish You had but that opinion of yourself Which every noble Roman bears of you . . . . *J. Cæsar* ii 1 91
So near will I be, That your best friends shall wish I had been further . ii 2 125
I wish your enterprise to-day may thrive . . . . . . iii 1 13
We shall have him well to friend.—I wish we may . . . . iii 1 144
Thither will I straight to visit him: He comes upon a wish . . iii 2 271
Hath given me some worthy cause to wish Things done, undone . iv 2 8
I wish your horses swift and sure of foot . . . . *Macbeth* iii 1 38
I gin to be aweary of the sun, And wish the estate o' the world were now undone . . . . v 5 50
Had I as many sons as I have hairs, I would not wish them to a fairer death . . . . v 8 49
That duty done, My thoughts and wishes bend again toward France *Ham.* i 2 55
I do wish That your good beauties be the happy cause Of Hamlet's wildness . . . . iii 1 38
Your virtues Will bring him to his wonted way again, To both your honours.—Madam, I wish it may . . . . iii 1 42
He could nothing do but wish and beg Your sudden coming o'er . iv 7 105
I cannot wish the fault undone, the issue of it being so proper *Lear* i 1 17
So will you wish on me, When the rash mood is on . . . . ii 4 171
Our wishes on the way May prove effects . . . . . . iv 2 14
Fled from her wish and yet said 'Now I may' . . . *Othello* ii 1 152
I could well wish courtesy would invent some other custom of entertainment . . . . ii 3 36
As men in rage strike those that wish them best . . . . ii 3 243
I could heartily wish this had not befallen; but, since it is as it is, mend it . . . . ii 3 303
And think it no addition, nor my wish, To have him see me woman'd . iii 4 194
You did wish that I would make her turn: Sir, she can turn . . iv 1 263
How many boys and wenches must I have?—If every of your wishes had a womb, And fertile every wish, a million . . *Ant. and Cleo.* i 2 38
You think none but your sheets are privy to your wishes . . . i 2 42
What our contempt doth often hurl from us, We wish it ours again . i 2 128
Tempt him not so too far; I wish, forbear . . . . . . i 3 11
You do wish yourself in Egypt?—Would I had never come from thence! ii 3 10
And her forehead As low as she would wish it . . . . . iii 3 37
He will fill thy wishes to the brim With principalities . . . ii 13 18
I wish I could be made so many men . . . . iv 2 16
Say that I wish he never find more cause To change a master . . iv 5 15
The hearts That spaniel'd me at heels, to whom I gave Their wishes, do discandy . . . . iv 12 22
I wish you all joy of the worm . . . . v 2 261; 281
Would there had been some hurt done!—I wish not so . . *Cymbeline* i 2 38
Quake in the present winter's state and wish That warmer days would come . . . . ii 4 5
So he wishes you all happiness, that remains loyal to his vow . . iii 2 46
Your valiant Britons have their wishes in it . . . . . . iii 5 20
I wish my brother make good time with him, You say he is so fell . iv 2 108

Wish. I speak against my present profit, but my wish hath a preferment in't . . . *Cymbeline* v 4 215
I know not how to wish A pair of worthier sons . . . v 5 355
To hear an old man sing May to your wishes pleasure bring *Pericles* i Gower 14
I life would wish, and that I might Waste it for you, like taper-light i Gower 15
Of all say'd yet, I wish thee happiness! . . . i 1 60
If all your beggars were whipped, I would wish no better office than to be beadle . . . ii 1 96
Were my fortunes equal to my desires, I could wish to make one there . ii 1 118
He loved me dearly, And for his sake I wish the having of it . . ii 1 145
Take I your wish, I leap into the seas, Where's hourly trouble for a minute's ease . . . ii 4 43
Sail seas in cockles, have an wish but for't . . . iv 4 2
What canst thou wish thine enemy to be?—Why, I could wish him to be my master, or rather, my mistress . . . iv 6 168
And die as I would do.—You wish me well . . . v 1 16
He will not speak To any.—Yet let me obtain my wish . . . v 1 35
I'ld wish no better choice, and think me rarely wed . . . v 1 69
Thy sacred physic shall receive such pay As thy desires can wish . v 1 75
In feather'd briefness sails are fill'd, And wishes fall out as they're will'd v 2 281
Wished. Should I have wish'd a thing, it had been he . *T. G. of Ver.* ii 4 82
Welcome hither, If this be he you oft have wish'd to hear from . ii 4 103
I wished your venison better; it was ill killed . *Mer. Wives* i 1 83
Nor wish'd to hold my peace.—I wish you now, then . *Meas. for Meas.* v 1 79
By the benefit of his wished light, The seas wax'd calm . *Com. of Errors* i 1 91
Death is the fairest cover for her shame That may be wish'd for *M. Ado* iv 1 118
And if a merry meeting may be wished, God prohibit it! . . v 1 335
And wish'd in silence that it were not his . . *Mer. of Venice* ii 8 32
Happily I have arrived at the last Unto the wished haven of my bliss
T. of Shrew v 1 131
This he wish'd: I after him do after him wish too . *All's Well* i 2 63
I was very late more near her than I think she wished me . . i 3 111
Remember who commended thy yellow stockings, and wished to see thee ever cross-gartered . . . *T. Night* ii 5 167; iii 4 55
False As o'er-dyed blacks, as wind, as waters, false As dice are to be wish'd by one that fixes No bourn 'twixt his and mine . *W. Tale* i 2 133
I never wish'd to see you sorry; now I trust I shall . . ii 1 123
But infirmity Which waits upon worn times hath something seized His wish'd ability . . . v 1 143
Your supply, which you have wish'd so long, Are cast away . *K. John* v 5 12
But when they seldom come, they wish'd for come . *1 Hen. IV.* i 2 230
His cousin king, That wish'd him on the barren mountains starve . i 3 159
Perceive how I will work To bring this matter to the wished end
1 Hen. VI. iii 3 28
I oft have been afear'd, Because I wish'd this world's eternity *2 Hen. VI.* ii 4 90
The sea received it, And so I wish'd thy body might my heart . iii 2 109
Blind and dusky spectacles, For losing ken of Albion's wished coast . iii 2 113
And to that end we wish'd your lordship here . *Richard III.* iii 5 67
This is the day that, in King Edward's time, I wish'd might fall on me v 1 14
This is the day wherein I wish'd to fall By the false faith of him I trusted most . . . v 1 16
They have sent me such a man I would have wish'd for . *Hen. VIII.* ii 2 101
You ever Have wish'd the sleeping of this business . . . ii 4 163
How often have I wished me thus!—Wished, my lord! . *Troi. and Cres.* iii 2 65
I wish'd myself a man, Or that we women had men's privilege . iii 2 135
We wish'd Coriolanus Had loved you as we did . . *Coriolanus* iv 6 24
If you do hold the same intent wherein You wish'd us parties . v 6 14
And they have wish'd that Lucius were their emperor . *T. Andron.* iv 4 77
I have often wished myself poorer, that I might come nearer to you
T. of Athens i 2 104
You are honourable,—But yet they could have wish'd—they know not ii 2 216
How rarely does it meet with this time's guise, When man was wish'd to love his enemies! . . . iv 3 473
Many . Have wish'd that noble Brutus had his eyes . *J. Cæsar* i 2 62
What said Popilius Lena?—He wish'd to-day our enterprise might thrive . . . iii 1 16
'Tis a consummation Devoutly to be wish'd . . *Hamlet* iii 1 64
'Twas wondrous pitiful: She wish'd she had not heard it, yet she wish'd That heaven had made her such a man . . *Othello* i 3 162
That he which is was wish'd until he were . *Ant. and Cleo.* i 4 42
She was bound to proffer: this She wish'd me to make known *Cymbeline* iii 5 50
Bloody cloth, I'll keep thee, for I wish'd Thou shouldst be colour'd thus v 1 1
Wisher. Sleep give thee all his rest!—With half that wish the wisher's eyes be press'd! . . . *M. N. Dream* ii 2 65
Yet come a little,—Wishers were ever fools . *Ant. and Cleo.* iv 15 37
Wishest. Shame take all!—And, in the number, thee that wishest shame!
2 Hen. VI. iii 1 308
Which rather thou dost fear to do Than wishest should be undone *Macb.* i 5 26
Wisheth. With A rising sigh he wisheth you in heaven . *1 Hen. IV.* iii 1 10
Wishful. To greet mine own land with my wishful sight . *3 Hen. VI.* iii 1 14
Wishing me with him, partner of his fortune . *T. G. of Ver.* i 3 59
Rather wishing a more strict restraint Upon the sisterhood . *M. for M.* i 4 4
Had time cohered with place or place with wishing . . ii 1 11
I cannot be a man with wishing, therefore I will die a woman with grieving . . . *Much Ado* iv 1 325
What's pity?—That wishing well had not a body in't . *All's Well* i 1 195
Wishing clocks more swift? Hours, minutes? noon, midnight? *W. Tale* i 2 289
Wishing his foot were equal with his eye . *3 Hen. VI.* iii 2 137
Wishing me to permit John de la Car, my chaplain, a choice hour
Hen. VIII. i 2 161
All viands that I eat do seem unsavoury, Wishing him my meat *Pericles* ii 3 32
Wishing it so much blood unto your life . . . ii 3 77
Wisp. A wisp of straw were worth a thousand crowns, To make this shameless callet know herself . . *3 Hen. VI.* ii 2 144
Wist. He thought no harm.—An if I wist he did,—but let it rest
1 Hen. VI. iv 1 180
Wistly. He wistly look'd on me; As who should say, 'I would thou wert the man' . . . *Richard II.* v 4 7
Wit. He's winding up the watch of his wit; by and by it will strike
Tempest ii 1 13
Out o' your wits and hearing too? A pox o' your bottle! . . iii 2 86
Wit shall not go unrewarded while I am king of this country . iv 1 242
Home-keeping youth have ever homely wits . . *T. G. of Ver.* i 1 2
But a folly bought with wit, Or else a wit by folly vanquished . i 1 34
So eating love Inhabits in the finest wits of all . . i 1 44
By love the young and tender wit Is turn'd to folly, blasting in the bud i 1 47
Made wit with musing weak, heart sick with thought . . i 1 69
You have a quick wit.—And yet it cannot overtake your slow purse . i 1 132
Borrows his wit from your ladyship's looks, and spends what he borrows kindly . . . ii 4 38

Wit. If you spend word for word with me, I shall make your wit bankrupt
T. G. of Ver. ii 4 42
And he wants wit that wants resolved will To learn his wit to exchange the bad for better . . . ii 6 12
Love, lend me wings to make my purpose swift, As thou hast lent me wit to plot this drift! . . . ii 6 43
I have the wit to think my master is a kind of a knave . . iii 1 262
She hath more hair than wit, and more faults than hairs . . iii 1 361
More hair than wit? It may be; I'll prove it . . . iii 1 368
The hair that covers the wit is more than the wit, for the greater hides the less . . . iii 1 371
If I had not had more wit than he, to take a fault upon me that he did iv 4 15
With wit or steel?—With both the humours, I . *Mer. Wives* i 3 102
Here's a fellow frights English out of his wits . . . ii 1 143
I will stare him out of his wits; I will awe him with my cudgel . ii 2 291
One that hath taught me more wit than ever I learned before . iv 5 61
I warrant they would whip me with their fine wits . . iv 5 102
My admirable dexterity of wit . . . delivered me . . iv 5 121
See now how wit may be made a Jack-a-Lent, when 'tis upon ill employment! . . . v 5 134
Are there not men in your ward sufficient to serve it?—Faith, sir, few of any wit in such matters . . *Meas. for Meas.* ii 1 282
Great men may jest with saints; 'tis wit in them . . ii 2 127
Thousand escapes of wit Make thee the father of their idle dreams . iv 1 63
Her wits, I fear me, are not firm . . . v 1 33
Hast thou or word, or wit, or impudence, That yet can do thee office? . v 1 368
Are my discourses dull? barren my wit? . . *Com. of Errors* ii 1 91
I shall seek my wit in my shoulders . . . ii 2 39
What he hath scanted men in hair he hath given them in wit . ii 2 82
There's many a man hath more hair than wit.—Not a man of those but he hath the wit to lose his hair . . . ii 2 84
Thou didst conclude hairy men plain dealers without wit . . ii 2 88
Every word by all my wit being scann'd, Want wit in all one word to understand . . . iii 2 152
I knew he was not in his perfect wits . . . v 1 42
Thy jealous fits Have scared thy husband from the use of wits . . v 1 86
It shall privilege him from your hands Till I have brought him to his wits again . . . v 1 96
They never meet but there's a skirmish of wit between them *Much Ado* i 1 64
In our last conflict four of his five wits went halting off . . i 1 66
If he have wit enough to keep himself warm, let him bear it for a difference between himself and his horse . . . i 1 68
Hath the fellow any wit that told you this?—A good sharp fellow . i 2 17
Do you think I do not know you by your excellent wit? . . ii 1 127
And that I had my good wit out of the 'Hundred Merry Tales' . . ii 1 135
The commendation is not in his wit, but in his villany . . ii 1 145
Despite of his quick wit and his queasy stomach, he shall fall in love . ii 1 399
Very wise.—He doth indeed show some sparks that are like wit . ii 3 194
It is no addition to her wit, nor no great argument of her folly . ii 3 242
I may chance have some odd quirks and remnants of wit broken on me ii 3 245
Her wit Values itself so highly that to her All matter else seems weak . iii 1 52
She would laugh me Out of myself, press me to death with wit . . iii 1 76
Having so swift and excellent a wit As she is prized to have . . iii 1 89
Doth not my wit become me rarely?—It is not seen enough . . iii 4 70
His wits are not so blunt as, God help, I would desire they were . iii 5 11
He will be talking: as they say, When the age is in, the wit is out . iii 5 37
We must do it wisely.—We will spare for no wit, I warrant you . iii 5 66
Wilt thou use thy wit?—It is in my scabbard: shall I draw it? . v 1 124
Dost thou wear thy wit by thy side?—Never any did so, though very many have been beside their wit . . . v 1 126
I shall meet your wit in the career, an you charge it against me . v 1 135
Sir, your wit ambles well; it goes easily . . . v 1 159
I'll tell thee how Beatrice praised thy wit the other day. I said, thou hadst a fine wit: 'True,' said she, 'a fine little one.' 'No,' said I, 'a great wit:' 'Right,' says she, 'a great gross one.' 'Nay,' said I, 'a good wit:' 'Just,' said she, 'it hurts nobody' . . v 1 161
What a pretty thing man is when he goes in his doublet and hose and leaves off his wit! . . . v 1 204
Thy wit is as quick as the greyhound's mouth; it catches . . v 2 11
A most manly wit, Margaret; it will not hurt a woman . . v 2 15
Thou hast frighted the word out of his right sense, so forcible is thy wit . . . v 2 56
Dainty bits Make rich the ribs, but bankrupt quite the wits *L. L. Lost* i 1 27
He surely affected her for her wit.—It was so, sir; for she had a green wit . . . i 2 93
My father's wit and my mother's tongue, assist me! . . . i 2 100
Yet was Solomon so seduced, and he had a very good wit . . i 2 181
Devise, wit; write, pen; for I am for whole volumes in folio . . i 2 191
Willing to be counted wise In spending your wit in the praise of mine ii 1 19
A sharp wit match'd with too blunt a will; Whose edge hath power to cut . . . ii 1 49
Such short-lived wits do wither as they grow . . . ii 1 54
For he hath wit to make an ill shape good, And shape to win grace though he had no wit . . . ii 1 59
His eye begets occasion for his wit . . . ii 1 69
Your wit's too hot, it speeds too fast, 'twill tire . . . ii 1 120
Good wits will be jangling; but, gentles, agree . . . ii 1 225
This civil war of wits were much better used . . . ii 1 226
An your waist, mistress, were as slender as my wit, One o' these maids' girdles for your waist should be fit . . . iv 1 49
O' my troth, most sweet jests! most incony vulgar wit! . . iv 1 144
That handful of wit! Ah, heavens, it is a most pathetical nit! . iv 1 149
Can you tell me by your wit What was a month old at Cain's birth, that's not five weeks old as yet? . . . iv 2 35
I will prove those verses to be very unlearned, neither savouring of poetry, wit, nor invention . . . iv 2 165
So they say the fool said, and so say I, and I the fool: well proved, wit! iv 3 6
Once more I'll mark how love can vary wit . . . iv 3 100
How will he spend his wit! How will he triumph, leap, and laugh at it! . . . iv 3 147
A sweet touch, a quick venue of wit! snip, snap, quick, and home! it rejoiceth my intellect: true wit! . . . v 1 62
Thou halfpenny purse of wit, thou pigeon-egg of discretion . . v 1 77
Well bandied both; a set of wit well play'd . . . v 2 29
Observe the times And spend his prodigal wits in bootless rhymes . v 2 64
None are so surely caught, when they are catch'd, As wit turn'd fool . v 2 70
The help of school And wit's own grace to grace a learned fool . v 2 72
Folly in fools bears not so strong a note As foolery in the wise, when wit doth dote; Since all the power thereof it doth apply To prove, by wit, worth in simplicity . . . v 2 76

Wit. Muster your wits; stand in your own defence; Or hide your heads like cowards . . . *L. L. Lost* v 2 85
Farewell, mad wenches; you have simple wits . . . v 2 264
Are these the breed of wits so wonder'd at?—Tapers they are . . . v 2 266
Well-liking wits they have; gross, gross; fat, fat.—O poverty in wit! . v 2 268
Well, better wits have worn plain statute-caps . . . v 2 281
This fellow pecks up wit as pigeons pease, And utters it again . . v 2 315
He is wit's pedler, and retails his wares At wakes and wassails . . v 2 317
Fair gentle sweet, Your wit makes wise things foolish . . . v 2 374
Thrust thy sharp wit quite through my ignorance; Cut me to pieces . v 2 398
Speak for yourselves; my wit is at an end . . . v 2 430
Welcome, pure wit! thou partest a fair fray . . . v 2 484
You on all estates will execute That lie within the mercy of your wit . v 2 856
Your task shall be, With all the fierce endeavour of your wit To enforce the pained impotent to smile . . . v 2 863
If that you should fright the ladies out of their wits, they would have no more discretion but to hang us . . . *M. N. Dream* i 2 82
Who would set his wit to so foolish a bird? . . . iii 1 137
If I had wit enough to get out of this wood, I have enough . . iii 1 152
I have had a dream, past the wit of man to say what dream it was . iv 1 211
He hath simply the best wit of any handicraft man in Athens . . iv 2 9
If my father had not scanted me And hedged me by his wit *Mer. of Ven.* ii 1 18
When they do choose, They have the wisdom by their wit to lose . . ii 9 81
From whom he bringeth sensible regreets, To wit . . . ii 9 90
Thou spend'st such high-day wit in praising him . . . ii 9 98
I think the best grace of wit will shortly turn into silence . . iii 5 49
Wilt thou show the whole wealth of thy wit in an instant? . . iii 5 61
Can no prayers pierce thee?—No, none that thou hast wit enough to make . . . iv 1 127
Repair thy wit, good youth, or it will fall To cureless ruin . . iv 1 141
Though Nature hath given us wit to flout at Fortune . *As Y. Like It* i 2 48
When Fortune makes Nature's natural the cutter-off of Nature's wit . i 2 53
Who perceiveth our natural wits too dull to reason . . . i 2 56
For always the dulness of the fool is the whetstone of the wits. How now, wit! whither wander you? . . . i 2 59
Since the little wit that fools have was silenced, the little foolery that wise men have makes a great show . . . i 2 95
How shall I answer you?—As wit and fortune will . . . i 2 110
I shall ne'er be ware of mine own wit till I break my shins against it . ii 4 60
He that hath learned no wit by nature nor art may complain of good breeding . . . iii 2 30
You have too courtly a wit for me: I'll rest.—Wilt thou rest damned? iii 2 72
You have a nimble wit: I think 'twas made of Atalanta's heels . . iii 2 293
When a man's verses cannot be understood, nor a man's good wit . . iii 3 13
Or I should think my honesty ranker than my wit . . . iv 1 86
She could not have the wit to do this: the wiser, the waywarder . . iv 1 161
Make the doors upon a woman's wit and it will out at the casement . iv 1 163
A man that had a wife with such a wit, he might say 'Wit, whither wilt?' . . . iv 1 167
Till you met your wife's wit going to your neighbour's bed.—And what wit could wit have to excuse that? . . . iv 1 170
We that have good wits have much to answer for; we shall be flouting . v 1 12
Art thou wise?—Ay, sir, I have a pretty wit . . . v 1 32
Or, to wit, I kill thee, make thee away, translate thy life into death . v 1 57
He uses his folly like a stalking-horse and under the presentation of that he shoots his wit . . . v 4 113
O, how we joy to see your wit restored! . . . *T. of Shrew* Ind. 2 79
If you love the maid, Bend thoughts and wits to achieve her . . . i 1 184
Her beauty and her wit, Her affability and bashful modesty . . ii 1 48
He had the wit which I can well observe To-day in our young lords *All's Well* i 2 32
Only shape thou thy silence to my wit . . . *T. Night* i 2 61
Sometimes I have no more wit than a Christian or an ordinary man has . . . i 3 89
I am a great eater of beef and I believe that does harm to my wit . . i 3 91
She'll not match above her degree, neither in estate, years, nor wit . i 3 117
Wit, an't be thy will, put me into good fooling! Those wits, that think they have thee, do very oft prove fools . . . i 5 35
What says Quinapalus? 'Better a witty fool than a foolish wit' . . i 5 40
Have you no wit, manners, nor honesty, but to gabble like tinkers? . ii 3 94
Do not think I have wit enough to lie straight in my bed: I know I can do it . . . ii 3 147
Follow me.—To the gates of Tartar, thou most excellent devil of wit! . ii 5 227
A sentence is but a cheveril glove to a good wit . . . iii 1 13
This fellow is wise enough to play the fool; And to do that well craves a kind of wit . . . iii 1 68
But wise men, folly-fall'n, quit taint their wit . . . iii 1 75
When wit and youth is come to harvest, Your wife is like to reap a proper man . . . iii 1 143
Maugre all thy pride, Nor wit nor reason can my passion hide . . iii 1 164
For, sure, the man is tainted in's wits . . . iii 4 14
Thou shalt hold the opinion of Pythagoras ere I will allow of thy wits . iv 2 63
Alas, sir, how fell you besides your five wits? . . . iv 2 93
I am as well in my wits, fool, as thou art.—But as well? then you are mad indeed, if you be no better in your wits than a fool . . iv 2 95
And do all they can to face me out of my wits . . . iv 2 101
Thy wits the heavens restore! endeavour thyself to sleep . . iv 2 103
I am as well in my wits as any man in Illyria . . . iv 2 114
I must have done no less with wit and safety . . . v 1 218
Prithee, read i' thy right wits.—So I do, madonna; but to read his right wits is to read thus . . . v 1 305
I'll use that tongue I have: if wit flow from't As boldness from my bosom, let't not be doubted I shall do good . . . *W. Tale* ii 2 52
Not he alone shall suffer what wit can make heavy and vengeance bitter iv 4 800
I will not keep this form upon my head, When there is such disorder in my wit . . . *K. John* iii 4 102
Where will doth mutiny with wit's regard . . . *Richard II.* ii 1 28
Though it [music] have holp madmen to their wits, In me it seems it will make wise men mad . . . v 5 62
He ambled up and down With shallow jesters and rash bavin wits *1 Hen. IV.* iii 2 61
I am not only witty in myself, but the cause that wit is in other men *2 Hen. IV.* i 2 12
Pregnancy is made a tapster, and hath his quick wit wasted in giving reckonings . . . i 2 193
Your wind short? your chin double? your wit single? . . . i 2 207
Yea; I thank your pretty sweet wit for it . . . i 2 231
A good wit will make use of any thing: I will turn diseases to commodity . . . i 2 277
It shall serve among wits of no higher breeding than thine . . ii 2 38

Wit. They say Poins has a good wit.—He a good wit? hang him, baboon! his wit's as thick as Tewksbury mustard . *2 Hen. IV.* ii 4 260
I would you had but the wit: 'twere better than your dukedom . iv 3 92
The tongue, which is the birth, becomes excellent wit . . . iv 3 110
Have you your wits? know you what 'tis you speak? . . . v 5 49
Establish'd then this law; to wit, no female Should be inheritrix *Hen. V.* i 2 50
His jest will savour but of shallow wit, When thousands weep . . i 2 295
Among foaming bottles and ale-washed wits . . . iii 6 83
The man hath no wit that cannot . . . vary deserved praise on my palfrey . . . iii 7 33
Leaving their wits with their wives . . . iii 7 160
Being in his right wits and his good judgements . . . iv 7 49
I have labour'd, With all my wits, my pains, and strong endeavours . v 2 25
A shepherd's daughter, My wit untrain'd in any kind of art . *1 Hen. VI.* i 2 73
Search out thy wit for secret policies, And we will make thee famous . iii 3 12
Thou mayst bereave him of his wits with wonder . . . v 3 195
Such as my wit affords And over-joy of heart doth minister . *2 Hen. VI.* i 1 30
Did my brother Bedford toil his wits, To keep by policy what Henry got? . . . i 1 83
And yet herein I judge mine own wit good . . . i 1 232
Lords, give us leave: I'll try this widow's wit . . . *3 Hen. VI.* iii 2 33
Her words do show her wit incomparable . . . iii 2 85
Away with scrupulous wit! now arms must rule . . . iv 7 61
Less than a mother's hope, To wit, an indigested and deformed lump . v 6 51
But, gentle Lady Anne, To leave this keen encounter of our wits *Rich. III.* i 2 115
Those whose dealings have deserved the place, And those who have the wit to claim the place . . . iii 1 50
With what his valour did enrich his wit, His wit set down to make his valour live . . . iii 1 85
With what a sharp-provided wit he reasons! . . . iii 1 132
Of an excellent And unmatch'd wit and judgement . . *Hen. VIII.* ii 4 47
With my weak wit, And to such men of gravity and learning . . iii 1 72
You know I am a woman, lacking wit To make a seemly answer . . iii 1 177
There was a haberdasher's wife of small wit near him . . . v 4 49
I will not dispraise your sister Cassandra's wit . *Troi. and Cres.* i 1 47
Hector shall not have his wit this year.—He shall not need it . . i 2 92
He has a shrewd wit, I can tell you; and he's a man good enough . i 2 206
Upon my wit, to defend my wiles; upon my secrecy, to defend mine honesty . . . i 2 285
When rank Thersites opes his mastic jaws, We shall hear music, wit, and oracle . . . i 3 74
I shall sooner rail thee into wit and holiness . . . ii 1 17
Thou art bought and sold among those of any wit, like a barbarian slave ii 1 52
What modicums of wit he utters! his evasions have ears thus long . ii 1 74
Who wears his wit in his belly and his guts in his head . . . ii 1 79
Has not so much wit . . . As will stop the eye of Helen's needle . ii 1 85
Will you set your wit to a fool's?—No, I warrant you; for a fool's will shame it . . . ii 1 94
A great deal of your wit, too, lies in your sinews . . . ii 1 108
Whose wit was mouldy ere your grandsires had nails on their toes . ii 1 115
I will keep where there is wit stirring and leave the faction of fools . ii 1 130
Take not that little less than little wit from them that they have! ii 3 15
An all men were o' my mind,—Wit would be out of fashion . . ii 3 226
Where is my wit? I know not what I speak . . . iii 2 158
For beauty, wit, High birth, vigour of bone, desert in service . . iii 3 171
As who should say 'There were wit in this head, an 'twould out' . . iii 3 255
The moral of my wit Is 'plain and true;' there's all the reach of it . iv 4 109
Wit larded with malice and malice forced with wit . . . v 1 63
Not that our heads are some brown, some black, some auburn, some bald, but that our wits are so diversely coloured . . *Coriolanus* ii 3 21
I think if all our wits were to issue out of one skull, they would fly east, west, north, south . . . ii 3 23
Which way do you judge my wit would fly?—Nay, your wit will not so soon out as another man's will; 'tis strongly wedged up in a block-head . . . ii 3 28
I'll try whether my old wit be in request With those that have but little iii 1 251
Why stay we to be baited With one that wants her wits? . . . iv 2 44
Upon her wit doth earthly honour wait . . . *T. Andron.* ii 1 10
Thy years want wit, thy wit wants edge, And manners . . . ii 1 26
With her sacred wit To villany and vengeance consecrate . . . ii 1 120
He that had wit would think that I had none . . . iii 3 1
And what an if His sorrows have so overwhelm'd his wits? . . . iv 4 10
She'll not be hit With cupid's arrow; she hath Dian's wit *Rom. and Jul.* i 1 215
Dost thou fall upon thy face? Thou wilt fall backward when thou hast more wit . . . i 3 42
Take our good meaning, for our judgement sits Five times in that ere once in our five wits . . . i 4 47
We mean well in going to this mask; But 'tis no wit to go . . . i 4 49
Come between us, good Benvolio; my wits faint . . . ii 4 72
If thy wits run the wild-goose chase, I have done, for thou hast more of the wild-goose in one of thy wits than, I am sure, I have in my whole five . . . ii 4 75
Thy wit is a very bitter sweeting; it is a most sharp sauce . . ii 4 83
Here's a wit of cheveril, that stretches from an inch narrow to an ell broad! . . . ii 4 87
Fie, fie, thou shamest thy shape, thy love, thy wit; Which, like a usurer, abound'st in all, And usest none in that true use indeed Which should bedeck thy shape, thy love, thy wit . . . iii 3 122
Thy wit, that ornament to shape and love . . . iii 3 130
Some grief shows much of love; But much of grief shows still some want of wit . . . iii 5 74
I already know thy grief; It strains me past the compass of my wits . iv 1 47
Pray you, put up your dagger, and put out your wit.—Then have at you with my wit! I will dry-beat you with an iron wit, and put up my iron dagger . . . iv 5 124
Wherefore?—That I had no angry wit to be a lord . . *T. of Athens* i 1 241
As much foolery as I have, so much wit thou lackest . . . ii 2 124
His wits Are drown'd and lost in his calamities . . . iv 3 88
This rudeness is a sauce to his good wit . . . *J. Cæsar* i 2 304
I have neither wit, nor words, nor worth, Action, nor utterance . . iii 2 225
Thou speak'st with all thy wit; and yet, i' faith, With wit enough for thee . . . *Macbeth* iv 2 42
That adulterate beast, With witchcraft of his wit . . . *Hamlet* i 5 43
O wicked wit and gifts, that have the power So to seduce! . . . i 5 44
Here's my drift; And, I believe, it is a fetch of wit . . . ii 1 38
Brevity is the soul of wit, And tediousness the limbs and outward flourishes . . . ii 2 90
They have a plentiful lack of wit, together with most weak hams . . ii 2 202
My wit's diseased: but, sir, such answer as I can make, you shall command . . . iii 2 334

Wit. Is't possible, a young maid's wits Should be as mortal as an old man's life? *Hamlet* iv 5 159
Hadst thou thy wits, and didst persuade revenge, It could not move thus iv 5 168
I like thy wit well, in good faith v 1 51
He shall recover his wits there; or, if he do not, it's no great matter there v 1 166
How came he mad?—Very strangely, they say.—How strangely?—Faith, e'en with losing his wits v 1 174
Let me, if not by birth, have lands by wit *Lear* i 2 199
Thou hadst little wit in thy bald crown, when thou gavest thy golden one away i 4 178
Fools had ne'er less wit in a year; For wise men are grown foppish, They know not how their wits to wear i 4 181
Thou hast pared thy wit o' both sides, and left nothing i' the middle i 4 205
I prithee, be merry; thy wit shall ne'er go slip-shod i 5 11
Having more man than wit about me ii 4 42
My wits begin to turn. Come on, my boy: how dost, my boy? art cold? iii 2 67
He that has and a little tiny wit,—With hey, ho, the wind and the rain iii 2 74
Bless thy five wits! Tom's a-cold,—O, do de, do de, do de iii 4 59
His wits begin to unsettle.—Canst thou blame him? His daughters seek his death iii 4 167
Truth to tell thee, The grief hath crazed my wits iii 4 175
All the power of his wits have given way to his impatience iii 6 4
Bless thy five wits!—O pity! iii 6 60
Trouble him not, his wits are gone iii 6 94
Poor Tom hath been scared out of his good wits iv 1 60
'Tis wonder that thy life and wits at once Had not concluded all iv 7 41
What, have you lost your wits? *Othello* i 1 92
Tying her duty, beauty, wit, and fortunes In an extravagant and wheeling stranger i 1 136
Be not too hard for my wits i 3 364
Fairness and wit, The one's for use, the other useth it ii 1 130
How if she be black and witty?—If she be black, and thereto have a wit, She'll find a white that shall her blackness fit ii 1 133
With no money at all and a little more wit, return again ii 3 375
We work by wit, and not by witchcraft; And wit depends on dilatory time ii 3 378
Witness that here Iago doth give up The execution of his wit iii 3 466
To do this is within the compass of man's wit; and therefore I will attempt the doing it iii 4 22
Bear some charity to my wit; do not think it so unwholesome iv 1 123
Of so high and plenteous wit and invention:—She's the worse for all this iv 1 201
He is much changed.—Are his wits safe? is he not light of brain? iv 1 280
Some such squire he was That turn'd your wit the seamy side without. iv 2 146
Your suspicion is not without wit and judgement iv 2 215
She's a good sign, but I have seen small reflection of her wit *Cymbeline* i 2 33
If his wit had been like him that broke it, it would have run all out ii 1 9
If you, born in these latter times, When wit's more ripe, accept my rhymes *Pericles* i Gower 12
Now please you wit The epitaph is for Marina writ iv 4 31

Witch. The foul witch Sycorax, who with age and envy Was grown into a hoop *Tempest* i 2 258
This damn'd witch Sycorax, . . . Thou know'st, was banish'd i 2 263
His mother was a witch, and one so strong That could control the moon v 1 269
He swears she's a witch; forbade her my house *Mer. Wives* iv 2 88
Let's go dress him like the witch of Brentford iv 2 100
A witch, a quean, an old cozening quean! iv 2 180
Come down, you witch, you hag, you; come down, I say! iv 2 187
Out of my door, you witch, you hag, you baggage! iv 2 194
Hang her, witch!—By yea and no, I think the 'oman is a witch indeed iv 2 201
I was like to be apprehended for the witch of Brentford iv 5 120
The knave constable had set me i' the stocks, i' the common stocks, for a witch iv 5 124
Soul-killing witches that deform the body *Com. of Errors* i 2 100
That I amazed ran from her as a witch iii 2 149
There's none but witches do inhabit here iii 2 161
I hope you do not mean to cheat me so.—Avaunt, thou witch! iv 3 80
I see these witches are afraid of swords iv 4 151
I could find in my heart to stay here still and turn witch iv 4 160
Beauty is a witch Against whose charms faith melteth into blood *M. Ado* ii 1 186
Out! A mankind witch! Hence with her! *W. Tale* ii 3 67
And witch the world with noble horsemanship 1 *Hen. IV.* iv 1 110
Chide the cripple tardy-gaited night Who, like a foul and ugly witch, doth limp So tediously away *Hen. V.* iv Prol. 21
Thou art a witch, And straightway give thy soul to him thou servest 1 *Hen. VI.* i 5 6
A witch, by fear, not force, like Hannibal, Drives back our troops i 5 21
Despairing of his own arm's fortitude, To join with witches! ii 1 18
Pucelle, that witch, that damned sorceress, Hath wrought this hellish mischief iii 2 38
See, how the ugly witch doth bend her brows! v 3 34
Hast thou as yet conferr'd With Margery Jourdain, the cunning witch? 2 *Hen. VI.* i 2 75
Dame Eleanor gives gold to bring the witch i 2 91
Dealing with witches and with conjurers ii 1 172
The witch in Smithfield shall be burn'd to ashes ii 3 7
And witch me, As Ascanius did When he to madding Dido would unfold His father's acts iii 2 116
And witch sweet ladies with my words and looks. O miserable thought! 3 *Hen. VI.* iii 2 150
Foul wrinkled witch, what makest thou in my sight? *Richard III.* i 3 164
Edward's wife, that monstrous witch, Consorted with that harlot strumpet iii 4 72
You whoreson cur!—Do, do.—Thou stool for a witch! *Troi. and Cres.* ii 1 46
Beshrew the witch! with venomous wights she stays As tediously as hell iv 2 12
You witch me in it; Surprise me to the very brink of tears *T. of Athens* v 1 158
'Aroint thee, witch!' the rump-fed ronyon cries *Macbeth* i 3 6
Scale of dragon, tooth of wolf, Witches' mummy iv 1 23
No fairy takes, nor witch hath power to charm *Hamlet* i 1 163
Bid her alight, And her troth plight, And, aroint thee, witch! *Lear* iii 4 129
Out, fool! I forgive thee for a witch *Ant. and Cleo.* i 2 40
Now the witch take me, if I meant it thus! Grace grow where those drops fall! iv 2 37
The witch shall die: To the young Roman boy she hath sold me iv 12 47
Such a holy witch That he enchants societies into him *Cymbeline* i 6 166

Witchcraft. A witchcraft drew me hither *T. Night* v 1 79
And thou, fresh piece Of excellent witchcraft *W. Tale* iv 4 434
This juggling witchcraft with revenue cherish *K. John* iii 1 169
You have witchcraft in your lips, Kate *Hen. V.* v 2 301
Tell me what they deserve That do conspire my death with devilish plots Of damned witchcraft? *Richard III.* iii 4 63
That by their witchcraft thus have marked me iii 4 74
He hath a witchcraft Over the king in 's tongue *Hen. VIII.* iii 2 18
I do not know what witchcraft's in him *Coriolanus* iv 7 2
Witchcraft celebrates Pale Hecate's offerings *Macbeth* ii 1 51
That adulterate beast, With witchcraft of his wit *Hamlet* i 5 43
But this gallant Had witchcraft in't; he grew unto his seat iv 7 86
For nature so preposterously to err, Being not deficient, blind, or lame of sense, Sans witchcraft could not *Othello* i 3 64
This only is the witchcraft I have used i 3 169
We work by wit, and not by witchcraft; And wit depends on dilatory time ii 3 378
He thought 'twas witchcraft—but I am much to blame iii 3 211
Let witchcraft join with beauty, lust with both! *Ant. and Cleo.* ii 1 22
No exorciser harm thee!—Nor no witchcraft charm thee! *Cymbeline* iv 2 277

Witched. Am I not witch'd like her? or thou not false like him? 2 *Hen. VI.* iii 2 119

Witching. 'Tis now the very witching time of night *Hamlet* iii 2 406

Wit-crackers. A college of wit-crackers cannot flout me out of my humour. Dost thou think I care for a satire? *Much Ado* v 4 102

With. Of any thing the image tell me that Hath kept with thy remembrance *Tempest* i 2 44
Thy vile race, Though thou didst learn, had that in't which good natures Could not abide to be with i 2 360
Will you grant with me That Ferdinand is drown'd? ii 1 243
I took him to be killed with a thunder-stroke ii 2 112
'Tis fresh morning with me When you are by at night iii 1 33
'Tis a custom with him, I' th' afternoon to sleep iii 2 95
I pray thee, out with't, and place it for her chief virtue *T. G. of Ver.* iii 1 339
'Out with the dog!' says one: 'What cur is that?' says another iv 4 22
Why do I pity him That with his very heart despiseth me? iv 4 99
What would you with her, if that I be she? iv 4 115
Pursue; up with your fights: Give fire *Mer. Wives* ii 2 142
To the forge with it then; shape it: I would not have things cool iv 2 239
I rather will suspect the sun with cold Than thee with wantonness iv 4 7
Heaven doth with us as we with torches do *Meas. for Meas.* i 1 33
Thus stands it with me i 2 149
Fie, brother! how the world is changed with you! *Com. of Errors* ii 2 154
For the which He did arrest me with an officer v 1 230
I will break with her and with her father And thou shalt have her *M. Ado* i 1 311
A vane blown with all winds iii 1 66
It were a better death than die with mocks iii 1 79
We had like to have had our two noses snapped off with two old men without teeth v 1 116
Which with,—O, with—but with this I passion to say wherewith *L. L. L.* i 1 263
With that, all laugh'd and clapp'd him on the shoulder v 2 107
Where art thou?—I will be with thee straight *M. N. Dream* iii 2 403
For aught I see, they are as sick that surfeit with too much as they that starve with nothing *Mer. of Venice* i 2 6
The magnificoes Of greatest port have all persuaded with him iii 2 283
I saw him put down the other day with an ordinary fool *T. Night* i 5 91
Be opposite with a kinsman, surly with servants ii 5 162; iii 4 76
The fool should be as oft with your master as with my mistress iii 1 45
Nay, an thou pass upon me, I'll no more with thee iii 1 49
This comes with seeking you: But there's no remedy iii 4 366
They're here with me already, whispering, rounding 'Sicilia is a so-forth:' 'tis far gone *W. Tale* i 2 217
He was torn to pieces with a bear v 2 68
Of Nature's gifts thou mayst with lilies boast *K. John* iii 1 53
Be stirring as the time; be fire with fire v 1 48
As a long-parted mother with her child Plays fondly with her tears and smiles in meeting *Richard II.* iii 2 8
I live with bread like you, feel want, Taste grief, need friends iii 2 175
Shall kin with kin and kind with kind confound iv 1 141
Nay, rather damn them with King Cerberus 2 *Hen. IV.* ii 4 181
If he be sick with joy, he'll recover without physic iv 5 14
God b' wi' you, and keep you, and heal your pate *Hen. V.* v 1 70
And wherefore crave you combat? or with whom?—With him, my lord 1 *Hen. VI.* iv 1 84
Cardinal, I am with you.—Why, how now! 2 *Hen. VI.* ii 1 48
He that can do all in all With her that hateth thee and hates us all ii 4 52
I feel remorse in myself with his words iv 7 111
Being suffer'd with the bear's fell paw, Hath clapp'd his tail between his legs v 1 153
Trod my title down, And with dishonour laid me on the ground 3 *Hen. VI.* iii 3 9
Since I am crept in favour with myself, I will maintain it with some little cost *Richard III.* i 2 259
When I parted with him, He hugg'd me in his arms i 4 251
'Tis better with me now Than when I met thee last where now we meet iii 2 100
The parents live, whose children thou hast butcher'd, Old wither'd plants, to wail it with their age iv 4 394
He would kiss you twenty with a breath *Hen. VIII.* i 4 30
I shall be with you presently, good master puppy v 4 29
Let him die, With every joint a wound, and that to-morrow! *T. and C.* iv 1 29
Trust ye? With every minute you do change a mind *Coriolanus* i 1 186
He is no with himself; let us withdraw *T. Andron.* i 1 368
Was I with you there for the goose?—Thou wast never with me for any thing when thou wast not there for the goose *Rom. and Jul.* ii 4 78
What wouldst thou have with me?—Good king of cats, nothing iii 1 79
Strange times, that weep with laughing, not with weeping! *T. of Athens* iv 3 493
The troubled Tiber chafing with her shores *J. Cæsar* i 2 101
I have seen The ambitious ocean swell and rage and foam, To be exalted with the threatening clouds i 3 8
Give him a statue with his ancestors iii 2 55
With meditating that she must die once, I have the patience to endure it now iv 3 191
How is't with me, when every noise appals me? *Macbeth* ii 2 58
It is an accustomed action with her, to seem thus washing her hands v 1 32
I have supp'd full with horrors v 5 13
How is it with you, lady?—Alas, how is't with you? *Hamlet* iii 4 115
O heavy deed! It had been so with us, had we been there iv 1 13
That we can let our beard be shook with danger And think it pastime iv 7 32
I'll pluck ye out, And cast you, with the waters that you lose *Lear* i 4 325
Return with her? Persuade me rather to be slave and sumpter ii 4 218
Are you there with me? No eyes in your head? iv 6 148
To-morrow with your earliest Let me have speech with you *Othello* ii 3 7
With your speediest bring us what she says *Ant. and Cleo.* v 1 67
Must I be unfolded With one that I have bred? v 2 171
A goodly day not to keep house, with such Whose roof's as low as ours! *Cymbeline* iii 3 1

With. And let the stinking elder, grief, untwine His perishing root with the increasing vine! . . . . *Cymbeline* iv 2 60
Bring me word how 'tis with her. A fever with the absence of her son, A madness, of which her life's in danger . . . . . iv 3 2
Withal. So glad of this as they I cannot be, Who are surprised withal *Tempest* iii 1 93
I fear me, he will scarce be pleased withal . . *T. G. of Ver.* ii 7 67
These banish'd men that I have kept withal . . . v 4 152
An honest, willing, kind fellow, as ever servant shall come in house withal, and, I warrant you, no tell-tale . . . *Mer. Wives* i 4 11
I'll entertain myself like one that I am not acquainted withal . . ii 1 90
Her cause and yours I'll perfect him withal . . *Meas. for Meas.* iv 3 146
Such a fellow is not to be talked withal . . . . . v 1 348
So befall my soul As this is false he burdens me withal! *Com. of Errors* v 1 209
I will acquaint my daughter withal, that she may be the better prepared *Much Ado* i 2 23
I have acquainted you withal, to the end to crave your assistance *L. L. Lost* v 1 122
They fell sick and died; I could not do withal . *Mer. of Venice* iii 4 72
I must have liberty Withal, as large a charter as the wind *As Y. Like It* ii 7 48
Why, nothing comes amiss, so money comes withal . . *T. of Shrew* i 2 82
Though he be merry, yet withal he's honest . . . . iii 2 25
Withal, full oft we see Cold wisdom waiting on superfluous folly *All's W.* i 1 115
If thou be pleased withal, Command thy son and daughter to join hands *K. John* ii 1 531
Yea, and myself and all, Will I withal endow a child of thine *Rich. III.* iv 4 249
I was moved withal.—I dare be sworn you were . . *Coriolanus* v 3 194
If he do bleed, I'll gild the faces of the grooms withal *Macbeth* ii 2 56
Withdraw thee, Valentine: who's this comes here? . *T. G. of Ver.* v 4 18
Let us withdraw together, And we may soon our satisfaction have *Meas. for Meas.* i 1 82
What's to do here, Thomas tapster? let's withdraw . . . i 2 117
Withdraw into a chamber by yourselves . . . . *Much Ado* v 4 11
Ladies, withdraw: the gallants are at hand . . . *L. L. Lost* v 2 308
If thou say so, withdraw, and prove it too . *M. N. Dream* iii 2 255
I pray now, call her. Withdraw yourselves . . . *W. Tale* ii 2 16
I must withdraw and weep Upon the spot of this enforced cause *K. John* v 2 29
Withdraw with us: and let the trumpets sound . . *Richard II.* i 3 121
Withdraw yourselves, and leave us here alone . . . . v 3 28
We'll withdraw awhile. Go to the king . . . *1 Hen. IV.* iv 3 107
I prithee, Harry, withdraw thyself; thou bleed'st too much . . v 4 2
Let us withdraw into the other room . . . *2 Hen. IV.* iv 5 18
And I'll withdraw me and my bloody power . . *1 Hen. VI.* iv 2 8
Withdraw you hence, my lord, I'll follow you . . *Richard III.* iii 4 43
Withdraw thee, wretched Margaret: who comes here? . . . iv 4 8
My kingdom for a horse!—Withdraw, my lord; I'll help you to a horse v 4 8
Whither, if it please you, we may now withdraw us . . . v 5 11
Withdraw Into your private chamber, we shall give you The full cause of our coming.—Speak it here . . . . . *Hen. VIII.* iii 1 27
Down with that sword! Tribunes, withdraw awhile . *Coriolanus* iii 1 226
Let us entreat . . . That you withdraw you and abate your strength *T. Andron.* i 1 43
He is not with himself; let us withdraw . . . . . i 1 368
I will withdraw: but this intrusion shall Now seeming sweet convert to bitter gall. . . . . *Rom. and Jul.* i 5 93
Withdraw it? for what purpose, love?—But to be frank, and give it thee again . . . . ii 2 130
Withdraw unto some private place, And reason coldly of your grievances iii 1 54
I hear him coming: let's withdraw, my lord . . *Hamlet* iii 1 55
To withdraw with you:—why do you go about to recover the wind of me? . . . . iii 2 360
Fear me not: withdraw, I hear him coming . . . . iii 4 7
Let us withdraw; 'twill be a storm . . . . . *Lear* ii 4 290
I will withdraw, To furnish me with some swift means of death *Othello* iii 3 476
Do you withdraw yourself a little while, He will recover straight . . iv 1 57
That's not amiss; But yet keep time in all. Will you withdraw? . iv 1 93
Let's withdraw; And meet the time as it seeks us . . *Cymbeline* iv 3 32
The knights are coming: we will withdraw Into the gallery . *Pericles* ii 2 58
Withdrawing. I believe I know the cause of his withdrawing *M. for M.* iii 2 140
Withdrawn. My brother is amorous on Hero and hath withdrawn her father to break with him about it . . . . *Much Ado* ii 1 162
Ah, Warwick, why hast thou withdrawn thyself? . *3 Hen. VI.* ii 3 14
Withdrew. When we withdrew, my liege, we left it here *2 Hen. IV.* iv 5 59
But advantageous care Withdrew me from the odds of multitude *Troi. and Cres.* v 4 23
Finger'd their packet, and in fine withdrew To mine own room again *Hamlet* v 2 15
Wither. Such short-lived wits do wither as they grow . *L. L. Lost* ii 1 54
But soft, but see, or rather do not see, My fair rose wither *Richard II.* v 1 8
Poor jade, is wrung in the withers out of all cess . *1 Hen. IV.* ii 1 7
A fair face will wither; a full eye will wax hollow . *Hen. V.* v 2 170
Will I for ever . . . wear, Until it wither with me to my grave *1 Hen. VI.* ii 4 110
Wither, garden; and be henceforth a burying-place . *2 Hen. VI.* iv 10 67
Wither one rose, and let the other flourish; If you contend, a thousand lives must wither. . . . . *3 Hen. VI.* ii 5 101
Why wither not the leaves the sap being gone? . *Richard III.* ii 2 42
Let two more summers wither in their pride, Ere we may think her ripe to be a bride. . . . . *Rom. and Jul.* i 2 10
Let prisons swallow 'em, Debts wither 'em to nothing! . *T. of Athens* iv 3 538
Let the galled jade wince, our withers are unwrung . *Hamlet* iii 2 253
She that herself will sliver and disbranch From her material sap, perforce must wither And come to deadly use . . . . *Lear* iv 2 35
When I have pluck'd the rose, I cannot give it vital growth again, It must needs wither . . . . *Othello* v 2 15
Age cannot wither her, nor custom stale Her infinite variety *A. and C.* ii 2 240
Withered. Thy food shall be The fresh-brook muscles, wither'd roots, and husks . . . . *Tempest* i 2 463
A withered serving-man [makes] a fresh tapster . . *Mer. Wives* i 3 19
Old, cold, withered, and of intolerable entrails . . . . v 5 161
A wither'd hermit, five-score winters worn . . *L. L. Lost* iv 3 242
Against her lips I bob And on her wither'd dewlap pour the ale *M. N. D.* ii 1 50
I am too young for you.—Yet you are wither'd . . *T. of Shrew* ii 1 239
A vengeance on your crafty wither'd hide! . . . . . ii 1 406
This is a man, old, wrinkled, faded, wither'd . . . . iv 5 43
Your old virginity is like one of our French withered pears . . .; marry, 'tis a withered pear; it was formerly better . . *All's Well* i 1 175
I, an old turtle, Will wing me to some wither'd bough . . *W. Tale* v 3 133
Like crooked age, To crop at once a too long wither'd flower *Richard II.* ii 1 134
The bay-trees in our country are all wither'd . . . . ii 4 8
I am withered like an old apple-john . . . . *1 Hen. IV.* iii 3 4

Withered. I will now take my leave of these six dry, round, old, withered knights . . . . *2 Hen. IV.* ii 4 8
Look, whether the withered elder hath not his poll clawed like a parrot . . . . ii 4 281
But health, alack, with youthful wings is flown From this bare wither'd trunk . . . . iv 5 230
Who twice a-day their wither'd hands hold up Toward heaven *Hen. V.* iv 1 316
Like to a wither'd vine That droops his sapless branches to the ground *1 Hen. VI.* ii 5 11
These eyes, that see thee now well coloured, Shall see thee wither'd . iv 2 38
She did corrupt frail nature with some bribe, To shrink mine arm up like a wither'd shrub . . . . *3 Hen. VI.* iii 2 156
Have done thy charm, thou hateful wither'd hag! . . *Richard III.* i 3 215
Why grow the branches now the root is wither'd? . . . . ii 2 41
Behold mine arm Is, like a blasted sapling, wither'd up . . . iii 4 71
And in my vantbrace put this wither'd brawn . . *Troi. and Cres.* i 3 297
You part in anger.—Doth that grieve thee? O wither'd truth! . v 2 46
As doth the honey-dew Upon a gather'd lily almost wither'd *T. Andron.* iii 1 113
Such wither'd herbs as these Are meet for plucking up . . . iii 1 178
What are these So wither'd and so wild in their attire? . . *Macbeth* i 3 40
Wither'd murder, Alarum'd by his sentinel, the wolf . . . ii 1 52
I would give you some violets, but they withered all when my father died . . . . *Hamlet* iv 5 185
O, wither'd is the garland of the war, The soldier's pole is fall'n *Ant. and Cleo.* iv 15 64
You were as flowers, now wither'd: even so These herblets shall *Cymb.* iv 2 286
A wither'd branch, that's only green at top; The motto, 'In hac spe vivo' . . . . *Pericles* ii 2 43
The fairest, sweet'st, and best lies here, Who wither'd in her spring of year . . . . iv 4 35
Withering. Long withering out a young man's revenue *M. N. Dream* i 1 7
Withering on the virgin thorn Grows, lives, and dies in single blessedness . . . . i 1 77
Withheld. To one his lands withheld, and to the other A land itself at large . . . . *As Y. Like It* v 4 174
To enforce these rights so forcibly withheld . . . *K. John* i 1 18
Oft have I seen a hot o'erweening cur Run back and bite, because he was withheld . . . . *2 Hen. VI.* v 1 152
The tender prince Would fain have come with me to meet your grace, But by his mother was perforce withheld . . *Richard III.* iii 1 30
Withhold. But she perforce withholds the loved boy *M. N. Dream* ii 1 26
And her withholds from me and other more, Suitors to her *T. of Shrew* i 2 121
Withhold thy speed, dreadful occasion! . . . . *K. John* iv 2 125
Withhold thine indignation, mighty heaven! . . . . . v 6 37
When that my care could not withhold thy riots, What wilt thou do when riot is thy care? . . . . *2 Hen. IV.* iv 5 135
Swearing that you withhold his levied host . . . *1 Hen. VI.* iv 4 31
Withhold revenge, dear God! 'tis not my fault . . . *3 Hen. VI.* ii 2 7
The fear of that withholds my present aid . . . *Richard III.* iv 5 5
Who should withhold me? Not fate, obedience, nor the hand of Mars *Troi. and Cres.* v 3 51
What cause withholds you then, to mourn for him? . *J. Cæsar* iii 2 108
Welcome hither: Your letters did withhold our breaking forth *Ant. and Cleo.* iii 6 79
The gods withhold me! Shall I do that? . . . . . . iv 14 69
The most high gods not minding longer To withhold the vengeance that they had in store . . . . *Pericles* ii 4 4
Within. I would Have sunk the sea within the earth . *Tempest* i 2 11
Within which space she died And left thee there . . . . i 2 279
Within this half hour will he be asleep . . . . . . iii 2 122
You are so without these follies, that these follies are within you *T. G. of Ver.* ii 1 40
He sent me word to stay within: I like his money well . *Mer. Wives* iii 5 59
At an instant?—Within a quarter of an hour . . . . iv 4 5
Search Windsor Castle, elves, within and out . . . . v 5 60
O, think on that; And mercy then will breathe within your lips *Meas. for Meas.* ii 2 78
O, what may man within him hide, Though angel on the outward side! iii 2 285
And then return and sleep within mine inn . . *Com. of Errors* i 2 14
I charge thee, Satan, housed within this man, To yield possession . iv 4 57
The fiend is strong within him.—Ay me, poor man! . . . iv 4 110
He is mad. Some get within him, take his sword away . . v 1 34
Within this hour I was his bondman, sir . . . . . . v 1 288
I Costard, running out, that was safely within, Fell over the threshold *L. L. Lost* iii 1 117
Why should a man, whose blood is warm within, Sit like his grandsire cut in alabaster? . . . . *Mer. of Venice* i 1 83
If the devil be within and that temptation without, I know he will choose it . . . . i 2 105
But here an angel in a golden bed Lies all within . . . . ii 7 59
I have within my mind A thousand raw tricks . . . . . iii 4 76
The spirit of my father, which I think is within me, begins to mutiny *As Y. Like It* i 1 24
Be the jacks fair within, the jills fair without? . . *T. of Shrew* iv 1 51
Which is within a very little of nothing . . . . *All's Well* ii 4 27
Yonder is heavy news within between two soldiers and my young lady iii 2 35
And then Let nature crush the sides o' the earth together And mar the seeds within! . . . . *W. Tale* iv 4 490
Go, stand within; let me alone with him . . . . *K. John* iv 1 85
What is the matter, my lord?—Ho! who is within there? *Richard II.* v 2 74
But this lies all within the will of God, To whom I do appeal *Hen. V.* i 2 289
Break a lance, And run a tilt at death within a chair *1 Hen. VI.* iii 2 51
If they perceive . . . that within ourselves we disagree . . . iv 1 140
Drown'd with grief, Whose flood begins to flow within mine eyes *2 Hen. VI.* iii 1 199
What ugly sights of death within mine eyes! . . . *Richard III.* i 4 23
Within these forty hours Surrey durst better Have burnt that tongue than said so . . . . *Hen. VIII.* iii 2 253
And yet will he, within three pound, lift as much as his brother *T. and C.* i 2 126
'Tis much pride For fair without the fair within to hide *Rom. and Jul.* i 3 90
The gods confound—hear me, you good gods all—The Athenians both within and out that wall! . . . . *T. of Athens* iv 1 38
Within the bond of marriage, tell me, Brutus, Is it excepted I should know no secrets That appertain to you? . . . . *J. Cæsar* ii 1 280
Help, ho! they murder Cæsar! Who's within? . . . . . ii 2 3
I'll call upon you straight: abide within. It is concluded *Macbeth* iii 1 140
'Tis better thee without than he within . . . . . . iii 4 14
When all that is within him does condemn Itself for being there . v 2 24
But I have that within which passeth show; These but the trappings and the suits of woe . . . . *Hamlet* i 2 85

Within. Whether aught, to us unknown, afflicts him thus, That, open'd, lies within our remedy . . . *Hamlet* ii 2 18
Whiles rank corruption, mining all within, Infects unseen . . . iii 4 148
Good madam, keep yourself within yourself . . . *Ant. and Cleo.* ii 5 75
I do not think So fair an outward and such stuff within Endows a man but he.—You speak him far.—I do extend him, sir, within himself *Cymbeline* i 1 23
When he was less furnished than now he is with that which makes him both without and within . . . . i 4 10
This will witness outwardly, As strongly as the conscience does within ii 2 36
Even when I wake, it is Without me, as within me; not imagined, felt iv 2 307
To shame the guise o' the world, I will begin The fashion, less without and more within . . . . v 1 33
Withold. S. Withold footed thrice the old; He met the night-mare *Lear* iii 4 125
Without. And deal in her command without her power *Tempest* v 1 271
Are all these things perceived in me?—They are all perceived without ye.—Without me? they cannot.—Without you? nay, that's certain, for, without you were so simple, none else would: but you are so without these follies, that these follies are within you *T. G. of Ver.* ii 1 35
Thou common friend, that's without faith or love . . . v 4 62
When I suddenly call you, come forth, and without any pause *M. Wives* iii 3 12
Such a one as a man may not speak of without he say 'Sir-reverence' *Com. of Errors* iii 2 92
He may stay him: marry, not without the prince be willing *Much Ado* iii 3 86
In the wood, a league without the town . . . . *M. N. Dream* i 1 165
Our intent Was to be gone from Athens, where we might, Without the peril of the Athenian law . . . . . . iv 1 158
Set a deep glass of rhenish wine on the contrary casket, for if the devil be within and that temptation without, I know he will choose it *Mer. of Venice* i 2 105
But didst thou hear without wondering? . . . *As Y. Like It* iii 2 181
Be the jacks fair within, the jills fair without? . . *T. of Shrew* iv 1 52
Businesses which none without thee can sufficiently manage *W. Tale* iv 2 16
What seal is that, that hangs without thy bosom? . *Richard II.* v 2 56
Not a man, for being simply man, Hath any honour, but honour for those honours That are without him . . . *Troi. and Cres.* iii 3 82
That man, how dearly ever parted, How much in having, or without or in iii 3 97
Most putrefied core, so fair without . . . . . v 8 1
'Tis much pride For fair without the fair within to hide . *Rom. and Jul.* i 3 90
There is no world without Verona walls, But purgatory . . . iii 3 17
Bring in thy ranks, but leave without thy rage . . *T. of Athens* v 4 39
They are, my lord, without the palace gate . . . *Macbeth* iii 1 47
'Tis better thee without than he within. Is he dispatch'd? . . iii 4 14
But where is he?—Without, my lord; guarded, to know your pleasure *Hamlet* iv 3 14
Sirs, stand you all without.—No, let's come in . . . iv 5 112
Some such squire he was That turn'd your wit the seamy side without *Othello* iv 2 146
You speak of him when he was less furnished than now he is with that which makes him both without and within . . *Cymbeline* i 4 10
Art thou a feodary for this act, and look'st So virgin-like without? . iii 2 22
The dream's here still: even when I wake, it is Without me, as within me . . . . iv 2 307
To shame the guise o' the world, I will begin The fashion, less without and more within . . . . v 1 33
Without-book. Nor no without-book prologue, faintly spoke After the prompter . . . . . . *Rom. and Jul.* i 4 7
Without-door. Praise her but for this her without-door form *W. Tale* ii 1 69
Withstand. They have won the bridge, killing all those that withstand them . . . . *2 Hen. VI.* iv 5 4
Stand by us?—Ay, in despite of all that shall withstand you *3 Hen. VI.* iv 1 146
Withstood. Rage must be withstood: Give me his gage . *Richard II.* i 1 173
Witless. Where youth, and cost, and witless bravery keeps *Meas. for Meas.* i 3 10
A witty mother! witless else her son . . . *T. of Shrew* ii 1 266
Behold, distraction, frenzy, and amazement, Like witless antics, one another meet . . . . . . *Troi. and Cres.* v 3 86
Witness. O heaven, O earth, bear witness to this sound! . *Tempest* iii 1 68
And Silvia—witness Heaven, that made her fair!—Shows Julia but a swarthy Ethiope . . . . . . *T. G. of Ver.* ii 6 25
To whom, thyself art witness, I am betroth'd . . . . iv 2 110
Which, if my augury deceive me not, Witness good bringing up . iv 4 74
Bear witness, Heaven, I have my wish for ever . . . v 4 119
Bear vitness that me have stay six or seven, two, tree hours . *Mer. Wives* iii 3 36
I suspect without cause, mistress, do I?—Heaven be my witness you do iv 2 139
With the warrant of womanhood and the witness of a good conscience . iv 2 220
Letters to Angelo,—The provost, he shall bear them,—whose contents Shall witness to him I am near at home . . . *Meas. for Meas.* iv 3 99
Is this the witness, friar? First, let her show her face, and after speak v 1 167
This is no witness for Lord Angelo.—Now I come to't . . v 1 193
And in the witness of his proper ear, To call him villain? . . v 1 310
That the world may witness that my end Was wrought by nature *C. of Er.* i 1 34
He's at two hands with me, and that my two ears can witness . ii 1 46
My bones bear witness, That since have felt the vigour of his rage . iv 4 80
I deliver'd it.—And I am witness with her that she did . . iv 4 92
God and the rope-maker bear me witness That I was sent for nothing but a rope! . . . . iv 4 93
Witness you, That he is borne about invisible . . . . v 1 186
That goldsmith there, were he not pack'd with her, Could witness it . v 1 220
In truth, thus far I witness with him, That he dined not at home . v 1 254
All these old witnesses—I cannot err—Tell me thou art my son . v 1 317
All that know me in the city Can witness with me that it is not so . v 1 324
It is the witness still of excellency To put a strange face on his own perfection . . . . *Much Ado* ii 3 48
They say the lady is fair; 'tis a truth, I can bear them witness . ii 3 240
I will disparage her no farther till you are my witnesses . . iii 2 132
Comes not that blood as modest evidence To witness simple virtue? . iv 1 39
Thou art full of piety, as shall be proved upon thee by good witness . iv 2 82
Praising myself, who, I myself will bear witness, is praiseworthy . v 2 89
An if my face were but as fair as yours, My favour were as great; be witness this . . . . *L. L. Lost* v 2 33
An evil soul producing holy witness Is like a villain with a smiling cheek, A goodly apple rotten at the heart . . . *Mer. of Venice* i 3 100
I am yours?—Heaven and thy thoughts are witness that thou art . ii 6 32
Lorenzo here Shall witness I set forth as soon as you . . v 1 271
As mine eye doth his effigies witness Most truly limn'd and living in your face, Be truly welcome hither . . . *As Y. Like It* ii 7 193
Hang there, my verse, in witness of my love . . . iii 2 1
Make mine eye the witness Of that report which I so oft have heard *T. of Shrew* ii 1 52
'Tis a match.—Amen, say we: we will be witnesses . . . ii 1 322

Witness. More Than words can witness, or your thoughts can guess *T. of Shrew* ii 1 338
And since mine eyes are witness of her lightness, I will with you . . iv 2 24
Take the priest, clerk, and some sufficient honest witnesses . . iv 4 95
Here's packing, with a witness, to deceive us all! . . . v 1 121
What is not holy, that we swear not by, But take the High'st to witness: then, pray you, tell me . . . . . . *All's Well* iv 2 24
Methought you said You saw one here in court could witness it . v 3 200
If I do feign, you witnesses above Punish my life! . . *T. Night* v 1 140
I witness to The times that brought them in . . . *W. Tale* iv 1 11
Five justices' hands at it, and witnesses more than my pack will hold . iv 4 288
A bargain! And, friends unknown, you shall bear witness to't . . iv 4 395
But, come on, Contract us 'fore these witnesses . . . iv 4 401
So be blest my spirit!—Then, good my lords, bear witness to his oath . v 1 72
I bring you witnesses, Twice fifteen thousand hearts of England's breed *K. John* ii 1 274
Then shall this hand and seal Witness against us to damnation! . . iv 2 218
May be a precedent and witness good . . . . *Richard II.* ii 1 130
And you can witness with me this is true . . . . iv 1 63
That he is old, the more the pity, his white hairs do witness it *1 Hen. IV.* ii 4 515
God witness with me, . . . How cold it struck my heart! *2 Hen. IV.* iv 5 150
Witness our too much memorable shame When Cressy battle fatally was struck, And all our princes captived . . . . . *Hen. V.* ii 4 53
Upon the which, I trust, Shall witness live in brass of this day's work iv 3 97
I hope your majesty is pear me testimony and witness . . . iv 8 38
Witness the night, your garments, your lowliness . . . iv 8 54
And bear me witness all, That here I kiss her as my sovereign queen . v 2 385
Fain would mine eyes be witness with mine ears . . *1 Hen. VI.* ii 3 9
Hark ye; not so: in witness, take ye that . . . . iii 4 37
You cannot witness for me, being slain . . . . . iv 5 43
Last time, I danced attendance on his will Till Paris was besieged, famisd'd and lost.—That can I witness . . . *2 Hen. VI.* i 3 176
God is my witness, I am falsely accused by the villain . . i 3 192
He did vow upon his knees he would be even with me: I have good witness . . . . i 3 204
For he hath witness of his servant's malice . . . . i 3 213
Witness my tears, I cannot stay to speak . . . . ii 4 86
I shall not want false witness to condemn me . . . . iii 1 168
'Tis meet that lucky ruler be employ'd; Witness the fortune he hath had iii 1 292
Heavens and honour be witness that no want of resolution in me makes me betake me to my heels . . . . iv 8 65
And be a witness That Bona shall be wife to the English king *3 Hen. VI.* iii 3 138
And, that I love the tree from whence thou sprang'st, Witness the loving kiss I give the fruit . . . . v 7 32
Tears in her eyes, The bleeding witness of her hatred by *Richard III.* i 2 234
Alas! alas! Witness my son, now in the shade of death . . i 3 267
Then be your eyes the witness of this ill: See how I am bewitch'd . iii 4 69
You come too late of our intents, Yet witness what you hear we did intend . . . . iii 5 70
Your mother lives a witness to that vow . . . . . iii 7 180
A dire induction am I witness to, And will to France . . . iv 4 5
Triumph not in my woes! God witness with me, I have wept for thine iv 4 60
Urged on the examinations, proofs, confessions Of divers witnesses *Hen. VIII.* ii 1 17
Yet, heaven bear witness, . . . if I be not faithful! . . . ii 1 59
Heaven witness, I have been to you a true and humble wife . . ii 4 22
His noble jury and foul cause can witness . . . . . iii 2 269
Bear witness, all that have not hearts of iron . . . . iii 2 424
He was most princely: ever witness for him Those twins of learning that he raised in you, Ipswich and Oxford! . . . . iv 2 57
It fits we thus proceed, or else no witness Would come against you . v 1 107
Ween you of better luck, I mean, in perjured witness, than your master? v 1 136
As, of late days, our neighbours, The upper Germany, can dearly witness v 3 30
And let heaven Witness, how dear I hold this confirmation . . v 3 174
Here's 'In witness whereof the parties interchangeably' *Troi. and Cres.* iii 2 61
Go to, a bargain made: seal it, seal it; I'll be the witness . . iii 2 205
Take his hand,—Witness the process of your speech . . . iv 1 8
Thereto witness may My surname, Coriolanus . . . *Coriolanus* iv 5 73
Witness of the malice and displeasure Which thou shouldst bear me . iv 5 78
You shall bear A better witness back than words . . . v 3 204
This is a witness that I am thy son . . . . *T. Andron.* ii 3 116
Witness the sorrow that their sister makes . . . . iii 1 119
Be, as your titles witness, Imperious and impatient of your wrongs . v 1 5
Well, let my deeds be witness of my worth . . . . v 1 103
Witness this wretched stump, witness these crimson lines; Witness these trenches made by grief and care; Witness the tiring day and heavy night; Witness all sorrow . . . . v 2 22
'Tis true, 'tis true; witness my knife's sharp point . . . v 3 63
My frosty signs and chaps of age, Grave witnesses of true experience . v 3 78
My scars can witness, dumb although they are, That my report is just v 3 114
The villain is alive in Titus' house, And as he is, to witness this is true v 3 124
I call the gods to witness, I will choose Mine heir from forth the beggars of the world, And dispossess her all . . . . *T. of Athens* i 1 137
I was sending to use Lord Timon myself, these gentlemen can witness iii 2 57
I'm weary of this charge, the gods can witness . . . . iii 4 25
The gods are witness, Ne'er did poor steward wear a truer grief . iv 3 486
Witness the hole you made in Cæsar's heart . . . *J. Cæsar* v 1 31
Be thou my witness that against my will, As Pompey was, am I compell'd to set Upon one battle all our liberties . . . . . v 1 74
Go get some water, And wash this filthy witness from your hand *Macb.* ii 2 47
Having no witness to confirm my speech . . . . . v 1 21
Till I may deliver, Upon the witness of these gentlemen, This marvel *Hamlet* i 2 194
Witness this army of such mass and charge . . . . iv 4 47
Witness the world, that I create thee here My lord and master . *Lear* v 3 77
Here comes the lady; let her witness it . . . . *Othello* i 3 170
Witness, you ever-burning lights above, You elements that clip us round about, Witness that here Iago doth give up The execution of his wit! . . . . iii 3 463
Now I find I had suborn'd the witness, And he's indicted falsely . iii 4 153
O, bear me witness, night,— What man is this? . *Ant. and Cleo.* iv 9 5
Be witness to me, O thou blessed moon, When men revolted shall upon record Bear hateful memory, poor Enobarbus did Before thy face repent! . . . . iv 9 7
This will witness outwardly, As strongly as the conscience does within . . . . *Cymbeline* ii 2 35
If you will make't an action, call witness to't . . . . ii 3 156
Alas, good lady!—I false! Thy conscience witness . . . iii 4 48
Do thou thy master's bidding: when thou see'st him, A little witness my obedience . . . . iii 4 68

Witness. Is not this true?—Our cheeks and hollow eyes do witness it *Pericles* i 4 51
Here comes my daughter, she can witness it ii 5 66
Witnessed. That every eye which in this forest looks Shall see thy virtue witness'd every where *As Y. Like It* iii 2 8
So looks the strand whereon the imperious flood Hath left a witness'd usurpation 2 *Hen. IV.* i 1 63
Which was to my belief witness'd the rather, For that I saw *Macbeth* iv 3 184
Witnesseth. Thou the beggar; for so witnesseth thy lowliness *L. L. Lost* iv 1 81
And all their minds transfigured so together, More witnesseth than fancy's images *M. N. Dream* v 1 25
Witnessing. Thy sun sets weeping in the lowly west, Witnessing storms to come. *Richard II.* ii 4 22
Pale they look with fear, as witnessing The truth on our side 1 *Hen. VI.* ii 4 63
Wit-old. It rejoiceth my intellect: true wit!—Offered by a child to an old man; which is wit-old *L. L. Lost* v 1 66
Wit-snapper. What a wit-snapper are you! *Mer. of Venice* iii 5 55
Wittenberg. For your intent In going back to school in Wittenberg, It is most retrograde to our desire *Hamlet* i 2 113
Let not thy mother lose her prayers, Hamlet: I pray thee, stay with us; go not to Wittenberg i 2 119
And what make you from Wittenberg, Horatio? Marcellus? i 2 164
But what, in faith, make you from Wittenberg?—A truant disposition. i 2 168
Wittiest. It is the wittiest partition that ever I heard discourse *M. N. Dream* v 1 168
Wittily. As the old hermit of Prague, that never saw pen and ink, very wittily said *T. Night* iv 2 16
Witting. Swift-winged with desire to get a grave, As witting I no other comfort have 1 *Hen. VI.* ii 5 16
Wittingly. Withhold revenge, dear God! 'tis not my fault, Nor wittingly have I infringed my vow 3 *Hen. VI.* ii 2 8
If I drown myself wittingly, it argues an act *Hamlet* v 1 11
Argal, she drowned herself wittingly.—Nay, but hear you v 1 13
Wittol!—Cuckold! the devil himself hath not such a name *Mer. Wives* ii 2 313
Wittolly. They say the jealous wittolly knave hath masses of money ii 2 283
Witty. Of excellent discourse, Pretty and witty *Com. of Errors* iii 1 110
A marvellous witty fellow, I assure you; but I will go about with him *Much Ado* iv 2 27
Pleasant without scurrility, witty without affection *L. L. Lost* v 1 4
It is extempore, from my mother-wit.—A witty mother! *T. of Shrew* ii 1 266
Go to, thou art a witty fool; I have found thee *All's Well* ii 4 32
Thou wert as witty a piece of Eve's flesh as any in Illyria *T. Night* i 5 30
What says Quinapalus? 'Better a witty fool than a foolish wit'. i 5 39
It is no matter how witty, so it be eloquent and full of invention iii 2 46
I am not only witty in myself, but the cause that wit is in other men 2 *Hen. IV.* i 2 11
They are soldiers, Witty, courteous, liberal, full of spirit 3 *Hen. VI.* i 2 43
The deep-revolving witty Buckingham *Richard III.* iv 2 42
Others, to hear the city Abused extremely, and to cry 'That's witty!' *Hen. VIII.* Epil. 6
She's making her ready, she'll come straight: you must be witty now *Troi. and Cres.* iii 2 32
Were our witty empress well afoot, She would applaud *T. Andron.* iv 2 29
Well praised! How if she be black and witty? *Othello* ii 1 132
Wived. An I could get me but a wife in the stews, I were manned, horsed, and wived 2 *Hen. IV.* i 2 61
But, good lieutenant, is your general wived?—Most fortunately *Othello* ii 1 60
So he thrived, That he is promised to be wived *Pericles* v 2 275
Wives. These that accuse him in his intent towards our wives are a yoke of his discarded men *Mer. Wives* ii 1 181
Our revolted wives share damnation together iii 2 40
Wives may be merry, and yet honest too iv 2 107
Let our wives . . . Appoint a meeting with this old fat fellow iv 4 13
Now, good Sir John, how like you Windsor wives? v 5 110
Money buys lands, and wives are sold by fate v 5 246
That we may lighten our own hearts and our wives' heels *Much Ado* v 4 121
Do not curst wives hold that self-sovereignty Only for praise sake? *L. L. Lost* iv 1 36
I had rather he should shrive me than wive me *Mer. of Venice* i 2 145
Here's a small trifle of wives: alas, fifteen wives is nothing! ii 2 170
When you shall please to play the thieves for wives, I'll watch as long for you then ii 6 23
The rest aloof are the Dardanian wives, With bleared visages iii 2 58
Have you not been acquainted with goldsmiths' wives, and conned them out of rings?—Not so *As Y. Like It* iii 2 288
Horns, which such as you are fain to be beholding to your wives for iv 1 60
Maids are May when they are maids, but the sky changes when they are wives iv 1 150
And I have thrust myself into this maze, Haply to wive and thrive as best I may *T. of Shrew* i 2 56
I come to wive it wealthily in Padua; If wealthily, then happily i 2 75
See where she comes and brings your froward wives As prisoners v 2 119
But when I came, alas! to wive, With hey, ho, &c. *T. Night* v 1 406
I wonder, sir, sith wives are monsters to you, . . . Yet you desire to marry *All's Well* v 3 155
Should all despair That have revolted wives, the tenth of mankind Would hang themselves *W. Tale* i 2 199
One Mistress Tale-porter, and five or six honest wives that were present iv 4 273
No more such wives; therefore, no wife: one worse, And better used v 1 56
Which fault lies on the hazards of all husbands That marry wives *K. John* i 1 120
And leave your children, wives, and you in peace ii 1 257
Let wives with child Pray that their burthens may not fall this day iii 1 89
Some poison'd by their wives; some sleeping kill'd *Richard II.* iii 2 159
Take no leave, For there will be a world of water shed Upon the parting of your wives and you 1 *Hen. IV.* iii 1 95
I'll haste the writer and withal Break with your wives of your departure iii 1 144
Here come our wives, and let us take our leave iii 1 191
Filthy dowlas: I have given them away to bakers' wives iii 3 80
Whiles the mad mothers with their howls confused Do break the clouds, as did the wives of Jewry *Hen. V.* iii 3 40
Leaving their wits with their wives iii 7 160
Some swearing, some crying for a surgeon, some upon their wives. iv 1 145
Let us our lives, our souls, Our debts, our careful wives, Our children, and our sins lay on the king! iv 1 248
The English beach Pales in the flood with men, with wives, and boys v Prol. 10
We and our wives and children all will fight 1 *Hen. VI.* iii 1 100
So worthless peasants bargain for their wives, As market-men for oxen v 5 53
I never read but England's kings have had Large sums of gold and dowries with their wives 2 *Hen. VI.* i 1 129
Even in their wives' and children's sight, Be hang'd up for example iv 2 189
Wives. And we charge and command that their wives be as free as heart can wish 2 *Hen. VI.* iv 7 132
Take your houses over your heads, ravish your wives and daughters iv 8 31
Wives for their husbands, And orphans for their parents' timeless death—Shall rue the hour that ever thou wast born. 3 *Hen. VI.* v 6 41
In change of lust; Which stretched to their servants, daughters, wives *Richard III.* iii 5 82
The insatiate greediness of his desires, And his enforcement of the city wives iii 7 8
If you do fight in safeguard of your wives, Your wives shall welcome home the conquerers v 3 259
You having lands, and blest with beauteous wives, They would restrain the one, distain the other v 3 321
Shall these enjoy our lands? lie with our wives? Ravish our daughters? v 3 336
Make wells and Niobes of the maids and wives *Troi. and Cres.* v 10 19
If you'll stand fast, we'll beat them to their wives. *Coriolanus* i 4 41
Lest that thy wives with spits and boys with stones In puny battle slay me. iv 4 5
Ourselves, our wives, and children, on our knees, Are bound to pray for you iv 6 22
You have holp . . . To see your wives dishonour'd to your noses iv 6 83
Men, wives, and children stare, cry out, and run, As it were doomsday *J. Cæsar* iii 1 97
Your wives, your daughters, Your matrons, and your maids, could not fill up The cistern of my lust *Macbeth* iv 3 61
And bid me, when my fate would have me wive, To give it her *Othello* iii 4 64
If she be not honest, chaste, and true, There's no man happy; the purest of their wives Is foul as slander iv 2 18
But I do think it is their husbands' faults If wives do fall iv 3 88
Let husbands know Their wives have sense like them iv 3 95
Would we had all such wives! *Ant. and Cleo.* ii 2 65
Enter the city, clip your wives, your friends, Tell them your feats iv 8 8
If each of you should take this course, how many Must murder wives much better than themselves For wrying but a little! *Cymbeline* v 1 4
Be it our wives, our children, or ourselves, The curse of heaven and men succeed their evils! *Pericles* i 4 103
Wiving. Hanging and wiving goes by destiny *Mer. of Venice* ii 9 83
Besides that hook of wiving, Fairness which strikes the eye *Cymbeline* v 5 167
Wizard. Peace, doting wizard, peace! I am not mad *Com. of Errors* iv 4 61
Wizards know their times: Deep night, dark night, the silent of the night 2 *Hen. VI.* i 4 18
Somerset Hath made the wizard famous in his death v 2 69
Says a wizard told him that by G His issue disinherited should be *Richard III.* i 1 56
Wode. And here am I, and wode within this wood *M. N. Dream* ii 1 192
Woe. There's no harm done.—O, woe the day! *Tempest* i 2 15
Our hint of woe Is common; every day some sailor's wife, The masters of some merchant, and the merchant, Have just our theme of woe. ii 1 3
I am woe for't, sir.—Irreparable is the loss v 1 139
I confess There is no woe to his correction *T. G. of Ver.* ii 4 138
I have fed upon this woe already, And now excess of it will make me surfeit iii 1 219
Wringing her hands, whose whiteness so became them As if but now they waxed pale for woe iii 1 228
To think upon her woes I do protest That I have wept a hundred several times iv 4 149
To the nightingale's complaining notes Tune my distresses and record my woes v 4 6
He's in prison.—Woe me! for what? *Meas. for Meas.* i 4 26
Pardon is still the nurse of second woe ii 1 298
My mirth it much displeased, but pleased my woe iv 1 13
Heaven shield your grace from woe! v 1 118
By the doom of death end woes and all *Com. of Errors* i 1 2
When your words are done, My woes end likewise with the evening sun i 1 28
Seeming as burdened With lesser weight but not with lesser woe i 1 109
Headstrong liberty is lash'd with woe ii 1 15
Whilst man and master laugh my woes to scorn ii 2 207
Converting all your sounds of woe Into Hey nonny, nonny *Much Ado* ii 3 70
Measure his woe the length and breadth of mine v 1 11
With songs of woe, Round about her tomb they go. v 3 14
And Hymen now with luckier issue speed's Than this for whom we render'd up this woe v 3 33
O short-lived pride! Not fair? alack for woe! *L. L. Lost* iv 1 15
So ridest thou triumphing in my woe iv 3 35
Never so weary, never so in woe, Bedabbled with the dew *M. N. Dream* iii 2 442
Puts the wretch that lies in woe In remembrance of a shroud v 1 384
Your husband, being troubled with a shrew, Measures my husband's sorrow by his woe *T. of Shrew* v 2 29
It shall become thee well to act my woes. *T. Night* i 4 26
Woe the while! O, cut my lace, lest my heart, cracking it, Break too! *W. Tale* iii 2 173
Cry 'woe!'—the queen, the queen, The sweet'st, dear'st creature's dead iii 2 201
Do not repent these things, for they are heavier Than all thy woes can stir iii 2 210
If all the world could have seen't, the woe had been universal v 2 100
Leave those woes alone which I alone Am bound to under-bear *K. John* iii 1 64
My reasonable part produces reason How I may be deliver'd of these woes iii 4 55
Let us pay the time but needful woe. v 7 110
Woe doth the heavier sit, Where it perceives it is but faintly borne *Rich. II.* i 3 280
Though death be poor, it ends a mortal woe ii 1 152
What it is, that is not yet known; what I cannot name; 'tis nameless woe, I wot ii 2 40
Have woe to woe, sorrow to sorrow join'd ii 2 66
What a tide of woes Comes rushing on this woeful land at once! ii 2 98
Thy sun sets weeping in the lowly west, Witnessing storms to come, woe, and unrest ii 4 22
Cry woe, destruction, ruin, and decay; The worst is death iii 2 102
Wise men ne'er sit and wail their woes, But presently prevent the ways to wail iii 2 178
There I'll pine away; A king, woe's slave, shall kingly woe obey iii 2 210
Alack, alack, for woe, That any harm should stain so fair a show! iii 3 70
Or shall we play the wantons with our woes, And make some pretty match with shedding tears? iii 3 164
Every one doth so Against a change; woe is forerun with woe iii 4 28
Come, ladies, go, To meet at London London's king in woe iii 4 97
For telling me these news of woe, Pray God the plants thou graft'st may never grow iii 4 100
Let it not be so, Lest child, child's children, cry against you 'woe!' iv 1 149
The woe's to come; the children yet unborn Shall feel this day iv 1 322

Woe. So two, together weeping, make one woe . . . *Richard II.* v 1 86
We make woe wanton with this fond delay: Once more, adieu . . v 1 101
My soul is full of woe, That blood should sprinkle me to make me grow v 6 45
Not in pleasure but in passion, not in words only, but in woes also *1 Hen. IV.* ii 4 459
Woe to my lord chief-justice!—Let vultures vile seize on his lungs! *2 Hen. IV.* v 3 145
Whose guiltless drops Are every one a woe, a sore complaint *Hen. V.* i 2 26
Many of our princes—woe the while!—Lie drown'd and soak'd in mercenary blood . . iv 7 78
And will be partner of your weal or woe . *1 Hen. VI.* iii 2 92
Ah, woe is me for Gloucester, wretched man!—Be woe for me, more wretched than he is . *2 Hen. VI.* iii 2 72
Nothing so heavy as these woes of mine . v 2 65
To triumph, like an Amazonian trull, Upon their woes . *3 Hen. VI.* i 4 115
To add more measure to your woes, I come to tell you things . ii 1 105
I, that did never weep, now melt with woe . ii 3 46
Would I were dead! if God's good will were so; For what is in this world but grief and woe? . ii 5 20
Woe above woe! grief more than common grief! . ii 5 94
Was ever king so grieved for subjects' woe? . ii 5 111
Their woes are parcell'd, mine are general *Richard III.* ii 2 81
Woe to that land that's govern'd by a child! . ii 3 11
You live that shall cry woe for this hereafter . iii 2 7
Woe, woe for England! not a whit for me . iii 4 82
Woe's scene, world's shame, grave's due by life usurp'd . iv 4 27
And let my woes frown on the upper hand . iv 4 37
If sorrow can admit society, Tell o'er your woes again by viewing mine iv 4 39
Triumph not in my woes! God witness with me, I have wept for thine iv 4 59
These English woes will make me smile in France . iv 4 115
Compare dead happiness with living woe . iv 4 119
Thy woes will make them [my words] sharp, and pierce like mine. iv 4 125
Why should calamity be full of words?—Windy attorneys to their client woes . iv 4 127
A serious brow, Sad, high, and working, full of state and woe *Hen. VIII.* Prol. 3
Ay, marry, There will be woe indeed . i 3 39
If the duke be guiltless, 'Tis full of woe . ii 1 140
Woe upon ye And all such false professors! . iii 1 114
Cry, Trojans, cry! a Helen and a woe: Cry, cry! *Troi. and Cres.* ii 2 111
With comfort go: Hope of revenge shall hide our inward woe . v 10 31
They have nursed this woe, in feeding life . *T. Andron.* iii 1 74
Here stands my other son, a banish'd man, And here my brother, weeping at my woes . iii 1 100
O, what a sympathy of woe is this, As far from help as Limbo is from bliss! . iii 1 148
If there were reason for these miseries, Then into limits could I bind my woes . iii 1 221
My bowels cannot hide her woes, But like a drunkard must I vomit them . iii 1 231
Woe is me to think upon thy woes More than remembrance of my father's death . iii 1 240
Eat no more Than will preserve just so much strength in us As will revenge these bitter woes of ours . iii 2 3
Thou map of woe, that thus dost talk in signs! . iii 2 12
We are all undone! Now help, or woe betide thee evermore! . iv 2 56
Woe to her chance, and damn'd her loathed choice! Accursed the offspring of so foul a fiend! . iv 2 78
Chief architect and plotter of these woes . v 3 122
May I govern so, To heal Rome's harms, and wipe away her woe! . v 3 148
Friends should associate friends in grief and woe . v 3 169
You sad Andronici, have done with woes . v 3 176
I cannot bound a pitch above dull woe *Rom. and Jul.* i 4 21
I have forgot that name, and that name's woe . ii 3 46
If e'er thou wast thyself and these woes thine, Thou and these woes were all for Rosaline: And art thou changed? . ii 3 78
This day's black fate on more days doth depend; This but begins the woe . iii 1 125
If he be slain, say 'I'; or if not, no: Brief sounds determine of my weal or woe . iii 2 51
These griefs, these woes, these sorrows make me old . iii 2 89
Your tributary drops belong to woe, Which you, mistaking, offer up to joy . iii 2 103
Tybalt's death Was woe enough, if it had ended there . iii 2 115
If sour woe delights in fellowship And needly will be rank'd with other griefs . iii 2 116
No words can that woe sound . iii 2 126
These times of woe afford no time to woo. . iii 4 8
More light and light; more dark and dark our woes! . iii 5 36
All these woes shall serve For sweet discourses in our time to come . iii 5 52
O woe! O woful, woful, woful day! Most lamentable day, most woful day! . iv 5 49
'My heart is full of woe:' O, play me some merry dump, to comfort me iv 5 107
O woe! thy canopy is dust and stones . v 3 13
We see the ground whereon these woes do lie; But the true ground of all these piteous woes We cannot without circumstance descry . v 3 180
What further woe conspires against mine age? . v 3 212
And then will I be general of your woes, And lead you even to death . v 3 219
For never was a story of more woe Than this of Juliet and her Romeo . v 3 309
But, woe the while! our fathers' minds are dead *J. Cæsar* i 3 82
Woe to the hand that shed this costly blood! . iii 1 258
Our royal master's murder'd!—Woe, alas! What, in our house? *Macbeth* ii 3 92
No mind that's honest But in it shares some woe . iv 3 198
And our whole kingdom To be contracted in one brow of woe *Hamlet* i 2 4
But I have that within which passeth show; These but the trappings and the suits of woe . i 2 86
We pray you, throw to earth This unprevailing woe . i 2 107
Woe is me, To have seen what I have seen, see what I see! . iii 1 168
But, woe is me, you are so sick of late, So far from cheer . iii 2 173
One woe doth tread upon another's heel, So fast they follow . iv 7 164
O, treble woe Fall ten times treble on that cursed head! . v 1 269
What is it ye would see? If aught of woe or wonder, cease your search v 2 374
Woe, that too late repents,—O, sir, are you come? *Lear* i 4 279
Shall of a corn cry woe, And turn his sleep to wake . iii 2 33
When we our betters see bearing our woes, We scarcely think our miseries our foes. Who alone suffers suffers most i' the mind . iii 6 109
And woes by wrong imaginations lose The knowledge of themselves . iv 6 290
Our present business Is general woe . v 3 319
Or, at the least, so prove it, . . . or woe upon thy life! *Othello* iii 3 366
The star is fall'n.—And time is at his period.—Alas, and woe! *Ant. and Cleo.* iv 14 107

Woe. Woe, woe are we, sir, you may not live to wear All your true followers out . *Ant. and Cleo.* iv 14 133
So it should be, that none but Antony Should conquer Antony; but woe 'tis so! . iv 15 17
Those that are betray'd Do feel the treason sharply, yet the traitor Stands in worse case of woe . *Cymbeline* iii 4 89
Malice and lucre in them Have laid this woe here . iv 2 325
I, in mine own woe charm'd, Could not find death where I did hear him groan . v 3 68
Woe is my heart That the poor soldier . . . cannot be found . v 5 2
As sick men do Who know the world, see heaven, but, feeling woe, Gripe not at earthly joys as erst they did *Pericles* i 1 48
Our tongues and sorrows do sound deep Our woes into the air . i 4 14
I'll then discourse our woes, felt several years . i 4 18
Omit we all their dole and woe . iii Gower 42
Thou hast a heart Than even cracks for woe! This chanced to-night . iii 2 77
How your favour's changed With this unprofitable woe! . iv 1 26
This borrow'd passion stands for true old woe . iv 4 24
Our scene must play His daughter's woe and heavy well-a-day . iv 4 49
I am great with woe, and shall deliver weeping . v 1 107
Perform my bidding, or thou livest in woe; Do it, and happy; by my silver bow! . v 1 248
Woe-begone. So dull, so dead in look, so woe-begone *2 Hen. IV.* i 1 71
Woeful. I am a woeful suitor to your honour *Meas. for Meas.* ii 2 27
And till that instant shut My woeful self up in a mourning house *L. L. Lost* v 2 818
This wide and universal theatre Presents more woeful pageants *As Y. Like It* ii 7 138
And then the lover, Sighing like furnace, with a woeful ballad ii 7 148
What a tide of woes Comes rushing on this woeful land at once! *Rich. II.* ii 2 99
A woeful pageant have we here beheld.—The woe's to come . iv 1 321
Let them tell thee tales Of woeful ages long ago betid . v 1 42
O Lord, have mercy on me, woful man! . *1 Hen. VI.* i 4 71
Accursed fatal hand That hath contrived this woful tragedy! . i 4 77
The most unnatural wounds, Which thou thyself hast given her woful breast . iii 3 51
That I may dew it with my mournful tears; Nor let the rain of heaven wet this place, To wash away my woful monuments *2 Hen. VI.* iii 2 342
A woful looker-on When as the noble Duke of York was slain *3 Hen. VI.* ii 1 45
How will the country for these woful chances Misthink the king! . ii 5 107
Sad-hearted men, much overgone with care, Here sits a king more woful ii 5 124
And made her widow to a woful bed . *Richard III.* i 2 249
My woful banishment, Could all but answer for that peevish brat? . i 3 193
Farewell, thou woful welcomer of glory! . iv 1 90
The cardinal Will have his will, and she must fall.—'Tis woful *Hen. VIII.* ii 1 167
A woful Cressid 'mongst the merry Greeks! . *Troi. and Cres.* iv 4 58
The woful fere And father of that chaste dishonour'd dame *T. Andron.* iv 1 89
Welcome, dread Fury, to my woful house . v 2 82
I am as woful as Virginius was, And have a thousand times more cause v 3 50
O woful sympathy! Piteous predicament! . *Rom. and Jul.* iii 3 85
O lamentable day!—O woful time! . iv 5 30
O woe! O woful, woful, woful day! Most lamentable day, most woful day! . iv 5 49
O noble Cæsar!—O woful day!—O traitors, villains! . *J. Cæsar* iii 2 204
Confused events New hatch'd to the woeful time . *Macbeth* ii 3 64
If there be more, more woeful, hold it in; For I am almost ready to dissolve . *Lear* v 3 202
The rough and woeful music that we have, Cause it to sound *Pericles* iii 2 88
His woeful queen we leave at Ephesus, Unto Diana there a votaress iv Gower 3
Woefullest. It will the woefullest division prove That ever fell upon this cursed earth . *Richard II.* iv 1 146
Take my heart with thee.—A jewel, lock'd into the woful'st cask That ever did contain a thing of worth *2 Hen. VI.* iii 2 409
My noble father, The woful'st man that ever lived in Rome *T. Andron.* iii 1 290
Woe-wearied. My woe-wearied tongue is mute and dumb *Richard III.* iv 4 18
Wo ha, ho! sola, sola!—Who calls? . *Mer. of Venice* v 1 39
Wolf. A wolf, nay, worse, a fellow all in buff *Com. of Errors* iv 2 36
On lion, bear, or wolf, or bull, On meddling monkey *M. N. Dream* ii 1 180
Now the hungry lion roars, And the wolf behowls the moon . v 1 379
You may as well use question with the wolf . *Mer. of Venice* iv 1 73
Thy currish spirit Govern'd a wolf . iv 1 134
How much the better To fall before the lion than the wolf! . *T. Night* iii 1 140
They have scared away two of my best sheep, which I fear the wolf will sooner find than the master . *W. Tale* iii 3 67
Since all is well, keep it so: wake not a sleeping wolf.—To wake a wolf is as bad as to smell a fox . *2 Hen. IV.* i 2 174
Thee I'll chase hence, thou wolf in sheep's array . *1 Hen. VI.* i 3 55
Sheep run not half so treacherous from the wolf . i 5 30
When thou didst keep my lambs a-field, I wish some ravenous wolf had eaten thee! . v 4 31
Is he a lamb? his skin is surely lent him, For he's inclined as is the ravenous wolf . *2 Hen. VI.* iii 1 78
I myself will hunt this wolf to death . *3 Hen. VI.* ii 4 13
And yonder is the wolf that makes this spoil . v 4 80
So flies the reckless shepherd from the wolf . v 6 7
Wilt thou, O God, fly from such gentle lambs, And throw them in the entrails of the wolf? . *Richard III.* iv 4 23
This holy fox, Or wolf, or both,—for he is equal ravenous As he is subtle, and as prone to mischief . *Hen. VIII.* i 1 159
And appetite, an universal wolf, So doubly seconded with will and power, Must make perforce an universal prey . *Troi. and Cres.* i 3 121
As false . . . As fox to lamb, as wolf to heifer's calf, Pard to the hind iii 2 200
Pray you, who does the wolf love?—The lamb . *Coriolanus* ii 1 8
Deserve such pity of him as the wolf Does of the shepherds . iv 6 110
If thou wert the ass, thy dulness would torment thee, and still thou livedst but as a breakfast to the wolf . *T. of Athens* iv 3 336
If thou wert the wolf, thy greediness would afflict thee, and oft thou shouldst hazard thy life for thy dinner . iv 3 337
He would not be a wolf, But that he sees the Romans are but sheep *J. Cæsar* i 3 104
Alarum'd by his sentinel, the wolf, Whose howl's his watch . *Macbeth* ii 1 53
Scale of dragon, tooth of wolf, Witches' mummy . iv 1 22
To be a comrade with the wolf and owl,—Necessity's sharp pinch! *Lear* ii 4 213
The lion and the belly-pinched wolf Keep their fur dry . iii 1 13
Hog in sloth, fox in stealth, wolf in greediness, dog in madness, lion in prey . iii 4 96
He's mad that trusts in the tameness of a wolf, a horse's health, a boy's love . iii 6 20
We are beastly, subtle as the fox for prey, Like warlike as the wolf for what we eat . *Cymbeline* iii 3 41

Wolsey. 'Tis well; for worthy Wolsey, Who cannot err, he did it *Hen. VIII.* i 1 173
For 'twas indeed his colour, but he came To whisper Wolsey . . i 1 179
O my Wolsey, The quiet of my wounded conscience . . . ii 2 74
There ye shall meet about this weighty business. My Wolsey, see it furnish'd . . . . ii 2 141
Wolsey, that once trod the ways of glory . . . . . iii 2 435
That the great child of honour, Cardinal Wolsey, Was dead . iv 2 6
Wolves. Thy groans Did make wolves howl . . . *Tempest* i 2 288
Put your torches out: The wolves have prey'd . . *Much Ado* v 3 25
'Tis like the howling of Irish wolves against the moon . *As Y. Like It* v 2 119
Wolves and bears, they say, Casting their savageness aside have done Like offices of pity . . . . *W. Tale* ii 3 187
O, thou wilt be a wilderness again, Peopled with wolves, thy old inhabitants! . . . . *2 Hen. IV.* iv 5 138
They will eat like wolves and fight like devils . . *Hen. V.* iii 7 162
Thus is the shepherd beaten from thy side And wolves are gnarling who shall gnaw thee first . . . . . . *2 Hen. VI.* iii 1 192
Loud-howling wolves arouse the jades That drag the tragic melancholy night . . . . iv 1 3
Such safety finds The trembling lamb environed with wolves *3 Hen. VI.* i 1 242
Fly, like ships before the wind Or lambs pursued by hunger-starved wolves . . . . i 4 5
She-wolf of France, but worse than wolves of France! . . . i 4 111
Courteous destroyers, affable wolves, meek bears! . . *T. of Athens* iii 6 105
O thou wall, That girdlest in those wolves, dive in the earth! . iv 1 2
Go great with tigers, dragons, wolves, and bears; Teem with new monsters! . . . . iv 3 189
If wolves had at thy gate howl'd that stern time, Thou shouldst have said 'Good porter, turn the key' . . . . . *Lear* iii 7 63
As salt as wolves in pride, and fools as gross As ignorance made drunk *Othello* iii 3 404

Wolvish. Thy desires Are wolvish, bloody, starved, and ravenous *Mer. of Venice* iv 1 138
When she shall hear this of thee, with her nails She'll flay thy wolvish visage . . . . *Lear* i 4 330
Wolvish-ravening lamb! Despised substance of divinest show! *R. and J.* iii 2 76
Woman. No woman's face remember, Save, from my glass, mine own *Tempest* iii 1 49
I never saw a woman, But only Sycorax my dam and she . . iii 2 108
A woman's reason; I think him so because I think him so *T. G. of Ver.* i 2 23
O, that she could speak now like a wood woman! . . . ii 3 31
In what habit will you go along?—Not like a woman . . . ii 7 40
Dumb jewels often in their silent kind More than quick words do move a woman's mind . . . . iii 1 91
A woman sometimes scorns what best contents her . . . iii 1 93
That man that hath a tongue, I say, is no man, If with his tongue he cannot win a woman . . . . iii 1 105
Nor who 'tis I love; and yet 'tis a woman; but what woman, I will not tell myself . . . . iii 1 267
To be slow in words is a woman's only virtue . . . . iii 1 338
Our youth got me to play the woman's part . . . . iv 4 165
He bears an honourable mind, And will not use a woman lawlessly . v 3 14
She has brown hair, and speaks small like a woman . . *Mer. Wives* i 1 49
But can you affection the 'oman? . . . . i 1 234
It is a 'oman that altogether's acquaintance with Mistress Anne Page . i 2 8
Never a woman in Windsor knows more of Anne's mind than I do . i 4 136
How now, good woman! how dost thou? . . . . . . i 4 142
What's the matter, woman?—O woman, if it were not for one trifling respect! . . . . ii 1 43
You are the happier woman . . . . ii 1 110
Here's a woman would speak with you.—Let her approach . . ii 2 32
Shall I vouchsafe your worship a word or two?—Two thousand, fair woman . . . . ii 2 43
The fairest, that would have won any woman's heart . . . ii 2 71
Alas! the sweet woman leads an ill life with him . . . . ii 2 92
I never knew a woman so dote upon a man . . . . . ii 2 106
If there be a kind woman in Windsor, she is one . . . . ii 2 126
See the hell of having a false woman! . . . . . . ii 2 305
She's a very tattling woman . . . . iii 3 99
Your husband's coming hither, woman, with all the officers in Windsor iii 3 114
Your wife is as honest a 'omans as I will desires among five thousand iii 3 236
A woman would run through fire and water for such a kind heart . iii 4 106
To build upon a foolish woman's promise . . . . . . iii 5 43
What I have suffered to bring this woman to evil for your good . iii 5 97
You are a very simplicity 'oman: I pray you, peace . . . iv 1 31
'Oman, art thou lunatics? hast thou no understandings for thy cases? iv 1 71
Why, woman, your husband is in his old lunes again . . . iv 2 21
What a woman are you!—Away with him! . . . . . iv 2 44
There is no woman's gown big enough for him . . . . . iv 2 72
My maid's aunt, the fat woman of Brentford, has a gown above . iv 2 77
He cannot abide the old woman of Brentford . . . . . iv 2 87
The honest woman, the modest wife, the virtuous creature . . iv 2 136
Mistress Page! come you and the old woman down . . . iv 2 175
Old woman! what old woman's that? . . . . . . iv 2 177
Good gentlemen, let him not strike the old woman . . . . iv 2 190
Are you not ashamed? I think you have killed the poor woman . iv 2 198
The 'oman is a witch indeed: I like not when a 'oman has a great peard iv 2 202
'Tis one of the best discretions of a 'oman as ever I did look upon . iv 4 2
He has been thrown in the rivers and has been grievously peaten as an old 'oman . . . . iv 4 23
There's an old woman, a fat woman, gone up into his chamber . iv 5 12
Ha! a fat woman! the knight may be robbed . . . . . iv 5 16
Here's a Bohemian-Tartar tarries the coming down of thy fat woman . iv 5 22
There was, mine host, an old fat woman even now with me; but she's gone . . . . iv 5 25
I spake with the old woman about it.—And what says she? . . iv 5 35
I would I could have spoken with the woman herself . . . iv 5 41
Was there a wise woman with thee?—Ay, that there was . . iv 5 59
My counterfeiting the action of an old woman delivered me . . iv 5 122
But I came from her, Master Brook, like a poor old woman . . v 1 18
He beat me grievously, in the shape of a woman . . . . v 1 22
If I had been married to him, for all he was in woman's apparel, I would not have had him . . . . v 5 204
What has he done?—A woman.—But what's his offence? *Meas. for Meas.* i 2 89
There's a woman with maid by him . . . . i 2 94
One that serves a bad woman . . . . ii 1 64
How? thy wife?—Ay, sir; whom, I thank heaven, is an honest woman ii 1 73
If she had been a woman cardinally given . . . . . ii 1 81
By the woman's means?—Ay, sir, by Mistress Overdone's means . . ii 1 84

Woman. A respected fellow; and his mistress is a respected woman *Meas. for Meas.* ii 1 171
The time is yet to come that she was ever respected with man, woman, or child . . . . ii 1 176
Can it be That modesty may more betray our sense Than woman's lightness? . . . . ii 2 170
Love you the man that wrong'd you?—Yes, as I love the woman that wrong'd him . . . . ii 3 25
Be that you are, That is, a woman . . . . ii 4 135
Is there none of Pygmalion's images, newly made woman, to be had now? iii 2 48
Angelo was not made by man and woman after this downright way of creation . . . . iii 2 112
If he be a married man, he's his wife's head, and I can never cut off a woman's head . . . . iv 2 5
And to set on this wretched woman here Against our substitute! . . v 1 132
First, hath this woman Most wrongfully accused your substitute . . v 1 139
For this woman, . . . Her shall you hear disproved to her eyes . . v 1 158
Know you this woman? . . . —My lord, I must confess I know this woman . . . . v 1 213
And thou pernicious woman, Compact with her that's gone . . . v 1 241
Say, wast thou e'er contracted to this woman?—I was . . . v 1 380
Proclaim it, provost, round about the city, Is any woman wrong'd . v 1 515
In Syracusa was I born, and wed Unto a woman . . *Com. of Errors* i 1 38
That very hour and in the self-same inn A meaner woman was delivered i 1 55
This woman that I mean, My wife—but, I protest, without desert—Hath oftentimes upbraided me withal . . . . iii 1 111
I am an ass, I am a woman's man, and besides myself.—What woman's man? and how besides thyself?—Marry, sir, besides myself, I am due to a woman . . . . iii 2 77
The venom clamours of a jealous woman Poisons more deadly than a mad dog's tooth . . . . v 1 69
Justice, sweet prince, against that woman there! . . . . v 1 197
A grievous fault! Say, woman, didst thou so?—No, my good lord . v 1 206
O perjured woman! They are both forsworn . . . . . v 1 212
This woman lock'd me out this day from dinner . . . . v 1 218
That a woman conceived me, I thank her . . . . *Much Ado* i 1 240
Such a man would win any woman in the world, if a' could get her good-will . . . . ii 1 17
Would it not grieve a woman to be overmastered with a piece of valiant dust? . . . . ii 1 63
One woman is fair, yet I am well; another is wise, yet I am well; another virtuous, yet I am well; but till all graces be in one woman, one woman shall not come in my grace . . . . ii 3 28
Nature never framed a woman's heart Of prouder stuff . . . iii 1 49
If he be not in love with some woman, there is no believing old signs iii 2 40
I cannot be a man with wishing, therefore I will die a woman with grieving . . . . iv 1 326
A most manly wit, Margaret; it will not hurt a woman . . . v 2 16
Study here three years. But there are other strict observances; As not to see a woman in that term . . . . . *L. L. Lost* i 1 37
That no woman shall come within a mile of my court . . . i 1 119
If any man be seen to talk with a woman within the term of three years i 1 131
It is the manner of a man to speak to a woman: for the form,—in some form . . . . i 1 213
A female; or, for thy more sweet understanding, a woman . . i 1 268
Who was Samson's love, my dear Moth?—A woman, master . . i 2 81
No woman may approach his silent court . . . . . . ii 1 24
What is she in the white?—A woman sometimes . . . . ii 1 198
A woman, that is like a German clock, Still a-repairing, ever out of frame . . . . iii 1 192
Are not you the chief woman? you are the thickest here . . iv 1 51
That was a woman when Queen Guinover of Britain was a little wench iv 1 125
A woman I forswore; but I will prove, Thou being a goddess, I forswore not thee . . . . iv 3 64
What you first did swear unto, To fast, to study, and to see no woman . iv 3 292
When would you, my lord, or you, or you, Have found the ground of study's excellence Without the beauty of a woman's face? . . iv 3 301
Not looking on a woman's face, You have in that forsworn the use of eyes . . . . iv 3 309
Where is any author in the world Teaches such beauty as a woman's eye? iv 3 313
Let not me play a woman; I have a beard coming . . *M. N. Dream* i 2 49
The juice of it on sleeping eye-lids laid Will make or man or woman madly dote Upon the next live creature that it sees . . . ii 1 171
I took him sleeping . . . And the Athenian woman by his side . . iii 2 39
This is the woman, but not this the man . . . . . . iii 2 42
He for a man, God warrant us; she for a woman, God bless us . v 1 326
Being an honest man's son, or rather an honest woman's son *Mer. of Ven.* ii 2 17
Well, if Fortune be a woman, she's a good wench . . . . ii 2 175
If my gossip Report be an honest woman of her word . . . iii 1 8
If she be less than an honest woman, she is indeed more than I took her for . . . . iii 5 46
He will, an if he live to be a man.—Ay, if a woman live to be a man . v 1 160
I'll die for't but some woman had the ring . . . . . v 1 208
By my soul, No woman had it, but a civil doctor . . . . v 1 210
The bountiful blind woman doth most mistake in her gifts to women *As Y. Like It* i 2 39
And—in my heart Lie there what hidden woman's fear there will . i 3 121
I could find in my heart to disgrace my man's apparel and to cry like a woman . . . . ii 4 5
What woman in the city do I name, When that I say the city-woman? . ii 7 74
Do you not know I am a woman? when I think, I must speak . . iii 2 263
I thank God I am not a woman, to be touched with so many giddy offences . . . . iii 2 366
Is there none here to give the woman?—I will not take her on gift of any man . . . . iii 3 68
You are a thousand times a properer man Than she a woman . . iii 5 52
A better jointure, I think, than you make a woman . . . iv 1 56
Certainly a woman's thought runs before her actions . . . iv 1 141
Make the doors upon a woman's wit and it will out at the casement . iv 1 163
O, that woman that cannot make her fault her husband's occasion! . iv 1 177
Can a woman rail thus?—Call you this railing? . . . . iv 3 42
Why, thy godhead laid apart, Warr'st thou with a woman's heart? . iv 3 45
He deserves no pity. Wilt thou love such a woman? . . . iv 3 67
The woman low And browner than her brother . . . . iv 3 88
I should have been a woman by right . . . . . . iv 3 177
Which he, sir?—He, sir, that must marry this woman . . . v 1 51
This female,—which in the common is woman . . . . . v 1 55
And I for Rosalind.—And I for no woman . . . . v 2 94; 99; 108
I will marry you, if ever I marry woman, and I'll be married to-morrow v 2 123
It is no dishonest desire to desire to be a woman of the world . v 3 5

Woman. I'll have no husband, if you be not he: Nor ne'er wed woman, if you be not she . . . *As Y. Like It* v 4 130

You to his love must accord, Or have a woman to your lord . . . v 4 140

If I were a woman I would kiss as many of you as had beards . . . Epil. 18

A woman's gift To rain a shower of commanded tears . . . *T. of Shrew* Ind. 1 124

Far more beautiful Than any woman in this waning age . . . Ind. 2 65

Cicely Hacket.—Ay, the woman's maid of the house . . . Ind. 2 92

And do you tell me of a woman's tongue? . . . i 2 208

And a woman's crupper of velure, which hath two letters for her name . . . iii 2 61

I see a woman may be made a fool, If she had not a spirit to resist . . . iii 2 222

Thou knowest, winter tames man, woman, and beast . . . iv 1 24

A' will make the man mad, to make a woman of him . . . iv 5 36

A woman moved is like a fountain troubled, Muddy, ill-seeming, thick . . . v 2 142

Such duty as the subject owes the prince Even such a woman oweth to her husband . . . v 2 156

Isbel the woman and I will do as we may . . . *All's Well* i 3 20

One good woman in ten, madam; which is a purifying o' the song . . . i 3 86

An we might have a good woman born but one every blazing star . . . i 3 91

That man should be at woman's command, and yet no hurt done! . . . i 3 96

I have felt so many quirks of joy and grief, That the first face of neither, on the start, Can woman me unto't . . . iii 2 53

A fool, sir, at a woman's service, and a knave at a man's . . . iv 5 25

What woman's that?—I am, my lord, a wretched Florentine . . . v 3 157

By him and by this woman here what know you? . . . v 3 237

Come, come, to the purpose: did he love this woman? . . . v 3 242

He did love her, sir, as a gentleman loves a woman.—How is that? . . . v 3 246

This woman's an easy glove, my lord; she goes off and on at pleasure . . . v 3 278

Thy small pipe Is as the maiden's organ, shrill and sound, And all is semblative a woman's part . . . *T. Night* i 4 34

My state is desperate for my master's love; As I am woman,—now alas! . . . ii 2 39

What kind of woman is't?—Of your complexion . . . ii 4 27

Let still the woman take An elder than herself . . . ii 4 30

No woman's sides Can bide the beating of so strong a passion As love doth give my heart; no woman's heart So big, to hold so much; they lack retention . . . ii 4 96

Make no compare Between that love a woman can bear me And that I owe . . . ii 4 105

My father had a daughter loved a man, As it might be, perhaps, were I a woman, I should your lordship . . . ii 4 111

I have one heart, one bosom, and one truth, And that no woman has . . . iii 1 171

No love-broker in the world can more prevail in man's commendation with woman than report of valour . . . iii 2 40

Carry his water to the wise woman . . . iii 4 114

Were you a woman, as the rest goes even, I should my tears let fall upon your cheek, And say 'Thrice-welcome!' . . . v 1 246

Thou hast said to me a thousand times Thou never shouldst love woman like to me . . . v 1 275

Let me see thee in thy woman's weeds . . . v 1 280

For every inch of woman in the world, Ay, every dram of woman's flesh is false, If she be . . . *W. Tale* ii 1 138

The office Becomes a woman best; I'll take't upon me . . . ii 2 32

Alas! I have show'd too much The rashness of a woman . . . iii 2 222

Now, good my liege, Sir, royal sir, forgive a foolish woman . . . iii 2 228

He hath songs for man or woman, of all sizes . . . iv 4 191

It was thought she was a woman and was turned into a cold fish . . . iv 4 283

For whose sight I have a woman's longing . . . iv 4 681

Or from the all that are took something good, To make a perfect woman . . . v 1 15

Women will love her, that she is a woman More worth than any man . . . v 1 110

He that perforce robs lions of their hearts May easily win a woman's . . . *K. John* i 1 269

A wicked will; A woman's will; a canker'd grandam's will! . . . ii 1 194

A widow, husbandless, subject to fears, A woman, naturally born to fears . . . iii 1 15

I am no woman, I'll not swoon at it . . . v 6 22

A woman's war, The bitter clamour of two eager tongues . . . *Richard II.* i 1 48

Join not with grief, fair woman, do not so . . . v 1 16

Peace, foolish woman.—I will not peace . . . v 2 80

Thou fond mad woman, Wilt thou conceal this dark conspiracy? . . . v 2 95

Away, fond woman! were he twenty times my son, I would appeach him . . . v 2 101

Make way, unruly woman! . . . v 2 110

What shrill-voiced suppliant makes this eager cry?—A woman . . . v 3 76

Thou frantic woman, what dost thou make here? . . . v 3 89

Why, what a wasp-stung and impatient fool Art thou to break into this woman's mood! . . . *1 Hen. IV.* i 3 237

For what offence have I this fortnight been A banish'd woman? . . . ii 3 42

Constant you are, But yet a woman . . . ii 3 112

That ever this fellow should have fewer words than a parrot, and yet the son of a woman! . . . ii 4 112

Bring him out that is but woman's son Can trace me in the tedious ways of art . . . iii 1 47

Then be still.—Neither; 'tis a woman's fault.—Now God help thee! . . . iii 1 245

Go to, you are a woman, go.—Who, I? no; I defy thee . . . iii 3 70

As I am a true woman, holland of eight shillings an ell . . . iii 3 82

Charge an honest woman with picking thy pocket! . . . iii 3 176

He will spare neither man, woman, nor child . . . *2 Hen. IV.* ii 1 18

A hundred mark is a long one for a poor lone woman to bear . . . ii 1 35

There is no honesty in such dealing; unless a woman should be made an ass . . . ii 1 40

Practised upon the easy-yielding spirit of this woman . . . ii 1 126

Answer in the effect of your reputation, and satisfy the poor woman . . . ii 1 143

Says he, 'you are an honest woman, and well thought on' . . . ii 4 100

What trade art thou, Feeble?—A woman's tailor, sir . . . iii 2 161

Wilt thou make as many holes in an enemy's battle as thou hast done in a woman's petticoat? . . . iii 2 166

Well said, good woman's tailor! well said, courageous Feeble! . . . iii 2 169

How swiftly will this Feeble the woman's tailor run off! . . . iii 2 287

No woman shall succeed in Salique land . . . *Hen. V.* i 2 39

A woman's voice may do some good, When articles too nicely urged be stood on . . . v 2 93

I fear no woman.—And while I live, I'll ne'er fly from a man . . . *1 Hen. VI.* i 2 102

Doubtless he shrives this woman to her smock . . . i 2 119

Woman, do what thou canst to save our honours; Drive them from Orleans . . . i 2 147

I cannot stay them; A woman clad in armour chaseth them . . . i 5 3

For when a world of men Could not prevail with all their oratory, Yet hath a woman's kindness over-ruled . . . ii 2 50

Wilt thou be daunted at a woman's sight? . . . v 3 69

She is a woman, therefore to be won . . . v 3 78

Art thou not second woman in the realm? . . . *2 Hen. VI.* i 2 43

Being a woman, I will not be slack To play my part . . . i 2 66

I have heard her reported to be a woman of an invincible spirit . . . i 4 9

What woman is this?—His wife, an't like your worship . . . ii 1 79

Woman. If it be fond, call it a woman's fear . . . *2 Hen. VI.* iii 1 36

Fie, coward woman and soft-hearted wretch! Hast thou not spirit to curse? . . . iii 2 307

Had I been there, which am a silly woman . . . *3 Hen. VI.* i 1 243

A woman's general; what should we fear? . . . i 2 69

O tiger's heart wrapt in a woman's hide! How couldst thou drain the life-blood of the child, To bid the father wipe his eyes withal, And yet be seen to bear a woman's face? . . . i 4 137

Ne'er was Agamemnon's brother wrong'd By that false woman, as this king by thee . . . ii 2 149

No, wrangling woman, we'll no longer stay . . . ii 2 176

She's a woman to be pitied much: Her sighs will make a battery in his breast . . . iii 1 36

A woman of this valiant spirit Should, if a coward heard her speak these words, Infuse his breast with magnanimity . . . v 4 39

Vouchsafe, divine perfection of a woman . . . *Richard III.* i 2 75

Was ever woman in this humour woo'd? Was ever woman in this humour won? . . . i 2 228

False-boding woman, end thy frantic curse . . . i 3 247

My woman's heart Grossly grew captive to his honey words . . . iv 1 79

Relenting fool, and shallow, changing woman! . . . iv 4 431

Not to deny her that A woman of less place might ask by law . . . *Hen. VIII.* ii 2 112

You, that have so fair parts of woman on you, Have too a woman's heart . . . ii 3 27

I am a most poor woman, and a stranger . . . ii 4 15

Of disposition gentle, and of wisdom O'ertopping woman's power . . . ii 4 88

I am a simple woman, much too weak To oppose your cunning . . . ii 4 106

What can be their business With me, a poor weak woman? . . . iii 1 20

Alas, I am a woman, friendless, hopeless! . . . iii 1 80

A wretched lady, A woman lost among ye, laugh'd at, scorn'd . . . iii 1 107

A woman, I dare say without vain-glory, Never yet branded with suspicion . . . iii 1 127

Bring me a constant woman to her husband, One that ne'er dream'd a joy beyond his pleasure; And to that woman, when she has done most, Yet will I add an honour, a great patience . . . iii 1 134

I am the most unhappy woman living . . . iii 1 147

You know I am a woman, lacking wit To make a seemly answer . . . iii 1 177

All my glories In that one woman I have lost for ever . . . iii 2 409

Thou hast forced me, Out of thy honest truth, to play the woman . . . iii 2 430

She is the goodliest woman That ever lay by man . . . iv 1 69

By her woman I sent your message . . . v 1 63

To pray for her? what, is she crying out?—So said her woman . . . v 1 68

I missed the meteor once, and hit that woman . . . v 4 53

I am weaker than a woman's tear, Tamer than sleep . . . *Troi. and Cres.* i 1 9

Fairer than ever I saw her look, or any woman else . . . i 1 33

Wherefore not afield?—Because not there: this woman's answer sorts . . . i 1 109

You are such a woman! one knows not at what ward you lie . . . i 2 282

O that I thought it could be in a woman—As, if it can, I will presume in you—To feed for aye her lamp and flames of love; To keep her constancy in plight and youth! . . . iii 2 165

A woman impudent and mannish grown Is not more loathed than an effeminate man In time of action . . . iii 3 217

I have a woman's longing, An appetite that I am sick withal . . . iii 3 237

A woman of quick sense . . . iv 5 54

In that day's feats, When he might act the woman in the scene, He proved best man i' the field . . . *Coriolanus* ii 2 100

Well said, noble woman! . . . iii 2 31

O heavens! O heavens!—Nay, I prithee, woman . . . iv 1 12

Not of a woman's tenderness to be, Requires nor child nor woman's face to see . . . v 3 129

She is a woman, therefore may be woo'd; She is a woman, therefore may be won; She is Lavinia, therefore must be loved . . . *T. Andron.* ii 1 82

O Tamora! thou bear'st a woman's face,— I will not hear her speak . . . ii 3 136

Do thou entreat her show a woman pity . . . ii 3 147

What begg'st thou, then? fond woman, let me go . . . ii 3 172

O most insatiate and luxurious woman! . . . v 1 88

I do love a woman.—I aim'd so near, when I supposed you loved . . . *R. and J.* i 1 210

I will tell her as much: Lord, Lord, she will be a joyful woman . . . ii 4 186

Unseemly woman in a seeming man! Or ill-beseeming beast in seeming both! . . . iii 3 112

I do not always follow lover, elder brother, and woman . . . *T. of Athens* ii 2 131

I love thee, Because thou art a woman, and disclaim'st Flinty mankind . . . iv 3 490

Surely, this man Was born of woman . . . iv 3 501

Lend me a fool's heart and a woman's eyes, And I'll beweep these comforts . . . v 1 160

I grant I am a woman; but withal A woman that Lord Brutus took to wife . . . *J. Cæsar* ii 1 292

I grant I am a woman; but withal A woman well-reputed . . . ii 1 294

I have a man's mind, but a woman's might . . . ii 4 8

Ay me, how weak a thing The heart of woman is! . . . ii 4 40

Come to my woman's breasts, And take my milk for gall! . . . *Macbeth* i 5 48

The repetition, in a woman's ear, Would murder as it fell . . . ii 3 90

A woman's story at a winter's fire, Authorized by her grandam . . . iii 4 65

Laugh to scorn The power of man, for none of woman born Shall harm Macbeth . . . iv 1 80

I am yet Unknown to woman, never was forsworn . . . iv 3 126

O, I could play the woman with mine eyes And braggart with my tongue! . . . iv 3 230

What's the boy Malcolm? Was he not born of woman? . . . v 3 4

No man that's born of woman Shall e'er have power upon thee . . . v 3 6

What's he That was not born of woman? Such a one Am I to fear, or none . . . v 7 3

Thou wast born of woman. But swords I smile at, weapons laugh to scorn, Brandish'd by man that's of a woman born . . . v 7 11

I bear a charmed life, which must not yield To one of woman born . . . v 8 13

Though Birnam wood be come to Dunsinane, And thou opposed, being of no woman born, Yet I will try the last . . . v 8 31

Frailty, thy name is woman! . . . *Hamlet* i 2 146

O most pernicious woman! O villain, villain, smiling, damned villain! . . . i 5 105

Man delights not me: no, nor woman neither . . . ii 2 322

'Tis brief, my lord.—As woman's love . . . iii 2 164

When these are gone, The woman will be out . . . iv 7 190

What man dost thou dig it for?—For no man, sir.—What woman, then? . . . v 1 143

One that was a woman, sir; but, rest her soul, she's dead . . . v 1 146

Such a kind of gain-giving, as would perhaps trouble a woman . . . v 2 226

Not so young, sir, to love a woman for singing . . . *Lear* i 4 40

There was never yet fair woman but she made mouths in a glass . . . iii 2 35

Wine loved I deeply, dice dearly; and in woman out-paramoured the Turk . . . iii 4 94

Let not the creaking of shoes nor the rustling of silks betray thy poor heart to woman . . . iii 4 99

O, the difference of man and man! To thee a woman's services are due . . . iv 2 27

Proper deformity seems not in the fiend So horrid as in woman . . . iv 2 61

Woman. Howe'er thou art a fiend, A woman's shape doth shield thee *Lear* iv 2 67
O undistinguish'd space of woman's will! . . . . iv 6 278
Her voice was ever soft, Gentle, and low, an excellent thing in woman . v 3 273
What praise couldst thou bestow on a deserving woman indeed? *Othello* ii 1 146
A pestilent complete knave; and the woman hath found him already . ii 1 252
Good name in man and woman, dear my lord, Is the immediate jewel of their souls . . . . iii 3 155
Go to, woman! Throw your vile guesses in the devil's teeth . . iii 4 183
I never knew woman love man so.—Alas, poor rogue! I think, i' faith, she loves me . . . . iv 1 111
And to see how he prizes the foolish woman your wife! . . . iv 1 186
A fine woman! a fair woman! a sweet woman! . . . . iv 1 189
O devil, devil! If that the earth could teem with woman's tears, Each drop she falls would prove a crocodile . . . . iv 1 256
I do not think there is any such woman.—Yes, a dozen . . iv 3 84
O perjured woman! thou dost stone my heart . . . . v 2 63
My husband!—What needs this iteration, woman? I say thy husband . v 2 150
He, woman; I say thy husband: dost understand the word? . . v 2 152
Fie! Your sword upon a woman? . . . . . . v 2 224
O murderous coxcomb! what should such a fool Do with so good a woman? . . . . v 2 234
The woman falls; sure, he hath kill'd his wife . . . . v 2 236
O, let him marry a woman that cannot go, sweet Isis! . *Ant. and Cleo.* i 2 66
There's some good news. What says the married woman? . . i 3 20
Our courteous Antony, Whom ne'er the word of 'No' woman heard speak ii 2 228
As well a woman with an eunuch play'd As with a woman . . ii 5 5
But there is never a fair woman has a true face . . . ii 6 104
Condemn myself to lack The courage of a woman . . . iv 14 60
E'en a woman, and commanded By such poor passion as the maid that milks . . . . iv 15 73
My resolution's placed, and I have nothing Of woman in me . . v 2 239
A very honest woman, but something given to lie; as a woman should not do . . . . v 2 252
You must not think I am so simple but I know the devil himself will not eat a woman: I know that a woman is a dish for the gods, if the devil dress her not . . . . v 2 275
A man worth any woman, overbuys me Almost the sum he pays *Cymb.* i 1 146
To think that man, who knows By history, report, or his own proof, What woman is, yea, what she cannot choose But must be, will his free hours languish for Assured bondage . . . . . i 6 71
A woman that Bears all down with her brain . . . . ii 1 58
Bid my woman Search for a jewel that too casually Hath left mine arm ii 3 145
Could I find out The woman's part in me! . . . . ii 5 20
There's no motion That tends to vice in man, but I affirm It is the woman's part: be it lying, note it, The woman's; flattering, hers; deceiving, hers . . . . ii 5 22
Go bid my woman feign a sickness . . . . . . iii 2 76
Well, then, here's the point: You must forget to be a woman . iii 4 157
Fear and niceness—The handmaids of all women, or, more truly, Woman it pretty self . . . . iii 4 160
She hath all courtly parts more exquisite Than lady, ladies, woman . iii 5 72
Were you a woman, youth, I should woo hard but be your groom . iii 6 69
'Tis said a woman's fitness comes by fits . . . . . iv 1 6
O most delicate fiend! Who is't can read a woman? . . . v 5 48
A shop of all the qualities that man Loves woman for . . . v 5 167
Hie thee, whiles I say A priestly farewell to her: suddenly, woman *Per.* iii 1 70
Are you a woman?—What would you have me be, an I be not a woman?—An honest woman, or not a woman . . . . . . iv 2 87

Womaned. And think it no addition, nor my wish, To have him see me woman'd . . . . *Othello* iii 4 195

Womanhood. May we, with the warrant of womanhood and the witness of a good conscience, pursue him? . . . *Mer. Wives* iv 2 220
There's neither faith, truth, nor womanhood in me else . 1 *Hen. IV.* iii 3 125
And for womanhood, Maid Marian may be the deputy's wife of the ward to thee . . . . iii 3 129
Setting thy womanhood aside, thou art a beast . . . . iii 3 139
Let it not be believed for womanhood! Think, we had mothers *T. and C.* v 2 129
Fond woman, let me go.—'Tis present death I beg; and one thing more That womanhood denies my tongue to tell . . *T. Andron.* ii 3 174
No womanhood? Ah, beastly creature! The blot and enemy to our general name! . . . . ii 3 182

Womanish. Lest resolution drop Out at mine eyes in tender womanish tears . . . . *K. John* iv 1 36
Relent! 'tis cowardly and womanish . . . *Richard III.* i 4 264
I do not think he fears death.—Sure, he does not: He never was so womanish; the cause He may a little grieve at . . *Hen. VIII.* ii 1 38
Wherefore not afield?—Because not there: this woman's answer sorts, For womanish it is to be from thence . . . *Troi. and Cres.* i 1 110
Art thou a man? . . . Thy tears are womanish . . *Rom. and Jul.* iii 3 110
If no inconstant toy, nor womanish fear, Abate thy valour in the acting it iv 1 119
Our yoke and sufferance show us womanish . . . *J. Cæsar* i 3 84

Womankind. O despiteful love! unconstant womankind! *T. of Shrew* iv 2 14

Womanly. Brings your froward wives As prisoners to her womanly persuasion . . . . v 2 120
Why then, alas, Do I put up that womanly defence, To say I have done no harm? . . . . *Macbeth* iv 2 78
Is not more manlike Than Cleopatra; nor the queen of Ptolemy More womanly than he . . . . . . *Ant. and Cleo.* i 4 7

Woman-post. But who comes in such haste in riding-robes? What woman-post is this? . . . . *K. John* i 1 218

Woman-queller. Thou art a honey-seed, a man-queller, and a woman-queller . . . . 2 *Hen. IV.* ii 1 58

Woman-tired. Thou dotard! thou art woman-tired, unroosted By thy dame Partlet here . . . . *W. Tale* ii 3 74

Womb. Good wombs have borne bad sons. . . . . *Tempest* i 2 120
Her plenteous womb Expresseth his full tilth and husbandry *M. for M.* i 4 43
Nourished in the womb of pia mater. . . . . *L. L. Lost* iv 2 71
Her womb then rich with my young squire . . . *M. N. Dream* ii 1 131
In that dimension grossly clad Which from the womb I did participate *T. Night* v 1 245
This child was prisoner to the womb . . . . *W. Tale* ii 2 59
For all the sun sees or The close earth wombs or the profound seas hide iv 4 501
But the second generation Removed from thy sin-conceiving womb *K. John* ii 1 182
Ugly and slanderous to thy mother's womb, Full of unpleasing blots . iii 1 44
The smallest thread That ever spider twisted from her womb . iv 3 128
You bloody Neroes, ripping up the womb Of your dear mother England v 2 152
That bed, that womb, That metal, that self mould, that fashion'd thee *Richard II.* i 2 22

Womb. This nurse, this teeming womb of royal kings . *Richard II.* ii 1 51
Gaunt as a grave, Whose hollow womb inherits nought but bones . . ii 1 83
Some unborn sorrow, ripe in fortune's womb, Is coming towards me . ii 2 10
Whose arms were moulded in their mothers' womb. . . 1 *Hen. IV.* i 1 23
The teeming earth Is with a kind of colic pinch'd . . . Within her womb iii 1 31
My womb, my womb, my womb, undoes me . . . 2 *Hen. IV.* iv 3 25
I pray God the fruit of her womb miscarry! . . . . v 4 15
Through the foul womb of night The hum of either army stilly sounds *Hen. V.* iv Prol. 4
Ay, rather than I'll shame my mother's womb . . 1 *Hen. VI.* iv 5 35
Murder not then the fruit within my womb . . . . v 4 63
Love forswore me in my mother's womb . . . 3 *Hen. VI.* iii 2 153
I the rather wean me from despair For love of Edward's offspring in my womb . . . . iv 4 18
Thou slander of thy mother's heavy womb! . . . *Richard III.* i 3 231
O my accursed womb, the bed of death! . . . . iv 1 54
From forth the kennel of thy womb hath crept A hell-hound . . iv 4 47
That excellent grand tyrant of the earth, That reigns in galled eyes of weeping souls, Thy womb let loose . . . . . . iv 4 54
Might have intercepted thee, By strangling thee in her accursed womb iv 4 138
If I have kill'd the issue of your womb, . . . I will beget Mine issue iv 4 296
Thou didst kill my children.—But in your daughter's womb I bury them iv 4 423
Who had Commanded nature, that my lady's womb, If it conceived a male child by me, should Do no more offices of life to't than The grave does to the dead . . . . *Hen. VIII.* ii 4 188
When yet he was but tender-bodied and the only son of my womb *Coriol.* i 3 7
My dear wife's estimate, her womb's increase, And treasure of my loins iii 3 114
To tread . . . on thy mother's womb, That brought thee to this world v 3 124
I may be pluck'd into the swallowing womb Of this deep pit *T. Andron.* ii 3 239
And from that womb where you imprison'd were He is enfranchised . iv 2 124
The earth that's nature's mother is her tomb; What is her burying grave that is her womb, And from her womb children of divers kind We sucking on her natural bosom find . . . *Rom. and Jul.* ii 3 10
Violently as hasty powder fired Doth hurry from the fatal cannon's womb v 1 65
Thou detestable maw, thou womb of death! . . . . v 3 45
Twinn'd brothers of one womb . . . . . *T. of Athens* iv 3 3
Whose womb unmeasurable, and infinite breast, Teems, and feeds all . iv 3 178
Ensear thy fertile and conceptious womb, Let it no more bring out ingrateful man! Go great with tigers! . . . . . iv 3 187
Macduff was from his mother's womb Untimely ripp'd . . *Macbeth* v 8 15
Of if thou hast uphoarded in thy life Extorted treasure in the womb of earth, . . . Speak of it . . . . . . *Hamlet* i 1 137
Into her womb convey sterility! Dry up in her the organs of increase! *Lear* i 4 300
There are many events in the womb of time which will be delivered *Oth.* i 3 377
How many boys and wenches must I have?—If every of your wishes had a womb, And fertile every wish, a million. . . *Ant. and Cleo.* i 2 38
Till by degrees the memory of my womb . . . Lie graveless . . iii 13 163
I died whilst in the womb he stay'd Attending nature's law . *Cymbeline* v 4 37
All love the womb that their first being bred, Then give my tongue like leave to love my head . . . . *Pericles* i 1 107
Thou hast as chiding a nativity As fire, air, water, earth, and heaven can make, To herald thee from the womb . . . . . iii 1 34

Womby. Caves and womby vaultages . . . . *Hen. V.* ii 4 124

Women. Had I not Four or five women once that tended me? *Tempest* i 2 47
All men idle, all; And women too, but innocent and pure . . ii 1 155
For several virtues Have I liked several women . . . . iii 1 43
Falsehood, cowardice, and poor descent, Three things that women highly hold in hate . . . . *T. G. of Ver.* iii 2 33
Provided that you do no outrages On silly women or poor passengers . iv 1 72
How many women would do such a message? . . . . iv 4 95
O, 'tis the curse in love, and still approved, When women cannot love where they're beloved! . . . . v 4 44
It is the lesser blot, modesty finds, Women to change their shapes than men their minds.—Than men their minds! . . . . . v 4 109
The women have so cried and shrieked at it, that it passed: but women, indeed, cannot abide 'em . . . . . . *Mer. Wives* i 1 309
And yet he would not swear; praised women's modesty . . . ii 1 58
We have some salt of our youth in us; we are the sons of women . ii 3 51
Lisping hawthorn-buds, that come like women in men's apparel . iii 3 78
Women are frail too.—Ay, as the glasses where they view themselves *Meas. for Meas.* ii 4 124
Women! Help Heaven! men their creation mar In profiting by them . ii 4 127
You will needs buy and sell men and women like beasts. . . iii 2 2
I never heard the absent duke much detected for women . . iii 2 130
Then ginger was not much in request, for the old women were all dead iv 3 9
These poor informal women are no more But instruments of some more mightier member That sets them on . . . . . . v 1 236
He indeed Hath set the women on to this complaint . . . v 1 251
Go darkly to work with her.—That's the way; for women are light at midnight . . . . v 1 280
Is't not enough thou hast suborn'd these women To accuse this worthy man? . . . . v 1 308
Fainting under The pleasing punishment that women bear *Com. of Errors* i 1 47
Alas, poor women! make us but believe, Being compact of credit, that you love us; Though others have the arm, show us the sleeve . iii 2 21
Truly, I love none.—A dear happiness to women . . *Much Ado* i 1 129
All women shall pardon me. Because I will not do them the wrong to mistrust any. . . . . i 1 244
Methinks you look with your eyes as other women do . . . ii 4 92
From women's eyes this doctrine I derive . . . *L. L. Lost* iv 3 302; 350
Then fools you were these women to forswear . . . . iv 3 355
Or for men's sake, the authors of these women, Or women's sake, by whom we men are men . . . . iv 3 359
By all the vows that ever men have broke, In number more than ever women spoke . . . . *M. N. Dream* i 1 176
And on the wager lay two earthly women . . . *Mer. of Venice* iii 5 85
The bountiful blind woman doth most mistake in her gifts to women *As Y. Like It* i 2 39
All the world's a stage, And all the men and women merely players . ii 7 140
Can you remember any of the principal evils that he laid to the charge of women?—There were none principal . . . . . iii 2 370
One of the points in the which women still give the lie to their consciences iii 2 409
Boys and women are for the most part cattle of this colour . . iii 2 434
There be some women . . . would have gone near To fall in love with him iii 5 124
Women's gentle brain Could not drop forth such giant-rude invention . iv 3 33
My way is to conjure you; and I'll begin with the women. I charge you, O women, for the love you bear to men . . . . . Epil. 12
I charge you, O men, for the love you bear to women . . . Epil. 16
Between you and the women the play may please . . . . Epil. 18

Women. Women are made to bear, and so are you . *T. of Shrew* ii 1 201
'Tis a world to see, How tame, when men and women are alone . ii 1 314
Kindness in women, not their beauteous looks, Shall win my love . iv 2 41
Tell these headstrong women What duty they do owe their lords . v 2 130
I am ashamed that women are so simple To offer war where they should kneel for peace, Or seek for rule . v 2 161
A harsh hearing when women are froward . v 2 183
If you could find out a country where but women were that had received so much shame . *All's Well* iv 3 362
Do you know these women?—My lord, I neither can nor will deny But that I know them . v 3 165
How easy is it for the proper-false In women's waxen hearts to set their forms! Alas, our frailty is the cause, not we! . *T. Night* ii 2 31
Our fancies are more giddy and unfirm, More longing, wavering, sooner lost and worn, Than women's are . ii 4 36
For women are as roses, whose fair flower Being once display'd, doth fall that very hour . ii 4 39
What dost thou know?—Too well what love women to men may owe . ii 4 108
Women say so, That will say any thing . *W. Tale* i 2 130
Black brows, they say, Become some women best . ii 1 9
Who taught you this?—I learnt it out of women's faces . ii 1 12
Beseech your highness, My women may be with me . ii 1 117
My women, come; you have leave . ii 1 124
Is't lawful, pray you, To see her women? any of them? . ii 2 12
The child-bed privilege denied, which 'longs To women of all fashion . iii 2 105
Make proselytes Of who she but bid follow.—How! not women? . v 1 109
Women will love her, that she is a woman More worth than any man; men, that she is The rarest of all women . v 1 110
Women and fools, break off your conference . *K. John* ii 1 150
Boys, with women's voices, Strive to speak big . *Richard II.* iii 2 113
Sup any women with him? . *2 Hen. IV.* ii 2 165
For the women?—For one of them, she is in hell already . ii 4 364
For women are shrews, both short and tall . v 3 36
Holding in disdain the German women For some dishonest manners . *Hen. V.* i 2 48
As ever you came of women, come in quickly . ii 1 122
They say he cried out of sack.—Ay, that a' did.—And of women . ii 3 31
A' said once, the devil would have him about women.—A' did in some sort, indeed, handle women . ii 3 38
Guarded with grandsires, babies, and old women . iii Prol. 20
And none but women left to wail the dead . *1 Hen. VI.* i 1 51
These women are shrewd tempters with their tongues . i 2 123
Tush, women have been captivate ere now . v 3 107
Her valiant courage and undaunted spirit, More than in women commonly is seen . v 5 71
Madam, the king is old enough himself To give his censure: these are no women's matters . *2 Hen. VI.* i 3 120
'Tis beauty that doth oft make women proud . *3 Hen. VI.* i 4 128
Women are soft, mild, pitiful, and flexible; Thou stern, obdurate . i 4 141
Why stand we like soft-hearted women here, Wailing our losses? . ii 3 25
Ay, Edward will use women honourably . iii 2 124
Women and children of so high a courage, And warriors faint! . v 4 50
And the women cried 'O, Jesus bless us, he is born with teeth!' . v 6 74
This it is, when men are ruled by women . *Richard III.* i 1 62
Let not the heavens hear these tell-tale women Rail on the Lord's anointed . iv 4 149
Two women placed together makes cold weather . *Hen. VIII.* i 4 22
Sir Thomas Bullen's daughter, . . . one of her highness' women . i 4 93
It was a gentle business, and becoming The action of good women . ii 3 55
Would all other women Could speak this with as free a soul as I do! . iii 1 31
You wrong your virtues With these weak women's fears . iii 1 169
More pangs and fears than wars or women have . iii 2 370
Great-bellied women, That had not half a week to go . iv 1 76
Have some pity Upon my wretched women, that so long Have follow'd both my fortunes faithfully . iv 2 140
You must not leave me yet: I must to bed; Call in more women . iv 2 167
Have we some strange Indian with the great tool come to court, the women so besiege us? . v 4 35
Only in The merciful construction of good women . Epil. 10
Go to—there were no more comparison between the women . *Tr. and Cr.* i 1 43
Women are angels, wooing: Things won are done . i 2 312
I wish'd myself a man, Or that we women had men's privilege Of speaking first . iii 2 136
Let all constant men be Troiluses, all false women Cressids! . iii 2 211
Tell these sad women 'Tis fond to wail inevitable strokes . *Coriolanus* iv 1 25
Think to front his revenges with the easy groans of old women? . v 2 45
How more unfortunate than all living women Are we come hither . v 3 97
At a few drops of women's rheum, which are As cheap as lies, he sold the blood and labour Of our great action . v 6 46
Women, being the weaker vessels, are ever thrust to the wall . *R. and J.* i 1 19
Women grow by men . i 3 95
Learns them first to bear, Making them women of good carriage . i 4 94
Women may fall, when there's no strength in men . ii 3 80
Hoy-day, what a sweep of vanity comes this way! They dance! they are mad women. Like madness is the glory of this life . *T. of Athens* i 2 138
Women are more valiant That stay at home, if bearing carry it . iii 5 47
If there sit twelve women at the table, let a dozen of them be—as they are . iii 6 88
What things in the world canst thou nearest compare to thy flatterers?—Women nearest; but men, men are the things themselves . iv 3 320
Soldiers, not thieves.—Both too; and women's sons . iv 3 417
I meddle with no tradesman's matters, nor women's matters . *J. Cæsar* i 1 26
A hundred ghastly women, Transformed with their fear . i 3 23
To kindle cowards and to steel with valour The melting spirits of women . ii 1 122
How hard it is for women to keep counsel! . ii 4 9
You should be women, And yet your beards forbid . *Macbeth* i 3 45
Thou hast it now: king, Cawdor, Glamis, all, As the weird women promised . iii 1 2
Your eye in Scotland Would create soldiers, make our women fight . iv 3 187
What is that noise?—It is the cry of women . v 5 8
Women's fear and love holds quantity; In neither aught, or in extremity . *Hamlet* iii 2 177
Let not women's weapons, water-drops, Stain my man's cheeks! . *Lear* ii 4 280
If she live long, And in the end meet the old course of death, Women will all turn monsters . iii 7 102
Down from the waist they are Centaurs, Though women all above . iv 6 127
He hath a person and a smooth dispose To be suspected, framed to make women false . *Othello* i 3 404
If I court moe women, you'll couch with moe men . iv 3 57
Dost thou in conscience think,—tell me, Emilia,—That there be women do abuse their husbands In such gross kind? . iv 3 62

Women. Then, we kill all our women: we see how mortal an unkindness is to them; if they suffer our departure, death's the word . *Ant. and Cleo.* i 2 137
Under a compelling occasion, let women die . i 2 141
If there were no more women but Fulvia, then had you indeed a cut . i 2 172
Would we had all such wives, that the men might go to wars with the women! . ii 2 66
Other women cloy The appetites they feed: but she makes hungry Where most she satisfies . ii 2 241
So our leader's led, And we are women's men . iii 7 71
Women are not In their best fortunes strong . iii 12 29
See, my women! Against the blown rose may they stop their nose . iii 13 38
Forborne the getting of a lawful race, And by a gem of women . iii 13 108
They weep; And I, an ass, am onion-eyed: for shame, Transform us not to women . iv 2 36
Help me, my women! O, he is more mad Than Telamon for his shield . iv 13 1
O, see, my women, The crown o' the earth doth melt. My lord! . iv 15 62
Ah, women, women, look, Our lamp is spent, it's out! . iv 15 84
Ah, women, women! come; we have no friend But resolution, and the briefest end . iv 15 90
You laugh when boys or women tell their dreams; Is't not your trick? v 2 74
Show me, my women, like a queen: go fetch My best attires . v 2 227
Rememberest thou any that have died on't?—Very many, men and women too . v 2 250
Devils do the gods great harm in their women; for in every ten that they make, the devils mar five . v 2 278
Take up her bed; And bear her women from the monument . v 2 360
Her women are about her: what If I do line one of their hands? *Cymb.* ii 3 71
I will make One of her women lawyer to me . ii 3 79
The vows of women Of no more bondage be, to where they are made, Than they are to their virtues; which is nothing . ii 4 110
Who knows if one of her women, being corrupted, Hath stol'n it from her? . ii 4 116
Is there no way for men to be but women Must be half-workers? . ii 5 1
O, Men's vows are women's traitors! . iii 4 56
Fear and niceness—The handmaids of all women . iii 4 159
I will report, so please you: these her women Can trip me, if I err . v 5 34
Heard you all this, her women?—We did, so please your highness . v 5 61
Men take women's gifts for impudence . *Pericles* ii 3 69
Nor let pity, which Even women have cast off, melt thee, but be A soldier . iv 1 7
Amongst honest women.—'Faith, my acquaintance lies little amongst them . iv 6 205

Women-kind. Will you not go the way of women-kind? . iv 6 159

Won. If haply won, perhaps a hapless gain; If lost, why then a grievous labour won . *T. G. of Ver.* i 1 32
The best and the fairest, that would have won any woman's heart . *Mer. Wives* ii 2 71
And never rise until my tears and prayers Have won his grace *Com. of Er.* v 1 116
Once before he won it of me with false dice . *Much Ado* ii 1 289
I have wooed in thy name, and fair Hero is won . ii 1 310
Small have continual plodders ever won Save base authority from others' books . *L. L. Lost* i 1 86
'Tis won as towns with fire, so won, so lost . i 1 147
Without the which I am not to be won . v 2 859
And won thy love, doing thee injuries . *M. N. Dream* i 1 17
Made love to Nedar's daughter, Helena, And won her soul . i 1 108
To trouble you with no more suit, unless you may be won by some other sort than your father's imposition . *Mer. of Venice* i 2 113
A Persian prince That won three fields of Sultan Solyman . ii 1 26
We are the Jasons, we have won the fleece.—I would you had won the fleece that he hath lost . iii 2 244
That flattering tongue of yours won me . *As Y. Like It* iv 1 189
Protesting oath on oath, That in a twink she won me to her love *T. of S.* ii 1 312
Go thy ways; the field is won.—Well, forward, forward! . iv 5 23
The wager thou hast won; and I will add Unto their losses . v 2 112
'Twas I won the wager, though you hit the white . v 2 186
That your daughter, ere she seems as won, Desires this ring . *All's Well* iii 7 31
You have won A wife of me, though there my hope be done . iv 2 64
A heaven on earth I have won by wooing thee . iv 2 66
Half won is match well made; match, and well make it . iv 3 254
Upon his many protestations to marry me when his wife was dead, I blush to say it, he won me . v 3 141
Will you be mine, now you are doubly won? . v 3 315
All is well ended, if this suit be won, That you express content . Epil. 336
Is he won yet?—He'll stay, my lord . *W. Tale* i 2 86
Near or far off, well won is still well shot . *K. John* i 1 174
But Fortune, O, She is corrupted, changed, and won from thee . iii 1 55
What he hath won, that hath he fortified . iii 4 10
What have you lost by losing of this day?—All days of glory, joy, and happiness.—If you had won it, certainly you had . iii 4 118
'Tis strange to think how much King John hath lost In this which he accounts so clearly won . iii 4 122
Spent not that Which his triumphant father's hand had won *Richard II.* ii 1 181
Dogs, easily won to fawn on any man! . iii 2 130
Your care is gain of care, by new care won . iv 1 197
Showed like a feast And won by rareness such solemnity . *1 Hen. IV.* iii 2 59
All's done, all's won; here breathless lies the king . v 3 16
I better brook the loss of brittle life Than those proud titles thou hast won of me . v 4 79
Since this business so fair is done, Let us not leave till all our own be won . v 5 44
O, such a day, So fought, so follow'd, and so fairly won! . *2 Hen. IV.* i 1 21
The sum of all Is that the king hath won . i 1 132
Had they been ruled by me, You should have won them dearer than you have . iv 3 73
You won it, wore it, kept it, gave it me . iv 5 222
There's nought in France That can be with a nimble galliard won *Hen. V.* i 2 252
You'll pay me the eight shillings I won of you at betting? . ii 1 98
Orleans is besieged, And how the English have the suburbs won *1 Hen. VI.* i 4 2
'Tis Joan, not we, by whom the day is won . i 6 17
Maine, Blois, Poictiers, and Tours, are won away . iv 3 45
Flight cannot stain the honour you have won . iv 5 26
Surely, by all the glory you have won . iv 6 50
She is a woman, therefore to be won . v 3 78
Whom I with pain have woo'd and won thereto . v 3 138
Thy plainness and thy housekeeping Hath won the greatest favour . *2 Hen. VI.* i 1 192
Till France be won into the Dauphin's hands . i 3 173
By flattery hath he won the commons' hearts . iii 1 28

Won. But all the honour Salisbury hath won Is, that he was the lord ambassador 2 *Hen. VI.* iii 2 275
They have won the bridge, killing all those that withstand them iv 5 3
Nor have we won one foot, If Salisbury be lost v 3 6
Saint Alban's battle won by famous York Shall be eternized in all age v 3 30
Many a battle have I won in France, When as the enemy hath been ten to one: Why should I not now? 3 *Hen. VI.* i 2 74
And Lewis a prince soon won with moving words iii 1 34
Warwick may lose, that now hath won the day iv 4 15
Was ever woman in this humour won? *Richard III.* i 2 229
O God, that seest it, do not suffer it; As it was won with blood, lost be it so! i 3 272
So loves the prince, That he will not be won to aught against him iii 1 166
And be not easily won to our request: Play the maid's part iii 7 50
Lead thy daughter to a conqueror's bed; To whom I will retail my conquest won iv 4 335
While we reason here, A royal battle might be won and lost iv 4 538
Things won are done; joy's soul lies in the doing *Troi. and Cres.* i 2 313
Though they be long ere they are wooed, they are constant being won iii 2 119
Hard to seem won: but I was won, my lord, With the first glance iii 2 125
I should freelier rejoice in that absence wherein he won honour *Coriol.* i 3 4
Where he hath won, With fame, a name to Caius Marcius ii 1 180
He cannot temperately transport his honours From where he should begin and end, but will Lose those he hath won ii 1 242
Abated captives to some nation That won you without blows iii 3 133
O my mother, mother! O! You have won a happy victory to Rome v 3 186
My lord, be ruled by me, be won at last *T. Andron.* i 1 442
She is a woman, therefore may be woo'd; She is a woman, therefore may be won ii 1 83
As sure a card as ever won the set v 1 100
If thou think'st I am too quickly won, I'll frown and be perverse and say thee nay, So thou wilt woo *Rom. and Jul.* ii 2 95
When the hurlyburly's done, When the battle's lost and won *Macbeth* i 1 4
What he hath lost noble Macbeth hath won i 2 67
Won to his shameful lust The will of my most seeming-virtuous queen *Hamlet* i 5 45
For such proceeding I am charged withal, I won his daughter *Othello* i 3 94
Cæsar and Antony have ever won More in their officer than person *Ant. and Cleo.* iii 1 16
Fall not a tear, I say; one of them rates All that is won and lost iii 11 70
The ring is won.—The stone's too hard to come by *Cymbeline* ii 4 45
Have patience, sir, And take your ring again; 'tis not yet won ii 4 114
Quite besides The government of patience! You have won ii 4 150
Woncot. William Visor of Woncot against Clement Perkes 2 *Hen. IV.* v 1 42
Wonder. My prime request, Which I do last pronounce, is, O you wonder! If you be maid or no?—No wonder, sir; But certainly a maid *Tempest* i 2 426
A single thing, as I am now, that wonders To hear thee speak i 2 432
A most ridiculous monster, to make a wonder of a poor drunkard! ii 2 170
All torment, trouble, wonder, and amazement Inhabits here v 1 104
I will requite you with as good a thing; At least bring forth a wonder v 1 170
O, wonder! How many goodly creatures are there here! v 1 181
Entreat thy company To see the wonders of the world abroad *T. G. of V.* i 1 6
I'll tell you as we pass along, That you will wonder what hath fortuned v 4 169
I have a letter from her Of such contents as you will wonder at *M. Wives* iv 6 13
Be you in the Park about midnight, at Herne's oak, and you shall see wonders v 1 13
But that frailty hath examples for his falling, I should wonder *Meas. for Meas.* iii 1 191
Sweet mistress,—what your name is else, I know not, Nor by what wonder you do hit of mine *Com. of Errors* iii 2 30
Less in your knowledge and your grace you show not Than our earth's wonder iii 2 32
This I wonder at, That he, unknown to me, should be in debt iv 2 47
I wonder much That you would put me to this shame and trouble v 1 13
I wonder that you will still be talking *Much Ado* i 1 117
I wonder that thou . . goest about to apply a moral medicine i 3 11
I do much wonder that one man, seeing how much another man is a fool when he dedicates his behaviours to love ii 3 8
Wonder not till further warrant: go but with me to-night iii 2 115
I wonder at it.—That shows thou art unconfirmed iii 3 123
I am so attired in wonder, I know not what to say iv 1 146
The supposition of the lady's death Will quench the wonder of her infamy iv 1 241
Meantime let wonder seem familiar v 4 70
Shall be the wonder of the world *L. L. Lost* i 1 12
Lord, how wise you are!—I will tell thee wonders.—With that face? i 2 144
A wonder, master! here's a costard broken in a shin iii 1 71
All ignorant that soul that sees thee without wonder iv 2 117
By heaven, the wonder in a mortal eye! iv 3 85
And wonder what they were and to what end Their shallow shows v 2 304
Some keep back The clamorous owl that nightly hoots and wonders At our quaint spirits *M. N. Dream* ii 2 6
I wonder if Titania be awaked iii 2 1
I wonder of their being here together iv 1 136
Masters, I am to discourse wonders: but ask me not what iv 2 29
Perchance you wonder at this show; But wonder on v 1 128
At the which let no man wonder v 1 135
I wonder if the lion be to speak.—No wonder, my lord v 1 154
I do wonder, Thou naughty gaoler, that thou art so fond *Mer. of Venice* iii 3 8
Should I anatomize him to thee as he is, I must blush and weep and thou must look pale and wonder *As Y. Like It* i 1 164
I was seven of the nine days out of the wonder before you came iii 2 185
Ay, and greater wonders than that v 2 31
That reason wonder may diminish, How thus we met v 4 145
And that's a wonder: fathers commonly Do get their children *T. of S.* ii 1 411
I must away to-day, before night come: Make it no wonder iii 2 193
Wonder not, Nor be not grieved: she is of good esteem iv 5 63
Here is a wonder, if you talk of a wonder.—And so it is: I wonder what it bodes v 2 106
'Tis a wonder, by your leave, she will be tamed so v 2 189
Bring in the admiration; that we with thee May spend our wonder too *All's Well* ii 1 92
'Tis the rarest argument of wonder that hath shot out in our latter times ii 3 7
Nay, I'll speak that Which you will wonder at iv 1 95
I wonder, sir, sith wives are monsters to you, And that you fly them as you swear them lordship, Yet you desire to marry v 3 155
Allowed your approach rather to wonder at you than to hear you *T. N.* i 5 210
I could not with such estimable wonder overfar believe that ii 1 29
Wonder. Wonder not, nor admire not in thy mind, why I do call thee so *T. Night* iii 4 165
Though 'tis wonder that enwraps me thus, Yet 'tis not madness iv 3 3
A very pretty barne! A boy or a child, I wonder? *W. Tale* iii 3 71
I shall have more than you can dream of yet; Enough then for your wonder iv 4 400
A couple, that 'twixt heaven and earth Might thus have stood begetting wonder v 1 133
A notable passion of wonder appeared in them v 2 17
Such a deal of wonder is broken out within this hour v 2 26
If I do not wonder how thou darest venture to be drunk v 2 184
I like your silence, it the more shows off Your wonder: but yet speak v 3 22
A wonder, lady! lo, upon thy wish, Our messenger Chatillon is arrived! *K. John* ii 1 50
In her eye I find A wonder, or a wondrous miracle ii 1 497
Thoughts tending to ambition, they do plot Unlikely wonders *Rich. II.* v 5 19
Yet let me wonder, Harry, At thy affections 1 *Hen. IV.* iii 2 29
I wonder much, Being men of such great leading as you are iv 3 16
And the mute wonder lurketh in men's ears *Hen. V.* i 1 49
Which is a wonder how his grace should glean it i 1 53
But thou, 'gainst all proportion, didst bring in Wonder to wait on treason ii 2 110
You'll find a difference, As we his subjects have in wonder found ii 4 135
To lay apart their particular functions and wonder at him iii 7 41
I once writ a sonnet in his praise and began thus: 'Wonder of nature' iii 7 43
Above human thought Enacted wonders with his sword and lance 1 *Hen. VI.* i 1 122
Whose life was England's glory, Gallia's wonder iv 7 48
Thou mayst bereave him of his wits with wonder v 3 195
A thing impossible To compass wonders but by help of devils v 4 48
A wonder and a pointing-stock To every idle rascal follower 2 *Hen. VI.* ii 4 46
These few days' wonder will be quickly worn ii 4 69
I wonder how the king escaped our hands 3 *Hen. VI.* i 1 1
I wonder how our princely father 'scaped, Or whether he be 'scaped ii 1 1
That would be ten days' wonder at the least.—That's a day longer than a wonder lasts.—By so much is the wonder in extremes iii 2 113
Leave off to wonder why I drew you hither iv 5 2
I wonder he is so fond To trust the mockery of unquiet slumbers *Richard III.* iii 2 26
He wonders to what end you have assembled Such troops iii 7 84
The king enacts more wonders than a man v 4 2
Each following day Became the next day's master, till the last Made former wonders its *Hen. VIII.* i 1 18
I wonder That such a keech can with his very bulk Take up the rays o' the beneficial sun i 1 54
This man so complete, Who was enroll'd 'mongst wonders i 2 119
Can thy spirit wonder A great man should decline? iii 2 374
But as when The bird of wonder dies, the maiden phœnix, Her ashes new create another heir v 5 41
Thou speakest wonders v 5 56
Ha! known!—Is that a wonder? *Troi. and Cres.* iii 3 195
A labour saved!—A wonder!—What? iii 3 242
I wonder now how yonder city stands iv 5 211
I do wonder His insolence can brook to be commanded *Coriolanus* i 1 265
Be still and wonder, When one but of my ordinance stood up To speak iii 2 11
And wonder greatly that man's face can fold In pleasing smiles such murderous tyranny *T. Andron.* ii 3 266
They may seize On the white wonder of dear Juliet's hand *Rom. and Jul.* iii 3 36
I wonder at this haste; that I must wed iii 5 119
I wonder men dare trust themselves with men *T. of Athens* i 2 44
Is not my lord seen yet?—Not yet.—I wonder on't. iii 4 10
O monument And wonder of good deeds evilly bestow'd! iv 3 467
Gaze And put on fear and cast yourself in wonder *J. Cæsar* i 3 60
I wonder none of you have thought of him ii 1 217
Of all the wonders that I yet have heard, It seems to me most strange ii 2 34
His wonders and his praises do contend Which should be thine or his *Macbeth* i 3 92
Whiles I stood rapt in the wonder of it i 5 6
Can such things be, And overcome us like a summer's cloud, Without our special wonder? iii 4 112
It harrows me with fear and wonder *Hamlet* i 1 44
Feeds on his wonder, keeps himself in clouds iv 5 89
What is it ye would see? If aught of woe or wonder, cease your search v 2 374
'Tis wonder that thy life and wits at once Had not concluded all *Lear* iv 7 41
The wonder is, he hath endured so long: He but usurp'd his life v 3 316
It gives me wonder great as my content To see you here before me *Oth.* ii 1 185
I wonder in my soul, What you would ask me, that I should deny iii 3 68
Sure, there's some wonder in this handkerchief iii 4 101
As for Cæsar, Kneel down, kneel down, and wonder *Ant. and Cleo.* iii 2 19
I wonder, doctor, Thou ask'st me such a question *Cymbeline* i 5 10
Whilst I am bound to wonder, I am bound To pity too i 6 81
No wonder, When rich ones scarce tell true iii 6 11
'Tis wonder That an invisible instinct should frame them To royalty unlearn'd iv 2 176
Do not wonder at it: you are made Rather to wonder at the things you hear Than to work any v 3 53
Upon his neck a mole, a sanguine star; It was a mark of wonder v 5 365
Her face was to mine eye beyond all wonder *Pericles* i 2 75
Like beauty's child, whom nature gat For men to see, and seeing wonder at ii 2 7
By Jove, I wonder, that is king of thoughts, These cates resist me, she but thought upon ii 3 28
The heavens, Through you, increase our wonder and set up Your fame for ever iii 2 97
All the grace, Which makes her both the heart and place Of general wonder iv Gower 11
Wondered. So rare a wonder'd father and a wife Makes this place Paradise *Tempest* iv 1 123
He wonder'd that your lordship Would suffer him *T. G. of Ver.* i 3 4
When men were fond, I smiled and wonder'd how *Meas. for Meas.* ii 2 187
Are these the breed of wits so wonder'd at? *L. L. Lost* v 2 266
Let no quarrel nor no brawl to come Taint the condition of this present hour, Which I have wonder'd at? *T. Night* v 1 366
Being wanted, he may be more wonder'd at 1 *Hen. IV.* i 2 225
I could not stir But like a comet I was wonder'd at iii 2 47
The contrary doth make thee wonder'd at 3 *Hen. VI.* i 4 131
And like the owl by day, If he arise, be mock'd and wonder'd at v 4 57
The midwife wonder'd and the women cried 'O, Jesus bless us!' v 6 74
Let us, that have our tongues, Plot some device of further misery, To make us wonder'd at in time to come *T. Andron.* iii 1 135

Wondered. Which I wonder'd Could be so rarely and exactly wrought *Cymbeline* ii 4 74
And strangers ne'er beheld but wonder'd at *Pericles* i 4 25
Like to gnats, Which make a sound, but kill'd are wonder'd at ii 3 63
Wonderful. You have brought her into such a canaries as 'tis wonderful *Mer. Wives* ii 2 62
Keep a gamester from the dice, and a good student from his book, and it is wonderful iii 1 39
And most wonderful that she should so dote *Much Ado* ii 3 98
O wonderful, wonderful, and most wonderful wonderful! and yet again wonderful, and after that, out of all hooping! *As Y. LikeIt* iii 2 201
That wench is stark mad or wonderful froward *T. of Shrew* i 1 69
This is wonderful.—Mistake no more iv 2 15
Nothing of that wonderful promise, to read him by his form *T. Night* iii 4 290
Most wonderful!—Do I stand there? v 1 232
'Tis wonderful What may be wrought out of their discontent *K. John* iii 4 178
It is a wonderful thing to see the semblable coherence of his men's spirits and his *2 Hen. IV.* v 1 72
What a beard ... will do ... is wonderful to be thought on *Hen. V.* iii 6 83
Take it, God, For it is none but thine!—'Tis wonderful! iv 8 117
O wonderful, when devils tell the truth!—More wonderful, when angels are so angry *Richard III.* i 2 73
So cunning and so young is wonderful iii 1 135
Saw you any thing more wonderful? *J. Cæsar* i 3 14
O, wonderful!—Good my lord, tell it.—No; you'll reveal it *Hamlet* i 5 118
O wonderful son, that can so astonish a mother! iii 2 340
Would I had never seen her!—O, sir, you had then left unseen a wonderful piece of work *Ant. and Cleo.* i 2 159
A wonderful sweet air, with admirable rich words to it *Cymbeline* ii 3 19
Wonderfully. The approbation of those that weep this lamentable divorce under her colours are wonderfully to extend him i 4 21
Wondering. Didst thou hear without wondering? *As Y. Like It* iii 2 181
That we with thee May spend our wonder too, or take off thine By wondering how thou took'st it *All's Well* ii 1 93
Now grown in grace Equal with wondering *W. Tale* iv 1 25
Makes me from wondering fall to weeping joys *2 Hen. VI.* i 1 34
Pages blush'd at him and men of heart Look'd wondering each at other *Coriolanus* v 6 100
Unto the white-upturned wondering eyes Of mortals *Rom. and Jul.* ii 2 29
Wonder-wounded. Makes them stand Like wonder-wounded hearers *Ham.* v 1 280
Wondrous heavy.—What a strange drowsiness possesses them! *Tempest* ii 1 198
I'll bear him no more sticks, but follow thee, Thou wondrous man ii 2 168
And yet is she a wondrous fat marriage *Com. of Errors* iii 2 94
That is, hot ice and wondrous strange snow *M. N. Dream* v 1 59
She is fair and, fairer than that word, Of wondrous virtues *Mer. of Ven.* i 1 163
With affection wondrous sensible He wrung Bassanio's hand ii 8 48
Her wondrous qualities and mild behaviour *T. of Shrew* ii 1 50
Wherefore gaze this goodly company, As if they saw some wondrous monument? iii 2 97
I spoke with her but once And found her wondrous cold *All's Well* iii 6 121
When I was like this maid, I found you wondrous kind v 3 311
In her eye I find A wonder, or a wondrous miracle *K. John* ii 1 497
Now, by my life, this day grows wondrous hot iii 2 1
Five moons were seen to-night; Four fixed, and the fifth did whirl about The other four in wondrous motion iv 2 184
Wondrous affable and as bountiful As mines of India *1 Hen. IV.* iii 1 168
And him, O wondrous him! O miracle of men! *2 Hen. IV.* ii 3 32
Fair maid, is't thou wilt do these wondrous feats? *1 Hen. VI.* i 2 64
Solicit Henry with her wondrous praise v 3 190
Your wondrous rare description ... hath astonish'd me v 5 1
'Tis wondrous strange, the like yet never heard of *3 Hen. VI.* ii 1 33
And thou, brave Oxford, wondrous well beloved iv 8 17
Confess yourselves wondrous malicious, Or be accused of folly *Coriolanus* i 1 91
Your helps are many, or else your actions would grow wondrous single ii 1 40
In troth, there's wondrous things spoke of him ii 1 152
Had you not by wondrous fortune come *T. Andron.* ii 3 112
O wondrous thing! How easily murder is discovered! ii 3 286
I'll show thee wondrous things, That highly may advantage thee to hear v 1 55
Prepare him up Against to-morrow: my heart is wondrous light, Since this same wayward girl is so reclaim'd *Rom. and Jul.* iv 2 46
O day and night, but this is wondrous strange! *Hamlet* i 5 164
And either ... the devil, or throw him out With wondrous potency iii 4 170
To such wondrous doing brought his horse, As had he been incorpsed iv 7 87
'Twas passing strange, 'Twas pitiful, 'twas wondrous pitiful *Othello* i 3 161
As a fair day in summer, wondrous fair *Pericles* ii 5 36
Whate'er it be, 'Tis wondrous heavy v 2 53
Wondrously. My lord leans wondrously to discontent *T. of Athens* iii 4 71
Wont. You were wont, when you laughed, to crow like a cock *T. G. of V.* ii 1 27
Or your own eyes had the lights they were wont to have ii 1 78
My tales of love were wont to weary you ii 4 126
I love him not as I was wont ii 4 204
You were wont to be a follower, but now you are a leader *Mer. Wives* iii 2 2
When were you wont to use my sister thus? *Com. of Errors* ii 2 155
I bear it on my shoulders, as a beggar wont her brat iv 4 40
He was wont to speak plain and to the purpose *Much Ado* ii 3 19
And when was he wont to wash his face? iii 2 56
When I was wont to think no harm all night *L. L. Lost* i 1 44
Where often you and I Upon faint primrose-beds were wont to lie *M. N. Dream* i 1 215
That same dew, which sometime on the buds Was wont to swell iv 1 59
Be as thou wast wont to be; See as thou wast wont to see iv 1 76
Was wont to tell me that I could do nothing without bidding *Mer. of Venice* ii 5 8
Let him look to his bond: he was wont to call me usurer iii 1 50
He was wont to lend money for a Christian courtesy iii 1 51
At whom so oft Your grace was wont to laugh *As Y. Like It* ii 2 9
I was wont To load my she with knacks *W. Tale* iv 4 359
That England, that was wont to conquer others *Richard II.* ii 1 65
Taste of it first, as thou art wont to do v 5 99
Talbot is taken, whom we wont to fear *1 Hen. VI.* i 2 14
Wont through a secret grate of iron bars ... to overpeer the city i 4 10
Where I was wont to feed you with my blood v 3 14
'Tis not his wont to be the hindmost man *2 Hen. VI.* iii 1 2
With his grumbling voice Was wont to cheer his dad in mutinies *3 Hen. VI.* i 4 77
Swear as thou wast wont.—What, not an oath? ii 6 76
I hope my holy humour will change; 'twas wont to hold me but while one would tell twenty *Richard III.* i 4 121
The people were not wont To be spoke to but by the recorder iii 7 29
Thou wert not wont to be so dull: Shall I be plain? iv 2 17
Wont. I have not that alacrity of spirit, Nor cheer of mind, that I was wont to have *Richard III.* v 3 74
Is he not wounded? he was wont to come home wounded *Coriolanus* ii 1 130
Who was wont To call them woollen vassals iii 2 8
When you were wont to say, If you had been the wife of Hercules iv 1 16
Here's he that was wont to thwack our general iv 5 188
There greet in silence, as the dead are wont *T. Andron.* i 1 90
When wert thou wont to walk alone, Dishonour'd thus? i 1 339
I wonder on't; he was wont to shine at seven *T. of Athens* iii 4 10
I do observe you now of late: I have not from your eyes that gentleness And show of love as I was wont to have *J. Cæsar* i 2 34
It draws near the season Wherein the spirit held his wont to walk *Hamlet* i 4 6
Even those you were wont to take delight in ii 2 341
Your flashes of merriment, that were wont to set the table on a roar v 1 210
Not entertained with that ceremonious affection as you were wont *Lear* i 4 64
When were you wont to be so full of songs? i 4 185
You were wont be civil *Othello* ii 3 190
She comes more nearer earth than she was wont, And makes men mad v 2 110
All is well yet. Sparkles this stone as it was wont? *Cymbeline* ii 4 40
Wonted. The spring, the summer, The childing autumn, angry winter, change Their wonted liveries *M. N. Dream* ii 1 113
And make his eyeballs roll with wonted sight iii 2 369
His wonted followers Shall all be very well provided for *2 Hen. IV.* v 5 104
How am I so poor? Or how haps it I seek not to advance Or raise myself, but keep my wonted calling? *1 Hen. VI.* iii 1 32
Entreat you to your wonted furtherance v 3 21
His wonted sleep under a fresh tree's shade *3 Hen. VI.* ii 5 49
You are to blame, Knowing she will not lose her wonted greatness *Hen. VIII.* iv 2 102
Their endeavour keeps in the wonted pace *Hamlet* ii 2 354
I hope your virtues Will bring him to his wonted way again iii 1 41
Promising To pay our wonted tribute *Cymbeline* v 5 462
Woo. She wooes you by a figure.—What figure?—By a letter, I should say *T. G. of Ver.* ii 1 154
Yet will I woo for him, but yet so coldly As, heaven it knows, I would not have him speed iv 4 111
I'll woo you like a soldier, at arms' end v 4 57
He wooes both high and low, both rich and poor *Mer. Wives* i 4 117
Anne Page is at a farm-house a-feasting; and thou shalt woo her ii 3 92
Let him woo for himself iii 4 51
I will never mistrust my wife again, till thou art able to woo her in good English v 5 142
Heard it agreed upon that the prince should woo Hero for himself *Much Ado* i 3 64
'Tis certain so; the prince wooes for himself ii 1 181
I pray thee, sing, and let me woo no more ii 3 50
Yet he wooes, Yet will he swear he loves ii 3 53
She will die, ere she make her love known, and she will die, if he woo her ii 3 183
I cannot woo in festival terms v 2 41
Thou and I are too wise to woo peaceably v 2 73
Shall we resolve to woo these girls of France? *L. L. Lost* iv 3 371
So shall your loves Woo contrary, deceived by these removes v 2 135
What shall we do, If they return in their own shapes to woo? v 2 299
Nor never come in vizard to my friend, Nor woo in rhyme v 2 405
We should be woo'd and were not made to woo *M. N. Dream* ii 1 242
You do me wrong, good sooth, you do, In such disdainful manner me to woo ii 2 130
Then will two at once woo one; That must needs be sport alone iii 2 118
Why should you think that I should woo in scorn? iii 2 122
Think no scorn To meet at Ninus' tomb, there, there to woo v 1 139
If I fail Of the right casket, never in my life To woo a maid in way of marriage *Mer. of Venice* ii 9 13
With one fool's head I came to woo, But I go away with two ii 9 75
Leave me alone to woo him *As Y. Like It* i 3 135
Nor did not with unbashful forehead woo The means of weakness ii 3 50
What a life is this, That your poor friends must woo your company? ii 7 10
He was to imagine me his love, his mistress; and I set him every day to woo me iii 2 429
Call me Rosalind and come every day to my cote and woo me iii 2 448
Chide a year together: I had rather hear you chide than this man woo iii 5 65
Come, woo me, woo me, for now I am in a holiday humour iv 1 68
Men are April when they woo, December when they wed iv 1 147
Whiles the eye of man did woo me, That could do no vengeance to me iv 3 47
But seeing you should love her? and loving woo? and, wooing, she should grant? v 2 3
That would thoroughly woo her, wed her, and bed her *T. of Shrew* i 1 149
Will undertake to woo curst Katharine, Yea, and to marry her i 2 184
But will you woo this wild-cat?—Will I live? i 2 197
Will he woo her? ay, or I'll hang her i 2 198
I may have welcome 'mongst the rest that woo ii 1 97
My business asketh haste, And every day I cannot come to woo ii 1 116
For I am rough and woo not like a babe.—Well mayst thou woo! ii 1 138
I will attend her here, And woo her with some spirit when she comes ii 1 170
Myself am moved to woo thee for my wife ii 1 195
He'll woo a thousand, 'point the day of marriage, Make feasts iii 2 15
Here I firmly vow Never to woo her more, but do forswear her iv 2 29
See that you come Not to woo honour, but to wed it *All's Well* ii 1 15
He wooes your daughter, Lays down his wanton siege before her beauty iii 7 17
My mother told me just how he would woo iv 2 69
'Accost' is front her, board her, woo her, assail her *T. Night* i 3 60
I'll do my best To woo your lady: yet, a barful strife! Whoe'er I woo, myself would be his wife i 4 41
Do not extort thy reasons from this clause, For that I woo iii 1 166
I'll reconcile me to Polixenes, New woo my queen *W. Tale* iii 2 157
Because he hath not the gift to woo in other places *Hen. V.* v 2 163
With an aspect of iron, that, when I come to woo ladies, I fright them v 2 245
Fain would I woo her, yet I dare not speak *1 Hen. VI.* v 3 65
I unworthy am To woo so fair a dame to be his wife v 3 124
Since thou dost deign to woo her little worth v 3 151
How canst thou woo her?—That would I learn of you *Richard III.* iv 4 268
Under what title shall I woo for thee? iv 4 340
Go to, go to; You take a precipice for no leap of danger, And woo your own destruction *Hen. VIII.* v 1 140
He's as tetchy to be woo'd to woo, As she is stubborn-chaste *T. and C.* i 1 99
Sweet Helen, I must woo you To help unarm our Hector iii 1 162
She is the hopeful lady of my earth: But woo her, gentle Paris, get her heart, My will to her consent is but a part *Rom. and Jul.* i 2 16
More inconstant than the wind, who wooes Even now the frozen bosom of the north i 4 100
I'll frown and be perverse and say thee nay, So thou wilt woo ii 2 97

Woo. These times of woe afford no time to woo . . *Rom. and Jul.* iii 4 8
I wonder at this haste; that I must wed Ere he, that should be husband, comes to woo . . . . . . iii 5 120
Grant I may ever love, and rather woo Those that would mischief me than those that do! *T. of Athens* iv 3 474
So did we woo Transformed Timon to our city's love By humble message . . . v 4 18
Virtue itself of vice must pardon beg, Yea, curb and woo for leave to do him good *Hamlet* iii 4 155
I should but teach him how to tell my story, And that would woo her *Othello* i 3 166
Keep it till you woo another wife, When Imogen is dead . *Cymbeline* i 1 113
So That our great king himself doth woo me oft For my confections . i 5 14
Were you a woman, youth, I should woo hard but be your groom . iii 6 70
You shall prevail, Were it to woo my daughter . *Pericles* v 1 263
Wood. He does make our fire, Fetch in our wood . . . *Tempest* i 2 312
There's wood enough within . . . . i 2 314
Here comes a spirit of his, and to torment me For bringing wood in slowly . . . . ii 2 16
Do not torment me, prithee; I'll bring my wood home faster . . ii 2 75
I'll pluck thee berries; I'll fish for thee and get thee wood enough . ii 2 165
O, that she could speak now like a wood woman! . *T. G. of Ver.* ii 3 30
Go thou with her to the west end of the wood . . . . v 3 9
Unfrequented woods, I better brook than flourishing peopled towns . v 4 2
Come, will this wood take fire? . *Mer. Wives* v 5 92
O wood divine! A wife of such wood were felicity . . *L. L. Lost* iv 3 248
In the wood, a league without the town . *M. N. Dream* i 1 165
In the wood, where often you and I Upon faint primrose-beds were wont to lie . . . . i 1 214
Then to the wood will he to-morrow night Pursue her . i 1 247
Meet me in the palace wood, a mile without the town . i 2 104
How long within this wood intend you stay? . ii 1 138
Thou told'st me they were stolen unto this wood; And here am I, and wode within this wood . . . . ii 1 191
Nor doth this wood lack worlds of company, For you in my respect are all the world . . . . ii 1 223
If thou follow me, do not believe But I shall do thee mischief in the wood ii 1 237
Fair love, you faint with wandering in the wood . ii 2 35
If I had wit enough to get out of this wood, I have enough . . iii 1 153
Out of this wood do not desire to go: Thou shalt remain here . iii 1 155
About the wood go swifter than the wind . . iii 2 94
I told him of your stealth unto this wood . . iii 2 310
Behind the wood, Seeking sweet favours for this hateful fool . iv 1 53
When in a wood of Crete they bay'd the bear . iv 1 118
Fair Helen told me of their stealth, Of this their purpose hither to this wood . . . . iv 1 166
Are not these woods More free from peril than the envious court? *As Y. Like It* ii 1 3
Whose antique root peeps out Upon the brook that brawls along this wood . . . . ii 1 32
Here we have no temple but the wood, no assembly but horn-beasts . iii 3 50
And to the skirts of this wild wood he came . v 4 165
And burn sweet wood to make the lodging sweet *T. of Shrew* Ind. 1 49
Or Daphne roaming through a thorny wood . Ind. 2 59
Dispark'd my parks and fell'd my forest woods *Richard II.* iii 1 23
My figured goblets for a dish of wood, My sceptre for a palmer's walking-staff . . . . iii 3 150
Our horses they shall not see; I'll tie them in the wood *1 Hen. IV.* i 2 199
He talks of wood: it is some carpenter . *1 Hen. VI.* v 3 90
These five days have I hid me in these woods . *2 Hen. VI.* iv 10 3
Like one lost in a thorny wood, That rends the thorns and is rent *3 Hen. VI.* iii 2 174
Brave followers, yonder stands the thorny wood . v 4 67
With our swords, upon a pile of wood, Let's hew his limbs *T. Andron.* i 1 128
The woods are ruthless, dreadful, deaf, and dull . ii 1 128
The morn is bright and grey, The fields are fragrant, and the woods are green . . . ii 2 2
The ruthless, vast, and gloomy woods . iv 1 53
He was ware of me And stole into the covert of the wood *Rom. and Jul.* i 1 132
Timon will to the woods; where he shall find The unkindest beast more kinder than mankind . *T. of Athens* iv 1 35
Shame not these woods, By putting on the cunning of a carper iv 3 208
Be men like blasted woods, And may diseases lick up their false bloods! iv 3 538
You are not wood, you are not stones, but men *J. Cæsar* iii 2 147
Light thickens; and the crow Makes wing to the rooky wood *Macbeth* iii 2 51
Until Great Birnam wood to high Dunsinane hill Shall come against him iv 1 93
Rebellion's head, rise never till the wood Of Birnam rise iv 1 97
Near Birnam wood Shall we well meet them . v 2 5
Till Birnam wood remove to Dunsinane, I cannot taint with fear . v 3 2
What wood is this before us?—The wood of Birnam . v 4 3
I look'd toward Birnam, and anon, methought, The wood began to move v 5 35
'Fear not, till Birnam wood Do come to Dunsinane:' and now a wood Comes toward Dunsinane . . . . v 5 44
Though Birnam wood be come to Dunsinane . v 8 30
Like the spring that turneth wood to stone . *Hamlet* iv 7 20
Woodbine. Even now Is couched in the woodbine coverture *Much Ado* iii 1 30
Quite over-canopied with luscious woodbine . *M. N. Dream* ii 1 251
So doth the woodbine the sweet honeysuckle Gently entwist . iv 1 47
Wood-birds. Begin these wood-birds but to couple now? . iv 1 145
Woodcock. Shall I not find a woodcock too? . *Much Ado* v 1 158
Four woodcocks in a dish! . *L. L. Lost* iv 3 82
O this woodcock, what an ass it is! . *T. of Shrew* i 2 161
We have caught the woodcock, and will keep him muffled *All's Well* iv 1 100
Now is the woodcock near the gin . *T. Night* ii 5 92
And fear to kill a woodcock, lest thou dispossess the soul of thy grandam . . . . iv 2 64
So strives the woodcock with the gin . *3 Hen. VI.* i 4 61
Springes to catch woodcocks . *Hamlet* i 3 115
As a woodcock to mine own springe, Osric; I am justly kill'd with mine own treachery . . . . v 2 317
Wooden. Would no more endure This wooden slavery than to suffer The flesh-fly blow my mouth . *Tempest* iii 1 62
Or may we cram Within this wooden O the very casques That did affright the air at Agincourt? *Hen. V.* Prol. 13
That every one may pare his nails with a wooden dagger . iv 4 77
Upon a wooden coffin we attend . *1 Hen. VI.* i 1 19
Tush, that's a wooden thing!—He talks of wood: it is some carpenter v 3 89
Doth think it rich To hear the wooden dialogue and sound *T. and C.* i 3 155
Pins, wooden pricks, nails, sprigs of rosemary . *Lear* ii 3 16
When a man's over-lusty at legs, then he wears wooden nether-stocks ii 4 10

Wooden. A man may serve seven years for the loss of a leg, and have not money enough in the end to buy him a wooden one *Pericles* iv 6 183
Woodland. I am a woodland fellow, sir, that always loved a great fire *All's Well* iv 5 49
Wood-leaves. With wild wood-leaves and weeds I ha' strew'd his grave, And on it said a century of prayers . *Cymbeline* iv 2 390
Woodman. Am I a woodman, ha? Speak I like Herne the hunter? *Mer. Wives* v 5 30
He's a better woodman than thou takest him for . *Meas. for Meas.* iv 3 170
You, Polydore, have proved best woodman and Are master of the feast *Cymbeline* iii 6 28
Woodmonger. I will pay you in cudgels: you shall be a woodmonger, and buy nothing of me but cudgels . *Hen. V.* v 1 69
Woodstock. Alas, the part I had in Woodstock's blood Doth more solicit me than your exclaims! . *Richard II.* i 2 1
Thomas of Woodstock, Duke of Gloucester . *2 Hen. VI.* ii 2 16
Woodvile. Faint-hearted Woodvile, prizest him 'fore me? . *1 Hen. VI.* i 3 22
Woodville. That good man of worship, Anthony Woodville *Richard III.* i 1 67
Wooed. Thy father's wealth Was the first motive that I woo'd thee *Mer. Wives* iii 4 14
The fault will be in the music, cousin, if you be not wooed *Much Ado* ii 1 73
I have wooed in thy name, and fair Hero is won . ii 1 309
As I wooed for thee to obtain her, I will join with thee to disgrace her iii 2 129
I have to-night wooed Margaret, the Lady Hero's gentlewoman . iii 3 154
And then we, Following the signs, woo'd but the sign of she *L. L. Lost* v 2 469
I woo'd thee with my sword, And won thy love *M. N. Dream* i 1 16
We should be woo'd and were not made to woo . ii 1 242
I had as lief be wooed of a snail.—Of a snail? . *As Y. Like It* iv 1 52
'Twas where you woo'd the gentlewoman so well *T. of Shrew* Ind. 1 85
Supposing it a thing impossible . . . That ever Katharina will be woo'd i 2 125
Who woo'd in haste and means to wed at leisure . iii 2 11
Yet never means to wed where he hath woo'd . iii 2 17
He'll have a lusty widow now, That shall be woo'd and wedded in a day iv 2 51
With wisdom I might fear, my Doricles, You woo'd me the false way *W. Tale* iv 4 151
O, thus she stood, Even with such life of majesty, warm life, As now it coldly stands, when first I woo'd her! . v 3 36
When she was young you woo'd her; now in age Is she become the suitor? . . . . v 3 108
And why rail I on this Commodity? But for because he hath not woo'd me yet . *K. John* ii 1 588
You took occasion to be quickly woo'd . *1 Hen. IV.* v 1 56
She's beautiful and therefore to be woo'd . *1 Hen. VI.* v 3 77
Whom I with pain have woo'd and won thereto . v 3 138
Was ever woman in this humour woo'd? . *Richard III.* i 2 228
Reflecting gems, Which woo'd the slimy bottom of the deep . i 4 32
He's as tetchy to be woo'd to woo, As she is stubborn-chaste *T. and C.* i 1 99
Though they be long ere they are wooed, they are constant being won . iii 2 118
But, though I loved you well, I woo'd you not . iii 2 134
O, let me clip ye In arms as sound as when I woo'd! . *Coriolanus* i 6 30
She is a woman, therefore may be woo'd . *T. Andron.* ii 1 82
We met, we woo'd, and made exchange of vow *Rom. and Jul.* ii 3 62
I see no sense for't, But his occasions might have woo'd me first *T. of A.* iii 3 15
Did Michael Cassio, when you woo'd my lady, Know of your love? *Oth.* iii 3 94
My wayward husband hath a hundred times Woo'd me to steal it . . iii 3 293
Having woo'd A villain to attempt it . *Pericles* v 1 174
Wooer. I will tell your worship more . . .; and of other wooers *M. W.* i 4 173
She mocks all her wooers out of suit . *Much Ado* ii 1 365
Many a wooer doth commence his suit To her he thinks not worthy . ii 3 52
I'll mark no words that smooth-faced wooers say *L. L. Lost* v 2 838
I am glad this parcel of wooers are so reasonable *Mer. of Venice* i 2 119
Whiles we shut the gates upon one wooer, another knocks at the door . i 2 147
Make one among these wooers . *T. of Shrew* i 1 252
Fair Leda's daughter had a thousand wooers . i 2 244
Thou with mildness entertain'st thy wooers, With gentle conference . ii 1 252
A foolish knight that you brought in one night here to be her wooer *T. N.* i 3 17
He is the bluntest wooer in Christendom . *3 Hen. VI.* iii 2 83
To her I go, a jolly thriving wooer . *Richard III.* iv 3 43
Prepare her ears to hear a wooer's tale . iv 4 327
Thou ever young, fresh, loved, and delicate wooer [gold]! *T. of Athens* iv 3 385
If she confess that she was half the wooer, Destruction on my head, if my bad blame Light on the man! . *Othello* i 3 176
A mother hourly coining plots, a wooer More hateful than the foul expulsion is Of thy dear husband . *Cymbeline* ii 1 64
Woof. Admits no orifex for a point as subtle As Ariachne's broken woof to enter . *Troi. and Cres.* v 2 152
Wooing. Use your art of wooing . *Mer. Wives* ii 2 244
We shall have the freer wooing . iii 2 86
Wooing thee, I found thee of more value Than stamps in gold . iii 4 15
Wooing, wedding, and repenting, is as a Scotch jig, a measure *M. Ado* ii 1 76
Because you talk of wooing, I will sing . ii 3 51
Henceforth my wooing mind shall be express'd In russet yeas and honest kersey noes . *L. L. Lost* v 2 412
Our wooing doth not end like an old play . v 2 884
Wooing here until I sweat again . *Mer. of Venice* iii 2 205
I remember the wooing of a peascod instead of her *As Y. Like It* ii 4 51
That but seeing you should love her? and loving woo? and, wooing, she should grant? . v 2 3
The small acquaintance, my sudden wooing . v 2 8
Would I had given him the best horse in Padua to begin his wooing! *T. of Shrew* i 1 148
As wealth is burden of my wooing dance . i 2 68
I promised we would be contributors And bear his charge of wooing . i 2 216
I would fain be doing.—I doubt it not, sir; but you will curse your wooing . . . . ii 1 75
But in this case of wooing, A child shall get a sire, if I fail not of my cunning . . . . ii 1 412
That Lucentio that comes a-wooing, 'Priami,' is my man Tranio . iii 1 35
A heaven on earth I have won by wooing thee . *All's Well* iv 2 66
Goes to the tune of 'Two maids wooing a man' . *W. Tale* iv 4 295
Wooing poor craftsmen with the craft of smiles . *Richard II.* i 4 28
In wooing sorrow let's be brief, Since, wedding it, there is such length in grief . . . . v 1 93
My wooing is fit for thy understanding . *Hen. V.* v 2 125
Women are angels, wooing: Things won are done . *Troi. and Cres.* i 2 312
What! Michael Cassio, That came a-wooing with you! . *Othello* iii 3 71
When I told thee he was of my counsel In my whole course of wooing, thou criedst 'Indeed!' . . . . iii 3 112
O, you have heard something of my power, and so stand aloof for more serious wooing . . *Pericles* iv 6 95

Wooingly. The heaven's breath Smells wooingly here . . *Macbeth* i 6 6
Wool. Fifteen hundred shorn, what comes the wool to? . *W. Tale* iv 3 35
Eye of newt and toe of frog, Wool of bat and tongue of dog *Macbeth* iv 1 15
Thou owest the worm no silk, the beast no hide, the sheep no wool *Lear* iii 4 109
Woollen. I had rather lie in the woollen . . *Much Ado* ii 1 33
Why he cannot abide a gaping pig; Why he, a harmless necessary cat; Why he, a woollen bag-pipe *Mer. of Venice* iv 1 56
Woollen vassals, things created To buy and sell with groats *Coriolanus* iii 2 9
Woolly. When the work of generation was Between these woolly breeders in the act *Mer. of Venice* i 3 84
My fleece of woolly hair that now uncurls Even as an adder *T. Andron.* ii 3 34
Wool-sack. How now, wool-sack! what mutter you? 1 *Hen. IV.* ii 4 148
Woolvish. Why in this woolvish toge should I stand here, To beg of Hob and Dick? *Coriolanus* ii 3 122
Woolward. I go woolward for penance . . *L. L. Lost* v 2 717
Woo't. Thou wo't, wo't thou? thou wo't, wo't ta? do, do, thou rogue! 2 *Hen. IV.* ii 1 63
Woo't weep? woo't fight? woo't fast? woo't tear thyself? Woo't drink up eisel? eat a crocodile? *Hamlet* v 1 298
Woo't thou fight well?—I'll strike, and cry 'Take all' *Ant. and Cleo.* iv 2 7
Noblest of men, woo't die? Hast thou no care of me? . iv 15 59
Worcester. At Worcester must his body be interr'd *K. John* v 7 99
The Earl of Worcester Hath broke his staff, resign'd his stewardship *Richard II.* ii 2 58
Young Harry Percy, Sent from my brother Worcester, whencesoever . ii 3 22
This is Worcester, Malevolent to you in all aspects 1 *Hen. IV.* i 1 96
Worcester, get thee gone; for I do see Danger and disobedience in thine eye . . . i 3 15
Worcester is stolen away to-night; thy father's beard is turned white . ii 4 392
Cousin Glendower, Will you sit down? And uncle Worcester . . iii 1 5
My good Lord of Worcester will set forth To meet your father . iii 1 84
There is more news: I learn'd in Worcester, as I rode along . iv 1 125
Your uncle Worcester's horse came but to-day . . iv 3 21
There is my Lord of Worcester and a head Of gallant warriors . iv 4 25
Worcester! 'tis not well That you and I should meet upon such terms . v 1 9
No, good Worcester, no, We love our people well . . v 1 103
Ill-spirited Worcester! did not we send grace, Pardon, and terms of love? v 5 2
Bear Worcester to the death and Vernon too . . v 5 14
Then was that noble Worcester Too soon ta'en prisoner . 2 *Hen. IV.* i 1 125
Word. I endow'd thy purposes With words that made them known *Tempest* i 2 358
A word, good sir; I fear you have done yourself some wrong: a word . i 2 442
Silence! one word more Shall make me chide thee, if not hate thee . i 2 475
His word is more than the miraculous harp . . ii 1 86
You cram these words into mine ears against The stomach of my sense ii 1 106
O, but one word . . . . . ii 1 296
Interrupt the monster one word further, and, by this hand, I'll turn my mercy out o' doors . . iii 2 77
I will pay thy graces Home both in word and deed . v 1 71
Their eyes do offices of truth, their words Are natural breath . v 1 156
Having nothing but the word 'noddy' for my pains *T. G. of Ver.* i 1 131
O hateful hands, to tear such loving words! . . i 2 105
Be calm, good wind, blow not a word away Till I have found each letter i 2 118
'Tis a word or two Of commendations . . i 3 52
Did you perceive her earnest?—She gave me none, except an angry word ii 1 164
What, gone without a word? Ay, so true love should do: it cannot speak; For truth hath better deeds than words to grace it . . ii 2 16
Now should not the shoe speak a word for weeping . . ii 3 28
Now the dog all this while sheds not a tear nor speaks a word . ii 3 35
A fine volley of words, gentlemen, and quickly shot off . ii 4 33
If you spend word for word with me, I shall make your wit bankrupt . ii 4 41
You have an exchequer of words, and, I think, no other treasure . ii 4 44
It appears, by their bare liveries, that they live by your bare words . ii 4 46
In a word, for far behind his worth Comes all the praises . ii 4 71
Thou wouldst as soon go kindle fire with snow As seek to quench the fire of love with words . . ii 7 20
His words are bonds, his oaths are oracles, His love sincere . ii 7 75
Win her with gifts, if she respect not words: Dumb jewels often in their silent kind More than quick words do move a woman's mind . iii 1 89
Friend Valentine, a word.—My ears are stopt . iii 1 204
Unless the next word that thou speak'st Have some malignant power upon my life . . iii 1 237
Well, your old vice still; mistake the word . . iii 1 284
She is slow in words.—O villain, that set this down among her vices! iii 1 336
To be slow in words is a woman's only virtue . iii 1 338
More wealth than faults.—Why, that word makes the faults gracious iii 1 377
Where your good word cannot advantage him, Your slander never can endamage him . . iii 2 42
I weep myself to think upon thy words . iv 4 180
If the gentle spirit of moving words Can no way change you . v 4 55
He hath wronged me; indeed he hath; at a word, he hath *Mer. Wives* i 1 109
Word of denial in thy labras here! Word of denial: froth and scum i 1 166
Come, coz; we stay for you. A word with you, coz; marry, this, coz. i 1 214
Let me see thee froth and lime: I am at a word . i 3 15
Speak a good word to Mistress Anne Page for my master i 4 88
Notwithstanding,—to tell you in your ear; I would have no words of it i 4 109
I would have sworn his disposition would have gone to the truth of his words . . ii 1 62
This is the very same; the very hand, the very words . ii 1 85
What he gets more of her than sharp words, let it lie on my head . ii 1 191
At a word, hang no more about me, I am no gibbet for you . ii 2 16
Shall I vouchsafe your worship a word or two?—Two thousand . ii 2 41
What, the sword and the word! do you study them both? . iii 1 44
I pray you, let-a me speak a word with your ear . iii 1 81
Master Slender would speak a word with you.—I come to him . iii 4 30
So I have promised, and I'll be as good as my word . iii 4 112
I must carry her word quickly: she'll make you amends . iii 5 48
He sent me word to stay within: I like his money well . iii 5 59
You do ill to teach the child such words . iv 1 68
He will seek there, on my word . iv 2 61
On my word, it will serve him . iv 2 79
How? to send him word they'll meet him in the park at midnight? . iv 4 18
To Master Brook you yet shall hold your word . v 5 258
Thus can the demigod Authority Make us pay down for our offence by weight The words of heaven *Meas. for Meas.* i 2 126
One word, good friend. Lucio, a word with you.—A hundred . i 2 146
Soon at night I'll send him certain word of my success . i 4 89
I, that do speak a word, May call it back again . ii 2 57
You but waste your words . ii 2 72
That in the captain's but a choleric word, Which in the soldier is flat blasphemy . ii 2 130

Word. When I would pray and think, I think and pray To several subjects. Heaven hath my empty words *Meas. for Meas.* ii 4 2
Let me be bold; I do arrest your words . ii 4 134
On mine honour, My words express my purpose . ii 4 148
My business is a word or two with Claudio.—And very welcome . iii 1 48
Provost, a word with you.—As many as you please . iii 1 50
Whose settled visage and deliberate word Nips youth i' the head . iii 1 90
I'll pray a thousand prayers for thy death, No word to save thee . iii 1 147
Vouchsafe a word, young sister, but one word.—What is your will? . iii 1 152
I have heard of the lady, and good words went with her name . iii 1 220
Is the world as it was, man? Which is the way? Is it sad, and few words? . iii 2 54
Away with her to prison! Go to; no more words . iii 2 218
I have not yet made known to Mariana A word of this . iv 1 50
Not a word: if you have any thing to say to me, come to my ward . iv 3 65
For certain words he spake against your grace In your retirement . v 1 129
As there comes light from heaven and words from breath, . . . I am affianced this man's wife as strongly As words could make up vows . v 1 225
The friar and you Must have a word anon . v 1 364
Hast thou or word, or wit, or impudence, That yet can do thee office? . v 1 368
When your words are done, My woes end likewise . *Com. of Errors* i 1 27
Many a man would take you at your word . i 2 17
What answer, sir? when spake I such a word? . ii 2 13
That never words were music to thine ear, . . . Unless I spake . ii 2 116
Who, every word by all my wit being scann'd, Want wit in all one word to understand . ii 2 152
Even her very words Didst thou deliver to me on the mart . ii 2 165
A man may break a word with you, sir, and words are but wind . iii 1 75
Ill deeds are doubled with an evil word . iii 2 20
The folded meaning of your words' deceit . iii 2 36
With what persuasion did he tempt thy love?—With words that in an honest suit might move . iv 2 14
Why, sir, I brought you word an hour since . iv 3 37
His word might bear my wealth at any time . v 1 8
And I to thee engaged a prince's word . v 1 162
Most mighty duke, vouchsafe me speak a word . v 1 282
I am not of many words, but I thank you *Much Ado* i 1 159
Thou wilt be like a lover presently And tire the hearer with a book of words . i 1 309
Answer, clerk.—No more words: the clerk is answered . ii 1 115
You are Signior Antonio.—At a word, I am not . ii 1 118
You are he, you are he.—At a word, I am not . ii 1 125
She speaks poniards, and every word stabs . ii 1 255
Rather than hold three words' conference with this harpy . ii 1 279
His words are a very fantastical banquet, just so many strange dishes . ii 3 21
One doth not know How much an ill word may empoison liking . iii 1 86
I have studied eight or nine wise words to speak to you . iii 2 74
The word is too good to paint out her wickedness . iii 2 112
I must leave you.—One word, sir . iii 5 49
I never tempted her with word too large . iv 1 53
O my father, Prove you . . . that I yesternight Maintain'd the change of words with any creature . iv 1 185
When he shall hear she died upon his words . iv 1 225
Will you not eat your word?—With no sauce that can be devised to it . iv 1 280
A word in your ear: sir, I say to you, it is thought you are false knaves iv 2 29
Count Claudio did mean, upon his words, to disgrace Hero . iv 2 56
Charm ache with air and agony with words . v 1 26
Show outward hideousness, And speak off half a dozen dangerous words v 1 97
Shall I speak a word in your ear? . v 1 144
Knowing what hath passed between you and Claudio.—Only foul words v 2 50
Foul words is but foul wind, and foul wind is but foul breath v 2 52
Thou hast frighted the word out of his right sense, so forcible is thy wit v 2 55
We'll have dancing afterward.—First, of my word . v 4 123
If I break faith, this word shall speak for me . *L. L. Lost* i 1 154
For interim to our studies shall relate In high-born words . i 1 173
A most illustrious wight, A man of fire-new words, fashion's own knight i 1 179
How low soever the matter, I hope in God for high words . i 1 195
No words!—Of other men's secrets, I beseech you . i 1 231
How easy it is to put 'years' to the word 'three,' and study three years in two words . i 2 55
It is not for prisoners to be too silent in their words . i 2 169
In such apt and gracious words That aged ears play truant at his tales ii 1 73
We arrest your word . ii 1 160
Not a word with him but a jest.—And every jest but a word . ii 1 216
It was well done of you to take him at his word . ii 1 217
To speak that in words which his eye hath disclosed . ii 1 250
Doth the inconsiderate take salve for l'envoy, and the word l'envoy for a salve? . iii 1 80
Remuneration! O, that's the Latin word for three farthings . iii 1 138
Remuneration! . . . I will never buy and sell out of this word . iii 1 143
Fair payment for foul words is more than due . iv 1 19
Thou fellow, a word: Who gave thee this letter?—I told you . iv 1 102
I am toiling in a pitch,—pitch that defiles: defile! a foul word . iv 3 4
O that I had my wish!— . . . Amen, so I had mine: is not that a good word? . iv 3 94
For wisdom's sake, a word that all men love, Or for love's sake, a word that loves all men . iv 3 357
They have lived long on the alms-basket of words . v 1 42
I marvel thy master hath not eaten thee for a word . v 1 43
The word is well culled, chose, sweet, and apt . v 1 98
Via, goodman Dull! thou hast spoken no word all this while . v 1 157
What's your dark meaning, mouse, of this light word? . v 2 19
White-handed mistress, one sweet word with thee . v 2 230
One word in secret.—Let it not be sweet . v 2 236
Will you vouchsafe with me to change a word?—Name it . v 2 238
Let's part the word.—No, I'll not be your half . v 2 249
Not one word more, my maids; break off, break off . v 2 262
The king was weeping-ripe for a good word . v 2 274
Command me any service to her thither.—That she vouchsafe me audience for one word.—I will; and so will she . v 2 313
They did not bless us with one happy word . v 2 370
But that you take what doth to you belong, It were a fault to snatch words from my tongue . v 2 382
The noble lord Most honourably doth uphold his word . v 2 449
I implore so much expense of thy royal sweet breath as will utter a brace of words . v 2 525
Honest plain words best pierce the ear of grief . v 2 763
I'll mark no words that smooth-faced wooers say . v 2 838
Cuckoo, cuckoo: O word of fear, Unpleasing to a married ear! . v 2 911; 920
The words of Mercury are harsh after the songs of Apollo . v 2 940

Word. Keep word, Lysander: we must starve our sight From lovers' food *M. N. Dream* i 1 222
O, how fit a word Is that vile name to perish on my sword! ii 2 106
What, out of hearing? gone? no sound, no word? Alack, where are you? ii 2 152
I am amazed at your passionate words iii 2 220
I will keep my word with thee.—I would I had your bond, for I perceive A weak bond holds you: I'll not trust your word iii 2 266
Let us hear, sweet Bottom.—Not a word of me iv 2 34
Some ten words long, Which is as brief as I have known a play; But by ten words, my lord, it is too long v 1 61
In all the play There is not one word apt, one player fitted v 1 65
Tongue, not a word: Come, trusty sword; Come, blade, my breast imbrue v 1 349
First, rehearse your song by rote, To each word a warbling note v 1 405
In a word, but even now worth this, And now worth nothing *Mer. of Ven.* i 1 35
And she is fair and, fairer than that word, Of wondrous virtues i 1 162
To choose me a husband. O me, the word 'choose!' i 2 24
Who brings word the prince his master will be here to-night i 2 138
His words were 'Farewell mistress;' nothing else ii 5 45
If my gossip Report be an honest woman of her word iii 1 8
In a word, The seeming truth which cunning times put on iii 2 99
You have bereft me of all words, Only my blood speaks to you in my veins iii 2 177
Here are a few of the unpleasant'st words That ever blotted paper! iii 2 254
And every word in it a gaping wound, Issuing life-blood iii 2 268
Waste no time in words, But get thee gone iii 4 54
How every fool can play upon the word! iii 5 48
Bid them prepare dinner.—That is done too, sir; only 'cover' is the word iii 5 57
O dear discretion, how his words are suited! iii 5 70
The fool hath planted in his memory An army of good words iii 5 72
That for a tricksy word Defy the matter iii 5 74
'Nearest his heart:' those are the very words iv 1 254
The words expressly are 'a pound of flesh:' Take then thy bond iv 1 307
A second Daniel! I thank thee, Jew, for teaching me that word iv 1 341
I bring word My mistress will before the break of day Be here v 1 28
Which speed, we hope, the better for our words v 1 115
You are very welcome to our house: It must appear in other ways than words v 1 140
My old master! he would not have spoke such a word *As Y. Like It* i 1 89
Not a word?—Not one to throw at a dog.—No, thy words are too precious to be cast away upon curs i 3 2
If their purgation did consist in words, They are as innocent as grace itself i 3 55
Upon mine honour, And in the greatness of my word, you die i 3 91
When shalt thou see him again? Answer me in one word iii 2 237
'Tis a word too great for any mouth of this age's size iii 2 239
I do not know what 'poetical' is: is it honest in deed and word? iii 3 18
The oath of a lover is no stronger than the word of a tapster iii 4 34
He writes brave verses, speaks brave words, swears brave oaths iii 4 44
I'll sauce her with bitter words iii 5 69
What care I for words? yet words do well When he that speaks them pleases iii 5 111
Pray thee, marry us.—I cannot say the words.—You must begin iv 1 128
Ethiope words, blacker in their effect Than in their countenance iv 3 35
Hence, and not a word; for here comes more company iv 3 74
Keep you your word, O duke, to give your daughter v 4 19
Keep your word, Phebe, that you'll marry me v 4 21
Keep your word, Silvius, that you'll marry her, If she refuse me v 4 23
He sent me word, if I said his beard was not cut well, he was in the mind it was v 4 74
If I sent him word again 'it was not well cut,' he would send me word, he cut it to please himself v 4 76
I will not eat my word, now thou art mine v 4 155
Let me have audience for a word or two v 4 157
But did I never speak of all that time?—O, yes, my lord, but very idle words *T. of Shrew* Ind. 2 85
Spake you not these words plain, 'Sirrah, knock me here?' i 2 40
'Twixt such friends as we Few words suffice i 2 66
O' my word, an she knew him as well as I do i 2 108
With more successful words Than you, unless you were a scholar i 2 158
A word ere you go; Are you a suitor to the maid you talk of? i 2 229
Is it any offence?—No; if without more words you will get you hence i 2 232
To what end are all these words? i 2 250
When did she cross thee with a bitter word?—Her silence flouts me ii 1 28
Be thou arm'd for some unhappy words ii 1 140
And, with that word, she struck me on the head ii 1 154
Say she be mute and will not speak a word; Then I'll commend her volubility ii 1 175
Love Bianca more Than words can witness, or your thoughts can guess ii 1 338
Means but well, Whatever fortune stays him from his word iii 2 23
I am come to keep my word, Though in some part enforced to digress iii 2 108
Ha' done with words: To me she's married, not unto my clothes iii 2 118
What, not a word? Nay, then thou lovest it not iv 3 42
I will be free Even to the uttermost, as I please, in words iv 3 80
Take no unkindness of his hasty words iv 3 169
You seem a sober ancient gentleman by your habit, but your words show you a madman v 1 76
For both our sakes, I would that word were true v 2 15
My mistress sends you word That she is busy and she cannot come v 2 80
To bandy word for word and frown for frown v 2 172
His plausive words He scatter'd not in ears *All's Well* i 2 53
And did communicate to herself her own words to her own ears i 3 112
Good sparks and lustrous, a word, good metals ii 1 41
If thou proceed As high as word, my deed shall match thy meed ii 1 213
The mere word 's a slave Debosh'd on every tomb, on every grave ii 3 144
You are not worth another word, else I'ld call you knave ii 3 280
What sharp stings are in her mildest words! iii 4 18
Let every word weigh heavy of her worth That he does weigh too light iii 4 31
I love not many words.—No more than a fish loves water iii 6 91
What to your sworn counsel I have spoken Is so from word to word iii 7 10
Your oaths Are words and poor conditions, but unseal'd iv 2 30
But with the word the time will bring on summer iv 4 31
I beseech your honour to hear me one single word.—You beg a single penny more: come, you shall ha't; save your word v 2 38
You beg more than 'word,' then. Cox my passion! give me your hand v 2 42
Whose words all ears took captive v 3 17
All is whole; Not one word more of the consumed time v 3 38
Speaks three or four languages word for word without book *T. Night* i 3 28

Word. He will not pass his word for two pence that you are no fool *T. N.* i 5 87
I hold the olive in my hand; my words are as full of peace as matter i 5 226
They that dally nicely with words may quickly make them wanton iii 1 17
Her name's a word; and to dally with that word might make my sister wanton iii 1 22
Indeed words are very rascals since bonds disgraced them iii 1 24
Thy reason, man?—Troth, sir, I can yield you none without words; and words are grown so false, I am loath to prove reason with them iii 1 28
I am indeed not her fool, but her corrupter of words iii 1 41
Out of my welkin, I might say 'element,' but the word is over-worn iii 1 66
Hob, nob, is his word; give't or take't iii 4 263
And, for that I promised you, I'll be as good as my word iii 4 357
Methinks his words do from such passion fly, That he believes himself iii 4 407
He has heard that word of some great man and now applies it to a fool iv 1 12
To him in thine own voice, and bring me word how thou findest him iv 2 72
Maintain no words with him, good fellow iv 2 107
But for thee, fellow; fellow, thy words are madness v 1 101
I Do come with words as medicinal as true *W. Tale* ii 3 37
Within this hour bring me word 'tis done, And by good testimony ii 3 136
Whose every word deserves To taste of thy most worst iii 2 179
If word nor oath Prevail not, go and see iii 2 204
Not a word, a word; we stand upon our manners iv 4 164
Forewarn him that he use no scurrilous words in's tunes iv 4 216
Clamour your tongues, and not a word more iv 4 251
Mark thou my words: Follow us to the court iv 4 442
For instance, sir, That you may know you shall not want, one word iv 4 605
He would not stir his pettitoes till he had both tune and words iv 4 620
I will tell the king all, every word, yea, and his son's pranks too iv 4 717
And the words that follow'd Should be 'Remember mine' v 1 66
They shoot but calm words folded up in smoke *K. John* ii 1 229
Our ears are cudgell'd; not a word of his But buffets better than a fist ii 1 464
I was never so bethump'd with words Since I first call'd my brother's father dad ii 1 466
Who, having no external thing to lose But the word 'maid,' cheats the poor maid of that ii 1 572
This Commodity, This bawd, this broker, this all-changing word ii 1 582
For thy word Is but the vain breath of a common man iii 1 7
Be these sad signs confirmers of thy words? Then speak again; not all thy former tale, But this one word, whether thy tale be true iii 1 24
Envenom him with words, or get thee gone And leave those woes alone iii 1 63
O, that a man should speak those words to me! iii 1 130
The latest breath that gave the sound of words Was deep-sworn faith iii 1 230
Using conceit alone, Without eyes, ears, and harmful sound of words iii 3 51
Walks up and down with me, Puts on his pretty looks, repeats his words iii 4 95
His words do take possession of my bosom iv 1 32
Many a poor man's son would have lien still And ne'er have spoke a loving word to you iv 1 51
I will not stir, nor wince, nor speak a word, Nor look upon the iron angerly iv 1 81
As bid me tell my tale in express words iv 2 234
Whate'er you think, good words, I think, were best iv 3 28
Our souls religiously confirm thy words iv 3 73
Now keep your holy word v 1 5
And send him word by me which way you go v 3 7
Let not my cold words here accuse my zeal *Richard II.* i 1 47
The hopeless word of 'never to return' Breathe I against thee i 3 152
How long a time lies in one little word! i 3 213
Thy word is current with him for my death i 3 231
To what purpose dost thou hoard thy words, That thou return'st no greeting to thy friends? i 3 253
My heart disdained that my tongue Should so profane the word i 4 13
Such grief That words seem'd buried in my sorrow's grave i 4 15
Would the word 'farewell' have lengthen'd hours And added years to his short banishment, He should have had a volume of farewells i 4 16
Where words are scarce, they are seldom spent in vain ii 1 7
They breathe truth that breathe their words in pain ii 1 8
These words hereafter thy tormentors be! ii 1 136
Impute his words To wayward sickliness and age in him ii 1 141
His tongue is now a stringless instrument; Words, life, and all, old Lancaster hath spent ii 1 150
Let him ne'er speak more That speaks thy words again to do thee harm! ii 1 231
Speaking so, Thy words are but as thoughts; therefore, be bold ii 1 276
For God's sake, speak comfortable words ii 2 76
Of much less value is my company Than your good words ii 3 20
I shall not need transport my words by you ii 3 81
That word 'grace' In an ungracious mouth is but profane ii 3 88
Let's fight with gentle words Till time lend friends iii 3 131
With words of sooth iii 3 136
If my word be sterling yet in England, Let it command a mirror hither straight iv 1 264
His words come from his mouth, ours from our breast v 3 102
If I were thy nurse, thy tongue to teach, 'Pardon' should be the first word v 3 114
I never long'd to hear a word till now v 3 115
The word is short, but not so short as sweet; No word like 'pardon' for kings' mouths so meet v 3 117
My hard-hearted lord, That set'st the word itself against the word! v 3 122
Didst thou not mark the king, what words he spake? v 4 1
These were his very words.—'Have I no friend?' quoth he v 4 3
As thoughts of things divine, are intermix'd With scruples and do set the word itself Against the word v 5 13
Neither my good word nor princely favour v 6 42
And sends me word, I shall have none *1 Hen. IV.* i 1 94
Sir John stands to his word, the devil shall have his bargain i 2 130
Then art thou damned for keeping thy word with the devil i 2 135
By how much better than my word I am, By so much shall I falsify men's hopes i 2 234
That ever this fellow should have fewer words than a parrot, and yet the son of a woman! ii 4 111
And, with a word, out-faced you from your prize ii 4 283
That thou art my son, I have partly thy mother's word, partly my own opinion ii 4 444
Not in pleasure but in passion, not in words only, but in woes also ii 4 459
If thou dost it half so gravely, so majestically, both in word and matter ii 4 479
I will engage my word to thee That I will ii 4 563
I cried 'hum,' and 'well, go to,' But mark'd him not a word iii 1 159
Hath sent word That Douglas and the English rebels met iii 2 164
Darest thou be as good as thy word now? iii 3 164
Either we or they must lower lie.—Rare words! brave world! iii 3 229
Nay, task me to my word; approve me lord iv 1 9

Word. There is not such a word Spoke of in Scotland as this term of fear *1 Hen. IV.* iv 1 84
Bring me word What he will do . . . . . . v 1 109
What is honour? a word. What is in that word honour? . . v 1 136
It cannot be, The king should keep his word in loving us . . v 2 5
That same word, rebellion, did divide The action of their bodies from their souls; And they did fight with queasiness . *2 Hen. IV.* i 1 194
It is not a confident brow, nor the throng of words . . ii 1 122
Come, no more words of it . . . . ii 1 151
No more words; let's have her . . . . . . ii 1 178
Make him eat it.—That's to make him eat twenty of his words . ii 2 150
No word to your master that I am yet come to town . . ii 2 177
You broke your word, When you were more endear'd to it than now ii 3 10
Sir John must not know of it: Bardolph hath brought word . ii 4 20
God's light, these villains will make the word as odious as the word 'occupy;' which was an excellent good word before it was ill sorted ii 4 160
These are very bitter words . . . . ii 4 185
When Richard, with his eye brimful of tears, . . . Did speak these words iii 1 69
Meet them like necessities: And that same word even now cries out on us iii 1 94
Pardon me, sir; I have heard the word. Phrase call you it? . iii 2 80
I will maintain the word with my sword to be a soldier-like word, and a word of exceeding good command . . . . . iii 2 82
I will not use many words with you . . . . . iii 2 309
Go to; I have spoke at a word. God keep you . . . iii 2 319
Every third word a lie, duer paid to the hearer than the Turk's tribute iii 2 330
Turning the word to sword and life to death . . . iv 2 10
I take your princely word for these redresses.—I give it you, and will maintain my word . . . . iv 2 66
The word of peace is render'd: hark, how they shout! . . iv 2 87
Not a tongue of them all speaks any other word but my name . iv 3 22
Believe not the word of the noble . . . . . . iv 3 59
'Tis needful that the most immodest word Be look'd upon and learn'd . iv 4 70
Will Fortune never come with both hands full, But write her fair words still in foulest letters? . . . . iv 4 104
So shall I live to speak my father's words . . . . v 2 107
Be it your charge, my lord, To see perform'd the tenour of our word v 5 75
I will be as good as my word . . . . v 5 90
Which I could with a ready guess declare, Before the Frenchman speak a word of it . . . . *Hen. V.* i 1 97
'Couple a gorge!' That is the word. I thee defy again . . ii 1 76
Let senses rule; the word is 'Pitch and Pay:' Trust none . . ii 3 51
By the means whereof a' breaks words, and keeps whole weapons . iii 2 37
He hath heard that men of few words are the best men . . iii 2 39
His few bad words are matched with as few good deeds . . iii 2 41
Quickly bring us word of England's fall . . . . iii 5 68
Uttered as prave words at the pridge as you shall see in a summer's day iii 6 66
If I live to see it, I will never trust his word after . . iv 1 208
Keep thy word: fare thee well . . . . . . iv 1 238
Description cannot suit itself in words To demonstrate the life of such a battle In life so lifeless as it shows itself . . . . iv 2 53
Our names, Familiar in his mouth as household words . . iv 3 52
Perpend my words, O Signieur Dew, and mark . . . iv 4 8
What are his words?—He prays you to save his life . . iv 4 46
Upon these words I came and cheer'd him up . . . iv 6 20
Then every soldier kill his prisoners; Give the word through . iv 6 38
As I judge By his blunt bearing he will keep his word . . iv 7 185
I have been as good as my word . . . . . . iv 8 34
And dare not avouch in your deeds any of your words . . v 1 77
For the one, I have neither words nor measure . . . v 2 139
And for my English moiety take the word of a king and a bachelor v 2 229
'I am thine:' which word thou shalt no sooner bless mine ear withal . v 2 256
By guileful fair words peace may be obtain'd . . *1 Hen. VI.* i 1 77
Believe my words, For they are certain and unfallible . . i 2 58
If thou vanquishest, thy words are true . . . . i 2 96
I will not answer thee with words, but blows . . . i 3 69
If thou spy'st any, run and bring me word . . . . i 4 19
Thus Joan la Pucelle hath perform'd her word . . . i 6 3
I'll maintain my words On any plot of ground in Christendom . ii 4 88
In argument upon a case, Some words there grew 'twixt Somerset and me . . . . ii 5 46
My fainting words do warrant death: Thou art my heir . . ii 5 95
When Gloucester says the word, King Henry goes . . . iii 1 184
Take heed, be wary how you place your words . . . iii 2 3
O, let no words, but deeds, revenge this treason! . . . iii 2 49
By fair persuasions mix'd with sugar'd words . . . iii 3 18
Speak, Pucelle, and enchant him with thy words . . . iii 3 40
She hath bewitch'd me with her words, Or nature makes me suddenly relent . . . . iii 3 58
These haughty words of hers Have batter'd me like roaring cannon-shot iii 3 78
Darest thou maintain the former words thou spakest? . . iii 4 31
He dies, we lose; I break my warlike word . . . . iv 3 31
The regent hath with Talbot broke his word . . . . iv 6 2
These words of yours draw life-blood from my heart . . iv 6 43
Submission, Dauphin! 'tis a mere French word . . . iv 7 54
Words sweetly placed and modestly directed . . . . v 3 179
Strumpet, thy words condemn thy brat and thee . . . v 4 84
Her grace in speech, Her words y-clad with wisdom's majesty *2 Hen. VI.* i 1 33
Are the cities, that I got with wounds, Deliver'd up again with peaceful words? . . . . i 1 122
Let not his smoothing words Bewitch your hearts; be wise and circumspect . . . . i 1 156
Seal up your lips, and give no words but mum . . . i 2 89
His words were these . . . . i 3 186
Say, man, were these thy words? . . . . . . i 3 189
Hang me, if ever I spake the words . . . . . . i 3 201
Reprove my allegation, if you can; Or else conclude my words effectual iii 1 41
And lowly words were ransom for their fault . . . iii 1 127
With ignominious words, though clerkly couch'd . . . iii 1 179
Say but the word, and I will be his priest . . . . iii 1 272
I thank thee, Meg; these words content me much . . . iii 2 26
I did dream to-night The duke was dumb and could not speak a word . iii 2 32
Hide not thy poison with such sugar'd words . . . . iii 2 45
Every word you speak in his behalf Is slander to your royal dignity iii 2 208
Dread lord, the commons send you word by me . . . iii 2 243
Had I but said, I would have kept my word, But when I swear, it is irrevocable . . . . iii 2 293
My tongue should stumble in mine earnest words . . . iii 2 316
First let my words stab him, as he hath me.—Base slave, thy words are blunt and so art thou . . . . iv 1 66
Thy words move rage and not remorse in me . . . . iv 1 112

Word. Will you credit this base drudge's words, That speaks he knows not what? . . . . *2 Hen. VI.* iv 2 159
Seeing gentle words will not prevail, Assail them with the army . iv 2 184
Be it a lordship, thou shalt have it for that word . . . iv 7 6
Such abominable words as no Christian ear can endure to hear . . iv 7 44
I feel remorse in myself with his words . . . . . iv 7 112
I think this word 'sallet' was born to do me good . . . iv 10 11
And now the word 'sallet' must serve me to feed on . . . iv 10 16
As for words, whose greatness answers words, Let this my sword report what speech forbears . . . . iv 10 56
I cannot give due action to my words, Except a sword or sceptre balance it . . . . v 1 8
His sons, he says, shall give their words for him . . . v 1 137
If our words will serve.—And if words will not, then our weapons shall v 1 139
By words or blows here let us win our right . . *3 Hen. VI.* i 1 37
Frowns, words, and threats Shall be the war that Henry means to use i 1 72
Urge it no more; lest that, instead of words, I send thee, Warwick, such a messenger As shall revenge his death . . . . . . i 1 98
O Clifford, how thy words revive my heart! . . . . i 1 163
Hear me but one word: Let me for this my life-time reign as king . i 1 170
My father's blood Hath stopp'd the passage where thy words should enter i 3 22
I will not bandy with thee word for word, But buckle with thee blows i 4 49
And at each word's deliverance Stab poniards in our flesh till all were told, The words would add more anguish than the wounds . . ii 1 97
The Duke of Norfolk sends you word by me, The queen is coming . ii 1 206
Have done with words, my lords, and hear me speak . . . ii 2 117
The wound that bred this meeting here Cannot be cured by words . ii 2 122
These words will cost ten thousand lives this day . . . ii 2 177
My tears shall wipe away these bloody marks; And no more words till they have flow'd their fill . . . . ii 5 72
Though before his face I speak the words, Your brother Richard mark'd him for the grave . . . . ii 6 39
If so thou think'st, vex him with eager words . . . . ii 6 68
Soon won with moving words . . . . iii 1 34
Her words do show her wit incomparable . . . . . iii 2 85
And witch sweet ladies with my words and looks. O miserable thought! iii 2 150
Those gracious words revive my drooping thoughts . . . iii 3 21
Heavens grant that Warwick's words bewitch him not! . . . iii 3 112
These words have turn'd my hate to love; And I forgive and quite forget iii 3 199
Few words, But such as I, without your special pardon, Dare not relate iv 1 86
Tell me their words as near as thou canst guess them . . iv 1 90
At my depart, these were his very words . . . . . iv 1 92
These were her words, utter'd with mild disdain . . . iv 1 98
In few words, If you'll not here proclaim yourself our king, I'll leave you . . . . iv 7 53
Speak gentle words and humbly bend thy knee . . . . v 1 22
A woman of this valiant spirit Should, if a coward heard her speak these words, Infuse his breast with magnanimity . . . . v 4 40
For every word I speak, Ye see, I drink the water of mine eyes . v 4 74
I will not hear them speak.—For my part, I'll not trouble thee with words . . . . v 5 5
Kneel thou, Whilst I propose the selfsame words to thee . . v 5 20
By heaven, brat, I'll plague ye for that word . . . . v 5 27
Why should she live, to fill the world with words? . . . v 5 44
Ah, kill me with thy weapon, not with words! . . . . v 6 26
And this word 'love,' which greybeards call divine, Be resident in men like one another And not in me . . . . v 6 81
My tongue could never learn sweet smoothing words . *Richard III.* i 2 169
That was in thy rage: Speak it again, and, even with the word . i 2 189
Entertain good comfort, And cheer his grace with quick and merry words i 3 5
The urging of that word 'judgement' hath bred a kind of remorse in me i 4 109
Attended to their sugar'd words, But look'd not on the poison of their hearts . . . . iii 1 13
Thus, like the formal vice, Iniquity, I moralize two meanings in one word iii 1 83
He sends you word He dreamt to-night the boar had razed his helm iii 2 10
Murder thy breath in middle of a word, And then begin again . iii 5 2
Your grace's word shall serve, As well as I had seen and heard him speak . . . . iii 5 62
The citizens are mum and speak not a word . . . . iii 7 3
No, so God help me, they spake not a word . . . . iii 7 24
My woman's heart Grossly grew captive to his honey words . . iv 1 80
My words are dull; O, quicken them with thine! . . . . iv 4 124
Why should calamity be full of words?—Windy attorneys to their client woes . . . . iv 4 126
And in the breath of bitter words let's smother My damned son . iv 4 133
Hear me a word; For I shall never speak to thee again . . iv 4 180
Conscience is but a word that cowards use . . . . v 3 309
Our ancient word of courage, fair Saint George, Inspire us! . . v 3 349
These very words I've heard him utter to his son-in-law . *Hen. VIII.* i 2 135
Who fed him every minute With words of sovereignty . . i 2 150
And that he doubted 'Twould prove the verity of certain words . i 2 159
Nor my prayers Are not words duly hallow'd . . . . i 3 68
Your words, Domestics to you, serve your will as't please Yourself . ii 4 113
Or ever Have to you . . . spake one the least word that might Be to the prejudice of her present state . . . . ii 4 153
'Tis a kind of good deed to say well: And yet words are no deeds . iii 2 154
He said he did; and with his deed did crown His word upon you . iii 2 156
Words cannot carry Authority so weighty . . . . . iii 2 233
Till I find more than will or words to do it . . . . iii 2 236
If I loved many words, lord, I should tell you You have as little honesty as honour . . . . iii 2 270
Honourably received him; To whom he gave these words . . iv 2 20
Ever double Both in his words and meaning . . . . iv 2 39
Your painted gloss discovers, To men that understand you, words and weakness . . . . v 3 72
The words I utter Let none think flattery, for they'll find 'em truth . v 5 16
But here's yet in the word 'hereafter' the kneading *Troi. and Cres.* i 1 23
Words, vows, gifts, tears, and love's full sacrifice, He offers in another's enterprise . . . . i 2 308
Great Agamemnon, Nestor shall apply Thy latest words . . i 3 33
Achilles shall have word of this intent . . . . . i 3 306
Good words, Thersites.—What's the quarrel? . . . . ii 1 97
No more words, Thersites; peace! . . . . . . ii 1 124
Friend, you! pray you, a word . . . . iii 1 1
Dear lord, you are full of fair words.—You speak your fair pleasure iii 1 50
My lord, will you vouchsafe me a word? . . . . . iii 1 64
Nay, I care not for such words; no, no . . . . . iii 1 83
You have bereft me of all words, lady.—Words pay no debts, give her deeds . . . . iii 2 57
Few words to fair faith . . . . iii 2 103

Word. You know now your hostages; your uncle's word and my firm faith *Troi. and Cres.* iii 2 116
Nay, I ll give my word for her too . iii 2 117
Bring word if Hector will to-morrow Be answer'd in his challenge . iii 3 34
Neither gave to me Good word nor look : what, are my deeds forgot? . iii 3 144
Since she could speak, She hath not given so many good words breath As for her Greeks and Trojans suffer'd death . iv 1 73
Matchless, firm of word, Speaking in deeds and deedless in his tongue . iv 5 97
I'll endeavour deeds to match these words . iv 5 259
The sun borrows of the moon, when Diomed keeps his word . v 1 102
Now, my sweet guardian! Hark, a word with you.—Yea, so familiar! v 2 7
Let your mind be coupled with your words . v 2 15
Hark, one word in your ear.—O plague and madness! . v 2 34
By hell and all hell's torments, I will not speak a word! . v 2 44
Nay, stay; by Jove, I will not speak a word . v 2 52
I will not keep my word.—Why, then, farewell . v 2 98
One cannot speak a word, But it straight starts you . v 2 100
Words, words, mere words, no matter from the heart . v 3 108
My love with words and errors still she feeds; But edifies another with her deeds . v 3 111
Hector's dead: There is a word will Priam turn to stone . v 10 18
And, in a word, Scare Troy out of itself . v 10 20
We have ever your good word.—He that will give good words to thee will flatter Beneath abhorring *Coriolanus* i 1 170
These are the words: I think I have the letter here . i 2 7
O' my word, the father's son! I'll swear, 'tis a very pretty boy . i 3 62
No, at a word, madam; indeed, I must not . i 3 122
Bring me word thither How the world goes . i 10 31
'Tis right.—It was his word . ii 1 253
Sir, I hope My words disbench'd you not.—No, sir: yet oft, When blows have made me stay, I fled from words . ii 2 75
No more words, we beseech you.—How! no more! . iii 1 75
So shall my lungs Coin words till their decay against those measles . iii 1 78
Let deeds express What's like to be their words . iii 1 133
Hear me one word; Beseech you, tribunes, hear me but a word . iii 1 215
If . . . I may be heard, I would crave a word or two . iii 1 283
But with such words that are but roted in Your tongue . iii 2 55
This no more dishonours you at all Than to take in a town with gentle words . iii 2 59
For they have pardons, being ask'd, as free As words to little purpose . iii 2 89
The word is 'mildly.' Pray you, let us go . iii 2 142
I would not buy Their mercy at the price of one fair word . iii 3 91
Banish him that struck more blows for Rome Than thou hast spoken words? . iv 2 20
More noble blows than ever thou wise words; And for Rome's good . iv 2 21
Thou'rt tired, then, in a word, I also am Longer to live most weary . iv 5 100
Each word thou hast spoke hath weeded from my heart A root of ancient envy . iv 5 108
If you had told as many lies in his behalf as you have uttered words in your own, you should not pass . v 2 26
Another word, Menenius, I will not hear thee speak . v 2 97
You shall bear A better witness back than words . v 3 204
Intends to appear before the people, hoping To purge himself with words v 6 8
Rest on my word, and let not discontent Daunt all your hopes *T. Andron.* i 1 267
True nobility Warrants these words in princely courtesy . i 1 272
O monstrous! what reproachful words are these? . i 1 308
These words are razors to my wounded heart . i 1 314
'And shall!' what villain was it spake that word? . i 1 359
These words, these looks, infuse new life in me . i 1 461
I have pass'd My word and promise to the emperor, That you will be more mild . i 1 469
Why should he despair that knows to court it With words, fair looks? . ii 1 92
And strike her home by force, if not by words . ii 1 118
Sweet lords, entreat her hear me but a word . ii 3 138
Let them not speak a word; the guilt is plain . ii 3 301
Cousin, a word; where is your husband? . ii 4 12
My lord the emperor Sends thee this word . iii 1 151
As if we should forget we had no hands, If Marcus did not name the word! . iii 2 33
I will go get a leaf of brass, And with a gad of steel will write these words . iv 1 103
But Pluto sends you word, If you will have Revenge from hell, you shall . iv 3 37
Of my word, I have written to effect; There's not a god left unsolicited iv 3 59
With words more sweet, and yet more dangerous, Than baits to fish . iv 4 90
Why dost not speak? what, deaf? not a word? A halter, soldiers! . v 1 46
I am come to talk with thee.—No, not a word . v 2 17
Stop close their mouths, let them not speak a word . v 2 165
Let them not speak to me; But let them hear what fearful words I utter v 2 169
If my frosty signs and chaps of age, Grave witnesses of true experience, Cannot induce you to attend my words . v 3 79
Gregory, o' my word, we'll not carry coals *Rom. and Jul.* i 1 1
What, drawn, and talk of peace! I hate the word, As I hate hell . i 1 77
Three civil brawls, bred of an airy word, By thee, old Capulet, and Montague . i 1 96
Bid a sick man in sadness make his will: Ah, word ill urged! . i 1 209
Tut, dun's the mouse, the constable's own word . i 4 40
Madam, your mother craves a word with you.—What is her mother? i 5 113
Speak to my gossip Venus one fair word, One nick-name for her purblind son . ii 1 11
Take all myself.—I take thee at thy word . ii 2 49
My name, dear saint, is hateful to myself, Because it is an enemy to thee; Had I it written, I would tear the word . ii 2 57
My ears have not yet drunk a hundred words Of that tongue's utterance, yet I know the sound . ii 2 58
I will take thy word: yet, if thou swear'st, Thou mayst prove false . ii 2 91
Three words, dear Romeo, and good night indeed . ii 2 142
Send me word to-morrow, By one that I'll procure to come to thee . ii 2 144
I stretch it out for that word 'broad' . ii 4 89
My words would bandy her to my sweet love, And his to me . ii 5 14
Close our hands with holy words, Then love-devouring death do what he dare . ii 6 6
Conceit, more rich in matter than in words, Brags of his substance . ii 6 30
Gentlemen, good den: a word with one of you.—And but one word with one of us? couple it with something; make it a word and a blow . iii 1 41
Some word there was, worser than Tybalt's death, That murder'd me . iii 2 108
That one word 'banished,' Hath slain ten thousand Tybalts . iii 2 113
'Romeo is banished,' to speak that word, Is father, mother, Tybalt, Romeo, Juliet, All slain, all dead . iii 2 122

Word. There is no end, no limit, measure, bound, In that word's death; no words can that woe sound *Rom. and Jul.* iii 2 126
The kind prince, Taking thy part, hath rush'd aside the law, And turn'd that black word death to banishment . iii 3 27
'Banished'? O friar, the damned use that word in hell . iii 3 47
How hast thou the heart . . . To mangle me with that word 'banished'? iii 3 51
Thou fond mad man, hear me but speak a word . iii 3 52
I'll give thee armour to keep off that word . iii 3 54
I beseech you on my knees, Hear me with patience but to speak a word iii 5 160
Talk not to me, for I'll not speak a word: Do as thou wilt . iii 5 204
What say'st thou? hast thou not a word of joy? . iii 5 213
Why, love, I say! madam! sweet-heart! why, bride! What, not a word? . iv 5 4
A thousand moral paintings I can show That shall demonstrate these quick blows of Fortune's More pregnantly than words *T. of Athens* i 1 92
O my friends, I have one word to say to you . i 2 174
I beseech your honour, Vouchsafe me a word; it does concern you near i 2 183
He owes For every word: he is so kind that he now Pays interest for't i 2 205
You gave Good words the other day of a bay courser I rode on: it is yours . i 2 217
You may take my word, my lord; I know, no man Can justly praise but what he does affect . i 2 220
My relief Must not be toss d and turn'd to me in words . ii 1 26
The world is but a word: Were it all yours to give it in a breath, How quickly were it gone! . ii 2 161
Will you befriend me so far, as to use mine own words to him? . iii 2 65
Your words have took such pains as if they labour'd . iii 5 26
Do you dare our anger? 'Tis in few words, but spacious in effect . iii 5 97
Not one word more: Thus part we rich in sorrow, parting poor . iv 2 28
I am rapt and cannot cover The monstrous bulk of this ingratitude With any size of words . v 1 69
Speak, and be hang'd: For each true word, a blister! . v 1 135
These words become your lips as they pass thorough them . v 1 198
Lips, let sour words go by and language end . v 1 223
'Tis most nobly spoken.—Descend, and keep your words . v 4 64
Upon the word, Accoutred as I was, I plunged in *J. Cæsar* i 2 104
I am glad that my weak words Have struck but thus much show of fire i 2 176
If I would not have taken him at a word, I would I might go to hell . i 2 270
Which gives men stomach to digest his words With better appetite . i 2 305
He did bid Antonius Send word to you he would be there to-morrow . i 3 38
Look in the calendar, and bring me word . ii 1 42
Shall I entreat a word? . ii 1 100
Secret Romans, that have spoke the word, And will not palter . ii 1 125
If you shall send them word you will not come, Their minds may change . ii 2 95
Bring me word, boy, if thy lord look well, For he went sickly forth . ii 4 13
Come to me again, And bring me word what he doth say to thee . ii 4 46
I mean, sweet words, Low-crooked court'sies, and base spaniel-fawning iii 1 42
Mark'd ye his words? He would not take the crown . iii 2 117
But yesterday the word of Cæsar might Have stood against the world . iii 2 123
I have neither wit, nor words, nor worth, Action, nor utterance . iii 2 225
Stand, ho!—Give the word, ho! and stand . iv 2 2
Stand, ho! Speak the word along . iv 2 33
Make forth; the generals would have some words . v 1 25
Words before blows: is it so, countrymen?—Not that we love words better . v 1 27
Good words are better than bad strokes . v 1 29
In your bad strokes, Brutus, you give good words . v 1 30
But for your words, they rob the Hybla bees, And leave them honeyless v 1 34
O Cassius, Brutus gave the word too early . v 3 5
Bring us word unto Octavius' tent How every thing is chanced . v 4 31
Slaying is the word; It is a deed in fashion . v 5 4
No, not for all the world.—Peace then! no words . v 5 7
List a word.—What says my lord? . v 5 15
So well thy words become thee as thy wounds *Macbeth* i 2 43
Went it not so?—To the selfsame tune and words . i 3 88
Cousins, a word, I pray you . i 3 127
When we can entreat an hour to serve, We would spend it in some words upon that business . ii 1 23
Words to the heat of deeds too cold breath gives . ii 1 61
Say to the king, I would attend his leisure For a few words . iii 2 4
Thou marvell'st at my words: but hold thee still . iii 2 54
From broad words and 'cause he fail'd His presence at the tyrant's feast, I hear Macduff lives in disgrace . iii 6 21
Two or three, my lord, that bring you word Macduff is fled to England iv 1 141
I have words That would be howl'd out in the desert air . iv 3 193
What, man! ne'er pull your hat upon your brows; Give sorrow words iv 3 209
There would have been a time for such a word . v 5 18
I have no words: My voice is in my sword . v 8 6
That keep the word of promise to our ear, And break it to our hope . v 8 21
Both in time, Form of the thing, each word made true and good *Hamlet* i 2 210
I would not, in plain terms, from this time forth, Have you so slander any moment leisure, As to give words or talk with the Lord Hamlet . i 3 134
I could a tale unfold whose lightest word Would harrow up thy soul . i 5 15
Now to my word; It is 'Adieu, adieu! remember me' . i 5 110
These are but wild and whirling words, my lord . i 5 133
Have you given him any hard words of late? . ii 1 107
What do you read, my lord?—Words, words, words . ii 2 194
Unpack my heart with words, And fall a-cursing, like a very drab . ii 2 614
The harlot's cheek . . . Is not more ugly to the thing that helps it Than is my deed to my most painted word . iii 1 53
Words of so sweet breath composed As made the things more rich . iii 1 98
Suit the action to the word, the word to the action . iii 2 20
These words are not mine.—No, nor mine now . iii 2 102
The lady doth protest too much, methinks.—O, but she'll keep her word . iii 2 241
I'll take the ghost's word for a thousand pound . iii 2 298
Vouchsafe me a word with you.—Sir, a whole history . iii 2 307
How in my words soever she be shent, To give them seals never, my soul, consent! . iii 2 416
My words fly up, my thoughts remain below: Words without thoughts never to heaven go . iii 3 97
As kill a king!—Ay, lady, 'twas my word . iii 4 30
Plucks The very soul, and sweet religion makes A rhapsody of words . iii 4 48
Speak to me no more; These words, like daggers, enter in mine ears . iii 4 95
If words be made of breath, And breath of life, I have no life to breathe What thou hast said . iii 4 197
Botch the words up fit to their own thoughts . iv 5 10
Let's have no words of this: but when they ask you what it means, say you this . iv 5 46

Word. Antiquity forgot, custom not known, The ratifiers and props of every word . . . *Hamlet* iv 5 105
I have words to speak in thine ear will make thee dumb . . . iv 6 25
To show yourself your father's son in deed More than in words . . . v 7 127
His purse is empty already; all's golden words are spent . . . v 2 137
I love you more than words can wield the matter . . . *Lear* i 1 56
Your large speeches may your deeds approve, That good effects may spring from words of love . . . i 1 188
As to the legitimate: fine word,—legitimate! . . . i 2 18
Found you no displeasure in him by word or countenance? . . . i 2 172
Have you heard of no likely wars toward . . . ?—Not a word . . . ii 1 13
If I would stand against thee, would the reposal Of any trust, virtue, or worth in thee Make thy words faith'd? . . . ii 1 72
To grudge my pleasures, to cut off my train, To bandy hasty words . . . ii 4 178
Have you no more to say?—Few words, but, to effect, more than all yet iii 1 52
When priests are more in word than matter . . . iii 2 81
Obey thy parents; keep thy word justly; swear not . . . iii 4 83
Swore as many oaths as I spake words, and broke them . . . iii 4 91
I'll talk a word with this same learned Theban . . . iii 4 162
Let me ask you one word in private.—Importune him once more to go iii 4 165
No words, no words: hush . . . iii 4 186
His word was still,—Fie, foh, and fum, I smell the blood of a British man . . . iii 4 188
Might not you Transport her purposes by word? . . . iv 5 20
Give the word.—Sweet marjoram.—Pass . . . iv 6 93
They are not men o' their words: they told me I was every thing; 'tis a lie . . . iv 6 106
If e'er your grace had speech with man so poor, Hear me one word . . . v 1 39
I will but spend a word here in the house, And go with you . . . *Othello* i 2 48
But words are words; I never yet did hear That the bruised heart was pierced through the ear . . . i 3 218
And weigh'st thy words before thou givest them breath . . . iii 3 119
Give thy worst of thoughts The worst of words . . . iii 3 133
In the due reverence of a sacred vow I here engage my words . . . iii 3 462
It is not words that shake me thus . . . iv 1 42
I understand a fury in your words, But not the words . . . iv 2 32
It doth abhor me now I speak the word . . . iv 2 162
Your words and performances are no kin together . . . iv 2 185
O, good my lord, I would speak a word with you! . . . v 2 90
I say thy husband: dost understand the word? My friend, thy husband, honest, honest Iago . . . v 2 153
What you know, you know: From this time forth I never will speak word . . . v 2 304
Soft you; a word or two before you go . . . v 2 338
If they suffer our departure, death's the word . . . *Ant. and Cleo.* i 2 139
Bid farewell, and go: when you sued staying, Then was the time for words . . . i 3 34
One word. Sir, you and I must part, but that's not it . . . i 3 86
I bring thee word, Menecrates and Menas . . . Make the sea serve them i 4 47
Their contestation Was theme for you, you were the word of war . . . ii 2 44
You may, when you hear no more words of Pompey, return it again . . . ii 2 105
Our courteous Antony, Whom ne'er the word of 'No' woman heard speak . . . ii 2 228
Let him not leave out The colour of her hair: bring me word quickly . . . ii 5 114
Bid you Alexas Bring me word how tall she is . . . ii 5 118
Most meet That first we come to words . . . ii 6 3
I have fair meanings, sir.—And fair words to them . . . ii 6 67
A word.—Say in mine ear: what is't?—Forsake thy seat, I do beseech thee, captain, And hear me speak a word . . . ii 7 42
The wild disguise hath almost Antick'd us all. What needs more words? . . . ii 7 132
Signify what in his name, That magical word of war, we have effected . iii 1 31
I'll bring thee word Straight, how 'tis like to go . . . iv 12 2
To the monument! There lock yourself, and send him word you are dead . . . iv 13 4
Say, that the last I spoke was 'Antony,' And word it, prithee, piteously iv 13 9
She sent you word she was dead; But, fearing since how it might work, hath sent Me to proclaim the truth . . . iv 14 124
He words me, girls, he words me, that I should not Be noble to myself v 2 191
I'll drink the words you send, Though ink be made of gall . . . *Cymbeline* i 1 100
That parting kiss which I had set Betwixt two charming words . . . i 3 35
Words him, I doubt not, a great deal from the matter . . . i 4 16
When thou shalt bring me word she loves my son, I'll tell thee on the instant thou art then As great as is thy master . . . i 5 49
Call my women: Think on my words . . . i 5 75
You are as welcome, worthy sir, as I Have words to bid you . . . i 6 30
Yes, I beseech; or I shall short my word By lengthening my return . . . i 6 200
A wonderful sweet air, with admirable rich words to it . . . ii 3 20
He sweats, Strains his young nerves and puts himself in posture That acts my words . . . iii 3 95
So tender of rebukes that words are strokes And strokes death to her . . . iii 5 40
Where is thy lady! In a word; or else Thou art straightway with the fiends . . . iii 5 82
Discover where thy mistress is at once, At the next word . . . iii 5 96
The words of your commission Will tie you to the numbers and the time Of their dispatch . . . iii 7 14
The rather—saving reverence of the word . . . iv 1 6
Thy words, I grant, are bigger, for I wear not My dagger in my mouth iv 2 78
Do not play in wench-like words with that Which is so serious . . . iv 2 230
Use like note and words . . . iv 2 237
I cannot sing: I'll weep, and word it with thee . . . iv 2 240
Again; and bring me word how 'tis with her . . . iv 3 1
All The rest do nothing—with this word 'Stand, stand' . . . v 3 31
'Tis strange he [death] hides him in fresh cups, soft beds, Sweet words v 3 72
Hanging is the word, sir: if you be ready for that, you are well cooked v 4 155
We'll learn our freeness of a son-in-law; Pardon's the word to all . . . v 5 422
I'll take thy word for faith, not ask thine oath . . . *Pericles* i 2 120
A better prince and benign lord, That will prove awful both in deed and word . . . ii Gower 4
To fulfil his prince' desire, Sends word of all that haps in Tyre . . . ii Gower 22
A black Ethiope reaching at the sun: The word, 'Lux tua vita mihi' . . . ii 2 21
I never spake bad word, nor did ill turn To any living creature . . . iv 1 76
Give me leave: a word, and I'll have done presently . . . iv 6 51
She has here spoken holy words to the Lord Lysimachus . . . iv 6 142
We have a maid in Mytilene, I durst wager, Would win some words of him . . . v 1 44
A word with you *Mer. Wives* ii 1; *All's Well* ii 3; 2 *Hen. IV.* i 2; ii 2; *Richard III.* iii 4; *Hen. VIII.* i 2; *J. Cæsar* iii 1; *Macbeth* iii 1
One word more *Much Ado* iii 3; *Richard II.* i 2; 2 *Hen. IV.* Epil.; *Coriolanus* iii 1; *Macbeth* iv 1; *Hamlet* iii 4

Word of mouth. I'll deliver thy indignation to him by word of mouth *T. Night* ii 3 141
I will deliver his challenge by word of mouth . . . iii 4 209
And bid me say to you by word of mouth . . . *J. Cæsar* iii 1 280
Wore. Is not, sir, my doublet as fresh as the first day I wore it? *Tempest* ii 1 103
I wore it at your daughter's marriage . . . ii 1 105
Which of the vizards was it that you wore?—Where? when? . *L. L. Lost* v 2 385
He wore none but a dishclout of Jaquenetta's, and that a' wears next his heart . . . v 2 720
And a chain, that you once wore, about his neck . . . *As Y. Like It* iii 2 191
Thy father's father wore it, And thy father bore it . . . iv 2 16
But on us both did haggish age steal on And wore us out of act *All's Well* i 2 30
I have served Prince Florizel and in my time wore three-pile *W. Tale* iv 3 14
You won it, wore it, kept it, gave it me . . . 2 *Hen. IV.* iv 5 222
Sixty and nine, that wore Their crownets regal . . . *Troi. and Cres.* Prol. 5
Doublets that hangmen would Bury with those that wore them *Coriol.* i 5 8
With a proud heart he wore his humble weeds . . . ii 3 161
Forget not With what contempt he wore the humble weed . . . ii 3 229
These eyes are not the same I wore in Rome . . . v 3 38
The last That wore the imperial diadem of Rome . . . *T. Andron.* i 1 6
Saw you not his face?—O, yes, my lord; he wore his beaver up *Hamlet* i 2 230
That curled my hair; wore gloves in my cap . . . *Lear* iii 4 88
I drunk him to his bed; Then put my tires and mantles on him, whilst I wore his sword Philippan . . . *Ant. and Cleo.* ii 5 23
He was my master; and I wore my life To spend upon his haters . . . v 1 8
The same suit he wore when he took leave of my lady . . . *Cymbeline* iii 5 128
But time hath nothing blurr'd those lines of favour Which then he wore iv 2 105
Many years, Though Cloten then but young, you see, not wore him From my remembrance . . . iv 4 23
A rider like myself, who ne'er wore rowel Nor iron on his heel . . . iv 4 39
And wager'd with him Pieces of gold 'gainst this which then he wore . v 5 183
Worest. Wert thou the devil, and worest it on thy horn, It should be challenged . . . *Troi. and Cres.* v 2 95
Work the peace of the present . . . *Tempest* i 1 24
Work you then . . . i 1 45
Ariel, thy charge Exactly is perform'd: but there's more work . . . i 2 238
Urchins Shall, for that vast of night that they may work, All exercise on thee . . . i 2 327
It works. Come on. Thou hast done well, fine Ariel! . . . i 2 493
I know it by thy trembling: now Prosper works upon thee . . . ii 2 84
My sweet mistress Weeps when she sees me work . . . iii 1 12
Alas, now, pray you, Work not so hard . . . iii 1 16
Let's follow it, and after do our work . . . iii 2 158
My high charms work And these mine enemies are all knit up . . . iii 3 88
Their great guilt, Like poison given to work a great time after . . . iii 3 105
Your father's in some passion That works him strongly . . . iv 1 144
At which time, my lord, You said our work should cease . . . v 1 5
Your charm so strongly works 'em . . . v 1 17
Which even now I do, To work mine end upon their senses . . . v 1 53
She works by charms, by spells, by the figure, and such daubery *M. W.* iv 2 185
I'll wink and couch: no man their works must eye . . . v 5 52
Then no more remains, But that to your sufficiency . . . as your worth is able, And let them work . . . *Meas. for Meas.* i 1 10
Correction and instruction must both work Ere this rude beast will profit . . . iii 2 33
I will go darkly to work with her.—That's the way . . . v 1 279
A very good piece of work, I assure you, and a merry . . . *M. N. Dream* i 2 14
Sweet Puck, You do their work, and they shall have good luck . . . ii 1 41
Rude mechanicals, That work for bread upon Athenian stalls . . . iii 2 10
Hard-handed men that work in Athens here . . . v 1 72
When the work of generation was Between these woolly breeders *M. of V.* i 3 83
Which therein works a miracle in nature . . . iii 2 90
You would be prouder of the work Than customary bounty can enforce you . . . iii 4 8
I have work in hand That you yet know not of . . . iii 4 57
This is not Fortune's work neither, but Nature's . . . *As Y. Like It* i 2 54
Alack, in me what strange effect Would they work in mild aspect! . iv 3 55
'Tis a very excellent piece of work, madam lady . . . *T. of Shrew* i 1 258
Ay, marry, sir, now it begins to work . . . iii 2 220
And death should have play for lack of work . . . *All's Well* i 1 24
I charge thee, As heaven shall work in me for thine avail, To tell me truly . . . i 3 190
He that of greatest works is finisher Oft does them by the weakest minister . . . ii 1 139
But I shall lose the grounds I work upon . . . iii 7 3
This has no holding, To swear by him whom I protest to love, That I will work against him . . . iv 2 29
On that vice in him will my revenge find notable cause to work *T. Night* ii 3 166
I know my physic will work with him . . . ii 3 188
Did not I say he would work it out? the cur is excellent at faults . . . ii 5 139
Does it work upon him?—Like aqua-vitæ with a midwife . . . ii 5 214
I'll go another way to work with him . . . iv 1 36
With no rash potion, But with a lingering dram that should not work Maliciously like poison . . . *W. Tale* i 2 320
How would he look, to see his work so noble Vilely bound up? . . . iv 4 21
He so chants to the sleeve-hand and the work about the square on't . iv 4 212
A good nose is requisite also, to smell out work for the other senses . iv 4 687
Every shop, church, session, hanging, yields a careful man work . . . iv 4 701
Had he himself eternity and could put breath into his work . . . v 2 107
Well then, to work . . . *K. John* ii 1 37
This toil of ours should be a work of thine . . . ii 1 93
This day hath made Much work for tears in many an English mother . . . ii 1 303
And pell-mell Make work upon ourselves, for heaven or hell . . . ii 1 407
It is a damned and a bloody work; The graceless action of a heavy hand, If that it be the work of any hand . . . iv 3 57
It is the shameful work of Hubert's hand . . . iv 3 62
Here's a good world! Knew you of this fair work? . . . iv 3 116
You look but on the outside of this work . . . v 2 109
Awhile to work, and after holiday . . . *Richard II.* iii 1 44
And toil'd with works of war, retired himself To Italy . . . iv 1 96
If all the year were playing holidays, To sport would be as tedious as to work; But when they seldom come, they wish'd for come 1 *Hen. IV.* i 2 229
Fie upon this quiet life! I want work . . . ii 4 118
In this great work, Which is almost to pluck a kingdom down 2 *Hen. IV.* i 3 48
How able such a work to undergo, To weigh against his opposite . . . i 3 54
Though it do work as strong As aconitum or rash gunpowder . . . iv 4 47
Let us, ciphers to this great accompt, On your imaginary forces work *Hen. V.* Prol. 18
And let another half stand laughing by, All out of work and cold for action! . . . i 2 114

Work. For so work the honey-bees, Creatures that by a rule in nature teach The act of order . . . . *Hen. V.* i 2 187
Many things, having full reference To one consent, may work contrariously . . . . i 2 206
Saw his heroical seed, and smiled to see him, Mangle the work of nature ii 4 60
Work, work your thoughts, and therein see a siege . . . . iii Prol. 25
The work ish give over, the trompet sound the retreat . . . iii 2 93
By my hand, I swear, and my father's soul, the work ish ill done . iii 2 95
There is throats to be cut, and works to be done . . . . . iii 2 120
There is not work enough for all our hands . . . . . . iv 2 19
O that we now had here But one ten thousand of those men in England That do no work to-day! . . . . iv 3 18
Upon the which, I trust, Shall witness live in brass of this day's work . iv 3 97
Thy heart-blood I will have for this day's work . . . . 1 *Hen. VI.* i 3 83
Perceive how I will work To bring this matter to the wished end . . iii 3 27
By inspiration of celestial grace, To work exceeding miracles on earth . v 4 41
So will I In England work your grace's full content . . 2 *Hen. VI.* i 3 70
Read you; and let us to our work . . . . i 4 15
That time best fits the work we have in hand . . . . . . i 4 23
To see how God in all his creatures works! . . . . . . ii 1 7
What mischiefs work the wicked ones, Heaping confusion on their own heads! . . . . ii 1 186
And too well given To dream on evil or to work my downfall . . . iii 1 73
And work in their shirt too; as myself, for example, that am a butcher iv 7 57
Work thou the way,—and thou shalt execute . . . 3 *Hen. VI.* v 7 25
Now have I done a good day's work . . . . . . *Richard III.* ii 1 1
Your honour hath no shriving work in hand . . . . . . iii 2 116
We smothered The most replenished sweet work of nature . . . iv 3 18
How holily he works in all his business! . . . . . *Hen. VIII.* ii 2 24
This imperious man will work us all From princes into pages . . ii 2 47
These sad thoughts, that work too much upon him . . . . . ii 2 58
I was set at work Among my maids . . . . iii 1 74
Has the king this?—Believe it.—Will this work? . . . . . iii 2 37
And durst commend a secret to your ear Much weightier than this work v 1 18
I was fain to draw mine honour in, and let 'em win the work . . . v 4 61
Do you with cheeks abash'd behold our works, And call them shames? *Troi. and Cres.* i 3 18
Do not these high strains Of divination in our sister work Some touches of remorse? . . . . ii 2 114
Spur them to ruthful work, rein them from ruth . . . . . v 3 48
Now here he fights on Galathe his horse, And there lacks work . . v 5 21
Now is my day's work done; I'll take good breath . . . . . v 8 3
O traitors and bawds, how earnestly are you set a-work! . . . . v 10 38
What work's, my countrymen, in hand? where go you With bats? *Cor.* i 1 56
Now, Mars, I prithee, make us quick in work! . . . . . . i 4 10
List, what work he makes Amongst your cloven army.—O, they are at it! . . . . i 4 20
Sir, praise me not; My work hath yet not warm'd me . . . . . i 5 18
Alone I fought in your Corioli walls, And made what work I pleased . i 8 9
If I should tell thee o'er this thy day's work, Thou 'ldst not believe thy deeds . . . . i 9 1
To report A little of that worthy work . . . . ii 2 49
Here's goodly work!—I would they were a-bed! . . . . . . iii 1 261
O, you have made good work! . . . . iv 6 80
You have made good work, You and your apron-men! . . . . . iv 6 95
You have made fair work! . . . . iv 6 100
Why, so: you have made good work! . . . . v 1 15
Murdering impossibility, to make What cannot be, slight work . . v 3 62
Out of that I'll work Myself a former fortune . . . . . . v 3 201
Revenge is come to join with him, And work confusion on his enemies *T. Andron.* v 2 8
How shall we be employ'd?—Tut, I have work enough for you to do . v 2 150
Come, come with me, and we will make short work . *Rom. and Jul.* ii 6 35
Day, night, hour, tide, time, work, play, Alone, in company . . . iii 5 178
Come, vial. What if this mixture do not work at all? . . . . iv 3 21
And bear this work of heaven with patience . . . . . . v 3 261
You are rapt, sir, in some work, some dedication . *T. of Athens* i 1 19
I have, in this rough work, shaped out a man . . . . . . i 1 43
I like your work; And you shall find I like it: wait attendance . . i 1 160
Wrought he not well that painted it?—He wrought better that made the painter; and yet he's but a filthy piece of work . . . . . i 1 202
Look in thy last work, where thou hast feigned him a worthy fellow . i 1 228
O, may diseases only work upon't! . . . . iii 1 63
Yet thanks I must you con That you are thieves profess'd, that you work not In holier shapes . . . . iv 3 429
Must thou needs stand for a villain in thine own work? . . . . v 1 40
Graves only be men's works and death their gain! Sun, hide thy beams! v 1 225
To wear out their shoes, to get myself into more work . . *J. Cæsar* i 1 34
What you would work me to, I have some aim . . . . . . i 2 163
The complexion of the element In favour's like the work we have in hand i 3 129
Let me work; For I can give his humour the true bent . . . . ii 1 209
Could it work so much upon your shape As it hath much prevail'd on your condition, I should not know you . . . . ii 1 253
What's to do?—A piece of work that will make sick men whole . . ii 1 327
Now let it work. Mischief, thou art afoot, Take thou what course thou wilt! . . . . iii 2 265
Well, to our work alive. What do you think Of marching to Philippi? iv 3 196
But this same day Must end that work the ides of March begun . . v 1 114
Let us meet, And question this most bloody piece of work . *Macbeth* ii 3 134
To leave no rubs nor botches in the work . . . . iii 1 134
With Him above To ratify the work . . . . iii 6 33
A most miraculous work in this good king . . . . iv 3 147
In what particular thought to work I know not . . . . *Hamlet* i 1 67
Well said, old mole! canst work i' the earth so fast? . . . . . i 5 162
No, I went round to work, And my young mistress thus I did bespeak . ii 2 139
What a piece of work is a man! how noble in reason! . . . . . ii 2 316
How now, my lord! will the king hear this piece of work? . . . . iii 2 52
'Tis a knavish piece of work: but what o' that? . . . . . . iii 2 251
Conceit in weakest bodies strongest works . . . . iii 4 114
Let it work; For 'tis the sport to have the enginer Hoist with his own petar . . . . iii 4 205
I will work him To an exploit, now ripe in my device . . . . iv 7 64
This is mere madness: And thus awhile the fit will work on him . . v 1 308
The point envenom'd too! Then, venom, to thy work . . . . . v 2 333
Briefness and fortune, work! Brother, a word . . . . . *Lear* ii 1 20
Of my land . . . I'll work the means To make thee capable . . . ii 1 86
How shall I live and work, To match thy goodness? . . . . . iv 7 1
I cannot draw a cart, nor eat dried oats; If it be man's work, I'll do't . v 3 39
He holds me well; The better shall my purpose work on him . *Othello* i 3 397
You rise to play and go to bed to work . . . . ii 1 116

Work. Thou know'st we work by wit, and not by witchcraft . *Othello* ii 3 378
That done, I will be walking on the works . . . . iii 2 3
I'll have the work ta'en out, And give't Iago . . . . . . iii 3 296
I should be wise, for honesty's a fool And loses that it works for . . iii 3 383
A sibyl . . . In her prophetic fury sew'd the work . . . . . iii 4 72
Take me this work out.—O Cassio, whence came this? . . . . . iii 4 180
I found it in my chamber. I like the work well . . . . . iii 4 189
Work on, My medicine, work! Thus credulous fools are caught . . iv 1 45
I must take out the work?—A likely piece of work, that you should find it! . . . . iv 1 156
This is some minx's token, and I must take out the work? . . . iv 1 159
Give it your hobby-horse: wheresoever you had it, I'll take out no work on't . . . . iv 1 161
Is it his use? Or did the letters work upon his blood? . . . . iv 1 286
She did gratify his amorous works With that recognizance . . . v 2 213
Look on the tragic loading of this bed; This is thy work . . . v 2 364
You had then left unseen a wonderful piece of work *Ant. and Cleo.* i 2 160
Mine honesty Shall not make poor my greatness, nor my power Work without it . . . . ii 2 94
Cæsar himself has work, and our oppression Exceeds what we expected iv 7 2
I have done my work ill, friends: O, make an end Of what I have begun . . . . iv 14 105
She sent you word she was dead; But, fearing since how it might work, hath sent Me to proclaim the truth . . . . iv 14 125
What work is here! Charmian, is this well done? . . . . . v 2 328
Here comes a flattering rascal; upon him Will I first work . *Cymbeline* i 5 28
Do thou work: When thou shalt bring me word she loves my son . . i 5 48
And every day that comes comes to decay A day's work in him . . i 5 57
A piece of work So bravely done, so rich, that it did strive In workmanship and value . . . . ii 4 72
The sweat of industry would dry and die, But for the end it works to . iii 6 32
The heavens still must work. Wherein I am false I am honest . . iv 3 41
Having work More plentiful than tools to do't . . . . . . v 3 8
You are made Rather to wonder at the things you hear Than to work any v 3 55
To work Her son into the adoption of the crown . . . . . v 5 55
There's other work in hand: I see a thing Bitter to me as death . . v 5 103
The sea works high, the wind is loud . . . . . *Pericles* iii 1 48
Give this to the 'pothecary, And tell me how it works . . . . iii 2 10
I can speak of the disturbances That nature works, and of her cures . iii 2 38
The gods are quick of ear, and I am sworn To do my work with haste . . . . iv 1 71
You must take some pains to work her to your manage . . . . iv 6 69
Worked. You have work'd for me; there's payment for you *T. of Athens* v 1 116
Working. In the working of your own affections . *Meas. for Meas.* ii 1 10
Be cunning in the working this, and thy fee is a thousand ducats *Much Ado* ii 2 54
By a familiar demonstration of the working . . . . *L. L. Lost* i 2 10
For praise, an outward part, We bend to that the working of the heart iv 1 33
His will hath in it a more modest working . . . . *As Y. Like It* i 2 215
Thy tyranny Together working with thy jealousies . . . *W. Tale* iii 2 181
Never did base and rotten policy Colour her working with such deadly wounds . . . . 1 *Hen. IV.* i 3 109
The very opener and intelligencer Between the grace, the sanctities of heaven, And our dull workings . . . . . . 2 *Hen. IV.* iv 2 22
His passions, like a whale on ground, Confound themselves with working . . . . iv 4 41
By whose fell working I was first advanced . . . . iv 5 207
Spurn at your most royal image And mock your workings in a second body . . . . v 2 90
Working so grossly in a natural cause . . . . . . *Hen. V.* ii 2 107
Not working with the eye without the ear, And but in purged judgement trusting neither . . . . ii 2 135
I am sick with working of my thoughts . . . . . 1 *Hen. VI.* v 5 86
A weighty and a serious brow, Sad, high, and working . *Hen. VIII.* Prol. 3
Sing, and disperse 'em, if thou canst: leave working . . . . iii 1 2
Limbs are his instruments, In no less working than are swords and bows Directive by the limbs . . . . . *Troi. and Cres.* i 3 355
By working wreakful vengeance on thy foes . . . *T. Andron.* v 2 32
As 'twere a thing a little soil'd i' the working . . . . . *Hamlet* ii 1 40
That from her working all his visage wann'd . . . . . . ii 2 580
Might in their working do you that offence, Which else were shame *Lear* i 4 231
They are close delations, working from the heart . . . . *Othello* iii 3 123
Gets more with begging than we can do with working . . *Pericles* ii 1 69
But are you flesh and blood? Have you a working pulse? . . . . v 1 155
Working-day. Unless I might have another for working-days *Much Ado* ii 1 341
O, how full of briers is this working-day world! . . *As Y. Like It* i 3 12
I have laid by my majesty And plodded like a man for working-days *Hen. V.* i 2 277
We are but warriors for the working-day . . . . iv 3 109
Working-house. In the quick forge and working-house of thought v Prol. 23
Workman. He, sir, 's a good workman, a very good tailor *All's Well* ii 5 21
When workmen strive to do better than well, They do confound their skill in covetousness . . . . *K. John* iv 2 28
The king's council are no good workmen . . . . 2 *Hen. VI.* iv 2 16
Do villany, do, since you protest to do't, Like workmen *T. of Athens* iv 3 438
Excellent workman! thou canst not paint a man so bad as is thyself . v 1 32
In respect of a fine workman, I am but, as you would say, a cobbler *J. Cæsar* i 1 10
That thou couldst see my wars to-day, and knew'st The royal occupation! thou shouldst see A workman in't . . . . . *Ant. and Cleo.* iv 4 18
Therein I must play the workman . . . . *Cymbeline* iv 1 7
Workmanly. So workmanly the blood and tears are drawn *T. of S.* Ind. 2 62
Workmanship. So bravely done, so rich, that it did strive In workmanship and value . . . . *Cymbeline* ii 4 74
Worky-day. Prithee, tell her but a worky-day fortune . *Ant. and Cleo.* i 2 55
World. He whom next thyself Of all the world I loved . . . *Tempest* i 2 69
The top of admiration! worth What's dearest to the world! . . . iii 1 39
I would not wish Any companion in the world but you . . . . . iii 1 55
I Beyond all limit of what else i' the world Do love, prize, honour you. iii 1 72
Destiny, That hath to instrument this lower world And what is in't . iii 3 54
I would not for the world . . . . v 1 173
How beauteous mankind is! O brave new world, That has such people in't! . . . . v 1 183
Entreat thy company, To see the wonders of the world abroad *T. G. of V.* i 1 6
Made me neglect my studies, lose my time, War with good counsel, set the world at nought . . . . i 1 68
He cannot be a perfect man, Not being tried and tutor'd in the world . i 3 21
Then let her alone.—Not for the world: why, man, she is mine own . ii 4 168
How will the world repute me For undertaking so unstaid a journey? . ii 7 59
And with thy daring folly burn the world . . . . iii 1 155

World. Then may I set the world on wheels, when she can spin for her living . . . *T. G. of Ver.* iii 1 317
I must never trust thee more, But count the world a stranger for thy sake . . . v 4 70
Dere is some simples in my closet, dat I vill not for the varld I shall leave behind . . . *Mer. Wives* i 4 66
What a Herod of Jewry is this! O wicked, wicked world! . . . ii 1 21
Why, then the world's mine oyster, Which I with sword will open . ii 2 2
Old folks, you know, have discretion, as they say, and know the world . . . ii 2 136
He is de coward Jack priest of de vorld; he is not show his face . . ii 3 33
O, what a world of vile ill-favour'd faults Looks handsome in three hundred pounds a-year! . . . iii 4 32
My son profits nothing in the world at his book . . . iv 1 15
I would all the world might be cozened; for I have been cozened . . iv 5 95
Why dost thou show me thus to the world? Bear me to prison *M. for M.* i 2 120
And void of all profanation in the world that good Christians ought to have . . . ii 1 56
But might you do't, and do the world no wrong? . . . ii 2 53
With an outstretch'd throat I'll tell the world aloud What man thou art ii 4 153
Perpetual durance, a restraint, Though all the world's vastidity you had iii 1 69
Blown with restless violence round about The pendent world . . iii 1 126
What a merit were it in death to take this poor maid from the world! . iii 1 241
We shall have all the world drink brown and white bastard . . iii 2 3
'Twas never merry world since, of two usuries, the merriest was put down . . . iii 2 6
Is the world as it was, man? Which is the way? Is it sad, and few words? . . . iii 2 52
What news abroad i' the world?—None . . . iii 2 234
Much upon this riddle runs the wisdom of the world . . . iii 2 243
He hath released him, Isabel, from the world: His head is off . iv 3 119
Wretched Isabel! Injurious world! most damned Angelo! . . iv 3 127
As thou believest There is another comfort than this world . . v 1 49
A stubborn soul, That apprehends no further than this world . . v 1 486
That the world may witness that my end Was wrought by nature *Com. of Errors* i 1 34
I to the world am like a drop of water That in the ocean seeks another drop . . . i 2 35
Lords of the wild world and wild watery seas . . . ii 1 21
Time himself is bald and therefore to the world's end will have bald followers . . . ii 2 108
Fie, brother! how the world is changed with you! . . . ii 2 154
If she lives till doomsday, she'll burn a week longer than the whole world . . . iii 2 102
We came into the world like brother and brother . . . v 1 424
The fashion of the world is to avoid cost, and you encounter it *Much Ado* i 1 98
Can the world buy such a jewel?—Yea, and a case to put it into . i 1 183
Hath not the world one man but he will wear his cap with suspicion? . i 1 200
Such a man would win any woman in the world, if a' could get her good-will . . . ii 1 17
That puts the world into her person, and so gives me out . . ii 1 216
Will your grace command me any service to the world's end? . . ii 1 272
Thus goes every one to the world but I, and I am sunburnt . . ii 1 331
The world must be peopled . . . ii 3 251
God help us! it is a world to see . . . iii 5 38
I do love nothing in the world so well as you . . . iv 1 269
Not for the wide world . . . iv 1 292
I will think nothing to any purpose that the world can say against it . v 4 107
Brave conquerors,—for so you are, That war against your own affections And the huge army of the world's desires . . *L. L. Lost* i 1 10
Navarre shall be the wonder of the world . . . i 1 12
The grosser manner of these world's delights He throws upon the gross world's baser slaves . . . i 1 29
A man in all the world's new fashion planted . . . i 1 165
Many a knight From tawny Spain lost in the world's debate . . i 1 174
The world was very guilty of such a ballad some three ages since . . i 2 116
Held precious in the world's esteem . . . ii 1 4
As Nature was in making graces dear When she did starve the general world beside And prodigally gave them all to you . . . ii 1 11
He'll be forsworn.—Not for the world, fair madam . . . ii 1 99
I do nothing in the world but lie, and lie in my throat . . iv 3 12
By the world, I would not care a pin, if the other three were in . iv 3 18
Rhetoric of thine eye, 'Gainst whom the world cannot hold argument . iv 3 61
Where is any author in the world Teaches such beauty as a woman's eye? iv 3 312
The academes, That show, contain, and nourish all the world . iv 3 353
An I had but one penny in the world, thou shouldst have it . . v 1 74
I must tell thee, it will please his grace, by the world . . v 1 107
By the world, I recount no fable . . . v 1 111
A soldier, a man of travel, that hath seen the world . . v 1 114
A world of torments though I should endure, I would not yield . v 2 353
And did value me Above this world . . . v 2 446
The whole world again Cannot pick out five such . . . v 2 547
When in the world I lived, I was the world's commander . . v 2 565
Some forlorn and naked hermitage, Remote from all the pleasures of the world . . . v 2 806
The world's large tongue Proclaims you for a man replete with mocks . v 2 852
Were the world mine, Demetrius being bated, The rest I'ld give to be to you translated . . . *M. N. Dream* i 1 190
The mazed world, By their increase, now knows not which is which . ii 1 113
Nor doth this wood lack worlds of company, For you in my respect are all the world: Then how can it be said I am alone, When all the world is here to look on me? . . . ii 1 223
How comes this gentle concord in the world? . . . iv 1 148
I have heard it over, And it is nothing, nothing in the world . . v 1 78
You have too much respect upon the world . . *Mer. of Venice* i 1 74
I hold the world but as the world, Gratiano; A stage where every man must play a part, And mine a sad one . . . i 1 77
Nor is the wide world ignorant of her worth . . . i 1 167
My little body is aweary of this great world . . . i 2 2
All the world desires her; From the four corners of the earth they come ii 7 38
I think he only loves the world for him . . . ii 8 50
The world is still deceived with ornament . . . iii 2 74
Nothing in the world Could turn so much the constitution Of any constant man . . . iii 2 248
The poor rude world Hath not her fellow . . . iii 5 87
The world thinks, and I think so too . . . iv 1 17
Life itself, my wife, and all the world, Are not with me esteem'd above thy life . . . iv 1 284
How far that little candle throws his beams! So shines a good deed in a naughty world . . . v 1 91

World. For all the world like cutler's poetry Upon a knife *Mer. of Venice* v 1 149
For the wealth That the world masters . . . v 1 174
And fleet the time carelessly, as they did in the golden world *As Y. L. It* i 1 125
Enchantingly beloved, and indeed so much in the heart of the world . i 1 175
Fortune reigns in gifts of the world, not in the lineaments of Nature . i 2 45
I shall do . . . the world no injury, for in it I have nothing; only in the world I fill up a place . . . i 2 203
The world esteem'd thy father honourable . . . i 2 238
All the world was of my father's mind . . . i 2 248
In a better world than this, I shall desire more love and knowledge of you . . . i 2 296
O, how full of briers is this working-day world! . . . i 3 12
He'll go along o'er the wide world with me; Leave me alone to woo him i 3 134
What a world is this, when what is comely Envenoms him that bears it! ii 3 14
How well in thee appears The constant service of the antique world! . ii 3 57
A miserable world! As I do live by food, I met a fool . . ii 7 13
'Thus we may see,' quoth he, 'how the world wags' . . ii 7 23
I will through and through Cleanse the foul body of the infected world ii 7 60
All the embossed sores . . . Wouldst thou disgorge into the general world . . . ii 7 69
All the world's a stage, And all the men and women merely players . ii 7 139
His youthful hose, well saved, a world too wide For his shrunk shank . ii 7 160
Her worth, being mounted on the wind, Through all the world bears Rosalind . . . iii 2 96
We two will rail against our mistress the world and all our misery . iii 2 296
I will chide no breather in the world but myself . . . iii 2 297
To forswear the full stream of the world and to live in a nook merely monastic . . . iii 2 440
'Tis such fools as you That makes the world full of ill-favour'd children iii 5 53
Though all the world could see, None could be so abused in sight as he iii 5 79
The poor world is almost six thousand years old . . . iv 1 95
Show the world what the bird hath done to her own nest . . iv 1 207
He hath no interest in me in the world . . . v 1 9
It is no dishonest desire to desire to be a woman of the world . v 3 5
Was converted Both from his enterprise and from the world . . v 4 168
Let the world slide . . . *T. of Shrew* Ind. 1 6
We can contain ourselves, Were he the veriest antic in the world . Ind. 1 101
She was the fairest creature in the world; And yet she is inferior to none . . . Ind. 2 68
Let the world slip: we shall ne'er be younger . . . Ind. 2 146
A merchant of great traffic through the world . . . i 1 12
There be good fellows in the world, an a man could light on them . i 1 132
Such wind as scatters young men through the world To seek their fortunes . . . i 2 50
And so am come abroad to see the world . . . i 2 58
Now, by the world, it is a lusty wench . . . ii 1 161
Why does the world report that Kate doth limp? O slanderous world! . . . ii 1 254
Yourself and all the world, That talk'd of her, have talk'd amiss of her ii 1 292
'Tis a world to see, How tame, when men and women are alone . . ii 1 313
The maid is mine from all the world, By your firm promise . . ii 1 386
Now must the world point at poor Katharine . . . iii 2 18
His lackey, for all the world caparisoned like the horse . . iii 2 66
Let all the world say no, I'll keep mine own, despite of all the world iii 2 143
Tell me, how goes the world?—A cold world . . . iv 1 36
Your mistress Bianca Loved none in the world so well as Lucentio iv 2 13
Would all the world but he had quite forsworn! . . . iv 2 35
He that is giddy thinks the world turns round . . . v 2 20
Unapt to toil and trouble in the world . . . v 2 166
With a world Of pretty, fond, adoptious christendoms . . *All's Well* i 1 187
If I may have your ladyship's good will to go to the world . . i 3 20
I have other holy reasons, such as they are.—May the world know them? i 3 36
Would God would serve the world so all the year! we'ld find no fault . i 3 88
My love hath in't a bond, Whereof the world takes note . . i 3 195
I may truly say, it is a novelty to the world . . . ii 3 23
She's very well and wants nothing i' the world . . . ii 4 5
Even to the world's pleasure and the increase of laughter . . ii 4 37
If there be breadth enough in the world, I will hold a long distance . iii 2 26
Do you think he will make no deed at all of this that so seriously he does address himself unto?—None in the world . . . iii 6 105
Which were the greatest obloquy i' the world In me to lose . . iv 2 44
You . . . can serve the world for no honest use; therefore you must die iv 3 341
One of the greatest in the Christian world Shall be my surety . iv 4 2
He is the prince of the world; let his nobility remain in's court . iv 5 52
With all the spots o' the world tax'd and debosh'd . . . v 3 206
O that I served that lady And might not be delivered to the world! *T. Night* i 2 42
I am a fellow o' the strangest mind i' the world . . . i 3 120
Is it a world to hide virtues in? . . . i 3 140
He that is well hanged in this world needs to fear no colours . i 5 6
If you will lead these graces to the grave And leave the world no copy . i 5 261
My love, more noble than the world, Prizes not quantity of dirty lands ii 4 84
'Twas never merry world Since lowly feigning was call'd compliment . iii 1 109
O world, how apt the poor are to be proud! . . . iii 1 138
There is no love-broker in the world can more prevail . . iii 2 39
I am afraid this great lubber, the world, will prove a cockney . iv 1 15
You wrong me, and the world shall know it . . . v 1 311
A great while ago the world begun, With hey, ho, the wind and the rain v 1 414
There is not in the world either malice or matter to alter it . *W. Tale* i 1 36
No tongue that moves, none, none i' the world, So soon as yours could win me . . . i 2 20
His folly, fear, Among the infinite doings of the world, Sometime puts forth . . . i 2 253
Is this nothing? Why, then the world and all that's in't is nothing . i 2 293
The most replenish'd villain in the world . . . ii 1 79
For every inch of woman in the world, Ay, every dram of woman's flesh is false, If she be . . . ii 1 137
Which is enough, I'll warrant, As this world goes, to pass for honest . ii 3 72
And will ignoble make you, Yea, scandalous to the world . . ii 3 121
If, one by one, you wedded all the world, . . . she you kill'd Would be unparallel'd . . . v 1 13
They looked as they had heard of a world ransomed, or one destroyed . v 2 16
If all the world could have seen't, the woe had been universal . v 2 99
No settled senses of the world can match The pleasure of that madness v 3 72
Till she had kindled France and all the world . . . *K. John* i 1 33
He came into the world Full fourteen weeks before the course of time . i 1 112
Your father might have kept This calf bred from his cow from all the world . . . i 1 124
That thou mayst be a queen, and check the world! . . . ii 1 123
Till that time Have we ramm'd up our gates against the world . ii 1 272

World. She in beauty, education, blood, Holds hand with any princess of the world . . . *K. John* ii 1 494
Mad world! mad kings! mad composition! . . . ii 1 561
Commodity, the bias of the world, The world, who of itself is peised well ii 1 574
The proud day, Attended with the pleasures of the world . . . iii 3 35
O, that my tongue were in the thunder's mouth! Then with a passion would I shake the world . . . iii 4 39
My fair son! My life, my joy, my food, my all the world! . . . iii 4 104
There's nothing in this world can make me joy . . . iii 4 107
And bitter shame hath spoil'd the sweet world's taste . . . iii 4 110
How green you are and fresh in this old world! . . . iii 4 145
Hubert, for the wealth of all the world, Will not offend thee . . . iv 1 131
Bad world the while! This must not be thus borne . . . iv 2 100
Now, what says the world To your proceedings? . . . iv 2 132
A holy vow, Never to taste the pleasures of the world . . . iv 3 68
Here's a good world! Knew you of this fair work? . . . iv 3 116
And lose my way Among the thorns and dangers of this world iv 3 141
Let not the world see fear and sad distrust Govern the motion of a kingly eye . . . v 1 46
Those baby eyes That never saw the giant world enraged . . . v 2 57
To any sovereign state throughout the world . . . v 2 82
And cull'd these fiery spirits from the world . . . v 2 114
According to the fair play of the world, Let me have audience . . . v 2 118
What in the world should make me now deceive? . . . v 4 26
What surety of the world, what hope, what stay, When this was now a king, and now is clay? . . . v 7 68
Come the three corners of the world in arms, And we shall shock them v 7 116
No way can I stray; Save back to England, all the world's my way *Richard II.* i 3 207
What a deal of world I wander from the jewels that I love . . . i 3 269
Where doth the world thrust forth a vanity—So it be new, there's no respect how vile—That is not quickly buzz'd into his ears? . . . ii 1 24
This little world, This precious stone set in the silver sea . . . ii 1 45
As is the sepulchre in stubborn Jewry Of the world's ransom . . . ii 1 56
This dear dear land, Dear for her reputation through the world . . . ii 1 58
Wert thou regent of the world, It were a shame to let this land by lease; But for thy world enjoying but this land, Is it not more than shame to shame it so? . . . ii 1 109
Leaving me no sign, Save men's opinions and my living blood, To show the world I am a gentleman . . . iii 1 27
When the searching eye of heaven is hid, Behind the globe, that lights the lower world, Then thieves and robbers range abroad . . . iii 2 38
As if the world were all dissolved to tears . . . iii 2 108
We'll play at bowls.—'Twill make me think the world is full of rubs . . . iii 4 4
As I intend to thrive in this new world . . . iv 1 78
Our holy lives must win a new world's crown . . . v 1 24
They shall not live within this world, I swear, But I will have them . . . v 3 142
I have been studying how I may compare This prison where I live unto the world: And for because the world is populous And here is not a creature but myself, I cannot do it . . . v 5 2
Thoughts people this little world, In humours like the people of this world . . . v 5 9
May tear a passage through the flinty ribs Of this hard world . . . v 5 21
And love to Richard Is a strange brooch in this all-hating world . . . v 5 66
To smother up his beauty from the world . . . *1 Hen. IV.* i 2 223
In the world's wide mouth Live scandalized and foully spoken of . . . i 3 153
Shall it be, That you a world of curses undergo? . . . i 3 164
Restore yourselves Into the good thoughts of the world again . . . i 3 182
He apprehends a world of figures here, But not the form . . . i 3 209
This is no world To play with mammets and to tilt with lips . . . ii 3 94
God help the while! a bad world, I say . . . ii 4 145
An I were at the strappado, or all the racks in the world, I would not tell you . . . ii 4 263
Could the world pick thee out three such enemies? . . . ii 4 403
Banish plump Jack, and banish all the world . . . ii 4 527
There will be a world of water shed Upon the parting of your wives and you . . . iii 1 94
For all the world As thou art to this hour was Richard then . . . iii 2 93
Either we or they must lower lie.—Rare words! brave world! . . . iii 3 229
Should go so general current through the world . . . iv 1 5
That daff'd the world aside, And bid it pass . . . iv 1 96
Wind a fiery Pegasus And witch the world with noble horsemanship . . . iv 1 110
The cankers of a calm world and a long peace . . . iv 2 32
Sick in the world's regard, wretched and low . . . iv 3 57
The Prince of Wales doth join with all the world In praise . . . v 1 86
Both together Are confident against the world in arms . . . v 1 117
Let me tell the world, If he outlive the envy of this day, England did never owe so sweet a hope . . . v 2 66
As speedy in your end As all the poisonous potions in the world . . . v 4 56
And time, that takes survey of all the world, Must have a stop . . . v 4 82
Lord, Lord, how this world is given to lying! . . . v 4 148
While covert enmity Under the smile of safety wounds the world *2 Hen. IV.* Ind. 10
Let this world no longer be a stage To feed contention in a lingering act! i 1 155
Since my exion is entered and my case so openly known to the world ii 1 33
Whereupon the world increases, and kindreds are mightily strengthened ii 2 29
Never a man's thought in the world keeps the road-way better than thine ii 2 62
No abuse, Ned, i' the world; honest Ned, none . . . ii 4 345
When a' was naked, he was, for all the world, like a forked radish iii 2 334
And put the world's whole strength Into one giant arm . . . iv 5 44
To show the incredulous world The noble change that I have purposed iv 5 154
'Gainst all the world will rightfully maintain . . . iv 5 225
I survive, To mock the expectation of the world, To frustrate prophecies v 2 126
I pray thee now, deliver them like a man of this world . . . v 3 102
A foutre for the world and worldlings base! I speak of Africa and golden joys . . . v 3 103
So shall the world perceive, That I have turn'd away my former self v 5 61
Look you, he must seem thus to the world . . . v 5 84
Till their conversations Appear more wise and modest to the world . . . v 5 107
Should with his lion gait walk the whole world . . . *Hen. V.* ii 2 122
He is an ass, as in the world: I will verify as much in his beard . . . iii 2 74
He will maintain his argument as well as any military man in the world iii 2 86
He is a man of no estimation in the world . . . iii 6 16
Tut! I have the best armour of the world. Would it were day! . . . iii 7 2
You are as well provided of both as any prince in the world . . . iii 7 10
A subject . . . for the world, familiar to us and unknown, to lay apart their particular functions and wonder at . . . iii 7 40
It is the greatest admiration in the universal world . . . iv 1 67
Nor the tide of pomp That beats upon the high shore of this world . . . iv 1 282
From this day to the ending of the world . . . iv 3 58

World. In the universal world, or in France, or in England! *Hen. V.* iv 8 11
In this best garden of the world Our fertile France . . . v 2 36
By which the world's best garden he achieved . . . Epil. 7
The sun with one eye vieweth all the world . . . *1 Hen. VI.* i 4 84
She hath beheld the man Whose glory fills the world with loud report . . . ii 2 43
For when a world of men Could not prevail with all their oratory, Yet hath a woman's kindness over-ruled . . . ii 2 48
Leave Lord Talbot?—Ay, All the Talbots in the world, to save my life iii 2 108
We will make thee famous through the world . . . iii 3 13
He, renowned noble gentleman, Yields up his life unto a world of odds iv 4 25
His fame lives in the world, his shame in you . . . iv 4 46
The world will say, he is not Talbot's blood, That basely fled . . . iv 5 16
It shall be thine, Let Henry fret and all the world repine . . . v 2 20
She hath lived too long, To fill the world with vicious qualities . . . v 4 35
Hast given me in this beauteous face A world of earthly blessings *2 Hen. VI.* i 1 22
Knit his brows, As frowning at the favours of the world . . . i 2 4
Enchased with all the honours of the world . . . i 2 8
Be my last breathing in this mortal world! . . . i 2 21
I think I have taken my last draught in this world . . . ii 3 74
Trow'st thou that e'er I'll look upon the world, Or count them happy that enjoy the sun? . . . ii 4 38
The world may laugh again . . . ii 4 82
My joy is death; Death, at whose name I oft have been afear'd, Because I wish'd this world's eternity . . . ii 4 90
This Gloucester should be quickly rid the world . . . iii 1 233
Upon thy eye-balls murderous tyranny Sits in grim majesty, to fright the world . . . iii 2 50
What know I how the world may deem of me? . . . iii 2 65
The world shall not be ransom for thy life . . . iii 2 297
For where thou art, there is the world itself, With every several pleasure in the world, And where thou art not, desolation . . . iii 2 362
Ay me! what is this world! what news are these! . . . iii 2 380
For wheresoe'er thou art in this world's globe, I'll have an Iris that shall find thee out . . . iii 2 406
And I proclaim'd a coward through the world! . . . iv 1 43
It was never merry world in England since gentlemen came up . . . iv 2 9
Exhort all the world to be cowards; for I, that never feared any, am vanquished . . . iv 10 79
O, let the vile world end, And the premised flames of the last day Knit earth and heaven together! . . . v 2 40
Hard-hearted Clifford, take me from the world . . . *3 Hen. VI.* i 4 167
Join our lights together And over-shine the earth as this the world ii 1 38
This world frowns, and Edward's sun is clouded . . . ii 3 7
Would I were dead! . . . For what is in this world but grief and woe? ii 5 20
The world goes hard When Clifford cannot spare his friends an oath ii 6 77
What other pleasure can the world afford? . . . iii 2 147
And, whiles I live, to account this world but hell . . . iii 2 169
Piercing as the mid-day sun, To search the secret treasons of the world v 2 18
So part we sadly in this troublous world, To meet with joy in sweet Jerusalem . . . v 5 7
Why should she live, to fill the world with words? . . . v 5 44
Teeth hadst thou in thy head when thou wast born, To signify thou camest to bite the world . . . v 6 54
I came into the world with my legs forward . . . v 6 71
For yet I am not look'd on in the world . . . v 7 22
Unfinish'd, sent before my time Into this breathing world . *Rich. III.* i 1 21
And leave the world for me to bustle in . . . i 1 152
Your beauty was the cause of that effect; Your beauty, which did haunt me in my sleep To undertake the death of all the world . . . i 2 123
As all the world is cheered by the sun, So I by that; it is my day . . . i 2 129
And yet to win her, all the world to nothing! . . . i 2 238
A lovelier gentleman . . . The spacious world cannot again afford . . . i 2 246
The world is grown so bad, That wrens make prey where eagles dare not perch . . . i 3 70
I am too childish-foolish for this world.—Hie thee to hell for shame, and leave the world, Thou cacodemon! . . . i 3 142
Hurl down their indignation On thee, the troubler of the poor world's peace! . . . i 3 221
I would not spend another such a night, Though 'twere to buy a world of happy days . . . i 4 6
For unfelt imagination, They often feel a world of restless cares . . . i 4 81
Are you call'd forth from out a world of men To slay the innocent? . . . i 4 186
From this world's thraldom to the joys of heaven . . . i 4 255
All-seeing heaven, what a world is this! . . . ii 1 82
Send forth plenteous tears to drown the world! Oh for my husband! . . . ii 2 70
I fear, I fear 'twill prove a troublous world . . . ii 3 5
Then, masters, look to see a troublous world . . . ii 3 9
The untainted virtue of your years Hath not yet dived into the world's deceit . . . iii 1 8
It is a reeling world, indeed, my lord; And I believe 'twill never stand upright . . . iii 2 38
How now, sirrah! how goes the world with thee? . . . iii 2 98
To avoid the carping censures of the world . . . iii 5 68
Here's a good world the while! . . . iii 6 10
Bad is the world; and all will come to nought, When such bad dealing must be seen in thought . . . iii 6 13
Would you enforce me to a world of care? . . . iii 7 223
A cockatrice hast thou hatch'd to the world . . . iv 1 55
And Anne my wife hath bid the world good night . . . iv 3 39
Woe's scene, world's shame, grave's due by life usurp'd! . . . iv 4 27
Now, by the world— 'Tis full of thy foul wrongs . . . iv 4 374
For further life in this world I ne'er hope, Nor will I sue *Hen. VIII.* ii 1 69
All That made me happy at one stroke has taken For ever from the world . . . ii 1 118
I would not be a queen For all the world . . . ii 3 46
That man i' the world who shall report he has A better wife, let him in nought be trusted, For speaking false in that . . . ii 4 134
Died where they were made, or shortly after This world had air'd them ii 4 193
My kingdom, Well worthy the best heir o' the world . . . ii 4 195
For no dislike i' the world against the person Of the good queen . . . ii 4 223
Before the primest creature That's paragon'd o' the world . . . ii 4 230
And will be—Though all the world should crack their duty to you iii 2 193
'Tis the account Of all that world of wealth I have drawn together iii 2 211
Vain pomp and glory of this world, I hate ye: I feel my heart new open'd iii 2 365
He gave his honours to the world again, His blessed part to heaven iv 2 29
By that you love the dearest in this world, As you wish Christian peace iv 2 155
Say his long trouble now is passing Out of this world . . . iv 2 163
That all the world may know I was a chaste wife to my grave . . . iv 2 169
Know you not How your state stands i' the world, with the whole world? v 1 127
Meant for his trial, And fair purgation to the world . . . v 3 152

World. Yet a virgin, A most unspotted lily shall she pass To the ground, and all the world shall mourn her . . . *Hen. VIII.* v 5 63
Hector's a gallant man.—As may be in the world . . *Troi. and Cres.* i 2 41
My lady Was fairer than his grandam and as chaste As may be in the world . . . i 3 300
Else might the world convince of levity As well my undertakings . ii 2 130
Whom, we know well, The world's large spaces cannot parallel . ii 2 162
Would not lose So rich advantage . . . For the wide world's revenue . ii 2 206
And never suffers matter of the world Enter his thoughts . ii 3 196
He is not emulous, as Achilles is.—Know the whole world, he is as valiant . . . ii 3 243
Let all pitiful goers-between be called to the world's end after my name iii 2 209
And here, to do you service, am become As new into the world . iii 3 12
One touch of nature makes the whole world kin . iii 3 175
With such a hell of pain and world of charge . iv 1 57
How the poor world is pestered with such waterflies! . v 1 38
A goodly medicine for my aching bones! O world! world! world! . v 10 36
Were half to half the world by the ears and he Upon my party, I'ld revolt, to make Only my wars with him . *Coriolanus* i 1 237
As if the world Were feverous and did tremble . i 4 60
Therefore, be it known, As to us, to all the world . i 9 59
Bring me word thither How the world goes, that to the pace of it I may spur on my journey . i 10 32
Of no more soul nor fitness for the world Than camels in the war . ii 1 266
The man I speak of cannot in the world Be singly counterpoised . ii 2 90
Look'd upon things precious as they were The common muck of the world . ii 2 130
His nature is too noble for the world . iii 1 255
Were to us all, that do't and suffer it, A brand to the end o' the world iii 1 304
Thus I turn my back: There is a world elsewhere . iii 3 135
So if the time thrust forth A cause for thy repeal, we shall not send O'er the vast world to seek a single man . iv 1 42
O world, thy slippery turns! . iv 4 12
Of all the men i' the world I would have 'voided thee . iv 5 87
He is simply the rarest man i' the world . iv 5 169
Then we shall have a stirring world again. This peace is nothing . iv 5 234
Here do we make his friends Blush that the world goes well . iv 6 5
Thrust forth his horns again into the world . iv 6 44
I neither care for the world nor your general . v 2 108
I prate, And the most noble mother of the world Leave unsaluted . v 3 49
To tread . . . on thy mother's womb, That brought thee to this world v 3 125
There's no man in the world More bound to's mother . v 3 158
Give me a staff of honour for mine age, But not a sceptre to control the world . . . *T. Andron.* i 1 199
King and commander of our commonweal, The wide world's emperor . i 1 248
By him that justly may Bear his betroth'd from all the world away . i 1 286
I care not, I, knew she and all the world: I love Lavinia more than all the world . ii 1 71
This before all the world do I prefer; This maugre all the world will I keep safe, Or some of you shall smoke for it . iv 2 109
Come down, and welcome me to this world's light; Confer with me of murder . v 2 33
My child is yet a stranger in the world . *Rom. and Jul.* i 2 8
The all-seeing sun Ne'er saw her match since first the world begun . i 2 98
Lady, such a man As all the world—why, he's a man of wax . i 3 76
I would not for the world they saw thee here . ii 2 74
I'll frown and be perverse and say thee nay, So thou wilt woo; but else, not for the world . ii 2 97
And all my fortunes at thy foot I'll lay And follow thee my lord throughout the world . ii 2 148
When I say so, she looks as pale as any clout in the versal world . ii 4 219
I am peppered, I warrant, for this world . iii 1 103
Make the face of heaven so fine That all the world will be in love with night . iii 2 24
From Verona art thou banished: Be patient, for the world is broad and wide . iii 3 16
There is no world without Verona walls, But purgatory, torture, hell itself . iii 3 17
Hence-banished is banish'd from the world, And world's exile is death . iii 3 19
And all the world to nothing, That he dares ne'er come back to challenge you . iii 5 215
The world is not thy friend nor the world's law; The world affords no law to make thee rich . v 1 72
Gold, worse poison to men's souls, Doing more murders in this loathsome world . v 1 81
How goes the world?—It wears, sir, as it grows . *T. of Athens* i 1 2
Whom this beneath world doth embrace and hug . i 1 44
I will choose Mine heir from forth the beggars of the world . i 1 138
How goes the world, that I am thus encounter'd With clamorous demands of date-broke bonds? . ii 2 37
The world is but a word: Were it all yours to give it in a breath, How quickly were it gone! . ii 2 161
Is't possible the world should so much differ, And we alive that lived? iii 1 49
This is the world's soul; and just of the same piece Is every flatterer's spirit . iii 2 71
Which indeed Is valour misbegot and came into the world When sects and factions were newly born . iii 5 29
Whom the world Voiced so regardfully . iv 3 80
The sweet degrees that this brief world affords To such as may the passive drugs of it Freely command . iv 3 253
Myself, Who had the world as my confectionary . iv 3 260
What things in the world canst thou nearest compare to thy flatterers? iv 3 318
What wouldst thou do with the world, Apemantus, if it lay in thy power? iv 3 322
I am sick of this false world, and will love nought But even the mere necessities upon't . iv 3 376
That beasts May have the world in empire! . iv 3 393
That same eye whose bend doth awe the world Did lose his lustre *J. Cæsar* i 2 123
So get the start of the majestic world And bear the palm alone . i 2 130
He doth bestride the narrow world Like a Colossus . i 2 135
I will do so: till then, think of the world . i 2 311
Else the world, too saucy with the gods, Incenses them to send destruction . i 3 12
If I know this, know all the world besides . i 3 98
These predictions Are to the world in general as to Cæsar . ii 2 29
They are all fire and every one doth shine, But there's but one in all doth hold his place: So in the world . iii 1 66
Made rich With the most noble blood of all this world . iii 1 156
O world, thou wast the forest to this hart; And this, indeed, O world, the heart of thee . iii 1 207
But yesterday the word of Cæsar might Have stood against the world . iii 2 124

World. Is it fit, The three-fold world divided, he should stand One of the three to share it? . *J. Cæsar* iv 1 14
That struck the foremost man of all this world . iv 3 22
Revenge yourselves alone on Cassius, For Cassius is aweary of the world iv 3 95
What, I, my lord? No, not for all the world . v 5 6
Thou seest the world, Volumnius, how it goes; Our enemies have beat us to the pit: It is more worthy to leap in ourselves . v 5 22
Nature might stand up And say to all the world 'This was a man!' . v 5 75
How goes the world, sir, now?—Why, see you not? . *Macbeth* ii 4 21
Whom the vile blows and buffets of the world Have so incensed that I am reckless what I do to spite the world . iii 1 109
But let the frame of things disjoint, both the worlds suffer, Ere we will eat our meal in fear . iii 2 16
I am in this earthly world; where to do harm Is often laudable . iv 2 75
I gin to be aweary of the sun, And wish the estate o' the world were now undone . v 5 50
Our valiant Hamlet—For so this side of our known world esteem'd him *Hamlet* i 1 85
Let the world take note, You are the most immediate to our throne . i 2 108
How weary, stale, flat, and unprofitable, Seem to me all the uses of this world! Fie on't! ah fie! 'tis an unweeded garden . i 2 134
To be honest, as this world goes, is to be one man picked out of ten thousand . ii 2 178
What's the news?—None, my lord, but that the world's grown honest ii 2 241
Denmark's a prison.—Then is the world one.—A goodly one . ii 2 250
The beauty of the world! the paragon of animals! . ii 2 320
The best actors in the world, either for tragedy, comedy, history . ii 2 415
And thirty dozen moons with borrow'd sheen About the world have times twelve thirties been . iii 2 168
Thou shalt live in this fair world behind, Honour'd, beloved . iii 2 185
This world is not for aye . iii 2 210
They do but jest, poison in jest; no offence i' the world . iii 2 245
For some must watch, while some must sleep: So runs the world away iii 2 285
When churchyards yawn and hell itself breathes out Contagion to this world . iii 2 408
In the corrupted currents of this world Offence's gilded hand may shove by justice, . . . but 'tis not so above . iii 3 57
Every god did seem to set his seal, To give the world assurance of a man iii 4 62
Whose whisper o'er the world's diameter, As level as the cannon to his blank, Transports his poison'd shot . iv 1 41
Says she hears There's tricks i' the world; and hems, and beats her heart iv 5 5
As the world were now but to begin, Antiquity forgot, custom not known iv 5 103
Both the worlds I give to negligence, Let come what comes . iv 5 134
Who shall stay you?—My will, not all the world . iv 5 137
I do not know from what part of the world I should be greeted, if not from Lord Hamlet . iv 6 4
The more pity that great folk should have countenance in this world to drown or hang themselves . v 1 31
O, that that earth, which kept the world in awe, Should patch a wall to expel the winter's flaw! . v 1 238
Thou art slain; No medicine in the world can do thee good . v 2 325
And in this harsh world draw thy breath in pain, To tell my story . v 2 359
Let me speak to the yet unknowing world How these things came about v 2 390
Came something saucily into the world before he was sent for . *Lear* i 1 22
Five days we do allot thee, for provision To shield thee from diseases of the world . i 1 177
This policy and reverence of age makes the world bitter to the best of our times . i 2 49
This is the excellent foppery of the world . i 2 129
I think the world's asleep . i 4 52
Thou must make a dullard of the world . ii 1 76
Whose disposition, all the world well knows, Will not be rubb'd nor stopp'd . ii 2 160
I will have such revenges on you both, That all the world shall . ii 4 283
Strives in his little world of man to out-scorn The to-and-fro-conflicting wind and rain . iii 1 10
All-shaking thunder, Smite flat the thick rotundity o' the world! . iii 2 7
World, world, O world! But that thy strange mutations make us hate thee, Life would not yield to age . iv 1 10
O you mighty gods! This world I do renounce . iv 6 35
This great world Shall so wear out to nought . iv 6 137
Yet you see how this world goes.—I see it feelingly . iv 6 151
A man may see how this world goes with no eyes. Look with thine ears iv 6 154
Your business of the world hath so an end, And machination ceases . v 1 45
Witness the world, that I create thee here My lord and master . v 3 77
What in the world he is That names me traitor, villain-like he lies . v 3 97
O, let him pass! he hates him much That would upon the rack of this tough world Stretch him out longer . v 3 314
Judge me the world, if 'tis not gross in sense That thou hast practised on her with foul charms . *Othello* i 2 72
An abuser of the world, a practiser Of arts inhibited and out of warrant i 2 78
And little of this great world can I speak, More than pertains to feats of broil and battle . i 3 86
My story being done, She gave me for my pains a world of sighs . i 3 159
My downright violence and storm of fortunes May trumpet to the world i 3 251
I have looked upon the world for four times seven years . i 3 313
Hell and night Must bring this monstrous birth to the world's light . i 3 410
The gravity and stillness of your youth The world hath noted . ii 3 192
Not poppy, nor mandragora, Nor all the drowsy syrups of the world . iii 3 331
O monstrous world! Take note, take note, O world, To be direct and honest is not safe . iii 3 377
By the world, I think my wife be honest and think she is not . iii 3 383
I will catechize the world for him . iii 4 16
A sibyl, that had number'd in the world The sun to course two hundred compasses . iii 4 70
O, the world hath not a sweeter creature . iv 1 194
Put in every honest hand a whip To lash the rascals naked through the world . iv 2 143
To do the act that might the addition earn Not the world's mass of vanity could make me . iv 2 164
Take me from this world with treachery and devise engines for my life iv 2 221
Wouldst thou do such a deed for all the world? . iv 3 64; 68
The world's a huge thing: it is a great price For a small vice . iv 3 69
But, for the whole world,—why, who would not make her husband a cuckold to make him a monarch? . iv 3 75
Beshrew me, if I would do such a wrong For the whole world.—Why, the wrong is but a wrong i' the world; and having the world for your labour, 'tis a wrong in your own world, and you might quickly make it right . iv 3 79
As many to the vantage as would store the world they played for . iv 3 86

World. What malice was between you?—None in the world . *Othello* v 1 103
If heaven would make me such another world Of one entire and perfect chrysolite, I'ld not have sold her for it . v 2 144
You shall see in him The triple pillar of the world transform'd Into a strumpet's fool . *Ant. and Cleo.* i 1 12
I bind, On pain of punishment, the world to weet We stand up peerless i 1 39
Whose quality, going on, The sides o' the world may danger . i 2 199
Thou, the greatest soldier of the world, Art turn'd the greatest liar . i 3 38
I Should say myself offended, and with you Chiefly i' the world . ii 2 33
The third o' the world is yours; which with a snaffle You may pace easy ii 2 63
If I knew What hoop should hold us stanch, from edge to edge O' the world I would pursue it . ii 2 118
The world and my great office will sometimes Divide me from your bosom ii 3 1
Read not my blemishes in the world's report . ii 3 5
The senators alone of this great world, Chief factors for the gods . ii 6 9
The least wind i' the world will blow them down . ii 7 3
What say'st thou?—Wilt thou be lord of the whole world? . ii 7 67
Though thou think me poor, I am the man Will give thee all the world ii 7 71
A' bears the third part of the world, man; see'st not?—The third part, then, is drunk . ii 7 96
Cup us, till the world go round, Cup us, till the world go round! . ii 7 124
Wars 'twixt you twain would be As if the world should cleave, and that slain men Should solder up the rift . iii 4 31
Then, world, thou hast a pair of chaps, no more . iii 5 14
The greater cantle of the world is lost With very ignorance . iii 10 6
I am so lated in the world, that I Have lost my way for ever . iii 11 3
With half the bulk o' the world play'd as I pleased, Making and marring fortunes . iii 11 64
When half to half the world opposed, he being The meered question . iii 13 9
From which the world should note Something particular . iii 13 21
Prove this a prosperous day, the three-nook'd world Shall bear the olive freely . iv 6 6
O thou day o' the world, Chain mine arm'd neck! . iv 8 13
Comest thou smiling from The world's great snare uncaught? . iv 8 18
Let the world rank me in register A master-leaver and a fugitive . iv 9 21
Blue promontory With trees upon't, that nod unto the world . iv 14 6
I, that with my sword Quarter'd the world . iv 14 58
That noble countenance, Wherein the worship of the whole world lies . iv 14 86
O sun, Burn the great sphere thou movest in! darkling stand The varying shore o' the world . iv 15 11
The greatest prince o' the world, The noblest . iv 15 54
Hast thou no care of me? shall I abide In this dull world, which in thy absence is No better than a sty? . iv 15 61
Tell them that this world did equal theirs Till they had stol'n our jewel iv 15 77
The round world Should have shook lions into civil streets . v 1 15
In the name lay A moiety of the world . v 1 19
We could not stall together In the whole world . v 1 40
Let the world see His nobleness well acted . v 2 44
His legs bestrid the ocean: his rear'd arm Crested the world . v 2 83
Sole sir o' the world, I cannot project mine own cause so well . v 2 120
I'll take my leave.—And may, through all the world: 'tis yours . v 2 134
If thus thou vanishest, thou tell'st the world It is not worth leave-taking v 2 300
What should I stay— In this vile world? . v 2 317
Not comforted to live, But that there is this jewel in the world That I may see again . *Cymbeline* i 1 91
What do you esteem it at?—More than the world enjoys . i 4 86
I durst attempt it against any lady in the world . i 4 123
That such a crafty devil as is his mother Should yield the world this ass! ii 1 58
They are people such That mend upon the world . ii 4 26
Britain is A world by itself; and we will nothing pay For wearing our own noses . iii 1 13
Swell'd so much that it did almost stretch The sides o' the world . iii 1 51
This story The world may read in me . iii 3 56
This twenty years This rock and these demesnes have been my world . iii 3 70
Rides on the posting winds and doth belie All corners of the world . iii 4 39
I' the world's volume Our Britain seems as of it, but not in't . iii 4 140
No companies abroad?—None in the world . iv 2 102
Yet reverence, That angel of the world, doth make distinction Of place iv 2 248
These flowers are like the pleasures of the world . iv 2 296
From this most bravest vessel of the world Struck the main-top! . iv 2 319
To shame the guise o' the world, I will begin The fashion, less without and more within . v 1 32
Moulded the stuff so fair, That he deserved the praise o' the world . v 4 50
Be not, as is our fangled world, a garment Nobler than that it covers . v 4 134
Being cruel to the world, concluded Most cruel to herself . v 5 32
Does the world go round?—How come these staggers on me? . v 5 232
The whole world shall not save him . v 5 321
And I must lose Two of the sweet'st companions in the world . v 5 349
Thou hast lost by this a kingdom.—No, my lord; I have got two worlds by't . v 5 374
I'll make my will then, and, as sick men do Who know the world, see heaven, but, feeling woe . *Pericles* i 1 48
He must not live to trumpet forth my infamy, Nor tell the world Antiochus doth sin . i 1 146
Knights come from all parts of the world to just and tourney for her love ii 1 115
Who, looking for adventures in the world, Was by the rough seas reft of ships . ii 3 83
If in the world he live, we'll seek him out; If in his grave he rest, we'll find him there . ii 4 29
By the four opposing coigns Which the world together joins . iii Gower 18
Thou art the rudeliest welcome to this world That ever was prince's child iii 1 30
The diamonds of a most praised water Do appear, to make the world twice rich . iii 2 103
What world is this?—Is not this strange?—Most rare . iii 2 106
Thou canst not do a thing in the world so soon, To yield thee so much profit . iv 1 3
This world to me is like a lasting storm, Whirring me from my friends . iv 1 20
You will not do't for all the world, I hope . iv 1 85
Were I chief lord of all this spacious world, I'ld give it to undo the deed iv 3 5
Time hath rooted out my parentage, And to the world and awkward casualties Bound me in servitude . v 1 94
Thou by some incensed god sent hither To make the world to laugh at me v 1 145
Worldlings. Thou makest a testament As worldlings do *As Y. Like It* ii 1 48
A foutre for the world and worldlings base! I speak of Africa *2 Hen. IV.* v 3 103
Worldly. Neglecting worldly ends, all dedicated To closeness *Tempest* i 2 89
My duty pricks me on to utter that Which else no worldly good should draw from me . *T. G. of Ver.* iii 1 9
The weariest and most loathed worldly life . *Meas. for Meas.* iii 1 129
The breath of worldly men cannot depose The deputy elected by the Lord . *Richard II.* iii 2 56
Worldy. The worst is worldly loss thou canst unfold. Say, is my kingdom lost? . *Richard II.* iii 2 94
Upon thy sight My worldly business makes a period . *2 Hen. IV.* iv 5 231
Hast thou not worldly pleasure at command? . *2 Hen. VI.* i 2 45
For with his soul fled all my worldly solace . iii 2 151
In common worldly things, 'tis call'd ungrateful . *Richard III.* ii 2 91
In no worldly suit would he be moved, To draw him from his holy exercise . iii 7 63
Repose you here in rest, Secure from worldly chances and mishaps! *T. Andron.* i 1 152
We worldly men Have miserable, mad, mistaking eyes . v 2 65
But life, being weary of these worldly bars, Never lacks power to dismiss itself . *J. Cæsar* i 3 96
I have but an hour Of love, of worldly matters, and direction *Othello* i 3 300
Thou thy worldly task hast done, Home art gone, and ta'en thy wages *Cymbeline* iv 2 260
World-sharers. These three world-sharers, these competitors *A. and C.* ii 7 76
World to come. True swains in love shall in the world to come Approve their truths by Troilus . *Troi. and Cres.* iii 2 180
World-wearied. And shake the yoke of inauspicious stars From this world-wearied flesh . *Rom. and Jul.* v 3 112
World-without-end. A time, methinks, too short To make a world-without-end bargain in . *L. L. Lost* v 2 799
Worm. Poor worm, thou art infected! This visitation shows it *Tempest* iii 1 31
Vile worm, thou wast o'erlook'd even in thy birth *Mer. Wives* v 5 87
Thou dost fear the soft and tender fork Of a poor worm *Meas. for Meas.* iii 1 17
Sigh for the toothache?—Where is but a humour or a worm *Much Ado* iii 2 27
If Don Worm, his conscience, find no impediment to the contrary . v 2 86
What grace hast thou, thus to reprove These worms for loving? *L. L. L.* iv 3 154
Beetles black, approach not near; Worm nor snail, do no offence *M. N. D.* ii 2 23
O brave touch! Could not a worm, an adder, do so much? . iii 2 71
Gilded tombs do worms infold . *Mer. of Venice* ii 7 69
Men have died from time to time and worms have eaten them *As Y. L. It* iv 1 108
Come, come, you froward and unable worms! . *T. of Shrew* v 2 169
She never told her love, But let concealment, like a worm i' the bud, Feed on her damask cheek . *T. Night* ii 4 114
And ring these fingers with thy household worms . *K. John* iii 4 31
Let's talk of graves, of worms, and epitaphs . *Richard II.* iii 2 145
Thou art dust, And food for— For worms . *1 Hen. IV.* v 4 87
Give that which gave thee life unto the worms . *2 Hen. IV.* iv 5 117
Civil dissension is a viperous worm . *1 Hen. VI.* iii 1 72
The mortal worm might make the sleep eternal . *2 Hen. VI.* iii 2 263
The smallest worm will turn being trodden on . *3 Hen. VI.* ii 2 17
The worm of conscience still begnaw thy soul! . *Richard III.* i 3 222
Which now, two tender playfellows for dust, Thy broken faith hath made a prey for worms . iv 4 386
And ever flourish, When I shall dwell with worms! . *Hen. VIII.* iv 2 126
As is the bud bit with an envious worm . *Rom. and Jul.* i 1 157
A round little worm Prick'd from the lazy finger of a maid . i 4 65
Here will I remain With worms that are thy chamber-maids . v 3 109
Engenders the black toad and adder blue, The gilded newt and eyeless venom'd worm . *T. of Athens* iv 3 182
The worm that's fled Hath nature that in time will venom breed *Macb.* iii 4 29
How will you live?—As birds do, mother.—What, with worms and flies? iv 2 32
A certain convocation of politic worms are e'en at him . *Hamlet* iv 3 21
Your worm is your only emperor for diet: we fat all creatures else to fat us . iv 3 22
A man may fish with the worm that hath eat of a king, and eat of the fish that hath fed of that worm . iv 3 28
And now my Lady Worm's; chapless, and knocked about the mazzard with a sexton's spade . v 1 97
Thou owest the worm no silk, the beast no hide, the sheep no wool *Lear* iii 4 108
I such a fellow saw; Which made me think a man a worm . iv 1 35
The worms were hallow'd that did breed the silk . *Othello* iii 4 73
Hast thou the pretty worm of Nilus there, That kills and pains not?—Truly, I have him . *Ant. and Cleo.* v 2 243
How she died of the biting of it, what pain she felt: truly, she makes a very good report o' the worm . v 2 256
But this is most fallible, the worm's an odd worm . v 2 258
I wish you all joy of the worm . v 2 261; 282
You must think this, look you, that the worm will do his kind . v 2 264
The worm is not to be trusted but in the keeping of wise people; for, indeed, there is no goodness in the worm . v 2 26
Slander . . . whose tongue Outvenoms all the worms of Nile *Cymbeline* iii 4 37
With female fairies will his tomb be haunted, And worms will not come to thee . iv 2 218
The blind mole casts Copp'd hills towards heaven, to tell the earth is throng'd By man's oppression; and the poor worm doth die for't *Pericles* i 1 102
I trod upon a worm against my will, But I wept for it . iv 1 79
She quickly pooped him, she made him roast-meat for worms . iv 2 26
Worm-eaten. Sometime like the shaven Hercules in the smirched worm-eaten tapestry . *Much Ado* iii 3 145
I do think him as concave as a covered goblet or a worm-eaten nut *As Y. Like It* iii 4 27
This worm-eaten hold of ragged stone . *2 Hen. IV.* Ind. 35
Worm-holes. Pick'd from the worm-holes of long-vanish'd days *Hen. V.* ii 4 86
Worms-meat. Most shallow man! thou worms-meat! . *As Y. Like It* iii 2 67
A plague o' both your houses! They have made worms' meat of me *Rom. and Jul.* iii 1 112
Wormwood. Weed this wormwood from your fruitful brain . *L. L. Lost* v 2 857
I had then laid wormwood to my dug . *Rom. and Jul.* i 3 26
When it did taste the wormwood on the nipple Of my dug and felt it bitter . i 3 30
None wed the second but who kill'd the first.—Wormwood, wormwood *Hamlet* iii 2 191
Wormy. Damned spirits all, That in crossways and floods have burial, Already to their wormy beds are gone . *M. N. Dream* iii 2 384
Worn. One that is well-nigh worn to pieces with age . *Mer. Wives* ii 1 21
You that have worn your eyes almost out in the service *Meas. for Meas.* i 1 80
Nineteen zodiacs have gone round And none of them been worn . i 2 173
The garland he might have worn himself . *Much Ado* ii 1 236
A wither'd hermit, five-score winters worn, Might shake off fifty *L. L. L.* iv 3 242
Well, better wits have worn plain statute-caps . v 2 281
Ay, and worn in the cap of a tooth-drawer . v 2 622
For the morning now is something worn . *M. N. Dream* iv 1 187
He should have worn the horns on his head . v 1 244
The rest have worn me out With several applications . *All's Well* i 2 73
And no sword worn But one to dance with! . ii 1 32
His right cheek is worn bare.—A scar nobly got . iv 5 103

Worn. Of six preceding ancestors, that gem, Conferr'd by testament to the sequent issue, Hath it been owed and worn . . *All's Well* v 3 198
Our fancies are more giddy and unfirm, More longing, wavering, sooner lost and worn, Than women's are . . . . . *T. Night* ii 4 35
Infirmity Which waits upon worn times . . . . *W. Tale* v 1 142
Alack the heavy day, That I have worn so many winters out! *Rich. II.* iv 1 258
Thou art fitter to be worn in my cap than to wait at my heels 2 *Hen. IV.* i 2 17
Like a rich armour worn in heat of day, That scalds with safety . iv 5 30
And time hath worn us into slovenry . . . . *Hen. V.* iv 3 114
And worn as a memorable trophy of predeceased valour . . . v 1 75
These few days' wonder will be quickly worn . . . . 2 *Hen. VI.* ii 4 69
That you might still have worn the petticoat . . . 3 *Hen. VI.* v 5 23
Their clothes are after such a pagan cut too, That, sure, they've worn out Christendom . . . . *Hen. VIII.* i 3 15
When waterdrops have worn the stones of Troy . *Troi. and Cres.* iii 2 193
They are worn, lord consul, so, That we shall hardly in our ages see Their banners wave again . . . . *Coriolanus* iii 1 6
I would have had you put your power well on, Before you had worn it out iii 2 18
Better than he have worn Vulcan's badge . . *T. Andron.* ii 1 89
I have seen the day That I have worn a visor . . *Rom. and Jul.* i 5 24
Follow me this jest now till thou hast worn out thy pump, that when the single sole of it is worn, the jest may remain after the wearing sole singular. . . . . ii 4 66
Meagre were his looks, Sharp misery had worn him to the bones . v 1 41
Which would be worn now in their newest gloss, Not cast aside so soon *Macbeth* i 7 34
In the cup an union shall he throw, Richer than that which four successive kings In Denmark's crown have worn . . . *Hamlet* v 2 285
When old robes are worn out, there are members to make new *Ant. and Cleo.* i 2 171
Draw that thy honest sword, which thou hast worn Most useful for thy country . . . . iv 14 79
That lady is not now living, or this gentleman's opinion by this worn out.—She holds her virtue still . . . . *Cymbeline* i 4 68
Not born where't grows, But worn a bait for ladies . . . iii 4 59

Worried. If we, with thrice such powers left at home, Cannot defend our own doors from the dog, Let us be worried . . *Hen. V.* i 2 219

Worry. Then again worries he his daughter with clipping her *W. Tale* v 2 58
That dog, that had his teeth before his eyes, To worry lambs and lap their gentle blood . . . . . . *Richard III.* iv 4 50

Worrying. Your own reasons turn into your bosoms, As dogs upon their masters, worrying you. . . . . . . *Hen. V.* ii 2 83

Worse. Why, they were no worse Than now they are . . *Tempest* ii 1 261
For some of you there present Are worse than devils . . . iii 3 36
Lingering perdition, worse than any death Can be at once . . iii 3 77
I would it were no worse.—I'll warrant you, 'tis as well *T. G. of Ver.* ii 1 169
That's far worse than none; better have none . . . . v 4 51
Well, heaven send Anne Page no worse fortune! . . *Mer. Wives* i 4 33
I shall think the worse of fat men, as long as I have an eye to make difference of men's liking . . . . ii 1 56
Or to be worse than worst Of those that lawless and incertain thought Imagine howling: 'tis too horrible! . . . *Meas. for Meas.* iii 1 126
Still thus, and thus; still worse! . . . . iii 2 55
You, indeed, spoke so of him; and much more, much worse . . . v 1 341
This may prove worse than hanging . . . . . . v 1 365
Foolish, blunt, unkind, Stigmatical in making, worse in mind *C. of Er.* iv 2 22
I think him better than I say, And yet would herein others' eyes were worse . . . . iv 2 26
He's in Tartar limbo, worse than hell . . . . . iv 2 32
Pitiless and rough; A wolf, nay, worse, a fellow all in buff . . . iv 2 36
It is the devil.—Nay, she is worse, she is the devil's dam . . iv 3 51
Scratching could not make it worse, an 'twere such a face as yours *Much Ado* i 1 137
He would make but a sport of it and torment the poor lady worse . ii 3 163
The word is too good to paint out her wickedness; I could say she were worse: think you of a worse title, and I will fit her to it . . iii 2 113
They are worse fools to purchase mocking so . . *L. L. Lost* v 2 59
That superfluous case That hid the worse and show'd the better face . v 2 388
'Tis some policy To have one show worse than the king's and his company v 2 514
Now I but chide; but I should use thee worse . *M. N. Dream* iii 2 45
The worst are no worse, if imagination amend them . . . v 1 214
If we imagine no worse of them than they of themselves, they may pass for excellent men . . . . v 1 218
When he is best, he is a little worse than a man . *Mer. of Venice* i 2 94
Never so rich a gem Was set in worse than gold . . . ii 7 55
I should then have told you That I was worse than nothing . . iii 2 263
I'll have no worse a name than Jove's own page . *As Y. Like It* i 3 126
Swearing that we Are mere usurpers, tyrants, and what's worse . ii 1 61
And betray themselves to every modern censure worse than drunkards iv 1 7
As curst and shrewd As Socrates' Xanthippe, or a worse . *T. of Shrew* i 2 71
It is worse for me than so . . . . iv 2 88
Neither art thou the worse For this poor furniture and mean array iv 3 181
And if you please to like No worse than I . . . . . iv 4 33
Pray God, sir, your wife send you not a worse. . . . . v 2 84
A goodly increase; and the principal itself not much the worse *All's Well* i 1 161
Nay, worse—if worse—extended With vilest torture let my life be ended ii 1 176
I ne'er had worse luck in my life in my 'O Lord, sir!' . . . ii 2 59
No worse man than Sir Toby to look to me! . . *T. Night* iii 4 72
If you tarry longer, I shall give worse payment . . . . iv 1 21
The better for my foes and the worse for my friends . . v 1 14; 25
The better for thy friends.—No, sir, the worse . . . . v 1 17
Thou shalt not be the worse for me: there's gold . . . v 1 30
Worse than the great'st infection That e'er was heard or read! *W. Tale* i 2 423
I have That honourable grief lodged here which burns Worse than tears drown . . . . ii 1 112
Might we lay the old proverb to your charge, So like you, 'tis the worse ii 3 97
Of this allow, If ever you have spent time worse ere now . . iv 1 30
No more such wives; therefore, no wife; one worse, And better used, would make her sainted spirit Again possess her corpse . . . v 1 56
A foot of honour better than I was; But many a many foot of land the worse . . . . *K. John* i 1 183
Oftentimes excusing of a fault Doth make the fault the worse by the excuse . . . . iv 2 31
Will I make good against thee, arm to arm, What I have spoke, or thou canst worse device . . . . *Richard II.* i 1 77
The apprehension of the good Gives but the greater feeling to the worse i 3 301
Now God in heaven forbid!—Ah, madam, 'tis too true: and that is worse ii 2 52
All goes worse than I have power to tell . . . . . iii 2 120
Three Judases, each one thrice worse than Judas! . . . . iii 2 132
Fear, and be slain; no worse can come to fight . . . . iii 2 183

Worse. Poor queen! so that thy state might be no worse, I would my skill were subject to thy curse . . . . . *Richard II.* iii 4 102
Yet a coward is worse than a cup of sack with lime in it . 1 *Hen. IV.* ii 4 139
As tedious As a tired horse, a railing wife; Worse than a smoky house . iii 1 161
Worse than the sun in March, This praise doth nourish agues . iv 1 111
Such as fear the report of a caliver worse than a struck fowl . . iv 2 21
To make that worse, suffer'd his kinsman March . . to be engaged in Wales . . . . iv 3 93
They wound my thoughts worse than thy sword my flesh . . . v 4 80
They bring smooth comforts false, worse than true wrongs 2 *Hen. IV.* Ind. 40
It is worse shame to beg than to be on the worst side, were it worse than the name of rebellion can tell how to make it . . . . i 2 88
Must I marry your sister?—God send the wench no worse fortune! . ii 2 152
By my troth; I am the worse, when one says swagger . . . ii 4 113
I am passing light in spirit.—So much the worse . . . . iv 2 86
They . . . will backbite.—No worse than they are backbitten . v 1 37
In thy maw, perdy, And, which is worse, within thy nasty mouth! *Hen. V.* ii 1 53
Entreat her not the worse in that I pray You use her well 2 *Hen. VI.* ii 4 81
Thy fortune, York, hadst thou been regent there, Might happily have proved far worse than his . . . . iii 1 306
Gall, worse than gall, the daintiest that they taste! . . . . iii 2 322
She-wolf of France, but worse than wolves of France! . 3 *Hen. VI.* i 4 111
What's worse than murderer, that I may name it? . . . . v 5 58
In that you brook it ill, it makes him worse . . *Richard III.* i 3 3
God grant that some less noble and less loyal . . . , Deserve not worse than wretched Clarence did! . . . . ii 1 93
Bettering thy loss makes the bad causer worse . . . . . iv 4 122
In him Sparing would show a worse sin than ill doctrine . *Hen. VIII.* i 3 60
All your studies Make me a curse like this.—Your fears are worse . iii 1 124
I'll startle you Worse than the sacring bell . . . . . iii 2 295
To fear the worst oft cures the worse . . . *Troi. and Cres.* iii 2 79
We know each other well.—We do; and long to know each other worse iv 1 31
The mouse ne'er shunn'd the cat as they did budge From rascals worse than they . . . . *Coriolanus* i 6 45
For I do hate thee Worse than a promise-breaker . . . . i 8 2
'Twere a concealment Worse than a theft, no less than a traducement . i 9 22
How is it less or worse, That it shall hold companionship in peace With honour, as in war? . . . . iii 2 48
The glorious gods sit in hourly synod about thy particular prosperity, and love thee no worse than thy old father! . . . . . v 2 75
Use her as you will, The worse to her, the better loved of me *T. Andron.* ii 3 167
O, keep me from their worse than killing lust . . . . ii 3 175
Were there worse end than death, That end upon them should be executed ii 3 302
For worse than Philomel you used my daughter, And worse than Progne I will be revenged . . . . v 2 195
Ten thousand worse than ever yet I did Would I perform, if I might . v 3 187
A thousand times good night!—A thousand times the worse, to want thy light . . . . *Rom. and Jul.* ii 2 156
I am the youngest of that name, for fault of a worse . . . ii 4 129
There is thy gold, worse poison to men's souls . . . . v 1 80
And now ingratitude makes it worse than stealth . . *T. of Athens* iii 4 27
I'm worse than mad . . . . iii 5 106
I love thee better now than e'er I did.—I hate thee worse . . iv 3 234
Best state, contentless, Hath a distracted and most wretched being, Worse than the worst, content . . . . iv 3 247
You blocks, you stones, you worse than senseless things! . . *J. Cæsar* i 1 40
Let Cæsar seat him sure; For we will shake him, or worse days endure i 2 326
Thy master is a wise and valiant Roman; I never thought him worse . iii 1 139
I fear there will a worse come in his place . . . . iii 2 116
And, which is worse, all you have done Hath been but for a wayward son, Spiteful and wrathful . . . . *Macbeth* iii 5 10
To do worse to you were fell cruelty, Which is too nigh your person iv 2 71
It would cost you a groaning to take off my edge.—Still better, and worse *Hamlet* iii 2 261
Thus bad begins and worse remains behind . . . . . iii 4 179
Methought I lay Worse than the mutines in the bilboes . . . v 2 6
Unnatural, detested, brutish villain! worse than brutish! . *Lear* i 2 82
If I like thee no worse after dinner, I will not part from thee yet . i 4 44
Much more worse, To have her gentleman abused, assaulted . . ii 2 155
They durst not do't; They could not, would not do't; 'tis worse than murder . . . . ii 4 23
There's a division betwixt the dukes; and a worse matter than that . iii 3 9
Who is't can say 'I am at the worst?' I am worse than e'er I was . iv 1 28
And worse I may be yet . . . . iv 1 29
I told him you were coming; His answer was 'The worse' . . iv 2 6
Thou worse than any name, read thine own evil . . . . v 3 156
I know my price, I am worth no worse a place . . . *Othello* i 1 11
With no worse nor better guard But with a knave of common hire, a gondolier . . . . i 1 125
She's the worse for all this.—O, a thousand thousand times . . iv 1 202
Let her die too, and give him a worse! and let worse follow worse, till the worst of all follow! . . . . *Ant. and Cleo.* i 2 68
Whose beauty claims No worse a husband than the best of men . ii 2 131
He has a cloud in's face.—He were the worse for that, were he a horse . iii 2 52
Many times, Doth ill deserve by doing well; what's worse, Must court'sy at the censure . . . . *Cymbeline* iii 3 54
Those that are betray'd Do feel the treason sharply, yet the traitor Stands in worse case of woe. . . . . iii 4 89
Falsehood Is worse in kings than beggars . . . . . . iii 6 14
His humour Was nothing but mutation, ay, and that From one bad thing to worse . . . . iv 2 134
For notes of sorrow out of tune are worse Than priests and fanes that lie iv 2 241
You some permit To second ills with ills, each elder worse . . v 1 14
The queen is dead.—Who worse than a physician Would this report become? . . . . v 5 27
Is there more?—More, sir, and worse . . . . . . v 5 49
That all the abhorred things o' the earth amend By being worse than they . . . . v 5 217
Bad child; worse father! to entice his own To evil *Pericles* i Gower 27
It is fit, What being more known grows worse, to smother it . . i 1 106
As well as we! ay, and better too; we offend worse . . . ii 2 42

Worse and worse. What, worse and worse! . . *Mer. of Venice* iii 2 250
She will not come; she bids you come to her.—Worse and worse *T. of S.* v 2 93
Speak not; he grows worse and worse; Question enrages him *Macbeth* iii 4 117
She'll find a white that shall her blackness fit.—Worse and worse *Othello* ii 1 135
Worse and worse, mistress; she has here spoken holy words *Pericles* iv 6 141

Worse at ease. I know the more one sickens the worse at ease he is *As Y. Like It* iii 2 25

Worse bested. I never saw a fellow worse bested . . 2 *Hen. VI.* ii 3 56

Worse bodied. Ill-faced, worse bodied, shapeless everywhere *Com. of Er.* iv 2 20

Worse hated. Who is of Rome worse hated than of you . . *Coriolanus* i 2 13
Worse issued. And thou his only heir And princess no worse issued *Temp.* i 2 59
Worse provided. Or it will seek me in another place And find me worse provided . . . . 2 *Hen. IV.* ii 3 50
Worser. The strong'st suggestion Our worser genius can, shall never melt Mine honour . . . . . . *Tempest* iv 1 27
It is so, it hath the worser sole . . . . . . *T. G. of Ver.* ii 3 19
And the worser allowed by order of law a furred gown *Meas. for Meas.* iii 2 7
What worser place can I beg in your love? . . *M. N. Dream* ii 1 208
Were my state far worser than it is, I would not wed her . *T. of Shrew* i 2 91
Changed to a worser shape thou canst not be . . . 1 *Hen. VI.* v 3 36
I wis your grandam had a worser match . . . *Richard III.* i 3 102
And where the worser is predominant, Full soon the canker death eats up that plant . . . . . . *Rom. and Jul.* ii 3 29
Some word there was, worser than Tybalt's death, That murder'd me iii 2 108
Thou hast cleft my heart in twain.—O, throw away the worser part of it, And live the purer with the other half . . *Hamlet* iii 4 157
Let not my worser spirit tempt me again To die before you please! *Lear* iv 6 222
Be better suited: These weeds are memories of those worser hours iv 7 7
My name is Roderigo.—The worser welcome . . . *Othello* i 1 95
How do you now, lieutenant?—The worser that you give me the addition Whose want even kills me . . . . iv 1 105
Our worser thoughts heavens mend! . . . . *Ant. and Cleo.* i 2 64
I cannot hate thee worser than I do, If thou again say 'Yes' . . ii 5 90
Worship. What a thrice-double ass Was I, to take this drunkard for a god And worship this dull fool! . . . . . *Tempest* v 1 297
Who bade you call her?—Your worship, sir; or else I mistook *T. G. of V.* ii 1 10
Do you know Madam Silvia?—She that your worship loves? . . ii 1 16
I read your fortune in your eye. Was this the idol that you worship so? ii 4 144
I did adore a twinkling star, But now I worship a celestial sun . . ii 6 10
Your falsehood shall become you well To worship shadows . . iv 2 131
I am glad to see your worships well . . . . *Mer. Wives* i 1 80
My father desires your worships' company.—I will wait on him . . i 1 271
Will't please your worship to come in, sir?—No, I thank you . . i 1 275
I may not go in without your worship: they will not sit till you come. i 1 288
How dost thou?—The better that it pleases your good worship to ask . i 4 145
Have not your worship a wart above your eye? . . . . . i 4 157
I will tell your worship more of the wart the next time we have confidence . . . . i 4 171
Give your worship good morrow.—Good morrow, good wife . . . ii 2 34
Shall I vouchsafe your worship a word or two?—Two thousand . ii 2 41
Your worship says very true: I pray your worship, come a little nearer ii 2 49
Your worship's a wanton! Well, heaven forgive you and all of us, I pray! . . . . ii 2 57
You say well. But I have another messenger to your worship . . ii 2 98
She bade me tell your worship that her husband is seldom from home . ii 2 104
And hath sent your worship a morning's draught of sack . . . ii 2 152
He knew your worship would kill him, if he came . . . . . ii 3 10
I thank your worship . . . . . . iv 5 56; *L. L. Lost* iii 1 151
Let not your worship think me the poor duke's officer . *Meas. for Meas.* ii 1 185
I thank your good worship for it. What is't your worship's pleasure I shall do? . . . . ii 1 191
Does your worship mean to geld and splay all the youth of the city? . ii 1 242
If your worship will take order for the drabs and the knaves, you need not to fear the bawds . . . . ii 1 246
To your worship's house, sir?—To my house . . . . . ii 1 288
I hope, sir, your good worship will be my bail.—No, indeed . . iii 2 75
If I should pay your worship those again, Perchance you will not bear them patiently . . . . *Com. of Errors* i 2 85
What mistress, slave, hast thou?—Your worship's wife . . . . i 2 88
You are tedious.—It pleases your worship to say so . . *Much Ado* iii 5 21
If I were as tedious as a king, I could find it in my heart to bestow it all of your worship . . . . iii 5 25
I hear as good exclamation on your worship as of any man in the city . iii 5 29
Excepting your worship's presence . . . . iii 5 34
We would have them this morning examined before your worship . . iii 5 52
Your worship speaks like a most thankful and reverend youth . . v 1 324
I leave an arrant knave with your worship; which I beseech your worship to correct yourself . . . . v 1 330
God keep your worship! I wish your worship well . . . . v 1 333
I will come to your worship to-morrow morning . . *L. L. Lost* iii 1 161
Show the sunshine of your face, That we, like savages, may worship it v 2 202
I cry your worships mercy, heartily: I beseech your worship's name *M. N. Dream* iii 1 182
Your worship was the last man in our mouths. . . *Mer. of Venice* i 3 61
We talk of young Master Launcelot.—Your worship's friend . . ii 2 58
To him, father.—God bless your worship! . . . . ii 2 127
His master and he, saving your worship's reverence, are scarce cater-cousins . . . . ii 2 138
I have here a dish of doves that I would bestow upon your worship . ii 2 145
The suit is impertinent to myself, as your worship shall know . . ii 2 147
Your worship was wont to tell me that I could do nothing without bidding . . . . ii 5 8
And so God keep your worship!—Farewell . . . *As Y. Like It* i 1 168
Nor your cheek of cream, That can entame my spirits to your worship . iii 5 48
Look upon him, love him; he worships you . . . . . . v 2 88
Whom should I knock? is there any man has rebused your worship? *T. of Shrew* i 2 7
As I before imparted to your worship, I am to get a man . . . iii 2 132
Here is the cap your worship did bespeak . . . . . . iv 3 63
She says your worship means to make a puppet of her . . . . iv 3 105
Thou hast marr'd her gown.—Your worship is deceived . . . iv 3 116
Is this all your worship's reason? . . . . . . *All's Well* i 3 33
Whom I from meaner form Have bench'd and rear'd to worship *W. Tale* i 2 314
Do not give us the lie.—Your worship had like to have given us one . iv 4 750
Pardon me all the faults I have committed to your worship . . v 2 161
He and his toothpick at my worship's mess . . . . *K. John* i 1 190
Since kings break faith upon commodity, Gain, be my lord, for I will worship thee. . . . . ii 1 598
Till I have set a glory to this hand, By giving it the worship of revenge iv 3 72
He shall render every glory up, Yea, even the slightest worship 1 *Hen. IV.* iii 2 151
He's gone into Smithfield to buy your worship a horse . . 2 *Hen. IV.* i 2 57
Give me your good hand, give me your worship's good hand . . . iii 2 91
Your good worship is welcome.—Fie! this is hot weather . . . iii 2 100
I grant your worship that he is a knave, sir . . . . . . v 1 47
I have served your worship truly, sir, this eight years . . . . v 1 51
I have but a very little credit with your worship . . . . . v 1 55
I beseech your worship, let him be countenanced . . . . . v 1 56
I am glad to see your worship.—I thank thee with all my heart . . v 1 63
Your worship! I'll be with you straight. . . . . . . v 3 46
Worship. God-den to your worship, good Captain James . . *Hen. V.* iii 2 89
How may I reverently worship thee enough? . . . 1 *Hen. VI.* i 2 145
Erect his statua and worship it, And make my image but an alehouse sign 2 *Hen. VI.* iii 2 80
That they may agree like brothers and worship me their lord . . iv 2 81
Ay, but give me worship and quietness; I like it better . 3 *Hen. VI.* iv 3 16
That good man of worship, Anthony Woodville . . . *Richard III.* i 1 66
I belong to worship and affect In honour honesty . . *Hen. VIII.* i 1 39
Then marvel not, thou great and complete man, That all the Greeks begin to worship Ajax . . . . *Troi. and Cres.* iii 3 182
I can't say your worships have delivered the matter well . *Coriolanus* ii 1 62
God-den to your worships . . . . ii 1 104
God save your good worships! . . . . ii 1 160
This double worship, Where one part does disdain with cause, the other Insult without all reason . . . . iii 1 142
He'll be your follower; Your worship in that sense may call him 'man' *Rom. and Jul.* iii 1 62
All the world will be in love with night And pay no worship to the garish sun . . . . iii 2 25
Fly, damned baseness, To him that worships thee! . . *T. of Athens* iii 1 51
What does his cashiered worship mutter?—No matter what; he's poor iii 4 61
To thee be worship! and thy saints for aye Be crown'd with plagues! . v 1 55
If he had done or said any thing amiss, he desired their worships to think it was his infirmity . . . . *J. Cæsar* i 2 273
And in the most exact regard support The worships of their name *Lear* i 4 288
Turn from me, then, that noble countenance, Wherein the worship of the whole world lies . . . . *Ant. and Cleo.* iv 14 86
All gold and silver rather turn to dirt! As 'tis no better reckon'd, but of those Who worship dirty gods . . . . . *Cymbeline* iii 6 56
An't like your worship *W. Tale* iv 4; v 2; 2 *Hen. VI.* ii 1
An't please your worship *M. W.* ii 2; 2 *Hen. IV.* v 3; *Rich. III.* i 1
Worshipful. What, my old worshipful old master? . . . *T. of Shrew* v 1 56
This is worshipful society And fits the mounting spirit like myself *K. John* i 1 205
Most worshipful lord, an't please your grace, I am a poor widow 2 *Hen. IV.* ii 1 75
What accites your most worshipful thought to think so? . . . ii 2 65
His master's son, as worshipful he terms it . . . *Richard III.* iii 4 41
Your very worshipful and loving friends . . . . . . iii 7 138
Worshipful mutiners, Your valour puts well forth . . . *Coriolanus* i 1 254
Worshipped. O thou senseless form, Thou shalt be worshipp'd, kiss'd, loved, and adored! . . . . *T. G. of Ver.* iv 4 204
But God is to be worshipped; all men are not alike . . *Much Ado* iii 5 43
Lord worshipped might he be! what a beard hast thou got! *Mer. of Ven.* ii 2 98
Canonized and worshipp'd as a saint . . . . . *K. John* iii 1 177
Not worshipp'd with a waxen epitaph . . . . . *Hen. V.* i 2 233
Shall he be worshipp'd Of that we hold an idol more than he? *T. and C.* ii 3 198
An hour before the worshipp'd sun Peer'd forth . . *Rom. and Jul.* i 1 125
What a god's gold, That he is worshipp'd in a baser temple Than where swine feed! . . . . *T. of Athens* v 1 51
Worshipper. I adore The sun, that looks upon his worshipper *All's Well* i 3 212
What kind of god art thou, that suffer'st more Of mortal griefs than do thy worshippers? . . . . *Hen. V.* iv 1 259
Worshippest. Thou worshippest Saint Nicholas as truly as a man of falsehood may . . . . 1 *Hen. IV.* ii 1 70
Worst. 'Mongst all foes that a friend should be the worst! *T. G. of Ver.* v 4 72
His worst fault is, that he is given to prayer . . . *Mer. Wives* i 4 13
His face is the worst thing about him . . . *Meas. for Meas.* ii 1 163; 164
Or to be worse than worst Of those that lawless and incertain thought Imagine howling: 'tis too horrible! . . . . iii 1 126
The best that ever I heard.—Ay, the best for the worst . . *L. L. Lost* i 1 283
Nay, to be perjured, which is worst of all; And, among three, to love the worst of all . . . . iii 1 196
That I may know The worst that may befall me in this case *M. N. Dream* i 1 63
The worst are no worse, if imagination amend them . . . . . v 1 214
When he is worst, he is little better than a beast: an the worst fall that ever fell, I hope I shall make shift to go without him *Mer. of Venice* i 2 95
Therefore, for fear of the worst, I pray thee, set a deep glass of rhenish wine on the contrary casket . . . . i 2 103
The worst fault you have is to be in love . . . *As Y. Like It* iii 2 299
My master is grown quarrelsome. I should knock you first, And then I know after who comes by the worst . . . . *T. of Shrew* i 2 14
Whom would to God I had well knock'd at first, Then had not Grumio come by the worst . . . . i 2 35
Katharine the curst! A title for a maid of all titles the worst . . i 2 130
Think it not the worst of all your fortunes . . . . . . iv 2 104
The worst is this, that, at so slender warning, You are like to have a thin and slender pittance . . . . iv 4 60
Would by combat make her good, so were I A man, the worst about you *W. Tale* ii 3 61
Whose every word deserves To taste of thy most worst . . . iii 2 180
Not the worst of the three but jumps twelve foot and a half by the squier . . . . iv 4 347
Though the pennyworth on his side be the worst, yet hold thee, there's some boot . . . . iv 4 651
But if you be afeard to hear the worst, Then let the worst unheard fall on your head . . . . *K. John* iv 2 135
Return and tell him so: we know the worst . . . . . . iv 3 27
Even in condition of the worst degree, In gross rebellion *Richard II.* ii 3 108
The worst is worldly loss thou canst unfold . . . . . iii 2 94
Cry woe, destruction, ruin, and decay; The worst is death . . iii 2 103
Those whom you curse Have felt the worst of death's destroying wound iii 2 139
By small and small To lengthen out the worst that must be spoken iii 2 199
Worst in this royal presence may I speak, Yet best beseeming me to speak the truth . . . . iv 1 115
Heavy news; Whose worst was, that the noble Mortimer . . . Was by the rude hands of that Welshman taken . . . 1 *Hen. IV.* i 1 38
That's the worst tidings that I hear of yet . . . . . . iv 1 127
And, to prevent the worst, Sir Michael, speed . . . . . iv 4 35
It is worse shame to beg than to be on the worst side . 2 *Hen. IV.* i 2 89
O thoughts of men accursed! Past and to come seems best; things present worst . . . . i 3 108
The worst that they can say of me is that I am a second brother . . ii 2 70
Therefore, thou best of gold art worst of gold . . . . . iv 5 161
O that the living Harry had the temper Of him, the worst of these three gentlemen! . . . . v 2 16
Or like to men proud of destruction Defy us to our worst . *Hen. V.* iii 3 5
Thou hast me, if thou hast me, at the worst . . . . . . v 2 250
Is that the worst this letter doth contain?—It is the worst . 1 *Hen. VI.* iv 1 66
She vaunted . . . , The very train of her worst wearing gown Was better worth than all my father's lands . . . . 2 *Hen. VI.* i 3 88
Yet am I arm'd against the worst can happen . . . . 3 *Hen. VI.* iv 1 128

Worst. To prevent the worst, Forthwith we'll send him hence *3 Hen. VI.* iv 6 96

Come, come, we fear the worst; all shall be well *Richard III.* ii 3 31

The two kings, Equal in lustre, were now best, now worst, As presence did present them . . . *Hen. VIII.* i 1 29

What we oft do best . . is Not ours, or not allow'd; what worst, as oft, Hitting a grosser quality, is cried up For our best act . . i 2 83

Your graces find me here part of a housewife, I would be all, against the worst may happen . . iii 1 25

Speak on, sir; I dare your worst objections . . ii 2 307

What news abroad?—The heaviest and the worst Is your displeasure . iii 2 391

You may, worst Of all this table, say so . . v 3 78

The tent that searches To the bottom of the worst . *Troi. and Cres.* ii 2 17

To fear the worst oft cures the worse . . iii 2 78

As what envy can say worst shall be a mock for his truth . iii 2 104

Thou go'st foremost: Thou rascal, that art worst in blood to run, Lead'st first to win some vantage . . *Coriolanus* i 1 163

He must come, Or what is worst will follow . . iii 1 336

Let your general do his worst. For you, be that you are, long! v 2 112

You say well.—Yea, is the worst well? very well took, i' faith *R. and J.* ii 4 131

You take us even at the best.—'Faith, for the worst is filthy *T. of Athens* i 2 158

He's truly valiant that can wisely suffer The worst that man can breathe iii 5 32

Strange, unusual blood, When man's worst sin is, he does too much good! . iv 2 39

Best state, contentless, Hath a distracted and most wretched being, Worse than the worst, content . . iv 3 247

If thou hadst not been born the worst of men, Thou hadst been a knave iv 3 275

I cannot choose but tell him, that I care not, And let him take't at worst . . v 1 181

I know, When thou didst hate him worst, thou lovedst him better Than ever thou lovedst Cassius . . *J. Cæsar* iv 3 106

Since the affairs of men rest still incertain, Let's reason with the worst that may befall . . v 1 97

And so of men. Now, if you have a station in the file, Not i' the worst rank of manhood, say't . . *Macbeth* iii 1 103

After life's fitful fever he sleeps well; Treason has done his worst . iii 2 24

Now I am bent to know, By the worst means, the worst . iii 4 135

Things at the worst will cease, or else climb upward To what they were before . . iv 2 24

In which there are many confines, wards, and dungeons, Denmark being one o' the worst . . *Hamlet* ii 2 253

Not being the worst Stands in some rank of praise . *Lear* ii 4 260

To be worst, The lowest and most dejected thing of fortune, Stands still in esperance, lives not in fear . . iv 1 2

The lamentable change is from the best; The worst returns to laughter iv 1 6

The wretch that thou hast blown unto the worst Owes nothing to thy blasts . . iv 1 8

Who is't can say 'I am at the worst'? I am worse than e'er I was . iv 1 27

The worst is not So long as we can say 'This is the worst' . iv 1 29

No, do thy worst, blind Cupid; I'll not love . . iv 6 140

We are not the first Who, with best meaning, have incurr'd the worst . v 3 4

Who, having seen me in my worst estate, Shunn'd my abhorr'd society v 3 209

When remedies are past, the griefs are ended By seeing the worst *Othello* i 3 203

O heavy ignorance! thou praisest the worst best . . ii 1 145

Give thy worst of thoughts The worst of words . . iii 3 132

That was not so well; yet would I knew That stroke would prove the worst! . . iv 1 285

She was too fond of her most filthy bargain.—Ha!—Do thy worst . v 2 159

And let worse follow worse, till the worst of all follow! *Ant. and Cleo.* i 2 68

Well, what worst?—The nature of bad news infects the teller . i 2 98

She's my good lady, and will conceive, I hope, But the worst of me. So, I leave you, sir, To the worst of discontent . . *Cymbeline* ii 3 159

You are music's master.—The worst of all her scholars *Pericles* ii 5 31

I do not fear the flaw; It hath done to me the worst . . iii 1 40

Of all the faults beneath the heavens, the gods Do like this worst. . iv 3 21

Worsted-stocking. Filthy, worsted-stocking knave *Lear* ii 2 17

Wort. Goot worts.—Good worts! good cabbage . *Mer. Wives* i 1 123

And if you grow so nice, Metheglin, wort, and malmsey. . *L. L. Lost* v 2 233

Worth What's dearest to the world! *Tempest* iii 1 38

'Tis an office of great worth And you an officer fit . *T. G. of Ver.* i 2 44

I know the gentleman To be of worth and worthy estimation . ii 4 56

Far behind his worth Comes all the praises that I now bestow . ii 4 71

Welcome him then according to his worth . . ii 4 83

His worth is warrant for his welcome hither . . ii 4 102

All I can is nothing To her whose worth makes other worthies nothing ii 4 166

Thou art an Hebrew, a Jew, and not worth the name of a Christian ii 5 58

A round hose, madam, now's not worth a pin, Unless you have a codpiece . . ii 7 55

Worth and qualities Beseeming such a wife as your fair daughter . iii 1 65

She I mean is promised by her friends Unto a youthful gentleman of worth . . iii 1 107

By praising me as much As you in worth dispraise Sir Valentine . iii 2 55

But that to your sufficiency . . . as your worth is able *Meas. for Meas.* i 1 9

If any in Vienna be of worth To undergo such ample grace and honour i 1 23

There's one yonder arrested and carried to prison was worth five thousand of you all . . i 2 61

Which once thou sworest was worth the looking on . . v 1 208

Were testimonies against his worth and credit . . v 1 244

Look that you love your wife; her worth worth yours . . v 1 502

Time is a very bankrupt and owes more than he's worth to season *Com. of Errors* iv 2 58

A ring he hath of mine worth forty ducats . . iv 3 84

There's not a note of mine that's worth the noting . . *Much Ado* ii 3 57

For a fine, quaint, graceful, and excellent fashion, yours is worth ten on't . . iii 4 23

Whose worth May counterpoise this rich and precious gift . . iv 1 28

What we have we prize not to the worth Whiles we enjoy it . iv 1 220

Shall relate In high-born words the worth of many a knight *L. L. Lost* i 1 173

I am less proud to hear you tell my worth . . ii 1 17

Although not valued to the money's worth . . ii 1 137

As jewels in crystal for some prince to buy; Who, tendering their own worth from where they were glass'd, Did point you to buy them, along as you pass'd . . ii 1 244

All the power thereof it doth apply To prove, by wit, worth in simplicity v 2 78

Great thanks, great Pompey.—'Tis not so much worth . v 2 561

The rich worth of your virginity . *M. N. Dream* ii 1 219

Even now worth this, And now worth nothing . *Mer. of Venice* i 1 35

Your worth is very dear in my regard . . i 1 62

You shall seek all day ere you find them, and when you have them, they are not worth the search . . i 1 118

Nor is the wide world ignorant of her worth . . i 1 167

Worth. There will come a Christian by, Will be worth a Jewess' eye *Mer. of Venice* ii 5 43

It is worth the pains . . ii 6 33

Thy lands and all things that thou dost call thine Worth seizure do we seize into our hands . . *As Y. Like It* iii 1 10

Her worth, being mounted on the wind, Through all the world bears Rosalind . . iii 2 95

Is his head worth a hat, or his chin worth a beard? . . iii 2 217

Every day Men of great worth resorted to this forest . . v 4 161

I would esteem him worth a dozen such . *T. of Shrew* Ind. 1 27

If you accept them, then their worth is great . . ii 1 102

[Virginity] the longer kept, the less worth . *All's Well* i 1 167

All that life can rate Worth name of life in thee hath estimate . ii 1 183

Yet art thou good for nothing but taking up; and that thou'rt scarce worth . . ii 3 219

You are not worth another word, else I'ld call you knave . ii 3 280

Where death and danger dogs the heels of worth . . iii 4 15

Let every word weigh heavy of her worth That he does weigh too light iii 4 31

To the worth Of the great count himself, she is too mean . iii 5 62

Titled goddess; And worth it, with addition! . . iv 2 3

It may be worth thy pains . . *T. Night* i 2 57

I can sing And speak to him in many sorts of music That will allow me very worth his service . . i 2 59

If it be worth stooping for, there it lies in your eye . ii 2 16

What kind of woman is't?—Of your complexion.—She is not worth thee, then . . ii 4 28

Were my worth as is my conscience firm, You should find better dealing iii 3 17

He hath better bethought him of his quarrel, and he finds that now scarce to be worth talking of . . iii 4 328

To his image, which methought did promise Most venerable worth, did I devotion . . iii 4 397

As it hath been to us rare, pleasant, speedy, The time is worth the use on't . . *W. Tale* iii 1 14

She is a woman More worth than any man . . v 1 111

To greet a man not worth her pains . . v 1 155

Sorry Your choice is not so rich in worth as beauty . v 1 214

She was more worth such gazes Than what you look on now . v 1 226

The dignity of this act was worth the audience of kings . v 2 86

Whose worth and honesty Is richly noted . . v 3 144

I am not worth this coil that's made for me . *K. John* ii 1 165

Lest I . . . forget Your worth, your greatness, and nobility . iv 3 86

By the glorious worth of my descent, This arm shall do it *Richard II.* i 1 107

By the worth and honour of himself . . iii 3 110

And to thy worth will add right worthy gains . . v 6 12

I know a trick worth two of that, i' faith . . *1 Hen. IV.* ii 1 41

It is worth the listening to . . ii 4 235

I have lost a seal-ring of my grandfather's worth forty mark . . iii 3 95

A thousand pound, Hal! a million: thy love is worth a million . iii 3 156

His health was never better worth than now . . iv 1 27

Welcome, by my soul.—Pray God my news be worth a welcome . iv 1 87

All the other gifts appertinent to man, as the malice of this age shapes them, are not worth a gooseberry . . *2 Hen. IV.* i 2 196

The German hunting in water-work is worth a thousand of these bed-hangings . . ii 1 158

A crown's worth of good interpretation . . ii 2 99

Why, that's well said; a good heart's worth gold . . ii 4 35

Thou art as valorous as Hector of Troy, worth five of Agamemnon . ii 4 237

A score of good ewes may be worth ten pounds . . iii 2 57

Let us swear That you are worth your breeding . . *Hen. V.* iii 1 28

What are thy comings in? O ceremony, show me but thy worth! . iv 1 261

More will I do; Though all that I can do is nothing worth . iv 1 320

Whose face is not worth sun-burning . . v 2 154

England ne'er lost a king of so much worth . . *1 Hen. VI.* i 1 7

My worth unknown, no loss is known in me . . iv 5 23

And give them burial as beseems their worth . . iv 7 86

Since thou dost deign to woo her little worth To be the princely bride of such a lord . . v 3 151

Marriage is a matter of more worth Than to be dealt in by attorneyship v 5 55

She vaunted . . . , The very train of her worst wearing gown Was better worth than all my father's lands . *2 Hen. VI.* i 3 89

What thou art Resign to death; it is not worth the enjoying . iii 1 334

Your loving uncle, twenty times his worth, They say, is shamefully bereft of life . . iii 2 268

A jewel, lock'd into the wofull'st cask That ever did contain a thing of worth . . iii 2 410

This small inheritance my father left me Contenteth me, and worth a monarchy . . iv 10 21

A wisp of straw were worth a thousand crowns . . *3 Hen. VI.* ii 2 144

A silly time To make prescription for a kingdom's worth . . iii 3 94

To ennoble those That scarce, some two days since, were worth a noble *Richard III.* i 3 82

A valiant crew; And many moe of noble fame and worth . iv 5 13

What were't worth to know The secret of your conference? *Hen. VIII.* ii 3 50

Nor my wishes More worth than empty vanities . . ii 3 69

His thinkings are below the moon, not worth His serious considering iii 2 134

How was it?—Well worth the seeing . . iv 1 61

Even so Doth valour's show and valour's worth divide *Troi. and Cres.* i 3 46

Having his ear full of his airy fame, Grows dainty of his worth . i 3 145

The worthiness of praise distains his worth, If that the praised himself bring the praise forth . . i 3 241

And dare avow her beauty and her worth In other arms than hers . i 3 271

The Grecian dames are sunburnt and not worth The splinter of a lance i 3 282

Lost so many tenths of ours, To guard a thing not ours nor worth to us ii 2 22

Weigh you the worth and honour of a king So great as our dread father in a scale Of common ounces? . . ii 2 26

She is not worth what she doth cost The holding . . ii 2 51

The Grecians keep our aunt: Is she worth keeping? . . ii 2 81

Disgrace to your great worths and shame to me . . ii 2 151

Imagined worth Holds in his blood such swoln and hot discourse . ii 3 182

Not for the worth that hangs upon our quarrel . . ii 3 217

Find out Something not worth in me such rich beholding . . iii 3 91

What things again most dear in the esteem And poor in worth! . iii 3 130

I'll nothing do on charge: to her own worth She shall be prized . iv 4 135

The glory of our Troy doth this day lie On his fair worth . iv 4 150

We'll forth and fight, Do deeds worth praise and tell you them at night v 3 93

That same dog-fox, Ulysses, is not proved worth a blackberry . v 4 13

It is not worth the wagging of your beards . . *Coriolanus* ii 1 96

Worth all your predecessors since Deucalion . . ii 1 101

He hath been used Ever to conquer, and to have his worth Of contradiction . . iii 3 26

Worth. Cats, that can judge as fitly of his worth As I can of those mysteries which heaven Will not have earth to know *Coriolanus* iv 2 34
By some chance, Some trick not worth an egg, shall grow dear friends iv 4 21
Worth six on him.—Nay, not so neither iv 5 174
What is that curt'sy worth? or those doves' eyes? v 3 27
Volumnia Is worth of consuls, senators, patricians, A city full v 4 56
Well, let my deeds be witness of my worth *T. Andron.* v 1 103
They are but beggars that can count their worth *Rom. and Jul.* ii 6 32
What dost thou think 'tis worth?—Not worth my thinking *T. of Athens* i 1 219
You have added worth unto 't and lustre i 2 154
I doubt whether their legs be worth the sums That are given for 'em i 2 238
I'ld rather than the worth of thrice the sum, Had sent to me first iii 3 22
Mindless of thy worth, Forgetting thy great deeds iv 3 93
Will you dine with me to-morrow?—Ay, if I be alive and your mind hold and your dinner worth the eating *J. Cæsar* i 2 296
Him and his worth and our great need of him You have right well conceited i 3 161
Nor no instrument Of half that worth as those your swords iii 1 155
I have neither wit, nor words, nor worth, Action, nor utterance iii 2 225
Mine eyes are made the fools o' the other senses, Or else worth all the rest *Macbeth* ii 1 45
Your cause of sorrow Must not be measured by his worth v 8 45
He's worth more sorrow, And that I'll spend for him.—He's worth no more v 8 50
Holding a weak supposal of our worth *Hamlet* i 2 18
From this time forth, My thoughts be bloody, or be nothing worth! iv 4 66
Whose worth, if praises may go back again, Stood challenger on mount of all the age For her perfections iv 7 27
Sir, I am made Of the self-same metal that my sister is, And prize me at her worth *Lear* i 1 72
And well are worth the want that you have wanted i 1 282
That these hot tears, which break from me perforce, Should make thee worth them i 4 321
Would the reposal Of any trust, virtue, or worth in thee Make thy words faith'd? ii 1 71
Your son . . . found this trespass worth The shame which here it suffers ii 4 44
I have been worth the whistle iv 2 29
You are not worth the dust which the rude wind Blows in your face iv 2 30
He that helps him take all my outward worth iv 4 10
In it a jewel Well worth a poor man's taking iv 6 29
I know my price, I am worth no worse a place *Othello* i 1 11
I would not my unhoused free condition Put into circumscription and confine For the sea's worth i 2 28
My fortunes against any lay worth naming ii 3 330
By the worth of man's eternal soul iii 3 361
Ne'er loved till ne'er worth love, Comes dear'd by being lack'd *A. and C.* i 4 43
Which do not be entreated to, but weigh What it is worth embraced ii 6 33
Come, come, and take a queen Worth many babes and beggars! v 2 48
Give it nothing, I pray you, for it is not worth the feeding.—Will it eat me? v 2 271
If thus thou vanishest, thou tell'st the world It is not worth leave-taking v 2 301
If this be worth your hearing, Mark it *Cymbeline* i 1 57
He is A man worth any woman i 1 146
I am no further your enemy; she is not worth our debate i 4 173
Such creatures as We count not worth the hanging i 5 20
If I had lost it, I should have lost the worth of it in gold ii 4 42
I slept not, but profess Had that was well worth watching ii 4 68
From whose so many weights of baseness cannot A dram of worth be drawn iii 5 89
Should not sooner Than thine own worth prefer thee iv 2 386
And struck Me, wretch more worth your vengeance v 1 11
Would so, had it been a carbuncle Of Phœbus' wheel, and might so safely, had it Been all the worth of 's car v 5 191
Wilt thou undo the worth thou art unpaid for, By tasting of our wrath? v 5 307
Your entertain shall be As doth befit our honour and your worth *Pericles* i 1 120
What mean you, sir?—To beg of you, kind friends, this coat of worth ii 1 142
To place upon the volume of your deeds, As in a title-page, your worth in arms, Were more than you expect, or more than's fit, Since every worth in show commends itself ii 3 4
Yon knight doth sit too melancholy, As if the entertainment in our court Had not a show might countervail his worth ii 3 56
And in your search spend your adventurous worth ii 4 51
I, King Pericles, have lost This queen, worth all our mundane cost iii 2 71
Whilst ours was blurted at and held a malkin Not worth the time of day iv 3 35
I had rather than twice the worth of her she had ne'er come here iv 6 1
Not worth a breakfast in the cheapest country under the cope iv 6 131
There's some of worth would come aboard; I pray ye, greet them fairly v 1 9
There well appears The worth that learned charity aye wears v 3 Gower 94

Worthied. And put upon him such a deal of man, That worthied him, got praises *Lear* ii 2 128

Worthier. He, none but he, shall have her, Though twenty thousand worthier come to crave her *Mer. Wives* iv 4 90
We shall employ thee in a worthier place *Meas. for Meas.* v 1 537
Wanting your father's voice, The other must be held the worthier *M. N. Dream* i 1 55
And reason says you are the worthier maid ii 2 116
I had made you merry, If worthier friends had not prevented me *Mer. of Venice* i 1 61
As a walled town is more worthier than a village *As Y. Like It* iii 3 60
Dispute not that: York is the worthier 2 *Hen. VI.* i 3 111
And worthier than himself Here tend the savage strangeness he puts on, Disguise the holy strength of their command *Troi. and Cres.* ii 3 134
There was never a worthier man *Coriolanus* ii 3 43
I'll give my reasons, More worthier than their voices iii 1 120
How many times shall Cæsar bleed in sport, That now on Pompey's basis lies along No worthier than the dust! *J. Cæsar* iii 1 116
Beseech you To avert your liking a more worthier way *Lear* i 1 214
I know not how to wish A pair of worthier sons *Cymbeline* v 5 356

Worthiest. Of all the fair resort of gentlemen That every day with parle encounter me, In thy opinion which is worthiest love? *T. G. of Ver.* i 2 6
We serve you, madam, In that and all your worthiest affairs *All's Well* iii 2 99
Care not for issue; The crown will find an heir: great Alexander Left his to the worthiest *W. Tale* v 1 48
Till you compound whose right is worthiest, We for the worthiest hold the right from both *K. John* ii 1 282
The worthiest of them tell me name by name *Troi. and Cres.* iv 5 160
Thou worthiest Marcius! Go sound thy trumpet in the market-place *Coriolanus* i 5 26

Worthiest. Have you not known The worthiest men have done't? *Cor.* ii 3 55
O worthiest cousin! The sin of my ingratitude even now Was heavy on me: thou art so far before *Macbeth* i 4 14
One that but performs The bidding of the fullest man, and worthiest To have command obey'd *Ant. and Cleo.* iii 13 87
With those hands, that grasp'd the heaviest club, Subdue my worthiest self iv 12 47
Blessed live you long! A lady to the worthiest sir that ever Country call'd his! and you his mistress, only For the most worthiest fit! *Cymbeline* i 6 160

Worthily. As my gift and thine own acquisition Worthily purchased, take my daughter *Tempest* iv 1 14
Thou and thy meaner fellows your last service Did worthily perform iv 1 36
We may pity, though not pardon thee.—O, had the gods done so, I had not now Worthily term'd them merciless to us! *Com. of Errors* i 1 100
Hast thou sounded him, If he appeal the duke on ancient malice; Or worthily, as a good subject should? *Richard II.* i 1 10
The souls of men May deem that you are worthily deposed iv 1 227
Wherefore the king, most worthily, hath caused every soldier to cut his prisoner's throat *Hen. V.* iv 7 9
How may he wound, And worthily, my falsehood! *Hen. VIII.* ii 4 97
He hath deserved worthily of his country *Coriolanus* ii 2 27
That's worthily As any ear can hear iv 1 53
Whom worthily you would have now succeed *T. Andron.* i 1 40
Let the presents Be worthily entertain'd *T. of Athens* i 2 191
The present need Speaks to atone you.—Worthily spoken *Ant. and Cleo.* ii 2 102
We had much more monstrous matter of feast, which worthily deserved noting ii 2 188
I desire to find him so, that I may worthily note him *Pericles* iv 6 56

Worthiness. Bold of your worthiness, we single you As our best-moving fair solicitor *L. L. Lost* ii 1 28
Much too little of that good I saw Is my report to his great worthiness ii 1 63
As honour without breach of honour may Make tender of to thy true worthiness ii 1 171
If you had known the virtue of the ring, Or half her worthiness that gave the ring, Or your own honour *Mer. of Venice* v 1 200
Whose worthiness would stir it up where it wanted *All's Well* i 1 10
Even to the utmost syllable of your worthiness iii 6 75
Quittance of desert and merit According to the weight and worthiness *Hen. V.* ii 2 35
Read them; and know, I know your worthiness ii 2 69
In confutation of which rude reproach And in defence of my lord's worthiness, I crave the benefit of law of arms 1 *Hen. VI.* iv 1 99
The worthiness of praise distains his worth, If that the praised himself bring the praise forth *Troi. and Cres.* i 3 241
As I do know the consul's worthiness, So can I name his faults *Coriol.* iii 1 278
It is very much lamented, Brutus, That you have no such mirrors as will turn Your hidden worthiness into your eye *J. Cæsar* i 2 57
That which would appear offence in us, His countenance, like richest alchemy, Will change to virtue and to worthiness i 3 160
His worthiness Does challenge much respect *Othello* ii 1 212
O noble strain! O worthiness of nature! breed of greatness! *Cymb.* iv 2 25

Worthless. I fear my Julia would not deign my lines, Receiving them from such a worthless post *T. G. of Ver.* i 1 161
Servant, you are welcome to a worthless mistress.—I'll die on him that says so but yourself.—That you are welcome?—That you are worthless ii 4 113
A little time . . . And worthless Valentine shall be forgot iii 2 10
Too true, too holy, To be corrupted with my worthless gifts iv 2 6
To these injunctions every one doth swear That comes to hazard for my worthless self *Mer. of Venice* ii 9 18
Even as a flattering dream or worthless fancy *T. of Shrew* Ind. 1 44
Kneeling at our feet, but a weak and worthless satisfaction *Hen. V.* iii 6 141
My ransom is this frail and worthless trunk iii 6 163
Keep off aloof with worthless emulation 1 *Hen. VI.* iv 4 21
So worthless peasants bargain for their wives, As market-men for oxen v 5 53
To affy a mighty lord Unto the daughter of a worthless king 2 *Hen. VI.* iv 1 81
How I scorn his worthless threats! 3 *Hen. VI.* i 1 101
Methinks I do digress too much, Citing my worthless praise *T. Andron.* v 3 117
A peevish schoolboy, worthless of such honour *J. Cæsar* v 1 61

Worthy. Remember I have done thee worthy service *Tempest* i 2 247
What might, Worthy Sebastian? O, what might?—No more ii 1 205
O king Stephano! O peer! O worthy Stephano! iv 1 221
And be in eye of every exercise Worthy his youth *T. G. of Ver.* i 3 33
I know the gentleman To be of worth and worthy estimation ii 4 56
He is as worthy for an empress' love As meet to be an emperor's counsellor ii 4 76
Too mean a servant To have a look of such a worthy mistress ii 4 108
Her whose worth makes other worthies nothing ii 4 166
A thousand times good morrow.—As many, worthy lady, to yourself iv 3 7
I do desire thy worthy company, Upon whose faith and honour I repose iv 3 25
And think thee worthy of an empress' love v 4 141
These banish'd men . . . Are men endued with worthy qualities v 4 153
'Tis fit, Worthy the owner, and the owner it *Mer. Wives* v 5 64
My very worthy cousin, fairly met! *Meas. for Meas.* v 1 1
O worthy prince, dishonour not your eye By throwing it on any other object v 1 22
O worthy duke, You bid me seek redemption of the devil v 1 28
To justify this worthy nobleman, So vulgarly and personally accused v 1 159
Is't not enough thou hast suborn'd these women To accuse this worthy man? v 1 309
Amen, if you love her; for the lady is very well worthy *Much Ado* i 1 224
That I love her, I feel.—That she is worthy, I know.—That I neither feel how she should be loved nor know how she should be worthy, is the opinion that fire cannot melt out of me i 1 231
Or to bind him up a rod, as being worthy to be whipped ii 1 227
Many a wooer doth commence his suit To her he thinks not worthy ii 3 53
Record it with your high and worthy deeds v 1 279
In her fair cheek, Where several worthies make one dignity *L. L. Lost* iv 3 236
Sir, you shall present before her the Nine Worthies v 1 125
I say none so fit as to present the Nine Worthies v 1 130
Where will you find men worthy enough? v 1 131
He is not quantity enough for that Worthy's thumb v 1 138
For the rest of the Worthies?—I will play three myself v 1 149
I will play On the tabor to the Worthies, and let them dance the hay v 1 161
They would know Whether the three Worthies shall come in or no v 2 486
It pleased them to think me worthy of Pompion the Great v 2 506
I know not the degree of the Worthy, but I am to stand for him v 2 508
Here is like to be a good presence of Worthies v 2 537

Worthy. If these four Worthies in their first show thrive, These four will change habits, and present the other five . . . . *L. L. Lost* v 2 541
My hat to a halfpenny, Pompey proves the best Worthy . . . v 2 564
He will be the ninth Worthy . . . v 2 582
There are Worthies a-coming will speak their mind in some other sort . v 2 588
Room for the incensed Worthies! . . . v 2 703
Worthies, away! the scene begins to cloud . . . v 2 730
Farewell, worthy lord! A heavy heart bears not a nimble tongue . . v 2 746
Was not that Hector?—The worthy knight of Troy . . . v 2 890
Demetrius is a worthy gentleman.—So is Lysander . *M. N. Dream* i 1 52
I remember him well, and I remember him worthy of thy praise *M. of V.* i 2 133
It doth appear you are a worthy judge; You know the law . . iv 1 236
Most worthy gentleman, I and my friend Have by your wisdom been this day acquitted Of grievous penalties . . . . iv 1 408
I think you would have begg'd The ring of me to give the worthy doctor v 1 222
O noble fool! A worthy fool! Motley 's the only wear *As Y. Like It* ii 7 34
O worthy fool! One that hath been a courtier . . . ii 7 36
Things of worthy memory, which now shall die in oblivion *T. of Shrew* iv 1 84
She is of good esteem, Her dowry wealthy, and of worthy birth . iv 5 65
Whether I live or die, be you the sons Of worthy Frenchmen *All's Well* ii 1 12
You give me most egregious indignity.—Ay, with all my heart; and thou art worthy of it . . . . ii 3 231
I do know him well, and common speech Gives him a worthy pass . ii 5 58
I am not worthy of the wealth I owe, Nor dare I say 'tis mine, and yet it is . . . . ii 5 84
But yet We'll strive to bear it for your worthy sake . . . iii 3 5
A countryman of yours That has done worthy service . . . iii 5 51
I will bestow some precepts of this virgin Worthy the note . . iii 5 104
The owner of no one good quality worthy your lordship's entertainment iii 6 13
I will grace the attempt for a worthy exploit . . . . iii 6 72
He has much worthy blame laid upon him . . . . iv 3 7
And not worthy to touch Fortune's fingers . . . *T. Night* ii 5 170
You know me, do you not?—For a worthy lady . . . *W. Tale* ii 2 5
Most worthy madam, Your honour and your goodness is so evident . ii 2 42
Thou art worthy to be hang'd, That wilt not stay her tongue . . ii 3 109
Hermione, queen to the worthy Leontes, king of Sicilia . . iii 2 12
And boasts himself To have a worthy feeding . . . . iv 4 169
Were I crown'd the most imperial monarch, Thereof most worthy . iv 4 384
And you, enchantment,—Worthy enough a herdsman . . . iv 4 446
There is none worthy, Respecting her that's gone . . . v 1 34
Your father's blest, As he from heaven merits it, with you Worthy his goodness . . . . v 1 176
I will not flatter you, my lord, That all I see in you is worthy love *K. John* ii 1 517
Hate turns one or both To worthy danger and deserved death *Rich. II.* v 1 68
And to thy worth will add right worthy gains . . . v 6 12
Wherein villanous, but in all things? wherein worthy, but in nothing? *1 Hen. IV.* ii 4 505
He is a worthy gentleman, Exceedingly well read . . . iii 1 165
He hath more worthy interest to the state Than thou the shadow of succession . . . . iii 2 98
'When Arthur first in court'—Empty the jordan.—'And was a worthy king' . . . . *2 Hen. IV.* ii 4 38
Ten times better than the Nine Worthies . . . . ii 4 238
Right joyous are we to behold your face, Most worthy brother *Hen. V.* v 2 10
A worthy leader, wanting aid, Unto his dastard foemen is betray'd *1 Hen. VI.* i 1 143
And should, if I were worthy to be judge, Be quite degraded . . iv 1 42
Knight of the noble order of Saint George, Worthy Saint Michael . . iv 7 69
This superficial tale Is but a preface of her worthy praise . . v 5 11
Whether your grace be worthy, yea or no, Dispute not that *2 Hen. VI.* i 3 110
To mow down thorns that would annoy our foot, Is worthy praise . iii 1 68
That he should die is worthy policy . . . . iii 1 235
We have but trivial argument, More than mistrust, that shows him worthy death . . . . iii 1 242
Here is my hand, the deed is worthy doing.—And so say I . . iii 1 278
Only for that cause they have been most worthy to live . . iv 7 50
The worthy gentleman did lose his life . . *3 Hen. VI.* iii 2 7
Fair Queen of England, worthy Margaret, Sit down with us . . iii 3 1
From worthy Edward, King of Albion, My lord and sovereign . . iii 3 49
Hath not our brother made a worthy choice? . . . iv 1 3
Thou art worthy of the sway . . . . iv 6 32
Nor were not worthy blame, If this foul deed were by to equal it . v 5 54
Thanks, noble Clarence; worthy brother, thanks . . . v 7 30
For doing worthy vengeance on thyself . . *Richard III.* i 2 87
I have bewept a worthy husband's death . . . . ii 2 49
'Tis well; for worthy Wolsey, Who cannot err, he did it . *Hen. VIII.* i 1 173
There should be one amongst 'em, by his person, More worthy this place i 4 79
That my kingdom, Well worthy the best heir o' the world, should not Be gladded in't by me . . . . ii 4 195
This same Cranmer's A worthy fellow . . . . iii 2 72
A man in much esteem with the king, and truly A worthy friend . iv 1 110
And brought me garlands, Griffith, which I feel I am not worthy yet to wear . . . . iv 2 92
Respect him; Take him, and use him well, he's worthy of it . . v 3 155
But, worthy Hector, She is a theme of honour and renown *Tr. and Cr.* ii 2 198
He beats me, and I rail at him: O, worthy satisfaction! . . ii 3 4
I come from the worthy Achilles . . . . iii 3 283
Worthy of arms! as welcome as to one That would be rid of such an enemy iv 5 163
And, worthy warrior, welcome to our tents . . . iv 5 200
May worthy Troilus be half attach'd With that which here his passion doth express? . . . . v 2 161
Your virtue is To make him worthy whose offence subdues him *Coriol.* i 1 179
We must follow you; Right worthy you priority . . . i 1 251
Worthy sir, thou bleed'st; Thy exercise hath been too violent . i 5 15
Nay, my good soldier, up; My gentle Marcius, worthy Caius . . ii 1 189
No more of him; he's a worthy man . . . . ii 2 39
To report A little of that worthy work perform'd . . . ii 2 49
Worthy man!—He cannot but with measure fit the honours . . ii 2 126
There's in all two worthy voices begg'd . . . . ii 3 86
God save thee, noble consul!—Worthy voices! . . . ii 3 145
His worthy deeds did claim no less Than what he stood for . . ii 3 194
Marcius is worthy Of present death . . . . iii 1 211
Put not your worthy rage into your tongue; One time will owe another iii 1 241
What has he done to Rome that's worthy death? . . . iii 1 298
Keep Rome in safety, and the chairs of justice Supplied with worthy men! . . . . iii 3 35
Receive so to heart the banishment of that worthy Coriolanus . iv 3 23
Caius Marcius was A worthy officer i' the war . . . . iv 6 30
The worthy fellow is our general: he's the rock, the oak . . v 2 116
Worthy. Worthy lords, have you with heed perused What I have written to you? . . . . *Coriolanus* v 6 62
Presents well worthy Rome's imperial lord . . . *T. Andron.* i 1 250
Then have I kept it to a worthy end . . . . iii 1 174
Worthy Andronicus, ill art thou repaid For that good hand . . iii 1 235
O worthy Goth, this is the incarnate devil That robb'd Andronicus . v 1 40
That we have wrought So worthy a gentleman to be her bridegroom *Rom. and Jul.* iii 5 146
O, 'tis a worthy lord.—Nay, that's most fix'd . . *T. of Athens* i 1 9
Look in thy last work, where thou hast feigned him a worthy fellow . i 1 229
He is worthy of thee, and to pay thee for thy labour: he that loves to be flattered is worthy o' the flatterer . . . . i 1 231
Hail to thee, worthy Timon, and to all That of his bounties taste! . i 2 128
Great Timon, noble, worthy, royal Timon! . . . . ii 2 177
It is a cause worthy my spleen and fury, That I may strike at Athens . iii 5 113
My worthy friends, will you draw near?—I'll tell you more anon . iii 6 66
My most worthy master; in whose breast Doubt and suspect, alas, are placed too late . . . . iv 3 518
Will you, indeed?—Doubt it not, worthy lord . . . v 1 95
Worthy Timon,— Of none but such as you, and you of Timon . . v 1 137
I'll beweep these comforts, worthy senators . . . v 1 161
Thoughts of great value, worthy cogitations . . *J. Cæsar* i 2 50
He will, after his sour fashion, tell you What hath proceeded worthy note to-day . . . . i 2 181
O ye gods, Render me worthy of this noble wife! . . . ii 1 303
If Brutus have in hand Any exploit worthy the name of honour . ii 1 317
Cæsar, all hail! good morrow, worthy Cæsar . . . ii 2 58
Is there no voice more worthy than my own, To sound more sweetly? . iii 1 49
His glory not extenuated, wherein he was worthy . . . iii 2 43
Hath given me some worthy cause to wish Things done, undone . iv 2 8
It is more worthy to leap in ourselves, Than tarry till they push us . v 5 24
The merciless Macdonwald—Worthy to be a rebel . . *Macbeth* i 2 10
O valiant cousin! worthy gentleman! . . . . i 2 24
Who comes here?—The worthy thane of Ross . . . i 2 45
Whence camest thou, worthy thane?—From Fife, great king . . i 2 48
In which addition, hail, most worthy thane! For it is thine . . i 3 106
Worthy Macbeth, we stay upon your leisure . . . i 3 148
My worthy Cawdor!—The Prince of Cumberland! that is a step . i 4 47
True, worthy Banquo; he is full so valiant . . . i 4 54
Great Glamis! worthy Cawdor! Greater than both, by the all-hail hereafter! . . . . i 5 55
Why, worthy thane, You do unbend your noble strength . . ii 2 44
Sit, worthy friends: my lord is often thus, And hath been from his youth iii 4 53
My worthy lord, Your noble friends do lack you . . . iii 4 83
Do not muse at me, my most worthy friends; I have a strange infirmity iii 4 85
There ran a rumour Of many worthy fellows that were out . . iv 3 183
You, worthy uncle, Shall, with my cousin, . . . Lead our first battle . v 6 2
Worthy Macduff and we Shall take upon's what else remains to do . v 6 4
Well said, old mole! canst work i' the earth so fast? A worthy pioner! *Hamlet* i 5 163
The noble duke my master, My worthy arch and patron . . *Lear* ii 1 61
I am glad on't; 'tis a worthy governor . . . *Othello* ii 1 30
King Stephen was a worthy peer, His breeches cost him but a crown . ii 3 92
Worthy Montano, you were wont be civil . . . . ii 3 190
Worthy Othello, I am hurt to danger . . . . ii 3 197
Cassio's my worthy friend—My lord, I see you're moved . . iii 3 223
Let me be thought too busy in my fears—As worthy cause I have to fear I am . . . . iii 3 254
Many worthy and chaste dames even thus, All guiltless, meet reproach iv 1 47
Save you, worthy general!—With all my heart . . . iv 1 229
This deed of thine is no more worthy heaven Than thou wast worthy her v 2 160
Know, worthy Pompey, That what they do delay, they not deny *A. and C.* ii 1 2
'Tis a worthy deed, And shall become you well . . . ii 2 1
Good fortune, worthy soldier; and farewell . . . . iii 2 22
Most worthy sir, you therein throw away The absolute soldiership you have . . . . iii 7 42
How now, worthy soldier!—O noble emperor, do not fight by sea . . iii 7 61
Rebukeable And worthy shameful check it were . . . iv 4 31
Mark Antony I served, who best was worthy Best to be served . . v 1 6
Hold, worthy lady, hold: Do not yourself such wrong . . . v 2 39
Hath referr'd herself Unto a poor but worthy gentleman . *Cymbeline* i 1 7
Expected to prove so worthy as since he hath been allowed the name of i 4 3
How worthy he is I will leave to appear hereafter . . . i 4 33
This worthy signior, I thank him, makes no stranger of me . . i 4 110
I doubt not you sustain what you're worthy of by your attempt . . i 4 126
The worthy Leonatus is in safety . . . . i 6 12
You are as welcome, worthy sir, as I Have words to bid you . . i 6 29
A worthy fellow, Albeit he comes on angry purpose now . . ii 3 60
Smiled at their lack of skill, but found their courage Worthy his frowning at . . . . ii 4 23
Under her breast—Worthy the pressing—lies a mole . . . ii 4 135
Leave not the worthy Lucius, good my lords, Till he have cross'd the Severn . . . . iii 5 16
O, my all-worthy lord!—All-worthy villain! Discover where thy mistress is at once, At the next word: no more of 'worthy lord!' . iii 5 96
I am son to the queen.—I am sorry for't; not seeming So worthy . iv 2 94
Why, worthy father, what have we to lose, But that he swore to take? iv 2 124
The ruin speaks that sometime It was a worthy building . . iv 2 355
They are worthy To inlay heaven with stars . . . . v 5 351
How many worthy princes' bloods were shed . . . *Pericles* i 2 88
Make the judgement good That thought you worthy of it . . iv 6 101
Wot. 'Twas I did the thing you wot of . . . *T. G. of Ver.* iv 4 30
You may come and see the picture, she says, that you wot of *Mer. Wives* ii 2 90
Such a one and such a one were past cure of the thing you wot of *Meas. for Meas.* ii 1 115
I wot not by what strong escape He broke from those *Com. of Errors* v 1 148
Have no more profit of their shining nights Than those that walk and wot not what they are . . . . *L. L. Lost* i 1 91
Well I wot Thou runn'st before me, shifting every place *M. N. Dream* iii 2 422
I wot not by what power,—But by some power it is . . . iv 1 169
As blanks, benevolences, and I wot not what . . *Richard II.* ii 1 250
That is not yet known; what I cannot name; 'tis nameless woe, I wot ii 2 40
I wot your love pursues A banish'd traitor . . . . ii 3 59
Shall not be forgot; Right noble is thy merit, well I wot . . v 6 18
In gross brain little wots What watch the king keeps to maintain the peace . . . . *Hen. V.* iv 1 299
O, too much folly is it, well I wot, To hazard all our lives in one small boat! . . . . *1 Hen. VI.* iv 6 32
'Tis a mere French word; We English warriors wot not what it means iv 7 55
For, well I wot, thou hast thy mother's tongue . . *3 Hen. VI.* ii 2 134

Wot. For well I wot that Henry is no soldier *3 Hen. VI.* iv 7 83
I need not add more fuel to your fire, For well I wot ye blaze to burn them out v 4 71
Stood the state so? No, no, good friends, God wot *Richard III.* ii 3 18
Wot you what, my lord? To-day the lords you talk of are beheaded iii 2 92
Wot you what I found There,—on my conscience, put unwittingly? *Hen. VIII.* iii 2 122
My mother, you wot well My hazards still have been your solace *Coriol.* iv 1 27
But a greater soldier than he, you wot one iv 5 171
Full well I wot the ground of all this grudge *T. Andron.* ii 1 48
More water glideth by the mill Than wots the miller of ii 1 86
Well I wot Thy napkin cannot drink a tear of mine iii 1 139
Well I wot the empress never wags But in her company there is a Moor v 2 87
I'll find Romeo To comfort you: I wot well where he is *Rom. and Jul.* iii 2 139
'As by lot, God wot,' and then, you know, 'It came to pass' *Hamlet* ii 2 435

Wottest. Do bravely, horse! for wot'st thou whom thou movest? *Ant. and Cleo.* i 5 22

Wotting. The gods themselves, Wotting no more than I, are ignorant *W. Tale* iii 2 77

Would. Now would I give a thousand furlongs of sea for an acre of barren ground *Tempest* i 1 69
The wills above be done! but I would fain die a dry death i 1 72
The sky, it seems, would pour down stinking pitch i 2 3
Would I might But ever see that man! i 2 168
For one thing she did They would not take her life i 2 267
That would not bless our Europe with your daughter, But rather lose her ii 1 124
No sovereignty;—Yet he would be king on't ii 1 156
I do think, a king; I would, not so! iii 1 61
What would my potent master? here I am iv 1 34
You play me false.—No, my dear'st love, I would not for the world v 1 173
For a score of kingdoms you should wrangle, And I would call it fair play v 1 175
And thrive therein, Even as I would when I to love begin *T. G. of Ver.* i 1 10
I would I knew his mind i 2 33
And yet I would I had o'erlooked the letter i 2 50
Should she thus be stol'n away from you, It would be much vexation iii 1 16
Unhappy messenger, To plead for that which I would not obtain iv 4 105
What would you with her, if that I be she? iv 4 115
That I would have sworn his disposition would have gone to the truth of his words *Mer. Wives* ii 1 60
I do relent: what would thou more of man? ii 2 31
To be what I would not shall not make me tame iii 5 153
I would my husband would meet him in this shape iv 2 86
There is our commission, From which we would not have you warp *Meas. for Meas.* i 1 15
Who I would be sorry should be thus foolishly lost i 2 195
I would to heaven I had your potency! ii 2 67
I would be glad to receive some instruction iv 2 18
Would yet he had lived! iv 4 35
Alack, when once our grace we have forgot, Nothing goes right: we would, and we would not iv 4 37
And would not rather Make rash remonstrance of my hidden power v 1 396
My dignity, Which princes, would they, may not disannul *Com. of Errors* i 1 145
You would all this time have proved there is no time for all things ii 2 101
I would not spare my brother in this case, If he should scorn me so iv 1 77
You dined at home; Where would you had remain'd until this time! iv 4 69
She that would be your wife now ran from you iv 4 152
I would to God some scholar would conjure her *Much Ado* ii 1 264
I would have thought her spirit had been invincible ii 3 119
I could wish he would modestly examine himself ii 3 213
Nothing becomes him ill that he would well *L. L. Lost* ii 1 46
What would these strangers? know their minds v 2 174
What would you with the princess?—Nothing but peace v 2 178
O that your frowns would teach my smiles such skill! *M. N. Dream* i 1 195
They would have stolen away; they would, Demetrius iv 1 161
I am aweary of this moon: would he would change! v 1 255
Is he yet possess'd How much ye would? *Mer. of Venice* i 3 66
He hath a great infection, sir, as one would say, to serve ii 2 134
One speak for both. What would you?—Serve you, sir ii 2 150
I would be loath to foil him, as I must, for my own honour *As Y. Like It* i 1 136
Were I my father, coz, would I do this? i 2 244
Heaven would that she these gifts should have iii 2 161
Alas! and would you take the letter of her? *All's Well* iii 4 1
I would it would make you invisible *T. Night* iii 1 34
I would you were as I would have you be!—Would it be better, madam, than I am? iii 1 154
Since all and every part of what we would Doth make a stand at what your highness will *K. John* iv 2 38
I would to God, So my untruth had not provoked him to it *Richard II.* ii 2 100
The time hath been, Would you have been so brief with him, he would Have been so brief with you iii 3 11
I would to God my name were not so terrible to the enemy as it is *2 Hen. IV.* i 2 243
We would, dear lords, unto the Holy Land iii 1 108
What would my lord and father?—Nothing but well to thee iv 4 18
He is very sick, and would to bed *Hen. V.* ii 1 87
I and my bosom must debate a while, And then I would no other company iv 1 32
If, Duke of Burgundy, you would the peace, . . . you must buy that peace v 2 68
If thou would have such a one, take me; and take me, take a soldier v 2 174
And thus he would: Open your city gates *1 Hen. VI.* iv 2 5
Give me leave to go; Sorrow would solace and mine age would ease *2 Hen. VI.* ii 3 21
I rather would have lost my life betimes iii 1 297
My soul's palace is become a prison: Ah, would she break from hence! *3 Hen. VI.* ii 1 75
Would all were well! but that will never be *Richard III.* i 3 40
I would to God my heart were flint, like Edward's i 3 140
I would not, as they term it, praise her: but I would somebody had heard her talk yesterday *Troi. and Cres.* i 1 44
Hark, what good sport is out of town to-day!—Better at home, if 'would I might' were 'may' i 1 117
As who should say 'There were wit in this head, an 'twould out' iii 3 256
Would the nobility lay aside their ruth, I'ld make a quarry *Cor.* i 1 201
If I could shake off but one seven years . . . , I'ld with thee every foot iv 1 57
Would half my wealth Would buy this for a lie! iv 6 160
As who would say, in Rome no justice were *T. Andron.* iv 4 20
Would none but I might venge my cousin's death! *Rom. and Jul.* iii 5 87
He would be crown'd: How that might change his nature, there's the question *J. Cæsar* ii 1 12

Would. For their dear causes Would to the bleeding and the grim alarm Excite the mortified man *Macbeth* v 2 4
'Well, well, we know,' or 'We could, and if we would' *Hamlet* i 5 176
That we would do, We should do when we would; for this 'would' changes And hath abatements and delays iv 7 119
Dost thou think, If I would stand against thee, would the reposal Of any trust, virtue, or worth in thee Make thy words faith'd? *Lear* ii 1 70
Being bid to ask what he would of the king, desired he might know none of his secrets *Pericles* i 3 6

Wouldst. What wouldst?—I myself reprehend his own person *L. L. Lost* i 1 183
Wouldst thou aught with me? *Mer. of Venice* ii 2 128
What wouldst thou think of me, if I should weep?—I would think thee a most princely hypocrite *2 Hen. IV.* ii 2 56
What wouldst thou of us, Trojan? make demand *Troi. and Cres.* iii 3 17
Thou wouldst be great; Art not without ambition *Macbeth* i 5 19
What thou wouldst highly, That wouldst thou holily; wouldst not play false, And yet wouldst wrongly win i 5 21

Wound. Sometime am I All wound with adders *Tempest* ii 2 13
May as well Wound the loud winds iii 3 63
Poor wounded name! my bosom as a bed Shall lodge thee till thy wound be throughly heal'd *T. G. of Ver.* i 2 115
The private wound is deepest: O time most accurst! v 4 71
What noise? That spirit's possess'd with haste That wounds the unsisting postern with these strokes *Meas. for Meas.* iv 2 92
Of this matter Is little Cupid's crafty arrow made, That only wounds by hearsay *Much Ado* iii 1 23
There's an eye Wounds like a leaden sword *L. L. Lost* v 2 481
Before milk-white, now purple with love's wound *M. N. Dream* ii 1 167
I see no blood, no wound. Lysander, if you live, good sir, awake. ii 2 101
Out, sword, and wound The pap of Pyramus v 1 301
And every word in it a gaping wound, Issuing life-blood *Mer. of Venice* iii 2 268
Have by some surgeon, Shylock, on your charge, To stop his wounds iv 1 258
Alas, poor shepherd! searching of thy wound, I have by hard adventure found mine own *As Y. Like It* ii 4 44
And if mine eyes can wound, now let them kill thee iii 5 16
Now show the wound mine eye hath made in thee iii 5 20
Then shall you know the wounds invisible That love's keen arrows make iii 5 30
Brief, I recover'd him, bound up his wound iv 3 151
Dart not scornful glances from those eyes, To wound thy lord *T. of S.* v 2 138
For then we wound our modesty *All's Well* i 3 5
Speak, is't so? If it be so, you have wound a goodly clew i 3 188
Thou dost shame thy mother And wound her honour *K. John* i 1 65
Win you this city without stroke or wound ii 1 418
And heal the inveterate canker of one wound By making many v 2 14
And wound our tattering colours clearly up, Last in the field v 5 7
Show me the very wound of this ill news: I am no woman v 6 21
His siege is now Against the mind, the which he pricks and wounds v 7 17
This England never did, nor never shall, Lie at the proud foot of a conqueror, But when it first did help to wound itself v 7 114
Ere my tongue Shall wound my honour with such feeble wrong *Rich. II.* i 1 191
The dire aspect Of civil wounds plough'd up with neighbours' sword i 3 128
Though rebels wound thee with their horses' hoofs iii 2 7
Those whom you curse Have felt the worst of death's destroying wound iii 2 139
He does me double wrong That wounds me with the flatteries of his tongue iii 2 216
Showers of blood Rain'd from the wounds of slaughter'd Englishmen iii 3 44
We at time of year Do wound the bark, the skin of our fruit-trees iii 4 58
Hath sorrow struck So many blows upon this face of mine, And made no deeper wounds? iv 1 279
The lion dying thrusteth forth his paw, And wounds the earth, if nothing else v 1 30
I then, all smarting with my wounds being cold *1 Hen. IV.* i 3 49
And talk so like a waiting-gentlewoman Of guns and drums and wounds i 3 56
All those wounds, Those mouthed wounds, which valiantly he took i 3 96
Never did base and rotten policy Colour her working with such deadly wounds i 3 109
May salve The long-grown wounds of my intemperance iii 2 156
How then? Can honour set to a leg? no: or an arm? no: or take away the grief of a wound? no v 1 134
They wound my thoughts worse than thy sword my flesh v 4 80
Therefore, sirrah, with a new wound in your thigh, come you along with me v 4 131
I'll take it upon my death, I gave him this wound in the thigh v 4 155
While covert enmity Under the smile of safety wounds the world *2 Hen. IV.* Ind. 10
You were advised his flesh was capable Of wounds and scars i 1 173
I am loath to gall a new-healed wound i 2 168
Thou didst swear to me then, as I was washing thy wound, to marry me ii 1 99
Whereby I told thee they were ill for a green wound ii 1 106
Let grievous, ghastly, gaping wounds Untwine the Sisters Three! ii 4 212
Show his scars, And say 'These wounds I had on Crispin's day' *Hen. V.* iv 3 48
By his bloody side, Yoke-fellow to his honour-owing wounds iv 6 9
It is good for your green wound and your ploody coxcomb v 1 44
Wounds will I lend the French instead of eyes, To weep *1 Hen. VI.* i 1 87
But, O! the treacherous Fastolfe wounds my heart i 4 35
As that slaughterer doth Which giveth many wounds when one will kill ii 5 110
Behold the wounds, the most unnatural wounds, Which thou thyself hast given her woful breast iii 3 50
O thou, whose wounds become hard-favour'd death, Speak to thy father! iv 7 23
And are the cities, that I got with wounds, Deliver'd up again with peaceful words? Mort Dieu! *2 Hen. VI.* i 1 121
Stop the rage betime, Before the wound do grow uncurable iii 1 286
Though parting be a fretful corrosive, It is applied to a deathful wound iii 2 404
Fear frames disorder, and disorder wounds Where it should guard v 2 32
Hold, Clifford! do not honour him so much To prick thy finger, though to wound his heart *3 Hen. VI.* i 4 55
Open Thy gate of mercy, gracious God! My soul flies through these wounds to seek out Thee i 4 178
The words would add more anguish than the wounds ii 1 99
The wound that bred this meeting here Cannot be cured by words ii 2 121
See what showers arise, Blown with the windy tempest of my heart, Upon thy wounds, that kill mine eye and heart! ii 5 87
Bootless are plaints, and cureless are my wounds ii 6 23
The air hath got into my deadly wounds, And much effuse of blood doth make me faint ii 6 27
My pity hath been balm to heal their wounds iv 8 41
This hand, fast wound about thy coal-black hair v 1 54
Stabb'd by the selfsame hand that made these wounds! *Richard III.* i 2 11
See, see! dead Henry's wounds Open their congeal'd mouths and bleed afresh! i 2 55

Wound. Lest, by a multitude, The new-heal'd wound of malice should break out *Richard III.* ii 2 125
Give me another horse: bind up my wounds v 3 177
Let them not live to taste this land's increase That would with treason wound this fair land's peace! v 5 39
Now civil wounds are stopp'd, peace lives again v 5 40
How may he wound, And worthily, my falsehood! *Hen. VIII.* ii 4 96
As honour, loss of time, travail, expense, Wounds, friends *Troi. and Cres.* ii 2 5
The wound of peace is surety, Surety secure ii 2 14
The shaft confounds, Not that it wounds, But tickles still the sore iii 1 129
Yet that which seems the wound to kill, Doth turn oh! oh! to ha! ha! he! iii 1 132
Those wounds heal ill that men do give themselves iii 3 229
Let him die, With every joint a wound, and that to-morrow! iv 1 29
That I may give the local wound a name iv 5 244
Who keeps the tent now?—The surgeon's box, or the patient's wound v 1 13
Look, how thy eye turns pale! Look, how thy wounds do bleed at many vents! v 3 82
Patroclus' wounds have roused his drowsy blood v 5 32
I have some wounds upon me, and they smart To hear themselves remember'd.—Should they not, Well might they fester *Coriolanus* i 9 28
The wounds become him.—On's brows ii 1 135
He had, before this last expedition, twenty-five wounds upon him ii 1 170
Showing, as the manner is, his wounds To the people, beg their stinking breaths ii 1 251
I had rather have my wounds to heal again Than hear say how I got them ii 2 73
I cannot Put on the gown, stand naked, and entreat them, For my wounds' sake, to give their suffrage ii 2 142
If he show us his wounds and tell us his deeds, we are to put our tongues into those wounds and speak for them ii 3 6
Look, sir, my wounds! I got them in my country's service ii 3 57
I have wounds to show you, which shall be yours in private ii 3 83
You have received many wounds for your country ii 3 113
Of wounds two dozen odd; battles thrice six I have seen and heard of ii 3 135
He should have show'd us His marks of merit, wounds received for's country ii 3 172
He said he had wounds, which he could show in private ii 3 174
The wounds his body bears, which show Like graves i' the holy churchyard iii 3 50
Good man, the wounds that he does bear for Rome! iv 2 28
Now to the bottom dost thou search my wound *T. Andron.* ii 3 262
Seeking to hide herself, as doth the deer That hath received some unrecuring wound iii 1 90
Ah, that this sight should make so deep a wound, And yet detested life not shrink thereat! iii 1 247
Wound it with sighing, girl, kill it with groans iii 2 15
With lines, That wound, beyond their feeling, to the quick iv 2 28
Brought the fatal engine in That gives our Troy, our Rome, the civil wound v 3 87
He jests at scars that never felt a wound *Rom. and Jul.* ii 2 1
I saw the wound, I saw it with mine eyes,—God save the mark!—here on his manly breast iii 2 52
Wash they his wounds with tears: mine shall be spent, When theirs are dry, for Romeo's banishment iii 2 130
When griping grief the heart doth wound iv 5 128
Made plenteous wounds!—He has made too much plenty with 'em *T. of Athens* iii 5 66
To sue, and be denied such common grace: My wounds ache at you iii 5 96
Is this the balsam that the usuring senate Pours into captains' wounds? iii 5 111
Giving myself a voluntary wound Here, in the thigh *J. Cæsar* ii 1 300
Had I as many eyes as thou hast wounds, Weeping as fast as they iii 1 200
Over thy wounds now do I prophesy,—Which, like dumb mouths, do ope their ruby lips iii 1 259
They would go and kiss dead Cæsar's wounds And dip their napkins in iii 2 137
Show you sweet Cæsar's wounds, poor poor dumb mouths, And bid them speak iii 2 229
Put a tongue In every wound of Cæsar that should move The stones of Rome iii 2 233
Never, till Cæsar's three and thirty wounds Be well avenged v 1 53
Except they meant to bathe in reeking wounds *Macbeth* i 2 39
So well thy words become thee as thy wounds; They smack of honour both i 2 43
Peace! the charm's wound up i 3 37
That my keen knife see not the wound it makes i 5 53
Each new day a gash Is added to her wounds iv 3 41
I thought you had received some bodily wound *Othello* ii 3 267
What wound did ever heal but by degrees? ii 3 377
Make the sea serve them, which they ear and wound With keels *Ant. and Cleo.* i 4 49
All this—It wounds thine honour that I speak it now i 4 69
When we debate Our trivial difference loud, we do commit Murder in healing wounds ii 2 22
Do you misdoubt This sword and these my wounds? iii 7 64
I had a wound here that was like a T, But now 'tis made an H iv 7 7
Whilst they with joyful tears Wash the congealment from your wounds iv 8 10
Come, then; for with a wound I must be cured iv 14 78
This is his sword; I robb'd his wound of it; behold it stain'd v 1 25
How fine this tyrant Can tickle where she wounds! *Cymbeline* i 1 85
And mine ear, Therein false struck, can take no greater wound iii 4 117
I have kill'd thy mistress; peace! I'll give no wound to thee v 1 21
Having found the back-door open Of the unguarded hearts, heavens, how they wound! v 3 46
She would with sharp needle wound The cambric *Pericles* iv Gower 23

Wounded. Here is writ 'love-wounded Proteus.' Poor wounded name! *T. G. of Ver.* i 2 114
Conceal her, As best befits her wounded reputation *Much Ado* iv 1 243
There lay he, stretched along, like a wounded knight *As Y. Like It* iii 2 254
I thought thy heart had been wounded with the claws of a lion.—Wounded it is, but with the eyes of a lady v 2 25
That maid Whose sudden sight hath thrall'd my wounded eye *T. of Shrew* i 1 225
How attentiveness wounded his daughter *W. Tale* v 2 94
It is the Count Melun.—Wounded to death *K. John* v 4 9
Too careless patient as thou art, Commit'st thy anointed body to the cure Of those physicians that first wounded thee *Richard II.* ii 1 99
The king is almost wounded to the death *2 Hen. IV.* i 1 14
Over Suffolk's neck He threw his wounded arm and kiss'd his lips *Hen. V.* iv 6 25
And their wounded steeds Fret fetlock deep in gore iv 7 81
So shall my name with slander's tongue be wounded *2 Hen. VI.* iii 2 68
Surprised our forts And sent the ragged soldiers wounded home iv 1 90
Duke of Buckingham Is either slain or wounded dangerously *3 Hen. VI.* i 1 11
O my Wolsey, The quiet of my wounded conscience *Hen. VIII.* ii 2 75
Is he not wounded? he was wont to come home wounded *Coriolanus* ii 1 130
O, he is wounded; I thank the gods for't.—So do I too, if it be not too much ii 1 133
Where is he wounded?—I' the shoulder and i' the left arm ii 1 162
When most struck home, being gentle wounded, craves A noble cunning iv 1 8
These words are razors to my wounded heart *T. Andron.* i 1 314
And, with these boys, mine honour thou hast wounded i 1 365
He that wounded her Hath hurt me more than had he kill'd me dead iii 1 91
The one is wounded with the bait, The other rotted with delicious feed iv 4 92
I have been feasting with mine enemy, Where on a sudden one hath wounded me, That's by me wounded *Rom and Jul.* ii 3 50
Weep you when you but behold Our Cæsar's vesture wounded? *J. Cæsar* iii 2 200
What a wounded name, Things standing thus unknown, shall live behind me! *Hamlet* v 2 355
I'll yet follow The wounded chance of Antony *Ant. and Cleo.* iii 10 36
Our Tarquin thus Did softly press the rushes, ere he waken'd The chastity he wounded *Cymbeline* ii 2 14

Wounding. Not wounding, pity would not let me do't; If wounding, then it was to show my skill *L. L. Lost* iv 1 27
Full of comparisons and wounding flouts v 2 854
Daily grew to quarrel and to bloodshed, Wounding supposed peace *2 Hen. IV.* iv 5 196
Look not upon me, for thine eyes are wounding *2 Hen. VI.* iii 2 51
Blasts and fogs upon thee! The untented woundings of a father's curse Pierce every sense about thee! *Lear* i 4 322
O Cæsar, what a wounding shame is this! *Ant. and Cleo.* v 2 159
To make the noble Leonatus mad, By wounding his belief *Cymbeline* v 5 202

Woundless. May miss our name, And hit the woundless air *Hamlet* iv 1 44

Woven. As they fly by them with their woven wings *Mer. of Venice* i 1 14
In her hairs The painter plays the spider and hath woven A golden mesh iii 2 121
No man living Could say 'This is my wife' there; all were woven So strangely in one piece *Hen. VIII.* iv 1 80

Wrack. Blow, wind! come, wrack! At least we'll die with harness on our back *Macbeth* v 5 51
That monster envy, oft the wrack Of earned praise *Pericles* iv Gower 12

Wrangle. For a score of kingdoms you should wrangle, And I would call it fair play *Tempest* v 1 174
It makes me almost ready to wrangle with mine own honesty *Mer. Wives* ii 1 88
You still wrangle with her *L. L. Lost* iv 1 119
I am ready to distrust mine eyes And wrangle with my reason *T. Night* iv 3 14
Let us not wrangle: bid them move away *J. Cæsar* iv 2 45
In such cases Men's natures wrangle with inferior things *Othello* iii 4 144
You shall have time to wrangle in when you have nothing else to do *Ant. and Cleo.* ii 2 106

Wrangler. He hath made a match with such a wrangler That all the courts of France will be disturb'd *Hen. V.* i 2 264
The seas and winds, old wranglers, took a truce *Troi. and Cres.* ii 2 75

Wrangling. You to a long and well-deserved bed: And you to wrangling *As Y. Like It* v 4 197
Wrangling pedant, this is The patroness of heavenly harmony *T. of S.* iii 1 4
As a scolding quean to a wrangling knave *All's Well* ii 2 27
Or else was wrangling Somerset in the error? *1 Hen. VI.* ii 4 6
No, wrangling woman, we'll no longer stay *3 Hen. VI.* ii 2 176
I can no longer hold me patient. Hear me, you wrangling pirates! *Richard III.* i 3 158
Unquiet wrangling days, How many of you have mine eyes beheld! ii 4 55
Fie, wrangling queen! Whom every thing becomes, to chide, to laugh, To weep *Ant. and Cleo.* i 1 48

Wrap. Weed wide enough to wrap a fairy in *M. N. Dream* ii 1 256
My often rumination wraps me in a most humorous sadness *As Y. L. It* iv 1 19
And wrap our bodies in black mourning gowns *3 Hen. VI.* ii 1 161
What dost thou wrap and fumble in thine arms? *T. Andron.* iv 2 58
Why do we wrap the gentleman in our more rawer breath? *Hamlet* v 2 128
Some dear cause Will in concealment wrap me up awhile *Lear* iv 3 54

Wrapp'd in sweet clothes, rings put upon his fingers *T. of Shrew* Ind. 1 38
From a casement thrown me, Wrapp'd in a paper *All's Well* v 3 94
I am wrapp'd in dismal thinkings v 3 128
Instead of bullets wrapp'd in fire, . . . They shoot but calm words folded up in smoke *K. John* ii 1 227
And sends them weapons wrapp'd about with lines *T. Andron.* iv 2 27

Wrapt. Unfold the evil which is here wrapt up In countenance! *Meas. for Meas.* v 1 117
O tiger's heart wrapt in a woman's hide! *3 Hen. VI.* i 4 137
I was much wrapt in this *Troi. and Cres.* iii 3 123

Wrath. Whose wraths to guard you from *Tempest* iii 3 79
My wrath shall far exceed the love I ever bore my daughter *T. G. of V.* iii 1 166
By penitence the Eternal's wrath's appeased v 4 81
Come not within the measure of my wrath v 4 127
Oberon is passing fell and wrath *M. N. Dream* ii 1 20
They are in the very wrath of love *As Y. Like It* v 2 44
Reprieve him from the wrath Of greatest justice *All's Well* iii 4 28
Your opposite hath in him what youth, strength, skill, and wrath can furnish man withal *T. Night* iii 4 254
In his rage and his wrath, Cries, ah, ha! to the devil iv 2 137
If thou refuse And wilt encounter with my wrath, say so *W. Tale* ii 3 138
So hence! Be thou the trumpet of our wrath *K. John* i 1 27
I am burn'd up with inflaming wrath iii 1 340
And pick strong matter of revolt and wrath iii 4 167
The vilest stroke That ever wall-eyed wrath or staring rage Presented iv 3 49
Harry Monmouth fell Under the wrath of noble Hotspur's sword *2 Hen. IV.* Ind. 30
Whose swift wrath beat down The never-daunted Percy to the earth i 1 109
In his rages, and his furies, and his wraths, and his cholers *Hen. V.* iv 7 37
Let my presumption not provoke thy wrath *1 Hen. VI.* i 3 70
Thou wilt but add increase unto my wrath *2 Hen VI.* iii 2 292
Heap of wrath, foul indigested lump, As crooked in thy manners as thy shape! v 1 157
Beauty that the tyrant oft reclaims Shall to my flaming wrath be oil and flax v 2 55
I am too mean a subject for thy wrath: Be thou revenged on men *3 Hen. VI.* i 3 19
Wrath makes him deaf: speak thou i 4 53
With fiery eyes sparkling for very wrath ii 5 131
And they shall feel the vengeance of my wrath iv 1 82
Thy cloudy wrath Hath in eternal darkness folded up *Richard III.* i 3 268
Execute thy wrath in me alone, O, spare my guiltless wife! i 4 71
All this from my remembrance brutish wrath Sinfully pluck'd ii 1 118
Put in their hands thy bruising irons of wrath! v 3 110

Wrath. To the field goes he; where every flower Did, as a prophet, weep what it foresaw In Hector's wrath . . *Troi. and Cres.* i 2 11
For Hector in his blaze of wrath subscribes To tender objects . . iv 5 105
They do disdain us much beyond our thoughts, Which makes me sweat with wrath . . . . . . *Coriolanus* i 4 27
But then Aufidius was within my view, And wrath o'erwhelm'd my pity i 9 86
I'll potch at him some way Or wrath or craft may get him . i 10 16
The good gods assuage thy wrath, and turn the dregs of it upon this varlet . . . . v 2 83
Highly moved to wrath To be controll'd in that he frankly gave *T. An.* i 1 419
When did the tiger's young ones teach the dam? O, do not learn her wrath . . . . ii 3 143
O, why should wrath be mute, and fury dumb? . . . . v 3 184
Wert thou the unicorn, pride and wrath would confound thee *T. of A.* iv 3 339
I'll teach them to prevent wild Alcibiades' wrath . . . v 1 206
And those kin Which in the bluster of thy wrath must fall . . v 4 41
To cut the head off and then hack the limbs, Like wrath in death and envy afterwards . . . . *J. Cæsar* ii 1 164
Let me endure your wrath, if't be not so . . . . *Macbeth* v 5 36
Roasted in wrath and fire, And thus o'er-sized with coagulate gore *Ham.* ii 2 483
Come not between the dragon and his wrath . . . *Lear* i 1 124
Without the form of justice, yet our power Shall do a courtesy to our wrath . . . . iii 7 26
O dear son Edgar, The food of thy abused father's wrath! . iv 1 24
It hath pleased the devil drunkenness to give place to the devil wrath *Othello* ii 3 298
Thou hadst been better have been born a dog Than answer my waked wrath! . . . . iii 3 363
I hear him mock The luck of Cæsar, which the gods give men To excuse their after wrath . . . *Ant. and Cleo.* v 2 290
I something fear my father's wrath; but nothing—Always reserved my holy duty—what His rage can do on me . *Cymbeline* i 1 86
Harm not yourself with your vexation: I am senseless of your wrath . i 1 135
Let's follow him, and pervert the present wrath He hath against himself ii 4 151
Your father's wrath, should he take me in his dominion, could not be so cruel . . . . iii 2 40
Wilt thou undo the worth thou art unpaid for, By tasting of our wrath? v 5 308
And testy wrath Could never be her mild companion . *Pericles* i 1 17
The pregnant instrument of wrath Prest for this blow . . iv Gower 44
Wrathful. Whiles we, God's wrathful agent, do correct Their proud contempt . . . . *K. John* ii 1 87
And grating shock of wrathful iron arms . . . . *Richard II.* i 3 136
As valiant as the wrathful dove or most magnanimous mouse *2 Hen. IV.* iii 2 171
His sparkling eyes, replete with wrathful fire . *1 Hen. VI.* i 1 12
Mad ire and wrathful fury makes me weep, That thus we die . iv 3 28
Barren winter, with his wrathful nipping cold . *2 Hen. VI.* ii 4 3
Took our state upon him To free us from his father's wrathful curse . iii 2 155
Your wrathful weapons drawn Here in our presence! dare you be so bold? . . . . iii 2 237
Angry, wrathful, and inclined to blood . . . . iv 2 134
Heart, be wrathful still: Priests pray for enemies, but princes kill . v 2 70
Let us depart, I pray you, Lest your displeasure should enlarge itself To wrathful terms . . . *Troi. and Cres.* v 2 38
Spiteful and wrathful, who, as others do, Loves for his own ends *Macb.* iii 5 12
The wrathful skies Gallow the very wanderers of the dark . *Lear* iii 2 43
Wrathfully. Let's kill him boldly, but not wrathfully . *J. Cæsar* ii 1 172
Wrath-kindled gentlemen, be ruled by me . . . *Richard II.* i 1 152
Wreak. Then if thou hast A heart of wreak in thee, that wilt revenge Thine own particular wrongs and stop those maims Of shame seen through thy country, speed thee straight . . *Coriolanus* iv 5 91
And with revengeful war Take wreak on Rome . *T. Andron.* iv 3 33
And move the gods To send down Justice for to wreak our wrongs iv 3 51
Shall we be thus afflicted in his wreaks, His fits, his frenzy? . . iv 4 11
To wreak the love I bore my cousin Upon his body . *Rom. and Jul.* iii 5 102
Wreakful. By working wreakful vengeance on thy foes *T. Andron.* v 2 32
Whose naked natures live in all the spite Of wreakful heaven *T. of A.* iv 3 229
Wreath. And we are graced with wreaths of victory . *3 Hen. VI.* v 3 2
Now are our brows bound with victorious wreaths *Richard III.* i 1 5
Did not they Put on my brows this wreath of victory? . *J. Cæsar* v 3 82
Like the wreath of radiant fire On flickering Phœbus' front . *Lear* ii 2 113
His device, a wreath of chivalry; The word, 'Me pompæ provexit apex' *Pericles* ii 2 29
This wreath of victory I give, And crown you king of this day's happiness . . . . ii 3 10
Wreathe. To wreathe your arms, like a malecontent *T. G. of Ver.* ii 1 19
Wreathed. Never lay his wreathed arms athwart His loving bosom *L. L. Lost* iv 3 135
About his neck A green and gilded snake had wreathed itself *As Y. L. It* iv 3 109
Each wreathed in the other's arms, Our pastimes done, possess a golden slumber . . . . *T. Andron.* ii 3 25
Wreck. The direful spectacle of the wreck . . . *Tempest* i 2 26
Sitting on a bank, Weeping again the king my father's wreck . i 2 390
This gallant which thou seest Was in the wreck . . . i 2 414
The weakness which I feel, The wreck of all my friends . . i 2 488
Go, go, be gone, to save your ship from wreck, Which cannot perish having thee aboard, Being destined to a drier death . *T. G. of Ver.* i 1 156
Hath he not lost much wealth by wreck of sea? . . *Com. of Errors* v 1 49
Besides her urging of her wreck at sea . . . . v 1 359
I spoke with some of the sailors that escaped the wreck . *Mer. of Venice* iii 1 110
That so terrible shows in the wreck of maidenhood . . *All's Well* iii 5 24
A wreck past hope he was: His life I gave him . . *T. Night* v 1 82
I shall have share in this most happy wreck . . . . v 1 273
On this day let seamen fear no wreck; No bargains break . *K. John* iii 1 92
We see the very wreck that we must suffer; And unavoided is the danger now, For suffering so the causes of our wreck . . *Richard II.* ii 1 267
As is the ooze and bottom of the sea With sunken wreck . *Hen. V.* i 2 165
Hence grew the general wreck and massacre . . *1 Hen. VI.* i 1 135
Moved with compassion of my country's wreck . . . iv 1 56
Hume's knavery will be the duchess' wreck . . *2 Hen. VI.* i 2 105
The commonwealth hath daily run to wreck . . . . i 3 127
Ay, as the rocks cheer them that fear their wreck . *3 Hen. VI.* ii 2 5
But keep our course, though the rough wind say no, From shelves and rocks that threaten us with wreck . . . . . . v 4 23
These eyes could never endure sweet beauty's wreck *Richard III.* i 2 127
Methought I saw a thousand fearful wrecks . . . . i 4 24
Found thee a way, out of his wreck, to rise in . . *Hen. VIII.* iii 2 437
And am not One that rejoices in the common wreck . *T. of Athens* v 1 195
He labour'd in his country's wreck . . . . *Macbeth* i 3 114
I fear'd he did but trifle, And meant to wreck thee . . *Hamlet* ii 1 113
A noble ship of Venice Hath seen a grievous wreck . . *Othello* ii 1 23

Wreck. What wreck discern you in me Deserves your pity? . *Cymbeline* i 6 84
What's thy interest In this sad wreck? How came it? Who is it? . iv 2 366
Even now Did the sea toss upon our shore this chest: 'Tis of some wreck.—Set't down, let's look upon't . . . *Pericles* iii 2 51
Wrecked. Supposing that they saw the king's ship wrecked . *Tempest* i 2 236
Who with mine eyes, never since at ebb, beheld The king my father wreck'd . . . . i 2 436
Who three hours since Were wreck'd upon this shore . . . v 1 137
Who most strangely Upon this shore, where you were wreck'd, was landed v 1 161
Her brother Frederick was wrecked at sea . . *Meas. for Meas.* iii 1 225
Hath a ship of rich lading wrecked on the narrow seas . *Mer. of Venice* iii 1 3
Wrecked the same instant of their master's death . *W. Tale* v 2 75
The great supply That was expected by the Dauphin here, Are wreck'd three nights ago on Goodwin Sands . . . *K. John* v 3 11
As men wrecked upon a sand, that look to be washed off the next tide *Hen. V.* iv 1 100
Was I for this nigh wreck'd upon the sea? . *2 Hen. VI.* iii 2 82
And each hour's joy wreck'd with a week of teen . *Richard III.* iv 1 97
Here I have a pilot's thumb, Wreck'd as homeward he did come *Macbeth* i 3 29
That the ship Should house him safe is wreck'd and split *Pericles* ii Gower 32
Wren. The wren with little quill . . . *M. N. Dream* iii 1 131
Would be thought No better a musician than the wren . *Mer. of Venice* v 1 106
Look, where the youngest wren of nine comes . . *T. Night* iii 2 70
And thinks he that the chirping of a wren, By crying comfort from a hollow breast, Can chase away the first-conceived sound? *2 Hen. VI.* iii 2 42
That wrens make prey where eagles dare not perch . *Richard III.* i 3 71
The poor wren, The most diminutive of birds, will fight . *Macbeth* iv 2 9
The wren goes to't, and the small gilded fly Does lecher in my sight *Lear* iv 6 114
If there be Yet left in heaven as small a drop of pity As a wren's eye, fear'd gods, a part of it! . . . . . *Cymbeline* iv 2 305
Be one of those that think The petty wrens of Tarsus will fly hence, And open this to Pericles . . . . *Pericles* iv 3 22
Wrench. With thy case, thy habit, Wrench awe from fools *M. for M.* ii 4 14
For thy revenge Wrench up thy power to the highest *Coriolanus* i 8 11
A noble nature May catch a wrench . . . *T. of Athens* ii 2 218
Wrench his sword from him . . . . . *Othello* v 2 288
'Tis wondrous heavy. Wrench it open straight . *Pericles* iii 2 53
Wrench it open; Soft! it smells most sweetly in my sense . iii 2 59
Wrenched. And put a barren sceptre in my gripe, Thence to be wrench'd with an unlineal hand . . . . *Macbeth* iii 1 63
Like an engine, wrench'd my frame of nature From the fix'd place *Lear* i 4 290
Wrenching. I am well acquainted with your manner of wrenching the true cause the false way . . . . *2 Hen. IV.* ii 1 120
Give me that mattock and the wrenching iron . . *Rom. and Jul.* v 3 22
Wrest. An bad thinking do not wrest true speaking . . *Much Ado* iii 4 33
I beseech you, Wrest once the law to your authority *Mer. of Venice* iv 1 215
That you should fashion, wrest, or bow your reading . *Hen. V.* i 2 14
He'll wrest the sense and hold us here all day . . *2 Hen. VI.* iii 1 186
But this Antenor, I know, is such a wrest in their affairs *Troi. and Cres.* iii 3 23
But I of these will wrest an alphabet . . . *T. Andron.* iii 2 44
Wrested. The imminent decay of wrested pomp . . *K. John* iv 3 154
Too lavishly Wrested his meaning and authority . . *2 Hen. IV.* iv 2 58
That doit that e'er I wrested from the king, Or any groat I hoarded to my use . . . . *2 Hen. VI.* iii 1 112
Wrestle. To wish him wrestle with affection . . . *Much Ado* iii 1 42
What, you wrestle to-morrow before the new duke? *As Y. Like It* i 1 126
To-morrow, sir, I wrestle for my credit . . . . . i 1 132
If ever he go alone again, I'll never wrestle for prize more . . i 1 167
Come, come, wrestle with thy affections . . . . . i 3 21
I'll wrestle with you in my strength of love . *Ant. and Cleo.* ii 2 62
Wrestled. The eldest of the three wrestled with Charles *As Y. Like It* i 2 133
You have wrestled well and overthrown More than your enemies . . i 2 266
Looks he as freshly as he did the day he wrestled? . . . iii 2 244
Wrestler. Was not Charles, the duke's wrestler, here to speak with me? i 1 94
But it shall not be so long; this wrestler shall clear all . . i 1 178
The eldest of the three wrestled with Charles, the duke's wrestler . i 2 134
Young man, have you challenged Charles the wrestler? . . . i 2 179
O, they take the part of a better wrestler than myself! . . . i 3 22
She secretly o'erheard Your daughter and her cousin much commend The parts and graces of the wrestler . . . . . . ii 2 13
Young Orlando, that tripped up the wrestler's heels and your heart . iii 2 225
Wrestling. 'Twill be a good way; and to-morrow the wrestling is . i 1 99
I would have told you of good wrestling, which you have lost the sight of i 2 116
Tell us the manner of the wrestling.—I will tell you the beginning . i 2 118
Shall we see this wrestling, cousin? . . . . . i 2 151
Here is the place appointed for the wrestling . . . . i 2 154
Are you crept hither to see the wrestling? . . . . . i 2 165
We will make it our suit to the duke that the wrestling might not go forward . . . . i 2 193
Which of the two was daughter of the duke That here was at the wrestling? . . . . i 2 282
Great affections wrestling in thy bosom Doth make an earthquake *K. John* v 2 41
Like an Olympian wrestling . . . . . *Troi. and Cres.* iv 5 194
Wretch. And so, good rest.—As wretches have o'ernight That wait for execution in the morn . . . . . *T. G. of Ver.* iv 2 133
O you beast! O faithless coward! O dishonest wretch! *Meas. for Meas.* iii 1 137
Whiles I Persuade this rude wretch willingly to die . . . iv 3 85
And you shall have your bosom on this wretch . . . . iv 3 139
By heaven, fond wretch, thou know'st not what thou speak'st . . v 1 105
Fie on thee, wretch! 'tis pity that thou livest . *Com. of Errors* v 1 27
A needy, hollow-eyed, sharp-looking wretch, A living-dead man . v 1 240
Visit the speechless sick and still converse With groaning wretches *L. L. L.* v 2 862
Whilst the screech-owl, screeching loud, Puts the wretch that lies in woe In remembrance of a shroud . . . . *M. N. Dream* v 1 384
A stony adversary, an inhuman wretch Uncapable of pity *Mer. of Ven.* iv 1 4
A meacock wretch can make the curstest shrew . . *T. of Shrew* ii 1 315
Ungracious wretch, Fit for the mountains and the barbarous caves! *T. N.* iv 1 51
Poor wretch, That for thy mother's fault art thus exposed! . *W. Tale* iii 3 49
O cursed wretch, That knew'st this was the prince! . . . iv 4 469
Never saw I Wretches so quake: they kneel, they kiss the earth . v 1 199
Thou wretch, thou coward! Thou little valiant, great in villany! *K. John* iii 1 115
How Camest thou by this ill tidings? speak, thou wretch *Richard II.* iii 4 80
The wretch . . . breaks like a fire Out of his keeper's arms . *2 Hen. IV.* i 1 140
As subject As are our wretches fetter'd in our prisons . *Hen. V.* i 2 243
Your too much love and care of me Are heavy orisons 'gainst this poor wretch! . . . . ii 2 53
Get you therefore hence, Poor miserable wretches, to your death . ii 2 178
That every wretch, pining and pale before, Beholding him, plucks comfort from his looks . . . . iv Prol. 41
Such a wretch, Winding up days with toil and nights with sleep . iv 1 295

Wretch. These fields, where, wretches, their poor bodies Must lie and fester . . . *Hen. V.* iv 3 87
Be these the wretches that we play'd at dice for? . . . . iv 5 8
Laughest thou, wretch? thy mirth shall turn to moan . 1 *Hen. VI.* ii 3 44
Decrepit miser! base ignoble wretch! I am descended of a gentler blood v 4 7
As the butcher takes away the calf And binds the wretch 2 *Hen. VI.* iii 1 211
Fie, coward woman and soft-hearted wretch! Hast thou not spirit to curse? . . . . . . iii 2 307
Eternal Mover of the heavens, Look with a gentle eye upon this wretch! iii 3 20
The busy meddling fiend That lays strong siege unto this wretch's soul iii 3 22
Die, damned wretch, the curse of her that bare thee . iv 10 83
Ah, timorous wretch! Thou hast undone thyself, thy son, and me 3 *Hen. VI.* i 1 231
So looks the pent-up lion o'er the wretch That trembles under his devouring paws; And so he walks . . . i 3 12
She, poor wretch, for grief can speak no more . . . . iii 1 47
More direful hap betide that hated wretch, That makes us wretched by the death of thee! . . . *Richard III.* i 2 17
Why do you look on us, and shake your head, And call us wretches? ii 2 6
From all the slaughters, wretch, that thou hast done! iv 4 139
This long-usurped royalty From the dead temples of this bloody wretch Have I pluck'd off . . . v 5 5
Was by that wretch betray'd, And without trial fell *Hen. VIII.* ii 1 110
Alas, poor wretch! ah, poor capocchia! hast not slept to-night? *T. and C.* iv 2 32
I have not wash'd My nose that bled, or foil'd some debile wretch *Coriol.* i 9 48
Thou wretch, despite o'erwhelm thee! . . . . iii 1 164
Sly frantic wretch, that holp'st to make me great *T. Andron.* iv 4 59
Hark, wretches! how I mean to martyr you . . . v 2 181
Die, frantic wretch, for this accursed deed! . . . v 3 64
Have done with woes: Give sentence on this execrable wretch v 3 177
The pretty wretch left crying and said 'Ay' . . *Rom. and Jul.* i 3 44
Hang thee, young baggage! disobedient wretch! . . iii 5 161
Here lives a caitiff wretch would sell it him . . . v 1 52
A wretch whose natural gifts were poor To those of mine! *Hamlet* i 5 51
But, look, where sadly the poor wretch comes reading . ii 2 168
Pull'd the poor wretch from her melodious lay To muddy death . iv 7 183
A wretch whom nature is ashamed Almost to acknowledge hers . *Lear* i 1 215
Such as basest and contemned'st wretches For pilferings and most common trespasses Are punish'd with . . . ii 2 150
Tremble, thou wretch, That hast within thee undivulged crimes iii 2 51
Poor naked wretches, wheresoe'er you are, That bide the pelting of this pitiless storm . . . iii 4 28
Take physic, pomp; Expose thyself to feel what wretches feel . iii 4 34
The wretch that thou hast blown unto the worst Owes nothing to thy blasts . . . . . iv 1 8
A sight most pitiful in the meanest wretch, Past speaking of in a king! iv 6 208
What profane wretch art thou? . . . . *Othello* i 1 115
Excellent wretch! Perdition catch my soul, But I do love thee! . iii 3 90
If any wretch have put this in your head, Let heaven requite it! . iv 2 15
This wretch hath part confess'd his villany: Did you and he consent? v 2 296
Come, thou mortal wretch, With thy sharp teeth this knot intrinsicate Of life at once untie . . *Ant. and Cleo.* v 2 306
The contract you pretend with that base wretch, One bred of alms . . it is no contract, none . . . *Cymbeline* ii 3 118
And struck Me, wretch more worth your vengeance . . v 1 11
Poor wretches that depend On greatness' favour dream as I have done v 4 127
Whereat I, wretch, Made scruple of his praise . . . v 5 181
Wretched Isabel! Injurious world! most damned Angelo! *Meas. for Meas.* iv 3 126
And to set on this wretched woman here Against our substitute! . v 1 132
O heaven, the vanity of wretched fools! . . . . v 1 164
A wretched soul, bruised with adversity . . *Com. of Errors* ii 1 34
Hast thou delight to see a wretched man Do outrage and displeasure to himself? . . . . . iv 4 118
Sit I in the sky, And wretched fools' secrets heedfully o'er-eye *L. L. Lost* iv 3 80
It is still her use To let the wretched man outlive his wealth *Mer. of Ven.* iv 1 269
The wretched animal heaved forth such groans . *As Y. Like It* ii 1 36
Who calls?—Your betters, sir.—Else are they very wretched . . ii 4 68
Who might be your mother, That you insult, exult, and all at once, Over the wretched? . . . . . iii 5 37
A wretched ragged man, o'ergrown with hair . . . iv 3 107
A wretched Florentine, Derived from the ancient Capilet *All's Well* v 3 158
In that thou seest thy wretched brother die . . *Richard II.* i 2 27
Wretched and low, A poor unminded outlaw sneaking home 1 *Hen. IV.* iv 3 57
What a wretched and peevish fellow is this king of England! *Hen. V.* iii 7 142
Not all these . . . Can sleep so soundly as the wretched slave . iv 1 285
Posterity, await for wretched years . . . 1 *Hen. VI.* i 1 48
O Lord, have mercy on us, wretched sinners! . . . i 4 70
Wretched shall France be only in my name . . . i 4 97
Ah, woe is me for Gloucester, wretched man!—Be woe for me, more wretched than he is . . . 2 *Hen. VI.* iii 2 72
For yet may England curse my wretched reign . . . iv 9 49
Ah, wretched man! would I had died a maid, And never seen thee! 3 *Hen. VI.* i 1 216
Weep, wretched man, I'll aid thee tear for tear . . . ii 5 76
More direful hap betide that hated wretch, That makes us wretched by the death of thee! . . . *Richard III.* i 2 18
Outlive thy glory, like my wretched self! . . . . i 3 203
God grant that some . . . Deserve not worse than wretched Clarence did! ii 1 93
Now thy heavy curse Is lighted on poor Hastings' wretched head! . iii 4 95
Miserable England! I prophesy the fearfull'st time to thee That ever wretched age hath look'd upon . . . . . iii 4 107
Withdraw thee, wretched Margaret: who comes here? . . iv 4 8
The wretched, bloody, and usurping boar, That spoil'd your summer fields . . . . v 2 7
That wretched Anne thy wife, That never slept a quiet hour with thee v 3 159
Which makes me A little happier than my wretched father *Hen. VIII.* ii 1 120
Is this your comfort? The cordial that ye bring a wretched lady? . iii 1 106
What will become of me now, wretched lady! . . . iii 1 146
O, how wretched Is that poor man that hangs on princes' favours! . iii 2 366
That his noble grace would have some pity Upon my wretched women iv 2 140
This way to death my wretched sons are gone . . *T. Andron.* iii 1 98
At your grief, See how my wretched sister sobs and weeps . . iii 1 137
If any power pities wretched tears, To that I call! . . . iii 1 209
And be this dismal sight The closing up of our most wretched eyes iii 1 263
Witness this wretched stump, witness these crimson lines . . v 2 22
And lively warrant For me, most wretched, to perform the like . v 3 45
Thou, wretched boy, that didst consort him here, Shalt with him hence *Rom. and Jul.* iii 1 135
A wretched puling fool, A whining mammet . . . iii 5 185
Accursed, unhappy, wretched, hateful day! . . . . iv 5 43

Wretched. 'Tis pity bounty had not eyes behind, That man might ne'er be wretched for his mind . . . . *T. of Athens* i 2 170
My dearest lord, bless'd, to be most accursed, Rich, only to be wretched iv 2 43
Best state, contentless, Hath a distracted and most wretched being . iv 3 246
Here lies a wretched corse, of wretched soul bereft: Seek not my name v 4 70
Cassius is A wretched creature and must bend his body . . *J. Cæsar* i 2 117
There are a crew of wretched souls That stay his cure . . *Macbeth* iv 3 141
I cannot strike at wretched kerns, whose arms Are hired to bear their staves . . . . v 7 17
And I, of ladies most deject and wretched . . . *Hamlet* iii 1 163
O wretched state! O bosom black as death! O limed soul! . . iii 3 67
Thou wretched, rash, intruding fool, farewell! I took thee for thy better iii 4 31
Wretched queen, adieu! You that look pale and tremble at this chance v 2 344
A poor old man, As full of grief as age; wretched in both! . . *Lear* ii 4 276
That I am wretched Makes thee the happier . . . . iv 1 68
Wretched though I seem, I can produce a champion . . . v 1 42
O wretched fool, That livest to make thine honesty a vice! *Othello* iii 3 375
It is my wretched fortune . . . . iv 2 128
O wretched villain!—Two or three groan: it is a heavy night . . v 1 41
Ay me, most wretched, That have my heart parted betwixt two friends That do afflict each other! . . . *Ant. and Cleo.* iii 6 76
You shall find me, wretched man, a thing The most disdain'd of fortune *Cymbeline* iii 4 19
O Jove! I think Foundations fly the wretched . . . . iii 6 7
Most wretched queen!—Here she lies, sir . . . *Pericles* iii 1 55
Wretchedest. He was the wretched'st thing when he was young *Richard III.* ii 4 18
Wretchedness. I love not to see wretchedness o'ercharged *M. N. Dream* v 1 85
My wretchedness unto a row of pins, They'll talk of state *Richard II.* iii 4 26
Whilst that my wretchedness doth bait myself . . . . iv 1 238
What can happen To me above this wretchedness? . . *Hen. VIII.* iii 1 123
Are ye all gone, And leave me here in wretchedness behind ye? . . iv 2 84
Art thou so bare and full of wretchedness, And fear'st to die? *R. and J.* v 1 68
O, the fierce wretchedness that glory brings us! . . *T. of Athens* iv 2 30
Is wretchedness deprived that benefit, To end itself by death? . *Lear* iv 6 61
Sinon's weeping Did scandal many a holy tear, took pity From most true wretchedness . . . . . . *Cymbeline* iii 4 63
Wring. It is a hint That wrings mine eyes to't . . . *Tempest* i 2 135
I wash, wring, brew, bake, scour, dress meat and drink . *Mer. Wives* i 4 101
Or wring redress from you. Hear me, O hear me, here! *Meas. for Meas.* v 1 32
No, no; 'tis all men's office to speak patience To those that wring under the load of sorrow . . . . . *Much Ado* v 1 28
O noble sir, Your over-kindness doth wring tears from me! . . v 1 302
Wrings his hapless hands And shakes his head . . 2 *Hen. VI.* i 1 226
The king is dead.—Rear up his body; wring him by the nose . iii 2 34
To wring the widow from her custom'd right . . . v 1 188
And wring the awful sceptre from his fist . . . 3 *Hen. VI.* ii 1 154
Why do you wring your hands, and beat your breast? *Richard III.* ii 2 3
Which God defend that I should wring from him! . . . iii 7 173
Why dost thou wring thy hands?—Ah, well-a-day! he's dead, he's dead! *Rom. and Jul.* iii 2 36
To wring From the hard hands of peasants their vile trash . *J. Cæsar* iv 3 73
Sit you down, And let me wring your heart . . . *Hamlet* iii 4 35
Then, sir, would he gripe and wring my hand, Cry 'O sweet creature!' *Othello* iii 3 421
He wrings at some distress.—Would I could free't! . *Cymbeline* iii 6 79
Wringer. His cook, or his laundry, his washer, and his wringer *M. Wives* i 2 5
Wringing. Our maid howling, our cat wringing her hands *T. G. of Ver.* ii 3 8
Wringing her hands, whose whiteness so became them As if but now they waxed pale for woe . . . . . . iii 1 227
Subject to the breath Of every fool, whose sense no more can feel But his own wringing! . . . . . *Hen. V.* iv 1 253
Doubts, wringing of the conscience, Fears, and despairs . *Hen VIII.* ii 2 28
Leave wringing of your hands: peace! sit you down . *Hamlet* iii 4 34
Wrinkle. With mirth and laughter let old wrinkles come *Mer. of Venice* i 1 80
So that you had her wrinkles and I her money . . *All's Well* ii 4 20
Hang'd in the frowning wrinkle of her brow! . . . *K. John* ii 1 505
Thou canst help time to furrow me with age, But stop no wrinkle in his pilgrimage . . . . . . *Richard II.* i 3 230
Have ever made me sour my patient cheek, Or bend one wrinkle . ii 1 170
Give me the glass, and therein will I read. No deeper wrinkles yet? . iv 1 277
The wrinkles in my brows, now fill'd with blood, Were liken'd oft to kingly sepulchres; For who lived king, but I could dig his grave? 3 *Hen. VI.* v 2 19
I have, as when the sun doth light a storm, Buried this sigh in wrinkle of a smile . . . . . . *Troi. and Cres.* i 1 38
Whose youth and freshness Wrinkles Apollo's, and makes stale the morning . . . . ii 2 79
And for these bitter tears, which now you see Filling the aged wrinkles in my cheeks; Be pitiful . . . . *T. Andron.* iii 1 7
Paint till a horse may mire upon your face. A pox of wrinkles! *T. of A.* iv 3 148
Let it stamp wrinkles in her brow of youth . . . *Lear* i 4 306
You shall paint when you are old.—Wrinkles forbid! . *Ant. and Cleo.* i 2 19
Wrinkled. Hath a purpose More grave and wrinkled than the aims and ends Of burning youth . . . . *Meas. for Meas.* i 3 5
To view with hollow eye and wrinkled brow An age of poverty *M. of V.* iv 1 270
This is a man, old, wrinkled, faded, wither'd . . *T. of Shrew* iv 5 43
Hermione was not so much wrinkled, nothing So aged as this *W. Tale* v 3 28
With wrinkled brows, with nods, with rolling eyes . . *K. John* iv 2 192
Grim-visaged war hath smooth'd his wrinkled front . *Richard III.* i 1 9
Foul wrinkled witch, what makest thou in my sight? . . . i 3 164
Virgins and boys, mid-age and wrinkled eld . . *Troi. and Cres.* ii 2 104
Slaves and fools, Pluck the grave wrinkled senate from the bench, And minister in their steads! . . . . *T. of Athens* iv 1 5
The satirical rogue says here that old men have grey beards, that their faces are wrinkled . . . . . . *Hamlet* ii 2 200
With Phœbus' amorous pinches black, And wrinkled deep in time *A. and C.* i 5 29
While I struck The lean and wrinkled Cassius . . . . iii 11 37
Wrist. And he that speaks doth gripe the hearer's wrist . *K. John* iv 2 190
What said he?—He took me by the wrist and held me hard . *Hamlet* ii 1 87
My conscience, thou art fetter'd More than my shanks and wrists *Cymb.* v 4 9
Writ. Some love of yours hath writ to you in rhyme . *T. G. of Ver.* i 2 79
Look, here is writ 'kind Julia.' Unkind Julia! . . . . i 2 109
And here is writ 'love-wounded Proteus.' Poor wounded name! . . i 2 113
Here in one line is his name twice writ, 'Poor forlorn Proteus' . i 2 123
Are they not lamely writ?—No, boy, but as well as I can do them . ii 1 97
I have writ your letter Unto the secret nameless friend of yours . ii 1 110
Being ignorant to whom it goes I writ at random, very doubtfully . ii 1 117
The lines are very quaintly writ; But since unwillingly, take them again ii 1 128
You writ them, sir, at my request; But I will none of them . . ii 1 132

Writ. I would have had them writ more movingly . *T. G. of Ver.* ii 1 134
When it's writ, for my sake read it over, And if it please you, so . ii 1 136
Why, she hath not writ to me?—What need she, when she hath made you write to yourself? . ii 1 157
She hath given you a letter.—That's the letter I writ to her friend ii 1 166
Often have you writ to her, and she, in modesty, Or else for want of idle time, could not again reply . ii 1 171
Thy letters may be here, . . . Which, being writ to me, shall be deliver'd iii 1 249
'Too liberal.'—Of her tongue she cannot, for that's writ down she is slow of . iii 1 357
I have writ me here a letter to her . *Mer. Wives* i 3 65
He hath a thousand of these letters, writ with blank space for different names . ii 1 76
The stealth of our most mutual entertainment With character too gross is writ on Juliet *Meas. for Meas.* i 2 159
But, by chance, nothing of what is writ . iv 2 218
Every letter he hath writ hath disvouched other . iv 4 1
There will she sit in her smock till she have writ a sheet of paper *M. Ado* ii 3 138
O, when she had writ it and was reading it over . ii 3 142
I should flout him, if he writ to me; yea, though I love him, I should . ii 3 150
They are both in a tale. Have you writ down, that they are none? iv 2 33
O that I had been writ down an ass! . iv 2 90
They have writ the style of gods And made a push at chance and sufferance . v 1 37
Writ in my cousin's hand, stolen from her pocket . v 4 89
I will have that subject newly writ o'er *L. L. Lost* i 2 120
This letter is mistook, it importeth none here; It is writ to Jaquenetta iv 1 58
Once more I'll read the ode that I have writ . iv 3 99
Writ o' both sides the leaf, margent and all . v 2 8
If he that writ it had played Pyramus *M. N. Dream* v 1 365
Whiter than the paper it writ on Is the fair hand that writ *Mer. of Venice* ii 4 13
Youth, you have done me much ungentleness, To show the letter that I writ to you *As Y. Like It* v 2 84
So holy writ in babes hath judgement shown *All's Well* ii 1 141
My mouth no more were broken than these boys', And writ as little beard ii 3 67
I have writ my letters, casketed my treasure . ii 5 26
Buried a wife, mourned for her; writ to my lady mother I am returning iv 3 102
And writ to me this other day to turn him out o' the band . iv 3 226
Will you give me a copy of the sonnet you writ to Diana? . iv 3 355
'Be not afraid of greatness:' 'twas well writ . *T. Night* iii 4 43
Has here writ a letter to you; I should have given't you to-day morning v 1 293
Maria writ The letter at Sir Toby's great importance . v 1 370
Yourself Have said and writ so, but your writing now Is colder *W. Tale* v 1 99
Can you not read it? is it not fair writ? . *K. John* iv 1 37
Writ in remembrance more than things long past *Richard II.* ii 1 14
The very book indeed Where all my sins are writ, and that's myself . iv 1 275
Crowing as if he had writ man ever since his father was a bachelor *2 Hen. IV.* i 2 30
Rotten opinion, who hath writ me down After my seeming . v 2 128
For in the book of Numbers is it writ . *Hen. V.* i 2 98
I once writ a sonnet in his praise . iii 7 42
A letter was deliver'd to my hands, Writ to your grace . *1 Hen. VI.* iv 1 12
His weapons holy saws of sacred writ . *2 Hen. VI.* i 3 61
Now, pray, my lord, let's see the devil's writ . i 4 60
This hand of mine hath writ in thy behalf . iv 1 63
Under the which is writ 'Invitis nubibus' . iv 1 99
Kent, in the Commentaries Cæsar writ, Is term'd the civil'st place of all this isle: Sweet is the country . iv 7 65
Let us pursue him ere the writs go forth . v 3 26
With old odd ends stolen out of holy writ *Richard III.* i 3 337
Let there be letters writ to every shire, Of the king's grace *Hen. VIII.* i 2 103
The letter, as I live, with all the business I writ to his holiness . iii 2 222
Your intercepted packets You writ to the pope against the king . iii 2 287
In all you writ to Rome, or else To foreign princes, 'Ego et Rex meus' Was still inscribed . iii 2 313
That therefore such a writ be sued against you . iii 2 341
Yet, for I loved thee, Take this along; I writ it for thy sake *Coriolanus* v 2 96
Whose chronicle thus writ: 'The man was noble' . v 3 145
Boy! false hound! If you have writ your annals true, 'tis there . v 6 114
Then all too late I bring this fatal writ *T. Andron.* ii 3 264
I have writ my name Without the help of any hand at all . iv 1 70
O, do ye read, my lord, what she hath writ? . iv 1 77
I am sent to find those persons whose names are here writ, and can never find what names the writing person hath here writ *Rom. and Jul.* i 2 43
And find delight writ there with beauty's pen . i 3 82
So many guests invite as here are writ . iv 2 1
What says Romeo? Or, if his mind be writ, give me his letter . v 2 4
O, give me thy hand, One writ with me in sour misfortune's book! . v 3 82
Meantime I writ to Romeo, That he should hither come . v 3 246
Are not within the leaf of pity writ . *T. of Athens* iv 3 117
Nor nothing in your letters writ of her?—Nothing *J. Cæsar* iv 3 183
We have here writ To Norway, uncle of young Fortinbras *Hamlet* i 2 27
We did think it writ down in our duty To let you know of it . ii 2 222
For the law of writ and the liberty, these are the only men . ii 2 421
The story is extant, and writ in choice Italian . iii 2 274
Is't writ in your revenge, That, swoopstake, you will draw both friend and foe? . iv 5 141
Folded the writ up in form of the other, Subscribed it . v 2 51
I know his heart. What he hath utter'd I have writ my sister *Lear* i 4 354
What, have you writ that letter to my sister? . i 4 357
Our father he hath writ, so hath our sister, Of differences . ii 1 124
My writ Is on the life of Lear and on Cordelia . v 3 245
Trifles light as air Are to the jealous confirmations strong As proofs of holy writ *Othello* iii 3 324
That self hand, Which writ his honour in the acts it did *Ant. and Cleo.* v 1 22
This is the tenour of the emperor's writ . *Cymbeline* iii 7 1
Where each man Thinks all is writ he speken can . *Pericles* ii Gower 12
Now please you wit The epitaph is for Marina writ . iv 4 32

Write. He writes How happily he lives, how well beloved *T. G. of Ver.* i 3 56
Last night she enjoined me to write some lines to one she loves . ii 1 93
I will write, Please you command, a thousand times as much . ii 1 119
Please you, I'll write your ladyship another . ii 1 135
That my master, being scribe, to himself should write the letter . ii 1 146
What need she, when she hath made you write to yourself? . ii 1 159
Herself hath taught her love himself to write unto her lover . ii 1 174
Write till your ink be dry, and with your tears Moist it again . iii 2 75
Who writes himself 'Armigero,' in any bill, warrant, quittance *M. Wives* i 1 9
He writes verses, he speaks holiday, he smells April and May . iii 2 69
And 'Honi soit qui mal y pense' write In emerald tufts . v 5 73

Write. We shall write to you, As time and our concernings shall importune *Meas. for Meas.* i 1 56
Let's write good angel on the devil's horn; 'Tis not the devil's crest . ii 4 16
Now will I write letters to Angelo,—The provost, he shall bear them . iv 3 97
In such great letters as they write 'Here is good horse to hire' *M. Ado* i 1 268
'Shall I,' says she, 'that have so oft encountered him with scorn, write to him?' . ii 3 133
This says she now when she is beginning to write to him . ii 3 136
That she should be so immodest to write to one that she knew would flout her . ii 3 148
They can write and read . iii 3 12
To write and read comes by nature . iii 3 16
Out on thee! Seeming! I will write against it . iv 1 57
And my name is Conrade.—Write down, master gentleman Conrade . iv 2 17
Write down, that they hope they serve God: and write God first . iv 2 20
Write down Prince John a villain . iv 2 43
Let him write down the prince's officer coxcomb . iv 2 73
O that he were here to write me down an ass! . iv 2 78
Will you then write me a sonnet in praise of my beauty? . v 2 4
And to the strict'st decrees I'll write my name *L. L. Lost* i 1 117
So to the laws at large I write my name . i 1 156
Devise, wit; write, pen; for I am for whole volumes in folio . i 2 191
Well, I will love, write, sigh, pray, sue, and groan . iii 1 206
These numbers will I tear, and write in prose . iv 3 57
When shall you see me write a thing in rhyme? . iv 3 181
Never durst poet touch a pen to write Until his ink were temper'd with Love's sighs . iv 3 346
Write, 'Lord have mercy on us' on those three . v 2 419
I have a device to make all well. Write me a prologue *M. N. Dream* iii 1 18
I will get Peter Quince to write a ballad of this dream . iv 1 220
You cannot better be employ'd, Bassanio, Than to live still and write mine epitaph *Mer. of Venice* iv 1 118
You hear the learn'd Bellario, what he writes . iv 1 167
At every sentence end, Will I Rosalinda write *As Y. Like It* iii 2 145
He writes brave verses, speaks brave words, swears brave oaths . iii 4 43
I'll write to him a very taunting letter, And thou shalt bear it . iii 5 134
I'll write it straight; The matter's in my head and in my heart . iii 5 136
Why writes she so to me? . iv 3 19
I know not the contents: Phebe did write it . iv 3 22
She Phebes me: mark how the tyrant writes . iv 3 39
I write man; to which title age cannot bring thee . *All's Well* ii 3 208
Write to the king That which I durst not speak . ii 3 305
Let me see what he writes, and when he means to come . iii 2 11
Then call me husband: but in such a 'then' I write a 'never' . iii 2 63
Write, write, that from the bloody course of war My dearest master, your dear son, may hie . iii 4 8
And yet she writes, Pursuit would be but vain . iii 4 24
Write, write, Rinaldo, To this unworthy husband of his wife . iii 4 29
Write loyal cantons of contemned love And sing them loud . *T. Night* i 5 289
I'll write thee a challenge; or I'll deliver thy indignation to him by word of mouth . ii 3 139
I can write very like my lady your niece . ii 3 173
Go, write it in a martial hand; be curst and brief . iii 2 45
Let there be gall enough in thy ink, though thou write with a goose-pen iii 2 53
Did he write this?—Ay, madam.—This savours not much of distraction v 1 320
Write from it, if you can, in hand or phrase . v 1 340
Things known betwixt us three, I'll write you down *W. Tale* iv 4 571
Nor never write, regreet, nor reconcile This louring tempest *Richard II.* i 3 186
And with rainy eyes Write sorrow on the bosom of the earth . iii 2 147
He writes me here, that inward sickness—And that his friends by deputation could not So soon be drawn . *1 Hen. IV.* iv 1 31
For, as he writes, there is no quailing now . iv 1 39
I must go write again To other friends; and so farewell . iv 4 40
And he holds his place; for look you how he writes . *2 Hen. IV.* ii 2 117
Will Fortune never come with both hands full, But write her fair words still in foulest letters? . iv 4 104
Having any occasion to write for matter of grant . *Hen. V.* v 2 365
It is the worst, and all, my lord, he writes . *1 Hen. VI.* iv 1 67
The Turk, that two and fifty kingdoms hath, Writes not so tedious a style . iv 7 74
I dare not speak: I'll call for pen and ink, and write my mind . v 3 66
And so will I and write home for it straight . *2 Hen. VI.* iv 1 24
He can write and read and cast accompt.—O monstrous! . iv 2 92
He can make obligations, and write court-hand . iv 2 100
Emmanuel.—They use to write it on the top of letters . iv 2 107
Dost thou use to write thy name? or hast thou a mark to thyself, like an honest plain-dealing man? . iv 2 109
I thank God, I have been so well brought up that I can write my name iv 2 113
That I'll write upon thy burgonet . v 1 200
And over the chair of state, where now he sits, Write up his title with usurping blood . *3 Hen. VI.* i 1 169
I'll write unto them and entreat them fair . i 1 271
Write in the dust this sentence with thy blood . v 1 56
With that grim ferryman which poets write of . *Richard III.* i 4 46
Eleven hours I spent to write it over . iii 6 5
Write to me very shortly, And you shall understand from me her mind iv 4 428
Men's evil manners live in brass; their virtues We write in water *Hen. VIII.* iv 2 46
Patience, is that letter, I caused you write, yet sent away? . iv 2 128
What are you reading?—A strange fellow here Writes me *Troi. and Cres.* iii 3 96
Ere we do repose us, we will write To Rome of our success . *Coriolanus* i 9 74
Titus Lartius writes, they fought together, but Aufidius got off . ii 1 140
Write down thy mind, bewray thy meaning so, An if thy stumps will let thee play the scribe . *T. Andron.* ii 4 3
In the dust I write My heart's deep languor and my soul's sad tears . iii 1 12
Write thou, good niece; and here display, at last, What God will have discover'd for revenge . iv 1 73
I will go get a leaf of brass, And with a gad of steel will write . iv 1 103
And now he writes to heaven for his redress: See, here's to Jove . iv 4 13
Any man that can write may answer a letter . *Rom. and Jul.* ii 4 10
Romeo Hath had no notice of these accidents; But I will write again . v 2 28
He writes that he did buy a poison Of a poor 'pothecary . v 3 288
And write in thee the figures of their love . *T. of Athens* v 1 157
That tongue of his that bade the Romans Mark him and write his speeches in their books . *J. Cæsar* i 2 126
Write them together, yours is as fair a name . i 2 144
Cæsar did write for him to come to Rome . iii 1 278
You wrong'd yourself to write in such a case . iv 3 6
Whereby he does receive Particular addition, from the bill That writes them all alike . *Macbeth* iii 1 101

Write. I have seen her . . . take forth paper, fold it, write upon't, read it, afterwards seal it . . . *Macbeth* v 1 7
I once did hold it, as our statists do, A baseness to write fair . . . *Hamlet* v 2 34
Had he a hand to write this? a heart and brain to breed it in? . . . *Lear* i 2 60
The effects he writes of succeed unhappily . . . i 2 156
I'll write straight to my sister, To hold my very course . . . i 3 25
Why should she write to Edmund? Might not you Transport her purposes by word? . . . iv 5 19
About it; and write happy when thou hast done . . . v 3 35
Write from us to him; post-post-haste dispatch . . . *Othello* i 3 46
You shall not write my praise.—No, let me not . . . ii 1 117
What wouldst thou write of me, if thou shouldst praise me? . . . ii 1 118
Was this fair paper, this most goodly book, Made to write 'whore' upon? . . . iv 2 72
Thou wilt write to Antony?—I'll humbly signify . . . *Ant. and Cleo.* iii 1 29
Scribes, bards, poets, cannot Think, speak, cast, write, sing, number, ho! iii 2 17
Thou shalt bring him to me Where I will write . . . iii 3 50
I'll write it: follow me . . . iii 13 28
Write to him—I will subscribe—gentle adieus and greetings . . . iv 5 13
Thither write, my queen, And with mine eyes I'll drink the words you send, Though ink be made of gall . . . *Cymbeline* i 1 99
If he should write, And I not have it, 'twere a paper lost, As offer'd mercy is . . . i 3 2
I will write. Send your trunk to me; it shall safe be kept . . . i 6 208
I will write all down: Such and such pictures; there the window . . . ii 2 24
Why should I write this down, that's riveted, Screw'd to my memory? ii 2 43
She writes so to you, doth she?—O, no, no, no! . . . ii 4 105
I'll write against them, Detest them, curse them . . . ii 5 32
Adultery? Wherefore write you not What monster's her accuser? . . . iii 2 1
I'll write to my lord she's dead . . . iii 5 104
To write and read Be henceforth treacherous! . . . iv 2 316
Writers say, as in the sweetest bud The eating canker dwells *T. G. of Ver.* i 1 42
And writers say, as the most forward bud Is eaten by the canker ere it blow . . . i 1 45
Only get the learned writer to set down our excommunication *Much Ado* iii 5 68
All your writers do consent that ipse is he . . . *As Y. Like It* v 1 47
This pitch, as ancient writers do report, doth defile . . . 1 *Hen. IV.* ii 4 455
I'll haste the writer and withal Break with your wives of your departure iii 1 143
Their writers say, King Pepin . . . Did . . . Make claim and title *Hen. V.* i 2 64
Their writers do them wrong, to make them exclaim against their own succession . . . *Hamlet* ii 2 366
Writhled. It cannot be this weak and writhled shrimp Should strike such terror to his enemies . . . 1 *Hen. VI.* ii 3 23
Writing. For your writing and reading, let that appear when there is no need of such vanity . . . *Much Ado* iii 3 21
It would neither serve for the writing nor the tune . . . *L. L. Lost* i 2 119
For the nomination of the party writing to the person written unto . . . iv 2 138
It is Biron's writing, and here is his name . . . iv 3 203
There is a written scroll! I'll read the writing . . . *Mer. of Venice* ii 7 64
And then the boy, his clerk, That took some pains in writing . . . v 1 182
Mar no more trees with writing love-songs in their barks *As Y. Like It* iii 2 277
I guess By the stern brow and waspish action Which she did use as she was writing of it, It bears an angry tenour . . . iv 3 10
And there it is in writing, fairly drawn . . . *T. of Shrew* iii 1 70
This is not my writing, Though, I confess, much like the character . . . *T. Night* v 1 353
Yourself Have said and writ so, but your writing now Is colder *W. Tale* v 1 99
Yea, look'st thou pale? let me see the writing . . . *Richard II.* v 2 57
Peruse this writing here, and thou shalt know . . . v 3 49
Think not, although in writing I preferr'd The manner of thy vile outrageous crimes, That therefore I have forged . . . 1 *Hen. VI.* iii 1 10
O, that her hand, In whose comparison all whites are ink, Writing their own reproach . . . *Troi. and Cres.* i 1 57
What he would do, He sent in writing after me . . . *Coriolanus* v 1 68
Writing destruction on the enemy's castle . . . *T. Andron.* iii 1 170
I am sent to find those persons whose names are here writ, and can never find what names the writing person hath here writ *R. and J.* i 2 44
Why, I was writing of my epitaph; It will be seen to-morrow *T. of Athens* v 1 188
In at his windows throw . . . Writings all tending to the great opinion That Rome holds of his name . . . *J. Cæsar* i 2 322
How calm and gentle I proceeded still In all my writings *Ant. and Cleo.* v 1 76
If you please To greet your lord with writing, do't to-night *Cymbeline* i 6 206
She thinks not so; peruse this writing else . . . *Pericles* ii 5 41
Written. But twice or thrice was 'Proteus' written down *T. G. of Ver.* i 2 117
There is written in your brow, provost, honesty and constancy *M. for M.* iv 2 162
It is written, they appear to men like angels of light *Com. of Errors* iv 3 55
And careful hours with time's deformed hand Have written strange defeatures in my face . . . v 1 299
Though it be not written down, yet forget not that I am an ass *M. Ado* iv 2 80
Here's a paper written in his hand, A halting sonnet . . . v 4 86
For the nomination of the party writing to the person written unto . . . *L. L. Lost* iv 2 138
Have you the lion's part written? . . . *M. N. Dream* i 2 68
Love's stories written in love's richest book . . . ii 2 122
It shall be written in eight and six.—No, make it two more; let it be written in eight and eight . . . iii 1 25
A carrion Death, within whose empty eye There is a written scroll! . . . *Mer. of Venice* ii 7 64
More I'll entreat you Written to bear along . . . *All's Well* iii 2 98
Having our fair order written down . . . *K. John* v 2 4
For divers reasons Which I shall send you written . . . 1 *Hen. IV.* i 3 263
That are written down old with all the characters of age . . . 2 *Hen. IV.* i 2 202
Whose memory is written on the earth With yet appearing blood . . . ii 1 81
With deep premeditated lines, With written pamphlets . . . 1 *Hen. VI.* iii 1 2
Have you with heed perused What I have written to you? *Coriolanus* v 6 63
I know There is enough written upon this earth To stir a mutiny in the mildest thoughts . . . *T. Andron.* iv 1 84
What's here? A scroll; and written round about? Let's see . . . iv 2 18
Of my word, I have written to effect; There's not a god left unsolicited iv 3 59
In bloody lines I have set down; And what is written shall be executed v 2 15
Find those persons out Whose names are written there . . . *Rom. and Jul.* i 2 36
Find them out whose names are written here! It is written, that the shoemaker should meddle with his yard . . . i 2 38
And what obscured in this fair volume lies Find written in the margent of his eyes . . . i 3 86
Had I it written, I would tear the word . . . ii 2 57
Raze out the written troubles of the brain . . . *Macbeth* v 3 42
Most meet That first we come to words; and therefore have we Our written purposes before us sent . . . *Ant. and Cleo.* ii 6 4
I crave our composition may be written, And seal'd between us . . . ii 6 59

Written. The record of what injuries you did us, Though written in our flesh, we shall remember As things but done by chance *A. and C.* v 2 119
Wrong. To sigh To the winds whose pity, sighing back again, Did us but loving wrong . . . *Tempest* i 2 151
I fear you have done yourself some wrong . . . i 2 443
With their high wrongs I am struck to the quick . . . v 1 25
I resign and do entreat Thou pardon me my wrongs . . . v 1 119
To wrong my friend, I shall be much forsworn *T. G. of Ver.* ii 6 3
Do him not that wrong To bear a hard opinion of his truth . . . ii 7 80
Art thou not ashamed To wrong him with thy importunacy? . . . iv 2 112
'You do him the more wrong,' quoth I; ''twas I did the thing' . . . iv 4 29
Though his false finger have profaned the ring, Mine shall not do his Julia so much wrong . . . iv 4 142
Poor gentlewoman! my master wrongs her much . . . iv 4 146
I will not go first; truly, la! I will not do you that wrong *Mer. Wives* i 1 323
You do yourself wrong, indeed, la! . . . i 1 326
Yet I wrong him to call him poor . . . ii 2 282
I shall not only receive this villanous wrong, but stand under the adoption of abominable terms, and by him that does me this wrong ii 2 308
Belike having received wrong by some person . . . iii 1 53
Be contented: you wrong yourself too much . . . iii 3 178
You do yourself mighty wrong . . . iii 3 221
You wrong me, sir, thus still to haunt my house . . . iii 4 73
Knowing my mind, you wrong me . . . iii 4 80
This is not well, Master Ford; this wrongs you . . . iv 2 161
Upon my life, then, you took the wrong.—What need you tell me that? v 5 201
I think I have done myself wrong, have I not? *Meas. for Meas.* i 2 41
It hath been great pains to you. They do you wrong to put you so oft upon't . . . ii 1 280
But might you do't, and do the world no wrong? . . . ii 2 53
And do him right that, answering one foul wrong, Lives not to act another . . . ii 2 103
Hooking both right and wrong to the appetite, To follow as it draws! ii 4 176
He would be drunk too; that let me inform you.—You do him wrong, surely . . . iii 2 137
I should wrong it, To lock it in the wards of covert bosom . . . v 1 9
Relate your wrongs; in what? by whom? be brief . . . v 1 26
You are i' the wrong To speak before your time . . . v 1 86
Unfeeling fools can with such wrongs dispense *Com. of Errors* ii 1 103
Be it my wrong you are from me exempt, But wrong not that wrong with a more contempt . . . ii 2 173
So it doth appear By the wrongs I suffer and the blows I bear . . . iii 1 16
'Tis double wrong, to truant with your bed And let her read it in thy looks . . . iii 2 17
You wrong me much to say so.—You wrong me more, sir, in denying it iv 1 66
You have done wrong to this my honest friend . . . v 1 19
A reverend lady: It cannot be that she hath done thee wrong . . . v 1 135
And sent him home, Whilst to take order for the wrongs I went . . . v 1 146
Beyond imagination is the wrong That she this day hath shameless thrown on me . . . v 1 201
Albeit my wrongs might make one wiser mad . . . v 1 217
And all . . . That by this sympathized one day's error Have suffer'd wrong, go keep us company . . . v 1 398
I will not do them the wrong to mistrust any . . . *Much Ado* i 1 245
But so I am apt to do myself wrong; I am not so reputed . . . ii 1 214
If they wrong her honour, The proudest of them shall well hear of it iv 1 193
Nor let no comforter delight mine ear But such a one whose wrongs do suit with mine . . . v 1 7
Who wrongs him?—Marry, thou dost wrong me; thou dissembler . . . v 1 52
Who I believe was pack'd in all this wrong, Hired to it . . . v 1 308
Death, in guerdon of her wrongs, Gives her fame which never dies . . . v 3 5
A man of complements, whom right and wrong Have chose as umpire . . . *L. L. Lost* i 1 169
You do the king my father too much wrong And wrong the reputation of your name . . . ii 1 154
O, pardon love this wrong, That sings heaven's praise with such an earthly tongue . . . iv 2 121
I have seen the day of wrong through the little hole of discretion . . . v 2 733
Your wrongs do set a scandal on my sex . . . *M. N. Dream* ii 1 240
Newts and blind-worms, do no wrong, Come not near our fairy queen . . . ii 2 11
You do me wrong, good sooth, you do, In such disdainful manner me to woo . . . ii 2 129
Made senseless things begin to do them wrong . . . iii 2 28
Then stir Demetrius up with bitter wrong . . . iii 2 361
You do me now more wrong In making question of my uttermost . . . *Mer. of Venice* i 1 155
And, for my love, I pray you wrong me not . . . i 3 171
If you choose wrong Never to speak to lady afterward In way of marriage ii 1 40
The very truth is that the Jew, having done me wrong . . . ii 2 141
If you poison us, do we not die? and if you wrong us, shall we not revenge? . . . iii 1 69
If a Jew wrong a Christian, what is his humility? Revenge. If a Christian wrong a Jew, what should his sufferance be by Christian example? . . . iii 1 71
For, in choosing wrong, I lose your company . . . iii 2 2
The substance of my praise doth wrong this shadow In underprizing it iii 2 128
What judgement shall I dread, doing no wrong? . . . iv 1 89
To do a great right, do a little wrong, And curb this cruel devil of his will . . . iv 1 216
By yonder moon I swear you do me wrong . . . v 1 142
Portia, forgive me this enforced wrong . . . v 1 240
I shall do my friends no wrong, for I have none to lament me *As Y. L. It* i 2 202
Good sister, wrong me not, nor wrong yourself . . . *T. of Shrew* ii 1 1
Why dost thou wrong her that did ne'er wrong thee? . . . ii 1 27
You are too blunt: go to it orderly.—You wrong me . . . ii 1 46
Accept of him, or else you do me wrong . . . ii 1 59
You do me double wrong, To strive for that which resteth in my choice iii 1 16
The more my wrong, the more his spite appears . . . iv 3 2
Love all, trust a few, Do wrong to none . . . *All's Well* i 1 74
I'll never do you wrong for your own sake . . . ii 3 96
I most unfeignedly beseech your lordship to make some reservation of your wrongs . . . ii 3 260
Go: The king has done you wrong: but, hush, 'tis so . . . ii 3 317
But to himself The greatest wrong of all . . . v 3 15
A common gamester to the camp.—He does me wrong, my lord . . . v 3 189
Of what nature the wrongs are thou hast done him, I know not *T. Night* iii 4 241
Who does beguile you? who does do you wrong? . . . v 1 143
You wrong me, and the world shall know it . . . v 1 310
Madam, you have done me wrong, Notorious wrong.—Have I? . . . v 1 336
You offer him, if this be so, a wrong Something unfilial . . . *W. Tale* iv 4 416

Wrong. I cannot forget My blemishes in them, and so still think of The wrong I did myself . . . *W. Tale* v 1 9
The wrongs I have done thee stir Afresh within me . . . v 1 148
Or else it must go wrong with you and me . . . . *K. John* i 1 41
That judge hath made me guardian to this boy : Under whose warrant I impeach thy wrong . . . ii 1 116
Oppress'd with wrongs and therefore full of fears . . . iii 1 13
Without my wrong There is no tongue hath power to curse him right . iii 1 182
When law can do no right, Let it be lawful that law bar no wrong . iii 1 186
Since law itself is perfect wrong, How can the law forbid my tongue to curse? . . . . iii 1 189
I must pocket up these wrongs . . . . iii 1 200
And thou possessed with a thousand wrongs . . . . iii 3 41
All things that you should use to do me wrong Deny their office . . iv 1 124
Your fears, which, as they say, attend The steps of wrong . . iv 2 57
We cannot deal but with the very hand Of stern injustice and confused wrong . . . . v 2 23
Ere my tongue Shall wound my honour with such feeble wrong *Rich. II.* i 1 191
O, sit my husband's wrongs on Hereford's spear! . . . i 2 47
You gave leave to my unwilling tongue Against my will to do myself this wrong . . . . i 3 246
How long Shall tender duty make me suffer wrong? . . . ii 1 164
Not Gaunt's rebukes, nor England's private wrongs . . . ii 1 166
'Tis shame such wrongs are borne In him . . . . . ii 1 238
I beseech your grace Look on my wrongs with an indifferent eye . . ii 3 116
To rouse his wrongs and chase them to the bay . . . . ii 3 128
I have had feeling of my cousin's wrongs And laboured all I could to do him right . . . . ii 3 141
To find out right with wrong, it may not be . . . . ii 3 145
With tears drawn from her eyes by your foul wrongs . . . iii 1 15
He does me double wrong That wounds me with the flatteries of his tongue . . . . iii 2 215
True noblesse would Learn him forbearance from so foul a wrong . . iv 1 120
May reasonably die and never rise To do him wrong . . *1 Hen. IV.* i 3 75
The unhappy king,—Whose wrongs in us God pardon! . . . i 3 149
You will not pocket up wrong : art thou not ashamed? . . . iii 3 184
Cries out upon abuses, seems to weep Over his country's wrongs . . iv 3 82
Broke oath on oath, committed wrong on wrong . . . . iv 3 101
They bring smooth comforts false, worse than true wrongs *2 Hen. IV.* Ind. 40
And make thee rich for doing me such wrong . . . . i 1 90
This strained passion doth you wrong, my lord . . . . i 1 161
Unless a woman should be made an ass and a beast, to bear every knave's wrong . . . . ii 1 41
You speak as having power to do wrong . . . . . ii 1 142
An you do not make him hanged among you, the gallows shall have wrong . . . . ii 2 105
Never, O never, do his ghost the wrong! . . . . . ii 3 39
See now, whether pure fear and entire cowardice doth not make thee wrong this virtuous gentlewoman? . . . . . . ii 4 353
Do not yourself wrong : they are your likeliest men . . . iii 2 273
I have in equal balance justly weigh'd What wrongs our arms may do, what wrongs we suffer. . . . . iv 1 68
We are denied access unto his person Even by those men that most have done us wrong . . . . iv 1 79
Go to; I say he shall have no wrong. Look about . . . v 1 58
Whose wrongs give edge unto the swords That make such waste *Hen. V.* i 2 27
Certainly she did you wrong; for you were troth-plight to her . . ii 1 21
It is plain pocketing up of wrongs . . . . . . iii 2 55
If his cause be wrong, our obedience to the king wipes the crime of it out of us . . . . iv 1 138
Fight valiantly to-day : And yet I do thee wrong to mind thee of it . iv 3 13
Thou know'st little of my wrongs . . . . *1 Hen. VI.* i 3 59
How much he wrongs his fame, Despairing of his own arm's fortitude! . ii 1 16
The argument you held was wrong in you . . . . . ii 4 57
Poor gentleman! his wrong doth equal mine . . . . ii 5 22
Thou dost then wrong me, as that slaughterer doth Which giveth many wounds when one will kill . . . . ii 5 109
Those wrongs, those bitter injuries, Which Somerset hath offer'd to my house, I doubt not but with honour to redress . . . . ii 5 124
So shall his father's wrongs be recompensed . . . . iii 1 161
Prick'd on by public wrongs sustain'd in France . . . iii 2 78
I'll unto his majesty, and crave I may have liberty to venge this wrong iii 4 42
He hath done me wrong.—And I with him; for he hath done me wrong.—What is that wrong whereof you both complain? . . iv 1 85
For that which we have fled During the life, let us not wrong it dead . iv 7 50
Thy wife too! that's some wrong, indeed . . . *2 Hen. VI.* i 3 22
Thou never didst them wrong nor no man wrong . . . . iii 1 209
No other reason for this wrong But that he was bound by a solemn oath? v 1 189
Be thy title right or wrong, Lord Clifford vows to fight in thy defence *3 Hen. VI.* i 1 159
What wrong is this unto the prince your son! . . . . i 1 176
Think but upon the wrong he did us all, And that will quickly dry thy melting tears . . . . i 4 173
If that be right which Warwick says is right, There is no wrong . . ii 2 132
Whiles Warwick tells his title, smooths the wrong, Inferreth arguments iii 1 48
Herein your highness wrongs both them and me . . . . iii 2 75
Yet heavens are just, and time suppresseth wrongs . . . . iii 3 77
I will revenge his wrong to Lady Bona And replant Henry . . . iii 3 197
He hath done me wrong, And therefore I'll uncrown him ere't be long . iii 3 231
I blame not her, she could say little less; She had the wrong . . iv 1 102
They do me wrong, and I will not endure it . . . *Richard III.* i 3 42
When have I injured thee? when done thee wrong? Or thee? or thee? . i 3 56
By God's holy mother, She hath had too much wrong . . . i 3 307
But you have all the vantage of her wrong . . . . . i 3 310
I do the wrong, and first begin to brawl . . . . . i 3 324
Wrong not her birth, she is of royal blood . . . . . iv 4 211
So in the Lethe of thy angry soul Thou drown the sad remembrance of those wrongs Which thou supposest I have done to thee . . . iv 4 251
Now, by the world— 'Tis full of thy foul wrongs . . . . iv 4 374
God's wrong is most of all . . . . iv 4 377
Shall I forget myself to be myself?—Ay, if yourself's remembrance wrong yourself . . . . iv 4 421
All-Souls' day to my fearful soul Is the determined respite of my wrongs . . . . v 1 19
Wrong hath but wrong, and blame the due of blame . . . v 1 29
Awake, and think our wrongs in Richard's bosom Will conquer him! . v 3 144
Madam, you do me wrong : I have no spleen against you *Hen. VIII.* ii 4 88
If he know That I am free of your report, he knows I am not of your wrong . . . . ii 4 100
Believe me, she has had much wrong . . . . . . iii 1 48

Wrong. Madam, you wrong the king's love with these fears *Hen. VIII.* iii 1 81
Why should we, good lady, Upon what cause, wrong you? . . . iii 1 156
You wrong your virtues With these weak women's fears . . . iii 1 168
I make as little doubt, as you do conscience In doing daily wrongs . v 3 68
Right and wrong, Between whose endless jar justice resides *Tr. and Cr.* i 3 116
More conduce To the hot passion of distemper'd blood Than to make up a free determination 'Twixt right and wrong . . . . . ii 2 171
To persist In doing wrong extenuates not wrong . . . . ii 2 187
Come, come, you'll do him wrong ere you're ware . . . . iv 2 57
We go wrong, we go wrong.—No, yonder 'tis . . . . . v 1 74
Revenge Thine own particular wrongs and stop those maims Of shame *Coriolanus* iv 5 92
I ever said we were i' the wrong when we banished him . . . iv 6 156
Think'st thou it honourable for a noble man Still to remember wrongs? v 3 155
And took some pride To do myself this wrong . . . . . v 6 38
Nor wrong mine age with this indignity . . . . *T. Andron.* i 1 8
May favour Tamora . . . To quit the bloody wrongs upon her foes . i 1 141
When wert thou wont to walk alone, Dishonour'd thus, and challenged of wrongs? . . . . ii 1 340
You shall know, my boys, Your mother's hand shall right your mother's wrong . . . . ii 3 121
And swear unto my soul to right your wrongs. The vow is made . . iii 1 279
If Lucius live, he will requite your wrongs . . . . . iii 1 297
He doth me wrong to feed me with delays . . . . . . iv 3 42
Steel to the very back, Yet wrung with wrongs more than our backs can bear . . . . iv 3 48
And move the gods To send down Justice for to wreak our wrongs . iv 3 51
What wrongs are these! was ever seen An emperor in Rome thus overborne? . . . . iv 4 1
Despiteful and intolerable wrongs! Shall I endure this monstrous villany? . . . . iv 4 50
Be, as your titles witness, Imperious and impatient of your wrongs . v 1 6
I am Revenge, sent from below To join with him and right his heinous wrongs . . . . v 2 4
Show me a thousand that have done thee wrong, And I will be revenged on them all . . . . v 2 96
And they, 'twas they, that did her all this wrong . . . . v 3 58
Wrongs, unspeakable, past patience, Or more than any living man could bear . . . . v 3 126
Soft! I will go along; An if you leave me so, you do me wrong *R. and J.* i 1 202
Good pilgrim, you do wrong your hand too much . . . . i 5 99
You do yourselves Much wrong, you bate too much of your own merits *T. of Athens* i 2 212
You do yourselves but wrong to stir me up; Let me pass quietly . . iii 4 53
And make his wrongs His outsides, to wear them like his raiment, carelessly . . . . iii 5 32
If wrongs be evils and enforce us kill, What folly 'tis to hazard life for ill! . . . . iii 5 36
'Tis honour with most lands to be at odds; Soldiers should brook as little wrongs as gods . . . . iii 5 117
Thus much of this [gold] will make black white, foul fair, Wrong right . iv 3 29
Ay, even such heaps and sums of love and wealth As shall to thee blot out what wrongs were theirs . . . . v 1 156
Now breathless wrong Shall sit and pant in your great chairs of ease . v 4 10
Old feeble carrions and such suffering souls That welcome wrongs *J. C.* ii 1 131
Know, Cæsar doth not wrong, nor without cause Will he be satisfied . iii 1 47
Pity to the general wrong of Rome—As fire drives out fire, so pity pity—Hath done this deed on Cæsar . . . . iii 1 170
It shall advantage more than do us wrong . . . . . . iii 1 242
If thou consider rightly of the matter, Cæsar has had great wrong . iii 2 115
If I were disposed to stir Your hearts and minds to mutiny and rage, I should do Brutus wrong, and Cassius wrong . . . . . iii 2 128
I will not do them wrong; I rather choose To wrong the dead, to wrong myself and you, Than I will wrong such honourable men . . . iii 2 130
I fear I wrong the honourable men Whose daggers have stabb'd Cæsar . iii 2 156
You have done me wrong.—Judge me, you gods! wrong I mine enemies? And, if not so, how should I wrong a brother? . . . . . iv 2 37
This sober form of yours hides wrongs . . . . . . iv 2 40
You wrong me every way; you wrong me, Brutus . . . . iv 3 55
I will not do thee so much wrong to wake thee . . . . iv 3 270
Wear thou thy wrongs; The title is affeer'd! . . . . *Macbeth* iv 3 33
We do it wrong, being so majestical, To offer it the show of violence *Hamlet* i 1 143
Their writers do them wrong, to make them exclaim against their own succession . . . . ii 2 367
The oppressor's wrong, the proud man's contumely . . . . iii 1 71
I've done you wrong; But pardon't, as you are a gentleman . . . v 2 237
If Hamlet from himself be ta'en away, And when he's not himself does wrong Laertes, Then Hamlet does it not . . . . . . v 2 246
I do receive your offer'd love like love, And will not wrong it . . v 2 263
Some villain hath done me wrong.—That's my fear . . . *Lear* i 2 180
By day and night he wrongs me . . . . i 3 3
I did her wrong . . . . i 5 25
He'll not feel wrongs Which tie him to an answer . . . . iv 2 13
Milk-liver'd man! That bear'st a cheek for blows, a head for wrongs . iv 2 51
You do me wrong to take me out o' the grave . . . . . iv 7 45
Your sisters Have, as I do remember, done me wrong : You have some cause . . . . iv 7 74
If this be known to you and your allowance, We then have done you bold and saucy wrongs . . . . *Othello* i 1 129
My brothers of the state Cannot but feel this wrong as 'twere their own i 2 97
That being anger'd, her revenge being nigh, Bade her wrong stay . ii 1 154
Yet, I persuade myself, to speak the truth Shall nothing wrong him . ii 3 224
Though Cassio did some little wrong to him, As men in rage strike those that wish them best . . . . ii 3 242
What, If I had said I had seen him do you wrong? Or heard him say . iv 1 24
His unbookish jealousy must construe Poor Cassio's smiles, gestures, and light behaviour, Quite in the wrong . . . . . . iv 1 104
Impudent strumpet!—By heaven, you do me wrong . . . . iv 2 81
Beshrew me, if I would do such a wrong For the whole world.—Why, the wrong is but a wrong i' the world; and having the world for your labour, 'tis a wrong in your own world, and you might quickly make it right . . . . iv 3 78
Honest and just, That hast such noble sense of thy friend's wrong! . v 1 32
You wrong this presence; therefore speak no more *Ant. and Cleo.* ii 2 111
Do not yourself such wrong, who are in this Relieved, but not betray'd v 2 40
I never do him wrong, But he does buy my injuries, to be friends *Cymb.* i 1 104
The wrongs he did me Were nothing prince-like . . . . . v 5 292
To lop that doubt, he'll fill this land with arms, And make pretence of wrong that I have done him . . . . *Pericles* i 2 91

Wrong. I do not doubt thy faith; But should he wrong my liberties in my absence? *Pericles* i 2 112
Wrong not your prince you love.—Wrong not yourself, then ii 4 25
I think thou said'st Thou hadst been toss'd from wrong to injury v 1 131
Wrong belief. For that she's in a wrong belief, I go to certify her *1 Hen. VI.* ii 3 31
Wrong imaginations. And woes by wrong imaginations lose The knowledge of themselves *Lear* iv 6 290
Wrong-incensed. Between these swelling wrong-incensed peers *Rich. III.* ii 1 51
Wrong led. We perceived, both how you were wrong led, And we in negligent danger *Ant. and Cleo.* iii 6 80
Wrong places. I have directed you to wrong places *Mer. Wives* iii 1 110
Wrong rebuke. But if you know not this, my manners tell me We have your wrong rebuke *Othello* i 1 131
Wrong side. So turns she every man the wrong side out *Much Ado* iii 1 68
How quickly the wrong side may be turned outward! *T. Night* iii 1 14
Call'd me sot, And told me I had turn'd the wrong side out *Lear* iv 2 9
Whom love hath turn'd almost the wrong side out *Othello* ii 3 54
Wrong surmise. By false intelligence, or wrong surmise *Richard III.* ii 1 54
Wrong thought. When false opinion, whose wrong thought defiles thee, In thy just proof, repeals and reconciles thee *Lear* iii 6 119
Wronged. Behold, sir king, The wronged Duke of Milan *Tempest* v 1 107
He hath wronged me, Master Page.—Sir, he doth in some sort confess it *Mer. Wives* i 1 105
He hath wronged me; indeed he hath; at a word, he hath, believe me: Robert Shallow, esquire, saith, he is wronged i 1 108
He hath wronged me in some humours ii 1 133
Love you the man that wrong'd you?—Yes, as I love the woman that wrong'd him *Meas. for Meas.* ii 3 24
You may most uprighteously do a poor wronged lady a merited benefit iii 1 206
We shall advise this wronged maid to stead up your appointment iii 1 260
Vail your regard Upon a wrong'd, I would fain have said, a maid! v 1 21
As I, thus wrong'd, hence unbelieved go! v 1 119
Whose salt imagination yet hath wrong'd Your well defended honour v 1 406
Is any woman wrong'd by this lewd fellow, . . . let her appear v 1 515
She, Claudio, that you wrong'd, look you restore v 1 531
Most mighty duke, behold a man much wrong'd *Com. of Errors* v 1 330
The gentleman that danced with her told her she is much wronged by you *Much Ado* ii 1 245
Tell him that he hath wronged his honour in marrying ii 2 23
Surely I do believe your fair cousin is wronged iv 1 262
She is wronged, she is slandered, she is undone iv 1 314
Think you in your soul the Count Claudio hath wronged Hero? iv 1 332
Thou hast so wrong'd mine innocent child and me v 1 63
Did ever keep your counsels, never wrong'd you *M. N. Dream* iii 2 308
Let me see wherein My tongue hath wrong'd him *As Y. Like It* ii 7 84
That you may well perceive I have not wrong'd you *All's Well* iv 4 1
Never was man thus wronged *T. Night* iv 2 32
Being wrong'd as we are by this peevish town *K. John* ii 1 402
My kinsman, whom the king hath wrong'd, Whom conscience and my kindred bids to right *Richard II.* ii 2 114
When we are wrong'd and would unfold our griefs, We are denied access unto his person *2 Hen. IV.* iv 1 77
I will subscribe and say I wrong'd the duke *2 Hen. VI.* iii 1 38
If ever lady wrong'd her lord so much iii 2 211
And ne'er was Agamemnon's brother wrong'd By that false woman, as this king by thee *3 Hen. VI.* ii 2 148
So thrive I . . . , As I intend more good to you and yours Than ever you or yours were by me wrong'd! *Richard III.* iv 4 238
Swear then by something that thou hast not wrong'd iv 4 373
The time to come.—That thou hast wronged in the time o'erpast iv 4 388
I myself have many tears to wash Hereafter time, for time past wrong'd by thee iv 4 390
The wronged souls Of butcher'd princes fight in thy behalf v 3 121
The wronged heirs of York do pray for thee: Good angels guard thy battle! v 3 137
The prayers of holy saints and wronged souls, Like high-rear'd bulwarks, stand before our faces v 3 241
Lord Titus here Is in opinion and in honour wrong'd *T. Andron.* i 1 416
Wert thou thus surprised, sweet girl, Ravish'd and wrong'd? iv 1 52
Beguiled, divorced, wronged, spited, slain! *Rom. and Jul.* iv 5 55
Decius Brutus loves thee not: thou hast wronged Caius Ligarius *J. C.* ii 3 5
That you have wrong'd me doth appear in this iv 3 1
You wrong'd yourself to write in such a case iv 3 6
Was't Hamlet wrong'd Laertes? Never Hamlet *Hamlet* v 2 244
Hamlet is of the faction that is wrong'd; His madness is poor Hamlet's enemy v 2 249
My duty cannot be silent when I think your highness wronged *Lear* i 4 71
Say you have wrong'd her, sir.—Ask her forgiveness? ii 4 154
I am no less in blood . . . ; If more, the more thou hast wrong'd me v 3 168
Thou dost conspire against thy friend, Iago, If thou but think'st him wrong'd and makest his ear A stranger to thy thoughts *Othello* iii 3 143
Witness that here Iago doth give up The execution of his wit, hands, heart, To wrong'd Othello's service! iii 3 467
Men's reports Give him much wrong'd *Ant. and Cleo.* iii 4 40
Where is he now?—My lord, in Athens.—No, my most wronged sister iii 6 65
Wronger. If you would know your wronger, look on me *Much Ado* v 1 272
That cuckold lives in bliss Who, certain of his fate, loves not his wronger *Othello* iii 3 168
Not the wronger Of her or you, having proceeded but By both your wills *Cymbeline* ii 4 54
Wrongest. Thou wrong'st thyself, if thou shouldst strive to choose *All's Well* ii 3 153
Now, by God's will, thou wrong'st him *1 Hen. VI.* ii 4 82
How much thou wrong'st me, heaven be my judge *2 Hen. VI.* iv 10 82
Wrongest. Therein thou wrong'st thy children mightily *3 Hen. VI.* iii 2 74
Thou wrong'st it, more than tears, with that report *Rom. and Jul.* iv 1 32
Thou wrong'st a gentleman, who is as far From thy report as thou from honour *Cymbeline* i 6 145
Wrongful. I despise thee for thy wrongful suit *T. G. of Ver.* iv 2 102
In wrongful quarrel you have slain your son *T. Andron.* i 1 293
Wrongfully. First, hath this woman Most wrongfully accused your substitute *Meas. for Meas.* v 1 140
He had received a thousand ducats of Don John for accusing the Lady Hero wrongfully *Much Ado* iv 2 51
The which if wrongfully, Let heaven revenge *Richard II.* i 2 39
If you do wrongfully seize Hereford's rights, Call in the letters patents ii 1 201
This poor fellow, Which he had thought to have murder'd wrongfully *2 Hen. VI.* ii 3 107
Have by my means been butcher'd wrongfully! *T. Andron.* iv 4 55
Over-heard them say . . . That Lucius' banishment was wrongfully iv 4 76
Wronging the ancientry, stealing, fighting *W. Tale* iii 3 62
Wrongly. Wouldst not play false, And yet wouldst wrongly win *Macbeth* i 5 23
Wrote. I wrote the letter that thy father found *T. Andron.* v 1 106
I sat me down, Devised a new commission, wrote it fair *Hamlet* v 2 32
Wilt thou know The effect of what I wrote? v 2 37
I hope, for my brother's justification, he wrote this but as an essay or taste of my virtue *Lear* i 2 47
He hath wrote this to feel my affection to your honour i 2 93
Not resting here, accuses him of letters he had formerly wrote *Ant. and Cleo.* iii 5 11
My emperor hath wrote, I must from hence *Cymbeline* iii 5 2
Lucius hath wrote already to the emperor How it goes here iii 5 21
I heard no letter from my master since I wrote him iv 3 37
Wroth. I'll keep my oath, Patiently to bear my wroth *Mer. of Venice* ii 9 78
Wrought. If my brother wrought by my pity, it should not be so with him *Meas. for Meas.* iii 2 222
His friends still wrought reprieves for him iv 2 140
That the world may witness that my end Was wrought by nature *Com. of Errors* i 1 35
As his wise mother wrought in his behalf *Mer. of Venice* i 3 74
Love wrought these miracles *T. of Shrew* v 1 127
If I had thought the sight of my poor image Would thus have wrought you,—for the stone is mine—I'ld not have show'd it *W. Tale* v 3 58
'Tis wonderful What may be wrought out of their discontent *K. John* iii 4 179
The best I had, a princess wrought it me iv 1 43
And those thy fears might have wrought fears in me iv 2 236
Of noble Gloucester's death, Who wrought it with the king *Richard II.* iv 1 4
Thou hast wrought A deed of slander with thy fatal hand Upon my head v 6 34
Knew that we ventured on such dangerous seas That if we wrought out life 'twas ten to one; And yet we ventured *2 Hen. IV.* i 1 182
The incessant care and labour of his mind Hath wrought the mure that should confine it in So thin that life looks through iv 4 119
Whatsoever cunning fiend it was That wrought upon thee *Hen. V.* ii 2 112
Hath the late overthrow wrought this offence? Be not dismay'd *1 Hen. VI.* i 2 49
That damned sorceress Hath wrought this hellish mischief unawares iii 2 39
The greatest miracle that e'er ye wrought v 4 66
O, let me view his visage, being dead, That living wrought me such exceeding trouble *2 Hen VI.* v 1 70
Many moe proud birds Have wrought the easy-melting king like wax *3 Hen. VI.* ii 1 171
Without the king's assent or knowledge, You wrought to be a legate *Hen. VIII.* iii 2 311
Hath beside well in his person wrought To be set high in place *Coriol.* iii 3 254
Chance of war hath wrought this change of cheer *T. Andron.* i 1 264
Grief has so wrought on him, He takes false shadows for true substances iii 2 79
Doth she not count her blest, Unworthy as she is, that we have wrought So worthy a gentleman to be her bridegroom? *Rom. and Jul.* iii 5 145
Took effect As I intended, for it wrought on her The form of death v 3 245
Wrought he not well that painted it?—He wrought better that made the painter; and yet he's but a filthy piece of work *T. of Athens* i 1 200
Thy honourable metal may be wrought From that it is disposed *J. Cæsar* i 2 313
My dull brain was wrought With things forgotten *Macbeth* i 3 149
Our will became the servant to defect; Which else should free have wrought ii 1 19
How you were borne in hand, how cross'd, the instruments, Who wrought with them iii 1 82
Great business must be wrought ere noon iii 5 22
My point and period will be throughly wrought, Or well or ill, as this day's battle's fought *Lear* iv 7 97
With some dram conjured to this effect He wrought upon her *Othello* i 3 106
There he dropp'd it for a special purpose Which wrought to his desire v 2 323
Of one not easily jealous, but being wrought Perplex'd in the extreme v 2 345
Which I wonder'd Could be so rarely and exactly wrought *Cymbeline* ii 4 75
Wrung. With affection wondrous sensible He wrung Bassanio's hand *Mer. of Venice* ii 8 49
Poor jade, is wrung in the withers out of all cess *1 Hen. IV.* ii 1 7
Thy place is fill'd, thy sceptre wrung from thee *3 Hen. VI.* iii 1 16
Yet wrung with wrongs more than our backs can bear *T. Andron.* iv 3 48
He hath, my lord, wrung from me my slow leave By laboursome petition *Hamlet* i 2 58
Wrying. How many Must murder wives much better than themselves For wrying but a little! *Cymbeline* v 1 5
Wry-necked. The vile squealing of the wry-neck'd fife *Mer. of Venice* ii 5 30
Wye. Thrice from the banks of Wye And sandy-bottom'd Severn have I sent him Bootless home *1 Hen. IV.* iii 1 65
There is also moreover a river at Monmouth: it is called Wye at Monmouth *Hen. V.* iv 7 29
All the water in Wye cannot wash your majesty's Welsh plood out of your pody iv 7 111

X

Xanthippe. As curst and shrewd As Socrates' Xanthippe *T. of Shrew* i 2 71

Y

Yard. On the topmast, The yards, and bowsprit, would I flame *Tempest* i 2 200
I will tell you what I am about.—Two yards, and more . *Mer. Wives* i 3 44
I am in the waist two yards about: but I am now about no waste . i 3 46
Loves her by the foot.—He may not by the yard . *L. L. Lost* v 2 676
Thou yard, three-quarters, half-yard, quarter, nail! *T. of Shrew* iv 3 109
Away, thou rag, thou quantity, thou remnant; Or I shall so be-mete thee with thy yard! . . . . iv 3 113
Eight yards of uneven ground is threescore and ten miles afoot with me; and the stony-hearted villains know it . . . . 1 *Hen. IV.* ii 2 26
A' should have sent me two and twenty yards of satin . 2 *Hen. IV.* i 2 50
The duke, look you, is digt himself four yard under the countermines *Hen. V.* iii 2 66
It is written, that the shoemaker should meddle with his yard *R. and J.* i 2 40
I will delve one yard below their mines, And blow them at the moon *Hamlet* iii 4 208
That fellow handles his bow like a crow-keeper: draw me a clothier's yard . . . . *Lear* iv 6 89
Yare. Cheerly, cheerly, my hearts! yare, yare! Take in the topsail *Temp.* i 1 7
Down with the topmast! yare! lower, lower! . . . i 1 37
Our ship . . . Is tight and yare and bravely rigg'd v 1 224
I do desire to learn, sir: and I hope, if you have occasion to use me for your own turn, you shall find me yare *Meas. for Meas.* iv 2 61
Be yare in thy preparation, for thy assailant is quick, skilful *T. Night* iii 4 244
Their ships are yare; yours, heavy: no disgrace Shall fall you *A. and C.* iii 7 39
Like A halter'd neck which does the hangman thank For being yare about him . . . . iii 13 131
Yare, yare, good Iras; quick. Methinks I hear Antony call . v 2 286
Yarely. Fall to't, yarely, or we run ourselves aground . *Tempest* i 1 4
Those flower-soft hands, That yarely frame the office . *Ant. and Cleo.* ii 2 216
Yarn. The web of our life is of a mingled yarn . *All's Well* iv 3 84
You would be another Penelope: yet, they say, all the yarn she spun in Ulysses' absence did but fill Ithaca full of moths *Coriolanus* i 3 93
Yaughan. Go, get thee to Yaughan: fetch me a stoup of liquor *Hamlet* v 1 68
Yaw. And yet but yaw neither, in respect of his quick sail . v 2 120
Yawn. Graves, yawn and yield your dead, Till death be uttered *Much Ado* v 3 19
Kisses the gashes That bloodily did yawn upon his face *Hen. V.* iv 6 14
To show bare heads In congregations, to yawn, be still, and wonder *Cor.* iii 2 11
When churchyards yawn and hell itself breathes out Contagion *Hamlet* iii 2 407
And that the affrighted globe Should yawn at alteration *Othello* v 2 101
Yawned. Graves have yawn'd, and yielded up their dead *J. Cæsar* ii 2 18
Yawning. Delivering o'er to executors pale The lazy yawning drone *Hen. V.* i 2 204
Now will I dam up this thy yawning mouth 2 *Hen. VI.* iv 1 73
Ere to black Hecate's summons The shard-borne beetle with his drowsy hums Hath rung night's yawning peal *Macbeth* iii 2 43
Y-clad. Her words y-clad with wisdom's majesty . 2 *Hen. VI.* i 1 33
Ycleped. It is ycleped thy park . . *L. L. Lost* i 1 242
Judas I am, ycliped Maccabæus v 2 602
Ye. A south-west blow on ye And blister you all o'er! . *Tempest* i 2 323
Ye elves of hills, brooks, standing lakes, and groves v 1 33
Bring forth a wonder, to content ye As much as me v 1 170
Yet he, of all the rest, I think, best loves ye *T. G. of Ver.* i 2 28
Will ye be gone?—That you may ruminate i 2 49
Are all these things perceived in me?—They are all perceived without ye ii 1 35
Stand, sir, and throw us that you have about ye iv 1 3
And love you 'gainst the nature of love,—force ye . v 4 58
Therefore, I promise ye, I fear you *Mer. of Venice* iii 5 3
God ye good even, William.—And good even to you, sir . *As Y. Like It* v 1 16
Fortunate mistress,—let my prophecy Come home to ye! *W. Tale* iv 4 663
But my love to ye Shall show itself more openly hereafter 2 *Hen. IV.* iv 2 75
This shall ye do, so help you righteous God! 1 *Hen. VI.* iv 1 8
Now help, ye charming spells and periapts; And ye choice spirits v 3 2
Ye familiar spirits, that are cull'd Out of the powerful regions under earth . . . . v 3 10
My Lord of Gloucester, now ye grow too hot . 2 *Hen. VI.* i 1 137
'Tis my presence that doth trouble ye . . . i 1 141
Give me my fan: what, minion! can ye not? I cry you mercy . i 3 141
Can you not see? or will ye not observe? . . . . iii 1 4
By heaven, brat, I'll plague ye for that word . . 3 *Hen. VI.* v 5 27
I tell ye all I am your better, traitors as ye are . . v 5 35
Didst thou not kill this king?—I grant ye *Richard III.* i 2 101
Look out there, some of ye *Hen. VIII.* i 4 50
The more shame for ye: holy men I thought ye . . iii 1 102
Therein, ye gods, you make the weak most strong *J. Cæsar* i 3 91
Are ye fantastical, or that indeed Which outwardly ye show? *Macbeth* i 3 53
I never loved you much; but I ha' praised ye . *Ant. and Cleo.* ii 6 78
Yea. Canst thou bring me to the party?—Yea, yea, my lord *Tempest* iii 2 68
The great globe itself, Yea, all which it inherit, shall dissolve iv 1 154
I thank you; by yea and no, I do . . *Mer. Wives* i 1 88
The very yea and the no is . . . . . i 4 98
By yea and no, I think the 'oman is a witch indeed. . iv 2 202
Did not I tell thee yea? hadst thou not order? . *Meas. for Meas.* ii 2 8
Yea, dost thou jeer and flout me in the teeth? . *Com. of Errors* ii 2 22
Mightst thou perceive . . . That he did plead in earnest? yea or no? . iv 2 3
By yea and nay, sir, then I swore in jest . . *L. L. Lost* i 1 54
My wooing mind shall be express'd In russet yeas and honest kersey noes . . . . v 2 413
Thine, by yea and no, which is as much as to say, as thou usest him 2 *Hen. IV.* ii 2 142
By yea and nay, sir, I dare say my cousin William is become a good scholar . . . . iii 2 10
Ask those on the banks If they were his assistants, yea or no *Richard III.* iv 4 526
Where gentry, title, wisdom, Cannot conclude but by the yea and no Of general ignorance . . . . . *Coriolanus* iii 1 145
Let me commend thee first to those that shall Say yea to thy desires . iv 5 151
Yea, is it come to this? Let it be so *Lear* i 4 326
Yead. Cost me two shilling and two pence a-piece of Yead Miller *M. Wives* i 1 160
Yea-forsooth. A rascally yea-forsooth knave! . 2 *Hen. IV.* i 2 41
Year. Then thou wast not Out three years old . . *Tempest* i 2 41
Twelve year since, Miranda, twelve year since, Thy father was the Duke i 2 53
Thou didst promise To bate me a full year . . . i 2 250
Imprison'd thou didst painfully remain A dozen years . . i 2 279
His years but young, but his experience old . . *T. G. of Ver.* ii 4 69

Year. That I do; and have done any time these three hundred years *Mer. Wives* i 1 13
Her grandsire . . . give, when she is able to overtake seventeen years old . . . . i 1 55
I have lived fourscore years and upward . . . iii 1 56
O, what a world of vile ill-favour'd faults Looks handsome in three hundred pounds a-year! . . . . iii 4 33
Three thousand dolours a year.—Ay, and more . . *Meas. for Meas.* i 2 50
Which for this nineteen years we have let slip . . i 3 21
A man of fourscore pound a year . . . . ii 1 128
Are you of fourscore pounds a year?—Yes, an't please you, sir . ii 1 204
Hang all that offend that way but for ten year together . ii 1 252
If this law hold in Vienna ten year, I'll rent the fairest house in it . ii 1 254
How long have you been in this place of constable?—Seven year and a half . . . . ii 1 274
You say, seven years together?—And a half, sir . . ii 1 277
A bawd of eleven years' continuance, may it please your honour . iii 2 208
His child is a year and a quarter old, come Philip and Jacob . iii 2 213
Compound with him by the year, and let him abide here with you . iv 2 25
One that is a prisoner nine years old . . . iv 2 135
A most notorious pirate, A man of Claudio's years . . iv 3 76
And five years since there was some speech of marriage . . v 1 217
Since which time of five years I never spake with her, saw her . v 1 222
My youngest boy . . . At eighteen years became inquisitive *Com. of Er.* i 1 126
Her sober virtue, years, and modesty, Plead on her part . iii 1 90
I buy a thousand pound a year: I buy a rope . . . iv 1 21
Hast thou so crack'd and splitted my poor tongue In seven short years? v 1 309
Seven years since, in Syracusa, boy, Thou know'st we parted . v 1 320
Twenty years Have I been patron to Antipholus . . v 1 326
Thirty-three years have I but gone in travail Of you, my sons . v 1 400
I think I told your lordship a year since . *Much Ado* ii 2 12
I know that Deformed; a' has been a vile thief this seven year . iii 3 134
Dost thou not suspect my place? dost thou not suspect my years? . iv 2 77
Have sworn for three years' term to live with me . *L. L. Lost* i 1 16
'Tis but a three years' fast: The mind shall banquet, though the body pine . . . . i 1 24
I have already sworn, That is, to live and study here three years . i 1 35
I only swore to study with your grace And stay here in your court for three years' space . . . . i 1 52
I'll keep what I have swore And bide the penance of each three years' day . . . . i 1 115
If any man be seen to talk with a woman within the term of three years i 1 131
All forsworn Three thousand times within this three years' space . i 1 151
And so to study, three years is but short . . . i 1 181
It was proclaimed a year's imprisonment, to be taken with a wench . i 1 289
I have promised to study three years with the duke.—You may do it in an hour . . . . i 2 37
And how easy it is to put 'years' to the word 'three,' and study three years in two words . . . . i 2 55
Navarre hath made a vow, Till painful study shall outwear three years ii 1 23
Go, tenderness of years . . . . . . iii 1 4
If thou marry, Hang me by the neck, if horns that year miscarry . iv 1 114
For he hath been five thousand years a boy . . . v 2 11
That smiles his cheek in years and knows the trick To make my lady laugh . . . . v 2 465
At the expiration of the year, Come challenge me . . v 2 814
To hold the plough for her sweet love three years . . v 2 894
Or else misgraffed in respect of years . . . *M. N. Dream* i 1 137
Nor is my whole estate Upon the fortune of this present year *M. of Ven.* i 1 44
Well, keep me company but two years moe, Thou shalt not know the sound of thine own tongue . . . . i 1 108
Falling out that year on Ash-Wednesday was four year, in the afternoon ii 5 26
Out upon it, old carrion! rebels it at these years? . . iii 1 39
Let his lack of years be no impediment to let him lack a reverend estimation . . . . iv 1 162
Young gentleman, your spirits are too bold for your years *As Y. Like It* i 2 184
From seventeen years till now almost fourscore Here lived I . ii 3 71
At seventeen years many their fortunes seek; But at fourscore it is too late . . . . ii 3 73
I'll rhyme you so eight years together . . . iii 2 101
Time's pace is so hard that it seems the length of seven year . iii 2 335
Sweet youth, I pray you, chide a year together . . iii 5 64
He is not very tall; yet for his years he's tall: His leg is but so so iii 5 118
The poor world is almost six thousand years old . . iv 1 95
Leander, he would have lived many a fair year, though Hero had turned nun, if it had not been for a hot midsummer night . . iv 1 101
I know you by description; Such garments and such years . iv 3 86
I have, since I was three year old, conversed with a magician . v 2 66
Who for this seven years hath esteemed him No better than a poor and loathsome beggar . . . . . . *T. of Shrew* Ind. 1 122
These fifteen years you have been in a dream . . .—These fifteen years! by my fay, a goodly nap. But did I never speak of all that time? Ind. 2 81
I have dream'd And slept above some fifteen year or more . Ind. 2 115
Myself am struck in years, I must confess . . . ii 1 362
Besides two thousand ducats by the year Of fruitful land . . ii 1 371
Two thousand ducats by the year of land! My land amounts not to so much in all . . . . ii 1 374
Near twenty years ago, in Genoa, Where we were lodgers at the Pegasus iv 4 4
I have brought him up ever since he was three years old . v 1 86
Within ten year it will make itself ten, which is a goodly increase *All's Well* i 1 159
Would God would serve the world so all the year! . . i 3 88
And kept a coil with 'Too young' and 'the next year' and ''tis too early' ii 1 28
In her sex, her years, profession, Wisdom, and constancy, hath amazed me. . . . . ii 1 86
The element itself, till seven years' heat, Shall not behold her face *T. N.* i 1 26
Why, he has three thousand ducats a year.—Ay, but he'll have but a year in all these ducats . . . . i 3 23
She'll not match above her degree, neither in estate, years, nor wit i 3 116
They shall yet belie thy happy years, That say thou art a man . i 4 30
Of what personage and years is he?—Not yet old enough for a man, nor young enough for a boy . . . . i 5 164
What years, i' faith?—About your years, my lord.—Too old . ii 4 28

Year. These wise men that give fools money get themselves a good report—after fourteen years' purchase . . . . . *T. Night* iv 1 24
Grew a twenty years removed thing While one would wink . . v 1 92
And died that day when Viola from her birth Had number'd thirteen years . . . . v 1 252
He finished indeed his mortal act That day that made my sister thirteen years . . . . v 1 255
Looking on the lines Of my boy's face, methoughts I did recoil Twenty-three years, and saw myself unbreech'd . . . . *W. Tale* i 2 155
A thousand knees Ten thousand years together, naked, fasting . iii 2 212
I slide O'er sixteen years and leave the growth untried . . . iv 1 6
It is fifteen years since I saw my country . . . . . iv 2 4
Heigh! the doxy over the dale, Why, then comes in the sweet o' the year . . . . iv 3 3
The year growing ancient, Not yet on summer's death . . . iv 4 79
There shall not at your father's house these seven years Be born another such . . . . iv 4 589
The gods do this year connive at us, and we may do any thing extempore iv 4 691
A piece many years in doing and now newly performed . . . v 2 104
Which lets go by some sixteen years and makes her As she lived now . v 3 31
Make me to think so twenty years together! . . . . . v 3 71
Shall I draw the curtain?—No, not these twenty years . . . v 3 84
A' pops me out At least from fair five hundred pound a year . *K. John* i 1 69
Your face hath got five hundred pound a year . . . . . i 1 152
Look upon the years Of Lewis the Dauphin and that lovely maid . ii 1 424
Many years of happy days befal My gracious sovereign! . *Richard II.* i 1 20
All the treasons for these eighteen years Complotted . . . i 1 95
My companion peers, Take from my mouth the wish of happy years . i 3 94
The language I have learn'd these forty years, My native English, now I must forego . . . . i 3 159
I am too old to fawn upon a nurse, Too far in years to be a pupil now i 3 171
Thy sad aspect Hath from the number of his banish'd years Pluck'd four away . . . . i 3 210
In regard of me He shortens four years of my son's exile . . i 3 217
Ere the six years that he hath to spend Can change their moons . i 3 219
Thou hast many years to live.—But not a minute, king, that thou canst give . . . . i 3 225
Six years we banish him, and he shall go . . . . . i 3 248
Would the word 'farewell' have lengthen'd hours And added years to his short banishment, He should have had a volume . . . i 4 17
Which, till my infant fortune comes to years, Stands for my bounty ii 3 66
We at time of year Do wound the bark, the skin of our fruit-trees . iii 4 57
His captain, steward, deputy-elect, Anointed, crowned, planted many years . . . . iv 1 127
And send him many years of sunshine days! . . . . . iv 1 221
I see some sparks of better hope, which elder years May happily bring forth . . . . v 3 21
Those blessed feet Which fourteen hundred years ago were nail'd For our advantage on the bitter cross . . . . *1 Hen. IV.* i 1 26
If all the year were playing holidays, To sport would be as tedious as to work . . . . i 2 228
I have forsworn his company hourly any time this two and twenty years ii 2 17
How long hast thou to serve, Francis?—Forsooth, five years . . ii 4 46
I did that I did not this seven year before, I blushed . . . ii 4 343
Villain, thou stolest a cup of sack eighteen years ago . . . ii 4 346
When I was about thy years, Hal, I was not an eagle's talon in the waist . . . . ii 4 363
That grey iniquity, that father ruffian, that vanity in years . . ii 4 500
And, being no more in debt to years than thou, Leads ancient lords . iii 2 103
Any time this two and thirty years . . . . . . iii 3 54
Whiles the big year, swoln with some other grief, Is thought with child by the stern tyrant war . . . . . . *2 Hen. IV.* Ind. 13
Is it not strange that desire should so many years outlive performance? ii 4 284
Saturn and Venus this year in conjunction! what says the almanac to that? . . . . ii 4 286
I have known thee these twenty nine years, come peascod-time . ii 4 413
'Tis not ten years gone Since . . . . iii 1 57
In two years after Were they at wars: it is but eight years since This Percy was the man nearest my soul . . . . . iii 1 59
You like well and bear your years very well . . . . . iii 2 92
That's fifty-five year ago . . . . iii 2 224
Let it go which way it will, he that dies this year is quit for the next iii 2 254
As the year Had found some months asleep and leap'd them over . iv 4 123
It hath been prophesied to me many years, I should not die but in Jerusalem . . . . iv 5 237
I have served your worship truly, sir, this eight years . . . v 1 52
We will eat a last year's pippin of my own graffing . . . v 3 2
Do nothing but eat, and make good cheer, And praise God for the merry year . . . . v 3 19
I will lay odds that, ere this year expire, We bear our civil swords and native fire As far as France . . . . . . v 5 111
Turning the accomplishment of many years Into an hour-glass *Hen. V.* Prol. 30
In the eleventh year of the last king's reign . . . . . i 1 2
A thousand pounds by the year: thus runs the bill . . . . i 1 19
Four hundred one and twenty years After defunction of King Pharamond i 2 57
Who died within the year of our redemption Four hundred twenty-six i 2 60
Charles the Great subdued the Saxons, and did seat the French Beyond the river Sala, in the year Eight hundred five . . . . i 2 63
The patterns that by God and by French fathers Had twenty years been made . . . . ii 4 62
And follows so the ever-running year, With profitable labour, to his grave . . . . iv 1 293
Ne'er throughout the year to church thou go'st . . *1 Hen. VI.* i 1 42
Posterity, await for wretched years . . . . . . i 1 48
I myself fight not once in forty year . . . . . . i 3 91
That hast by tyranny these many years Wasted our country . . i 3 40
Would some part of my young years Might but redeem the passage of your age! . . . . ii 5 107
My tender years can tell Civil dissension is a viperous worm . . iii 1 71
O, think upon the conquest of my father, My tender years! . . iv 1 149
This seven years did not Talbot see his son; And now they meet where both their lives are done . . . . iv 3 37
Marriage, uncle! alas, my years are young! And fitter is my study . v 1 21
I saw not better sport these seven years' day . . *2 Hen. VI.* ii 1 2
I see no reason why a king of years Should be to be protected like a child . . . . ii 3 28
Nothing but claret wine this first year of our reign . . . iv 6 5
If I might have a lease of my life for a thousand years I could stay no longer . . . . iv 10 6
I would break a thousand oaths to reign one year . . *3 Hen. VI.* i 2 17

Year. How many days will finish up the year; How many years a mortal man may live . . . . *3 Hen. VI.* ii 5 28
So many years ere I shall shear the fleece . . . . . ii 5 37
So minutes, hours, days, months, and years, Pass'd over to the end they were created, Would bring white hairs unto a quiet grave . ii 5 38
But for the rest, you tell a pedigree Of threescore and two years . iii 3 93
Canst thou speak against thy liege, Whom thou obeyed'st thirty and six years? . . . . iii 3 96
Even in the downfall of his mellow'd years . . . . . iii 3 104
Well struck in years, fair, and not jealous . . . *Richard III.* i 1 92
In his nonage council under him, And in his full and ripen'd years himself, No doubt, shall then and till then, govern well . . ii 3 14
He could gnaw a crust at two hours old: 'Twas full two years ere I could get a tooth . . . . ii 4 29
The untainted virtue of your years Hath not yet dived into the world's deceit . . . . iii 1 7
Eighty odd years of sorrow have I seen . . . . . . iv 1 96
Make bold her bashful years with your experience . . . . iv 4 326
Can make seem pleasing to her tender years . . . . . iv 4 342
May he live Longer than I have time to tell his years! . *Hen. VIII.* ii 1 91
That, like a jewel, has hung twenty years About his neck . . ii 2 32
A thousand pound a year, annual support, Out of his grace he adds . ii 3 64
I have been begging sixteen years in court, Am yet a courtier beggarly ii 3 82
A thousand pounds a year for pure respect! No other obligation! . ii 3 95
I have been your wife, in this obedience, Upward of twenty years . ii 4 36
The wisest prince that there had reign'd by many A year before . ii 4 50
Hector shall not have his wit this year . . . *Troi. and Cres.* i 2 92
After seven years' siege yet Troy walls stand . . . . i 3 12
Lend you him I will For half a hundred years . . . *Coriolanus* i 4 7
A letter for me! it gives me an estate of seven years' health . . ii 1 126
At sixteen years . . . he fought Beyond the mark of others . . ii 2 91
Thou hast years upon thee; and thou art too full Of the wars' surfeits iv 1 45
If I could shake off but one seven years From these old arms and legs, by the good gods, I'ld with thee every foot . . . . iv 1 55
Ten years are spent since first he undertook This cause of Rome *T. Andron.* i 1 31
Rome, I have been thy soldier forty years . . . . . i 1 193
This monument five hundred years hath stood . . . . . i 1 350
Thy years want wit, thy wit wants edge, And manners . . . ii 1 26
'Tis not the difference of a year or two Makes me less gracious . ii 1 31
My child is yet a stranger in the world; She hath not seen the change of fourteen years . . . . *Rom. and Jul.* i 2 9
Now, by my maidenhead, at twelve year old, I bade her come . . i 3 2
Of all days in the year, Come Lammas-eve at night shall she be fourteen i 3 16
I remember it well. 'Tis since the earthquake now eleven years . i 3 23
I never shall forget it,—Of all the days of the year, upon that day . i 3 25
And since that time it is eleven years; For then she could stand alone i 3 35
I warrant, an I should live a thousand years, I never should forget it . i 3 46
I was your mother much upon these years That you are now a maid . i 3 72
How long is't now since last yourself and I Were in a mask?—By'r lady, thirty years.—What, man! 'tis not so much . . . . i 5 35
Come pentecost as quickly as it will, Some five and twenty years . i 5 39
His son was but a ward two years ago . . . . . . i 5 42
At what o'clock to-morrow Shall I send to thee?—At the hour of nine. —I will not fail: 'tis twenty years till then . . . . ii 2 170
O, by this count I shall be much in years Ere I again behold my Romeo! iii 5 46
Arbitrating that Which the commission of thy years and art Could to no issue of true honour bring . . . . iv 1 64
An ancient receptacle, Where, for these many hundred years, the bones Of all my buried ancestors are pack'd . . . . . . iv 3 40
Doors, that were ne'er acquainted with their wards Many a bounteous year, Must be employ'd Now . . . . . *T. of Athens* iii 3 39
Growing on the south, Weighing the youthful season of the year *J. C.* ii 1 108
He that cuts off twenty years of life Cuts off so many years of fearing death . . . . iii 1 101
Live a thousand years, I shall not find myself so apt to die . . iii 1 159
Love, and be friends, as two such men should be; For I have seen more years, I'm sure, than ye . . . . iv 3 132
There's hope a great man's memory may outlive his life half a year *Ham.* iii 2 141
These three years I have taken note of it . . . . . v 1 150
Of all the days i' the year, I came to't that day . . . . v 1 155
I have been sexton here, man and boy, thirty years . . . . v 1 177
Some eight year or nine year: a tanner will last you nine year . v 1 183
Here's a skull now; this skull has lain in the earth three and twenty years . . . . v 1 191
I have, sir, a son by order of law, some year elder than this . *Lear* i 1 20
He hath been out nine years, and away he shall again . . . i 1 33
The unruly waywardness that infirm and choleric years bring with them i 1 302
I have years on my back forty-eight . . . . . . i 4 42
Fools had ne'er less wit in a year; For wise men are grown foppish i 4 181
Thou shalt have as many dolours for thy daughters as thou canst tell in a year . . . . ii 4 55
Mice and rats, and such small deer, Have been Tom's food for seven long year . . . . iii 4 145
I have been your tenant, and your father's tenant, these fourscore years iv 1 15
You shall more command with years Than with your weapons *Othello* i 2 60
Since these arms of mine had seven years' pith, Till now some nine moons i 3 83
In spite of nature, Of years, of country, credit, every thing . . i 3 97
Still question'd me the story of my life, From year to year . . i 3 130
I have looked upon the world for four times seven years . . i 3 313
Loveliness in favour, sympathy in years, manners, and beauties . ii 1 232
I am declined Into the vale of years,—yet that's not much . . iii 3 266
'Tis not a year or two shows us a man: They are all but stomachs . iii 4 103
I would have him nine years a-killing . . . . . . iv 1 188
Like to the time o' the year between the extremes Of hot and cold *Ant. and Cleo.* i 5 51
Bid him Report the feature of Octavia, her years, Her inclination . ii 5 112
That year, indeed, he was troubled with a rheum . . . . iii 2 57
Guess at her years, I prithee . . . . iii 3 29
The eldest of them at three years old, I' the swathing-clothes the other, from their nursery Were stol'n . . . . . *Cymbeline* i 1 58
How long is this ago?—Some twenty years . . . . . i 1 62
Disloyal thing, That shouldst repair my youth, thou heap'st A year's age on me . . . . i 1 133
This twenty years This rock and these demesnes have been my world . iii 3 69
At three and two years old, I stole these babes . . . . iii 3 101
I saw him not these many years, and yet I know 'tis he . . . iv 2 66
I had rather Have skipp'd from sixteen years of age to sixty . . iv 2 199
Many years, Though Cloten then but young, you see, not wore him From my remembrance . . . . iv 4 22

Year. Lopped branches, which, being dead many years, shall after revive *Cymbeline* v 4 142; v 5 439
These gentle princes . . . these twenty years Have I train'd up v 5 337
For many years thought dead, are now revived v 5 456
Tyrants' fears Decrease not, but grow faster than the years *Pericles* i 2 85
I'll then discourse our woes, felt several years i 4 18
The fairest, sweet'st, and best lies here, Who wither'd in her spring of year iv 4 35
Go to the wars, would you? where a man may serve seven years for the loss of a leg? iv 6 182
Who at fourteen years He sought to murder v 3 8
And what this fourteen years no razor touch'd, To grace thy marriage-day, I'll beautify v 3 75
Yearly. Unto thy bones good night! Yearly will I do this rite *Much Ado* v 3 23
The yearly course that brings this day about Shall never see it but a holiday.—A wicked day! *K. John* iii 1 81
Five hundred poor I have in yearly pay *Hen. V.* iv 1 315
Will yearly on the vigil feast his neighbours iv 3 45
Granted Rome a tribute, Yearly three thousand pounds *Cymbeline* iii 1 9
Yearn. She laments, sir, for it, that it would yearn your heart to see it *Mer. Wives* iii 5 45
My manly heart doth yearn *Hen. V.* ii 3 3
Falstaff he is dead, And we must yearn therefore ii 3 6
It yearns me not if men my garments wear iv 3 26
That every like is not the same, O Cæsar, The heart of Brutus yearns to think upon! *J. Cæsar* ii 2 129
Yearned. O, how it yearn'd my heart when I beheld! *Richard II.* v 5 76
Yedward. Hear ye, Yedward; if I tarry at home and go not, I'll hang you for going *1 Hen. IV.* i 2 149
Yell. The dogs did yell *L. L. Lost* iv 2 60
Nor yells of mothers, maids, nor babes, . . . Shall pierce a jot *T. of A.* iv 3 124
With like timorous accent and dire yell As when, by night and negligence, the fire Is spied in populous cities *Othello* i 1 75
Yelled. And yell'd out Like syllable of dolour *Macbeth* iv 3 7
Yellow. Come unto these yellow sands, And then take hands *Tempest* i 2 376
Her hair is auburn, mine is perfect yellow *T. G. of Ver.* iv 4 194
A little wee face, with a little yellow beard, a Cain-coloured beard *M. W.* i 4 23
Cuckoo-buds of yellow hue Do paint the meadows with delight *L. L. Lost* v 2 906
Your French-crown-colour beard, your perfect yellow *M. N. Dream* i 2 98
And sat with me on Neptune's yellow sands ii 1 126
Turns into yellow gold his salt green streams iii 2 393
This cherry nose, These yellow cowslip cheeks, Are gone v 1 339
With a green and yellow melancholy She sat like patience on a monument, Smiling at grief *T. Night* ii 4 116
Remember who commended thy yellow stockings ii 5 166; iii 4 52
She did commend my yellow stockings of late ii 5 181
I will be strange, stout, in yellow stockings, and cross-gartered ii 5 186
He will come to her in yellow stockings, and 'tis a colour she abhors ii 5 219
Not black in my mind, though yellow in my legs iii 4 28
Bade me come smiling and cross-garter'd to you, To put on yellow stockings v 1 346
If thou hast The ordering of the mind too, 'mongst all colours No yellow in't, lest she suspect! *W. Tale* ii 3 107
Have you not a moist eye? a dry hand? a yellow cheek? *2 Hen. IV.* i 2 204
A fellow In a long motley coat guarded with yellow *Hen. VIII.* Prol. 16
With reeky shanks and yellow chapless skulls *Rom. and Jul.* iv 1 83
What is here? Gold? yellow, glittering, precious gold? *T. of Athens* iv 3 26
This yellow slave [gold] Will knit and break religions, bless the accursed iv 3 33
My way of life Is fall'n into the sear, the yellow leaf *Macbeth* v 3 23
O, all the devils! This yellow Iachimo, in an hour,—was't not? *Cymbeline* ii 5 14
The yellows, blues, The purple violets, and marigolds *Pericles* iv 1 15
Yellowness. I will possess him with yellowness, for the revolt of mine is dangerous *Mer. Wives* i 3 111
Yellows. Rayed with the yellows, past cure of the fives *T. of Shrew* iii 2 54
Yelping. Mazed with a yelping kennel of French curs! *1 Hen. VI.* iv 2 47
Let us sit down and mark their yelping noise *T. Andron.* ii 3 20
Yeoman. The lady of the Strachy married the yeoman of the wardrobe *T. Night* ii 5 45
I press me none but good householders, yeomen's sons *1 Hen. IV.* iv 2 16
Where's your yeoman? Is't a lusty yeoman? will a' stand to't? *2 Hen. IV.* ii 1 4
And you, good yeomen, Whose limbs were made in England, show us here The mettle of your pasture *Hen. V.* iii 1 25
We grace the yeoman by conversing with him *1 Hen. VI.* ii 4 81
Spring crestless yeomen from so deep a root? ii 4 85
And, till thou be restored, thou art a yeoman ii 4 95
Yet not so wealthy as an English yeoman *3 Hen. VI.* i 4 123
Fight, gentlemen of England! fight, bold yeomen! *Richard III.* v 3 338
But, sir, now It did me yeoman's service *Hamlet* v 2 36
Prithee, nuncle, tell me whether a madman be a gentleman or a yeoman? *Lear* iii 6 11
He's a yeoman that has a gentleman to his son; for he's a mad yeoman that sees his son a gentleman before him iii 6 13
Yerk. And with wild rage Yerk out their armed heels *Hen. V.* iv 7 83
Yerked. I had thought to have yerk'd him here under the ribs *Othello* i 2 5
Yes. Alack, for mercy!—Yes, faith, and all his lords *Tempest* i 2 437
I would not for the world.—Yes, for a score of kingdoms you should wrangle v 1 174
Do you not like it?—Yes, yes: the lines are very quaintly writ *T. G. of V.* ii 1 128
That cannot be so neither: yes, it is so, it is so ii 3 18
Surely I think you have charms, la; yes, in truth *Mer. Wives* ii 2 108
Yes, truly: I speak not as desiring more *Meas. for Meas.* i 4 3
I would not tell you what I would, my lord: Faith, yes *All's Well* ii 5 90
Yes, if this present quality of war, Indeed the instant action *2 Hen. IV.* i 3 36
I say, take heed; Yes, heartily beseech you *Hen. VIII.* i 2 176
My quarrel was not altogether slight.—Faith, yes *Cymbeline* i 4 52
Yest. And anon swallowed with yest and froth, as you'ld thrust a cork into a hogshead *W. Tale* iii 3 94
Yesterday. There was one conveyed out of my house yesterday *M. Wives* iv 2 152
Went you not to her yesterday, sir, as you told me? v 1 14
I reason'd with a Frenchman yesterday *Mer. of Venice* ii 8 27
I'll give you a verse to this note that I made yesterday *As Y. Like It* ii 5 49
I met the duke yesterday and had much question with him iii 4 38
I heard my lady talk of it yesterday *T. Night* i 3 15
Since the birth of Cain, the first male child, To him that did but yesterday suspire *K. John* iii 4 80
O, call back yesterday, bid time return! *Richard II.* iii 2 69
Enlarge the man committed yesterday *Hen. V.* ii 2 40
Methought yesterday your mistress shrewdly shook your back iii 7 51
Five hundred were but yesterday dubb'd knights iv 8 91
He is come to me and prings me pread and salt yesterday v 1 9
Yesterday. You called me yesterday mountain-squire *Hen. V.* v 1 36
I would somebody had heard her talk yesterday, as I did *Troi. and Cres.* i 1 46
They say he yesterday coped Hector in the battle i 2 34
I told you a thing yesterday; think on't i 2 185
You have a Trojan prisoner, call'd Antenor, Yesterday took iii 3 19
And but one half of what he was yesterday *Coriolanus* iv 5 211
Yesterday the bird of night did sit Even at noon-day upon the market-place, Hooting and shrieking *J. Cæsar* i 3 26
But yesterday the word of Cæsar might Have stood against the world iii 2 123
Was it not yesterday we spoke together?—It was *Macbeth* iii 1 74
And all our yesterdays have lighted fools The way to dusty death v 5 22
I saw him yesterday, or t'other day, Or then, or then *Hamlet* ii 1 56
To that sweet sleep Which thou owedst yesterday *Othello* iii 3 333
This is his second fit; he had one yesterday iv 1 52
I heard of one of them no longer than yesterday *Ant. and Cleo.* v 2 251
Yesternight, my lord, she and that friar, I saw them *Meas. for Meas.* v 1 134
What man was he talk'd with you yesternight? *Much Ado* iv 1 84
Prove you . . . that I yesternight Maintain'd the change of words with any creature iv 1 184
What yesternight our council did decree *1 Hen. IV.* i 1 32
And many limits of the charge set down But yesternight i 1 36
It holds current that I told you yesternight ii 1 59
For yesternight by Catesby was it brought me *Richard III.* iii 6 6
She looked yesternight fairer than ever I saw her look *Troi. and Cres.* i 1 32
His wife but yesternight was brought to bed *T. Andron.* iv 2 153
Was stay'd by accident, and yesternight Return'd my letter back *Rom. and Jul.* v 3 251
Yesternight, at supper, You suddenly arose, and walk'd about *J. Cæsar* ii 1 238
I think I saw him yesternight *Hamlet* i 2 189
Yesty. Though the yesty waves Confound and swallow navigation up *Macbeth* iv 1 53
A kind of yesty collection, which carries them through and through *Ham.* v 2 199
Yet. He'll be hang'd yet *Tempest* i 1 61
Left me to a bootless inquisition, Concluding 'Stay: not yet' i 2 36
Thou dost me yet but little hurt; thou wilt anon ii 2 82
Not one of them That yet looks on me, or would know me v 1 83
I shall miss thee; But yet thou shalt have freedom v 1 96
No more yet of this; For 'tis a chronicle of day by day v 1 162
A quick wit.—And yet it cannot overtake your slow purse *T. G. of Ver.* i 1 133
And yet— A pretty period! ii 1 121
I guess the sequel; And yet I will not name it; and yet I care not; And yet take this again; and yet I thank you, Meaning henceforth to trouble you no more.—And yet you will; and yet another 'yet' ii 1 123
Yet did not this cruel-hearted cur shed one tear ii 3 9
Begin to love her! 'Tis but her picture I have yet beheld ii 4 209
Not so; but yet so false that he grieves my very heart-strings iv 2 61
Yet heaven may decrease it upon better acquaintance *Mer. Wives* i 1 254
I keep but three men and a boy yet, till my mother be dead i 1 285
The time is yet to come that she was ever respected with man *M. for M.* ii 1 176
What's yet in this That bears the name of life? iii 1 38
This forenamed maid hath yet in her the continuance of her first affection iii 1 248
But tell me yet, dost thou not know my voice? *Com. of Errors* v 1 300
Since you could not be my son-in-law, Be yet my nephew *Much Ado* v 1 297
What was a month old at Cain's birth, that's not five weeks old as yet?—Dictynna, goodman Dull *L. L. Lost* iv 2 36
But as yet, I swear, I cannot truly say how I came here *M. N. Dream* iv 1 152
Is he yet possess'd How much ye would? *Mer. of Venice* i 3 65
Hear me yet, good Shylock.—I'll have my bond iii 3 3
What, are you answer'd yet? iv 1 46
My soul, yet I know not why, hates nothing more than he *As Y. Like It* i 1 171
I will not trouble you As yet, to question you ii 7 172
The time was that I hated thee, And yet it is not that I bear thee love iii 5 93
For yet his honour never heard a play *T. of Shrew* Ind. 1 96
She was the fairest creature in the world; And yet she is inferior to none Ind. 2 69
Did you yet ever see Baptista's daughter? i 2 252
I'll watch you better yet iii 1 50
In time I may believe, yet I mistrust.—Mistrust it not iii 1 51
I am yours Upon your will to suffer.—Yet, I pray you *All's Well* iv 4 30
And I am yet so near the manners of my mother *T. Night* ii 1 41
Hardly Will he endure your sight as yet, I fear *W. Tale* iv 4 481
Whose party do the townsmen yet admit? *K. John* ii 1 361
Have you inquired yet who picked my pocket? *1 Hen. IV.* iii 3 61
Yet all goes well, yet all our joints are whole iv 1 83
A man may prophesy, With a near aim, of the main chance of things As yet not come to life *2 Hen. IV.* iii 1 84
How yet resolves the governor of the town? *Hen. V.* iii 3 1
His powers are yet not ready To raise so great a siege iii 3 46
Helen, . . . Nor yet Saint Philip's daughters, were like thee *1 Hen. VI.* i 2 143
Her mother liveth yet, can testify v 4 12
For yet is hope of life and victory. Forslow no longer *3 Hen. VI.* ii 3 55
When I know; for I protest As yet I do not *Richard III.* i 1 53
I then did feel full sick, and yet not well *Hen. VIII.* ii 4 204
But here's yet in the word 'hereafter' the kneading *Troi. and Cres.* i 1 22
Know'st thou me yet?—I know thee not *Coriolanus* iv 5 69
O Julius Cæsar, thou art mighty yet! *J. Cæsar* v 3 94
Let me speak to the yet unknowing world How these things came about *Hamlet* v 2 390
If I like thee no worse after dinner, I will not part from thee yet *Lear* i 4 45
I will do such things,—What they are, yet I know not ii 4 284
Yet to be known shortens my made intent iv 7 9
'Tis yet to know,—Which, when I know that boasting is an honour, I shall promulgate *Othello* i 2 19
Nay, yet there's more in this: I prithee, speak to me as to thy thinkings iii 3 130
Or that I do not yet, and ever did, And ever will . . . love him dearly iv 2 156
If you bethink yourself of any crime Unreconciled as yet to heaven v 2 27
You shall be yet far fairer than you are *Ant. and Cleo.* i 2 16
We yet not know. Be't as our gods will have't! ii 1 49
But yet, madam,— I do not like 'But yet,' it does allay The good precedence; fie upon 'But yet!' 'But yet' is as a goaler to bring forth Some monstrous malefactor ii 5 49
He's very knowing; I do perceive't: there's nothing in her yet iii 3 27
Have you done yet? iii 13 153
Whence are you?—A poor Egyptian yet v 1 52
For I yet not understand the case myself *Cymbeline* ii 3 80
She stripp'd it from her arm; I see her yet ii 4 101
We wept after her hearse, And yet we mourn *Pericles* iv 3 42
Yet a while. But I must make fair weather yet a while *2 Hen. VI.* v 1 30
Yet again! what do you here? *Tempest* i 1 41
Bid every noise be still: peace yet again! *J. Cæsar* i 2 14

Yet again. Yet again your fingers to your lips? *Othello* ii 1 177
Yet appearing. Whose memory is written on the earth With yet appearing blood . . . *2 Hen. IV.* iv 1 82
Yet once again, to make us public sport, Appoint a meeting *Mer. Wives* iv 4 14
Yet once again proclaim it publicly . . . *Com. of Errors* v 1 130
Yet once more, I hold my most malicious foe . . . *Hen. VIII.* iii 2 82
Yew. My shroud of white, stuck all with yew, O, prepare it! . *T. Night* ii 4 56
Bend their bows Of double-fatal yew against thy state . *Richard II.* iii 2 117
They told me they would bind me here Unto the body of a dismal yew, And leave me to this miserable death . . . *T. Andron.* ii 3 107
Gall of goat, and slips of yew Sliver'd in the moon's eclipse *Macbeth* iv 1 27
Yew tree. Under yond yew-trees lay thee all along, Holding thine ear close to the hollow ground . . . *Rom. and Jul.* v 3 3
As I did sleep under this yew-tree here, I dreamt . . . v 3 137
Yield. My slave, who never Yields us kind answer *Tempest* i 2 309
A birth indeed Which throes thee much to yield . . . ii 1 231
I'll yield him thee asleep, Where thou mayst knock a nail into his head iii 2 68
Injurious wasps, to feed on such sweet honey And kill the bees that yield it with your stings! . . . *T. G. of Ver.* i 2 107
I'll force thee yield to my desire . . . v 4 59
And makes milch-kine yield blood and shakes a chain *Mer. Wives* iv 4 33
And strip myself to death, as to a bed That longing have been sick for, ere I'ld yield My body up to shame . *Meas. for Meas.* ii 4 103
Had he twenty heads . . . , he'ld yield them up, Before his sister should her body stoop To such abhorr'd pollution . . . ii 4 181
If I would yield him my virginity, Thou mightst be freed . . iii 1 98
Leave me your snatches, and yield me a direct answer . . iv 2 7
Our soul Cannot but yield you forth to public thanks . . v 1 7
My sisterly remorse confutes mine honour, And I did yield to him . v 1 101
Transform me then, and to your power I'll yield . *Com. of Errors* iii 2 40
Yield possession to my holy prayers . . . iv 4 58
Graves, yawn and yield your dead, Till death be uttered . *Much Ado* v 3 19
I yield upon great persuasion; and partly to save your life . . v 4 95
If you prove it, I'll repay it back Or yield up Aquitaine . *L. L. Lost* ii 1 160
At which interview All liberal reason I will yield unto . . ii 1 168
I would not yield to be your house's guest . . . v 2 354
Whether, if you yield not to your father's choice, You can endure the livery of a nun . . . *M. N. Dream* i 1 69
So die, so die, my lord, Ere I will yield my virgin patent up . . i 1 80
Yield Thy crazed title to my certain right . . . i 1 91
Or else the law of Athens yields you up . . . i 1 119
With all my heart, In Hermia's love I yield you up my part . . iii 2 165
To yield myself His wife who wins me by that means I told you *Mer. of Venice* ii 1 18
To shake the head, relent, and sigh, and yield To Christian intercessors iii 3 15
But of force Must yield to such inevitable shame . . . iv 1 57
You press me far, and therefore I will yield . . . iv 1 425
A rotten tree, That cannot so much as a blossom yield . *As Y. Like It* ii 3 64
If this uncouth forest yield any thing savage, I will either be food for it or bring it for food to thee . . . ii 6 6
Truly, the tree yields bad fruit.—I'll graff it with you . . iii 2 123
So I to her and so she yields to me . . . *T. of Shrew* ii 1 137
The reasons of our state I cannot yield . . . *All's Well* iii 1 10
Thy reason, man?—Troth, sir, I can yield you none . *T. Night* iii 1 27
Give thy reason.—You must needs yield your reason . . iii 2 4
Every 'leven wether tods; every tod yields pound and odd shilling *W. Tale* iv 3 34
I yield all this; But for some other reasons, my grave sir . . iv 4 421
Every shop, church, session, hanging, yields a careful man work . iv 4 701
Yield thee to my hand; And out of my dear love I'll give thee more *K. John* ii 1 156
It [the world] yields nought but shame and bitterness . . iii 4 111
On that day at noon, whereon he says I shall yield up my crown, let him be hang'd . . . iv 2 157
Ere further leisure yield them further means For their advantage *Rich. II.* i 4 40
Yield stinging nettles to mine enemies . . . iii 2 18
The means that heaven yields must be embraced, And not neglected . iii 2 29
What, will not this castle yield?—The castle royally is mann'd . . iii 3 20
His high sceptre yields To the possession of thy royal hand . . iv 1 109
Villain, thy own hand yields thy death's instrument . . v 5 107
If he will not yield, Rebuke and dread correction wait on us *1 Hen. IV.* v 1 110
This sword hath ended him: so shall it thee, Unless thou yield thee . v 3 10
O earth, yield us that king again, And take thou this! . *2 Hen. IV.* i 3 106
Do ye yield, sir? or shall I sweat for you? . . . iv 3 13
I think you are Sir John Falstaff, and in that thought yield me . iv 3 19
Here he is, and here I yield him . . . iv 3 49
This bitter taste Yield his engrossments to the ending father . . iv 5 80
He'll yield the crow a pudding one of these days . *Hen. V.* ii 1 91
What say you? will you yield, and this avoid? . . . iii 3 42
We yield our town and lives to thy soft mercy . . . iii 3 48
That England shall couch down in fear and yield . . iv 2 37
Which if they have as I will leave 'em them, Shall yield them little . iv 3 125
Yield, cur!—Je pense que vous êtes gentilhomme de bonne qualité . iv 4 1
Yet they do wink and yield, as love is blind and enforces . . v 2 327
Hung be the heavens with black, yield day to night! . *1 Hen. VI.* i 1 1
These news would cause him once more yield the ghost . . i 1 67
I must not yield to any rites of love, For my profession's sacred . i 2 113
He upon whose side The fewest roses are cropp'd from the tree Shall yield the other in the right opinion . . . ii 4 42
Yield, my lord protector; yield, Winchester . . . iii 1 112
He shall submit, or I will never yield . . . iii 1 118
I will yield to thee; Love for thy love and hand for hand I give . iii 1 134
And made me almost yield upon my knees . . . iii 3 80
He, renowned noble gentleman, Yields up his life unto a world of odds iv 4 25
Speak to thy father ere thou yield thy breath! . . . iv 7 24
Henry is youthful and will quickly yield . . . v 3 99
Then yield, my lords; and here conclude with me . . v 5 77
And, force perforce, I'll make him yield the crown . *2 Hen. VI.* i 1 258
Let York be regent; I will yield to him . . . i 3 109
Vanquish'd as I am, I yield to thee, Or to the meanest groom . iii 1 184
Wrathful, and inclined to blood, If you go forward; therefore yield, or die . . . iv 2 135
Will ye relent, And yield to mercy whilst 'tis offer'd you? . . iv 8 12
He is fled, my lord, and all his powers do yield . . . iv 9 10
I'll yield myself to prison willingly, Or unto death, to do my country good . . . iv 9 42
They seek revenge and therefore will not yield . *3 Hen. VI.* i 1 190
Yield to our mercy, proud Plantagenet . . . i 4 30
So true men yield, with robbers so o'ermatch'd . . . i 4 64
But Hercules himself must yield to odds . . . ii 1 53
Yield. Being a king, blest with a goodly son, Didst yield consent to disinherit him . . . *3 Hen. VI.* ii 2 24
What say'st thou, Henry, wilt thou yield the crown? . . . ii 2 101
A thousand men have broke their fasts to-day, That ne'er shall dine unless thou yield the crown . . . ii 2 128
May yet ere night yield both my life and them To some man else . ii 5 59
And what he will, I humbly yield unto . . . iii 1 101
And that is more than I will yield unto . . . iii 2 96
Yield not thy neck To fortune's yoke . . . iii 3 16
Tell thy grief; It shall be eased, if France can yield relief . . iii 3 20
Yet shall you have all kindness at my hand That your estate requires and mine can yield . . . iii 3 150
Therefore I yield thee my free consent . . . iv 6 36
That he consents, if Warwick yield consent . . . iv 6 46
Doubtless Burgundy will yield him help, And we shall have more wars iv 6 90
Yield me up the keys; For Edward will defend the town . . iv 7 37
My sick heart shows That I must yield my body to the earth . . v 2 9
Thus yields the cedar to the axe's edge . . . v 2 11
So first the harmless sheep doth yield his fleece And next his throat v 6 8
I do find more pain in banishment Than death can yield me here *Richard III.* i 3 169
And often did I strive To yield the ghost . . . i 4 37
What shall we do, if we perceive Lord Hastings will not yield? . iii 1 192
Take it not amiss; I cannot nor I will not yield to you . . iii 7 207
O, that thou wouldst as well afford a grave As thou canst yield a melancholy seat! Then would I hide my bones . . . iv 4 32
Day, yield me not thy light; nor, night, thy rest! . . . iv 4 401
Fainting, despair; despairing, yield thy breath! . . . v 3 172
Bull-bearing Milo his addition yield To sinewy Ajax . *Troi. and Cres.* ii 3 258
O Priam, yield not to him!—Do not, dear father . . . v 3 76
If they would yield us but the superfluity, while it were wholesome *Coriolanus* i 1 17
We do request your kindest ears, and after, Your loving motion toward the common body, To yield what passes here . . . ii 2 58
Of such childish friendliness To yield your voices . . . ii 3 184
Must these have voices, that can yield them now And straight disclaim? iii 1 34
Seize him!—Yield, Marcius, yield!—Hear me one word . . . iii 1 215
All places yield to him ere he sits down . . . iv 7 28
Bound with an oath to yield to his conditions . . . v 1 69
Be chosen with proclamations to-day, To-morrow yield up rule *T. An.* i 1 191
Yield at entreats; and then let me alone . . . i 1 449
Yield to his humour, smooth and speak him fair . . . v 2 140
Nor will he know his purse, or yield me this, To show him what a beggar his heart is . . . *T. of Athens* i 2 200
All covered dishes!—Royal cheer, I warrant you.—Doubt not that, if money and the season can yield it . . . iii 6 58
Earth, yield me roots! Who seeks for better of thee, sauce his palate With thy most operant poison! . . . iv 3 23
Yield him, who all thy human sons doth hate, . . . one poor root! . iv 3 185
And the man entire Upon the next encounter yields him ours *J. Cæsar* i 3 156
How foolish do your fears seem now, Calpurnia! I am ashamed I did yield to them . . . ii 2 106
Yield, or thou diest.—Only I yield to die . . . v 4 12
If good, why do I yield to that suggestion Whose horrid image doth unfix my hair? . . . *Macbeth* i 3 134
God 'ild us for your pains, And thank us for your trouble . . i 6 13
I bear a charmed life, which must not yield To one of woman born . v 8 12
Then yield thee, coward, And live to be the show and gaze o' the time . v 8 23
I will not yield, To kiss the ground before young Malcolm's feet . v 8 27
Nor will it yield to Norway or the Pole A ranker rate *Hamlet* iv 4 21
Which, as her winks, and nods, and gestures yield them . . iv 5 11
Now quit you well. Yield: come before my father . *Lear* ii 1 33
O world! But that thy strange mutations make us hate thee, Life would not yield to age . . . iv 1 12
And by no means Will yield to see his daughter . . . iv 3 43
And yet I know not how conceit may rob The treasury of life, when life itself Yields to the theft . . . iv 6 44
Yield up, O love, thy crown and hearted throne To tyrannous hate! *Othello* iii 3 448
But well and free, If thou so yield him, there is gold *Ant. and Cleo.* ii 5 28
He'll never yield to that.—Nor must not then be yielded to in this . iii 6 37
The queen shall then have courtesy, so she Will yield us up . . iii 13 16
Tend me to-night two hours, I ask no more, And the gods yield you for't! . . . iv 2 33
Bid him yield; Being so frustrate, tell him he mocks The pauses that he makes . . . v 1 1
If thou please To take me to thee, as I was to him I'll be to Cæsar; if thou pleasest not, I yield thee up my life . . . v 1 12
Hired with that self exhibition Which your own coffers yield! *Cymbeline* i 6 123
That such a crafty devil as is his mother Should yield the world this ass! ii 1 58
Makes Diana's rangers false themselves, yield up Their deer . . ii 3 74
But that you shall not say I yield being silent, I would not speak . ii 3 99
Thou art a robber, A law-breaker, a villain: yield thee, thief . iv 2 75
Say what thou art, Why I should yield to thee? . . . iv 2 80
Yield, rustic mountaineer . . . iv 2 100
Valour That wildly grows in them, but yields a crop As if it had been sow'd . . . iv 2 180
Nor hear I from my mistress, who did promise To yield me often tidings iv 3 39
Fight I will no more, But yield me to the veriest hind that shall Once touch my shoulder . . . v 3 77
Wind, rain, and thunder, remember, earthly man Is but a substance that must yield to you . . . *Pericles* ii 1 3
To wisdom he's a fool that will not yield . . . ii 4 54
Briefly yield her; for she must overboard straight . . . iii 1 53
Thou canst not do a thing in the world so soon, To yield thee so much profit . . . iv 1 4
How have I offended, Wherein my death might yield her any profit? . iv 1 81
I doubt not but this populous city will Yield many scholars . . iv 6 198
Yielded. Thus lorded, Not only with what my revenue yielded *Tempest* i 2 98
He doth deserve As much as may be yielded to a man . *Much Ado* iii 1 48
I have yielded: Instruct my daughter how she shall persever *All's Well* iii 7 36
And left them More rich for what they yielded . . *W. Tale* v 1 55
Thus have I yielded up into your hand The circle of my glory *K. John* v 1 1
All Kent hath yielded; nothing there holds out But Dover castle . v 1 30
Shall I now give o'er the yielded set? . . . v 2 107
Warr'd he hath not, But basely yielded upon compromise That which his noble ancestors achieved with blows . . *Richard II.* ii 1 253
And all your northern castles yielded up . . . iii 2 201
Hath yielded up his body to the grave . . . v 6 21
But what of that? he saw me, and yielded . . *2 Hen. IV.* iv 3 44

Yielded. Is Paris lost? is Rouen yielded up? . . . 1 *Hen. VI.* i 1 65
France should have torn and rent my very heart, Before I would have yielded to this league . . . 2 *Hen. VI.* i 1 127
The king hath yielded unto thy demand . . . v 1 40
And look to have it yielded with all willingness . . . *Richard III.* iii 1 198
You might haply think Tongue-tied ambition, not replying, yielded . . . iii 7 145
For they had so vilely Yielded the town . . . *Coriolanus* iii 1 11
To grace him only . . . a very little I have yielded to . . . v 3 17
Graves have yawn'd, and yielded up their dead . . . *J. Cæsar* ii 2 18
He'll never yield to that.—Nor must not then be yielded to in this . . . *Ant. and Cleo.* iii 6 38
Mine honour was not yielded, But conquer'd merely . . . iii 13 61
This foul Egyptian hath betrayed me: My fleet hath yielded to the foe iv 12 11
Send your trunk to me; it shall safe be kept, And truly yielded you *Cymb.* i 6 210
And call'd Marina For she was yielded there . . . *Pericles* v 3 48
Yielder. Some sleeves, some hats, from yielders all things catch *M. N. D.* iii 2 30
I was not born a yielder, thou proud Scot . . . 1 *Hen. IV.* v 3 11
The block of death, Treason's true bed and yielder up of breath 2 *Hen. IV.* iv 2 123
Yielding. Redeem thy brother By yielding up thy body to my will . . . *Meas. for Meas.* ii 4 164
And yielding to him humours well his frenzy . . . *Com. of Errors* iv 4 84
How well this yielding rescues thee from shame! . . . *L. L. Lost* i 1 118
Were not his requests so far From reason's yielding, your fair self should make A yielding 'gainst some reason in my breast . . . ii 1 151
This weak and idle theme, No more yielding but a dream . . . *M. N. D.* v 1 435
I see a yielding in the looks of France . . . *K. John* ii 1 474
Be he the fire, I'll be the yielding water . . . *Richard II.* iii 3 58
Therefore, patiently and yielding . . . *Hen. V.* v 2 301
Obeying with my wind when I do blow, And yielding to another when it blows, Commanded always by the greater gust . . . 3 *Hen. VI.* iii 1 87
What merit's in that reason which denies The yielding of her up? . . . *Troi. and Cres.* ii 2 25
Making a treaty where There was a yielding . . . *Coriolanus* v 6 69
Pardon me, And not impute this yielding to light love . . . *Rom. and Jul.* ii 2 105
Unto the voice and yielding of that body Whereof he is the head *Hamlet* i 3 23
To Cæsar will I render My legions and my horse: Six kings already Show me the way of yielding . . . *Ant. and Cleo.* iii 10 35
Make her go back, even to the yielding . . . *Cymbeline* i 4 115
Yoke. These that accuse him in his intent towards our wives are a yoke of his discarded men . . . *Mer. Wives* ii 1 181
Do not these fair yokes Become the forest better than the town? . . . v 5 111
An thou wilt needs thrust thy neck into a yoke, wear the print of it . . . *Much Ado* i 1 203
In time the savage bull doth bear the yoke . . . i 1 263
Whose unwished yoke My soul consents not to give sovereignty *M. N. D.* i 1 81
The ox hath therefore stretch'd his yoke in vain . . . ii 1 93
Whose souls do bear an equal yoke of love . . . *Mer. of Venice* iii 4 13
If then we shall shake off our slavish yoke . . . *Richard II.* ii 1 291
How a good yoke of bullocks at Stamford fair? . . . 2 *Hen. IV.* iii 2 42
Pause us, till these rebels, now afoot, Come underneath the yoke of government . . . iv 4 10
Quell the Dauphin utterly, Or bring him in obedience to your yoke . . . 1 *Hen. VI.* ii 1 164
Can I bear this shameful yoke? . . . 2 *Hen. VI.* ii 4 37
Yield not thy neck To fortune's yoke . . . 3 *Hen. VI.* iii 3 17
'Twere pity To sunder them that yoke so well together . . . iv 1 23
We'll yoke together, like a double shadow . . . iv 6 49
Yielded To bear the golden yoke of sovereignty . . . *Richard III.* iii 7 146
Now thy proud neck bears half my burthen'd yoke . . . iv 4 111
My most loving friends, Bruised underneath the yoke of tyranny . . . v 2 2
And ever may your highness yoke together, As I will lend you cause, my doing well With my well saying! . . . *Hen. VIII.* iii 2 150
Yoke you like draught-oxen and make you plough up the wars *T. and C.* ii 1 116
Never be so noble as a consul, Nor yoke with him for tribune *Coriol.* iii 1 57
And brought to yoke, the enemies of Rome . . . *T. Andron.* i 1 69
To beautify thy triumphs and return, Captive to thee and to thy Roman yoke . . . i 1 111
Their mother's bed-chamber should not be safe For these bad bondmen to the yoke of Rome . . . iv 1 109
And shake the yoke of inauspicious stars From this world-wearied flesh. Eyes, look your last! . . . *Rom. and Jul.* v 3 111
Groaning underneath this age's yoke . . . *J. Cæsar* i 2 61
Our yoke and sufferance show us womanish . . . i 3 84
Our country sinks beneath the yoke; It weeps, it bleeds . . . *Macbeth* iv 3 39
Against all colour here Did put the yoke upon's; which to shake off Becomes a warlike people . . . *Cymbeline* iii 1 52
Our subjects, sir, Will not endure his yoke . . . iii 5 5
If it be sin to say so, sir, I yoke me In my good brother's fault iv 2 19
Nobly he yokes A smiling with a sigh . . . iv 2 51
I shall with aged patience bear your yoke . . . *Pericles* ii 4 48
Yoked. He that is so yoked by a fool, Methinks, should not be chronicled for wise . . . *T. G. of Ver.* i 1 40
My name Be yoked with his that did betray the Best! . . . *W. Tale* i 2 419
With his sons, a terror to our foes, Hath yoked a nation strong *T. An.* i 1 30
O Cassius, you are yoked with a lamb That carries anger as the flint bears fire . . . *J. Cæsar* iv 3 110
Think every bearded fellow that's but yoked May draw with you *Oth.* iv 1 67
Yoke-devils. Kept together, As two yoke-devils sworn to either's purpose . . . *Hen. V.* ii 2 106
Yoke-fellows in arms, Let us to France; like horse-leeches, my boys ii 3 56
By his bloody side, Yoke-fellow to his honour-owing wounds . . . iv 6 9
Take thy place; And thou, his yoke-fellow of equity, Bench by his side . . . *Lear* iii 6 39
Yoketh. He yoketh your rebellious necks, Razeth your cities 1 *Hen. VI.* ii 3 64
Yon. Who more engilds the night Than all yon fiery oes and eyes of light . . . *M. N. Dream* iii 2 188
Nerissa, cheer yon stranger; bid her welcome . . . *Mer. of Venice* iii 2 240
There are some shrewd contents in yon same paper . . . iii 2 246
Yon green boy shall have no sun to ripe The bloom . . . *K. John* ii 1 472
Throw thine eye On yon young boy . . . iii 3 60
There stands the castle, by yon tuft of trees . . . *Richard II.* ii 3 53
King Richard lies Within the limits of yon lime and stone . . . iii 3 26
That laid the sentence of dread banishment On yon proud man . . . iii 3 135
Go, bind thou up yon dangling apricocks . . . iii 4 29
Do but behold yon poor and starved band . . . *Hen. V.* iv 2 16
Yon island carrions, desperate of their bones . . . iv 2 39
Ride thou unto the horsemen on yon hill . . . iv 7 60
But first I'll turn yon fellow in his grave . . . *Richard III.* i 2 261
See you yond coign o' the Capitol, yon corner-stone? . . . *Coriolanus* v 4 1
Nightly she sings on yon pomegranate-tree . . . *Rom. and Jul.* iii 5 4
Yon. Yon light is not day-light, I know it, I . . . *Rom. and Jul.* iii 5 12
I'll say yon grey is not the morning's eye . . . iii 5 19
Yon gray lines That fret the clouds are messengers of day *J. Cæsar* ii 1 103
But, look, the morn, in russet mantle clad, Walks o'er the dew of yon high eastward hill . . . *Hamlet* i 1 167
Yon ribaudred nag of Egypt,—Whom leprosy o'ertake! *Ant. and Cleo.* iii 10 10
For her many a wight did die, As yon grim looks do testify *Pericles* i Gower 40
To taste the fruit of yon celestial tree, Or die in the adventure . . . i 1 21
Without covering, save yon field of stars . . . ii 1 37
Yon king's to me like to my father's picture . . . ii 3 37
Yon knight doth sit too melancholy . . . ii 3 54
Yond. And say what thou seest yond . . . *Tempest* i 2 409
Yond same black cloud, yond huge one, looks like a foul bombard . . . ii 2 20
Yond same cloud cannot choose but fall by pailfuls . . . ii 2 24
For 'tis no trusting to yond foolish lout . . . *T. G. of Ver.* iv 4 71
Good mother, do not marry me to yond fool . . . *Mer. Wives* iii 4 87
Question yond man If he for gold will give us any food *As Y. Like It* ii 4 64
Yond's that same knave That leads him to these places . . . *All's Well* iii 5 85
Yond young fellow swears he will speak with you . . . *T. Night* i 5 147
Get thee to yond same sovereign cruelty . . . ii 4 83
Yond gull Malvolio is turned heathen, a very renegado . . . iii 2 73
I will tell it softly; Yond crickets shall not hear it . . . *W. Tale* ii 1 31
Tell Bolingbroke—for yond methinks he stands . . . *Richard II.* iii 3 91
Agreed: I'll to yond corner.—And I to this . . . 1 *Hen. VI.* ii 1 33
Is not yond Diomed, with Calchas' daughter? . . . *Troi. and Cres.* iv 5 13
Yond towers, whose wanton tops do buss the clouds, Must kiss their own feet . . . iv 5 220
By all Diana's waiting-women yond, And by herself . . . v 2 91
Here's a letter come from yond poor girl.—Let me read . . . v 3 99
By yond clouds, Let me deserve so ill as you . . . *Coriolanus* iii 1 50
If Jupiter Should from yond cloud speak divine things . . . iv 5 110
Come hither, nurse. What is yond gentleman? . . . *Rom. and Jul.* i 5 130
Under yond yew-trees lay thee all along . . . v 3 3
What torch is yond, that vainly lends his light To grubs? . . . v 3 125
'Ira furor brevis est;' but yond man is ever angry . . . *T. of Athens* i 2 29
Is yond despised and ruinous man my lord? . . . iv 3 465
Yond Cassius has a lean and hungry look . . . *J. Cæsar* i 2 194
That I may rest assured Whether yond troops are friend or enemy . . . v 3 18
When yond same star that's westward from the pole Had made his course . . . *Hamlet* i 1 36
Yond tall anchoring bark, Diminish'd to her cock . . . *Lear* iv 6 18
Behold yond simpering dame, Whose face between her forks presages snow . . . iv 6 120
See how yond justice rails upon yond simple thief . . . iv 6 155
But, look! what lights come yond? . . . *Othello* i 2 28
Now, by yond marble heaven, In the due reverence of a sacred vow . . . iii 3 460
Set we our squadrons on yond side o' the hill *Ant. and Cleo.* iii 9 1
Where yond pine does stand, I shall discover all . . . iv 12 1
Now for our mountain sport: up to yond hill . . . *Cymbeline* iii 3 10
Which is the way?—I thank you.—By yond bush? . . . iv 2 292
Yonder is Silvia; and Silvia's mine . . . *T. G. of Ver.* v 4 125
Look who comes yonder: she shall be our messenger *Mer. Wives* ii 1 163
Yonder he is coming, this way . . . iii 1 27
Yonder is a most reverend gentleman . . . iii 1 52
He so takes on yonder with my husband . . . iv 2 22
I came yonder at Eton to marry Mistress Anne Page . . . v 5 194
There's one yonder arrested and carried to prison *Meas. for Meas.* i 2 60
Yonder man is carried to prison.—Well; what has he done? . . . i 2 87
But, soft! who wafts us yonder? . . . *Com. of Errors* ii 2 111
Come, go along; my wife is coming yonder . . . iv 4 43
Speak softly: yonder, as I think, he walks . . . v 1 9
I came yonder from a great supper . . . *Much Ado* i 3 44
Yonder's old coil at home . . . v 2 98
Hereby, upon the edge of yonder coppice . . . *L. L. Lost* iv 1 9
As bright, as clear, As yonder Venus in her glimmering sphere *M. N. D.* iii 2 61
Look, where thy love comes; yonder is thy dear . . . iii 2 176
And yonder shines Aurora's harbinger . . . iii 2 380
It will fall pat as I told you. Yonder she comes . . . v 1 188
Where is your master?—Yonder, sir, he walks . . . *Mer. of Venice* ii 2 183
By yonder moon I swear you do me wrong . . . v 1 142
Yonder comes my master, your brother . . . *As Y. Like It* i 1 28
Yonder they lie; the poor old man, their father, making such pitiful dole . . . i 2 137
Yonder, sure, they are coming: let us now stay and see it . . . i 2 156
Is yonder the man?—Even he, madam . . . i 2 160
Yonder he is: deny him, forswear him, or else we are all undone *T. of S.* v 1 113
O madam, yonder is heavy news within! . . . *All's Well* iii 2 35
Yonder's my lord your son with a patch of velvet on's face . . . iv 5 99
He has been yonder i' the sun practising behaviour to his own shadow . . . *T. Night* ii 5 20
He will not now be pacified: Fabian can scarce hold him yonder . . . iii 4 310
Demand of yonder champion The cause of his arrival here *Richard II.* i 3 7
Ask yonder knight in arms, Both who he is and why he cometh hither . . . i 3 26
Yonder he comes; and that arrant malmsey-nose knave . . . 2 *Hen. IV.* ii 1 41
Is not that the morning which breaks yonder?—I think it be *Hen. V.* iv 1 88
We see yonder the beginning of the day, but I think we shall never see the end of it . . . iv 1 91
Call yonder fellow hither.—Soldier, you must come to the king . . . iv 7 123
In yonder tower to overpeer the city . . . 1 *Hen. VI.* i 4 11
By thrusting out a torch from yonder tower . . . iii 2 23
The burning torch in yonder turret stands . . . iii 2 30
Yonder's the head of that arch-enemy . . . 3 *Hen. VI.* ii 2 2
Brave followers, yonder stands the thorny wood . . . v 4 67
And yonder is the wolf that makes this spoil . . . v 4 80
Take heed of yonder dog! Look, when he fawns, he bites *Richard III.* i 3 289
Yonder comes Paris. Look ye yonder, niece . . . *Troi. and Cres.* i 2 230
What sneaking fellow comes yonder?—Where? yonder? . . . i 2 246
The Trojans' trumpet.—Yonder comes the troop . . . iv 5 64
I have said to some my standers by 'Lo, Jupiter is yonder, dealing life!' . . . iv 5 191
I wonder now how yonder city stands When we have here her base and pillar . . . iv 5 211
Yonder walls, that pertly front your town, . . . Must kiss their own feet iv 5 219
We go wrong, we go wrong.—No, yonder 'tis . . . v 1 74
Then is he yonder, And there the strawy Greeks, ripe for his edge, Fall down . . . v 5 23
No, by the flame of yonder glorious heaven, He shall not carry him . . . v 6 23
Yonder comes news. A wager they have met . . . *Coriolanus* i 4 1
Who's yonder, That does appear as he were flay'd? . . . i 6 21
Empress I am, but yonder sits the emperor . . . *T. Andron.* iv 4 41
What lady is that, which doth enrich the hand Of yonder knight? . . . *Rom. and Jul.* i 5 44

Yonder. So shows a snowy dove trooping with crows, As yonder lady o'er her fellows shows . . . . *Rom. and Jul.* i 5 51
But, soft! what light through yonder window breaks? It is the east . ii 2 2
Lady, by yonder blessed moon I swear . . . . . . ii 2 107
Look, love, what envious streaks Do lace the severing clouds in yonder east . . . . iii 5 8
Bid me leap, rather than marry Paris, From off the battlements of yonder tower . . . . iv 1 78
See, by good hap, yonder's my lord . . . . . *T. of Athens* iii 2 27
Yonder comes a poet and a painter: the plague of company light upon thee! . . . . iv 3 356
Darest thou, Cassius, now Leap in with me into this angry flood, And swim to yonder point? . . . . . . *J. Cæsar* i 2 104
Hide thy spurs in him, Till he have brought thee up to yonder troops . v 3 16
Where, where, Messala, doth his body lie?—Lo, yonder . . . v 3 92
Do you see yonder cloud that's almost in shape of a camel? . *Hamlet* iii 2 393
So would I ha' done, by yonder sun . . . . . . iv 5 65
O, my good lord, yonder's foul murders done! . . . *Othello* v 2 106
Here comes The noble Antony.—And yonder, Cæsar . *Ant. and Cleo.* ii 2 14
Yonder They cast their caps up and carouse together Like friends long lost . . . . iv 12 11
Sir, yonder is your place.—Some other is more fit . . . *Pericles* ii 3 23
Yorick. This same skull, sir, was Yorick's skull, the king's jester *Ham.* v 1 198
Alas, poor Yorick! I knew him, Horatio: a fellow of infinite jest . v 1 203
York. Commend me to thy brother, Edmund York . . . *Richard II.* i 2 62
And what shall good old York there see But empty lodgings? . . . i 2 67
Be York the next that must be bankrupt so! . . . . . ii 1 151
York is too far gone with grief, Or else he never would compare between ii 1 184
Here comes the Duke of York.—With signs of war about his aged neck ii 2 73
Ne'er shall meet again.—That's as York thrives to beat back Bolingbroke ii 2 144
What stir Keeps good old York there with his men of war? . . . ii 3 52
From the most gracious regent of this land, The Duke of York . . ii 3 78
I know my uncle York Hath power enough to serve our turn . . iii 2 89
York is join'd with Bolingbroke, And all your northern castles yielded up iii 2 200
Letters came last night To a dear friend of the good Duke of York's . iii 4 70
Why, York, what wilt thou do? Wilt thou not hide the trespass of thine own? . . . . v 2 88
Sweet York, sweet husband, be not of that mind . . . . v 2 107
Though I be old, I doubt not but to ride as fast as York . . . v 2 115
Sweet York, be patient. Hear me, gentle liege . . . . v 3 91
Travelling towards York, With much ado at length have gotten leave . v 5 73
'Twas where the madcap duke his uncle kept, His uncle York *1 Hen. IV.* i 3 245
That same noble prelate, well beloved, The archbishop.—Of York, is it not? . . . . i 3 269
And then the power of Scotland and of York, To join with Mortimer, ha? i 3 280
Why, my lord of York commends the plot . . . . . ii 3 22
The Archbishop's grace of York, Douglas, Mortimer, Capitulate against us iii 2 119
Westmoreland Towards York shall bend you with your dearest speed . v 5 36
The gentle Archbishop of York is up With well-appointed powers *2 Hen. IV.* i 1 189
You should have been well on your way to York . . . . ii 1 73
My Lord of York, it better show'd with you When that your flock, assembled by the bell, Encircled you . . . . . . iv 2 4
Send Colevile with his confederates To York, to present execution . iv 3 80
I beg The leading of the vaward.—Take it, brave York . *Hen. V.* iv 3 131
York, all haggled over, Comes to him, where in gore he lay insteep'd . iv 6 11
And if thou be not then created York, I will not live to be accounted Warwick . . . . *1 Hen. VI.* ii 4 119
Sweet stem from York's great stock . . . . . . ii 5 41
Derived From famous Edmund Langley, Duke of York . . . ii 5 85
The whole inheritance I give That doth belong unto the house of York iii 1 165
I gird thee with the valiant sword of York . . . . . iii 1 171
Welcome, high prince, the mighty Duke of York!—Perish, base prince, ignoble Duke of York! . . . . iii 1 177
These colours that I wear In honour of my noble Lord of York . . iii 4 30
Why, what is he? as good a man as York.—Hark ye; not so . . iii 4 36
A certain question in the law Argued betwixt the Duke of York and him iv 1 96
Your private grudge, my Lord of York, will out . . . . iv 1 109
Good cousins both, of York and Somerset, Quiet yourselves, I pray . iv 1 114
I see no reason, if I wear this rose, That any one should therefore be suspicious I more incline to Somerset than York . . . . iv 1 154
Cousin of York, we institute your grace To be our regent . . . iv 1 162
To Bourdeaux, York! Else, farewell Talbot, France, and England's honour . . . . iv 3 22
This expedition was by York and Talbot Too rashly plotted . . iv 4 2
That, Talbot dead, great York might bear the name . . . iv 4 9
Ring'd about with bold adversity, Cries out for noble York and Somerset iv 4 15
York set him on; York should have sent him aid.—And York as fast upon your grace exclaims . . . . iv 4 29
York lies; he might have sent and had the horse; I owe him little duty . . . . iv 4 33
Had York and Somerset brought rescue in, We should have found a bloody day . . . . iv 7 33
Cousin of York, We here discharge your grace from being regent *2 Hen. VI.* i 1 65
Brave York, Salisbury, and victorious Warwick, Received deep scars . i 1 86
Brother York, thy acts in Ireland, In bringing them to civil discipline i 1 194
And so says York, for he hath greatest cause . . . . i 1 207
So York must sit and fret and bite his tongue, While his own lands are bargain'd for and sold . . . . i 1 230
A day will come when York shall claim his own . . . . i 1 239
Then, York, be still awhile, till time do serve: Watch thou and wake . i 1 248
Bear the arms of York, To grapple with the house of Lancaster . . i 1 256
Somerset, Buckingham, And grumbling York . . . . . i 3 73
For the Duke of York, this late complaint Will make but little for his benefit . . . . i 3 100
I care not which; Or Somerset or York, all's one to me . . . i 3 105
If York have ill demean'd himself in France, Then let him be denay'd the regentship . . . . i 3 106
If Somerset be unworthy of the place, Let York be regent . . . i 3 109
Dispute not that: York is the worthier . . . . . . i 3 111
York is meetest man To be your regent in the realm of France . . i 3 163
Give me leave To show some reason, of no little force, That York is most unmeet of any man . . . . i 3 167
Pray God the Duke of York excuse himself!—Doth any one accuse York for a traitor? . . . . i 3 181
One night, as we were scouring my Lord of York's armour . . . i 3 195
Let Somerset be regent o'er the French, Because in York this breeds suspicion . . . . i 3 210
Sweet York, begin: and if thy claim be good, The Nevils are thy subjects ii 2 7

York. The fifth [son of Edward III.] was Edmund Langley, Duke of York *2 Hen VI.* ii 2 15
York claims it from the third [son] . . . . ii 2 55
They in seeking that Shall find their deaths, if York can prophesy . ii 2 76
The Earl of Warwick Shall one day make the Duke of York a king . ii 2 79
Touching the Duke of York, I will take my death, I never meant him any ill . . . . ii 3 90
York and impious Beaufort, that false priest, Have all limed bushes . ii 4 53
And dogged York, that reaches at the moon . . . . . iii 1 158
'Tis York that hath more reason for his death . . . . . iii 1 245
If York, with all his far-fet policy, Had been the regent there instead of me . . . . iii 1 293
No more, good York; sweet Somerset, be still: Thy fortune, York, hadst thou been regent there, Might happily have proved far worse than his . . . . iii 1 304
Now, York, or never, steel thy fearful thoughts . . . . iii 1 331
Perceive the commons' mind, How they affect the house and claim of York . . . . iii 1 375
The house of York, thrust from the crown By shameful murder . . iv 1 94
Jack Cade, the Duke of York hath taught you this . . . . iv 2 162
Thus stands my state, 'twixt Cade and York distress'd . . . iv 9 31
Now is Cade driven back, his men dispersed; And now is York in arms iv 9 35
From Ireland thus comes York to claim his right . . . . v 1 1
York, if thou meanest well, I greet thee well . . . . . v 1 14
Doth York intend no harm to us, That thus he marcheth with thee arm in arm? . . . . v 1 56
For thousand Yorks he shall not hide his head . . . . . v 1 85
Is Somerset at liberty? Then, York, unloose thy long-imprison'd thoughts . . . . v 1 88
I arrest thee, York, Of capital treason 'gainst the king and crown . v 1 106
The bastard boys of York Shall be the surety for their traitor father . v 1 115
The sons of York, thy betters in their birth, Shall be their father's bail v 1 119
This is my king, York, I do not mistake; But thou mistakest . . v 1 129
Then, nobly, York; 'tis for a crown thou fight'st . . . . v 2 16
York not our old men spares; No more will I their babes . . v 2 51
Meet I an infant of the house of York, Into as many gobbets will I cut it As wild Medea young Absyrtus did . . . . . . v 2 57
Saint Alban's battle won by famous York Shall be eternized in all age . v 3 30
Victorious Prince of York, Before I see thee seated in that throne . . . I vow by heaven these eyes shall never close . . . *3 Hen. VI.* i 1 21
This the regal seat: possess it, York; For this is thine . . . i 1 26
Here in the parliament Let us assail the family of York . . . i 1 65
Thou factious Duke of York, descend my throne, And kneel for grace . i 1 74
He made thee Duke of York.—'Twas my inheritance, as the earldom was i 1 77
Do right unto this princely Duke of York . . . . . . i 1 166
Be thou a prey unto the house of York, And die in bands for this! . i 1 185
Now York and Lancaster are reconciled . . . . . . i 1 204
And given unto the house of York such head . . . . . i 1 233
To thy foul disgrace And utter ruin of the house of York . . . i 1 254
The sight of any of the house of York Is as a fury to torment my soul . i 3 30
Alas, poor York! but that I hate thee deadly, I should lament thy miserable state . . . . i 4 84
I prithee, grieve, to make me merry, York . . . . . . i 4 86
York cannot speak, unless he wear a crown. A crown for York! . . i 4 93
Off with his head, and set it on York gates; So York may overlook the town of York . . . . i 4 179
That was a woful looker-on When as the noble Duke of York was slain ii 1 46
They took his head, and on the gates of York They set the same . ii 1 65
Sweet Duke of York, our prop to lean upon, Now thou art gone, we have no staff, no stay . . . . ii 1 68
O valiant lord, the Duke of York is slain!—O Warwick, Warwick! . ii 1 100
No longer Earl of March, but Duke of York . . . . . ii 1 192
Welcome, my lord, to this brave town of York . . . . ii 2 1
Ambitious York did level at thy crown, Thou smiling . . . ii 2 19
Ah, cousin York! would thy best friends did know How it doth grieve me that thy head is here! . . . . ii 2 54
Comes Warwick, backing of the Duke of York . . . . . ii 2 69
'Twas you that kill'd young Rutland, was it not?—Ay, and old York . ii 2 99
Their blood upon thy head; For York in justice puts his armour on . ii 2 130
Suppose this arm is for the Duke of York, And this for Rutland . . ii 4 2
This is the hand that stabb'd thy father York . . . . . ii 4 6
Came on the part of York, press'd by his master . . . . ii 5 66
Impairing Henry, strengthening misproud York . . . . . ii 6 7
Giving no ground unto the house of York . . . . . . ii 6 16
From off the gates of York fetch down the head, Your father's head . ii 6 52
Thou didst love York, and I am son to York . . . . . ii 6 73
Whose unstanched thirst York and young Rutland could not satisfy . ii 6 84
In quarrel of the house of York The worthy gentleman did lose his life iii 2
This arm upholds the house of Lancaster.—And I the house of York . iii 3 108
Did I forget that by the house of York My father came untimely to his death? . . . . iii 3 186
I degraded you from being king, And come now to create you Duke of York . . . . iv 3 34
The Bishop of York, Fell Warwick's brother and by that our foe . . iv 4 11
Being thus arrived From Ravenspurgh haven before the gates of York . iv 7 8
If Henry be your king, Yet Edward at the least is Duke of York . . iv 7 21
Now, for this night, let's harbour here in York . . . . iv 7 79
Be penitent? And thou shalt still remain the Duke of York . . v 1 28
Both Dukes of Somerset Have sold their lives unto the house of York . v 1 74
Come to me, friend or foe, And tell me who is victor, York or Warwick? v 2 6
Speak like a subject, proud ambitious York! . . . . . . v 5 17
Now is the winter of our discontent Made glorious summer by this sun of York . . . . *Richard III.* i 1 2
York and Edward wept, To hear the piteous moan that Rutland made . i 2 157
Did York's dread curse prevail so much with heaven? . . . . i 3 191
Cited up a thousand fearful times, During the wars of York and Lancaster i 4 15
When that our princely father York Bless'd his three sons . . i 4 241
They say my son of York Hath almost overta'en him in his growth . ii 4 6
I pray thee, pretty York, who told thee this? . . . . . ii 4 31
I thought my mother, and my brother York, Would long ere this have met us . . . . iii 1 20
The queen your mother, and your brother York, Have taken sanctuary . iii 1 27
Persuade the queen to send the Duke of York Unto his princely brother . . . . iii 1 33
If my weak oratory Can from his mother win the Duke of York . . iii 1 38
My Lord of York will still be cross in talk . . . . . . iii 1 126
Think you, my lord, this little prating York Was not incensed by his subtle mother? . . . . iii 1 151
Noble York My princely father then had wars in France . . . iii 5 87
One hour hence, And I'll salute your grace of York as mother . . iv 1 30

York. Young York he is but boot, because both they Match not the high perfection of my loss . . . . . . *Richard III.* iv 4 65
Farewell, York's wife, and queen of sad mischance . . . iv 4 114
A pair of bleeding hearts; thereon engrave Edward and York . iv 4 273
What heir of York is there alive but we? And who is England's king but great York's heir? . . . . iv 4 472
Lancaster, The wronged heirs of York do pray for thee . . . v 3 137
All this divided York and Lancaster, Divided in their dire division . v 5 27
By the good discretion Of the right reverend Cardinal of York *Hen. VIII.* i 1 51
You, my lord Cardinal of York, are join'd with me their servant . ii 2 106
The stout Earl Northumberland Arrested him at York . . . iv 2 13
York-place. With the same full state paced back again To York-place . iv 1 94
You must no more call it York-place, that's past . . . iv 1 95
Yorkshire. Are by the sheriff of Yorkshire overthrown . 2 *Hen. IV.* iv 4 99
Sir Thomas Lovel and Lord Marquis Dorset, 'Tis said, my liege, in Yorkshire are in arms . . . . *Richard III.* iv 4 521
You. Come on, you madcap, I'll to the alehouse with you *T. G. of Ver.* ii 5 8
Notwithstanding, man, I'll do you your master what good I can *M. W.* i 4 97
In these times you stand on distance, your passes, stoccadoes . ii 1 233
That will not miss you morning nor evening prayer . . . ii 2 102
Come down, you witch, you hag, you; come down, I say! . . iv 2 188
What offence hath this man made you, sir? *Meas. for Meas.* iii 2 15
Keep your instruction, And hold you ever to our special drift . iv 5 4
She will sit you, you heard my daughter tell you how . . *Much Ado* ii 3 116
You have among you killed a sweet and innocent lady . . . v 1 194
But, soft you, let me be: pluck up, my heart, and be sad . . v 1 207
Fie, fie! you counterfeit, you puppet, you! . . *M. N. Dream* iii 2 288
That you should here repent you, The actors are at hand . . v 1 115
Master young man, you, I pray you, which is the way? . *Mer. of Venice* ii 2 34
Will you prepare you for this masque to-night? . . . . ii 4 23
Therefore, put you in your best array; bid your friends *As Y. Like It* v 2 79
Welcome, you;—how now, you;—what, you;—fellow, you *T. of Shrew* iv 1 114
You, sir! why, what are you? . . . . *T. Night* iii 4 346
To your own bents dispose you: you'll be found, Be you beneath the sky . . . . *W. Tale* i 2 179
John lays you plots; the times conspire with you . . *K. John* iii 4 146
They will learn you by rote where services were done . . . *Hen. V.* iii 6 74
Prepare you, lords, for Edward is at hand, Ready to fight . 3 *Hen. VI.* v 4 60
He will weep you, an 'twere a man born in April . . *Troi. and Cres.* i 2 188
Mistress minion, you, Thank me no thankings . . . *Rom. and Jul.* iii 5 152
You blocks, you stones, you worse than senseless things! . . *J. Cæsar* i 1 40
Prepare you, generals: The enemy comes on in gallant show . . v 1 12
Soft you now! The fair Ophelia! . . . . *Hamlet* iii 1 88
Soft you; a word or two before you go . . . . . *Othello* v 2 338
Young. By love the young and tender wit Is turn'd to folly *T. G. of Ver.* i 1 47
His years but young, but his experience old; His head unmellow'd . ii 4 69
O' my life, if I were young again, the sword should end it . *Mer. Wives* i 1 40
Would I were young for your sake, Mistress Anne! . . . i 1 268
You are not young, no more am I; go to then, there's sympathy . ii 1 6
Sir John affects thy wife.—Why, sir, my wife is not young . . ii 1 116
He wooes both high and low, both rich and poor, Both young and old . ii 1 118
How wise, how noble, young, how rarely featured . . *Much Ado* iii 1 60
To brag What I have done being young, or what would do Were I not old v 1 61
Had we fought, I doubt we should have been too young for them . v 1 119
Say, can you fast? your stomachs are too young . . . *L. L. Lost* iv 3 294
Few taller are so young . . . . v 2 846
O spite! too old to be engaged to young . . . . *M. N. Dream* i 1 138
Things growing are not ripe until their season: So I, being young, till now ripe not to reason . . . . ii 2 118
Pluck the young sucking cubs from the she-bear . . *Mer. of Venice* ii 1 29
Had you been as wise as bold, Young in limbs, in judgement old . ii 7 71
Doth commend A young and learned doctor . . . . . iv 1 144
I never knew so young a body with so old a head . . . . iv 1 163
Come, come, elder brother, you are too young in this . *As Y. Like It* i 1 57
Your brother is but young and tender; and, for your love, I would be loath to foil him, as I must. . . . . i 1 135
There is not one so young and so villanous this day living . . i 1 161
His mouth full of news.—Which he will put on us, as pigeons feed their young . . . . i 2 100
Alas, he is too young! yet he looks successfully . . . . i 2 162
I was too young that time to value her; But now I know her . . i 3 73
And says, if ladies be but young and fair, They have the gift to know it ii 7 37
I perish, Tranio, If I achieve not this young modest girl . *T. of Shrew* i 1 161
A wife With wealth enough and young and beauteous . . . . i 2 86
I will not burden thee; For, knowing thee to be but young and light . ii 1 204
He is old, I young.—And may not young men die, as well as old? . ii 1 393
Young budding virgin, fair and fresh and sweet . . . . iv 5 37
Even so it was with me when I was young . . . . *All's Well* i 3 134
And kept a coil with 'Too young' and 'the next year' and ''tis too early' ii 1 28
To be young again, if we could . . . . ii 2 40
You are too young, too happy, and too good . . . . . ii 3 102
She is young, wise, fair; In these to nature she's immediate heir . ii 3 138
I long to talk with the young noble soldier . . . . . iv 5 109
Not yet old enough for a man, nor young enough for a boy . *T. Night* i 5 165
Young though thou art, thine eye Hath stay'd upon some favour that it loves . . . . ii 4 24
Sooth, when I was young And handed love as you do . . . *W. Tale* iv 4 358
She shall not be so young As was your former. . . . . . v 1 78
When she was young you woo'd her; now in age Is she become the suitor? v 3 108
But lusty, young, and cheerly drawing breath . . . . *Richard II.* i 3 66
For young hot colts being raged do rage the more . . . . ii 1 70
Never gentle lamb more mild, Than was that young and princely gentleman ii 1 175
I tender you my service, Such as it is, being tender, raw, and young . ii 3 42
Both young and old rebel, And all goes worse than I have power to tell iii 2 119
I am too young to be your father, Though you are old enough to be my heir . . . . iii 3 204
The very windows spake, So many greedy looks of young and old . v 2 13
Being but young, I framed to the harp Many an English ditty 1 *Hen. IV.* iii 1 123
You that are old consider not the capacities of us that are young 2 *Hen. IV.* i 2 197
Blasted with antiquity? and will you yet call yourself young? . . i 2 209
A good-limbed fellow; young, strong, and of good friends . . iii 2 114
This same young sober-blooded boy doth not love me . . . iv 3 94
As young as I am, I have observed these three swashers . *Hen. V.* iii 2 29
When I was young, as yet I am not old, I do remember . 1 *Hen. VI.* iii 4 17
Marriage, uncle! alas, my years are young! And fitter is my study . v 1 21
Whose hand is that the forest bear doth lick? Not his that spoils her young before her face . . . . 3 *Hen. VI.* ii 2 14
Unreasonable creatures feed their young . . . . . . ii 2 26
Offering their own lives in their young's defence . . . . ii 2 32
So many days my ewes have been with young . . . . . ii 5 35
Young. What! can so young a thorn begin to prick? . 3 *Hen. VI.* v 5 13
Have now the fatal object in my eye Where my poor young was limed . v 6 17
Framed in the prodigality of nature, Young, valiant, wise *Richard III.* i 2 245
He is young, and his minority Is put unto the trust of Richard Gloucester ii 3 11
He was the wretched'st thing when he was young, So long a-growing ii 4 18
So wise so young, they say, do never live long . . . . iii 1 79
He prettily and aptly taunts himself: So cunning and so young is wonderful . . . . iii 1 135
'Be thou,' quoth I, 'accursed, For making me, so young, so old a widow!' iv 1 73
You are young, Sir Harry Guildford . . . . . *Hen. VIII.* i 4 9
They were young and handsome, and of the best breed in the north ii 2 3
This is yet but young, and may be left To some ears unrecounted . . iii 2 47
She is young, and of a noble modest nature, I hope she will deserve well iv 2 135
If I spared any That had a head to hit, either young or old, He or she . v 4 24
He is very young: and yet will he, within three pound, lift as much as his brother . . . . *Troi. and Cres.* i 2 125
Is he so young a man and so old a lifter? . . . . . . i 2 128
That same young Trojan ass . . . . v 4 6
Help, You that be noble; help him, young and old! . *Coriolanus* iii 1 228
Thy sight is young, And thou shalt read when mine begin to dazzle *T. Andron.* iii 2 84
Good morrow, cousin.—Is the day so young? . . . *Rom. and Jul.* i 1 166
A very gross kind of behaviour, as they say: for the gentlewoman is young . . . . ii 4 178
Wert thou as young as I, Juliet thy love, An hour but married . . iii 3 65
I'll not wed; I cannot love, I am too young; I pray you, pardon me . iii 5 188
She's best married that dies married young . . . . . iv 5 78
She is young and apt: Our own precedent passions do instruct us What levity's in youth . . . . *T. of Athens* i 1 132
Thus much of this [gold] will make black white, foul fair, Wrong right, base noble, old young . . . . iv 3 29
Thou ever young, fresh, loved, and delicate wooer [gold]! . . iv 3 385
An aged interpreter, though young in days . . . . . v 3 8
Noble and young, When thy first griefs were but a mere conceit . v 4 13
My strange and self-abuse Is the initiate fear that wants hard use: We are yet but young in deed . . . . *Macbeth* iii 4 144
I am young; but something You may deserve of him through me . . iv 3 14
Believe so much in him, that he is young, And with a larger tether may he walk Than may be given you . . . . . . *Hamlet* i 3 124
So young, and so untender?—So young, my lord, and true . *Lear* i 1 108
Not so young, sir, to love a woman for singing, nor so old to dote on her for any thing . . . . i 4 40
You know, nuncle, The hedge-sparrow fed the cuckoo so long, That it had it head bit off by it young . . . . i 4 236
The oldest hath borne most: we that are young Shall never see so much v 3 325
The knave is handsome, young, and hath all those requisites in him that folly and green minds look after . . . . *Othello* ii 1 250
She that, so young, could give out such a seeming . . . . iii 3 209
Here's a young and sweating devil here, That commonly rebels . . iii 4 42
Patience, thou young and rose-lipp'd cherubin! . . . . iv 2 63
Up to yond hill; Your legs are young; I'll tread these flats *Cymbeline* iii 3 11
The lines of my body are as well drawn as his; no less young, more strong iv 1 11
All lovers young, all lovers must Consign to thee, and come to dust . iv 2 274
Many years, Though Cloten then but young, you see, not wore him From my remembrance . . . . iv 4 23
Here is a thing too young for such a place . . . . *Pericles* iii 1 15
That excellent complexion, which did steal The eyes of young and old . iv 1 42
You're a young foolish sapling, and must be bowed . . . iv 2 93
Did you go to't so young? Were you a gamester at five or at seven? . iv 6 80
Young Adam Cupid, he that shot so trim . . . *Rom. and Jul.* ii 1 13
Young affection. And young affection gapes to be his heir ii Prol. 2
Young affects. Nor to comply with heat—the young affects In me defunct—and proper satisfaction . . . . *Othello* i 3 264
Young Alcides. With much more love Than young Alcides *Mer. of Ven.* iii 2 55
Young ambition. Lowliness is young ambition's ladder . *J. Cæsar* ii 1 22
Young Arthur. And put the same into young Arthur's hand . *K. John* i 1 14
Open wide your gates, And let young Arthur, Duke of Bretagne, in . ii 1 301
We will heal up all; For we'll create young Arthur Duke of Bretagne . ii 1 551
I was Geffrey's wife; Young Arthur is my son . . . . iii 4 47
But what shall I gain by young Arthur's fall? . . . . . iii 4 141
May be he will not touch young Arthur's life . . . . . iii 4 160
Young Arthur's death is common in their mouths . . . . iv 2 187
Why urgest thou so oft young Arthur's death? . . . . . iv 2 204
Young Arthur is alive: this hand of mine Is yet a maiden and an innocent hand . . . . iv 2 251
After young Arthur, claim this land for mine . . . . . v 2 94
Young babes. Those that do teach young babes Do it with gentle means and easy tasks . . . . *Othello* iv 2 111
Young baggage! disobedient wretch! . . . . *Rom. and Jul.* iii 5 161
Young baron. Falconbridge, the young baron of England *Mer. of Venice* i 2 72
Young blood doth not obey an old decree . . . . *L. L. Lost* iv 3 217
I know young bloods look for a time of rest . . . . *J. Cæsar* iv 3 262
Would harrow up thy soul, freeze thy young blood . . . . *Hamlet* i 5 16
Young bones. Strike her young bones, You taking airs, with lameness! *Lear* ii 4 165
Young boy. To beguile the supposition of that lascivious young boy *All's Well* iv 3 333
Hubert, throw thine eye On yon young boy . . . . *K. John* iii 3 60
Must you with hot irons burn out both mine eyes?—Young boy, I must iv 1 40
I love thee better than I love e'er a scurvy young boy of them all 2 *Hen. IV.* ii 4 296
And my young boy Hath an aspect of intercession . . . *Coriolanus* v 3 31
Young boys and girls Are level now with men; the odds is gone *A. and C.* iv 15 65
Young bulls. Wanton as youthful goats, wild as young bulls 1 *Hen. IV.* iv 1 103
Young Charbon the puritan and old Poysam the papist . . *All's Well* i 3 55
Young clerk. I'll mar the young clerk's pen . . *Mer. of Venice* v 1 237
Young cockerel. A bump as big as a young cockerel's stone *Rom. and Jul.* i 3 53
Young conception. I have a young conception in my brain *Tr. and Cr.* i 3 312
Young count. I knew the young count to be a dangerous and lascivious boy . . . . *All's Well* iv 3 248
I would not be a young count in your way . . . . *Hen. VIII.* ii 3 41
Young couple. I must Bestow upon the eyes of this young couple Some vanity of mine art . . . . *Tempest* iv 1 40
Young cousin. Why, my young cousin, it is good to grow *Richard III.* ii 4 9
Young Cupid. I might see young Cupid's fiery shaft . *M. N. Dream* ii 1 161
Yet You clasp young Cupid's tables . . . . . . *Cymbeline* iii 2 39
Young dace. If the young dace be a bait for the old pike 2 *Hen. IV.* iii 2 355
Young daughter. I have commended to his goodness The model of our chaste loves, his young daughter . . . . . . *Hen. VIII.* iv 2 132
Young Dauphin. Is the young Dauphin every way complete . *K. John* ii 1 433

Young days. Thy young days, which we may nominate tender *L. L. Lost* i 2 15
God forbid I should be so bold to press to heaven in my young days *T. Andron.* iv 3 91
Being of so young days brought up with him . *Hamlet* ii 2 11
Young doctor. A young doctor of Rome; his name is Balthasar *M. of V.* iv 1 153
Young down. Smooth as oil, soft as young down . *1 Hen. IV.* i 3 7
Young earl. A filthy officer he is in those suggestions for the young earl. Beware of them . . . . *All's Well* iii 5 19
Young Edward. And all the unlook'd for issue of their bodies *3 Hen. VI.* iii 2 130
Nay, now dispatch; 'twas I that stabb'd young Edward *Richard III.* i 2 182
Young Edward lives: think now what I would say . . iv 2 10
Young-eyed. Still quiring to the young-eyed cherubins . *Mer. of Venice* v 1 62
Young fellow. It is the stubbornest young fellow of France *As Y. Like It* i 1 148
Madam, yond young fellow swears he will speak with you *T. Night* i 5 147
A good shallow young fellow . . . . *2 Hen. IV.* ii 4 258
I cannot conceive you.—Sir, this young fellow's mother could . *Lear* i 1 13
Young folks. How the young folks lay their heads together! *T. of Shrew* i 2 139
Young fry. What, you egg! Young fry of treachery! . *Macbeth* iv 2 84
Young gallant. One that is well-nigh worn to pieces with age to show himself a young gallant! . . . . . *Mer. Wives* ii 1 22
Come, where is this young gallant that is so desirous to lie with his mother earth? . . . . *As Y. Like It* i 2 212
Young gamester, your father were a fool To give thee all *T. of Shrew* ii 1 402
Young gentleman. Master young gentleman, I pray you, which is the way? . . . . *Mer. of Venice* ii 2 40
They say many young gentlemen flock to him every day *As Y. Like It* i 1 123
Young gentleman, your spirits are too bold for your years . i 2 183
At the gate a young gentleman much desires to speak with you *T. Night* i 5 107
The young gentleman of the Count Orsino's is returned . . iii 4 62
The behaviour of the young gentleman gives him out to be of good capacity iii 4 203
If this young gentleman Have done offence, I take the fault on me . iii 4 343
When I was in France, Young gentlemen would be as sad as night *K. John* iv 1 15
These two young gentlemen, that call me father And think they are my sons, are none of mine . . . . . *Cymbeline* v 5 328
Young gentlewoman. I know the young gentlewoman . . *Mer. Wives* i 1 63
This young gentlewoman had a father,—O, that 'had'! . . *All's Well* i 1 19
He hath perverted a young gentlewoman here . . . . iv 3 17
Young George. If I revolt, off goes young George's head *Richard III.* iv 5 4
But, tell me, is young George Stanley living? . . . . v 5 9
Young German. How like you the young German? . *Mer. of Venice* i 2 90
Young gibbets. Unless a man would marry a gallows and beget young gibbets . . . . *Cymbeline* v 4 207
Young guest. My young guest, methinks you're allycholly *T. G. of V.* iv 2 26
Young Harry. See riot and dishonour stain the brow Of my young Harry *1 Hen. IV.* i 1 86
I saw young Harry, with his beaver on . . . . iv 1 104
Said he young Harry Percy's spur was cold? . *2 Hen. IV.* i 1 49
Young Henry. I will proclaim young Henry king . . *1 Hen. VI.* i 1 169
Depart to Paris to the king, For there young Henry with his nobles lie iii 2 129
It is young Henry, earl of Richmond . . . *3 Hen. VI.* iv 6 67
Young Hotspur. Who in a bloody field by Shrewsbury Hath beaten down young Hotspur and his troops . . . *2 Hen. IV.* Ind. 25
It was young Hotspur's case at Shrewsbury . . . . i 3 26
Young huntsman. You are a young huntsman, Marcus . *T. Andron.* iv 1 101
Young John Talbot. Then God take mercy on brave Talbot's soul; And on his son young John! . . . . *1 Hen. VI.* iv 3 35
Young John Talbot! I did send for thee To tutor thee in stratagems of war iv 5 1
Before young Talbot from old Talbot fly, The coward horse that bears me fall and die! . . . . iv 6 46
O, where's young Talbot? where is valiant John? Triumphant death, smear'd with captivity, Young Talbot's valour makes me smile at thee . . . . iv 7 2
I have what I would have, Now my old arms are young John Talbot's grave . . . . iv 7 32
Young Talbot was not born To be the pillage of a giglot wench . iv 7 40
Young judge. O wise young judge, how I do honour thee! *Mer. of Ven.* iv 1 224
Young king. Indeed I think the young king loves you not . *2 Hen. IV.* v 2 9
I know the young king is sick for me . . . . v 3 141
Young knave. What! a young knave, and begging! . . . i 2 84
That same scurvy doting foolish young knave's sleeve of Troy *T. and C.* v 4 4
Young lad, come forth; I have to say with you . *K. John* iv 1 8
Here's a young lad framed of another leer . . *T. Andron.* iv 2 119
Young lady. Is she not a modest young lady? . . . *Much Ado* i 1 166
Your grace had got the good will of this young lady . . ii 1 224
Yonder is heavy news within between two soldiers and my young lady! *All's Well* iii 2 36
A man, young lady! lady, such a man As all the world . *Rom. and Jul.* i 3 75
Supper served up, you called, my young lady asked for . . i 3 101
My young lady bade me inquire you out . . . . ii 4 173
What, my young lady and mistress! . . . . *Hamlet* ii 2 444
Since my young lady's going into France, sir, the fool hath much pined away . . . . *Lear* i 4 79
Young limbs. A man can no more separate age and covetousness than a' can part young limbs and lechery . . . *2 Hen. IV.* i 2 257
Young lion. The young lion repents; marry, not in ashes . . i 2 221
Young lord. In his youth He had the wit which I can well observe To-day in our young lords . . . . . *All's Well* i 2 33
Farewell, young lords; these warlike principles Do not throw from you ii 1 1
I take my young lord to be a very melancholy man . . iii 2 3
The young lord Did to his majesty, his mother, and his lady Offence . v 3 12
Young lords, beware! an should the empress know This discord's ground, the music would not please . . . *T. Andron.* ii 1 69
Now, young lords, was't not a happy star Led us to Rome? . iv 2 32
Young love. To whose young love The vines of France and milk of Burgundy Strive to be interess'd . . . . . *Lear* i 1 85
Young maid. Here's a young maid with travel much oppress'd And faints for succour . . . . . . *As Y. Like It* ii 4 74
[Time] trots hard with a young maid between the contract of her marriage and the day it is solemnized . . . . . iii 2 331
This young maid might do her A shrewd turn . . . *All's Well* iii 5 70
A fair young maid that yet wants baptism . . *Hen. VIII.* v 3 162
O heavens! is't possible, a young maid's wits Should be as mortal as an old man's life? . . . . *Hamlet* iv 5 159
Did you by indirect and forced courses Subdue and poison this young maid's affections? . . . . *Othello* i 3 112
Young man. Run in here, good young man; go into this closet *M. Wives* i 4 39
If he had found the young man, he would have been horn-mad . i 4 51
Ay me, he'll find the young man there, and be mad! . . i 4 68
The young man is an honest man . . . . . i 4 75
I'll but bring my young man here to school . . . . iv 1 8
Young man. A young man More fit to do another such offence Than die for this . . . . *Meas. for Meas.* ii 3 13
A dowager Long withering out a young man's revenue . *M. N. Dream* i 1 6
Is't not enough, young man, That I did never, no, nor never can? . ii 2 125
Master young man, you, I pray you, which is the way? *Mer. of Venice* ii 2 34
When we are both accoutred like young men, I'll prove the prettier fellow . . . . iii 4 63
O noble judge! O excellent young man! . . . . . iv 1 246
Three proper young men, of excellent growth and presence *As Y. Like It* i 2 129
Young man, have you challenged Charles the wrestler? . . i 2 178
Now Hercules be thy speed, young man! . . . . i 2 222
O excellent young man! . . . . i 2 225
What is thy name, young man? . . . . . . i 2 233
Had I before known this young man his son, I should have given him tears . . . . i 2 249
Look you, who comes here; a young man and an old in solemn talk ii 4 20
Welcome, young man; Thou offer'st fairly to thy brothers' wedding v 4 172
Scatters young men through the world To seek their fortunes *T. of Shrew* i 2 50
By good fortune I have lighted well On this young man . . i 2 169
He is old, I young.—And may not young men die, as well as old? . ii 1 393
A young man married is a man that's marr'd . *All's Well* ii 3 315
'Tis a fair young man, and well attended . . . *T. Night* i 5 110
Leave this young man in pawn till I bring it you . *W. Tale* iv 4 838
He that wins of all, Of kings, of beggars, old men, young men, maids *K. John* ii 1 570
What, ye knaves! young men must live . . . *1 Hen. IV.* ii 2 96
Young men, whom Aristotle thought Unfit to hear moral philosophy *Troi. and Cres.* ii 2 166
Never did young man fancy With so eternal and so fix'd a soul . v 2 165
How now, young man! mean'st thou to fight to-day? . . . v 3 29
I do remit these young men's heinous faults . . *T. Andron.* i 1 484
Such comfort as do lusty young men feel . . . *Rom. and Jul.* i 2 26
Young men's love then lies Not truly in their hearts, but in their eyes ii 3 67
Young man, thou couldst not die more honourable . . *J. Cæsar* v 1 60
Whose providence Should have kept short, restrain'd, and out of haunt, This mad young man . . . . *Hamlet* iv 1 19
Young men will do't, if they come to't; By cock, they are to blame iv 5 61
Now I must To the young man send humble treaties *Ant. and Cleo.* iii 11 62
Young Mars. The Black Prince, that young Mars of men *Richard II.* ii 3 101
Young master. My young master doth expect your reproach *M. of Ven.* ii 5 19
What, my young master? O my gentle master! . *As Y. Like It* ii 3 2
Come, I'll flesh ye; come on, young master . . . *Lear* ii 2 49
Young mistress. And my young mistress thus I did bespeak *Hamlet* ii 2 140
He'll be as full of quarrel and offence As my young mistress' dog *Othello* ii 3 53
Young Ned, for thee, thine uncles and myself Have in our armours watch'd the winter's night . . . . . . *3 Hen. VI.* v 7 16
Young nephew. When your young nephew Titus lost his leg . *T. Night* v 1 66
Young nerves. He sweats, Strains his young nerves . *Cymbeline* iii 3 94
Young nobility. O, that your young nobility could judge! *Richard III.* i 3 257
Young Octavius. Thou shalt discourse To young Octavius of the state of things . . . . *J. Cæsar* iii 1 296
Young Octavius with Mark Antony Have made themselves so strong . iv 3 153
Young Octavius and Mark Antony Come down upon us . . . iv 3 168
Young one. Well aim'd of such a young one.—Now, by Saint George, I am too young for you . . . . *T. of Shrew* ii 1 237
Dead though she be, she feels her young one kick . *All's Well* v 3 303
What say these young ones? What say you, my niece? . *K. John* ii 1 521
As the dam runs lowing up and down, Looking the way her harmless young one went, And can do nought but wail . *2 Hen. VI.* iii 1 215
I long To have this young one made a Christian . . *Hen. VIII.* v 3 180
When did the tiger's young ones teach the dam? . *T. Andron.* ii 3 142
The poor wren, The most diminutive of birds, will fight, Her young ones in her nest, against the owl . . . . . . *Macbeth* iv 2 11
Young one, Inform us of thy fortunes . . . *Cymbeline* iv 2 360
Come, young one, I like the manner of your garments well *Pericles* iv 2 144
Young Paris. Read o'er the volume of young Paris' face *Rom. and Jul.* i 3 81
Young Petrucio. Marry, that, I think, be young Petrucio . . i 5 133
Young Phœbus. His brave fleet With silken streamers the young Phœbus fanning . . . . *Hen. V.* iii Prol. 6
Young pigeons. William cook: are there no young pigeons? *2 Hen. IV.* v 1 18
Young plants. Abuses our young plants with carving . *As Y. Like It* iii 2 378
Young play-fellow. Your precious self had then not cross'd the eyes Of my young play-fellow . . . . *W. Tale* i 2 80
Young prince. You have an unspeakable comfort of your young prince i 1 38
Are you so fond of your young prince as we Do seem to be of ours? . i 2 164
Nor is't directly laid to thee, the death Of the young prince . . iii 2 196
Having both their country quitted With this young prince . . v 1 193
Which you truly owe To him that owes it, namely this young prince *K. John* ii 1 248
Young princes, close your hands.—And your lips too . . ii 1 533
The most comparative, rascalliest, sweet young prince . *1 Hen. IV.* i 2 91
Nay, I'll tickle ye for a young prince, i' faith . . . ii 4 489
The young prince hath misled me . . . . *2 Hen. IV.* i 2 164
You follow the young prince up and down, like his ill angel . . i 2 185
How many good young princes would do so? . . . . ii 2 33
If our queen and this young prince agree, I'll join mine eldest daughter and my joy To him . . . . . . *3 Hen. VI.* iii 3 241
O brave young prince! thy famous grandfather Doth live again in thee v 4 52
So cut off As, deathsmen, you have rid this sweet young prince! . . v 5 67
Bethink you, like a careful mother, Of the young prince *Richard III.* ii 2 97
Forthwith from Ludlow the young prince be fetch'd Hither to London ii 2 121
The devil take Antenor! the young prince will go mad *Troi. and Cres.* iv 2 77
Young prince of Tyre, you have at large received The danger of the task *Pericles* i 1 1
Young quat. I have rubb'd this young quat almost to the sense, And he grows angry . . . . *Othello* v 1 11
Young ravens must have food . . . . *Mer. Wives* i 3 38
Young remembrance. 'Twas a rough night.—My young remembrance cannot parallel A fellow to it . . . . . *Macbeth* ii 3 67
Young Romeo is it?—'Tis he, that villain Romeo *Rom. and Jul.* i 5 66
Can any of you tell me where I may find the young Romeo? . . ii 4 125
Young Romeo will be older when you have found him than he was when you sought him . . . . ii 4 126
There lies the man, slain by young Romeo, That slew thy kinsman . iii 1 149
Young rover. Next to thyself and my young rover, he's Apparent to my heart . . . . *W. Tale* i 2 176
Young scamels. I'll get thee Young scamels from the rock . *Tempest* ii 2 176
Young scholar. Freely give unto you this young scholar *T. of Shrew* ii 1 79
Young sir. Give over this attempt.—Do, young sir . *As Y. Like It* i 2 191
Mark your divorce, young sir, Whom son I dare not call *W. Tale* iv 4 428

Young sister. Vouchsafe a word, young sister, but one word *M. for M.* iii 1 152
Young soldier. Come, my young soldier, put up your iron *T. Night* iv 1 42
Young son. Alas, what joy shall noble Talbot have To bid his young son welcome to his grave? 1 *Hen. VI.* iv 3 40
How doth the prince, and my young son of York? *Richard III.* iv 1 14
What early tongue so sweet saluteth me? Young son, it argues a distemper'd head So soon to bid good morrow to thy bed *Rom. and Jul.* ii 3 33
Young squarer. Is there no young squarer now that will make a voyage with him to the devil? *Much Ado* i 1 82
Young squire. Her womb then rich with my young squire *M. N. Dream* ii 1 131
Young start-up. That young start-up hath all the glory of my overthrow *Much Ado* i 3 68
Young swain. That young swain that you saw here but erewhile, That little cares for buying any thing *As Y. Like It* ii 4 89
How prettily the young swain seems to wash The hand was fair before! *W. Tale* iv 4 377
Young traveller. I was then a young traveller *Cymbeline* i 4 46
Young Venetian. There is alighted at your gate A young Venetian *Mer. of Venice* ii 9 87
Cassio, my lord, hath kill'd a young Venetian *Othello* v 2 112
Young wanton and effeminate boy *Richard II.* v 3 10
Young waverer, come, go with me *Rom. and Jul.* ii 3 89
Young wench. To weep, like a young wench that had buried her grandam; to fast, like one that takes diet *T. G. of Ver.* ii 1 24
Young whelp. The young whelp of Talbot's, raging-wood 1 *Hen. VI.* iv 7 35
Young years. Would some part of my young years Might but redeem the passage of your age! ii 5 107
Young York he is but boot *Richard III.* iv 4 65
Younger. He looks younger than he did, by the loss of a beard *M. Ado* iii 2 48
That aged ears play truant at his tales And younger hearings are quite ravished *L. L. Lost* ii 1 75
The old duke is banished by his younger brother *As Y. Like It* i 1 105
Your younger brother Orlando hath a disposition to come in disguised against me i 1 130
I'll do the service of a younger man In all your business ii 3 54
For simply your having in beard is a younger brother's revenue iii 2 397
Let the world slip: we shall ne'er be younger *T. of Shrew* Ind. 2 147
Until the elder sister first be wed: The younger then is free i 2 264
Achieve the elder, set the younger free For our access i 2 268
Proceed in practice with my younger daughter; She's apt to learn ii 1 165
Such a man Might be a copy to these younger times *All's Well* i 2 46
'Let me not live,' quoth he, 'After my flame lacks oil, to be the snuff Of younger spirits' i 2 60
If I were but two hours younger, I'ld beat thee ii 3 269
I am sure the younger of our nature, That surfeit on their ease, will day by day Come here for physic iii 1 17
Then let thy love be younger than thyself, Or thy affection cannot hold the bent; For women are as roses *T. Night* ii 4 37
Why, being younger born, Doth he lay claim to thine inheritance? *K. John* i 1 71
Thy place in council thou hast rudely lost, Which by thy younger brother is supplied 1 *Hen. IV.* iii 2 33
Younger sons to younger brothers, revolted tapsters and ostlers iv 2 30
Violation of all faith and troth Sworn to us in your younger enterprise. v 1 71
If the issue of the elder son Succeed before the younger, I am king 2 *Hen. VI.* ii 2 52
Young Prince Edward marries Warwick's daughter.—Belike the elder; Clarence will have the younger 3 *Hen. VI.* iv 1 118
Thy tears are salter than a younger man's *Coriolanus* iv 1 22
Younger than she are happy mothers made *Rom. and Jul.* i 2 12
Younger than you, Here in Verona, ladies of esteem, Are made already mothers i 3 69
It is common for the younger sort To lack discretion *Hamlet* ii 1 116
Conferring them on younger strengths *Lear* i 1 41
The younger rises when the old doth fall iii 3 26
Though grey Do something mingle with our younger brown, yet ha' we A brain that nourishes our nerves *Ant. and Cleo.* iv 8 20
The younger brother, Cadwal, Once Arviragus *Cymbeline* iii 3 95
This gentleman, my Cadwal, Arviragus, Your younger princely son v 5 360
Those palates who, not yet two summers younger, Must have inventions *Pericles* i 4 39
How dost thou find the inclination of the people, especially of the younger sort? iv 2 105
Youngest. My youngest boy, and yet my eldest care *Com. of Errors* i 1 125
I am the youngest son of Sir Rowland de Boys *As Y. Like It* i 1 59; i 2 234
I am more proud to be Sir Rowland's son, His youngest son i 2 246
Is it possible, on such a sudden, you should fall into so strong a liking with old Sir Rowland's youngest son? i 3 28
That is, not to bestow my youngest daughter Before I have a husband for the elder *T. of Shrew* i 1 50
By helping Baptista's eldest daughter to a husband we set his youngest free i 1 142
The next wish after, That Lucentio indeed had Baptista's youngest daughter i 1 245
His youngest daughter, beautiful Bianca i 2 120
The youngest daughter whom you hearken for Her father keeps from all access of suitors i 2 260
Look, where the youngest wren of nine comes *T. Night* iii 2 70
Thus Eleanor's pride dies in her youngest days 2 *Hen. VI.* ii 3 46
Brother, though I be youngest, give me leave 3 *Hen. VI.* i 2 1
Then I'll marry Warwick's youngest daughter *Richard III.* i 1 153
The youngest son of Priam, a true knight, Not yet mature *Tr. and Cr.* iv 5 96
O, well fought, my youngest brother! v 6 12
Vows revenge as spacious as between The young'st and oldest thing *Cor.* iv 6 68
With his own hand did slay his youngest son *T. Andron.* i 1 418
I am the youngest of that name, for fault of a worse *Rom. and Jul.* ii 4 128
The maid is fair, o' the youngest for a bride *T. of Athens* i 1 123
Great rivals in our youngest daughter's love *Lear* i 1 47
Answer my life my judgement, Thy youngest daughter does not love thee least i 1 154
The hot-blooded France, that dowerless took Our youngest born ii 4 216
Most praised, most loved, A sample to the youngest *Cymbeline* i 1 48
Youngling, thou canst not love so dear as I.—Greybeard, thy love doth freeze.—But thine doth fry *T. of Shrew* ii 1 339
Youngling, learn thou to make some meaner choice *T. Andron.* ii 1 73
I tell you, younglings, not Enceladus Shall seize this prey iv 2 93
Youngly. How youngly he began to serve his country *Coriolanus* ii 3 244
Younker. How like a younker or a prodigal The scarfed bark puts from her native bay! *Mer. of Venice* ii 6 14
What, will you make a younker of me? 1 *Hen. IV.* iii 3 92
Trimm'd like a younker prancing to his love! 3 *Hen. VI.* ii 1 24

Your beggar of fifty *Meas. for Meas.* iii 2 133
Every true man's apparel fits your thief iv 2 46
There is not a more fearful wild-fowl than your lion living *M. N. Dream* iii 1 33
I could munch your good dry oats iv 1 36
Your chestnut was ever the only colour *As Y. Like It* iii 4 12
As your pearl in your foul oyster v 4 63
Your marriage comes by destiny, Your cuckoo sings by kind *All's Well* i 3 66
Your worm is your only emperor for diet *Hamlet* iv 3 22
Your fat king and your lean beggar is but variable service iv 3 24
Your Dane, your German, and your swag-bellied Hollander *Othello* ii 3 79
Is your Englishman so expert in his drinking? ii 3 82
That remains loyal to his vow, and your, increasing in love *Cymbeline* iii 2 47
Yours. What to come In yours and my discharge *Tempest* ii 1 254
My good will is to it, And yours it is against iii 1 31
The king, His brother, and yours, abide all three distracted v 1 12
Gentle breath of yours my sails Must fill, or else my project fails Epil. 11
Some love of yours hath writ to you in rhyme *T. G. of Ver.* i 2 79
Not mine; my gloves are on.—Why, then, this may be yours ii 1 2
You swinged me for my love, which makes me the bolder to chide you for yours ii 1 89
I have writ your letter Unto the secret nameless friend of yours ii 1 111
That done, our day of marriage shall be yours v 4 172
What's mine is yours and what is yours is mine *Meas. for Meas.* v 1 543
That flattering tongue of yours won me *As Y. Like It* iv 1 189
I am yours Upon your will to suffer *All's Well* iv 4 29
If you would seek us, We are yours i' the garden *W. Tale* i 2 178
Whenever Buckingham doth turn his hate On you or yours *Richard III.* ii 1 33
O God, I fear thy justice will take hold On me, and you, and mine, and yours for this! ii 1 132
And so betide to me As well I tender you and all of yours! ii 4 72
And stand unshaken yours *Hen. VIII.* iii 2 199
I have wounds to show you, which shall be yours in private *Coriolanus* ii 3 83
This sober form of yours hides wrongs *J. Cæsar* iv 2 40
Whose heavy hand hath bow'd you to the grave And beggar'd yours for ever *Macbeth* iii 1 91
Fear not yet To take upon you what is yours iv 3 70
Make your soonest haste; So your desires are yours *Ant. and Cleo.* iv 4 28
O, behold, How pomp is follow'd! mine will now be yours; And, should we shift estates, yours would be mine v 2 151
Yourself. Make yourself ready in your cabin for the mischance *Tempest* i 1 27
I fear you have done yourself some wrong i 2 443
You may thank yourself for this great loss ii 1 123
My father Is hard at study; pray now, rest yourself iii 1 20
Nor can imagination form a shape, Besides yourself, to like of iii 1 57
Henceforth carry your letters yourself *T. G. of Ver.* i 1 154
What are you reasoning with yourself?—Nay, I was rhyming ii 1 148
Who is that, servant?—Yourself, sweet lady ii 4 37
A thousand times good morrow.—As many, worthy lady, to yourself iv 3 7
Yourself shall go first.—Not I, sir; pray you, keep on *Mer. Wives* i 1 320
You yourself know how easy it is to be such an offender ii 2 195
Finding yourself desired of such a person *Meas. for Meas.* ii 4 91
I know this to be true; therefore prepare yourself to death iii 1 169
I will call upon you anon, for some advantage to yourself iv 1 24
You bid me seek redemption of the devil: Hear me yourself v 1 30
About evening come yourself alone To know the reason *Com. of Errors* iii 1 96
What is your will that I shall do with this?—What please yourself iii 2 175
Joshua, yourself; myself and this gallant gentleman, Judas *L. L. Lost* v 1 133
Madam, yourself are not exempt in this, Nor your son *Richard III.* ii 1 18
Be to yourself As you would to your friend *Hen. VIII.* i 1 135
Unfold to me, yourself, your half, Why you are heavy *J. Cæsar* ii 1 274
Am I yourself But, as it were, in sort or limitation? ii 1 282
Yourselves. How answer you for yourselves? *Much Ado* iv 2 25
Withdraw into a chamber by yourselves v 4 11
We can afford no more at such a price.—Prize you yourselves *L. L. Lost* v 2 224
Speak for yourselves; my wit is at an end v 2 430
Masters, spread yourselves *M. N. Dream* i 2 17
Masters, you ought to consider with yourselves iii 1 31
Feed yourselves with questioning *As Y. Like It* v 4 144
If you . . . will laugh yourselves into stitches, follow me *T. Night* iii 2 73
Our part therein we banish with yourselves *Richard II.* i 3 181
We come to be informed by yourselves 1 *Hen. VI.* v 4 118
Now show yourselves men; 'tis for liberty 2 *Hen. VI.* iv 2 193
Though he be infortunate, Assure yourselves, will never be unkind v 9 19
Love not yourselves: away, Rob one another *T. of Athens* iv 3 447
Youth. Home-keeping youth have ever homely wits *T. G. of Ver.* i 1 2
Living dully sluggardized at home, Wear out thy youth with shapeless idleness i 1 8
To whisper and conspire against my youth? i 2 43
He wonder'd that your lordship Would suffer him to spend his youth at home i 3 5
Great impeachment to his age, In having known no travel in his youth i 3 16
And be in eye of every exercise Worthy his youth and nobleness of birth i 3 33
Forswear not thyself, sweet youth, for I am not welcome ii 5 3
To be fantastic may become a youth Of greater time than I shall show to be ii 7 47
Perceive my fear of this, Knowing that tender youth is soon suggested iii 1 34
Such as the fury of ungovern'd youth Thrust from the company of awful men iv 1 45
The musician likes me not.—Why, my pretty youth? iv 2 58
I have need of such a youth That can with some discretion do my business iv 4 69
Our youth got me to play the woman's part iv 4 165
She is beholding to thee, gentle youth iv 4 178
Here, youth, there is my purse; I give thee this For thy sweet mistress' sake iv 4 181
We have some salt of our youth in us *Mer. Wives* ii 3 50
He capers, he dances, he has eyes of youth, he writes verses iii 2 68
Somebody call my wife. Youth in a basket! O you pandarly rascals! iv 2 122
In her youth There is a prone and speechless dialect *Meas. for Meas.* i 2 187
More grave and wrinkled than the aims and ends Of burning youth i 3 6
To haunt assemblies Where youth, and cost, and witless bravery keeps i 3 10
Does your worship mean to geld and splay all the youth of the city? ii 1 243
Who, falling in the flaws of her own youth, Hath blister'd her report ii 3 11
Thou hast nor youth nor age, But, as it were, an after-dinner's sleep, Dreaming on both; for all thy blessed youth Becomes as aged, and doth beg the alms Of palsied eld iii 1 32
Nips youth i' the head and follies doth emmew As falcon doth the fowl iii 1 91
His riotous youth, with dangerous sense, Might in the times to come have ta'en revenge iv 4 32
I see by you I am a sweet-faced youth *Com. of Errors* v 1 418

Youth. He that hath a beard is more than a youth . . . *Much Ado* ii 1 39
He that is more than a youth is not for me, and he that is less than a man, I am not for him . . . . . ii 1 40
A man loves the meat in his youth that he cannot endure in his age ii 3 248
That's as much as to say, the sweet youth's in love . . . iii 2 53
Have vanquish'd the resistance of her youth . . . . iv 1 47
His active practice, His May of youth and bloom of lustihood v 1 76
Your worship speaks like a most thankful and reverend youth . v 1 325
A well-accomplish'd youth, Of all that virtue love for virtue loved *L. L. L.* ii 1 56
Vow, alack, for youth unmeet, Youth so apt to pluck a sweet! iv 3 113
To see no woman; Flat treason 'gainst the kingly state of youth iv 3 293
Do you not educate youth at the charge-house on the top of the mountain? v 1 87
The blood of youth burns not with such excess As gravity's revolt to wantonness . . . . . . v 2 73
Stir up the Athenian youth to merriments . . . *M. N. Dream* i 1 13
Nosegays, sweetmeats, messengers Of strong prevailment in unharden'd youth . . . . . . i 1 35
Question your desires; Know of your youth, examine well your blood . i 1 68
The green corn Hath rotted ere his youth attain'd a beard . . ii 1 95
A sweet Athenian lady is in love With a disdainful youth . . ii 1 261
Helena is here at hand; And the youth, mistook by me . . iii 2 112
Anon comes Pyramus, sweet youth and tall . . . v 1 145
I owe you much, and, like a wilful youth, That which I owe is lost *M. of V.* i 1 146
Such a hare is madness the youth, to skip o'er the meshes of good counsel the cripple . . . . . i 2 21
Being so full of unmannerly sadness in his youth . . . i 2 55
If that the youth of my new interest here Have power to bid you welcome . . . . iii 2 224
And speak of frays Like a fine bragging youth . . . . iii 4 69
Repair thy wit, good youth, or it will fall To cureless ruin . iv 1 141
Furthermore, I pray you, show my youth old Shylock's house . iv 2 11
I gave it to a youth, A kind of boy, a little scrubbed boy . . v 1 161
Come on: since the youth will not be entreated, his own peril on his forwardness . . . . . . *As Y. Like It* i 2 158
In pity of the challenger's youth I would fain dissuade him . . i 2 170
I come but in, as others do, to try with him the strength of my youth i 2 182
Thou art a gallant youth: I would thou hadst told me of another father i 2 242
Wherever they are gone, That youth is surely in their company . ii 2 16
O unhappy youth! Come not within these doors . . . ii 3 16
In my youth I never did apply Hot and rebellious liquors in my blood . ii 3 48
In thy youth thou wast as true a lover As ever sigh'd . . . ii 4 26
Where dwell you, pretty youth?—With this shepherdess, my sister . iii 2 352
Who was in his youth an inland man . . . . . iii 2 363
Fair youth, I would I could make thee believe I love . . . iii 2 404
I swear to thee, youth, by the white hand of Rosalind . . . iii 2 413
At which time would I, being but a moonish youth, grieve, be effeminate iii 2 430
I would not be cured, youth.—I would cure you . . . . iii 2 445
Will you go?—With all my heart, good youth . . . . iii 2 454
All's brave that youth mounts and folly guides . . . . iii 4 48
Sweet youth, I pray you, chide a year together . . . iii 5 64
Know'st thou the youth that spoke to me erewhile? . . . iii 5 105
It is a pretty youth: not very pretty: But, sure, he's proud . iii 5 113
I prithee, pretty youth, let me be better acquainted with thee . iv 1 1
My errand is to you, fair youth . . . . . . iv 3 6
Whether that thy youth and kind Will the faithful offer take . iv 3 59
To that youth he calls his Rosalind He sends this bloody napkin . iv 3 93
Give this napkin Dyed in his blood unto the shepherd youth . iv 3 156
Be of good cheer, youth: you a man! you lack a man's heart . iv 3 164
There is a youth here in the forest lays claim to you . . v 1 7
Youth, you have done me much ungentleness, To show the letter . v 2 83
Good shepherd, tell this youth what 'tis to love . . . v 2 89
Schoolmasters will I keep within my house, Fit to instruct her youth *T. of Shrew* i 1 95
'Tis age that nourisheth.—But youth in ladies' eyes that flourisheth ii 1 342
Youth, thou bear'st thy father's face; Frank nature, rather curious than in haste, Hath well composed thee . . *All's Well* i 2 19
In his youth He had the wit which I can well observe To-day . i 2 31
This thorn Doth to our rose of youth rightly belong . . . i 3 136
It is the show and seal of nature's truth, Where love's strong passion is impress'd in youth . . . . i 3 139
Yourself, Whose aged honour cites a virtuous youth . . . i 3 216
Youth, beauty, wisdom, courage, all That happiness and prime can happy call . . . . ii 1 184
If thou be'st not an ass, I am a youth of fourteen . . . ii 3 107
Into the staggers and the careless lapse Of youth and ignorance . ii 3 171
If the quick fire of youth light not your mind, You are no maiden iv 2 5
Would have made all the unbaked and doughy youth of a nation in his colour . . . . iv 5 4
Natural rebellion, done i' the blaze of youth . . . . v 3 6
And boarded her i' the wanton way of youth . . . . v 3 211
Therefore, good youth, address thy gait unto her . . *T. Night* i 4 15
She will attend it better in thy youth Than in a nuncio's of more grave aspect . . . . i 4 27
Noble, Of great estate, of fresh and stainless youth . . . i 5 278
Methinks I feel this youth's perfections With an invisible and subtle stealth . . . . i 5 315
If that the youth will come this way to-morrow, I'll give him reasons for't . . . . i 5 324
Come kiss me, sweet and twenty, Youth's a stuff will not endure . ii 3 53
Since the youth of the count's was to-day with my lady, she is much out of quiet . . . . ii 3 143
That youth's a rare courtier . . . . iii 1 97
Good youth, I will not have you: And yet, when wit and youth is come to harvest, Your wife is like to reap a proper man . . . iii 1 142
By innocence I swear, and by my youth, I have one heart . . iii 1 169
She did show favour to the youth in your sight only to exasperate you iii 2 19
You should have banged the youth into dumbness . . . iii 2 25
Challenge me the count's youth to fight with him . . . iii 2 37
By all means stir on the youth to an answer . . . . iii 2 63
The youth bears in his visage no great presage of cruelty . . iii 2 68
Youth is bought more oft than begg'd or borrow'd . . . iii 4 3
Youth, whatsoever thou art, thou art but a scurvy fellow . . iii 4 162
This letter, being so excellently ignorant, will breed no terror in the youth iii 4 207
And drive the gentleman, as I know his youth will aptly receive it, into a most hideous opinion of his rage . . . . . . iii 4 211
Hath in him what youth, strength, skill, and wrath can furnish man withal . . . . iii 4 254
I have persuaded him the youth's a devil . . . . . iii 4 321
This youth that you see here I snatch'd one half out of the jaws of death iii 4 393
Three months this youth hath tended upon me . . . . v 1 102

Youth. Unfold . . . what thou dost know Hath newly pass'd between this youth and me . . . . *T. Night* v 1 158
I would there were no age between sixteen and three-and-twenty, or that youth would sleep out the rest . . . . *W. Tale* iii 3 60
If the sins of your youth are forgiven you, you're well to live . iii 3 125
No more than were I painted I would wish This youth should say 'twere well . . . . iv 4 102
Your youth, And the true blood which peepeth fairly through't . iv 4 147
Were I the fairest youth That ever made eye swerve . . . iv 4 384
Your eye hath too much youth in't . . . . . . v 1 225
Deny his youth The rich advantage of good exercise . . *K. John* iv 2 59
I do commit his youth To your direction . . . . . iv 2 67
By all the blood that ever fury breathed, The youth says well . v 2 128
Had I thy youth and cause, I would not stay . . *Richard II.* i 3 305
That I may breathe my last In wholesome counsel to his unstaid youth ii 1 2
He that no more must say is listen'd more Than they whom youth and ease have taught to glose . . . . ii 1 10
Lascivious metres, to whose venom sound The open ear of youth doth always listen; Report of fashions . . . . . . ii 1 20
Deal mildly with his youth; For young hot colts being raged do rage the more . . . . ii 1 69
Were I but now the lord of such hot youth . . . . ii 3 99
Which makes him prune himself, and bristle up The crest of youth *1 Hen. IV.* i 1 99
Bacon-fed knaves! they hate us youth: down with them: fleece them ii 2 89
Youth, the more it is wasted the sooner it wears . . . ii 4 442
That villanous abominable misleader of youth . . . . ii 4 509
Wherein my youth Hath faulty wander'd and irregular . . . iii 2 26
The time will come, That I shall make this northern youth exchange His glorious deeds for my indignities . . . . . . iii 2 145
It hath the excuse of youth and heat of blood . . . . v 2 17
And chid his truant youth with such a grace . . . . v 2 63
O, Harry, thou hast robb'd me of my youth! . . . . v 4 77
Your lordship, Though not clean past your youth, hath yet some smack of age in you . . . . *2 Hen. IV.* i 2 110
We that are in the vaward of our youth, I must confess, are wags . i 2 200
Do you set down your name in the scroll of youth? . . . i 2 202
To approve my youth further, I will not . . . . . i 2 214
He was indeed the glass Wherein the noble youth did dress themselves ii 3 22
The happiest youth, viewing his progress through, What perils past, what crosses to ensue, Would shut the book . . . . iii 1 54
Hath done nothing but prate to me of the wildness of his youth . iii 2 328
Base and abject routs, Led on by bloody youth, guarded with rags . iv 1 34
We will our youth lead on to higher fields . . . . . iv 4 3
And he, the noble image of my youth . . . . . . iv 4 55
O foolish youth! Thou seek'st the greatness that will overwhelm thee iv 5 97
There is my hand. You shall be as a father to my youth . . v 2 118
The courses of his youth promised it not . . . *Hen. V.* i 1 24
Is in the very May-morn of his youth, Ripe for exploits . . i 2 120
Our master Says that you savour too much of your youth . . i 2 250
All the youth of England are on fire, And silken dalliance in the wardrobe lies . . . . ii Prol. 1
A vain, giddy, shallow, humorous youth . . . . . ii 4 28
As matching to his youth and vanity, I did present him with the Paris balls . . . . ii 4 130
Whiles a more frosty people Sweat drops of gallant youth in our rich fields! . . . . iii 5 25
And they will give Their bodies to the lust of English youth . . iii 5 30
Detain'd me all my flowering youth Within a loathsome dungeon *1 Hen. VI.* ii 5 56
And shall my youth be guilty of such blame? . . . . iv 5 47
My death's revenge, thy youth, and England's fame . . . iv 6 39
My tender youth was never yet attaint With any passion of inflaming love . . . . v 5 81
What! did my brother Henry spend his youth, His valour, coin, and people, in the wars? . . . . *2 Hen. VI.* i 1 78
And wouldst climb a tree?—But that in all my life, when I was a youth ii 1 99
Thou hast most traitorously corrupted the youth of the realm . iv 7 36
Wast thou ordain'd, dear father, To lose thy youth in peace? . v 2 46
And, like a gallant in the brow of youth, Repairs him with occasion v 3 4
How well resembles it the prime of youth, Trimm'd like a younker prancing to his love! . . . . *3 Hen. VI.* ii 1 23
You will have leave, Till youth take leave and leave you to the crutch iii 2 35
What youth is that, Of whom you seem to have so tender care? . iv 6 65
If you ever chance to have a child, Look in his youth to have him so cut off! . . . . v 5 66
Die in his youth by like untimely violence! . . *Richard III.* i 3 201
Your children were vexation to your youth . . . . . iv 4 305
The children live, whose parents thou hast slaughter'd, Ungovern'd youth, to wail it in their age . . . . iv 4 392
Think, how thou stab'dst me in my prime of youth . . . v 3 119
These are the youths that thunder at a playhouse . . *Hen. VIII.* v 4 63
O admirable youth! he ne'er saw three and twenty . *Troi. and Cres.* i 2 255
Gentleness, virtue, youth, liberality, and such like, the spice and salt that season a man . . . . i 2 277
His youth in flood, I'll prove this truth with my three drops of blood i 3 300
Now heavens forbid such scarcity of youth! . . . . i 3 302
Whose youth and freshness Wrinkles Apollo's, and makes stale the morning . . . . ii 2 78
To keep her constancy in plight and youth . . . . . iii 2 168
The Grecian youths are full of quality . . . . . iv 4 78
One that knows the youth Even to his inches . . . . iv 5 110
I have, thou gallant Trojan, seen thee oft Labouring for destiny make cruel way Through ranks of Greekish youth . . . . iv 5 185
Doff thy harness, youth; I am to-day i' the vein of chivalry . v 3 31
Make wells and Niobes of the maids and wives, Cold statues of the youth . . . . v 10 20
When youth with comeliness plucked all gaze his way . *Coriolanus* i 3 7
Hark! our drums Are bringing forth our youth . . . . i 4 16
She will a handmaid be to his desires, A loving nurse, a mother to his youth . . . . *T. Andron.* i 1 332
For pity of mine age, whose youth was spent In dangerous wars . iii 1 2
My youth can better spare my blood than you . . . . iii 1 166
And would not, but in fury, fright my youth . . . . iv 1 24
To gratify your honourable youth, The hope of Rome . . . iv 2 12
This myself, The vigour and the picture of my youth . . . iv 2 108
Verona brags of him To be a virtuous and well govern'd youth *R. and J.* i 5 70
Where unbruised youth with unstuff'd brain Doth couch his limbs . ii 3 37
Good gentle youth, tempt not a desperate man; Fly hence, and leave me v 3 59
Youth, Put not another sin upon my head, By urging me to fury . v 3 61

Youth. I'll bury thee in a triumphant grave; A grave? O, no! a lantern, slaughter'd youth *Rom. and Jul.* v 3 84
O, what more favour can I do to thee, Than with that hand that cut thy youth in twain To sunder his that was thine enemy? v 3 99
Our own precedent passions do instruct us What levity's in youth *T. of Athens* i 1 134
Lust and liberty Creep in the minds and marrows of our youth! iv 1 26
Bring down rose-cheeked youth To the tub-fast and the diet iv 3 86
Melted down thy youth In different beds of lust iv 3 256
A discovery of the infinite flatteries that follow youth and opulency v 1 38
In pity of our aged and our youth, I cannot choose but tell him v 1 179
Our youths and wildness shall no whit appear, But all be buried in his gravity *J. Cæsar* ii 1 148
My lord is often thus, And hath been from his youth *Macbeth* iii 4 54
Many unrough youths that even now Protest their first of manhood v 2 10
A violet in the youth of primy nature, Forward, not permanent *Hamlet* i 3 7
In the morn and liquid dew of youth Contagious blastments are most imminent i 3 41
Best safety lies in fear: Youth to itself rebels, though none else near i 3 44
Noble youth, The serpent that did sting thy father's life Now wears his crown i 5 38
All forms, all pressures past, That youth and observation copied there i 5 101
Wild and usual slips As are companions noted and most known To youth ii 1 24
Having ever seen in the prenominate crimes The youth you breathe of guilty ii 1 44
Brought up with him, And sith so neighbour'd to his youth and haviour ii 2 12
Truly in my youth I suffered much extremity for love ii 2 191
By the consonancy of our youth, by the obligation of our ever-preserved love ii 2 295
That unmatch'd form and feature of blown youth Blasted with ecstasy iii 1 167
To flaming youth let virtue be as wax, And melt in her own fire iii 4 84
A very riband in the cap of youth, Yet needful too iv 7 78
Youth no less becomes The light and careless livery that it wears Than settled age his sables iv 7 79
In youth, when I did love, did love, Methought it was very sweet v 1 69
That is Laertes, A very noble youth v 1 247
Let it stamp wrinkles in her brow of youth *Lear* i 4 306
I protest, Maugre thy strength, youth, place, and eminence v 3 131
Is there not charms By which the property of youth and maidhood May be abused? *Othello* i 1 173
Abused her delicate youth with drugs or minerals That weaken motion i 2 74
When I did speak of some distressful stroke That my youth suffer'd i 3 158
She must change for youth: when she is sated with his body, she will find the error of her choice i 3 356
The gravity and stillness of your youth The world hath noted ii 3 191
The borders maritime Lack blood to think on 't, and flush youth revolt *Ant. and Cleo.* i 4 52
And carry back to Sicily much tall youth That else must perish here ii 6 7
Tell him he wears the rose Of youth upon him iii 13 21
Like the spirit of a youth That means to be of note, begins betimes iv 4 26
Yet ha' we A brain that nourishes our nerves, and can Get goal for goal of youth iv 8 22

Youth. O disloyal thing, That shouldst repair my youth, thou heap'st A year's age on me *Cymbeline* i 1 132
My youth I spent Much under him; of him I gather'd honour iii 1 70
And with what imitation you can borrow From youth of such a season iii 4 175
Money, youth?—All gold and silver rather turn to dirt! iii 6 53
Prithee, fair youth, Think us no churls iii 6 64
Were you a woman, youth, I should woo hard but be your groom iii 6 69
Fair youth, come in: Discourse is heavy, fasting iii 6 90
I know not why I love this youth iv 2 21
A demand who is't shall die, I'ld say 'My father, not this youth' iv 2 24
This youth, howe'er distress'd, appears he hath had Good ancestors iv 2 46
'Lack, good youth! Thou movest no less with thy complaining iv 2 374
So please you entertain me.—Ay, good youth iv 2 394
Thou'rt my good youth, my page; I'll be thy master v 5 118
Though you did love this youth, I blame ye not; You had a motive for't v 5 267
Prithee, valiant youth, Deny 't again.—I have spoke it, and I did it v 5 289
If in our youths we could pick up some pretty estate, 'twere not amiss to keep our door hatched *Pericles* iv 2 35
Youthful Valentine Attends the emperor in his royal court *T. G. of Ver.* i 3 26
The youthful lover now is gone And this way comes he iii 1 41
But she I mean is promised by her friends Unto a youthful gentleman iii 1 107
Have you the tongues?—My youthful travel therein made me happy iv 1 34
Youthful still! in your doublet and hose this raw rheumatic day! *M. W.* iii 1 46
A sin prevailing much in youthful men *Com. of Errors* v 1 52
Youthful and unhandled colts, Fetching mad bounds *Mer. of Venice* v 1 72
And ere we have thy youthful wages spent, We'll light upon some settled low content *As Y. Like It* ii 3 67
His youthful hose, well saved, a world too wide For his shrunk shank ii 7 160
This youthful parcel Of noble bachelors *All's Well* ii 3 58
Your mind is all as youthful as your blood *K. John* iii 4 125
O thou, the earthly author of my blood, Whose youthful spirit, in me regenerate, Doth with a twofold vigour lift me up *Richard II.* i 3 70
Rouse up thy youthful blood, be valiant and live i 3 83
Wanton as youthful goats, wild as young bulls 1 *Hen. IV.* iv 1 103
You have misled the youthful prince 2 *Hen. IV.* i 2 163
Like youthful steers unyoked, they take their courses East, west, north, south iv 2 103
But health, alack, with youthful wings is flown From this bare wither'd trunk iv 5 229
Leaden age, Quicken'd with youthful spleen and warlike rage 1 *Hen. VI.* iv 6 13
Henry is youthful and will quickly yield v 3 99
Thus he goes, As did the youthful Paris once to Greece v 5 104
And lo, where youthful Edward comes! 3 *Hen. VI.* v 5 11
Modest as morning when she coldly eyes The youthful Phœbus *T. and C.* i 3 230
Troy burns, or else let Helen go.—Now, youthful Troilus ii 2 113
Than youthful April shall with all his showers *T. Andron.* iii 1 18
Had she affections and warm youthful blood, She would be as swift in motion as a ball *Rom. and Jul.* ii 5 12
Youthful, and nobly train'd, Stuff'd, as they say, with honourable parts iii 5 182
I met the youthful lord at Laurence' cell iv 2 25
Weighing the youthful season of the year *J. Cæsar* ii 1 108
Y-ravished the regions round, And every one with claps can sound *Pericles* iii Gower 35
Yslaked. Now sleep yslaked hath the rout; No din but snores iii Gower 1

Z

Zany. Some carry-tale, some please-man, some slight zany *L. L. Lost* v 2 463
These set kind of fools, no better than the fools' zanies *T. Night* i 5 96
Zeal. Methinks my zeal to Valentine is cold, And that I love him not as I was wont *T. G. of Ver.* ii 4 203
Intend a kind of zeal *Much Ado* ii 2 36
What will Biron say when that he shall hear Faith so infringed, which such zeal did swear? *L. L. Lost* iv 3 146
What zeal, what fury hath inspired thee now? iv 3 229
Where zeal strives to content, and the contents Dies in the zeal of that which it presents v 2 518
If you had pleased to have defended it With any terms of zeal *Mer. of Venice* v 1 205
Would she begin a sect, might quench the zeal Of all professors else *W. T.* v 1 107
No further enemy to you Than the constraint of hospitable zeal *K. John* ii 1 244
Lest zeal, now melted by the windy breath Of soft petitions, pity, and remorse, Cool and congeal ii 1 477
Whom zeal and charity brought to the field ii 1 565
Shall cool the hearts Of all his people and freeze up their zeal iii 4 150
We swear A voluntary zeal and an unurged faith To your proceedings v 2 10
Let not my cold words here accuse my zeal *Richard II.* i 1 47
His prayers are full of false hypocrisy; Ours of true zeal v 3 108
Beg his peace, With tears of innocency and terms of zeal 1 *Hen. IV.* iv 3 63
If thou wert sensible of courtesy, I should not make so dear a show of zeal v 4 95
Or honest Bardolph, whose zeal burns in his nose 2 *Hen. IV.* ii 4 357
Under the counterfeited zeal of God iv 2 27
This doth infer the zeal I had to see him v 5 14
And do serve you With hearts create of duty and of zeal *Hen. V.* ii 2 31
'Twill make them cool in zeal unto your grace 2 *Hen. VI.* iii 1 177
With whom an upright zeal to right prevails 3 *Hen. VI.* v 1 78
This do I beg of God, When I am cold in zeal to you or yours *Rich. III.* ii 1 40

Zeal. Pardon us the interruption Of thy devotion and right Christian zeal *Richard III.* iii 7 103
As, in love and zeal, Loath to depose the child, your brother's son iii 7 208
How holily he works in all his business! And with what zeal! *Hen. VIII.* ii 2 25
Out of his noble nature, Zeal, and obedience he still bore your grace iii 1 63
Had I but served my God with half the zeal I served my king iii 2 455
As angry with my fancy, More bright in zeal than the devotion which Cold lips blow to their deities *Troi. and Cres.* iv 4 28
Thou dost not use me courteously, To shame the zeal of my petition to thee iv 4 124
With his own hand did slay his youngest son, In zeal to you *T. Andron.* i 1 419
That you would once use our hearts, whereby we might express some part of our zeals *T. of Athens* i 2 89
Like those that under hot ardent zeal would set whole realms on fire iii 3 33
That which I show, heaven knows, is merely love, Duty, and zeal iv 3 523
Zealous. With that, they all did tumble on the ground, With such a zealous laughter *L. L. Lost* v 2 116
Whilst I from far His name with zealous fervour sanctify *All's Well* iii 4 11
Upon thy cheek lay I this zealous kiss *K. John* ii 1 19
If zealous love should go in search of virtue, Where should he find it purer? ii 1 428
So sweet is zealous contemplation *Richard III.* iii 7 94
Zed. Thou whoreson zed! thou unnecessary letter! *Lear* ii 2 69
Zenelophon. The pernicious and indubitate beggar Zenelophon *L. L. Lost* iv 1 67
Zenith. My zenith doth depend upon A most auspicious star *Tempest* i 2 181
Zephyrs. They are as gentle As zephyrs blowing below the violet *Cymb.* iv 2 172
Zodiac. So long that nineteen zodiacs have gone round *Meas. for Meas.* i 2 172
Gallops the zodiac in his glistering coach *T. Andron.* ii 1 7
Zone. Till our ground, Singeing his pate against the burning zone, Make Ossa like a wart! *Hamlet* v 1 305
Zwaggered. An chud ha' bin zwaggered out of my life *Lear* iv 6 243

CONCORDANCE

TO THE

POEMS OF SHAKESPEARE

A

Abate. As air and water do abate the fire . . . *Ven. and Adon.* 654
Abettor. Thou foul abettor! thou notorious bawd! . . . *Lucrece* 886
Abhor. But having no defects, why dost abhor me? *Ven. and Adon.* 138
Let fair humanity abhor the deed . . . . . . *Lucrece* 195
I must deflower: The powers to whom I pray abhor this fact 349
O, though I love what others do abhor, With others thou shouldst not abhor my state . . . . *Sonnet* 150 11
Age, I do abhor thee; youth, I do adore thee . . *Pass. Pil.* 165
Abide. Where thou with patience must my will abide *Lucrece* 486
Small lights are soon blown out, huge fires abide . . 647
Blood untainted still doth red abide 1749
My thoughts, from far where I abide, Intend a zealous pilgrimage to thee . . . . *Sonnet* 27 5
Slight air and purging fire, Are both with thee, wherever I abide. 45 2
And when in his fair parts she did abide, She was new lodged *Lov. Comp.* 83
A-billing. Show'd like two silver doves that sit a-billing *Ven. and Adon.* 366
Able. Still cry 'Amen' To every hymn that able spirit affords *Sonnet* 85 7
Abomination. Drunken Desire must vomit his receipt, Ere he can see his own abomination . . . . *Lucrece* 704
Guilty of treason, forgery, and shift, Guilty of incest, that abomination . 921
That they will suffer these abominations 1832
About. His testy master goeth about to take him *Ven. and Adon.* 319
Some twine about her thigh to make her stay . . . 873
About he walks, Rolling his greedy eyeballs in his head *Lucrece* 367
Like a foul usurper, went about From this fair throne to heave the owner out 412
Ere he go to bed, Knit poisonous clouds about his golden head 777
About him were a press of gaping faces 1408
She throws her eyes about the painting round . . . 1499
Round about her tear-distained eye Blue circles stream'd . 1586
About the mourning and congealed face Of that black blood a watery rigol goes 1744
That which governs me to go about Doth part his function *Sonnet* 113 2
Above. The field's chief flower, sweet above compare, Stain to all nymphs, more lovely than a man . . . *Ven. and Adon.* 8
By spirits taught to write Above a mortal pitch, that struck me dead *Sonnet* 86 6
Every humour hath his adjunct pleasure, Wherein it finds a joy above the rest 91 6
But, by all above, These blenches gave my heart another youth 110 6
Which shall above that idle rank remain Beyond all date 122 3
Gave the tempter place, Which like a cherubin above them hover'd *Lov. Comp.* 319
Abridgement. This brief abridgement of my will I make *Lucrece* 1198
Abroad. The goodly objects which abroad they find *Lov. Comp.* 137
All my offences that abroad you see Are errors of the blood . 183
Absence. O absence, what a torment wouldst thou prove . *Sonnet* 39 9
Nor think the bitterness of absence sour 57 7
O, let me suffer, being at your beck, The imprison'd absence of your liberty 58 6
How like a winter hath my absence been From thee! . . 97 1
Though absence seem'd my flame to qualify . . . 109 2
And makes her absence valiant, not her might *Lov. Comp.* 245
Absent. When I am sometime absent from thy heart *Sonnet* 41 2
I will acquaintance strangle and look strange, Be absent from thy walks 89 9
From you have I been absent in the spring . . . 98 1
Absolute. No perfection is so absolute, That some impurity doth not pollute . . . . *Lucrece* 853
Absolution. The blackest sin is clear'd with absolution . . 354
Abstaining. Though weak-built hopes persuade him to abstaining 130
Abundance. Making a famine where abundance lies . *Sonnet* 1 7
Whose strength's abundance weakens his own heart . . 23 4
I in thy abundance am sufficed And by a part of all thy glory live 37 11
And in abundance addeth to his store 135 10
Abundant. Yet this abundant issue seem'd to me But hope of orphans 97 9
Abuse. Things growing to themselves are growth's abuse *Ven. and Adon.* 166
O strange excuse, When reason is the bawd to lust's abuse! . 792
Poor wretches have remorse in poor abuses . . . *Lucrece* 269
Who in their pride do presently abuse it 864
To hide the truth of this false night's abuses . . . 1075
O, let it not be hild Poor women's faults, that they are so fulfill'd With men's abuses 1259
Who cannot abuse a body dead? 1267
Lest he should hold it her own gross abuse 1315
Though my gross blood be stain'd with this abuse . . . 1655
Why dost thou abuse The bounteous largess given thee to give? *Sonnet* 4 5
And for my sake even so doth she abuse me . . . 42 7
I am that I am, and they that level At my abuses reckon up their own 121 10
So him I lose through my unkind abuse 134 12

Abused. Saying, some shape in Sinon's was abused. . . *Lucrece* 1529
Their gross painting might be better used Where cheeks need blood; in thee it is abused . . . . *Sonnet* 82 14
Abusing. And ever let his unrecalling crime Have time to wail th' abusing of his time . . . . *Lucrece* 994
Abysm. In so profound abysm I throw all care Of others' voices *Sonnet* 112 9
Accent. So her accent breaks, That twice she doth begin ere once she speaks *Lucrece* 566
After many accents and delays, Untimely breathings . . . 1719
In other accents do this praise confound . . . *Sonnet* 69 7
Acceptable. What acceptable audit canst thou leave? . . 4 12
Acceptance. And in my will no fair acceptance shine . . 135 8
I have received from many a several fair, Their kind acceptance *Lov. Comp.* 207
Accessary. An accessary by thine inclination To all sins past *Lucrece* 922
That was not forced; that never was inclined To accessary yieldings 1658
That I an accessary needs must be To that sweet thief . *Sonnet* 35 13
Accident. Time, whose million'd accidents Creep in 'twixt vows and change decrees of kings 115 5
No, it was builded far from accident 124 5
The accident which brought me to her eye Upon the moment did her force subdue . . . . *Lov. Comp.* 247
Accidental. He takes for accidental things of trial . . *Lucrece* 326
Accomplish'd in himself, not in his case . . . *Lov. Comp.* 116
Accomplishment. So fares it with this faultful lord of Rome, Who this accomplishment so hotly chased . . . . . *Lucrece* 716
Accorded. My spirits to attend this double voice accorded *Lov. Comp.* 3
Account. Tell o'er The sad account of fore-bemoaned moan . *Sonnet* 30 11
Or at your hand the account of hours to crave . . . 58 3
No face so gracious is as mine, No shape so true, no truth of such account 62 6
Let me pass untold, Though in thy stores' account I one must be 136 10
Accounted. No more than wax shall be accounted evil Wherein is stamp'd the semblance of a devil . . . . *Lucrece* 1245
Accumulate. And on just proof surmise accumulate . . *Sonnet* 117 10
Accurst. Never did he bless My youth with his; the more am I accurst *Ven. and Adon.* 1120
Accuse. Accuse me thus: that I have scanted all . *Sonnet* 117 1
But why of two oaths' breach do I accuse thee, When I break twenty? 152 5
Accusing. And patience, tame to sufferance, bide each check, Without accusing you of injury 58 8
Ache. Like a milch doe, whose swelling dugs do ache *Ven. and Adon.* 875
To see the salve doth make the wound ache more . . *Lucrece* 1116
Achieve. That sin by him advantage should achieve And lace itself with his society . . . . *Sonnet* 67 3
Achilles. That for Achilles' image stood his spear, Griped in an armed hand . . . . *Lucrece* 1424
Acknowledge. I may not evermore acknowledge thee . *Sonnet* 36 9
Acquaintance. Like old acquaintance in a trance, Met far from home *Lucr.* 1595
Thou shalt find Those children nursed, deliver'd from thy brain, To take a new acquaintance of thy mind . . . . . . *Sonnet* 77 12
Knowing thy will, I will acquaintance strangle and look strange 89 8
And haply of our old acquaintance tell 89 12
Acquainted. A woman's gentle heart, but not acquainted With shifting change 20 3
With mine own weakness being best acquainted . . . 88 5
Acquit. Till life to death acquit my forced offence . . *Lucrece* 1071
May any terms acquit me from this chance? 1706
Across. With sad set eyes, and wretched arms across . . . 1662
Act. And all this dumb play had his acts made plain With tears *Ven. and Adon.* 359
I did but act, he's author of thy slander 1006
O impious act, including all foul harms! . . . . . *Lucrece* 199
The powers to whom I pray abhor this fact, How can they then assist me in the act? 350
And swear I found you where you did fulfil The loathsome act of lust . . 1636
This act will be My fame and thy perpetual infamy . . . 1637
May my pure mind with the foul act dispense 1704
Is it revenge to give thyself a blow For his foul act? 1824
In act thy bed-vow broke and new faith torn . . *Sonnet* 152 3
'He seized on my lips,' And with her lips on his did act the seizure *Pass. Pil.* 152
Action. She would not blot the letter With words, till action might become them better . . . . *Lucrece* 1323
Making such sober action with his hand 1403
And to their hope they such odd action yield 1433
Whose action is no stronger than a flower . . . *Sonnet* 65 4
The expense of spirit in a waste of shame Is lust in action; and till action, lust Is perjured 129 2

Active. As a decrepit father takes delight To see his active child do deeds of youth *Sonnet* 37 2
Actor. No outrageous thing From vassal actors can be wiped away *Lucrece* 608
As an unperfect actor on the stage Who with his fear is put besides his part *Sonnet* 23 1
Acture. With acture they may be, Where neither party is nor true nor kind *Lov. Comp.* 185
Add. Now she adds honours to his hateful name *Ven. and Adon.* 994
To add a more rejoicing to the prime, And give the sneaped birds more cause to sing *Lucrece* 332
Which to her oratory adds more grace 564
Their fresh falls' haste Add to his flow, but alter not his taste 651
To thy fair flower add the rank smell of weeds *Sonnet* 69 12
You to your beauteous blessings add a curse 84 13
'Tis so, 'tis true, And to the most of praise add something more 85 10
Add to thy 'Will' One will of mine, to make thy large 'Will' more 135 11
Added. Rain added to a river that is rank Perforce will force it overflow the bank *Ven. and Adon.* 71
Have added feathers to the learned's wing *Sonnet* 78 7
Is of more worth Than when it hath my added praise beside 103 4
Now are minutes added to the hours; To spite me now, each minute seems a moon *Pass. Pil.* 206
Adder. Like one that spies an adder Wreathed up in fatal folds just in his way *Ven. and Adon.* 878
The adder hisses where the sweet birds sing *Lucrece* 871
My adder's sense To critic and to flatterer stopped are *Sonnet* 112 10
Addeth. And in abundance addeth to his store 135 10
Addict. If he be addict to vice, Quickly him they will entice *Pass. Pil.* 415
Adding. Me of thee defeated, By adding one thing to my purpose nothing *Sonnet* 20 12
Addition. By addition me of thee defeated, By adding one thing to my purpose nothing 20 11
To thy sweet will making addition thus 135 4
All aids, themselves made fairer by their place, Came for additions *L. Comp.* 118
Addressed. At length address'd to answer his desire, She modestly prepares to let them know *Lucrece* 1606
Adieu. Ere he says 'Adieu,' The honey fee of parting tender'd is *V. and A.* 537
When you have bid your servant once adieu *Sonnet* 57 8
Adjunct. Though death be adjunct, there's no death supposed *Lucrece* 133
Every humour hath his adjunct pleasure, Wherein it finds a joy *Sonnet* 91 5
To keep an adjunct to remember thee Were to import forgetfulness 122 13
Admiration. With more than admiration he admired Her azure veins *Lucr.* 418
Admire. We admire What thou dost foist upon us that is old *Sonnet* 123 5
Which is to me some praise, that I thy parts admire *Pass. Pil.* 66
Admired. She lies, To be admired of lewd unhallow'd eyes *Lucrece* 392
With more than admiration he admired Her azure veins 418
Making his style admired every where *Sonnet* 84 12
Admiring. The wits of former days To subjects worse have given admiring praise 59 14
Admit. His ear her prayers admits *Lucrece* 558
Let me not to the marriage of true minds Admit impediments *Sonnet* 116 2
Admitted. I was thy 'Will,' And will, thy soul knows, is admitted there 136 3
Ado. Ceasing their clamorous cry till they have singled With much ado the cold fault cleanly out *Ven. and Adon.* 694
Adon. 'Nay, then,' quoth Adon, 'you will fall again' 769
'And yet,' quoth she, 'behold two Adons dead!' 1070
By a brook, A brook where Adon used to cool his spleen *Pass. Pil.* 76
Paler for sorrow than her milk-white dove, For Adon's sake 120
Adonis. Rose-cheek'd Adonis hied him to the chase *Ven. and Adon.* 3
Look, how a bird lies tangled in a net, So fasten'd in her arms Adonis lies 68
Wishing Adonis had his team to guide, So he were like him and by Venus' side 179
And now Adonis, with a lazy spright, And with a heavy, dark, disliking eye 181
At this Adonis smiles as in disdain, That in each cheek appears a pretty dimple 241
A breeding jennet, lusty, young, and proud, Adonis' trampling courser doth espy 261
With her the horse, and left Adonis there: As they were mad 322
All swoln with chafing, down Adonis sits 325
Because Adonis' heart hath made mine hard 378
Reviving joy bids her rejoice, And flatters her it is Adonis voice 978
Adonis lives, and Death is not to blame 992
Thus hoping that Adonis is alive, Her rash suspect she doth extenuate 1009
But when Adonis lived, sun and sharp air Lurk'd like two thieves 1085
Then would Adonis weep; And straight, in pity of his tender years, They both would strive who first should dry his tears 1090
Thus was Adonis slain: He ran upon the boar with his sharp spear 1111
Comparing it to her Adonis' breath 1172
Describe Adonis, and the counterfeit Is poorly imitated after you *Son.* 53 5
Sweet Cytherea, sitting by a brook, With young Adonis *Pass. Pil.* 44
Cytherea, all in love forlorn, A longing tarriance for Adonis made 74
Anon Adonis comes with horn and hounds 122
Venus, with young Adonis sitting by her Under a myrtle shade 143
And then she clipp'd Adonis in her arms 148
Adore. By the Capitol that we adore, And by this chaste blood *Lucrece* 1835
Yet mortal looks adore his beauty still *Sonnet* 7 7
Age, I do abhor thee; youth, I do adore thee *Pass. Pil.* 165
Adored. This earthly saint, adored by this devil, Little suspecteth *Lucrece* 85
Adorn. Canopied in darkness sweetly lay, Till they might open to adorn the day 399
A-doting. Nature, as she wrought thee, fell a-doting *Sonnet* 20 10
Adulterate. And never be forgot in mighty Rome Th' adulterate death of Lucrece and her groom *Lucrece* 1645
For why should others' false adulterate eyes Give salutation? *Sonnet* 121 5
And bastards of his foul adulterate heart *Lov. Comp.* 175
Advance. May my pure mind with the foul act dispense, My low-declined honour to advance? *Lucrece* 1705
Thou art all my art and dost advance As high as learning my rude ignorance *Sonnet* 78 13
O, then, advance of yours that phraseless hand *Lov. Comp.* 225
Advantage. Make use of time, let not advantage slip *Ven. and Adon.* 129
I heartily beseech thee, To take advantage on presented joy 405
What may a heavy groan advantage thee? 950
I have seen the hungry ocean gain Advantage on the kingdom of the shore *Sonnet* 64 6
That sin by him advantage should achieve And lace itself with his society 67 3
A maid of Dian's this advantage found 153 2
Reason strong, For his advantage still did wake and sleep *Lov. Comp.* 123
Adverse. Thy adverse party is thy advocate—And 'gainst myself a lawful plea commence *Sonnet* 35 10
Advice. Advice is sporting while infection breeds *Lucrece* 907
A press of gaping faces, Which seem'd to swallow up his sound advice 1409
Advice is often seen By blunting us to make our wits more keen *Lov. Comp.* 160
Advised. O, be advised! thou know'st not what it is With javelin's point a churlish swine to gore *Ven. and Adon.* 615
When they had sworn to this advised doom *Lucrece* 1849
His utmost sum, Call'd to that audit by advised respects *Sonnet* 49 4
Advisedly. This ill presage advisedly she marketh *Ven. and Adon.* 457
And to the flame thus speaks advisedly *Lucrece* 180
This picture she advisedly perused, And chid the painter 1527
And arm'd his long-hid wits advisedly 1816
Advocate. Thy adverse party is thy advocate—And 'gainst myself a lawful plea commence *Sonnet* 35 10
Ætna. So vanisheth As smoke from Ætna, that in air consumes *Lucrece* 1042
Afar. And Tarquin's eye may read the mot afar 830
Whilst I thy babe chase thee afar behind *Sonnet* 143 10
Afeard. And wast afeard to scratch her wicked foe *Lucrece* 1035
Affable. He, nor that affable familiar ghost Which nightly gulls him *Son.* 86 9
Affairs. His honour, his affairs, his friends, his state, Neglected all *Lucrece* 45
Nor dare I question with my jealous thought Where you may be, or your affairs suppose *Sonnet* 57 10
To stand in thy affairs, fall by thy side 151 12
Affected. Is thine own heart to thine own face affected? *Ven. and Adon.* 157
Affectedly Enswathed, and seal'd to curious secrecy *Lov. Comp.* 48
Affection is a coal that must be cool'd; Else, suffer'd, it will set the heart on fire *Ven. and Adon.* 387
Affection faints not like a pale-faced coward 569
Disturbing Jealousy Doth call himself Affection's sentinel 650
Affection is my captain, and he leadeth *Lucrece* 271
But nothing can affection's course control 500
I will not wrong thy true affection so, To flatter thee with an infringed oath 1060
Sold cheap what is most dear, Made old offences of affections new *Son.* 110 4
And nice affections wavering stood in doubt *Lov. Comp.* 97
Threw my affections in his charmed power 146
Or my affection put to the smallest teen, Or any of my leisures ever charm'd 192
All these trophies of affections hot, Of pensived and subdued desires the tender 218
Afflict. Afflict him in his bed with bedrid groans *Lucrece* 975
Afflicted. Observed as they flew—Towards this afflicted fancy fastly drew *Lov. Comp.* 61
Afford. Sometime her grief is dumb and hath no words; Sometime 'tis mad and too much talk affords *Lucrece* 1106
Vouchsafe t' afford—If ever, love, thy Lucrece thou wilt see—Some present speed to come and visit me 1305
He can afford No praise to thee but what in thee doth live *Sonnet* 79 11
Still cry 'Amen' To every hymn that able spirit affords 85 7
Three themes in one, which wondrous scope affords 105 12
Afloat. Your shallowest help will hold me up afloat 80 9
Afraid. 'Tis a causeless fantasy, And childless error, that they are afraid *Ven. and Adon.* 898
And be not of my holy vows afraid *Lov. Comp.* 179
My curtail dog, that wont to have play'd, Plays not at all, but seems afraid *Pass. Pil.* 274
Afresh. And weep afresh love's long since cancell'd woe *Sonnet* 30 7
Affright. Let ghastly shadows his lewd eyes affright *Lucrece* 971
Against my heart Will fix a sharp knife to affright mine eye 1138
After. Love comforteth like sunshine after rain, But Lust's effect is tempest after sun *Ven. and Adon.* 799
So glides he in the night from Venus' eye; Which after him she darts 817
They answer all ''Tis so:' And would say after her, if she said 'No' 852
Long after fearing to creep forth again 1036
For, after supper, long he questioned With modest Lucrece *Lucrece* 122
'But tell me girl, when went'—and there she stay'd Till after a deep groan—'Tarquin from hence?' 1276
Sinon, whose enchanting story The credulous old Priam after slew 1522
After many accents and delays, Untimely breathings 1719
Then you were Yourself again after yourself's decease *Sonnet* 13 7
After a thousand victories once foil'd 25 10
Describe Adonis, and the counterfeit Is poorly imitated after you 53 6
Lest the wise world should look into your moan And mock you with me after I am gone 71 14
What merit lived in me, that you should love After my death 72 3
The twilight of such day As after sunset fadeth in the west 73 6
Like widow'd wombs after their lords' decease 97 8
They were but sweet, but figures of delight, Drawn after you 98 12
So runn'st thou after that which flies from thee 143 9
New faith torn In vowing new hate after new love bearing 152 4
After-loss. Make be bow, And do not drop in for an after-loss 90 4
Afterwards. My most full flame should afterwards burn clearer 115 4
Again. Then with her windy sighs and golden hairs To fan and blow them dry again she seeks *Ven. and Adon.* 52
Then wink again, And I will wink; so shall the day seem night 121
Give me one kiss, I'll give it thee again, And one for interest 209
His nostrils drink the air, and forth again 273
The lesson is but plain, And once made perfect, never lost again 408
Till his breath breatheth life in her again 474
O, thou didst kill me: kill me once again 499
You will fall again Into your idle over-handled theme 769
She treads the path that she untreads again 908
And sighing it again, exclaims on Death 930
And with his strong course opens them again 960
Sighs dry her cheeks, tears make them wet again 966
With him is beauty slain, And, beauty dead, black chaos comes again 1020
Long after fearing to creep forth again 1036
And never wound the heart with looks again 1042
He ran upon the boar with his sharp spear, Who did not whet his teeth at him again 1113
Return again in haste; Thou see'st our mistress' ornaments are chaste *Lucr.* 321
Then Collatine again, by Lucrece' side, In his clear bed might have reposed still 381
And he hath won what he would lose again 688
Through Night's black bosom should not peep again 788
Long she thinks till he return again, And yet the duteous vassal scarce is gone 1359
Their ranks began To break upon the galled shore, and than Retire again 1441
What he breathes out his breath drinks up again 1666
The poison'd fountain clears itself again 1707
Live again and see Thy father die, and not thy father thee! 1770
That deep vow, which Brutus made before, He doth again repeat 1848
Then you were Yourself again after yourself's decease *Sonnet* 13 7

Again. Thou gavest me thine, not to give back again . . . *Sonnet* 22 14
Who even but now come back again, assured Of thy fair health . . 45 11
No longer glad, I send them back again and straight grow sad . . 45 14
To-morrow see again, and do not kill The spirit of love . . 56 7
Spending again what is already spent . . 76 12
Yet what of thee thy poet doth invent He robs thee of and pays it thee again . . 79 8
And so my patent back again is swerving . . 87 8
So thy great gift, upon misprision growing, Comes home again . . 87 12
If I have ranged, Like him that travels I return again . . 109 6
When he again desires her, being sat, Her grievance with his hearing to divide . . *Lov. Comp.* 66
And yet do question make What I should do again for such a sake . . 322
O, all that borrow'd motion seeming owed, Would yet again betray the fore-betray'd! . . 328
'Farewell,' quoth she, 'and come again to-morrow' . . *Pass. Pil.* 185
'T may be, again to make me wander thither . . 190
Against. And all in vain you strive against the stream . . *Ven. and Adon.* 772
Licking of his wound, 'Gainst venom'd sores the only sovereign plaster . . 916
Against the welkin volleys out his voice . . 921
Against the golden splendour of the sun . . *Lucrece* 25
Against love's fire fear's frost hath dissolution . . 355
And dotes on what he looks, 'gainst law or duty . . 497
Thou back'st reproach against long-living laud . . 622
For now against himself he sounds this doom . . 717
Here she exclaims against repose and rest . . 757
Thus breathes she forth her spite Against the unseen secrecy of night . . 763
Make war against proportion'd course of time . . 774
Let him have time against himself to rave . . 982
Whiles against a thorn thou bear'st thy part . . 1135
Against my heart Will fix a sharp knife to affright mine eye . . 1137
No man inveigh against the wither'd flower . . 1254
And then against my heart he sets his sword . . 1640
That 'gainst thyself thou stick'st not to conspire . . *Sonnet* 10 6
And nothing 'gainst Time's scythe can make defence . . 12 13
Against this coming end you should prepare . . 13 3
Might uphold Against the stormy gusts of winter's day . . 13 11
And 'gainst myself a lawful plea commence . . 35 11
If aught in me Worthy perusal stand against thy sight . . 38 6
Against that time, if ever that time come, When I shall see thee frown . . 49 1
Against that time when thou shalt strangely pass And scarcely greet me . . 49 5
Against that time do I ensconce me here . . 49 9
And this my hand against myself uprear . . 49 11
'Gainst death and all-oblivious enmity Shall you pace forth . . 55 9
Crooked eclipses 'gainst his glory fight . . 60 7
Against my love shall be, as I am now, With Time's injurious hand crush'd and o'erworn . . 63 1
For such a time do I now fortify Against confounding age's cruel knife . . 63 10
Against the wreckful siege of battering days . . 65 6
Upon those boughs which shake against the cold . . 73 3
Upon thy side against myself I'll fight And prove thee virtuous . . 88 3
I straight will halt, Against thy reasons making no defence . . 89 4
For thee against myself I'll vow debate . . 89 13
I will drink Potions of eisel 'gainst my strong infection . . 111 10
When I against myself with thee partake . . 149 2
Gave eyes to blindness, Or made them swear against the thing they see . . 152 12
More perjured I, To swear against the truth so foul a lie! . . 152 14
Which yet men prove Against strange maladies a sovereign cure . . 153 8
Or forced examples, 'gainst her own content . . *Lov. Comp.* 157
Love's arms are peace, 'gainst rule, 'gainst sense, 'gainst shame . . 271
Against the thing he sought he would exclaim . . 313
Age. Thy mark is feeble age, but thy false dart Mistakes that aim . . *Ven. and Adon.* 941
Teaching decrepit age to tread the measures . . 1148
Beauty's red, Which virtue gave the golden age . . *Lucrece* 60
To nurse the life With honour, wealth, and ease, in waning age . . 142
Respect and reason, wait on wrinkled age! . . 275
How will thy shame be seeded in thine age! . . 603
One poor retiring minute in an age Would purchase thee a thousand thousand friends . . 962
Even so this pattern of the worn-out age Pawn'd honest looks . . 1350
I often did behold In thy sweet semblance my old age new born . . 1759
So thou through windows of thine age shalt see . . *Sonnet* 3 11
Resembling strong youth in his middle age . . 7 6
Like feeble age, he reeleth from the day . . 7 10
Herein lives wisdom, beauty, and increase; Without this, folly, age, and cold decay . . 11 6
The age to come would say 'This poet lies' . . 17 7
So should my papers yellow'd with their age Be scorn'd . . 17 9
Had my friend's Muse grown with this growing age . . 32 10
Painting my age with beauty of thy days . . 62 14
When his youthful morn Hath travell'd on to age's steepy night . . 63 5
For such a time do I now fortify Against confounding age's cruel knife . . 63 10
The rich proud cost of outworn buried age . . 64 2
Anon Doubting the filching age will steal his treasure . . 75 6
And to be praised of ages yet to be . . 101 12
For fear of which, hear this, thou age unbred . . 104 13
And peace proclaims olives of endless age . . 107 8
Eternal love in love's fresh case Weighs not the dust and injury of age . . 108 10
In the old age black was not counted fair . . 127 1
And age in love loves not to have years told . . 138 12; *Pass. Pil.* 12
Some beauty peep'd through lattice of sear'd age . . *Lov. Comp.* 14
Privileged by age, desires to know In brief the grounds . . 62
'Tis promised in the charity of age . . 70
Not age, but sorrow, over me hath power . . 74
Crabbed age and youth cannot live together: Youth is full of pleasance, age is full of care . . *Pass. Pil.* 157
Age like winter weather; Youth like summer brave, age like winter bare . . 159
Youth is full of sport, age's breath is short; Youth is nimble, age is lame . . 161
Youth is hot and bold, age is weak and cold; Youth is wild, and age is tame . . 163
Age, I do abhor thee; youth, I do adore thee . . 165
O, my love, my love is young! Age, I do defy thee . . 167
There is no heaven, by holy then, When time with age doth them attaint . . 344
Aged. The aged man that coffers-up his gold Is plagued with cramps . . *Lucr.* 855
To stamp the seal of time in aged things . . 941
Agents. His other agents aim at like delight . . *Ven. and Adon.* 400
Aggravate. Then, soul, live thou upon thy servant's loss, And let that pine to aggravate thy store . . *Sonnet* 146 10
Agree. He sees his love, and nothing else he sees, For nothing else with his proud sight agrees . . *Ven. and Adon.* 288
Agree. As a child, Who wayward once, his mood with nought agrees . . *Lucrece* 1095
If music and sweet poetry agree, As they must needs . . *Pass. Pil.* 103
Agreeing. Mine eye well knows what with his gust is 'greeing . . *Sonnet* 114 11
Agues. Agues pale and faint, Life-poisoning pestilence . . *Ven. and Adon.* 739
Aid. By whose swift aid Their mistress mounted through the empty skies . . 1190
When Truth and Virtue have to do with thee, A thousand crosses keep them from thy aid . . *Lucrece* 912
With noble disposition Each present lord began to promise aid . . 1696
Through his lips do throng Weak words, so thick come in his poor heart's aid . . 1784
Whilst I alone did call upon thy aid, My verse alone had all thy gentle grace . . *Sonnet* 79 1
No, neither he, nor his compeers by night Giving him aid, my verse astonished . . 86 8
All aids, themselves made fairer by their place, Came for additions . . *L. Comp.* 117
Aidance. For lovers say, the heart hath treble wrong When it is barr'd the aidance of the tongue . . *Ven. and Adon.* 330
Aim. His other agents aim at like delight . . 400
Thy false dart Mistakes that aim and cleaves an infant's heart . . 942
The aim of all is but to nurse the life With honour, wealth, and ease . . *Lucr.* 141
In this aim there is such thwarting strife, That one for all, or all for one we gage . . 143
End thy ill aim before thy shoot be ended . . 579
Not a heart . . . Could 'scape the hail of his all-hurting aim . . *Lov. Comp.* 310
Air. And calls it heavenly moisture, air of grace . . *Ven. and Adon.* 64
His nostrils drink the air, and forth again . . 273
Distempering gentle Love in his desire, As air and water do abate the fire . . 654
Sun and sharp air Lurk'd like two thieves, to rob him of his fair . . 1085
With rotten damps ravish the morning air . . *Lucrece* 778
So vanisheth As smoke from Ætna, that in air consumes . . 1042
'My daughter' and 'my wife' with clamours fill'd The dispersed air . . 1805
And all things rare That heaven's air in this huge rondure hems . . *Sonnet* 21 8
Though not so bright As those gold candles fix'd in heaven's air . . 21 12
Slight air and purging fire Are both with thee, wherever I abide . . 45 1
The ornament of beauty is suspect, A crow that flies in heaven's sweetest air . . 70 4
Spied a blossom passing fair, Playing in the wanton air . . *Pass. Pil.* 230
'Air,' quoth he, 'thy cheeks may blow; Air, would I might triumph so!' . . 235
Airy. That phraseless hand, Whose white weighs down the airy scale of praise . . *Lov. Comp.* 226
Ajax. In Ajax and Ulysses, O, what art Of physiognomy might one behold? The face of either cipher'd either's heart . . *Lucrece* 1394
In Ajax' eyes blunt rage and rigour roll'd . . 1398
Alabaster. A lily prison'd in a gaol of snow, Or ivory in an alabaster band . . *Ven. and Adon.* 363
Her alabaster skin, Her coral lips, her snow-white dimpled chin . . *Lucrece* 419
Alack. 'To kill myself,' quoth she, 'alack, what were it?' . . 1156
But out, alack! he was but one hour mine . . *Sonnet* 33 11
Where, alack, Shall Time's best jewel from Time's chest lie hid? . . 65 9
Alack, what poverty my Muse brings forth! . . 103 1
Bright orient pearl, alack, too timely shaded! . . *Pass. Pil.* 133
On a day, alack the day! Love, whose month was ever May . . 227
Vow, alack! for youth unmeet: Youth, so apt to pluck a sweet . . 239
Alarm. Remove your siege from my unyielding heart; To love's alarms it will not ope the gate . . *Ven. and Adon.* 424
Gives false alarms, suggesteth mutiny . . 651
Peers her whiter chin, The reason of this rash alarm to know . . *Lucrece* 473
Alarum. Anon their loud alarums he doth hear . . *Ven. and Adon.* 700
Anon his beating heart, alarum striking, Gives the hot charge . . *Lucrece* 433
Alas. Alas, he nought esteems that face of thine . . *Ven. and Adon.* 631
Alas, poor world, what treasure hast thou lost! . . 1075
Alas, how many bear such shameful blows! . . *Lucrece* 832
From that, alas, thy Lucrece is not free . . 1624
Alas, 'tis true I have gone here and there . . *Sonnet* 110 1
Alas, why, fearing of time's tyranny, Might I not then say . . 115 9
Alas, it was a spite Unto the silly damsel! . . *Pass. Pil.* 217
The trusty knight was wounded with disdain: Alas, she could not help it! . . 222
Alchemy. Gilding pale streams with heavenly alchemy . . *Sonnet* 33 4
And that your love taught it this alchemy . . 114 4
Alien. Every alien pen hath got my use And under thee their poesy disperse . . 78 3
Alight. Vouchsafe, thou wonder, to alight thy steed . . *Ven. and Adon.* 13
Alike. Since all alike my songs and praises be To one, of one . . *Sonnet* 105 3
Alive. Thou dost survive, In that thy likeness still is left alive . . *V. and A.* 174
Thus hoping that Adonis is alive, Her rash suspect she doth extenuate . . 1009
What face remains alive that's worth the viewing? Whose tongue is music now? . . 1076
Leave the faltering feeble souls alive . . *Lucrece* 1768
Were some child of yours alive that time, You should live twice . . *Sonnet* 17 13
None else to me, nor I to none alive . . 112 7
Even so, poor bird, like thee, None alive will pity me . . *Pass. Pil.* 400
All. Shaking her wings, devouring all in haste . . *Ven. and Adon.* 57
Her contending tears, Which long have rain'd, making her cheeks all wet . . 83
Love is a spirit all compact of fire, Not gross to sink . . 149
All swoln with chafing, down Adonis sits . . 325
For all askance he holds her in his eye . . 342
And all this dumb play had his acts made plain With tears . . 359
My heart all whole as thine, thy heart my wound . . 370
For all my mind, my thought, my busy care, Is how to get my palfrey . . 383
That laughs and weeps, and all but with a breath . . 414
And all amazed brake off his late intent . . 469
He cheers the morn and all the earth relieveth . . 484
While she takes all she can, not all she listeth . . 564
All is imaginary she doth prove, He will not manage her . . 597
But all in vain; good queen, it will not be . . 607
'In night,' quoth she, 'desire sees best of all' . . 720
And all is but to rob thee of a kiss . . 723
And all in vain you strive against the stream . . 772
Love is all truth, Lust full of forged lies . . 804
She says ''Tis so:' they answer all ''Tis so' . . 851
And all in haste she coasteth to the cry . . 870
Whose frothy mouth, bepainted all with red . . 901
Full of respects, yet nought at all respecting; In hand with all things, nought at all effecting . . 911
All entertain'd, each passion labours so . . 969
Then join they all together, Like many clouds consulting for foul weather . . 971
From the besieged Ardea all in post . . *Lucrece* 1
His honour, his affairs, his friends, his state, Neglected all . . 46
Which, having all, all could not satisfy . . 96
The aim of all is but to nurse the life With honour, wealth, and ease . . 141

All. Such thwarting strife, That one for all, or all for one we gage *Lucrece* 144
Oft that wealth doth cost The death of all, and all together lost 147
And, all for want of wit, Make something nothing by augmenting it 153
The help that thou shalt lend me Comes all too late 1686
They all at once began to say, Her body's stain her mind untainted clears 1709
And all in war with Time for love of you *Sonnet* 15 13
Their images I loved I view in thee, And thou, all they, hast all the all of me 31 14
Any of these all, or all, or more, Entitled in thy parts do crowned sit 37 6
Take all my loves, my love, yea, take them all 40 1
Lascivious grace in whom all ill well shows, Kill me with spites 40 13
Then do mine eyes best see, For all the day they view things unrespected 43 2
From me far off, with others all too near 61 14
Sin of self-love possesseth all mine eye And all my soul and all my every part 62 1
And for myself mine own worth do define, As I all other in all worths surmount 62 8
When that fell arrest Without all bail shall carry me away 74 2
Thus do I pine and surfeit day by day, Or gluttoning on all, or all away 75 14
Though I, once gone, to all the world must die 81 6
For nothing this wide universe I call, Save thou, my rose; in it thou art my all 109 14
Now all is done, have what shall have no end 110 9
You are my all the world 112 5
That all the world besides methinks are dead 112 14
Think all but one, and me in that one 'Will' 135 14
Sets down her babe and makes all swift dispatch 143 3
Time had not scythed all that youth begun, Nor youth all quit *L. Comp.* 12
For thou art all, and all things else are thine 266
Allayed. Than appetite, Which but to-day by feeding is allay'd *Sonnet* 56 3
All-eating. Were an all-eating shame and thriftless praise 2 8
Allege. Thou hast the strength of laws, Since why to love I can allege no cause 49 14
All-hiding. Let not the jealous Day behold that face Which underneath thy black all-hiding cloak Immodestly lies *Lucrece* 801
All-hurting. That not a heart which in his level came Could 'scape the hail of his all-hurting aim *Lov. Comp.* 310
All-oblivious. 'Gainst death and all-oblivious enmity Shall you pace forth *Sonnet* 55 9
Allotted. And undeserved reproach to him allotted That is as clear from this attaint of mine As I, ere this, was pure to Collatine *Lucrece* 824
Allow. Who, wondering at him, did his words allow 1845
Him in thy course untainted do allow For beauty's pattern to succeeding men *Sonnet* 19 11
So you o'er-green my bad, my good allow 112 4
All-to. It was not she that call'd him all-to naught *Ven. and Adon.* 993
All-too-timeless. Did instigate His all-too-timeless speed *Lucrece* 44
All-triumphant. With all-triumphant splendour on my brow *Sonnet* 33 10
Allure. She show'd him favours to allure his eye *Pass. Pil.* 48
Almighty. She conjures him by high almighty Jove, By knighthood *Lucrece* 568
Almost. So heedful fear Is almost choked by unresisted lust 282
The scalps of many, almost hid behind, To jump up higher seem'd, to mock the mind 1413
Yet in these thoughts myself almost despising, Haply I think on thee *Son.* 29 9
That every word doth almost tell my name 76 7
And almost thence my nature is subdued To what it works in, like the dyer's hand 111 6
Alms. One that by alms doth live Disdain to him disdained scraps to give *Lucr.* 986
Aloes. And sweetens, in the suffering pangs it bears, The aloes of all forces, shocks, and fears *Lov. Comp.* 273
Aloft. This said, he shakes aloft his Roman blade *Lucrece* 505
Thine eyes that taught the dumb on high to sing And heavy ignorance aloft to fly *Sonnet* 78 6
Alone. Well-painted idol, image dull and dead, Statue contenting but the eye alone *Ven. and Adon.* 213
I pray you hence, and leave me here alone 382
My heart longs not to groan, But soundly sleeps, while now it sleeps alone 786
But I alone alone must sit and pine *Lucrece* 795
Let sin, alone committed, light alone Upon his head that hath transgressed so 1480
Having traffic with thyself alone, Thou of thyself thy sweet self dost deceive *Sonnet* 4 9
I all alone beweep my outcast state 29 2
That due of many now is thine alone 31 12
So shall those blots that do with me remain Without thy help by me be borne alone 36 4
By this separation I may give That due to thee which thou deservest alone 39 8
Sweet flattery! then she loves but me alone 42 14
My life, being made of four, with two alone Sinks down to death 45 7
From these would I be gone, Save that, to die, I leave my love alone 66 14
Then thou alone kingdoms of hearts shouldst owe 70 14
Now counting best to be with you alone 75 7
Whilst I alone did call upon thy aid, My verse alone had all thy gentle grace 79 1
Which can say more Than this rich praise, that you alone are you? 84 2
Wretched in this alone, that thou mayst take All this away 91 13
Fair, kind, and true, have often lived alone 105 13
But all alone stands hugely politic 124 11
To say they err I dare not be so bold, Although I swear it to myself alone 131 8
Is't not enough to torture me alone? 133 3
Nor taste, nor smell, desire to be invited To any sensual feast with thee alone 141 8
He saw more wounds than one, And blushing fled, and left her all alone *Pass. Pil.* 130
Poor Corydon Must live alone 297
Every thing did banish moan, Save the nightingale alone 380
Along. So soon was she along as he was down *Ven. and Adon.* 43
To see his face the lion walk'd along Behind some hedge 1093
Aloof. O appetite, from judgement stand aloof! *Lov. Comp.* 166
Aloud. And forth she rushes, snorts, and neighs aloud *Ven. and Adon.* 262
In one place, Where fearfully the dogs exclaim aloud 886
Already. These water-galls in her dim element Foretell new storms to those already spent *Lucrece* 1589
Spending again what is already spent *Sonnet* 76 12
Altar. Over my altars hath he hung his lance, His batter'd shield, his uncontrolled crest *Ven. and Adon.* 103
For these, of force, must your oblations be, Since I their altar, you enpatron me *Lov. Comp.* 224
Alter. Their fresh falls' haste Add to his flow, but alter not his taste *Lucr.* 651
To blot old books and alter their contents 948
Though it alter not love's sole effect, Yet doth it steal sweet hours *Son.* 36 7
Alter. Love is not love Which alters when it alteration finds *Sonnet* 116 3
Love alters not with his brief hours and weeks 116 11
Alteration. Love is not love Which alters when it alteration finds 116 3
Altered. So love's face May still seem love to me, though alter'd new 93 3
'I hate,' she alter'd with an end, That follow'd it as gentle day 145 9
Altering. Divert strong minds to the course of altering things 115 8
Although. He will not manage her, although he mount her *Ven. and Adon.* 598
We two must be twain, Although our undivided loves are one *Sonnet* 36 2
I do forgive thy robbery, gentle thief, Although thou steal thee all my poverty 40 10
No matter then although my foot did stand Upon the farthest earth removed from thee 44 5
Although to-day thou fill Thy hungry eyes even till they wink with fullness 56 5
Their thoughts, although their eyes were kind, To thy fair flower add the rank smell of weeds 69 11
From hence your memory death cannot take, Although in me each part will be forgotten 81 4
Whose worth's unknown, although his height be taken 116 8
I dare not be so bold, Although I swear it to myself alone 131 8
Although she knows my days are past the best 138 6
Although I know my years be past the best *Pass. Pil.* 6
Altogether. Make slow pursuit, or altogether balk The prey *Lucrece* 696
Always. Love's gentle spring doth always fresh remain *Ven. and Adon.* 801
I always write of you, And you and love are still my argument *Sonnet* 76 9
Serve always with assured trust, And in thy suit be humble true *Pass. Pil.* 329
Am. I am that I am, and they that level At my abuses reckon up their own *Sonnet* 121 9
Amain. Sick-thoughted Venus makes amain unto him *Ven. and Adon.* 5
Amaze. Whose full perfection all the world amazes 634
Are like a labyrinth to amaze his foes 684
Amazed. And all amazed brake off his late intent 469
Amazed, as one that unaware Hath dropp'd a precious jewel in the flood 823
Look, how the world's poor people are amazed At apparitions 925
She, much amazed, breaks ope her lock'd-up eyes *Lucrece* 446
Her earnest eye did make him more amazed 1356
Amazedly. Which when her sad-beholding husband saw, Amazedly in her sad face he stares 1591
Amazeth. Which steals men's eyes and women's souls amazeth *Sonnet* 20 8
Amber. Favours . . . Of amber, crystal, and of beaded jet *Lov. Comp.* 37
A belt of straw and ivy buds, With coral clasps and amber studs *Pass. Pil.* 366
Ambition. Yet their ambition makes them still to fight *Lucrece* 68
These worlds in Tarquin new ambition bred 411
Ambitious. This ambitious foul infirmity, In having much, torments us with defect Of that we have 150
Ambush. Had Collatinus kill'd my son or sire, Or lain in ambush to betray my life 233
Thou hast pass'd by the ambush of young days *Sonnet* 70 9
Amen. Like unletter'd clerk still cry 'Amen' To every hymn 85 6
Amend. Unless thou couldst return to make amends *Lucrece* 961
What shall be thy amends For thy neglect of truth in beauty dyed? *Sonnet* 101 1
The deep-green emerald, in whose fresh regard Weak sights their sickly radiance do amend *Lov. Comp.* 214
Amended. Mar not the thing that cannot be amended *Lucrece* 578
Amending. Where no excuse can give the fault amending 1614
Amid. And yet not cloy thy lips with loathed satiety, But rather famish them amid their plenty *Ven. and Adon.* 20
Amiss. Salving thy amiss, Excusing thy sins more than thy sins are *Son.* 35 7
Labouring for invention, bear amiss The second burthen of a former child 59 3
Then, gentle cheater, urge not my amiss 151 3
My ewes breed not, My rams speed not, All is amiss *Pass. Pil.* 248
Among. Sometime he runs among a flock of sheep, To make the cunning hounds mistake their smell *Ven. and Adon.* 685
Thou among the wastes of time must go *Sonnet* 12 10
Weeds among weeds, or flowers with flowers gather'd 124 4
With ease we prove Among a number one is reckon'd none 136 8
Among the many that mine eyes have seen *Lov. Comp.* 190
And mine I pour your ocean all among 256
Amorous. The foil Of this false jewel, and his amorous spoil 154
Amorously. Behold these talents of their hair, With twisted metal amorously impleach'd 205
Amplify. Deep-brain'd sonnets that did amplify Each stone's dear nature 209
Anatomized. In her the painter had anatomized Time's ruin, beauty's wreck *Lucrece* 1450
Anchored. If eyes corrupt by over-partial looks Be anchor'd in the bay where all men ride *Sonnet* 137 6
Ancient. To pluck the quills from ancient ravens' wings *Lucrece* 949
Anew. And where she ends she doth anew begin *Ven. and Adon.* 60
And therefore art enforced to seek anew Some fresher stamp *Sonnet* 82 7
And ruin'd love, when it is built anew, Grows fairer than at first 119 11
And taught it thus anew to greet 145 8
Unless thy lady prove unjust, Press never thou to choose anew *Pass. Pil.* 332
Angel. The better angel is a man right fair *Sonnet* 144 3
My female evil Tempteth my better angel from my side 144 6; *Pass. Pil.* 20
Whether that my angel be turn'd fiend Suspect I may *Sonnet* 144 9
I guess one angel in another's hell 144 12
But live in doubt, Till my bad angel fire my good one out 144 14; *Pass. Pil.* 28
My better angel is a man right fair, My worser spirit a woman colour'd ill *Pass. Pil.* 17
Whether that my angel be turn'd fiend, Suspect I may, yet not directly tell 23
Being both to me, both to each friend, I guess one angel in another's hell 26
Anger. Still is he sullen, still he lours and frets, 'Twixt crimson shame and anger ashy-pale *Ven. and Adon.* 76
The colour in thy face, That even for anger makes the lily pale *Lucrece* 478
The bloody spur cannot provoke him on That sometimes anger thrusts into his hide *Sonnet* 50 10
Which, not to anger bent, is music and sweet fire *Pass. Pil.* 68
Angry. Pure shame and awed resistance made him fret, Which bred more beauty in his angry eyes *Ven. and Adon.* 70
What recketh he his rider's angry stir, His flattering 'Holla,' or his 'Stand, I say'? 283
And with his bonnet hides his angry brow 339
Who, therefore angry, seems to part in sunder *Lucrece* 388
Who, angry that the eyes fly from their lights, In darkness daunts them with more dreadful sights 461
It seem'd they would debate with angry swords 1421
With my knife scratch out the angry eyes Of all the Greeks 1469
The physician to my love, Angry that his prescriptions are not kept *Sonnet* 147 6

Angry-chafing. The picture of an angry-chafing boar *Ven. and Adon.* 662
Annexed. And to his robbery had annex'd thy breath *Sonnet* 99 11
Annexions. With the annexions of fair gems enriched *Lov. Comp.* 208
Annoy. But now I lived, and life was death's annoy *Ven. and Adon.* 497
That worse than Tantalus' is her annoy, To clip Elysium and to lack her joy 599
For mirth doth search the bottom of annoy *Lucrece* 1109
Threatening cloud-kissing Ilion with annoy 1370
Why lovest thou that which thou receivest not gladly, Or else receivest with pleasure thine annoy? *Sonnet* 8 4
Anon he rears upright, curvets and leaps *Ven. and Adon.* 279
There he stares; Anon he starts at stirring of a feather 302
Anon their loud alarums he doth hear 700
Anon she hears them chant it lustily, And all in haste she coasteth to the cry 869
Anon his beating heart, alarum striking, Gives the hot charge *Lucrece* 433
Anon permit the basest clouds to ride With ugly rack *Sonnet* 33 5
Anon Doubting the filching age will steal his treasure 75 5
Anon their gazes lend To every place at once, and, nowhere fix'd *Lov. Comp.* 26
Anon he comes, and throws his mantle by, And stood stark naked *Pass. Pil.* 79
Anon Adonis comes with horn and hounds 122
Another. He winks, and turns his lips another way *Ven. and Adon.* 90
Then do they spend their mouths: Echo replies, As if another chase were in the skies 696
And there another licking of his wound 915
Here she meets another sadly scowling, To whom she speaks 917
Another flap-mouth'd mourner, black and grim 920
Another and another answer him 922
But his hot heart, which fond desire doth scorch, Puffs forth another wind that fires the torch *Lucrece* 315
Think but how vile a spectacle it were, To view thy present trespass in another 632
The branches of another root are rotted 823
And as one shifts, another straight ensues 1104
Here one man's hand lean'd on another's head 1415
Another smother'd seems to pelt and swear 1418
Swearing, unless I took all patiently, I should not live to speak another word 1642
Dear lord, thy sorrow to my sorrow lendeth Another power 1677
Now is the time that face should form another *Sonnet* 3 2
That's for thyself to breed another thee 6 7
The eyes, 'fore duteous, now converted are From his low tract and look another way 7 12
Mark how one string, sweet husband to another 8 9
Make thee another self, for love of me 10 13
Another time mine eye is my heart's guest 47 7
Ere beauty's dead fleece made another gay 68 8
Making no summer of another's green 68 11
But now my gracious numbers are decay'd And my sick Muse doth give another place 79 4
One blushing shame, another white despair 99 9
By all above, These blenches gave my heart another youth 110 7
A thousand groans, but thinking on thy face, One on another's neck, do witness bear 131 11
I guess one angel in another's hell 144 12
Being both to me, both to each friend, I guess one angel in another's hell *Pass. Pil.* 26
Were kisses all the joys in bed, One woman would another wed 346
Answer. She answers him as if she knew his mind *Ven. and Adon.* 308
And still the choir of echoes answer so 840
She says 'Tis so:' they answer all 'Tis so' 851
Another and another answer him 922
Answers with surmise, In silent wonder of still-gazing eyes *Lucrece* 83
Who nothing wants to answer her but cries, And bitter words to ban her cruel foes 1459
At length address'd to answer his desire, She modestly prepares 1606
Begins to blow The grief away that stops his answer so 1664
If thou couldst answer 'This fair child of mine Shall sum my count' *Sonnet* 2 10
Which heavily he answers with a groan 50 11
How like Eve's apple doth thy beauty grow, If thy sweet virtue answer not thy show! 93 14
Make answer, Muse; wilt thou not haply say 'Truth needs no colour?' 101 5
Answered. The dispersed air, who, holding Lucrece' life, Answer'd their cries *Lucrece* 1806
Her audit, though delay'd, answer'd must be *Sonnet* 126 11
Answering. Like shrill-tongued tapsters answering every call *V. and A.* 849
Anthem. Her heavy anthem still concludes in woe 839
Here the anthem doth commence: Love and constancy is dead *Ph. and Tur.* 21
Anticipate. Thus policy in love, to anticipate The ills that were not *Son.* 118 9
Antics. There appears Quick-shifting antics, ugly in her eyes *Lucrece* 459
Antique. A poet's rage And stretched metre of an antique song *Sonnet* 17 12
Nor draw no lines there with thine antique pen 19 10
Show me your image in some antique book 59 7
In him those holy antique hours are seen, Without all ornament 68 9
I see their antique pen would have express'd Even such a beauty as you master now 106 7
Antiquity. To spoil antiquities of hammer'd steel *Lucrece* 951
Beated and chopp'd with tann'd antiquity *Sonnet* 62 10
But makes antiquity for aye his page 108 12
Any. As apt as new-fall'n snow takes any dint *Ven. and Adon.* 354
If springing things be any jot diminish'd, They wither in their prime, prove nothing worth 417
If any love you owe me, Measure my strangeness with my unripe years 523
For misery is trodden on by many, And being low never relieved by any 708
What canst thou boast Of things long since, or any thing ensuing? 1078
Poor bird, thou sing'st not in the day, As shaming any eye should thee behold *Lucrece* 1143
May any terms acquit me from this chance? 1706
Deny that thou bear'st love to any, Who for thyself art so unprovident *Sonnet* 10 1
Then believe me, my love is as fair As any mother's child 21 11
Any of these all, or all, or more, Entitled in thy parts do crowned sit 37 6
Thee have I not lock'd up in any chest, Save where thou art not 48 9
So true a fool is love that in your will, Though you do any thing, he thinks no ill 57 14
I was not sick of any fear from thence 86 12
Nor the lays of birds ... Could make me any summer's story tell 98 7
If Time have any wrinkle graven there; If any, be a satire to decay 100 10
I think my love as rare As any she belied with false compare 130 14
Desire to be invited To any sensual feast with thee alone 141 8
Or any of my leisures ever charm'd *Lov. Comp.* 193

Apace. And homeward through the dark laund runs apace *Ven. and Adon.* 813
A fount With brinish current downward flow'd apace *Lov. Comp.* 284
Appaid. Thou art well appaid As well to hear as grant what he hath said *Lucr.* 914
Appalled. Property was thus appalled, That the self was not the same *Ph. and Tur.* 37
Appals. The timorous yelping of the hounds Appals her senses *Ven. and Adon.* 882
Apparel. And puts apparel on my tatter'd loving *Sonnet* 26 11
Apparitions. Look, how the world's poor people are amazed At apparitions *Ven. and Adon.* 926
Appeal. But with a pure appeal seeks to the heart *Lucrece* 293
To thee, my heaved-up hands appeal, Not to seducing lust 638
Since my appeal says I did strive to prove *Sonnet* 117 13
Appear. That in each cheek appears a pretty dimple *Ven. and Adon.* 242
She crops the stalk, and in the breach appears Green dropping sap 1175
No cloudy show of stormy blustering weather Doth yet in his fair welkin once appear *Lucrece* 116
She dares not look; yet, winking, there appears Quick-shifting antics 458
Men's faults do seldom to themselves appear 633
From the towers of Troy there would appear The very eyes of men through loop-holes thrust 1382
Seemed to appear, Like bright things stain'd, a kind of heavy fear 1434
Which now appear But things removed that hidden in thee lie *Sonnet* 31 7
One doth shadow of your beauty show, The other as your bounty doth appear 53 11
My saucy bark inferior far to his On your broad main doth wilfully appear 80 8
I love not less, though less the show appear 102 2
Look in your glass, and there appears a face 103 6
His phœnix down began but to appear Like unshorn velvet *Lov. Comp.* 93
Appear to him, as he to me appears, All melting 299
Appearance. The defendant doth that plea deny And says in him thy fair appearance lies *Sonnet* 46 8
Appertainings. His real habitude gave life and grace To appertainings and to ornament *Lov. Comp.* 115
Appetite. With leaden appetite, unapt to toy *Ven. and Adon.* 34
Unhappily set This bateless edge on his keen appetite *Lucrece* 9
Nor aught obeys but his foul appetite 546
Be it not said Thy edge should blunter be than appetite *Sonnet* 56 2
Mine appetite I never more will grind On newer proof 110 10
To make our appetites more keen, With eager compounds 118 1
The uncertain sickly appetite to please 147 4
O appetite, from judgement stand aloof! *Lov. Comp.* 166
Apple. How like Eve's apple doth thy beauty grow! *Sonnet* 93 13
Applied. Being so applied, His venom in effect is purified *Lucrece* 531
If that from him there may be aught applied *Lov. Comp.* 68
In him a plenitude of subtle matter, Applied to cautels, all strange forms receives 303
Applying this to that, and so to so; For love can comment upon every woe *Ven. and Adon.* 713
Applying fears to hopes and hopes to fears *Sonnet* 119 3
Like usury, applying wet to wet, Or monarch's hands that let not bounty fall *Lov. Comp.* 40
Approach. Welcomes the warm approach of sweet desire *Ven. and Adon.* 386
Hot was the day; she hotter that did look For his approach *Pass. Pil.* 78
Approve. Suffering my friend for my sake to approve her *Sonnet* 42 8
So thou be good, slander doth but approve Thy worth the greater 70 5
I desperate now approve Desire is death, which physic did except 147 7
Apologies. What needeth then apologies be made? *Lucrece* 31
April. Whose perfect white Show'd like an April daisy on the grass 395
She in thee Calls back the lovely April of her prime *Sonnet* 3 10
With earth and sea's rich gems, With April's first-born flowers 21 7
When proud-pied April dress'd in all his trim Hath put a spirit of youth in every thing 98 2
Three April perfumes in three hot Junes burn'd, Since first I saw you fresh 104 7
Such a storm As oft 'twixt May and April is to see *Lov. Comp.* 102
Apt. As apt as new-fall'n snow takes any dint *Ven. and Adon.* 354
Vow, alack! for youth unmeet: Youth, so apt to pluck a sweet *Pass. Pil.* 240
Aptly. Leave me, and then the story aptly ends: The night is spent *Ven. and Adon.* 716
What's sweet to do, to do will aptly find *Lov. Comp.* 88
Blushes, aptly understood In bloodless white and the encrimson'd mood 200
Aptness. And he takes and leaves, In either's aptness, as it best deceives 306
Arabian. The bird of loudest lay On the sole Arabian tree *Ph. and Tur.* 2
Arbitrators. Unprofitable sounds, weak arbitrators *Lucrece* 1017
Arch. As through an arch the violent roaring tide Outruns the eye that doth behold his haste 1667
Ardea. From the besieged Ardea all in post 1
And on it writ 'At Ardea to my lord with more than haste' 1332
Argued. This heraldry in Lucrece' face was seen, Argued by beauty's red and virtue's white 65
Argument. I force not argument a straw, Since that my case is past the help of law 1021
That pour'st into my verse Thine own sweet argument *Sonnet* 38 3
I always write of you, And you and love are still my argument 76 10
Thy lovely argument Deserves the travail of a worthier pen 79 5
And gives thy pen both skill and argument 100 8
The argument all bare is of more worth Than when it hath my added praise beside! 103 3
'Fair, kind, and true' is all my argument, 'Fair, kind, and true' 105 9
All kind of arguments and question deep *Lov. Comp.* 121
'Gainst whom the world could not hold argument *Pass. Pil.* 30
Aright. Where is my judgement fled, That censures falsely what they see aright? *Sonnet* 148 4
Arise. He doth debate What following sorrow may on this arise *Lucrece* 186
'Thou wronged lord of Rome,' quoth he, 'arise' 1818
So, till the judgement that yourself arise, You live in this *Sonnet* 55 13
Ariseth. The sun ariseth in his majesty *Ven. and Adon.* 856
Arising. Like to the lark at break of day arising *Sonnet* 29 11
Arm. Over one arm the lusty courser's rein, Under her other was the tender boy *Ven. and Adon.* 31
Look, how a bird lies tangled in a net, So fasten'd in her arms Adonis lies 68
Making my arms his field, his tent my bed 108
Sometimes her arms infold him like a band: She would, he will not in her arms be bound 225
And from her twining arms doth urge releasing 256
Her arms do lend his neck a sweet embrace 539
And on his neck her yoking arms she throws 592
With this, he breaketh from the sweet embrace, Of those fair arms 812
Honour and beauty, in the owner's arms *Lucrece* 27
With bruised arms and wreaths of victory 110

Arm. Throwing his mantle rudely o'er his arm *Lucrece* 170
O shame to knighthood and to shining arms! 197
And in thy dead arms do I mean to place him 517
To cross their arms and hang their heads with mine 793
With sad set eyes, and wretched arms across 1662
'Tis a meritorious fair design To chase injustice with revengeful arms 1693
By our strong arms from forth her fair streets chased 1834
Love's arms are peace, 'gainst rule, 'gainst sense, 'gainst shame *Lov. Comp.* 271
And then she clipp'd Adonis in her arms *Pass. Pil.* 148
Thus art with arms contending was victor of the day 223
Armed. His brawny sides, with hairy bristles arm'd, Are better proof than thy spear's point can enter *Ven. and Adon.* 625
My heart stands armed in mine ear, And will not let a false sound enter there 779
That for Achilles' image stood his spear, Griped in an armed hand *Lucrece* 1425
As if with grief or travail he had fainted, To me came Tarquin armed 1544
And arm'd his long-hid wits advisedly 1816
Armies. The coward captive vanquished doth yield To those two armies 76
Armour. He doth despise His naked armour of still slaughter'd lust 188
Array. Like the fair sun, when in his fresh array He cheers the morn and all the earth relieveth *Ven. and Adon.* 483
Poor soul, the centre of my sinful earth, . . . these rebel powers that thee array *Sonnet* 146 2
Arrest. Hath served a dumb arrest upon his tongue *Lucrece* 1780
When that fell arrest Without all bail Shall carry me away *Sonnet* 74 1
Arrive. Ere he arrive his weary noon-tide prick *Lucrece* 781
Arrived. When at Collatium this false lord arrived, Well was he welcomed 50
Arrow. Love's golden arrow at him should have fled *Ven. and Adon.* 947
Art thou ashamed to kiss? then wink again, And I will wink 121
Art thou obdurate, flinty, hard as steel, Nay, more than flint? 199
Art thou a woman's son, and canst not feel What 'tis to love? 201
His art with nature's workmanship at strife 291
In scorn of nature, art gave lifeless life *Lucrece* 1374
In Ajax and Ulysses, O, what art Of physiognomy might one behold! 1394
In them I read such art As truth and beauty shall together thrive *Son.* 14 10
And perspective it is best painter's art 24 4
Yet eyes this cunning want to grace their art 24 13
Desiring this man's art and that man's scope 29 7
On Helen's cheek all art of beauty set 53 7
And art made tongue-tied by authority 66 9
And him as for a map doth nature store, To show false Art 68 14
And arts with thy sweet graces graced be 78 12
Thou art all my art and dost advance As high as learning my rude ignorance 78 13
Which is not mix'd with seconds, knows no art 125 11
Fairing the foul with art's false borrow'd face 127 6
Thou art as tyrannous, so as thou art 131 1
Use power with power and slay me not by art 139 4
What with his art in youth, and youth in art *Lov. Comp.* 145
Thought characters and words merely but art 174
His passion, but an art of craft, Even there resolved my reason into tears 295
Where all those pleasures live that art can comprehend *Pass. Pil.* 62
Thus art with arms contending was victor of the day 223
As. Backward she push'd him, as she would be thrust *Ven. and Adon.* 41
So soon was she along as he was down, Each leaning on their elbows 43
Even as an empty eagle, sharp by fast, Tires with her beak on feathers 55
She feedeth on the steam as on a prey, And calls it heavenly moisture 63
The kiss shall be thine own as well as mine 117
My beauty as the spring doth yearly grow, My flesh is soft and plump 141
At this Adonis smiles as in disdain 241
As from a furnace, vapours doth he send 274
Sometime he trots, as if he told the steps, With gentle majesty 277
As who should say 'Lo, thus my strength is tried' 280
As if the dead the living should exceed 292
She answers him as if she knew his mind 308
With her the horse, and left Adonis there: As they were mad 323
The client breaks, as desperate in his suit 336
Begins to glow, Even as a dying coal revives with wind 338
Her soft hand's print, As apt as new-fall'n snow takes any dint 354
His eyes saw her eyes as they had not seen them 357
Even as the wind is hush'd before it raineth 458
For on the grass she lies as she were slain 473
As if from thence they borrow'd all their shine 488
Even as poor birds, deceived with painted grapes 601
As those poor birds that helpless berries saw 604
She hath assay'd as much as may be proved 608
As air and water do abate the fire 654
Echo replies, As if another chase were in the skies 696
As one that unaware Hath dropp'd a precious jewel in the flood 823
Shaking their scratch'd ears, bleeding as they go 924
As one full of despair, She vail'd her eyelids 955
As striving who should best become her grief 968
Yet pardon me I felt a kind of fear When as I met the boar 999
So full of fear As one with treasure laden, hemm'd with thieves 1022
As falcon to the lure, away she flies 1027
Her eyes, as murder'd with the view, Like stars ashamed of day 1031
As when the wind, imprison'd in the ground, Struggling for passage 1046
Whispers in his ears a heavy tale, As if they heard the woeful words 1126
But know, it is as good To wither in my breast as in his blood 1181
As one of which doth Tarquin lie revolving The sundry dangers *Lucrece* 127
As from this cold flint I enforced this fire, So Lucrece must I force to my desire 181
To pray he doth begin, As if the heavens should countenance his sin 343
As if between them twain there were no strife 405
Seem so As winter meads when sun doth melt their snow 1218
As truth and beauty shall together thrive *Sonnet* 14 11
When I perceive that men as plants increase 15 5
I love thee in such sort As, thou being mine, mine is my good report 36 14
As thus; mine eye's due is thy outward part 46 13
For restful death I cry, As, to behold desert a beggar born 66 2
As every alien pen hath got my use 78 3
Like as, to make our appetites more keen 118 1
Thou art as tyrannous, so as thou art, As those whose beauties proudly make them cruel 131 1
Her levell'd eyes their carriage ride, As they did battery *Lov. Comp.* 23
As if the boy should use like loving charms *Pass. Pil.* 150
As it fell upon a day In the merry month of May 373
A-shaking. Whose grim aspect sets every joint a-shaking *Lucrece* 452
Ashamed. Art thou ashamed to kiss? then wink again, And I will wink; so shall the day seem night *Ven. and Adon.* 121
Like stars ashamed of day, themselves withdrew 1032

Ashes. So of shame's ashes shall my fame be bred *Lucrece* 1188
Such fire That on the ashes of his youth doth lie *Sonnet* 73 10
Ashy. And dying eyes gleam'd forth their ashy lights *Lucrece* 1378
Ashy-pale. Still is he sullen, still he lours and frets, 'Twixt crimson shame and anger ashy-pale *Ven. and Adon.* 76
No guilty instance gave, Nor ashy-pale the fear that false hearts have *Lucr.* 1512
Aside. Who sees the lurking serpent steps aside 362
Why with the time do I not glance aside? *Sonnet* 76 3
In my sight, Dear heart, forbear to glance thine eye aside 139 6
Ask. And asks the weary caitiff for his master *Ven. and Adon.* 914
To whose weak ruins muster troops of cares, To ask the spotted princess how she fares *Lucrece* 721
Durst not ask of her audaciously Why her two suns were cloud-eclipsed so 1223
He hath no power to ask her how she fares 1594
Askance. For all askance he holds her in his eye *Ven. and Adon.* 342
That from their own misdeeds askance their eyes *Lucrece* 637
Most true it is that I have look'd on truth Askance and strangely *Son.* 110 6
Asked. Then being ask'd where all thy beauty lies 2 5
Ask'd their own wills, and made their wills obey *Lov. Comp.* 133
Asleep. Cupid laid by his brand, and fell asleep *Sonnet* 153 1
The little Love-god lying once asleep 154 1
Aspect. With pure aspects did him peculiar duties *Lucrece* 14
Whose grim aspect sets every joint a-shaking 452
Whatsoever star that guides my moving Points on me graciously with fair aspect *Sonnet* 26 10
Aspire. Not gross to sink, but light, and will aspire *Ven. and Adon.* 150
The lightless fire Which, in pale embers hid, lurks to aspire *Lucrece* 5
Aspiring. In his dim mist the aspiring mountains hiding 548
Assail. Such passion her assails, That patience is quite beaten from her breast 1562
Dieted in grace, Believed her eyes when they to assail begun *Lov. Comp.* 262
Assailed. When shame assail'd, the red should fence the white *Lucrece* 63
Assail'd by night with circumstances strong Of present death 1262
Beauteous thou art, therefore to be assailed *Sonnet* 41 6
Either not assail'd or victor being charged 70 10
Assault. If, Collatine, thine honour lay in me, From me by strong assault it is bereft *Lucrece* 835
Assay. Untimely breathings, sick, and short assays 1720
The destined ill she must herself assay *Lov. Comp.* 156
Assayed. She hath assay'd as much as may be proved *Ven. and Adon.* 608
Assemble. As fast as objects to his beams assemble *Sonnet* 114 8
Assigned. Of lands and mansions, theirs in thought assign'd *Lov. Comp.* 138
Assist. The powers to whom I pray abhor this fact, How can they then assist me in the act? *Lucrece* 350
Assistance. And found such fair assistance in my verse *Sonnet* 78 2
Assuage. Free vent of words love's fire doth assuage *Ven. and Adon.* 334
Fellowship in woe doth woe assuage *Lucrece* 790
Which may her suffering ecstasy assuage *Lov. Comp.* 69
Assuaged. Grew kinder, and his fury was assuaged *Ven. and Adon.* 318
Assure. For one sweet look thy help I would assure thee 371
I assure ye Even that your pity is enough to cure me *Sonnet* 111 13
Assured. Assured Of thy fair health, recounting it to me 45 11
For term of life thou art assured mine 92 2
Incertainties now crown themselves assured 107 7
To anticipate The ills that were not, grew to faults assured 118 10
Serve always with assured trust, And in thy suit be humble true *Pass. Pil.* 329
Astonished. Or 'stonished as night-wanderers often are, Their light blown out *Ven. and Adon.* 825
Stone-still, astonish'd with this deadly deed, Stood Collatine *Lucrece* 1730
No, neither he, nor his compeers by night Giving him aid, my verse astonished *Sonnet* 86 8
Astronomy. Methinks I have astronomy, But not to tell of good or evil luck 14 2
Asunder. And now his woven girths he breaks asunder *Ven. and Adon.* 266
Hearts remote, yet not asunder *Ph. and Tur.* 29
At this Adonis smiles as in disdain *Ven. and Adon.* 241
Anon he starts at stirring of a feather 302
And at his look she flatly falleth down 463
And yields at last to every light impression 566
Yet love breaks through and picks them all at last 576
Uncouple at the timorous flying hare 674
By this, she hears the hounds are at a bay 877
Full of respects, yet nought at all respecting; In hand with all things, nought at all effecting 911
Love's golden arrow at him should have fled, And not Death's ebon dart 947
Who did not whet his teeth at him again 1113
Like a troubled ocean, Beat at thy rocky and wreck-threatening heart *Lucr.* 590
Soft pity enters at an iron gate 595
As the poor frighted deer, that stands at gaze 1149
At last she thus begins: 'Thou worthy lord' 1303
At Ardea to my lord with more than haste 1332
At last she calls to mind where hangs a piece Of skilful painting 1366
They join and shoot their foam at Simois' banks 1442
At last she sees a wretched image bound 1501
At last she smilingly with this gives o'er 1567
At last he takes her by the bloodless hand 1597
At last it rains, and busy winds give o'er 1790
Their fair leaves spread But as the marigold at the sun's eye *Sonnet* 25 6
I have no precious time at all to spend, Nor services to do, till you require 57 3
Shoot not at me in your waken'd hate 117 12
At the least, so long as brain and heart Have faculty 122 5
Plays not at all, but seems afraid *Pass. Pil.* 274
Attaint. The marrow-eating sickness, whose attaint Disorder breeds *Ven. and Adon.* 741
As clear from this attaint of mine As I, ere this, was pure to Collatine *Lucr.* 825
I will not poison thee with my attaint 1072
And therefore mayst without attaint o'erlook *Sonnet* 82 2
There is no heaven, by holy then, When time with age doth them attaint *Pass. Pil.* 344
Attainted. Wherein I am attainted, That thou in losing me shalt win much glory *Sonnet* 88 7
Attempt. I see what crosses my attempt will bring *Lucrece* 491
Attend. Sorrow on love hereafter shall attend *Ven. and Adon.* 1136
'So, so,' quoth he, 'these lets attend the time, Like little frosts' *Lucrece* 330
Will tie the hearers to attend each line 818
The post attends, and she delivers it 1333
Attend me: Be suddenly revenged on my foe, Thine, mine, his own 1682
I must attend time's leisure with my moan *Sonnet* 44 12
My spirits to attend this double voice accorded *Lov. Comp.* 3

Attended. Mine ears, that to your wanton talk attended, Do burn *V. and A.* 809
But, woe is me! too early I attended A youthful suit . . *Lov. Comp.* 78
Attendeth. Which speechless woe of his poor she attendeth . . *Lucrece* 1674
Attending. Attending on his golden pilgrimage . . *Sonnet* 7 8
And simple truth miscall'd simplicity, And captive good attending captain ill 66 12
Attention. Making such sober action with his hand, That it beguiled attention . . . . *Lucrece* 1404
Collatine and his consorted lords With sad attention long to hear her words 1610
Attired. Why art thou thus attired in discontent? 1601
Attorney. But when the heart's attorney once is mute, The client breaks *Ven. and Adon.* 335
A-turning. She bade love last, and yet she fell a-turning . *Pass. Pil.* 100
Till looking on an Englishman, the fair'st that eye could see, Her fancy fell a-turning 214
A-twain. Tearing of papers, breaking rings a-twain . . *Lov. Comp.* 6
Audaciously. But durst not ask of her audaciously . . *Lucrece* 1223
Audacity. God wot, it was defect Of spirit, life, and bold audacity . 1346
Audience. Their copious stories oftentimes begun End without audience *Ven. and Adon.* 846
Lending soft audience to my sweet design . . *Lov. Comp.* 278
Audit. What acceptable audit canst thou leave? . . . *Sonnet* 4 12
His utmost sum, Call'd to that audit by advised respects . . 49 4
Her audit, though delay'd, answer'd must be 126 11
And to your audit comes Their distract parcels in combined sums *Lov. Comp.* 230
Aught. Nor aught obeys but his foul appetite . . . *Lucrece* 546
O, give thyself the thanks, if aught in me Worthy perusal stand against thy sight . . . . *Sonnet* 38 5
Were't aught to me I bore the canopy, With my extern the outward honouring? 125 1
If that from him there may be aught applied . . . *Lov. Comp.* 68
Augmenting. For want of wit, Make something nothing by augmenting it *Lucrece* 154
Augur. And the sad augurs mock their own presage . . *Sonnet* 107 6
Augur of the fever's end, To this troop come thou not near! *Ph. and Tur.* 7
Auspicious. And they would stand auspicious to the hour *Lucrece* 347
Author. I did but act, he's author of thy slander *Ven. and Adon.* 1006
And thou, the author of their obloquy . . . *Lucrece* 523
Then call them not the authors of their ill . . . 1244
Authority. Wilt thou be glass wherein it shall discern Authority for sin? 620
And art made tongue-tied by authority . . . *Sonnet* 66 9
Authorized. His rudeness so with his authorized youth Did livery falseness in a pride of truth . . . . . . *Lov. Comp.* 104
Authorizing thy trespass with compare, Myself corrupting . *Sonnet* 35 6
Autumn. The teeming autumn, big with rich increase . . 97 6
Three beauteous springs to yellow autumn turn'd . . . 104 5
Avails. Know, gentle wench, it small avails my mood . *Lucrece* 1273
Avaunt. Then, childish fear, avaunt! debating, die! . . . 274
Awake. And softly cried 'Awake, thou Roman dame, And entertain my love' 1628
Thy picture in my sight Awakes my heart to heart's and eye's delight *Son.* 47 14
It is my love that keeps mine eye awake 61 10
Awaketh. And his untimely frenzy thus awaketh . . *Lucrece* 1675
Awards. I count my gain, That she that makes me sin awards me pain *Sonnet* 141 14
Away. The time is spent, her object will away . . *Ven. and Adon.* 255
Away. Away he springs and hasteth to his horse . . *Ven. and Adon.* 258
So in thyself thyself art made away 763
Therefore, in sadness, now I will away 807
As falcon to the lure, away she flies 1027
My sighs are blown away, my salt tears gone 1071
Away she hies, And yokes her silver doves 1189
Beaten away by brain-sick rude desire . . . . *Lucrece* 175
First red as roses that on lawn we lay, Then white as lawn, the roses took away 259
Away he steals with open listening ear 283
No outrageous thing From vassal actors can be wiped away . . 608
Bearing away the wound that nothing healeth 731
The crow may bathe his coal-black wings in mire, And unperceived fly with the filth away 1010
Poor helpless help, the treasure stol'n away 1056
So must my soul, her bark being peel'd away 1169
Ere the break of day, And, ere I rose, was Tarquin gone away . 1281
From lips new-waxen pale begins to blow The grief away . . 1664
While with a joyless smile she turns away The face . . . 1711
Do not take away My sorrow's interest 1796
And threescore year would make the world away . . *Sonnet* 11 8
To give away yourself keeps yourself still 16 13
Either by thy picture or my love, Thyself away art present still with me 47 10
Stealing away the treasure of his spring 63 8
Thus to ruminate That Time will come and take my love away . 64 12
The right of sepulchres, were shorn away, To live a second life on second head 68 6
Which by and by black night doth take away, Death's second self . 73 7
When that fell arrest Without all bail shall carry me away . . 74 2
Thus do I pine and surfeit day by day, Or gluttoning on all, or all away 75 14
Then if he thrive and I be cast away, The worst was this . . 80 13
Thou mayst take All this away and me most wretched make . . 91 14
But do thy worst to steal thyself away 92 1
How many gazers mightst thou lead away! 96 11
And, thou away, the very birds are mute 97 12
Yet seem'd it winter still, and, you away 98 13
Lo! as a careful housewife runs to catch One of her feather'd creatures broke away 143 2
Who like a fiend From heaven to hell is flown away . . . 145 12
'I hate' from hate away she threw, And saved my life, saying 'not you' 145 13
He rose and ran away; ah, fool too froward! . . . *Pass. Pil.* 56
And as she fetched breath, away he skips 153
Ah, that I had my lady at this bay, To kiss and clip me till I run away! . 156
She bade good night that kept my rest away 182
And drives away dark dismal-dreaming night 200
Which by a gift of learning did bear the maid away . . . 224
And twice desire, ere it be day, That which with scorn she put away . 316
Awe. Shall by a painted cloth be kept in awe . . . *Lucrece* 245
Awed. Pure shame and awed resistance made him fret . *Ven. and Adon.* 69
Awhile. Counsel may stop awhile what will not stay . *Lov. Comp.* 159
A-work. So Lucrece set a-work, sad tales doth tell . . . *Lucrece* 1496
'Ay me,' quoth Venus, 'young, and so unkind?' . *Ven. and Adon.* 187
'Ay me!' she cries, and twenty times 'Woe, woe!' . . . 833
Aye. But makes antiquity for aye his page . . . *Sonnet* 108 12
Azure. With more than admiration he admired Her azure veins . *Lucrece* 419

B

Babe. A nurse's song ne'er pleased her babe so well . *Ven. and Adon.* 974
And fright her crying babe with Tarquin's name . . *Lucrece* 814
That mother tries a merciless conclusion Who, having two sweet babes, when death takes one, Will slay the other and be nurse to none . 1161
Which I will keep so chary As tender nurse her babe from faring ill *Son.* 22 12
Love is a babe 115 13
Sets down her babe and makes all swift dispatch . . . 143 3
Whilst I thy babe chase thee afar behind 143 10
Back. Look, what a horse should have he did not lack, Save a proud rider on so proud a back . . . . . . *Ven. and Adon.* 300
Enfranchising his mouth, his back, his breast 396
Planting oblivion, beating reason back 557
He on her belly falls, she on her back 594
On his back doth lie An image like thyself, all stain'd with gore . 663
Leaves Love upon her back deeply distress'd 814
This way she runs, and now she will no further, But back retires . 906
Coming from thee, I could not put him back . . . *Lucrece* 843
O, this dread night, wouldst thou one hour come back! . . . 965
Here one being throng'd bears back, all boll'n and red . . . 1417
The mindful messenger, come back, Brings home his lord and other company 1583
The eddy boundeth in his pride Back to the strait that forced him on so fast 1670
His sighs, his sorrows, make a saw, To push grief on, and back the same grief draw 1673
Held back his sorrow's tide, to make it more 1789
She in thee Calls back the lovely April of her prime . . *Sonnet* 3 10
Thou gavest me thine, not to give back again 22 14
Who even but now come back again, assured Of thy fair health . . 45 11
No longer glad, I send them back again and straight grow sad . . 45 14
What strong hand can hold his swift foot back? 65 11
And so my patent back again is swerving 87 8
Nature, . . . As thou goest onwards, still will pluck thee back . 126 6
Turn back to me, And play the mother's part, kiss me, be kind . 143 11
Thou mayst have thy 'Will,' If thou turn back, and my loud crying still 143 14
Then fell she on her back, fair queen, and toward . . *Pass. Pil.* 55
Nymphs back peeping Fearfully 287
Be thou not slack To proffer, though she put thee back . . . 334
Backed. The colt that's back'd and burden'd being young Loseth his pride and never waxeth strong . . . . . *Ven. and Adon.* 419
My will is back'd with resolution: Thoughts are but dreams . *Lucrece* 352
Backest. Thou back'st reproach against long-living laud . . . 622
Backward she push'd him, as she would be thrust . *Ven. and Adon.* 41
Backward. Till, breathless, he disjoin'd, and backward drew *Ven. and Adon.* 541
The snail, whose tender horns being hit, Shrinks backward in his shelly cave 1034
A backward look, Even of five hundred courses of the sun . . *Sonnet* 59 5
Bad. How comes it then, vile Opportunity, Being so bad, such numbers seek for thee? . . . . *Lucrece* 896
Lending him wit that to bad debtors lends 964
O Time, thou tutor both to good and bad! 995
What wealth she had In days long since, before these last so bad . *Sonnet* 67 14
So you o'er-green my bad, my good allow 112 4
Creating every bad a perfect best, As fast as objects to his beams assemble 114 7
Which in their wills count bad what I think good . . . 121 8
Unless this general evil they maintain, All men are bad . . 121 14
Now this ill-wresting world is grown so bad 140 11
But live in doubt, Till my bad angel fire my good one out 144 14; *Pass. Pil.* 28
Bad in the best, though excellent in neither 102
Bade. She bade love last, and yet she fell a-turning 100
She bade good night that kept my rest away 182
For why, she sigh'd and bade me come to-morrow . . . 204
Badge. To clear this spot by death, at least I give A badge of fame to slander's livery . . . . *Lucrece* 1054
Heavy tears, badges of either's woe . . . . . *Sonnet* 44 14
Badness. Unless this general evil they maintain, All men are bad, and in their badness reign 121 14
Bail. That blow did bail it from the deep unrest Of that polluted prison where it breathed . . . . *Lucrece* 1725
When that fell arrest Without all bail shall carry me away . . *Sonnet* 74 2
Then my friend's heart let my poor heart bail 133 10
Bait. She touch'd no unknown baits, nor fear'd no hooks . *Lucrece* 103
No sooner had Past reason hated, as a swallow'd bait . *Sonnet* 129 7
The tender nibbler would not touch the bait . . . *Pass. Pil.* 53
Balk. Make slow pursuit, or altogether balk The prey . . *Lucrece* 696
Ball. Those round clear pearls of his, that move thy pity, Are balls of quenchless fire 1554
Sometime diverted their poor balls are tied To the orbed earth *Lov. Comp.* 24
Balm. Calls it balm, Earth's sovereign salve to do a goddess good *Ven. and Adon.* 27
And drop sweet balm in Priam's painted wound . . *Lucrece* 1466
Balmy. Now with the drops of this most balmy time My love looks fresh *Sonnet* 107 9
Ban. And bitter words to ban her cruel foes . . . . *Lucrece* 1460
What though she strive to try her strength, And ban and brawl *Pass. Pil.* 318

Bearing. The bearing earth with his hard hoof he wounds *Ven. and Adon.* 267
I had my load before, now press'd with bearing 430
Unconquered, Save of their lord no bearing yoke they knew *Lucrece* 409
Bearing away the wound that nothing healeth 731
In youth, quick bearing and dexterity 1389
Bearing thy heart, which I will keep so chary *Sonnet* 22 11
Bearing the wanton burthen of the prime 97 7
New faith torn In vowing new hate after new love bearing 152 4
Beast. Banning his boisterous and unruly beast *Ven. and Adon.* 326
That bloody beast, Which knows no pity, but is still severe 999
The rough beast that knows no gentle right *Lucrece* 545
Since men prove beasts, let beasts bear gentle minds 1148
The beast that bears me, tired with my woe, Plods dully on *Sonnet* 50 5
O, what excuse will my poor beast then find, When swift extremity can seem but slow? 51 5
Beasts did leap, and birds did sing, Trees did grow, and plants did spring *Pass. Pil.* 377
Ruthless beasts they will not cheer thee 394
Beat. My boding heart pants, beats, and takes no rest *Ven. and Adon.* 647
And now she beats her heart, whereat it groans 829
My part is youth, and beats these from the stage *Lucrece* 278
But as reproof and reason beat it dead, By thy bright beauty was it newly bred 489
Beat at thy rocky and wreck-threatening heart, To soften it 590
The strongest castle, tower, and town, The golden bullet beats it down *Pass. Pil.* 328
Beated. Beated and chopp'd with tann'd antiquity *Sonnet* 62 10
Beaten away by brain-sick rude desire *Lucrece* 175
Such passion her assails, That patience is quite beaten from her breast 1563
Beating. Beating his kind embracements with her heels *Ven. and Adon.* 312
Planting oblivion, beating reason back 557
Anon his beating heart, alarum striking, Gives the hot charge *Lucrece* 433
May feel her heart—poor citizen!—distress'd, Wounding itself to death, rise up and fall, Beating her bulk, that his hand shakes withal 467
She wakes her heart by beating on her breast, And bids it leap from thence 759
Beauteous. This beauteous combat, wilful and unwilling, Show'd like two silver doves that sit a-billing *Ven. and Adon.* 365
Each lamp and shining star doth borrow The beauteous influence that makes him bright 862
Ne'er saw the beauteous livery that he wore 1107
In the possession of his beauteous mate *Lucrece* 18
Beauteous niggard, why dost thou abuse The bounteous largess given thee to give? *Sonnet* 4 5
Seeking that beauteous roof to ruinate 10 7
Makes black night beauteous and her old face new 27 12
Why didst thou promise such a beauteous day? 34 1
Beauteous thou art, therefore to be assailed 41 6
O, how much more doth beauty beauteous seem By that sweet ornament which truth doth give! 54 1
And so of you, beauteous and lovely youth 54 13
You to your beauteous blessings add a curse 84 13
Three beauteous springs to yellow autumn turn'd 104 5
His qualities were beauteous as his form *Lov. Comp.* 99
Beautiful. Beauty making beautiful old rhyme In praise of ladies *Sonnet* 106 3
The diamond,—why, 'twas beautiful and hard *Lov. Comp.* 211
Beautify. Each in her sleep themselves so beautify *Lucrece* 404
Beauty. Pure shame and awed resistance made him fret, Which bred more beauty in his angry eyes *Ven. and Adon.* 70
Look in mine eye-balls, there thy beauty lies 119
Beauty within itself should not be wasted 130
My beauty as the spring doth yearly grow 141
Fresh beauty for the use, Herbs for their smell, and sappy plants to bear 164
Seeds spring from seeds and beauty breedeth beauty 167
Had I no eyes but ears, my ears would love That inward beauty and invisible 434
Were beauty under twenty locks kept fast, Yet love breaks through and picks them all at last 575
Would root these beauties as he roots the mead 636
Beauty hath nought to do with such foul fiends 638
To mingle beauty with infirmities, And pure perfection with impure defeature 735
But in one minute's fight brings beauty under 746
He hath fed Upon fresh beauty, blotting it with blame 796
Dost thou mean To stifle beauty and to steal his breath? 934
His breath and beauty set Gloss on the rose, smell to the violet 935
If he be dead,—O no, it cannot be, Seeing his beauty, thou shouldst strike at it:—O yes, it may 938
And that his beauty may the better thrive, With Death she humbly doth insinuate 1011
For he being dead, with him is beauty slain, And, beauty dead, black chaos comes again 1019
But true-sweet beauty lived and died with him 1080
And every beauty robb'd of his effect 1132
Mortal stars, as bright as heaven's beauties *Lucrece* 13
Honour and beauty, in the owner's arms 27
Beauty itself doth of itself persuade The eyes of men without an orator 29
Within whose face beauty and virtue strived 52
When virtue bragg'd, beauty would blush for shame 54
When beauty boasted blushes, in despite Virtue would stain that o'er with silver white 55
But beauty, in that white intituled, From Venus' doves doth challenge that fair field 57
Then virtue claims from beauty beauty's red, Which virtue gave 59
This heraldry in Lucrece' face was seen, Argued by beauty's red and virtue's white 65
In that high task hath done her beauty wrong 80
All orators are dumb when beauty pleadeth 268
Desire my pilot is, beauty my prize 279
Thy beauty hath ensnared thee to this night 485
By thy bright beauty was it newly bred 490
Only he hath an eye to gaze on beauty, And dotes on what he looks 496
Time's ruin, beauty's wreck, and grim care's reign 1451
That with my nails her beauty I may tear 1472
That my poor beauty hath purloin'd his eyes 1651
And shiver'd all the beauty of my glass 1763
That thereby beauty's rose might never die *Sonnet* 1 2
And dig deep trenches in thy beauty's field 2 2
Then being ask'd where all thy beauty lies 2 5
How much more praise deserved thy beauty's use 2 9
Proving his beauty by succession thine 2 12
Why dost thou spend Upon thyself thy beauty's legacy? 4 2
Thy unused beauty must be tomb'd with thee 4 13
Beauty o'ersnow'd and bareness every where 5 8
Beauty. Beauty's effect with beauty were bereft, Nor it nor no remembrance what it was *Sonnet* 5 11
Treasure thou some place With beauty's treasure, ere it be self-kill'd 6 4
Yet mortal looks adore his beauty still 7 7
Beauty's waste hath in the world an end 9 11
That beauty still may live in thine or thee 10 14
Herein lives wisdom, beauty, and increase 11 5
Of thy beauty do I question make, That thou among the wastes of time must go 12 9
Since sweets and beauties do themselves forsake And die 12 11
So should that beauty which you hold in lease Find no determination 13 5
In them I read such art As truth and beauty shall together thrive 14 11
Thy end is truth's and beauty's doom and date 14 14
If I could write the beauty of your eyes 17 5
Him in thy course untainted do allow For beauty's pattern to succeeding men 19 12
Stirr'd by a painted beauty to his verse 21 2
For all that beauty that doth cover thee Is but the seemly raiment of my heart 22 5
And hath stell'd Thy beauty's form in table of my heart 24 2
For whether beauty, birth, or wealth, or wit, Or any of these all 37 5
Thy beauty and thy years full well befits, For still temptation follows where thou art 41 3
And chide thy beauty and thy straying youth, Who lead thee in their riot 41 10
Hers, by thy beauty tempting her to thee, Thine, by thy beauty being false to me 41 13
On Helen's cheek all art of beauty set 53 7
The one doth shadow of your beauty show 53 10
O, how much more doth beauty beauteous seem By that sweet ornament which truth doth give! 54 1
And delves the parallels in beauty's brow 60 10
Painting my age with beauty of thy days 62 14
All those beauties whereof now he's king Are vanishing or vanish'd out of sight 63 6
That he shall never cut from memory My sweet love's beauty 63 12
His beauty shall in these black lines be seen, And they shall live 63 13
How with this rage shall beauty hold a plea? 65 3
Or who his spoil of beauty can forbid? 65 12
Why should poor beauty indirectly seek Roses of shadow? 67 7
When beauty lived and died as flowers do now 68 2
Ere beauty's dead fleece made another gay 68 8
Robbing no old to dress his beauty new 68 12
To show false Art what beauty was of yore 68 14
They look into the beauty of thy mind 69 9
The ornament of beauty is suspect, A crow that flies in heaven's sweetest air 70 3
Thy glass will show thee how thy beauties wear 77 1
Beauty doth he give And found it in thy cheek 79 10
I impair not beauty being mute, When others would give life and bring a tomb 83 11
How like Eve's apple doth thy beauty grow! 93 13
Which, like a canker in the fragrant rose, Doth spot the beauty 95 3
Where beauty's veil doth cover every blot 95 11
What shall be thy amends For thy neglect of truth in beauty dyed? 101 2
Both truth and beauty on my love depends 101 3
Beauty no pencil [needs], beauty's truth to lay 101 7
For as you were when first your eye I eyed, Such seems your beauty still 104 3
Yet doth beauty, like a dial-hand, Steal from his figure 104 9
Ere you were born was beauty's summer dead 104 14
Beauty making beautiful old rhyme In praise of ladies 106 3
Sweet beauty's best, Of hand, of foot, of lip, of eye, of brow 106 5
I see their antique pen would have express'd Even such a beauty as you master now 106 8
Tan sacred beauty, blunt the sharp'st intents, Divert strong minds 115 7
Black was not counted fair, Or if it were, it bore not beauty's name 127 2
But now is black beauty's successive heir, And beauty slander'd with a bastard shame 127 3
Sweet beauty hath no name, no holy bower, But is profaned 127 7
No beauty lack, Slandering creation with a false esteem 127 11
Becoming of their woe, That every tongue says beauty should look so 127 14
So as thou art, As those whose beauties proudly make them cruel 131 2
Beauty herself is black And all they foul that thy complexion lack 132 13
The statute of thy beauty thou wilt take, Thou usurer 134 9
They know what beauty is, see where it lies 137 3
The carcass of a beauty spent and done *Lov. Comp.* 11
Some beauty peep'd through lattice of sear'd age 14
Such looks as none could look but beauty's queen *Pass. Pil.* 46
O never faith could hold, if not to beauty vow'd 58
Beauty is but a vain and doubtful good; A shining gloss that vadeth suddenly 169
So beauty blemish'd once 's for ever lost 179
Beauty, truth, and rarity, Grace in all simplicity *Ph. and Tur.* 53
Beauty brag, but 'tis not she; Truth and beauty buried be 63
Became. Whether the horse by him became his deed, Or he his manage by the well-doing steed *Lov. Comp.* 111
Because. Because Adonis' heart hath made mine hard *Ven. and Adon.* 378
Because the cry remaineth in one place 885
The lion walk'd along Behind some hedge, because he would not fear him 1094
That rich jewel he should keep unknown From thievish ears, because it is his own *Lucrece* 35
Thou dost love her, because thou know'st I love her *Sonnet* 42 6
Because he needs no praise, wilt thou be dumb? Excuse not silence so 101 9
I sometime hold my tongue, Because I would not dull you with my song 102 14
Because thou lovest the one, and I the other *Pass. Pil.* 106
Bechance. Let there bechance him pitiful mischances, To make him moan *Lucrece* 976
Beck. O, let me suffer, being at your beck, The imprison'd absence of your liberty *Sonnet* 58 5
Become. As striving who should best become her grief *Ven. and Adon.* 968
Make the young old, the old become a child 1152
She would not blot the letter With words, till action might become them better *Lucrece* 1323
Why should the private pleasure of some one Become the public plague of many moe? 1479
Your trespass now becomes a fee *Sonnet* 120 13
Truly not the morning sun of heaven Better becomes the grey cheeks of the east 132 6
As those two mourning eyes become thy face 132 9
Becoming. Yet so they mourn, becoming of their woe 127 13
Whence hast thou this becoming of things ill? 150 5
Bed. Making my arms his field, his tent my bed *Ven. and Adon.* 108

Bed. Who sees his true-love in her naked bed *Ven. and Adon.* 397
From their dark beds once more leap her eyes 1050
Here was thy father's bed, here in my breast 1183
For then is Tarquin brought unto his bed, Intending weariness *Lucrece* 120
And now this lustful lord leap'd from his bed 169
Thus madly led, The Roman lord marcheth to Lucrece' bed 301
Wickedly he stalks, And gazeth on her yet unstained bed 366
By Lucrece' side, In his clear bed might have reposed still 382
Without the bed her other fair hand was, On the green coverlet 393
Force must work my way, For in thy bed I purpose to destroy thee 514
That to his borrow'd bed he make retire, And stoop to honour, not to foul desire 573
I mean to bear thee Unto the base bed of some rascal groom 671
O, that prone lust should stain so pure a bed! 684
Yet ere he go to bed, Knit poisonous clouds about his golden head 776
To eat up errors by opinion bred, Not spend the dowry of a lawful bed 938
Afflict him in his bed with bedrid groans 975
Dear husband, in the interest of thy bed A stranger came 1619
Weary with toil, I haste me to my bed *Sonnet* 27 1
Robb'd others' beds' revenues of their rents 142 8
Were kisses all the joys in bed, One woman would another wed *Pass. Pil.* 345
There will I make thee a bed of roses, With a thousand fragrant posies 361
Bedchamber. In his bedchamber to be barr'd of rest *Ven. and Adon.* 784
Bedrid. Afflict him in his bed with bedrid groans *Lucrece* 975
Bed-vow. In act thy bed-vow broke and new faith torn *Sonnet* 152 3
Bee. My honey lost, and I, a drone-like bee *Lucrece* 836
And suck'd the honey which thy chaste bee kept 840
The old bees die, the young possess their hive 1769
Been. I have been woo'd, as I entreat thee now, Even by the stern and direful god of war *Ven. and Adon.* 97
Yet hath he been my captive and my slave 101
'Thou hadst been gone,' quoth she, 'sweet boy, ere this, But that thou told'st me thou wouldst hunt the boar' 613
Had I been tooth'd like him, I must confess, With kissing him I should have kill'd him first 1117
And hold it for no sin To wish that I their father had not been *Lucrece* 210
I could not put him back, For it had been dishonour to disdain him 844
Troy had been bright with fame and not with fire 1491
But that which is Hath been before, how are our brains beguiled *Sonnet* 59 2
How like a winter hath my absence been From thee 97 1
From you have I been absent in the spring 98 1
That I have frequent been with unknown minds 117 5
How have mine eyes out of their spheres been fitted! 119 7
My love well knows Her pretty looks have been mine enemies 139 10
I might as yet have been a spreading flower *Lov. Comp.* 75
For feasts of love I have been call'd unto, Till now did ne'er invite 181
She hotter that did look For his approach, that often there had been *Pass. Pil.* 78
Had women been so strong as men, In faith, you had not had it then 321
Befallen. What uncouth ill event Hath thee befall'n, that thou dost trembling stand? *Lucrece* 1599
Befit. Thy beauty and thy years full well befits, For still temptation follows where thou art *Sonnet* 41 3
Before. Being mad before, how doth she now for wits? *Ven. and Adon.* 249
Now was she just before him as he sat 349
Who plucks the bud before one leaf put forth? 416
I had my load before, now press'd with bearing 430
Even as the wind is hush'd before it raineth 458
Or as the wolf doth grin before he barketh, Or as the berry breaks before it staineth 459
Before I know myself, seek not to know me 525
For he the night before, in Tarquin's tent, Unlock'd the treasure *Lucrece* 15
Before you blot With your uncleanness that which is divine 192
End thy ill aim before thy shoot be ended 579
When thus thy vices bud before thy spring 604
And Lust, the thief, far poorer than before 693
Much like a press of people at a door, Throng her inventions, which shall go before 1302
To hie as fast As lagging fowls before the northern blast 1335
Before the which is drawn the power of Greece 1368
That deep vow, which Brutus made before, He doth again repeat 1847
Sets you most rich in youth before my sight *Sonnet* 15 10
Which I new pay as if not paid before 30 12
What hast thou then more than thou hadst before? 40 2
All mine was thine before thou hadst this more 40 4
If there be nothing new, but that which is Hath been before 59 2
Each changing place with that which goes before 60 3
What wealth she had In days long since, before these last so bad 67 14
Before these bastard signs of fair were born 68 3
Before the golden tresses of the dead, The right of sepulchres, were shorn away 68 5
Though words come hindmost, holds his rank before 85 12
Were it not sinful then, striving to mend, To mar the subject that before was well? 103 10
Those lines that I before have writ do lie 115 1
Than think that we before have heard them told 123 8
Before, a joy proposed; behind, a dream 129 12
Whose busy care is bent To follow that which flies before her face 143 7
And falls, through wind, before the fall should be *Pass. Pil.* 136
They that fawn'd on him before Use his company no more 421
Beforehand. All this beforehand counsel comprehends *Lucrece* 494
Befriends. That you were once unkind befriends me now *Sonnet* 120 1
Beg. Flint-hearted boy! 'Tis but a kiss I beg; why art thou coy? *V. and A.* 96
There is no hate in loving: I'll beg her love *Lucrece* 241
Where want cries some, but where excess begs all *Lov. Comp.* 42
Began. 'Thrice-fairer than myself,' thus she began *Ven. and Adon.* 7
'O, pity,' 'gan she cry, 'flint-hearted boy!' 95
By this the love-sick queen began to sweat 175
Once more the engine of her thoughts began 367
Her tears began to turn their tide, Being prison'd in her eye 979
Their ranks began To break upon the galled shore, and than Retire again *Lucrece* 1439
Show me the strumpet that began this stir 1471
With noble disposition Each present lord began to promise aid 1696
They all at once began to say, Her body's stain her mind untainted clears 1709
Began to clothe his wit in state and pride 1809
His phœnix down began but to appear Like unshorn velvet *Lov. Comp.* 93
Venus, with young Adonis sitting by her Under a myrtle shade, began to woo him *Pass. Pil.* 144
Begets. But gold that's put to use more gold begets *Ven. and Adon.* 768
Begets. The mightier man, the mightier is the thing That makes him honour'd, or begets him hate *Lucrece* 1005
Beggar. Or what fond beggar, but to touch the crown, Would with the sceptre straight be strucken down? 216
Poor, and meek, Like to a bankrupt beggar wails his case 711
Let him have time a beggar's orts to crave 985
As, to behold desert a beggar born, And needy nothing trimm'd in jollity *Sonnet* 66 2
Beggared. Beggar'd of blood to blush through lively veins 67 10
Begged. And begg'd for that which thou unask'd shalt have *Ven. and Adon.* 102
Begin. And like a bold-faced suitor 'gins to woo him 6
The steed is stalled up, and even now To tie the rider she begins to prove 40
Now doth he frown, And 'gins to chide, but soon she stops his lips 46
And where she ends she doth anew begin 60
He sees her coming, and begins to glow 337
With blindfold fury she begins to forage 554
She marking them begins a wailing note 835
That for his prey to pray he doth begin *Lucrece* 342
First, like a trumpet, doth his tongue begin To sound a parley 470
So her accent breaks, That twice she doth begin ere once she speaks 567
At last she thus begins: 'Thou worthy lord' 1303
Begins the sad dirge of her certain ending 1612
With this, I did begin to start and cry 1639
From lips new-waxen pale begins to blow The grief away 1663
Begins to talk; but through his lips do throng Weak words 1783
Then begins a journey in my head, To work my mind *Sonnet* 27 3
'Tis the lesser sin That mine eye loves it and doth first begin 114 14
Beginning. Find sweet beginning, but unsavoury end *Ven. and Adon.* 1138
Begot. Thou wast begot; to get it is thy duty 168
Begrimed with sweat, and smeared all with dust *Lucrece* 1381
Beguile. O'erstraw'd With sweets that shall the truest sight beguile *V. and A.* 1144
Thou dost beguile the world, unbless some mother *Sonnet* 3 4
Beguiled. To mock the subtle in themselves beguiled *Lucrece* 957
Making such sober action with his hand, That it beguiled attention 1404
Beguiled With outward honesty, but yet defiled With inward vice 1544
How are our brains beguiled, Which, labouring for invention, bear amiss *Sonnet* 59 2
Whilst as fickle Fortune smiled, Thou and I were both beguiled *Pass. Pil.* 402
Beguiling. And knew the patterns of his foul beguiling *Lov. Comp.* 170
Begun. His meaning struck her ere his words begun *Ven. and Adon.* 462
Their copious stories oftentimes begun End without audience 845
An expired date, cancell'd ere well begun *Lucrece* 26
Even so, the curtain drawn, his eyes begun To wink 374
Time had not scythed all that youth begun, Nor youth all quit *Lov. Comp.* 12
Dieted in grace, Believed her eyes when they to assail begun 262
Behaviour. Her sad behaviour feeds his vulture folly *Lucrece* 556
He lends thee virtue and he stole that word From thy behaviour *Sonnet* 79 10
Beheld. When he beheld his shadow in the brook, The fishes spread on it their golden gills *Ven. and Adon.* 1099
Two glasses, where herself herself beheld A thousand times 1129
What he beheld, on that he firmly doted *Lucrece* 416
That thinks she hath beheld some ghastly sprite 451
Till she despairing Hecuba beheld 1447
Behests. Or kings be breakers of their own behests 852
Behind. To see his face the lion walk'd along Behind some hedge *V. and A.* 1094
She bears the load of lust he left behind *Lucrece* 734
The scalps of many, almost hid behind, To jump up higher seem'd, to mock the mind 1413
An armed hand: himself, behind, Was left unseen, save to the eye of mind 1425
And still weep That thou no form of thee hast left behind *Sonnet* 9 6
My grief lies onward and my joy behind 50 14
Before, a joy proposed; behind, a dream 129 12
Whilst I thy babe chase thee afar behind 143 10
Behold. Who doth the world so gloriously behold That cedar-tops and hills seem burnish'd gold *Ven. and Adon.* 857
'And yet,' quoth she, 'behold two Adons dead!' 1070
That eye which him beholds, as more divine, Unto a view so false will not incline *Lucrece* 291
Who, peeping forth this tumult to behold, Are by his flaming torch dimm'd and controll'd 447
She prays she never may behold the day 746
They think not but that every eye can see The same disgrace which they themselves behold 751
Let not the jealous Day behold that face 800
And scarce hath eyes his treasure to behold 857
Poor bird, thou sing'st not in the day, As shaming any eye should thee behold 1143
The eye interprets to the ear The heavy motion that it doth behold 1326
They whose guilt within their bosoms lie Imagine every eye beholds their blame 1343
Grace and majesty You might behold, triumphing in their faces 1388
In Ajax and Ulysses, O, what art Of physiognomy might one behold! 1395
The violent roaring tide Outruns the eye that doth behold his haste 1668
Lucrece' father that beholds her bleed, Himself on her self-slaughter'd body threw 1732
I often did behold In thy sweet semblance my old age new born 1758
When I behold the violet past prime *Sonnet* 12 3
When in thee time's furrows I behold 22 3
As, to behold desert a beggar born, And needy nothing trimm'd in jollity 66 2
That time of year thou mayst in me behold 73 1
We, which now behold these present days, Have eyes to wonder 106 13
Some say that thee behold Thy face hath not the power to make love groan 131 5
Love, what dost thou to mine eyes, That they behold, and see not what they see? 137 2
In me you behold The injury of many a blasting hour *Lov. Comp.* 71
Behold these talents of their hair, With twisted metal amorously impleach'd 204
Beholding. He ten times pines that pines beholding food *Lucrece* 1115
Behoof. For fear of harms that preach in our behoof *Lov. Comp.* 165
Being. Here come and sit, where never serpent hisses, And being set, I'll smother thee with kisses *Ven. and Adon.* 18
A summer's day will seem an hour but short, Being wasted in such time-beguiling sport 24
Being so enraged, desire doth lend her force Courageously to pluck him from his horse 29
Being red, she loves him best: and being white, Her best is better'd with a more delight 77
Like a dive-dapper peering through a wave, Who, being look'd on, ducks as quickly in 87
Being judge in love, she cannot right her cause 220
Being mad before, how doth she now for wits? 249

Being. The strong-neck'd steed, being tied unto a tree, Breaketh his rein, and to her straight goes he . . . . . *Ven. and Adon.* 263
Being proud, as females are, to see him woo her . . . 309
And being steel'd, soft sighs can never grave it . . . 376
Who is so faint, that dare not be so bold To touch the fire, the weather being cold? . . . 402
The colt that's back'd and burden'd being young Loseth his pride and never waxeth strong . . . 419
What banquet wert thou to the taste, Being nurse and feeder of the other four! . . . 446
Or being early pluck'd is sour to taste . . . 528
Like a wild bird being tamed with too much handling . . . 560
Like lawn being spread upon the blushing rose, Usurps her cheek . . . 590
Being moved, he strikes whate'er is in his way . . . 623
Being ireful, on the lion he will venture . . . 628
Whose blood upon the fresh flowers being shed Doth make them droop . . . 665
For there his smell with others being mingled, The hot scent-snuffing hounds are driven to doubt . . . 691
For misery is trodden on by many, And being low never relieved by any . . . 708
Like milk and blood being mingled both together . . . 902
Her tears began to turn their tide, Being prison'd in her eye . . . 980
For he being dead, with him is beauty slain . . . 1019
Or, as the snail, whose tender horns being hit, Shrinks backward . . . 1033
Once more leap her eyes; And, being open'd, threw unwilling light . . . 1051
For oft the eye mistakes, the brain being troubled . . . 1068
The wind would blow it off and, being gone, Play with his locks . . . 1089
This is my spite, That, thou being dead, the day should yet be light . . . 1134
The sovereignty of either being so great . . . *Lucrece* 69
He makes excuses for his being there . . . 114
The guilt being great, the fear doth still exceed . . . 229
And how her hand, in my hand being lock'd, Forced it to tremble! . . . 260
And being lighted, by the light he spies Lucretia's glove . . . 316
The curtains being close, about he walks, Rolling his greedy eyeballs . . . 367
His eyes begun To wink, being blinded with a greater light . . . 375
Being so applied, His venom in effect is purified . . . 531
The flesh being proud, Desire doth fight with Grace, For there it revels . . . 712
How comes it then, vile Opportunity, Being so bad, such numbers seek for thee? . . . 896
The moon being clouded presently is miss'd . . . 1007
Like a gentle flood, Who, being stopp'd, the bounding banks o'erflows . . . 1119
So must my soul, her bark being peel'd away . . . 1169
'Tis honour to deprive dishonour'd life; The one will live, the other being dead . . . 1187
But as the earth doth weep, the sun being set . . . 1226
Sorrow ebbs, being blown with wind of words . . . 1330
His nose being shadow'd by his neighbour's ear . . . 1416
Here one being throng'd bears back, all boll'n and red . . . 1417
Being from the feeling of her own grief brought By deep surmise of others' detriment . . . 1578
In rage sent out, recall'd in rage, being past . . . 1671
Being constrain'd with dreadful circumstance . . . 1703
Which being done with speedy diligence, The Romans plausibly did give consent . . . 1853
Then being ask'd where all thy beauty lies . . . *Sonnet* 2 5
Being frank she lends to those are free . . . 4 4
Whose speechless song, being many, seeming one, Sings this to thee . . . 8 13
I love thee in such sort As, thou being mine, mine is thy good report . . . 36 14
Hers, by thy beauty tempting her to thee, Thine, by thy beauty being false to me . . . 41 14
My life, being made of four, with two alone Sinks down to death . . . 45 7
As if by some instinct the wretch did know His rider loved not speed, being made from thee . . . 50 8
Desire, of perfect'st love being made, Shall neigh . . . 51 10
Being had, to triumph, being lack'd, to hope . . . 52 14
Else call it winter, which being full of care Makes summer's welcome thrice more wish'd, more rare . . . 56 13
Being your slave, what should I do but tend Upon the hours? . . . 57 1
Being your vassal, bound to stay your leisure . . . 58 4
O, let me suffer, being at your beck, The imprison'd absence of your liberty . . . 58 5
Being crown'd, Crooked eclipses 'gainst his glory fight . . . 60 6
So thou be good, slander doth but approve Thy worth the greater, being woo'd of time . . . 70 6
Either not assail'd or victor being charged . . . 70 10
My body being dead, The coward conquest of a wretch's knife . . . 74 10
Being wreck'd, I am a worthless boat, He of tall building and of goodly pride . . . 80 11
And tongues to be your being shall rehearse . . . 81 11
That you yourself being extant well might show How far a modern quill doth come too short . . . 83 6
Which shall be most my glory, being dumb . . . 83 10
I impair not beauty being mute, When others would give life and bring a tomb . . . 83 11
Being fond on praise, which makes your praises worse . . . 84 14
With mine own weakness being best acquainted . . . 88 5
I love thee in such sort As, thou being mine, mine is thy good report . . . 96 14
My mind being crown'd with you, Drink up the monarch's plague . . . 114 1
Even so, being full of your ne'er-cloying sweetness . . . 118 5
'Tis better to be vile than vile esteem'd, When not to be receives reproach of being . . . 121 2
For I, being pent in thee, Perforce am thine, and all that is in me . . . 133 13
So thou, being rich in 'Will,' add to thy 'Will' One will of mine . . . 135 11
But being both from me, both to each friend, I guess one angel in another's hell . . . 144 11; *Pass. Pil.* 25
When he again desires her, being sat, Her grievance with his hearing to divide . . . *Lov. Comp.* 66
Yet did I not, as some my equals did, Demand of him, nor being desired yielded . . . 149
I strong o'er them, and you o'er me being strong . . . 257
I forswore; but I will prove, Thou being a goddess, I forswore not thee . . . 34
Thy grace being gain'd cures all disgrace in me . . . 36
Beldam. To show the beldam daughters of her daughter . . . *Lucrece* 953
And shapes her sorrow to the beldam's woes . . . 1458
Belied. She concludes the picture was belied . . . 1533
I think my love as rare As any she belied with false compare . . . *Sonnet* 130 14
That I may not be so, nor thou belied, Bear thine eyes straight . . . 140 13
Believe. How strange it seems Not to believe, and yet too credulous . . . *Ven. and Adon.* 986
Who will believe my verse in time to come? . . . *Sonnet* 17 1
Then believe me, my love is as fair As any mother's child . . . 21 10
Believe. Never believe, though in my nature reign'd All frailties . . . *Sonnet* 109 9
I do believe her, though I know she lies . . . 138 2; *Pass. Pil.* 2
Believed. Mad slanderers by mad ears believed be . . . *Sonnet* 140 12
Dieted in grace, Believed her eyes when they to assail begun . . . *Lov. Comp.* 262
Believing. The silly boy, believing she is dead, Claps her pale cheek, till clapping makes it red . . . *Ven. and Adon.* 467
Bell. Marking what he tells With trembling fear, as fowl hear falcon's bells . . . *Lucrece* 511
Like a heavy-hanging bell, Once set on ringing, with his own weight goes . . . 1493
No longer mourn for me when I am dead Than you shall hear the surly sullen bell . . . *Sonnet* 71 2
My wether's bell rings doleful knell . . . *Pass. Pil.* 272
Belly. He on her belly falls, she on her back . . . *Ven. and Adon.* 594
Belong. Such danger to resistance did belong . . . *Lucrece* 1265
To hear with eyes belongs to love's fine wit . . . *Sonnet* 23 14
To you it doth belong Yourself to pardon of self-doing crime . . . 58 11
To thee I so belong, That for thy right myself will bear all wrong . . . 88 13
A better state to me belongs Than that which on thy humour doth depend . . . 92 7
The broken bosoms that to me belong Have emptied all their fountains in my well . . . *Lov. Comp.* 254
Beloved. Fearing some hard news from the warlike band, Where her beloved Collatinus lies . . . *Lucrece* 256
Thou art beloved of many, But that thou none lovest is most evident . . . *Sonnet* 10 3
Then happy I, that love and am beloved . . . 25 13
In my tongue Thy sweet beloved name no more shall dwell . . . 89 10
Let not my love be call'd idolatry, Nor my beloved as an idol show . . . 105 2
More worthy I to be beloved of thee . . . 150 14
Below. Clapping their proud tails to the ground below . . . *Ven. and Adon.* 923
Which, like a falcon towering in the skies, Coucheth the fowl below *Lucrece* 507
Belt. A belt of straw and ivy buds, With coral clasps and amber studs . . . *Pass. Pil.* 365
Bend. He bends her fingers, holds her pulses hard, He chafes her lips . . . *Ven. and Adon.* 476
He is no woodman that doth bend his bow To strike a poor unseasonable doe . . . *Lucrece* 580
Or bends with the remover to remove . . . *Sonnet* 116 4
Bending. Throwing the base thong from his bending crest *Ven. and Adon.* 395
A gainer too; For bending all my loving thoughts on thee . . . *Sonnet* 88 10
Love's not Time's fool, though rosy lips and cheeks Within his bending sickle's compass come . . . 116 10
Benefit. How can I then return in happy plight, That am debarr'd the benefit of rest? . . . 28 2
O benefit of ill! now I find true That better is by evil still made better 119 9
Bent. Like to a mortal butcher bent to kill . . . *Ven. and Adon.* 618
While the world is bent my deeds to cross, Join with the spite of fortune . . . *Sonnet* 90 2
Whose busy care is bent To follow that which flies before her face 143 6
Which, not to anger bent, is music and sweet fire . . . *Pass. Pil.* 68
What though her frowning brows be bent . . . 311
If to women he be bent, They have at commandement . . . 417
Bepainted. Whose frothy mouth, bepainted all with red *Ven. and Adon.* 901
Bequeath. Bequeath not to their lot The shame that from them no device can take . . . *Lucrece* 534
My stained blood to Tarquin I'll bequeath . . . 1181
My honour I'll bequeath unto the knife That wounds my body . . . 1184
Dear lord of that dear jewel I have lost, What legacy shall I bequeath to thee? 1192
I pardon crave of thee, Thy discontent thou didst bequeath to me *Pass. Pil.* 142
Bequeathed. Her contrite sighs unto the clouds bequeathed Her winged sprite . . . *Lucrece* 1727
Bequest. Nature's bequest gives nothing but doth lend . . . *Sonnet* 4 3
Bereaves. And soon bereaves, As caterpillars do the tender leaves . . . *Ven. and Adon.* 797
As the fair and fiery-pointed sun, Rushing from forth a cloud, bereaves our sight . . . *Lucrece* 373
Bereft. My horse is gone, And 'tis your fault I am bereft him so . . . *Ven. and Adon.* 381
Say, that the sense of feeling were bereft me . . . 439
If, Collatine, thine honour lay in me, From me by strong assault it is bereft . . . *Lucrece* 835
Beauty's effect with beauty were bereft, Nor it nor no remembrance what it was . . . *Sonnet* 5 11
Berry. Or as the berry breaks before it staineth, Or like the deadly bullet of a gun . . . *Ven. and Adon.* 460
As those poor birds that helpless berries saw . . . 604
He fed them with his sight, they him with berries . . . 1104
Beseech. I heartily beseech thee, To take advantage on presented joy . . . 404
Beseeched. I have received from many a several fair, Their kind acceptance weepingly beseech'd . . . *Lov. Comp.* 207
Beseechers. Let no unkind, no fair beseechers kill . . . *Sonnet* 135 13
Beseem. Sad pause and deep regard beseem the sage . . . *Lucrece* 277
O, let it then as well beseem thy heart To mourn for me . . . *Sonnet* 132 10
Beset. She is dreadfully beset, And fright her with confusion of their cries . . . *Lucrece* 444
Beshrew. Beshrew that heart that makes my heart to groan . . . *Sonnet* 133 1
Beside. Yet sometimes falls an orient drop beside, Which her cheek melts . . . *Ven. and Adon.* 981
Is of more worth Than when it hath my added praise beside *Sonnet* 103 4
Hanging her pale and pined cheek beside . . . *Lov. Comp.* 32
If I had self-applied Love to myself and to no love beside . . . 77
Besides. Besides, his soul's fair temple is defaced . . . *Lucrece* 719
Besides, of weariness he did complain him, And talk'd of virtue . . . 845
Besides, the life and feeling of her passion She hoards . . . 1317
As an unperfect actor on the stage Who with his fear is put besides his part . . . *Sonnet* 23 2
That all the world besides methinks are dead . . . 112 14
Besiege. When forty winters shall besiege thy brow . . . 2 1
All frailties that besiege all kinds of blood . . . 109 10
Long upon these terms I held my city, Till thus he gan besiege me *L. Comp.* 177
Besieged. From the besieged Ardea all in post . . . *Lucrece* 1
Besmeared. More bright in these contents Than unswept stone besmear'd with sluttish time . . . *Sonnet* 55 4
Best. Being red, she loves him best: and being white, Her best is better'd with a more delight . . . *Ven. and Adon.* 77
But then woos best when most his choice is froward . . . 570
'In night,' quoth she, 'desire sees best of all' . . . 720
Since her best work is ruin'd with thy rigour . . . 954
As striving who should best become her grief . . . 968
Every present sorrow seemeth chief, But none is best . . . 971
They that love best their loves shall not enjoy . . . 1164

Best. Grief best is pleased with grief's society . . . *Lucrece* 1111
'Few words,' quoth she, 'shall fit the trespass best' . . . 1613
Look, whom she best endow'd she gave the more . . . *Sonnet* 11 11
And perspective it is best painter's art . . . 24 4
Look, what is best, that best I wish in thee : This wish I have . . . 37 13
Then do mine eyes best see, For all the day they view things unrespected 43 1
Thou, best of dearest and mine only care . . . 48 7
Where, alack, Shall Time's best jewel from Time's chest lie hid? . . . 65 10
Now counting best to be with you alone . . . 75 7
So all my best is dressing old words new . . . 76 11
With mine own weakness being best acquainted . . . 88 5
All these I better in one general best . . . 91 8
But best is best, if never intermix'd . . . 101 8
Sweet beauty's best, Of hand, of foot, of lip, of eye, of brow . . . 106 5
And worse essays proved thee my best of love . . . 110 8
Then give me welcome, next my heaven the best . . . 110 13
Creating every bad a perfect best, As fast as objects to his beams assemble 114 7
Fearing of time's tyranny, Might I not then say 'Now I love you best?' 115 10
Yet what the best is take the worst to be . . . 137 4
Although she knows my days are past the best . . . 138 6
O, love's best habit is in seeming trust . . . 138 11
When all my best doth worship thy defect . . . 149 11
That, in my mind, thy worst all best exceeds . . . 150 8
Stood in doubt If best were as it was, or best without . . . *Lov. Comp.* 98
And he takes and leaves, In either's aptness, as it best deceives . . . 306
Although I know my years be past the best . . . *Pass. Pil.* 6
O, love's best habit is a soothing tongue . . . 11
Bad in the best, though excellent in neither . . . 102
Bestow. I hope some good conceit of thine In thy soul's thought, all naked, will bestow it . . . *Sonnet* 26 8
Labouring in moe pleasures to bestow them Than the true gouty landlord which doth owe them . . . *Lov. Comp.* 139
Bestowed. The kiss I gave you is bestow'd in vain . . . *Ven. and Adon.* 771
O, that sad breath his spongy lungs bestow'd! . . . *Lov. Comp.* 326
Bestowest. That fresh blood which youngly thou bestowest Thou mayst call thine . . . *Sonnet* 11 3
Betake. And every one to rest themselves betake, Save thieves . . . *Lucrece* 125
But honest fear, bewitch'd with lust's foul charm, Doth too too oft betake him to retire . . . 174
I in deep delight am chiefly drown'd Whenas himself to singing he betakes . . . *Pass. Pil.* 114
Bethinking. Thy coward heart with false bethinking grieves *Ven. and Adon.* 1024
Betokened. Like a red morn, that ever yet betoken'd Wreck to the seaman . . . 453
Betray. When he himself himself confounds, betrays To slanderous tongues . . . *Lucrece* 160
Had Collatinus kill'd my son or sire, Or lain in ambush to betray my life . . . 233
The fault is thine, For those thine eyes betray thee unto mine . . . 483
How many lambs might the stern wolf betray! . . . *Sonnet* 96 9
I do betray My nobler part to my gross body's treason . . . 151 5
O, all that borrow'd motion seeming owed, Would yet again betray the fore-betray'd! . . . *Lov. Comp.* 328
Betrayed. Why hath thy servant, Opportunity, Betray'd the hours thou gavest me to repose? . . . *Lucrece* 933
Betraying. For, thou betraying me, I do betray My nobler part to my gross body's treason . . . *Sonnet* 151 5
Better. Are better proof than thy spear's point can enter *Ven. and Adon.* 626
And that his beauty may the better thrive, With Death she humbly doth insinuate . . . 1011
While thou on Tereus descant'st better skill . . . *Lucrece* 1134
To live or die which of the twain were better, When life is shamed . . . 1154
The better so to clear her From that suspicion which the world might bear her . . . 1320
She would not blot the letter With words, till action might become them better . . . 1323
A dearer birth than this his love had brought, To march in ranks of better equipage . . . *Sonnet* 32 12
Since he died and poets better prove, Theirs for their style I'll read . . . 32 13
When thou art all the better part of me . . . 39 2
Whether we are mended, or whether better they . . . 59 11
My spirit is thine, the better part of me . . . 74 8
Knowing a better spirit doth use your name . . . 80 2
Their gross painting might be better used Where cheeks need blood . . . 82 13
So thy great gift, upon misprision growing, Comes home again, on better judgement making . . . 87 12
All these I better in one general best . . . 91 8
Thy love is better than high birth to me, Richer than wealth . . . 91 9
A better state to me belongs Than that which on thy humour doth depend . . . 92 7
That did not better for my life provide Than public means . . . 111 3
Now I find true That better is by evil still made better . . . 119 10
'Tis better to be vile than vile esteem'd . . . 121 1
Truly not the morning sun of heaven Better becomes the grey cheeks of the east . . . 132 6
Better it were, Though not to love, yet, love, to tell me so . . . 140 5
The better angel is a man right fair . . . 144 3
My female evil Tempteth my better angel from my side . . . 144 6
My better angel is a man right fair, My worser spirit a woman colour'd ill . . . *Pass. Pil.* 17
My female evil Tempteth my better angel from my side . . . 20
Bettered. Being red, she loves him best: and being white, Her best is better'd with a more delight . . . *Ven. and Adon.* 78
Then better'd that the world may see my pleasure . . . *Sonnet* 75 8
Bettering. Compare them with the bettering of the time . . . 32 5
Be-tumbled. This said, from her be-tumbled couch she starteth . . . *Lucrece* 1037
Between. And, lo, I lie between that sun and thee . . . *Ven. and Adon.* 194
And were I not immortal, life were done Between this heavenly and earthly sun . . . 198
The iron bit he crusheth 'tween his teeth . . . 269
O, what a war of looks was then between them! . . . 355
Where, lest between them both it should be kill'd, The coward captive vanquished doth yield . . . *Lucrece* 74
Is madly toss'd between desire and dread . . . 171
'Tween frozen conscience and hot-burning will . . . 247
The locks between her chamber and his will, Each one by him enforced . . . 302
Between whose hills her head entombed is . . . 390
As if between them twain there were no strife . . . 405
Between each kiss her oaths of true love swearing . . . *Pass. Pil.* 92
So between them love did shine . . . *Ph. and Tur.* 33
Betwixt. 'Twixt crimson shame and anger ashy-pale . . . *Ven. and Adon.* 76
And set dissension 'twixt the son and sire . . . 1160
Betwixt. Betwixt mine eye and heart a league is took, And each doth good turns . . . *Sonnet* 47 1
Such strife As 'twixt a miser and his wealth is found . . . 75 4
Such a storm As oft 'twixt May and April is to see . . . *Lov. Comp.* 102
Then must the love be great 'twixt thee and me . . . *Pass Pil.* 105
Bevel. I may be straight, though they themselves be bevel *Sonnet* 121 11
Bewailed. Lest my bewailed guilt should do thee shame . . . 36 10
Beware. Hadst thou but bid beware, then he had spoke . . . *Ven. and Adon.* 943
Beweep. I all alone beweep my outcast state . . . *Sonnet* 29 2
Bewitched. But honest fear, bewitch'd with lust's foul charm, Doth too too oft betake him to retire . . . *Lucrece* 173
Consents bewitch'd, ere he desire, have granted . . . *Lov. Comp.* 131
Bewitching like the wanton mermaid's songs . . . *Ven. and Adon.* 777
Bewrayed. Longing to hear the hateful foe bewray'd . . . *Lucrece* 1698
Yet will she blush, here be it said, To hear her secrets so bewray'd *Pass. Pil.* 352
Beyond. Devise extremes beyond extremity, To make him curse . . . *Lucrece* 969
Beyond all date, even to eternity . . . *Sonnet* 122 4
Bias. Study his bias leaves, and makes his book thine eyes . . . *Pass. Pil.* 61
Bid. Bid me discourse, I will enchant thine ear . . . *Ven. and Adon.* 145
To bid the wind a base he now prepares . . . 303
And bid Suspicion double-lock the door . . . 448
And coal-black clouds that shadow heaven's light Do summon us to part and bid good night . . . 534
Bids him farewell, and look well to her heart . . . 580
Bids them leave quaking, bids them fear no more . . . 899
Hadst thou but bid beware, then he had spoke . . . 943
They bid thee crop a weed, thou pluck'st a flower . . . 946
Reviving joy bids her rejoice, And flatters her it is Adonis' voice . . . 977
Who bids them still consort with ugly night . . . 1041
Anon his beating heart, alarum striking, Gives the hot charge and bids them do their liking . . . *Lucrece* 434
And bids her eyes hereafter still be blind . . . 758
She wakes her heart by beating on her breast, And bids it leap from thence . . . 760
By this, mild patience bid fair Lucrece speak . . . 1268
One of my husband's men Bid thou be ready, by and by . . . 1292
Bid him with speed prepare to carry it . . . 1294
And bids Lucretius give his sorrow place . . . 1773
Till manly shame bids him possess his breath . . . 1777
My eye doth feast And to the painted banquet bids my heart *Sonnet* 47 6
When you have bid your servant once adieu . . . 57 8
Biding. Which blows these pitchy vapours from their biding *Lucrece* 550
Bidding them find their sepulchres in mud . . . *Lov. Comp.* 46
Bide. And patience, tame to sufferance, bide each check, Without accusing you of injury . . . *Sonnet* 58 7
When thy might Is more than my o'er-press'd defence can bide . . . 139 8
Some in her threaden fillet still did bide . . . *Lov. Comp.* 33
Bier. Borne on the bier with white and bristly beard . . . *Sonnet* 12 8
Big. The teeming autumn, big with rich increase . . . 97 6
The lines she rents, Big discontent so breaking their contents *Lov. Comp.* 56
Bills. The birds such pleasure took, That some would sing, some other in their bills Would bring him mulberries . . . *Ven. and Adon.* 1102
Bind. Under that bond that him as fast doth bind . . . *Sonnet* 134 8
Bird. Look, how a bird lies tangled in a net, So fasten'd in her arms Adonis lies . . . *Ven. and Adon.* 67
Sorrow to shepherds, woe unto the birds . . . 455
The sheep are gone to fold, birds to their nest . . . 532
Like a wild bird being tamed with too much handling . . . 560
Even as poor birds, deceived with painted grapes . . . 601
As those poor birds that helpless berries saw . . . 604
When he was by, the birds such pleasure took, That some would sing . . . 1101
Birds never limed no secret bushes fear . . . *Lucrece* 88
And give the sneaped birds more cause to sing . . . 333
Like to a new-kill'd bird she trembling lies . . . 457
The adder hisses where the sweet birds sing . . . 871
The little birds that tune their morning's joy Make her moans mad with their sweet melody . . . 1107
'You mocking birds,' quoth she . . . 1121
'Poor bird, thou sing'st not in the day, As shaming any eye should thee behold . . . 1142
Bare ruin'd choirs, where late the sweet birds sang . . . *Sonnet* 73 4
And, thou away, the very birds are mute . . . 97 12
Yet nor the lays of birds nor the sweet smell Of different flowers . . . 98 5
For it no form delivers to the heart Of bird, of flower, or shape . . . 113 6
Clear wells spring not, Sweet birds sing not . . . *Pass. Pil.* 282
By shallow rivers, by whose falls Melodious birds sing madrigals . . . 360
Beasts did leap, and birds did sing, Trees did grow, and plants did spring . . . 377
She, poor bird, as all forlorn, Lean'd her breast up-till a thorn . . . 381
All thy fellow birds do sing, Careless of thy sorrowing . . . 397
Even so, poor bird, like thee, None alive will pity me . . . 399
The bird of loudest lay, On the sole Arabian tree . . . *Ph. and Tur.* 1
For these dead birds sigh a prayer . . . 67
Birth. A dearer birth than this his love had brought . . . *Sonnet* 32 11
For whether beauty, birth, or wealth, or wit, Or any of these all . . . 37 5
Every word doth almost tell my name, Showing their birth and where they did proceed . . . 76 8
Some glory in their birth, some in their skill, Some in their wealth . . . 91 1
Thy love is better than high birth to me, Richer than wealth . . . 91 9
Birth-hour. Worse than a slavish wipe or birth-hour's blot . . . *Lucrece* 537
Bit. The iron bit he crusheth 'tween his teeth . . . *Ven. and Adon.* 269
Bites. He stamps and bites the poor flies in his fume . . . 316
Bitter. Thy sugar'd tongue to bitter wormwood taste . . . *Lucrece* 893
And bitter words to ban her cruel foes . . . 1460
No bitterness that I will bitter think, Nor double penance . . . *Sonnet* 111 11
To bitter sauces did I frame my feeding . . . 118 6
Bitterness. Nor think the bitterness of absence sour . . . 57 7
No bitterness that I will bitter think, Nor double penance . . . 111 11
Blab. These blue-vein'd violets whereon we lean Never can blab, nor know not what we mean . . . *Ven. and Adon.* 126
Black. Another flap-mouth'd mourner, black and grim . . . 920
With him is beauty slain, And, beauty dead, black chaos comes again . . . 1020
What excuse can my invention make, When thou shalt charge me with so black a deed? . . . *Lucrece* 226
Reward not hospitality With such black payment . . . 576
There falls into thy boundless flood Black lust, dishonour, shame . . . 654
Black stage for tragedies and murders fell! . . . 766
Through Night's black bosom should not peep again . . . 788
Which underneath thy black all-hiding cloak Immodestly lies . . . 801
Her blue blood changed to black in every vein . . . 1454
Who finds his Lucrece clad in mourning black . . . 1585
Some of her blood still pure and red remain'd, And some look'd black . . . 1743

Black. About the mourning and congealed face Of that black blood a watery rigol goes . . . . *Lucrece* 1745
Makes black night beauteous and her old face new . . *Sonnet* 27 12
His beauty shall in these black lines be seen, And they shall live . 63 13
That in black ink my love may still shine bright . . . 65 14
Which by and by black night doth take away, Death's second self . 73 7
In the old age black was not counted fair 127 1
But now is black beauty's successive heir 127 3
My mistress' brows are raven black, Her eyes so suited . . 127 9
If hairs be wires, black wires grow on her head 130 4
Do witness bear Thy black is fairest in my judgement's place . . 131 12
In nothing art thou black save in thy deeds 131 13
Have put on black and loving mourners be 132 3
Beauty herself is black And all they foul that thy complexion lack . 132 13
And thought thee bright, Who art as black as hell, as dark as night . 147 14
Ink would have seem'd more black and damned here ! . . *Lov. Comp.* 54
In black mourn I, All fears scorn I, Love hath forlorn me, Living in thrall *Pass. Pil.* 263

Blackest. The blackest sin is clear'd with absolution . . *Lucrece* 354

Black-faced. For by this black-faced night, desire's foul nurse, Your treatise makes me like you worse and worse *Ven. and Adon.* 773
But when a black-faced cloud the world doth threat . . . *Lucrece* 547
Should thrust Into so bright a day such black-faced storms . . . 1518

Blade. This said, he shakes aloft his Roman blade 505

Blame. He saith she is immodest, blames her 'miss *Ven. and Adon.* 53
He hath fed Upon fresh beauty, blotting it with blame 796
Adonis lives, and Death is not to blame 992
Whose crime will bear an ever-during blame . . . . *Lucrece* 224
Warrant for blame, To privilege dishonour in thy name . . . 620
Vast sin-concealing chaos ! nurse of blame ! Blind muffled bawd ! . . 767
Not that devour'd, but that which doth devour, Is worthy blame . 1257
Those proud lords, to blame, Make weak-made women tenants to their shame 1259
Replied the maid, 'The more to blame my sluggard negligence' . 1278
They whose guilt within their bosoms lie Imagine every eye beholds their blame 1343
I cannot blame thee for my love thou usest . . . *Sonnet* 40 6
Not blame your pleasure, be it ill or well 58 14
O, blame me not, if I no more can write ! 103 5
Till action, lust Is perjured, murderous, bloody, full of blame . 129 3
Let reason rule things worthy blame, As well as fancy partial might *Pass. Pil.* 301

Blamed. But yet be blamed, if thou thyself deceivest By wilful taste of what thyself refusest . . . . *Sonnet* 40 7
That thou art blamed shall not be thy defect 70 1

Blanks. What thy memory can not contain Commit to these waste blanks 77 10

Blast. Thy hasty spring still blasts, and ne'er grows old . . *Lucrece* 49
Unruly blasts wait on the tender spring 869
To hie as fast As lagging fowls before the northern blast . . 1335

Blasted. Bud and be blasted in a breathing-while . *Ven. and Adon.* 1142

Blasting. In me you behold The injury of many a blasting hour *Lov. Comp.* 72

Blaze. Red cheeks and fiery eyes blaze forth her wrong . *Ven. and Adon.* 219

Blazed. Two red fires in both their faces blazed . . . *Lucrece* 1353

Blazon. In the blazon of sweet beauty's best . . . *Sonnet* 106 5

Blazoned. Each several stone, With wit well blazon'd, smiled or made some moan . . . . *Lov. Comp.* 217

Bleed. The thought of it doth make my faint heart bleed *Ven. and Adon.* 669
No grass, herb, leaf, or weed, But stole his blood and seem'd with him to bleed 1056
My frail joints shake, Mine eyes forego their light, my false heart bleed *Lucrece* 228
For every tear he falls a Trojan bleeds 1551
Lucrece' father, that beholds her bleed, Himself on her self-slaughter'd body threw 1732
For his foul act by whom thy fair wife bleeds 1824

Bleeding. Shaking their scratch'd ears, bleeding as they go *Ven. and Adon.* 924
Which bleeding under Pyrrhus' proud foot lies . . . *Lucrece* 1449
Then in key-cold Lucrece' bleeding stream He falls . . . 1774
To show her bleeding body thorough Rome 1851
Now all these hearts that do on mine depend, Feeling it break, with bleeding groans they pine . . . . . . *Lov. Comp.* 275
Heart is bleeding, All help needing, O cruel speeding, Fraughted with gall *Pass. Pil.* 267

Blemish. From them no device can take, The blemish that will never be forgot . . . . *Lucrece* 536
The more she thought he spied in her some blemish . . . 1358

Blemished. Let it not be call'd impiety, If in this blemish'd fort I make some hole 1175
So beauty blemish'd once's for ever lost . . . *Pass. Pil.* 179

Blenches. By all above, These blenches gave my heart another youth *Son.* 110 7

Blend. The heaven-hued sapphire and the opal blend With objects manifold *Lov. Comp.* 215

Bless. Never did he bless My youth with his ; the more am I accurst *Ven. and Adon.* 1119
Naming thy name blesses an ill report . . . . *Sonnet* 95 8

Blessed. But blessed bankrupt, that by love so thriveth ! *Ven. and Adon.* 466
Hath barr'd him from the blessed thing he sought . . . *Lucrece* 340
But they must ope, this blessed league to kill 383
With means more blessed than my barren rhyme . . *Sonnet* 16 4
How would, I say, mine eyes be blessed made By looking on thee in the living day ! 43 9
Whose blessed key Can bring him to his sweet up-locked treasure . 52 1
Blessed are you, whose worthiness gives scope, Being had, to triumph 52 13
And you in every blessed shape we know 53 12
Whilst it hath thought itself so blessed never 119 6
When thou, my music, music play'st, Upon that blessed wood . 128 2

Blessed-fair. But what's so blessed-fair that fears no blot? . . 92 13

Blessing. The dedicated words which writers use Of their fair subject, blessing every book 82 4
You to your beauteous blessings add a curse 84 13

Blest. That love-sick Love by pleading may be blest *Ven. and Adon.* 328
To make some special instant special blest, By new unfolding his imprison'd pride . . . . *Sonnet* 52 11
That, when they see Return of love, more blest may be the view . 56 12
Making dead wood more blest than living lips 128 12

Blind. But blind they are, and keep themselves enclosed . . *Lucrece* 378
Shame folded up in blind concealing night 675
And bids her eyes hereafter still be blind 758
Blind muffled bawd ! dark harbour for defame ! Grim cave of death ! . 768
The poor, lame, blind, halt, creep, cry out for thee 902
Looking on darkness which the blind do see . . . *Sonnet* 27 8

Blind. That which governs me to go about Doth part his function and is partly blind . . . . *Sonnet* 113 3
Swear to thy blind soul that I was thy 'Will' 136 2
Thou blind fool, Love, what dost thou to mine eyes? 137 1
O cunning Love ! with tears thou keep'st me blind . . . 148 13
Those that can see thou lovest, and I am blind 149 14

Blinded. His eyes begun To wink, being blinded with a greater light *Lucrece* 375

Blindfold. With blindfold fury she begins to forage . *Ven. and Adon.* 554

Blindness. Gave eyes to blindness, Or made them swear against the thing they see . . . . *Sonnet* 152 11

Bliss. Seems to part in sunder, Swelling on either side to want his bliss *Lucrece* 389
A bliss in proof, and proved, a very woe . . . . *Sonnet* 129 11

Blood. Her face doth reek and smoke, her blood doth boil *Ven. and Adon.* 555
Whose blood upon the fresh flowers being shed Doth make them droop 665
Whose attaint Disorder breeds by heating of the blood . . . 742
Bepainted all with red, Like milk and blood being mingled both together . 902
No flower was nigh, no grass, herb, leaf, or weed, But stole his blood . 1056
And stains her face with his congealed blood 1122
And in his blood that on the ground lay spill'd, A purple flower sprung up 1167
His pale cheeks and the blood Which in round drops upon their whiteness stood 1169
It is as good To wither in my breast as in his blood 1182
Thou art the next of blood, and 'tis thy right 1184
Who seek to stain the ocean of thy blood . . . . *Lucrece* 655
Such wretched hands such wretched blood should spill . . . 999
The remedy indeed to do me good Is to let forth my foul-defiled blood . 1029
My stained blood to Tarquin I'll bequeath 1181
My blood shall wash the slander of mine ill 1207
Ere she with blood had stain'd her stain'd excuse 1316
The more she saw the blood his cheeks replenish, The more she thought he spied in her some blemish 1357
The red blood reek'd, to show the painter's strife 1377
To Simois' reedy banks the red blood ran 1437
Her blue blood changed to black in every vein 1454
Though my gross blood be stain'd with this abuse, Immaculate and spotless is my mind 1655
From the purple fountain Brutus drew The murderous knife, and, as it left the place, Her blood, in poor revenge, held it in chase . . . 1736
The crimson blood Circles her body in on every side 1738
Some of her blood still pure and red remain'd, And some look'd black . 1742
About the mourning and congeal'd face, Of that black blood a watery rigol goes 1745
As pitying Lucrece' woes, Corrupted blood some watery token shows . 1748
Blood untainted still doth red abide, Blushing at that which is so putrified 1749
By the Capitol that we adore, And by this chaste blood so unjustly stain'd 1836
And see thy blood warm when thou feel'st it cold . . *Sonnet* 2 14
That fresh blood which youngly thou bestowest Thou mayst call thine 11 3
Burn the long-lived Phœnix in her blood 19 4
When hours have drain'd his blood and fill'd his brow With lines and wrinkles 63 3
Now Nature bankrupt is, Beggar'd of blood to blush through lively veins 67 10
Their gross painting might be better used Where cheeks need blood . 82 14
Though in my nature reign'd All frailties that besiege all kinds of blood 109 10
Why should others' false adulterate eyes Give salutation to my sportive blood? 121 6
Found yet moe letters sadly penn'd in blood . . . *Lov. Comp.* 47
O false blood, thou register of lies, What unapproved witness dost thou bear ! 52
Nor gives it satisfaction to our blood, That we must curb it upon others' proof 162
All my offences that abroad you see Are errors of the blood . . . 184
What tributes wounded fancies sent me, Of paled pearls and rubies red as blood 198

Bloodless. Overcome by doubt and bloodless fear . *Ven. and Adon.* 891
At last he takes her by the bloodless hand . . . . *Lucrece* 1597
In bloodless white and the encrimson'd mood . . . *Lov. Comp.* 201

Bloody. That bloody beast, Which knows no pity, but is still severe *Ven. and Adon.* 999
At his bloody view, her eyes are fled Into the deep dark cabins of her head 1037
Obdurate vassals fell exploits effecting, In bloody death . . *Lucrece* 430
Here Troilus swounds, Here friend by friend in bloody channel lies . 1487
My bloody judge forbade my tongue to speak 1648
By this bloody knife, We will revenge the death of this true wife . 1840
Make war upon this bloody tyrant, Time . . . *Sonnet* 16 2
The bloody spur cannot provoke him on 50 9
Till action, lust Is perjured, murderous, bloody, full of blame . 129 3
Like a thousand vanquish'd men in bloody fight ! . . *Pass. Pil.* 280

Blossom. Whose rarest havings made the blossoms dote . . *Lov. Comp.* 235
Spied a blossom passing fair, Playing in the wanton air . . *Pass. Pil.* 229

Blot. Like misty vapours when they blot the sky . *Ven. and Adon.* 184
And die, unhallow'd thoughts, before you blot With your uncleanness that which is divine . . . . *Lucrece* 192
Worse than a slavish wipe or birth-hour's blot 537
To blot old books and alter their contents 948
To shun this blot, she would not blot the letter With words . . . 1322
Or blot with hell-born sin such saint-like forms 1519
And dost him grace when clouds do blot the heaven . . *Sonnet* 28 10
So shall those blots that do with me remain Without thy help by me be borne alone 36 3
But what's so blessed-fair that fears no blot? 92 13
Where beauty's veil doth cover every blot 95 11

Blotted. What wit sets down is blotted straight with will . *Lucrece* 1299

Blotting. He hath fed Upon fresh beauty, blotting it with blame *Ven. and Adon.* 796

Blow. Then with her windy sighs and golden hairs To fan and blow them dry again she seeks 52
The wind would blow it off and, being gone, Play with his locks . . 1089
The wind wars with his torch to make him stay, And blows the smoke of it into his face . . . . *Lucrece* 312
Some gentle gust doth get, Which blows these pitchy vapours . . . 550
Alas, how many bear such shameful blows ! 832
From lips new-waxen pale begins to blow The grief away . . . 1663
That blow did bail it from the deep unrest Of that polluted prison . 1725
This windy tempest, till it blow up rain, Held back his sorrow's tide . 1788
Is it revenge to give thyself a blow For his foul act? 1823
Nor falls Under the blow of thralled discontent . . *Sonnet* 124 7
'Air,' quoth he, 'thy cheeks may blow ; Air, would I might triumph so !' *Pass. Pil.* 235

Blowest. Thou blow'st the fire when temperance is thaw'd . . *Lucrece* 384

Blown. Yet from mine ear the tempting tune is blown . . *Ven. and Adon.* 778
As night-wanderers often are, Their light blown out in some mistrustful wood . . . 826
My sighs are blown away, my salt tears gone, Mine eyes are turn'd to fire . 1071
Small lights are soon blown out, huge fires abide . . . *Lucrece* 647
Sorrow ebbs, being blown with wind of words . . . 1330
Blue. Her two blue windows faintly she up-heaveth, Like the fair sun, when in his fresh array He cheers the morn . . *Ven. and Adon.* 482
Her breasts, like ivory globes circled with blue . . . *Lucrece* 407
Whose ranks of blue veins, as his hand did scale, Left their round turrets destitute and pale . . . 440
Her blue blood changed to black in every vein . . . 1454
Round about her tear-distained eye Blue circles stream'd . . 1587
Blue-veined. These blue-vein'd violets whereon we lean Never can blab, nor know not what we mean . . *Ven. and Adon.* 125
Blunt. She knows it is no gentle chase, But the blunt boar, rough bear, or lion proud . . . 884
This is too curious-good, this blunt and ill . . . *Lucrece* 1300
In Ajax' eyes blunt rage and rigour roll'd . . . 1398
Onward to Troy with the blunt swains he goes . . . 1504
Devouring Time, blunt thou the lion's paws . . . *Sonnet* 19 1
There appears a face That over-goes my blunt invention quite . 103 7
Tan sacred beauty, blunt the sharp'st intents, Divert strong minds . 115 7
Blunter. Be it not said Thy edge should blunter be than appetite . 56 2
Blunting the fine point of seldom pleasure . . . 52 4
For when we rage, advice is often seen By blunting us to make our wits more keen . . . *Lov. Comp.* 161
Blur. This blur to youth, this sorrow to the sage, This dying virtue *Lucrece* 222
Blurred. Thy issue blurr'd with nameless bastardy . . . 522
Blush. Forgetting shame's pure blush and honour's wrack *Ven. and Adon.* 558
When virtue bragg'd, beauty would blush for shame . . *Lucrece* 54
When beauty boasted blushes, in despite Virtue would stain that o'er with silver white . . . 55
Makes the lily pale, And the red rose blush at her own disgrace . 479
Where now I have no one to blush with me . . . 792
Beggar'd of blood to blush through lively veins . . *Sonnet* 67 10
Figuring that they their passions likewise lent me Of grief and blushes . . . *Lov. Comp.* 200
Of burning blushes, or of weeping water, Or swooning paleness . 304
To blush at speeches rank, to weep at woes . . . 307
Yet will she blush, here be it said . . . *Pass. Pil.* 351
Blushed. Who blush'd and pouted in a dull disdain, With leaden appetite, unapt to toy . . . *Ven. and Adon.* 33
Lucrece thought he blush'd to see her shame . . . *Lucrece* 1344
She thought he blush'd, as knowing Tarquin's lust . . . 1354
Blushing. Like lawn being spread upon the blushing rose *Ven. and Adon.* 590
The blushing morrow Lends light to all fair eyes that light will borrow *Lucrece* 1082
Blushing on her, with a steadfast eye Receives the scroll . . 1339
Blushing with him, wistly on him gazed . . . 1355
That blushing red no guilty instance gave . . . 1511
Blood untainted still doth red abide, Blushing at that which is so putrified 1750
The roses fearfully on thorns did stand, One blushing shame *Sonnet* 99 9
My poor lips, . . . At the wood's boldness by thee blushing stand . 128 8
He saw more wounds than one, And blushing fled, and left her all alone *Pass. Pil.* 130
Blusterer. Sometime a blusterer, that the ruffle knew Of court, of city *Lov. Comp.* 58
Blustering. No cloudy show of stormy blustering weather . *Lucrece* 115
Boar. 'I know not love,' quoth he, 'nor will not know it, Unless it be a boar, and then I chase it' . . . *Ven. and Adon.* 410
He intends To hunt the boar with certain of his friends. 'The boar!' quoth she . . . 588
But that thou told'st me thou wouldst hunt the boar . . . 614
When thou didst name the boar, not to dissemble, I fear'd thy fortune 641
The picture of an angry-chafing boar . . . 662
My living sorrow, If thou encounter with the boar to-morrow . . 672
To make thee hate the hunting of the boar, Unlike myself thou hear'st me moralize . . . 711
She knows it is no gentle chase, But the blunt boar, rough bear, or lion proud . . . 884
And with that word she spied the hunted boar . . . 900
She will no further, But back retires to rate the boar for murther . 906
Yet pardon me I felt a kind of fear When as I met the boar . . 999
The boar provoked my tongue; Be wreak'd on him, invisible commander 1003
And in her haste unfortunately spies The foul boar's conquest . . 1030
The wide wound that the boar had trench'd In his soft flank . . 1052
Urchin-snouted boar, Whose downward eye still looketh for a grave . 1105
Thus was Adonis slain: He ran upon the boar with his sharp spear . 1112
Deep-wounded with a boar, Deep in the thigh, a spectacle of ruth! *Pass. Pil.* 126
Boast. What canst thou boast Of things long since, or any thing ensuing? *Ven. and Adon.* 1077
Perchance his boast of Lucrece' sovereignty Suggested this proud issue of a king . . . *Lucrece* 36
He shall not boast who did thy stock pollute That thou art doting father of his fruit . . . 1063
My resolution, love, shall be thy boast . . . 1193
Of public honour and proud titles boast . . . *Sonnet* 25 2
Then may I dare to boast how I do love thee; Till then not show my head 26 13
As victors of my silence cannot boast . . . 86 11
And having thee, of all men's pride I boast . . . 91 12
No, Time, thou shalt not boast that I do change . . . 123 1
O, pardon me, in that my boast is true . . . *Lov. Comp.* 246
Boasted. When beauty boasted blushes, in despite Virtue would stain that o'er with silver white . . . *Lucrece* 55
Boat. Being wreck'd, I am a worthless boat, He of tall building and of goodly pride . . . *Sonnet* 80 11
Boding. My boding heart pants, beats, and takes no rest *Ven. and Adon.* 647
Body. Though nothing but my body's bane would cure thee . . 372
What is thy body but a swallowing grave? . . . 757
The strongest body shall it make most weak, Strike the wise dumb . 1145
What were it, But with my body my poor soul's pollution? . *Lucrece* 1157
My body or my soul, which was the dearer, When the one pure, the other made divine? . . . 1163
My honour I'll bequeath unto the knife That wounds my body so dishonoured . . . 1185
My soul and body to the skies and ground . . . 1199
That dying fear through all her body spread; And who cannot abuse a body dead? . . . 1266
Show'd life imprison'd in a body dead . . . 1456
Body. Her body's stain her mind untainted clears . . . *Lucrece* 1710
Himself on her self-slaughter'd body threw . . . 1733
The crimson blood Circles her body in on every side . . . 1739
They did conclude to bear dead Lucrece thence: To show her bleeding body thorough Rome . . . 1851
My body is the frame wherein 'tis held . . . *Sonnet* 24 3
Then begins a journey in my head, To work my mind, when body's work's expired . . . 27 4
My name be buried where my body is . . . 72 11
My body being dead, The coward conquest of a wretch's knife . 74 10
Some [glory] in their bodies' force, Some in their garments . . 91 2
Shall worms, inheritors of this excess, Eat up thy charge? is this thy body's end? . . . 146 8
I do betray My nobler part to my gross body's treason . . 151 6
My soul doth tell my body that he may Triumph in love . . 151 7
Boil. Her face doth reek and smoke, her blood doth boil *Ven. and Adon.* 555
Boisterous. Banning his boisterous and unruly beast . . . 326
Bold. Be bold to play, our sport is not in sight . . . 124
Who is so faint, that dare not be so bold To touch the fire, the weather being cold? . . . 401
Though men can cover crimes with bold stern looks . . *Lucrece* 1252
If your maid may be so bold, She would request to know your heaviness 1282
God wot, it was defect Of spirit, life, and bold audacity . . 1346
When their brave hope, bold Hector, march'd to field . . 1430
These contraries such unity do hold, Only to flatter fools and make them bold . . . 1559
Therefore to give them from me was I bold, To trust those tables? *Son.* 122 11
To say they err I dare not be so bold, Although I swear it to myself alone 131 7
Youth is hot and bold, age is weak and cold; Youth is wild, and age is tame *Pass. Pil.* 163
Bold-faced. And like a bold-faced suitor 'gins to woo him *Ven. and Adon.* 6
Boldness. My poor lips, which should that harvest reap, At the wood's boldness by thee blushing stand . . . *Sonnet* 128 8
Bollen. Here one being throng'd bears back, all boll'n and red . *Lucrece* 1417
Bond. That which they possess They scatter and unloose it from their bond 136
My bonds in thee are all determinate . . . *Sonnet* 87 4
Whereto all bonds do tie me day by day . . . 117 4
Under that bond that him as fast doth bind . . . 134 8
And seal'd false bonds of love as oft as mine . . . 142 7
Vow, bond, nor space, In thee hath neither sting, knot, nor confine *L. Comp.* 264
Bondage. He held such petty bondage in disdain . *Ven. and Adon.* 394
And true to bondage would not break from thence . *Lov. Comp.* 34
Bone. Even as an empty eagle, sharp by fast, Tires with her beak on feathers, flesh, and bone . . . *Ven. and Adon.* 56
In shape, in courage, colour, pace, and bone . . . 294
Posterity, shamed with the note, Shall curse my bones . . *Lucrece* 209
When that churl Death my bones with dust shall cover. . *Sonnet* 32 2
Crack'd many a ring of posied gold and bone . . *Lov. Comp.* 45
Bonnet. And with his bonnet hides his angry brow *Ven. and Adon.* 339
Bonnet nor veil henceforth no creature wear! . . . 1081
And therefore would he put his bonnet on . . . 1087
Book. Secrecies Writ in the glassy margents of such books *Lucrece* 102
Princes are the glass, the school, the book, Where subjects' eyes do learn 615
That know not how To cipher what is writ in learned books . 811
To blot old books and alter their contents . . . 948
Poor women's faces are their own faults' books . . . 1253
O, let my books be then the eloquence And dumb presagers of my speaking breast . . . *Sonnet* 23 9
Once foil'd, Is from the book of honour razed quite . . 25 11
Show me your image in some antique book . . . 59 7
The vacant leaves thy mind's imprint will bear, And of this book this learning mayst thou taste . . . 77 4
So oft as thou wilt look, Shall profit thee and much enrich thy book 77 14
The dedicated words which writers use Of their fair subject, blessing every book . . . 82 4
Book both my wilfulness and errors down . . . 117 9
Study his bias leaves, and makes his book thine eyes . *Pass. Pil.* 61
Boot. Thou hast thy 'Will,' And 'Will' to boot, and 'Will' in overplus *Sonnet* 135 2
Bootless. Let us part, And leave this idle theme, this bootless chat *Ven. and Adon.* 422
And trouble deaf heaven with my bootless cries . . *Sonnet* 29 3
Bore. I bore the canopy, With my extern the outward honouring . 125 1
Black was not counted fair, Or if it were, it bore not beauty's name 127 2
Our drops this difference bore, His poison'd me, and mine did him restore *Lov. Comp.* 300
Born. I often did behold In thy sweet semblance my old age new born *Lucr.* 1759
As, to behold desert a beggar born, And needy nothing trimm'd in jollity *Sonnet* 66 2
Before these bastard signs of fair were born . . . 68 3
Whose influence is thine and born of thee . . . 78 10
Ere you were born was beauty's summer dead . . . 104 14
And rather make them born to our desire . . . 123 7
They mourners seem At such who, not born fair, no beauty lack . 127 11
Yet who knows not conscience is born of love? . . . 151 2
Borne. O, had thy mother borne so hard a mind, She had not brought forth thee . . . *Ven. and Adon.* 203
Borne by the trustless wings of false desire . . . *Lucrece* 2
Borne on the bier with white and bristly beard . . *Sonnet* 12 8
So shall those blots that do with me remain Without thy help by me be borne alone . . . 36 4
Borrow. 'Tis much to borrow, and I will not owe it . *Ven. and Adon.* 411
Patron of all light, From whom each lamp and shining star doth borrow 861
O, how her eyes and tears did lend and borrow . . . 961
The blushing morrow Lends light to all fair eyes that light will borrow *Lucrece* 1083
She lends them words, and she their looks doth borrow . . 1498
Pack night, peep day; good day, of night now borrow . . *Pass. Pil.* 209
Borrowed. Whose beams upon his hairless face are fix'd, As if from thence they borrow'd all their shine . . . *Ven. and Adon.* 488
That to his borrow'd bed he make retire, And stoop to honour . *Lucrece* 573
Priam wets his eyes, To see those borrow'd tears that Sinon sheds . 1549
Fairing the foul with art's false borrow'd face. . *Sonnet* 127 6
Which borrow'd from this holy fire of Love A dateless lively heat . 153 5
O, all that borrow'd motion seeming owed, Would yet again betray the fore-betray'd! . . . *Lov. Comp.* 327
Bosom. She swears, From his soft bosom never to remove *Ven. and Adon.* 81
Within my bosom, whereon thou dost lie, My boding heart pants . 646
In the sweet channel of her bosom dropt . . . 958
And says, within her bosom it shall dwell . . . 1173

Bosom. Through Night's black bosom should not peep again . *Lucrece* 788
They whose guilt within their bosoms lie Imagine every eye beholds their blame 1342
No love toward others in that bosom sits . *Sonnet* 9 13
Which in my bosom's shop is hanging still . 24 7
Thy bosom is endeared with all hearts . 31 1
Then tender'd The humble salve which wounded bosoms fits . 120 12
Prison my heart in thy steel bosom's ward . 133 9
He did in the general bosom reign Of young, of old . *Lov. Comp.* 127
The broken bosoms that to me belong Have emptied all their fountains in my well 254
Both. Both favour, savour, hue, and qualities . *Ven. and Adon.* 747
Bepainted all with red, Like milk and blood being mingled both together . 902
Both crystals, where they view'd each other's sorrow . 963
Thy weal and woe are both of them extremes . 987
Grief hath two tongues, and never woman yet Could rule them both without ten women's wit . 1008
They both would strive who first should dry his tears . 1092
Beauty and virtue strived Which of them both should underprop her fame *Lucrece* 53
Where, lest between them both it should be kill'd, The coward captive vanquished doth yield 74
Both which, as servitors to the unjust, So cross him . 285
By heaven and earth, and all the power of both . 572
O Time, thou tutor both to good and bad, Teach me to curse! 995
Kill both thyself and her for yielding so . 1036
When both were kept for heaven and Collatine . 1166
Thou dead, both die, and both shall victors be . 1211
Two red fires in both their faces blazed . 1353
She looks for night, and then she longs for morrow, And both she thinks too long with her remaining . 1572
Both stood, like old acquaintance in a trance, Met far from home . 1595
Clouds and eclipses stain both moon and sun . *Sonnet* 35 3
Both find each other, and I lose both twain, And both for my sake lay on me this cross . 42 11
For nimble thought can jump both sea and land . 44 7
Slight air and purging fire, Are both with thee, wherever I abide . 45 2
Than both your poets can in praise devise . 83 14
Both grace and faults are loved of more and less . 96 3
A third, nor red nor white, had stol'n of both . 99 10
And gives thy pen both skill and argument . 100 8
Both truth and beauty on my love depends . 101 3
Book both my wilfulness and errors down . 117 9
Thy registers and thee I both defy . 123 9
Thou hast both him and me: He pays the whole, and yet am I not free 134 13
On both sides thus is simple truth suppress'd . 138 8
But being both from me, both to each friend, I guess one angel in another's hell . 144 11; *Pass. Pil.* 25
In clamours of all size, both high and low . *Lov. Comp.* 21
And sexes both enchanted, To dwell with him in thoughts . 128
Cold modesty, hot wrath, Both fire from hence and chill extincture hath . 294
Showing fair nature is both kind and tame . 311
One god is god of both, as poets feign; One knight loves both, and both in thee remain . *Pass. Pil.* 115
More mickle was the pain That nothing could be used to turn them both to gain 220
Whilst as fickle Fortune smiled, Thou and I were both beguiled . 402
Bottom. The bottom poison, and the top o'erstraw'd With sweets *Ven. and Adon.* 1143
For mirth doth search the bottom of annoy . *Lucrece* 1109
Bottom-grass. Sweet bottom-grass and high delightful plain *Ven. and Adon.* 236
Bottomless. O, deeper sin than bottomless conceit Can comprehend in still imagination! *Lucrece* 701
Bough. The studded bridle on a ragged bough Nimbly she fastens:—O, how quick is love! *Ven. and Adon.* 37
Upon those boughs which shake against the cold . *Sonnet* 73 3
That wild music burthens every bough . 102 11
Bought. Thou shalt know thy interest was not bought Basely with gold *Lucrece* 1067
Bounced. He, spying her, bounced in, whereas he stood . *Pass. Pil.* 83
Bound. By law of nature thou art bound to breed . *Ven. and Adon.* 171
She would, he will not in her arms be bound . 226
Imperiously he leaps, he neighs, he bounds . 265
The sea hath bounds, but deep desire hath none . 389
From the sweet embrace, Of those fair arms which bound him to her breast 812
At last she sees a wretched image bound . *Lucrece* 1501
As bound in knighthood to her imposition . 1697
Being your vassal, bound to stay your leisure . *Sonnet* 58 4
Bound for the prize of all too precious you . 86 2
What rounds, what bounds, what course, what stop he makes! *Lov. Comp.* 109
Boundeth in his pride Back to the strait that forced him on so fast *Lucrece* 1669
Bounding. Like a gentle flood, Who, being stopp'd, the bounding banks o'erflows . 1119
Boundless. There falls into thy boundless flood Black lust, dishonour . 653
Brass, nor stone, nor earth, nor boundless sea . *Sonnet* 65 1
Bounteous. Why dost thou abuse The bounteous largess given thee to give? . 4 6
Which bounteous gift thou shouldst in bounty cherish . 11 12
Bountiful. If that one be prodigal, Bountiful they will him call . *Pass. Pil.* 412
Bounty. Which bounteous gift thou shouldst in bounty cherish . *Sonnet* 11 12
One doth shadow of your beauty show, The other as your bounty doth appear . 53 11
Or monarch's hands that let not bounty fall . *Lov. Comp.* 41
Bow. Whose sinewy neck in battle ne'er did bow . *Ven. and Adon.* 99
Her heart, The which, by Cupid's bow she doth protest, He carries thence incaged in his breast . 581
Her voice is stopt, her joints forget to bow; Her eyes are mad . 1061
She bows her head, the new-sprung flower to smell . 1171
He is no woodman that doth bend his bow To strike a poor unseasonable doe *Lucrece* 580
Then jointly to the ground their knees they bow . 1846
Make me bow, And do not drop in for an after-loss . *Sonnet* 90 3
Needs must I under my transgression bow . 120 3
Bow-back. On his bow-back he hath a battle set Of bristly pikes *Ven. and Adon.* 619
Bowed. So proud, As heaven, it seem'd to kiss the turrets bow'd . *Lucrece* 1372
Those thoughts, to me like oaks, to thee like osiers bow'd . *Pass. Pil.* 60
Bower. Sweet beauty hath no name, no holy bower, But is profaned *Son.* 127 7
Boy. Over one arm the lusty courser's rein, Under her other was the tender boy *Ven. and Adon.* 32
Flint-hearted boy! 'Tis but a kiss I beg; why art thou coy? . *Son.* 95
Is love so light, sweet boy, and may it be That thou shouldst think it heavy unto thee? . *Ven. and Adon.* 155
Wistly to view How she came stealing to the wayward boy . 344
Let me excuse thy courser, gentle boy; And learn of him . 403
The silly boy, believing she is dead, Claps her pale cheek, till clapping makes it red 467
'Sweet boy,' she says, 'this night I'll waste in sorrow' . 583
'Thou hadst been gone,' quoth she, 'sweet boy, ere this' . 613
The boy that by her side lay kill'd Was melted like a vapour from her sight 1165
What new to register, That may express my love or thy dear merit? Nothing, sweet boy . *Sonnet* 108 5
O thou, my lovely boy, who in thy power Dost hold Time's fickle glass! 126 1
The boy for trial needs would touch my breast . 153 10
She, silly queen, with more than love's good will, Forbade the boy he should not pass those grounds . *Pass. Pil.* 124
As if the boy should use like loving charms . 150
Brag. Brag not of thy might, For mastering her that foil'd the god of fight *Ven. and Adon.* 113
Nor shall Death brag thou wander'st in his shade . *Sonnet* 18 11
Beauty brag, but 'tis not she; Truth and beauty buried be . *Ph. and Tur.* 63
Bragged. When virtue bragg'd, beauty would blush for shame . *Lucrece* 54
Braided. His braided hanging mane Upon his compass'd crest now stand on end . *Ven. and Adon.* 271
Though slackly braided in loose negligence . *Lov. Comp.* 35
Brain. Like the proceedings of a drunken brain . *Ven. and Adon.* 910
To the disposing of her troubled brain . 1040
For oft the eye mistakes, the brain being troubled . 1068
Such shadows are the weak brain's forgeries . *Lucrece* 460
How are our brains beguiled, Which, labouring for invention, bear amiss *Sonnet* 59 2
Thou shalt find Those children nursed, deliver'd from thy brain . 77 11
That did my ripe thoughts in my brain inhearse . 86 3
What's in the brain that ink may character? . 108 1
Thy gift, thy tables, are within my brain Full character'd . 122 1
So long as brain and heart Have faculty by nature to subsist . 122 5
Brain-sick. Beaten away by brain-sick rude desire . *Lucrece* 175
Brake. Round rising hillocks, brakes obscure and rough *Ven. and Adon.* 237
And all amazed brake off his late intent . 469
Hasting to feed her fawn hid in some brake . 876
Here kennell'd in a brake she finds a hound . 913
'Once,' quoth she, 'did I see a fair sweet youth Here in these brakes' *Pass. Pil.* 126
Brambles. The thorny brambles and embracing bushes *Ven. and Adon.* 629
Branches. The branches of another root are rotted . *Lucrece* 823
Brand not my forehead with thy piercing light . 1091
Thence comes it that my name receives a brand . *Sonnet* 111 5
Cupid laid by his brand, and fell asleep . 153 1
Love's brand new-fired, The boy for trial needs would touch my breast 153 9
Laid by his side his heart-inflaming brand . 154 2
This brand she quenched in a cool well by . 154 9
Brass. Lofty towers I see down-razed And brass eternal slave to mortal rage . 64 4
Brass, nor stone, nor earth, nor boundless sea . 65 1
When tyrants' crests and tombs of brass are spent . 107 14
Unless my nerves were brass or hammer'd steel . 120 4
Brave. When their brave hope, bold Hector, march'd to field . *Lucrece* 1430
And see the brave day sunk in hideous night . *Sonnet* 12 2
Nothing 'gainst Time's scythe can make defence Save breed, to brave him when he takes thee hence . 12 14
And wear their brave state out of memory . 15 8
Youth like summer brave, age like winter bare . *Pass. Pil.* 160
Bravery. Hiding thy bravery in their rotten smoke . *Sonnet* 34 4
Braving compare, disdainfully did sting His high-pitch'd thoughts *Lucrece* 40
Brawl. What though she strive to try her strength, And ban and brawl, and say thee nay . *Pass. Pil.* 318
Brawny. His brawny sides, with hairy bristles arm'd, Are better proof than thy spear's point can enter . *Ven. and Adon.* 625
Breach. Her mangling eye, That makes more gashes where no breach should be 1066
She crops the stalk, and in the breach appears Green dropping sap . 1175
This moves in him more rage and lesser pity, To make the breach *Lucrece* 469
The impious breach of holy wedlock vow . 809
But why of two oaths' breach do I accuse thee, When I break twenty? *Sonnet* 152 5
Break. And now her sobs do her intendments break . *Ven. and Adon.* 222
And now his woven girths he breaks asunder . 266
The client breaks, as desperate in his suit . 336
Or as the berry breaks before it staineth, Or like the deadly bullet of a gun 460
Yet love breaks through and picks them all at last . 576
But through the flood-gates breaks the silver rain . 959
She, much amazed, breaks ope her lock'd-up eyes . *Lucrece* 446
So her accent breaks, That twice she doth begin ere once she speaks . 566
And then they drown their eyes or break their hearts . 1239
'My girl,' quoth she, 'on what occasion break Those tears from thee?' . 1270
Ere the break of day, And, ere I rose, was Tarquin gone away . 1280
Their ranks began To break upon the galled shore, and than Retire again . 1440
As if her heart would break, She throws forth Tarquin's name . 1716
Like to the lark at break of day arising . *Sonnet* 29 11
'Tis not enough that through the cloud thou break . 34 5
Even there Where thou art forced to break a twofold truth . 41 12
But why of two oaths' breach do I accuse thee, When I break twenty? 152 6
And true to bondage would not break from thence . *Lov. Comp.* 34
Now all these hearts that do on mine depend, Feeling it break . 275
What fool is not so wise To break an oath, to win a paradise? *Pass. Pil.* 42
Breakers. Or kings be breakers of their own behests . *Lucrece* 852
Breaketh. The strong-neck'd steed, being tied unto a tree, Breaketh his rein *Ven. and Adon.* 264
With this, he breaketh from the sweet embrace, Of those fair arms . 811
She wildly breaketh from their strict embrace . 874
Breaking. Tearing of papers, breaking rings a-twain . *Lov. Comp.* 6
The lines she rents, Big discontent so breaking their contents . 56
Breast. Broad breast, full eye, small head, and nostril wide, High crest, short ears, straight legs, and passing strong . *Ven. and Adon.* 296
Enfranchising his mouth, his back, his breast . 396
The which . . . He carries thence incaged in his breast . 582
But, like an earthquake, shakes thee on my breast . 648
Should run Into the quiet closure of my breast . 782
Of those fair arms which bound him to her breast . 812
From whose silver breast The sun ariseth in his majesty . 855
It is as good To wither in my breast as in his blood . 1182
Here was thy father's bed, here in my breast; Thou art the next of blood 1183

Breast. Her breasts, like ivory globes, circled with blue *Lucrece* 407
Smoking with pride, march'd on to make his stand On her bare breast 439
His hand, that yet remains upon her breast,—Rude ram! 463
She wakes her heart by beating on her breast, And bids it leap from thence 759
Or tyrant folly lurk in gentle breasts 851
Your tunes entomb Within your hollow-swelling feather'd breasts 1122
Such passion her assails, That patience is quite beaten from her breast 1563
She sheathed in her harmless breast A harmful knife 1723
Bubbling from her breast, it doth divide In two slow rivers 1737
He struck his hand upon his breast, And kiss'd the fatal knife 1842
Is but the seemly raiment of my heart, Which in thy breast doth live *Son.* 22 7
Dumb presagers of my speaking breast, Who plead for love 23 10
Mine eyes have drawn thy shape, and thine for me Are windows to my breast 24 11
Though I feel thou art, Within the gentle closure of my breast 48 11
As easy might I from myself depart As from my soul, which in thy breast doth lie 109 4
Next my heaven the best, Even to thy pure and most most loving breast 110 14
If snow be white, why then her breasts are dun 130 3
Love's brand new-fired, The boy for trial needs would touch my breast 153 10
As compound love to physic your cold breast *Lov. Comp.* 259
What breast so cold that is not warmed here? 292
She, poor bird, as all forlorn, Lean'd her breast up-till a thorn *Pass. Pil.* 382
And the turtle's loyal breast To eternity doth rest *Ph. and Tur.* 57
Breath. I'll sigh celestial breath, whose gentle wind Shall cool the heat of this descending sun *Ven. and Adon.* 189
It is a life in death, That laughs and weeps, and all but with a breath 414
Comes breath perfumed that breedeth love by smelling 444
She lies as she were slain, Till his breath breatheth life in her again 474
That the star-gazers, having writ on death, May say, the plague is banish'd by thy breath 510
So she at these sad signs draws up her breath 929
Dost thou mean To stifle beauty and to steal his breath? 934
His breath and beauty set Gloss on the rose, smell to the violet 935
Comparing it to her Adonis' breath 1172
A dream, a breath, a froth of fleeting joy *Lucrece* 212
Her hair, like golden threads, play'd with her breath; O modest wantons! 400
Let their exhaled unwholesome breaths make sick The life of purity 779
No tool imparteth To make more vent for passage of her breath 1040
Revenge on him that made me stop my breath 1180
From his lips did fly Thin winding breath, which purl'd up to the sky 1407
He strives in vain; What he breathes out his breath drinks up again 1666
Till manly shame bids him possess his breath And live to be revenged 1777
When summer's breath their masked buds discloses *Sonnet* 54 8
O, how shall summer's honey breath hold out Against the wreckful siege? 65 5
Such virtue hath my pen—Where breath most breathes, even in the mouths of men 81 14
Others for the breath of words respect, Me for my dumb thoughts 85 13
Whence didst thou steal thy sweet that smells, If not from my love's breath? 99 3
And to his robbery had annex'd thy breath 99 11
In some perfumes is there more delight Than in the breath that from my mistress reeks 130 8
O, that sad breath his spongy lungs bestow'd! *Lov. Comp.* 326
My vow was breath, and breath a vapour is *Pass. Pil.* 37
And as she fetched breath, away he skips, And would not take her meaning 153
Youth is full of sport, age's breath is short; Youth is nimble, age is lame 161
That the lover, sick to death, Wish'd himself the heaven's breath 234
With the breath thou givest and takest, 'Mongst our mourners shalt thou go *Ph. and Tur.* 19
Breathe. Frantic with grief thus breathes she forth her spite *Lucrece* 762
He strives in vain; What he breathes out his breath drinks up again 1666
So long as men can breathe or eyes can see, So long lives this *Sonnet* 18 13
How can my Muse want subject to invent, While thou dost breathe? 38 2
Such virtue hath my pen—Where breath most breathes, even in the mouths of men 81 14
When winds breathe sweet, unruly though they be *Lov. Comp.* 103
Breathed. That blow did bail it from the deep unrest Of that polluted prison where it breathed *Lucrece* 1726
Those lips that Love's own hand did make Breathed forth the sound that said 'I hate' *Sonnet* 145 2
Breathers. Your being shall rehearse When all the breathers of this world are dead 81 12
Breatheth. Panting he lies and breatheth in her face *Ven. and Adon.* 62
She lies as she were slain, Till his breath breatheth life in her again 474
Breathings. Untimely breathings, sick, and short assays *Lucrece* 1720
Breathing-while. Bud and be blasted in a breathing-while *Ven. and Adon.* 1142
Breathless. Till, breathless, he disjoin'd, and backward drew 541
Bred. Pure shame and awed resistance made him fret, Which bred more beauty in his angry eyes 70
Contenting but the eye alone, Thing like a man, but of no woman bred! 214
These worlds in Tarquin new ambition bred *Lucrece* 411
By thy bright beauty was it newly bred 490
To eat up errors by opinion bred, Not spend the dowry of a lawful bed 937
So of shame's ashes shall my fame be bred 1188
Finding the first conceit of love there bred *Sonnet* 108 13
You are so strongly in my purpose bred That all the world besides methinks are dead 112 13
Breed. By law of nature thou art bound to breed *Ven. and Adon.* 171
Whose attaint Disorder breeds by heating of the blood 742
Self-loving nuns, That on the earth would breed a scarcity 753
What wrong, what shame, what sorrow I shall breed *Lucrece* 499
This momentary joy Breeds months of pain 690
What virtue breeds iniquity devours 872
Advice is sporting while infection breeds 907
By heaven's fair sun that breeds the fat earth's store, By all our country rights 1837
That's for thyself to breed another thee *Sonnet* 6 7
Nothing 'gainst Time's scythe can make defence Save breed, to brave him 12 14
That did not better for my life provide Than public means which public manners breeds 111 4
My ewes breed not, My rams speed not, All is amiss *Pass. Pil.* 246
Breeder. And this I do to captivate the eye Of the fair breeder that is standing by *Ven. and Adon.* 282
The unback'd breeder, full of fear, Jealous of catching 320
Breedeth. Seeds spring from seeds and beauty breedeth beauty 167
Comes breath perfumed that breedeth love by smelling 444
Breeding. A breeding jennet, lusty, young, and proud 260
Bribed. And therefore hath she bribed the Destinies 733
Bridle. The studded bridle on a ragged bough Nimbly she fastens 37
Brief. This brief abridgement of my will I make *Lucrece* 1198

Brief. My woes are tedious, though my words are brief *Lucrece* 1309
Nor can I fortune to brief minutes tell *Sonnet* 14 5
Love alters not with his brief hours and weeks 116 11
Our dates are brief, and therefore we admire What thou dost foist upon us 123 5
Desires to know In brief the grounds and motives of her woe *Lov. Comp.* 63
Brier. Each envious brier his weary legs doth scratch *Ven. and Adon.* 705
Bright. Mine eyes are gray and bright and quick in turning 140
And as the bright sun glorifies the sky, So is her face illumined with her eye 485
Look, how a bright star shooteth from the sky, So glides he in the night 815
Each lamp and shining star doth borrow The beauteous influence that makes him bright 862
Mortal stars, as bright as heaven's beauties *Lucrece* 13
Whether it is that she reflects so bright, That dazzleth them, or else some shame supposed 376
By thy bright beauty was it newly bred 490
And wiped the brinish pearl from her bright eyes 1213
Sharing joy To see their youthful sons bright weapons wield 1432
Seemed to appear, Like bright things stain'd, a kind of heavy fear 1435
Had doting Priam check'd his son's desire, Troy had been bright with fame 1491
Should thrust Into so bright a day such black-faced storms 1518
But thou, contracted to thine own bright eyes *Sonnet* 1 5
An eye more bright than theirs, less false in rolling 20 5
Though not so bright As those gold candles fix'd in heaven's air 21 11
I tell the day, to please him thou art bright 28 9
And darkly bright are bright in dark directed 43 4
Thou, whose shadow shadows doth make bright 43 5
All days are nights to see till I see thee, And nights bright days when dreams do show thee me 43 14
But you shall shine more bright in these contents Than unswept stone 55 3
Unless this miracle have might, That in black ink my love may still shine bright 65 14
I have sworn thee fair and thought thee bright, Who art as black as hell 147 13
Bright orient pearl, alack, too timely shaded! *Pass. Pil.* 133
Brighter. Brighter than glass, and yet, as glass is, brittle 87
Brightness. And swear that brightness doth not grace the day *Sonnet* 150 4
Brim. He put his bonnet on, Under whose brim the gaudy sun would peep *Ven. and Adon.* 1088
And stood stark naked on the brook's green brim *Pass. Pil.* 80
Brine. Seasoning the earth with showers of silver brine *Lucrece* 796
Laundering the silken figures in the brine That season'd woe had pelleted in tears *Lov. Comp.* 17
Bring. That sometime true news, sometime false doth bring *Ven. and Adon.* 658
But in one minute's fight brings beauty under 746
Would bring him mulberries and ripe-red cherries 1103
I see what crosses my attempt will bring *Lucrece* 491
Be the humble suppliant's friend, And bring him where his suit may be obtain'd 898
And bring truth to light, To stamp the seal of time in aged things 940
The mindful messenger, come back, Brings home his lord and other company 1584
For thy sweet love remember'd such wealth brings *Sonnet* 29 13
To thy sensual fault I bring in sense—Thy adverse party is thy advocate 35 9
Let him bring forth Eternal numbers to outlive long date 38 11
What can mine own praise to mine own self bring? 39 3
Whose blessed key Can bring him to his sweet up-locked treasure 52 2
For I am shamed by that which I bring forth, And so should you 72 13
I impair not beauty being mute, When others would give life and bring a tomb 83 12
Alack, what poverty my Muse brings forth! 103 1
So that myself bring water for my stain 109 8
Bring me within the level of your frown, But shoot not at me 117 11
Green plants bring not Forth their dye *Pass. Pil.* 283
Brinish. And wiped the brinish pearl from her bright eyes *Lucrece* 1213
A fount With brinish current downward flow'd apace *Lov. Comp.* 284
Bristles. His brawny sides, with hairy bristles arm'd *Ven. and Adon.* 625
Bristly. On his bow-back he hath a battle set Of bristly pikes 620
Borne on the bier with white and bristly beard *Sonnet* 12 8
Brittle. Brighter than glass, and yet, as glass is, brittle *Pass. Pil.* 87
A brittle glass that's broken presently: A doubtful good 172
Broad breast, full eye, small head, and nostril wide, High crest, short ears, straight legs, and passing strong *Ven. and Adon.* 296
Thin mane, thick tail, broad buttock, tender hide 298
My saucy bark inferior far to his On your broad main doth wilfully appear *Sonnet* 80 8
Broils. And broils root out the work of masonry 55 6
Broke. Lo! as a careful housewife runs to catch One of her feather'd creatures broke away 143 2
To me love swearing, In act thy bed-vow broke and new faith torn 152 3
Vows for thee broke deserve not punishment *Pass. Pil.* 32
If by me broke, what fool is not so wise To break an oath, to win a paradise? 41
Broken. And kissing speaks, with lustful language broken *Ven. and Adon.* 47
Poor broken glass, I often did behold In thy sweet semblance my old age new born *Lucrece* 1758
Dost thou desire my slumbers should be broken? *Sonnet* 61 3
The broken bosoms that to me belong Have emptied all their fountains in my well *Lov. Comp.* 254
In thee it is: If broken, then it is no fault of mine *Pass. Pil.* 40
A brittle glass that's broken presently: A doubtful good 172
A glass, a flower, Lost, vaded, broken, dead within an hour 174
As broken glass no cement can redress, So beauty blemish'd once 's for ever lost 178
Brokers. Knew vows were ever brokers to defiling *Lov. Comp.* 173
Brood. Draw not thy sword to guard iniquity, For it was lent thee all that brood to kill *Lucrece* 627
Make the earth devour her own sweet brood *Sonnet* 19 2
Brook. And died to kiss his shadow in the brook *Ven. and Adon.* 162
When he beheld his shadow in the brook The fishes spread on it their golden gills 1099
A woeful hostess brooks not merry guests *Lucrece* 1125
Sweet Cytherea, sitting by a brook, With young Adonis *Pass. Pil.* 43
By a brook, A brook where Adon used to cool his spleen 75
And stood stark naked on the brook's green brim 80
Brother. This guilt would seem death-worthy in thy brother *Lucrece* 635
If music and sweet poetry agree, As they must needs, the sister and the brother *Pass. Pil.* 104
Brought. O, had thy mother borne so hard a mind, She had not brought forth thee *Ven. and Adon.* 204
For then is Tarquin brought unto his bed, Intending weariness *Lucrece* 120
And by their mortal fault brought in subjection Her immortality 724
Being from the feeling of her own grief brought By deep surmise of others' detriment 1578
A dearer birth than this his love had brought *Sonnet* 32 11

Brought. Despite of space I would be brought, From limits far remote, where thou dost stay *Sonnet* 44 3
And brought to medicine a healthful state 118 11
The accident which brought me to her eye Upon the moment did her force subdue *Lov. Comp.* 247
Brow. Even so she kissed his brow, his cheek, his chin *Ven. and Adon.* 59
Thou canst not see one wrinkle in my brow; Mine eyes are gray 139
Disliking eye, His louring brows o'erwhelming his fair sight 183
And with his bonnet hides his angry brow 339
Were never four such lamps together mix'd, Had not his clouded with his brow's repine 490
With heavy eye, knit brow, and strengthless pace *Lucrece* 709
My true eyes have never practised how To cloak offences with a cunning brow 749
To mask their brows and hide their infamy 794
The light will show, character'd in my brow, The story of sweet chastity's decay 807
Eyes wailing still, A brow unbent, that seem'd to welcome woe 1509
When forty winters shall besiege thy brow *Sonnet* 2 1
O, carve not with thy hours my love's fair brow, Nor draw no lines there 19 9
With all-triumphant splendour on my brow 33 10
Time doth transfix the flourish set on youth And delves the parallels in beauty's brow 60 10
When hours have drain'd his blood and fill'd his brow With lines and wrinkles 63 3
Before these bastard signs of fair were born, Or durst inhabit on a living brow 68 4
Sweet beauty's best, Of hand, of foot, of lip, of eye, of brow 106 6
Which vulgar scandal stamp'd upon my brow 112 2
My mistress' brows are raven black, Her eyes so suited 127 9
What though her frowning brows be bent, Her cloudy looks will calm ere night *Pass. Pil.* 311
Browny. His browny locks did hang in crooked curls *Lov. Comp.* 85
Bruised. With bruised arms and wreaths of victory *Lucrece* 110
Brutus. From the purple fountain Brutus drew The murderous knife 1734
Brutus, who pluck'd the knife from Lucrece' side 1807
That deep vow, which Brutus made before, He doth again repeat 1847
Bubbling from her breast, it doth divide In two slow rivers 1737
Bud. Who plucks the bud before one leaf put forth? *Ven. and Adon.* 416
Bud and be blasted in a breathing-while 1142
When thus thy vices bud before thy spring *Lucrece* 604
Why should the worm intrude the maiden bud? 848
Within thine own bud buriest thy content *Sonnet* 1 11
Rough winds do shake the darling buds of May 18 3
Loathsome canker lives in sweetest bud 35 4
Play as wantonly When summer's breath their masked buds discloses 54 8
For canker vice the sweetest buds doth love 70 7
And buds of marjoram had stol'n thy hair 99 7
Soon vaded, Pluck'd in the bud, and vaded in the spring *Pass. Pil.* 132
A flower that dies when first it gins to bud 171
A belt of straw and ivy buds, With coral clasps and amber studs 365
Budding. Which, like a canker in the fragrant rose, Doth spot the beauty of thy budding name *Sonnet* 95 3
Builded. No, it was builded far from accident 124 5
Experience for me many bulwarks builded *Lov. Comp.* 152
Building. To ruinate proud buildings with thy hours *Lucrece* 944
He of tall building and of goodly pride *Sonnet* 80 12
Built. And ruin'd love, when it is built anew, Grows fairer than at first 119 11
Thy pyramids built up with newer might To me are nothing novel 123 2
Bulk. May feel her heart . . . rise up and fall, Beating her bulk, that his hand shakes withal *Lucrece* 467
Bullet. Or like the deadly bullet of a gun, His meaning struck her ere his words begun *Ven. and Adon.* 461
The strongest castle, tower, and town, The golden bullet beats it down *Pass. Pil.* 328
Bulwarks. Experience for me many bulwarks builded *Lov. Comp.* 152
Burden. O'ercharged with burden of mine own love's might *Sonnet* 23 8
Burdened. The colt that's back'd and burden'd being young Loseth his pride and never waxeth strong *Ven. and Adon.* 419
Burden-wise. For burden-wise I'll hum on Tarquin still *Lucrece* 1133
Buried. He might be buried in a tomb so simple *Ven. and Adon.* 244
And in themselves their pride lies buried *Sonnet* 25 7
All love's loving parts, And all those friends which I thought buried 31 4
Thou art the grave where buried love doth live 31 9
The rich proud cost of outworn buried age 64 2
My name be buried where my body is, And live no more to shame nor me nor you 72 11
Beauty brag, but 'tis not she; Truth and beauty buried be *Ph. and Tur.* 64
Buriest. Within thine own bud buriest thy content *Sonnet* 1 11
Burn. He burns with bashful shame: she with her tears Doth quench the maiden burning of his cheeks *Ven. and Adon.* 49
She bathes in water, yet her fire must burn 94
No more of love! The sun doth burn my face; I must remove 186
I'll make a shadow for thee of my hairs; If they burn too, I'll quench them with my tears 192
The lamp that burns by night Dries up his oil to lend the world his light 755
Mine ears, that to your wanton talk attended, Do burn themselves 810
Fair torch, burn out thy light, and lend it not *Lucrece* 190
Poor helpless help, the treasure stol'n away, To burn the guiltless casket where it lay! 1057
And with my tears quench Troy that burns so long 1468
Those round clear pearls of his, that move thy pity, Are balls of quenchless fire to burn thy city 1554
False Sinon's tears doth flatter, That he finds means to burn his Troy with water 1561
Pluck the keen teeth from the fierce tiger's jaws, And burn the long-lived phœnix in her blood *Sonnet* 19 4
Nor war's quick fire shall burn The living record of your memory 55 7
Knew no reason why My most full flame should afterwards burn clearer 115 4
Burned. Three April perfumes in three hot Junes burn'd, Since first I saw you fresh, which yet are green 104 7
When he most burn'd in heart-wish'd luxury, He preach'd pure maid, and praised cold chastity *Lov. Comp.* 314
She burn'd with love, as straw with fire flameth; She burn'd out love *Pass. Pil.* 97
Burneth. Thine eye darts forth the fire that burneth me *Ven. and Adon.* 196
An oven that is stopp'd, or river stay'd, Burneth more hotly, swelleth with more rage 332
Thy eye kindled the fire that burneth here *Lucrece* 1475
Burning. She with her tears Doth quench the maiden burning of his cheeks *Ven. and Adon.* 50
My beauty as the spring doth yearly grow, My flesh is soft and plump, my marrow burning 142
Titan, tired in the mid-day heat, With burning eye did hotly overlook them 178
As burning fevers, agues pale and faint, Life-poisoning pestilence 739
His drumming heart cheers up his burning eye *Lucrece* 435
Fond Paris, did incur This load of wrath that burning Troy doth bear 1474
In the orient when the gracious light Lifts up his burning head *Sonnet* 7 2
Hallow'd with sighs that burning lungs did raise *Lov. Comp.* 228
Of burning blushes, or of weeping water, Or swooning paleness 304
Burnished. That cedar-tops and hills seem burnish'd gold *Ven. and Adon.* 858
Burnt. His eyes, Where, lo, two lamps, burnt out, in darkness lies 1128
And dying eyes gleam'd forth their ashy lights, Like dying coals burnt out in tedious nights *Lucrece* 1379
Whose words like wildfire burnt the shining glory Of rich-built Ilion 1523
Burthen. She bears the load of lust he left behind, And he the burthen of a guilty mind 735
How are our brains beguiled, Which labouring for invention, bear amiss The second burthen of a former child *Sonnet* 59 4
Big with rich increase, Bearing the wanton burthen of the prime 97 7
That wild music burthens every bough 102 11
Bury. Seeming to bury that posterity Which by the rights of time thou needs must have *Ven. and Adon.* 758
Burying in Lucrece' wound his folly's show *Lucrece* 1810
Bush. The thorny brambles and embracing bushes, As fearful of him, part, through whom he rushes *Ven. and Adon.* 629
The bushes in the way Some catch her by the neck 871
Birds never limed no secret bushes fear *Lucrece* 88
Shape every bush a hideous shapeless devil 973
Busy. All my mind, my thought, my busy care *Ven. and Adon.* 383
Busy yourselves in skill-contending schools *Lucrece* 1018
At last it rains, and busy winds give o'er 1790
Whose busy care is bent To follow that which flies before her face *Son.* 143 6
But. A summer's day will seem an hour but short, Being wasted in such time-beguiling sport *Ven. and Adon.* 23
Look how he can, she cannot choose but love 79
Flint-hearted boy! 'Tis but a kiss I beg; why art thou coy? 96
Touch but my lips with those fair lips of thine 115
The sun that shines from heaven shines but warm 193
But, lo, from forth a copse that neighbours by, A breeding jennet 259
But when the heart's attorney once is mute, The client breaks 335
But now her cheek was pale, and by and by It flash'd forth fire 347
My love to love is love but to disgrace it 412
That laughs and weeps, and all but with a breath 414
Had I no eyes but ears, my ears would love That inward beauty 433
But, O, what banquet wert thou to the taste! 445
But now I lived, and life was death's annoy; But now I died, and death was lively joy 497
She seeks to kindle with continual kissing. But all in vain 607
But that thou told'st me thou wouldst hunt the boar 614
But, like an earthquake, shakes thee on my breast 648
And all is but to rob thee of a kiss 723
Hadst thou but bid beware, then he had spoke 943
But like a stormy day, now wind, now rain, Sighs dry her cheeks 965
Whereat she leaps that was but late forlorn 1026
O happiness enjoy'd but of a few *Lucrece* 22
And so, by hoping more, they have but less 137
What could he see but mightily he noted? 414
They think not but that every eye can see 750
They draw but what they see, know not the heart *Sonnet* 24 14
But out, alack! he was but one hour mine 33 11
But that so much of earth and water wrought 44 11
Butcher. Like to a mortal butcher bent to kill *Ven. and Adon.* 618
Butcher-sire. Or butcher-sire that reaves his son of life 766
Buttock. Thin mane, thick tail, broad buttock, tender hide 298
He vails his tail that, like a falling plume, Cool shadow to his melting buttock lent 315
Buy. So thou wilt buy and pay and use good dealing 514
A thousand kisses buys my heart from me 517
Who buys a minute's mirth to wail a week? Or sells eternity to get a toy? *Lucrece* 213
They buy thy help; but Sin ne'er gives a fee, He gratis comes 913
Buy terms divine in selling hours of dross *Sonnet* 146 11
By. Even as an empty eagle, sharp by fast *Ven. and Adon.* 55
By law of nature thou art bound to breed 171
By this, the love-sick queen began to sweat 175
So he were like him and by Venus' side 180
But, lo, from forth a copse that neighbours by, A breeding jennet, lusty, young, and proud 259
And this I do to captivate the eye Of the fair breeder that is standing by 282
But now her cheek was pale, and by and by It flash'd forth fire 347
And pay them at thy leisure, one by one 518
By this, poor Wat, far off upon a hill, Stands on his hinder legs 697
By this, she hears the hounds are at a bay 877
By this, far off she hears some huntsman hollo 973
When he was by, the birds such pleasure took, That some would sing 1101
By this, the boy that by her side lay kill'd Was melted like a vapour from her sight 1165
For by our ears our hearts oft tainted be *Lucrece* 38
Sits Sin, to seize the souls that wander by him 882
The life and feeling of her passion She hoards, to spend when he is by 1318
But now he throws that shallow habit by 1814
Which by and by black night doth take away, Death's second self *Son.* 73 7
Consumed with that which it was nourish'd by 73 12
All full with feasting on your sight And by and by clean starved for a look 75 10
And I by this will be a gainer too 88 9
This brand she quenched in a cool well by 154 9
'Fie, fie, fie,' now would she cry; 'Tereu, tereu!' by and by *Pass. Pil.* 386
By-past. 'Gainst her own content, To put the by-past perils in her way *Lov. Comp.* 158

C

Cabin. O, let him keep his loathsome cabin still . . . *Ven. and Adon.* 637
Her eyes are fled Into the deep dark cabins of her head 1038
And daff'd me to a cabin hang'd with care . . . . *Pass. Pil.* 183
Cabinet. The gentle lark, weary of rest, From his moist cabinet mounts up on high . . . . *Ven. and Adon.* 854
They, mustering to the quiet cabinet Where their dear governess and lady lies *Lucrece* 442
Caged. And now she would the caged cloister fly . . . *Lov. Comp.* 249
Caitiff. And asks the weary caitiff for his master . . *Ven. and Adon.* 914
Call. In her passion, calls it balm, Earth's sovereign salve 27
And calls it heavenly moisture, air of grace 64
Disturbing Jealousy Doth call himself Affection's sentinel . . . 650
Call it not love, for Love to heaven is fled 793
Like shrill-tongued tapsters answering every call 849
Turn to loathed sours Even in the moment that we call them ours *Lucrece* 868
She hoarsely calls her maid, Whose swift obedience to her mistress hies . 1214
Then call them not the authors of their ill 1244
At last she calls to mind where hangs a piece Of skilful painting . . 1366
One doth call her his, the other his, Yet neither may possess the claim . 1793
She in thee Calls back the lovely April of her prime . . . *Sonnet* 3 10
Then how, when nature calls thee to be gone? 4 11
That fresh blood which youngly thou bestowest Thou mayst call thine when thou from youth convertest 11 4
He that calls on thee, let him bring forth Eternal numbers to outlive long date 38 11
No love, my love, that thou mayst true love call 40 3
Else call it winter, which being full of care Makes summer's welcome thrice more wish'd, more rare 56 13
Whilst I alone did call upon thy aid, My verse alone had all thy gentle grace 79 1
For nothing this wide universe I call, Save thou, my rose . . . 109 13
For what care I who calls me well or ill, So you o'er-green my bad? . 112 3
Forgot upon your dearest love to call, Whereto all bonds do tie me . 117 3
Whereto the inviting time our fashion calls 124 8
To this I witness call the fools of time, Which die for goodness . . 124 13
Call not me to justify the wrong That thy unkindness lays upon my heart 139 1
Who hateth thee that I do call my friend? 149 5
No want of conscience hold it that I call Her 'love' . . . 151 13
If that one be prodigal, Bountiful they will him call . . *Pass. Pil.* 412
Called. It was not she that call'd him all-to naught . . *Ven. and Adon.* 993
Beauty's red, Which virtue gave the golden age to gild Their silver cheeks, and call'd it then their shield . . . . *Lucrece* 61
Let it not be call'd impiety, If in this blemish'd fort I make some hole . 1174
That deep torture may be call'd a hell 1287
His utmost sum, Call'd to that audit by advised respects . . *Sonnet* 49 4
Let not my love be call'd idolatry, Nor my beloved as an idol show . 105 1
For feasts of love I have been call'd unto . . . *Lov. Comp.* 181
Single nature's double name Neither two nor one was called . *Ph. and Tur.* 40
Calm. Time's glory is to calm contending kings . . . . *Lucrece* 939
And give the harmless show An humble gait, calm looks, eyes wailing still 1508
Her cloudy looks will calm ere night . . . . . *Pass. Pil.* 312
Came. Foreknowing well, if there he came to lie, Why, there Love lived and there he could not die . . . . *Ven. and Adon.* 245
Wistly to view How she came stealing to the wayward boy . . . 344
But Tarquin's shape came in her mind the while . . . *Lucrece* 1536
As if with grief or travail he had fainted, To me came Tarquin armed . 1544
Dear husband, in the interest of thy bed A stranger came . . . 1620
With shining falchion in my chamber came A creeping creature . . 1626
His scarlet lust came evidence to swear That my poor beauty had purloin'd his eyes 1650
'You fair lords,' quoth she, Speaking to those that came with Collatine . 1689
Thou usurer, that put'st forth all to use, And sue a friend came debtor for my sake . . . . *Sonnet* 134 11
Whilst many nymphs that vow'd chaste life to keep Came tripping by . 154 4
But I, my mistress' thrall, Came there for cure 154 13
All aids, themselves made fairer by their place, Came for additions *L. Comp.* 118
That not a heart which in his level came Could 'scape 309
Can. Look how he can, she cannot choose but love . . *Ven. and Adon.* 79
These blue-vein'd violets whereon we lean Never can blab . . . 126
Can thy right hand seize love upon thy left? Then woo thyself . . 158
And being steel'd, soft sighs can never grave it 376
Fair fall the wit that can so well defend her! 472
To sell myself I can be well contented, So thou wilt buy . . . 513
No more resisteth, While she takes all she can, not all she listeth . . 564
For pity now she can no more detain him 577
With hairy bristles arm'd, Are better proof than thy spear's point can enter 626
For love can comment upon every woe 714
O, what excuse can my invention make . . . . . *Lucrece* 225
The fear doth still exceed; And extreme fear can neither fight nor fly . . 230
How can they then assist me in the act? 350
Nothing can affection's course control, Or stop the headlong fury . . 500
Bequeath not to their lot The shame that from them no device can take . 535
No outrageous thing From vassal actors can be wiped away . . . 608
O, deeper sin than bottomless conceit Can comprehend in still imagination! 702
Drunken Desire must vomit his receipt, Ere he can see his own abomination 704
While Lust is in his pride, no exclamation Can curb his heat . . . 706
They think not but that every eye can see The same disgrace . . . 750
We have no good that we can say is ours, But ill-annexed Opportunity . 873
Thy violent vanities can never last 894
Though men can cover crimes with bold stern looks 1252
Yet with the fault I thus far can dispense 1279
Repetition cannot make it less; For more it is than I can well express . 1286
'It cannot be,' quoth she, 'that so much guile'—She would have said 'can lurk in such a look' 1535
And from her tongue 'can lurk' from 'cannot' took 1537
Ere once she can discharge one word of woe 1605
Where no excuse can give the fault amending 1614
That I no more can see what once I was 1764
Nothing 'gainst Time's scythe can make defence Save breed . *Sonnet* 12 13
Nor can I fortune to brief minutes tell 14 5
Time's pencil, or my pupil pen, Neither in inward worth nor outward fair, Can make you live yourself in eyes of men 16 12
So long as men can breathe or eyes can see, So long lives this . . 18 13

Can. How can I then be elder than thou art? . . . *Sonnet* 22 8
How can I then return in happy plight, That am debarr'd the benefit of rest? 28 1
Then can I drown an eye, unused to flow, For precious friends . . 30 5
Then can I grieve at grievances foregone 30 9
For no man well of such a salve can speak 34 7
Nor can thy shame give physic to my grief 34 9
How can my Muse want subject to invent, While thou dost breathe? . . 38 1
What can mine own praise to mine own self bring? 39 3
For nimble thought can jump both sea and land As soon as think the place where he would be 44 7
Thou hast the strength of laws, Since why to love I can allege no cause 49 14
Thus can my love excuse the slow offence Of my dull bearer . . . 51 1
When swift extremity can seem but slow 51 6
Then can no horse with my desire keep pace 51 9
Whose blessed key Can bring him to his sweet up-locked treasure . . 52 2
Since every one hath, every one, one shade, And you, but one, can every shadow lend 53 4
What strong hand can hold his swift foot back? Or who his spoils of beauty can forbid? 65 11
Want nothing that the thought of hearts can mend 69 2
Dear love, forget me quite, For you in me can nothing worthy prove . 72 4
The earth can have but earth, which is his due 74 7
What thy memory can not contain Commit to these waste blanks . . 77 9
He can afford No praise to thee but what in thee doth live . . . 79 11
The earth can yield me but a common grave 81 7
When they have devised What strained touches rhetoric can lend . . 82 10
There lives more life in one of your fair eyes Than both your poets can in praise devise 83 14
Which can say more Than this rich praise, that you alone are you? . . 84 1
If he can tell That you are you, so dignifies his story 84 7
Upon thy part I can set down a story Of faults conceal'd . . . 88 6
For there can live no hatred in thine eye 93 5
And all things turn to fair that eyes can see 95 12
O, blame me not, if I no more can write! 103 5
And more, much more, than in my verse can sit Your own glass shows . 103 13
To me, fair friend, you never can be old 104 1
Till each to razed oblivion yield his part Of thee, thy record never can be miss'd 122 8
When thy might Is more than my o'er-press'd defence can bide . . 139 8
But my five wits nor my five senses can Dissuade one foolish heart from serving thee 141 9
How can it? O, how can Love's eye be true? 148 9
Those that can see thou lovest, and I am blind 149 14
Where all those pleasures live that art can comprehend . *Pass. Pil.* 62
Well learned is that tongue that well can thee commend . . . 64
As broken glass no cement can redress 178
My shepherd's pipe can sound no deal 271
A cripple soon can find a halt 308
Let the priest in surplice white, That defunctive music can, Be the death-divining swan . . . . *Ph. and Tur.* 14
Love hath reason, reason none, If what parts can so remain . . . 48
Cancelled. An expired date, cancell'd ere well begun . . . *Lucrece* 26
Cancell'd my fortunes, and enchained me To endless date . . . 934
Doth fly Life's lasting date from cancell'd destiny 1729
And weep afresh love's long since cancell'd woe . . . *Sonnet* 30 7
Candles. Though not so bright As those gold candles fix'd in heaven's air 21 12
Canker. This canker that eats up Love's tender spring . *Ven. and Adon.* 656
Loathsome canker lives in sweetest bud . . . . . *Sonnet* 35 4
For canker vice the sweetest buds doth love 70 7
Which, like a canker in the fragrant rose, Doth spot the beauty . . 95 2
In pride of all his growth A vengeful canker eat him up to death . . 99 13
Canker-blooms have full as deep a dye As the perfumed tincture of the roses 54 5
Cannon. As smoke from Ætna, that in air consumes, Or that which from discharged cannon fumes . . . . *Lucrece* 1043
Cannot. Look how he can, she cannot choose but love . *Ven. and Adon.* 79
Her help she sees, but help she cannot get 93
Being judge in love, she cannot right her cause 220
His short thick neck cannot be easily harm'd 627
What have you urged that I cannot reprove? 787
If he be dead,—O no, it cannot be, Seeing his beauty, thou shouldst strike at it—O yes, it may 937
My tongue cannot express my grief for one 1069
Mar not the thing that cannot be amended . . . . *Lucrece* 578
Then kings' misdeeds cannot be hid in clay 609
Having no other pleasure of his gain But torment that it cannot cure his pain 861
So then he hath it when he cannot use it 862
O no, that cannot be; Of that true type hath Tarquin rifled me . . 1049
One . . . , That cannot tread the way out readily 1152
Who cannot abuse a body dead? 1267
If it should be told, The repetition cannot make it less . . . 1285
The weary time she cannot entertain, For now 'tis stale to sigh . . 1361
'It cannot be,' quoth she, 'that so much guile'—She would have said 'can lurk in such a look' 1534
And from her tongue 'can lurk' from 'cannot' took: 'It cannot be' she in that sense forsook, And turn'd it thus, 'It cannot be,' I find, But such a face should bear a wicked mind 1537
Who's so dumb that cannot write to thee? . . . . . *Sonnet* 38 7
I cannot blame thee for my love thou usest 40 6
The bloody spur cannot provoke him on 50 9
This thought is as a death, which cannot choose But weep . . . 64 13
Yet this thy praise cannot be so thy praise To tie up envy . . . 70 11
From hence your memory death cannot take 81 3
As victors of my silence cannot boast 86 11
Therefore in that I cannot know thy change 93 6
Cannot dispraise but in a kind of praise 95 7
Crabbed age and youth cannot live together . . . . *Pass. Pil.* 157
As take the pain, but cannot pluck the pelf 192
Senseless trees they cannot hear thee 393
If thou sorrow, he will weep; If thou wake, he cannot sleep . . . 426
Truth may seem, but cannot be: Beauty brag, but 'tis not she *Ph. and Tur.* 62
Canopied in darkness sweetly lay, Till they might open to adorn the day *Lucr.* 398

Canopy. When lofty trees I see barren of leaves Which erst from heat did canopy the herd . . . . *Sonnet* 12 6
I bore the canopy, With my extern the outward honouring . . 125 1
Canst. Thou canst not see one wrinkle in my brow . *Ven. and Adon.* 139
Art thou a woman's son, and canst not feel What 'tis to love? 201
'What! canst thou talk?' quoth she, 'hast thou a tongue?' . . 427
What canst thou boast Of things long since, or any thing ensuing? . 1077
Thy princely office how canst thou fulfil? . . . . *Lucrece* 628
So great a sum of sums, yet canst not live? . . . . *Sonnet* 4 8
What acceptable audit canst thou leave? 4 12
For thou not farther than my thoughts canst move . . . 47 11
Thou canst not, love, disgrace me half so ill 89 5
Thou canst not vex me with inconstant mind 92 9
Thou canst not then use rigour in my gaol; And yet thou wilt . 133 12
Canst thou, O cruel! say I love thee not? 149 1
Cap. A cap of flowers, and a kirtle Embroider'd all with leaves of myrtle *Pass. Pil.* 363
Caparisons. What cares he now for curb or pricking spur? For rich caparisons or trapping gay? . . . . . *Ven. and Adon.* 286
Capitol. By the Capitol that we adore, And by this chaste blood . *Lucrece* 1835
Captain. Like soldiers, when their captain once doth yield, They basely fly and dare not stay the field . . . . . *Ven. and Adon.* 893
Affection is my captain, and he leadeth . . . . *Lucrece* 271
And as their captain, so their pride doth grow 298
Like stones of worth they thinly placed are, Or captain jewels in the carcanet . . . . *Sonnet* 52 8
And simple truth miscall'd simplicity, And captive good attending captain ill 66 12
Captivate. And this I do to captivate the eye Of the fair breeder that is standing by . . . . *Ven. and Adon.* 281
Captive. Yet hath he been my captive and my slave 101
The coward captive vanquished doth yield To those two armies . *Lucrece* 75
A captive victor that hath lost in gain 730
And simple truth miscall'd simplicity, And captive good attending captain ill . . . . *Sonnet* 66 12
Car. With weary car, Like feeble age, he reeleth from the day . 7 9
Carcanet. Like stones of worth they thinly placed are, Or captain jewels in the carcanet 52 8
Carcass. The carcass of a beauty spent and done . . *Lov. Comp.* 11
Care. What cares he now for curb or pricking spur? For rich caparisons or trapping gay? . . . . . . *Ven. and Adon.* 285
All my mind, my thought, my busy care, Is how to get my palfrey . 383
How he outruns the wind and with what care 681
Now Nature cares not for thy mortal vigour 953
Save thieves, and cares, and troubled minds, that wake . *Lucrece* 126
To whose weak ruins muster troops of cares 720
Swift subtle post, carrier of grisly care, Eater of youth . . . 926
So she, deep-drenched in a sea of care, Holds disputation . . . 1100
Many she sees where cares have carved some 1445
Time's ruin, beauty's wreck, and grim care's reign 1451
His face, though full of cares, yet show'd content 1503
Her lively colour kill'd with deadly cares 1593
Thou, best of dearest and mine only care . . . . *Sonnet* 48 7
Else call it winter, which being full of care Makes summer's welcome thrice more wish'd, more rare 56 13
For what care I who calls me well or ill? 112 3
In so profound abysm I throw all care Of others' voices . . . 112 9
Whose busy care is bent To follow that which flies before her face . 143 6
Past cure I am, now reason is past care, And frantic-mad . . 147 9
Youth is full of pleasance, age is full of care . . . *Pass. Pil.* 158
And daff'd me to a cabin hang'd with care 183
Careful. How careful was I, when I took my way . . *Sonnet* 48 1
Lo! as a careful housewife runs to catch One of her feather'd creatures broke away 143 1
Careless. And careless lust stirs up a desperate courage *Ven. and Adon.* 556
Proclaim'd in her a careless hand of pride . . . *Lov. Comp.* 30
All thy fellow birds do sing, Careless of thy sorrowing . *Pass. Pil.* 398
Carriage. Sometimes her levell'd eyes their carriage ride *Lov. Comp.* 22
Carrier. Swift subtle post, carrier of grisly care, Eater of youth *Lucrece* 926
Carry. The which . . . He carries thence incaged in his breast *V. and A.* 582
Bid him with speed prepare to carry it . . . . . *Lucrece* 1294
When that fell arrest Without all bail shall carry me away . *Sonnet* 74 2
Carry-tale. This carry-tale, dissentious Jealousy . *Ven. and Adon.* 657
Carve. O, carve not with thy hours my love's fair brow . *Sonnet* 19 9
Carved. Many she sees where cares have carved some . . *Lucrece* 1445
The face, that map which deep impression bears Of hard misfortune, carved in it with tears 1713
She carved thee for her seal, and meant thereby Thou shouldst print more, not let that copy die . . . . *Sonnet* 11 13
Case. Extinguishing his conduct in this case . . . . *Lucrece* 313
Poor, and meek, Like to a bankrupt beggar wails his case . . . 711
Since that my case is past the help of law 1022
Eternal love in love's fresh case Weighs not the dust and injury of age *Son.* 108 9
Accomplish'd in himself, not in his case . . . . *Lov. Comp.* 116
Casket. Poor helpless help, the treasure stol'n away, To burn the guiltless casket where it lay! . . . . *Lucrece* 1057
Cast. Why hast thou cast into eternal sleeping Those eyes? *Ven. and Adon.* 951
When as thy love hath cast his utmost sum . . . . *Sonnet* 49 3
Then if he thrive and I be cast away, The worst was this . . 80 13
Castaway. She there remains a hopeless castaway . . . *Lucrece* 744
Castle. The strongest castle, tower, and town, The golden bullet beats it down . . . . *Pass. Pil.* 327
Cat. Yet, foul night-waking cat, he doth but dally . . . *Lucrece* 554
Catch. The bushes in the way Some catch her by the neck *Ven. and Adon.* 872
The dove sleeps fast that this night-owl will catch . . . *Lucrece* 360
Nor his own vision holds what it doth catch . . . *Sonnet* 113 8
Lo! as a careful housewife runs to catch One of her feather'd creatures broke away 143 1
Whilst her neglected child holds her in chase, Cries to catch her . 143 6
But if thou catch thy hope, turn back to me 143 11
Catching. Jealous of catching, swiftly doth forsake him *Ven. and Adon.* 321
Catching all passions in his craft of will . . . . *Lov. Comp.* 126
Caterpillars. And soon bereaves, As Caterpillars do the tender leaves *Ven. and Adon.* 798
Cattle. A reverend man that grazed his cattle nigh . . *Lov. Comp.* 57
Caught. Now quick desire hath caught the yielding prey *Ven. and Adon.* 547
Cause. Being judge in love, she cannot right her cause 220
It shall suspect where is no cause of fear 1153
It shall be cause of war and dire events 1159
And give the sneaped birds more cause to sing . . . . *Lucrece* 333
Cause. Die I will not till my Collatine Have heard the cause of my untimely death . . . . *Lucrece* 1178
The other takes in hand No cause, but company, of her drops spilling . 1236
The cause craves haste, and it will soon be writ 1295
Thou hast the strength of laws, Since why to love I can allege no cause *Sonnet* 49 14
The cause of this fair gift in me is wanting 87 7
The more I hear and see just cause of hate 150 10
I weep for thee, and yet no cause I have . . . . . *Pass. Pil.* 137
Thy like ne'er was For a sweet content, the cause of all my moan . 295
Causeless. She tells them 'tis a causeless fantasy, And childish error *Ven. and Adon.* 897
Causer. Love's denying, Faith's defying, Heart's renying, Causer of this *Pass. Pil.* 252
Cautels. In him a plenitude of subtle matter, Applied to cautels, all strange forms receives . . . . *Lov. Comp.* 303
Cave. These lovely caves, these round enchanting pits, Open'd their mouths to swallow Venus' liking . . . . . . *Ven. and Adon.* 247
The neighbour caves, as seeming troubled, Make verbal repetition of her moans 830
Shrinks backward in his shelly cave with pain 1034
Dark harbour for defame! Grim cave of death! . . . *Lucrece* 769
Cave-keeping evils that obscurely sleep 1250
Cavil. In vain I cavil with mine infamy, In vain I spurn at my confirm'd despite 1025
Thus cavils she with every thing she sees 1093
Cease. O time, cease thou thy course and last no longer . . . 1765
If all were minded so, the times should cease . . . *Sonnet* 11 9
Ceased. When he hath ceased his ill-resounding noise *Ven. and Adon.* 919
Ceaseless. Thou ceaseless lackey to eternity . . . . *Lucrece* 967
Ceasing their clamorous cry till they have singled With much ado the cold fault cleanly out . . . . *Ven. and Adon.* 693
Cedar. The cedar stoops not to the base shrub's foot, But low shrubs wither at the cedar's root . . . . *Lucrece* 664
Cedar-tops. That cedar-tops and hills seem burnish'd gold *Ven. and Adon.* 858
Celestial. I'll sigh celestial breath, whose gentle wind Shall cool the heat of this descending sun 189
Anon permit the basest clouds to ride With ugly rack on his celestial face *Sonnet* 33 6
Celestial as thou art, O do not love that wrong . . . *Pass. Pil.* 69
Cell. In thy shady cell, where none may spy him Sits Sin . . *Lucrece* 881
Cement. As broken glass no cement can redress . . . *Pass. Pil.* 178
Censures. Where is my judgement fled, That censures falsely what they see aright? . . . . *Sonnet* 148 4
Centre. Poor soul, the centre of my sinful earth 146 1
Ceremony. The perfect ceremony of love's rite 23 6
Certain. He intends To hunt the boar with certain of his friends *V. and A.* 588
Here folds she up the tenour of her woe, Her certain sorrow writ uncertainly *Lucrece* 1311
Begins the sad dirge of her certain ending 1612
When I was certain o'er incertainty, Crowning the present *Sonnet* 115 11
These are certain signs to know Faithful friend from flattering foe *Pass. Pil.* 429
Chafes. He bends her fingers, holds her pulses hard, He chafes her lips *Ven. and Adon.* 477
Chafing. All swoln with chafing, down Adonis sits 325
Chain. Leading him prisoner in a red-rose chain 110
Chained. Or free that soul which wretchedness hath chain'd *Lucrece* 900
Challenge. But beauty, in that white intituled, From Venus' doves doth challenge that fair field 58
Chamber. The locks between her chamber and his will, Each one by him enforced retires his ward 302
Now is he come unto the chamber door 337
Into the chamber wickedly he stalks, And gazeth on her 365
With shining falchion in my chamber came A creeping creature . 1626
Champaign. Like a goodly champaign plain, Lays open all the little worms that creep 1247
Champion. Her champion mounted for the hot encounter *Ven. and Adon.* 596
Chance. Met far from home, wondering each other's chance . *Lucrece* 1596
May any terms acquit me from this chance? 1706
Every fair from fair sometime declines, By chance or nature's changing course untrimm'd . . . . *Sonnet* 18 8
Change. If all these petty ills shall change thy good . *Lucrece* 656
There we will unfold To creatures stern sad tunes, to change their kinds . 1147
O, change thy thought, that I may change my mind! . . *Sonnet* 10 9
Where wasteful Time debateth with Decay, To change your day of youth to sullied night 15 12
A woman's gentle heart, but not acquainted With shifting change . 20 4
Such wealth brings That then I scorn to change my state with kings . 29 14
Why is my verse so barren of new pride, So far from variation or quick change? 76 2
Thou canst not, love, disgrace me half so ill, To set a form upon desired change, As I'll myself disgrace 89 6
Therefore in that I cannot know thy change 93 6
And in this change is my invention spent 105 11
Nor I to none alive, That my steel'd sense or changes right or wrong . 112 8
Million'd accidents Creep in 'twixt vows and change decrees of kings . 115 6
No, Time, thou shalt not boast that I do change 123 1
To be so tickled, they would change their state And situation . . 128 9
Changed. Her blue blood changed to black in every vein . *Lucrece* 1454
Sorrow changed to solace, solace mix'd with sorrow . *Pass. Pil.* 203
Changing. Every fair from fair sometime declines, By chance or nature's changing course untrimm'd . . . . *Sonnet* 18 8
Each changing place with that which goes before 60 3
Channel. In the sweet channel of her bosom dropt . . *Ven. and Adon.* 958
Here friend by friend in bloody channel lies . . . *Lucrece* 1487
O, how the channel to the stream gave grace! . . *Lov. Comp.* 285
Chant. Anon she hears them chant it lustily, And all in haste she coasteth to the cry . . . . *Ven. and Adon.* 869
Chaos. With him is beauty slain, And, beauty dead, black chaos comes again 1020
Vast sin-concealing chaos! nurse of blame! . . . . *Lucrece* 767
Chaps. Her cheeks with chaps and wrinkles were disguised . . . 1452
Character. Since mind at first in character was done . *Sonnet* 59 8
While comments of your praise, richly compiled, Reserve their character with golden quill 85 3
What's in the brain that ink may character? 108 1
Oft did she heave her napkin to her eyne, Which on it had conceited characters . . . . *Lov. Comp.* 16
Thought characters and words merely but art 174
Charactered. The light will show, character'd in my brow, The story *Lucr.* 807
Thy gift, thy tables, are within my brain Full character'd . *Sonnet* 122 2

Charge. What excuse can my invention make, When thou shalt charge me with so black a deed? *Lucrece* 226
Anon his beating heart, alarum striking, Gives the hot charge 434
Shall worms, inheritors of this excess, Eat up thy charge? *Sonnet* 146 8
Lord, how mine eyes throw gazes to the east! My heart doth charge the watch *Pass. Pil.* 194
Charged. Either not assail'd or victor being charged *Sonnet* 70 10
Nature hath charged me that I hoard them not, But yield them up *Lov. Comp.* 220
Charging the sour-faced groom to hie as fast As lagging fowls before the northern blast *Lucrece* 1334
Chariot. By whose swift aid Their mistress mounted through the empty skies In her light chariot quickly is convey'd *Ven. and Adon.* 1192
Charitable. Thou grant'st no time for charitable deeds *Lucrece* 908
Charity. 'Tis promised in the charity of age *Lov. Comp.* 70
Charm. But honest fear, bewitch'd with lust's foul charm, Doth too too oft betake him to retire *Lucrece* 173
For my sake, when I might charm thee so For she that was thy Lucrece, now attend me 1681
My parts had power to charm a sacred nun *Lov. Comp.* 260
As if the boy should use like loving charms *Pass. Pil.* 150
Charmed. That it beguiled attention, charm'd the sight *Lucrece* 1404
Threw my affections in his charmed power *Lov. Comp.* 146
Or my affection put to the smallest teen, Or any of my leisures ever charm'd 193
Charter. Your charter is so strong That you yourself may privilege your time *Sonnet* 58 9
The charter of thy worth gives thee releasing 87 3
Chary. Bearing thy heart, which I will keep so chary 22 11
Chase. Rose-cheek'd Adonis hied him to the chase *Ven. and Adon.* 3
'I know not love,' quoth he, 'nor will not know it, Unless it be a boar, and then I chase it' 410
Then do they spend their mouths: Echo replies, As if another chase were in the skies 696
For now she knows it is no gentle chase 883
'Tis a meritorious fair design To chase injustice with revengeful arms *Lucr.* 1693
From the purple fountain Brutus drew The murderous knife, and as it left the place, Her blood, in poor revenge, held it in chase 1736
Whilst her neglected child holds her in chase, Cries to catch her *Sonnet* 143 5
Whilst I thy babe chase thee afar behind 143 10
Chased. So fares it with this faultful lord of Rome, Who this accomplishment so hotly chased *Lucrece* 716
By our strong arms from forth her fair streets chased 1834
Chasing. Or as the fleet-foot roe that's tired with chasing *Ven. and Adon.* 561
Chaste. Lucrece the chaste. Haply that name of 'chaste' *Lucrece* 7
Thou see'st our mistress' ornaments are chaste 322
And suck'd the honey which thy chaste bee kept 840
By the Capitol that we adore, And by this chaste blood 1836
By chaste Lucrece' soul that late complain'd Her wrongs to us 1839
Whilst many nymphs that vow'd chaste life to keep Came tripping by *Sonnet* 154 3
Herald sad and trumpet be, To whose sound chaste wings obey *Ph. and Tur.* 4
Chastest. The chastest tears That ever modest eyes with sorrow shed *Lucr.* 682
Chastity. Despite of fruitless chastity, Love-lacking vestals *Ven. and Adon.* 751
Pure Chastity is rifled of her store *Lucrece* 692
The story of sweet chastity's decay 808
There my white stole of chastity I daff'd *Lov. Comp.* 297
He preach'd pure maid, and praised cold chastity 315
Touches so soft still conquer chastity *Pass. Pil.* 50
'Twas not their infirmity, It was married chastity *Ph. and Tur.* 61
Chat. Let us part, And leave this idle theme, this bootless chat *V. and A.* 422
As palmers' chat makes short their pilgrimage *Lucrece* 791
Cheap. Sold cheap what is most dear, Made old offences of affections new *Sonnet* 110 3
Cheater. Then, gentle cheater, urge not my amiss 151 3
Check. To check the tears in Collatinus' eyes *Lucrece* 1817
And patience, tame to sufferance, bide each check, Without accusing you of injury *Sonnet* 58 7
If thy soul check thee that I come so near, Swear to thy blind soul. 136 1
Checked. Had doting Priam check'd his son's desire, Troy had been bright with fame *Lucrece* 1490
Sap check'd with frost and lusty leaves quite gone. *Sonnet* 5 7
Cheered and check'd even by the self-same sky 15 6
Cheek. Now doth she stroke his cheek, now doth he frown *Ven. and Adon.* 45
She with her tears Doth quench the maiden burning of his cheeks 50
Even so she kissed his brow, his cheek, his chin 59
Wishing her cheeks were gardens full of flowers 65
Her contending tears, Which long have rain'd, making her cheeks all wet 83
Souring his cheeks cries 'Fie, no more of love!' 185
Red cheeks and fiery eyes blaze forth her wrong 219
That in each cheek appears a pretty dimple 242
To love a cheek that smiles at thee in scorn! 252
But now her cheek was pale, and by and by It flashed forth fire 347
Her other tender hand his fair cheek feels: His tenderer cheek receives her soft hand's print 352
Claps her pale cheek, till clapping makes it red 468
He wrings her nose, he strikes her on the cheeks, He bends her fingers 475
Like lawn being spread upon the blushing rose, Usurps her cheek 591
The crystal tide that from her two cheeks fair In the sweet channel of her bosom dropt 957
Sighs dry her cheeks, tears make them wet again 966
Yet sometimes falls an orient drop beside, Which her cheek melts 982
Chequer'd with white, Resembling well his pale cheeks 1169
Which virtue gave the golden age to gild Their silver cheeks *Lucrece* 61
Her lily hand her rosy cheek lies under, Cozening the pillow of a lawful kiss 386
With lank and lean discolour'd cheek, With heavy eye 708
And grave, like water that doth eat in steel, Upon my cheeks 756
Poor Lucrece' cheeks unto her maid seem so As winter meads 1217
Nor why her fair cheeks over-wash'd with woe 1225
On what occasion break Those tears from thee, that down thy cheeks are raining? 1271
The more she saw the blood his cheeks replenish, The more she thought he spied in her some blemish 1357
Her cheeks with chaps and wrinkles were disguised 1452
Cheeks neither red nor pale, but mingled so That blushing red no guilty instance gave 1510
O, from thy cheeks my image thou hast torn! 1762
On Helen's cheek all art of beauty set *Sonnet* 53 7
Why should false painting imitate his cheek? 67 5
Thus is his cheek the map of days outworn 68 1
Beauty doth he give And found it in thy cheek 79 11
Cheek. Their gross painting might be better used Where cheeks need blood *Sonnet* 82 14
The purple pride Which on thy soft cheek for complexion dwells. 99 4
Love's not Time's fool, though rosy lips and cheeks Within his bending sickle's compass come 116 9
Roses damask'd, red and white, But no such roses see I in her cheeks. 130 6
Truly not the morning sun of heaven Better becomes the grey cheeks of the east 132 6
Hanging her pale and pined cheek beside *Lov. Comp.* 32
Each cheek a river running from a fount 283
O, that false fire which in his cheek so glow'd! 324
'Air,' quoth he, 'thy cheeks may blow; Air, would I might triumph so!' *Pass. Pil.* 235
Cheer. He cheers the morn and all the earth relieveth *Ven. and Adon.* 484
So guiltless she securely gives good cheer And reverend welcome *Lucrece* 89
Whereat she smiled with so sweet a cheer 264
His drumming heart cheers up his burning eye 435
To cheer the ploughman with increaseful crops 958
With so dull a cheer That leaves look pale, dreading the winter's near *Sonnet* 97 13
Ruthless beasts they will not cheer thee *Pass. Pil.* 394
Cheered. Cheered and check'd even by the self-same sky *Sonnet* 15 6
Cheering up her senses all dismay'd, She tells them 'tis a causeless fantasy *Ven. and Adon.* 896
Chequered. A purple flower sprung up, chequer'd with white 1168
Cherish. To dry the old oak's sap and cherish springs *Lucrece* 950
As Priam him did cherish, So did I Tarquin; so my Troy did perish 1546
Which bounteous gift thou shouldst in bounty cherish *Sonnet* 11 12
Cherries. Mulberries and ripe-red cherries *Ven. and Adon.* 1103
Cherubin. Such cherubins as your sweet self resemble *Sonnet* 114 6
Gave the tempter place, Which like a cherubin above them hover'd *L. Comp.* 319
Chest. She wakes her heart by beating on her breast, And bids it leap from thence, where it may find Some purer chest to close so pure a mind *Lucrece* 761
Thee have I not lock'd up in any chest, Save where thou art not *Sonnet* 48 9
So is the time that keeps you as my chest 52 9
Where, alack, Shall Time's best jewel from Time's chest lie hid? 65 10
Chid. And chid the painter for his wondrous skill *Lucrece* 1528
Chide. Now doth he frown, And 'gins to chide, but soon she stops his lips *Ven. and Adon.* 46
If thou wilt chide, thy lips shall never open 48
Hateful divorce of love,—thus chides she Death 932
Thus I forestall thee, if thou mean to chide *Lucrece* 484
He runs, and chides his vanish'd, loathed delight 742
But chide rough winter that the flower hath kill'd 1255
They do but sweetly chide thee, who confounds In singleness the parts that thou shouldst bear *Sonnet* 8 7
And chide thy beauty and thy straying youth, Who lead thee in their riot 41 10
Nor dare I chide the world-without-end hour 57 5
The forward violet thus did I chide: Sweet thief 99 1
With Fortune chide, The guilty goddess of my harmful deeds 111 1
Chiding. Chiding that tongue that ever sweet Was used in giving gentle doom, And taught it thus anew to greet 145 6
Chief. The field's chief flower, sweet above compare, Stain to all nymphs *Ven. and Adon.* 8
Every present sorrow seemeth chief, But none is best 970
Seeking that beauteous roof to ruinate Which to repair should be thy chief desire *Sonnet* 10 8
That she hath thee, is of my wailing chief 42 3
Chiefly in love, whose leave exceeds commission *Ven. and Adon.* 568
I in deep delight am chiefly drown'd Whenas himself to singing he betakes *Pass. Pil.* 113
Spare not to spend, and chiefly there Where thy desert may merit praise 324
Child. Make the young old, the old become a child *Ven. and Adon.* 1152
Were Tarquin Night, as he is but Night's child *Lucrece* 785
The nurse, to still her child, will tell my story 813
To make the child a man, the man a child 954
True grief is fond and testy as a child 1094
If in the child the father's image lies, Where shall I live now Lucrece is unlived 1753
This fair child of mine Shall sum my count *Sonnet* 2 10
Resembling sire and child and happy mother 8 11
Were some child of yours alive that time, You should live twice 17 13
Then believe me, my love is as fair As any mother's child 21 11
As a decrepit father takes delight To see his active child do deeds of youth 37 2
Labouring for invention, bear amiss The second burthen of a former child 59 4
If my dear love were but the child of state 124 1
Whilst her neglected child holds her in chase, Cries to catch her 143 5
Childish. 'Tis a causeless fantasy, And childless error, that they are afraid *Ven. and Adon.* 898
Then, childish fear, avaunt! debating, die! *Lucrece* 274
Such childish humour from weak minds proceeds 1825
Children. Nor children's tears nor mothers' groans respecting, Swell in their pride 431
Cited up in rhymes, and sung by children in succeeding times 525
Then, for thy husband and thy children's sake, Tender my suit 533
If children pre-decease progenitors, We are their offspring 1756
Every private widow well may keep By children's eyes her husband's shape in mind *Sonnet* 9 8
Thou shalt find Those children nursed, deliver'd from thy brain 77 11
Chill. Cold modesty, hot wrath, Both fire from hence and chill extincture hath *Lov. Comp.* 294
Chin. Even so she kissed his brow, his cheek, his chin *Ven. and Adon.* 59
Upon this promise did he raise his chin 85
Her alabaster skin, Her coral lips, her snow-white dimpled chin *Lucrece* 420
Who o'er the white sheet peers her whiter chin, The reason of this rash alarm to know 472
Small show of man was yet upon his chin *Lov. Comp.* 92
Chips. Those dancing chips, O'er whom thy fingers walk with gentle gait *Sonnet* 128 10
Chivalry. Collatine's high name, Made glorious by his manly chivalry *Lucr.* 109
Choice. But then woos best when most his choice is froward *Ven. and Adon.* 570
Choir. Still concludes in woe, And still the choir of echoes answer so 840
Bare ruin'd choirs, where late the sweet birds sang *Sonnet* 73 4
Chokes. This said, impatience chokes her pleading tongue *Ven. and Adon.* 217
Choked. So heedful fear Is almost choked by unresisted lust *Lucrece* 282
Choose. Look how he can, she cannot choose but love *Ven. and Adon.* 79
This thought is as a death, which cannot choose But weep *Sonnet* 64 13
Unless thy lady prove unjust, Press never thou to choose anew *Pass. Pil.* 332

Chopped. Beated and chopp'd with tann'd antiquity . . . *Sonnet* 62 10
Chorus. The phœnix and the dove, Co-supremes and stars of love, As chorus to their tragic scene . . . . *Ph. and Tur.* 52
Chorus-like. With tears, which, chorus-like, her eyes did rain *V. and A.* 360
Chose. O, what a mansion have those vices got Which for their habitation chose out thee! . . . . *Sonnet* 95 10
When as thine eye hath chose the dame . . . . . *Pass. Pil.* 299
Chronicle. When in the chronicle of wasted time I see . *Sonnet* 106 1
Churl. And, tender churl, makest waste in niggarding 1 12
When that churl Death my bones with dust shall cover . . 32 2
Then, churls, their thoughts, although their eyes were kind . . 69 11
Churlish. Scorning his churlish drum and ensign red . *Ven. and Adon.* 107
Ill-nurtured, crooked, churlish, harsh in voice, O'erworn, despised . . 134
Thou know'st not what it is With javelin's point a churlish swine to gore . 616
'Cide. To 'cide this title is impanneled A quest of thoughts . . *Sonnet* 46 9
Cinders. Grace in all simplicity, Here enclosed in cinders lie *Ph. and Tur.* 55
Cipher. Some loathsome dash the herald will contrive, To cipher me *Lucrece* 207
The illiterate, that know not how To cipher what is writ . . 811
Ciphered. The face of either cipher'd either's heart . . . 1396
Circle. Round about her tear-distained eye Blue circles stream'd . . . 1587
The crimson blood Circles her body in on every side . . . 1739
Circled. Her breasts, like ivory globes circled with blue . . . 407
Her circled eyne, enforced by sympathy Of those fair suns . . 1229
Circuit. Within the circuit of this ivory pale . . *Ven. and Adon.* 230
Circumstance. In such-like circumstance, with such-like sport . . 844
With circumstances strong Of present death, and shame . . *Lucrece* 1262
Being constrain'd with dreadful circumstance 1703
Cisterns. Like ivory conduits coral cisterns filling 1234
Cite. The morning rise Doth cite each moving sense from idle rest *Pass. Pil.* 195
Cited up in rhymes, And sung by children in succeeding times . *Lucrece* 524
Citizen. May feel her heart—poor citizen!—distress'd, Wounding itself to death, rise up and fall 465
City. This moves in him more rage and lesser pity, To make the breach and enter this sweet city 469
For Helen's rape the city to destroy 1369
Those round clear pearls of his, that move thy pity, Are balls of quenchless fire to burn thy city 1554
Sometime a blusterer, that the ruffle knew Of court, of city . *Lov. Comp.* 59
Long upon these terms I held my city, Till thus he gan besiege me . 176
Civil. A mischief worse than civil home-bred strife . *Ven. and Adon.* 764
Such civil war is in my love and hate . . . . *Sonnet* 35 12
Shook off my sober guards and civil fears . . . *Lov. Comp.* 298
Clad. Who finds his Lucrece clad in mourning black . . *Lucrece* 1585
Claim. Then virtue claims from beauty beauty's red, Which virtue gave . 59
No dame, hereafter living, By my excuse shall claim excuse's giving . . 1715
One doth call her his, the other his, Yet neither may possess the claim . 1794
Clamorous. Ceasing their clamorous cry till they have singled With much ado the fault cleanly out . . . . . . *Ven. and Adon.* 693
Clamour. With the nightly linen that she wears He pens her piteous clamours in her head . . . . *Lucrece* 681
'My daughter' and 'my wife' with clamours fill'd The dispersed air . . 1804
In clamours of all size, both high and low . . . *Lov. Comp.* 21
Clapping. Claps her pale cheek, till clapping makes it red *Ven. and Adon.* 468
Clapping their proud tails to the ground below 923
Claps. Claps her pale cheek, till clapping makes it red . . . 468
Clasp. A belt of straw and ivy buds, With coral clasps and amber studs *Pass. Pil.* 366
Claws. Like a white hind under the gripe's sharp claws, Pleads . *Lucrece* 543
Clay. Then kings' misdeeds cannot be hid in clay 609
When I perhaps compounded am with clay . . . . *Sonnet* 71 10
Clean. All full with feasting on your sight And by and by clean starved for a look 75 10
Cleanly. Ceasing their clamorous cry till they have singled With much ado the cold fault cleanly out . . . . *Ven. and Adon.* 694
Cleanly-coined. Nor fold my fault in cleanly-coin'd excuses . *Lucrece* 1073
Clear. O thou clear god, and patron of all light . . *Ven. and Adon.* 860
Did not let To praise the clear unmatched red and white . *Lucrece* 11
By Lucrece' side, In his clear bed might have reposed still . . 382
As clear from this attaint of mine As I, ere this, was pure to Collatine . 825
To clear this spot by death, at least I give A badge of fame to slander's livery 1053
To clear her From that suspicion which the world might bear her . . 1320
Those round clear pearls of his, that move thy pity, Are balls of quenchless fire 1553
The poison'd fountain clears itself again 1707
Her body's stain her mind untainted clears 1710
How would thy shadow's form form happy show To the clear day! *Son.* 43 7
By their verdict is determined The clear eye's moiety . . . 46 12
Not making worse what nature made so clear 84 10
The sun itself sees not till heaven clears 148 12
Clear wells spring not, Sweet birds sing not . . . *Pass. Pil.* 281
Cleared. The blackest sin is cleared with absolution . *Lucrece* 354
Clearer. How would thy shadow's form form happy show To the clear day with thy much clearer light, When to unseeing eyes thy shade shines so! *Sonnet* 43 7
My most full flame should afterwards burn clearer . . . 115 4
Cleaves. Thy false dart Mistakes that aim and cleaves an infant's heart *Ven. and Adon.* 942
Cleft. O cleft effect! cold modesty, hot wrath . . . *Lov. Comp.* 293
Clepes. She clepes him king of graves and grave for kings *Ven. and Adon.* 995
Clerk. Like unletter'd clerk still cry 'Amen' To every hymn . *Sonnet* 85 6
Client. The client breaks, as desperate in his suit . *Ven. and Adon.* 336
To trembling clients be you mediators . . . . *Lucrece* 1020
Climb. Or if thou wilt permit the sun to climb His wonted height . . 775
Climbed. Having climb'd the steep-up heavenly hill . . *Sonnet* 7 5
Clip. To clip Elysium and to lack her joy . . . *Ven. and Adon.* 600
Ah, that I had my lady at this bay, To kiss and clip me . *Pass. Pil.* 156
Clipped. And then she clipp'd Adonis in her arms 148
Cloak. My true eyes have never practised how To cloak offences . *Lucrece* 749
Which underneath thy black all-hiding cloak Immodestly lies . . 801
And make me travel forth without my cloak . . . . *Sonnet* 34 2
Clock. When I do count the clock that tells the time . . . 12 1
Whilst I, my sovereign, watch the clock for you 57 6
Cloister. And now she would the caged cloister fly . . *Lov. Comp.* 249
Cloistered. Shames herself to see, And therefore still in night would cloister'd be . . . . *Lucrece* 1085
Close. She lifts the coffer-lids that close his eyes . *Ven. and Adon.* 1127
The curtains being close, about he walks, Rolling his greedy eyeballs *Lucr.* 367
She wakes her heart by beating on her breast, And bids it leap from thence, where it may find Some purer chest to close so pure a mind . . 761
Closed. When heavy sleep had closed up mortal eyes . . *Lucrece* 163
Closet. But still pure Doth in her poison'd closet yet endure . . 1659
A closet never pierced with crystal eyes . . . . *Sonnet* 46 6
Close-tongued. With close-tongued treason and the ravisher . *Lucrece* 770
Closure. Should run Into the quiet closure of my breast *Ven. and Adon.* 782
Though I feel thou art, Within the gentle closure of my breast . *Sonnet* 48 11
Cloth. Shall by a painted cloth be kept in awe . . . *Lucrece* 245
Clothe. Began to clothe his wit in state and pride 1809
Cloud. And coal-black clouds that shadow heaven's light Do summon us to part and bid good night . . . . . . *Ven. and Adon.* 533
Whose ridges with the meeting clouds contend 820
Then join they all together, Like many clouds consulting for foul weather . 972
To draw the cloud that hides the silver moon . . . *Lucrece* 371
As the fair and fiery-pointed sun, Rushing from forth a cloud, bereaves our sight 373
But when a black-faced cloud the world doth threat 547
Ere he go to bed, Knit poisonous clouds about his golden head . . 777
Her contrite sighs unto the clouds bequeathed Her winged sprite . . 1727
And dost him grace when clouds do blot the heaven . . *Sonnet* 28 10
Anon permit the basest clouds to ride With ugly rack 33 5
The region cloud hath mask'd him from me now 33 12
To let base clouds o'ertake me in my way 34 3
'Tis not enough that through the cloud thou break 34 5
Clouds and eclipses stain both moon and sun 35 3
Cloud-eclipsed. Why her two suns were cloud-eclipsed so . *Lucrece* 1224
Clouded. Were never four such lamps together mix'd, Had not his clouded with his brow's repine . . . . . *Ven. and Adon.* 490
The moon being clouded presently is miss'd . . . *Lucrece* 1007
Cloud-kissing. Threatening cloud-kissing Ilion with annoy . . 1370
Cloudy. So do thy lips Make modest Dian cloudy and forlorn *Ven. and Adon.* 725
No cloudy show of stormy blustering weather . . . *Lucrece* 115
Cloudy Lucrece shames herself to see 1084
Her cloudy looks will calm ere night . . . . *Pass. Pil.* 312
Cloy. And yet not cloy thy lips with loathed satiety *Ven. and Adon.* 19
Cloyed. That, cloy'd with much, he pineth still for more . *Lucrece* 98
Coal. She red and hot as coals of glowing fire . . *Ven. and Adon.* 35
Even as a dying coal revives with wind 338
Affection is a coal that must be cool'd; Else, suffer'd it will set the heart on fire 387
He goes To quench the coal which in his liver glows . . *Lucrece* 47
Like dying coals burnt out in tedious nights 1379
Coal-black. And coal-black clouds that shadow heaven's light Do summon us to part and bid good night . . . . *Ven. and Adon.* 533
The crow may bathe his coal-black wings in mire . . *Lucrece* 1009
Coasteth. And all in haste she coasteth to the cry . *Ven. and Adon.* 870
Coat. The scandal will survive, And be an eye-sore in my golden coat *Lucrece* 205
She was sought by spirits of richest coat, But kept cold distance *Lov. Comp.* 236
Cock. The cock that treads them shall not know . . . *Pass. Pil.* 338
Cockatrice. With a cockatrice' dead-killing eye He rouseth up himself *Lucrece* 540
Coffer-lids. She lifts the coffer-lids that close his eyes . *Ven. and Adon.* 1127
Coffers-up. The aged man that coffers-up his gold Is plagued with cramps and gouts and painful fits . . . . *Lucrece* 855
Coined. How many tales to please me hath she coined! . . *Pass. Pil.* 93
Cold. O'erworn, despised, rheumatic, and cold . . *Ven. and Adon.* 135
Fie, lifeless picture, cold and senseless stone, Well-painted idol . . 211
Who is so faint, that dare not be so bold To touch the fire, the weather being cold 402
Ceasing their clamorous cry till they have singled With much ado the cold fault cleanly out 694
Earth's foundation shakes, Which with cold terror doth men's minds confound 1048
She takes him by the hand, and that is cold; She whispers in his ears . 1124
O rash false heat, wrapp'd in repentant cold! . . . . *Lucrece* 48
On a flint he softly smiteth, That from the cold stone sparks of fire do fly . 177
As from this cold flint I enforced this fire, So Lucrece must I force to my desire 181
This hot desire converts to cold disdain 691
That knows not parching heat nor freezing cold 1145
Sinon in his fire doth quake with cold, And in that cold hot-burning fire doth dwell 1556
And see thy blood warm when thou feel'st it cold . . . *Sonnet* 2 14
Herein lives wisdom, beauty, and increase; Without this, folly, age, and cold decay 11 6
Barren rage of death's eternal cold 13 12
Upon those boughs which shake against the cold 73 3
Who, moving others, are themselves as stone, Unmoved, cold . . 94 4
Three winters cold Have from the forests shook three summers' pride . 104 3
In a cold valley-fountain of that ground 153 4
She was sought by spirits of richest coat, But kept cold distance *Lov. Comp.* 237
As compound love to physic your cold breast 259
What breast so cold that is not warmed here? 292
Cold modesty, hot wrath, Both fire from hence and chill extincture hath . 293
He preach'd pure maid, and praised cold chastity 315
Youth is hot and bold, age is weak and cold; Youth is wild, and age is tame *Pass. Pil.* 163
Coldly. When thou wilt inflame, How coldly those impediments stand forth Of wealth, of filial fear, law, kindred, fame! . . *Lov. Comp.* 269
Cold-pale. With cold-pale weakness numbs each feeling part *Ven. and Adon.* 892
Collatine. The waist Of Collatine's fair love, Lucrece the chaste . *Lucrece* 7
Collatine unwisely did not let To praise the clear unmatched red and white 10
Why is Collatine the publisher Of that rich jewel he should keep unknown? 33
Therefore that praise which Collatine doth owe Enchanted Tarquin answers with surmise 82
And decks with praises Collatine's high name. 108
And in the self-same seat sits Collatine 289
Then Collatine again, by Lucrece' side, In his clear bed might have reposed still 381
Attend each line, How Tarquin wronged me, I Collatine . . . 819
Let my good name, that senseless reputation, For Collatine's dear love be kept unspotted 821
As clear from this attaint of mine As I, ere this, was pure to Collatine . 826
If, Collatine, thine honour lay in me, From me by strong assault it is bereft 834
My Collatine would else have come to me When Tarquin did . . 916
Dear Collatine, thou shalt not know The stained taste of violated troth . 1058
When both were kept for heaven and Collatine 1166
Die I will not till my Collatine Have heard the cause of my untimely death 1177
Thou, Collatine, shalt oversee this will 1205
By this short schedule Collatine may know Her grief . . . 1312
Collatine and his consorted lords With sad attention long to hear her words 1609

Compound. To make our appetites more keen, With eager compounds we our palate urge *Sonnet* 118 2
Paying too much rent, For compound sweet forgoing simple savour 125 7
As compound love to physic your cold breast *Lov. Comp.* 259
Compounded. When I perhaps compounded am with clay *Sonnet* 71 10
To themselves yet either neither, Simple were so well compounded *Ph. and Tur.* 44
Comprehend. All this beforehand counsel comprehends *Lucrece* 494
O, deeper sin than bottomless conceit Can comprehend in still imagination! 702
Where all those pleasures live that art can comprehend *Pass. Pil.* 62
Concave. From off a hill whose concave womb re-worded A plaintful story from a sistering vale *Lov. Comp.* 1
Concealed. So of concealed sorrow may be said; Free vent of words love's fire doth assuage *Ven. and Adon.* 333
Upon thy part I can set down a story Of faults conceal'd *Sonnet* 88 7
With the garment of a Grace The naked and concealed fiend he cover'd *Lov. Comp.* 317
Concealing. Shame folded up in blind concealing night *Lucrece* 675
Conceit. O, deeper sin than bottomless conceit Can comprehend in still imagination! 701
Conceit and grief an eager combat fight 1298
Conceit deceitful, so compact, so kind, That for Achilles' image stood his spear 1423
The conceit of this inconstant stay Sets you most rich in youth *Sonnet* 15 9
I hope some good conceit of thine In thy soul's thought, all naked, will bestow it 26 7
Finding the first conceit of love there bred 108 13
Whether unripe years did want conceit *Pass. Pil.* 51
Whose deep conceit is such As, passing all conceit, needs no defence 109
Conceited. Which the conceited painter drew so proud, As heaven *Lucrece* 1371
Oft did she heave her napkin to her eyne, Which on it had conceited characters *Lov. Comp.* 16
Conclude. Her heavy anthem still concludes in woe *Ven. and Adon.* 839
She concludes the picture was belied *Lucrece* 1533
They did conclude to bear dead Lucrece thence 1850
Conclusion. That mother tries a merciless conclusion Who, having two sweet babes, when death takes one, Will slay the other and be nurse to none 1160
Concord. If the true concord of well-tuned sounds, By unions married, do offend thine ear *Sonnet* 8 5
When thou gently sway'st The wiry concord that mine ear confounds 128 4
Concordant. That it cried, How true a twain Seemeth this concordant one! *Ph. and Tur.* 46
Condemned. Till forging Nature be condemn'd of treason *Ven. and Adon.* 729
The lily I condemned for thy hand *Sonnet* 99 6
Conduct. Extinguishing his conduct in this case *Lucrece* 313
Conduits. Like ivory conduits coral cisterns filling 1234
Confess. Truth I must confess,—I rail'd on thee, fearing my love's decease *Ven. and Adon.* 1001
I must confess, With kissing him I should have kill'd him first 1117
Let me confess that we two must be twain *Sonnet* 36 1
Confessed. So, now I have confess'd that he is thine 134 1
Confine. In whose confine immured is the store 84 3
Vow, bond, nor space, In thee hath neither sting, knot, nor confine *L. Comp.* 265
Confined. Therefore my verse to constancy confined, One thing expressing *Sonnet* 105 7
Supposed as forfeit to a confined doom 107 4
A god in love, to whom I am confined 110 12
Confirmed. In vain I cavil with mine infamy, In vain I spurn at my confirm'd despite *Lucrece* 1026
Like a constant and confirmed devil 1513
Conflict. To note the fighting conflict of her hue, How white and red each other did destroy! *Ven. and Adon.* 345
Confound. Appals her senses and her spirit confounds 882
Which with cold terror doth men's minds confound 1048
When he himself himself confounds, betrays To slanderous tongues *Lucrece* 160
Which in a moment doth confound and kill All pure effects 250
That eye which looks on her confounds his wits 290
My shame be his that did my fame confound 1202
And one man's lust these many lives confounds 1489
Never-resting time leads summer on To hideous winter and confounds him there *Sonnet* 5 6
They do but sweetly chide thee, who confounds In singleness the parts that thou shouldst bear 8 7
And Time that gave doth now his gift confound 60 8
In other accents do this praise confound 69 7
When thou gently sway'st The wiry concord that mine ear confounds 128 4
Confounded. Even so confounded in the dark she lay *Ven. and Adon.* 827
Wrapp'd and confounded in a thousand fears *Lucrece* 456
I have seen such interchange of state, Or state itself confounded to decay *Sonnet* 64 10
Reason, in itself confounded, Saw division grow together *Ph. and Tur.* 41
Confounding. For such a time do I now fortify Against confounding age's cruel knife *Sonnet* 63 10
Confusion. And fright her with confusion of their cries *Lucrece* 445
They that lose half with greater patience bear it Than they whose whole is swallow'd in confusion 1159
Congealed. And stains her face with his congealed blood *Ven. and Adon.* 1122
About the mourning and congealed face Of that black blood a watery rigol goes *Lucrece* 1744
Congest. Must for your victory us all congest, As compound love to physic your cold breast *Lov. Comp.* 258
Conjures. She conjures him by high almighty Jove, By knighthood *Lucrece* 568
Conquer. Who conquers where he comes in every jar *Ven. and Adon.* 100
Which I to conquer sought with all my might *Lucrece* 488
Yield to my hand; my hand shall conquer thee 1210
Touches so soft still conquer chastity *Pass. Pil.* 50
Conquered. Ah, do not, when my heart hath 'scaped this sorrow, Come in the rearward of a conquer'd woe *Sonnet* 90 6
Conquerors. Her lips are conquerors, his lips obey *Ven. and Adon.* 549
Conquest. And in her haste unfortunately spies The foul boar's conquest on her fair delight 1030
As the grim lion fawneth o'er his prey, Sharp hunger by the conquest satisfied *Lucrece* 422
Shall rotten death make conquest of the stronger? 1767
Thou art much too fair To be death's conquest and make worms thine heir *Sonnet* 6 14
At a mortal war How to divide the conquest of thy sight 46 2
My body being dead, The coward conquest of a wretch's knife 74 11
Conscience. 'Tween frozen conscience and hot-burning will *Lucrece* 247
Love is too young to know what conscience is; Yet who knows not conscience is born of love? *Sonnet* 151 1

Conscience. No want of conscience hold it that I call Her 'love' *Sonnet* 151 13
Consecrate. Thou dost review The very part was consecrate to thee 74 6
Consecrated. Have batter'd down her consecrated wall *Lucrece* 723
Consecrations. All vows and consecrations giving place *Lov. Comp.* 263
Consent. The Romans plausibly did give consent *Lucrece* 1854
Do in consent shake hands to torture me *Sonnet* 28 6
Consents bewitch'd, ere he desire, have granted *Lov. Comp.* 131
Consider. When I consider every thing that grows Holds in perfection but a little moment *Sonnet* 15 1
Consort. Who bids them still consort with ugly night *Ven. and Adon.* 1041
Consorted. Collatine and his consorted lords With sad attention long to hear her words *Lucrece* 1609
Conspirator. Whispering conspirator With close-tongued treason and the ravisher! 769
Conspire. 'Gainst thyself thou stick'st not to conspire *Sonnet* 10 6
Constancy. Therefore my verse to constancy confined, One thing expressing, leaves out difference 105 7
I did strive to prove The constancy and virtue of your love 117 14
Oaths of thy love, thy truth, thy constancy 152 10
Here the anthem doth commence: Love and constancy is dead *Ph. and Tur.* 22
Constant. Variable passions throng her constant woe *Ven. and Adon.* 967
Like a constant and confirm'd devil *Lucrece* 1513
From thine eyes my knowledge I derive, And, constant stars *Sonnet* 14 10
But you like none, none you, for constant heart 53 14
Still constant in a wondrous excellence 105 6
Though to myself forsworn, to thee I'll constant prove *Pass. Pil.* 59
Constrained. Being constrain'd with dreadful circumstance *Lucrece* 1703
Construe. He in the worst sense construes their denial 324
In scorn or friendship, nill I construe whether *Pass. Pil.* 188
Consulting. Like many clouds consulting for foul weather *Ven. and Adon.* 972
Consume. Fair flowers that are not gather'd in their prime Rot and consume themselves in little time 132
So vanisheth As smoke from Ætna, that in air consumes *Lucrece* 1042
Consumed. Consumed with that which it was nourish'd by *Sonnet* 73 12
Consumest. Is it for fear to wet a widow's eye That thou consumest thyself in single life? 9 2
Contain. The worth of that is that which it contains 74 13
What thy memory can not contain Commit to these waste blanks 77 9
By how much of me their reproach contains *Lov. Comp.* 189
Contemn. What am I, that thou shouldst contemn me this? *Ven. and Adon.* 205
Contend. Whose ridges with the meeting clouds contend 820
In sequent toil all forwards do contend *Sonnet* 60 4
Contending. Till he take truce with her contending tears, Which long have rain'd, making her cheeks all wet *Ven. and Adon.* 82
Time's glory is to calm contending kings *Lucrece* 939
Thus art with arms contending was victor of the day *Pass. Pil.* 223
Content. Forced to content, but never to obey *Ven. and Adon.* 61
To blot old books and alter their contents *Lucrece* 948
His face, though full of cares, yet show'd content 1503
Within thine own bud buriest thy content *Sonnet* 1 11
But you shall shine more bright in these contents 55 3
So I return rebuked to my content And gain by ill thrice more 119 13
And often reading what contents it bears *Lov. Comp.* 19
The lines she rents, Big discontent so breaking their contents 56
Or forced examples, 'gainst her own content 157
Thy like ne'er was For a sweet content, the cause of all my moan *Pass. Pil.* 295
Contented. To sell myself I can be well contented, So thou wilt buy *V. and A.* 513
With what I most enjoy contented least *Sonnet* 29 8
But be contented: when that fell arrest Without all bail shall carry me away 74 1
Proud of this pride, He is contented thy poor drudge to be 151 11
Contenting. Well-painted idol, image dull and dead, Statue contenting but the eye alone *Ven. and Adon.* 213
Continual. She seeks to kindle with continual kissing 606
Like a troubled ocean, Beat at thy rocky and wreck-threatening heart, To soften it with their continual motion *Lucrece* 591
What we see doth lie, Made more or less by thy continual haste *Sonnet* 123 12
Continuance tames the one; the other wild, Like an unpractised swimmer *Lucrece* 1097
Contracted. Thou, contracted to thine own bright eyes, Feed'st thy light's flame *Sonnet* 1 5
Where two contracted new Come daily to the banks 56 10
Contradict. If thou my love's desire do contradict *Lucrece* 1631
Contrary. These contraries such unity do hold, Only to flatter fools 1558
Mine own self-love quite contrary I read *Sonnet* 62 11
Contrite. Her contrite sighs unto the clouds bequeathed Her winged sprite *Lucrece* 1727
Contrive. Some loathsome dash the herald will contrive, To cipher me 206
She that her fame so to herself contrives, The scars of battle 'scapeth by the flight *Lov. Comp.* 243
Control. And justly thus controls his thoughts unjust *Lucrece* 189
Nothing can affections course control, Or stop the headlong fury 500
Mad that sorrow should his use control 1781
God forbid that made me first your slave, I should in thought control your times of pleasure *Sonnet* 58 2
Can yet the lease of my true love control 107 3
A true soul When most impeach'd stands least in thy control 125 14
Controlled. Controlling what he was controlled with *Ven. and Adon.* 270
Her lock'd-up eyes, ... Are by his flaming torch dimm'd and controll'd *Lucr.* 448
Her own white fleece her voice controll'd Entombs her outcry 678
She controlled still, But her foresight could not forestall their will 727
Controlling what he was controlled with *Ven. and Adon.* 270
A man in hue, all 'hues' in his controlling, Which steals men's eyes *Son.* 20 7
And folly doctor-like controlling skill 66 10
Controversy. And controversy hence a question takes *Lov. Comp.* 110
Convert. For stones dissolved to water do convert *Lucrece* 592
This hot desire converts to cold disdain 691
If from thyself to store thou wouldst convert *Sonnet* 14 12
Converted. The eyes, 'fore duteous, now converted are From his low tract 7 11
When love, converted from the thing it was, Shall reasons find 49 7
Convertest. That fresh blood which youngly thou bestowest Thou mayst call thine when thou from youth convertest 11 4
Convertite. He thence departs a heavy convertite *Lucrece* 743
Convey. Make some hole Through which I may convey this troubled soul 1176
Conveyed. Through the empty skies In her light chariot quickly is convey'd *Ven. and Adon.* 1192
Conies. And sometime where earth-delving conies keep 687
Cool. I'll sigh celestial breath, whose gentle wind Shall cool the heat of this descending sun 190

Cool. He vails his tail that, like a falling plume, Cool shadow to his melting buttock lent . *Ven. and Adon.* 315
This brand she quenched in a cool well by . *Sonnet* 154 9
This by that I prove, Love's fire heats water, water cools not love . 154 14
By a brook, A brook where Adon used to cool his spleen *Pass. Pil.* 76
Cooled. Affection is a coal that must be cool'd ; Else, suffer'd, it will set the heart on fire *Ven. and Adon.* 387
Cooling his hot face in the chastest tears That ever modest eyes with sorrow shed . . . . . *Lucrece* 682
Co-partners. So should I have co-partners in my pain . 789
Cope. They all strain courtesy who shall cope him first . *Ven. and Adon.* 888
Coped. But she, that never coped with stranger eyes, Could pick no meaning from their parling looks . . . . . . *Lucrece* 99
Copesmate. Mis-shapen Time, copesmate of ugly Night, Swift subtle post 925
Copious. Their copious stories oftentimes begun End without audience *Ven. and Adon.* 845
Copse. But, lo, from forth a copse that neighbours by, A breeding jennet 259
Copy. Meant thereby Thou shouldst print more, not let that copy die *Son.* 11 14
Let him but copy what in you is writ . 84 9
Coral. That sweet coral mouth, Whose precious taste her thirsty lips well knew . . . . . *Ven. and Adon.* 542
Her alabaster skin, Her coral lips, her snow-white dimpled chin . *Lucrece* 420
Like ivory conduits coral cisterns filling . 1234
Coral is far more red than her lips' red . *Sonnet* 130 2
A belt of straw and ivy buds, With coral clasps and amber studs *Pass. Pil.* 366
Corn. As corn o'ergrown by weeds, so heedful fear Is almost choked *Lucrece* 281
Correct. No bitterness that I will bitter think, Nor double penance, to correct correction . *Sonnet* 111 12
Correction. No bitterness that I will bitter think, Nor double penance, to correct correction . 111 12
Correspondence. Which have no correspondence with true sight . 148 2
Corrupt. If eyes corrupt by over-partial looks Be anchor'd in the bay 137 5
And would corrupt my saint to be a devil, Wooing his purity 144 7 ; *Pass. Pil.* 21
Corrupted. But with a pure appeal seeks to the heart, Which once corrupted takes the worser part . *Lucrece* 294
Spotted, spoil'd, corrupted, Grossly engirt with daring infamy . 1172
As pitying Lucrece' woes, Corrupted blood some watery token shows . 1748
Corrupting. Authorizing thy trespass with compare, Myself corrupting *Sonnet* 35 7
Corydon. Poor Corydon Must live alone . *Pass. Pil.* 296
Cost. Oft that wealth doth cost The death of all, and all together lost *Lucr.* 146
The rich proud cost of outworn buried age . *Sonnet* 64 2
Prouder than garments' cost, Of more delight than hawks or horses be 91 10
Why so large cost, having so short a lease? . 146 5
Yet show'd his visage by that cost more dear . *Lov. Comp.* 96
For ever lost, In spite of physic, painting, pain, and cost . *Pass. Pil.* 180
Costly. Painting thy outward walls so costly gay *Sonnet* 146 4
Co-supremes and stars of love, As chorus to their tragic scene *Ph. and Tur.* 51
Couch. This said, from her be-tumbled couch she starteth *Lucrece* 1037
Coucheth. Which, like a falcon towering in the skies, Coucheth the fowl below 507
Could. Why, there Love lived and there he could not die *Ven. and Adon.* 246
More I could tell, but more I dare not say . 805
Grief hath two tongues, and never woman yet Could rule them both without ten women's wit . 1008
What could he see but mightily he noted? . *Lucrece* 414
That not a heart which in his level came Could 'scape . *Lov. Comp.* 310
Couldst. Unless thou couldst return to make amends *Lucrece* 961
Since thou couldst not defend thy loyal dame . 1034
Counsel. They that thrive well take counsel of their friends *Ven. and Adon.* 640
All this beforehand counsel comprehends . *Lucrece* 494
Counsel may stop awhile what will not stay . *Lov. Comp.* 159
Take counsel of some wiser head, Neither too young nor yet unwed *Pass. Pil.* 303
Count. Shall sum my count and make my old excuse . *Sonnet* 2 11
When I do count the clock that tells the time . 12 1
Which in their wills count bad what I think good . 121 8
Only my plague thus far I count my gain . 141 13
Counted. In the old age black was not counted fair . 127 1
Countenance. To pray he doth begin, As if the heavens should countenance his sin . *Lucrece* 343
When your countenance fill'd up his line, Then lack'd I matter *Sonnet* 86 13
Counterfeit. Bid fair Lucrece speak To the poor counterfeit of her complaining . *Lucrece* 1269
And counterfeits to die with her a space . 1776
Living flowers, Much liker than your painted counterfeit . *Sonnet* 16 8
Describe Adonis, and the counterfeit Is poorly imitated after you . 53 5
Countermand. My heart shall never countermand mine eye *Lucrece* 276
Counterpart. And such a counterpart shall fame his wit . *Sonnet* 84 11
Counting. Now counting best to be with you alone . 75 7
Counting no old thing old, thou mine, I thine . 108 7
Countless. And one sweet kiss shall pay this countless debt *Ven. and Adon.* 84
Country. By all our country rights in Rome maintain'd . *Lucrece* 1838
Couple. The orator, to deck his oratory, Will couple my reproach to Tarquin's shame . 816
Couplement. Making a couplement of proud compare, With sun and moon, with earth and sea's rich gems . *Sonnet* 21 5
Courage. Shows his hot courage and his high desire . *Ven. and Adon.* 276
So did this horse excel a common one In shape, in courage, colour . 294
Her blood doth boil, And careless lust stirs up a desperate courage . 556
Put fear to valour, courage to the coward . 1158
Courageous Roman, do not steep thy heart In such relenting dew of lamentations . *Lucrece* 1828
Courageously. Being so enraged, desire doth lend her force Courageously to pluck him from his horse . *Ven. and Adon.* 30
Course. And with his strong course opens them again . 960
Holding their course to Paphos, where their queen Means to immure herself 1193
As those bars which stop the hourly dial, Who with a lingering stay his course doth let . *Lucrece* 328
Nothing can affection's course control, Or stop the headlong fury . 500
Make war against proportion'd course of time . 774
O time, cease thou thy course and last no longer . 1765
Every fair from fair sometime declines, By chance or nature's changing course untrimm'd . *Sonnet* 18 8
Him in thy course untainted do allow For beauty's pattern to succeeding men . 19 11
A backward look, Even of five hundred courses of the sun . 59 6
Divert strong minds to the course of altering things . 115 8
What rounds, what bounds, what course, what stop he makes! *Lov. Comp.* 109
Courser. Over one arm the lusty courser's rein, Under her other was the tender boy . *Ven. and Adon.* 31
Courser. A breeding jennet, lusty, young, and proud, Adonis' trampling courser doth espy . *Ven. and Adon.* 261
Let me excuse thy courser, gentle boy ; And learn of him . 403
Court. Sometime a blusterer, that the ruffle knew Of court, of city *Lov. Comp.* 59
Which late her noble suit in court did shun . 234
Did court the lad with many a lovely look . *Pass. Pil.* 45
Courtesy. They all strain courtesy who shall cope him first *Ven. and Adon.* 888
The homely villain court'sies to her low . *Lucrece* 1338
Cover. Misty night Covers the shame that follows sweet delight . 357
Though men can cover crimes with bold stern looks . 1252
For all that beauty that doth cover thee Is but the seemly raiment of my heart . *Sonnet* 22 5
When that churl Death my bones with dust shall cover . 32 2
Where beauty's veil doth cover every blot, And all things turn to fair . 95 11
Covered. With the garment of a Grace The naked and concealed fiend he cover'd . *Lov. Comp.* 317
Coverlet. Without the bed her other fair hand was, On the green coverlet *Lucrece* 394
Covet. Those that much covet are with gain so fond, For what they have not 134
Covetous. Nor he will not be free, For thou art covetous and he is kind *Sonnet* 134 6
Coward. Affection faints not like a pale-faced coward *Ven. and Adon.* 569
Thy coward heart with false bethinking grieves . 1024
Put fear to valour, courage to the coward . 1158
The coward captive vanquished doth yield to those two armies . *Lucrece* 75
And when his gaudy banner is display'd, The coward fights and will not be dismay'd . 273
The painter interlaces Pale cowards, marching on with trembling paces 1391
My body being dead, The coward conquest of a wretch's knife . *Sonnet* 74 11
Coward-like. But coward-like with trembling terror die . *Lucrece* 231
Coy. Flint-hearted boy! 'Tis but a kiss I beg ; why art thou coy? *V. and A.* 96
Yet was he servile to my coy disdain . 112
Enforced hate, Instead of love's coy touch, shall rudely tear thee *Lucrece* 669
Cozening. Her rosy cheek lies under, Cozening the pillow of a lawful kiss 387
Crabbed. Crabbed age and youth cannot live together *Pass. Pil.* 157
Crack'd many a ring of posied gold and bone . *Lov. Comp.* 45
Cradle. Lo, in this hollow cradle take thy rest . *Ven. and Adon.* 1185
Craft. Jealousy itself could not mistrust False-creeping craft and perjury *Lucrece* 1517
Catching all passions in his craft of will . *Lov. Comp.* 126
His passion, but an art of craft, Even there resolved my reason into tears 295
When craft hath taught her thus to say . *Pass. Pil.* 320
Craggy. We will all the pleasures prove That hills and valleys, dales and fields, And all the craggy mountains yields . 356
Cramps. Is plagued with cramps and gouts and painful fits *Lucrece* 856
Cranks. He cranks and crosses with a thousand doubles *Ven. and Adon.* 682
Cranny. Through little vents and crannies of the place . *Lucrece* 310
Revealing day through every cranny spies . 1086
Crave. So offers he to give what she did crave . *Ven. and Adon.* 88
Let him have time a beggar's orts to crave . *Lucrece* 985
The cause craves haste, and it will soon be writ . 1295
Or at your hand the account of hours to crave . *Sonnet* 58 3
And yet thou left'st me more than I did crave *Pass. Pil.* 139
I pardon crave of thee, Thy discontent thou didst bequeath to me . 141
Craved. For why I craved nothing of thee still . 140
Crawls. Nativity, once in the main of light, Crawls to maturity *Sonnet* 60 6
Created. And for a woman wert thou first created . 20 9
My gentle verse, Which eyes not yet created shall o'er-read . 81 10
Creating every bad a perfect best . 114 7
Creation. From the creation to the general doom . *Lucrece* 924
Heaven in thy creation did decree That in thy face sweet love should ever dwell . *Sonnet* 93 9
No beauty lack, Slandering creation with a false esteem . 127 12
Creature. Pursue these fearful creatures o'er the downs *Ven. and Adon.* 677
'Tis he, foul creature, that hath done thee wrong . 1005
Bonnet nor veil henceforth no creature wear! . 1081
There we will unfold To creatures stern sad tunes, to change their kinds *Lucrece* 1147
These pretty creatures stand Like ivory conduits coral cisterns filling . 1233
Such harmless creatures have a true respect To talk in deeds . 1347
In my chamber came A creeping creature, with a flaming light . 1627
From fairest creatures we desire increase . *Sonnet* 1 1
The most sweet favour or deformed'st creature . 113 10
Lo! as a careful housewife runs to catch One of her feather'd creatures broke away . 143 2
Fair creature, kill'd too soon by death's sharp sting! . *Pass. Pil.* 134
Credent. Lending soft audience to my sweet design, And credent soul to that strong-bonded oath . *Lov. Comp.* 279
Credit. Simply I credit her false-speaking tongue . *Sonnet* 138 7
I smiling credit her false-speaking tongue . *Pass. Pil.* 7
Credulous. How strange it seems Not to believe, and yet too credulous *Ven. and Adon.* 986
Sinon, whose enchanting story The credulous old Priam after slew *Lucrece* 1522
Creep. Long after fearing to creep forth again . *Ven. and Adon.* 1036
He like a thievish dog creeps sadly thence . *Lucrece* 736
The poor, lame, blind, halt, creep, cry out for thee . 902
Like a goodly champaign plain, Lays open all the little worms that creep 1248
They that watch see time how slow it creeps . 1575
Million'd accidents Creep in 'twixt vows and change decrees *Sonnet* 115 6
Creeping. They all rate his ill, Which drives the creeping thief to some regard . *Lucrece* 305
In my chamber came A creeping creature, with a flaming light . 1627
Crept. In thy weak hive a wandering wasp hath crept . 839
Crest. His batter'd shield, his uncontrolled crest *Ven. and Adon.* 104
His braided hanging mane Upon his compass'd crest now stand on end 272
High crest, short ears, straight legs, and passing strong, Thin mane, thick tail, broad buttock, tender hide . 297
Throwing the base thong from his bending crest, Enfranchising his mouth 395
When tyrants' crests and tombs of brass are spent. *Sonnet* 107 14
Crest-wounding. O unfelt sore! crest-wounding, private scar! *Lucrece* 828
Crew. Stood Collatine and all his lordly crew . 1731
Cried. And softly cried 'Awake, thou Roman dame, And entertain my love' 1628
Cried 'O false blood, thou register of lies!' . *Lov. Comp.* 52
That it cried, How true a twain Seemeth this concordant one! *Ph. and Tur.* 45
Crime. Whose crime will bear an ever-during blame *Lucrece* 224
Foggy Night! Since thou art guilty of my cureless crime, Muster thy mists to meet the eastern light . 772
Be guilty of my death, since of my crime . 931
And ever let his unrecalling crime Have time to wail . 993
Though men can cover crimes with bold stern looks . 1252

Crime. But I forbid thee one most heinous crime . . . *Sonnet* 19 8
To you it doth belong Yourself to pardon of self-doing crime . 58 12
Have no leisure taken To weigh how once I suffer'd in your crime . 120 8
The fools of time, Which die for goodness, who have lived for crime . 124 14
Crimeful. To make him curse this cursed crimeful night *Lucrece* 970
Crimson. Still is he sullen, still he lours and frets, 'Twixt crimson shame and anger ashy-pale . . . *Ven. and Adon.* 76
O, never let their crimson liveries wear! 506
The crimson blood Circles her body in on every side . . *Lucrece* 1738
Cripple. A cripple soon can find a halt . . . *Pass. Pil.* 308
Critic. My adder's sense To critic and to flatterer stopped are *Sonnet* 112 11
Crooked. Ill-nurtured, crooked, churlish, harsh in voice *Ven. and Adon.* 134
He strikes whate'er is in his way, And whom he strikes his crooked tushes slay 624
Whose crooked beak threats if he mount he dies . . *Lucrece* 508
Being crown'd, Crooked eclipses 'gainst his glory fight . . *Sonnet* 60 7
Give my love fame faster than Time wastes life; So thou prevent'st his scythe and crooked knife 100 14
His browny locks did hang in crooked curls . . . . *Lov. Comp.* 85
Crop. They bid thee crop a weed, thou pluck'st a flower *Ven. and Adon.* 946
She crops the stalk, and in the breach appears Green dropping sap 1175
To cheer the ploughman with increaseful crops . . *Lucrece* 958
Cross. He cranks and crosses with a thousand doubles . *Ven. and Adon.* 682
To cross the curious workmanship of nature, To mingle beauty with infirmities 734
So cross him with their opposite persuasion . . . *Lucrece* 286
I see what crosses my attempt will bring 491
I have no one to blush with me, To cross their arms and hang their heads with mine 793
When Truth and Virtue have to do with thee, A thousand crosses keep them from thy aid 912
With some mischance cross Tarquin in his flight . . . 968
But weak relief To him that bears the strong offence's cross . . *Sonnet* 34 12
I lose both twain, And both for my sake lay on me this cross . . 42 12
Now, while the world is bent my deeds to cross, Join with the spite of fortune 90 2
One silly cross Wrought all my loss; O frowning Fortune! . . *Pass. Pil.* 257
Crossed. A torment thrice threefold thus to be cross'd . . *Sonnet* 133 8
Crow. Out-stripping crows that strive to over-fly them . *Ven. and Adon.* 324
The crow may bathe his coal-black wings in mire . . *Lucrece* 1009
The ornament of beauty is suspect, A crow that flies in heaven's sweetest air *Sonnet* 70 4
The mountain or the sea, the day or night, The crow or dove . 113 12
And thou treble-dated crow, That thy sable gender makest . *Ph. and Tur.* 17
Crown. Or what fond beggar, but to touch the crown, Would with the sceptre straight be strucken down? . . . . . *Lucrece* 216
Incertainties now crown themselves assured . . . *Sonnet* 107 7
But if store of crowns be scant, No man will supply thy want *Pass. Pil.* 409
Crowned. Any of these all, or all, or more, Entitled in thy parts do crowned sit . . . . *Sonnet* 37 7
Being crown'd, Crooked eclipses 'gainst his glory fight . . 60 6
Thy outward thus with outward praise is crown'd . . . 69 5
Or whether doth my mind, being crown'd with you, Drink up the monarch's plague, this flattery? 114 1
Crowning. Crowning the present, doubting of the rest . . 115 12
Cruel. And bitter words to ban her cruel foes . . . *Lucrece* 1460
Thyself thy foe, to thy sweet self too cruel . . . *Sonnet* 1 8
My verse shall stand, Praising thy worth, despite his cruel hand . 60 14
For such a time do I now fortify Against confounding age's cruel knife 63 10
Bloody, full of blame, Savage, extreme, rude, cruel, not to trust . 129 4
So as thou art, As those whose beauties proudly make them cruel 131 2
Me from myself thy cruel eye hath taken 133 5
Be wise as thou art cruel; do not press My tongue-tied patience . 140 1
Canst thou, O cruel! say I love thee not? 149 1
Heart is bleeding, All help needing, O cruel speeding, Fraughted with gall *Pass. Pil.* 269
Crush. 'Fie, fie,' he says, 'you crush me; let me go' *Ven. and Adon.* 611
Crushed. With Time's injurious hand crush'd and o'erworn . *Sonnet* 63 2
Crusheth. The iron bit he crusheth 'tween his teeth *Ven. and Adon.* 269
Cry. 'O, pity,' 'gan she cry, 'flint-hearted boy! 'Tis but a kiss I beg' . 95
Souring his cheeks cries 'Fie, no more of love!' . . . 185
'Pity,' she cries, 'some favour, some remorse!' . . . 257
'For shame,' he cries, 'let go, and let me go; My day's delight is past' 379
Suggesteth mutiny, And in a peaceful hour doth cry 'Kill, kill!' . 652
Ceasing their clamorous cry till they have singled With much ado the cold fault cleanly out 693
'Ay me!' she cries, and twenty times 'Woe, woe!' And twenty echoes twenty times cry so 833
She hears them chant it lustily, And all in haste she coasteth to the cry . 870
It is no gentle chase, . . . Because the cry remaineth in one place . 885
This dismal cry rings sadly in her ear 889
No noise but owls' and wolves' death-boding cries . . . *Lucrece* 165
And fright her with confusion of their cries 445
The wolf hath seized his prey, the poor lamb cries . . . 677
The poor, lame, blind, halt, creep, cry out for thee . . . 902
Who nothing wants to answer her but cries, And bitter words to ban her cruel foes 1459
With this, I did begin to start and cry 1639
'Daughter, dear daughter,' old Lucretius cries 1751
Cry. The dispersed air, who, holding Lucrece' life, Answer'd their cries *Lucrece* 1806
And trouble deaf heaven with my bootless cries . . . *Sonnet* 29 3
Tired with all these, for restful death I cry 66 1
Like unletter'd clerk still cry 'Amen' To every hymn . . 85 6
Whilst her neglected child holds her in chase, Cries to catch her . 143 6
Where want cries some, but where excess begs all . . *Lov. Comp.* 42
Though Reason weep, and cry 'It is thy last' 168
'Fie, fie, fie,' now would she cry; 'Tereu, tereu!' by and by . *Pass. Pil.* 385
Crying. And fright her crying babe with Tarquin's name . *Lucrece* 814
Thou mayst have thy 'Will,' If thou turn back, and my loud crying still *Sonnet* 143 14
Crystal. The crystal tears gave light, Shone like the moon in water seen by night . . . . *Ven. and Adon.* 491
Nor thy soft hands, sweet lips, and crystal eyne 633
The crystal tide that from her two cheeks fair In the sweet channel of her bosom dropt 957
Both crystals, where they view'd each other's sorrow . . . 963
Through crystal walls each little mote will peep . . *Lucrece* 1251
A closet never pierced with crystal eyes . . . *Sonnet* 46 6
Favours . . . Of amber, crystal, and of beaded jet . . . *Lov. Comp.* 37
Who glazed with crystal gate the glowing roses 286
Cuckoos. Or hateful cuckoos hatch in sparrows' nests? . . *Lucrece* 849
Cunning. Which cunning love did wittily prevent . *Ven. and Adon.* 471
To make the cunning hounds mistake their smell . . . 686
My true eyes have never practised how To cloak offences with a cunning brow . . . . *Lucrece* 749
Yet eyes this cunning want to grace their art . . . *Sonnet* 24 13
What need'st thou wound with cunning when thy might Is more than my o'er-press'd defence can bide? 139 7
O cunning Love! with tears thou keep'st me blind . . . 148 13
Cup. And to his palate doth prepare the cup 114 12
Cupid. Her heart, The which, by Cupid's bow she doth protest, He carries thence incaged in his breast . . . *Ven. and Adon.* 581
Cupid laid by his brand, and fell asleep . . . *Sonnet* 153 1
The bath for my help lies Where Cupid got new fire—my mistress' eyes 153 14
Curb. What cares he now for curb or pricking spur? For rich caparisons or trapping gay? . . . . *Ven. and Adon.* 285
While Lust is in his pride, no exclamation Can curb his heat *Lucrece* 706
Nor gives it satisfaction to our blood, That we must curb it upon others' proof . . . . *Lov. Comp.* 163
Cure. Though nothing but my body's bane would cure thee *Ven. and Adon.* 372
Long may they kiss each other, for this cure 505
The scar that will, despite of cure, remain . . . *Lucrece* 732
Having no other pleasure of his gain But torment that it cannot cure his pain 861
Why, Collatine, is woe the cure for woe? 1821
That heals the wound and cures not the disgrace . . *Sonnet* 34 8
I assure ye Even that your pity is enough to cure me . . . 111 14
Past cure I am, now reason is past care, And frantic-mad . . 147 9
Which yet men prove Against strange maladies a sovereign cure . 153 8
And thither hied, a sad distemper'd guest, But found no cure . 153 13
But I, my mistress' thrall, Came there for cure . . . 154 13
Thy grace being gain'd cures all disgrace in me . . *Pass. Pil.* 36
Cured. It easeth some, though none it ever cured, To think their dolour others have endured . . . . *Lucrece* 1581
A healthful state Which, rank of goodness, would by ill be cured *Sonnet* 118 12
Cureless. Since thou art guilty of my cureless crime, Muster thy mists to meet the eastern light . . . . *Lucrece* 772
Curious. To cross the curious workmanship of nature *Ven. and Adon.* 734
If my slight Muse do please these curious days, The pain be mine *Sonnet* 38 13
Affectedly Enswathed, and seal'd to curious secrecy . . *Lov. Comp.* 49
Curious-good. This is too curious-good, this blunt and ill . *Lucrece* 1300
Curl. And sable curls all silver'd o'er with white . . *Sonnet* 12 4
His browny locks did hang in crooked curls . . . *Lov. Comp.* 85
Curled. Let him have time to tear his curled hair . . *Lucrece* 981
Current. Thus ebbs and flows the current of her sorrow . . 1569
A fount With brinish current downward flow'd apace . *Lov. Comp.* 284
Curse. The Destinies will curse thee for this stroke *Ven. and Adon.* 945
Posterity, shamed with the note, Shall curse my bones . . *Lucrece* 209
To make him curse this cursed crimeful night 970
Teach me to curse him that thou taught'st this ill! . . . 996
And look upon myself and curse my fate. . . . *Sonnet* 29 4
You to your beauteous blessings add a curse 84 13
Cursed. To make him curse this cursed crimeful night . *Lucrece* 970
O frowning Fortune, cursed, fickle dame! . . . *Pass. Pil.* 259
Cursed-blessed. And they too strong, To hold their cursed-blessed fortune long . . . . *Lucrece* 866
Curst. Finding their enemy to be so curst, They all strain courtesy who shall cope him first . . . . . . *Ven. and Adon.* 887
Curtail. My curtail dog, that wont to have play'd, Plays not at all *Pass. Pil.* 273
Curtain. The curtains being close, about he walks, Rolling his greedy eye-balls . . . . *Lucrece* 367
Even so, the curtain drawn, his eyes begun To wink . . . 374
Curvets. Anon he rears upright, curvets and leaps . *Ven. and Adon.* 279
Cut. That he shall never cut from memory My sweet love's beauty *Sonnet* 63 11
Cynthia for shame obscures her silver shine . *Ven. and Adon.* 728
Cytherea. Sweet Cytherea, sitting by a brook With young Adonis *Pass. Pil.* 43
When Cytherea, all in love forlorn, A longing tarriance for Adonis made . 73

D

Daffed. There my white stole of chastity I daff'd . . . *Lov. Comp.* 297
And daff'd me to a cabin hang'd with care . . . *Pass. Pil.* 183
Daily. The petty streams that pay a daily debt To their salt sovereign *Lucr.* 649
But day doth daily draw my sorrows longer . . . *Sonnet* 28 13
Where two contracted new Come daily to the banks . . . 56 11
For as the sun is daily new and old, So is my love . . . 76 13
Dainties. Torches are made to light, jewels to wear, Dainties to taste, fresh beauty for the use . . . . . . *Ven. and Adon.* 164
Daisy. Whose perfect white Show'd like an April daisy on the grass *Lucrece* 395
Dale. Feed where thou wilt, on mountain or in dale *Ven. and Adon.* 232
As from a mountain-spring that feeds a dale . . . *Lucrece* 1077
We will all the pleasures prove That hills and valleys, dales and fields, And all the craggy mountains yields . . . . . *Pass. Pil.* 355
Dallied. Grief dallied with nor law nor limit knows . . *Lucrece* 1120
Dally. To sport and dance, To toy, to wanton, dally, smile, and jest *Ven. and Adon.* 106
Yet, foul night-waking cat, he doth but dally. . . . *Lucrece* 554
Damask. A lily pale, with damask dye to grace her, None fairer *Pass. Pil.* 89

Damasked. I have seen roses damask'd, red and white *Sonnet* 130 5
Dame. Kings might be espoused to more fame, But king nor peer to such a peerless dame *Lucrece* 21
Well was he welcomed by the Roman dame 51
Since thou couldst not defend thy loyal dame 1034
For trespass of thine eye, The sire, the son, the dame, and daughter die 1477
And softly cried 'Awake, thou Roman dame, And entertain my love' 1628
No dame, hereafter living, By my excuse shall claim excuse's giving 1714
O frowning Fortune, cursed, fickle dame! *Pass. Pil.* 259
When as thine eye hath chose the dame 299
Dammed. With head declined, and voice damm'd up with woe *Lucrece* 1661
Damned. Surfeits, imposthumes, grief, and damn'd despair *Ven. and Adon.* 743
Ink would have seem'd more black and damned here! *Lov. Comp.* 54
Damps. With rotten damps ravish the morning air *Lucrece* 778
Damsel. To put in practice either, alas, it was a spite Unto the silly damsel! *Pass. Pil.* 218
Dance. To sport and dance, To toy, to wanton, dally, smile, and jest *Ven. and Adon.* 105
Or, like a nymph, with long dishevell'd hair, Dance on the sands, and yet no footing seen 148
Dancing. Those dancing chips, O'er whom thy fingers walk with gentle gait *Sonnet* 128 10
Dandling. Or like the froward infant still'd with dandling *Ven. and Adon.* 562
Danger. Or what great danger dwells upon my suit? 206
Come not within his danger by thy will 639
Danger deviseth shifts; wit waits on fear 690
The path is smooth that leadeth on to danger 788
Revolving The sundry dangers of his will's obtaining *Lucrece* 128
He doth premeditate The dangers of his loathsome enterprise 184
Such danger to resistance did belong 1265
Dangerous. To drive infection from the dangerous year *Ven. and Adon.* 508
Dank. The dank earth weeps at thy languishment *Lucrece* 1130
Dardan. From the strand of Dardan, where they fought, To Simois' reedy banks 1436
Dare. Who is so faint, that dare not be so bold To touch the fire, the weather being cold? *Ven. and Adon.* 401
Or at the roe which no encounter dare 676
More I could tell, but more I dare not say; The text is old 805
They basely fly and dare not stay the field 894
She dares not look; yet, winking, there appears Quick-shifting antics *Lucr.* 458
She dares not thereof make discovery 1314
Then may I dare to boast how I do love thee *Sonnet* 26 13
Nor dare I chide the world-without-end hour 57 5
Nor dare I question with my jealous thought Where you may be 57 9
To say they err I dare not be so bold, Although I swear it to myself alone 131 7
Darest. If in thy hope thou darest do such outrage, What darest thou not when once thou art a king? *Lucrece* 605
Daring. Grossly engirt with daring infamy 1173
Not daring trust the office of mine eyes *Pass. Pil.* 196
Dark. With a lazy spright, And with a heavy, dark, disliking eye *V. and A.* 182
And now 'tis dark, and going I shall fall 719
Now of this dark night I perceive the reason 727
If thou destroy them not in dark obscurity 760
And homeward through the dark laund runs apace 813
Even so confounded in the dark she lay 827
Her eyes are fled Into the deep dark cabins of her head 1038
From their dark beds once more leap her eyes 1050
From earth's dark womb some gentle gust doth get *Lucrece* 549
Even in this thought through the dark night he stealeth 729
Dark harbour for defame! Grim cave of death! whispering conspirator! 768
Some dark deep desert, seated from the way 1144
In the dreadful dead of dark midnight 1625
And darkly bright are bright in dark directed *Sonnet* 43 4
What freezings have I felt, what dark days seen! 97 3
And thought thee bright, Who art as black as hell, as dark as night 147 14
And drives away dark dismal-dreaming night *Pass. Pil.* 200
Darken. Burn out thy light, and lend it not To darken her whose light excelleth thine *Lucrece* 191
Darkening. Darkening thy power to lend base subjects light *Sonnet* 100 4
Darkly. And darkly bright are bright in dark directed 43 4
Darkness. His eyes, Where, lo, two lamps, burnt out, in darkness lies *Ven. and Adon.* 1128
Till sable Night, . . . Upon the world dim darkness doth display *Lucrece* 118
Canopied in darkness sweetly lay, Till they might open to adorn the day 398
In darkness daunts them with more dreadful sights 462
Therefore would they still in darkness be 752
Looking on darkness which the blind do see *Sonnet* 27 8
Darksome. O, had they in that darksome prison died! *Lucrece* 379
Darling. Rough winds do shake the darling buds of May *Sonnet* 18 3
Dart. Thine eye darts forth the fire that burneth me *Ven. and Adon.* 196
So glides he in the night from Venus' eye; Which after him she darts 817
Thy mark is feeble age, but thy false dart Mistakes that aim 941
Love's golden arrow at him should have fled, And not Death's ebon dart, to strike him dead 948
She turns my foes, That they elsewhere might dart their injuries *Son.* 139 12
Dash. Some loathsome dash the herald will contrive, To cipher me *Lucrece* 206
Date. An expired date, cancell'd ere well begun 26
Enchained me To endless date of never-ending woes 935
Through her wounds doth fly Life's lasting date 1729
Thy end is truth's and beauty's doom and date *Sonnet* 14 14
Summer's lease hath all too short a date 18 4
So long as youth and thou are of one date 22 2
Let him bring forth Eternal numbers to outlive long date 38 12
Beyond all date, even to eternity 122 4
Our dates are brief, and therefore we admire 123 5
Dateless. For precious friends hid in death's dateless night 30 6
Which borrow'd from this holy fire of Love A dateless lively heat 153 6
Daughter. And barren dearth of daughters and of sons, Be prodigal *V. and A.* 754
To show the beldam daughters of her daughter *Lucrece* 953
For trespass of thine eye, The sire, the son, the dame, and daughter die 1477
'Daughter, dear daughter,' old Lucretius cries 1751
With equal strife Who should weep most, for daughter or for wife 1792
'My daughter' and 'my wife' with clamours fill'd The dispersed air 1804
The dispersed air, . . . Answer'd their cries 'my daughter' and 'my wife' 1806
It was a lording's daughter, the fairest one of three *Pass. Pil.* 211
Daunts. In darkness daunts them with more dreadful sights *Lucrece* 462
Day. A summer's day will seem an hour but short *Ven. and Adon.* 23
Then wink again, And I will wink; so shall the day seem night 122
He cries, 'let go, and let me go; My day's delight is past' 380

Day. The night of sorrow now is turn'd to day *Ven. and Adon.* 481
With weary gait, His day's hot task hath ended in the west 530
To shame the sun by day and her by night 732
But like a stormy day, now wind, now rain, Sighs dry her cheeks 965
Like stars ashamed of day, themselves withdrew 1032
The wolf would leave his prey And never fright the silly lamb that day 1098
This is my spite, That, thou being dead, the day should yet be light 1134
My throbbing heart shall rock thee day and night 1186
Till sable Night, . . . in her vaulty prison stows the Day *Lucrece* 119
Betrays To slanderous tongues and wretched hateful days 161
Canopied in darkness sweetly lay, Till they might open to adorn the day 399
She prays she never may behold the day, 'For day,' quoth she, 'night's scapes doth open lay' 746
Let not the jealous Day behold that face 800
Make me not object to the tell-tale Day! The light will show 806
Poor grooms are sightless night, kings glorious day 1013
Revealing day through every cranny spies 1086
For day hath nought to do what's done by night 1092
Poor bird, thou sing'st not in the day, As shaming any eye should thee behold 1142
Ere the break of day, And, ere I rose, was Tarquin gone away 1280
Should thrust Into so bright a day such black-faced storms 1518
Where all the treasure of thy lusty days *Sonnet* 2 6
With weary car, Like feeble age, he reeleth from the day 7 10
And see the brave day sunk in hideous night 12 2
Might uphold Against the stormy gusts of winter's day 13 11
Where wasteful Time debateth with Decay, To change your day of youth to sullied night 15 12
Shall I compare thee to a summer's day? 18 1
Then look I death my days should expiate 22 4
By day my limbs, by night my mind, For thee and for myself no quiet find 27 13
When day's oppression is not eased by night, But day by night, and night by day oppress'd 28 3
But day doth daily draw my sorrows longer 28 13
Like to the lark at break of day arising From sullen earth 29 11
My well-contented day, When that churl Death my bones with dust shall cover 32 1
Why didst thou promise such a beauteous day? 34 1
If my slight Muse do please these curious days, The pain be mine 38 13
Then do mine eyes best see, For all the day they view things unrespected 43 2
How would thy shadow's form form happy show To the clear day! 43 7
How would, I say, mine eyes be blessed made By looking on thee in the living day! 43 10
All days are nights to see till I see thee, And nights bright days when dreams do show thee me 43 13
The wits of former days To subjects worse have given admiring praise 59 13
Painting my age with beauty of thy days 62 14
Against the wreckful siege of battering days 65 6
What wealth she had In days long since, before these last so bad 67 14
Thus is his cheek the map of days outworn, When beauty lived 68 1
Thou hast pass'd by the ambush of young days 70 9
The twilight of such day As after sunset fadeth in the west 73 5
Thus do I pine and surfeit day by day, Or gluttoning on all, or all away 75 13
Seek anew Some fresher stamp of the time-bettering days 82 8
That tongue that tells the story of thy days 95 5
What freezings have I felt, what dark days seen! 97 3
And stops her pipe in growth of riper days 102 8
We, which now behold these present days, Have eyes to wonder 106 13
Like prayers divine, I must each day say o'er the very same 108 6
The mountain or the sea, the day or night, The crow or dove 113 11
Whereto all bonds do tie me day by day 117 4
She thinks me young, Although she knows my days are past the best 138 6
That follow'd it as gentle day Doth follow night 145 10
And swear that brightness doth not grace the day 150 4
Hot was the day; she hotter that did look For his approach *Pass. Pil.* 77
Pack night; peep day; good day, of night now borrow 209
Thus art with arms contending was victor of the day 223
On a day, alack the day! Love, whose month was ever May 227
And twice desire, ere it be day, That which with scorn she put away 315
As it fell upon a day In the merry month of May 373
Daylight. Like the lark; For she doth welcome daylight with her ditty 199
Dazzleth. Whether it is that she reflects so bright, That dazzleth them, or else some shame supposed *Lucrece* 377
Dazzling. That her sight dazzling makes the wound seem three *V. and A.* 1064
Dead. Thou art bound to breed, That thine may live when thou thyself art dead 172
Well-painted idol, image dull and dead, Statue contenting but the eye alone 212
How doth she now for wits? Struck dead at first, what needs a second striking? 250
His art with nature's workmanship at strife, As if the dead the living should exceed 292
The silly boy, believing she is dead, Claps her pale cheek, till clapping makes it red 467
If he be dead,—O no, it cannot be, Seeing his beauty, thou shouldst strike at it:—O yes, it may 937
Love's golden arrow at him should have fled, And not Death's ebon dart, to strike him dead 948
For he being dead, with him is beauty slain, And, beauty dead, black chaos comes again 1019
Franticly she doteth; She thinks he could not die, he is not dead 1060
Behold two Adons dead! My sighs are blown away 1070
But he is dead, and never did he bless My youth with his 1119
This is my spite, That, thou being dead, the day should yet be light 1134
Since thou art dead, lo, here I prophesy 1135
Now stole upon the time the dead of night *Lucrece* 162
Pure thoughts are dead and still, While lust and murder wake to stain and kill 167
As one in dead of night From forth dull sleep by dreadful fancy waking 449
But as reproof and reason beat it dead, By thy bright beauty was it newly bred 489
And in thy dead arms do I mean to place him 517
'Tis honour to deprive dishonour'd life; The one will live, the other being dead 1187
My shame so dead, mine honour is new-born 1190
Thou dead, both die, and both shall victors be 1211
Who cannot abuse a body dead? 1267
Show'd life imprison'd in a body dead 1456
In the dreadful dead of dark midnight 1625
They did conclude to bear dead Lucrece thence 1850

Dead. Which I by lacking have supposed dead . . . . *Sonnet* 31 2
How many a holy and obsequious tear Hath dear religious love stol'n from mine eye As interest of the dead 31 7
When in dead night thy fair imperfect shade Through heavy sleep on sightless eyes doth stay 43 11
And steal dead seeing of his living hue 67 6
Before the golden tresses of the dead, The right of sepulchres, were shorn away 68 5
Ere beauty's dead fleece made another gay 68 8
No longer mourn for me when I am dead Than you shall hear the surly sullen bell 71 1
My body being dead, The coward conquest of a wretch's knife . 74 10
When all the breathers of this world are dead 81 12
By spirits taught to write Above a mortal pitch, that struck me dead . 86 6
Ere you were born was beauty's summer dead 104 14
Old rhyme In praise of ladies dead and lovely knights . . 106 4
Where time and outward form would show it dead . . . 108 14
That all the world besides methinks are dead 112 14
Making dead wood more blest than living lips 128 12
And Death once dead, there's no more dying then 146 14
Lost, vaded, broken, dead within an hour . . . *Pass. Pil.* 174
As flowers dead lie wither'd on the ground 177
All our evening sport from us is fled, All our love is lost, for Love is dead . 292
King Pandion he is dead; All thy friends are lapp'd in lead . . 395
Here the anthem doth commence: Love and constancy is dead *Ph. and Tur.* 22
For these dead birds sigh a prayer 67
Dead-killing. With a cockatrice' dead-killing eye He rouseth up . *Lucrece* 540
Deadly. Or like the deadly bullet of a gun, His meaning struck her ere his words begun . . . . *Ven. and Adon.* 461
By their suggestion gives a deadly groan 1044
Repentant tears ensue the deed, Reproach, disdain, and deadly enmity *Lucr.* 503
He sets his foot upon the light, For light and lust are deadly enemies . 674
Her lively colour kill'd with deadly cares 1593
Stone-still, astonish'd with this deadly deed, Stood Collatine . . 1730
Deaf. Or were I deaf, thy outward parts would move Each part in me that were but sensible . . . . . . *Ven. and Adon.* 435
But will is deaf and hears no heedful friends . . . . *Lucrece* 495
And trouble deaf heaven with my bootless cries . . . *Sonnet* 29 3
Deal. My shepherd's pipe can sound no deal . . . *Pass. Pil.* 271
Dealing. So thou wilt buy and pay and use good dealing *Ven. and Adon.* 514
Dear. Or were he not my dear friend, this desire Might have excuse to work upon his wife . . . . *Lucrece* 234
But as he is my kinsman, my dear friend, The shame and fault finds no excuse nor end 237
The quiet cabinet Where their dear governess and lady lies . . 443
Let my good name, that senseless reputation, For Collatine's dear love be kept unspotted 821
Dear Collatine, thou shalt not know The stained taste of violated troth . 1058
Dear lord of that dear jewel I have lost What legacy shall I bequeath to thee? 1191
By and by, to bear A letter to my lord, my love, my dear . . 1293
Unmask, dear dear, this moody heaviness, And tell thy grief . . 1602
Dear husband, in the interest of thy bed A stranger came . . 1619
Dear lord, thy sorrow to my sorrow lendeth Another power . . 1676
'Daughter, dear daughter,' old Lucretius cries 1751
Dear my love, you know You had a father: let your son say so *Sonnet* 13 13
My bed, The dear repose for limbs with travel tired . . . 27 2
And with old woes new wail my dear time's waste . . . 30 4
But if the while I think on thee, dear friend, All losses are restored . 30 13
How many a holy and obsequious tear Hath dear religious love stol'n from mine eye As interest of the dead 31 6
Even for this let us divided live, And our dear love lose name of single one 39 6
The clear eye's moiety and the dear heart's part . . . 46 12
Thou wilt be stol'n, I fear, For truth proves thievish for a prize so dear 48 14
Dear love, forget me quite, For you in me can nothing worthy prove . 72 3
Farewell! thou art too dear for my possessing 87 1
Take heed, dear heart, of this large privilege 95 13
And sweets grown common lose their dear delight . . . 102 12
What new to register, That may express my love or thy dear merit? . 108 4
Sold cheap what is most dear, Made old offences of affections new . 110 3
Pity me then, dear friend, and I assure ye Even that your pity is enough to cure me 111 13
Nor need I tallies thy dear love to score 122 10
If my dear love were but the child of state 124 1
To my dear doting heart Thou art the fairest and most precious jewel . 131 3
In my sight, Dear heart, forbear to glance thine eye aside . . 139 6
Love is my sin and thy dear virtue hate, Hate of my sin . . 142 1
I call Her 'love' for whose dear love I rise and fall . . . 151 14
Yet show'd his visage by that cost more dear . . . *Lov. Comp.* 96
Effects of terror and dear modesty, Encamp'd in hearts . . . 202
Deep-brain'd sonnets that did amplify Each stone's dear nature . . 210
Dowland to thee is dear, whose heavenly touch Upon the lute doth ravish human sense . . . . *Pass. Pil.* 107
O yes, dear friend, I pardon crave of thee 141
Dearer. But she hath lost a dearer thing than life . . *Lucrece* 687
My body or my soul, which was the dearer, When the one pure, the other made divine? 1163
A dearer birth than this his love had brought . . . *Sonnet* 32 11
Even those that said I could not love you dearer 115 2
Dearest. So I, made lame by fortune's dearest spite . . . 37 3
Thou, best of dearest and mine only care 48 7
Forgot upon your dearest love to call 117 3
Dearly. And yet it may be said I loved her dearly 42 2
Dear-purchased. And given to time your own dear-purchased right . 117 6
Dearth. He with her plenty press'd, she faint with dearth *Ven. and Adon.* 545
And barren dearth of daughters and of sons, Be prodigal . . . 754
Of good or evil luck, Of plagues, of dearths, or seasons' quality *Sonnet* 14 4
Why dost thou pine within and suffer dearth? 146 3
Death. And so, in spite of death, thou dost survive, In that thy likeness still is left alive . . . . *Ven. and Adon.* 173
For I have heard it is a life in death 413
But now I lived, and life was death's annoy; But now I died, and death was lively joy 497
That the star-gazers, having writ on death, May say, the plague is banish'd by thy breath 509
Whispers in mine ear That if I love thee, I thy death should fear . . 660
I prophesy thy death, my living sorrow 671
Grief, and damn'd despair, Swear Nature's death for framing thee so fair 744
Draws up her breath And sighing it again, exclaims on Death . . 930
Meagre, lean, Hateful divorce of love,—thus chides she Death . . 932
Death. Love's golden arrow at him should have fled, And not Death's ebon dart . . . . *Ven. and Adon.* 948
Adonis lives, and Death is not to blame 992
Sweet Death, I did but jest; Yet pardon me I felt a kind of fear . . 997
With Death she humbly doth insinuate; Tells him of trophies . . 1012
To wail his death who lives and must not die 1017
Sith in his prime Death doth my love destroy 1163
Since he himself is reft from her by death 1174
Though death be adjunct, there's no death supposed . . . *Lucrece* 133
Oft that wealth doth cost The death of all, and all together lost . 147
Showing life's triumph in the map of death, And death's dim look in life's mortality 402
There were no strife, But that life lived in death, and death in life . . 406
Obdurate vassals fell exploits effecting, In bloody death . . . 430
May feel her heart—poor citizen!—distress'd, Wounding itself to death, rise up and fall 466
And made her thrall To living death and pain perpetual . . . 726
Dark harbour for defame! Grim cave of death! whispering conspirator! . 769
Shifting Time! Be guilty of my death, since of my crime . . . 931
She starteth, To find some desperate instrument of death . . . 1038
To clear this spot by death, at least I give A badge of fame to slander's livery 1053
Never will dispense, Till life to death acquit my forced offence . . 1071
'Tis double death to drown in ken of shore 1114
When life is shamed, and death reproach's debtor 1155
That mother tries a merciless conclusion Who, having two sweet babes, when death takes one, Will slay the other and be nurse to none . . 1161
Die I will not till my Collatine Have heard the cause of my untimely death 1178
For in my death I murder shameful scorn 1189
This plot of death when sadly she had laid 1212
With circumstances strong Of present death, and shame that might ensue . 1263
And shame that might ensue By that her death, to do her husband wrong . 1264
And never be forgot in mighty Rome Th' adulterate death of Lucrece and her groom 1645
That fair fresh mirror, dim and old, Shows me a bare-boned death . . 1761
Shall rotten death make conquest of the stronger? 1767
And live to be revenged on her death 1778
By this bloody knife, We will revenge the death of this true wife . . 1841
What could death do, if thou shouldst depart, Leaving thee living in posterity? . . . . *Sonnet* 6 11
Thou art much too fair To be death's conquest and make worms thine heir 6 14
Gusts of winter's day and barren rage of death's eternal cold . . 13 12
Nor shall Death brag thou wander'st in his shade 18 11
Then look I death my days should expiate 22 4
For precious friends hid in death's dateless night 30 6
When that churl Death my bones with dust shall cover . . . 32 2
Sinks down to death, oppress'd with melancholy 45 8
Sweet roses do not so; Of their sweet deaths are sweetest odours made . 54 12
'Gainst death and all-oblivious enmity Shall you pace forth . . 55 9
This thought is as a death, which cannot choose But weep . . . 64 13
Tired with all these, for restful death I cry 66 1
What merit lived in me, that you should love After my death . . 72 3
Which by and by black night doth take away, Death's second self . . 73 8
From hence your memory death cannot take 81 3
In pride of all his growth A vengeful canker eat him up to death . . 99 13
My love looks fresh, and Death to me subscribes 107 10
As testy sick men, when their deaths be near, No news but health from their physicians know 140 7
So shalt thou feed on Death, that feeds on men, And Death once dead, there's no more dying then 146 13
I desperate now approve Desire is death, which physic did except . . 147 8
Fair creature, kill'd too soon by death's sharp sting! . . *Pass. Pil.* 134
That the lover, sick to death, Wish'd himself the heaven's breath . . 233
Death is now the phœnix' nest; And the turtle's loyal breast To eternity doth rest . . . . *Ph. and Tur.* 56
Death-bed. As the death-bed whereon it must expire . . *Sonnet* 73 11
Death-boding. No noise but owls' and wolves' death-boding cries . *Lucrece* 165
Death-divining. Let the priest in surplice white, That defunctive music can, Be the death-divining swan . . . . *Ph. and Tur.* 15
Deathsman. As slanderous deathsman to so base a slave . . *Lucrece* 1001
Death-worthy. This guilt would seem death-worthy in thy brother . 635
Debarred. How can I then return in happy plight, That am debarr'd the benefit of rest? . . . . *Sonnet* 28 2
Debate. He doth debate What following sorrow may on this arise *Lucrece* 185
Debate where leisure serves with dull debaters 1019
It seem'd they would debate with angry swords 1421
For thee against myself I'll vow debate . . . . . *Sonnet* 89 13
Debated. I have debated, even in my soul, What wrong . . . *Lucrece* 498
Debaters. Debate where leisure serves with dull debaters . . . 1019
Debateth. Where wasteful Time debateth with Decay . . . *Sonnet* 15 11
Debating. Then, childish fear, avaunt! debating, die! . . . *Lucrece* 274
Debt. And one sweet kiss shall pay this countless debt . *Ven. and Adon.* 84
Say, for non-payment that the debt should double 521
Till every minute pays the hour his debt . . . . . *Lucrece* 329
The petty streams that pay a daily debt To their salt sovereign . . 649
You did exceed The barren tender of a poet's debt . . . *Sonnet* 83 4
Debtor. Lending him wit that to bad debtors lends . . . *Lucrece* 964
When life is shamed, and death reproach's debtor 1155
Thou usurer, that put'st forth all to use, And sue a friend came debtor for my sake . . . . *Sonnet* 134 11
Decay. To kill thine honour with thy life's decay . . . *Lucrece* 516
When that decays, The guilty rebel for remission prays 713
The story of sweet chastity's decay 808
To feed oblivion with decay of things, To blot old books 947
The bark peel'd from the lofty pine, His leaves will wither and his sap decay 1168
Herein lives wisdom, beauty, and increase; Without this, folly, age, and cold decay . . . . *Sonnet* 11 6
Who lets so fair a house fall to decay? 13 9
Where wasteful Time debateth with Decay 15 11
Fortify yourself in your decay With means more blessed 16 3
In mine own love's strength seem to decay 23 7
I have seen such interchange of state, Or state itself confounded to decay 64 10
Nor gates of steel so strong, but Time decays 65 8
But let your love even with my life decay 71 12
The worst was this; my love was my decay 80 14
Be a satire to decay, And make Time's spoils despised every where . 100 11
To descant on the doubts of my decay . . . . . *Pass. Pil.* 184
Decayed. As soon decay'd and done As is the morning's silver-melting dew Against the golden splendour of the sun . . . . . *Lucrece* 23
But now my gracious numbers are decay'd . . . . . *Sonnet* 79 3

Decease. I must confess,—I rail'd on thee, fearing my love's decease *Ven. and Adon.* 1002
But as the riper should by time decease . . . . . *Sonnet* 1 3
Then you were Yourself again after yourself's decease 13 7
Like widow'd wombs after their lords' decease 97 8
Deceased. Once more re-survey These poor rude lines of thy deceased lover 32 4
And hang more praise upon deceased I Than niggard truth would willingly impart 72 7
Deceit. Thou look'st not like deceit; do not deceive me . *Lucrece* 585
In him the painter labour'd with his skill To hide deceit . . . 1507
Saw how deceits were gilded in his smiling . . *Lov. Comp.* 172
Deceitful. Conceit deceitful, so compact, so kind, That for Achilles' image stood his spear . . . . . . *Lucrece* 1423
Deceive. Thou look'st not like deceit; do not deceive me . . 585
Thou of thyself thy sweet self dost deceive . . . *Sonnet* 4 10
Which time and thoughts so sweetly doth deceive . . . 39 12
And he takes and leaves, In either's aptness, as it best deceives *Lov. Comp.* 306
Deceived. Even as poor birds, deceived with painted grapes *Ven. and Adon.* 601
So shall I live, supposing thou art true, Like a deceived husband *Sonnet* 93 2
Mine eye may be deceived: For fear of which, hear this . 104 12
Deceivest. But yet be blamed, if thou thyself deceivest By wilful taste 40 7
Deceiving. Lest the deceiving harmony should run Into the quiet closure of my breast . . . . . . *Ven. and Adon.* 781
Too severe, And most deceiving when it seems most just . 1156
December. What old December's bareness every where! . *Sonnet* 97 4
Deck. And decks with praises Collatine's high name . *Lucrece* 108
The orator, to deck his oratory, Will couple my reproach to Tarquin's shame 815
Declines. Every fair from fair sometime declines, By chance . *Sonnet* 18 7
Declined. With head declined, and voice damm'd up with woe . *Lucrece* 1661
Decrease. Vaunt in their youthful sap, at height decrease *Sonnet* 15 7
Decree. Poor hand, why quiver'st thou at this decree? . *Lucrece* 1030
Heaven in thy creation did decree That in thy face sweet love should ever dwell . . . . . . *Sonnet* 93 9
Million'd accidents Creep in 'twixt vows and change decrees of kings . 115 6
Decrepit. Teaching decrepit age to tread the measures *Ven. and Adon.* 1148
As a decrepit father takes delight To see his active child do deeds of youth *Sonnet* 37 1
Dedicated. The dedicated words which writers use Of their fair subject 82 3
Deed. Let fair humanity abhor the deed . . . *Lucrece* 195
What excuse can my invention make, When thou shalt charge me with so black a deed? 226
And doth so far proceed, That what is vile shows like a virtuous deed . 252
Repentant tears ensue the deed, Reproach, disdain, and deadly enmity . 502
This deed will make thee only loved for fear 610
Thou grant'st no time for charitable deeds 908
To shame his hope with deeds degenerate 1003
My life's foul deed, my life's fair end shall free it . . . 1208
Such harmless creatures have a true respect To talk in deeds . 1348
Comparing him to that unhappy guest Whose deed hath made herself herself detest 1566
And so did kill The lechers in their deed 1637
Stone-still, astonish'd with this deadly deed, Stood Collatine . 1730
Do wounds help wounds, or grief help grievous deeds? . . . 1822
And they are rich and ransom all ill deeds . . . *Sonnet* 34 14
As a decrepit father takes delight To see his active child do deeds of youth 37 2
Is it thy spirit that thou send'st from thee So far from home into my deeds to pry? 61 6
They look into the beauty of thy mind, And that, in guess, they measure by thy deeds 69 10
Now, while the world is bent my deeds to cross, Join with the spite of fortune 90 2
Sweetest things turn sourest by their deeds 94 13
With Fortune chide, The guilty goddess of my harmful deeds . . 111 2
By their rank thoughts my deeds must not be shown . . . 121 12
In nothing art thou black save in thy deeds 131 13
That in the very refuse of thy deeds There is such strength . . 150 6
Whether the horse by him became his deed, Or he his manage by the well-doing steed . . . . . . *Lov. Comp.* 111
Deem. Speed more than speed but dull and slow she deems . *Lucrece* 1336
The rose looks fair, but fairer we it deem For that sweet odour *Sonnet* 54 3
Deemed. So are those errors that in thee are seen To truths translated and for true things deem'd 96 8
And the just pleasure lost which is so deem'd Not by our feeling but by others' seeing 121 3
Deep. Then love's deep groans I never shall regard *Ven. and Adon.* 377
The sea hath bounds, but deep desire hath none . . . 389
Her eyes are fled Into the deep dark cabins of her head . . 1038
Sad pause and deep regard beseem the sage . . . *Lucrece* 277
Deep woes roll forward like a gentle flood 1118
And with deep groans the diapason bear 1132
Some dark deep desert, seated from the way 1144
'When went'—and there she stay'd Till after a deep groan—'Tarquin from hence?' 1276
That deep torture may be call'd a hell 1287
Deep sounds make lesser noise than shallow fords . . . 1329
Show'd deep regard and smiling government 1400
Being from the feeling of her own grief brought By deep surmise of other's detriment 1579
The face, that map which deep impression bears Of hard misfortune . 1712
That blow did bail it from the deep unrest Of that polluted prison . 1725
The deep vexation of his inward soul Hath served a dumb-arrest upon his tongue 1779
Wherein deep policy did him disguise 1815
That deep vow, which Brutus made before, He doth again repeat . 1847
And dig deep trenches in thy beauty's field . . . *Sonnet* 2 2
As deep a dye As the perfumed tincture of the roses . . 54 5
Whilst he upon your soundless deep doth ride . . . 80 10
Nor did I wonder at the lily's white, Nor praise the deep vermilion in the rose 98 10
That makes my heart to groan For that deep wound it gives my friend and me 133 2
For I have sworn deep oaths of thy deep kindness, Oaths of thy love . 152 9
All kind of arguments and question deep . . *Lov. Comp.* 121
Whose deep conceit is such As, passing all conceit, needs no defence *Pass. Pil.* 109
I in deep delight am chiefly drown'd Whenas himself to singing he betakes 113
Deep-wounded with a boar, Deep in the thigh, a spectacle of ruth! . . 127
My sighs so deep Procure to weep, In howling wise 275

Deep-brained. Deep-brain'd sonnets that did amplify Each stone's dear nature . . . . *Lov. Comp.* 209
Deep-drenched. So she, deep-drenched in a sea of care, Holds disputation *Lucrece* 1100
Deeper. O, deeper sin than bottomless conceit Can comprehend in still imagination! 701
Deepest. O, that our night of woe might have remember'd My deepest sense *Sonnet* 120 10
Deep-green. The deep-green emerald, in whose fresh regard Weak sights their sickly radiance do amend . . . *Lov. Comp.* 213
Deeply. Leaves Love upon her back deeply distress'd *Ven. and Adon.* 814
Passion on passion deeply is redoubled 832
Deep-sore. Ear's deep-sweet music, and heart's deep-sore wounding . . 432
Deep-sunken. To say, within thine own deep-sunken eyes . . *Sonnet* 2 7
Deep-sweet. Ear's deep-sweet music, and heart's deep-sore wounding *Ven. and Adon.* 432
Deep-wounded with a boar, Deep in the thigh, a spectacle of ruth! *Pass. Pil.* 126
Deer. I'll be a park, and thou shalt be my deer *Ven. and Adon.* 231
Then be my deer, since I am such a park; No dog shall rouse thee . . 239
And sometime sorteth with a herd of deer 689
As the poor frighted deer, that stands at gaze . . *Lucrece* 1149
And stall'd the deer that thou shouldst strike . . *Pass. Pil.* 300
Deface. Let not winter's ragged hand deface In thee thy summer *Sonnet* 6 1
None fairer, nor none falser to deface her . . . *Pass. Pil.* 90
Defaced. Besides, his soul's fair temple is defaced . . *Lucrece* 719
When I have seen by Time's fell hand defaced The rich proud cost of outworn buried age . . . . . . *Sonnet* 64 1
Defame. Dark harbour for defame! Grim cave of death . *Lucrece* 768
Feast-finding minstrels, tuning my defame, Will tie the hearers to attend each line 817
But if I live, thou livest in my defame 1033
Defeat. Mine own true love that doth my rest defeat . *Sonnet* 61 11
Defeated. By addition me of thee defeated, By adding one thing to my purpose nothing 20 11
Defeature. And pure perfection with impure defeature . *Ven. and Adon.* 736
Defect. But having no defects, why dost abhor me? . . . 138
This ambitious foul infirmity, In having much, torments us with defect Of that we have . . . . . . *Lucrece* 151
God wot, it was defect Of spirit, life, and bold audacity . . 1345
If ever that time come, When I shall see thee frown on my defects *Sonnet* 49 2
That thou art blamed shall not be thy defect . . . 70 1
When all my best doth worship thy defect . . . 149 11
Defence. Nothing 'gainst Time's scythe can make defence Save breed 12 13
I straight will halt, Against thy reasons making no defence . 89 4
When thy might Is more than my o'erpress'd defence can bide . 139 8
Whose deep conceit is such As, passing all conceit needs no defence *Pass. Pil.* 110
Defend. Fair fall the wit that can so well defend her! . *Ven. and Adon.* 472
I know what thorns the growing rose defends . . . *Lucrece* 492
Since thou couldst not defend thy loyal dame . . . 1034
Suppose thou dost defend me From what is past . . . 1684
Defendant. The defendant doth that plea deny And says in him thy fair appearance lies . . . . . . *Sonnet* 46 7
Defiled. The silver-shining queen he would distain; Her twinkling handmaids too, by him defiled . . . . . *Lucrece* 787
Beguiled With outward honesty, but yet defiled With inward vice . 1545
Defiling. Knew vows were ever brokers to defiling . . *Lov. Comp.* 173
Define. And for myself mine own worth do define As I all other in all worths surmount . . . . . . *Sonnet* 62 7
Deflower. I must deflower: The powers to whom I pray abhor this fact *Lucrece* 348
Deformed'st. The most sweet favour or deformed'st creature *Sonnet* 113 10
Defunctive. Let the priest in surplice white, That defunctive music can, Be the death-divining swan . . . . *Ph. and Tur.* 14
Defy. Thy registers and thee I both defy . . . *Sonnet* 123 9
O, my love, my love is young! Age, I do defy thee . *Pass. Pil.* 167
Defying. Love's denying, Faith's defying, Heart's renying, Causer of this 250
Degenerate. To shame his hope with deeds degenerate . *Lucrece* 1003
Deified. She was new lodged and newly deified . . *Lov. Comp.* 84
Deign. If thou wilt deign this favour, for thy meed A thousand honey secrets shalt thou know . . . . . *Ven. and Adon.* 15
Delay. Her more than haste is mated with delays . . . 909
The doors, the wind, the glove, that did delay him, He takes for accidental things of trial . . . . *Lucrece* 325
So his unhallow'd haste her words delays 552
After many accents and delays, Untimely breathings . . . 1719
Delayed. Her audit, though delay'd, answer'd must be . *Sonnet* 126 11
Delicious. His taste delicious, in digestion souring, Devours his will *Lucr.* 699
Delight. Being red, she loves him best: and being white, Her best is better'd with a more delight . . . . *Ven. and Adon.* 78
He cries, 'let go, and let me go; My day's delight is past' . . 380
His other agents aim at like delight 400
Do I delight to die, or life desire? 496
Others, they think, delight In such-like circumstance, with such-like sport 843
And in her haste unfortunately spies The foul boar's conquest on her fair delight 1030
Which triumph'd in that sky of his delight . . . *Lucrece* 12
Misty night Covers the shame that follows sweet delight . . 357
Lucrece to their sight Must sell her joy, her life, her world's delight . 385
My will that marks thee for my earth's delight . . . 487
Or altogether balk The prey wherein by nature they delight . . 697
He runs, and chides his vanish'd, loathed delight . . . 742
Carrier of grisly care, Eater of youth, false slave to false delight . 927
Sweets with sweets war not, joy delights in joy . . *Sonnet* 8 2
Where-through the sun Delights to peep, to gaze therein on thee . 24 12
Yet doth it steal sweet hours from love's delight . . . 36 8
As a decrepit father takes delight To see his active child do deeds of youth 37 1
Thy picture in my sight Awakes my heart to heart's and eye's delight 47 14
Possessing or pursuing no delight, Save what is had or must from you be took 75 11
Prouder than garments' cost, Of more delight than hawks or horses be 91 11
They were but sweet, but figures of delight, Drawn after you . 98 11
And sweets grown common lose their dear delight . . . 102 12
In some perfumes is there more delight Than in the breath that from my mistress reeks 130 7
She told him stories to delight his ear; She show'd him favours *Pass. Pil.* 47
I in deep delight am chiefly drown'd Whenas himself to singing he betakes 113
Then too late she will repent That thus dissembled her delight . . 314
Delighted. Nor are mine ears with thy tongue's tune delighted *Sonnet* 141 5
Delightful. Sweet bottom-grass and high delightful plain *Ven. and Adon.* 236
Delighting. In bloody death and ravishment delighting . . *Lucrece* 430

Deliver. The post attends, and she delivers it . . . . . *Lucrece* 1333
For it no form delivers to the heart Of bird, of flower, or shape *Sonnet* 113 5
Delivered. Thou shalt find Those children nursed, deliver'd from thy brain 77 11
Delves. And delves the parallels in beauty's brow . . . 60 10
Demand. Yet did I not, as some my equals did, Demand of him, nor being desired yielded . . . *Lov. Comp.* 149
Demeanour. Which he by dumb demeanour seeks to show . *Lucrece* 474
Demure. Her mistress she doth give demure good-morrow . 1219
Denial. But she is not her own: The worst is but denial and reproving 242
He in the worst sense construes their denial . . . 324
Denied. By self-example mayst thou be denied *Sonnet* 142 14
Denote. Then love doth well denote Love's eye is not so true as all men's 'No' 148 7
Deny. If thou deny, then force must work my way *Lucrece* 513
Deny that thou bear'st love to any, Who for thyself art so unprovident *Sonnet* 10 1
The defendant doth that plea deny And says in him thy fair appearance lies 46 7
And deny himself for Jove, Turning mortal for thy love *Pass. Pil.* 243
Denying. Love's denying, Faith's defying, Heart's renying, Causer of this 249
Depart. The poor fool prays her that he may depart *Ven. and Adon.* 578
He thence departs a heavy convertite . . . *Lucrece* 743
What could death do, if thou shouldst depart, Leaving thee living in posterity *Sonnet* 6 11
As easy might I from myself depart As from my soul . . . 109 3
Departest. As fast as thou shalt wane, so fast thou growest In one of thine, from that which thou departest . . . 11 2
Depend. Life no longer than thy love will stay, For it depends upon that love of thine 92 4
A better state to me belongs Than that which on thy humour doth depend 92 8
Both truth and beauty on my love depends . . . 101 3
Now all these hearts that do on mine depend, Feeling it break, with bleeding groans they pine . . . *Lov. Comp.* 274
Depending. In me moe woes than words are now depending *Lucrece* 1615
Deprive. 'Tis honour to deprive dishonour'd life; The one will live, the other being dead 1186
Deprived. That life was mine which thou hast here deprived 1752
Derive. From thine eyes my knowledge I derive, And, constant stars *Son.* 14 9
Derived. Thou wast not to this end from me derived *Lucrece* 1755
Descant. To descant on the doubts of my decay . *Pass. Pil.* 184
Descantest. While thou on Tereus descant'st better skill *Lucrece* 1134
Descended. Solemn night with slow sad gait descended To ugly hell 1081
For some, untuck'd, descended her sheaved hat *Lov. Comp.* 31
Descending. I'll sigh celestial breath, whose gentle wind Shall cool the heat of this descending sun . . . *Ven. and Adon.* 190
Describe. Describe Adonis, and the counterfeit Is poorly imitated after you *Sonnet* 53 5
Descried. For marks descried in men's nativity Are nature's faults *Lucrece* 538
Descriptions. When in the chronicle of wasted time I see descriptions of the fairest wights . . . . . . *Sonnet* 106 2
Desert. Some dark deep desert, seated from the way *Lucrece* 1144
Who will believe my verse in time to come, If it were fill'd with your most high deserts? . . . . *Sonnet* 17 2
I ensconce me here Within the knowledge of mine own desert 49 10
As, to behold desert a beggar born, And needy nothing trimm'd in jollity 66 2
To do more for me than mine own desert . . . 72 6
I have scanted all Wherein I should your great deserts repay 117 2
Spare not to spend, and chiefly there Where thy desert may merit praise *Pass. Pil.* 325
Deserve. Thy lovely argument Deserves the travail of a worthier pen *Son.* 79 6
Root pity in thy heart, that when it grows Thy pity may deserve to pitied be 142 12
Vows for thee broke deserve not punishment . *Pass. Pil.* 32
Deserved. Her pleading hath deserved a greater fee *Ven. and Adon.* 609
How much more praise deserved thy beauty's use . . *Sonnet* 2 9
Deservest. By this separation I may give That due to thee which thou deservest alone 39 8
Deserving. And for that riches where is my deserving? . . 87 6
Design. 'Tis a meritorious fair design To chase injustice with revengeful arms *Lucrece* 1692
Lending soft audience to my sweet design . *Lov. Comp.* 278
Desire. Being so enraged, desire doth lend her force Courageously to pluck him from his horse . . . *Ven. and Adon.* 29
He red for shame, but frosty in desire . . . 36
Shows his hot courage and his high desire . . 276
Thy palfrey, as he should, Welcomes the warm approach of sweet desire . 386
The sea hath bounds, but deep desire hath none . . 389
Do I delight to die, or life desire? 496
Now quick desire hath caught the yielding prey . . 547
Distempering gentle Love in his desire, As air and water do abate the fire . 653
'In night,' quoth she, 'desire sees best of all' . . 720
By this black-faced night, desires foul nurse . . 773
So shall I die by drops of hot desire 1074
To grow unto himself was his desire, And so 'tis thine . . 1180
Borne by the trustless wings of false desire . *Lucrece* 2
Is madly toss'd between desire and dread . . . 171
Beaten away by brain-sick rude desire . . . 175
So Lucrece must I force to my desire . . . 182
This desire Might have excuse to work upon his wife . . 234
Desire my pilot is, beauty my prize 279
By reprobate desire thus madly led, The Roman lord marcheth to Lucrece' bed 300
But his hot heart, which fond desire doth scorch, Puffs forth another wind 314
That to his borrow'd bed he make retire, And stoop to honour, not to foul desire 574
His true respect will prison false desire . . . 642
This hot desire converts to cold disdain . . . 691
Drunken Desire must vomit his receipt . . . 703
No exclamation Can curb his heat or rein his rash desire . . 706
Feeble Desire, all recreant, poor, and meek, Like to a bankrupt beggar 710
Desire doth fight with Grace, For there it revels . . 712
But if the like the snow-white swan desire, The stain upon his silver down will stay 1011
Had doting Priam check'd his son's desire, Troy had been bright with fame 1490
At length address'd to answer his desire, She modestly prepares . . 1606
If thou my love's desire do contradict . . . 1631
From fairest creatures we desire increase . . *Sonnet* 1 1
Seeking that beauteous roof to ruinate Which to repair should be thy chief desire 10 8
The first my thought, the other my desire . . . 45 3
Then can no horse with my desire keep pace . . . 51 9
Desire. Desire, of perfect'st love being made, Shall neigh *Sonnet* 51 10
What should I do but tend Upon the hours and times of your desire? . 57 2
Dost thou desire my slumbers should be broken? . . 61 3
And rather make them born to our desire . . . 123 7
Nor taste, nor smell, desire to be invited To any sensual feast with thee alone 141 7
I desperate now approve Desire is death, which physic did except 147 8
And so the general of hot desire Was sleeping by a virgin hand disarm'd 154 7
Desires to know In brief the grounds and motives of her woe *Lov. Comp.* 62
When he again desires her, being sat, Her grievance with his hearing to divide 66
Consents bewitch'd, ere he desire, have granted . . 131
All these trophies of affections hot, Of pensived and subdued desires the tender 219
And twice desire, ere it be day, That which with scorn she put away *Pass. Pil.* 315
Desired. What did he note but strongly he desired . *Lucrece* 415
Thou canst not, love, disgrace me half so ill, To set a form upon desired change . . . . *Sonnet* 89 6
I, sick withal, the help of bath desired, And thither hied . 153 11
Yet did I not, as some my equals did, Demand of him, nor being desired yielded . . . . *Lov. Comp.* 149
Desiring. Desiring this man's art and that man's scope . *Sonnet* 29 7
Despair. Surfeits, imposthumes, grief, and damn'd despair *Ven. and Adon.* 743
As one full of despair, She vail'd her eyelids . . 955
Despair and hope makes thee ridiculous . . . 988
Despair to gain doth traffic oft for gaining . *Lucrece* 131
Let him have time of Time's help to despair . . 983
One blushing shame, another white despair . . *Sonnet* 99 9
For if I should despair, I should grow mad . . . 140 9
Two loves I have, of comfort and despair, Which like two spirits do suggest me still . . . . 144 1; *Pass. Pil.* 15
Despairing. Till she despairing Hecuba beheld . *Lucrece* 1447
Desperate. The client breaks, as desperate in his suit . *Ven. and Adon.* 336
And careless lust stirs up a desperate courage . . 556
Or theirs whose desperate hands themselves do slay . 765
Will he not wake, and in a desperate rage Post hither? . *Lucrece* 219
She, desperate, with her nails her flesh doth tear . . 739
She starteth, To find some desperate instrument of death 1038
I desperate now approve Desire is death, which physic did except *Son.* 147 7
Despise. Looking scornfully, he doth despise His naked armour *Lucrece* 187
But 'tis my heart that loves what they despise *Sonnet* 141 3
What merit do I in myself respect, That is so proud thy service to despise? 149 10
Despised. O'erworn, despised, rheumatic, and cold *Ven. and Adon.* 135
So then I am not lame, poor, nor despised . . *Sonnet* 37 9
And make Time's spoils despised every where . . 100 12
Enjoy'd no sooner but despised straight . . . 129 5
Despising. Yet in these thoughts myself almost despising, Haply I think on thee 29 9
Despite. Wherein she framed thee in high heaven's despite *Ven. and Adon.* 731
Despite of fruitless chastity, Love-lacking vestals and self-loving nuns . 751
When beauty boasted blushes, in despite Virtue would stain that o'er with silver white . . . . *Lucrece* 55
The scar that will, despite of cure, remain . . 732
In vain I cavil with mine infamy, In vain I spurn at my confirm'd despite . 1026
Shalt see Despite of wrinkles this thy golden time . *Sonnet* 3 12
Despite thy wrong, My love shall in my verse ever live young . 19 13
Despite of space I would be brought, From limits far remote, where thou dost stay 44 3
My verse shall stand, Praising thy worth, despite his cruel hand . . 60 14
I will be true, despite thy scythe and thee . . 123 14
Who in despite of view is pleased to dote . . . 141 4
Despitefully I mean to bear thee Unto the base bed of some rascal groom *Lucrece* 670
Destined. The destined ill she must herself assay . *Lov. Comp.* 156
Destiny. And therefore hath she bribed the Destinies . *Ven. and Adon.* 733
The Destinies will curse thee for this stroke . . 945
Doth fly Life's lasting date from cancell'd destiny *Lucrece* 1729
Destitute. Left their round turrets destitute and pale . 441
Destroy. To note the fighting conflict of her hue, How white and red each other did destroy! . . . . *Ven. and Adon.* 346
Seeming to bury that posterity Which by the rights of time thou needs must have, If thou destroy them not in dark obscurity . . . 760
Sith in his prime Death doth my love destroy . . . 1163
For one sweet grape who will the vine destroy? . *Lucrece* 215
For in thy bed I purpose to destroy thee . . . 514
For Helen's rape the city to destroy 1369
Beauty's waste hath in the world an end, And kept unused, the user so destroys it . . . . *Sonnet* 9 12
Detain. For pity now she can no more detain him . *Ven. and Adon.* 577
She may detain, but not still keep, her treasure . . *Sonnet* 126 10
Determinate. My bonds in thee are all determinate . . 87 4
Determination. So should that beauty which you hold in lease Find no determination 13 6
Determined. By their verdict is determined The clear eye's moiety 46 11
Determining. Stands at gaze, Wildly determining which way to fly *Lucr.* 1150
Detest. Comparing him to that unhappy guest Whose deed hath made herself herself detest 1566
Detriment. Being from the feeling of her own grief brought By deep surmise of others' detriment 1579
Device. I hate not love, but your device in love *Ven. and Adon.* 789
Bequeath not to their lot The shame that from them no device can take *Lucrece* 535
This device was sent me from a nun, Or sister sanctified . *Lov. Comp.* 232
Devil. This earthly saint, adored by this devil, Little suspecteth . *Lucrece* 85
O unlook'd-for evil, When virtue is profaned in such a devil! . 847
Shape every bush a hideous shapeless devil . . . 973
Wherein is stamp'd the semblance of a devil . . . 1246
Like a constant and confirmed devil, He entertain'd a show so seeming just 1513
Such devils steal effects from lightless hell . . . 1555
And would corrupt my saint to be a devil *Sonnet* 144 7; *Pass. Pil.* 21
Devise extremes beyond extremity, To make him curse *Lucrece* 969
Unless you would devise some virtuous lie . . *Sonnet* 72 5
There lives more life in one of your fair eyes Than both your poets can in praise devise 83 14
Devised. When they have devised What strained touches rhetoric can lend 82 9
Deviseth. Danger deviseth shifts; wit waits on fear *Ven. and Adon.* 690
Devour. His taste delicious, in digestion souring, Devours his will *Lucrece* 700

Devour. What virtue breeds iniquity devours *Lucrece* 872
Not that devour'd, but that which doth devour, Is worthy blame 1256
Make the earth devour her own sweet brood *Sonnet* 19 2
Devoured. Not that devour'd, but that which doth devour, Is worthy blame *Lucrece* 1256
Devouring. Shaking her wings, devouring all in haste *Ven. and Adon.* 57
His taste delicious, in digestion souring, Devours his will, that lived by foul devouring *Lucrece* 700
Devouring Time, blunt thou the lion's paws *Sonnet* 19 1
Dew. Soon decay'd and done As is the morning's silver-melting dew *Lucrece* 24
With pearly sweat, resembling dew of night 396
Do not steep thy heart In such relenting dew of lamentations 1829
Dew-bedabbled. Then shalt thou see the dew-bedabbled wretch Turn, and return, indenting with the way *Ven. and Adon.* 703
Dewed. Wishing her cheeks were gardens full of flowers, So they were dew'd with such distilling showers 66
Dewy. Which makes the maid weep like the dewy night *Lucrece* 1232
Scarce had the sun dried up the dewy morn *Pass. Pil.* 71
Dexterity. In youth, quick bearing and dexterity *Lucrece* 1389
Dial. Or as those bars which stop the hourly dial 327
Thy glass will show thee how thy beauties wear, Thy dial how thy precious minutes waste *Sonnet* 77 2
Thou by thy dial's shady stealth mayst know Time's thievish progress 77 7
Dialect. He had the dialect and different skill *Lov. Comp.* 125
Dial-hand. Yet doth beauty, like a dial-hand, Steal from his figure *Sonnet* 104 9
Dialogued. And dialogued for him what he would say *Lov. Comp.* 132
Diamond. The diamond,—why, 'twas beautiful and hard 211
Dian. So do thy lips Make modest Dian cloudy and forlorn *Ven. and Adon.* 725
A maid of Dian's this advantage found *Sonnet* 153 2
Diapason. And with deep groans the diapason bear *Lucrece* 1132
Did. So did the merciless and pitchy night Fold in the object that did feed her sight *Ven. and Adon.* 821
I did but act, he's author of thy slander 1006
My Collatine would else have come to me When Tarquin did *Lucrece* 917
As Priam him did cherish, So did I Tarquin ; so my Troy did perish 1546
Beasts did leap, and birds did sing, Trees did grow, and plants did spring *Pass. Pil.* 377
Didst. O, thou didst kill me : kill me once again *Ven. and Adon.* 499
When thou didst name the boar, not to dissemble, I fear'd thy fortune 641
Didst thou not mark my face? was it not white? 643
Foul sin may say, He learn'd to sin, and thou didst teach the way *Lucrece* 630
Die. Why, there Love lived and there he could not die *Ven. and Adon.* 246
Do I delight to die, or life desire? 496
Lest she should steal a kiss and die forsworn 726
Lust like a glutton dies ; Love is all truth, Lust full of forged lies 803
To wail his death who lives and must not die 1017
She thinks he could not die, he is not dead 1060
So shall I die by drops of hot desire 1074
And die, unhallow'd thoughts, before you blot With your uncleanness that which is divine *Lucrece* 192
Yea, though I die, the scandal will survive, And be an eye-sore 204
But coward-like with trembling terror die 231
Then, childish fear, avaunt! debating, die! 274
Whose crooked beak threats if he mount he dies 508
The patient dies while the physician sleeps 904
For if I die, my honour lives in thee 1032
And therefore now I need not fear to die 1052
Shall thereon fall and die 1139
To live or die which of the twain were better, When life is shamed 1154
Die I will not till my Collatine Have heard the cause of my untimely death 1177
Thou dead, both die, and both shall victors be 1211
For trespass of thine eye, The sire, the son, the dame, and daughter die 1477
Lo, here weeps Hecuba, here Priam dies 1485
And when the judge is robb'd the prisoner dies 1652
The help that thou shalt lend me Comes all too late, yet let the traitor die 1686
The old bees die, the young possess their hive 1769
Live again and see Thy father die, and not thy father thee! 1771
And counterfeits to die with her a space 1776
That thereby beauty's rose might never die *Sonnet* 1 2
Die single, and thine image dies with thee 3 14
If thou issueless shalt hap to die, The world will wail thee 9 3
Meant thereby Thou shouldst print more, not let that copy die 11 14
Beauties do themselves forsake And die as fast as they see others grow 12 12
For at a frown they in their glory die 25 8
They live unwoo'd and unrespected fade, Die to themselves 54 11
From these would I be gone, Save that, to die, I leave my love alone 66 14
Though I, once gone, to all the world must die 81 6
O, what a happy title do I find, Happy to have thy love, happy to die! 92 12
The summer's flower is to the summer sweet, Though to itself it only live and die 94 10
The fools of time, Which die for goodness, who have lived for crime 124 14
A flower that dies when first it gins to bud *Pass. Pil.* 171
Died. And died to kiss his shadow in the brook *Ven. and Adon.* 162
O, had thy mother borne so hard a mind, She had not brought forth thee, but died unkind 204
But now I died, and death was lively joy. O, thou didst kill me 498
But true-sweet beauty lived and died with him 1080
O, had they in that darksome prison died! *Lucrece* 379
Since he died and poets better prove, Theirs for their style I'll read *Son.* 32 13
When beauty lived and died as flowers do now 68 2
Diest. So thou, thyself out-going in thy noon, Unlook'd on diest 7 14
Dieted. Who, disciplined, ay, dieted in grace, Believed her eyes when they to assail begun *Lov. Comp.* 261
Difference. One thing expressing, leaves out difference *Sonnet* 105 8
Our drops this difference bore, His poison'd me, and mine did him restore *Lov. Comp.* 300
Different. Nor the sweet smell Of different flowers in odour and in hue Could make me any summer's story tell *Sonnet* 98 6
He had the dialect and different skill *Lov. Comp.* 125
Dig. His snout digs sepulchres where'er he goes *Ven. and Adon.* 622
And dig deep trenches in thy beauty's field *Sonnet* 2 2
Digestion. His taste delicious, in digestion souring, Devours his will *Lucr.* 699
Dignified. Thou nobly base, they basely dignified 660
Both truth and beauty on my love depends ; So dost thou too, and therein dignified *Sonnet* 101 4
Dignifies. If he can tell That you are you, so dignifies his story 84 8
Dignity. His hand, as proud of such a dignity, Smoking with pride, march'd on to make his stand *Lucrece* 437
But if that flower with base infection meet, The basest weed outbraves his dignity *Sonnet* 94 12
Digression. Then my digression is so vile, so base, That it will live engraven in my face *Lucrece* 202
Diligence. Which being done with speedy diligence, The Romans plausibly did give consent 1853
Dim. Till sable Night, . . . Upon the world dim darkness doth display 118
Showing life's triumph in the map of death, And death's dim look in life's mortality 403
In his dim mist the aspiring mountains hiding 548
Wipe the dim mist from thy doting eyne 643
O comfort-killing Night, image of hell! Dim register and notary of shame! 765
These water-galls in her dim element Foretell new storms to those already spent 1588
That fair fresh mirror, dim and old, Shows me a bare-boned death 1760
Diminished. If springing things be any jot diminish'd, They wither in their prime, prove nothing worth *Ven. and Adon.* 417
Dimmed. Are by his flaming torch dimm'd and controll'd *Lucrece* 448
Sometime too hot the eye of heaven shines, And often is his gold complexion dimm'd *Sonnet* 18 6
Dimple. That in each cheek appears a pretty dimple *Ven. and Adon.* 242
Dimpled. Her azure veins, her alabaster skin, Her coral lips, her snow-white dimpled chin *Lucrece* 420
Dint. As apt as new-fall'n snow takes any dint *Ven. and Adon.* 354
Dire. The dire imagination she did follow This sound of hope doth labour to expel 975
It shall be cause of war and dire events 1159
And the dire thought of his committed evil Shape every bush a hideous shapeless devil *Lucrece* 972
Directed. And darkly bright are bright in dark directed *Sonnet* 43 4
Direction. For men will kiss even by their own direction *Ven. and Adon.* 216
Directly. Suspect I may, yet not directly tell *Sonnet* 144 10
Whether that my angel be turn'd fiend, Suspect I may, yet not directly tell *Pass. Pil.* 24
Direful. The stern and direful god of war, Whose sinewy neck in battle ne'er did bow *Ven. and Adon.* 98
She stays, exclaiming on the direful night *Lucrece* 741
Dirge. Begins the sad dirge of her certain ending 1612
Disabled. And strength by limping sway disabled *Sonnet* 66 8
Disarmed. And so the general of hot desire Was sleeping by a virgin hand disarm'd 154 8
Disbursed. And all my fame that lives disbursed be To those that live *Lucr.* 1203
Discern. Wilt thou be glass wherein it shall discern Authority for sin? 619
Discharge. Ere once she can discharge one word of woe 1605
Discharged. As smoke from Ætna, that in air consumes, Or that which from discharged cannon fumes 1043
Disciplined. Who, disciplined, ay, dieted in grace, Believed her eyes *L. Comp.* 261
Discloses. When summer's breath their masked buds discloses *Sonnet* 54 8
Discoloured. With lank and lean discolour'd cheek, With heavy eye *Lucrece* 706
Discontent. Subject and servile to all discontents, As dry combustious matter is to fire *Ven. and Adon.* 1161
Losing her woes in shows of discontent *Lucrece* 1580
Why art thou thus attired in discontent? 1601
Nor falls Under the blow of thralled discontent *Sonnet* 124 7
Not prizing her poor infant's discontent 143 8
The lines she rents, Big discontent so breaking their contents *Lov. Comp.* 56
I pardon crave of thee, Thy discontent thou didst bequeath to me *Pass. Pil.* 142
Discord. Melodious discord, heavenly tune harsh-sounding *Ven. and Adon.* 431
My restless discord loves no stops nor rests *Lucrece* 1124
Discourse. Bid me discourse, I will enchant thine ear *Ven. and Adon.* 145
My thoughts and my discourse as madmen's are *Sonnet* 147 11
Discovery. In the dark she lay, Having lost the fair discovery of her way *Ven. and Adon.* 828
She dares not thereof make discovery *Lucrece* 1314
Disdain. Who blush'd and pouted in a dull disdain, With leaden appetite, unapt to toy *Ven. and Adon.* 33
Yet was he servile to my coy disdain 112
At this Adonis smiles as in disdain, That in each cheek appears a pretty dimple 241
He held such petty bondage in disdain 394
That hard heart of thine, Hath taught them scornful tricks and such disdain 501
The world will hold thee in disdain, Sith in thy pride so fair a hope is slain 761
Repentant tears ensue the deed, Reproach, disdain, and deadly enmity *Lucr.* 503
Thy kinsmen hang their heads at this disdain 521
This hot desire converts to cold disdain 691
For it had been dishonour to disdain him 844
One that by alms doth live Disdain to him disdained scraps to give 987
Where is she so fair whose unear'd womb Disdains the tillage of thy husbandry? *Sonnet* 3 6
Knowing thy heart torments me with disdain 132 2
Do not press My tongue-tied patience with too much disdain 140 2
For of the two the trusty knight was wounded with disdain *Pass. Pil.* 221
Disdained. Her eyes woo'd still, his eyes disdain'd the wooing *Ven. and Adon.* 358
One that by alms doth live Disdain to him disdained scraps to give *Lucrece* 987
Disdaineth. Yet him for this my love no whit disdaineth *Sonnet* 33 13
Disdainfully did sting His high-pitch'd thoughts *Lucrece* 40
Disease. My love is as a fever, longing still For that which longer nurseth the disease *Sonnet* 147 2
Diseased. A kind of meetness To be diseased ere that there was true needing 118 8
Growing a bath and healthful remedy For men diseased 154 12
Disgrace. My love to love is love but to disgrace it *Ven. and Adon.* 412
Makes the lily pale, And the red rose blush at her own disgrace *Lucrece* 479
They think not but that every eye can see The same disgrace which they themselves behold 751
Immodestly lies martyr'd with disgrace 802
O unseen shame! invisible disgrace! O unfelt sore! 827
When sighs and groans and tears may grace the fashion Of her disgrace 1320
In disgrace with fortune and men's eyes *Sonnet* 29 1
Stealing unseen to west with this disgrace 33 8
That heals the wound and cures not the disgrace 34 8
Thou canst not, love, disgrace me half so ill, To set a form upon desired change, As I'll myself disgrace 89 5
Dulling my lines and doing me disgrace 103 8
Her skill May time disgrace and wretched minutes kill 126 8
No holy bower, But is profaned, if not lives in disgrace 127 8
Thy grace being gain'd cures all disgrace in me *Pass. Pil.* 36
Disgraced. Through the length of times he stands disgraced *Lucrece* 718
Since Rome herself in them doth stand disgraced 1833
And right perfection wrongfully disgraced *Sonnet* 66 7
Disguise. Wherein deep policy did him disguise *Lucrece* 1815
Disguised. Her cheeks with chaps and wrinkles were disguised 1452

Dishevelled. Or, like a nymph, with long dishevell'd hair, Dance on the sands, and yet no footing seen . . . *Ven. and Adon.* 147

Make thy sad grove in my dishevell'd hair . . . *Lucrece* 1129

Dishonour. O foul dishonour to my household's grave! . . . 198

Warrant for blame, To privilege dishonour in thy name . . . 621

There falls into thy boundless flood Black lust, dishonour, shame 654

For it had been dishonour to disdain him . . . 844

Dishonoured. My honour I'll bequeath unto the knife That wounds my body so dishonoured . . . 1185

'Tis honour to deprive dishonour'd life; The one will live, the other being dead . . . 1186

Disjoined. Till, breathless, he disjoin'd, and backward drew *Ven. and Adon.* 541

Disliking. With a lazy spright, And with a heavy, dark, disliking eye . . . 182

Dismal. This dismal cry rings sadly in her ear . . . 889

Dismal-dreaming. And drives away dark dismal-dreaming night *Pass. Pil.* 200

Dismayed. Cheering up her senses all dismay'd, She tells them 'tis a causeless fantasy . . . *Ven. and Adon.* 896

And when his gaudy banner is display'd, The coward fights and will not be dismay'd . . . *Lucrece* 273

Dismiss your vows, your feigned tears, your flattery . . . *Ven. and Adon.* 425

Dismount. This said, his watery eyes he did dismount . . . *Lov. Comp.* 281

Disorder. Whose attaint Disorder breeds by heating of the blood *V. and A.* 742

Dispatch. Sets down her babe and makes all swift dispatch *Sonnet* 143 3

Dispensation. With good thoughts makes dispensation, Urging the worser sense for vantage still . . . *Lucrece* 248

Dispense. I am the mistress of my fate, And with my trespass never will dispense . . . 1070

Yet with the fault I thus far can dispense . . . 1279

May my pure mind with the foul act dispense . . . 1704

Mark how with my neglect I do dispense . . . *Sonnet* 112 12

Disperse. Every alien pen hath got my use And under thee their poesy disperse . . . 78 4

Dispersed. Thy sea within a puddle's womb is hearsed, And not the puddle in thy sea dispersed . . . *Lucrece* 658

'My daughter' and 'my wife' with clamours fill'd The dispersed air . . . 1805

Displacest. Thou plantest scandal and displacest laud . . . 887

Display. Till sable Night, . . . Upon the world dim darkness doth display . . . 118

Displayed. And when his gaudy banner is display'd, The coward fights and will not be dismay'd . . . 272

Disposed. When thou shalt be disposed to set me light . . . *Sonnet* 88 1

Disposing. To the disposing of her troubled brain *Ven. and Adon.* 1040

Disposition. With noble disposition Each present lord began to promise aid *Lucrece* 1695

Dispraise. Cannot dispraise but in a kind of praise . . . *Sonnet* 95 7

Disputation. Thus, graceless, holds he disputation . . . *Lucrece* 246

If that be made a theme for disputation . . . 822

Holds disputation with each thing she views . . . 1101

Dissemble. When thou didst name the boar, not to dissemble, I fear'd thy fortune . . . *Ven. and Adon.* 641

Dissembled. Then too late she will repent That thus dissembled her delight *Pass. Pil.* 314

Wiles and guiles that women work, Dissembled with an outward show 336

Dissension. And set dissension 'twixt the son and sire *Ven. and Adon.* 1160

Dissentious. This carry-tale, dissentious Jealousy . . . 657

Dissolution. Against love's fire fear's frost hath dissolution . . . *Lucrece* 355

Dissolve. My smooth moist hand, were it with thy hand felt, Would in thy palm dissolve, or seem to melt . . . *Ven. and Adon.* 144

What wax so frozen but dissolves with tempering? . . . 565

Dissolved. For stones dissolved to water do convert . . . *Lucrece* 592

Dissuade. But my five wits nor my five senses can Dissuade one foolish heart from serving thee . . . *Sonnet* 141 10

Distain. The silver-shining queen he would distain; Her twinkling handmaids too . . . *Lucrece* 786

Distance. Injurious distance should not stop my way . . . *Sonnet* 44 2

With safest distance I mine honour shielded . . . *Lov. Comp.* 151

She was sought by spirits of richest coat, But kept cold distance . . . 237

Distance, and no space was seen 'Twixt the turtle and his queen *Ph. and Tur.* 30

Distempered. And thither hied, a sad distemper'd guest, But found no cure *Sonnet* 153 12

Distempering gentle Love in his desire, As air and water do abate the fire *Ven. and Adon.* 653

Distills. When that shall fade, my verse distills your truth *Sonnet* 54 14

Distillation. Then, were not summer's distillation left, A liquid prisoner 5 9

Distilled. Flowers distill'd, though they with winter meet, Leese but their show . . . 5 13

Let not winter's ragged hand deface In thee thy summer, ere thou be distill'd . . . 6 2

Siren tears, Distill'd from limbecks foul as hell within . . . 119 2

Distilling. Wishing her cheeks were gardens full of flowers, So they were dew'd with such distilling showers . . . *Ven. and Adon.* 66

Distincts. Two distincts, division none: Number there in love was slain *Ph. and Tur.* 27

Distinguish. No man could distinguish what he said . . . *Lucrece* 1785

Distract. And to your audit comes Their distract parcels in combined sums *Lov. Comp.* 231

Distractedly. The mind and sight distractedly commix'd . . . 28

Distraction. In the distraction of this madding fever . . . *Sonnet* 119 8

Distress. Distress likes dumps when time is kept with tears . . . *Lucrece* 1127

To find a face where all distress is stell'd . . . 1444

But none where all distress and dolour dwell'd . . . 1446

Distressed. Leaves Love upon her back deeply distress'd *Ven. and Adon.* 814

May feel her heart—poor citizen!—distress'd, Wounding itself to death, rise up and fall . . . *Lucrece* 465

Disturb. Lest jealousy, that sour unwelcome guest, Should, by his stealing in, disturb the feast . . . *Ven. and Adon.* 450

Disturb his hours of rest with restless trances . . . *Lucrece* 974

Disturbed. Looks on the dull earth with disturbed mind *Ven. and Adon.* 340

From sleep disturbed, heedfully doth view The sight . . . *Lucrece* 454

Disturbing. Disturbing Jealousy Doth call himself Affection's sentinel *Ven. and Adon.* 649

Ditty. And sings extemporally a woeful ditty . . . 836

Like the lark; For she doth welcome daylight with her ditty *Pass. Pil.* 199

And there sung the dolefull'st ditty, That to hear it was great pity . . . 383

Dive-dapper. Like a dive-dapper peering through a wave, Who, being look'd on, ducks as quickly in . . . *Ven. and Adon.* 86

Divert. Divert strong minds to the course of altering things . . . *Sonnet* 115 8

Diverted. Sometime diverted their poor balls are tied To the orbed earth *Lov. Comp.* 24

Divide. Bubbling from her breast, it doth divide In two slow rivers *Lucrece* 1737

At a mortal war How to divide the conquest of thy sight . . . *Sonnet* 46 2

Divide. When he again desires her, being sat, Her grievance with his hearing to divide . . . *Lov. Comp.* 67

Divided. Even for this let us divided live, And our dear love lose name of single one . . . *Sonnet* 39 5

Dividing. Hindering their present fall by this dividing . . . *Lucrece* 551

Divination. It doth make my faint heart bleed, And fear doth teach it divination . . . *Ven. and Adon.* 670

Divine. For stealing moulds from heaven that were divine . . . 730

And die, unhallow'd thoughts, before you blot With your uncleanness that which is divine . . . *Lucrece* 193

That eye which him beholds, as more divine, Unto a view so false will not incline . . . 291

My body or my soul, which was the dearer, When the one pure, the other made divine? . . . 1164

Like prayers divine, I must each day say o'er the very same . . . *Sonnet* 108 5

Buy terms divine in selling hours of dross . . . 146 11

Divining. For they look'd but with divining eyes . . . 106 11

Division. Two distincts, division none: Number there in love was slain *Ph. and Tur.* 27

Reason, in itself confounded, Saw division grow together . . . 42

Divorce. Ugly, meagre, lean, Hateful divorce of love *Ven. and Adon.* 932

Do I delight to die, or life desire? . . . 496

Beauty hath nought to do with such foul fiends . . . 638

What should I do, seeing thee so indeed, That tremble at the imagination? 667

And soon bereaves, As caterpillars do the tender leaves . . . 798

When Truth and Virtue hath to do with thee . . . *Lucrece* 911

For day hath nought to do what's done by night . . . 1092

If tears could help, mine own would do me good . . . 1274

When beauty lived and died as flowers do now . . . *Sonnet* 68 2

To do more for me than mine own desert . . . 72 6

That do not do the thing they most do show . . . 94 2

Then do thy office, Muse; I teach thee how . . . 101 13

What's sweet to do, to do will aptly find . . . *Lov. Comp.* 88

And yet do question make What I should do again for such a sake . . . 321

Doctor-like. And folly doctor-like controlling skill . . . *Sonnet* 66 10

Doe. Like a milch doe, whose swelling dugs do ache *Ven. and Adon.* 875

He is no woodman that doth bend his bow To strike a poor unseasonable doe *Lucrece* 581

Dog. No dog shall rouse thee, though a thousand bark . . . *Ven. and Adon.* 240

In one place, Where fearfully the dogs exclaim aloud . . . 886

He like a thievish dog creeps sadly thence . . . *Lucrece* 736

My curtail dog, that wont to have play'd, Plays not at all *Pass. Pil.* 273

Doing. The injuries that to myself I do, Doing thee vantage, double-vantage me *Sonnet* 88 12

Dulling my lines and doing me disgrace . . . 103 8

Doleful. Then little strength rings out the doleful knell . . . *Lucrece* 1495

My wether's bell rings doleful knell . . . *Pass. Pil.* 272

Procure to weep, In howling wise, to see my doleful plight . . . 277

Dolefullest. And there sung the dolefull'st ditty, That to hear it was great pity . . . 383

Dolour. But none where all distress and dolour dwell'd . . . *Lucrece* 1446

It easeth some, though none it ever cured, To think their dolour others have endured . . . 1582

Done. And were I not immortal, life were done Between this heavenly and earthly sun . . . *Ven. and Adon.* 197

Her words are done, her woes the more increasing; The time is spent . . . 254

Thy mermaid's voice hath done me double wrong; I had my load before . . . 429

Thaw'd and done, As mountain-snow melts with the mid-day sun . . . 749

Lust's winter comes ere summer half be done . . . 802

Stories oftentimes begun End without audience and are never done . . . 846

'Tis he, foul creature, that hath done thee wrong . . . 1005

As soon decay'd and done As is the morning's silver-melting dew . . . *Lucrece* 23

That done, some worthless slave of thine I'll slay, To kill thine honour . . . 515

A little harm done to a great good end For lawful policy remains enacted . . . 528

'Have done,' quoth he: 'my uncontrolled tide Turns not' . . . 645

That done, despitefully I mean to bear thee Unto the base bed of some rascal groom . . . 670

For day hath nought to do what's done by night . . . 1092

And rail on Pyrrhus that hath done him wrong . . . 1467

What wrong else may be imagined By foul enforcement might be done to me 1623

Which being done with speedy diligence, The Romans plausibly did give consent . . . 1853

Now see what good turns eyes for eyes have done . . . *Sonnet* 24 9

No more be grieved at that which thou hast done . . . 35 1

Since mind at first in character was done . . . 59 8

Now all is done, have what shall have no end . . . 110 9

The carcass of a beauty spent and done . . . *Lov. Comp.* 11

Harm have I done to them, but ne'er was harm'd . . . 194

Doom. Some rascal groom, To be thy partner in this shameful doom *Lucrece* 672

For now against himself he sounds this doom . . . 717

And all that are to come, From the creation to the general doom . . . 924

When they had sworn to this advised doom . . . 1849

Thy end is truth's and beauty's doom and date . . . *Sonnet* 14 14

All posterity That wear this world out to the ending doom . . . 55 12

Supposed as forfeit to a confined doom . . . 107 4

But bears it out even to the edge of doom . . . 116 12

That tongue that ever sweet Was used in giving gentle doom . . . 145 7

Door. And bid Suspicion double-lock the door . . . *Ven. and Adon.* 448

The threshold grates the door to have him heard . . . *Lucrece* 306

The doors, the wind, the glove, that did delay him, He takes for accidental things of trial . . . 325

Now is he come unto the chamber door . . . 337

Pluck'd up the latch, And with his knee the door he opens wide . . . 359

Much like a press of people at a door, Throng her inventions . . . 1301

Dost. But having no defects, why dost abhor me? . . . *Ven. and Adon.* 138

Both truth and beauty on my love depends; So dost thou too *Sonnet* 101 4

Dote. How love makes young men thrall and old men dote *Ven. and Adon.* 837

The herald will contrive, To cipher me how fondly I did dote *Lucrece* 207

He hath an eye to gaze on beauty, And dotes on what he looks . . . 497

Who in despite of view is pleased to dote . . . *Sonnet* 141 4

If that be fair whereon my false eyes dote, What means the world to say it is not so? . . . 148 5

Whose rarest havings made the blossoms dote . . . *Lov. Comp.* 235

Doted. What he beheld, on that he firmly doted . . . *Lucrece* 416

Doteth. Dumbly she passions, franticly she doteth *Ven. and Adon.* 1059

Doth. Now doth she stroke his cheek, now doth he frown . . . 45

Being mad before, how doth she now for wits? . . . 249

Nor that full star that ushers in the even Doth half that glory to the sober west . . . *Sonnet* 132 8

Doting. Such hazard now must doting Tarquin make . . . *Lucrece* 155

Doting. Wipe the dim mist from thy doting eyne, That thou shalt see *Lucrece* 643
He shall not boast who did thy stock pollute That thou art doting father of his fruit 1064
Had doting Priam check'd his son's desire, Troy had been bright with fame 1490
Nature, as she wrought thee, fell a-doting *Sonnet* 20 10
To my dear doting heart Thou art the fairest and most precious jewel 131 3
Double. Thy mermaid's voice hath done me double wrong *Ven. and Adon.* 429
Say, for non-payment that the debt should double 521
With what care He cranks and crosses with a thousand doubles 682
'Tis double death to drown in ken of shore *Lucrece* 1114
And given grace a double majesty *Sonnet* 78 8
No bitterness that I will bitter think, Nor double penance 111 12
My spirits to attend this double voice accorded *Lov. Comp.* 3
Single nature's double name Neither two nor one was called *Ph. and Tur.* 39
Doubled. His face seems twain, each several limb is doubled *Ven. and Adon.* 1067
Double-lock. And bid Suspicion double-lock the door 448
Double-vantage. The injuries that to myself I do, Doing thee vantage, double-vantage me *Sonnet* 88 12
Doubt. The hot scent-snuffing hounds are driven to doubt *Ven. and Adon.* 692
Overcome by doubt and bloodless fear, With cold-pale weakness 891
Yet this shall I ne'er know, but live in doubt *Sonnet* 144 13
And nice affections wavering stood in doubt If best were as it was *L. Comp.* 97
But live in doubt, Till my bad angel fire my good one out *Pass. Pil.* 27
To descant on the doubts of my decay 184
Doubtful. Beauty is but a vain and doubtful good; A shining gloss that vadeth suddenly 169
A doubtful good, a gloss, a glass, a flower 173
Long was the combat doubtful that love with love did fight 215
Doubting. Anon Doubting the filching age will steal his treasure *Sonnet* 75 6
Crowning the present, doubting of the rest 115 12
Dove. More white and red than doves or roses are *Ven. and Adon.* 10
Two strengthless doves will draw me through the sky 153
Wilful and unwilling, Show'd like two silver doves that sit a-billing 366
Weary of the world, away she hies, And yokes her silver doves 1190
But beauty, in that white intituled, From Venus' doves doth challenge that fair field *Lucrece* 58
The dove sleeps fast that this night-owl will catch 360
The mountain or the sea, the day or night, The crow or dove *Sonnet* 113 12
Mild as a dove, but neither true nor trusty *Pass. Pil.* 86
Paler for sorrow than her milk-white dove, For Adon's sake 119
Whereupon it made this threne To the phœnix and the dove *Ph. and Tur.* 50
Dowland. Dowland to thee is dear, whose heavenly touch Upon the lute doth ravish human sense *Pass. Pil.* 107
Down. So soon was she along as he was down *Ven. and Adon.* 43
Down Adonis sits, Banning his boisterous and unruly beast 325
And like a lowly lover down she kneels 350
She flatly falleth down, For looks kill love and love by looks reviveth 463
She sinketh down, still hanging by his neck, He on her belly falls 593
Pursue these fearful creatures o'er the downs 677
Pluck down the rich, enrich the poor with treasures 1150
Would with the sceptre straight be strucken down *Lucrece* 217
With foul insurrection, Have batter'd down her consecrated wall 723
The stain upon his silver down will stay 1012
On what occasion break Those tears from thee, that down thy cheeks are raining? 1271
What wit sets down is blotted straight with will 1299
In speech, it seem'd, his beard, all silver white, Wagg'd up and down 1406
Sinks down to death, oppress'd with melancholy *Sonnet* 45 8
Upon thy part I can set down a story Of faults conceal'd 88 6
Book both my wilfulness and errors down 117 9
Sets down her babe and makes all swift dispatch In pursuit 143 3
And down I laid to list the sad-tuned tale *Lov. Comp.* 4
So slides he down upon his grained bat, And comely-distant sits 64
His phœnix down began but to appear Like unshorn velvet 93
That phraseless hand, Whose white weighs down the airy scale of praise 226
The strongest castle, tower, and town, The golden bullet beats it down *Pass. Pil.* 328
Down-razed. When sometime lofty towers I see down-razed *Sonnet* 64 3
Downright. Grew I not faint? and fell I not downright? *Ven. and Adon.* 645
Downward. Whose downward eye still looketh for a grave 1106
A fount With brinish current downward flow'd apace *Lov. Comp.* 284
Dowry. Not spend the dowry of a lawful bed *Lucrece* 938
Drained. When hours have drain'd his blood and fill'd his brow With lines and wrinkles *Sonnet* 63 3
Draw. Two strengthless doves will draw me through the sky *Ven. and Adon.* 153
That she will draw his lips' rich treasure dry 552
Draws up her breath And sighing it again, exclaims on Death 929
To draw the cloud that hides the silver moon *Lucrece* 371
Draw not thy sword to guard iniquity 626
His sighs, his sorrows, make a saw, To push grief on, and back the same grief draw 1673
Nor draw no lines there with thine antique pen *Sonnet* 19 10
They draw but what they see, know not the heart 24 14
But day doth daily draw my sorrows longer 28 13
Drawn. Even so, the curtain drawn, his eyes begun To wink *Lucrece* 374
Before the which is drawn the power of Greece 1368
My laments would be drawn out too long, To tell them all 1616
You must live, drawn by your own sweet skill *Sonnet* 16 14
Mine eyes have drawn thy shape, and thine for me Are windows to my breast 24 10
They were but sweet, but figures of delight, Drawn after you 98 12
On his visage was in little drawn What largeness thinks in Paradise was sawn *Lov. Comp.* 90
Dread. But having thee at vantage,—wondrous dread! *Ven. and Adon.* 635
Sable Night, mother of Dread and Fear *Lucrece* 117
Is madly toss'd between desire and dread 171
O, this dread night, wouldst thou one hour come back! 965
Dreadeth. Love thrives not in the heart that shadows dreadeth 270
Dreadful. Infusing them with dreadful prophecies *Ven. and Adon.* 928
From forth dull sleep by dreadful fancy waking *Lucrece* 450
In darkness daunts them with more dreadful sights 462
In the dreadful dead of dark midnight 1625
Being constrain'd with dreadful circumstance 1703
Thine eye Jove's lightning seems, thy voice his dreadful thunder *Pass. Pil.* 67
Dreadfully. They, . . . Do tell her, she is dreadfully beset, And fright her with confusion of their cries *Lucrece* 444
Dreading. That leaves look pale, dreading the winter's near *Sonnet* 97 14
Dreading my love, the loss thereof still fearing *Pass. Pil.* 94
Dream. For unstain'd thoughts do seldom dream on evil *Lucrece* 87
A dream, a breath, a froth of fleeting joy 212

Dream. If Collatinus dream of my intent, Will he not wake? *Lucrece* 218
Thoughts are but dreams till their effects be tried 353
By this, starts Collatine as from a dream 1772
When I sleep, in dreams they look on thee *Sonnet* 43 3
All days are nights to see till I see thee, And nights bright days when dreams do show thee me 43 14
Thus have I had thee, as a dream doth flatter, In sleep a king 87 13
A very woe; Before, a joy proposed; behind, a dream 129 12
Dreaming. The prophetic soul Of the wide world dreaming on things to come 107 2
Dregs. So then thou hast but lost the dregs of life, The prey of worms. 74 9
Drenched. 'O, where am I?' quoth she, 'in earth or heaven, Or in the ocean drench'd, or in the fire?' *Ven. and Adon.* 494
Whose wonted lily white With purple tears, that his wound wept, was drench'd 1054
Dress. Robbing no old to dress his beauty new *Sonnet* 68 12
Dressed. When proud-pied April dress'd in all his trim Hath put a spirit of youth in every thing 98 2
Dressing. So all my best is dressing old words new 76 11
They are but dressings of a former sight 123 4
Drew. Till, breathless, he disjoin'd, and backward drew *Ven. and Adon.* 541
Which the conceited painter drew so proud, As heaven *Lucrece* 1371
The well-skill'd workman this mild image drew For perjured Sinon 1520
From the purple fountain Brutus drew The murderous knife 1734
A thousand favours from a maund she drew *Lov. Comp.* 36
Observed as they flew—Towards this afflicted fancy fastly drew 61
Dried. Scarce had the sun dried up the dewy morn *Pass. Pil.* 71
Drink. Never did passenger in summer's heat More thirst for drink *V. and A.* 92
His nostrils drink the air, and forth again 273
Dost thou drink tears, that thou provokest such weeping? 949
Mud not the fountain that gave drink to thee *Lucrece* 577
What he breathes out his breath drinks up again 1666
I will drink Potions of eisel 'gainst my strong infection *Sonnet* 111 9
Drink up the monarch's plague, this flattery 114 2
And my great mind most kingly drinks it up 114 10
Drive. To drive infection from the dangerous year *Ven. and Adon.* 508
They all rate his ill, Which drives the creeping thief to some regard *Lucrece* 305
And drives away dark dismal-dreaming night *Pass. Pil.* 200
Driven. The hot scent-snuffing hounds are driven to doubt *Ven. and Adon.* 692
Drone-like. My honey lost, and I, a drone-like bee *Lucrece* 836
Droop. Doth make them droop with grief and hang the head *Ven. and Adon.* 666
Drooping. And keep my drooping eyelids open wide *Sonnet* 27 7
Drop. Yet sometimes falls an orient drop beside, Which her cheek melts *Ven. and Adon.* 981
So shall I die by drops of hot desire 1074
His pale cheeks and the blood Which in round drops upon their whiteness stood 1170
The spots whereof could weeping purify, Her tears should drop on them *Lucrece* 686
Even so the maid with swelling drops gan wet 1228
The other takes in hand No cause, but company, of her drops spilling 1236
Many a dry drop seem'd a weeping tear 1375
And drop sweet balm in Priam's painted wound 1466
His eye drops fire, no water thence proceeds 1552
Make me bow, And do not drop in for an after-loss *Sonnet* 90 4
Now with the drops of this most balmy time My love looks fresh 107 9
Our drops this difference bore, His poison'd me, and mine did him restore *Lov. Comp.* 300
Dropped. As one that unaware Hath dropp'd a precious jewel in the flood *Ven. and Adon.* 824
Dropping. She crops the stalk, and in the breach appears Green dropping sap 1176
Dropt. In the sweet channel of her bosom dropt 958
Dross. Buy terms divine in selling hours of dross *Sonnet* 146 11
Drouth. Whereon they surfeit, yet complain on drouth *Ven. and Adon.* 544
Drown. With too much labour drowns for want of skill *Lucrece* 1099
'Tis double death to drown in ken of shore 1114
And then they drown their eyes or break their hearts 1239
Let it then suffice To drown one woe, one pair of weeping eyes 1680
Then can I drown an eye, unused to flow, For precious friends *Sonnet* 30 5
That it nor grows with heat nor drowns with showers 124 12
Drowned. To wash the foul face of the sluttish ground, Who is but drunken when she seemeth drown'd *Ven. and Adon.* 984
That had Narcissus seen her as she stood, Self-love had never drown'd him in the flood *Lucrece* 266
I in deep delight am chiefly drown'd Whenas himself to singing he betakes *Pass. Pil.* 113
Drudge. Proud of this pride, He is contented thy poor drudge to be *Son.* 151 11
Drugs. And find the lesson true, Drugs poison him that so fell sick of you 118 14
Drum. Scorning his churlish drum and ensign red *Ven. and Adon.* 107
Drumming. His drumming heart cheers up his burning eye *Lucrece* 435
Drunk. What potions have I drunk of Siren tears, Distill'd from limbecks foul as hell within *Sonnet* 119 1
Drunken. Like the proceedings of a drunken brain *Ven. and Adon.* 910
To wash the foul face of the sluttish ground, Who is but drunken when she seemeth drown'd 984
Drunken Desire must vomit his receipt *Lucrece* 703
Dry. Then with her windy sighs and golden hairs To fan and blow them dry again she seeks *Ven. and Adon.* 52
Graze on my lips; and if those hills be dry, Stray lower, where the pleasant fountains lie 233
That she will draw his lips' rich treasure dry 552
The lamp that burns by night Dries up his oil to lend the world his light 756
Sorrow that friendly sighs sought still to dry 964
Sighs dry her cheeks, tears make them wet again 966
They both would strive who first should dry his tears 1092
Subject and servile to all discontents, As dry combustious matter is to fire 1162
To dry the old oak's sap and cherish springs *Lucrece* 950
Many a dry drop seem'd a weeping tear 1375
To dry the rain on my storm-beaten face *Sonnet* 34 6
Ducks. Like a dive-dapper peering through a wave, Who, being look'd on, ducks as quickly in *Ven. and Adon.* 87
Due. And as his due writ in my testament *Lucrece* 1183
Pity the world, or else this glutton be, To eat the world's due *Sonnet* 1 14
That due of many now is thine alone 31 12
By this separation I may give That due to thee which thou deservest alone 39 8
Mine eye's due is thy outward part 46 13
All tongues, the voice of souls, give thee that due, Uttering bare truth 69 3
The earth can have but earth, which is his due 74 7
Dugs. Like a milch doe, whose swelling dugs do ache *Ven. and Adon.* 875

E

Early. Even so my sun one early morn did shine . . . *Sonnet* 33 9
But, woe is me! too early I attended A youthful suit . . . *Lov. Comp.* 78
Earnest. Her earnest eye did make him more amazed . . . *Lucrece* 1356
Earth. Calls it balm, Earth's sovereign salve to do a goddess good *V. and A.* 28
Upon the earth's increase why shouldst thou feed, Unless the earth with thy increase be fed? . . . 169
The bearing earth with his hard hoof he wounds . . . 267
Looks on the dull earth with disturbed mind . . . 340
In his fresh array He cheers the morn and all the earth relieveth . . . 484
'O, where am I?' quoth she, 'in earth or heaven, Or in the ocean?' . . . 493
She faint with dearth, Their lips together glued, fall to the earth . . . 546
Then imagine this, The earth, in love with thee, thy footing trips . . . 722
Self-loving nuns, That on the earth would breed a scarcity . . . 753
Love to heaven is fled, Since sweating Lust on earth usurp'd his name . . . 794
Grim-grinning ghost, earth's worm, what dost thou mean To stifle beauty? 933
Struggling for passage, earth's foundation shakes . . . 1047
My will that marks thee for my earth's delight . . . *Lucrece* 487
From earth's dark womb some gentle gust doth get . . . 549
By heaven and earth, and all the power of both . . . 572
Seasoning the earth with showers of silver brine . . . 796
The dank earth weeps at thy languishment . . . 1130
But as the earth doth weep, the sun being set, Each flower moisten'd like a melting eye . . . 1226
By heaven's fair sun that breeds the fat earth's store . . . 1837
Make the earth devour her own sweet brood . . . *Sonnet* 19 2
With earth and sea's rich gems, With April's first-born flowers . . . 21 6
Like to the lark at break of day arising From sullen earth, sings hymns at heaven's gate . . . 29 12
No matter then although my foot did stand Upon the farthest earth removed from thee . . . 44 6
But that so much of earth and water wrought I must attend time's leisure with my moan . . . 44 11
Brass, nor stone, nor earth, nor boundless sea . . . 65 1
The earth can have but earth, which is his due; My spirit is thine . . . 74 7
I shall live your epitaph to make, Or you survive when I in earth am rotten . . . 81 2
The earth can yield me but a common grave . . . 81 7
Poor soul, the centre of my sinful earth . . . 146 1
Sometime diverted their poor balls are tied To the orbed earth *Lov. Comp.* 25
Then, thou fair sun, that on this earth doth shine, Exhale this vapour vow *Pass. Pil.* 38
Earth-delving. And sometime where earth-delving conies keep *V. and A.* 687
Earthly. And were I not immortal, life were done Between this heavenly and earthly sun . . . 198
There lives a son that suck'd an earthly mother, May lend thee light . . . 863
This earthly saint, adored by this devil, Little suspecteth . . . *Lucrece* 85
Such heavenly touches ne'er touch'd earthly faces . . . *Sonnet* 17 8
My vow was earthly, thou a heavenly love . . . *Pass. Pil.* 35
O do not love that wrong, To sing heaven's praise with such an earthly tongue . . . 70
Earthquake. But, like an earthquake, shakes thee on my breast *V. and A.* 648
Ease. The aim of all is but to nurse the life With honour, wealth, and ease *Lucrece* 142
Give physic to the sick, ease to the pain'd . . . 901
My weary travel's end, Doth teach that ease and that repose . *Sonnet* 50 3
With ease we prove Among a number one is reckon'd none . . . 136 7
Eased. When day's oppression is not eased by night . . . 28 3
Easeth. It easeth some, though none it ever cured, To think their dolour others have endured . . . *Lucrece* 1581
Easily. His short thick neck cannot be easily harm'd *Ven. and Adon.* 627
East. Truly not the morning sun of heaven Better becomes the grey cheeks of the east . . . *Sonnet* 132 6
Lord, how mine eyes throw gazes to the east! My heart doth charge the watch . . . *Pass. Pil.* 193
Eastern. Foggy Night! Since thou art guilty of my cureless crime, Muster thy mists to meet the eastern light . . . *Lucrece* 773
Easy. As easy might I from myself depart As from my soul . *Sonnet* 109 3
Words are easy, like the wind; Faithful friends are hard to find *Pass. Pil.* 405
Eat. This canker that eats up Love's tender spring . *Ven. and Adon.* 656
And grave, like water that doth eat in steel, Upon my cheeks *Lucrece* 755
To eat up errors by opinion bred, Not spend the dowry of a lawful bed . 937
Pity the world, or else this glutton be, To eat the world's due . *Sonnet* 1 14
In pride of all his growth A vengeful canker eat him up to death . . 99 13
Shall worms, inheritors of this excess, Eat up thy charge? . . 146 8
Eater. Carrier of grisly care, Eater of youth, false slave to false delight *Lucrece* 927
Ebb. Sorrow ebbs, being blown with wind of words . . . 1330
Thus ebbs and flows the current of her sorrow . . . 1569
Ebon. Love's golden arrow at him should have fled, And not Death's ebon dart, to strike him dead . . . *Ven. and Adon.* 948
Echo. Then do they spend their mouths: Echo replies, As if another chase were in the skies . . . 695
'Ay me!' she cries, and twenty times 'Woe, woe!' And twenty echoes twenty times cry so . . . 834
And still the choir of echoes answer so . . . 840
Eclipse. Clouds and eclipses stain both moon and sun . *Sonnet* 35 3
Being crown'd, Crooked eclipses 'gainst his glory fight . . . 60 7
The mortal moon hath her eclipse endured . . . 107 5
Ecstasy. Thus stands she in a trembling ecstasy . . *Ven. and Adon.* 895
Which may her suffering ecstasy assuage . . . *Lov. Comp.* 69
Eddy. Yet in the eddy boundeth in his pride Back to the strait that forced him on so fast . . . *Lucrece* 1669
Edge. Unhappily set This bateless edge on his keen appetite . . . 9
Be it not said Thy edge should blunter be than appetite . *Sonnet* 56 2
The hardest knife ill-used doth lose his edge . . . 95 14
But bears it out even to the edge of doom . . . 116 12
Effect. The warm effects which she in him finds missing She seeks to kindle with continual kissing . . . *Ven. and Adon.* 605
Love comforteth like sunshine after rain, But Lust's effect is tempest after sun . . . 800
And every beauty robb'd of his effect . . . 1132
Which in a moment doth confound and kill All pure effects . . *Lucrece* 251
Thoughts are but dreams till their effects be tried . . . 353
Being so applied, His venom in effect is purified . . . 532
Such devils steal effects from lightless hell . . . 1555
Beauty's effect with beauty were bereft, Nor it nor no remembrance what it was . . . *Sonnet* 5 11
Though it alter not love's sole effect, Yet doth it steal sweet hours . 36 7
Then others for the breath of words respect, Me for my dumb thoughts, speaking in effect . . . 85 14
Effect. Effects of terror and dear modesty, Encamp'd in hearts *Lov. Comp.* 202
O cleft effect! cold modesty, hot wrath . . . 293
Effecting. In hand with all things, nought at all effecting *Ven. and Adon.* 912
Obdurate vassals fell exploits effecting, In bloody death . . *Lucrece* 429
Effectually. Is partly blind, Seems seeing, but effectually is out *Sonnet* 113 4
Eisel. I will drink Potions of eisel 'gainst my strong infection . . 111 10
Either. Till either gorge be stuff'd or prey be gone . *Ven. and Adon.* 58
Of either's colour was the other queen . . . *Lucrece* 66
The sovereignty of either being so great . . . 69
Seems to part in sunder, Swelling on either side to want his bliss . . 389
Whose love of either to myself was nearer . . . 1165
The face of either cipher'd either's heart . . . 1396
And each, though enemies to either's reign, Do in consent shake hands to torture me . . . *Sonnet* 28 5
Heavy tears, badges of either's woe . . . 44 14
Either by thy picture or my love, Thyself away art present still with me . . . 47 9
Either not assail'd or victor being charged . . . 70 10
And he takes and leaves, In either's aptness, as it best deceives *Lov. Comp.* 306
To put in practice either, alas, it was a spite Unto the silly damsel! *Pass. Pil.* 217
Either was the other's mine . . . *Ph. and Tur.* 36
To themselves yet either neither, Simple were so well compounded . . 43
To this urn let those repair That are either true or fair . . . 66
Elbows. Each leaning on their elbows and their hips . *Ven. and Adon.* 44
Elder. How can I then be elder than thou art? . . . *Sonnet* 22 8
Element. These water-galls in her dim element Foretell new storms to those already spent . . . *Lucrece* 1588
Receiving nought by elements so slow But heavy tears . . *Sonnet* 44 13
When these quicker elements are gone In tender embassy of love to thee . . . 45 5
Eloquence. Her modest eloquence with sighs is mixed . . *Lucrece* 563
Let my books be then the eloquence And dumb presagers of my speaking breast . . . *Sonnet* 23 9
Else. Speak, fair; but speak fair words, or else be mute *Ven. and Adon.* 208
He sees his love, and nothing else he sees, For nothing else with his proud sight agrees . . . 287
Affection is a coal that must be cool'd; Else, suffer'd, it will set the heart on fire . . . 388
Whether it is that she reflects so bright, That dazzleth them, or else some shame supposed . . . *Lucrece* 377
We have no good that we can say is ours, But ill-annexed Opportunity Or kills his life or else his quality . . . 875
My Collatine would else have come to me When Tarquin did . . . 916
What wrong else may be imagined By foul enforcement might be done to me 1622
Else lasting shame On thee and thine this night I will inflict . . . 1629
Pity the world, or else this glutton be, To eat the world's due . *Sonnet* 1 13
Or else of thee this I prognosticate . . . 14 13
Else call it winter, which being full of care Makes summer's welcome thrice more wish'd, more rare . . . 56 13
Or me, to whom thou gavest it, else mistaking . . . 87 10
None else to me, nor I to none alive . . . 112 7
For thou art all, and all things else are thine . . . *Lov. Comp.* 266
Elsewhere. For thee watch I whilst thou dost wake elsewhere, From me far off . . . *Sonnet* 61 13
Tell me thou lovest elsewhere, but in my sight, Dear heart, forbear to glance thine eye aside . . . 139 5
She turns my foes, That they elsewhere might dart their injuries . . 139 12
Elysium. To clip Elysium and to lack her joy . . *Ven. and Adon.* 600
Embassage. To thee I send this written embassage, To witness duty *Son.* 26 3
Embassy. When these quicker elements are gone In tender embassy of love to thee . . . 45 6
Embers. The lightless fire Which, in pale embers hid, lurks to aspire *Lucr.* 5
Embrace. Her arms do lend his neck a sweet embrace . *Ven. and Adon.* 539
With this, he breaketh from the sweet embrace, Of those fair arms . 811
She wildly breaketh from their strict embrace . . . 874
Yet strive I to embrace mine infamy . . . *Lucrece* 504
Swearing I slew him, seeing thee embrace him . . . 518
Embraced. 'Even thus,' quoth she, 'the warlike god embraced me' *Pass. Pil.* 147
Embracements. 'eating his kind embracements with her heels *V. and A.* 312
Your device in ⸱ve, That lends embracements unto every stranger . 790
Embracing. Hot, faint, and weary, with her hard embracing . . 559
The thorny brambles and embracing bushes . . . 629
Girdle with embracing flames the waist Of Collatine's fair love . *Lucrece* 6
Embroidered. A cap of flowers, and a kirtle Embroider'd all with leaves of myrtle . . . *Pass. Pil.* 364
Emerald. The deep-green emerald, in whose fresh regard Weak sights their sickly radiance do amend . . . *Lov. Comp.* 213
Emptied. The broken bosoms that to me belong Have emptied all their fountains in my well . . . 255
Empty. Even as an empty eagle, sharp by fast, Tires with her beak on feathers, flesh, and bone . . . *Ven. and Adon.* 55
Through the empty skies In her light chariot quickly is convey'd . . 1191
Emulation. Seeing such emulation in their woe . . . *Lucrece* 1808
Enacted. A little harm done to a great good end For lawful policy remains enacted . . . 529
Encamped. Effects of terror and dear modesty, Encamp'd in hearts *L. Comp.* 203
Enchained me To endless date of never-ending woes . . . *Lucrece* 934
Enchant. Bid me discourse, I will enchant thine ear . *Ven. and Adon.* 145
Each eye that saw him did enchant the mind . . . *Lov. Comp.* 89
Enchanted Tarquin answers with surmise, In silent wonder . *Lucrece* 83
And sexes both enchanted, To dwell with him in thoughts . *Lov. Comp.* 128
Enchanting. These lovely caves, these round enchanting pits, Open'd their mouths to swallow Venus' liking . . . *Ven. and Adon.* 247
Sinon, whose enchanting story The credulous old Priam after slew *Lucrece* 1521
Enclose. In their pure ranks his traitor eye encloses . . . 73
O, in what sweets dost thou thy sins enclose! . . . *Sonnet* 95 4
The glowing roses That flame through water which their hue encloses *Lov. Comp.* 287
Enclosed. But blind they are, and keep themselves enclosed . . *Lucrece* 378
Grace in all simplicity, Here enclosed in cinders lie . . *Ph. and Tur.* 55
Encompassed. Or one encompass'd with a winding maze . . *Lucrece* 1151
Encounter. Her champion mounted for the hot encounter *Ven. and Adon.* 596
If thou encounter with the boar to-morrow . . . 672
Or at the roe which no encounter dare . . . 676
Encouraging. As 'twere encouraging the Greeks to fight . . *Lucrece* 1402
Encrimsoned. In bloodless white and the encrimson'd mood . *Lov. Comp.* 201
End. And where she ends she doth anew begin . . *Ven. and Adon.* 60
His braided hanging mane Upon his compass'd crest now stand on end . 272
Leave me, and then the story aptly ends: The night is spent . . 716
Their copious stories oftentimes begun End without audience . . 846

End. Find sweet beginning, but unsavoury end *Ven. and Adon.* 1138
The shame and fault finds no excuse nor end *Lucrece* 238
A little harm done to a great good end For lawful policy remains enacted 528
End thy ill aim before thy shoot be ended 579
When wilt thou sort an hour great strifes to end? 899
I live, and seek in vain Some happy mean to end a hapless life 1045
My life's foul deed, my life's fair end shall free it 1208
Thou wast not to this end from me derived 1755
And kiss'd the fatal knife, to end his vow 1843
Beauty's waste hath in the world an end *Sonnet* 9 11
Against this coming end you should prepare 13 3
Thy end is truth's and beauty's doom and date 14 14
All losses are restored and sorrows end 30 14
When what I seek, my weary travel's end, Doth teach that ease 50 2
So do our minutes hasten to their end 60 2
Then need I not to fear the worst of wrongs, When in the least of them my life hath end 92 6
Now all is done, have what shall have no end 110 9
'I hate' she alter'd with an end 145 9
Shall worms, inheritors of this excess, Eat up thy charge? is this thy body's end? 146 8
Augur of the fever's end, To this troop come thou not near! *Ph. and Tur.* 7
Endeared. Thy bosom is endeared with all hearts *Sonnet* 31 1
Ended. His day's hot task hath ended in the west *Ven. and Adon.* 530
End thy ill aim before thy shoot be ended *Lucrece* 579
Philomel had ended The well-tuned warble of her nightly sorrow 1079
Then, lullaby, the learned man hath got the lady gay; For now my song is ended *Pass. Pil.* 226
Ender. Where I myself must render, That is, to you, my origin and ender *Lov. Comp.* 222
Ending. Nature that made thee, with herself at strife, Saith that the world hath ending with thy life *Ven. and Adon.* 12
Begins the sad dirge of her certain ending *Lucrece* 1612
All posterity That wear this world out to the ending doom *Sonnet* 55 12
Endless. Enchained me To endless date of never-ending woes *Lucrece* 935
And peace proclaims olives of endless age *Sonnet* 107 8
Endowed. Look, whom she best endow'd she gave the more 11 11
Endure. And as they last, their verdure still endure *Ven. and Adon.* 507
But still pure Doth in her poison'd closet yet endure *Lucrece* 1659
A dateless lively heat, still to endure, And grew a seething bath *Sonnet* 153 6
Endured. It easeth some, though none it ever cured, To think their dolour others have endured *Lucrece* 1582
The mortal moon hath her eclipse endured *Sonnet* 107 5
Enemy. Finding their enemy to be so curst, They all strain courtesy who shall cope him first *Ven. and Adon.* 887
He sets his foot upon the light, For light and lust are deadly enemies *Lucr.* 674
Her quiet interrupted, Her mansion batter'd by the enemy 1171
Scratch out the angry eyes Of all the Greeks that are thine enemies 1470
Mine enemy was strong, my poor self weak, And far the weaker with so strong a fear 1646
And each, though enemies to either's reign, Do in consent shake hands to torture me *Sonnet* 28 5
My love well knows Her pretty looks have been mine enemies 139 10
Enfeebled. But when your countenance fill'd up his line, Then lack'd I matter; that enfeebled mine 86 14
Enforced. As from this cold flint I enforced this fire, So Lucrece must I force to my desire *Lucrece* 181
The locks between her chamber and his will, Each one by him enforced 303
Enforced hate, Instead of love's coy touch, shall rudely tear thee 668
Her circled eyne, enforced by sympathy Of those fair suns 1229
And therefore art enforced to seek anew Some fresher stamp *Sonnet* 82 7
Enforcement. What wrong else may be imagined By foul enforcement might be done to me *Lucrece* 1623
Enfranchising his mouth, his back, his breast *Ven. and Adon.* 396
Engine. Once more the engine of her thoughts began 367
Engirt. So white a friend engirts so white a foe 364
This siege that hath engirt his marriage, This blur to youth *Lucrece* 221
Grossly engirt with daring infamy 1173
Englishman. Till looking on an Englishman, the fair'st that eye could see Her fancy fell a-turning *Pass. Pil.* 213
Engraft. And all in war with Time for love of you, As he takes from you, I engraft you new *Sonnet* 15 14
Engrafted. I make my love engrafted to this store 37 8
Engraven. So vile, so base, That it will live engraven in my face *Lucrece* 203
Engrossed. My next self thou harder hast engross'd *Sonnet* 133 6
Enjoy. They that love best their loves shall not enjoy *Ven. and Adon.* 1164
'Lucrece,' quoth he, 'this night I must enjoy thee' *Lucrece* 512
Look, what an unthrift in the world doth spend Shifts but his place, for still the world enjoys it *Sonnet* 9 10
With what I most enjoy contented least 29 8
Enjoyed. O happiness enjoy'd but of a few! And, if possess'd, as soon decay'd *Lucrece* 22
Enjoy'd no sooner but despised straight *Sonnet* 129 5
Enjoyer. Now proud as an enjoyer and anon Doubting the filching age will steal his treasure 75 5
Enlarged. Yet this thy praise cannot be so thy praise, To tie up envy evermore enlarged 70 12
Enlighten. And, to enlighten thee, gave eyes to blindness 152 11
Enmity. Repentant tears ensue the deed, Reproach, disdain, and deadly enmity *Lucrece* 503
'Gainst death and all-oblivious enmity Shall you pace forth *Sonnet* 55 9
Enough. Within this limit is relief enough *Ven. and Adon.* 235
'Tis not enough that through the cloud thou break *Sonnet* 34 5
And like enough thou know'st thy estimate 87 2
They had not skill enough your worth to sing 106 12
I assure ye Even that your pity is enough to cure me 111 14
Is't not enough to torture me alone? 133 3
More than enough am I that vex thee still 135 3
Enough, too much, I fear; Lest that my mistress hear my song *Pass. Pil.* 347
Enpatron. For these, of force, must your oblations be, Since I their altar, you enpatron me *Lov. Comp.* 224
Enraged. Being so enraged, desire doth lend her force Courageously to pluck him from his horse *Ven. and Adon.* 29
His love, perceiving how he is enraged, Grew kinder 317
Here, all enraged, such passion her assails, That patience is quite beaten from her breast *Lucrece* 1562
Enrich. Pluck down the rich, enrich the poor with treasures *Ven. and Adon.* 1150
Shall profit thee and much enrich thy book *Sonnet* 77 14
Enriched. With the annexions of fair gems enrich'd *Lov. Comp.* 208
Ensconce. Against that time do I ensconce me here *Sonnet* 49 9

Ensconced. And therein so ensconced his secret evil *Lucrece* 1515
Ensign. Scorning his churlish drum and ensign red *Ven. and Adon.* 107
Ensnare. Do not then ensnare me: Thou look'st not like deceit *Lucrece* 584
Ensnared. Thy beauty hath ensnared thee to this night 485
Ensue. Repentant tears ensue the deed, Reproach, disdain, and deadly enmity 502
And as one shifts, another straight ensues 1104
With circumstances strong Of present death, and shame that might ensue 1263
Ensuing. What canst thou boast Of things long since, or any thing ensuing? *Ven. and Adon.* 1078
Enswathed. Affectedly Enswathed, and seal'd to curious secrecy *Lov. Comp.* 49
Enter. Are better proof than thy spear's point can enter *Ven. and Adon.* 626
And will not let a false sound enter there 780
This dismal cry rings sadly in her ear, Through which it enters to surprise her heart 890
This moves in him more rage and lesser pity, To make the breach and enter this sweet city *Lucrece* 469
Soft pity enters at an iron gate 595
Enterprise. He doth premeditate The dangers of his loathsome enterprise 184
Entertain. In Tarquin's likeness I did entertain thee 596
Yet am I guilty of thy honour's wrack; Yet for thy honour did I entertain him 842
The weary time she cannot entertain, For now 'tis stale to sigh 1361
And softly cried 'Awake, thou Roman dame, And entertain my love' 1629
Thy sour leisure gave sweet leave To entertain the time with thoughts of love *Sonnet* 39 11
Entertained. All entertain'd, each passion labours so *Ven. and Adon.* 969
He entertain'd a show so seeming just *Lucrece* 1514
Entertainment. Witness the entertainment that he gave *Ven. and Adon.* 1108
Entice. As if some mermaid did their ears entice *Lucrece* 1411
If he be addict to vice, Quickly him they will entice *Pass. Pil.* 416
Entitled. Any of these all, or all, or more, Entitled in thy parts do crowned sit *Sonnet* 37 7
Entomb. Her voice controll'd Entombs her outcry in her lips' sweet fold *Lucrece* 679
Your tunes entomb Within your hollow-swelling feather'd breasts 1121
Entombed. Between whose hills her head entombed is 390
When you entombed in men's eyes shall lie *Sonnet* 81 8
Entrance. His heart granteth No penetrable entrance to her plaining *Lucr.* 559
Entreat. Still she entreats, and prettily entreats, For to a pretty ear she tunes her tale *Ven. and Adon.* 73
I have been woo'd, as I entreat thee now, Even by the stern and direful god of war 97
Envious. Each envious brier his weary legs doth scratch 705
Envy. Perchance that envy of so rich a thing, Braving compare, disdainfully did sting *Lucrece* 39
Wrath, envy, treason, rape, and murder's rages 909
Yet this thy praise cannot be so thy praise, To tie up envy evermore enlarged *Sonnet* 70 12
Do I envy those jacks that nimble leap To kiss the tender inward of thy hand! 128 5
Epitaph. Or I shall live your epitaph to make, Or you survive 81 1
Equal. Son and father weep with equal strife Who should weep most *Lucr.* 1791
The store Which should example where your equal grew *Sonnet* 84 4
Yet did I not, as some my equals did, Demand of him, nor being desired yielded *Lov. Comp.* 148
Equally. Ne'er settled equally, but high or low, That all love's pleasure shall not match his woe *Ven. and Adon.* 1139
Equipage. A dearer birth than this his love had brought, To march in ranks of better equipage *Sonnet* 32 12
Ere. His meaning struck her ere his words begun *Ven. and Adon.* 462
Ere he says 'Adieu,' The honey fee of parting tender'd is 537
'Thou hadst been gone,' quoth she, 'sweet boy, ere this' 613
Lust's winter comes ere summer half be done 802
An expired date, cancell'd ere well begun *Lucrece* 26
Shelves and sands, The merchant fears, ere rich at home he lands 336
Thus treason works ere traitors be espied 361
So her accent breaks, That twice she doth begin ere once she speaks 567
Drunken Desire must vomit his receipt, Ere he can see his own abomination 704
Yet ere he go to bed, Knit poisonous clouds about his golden head 776
Ere he arrive his weary noon-tide prick 781
As clear from this attaint of mine As I, ere this, was pure to Collatine 826
Myself was stirring ere the break of day, And, ere I rose, was Tarquin gone away 1280
Ere she with blood had stain'd her stain'd excuse 1316
Ere once she can discharge one word of woe 1605
'But ere I name him, you fair lords,' quoth she, Speaking to those that came with Collatine 1688
Ere thou be distill'd: Make sweet some vial *Sonnet* 6 2
Treasure thou some place With beauty's treasure, ere it be self-kill'd 6 4
Ere beauty's dead fleece made another gay 68 8
Which makes thy love more strong, To love that well which thou must leave ere long 73 14
Ere you were born was beauty's summer dead 104 14
A kind of meetness To be diseased ere that there was true needing 118 8
Ere long espied a fickle maid full pale, Tearing of papers *Lov. Comp.* 5
Consents bewitch'd, ere he desire, have granted 131
Her cloudy looks will calm ere night *Pass. Pil.* 312
And twice desire, ere it be day, That which with scorn she put away 315
Err. To say they err I dare not be so bold, Although I swear it to myself alone *Sonnet* 131 7
Erred. In things right true my heart and eyes have erred 137 13
Error. 'Tis a causeless fantasy, And childish error, that they are afraid *Ven. and Adon.* 898
To eat up errors by opinion bred, Not spend the dowry of a lawful bed *Lucr.* 937
So are those errors that in thee are seen To truths translated *Sonnet* 96 7
If this be error and upon me proved, I never writ, nor no man ever loved 116 13
Book both my wilfulness and errors down 117 9
What wretched errors hath my heart committed! 119 5
I do not love thee with mine eyes, For they in thee a thousand errors note 141 2
All my offences that abroad you see Are errors of the blood *Lov. Comp.* 184
Erst. When lofty trees I see barren of leaves Which erst from heat did canopy the herd *Sonnet* 12 6
Espied. Thus treason works ere traitors be espied *Lucrece* 361
Ere long espied a fickle maid full pale, Tearing of papers *Lov. Comp.* 5
Espoused. That kings might be espoused to more fame *Lucrece* 20
Espy. A breeding jennet, lusty, young, and proud, Adonis' trampling courser doth espy *Ven. and Adon.* 261
Essays. And worse essays proved thee my best of love *Sonnet* 110 8

Essence. So they loved, as love in twain Had the essence but in one *Ph. and Tur.* 26
Estate. For that he colour'd with his high estate *Lucrece* 92
Esteem. Alas, he nought esteems that face of thine *Ven. and Adon.* 631
Sing to the ear that doth thy lays esteem *Sonnet* 100 7
No beauty lack, Slandering creation with a false esteem 127 12
Esteemed. Was esteemed so As silly-jeering idiots are with kings *Lucrece* 1811
As on the finger of a throned queen The basest jewel will be well esteem'd *Sonnet* 96 6
'Tis better to be vile than vile esteem'd 121 1
Esteeming. Whose rich esteeming The owner's tongue doth publish every where 102 3
Estimate. And like enough thou know'st thy estimate 87 2
Eternal. Why hast thou cast into eternal sleeping Those eyes? *V. and A.* 951
Having solicited th' eternal power That his foul thoughts might compass his fair fair *Lucrece* 345
Barren rage of death's eternal cold *Sonnet* 13 12
But thy eternal summer shall not fade 18 9
When in eternal lines to time thou growest 18 12
Let him bring forth Eternal numbers to outlive long date 38 12
Lofty towers I see down-razed And brass eternal slave to mortal rage 64 4
Eternal love in love's fresh case Weighs not the dust and injury of age 108 9
And did thence remove, To spend her living in eternal love *Lov. Comp.* 238
Eternity. Who buys a minute's mirth to wail a week? Or sells eternity to get a toy? *Lucrece* 214
Thou ceaseless lackey to eternity 967
Thou by thy dial's shady stealth mayst know Time's thievish progress to eternity *Sonnet* 77 8
Beyond all date, even to eternity 122 4
Or laid great bases for eternity 125 3
And the turtle's loyal breast To eternity doth rest *Ph. and Tur.* 58
Ethiope. Thou for whom Jove would swear Juno but an Ethiope were *Pass. Pil.* 242
Eve. How like Eve's apple doth thy beauty grow! *Sonnet* 93 13
Even as the sun with purple-colour'd face Had ta'en his last leave of the weeping morn *Ven. and Adon.* 1
The steed is stalled up, and even now To tie the rider she begins to prove 39
Even as an empty eagle, sharp by fast, Tires with her beak on feathers, flesh, and bone 55
Even so she kissed his brow, his cheek, his chin 59
I have been woo'd, as I entreat thee now, Even by the stern and direful god of war 98
From morn till night, even where I list to sport me 154
For men will kiss even by their own direction 216
And begins to glow, Even as a dying coal revives with wind 338
Even as the wind is hush'd before it raineth 458
What hour is this? or morn or weary even? Do I delight to die, or life desire? 495
Even as poor birds, deceived with painted grapes 601
Even so she languisheth in her mishaps 603
Even so confounded in the dark she lay, Having lost the fair discovery of her way 827
Even so the timorous yelping of the hounds Appals her senses 881
Even at this word she hears a merry horn, Whereat she leaps 1025
Even there he starts: quoth he, 'I must deflower' *Lucrece* 348
Even so, the curtain drawn, his eyes begun To wink 374
The colour in thy face, That even for anger makes the lily pale 478
I have debated, even in my soul, What wrong, what shame 498
His vulture folly, A swallowing gulf that even in plenty wanteth 557
Even in this thought through the dark night he stealeth 729
Turn to loathed sours Even in the moment that we call them ours 868
Even so the maid with swelling drops gan wet Her circled eyne 1228
Even so this pattern of the worn-out age Pawn'd honest looks 1350
Even as subtle Sinon here is painted, So sober-sad, so weary, and so mild 1541
Even so his sighs, his sorrows, make a saw, To push grief on 1672
Even here she sheathed in her harmless breast A harmful knife 1723
Cheered and check'd even by the self-same sky *Sonnet* 15 6
When sparkling stars twire not thou gild'st the even 28 12
Even so my sun one early morn did shine 33 9
All men make faults, and even I in this 35 5
Even for this let us divided live, And our dear love lose name of single one 39 5
Even there Where thou art forced to break a twofold truth 41 11
And for my sake even so doth she abuse me 42 7
Who even but now come back again, assured Of thy fair health 45 11
And even thence thou wilt be stol'n, I fear, For truth proves thievish 48 13
Your praise shall still find room Even in the eyes of all posterity 55 11
Although to-day thou fill Thy hungry eyes even till they wink with fullness 56 6
A backward look, Even of five hundred courses of the sun 59 6
Uttering bare truth, even so as foes commend 69 4
But let your love even with my life decay 71 12
Where breath most breathes, even in the mouths of men 81 14
Even such a beauty as you master now 106 8
Thou mine, I thine, Even as when first I hallow'd thy fair name 108 8
Even to thy pure and most most loving breast 110 14
I assure ye Even that your pity is enough to cure me 111 14
Do lie, Even those that said I could not love you dearer 115 2
But bears it out even to the edge of doom 116 12
Even so, being full of your ne'er-cloying sweetness 118 5
Beyond all date, even to eternity 122 4
Nor that full star that ushers in the even 132 7
His passion, but an art of craft, Even there resolved my reason into tears *Lov. Comp.* 296
'Even thus,' quoth she, 'the warlike god embraced me' *Pass. Pil.* 147
'Even thus,' quoth she, 'the warlike god unlaced me' 149
'Even thus,' quoth she, 'he seized on my lips' 151
Even so, poor bird, like thee, None alive will pity me 399
Evening. All our evening sport from us is fled, All our love is lost 291
Event. It shall be cause of war and dire events *Ven. and Adon.* 1159
What uncouth ill event Hath thee befall'n, that thou dost trembling stand? *Lucrece* 1598
Ever. Would they not wish the feast might ever last? *Ven. and Adon.* 447
Like a red morn, that ever yet betoken'd Wreck to the seaman 453
He hath a battle set Of bristly pikes, that ever threat his foes 620
Nor sun nor wind will ever strive to kiss you 1082
Yet ever to obtain his will resolving *Lucrece* 129
If ever man were moved with woman's moans, Be moved with my tears 587
The chastest tears That ever modest eyes with sorrow shed 683
And ever let his unrecalling crime Have time to wail 993
Ever. Vouchsafe t' afford—If ever, love, thy Lucrece thou wilt see—Some present speed to come and visit me *Lucrece* 1306
It easeth some, though none it ever cured, To think their dolour others have endured 1581
And ever since, as pitying Lucrece' woes, Corrupted blood some watery token shows 1747
Despite thy wrong, My love shall in my verse ever live young *Sonnet* 19 14
Against that time, if ever that time come, When I shall see thee frown 49 1
To play the watchman ever for thy sake 61 12
Not be thy defect, For slander's mark was ever yet the fair 70 2
Why write I still all one, ever the same, And keep invention in a noted weed? 76 5
If ever, now; Now, while the world is bent my deeds to cross 90 1
Heaven in thy creation did decree That in thy face sweet love should ever dwell 93 10
My songs and praises be To one, of one, still such, and ever so 105 4
If this be error and upon me proved, I never writ, nor no man ever loved 116 14
This I do vow and this shall ever be; I will be true 123 13
That tongue that ever sweet Was used in giving gentle doom 145 6
Who ever shunn'd by precedent The destined ill she must herself assay? *Lov. Comp.* 155
Knew vows were ever brokers to defiling 173
That's to ye sworn to none was ever said 180
To the smallest teen, Or any of my leisures ever charm'd 193
So beauty blemish'd once's for ever lost *Pass. Pil.* 179
Love, whose month was ever May, Spied a blossom passing fair 228
Ever-during. Whose crime will bear an ever-during blame *Lucrece* 224
Ever-fixed. It is an ever-fixed mark That looks on tempests and is never shaken *Sonnet* 116 5
Everlasting. To Tarquin's everlasting banishment *Lucrece* 1855
Evermore. I may not evermore acknowledge thee *Sonnet* 36 9
Yet this thy praise cannot be so thy praise, To tie up envy evermore enlarged 70 12
Reason is past care, And frantic-mad with evermore unrest 147 10
Every. Who conquers where he comes in every jar *Ven. and Adon.* 100
Dissolves with tempering, And yields at last to every light impression 566
And so to so; For love can comment upon every woe 714
Twenty thousand tongues, And every tongue more moving than your own 776
Your device in love, That lends embracements unto every stranger 790
Like shrill-tongued tapsters answering every call 849
Every present sorrow seemeth chief, But none is best 970
And every beauty robb'd of his effect 1132
Sweet issue of a more sweet-smelling sire—For every little grief to wet his eyes 1179
And every one to rest themselves betake, Save thieves *Lucrece* 125
His course doth let, Till every minute pays the hour his debt 329
Some ghastly sprite, Whose grim aspect sets every joint a-shaking 452
Shall remain The scornful mark of every open eye 520
Thou art, a god, a king; For kings like gods should govern every thing 602
They think not but that every eye can see The same disgrace 750
Thought of his committed evil Shape every bush a hideous shapeless devil 973
Let the thief run mad, Himself himself seek every hour to kill! 998
Gnats are unnoted wheresoe'er they fly, But eagles gazed upon with every eye 1015
Revealing day through every cranny spies 1086
Thus cavils she with every thing she sees 1093
When every part a part of woe doth bear 1327
They whose guilt within their bosoms lie Imagine every eye beholds their blame 1343
Her blue blood changed to black in every vein 1454
For every tear he falls a Trojan bleeds 1551
The crimson blood Circles her body in on every side 1739
The lovely gaze where every eye doth dwell *Sonnet* 5 2
Leaves quite gone, Beauty o'ersnow'd and bareness every where 5 8
Every private widow well may keep By children's eyes her husband's shape in mind 9 7
Every thing that grows Holds in perfection but a little moment 15 1
Every fair from fair sometime declines By chance 18 7
And every fair with his fair doth rehearse 21 4
Though they be outstripp'd by every pen, Reserve them for my love 32 6
Too excellent For every vulgar paper to rehearse 38 4
Mine only care, Art left the prey of every vulgar thief 48 8
The which he will not every hour survey, For blunting the fine point of seldom pleasure 52 3
Since every one hath, every one, one shade, And you, but one, can every shadow lend 53 3
Your bounty doth appear; And you in every blessed shape we know 53 12
All mine every And all my soul and all my every part 62 2
That every word doth almost tell my name 76 7
Every alien pen hath got my use And under thee their poesy disperse 78 3
The dedicated words which writers use Of their fair subject, blessing every book 82 4
Making his style admired every where 84 12
Like unletter'd clerk still cry 'Amen' To every hymn 85 7
Every humour hath his adjunct pleasure, Wherein it finds a joy 91 5
Where beauty's veil doth cover every blot 95 11
What dark days seen! What old December's bareness every where! 97 4
Hath put a spirit of youth in every thing 98 3
And make Time's spoils despised every where 100 12
Whose rich esteeming The owner's tongue doth publish every where 102 4
That wild music burthens every bough 102 11
Creating every bad a perfect best, As fast as objects to his beams assemble 114 7
It is the star to every wandering bark, Whose worth's unknown 116 7
Becoming of their woe, That every tongue says beauty should look so 127 14
And suit thy pity like in every part 132 12
Anon their gazes lend To every place at once, and, nowhere fix'd *L. Comp.* 27
And every light occasion of the wind Upon his lips their silken parcels hurls 86
Would not touch the bait, But smile and jest at every gentle offer *Pass. Pil.* 54
And truth in every shepherd's tongue 370
Every thing did banish moan, Save the nightingale alone 379
Every one that flatters thee Is no friend in misery 403
Every man will be thy friend Whilst thou hast wherewith to spend 407
Thus of every grief in heart He with thee doth bear a part 427
From this session interdict Every fowl of tyrant wing *Ph. and Tur.* 10
Evidence. His scarlet lust came evidence to swear That my poor beauty had purloin'd his eyes *Lucrece* 1650
Evident. Thou art beloved of many, But that thou none lovest is most evident *Sonnet* 10 4
Evil. For unstain'd thoughts do seldom dream on evil *Lucrece* 87
O unlook'd-for evil, When virtue is profaned in such a devil! 846

Evil. And the dire thought of his committed evil Shape every bush a hideous shapeless devil . . . . *Lucrece* 972
No more than wax shall be accounted evil Wherein is stamp'd the semblance of a devil 1245
Cave-keeping evils that obscurely sleep 1250
So ensconced his secret evil, That jealousy itself could not mistrust . 1515
Methinks I have astronomy, But not to tell of good or evil luck *Sonnet* 14 3
Now I find true That better is by evil still made better 119 10
Unless this general evil they maintain, All men are bad . . . 121 13
My female evil Tempteth my better angel from my side . 144 5 ; *Pass. Pil.* 19
Ewes. My ewes breed not, My rams speed not, All is amiss . . . 246
Example. By whose example thou revenged mayst be . . . *Lucrece* 1194
The store Which should example where your equal grew . *Sonnet* 84 4
Or forced examples, 'gainst her own content . . *Lov. Comp.* 157
When thou impressest, what are precepts worth Of stale example? . . 268
Exceed. His art with nature's workmanship at strife, As if the dead the living should exceed . . . . *Ven. and Adon.* 292
Chiefly in love, whose leave exceeds commission 568
Which far exceeds his barren skill to show . . . . *Lucrece* 81
The guilt being great, the fear doth still exceed 229
I found you did exceed The barren tender of a poet's debt . *Sonnet* 83 3
That, in my mind, thy worst all best exceeds 150 8
Exceeded. Exceeded by the height of happier men 32 8
Excel. So did this horse excel a common one In shape, in courage *V. and A.* 293
And that unfair which fairly doth excel . . . . *Sonnet* 5 4
Excelled. Their virtue lost, wherein they late excell'd *Ven. and Adon.* 1131
Excellence. They are the lords and owners of their faces, Others but stewards of their excellence . . . . *Sonnet* 94 8
Still constant in a wondrous excellence 105 6
Excellent. Too excellent For every vulgar paper to rehearse . . 38 3
Bad in the best, though excellent in neither . . . . *Pass. Pil.* 102
Excelleth. Fair torch, burn out thy light, and lend it not To darken her whose light excelleth thine . . . . *Lucrece* 191
Excelling. For from the stillitory of thy face excelling Comes breath perfumed that breedeth love by smelling . . . . *Ven. and Adon.* 443
Except. I desperate now approve Desire is death, which physic did except *Sonnet* 147 8
Excess. Gaining more, the profit of excess Is but to surfeit . . *Lucrece* 138
Shall worms, inheritors of this excess, Eat up thy charge? . *Sonnet* 146 7
Where want cries some, but where excess begs all . . *Lov. Comp.* 42
Exchanged. Just to the time, not with the time exchanged . *Sonnet* 109 7
Exchequer. She hath no exchequer now but his, And, proud of many, lives upon his gains 67 11
Exclaim. In one place, Where fearfully the dogs exclaim aloud *V. and A.* 886
Draws up her breath And sighing it again, exclaims on Death . . . 930
Here she exclaims against repose and rest . . . . *Lucrece* 757
Against the thing he sought he would exclaim . . . *Lov. Comp.* 313
Exclaiming. She stays, exclaiming on the direful night . . . *Lucrece* 741
Exclamation. While Lust is in his pride, no exclamation Can curb his heat 705
Excuse. What bare excuses makest thou to be gone! . *Ven. and Adon.* 188
Let me excuse thy courser, gentle boy ; And learn of him 403
O strange excuse, When reason is the bawd to lust's abuse! 791
He makes excuses for his being there . . . . . . *Lucrece* 114
What excuse can my invention make, When thou shalt charge me with so black a deed? 225
This desire Might have excuse to work upon his wife 235
My dear friend, The shame and fault finds no excuse nor end . . . 238
Why hunt I then for colour or excuses? 267
Nor fold my fault in cleanly-coin'd excuses 1073
Ere she with blood had stain'd her stain'd excuse 1316
Where no excuse can give the fault amending 1614
O, teach me how to make mine own excuse! 1653
No dame, hereafter living, By my excuse shall claim excuse's giving . . 1715
Shall sum my count and make my old excuse . . . . *Sonnet* 2 11
Loving offenders, thus I will excuse ye 42 5
Thus can my love excuse the slow offence Of my dull bearer . . 51 1
O, what excuse will my poor beast then find, When swift extremity can seem but slow? 51 5
But love, for love, thus shall excuse my jade 51 12
Because he needs no praise, wilt thou be dumb? Excuse not silence so 101 10
Let me excuse thee : ah! my love well knows Her pretty looks have been mine enemies 139 9
Excusing. Salving thy amiss, Excusing thy sins more than thy sins are 35 8
Executest. O Opportunity, thy guilt is great! 'Tis thou that executest the traitor's treason . . . . *Lucrece* 877
Executor. Thy unused beauty must be tomb'd with thee, Which, used, lives th' executor to be . . . . *Sonnet* 4 14
Exhale. Then, thou fair sun, that on this earth doth shine, Exhale this vapour vow . . . . *Pass. Pil.* 39
Exhaled. Let their exhaled unwholesome breaths make sick The life of purity, the supreme fair . . . . *Lucrece* 779
Exile. 'T may be, she joy'd to jest at my exile . . . *Pass. Pil.* 189
Exiled. I sue for exiled majesty's repeal ; Let him return . . *Lucrece* 640
Expect. We leave to be The things we are for that which we expect . 149
Expected. 'I am,' quoth he, 'expected of my friends' . *Ven. and Adon.* 718
Expecting. Swell in their pride, the onset still expecting . . *Lucrece* 432
Expel. The dire imagination she did follow This sound of hope doth labour to expel . . . . *Ven. and Adon.* 976
Expense. And moan the expense of many a vanish'd sight . . *Sonnet* 30 8
And husband nature's riches from expense 94 6
The expense of spirit in a waste of shame Is lust in action . . . 129 1
Experience. Experience for me many bulwarks builded . *Lov. Comp.* 152
Expiate. Then look I death my days should expiate . . *Sonnet* 22 4
Expire. As the death-bed whereon it must expire 73 11
Expired. An expired date, cancell'd ere well begun . . . *Lucrece* 26
To work my mind, when body's work's expired . . . *Sonnet* 27 4
Exploits. Obdurate vassals fell exploits effecting, In bloody death *Lucrece* 429
Express. My tongue cannot express my grief for one *Ven. and Adon.* 1069
Her joy with heaved-up hand she doth express . . . . *Lucrece* 111
For more it is than I can well express 1286
What's new to speak, what new to register, That may express my love? *Sonnet* 108 4
And words express The manner of my pity-wanting pain . . . 140 3
Expressed. Whose inward ill no outward harm express'd . . *Lucrece* 91
More than that tongue that more hath more express'd . . *Sonnet* 23 12
I see their antique pen would have express'd Even such a beauty as you master now 106 7
At random from the truth vainly express'd 147 12
Expressing. Therefore my verse to constancy confined, One thing expressing 105 8

Expressly. Their face their manners most expressly told . . *Lucrece* 1397
Extant. That you yourself being extant well might show How far a modern quill doth come too short . . . . *Sonnet* 83 6
Extemporally. And sings extemporally a woeful ditty . *Ven. and Adon.* 836
Extend. Sometimes they do extend Their view right on . . *Lov. Comp.* 25
And supplicant their sighs to you extend 276
Extenuate. Her rash suspect she doth extenuate . . *Ven. and Adon.* 1010
Extern. I bore the canopy, With my extern the outward honouring *Son.* 125 2
External. In all external grace you have some part 53 13
Extincture. Cold modesty, hot wrath, Both fire from hence and chill extincture hath . . . . *Lov. Comp.* 294
Extinguishing his conduct in this case . . . . . . *Lucrece* 313
Extreme. Thy weal and woe are both of them extremes *Ven. and Adon.* 987
Extreme fear can neither fight nor fly . . . . . . *Lucrece* 230
Devise extremes beyond extremity, To make him curse 969
Extremity still urgeth such extremes 1337
Savage, extreme, rude, cruel, not to trust . . . *Sonnet* 129 4
Had, having, and in quest to have, extreme 129 10
Extremity. Devise extremes beyond extremity, To make him curse *Lucrece* 969
Extremity still urgeth such extremes 1337
When swift extremity can seem but slow . . . . . *Sonnet* 51 6
Eye. Pure shame and awed resistance made him fret, Which bred more beauty in his angry eyes . . . . *Ven. and Adon.* 70
Then why not lips on lips, since eyes in eyes? 120
Mine eyes are gray and bright and quick in turning 140
Titan . . . With burning eye did hotly overlook them 178
With a lazy spright, And with a heavy, dark, disliking eye 182
Thine eye darts forth the fire that burneth me 196
Well-painted idol, image dull and dead, Statue contenting but the eye alone 213
Red cheeks and fiery eyes blaze forth her wrong 219
His eye, which scornfully glisters like fire, Shows his hot courage . . 275
And this I do to captivate the eye Of the fair breeder that is standing by 281
Broad breast, full eye, small head, and nostril wide, High crest, short ears 296
For all askance he holds her in his eye 342
Her eyes petitioners to his eyes suing 356
His eyes saw her eyes as they had not seen them ; Her eyes woo'd still, his eyes disdain'd the wooing 357
His acts made plain With tears, which, chorus-like, her eyes did rain . 360
But, when his glutton eye so full hath fed, His other agents aim at like delight 399
Had I no eyes but ears, my ears would love That inward beauty and invisible 433
Though neither eyes nor ears, to hear nor see, Yet should I be in love by touching thee 437
As the bright sun glorifies the sky, So is her face illumined with her eye . 486
Thy eyes' shrewd tutor, that hard heart of thine, Hath taught them scornful tricks 500
And these mine eyes, true leaders to their queen, But for thy piteous lips no more had seen 503
This night I'll waste in sorrow, For my sick heart commands mine eyes to watch 584
Even as poor birds, . . . Do surfeit by the eye and pine the maw . . . 602
His eyes, like glow-worms, shine when he doth fret ; His snout digs sepulchres 621
That face of thine, To which Love's eyes pay tributary gazes . . . 632
Saw'st thou not signs of fear lurk in mine eye? Grew I not faint? . . 644
And more than so, presenteth to mine eye The picture of an angry-chafing boar 661
So glides he in the night from Venus' eye ; Which after him she darts . 816
Signs and prodigies, Whereon with fearful eyes they long have gazed . . 927
Thou hast no eyes to see, But hatefully at random dost thou hit . . . 939
Those eyes that taught all other eyes to see 952
O, how her eyes and tears did lend and borrow! Her eyes seen in the tears, tears in her eye 961
Her tears began to turn their tide, Being prison'd in her eye 980
Trifles, unwitnessed with eye or ear 1023
Her eyes, as murder'd with the view, Like stars ashamed of day, themselves withdrew 1031
Her eyes are fled Into the deep dark cabins of her head 1037
Doth so surprise That from their dark beds once more leap her eyes . . 1050
Her eyes are mad that they have wept till now 1062
And then she reprehends her mangling eye 1065
For oft the eye mistakes, the brain being troubled 1068
Mine eyes are turn'd to fire, my heart to lead : Heavy heart's lead, melt at mine eyes' red fire! 1072
Urchin-snouted boar, Whose downward eye still looketh for a grave . . 1106
She lifts the coffer-lids that close his eyes 1127
Sweet issue of a more sweet-smelling sire—For every little grief to wet his eyes 1179
Beauty itself doth of itself persuade The eyes of men without an orator *Lucrece* 30
In their pure ranks his traitor eye encloses 73
Answers with surmise, In silent wonder of still-gazing eyes 84
That nothing in him seem'd inordinate, Save sometime too much wonder of his eye 95
But she, that never coped with stranger eyes, Could pick no meaning from their parling looks 99
Nor could she moralize his wanton sight, More than his eyes were open'd to the light 105
The dead of night, When heavy sleep had closed up mortal eyes . . . 163
Which must be lode-star to his lustful eye 179
My frail joints shake, Mine eyes forego their light, my false heart bleed 228
She took me kindly by the hand, And gazed for tidings in my eager eyes . 254
My heart shall never countermand mine eye 276
That eye which looks on her confounds his wits 290
That eye which him beholds, as more divine, Unto a view so false will not incline 291
The eye of heaven is out, and misty night Covers the shame that follows sweet delight 356
Even so, the curtain drawn, his eyes begun To wink 374
She lies, To be admired of lewd unhallow'd eyes 392
Her eyes, like marigolds, had sheathed their light 397
On that he firmly doted, And in his will his wilful eye he tired . . . 417
His eye, which late this mutiny restrains, Unto a greater uproar tempts his veins 426
His drumming heart cheers up his burning eye, His eye commends the leading to his hand 435
She, much amazed, breaks ope her lock'd-up eyes 446
There appears Quick-shifting antics, ugly in her eyes 459
Who, angry that the eyes fly from their lights, In darkness daunts them with more dreadful sights 461
The fault is thine, For those thine eyes betray thee unto mine . . . 483
Only he hath an eye to gaze on beauty, And dotes on what he looks . . 496
Shall remain The scornful mark of every open eye 520
With a cockatrice' dead-killing eye He rouseth up himself 540

Eye. Her pity-pleading eyes are sadly fixed In the remorseless wrinkles of his face *Lucrece* 561
Princes are the glass, the school, the book, Where subjects' eyes do learn 616
Wrapp'd in with infamies That from their own misdeeds askance their eyes 637
The chastest tears That ever modest eyes with sorrow shed 683
Discolour'd cheek, With heavy eye, knit brow, and strengthless pace 709
My true eyes have never practised how To cloak offences 748
They think not but that every eye can see the same disgrace 750
And bids her eyes hereafter still be blind 758
Tarquin's eye may read the mot afar, How he in peace is wounded 830
Scarce hath eyes his treasure to behold, But like still-pining Tantalus he sits 857
Let ghastly shadows his lewd eyes affright 971
Gnats are unnoted wheresoe'er they fly, But eagles gazed upon with every eye 1015
Mine eyes, like sluices, As from a mountain-spring that feeds a dale 1076
The blushing morrow Lends light to all fair eyes that light will borrow 1083
O eye of eyes, Why pry'st thou through my window? leave thy peeping 1088
Leave thy peeping: Mock with thy tickling beams eyes that are sleeping 1090
Against my heart Will fix a sharp knife to affright mine eye 1138
Poor bird, thou sing'st not in the day, As shaming any eye should thee behold 1143
And wiped the brinish pearl from her bright eyes 1213
The sun being set, Each flower moisten'd like a melting eye 1227
And then they drown their eyes or break their hearts 1239
The eye interprets to the ear The heavy motion that it doth behold 1325
With a steadfast eye Receives the scroll without or yea or no 1339
They whose guilt within their bosoms lie Imagine every eye beholds their blame 1343
Her earnest eye did make him more amazed 1356
And dying eyes gleam'd forth their ashy lights, Like dying coals 1378
There would appear The very eyes of men through loop-holes thrust 1383
That one might see those far-off eyes look sad 1386
In Ajax' eyes blunt rage and rigour roll'd 1398
Himself, behind, Was left unseen, save to the eye of mind 1426
Staring on Priam's wounds with her old eyes 1448
On this sad shadow Lucrece spends her eyes 1457
With my knife scratch out the angry eyes Of all the Greeks 1469
Thy eye kindled the fire that burneth here 1475
For trespass of thine eye, The sire, the son, the dame, and daughter die 1476
She throws her eyes about the painting round 1499
And give the harmless show An humble gait, calm looks, eyes wailing still 1508
Priam wets his eyes, To see those borrow'd tears that Sinon sheds 1548
His eye drops fire, no water thence proceeds 1552
Round about her tear-distained eye Blue circles stream'd 1586
Her eyes, though sod in tears, look'd red and raw 1592
To swear That my poor beauty had purloin'd his eyes 1651
With sad set eyes, and wretched arms across 1662
The violent roaring tide Outruns the eye that doth behold his haste 1668
Let it then suffice To drown one woe, one pair of weeping eyes 1680
To check the tears in Collatinus' eyes 1817
But thou, contracted to thine own bright eyes *Sonnet* 1 5
To say, within thine own deep-sunken eyes, Were an all-eating shame 2 7
The lovely gaze where every eye doth dwell 5 2
Each under eye Doth homage to his new-appearing sight 7 2
The eyes, 'fore duteous, now converted are From his low tract 7 11
Is it for fear to wet a widow's eye That thou consumest thyself in single life! 9 1
Every private widow well may keep By children's eyes her husband's shape in mind 9 8
From thine eyes my knowledge I derive, And, constant stars, in them I read such art As truth and beauty shall together thrive 14 9
Time's pencil, or my pupil pen, Neither in inward worth nor outward fair, Can make you live yourself in eyes of men 16 12
If I could write the beauty of your eyes And in fresh numbers number all your graces 17 5
Sometime too hot the eye of heaven shines 18 5
So long as men can breathe or eyes can see, So long lives this 18 13
An eye more bright than theirs, less false in rolling 20 5
Which steals men's eyes and women's souls amazeth 20 8
To hear with eyes belongs to love's fine wit 23 14
Mine eye hath play'd the painter and hath stell'd Thy beauty's form 24 1
That hath his windows glazed with thine eyes 24 8
Now see what good turns eyes for eyes have done 24 9
Mine eyes have drawn thy shape, and thine for me Are windows to my breast 24 10
Yet eyes this cunning want to grace their art; They draw but what they see, know not the heart 24 13
Their fair leaves spread But as the marigold at the sun's eye 25 6
In disgrace with fortune and men's eyes, I all alone beweep 29 1
Then can I drown an eye, unused to flow, For precious friends 30 5
How many a holy and obsequious tear Hath dear religious love stol'n from mine eye As interest of the dead 31 6
Full many a glorious morning have I seen Flatter the mountain-tops with sovereign eye 33 2
Then do mine eyes best see, For all the day they view things unrespected 43 1
How would thy shadow's form form happy show To the clear day with thy much clearer light, When to unseeing eyes thy shade shines so! 43 8
How would, I say, mine eyes be blessed made By looking on thee in the living day! 43 9
Thy fair imperfect shade Through heavy sleep on sightless eyes doth stay 43 12
Mine eye and heart are at a mortal war How to divide the conquest of thy sight 46 1
Mine eye my heart thy picture's sight would bar, My heart mine eye the freedom of that right 46 3
A closet never pierced with crystal eyes 46 6
By their verdict is determined The clear eye's moiety 46 12
Mine eye's due is thy outward part, And my heart's right thy inward love 46 13
Betwixt mine eye and heart a league is took, And each doth good turns 47 1
When that mine eye is famish'd for a look, Or heart in love 47 3
With my love's picture then my eye doth feast 47 5
Another time mine eye is my heart's guest 47 7
Thy picture in my sight Awakes my heart to heart's and eye's delight 47 14

Eye. Thou shalt strangely pass And scarcely greet me with that sun, thine eye *Sonnet* 49 6
Your praise shall still find room Even in the eyes of all posterity 55 11
You live in this, and dwell in lovers' eyes 55 14
Although to-day thou fill Thy hungry eyes even till they wink with fullness 56 6
It is my love that keeps mine eye awake 61 10
Sin of self-love possesseth all mine eye And all my soul 62 1
Those parts of thee that the world's eye doth view Want nothing that the thought of hearts can mend 69 1
By seeing farther than the eye hath shown 69 8
Their thoughts, although their eyes were kind, To thy fair flower add the rank smell of weeds 69 11
Thine eyes that taught the dumb on high to sing 78 5
When you entombed in men's eyes shall lie 81 8
My gentle verse, Which eyes not yet created shall o'er-read 81 10
There lives more life in one of your fair eyes Than both your poets can in praise devise 83 13
To set me light And place my merit in the eye of scorn 88 2
For there can live no hatred in thine eye 93 5
And all things turn to fair that eyes can see 95 12
For as you were when first your eye I eyed, Such seems your beauty still 104 2
Mine eye may be deceived: For fear of which, hear this 104 12
Sweet beauty's best, Of hand, of foot, of lip, of eye, of brow 106 6
For they look'd but with divining eyes, They had not skill enough your worth to sing 106 11
We, which now behold these present days, Have eyes to wonder 106 14
Since I left you, mine eye is in my mind 113 1
My most true mind thus makes mine eye untrue 113 14
Shall I say, mine eye saith true, And that your love taught it this alchemy? 114 3
Mine eye well knows what with his gust is 'greeing 114 11
'Tis the lesser sin That mine eye loves it and doth first begin 114 14
How have mine eyes out of their spheres been fitted! 119 7
For why should others' false adulterate eyes Give salutation? 121 5
My mistress' brows are raven black, Her eyes so suited 127 10
My mistress' eyes are nothing like the sun 130 1
Thine eyes I love, and they, as pitying me, Knowing thy heart torments me with disdain 132 1
As those two mourning eyes become thy face 132 9
Me from myself thy cruel eye hath taken 133 5
Love, what dost thou to mine eyes, That they behold, and see not what they see? 137 1
If eyes corrupt by over-partial looks Be anchor'd in the bay 137 5
Why of eyes' falsehood hast thou forged hooks, Whereto the judgement of my heart is tied? 137 7
Mine eyes seeing this, say this is not, To put fair truth upon so foul a face 137 11
In things right true my heart and eyes have erred 137 13
Wound me not with thine eye but with thy tongue 139 3
In my sight, Dear heart, forbear to glance thine eye aside 139 6
Bear thine eyes straight, though thy proud heart go wide 140 14
In faith, I do not love thee with mine eyes 141 1
As thou lovest those Whom thine eyes woo as mine importune thee 142 10
O me, what eyes hath Love put in my head! 148 1
If that be fair whereon my false eyes dote, What means the world to say it is not so? 148 5
Then love doth well denote Love's eye is not so true as all men's 'No' 148 8
How can Love's eye be true, That is so vex'd with watching? 148 9
Thou keep'st me blind, Lest eyes well-seeing thy foul faults should find 148 14
Commanded by the motion of thine eyes 149 12
Gave eyes to blindness, Or made them swear against the thing they see 152 11
But at my mistress' eye Love's brand new-fired, The boy for trial needs would touch my breast 153 9
The bath for my help lies Where Cupid got new fire—my mistress' eyes 153 14
Sometimes her levell'd eyes their carriage ride *Lov. Comp.* 22
These often bathed she in her fluxive eyes, And often kiss'd 50
So commended, That maidens' eyes stuck over all his face 81
Each eye that saw him did enchant the mind 89
Many there were that did his picture get, To serve their eyes 135
Among the many that mine eyes have seen 190
The accident which brought me to her eye Upon the moment did her force subdue 247
Religious love put out Religion's eye 250
Dieted in grace, Believed her eyes when they to assail begun 262
This said, his watery eyes he did dismount 281
But with the inundation of the eyes What rocky heart to water will not wear? 290
O, that infected moisture of his eye! 323
Did not the heavenly rhetoric of thine eye, . . . Persuade my heart to this false perjury? *Pass. Pil.* 29
She show'd him favours to allure his eye 48
Study his bias leaves, and makes his book thine eyes 61
Thine eye Jove's lightning seems, thy voice his dreadful thunder 67
The sun look'd on the world with glorious eye 81
Lord, how mine eyes throw gazes to the east! My heart doth charge the watch 193
Not daring trust the office of mine eyes 196
Heart hath his hope, and eyes their wished sight 202
When as thine eye hath chose the dame 299

Eye-ball. Look in mine eye-balls, there thy beauty lies *Ven. and Adon.* 119
About he walks, Rolling his greedy eyeballs in his head *Lucrece* 368

Eyed. For as you were when first your eye I eyed, Such seems your beauty still *Sonnet* 104 2

Eyelid. As one full of despair, She vail'd her eyelids *Ven. and Adon.* 956
And keep my drooping eyelids open wide *Sonnet* 27 7
Is it thy will thy image should keep open My heavy eyelids? 61 2

Eyne. Nor thy soft hands, sweet lips, and crystal eyne *Ven. and Adon.* 633
Wipe the dim mist from thy doting eyne *Lucrece* 643
Her circled eyne, enforced by sympathy Of those fair suns 1229
Oft did she heave her napkin to her eyne *Lov. Comp.* 15

Eye-sore. The scandal will survive, And be an eye-sore in my golden coat *Lucrece* 205

F

Face. Even as the sun with purple-colour'd face Had ta'en his last leave of the weeping morn *Ven. and Adon.* 1
Panting he lies and breatheth in her face 62
Is thine own heart to thine own face affected? 157
No more of love! The sun doth burn my face; I must remove 186
For from the stillitory of thy face excelling Comes breath perfumed 443
So is her face illumined with her eye; Whose beams upon his hairless face are fix'd 486
Incorporate then they seem; face grows to face 540
Her face doth reek and smoke, her blood doth boil 555
Alas, he nought esteems that face of thine 631
Didst thou not mark my face? was it not white? Saw'st thou not signs of fear? 643
Now I will away; My face is full of shame, my heart of teen 808
Some kiss her face, Some twine about her thigh to make her stay 872
To wash the foul face of the sluttish ground 983
His face seems twain, each several limb is doubled 1067
What face remains alive that's worth the viewing? Whose tongue is music now? 1076
To see his face the lion walk'd along Behind some hedge 1093
If he did see his face, why then I know He thought to kiss him 1109
And stains her face with his congealed blood 1122
Within whose face beauty and virtue strived *Lucrece* 52
This heraldry in Lucrece' face was seen, Argued by beauty's red and virtue's white 64
Their silent war of lilies and of roses, Which Tarquin view'd in her fair face's field, In their pure ranks his traitor eye encloses 72
So vile, so base, That it will live engraven in my face 203
The wind wars with his torch to make him stay, And blows the smoke of it into his face 312
The colour in thy face, That even for anger makes the lily pale 477
Her pity-pleading eyes are sadly fixed In the remorseless wrinkles of his face 562
Cooling his hot face in the chastest tears That ever modest eyes with sorrow shed 682
Let not the jealous Day behold that face 800
Reproach is stamp'd in Collatinus' face 829
For why her face wore sorrow's livery 1222
Poor women's faces are their own faults' books 1253
Two red fires in both their faces blazed 1353
Grace and majesty You might behold, triumphing in their faces 1388
The face of either cipher'd either's heart; Their face their manners most expressly told 1396
A press of gaping faces, Which seem'd to swallow up his sound advice 1408
A hand, a foot, a face, a leg, a head, Stood for the whole to be imagined 1427
Come, To find a face where all distress is stell'd 1444
His face, though full of cares, yet show'd content 1503
When their glass fell wherein they view'd their faces 1526
Such signs of truth in his plain face she spied 1532
It cannot be, I find, But such a face should bear a wicked mind 1540
Which when her sad-beholding husband saw, Amazedly in her sad face he stares 1591
The face, that map which deep impression bears Of hard misfortune 1712
About the mourning and congealed face Of that black blood a watery rigol goes 1744
He falls, and bathes the pale fear in his face 1775
Look in thy glass, and tell the face thou viewest Now is the time that face should form another *Sonnet* 3 1
Such heavenly touches ne'er touch'd earthly faces 17 8
A woman's face with Nature's own hand painted Hast thou 20 1
Makes black night beauteous and her old face new 27 12
Kissing with golden face the meadows green 33 3
Anon permit the basest clouds to ride With ugly rack on his celestial face 33 6
To dry the rain on my storm-beaten face 34 6
Methinks no face so gracious is as mine, No shape so true 62 5
So love's face May still seem love to me, though alter'd new 93 2
Heaven in thy creation did decree That in thy face sweet love should ever dwell 93 10
They are the lords and owners of their faces 94 7
My love's sweet face survey, If Time have any wrinkle graven there 100 9
Look in your glass, and there appears a face 103 6
Fairing the foul with art's false borrow'd face 127 6
Thy face hath not the power to make love groan 131 6
A thousand groans, but thinking on thy face, One on another's neck, do witness bear 131 10
Say this is not, To put fair truth upon so foul a face 137 12
And therefore from my face she turns my foes 139 11
Whose busy care is bent To follow that which flies before her face 143 7
So commended, That maidens' eyes stuck over all his face *Lov. Comp.* 81
Whose sights till then were levell'd on my face 282

Fact. Shameful it is; ay, if the fact be known *Lucrece* 239
I must deflower: The powers to whom I pray abhor this fact 349

Faculty. So long as brain and heart Have faculty by nature to subsist *Sonnet* 122 6

Fade. But thy eternal summer shall not fade 18 9
They live unwoo'd and unrespected fade, Die to themselves 54 10
When that shall fade, my verse distills your truth 54 14

Fadeth. The twilight of such day As after sunset fadeth in the west 73 6

Fading. To the wide world and all her fading sweets 19 7
Why so large cost, having so short a lease, Dost thou upon thy fading mansion spend? 146 6

Fain. And now she weeps, and now she fain would speak *Ven. and Adon.* 221

Faint. Who is so faint, that dare not be so bold To touch the fire, the weather being cold? 401
He with her plenty press'd, she faint with dearth 545
Hot, faint, and weary, with her hard embracing 559
Affection faints not like a pale-faced coward 569
Saw'st thou not signs of fear lurk in mine eye? Grew I not faint? 645
The thought of it doth make my faint heart bleed, And fear doth teach it divination 669
Agues pale and faint, Life-poisoning pestilence and frenzies wood 739
Faint not, faint heart, but stoutly say 'So be it' *Lucrece* 1209
Here manly Hector faints, here Troilus swounds 1486
O, how I faint when I of you do write! *Sonnet* 80 1

Fainted. As if with grief or travail he had fainted, To me came Tarquin armed *Lucrece* 1543

Faintly. Her two blue windows faintly she up-heaveth, Like the fair sun, when in his fresh array He cheers the morn *Ven. and Adon.* 482
He faintly flies, sweating with guilty fear *Lucrece* 740

Fair. And by her fair immortal hand she swears, From his soft bosom never to remove *Ven. and Adon.* 80
Touch but my lips with those fair lips of thine,—Though mine be not so fair, yet are they red 115
Fair flowers that are not gather'd in their prime Rot and consume themselves in little time 131
His louring brows o'erwhelming his fair sight Like misty vapours 183
Speak, fair; but speak fair words, or else be mute: Give me one kiss 208
And this I do to captivate the eye Of the fair breeder that is standing by 282
With one fair hand she heaveth up his hat, Her other tender hand his fair cheek feels 351
But when he saw his love, his youth's fair fee, He held such petty bondage in disdain 393
Fair fall the wit that can so well defend her! 472
Like the fair sun, when in his fresh array He cheers the morn and all the earth relieveth 483
'Fair queen,' quoth he, 'if any love you owe me, Measure my strangeness with my unripe years 523
Swear Nature's death for framing thee so fair 744
Sith in thy pride so fair a hope is slain 762
With this, he breaketh from the sweet embrace, Of those fair arms 812
In the dark she lay, Having lost the fair discovery of her way 828
Venus salutes him with this fair good-morrow: 'O thou clear god' 859
The crystal tide that from her two cheeks fair In the sweet channel of her bosom dropt 957
And in her haste unfortunately spies The foul boar's conquest on her fair delight 1030
Having no fair to lose, you need not fear; The sun doth scorn you 1083
Sun and sharp air Lurk'd like two thieves, to rob him of his fair 1086
The waist Of Collatine's fair love, Lucrece the chaste *Lucrece* 7
But beauty, in that white intituled, From Venus' doves doth challenge that fair field 58
Their silent war of lilies and of roses, Which Tarquin view'd in her fair face's field, In their pure ranks his traitor eye encloses 72
No cloudy show of stormy blustering weather Doth yet in his fair welkin once appear 116
Fair torch, burn out thy light, and lend it not 190
Let fair humanity abhor the deed 195
That his foul thoughts might compass his fair fair 346
As the fair and fiery-pointed sun, Rushing from forth a cloud, bereaves our sight 372
Without the bed her other fair hand was, On the green coverlet 393
Went about From this fair throne to heave the owner out 413
And makest fair reputation but a bawd 623
Thou their fair life, and they thy fouler grave 661
Besides, his soul's fair temple is defaced 719
The life of purity, the supreme fair 780
Or toads infect fair founts with venom mud 850
The blushing morrow Lends light to all fair eyes that light will borrow 1083
My life's foul deed, my life's fair end shall free it 1208
Nor why her fair cheeks over-wash'd with woe 1225
Enforced by sympathy Of those fair suns set in her mistress' sky 1230
By this, mild patience bid fair Lucrece speak 1268
So fair a form lodged not a mind so ill 1530
Sweet love, what spite hath thy fair colour spent? 1600
'You fair lords,' quoth she, Speaking to those that came with Collatine 1688
'Tis a meritorious fair design To chase injustice with revengeful arms 1692
He, he, fair lords, 'tis he, That guides this hand to give this wound 1721
That fair fresh mirror, dim and old, Shows me a bare-boned death 1760
For his foul act by whom thy fair wife bleeds 1824
By our strong arms from forth her fair streets chased 1834
By heaven's fair sun that breeds the fat earth's store 1837
This fair child of mine Shall sum my count *Sonnet* 2 10
For where is she so fair whose unear'd womb Disdains the tillage of thy husbandry? 3 5
Thou art much too fair To be death's conquest and make worms thine heir 6 13
Who lets so fair a house fall to decay? 13 9
Neither in inward worth nor outward fair 16 11
Every fair from fair sometime declines, By chance 18 7
Thy eternal summer shall not fade Nor lose possession of that fair thou owest 18 10
O, carve not with thy hours my love's fair brow 19 9
And every fair with his fair doth rehearse 21 4
Then believe me, my love is as fair As any mother's child 21 10
Great princes' favourites their fair leaves spread 25 5
Whatsoever star that guides my moving Points on me graciously with fair aspect 26 10
Thy fair imperfect shade Through heavy sleep on sightless eyes doth stay 43 11
Who even but now come back again, assured Of thy fair health 45 12
The defendant doth that plea deny And says in him thy fair appearance lies 46 8
The rose looks fair, but fairer we it deem For that sweet odour 54 3
Before these bastard signs of fair were born 68 3
To thy fair flower add the rank smell of weeds 69 12
For slander's mark was ever yet the fair 70 2
And found such fair assistance in my verse 78 2
The dedicated words which writers use Of their fair subject 82 4
Thou art as fair in knowledge as in hue 82 5
Thou truly fair wert truly sympathized In true plain words 82 11
I never saw that you did painting need And therefore to your fair no painting set 83 2
There lives more life in one of your fair eyes 83 13
The cause of this fair gift in me is wanting 87 7
And all things turn to fair that eyes can see 95 12
To me, fair friend, you never can be old 104 1
'Fair, kind, and true' is all my argument, 'Fair, kind, and true' 105 9

Fair. 'Fair, kind, and true,' have often lived alone *Sonnet* 105 13
Thou mine, I thine, Even as when first I hallow'd thy fair name 108 8
In the old age black was not counted fair 127 1
At such who, not born fair, no beauty lack 127 11
And in my will no fair acceptance shine 135 8
Let no unkind, no fair beseechers kill 135 13
Say this is not, To put fair truth upon so foul a face 137 12
The better angel is a man right fair 144 3
I have sworn thee fair and thought thee bright, Who art as black as hell 147 13
If that be fair whereon my false eyes dote, What means the world to say it is not so? 148 5
For I have sworn thee fair; more perjured I 152 13
And when in his fair parts she did abide, She was new lodged *Lov. Comp.* 83
I have received from many a several fair, Their kind acceptance 206
With the annexions of fair gems enrich'd 208
Showing fair nature is both kind and tame 311
My better angel is a man right fair, My worser spirit a woman colour'd ill *Pass. Pil.* 17
Wooing his purity with her fair pride 22
Then, thou fair sun, that on this earth doth shine, Exhale this vapour vow 38
Then fell she on her back, fair queen, and toward: He rose and ran away 55
Fair is my love, but not so fair as fickle; Mild as a dove 85
Fair was the morn when the fair queen of love 117
'Once,' quoth she, 'did I see a fair sweet youth Here in these brakes'. 125
Sweet rose, fair flower, untimely pluck'd, soon vaded, Pluck'd in the bud 131
Fair creature, kill'd too soon by death's sharp sting! 134
Spied a blossom passing fair, Playing in the wanton air. 229
To this urn let those repair That are either true or fair *Ph. and Tur.* 66
Fairer. Shall hate be fairer lodged than gentle love? *Sonnet* 10 10
The rose looks fair, but fairer we it deem For that sweet odour 54 3
And ruin'd love, when it is built anew, Grows fairer than at first 119 12
All aids, themselves made fairer by their place, Came for additions *L. Comp.* 117
None fairer, nor none falser to deface her *Pass. Pil.* 90
Fairest. O fairest mover on this mortal round *Ven. and Adon.* 368
From fairest creatures we desire increase *Sonnet* 1 1
When in the chronicle of wasted time I see descriptions of the fairest wights 106 2
To my dear doting heart Thou art the fairest and most precious jewel 131 4
Do witness bear Thy black is fairest in my judgement's place 131 12
The fairest votary took up that fire Which many legions of true hearts had warm'd 154 5
It was a lording's daughter, the fairest one of three *Pass. Pil.* 211
Till looking on an Englishman, the fair'st that eye could see 213
Fairing. Fairing the foul with art's false borrow'd face *Sonnet* 127 6
Fairly. And that unfair which fairly doth excel 5 4
Fairy. Or, like a fairy, trip upon the green *Ven. and Adon.* 146
Faith. Plight your honourable faiths to me, With swift pursuit to venge this wrong *Lucrece* 1690
Purest faith unhappily forsworn, And gilded honour shamefully misplaced *Sonnet* 66 4
Yet, in good faith, some say that thee behold Thy face hath not the power to make love groan 131 5
In faith, I do not love thee with mine eyes 141 1
In act thy bed-vow broke and new faith torn 152 3
And all my honest faith in thee is lost 152 8
O never faith could hold, if not to beauty vow'd *Pass. Pil.* 58
Her faith, her oaths, her tears, and all were jestings 96
Love's denying, Faith's defying, Heart's renying, Causer of this 250
Where her faith was firmly fix'd in love, There a nay is placed 255
Had women been so strong as men, In faith, you had not had it then 322
Faithful. Words are easy, like the wind; Faithful friends are hard to find 406
These are certain signs to know Faithful friend from flattering foe 430
Falchion. His falchion on a flint he softly smiteth, That from the cold stone sparks of fire do fly *Lucrece* 176
So under his insulting falchion lies Harmless Lucretia 509
I fear'd by Tarquin's falchion to be slain 1046
With shining falchion in my chamber came A creeping creature 1626
Falcon. As falcon to the lure, away she flies *Ven. and Adon.* 1027
Which, like a falcon towering in the skies, Coucheth the fowl below *Lucrece* 506
Marking what he tells With trembling fear, as fowl hear falcon's bells. 511
Fall. Fair fall the wit that can so well defend her! *Ven. and Adon.* 472
The mellow plum doth fall, the green sticks fast 527
She faint with dearth, Their lips together glued, fall to the earth 546
Still hanging by his neck, He on her belly falls, she on her back 594
And now 'tis dark, and going I shall fall 719
But if thou fall, O, then imagine this 721
You will fall again Into your idle over-handled theme 769
Yet sometimes falls an orient drop beside, Which her cheek melts 981
May feel her heart . . . rise up and fall, Beating her bulk, that his hand shakes withal *Lucrece* 466
Hindering their present fall by this dividing 551
Their fresh falls' haste Add to his flow, but alter not his taste 650
There falls into thy boundless flood Black lust, dishonour, shame 653
Shall thereon fall and die 1139
For one's offence why should so many fall? 1483
For every tear he falls a Trojan bleeds 1551
He falls, and bathes the pale fear in his face 1775
Who lets so fair a house fall to decay? *Sonnet* 13 9
Nor falls Under the blow of thralled discontent 124 6
To stand in thy affairs, fall by thy side 151 12
I call Her 'love' for whose dear love I rise and fall 151 14
Or monarch's hands that let not bounty fall *Lov. Comp.* 41
And falls, through wind, before the fall should be *Pass. Pil.* 136
By shallow rivers, by whose falls Melodious birds sing madrigals 359
Falleth. And at his look she flatly falleth down *Ven. and Adon.* 463
With this, she falleth in the place she stood 1121
Falling. He vails his tail that, like a falling plume, Cool shadow to his melting buttock lent 314
False. Gives false alarms, suggesteth mutiny 651
That sometime true news, sometime false doth bring 658
My heart stands armed in mine ear, And will not let a false sound enter there 780
Thy mark is feeble age, but thy false dart Mistakes that aim 941
Thy coward heart with false bethinking grieves 1024
It shall be fickle, false, and full of fraud 1141
Borne by the trustless wings of false desire *Lucrece* 2
O rash false heat, wrapp'd in repentant cold! 48
When at Collatium this false lord arrived, Well was he welcomed 50
Would let him go, Rather than triumph in so false a foe 77
Little suspecteth the false worshipper 86
My frail joints shake, Mine eyes forego their light, my false heart bleed 228
False. That eye which him beholds, as more divine, Unto a view so false will not incline *Lucrece* 292
His true respect will prison false desire 642
Thou ravisher, thou traitor, thou false thief, Thy honey turns to gall 888
Carrier of grisly care, Eater of youth, false slave to false delight 927
I will not paint, To hide the truth of this false night's abuses 1075
And for my sake serve thou false Tarquin so 1197
No guilty instance gave, Nor ashy pale the fear that false hearts have 1512
So Priam's trust false Sinon's tears doth flatter 1560
Some of her blood still pure and red remain'd, And some look'd black, and that false Tarquin stain'd 1743
But not acquainted With shifting change, as is false women's fashion *Son.* 20 4
An eye more bright than theirs, less false in rolling 20 5
Hers, by thy beauty tempting her to thee, Thine, by thy beauty being false to me 41 14
Why should false painting imitate his cheek? 67 5
And him as for a map doth Nature store, To show false Art 68 14
Lest your true love may seem false in this 72 9
Thou mayst be false, and yet I know it not 92 14
In many's looks the false heart's history Is writ 93 7
O, never say that I was false of heart 109 1
For why should others' false adulterate eyes Give salutation? 121 5
Fairing the foul with art's false borrow'd face 127 6
No beauty lack, Slandering creation with a false esteem 127 12
I think my love as rare As any she belied with false compare 130 14
And, to be sure that is not false I swear 131 9
And to this false plague are they now transferr'd 137 14
Some untutor'd youth, Unlearned in the world's false subtleties 138 4
And seal'd false bonds of love as oft as mine 142 7
If that be fair whereon my false eyes dote, What means the world to say it is not so? 148 5
Cried 'O false blood, thou register of lies!' *Lov. Comp.* 52
The foil Of this false jewel, and his amorous spoil 154
O, that false fire which in his cheek so glow'd! 324
Untutor'd youth, Unskilful in the world's false forgeries *Pass. Pil.* 4
Did not the heavenly rhetoric of thine eye, 'Gainst whom the world could not hold argument, Persuade my heart to this false perjury? 31
False-creeping. Jealousy itself could not mistrust False-creeping craft *Lucr.* 1517
Falsehood. To unmask falsehood and bring truth to light 940
Unused stay From hands of falsehood, in sure wards of trust *Sonnet* 48 4
Why of eyes' falsehood hast thou forged hooks? 137 7
Falsely. Where is my judgement fled, That censures falsely what they see aright? 148 4
Falseness. His rudeness so with his authorized youth Did livery falseness in a pride of truth *Lov. Comp.* 105
Falser. None fairer, nor none falser to deface her *Pass. Pil.* 90
False-speaking. Simply I credit her false-speaking tongue *Sonnet* 138 7
I smiling credit her false-speaking tongue *Pass. Pil.* 7
Faltering. Leave the faltering feeble souls alive *Lucrece* 1768
Fame. That kings might be espoused to more fame 20
Beauty and virtue strived Which of them both should underprop her fame 53
He stories to her ears her husband's fame, Won in the fields of fruitful Italy 106
To clear this spot by death, at least I give A badge of fame to slander's livery 1054
So of shame's ashes shall my fame be bred 1188
My shame be his that did my fame confound 1202
And all my fame that lives disbursed be To those that live 1203
Had doting Priam check'd his son's desire, Troy had been bright with fame and not with fire 1491
This act will be My fame and thy perpetual infamy 1638
To make me tongue-tied, speaking of your fame *Sonnet* 80 4
And such a counterpart shall fame his wit 84 11
Give my love fame faster than Time wastes life 100 13
She that her fame so to herself contrives, The scars of battle 'scapeth by the flight *Lov. Comp.* 243
Of wealth, of filial fear, law, kindred, fame 270
Familiar. He, nor that affable familiar ghost Which nightly gulls him *Son.* 86 9
Famine. Making a famine where abundance lies 1 7
Famish. And yet not cloy thy lips with loathed satiety, But rather famish them amid their plenty *Ven. and Adon.* 20
Famished. When that mine eye is famish'd for a look, Or heart in love *Son.* 47 3
Famoused. The painful warrior famoused for fight 25 9
Fan. Then with her windy sighs and golden hairs To fan and blow them dry again she seeks *Ven. and Adon.* 52
Fancy. A martial man to be soft fancy's slave! *Lucrece* 200
In dead of night From forth dull sleep by dreadful fancy waking 450
Observed as they flew—Towards this afflicted fancy fastly drew *Lov. Comp.* 61
Look here, what tributes wounded fancies sent me, Of paled pearls 197
Till looking on an Englishman, the fair'st that eye could see, Her fancy fell a-turning *Pass. Pil.* 214
Let reason rule things worthy blame, As well as fancy partial might 302
Fangs. Under whose sharp fangs on his back doth lie An image like thyself, all stain'd with gore *Ven. and Adon.* 663
Fanning the hairs, who wave like feather'd wings 306
Fantastic. Soothing the humour of fantastic wits 850
Fantasy. She tells them 'tis a causeless fantasy, And childless error 897
Far. Sometime he scuds far off and there he stares 301
By this, poor Wat, far off upon a hill, Stands on his hinder legs 697
By this, far off she hears some huntsman hollo 973
Which far exceeds his barren skill to show *Lucrece* 81
Far from the purpose of his coming hither, He makes excuses 113
And doth so far proceed, That what is vile shows like a virtuous deed 251
Pure Chastity is rifled of her store, And Lust, the thief, far poorer than before 693
Yet with the fault I thus far can dispense 1279
Both stood, like old acquaintance in a trance, Met far from home 1596
Mine enemy was strong, my poor self weak, And far the weaker with so strong a fear 1647
My thoughts, from far where I abide, Intend a zealous pilgrimage to thee *Sonnet* 27 5
How far I toil, still farther off from thee 28 8
I would be brought, From limits far remote, where thou dost stay 44 4
Thus far the miles are measured from thy friend 50 4
Is it thy spirit that thou send'st from thee So far from home? 61 6
From me far off, with others all too near 61 14
Why is my verse so barren of new pride, So far from variation or quick change? 76 2
My saucy bark inferior far to his On your broad main doth wilfully appear 80 7
Well might show How far a modern quill doth come too short 83 7
Lilies that fester smell far worse than weeds 94 14
Grows fairer than at first, more strong, far greater 119 12

Far. No, it was builded far from accident . . . . *Sonnet* 124 5
Coral is far more red than her lips' red 130 2
Yet well I know That music hath a far more pleasing sound . . 130 10
Thus far for love my love-suit, sweet, fulfil 136 4
Only my plague thus far I count my gain 141 13
Fare. So surfeit-taking Tarquin fares this night . . *Lucrece* 698
So fares it with this faultful lord of Rome 715
To whose weak ruins muster troops of cares, To ask the spotted princess how she fares 721
He hath no power to ask her how she fares 1594
Fare well I could not, for I supp'd with sorrow . . *Pass. Pil.* 186
Farewell. Bids him farewell, and look well to her heart. *Ven. and Adon.* 580
Farewell! thou art too dear for my possessing . . . *Sonnet* 87 1
'Farewell,' quoth she, 'and come again to-morrow:' Fare well I could not, for I supp'd with sorrow . . . . . *Pass. Pil.* 185
Farewell, sweet lass, Thy like ne'er was For a sweet content . . 293
But if Fortune once do frown, Then farewell his great renown . 420
Faring. Which I will keep so chary As tender nurse her babe from faring ill *Sonnet* 22 12
Far-off. That one might see those far-off eyes look sad . . *Lucrece* 1386
Farther. How far I toil, still farther off from thee . . *Sonnet* 28 8
For thou not farther than my thoughts canst move . . . 47 11
By seeing farther than the eye hath shown 69 8
My soul doth tell my body that he may Triumph in love; flesh stays no farther reason 151 8
Farthest. No matter then although my foot did stand Upon the farthest earth removed from thee 44 6
The winds Which should transport me farthest from your sight . . 117 8
Fashion. When sighs and groans and tears may grace the fashion Of her disgrace . . . . *Lucrece* 1319
But not acquainted With shifting change, as is false women's fashion *Son.* 20 4
Whereto the inviting time our fashion calls 124 8
Fast. Even as an empty eagle, sharp by fast, Tires with her beak on feathers, flesh, and bone . . . . . . *Ven. and Adon.* 55
The mellow plum doth fall, the green sticks fast 527
Were beauty under twenty locks kept fast, Yet love breaks through and picks them all at last 575
The dove sleeps fast that this night-owl will catch . . . *Lucrece* 360
Thy secret pleasure turns to open shame, Thy private feasting to a public fast 891
To hie as fast As lagging fowls before the northern blast . . 1334
The eddy boundeth in his pride Back to the strait that forced him on so fast 1670
As fast as thou shalt wane, so fast thou growest In one of thine *Sonnet* 11 1
Beauties do themselves forsake And die as fast as they see others grow 12 12
Creating every bad a perfect best; As fast as objects to his beams assemble 114 8
To write for me Under that bond that him as fast doth bind . . 134 8
Fastened. Look, how a bird lies tangled in a net, So fasten'd in her arms Adonis lies . . . . *Ven. and Adon.* 68
Fastens. The studded bridle on a ragged bough Nimbly she fastens . 38
Faster. Her loyal fear! Which struck her sad, and then it faster rock'd *Lucr.* 262
Give my love fame faster than Time wastes life . . . *Sonnet* 100 13
Fastly. Observed as they flew—Towards this afflicted fancy fastly drew *Lov. Comp.* 61
Fat. By heaven's fair sun that breeds the fat earth's store . . *Lucrece* 1837
Fatal. Like one that spies an adder Wreathed up in fatal folds just in his way *Ven. and Adon.* 879
And kiss'd the fatal knife, to end his vow . . . . *Lucrece* 1843
Fate. I am the mistress of my fate, And with my trespass never will dispense 1069
And look upon myself and curse my fate . . . . *Sonnet* 29 4
Father. 'Poor flower,' quoth she, 'this was thy father's guise' *Ven. and Adon.* 1177
Here was thy father's bed, here in my breast 1183
And hold it for no sin To wish that I their father had not been *Lucrece* 210
Their father was too weak, and they too strong 865
He shall not boast who did thy stock pollute That thou art doting father of his fruit 1064
Lucrece' father, that beholds her bleed, Himself on her self-slaughter'd body threw 1732
If in the child the father's image lies, Where shall I live now Lucrece is unlived? 1753
Live again and see Thy father die, and not thy father thee . . 1771
Son and father weep with equal strife Who should weep most . . 1791
The father says 'She's mine.' 'O, mine she is,' Replies her husband . 1795
My love, you know You had a father: let your son say so . . *Sonnet* 13 14
As a decrepit father takes delight To see his active child do deeds of youth 37 1
'Father,' she says, 'though in me you behold The injury of many a blasting hour, Let it not tell your judgement I am old . . *Lov. Comp.* 71
O father, what a hell of witchcraft lies In the small orb of one particular tear! 288
Fault. My horse is gone, And 'tis your fault I am bereft him so *V. and A.* 381
Ceasing their clamorous cry till they have singled With much ado the cold fault cleanly out 694
'Tis not my fault: the boar provoked my tongue; Be wreak'd on him . . 1003
The shame and fault finds no excuse nor end . . . . *Lucrece* 238
The fault is thine, For those thine eyes betray thee unto mine . 482
The fault unknown is as a thought unacted 527
For marks descried in men's nativity Are nature's faults . . . 539
When, pattern'd by thy fault, foul sin may say, He learn'd to sin, and thou didst teach the way 630
Men's faults do seldom to themselves appear 633
And by their mortal fault brought in subjection Her immortality . . 724
That all the faults which in thy reign are made May likewise be sepulchred in thy shade 804
Nor fold my fault in cleanly-coin'd excuses 1073
Poor women's faces are their own faults' books 1253
O, let it not be hild Poor women's faults, that they are so fulfill'd With men's abuses 1258
Yet with the fault I thus far can dispense 1279
Where no excuse can give the fault amending 1614
All men make faults, and even I in this . . . . *Sonnet* 35 5
To thy sensual fault I bring in sense—Thy adverse party is thy advocate 35 9
Upon thy part I can set down a story Of faults conceal'd . . 88 7
Say that thou didst forsake me for some fault 89 1
Some say thy fault is youth, some wantonness 96 1
Both grace and faults are loved of more and less; Thou makest faults graces that to thee resort 96 3
To anticipate The ills that were not, grew to faults assured . . 118 10
And in our faults by lies we flatter'd be 138 14
Thou keep'st me blind, Lest eyes well-seeing thy foul faults should find 148 14
Urge not my amiss, Lest guilty of my faults thy sweet self prove . 151 4

Fault. Outfacing faults in love with love's ill rest . . . *Pass. Pil.* 8
Love with me, Since that our faults in love thus smother'd be . . 14
Exhale this vapour vow; in thee it is: If broken, then it is no fault of mine 40
Faultful. So fares it with this faultful lord of Rome . . . *Lucrece* 715
Favour. If thou wilt deign this favour, for thy meed A thousand honey secrets shalt thou know . . . . . . *Ven. and Adon.* 15
'Pity,' she cries, 'some favour, some remorse!' Away he springs . . 257
Both favour, savour, hue, and qualities 747
Let those who are in favour with their stars Of public honour and proud titles boast . . . . *Sonnet* 25 1
The most sweet favour or deformed'st creature, The mountain or the sea 113 10
Have I not seen dwellers on form and favour Lose all, and more? . . 125 5
A thousand favours from a maund she drew . . . *Lov. Comp.* 36
She show'd him favours to allure his eye . . . . . *Pass. Pil.* 48
Favourites. Great princes' favourites their fair leaves spread . . *Sonnet* 25 5
Fawn. Hasting to feed her fawn hid in some brake . *Ven. and Adon.* 876
On whom frown'st thou that I do fawn upon? . . . *Sonnet* 149 6
Fawned. They that fawn'd on him before Use his company no more *Pass. Pil.* 421
Fawneth. As the grim lion fawneth o'er his prey, Sharp hunger by the conquest satisfied, So o'er this sleeping soul doth Tarquin stay *Lucrece* 421
Fear. When, lo, the unback'd breeder, full of fear, Jealous of catching, swiftly doth forsake him . . . . . . *Ven. and Adon.* 320
Which purchase if thou make, for fear of slips Set thy seal-manual on my wax-red lips 515
Saw'st thou not signs of fear lurk in mine eye? Grew I not faint? . 644
Whispers in mine ear That if I love thee, I thy death should fear . . 660
It doth make my faint heart bleed, And fear doth teach it divination . . 670
Danger deviseth shifts; wit waits on fear 690
The fear whereof doth make him shake and shudder 880
Overcome by doubt and bloodless fear, With cold-pale weakness . . 891
Bids them leave quaking, bids them fear no more 899
A second fear through all her sinews spread, Which madly hurries her . 903
Yet pardon me I felt a kind of fear When as I met the boar . . 998
Thou art so full of fear As one with treasure laden, hemm'd with thieves . 1021
Having no fair to lose, you need not fear; The sun doth scorn you . . 1083
The lion walk'd along Behind some hedge, because he would not fear him . 1094
It shall suspect where is no cause of fear; It shall not fear where it should most mistrust 1153
Put fear to valour, courage to the coward 1158
Birds never limed no secret bushes fear . . . . . *Lucrece* 88
Sable Night, mother of Dread and Fear 117
But honest fear, bewitch'd with lust's foul charm, Doth too too oft betake him to retire 173
Here pale with fear he doth premeditate the dangers 183
The guilt being great, the fear doth still exceed 229
Extreme fear can neither fight nor fly 230
Who fears a sentence or an old man's saw Shall by a painted cloth be kept in awe 244
O, how her fear did make her colour rise! First red as roses . . 257
And how her hand, in my hand being lock'd, Forced it to tremble with her loyal fear! 261
Then, childish fear, avaunt! debating, die! 274
Then who fears sinking where such treasure lies? 280
So heedful fear Is almost choked by unresisted lust 281
They fright him, yet he still pursues his fear 308
Shelves and sands, The merchant fears, ere rich at home he lands . . 336
Against love's fire fear's frost hath dissolution 355
Wrapp'd and confounded in a thousand fears 456
Marking what he tells With trembling fear, as fowl hear falcon's bells . 511
This deed will make thee only loved for fear 610
If but for fear of this, thy will remove 614
He faintly flies, sweating with guilty fear; She stays 740
And therefore now I need not fear to die 1052
That dying fear through all her body spread 1266
Seemed to appear, Like bright things stain'd a kind of heavy fear . . 1435
No guilty instance gave, Nor ashy pale the fear that false hearts have . 1512
Mine enemy was strong, my poor self weak, And far the weaker with so strong a fear 1647
He falls, and bathes the pale fear in his face, And counterfeits to die . 1775
Is it for fear to wet a widow's eye That thou consumest thyself in single life? *Sonnet* 9 1
As an unperfect actor on the stage Who with his fear is put besides his part 23 2
So I, for fear of trust, forget to say The perfect ceremony of love's rite 23 5
And even thence thou wilt be stol'n, I fear, For truth proves thievish 48 13
Which cannot choose But weep to have that which it fears to lose 64 14
I was not sick of any fear from thence 86 12
Then need I not to fear the worst of wrongs 92 5
But what's so blessed-fair that fears no blot? 92 13
For fear of which, hear this, thou age unbred 104 13
Not mine own fears, nor the prophetic soul Of the wide world . . 107 1
Applying fears to hopes and hopes to fears 119 3
It fears not policy, that heretic, Which works on leases of short-number'd hours 124 9
Yet fear her, O thou minion of her pleasure! 126 9
Forbod the sweets that seem so good, For fear of harms . *Lov. Comp.* 165
How coldly those impediments stand forth Of wealth, of filial fear . 270
The aloes of all forces, shocks, and fears 273
Shook off my sober guards and civil fears 298
In black mourn I, All fears scorn I, Love hath forlorn me, Living in thrall *Pass. Pil.* 264
Enough, too much, I fear; Lest that my mistress hear my song . . 347
Feared. I fear'd thy fortune, and my joints did tremble . *Ven. and Adon.* 642
She touch'd no unknown baits, nor fear'd no hooks . . . *Lucrece* 103
But happy monarchs still are fear'd for love 611
I fear'd by Tarquin's falchion to be slain 1046
But when I fear'd I was a loyal wife: So am I now 1048
Feareth. Th' one sweetly flatters, th' other feareth harm . . . 172
Fearful. Embracing bushes, As fearful of him, part, through whom he rushes *Ven. and Adon.* 630
Pursue these fearful creatures o'er the downs 677
Prodigies, Whereon with fearful eyes they long have gazed . . . 927
Stood Bare and unpeopled in this fearful flood . . . . *Lucrece* 1741
O fearful meditation! where, alack, Shall Time's best jewel from Time's chest lie hid? . . . . *Sonnet* 65 9
Fearfully. In one place, Where fearfully the dogs exclaim aloud *V. and A.* 886
The roses fearfully on thorns did stand, One blushing shame . *Sonnet* 99 8
Nymphs back peeping Fearfully . . . . *Pass. Pil.* 288
Fearing. I must confess,—I rail'd on thee, fearing my love's decease *V. and A.* 1002
In shade doth sit, Long after fearing to creep forth again . . . 1036

Fearing. Fearing some hard news from the warlike band . . . *Lucrece* 255
Fearing no such thing, Lies at the mercy of his mortal sting . . 363
Alas, why, fearing of time's tyranny, Might I not then say? . *Sonnet* 115 9
Dreading my love, the loss thereof still fearing . . . *Pass. Pil.* 94
Feast. Would they not wish the feast might ever last? . *Ven. and Adon.* 447
Lest Jealousy, that sour unwelcome guest, Should, by his stealing in, disturb the feast 450
With my love's picture then my eye doth feast . . . *Sonnet* 47 5
Therefore are feasts so solemn and so rare, Since, seldom coming . 52 5
Nor taste, nor smell, desire to be invited To any sensual feast with thee alone 141 8
For feasts of love I have been call'd unto . . . *Lov. Comp.* 181
Feast-finding minstrels, tuning my defame, Will tie the hearers to attend each line . . . . *Lucrece* 817
Feasting. Turns to open shame, Thy private feasting to a public fast . 891
Justice is feasting while the widow weeps 906
Sometime all full with feasting on your sight . . . *Sonnet* 75 9
Feat. With sleided silk feat and affectedly Enswathed . . *Lov. Comp.* 48
Feather. Even as an empty eagle, sharp by fast, Tires with her beak on feathers, flesh, and bone . . . . *Ven. and Adon.* 56
There he stares; Anon he starts at stirring of a feather . . . 302
Fleet-wing'd duty with thought's feathers flies . . . *Lucrece* 1216
Have added feathers to the learned's wing . . . . *Sonnet* 78 7
Feathered. Fanning the hairs, who wave like feather'd wings *Ven. and Adon.* 306
Your tunes entomb Within your hollow-swelling feather'd breasts *Lucrece* 1122
Lo! as a careful housewife runs to catch One of her feather'd creatures broke away . . . . *Sonnet* 143 2
Every fowl of tyrant wing, Save the eagle, feather'd king . *Ph. and Tur.* 11
Feature. For if it see the rudest or gentlest sight, . . . it shapes them to your feature . . . . *Sonnet* 113 12
Featured. Featured like him, like him with friends possess'd . 29 6
Featureless. Let those whom Nature hath not made for store, Harsh featureless and rude, barrenly perish 11 10
Fed. Upon the earth's increase why shouldst thou feed, Unless the earth with thy increase be fed? . . . . *Ven. and Adon.* 170
But, when his glutton eye so full hath fed, His other agents aim at like delight 399
Under whose simple semblance he hath fed Upon fresh beauty . . 795
He fed them with his sight, they him with berries 1104
Wanting the spring that those shrunk pipes had fed . *Lucrece* 1455
Within be fed, without be rich no more . . . . *Sonnet* 146 12
Fee. But when he saw his love, his youth's fair fee, He held such petty bondage in disdain . . . . . . *Ven. and Adon.* 393
Ere he says 'Adieu,' The honey fee of parting tender'd is . . 538
Her pleading hath deserved a greater fee 609
They buy thy help; but Sin ne'er gives a fee, He gratis comes *Lucrece* 913
Your trespass now becomes a fee . . . . . *Sonnet* 120 13
Feeble. Thy mark is feeble age, but thy false dart Mistakes that aim *V. and A.* 941
Feeble Desire, all recreant, poor, and meek . . . *Lucrece* 710
Leave the faltering feeble souls alive 1768
Like feeble age, he reeleth from the day . . . . *Sonnet* 7 10
Her feeble force will yield at length . . . . *Pass. Pil.* 319
Feed. Upon the earth's increase why shouldst thou feed? *Ven. and Adon.* 169
Feed where thou wilt, on mountain or in dale: Graze on my lips . 232
And glutton-like she feeds, yet never filleth 548
So did the merciless and pitchy night Fold in the object that did feed her sight 822
Hasting to feed her fawn hid in some brake 876
Her sad behaviour feeds his vulture folly . . . . *Lucrece* 556
The orphan pines while the oppressor feeds; Justice is feasting . 905
To feed oblivion with decay of things, To blot old books . . 947
As from a mountain-spring that feeds a dale, Shall gush pure streams. 1077
Let the traitor die; For sparing justice feeds iniquity . . . 1687
Feeds on the rarities of nature's truth . . . . *Sonnet* 60 11
So shalt thou feed on Death, that feeds on men . . . 146 13
My flocks feed not, My ewes breed not, . . All is amiss *Pass. Pil.* 245
There will we sit upon the rocks, And see the shepherds feed their flocks . 358
Feeder. What banquet wert thou to the taste, Being nurse and feeder of the other four . . . . *Ven. and Adon.* 446
Feedest. Feed'st thy light's flame with self-substantial fuel . *Sonnet* 1 6
Feedeth. She feedeth on the steam as on a prey, And calls it heavenly moisture, air of grace . . . . . *Ven. and Adon.* 63
Feeding. Than appetite, Which but to-day by feeding is allay'd *Sonnet* 56 3
To bitter sauces did I frame my feeding 118 6
Feeding on that which doth preserve the ill 147 3
Feel. Art thou a woman's son, and canst not feel What 'tis to love? how want of love tormenteth? . . . . . *Ven. and Adon.* 201
Seems unkind, Spurns at his love and scorns the heat he feels . 311
Her other tender hand his fair cheek feels 352
'Give me my hand,' saith he, 'why dost thou feel it?' . . . 373
May feel her heart—poor citizen!—distress'd, Wounding itself to death, rise up and fall . . . . *Lucrece* 465
And grave, like water that doth eat in steel, Upon my cheeks what helpless shame I feel 756
Though I feel thou art, Within the gentle closure of my breast *Sonnet* 48 10
And for that sorrow which I then did feel Needs must I under my transgression bow 120 2
Feelest. And see thy blood warm when thou feel'st it cold . . 2 14
Feeling. Say, that the sense of feeling were bereft me *Ven. and Adon.* 439
Bloodless fear, With cold-pale weakness numbs each feeling part . 892
The life and feeling of her passion She hoards, to spend when he is by *Lucr.* 1317
Being from the feeling of her own grief brought By deep surmise of others' detriment 1578
Which is so deem'd Not by our feeling but by others' seeing . *Sonnet* 121 4
Nor tender feeling, to base touches prone 141 6
Gentle maid, Have of my suffering youth some feeling pity . *Lov. Comp.* 178
Now all these hearts that do on mine depend, Feeling it break, with bleeding groans they pine 275
Feelingly. True sorrow then is feelingly sufficed . . *Lucrece* 1112
Here feelingly she weeps Troy's painted woes 1492
Feeling-painful. My woe too sensible thy passion maketh More feeling-painful 1679
Fee-simple. And was my own fee-simple, not in part . *Lov. Comp.* 144
Feign. One god is god of both, as poets feign . . . *Pass. Pil.* 115
Feigned. Dismiss your vows, your feigned tears, your flattery *V. and A.* 425
Fell. Grew I not faint? and fell I not downright? 645
As life for honour in fell battle's rage; Honour for wealth . *Lucrece* 145
Obdurate vassals fell exploits effecting, In bloody death . . . 429
Black stage for tragedies and murders fell! Vast sin-concealing chaos! . 766
When their glass fell wherein they view'd their faces 1526
Fell. Nature, as she wrought thee, fell a-doting . . . . *Sonnet* 20 10
When I have seen by Time's fell hand defaced The rich proud cost of outworn buried age 64 1
When that fell arrest Without all bail shall carry me away . . 74 1
And find the lesson true, Drugs poison him that so fell sick of you 118 14
Cupid laid by his brand, and fell asleep 153 1
But, spite of heaven's fell rage, Some beauty peep'd through lattice of sear'd age . . . . *Lov. Comp.* 13
Ay me! I fell; and yet do question make What I should do again for such a sake 321
Then fell she on her back, fair queen, and toward . . *Pass. Pil.* 55
She bade love last, and yet she fell a-turning 100
God Mars did try her, And as he fell to her, so fell she to him . 146
Till looking on an Englishman, the fair'st that eye could see, Her fancy fell a-turning 214
As it fell upon a day In the merry month of May 373
Fellow. All thy fellow birds do sing, Careless of thy sorrowing . 397
Fellowship in woe doth woe assuage . . . . . *Lucrece* 790
Felt. My smooth moist hand, were it with thy hand felt, Would in thy palm dissolve, or seem to melt . . . . . *Ven. and Adon.* 143
And having felt the sweetness of the spoil, With blindfold fury she begins to forage 553
Yet pardon me I felt a kind of fear When as I met the boar . . 998
When more is felt than one hath power to tell . . . *Lucrece* 1288
What freezings have I felt, what dark days seen! . . . . *Sonnet* 97 3
Female. Being proud, as females are, to see him woo her *Ven. and Adon.* 309
My female evil Tempteth my better angel from my side *Son.* 144 5; *Pass. Pil.* 19
Fence. When shame assail'd, the red should fence the white . *Lucrece* 63
Fester. Lilies that fester smell far worse than weeds . . *Sonnet* 94 14
Fetched. And as she fetched breath, away he skips . . *Pass. Pil.* 153
Fetlocks. Round-hoof'd, short-jointed, fetlocks shag and long *V. and A.* 295
Fever. Burning fevers, agues pale and faint, Life-poisoning pestilence . 739
In the distraction of this madding fever . . . . *Sonnet* 119 8
My love is as a fever, longing still For that which longer nurseth the disease 147 1
Augur of the fever's end, To this troop come thou not near! *Ph. and Tur.* 7
Few. O happiness enjoy'd but of a few! And, if possess'd, as soon decay'd *Lucrece* 22
'Few words,' quoth she, 'shall fit the trespass best' 1613
When yellow leaves, or none, or few, do hang Upon those boughs *Sonnet* 73 2
Fickle. It shall be fickle, false, and full of fraud . *Ven. and Adon.* 1141
Who in thy power Dost hold Time's fickle glass, his sickle, hour *Sonnet* 126 2
Ere long espied a fickle maid full pale, Tearing of papers . *Lov. Comp.* 5
Fair is my love, but not so fair as fickle . . . . *Pass. Pil.* 85
O frowning Fortune, cursed, fickle dame! 259
Whilst as fickle Fortune smiled, Thou and I were both beguiled . 401
Fie. Souring his cheeks cries 'Fie, no more of love! . *Ven. and Adon.* 185
Fie, lifeless picture, cold and senseless stone, Well-painted idol . . 211
'Fie, fie,' he says, 'you crush me; let me go' 611
Fie, fie, fond love, thou art so full of fear 1021
'Fie, fie, fie,' now would she cry; 'Tereu, tereu!' by and by *Pass. Pil.* 385
Field. The field's chief flower, sweet above compare, Stain to all nymphs, more lovely than a man . . . . *Ven. and Adon.* 8
Making my arms his field, his tent my bed 108
Like a red morn, that ever yet betoken'd Wreck to the seaman, tempest to the field 454
They basely fly and dare not stay the field 894
But beauty, in that white intituled, From Venus' doves doth challenge that fair field . . . . *Lucrece* 58
Their silent war of lilies and of roses, Which Tarquin view'd in her fair face's field, In their pure ranks his traitor eye encloses 72
Her husband's fame, Won in the fields of fruitful Italy . . . 107
When their brave hope, bold Hector, march'd to field . . . 1430
And dig deep trenches in thy beauty's field . . . . *Sonnet* 2 2
That hills and valleys, dales and fields, and all the craggy mountains yields *Pass. Pil.* 355
Fiend. Beauty hath nought to do with such foul fiends . *Ven. and Adon.* 638
Whether that my angel be turn'd fiend Suspect I may . . *Sonnet* 144 9
Who like a fiend From heaven to hell is flown away . . . 145 11
With the garment of a Grace The naked and concealed fiend he cover'd *Lov. Comp.* 317
Whether that my angel be turn'd fiend, Suspect I may, yet not directly tell *Pass. Pil.* 23
Thou shrieking harbinger, Foul precurrer of the fiend . . *Ph. and Tur.* 6
Fierce. Pluck the keen teeth from the fierce tiger's jaws . *Sonnet* 19 3
Some fierce thing replete with too much rage 23 3
Fiery. Red cheeks and fiery eyes blaze forth her wrong . *Ven. and Adon.* 219
Desire, of perfect'st love being made, Shall neigh—no dull flesh—in his fiery race . . . . *Sonnet* 51 11
Fiery-pointed. As the fair and fiery-pointed sun, Rushing from forth a cloud, bereaves our sight . . . . *Lucrece* 372
Fight. Brag not of thy might, For mastering her that foil'd the god of fight *Ven. and Adon.* 114
But in one minute's fight brings beauty under 746
Teaching them thus to use it in the fight . . . . . *Lucrece* 62
Yet their ambition makes them still to fight 68
Now leaden slumber with life's strength doth fight 124
The fear doth still exceed; And extreme fear can neither fight nor fly . 230
And when his gaudy banner is display'd, The coward fights and will not be dismay'd 273
Desire doth fight with Grace, For there it revels 712
Conceit and grief an eager combat fight 1298
See grave Nestor stand, As 'twere encouraging the Greeks to fight . 1402
The painful warrior famoused for fight . . . . . *Sonnet* 25 9
Being crown'd, Crooked eclipses 'gainst his glory fight . . . 60 7
Upon thy side against myself I'll fight And prove thee virtuous . 88 3
Long was the combat doubtful that love with love did fight *Pass. Pil.* 215
Like a thousand vanquish'd men in bloody fight! 280
Fighting. To note the fighting conflict of her hue, How white and red each other did destroy! . . . . *Ven. and Adon.* 345
And they, like straggling slaves for pillage fighting . *Lucrece* 428
Effects of terror and dear modesty, Encamp'd in hearts, but fighting outwardly . . . . *Lov. Comp.* 203
Figure. They were but sweet, but figures of delight, Drawn after you *Son.* 98 11
Like a dial-hand, Steal from his figure and no pace perceived . 104 10
Laundering the silken figures in the brine That season'd woe had pelleted in tears . . . . *Lov. Comp.* 17
Figured. What's in the brain that ink may character Which hath not figured to thee my true spirit? . . . . *Sonnet* 108 2
He refused to take her figured proffer . . . . . *Pass. Pil.* 52

Figuring. Figuring that they their passions likewise lent me Of grief and blushes . . . . *Lov. Comp.* 199
Filching. Anon Doubting the filching age will steal his treasure *Sonnet* 75 6
Filed. And precious phrase by all the Muses filed . . . 85 4
And when thou comest thy tale to tell, Smooth not thy tongue with filed talk . . . . *Pass. Pil.* 306
Filial. Of wealth, of filial fear, law, kindred, fame . *Lov. Comp.* 270
Fill. Stuff up his lust, as minutes fill up hours . . *Lucrece* 297
To fill with worm-holes stately monuments 946
Although to-day thou fill Thy hungry eyes even till they wink with fullness, To-morrow see again . . . . *Sonnet* 56 5
Your love and pity doth the impression fill 112 1
Ay, fill it full with wills, and my will one . . . 136 6
Filled. 'My daughter' and 'my wife' with clamours fill'd The dispersed air *Lucrece* 1804
Who will believe my verse in time to come, If it were fill'd with your most high deserts? . . . . *Sonnet* 17 2
When hours have drain d his blood and fill'd his brow With lines and wrinkles 63 3
When your countenance fill'd up his line, Then lack'd I matter 86 13
Fillet. Some in her threaden fillet still did bide . *Lov. Comp.* 33
Filleth. And glutton-like she feeds, yet never filleth . *Ven. and Adon.* 548
Filling. Like ivory conduits coral cisterns filling . *Lucrece* 1234
Filth. The crow may bathe his coal-black wings in mire, And unperceived fly with the filth away 1010
Find. The warm effects which she in him finds missing She seeks to kindle with continual kissing . . . *Ven. and Adon.* 605
Here kennell'd in a brake she finds a hound 913
Find sweet beginning, but unsavoury end 1138
When shall he think to find a stranger just, When he himself himself confounds? . . . . *Lucrece* 159
My dear friend, The shame and fault finds no excuse nor end . 238
She wakes her heart by beating on her breast, And bids it leap from thence, where it may find Some purer chest to close so pure a mind . . 760
She starteth, To find some desperate instrument of death . . 1038
Come, To find a face where all distress is stell'd . . . 1444
And whom she finds forlorn she doth lament . . . 1500
It cannot be, I find, But such a face should bear a wicked mind . 1539
That he finds means to burn his Troy with water . . 1561
Who finds his Lucrece clad in mourning black . . . 1585
Or at the least this refuge let me find 1654
So should that beauty which you hold in lease Find no determination *Sonnet* 13 6
Or say with princes if it shall go well, By oft predict that I in heaven find 14 8
To find where your true image pictured lies . . . 24 6
By night my mind, For thee and for myself no quiet find . 27 14
Both find each other, and I lose both twain . . . 42 11
When love, converted from the thing it was, Shall reasons find 49 8
O, what excuse will my poor beast then find, When swift extremity can seem but slow? 51 5
Your praise shall still find room Even in the eyes of all posterity . 55 10
To find out shames and idle hours in me, The scope and tenour of thy jealousy? 61 7
Thou shalt find Those children nursed, deliver'd from thy brain . 77 10
Every humour hath his adjunct pleasure, Wherein it finds a joy . 91 6
O, what a happy title do I find, Happy to have thy love, happy to die! 92 11
And thou in this shalt find thy monument . . . 107 13
Love is not love Which alters when it alteration finds . . 116 3
But thence I learn, and find the lesson true . . . 118 13
Now I find true That better is by evil still made better . . 119 9
And thou shalt find it merits not reproving . . . 142 4
Thou keep'st me blind, Lest eyes well-seeing thy foul faults should find 148 14
Bidding them find their sepulchres in mud . . . *Lov. Comp.* 46
What's sweet to do, to do will aptly find . . . 88
The goodly objects which abroad they find Of lands and mansions . 137
They sought their shame that so their shame did find . . 187
Through the velvet leaves the wind, All unseen 'gan passage find *Pass. Pil.* 232
A cripple soon can find a halt 308
Words are easy, like the wind; Faithful friends are hard to find . . 406
Finding their enemy to be so curst, They all strain courtesy who shall cope him first . . . . *Ven. and Adon.* 887
Finding thy worth a limit past my praise . . . *Sonnet* 82 6
Finding the first conceit of love there bred . . . 108 13
Finding myself in honour so forbid, With safest distance I mine honour shielded . . . . *Lov. Comp.* 150
Fine. Time's office is to fine the hate of foes . . . *Lucrece* 936
To hear with eyes belongs to love's fine wit . . *Sonnet* 23 14
Blunting the fine point of seldom pleasure . . . 52 4
Finger. She locks her lily fingers one in one . . *Ven. and Adon.* 228
He bends her fingers, holds her pulses hard, He chafes her lips . 476
And griping it, the needle his finger pricks . . . *Lucrece* 319
As on the finger of a throned queen The basest jewel will be well esteem'd *Sonnet* 96 5
That blessed wood whose motion sounds With thy sweet fingers . 128 3
Those dancing chips, O'er whom thy fingers walk with gentle gait 128 11
Give them thy fingers, me thy lips to kiss . . . 128 14
Fire. She red and hot as coals of glowing fire, He red for shame, but frosty in desire . . . . *Ven. and Adon.* 35
She bathes in water, yet her fire must burn: 'O, pity,' 'gan she cry! . . 94
Love is a spirit all compact of fire, Not gross to sink . . . 149
Thine eye darts forth the fire that burneth me . . . 196
His eye, which scornfully glisters like fire, Shows his hot courage . 275
Free vent of words love's fire doth assuage 334
But now her cheek was pale, and by and by It flash'd forth fire . 348
Affection is a coal that must be cool'd; Else, suffer'd, it will set the heart on fire 388
Who is so faint, that dare not be so bold To touch the fire, the weather being cold? 402
In earth or heaven, Or in the ocean drench'd, or in the fire? . . 494
As air and water do abate the fire 654
Mine eyes are turn'd to fire, my heart to lead: Heavy heart's lead, melt at mine eyes' red fire! 1072
Subject and servile to all discontents, As dry combustious matter is to fire. 1162
To Collatium bears the lightless fire . . . . *Lucrece* 4
That from the cold stone sparks of fire do fly . . . 177
As from this cold flint I enforced this fire, So Lucrece must I force to my desire 181
But his hot heart, which fond desire doth scorch, Puffs forth another wind that fires the torch 315
Fire. Against love's fire fear's frost hath dissolution . . . *Lucrece* 355
Small lights are soon blown out, huge fires abide . . . 647
Thou blow'st the fire when temperance is thaw'd; Thou smother'st honesty 884
Two red fires in both their faces blazed; She thought he blush'd . 1353
Thy eye kindled the fire that burneth here 1475
Troy had been bright with fame and not with fire . . . 1491
His eye drops fire, no water thence proceeds . . . 1552
Those round clear pearls of his, that move thy pity, Are balls of quenchless fire 1554
Sinon in his fire doth quake with cold, And in that cold hot-burning fire doth dwell 1556
Three times with sighs she gives her sorrow fire . . . 1604
Slight air and purging fire, Are both with thee, wherever I abide *Sonnet* 45 1
Nor war's quick fire shall burn The living record of your memory . 55 7
In me thou see'st the glowing of such fire . . . 73 9
But live in doubt, Till my bad angel fire my good one out 144 14; *Pass. Pil.* 28
His love-kindling fire did quickly steep In a cold valley-fountain *Sonnet* 153 3
Which borrow'd from this holy fire of Love a dateless lively heat 153 5
The bath for my help lies Where Cupid got new fire—my mistress' eyes 153 14
That fire Which many legions of true hearts had warm'd . 154 5
This brand she quenched in a cool well by, Which from Love's fire took heat perpetual 154 10
Love's fire heats water, water cools not love . . . 154 14
Cold modesty, hot wrath, Both fire from hence and chill extincture hath *Lov. Comp.* 294
O, that false fire which in his cheek so glow'd! 324
Which, not to anger bent, is music and sweet fire . . . *Pass. Pil.* 68
She burn'd with love, as straw with fire flameth . . . 97
Firm. And the firm soil win of the watery main, Increasing store *Sonnet* 64 7
Firmly. What he beheld, on that he firmly doted . . *Lucrece* 416
Where her faith was firmly fix'd in love, There a nay is placed *Pass. Pil.* 255
First. Struck dead at first, what needs a second striking? *Ven. and Adon.* 250
They all strain courtesy who shall cope him first . . . 888
They both would strive who first should dry his tears . . 1092
I must confess, With kissing him I should have kill'd him first . 1118
First red as roses that on lawn we lay, Then white as lawn, the roses took away . . . . *Lucrece* 258
First, like a trumpet, doth his tongue begin To sound a parley . 470
She prepares to write, First hovering o'er the paper with her quill . 1297
And for a woman wert thou first created . . . *Sonnet* 20 9
The first my thought, the other my desire . . . 45 3
That God forbid that made me first your slave . . . 58 1
Since mind at first in character was done . . . 59 8
So shall I taste At first the very worst of fortune's might . 90 12
For as you were when first your eye I eyed, Such seems your beauty still 104 2
Three hot Junes burn'd, Since first I saw you fresh, which yet are green 104 8
Thou mine, I thine, Even as when first I hallow'd thy fair name . 108 8
Finding the first conceit of love there bred . . . 108 13
'Tis the lesser sin That mine eye loves it and doth first begin . 114 14
And ruin'd love, when it is built anew, Grows fairer than at first . 119 12
A flower that dies when first it gins to bud . . . *Pass Pil.* 171
First-born. With earth and sea's rich gems, With April's first-born flowers *Sonnet* 21 7
Fishes. When he beheld his shadow in the brook, The fishes spread on it their golden gills . . . . *Ven. and Adon.* 1100
Fisher. No fisher but the ungrown fry forbears . . . 526
Fit. And now the happy season once more fits 327
Is plagued with cramps and gouts and painful fits . . *Lucrece* 856
'Few words,' quoth she, 'shall fit the trespass best' . . 1613
Then tender'd The humble salve which wounded bosoms fits *Sonnet* 120 12
Fitted. How have mine eyes out of their spheres been fitted! . 119 7
Five. A backward look, Even of five hundred courses of the sun . 59 6
But my five wits nor my five senses can Dissuade one foolish heart from serving thee 141 9
Fix. Against my heart Will fix a sharp knife to affright mine eye . *Lucrece* 1138
Fixed. Whose beams upon his hairless face are fix'd . *Ven. and Adon.* 487
Her pity-pleading eyes are sadly fixed In the remorseless wrinkles of his face *Lucrece* 561
The skies were sorry, And little stars shot from their fixed places . 1525
Though not so bright As those gold candles fix'd in heaven's air *Sonnet* 21 12
Truth needs no colour, with his colour fix'd . . . 101 6
Anon their gazes lend To every place at once, and, nowhere fix'd *Lov. Comp.* 27
Where her faith was firmly fix'd in love, There a nay is placed *Pass. Pil.* 255
Flame. Girdle with embracing flames the waist Of Collatine's fair love *Lucrece* 6
And to the flame thus speaks advisedly 180
Feed'st thy light's flame with self-substantial fuel . . *Sonnet* 1 6
Though absence seem'd my flame to qualify . . . 109 2
No reason why My most full flame should afterwards burn clearer 115 4
Not one whose flame my heart so much as warm'd . . *Lov. Comp.* 191
The glowing roses That flame through water which their hue encloses . 287
Phœnix and the turtle fled In a mutual flame from hence *Ph. and Tur.* 24
Flameth. She burn'd with love, as straw with fire flameth . *Pass. Pil.* 97
Flaming. Are by his flaming torch dimm'd and controll'd . *Lucrece* 448
A creeping creature, with a flaming light 1627
The turtle saw his right Flaming in the phœnix' sight . *Ph. and Tur.* 35
Flank. The wide wound that the boar had trench'd In his soft flank *Ven. and Adon.* 1053
And nuzzling in his flank, the loving swine Sheathed unaware the tusk in his soft groin 1115
Flap-mouthed. Another flap-mouth'd mourner, black and grim . 920
Fashed. But now her cheek was pale, and by and by It flash'd forth fire, as lightning from the sky 348
Flatly. And at his look she flatly falleth down 463
Flatter. Reviving joy bids her rejoice, And flatters her it is Adonis' voice . 978
The one doth flatter thee in thoughts unlikely, In likely thoughts the other kills thee quickly 989
Th' one sweetly flatters, th' other feareth harm . . *Lucrece* 172
I will not wrong thy true affection so, To flatter thee with an infringed oath 1061
These contraries such unity do hold, Only to flatter fools and make them bold 1559
So Priam's trust false Sinon's tears doth flatter . . . 1560
So flatter I the swart-complexion'd night . . . *Sonnet* 28 11
Full many a glorious morning have I seen Flatter the mountain-tops . 33 2
Thus have I had thee, as a dream doth flatter, In sleep a king . 87 13
Every one that flatters thee Is no friend in misery . . *Pass. Pil.* 403
Flattered. Who, flatter'd by their leader's jocund show, Stuff up his lust, as minutes fill up hours . . . . *Lucrece* 296
And in our faults by lies we flatter'd be . . . *Sonnet* 138 14
Flatterer. My adder's sense To critic and to flatterer stopped are . 112 11

Flattering. His flattering 'Holla,' or his 'Stand, I say'. *Ven. and Adon.* 284
Let him return, and flattering thoughts retire. . . . *Lucrece* 641
And with such-like flattering, 'Pity but he were a king' *Pass. Pil.* 413
These are certain signs to know Faithful friend from flattering foe 430
Flattery. Dismiss your vows, your feigned tears, your flattery *Ven. and Adon.* 425
Sweet flattery ! then she loves but me alone . . *Sonnet* 42 14
Drink up the monarch's plague, this flattery 114 2
'Tis flattery in my seeing, And my great mind most kingly drinks it up 114 9
Flaws. Gusts and foul flaws to herdmen and to herds . *Ven. and Adon.* 456
Fled. Call it not love, for Love to heaven is fled 793
Love's golden arrow at him should have fled, And not Death's ebon dart . 947
Her eyes are fled Into the deep dark cabins of her head . . . 1037
Give warning to the world that I am fled From this vile world . *Sonnet* 71 3
Where is my judgement fled, That censures falsely what they see aright? 148 3
He saw more wounds than one, And blushing fled, and left her all alone *Pass. Pil.* 130
All our evening sport from us is fled, All our love is lost . . 291
Phœnix and the turtle fled In a mutual flame from hence . *Ph. and Tur.* 23
Fleece. The poor lamb cries; Till with her own white fleece her voice controll'd Entombs her outcry in her lips' sweet fold *Lucrece* 678
Ere beauty's dead fleece made another gay . . . *Sonnet* 68 8
Fleet-foot. Or as the fleet-foot roe that's tired with chasing *Ven. and Adon.* 561
Fleeting. A dream, a breath, a froth of fleeting joy . *Lucrece* 212
How like a winter hath my absence been From thee, the pleasure of the fleeting year! . . . . . *Sonnet* 97 2
Fleets. Make glad and sorry seasons as thou fleets . . . 19 5
Fleet-winged. Fleet-wing'd duty with thought's feathers flies *Lucrece* 1216
Flesh. Even as an empty eagle, sharp by fast, Tires with her beak on feathers, flesh, and bone . . . *Ven. and Adon.* 56
My flesh is soft and plump, my marrow burning . . . 142
The flesh being proud, Desire doth fight with Grace, For there it revels *Lucrece* 712
She, desperate, with her nails her flesh doth tear; He faintly flies . 739
If the dull substance of my flesh were thought, Injurious distance should not stop my way . . . . . . *Sonnet* 44 1
Desire, of perfect'st love being made, Shall neigh—no dull flesh—in his fiery race 51 11
My soul doth tell my body that he may Triumph in love; flesh stays no farther reason 151 8
Flew. Observed as they flew—Towards this afflicted fancy fastly drew *Lov. Comp.* 60
Flight. Unapt for tender smell or speedy flight . . *Lucrece* 695
With some mischance cross Tarquin in his flight . . . 968
The scars of battle 'scapeth by the flight. . *Lov. Comp.* 244
Flint. Art thou obdurate, flinty, hard as steel, Nay, more than flint? *Ven. and Adon.* 200
His falchion on a flint he softly smiteth, That from the cold stone sparks of fire do fly . . . . . *Lucrece* 176
As from this cold flint I enforced this fire, So Lucrece must I force to my desire 181
Flint-hearted boy! 'Tis but a kiss I beg; why art thou coy? *Ven. and Adon.* 95
Flinty. Art thou obdurate, flinty, hard as steel, Nay, more than flint? . 199
Flock. Sometime he runs among a flock of sheep, To make the cunning hounds mistake their smell 685
My flocks feed not, My ewes breed not, . . . All is amiss *Pass. Pil.* 245
Herds stand weeping, Flocks all sleeping, Nymphs back peeping . 286
There will we sit upon the rocks, And see the shepherds feed their flocks . 358
Flood. As one that unaware Hath dropp'd a precious jewel in the flood *Ven. and Adon.* 824
That had Narcissus seen her as she stood, Self-love had never drown'd him in the flood . . . . . *Lucrece* 266
There falls into thy boundless flood Black lust, dishonour, shame . 653
Deep woes roll forward like a gentle flood . . . 1118
Thy sorrow to my sorrow lendeth Another power, no flood by raining slaketh. 1677
Vastly stood Bare and unpeopled in this fearful flood . . . 1741
Which she perused, sigh'd, tore, and gave the flood . . *Lov. Comp.* 44
O Jove, quoth she, why was not I a flood! . . . *Pass. Pil.* 84
Flood-gates. But through the flood-gates breaks the silver rain *V. and A.* 959
Flourish. Time doth transfix the flourish set on youth . *Sonnet* 60 9
Flow. Their fresh falls' haste Add to his flow, but alter not his taste *Lucrece* 651
Thus ebbs and flows the current of her sorrow . . . 1569
Then can I drown an eye, unused to flow, For precious friends . *Sonnet* 30 5
Flowed. A fount With brinish current downward flow'd apace *Lov. Comp.* 284
Flower. The field's chief flower, sweet above compare *Ven. and Adon.* 8
Wishing her cheeks were gardens full of flowers . . . 65
Fair flowers that are not gather'd in their prime Rot and consume themselves 131
These forceless flowers like sturdy trees support me . . . 152
Whose blood upon the fresh flowers being shed Doth make them droop . 665
They bid thee crop a weed, thou pluck'st a flower . . . 946
No flower was nigh, no grass, herb, leaf, or weed, But stole his blood . 1055
The flowers are sweet, their colours fresh and trim . . . 1079
A purple flower sprung up, chequer'd with white . . . 1168
She bows her head, the new-sprung flower to smell . . . 1171
'Poor flower,' quoth she, 'this was thy father's guise' . . 1177
There shall not be one minute in an hour Wherein I will not kiss my sweet love's flower 1188
Unwholesome weeds take root with precious flowers . . *Lucrece* 870
The sun being set, Each flower moisten'd like a melting eye . . 1227
No man inveigh against the wither'd flower, But chide rough winter that the flower hath kill'd 1254
Flowers distill'd, though they with winter meet, Leese but their show; their substance still lives sweet. . . . *Sonnet* 5 13
Living flowers, Much liker than your painted counterfeit . 16 7
With earth and sea's rich gems, With April's first-born flowers . 21 7
Whose action is no stronger than a flower 65 4
When beauty lived and died as flowers do now . . . 68 2
To thy fair flower add the rank smell of weeds . . . 69 12
The summer's flower is to the summer sweet, Though to itself it only live and die 94 9
But if that flower with base infection meet, The basest weed outbraves his dignity 94 11
Nor the sweet smell Of different flowers in odour and in hue . 98 6
More flowers I noted, yet I none could see But sweet or colour it had stol'n from thee 99 14
For it no form delivers to the heart Of bird, of flower, or shape . 113 6
Weeds among weeds, or flowers with flowers gather'd . . 124 4
I might as yet have been a spreading flower, Fresh to myself *Lov. Comp.* 75
Flower. Reserved the stalk and gave him all my flower *Lov. Comp.* 147
Sweet rose, fair flower, untimely pluck'd, soon vaded, Pluck'd in the bud, and vaded in the spring! . . . . *Pass. Pil.* 131
A flower that dies when first it gins to bud 171
A doubtful good, a gloss, a glass, a flower 173
As flowers dead lie wither'd on the ground 177
Yet not for me, shine sun to succour flowers 208
A cap of flowers, and a kirtle Embroider'd all with leaves of myrtle . 363
Flown. Who like a fiend From heaven to hell is flown away *Sonnet* 145 12
Fluxive. These often bathed she in her fluxive eyes, And often kiss'd *L. Comp.* 50
Fly. And whether he run or fly they know not whether *Ven. and Adon.* 304
He stamps and bites the poor flies in his fume . . . 316
Like soldiers, when their captain once doth yield, They basely fly . 894
As falcon to the lure, away she flies; The grass stoops not . . 1027
That from the cold stone sparks of fire do fly . . . *Lucrece* 177
Extreme fear can neither fight nor fly 230
Who, angry that the eyes fly from their lights, In darkness daunts them with more dreadful sights 461
He faintly flies, sweating with guilty fear; She stays . . . 740
The crow may bathe his coal-black wings in mire, And unperceived fly with the filth away 1010
Gnats are unnoted wheresoe'er they fly 1014
Stands at gaze, Wildly determining which way to fly . . . 1150
Fleet-wing'd duty with thought's feathers flies . . . 1216
From his lips did fly Thin winding breath, which purl'd up to the sky . 1406
Through her wounds doth fly Life's lasting date . . . 1728
The ornament of beauty is suspect, A crow that flies in heaven's sweetest air *Sonnet* 70 4
Thine eyes that taught the dumb on high to sing And heavy ignorance aloft to fly 78 6
Whose busy care is bent to follow that which flies before her face 143 7
So runn'st thou after that which flies from thee . . . 143 9
And now she would the caged cloister fly . . *Lov. Comp.* 249
O, that forced thunder from his heart did fly! . . . 325
Flying. Uncouple at the timorous flying hare *Ven. and Adon.* 674
Foam. They join and shoot their foam at Simois' banks . *Lucrece* 1442
Foe. So white a friend engirts so white a foe *Ven. and Adon.* 364
He hath a battle set Of bristly pikes, that ever threat his foes . 620
Are like a labyrinth to amaze his foes 684
Stands on his hinder legs with listening ear, To hearken if his foes pursue him still 699
Would let him go, Rather than triumph in so false a foe . *Lucrece* 77
First, like a trumpet, doth his tongue begin To sound a parley to his heartless foe 471
Time's office is to fine the hate of foes 936
Let him have time to see his friends his foes . . . 988
And wast afeard to scratch her wicked foe 1035
Myself, thy friend, will kill myself, thy foe . . . 1196
And bitter words to ban her cruel foes 1460
She modestly prepares to let them know Her honour is ta'en prisoner by the foe 1608
Attend me: Be suddenly revenged on my foe, Thine, mine, his own . 1683
Longing to hear the hateful foe bewray'd 1698
Mistook the matter so, To slay herself that should have slain her foe . 1827
Thyself thy foe, to thy sweet self too cruel . . . *Sonnet* 1 8
Lascivious grace, in whom all ill well shows, Kill me with spites; yet we must not be foes 40 14
Uttering bare truth, even so as foes commend . . . 69 4
She turns my foes, That they elsewhere might dart their injuries . 139 11
These are certain signs to know Faithful friend from flattering foe *Pass. Pil.* 430
Foggy. O hateful, vaporous, and foggy Night! . . *Lucrece* 771
Foil. The foil Of this false jewel, and his amorous spoil . *Lov. Comp.* 153
Foiled. Brag not of thy might, For mastering her that foil'd the god of fight *Ven. and Adon.* 114
After a thousand victories once foil'd, Is from the book of honour razed quite *Sonnet* 25 10
She framed the love, and yet she foil'd the framing . *Pass. Pil.* 99
Foison. Speak of the spring and foison of the year . . *Sonnet* 53 9
Foist. We admire What thou dost foist upon us that is old . 123 6
Fold. The sheep are gone to fold, birds to their nest *Ven. and Adon.* 532
So did the merciless and pitchy night Fold in the object that did feed her sight 822
Like one that spies an adder Wreathed up in fatal folds just in his way . 879
Her voice controll'd Entombs her outcry in her lips' sweet fold . *Lucrece* 679
Nor fold my fault in cleanly-coin'd excuses 1073
Here folds she up the tenour of her woe, Her certain sorrow writ uncertainly 1310
Folded. Shame folded up in blind concealing night . . . 675
Of folded schedules had she many a one, Which she perused . *Lov. Comp.* 43
Follow. What follows more she murders with a kiss . *Ven. and Adon.* 54
The dire imagination she did follow This sound of hope doth labour to expel 975
Misty night Covers the shame that follows sweet delight . *Lucrece* 357
Thy beauty and thy years full well befits, For still temptation follows where thou art . . . . *Sonnet* 41 4
Whose busy care is bent To follow that which flies before her face 143 7
That follow'd it as gentle day Doth follow night . . . 145 11
Followed. That follow'd it as gentle day Doth follow night . . 145 10
Following. He doth debate What following sorrow may on this arise *Lucr.* 186
To remain In personal duty, following where he haunted *Lov. Comp.* 130
Folly. How love is wise in folly, foolish-witty . . *Ven. and Adon.* 838
Her sad behaviour feeds his vulture folly . . . *Lucrece* 556
Or tyrant folly lurk in gentle breasts 851
How swift and short His time of folly and his time of sport . . 992
Burying in Lucrece' wound his folly's show 1810
Herein lives wisdom, beauty, and increase; Without this, folly, age, and cold decay . . . . *Sonnet* 11 6
And folly doctor-like controlling skill 66 10
Fond. Fie, fie, fond love, thou art so full of fear *Ven. and Adon.* 1021
Those that much covet are with gain so fond, For what they have not *Lucr.* 134
Or what fond beggar, but to touch the crown, Would with the sceptre straight be strucken down? 216
Full of foul hope and full of fond mistrust 284
But his hot heart, which fond desire doth scorch, Puffs forth another wind 314
True grief is fond and testy as a child 1094
Thy heat of lust, fond Paris, did incur This load of wrath . . 1473
Who is he so fond will be the tomb Of his self-love, to stop posterity? *Son.* 3 7
Being fond on praise, which makes your praises worse . . . 84 14
'Fondling,' she saith, 'since I have hemm'd thee here Within the circuit of this ivory pale, I'll be a park, and thou shalt be my deer' *V. and A.* 229
Fondly. The herald will contrive, To cipher me how fondly I did dote *Lucr.* 207
Food. He ten times pines that pines beholding food . . . 1115
So are you to my thoughts as food to life . . . *Sonnet* 75 1

Fool. The poor fool prays her that he may depart *Ven. and Adon.* 578
How much a fool was I To be of such a weak and silly mind 1015
Strike the wise dumb and teach the fool to speak 1146
And merry fools to mock at him resort *Lucrece* 989
Out, idle words, servants to shallow fools! 1016
These contraries such unity do hold, Only to flatter fools and make them bold 1559
'Fool, fool!' quoth she, 'his wounds will not be sore' 1568
Let my unsounded self, supposed a fool, Now set thy long-experienced wit to school 1819
So true a fool is love that in your will, Though you do any thing, he thinks no ill *Sonnet* 57 13
Love's not Time's fool, though rosy lips and cheeks Within his bending sickle's compass come 116 9
The fools of time, Which die for goodness, who have lived for crime . 124 13
Thou blind fool, Love, what dost thou to mine eyes? 137 1
Like fools that in th' imagination set The goodly objects which abroad they find *Lov. Comp.* 136
What fool is not so wise To break an oath, to win a paradise? *Pass. Pil.* 41
He rose and ran away; ah, fool too froward! 56
Foolish. For sportive words and uttering foolish things . *Lucrece* 1813
But my five wits nor my five senses can Dissuade one foolish heart from serving thee . . . . . . *Sonnet* 141 10
Foolish-witty. How love is wise in folly, foolish-witty *Ven. and Adon.* 838
Foot. And when thou hast on foot the purblind hare, Mark the poor wretch 679
He doth but dally, While in his hold-fast foot the weak mouse panteth *Lucrece* 555
The cedar stoops not to the base shrub's foot 664
He sets his foot upon the light, For light and lust are deadly enemies . 673
A hand, a foot, a face, a leg, a head, Stood for the whole to be imagined 1427
Which bleeding under Pyrrhus' proud foot lies 1449
No matter then although my foot did stand Upon the farthest earth removed from thee . . . . *Sonnet* 44 5
What strong hand can hold his swift foot back? 65 11
Sweet beauty's best, Of hand, of foot, of lip, of eye, of brow . . 106 6
Footing. Or, like a nymph, with long dishevell'd hair, Dance on the sands, and yet no footing seen *Ven. and Adon.* 148
The earth, in love with thee, thy footing trips 722
For. She red and hot as coals of glowing fire, He red for shame . . 36
For all askance he holds her in his eye 342
But for thy piteous lips no more had seen 504
Long may they kiss each other, for this cure! 505
For know, my heart stands armed in mine ear 779
For now she knows it is no gentle chase 883
For now reviving joy bids her rejoice 977
For by our ears our hearts oft tainted be . . . . *Lucrece* 38
For that he colour'd with his high estate 92
The colour in thy face, That even for anger makes the lily pale . . 478
If but for fear of this, thy will remove 614
The sweets we wish for turn to loathed sours 867
For me, I force not argument a straw, Since that my case is past . 1021
And for, poor bird, thou sing'st not in the day, As shaming any eye should thee behold 1142
A piece Of skilful painting, made for Priam's Troy 1367
That for Achilles' image stood his spear 1424
Unlook'd for joy in that I honour most . . . . *Sonnet* 25 4
But, for their virtue only is their show, They live unwoo'd . 54 9
But, for his theft, in pride of all his growth A vengeful canker eat him up 99 12
And, for they look'd but with divining eyes 106 11
For we, which now behold these present days, Have eyes to wonder . 106 13
For now I see Inconstancy More in women than in men remain *Pass. Pil.* 260
Think women still to strive with men, To sin and never for to saint . 342
Forage. With blindfold fury she begins to forage *Ven. and Adon.* 554
Forbade. My bloody judge forbade my tongue to speak . *Lucrece* 1648
She, silly queen, with more than love's good will, Forbade the boy he should not pass those grounds . . . . . *Pass. Pil.* 124
Forbear. No fisher but the ungrown fry forbears *Ven. and Adon.* 526
Ay me! but yet thou mightst my seat forbear . . . *Sonnet* 41 9
In my sight, Dear heart, forbear to glance thine eye aside . . 139 6
Forbid. But I forbid thee one most heinous crime 19 8
That God forbid that made me first your slave 58 1
Or who his spoil of beauty can forbid? 65 12
Finding myself in honour so forbid, With safest distance I mine honour shielded *Lov. Comp.* 150
Forbidden. That use is not forbidden usury Which happies those that pay the willing loan *Sonnet* 6 5
Forbiddings But all these poor forbiddings could not stay him *Lucrece* 323
Forbod. To be forbod the sweets that seem so good *Lov. Comp.* 164
Force. Being so enraged, desire doth lend her force Courageously to pluck him from his horse *Ven. and Adon.* 29
Rain added to a river that is rank Perforce will force it overflow the bank 72
So Lucrece must I force to my desire *Lucrece* 182
If thou deny, then force must work my way 513
This forced league doth force a further strife 689
I force not argument a straw, Since that my case is past the help of law 1021
Impression of strange kinds Is form'd in them by force, by fraud, or skill 1243
Sweet love, renew thy force; be it not said Thy edge should blunter be than appetite *Sonnet* 56 1
Some [glory] in their bodies' force, Some in their garments . . 91 2
For these, of force, must your oblations be, Since I their altar, you enpatron me *Lov. Comp.* 223
The accident which brought me to her eye Upon the moment did her force subdue 248
And sweetens, in the suffering pangs it bears, The aloes of all forces . 273
Her feeble force will yield at length . . . . *Pass. Pil.* 319
Forced. Forced to content, but never to obey . . *Ven. and Adon.* 61
And how her hand, in my hand being lock'd, Forced it to tremble! *Lucrece* 261
This forced league doth force a further strife 689
Till life to death acquit my forced offence 1071
That was not forced; that never was inclined To accessary yieldings . 1657
The eddy boundeth in his pride Back to the strait that forced him on so fast 1670
How may this forced stain be wiped from me? 1701
Even there Where thou art forced to break a twofold truth . *Sonnet* 41 12
Or forced examples, 'gainst her own content . . . *Lov. Comp.* 157
O, that forced thunder from his heart did fly! 325
Forceless. These forceless flowers like sturdy trees support me *V. and A.* 152
Fords. Deep sounds make lesser noise than shallow fords . *Lucrece* 1329
'Fore. The eyes, 'fore duteous, now converted are From his low tract *Son.* 7 11
Fore-bemoaned. The sad account of fore-bemoaned moan . . . 30 11
Fore-betrayed. O, all that borrow'd motion seeming owed, Would yet again betray the fore-betray'd! . . . . *Lov. Comp.* 328

Forego. My frail joints shake, Mine eyes forego their light, my false heart bleed *Lucrece* 228
Foregone. Then can I grieve at grievances foregone . . *Sonnet* 30 9
Forehead. Brand not my forehead with thy piercing light . *Lucrece* 1091
Foreknowing well, if there he came to lie, Why, there Love lived and there he could not die . . . . *Ven. and Adon.* 245
Foresight. But her foresight could not forestall their will . *Lucrece* 728
Forests. Three winters cold Have from the forests shook three summers' pride *Sonnet* 104 4
Forestall. Thus I forestall thee, if thou mean to chide . . *Lucrece* 484
But her foresight could not forestall their will 728
Foretell. These water-galls in her dim element Foretell new storms . 1589
Forfeit. Supposed as forfeit to a confined doom . . . *Sonnet* 107 4
I myself am mortgaged to thy will, Myself I'll forfeit . . . 134 3
Forged. Love is all truth, Lust full of forged lies . *Ven. and Adon.* 804
Why of eyes' falsehood hast thou forged hooks? . . . *Sonnet* 137 7
Forgery. Such shadows are the weak brain's forgeries . *Lucrece* 460
Guilty of treason, forgery, and shift, Guilty of incest, that abomination 920
Untutor'd youth, Unskilful in the world's false forgeries . *Pass. Pil.* 4
Forget. Her voice is stopt, her joints forget to bow; Her eyes are mad that they have wept till now . . . . . *Ven. and Adon.* 1061
So I, for fear of trust, forget to say . . . . . . *Sonnet* 23 5
Dear love, forget me quite, For you in me can nothing worthy prove . 72 3
Forgetest. Where art thou, Muse, that thou forget'st so long To speak? 100 1
Forgetful. Return, forgetful Muse, and straight redeem In gentle numbers time so idly spent 100 5
Forgetfulness. To keep an adjunct to remember thee Were to import forgetfulness in me 122 14
Forgetting shame's pure blush and honour's wrack . . *Ven. and Adon.* 558
Forging. Till forging Nature be condemn'd of treason 729
Forgive. I do forgive thy robbery, gentle thief, Although thou steal thee all my poverty . . . . *Sonnet* 40 9
Forgoing. Paying too much rent, For compound sweet forgoing simple savour 125 7
Forgot. From them no device can take, The blemish that will never be forgot *Lucrece* 536
And never be forgot in mighty Rome Th' adulterate death of Lucrece and her groom 1644
And all the rest forgot for which he toil'd . . . *Sonnet* 25 12
I in your sweet thoughts would be forgot If thinking on me then should make you woe 71 7
Forgot upon your dearest love to call 117 3
Do I not think on thee, when I forgot Am of myself, all tyrant, for thy sake? 149 3
All my merry jigs are quite forgot, All my lady's love is lost, God wot *Pass. Pil.* 253
Forgotten. From hence your memory death cannot take, Although in me each part will be forgotten . . . . . . *Sonnet* 81 4
Forlorn. Poor queen of love, in thine own law forlorn *Ven. and Adon.* 251
So do thy lips Make modest Dian cloudy and forlorn 725
Whereat she leaps that was but late forlorn 1026
And whom she finds forlorn she doth lament . . . . *Lucrece* 1500
And from the forlorn world his visage hide . . . *Sonnet* 33 7
When Cytherea, all in love forlorn, A longing tarriance for Adonis made *Pass. Pil.* 73
In black mourn I, All fears scorn I, Love hath forlorn me, Living in thrall 265
She, poor bird, as all forlorn, Lean'd her breast up-till a thorn . 381
Form. Or blot with hell-born sin such saint-like forms . *Lucrece* 1519
So fair a form lodged not a mind so ill 1530
Now is the time that face should form another . . *Sonnet* 3 2
And still weep That thou no form of thee hast left behind . . 9 6
When your sweet issue your sweet form should bear . . . 13 8
And hath stell'd Thy beauty's form in table of my heart . . 24 2
How would thy shadow's form form happy show To the clear day with thy much clearer light, When to unseeing eyes thy shade shines so! 43 6
In polish'd form of well-refined pen 85 8
Thou canst not, love, disgrace me half so ill, To set a form upon desired change, As I'll myself disgrace 89 6
Where time and outward form would show it dead . . . 108 14
For it no form delivers to the heart Of bird, of flower, or shape . 113 5
Have I not seen dwellers on form and favour Lose all, and more? . 125 5
His qualities were beauteous as his form . . . *Lov. Comp.* 99
Playing the place which did no form receive 241
In him a plenitude of subtle matter, Applied to cautels, all strange forms receives 303
Formal. Her hair, nor loose nor tied in formal plat 29
Formed. And therefore are they form'd as marble will . *Lucrece* 1241
Impression of strange kinds Is form'd in them by force, by fraud, or skill 1243
Former. To-morrow sharpen'd in his former might . *Sonnet* 56 4
Labouring for invention, bear amiss The second burthen of a former child 59 4
The wits of former days To subjects worse have given admiring praise 59 13
They are but dressings of a former sight 123 4
Forsake. Jealous of catching, swiftly doth forsake him . *Ven. and Adon.* 321
And for himself himself he must forsake . . . . *Lucrece* 157
Since sweets and beauties do themselves forsake And die . *Sonnet* 12 11
Say that thou didst forsake me for some fault 89 1
Forsaken. Of him, myself, and thee, I am forsaken 133 7
Forsook. Narcissus so himself himself forsook, And died to kiss his shadow in the brook *Ven. and Adon.* 161
For where they lay the shadow had forsook them 176
'It cannot be' she in that sense forsook, And turn'd it thus . *Lucrece* 1538
Forswore. I forswore; but I will prove, Thou being a goddess, I forswore not thee . . . . *Pass. Pil.* 33
Forsworn. Lest she should steal a kiss and die forsworn *Ven. and Adon.* 726
Purest faith unhappily forsworn, And gilded honour shamefully misplaced *Sonnet* 66 4
And prove thee virtuous, though thou art forsworn . . . 88 4
In loving thee thou know'st I am forsworn, But thou art twice forsworn, to me love swearing 152 1
If love make me forsworn, how shall I swear to love? . *Pass. Pil.* 57
Though to myself forsworn, to thee I'll constant prove . . 59
Fort. Under that colour am I come to scale Thy never-conquer'd fort *Lucrece* 482
Let it not be call'd impiety, If in this blemish'd fort I make some hole 1175
Forth. Thine eye darts forth the fire that burneth me *Ven. and Adon.* 196
O, had thy mother borne so hard a mind, She had not brought forth thee . 204
Red cheeks and fiery eyes blaze forth her wrong 219
But, lo, from forth a copse that neighbours by, A breeding jennet . . 259
And forth she rushes, snorts, and neighs aloud 262
His nostrils drink the air, and forth again 273

Forth. But now her cheek was pale, and by and by It flash'd forth fire, as lightning from the sky *Ven. and Adon.* 348
Who plucks the bud before one leaf put forth? 416
In shade doth sit, Long after fearing to creep forth again 1036
What needeth then apologies be made, To set forth that which is so singular? *Lucrece* 32
But his hot heart, which fond desire doth scorch, Puffs forth another wind 315
As the fair and fiery-pointed sun, Rushing from forth a cloud, bereaves our sight 373
Who, peeping forth this tumult to behold, Are by his flaming torch dimm'd and controll'd 447
As one in dead of night From forth dull sleep by dreadful fancy waking 450
Frantic with grief thus breathes she forth her spite 762
The remedy indeed to do me good Is to let forth my foul-defiled blood 1029
Thy interest was not bought Basely with gold, but stol'n from forth thy gate 1068
And forth with bashful innocence doth hie 1341
And dying eyes gleam'd forth their ashy lights 1378
As if her heart would break, She throws forth Tarquin's name 1717
By our strong arms from forth her fair streets chased 1834
And make me travel forth without my cloak *Sonnet* 34 2
Let him bring forth Eternal numbers to outlive long date 38 11
'Gainst death and all-oblivious enmity Shall you pace forth 55 10
For I am shamed by that which I bring forth, And so should you 72 13
Alack, what poverty my Muse brings forth! 103 1
Thou usurer, that put'st forth all to use 134 10
Those lips that Love's own hand did make Breathed forth the sound that said 'I hate' 145 2
When thou wilt inflame, How coldly those impediments stand forth! *Lov. Comp.* 269
Green plants bring not Forth their dye *Pass. Pil.* 284
But plainly say thou lovest her well, And set thy person forth to sell 310
Forthwith. Whereat a waxen torch forthwith he lighteth *Lucrece* 178
Fortified. A platted hive of straw, Which fortified her visage from the sun *Lov. Comp.* 9
Fortify. Fortify yourself in your decay With means more blessed *Sonnet* 16 3
For such a time do I now fortify Against confounding age's cruel knife 63 9
Fortressed. Honour and beauty, in the owner's arms, Are weakly fortress'd from a world of harms *Lucrece* 28
Fortune. I fear'd thy fortune, and my joints did tremble *Ven. and Adon.* 642
Reckoning his fortune at such high-proud rate *Lucrece* 19
Then Love and Fortune be my gods, my guide! 351
And they too strong, To hold their cursed-blessed fortune long 866
Cancell'd my fortunes, and enchained me To endless date 934
And turn the giddy round of Fortune's wheel 952
Nor can I fortune to brief minutes tell *Sonnet* 14 5
Whilst I, whom fortune of such triumph bars, Unlook'd for joy 25 3
In disgrace with fortune and men's eyes, I all alone beweep 29 1
And shalt by fortune once more re-survey These poor rude lines 32 3
So I, made lame by fortune's dearest spite 37 3
Now, while the world is bent my deeds to cross, Join with the spite of fortune 90 3
So shall I taste At first the very worst of fortune's might 90 12
Do you with Fortune chide, The guilty goddess of my harmful deeds 111 1
It might for Fortune's bastard be unfather'd 124 2
One silly cross Wrought all my loss; O frowning Fortune! *Pass. Pil.* 259
Whilst as fickle Fortune smiled, Thou and I were both beguiled 401
But if Fortune once do frown, Then farewell his great renown 419
Forty. When forty winters shall besiege thy brow *Sonnet* 2 1
Forward. Deep woes roll forward like a gentle flood *Lucrece* 1118
In sequent toil all forwards do contend *Sonnet* 60 4
The forward violet thus did I chide: Sweet thief 99 1
Fought. From the strand of Dardan, where they fought, To Simois' reedy banks *Lucrece* 1436
Foul. Were I hard-favour'd, foul, or wrinkled-old *Ven. and Adon.* 133
Gusts and foul flaws to herdmen and to herds 456
Foul words and frowns must not repel a lover 573
Beauty hath nought to do with such foul fiends 638
By this black-faced night, desire's foul nurse 773
Like many clouds consulting for foul weather 972
To wash the foul face of the sluttish ground 983
'Tis he, foul creature, that hath done thee wrong 1005
And in her haste unfortunately spies The foul boar's conquest 1030
This foul, grim, and urchin-snouted boar 1105
This ambitious foul infirmity, In having much, torments us with defect Of that we have *Lucrece* 150
But honest fear, bewitch'd with lust's foul charm, Doth too too oft betake him to retire 173
O foul dishonour to my household's grave! O impious act, including all foul harms! 198
Full of foul hope and full of fond mistrust 284
That his foul thoughts might compass his fair fair 346
Like a foul usurper, went about From this fair throne to heave the owner out 412
Nor aught obeys but his foul appetite 546
Yet, foul night-waking cat, he doth but dally 554
That to his borrow'd bed he make retire, And stoop to honour, not to foul desire 574
With foul offenders thou perforce must bear 612
Foul sin may say, He learn'd to sin, and thou didst teach the way 629
His taste delicious, in digestion souring, Devours his will, that lived by foul devouring 700
Her subjects with foul insurrection Have batter'd down her consecrated wall 722
Thou murder'st troth: Thou foul abettor! thou notorious bawd! 886
My life's foul deed, my life's fair end shall free it 1208
What wrong else may be imagined By foul enforcement might be done to me 1623
May my pure mind with the foul act dispense 1704
Is it revenge to give thyself a blow For his foul act? 1824
And so to publish Tarquin's foul offence 1852
Siren tears, Distill'd from limbecks foul as hell within *Sonnet* 119 2
Fairing the foul with art's false borrow'd face 127 6
Beauty herself is black And all they foul that thy complexion lack 132 14
Say this is not, To put fair truth upon so foul a face 137 12
Wooing his purity with her foul pride 144 8
Thou keep'st me blind, Lest eyes well-seeing thy foul faults should find 148 14
More perjured I, To swear against the truth so foul a lie! 152 14
And knew the patterns of his foul beguiling *Lov. Comp.* 170
And bastards of his foul adulterate heart 175
Thou shrieking harbinger, Foul precurrer of the fiend *Ph. and Tur.* 6
Foul-cankering rust the hidden treasure frets *Ven. and Adon.* 767
Foul-defiled. The remedy indeed to do me good Is to let forth my foul-defiled blood *Lucrece* 1029
Fouler. Thou their fair life, and they thy fouler grave 661
Foul-reeking. O Night, thou furnace of foul-reeking smoke! 799
Found. And swear I found you where you did fulfil The loathsome act of lust 1635
If I lose thee, my loss is my love's gain, And losing her, my friend hath found that loss *Sonnet* 42 10
I hold such strife As 'twixt a miser and his wealth is found 75 4
And found such fair assistance in my verse 78 2
Beauty doth he give And found it in thy cheek 79 11
I found, or thought I found, you did exceed The barren tender of a poet's debt 83 3
And, sick of welfare, found a kind of meetness To be diseased 118 7
A maid of Dian's this advantage found 153 2
And thither hied, a sad distemper'd guest, But found no cure 153 13
Found yet moe letters sadly penn'd in blood *Lov. Comp.* 47
As goods lost are seld or never found, As vaded gloss no rubbing will refresh *Pass. Pil.* 175
Foundation. Struggling for passage, earth's foundation shakes *V. and A.* 1047
Fount. Or toads infect fair founts with venom mud *Lucrece* 850
Each cheek a river running from a fount *Lov. Comp.* 283
Fountain. Graze on my lips; and if those hills be dry, Stray lower, where the pleasant fountains lie *Ven. and Adon.* 234
Mud not the fountain that gave drink to thee *Lucrece* 577
The poison'd fountain clears itself again 1707
From the purple fountain Brutus drew The murderous knife 1734
Roses have thorns, and silver fountains mud *Sonnet* 35 2
The broken bosoms that to me belong Have emptied all their fountains in my well *Lov. Comp.* 255
Four. What banquet wert thou to the taste, Being nurse and feeder of the other four! *Ven. and Adon.* 446
Were never four such lamps together mix'd, Had not his clouded with his brow's repine 489
My life, being made of four, with two alone Sinks down to death *Sonnet* 45 7
Fowl. Which, like a falcon towering in the skies, Coucheth the fowl below *Lucrece* 507
Marking what he tells With trembling fear, as fowl hear falcon's bells 511
To hie as fast As lagging fowls before the northern blast 1335
From this session interdict Every fowl of tyrant wing *Ph. and Tur.* 10
Fox. Or at the fox which lives by subtlety *Ven. and Adon.* 675
Fragrant. Which, like a canker in the fragrant rose, Doth spot the beauty of thy budding name! *Sonnet* 95 2
There will I make thee a bed of roses, With a thousand fragrant posies *Pass. Pil.* 362
Frail. Will not my tongue be mute, my frail joints shake? *Lucrece* 227
Frailer. On my frailties why are frailer spies, Which in their wills count bad what I think good? *Sonnet* 121 7
Frailties. All frailties that besiege all kinds of blood 109 10
On my frailties why are frailer spies, Which in their wills count bad what I think good? 121 7
Frame. Those hours, that with gentle work did frame The lovely gaze 5 1
My body is the frame wherein 'tis held 24 3
What the old world could say To this composed wonder of your frame 59 10
To bitter sauces did I frame my feeding 118 6
And to her will frame all thy ways *Pass. Pil.* 323
Framed. Wherein she framed thee in high heaven's despite *Ven. and Adon.* 731
She framed the love, and yet she foil'd the framing *Pass. Pil.* 99
Framing. Swear Nature's death for framing thee so fair *Ven. and Adon.* 744
She framed the love, and yet she foil'd the framing *Pass. Pil.* 99
Frank. Being frank she lends to those are free *Sonnet* 4 4
Frantic with grief thus breathes she forth her spite *Lucrece* 762
Franticly. Dumbly she passions, franticly she doteth *Ven. and Adon.* 1059
Frantic-mad. And frantic-mad with evermore unrest *Sonnet* 147 10
Fraud. It shall be fickle, false, and full of fraud *Ven. and Adon.* 1141
Impression of strange kinds Is form'd in them by force, by fraud, or skill *Lucrece* 1243
Fraughted. O cruel speeding, Fraughted with gall *Pass. Pil.* 270
Free. Free vent of words love's fire doth assuage *Ven. and Adon.* 334
Or free that soul which wretchedness hath chain'd *Lucrece* 900
My life's foul deed, my life's fair end shall free it 1208
From that, alas, thy Lucrece is not free 1624
Being frank she lends to those are free *Sonnet* 4 4
Take thou my oblation, poor but free 125 10
Nor he will not be free, For thou art covetous and he is kind 134 5
He pays the whole, and yet am I not free 134 14
For maiden-tongued he was, and thereof free *Lov. Comp.* 100
Kept hearts in liveries, but mine own was free 195
Freed. Let guiltless souls be freed from guilty woe *Lucrece* 1482
Freedom. Steal thine own freedom and complain on theft *Ven. and Adon.* 160
Mine eye my heart thy picture's sight would bar, My heart mine eye the freedom of that right *Sonnet* 46 4
My woeful self, that did in freedom stand *Lov. Comp.* 143
Freezing. That knows not parching heat nor freezing cold *Lucrece* 1145
What freezings have I felt, what dark days seen! *Sonnet* 97 3
Frenzy. Life-poisoning pestilence and frenzies wood *Ven. and Adon.* 740
And his untimely frenzy thus awaketh *Lucrece* 1675
Frequent. That I have frequent been with unknown minds *Sonnet* 117 5
Fresh. Making them red and pale with fresh variety *Ven. and Adon.* 21
Fresh beauty for the use, Herbs for their smell, and sappy plants to bear 164
Like the fair sun, when in his fresh array He cheers the morn and all the earth relieveth 483
Whose blood upon the fresh flowers being shed Doth make them droop 665
He hath fed Upon fresh beauty, blotting it with blame 796
Love's gentle spring doth always fresh remain 801
The flowers are sweet, their colours fresh and trim 1079
Their fresh falls' haste Add to his flow, but alter not his taste *Lucrece* 650
That fair fresh mirror, dim and old, Shows me a bare-boned death 1760
Thou that art now the world's fresh ornament *Sonnet* 1 9
Whose fresh repair if now thou not renewest, Thou dost beguile the world 3 3
That fresh blood which youngly thou bestowest Thou mayst call thine 11 3
And in fresh numbers number all your graces 17 6
Three hot Junes burn'd, Since first I saw you fresh, which yet are green 104 8
Now with the drops of this most balmy time My love looks fresh 107 10
Eternal love in love's fresh case Weighs not the dust and injury of age 108 9
I might as yet have been a spreading flower, Fresh to myself *Lov. Comp.* 76
The deep-green emerald, in whose fresh regard Weak sights their sickly radiance do amend 213
Sitting by a brook With young Adonis, lovely, fresh, and green *Pass. Pil.* 44

Fresher. Seek anew Some fresher stamp of the time-bettering days *Son.* 82 8
Fret. Pure shame and awed resistance made him fret *Ven. and Adon.* 69
Still is he sullen, still he lours and frets, 'Twixt crimson shame and anger ashy-pale 75
His eyes, like glow-worms, shine when he doth fret . . . 621
Foul-cankering rust the hidden treasure frets 767
Huge fires abide, And with the wind in greater fury fret *Lucrece* 648
These means, as frets upon an instrument, Shall tune our heart-strings 1140
Friend. So white a friend engirts so white a foe . . *Ven. and Adon.* 364
He intends To hunt the boar with certain of his friends 588
They that thrive well take counsel of their friends 640
'I am,' quoth he, 'expected of my friends' 718
As one on shore Gazing upon a late-embarked friend 818
His honour, his affairs, his friends, his state, Neglected all . *Lucrece* 45
Or were he not my dear friend, this desire Might have excuse to work upon his wife 234
But as he is my kinsman, my dear friend, The shame and fault finds no excuse nor end 237
But will is deaf and hears no heedful friends 495
I rest thy secret friend: The fault unknown is as a thought unacted . 526
My husband is thy friend; for his sake spare me: Thyself art mighty . 582
When wilt thou be the humble suppliant's friend? 897
One poor retiring minute in an age Would purchase thee a thousand thousand friends 963
Let him have time to see his friends his foes 988
Myself, thy friend, will kill myself, thy foe 1196
Here friend by friend in bloody channel lies And friend to friend gives unadvised wounds 1487
Featured like him, like him with friends possess'd. . *Sonnet* 29 6
For precious friends hid in death's dateless night . . . 30 6
But if the while I think on thee, dear friend, All losses are restored . 30 13
And all those friends which I thought buried 31 4
Had my friend's Muse grown with this growing age . . . 32 10
So doth she abuse me, Suffering my friend for my sake to approve her 42 8
If I lose thee, my loss is my love's gain, And losing her, my friend hath found that loss 42 10
But here's the joy; my friend and I are one; Sweet flattery! . 42 13
Thus far the miles are measured from thy friend . . . 50 4
Sympathized In true plain words by thy true-telling friend . 82 12
To me, fair friend, you never can be old 104 1
Mine appetite I never more will grind On newer proof, to try an older friend 110 11
Pity me then, dear friend, and I assure ye Even that your pity is enough to cure me 111 13
That makes my heart to groan For that deep wound it gives my friend and me! 133 2
But slave to slavery my sweet'st friend must be . . . 133 4
But then my friend's heart let my poor heart bail . . . 133 10
That put'st forth all to use, And sue a friend came debtor for my sake 134 11
But being both from me, both to each friend, I guess one angel in another's hell . . . . 144 11; *Pass. Pil.* 25
Who hateth thee that I do call my friend? . . . *Sonnet* 149 5
O yes, dear friend, I pardon crave of thee . . . *Pass. Pil.* 141
King Pandion he is dead; All thy friends are lapp'd in lead . . 396
Every one that flatters thee Is no friend in misery . . . 404
Faithful friends are hard to find: Every man will be thy friend Whilst thou hast wherewith to spend 406
He that is thy friend indeed, He will help thee in thy need . . 423
These are certain signs to know Faithful friend from flattering foe . 430
Friendly. Sorrow that friendly sighs sought still to dry . *Ven. and Adon.* 964
Friendship. By knighthood, gentry, and sweet friendship's oath . *Lucrece* 569
In scorn or friendship, nill I construe whether . . *Pass. Pil.* 188
Fright. The wolf would leave his prey And never fright the silly lamb that day *Ven. and Adon.* 1098
They fright him, yet he still pursues his fear . . . *Lucrece* 308
And fright her with confusion of their cries 445
And fright her crying babe with Tarquin's name . . . 814
Frighted. As the poor frighted deer, that stands at gaze . . . 1149
From. Desire doth lend her force Courageously to pluck him from his horse *Ven. and Adon.* 30
But, lo, from forth a copse that neighbours by, A breeding jennet . 259
As from a furnace, vapours doth he send 274
A thousand kisses buys my heart from me 517
On a flint he softly smiteth, That from the cold stone sparks of fire do fly *Lucrece* 177
That from their own misdeeds askance their eyes . . . 637
So, I commend me from our house in grief 1308
Front. As Philomel in summer's front doth sing . . *Sonnet* 102 7
Frost. Like little frosts that sometime threat the spring . *Lucrece* 331
Against love's fire fear's frost hath dissolution . . . 355
Sap check'd with frost and lusty leaves quite gone . *Sonnet* 5 7
Frosty. He red for shame, but frosty in desire . *Ven. and Adon.* 36
Froth. A dream, a breath, a froth of fleeting joy . . *Lucrece* 212
Frothy. Whose frothy mouth, bepainted all with red *Ven. and Adon.* 901
Froward. Or like the froward infant still'd with dandling . . 562
But then woos best when most his choice is froward . . . 570
He rose and ran away; ah, fool too froward! . . . *Pass. Pil.* 56

Frown. Now doth he frown, And 'gins to chide, but soon she stops his lips *Ven. and Adon.* 45
A smile recures the wounding of a frown 465
When he did frown, O, had she then gave over, Such nectar from his lips she had not suck'd 571
Foul words and frowns must not repel a lover 573
For at a frown they in their glory die . . . *Sonnet* 25 8
If ever that time come, When I shall see thee frown on my defects . 49 2
The false heart's history Is writ in moods and frowns and wrinkles strange 93 8
Bring me within the level of your frown 117 11
But if Fortune once do frown, Then farewell his great renown *Pass. Pil.* 419
Frownest. On whom frown'st thou that I do fawn upon? *Sonnet* 149 6
Frowning. One silly cross Wrought all my loss; O frowning Fortune! *Pass. Pil.* 259
What though her frowning brows be bent 311
Frozen. What wax so frozen but dissolves with tempering? *Ven. and Adon.* 565
'Tween frozen conscience and hot-burning will . . *Lucrece* 247
Fruit. He shall not boast who did thy stock pollute That thou art doting father of his fruit 1064
Yet this abundant issue seem'd to me But hope of orphans and unfather'd fruit . . . . *Sonnet* 97 10
Fruitful. Her husband's fame, Won in the fields of fruitful Italy . *Lucrece* 107
Fruitless. Despite of fruitless chastity, Love-lacking vestals *Ven. and Adon.* 751
Fry. No fisher but the ungrown fry forbears 526
Fuel. Feed'st thy light's flame with self-substantial fuel . *Sonnet* 1 6
Fulfil. Thy princely office how canst thou fulfil? . . *Lucrece* 628
And swear I found you where you did fulfil The loathsome act of lust . 1635
Thus far for love my love-suit, sweet, fulfil . . . *Sonnet* 136 4
'Will' will fulfil the treasure of thy love 136 5
Fulfilled. O, let it not be hild Poor women's faults, that they are so fulfill'd With men's abuses . . . . *Lucrece* 1258
Full. Wishing her cheeks were gardens full of flowers *Ven. and Adon.* 65
Broad breast, full eye, small head, and nostril wide, High crest, short ears 296
When, lo, the unback'd breeder, full of fear, Jealous of catching, swiftly doth forsake him 320
Full gently now she takes him by the hand 361
But, when his glutton eye so full hath fed, His other agents aim at like delight 399
Crystal eyne, Whose full perfection all the world amazes . . . 634
Love is all truth, Lust full of forged lies 804
Now I will away; My face is full of shame, my heart of teen . . 808
Full of respects, yet nought at all respecting 911
As one full of despair, She vail'd her eyelids 955
Fie, fie, fond love, thou art so full of fear 1021
It shall be fickle, false, and full of fraud 1141
It shall be sparing and too full of riot 1147
Full of foul hope and full of fond mistrust . . . *Lucrece* 284
Which gives the watch-word to his hand full soon . . . 370
His face, though full of cares, yet show'd content . . . 1503
Full many a glorious morning have I seen Flatter the mountain-tops *Son.* 33 1
Thy beauty and thy years full well befits, For still temptation follows where thou art 41 3
The canker-blooms have full as deep a dye As the perfumed tincture of the roses 54 5
Else call it winter, which being full of care Makes summer's welcome thrice more wish'd, more rare 56 13
Sometime all full with feasting on your sight . . . 75 9
Was it the proud full sail of his great verse? . . . 86 1
No reason why My most full flame should afterwards burn clearer . 115 4
To give full growth to that which still doth grow . . . 115 14
Even so, being full of your ne'er-cloying sweetness . . . 118 5
Thy gift, thy tables, are within my brain Full character'd . . 122 2
Till action, lust Is perjured, murderous, bloody, full of blame . 129 3
Nor that full star that ushers in the even 132 7
Ay, fill it full with wills, and my will one . . . 136 6
Ere long espied a fickle maid full pale, Tearing of papers . *Lov. Comp.* 5
Youth is full of pleasance, age is full of care . . *Pass. Pil.* 158
Youth is full of sport, age's breath is short; Youth is nimble, age is lame 161
Have you not heard it said full oft, A woman's nay doth stand for nought? 339
Full-fed. As the full-fed hound or gorged hawk, . . . Make slow pursuit *Lucr.* 694
Fullness. Although to-day thou fill Thy hungry eyes even till they wink with fullness . . . . *Sonnet* 56 6
Fume. He stamps and bites the poor flies in his fume *Ven. and Adon.* 316
As smoke from Ætna, that in air consumes, Or that which from discharged cannon fumes . . . . *Lucrece* 1043
Function. That which governs me to go about Doth part his function *Son.* 113 3
Furnace. As from a furnace, vapours doth he send . *Ven. and Adon.* 274
O Night, thou furnace of foul-reeking smoke! . . . *Lucrece* 799
Furrows. When in thee time's furrows I behold . . . *Sonnet* 22 3
Further. This way she runs, and now she will no further, But back retires *Ven. and Adon.* 905
This forced league doth force a further strife . . . *Lucrece* 689
For further I could say 'This man's untrue' . . . *Lov. Comp.* 169
Fury. Grew kinder, and his fury was assuaged . *Ven. and Adon.* 318
With blindfold fury she begins to forage 554
Or stop the headlong fury of his speed . . . . *Lucrece* 501
Huge fires abide, And with the wind in greater fury fret . . 648
Spend'st thou thy fury on some worthless song? . . . *Sonnet* 100 3

G

Gage. Such thwarting strife, That one for all, or all for one we gage *Lucrece* 144
Pawn'd honest looks, but laid no words to gage 1351
Gain. Despair to gain doth traffic oft for gaining 131
Those that much covet are with gain so fond, For what they have not . 134
Such griefs sustain, That they prove bankrupt in this poor-rich gain . 140
What win I, if I gain the thing I seek? A dream, a breath . . 211
A captive victor that hath lost in gain 730
Having no other pleasure of his gain But torment 860
If I lose thee, my loss is my love's gain, And losing her, my friend hath found that loss . . . . *Sonnet* 42 9

Gain. I have seen the hungry ocean gain Advantage on the kingdom of the shore 64 5
She hath no exchequer now but his, And, proud of many, lives upon his gains 67 12
And gain by ill thrice more than I have spent . . . 119 14
I count my gain, That she that makes me sin awards me pain . 141 13
It was to gain my grace—Of one by nature's outwards so commended *Lov. Comp.* 79
More mickle was the pain That nothing could be used to turn them both to gain . . . . *Pass. Pil.* 220

Gained. Thy grace being gain'd cures all disgrace in me *Pass. Pil.* 36
Gainer. And I by this will be a gainer too *Sonnet* 88 9
Gaining. Despair to gain doth traffic oft for gaining *Lucrece* 131
Gaining more, the profit of excess Is but to surfeit 138
'Gainst venom'd sores the only sovereign plaster *Ven. and Adon.* 916
And dotes on what he looks, 'gainst law or duty *Lucrece* 497
That 'gainst thyself thou stick'st not to conspire *Sonnet* 10 6
Nothing 'gainst Time's scythe can make defence Save breed 12 13
Thy adverse party is thy advocate—And 'gainst myself a lawful plea commence 35 11
'Gainst death and all-oblivious enmity Shall you pace forth 55 9
Being crown'd, Crooked eclipses 'gainst his glory fight 60 7
I will drink Potions of eisel 'gainst my strong infection 111 10
Or forced examples, 'gainst her own content *Lov. Comp.* 157
Love's arms are peace, 'gainst rule, 'gainst sense, 'gainst shame 271
And supplicant their sighs to you extend, To leave the battery that you make 'gainst mine 277
'Gainst whom the world could not hold argument *Pass. Pil.* 30
Gait. Look, the world's comforter, with weary gait, His day's hot task hath ended in the west *Ven. and Adon.* 529
Solemn night with slow sad gait descended To ugly hell *Lucrece* 1081
And give the harmless show An humble gait, calm looks, eyes wailing still 1508
Those dancing chips, O'er whom thy fingers walk with gentle gait *Sonnet* 128 11
Gall. Thou false thief, Thy honey turns to gall, thy joy to grief! *Lucrece* 889
O cruel speeding, Fraughted with gall *Pass. Pil.* 270
Gallant. To leave the master loveless, or kill the gallant knight 216
Galled. Their ranks began To break upon the galled shore, and than Retire again *Lucrece* 1440
'Gan. 'O, pity,' 'gan she cry, 'flint-hearted boy! 'Tis but a kiss I beg' *Ven. and Adon.* 95
Even so the maid with swelling drops gan wet *Lucrece* 1228
And often kiss'd, and often gan to tear *Lov. Comp.* 51
Long upon these terms I held my city, Till thus he gan besiege me 177
Through the velvet leaves the wind, All unseen, gan passage find *Pass. Pil.* 232
Gaol. A lily prison'd in a gaol of snow, Or ivory in an alabaster band *Ven. and Adon.* 362
Thou canst not then use rigour in my gaol: And yet thou wilt *Sonnet* 133 12
Gaping. A press of gaping faces, Which seem'd to swallow up his sound advice *Lucrece* 1408
Gardens. Wishing her cheeks were gardens full of flowers *Ven. and Adon.* 65
Many maiden gardens yet unset With virtuous wish *Sonnet* 16 6
Garment. Who wears a garment shapeless and unfinish'd *Ven and Adon.* 415
Some [glory] in their garments, though new-fangled ill *Sonnet* 91 3
Prouder than garments' cost, Of more delight than hawks or horses be 91 10
With the garment of a Grace The naked and concealed fiend he cover'd *Lov. Comp.* 316
Gashes. Her mangling eye, That makes more gashes where no breach should be *Ven. and Adon.* 1066
Gate. Remove your siege from my unyielding heart; To love's alarms it will not ope the gate 424
Soft pity enters at an iron gate *Lucrece* 595
Thy interest was not bought Basely with gold, but stol'n from forth thy gate 1068
Like to the lark at break of day arising From sullen earth, sings hymns at heaven's gate *Sonnet* 29 12
Nor gates of steel so strong, but Time decays 65 8
Who glazed with crystal gate the glowing roses *Lov. Comp.* 286
Gathered. Fair flowers that are not gather'd in their prime, Rot and consume themselves in little time *Ven. and Adon.* 131
Weeds among weeds, or flowers with flowers gather'd *Sonnet* 124 4
Gaudy. He put his bonnet on, Under whose brim the gaudy sun would peep *Ven. and Adon.* 1088
And when his gaudy banner is display'd, The coward fights and will not be dismay'd *Lucrece* 272
The world's fresh ornament And only herald to the gaudy spring *Sonnet* 1 10
Gave. But hers, which through the crystal tears gave light, Shone like the moon in water seen by night *Ven. and Adon.* 491
Had she then gave over, Such nectar from his lips she had not suck'd 571
The kiss I gave you is bestow'd in vain 771
Witness the entertainment that he gave 1108
Virtue claims from beauty beauty's red, Which virtue gave the golden age *Lucrece* 60
Mud not the fountain that gave drink to thee 577
By him that gave it thee, From a pure heart command thy rebel will 624
In scorn of nature, art gave lifeless life 1374
That blushing red no guilty instance gave 1511
Look, whom she best endow'd she gave the more *Sonnet* 11 11
Were it not thy sour leisure gave sweet leave To entertain the time 39 10
And Time that gave doth now his gift confound 60 8
By all above, These blenches gave my heart another youth 110 7
Gave eyes to blindness, Or made them swear against the thing they see 152 11
Which she perused, sigh'd, tore, and gave the flood *Lov. Comp.* 44
His real habitude gave life and grace To appertainings 114
Reserved the stalk and gave him all my flower 147
O, how the channel to the stream gave grace! 285
Gave the tempter place, Which like a cherubin above them hover'd 318
Gavest. Why hath thy servant, Opportunity, Betray'd the hours thou gavest me to repose? *Lucrece* 933
Thou gavest me thine, not to give back again *Sonnet* 22 14
Thyself thou gavest, thy own worth then not knowing, Or me, to whom thou gavest it, else mistaking 87 9
Gay. What cares he now for curb or pricking spur? For rich caparisons or trapping gay? *Ven. and Adon.* 286
Ere beauty's dead fleece made another gay *Sonnet* 68 8
Painting thy outward walls so costly gay 146 4
Then, lullaby, the learned man hath got the lady gay *Pass. Pil.* 225
Gaze. To which Love's eyes pay tributary gazes *Ven. and Adon.* 632
Only he hath an eye to gaze on beauty, And dotes on what he looks *Lucrece* 496
As the poor frighted deer, that stands at gaze 1149
The lovely gaze where every eye doth dwell *Sonnet* 5 2
Where-through the sun Delights to peep, to gaze therein on thee 24 12
Anon their gazes lend To every place at once, and, nowhere fix'd *Lov. Comp.* 26
Lord, how mine eyes throw gazes to the east! My heart doth charge the watch *Pass. Pil.* 193
Gazed. Whereon with fearful eyes they long have gazed *Ven. and Adon.* 927
She took me kindly by the hand, And gazed for tidings in my eager eyes *Lucr.* 254
Gnats are unnoted wheresoe'er they fly, But eagles gazed upon with every eye 1015
Blushing with him, wistly on him gazed 1355
So fair a form lodged not a mind so ill: And still on him she gazed 1531
Thy youth's proud livery, so gazed on now, Will be a tatter'd weed *Sonnet* 2 3
Gazer. Whereat the impartial gazer late did wonder *Ven. and Adon.* 748
How many gazers mightst thou lead away! *Sonnet* 96 11
Gazeth. Now gazeth she on him, now on the ground *Ven. and Adon.* 224
Wickedly he stalks, And gazeth on her yet unstained bed *Lucrece* 366
An eye more bright . . . , Gilding the object whereupon it gazeth *Sonnet* 20 6
Gazing. As one on shore Gazing upon a late-embarked friend *V. and A.* 818
His rage of lust by gazing qualified; Slack'd, not suppress'd *Lucrece* 424
Gazing upon the Greeks with little lust 1384
And gazing still, Such signs of truth in his plain face she spied 1531
Pitiful thrivers, in their gazing spent *Sonnet* 125 8
Gems. With earth and sea's rich gems, With April's first-born flowers 21 6
With the annexions of fair gems enrich'd *Lov. Comp.* 208
Gender. And thou treble-dated crow, That thy sable gender makest *Ph. and Tur.* 18
General. From the creation to the general doom *Lucrece* 924
Why should so many fall, To plague a private sin in general? 1484
All these I better in one general best *Sonnet* 91 8
Unless this general evil they maintain, All men are bad 121 13
And so the general of hot desire Was sleeping by a virgin hand disarm'd 154 7
He did in the general bosom reign Of young, of old *Lov. Comp.* 127
Gentle. I'll sigh celestial breath, whose gentle wind Shall cool the heat of this descending sun *Ven. and Adon.* 189
With gentle majesty and modest pride 278
Let me excuse thy courser, gentle boy; And learn of him 403
Distempering gentle Love in his desire, As air and water do abate the fire 653
Love's gentle spring doth always fresh remain 801
The gentle lark, weary of rest, From his moist cabinet mounts up on high 853
For now she knows it is no gentle chase, But the blunt boar 883
Gentle shadow,—truth I must confess,—I rail'd on thee 1001
The rough beast that knows no gentle right *Lucrece* 545
From earth's dark womb some gentle gust doth get 549
Or tyrant folly lurk in gentle breasts 851
Deep woes roll forward like a gentle flood 1118
Since men prove beasts, let beasts bear gentle minds 1148
Their gentle sex to weep are often willing 1237
Know, gentle wench, it small avails my mood 1273
Those hours, that with gentle work did frame The lovely gaze *Sonnet* 5 1
Shall hate be fairer lodged than gentle love? 10 10
A woman's gentle heart, but not acquainted With shifting change 20 3
I do forgive thy robbery, gentle thief, Although thou steal thee all my poverty 40 9
Gentle thou art and therefore to be won 41 5
Though I feel thou art, Within the gentle closure of my breast 48 11
My verse alone had all thy gentle grace 79 2
Your monument shall be my gentle verse 81 9
Some say thy grace is youth and gentle sport 96 2
And straight redeem In gentle numbers time so idly spent 100 6
Those dancing chips, O'er whom thy fingers walk with gentle gait 128 11
That tongue that ever sweet Was used in giving gentle doom 145 7
That follow'd it as gentle day Doth follow night 145 10
Then, gentle cheater, urge not my amiss 151 3
Gentle maid, Have of my suffering youth some feeling pity *Lov. Comp.* 177
Would not touch the bait, But smile and jest at every gentle offer *Pass. Pil.* 54
Gentlest. For if it see the rudest or gentlest sight, . . . it shapes them to your feature *Sonnet* 113 9
Gently. Full gently now she takes him by the hand *Ven. and Adon.* 361
The tiger would be tame and gently hear him 1096
When thou gently sway'st The wiry concord that mine ear confounds *Sonnet* 128 3
Gentry. By knighthood, gentry, and sweet friendship's oath *Lucrece* 569
Get. Her help she sees, but help she cannot get *Ven. and Adon.* 93
Thou wast begot; to get it is thy duty 168
All my mind, my thought, my busy care, Is how to get my palfrey 384
Who buys a minute's mirth to wail a week? Or sells eternity to get a toy? *Lucrece* 214
From earth's dark womb some gentle gust doth get 549
Thou set'st the wolf where he the lamb may get 878
Go, get me hither paper, ink, and pen 1289
Unlook'd on diest, unless thou get a son *Sonnet* 7 14
Many there were that did his picture get, To serve their eyes *Lov. Comp.* 134
Ghastly. That thinks she hath beheld some ghastly sprite *Lucrece* 451
Let ghastly shadows his lewd eyes affright 971
Like a jewel hung in ghastly night *Sonnet* 27 11
Ghost. Grim-grinning ghost, earth's worm, what dost thou mean To stifle beauty? *Ven. and Adon.* 933
He, nor that affable familiar ghost Which nightly gulls him *Sonnet* 86 9
Giddy. And turn the giddy round of Fortune's wheel *Lucrece* 952
Gift. Which bounteous gift thou shouldst in bounty cherish *Sonnet* 11 12
And Time that gave doth now his gift confound 60 8
The cause of this fair gift in me is wanting 87 7
So thy great gift, upon misprision growing, Comes home again 87 11
For to no other pass my verses tend Than of your graces and your gifts to tell 103 12
Thy gift, thy tables, are within my brain Full character'd 122 1
Which by a gift of learning did bear the maid away *Pass. Pil.* 224
Gild. Which virtue gave the golden age to gild Their silver cheeks *Lucrece* 60
Gilded. Nor the gilded monuments Of princes, shall outlive this powerful rhyme *Sonnet* 55 1
And gilded honour shamefully misplaced 66 5
It lies in thee To make him much outlive a gilded tomb 101 11
Saw how deceits were gilded in his smiling *Lov. Comp.* 172
Gildest. When sparkling stars twire not thou gild'st the even *Sonnet* 28 12
Gilding. An eye more bright than theirs, less false in rolling, Gilding the object whereupon it gazeth 20 6
Gilding pale streams with heavenly alchemy 33 4
Gills. When he beheld his shadow in the brook, The fishes spread on it their golden gills *Ven. and Adon.* 1100
'Gins. And like a bold-faced suitor 'gins to woo him 6
Now doth he frown, And 'gins to chide, but soon she stops his lips 46
A flower that dies when first it gins to bud *Pass. Pil.* 171
Girded. And summer's green all girded up in sheaves *Sonnet* 12 7
Girdle with embracing flames the waist Of Collatine's fair love *Lucrece* 6
Girl. 'My girl,' quoth she, 'on what occasion break Those tears from thee?' 1270
'But tell me, girl, when went'—and there she stay'd Till after a deep groan—'Tarquin from hence?' 1275
Girths. And now his woven girths he breaks asunder *Ven. and Adon.* 266
Give. So offers he to give what she did crave 88
Give me one kiss, I'll give it thee again, And one for interest 209
'Give me my hand,' saith he, 'why dost thou feel it?' 'Give me my heart,' saith she, 'and thou shalt have it' 373

Give. O, give it me, lest thy hard heart do steel it *Ven. and Adon.* 375
Gives false alarms, suggesteth mutiny 651
By their suggestion gives a deadly groan 1044
So guiltless she securely gives good cheer And reverend welcome *Lucrece* 89
And give the sneaped birds more cause to sing 333
Which gives the watch-word to his hand full soon 370
Anon his beating heart, alarum striking, Gives the hot charge 434
Alas, how many bear such shameful blows, Which not themselves, but he that gives them knows! 833
Give physic to the sick, ease to the pain'd 901
They buy thy help; but Sin ne'er gives a fee, He gratis comes 913
One that by alms doth live Disdain to him disdained scraps to give 987
To clear this spot by death, At least I give A badge of fame to slander's livery 1053
Her mistress she doth give demure good-morrow 1219
He did her wrong, To give her so much grief and not a tongue 1463
And friend to friend gives unadvised wounds 1488
And give the harmless show An humble gait, calm looks, eyes wailing still 1507
At last she smilingly with this gives o'er 1567
Tell thy grief, that we may give redress 1603
Three times with sighs she gives her sorrow fire 1604
Where no excuse can give the fault amending 1614
'Tis he, That guides this hand to give this wound to me 1722
And bids Lucretius give his sorrow place 1773
At last it rains, and busy winds give o'er 1790
I did give that life Which she too early and too late hath spill'd 1800
Is it revenge to give thyself a blow For his foul act? 1823
The Romans plausibly did give consent 1854
Nature's bequest gives nothing but doth lend *Sonnet* 4 3
Why dost thou abuse The bounteous largess given thee to give? 4 6
Your sweet semblance to some other give 13 4
To give away yourself keeps yourself still 16 13
So long lives this and this gives life to thee 18 14
Thou gavest me thine, not to give back again 22 14
My lovers gone, Who all their parts of me to thee did give 31 11
Nor can thy shame give physic to my grief 34 9
Whilst that this shadow doth such substance give 37 10
O, give thyself the thanks, if aught in me Worthy perusal stand against thy sight 38 5
Who's so dumb that cannot write to thee, When thou thyself dost give invention light? 38 8
By this separation I may give That due to thee which thou deservest alone 39 7
Towards thee I'll run, and give him leave to go 51 14
Blessed are you, whose worthiness gives scope, Being had, to triumph 52 13
By that sweet ornament which truth doth give 54 2
All tongues, the voice of souls, give thee that due, Uttering bare truth 69 3
Those same tongues that give thee so thine own In other accents do this praise confound 69 6
Give warning to the world that I am fled From this vile world 71 3
The wrinkles which thy glass will truly show Of mouthed graves will give thee memory 77 6
But now my gracious numbers are decay'd And my sick Muse doth give another place 79 4
Beauty doth he give And found it in thy cheek 79 10
I impair not beauty being mute, When others would give life and bring a tomb 83 12
The charter of thy worth gives thee releasing 87 3
Give not a windy night a rainy morrow 90 7
Thou forget'st so long To speak of that which gives thee all thy might 100 2
And gives thy pen both skill and argument 100 8
Give my love fame faster than Time wastes life 100 13
Nor gives to necessary wrinkles place 108 11
Then give me welcome, next my heaven the best 110 13
To give full growth to that which still doth grow 115 14
For why should others' false adulterate eyes Give salutation? 121 6
Therefore to give them from me was I bold, To trust those tables 122 11
Give them thy fingers, me thy lips to kiss 128 14
That makes my heart to groan For that deep wound it gives my friend and me 133 2
To make me give the lie to my true sight 150 3
Nor gives it satisfaction to our blood, That we must curb it upon others' proof *Lov. Comp.* 162
Given. Why dost thou abuse The bounteous largess given thee to give? *Sonnet* 4 6
The wits of former days To subjects worse have given admiring praise 59 14
And given grace a double majesty 78 8
And given to time your own dear-purchased right 117 6
Givest. With the breath thou givest and takest, 'Mongst our mourners shalt thou go *Ph. and Tur.* 19
Giving. No dame, hereafter living, By my excuse shall claim excuse's giving *Lucrece* 1715
No, neither he, nor his compeers by night Giving him aid, my verse astonished *Sonnet* 86 8
That tongue that ever sweet Was used in giving gentle doom 145 7
All vows and consecrations giving place *Lov. Comp.* 263
Glad. Make glad and sorry seasons as thou fleets *Sonnet* 19 5
No longer glad, I send them back again and straight grow sad 45 13
Gladly. Why lovest thou that which thou receivest not gladly? 8 3
Glance. The mild glance that sly Ulysses lent Show'd deep regard *Lucrece* 1399
Why with the time do I not glance aside? *Sonnet* 76 3
In my sight, Dear heart, forbear to glance thine eye aside 139 6
Glass. Her tears began to turn their tide, Being prison'd in her eye like pearls in glass *Ven. and Adon.* 980
Two glasses, where herself herself beheld A thousand times 1129
Princes are the glass, the school, the book, Where subjects' eyes do learn *Lucrece* 615
Wilt thou be glass wherein it shall discern Authority for sin? 619
When their glass fell wherein they view'd their faces 1526
Poor broken glass, I often did behold In thy sweet semblance my old age new born 1758
And shiver'd all the beauty of my glass 1763
Look in thy glass, and tell the face thou viewest *Sonnet* 3 1
Thou art thy mother's glass, and she in thee Calls back the lovely April of her prime 3 9
A liquid prisoner pent in walls of glass 5 10
My glass shall not persuade me I am old 22 1
But when my glass shows me myself indeed 62 9
Thy glass will show thee how thy beauties wear 77 1
Glass. The wrinkles which thy glass will truly show Of mouthed graves will give thee memory *Sonnet* 77 5
Look in your glass, and there appears a face 103 6
Your own glass shows you when you look in it 103 14
Who in thy power Dost hold Time's fickle glass, his sickle, hour 126 2
Brighter than glass, and yet, as glass is, brittle *Pass. Pil.* 87
A brittle glass that's broken presently 172
A doubtful good, a gloss, a glass, a flower 173
As broken glass no cement can redress 178
Glassy. Secrecies Writ in the glassy margents of such books *Lucrece* 102
Glazed. That hath his windows glazed with thine eyes *Sonnet* 24 8
Who glazed with crystal gate the glowing roses *Lov. Comp.* 286
Gleamed. And dying eyes gleam'd forth their ashy lights *Lucrece* 1378
Glides. So glides he in the night from Venus' eye; Which after him she darts *Ven. and Adon.* 816
Glisters. His eye, which scornfully glisters like fire, Shows his hot courage and his high desire 275
Glittering. And smear with dust their glittering golden towers *Lucrece* 945
Globes. Her breasts, like ivory globes circled with blue 407
Gloomy. Keep still possession of thy gloomy place 803
Glorifies. And as the bright sun glorifies the sky, So is her face illumined with her eye *Ven. and Adon.* 485
Glorious. Collatine's high name, Made glorious by his manly chivalry *Lucr.* 109
Poor grooms are sightless night, kings glorious day 1013
Full many a glorious morning have I seen Flatter the mountain-tops *Son.* 33 1
The sun look'd on the world with glorious eye *Pass. Pil.* 81
Gloriously. Who doth the world so gloriously behold That cedar-tops and hills seem burnish'd gold *Ven. and Adon.* 857
Glory. His victories, his triumphs, and his glories 1014
Time's glory is to calm contending kings *Lucrece* 939
Whose words like wildfire burnt the shining glory Of rich-built Ilion 1523
For at a frown they in their glory die *Sonnet* 25 8
I in thy abundance am sufficed And by a part of all thy glory live 37 12
Being crown'd, Crooked eclipses 'gainst his glory fight 60 7
Which shall be most my glory, being dumb 83 10
That to his subject lends not some small glory 84 6
Wherein I am attainted, That thou in losing me shalt win much glory 88 8
Some glory in their birth, some in their skill, Some in their wealth 91 1
Nor that full star that ushers in the even Doth half that glory to the sober west 132 8
Gloss. His breath and beauty set Gloss on the rose, smell to the violet *Ven. and Adon.* 936
Beauty is but a vain and doubtful good; A shining gloss that vadeth suddenly *Pass. Pil.* 170
A doubtful good, a gloss, a glass, a flower 173
As vaded gloss no rubbing will refresh 176
Glove. And being lighted, by the light he spies Lucretia's glove *Lucrece* 317
As who should say 'This glove to wanton tricks Is not inured' 320
The doors, the wind, the glove, that did delay him, He takes for accidental things of trial 325
Glow. He sees her coming, and begins to glow *Ven. and Adon.* 337
He goes To quench the coal which in his liver glows *Lucrece* 47
Glowed. O, that false fire which in his cheek so glow'd! *Lov. Comp.* 324
Glowing. She red and hot as coals of glowing fire, He red for shame, but frosty in desire *Ven. and Adon.* 35
In me thou see'st the glowing of such fire *Sonnet* 73 9
Who glazed with crystal gate the glowing roses *Lov. Comp.* 286
Glow-worms. His eyes, like glow-worms, shine when he doth fret *V. and A.* 621
Glued. Their lips together glued, fall to the earth 546
Glutton. But, when his glutton eye so full hath fed, His other agents aim at like delight 399
Lust like a glutton dies, Love is all truth, Lust full of forged lies 803
Pity the world, or else this glutton be, To eat the world's due *Sonnet* 1 13
Gluttoning. Thus do I pine and surfeit day by day, Or gluttoning on all, or all away 75 14
Glutton-like. And glutton-like she feeds, yet never filleth *Ven. and Adon.* 548
Gnats are unnoted wheresoe'er they fly *Lucrece* 1014
Go. The strong-neck'd steed, being tied unto a tree, Breaketh his rein, and to her straight goes he *Ven. and Adon.* 264
He cries, 'let go, and let me go; My day's delight is past' 379
'Fie, fie,' he says, 'you crush me; let me go' 611
His snout digs sepulchres where'er he goes 622
The many musets through the which he goes Are like a labyrinth 683
Shaking their scratch'd ears, bleeding as they go 924
With swift intent he goes To quench the coal *Lucrece* 46
Would let him go, Rather than triumph in so false a foe 76
Yet ere he go to bed, Knit poisonous clouds about his golden head 776
Let him have time to mark how slow time goes In time of sorrow 990
Go, get me hither paper, ink, and pen 1289
Much like a press of people at a door, Throng her inventions, which shall go before 1302
Like a heavy-hanging bell, Once set on ringing, with his own weight goes 1494
Onward to Troy with the blunt swains he goes 1504
A watery rigol goes, Which seems to weep upon the tainted place 1745
Thou among the wastes of time must go *Sonnet* 12 10
Or say with princes if it shall go well, By oft predict that I in heaven find 14 7
Towards thee I'll run, and give him leave to go 51 14
Each changing place with that which goes before 60 3
That which governs me to go about Doth part his function 113 2
I grant I never saw a goddess go 130 11
Bear thine eyes straight, though thy proud heart go wide 140 14
And had let go by The swiftest hours *Lov. Comp.* 59
With the breath thou givest and takest, 'Mongst our mourners shalt thou go *Ph. and Tur.* 20
God. The stern and direful god of war, Whose sinewy neck in battle ne'er did bow *Ven. and Adon.* 98
Brag not of thy might, For mastering her that foil'd the god of fight 114
O thou clear god, and patron of all light 860
Then Love and Fortune be my gods, my guide! *Lucrece* 351
Thou seem'st not what thou art, a god, a king 601
For kings like gods should govern every thing 602
God wot, it was defect Of spirit, life, and bold audacity 1345
The painter was no god to lend her those 1461
To rouse our Roman gods with invocations 1831
That God forbid that made me first your slave *Sonnet* 58 1
A god in love, to whom I am confined 110 12
One god is god of both, as poets feign *Pass. Pil.* 115
She told the youngling how god Mars did try her 145
'Even thus,' quoth she, 'the warlike god embraced me 147
'Even thus,' quoth she, 'the warlike god unlaced me' 149

God. All my merry jigs are quite forgot, All my lady's love is lost, God wot . *Pass. Pil.* 254
Goddess. Calls it balm, Earth's sovereign salve to do a goddess good *Ven. and Adon.* 28
With Fortune chide, The guilty goddess of my harmful deeds *Sonnet* 111 2
I grant I never saw a goddess go 130 11
I forswore; but I will prove, Thou being a goddess, I forswore not thee *Pass. Pil.* 34
Goest. Nature, sovereign mistress over wrack, As thou goest onwards, still will pluck thee back . . . . . *Sonnet* 126 6
Goeth. His testy master goeth about to take him . *Ven. and Adon.* 319
Going. And now 'tis dark, and going I shall fall 719
Since from thee going he went wilful-slow, Towards thee I'll run *Sonnet* 51 13
Gold. But gold that's put to use more gold begets . *Ven. and Adon.* 768
That cedar-tops and hills seem burnish'd gold 858
The aged man that coffers-up his gold Is plagued with cramps . *Lucrece* 855
Thy interest was not bought Basely with gold, but stol'n from forth thy gate 1068
Sometime too hot the eye of heaven shines, And often is his gold complexion dimm'd . . . . *Sonnet* 18 6
Though not so bright As those gold candles fix'd in heaven's air . 21 12
Crack'd many a ring of posied gold and bone . *Lov. Comp.* 45
Golden. Then with her windy sighs and golden hairs To fan and blow them dry again she seeks . *Ven. and Adon.* 51
Love's golden arrow at him should have fled 947
When he beheld his shadow in the brook, The fishes spread on it their golden gills 1100
Against the golden splendour of the sun . . . . *Lucrece* 25
That meaner men should vaunt That golden hap which their superiors want 42
Beauty's red, Which virtue gave the golden age to gild . . . 60
The scandal will survive, And be an eye-sore in my golden coat 205
Her hair, like golden threads, play'd with her breath . . . 400
Ere he go to bed, Knit poisonous clouds about his golden head . 777
And smear with dust their glittering golden towers . . . 945
But for loss of Nestor's golden words, It seem'd they would debate with angry swords 1420
Shalt see Despite of wrinkles this thy golden time . *Sonnet* 3 12
Attending on his golden pilgrimage 7 8
Kissing with golden face the meadows green 33 3
Before the golden tresses of the dead, The right of sepulchres, were shorn away 68 5
While comments of your praise, richly compiled, Reserve their character with golden quill 85 3
The strongest castle, tower, and town, The golden bullet beats it down *Pass. Pil.* 328
Gone. Till either gorge be stuff'd or prey be gone . . *Ven. and Adon.* 58
Young, and so unkind? What bare excuses makest thou to be gone! . 188
And when from thence he struggles to be gone, She locks her lily fingers one in one 227
My horse is gone, And 'tis your fault I am bereft him so . . 380
Therefore no marvel though thy horse be gone 390
Are they not quickly told and quickly gone? 520
''Tis very late;' The sheep are gone to fold, birds to their nest . 532
'Thou hadst been gone,' quoth she, 'sweet boy, ere this, But that thou told'st me thou wouldst hunt the boar' 613
My sighs are blown away, my salt tears gone 1071
The wind would blow it off and, being gone, Play with his locks . 1089
O, that is gone for which I sought to live . . . *Lucrece* 1051
Ere the break of day, And, ere I rose, was Tarquin gone away . 1281
Her maid is gone, and she prepares to write 1296
And yet the duteous vassal scarce is gone 1360
Then how, when nature calls thee to be gone? . . . *Sonnet* 4 11
Sap check'd with frost and lusty leaves quite gone . . . 5 7
Hung with the trophies of my lovers gone 31 10
Thought kills me that I am not thought, To leap large lengths of miles when thou art gone 44 10
When these quicker elements are gone In tender embassy of love to thee 45 5
Tired with all these, from these would I be gone . . . 66 13
Lest the wise world should look into your moan And mock you with me after I am gone 71 14
Though I, once gone, to all the world must die . . . 81 6
I have gone here and there And made myself a motley to the view . 110 1
And scarce the herd gone to the hedge for shade . *Pass. Pil.* 72
Good. Calls it balm, Earth's sovereign salve to do a goddess good *V. and A.* 28
Never did passenger in summer's heat More thirst for drink than she for this good turn 92
She, by her good will, Will never rise, so he will kiss her still . 479
So thou wilt buy and pay and use good dealing 514
And coal-black clouds that shadow heaven's light Do summon us to part and bid good night 534
'Good night,' and so say you; If you will say so, you shall have a kiss . 535
'Good night,' quoth she, and, ere he says 'Adieu,' The honey fee of parting tender'd is 537
But all in vain; good queen, it will not be 607
But know, it is as good To wither in my breast as in his blood . 1181
So guiltless she securely gives good cheer And reverend welcome *Lucrece* 89
With good thoughts makes dispensation, Urging the worser sense for vantage still 248
A little harm done to a great good end For lawful policy remains enacted . 528
If all these petty ills shall change thy good 656
Let my good name, that senseless reputation, For Collatine's dear love be kept unspotted 820
We have no good that we can say is ours, But ill-annexed Opportunity Or kills his life or else his quality 873
O Time, thou tutor both to good and bad, Teach me to curse him! . . 995
The remedy indeed to do me good Is to let forth my foul-defiled blood . 1028
Great grief grieves most at that would do it good . . . 1117
If tears could help, mine own would do me good . . . 1274
Methinks I have astronomy, But not to tell of good or evil luck *Sonnet* 14 3
Now see what good turns eyes for eyes have done . . . 24 9
I hope some good conceit of thine In thy soul's thought, all naked, will bestow it 26 7
I love thee in such sort As, thou being mine, mine is thy good report 36 14; 96 14
A league is took, And each doth good turns now unto the other . 47 2
And simple truth miscall'd simplicity, And captive good attending captain ill 66 12
So thou be good, slander doth but approve Thy worth the greater . 70 5
I think good thoughts whilst other write good words . . . 85 5
To leave for nothing all thy sum of good 109 12
Well or ill, So you o'er-green my bad, my good allow . . . 112 4
Good. Which in their wills count bad what I think good . *Sonnet* 121 8
Yet, in good faith, some say that thee behold Thy face hath not the power to make love groan 131 5
But live in doubt, Till my bad angel fire my good one out 144 14; *Pass. Pil.* 28
To be forbod the sweets that seem so good . . . *Lov. Comp.* 164
She, silly queen, with more than love's good will, Forbade the boy he should not pass those grounds . . . . . *Pass. Pil.* 123
Beauty is but a vain and doubtful good; A shining gloss that vadeth suddenly 169
A doubtful good, a gloss, a glass, a flower 173
As goods lost are seld or never found, As vaded gloss no rubbing will refresh 175
Good night, good rest. Ah, neither be my share: She bade good night that kept my rest away 181
Pack night, peep day; good day, of night now borrow . . . 209
Goodly. Like a goodly champaign plain, Lays open all the little worms that creep . . . . *Lucrece* 1247
He of tall building and of goodly pride . . . . *Sonnet* 80 12
The goodly objects which abroad they find . . . *Lov. Comp.* 137
Good-morrow. Venus salutes him with this fair good-morrow *V. and A.* 859
Her mistress she doth give demure good-morrow . . . *Lucrece* 1219
Goodness. A healthful state Which, rank of goodness, would by ill be cured *Sonnet* 118 12
The fools of time, Which die for goodness, who have lived for crime . 124 14
Gore. Thou know'st not what it is With javelin's point a churlish swine to gore . . . . *Ven. and Adon.* 616
An image like thyself, all stain'd with gore 664
Gored. Gored mine own thoughts, sold cheap what is most dear *Sonnet* 110 3
Gorge. Till either gorge be stuff'd or prey be gone . *Ven. and Adon.* 58
Gorged. As the full-fed hound or gorged hawk, Unapt for tender smell or speedy flight Make slow pursuit . . . . *Lucrece* 694
Got. Every alien pen hath got my use And under thee their poesy disperse *Sonnet* 78 3
O, what a mansion have those vices got! 95 9
The bath for my help lies Where Cupid got new fire—my mistress' eyes 153 14
Then, lullaby, the learned man hath got the lady gay . *Pass. Pil.* 225
Gouts. Is plagued with cramps and gouts and painful fits . *Lucrece* 856
Gouty. Than the true gouty landlord which doth owe them . *Lov. Comp.* 140
Govern. For kings like gods should govern every thing . *Lucrece* 602
That which governs me to go about Doth part his function . *Sonnet* 113 2
Governed. And govern'd him in strength, though not in lust . *V. and A.* 42
Governess. The quiet cabinet Where their dear governess and lady lies *Lucr.* 443
Government. Show'd deep regard and smiling government . . 1400
Grace. And calls it heavenly moisture, air of grace . *Ven. and Adon.* 64
Which to her oratory adds more grace . . . . *Lucrece* 564
Desire doth fight with Grace, For there it revels . . . 712
When sighs and groans and tears may grace the fashion Of her disgrace 1319
In great commanders grace and majesty You might behold . . 1387
All jointly listening, but with several graces 1410
And in fresh numbers number all your graces . . . *Sonnet* 17 6
Yet eyes this cunning want to grace their art . . . 24 13
And dost him grace when clouds do blot the heaven . . . 28 10
Lascivious grace, in whom all ill well shows, Kill me with spites . 40 13
In all external grace you have some part 53 13
And with his presence grace impiety 67 2
And given grace a double majesty 78 8
And arts with thy sweet graces graced be 78 12
My verse alone had all thy gentle grace 79 2
And to temptation slow, They rightly do inherit heaven's graces . 94 5
Some say thy grace is youth and gentle sport 96 2
Both grace and faults are loved of more and less; Thou makest faults graces that to thee resort 96 3
For to no other pass my verses tend Than of your graces and your gifts to tell 103 12
Mourn for me, since mourning doth thee grace 132 11
And swear that brightness doth not grace the day . . . 150 4
It was to gain my grace—Of one by nature's outwards so commended *Lov. Comp.* 79
His real habitude gave life and grace To appertainings . . . 114
Their purposed trim Pieced not his grace, but were all graced by him . 119
Dieted in grace, Believed her eyes when they to assail begun . 261
O, how the channel to the stream gave grace! 285
With the garment of a Grace The naked and concealed fiend he cover'd 316
Thy grace being gain'd cures all disgrace in me . . *Pass. Pil.* 36
A lily pale, with damask dye to grace her, None fairer . . . 89
Grace in all simplicity, Here enclosed in cinders lie . . *Ph. and Tur.* 54
Graced. And arts with thy sweet graces graced be . . *Sonnet* 78 12
Their purposed trim Pieced not his grace, but were all graced by him *Lov. Comp.* 119
Graceless, holds he disputation 'Tween frozen conscience and hot-burning will . . . . *Lucrece* 246
Gracious. In the orient when the gracious light Lifts up his burning head, each under eye Doth homage to his new-appearing sight . *Sonnet* 7 1
Be, as thy presence is, gracious and kind 10 11
Methinks no face so gracious is as mine, No shape so true . . 62 5
But now my gracious numbers are decay'd 79 3
Shall will in others seem right gracious? 135 7
Graciously. Till whatsoever star that guides my moving Points on me graciously 26 10
Graff. This bastard graff shall never come to growth . . *Lucrece* 1062
Grained. So slides he down upon his grained bat . . *Lov. Comp.* 64
Grant. Thou art well appaid As well to hear as grant what he hath said *Lucrece* 915
Grant, if thou wilt, thou art beloved of many . . . *Sonnet* 10 3
I grant, sweet love, thy lovely argument Deserves the travail of a worthier pen 79 5
I grant thou wert not married to my Muse 82 1
I grant I never saw a goddess go 130 11
Granted. Consents bewitch'd, ere he desire, have granted . *Lov. Comp.* 131
Grantest. Thou grant'st no time for charitable deeds . . *Lucrece* 908
Granteth. His heart granteth No penetrable entrance to her plaining . 558
Granting. For how do I hold thee but by thy granting? . *Sonnet* 87 5
Grape. Even as poor birds, deceived with painted grapes *Ven. and Adon.* 601
For one sweet grape who will the vine destroy! . . . *Lucrece* 215
Grass. For on the grass she lies as she were slain . *Ven. and Adon.* 473
The grass stoops not, she treads on it so light 1028
No flower was nigh, no grass, herb, leaf, or weed, But stole his blood . 1055
Whose perfect white Show'd like an April daisy on the grass . *Lucrece* 395
Grates. The threshold grates the door to have him heard . . . 306
Gratis. They buy thy help; but Sin ne'er gives a fee, He gratis comes . . 914

Grave. And being steel'd, soft sighs can never grave it . *Ven. and Adon.* 376
What is thy body but a swallowing grave? 757
She clepes him king of graves and grave for kings . . . 995
Whose downward eye still looketh for a grave 1106
O foul dishonour to my household's grave! . . . . *Lucrece* 198
Thou their fair life, and they thy fouler grave 661
And grave, like water that doth eat in steel, Upon my cheeks . . 755
There pleading might you see grave Nestor stand . . . 1401
This glutton be, To eat the world's due, by the grave and thee *Sonnet* 1 14
Thou art the grave where buried love doth live . . . 31 9
The wrinkles which thy glass will truly show Of mouthed graves will give thee memory . . . 77 6
The earth can yield me but a common grave . . . 81 7
Graven. My love's sweet face survey, If Time have any wrinkle graven there . . . 100 10
Gravity. When love, . . . Shall reasons find of settled gravity 49 8
Gray. Mine eyes are gray and bright and quick in turning *Ven. and Adon.* 140
Truly not the morning sun of heaven Better becomes the grey cheeks of the east . . . *Sonnet* 132 6
Graze. Graze on my lips; and if those hills be dry, Stray lower, where the pleasant fountains lie . . . *Ven. and Adon.* 233
Grazed. A reverend man that grazed his cattle nigh . . *Lov. Comp.* 57
Great. Or what great danger dwells upon my suit? . *Ven. and Adon.* 206
The sovereignty of either being so great . . . *Lucrece* 69
When great treasure is the meed proposed, Though death be adjunct, there's no death supposed . . . 132
The guilt being great, the fear doth still exceed . . . 229
A little harm done to a great good end For lawful policy remains enacted 528
O Opportunity, thy guilt is great! 'Tis thou that executest the traitor's treason . . . 876
When wilt thou sort an hour great strifes to end? . . . 899
Great grief grieves most at that would do it good . . . 1117
In great commanders grace and majesty You might behold . . 1387
Why dost thou use So great a sum of sums, yet canst not live? . *Sonnet* 4 8
Great princes' favourites their fair leaves spread . . 25 5
Duty so great, which wit so poor as mine May make seem bare, in wanting words to show it . . . 26 5
Thy love, though much, is not so great: It is my love that keeps mine eye awake . . . 61 9
Was it the proud full sail of his great verse? . . . 86 1
So thy great gift, upon misprision growing, Comes home again 87 11
And my great mind most kingly drinks it up . . . 114 10
I have scanted all Wherein I should your great deserts repay . 117 2
Or laid great bases for eternity 125 3
In things of great receipt with ease we prove Among a number one is reckon'd none . . . 136 7
Then must the love be great 'twixt thee and me . . *Pass. Pil.* 105
And there sung the dolefull'st ditty, That to hear it was great pity 384
But if Fortune once do frown, Then farewell his great renown . 420
Greater. Her pleading hath deserved a greater fee . *Ven. and Adon.* 609
His eyes begun To wink, being blinded with a greater light *Lucrece* 375
Unto a greater uproar tempts his veins 427
Huge fires abide, And with the wind in greater fury fret . . 648
The lesser thing should not the greater hide . . . 663
Leaving his spoil perplex'd in greater pain . . . 733
They that lose half with greater patience bear it Than they whose whole is swallow'd in confusion . . . 1158
Till, meeting greater ranks, They join and shoot their foam at Simois' banks 1441
It is a greater grief To bear love's wrong than hate's known injury *Sonnet* 40 11
So thou be good, slander doth but approve Thy worth the greater 70 6
Grows fairer than at first, more strong, far greater . . 119 12
Greatest. For greatest scandal waits on greatest state . *Lucrece* 1006
Most worthy comfort, now my greatest grief . . *Sonnet* 48 6
Grecian. And you in Grecian tires are painted new . . 53 8
Greece. Before the which is drawn the power of Greece . *Lucrece* 1368
Greedy. About he walks, Rolling his greedy eyeballs in his head 368
'Greeing. Mine eye well knows what with his gust is 'greeing *Sonnet* 114 11
Greeks. Gazing upon the Greeks with little lust . . *Lucrece* 1384
As 'twere encouraging the Greeks to fight . . . 1402
Scratch out the angry eyes Of all the Greeks that are thine enemies 1470
Green. Or, like a fairy, trip upon the green . . *Ven. and Adon.* 146
The mellow plum doth fall, the green sticks fast . . 527
The text is old, the orator too green 806
She crops the stalk, and in the breach appears Green dropping sap 1176
Without the bed her other fair hand was, On the green coverlet *Lucrece* 394
And summer's green all girded up in sheaves . . *Sonnet* 12 7
Kissing with golden face the meadows green . . . 33 3
His beauty shall in these black lines be seen, And they shall live, and he in them still green . . . 63 14
Making no summer of another's green 68 11
Three hot Junes burn'd, Since first I saw you fresh, which yet are green 104 8
Sitting by a brook With young Adonis, lovely, fresh, and green *Pass. Pil.* 44
And stood stark naked on the brook's green brim . . 80
Like a green plum that hangs upon a tree, And falls, through wind 135
Green plants bring not Forth their dye 283
Greet. And, wordless, so greets heaven for his success . *Lucrece* 112
Thou shalt strangely pass And scarcely greet me with that sun, thine eye *Sonnet* 49 6
In the spring When I was wont to greet it with my lays . 102 6
And taught it thus anew to greet 145 8
Greeteth. Thou worthy lord Of that unworthy wife that greeteth thee *Lucrece* 1304
Grew. Grew kinder, and his fury was assuaged . *Ven. and Adon.* 318
Grew I not faint? and fell I not downright? . . . 645
The store Which should example where your equal grew . *Sonnet* 84 4
Making their tomb the womb wherein they grew . . 86 4
Or from their proud lap pluck them where they grew . . 98 8
To anticipate The ills that were not, grew to faults assured . 118 10
A dateless lively heat, still to endure, And grew a seething bath . 153 7
Heard where his plants in others' orchards grew . . *Lov. Comp.* 171
Grief. Doth make them droop with grief and hang the head *Ven. and Adon.* 666
Now his grief may be compared well To one sore sick that hears the passing-bell . . . 701
Surfeits, imposthumes, grief, and damn'd despair . . 743
As striving who should best become her grief . . . 968
Grief hath two tongues, and never woman yet Could rule them both without ten women's wit . . . 1007
My tongue cannot express my grief for one . . . 1069
Sweet issue of a more sweet-smelling sire—For every little grief to wet his eyes . . . 1179

Grief. Such griefs sustain, That they prove bankrupt in this poor-rich gain *Lucrece* 139
Frantic with grief thus breathes she forth her spite . . 762
Mingling my talk with tears, my grief with groans . . 797
Thou false thief, Thy honey turns to gall, thy joy to grief . 889
True grief is fond and testy as a child 1094
Sometime her grief is dumb and hath no words; Sometime 'tis mad 1105
Grief best is pleased with grief's society . . . 1111
Great grief grieves most at that would do it good . . 1117
Grief dallied with nor law nor limit knows . . . 1120
If thou dost weep for grief of my sustaining, . . . it small avails my mood 1272
Conceit and grief an eager combat fight 1298
So, I commend me from our house in grief . . . 1308
By this short schedule Collatine may know Her grief, but not her grief's true quality . . . 1313
He did her wrong, To give her so much grief and not a tongue . 1463
As if with grief or travail he had fainted, To me came Tarquin armed . 1543
Being from the feeling of her own grief brought By deep surmise of others' detriment . . . 1578
Tell thy grief, that we may give redress 1603
From lips new-waxen pale begins to blow The grief away . . 1664
Even so his sighs, his sorrows, make a saw, To push grief on, and back the same grief draw . . . 1673
Do wounds help wounds, or grief help grievous deeds? . . 1822
Night doth nightly make grief's strength seem stronger . . *Sonnet* 28 14
Nor can thy shame give physic to my grief . . . 34 9
It is a greater grief To bear love's wrong than hate's known injury 40 11
That thou hast her, it is not all my grief . . . 42 1
Most worthy comfort, now my greatest grief . . . 48 6
My grief lies onward and my joy behind 50 14
Do not leave me last, When other petty griefs have done their spite 90 10
Figuring that they their passions likewise lent me Of grief and blushes *Lov. Comp.* 200
For her griefs, so lively shown, Made me think upon mine own *Pass. Pil.* 389
Thus of every grief in heart He with thee doth bear a part . 427
Grievance. Then can I grieve at grievances foregone . *Sonnet* 30 9
When he again desires her, being sat, Her grievance with his hearing to divide *Lov. Comp.* 67
Grieve. Thy coward heart with false bethinking grieves *Ven. and Adon.* 1024
Great grief grieves most at that would do it good . *Lucrece* 1117
Then can I grieve at grievances foregone . . *Sonnet* 30 9
Grieved. No more be grieved at that which thou hast done . 35 1
Grieving themselves to guess at others' smarts . . *Lucrece* 1238
Grievous. Do wounds help wounds, or grief help grievous deeds? 1822
Grim. Another flap-mouth'd mourner, black and grim *Ven. and Adon.* 920
This foul, grim, and urchin-snouted boar . . . 1105
As the grim lion fawneth o'er his prey, Sharp hunger by the conquest satisfied . . . *Lucrece* 421
Whose grim aspect sets every joint a-shaking . . . 452
Dark harbour for defame! Grim cave of death! . . . 769
Time's ruin, beauty's wreck, and grim care's reign . . 1451
Grim-grinning ghost, earth's worm, what dost thou mean To stifle beauty? *Ven. and Adon.* 933
Grin. Or as the wolf doth grin before he barketh, Or as the berry breaks before it staineth . . . 459
Grind. Mine appetite I never more will grind On newer proof *Sonnet* 110 10
Gripe. Like a white hind under the gripe's sharp claws, Pleads *Lucrece* 543
Griped. That for Achilles' image stood his spear, Griped in an armed hand 1425
Griping. And griping it, the needle his finger pricks . . 319
Grisly. Swift subtle post, carrier of grisly care, Eater of youth 926
Groan. Then love's deep groans I never shall regard *Ven. and Adon.* 377
My heart longs not to groan, But soundly sleeps, while now it sleeps alone 785
And now she beats her heart, whereat it groans . . 829
What may a heavy groan advantage thee? 950
By their suggestion gives a deadly groan 1044
Nor children's tears nor mothers' groans respecting, Swell in their pride, the onset still expecting . . . *Lucrece* 431
Be moved with my tears, my sighs, my groans . . . 588
Mingling my talk with tears, my grief with groans . . 797
Afflict him in his bed with bedrid groans . . . 975
And with deep groans the diapason bear 1132
'When went'—and there she stay'd Till after a deep groan—'Tarquin from hence?' . . . 1276
When sighs and groans and tears may grace the fashion Of her disgrace 1319
For now 'tis stale to sigh, to weep, and groan . . . 1362
Which heavily he answers with a groan . . . *Sonnet* 50 11
For that same groan doth put this in my mind . . 50 13
Thy face hath not the power to make love groan . . 131 6
A thousand groans, but thinking on thy face, One on another's neck, do witness bear . . . 131 10
Beshrew that heart that makes my heart to groan! . . 133 1
Now all these hearts that do on mine depend, Feeling it break, with bleeding groans they pine . . . *Lov. Comp.* 275
Groin. The loving swine Sheathed unaware the tusk in his soft groin *Ven. and Adon.* 1116
Groom. I mean to bear thee Unto the base bed of some rascal groom *Lucrece* 671
Poor grooms are sightless night, kings glorious day . . 1013
Charging the sour-faced groom to hie as fast As lagging fowls before the northern blast . . . 1334
Silly groom! God wot, it was defect Of spirit, life, and bold audacity . 1345
'Some hard-favour'd groom of thine,' quoth he, . . . 'I'll murder straight' 1632
And never be forgot in mighty Rome Th' adulterate death of Lucrece and her groom . . . 1645
Gross. Not gross to sink, but light, and will aspire . *Ven. and Adon.* 150
Lest he should hold it her own gross abuse . . . *Lucrece* 1315
Though my gross blood be stain'd with this abuse . . 1655
Their gross painting might be better used Where cheeks need blood *Son.* 82 13
I do betray My nobler part to my gross body's treason . 151 6
Grossly engirt with daring infamy . . . . *Lucrece* 1173
In my love's veins thou hast too grossly dyed . . *Sonnet* 99 5
Ground. What seest thou in the ground? hold up thy head *Ven. and Adon.* 118
Now gazeth she on him, now on the ground . . . 224
Clapping their proud tails to the ground below . . . 923
To wash the foul face of the sluttish ground . . . 983
As when the wind, imprison'd in the ground . . . 1046
And in his blood that on the ground lay spill'd, A purple flower sprung up . 1167
My sable ground of sin I will not paint, To hide the truth . *Lucrece* 1074
My will I make: My soul and body to the skies and ground . 1199
Then jointly to the ground their knees they bow . . 1846
As sweet-season'd showers are to the ground . . *Sonnet* 75 2

Ground. My mistress, when she walks, treads on the ground *Sonnet* 130 12
In a cold valley-fountain of that ground 153 4
Desires to know In brief the grounds and motives of her woe *Lov. Comp.* 63
She, silly queen, with more than love's good will, Forbade the boy he should not pass those grounds . . . . . . *Pass. Pil.* 124
As flowers dead lie wither'd on the ground 177
How sighs resound Through heartless ground 279
Grounded. It is so grounded inward in my heart . . . *Sonnet* 62 4
Hate of my sin, grounded on sinful loving 142 2
Grove. This said, she hasteth to a myrtle grove *Ven. and Adon.* 865
Make thy sad grove in my dishevell'd hair . . . . *Lucrece* 1129
In men, as in a rough-grown grove, remain Cave-keeping evils that obscurely sleep 1249
Sitting in a pleasant shade Which a grove of myrtles made *Pass. Pil.* 376
Grow. My beauty as the spring doth yearly grow . *Ven. and Adon.* 141
Incorporate then they seem; face grows to face 540
To grow unto himself was his desire, And so 'tis thine 1180
Thy hasty spring still blasts, and ne'er grows old . . . *Lucrece* 49
So their pride doth grow, Paying more slavish tribute than they owe . 298
Beauties do themselves forsake And die as fast as they see others grow *Sonnet* 12 12
Every thing that grows Holds in perfection but a little moment . 15 1
No longer glad, I send them back again and straight grow sad . 45 14
But why thy odour matcheth not thy show, The solve is this, that thou dost common grow 69 14
Speaking of worth, what worth in you doth grow 83 8
How like Eve's apple doth thy beauty grow! 93 13
To give full growth to that which still doth grow 115 14
And ruin'd love, when it is built anew, Grows fairer than at first . 119 12
That it nor grows with heat nor drowns with showers . . . 124 12
If hairs be wires, black wires grow on her head 130 4
For if I should despair, I should grow mad 140 9
Root pity in thy heart, that when it grows Thy pity may deserve to pitied be 142 11
Beasts did leap, and birds did sing, Trees did grow, and plants did spring *Pass. Pil.* 378
Reason, in itself confounded, Saw division grow together *Ph. and Tur.* 42
Growest. As fast as thou shalt wane, so fast thou growest In one of thine, from that which thou departest . . . . . . *Sonnet* 11 1
When in eternal lines to time thou growest 18 12
And therein show'st Thy lovers withering as thy sweet self grow'st 126 4
Growing. Things growing to themselves are growth's abuse *Ven. and Adon.* 166
I know what thorns the growing rose defends . . . . *Lucrece* 492
Had my friend's Muse grown with this growing age . *Sonnet* 32 10
So thy great gift, upon misprision growing, Comes home again . 87 11
Growing a bath and healthful remedy For men diseased . . . 154 11
Under an osier growing by a brook, A brook where Adon used to cool his spleen . . . . *Pass. Pil.* 75
Grown. Had my friend's Muse grown with this growing age *Sonnet* 32 10
And sweets grown common lose their dear delight 102 12
Who hast by waning grown 126 3
Now this ill-wresting world is grown so bad 140 11
Growth. Things growing to themselves are growth's abuse *Ven. and Adon.* 166
This bastard graff shall never come to growth . . . *Lucrece* 1062
In pride of all his growth A vengeful canker eat him up to death *Sonnet* 99 12
And stops her pipe in growth of riper days 102 8
To give full growth to that which still doth grow 115 14
Guard. Draw not thy sword to guard iniquity . . . *Lucrece* 626
To guard the lawful reasons on thy part . . . . *Sonnet* 49 12
Whoe'er keeps me, let my heart be his guard 133 11
Shook off my sober guards and civil fears . . . *Lov. Comp.* 298
Guarded. I think the honey guarded with a sting . . *Lucrece* 493
Guess. Grieving themselves to guess at others' smarts 1238

Guess. They look into the beauty of thy mind, And that, in guess, they measure by thy deeds . . . . *Sonnet* 69 10
I guess one angel in another's hell 144 12
Being both to me, both to each friend, I guess one angel in another's hell *Pass. Pil.* 26
Guest. Lest Jealousy, that sour unwelcome guest, Should, by his stealing in, disturb the feast . . . . *Ven. and Adon.* 449
Gives good cheer And reverend welcome to her princely guest *Lucrece* 90
A woeful hostess brooks not merry guests 1125
Comparing him to that unhappy guest Whose deed hath made herself herself detest 1565
Another time mine eye is my heart's guest . . . *Sonnet* 47 7
And thither hied, a sad distemper'd guest, But found no cure . 153 12
Guide. Wishing Adonis had his team to guide, So he were like him and by Venus' side . . . . *Ven. and Adon.* 179
Then Love and Fortune be my gods, my guide! . . . *Lucrece* 351
'Tis he, That guides this hand to give this wound to me . . . 1722
Till whatsoever star that guides my moving Points on me graciously *Son.* 26 9
Guile. 'It cannot be,' quoth she, 'that so much guile'—She would have said 'can lurk in such a look' . . . . *Lucrece* 1534
Wiles and guiles that women work, Dissembled with an outward show *Pass. Pil.* 335
Guilt. The guilt being great, the fear doth still exceed . *Lucrece* 229
This guilt would seem death-worthy in thy brother 635
For they their guilt with weeping will unfold 754
O Opportunity, thy guilt is great! 'Tis thou that executest the traitor's treason 876
They whose guilt within their bosoms lie Imagine every eye beholds their blame 1342
Lest my bewailed guilt should do thee shame . . . . . *Sonnet* 36 10
Guiltless. So guiltless she securely gives good cheer And reverend welcome *Lucrece* 89
Poor helpless help, the treasure stol'n away, To burn the guiltless casket where it lay! 1057
Let guiltless souls be freed from guilty woe 1482
Guilty. This said, his guilty hand pluck'd up the latch 358
The guilty rebel for remission prays 714
She bears the load of lust he left behind, And he the burthen of a guilty mind 735
He faintly flies, sweating with guilty fear 740
Foggy Night! Since thou art guilty of my cureless crime, Muster thy mists to meet the eastern light 772
Yet am I guilty of thy honour's wrack; Yet for thy honour did I entertain him 841
Guilty thou art of murder and of theft, Guilty of perjury and subornation, Guilty of treason, forgery, and shift, Guilty of incest, that abomination 918
Be guilty of my death, since of my crime 931
Let guiltless souls be freed from guilty woe 1482
That blushing red no guilty instance gave 1511
With Fortune chide, The guilty goddess of my harmful deeds *Sonnet* 111 2
Then, gentle cheater, urge not my amiss, Lest guilty of my faults thy sweet self prove 151 4
Guise. 'Poor flower,' quoth she, 'this was thy father's guise' *Ven. and Adon.* 1177
Gulf. A swallowing gulf that even in plenty wanteth . . *Lucrece* 557
Gull. That affable familiar ghost Which nightly gulls him with intelligence *Sonnet* 86 10
Gun. Or like the deadly bullet of a gun, His meaning struck her ere his words begun . . . . *Ven. and Adon.* 461
Gush. Shall gush pure streams to purge my impure tale *Lucrece* 1078
Gusts and foul flaws to herdmen and to herds *Ven. and Adon.* 456
From earth's dark womb some gentle gust doth get . . *Lucrece* 549
Might uphold Against the stormy gusts of winter's day *Sonnet* 13 11
Mine eye well knows what with his gust is 'greeing . . . 114 11
Gyves. Playing patient sports in unconstrained gyves *Lov. Comp.* 242

H

Habit. But now he throws that shallow habit by . . *Lucrece* 1814
O, love's best habit is in seeming trust . . . *Sonnet* 138 11
O, love's best habit is a soothing tongue . . . . *Pass. Pil.* 11
Habitation. O, what a mansion have those vices got Which for their habitation chose out thee! . . . . *Sonnet* 95 10
Habitude. His real habitude gave life and grace To appertainings *L. Comp.* 114
Had. Wishing Adonis had his team to guide, So he were like him *V. and A.* 179
O, had thy mother borne so hard a mind, She had not brought forth thee 203
His eyes saw her eyes as they had not seen them 357
And all this dumb play had his acts made plain With tears . . . 359
Hast thou a tongue? O, would thou hadst not, or I had no hearing! 428
I had my load before, now press'd with bearing 430
Had I no eyes but ears, my ears would love That inward beauty and invisible 433
Had she then gave over, Such nectar from his lips she had not suck'd . 571
Hadst thou but bid beware, then he had spoke 943
O, had they in that darksome prison died! Then had they seen the period of their ill . . . . *Lucrece* 379
Such sweet observance in this work was had 1385
Save what is had or must from you be took . . . . *Sonnet* 75 12
Past reason hunted, and no sooner had Past reason hated . . 129 6
Had, having, and in quest to have, extreme 129 10
Had women been so strong as men, In faith, you had not had it then *Pass. Pil.* 321
Hadst. Hast thou a tongue? O, would thou hadst not, or I had no hearing! *Ven. and Adon.* 428
'Thou hadst been gone,' quoth she, 'sweet boy, ere this, But that thou told'st me thou wouldst hunt the boar' 613
Hail. Not a heart . . . Could 'scape the hail of his all-hurting aim *L. Comp.* 310
Hair. Then with her windy sighs and golden hairs To fan and blow them dry again she seeks . . . . *Ven. and Adon.* 51
Or, like a nymph, with long dishevell'd hair 147
I'll make a shadow for thee of my hairs 191
Fanning the hairs, who wave like feather'd wings 306
Her hair, like golden threads, play'd with her breath . . . *Lucrece* 400
Let him have time to tear his curled hair 981

Hair. Make thy sad grove in my dishevell'd hair . . . *Lucrece* 1129
And buds of marjoram had stol'n thy hair . . . . *Sonnet* 99 7
If hairs be wires, black wires grow on her head 130 4
Her hair, nor loose nor tied in formal plat . . . *Lov. Comp.* 29
Behold these talents of their hair, With twisted metal amorously impleach'd 204
Hairless. Whose beams upon his hairless face are fix'd *Ven. and Adon.* 487
Hairy. His brawny sides, with hairy bristles arm'd, Are better proof than thy spear's point can enter 625
Half. Lust's winter comes ere summer half be done 802
They that lose half with greater patience bear it Than they whose whole is swallow'd in confusion . . . . *Lucrece* 1158
It is but as a tomb Which hides your life and shows not half your parts *Sonnet* 17 4
Thou canst not, love, disgrace me half so ill 89 5
Nor that full star that ushers in the even Doth half that glory to the sober west 132 8
Hallowed. Even as when first I hallow'd thy fair name . . . 108 8
Hallow'd with sighs that burning lungs did raise . . *Lov. Comp.* 228
Halt. The poor, lame, blind, halt, creep, cry out for thee *Lucrece* 902
Speak of my lameness, and I straight will halt, Against thy reasons *Son.* 89 3
A cripple soon can find a halt . . . . *Pass. Pil.* 308
Hammered. To spoil antiquities of hammer'd steel . . . *Lucrece* 951
Unless my nerves were brass or hammer'd steel . . *Sonnet* 120 4
Hand. And by her fair immortal hand she swears, From his soft bosom never to remove . . . . *Ven. and Adon.* 80
My smooth moist hand, were it with thy hand felt, Would in thy palm dissolve, or seem to melt 143
Can thy right hand seize love upon thy left? 158
Sometimes she shakes her head and then his hand 223
With one fair hand she heaveth up his hat, Her other tender hand his fair cheek feels 351
His tenderer cheek receives her soft hand's print 353
She takes him by the hand, A lily prison'd in a gaol of snow . . 361
'Give me my hand,' saith he, 'why dost thou feel it?' 373

Hand. You hurt my hand with wringing; let us part, And leave this idle theme . . . *Ven. and Adon.* 421
Nor thy soft hands, sweet lips, and crystal eyne . 633
Or theirs whose desperate hands themselves do slay . 765
In hand with all things, nought at all effecting . 912
She takes him by the hand, and that is cold; She whispers in his ears 1124
Her joy with heaved-up hand she doth express . *Lucrece* 111
She took me kindly by the hand, And gazed for tidings in my eager eyes . 253
And how her hand, in my hand being lock'd, Forced it to tremble! 260
His guilty hand pluck'd up the latch, And with his knee the door he opens 358
Which gives the watch-word to his hand full soon . 370
Her lily hand her rosy cheek lies under, Cozening the pillow of a lawful kiss 386
Without the bed her other fair hand was, On the green coverlet . 393
His eye commends the leading to his hand . 436
His hand, as proud of such a dignity, Smoking with pride, march'd on to make his stand . 437
Whose ranks of blue veins, as his hand did scale, Left their round turrets destitute and pale . 440
His hand, that yet remains upon her breast,—Rude ram! 463
May feel her heart— . . . rise up and fall, Beating her bulk, that his hand shakes withal . 467
To thee, to thee, my heaved-up hands appeal, Not to seducing lust, thy rash relier . 638
Such wretched hands such wretched blood should spill . 999
Poor hand, why quiver'st thou at this decree? . 1030
Yield to my hand; my hand shall conquer thee . 1210
The other takes in hand No cause, but company, of her drops spilling . 1235
Making such sober action with his hand, That it beguiled attention . 1403
Here one man's hand lean'd on another's head . 1415
That for Achilles' image stood his spear, Griped in an armed hand . 1425
A hand, a foot, a face, a leg, a head, Stood for the whole to be imagined 1427
At last he takes her by the bloodless hand . 1597
'Tis he, That guides this hand to give this wound to me . 1722
This said, he struck his hand upon his breast . 1842
Let not winter's ragged hand deface In thee thy summer . *Sonnet* 6 1
A woman's face with Nature's own hand painted Hast thou . 20 1
Do in consent shake hands to torture me . 28 6
Unused stay From hands of falsehood, in sure wards of trust . 48 4
And this my hand against myself uprear . 49 11
Or at your hand the account of hours to crave . 58 3
My verse shall stand, Praising thy worth, despite his cruel hand . 60 14
With Time's injurious hand crush'd and o'erworn . 63 2
When I have seen by Time's fell hand defaced The rich proud cost of outworn buried age . 64 1
What strong hand can hold his swift foot back? . 65 11
If you read this line, remember not The hand that writ it . 71 6
The lily I condemned for thy hand . 99 6
Sweet beauty's best, Of hand, of foot, of lip, of eye, of brow . 106 6
My nature is subdued To what it works in, like the dyer's hand . 111 7
Since each hand hath put on nature's power . 127 5
Jacks that nimble leap To kiss the tender inward of thy hand . 128 6
Those lips that Love's own hand did make . 145 1
But in her maiden hand The fairest votary took up that fire . 154 4
And so the general of hot desire Was sleeping by a virgin hand disarm'd 154 8
Proclaim'd in her a careless hand of pride . *Lov. Comp.* 30
Or monarch's hands that let not bounty fall Where want cries some . 41
So many have, that never touch'd his hand, Sweetly supposed . 141
O, then, advance of yours that phraseless hand . 225
My hand hath sworn Ne'er to pluck thee from thy thorn . *Pass. Pil.* 237
Handling. Like a wild bird being tamed with too much handling *V. and A.* 560
Handmaids. The silver-shining queen he would distain; Her twinkling handmaids too . *Lucrece* 787
Hang. Doth make them droop with grief and hang the head *Ven. and Adon.* 666
Over one shoulder doth she hang her head . 1058
Thy kinsmen hang their heads at this disdain . *Lucrece* 521
No one to blush with me, To cross their arms and hang their heads with mine 793
At last she calls to mind where hangs a piece Of skilful painting . 1366
Hang on such thorns and play as wantonly . *Sonnet* 54 7
And hang more praise upon deceased I Than niggard truth would willingly impart . 72 7
When yellow leaves, or none, or few, do hang Upon those boughs . 73 2
His browny locks did hang in crooked curls . *Lov. Comp.* 85
Like a green plum that hangs upon a tree, And falls, through wind *Pass. Pil.* 135
Hanged. And daff'd me to a cabin hang'd with care . 183
Hanging. His braided hanging mane Upon his compass'd crest now stand on end . *Ven. and Adon.* 271
She sinketh down, still hanging by his neck . 593
Which in my bosom's shop is hanging still . *Sonnet* 24 7
Hanging her pale and pined cheek beside . *Lov. Comp.* 32
Hap. That meaner men should vaunt That golden hap which their superiors want . *Lucrece* 42
If thou issueless shalt hap to die, The world will wail thee . *Sonnet* 9 3
Hapless. I live, and seek in vain Some happy mean to end a hapless life *Lucr.* 1045
Haply that name of 'chaste' unhappily set . 8
Yet in these thoughts myself almost despising, Haply I think on thee *Sonnet* 29 10
And haply of our old acquaintance tell . 89 12
Haply say 'Truth needs no colour, with his colour fix'd' . 101 5
Happier. To breed another thee, Or ten times happier, be it ten for one 6 8
Ten times thyself were happier than thou art, If ten of thine ten times refigured thee . 6 9
Exceeded by the height of happier men . 32 8
Happiness. O happiness enjoy'd but of a few! And, if possess'd, as soon decay'd . *Lucrece* 22
Happy. And now the happy season once more fits . *Ven. and Adon.* 327
In Tarquin's tent, Unlock'd the treasure of his happy state . *Lucrece* 16
But happy monarchs still are fear'd for love . 611
I live, and seek in vain Some happy mean to end a hapless life . 1045
Which happies those that pay the willing loan . *Sonnet* 6 6
Resembling sire and child and happy mother . 8 11
Now stand you on the top of happy hours . 16 5
Then happy I, that love and am beloved . 25 13
How can I then return in happy plight, That am debarr'd the benefit of rest? . 28 1
This wish I have; then ten times happy me! . 37 14
How would thy shadow's form form happy show To the clear day! . 43 6
Think of nought Save, where you are how happy you make those . 57 12
O, what a happy title do I find, Happy to have thy love, happy to die! 92 11
Since saucy jacks so happy are in this, Give them thy fingers . 128 13
Harbinger. Thou shrieking harbinger, Foul precurrer of the fiend *Ph. and Tur.* 5

Harbour. Dark harbour for defame! Grim cave of death! . *Lucrece* 768
Hard. Art thou obdurate, flinty, hard as steel, Nay, more than flint, for stone at rain relenteth? . *Ven. and Adon.* 199
O, had thy mother borne so hard a mind, She had not brought forth thee 203
The bearing earth with his hard hoof he wounds . 267
O, give it me, lest thy hard heart do steel it . 375
Because Adonis' heart hath made mine hard . 378
For where a heart is hard they make no battery . 426
He bends her fingers, holds her pulses hard, He chafes her lips . 476
That hard heart of thine, Hath taught them scornful tricks and such disdain 500
Hot, faint, and weary, with her hard embracing . 559
Fearing some hard news from the warlike band . *Lucrece* 255
The face, that map which deep impression bears Of hard misfortune . 1713
How hard true sorrow hits, And soon to you, as you to me! . *Sonnet* 120 10
The diamond,—why, 'twas beautiful and hard . *Lov. Comp.* 211
Words are easy, like the wind; Faithful friends are hard to find *Pass. Pil.* 406
Hard-believing. O hard-believing love, how strange it seems Not to believe, and yet too credulous! . *Ven. and Adon.* 985
Harden. Tears harden lust, though marble wear with raining . *Lucrece* 560
Hardened. Stone him with harden'd hearts, harder than stones . 978
Harder. O, if no harder than a stone thou art, Melt at my tears! . 593
Stone him with harden'd hearts, harder than stones . 978
My next self thou harder hast engross'd . *Sonnet* 133 6
Hardest. The hardest knife ill-used doth lose his edge . 95 14
Hard-favoured. Were I hard-favour'd, foul, or wrinkled-old *Ven. and Adon.* 133
Hard-favour'd tyrant, ugly, meagre, lean, Hateful divorce of love . 931
'Some hard-favour'd groom of thine,' quoth he, 'Unless thou yoke thy liking to my will, I'll murder straight' . *Lucrece* 1632
Hare. Uncouple at the timorous flying hare . *Ven. and Adon.* 674
And when thou hast on foot the purblind hare, Mark the poor wretch . 679
Harm. The heat I have from thence doth little harm . 195
Honour and beauty, in the owner's arms, Are weakly fortress'd from a world of harms . *Lucrece* 28
Whose inward ill no outward harm express'd . 91
Th' one sweetly flatters, th' other feareth harm . 172
O impious act, including all foul harms! . 199
A little harm done to a great good end For lawful policy remains enacted . 528
Knights, by their oaths, should right poor ladies' harms . 1694
For fear of harms that preach in our behoof . *Lov. Comp.* 165
Harm have I done to them, but ne'er was harm'd . 194
Harmed. His short thick neck cannot be easily harm'd . *Ven. and Adon.* 627
Harm have I done to them, but ne'er was harm'd . *Lov. Comp.* 194
Harmful. She sheathed in her harmless breast A harmful knife *Lucrece* 1724
With Fortune chide, The guilty goddess of my harmful deeds *Sonnet* 111 2
Harmless. So under his insulting falchion lies Harmless Lucretia *Lucrece* 510
Such harmless creatures have a true respect To talk in deeds . 1347
And give the harmless show An humble gait, calm looks, eyes wailing still 1507
She sheathed in her harmless breast A harmful knife . 1723
Harmony. Lest the deceiving harmony should run Into the quiet closure of my breast . *Ven. and Adon.* 781
Harsh. Ill-nurtured, crooked, churlish, harsh in voice . 134
Let those whom Nature hath not made for store, Harsh featureless and rude, barrenly perish . *Sonnet* 11 10
Harsh-sounding. Melodious discord, heavenly tune harsh-sounding *V. and A.* 431
Harvest. And useless barns the harvest of his wits . *Lucrece* 859
Whilst my poor lips, which should that harvest reap, At the wood's boldness by thee blushing stand . *Sonnet* 128 7
Hast. Hast thou a tongue? O, would thou hadst not, or I had no hearing! *Ven. and Adon.* 427
And when thou hast on foot the purblind hare, Mark the poor wretch . 679
Thou hast no eyes to see, But hatefully at random dost thou hit . 939
Why hast thou cast into eternal sleeping Those eyes? . 951
Alas, poor world, what treasure hast thou lost! . 1075
That thou hast her, it is not all my grief . *Sonnet* 42 1
Every man will be thy friend Whilst thou hast wherewith to spend *Pass. Pil.* 408
Haste. Shaking her wings, devouring all in haste . *Ven. and Adon.* 57
And all in haste she coasteth to the cry . 870
Her more than haste is mated with delays . 909
And in her haste unfortunately spies The foul boar's conquest . 1029
Return again in haste; Thou see'st our mistress' ornaments are chaste *Lucr.* 321
So his unhallow'd haste her words delays . 552
Their fresh falls' haste Add to his flow, but alter not his taste . 650
The cause craves haste, and it will soon be writ . 1295
And on it writ 'At Ardea to my lord with more than haste' . 1332
The violent roaring tide Outruns the eye that doth behold his haste . 1668
Weary with toil, I haste me to my bed . *Sonnet* 27 1
From where thou art why should I haste me thence? . 51 3
What we see doth lie, Made more or less by thy continual haste . 123 12
Hasten. So do our minutes hasten to their end . 60 2
Hasteth. Away he springs and hasteth to his horse . *Ven. and Adon.* 258
This said, she hasteth to a myrtle grove . 865
Hasting to feed her fawn hid in some brake . 876
Hasty. Thy hasty spring still blasts, and ne'er grows old . *Lucrece* 49
Hat. With one fair hand she heaveth up his hat . *Ven. and Adon.* 351
For some, untuck'd, descended her sheaved hat . *Lov. Comp.* 31
Hatch. Or hateful cuckoos hatch in sparrows' nests? . *Lucrece* 849
Hate. To make thee hate the hunting of the boar, Unlike myself thou hear'st me moralize . *Ven. and Adon.* 711
I hate not love, but your device in love . 789
There is no hate in loving: I'll beg her love . *Lucrece* 240
Enforced hate, Instead of love's coy touch, shall rudely tear thee . 668
He scowls and hates himself for his offence . 738
Time's office is to fine the hate of foes . 936
The mightier man, the mightier is the thing That makes him honour'd, or begets him hate . 1005
Thou art so possess'd with murderous hate . *Sonnet* 10 5
Shall hate be fairer lodged than gentle love? . 10 10
Such civil war is in my love and hate . 35 12
It is a greater grief To bear love's wrong than hate's known injury . 40 12
For I must ne'er love him whom thou dost hate. Then hate me when thou wilt . 89 14
But shoot not at me in your waken'd hate . 117 12
As subject to Time's love or to Time's hate . 124 3
Love is my sin and thy dear virtue hate, Hate of my sin . 142 1
Those lips that Love's own hand did make Breathed forth the sound that said 'I hate' . 145 2
'I hate' she alter'd with an end That follow'd it as gentle day . 145 9
'I hate' from hate away she threw, And saved my life, saying 'not you' . 145 13
But, love hate on, for now I know thy mind . 149 13

Hate. The more I hear and see just cause of hate . . . *Sonnet* 150 10
New faith torn In vowing new hate after new love bearing . . 152 4
Hated. Past reason hunted, and no sooner had Past reason hated . . 129 7
Hateful. Ugly, meagre, lean, Hateful divorce of love . . *Ven. and Adon.* 932
Now she adds honours to his hateful name 994
Betrays To slanderous tongues and wretched hateful days . *Lucrece* 161
Hateful it is; there is no hate in loving: I'll beg her love . . 240
O hateful, vaporous, and foggy Night! 771
Or hateful cuckoos hatch in sparrows' nests? 849
Longing to hear the hateful foe bewray'd 1698
Hatefully. But hatefully at random dost thou hit . *Ven. and Adon.* 940
Hateth. Who hateth thee that I do call my friend? . *Sonnet* 149 5
Hath. The heart hath treble wrong When it is barr'd the aidance of the tongue . . . . *Ven. and Adon.* 329
But, when his glutton eye so full hath fed, His other agents aim at like delight 399
Thy mermaid's voice hath done me double wrong 429
That hard heart of thine, Hath taught them scornful tricks . . 501
Now quick desire hath caught the yielding prey 547
For who hath she to spend the night withal But idle sounds resembling parasites 847
So then he hath it when he cannot use it . . . *Lucrece* 862
That she hath thee, is of my wailing chief . . . *Sonnet* 42 3
Hatred. For there can live no hatred in thine eye . . . 93 5
Haunted. To remain In personal duty, following where he haunted *Lov. Comp.* 130
Have. Her contending tears, Which long have rain'd, making her cheeks all wet . . . . *Ven. and Adon.* 83
I have been woo'd, as I entreat thee now, Even by the stern and direful god of war 97
And begg'd for that which thou unask'd shalt have . . . 102
The heat I have from thence doth little harm 195
Look, what a horse should have he did not lack . . . 299
For I have heard it is a life in death 413
That they have murder'd this poor heart of mine . . . 502
Seeming to bury that posterity Which by the rights of time thou needs must have 759
Till the wild waves will have him seen no more . . . 819
Torments us with defect Of that we have . . . *Lucrece* 152
So then we do neglect The thing we have 153
The threshold grates the door to have him heard . . . 306
'Have done,' quoth he: 'my uncontrolled tide Turns not' . . 645
For who so base would such an office have? 1000
Methinks I have astronomy, But not to tell of good or evil luck *Sonnet* 14 2
Thus have I had thee, as a dream doth flatter, In sleep a king . 87 13
Now all is done, have what shall have no end . . . 110 9
Had, having, and in quest to have, extreme . . . 129 10
I might as yet have been a spreading flower, Fresh to myself *Lov. Comp.* 75
Gentle maid, Have of my suffering youth some feeling pity . . 178
But, O my sweet, what labour is't to leave The thing we have not . 240
And age, in love, loves not to have years told . . *Pass. Pil.* 12
Having. But having no defects, why dost abhor me? *Ven. and Adon.* 138
But having thee at vantage,—wondrous dread! 635
Mine ears, that to your wanton talk attended, Do burn themselves for having so offended 810
Having no fair to lose, you need not fear 1083
Which, having all, all could not satisfy . . . *Lucrece* 96
This ambitious foul infirmity, In having much, torments us with defect Of that we have 151
Had, having, and in quest to have, extreme . . . *Sonnet* 129 10
Why so large cost, having so short a lease? . . . 146 5
Whose rarest havings made the blossoms dote . . *Lov. Comp.* 235
Hawk. As the full-fed hound or gorged hawk, . . . Make slow pursuit *Lucr.* 694
Some [glory] in their hawks and hounds, some in their horse . *Sonnet* 91 4
Prouder than garments' cost, Of more delight than hawks or horses be 91 11
Hazard. Such hazard now must doting Tarquin make . . *Lucrece* 155
He. He burns with bashful shame: she with her tears Doth quench the maiden burning of his cheeks . . . *Ven. and Adon.* 49
Thus he that overruled I overway'd 109
He might be buried in a tomb so simple 244
Breaketh his rein, and to her straight goes he . . . 264
Imperiously he leaps, he neighs, he bounds 265
What recketh he his rider's angry stir? 283
He sees his love, and nothing else he sees 287
He wrings her nose, he strikes her on the cheeks, He bends her fingers 475
He with her plenty press'd, she faint with dearth . . . 545
Hadst thou but bid beware, then he had spoke . . . 943
'He, he,' she says, But more than 'he' her poor tongue could not speak *Lucrece* 1717
He, he, fair lords, 'tis he, That guides this hand to give this wound to me . 1721
But he that writes of you, if he can tell That you are you, so dignifies his story . . . . *Sonnet* 84 7
Head. Vouchsafe, thou wonder, to alight thy steed, And rein his proud head to the saddle-bow . . . . *Ven. and Adon.* 14
What seest thou in the ground? hold up thy head: Look in mine eye-balls 118
Sometimes she shakes her head and then his hand, Now gazeth she on him 223
Broad breast, full eye, small head, and nostril wide, High crest, short ears 296
Doth make them droop with grief and hang the head . . . 666
Her eyes are fled Into the deep dark cabins of her head . . 1038
Over one shoulder doth she hang her head; Dumbly she passions . 1058
She bows her head, the new-sprung flower to smell . . . 1171
About he walks, Rolling his greedy eyeballs in his head . *Lucrece* 368
Between whose hills her head entombed is 390
Thy kinsmen hang their heads at this disdain 521
With the nightly linen that she wears He pens her piteous clamours in her head 681
Ere he go to bed, Knit poisonous clouds about his golden head . 777
No one to blush with me, To cross their arms and hang their heads with mine 793
Here one man's hand lean'd on another's head 1415
A hand, a foot, a face, a leg, a head, Stood for the whole to be imagined . 1427
Let sin, alone committed, light alone Upon his head that hath transgressed so 1481
And on that pillow lay Where thou wast wont to rest thy weary head . 1621
With head declined, and voice damm'd up with woe . . . 1661
In the orient when the gracious light Lifts up his burning head *Sonnet* 7 2
Till then not show my head where thou mayst prove me . . 26 14
Then begins a journey in my head, To work my mind . . 27 3
The right of sepulchres, were shorn away, To live a second life on second head 68 7

Head. If hairs be wires, black wires grow on her head . *Sonnet* 130 4
O me, what eyes hath Love put in my head! 148 1
Upon her head a platted hive of straw . . . . *Lov. Comp.* 8
Take counsel of some wiser head, Neither too young nor yet unwed *Pass. Pil.* 303
Headlong. Or stop the headlong fury of his speed . . *Lucrece* 501
Healeth. Bearing away the wound that nothing healeth . . . 731
Heals. That heals the wound and cures not the disgrace . *Sonnet* 34 8
Health. Thou worthy lord Of that unworthy wife that greeteth thee, Health to thy person! . . . . *Lucrece* 1305
Who even but now come back again, assured Of thy fair health . *Sonnet* 45 12
As testy sick men, when their deaths be near, No news but health from their physicians know 140 8
Healthful. And brought to medicine a healthful state . . 118 11
Growing a bath and healthful remedy For men diseased . . 154 11
Hear. Though neither eyes nor ears, to hear nor see *Ven. and Adon.* 437
And that I could not see, nor hear, nor touch 440
Anon their loud alarums he doth hear 700
To one sore sick that hears the passing-bell 702
Lie quietly, and hear a little more; Nay, do not struggle . . 709
And yet she hears no tidings of her love 867
Anon she hears them chant it lustily, And all in haste she coasteth to the cry 869
By this, she hears the hounds are at a bay, Whereat she starts . 877
By this, far off she hears some huntsman hollo . . . 973
Even at this word she hears a merry horn, Whereat she leaps . 1025
When he hath sung, The tiger would be tame and gently hear him . 1096
Until her husband's welfare she did hear . . . *Lucrece* 263
But will is deaf and hears no heedful friends 495
Marking what he tells With trembling fear, as fowl hear falcon's bells . 511
By heaven, I will not hear thee: Yield to my love . . . 667
Thou art well appaid As well to hear as grant what he hath said . 915
O, hear me then, injurious, shifting Time! 930
The life and feeling of her passion She hoards, to spend when he is by to hear her 1318
To see sad sights moves more than hear them told . . . 1324
'Tis but a part of sorrow that we hear 1328
Collatine and his consorted lords With sad attention long to hear her words 1610
Longing to hear the hateful foe bewray'd 1698
Music to hear, why hear'st thou music sadly? . . . *Sonnet* 8 1
To hear with eyes belongs to love's fine wit . . . 23 14
No longer mourn for me when I am dead Than you shall hear the surly sullen bell 71 2
For fear of which, hear this, thou age unbred . . . 104 13
I love to hear her speak, yet well I know That music hath a far more pleasing sound 130 9
The more I hear and see just cause of hate 150 10
How mighty then you are, O, hear me tell! . . . *Lov. Comp.* 253
Thou lovest to hear the sweet melodious sound That Phœbus' lute, the queen of music, makes . . . . *Pass. Pil.* 111
Enough, too much, I fear; Lest that my mistress hear my song . . 348
Yet will she blush, here be it said, To hear her secrets so bewray'd . 352
And there sung the dolefull'st ditty, That to hear it was great pity . 384
That to hear her so complain, Scarce I could from tears refrain . 387
Senseless trees they cannot hear thee 393
Heard. For I have heard it is a life in death . . *Ven. and Adon.* 413
Whispers in his ears . . . , As if they heard the woeful words . . 1126
The threshold grates the door to have him heard . . *Lucrece* 306
Die I will not till my Collatine Have heard the cause of my untimely death 1178
Than think that we before have heard them told . . *Sonnet* 123 8
Heard where his plants in others' orchards grew . . *Lov. Comp.* 171
Have you not heard it said full oft, A woman's nay doth stand for nought? *Pass. Pil.* 339
Hearers. Will tie the hearers to attend each line . . *Lucrece* 818
Hearest. Unlike myself thou hear'st me moralize . *Ven. and Adon.* 712
Music to hear, why hear'st thou music sadly? . . . *Sonnet* 8 1
Hearing. Hast a thou tongue? O, would thou hadst not, or I had no hearing! . . . . *Ven. and Adon.* 428
Hearing him, thy power had lost his power 944
And in my hearing be you mute and dumb . . . *Lucrece* 1123
Hearing you praised, I say ''Tis so, 'tis true' . . *Sonnet* 85 9
When he again desires her, being sat, Her grievance with his hearing to divide *Lov. Comp.* 67
Hearken. Stands on his hinder legs with listening ear, To hearken *V. and A.* 699
She hearkens for his hounds and for his horn 868
Hearsay. Let them say more that like of hearsay well . *Sonnet* 21 13
Hearsed. Thy sea within a puddle's womb is hearsed . . *Lucrece* 657
Heart. Is thine own heart to thine own face affected? *Ven. and Adon.* 157
For lovers say, the heart hath treble wrong When it is barr'd the aidance of the tongue 329
But when the heart's attorney once is mute, The client breaks . . 335
My heart all whole as thine, thy heart my wound . . . 370
'Give me my heart,' saith she, 'and thou shalt have it; O, give it me, lest thy hard heart do steel it' 374
Because Adonis' heart hath made mine hard 378
Affection is a coal that must be cool'd; Else, suffer'd, it will set the heart on fire 388
Remove your siege from my unyielding heart 423
For where a heart is hard they make no battery . . . 426
Ear's deep-sweet music, and heart's deep-sore wounding . . 432
That hard heart of thine Hath taught them scornful tricks and such disdain 500
That they have murder'd this poor heart of mine . . . 502
A thousand kisses buys my heart from me 517
Bids him farewell, and look well to her heart 580
I'll waste in sorrow, For my sick heart commands mine eyes to watch . 584
My boding heart pants, beats, and takes no rest . . . 647
Knocks at my heart and whispers in mine ear 659
The thought of it doth make my faint heart bleed, And fear doth teach it divination 669
My heart stands armed in mine ear, And will not let a false sound enter there 779
And then my little heart were quite undone 783
My heart longs not to groan, But soundly sleeps, while now it sleeps alone 785
Now I will away; My face is full of shame, my heart of teen . 808
And now she beats her heart, whereat it groans . . . 829
This dismal cry rings sadly in her ear, Through which it enters to surprise her heart 890
Thy false dart Mistakes that aim and cleaves an infant's heart . . 942
Thy coward heart with false bethinking grieves . . . 1024
And never wound the heart with looks again 1042
Mine eyes are turn'd to fire, my heart to lead: Heavy heart's lead, melt at mine eyes' red fire! 1072

Heart. My throbbing heart shall rock thee day and night *Ven. and Adon.* 1186
For by our ears our hearts oft tainted be *Lucrece* 38
My frail joints shake, Mine eyes forego their light, my false heart bleed 228
Love thrives not in the heart that shadows dreadeth 270
My heart shall never countermand mine eye 276
But with a pure appeal seeks to the heart, Which once corrupted takes the worser part 293
But his hot heart, which fond desire doth scorch, Puffs forth another wind 314
By their high treason is his heart misled 369
Anon his beating heart, alarum striking, Gives the hot charge 433
His drumming heart cheers up his burning eye 435
Her bare breast, the heart of all her land 439
May feel her heart—poor citizen!—distress'd, Wounding itself to death, rise up and fall 465
His heart granteth No penetrable entrance to her plaining 558
Beat at thy rocky and wreck-threatening heart, To soften it 590
By him that gave it thee, From a pure heart command thy rebel will 625
She wakes her heart by beating on her breast, And bids it leap from thence 759
Pity not his moans: Stone him with harden'd hearts, harder than stones 978
Against my heart Will fix a sharp knife to affright mine eye 1137
Faint not, faint heart, but stoutly say 'So be it:' Yield to my hand 1209
And then they drown their eyes or break their hearts 1239
The face of either cipher'd either's heart 1396
No guilty instance gave, Nor ashy pale the fear that false hearts have 1512
And then against my heart he set his sword 1640
As if her heart would break, She throws forth Tarquin's name 1716
Through his lips do throng Weak words, so thick come in his poor heart's aid 1784
Do not steep thy heart In such relenting dew of lamentations 1828
A woman's gentle heart, but not acquainted With shifting change *Sonnet* 20 3
For all that beauty that doth cover thee Is but the seemly raiment of my heart 22 6
Bearing thy heart, which I will keep so chary As tender nurse her babe 22 11
Presume not on thy heart when mine is slain 22 13
Whose strength's abundance weakens his own heart 23 4
And hath stell'd Thy beauty's form in table of my heart 24 2
They draw but what they see, know not the heart 24 14
Thy bosom is endeared with all hearts 31 1
When I am sometime absent from thy heart 41 2
Mine eye and heart are at a mortal war How to divide the conquest 46 1
Mine eye my heart thy picture's sight would bar, My heart mine eye the freedom of that right 46 3
My heart doth plead that thou in him dost lie 46 5
A quest of thoughts, all tenants to the heart 46 10
The clear eye's moiety and the dear heart's part 46 12
Mine eye's due is thy outward part, And my heart's right thy inward love of heart 46 14
Betwixt mine eye and heart a league is took, And each doth good turns 47 1
Or heart in love with sighs himself doth smother 47 4
My eye doth feast And to the painted banquet bids my heart 47 6
Another time mine eye is my heart's guest 47 7
Thy picture in my sight Awakes my heart to heart's and eye's delight 47 14
But you like none, none you, for constant heart 53 14
There is no remedy, It is so grounded inward in my heart 62 4
Want nothing that the thought of hearts can mend 69 2
Then thou alone kingdoms of hearts shouldst owe 70 14
Ah, do not, when my heart hath 'scaped this sorrow, Come in the rearward of a conquer'd woe 90 5
Though alter'd new; Thy looks with me, thy heart in other place 93 4
In many's looks the false heart's history Is writ in moods 93 7
Whate'er thy thoughts or thy heart's workings be 93 11
Take heed, dear heart, of this large privilege 95 13
O, never say that I was false of heart 109 1
By all above, These blenches gave my heart another youth 110 7
For it no form delivers to the heart Of bird, of flower, or shape 113 5
What wretched errors hath my heart committed! 119 5
So long as brain and heart Have faculty by nature to subsist 122 5
Let me be obsequious in thy heart, And take thou my oblation 125 9
To my dear doting heart Thou art the fairest and most precious jewel 131 3
Knowing thy heart torments me with disdain 132 2
O, let it then as well beseem thy heart To mourn for me 132 10
Beshrew that heart that makes my heart to groan! 133 1
Prison my heart in thy steel bosom's ward, But then my friend's heart let my poor heart bail 133 9
Whoe'er keeps me, let my heart be his guard 133 11
Hooks, Whereto the judgement of my heart is tied 137 8
Why should my heart think that a several plot Which my heart knows the wide world's common place? 137 9
In things right true my heart and eyes have erred 137 13
Call not me to justify the wrong That thy unkindness lays upon my heart 139 2
In my sight, Dear heart, forbear to glance thine eye aside 139 6
Bear thine eyes straight, though thy proud heart go wide 140 14
But 'tis my heart that loves what they despise 141 3
But my five wits nor my five senses can Dissuade one foolish heart from serving thee 141 10
Thy proud heart's slave and vassal wretch to be 141 12
Root pity in thy heart, that when it grows Thy pity may deserve to pitied be 142 11
Straight in her heart did mercy come 145 5
This powerful might With insufficiency my heart to sway 150 2
That fire Which many legions of true hearts had warm'd 154 6
Sweetly supposed them mistress of his heart *Lov. Comp.* 142
And bastards of his foul adulterate heart 175
Not one whose flame my heart so much as warm'd 191
Kept hearts in liveries, but mine own was free 195
Effects of terror and dear modesty, Encamp'd in hearts 203
Now all these hearts that do on mine depend, Feeling it break, with bleeding groans they pine 274
But with the inundation of the eyes What rocky heart to water will not wear? 291
That not a heart which in his level came Could 'scape 309
O, that forced thunder from his heart did fly! 325
Did not the heavenly rhetoric of thine eye, . . . Persuade my heart to this false perjury? *Pass. Pil.* 31
To win his heart, she touch'd him here and there 49
Lord, how mine eyes throw gazes to the east! My heart doth charge the watch 194
Heart hath his hope, and eyes their wished sight 202
Love's denying, Faith's defying, Heart's renying, Causer of this 251
Heart is bleeding, All help needing, O cruel speeding, Fraughted with gall 267
Thus of every grief in heart He with thee doth bear a part 427
Hearts remote, yet not asunder *Ph. and Tur.* 29

Heart-easing. Who, mad that sorrow should his use control, Or keep him from heart-easing words so long, Begins to talk *Lucrece* 1782
Heartens. And therein heartens up his servile powers 295
Heartily. I heartily beseech thee, To take advantage on presented joy *Ven. and Adon.* 404
Heart-inflaming. Laid by his side his heart-inflaming brand *Sonnet* 154 2
Heartless. First, like a trumpet, doth his tongue begin To sound a parley to his heartless foe *Lucrece* 471
Which heartless peasants did so well resemble 1392
How sighs resound Through heartless ground *Pass. Pil.* 279
Heart-strings. These means, as frets upon an instrument, Shall tune our heart-strings *Lucrece* 1141
Heart-wished. When he most burn'd in heart-wish'd luxury *Lov. Comp.* 314
Heat. Never did passenger in summer's heat More thirst for drink *V. and A.* 91
And Titan, tired in the mid-day heat, With burning eye did hotly overlook them 177
I'll sigh celestial breath, whose gentle wind Shall cool the heat of this descending sun 190
The heat I have from thence doth little harm 195
Seems unkind, Spurns at his love and scorns the heat he feels 311
O rash false heat, wrapp'd in repentant cold! *Lucrece* 48
While Lust is in his pride, no exclamation Can curb his heat 706
That knows not parching heat nor freezing cold 1145
Thy heat of lust, fond Paris, did incur This load of wrath 1473
When lofty trees I see barren of leaves Which erst from heat did canopy the herd *Sonnet* 12 6
That it nor grows with heat nor drowns with showers 124 12
Which borrow'd from this holy fire of Love A dateless lively heat 153 6
This brand she quenched in a cool well by, Which from Love's fire took heat perpetual 154 10
Love's fire heats water, water cools not love 154 14
Heating. Whose attaint Disorder breeds by heating of the blood *V. and A.* 742
Heave. Went about From this fair throne to heave the owner out *Lucrece* 413
My sighs, like whirlwinds, labour hence to heave thee 586
Oft did she heave her napkin to her eyne *Lov. Comp.* 15
Heaved-up. Her joy with heaved-up hand she doth express *Lucrece* 111
To thee, to thee, my heaved-up hands appeal 638
Heaven. The sun that shines from heaven shines but warm *Ven. and Adon.* 193
The bearing earth . . . Whose hollow womb resounds like heaven's thunder 268
'O, where am I?' quoth she, 'in earth or heaven, Or in the ocean?' 493
And coal-black clouds that shadow heaven's light Do summon us to part 533
Condemn'd of treason, For stealing moulds from heaven that were divine 730
Wherein she framed thee in high heaven's despite, To shame the sun 731
Love to heaven is fled, Since sweating Lust on earth usurp'd his name 793
Mortal stars, as bright as heaven's beauties *Lucrece* 13
What priceless wealth the heavens had him lent 17
And, wordless, so greets heaven for his success 112
The chamber door, That shuts him from the heaven of his thought 338
To pray he doth begin, As if the heavens should countenance his sin 343
The eye of heaven is out, and misty night Covers the shame 356
By heaven and earth, and all the power of both 572
To all the host of heaven I complain me, Thou wrong'st his honour 598
By heaven, I will not hear thee: Yield to my love 667
When both were kept for heaven and Collatine 1166
So proud, As heaven, it seem'd, to kiss the turrets bow'd 1372
By heaven's fair sun that breeds the fat earth's store 1837
Or say with princes if it shall go well, By oft predict that I in heaven find *Sonnet* 14 8
Heaven knows, it is but as a tomb Which hides your life 17 3
Sometime too hot the eye of heaven shines 18 5
Who heaven itself for ornament doth use 21 3
And all things rare That heaven's air in this huge rondure hems 21 8
Though not so bright As those gold candles fix'd in heaven's air 21 12
And dost him grace when clouds do blot the heaven 28 10
And trouble deaf heaven with my bootless cries 29 3
Like to the lark at break of day arising From sullen earth, sings hymns at heaven's gate 29 12
Suns of the world may stain when heaven's sun staineth 33 14
The ornament of beauty is suspect, A crow that flies in heaven's sweetest air 70 4
Heaven in thy creation did decree That in thy face sweet love should ever dwell 93 9
And to temptation slow, They rightly do inherit heaven's graces 94 5
Then give me welcome, next my heaven the best 110 13
Yet none knows well To shun the heaven that leads men to this hell 129 14
By heaven, I think my love as rare As any she belied with false compare 130 13
Truly not the morning sun of heaven Better becomes the grey cheeks of the east 132 5
Who like a fiend From heaven to hell is flown away 145 12
The sun itself sees not till heaven clears 148 12
But, spite of heaven's fell rage, Some beauty peep'd through lattice of sear'd age *Lov. Comp.* 13
O do not love that wrong, To sing heaven's praise with such an earthly tongue *Pass. Pil.* 70
That the lover, sick to death, Wish'd himself the heaven's breath 234
There is no heaven, by holy then, When time with age doth them attaint 343
Heaven-hued. The heaven-hued sapphire and the opal blend With objects manifold *Lov. Comp.* 215
Heavenly. And calls it heavenly moisture, air of grace *Ven. and Adon.* 64
And were I not immortal, life were done Between this heavenly and earthly sun 198
Melodious discord, heavenly tune harsh-sounding 431
Till, breathless, he disjoin'd, and backward drew The heavenly moisture 542
Within his thought her heavenly image sits *Lucrece* 288
Having climb'd the steep-up heavenly hill *Sonnet* 7 5
Such heavenly touches ne'er touch'd earthly faces 17 8
Gilding pale streams with heavenly alchemy 33 4
Did not the heavenly rhetoric of thine eye, . . . Persuade my heart to this false perjury? *Pass. Pil.* 29
My vow was earthly, thou a heavenly love 35
Whose heavenly touch Upon the lute doth ravish human sense 107
Heaveth. With one fair hand she heaveth up his hat *Ven. and Adon.* 351
Heavily. And heavily from woe to woe tell o'er The sad account *Sonnet* 30 10
Which heavily he answers with a groan 50 11
Heaviness. If your maid may be so bold, She would request to know your heaviness *Lucrece* 1283
Unmask, dear dear, this moody heaviness, And tell thy grief 1602
Heavy. Is love so light, sweet boy, and may it be That thou shouldst think it heavy unto thee? *Ven. and Adon.* 156
With a lazy spright, And with a heavy, dark, disliking eye 182
Her heavy anthem still concludes in woe 839

Heavy. What may a heavy groan advantage thee? *Ven. and Adon.* 950
Heavy heart's lead, melt at mine eyes' red fire! . . . 1073
She whispers in his ears a heavy tale . . . 1125
Intending weariness with heavy spright . *Lucrece* 121
When heavy sleep had closed up mortal eyes . . . 163
With heavy eye, knit brow, and strengthless pace . . . 709
He thence departs a heavy convertite . . . 743
The eye interprets to the ear The heavy motion that it doth behold . 1326
Seem'd to appear, Like bright things stain'd, a kind of heavy fear . 1435
Though woe be heavy, yet it seldom sleeps . . . 1574
Thy fair imperfect shade Through heavy sleep on sightless eyes doth stay *Sonnet* 43 12
Heavy tears, badges of either's woe . . . 44 14
How heavy do I journey on the way . . . 50 1
Is it thy will thy image should keep open My heavy eyelids? . 61 2
Thine eyes that taught the dumb on high to sing And heavy ignorance aloft to fly . . . 78 6
That heavy Saturn laugh'd and leap'd with him . . . 98 4
Heavy-hanging. Like a heavy-hanging bell, Once set on ringing, with his own weight goes . . . *Lucrece* 1493
Hector. When their brave hope, bold Hector, march'd to field . . 1430
Here manly Hector faints, here Troilus swounds . . . 1486
Hecuba. Till she despairing Hecuba beheld . . . 1447
Lo, here weeps Hecuba, here Priam dies . . . 1485
Hedge. To see his face the lion walk'd along Behind some hedge *Ven. and Adon.* 1094
And scarce the herd gone to the hedge for shade . . . *Pass. Pil.* 72
Heed. Take heed, dear heart, of this large privilege . *Sonnet* 95 13
Heedful. So heedful fear Is almost choked by unresisted lust . *Lucrece* 281
But will is deaf and hears no heedful friends . . . 495
Heedfully doth view The sight which makes supposed terror true . 454
Heels. Beating his kind embracements with her heels *Ven. and Adon.* 312
Height. Or if thou wilt permit the sun to climb His wonted height *Lucrece* 776
Vaunt in their youthful sap, at height decrease . *Sonnet* 15 7
Exceeded by the height of happier men . . . 32 8
Whose worth's unknown, although his height be taken . . 116 8
Heinous. Thy heinous hours wait on them as their pages *Lucrece* 910
But I forbid thee one most heinous crime . . *Sonnet* 19 8
Heir. His tender heir might bear his memory . . . 1 4
Thou art much too fair To be death's conquest and make worms thine heir . . . 6 14
But now is black beauty's successive heir . . . 127 3
Held. He held such petty bondage in disdain *Ven. and Adon.* 394
From the purple fountain Brutus drew The murderous knife, and, as it left the place, Her blood, in poor revenge, held it in chase . *Lucrece* 1736
Held back his sorrow's tide, to make it more . . . 1789
A tatter'd weed, of small worth held . . . *Sonnet* 2 4
My body is the frame wherein 'tis held . . . 24 3
Long upon these terms I held my city, Till thus he gan besiege *Lov. Comp.* 176
Helen. For Helen's rape the city to destroy . . *Lucrece* 1369
On Helen's cheek all art of beauty set . . . *Sonnet* 53 7
Hell. O comfort-killing Night, image of hell! Dim register and notary of shame! . . . *Lucrece* 764
Solemn night with slow sad gait descended To ugly hell . . 1082
That deep torture may be call'd a hell . . . 1287
Such devils steal effects from lightless hell . . . 1555
I am to wait, though waiting so be hell . . *Sonnet* 58 13
Siren tears, Distill'd from limbecks foul as hell within . . 119 2
For if you were by my unkindness shaken As I by yours, you've pass'd a hell of time . . . 120 6
Yet none knows well To shun the heaven that leads men to this hell . 129 14
To win me soon to hell, my female evil Tempteth my better angel from my side . . . 144 5; *Pass. Pil.* 19
Being both to me, both to each friend, I guess one angel in another's hell *Sonnet* 144 12; *Pass. Pil.* 26
Who like a fiend From heaven to hell is flown away . . *Sonnet* 145 12
And thought thee bright, Who art as black as hell, as dark as night . 147 14
What a hell of witchcraft lies In the small orb of one particular tear! *Lov. Comp.* 288
Hell-born. Or blot with hell-born sin such saint-like forms . . *Lucrece* 1519
Help. Her help she sees, but help she cannot get . *Ven. and Adon.* 93
For one sweet look thy help I would assure thee . . . 371
They buy thy help; but Sin ne'er gives a fee, He gratis comes *Lucrece* 913
Let him have time of Time's help to despair . . . 983
Since that my case is past the help of law . . . 1022
Poor helpless help, the treasure stol'n away . . . 1056
If tears could help, mine own would do me good . . . 1274
The help that thou shalt lend me Comes all too late, yet let the traitor die . 1685
Do wounds help wounds, or grief help grievous deeds? . . 1822
Kneel with me and help to bear thy part . . . 1830
So shall those blots that do with me remain Without thy help by me be borne alone . . . *Sonnet* 36 4
Your shallowest help will hold me up afloat . . . 80 9
I, sick withal, the help of bath desired, And thither hied . . 153 11
The bath for my help lies Where Cupid got new fire—my mistress' eyes 153 13
The trusty knight was wounded with disdain: Alas, she could not help it! *Pass. Pil.* 222
Heart is bleeding, All help needing, O cruel speeding, Fraughted with gall 268
Other help for him I see that there is none . . . 298
He that is thy friend indeed, He will help thee in thy need . . 424
Helpless. As those poor birds that helpless berries saw . *Ven. and Adon.* 604
And grave, like water that doth eat in steel, Upon my cheeks what helpless shame I feel . . . *Lucrece* 756
This helpless smoke of words doth me no right . . . 1027
Poor helpless help, the treasure stol'n away . . . 1056
Hemmed. Since I have hemm'd thee here Within the circuit of this ivory pale . . . *Ven. and Adon.* 229
So full of fear As one with treasure laden, hemm'd with thieves . . 1022
Hems. And all things rare That heaven's air in this huge rondure hems *Sonnet* 21 8
Hence. I pray you hence, and leave me here alone . *Ven. and Adon.* 382
My sighs, like whirlwinds, labour hence to heave thee . . *Lucrece* 586
'When went'—and there she stay'd Till after a deep groan—'Tarquin from hence?' . . . 1276
Nothing 'gainst Time's scythe can make defence Save breed, to brave him when he takes thee hence . . . *Sonnet* 12 14
Thou teachest how to make one twain, By praising him here who doth hence remain . . . 39 14
From hence your memory death cannot take . . . 81 3
Your name from hence immortal life shall have . . . 81 5
Hence. I teach thee how To make him seem long hence as he shows now *Sonnet* 101 14
Hence, thou suborn'd informer! . . . 125 13
And controversy hence a question takes . . . *Lov. Comp.* 110
Cold modesty, hot wrath, Both fire from hence and chill extincture hath . 294
Phœnix and the turtle fled In a mutual flame from hence . *Ph. and Tur.* 24
Henceforth. Bonnet nor veil henceforth no creature wear! *Ven. and Adon.* 1081
Her. And trembling in her passion, calls it balm . . . 27
Her words are done, her woes the more increasing . . . 254
Her eyes petitioners to his eyes suing . . . 356
His eyes saw her eyes as they had not seen them; Her eyes woo'd still, his eyes disdain'd the wooing . . . 357
But hers, which through the crystal tears gave light, Shone like the moon . 491
Her voice is stopt, her joints forget to bow; Her eyes are mad . . 1061
Lucrece to their sight Must sell her joy, her life, her world's delight *Lucr.* 385
Her azure veins, her alabaster skin, Her coral lips, her snow-white dimpled chin . . . 419
Such passion her assails, That patience is quite beaten from her breast . 1562
Herald. The owl, night's herald, shrieks, ''Tis very late' *Ven. and Adon.* 531
Some loathsome dash the herald will contrive, To cipher me . *Lucrece* 206
The world's fresh ornament And only herald to the gaudy spring *Sonnet* 1 10
Herald sad and trumpet be, To whose sound chaste wings obey *Ph. and Tur.* 3
Heraldry. This heraldry in Lucrece' face was seen, Argued by beauty's red and virtue's white . . . *Lucrece* 64
Herb. Dainties to taste, fresh beauty for the use, Herbs for their smell, and sappy plants to bear . . . *Ven. and Adon.* 165
No flower was nigh, no grass, herb, leaf, or weed, But stole his blood . 1055
Herd. Gusts and foul flaws to herdmen and to herds . . . 456
And sometime sorteth with a herd of deer . . . 689
When lofty trees I see barren of leaves Which erst from heat did canopy the herd . . . *Sonnet* 12 6
And scarce the herd gone to the hedge for shade . . . *Pass. Pil.* 72
Herds stand weeping, Flocks all sleeping . . . 285
Herdmen. Gusts and foul flaws to herdmen and to herds *Ven. and Adon.* 456
Here come and sit, where never serpent hisses . . . 17
Since I have hemm'd thee here Within the circuit of this ivory pale . . 229
I pray you hence, and leave me here alone . . . 382
Here the gentle lark, weary of rest, From his moist cabinet mounts up on high . . . 853
Here kennell'd in a brake she finds a hound . . . 913
Here she meets another sadly scowling, To whom she speaks . . 917
Here overcome, as one full of despair, She vail'd her eyelids . . 955
Since thou art dead, lo, here I prophesy . . . 1135
Here was thy father's bed, here in my breast . . . 1183
Here pale with fear he doth premeditate The dangers . . *Lucrece* 183
Here with a cockatrice' dead-killing eye He rouseth up himself . . 540
Here she exclaims against repose and rest . . . 757
Get me hither paper, ink, and pen: Yet save that labour, for I have them here . . . 1290
Here folds she up the tenour of her woe, Her certain sorrow writ uncertainly 1310
And here and there the painter interlaces Pale cowards . . . 1390
Here one man's hand lean'd on another's head . . . 1415
Here one being throng'd bears back, all boll'n and red . . . 1417
Thy eye kindled the fire that burneth here . . . 1475
Here in Troy, for trespass of thine eye, The sire, the son, the dame, and daughter die . . . 1476
Here weeps Hecuba, here Priam dies, Here manly Hector faints . . 1485
Here Troilus swounds, Here friend by friend in bloody channel lies . 1486
Here feelingly she weeps Troy's painted woes . . . 1492
Sinon here is painted, So sober-sad, so weary, and so mild . . 1541
Here, all enraged, such passion her assails, That patience is quite beaten . 1562
Lo, here, the hopeless merchant of this loss, With head declined . . 1660
Here with a sigh, as if her heart would break, She throws forth Tarquin's name . . . 1716
Even here she sheathed in her harmless breast A harmful knife . . 1723
That life was mine which thou hast here deprived . . . 1752
But, love, you are No longer yours than you yourself here live . *Sonnet* 13 2
Thou teachest how to make one twain, By praising him here who doth hence remain . . . 39 14
But here's the joy; my friend and I are one; Sweet flattery . 42 13
I ensconce me here Within the knowledge of mine own desert . 49 9
I have gone here and there And made myself a motley to the view 110 1
Ink would have seem'd more black and damned here . *Lov. Comp.* 54
Look here, what tributes wounded fancies sent me, Of paled pearls . 197
What breast so cold that is not warmed here? O cleft effect! . 292
She touch'd him here and there,—Touches so soft still conquer chastity *Pass. Pil.* 49
I see a fair sweet youth Here in these brakes deep-wounded . . 126
Yet will she blush, here be it said, To hear her secrets so bewray'd . 351
Here the anthem doth commence: Love and constancy is dead *Ph. and Tur.* 21
Grace in all simplicity, Here enclosed in cinders lie . . . 55
Hereafter. Sorrow on love hereafter shall attend . *Ven. and Adon.* 1136
And bids her eyes hereafter still be blind . . . *Lucrece* 758
No dame, hereafter living, By my excuse shall claim excuse's giving . 1714
Herein. Herein lives wisdom, beauty, and increase . . *Sonnet* 11 5
Heretic. That heretic, Which works on leases of short-number'd hours 124 9
Herself. Nature that made thee, with herself at strife, Saith that the world hath ending with thy life . . . *Ven. and Adon.* 11
Two glasses, where herself herself beheld A thousand times . . 1129
Means to immure herself and not be seen . . . 1194
Cloudy Lucrece shames herself to see . . . *Lucrece* 1084
And to herself all sorrow doth compare . . . 1102
So with herself is she in mutiny To live or die . . . 1153
Comparing him to that unhappy guest Whose deed hath made herself her-self detest . . . 1566
Thy wretched wife mistook the matter so, To slay herself . . 1827
Since Rome herself in them doth stand disgraced . . . 1833
I swear beauty herself is black And all they foul that thy complexion lack *Sonnet* 132 13
Who ever shunn'd by precedent The destined ill she must herself assay? *Lov. Comp.* 156
She that her fame so to herself contrives, The scars of battle . . 243
Hid. Hasting to feed her fawn hid in some brake . *Ven. and Adon.* 876
The lightless fire Which, in pale embers hid, lurks to aspire . *Lucrece* 5
Then kings' misdeeds cannot be hid in clay . . . 609
The scalps of many, almost hid behind, To jump up higher seem'd, to mock the mind . . . 1414
For precious friends hid in death's dateless night . . *Sonnet* 30 6
Where, alack, Shall Time's best jewel from Time's chest lie hid? . . 65 10
Hidden. Foul-cankering rust the hidden treasure frets . *Ven. and Adon.* 767

Hidden. Which now appear But things removed that hidden in thee lie *Sonnet* 31 8

Hide. Thin mane, thick tail, broad buttock, tender hide *Ven. and Adon.* 298
And with his bonnet hides his angry brow 339
To draw the cloud that hides the silver moon . *Lucrece* 371
The lesser thing should not the greater hide 663
To mask their brows and hide their infamy 794
Little stars may hide them when they list 1008
My sable ground of sin I will not paint, To hide the truth 1075
In him the painter labour'd with his skill To hide deceit 1507
It is but as a tomb Which hides your life and shows not half your parts *Sonnet* 17 4
And from the forlorn world his visage hide . . 33 7
The bloody spur cannot provoke him on That sometimes anger thrusts into his hide 50 10
As my chest, Or as the wardrobe which the robe doth hide . 52 10
Not once vouchsafe to hide my will in thine . . 135 6
If thou dost seek to have what thou dost hide, By self-example mayst thou be denied 142 13

Hideous. Shape every bush a hideous shapeless devil . . *Lucrece* 973
For never-resting time leads summer on To hideous winter *Sonnet* 5 6
And see the brave day sunk in hideous night . . . 12 2

Hiding base sin in plaits of majesty . . *Lucrece* 93
In his dim mist the aspiring mountains hiding . . . 548
Hiding thy bravery in their rotten smoke . . *Sonnet* 34 4

Hie. Unto the wood they hie them, Out-stripping crows that strive to over-fly them . . . *Ven. and Adon.* 323
Weary of the world, away she hies, And yokes her silver doves . . 1189
Calls her maid, Whose swift obedience to her mistress hies *Lucrece* 1215
To hie as fast As lagging fowls before the northern blast . . 1334
And forth with bashful innocence doth hie 1341
O, sweet shepherd, hie thee, For methinks thou stay'st too long . *Pass. Pil.* 167

Hied. Rose-cheek'd Adonis hied him to the chase *Ven. and Adon.* 3
And thither hied, a sad distemper'd guest, But found no cure *Sonnet* 153 12

High. Sweet bottom-grass and high delightful plain *Ven. and Adon.* 236
Shows his hot courage and his high desire 276
High crest, short ears, straight legs, and passing strong . . 297
For through his mane and tail the high wind sings, Fanning the hairs . 305
Whose vulture thought doth pitch the price so high, That she will draw his lips' rich treasure dry 551
Wherein she framed thee in high heaven's despite . . . 731
The gentle lark, weary of rest, From his moist cabinet mounts up on high . 854
But high or low, That all love's pleasure shall not match his woe . 1139
In that high task hath done her beauty wrong . . *Lucrece* 80
For that he colour'd with his high estate 92
And decks with praises Collatine's high name . . . 108
Huge rocks, high winds, strong pirates, shelves, and sands, The merchant fears, ere rich at home he lands 335
By their high treason is his heart misled 369
She conjures him by high almighty Jove, By knighthood . . 568
Some high, some low, the painter was so nice . . . 1412
Who will believe my verse in time to come, If it were fill'd with your most high deserts? . . *Sonnet* 17 2
Thine eyes that taught the dumb on high to sing . . 78 5
Thou art all my art and dost advance As high as learning my rude ignorance . . . 78 14
Thy love is better than high birth to me, Richer than wealth . 91 9
In clamours of all size, both high and low . *Lov. Comp.* 21

Higher. My uncontrolled tide Turns not, but swells the higher by this let *Lucrece* 646
The scalps of many, almost hid behind, To jump up higher seem'd, to mock the mind 1414

Highmost. But when from highmost pitch, with weary car, Like feeble age, he reeleth from the day *Sonnet* 7 9

High-pitched. Did sting His high-pitch'd thoughts . . *Lucrece* 41

High-proud. Reckoning his fortune at such high-proud rate . . 19

Hild. O, let it not be hild Poor women's faults, that they are so fulfill'd With men's abuses 1257

Hill. Graze on my lips; and if those hills be dry, Stray lower, where the pleasant fountains lie . . . *Ven. and Adon.* 233
By this, poor Wat, far off upon a hill, Stands on his hinder legs . 697
That cedar-tops and hills seem burnish'd gold . . . 858
Between whose hills her head entombed is . . *Lucrece* 390
Having climb'd the steep-up heavenly hill . . *Sonnet* 7 5
From off a hill whose concave womb re-worded A plaintful story *Lov. Comp.* 1
Her stand she takes upon a steep-up hill . . *Pass. Pil.* 121
That hills and valleys, dales and fields, And all the craggy mountains yields 355

Hillocks. Round rising hillocks, brakes obscure and rough *Ven. and Adon.* 237

Him. Rose-cheek'd Adonis hied him to the chase . . . 3
And 'tis your fault I am bereft him so 381
They all strain courtesy who shall cope him first . . 888
Love's golden arrow at him should have fled . . . 947
He fed them with his sight, they him with berries . . . 1104
Had I been tooth'd like him, I must confess, With kissing him I should have kill'd him first 1117
I tell the day, to please him thou art bright . . *Sonnet* 28 9
Featured like him, like him with friends possess'd . . 29 6
Him have I lost; thou hast both him and me . . 134 13

Himself. Narcissus so himself himself forsook, And died to kiss his shadow in the brook . . . *Ven. and Adon.* 161
Love made those hollows, if himself were slain, He might be buried in a tomb so simple 243
Disturbing Jealousy Doth call himself Affection's sentinel . . 650
To recreate himself when he hath sung, The tiger would be tame . 1095
Since he himself is reft from her by death . . . 1174
To grow unto himself was his desire, And so 'tis thine . . 1180
And for himself himself he must forsake . . *Lucrece* 157
When he himself himself confounds, betrays To slanderous tongues . 160
So from himself impiety hath wrought 341
He rouseth up himself and makes a pause 541
Till like a jade Self-will himself doth tire 707
For now against himself he sounds this doom . . . 717
Let the thief run mad, Himself himself seek every hour to kill! . 998
Himself, behind, Was left unseen, save to the eye of mind . . 1425
Himself on her self-slaughter'd body threw 1733
That on himself such murderous shame commits . *Sonnet* 9 14
Or heart in love with sighs himself doth smother, With my love's picture 47 4
Accomplish'd in himself, not in his case . . *Lov. Comp.* 116

Himself. I in deep delight am chiefly drown'd Whenas himself to singing he betakes . . . . *Pass. Pil.* 114
That the lover, sick to death, Wish'd himself the heaven's breath 234
And deny himself for Jove, Turning mortal for thy love . . 243

Hind. Like a white hind under the gripe's sharp claws, Pleads *Lucrece* 543

Hinder. Stands on his hinder legs with listening ear, To hearken *V. and A.* 698

Hindering their present fall by this dividing . . *Lucrece* 551

Hindmost. Though words come hindmost, holds his rank before *Sonnet* 85 12

Hips. Each leaning on their elbows and their hips *Ven. and Adon.* 44

His. Now doth she stroke his cheek, now doth he frown, And 'gins to chide 45
His louring brows o'erwhelming his fair sight, Like misty vapours . 183
His ears up-prick'd; his braided hanging mane Upon his compass'd crest now stand on end 271
His eye, which scornfully glisters like fire, Shows his hot courage and his high desire 275
His eyes saw her eyes as they had not seen them; Her eyes woo'd still, his eyes disdain'd the wooing 357
Enfranchising his mouth, his back, his breast . . . 396
Were never four such lamps together mix'd, Had not his clouded with his brow's repine 490
Then he had spoke, And, hearing him, thy power had lost his power . 944
Never did he bless My youth with his; the more am I accurst . 1120
No comfortable star did lend his light, No noise but owls' . *Lucrece* 164
The locks between her chamber and his will Each one by him enforced retires his ward 302
She puts the period often from his place 565
The bark peel'd from the lofty pine, His leaves will wither and his sap decay 1168
One doth call her his, the other his, Yet neither may possess the claim 1793
Sometime too hot the eye of heaven shines, And often is his gold complexion dimm'd . . . . *Sonnet* 18 6
Nor Mars his sword nor war's quick fire shall burn The living record of your memory 55 7

Hiss. Here come and sit, where never serpent hisses *Ven. and Adon.* 17
The sun doth scorn you and the wind doth hiss you . . 1084
The adder hisses where the sweet birds sing . . *Lucrece* 871

History. In many's looks the false heart's history Is writ . *Sonnet* 93 7

Hit. But hatefully at random dost thou hit . . *Ven. and Adon.* 940
The snail, whose tender horns being hit, Shrinks backward in his shelly cave 1033
How hard true sorrow hits, And soon to you, as you to me! *Sonnet* 120 10

Hither. Far from the purpose of his coming hither, He makes excuses *Lucr.* 113
And in a desperate rage Post hither, this vile purpose to prevent . . 220
Go, get me hither paper, ink, and pen 1289

Hive. In thy weak hive a wandering wasp hath crept . . . 839
The old bees die, the young possess their hive . . . 1769
Upon her head a platted hive of straw . . . *Lov. Comp.* 8

Hoard. The life and feeling of her passion She hoards, to spend when he is by *Lucrece* 1318
Nature hath charged me that I hoard them not, But yield them up *L. Comp.* 220

Hoarsely. With untuned tongue she hoarsely calls her maid . *Lucrece* 1214

Hoisted. I have hoisted sail to all the winds Which should transport me *Sonnet* 117 7

Hold. What seest thou in the ground? hold up thy head *Ven. and Adon.* 118
For all askance he holds her in his eye 342
He bends her fingers, holds her pulses hard, He chafes her lips . 476
The world will hold thee in disdain, Sith in thy pride so fair a hope is slain 761
And hold it for no sin To wish that I their father had not been *Lucrece* 209
Thus, graceless, holds he disputation 'Tween frozen conscience . 246
And they too strong, To hold their cursed-blessed fortune long . 866
In a sea of care, Holds disputation with each thing she views . 1101
She dares not thereof make discovery, Lest he should hold it her own gross abuse 1315
These contraries such unity do hold, Only to flatter fools and make them bold 1558
So should that beauty which you hold in lease Find no determination *Sonnet* 13 5
Every thing that grows Holds in perfection but a little moment . 15 2
How with this rage shall beauty hold a plea? . . . 65 3
O, how shall summer's honey breath hold out? . . . 65 5
What strong hand can hold his swift foot back? . . . 65 11
I hold such strife As 'twixt a miser and his wealth is found . 75 3
Your shallowest help will hold me up afloat . . . 80 9
My tongue-tied Muse in manners holds her still . . 85 1
Though words come hindmost, holds his rank before . . 85 12
For how do I hold thee but by thy granting? . . . 87 5
I sometime hold my tongue, Because I would not dull you with my song 102 13
Nor his own vision holds what it doth catch . . . 113 8
That poor retention could not so much hold . . . 122 9
Who in thy power Dost hold Time's fickle glass, his sickle, hour . 126 2
For nothing hold me, so it please thee hold That nothing me . 136 11
Whilst her neglected child holds her in chase, Cries to catch her . 143 5
No want of conscience hold it that I call Her 'love' . . 151 13
'Gainst whom the world could not hold argument . . *Pass. Pil.* 30
O never faith could hold, if not to beauty vow'd . . . 58

Hold-fast. While in his hold-fast foot the weak mouse panteth *Lucrece* 555

Holding their course to Paphos, where their queen Means to immure herself *Ven. and Adon.* 1193
The dispersed air, who, holding Lucrece' life, Answer'd their cries *Lucrece* 1805

Hole. Let it not be call'd impiety, If in this blemish'd fort I make some hole 1175

Holiest. This device was sent me from a nun, Or sister sanctified, of holiest note . . . . *Lov. Comp.* 233

Holla. What recketh he his rider's angry stir, His flattering 'Holla,' or his 'Stand, I say'? . . . *Ven. and Adon.* 284

Hollo. She hears some huntsman hollo; A nurse's song ne'er pleased her babe so well 973

Hollow. Love made those hollows, if himself were slain, He might be buried in a tomb so simple 243
The bearing earth . . ., Whose hollow womb resounds like heaven's thunder 268
Lo, in this hollow cradle take thy rest 1185

Hollow-swelling. Your tunes entomb Within your hollow-swelling feather'd breasts . . . . *Lucrece* 1122

Holy. By holy human law, and common troth, By heaven and earth . 571
Sweet chastity's decay, The impious breach of holy wedlock vow . 809
How many a holy and obsequious tear Hath dear religious love stol'n from mine eye As interest of the dead . . . *Sonnet* 31 5
In him those holy antique hours are seen, Without all ornament . 68 9
Sweet beauty hath no name, no holy bower, But is profaned . 127 7
Which borrow'd from this holy fire of Love A dateless lively heat . 153 5
And be not of my holy vows afraid . . . *Lov. Comp.* 179
There is no heaven, by holy then, When time with age doth them attaint *Pass. Pil.* 343

Holy-thoughted Lucrece to their sight Must sell her joy *Lucrece* 384
Homage. Each under eye Doth homage to his new-appearing sight *Sonnet* 7 3
Home. Huge rocks, high winds, strong pirates, shelves and sands, The merchant fears, ere rich at home he lands *Lucrece* 336
The mindful messenger, come back, Brings home his lord and other company 1584
Both stood, like old acquaintance in a trance, Met far from home 1596
Is it thy spirit that thou send'st from thee So far from home? *Sonnet* 61 6
So thy great gift, upon misprision growing, Comes home again 87 12
Which in thy breast doth lie: That is my home of love 109 5
Home-bred. A mischief worse than civil home-bred strife *Ven. and Adon.* 764
Homely. The homely villain court'sies to her low *Lucrece* 1338
Homeward. And homeward through the dark laund runs apace *V. and A.* 813
Honest. But honest fear, bewitch'd with lust's foul charm, Doth too too oft betake him to retire *Lucrece* 173
Pawn'd honest looks, but laid no words to gage 1351
And all my honest faith in thee is lost *Sonnet* 152 8
Honesty. Thou smother'st honesty, thou murder'st troth *Lucrece* 885
Beguiled With outward honesty, but yet defiled With inward vice 1545
Honey. For thy meed A thousand honey secrets shalt thou know *V. and A.* 16
Once more the ruby-colour'd portal open'd, Which to his speech did honey passage yield 452
Ere he says 'Adieu,' The honey fee of parting tender'd is 538
I think the honey guarded with a sting *Lucrece* 493
My honey lost, and I, a drone-like bee 836
And suck'd the honey which thy chaste bee kept 840
Thou false thief, Thy honey turns to gall, thy joy to grief! 889
O, how shall summer's honey breath hold out? *Sonnet* 65 5
Honour. Forgetting shame's pure blush and honour's wrack *Ven. and Adon.* 558
Now she adds honours to his hateful name 994
Honour and beauty in the owner's arms *Lucrece* 27
His honour, his affairs, his friends, his state, Neglected all 45
The aim of all is but to nurse the life With honour, wealth, and ease 142
As life for honour in fell battle's rage; Honour for wealth 145
Pawning his honour to obtain his lust 156
To kill thine honour with thy life's decay 516
That to his borrow'd bed he make retire, And stoop to honour, not to foul desire 574
Thou wrong'st his honour, wound'st his princely name 599
If, Collatine, thine honour lay in me, From me by strong assault it is bereft 834
Yet am I guilty of thy honour's wrack; Yet for thy honour did I entertain him 841
Honour thyself to rid me of this shame; For if I die, my honour lives in thee 1031
My honour I'll bequeath unto the knife That wounds my body 1184
'Tis honour to deprive dishonour'd life; The one will live, the other being dead 1186
My shame so dead, mine honour is new-born 1190
Mine honour be the knife's that makes my wound 1201
She modestly prepares to let them know Her honour is ta'en prisoner 1608
May my pure mind with the foul act dispense, My low-declined honour to advance? 1705
Which husbandry in honour might uphold Against the stormy gusts *Son.* 13 10
Of public honour and proud titles boast 25 2
Unlook'd for joy in that I honour most 25 4
Once foil'd, Is from the book of honour razed quite 25 11
Nor thou with public kindness honour me, Unless thou take that honour from thy name 36 11
And gilded honour shamefully misplaced 66 5
Finding myself in honour so forbid, With safest distance I mine honour shielded *Lov. Comp.* 150
Honourable. Plight your honourable faiths to me, With swift pursuit to venge this wrong *Lucrece* 1690
Honoured. And him by oath they truly honoured 410
The mightier man, the mightier is the thing That makes him honour'd 1005
Honouring. I bore the canopy, With my extern the outward honouring *Sonnet* 125 2
Hoof. The bearing earth with his hard hoof he wounds *Ven. and Adon.* 267
Hooks. She touch'd no unknown baits, nor fear'd no hooks *Lucrece* 103
Hooks, Whereto the judgement of my heart is tied *Sonnet* 137 7
Hope. Things out of hope are compass'd oft with venturing *Ven. and Adon.* 567
Sith in thy pride so fair a hope is slain 762
The dire imagination she did follow This sound of hope doth labour to expel 976
Despair and hope makes thee ridiculous 988
Though weak-built hopes persuade him to abstaining *Lucrece* 130
Full of foul hope and full of fond mistrust 284
If in thy hope thou darest do such outrage 605
To shame his hope with deeds degenerate 1003
When their brave hope, bold Hector, march'd to field 1430
And to their hope they such odd action yield 1433
I hope some good conceit of thine In thy soul's thought, all naked, will bestow it *Sonnet* 26 7
Wishing me like to one more rich in hope, Featured like him 29 5
Being had, to triumph, being lack'd, to hope 52 14
And yet to times in hope my verse shall stand, Praising thy worth 60 13
Yet this abundant issue seem'd to me But hope of orphans 97 10
Applying fears to hopes and hopes to fears 119 3
But if thou catch thy hope, turn back to me 143 11
Heart hath his hope, and eyes their wished sight *Pass. Pil.* 202
Hopeless. She there remains a hopeless castaway *Lucrece* 744
Lo, here, the hopeless merchant of this loss, With head declined 1660
Hoping. Thus hoping that Adonis is alive, Her rash suspect she doth extenuate *Ven. and Adon.* 1009
And so, by hoping more, they have but less *Lucrece* 137
Horn. She hearkens for his hounds and for his horn *Ven. and Adon.* 868
Even at this word she hears a merry horn 1025
As the snail, whose tender horns being hit, Shrinks backward 1033
Anon Adonis comes with horn and hounds *Pass. Pil.* 122
Horse. Being so enraged, desire doth lend her force Courageously to pluck him from his horse *Ven. and Adon.* 30
Away he springs and hasteth to his horse 258
So did this horse excel a common one In shape, in courage 293
Look, what a horse should have he did not lack 299
With her the horse, and left Adonis there: As they were mad 322
My horse is gone, And 'tis your fault I am bereft him so 380
Therefore no marvel though thy horse be gone 390
And on thy well-breath'd horse keep with thy hounds 678
Then can no horse with my desire keep pace *Sonnet* 51 9
Some [glory] in their hawks and hounds, some in their horse 91 4
Prouder than garments' cost, Of more delight than hawks or horses be 91 11

Horse. Often men would say That horse his mettle from his rider takes *Lov. Comp.* 107
Whether the horse by him became his deed, Or he his manage by the well-doing steed 111
Hospitality. Reward not hospitality With such black payment *Lucrece* 575
Host. Lust-breathed Tarquin leaves the Roman host 3
To all the host of heaven I complain me, Thou wrong'st his honour 598
Hostess. A woeful hostess brooks not merry guests 1125
Hot. She red and hot as coals of glowing fire, He red for shame, but frosty in desire *Ven. and Adon.* 35
Shows his hot courage and his high desire 276
With weary gait, His day's hot task hath ended in the west 530
Hot, faint, and weary, with her hard embracing 559
In the very lists of love, Her champion mounted for the hot encounter 596
The hot scent-snuffing hounds are driven to doubt, Ceasing their clamorous cry 692
The hot tyrant stains and soon bereaves, As caterpillars do the tender leaves 797
So shall I die by drops of hot desire 1074
But his hot heart, which fond desire doth scorch, Puffs forth another wind *Lucrece* 314
Anon his beating heart, alarum striking, Gives the hot charge 434
Cooling his hot face in the chastest tears That ever modest eyes with sorrow shed 682
This hot desire converts to cold disdain 691
Sometime too hot the eye of heaven shines *Sonnet* 18 5
Three April perfumes in three hot Junes burn'd, Since first I saw you fresh 104 7
And so the general of hot desire Was sleeping by a virgin hand disarm'd 154 7
All these trophies of affections hot, Of pensived and subdued desires the tender *Lov. Comp.* 218
Cold modesty, hot wrath, Both fire from hence and chill extincture hath 293
Hot was the day; she hotter that did look For his approach *Pass. Pil.* 77
Youth is hot and bold, age is weak and cold; Youth is wild, and age is tame 163
Hot-burning. 'Tween frozen conscience and hot-burning will. *Lucrece* 247
And in that cold hot-burning fire doth dwell 1557
Hotly. Titan . . . With burning eye did hotly overlook them *Ven. and Adon.* 178
An oven that is stopp'd, or river stay'd, Burneth more hotly, swelleth with more rage 332
So fares it with this faultful lord of Rome, Who this accomplishment so hotly chased *Lucrece* 716
Hotter. Hot was the day; she hotter that did look For his approach *Pass. Pil.* 77
Hound. And on thy well-breath'd horse keep with thy hounds *V. and A.* 678
He runs among a flock of sheep, To make the cunning hounds mistake their smell 686
The hot scent-snuffing hounds are driven to doubt, Ceasing their clamorous cry 692
She hearkens for his hounds and for his horn: Anon she hears them 868
By this, she hears the hounds are at a bay; Whereat she starts 877
Even so the timorous yelping of the hounds Appals her senses 881
In a brake she finds a hound, And asks the weary caitiff for his master 913
As the full-fed hound or gorged hawk, Unapt for tender smell *Lucrece* 694
Some [glory] in their hawks and hounds, some in their horse *Sonnet* 91 4
Anon Adonis comes with horn and hounds *Pass. Pil.* 122
Hour. A summer's day will seem an hour but short, Being wasted in such time-beguiling sport *Ven. and Adon.* 23
What hour is this? or morn or weary even? Do I delight to die, or life desire? 495
Suggesteth mutiny, And in a peaceful hour doth cry 'Kill, kill!' 652
For lovers' hours are long, though seeming short 842
There shall not be one minute in an hour Wherein I will not kiss my sweet love's flower 1187
Stuff up his lust, as minutes fill up hours *Lucrece* 297
Till every minute pays the hour his debt 329
And they would stand auspicious to the hour 347
When wilt thou sort an hour great strifes to end? 899
Rape and murder's rages, Thy heinous hours wait on them as their pages 910
Why hath thy servant, Opportunity, Betray'd the hours thou gavest me to repose? 933
To ruinate proud buildings with thy hours 944
O, this dread night, wouldst thou one hour come back! 965
Disturb his hours of rest with restless trances, Afflict him in his bed 974
Let the thief run mad, Himself himself seek every hour to kill! 998
That he may vow, in that sad hour of mine, Revenge on him that made me stop my breath 1179
Those hours, that with gentle work did frame The lovely gaze *Sonnet* 5 1
Now stand you on the top of happy hours 16 5
O, carve not with thy hours my love's fair brow, Nor draw no lines there 19 9
He was but one hour mine; The region cloud hath mask'd him from me now 33 11
Yet doth it steal sweet hours from love's delight 36 8
The which he will not every hour survey, For blunting the fine point of seldom pleasure 52 3
What should I do but tend Upon the hours and times of your desire? 57 2
Nor dare I chide the world-without-end hour 57 5
Or at your hand the account of hours to crave 58 3
To find out shames and idle hours in me, The scope and tenour of thy jealousy? 61 7
When hours have drain'd his blood and fill'd his brow With lines and wrinkles 63 3
In him those holy antique hours are seen, Without all ornament 68 9
Love alters not with his brief hours and weeks, But bears it out 116 11
That heretic, Which works on leases of short-number'd hours 124 10
Who in thy power Dost hold Time's fickle glass, his sickle, hour 126 2
Buy terms divine in selling hours of dross 146 11
And had let go by The swiftest hours *Lov. Comp.* 60
In me you behold The injury of many a blasting hour 72
Lost, vaded, broken, dead within an hour *Pass. Pil.* 174
Now are minutes added to the hours; To spite me now, each minute seems a moon 206
Hourly. Or as those bars which stop the hourly dial *Lucrece* 327
House. Her house is sack'd, her quiet interrupted, Her mansion batter'd 1170
So, I commend me from our house in grief 1308
Who lets so fair a house fall to decay? *Sonnet* 13 9
Household. O foul dishonour to my household's grave! O impious act! *Lucrece* 198
Housewife. Lo! as a careful housewife runs to catch One of her feather'd creatures broke away *Sonnet* 143 1
Hovered. Gave the tempter place, Which like a cherubin above them hover'd *Lov. Comp.* 319

Hovering. She prepares to write, First hovering o'er the paper with her quill *Lucrece* 1297
How. Look, how a bird lies tangled in a net . . . *Ven. and Adon.* 67
Look how he can, she cannot choose but love 79
Being mad before, how doth she now for wits? 249
Wistly to view How she came stealing to the wayward boy 344
To note the fighting conflict of her hue, How white and red each other did destroy! 346
For all my mind, my thought, my busy care, Is how to get my palfrey . 384
How like a jade he stood, tied to the tree, Servilely master'd! . . . 391
To overshoot his troubles How he outruns the wind and with what care 681
Look, how a bright star shooteth from the sky, So glides he in the night 815
How love makes young men thrall and old men dote; How love is wise in folly, foolish-witty 837
O, how her eyes and tears did lend and borrow! 961
How strange it seems Not to believe, and yet too credulous . . . 985
How much a fool was I To be of such a weak and silly mind . . . 1015
O, how her fear did make her colour rise! . . . . *Lucrece* 257
And how her hand, in my hand being lock'd, Forced it to tremble! . . 260
My true eyes have never practised how To cloak offences . . . 748
How Tarquin must be used, read it in me 1195
How was I overseen that thou shalt see it! 1206
How like Eve's apple doth thy beauty grow! . . . *Sonnet* 93 13
I teach thee how To make him seem long hence as he shows now . . 101 13
Howling. To whom she speaks, and he replies with howling *Ven. and Adon.* 918
My sighs so deep Procure to weep, In howling wise . . *Pass. Pil.* 277
Hue. To note the fighting conflict of her hue, How white and red each other did destroy! . . . . . . *Ven. and Adon.* 345
In her naked bed, Teaching the sheets a whiter hue than white . . 398
Brings beauty under: Both favour, savour, hue, and qualities . . 747
A man in hue, all 'hues' in his controlling . . . *Sonnet* 20 7
Why should false painting imitate his cheek And steal dead seeing of his living hue? 67 6
Thou art as fair in knowledge as in hue 82 5
Nor the sweet smell Of different flowers in odour and in hue . . 98 6
So your sweet hue, which methinks still doth stand, Hath motion . 104 11
The glowing roses That flame through water which their hue encloses *Lov. Comp.* 287
Huge rocks, high winds, strong pirates, shelves, and sands, The merchant fears, ere rich at home he lands . . . . . *Lucrece* 335
Small lights are soon blown out, huge fires abide 647
And waste huge stones with little water-drops 959
This huge stage presenteth nought but shows . . . *Sonnet* 15 3
And all things rare That heaven's air in this huge rondure hems . 21 8
Hugely. But all alone stands hugely politic 124 11
Hum. For burden-wise I'll hum on Tarquin still . . . *Lucrece* 1133
Human. By holy human law, and common troth, By heaven and earth 571
Whose heavenly touch Upon the lute doth ravish human sense *Pass. Pil.* 108
Humanity. Let fair humanity abhor the deed . . . *Lucrece* 195
Humble. When wilt thou be the humble suppliant's friend? . . . 897
And give the harmless show An humble gait, calm looks, eyes wailing still 1508
Wide as the ocean is, The humble as the proudest sail doth bear *Sonnet* 80 6
Then tender'd The humble salve which wounded bosoms fits . . 120 12
Serve always with assured trust, And in thy suit be humble true *Pass. Pil.* 330
Humbly. With Death she humbly doth insinuate . . *Ven. and Adon.* 1012
Humour. Soothing the humour of fantastic wits 850
Such childish humour from weak minds proceeds . . . *Lucrece* 1825
Every humour hath his adjunct pleasure, Wherein it finds a joy *Sonnet* 91 5
A better state to me belongs Than that which on thy humour doth depend 92 8

Hundred. What is ten hundred touches unto thee? . . *Ven. and Adon.* 519
Is twenty hundred kisses such a trouble? 522
A backward look, Even of five hundred courses of the sun . *Sonnet* 59 6
Hung. Over my altars hath he hung his lance, His batter'd shield, his uncontrolled crest . . . . *Ven. and Adon.* 103
Like a jewel hung in ghastly night . . . . . *Sonnet* 27 11
Hung with the trophies of my lovers gone 31 10
Hunger. As the grim lion fawneth o'er his prey, Sharp hunger by the conquest satisfied . . . . *Lucrece* 422
Hungry. Although to-day thou fill Thy hungry eyes even till they wink with fullness . . . . *Sonnet* 56 6
I have seen the hungry ocean gain Advantage on the kingdom of the shore 64 5
Hunt. He intends To hunt the boar with certain of his friends *V. and A.* 588
But that thou told'st me thou wouldst hunt the boar 614
But if thou needs will hunt, be ruled by me 673
Why hunt I then for colour or excuses? . . . . *Lucrece* 267
Hunted. And with that word she spied the hunted boar *Ven. and Adon.* 900
Past reason hunted, and no sooner had Past reason hated *Sonnet* 129 6
Hunting he loved, but love he laugh'd to scorn . . *Ven. and Adon.* 4
To make thee hate the hunting of the boar, Unlike myself thou hear'st me moralize 711
Huntsman. By this, far off she hears some huntsman hollo . . 973
Hurls. The wind Upon his lips their silken parcels hurls . *Lov. Comp.* 87
Hurries. Which madly hurries her she knows not whither *Ven. and Adon.* 904
Hurt. You hurt my hand with wringing; let us part 421
He seeks To mend the hurt that his unkindness marr'd 478
Upon his hurt she looks so steadfastly 1063
They that have power to hurt and will do none . . . *Sonnet* 94 1
Husband. Her husband's shallow tongue . . . hath done her beauty wrong *Lucrece* 78
He stories to her ears her husband's fame 106
Until her husband's welfare she did hear 263
So thy surviving husband shall remain The scornful mark . . . 519
Then, for thy husband and thy children's sake, Tender my suit . . 533
By her untimely tears, her husband's love, By holy human law . . 570
My husband is thy friend; for his sake spare me 582
My resolution, husband, do thou take 1200
And shame that might ensue By that her death, to do her husband wrong . 1264
One of my husband's men Bid thou be ready, by and by . . . 1291
A weeping tear, Shed for the slaughter'd husband by the wife . . 1376
Which when her sad-beholding husband saw, Amazedly in her sad face he stares 1590
Dear husband, in the interest of thy bed A stranger came . . . 1619
The father says 'She's mine.' 'O, mine she is,' Replies her husband . 1796
Mark how one string, sweet husband to another, Strikes each in each by mutual ordering . . . . *Sonnet* 8 9
Every private widow well may keep By children's eyes her husband's shape in mind 9 8
So shall I live, supposing thou art true, Like a deceived husband . 93 2
And husband nature's riches from expense 94 6
Husbandry. Where is she so fair whose unear'd womb Disdains the tillage of thy husbandry? 3 6
Which husbandry in honour might uphold 13 10
Hush. When her mournful hymns did hush the night . . . 102 10
Hushed. Even as the wind is hush'd before it raineth *Ven. and Adon.* 458
Hymn. Like to the lark at break of day arising From sullen earth, sings hymns at heaven's gate . . . . *Sonnet* 29 12
Like unletter'd clerk still cry 'Amen' To every hymn . . . 85 7
When her mournful hymns did hush the night 102 10

I

Idiots. Esteemed so As silly-jeering idiots are with kings . *Lucrece* 1812
Idle. Let us part, And leave this idle theme, this bootless chat *V. and A.* 422
You will fall again Into your idle over-handled theme 770
Idle sounds resembling parasites, Like shrill-tongued tapsters . . 848
Out, idle words, servants to shallow fools! Unprofitable sounds! *Lucrece* 1016
To find out shames and idle hours in me, The scope and tenour of thy jealousy? . . . . *Sonnet* 61 7
Which shall above that idle rank remain Beyond all date . . . 122 3
The morning rise Doth cite each moving sense from idle rest . *Pass. Pil.* 195
Idly. And straight redeem In gentle numbers time so idly spent *Sonnet* 100 6
Idol. Well-painted idol, image dull and dead, Statue contenting but the eye alone . . . . *Ven. and Adon.* 212
Let not my love be call'd idolatry, Nor my beloved as an idol show *Sonnet* 105 2
Idolatry. Let not my love be call'd idolatry, Nor my beloved as an idol show 105 1
If thou wilt chide, thy lips shall never open . . *Ven. and Adon.* 48
If springing things be any jot diminish'd 417
As if from thence they borrow'd all their shine 488
My living sorrow, If thou encounter with the boar to-morrow . . 672
But if thou needs wilt hunt, be ruled by me 673
As if another chase were in the skies 696
If so, the world will hold thee in disdain 761
If he had spoke, the wolf would leave his prey 1097
Wavering stood in doubt If best were as it was, or best without *Lov. Comp.* 98
If that the world and love were young . . . . *Pass. Pil.* 369
Ignorance. Thine eyes that taught the dumb on high to sing And heavy ignorance aloft to fly . . . . *Sonnet* 78 6
Thou art all my art and dost advance As high as learning my rude ignorance 78 14
Ignorant. All ignorant that soul that sees thee without wonder *Pass. Pil.* 65
Ilion. Threatening cloud-kissing Ilion with annoy . . . *Lucrece* 1370
Whose words like wildfire burnt the shining glory Of rich-built Ilion . 1524
Ill. This ill presage advisedly she marketh . . *Ven. and Adon.* 457
Whose inward ill no outward harm express'd . . . *Lucrece* 91
In venturing ill we leave to be The things we are for that which we expect 148
They all rate his ill, Which drives the creeping thief to some regard . 304
Then had they seen the period of their ill 380
Urgeth still Under what colour he commits this ill 476

Ill. End thy ill aim before thy shoot be ended . . . . *Lucrece* 579
If all these petty ills shall change thy good 656
Teach me to curse him that thou taught'st this ill! 996
My blood shall wash the slander of mine ill 1207
Then call them not the authors of their ill 1244
This is too curious-good, this blunt and ill 1300
So fair a form lodged not a mind so ill 1530
What uncouth ill event Hath thee befall'n, that thou dost trembling stand 1598
Which I will keep so chary As tender nurse her babe from faring ill *Son.* 22 12
And they are rich and ransom all ill deeds 34 14
Lascivious grace, in whom all ill well shows, Kill me with spites . 40 13
So true a fool is love that in your will, Though you do any thing, he thinks no ill 57 14
Not blame your pleasure, be it ill or well 58 14
And simple truth miscall'd simplicity, And captive good attending captain ill 66 12
If some suspect of ill mask'd not thy show 70 13
Thou canst not, love, disgrace me half so ill 89 5
Some glory in their birth, . . . Some in their garments, though new-fangled ill 91 4
Naming thy name blesses an ill report 95 8
For what care I who calls me well or ill? 112 3
To anticipate The ills that were not, grew to faults assured . . 118 10
A healthful state Which, rank of goodness, would by ill be cured . 118 12
O benefit of ill! now I find true That better is by evil still made better 119 9
And gain by ill thrice more than I have spent 119 14
I should grow mad, And in my madness might speak ill of thee . 140 10
The better angel is a man right fair, The worser spirit a woman colour'd ill . . . . 144 4; *Pass. Pil.* 18
Feeding on that which doth preserve the ill . . . . *Sonnet* 147 3
Whence hast thou this becoming of things ill? 150 5
The destined ill she must herself assay . . . . *Lov. Comp.* 156
Outfacing faults in love with love's ill rest . . . *Pass. Pil.* 8
Ill-annexed. We have no good that we can say is ours, But ill-annexed Opportunity Or kills his life or else his quality . . . *Lucrece* 874
Illiterate. The illiterate, that know not how To cipher what is writ . 810
Ill-nurtured, crooked, churlish, harsh in voice . . . *Ven. and Adon.* 134

Ill-resounding. When he hath ceased his ill-resounding noise *V. and A.* 919
Illumined. So is her face illumined with her eye 486
Ill-used. The hardest knife ill-used doth lose his edge *Sonnet* 95 14
Ill-wresting. Now this ill-wresting world is grown so bad 140 11
Image. Well-painted idol, image dull and dead, Statue contenting but the eye alone *Ven. and Adon.* 212
An image like thyself, all stain'd with gore 664
Within his thought her heavenly image sits *Lucrece* 288
O comfort-killing Night, image of hell! Dim register and notary of shame! 764
That for Achilles' image stood his spear, Griped in an armed hand 1424
At last she sees a wretched image bound 1501
The well-skill'd workman this mild image drew For perjured Sinon 1520
Overslipp'd her thought, That she with painted images hath spent 1577
If in the child the father's image lies, Where shall I live now Lucrece is unlived? 1753
O, from thy cheeks my image thou hast torn! 1762
Die single, and thine image dies with thee *Sonnet* 3 14
For through the painter must you see his skill, To find where your true image pictured lies 24 6
Their images I loved I view in thee, And thou, all they, hast all the all of me 31 13
Show me your image in some antique book 59 7
Is it thy will thy image should keep open My heavy eyelids? 61 1
Imaginary. All is imaginary she doth prove, He will not manage her *Ven. and Adon.* 597
Much imaginary work was there; Conceit deceitful, so compact, so kind *Lucrece* 1422
Save that my soul's imaginary sight Presents thy shadow *Sonnet* 27 9
Imagination. What should I do, seeing thee so indeed, That tremble at the imagination? *Ven. and Adon.* 668
The dire imagination she did follow This sound of hope doth labour to expel 975
O, deeper sin than bottomless conceit Can comprehend in still imagination! *Lucrece* 702
Like fools that in th' imagination set The goodly objects which abroad they find *Lov. Comp.* 136
Imagine. But if thou fall, O, then imagine this *Ven. and Adon.* 721
Imagine her as one in dead of night From forth dull sleep by dreadful fancy waking *Lucrece* 449
They whose guilt within their bosoms lie Imagine every eye beholds their blame 1343
Imagined. A hand, a foot, a face, a leg, a head, Stood for the whole to be imagined 1428
What wrong else may be imagined By foul enforcement might be done 1622
Imitate. Wretched I, To imitate thee well, against my heart Will fix a sharp knife 1137
Whose waves to imitate the battle sought With swelling ridges 1438
Why should false painting imitate his cheek? *Sonnet* 67 5
Imitated. Describe Adonis, and the counterfeit Is poorly imitated after you 53 6
Immaculate and spotless is my mind; That was not forced *Lucrece* 1656
Immodest. He saith she is immodest, blames her 'miss *Ven. and Adon.* 53
Immodestly lies martyr'd with disgrace *Lucrece* 802
Immortal. And by her fair immortal hand she swears, From his soft bosom never to remove *Ven. and Adon.* 80
And were I not immortal, life were done Between this heavenly and earthly sun 197
Your name from hence immortal life shall have *Sonnet* 81 5
Immortality. And by their mortal fault brought in subjection Her immortality *Lucrece* 725
Immure. Their queen Means to immure herself and not be seen *V. and A.* 1194
Immured. In whose confine immured is the store *Sonnet* 84 3
Not to be tempted, would she be immured *Lov. Comp.* 251
Impair. I impair not beauty being mute, When others would give life and bring a tomb *Sonnet* 83 11
Impanneled. To 'cide this title is impanneled A quest of thoughts 46 9
Impart. And hang more praise upon deceased I Than niggard truth would willingly impart 72 8
Imparteth. But this no slaughterhouse no tool imparteth *Lucrece* 1039
Impartial. Whereat the impartial gazer late did wonder *Ven. and Adon.* 748
Impatience. This said, impatience chokes her pleading tongue 217
Impeached. A true soul When most impeach'd stands least in thy control *Sonnet* 125 14
Impediment. Let me not to the marriage of true minds Admit impediments 116 2
When thou wilt inflame, How coldly those impediments stand forth! *Lov. Comp.* 269
Imperfect. Thy fair imperfect shade Through heavy sleep on sightless eyes doth stay *Sonnet* 43 11
Imperious supreme of all mortal things *Ven. and Adon.* 996
Imperiously he leaps, he neighs, he bounds 265
Impiety. So from himself impiety hath wrought *Lucrece* 341
Let it not be call'd impiety, If in this blemish'd fort I make some hole 1174
Should he live, And with his presence grace impiety *Sonnet* 67 2
Impious. O impious act, including all foul harms! *Lucrece* 199
The impious breach of holy wedlock vow 809
Impleached. Behold these talents of their hair, With twisted metal amorously impleach'd *Lov. Comp.* 205
Import. To keep an adjunct to remember thee Were to import forgetfulness in me *Sonnet* 122 14
Importune. As thou lovest those Whom thine eyes woo as mine importune thee 142 10
Imposition. As bound in knighthood to her imposition *Lucrece* 1697
Imposthumes. Surfeits, imposthumes, grief, and damn'd despair *V. and A.* 743
Impregnable. When rocks impregnable are not so stout, Nor gates of steel so strong *Sonnet* 65 7
Impressest. When thou impressest, what are precepts worth Of stale example? *Lov. Comp.* 267
Impression. And yields at last to every light impression *Ven. and Adon.* 566
Impression of strange kinds Is form'd in them by force, by fraud, or skill *Lucrece* 1242
The face, that map which deep impression bears Of hard misfortune 1712
Your love and pity doth the impression fill *Sonnet* 112 1
Imprint. The vacant leaves thy mind's imprint will bear 77 3
Imprinted. Pure lips, sweet seals in my soft lips imprinted *Ven. and Adon.* 511
Imprisoned. As when the wind, imprison'd in the ground, Struggling for passage, earth's foundation shakes 1046
Show'd life imprison'd in a body dead *Lucrece* 1456
To make some special instant special blest, By new unfolding his imprison'd pride *Sonnet* 52 12
Imprisoned. O, let me suffer, being at your beck, The imprison'd absence of your liberty *Sonnet* 58 6
Impure. And pure perfection with impure defeature *Ven. and Adon.* 736
Shall gush pure streams to purge my impure tale *Lucrece* 1078
Impurity. No perfection is so absolute, That some impurity doth not pollute 854
Impute. This silence for my sin you did impute, Which shall be most my glory *Sonnet* 83 9
In. Being wasted in such time-beguiling sport *Ven. and Adon.* 24
Who blush'd and pouted in a dull disdain 33
Shaking her wings, devouring all in haste 57
Like a dive-dapper peering through a wave, Who, being look'd on, ducks as quickly in 87
Never did passenger in summer's heat More thirst for drink 91
She bathes in water, yet her fire must burn 94
Whose sinewy neck in battle ne'er did bow, Who conquers where he comes in every jar 99
What seest thou in the ground? hold up thy head 118
In spite of death, thou dost survive, In that thy likeness still is left alive 173
In shape, in courage, colour, pace, and bone 294
'In night,' quoth she, 'desire sees best of all' 720
In hand with all things, nought at all effecting 912
Who, like a king perplexed in his throne, By their suggestion gives a deadly groan 1043
Who, therefore angry, seems to part in sunder *Lucrece* 388
Wit so poor as mine May make seem bare, in wanting words to show it *Sonnet* 26 6
Incaged. The which, by Cupid's bow she doth protest, He carries thence incaged in his breast *Ven. and Adon.* 582
Incapable. Incapable of more, replete with you *Sonnet* 113 13
Incense. Offer pure incense to so pure a shrine *Lucrece* 194
Incertainty. Incertainties now crown themselves assured *Sonnet* 107 7
When I was certain o'er incertainty, Crowning the present 115 11
Incest. Guilty of treason, forgery, and shift, Guilty of incest, that abomination *Lucrece* 921
Inclination. An accessary by thine inclination To all sins past, and all that are to come 922
Incline. That eye which him beholds, as more divine, Unto a view so false will not incline 292
Inclined. That was not forced; that never was inclined To accessary yieldings 1657
Including. O impious act, including all foul harms! 199
Income. Pain pays the income of each precious thing 334
Inconstancy. For now I see Inconstancy More in women than in men remain *Pass. Pil.* 261
Inconstant. The conceit of this inconstant stay Sets you most rich in youth before my sight *Sonnet* 15 9
Thou canst not vex me with inconstant mind 92 9
Incorporate then they seem; face grows to face *Ven. and Adon.* 540
Increase. Upon the earth's increase why shouldst thou feed, Unless the earth with thy increase be fed? 169
You do it for increase: O strange excuse, When reason is the bawd to lust's abuse! 791
From fairest creatures we desire increase *Sonnet* 1 1
Herein lives wisdom, beauty, and increase 11 5
I perceive that men as plants increase, Cheered and check'd even by the self-same sky 15 5
The teeming autumn, big with rich increase 97 6
Increaseful. To cheer the ploughman with increaseful crops *Lucrece* 958
Increasing. Her words are done, her woes the more increasing *V. and A.* 254
And the firm soil win of the watery main, Increasing store *Sonnet* 64 8
Incur. Thy heat of lust, fond Paris, did incur This load of wrath *Lucrece* 1473
Indeed. What should I do, seeing thee so indeed? *Ven. and Adon.* 667
The remedy indeed to do me good Is to let forth my foul-defiled blood *Lucr.* 1028
But when my glass shows me myself indeed *Sonnet* 62 9
He that is thy friend indeed, He will help thee in thy need *Pass. Pil.* 423
Indenting. Turn, and return, indenting with the way *Ven. and Adon.* 704
Indigest. To make of monsters and things indigest Such cherubins *Son.* 114 5
Indirectly. Why should poor beauty indirectly seek Roses of shadow? 67 7
Infamy. Yet strive I to embrace mine infamy *Lucrece* 504
Are nature's faults, not their own infamy 539
O, how are they wrapp'd in with infamies That from their own misdeeds askance their eyes! 636
To mask their brows and hide their infamy 794
In vain I cavil with mine infamy, In vain I spurn at my confirm'd despite 1025
A dying life to living infamy 1055
Spoil'd, corrupted, Grossly engirt with daring infamy 1173
This act will be My fame and thy perpetual infamy 1638
Infant. Or like the froward infant still'd with dandling *Ven. and Adon.* 562
Thy false dart Mistakes that aim and cleaves an infant's heart 942
Old woes, not infant sorrows, bear them mild *Lucrece* 1096
Not prizing her poor infant's discontent *Sonnet* 143 8
Infect. Or toads infect fair founts with venom mud *Lucrece* 850
Infected. O, that infected moisture of his eye! *Lov. Comp.* 323
Infection. To drive infection from the dangerous year *Ven. and Adon.* 508
Advice is sporting while infection breeds *Lucrece* 907
Ah! wherefore with infection should he live? *Sonnet* 67 1
But if that flower with base infection meet, The basest weed outbraves his dignity 94 11
I will drink Potions of eisel 'gainst my strong infection 111 10
Inferior. My saucy bark inferior far to his 80 7
Infirmity. To mingle beauty with infirmities *Ven. and Adon.* 735
This ambitious foul infirmity, In having much, torments us with defect Of that we have *Lucrece* 150
'Twas not their infirmity, It was married chastity *Ph. and Tur.* 60
Inflame. When thou wilt inflame, How coldly those impediments stand forth! *Lov. Comp.* 268
Inflict. Else lasting shame On thee and thine this night I will inflict *Lucr.* 1630
Influence. Each lamp and shining star doth borrow The beauteous influence that makes him bright *Ven. and Adon.* 862
This huge stage presenteth nought but shows Whereon the stars in secret influence comment *Sonnet* 15 4
Whose influence is thine and born of thee 78 10
Infold. Sometimes her arms infold him like a band *Ven. and Adon.* 225
Informer. This sour informer, this bate-breeding spy 655
Hence, thou suborn'd informer! *Sonnet* 125 13
Infringed. I will not wrong thy true affection so, To flatter thee with an infringed oath *Lucrece* 1061
Infusing them with dreadful prophecies *Ven. and Adon.* 928

Inhabit. Before these bastard signs of fair were born, Or durst inhabit on a living brow *Sonnet* 68 4
Inhearse. That did my ripe thoughts in my brain inhearse 86 3
Inherit. And to temptation slow, They rightly do inherit heaven's graces 94 5
Inheritors. Shall worms, inheritors of this excess, Eat up thy charge? 146 7
Iniquity. Draw not thy sword to guard iniquity *Lucrece* 626
What virtue breeds iniquity devours: We have no good that we can say is ours 872
Let the traitor die; For sparing justice feeds iniquity 1687
Mine own self-love quite contrary I read; Self so self-loving were iniquity *Sonnet* 62 12
Injurious. Robb'd and ransack'd by injurious theft *Lucrece* 838
O, hear me then, injurious, shifting Time! 930
Injurious distance should not stop my way *Sonnet* 44 2
With Time's injurious hand crush'd and o'erworn 63 2
Injury. It is a greater grief To bear love's wrong than hate's known injury 40 12
And patience, tame to sufferance, bide each check, Without accusing you of injury 58 8
The injuries that to myself I do, Doing thee vantage, double-vantage me 88 11
Eternal love in love's fresh case Weighs not the dust and injury of age 108 10
She turns my foes, That they elsewhere might dart their injuries 139 12
In me you behold The injury of many a blasting hour *Lov. Comp.* 72
Injustice. 'Tis a meritorious fair design To chase injustice with revengeful arms *Lucrece* 1693
Ink. Go, get me hither paper, ink, and pen 1289
That in black ink my love may still shine bright *Sonnet* 65 14
What's in the brain that ink may character? 108 1
Ink would have seem'd more black and damned here! *Lov. Comp.* 54
Innocence. And forth with bashful innocence doth hie *Lucrece* 1341
Inordinate. That nothing in him seem'd inordinate, Save sometime too much wonder of his eye 94
Insinuate. With Death she humbly doth insinuate *Ven. and Adon.* 1012
Instance. That blushing red no guilty instance gave *Lucrece* 1511
Instant. To make some special instant special blest, By new unfolding his imprison'd pride *Sonnet* 52 11
Instead. Enforced hate, Instead of love's coy touch, shall rudely tear thee *Lucrece* 669
Instigate. Some untimely thought did instigate His all-too-timeless speed 43
Instinct. As if by some instinct the wretch did know His rider loved not speed *Sonnet* 50 7
Instrument. She starteth, To find some desperate instrument of death *Lucrece* 1038
These means, as frets upon an instrument, Shall tune our heart-strings 1140
'Poor instrument,' quoth she, 'without a sound, I'll tune thy woes' 1464
Insufficiency. O, from what power hast thou this powerful might With insufficiency my heart to sway? *Sonnet* 150 2
Insults. I'll live in this poor rhyme, While he insults o'er dull and speechless tribes 107 12
Insulter. Paying what ransom the insulter willeth *Ven. and Adon.* 550
Insulting. So under his insulting falchion lies Harmless Lucretia *Lucrece* 509
Insurrection. Her subjects with foul insurrection Have batter'd down her consecrated wall 722
Intelligence. That affable familiar ghost Which nightly gulls him with intelligence *Sonnet* 86 10
Intend. To-morrow he intends To hunt the boar with certain of his friends *Ven. and Adon.* 587
My thoughts, from far where I abide, Intend a zealous pilgrimage to thee *Sonnet* 27 6
Sometimes her levell'd eyes their carriage ride, As they did battery to the spheres intend *Lov. Comp.* 23
Intending weariness with heavy spright *Lucrece* 121
Intendments. And now her sobs do her intendments break *Ven. and Adon.* 222
Intent. And all amazed brake off his late intent 469
With swift intent he goes To quench the coal *Lucrece* 46
If Collatinus dream of my intent, Will he not wake? 218
Tan sacred beauty, blunt the sharp'st intents, Divert strong minds *Son.* 115 7
Interchange. That oft they interchange each other's seat *Lucrece* 70
I have seen such interchange of state, Or state itself confounded to decay *Sonnet* 64 9
Interdict. From this session interdict Every fowl of tyrant wing, Save the eagle, feather'd king *Ph. and Tur.* 9
Interest. Give me one kiss, I'll give it thee again, And one for interest *Ven. and Adon.* 210
Thy interest was not bought Basely with gold, but stol'n from forth thy gate *Lucrece* 1067
Dear husband, in the interest of thy bed A stranger came 1619
Do not take away My sorrow's interest 1797
How many a holy and obsequious tear Hath dear religious love stol'n from mine eye As interest of the dead *Sonnet* 31 7
My life hath in this line some interest 74 3
Interim. Let this sad interim like the ocean be Which parts the shore 56 9
Interlaces. Here and there the painter interlaces Pale cowards *Lucrece* 1390
Intermixed. But best is best, if never intermix'd 101 8
Interprets. The eye interprets to the ear The heavy motion that it doth behold *Lucrece* 1325
Interrupted. Her quiet interrupted, Her mansion batter'd by the enemy 1170
Intituled. But beauty, in that white intituled, From Venus' doves doth challenge that fair field 57
Into. You will fall again Into your idle over-handled theme *Ven. and Adon.* 770
Lest the deceiving harmony should run Into the quiet closure of my breast 782
Why hast thou cast into eternal sleeping Those eyes? 951
Her eyes are fled Into the deep dark cabins of her head 1038
The wind wars with his torch to make him stay, And blows the smoke of it into his face *Lucrece* 312
Into the chamber wickedly he stalks, And gazeth on her yet unstained bed 365
There falls into thy boundless flood Black lust, dishonour, shame 653
And perjury should thrust Into so bright a day such black-faced storms 1518
That pour'st into my verse Thine own sweet argument *Sonnet* 38 2
The bloody spur cannot provoke him on That sometimes anger thrusts into his hide 50 10
Into my deeds to pry, To find out shames and idle hours in me 61 6
They look into the beauty of thy mind, And that, in guess, they measure by thy deeds *Sonnet* 69 9
Lest the wise world should look into your moan And mock you with me after I am gone 71 13
But an art of craft, Even there resolved my reason into tears *Lov. Comp.* 296
Intrude. Why should the worm intrude the maiden bud? *Lucrece* 848
Inundation. But with the inundation of the eyes What rocky heart to water will not wear? *Lov. Comp.* 290
Inured. As who should say 'This glove to wanton tricks Is not inured' *Lucrece* 321
Invasion. That now he vows a league, and now invasion 287
Inveigh. No man inveigh against the wither'd flower 1254
Invent. How can my Muse want subject to invent, While thou dost breathe? *Sonnet* 38 1
Yet what of thee thy poet doth invent He robs thee of and pays it thee again 79 7
Invention. O, what excuse can my invention make? *Lucrece* 225
Much like a press of people at a door, Throng her inventions 1302
Who's so dumb that cannot write to thee, When thou thyself dost give invention light? *Sonnet* 38 8
How are our brains beguiled, Which, labouring for invention, bear amiss 59 3
Why write I still all one, ever the same, And keep invention in a noted weed? 76 6
There appears a face That over-goes my blunt invention quite 103 7
And in this change is my invention spent 105 11
Invised. The diamond,—why, 'twas beautiful and hard, Whereto his invised properties did tend *Lov. Comp.* 212
Invisible. Had I no eyes but ears, my ears would love That inward beauty and invisible *Ven. and Adon.* 434
Be wreak'd on him, invisible commander 1004
O unseen shame! invisible disgrace! O unfelt sore! *Lucrece* 827
Invite. Till now did ne'er invite, nor never woo *Lov. Comp.* 182
Invited. Nor taste, nor smell, desire to be invited To any sensual feast with thee alone *Sonnet* 141 7
Inviting. Whereto the inviting time our fashion calls 124 8
Invocate. Be thou the tenth Muse, ten times more in worth Than those old nine which rhymers invocate 38 10
Invocations. To rouse our Roman gods with invocations *Lucrece* 1831
Invoked. So oft have I invoked thee for my Muse And found such fair assistance *Sonnet* 78 1
Inward. Had I no eyes but ears, my ears would love That inward beauty and invisible *Ven. and Adon.* 434
Whose inward ill no outward harm express'd *Lucrece* 91
In his inward mind he doth debate What following sorrow may on this arise 185
Beguiled With outward honesty, but yet defiled With inward vice 1546
The deep vexation of his inward soul Hath served a dumb arrest upon his tongue 1779
Neither in inward worth nor outward fair *Sonnet* 16 11
Mine eye's due is thy outward part, And my heart's right thy inward love of heart 46 14
It is so grounded inward in my heart 62 4
Do I envy those jacks that nimble leap To kiss the tender inward of thy hand 128 6
Ireful. Being ireful, on the lion he will venture *Ven. and Adon.* 628
Iron. The iron bit he crusheth 'tween his teeth 269
Be compassionate! Soft pity enters at an iron gate *Lucrece* 595
Softer than wax, and yet, as iron, rusty *Pass. Pil.* 88
Is. What is ten hundred touches unto thee? *Ven. and Adon.* 519
Is twenty hundred kisses such a trouble? 522
If there be nothing new, but that which is Hath been before *Sonnet* 59 1
Island. Like a late-sack'd island, vastly stood Bare and unpeopled *Lucrece* 1740
Issue. Sweet issue of a more sweet-smelling sire *Ven. and Adon.* 1178
Perchance his boast of Lucrece' sovereignty Suggested this proud issue of a king *Lucrece* 37
Thy issue blurr'd with nameless bastardy 522
When your sweet issue your sweet form should bear *Sonnet* 13 8
Yet this abundant issue seem'd to me But hope of orphans 97 9
Issueless. If thou issueless shalt hap to die, The world will wail thee 9 3
It. And may it be That thou shouldst think it heavy unto thee *V. and A.* 155
She hears them chant it lustily, And all in haste she coasteth 869
The strongest body shall it make most weak 1145
The staring ruffian shall it keep in quiet 1149
Nor it nor no remembrance what it was *Sonnet* 5 12
And perspective it is best painter's art 24 4
Italy. Her husband's fame, Won in the fields of fruitful Italy *Lucrece* 107
Itself. Beauty within itself should not be wasted *Ven. and Adon.* 130
Beauty itself doth of itself persuade The eyes of men without an orator *Lucrece* 29
Wounding itself to death, rise up and fall, Beating her bulk 466
So ensconced his secret evil, That jealousy itself could not mistrust 1516
The poison'd fountain clears itself again 1707
Who heaven itself for ornament doth use *Sonnet* 21 3
Such interchange of state, Or state itself confounded to decay 64 10
That sin by him advantage should achieve And lace itself with his society 67 4
In him those holy antique hours are seen, Without all ornament, itself and true 68 10
Whilst it hath thought itself so blessed never 119 6
The sun itself sees not till heaven clears 148 12
Reason, in itself confounded, Saw division grow together *Ph. and Tur.* 41
Ivory. Within the circuit of this ivory pale, I'll be a park, and thou shalt be my deer *Ven. and Adon.* 230
A lily prison'd in a gaol of snow, Or ivory in an alabaster band 363
Her breasts, like ivory globes circled with blue, A pair of maiden worlds unconquered *Lucrece* 407
His hand, that yet remains upon her breast,—Rude ram, to batter such an ivory wall! 464
A pretty while these pretty creatures stand, Like ivory conduits coral cisterns filling 1234
Ivy. A belt of straw and ivy buds, With coral clasps and amber studs *Pass. Pil.* 365

J

Jacks. Do I envy those jacks that nimble leap To kiss the tender inward of thy hand! *Sonnet* 128 5

Since saucy jacks so happy are in this, Give them thy fingers 128 13

Jade. How like a jade he stood, tied to the tree! *Ven. and Adon.* 391

Till like a jade Self-will himself doth tire *Lucrece* 707

But love, for love, thus shall excuse my jade *Sonnet* 51 12

Jar. Who conquers where he comes in every jar *Ven. and Adon.* 100

Javelin. Thou know'st not what it is With javelin's point a churlish swine to gore 616

Jaws. Pluck the keen teeth from the fierce tiger's jaws *Sonnet* 19 3

Jealous of catching, swiftly doth forsake him *Ven. and Adon.* 321

Let not the jealous Day behold that face *Lucrece* 800

Nor dare I question with my jealous thought Where you may be *Sonnet* 57 9

Jealousy. Lest Jealousy, that sour unwelcome guest, Should, by his stealing in, disturb the feast *Ven. and Adon.* 449

Disturbing Jealousy Doth call himself Affection's sentinel 649

This carry-tale, dissentious Jealousy 657

It shall be waited on with jealousy 1137

So ensconced his secret evil, That jealousy itself could not mistrust *Lucrece* 1516

To find out shames and idle hours in me, The scope and tenour of thy jealousy? *Sonnet* 61 8

Jennet. A breeding jennet, lusty, young, and proud *Ven. and Adon.* 260

Jest. To sport and dance, To toy, to wanton, dally, smile, and jest 106

'No, no,' quoth she, 'sweet Death, I did but jest; Yet pardon me' 997

Would not touch the bait, But smile and jest at every gentle offer *Pass. Pil.* 54

'T may be, she joy'd to jest at my exile 189

Jestings. Her faith, her oaths, her tears, and all were jestings 96

Jet. From a maund she drew Of amber, crystal, and of beaded jet *L. Comp.* 37

Jewel. Torches are made to light, jewels to wear, Dainties to taste, fresh beauty for the use *Ven. and Adon.* 163

As one that unaware Hath dropp'd a precious jewel in the flood 824

Why is Collatine the publisher Of that rich jewel? *Lucrece* 34

Dear lord of that dear jewel I have lost, What legacy shall I bequeath to thee? 1191

Like a jewel hung in ghastly night, Makes black night beauteous *Sonnet* 27 11

Thou, to whom my jewels trifles are, Most worthy comfort 48 5

Like stones of worth they thinly placed are, Or captain jewels in the carcanet 52 8

Where, alack, Shall Time's best jewel from Time's chest lie hid 65 10

As on the finger of a throned queen The basest jewel will be well esteem'd 96 6

To my dear doting heart Thou art the fairest and most precious jewel 131 4

The foil Of this false jewel, and his amorous spoil *Lov. Comp.* 154

Jigs. All my merry jigs are quite forgot, All my lady's love is lost, God wot *Pass. Pil.* 253

Jocund. Who, flatter'd by their leader's jocund show, Stuff up his lust *Lucr.* 296

Join. Then join they all together, Like many clouds *Ven. and Adon.* 971

They join and shoot their foam at Simois' banks *Lucrece* 1442

While the world is bent my deeds to cross, Join with the spite of fortune *Sonnet* 90 3

Joined. Her lips to mine how often hath she joined! *Pass. Pil.* 91

Joint. I fear'd thy fortune, and my joints did tremble *Ven. and Adon.* 642

Her voice is stopt, her joints forget to bow; Her eyes are mad 1061

Will not my tongue be mute, my frail joints shake? *Lucrece* 227

Whose grim aspect sets every joint a-shaking 452

Jointly. All jointly listening, but with several graces 1410

Then jointly to the ground their knees they bow 1846

Jollity. As, to behold desert a beggar born, And needy nothing trimm'd in jollity *Sonnet* 66 3

Jot. If springing things be any jot diminish'd, They wither in their prime, prove nothing worth *Ven. and Adon.* 417

Journey. Then begins a journey in my head, To work my mind *Sonnet* 27 3

How heavy do I journey on the way 50 1

Jove. 'O Jove,' quoth she, 'how much a fool was I!' *Ven. and Adon.* 1015

She conjures him by high almighty Jove, By knighthood *Lucrece* 568

Thine eye Jove's lightning seems, thy voice his dreadful thunder *Pass. Pil.* 67

'O Jove,' quoth she, 'why was not I a flood!' 84

Jove. Thou for whom Jove would swear Juno but an Ethiope were *Pass. Pil.* 241

And deny himself for Jove, Turning mortal for thy love 243

Joy. I heartily beseech thee, To take advantage on presented joy *V. and A.* 405

But now I died, and death was lively joy. O, thou didst kill me 498

To clip Elysium and to lack her joy 600

Reviving joy bids her rejoice, And flatters her it is Adonis' voice 977

Her joy with heaved-up hand she doth express *Lucrece* 111

A dream, a breath, a froth of fleeting joy 212

Lucrece to their sight Must sell her joy, her life, her world's delight 385

This momentary joy breeds months of pain 690

Thy honey turns to gall, thy joy to grief 889

The little birds that tune their morning's joy Make her moans mad with their sweet melody 1107

Sharing joy To see their youthful sons bright weapons wield 1431

Through their light joy seem'd to appear, Like bright things stain'd, a kind of heavy fear 1434

Sweets with sweets war not, joy delights in joy *Sonnet* 8 2

Whilst I, whom fortune of such triumph bars, Unlook'd for joy in that I honour most 25 4

But here's the joy; my friend and I are one 42 13

This told, I joy; but then no longer glad, I send them back again 45 13

My grief lies onward and my joy behind 50 14

Every humour hath his adjunct pleasure, Wherein it finds a joy 91 6

Before, a joy proposed; behind, a dream 129 12

Were kisses all the joys in bed, One woman would another wed *Pass. Pil.* 345

Joyed. 'T may be, she joy'd to jest at my exile 189

Joyless. While with a joyless smile she turns away The face *Lucrece* 1711

Judge. Being judge in love, she cannot right her cause *Ven. and Adon.* 220

My bloody judge forbade my tongue to speak *Lucrece* 1648

And when the judge is robb'd the prisoner dies 1652

Judgement. Not from the stars do I my judgement pluck *Sonnet* 14 1

So, till the judgement that yourself arise, You live in this 55 13

So thy great gift, upon misprision growing, Comes home again, on better judgement making 87 12

Yet then my judgement knew no reason why 115 3

Do witness bear Thy black is fairest in my judgement's place 131 12

Hooks, Whereto the judgement of my heart is tied 137 8

Where is my judgement fled, That censures falsely what they see aright? 148 3

Let it not tell your judgement I am old *Lov. Comp.* 73

O appetite, from judgement stand aloof! 166

Juice. Thick-sighted, barren, lean, and lacking juice *Ven. and Adon.* 136

Jump. The scalps of many, almost hid behind, To jump up higher seem'd, to mock the mind *Lucrece* 1414

For nimble thought can jump both sea and land As soon as think the place where he would be *Sonnet* 44 7

Junes. Three April perfumes in three hot Junes burn'd, Since first I saw you fresh 104 7

Juno. Thou for whom Jove would swear Juno but an Ethiope were *Pass. Pil.* 242

Just. Now was she just before him as he sat *Ven. and Adon.* 349

Like one that spies an adder Wreathed up in fatal folds just in his way 879

Too severe, And most deceiving when it seems most just 1156

When shall he think to find a stranger just, When he himself himself confounds? *Lucrece* 159

He entertain'd a show so seeming just 1514

Just to the time, not with the time exchanged *Sonnet* 109 7

And on just proof surmise accumulate 117 10

And the just pleasure lost which is so deem'd, Not by our feeling but by others' seeing 121 3

The more I hear and see just cause of hate 150 10

Justice. Justice is feasting while the widow weeps *Lucrece* 906

No rightful plea might plead for justice there 1649

Let the traitor die; For sparing justice feeds iniquity 1687

Justify. Call not me to justify the wrong That thy unkindness lays upon my heart *Sonnet* 139 1

Justly. And justly thus controls his thoughts unjust *Lucrece* 189

One justly weeps; the other takes in hand No cause 1235

K

Keen. Unhappily set This bateless edge on his keen appetite *Lucrece* 9

Pluck the keen teeth from the fierce tiger's jaws *Sonnet* 19 3

To make our appetites more keen, With eager compounds 118 1

Advice is often seen By blunting us to make our wits more keen *Lov. Comp.* 161

Keep. Love keeps his revels where there are but twain *Ven. and Adon.* 123

O, let him keep his loathsome cabin still 637

And on thy well-breath'd horse keep with thy hounds 678

And sometime where earth-delving conies keep 687

The staring ruffian shall it keep in quiet 1149

That rich jewel he should keep unknown From thievish ears *Lucrece* 34

But blind they are, and keep themselves enclosed 378

Keep still possession of thy gloomy place 803

When Truth and Virtue have to do with thee, A thousand crosses keep them from thy aid 912

Thou bear'st thy part, To keep thy sharp woes waking 1136

Who, mad that sorrow should his use control, Or keep him from heart-easing words so long, Begins to talk 1782

Every private widow well may keep By children's eyes her husband's shape in mind *Sonnet* 9 7

To give away yourself keeps yourself still 16 13

Bearing thy heart, which I will keep so chary As tender nurse her babe 22 11

And keep my drooping eyelids open wide 27 7

Then can no horse with my desire keep pace 51 9

Keep. So is the time that keeps you as my chest *Sonnet* 52 9

Is it thy will thy image should keep open My heavy eyelids? 61 1

It is my love that keeps mine eye awake 61 10

Why write I still all one, ever the same, And keep invention in a noted weed? 76 6

To keep an adjunct to remember thee Were to import forgetfulness in me 122 13

She keeps thee to this purpose, that her skill May time disgrace 126 7

She may detain, but not still keep, her treasure 126 10

Whoe'er keeps me, let my heart be his guard 133 11

Whilst many nymphs that vow'd chaste life to keep Came tripping by 154 3

Keep the obsequy so strict *Ph. and Tur.* 12

Keepest. O cunning Love! with tears thou keep'st me blind *Sonnet* 148 13

Ken. 'Tis double death to drown in ken of shore *Lucrece* 1114

Kennelled. Here kennell'd in a brake she finds a hound *Ven. and Adon.* 913

Kept. Were beauty under twenty locks kept fast, Yet love breaks through and picks them all at last 575

Shall by a painted cloth be kept in awe *Lucrece* 245

Let my good name, that senseless reputation, For Collatine's dear love be kept unspotted 821

And suck'd the honey which thy chaste bee kept 840

Distress likes dumps when time is kept with tears 1127

When both were kept for heaven and Collatine 1166

Kept. Beauty's waste hath in the world an end, And kept unused, the user so destroys it . . . . . . *Sonnet* 9 12
'Fair, kind, and true,' have often lived alone, Which three till now never kept seat in one . . . 105 14
My reason, the physician to my love, Angry that his prescriptions are not kept . . . 147 6
Kept hearts in liveries, but mine own was free . . *Lov. Comp.* 195
She was sought by spirits of richest coat, But kept cold distance . . 237
She bade good night that kept my rest away . . *Pass. Pil.* 182

Key. So am I as the rich, whose blessed key Can bring him to his sweet up-locked treasure . . . *Sonnet* 52 1

Key-cold. Then in key-cold Lucrece' bleeding stream He falls *Lucrece* 1774

Kill. For looks kill love and love by looks reviveth . *Ven. and Adon.* 464
O, thou didst kill me : kill me once again . . . 499
Like to a mortal butcher bent to kill . . . 618
Suggesteth mutiny, And in a peaceful hour doth cry 'Kill, kill!' . 652
The one doth flatter thee in thoughts unlikely, In likely thoughts the other kills thee quickly . . . 990
While lust and murder wake to stain and kill . . *Lucrece* 168
Which in a moment doth confound and kill All pure effects . . 250
But they must ope, this blessed league to kill . . . 383
To kill thine honour with thy life's decay . . . 516
Draw not thy sword to guard iniquity, For it was lent thee all that brood to kill . . . 627
We have no good that we can say is ours, But ill-annexed Opportunity Or kills his life or else his quality . . . 875
Let the thief run mad, Himself himself seek every hour to kill! . 998
Kill both thyself and her for yielding so . . . 1036
'To kill myself,' quoth she, 'alack, what were it?' . . . 1156
Myself, thy friend, will kill myself, thy foe . . . 1196
And so did kill The lechers in their deed . . . 1636
Lascivious grace, in whom all ill well shows, Kill me with spites *Son.* 40 14
Thought kills me that I am not thought, To leap large lengths of miles when thou art gone . . . 44 9
Do not kill The spirit of love with a perpetual dullness . . 56 7
Her skill May time disgrace and wretched minutes kill . . 126 8
Let no unkind, no fair beseechers kill . . . 135 13
Kill me outright with looks and rid my pain . . . 139 14
To leave the master loveless, or kill the gallant knight . . *Pass. Pil.* 216

Killed. He thought to kiss him, and hath kill'd him so. 'Tis true *V. and A.* 1110
I must confess, With kissing him I should have kill'd him first . 1118
The boy that by her side lay kill'd Was melted like a vapour from her sight 1165
Where, lest between them both it should be kill'd, The coward captive vanquished doth yield . . . *Lucrece* 74
Had Collatinus kill'd my son or sire, Or lain in ambush to betray my life . 232
But chide rough winter that the flower hath kill'd . . . 1255
Her lively colour kill'd with deadly cares . . . 1593
She was my wife, I owed her, and 'tis mine that she hath kill'd . 1803
Fair creature, kill'd too soon by death's sharp sting! *Pass. Pil.* 134

Kind. Beating his kind embracements with her heels *Ven. and Adon.* 312
Yet pardon me I felt a kind of fear When as I met the boar . . 998
And must not die Till mutual overthrow of mortal kind . . 1018
There we will unfold To creatures stern sad tunes, to change their kinds *Lucrece* 1147
The impression of strange kinds Is form'd in them by force, by fraud, or skill . . . 1242
Conceit deceitful, so compact, so kind, That for Achilles' image stood his spear . . . 1423
Seemed to appear, Like bright things stain'd, a kind of heavy fear 1435
Be, as thy presence is, gracious and kind . . *Sonnet* 10 11
Their thoughts, although their eyes were kind, To thy fair flower add the rank smell of weeds . . . 69 11
Cannot dispraise but in a kind of praise . . . 95 7
Kind is my love to-day, to-morrow kind, Still constant . . 105 5
'Fair, kind, and true' is all my argument, 'Fair, kind, and true' . 105 9
'Fair, kind, and true,' have often lived alone . . 105 13
All frailties that besiege all kinds of blood . . 109 10
And, sick of welfare, found a kind of meetness To be diseased . 118 7
Nor he will not be free, For thou art covetous and he is kind . 134 6
Turn back to me, And play the mother's part, kiss me, be kind . 143 12
All kind of arguments and question deep . . *Lov. Comp.* 121
With acture they may be, Where neither party is nor true nor kind . 186
I have received from many a several fair, Their kind acceptance . 207
Showing fair nature is both kind and tame . . . 311

Kinder. Grew kinder, and his fury was assuaged . *Ven. and Adon.* 318

Kind-hearted. Be, as thy presence is, gracious and kind, Or to thyself at least kind-hearted prove . . . *Sonnet* 10 12

Kindle. She seeks to kindle with continual kissing *Ven. and Adon.* 606

Kindled. His kindled duty kindled her mistrust . . *Lucrece* 1352
Thy eye kindled the fire that burneth here . . . 1475

Kindly. She took me kindly by the hand, And gazed for tidings in my eager eyes . . . 253

Kindness. Nor thou with public kindness honour me . . *Sonnet* 36 11
For I have sworn deep oaths of thy deep kindness, Oaths of thy love . 152 9

Kindred. Of wealth, of filial fear, law, kindred, fame . *Lov. Comp.* 270

King. She clepes him king of graves and grave for kings *Ven. and Adon.* 995
Who, like a king perplexed in his throne, By their suggestion gives a deadly groan . . . 1043
That kings might be espoused to more fame, But king nor peer to such a peerless dame . . . *Lucrece* 20
Perchance his boast of Lucrece' sovereignty Suggested this proud issue of a king . . . 37
Thou seem'st not what thou art, a god, a king . . . 601
For kings like gods should govern every thing . . . 602
What darest thou not when once thou art a king? . . . 606
Then kings' misdeeds cannot be hid in clay . . . 609
'Thou art,' quoth she, 'a sea, a sovereign king' . . . 652
So shall these slaves be king, and thou their slave . . . 659
Or kings be breakers of their own behests . . . 852
Time's glory is to calm contending kings, To unmask falsehood . 939
The baser is he, coming from a king . . . 1002
Poor grooms are sightless night, kings glorious day . . 1013
Esteemed so As silly-jeering idiots are with kings . . . 1812
Such wealth brings That then I scorn to change my state with kings *Son.* 29 14
All those beauties whereof now he's king Are vanishing or vanish'd out of sight . . . 63 6
Thus have I had thee, as a dream doth flatter, In sleep a king . 87 14
Million'd accidents Creep in 'twixt vows and change decrees of kings 115 6
King Pandion he is dead ; All thy friends are lapp'd in lead . *Pass. Pil.* 395
And with such like flattering, 'Pity but he were a king' . . 414
King. Every fowl of tyrant wing, Save the eagle, feather'd king *Ph. and Tur.* 11

Kingdom. I have seen the hungry ocean gain Advantage on the kingdom of the shore . . . *Sonnet* 64 6
Then thou alone kingdoms of hearts shouldst owe . . 70 14

Kingly. And my great mind most kingly drinks it up . 114 10

Kinsman. But as he is my kinsman, my dear friend, The shame and fault finds no excuse nor end . . . *Lucrece* 237
Thy kinsmen hang their heads at this disdain . . . 521

Kirtle. A cap of flowers, and a kirtle Embroider'd all with leaves of myrtle *Pass. Pil.* 363

Kiss. I'll smother thee with kisses . . *Ven. and Adon.* 18
Ten kisses short as one, one long as twenty . . . 22
What follows more she murders with a kiss . . . 54
And one sweet kiss shall pay this countless debt . . . 84
Flint-hearted boy! 'Tis but a kiss I beg ; why art thou coy? . 96
The kiss shall be thine own as well as mine . . . 117
Art thou ashamed to kiss? then wink again, And I will wink . 121
Narcissus so himself himself forsook, And died to kiss his shadow in the brook . . . 162
What were thy lips the worse for one poor kiss? Speak, fair . 207
Give me one kiss, I'll give it thee again, And one for interest . 209
For men will kiss even by their own direction . . . 216
He kisses her ; and she, by her good will, Will never rise, so he will kiss her still . . . 479
Long may they kiss each other, for this cure . . . 505
A thousand kisses buys my heart from me . . . 517
Is twenty hundred kisses such a trouble? . . . 522
'Good night,' and so say you ; If you will say so, you shall have a kiss 536
And all is but to rob thee of a kiss . . . 723
Make modest Dian cloudy and forlorn, Lest she should steal a kiss and die forsworn . . . 726
The kiss I gave you is bestow'd in vain . . . 771
Some kiss her face, Some twine about her thigh to make her stay . 872
Nor sun nor wind will ever strive to kiss you . . . 1082
He thought to kiss him, and hath kill'd him so. 'Tis true, tis true . 1110
But by a kiss thought to persuade him there . . . 1114
There shall not be one minute in an hour Wherein I will not kiss my sweet love's flower . . . 1188
Her rosy cheek lies under, Cozening the pillow of a lawful kiss . *Lucrece* 387
So proud, As heaven, it seem'd, to kiss the turrets bow'd . . 1372
To kiss the tender inward of thy hand . . *Sonnet* 128 6
Give them thy fingers, me thy lips to kiss . . . 128 14
Turn back to me, And play the mother's part, kiss me, be kind . 143 12
Between each kiss her oaths of true love swearing . . *Pass. Pil.* 92
Ah, that I had my lady at this bay, To kiss and clip me till I run away! . 156
Were kisses all the joys in bed, One woman would another wed . 345

Kissed. Even so she kissed his brow, his cheek, his chin *Ven. and Adon.* 59
And kiss'd the fatal knife, to end his vow . . *Lucrece* 1843
These often bathed she in her fluxive eyes, And often kiss'd *Lov. Comp.* 51

Kissing. And kissing speaks, with lustful language broken *Ven. and Adon.* 47
She seeks to kindle with continual kissing . . . 606
I must confess, With kissing him I should have kill'd him first . 1118
Kissing with golden face the meadows green . . *Sonnet* 33 3

Knee. And with his knee the door he opens wide . . *Lucrece* 359
Then jointly to the ground their knees they bow . . . 1846

Kneel. And like a lowly lover down she kneels . *Ven. and Adon.* 350
Kneel with me and help to bear thy part . . *Lucrece* 1830

Knell. Then little strength rings out the doleful knell . . 1495
My wether's bell rings doleful knell . . *Pass. Pil.* 272

Knew. She answers him as if she knew his mind . *Ven. and Adon.* 308
Whose precious taste her thirsty lips well knew . . . 543
Unconquered, Save of their lord no bearing yoke they knew . *Lucrece* 409
Yet then my judgement knew no reason why . . *Sonnet* 115 3
Sometime a blusterer, that the ruffle knew Of court, of city *Lov. Comp.* 58
And knew the patterns of his foul beguiling . . . 170
Knew vows were ever brokers to defiling . . . 173

Knife. Yet for the self-same purpose seek a knife . . *Lucrece* 1047
Against my heart Will fix a sharp knife to affright mine eye . . 1138
My honour I'll bequeath unto the knife That wounds my body . 1184
Mine honour be the knife's that makes my wound . . . 1201
With my knife scratch out the angry eyes Of all the Greeks . . 1469
She sheathed in her harmless breast A harmful knife . . . 1724
From the purple fountain Brutus drew The murderous knife . . 1735
Brutus, who pluck'd the knife from Lucrece' side . . . 1807
By this bloody knife, We will revenge the death of this true wife . 1840
And kiss'd the fatal knife, to end his vow . . . 1843
For such a time do I now fortify Against confounding age's cruel knife *Sonnet* 63 10
My body being dead, The coward conquest of a wretch's knife . 74 11
The hardest knife ill-used doth lose his edge . . . 95 14
Give my love fame faster than Time wastes life ; So thou prevent'st his scythe and crooked knife . . . 100 14

Knight. Knights, by their oaths, should right poor ladies' harms *Lucrece* 1694
Old rhyme In praise of ladies dead and lovely knights . *Sonnet* 106 4
One knight loves both, and both in thee remain . . *Pass. Pil.* 116
To leave the master loveless, or kill the gallant knight . . 216
For of the two the trusty knight was wounded with disdain . . 221

Knighthood. O shame to knighthood and to shining arms! . *Lucrece* 197
By knighthood, gentry, and sweet friendship's oath . . . 569
As bound in knighthood to her imposition . . . 1697

Knit. With heavy eye, knit brow, and strengthless pace . . . 709
Ere he go to bed, Knit poisonous clouds about his golden head . . 777
To whom in vassalage Thy merit hath my duty strongly knit *Sonnet* 26 2

Knocks at my heart and whispers in mine ear . *Ven. and Adon.* 659

Knot. O most potential love! vow, bond, nor space, In thee hath neither sting, knot, nor confine . . . *Lov. Comp.* 265

Know. For thy meed A thousand honey secrets shalt thou know *V. and A.* 16
Violets whereon we lean Never can blab, nor know not what we mean . 126
He now prepares, And whether he run or fly they know not whether . 304
'I know not love,' quoth he, 'nor will not know it' . . . 409
Before I know myself, seek not to know me . . . 525
For know, my heart stands armed in mine ear . . . 779
For now she knows it is no gentle chase, But the blunt boar . . 883
Which madly hurries her she knows not whither . . . 904
That bloody beast, Which knows no pity, but is still severe . . 1000
Why then I know He thought to kiss him, and hath kill'd him so . 1109
But know, it is as good To wither in my breast as in his blood . 1181
Peers her whiter chin, The reason of this rash alarm to know . *Lucrece* 473
I know what thorns the growing rose defends . . . 492
I know repentant tears ensue the deed, Reproach, disdain . . 502

Know. Pleads . . . To the rough beast that knows no gentle right *Lucrece* 545
The illiterate, that know not how To cipher what is writ in learned books 810
Alas, how many bear such shameful blows, Which not themselves, but he that gives them knows! 833
Dear Collatine, thou shalt not know The stained taste of violated troth 1058
But thou shalt know thy interest was not bought Basely with gold 1067
Grief dallied with nor law nor limit knows 1120
That knows not parching heat nor freezing cold 1145
Know, gentle wench, it small avails my mood 1273
If your maid may be so bold, She would request to know your heaviness 1283
By this short schedule Collatine may know Her grief 1312
She modestly prepares to let them know Her honour is ta'en prisoner 1607
My love, you know You had a father: let your son say so *Sonnet* 13 13
Heaven knows, it is but as a tomb Which hides your life 17 3
They draw but what they see, know not the heart 24 14
And yet, love knows, it is a greater grief To bear love's wrong than hate's known injury 40 11
As if by some instinct the wretch did know His rider loved not speed 50 7
In winged speed no motion shall I know 51 8
And you in every blessed shape we know 53 12
O, know, sweet love, I always write of you 76 9
Thou by thy dial's shady stealth mayst know Time's thievish progress 77 7
Thou mayst be false, and yet I know it not 92 14
Therefore in that I cannot know thy change 93 6
I must strive To know my shames and praises from your tongue 112 6
Mine eye well knows what with his gust is 'greeing 114 11
Which is not mix'd with seconds, knows no art, But mutual render 125 11
All this the world well knows; yet none knows well To shun the heaven that leads men to this hell 129 13
Yet well I know That music hath a far more pleasing sound 130 9
I was thy 'Will,' And will, thy soul knows, is admitted there 136 3
They know what beauty is, see where it lies 137 3
Which my heart knows the wide world's common place 137 10
I do believe her, though I know she lies 138 2

Know. She thinks me young, Although she knows my days are past the best *Sonnet* 138 6
My love well knows Her pretty looks have been mine enemies 139 9
As testy sick men, when their deaths be near, No news but health from their physicians know 140 8
Yet this shall I ne'er know, but live in doubt 144 13
But, love, hate on, for now I know thy mind 149 13
Love is too young to know what conscience is; Yet who knows not conscience is born of love? 151 1
Desires to know In brief the grounds and motives of her woe *Lov. Comp.* 62
I do believe her, though I know she lies *Pass. Pil.* 2
She thinks me young, Although I know my years be past the best 6
The truth I shall not know, but live in doubt 27
If knowledge be the mark, to know thee shall suffice 63
The cock that treads them shall not know 338
These are certain signs to know Faithful friend from flattering foe 429
Knowest. Thou know'st not what it is With javelin's point a churlish swine to gore *Ven. and Adon.* 615
Thou dost love her, because thou know'st I love her *Sonnet* 42 6
And like enough thou know'st thy estimate 87 2
For well thou know'st to my dear doting heart Thou art the fairest 131 3
In loving thee thou know'st I am forsworn 152 1
Knowing. She thought he blush'd, as knowing Tarquin's lust *Lucrece* 1354
Knowing a better spirit doth use your name *Sonnet* 80 2
Thyself thou gavest, thy own worth then not knowing 87 9
Knowing thy will, I will acquaintance strangle and look strange 89 7
Knowing thy heart torments me with disdain 132 2
Knowledge. From thine eyes my knowledge I derive, And, constant stars, in them I read such art 14 9
I ensconce me here Within the knowledge of mine own desert 49 10
Thou art as fair in knowledge as in hue 82 5
If knowledge be the mark, to know thee shall suffice *Pass. Pil.* 63
Known. Shameful it is; ay, if the fact be known *Lucrece* 239
It is a greater grief To bear love's wrong than hate's known injury *Sonnet* 40 12
All our pleasure known to us poor swains *Pass. Pil.* 289

L

Labour. Each passion labours so, That every present sorrow seemeth chief *Ven. and Adon.* 969
The dire imagination she did follow This sound of hope doth labour to expel 976
My sighs, like whirlwinds, labour hence to heave thee *Lucrece* 586
Like an unpractised swimmer plunging still, With too much labour drowns 1099
Get me hither paper, ink, and pen: Yet save that labour, for I have them here 1290
But, O my sweet, what labour is't to leave The thing we have not *Lov. Comp.* 239
Laboured. In him the painter labour'd with his skill To hide deceit *Lucrece* 1506
Labouring. There might you see the labouring pioner 1380
How are our brains beguiled, Which, labouring for invention, bear amiss *Sonnet* 59 3
Labouring in moe pleasures to bestow them Than the true gouty landlord which doth owe them *Lov. Comp.* 139
Labyrinth. The many musets through the which he goes Are like a labyrinth to amaze his foes *Ven. and Adon.* 684
Lace. That sin by him advantage should achieve And lace itself with his society *Sonnet* 67 4
Lack. Look, what a horse should have he did not lack *Ven. and Adon.* 299
To clip Elysium and to lack her joy 600
I sigh the lack of many a thing I sought *Sonnet* 30 3
Have eyes to wonder, but lack tongues to praise 106 14
No beauty lack, Slandering creation with a false esteem 127 11
Beauty herself is black And all they foul that thy complexion lack 132 14
Be the death-divining swan, Lest the requiem lack his right *Ph. and Tur.* 16
Lacked. Being had, to triumph, being lack'd, to hope *Sonnet* 52 14
When your countenance fill'd up his line, Then lack'd I matter 86 14
Love lack'd a dwelling, and made him her place *Lov. Comp.* 82
Lackey. Thou ceaseless lackey to eternity, With some mischance cross *Lucr.* 967
Lacking. Thick-sighted, barren, lean, and lacking juice *Ven. and Adon.* 136
Which I by lacking have supposed dead *Sonnet* 31 2
Lad. Did court the lad with many a lovely look *Pass. Pil.* 45
Laden. So full of fear As one with treasure laden, hemm'd with thieves *Ven. and Adon.* 1022
Lady. No, lady, no; my heart longs not to groan, But soundly sleeps 785
The quiet cabinet Where their dear governess and lady lies *Lucrece* 443
And sorts a sad look to her lady's sorrow 1221
But, lady, if your maid may be so bold 1282
Knights, by their oaths, should right poor ladies' harms 1694
Old rhyme In praise of ladies dead and lovely knights *Sonnet* 106 4
Ah, that I had my lady at this bay, To kiss and clip me till I run away! *Pass. Pil.* 155
Then, lullaby, the learned man hath got the lady gay 225
All my merry jigs are quite forgot, All my lady's love is lost, God wot 254
Where thy desert may merit praise, By ringing in thy lady's ear 326
Unless thy lady prove unjust, Press never thou to choose anew 331
Lagging. To hie as fast As lagging fowls before the northern blast *Lucrece* 1335
Laid. This plot of death when sadly she had laid 1212
Pawn'd honest looks, but laid no words to gage 1351
Or laid great bases for eternity, Which prove more short than waste *Son.* 125 3
A swallow'd bait On purpose laid to make the taker mad 129 8
Cupid laid by his brand, and fell asleep 153 1
Once asleep Laid by his side his heart-inflaming brand 154 2
And down I laid to list the sad-tuned tale *Lov. Comp.* 4
Lain. Had Collatinus kill'd my son or sire, Or lain in ambush to betray my life *Lucrece* 233
Lamb. The wolf would leave his prey And never fright the silly lamb that day *Ven. and Adon.* 1098
Now serves the season that they may surprise The silly lambs *Lucrece* 167
The wolf hath seized his prey, the poor lamb cries 677
She like a wearied lamb lies panting there 737
Thou set'st the wolf where he the lamb may get 878

Lamb. How many lambs might the stern wolf betray, If like a lamb he could his looks translate! *Sonnet* 96 9
Lame. The poor, lame, blind, halt, creep, cry out for thee *Lucrece* 902
So I, made lame by fortune's dearest spite *Sonnet* 37 3
So then I am not lame, poor, nor despised 37 9
Youth is full of sport, age's breath is short; Youth is nimble, age is lame *Pass. Pil.* 162
Lameness. Speak of my lameness, and I straight will halt, Against thy reasons making no defence *Sonnet* 89 3
Lament. And whom she finds forlorn she doth lament *Lucrece* 1500
My laments would be drawn out too long, To tell them all 1616
Lamentable. A thousand lamentable objects there, In scorn of nature 1373
Lamentations. Do not steep thy heart In such relenting dew of lamentations 1829
Lamenting Philomel had ended The well-tuned warble of her nightly sorrow 1079
I'll tune thy woes with my lamenting tongue 1465
Lamp. Were never four such lamps together mix'd, Had not his clouded with his brow's repine *Ven. and Adon.* 489
The lamp that burns by night Dries up his oil to lend the world his light 755
Patron of all light, From whom each lamp and shining star doth borrow 861
His eyes, Where, lo, two lamps, burnt out, in darkness lies 1128
Lance. Over my altars hath he hung his lance, His batter'd shield, his uncontrolled crest 103
Land. Huge rocks, high winds, strong pirates, shelves and sands, The merchant fears, ere rich at home he lands *Lucrece* 336
Her bare breast, the heart of all her land 439
For nimble thought can jump both sea and land As soon as think the place where he would be *Sonnet* 44 7
Of lands and mansions, theirs in thought assign'd *Lov. Comp.* 138
Landlord. Than the true gouty landlord which doth owe them 140
Language. And kissing speaks, with lustful language broken *Ven. and Adon.* 47
Languished. To me that languish'd for her sake *Sonnet* 145 3
Languisheth. Even so she languisheth in her mishaps *Ven. and Adon.* 603
Languishment. The dank earth weeps at thy languishment *Lucrece* 1130
Shall tune our heart-strings to true languishment 1141
Lank. With lank and lean discolour'd cheek, With heavy eye 708
Lap. Or from their proud lap pluck them where they grew *Sonnet* 98 8
Lapped. King Pandion he is dead; All thy friends are lapp'd in lead *Pass. Pil.* 396
Large. Thought kills me that I am not thought, To leap large lengths of miles when thou art gone *Sonnet* 44 10
Take heed, dear heart, of this large privilege 95 13
Wilt thou, whose will is large and spacious, Not once vouchsafe to hide my will in thine? 135 5
Add to thy 'Will' One will of mine, to make thy large 'Will' more 135 12
Why so large cost, having so short a lease? 146 5
Largeness. What largeness thinks in Paradise was sawn *Lov. Comp.* 91
Largess. Why dost thou abuse The bounteous largess given thee to give? *Sonnet* 4 6
Lark. Lo, here the gentle lark, weary of rest, From his moist cabinet mounts up on high *Ven. and Adon.* 853
Like to the lark at break of day arising *Sonnet* 29 11
I sit and mark, And wish her lays were tuned like the lark *Pass. Pil.* 198
Lascivious. Lascivious grace, in whom all ill well shows, Kill me with spites; yet we must not be foes *Sonnet* 40 13
Making lascivious comments on thy sport 95 6
Lass. Farewell, sweet lass, Thy like ne'er was For a sweet content *Pass. Pil.* 293
Last. Even as the sun with purple-colour'd face Had ta'en his last leave of the weeping morn *Ven. and Adon.* 2
Would they not wish the feast might ever last? 447
And as they last, their verdure still endure 507
Dissolves with tempering, And yields at last to every light impression 566
Yet love breaks through and picks them all at last 576

Last. Thy violent vanities can never last . . . . . *Lucrece* 894
At last she thus begins : 'Thou worthy lord Of that unworthy wife' . . 1303
At last she calls to mind where hangs a piece Of skilful painting . . 1366
At last she sees a wretched image bound, That piteous looks . . 1501
At last she smilingly with this gives o'er 1567
At last he takes her by the bloodless hand, And thus begins . . 1597
O time, cease thou thy course and last no longer 1765
At last it rains, and busy winds give o'er 1790
What wealth she had In days long since, before these last so bad *Sonnet* 67 14
If thou wilt leave me, do not leave me last 90 9
Though Reason weep, and cry 'It is thy last' . . . *Lov. Comp.* 168
She bade love last, and yet she fell a-turning . . . . *Pass. Pil.* 100
Lasting. Poor wasting monuments of lasting moans . . . *Lucrece* 798
Else lasting shame On thee and thine this night I will inflict . . 1629
Through her wounds doth fly Life's lasting date 1729
Full character'd with lasting memory . . . . *Sonnet* 122 2
Latch. Which with a yielding latch, and with no more, Hath barr'd him from the blessed thing he sought . . . . . *Lucrece* 339
This said, his guilty hand pluck'd up the latch 358
For it no form delivers to the heart Of bird, of flower, or shape, which it doth latch . . . . *Sonnet* 113 6
Late. And all amazed brake off his late intent . . *Ven. and Adon.* 469
The owl, night's herald, shrieks, ''Tis very late' 531
Whereat the impartial gazer late did wonder 748
She hears a merry horn, Whereat she leaps that was but late forlorn . . 1026
Their virtue lost, wherein they late excell'd 1131
His eye, which late this mutiny restrains, Unto a greater uproar tempts his veins . . . . *Lucrece* 426
The help that thou shalt lend me Comes all too late, yet let the traitor die . 1686
I did give that life Which she too early and too late hath spill'd . 1801
By chaste Lucrece' soul that late complain'd Her wrongs to us . . 1839
Bare ruin'd choirs, where late the sweet birds sang . . *Sonnet* 73 4
Which late her noble suit in court did shun . . . *Lov. Comp.* 234
Then too late she will repent That thus dissembled her delight . *Pass. Pil.* 313
Late-embarked. Gazing upon a late-embarked friend . . *Ven. and Adon.* 818
Late-sacked. Like a late-sack'd island, vastly stood Bare . . *Lucrece* 1740
Lattice. Some beauty peep'd through lattice of sear'd age . *Lov. Comp.* 14
Laud. Thou back'st reproach against long-living laud . . *Lucrece* 622
Thou plantest scandal and displacest laud 887
Laugh. That laughs and weeps, and all but with a breath *Ven. and Adon.* 414
Nor laugh with his companions at thy state . . . *Lucrece* 1066
To make the weeper laugh, the laugher weep . . . *Lov. Comp.* 124
Laughed. Hunting he loved, but love he laugh'd to scorn *Ven. and Adon.* 4
That heavy Saturn laugh'd and leap'd with him . . . *Sonnet* 98 4
Laugher. To make the weeper laugh, the laugher weep . . *Lov. Comp.* 124
Laund. And homeward through the dark laund runs apace *Ven. and Adon.* 813
Laundering the silken figures in the brine That season'd woe had pelleted in tears . . . . *Lov. Comp.* 17
Law. By law of nature thou art bound to breed . . *Ven. and Adon.* 171
Poor queen of love, in thine own law forlorn, To love a cheek that smiles at thee in scorn ! 251
And dotes on what he looks, 'gainst law or duty . . . *Lucrece* 497
Pleads, in a wilderness where are no laws, To the rough beast . . 544
By holy human law, and common troth, By heaven and earth . . . 571
'Tis thou that spurn'st at right, at law, at reason 880
Since that my case is past the help of law 1022
Grief dallied with nor law nor limit knows 1120
To leave poor me thou hast the strength of laws . . . *Sonnet* 49 13
Of wealth, of filial fear, law, kindred, fame . . . *Lov. Comp.* 270
Lawful. Her rosy cheek lies under, Cozening the pillow of a lawful kiss *Lucrece* 387
A little harm done to a great good end For lawful policy remains enacted . 529
To eat up errors by opinion bred, Not spend the dowry of a lawful bed . 938
Thy adverse party is thy advocate—And 'gainst myself a lawful plea commence . . . . *Sonnet* 35 11
To guard the lawful reasons on thy part 49 12
Be it lawful I love thee, as thou lovest those Whom thine eyes woo . 142 9
Lawn. A sudden pale, Like lawn being spread upon the blushing rose, Usurps her cheek . . . . *Ven. and Adon.* 590
First red as roses that on lawn we lay, Then white as lawn, the roses took away . . . . *Lucrece* 258
Lay. For where they lay the shadow had forsook them . *Ven. and Adon.* 176
Even so confounded in the dark she lay 827
The boy that by her side lay kill'd Was melted like a vapour from her sight 1165
And in his blood that on the ground lay spill'd, A purple flower sprung up 1167
First red as roses that on lawn we lay, Then white as lawn, the roses took away . . . . *Lucrece* 258
Canopied in darkness sweetly lay, Till they might open to adorn the day . 398
'For day,' quoth she, 'night's scapes doth open lay' 747
If, Collatine, thine honour lay in me, From me by strong assault it is bereft 834
Poor helpless help, the treasure stol'n away, To burn the guiltless casket where it lay ! 1057
Like a goodly champaign plain, Lays open all the little worms that creep . 1248
And on that pillow lay Where thou wast wont to rest thy weary head . 1620
One doth call her his, the other his, Yet neither may possess the claim they lay 1794
And both for my sake lay on me this cross . . . *Sonnet* 42 12
Yet nor the lays of birds nor the sweet smell Of different flowers . 98 5
Sing to the ear that doth thy lays esteem 100 7
Beauty no pencil [needs], beauty's truth to lay 101 7
In the spring When I was wont to greet it with my lays . . . 102 6
Call not me to justify the wrong That thy unkindness lays upon my heart 139 2
I sit and mark, And wish her lays were tuned like the lark . . *Pass. Pil.* 198
The bird of loudest lay On the sole Arabian tree . . . *Ph. and Tur.* 1
Lazy. With a lazy spright, And with a heavy, dark, disliking eye *V. and A.* 181
Lead. Mine eyes are turn'd to fire, my heart to lead : Heavy heart's lead, melt at mine eyes' red fire ! 1072
For never-resting time leads summer on To hideous winter . . *Sonnet* 5 5
And chide thy beauty and thy straying youth, Who lead thee in their riot 41 11
How many gazers mightst thou lead away ! 96 11
Yet none knows well To shun the heaven that leads men to this hell . 129 14
King Pandion he is dead ; All thy friends are lapp'd in lead . . *Pass. Pil.* 396
Leaden. With leaden appetite, unapt to toy . . . *Ven. and Adon.* 34
Now leaden slumber with life's strength doth fight . . . *Lucrece* 124
Leader. And these mine eyes, true leaders to their queen, But for thy piteous lips no more had seen . . . . . . *Ven. and Adon.* 503
Who, flatter'd by their leader's jocund show, Stuff up his lust . *Lucrece* 296
Leadeth. The path is smooth that leadeth on to danger . *Ven. and Adon.* 788
Leadeth. Affection is my captain, and he leadeth . . . . *Lucrece* 271
Leading. Leading him prisoner in a red-rose chain . . *Ven. and Adon.* 110
His eye commends the leading to his hand . . . . *Lucrece* 436
Leaf. Who plucks the bud before one leaf put forth ? . *Ven. and Adon.* 416
And soon bereaves, As caterpillars do the tender leaves . . . 798
No flower was nigh, no grass, herb, leaf, or weed, But stole his blood . 1055
The bark peel'd from the lofty pine, His leaves will wither . . *Lucrece* 1168
Sap check'd with frost and lusty leaves quite gone . . . *Sonnet* 5 7
When lofty trees I see barren of leaves 12 5
Great princes' favourites their fair leaves spread 25 5
When yellow leaves, or none, or few, do hang Upon those boughs . 73 2
The vacant leaves thy mind's imprint will bear 77 3
With so dull a cheer That leaves look pale, dreading the winter's near . 97 14
Study his bias leaves, and makes his book thine eyes . . *Pass. Pil.* 61
Through the velvet leaves the wind, All unseen, gan passage find . . 231
A cap of flowers, and a kirtle Embroider'd all with leaves of myrtle . . 364
League. That now he vows a league, and now invasion . . *Lucrece* 287
But they must ope, this blessed league to kill 383
This forced league doth force a further strife 689
Betwixt mine eye and heart a league is took . . . *Sonnet* 47 1
Lean. These blue-vein'd violets whereon we lean Never can blab, nor know not what we mean . . . . *Ven. and Adon.* 125
Rheumatic and cold, Thick-sighted, barren, lean, and lacking juice . . 136
'Ugly, meagre, lean, Hateful divorce of love,'—thus chides she Death . 931
With lank and lean discolour'd cheek, With heavy eye . . . *Lucrece* 708
Lean penury within that pen doth dwell . . . . *Sonnet* 84 5
Leaned. Here one man's hand lean'd on another's head . . *Lucrece* 1415
She, poor bird, as all forlorn, Lean'd her breast up-till a thorn *Pass. Pil.* 382
Leaning. Each leaning on their elbows and their hips *Ven. and Adon.* 44
Leap. Imperiously he leaps, he neighs, he bounds 265
Anon he rears upright, curvets, and leaps 279
She hears a merry horn, Whereat she leaps that was but late forlorn . 1026
From their dark beds once more leap her eyes 1050
She wakes her heart by beating on her breast, And bids it leap from thence *Lucrece* 760
Thought kills me that I am not thought, To leap large lengths of miles when thou art gone . . . . *Sonnet* 44 10
Do I envy those jacks that nimble leap To kiss the tender inward of thy hand ! 128 5
Beasts did leap, and birds did sing, Trees did grow, and plants did spring *Pass. Pil.* 377
Leaped. And now this lustful lord leap'd from his bed . . *Lucrece* 169
That heavy Saturn laugh'd and leap'd with him . . . *Sonnet* 98 4
Learn of him, I heartily beseech thee, To take advantage on presented joy *Ven. and Adon.* 404
O, learn to love ; the lesson is but plain, And once made perfect, never lost again 407
Princes are the glass, the school, the book, Where subjects' eyes do learn, do read, do look . . . . *Lucrece* 616
And wilt thou be the school where Lust shall learn ? 617
O, learn to read what silent love hath writ . . . . *Sonnet* 23 13
But thence I learn, and find the lesson true 118 13
Learned. And for my sake hath learn'd to sport and dance, To toy, to wanton, dally, smile, and jest . . . . . *Ven. and Adon.* 105
Foul sin may say, He learn'd to sin, and thou didst teach the way *Lucrece* 630
That know not how To cipher what is writ in learned books . . . 811
Have added feathers to the learned's wing . . . . *Sonnet* 78 7
He learn'd but surety-like to write for me 134 7
Well learned is that tongue that well can thee commend . . *Pass. Pil.* 64
Then, lullaby, the learned man hath got the lady gay 225
Learning. The vacant leaves thy mind's imprint will bear, And of this book this learning mayst thou taste . . . . . . *Sonnet* 77 4
Thou art all my art and dost advance As high as learning my rude ignorance 78 14
Which by a gift of learning did bear the maid away . . . *Pass. Pil.* 224
Lease. So should that beauty which you hold in lease Find no determination *Sonnet* 13 5
Summer's lease hath all too short a date 18 4
Can yet the lease of my true love control 107 3
That heretic, Which works on leases of short-number'd hours . . 124 10
Why so large cost, having so short a lease ? 146 5
Least. Not the least of all these maladies But in one minute's fight brings beauty under . . . . *Ven. and Adon.* 745
To clear this spot by death, At least I give A badge of fame to slander's livery . . . . *Lucrece* 1053
Or at the least this refuge let me find 1654
Be, as thy presence is, gracious and kind, Or to thyself at least kind-hearted prove . . . . *Sonnet* 10 12
With what I most enjoy contented least 29 8
Then need I not to fear the worst of wrongs, When in the least of them my life hath end 92 6
Or at the least, so long as brain and heart Have faculty by nature to subsist 122 5
A true soul When most impeach'd stands least in thy control . . 125 14
Leathern. Servilely master'd with a leathern rein ! . . *Ven. and Adon.* 392
Leave. Even as the sun with purple-colour'd face Had ta'en his last leave of the weeping morn 2
I pray you hence, and leave me here alone 382
Let us part, And leave this idle theme, this bootless chat . . . 422
Chiefly in love, whose leave exceeds commission 568
'Where did I leave ?' 'No matter where ;' quoth he, 'Leave me' . . 715
Leaves Love upon her back deeply distress'd 814
Bids them leave quaking, bids them fear no more 899
If he had spoke, the wolf would leave his prey 1097
Lust-breathed Tarquin leaves the Roman host . . . . *Lucrece* 3
In venturing ill we leave to be The things we are for that which we expect . 148
Thyself art mighty ; for thine own sake leave me : Myself a weakling . 583
He cannot use it, And leaves it to be master'd by his young . . . 863
Why pry'st thou through my window ? leave thy peeping . . . 1089
Leave the faltering feeble souls alive 1768
What acceptable audit canst thou leave ? . . . . . *Sonnet* 4 12
Were it not thy sour leisure gave sweet leave To entertain the time . 39 10
When a woman woos, what woman's son Will sourly leave her till she have prevailed ? 41 8
To leave poor me thou hast the strength of laws 49 13
Towards thee I'll run, and give him leave to go 51 14
From these would I be gone, Save that, to die, I leave my love alone . 66 14
Which makes thy love more strong, To love that well which thou must leave ere long 73 14
If thou wilt leave me, do not not leave me last 90 9

Leave. My verse to constancy confined, One thing expressing, leaves out difference *Sonnet* 105 8
To leave for nothing all thy sum of good 109 12
Who leaves unsway'd the likeness of a man 141 11
But, O my sweet, what labour is't to leave The thing we have not *L. Comp.* 239
And supplicant their sighs to you extend, To leave the battery that you make 'gainst mine 277
And he takes and leaves, In either's aptness, as it best deceives 305
To leave the master loveless, or kill the gallant knight *Pass. Pil.* 216
Leaving. Leaving his spoil perplex'd in greater pain *Lucrece* 733
If thou shouldst depart, Leaving thee living in posterity *Sonnet* 6 12
To eternity doth rest, Leaving no posterity *Ph. and Tur.* 59
Lecher. And so did kill The lechers in their deed *Lucrece* 1637
She fell a-turning. Was this a lover, or a lecher whether? *Pass. Pil.* 101
Lectures. Must he in thee read lectures of such shame? *Lucrece* 618
Led. Thus madly led, The Roman lord marcheth to Lucrece' bed 300
Leese. Flowers distill'd, though they with winter meet, Leese but their show *Sonnet* 5 14
Left. Can thy right hand seize love upon thy left? *Ven. and Adon.* 158
Thou dost survive, In that thy likeness still is left alive 174
With her the horse, and left Adonis there, As they were mad 322
And nothing but the very smell were left me 441
Left their round turrets destitute and pale *Lucrece* 441
She bears the load of lust he left behind 734
I, a drone-like bee, Have no perfection of my summer left 837
Himself, behind, Was left unseen, save to the eye of mind 1426
From the purple fountain Brutus drew The murderous knife, and as it left the place, Her blood, in poor revenge, held it in chase 1735
Then, were not summer's distillation left, A liquid prisoner *Sonnet* 5 9
And still weep That thou no form of thee hast left behind 9 6
Mine only care, Art left the prey of every vulgar thief 48 8
Since I left you, mine eye is in my mind 113 1
Angry that his prescriptions are not kept, Hath left me 147 7
He saw more wounds than one, And blushing fled, and left her all alone *Pass. Pil.* 130
Leftest. For why thou left'st me nothing in thy will: And yet thou left'st me more than I did crave 138
Leg. High crest, short ears, straight legs, and passing strong *Ven. and Adon.* 297
Stands on his hinder legs with listening ear, To hearken 698
Each envious brier his weary legs doth scratch, Each shadow makes him stop 705
A hand, a foot, a face, a leg, a head, Stood for the whole to be imagined *Lucrece* 1427
Legacy. Dear lord of that dear jewel I have lost, What legacy shall I bequeath to thee? 1192
Why dost thou spend Upon thyself thy beauty's legacy? *Sonnet* 4 2
Legions. That fire Which many legions of true hearts had warm'd 154 6
Leisure. And pay them at thy leisure, one by one *Ven. and Adon.* 518
Debate where leisure serves with dull debaters *Lucrece* 1019
Were it not thy sour leisure gave sweet leave To entertain the time *Son.* 39 10
I must attend time's leisure with my moan 44 12
Being your vassal, bound to stay your leisure 58 4
And I, a tyrant, have no leisure taken 120 7
Or my affection put to the smallest teen, Or any of my leisures ever charm'd *Lov. Comp.* 193
Leisurely. While others saucily Promise more speed, but do it leisurely *Lucrece* 1349
Lend. Being so enraged, desire doth lend her force Courageously to pluck him from his horse *Ven. and Adon.* 29
Her arms do lend his neck a sweet embrace; Incorporate then they seem 539
The lamp that burns by night Dries up his oil to lend the world his light 756
Your device in love, That lends embracements unto every stranger 790
There lives a son . . . May lend thee light, as thou dost lend to other 864
O, how her eyes and tears did lend and borrow! 961
No comfortable star did lend his light *Lucrece* 164
Fair torch, burn out thy light, and lend it not 190
Lending him wit that to bad debtors lends 964
The blushing morrow Lends light to all fair eyes that light will borrow 1083
The painter was no god to lend her those 1461
She lends them words, and she their looks doth borrow 1498
The help that thou shalt lend me Comes all too late, yet let the traitor die 1685
Nature's bequest gives nothing but doth lend, And being frank she lends to those are free *Sonnet* 4 3
The offender's sorrow lends but weak relief 34 11
Since every one hath, every one, one shade, And you, but one, can every shadow lend 53 4
He lends thee virtue and he stole that word From thy behaviour 79 9
When they have devised What strained touches rhetoric can lend 82 10
That to his subject lends not some small glory 84 6
Some worthless song, Darkening thy power to lend base subjects light 100 4
Lest sorrow lend me words and words express The manner of my pity-wanting pain 140 3
Anon their gazes lend To every place at once, and, nowhere fix'd *Lov. Comp.* 26
Lendeth. Dear lord, thy sorrow to my sorrow lendeth Another power *Lucr.* 1676
Lending him wit that to bad debtors lends 964
Lending soft audience to my sweet design *Lov. Comp.* 278
Length. Through the length of times he stands disgraced *Lucrece* 718
At length address'd to answer his desire, She modestly prepares 1606
Thought kills me that I am not thought, To leap large lengths of miles when thou art gone *Sonnet* 44 10
Short, night, to-night, and length thyself to-morrow *Pass. Pil.* 210
Her feeble force will yield at length, When craft hath taught her 319
Lent. He vails his tail that, like a falling plume, Cool shadow to his melting buttock lent *Ven. and Adon.* 315
If love have lent you twenty thousand tongues 775
What priceless wealth the heavens had him lent *Lucrece* 17
Draw not thy sword to guard iniquity, For it was lent thee all that brood to kill 627
The mild glance that sly Ulysses lent Show'd deep regard 1399
A wretched image bound, That piteous looks to Phrygian shepherds lent 1502
Figuring that they their passions likewise lent me Of grief and blushes, aptly understood *Lov. Comp.* 199
Less. And so, by hoping more, they have but less *Lucrece* 137
If it should be told, The repetition cannot make it less 1285
Be scorn'd like old men of less truth than tongue *Sonnet* 17 10
An eye more bright than theirs, less false in rolling 20 5
Both grace and faults are loved of more and less 96 3
I love not less, though less the show appear 102 2
Not that the summer is less pleasant now 102 9
What we see doth lie, Made more or less by thy continual haste 123 12
Less. And so much less of shame in me remains *Lov. Comp.* 188
Lesser. This moves in him more rage and lesser pity, To make the breach and enter this sweet city *Lucrece* 468
The lesser thing should not the greater hide 663
Deep sounds make lesser noise than shallow fords 1329
'Tis the lesser sin That mine eye loves it and doth first begin *Sonnet* 114 13
Lesson. The lesson is but plain, And once made perfect, never lost again *Ven. and Adon.* 407
But thence I learn, and find the lesson true *Sonnet* 118 13
Lest. O, give it me, lest thy hard heart do steel it *Ven. and Adon.* 375
Lest Jealousy, that sour unwelcome guest, Should, by his stealing in, disturb the feast 449
Make modest Dian cloudy and forlorn, Lest she should steal a kiss 726
Lest the deceiving harmony should run Into the quiet closure of my breast 781
Where, lest between them both it should be kill'd, The coward captive vanquished doth yield *Lucrece* 74
Lest he should hold it her own gross abuse 1315
Lest my bewailed guilt should do thee shame *Sonnet* 36 10
Lest the wise world should look into your moan And mock you 71 13
Lest the world should task you to recite What merit lived in me 72 1
Lest your true love may seem false in this 72 9
Lest I, too much profane, should do it wrong 89 11
Lest sorrow lend me words and words express The manner of my pity-wanting pain 140 3
Thou keep'st me blind, Lest eyes well-seeing thy foul faults should find 148 14
Urge not my amiss, Lest guilty of my faults thy sweet self prove 151 4
Smooth not thy tongue with filed talk, Lest she some subtle practice smell *Pass. Pil.* 307
Enough, too much, I fear; Lest that my mistress hear my song 348
Be the death-divining swan, Lest the requiem lack his right *Ph. and Tur.* 16
Let. Make use of time, let not advantage slip *Ven. and Adon.* 129
He cries, 'let go, and let me go; My day's delight is past' 379
Let me excuse thy courser, gentle boy; And learn of him 403
Let us part, And leave this idle theme, this bootless chat 421
O, never let their crimson liveries wear! 506
Now let me say 'Good night,' and so say you; If you will say so. 535
Let me go; You have no reason to withhold me so. 611
O, let him keep his loathsome cabin still. 637
My heart stands armed in mine ear, And will not let a false sound enter there 780
Unwisely did not let To praise the clear unmatched red and white *Lucrece* 10
Would let him go, Rather than triumph in so false a foe 76
Let fair humanity abhor the deed 195
As those bars which stop the hourly dial, Who with a lingering stay his course doth let 328
'So, so,' quoth he, 'these lets attend the time, Like little frosts' 330
Let him return, and flattering thoughts retire 641
My uncontrolled tide Turns not, but swells the higher by this let 646
So let thy thoughts, low vassals to thy state 666
Let their exhaled unwholesome breaths make sick The life of purity 779
Let thy misty vapours march so thick 782
Let my good name, that senseless reputation, For Collatine's dear love be kept unspotted 820
Let ghastly shadows his lewd eyes affright 971
Let there bechance him pitiful mischances, To make him moan 976
Let mild women to him lose their mildness 979
Let him have time to tear his curled hair, Let him have time against himself to rave 981
Let him have time of Time's help to despair, Let him have time to live a loathed slave 983
Let him have time a beggar's orts to crave 985
Let him have time to see his friends his foes 988
Let him have time to mark how slow time goes In time of sorrow 990
And ever let his unrecalling crime Have time to wail 993
At his own shadow let the thief run mad 997
The remedy indeed to do me good Is to let forth my foul-defiled blood 1029
Since men prove beasts, let beasts bear gentle minds 1148
Let it not be call'd impiety, If in this blemish'd fort I make some hole 1174
O, let it not be hild Poor women's faults, that they are so fulfill'd With men's abuses 1257
Let sin, alone committed, light alone Upon his head that hath transgressed so 1480
Let guiltless souls be freed from guilty woe 1482
She modestly prepares to let them know Her honour is ta'en prisoner 1607
This refuge let me find; Though my gross blood be stain'd with this abuse 1654
Let it then suffice To drown one woe, one pair of weeping eyes 1679
Let no mourner say He weeps for her, for she was only mine 1797
Let not winter's ragged hand deface In thee thy summer *Sonnet* 6 1
Thou shouldst print more, not let that copy die 11 14
Who lets so fair a house fall to decay? 13 9
My love you know You had a father: let your son say so 13 14
O, let me, true in love, but truly write, And then believe me 21 9
Let them say more that like of hearsay well 21 13
Let my books be then the eloquence And dumb presagers 23 9
Let those who are in favour with their stars Of public honour and proud titles boast 25 1
To let base clouds o'ertake me in my way 34 3
Let this sad interim like the ocean be Which parts the shore 56 9
But let your love even with my life decay 71 12
Let him but copy what in you is writ 84 9
Let not my love be call'd idolatry, Nor my beloved as an idol show 105 1
Let me not to the marriage of true minds Admit impediments 116 1
Let me be obsequious in thy heart, And take thou my oblation 125 9
O, let it then as well beseem thy heart To mourn for me 132 10
Let no unkind, no fair beseechers kill 135 13
Let me excuse thee: ah! my love well knows Her pretty looks have been mine enemies 139 9
Like usury, applying wet to wet, Or monarch's hands that let not bounty fall Where want cries some *Lov. Comp.* 41
And had let go by The swiftest hours 59
Let it not tell your judgement I am old 73
Letter. By and by, to bear A letter to my lord, my love, my dear *Lucrece* 1293
To shun this blot, she would not blot the letter with words 1322
Her letter now is seal'd, and on it writ 'At Ardea to my lord' 1331
Found yet moe letters sadly penn'd in blood *Lov. Comp.* 47
Level. Bring me within the level of your frown *Sonnet* 117 11
I am that I am, and they that level At my abuses reckon up their own 121 9
That not a heart which in his level came Could 'scape *Lov. Comp.* 309
Levelled. Sometimes her levell'd eyes their carriage ride 22
Whose sights till then were levell'd on my face 282

Lewd. She lies, To be admired of lewd unhallow'd eyes *Lucrece* 392
Let ghastly shadows his lewd eyes affright 971
Liberty. Those pretty wrongs that liberty commits *Sonnet* 41 1
O, let me suffer, being at your beck, The imprison'd absence of your liberty 58 6
And now, to tempt, all liberty procured *Lov. Comp.* 252
Licking. And there another licking of his wound *Ven. and Adon.* 915
Lie. Panting he lies and breatheth in her face 62
Look, how a bird lies tangled in a net, So fasten'd in her arms Adonis lies 67
Hold up thy head: Look in mine eye-balls, there thy beauty lies 119
Witness this primrose bank whereon I lie 151
And, lo, I lie between that sun and thee 194
Graze on my lips; and if those hills be dry, Stray lower, where the pleasant fountains lie 234
Foreknowing well, if there he came to lie, Why, there Love lived and there he could not die 245
On the grass she lies as she were slain, Till his breath breatheth life in her again 473
Within my bosom, whereon thou dost lie, My boding heart pants 646
On his back doth lie An image like thyself, all stain'd with gore 663
Lie quietly, and hear a little more; Nay, do not struggle 709
Love is all truth, Lust full of forged lies 804
His eyes, Where, lo, two lamps, burnt out, in darkness lies 1128
As one of which doth Tarquin lie revolving The sundry dangers *Lucrece* 127
Fearing some hard news from the warlike band, Where her beloved Collatinus lies 256
Then who fears sinking where such treasure lies? 280
He takes it from the rushes where it lies 318
Fearing no such thing, Lies at the mercy of his mortal sting 364
Her lily hand her rosy cheek lies under, Cozening the pillow of a lawful kiss 386
Where, like a virtuous monument, she lies, To be admired 391
The quiet cabinet Where their dear governess and lady lies 443
Like to a new-kill'd bird she trembling lies; She dares not look 457
So under his insulting falchion lies Harmless Lucretia 509
She like a wearied lamb lies panting there 737
Immodestly lies martyr'd with disgrace 802
They whose guilt within their bosoms lie Imagine every eye beholds their blame 1342
Which bleeding under Pyrrhus' proud foot lies 1449
Here friend by friend in bloody channel lies 1487
If in the child the father's image lies, Where shall I live now Lucrece is unlived? 1753
Making a famine where abundance lies *Sonnet* 1 7
Where all thy beauty lies, Where all the treasure of thy lusty days 2 5
The age to come would say 'This poet lies' 17 7
To find where your true image pictured lies 24 6
And in themselves their pride lies buried 25 7
Which now appear But things removed that hidden in thee lie 31 8
My heart doth plead that thou in him dost lie 46 5
The defendant doth that plea deny And says in him thy fair appearance lies 46 8
My grief lies onward and my joy behind 50 14
Where, alack, Shall Time's best jewel from Time's chest lie hid? 65 10
Unless you would devise some virtuous lie, To do more for me 72 5
Such fire That on the ashes of his youth doth lie 73 10
When you entombed in men's eyes shall lie 81 8
Thou canst not vex me with inconstant mind, Since that my life on thy revolt doth lie 92 10
'T lies in thee To make him much outlive a gilded tomb 101 10
As easy might I from myself depart As from my soul, which in thy breast doth lie 109 4
Those lines that I before have writ do lie 115 1
For thy records and what we see doth lie 123 11
See where it lies, Yet what the best is take the worst to be 137 3
I do believe her, though I know she lies 138 2
Therefore I lie with her and she with me, And in our faults by lies we flatter'd be 138 13
To make me give the lie to my true sight 150 3
More perjured I, To swear against the truth so foul a lie! 152 14
The bath for my help lies Where Cupid got new fire—my mistress' eyes 153 13
Thou register of lies, What unapproved witness dost thou bear! *Lov. Comp.* 52
What a hell of witchcraft lies In the small orb of one particular tear! 288
I do believe her, though I know she lies *Pass. Pil.* 2
Therefore I'll lie with love, and love with me 13
As flowers dead lie wither'd on the ground 177
Grace in all simplicity, Here enclosed in cinders lie *Ph. and Tur.* 55
Life. Nature that made thee, with herself at strife, Saith that the world hath ending with thy life *Ven. and Adon.* 12
And were I not immortal, life were done Between this heavenly and earthly sun 197
Look, when a painter would surpass the life, In limning out a well-proportion'd steed 289
For I have heard it is a life in death, That laughs and weeps 413
Till his breath breatheth life in her again 474
Do I delight to die, or life desire? But now I lived, and life was death's annoy 496
Or butcher-sire that reaves his son of life 766
Now leaden slumber with life's strength doth fight *Lucrece* 124
The aim of all is but to nurse the life With honour, wealth, and ease 141
As life for honour in fell battle's rage; Honour for wealth 145
Had Collatinus kill'd my son or sire, Or lain in ambush to betray my life 233
Lucrece to their sight Must sell her joy, her life, her world's delight 385
Showing life's triumph in the map of death, And death's dim look in life's mortality 402
There were no strife, But that life lived in death, and death in life 406
To kill thine honour with thy life's decay 516
Thou their fair life, and they thy fouler grave 661
But she hath lost a dearer thing than life 687
The life of purity, the supreme fair 780
We have no good that we can say is ours, But ill-annexed Opportunity Or kills his life or else his quality 875
I live, and seek in vain Some happy mean to end a hapless life 1045
A badge of fame to slander's livery; A dying life to living infamy 1055
Till life to death acquit my forced offence 1071
To live or die which of the twain were better, When life is shamed 1155
'Tis honour to deprive dishonour'd life; The one will live, the other being dead 1186
My life's foul deed, my life's fair end shall free it 1208
The life and feeling of her passion She hoards, to spend when he is by. 1317
God wot, it was defect Of spirit, life, and bold audacity 1346
Life. In scorn of nature, art gave lifeless life *Lucrece* 1374
Show'd life imprison'd in a body dead 1456
And one man's lust these many lives confounds 1489
Through her wounds doth fly Life's lasting date 1729
That life was mine which thou hast here deprived 1752
I did give that life Which she too early and too late hath spill'd 1800
The dispersed air, who, holding Lucrece' life, Answer'd their cries 1805
Is it for fear to wet a widow's eye That thou consumest thyself in single life? *Sonnet* 9 2
So should the lines of life that life repair 16 9
It is but as a tomb Which hides your life and shows not half your parts 17 4
So long lives this and this gives life to thee 18 14
In our two loves there is but one respect, Though in our lives a separable spite 36 6
My life, being made of four, with two alone Sinks down to death 45 7
Until life's composition be recured By those swift messengers return'd from thee 45 9
That he shall never cut from memory My sweet love's beauty, though my lover's life 63 12
The right of sepulchres, were shorn away, To live a second life on second head 68 7
But let your love even with my life decay 71 12
My life hath in this line some interest 74 3
So then thou hast but lost the dregs of life, The prey of worms 74 9
So are you to my thoughts as food to life 75 1
Your name from hence immortal life shall have 81 5
I impair not beauty being mute, When others would give life and bring a tomb 83 12
There lives more life in one of your fair eyes 83 13
For term of life thou art assured mine, And life no longer than thy love will stay 92 2
Then need I not to fear the worst of wrongs, When in the least of them my life hath end 92 6
Thou canst not vex me with inconstant mind, Since that my life on thy revolt doth lie 92 10
Give my love fame faster than Time wastes life 100 13
That did not better for my life provide Than public means 111 3
'I hate' from hate away she threw, And saved my life, saying 'not you' 145 14
Whilst many nymphs that vow'd chaste life to keep Came tripping by 154 3
His real habitude gave life and grace To appertainings *Lov. Comp.* 114
Lifeless. Fie, lifeless picture, cold and senseless stone *Ven. and Adon.* 211
In scorn of nature, art gave lifeless life *Lucrece* 1374
Life-poisoning pestilence and frenzies wood *Ven. and Adon.* 740
Lift. She lifts the coffer-lids that close his eyes 1127
In the orient when the gracious light Lifts up his burning head *Sonnet* 7 2
Light. Not gross to sink, but light, and will aspire *Ven. and Adon.* 150
Is love so light, sweet boy, and may it be That thou shouldst think it heavy unto thee? 155
Torches are made to light, jewels to wear, Dainties to taste 163
But hers, which through the crystal tears gave light, Shone like the moon in water seen by night 491
And coal-black clouds that shadow heaven's light Do summon us to part 533
Dissolves with tempering, And yields at last to every light impression 566
The lamp that burns by night Dries up his oil to lend the world his light 756
Their light blown out in some mistrustful wood 826
Patron of all light, From whom each lamp and shining star doth borrow 860
There lives a son ... May lend thee light, as thou dost lend to other 864
Away she flies; The grass stoops not, she treads on it so light 1028
Where they resign their office and their light 1039
Once more leap her eyes; And, being open'd, threw unwilling light 1051
This is my spite, That, thou being dead, the day should yet be light 1134
Through the empty skies In her light chariot quickly is convey'd 1192
Nor could she moralize his wanton sight, More than his eyes were open'd to the light *Lucrece* 105
No comfortable star did lend his light, No noise but owls' 164
Fair torch, burn out thy light, and lend it not To darken her whose light excelleth thine 190
My frail joints shake, Mine eyes forego their light, my false heart bleed 228
And being lighted, by the light he spies Lucretia's glove 316
His eyes begun To wink, being blinded with a greater light 375
Her eyes, like marigolds, had sheathed their light 397
Who, angry that the eyes fly from their lights, In darkness daunts them with more dreadful sights 461
Small lights are soon blown out, huge fires abide 647
He sets his foot upon the light, For light and lust are deadly enemies 673
He in his speed looks for the morning light 745
Foggy Night! ... Muster thy mists to meet the eastern light 773
That in their smoky ranks his smother'd light May set at noon 783
The light will show, character'd in my brow, The story 807
To unmask falsehood and bring truth to light 940
The blushing morrow Lends light to all fair eyes that light will borrow 1083
Brand not my forehead with thy piercing light 1091
Who in a salt-waved ocean quench their light 1231
And dying eyes gleam'd forth their ashy lights 1378
Through their light joy seem'd to appear, Like bright things stain'd, a kind of heavy fear 1434
Let sin, alone committed, light alone Upon his head that hath transgressed so 1480
In my chamber came A creeping creature, with a flaming light 1627
Feed'st thy light's flame with self-substantial fuel *Sonnet* 1 6
In the orient when the gracious light Lifts up his burning head 7 1
Who's so dumb that cannot write to thee, When thou thyself dost give invention light? 38 8
How would thy shadow's form form happy show To the clear day with thy much clearer light, When to unseeing eyes thy shade shines so! 43 7
Nativity, once in the main of light, Crawls to maturity 60 5
To set me light And place my merit in the eye of scorn 88 1
Darkening thy power to lend base subjects light 100 4
And every light occasion of the wind Upon his lips their silken parcels hurls *Lov. Comp.* 86
Lighted. And being lighted, by the light he spies Lucretia's glove *Lucrece* 316
Lighteth. Whereat a waxen torch forthwith he lighteth 178
Lightless. To Collatium bears the lightless fire 4
Such devils steal effects from lightless hell 1555
Lightning. But now her cheek was pale, and by and by It flash'd forth fire, as lightning from the sky *Ven. and Adon.* 348
Thine eye Jove's lightning seems, thy voice his dreadful thunder *Pass. Pil.* 67
Like. And like a bold-faced suitor 'gins to woo him. *Ven. and Adon.* 6
Like a dive-dapper peering through a wave, Who, being look'd on, ducks as quickly in 86

Like. Or, like a fairy, trip upon the green . . . *Ven. and Adon.* 146
Or, like a nymph, with long dishevell'd hair, Dance on the sands . 147
These forceless flowers like sturdy trees support me 152
Wishing Adonis had his team to guide, So he were like him and by Venus' side 180
His louring brows o'erwhelming his fair sight, Like misty vapours . 184
Thing like a man, but of no woman bred! Thou art no man . . 214
Sometimes her arms infold him like a band 225
The bearing earth . . . Whose hollow womb resounds like heaven's thunder 268
His eye, which scornfully glisters like fire, Shows his hot courage . 275
The high wind sings, Fanning the hairs, who wave like feather'd wings . 306
Then, like a melancholy malcontent, He vails his tail that, like a falling plume, Cool shadow to his melting buttock lent 313
And like a lowly lover down she kneels 350
Wilful and unwilling, Show'd like two silver doves that sit a-billing 366
How like a jade he stood, tied to the tree, Servilely master'd . . 391
When his glutton eye so full hath fed, His other agents aim at like delight . 400
Like a red morn, that ever yet betoken'd Wreck to the seaman . . 453
Or like the deadly bullet of a gun, His meaning struck her ere his words begun 461
Like the fair sun, when in his fresh array He cheers the morn and all the earth relieveth 483
The crystal tears gave light, Shone like the moon in water seen by night . 492
Like a wild bird being tamed with too much handling . . . 560
Or like the froward infant still'd with dandling, He now obeys . . 562
Affection faints not like a pale-faced coward 569
Like lawn being spread upon the blushing rose, Usurps her cheek . 590
He whetteth still, Like to a mortal butcher bent to kill . . . 618
His eyes, like glow-worms, shine when he doth fret . . . 621
Takes no rest, But, like an earthquake, shakes thee on my breast . 648
On his back doth lie An image like thyself, all stain'd with gore . 664
The many musets through the which he goes Are like a labyrinth . 684
Your treatise makes me like you worse and worse 774
Bewitching like the wanton mermaid's songs 777
Love comforteth like sunshine after rain, But Lust's effect is tempest after sun 799
Lust like a glutton dies; Love is all truth, Lust full of forged lies . 803
Like shrill-tongued tapsters answering every call 849
Like a milch doe, whose swelling dugs do ache, Hasting to feed her fawn . 875
Like one that spies an adder Wreathed up in fatal folds just in his way . 878
Like soldiers, when their captain once doth yield, They basely fly . 893
Bepainted all with red, Like milk and blood being mingled both together . 902
Haste is mated with delays, Like the proceedings of a drunken brain . 910
She vail'd her eyelids, who, like sluices, stopt The crystal tide . 956
But like a stormy day, now wind, now rain, Sighs dry her cheeks . 965
Then join they all together, Like many clouds consulting for foul weather . 972
Her tears began to turn their tide, Being prison'd in her eye like pearls in glass 980
Like stars ashamed of day, themselves withdrew 1032
Who, like a king perplexed in his throne, By their suggestion gives a deadly groan 1043
Sun and sharp air Lurk'd like two thieves, to rob him of his fair . 1086
Had I been tooth'd like him, I must confess, With kissing him I should have kill'd him first 1117
The boy that by her side lay kill'd Was melted like a vapour from her sight 1166
And doth so far proceed, That what is vile shows like a virtuous deed *Lucr.* 252
These lets attend the time, Like little frosts that sometime threat the spring 331
Like a virtuous monument, she lies, To be admired of lewd unhallow'd eyes 391
Whose perfect white Show'd like an April daisy on the grass . . 395
Her eyes, like marigolds, had sheathed their light 397
Her hair, like golden threads, play'd with her breath; O modest wantons! . 400
Her breasts, like ivory globes circled with blue, A pair of maiden worlds . 407
Like a foul usurper, went about From this fair throne to heave the owner out 412
And they, like straggling slaves for pillage fighting . . . 428
In a thousand fears, Like to a new-kill'd bird she trembling lies . 457
First, like a trumpet, doth his tongue begin To sound a parley . 470
Which, like a falcon towering in the skies, Coucheth the fowl below . 506
Like a white hind under the gripe's sharp claws, Pleads, in a wilderness where are no laws 543
Do not then ensnare me: Thou look'st not like deceit; do not deceive me . 585
My sighs, like whirlwinds, labour hence to heave thee . . . 586
Like a troubled ocean, Beat at thy rocky and wreck-threatening heart . 589
For kings like gods should govern every thing 602
Thou perforce must bear, When they in thee the like offences prove . 613
Till like a jade Self-will himself doth tire 707
Poor, and meek, Like to a bankrupt beggar wails his case . . 711
He like a thievish dog creeps sadly thence; She like a wearied lamb lies panting there 736
And grave, like water that doth eat in steel, Upon my cheeks . . 755
Like still-pining Tantalus he sits, And useless barns the harvest of his wits 858
But if the like the snow-white swan desire, The stain upon his silver down will stay 1011
Mine eyes, like sluices, As from a mountain-spring that feeds a dale . 1076
Like an unpractised swimmer plunging still With too much labour drowns . 1098
True sorrow then is feelingly sufficed When with like semblance it is sympathized 1113
Like a gentle flood, Who, being stopp'd, the bounding banks o'erflows . 1118
Distress likes dumps when time is kept with tears 1127
The sun being set, Each flower moisten'd like a melting eye . . 1227
Which makes the maid weep like the dewy night 1232
Like ivory conduits coral cisterns filling 1234
Like a goodly champaign plain, Lays open all the little worms that creep 1247
Much like a press of people at a door, Throng her inventions . . 1301
Like dying coals burnt out in tedious nights 1379
Seemed to appear, Like bright things stain'd, a kind of heavy fear . 1435
Like a heavy-hanging bell, Once set on ringing, with his own weight goes . 1493
Like a constant and confirmed devil, He entertain'd a show so seeming just 1513
Whose words like wildfire burnt the shining glory Of rich-built Ilion . 1523
Blue circles stream'd like rainbows in the sky 1587
Both stood, like old acquaintance in a trance, Met far from home . 1595
Like a late-sack'd island, vastly stood Bare and unpeopled . . 1740
With weary car, Like feeble age, he reeleth from the day . . *Sonnet* 7 10
The world will wail thee, like a makeless wife 9 4
Be scorn'd like old men of less truth than tongue 17 10
Let them say more that like of hearsay well 21 13
Like a jewel hung in ghastly night, Makes black night beauteous . . 27 11
Wishing me like to one more rich in hope, Featured like him, like him with friends possess'd. 29 5
Like to the lark at break of day arising From sullen earth . . . 29 11

Like. Like stones of worth they thinly placed are, Or captain jewels in the carcanet . . . . *Sonnet* 52 7
But you like none, none you, for constant heart 53 14
Let this sad interim like the ocean be Which parts the shore . . 56 9
Like a sad slave, stay and think of nought Save, where you are . . 57 11
Like as the waves make towards the pebbled shore 60 1
While shadows like to thee do mock my sight 61 4
Like unletter'd clerk still cry 'Amen' To every hymn . . . 85 6
And like enough thou know'st thy estimate 87 2
So shall I live, supposing thou art true, Like a deceived husband . 93 2
How like Eve's apple doth thy beauty grow! 93 13
Which, like a canker in the fragrant rose, Doth spot the beauty . 95 2
How many lambs might the stern wolf betray, If like a lamb he could his looks translate! 96 10
How like a winter hath my absence been From thee! 97 1
Like widow'd wombs after their lords' decease 97 8
Therefore like her I sometime hold my tongue 102 13
Yet doth beauty, like a dial-hand, Steal from his figure . . . 104 9
Like prayers divine, I must each day say o'er the very same. . . 108 5
If I have ranged, Like him that travels I return again . . . 109 6
My nature is subdued To what it works in, like the dyer's hand . 111 7
Whilst, like a willing patient, I will drink Potions of eisel . . 111 9
Like as, to make our appetites more keen, With eager compounds . 118 1
My mistress' eyes are nothing like the sun 130 1
And suit thy pity like in every part. 132 12
Which like two spirits do suggest me still 144 2
Who like a fiend From heaven to hell is flown away . . . 145 11
Like usury, applying wet to wet, Or monarch's hands that let not bounty fall . . . . *Lov. Comp.* 40
His phœnix down began but to appear Like unshorn velvet . . . 94
Like fools that in th' imagination set The goodly objects which abroad they find 136
Gave the tempter place, Which like a cherubin above them hover'd . 319
Two loves I have, of comfort and despair, That like two spirits do suggest me still . . . . *Pass. Pil.* 16
Those thoughts, to me like oaks, to thee like osiers bow'd . . . 60
Like a green plum that hangs upon a tree, And falls, through wind . 135
As if the boy should use like loving charms 150
Youth like summer morn, age like winter weather; Youth like summer brave, age like winter bare 159
'Wander,' a word for shadows like myself 191
I sit and mark, And wish her lays were tuned like the lark . . . 198
Like a thousand vanquish'd men in bloody fight 280
Thy like ne'er was For a sweet content, the cause of all my moan . 294
Even so, poor bird, like thee, None alive will pity me . . . 399
Words are easy, like the wind; Faithful friends are hard to find . 405
Liked. The fairest one of three, That liked of her master as well as well might be 212
Likely. The one doth flatter thee in thoughts unlikely, In likely thoughts the other kills thee quickly . . . . . *Ven. and Adon.* 990
Likeness. Thou dost survive, In that thy likeness still is left alive . 174
In Tarquin's likeness I did entertain thee . . . . *Lucrece* 596
Who leaves unsway'd the likeness of a man . . . *Sonnet* 141 11
Liker. Living flowers, Much liker than your painted counterfeit . . 16 8
Likewise. That all the faults which in thy reign are made May likewise be sepulchred in thy shade . . . . *Lucrece* 805
Figuring that they their passions likewise lent me Of grief and blushes *Lov. Comp.* 199
Liking. These lovely caves, these round enchanting pits, Open'd their mouths to swallow Venus' liking . . . . . . *Ven. and Adon.* 248
Anon his beating heart, alarum striking, Gives the hot charge and bids them do their liking . . . . *Lucrece* 434
Unless thou yoke thy liking to my will, I'll murder straight . . . 1633
Lily. She locks her lily fingers one in one. . . . *Ven. and Adon.* 228
A lily prison'd in a gaol of snow, Or ivory in an alabaster band . 362
Whose wonted lily white With purple tears, that his wound wept, was drench'd 1053
Their silent war of lilies and of roses . . . . . . *Lucrece* 71
Her lily hand her rosy cheek lies under, Cozening the pillow of a lawful kiss 386
The colour in thy face, That even for anger makes the lily pale . . 478
Lilies that fester smell far worse than weeds . . . *Sonnet* 94 14
Nor did I wonder at the lily's white, Nor praise the deep vermilion in the rose 98 9
The lily I condemned for thy hand 99 6
A lily pale, with damask dye to grace her, None fairer . . *Pass. Pil.* 89
Limb. His face seems twain, each several limb is doubled *Ven. and Adon.* 1067
My bed, The dear repose for limbs with travel tired . . . *Sonnet* 27 2
By day my limbs, by night my mind, For thee and for myself no quiet find 27 13
Limbecks. Siren tears, Distill'd from limbecks foul as hell within . . 119 2
Limed. Birds never limed no secret bushes fear . . . . *Lucrece* 88
Limit. Within this limit is relief enough . . . . *Ven. and Adon.* 235
Grief dallied with nor law nor limit knows . . . . *Lucrece* 1120
Despite of space I would be brought, From limits far remote, where thou dost stay . . . . *Sonnet* 44 4
Finding thy worth a limit past my praise 82 6
Limning. Look, when a painter would surpass the life, In limning out a well-proportion'd steed . . . . *Ven. and Adon.* 290
Limping. And strength by limping sway disabled . . . *Sonnet* 66 8
Line. Will tie the hearers to attend each line . . . . *Lucrece* 818
So should the lines of life that life repair . . . . *Sonnet* 16 9
When in eternal lines to time thou growest 18 12
Nor draw no lines there with thine antique pen 19 10
Once more re-survey These poor rude lines of thy deceased lover . 32 4
When hours have drain'd his blood and fill'd his brow With lines and wrinkles 63 4
His beauty shall in these black lines be seen, And they shall live . 63 13
If you read this line, remember not The hand that writ it . . . 71 5
My life hath in this line some interest 74 3
When your countenance fill'd up his line, Then lack'd I matter . . 86 13
Dulling my lines and doing me disgrace 103 8
Those lines that I before have writ do lie 115 1
The lines she rents, Big discontent so breaking their contents *Lov. Comp.* 55
Linen. With the nightly linen that she wears He pens her piteous clamours in her head . . . . *Lucrece* 680
Linger. Give not a windy night a rainy morrow, To linger out a purposed overthrow . . . . *Sonnet* 90 8
Lingering. As those bars which stop the hourly dial, Who with a lingering stay his course doth let . . . . *Lucrece* 328
Lion. Being ireful, on the lion he will venture . . . *Ven. and Adon.* 628

Lion. She knows it is no gentle chase, But the blunt boar, rough bear, or lion proud *Ven. and Adon.* 884
To see his face the lion walk'd along Behind some hedge 1093
As the grim lion fawneth o'er his prey, Sharp hunger by the conquest satisfied *Lucrece* 421
To tame the unicorn and lion wild 956
Devouring Time, blunt thou the lion's paws *Sonnet* 19 1
Lip. And yet not cloy thy lips with loathed satiety *Ven. and Adon.* 19
Now doth he frown, And 'gins to chide, but soon she stops his lips 46
If thou wilt chide, thy lips shall never open 48
But when her lips were ready for his pay, He winks, and turns his lips another way 89
Touch but my lips with those fair lips of thine 115
Then why not lips on lips, since eyes in eyes? 120
The tender spring upon thy tempting lip Shows thee unripe 127
What were thy lips the worse for one poor kiss? Speak, fair 207
Graze on my lips; and if those hills be dry, Stray lower, where the pleasant fountains lie 233
He bends her fingers, holds her pulses hard, He chafes her lips 477
These mine eyes, true leaders to their queen, But for thy piteous lips no more had seen 504
Pure lips, sweet seals in my soft lips imprinted 511
For fear of slips Set thy seal-manual on my wax-red lips 516
That sweet coral mouth, Whose precious taste her thirsty lips well knew 543
Their lips together glued, fall to the earth 546
Her lips are conquerors, his lips obey, Paying what ransom the insulter willeth 549
That she will draw his lips' rich treasure dry 552
Had she then gave over, Such nectar from his lips she had not suck'd 572
Nor thy soft hands, sweet lips, and crystal eyne 633
So do thy lips Make modest Dian cloudy and forlorn 724
She looks upon his lips, and they are pale; She takes him by the hand 1123
Her alabaster skin, Her coral lips, her snow-white dimpled chin *Lucrece* 420
Her voice controll'd Entombs her outcry in her lips' sweet fold 679
Which, thronging through her lips, so vanisheth As smoke from Ætna 1041
From his lips did fly Thin winding breath, which purl'd up to the sky 1406
From lips new-waxen pale begins to blow The grief away 1663
Through his lips do throng Weak words, so thick come in his poor heart's aid 1783
Sweet beauty's best, Of hand, of foot, of lip, of eye, of brow *Sonnet* 106 6
Love's not Time's fool, though rosy lips and cheeks Within his bending sickle's compass come 116 9
Whilst my poor lips, which should that harvest reap, At the wood's boldness by thee blushing stand 128 7
Making dead wood more blest than living lips 128 12
Give them thy fingers, me thy lips to kiss 128 14
Coral is far more red than her lips' red 130 2
Not from those lips of thine, That have profaned their scarlet ornaments 142 5
Those lips that Love's own hand did make 145 1
The wind Upon his lips their silken parcels hurls *Lov. Comp.* 87
Her lips to mine how often hath she joined *Pass. Pil.* 91
'He seized on my lips,' And with her lips on his did act the seizure 151
Liquid. A liquid prisoner pent in walls of glass *Sonnet* 5 10
List. From morn till night, even where I list to sport me *Ven. and Adon.* 154
Now is she in the very lists of love, Her champion mounted 595
Little stars may hide them when they list *Lucrece* 1008
Be where you list, your charter is so strong That you yourself may privilege your time To what you will *Sonnet* 58 9
And down I laid to list the sad-tuned tale *Lov. Comp.* 4
Listening. Stands on his hinder legs with listening ear To hearken *V. and A.* 698
Away he steals with open listening ear *Lucrece* 283
All jointly listening, but with several graces 1410
Listening Priam wets his eyes, To see those borrow'd tears that Sinon sheds 1548
Listeth. While she takes all she can, not all she listeth *Ven. and Adon.* 564
Little. Fair flowers that are not gather'd in their prime Rot and consume themselves in little time 132
The heat I have from thence doth little harm 195
Lie quietly, and hear a little more; Nay, do not struggle 709
And then my little heart were quite undone 783
Sweet issue of a more sweet-smelling sire—For every little grief to wet his eyes 1179
Little suspecteth the false worshipper *Lucrece* 86
Through little vents and crannies of the place The wind wars 310
These lets attend the time, Like little frosts that sometime threat the spring 331
A little harm done to a great good end For lawful policy remains enacted 528
And waste huge stones with little water-drops 959
Little stars may hide them when they list 1008
The little birds that tune their morning's joy Make her moans mad with their sweet melody 1107
Like a goodly champaign plain, Lays open all the little worms that creep 1248
Through crystal walls each little mote will peep 1251
That she her plaints a little while doth stay 1364
Gazing upon the Greeks with little lust 1384
Then little strength rings out the doleful knell 1495
The skies were sorry, And little stars shot from their fixed places 1525
Every thing that grows Holds in perfection but a little moment *Sonnet* 15 2
The little Love-god lying once asleep 154 1
On his visage was in little drawn What largeness thinks in Paradise was sawn *Lov. Comp.* 90
Live. Thou art bound to breed, That thine may live when thou thyself art dead *Ven. and Adon.* 172
Or at the fox which lives by subtlety 675
There lives a son that suck'd an earthly mother, May lend thee light 863
Adonis lives, and Death is not to blame 992
A weak and silly mind To wail his death who lives and must not die 1017
So vile, so base, That it will live engraven in my face *Lucrece* 203
To slay the tiger that doth live by slaughter 955
Let him have time to live a loathed slave 984
One that by alms doth live Disdain to him disdained scraps to give 986
For if I die, my honour lives in thee; But if I live, thou livest in my defame 1032
I live, and seek in vain Some happy mean to end a hapless life 1044
O, that is gone for which I sought to live 1051
To live or die which of the twain were better, When life is shamed 1154
'Tis honour to deprive dishonour'd life; The one will live, the other being dead 1187
And all my fame that lives disbursed be To those that live 1203
Swearing, unless I took all patiently, I should not live to speak 1642
Where shall I live now Lucrece is unlived? 1754
Then live, sweet Lucrece, live again and see Thy father die 1770
And live to be revenged on her death 1778
Live. But if thou live, remember'd not to be, Die single *Sonnet* 3 13
Why dost thou use So great a sum of sums, yet canst not live? 4 8
Thy unused beauty must be tomb'd with thee, Which, used, lives th' executor to be 4 14
Flowers distill'd, though they with winter meet, Leese but their show; their substance still lives sweet 5 14
That beauty still may live in thine or thee 10 14
Herein lives wisdom, beauty, and increase 11 5
But, love, you are No longer yours than you yourself here live 13 2
Time's pencil, or my pupil pen, Neither in inward worth nor outward fair, Can make you live yourself in eyes of men 16 12
You must live, drawn by your own sweet skill 16 14
Were some child of yours alive that time, You should live twice 17 14
So long as men can breathe or eyes can see, So long lives this 18 14
Despite thy wrong, My love shall in my verse ever live young 19 14
Which in thy breast doth live, as thine in me 22 7
Thou art the grave where buried love doth live 31 9
Loathsome canker lives in sweetest bud 35 4
I in thy abundance am sufficed And by a part of all thy glory live 37 12
Even for this let us divided live, And our dear love lose name of single one 39 5
The rose looks fair, but fairer we it deem For that sweet odour which doth in it live 54 4
They live unwoo'd and unrespected fade, Die to themselves 54 10
You live in this, and dwell in lovers' eyes 55 14
His beauty shall in these black lines be seen, And they shall live 63 14
Ah! wherefore with infection should he live? 67 1
Why should he live, now Nature bankrupt is? 67 9
She hath no exchequer now but his, And, proud of many, lives upon his gains 67 12
The right of sepulchres, were shorn away, To live a second life on second head 68 7
And live no more to shame nor me nor you 72 12
He can afford No praise to thee but what in thee doth live 79 12
Or I shall live your epitaph to make, Or you survive 81 1
You still shall live—such virtue hath my pen 81 13
There lives more life in one of your fair eyes 83 13
So shall I live, supposing thou art true, Like a deceived husband 93 1
For there can live no hatred in thine eye 93 5
The summer's flower is to the summer sweet, Though to itself it only live and die 94 10
Since, spite of him, I'll live in this poor rhyme 107 11
No holy bower, But is profaned, if not lives in disgrace 127 8
Yet this shall I ne'er know, but live in doubt 144 13
Then, soul, live thou upon thy servant's loss 146 9
But live in doubt, Till my bad angel fire my good one out *Pass. Pil.* 27
Where all those pleasures live that art can comprehend 62
Crabbed age and youth cannot live together 157
Poor Corydon Must live alone 297
Live with me, and be my love, And we will all the pleasures prove 353
And if these pleasures may thee move, Then live with me and be my love 368
These pretty pleasures might me move To live with thee and be thy love 372
Lived. Why, there Love lived and there he could not die *Ven. and Adon.* 246
But now I lived, and life was death's annoy 497
Who when he lived, his breath and beauty set Gloss on the rose 935
But true-sweet beauty lived and died with him 1080
But when Adonis lived, sun and sharp air Lurk'd like two thieves 1085
There were no strife, But that life lived in death, and death in life *Lucrece* 406
His taste delicious, in digestion souring, Devours his will, that lived by foul devouring 700
When beauty lived and died as flowers do now *Sonnet* 68 2
Lest the world should task you to recite What merit lived in me 72 2
'Fair, kind, and true,' have often lived alone 105 13
The fools of time, Which die for goodness, who have lived for crime 124 14
Livelihood. With this she seizeth on his sweating palm, The precedent of pith and livelihood *Ven. and Adon.* 26
Lively. But now I died, and death was lively joy. O, thou didst kill me 498
Her lively colour kill'd with deadly cares *Lucrece* 1593
Beggar'd of blood to blush through lively veins *Sonnet* 67 10
Which borrow'd from this holy fire of Love A dateless lively heat 153 6
For her griefs, so lively shown, Made me think upon mine own *Pass. Pil.* 389
Liver. He goes To quench the coal which in his liver glows *Lucrece* 47
Livery. O, never let their crimson liveries wear! *Ven. and Adon.* 506
Ne'er saw the beauteous livery that he wore 1107
To clear this spot by death, at least I give A badge of fame to slander's livery *Lucrece* 1054
For why her face wore sorrow's livery 1222
Thy youth's proud livery, so gazed on now, Will be a tatter'd weed *Sonnet* 2 3
His rudeness so with his authorized youth Did livery falseness in a pride of truth *Lov. Comp.* 105
Kept hearts in liveries, but mine own was free 195
Livest. But if I live, thou livest in my defame *Lucrece* 1033
Living. His art with nature's workmanship at strife, As if the dead the living should exceed *Ven. and Adon.* 292
I prophesy thy death, my living sorrow 671
And made her thrall To living death and pain perpetual *Lucrece* 726
A dying life to living infamy 1055
No dame, hereafter living, By my excuse shall claim excuse's giving 1714
If thou shouldst depart, Leaving thee living in posterity *Sonnet* 6 12
Living flowers, Much liker than your painted counterfeit 16 7
How would, I say, mine eyes be blessed made By looking on thee in the living day! 43 10
Nor war's quick fire shall burn The living record of your memory 55 8
Why should false painting imitate his cheek And steal dead seeing of his living hue? 67 6
Before these bastard signs of fair were born, Or durst inhabit on a living brow 68 4
Making dead wood more blest than living lips 128 12
And did thence remove, To spend her living in eternal love *Lov. Comp.* 238
In black mourn I, All fears scorn I, Love hath forlorn me, Living in thrall *Pass. Pil.* 266
Lo. And, lo, I lie between that sun and thee *Ven. and Adon.* 194
But, lo, from forth a copse that neighbours by, A breeding jennet 259
Curvets and leaps, As who should say 'Lo, thus my strength is tried' 280
When, lo, the unback'd breeder, full of fear, Jealous of catching, swiftly doth forsake him 320
Lo, here the gentle lark, weary of rest, From his moist cabinet mounts up on high 853
His eyes, Where, lo, two lamps burnt out, in darkness lies 1128
Lo, here I prophesy: Sorrow on love hereafter shall attend 1135

Lo. Lo, in this hollow cradle take thy rest . *Ven. and Adon.* 1185
And, lo, there falls into thy boundless flood, Black lust, dishonour *Lucrece* 653
Lo, here weeps Hecuba, here Priam dies . . 1485
Load. I had my load before, now press'd with bearing . *Ven. and Adon.* 430
She bears the load of lust he left behind . . *Lucrece* 734
This load of wrath that burning Troy doth bear . . 1474
Loan. Which happies those that pay the willing loan . *Sonnet* 6 6
Loathed. And yet not cloy thy lips with loathed satiety *Ven. and Adon.* 19
Thou loathed in their shame, they in thy pride . *Lucrece* 662
He runs, and chides his vanish'd, loathed delight . . 742
The sweets we wish for turn to loathed sours . . 867
Let him have time to live a loathed slave . . 984
Loathsome. O, let him keep his loathsome cabin still . *Ven. and Adon.* 637
He doth premeditate The dangers of his loathsome enterprise *Lucrece* 184
Some loathsome dash the herald will contrive, To cipher me . 206
Will quote my loathsome trespass in my looks . . 812
And swear I found you where you did fulfil The loathsome act of lust . 1636
Loathsome canker lives in sweetest bud . . *Sonnet* 35 4
Lock. She locks her lily fingers one in one . *Ven. and Adon.* 228
Were beauty under twenty locks kept fast, Yet love breaks through and picks them all at last 575
The wind would blow it off and, being gone, Play with his locks . 1090
The locks between her chamber and his will, Each one by him enforced, retires his ward . . . . . *Lucrece* 302
His browny locks did hang in crooked curls . *Lov. Comp.* 85
Locked. And how her hand, in my hand being lock'd, Forced it to tremble with her loyal fear ! . . . . *Lucrece* 260
Thee have I not lock'd up in any chest, Save where thou art not *Sonnet* 48 9
Locked-up. She, much amazed, breaks ope her lock'd-up eyes . *Lucrece* 446
Lode-star. Which must be lode-star to his lustful eye . . 179
Lodged. So fair a form lodged not a mind so ill . . 1530
Shall hate be fairer lodged than gentle love ? . . *Sonnet* 10 10
And when in his fair parts she did abide, She was new lodged *Lov. Comp.* 84
Lofty. The bark peel'd from the lofty pine, His leaves will wither *Lucrece* 1167
When lofty trees I see barren of leaves . . *Sonnet* 12 5
When sometime lofty towers I see down-razed . . 64 3
Long. Ten kisses short as one, one long as twenty . *Ven. and Adon.* 22
Her contending tears, Which long have rain'd, making her cheeks all wet . 83
Or, like a nymph, with long dishevell'd hair, Dance on the sands . 147
Round-hoof'd, short-jointed, fetlocks shag and long . . 295
Long may they kiss each other, for this cure ! . . 505
My heart longs not to groan, But soundly sleeps, while now it sleeps alone 785
For lovers' hours are long, though seeming short . . 842
Whereon with fearful eyes they long have gazed . . 927
In shade doth sit, Long after fearing to creep forth again . 1036
What canst thou boast Of things long since, or any thing ensuing ? . 1078
Long he questioned With modest Lucrece, and wore out the night *Lucrece* 122
And they too strong, To hold their cursed-blessed fortune long . 866
Long she thinks till he return again, And yet the duteous vassal scarce is gone 1359
And with my tears quench Troy that burns so long . . 1468
She looks for night, and then she longs for morrow, And both she thinks too long with her remaining 1571
Short time seems long in sorrow's sharp sustaining . . 1573
Collatine and his consorted lords With sad attention long to hear her words 1610
My laments would be drawn out too long, To tell them all . . 1616
Who, mad that sorrow should his use control, Or keep him from heart-easing words so long, Begins to talk 1782
So long as men can breathe or eyes can see, So long lives this *Sonnet* 18 13
So long as youth and thou are of one date . . 22 2
And weep afresh love's long since cancell'd woe . . 30 7
Let him bring forth Eternal numbers to outlive long date . 38 12
Therefore are feasts so solemn and so rare, Since, seldom coming, in the long year set 52 6
What wealth she had In days long since, before these last so bad . 67 14
Which makes thy love more strong, To love that well which thou must leave ere long 73 14
Where art thou, Muse, that thou forget'st so long To speak ? . 100 1
I teach thee how To make him seem long hence as he shows now . 101 14
So long as brain and heart Have faculty by nature to subsist . 122 5
Ere long espied a fickle maid full pale, Tearing of papers *Lov. Comp.* 5
Long upon these terms I held my city, Till thus he gan besiege me . 176
O, sweet shepherd, hie thee, For methinks thou stay'st too long *Pass. Pil.* 168
Long was the combat doubtful that love with love did fight . . 215
She will not stick to round me i' the ear, To teach my tongue to be so long 350
Longer. She is resolved no longer to restrain him . *Ven. and Adon.* 579
O time, cease thou thy course and last no longer . *Lucrece* 1765
You are No longer yours than you yourself here live . *Sonnet* 13 2
But day doth daily draw my sorrows longer . . 28 13
No longer glad, I send them back again and straight grow sad . 45 13
No longer mourn for me when I am dead Than you shall hear the surly sullen bell 71 1
Life no longer than thy love will stay . . . 92 3
My love is as a fever, longing still For that which longer nurseth the disease 147 2
Long-experienced. Now set thy long-experienced wit to school . *Lucrece* 1820
Long-hid. And arm'd his long-hid wits advisedly . . 1816
Longing. Longing to hear the hateful foe bewray'd . . 1698
My love is as a fever, longing still For that which longer nurseth the disease . . . . *Sonnet* 147 1
Cytherea, all in love forlorn, A longing tarriance for Adonis made *Pass. Pil.* 74
Long-lived. Burn the long-lived phœnix in her blood . *Sonnet* 19 4
Long-living. Thou back'st reproach against long-living laud . *Lucrece* 622
Look. Look, how a bird lies tangled in a net, So fasten'd in her arms Adonis lies . . . . *Ven. and Adon.* 67
Look how he can, she cannot choose but love . . 79
Look in mine eye-balls, there thy beauty lies . . 119
Look, when a painter would surpass the life, In limning out a well-proportion'd steed 289
Look, what a horse should have he did not lack, Save a proud rider . 299
He looks upon his love and neighs unto her ; She answers him . 307
Looks on the dull earth with disturbed mind, Taking no notice . 340
O, what a war of looks was then between them ! Her eyes petitioners to his eyes 355
For one sweet look thy help I would assure thee . . 371
And at his look she flatly falleth down, For looks kill love and love by looks reviveth 463
Look, the world's comforter, with weary gait, His day's hot task hath ended in the west 529
Bids him farewell, and look well to her heart . . 580
Look. Look, how a bright star shooteth from the sky, So glides he in the night . . . . *Ven. and Adon.* 815
Look, how the world's poor people are amazed At apparitions . 925
And never wound the heart with looks again . . 1042
Upon his hurt she looks so steadfastly . . . 1063
She looks upon his lips, and they are pale ; She takes him by the hand . 1123
But she, that never coped with stranger eyes, Could pick no meaning from their parling looks . . . . . . *Lucrece* 100
That eye which looks on her confounds his wits . . 290
Look, as the fair and fiery-pointed sun, Rushing from forth a cloud, bereaves our sight 372
Showing life's triumph in the map of death, And death's dim look in life's mortality 403
She dares not look ; yet, winking, there appears Quick-shifting antics . 458
Only he hath an eye to gaze on beauty, And dotes on what he looks . 497
Princes are the glass, the school, the book, Where subjects' eyes do learn, do read, do look 616
Look, as the full-fed hound or gorged hawk, . . . Make slow pursuit . 694
He in his speed looks for the morning light . . 745
Will quote my loathsome trespass in my looks . . 812
And sorts a sad look to her lady's sorrow . . 1221
Though men can cover crimes with bold stern looks . . 1252
Pawn'd honest looks, but laid no words to gage . . 1351
That one might see those far-off eyes look sad . . 1386
She lends them words, and she their looks doth borrow . . 1498
A wretched image bound, That piteous looks to Phrygian shepherds lent . 1502
And give the harmless show An humble gait, calm looks, eyes wailing still . 1508
'It cannot be,' quoth she, 'that so much guile'—She would have said 'can lurk in such a look' 1535
Look, look, how listening Priam wets his eyes ! . . 1548
She looks for night, and then she longs for morrow . . 1571
Look in thy glass, and tell the face thou viewest . *Sonnet* 3 1
Serving with looks his sacred majesty . . . 7 4
Yet mortal looks adore his beauty still . . . 7 7
The eyes, 'fore duteous, now converted are From his low tract and look another way 7 12
Look, what an unthrift in the world doth spend Shifts but his place . 9 9
Look, whom she best endow'd she gave the more . . 11 11
Then look I death my days should expiate . . . 22 4
Who plead for love and look for recompense . . 23 11
And look upon myself and curse my fate . . . 29 4
Look, what is best, that best I wish in thee : This wish I have . 37 13
When I sleep, in dreams they look on thee . . 43 3
When that mine eye is famish'd for a look, Or heart in love . 47 3
The rose looks fair, but fairer we it deem For that sweet odour . 54 3
A backward look, Even of five hundred courses of the sun . 59 6
They look into the beauty of thy mind . . . 69 9
O, if, I say, you look upon this verse When I perhaps compounded am with clay 71 9
Lest the wise world should look into your moan . . 71 13
All full with feasting on your sight And by and by clean starved for a look 75 10
Look, what thy memory can not contain Commit to these waste blanks 77 9
These offices, so oft as thou wilt look, Shall profit thee . 77 13
Knowing thy will, I will acquaintance strangle and look strange . 89 8
Thy looks with me, thy heart in other place . . 93 4
In many's looks the false heart's history Is writ . . 93 7
Thy looks should nothing thence but sweetness tell . . 93 12
How many lambs might the stern wolf betray, If like a lamb he could his looks translate ! 96 10
With so dull a cheer That leaves look pale, dreading the winter's near 97 14
Look in your glass, and there appears a face . . 103 6
Your own glass shows you when you look in it . . 103 14
Now with the drops of this most balmy time My love looks fresh . 107 10
It is an ever-fixed mark That looks on tempests and is never shaken . 116 6
Becoming of their woe, That every tongue says beauty should look so . 127 14
If eyes corrupt by over-partial looks Be anchor'd in the bay . 137 5
My love well knows Her pretty looks have been mine enemies . 139 10
Kill me outright with looks and rid my pain . . 139 14
Look here, what tributes wounded fancies sent me . *Lov. Comp.* 197
Did court the lad with many a lovely look, Such looks as none could look but beauty's queen . . . . *Pass. Pil.* 45
Hot was the day ; she hotter that did look For his approach . 77
Her cloudy looks will calm ere night . . . 312
Looked. Like a dive-dapper peering through a wave, Who, being look'd on, ducks as quickly in . . . . . *Ven. and Adon.* 87
Her eyes, though sod in tears, look'd red and raw . *Lucrece* 1592
Some of her blood still pure and red remain'd, And some look'd black . 1743
For they look'd but with divining eyes . . . *Sonnet* 106 11
Most true it is that I have look'd on truth Askance and strangely . 110 5
The sun look'd on the world with glorious eye . . *Pass. Pil.* 81
Lookest. Thou look'st not like deceit ; do not deceive me . *Lucrece* 585
Looketh. Whose downward eye still looketh for a grave *Ven. and Adon.* 1106
Looking. Looking scornfully, he doth despise His naked armour . *Lucrece* 187
Looking on darkness which the blind do see . . *Sonnet* 27 8
How would, I say, mine eyes be blessed made By looking on thee in the living day ! 43 10
Looking with pretty ruth upon my pain . . . 132 4
Till looking on an Englishman, the fair'st that eye could see *Pass. Pil.* 213
Loop-holes. There would appear The very eyes of men through loop-holes thrust . . . . *Lucrece* 1383
Loose. Her hair, nor loose nor tied in formal plat . *Lov. Comp.* 29
Though slackly braided in loose negligence . . . 35
Lord. When at Collatium this false lord arrived, Well was he welcomed *Lucrece* 50
And now this lustful lord leap'd from his bed . . 169
Thus madly led, The Roman lord marcheth to Lucrece' bed . 301
Unconquered, Save of their lord no barring yoke they knew . 409
So fares it with this faultful lord of Rome . . 715
Dear lord of that dear jewel I have lost, What legacy shall I bequeath to thee ? 1191
Those proud lords, to blame, Make weak-made women tenants to their shame 1259
By and by, to bear A letter to my lord, my love, my dear . 1293
Thou worthy lord Of that unworthy wife that greeteth thee . . 1303
And on it writ 'At Ardea to my lord with more than haste . 1332
The mindful messenger, come back, Brings home his lord and other company 1584
Collatine and his consorted lords With sad attention long to hear her words 1609
Dear lord, thy sorrow to my sorrow lendeth Another power . . 1676
'You fair lords,' quoth she, Speaking to those that came with Collatine 1688
With noble disposition Each present lord began to promise aid . 1696
He, he, fair lords, 'tis he, That guides this hand to give this wound . 1721

Lord. 'Thou wronged lord of Rome,' quoth he, 'arise' *Lucrece* 1818
Lord of my love, to whom in vassalage Thy merit hath my duty strongly knit *Sonnet* 26 1
They are the lords and owners of their faces 94 7
Like widow'd wombs after their lords' decease 97 8
Lord, how mine eyes throw gazes to the east! My heart doth charge the watch *Pass. Pil.* 193
Lording. It was a lording's daughter, the fairest one of three 211
Lordly. Stood Collatine and all his lordly crew *Lucrece* 1731
Lose. Having no fair to lose, you need not fear *Ven. and Adon.* 1083
And he hath won what he would lose again *Lucrece* 688
Let mild women to him lose their mildness 979
They that lose half with greater patience bear it Than they whose whole is swallow'd in confusion 1158
Thy eternal summer shall not fade Nor lose possession of that fair thou owest *Sonnet* 18 10
Even for this let us divided live, And our dear love lose name of single one 39 6
If I lose thee, my loss is my love's gain 42 9
Both find each other, and I lose both twain 42 11
Which cannot choose But weep to have that which it fears to lose 64 14
The hardest knife ill-used doth lose his edge 95 14
And sweets grown common lose their dear delight 102 12
Have I not seen dwellers on form and favour Lose all, and more? 125 6
So him I lose through my unkind abuse 134 12
Loseth. The colt that's back'd and burden'd being young Loseth his pride and never waxeth strong *Ven. and Adon.* 420
Losing. Losing her woes in shows of discontent *Lucrece* 1580
If I lose thee, my loss is my love's gain, And losing her, my friend hath found that loss *Sonnet* 42 10
Wherein I am attainted, That thou in losing me shalt win much glory 88 8
Still losing when I saw myself to win 119 4
Loss. But for loss of Nestor's golden words, It seem'd they would debate with angry swords *Lucrece* 1420
Lo, here, the hopeless merchant of this loss, With head declined 1660
All losses are restored and sorrows end *Sonnet* 30 14
Though thou repent, yet I have still the loss 34 10
A loss in love that touches me more nearly 42 4
If I lose thee, my loss is my love's gain, And losing her, my friend hath found that loss 42 9
And the firm soil win of the watery main, Increasing store with loss and loss with store 64 8
And other strains of woe, which now seem woe, Compared with loss of thee will not seem so 90 14
Then, soul, live thou upon thy servant's loss 146 9
Dreading my love, the loss thereof still fearing! *Pass. Pil.* 94
One silly cross Wrought all my loss; O frowning Fortune! 258
Lost. The lesson is but plain, And once made perfect, never lost again *Ven. and Adon.* 408
In the dark she lay, Having lost the fair discovery of her way 828
Hearing him, thy power had lost his power 944
Alas, poor world, what treasure hast thou lost! 1075
Their virtue lost, wherein they late excell'd 1131
Oft that wealth doth cost The death of all, and all together lost *Lucrece* 147
But she hath lost a dearer thing than life 687
A captive victor that hath lost in gain 730
My honey lost, and I, a drone-like bee 836
Dear lord of that dear jewel I have lost, What legacy shall I bequeath to thee? 1191
So then thou hast but lost the dregs of life, The prey of worms *Sonnet* 74 9
And the just pleasure lost which is so deem'd Not by our feeling but by others' seeing 121 3
Him have I lost; thou hast both him and me 134 13
And all my honest faith in thee is lost 152 8
Lost, vaded, broken, dead within an hour *Pass. Pil.* 174
As goods lost are seld or never found, As vaded gloss no rubbing will refresh 175
So beauty blemish'd once's for ever lost 179
All my merry jigs are quite forgot, All my lady's love is lost, God wot 254
All our evening sport from us is fled, All our love is lost, for Love is dead 292
Lot. Bequeath not to their lot The shame that from them no device can take *Lucrece* 534
Loud. To stop the loud pursuers in their yell *Ven. and Adon.* 688
Anon their loud alarums he doth hear 700
Thou mayst have thy 'Will,' If thou turn back, and my loud crying still *Sonnet* 143 14
Loudest. The bird of loudest lay, On the sole Arabian tree *Ph. and Tur.* 1
Lours. Still is he sullen, still he lours and frets, 'Twixt crimson shame and anger ashy-pale *Ven. and Adon.* 75
Lourest. If thou lour'st on me, do I not spend Revenge upon myself? *Sonnet* 149 7
Louring. His louring brows o'erwhelming his fair sight *Ven. and Adon.* 183
Love. Hunting he loved, but love he laugh'd to scorn 4
O, how quick is love! 38
Being red, she loves him best; and being white, Her best is better'd with a more delight 77
Look how he can, she cannot choose but love 79
Love keeps his revels where there are but twain 123
Love is a spirit all compact of fire, Not gross to sink, but light, and will aspire 149
Is love so light, sweet boy, and may it be That thou shouldst think it heavy unto thee? 155
Can thy right hand seize love upon thy left? 158
Cries 'Fie, no more of love!' The sun doth burn my face 185
Art thou a woman's son, and canst not feel What 'tis to love? how want of love tormenteth? 202
Being judge in love, she cannot right her cause 220
Love made those hollows, if himself were slain, He might be buried in a tomb so simple 243
Why, there Love lived and there he could not die 246
Poor queen of love, in thine own law forlorn, To love a cheek that smiles at thee in scorn! 251
He sees his love, and nothing else he sees 287
He looks upon his love and neighs unto her; She answers him 307
Seems unkind, Spurns at his love and scorns the heat he feels 311
His love, perceiving how he is enraged, Grew kinder 317
Once more fits, That love-sick Love by pleading may be blest 328
Free vent of words love's fire doth assuage 334
Then love's deep groans I never shall regard 377
But when he saw his love, his youth's fair fee, He held such petty bondage in disdain 393
O, learn to love; the lesson is but plain, And once made perfect, never lost again 407
'I know not love,' quoth he, 'nor will not know it' 409
Love. My love to love is love but to disgrace it *Ven. and Adon.* 412
Remove your siege from my unyielding heart; To love's alarms it will not ope the gate 424
Had I no eyes but ears, my ears would love That inward beauty and invisible 433
Yet should I be in love by touching thee 438
Yet would my love to thee be still as much 442
Comes breath perfumed that breedeth love by smelling 444
For looks kill love and love by looks reviveth 464
But blessed bankrupt, that by love so thriveth! 466
He did think to reprehend her, Which cunning love did wittily prevent 471
If any love you owe me, Measure my strangeness with my unripe years 523
Things out of hope are compass'd oft with venturing, Chiefly in love 568
Yet love breaks through and picks them all at last 576
Tell me, Love's master, shall we meet to-morrow? Say, shall we? 585
Now is she in the very lists of love, Her champion mounted 595
She's Love, she loves, and yet she is not loved 610
That face of thine, To which Love's eyes pay tributary gazes 632
For where Love reigns, disturbing Jealousy Doth call himself Affection's sentinel 649
Distempering gentle Love in his desire, As air and water do abate the fire 653
This bate-breeding spy, This canker that eats up Love's tender spring 656
Whispers in mine ear That if I love thee, I thy death should fear 660
Applying this to that, and so to so, For love can comment upon every woe 714
The earth, in love with thee, thy footing trips 722
If love have lent you twenty thousand tongues 775
I hate not love, but your device in love, That lends embracements 789
Call it not love, for Love to heaven is fled 793
Love comforteth like sunshine after rain, But Lust's effect is tempest after sun 799
Love's gentle spring doth always fresh remain 801
Love surfeits not, Lust like a glutton dies; Love is all truth, Lust full of forged lies 803
Leaves Love upon her back deeply distress'd 814
How love makes young men thrall and old men dote; How love is wise in folly, foolish-witty 837
And yet she hears no tidings of her love: She hearkens 867
Hard-favour'd tyrant, ugly, meagre, lean, Hateful divorce of love 932
Love's golden arrow at him should have fled, And not Death's ebon dart 947
O hard-believing love, how strange it seems Not to believe 985
Truth I must confess,—I rail'd on thee, fearing my love's decease 1002
Fie, fie, fond love, thou art so full of fear As one with treasure laden 1021
Here I prophesy: Sorrow on love hereafter shall attend 1136
High or low, That all love's pleasure shall not match his woe 1140
Sith in his prime Death doth my love destroy, They that love best their loves shall not enjoy 1163
There shall not be one minute in an hour Wherein I will not kiss my sweet love's flower 1188
The waist Of Collatine's fair love, Lucrece the chaste *Lucrece* 7
Abhor the deed That spots and stains love's modest snow-white weed 196
There is no hate in loving: I'll beg her love; but she is not her own 241
Love thrives not in the heart that shadows dreadeth 270
Love and Fortune be my gods, my guide! My will is back'd with resolution 351
Against love's fire fear's frost hath dissolution 355
By her untimely tears, her husband's love, By holy human law 570
Only loved for fear; But happy monarchs still are fear'd for love 611
Yield to my love; if not, enforced hate, Instead of love's coy touch, shall rudely tear thee 669
Let my good name, that senseless reputation, For Collatine's dear love be kept unspotted 821
My restless discord loves no stops nor rests 1124
Whose love of either to myself was nearer 1165
My resolution, love, shall be thy boast, By whose example thou revenged mayst be 1193
By and by, to bear A letter to my lord, my love, my dear 1293
Vouchsafe t' afford—If ever, love, thy Lucrece thou wilt see—Some present speed to come and visit me 1306
Sweet love, what spite hath thy fair colour spent? 1600
And softly cried 'Awake, thou Roman dame, And entertain my love' 1629
If thou my love's desire do contradict 1631
No love toward others in that bosom sits *Sonnet* 9 13
Deny that thou bear'st love to any, Who for thyself art so unprovident 10 1
Shall hate be fairer lodged than gentle love? 10 10
Make thee another self, for love of me 10 13
But, love, you are No longer yours than you yourself here live 13 1
My love, you know You had a father: let your son say so 13 13
And all in war with Time for love of you 15 13
O, carve not with thy hours my love's fair brow 19 9
Despite thy wrong, My love shall in my verse ever live young 19 14
Mine be thy love and thy love's use their treasure 20 14
O, let me, true in love, but truly write, And then believe me, my love is as fair As any mother's child 21 9
O, therefore, love, be of thyself so wary As I, not for myself, but for thee will 22 9
So I, for fear of trust, forget to say The perfect ceremony of love's rite 23 6
In mine own love's strength seem to decay, O'ercharged with burden of mine own love's might 23 7
Who plead for love and look for recompense 23 11
O, learn to read what silent love hath writ: To hear with eyes belongs to love's fine wit 23 13
Then happy I, that love and am beloved 25 13
Lord of my love, to whom in vassalage Thy merit hath my duty strongly knit 26 1
Then may I dare to boast how I do love thee 26 13
For thy sweet love remember'd such wealth brings 29 13
And weep afresh love's long since cancell'd woe 30 7
And there reigns love and all love's loving parts 31 3
How many a holy and obsequious tear Hath dear religious love stol'n from mine eye As interest of the dead 31 6
Thou art the grave where buried love doth live 31 9
Outstripp'd by every pen, Reserve them for my love, not for their rhyme 32 7
A dearer birth than this his love had brought 32 11
Since he died and poets better prove, Theirs for their style I'll read, his for his love 32 14
Yet him for this my love no whit disdaineth 33 13
Ah! but those tears are pearl which thy love sheds 34 13
Such civil war is in my love and hate 35 12
We two must be twain, Although our undivided loves are one 36 2
In our two loves there is but one respect 36 5
Though it alter not love's sole effect, Yet doth it steal sweet hours from love's delight 36 7
I love thee in such sort As, thou being mine, mine is thy good report 36 13

Love. I make my love engrafted to this store . . . *Sonnet* 37 8
Even for this let us divided live, And our dear love lose name of single one 39 6
Thy sour leisure gave sweet leave To entertain the time with thoughts of love 39 11
Take all my loves, my love, yea, take them all 40 1
No love, my love, that thou mayst true love call 40 3
Then if for my love thou my love receivest, I cannot blame thee for my love thou usest 40 5
And yet, love knows, it is a greater grief To bear love's wrong than hate's known injury 40 11
A loss in love that touches me more nearly 42 4
Thou dost love her, because thou know'st I love her 42 6
If I lose thee, my loss is my love's gain, And losing her, my friend hath found that loss 42 9
My friend and I are one; Sweet flattery! then she loves but me alone 42 14
When these quicker elements are gone In tender embassy of love to thee 45 6
Mine eye's due is thy outward part, And my heart's right thy inward love of heart 46 14
Or heart in love with sighs himself doth smother, With my love's picture then my eye doth feast 47 4
Mine eye is my heart's guest And in his thoughts of love doth share a part 47 8
Either by thy picture or my love, Thyself away art present still with me 47 9
When as thy love hath cast his utmost sum 49 3
When love, converted from the thing it was, Shall reasons find 49 7
Thou hast the strength of laws, Since why to love I can allege no cause 49 14
Thus can my love excuse the slow offence Of my dull bearer 51 1
Desire, of perfect'st love being made, Shall neigh 51 10
But love, for love, thus shall excuse my jade 51 12
Sweet love, renew thy force; be it not said Thy edge should blunter be than appetite 56 1
So, love, be thou; although to-day thou fill Thy hungry eyes till they wink 56 5
Do not kill The spirit of love with a perpetual dullness 56 8
That, when they see Return of love, more blest may be the view 56 12
So true a fool is love that in your will, Though you do any thing, he thinks no ill 57 13
Thy love, though much, is not so great: It is my love that keeps mine eye awake 61 9
Mine own true love that doth my rest defeat, To play the watchman 61 11
Against my love shall be, as I am now, With Time's injurious hand crush'd and o'erworn 63 1
That he shall never cut from memory My sweet love's beauty 63 12
Thus to ruminate That Time will come and take my love away 64 12
That in black ink my love may still shine bright 65 14
From these would I be gone, Save that, to die, I leave my love alone 66 14
For canker vice the sweetest buds doth love 70 7
For I love you so That I in your sweet thoughts would be forgot If thinking on me then should make you woe 71 6
But let your love even with my life decay 71 12
What merit lived in me, that you should love After my death, dear love, forget me quite 72 2
Lest your true love may seem false in this, That you for love speak well of me untrue 72 9
I am shamed by that which I bring forth, And so should you, to love things nothing worth 72 14
Which makes thy love more strong, To love that well which thou must leave ere long 73 13
Sweet love, I always write of you, And you and love are still my argument 76 9
For as the sun is daily new and old, So is my love 76 14
I grant, sweet love, thy lovely argument Deserves the travail of a worthier pen 79 5
The worst was this; my love was my decay 80 14
Do so, love; yet when they have devised What strained touches rhetoric can lend 82 9
But that is in my thought, whose love to you, Though words come hindmost, holds his rank before 85 11
Such is my love, to thee I so belong, That for thy right myself will bear all wrong 88 13
Thou canst not, love, disgrace me half so ill 89 5
For I must ne'er love him whom thou dost hate 89 14
Thy love is better than high birth to me, Richer than wealth 91 9
Life no longer than thy love will stay, For it depends upon that love of thine 92 3
O, what a happy title do I find, Happy to have thy love, happy to die! 92 12
So love's face May still seem love to me, though alter'd new 93 2
Heaven in thy creation did decree That in thy face sweet love should ever dwell 93 10
I love thee in such sort As, thou being mine, mine is thy good report 96 13
Whence didst thou steal thy sweet that smells, If not from my love's breath? 99 3
In my love's veins thou hast too grossly dyed 99 5
My love's sweet face survey, If Time have any wrinkle graven there 100 9
Give my love fame faster than Time wastes life 100 13
Both truth and beauty on my love depends; So dost thou too 101 3
My love is strengthen'd, though more weak in seeming; I love not less 102 1
That love is merchandized whose rich esteeming The owner's tongue doth publish every where 102 3
Our love was new and then but in the spring 102 5
Let not my love be call'd idolatry, Nor my beloved as an idol show 105 1
Kind is my love to-day, to-morrow kind, Still constant 105 5
Can yet the lease of my true love control 107 3
Now with the drops of this most balmy time My love looks fresh 107 10
What's new to speak, what new to register, That may express my love? 108 4
Eternal love in love's fresh case Weighs not the dust and injury of age 108 9
Finding the first conceit of love there bred 108 13
Which in thy breast doth lie: That is my home of love 109 5
And worse essays proved thee my best of love 110 8
A god in love, to whom I am confined 110 12
Your love and pity doth the impression fill 112 1
Mine eye saith true, And that your love taught it this alchemy 114 4
'Tis the lesser sin That mine eye loves it and doth first begin 114 14
Even those that said I could not love you dearer 115 2
Fearing of time's tyranny, Might I not then say 'Now I love you best?' 115 10
Love is a babe; then might I not say so, To give full growth to that which still doth grow? 115 13
Love is not love Which alters when it alteration finds 116 2
Love's not Time's fool, though rosy lips and cheeks Within his bending sickle's compass come 116 9
Love alters not with his brief hours and weeks 116 11

Love. Forgot upon your dearest love to call . . . *Sonnet* 117 3
I did strive to prove The constancy and virtue of your love 117 14
Thus policy in love, to anticipate The ills that were not 118 9
And ruin'd love, when it is built anew, Grows fairer than at first 119 11
Nor need I tallies thy dear love to score 122 10
If my dear love were but the child of state 124 1
As subject to Time's love or to Time's hate 124 3
I love to hear her speak, yet well I know That music hath a far more pleasing sound 130 9
I think my love as rare As any she belied with false compare 130 13
Some say that thee behold Thy face hath not the power to make love groan 131 6
Thine eyes I love, and they, as pitying me, Knowing thy heart torments me with disdain 132 1
Thus far for love my love-suit, sweet, fulfil 136 4
'Will' will fulfil the treasure of thy love, Ay, fill it full with wills 136 5
Make but my name thy love, and love that still, And then thou lovest me 136 13
Love, what dost thou to mine eyes, That they behold, and see not what they see? 137 1
When my love swears that she is made of truth I do believe her 138 1
O, love's best habit is in seeming trust, And age in love loves not to have years told 138 11
My love well knows Her pretty looks have been mine enemies 139 9
Better it were, Though not to love, yet, love, to tell me so 140 6
In faith, I do not love thee with mine eyes 141 1
But 'tis my heart that loves what they despise 141 3
Love is my sin and thy dear virtue hate, Hate of my sin 142 1
And seal'd false bonds of love as oft as mine 142 7
Be it lawful I love thee, as thou lovest those Whom thine eyes woo 142 9
Two loves I have of comfort and despair 144 1
Those lips that Love's own hand did make 145 1
My love is as a fever, longing still For that which longer nurseth the disease 147 1
My reason, the physician to my love 147 5
O me, what eyes hath Love put in my head! 148 1
Then love doth well denote Love's eye is not so true as all men's 'No' 148 7
How can Love's eye be true, That is so vex'd with watching? 148 9
O cunning Love! with tears thou keep'st me blind 148 13
Canst thou, O cruel! say I love thee not? 149 1
But, love, hate on, for now I know thy mind 149 13
Who taught thee how to make me love thee more? 150 9
O, though I love what others do abhor, With others thou shouldst not abhor my state 150 11
If thy unworthiness raised love in me, More worthy I to be beloved of thee 150 13
Love is too young to know what conscience is; Yet who knows not conscience is born of love? 151 1
My soul doth tell my body that he may Triumph in love 151 8
No want of conscience hold it that I call Her 'love' for whose dear love I rise and fall 151 14
I am forsworn, But thou art twice forsworn, to me love swearing 152 2
New faith torn In vowing new hate after new love bearing 152 4
Oaths of thy love, thy truth, thy constancy 152 10
Which borrow'd from this holy fire of Love A dateless lively heat 153 5
But at my mistress' eye Love's brand new-fired, The boy for trial needs would touch my breast 153 9
This brand she quenched in a cool well by, Which from Love's fire took heat perpetual 154 10
Love's fire heats water, water cools not love 154 14
If I had self-applied Love to myself and to no love beside . . . *Lov. Comp.* 77
Love lack'd a dwelling, and made him her place 82
For feasts of love I have been call'd unto, Till now did ne'er invite 181
Errors of the blood, none of the mind; Love made them not 185
And did thence remove, To spend her living in eternal love 238
Religious love put out Religion's eye 250
As compound love to physic your cold breast 259
O most potential love! vow, bond, nor space, In thee hath neither sting, knot, nor confine 264
Love's arms are peace, 'gainst rule, 'gainst sense, 'gainst shame 271
When my love swears that she is made of truth, I do believe her . . . *Pass. Pil.* 1
False-speaking tongue, Outfacing faults in love with love's ill rest 8
But wherefore says my love that she is young? 9
O, love's best habit is a soothing tongue, And age, in love, loves not to have years told 11
Therefore I'll lie with love, and love with me, Since that our faults in love thus smother'd be 13
Two loves I have, of comfort and despair, That like two spirits do suggest me still 15
My vow was earthly, thou a heavenly love 35
If love make me forsworn, how shall I swear to love? 57
Celestial as thou art, O do not love that wrong 69
When Cytherea, all in love forlorn, A longing tarriance for Adonis made 73
Fair is my love, but not so fair as fickle; Mild as a dove 85
Between each kiss her oaths of true love swearing 92
How many tales to please me hath she coined, Dreading my love! 94
She burn'd with love, as straw with fire flameth; She burn'd out love 97
She framed the love, and yet she foil'd the framing; She bade love last, and yet she fell a-turning 99
Then must the love be great 'twixt thee and me 105
One knight loves both, and both in thee remain 116
Fair was the morn when the fair queen of love 117
She, silly queen, with more than love's good will, Forbade the boy he should not pass those grounds 123
O, my love, my love is young! Age, I do defy thee 166
Long was the combat doubtful that love with love did fight 215
Love, whose month was ever May, Spied a blossom passing fair 228
And deny himself for Jove, Turning mortal for thy love 244
Love's denying, Faith's defying, Heart's renying, Causer of this 249
All my merry jigs are quite forgot, All my lady's love is lost, God wot 254
Where her faith was firmly fix'd in love, There a nay is placed 255
In black mourn I, All fears scorn I, Love hath forlorn me, Living in thrall 265
All our evening sport from us is fled, All our love is lost, for Love is dead 292
Live with me, and be my love, And we will all the pleasures prove 353
And if these pleasures may thee move, Then live with me and be my love 368
If that the world and love were young, And truth in every shepherd's tongue 369
These pretty pleasures might me move To live with thee and be thy love 372
Here the anthem doth commence: Love and constancy is dead . . . *Ph. and Tur.* 22
So they loved, as love in twain Had the essence but in one 25

Love. Two distincts, division none: Number there in love was slain *Ph. and Tur.* 28
So between them love did shine 33
Love hath reason, reason none, If what parts can so remain . . 47
Co-supremes and stars of love, As chorus to their tragic scene . 51
Loved. Hunting he loved, but love he laugh'd to scorn *Ven. and Adon.* 4
She's Love, she loves, and yet she is not loved . . . 610
This deed will make thee only loved for fear . . *Lucrece* 610
Their images I loved I view in thee, And thou, all they, hast all the all of me *Sonnet* 31 13
And yet it may be said I loved her dearly . . . 42 2
As if by some instinct the wretch did know His rider loved not speed . 50 8
Both grace and faults are loved of more and less . . 96 3
If this be error and upon me proved, I never writ, nor no man ever loved 116 14
So they loved, as love in twain Had the essence but in one . *Ph. and Tur.* 25
Love-god. The little Love-god lying once asleep . . *Sonnet* 154 1
Love-kindling. And his love-kindling fire did quickly steep . 153 3
Love-lacking vestals and self-loving nuns, That on the earth would breed a scarcity . . . . *Ven. and Adon.* 752
Loveless. To leave the master loveless, or kill the gallant knight *Pass. Pil.* 216
Loveliness. Unthrifty loveliness, why dost thou spend Upon thyself thy beauty's legacy? . . . . *Sonnet* 4 1
Lovely. More lovely than a man, More white and red than doves or roses are . . . . *Ven. and Adon.* 9
These lovely caves, these round enchanting pits, Open'd their mouths to swallow Venus' liking 247
She in thee Calls back the lovely April of her prime . *Sonnet* 3 10
The lovely gaze where every eye doth dwell . . . 5 2
Shall I compare thee to a summer's day? Thou art more lovely and more temperate 18 2
And so of you, beauteous and lovely youth . . . 54 13
Thy lovely argument Deserves the travail of a worthier pen . . 79 5
How sweet and lovely dost thou make the shame . . 95 1
Old rhyme In praise of ladies dead and lovely knights . . 106 4
O thou, my lovely boy, who in thy power Dost hold Time's fickle glass! 126 1
Sweet Cytherea, sitting by a brook With young Adonis, lovely, fresh, and green, Did court the lad with many a lovely look . . *Pass. Pil.* 44
Lover. For lovers say, the heart hath treble wrong When it is barr'd the aidance of the tongue . . . . . . *Ven. and Adon.* 329
And like a lowly lover down she kneels 350
Foul words and frowns must not repel a lover . . . 573
Her song was tedious and outwore the night, For lovers' hours are long 842
Hung with the trophies of my lovers gone . . . *Sonnet* 31 10
Once more re-survey These poor rude lines of thy deceased lover . 32 4
You live in this, and dwell in lovers' eyes . . . 55 14
That he shall never cut from memory My sweet love's beauty, though my lover's life 63 12
And therein show'st Thy lovers withering as thy sweet self grow'st 126 4
She fell a-turning. Was this a lover, or a lecher whether? . *Pass. Pil.* 101
That the lover, sick to death, Wish'd himself the heaven's breath 233
Lovered. Who, young and simple, would not be so lover'd? . *Lov. Comp.* 320
Love-sick. By this the love-sick queen began to sweat . *Ven. and Adon.* 175
That love-sick Love by pleading may be blest . . . 328
Lovest. Why lovest thou that which thou receivest not gladly? . *Sonnet* 8 3
Thou art beloved of many, But that thou none lovest is most evident . 10 4
Make but my name thy love, and love that still, And then thou lovest me, for my name is 'Will' 136 14
Tell me thou lovest elsewhere, but in my sight, Dear heart, forbear to glance thine eye aside 139 5
As thou lovest those Whom thine eyes woo as mine importune thee . 142 9
Those that can see thou lovest, and I am blind . . 149 14
Because thou lovest the one, and I the other . . *Pass. Pil.* 106
Thou lovest to hear the sweet melodious sound That Phœbus' lute, the queen of music, makes 111
But plainly say thou lovest her well, And set thy person forth to sell . 309
Love-suit. Thus far for love my love-suit, sweet, fulfil *Sonnet* 136 4
Loving. The loving swine Sheathed unaware the tusk in his soft groin *Ven. and Adon.* 1115
There is no hate in loving: I'll beg her love: but she is not her own *Lucr.* 240
The colour in thy face, . . . Shall plead for me and tell my loving tale 480
And puts apparel on my tatter'd loving . . . *Sonnet* 26 11
And there reigns love and all love's loving parts . . 31 3
O, then vouchsafe me but this loving thought . . 32 9
Loving offenders, thus I will excuse ye . . . 42 5
A gainer too; For bending all my loving thoughts on thee . . 88 10
Even to thy pure and most most loving breast . . 110 14
Have put on black and loving mourners be . . . 132 3
Hate of my sin, grounded on sinful loving . . . 142 2
In loving thee thou know'st I am forsworn . . . 152 1
As if the boy should use like loving charms . . *Pass. Pil.* 150
Low. For misery is trodden on by many, And being low never relieved by any *Ven. and Adon.* 708
But high or low, That all love's pleasure shall not match his woe . 1139
But low shrubs wither at the cedar's root. So let thy thoughts, low vassals to thy state . . . . *Lucrece* 665
The homely villain court'sies to her low 1338
Some high, some low, the painter was so nice . . . 1412
The eyes, 'fore duteous, now converted are From his low tract . *Sonnet* 7 12
In clamours of all size, both high and low . . *Lov. Comp.* 21
Low-declined. May my pure mind with the foul act dispense, My low-declined honour to advance? . . . . . . *Lucrece* 1705
Lower. Graze on my lips; and if those hills be dry, Stray lower, where the pleasant fountains lie . . . . . *Ven. and Adon.* 234
Lowly. And like a lowly lover down she kneels . . . 350
Loyal. And how her hand, in my hand being lock'd, Forced it to tremble with her loyal fear! . . . . *Lucrece* 261
Since thou couldst not defend thy loyal dame . . . 1034
But when I fear'd I was a loyal wife: So am I now . . 1048
And the turtle's loyal breast To eternity doth rest . *Ph. and Tur.* 57
Luck. Methinks I have astronomy, But not to tell of good or evil luck *Son.* 14 3
Lucrece. The waist Of Collatine's fair love, Lucrece the chaste . *Lucrece* 7
Perchance his boast of Lucrece' sovereignty Suggested this proud issue of a king 36
This heraldry in Lucrece' face was seen, Argued by beauty's red and virtue's white 64
Long he questioned With modest Lucrece, and wore out the night . 123

Lucrece. So Lucrece must I force to my desire . . . *Lucrece* 182
Thus madly led, The Roman lord marcheth to Lucrece' bed . . 301
Then Collatine again, by Lucrece' side, In his clear bed might have reposed still 381
Holy-thoughted Lucrece to their sight Must sell her joy . . 384
'Lucrece,' quoth he, 'this night I must enjoy thee' . . . 512
Cloudy Lucrece shames herself to see, And therefore still in night would cloister'd be 1084
Poor Lucrece' cheeks unto her maid seem so As winter meads . 1217
The precedent whereof in Lucrece view, Assail'd by night . . 1261
By this, mild patience bid fair Lucrece speak . . . 1268
Quoth Lucrece: 'if it should be told, The repetition cannot make it less' . 1284
Vouchsafe t' afford—If ever, love, thy Lucrece thou wilt see—Some present speed to come and visit me 1306
Lucrece thought he blush'd to see her shame . . . 1344
To this well-painted piece is Lucrece come, To find a face where all distress is stell'd 1443
On this sad shadow Lucrece spends her eyes . . . 1457
Lucrece swears he did her wrong, To give her so much grief and not a tongue 1462
So Lucrece, set a-work, sad tales doth tell . . . 1496
Who finds his Lucrece clad in mourning black . . . 1585
From that, alas, thy Lucrece is not free 1624
And never be forgot in mighty Rome Th' adulterate death of Lucrece and her groom 1645
For my sake, when I might charm thee so For she that was thy Lucrece, now attend me 1682
Lucrece' father, that beholds her bleed, Himself on her self-slaughter'd body threw 1732
As pitying Lucrece' woes, Corrupted blood some watery token shows . 1747
Where shall I live now Lucrece is unlived? 1754
Then live, sweet Lucrece, live again and see Thy father die . . 1770
Then in key-cold Lucrece' bleeding stream He falls . . . 1774
The dispersed air, who, holding Lucrece' life, Answer'd their cries . 1805
Brutus, who pluck'd the knife from Lucrece' side . . . 1807
Burying in Lucrece' wound his folly's show 1810
By chaste Lucrece' soul that late complain'd Her wrongs to us . 1839
They did conclude to bear dead Lucrece thence . . . 1850
Lucretia. And being lighted, by the light he spies Lucretia's glove . 317
So under his insulting falchion lies Harmless Lucretia . . 510
Lucretius. 'Daughter, dear daughter,' old Lucretius cries . . 1751
And bids Lucretius give his sorrow place 1773
Quoth Lucretius, 'I did give that life Which she too early and too late hath spill'd' 1800
Lullaby. Then, lullaby, the learned man hath got the lady gay . *Pass. Pil.* 225
Lung. Hallow'd with sighs that burning lungs did raise . *Lov. Comp.* 228
O, that sad breath his spongy lungs bestow'd! . . . 326
Lure. As falcon to the lure, away she flies . . *Ven. and Adon.* 1027
Lurk. Saw'st thou not signs of fear lurk in mine eye? . . . 644
The lightless fire Which, in pale embers hid, lurks to aspire . *Lucrece* 5
Or tyrant folly lurk in gentle breasts 851
'It cannot be,' quoth she, 'that so much guile'—She would have said 'can lurk in such a look' 1535
And from her tongue 'can lurk' from 'cannot' took . . . 1537
The tricks and toys that in them lurk . . . . *Pass. Pil.* 337
Lurked. Sun and sharp air Lurk'd like two thieves . *Ven. and Adon.* 1086
Lurking. Who sees the lurking serpent steps aside . . *Lucrece* 362
Lust. And govern'd him in strength, though not in lust . *Ven. and Adon.* 42
And careless lust stirs up a desperate courage . . . 556
O strange excuse, When reason is the bawd to lust's abuse! . . 792
Love to heaven is fled, Since sweating Lust on earth usurp'd his name . 794
Love comforteth like sunshine after rain, But Lust's effect is tempest after sun 800
Lust's winter comes ere summer half be done . . . 802
Lust like a glutton dies; Love is all truth, Lust full of forged lies . 803
Pawning his honour to obtain his lust . . . . *Lucrece* 156
While lust and murder wake to stain and kill . . . 168
But honest fear, bewitch'd with lust's foul charm, Doth too too oft betake him to retire 173
He doth despise His naked armour of still-slaughter'd lust . . 188
So heedful fear Is almost choked by unresisted lust . . . 282
Stuff up his lust, as minutes fill up hours 297
His rage of lust by gazing qualified; Slack'd, not suppress'd . . 424
Tears harden lust, though marble wear with raining . . . 560
And wilt thou be the school where Lust shall learn? . . . 617
To thee, my heaved-up hands appeal, Not to seducing lust, thy rash relier 639
There falls into thy boundless flood Black lust, dishonour, shame . 654
He sets his foot Upon the light, For light and lust are deadly enemies . 674
O, that prone lust should stain so pure a bed! . . . 684
And Lust, the thief, far poorer than before . . . 693
While Lust is in his pride, no exclamation Can curb his heat . . 705
She bears the load of lust he left behind 734
She thought he blush'd, as knowing Tarquin's lust . . . 1354
Gazing upon the Greeks with little lust 1384
Thy heat of lust, fond Paris, did incur This load of wrath . . 1473
And one man's lust these many lives confounds . . . 1489
And swear I found you where you did fulfil The loathsome act of lust . 1636
His scarlet lust came evidence to swear That my poor beauty had purloin'd his eyes 1650
The expense of spirit in a waste of shame Is lust in action; and till action, lust Is perjured . . . . *Sonnet* 129 2
Lust-breathed Tarquin leaves the Roman host . . *Lucrece* 3
Lustful. And kissing speaks, with lustful language broken *Ven. and Adon.* 47
And now this lustful lord leap'd from his bed . . *Lucrece* 169
Which must be lode-star to his lustful eye 179
Lustily. Anon she hears them chant it lustily, And all in haste she coasteth to the cry . . . . *Ven. and Adon.* 869
Lusty. Over one arm the lusty courser's rein, Under her other was the tender boy 31
A breeding jennet, lusty, young, and proud 260
Where all the treasure of thy lusty days . . . *Sonnet* 2 6
Sap check'd with frost and lusty leaves quite gone . . 5 7
Lute. Whose heavenly touch Upon the lute doth ravish human sense *Pass. Pil.* 108
Sweet melodious sound That Phœbus' lute, the queen of music, makes 112
Luxury. When he most burn'd in heart-wish'd luxury, He preach'd pure maid *Lov. Comp.* 314
Lying. The little Love-god lying once asleep . . *Sonnet* 154 1

M

Mad. Being mad before, how doth she now for wits? *Ven. and Adon.* 249
With her the horse, and left Adonis there, As they were mad 323
Making it subject to the tyranny Of mad mischances and much misery 738
Her eyes are mad that they have wept till now 1062
At his own shadow let the thief run mad *Lucrece* 997
Sometime her grief is dumb and hath no words ; Sometime 'tis mad 1106
The little birds . . . Make her moans mad with their sweet melody 1108
Mad that sorrow should his use control 1781
On purpose laid to make the taker mad ; Mad in pursuit and in possession so *Sonnet* 129 8
For if I should despair, I should grow mad 140 9
Mad slanderers by mad ears believed be 140 12
'Madam, ere I was up,' replied the maid *Lucrece* 1277
Madding. In the distraction of this madding fever *Sonnet* 119 8
Made. Nature that made thee, with herself at strife, Saith that the world hath ending with thy life *Ven. and Adon.* 11
Pure shame and awed resistance made him fret 69
Torches are made to light, jewels to wear, Dainties to taste 163
Love made those hollows, if himself were slain, He might be buried in a tomb so simple 243
And all this dumb play had his acts made plain With tears 359
Groans I never shall regard, Because Adonis' heart hath made mine hard 378
The lesson is but plain, And once made perfect, never lost again 408
So in thyself thyself art made away 763
What needeth then apologies be made? *Lucrece* 31
Collatine's high name, Made glorious by his manly chivalry 109
And made her thrall To living death and pain perpetual 725
That all the faults which in thy reign are made May likewise be sepulchred in thy shade 804
If that be made a theme for disputation 822
My body or my soul, which was the dearer, When the one pure, the other made divine? 1164
Revenge on him that made me stop my breath 1180
A piece Of skilful painting, made for Priam's Troy 1367
Comparing him to that unhappy guest Whose deed hath made herself herself detest 1566
That deep vow, which Brutus made before, He doth again repeat 1847
This were to be new made when thou art old *Sonnet* 2 13
Let those whom Nature hath not made for store, Harsh featureless and rude, barrenly perish 11 9
So I, made lame by fortune's dearest spite 37 3
How would, I say, mine eyes be blessed made By looking on thee in the living day! 43 9
My life, being made of four, with two alone Sinks down to death 45 7
As if by some instinct the wretch did know His rider loved not speed, being made from thee 50 8
Desire, of perfect'st love being made, Shall neigh 51 10
Whereof are you made, That millions of strange shadows on you tend? 53 1
Sweet roses do not so ; Of their sweet deaths are sweetest odours made 54 12
That God forbid that made me first your slave 58 1
And art made tongue-tied by authority 66 9
Ere beauty's dead fleece made another gay 68 8
Not making worse what nature made so clear 84 10
I have gone here and there And made myself a motley to the view 110 2
Sold cheap what is most dear, Made old offences of affections new 110 4
Now I find true That better is by evil still made better 119 10
What we see doth lie, Made more or less by thy continual haste 123 12
When my love swears that she is made of truth I do believe her 138 1
Gave eyes to blindness, Or made them swear against the thing they see 152 12
Love lack'd a dwelling, and made him her place *Lov. Comp.* 82
All aids, themselves made fairer by their place, Came for additions 117
Ask'd their own wills, and made their wills obey 133
Errors of the blood, none of the mind ; Love made them not 185
Each several stone, With wit well blazon'd, smiled or made some moan 217
Whose rarest havings made the blossoms dote 235
When my love swears that she is made of truth, I do believe her *Pass. Pil.* 1
Cytherea, all in love forlorn, A longing tarriance for Adonis made 74
Sitting in a pleasant shade Which a grove of myrtles made 376
For her griefs, so lively shown, Made me think upon mine own 390
Whereupon it made this threne To the phœnix and the dove *Ph. and Tur.* 49
Madly. Which madly hurries her she knows not whither *Ven. and Adon.* 904
Is madly toss'd between desire and dread *Lucrece* 171
Thus madly led The Roman lord marcheth to Lucrece' bed 300
Madmen. My thoughts and my discourse as madmen's are *Sonnet* 147 11
Madness. And in my madness might speak ill of thee 140 10
Madrigals. By shallow rivers, by whose falls Melodious birds sing madrigals *Pass. Pil.* 360
Maid. Calls her maid, Whose swift obedience to her mistress hies *Lucrece* 1214
Poor Lucrece' cheeks unto her maid seem so As winter meads 1217
Even so the maid with swelling drops gan wet 1228
Which makes the maid weep like the dewy night 1232
Replied the maid, 'The more to blame my sluggard negligence' 1277
If your maid may be so bold, She would request to know your heaviness 1282
Her maid is gone, and she prepares to write 1296
A maid of Dian's this advantage found *Sonnet* 153 2
Ere long espied a fickle maid full pale, Tearing of papers *Lov. Comp.* 5
Gentle maid, Have of my suffering youth some feeling pity 177
He preach'd pure maid, and praised cold chastity 315
And new pervert a reconciled maid 329
Which by a gift of learning did bear the maid away *Pass. Pil.* 224
Maiden. She with her tears Doth quench the maiden burning of his cheeks *Ven. and Adon.* 50
A pair of maiden worlds unconquered, Save of their lord *Lucrece* 408
Why should the worm intrude the maiden bud? 848
Many maiden gardens yet unset With virtuous wish *Sonnet* 16 6
And maiden virtue rudely strumpeted 66 6
But in her maiden hand The fairest votary took up that fire 154 4
So commended, That maidens' eyes stuck over all his face *Lov. Comp.* 81
Maiden-tongued. For maiden-tongued he was, and thereof free 100
Maim. And, veil'd in them, did win whom he would maim 312
Main. Nativity, once in the main of light, Crawls to maturity *Sonnet* 60 5
And the firm soil win of the watery main, Increasing store 64 7
My saucy bark inferior far to his On your broad main doth wilfully appear 80 8

Maintain. Unless this general evil they maintain, All men are bad *Son.* 121 13
Maintained. By all our country rights in Rome maintain'd *Lucrece* 1838
Majesty. With gentle majesty and modest pride *Ven. and Adon.* 278
The sun ariseth in his majesty 856
Hiding base sin in plaits of majesty *Lucrece* 93
I sue for exiled majesty's repeal ; Let him return 640
In great commanders grace and majesty You might behold 1387
Serving with looks his sacred majesty *Sonnet* 7 4
And given grace a double majesty 78 8
Make. Sick-thoughted Venus makes amain unto him *Ven. and Adon.* 5
Make use of time, let not advantage slip 129
I'll make a shadow for thee of my hairs 191
For where a heart is hard they make no battery 426
Claps her pale cheek, till clapping makes it red 468
What bargains may I make, still to be sealing? 512
Which purchase if thou make, for fear of slips Set thy seal-manual on my wax-red lips 515
Wilt thou make the match? He tells her, no 586
Doth make them droop with grief and hang the head 666
The thought of it doth make my faint heart bleed, And fear doth teach it divination 669
To make the cunning hounds mistake their smell 686
Each shadow makes him stop, each murmur stay 706
To make thee hate the hunting of the boar, Unlike myself thou hear'st me moralize 711
Rich preys make true men thieves 724
So do thy lips Make modest Dian cloudy and forlorn 725
Your treatise makes me like you worse and worse 774
The neighbour caves, as seeming troubled, Make verbal repetition of her moans 831
How love makes young men thrall and old men dote 837
Each lamp and shining star doth borrow The beauteous influence that makes him bright 862
The bushes in the way . . . Some twine about her thigh to make her stay 873
The fear whereof doth make him shake and shudder 880
Sighs dry her cheeks, tears make them wet again 966
Despair and hope makes thee ridiculous 988
That her sight dazzling makes the wound seem three 1064
Her mangling eye, That makes more gashes where no breach should be 1066
The strongest body shall it make most weak 1145
Make the young old, the old become a child 1152
Yet their ambition makes them still to fight *Lucrece* 68
He makes excuses for his being there 114
For want of wit, Make something nothing by augmenting it 154
Such hazard now must doting Tarquin make 155
What excuse can my invention make, When thou shalt charge me with so black a deed? 225
With good thoughts makes dispensation, Urging the worser sense for vantage still 248
O, how her fear did make her colour rise! 257
The wind wars with his torch to make him stay 311
Smoking with pride, march'd on to make his stand On her bare breast 438
Heedfully doth view The sight which makes supposed terror true 455
This moves in him more rage and lesser pity, To make the breach 469
The colour in thy face, That even for anger makes the lily pale 478
He rouseth up himself and makes a pause 541
That to his borrow'd bed he make retire, And stoop to honour, not to foul desire 573
This deed will make thee only loved for fear 610
Make slow pursuit, or altogether balk The prey 696
Make war against proportion'd course of time 774
Let their exhaled unwholesome breaths make sick The life of purity 779
His smother'd light May set at noon and make perpetual night 784
As palmers' chat makes short their pilgrimage 791
Make me not object to the tell-tale Day! 806
To make the child a man, the man a child 954
Unless thou couldst return to make amends 961
To make him curse this cursed crimeful night 970
Let there bechance him pitiful mischances, To make him moan 977
The mightier man, the mightier is the thing that makes him honour'd 1005
No tool imparteth To make more vent for passage of her breath 1040
The little birds . . . Make her moans mad with their sweet melody 1108
To see the salve doth make the wound ache more 1116
Make thy sad grove in my dishevell'd hair 1129
Let it not be call'd impiety, If in this blemish'd fort I make some hole 1175
This brief abridgement of my will I make 1198
Mine honour be the knife's that makes my wound 1201
Which makes the maid weep like the dewy night 1232
Those proud lords, to blame, Make weak-made women tenants to their shame 1260
If it should be told, The repetition cannot make it less 1285
She dares not thereof make discovery 1314
Deep sounds make lesser noise than shallow fords 1329
Her earnest eye did make him more amazed 1356
These contraries such unity do hold, Only to flatter fools and make them bold 1559
O, teach me how to make mine own excuse! 1653
His sighs, his sorrows, make a saw, To push grief on 1672
Shall rotten death make conquest of the stronger? 1767
Held back his sorrow's tide, to make it more 1789
Shall sum my count and make my old excuse *Sonnet* 2 11
Make sweet some vial ; treasure thou some place With beauty's treasure 6 3
Thou art much too fair To be death's conquest and make worms thine heir 6 14
Make thee another self, for love of me 10 13
And threescore year would make the world away 11 8
Of thy beauty do I question make, That thou among the wastes of time must go 12 9
Nothing 'gainst Time's scythe can make defence Save breed 12 13
Make war upon this bloody tyrant, Time 16 2
Time's pencil, or my pupil pen, Neither in inward worth nor outward fair, Can make you live yourself in eyes of men 16 12
Make the earth devour her own sweet brood 19
Make glad and sorry seasons as thou fleets 19 5
Wit so poor as mine May make seem bare, in wanting words to show it 26 6
Makes black night beauteous and her old face new 27 12
And night doth nightly make grief's strength seem stronger 28 14

Make. And make me travel forth without my cloak *Sonnet* 34 2
All men make faults, and even I in this 35 5
I make my love engrafted to this store 37 8
Thou teachest how to make one twain 39 13
To make some special instant special blest, By new unfolding his imprison'd pride 52 11
Makes summer's welcome thrice more wish'd, more rare 56 14
Think of nought Save, where you are how happy you make those 57 12
Like as the waves make towards the pebbled shore 60 1
I in your sweet thoughts would be forgot If thinking on me then should make you woe 71 8
Which makes thy love more strong, To love that well which thou must leave ere long 73 13
To make me tongue-tied, speaking of your fame 80 4
Or I shall live your epitaph to make, Or you survive 81 1
Being fond on praise, which makes your praises worse 84 14
My deeds to cross, Join with the spite of fortune, make me bow 90 3
Thou mayst take All this away and me most wretched make 91 14
How sweet and lovely dost thou make the shame 95 1
Nor the lays of birds . . . Could make me any summer's story tell 98 7
And make Time's spoils despised every where 100 12
Make answer, Muse: wilt thou not haply say 'Truth needs no colour' 101 5
'T lies in thee To make him much outlive a gilded tomb 101 11
I teach thee how To make him seem long hence as he shows now 101 14
But makes antiquity for aye his page 108 12
My most true mind thus makes mine eye untrue 113 14
To make of monsters and things indigest Such cherubins 114 5
To make our appetites more keen, With eager compounds 118 1
And rather make them born to our desire 123 7
On purpose laid to make the taker mad 129 8
So as thou art, As those whose beauties proudly make them cruel 131 2
Thy face hath not the power to make love groan 131 6
Beshrew that heart that makes my heart to groan! 133 1
Add to thy 'Will' One will of mine, to make thy large 'Will' more 135 12
Make but my name thy love, and love that still, And then thou lovest me 136 13
I count my gain, That she that makes me sin awards me pain 141 14
Sets down her babe and makes all swift dispatch 143 3
Those lips that Love's own hand did make Breathed forth the sound 145 1
To make me give the lie to my true sight 150 3
Who taught thee how to make me love thee more? 150 9
What rounds, what bounds, what course, what stop he makes! *Lov. Comp.* 109
To make the weeper laugh, the laugher weep, He had the dialect 124
Advice is often seen By blunting us to make our wits more keen 161
And makes her absence valiant, not her might 245
And supplicant their sighs to you extend, To leave the battery that you make 'gainst mine 277
And yet do question make What I should do again for such a sake 321
If love make me forsworn, how shall I swear to love? *Pass. Pil.* 57
Study his bias leaves, and makes his book thine eyes 61
Sweet melodious sound That Phœbus' lute, the queen of music, makes 112
'T may be, again to make me wander thither 190
There will I make thee a bed of roses, With a thousand fragrant posies 361
Makeless. The world will wail thee, like a makeless wife *Sonnet* 9 4
Makest. What bare excuses makest thou to be gone! *Ven. and Adon.* 188
And makest fair reputation but a bawd *Lucrece* 623
Thou makest the vestal violate her oath 883
And, tender churl, makest waste in niggarding *Sonnet* 1 12
Thou makest faults graces that to thee resort 96 4
And thou treble-dated crow, That thy sable gender makest *Ph. and Tur.* 18
Maketh. My woe too sensible thy passion maketh More feeling-painful *Lucr.* 1678
Making them red and pale with fresh variety *Ven. and Adon.* 21
Her contending tears, Which long have rain'd, making her cheeks all wet 83
Making my arms his field, his tent my bed 108
Making it subject to the tyranny Of mad mischances and much misery 737
Making such sober action with his hand, That it beguiled attention *Lucrece* 1403
Making a famine where abundance lies *Sonnet* 1 7
Making a couplement of proud compare, With sun and moon 21 5
Itself and true, Making no summer of another's green 68 11
Not making worse what nature made so clear 84 10
Making his style admired every where 84 12
Making their tomb the womb wherein they grew 86 4
So thy great gift, upon misprision growing, Comes home again, on better judgement making 87 12
I straight will halt, Against thy reasons making no defence 89 4
Making lascivious comments on thy sport, Cannot dispraise 95 6
Beauty making beautiful old rhyme In praise of ladies 106 3
Making dead wood more blest than living lips 128 12
I that vex thee still, To thy sweet will making addition thus 135 4
Maladies. Not the least of all these maladies But in one minute's fight brings beauty under *Ven. and Adon.* 745
To prevent our maladies unseen, We sicken to shun sickness when we purge *Sonnet* 118 3
Which yet men prove Against strange maladies a sovereign cure 153 8
Malcontent. Then, like a melancholy malcontent, He vails his tail *V. and A.* 313
Man. More lovely than a man, More white and red than doves or roses are 9
Thing like a man, but of no woman bred! 214
Thou art no man, though of a man's complexion 215
Would thou wert as I am, and I a man, My heart all whole as thine 369
How love makes young men thrall and old men dote 837
A martial man to be soft fancy's slave! *Lucrece* 200
Who fears a sentence or an old man's saw Shall by a painted cloth be kept in awe 244
If ever man were moved with woman's moans, Be moved with my tears 587
The aged man that coffers-up his gold Is plagued with cramps 855
To make the child a man, the man a child 954
The mightier man, the mightier is the thing That makes him honour'd 1004
No man inveigh against the wither'd flower 1254
Here one man's hand lean'd on another's head 1415
And one man's lust these many lives confounds 1489
No man could distinguish what he said 1785
A man in hue, all 'hues' in his controlling, Which steals men's eyes *Son.* 20 7
Like him with friends possess'd, Desiring this man's art and that man's scope 29 7
For no man well of such a salve can speak 34 7
If this be error and upon me proved, I never writ, nor no man ever loved 116 14
Who leaves unsway'd the likeness of a man, Thy proud heart's slave 141 11
The better angel is a man right fair 144 3
A reverend man that grazed his cattle nigh—Sometime a blusterer *L. Comp.* 57
Small show of man was yet upon his chin 92
Man. This man's untrue, And knew the patterns of his foul beguiling *Lov. Comp.* 169
My better angel is a man right fair, My worser spirit a woman colour'd ill *Pass. Pil.* 17
Then, lullaby, the learned man hath got the lady gay 225
Every man will be thy friend Whilst thou hast wherewith to spend 407
But if store of crowns be scant, No man will supply thy want 410
Manage. He will not manage her, although he mount her *Ven. and Adon.* 598
Whether the horse by him became his deed, Or he his manage by the well-doing steed *Lov. Comp.* 112
Mane. His braided hanging mane Upon his compass'd crest now stand on end *Ven. and Adon.* 271
Thin mane, thick tail, broad buttock, tender hide 298
For through his mane and tail the high wind sings, Fanning the hairs 305
Mangling. And then she reprehends her mangling eye 1065
Manifold. The heaven-hued sapphire and the opal blend With objects manifold *Lov. Comp.* 216
Manly. Collatine's high name, Made glorious by his manly chivalry *Lucrece* 109
Here Priam dies, Here manly Hector faints, here Troilus swounds 1486
Till manly shame bids him possess his breath 1777
Manner. Their face their manners most expressly told 1397
O, how thy worth with manners may I sing? *Sonnet* 39 1
My tongue-tied Muse in manners holds her still 85 1
That did not better for my life provide Than public means which public manners breeds 111 4
And words express The manner of my pity-wanting pain 140 4
Mansion. Her quiet interrupted, Her mansion batter'd by the enemy *Lucrece* 1171
O, what a mansion have those vices got! *Sonnet* 95 9
Why so large cost, having so short a lease, Dost thou upon thy fading mansion spend? 146 6
The goodly objects which abroad they find Of lands and mansions *L. Comp.* 138
Mantle. Throwing his mantle rudely o'er his arm *Lucrece* 170
Anon he comes, and throws his mantle by, And stood stark naked *Pass. Pil.* 79
Many. The many musets through the which he goes Are like a labyrinth to amaze his foes *Ven. and Adon.* 683
For misery is trodden on by many, And being low never relieved by any 707
Join they all together, Like many clouds consulting for foul weather 972
Alas, how many bear such shameful blows! *Lucrece* 832
Many a dry drop seem'd a weeping tear 1375
The scalps of many, almost hid behind, To jump up higher seem'd, to mock the mind 1413
Stood many Trojan mothers, sharing joy To see their youthful sons bright weapons wield 1431
Many she sees where cares have carved some 1445
Why should the private pleasure of some one Become the public plague of many moe? 1479
Why should so many fall, To plague a private sin in general? 1483
And one man's lust these many lives confounds 1489
After many accents and delays, Untimely breathings 1719
Whose speechless song, being many, seeming one, Sings this to thee: 'thou single wilt prove none' *Sonnet* 8 13
Thou art beloved of many, But that thou none lovest is most evident 10 3
Many maiden gardens yet unset With virtuous wish 16 6
I sigh the lack of many a thing I sought 30 3
And moan the expense of many a vanish'd sight 30 8
How many a holy and obsequious tear Hath dear religious love stol'n from mine eye As interest of the dead 31 5
That due of many now is thine alone 31 12
Full many a glorious morning have I seen Flatter the mountain-tops 33 1
She hath no exchequer now but his, And, proud of many, lives upon his gains 67 12
In many's looks the false heart's history Is writ in moods and frowns 93 7
How many lambs might the stern wolf betray, If like a lamb he could his looks translate! 96 9
How many gazers mightst thou lead away, If thou wouldst use the strength of all thy state! 96 11
Whilst many nymphs that vow'd chaste life to keep Came tripping by 154 3
That fire Which many legions of true hearts had warm'd 154 6
Of folded schedules had she many a one, Which she perused *Lov. Comp.* 43
Crack'd many a ring of posied gold and bone, Bidding them find their sepulchres in mud 45
In me you behold The injury of many a blasting hour 72
Many there were that did his picture get, To serve their eyes 134
So many have, that never touch'd his hand, Sweetly supposed 141
Experience for me many bulwarks builded Of proofs new-bleeding 152
Among the many that mine eyes have seen 190
I have received from many a several fair, Their kind acceptance 206
Did court the lad with many a lovely look *Pass. Pil.* 45
How many tales to please me hath she coined! 93
Map. Showing life's triumph in the map of death *Lucrece* 402
The face, that map which deep impression bears Of hard misfortune 1712
Thus is his cheek the map of days outworn *Sonnet* 68 1
And him as for a map doth Nature store, To show false Art 68 13
Mar not the thing that cannot be amended. *Lucrece* 578
Were it not sinful then, striving to mend, To mar the subject? *Sonnet* 103 10
Marble. Tears harden lust, though marble wear with raining. *Lucrece* 560
Men have marble, women waxen, minds, And therefore are they form'd as marble will 1240
Not marble, nor the gilded monuments Of princes *Sonnet* 55 1
March. Let thy misty vapours march so thick *Lucrece* 782
A dearer birth than this his love had brought, To march in ranks of better equipage *Sonnet* 32 12
Marched. Smoking with pride, march'd on to make his stand On her bare breast *Lucrece* 438
When their brave hope, bold Hector, march'd to field 1430
Marcheth. Thus madly led, The Roman lord marcheth to Lucrece' bed 301
Marching. Pale cowards, marching on with trembling paces 1391
Mare. My busy care, Is how to get my palfrey from the mare *Ven. and Adon.* 384
Margent. Secrecies Writ in the glassy margents of such books *Lucrece* 102
She in a river threw, Upon whose weeping margent she was set *Lov. Comp.* 39
Marigold. Her eyes, like marigolds, had sheathed their light. *Lucrece* 397
Their fair leaves spread But as the marigold at the sun's eye. *Sonnet* 25 6
Marjoram. And buds of marjoram had stol'n thy hair 99 7
Mark. Didst thou not mark my face? was it not white? *Ven. and Adon.* 643
And when thou hast on foot the purblind hare, Mark the poor wretch 680
Thy mark is feeble age, but thy false dart Mistakes that aim 941
My will that marks thee for my earth's delight *Lucrece* 487
Shall remain The scornful mark of every open eye 520
For marks descried in men's nativity Are nature's faults 538
Let him have time to mark how slow time goes In time of sorrow 990

Mark. With soft-slow tongue, true mark of modesty . . . *Lucrece* 1220
Mark how one string, sweet husband to another . . . *Sonnet* 8 9
For slander's mark was ever yet the fair . . . 70 2
Mark how with my neglect I do dispense . . . 112 12
It is an ever-fixed mark That looks on tempests and is never shaken 116 5
If knowledge be the mark, to know thee shall suffice *Pass. Pil.* 63
I sit and mark, And wish her lays were tuned like the lark . 197
Marketh. This ill presage advisedly she marketh *Ven. and Adon.* 457
Marking. She marking them begins a wailing note And sings 835
Marking what he tells With trembling fear, as fowl hear falcon's bells *Lucr.* 510
Marred. He seeks To mend the hurt that his unkindness marr'd *V. and A.* 478
Marriage. This siege that hath engirt his marriage, This blur to youth *Lucr.* 221
Let me not to the marriage of true minds Admit impediments *Sonnet* 116 1
Married. If the true concord of well-tuned sounds, By unions married, do offend thine ear 8 6
I grant thou wert not married to my Muse 82 1
'Twas not their infirmity, It was married chastity . *Ph. and Tur.* 61
Marrow. My flesh is soft and plump, my marrow burning *Ven. and Adon.* 142
Marrow-eating sickness, whose attaint Disorder breeds 741
Mars. Nor Mars his sword nor war's quick fire shall burn *Sonnet* 55 7
She told the youngling how god Mars did try her *Pass. Pil.* 145
Martial. A martial man to be soft fancy's slave! *Lucrece* 200
Martyred. Immodesty lies martyr'd with disgrace 802
Marvel. Therefore no marvel though thy horse be gone . *Ven. and Adon.* 390
No marvel then, though I mistake my view *Sonnet* 148 11
Mask. To mask their brows and hide their infamy *Lucrece* 794
Masked. The region cloud hath mask'd him from me now *Sonnet* 33 12
When summer's breath their masked buds discloses 54 8
If some suspect of ill mask'd not thy show 70 13
Masonry. And broils root out the work of masonry 55 6
Master. His testy master goeth about to take him *Ven. and Adon.* 319
Tell me, Love's master, shall we meet to-morrow? 585
And asks the weary caitiff for his master. 914
I see their antique pen would have express'd Even such a beauty as you master now *Sonnet* 106 8
The fairest one of three, That liked of her master as well as well might be *Pass. Pil.* 212
To leave the master loveless, or kill the gallant knight . 216
Mastered. Servilely master'd with a leathern rein! *Ven. and Adon.* 392
He cannot use it, And leaves it to be master'd by his young . *Lucrece* 863
Mastering. O, be not proud, nor brag not of thy might, For mastering her that foil'd the god of fight! *Ven. and Adon.* 114
What labour is't to leave The thing we have not, mastering what not strives *Lov. Comp.* 240
Master-mistress. A woman's face with Nature's own hand painted Hast thou, the master-mistress of my passion *Sonnet* 20 2
Match. Wilt thou make the match? He tells her, no *Ven. and Adon.* 586
That all love's pleasure shall not match his woe 1140
Matcheth. But why thy odour matcheth not thy show, The solve is this *Sonnet* 69 13
Mate. In the possession of his beauteous mate *Lucrece* 18
Mated. Her more than haste is mated with delays *Ven. and Adon.* 909
Matter. 'Where did I leave?' 'No matter where;' quoth he, 'Leave me' 715
Subject and servile to all discontents, As dry combustious matter is to fire 1162
Thy wretched wife mistook the matter so, To slay herself *Lucrece* 1826
No matter then although my foot did stand Upon the farthest earth removed from thee *Sonnet* 44 5
When your countenance fill'd up his line, Then lack'd I matter 86 14
As a dream doth flatter, In sleep a king, but waking no such matter 87 14
In him a plenitude of subtle matter, Applied to cautels, all strange forms receives *Lov. Comp.* 302
Maturity. Nativity, once in the main of light, Crawls to maturity *Son.* 60 6
Maund. A thousand favours from a maund she drew *Lov. Comp.* 36
Maw. Even as poor birds, deceived with painted grapes, Do surfeit by the eye and pine the maw *Ven. and Adon.* 602
May. And may it be That thou shouldst think it heavy unto thee 155
Thou art bound to breed, That thine may live when thou thyself art dead 172
That love-sick Love by pleading may be blest 328
So of concealed sorrow may be said 333
Long may they kiss each other, for this cure! 505
The star-gazers, . . . May say, the plague is banish'd by thy breath 510
What bargains may I make, still to be sealing? 512
She hath assay'd as much as may be proved 608
What may a heavy groan advantage thee? 950
If your maid may be so bold, She would request to know your heaviness *Lucrece* 1282
And tell thy grief, that we may give redress 1603
May my pure mind with the foul act dispense 1704
May any terms acquit me from this chance? 1706
Rough winds do shake the darling buds of May *Sonnet* 18 3
Then may I dare to boast how I do love thee 26 13
I may not evermore acknowledge thee 36 9
What's in the brain that ink may character? 108 1
I may be straight, though they themselves be bevel 121 11
That I may not be so, nor thou belied, Bear thine eyes straight 140 13
Whether that my angel be turn'd fiend Suspect I may 144 10
Such a storm As oft 'twixt May and April is to see *Lov. Comp.* 102
'T may be, she joy'd to jest at my exile, 'T may be, again to make me wander thither *Pass. Pil.* 189
Love, whose month was ever May, Spied a blossom passing fair 228
As it fell upon a day In the merry month of May 374
Mayst. By whose example thou revenged mayst be. *Lucrece* 1194
Thou mayst take All this away and me most wretched make *Sonnet* 91 13
Thou mayst be false, and yet I know it not 92 14
By self-example mayst thou be denied 142 14
Maze. Or one encompass'd with a winding maze *Lucrece* 1151
Mead. Would root these beauties as he roots the mead *Ven. and Adon.* 636
As winter meads when sun doth melt their snow *Lucrece* 1218
Meadows. Kissing with golden face the meadows green *Sonnet* 33 3
Meagre, lean, Hateful divorce of love,—thus chides she Death *Ven. and Adon.* 931
Mean. Never can blab, nor know not what we mean 126
Dost thou mean To stifle beauty and to steal his breath. 933
Where their queen Means to immure herself and not be seen 1194
Thus I forestall thee, if thou mean to chide *Lucrece* 484
And in thy dead arms do I mean to place him. 517
I mean to bear thee Unto the base bed of some rascal groom 670
I live, and seek in vain Some happy mean to end a hapless life 1045
These means, as frets upon an instrument, Shall tune our heart-strings 1140
Pausing for means to mourn some newer way 1365
That he finds means to burn his Troy with water 1561

Mean. With means more blessed than my barren rhyme . *Sonnet* 16 4
That did not better for my life provide Than public means . 111 4
What means the world to say it is not so? 148 6
Meaner. That meaner men should vaunt That golden hap which their superiors want *Lucrece* 41
Meaning. His meaning struck her ere his words begun *Ven. and Adon.* 462
But she, that never coped with stranger eyes, Could pick no meaning from their parling looks *Lucrece* 100
And would not take her meaning nor her pleasure *Pass. Pil.* 154
Meant. She carved thee for her seal, and meant thereby Thou shouldst print more, not let that copy die *Sonnet* 11 13
Measure my strangeness with my unripe years . *Ven. and Adon.* 524
Teaching decrepit age to tread the measures 1148
They look into the beauty of thy mind, And that, in guess, they measure by thy deeds *Sonnet* 69 10
But these particulars are not my measure 91 7
Measured. Thus far the miles are measured from thy friend 50 4
Mediators. To trembling clients be you mediators *Lucrece* 1020
Medicine. And brought to medicine a healthful state *Sonnet* 118 11
Meditation. O fearful meditation! where, alack, Shall Time's best jewel from Time's chest lie hid? 65 9
Meed. For thy meed A thousand honey secrets shalt thou know *V. and A.* 15
When great treasure is the meed proposed, Though death be adjunct, there's no death supposed *Lucrece* 132
Meek. Feeble Desire, all recreant, poor, and meek . 710
Meet. Tell me, Love's master, shall we meet to-morrow? *Ven. and Adon.* 585
Here she meets another sadly scowling, To whom she speaks 917
Foggy Night! . . . Muster thy mists to meet the eastern light *Lucrece* 773
But they ne'er meet with Opportunity 903
Flowers distill'd, though they with winter meet, Leese but their show; their substance still lives sweet *Sonnet* 5 13
But if that flower with base infection meet, The basest weed outbraves his dignity 94 11
Meeting. Whose ridges with the meeting clouds contend *Ven. and Adon.* 820
Till, meeting greater ranks, They join and shoot their foam at Simois' banks *Lucrece* 1441
All our merry meetings on the plains *Pass. Pil.* 290
Meetness. And, sick of welfare, found a kind of meetness To be diseased ere that there was true needing *Sonnet* 118 7
Melancholy. Then, like a melancholy malcontent, He vails his tail *V. and A.* 313
Sinks down to death, oppress'd with melancholy *Sonnet* 45 8
Mellow. The mellow plum doth fall, the green sticks fast *Ven. and Adon.* 527
Melodious discord, heavenly tune harsh-sounding 431
Sweet melodious sound That Phœbus' lute, the queen of music, makes *Pass. Pil.* 111
By shallow rivers, by whose falls Melodious birds sing madrigals 360
Melody. The little birds that tune their morning's joy Make her moans mad with their sweet melody *Lucrece* 1108
Melt. My smooth moist hand, were it with thy hand felt, Would in thy palm dissolve, or seem to melt *Ven. and Adon.* 144
As mountain-snow melts with the midday sun 750
Yet sometimes falls an orient drop beside, Which her cheek melts 982
Heavy heart's lead, melt at mine eyes' red fire! 1073
O, if no harder than a stone thou art, Melt at my tears! *Lucrece* 594
Seem so As winter meads when sun doth melt their snow 1218
Melted. The boy that by her side lay kill'd Was melted like a vapour from her sight *Ven. and Adon.* 1166
Melting. He vails his tail that, like a falling plume, Cool shadow to his melting buttock lent 315
Each flower moisten'd like a melting eye. *Lucrece* 1227
Appear to him, as he to me appears, All melting *Lov. Comp.* 300
Memorial. Some interest, Which for memorial still with thee shall stay *Sonnet* 74 4
Memory. His tender heir might bear his memory 1 4
And wear their brave state out of memory 15 8
Nor war's quick fire shall burn The living record of your memory 55 8
That he shall never cut from memory My sweet love's beauty 63 11
The wrinkles which thy glass will truly show Of mouthed graves will give thee memory 77 6
What thy memory can not contain Commit to these waste blanks 77 9
From hence your memory death cannot take 81 3
Full character'd with lasting memory 122 2
Men. For men will kiss even by their own direction *Ven. and Adon.* 216
Rich preys make true men thieves 724
Which with cold terror doth men's minds confound 1048
Beauty itself doth of itself persuade The eyes of men without an orator *Lucr.* 30
That meaner men should vaunt That golden hap which their superiors want 41
For marks descried in men's nativity Are nature's faults 538
Men's faults do seldom to themselves appear 633
Since men prove beasts, let beasts bear gentle minds 1148
For men have marble, women waxen, minds 1240
In men, as in a rough-grown grove, remain Cave keeping evils that obscurely sleep 1249
Though men can cover crimes with bold stern looks 1252
O, let it not be hild Poor women's faults, that they are so fulfill'd With men's abuses 1259
One of my husband's men Bid thou be ready, by and by 1291
There would appear The very eyes of men through loop-holes thrust 1383
I perceive that men as plants increase, Cheered and check'd even by the self-same sky *Sonnet* 15 5
Time's pencil, or my pupil pen, Neither in inward worth nor outward fair, Can make you live yourself in eyes of men 16 12
Be scorn'd like old men of less truth than tongue 17 10
So long as men can breathe or eyes can see, So long lives this 18 13
Him in thy course untainted do allow For beauty's pattern to succeeding men 19 12
Which steals men's eyes and women's souls amazeth 20 8
In disgrace with fortune and men's eyes 29 1
Exceeded by the height of happier men 32 8
All men make faults, and even I in this 35 5
When you entombed in men's eyes shall lie 81 8
Where breath most breathes, even in the mouths of men 81 14
And having thee, of all men's pride I boast 91 12
Unless this general evil they maintain, All men are bad 121 14
Yet none knows well To shun the heaven that leads men to this hell 129 14
Be anchor'd in the bay where all men ride 137 6
As testy sick men, when their deaths be near, No news but health from their physicians know 140 7
So shalt thou feed on Death, that feeds on men 146 13
Then love doth well denote Love's eye is not so true as all men's 'No' 148 8

Men. Which yet men prove Against strange maladies a sovereign cure *Sonnet* 153 7
Growing a bath and healthful remedy For men diseased . . 154 12
Yet, if men moved him, was he such a storm . *Lov. Comp.* 101
Often men would say 'That horse his mettle from his rider takes' . 106
For now I see Inconstancy More in women than in men remain *Pass. Pil.* 262
Like a thousand vanquish'd men in bloody fight! . . . 280
Had women been so strong as men, In faith, you had not had it then . 321
Think women still to strive with men, To sin and never for to saint 341
Mend. He seeks To mend the hurt that his unkindness marr'd *Ven. and Adon.* 478
Want nothing that the thought of hearts can mend . *Sonnet* 69 2
In others' works thou dost but mend the style 78 11
Were it not sinful then, striving to mend, To mar the subject? 103 9
Mended. Whether we are mended, or whether better they 59 11
Merchandized. That love is merchandized whose rich esteeming The owner's tongue doth publish every where 102 3
Merchant. Shelves and sands, The merchant fears, ere rich at home he lands *Lucrece* 336
Lo, here, the hopeless merchant of this loss, With head declined . 1660
Merciful. It shall be merciful and too severe *Ven. and Adon.* 1155
Merciless. So did the merciless and pitchy night Fold in the object that did feed her sight 821
That mother tries a merciless conclusion Who, having two sweet babes, when death takes one, Will slay the other and be nurse to none *Lucrece* 1160
Mercy. Fearing no such thing, Lies at the mercy of his mortal sting 364
Straight in her heart did mercy come *Sonnet* 145 5
Merely. Thought characters and words merely but art *Lov. Comp.* 174
Thus merely with the garment of a Grace The naked and concealed fiend he cover'd 316
Merit. To whom in vassalage Thy merit hath my duty strongly knit *Sonnet* 26 2
Lest the world should task you to recite What merit lived in me . 72 2
To set me light And place my merit in the eye of scorn 88 2
What new to register, That may express my love or thy dear merit? 108 4
And thou shalt find it merits not reproving 142 4
What merit do I in myself respect, That is so proud thy service to despise? 149 9
Spare not to spend, and chiefly there Where thy desert may merit praise *Pass. Pil.* 325
Meritorious. 'Tis a meritorious fair design To chase injustice with revengeful arms *Lucrece* 1692
Mermaid. Thy mermaid's voice hath done me double wrong *Ven. and Adon.* 429
Bewitching like the wanton mermaid's songs 777
As if some mermaid did their ears entice *Lucrece* 1411
Merry. Even at this word see hears a merry horn *Ven. and Adon.* 1025
And merry fools to mock at him resort *Lucrece* 989
Sad souls are slain in merry company 1110
A woeful hostess brooks not merry guests 1125
All my merry jigs are quite forgot, All my lady's love is lost, God wot *Pass. Pil.* 253
All our merry meetings on the plains 290
As it fell upon a day In the merry month of May 374
Messenger. The mindful messenger, come back, Brings home his lord *Lucr.* 1583
By those swift messengers return'd from thee . *Sonnet* 45 10
Met. Yet pardon me I felt a kind of fear When as I met the boar *V. and A.* 999
Both stood, like old acquaintance in a trance, Met far from home *Lucrece* 1596
Metal. Behold these talents of their hair, With twisted metal amorously impleach'd *Lov. Comp.* 205
Methinks. Methinks I have astronomy, But not to tell of good or evil luck *Sonnet* 14 2
Methinks no face so gracious is as mine, No shape so true 62 5
So your sweet hue, which methinks still doth stand, Hath motion 104 11
That all the world besides methinks are dead 112 14
O, sweet shepherd, hie thee, For methinks thou stay'st too long *Pass. Pil.* 168
Methods. To new-found methods and to compounds strange . *Sonnet* 76 4
Metre. A poet's rage And stretched metre of an antique song 17 12
Mettle. Often men would say That horse his mettle from his rider takes *Lov. Comp.* 107
Mickle. More mickle was the pain That nothing could be used to turn them both to gain *Pass. Pil.* 219
Mid-day. And Titan, tired in the mid-day heat, With burning eye did hotly overlook them *Ven. and Adon.* 177
As mountain-snow melts with the midday sun 750
Middle. Resembling strong youth in his middle age *Sonnet* 7 6
Midnight. In the dreadful dead of dark midnight *Lucrece* 1625
Midst. But in the midst of his unfruitful prayer 344
And midst the sentence so her accent breaks, That twice she doth begin ere once she speaks 566
In the midst of all her pure protestings *Pass. Pil.* 95
Might. Brag not of thy might, For mastering her that foil'd the god of fight *Ven. and Adon.* 113
He might be buried in a tomb so simple 244
Would they not wish the feast might ever last? 447
Kings might be espoused to more fame, But king nor peer to such a peerless dame *Lucrece* 20
This desire Might have excuse to work upon his wife 235
That his foul thoughts might compass his fair fair 346
By Lucrece' side, In his clear bed might have reposed still 382
Canopied in darkness sweetly lay, Till they might open to adorn the day 399
Which I to conquer sought with all my might 488
Circumstances strong Of present death, and shame that might ensue . 1263
To clear her From that suspicion which the world might bear her 1321
She would not blot the letter With words, till action might become them better 1323
There might you see the labouring pioner Begrimed with sweat 1380
That one might see those far-off eyes look sad 1386
In great commanders grace and majesty You might behold 1388
In Ajax and Ulysses, O, what art Of physiognomy might one behold? 1395
There pleading might you see grave Nestor stand 1401
What wrong else may be imagined By foul enforcement might be done to me 1623
No rightful plea might plead for justice there 1649
We desire increase, That thereby beauty's rose might never die *Sonnet* 1 2
Which husbandry in honour might uphold 13 10
O'ercharged with burden of mine own love's might 23 8
That to my use it might unused stay From hands of falsehood 48 3
To-morrow sharpen'd in his former might 56 4
That I might see what the old world could say 59 9
Unless this miracle have might, That in black ink my love may still shine bright 65 13
In the praise thereof spends all his might, To make me tongue-tied 80 3
Well might show How far a modern quill doth come too short 83 6

Might. So shall I taste At first the very worst of fortune's might *Sonnet* 90 12
How many lambs might the stern wolf betray! 96 9
Thou forget'st so long To speak of that which gives thee all thy might 100 2
O, that our night of woe might have remember'd My deepest sense 120 9
Thy pyramids built up with newer might To me are nothing novel 123 2
What need'st thou wound with cunning when thy might Is more than my o'er-press'd defence can bide? 139 7
O, from what power hast thou this powerful might? 150 1
I might as yet have been a spreading flower, Fresh to myself *Lov. Comp.* 75
And makes her absence valiant, not her might 245
The fairest one of three, That liked of her master as well as well might be *Pass. Pil.* 212
Let reason rule things worthy blame, As well as fancy partial might 302
These pretty pleasures might me move To live with thee and be thy love . 371
Mightier. The mightier man, the mightier is the thing That makes him honour'd *Lucrece* 1004
Wherefore do not you a mightier way Make war? . *Sonnet* 16 1
Mightily. What could he see but mightily he noted? *Lucrece* 414
Mightst. Then mightst thou pause, for then I were not for thee *V. and A.* 137
Ay me! but yet thou mightst my seat forbear *Sonnet* 41 9
How many gazers mightst thou lead away! 96 11
Mighty. Thyself art mighty; for thine own sake leave me: Myself a weakling *Lucrece* 583
And never be forgot in mighty Rome Th' adulterate death of Lucrece and her groom 1644
How mighty then you are, O, hear me tell! *Lov. Comp.* 253
Milch. Like a milch doe, whose swelling dugs do ache *Ven. and Adon.* 875
Mild. Let mild women to him lose their mildness *Lucrece* 979
Old woes, not infant sorrows, bear them mild 1096
By this, mild patience bid fair Lucrece speak 1268
The mild glance that sly Ulysses lent Show'd deep regard 1399
So mild, that Patience seem'd to scorn his woes 1505
The well-skill'd workman this mild image drew For perjured Sinon 1520
Even as subtle Sinon is painted, So sober-sad, so weary, and so mild 1542
Mild as a dove, but neither true nor trusty *Pass. Pil.* 86
Mildness. Let mild women to him lose their mildness *Lucrece* 979
Miles. Thought kills me that I am not thought, To leap large lengths of miles when thou art gone *Sonnet* 44 10
Thus far the miles are measured from thy friend 50 4
Milk. Like milk and blood being mingled both together . *Ven. and Adon.* 902
Milk-white. Paler for sorrow than her milk-white dove, For Adon's sake *Pass. Pil.* 119
Millions. Whereof are you made, That millions of strange shadows on you tend? *Sonnet* 53 2
Million'd accidents Creep in 'twixt vows and change decrees of kings . 115 5
Mind. O, had thy mother borne so hard a mind, She had not brought forth thee *Ven. and Adon.* 203
She answers him as if she knew his mind 308
Looks on the dull earth with disturbed mind 340
For all my mind, my thought, my busy care, Is how to get my palfrey 383
How much a fool was I To be of such a weak and silly mind 1016
Which with cold terror doth men's minds confound 1048
Save thieves, and cares, and troubled minds, that wake *Lucrece* 126
In his inward mind he doth debate What following sorrow may on this arise 185
She bears the load of lust he left behind, And he the burthen of a guilty mind 735
She wakes her heart by beating on her breast, And bids it leap from thence, where it may find Some purer chest to close so pure a mind 761
Since men prove beasts, let beasts bear gentle minds 1148
For men have marble, women waxen, minds 1240
At last she calls to mind where hangs a piece Of skilful painting 1366
The scalps of many, almost hid behind, To jump up higher seem'd to mock the mind 1414
Himself, behind, Was left unseen, save to the eye of mind 1426
So fair a form lodged not a mind so ill 1530
But Tarquin's shape came in her mind the while 1536
It cannot be, I find, But such a face should bear a wicked mind 1540
Immaculate and spotless is my mind 1656
May my pure mind with the foul act dispense 1704
Her body's stain her mind untainted clears 1710
Such childish humour from weak minds proceeds 1825
Every private widow well may keep By children's eyes her husband's shape in mind *Sonnet* 9 8
O, change thy thought, that I may change my mind! 10 9
Then begins a journey in my head, To work my mind 27 4
By day my limbs, by night my mind, For thee and for myself no quiet find 27 13
For that same groan doth put this in my mind 50 13
Since mind at first in character was done 59 8
They look into the beauty of thy mind 69 9
The vacant leaves thy mind's imprint will bear 77 3
Thou shalt find Those children nursed, deliver'd from thy brain, To take a new acquaintance of thy mind 77 12
Thou canst not vex me with inconstant mind 92 9
Since I left you, mine eye is in my mind 113 1
Of his quick objects hath the mind no part 113 7
My most true mind thus makes mine eye untrue 113 14
Or whether doth my mind, being crown'd with you, Drink up the monarch's plague, this flattery? 114 1
And my great mind most kingly drinks it up 114 10
Divert strong minds to the course of altering things 115 8
Let me not to the marriage of true minds Admit impediments 116 1
That I have frequent been with unknown minds 117 5
But, love, hate on, for now I know thy mind 149 13
That, in my mind, thy worst all best exceeds 150 8
The mind and sight distractedly commix'd *Lov. Comp.* 28
Each eye that saw him did enchant the mind 89
Many there were that did his picture get, To serve their eyes, and in it put their mind 135
All my offences that abroad you see Are errors of the blood, none of the mind 184
Minded. If all were minded so, the times should cease . *Sonnet* 11 7
Mindful. The mindful messenger, come back, Brings home his lord *Lucrece* 1583
Mine. Touch but my lips with those fair lips of thine,—Though mine be not so fair, yet are they red *Ven. and Adon.* 116
The kiss shall be thine own as well as mine 117
Hold up thy head: Look in mine eye-balls, there thy beauty lies 119
Mine eyes are gray and bright and quick in turning 140
Because Adonis' heart hath made mine hard 378
That they have murder'd this poor heart of mine 502
And these mine eyes, true leaders to their queen, But for thy piteous lips no more had seen 503
Yet from mine ear the tempting tune is blown 778

Mine. My heart stands armed in mine ear, And will not let a false sound enter there . . . . *Ven. and Adon.* 779
Mine ears, that to your wanton talk attended, Do burn themselves 809
My heart shall never countermand mine eye . . *Lucrece* 276
The father says 'She's mine' 'O, mine she is,' Replies her husband . 1795
I love thee in such sort As, thou being mine, mine is thy good report *Sonnet* 36 14 ; 96 14
The pain be mine, but thine shall be the praise . . 38 14
All mine was thine before thou hadst this more . . 40 4
Myself I'll forfeit, so that other mine Thou wilt restore . . 134 3
Either was the other's mine . . . . *Ph. and Tur.* 36
Mingle. To mingle beauty with infirmities . . . *Ven. and Adon.* 735
Mingled. For there his smell with others being mingled, The hot scent-snuffing hounds are driven to doubt 691
Like milk and blood being mingled both together 902
Cheeks neither red nor pale, but mingled so That blushing red no guilty instance gave . . . . *Lucrece* 1510
Mingling my talk with tears, my grief with groans . . . 797
Minion. Yet fear her, O thou minion of her pleasure ! *Sonnet* 126 9
Minister. What me your minister, for you obeys, Works under you *L. Comp.* 229
Minority. Proving from world's minority their right . *Lucrece* 67
Minstrels. Feast-finding minstrels, tuning my defame, Will tie the hearers to attend each line 817
Minute. But in one minute's fight brings beauty under . *Ven. and Adon.* 746
There shall not be one minute in an hour Wherein I will not kiss my sweet love's flower 1187
Who buys a minute's mirth to wail a week ? Or sells eternity to get a toy ? *Lucrece* 213
Stuff up his lust, as minutes fill up hours 297
Till every minute pays the hour his debt 329
One poor retiring minute in an age Would purchase thee a thousand thousand friends 962
Nor can I fortune to brief minutes tell . . . *Sonnet* 14 5
So do our minutes hasten to their end 60 2
Thy glass will show thee how thy beauties wear, Thy dial how thy precious minutes waste 77 2
Her skill May time disgrace and wretched minutes kill . . 126 8
Now are minutes added to the hours ; To spite me now, each minute seems a moon . . . . *Pass. Pil.* 206
Miracle. Unless this miracle have might, That in black ink my love may still shine bright . . . . *Sonnet* 65 13
Mire. The crow may bathe his coal-black wings in mire . *Lucrece* 1009
Mirror. That fair fresh mirror, dim and old, Shows me a bare-boned death 1760
Mirth. Who buys a minute's mirth to wail a week ? Or sells eternity to get a toy ? 213
For mirth doth search the bottom of annoy 1109
Miscalled. And simple truth miscall'd simplicity, And captive good attending captain ill . . . . *Sonnet* 66 11
Mischance. Making it subject to the tyranny Of mad mischances and much misery . . . . *Ven. and Adon.* 738
With some mischance cross Tarquin in his flight . *Lucrece* 968
Let there bechance him pitiful mischances, To make him moan . . 976
Mischief. A mischief worse than civil home-bred strife *Ven. and Adon.* 764
Why work'st thou mischief in thy pilgrimage ? . *Lucrece* 960
Misdeeds. Then kings' misdeeds cannot be hid in clay . . 609
That from their own misdeeds askance their eyes . . . 637
Miser. I hold such strife As 'twixt a miser and his wealth is found *Sonnet* 75 4
Misery. For misery is trodden on by many, And being low never relieved by any . . . . *Ven. and Adon.* 707
Making it subject to the tyranny Of mad mischances and much misery . 738
Every one that flatters thee Is no friend in misery . . *Pass. Pil.* 404
Misfortune. That map which deep impression bears Of hard misfortune, carved in it with tears . . . . *Lucrece* 1713
Misgoverning. Black lust, dishonour, shame, misgoverning . . 654
Mishaps. Even so she languisheth in her mishaps *Ven. and Adon.* 603
Misled. By their high treason is his heart misled . *Lucrece* 369
Misplaced. And gilded honour shamefully misplaced . *Sonnet* 66 5
Misprision. So thy great gift, upon misprision growing, Comes home again 87 11
'Miss. He saith she is immodest, blames her 'miss *Ven. and Adon.* 53
Missed. The moon being clouded presently is miss'd . *Lucrece* 1007
Till each to razed oblivion yield his part Of thee, thy record never can be miss'd . . . . *Sonnet* 122 8
Mis-shapen Time, copesmate of ugly Night, Swift subtle post . *Lucrece* 925
Missing. The warm effects which she in him finds missing She seeks to kindle with continual kissing . . . . *Ven. and Adon.* 605
Mist. In his dim mist the aspiring mountains hiding . *Lucrece* 548
Wipe the dim mist from thy doting eyne 643
Foggy Night ! . . . Muster thy mists to meet the eastern light . 773
Mistake. To make the cunning hounds mistake their smell *Ven. and Adon.* 686
Thy false dart Mistakes that aim and cleaves an infant's heart . 942
For oft the eye mistakes, the brain being troubled . . . 1068
No marvel then, though I mistake my view . . *Sonnet* 148 11
Mistaking. Or me, to whom thou gavest it, else mistaking . 87 10
Mistook. Thy wretched wife mistook the matter so, To slay herself *Lucrece* 1826
Mistress. By whose swift aid Their mistress mounted through the empty skies *Ven. and Adon.* 1191
Thou see'st our mistress' ornaments are chaste . . *Lucrece* 322
I am the mistress of my fate, And with my trespass never will dispense . 1069
Calls her maid, Whose swift obedience to her mistress hies . . 1215
Her mistress she doth give demure good-morrow . . . 1219
Enforced by sympathy Of those fair suns set in her mistress' sky . 1230
Nature, sovereign mistress over wrack . . . *Sonnet* 126 5
My mistress' brows are raven black, Her eyes so suited . . 127 9
My mistress' eyes are nothing like the sun . . . 130 1
In some perfumes is there more delight Than in the breath that from my mistress reeks 130 8
My mistress, when she walks, treads on the ground . . 130 12
But at my mistress' eye Love's brand new-fired, The boy for trial needs would touch my breast 153 9
The bath for my help lies Where Cupid got new fire—my mistress' eyes 153 14
But I, my mistress' thrall, Came there for cure . . . 154 12
Sweetly supposed them mistress of his heart . . *Lov. Comp.* 142
Enough, too much, I fear ; Lest that my mistress hear my song *Pass. Pil.* 348
Mistrust. It shall not fear where it should most mistrust *Ven. and Adon.* 1154
Full of foul hope and full of fond mistrust . . *Lucrece* 284
His kindled duty kindled her mistrust 1352
So ensconced his secret evil, That jealousy itself could not mistrust . 1516
Mistrustful. Their light blown out in some mistrustful wood *V. and A.* 826
Misty. Like misty vapours when they blot the sky . . . 184
Misty night Covers the shame that follows sweet delight . *Lucrece* 356
Misty. Let thy misty vapours march so thick . . . *Lucrece* 782
Misuse. I am perjured most ; For all my vows are oaths but to misuse thee *Sonnet* 152 7
Mixed. Were never four such lamps together mix'd, Had not his clouded with his brow's repine . . . . . . *Ven. and Adon.* 489
Her modest eloquence with sighs is mixed . . . *Lucrece* 563
Which is not mix'd with seconds, knows no art . . *Sonnet* 125 11
Sorrow changed to solace, solace mix'd with sorrow . *Pass. Pil.* 203
Moan. The neighbour caves, as seeming troubled, Make verbal repetition of her moans . . . . *Ven. and Adon.* 831
If ever man were moved with woman's moans, Be moved with my tears *Lucr.* 587
Poor wasting monuments of lasting moans 798
Let there bechance him pitiful mischances, To make him moan ; but pity not his moans 977
The little birds . . . Make her moans mad with their sweet melody . 1108
So woe hath wearied woe, moan tired moan 1363
And moan the expense of many a vanish'd sight . . *Sonnet* 30 8
Tell o'er The sad account of fore-bemoaned moan . . . 30 11
I must attend time's leisure with my moan 44 12
Lest the wise world should look into your moan And mock you . 71 13
Do I not spend Revenge upon myself with present moan ? . . 149 8
Each several stone, With wit well blazon'd, smiled or made some moan *Lov. Comp.* 217
Thy like ne'er was For a sweet content, the cause of all my moan *Pass. Pil.* 295
Every thing did banish moan, Save the nightingale alone . . 379
Mock. To mock the subtle in themselves beguiled . . *Lucrece* 957
And merry fools to mock at him resort 989
Mock with thy tickling beams eyes that are sleeping . . . 1090
The scalps of many, almost hid behind, To jump up higher seem'd, to mock the mind 1414
While shadows like to thee do mock my sight . . . *Sonnet* 61 4
Lest the wise world should look into your moan And mock you with me after I am gone 71 14
And the sad augurs mock their own presage 107 6
Mocking. 'You mocking birds,' quoth she . . . *Lucrece* 1121
Modern. Well might show How far a modern quill doth come too short *Sonnet* 83 7
Modest. With gentle majesty and modest pride . *Ven. and Adon.* 278
So do thy lips Make modest Dian cloudy and forlorn . . . 725
Long he questioned With modest Lucrece, and wore out the night *Lucrece* 123
Abhor the deed That spots and stains love's modest snow-white weed . 196
O modest wantons ! wanton modesty ! 401
Her modest eloquence with sighs is mixed 563
The chastest tears That ever modest eyes with sorrow shed . . 683
Modestly. She modestly prepares to let them know Her honour is ta'en prisoner 1607
Modesty. O modest wantons ! wanton modesty ! 401
With soft-slow tongue, true mark of modesty 1220
Effects of terror and dear modesty, Encamp'd in hearts . *Lov. Comp.* 202
Cold modesty, hot wrath, Both fire from hence and chill extincture hath 293
Moe. Why should the private pleasure of some one Become the public plague of many moe ? . . . . *Lucrece* 1479
In me moe woes than words are now depending 1615
Found yet moe letters sadly penn'd in blood . . *Lov. Comp.* 47
Labouring in moe pleasures to bestow them Than the true gouty landlord which doth owe them 139
Moiety. By their verdict is determined The clear eye's moiety *Sonnet* 46 12
Moist. My smooth moist hand, were it with thy hand felt, Would in thy palm dissolve, or seem to melt . . . . . *Ven. and Adon.* 143
The gentle lark, weary of rest, From his moist cabinet mounts up on high . 854
Moistened. Each flower moisten'd like a melting eye . *Lucrece* 1227
Moisture. And calls it heavenly moisture, air of grace *Ven. and Adon.* 64
Till, breathless, he disjoin'd, and backward drew The heavenly moisture 542
O, that infected moisture of his eye ! . . . *Lov. Comp.* 323
Moment. Which in a moment doth confound and kill All pure effects *Lucr.* 250
Turn to loathed sours Even in the moment that we call them ours . 868
Every thing that grows Holds in perfection but a little moment *Sonnet* 15 2
The accident which brought me to her eye Upon the moment did her force subdue . . . . *Lov. Comp.* 248
Momentary. This momentary joy breeds months of pain *Lucrece* 690
Monarch. But happy monarchs still are fear'd for love . . 611
Drink up the monarch's plague, this flattery . . *Sonnet* 114 2
Or monarch's hands that let not bounty fall . . *Lov. Comp.* 41
Monarchy. And reign'd, commanding in his monarchy . . . 196
'Mongst. With the breath thou givest and takest, 'Mongst our mourners shalt thou go . . . . *Ph. and Tur.* 20
Monsters. To make of monsters and things indigest Such cherubins *Son.* 114 5
Month. This momentary joy breeds months of pain . . *Lucrece* 690
Love, whose month was ever May, Spied a blossom passing fair *Pass. Pil.* 228
As it fell upon a day In the merry month of May . . . 374
Monument. Where, like a virtuous monument, she lies, To be admired *Lucrece* 391
Poor wasting monuments of lasting moans 798
To fill with worm-holes stately monuments 946
Not marble, nor the gilded monuments Of princes . . . *Sonnet* 55 1
Your monument shall be my gentle verse 81 9
And thou in this shalt find thy monument 107 13
Mood. As a child, Who wayward once, his mood with nought agrees *Lucrece* 1095
Know, gentle wench, it small avails my mood 1273
The false heart's history Is writ in moods and frowns and wrinkles strange *Sonnet* 93 8
In bloodless white and the encrimson'd mood . . *Lov. Comp.* 201
Moody. And moody Pluto winks while Orpheus plays . *Lucrece* 553
Unmask, dear dear, this moody heaviness, And tell thy grief . . 1602
Moon. Shone like the moon in water seen by night . *Ven. and Adon.* 492
To draw the cloud that hides the silver moon . . *Lucrece* 371
The moon being clouded presently is miss'd 1007
Making a couplement of proud compare, With sun and moon . *Sonnet* 21 6
Clouds and eclipses stain both moon and sun 35 3
The mortal moon hath her eclipse endured 107 5
Now are minutes added to the hours ; To spite me now, each minute seems a moon . . . . *Pass. Pil.* 207
Moralize. Unlike myself thou hear'st me moralize . *Ven. and Adon.* 712
Nor could she moralize his wanton sight . . . *Lucrece* 104
More lovely than a man, More white and red than doves or roses are *V. and A.* 9
What follows more she murders with a kiss 54
Pure shame and awed resistance made him fret, Which bred more beauty in his angry eyes 70
Being red, she loves him best : and being white, Her best is better'd with a more delight 78
Never did passenger in summer's heat More thirst for drink . . . 92

More. Souring his cheeks cries 'Fie, no more of love!' *Ven. and Adon.* 185
Art thou obdurate, flinty, hard as steel, Nay, more than flint? 200
Her words are done, her woes the more increasing 254
And now the happy season once more fits 327
An oven that is stopp'd, or river stay'd, Burneth more hotly, swelleth with more rage 332
Once more the engine of her thoughts began 367
Once more the ruby-colour'd portal open'd 451
These mine eyes, true leaders to their queen, But for thy piteous lips no more had seen 504
He now obeys, and now no more resisteth, While she takes all she can 563
For pity now she can no more detain him 577
And more than so, presenteth to mine eye The picture of an angry-chafing boar 661
Lie quietly, and hear a little more; Nay, do not struggle 709
But gold that's put to use more gold begets 768
And every tongue more moving than your own 776
More I could tell, but more I dare not say; The text is old 805
Till the wild waves will have him seen no more 819
Bids them leave quaking, bids them fear no more 899
Her more than haste is mated with delays 909
From their dark beds once more leap her eyes 1050
Her mangling eye, That makes more gashes where no breach should be 1066
Never did he bless My youth with his; the more am I accurst 1120
Two glasses, where herself herself beheld A thousand times, and now no more reflect 1130
Sweet issue of a more sweet-smelling sire—For every little grief to wet his eyes 1178
That kings might be espoused to more fame *Lucrece* 20
That, cloy'd with much, he pineth still for more 98
Nor could she moralize his wanton sight, More than his eyes were open'd to the light 105
And so, by hoping more, they have but less 137
Gaining more, the profit of excess Is but to surfeit 138
That eye which him beholds, as more divine, Unto a view so false will not incline 291
So their pride doth grow, Paying more slavish tribute than they owe 299
To add a more rejoicing to the prime, And give the sneaped birds more cause to sing 332
Which with a yielding latch, and with no more, Hath barr'd him from the blessed thing he sought 339
With more than admiration he admired Her azure veins 418
In darkness daunts them with more dreadful sights 462
This moves in him more rage and lesser pity, To make the breach 468
Which to her oratory adds more grace 564
'No more,' quoth he; 'by heaven, I will not hear thee' 667
No tool imparteth To make more vent for passage of her breath 1040
To see the salve doth make the wound ache more 1116
No more than wax shall be accounted evil Wherein is stamp'd the semblance of a devil 1245
Replied the maid, 'The more to blame my sluggard negligence' 1278
For more it is than I can well express 1286
When more is felt than one hath power to tell 1288
To see sad sights moves more than hear them told 1324
And on it writ 'At Ardea to my lord with more than haste' 1332
Speed more than speed but dull and slow she deems 1336
While others saucily Promise more speed, but do it leisurely 1349
Her earnest eye did make him more amazed 1356
The more she saw the blood his cheeks replenish, The more she thought he spied in her some blemish 1357
My woe too sensible thy passion maketh More feeling-painful 1679
But more than 'he' her poor tongue could not speak 1718
That I no more can see what once I was 1764
Held back his sorrow's tide, to make it more 1789
How much more praise deserved thy beauty's use *Sonnet* 2 9
Look, whom she best endow'd she gave the more 11 11
Meant thereby Thou shouldst print more, not let that copy die 11 14
With means more blessed than my barren rhyme 16 4
Shall I compare thee to a summer's day? Thou art more lovely and more temperate 18 2
An eye more bright than theirs, less false in rolling 20 5
Let them say more that like of hearsay well 21 13
More than that tongue that more hath more express'd 23 12
Wishing me like to one more rich in hope, Featured like him 29 5
And shalt by fortune once more re-survey These poor rude lines 32 3
No more be grieved at that which thou hast done 35 1
Salving thy amiss, Excusing thy sins more than thy sins are 35 8
Any of these all, or all, or more, Entitled in thy parts do crowned sit 37 6
Be thou the tenth Muse, ten times more in worth Than those old nine 38 9
What hast thou then more than thou hadst before? 40 2
All mine was thine before thou hadst this more 40 4
A loss in love that touches me more nearly 42 4
He answers with a groan, More sharp to me than spurring to his side 50 12
O, how much more doth beauty beauteous seem By that sweet ornament which truth doth give! 54 1
But you shall shine more bright in these contents 55 3
That, when they see Return of love, more blest may be the view 56 12
Makes summer's welcome thrice more wish'd, more rare 56 14
To do more for me than mine own desert 72 6
And hang more praise upon deceased I Than niggard truth would willingly impart 72 7
And live no more to shame nor me nor you 72 12
Which makes thy love more strong, To love that well which thou must leave ere long 73 13
There lives more life in one of your fair eyes 83 13
Which can say more Than this rich praise, that you alone are you? 84 1
''Tis so, 'tis true,' And to the most of praise add something more 85 10
In my tongue Thy sweet beloved name no more shall dwell 89 10
Prouder than garments' cost, Of more delight than hawks or horses be 91 11
Both grace and faults are loved of more and less 96 3
More flowers I noted, yet I none could see But sweet or colour it had stol'n from thee 99 14
My love is strengthened, though more weak in seeming 102 1
Is of more worth Than when it hath my added praise beside 103 3
O, blame me not, if I no more can write! 103 5
And more, much more, than in my verse can sit Your own glass shows 103 13
Mine appetite I never more will grind On newer proof 110 10
Incapable of more, replete with you 113 13
To make our appetites more keen, With eager compounds 118 1
Grows fairer than at first, more strong, far greater 119 12
And gain by ill thrice more than I have spent 119 14
Was I bold, To trust those tables that receive thee more? 122 12

More. What we see doth lie, Made more or less by thy continual haste *Sonnet* 123 12
Which prove more short than waste or ruining 125 4
Have I not seen dwellers on form and favour Lose all, and more? 125 6
Making dead wood more blest than living lips 128 12
Coral is far more red than her lips' red 130 2
In some perfumes is there more delight Than in the breath that from my mistress reeks 130 7
Yet well I know That music hath a far more pleasing sound 130 10
More than enough am I that vex thee still 135 3
Add to thy 'Will' One will of mine, to make thy large 'Will' more 135 12
When thy might Is more than my o'er-press'd defence can bide 139 8
Within be fed, without be rich no more 146 12
And Death once dead, there's no more dying then 146 14
Who taught thee how to make me love thee more The more I hear and see just cause of hate? 150 9
More worthy I to be beloved of thee 150 14
Ink would have seem'd more black and damned here! *Lov. Comp.* 54
Yet show'd his visage by that cost more dear 96
Advice is often seen By blunting us to make our wits more keen 161
She, silly queen, with more than love's good will, Forbade the boy he should not pass those grounds *Pass. Pil.* 123
He saw more wounds than one, And blushing fled, and left her all alone 129
And yet thou left'st me more than I did crave 139
More mickle was the pain That nothing could be used to turn them both to gain 219
For now I see Inconstancy More in women than in men remain 262
They that fawn'd on him before Use his company no more 422
Morn. Even as the sun with purple-colour'd face Had ta'en his last leave of the weeping morn *Ven. and Adon.* 2
From morn till night, even where I list to sport me 154
Like a red morn, that ever yet betoken'd Wreck to the seaman 453
He cheers the morn and all the earth relieveth 484
What hour is this? or morn or weary even? Do I delight to die, or life desire? 495
To wake the morn and sentinel the night *Lucrece* 942
Even so my sun one early morn did shine *Sonnet* 33 9
When his youthful morn Hath travell'd on to age's steepy night 63 4
Scarce had the sun dried up the dewy morn *Pass. Pil.* 71
Fair was the morn when the fair queen of love 117
Youth like summer morn, age like winter weather 159
Morning. And wakes the morning, from whose silver breast The sun ariseth in his majesty *Ven. and Adon.* 855
Musing the morning is so much o'erworn 866
Soon decay'd and done As is the morning's silver-melting dew *Lucrece* 24
He in his speed looks for the morning light 745
With rotten damps ravish the morning air 778
The little birds that tune their morning's joy Make her moans mad with their sweet melody 1107
Full many a glorious morning have I seen Flatter the mountain-tops with sovereign eye *Sonnet* 33 1
Truly not the morning sun of heaven Better becomes the grey cheeks of the east 132 5
The morning rise Doth cite each moving sense from idle rest *Pass. Pil.* 194
Morrow. The blushing morrow Lends light to all fair eyes that light will borrow *Lucrece* 1082
She looks for night, and then she longs for morrow 1571
Give not a windy night a rainy morrow *Sonnet* 90 7
Mortal. O fairest mover on this mortal round *Ven. and Adon.* 368
Like to a mortal butcher bent to kill 618
Now Nature cares not for thy mortal vigour 953
Imperious supreme of all mortal things 996
And must not die Till mutual overthrow of mortal kind 1018
Mortal stars, as bright as heaven's beauties *Lucrece* 13
When heavy sleep had closed up mortal eyes 163
Fearing no such thing, Lies at the mercy of his mortal sting 364
And by their mortal fault brought in subjection Her immortality 724
Yet mortal looks adore his beauty still *Sonnet* 7 7
Mine eye and heart are at a mortal war How to divide the conquest 46 1
Lofty towers I see down-razed And brass eternal slave to mortal rage 64 4
By spirits taught to write Above a mortal pitch, that struck me dead 86 6
The mortal moon hath her eclipse endured 107 5
And deny himself for Jove, Turning mortal for thy love *Pass. Pil.* 244
Mortality. Showing life's triumph in the map of death, And death's dim look in life's mortality *Lucrece* 403
Sad mortality o'er-sways their power *Sonnet* 65 2
Mortgaged. He is thine, And I myself am mortgaged to thy will 134 2
Most. But then woos best when most his choice is froward *Ven. and Adon.* 570
The strongest body shall it make most weak 1145
It shall not fear where it should most mistrust 1154
Too severe, And most deceiving when it seems most just 1156
Perverse it shall be where it shows most toward 1157
Shame folded up in blind concealing night, When most unseen, then most doth tyrannize *Lucrece* 676
Great grief grieves most at that would do it good 1117
Their face their manners most expressly told 1397
Son and father weep with equal strife Who should weep most 1792
Thou art beloved of many, But that thou none lovest is most evident *Sonnet* 10 4
Sets you most rich in youth before my sight 15 10
Who will believe my verse in time to come, If it were fill'd with your most high deserts? 17 2
But I forbid thee one most heinous crime 19 8
Whilst I, . . . Unlook'd for joy in that I honour most 25 4
With what I most enjoy contented least 29 8
When most I wink, then do mine eyes best see, For all the day they view things unrespected 43 1
But thou, to whom my jewels trifles are, Most worthy comfort 48 6
Yet be most proud of that which I compile 78 9
Where breath most breathes, even in the mouths of men 81 14
Which shall be most my glory, being dumb 83 10
Who is it that says most? which can say more Than this rich praise? 84 1
''Tis so, 'tis true,' And to the most of praise add something more 85 10
Thou mayst take All this away and me most wretched make 91 14
That do not do the thing they most do show 94 2
Now with the drops of this most balmy time My love looks fresh 107 9
Sold cheap what is most dear, Made old offences of affections new 110 3
Most true it is that I have look'd on truth Askance and strangely 110 5
Even to thy pure and most most loving breast 110 14
The most sweet favour or deformed'st creature 113 10

Most. My most true mind thus makes mine eye untrue *Sonnet* 113 14
And my great mind most kingly drinks it up 114 10
My most full flame should afterwards burn clearer 115 4
A true soul When most impeach'd stands least in thy control 125 14
To my dear doting heart Thou art the fairest and most precious jewel 131 4
I am perjured most; For all my vows are oaths but to misuse thee 152 6
O most potential love! vow, bond, nor space, In thee hath neither sting, knot, nor confine *Lov. Comp.* 264
When he most burn'd in heart-wish'd luxury, He preach'd pure maid 314
Mot. And Tarquin's eye may read the mot afar *Lucrece* 830
Mote. Through crystal walls each little mote will peep 1251
Mother. O, had thy mother borne so hard a mind, She had not brought forth thee *Ven. and Adon.* 203
There lives a son that suck'd an earthly mother, May lend thee light 863
Sable Night, mother of Dread and Fear *Lucrece* 117
Nor children's tears nor mothers' groans respecting, Swell in their pride 431
That mother tries a merciless conclusion Who, having two sweet babes, when death takes one, Will slay the other and be nurse to none 1160
Many Trojan mothers, sharing joy To see their youthful sons bright weapons wield 1431
Thou dost beguile the world, unbless some mother *Sonnet* 3 4
Thou art thy mother's glass, and she in thee Calls back the lovely April of her prime 3 9
Resembling sire and child and happy mother 8 11
Then believe me, my love is as fair As any mother's child 21 11
Turn back to me, And play the mother's part, kiss me, be kind 143 12
Motion. Like a troubled ocean, Beat at thy rocky and wreck-threatening heart, To soften it with their continual motion *Lucrece* 591
The eye interprets to the ear The heavy motion that it doth behold 1326
These present-absent with swift motion slide *Sonnet* 45 4
In winged speed no motion shall I know 51 8
So your sweet hue, which methinks still doth stand, Hath motion 104 12
That blessed wood whose motion sounds With thy sweet fingers 128 2
Commanded by the motion of thine eyes 149 12
O, all that borrow'd motion seeming owed, Would yet again betray the fore-betray'd! *Lov. Comp.* 327
Motives. Desires to know In brief the grounds and motives of her woe 63
Motley. I have gone here and there And made myself a motley to the view *Sonnet* 110 2
Moulds. For stealing moulds from heaven that were divine *Ven. and Adon.* 730
Mount. He will not manage her, although he mount her 598
The gentle lark, weary of rest, From his moist cabinet mounts up on high 854
Whose crooked beak threats if he mount he dies *Lucrece* 508
Mountain. Feed where thou wilt, on mountain or in dale *Ven. and Adon.* 232
In his dim mist the aspiring mountains hiding *Lucrece* 548
The mountain or the sea, the day or night, The crow or dove *Sonnet* 113 11
And we will all the pleasures prove That hills and valleys, dales and fields, And all the craggy mountains yields. *Pass. Pil.* 356
Mountain-snow. As mountain-snow melts with the midday sun *V. and A.* 750
Mountain-spring. As from a mountain-spring that feeds a dale, Shall gush pure streams to purge my impure tale *Lucrece* 1077
Mountain-tops. Full many a glorious morning have I seen Flatter the mountain-tops with sovereign eye *Sonnet* 33 2
Mounted. Her champion mounted for the hot encounter *Ven. and Adon.* 596
By whose swift aid Their mistress mounted through the empty skies 1191
Then should I spur, though mounted on the wind *Sonnet* 51 7
Mourn. Pausing for means to mourn some newer way *Lucrece* 1365
No longer mourn for me when I am dead Than you shall hear the surly sullen bell *Sonnet* 71 1
Yet so they mourn, becoming of their woe 127 13
O, let it then as well beseem thy heart To mourn for me 132 11
In black mourn I, All fears scorn I, Love hath forlorn me, Living in thrall *Pass. Pil.* 263
Mourner. Another flap-mouth'd mourner, black and grim *Ven. and Adon.* 920
Let no mourner say He weeps for her, for she was only mine *Lucrece* 1797
My mistress' brows are raven black, Her eyes so suited, and they mourners seem *Sonnet* 127 10
Have put on black and loving mourners be 132 3
With the breath thou givest and takest, 'Mongst our mourners shalt thou go *Ph. and Tur.* 20
Mournest. Ah, thought I, thou mourn'st in vain! None takes pity on thy pain *Pass. Pil.* 391
Mournful. When her mournful hymns did hush the night *Sonnet* 102 10
Mourning. Who finds his Lucrece clad in mourning black *Lucrece* 1585
About the mourning and congealed face Of that black blood a watery rigol goes 1744
As those two mourning eyes become thy face *Sonnet* 132 9
Mourn for me, since mourning doth thee grace 132 11
Mouse. He doth but dally, While in his hold-fast foot the weak mouse panteth *Lucrece* 555
Mouth. These lovely caves, these round enchanting pits, Open'd their mouths to swallow Venus' liking *Ven. and Adon.* 248
Enfranchising his mouth, his back, his breast 396
That sweet coral mouth, Whose precious taste her thirsty lips well knew 542
Then do they spend their mouths: Echo replies, As if another chase were in the skies 695
Whose frothy mouth, bepainted all with red, Like milk and blood 901
Where breath most breathes, even in the mouths of men *Sonnet* 81 14
Mouthed. The wrinkles which thy glass will truly show Of mouthed graves will give thee memory 77 6
Move. Or were I deaf, thy outward parts would move Each part in me that were but sensible *Ven. and Adon.* 435
This moves in him more rage and lesser pity, To make the breach *Lucrece* 468
To see sad sights moves more than hear them told 1324
Those round clear pearls of his, that move thy pity, Are balls of quenchless fire 1553
For thou not farther than my thoughts canst move *Sonnet* 47 11
And if these pleasures may thee move, Then live with me and be my love *Pass. Pil.* 367
These pretty pleasures might me move To live with thee and be thy love 371
Moved. Being moved, he strikes whate'er is in his way *Ven. and Adon.* 623
If ever man were moved with woman's moans, Be moved with my tears *Lucrece* 587
Yet, if men moved him, was he such a storm *Lov. Comp.* 101
Mover. O fairest mover on this mortal round *Ven. and Adon.* 368
Moving. And every tongue more moving than your own 776
Till whatsoever star that guides my moving Points on me graciously *Sonnet* 26 9
Who, moving others, are themselves as stone, Unmoved, cold 94 3
The morning rise Doth cite each moving sense from idle rest *Pass. Pil.* 195
Mow. Nothing stands but for his scythe to mow *Sonnet* 60 12
Much. 'Tis much to borrow, and I will not owe it *Ven. and Adon.* 411
Yet would my love to thee be still as much 442
Like a wild bird being tamed with too much handling 560
She hath assay'd as much as may be proved 608
Ceasing their clamorous cry till they have singled With much ado the cold fault cleanly out 694
Making it subject to the tyranny Of mad mischances and much misery 738
Musing the morning is so much o'erworn 866
How much a fool was I To be of such a weak and silly mind 1015
That nothing in him seem'd inordinate, Save sometime too much wonder of his eye *Lucrece* 95
That, cloy'd with much, he pineth still for more 98
Those that much covet are with gain so fond, For what they have not 134
This ambitious foul infirmity, In having much, torments us with defect Of that we have 151
She, much amazed, breaks ope her lock'd-up eyes 446
With too much labour drowns for want of skill 1099
Sometime her grief is dumb and hath no words; Sometime 'tis mad and too much talk affords 1106
Much like a press of people at a door, Throng her inventions 1301
Much imaginary work was there; Conceit deceitful, so compact, so kind 1422
He did her wrong, To give her so much grief and not a tongue 1463
'It cannot be,' quoth she, 'that so much guile'—She would have said 'can lurk in such a look' 1534
How much more praise deserved thy beauty's use *Sonnet* 2 9
Thou art much too fair To be death's conquest and make worms thine heir 6 13
Living flowers, Much liker than your painted counterfeit 16 8
Some fierce thing replete with too much rage 23 3
How would thy shadow's form form happy show To the clear day with thy much clearer light! 43 7
But that so much of earth and water wrought I must attend time's leisure with my moan 44 11
O, how much more doth beauty beauteous seem By that sweet ornament which truth doth give! 54 1
Thy love, though much, is not so great: It is my love that keeps mine eye awake 61 9
Do not so much as my poor name rehearse 71 11
So oft as thou wilt look, Shall profit thee and much enrich thy book 77 14
Wherein I am attainted, That thou in losing me shalt win much glory 88 8
Lest I, too much profane, should do it wrong 89 11
'T lies in thee To make him much outlive a gilded tomb 101 11
And more, much more, than in my verse can sit 103 13
That poor retention could not so much hold 122 9
Paying too much rent, For compound sweet forgoing simple savour 125 6
Do not press My tongue-tied patience with too much disdain 140 2
And so much less of shame in me remains, By how much of me their reproach contains *Lov. Comp.* 188
Not one whose flame my heart so much as warm'd 191
Enough, too much, I fear; Lest that my mistress hear my song *Pass. Pil.* 347
Mud not the fountain that gave drink to thee *Lucrece* 577
Or toads infect fair founts with venom mud 850
Roses have thorns, and silver fountains mud *Sonnet* 35 2
Bidding them find their sepulchres in mud *Lov. Comp.* 46
Muffled. Blind muffled bawd! dark harbour for defame! *Lucrece* 768
Mulberries. Some other in their bills Would bring him mulberries and ripe-red cherries *Ven. and Adon.* 1103
Murder. What follows more she murders with a kiss 54
But back retires to rate the boar for murther 906
While lust and murder wake to stain and kill *Lucrece* 168
Black stage for tragedies and murders fell! 766
Wrath, envy, treason, rape, and murder's rages 909
Guilty thou art of murder and of theft, Guilty of perjury and subornation 918
For in my death I murder shameful scorn 1189
I'll murder straight, and then I'll slaughter thee 1634
Murdered. That they have murder'd this poor heart of mine *Ven. and Adon.* 502
Her eyes, as murder'd with the view, Like stars ashamed of day, themselves withdrew 1031
Murderest. Thou smother'st honesty, thou murder'st troth *Lucrece* 885
Thou nursest all and murder'st all that are 929
Murderous. From the purple fountain Brutus drew The murderous knife 1735
No love toward others in that bosom sits That on himself such murderous shame commits *Sonnet* 9 14
Thou art so possess'd with murderous hate That 'gainst thyself thou stick'st not to conspire 10 5
Till action, lust Is perjured, murderous, bloody, full of blame 129 3
Murmur. Each shadow makes him stop, each murmur stay *Ven. and Adon.* 706
Muse. As with that Muse Stirr'd by a painted beauty to his verse *Sonnet* 21 1
Had my friend's Muse grown with this growing age 32 10
How can my Muse want subject to invent, While thou dost breathe? 38 1
Be thou the tenth Muse, ten times more in worth Than those old nine 38 9
If my slight Muse do please these curious days, The pain be mine 38 13
So oft have I invoked thee for my Muse And found such fair assistance 78 1
But now my gracious numbers are decay'd And my sick Muse doth give another place 79 4
I grant thou wert not married to my Muse 82 1
My tongue-tied Muse in manners holds her still 85 1
And precious phrase by all the Muses filed 85 4
Where art thou, Muse, that thou forget'st so long To speak? 100 1
Return, forgetful Muse, and straight redeem In gentle numbers time so idly spent 100 5
Rise, resty Muse, my love's sweet face survey 100 9
O truant Muse, what shall be thy amends For thy neglect? 101 1
Make answer, Muse; wilt thou not haply say Truth needs no colour? 101 5
Then do thy office, Muse; I teach thee how 101 13
Alack, what poverty my Muse brings forth! 103 1
Musets. The many musets through the which he goes Are like a labyrinth to amaze his foes *Ven. and Adon.* 683
Music. Ear's deep-sweet music, and heart's deep-sore wounding 432
What face remains alive that's worth the viewing? Whose tongue is music now? 1077
Music to hear, why hear'st thou music sadly? *Sonnet* 8 1
That wild music burthens every bough 102 11
When thou, my music, music play'st, Upon that blessed wood 128 1
Yet well I know That music hath a far more pleasing sound 130 10
Which, not to anger bent, is music and sweet fire *Pass. Pil.* 68
If music and sweet poetry agree, As they must needs 103
Sweet melodious sound That Phœbus' lute, the queen of music, makes 112

Music. Let the priest in surplice white, That defunctive music can, Be the death-divining swan *Ph. and Tur.* 14
Musing the morning is so much o'erworn *Ven. and Adon.* 866
Must. She bathes in water, yet her fire must burn 94
The sun doth burn my face; I must remove 186
Affection is a coal that must be cool'd; Else, suffer'd, it will set the heart on fire 387
Foul words and frowns must not repel a lover 573
Seeming to bury that posterity Which by the rights of time thou needs must have 759
Truth I must confess,—I rail'd on thee, fearing my love's decease 1001
To wail his death who lives and must not die 1017
I must confess, With kissing him I should have kill'd him 1117
Such hazard now must doting Tarquin make *Lucrece* 155
And for himself himself he must forsake 157
So Lucrece must I force to my desire 182
I must deflower: The powers to whom I pray abhor this fact 348
But they must ope, this blessed league to kill 383
Lucrece to their sight Must sell her joy, her life, her world's delight 385
Where thou with patience must my will abide 486
'Lucrece,' quoth he, 'this night I must enjoy thee' 512
If thou deny, then force must work my way 513
With foul offenders thou perforce must bear 612
Must he in thee read lectures of such shame? 618
Drunken Desire must vomit his receipt 703
So must my soul, her bark being peel'd away 1169
How Tarquin must be used, read it in me 1195
She was only mine, And only must be wail'd by Collatine 1799
Thy unused beauty must be tomb'd with thee *Sonnet* 4 13
Thou among the wastes of time must go 12 10
You must live, drawn by your own sweet skill 16 14
For through the painter must you see his skill 24 5
I an accessary needs must be To that sweet thief which sourly robs from me 35 13
We two must be twain, Although our undivided loves are one 36 1
Lascivious grace, in whom all ill well shows, Kill me with spites; yet we must not be foes 40 14
I must attend time's leisure with my moan 44 12
As the death-bed whereon it must expire 73 11
Which makes thy love more strong, To love that well which thou must leave ere long 73 14
Possessing or pursuing no delight, Save what is had or must from you be took 75 12
Though I, once gone, to all the world must die 81 6
For I must ne'er love him whom thou dost hate 89 14
Like prayers divine, I must each day say o'er the very same 108 6
Needs must I under my transgression bow 120 3
Mine ransoms yours, and yours must ransom me 120 14
By their rank thoughts my deeds must not be shown 121 12
Her audit, though delay'd, answer'd must be 126 11
But slave to slavery my sweet'st friend must be 133 4

Must. The destined ill she must herself assay *Lov. Comp.* 156
Nor gives it satisfaction to our blood, That we must curb it upon others' proof 163
Where I myself must render, That is, to you, my origin and ender 221
For these, of force, must your oblations be, Since I their altar 223
Must for your victory us all congest, As compound love to physic your cold breast 258
If music and sweet poetry agree, As they must needs *Pass. Pil.* 104
Then must the love be great 'twixt thee and me 105
But one must be refused; more mickle was the pain 219
Poor Corydon Must live alone 297
Muster. To whose weak ruins muster troops of cares *Lucrece* 720
Foggy Night! . . . Muster thy mists to meet the eastern light 773
Mustering. They, mustering to the quiet cabinet Where their dear governess and lady lies 442
Mute. Speak, fair; but speak fair words, or else be mute *Ven. and Adon.* 208
But when the heart's attorney once is mute, The client breaks 335
Will not my tongue be mute, my frail joints shake? *Lucrece* 227
And in my hearing be you mute and dumb 1123
I impair not beauty being mute, When others would give life and bring a tomb *Sonnet* 83 11
And, thou away, the very birds are mute 97 12
Mutiny. Gives false alarms, suggesteth mutiny *Ven. and Adon.* 651
This mutiny each part doth so surprise 1049
His eye, which late this mutiny restrains, Unto a greater uproar tempts his veins *Lucrece* 426
So with herself is she in mutiny, To live or die 1153
Mutual. And must not die Till mutual overthrow of mortal kind *Ven. and Adon.* 1018
Strikes each in each by mutual ordering *Sonnet* 8 10
Knows no art, But mutual render, only me for thee 125 12
Phœnix and the turtle fled In a mutual flame from hence *Ph. and Tur.* 24
Myrtle. This said, she hasteth to a myrtle grove *Ven. and Adon.* 865
Venus, with young Adonis sitting by her Under a myrtle shade *Pass. Pil.* 144
A cap of flowers, and a kirtle Embroider'd all with leaves of myrtle 364
Sitting in a pleasant shade Which a grove of myrtles made 376
Myself. 'Thrice-fairer than myself,' thus she began, 'The field's chief flower, sweet above compare *Ven. and Adon.* 7
To sell myself I can be well contented 513
Before I know myself, seek not to know me 525
Unlike myself thou hear'st me moralize 712
Thyself art mighty; for thine own sake leave me: Myself a weakling *Lucr.* 584
'To kill myself,' quoth she, 'alack, what were it?' 1156
Whose love of either to myself was nearer 1165
Myself, thy friend, will kill myself, thy foe 1196
Myself was stirring ere the break of day 1280
'Tis thee, myself, that for myself I praise *Sonnet* 62 13
So that myself bring water for my stain 109 8
Me from myself thy cruel eye hath taken 133 5
Of him, myself, and thee, I am forsaken 133 7
I myself am mortgaged to thy will, Myself I'll forfeit 134 2

N

Nails. She, desperate, with her nails her flesh doth tear *Lucrece* 739
That with my nails her beauty I may tear 1472
She tears the senseless Sinon with her nails 1564
Naked. Who sees his true-love in her naked bed *Ven. and Adon.* 397
He doth despise His naked armour of still-slaughter'd lust *Lucrece* 188
I hope some good conceit of thine In thy soul's thought, all naked, will bestow it *Sonnet* 26 8
With the garment of a Grace The naked and concealed fiend he cover'd *Lov. Comp.* 317
And stood stark naked on the brook's green brim *Pass. Pil.* 80
Name. When thou didst name the boar, not to dissemble, I fear'd thy fortune *Ven. and Adon.* 641
Love to heaven is fled, Since sweating Lust on earth usurp'd his name 794
Now she adds honours to his hateful name 994
Haply that name of 'chaste' unhappily set *Lucrece* 8
And decks with praises Collatine's high name 108
Thou wrong'st his honour, wound'st his princely name 599
Warrant for blame, To privilege dishonour in thy name 621
And fright her crying babe with Tarquin's name 814
Let my good name, that senseless reputation, For Collatine's dear love be kept unspotted 820
Thy smoothing titles to a ragged name 892
'Ere I name him, you fair lords,' quoth she, Speaking to those that came with Collatine 1688
As if her heart would break, She throws forth Tarquin's name 1717
'Tarquin' was pronounced plain, But through his teeth, as if the name he tore 1787
Unless thou take that honour from thy name *Sonnet* 36 12
Even for this let us divided live, And our dear love lose name of single one 39 6
Do not so much as my poor name rehearse 71 11
My name be buried where my body is 72 11
That every word doth almost tell my name 76 7
Knowing a better spirit doth use your name 80 2
Your name from hence immortal life shall have 81 5
In my tongue Thy sweet beloved name no more shall dwell 89 10
Which, like a canker in the fragrant rose, Doth spot the beauty of thy budding name 95 3
Naming thy name blesses an ill report 95 8
Thou mine, I thine, Even as when first I hallow'd thy fair name 108 8
Thence comes it that my name receives a brand 111 5
Black was not counted fair, Or if it were, it bore not beauty's name 127 2
Sweet beauty hath no name, no holy bower, But is profaned 127 7
Make but my name thy love, and love that still, And then thou lovest me, for my name is 'Will' 136 13
But, rising at thy name, doth point out thee As his triumphant prize 151 9

Name. Single nature's double name Neither two nor one was called *Ph. and Tur.* 39
Nameless. Thy issue blurr'd with nameless bastardy *Lucrece* 522
Naming. Naming thy name blesses an ill report *Sonnet* 95 8
Napkin. Oft did she heave her napkin to her eyne *Lov. Comp.* 15
Narcissus so himself himself forsook, And died to kiss his shadow in the brook *Ven. and Adon.* 161
That had Narcissus seen her as she stood, Self-love had never drown'd him in the flood *Lucrece* 265
Nativity. For marks descried in men's nativity Are nature's faults 538
Nativity, once in the main of light, Crawls to maturity *Sonnet* 60 5
Nature that made thee, with herself at strife, Saith that the world hath ending with thy life *Ven. and Adon.* 11
By law of nature thou art bound to breed 171
His art with nature's workmanship at strife 291
Till forging Nature be condemn'd of treason 729
To cross the curious workmanship of nature 734
Swear Nature's death for framing thee so fair 744
Now Nature cares not for thy mortal vigour 953
For marks descried in men's nativity Are nature's faults *Lucrece* 539
Or altogether balk The prey wherein by nature they delight 697
In scorn of nature, art gave lifeless life 1374
Nature's bequest gives nothing but doth lend *Sonnet* 4 3
Then how, when nature calls thee to be gone 4 11
Let those whom Nature hath not made for store, Harsh featureless and rude, barrenly perish 11 9
Every fair from fair sometime declines, By chance or nature's changing course untrimm'd 18 8
A woman's face with Nature's own hand painted Hast thou 20 1
Nature, as she wrought thee, fell a-doting 20 10
Feeds on the rarities of nature's truth 60 11
Why should he live, now Nature bankrupt is? 67 9
And him as for a map doth Nature store, To show false Art 68 13
Not making worse what nature made so clear 84 10
And husband nature's riches from expense 94 6
Never believe, though in my nature reign'd All frailties 109 9
My nature is subdued To what it works in, like the dyer's hand 111 6
So long as brain and heart Have faculty by nature to subsist 122 6
Nature, sovereign mistress over wrack 126 5
Since each hand hath put on nature's power 127 5
One by nature's outwards so commended, That maidens' eyes stuck over all his face *Lov. Comp.* 80
Deep-brain'd sonnets that did amplify Each stone's dear nature 210
Nature hath charged me that I hoard them not, But yield them up 220
Showing fair nature is both kind and tame 311
Single nature's double name Neither two nor one was called *Ph. and Tur.* 39

Nay. Art thou obdurate, flinty, hard as steel, Nay, more than flint? *Ven. and Adon.* 200
Nay, do not struggle, for thou shalt not rise 710
'Nay, then,' quoth Adon, 'you will fall again' 769
Nay, if you read this line, remember not The hand that writ it *Sonnet* 71 5
Where her faith was firmly fix'd in love, There a nay is placed *Pass Pil.* 256
What though she strive to try her strength, And ban and brawl, and say thee nay 318
A woman's nay doth stand for nought 340
Near. From me far off, with others all too near *Sonnet* 61 14
That leaves look pale, dreading the winter's near 97 14
If thy soul check thee that I come so near, Swear to thy blind soul 136 1
But since I am near slain, Kill me outright with looks and rid my pain 139 13
As testy sick men, when their deaths be near, No news but health from their physicians know 140 7
Augur of the fever's end, To this troop, come thou not near! *Ph. and Tur.* 8
Nearer. Whose love of either to myself was nearer *Lucrece* 1165
Nearly. A loss in love that touches me more nearly *Sonnet* 42 4
Necessary. Nor gives to necessary wrinkles place 108 11
Neck. Whose sinewy neck in battle ne'er did bow *Ven. and Adon.* 99
Her arms do lend his neck a sweet embrace 539
And on his neck her yoking arms she throws, She sinketh down, still hanging by his neck 592
His short thick neck cannot be easily harm'd 627
The bushes in the way Some catch her by the neck 872
A thousand groans, but thinking on thy face, One on another's neck, do witness bear *Sonnet* 131 11
Nectar. Such nectar from his lips she had not suck'd *Ven. and Adon.* 572
Need. Struck dead at first, what needs a second striking? 250
But if thou needs wilt hunt, be ruled by me 673
Seeming to bury that posterity Which by the rights of time thou needs must have 759
Having no fair to lose, you need not fear. 1083
And therefore now I need not fear to die. *Lucrece* 1052
I an accessary needs must be To that sweet thief which sourly robs from me *Sonnet* 35 13
Why should I haste me thence? Till I return, of posting is no need 51 4
Their gross painting might be better used Where cheeks need blood 82 14
I never saw that you did painting need 83 1
Then need I not to fear the worst of wrongs? 92 5
Truth needs no colour, with his colour fix'd 101 6
Because he needs no praise, wilt thou be dumb? Excuse not silence so 101 9
Needs must I under my transgression bow 120 3
Nor need I tallies thy dear love to score 122 10
The boy for trial needs would touch my breast 153 10
The one a palate hath that needs will taste *Lov. Comp.* 167
If music and sweet poetry agree, As they must needs *Pass. Pil.* 104
Whose deep conceit is such As, passing all conceit, needs no defence 110
He that is thy friend indeed, He will help thee in thy need 424
Needest. What need'st thou wound with cunning when thy might Is more than my o'er-press'd defence can bide? *Sonnet* 139 7
Needeth. What needeth then apologies be made? *Lucrece* 31
Needing. A kind of meetness To be diseased ere that there was true needing *Sonnet* 118 8
Heart is bleeding, All help needing, O cruel speeding *Pass. Pil.* 268
Needle. By the light he spies Lucretia's glove, wherein her needle sticks *Lucrece* 317
And griping it, the needle his finger pricks 319
Needy. As, to behold desert a beggar born, And needy nothing trimm'd in jollity *Sonnet* 66 3
Neglect. So then we do neglect The thing we have *Lucrece* 152
What shall be thy amends For thy neglect of truth in beauty dyed? *Son.* 101 2
Mark how with my neglect I do dispense 112 12
Neglected. His honour, his affairs, his friends, his state, Neglected all *Lucr.* 46
Whilst her neglected child holds her in chase, Cries to catch her *Sonnet* 143 5
Negligence. Replied the maid, 'The more to blame my sluggard negligence' *Lucrece* 1278
Though slackly braided in loose negligence *Lov. Comp.* 35
Neigh. And forth she rushes, snorts, and neighs aloud *Ven. and Adon.* 262
Imperiously he leaps, he neighs, he bounds 265
He looks upon his love and neighs unto her 307
Desire, of perfect'st love being made, Shall neigh *Sonnet* 51 11
Neighbour. But, lo, from forth a copse that neighbours by, A breeding jennet, lusty, young, and proud *Ven. and Adon.* 259
The neighbour caves, as seeming troubled, Make verbal repetition of her moans 830
His nose being shadow'd by his neighbour's ear *Lucrece* 1416
Neither. Though neither eyes nor ears, to hear nor see, Yet should I be in love by touching thee *Ven. and Adon.* 437
Extreme fear can neither fight nor fly *Lucrece* 230
Cheeks neither red nor pale, but mingled so That blushing red no guilty instance gave 1510
One doth call her his, the other his, Yet neither may possess the claim 1794
Neither in inward worth nor outward fair *Sonnet* 16 11
No, neither he, nor his compeers by night Giving him aid, my verse astonished 86 7
With acture they may be, Where neither party is nor true nor kind *L. Comp.* 186
Vow, bond, nor space, In thee hath neither sting, knot, nor confine 265
Mild as a dove, but neither true nor trusty *Pass. Pil.* 86
Bad in the best, though excellent in neither 102
Good night, good rest. Ah, neither be my share 181
Take counsel of some wiser head, Neither too young nor yet unwed 304
Single nature's double name Neither two nor one was called *Ph. and Tur.* 40
To themselves yet either neither, Simple were so well compounded 43
Nerves. Unless my nerves were brass or hammer'd steel. *Sonnet* 120 4
Nest. The sheep are gone to fold, birds to their nest *Ven. and Adon.* 532
Or hateful cuckoos hatch in sparrows' nests *Lucrece* 849
Now this pale swan in her watery nest Begins the sad dirge of her certain ending 1611
Death is now the phœnix' nest: And the turtle's loyal breast To eternity doth rest *Ph. and Tur.* 56
Nestor. There pleading might you see grave Nestor stand *Lucrece* 1401
But for loss of Nestor's golden words, It seem'd they would debate with angry swords 1420
Net. Look, how a bird lies tangled in a net, So fasten'd in her arms Adonis lies *Ven. and Adon.* 67
Never. Here come and sit, where never serpent hisses 17
If thou wilt chide, thy lips shall never open 48
Forced to content, but never to obey 61
She swears, From his soft bosom never to remove 81
Never. Never did passenger in summer's heat More thirst for drink than she for this good turn *Ven. and Adon.* 91
Whose sinewy neck in battle ne'er did bow 99
These blue-vein'd violets whereon we lean Never can blab 126
And being steel'd, soft sighs can never grave it 376
Then love's deep groans I never shall regard 377
The lesson is but plain, And once made perfect, never lost again 408
The colt that's back'd and burden'd being young Loseth his pride and never waxeth strong 420
She, by her good will, Will never rise, so he will kiss her still 480
Were never four such lamps together mix'd, Had not his clouded with his brow's repine 489
O, never let their crimson liveries wear! 506
And glutton-like she feeds, yet never filleth 548
Whose tushes never sheathed he whetteth still 617
For misery is trodden on by many, And being low never relieved by any 708
End without audience and are never done 846
A nurse's song ne'er pleased her babe so well 974
Grief hath two tongues, and never woman yet Could rule them both without ten women's wit 1007
And never wound the heart with looks again 1042
The wolf would leave his prey And never fright the silly lamb that day 1098
Ne'er saw the beauteous livery that he wore 1107
Never did he bless My youth with his; the more am I accurst 1119
Ne'er settled equally, but high or low, That all love's pleasure shall not match his woe 1139
Thy hasty spring still blasts, and ne'er grows old *Lucrece* 49
Birds never limed no secret bushes fear 88
She, that never coped with stranger eyes, Could pick no meaning 99
That had Narcissus seen her as she stood, Self-love had never drown'd him in the flood 266
My heart shall never countermand mine eye 276
From them no device can take, The blemish that will never be forgot 536
She prays she never may behold the day 746
My true eyes have never practised how To cloak offences 748
Thy violent vanities can never last 894
This bastard graff shall never come to growth 1062
I am the mistress of my fate, And with my trespass never will dispense 1070
And never be forgot in mighty Rome, Th' adulterate death of Lucrece and her groom 1644
That never was inclined To accessary yieldings 1657
We desire increase, That thereby beauty's rose might never die *Sonnet* 1 2
Such heavenly touches ne'er touch'd earthly faces 17 8
A closet never pierced with crystal eyes 46 6
He shall never cut from memory My sweet love's beauty 63 11
I never saw that you did painting need 83 1
But best is best, if never intermix'd 101 8
To me, fair friend, you never can be old 104 1
O, never say that I was false of heart 109 1
Never believe, though in my nature reign'd All frailties 109 9
Mine appetite I never more will grind On newer proof 110 10
An ever-fixed mark That looks on tempests and is never shaken 116 6
If this be error and upon me proved, I never writ, nor no man ever loved 116 14
Whilst it hath thought itself so blessed never 119 6
Till now did ne'er invite, nor never woo *Lov. Comp.* 182
O never faith could hold, if not to beauty vow'd *Pass. Pil.* 58
As goods lost are seld or never found, As vaded gloss no rubbing will refresh 175
Unless thy lady prove unjust, Press never thou to choose anew 332
Think women still to strive with men, To sin and never for to saint 342
Never-cloying. Even so, being full of your ne'er-cloying sweetness *Sonnet* 118 5
Never-conquered. Under that colour am I come to scale Thy never-conquer'd fort *Lucrece* 482
Never-ending. Enchained me To endless date of never-ending woes 935
Never-resting. For never-resting time leads summer on To hideous winter and confounds him there *Sonnet* 5 5
New. These worlds in Tarquin new ambition bred *Lucrece* 411
These water-galls in her dim element Foretell new storms to those already spent 1589
I often did behold In thy sweet semblance my old age new born 1759
This were to be new made when thou art old *Sonnet* 2 13
And all in war with Time for love of you, As he takes from you, I engraft you new 15 14
Makes black night beauteous and her old face new 27 12
And with old woes new wail my dear time's waste 30 4
Which I new pay as if not paid before 30 12
To make some special instant special blest, By new unfolding his imprison'd pride 52 12
And you in Grecian tires are painted new 53 8
Where two contracted new Come daily to the banks 56 10
If there be nothing new, but that which is Hath been before 59 1
Robbing no old to dress his beauty new 68 12
Why is my verse so barren of new pride, So far from variation or quick change? 76 1
So all my best is dressing old words new 76 11
For as the sun is daily new and old, So is my love 76 13
Thou shalt find Those children nursed, deliver'd from thy brain, To take a new acquaintance of thy mind 77 12
So love's face May still seem love to me, though alter'd new 93 3
Our love was new and then but in the spring 102 5
What's new to speak, what new to register, That may express my love? 108 3
Sold cheap what is most dear, Made old offences of affections new 110 4
New faith torn In vowing new hate after new love bearing 152 3
The bath for my help lies Where Cupid got new fire—my mistress' eyes 153 14
And when in his fair parts she did abide, She was new lodged *Lov. Comp.* 84
And new pervert a reconciled maid 329
New-appearing. Doth homage to his new-appearing sight *Sonnet* 7 3
New-bleeding. Of proofs new-bleeding, which remain'd the foil Of this false jewel *Lov. Comp.* 153
New-born. My shame so dead, mine honour is new-born *Lucrece* 1190
Newer. Pausing for means to mourn some newer way 1365
Mine appetite I never more will grind On newer proof *Sonnet* 110 11
Thy pyramids built up with newer might To me are nothing novel 123 2
New-fallen. As apt as new-fall'n snow takes any dint *Ven. and Adon.* 354
New-fangled. Some [glory] in their garments, though new-fangled ill *Son.* 91 3
New-fired. But at my mistress' eye Love's brand new-fired, The boy for trial needs would touch my breast 153 9
New-found. To new-found methods and to compounds strange 76 4
New-killed. Like to a new-kill'd bird she trembling lies *Lucrece* 457
Newly. By thy bright beauty was it newly bred 490
She was new lodged and newly deified *Lov. Comp.* 84

News. That sometime true news, sometime false doth bring *Ven. and Adon.* 658

Fearing some hard news from the warlike band . . . *Lucrece* 255

As testy sick men, when their deaths be near, No news but health from their physicians know . . . *Sonnet* 140 8

New-sprung. She bows her head, the new-sprung flower to smell *V. and A.* 1171

New-waxen. From lips new-waxen pale begins to blow The grief away *Lucr.* 1663

Next. Thou art the next of blood, and 'tis thy right *Ven. and Adon.* 1184

Next vouchsafe t' afford—If ever, love, thy Lucrece thou wilt see—Some present speed to come and visit me *Lucrece* 1305

Then give me welcome, next my heaven the best *Sonnet* 110 13

My next self thou harder hast engross'd 133 6

Nibbler. The tender nibbler would not touch the bait *Pass. Pil.* 53

Nice. Some high, some low, the painter was so nice *Lucrece* 1412

And nice affections wavering stood in doubt *Lov. Comp.* 97

Niggard. The niggard prodigal that praised her so *Lucrece* 79

Beauteous niggard, why dost thou abuse The bounteous largess given thee to give *Sonnet* 4 5

And hang more praise upon deceased I Than niggard truth would willingly impart 72 8

Niggarding. And, tender churl, makest waste in niggarding 1 12

Nigh. Taking no notice that she is so nigh, For all askance he holds her in his eye *Ven. and Adon.* 341

No flower was nigh, no grass, herb, leaf, or weed, But stole his blood 1055

A reverend man that grazed his cattle nigh *Lov. Comp.* 57

Night. Then wink again, And I will wink; so shall the day seem night *V. and A.* 122

From morn till night, even where I list to sport me 154

The night of sorrow now is turn'd to day 481

Shone like the moon in water seen by night 492

The owl, night's herald, shrieks, ''Tis very late' 531

And coal-black clouds that shadow heaven's light Do summon us to part and bid good night 534

'Good night,' and so say you; If you will say so, you shall have a kiss 535

'Good night,' quoth she, and, ere he says 'Adieu,' The honey fee of parting tender'd is 537

'Sweet boy,' she says, 'this night I'll waste in sorrow' 583

'The night is spent.' 'Why, what of that?' quoth she 717

'In night,' quoth she, 'desire sees best of all' 720

Now of this dark night I perceive the reason 727

To shame the sun by day and her by night 732

The lamp that burns by night Dries up his oil to lend the world his light 755

By this black-faced night, desire's foul nurse 773

So glides he in the night from Venus' eye; Which after him she darts 816

So did the merciless and pitchy night Fold in the object that did feed her sight 821

Her song was tedious and outwore the night, For lovers' hours are long 841

For who hath she to spend the night withal But idle sounds resembling parasites 847

Who bids them still consort with ugly night 1041

My throbbing heart shall rock thee day and night 1186

For he the night before, in Tarquin's tent, Unlock'd the treasure *Lucrece* 15

Sable Night, mother of Dread and Fear 117

Long he questioned With modest Lucrece, and wore out the night 123

Now stole upon the time the dead of night 162

Misty night Covers the shame that follows sweet delight 356

With pearly sweat, resembling dew of night 396

As one in dead of night From forth dull sleep by dreadful fancy waking 449

Thy beauty hath ensnared thee to this night 485

'Lucrece,' quoth he, 'this night I must enjoy thee' 512

Shame folded up in blind concealing night 675

So surfeit-taking Tarquin fares this night 698

Even in this thought through the dark night he stealeth 729

She stays, exclaiming on the direful night 741

'For day,' quoth she, 'night's scapes doth open lay' 747

Thus breathes she forth her spite Against the unseen secrecy of night 763

O comfort-killing Night, image of hell! Dim register and notary of shame! 764

O hateful, vaporous, and foggy Night! 771

His smother'd light May set at noon and make perpetual night 784

Were Tarquin Night, as he is but Night's child 785

Through Night's black bosom should not peep again 788

O Night, thou furnace of foul-reeking smoke! 799

Mis-shapen Time, copesmate of ugly Night, Swift subtle post 925

To wake the morn and sentinel the night 942

O, this dread night, wouldst thou one hour come back! 965

To make him curse this cursed crimeful night 970

Poor grooms are sightless night, kings glorious day 1013

I rail at Opportunity, At Time, at Tarquin, and uncheerful Night 1024

To hide the truth of this false night's abuses 1075

Solemn night with slow sad gait descended To ugly hell 1081

Shames herself to see, And therefore still in night would cloister'd be 1085

For day hath nought to do what's done by night 1092

Which makes the maid weep like the dewy night 1232

Assail'd by night with circumstances strong Of present death 1262

Like dying coals burnt out in tedious nights 1379

She looks for night, and then she longs for morrow 1571

Else lasting shame On thee and thine this night I will inflict 1630

And see the brave day sunk in hideous night *Sonnet* 12 2

Where wasteful Time debateth with Decay, To change your day of youth to sullied night 15 12

Like a jewel hung in ghastly night, Makes black night beauteous and her old face new 27 11

By day my limbs, by night my mind, For thee and for myself no quiet find 27 13

When day's oppression is not eased by night, But day by night, and night by day, oppress'd 28 3

So flatter I the swart-complexion'd night 28 11

And night doth nightly make grief's strength seem stronger. 28 14

For precious friends hid in death's dateless night 30 6

When in dead night thy fair imperfect shade Through heavy sleep on sightless eyes doth stay 43 11

All days are nights to see till I see thee, And nights bright days when dreams do show thee me 43 13

Is it thy will thy image should keep open My heavy eyelids to the weary night? 61 2

When his youthful morn Hath travell'd on to age's steepy night 63 5

Which by and by black night doth take away, Death's second self 73 7

No, neither he, nor his compeers by night Giving him aid, my verse astonished 86 7

Give not a windy night a rainy morrow 90 7

When her mournful hymns did hush the night 102 10

The mountain or the sea, the day or night, The crow or dove 113 11

Night. O, that our night of woe might have remember'd My deepest sense, how hard true sorrow hits *Sonnet* 120 9

That follow'd it as gentle day Doth follow night 145 11

And thought thee bright, Who art as black as hell, as dark as night 147 14

Good night, good rest. Ah, neither be my share: She bade good night that kept my rest away *Pass. Pil.* 181

And drives away dark dismal-dreaming night 200

The night so pack'd, I post unto my pretty 201

Were I with her, the night would post too soon 205

Pack night, peep day; good day, of night now borrow: Short, night, to-night, and length thyself to-morrow 209

Her cloudy looks will calm ere night 312

Nightingale. Every thing did banish moan, Save the nightingale alone 380

Nightly. With the nightly linen that she wears He pens her piteous clamours in her head *Lucrece* 680

The well-tuned warble of her nightly sorrow 1080

And night doth nightly make grief's strength seem stronger. *Sonnet* 28 14

That affable familiar ghost Which nightly gulls him with intelligence 86 10

Night-owl. The dove sleeps fast that this night-owl will catch *Lucrece* 360

Night-waking. Yet, foul night-waking cat, he doth but dally 554

Night-wanderers. Or stonish'd as night-wanderers often are, Their light blown out in some mistrustful wood *Ven. and Adon.* 825

Night-wandering weasels shriek to see him there *Lucrece* 307

Nill. In scorn or friendship, nill I construe whether *Pass. Pil.* 188

Nimble. Relish your nimble notes to pleasing ears *Lucrece* 1126

For nimble thought can jump both sea and land As soon as think the place where he would be *Sonnet* 44 7

Do I envy those jacks that nimble leap To kiss the tender inward of thy hand! 128 5

Youth is full of sport, age's breath is short; Youth is nimble, age is lame *Pass. Pil.* 162

Nimbly. The studded bridle on a ragged bough Nimbly she fastens *V. and A.* 38

Nine. Be thou the tenth Muse, ten times more in worth Than those old nine *Sonnet* 38 10

No. But having no defects, why dost abhor me? *Ven. and Adon.* 138

Thing like a man, but of no woman bred! 214

No dog shall rouse thee, though a thousand bark 240

Therefore no marvel though thy horse be gone 390

For where a heart is hard they make no battery 426

No fisher but the ungrown fry forbears 526

Wilt thou make the match? He tells her, no 587

'Where did I leave?' 'No matter where;' quoth he 715

No, lady, no; my heart longs not to groan, But soundly sleeps 785

They answer all ''Tis so:' And would say after her, if she said 'No' 852

'No, no,' quoth she, 'sweet Death, I did but jest' 997

No flower was nigh, no grass, herb, leaf, or weed, But stole his blood 1055

We have no good that we can say is ours *Lucrece* 873

But this no slaughterhouse no tool imparteth 1039

With a steadfast eye Receives the scroll without or yea or no 1340

Then love doth well denote Love's eye is not so true as all men's 'No' *Sonnet* 148 8

Noble. With noble disposition Each present lord began to promise aid *Lucr.* 1695

Proud of subjection, noble by the sway *Lov. Comp.* 108

Which late her noble suit in court did shun 234

Nobler. I do betray My nobler part to my gross body's treason *Sonnet* 151 6

Nobly. Thou nobly base, they basely dignified *Lucrece* 660

Noise. When he hath ceased his ill-resounding noise *Ven. and Adon.* 919

No noise but owls' and wolves' death-boding cries *Lucrece* 165

Deep sounds make lesser noise than shallow fords 1329

None. The sea hath bounds, but deep desire hath none *Ven. and Adon.* 389

Every present sorrow seemeth chief, But none is best 971

Some untimely thought did instigate His all-too-timeless speed, if none of those *Lucrece* 44

In thy shady cell, where none may spy him, Sits Sin 881

That mother tries a merciless conclusion Who, having two sweet babes, when death takes one, Will slay the other and be nurse to none 1162

But none where all distress and dolour dwell'd 1446

It easeth some, though none it ever cured, To think their dolour others have endured 1581

If children pre-decease progenitors, We are their offspring, and they none of ours 1757

Sings this to thee: 'thou single wilt prove none' *Sonnet* 8 14

Thou art beloved of many, But that thou none lovest is most evident 10 4

O, none but unthrifts! Dear my love, you know You had a father 13 13

But you like none, none you, for constant heart 53 14

Or who his spoil of beauty can forbid? O, none, unless this miracle have might 65 13

When yellow leaves, or none, or few, do hang Upon those boughs 73 2

They that have power to hurt and will do none 94 1

Yet I none could see But sweet or colour it had stol'n from thee 99 14

None else to me, nor I to none alive 112 7

Yet none knows well To shun the heaven that leads men to this hell 129 13

With ease we prove Among a number one is reckon'd none 136 8

That's to ye sworn to none was ever said *Lov. Comp.* 180

All my offences that abroad you see Are errors of the blood, none of the mind 184

Such looks as none could look but beauty's queen *Pass. Pil.* 46

None fairer, nor none falser to deface her 90

Other help for him I see that there is none 298

Ah, thought I, thou mourn'st in vain! None takes pity on thy pain 392

Even so, poor bird, like thee, None alive will pity me 400

Two distincts, division none: Number there in love was slain *Ph. and Tur.* 27

Love hath reason, reason none, If what parts can so remain 47

Non-payment. Say, for non-payment that the debt should double *V. and A.* 521

Noon. That in their smoky ranks his smother'd light May set at noon *Lucr.* 784

So thou, thyself out-going in thy noon, Unlook'd on diest *Sonnet* 7 13

Noon-tide. Ere he arrive his weary noon-tide prick *Lucrece* 781

Nor. Though neither eyes nor ears, to hear nor see, Yet should I be in love by touching thee *Ven. and Adon.* 437

And that I could not see, nor hear, nor touch 440

Nor sun nor wind will ever strive to kiss you 1082

Nor children's tears nor mothers' groans respecting *Lucrece* 431

Grief dallied with nor law nor limit knows 1120

That knows not parching heat nor freezing cold 1145

And live no more to shame nor me nor you *Sonnet* 72 12

Northern. To hie as fast As lagging fowls before the northern blast *Lucrece* 1335

Nose. He wrings her nose, he strikes her on the cheeks, He bends her fingers *Ven. and Adon.* 475

His nose being shadow'd by his neighbour's ear *Lucrece* 1416

Nostril. His nostrils drink the air, and forth again *Ven. and Adon.* 273

Nostril. Broad breast, full eye, small head, and nostril wide *Ven. and Adon.* 296
Not. I'll smother thee with kisses; And yet not cloy thy lips 19
And govern'd him in strength, though not in lust 42
O, be not proud, nor brag not of thy might! 113
Not gross to sink, but light, and will aspire 150
And whether he run or fly they know not whether 304
'I know not love,' quoth he, 'nor will not know it' 409
Would they not wish the feast might ever last? 447
Are they not quickly told and quickly gone? 520
Before I know myself, seek not to know me 525
Didst thou not mark my face? was it not white? 643
Saw'st thou not signs of fear lurk in mine eye? Grew I not faint? 644
My heart longs not to groan, But soundly sleeps 785
Call it not love, for Love to heaven is fled 793
How strange it seems Not to believe, and yet too credulous 986
Do not then ensnare me: Thou look'st not like deceit; do not deceive me *Lucrece* 585
They think not but that every eye can see The same disgrace 750
Notary. O comfort-killing Night, image of hell! Dim register and notary of shame! 765
Note. To note the fighting conflict of her hue, How white and red each other did destroy! *Ven. and Adon.* 345
She marking them begins a wailing note 835
Posterity, shamed with the note, Shall curse my bones *Lucrece* 208
What did he note but strongly he desired 415
Relish your nimble notes to pleasing ears 1126
Who all in one, one pleasing note do sing *Sonnet* 8 12
I do not love thee with mine eyes, For they in thee a thousand errors note 141 2
This device was sent me from a nun, Or sister sanctified, of holiest note *Lov. Comp.* 233
Noted. What could he see but mightily he noted? *Lucrece* 414
Why write I still all one, ever the same, And keep invention in a noted weed? *Sonnet* 76 6
More flowers I noted, yet I none could see But sweet or colour it had stol'n from thee 99 14
Noteth. This solemn sympathy poor Venus noteth *Ven. and Adon.* 1057
Nothing. He sees his love, and nothing else he sees, For nothing else with his proud sight agrees 287
Though nothing but my body's bane would cure thee 372
If springing things be any jot diminish'd, They wither in their prime, prove nothing worth 418
And nothing but the very smell were left me 441
That nothing in him seem'd inordinate, Save sometime too much wonder of his eye *Lucrece* 94
For want of wit, Make something nothing by augmenting it 154
But nothing can affection's course control 500
Bearing away the wound that nothing healeth 731
Who nothing wants to answer her but cries, And bitter words 1459
Nature's bequest gives nothing but doth lend *Sonnet* 4 3
Nothing 'gainst Time's scythe can make defence Save breed 12 13
Me of thee defeated, By adding one thing to my purpose nothing 20 12
If there be nothing new, but that which is Hath been before 59 1
Nothing stands but for his scythe to mow 60 12
As, to behold desert a beggar born, And needy nothing trimm'd in jollity 66 3
Those parts of thee that the world's eye doth view Want nothing 69 2
Dear love, forget me quite, For you in me can nothing worthy prove 72 4
I am shamed by that which I bring forth, And so should you, to love things nothing worth 72 14
Thy looks should nothing thence but sweetness tell 93 12
What new to register, That may express my love or thy dear merit? Nothing, sweet boy 108 5
To leave for nothing all thy sum of good 109 12
For nothing this wide universe I call, Save thou, my rose 109 13
To me are nothing novel, nothing strange 123 3
My mistress' eyes are nothing like the sun 130 1
In nothing art thou black save in thy deeds 131 13
For nothing hold me, so it please thee hold That nothing me, a something sweet to thee 136 11
For why thou left'st me nothing in thy will *Pass. Pil.* 138
For why I craved nothing of thee still 140
More mickle was the pain That nothing could be used to turn them both to gain 220
Notice. Taking no notice that she is so nigh, For all askance he holds her in his eye *Ven. and Adon.* 341
Notorious. Thou foul abettor! thou notorious bawd! *Lucrece* 886
Nought. Alas, he nought esteems that face of thine *Ven. and Adon.* 631
Beauty hath nought to do with such foul fiends 638

Nought. Full of respects, yet nought at all respecting; In hand with all things, nought at all effecting *Ven. and Adon.* 911
It was not she that call'd him all-to naught 993
For day hath nought to do what's done by night *Lucrece* 1092
As a child, Who wayward once, his mood with nought agrees 1095
This huge stage presenteth nought but shows *Sonnet* 15 3
Receiving nought by elements so slow But heavy tears 44 13
Think of nought Save, where you are how happy you make those 57 11
A woman's nay doth stand for nought *Pass. Pil.* 340
Nourished. Consumed with that which it was nourish'd by *Sonnet* 73 12
Novel. To me are nothing novel, nothing strange 123 3
Now. The steed is stalled up, and even now To tie the rider she begins to prove *Ven. and Adon.* 39
Now doth she stroke his cheek, now doth he frown 45
I have been woo'd, as I entreat thee now, Even by the stern and direful god of war 97
And now Adonis, with a lazy spright, And with a heavy, dark, disliking eye 181
And now she weeps, and now she fain would speak, And now her sobs do her intendments break 221
Now gazeth she on him, now on the ground 224
Being mad before, how doth she now for wits? 249
Now which way shall she turn? what shall she say? 253
And now his woven girths he breaks asunder 266
What cares he now for curb or pricking spur? For rich caparisons? 285
To bid the wind a base he now prepares 303
But now her cheek was pale, and by and by It flash'd forth fire 347
Now was she just before him as he sat 349
But now I lived, and life was death's annoy; But now I died, and death was lively joy 497
Now let me say 'Good night,' and so say you; If you will say so 535
For pity now she can no more detain him 577
Now of this dark night I perceive the reason 727
My heart longs not to groan, But soundly sleeps, while now it sleeps alone 786
For now she knows it is no gentle chase 883
This way she runs, and now she will no further 905
But like a stormy day, now wind, now rain, Sighs dry her cheeks 965
Her eyes are mad that they have wept till now 1062
If ever, now; Now, while the world is bent my deeds to cross *Sonnet* 90 1
Now all is done, have what shall have no end 110 9
Now are minutes added to the hours; To spite me now, each minute seems a moon *Pass. Pil.* 206
Nowhere. Anon their gazes lend To every place at once, and, nowhere fix'd *Lov. Comp.* 27
Numbs. With cold-pale weakness numbs each feeling part *Ven. and Adon.* 892
Number. How comes it then, vile Opportunity, Being so bad, such numbers seek for thee? *Lucrece* 896
And in fresh numbers number all your graces *Sonnet* 17 6
Let him bring forth Eternal numbers to outlive long date 38 12
But now my gracious numbers are decay'd 79 3
And straight redeem In gentle numbers time so idly spent 100 6
With ease we prove Among a number one is reckon'd none 136 8
Then in the number let me pass untold 136 9
Two distincts, division none: Number there in love was slain *Ph. and Tur.* 28
Nun. Self-loving nuns, That on the earth would breed a scarcity *V. and A.* 752
This device was sent me from a nun, Or sister sanctified *Lov. Comp.* 232
My parts had power to charm a sacred nun 260
Nurse. What banquet wert thou to the taste, Being nurse and feeder of the other four! *Ven. and Adon.* 446
By this black-faced night, desire's foul nurse 773
A nurse's song ne'er pleased her babe so well 974
The aim of all is but to nurse the life With honour, wealth, and ease *Lucr.* 141
Vast sin-concealing chaos! nurse of blame! 767
The nurse, to still her child, will tell my story 813
That mother tries a merciless conclusion Who, having two sweet babes, when death takes one, Will slay the other and be nurse to none 1162
Which I will keep so chary As tender nurse her babe from faring ill *Son.* 22 12
Nursed. Thou shalt find Those children nursed, deliver'd from thy brain 77 11
Nursest. Thou nursest all and murder'st all that are *Lucrece* 929
Nurseth. My love is as a fever, longing still For that which longer nurseth the disease *Sonnet* 147 2
Nuzzling. And nuzzling in his flank, the loving swine Sheathed unaware the tusk in his soft groin *Ven. and Adon.* 1115
Nymph. The field's chief flower, sweet above compare, Stain to all nymphs 9
Or, like a nymph, with long dishevell'd hair, Dance on the sands, and yet no footing seen 147
Whilst many nymphs that vow'd chaste life to keep Came tripping by *Sonnet* 154 3
Nymphs back peeping Fearfully *Pass. Pil.* 287

O

Oak. To dry the old oak's sap and cherish springs *Lucrece* 950
Those thoughts, to me like oaks, to thee like osiers bow'd *Pass. Pil.* 60
Oath. And him by oath they truly honoured *Lucrece* 410
By knighthood, gentry, and sweet friendship's oath 569
Thou makest the vestal violate her oath 883
I will not wrong thy true affection so, To flatter thee with an infringed oath 1061
Knights, by their oaths, should right poor ladies' harms 1694
But why of two oaths' breach do I accuse thee, When I break twenty? *Sonnet* 152 5
I am perjured most; For all my vows are oaths but to misuse thee 152 7
For I have sworn deep oaths of thy deep kindness, Oaths of thy love 152 9
That strong-bonded oath That shall prefer and undertake my troth *Lov. Comp.* 279
What fool is not so wise To break an oath, to win a paradise? *Pass. Pil.* 42
Between each kiss her oaths of true love swearing 92
Her faith, her oaths, her tears, and all were jestings 96
Obdurate. Art thou obdurate, flinty, hard as steel, Nay more than flint? *Ven. and Adon.* 199
Obdurate vassals fell exploits effecting, In bloody death *Lucrece* 429
Obedience. Calls her maid, Whose swift obedience to her mistress hies 1215

Obey. Forced to content, but never to obey *Ven. and Adon.* 61
His lips obey, Paying what ransom the insulter willeth 549
He now obeys, and now no more resisteth, While she takes all she can 563
Nor aught obeys but his foul appetite *Lucrece* 546
Ask'd their own wills, and made their wills obey *Lov. Comp.* 133
What me your minister, for you obeys, Works under you 229
Herald sad and trumpet be, To whose sound chaste wings obey *Ph. and Tur.* 4
Obeyed. Strong-tempered steel his stronger strength obey'd *Ven. and Adon.* 111
Object. The time is spent, her object will away, And from her twining arms doth urge releasing 255
So did the merciless and pitchy night Fold in the object that did feed her sight 822
Make me not object to the tell-tale Day! *Lucrece* 806
No object but her passion's strength renews 1103
A thousand lamentable objects there, In scorn of nature 1373
An eye more bright . . . , Gilding the object whereupon it gazeth *Sonnet* 20 6
Of his quick objects hath the mind no part 113 7
As fast as objects to his beams assemble 114 8
The goodly objects which abroad they find *Lov. Comp.* 137

Object. The heaven-hued sapphire and the opal blend With objects manifold *Lov. Comp.* 216
Oblation. Take thou my oblation, poor but free . . . *Sonnet* 125 10
For these, of force, must your oblations be, Since I their altar, you enpatron me . . . . *Lov. Comp.* 223
Oblivion. Planting oblivion, beating reason back . . *Ven. and Adon.* 557
To feed oblivion with decay of things . . . *Lucrece* 947
Till each to razed oblivion yield his part . . *Sonnet* 122 7
Obloquy. And thou, the author of their obloquy . . *Lucrece* 523
Obscure. Round rising hillocks, brakes obscure and rough *Ven. and Adon.* 237
Cynthia for shame obscures her silver shine . . 728
Obscurely. Cave-keeping evils that obscurely sleep . *Lucrece* 1250
Obscurity. Seeming to bury that posterity Which by the rights of time thou needs must have, If thou destroy them not in dark obscurity *Ven. and Adon.* 760
Obsequious. How many a holy and obsequious tear Hath dear religious love stol'n from mine eye As interest of the dead . . *Sonnet* 31 5
Let me be obsequious in thy heart, And take thou my oblation 125 9
Obsequy. Keep the obsequy so strict . . *Ph. and Tur.* 12
Observance. Such sweet observance in this work was had *Lucrece* 1385
Observed. Observed as they flew—Towards this afflicted fancy fastly drew *Lov. Comp.* 60
Obtain. Yet ever to obtain his will resolving *Lucrece* 129
Pawning his honour to obtain his lust 156
Obtained. Bring him where his suit may be obtain'd 898
Obtaining. Revolving The sundry dangers of his will's obtaining . 128
Occasion. 'My girl,' quoth she, 'on what occasion break Those tears from thee?' 1270
And every light occasion of the wind Upon his lips their silken parcels hurls *Lov. Comp.* 86
Ocean. 'O, where am I?' quoth she, 'in earth or heaven, Or in the ocean?' *Ven. and Adon.* 494
All which together, like a troubled ocean *Lucrece* 589
Who seek to stain the ocean of thy blood 655
Who in a salt-waved ocean quench their light . 1231
Let this sad interim like the ocean be Which parts the shore . *Sonnet* 56 9
I have seen the hungry ocean gain Advantage on the kingdom of the shore . . . 64 5
Wide as the ocean is, The humble as the proudest sail doth bear . 80 5
And mine I pour your ocean all among *Lov. Comp.* 256
Odd. And to their hope they such odd action yield . *Lucrece* 1433
Odour. The rose looks fair, but fairer we it deem For that sweet odour, which doth in it live . . *Sonnet* 54 4
Sweet roses do not so; Of their sweet deaths are sweetest odours made 54 12
But why thy odour matcheth not thy show, The solve is this 69 13
Nor the sweet smell Of different flowers in odour and in hue . 98 6
Of. The precedent of pith and livelihood *Ven. and Adon.* 26
Love is a spirit all compact of fire 149
By law of nature thou art bound to breed 171
A lily prison'd in a gaol of snow, Or ivory in an alabaster band 362
Now is she in the very lists of love, Her champion mounted 595
'I am,' quoth he, 'expected of my friends; And now 'tis dark' 718
O happiness enjoy'd but of a few! And, if possess'd, as soon decay'd *Lucr.* 22
Beauty itself doth of itself persuade The eyes of men 29
Off. Sometime he scuds far off and there he stares *Ven. and Adon.* 301
And all amazed brake off his late intent 469
By this, poor Wat, far off upon a hill, Stands on his hinder legs 697
By this, far off she hears some huntsman hollo 973
The wind would blow it off and, being gone, Play with his locks 1089
How far I toil, still farther off from thee . *Sonnet* 28 8
From me far off, with others all too near . 61 14
From off a hill whose concave womb re-worded A plaintful story *Lov. Comp.* 1
Shook off my sober guards and civil fears 298
Offence. When they in thee the like offences prove *Lucrece* 613
He scowls and hates himself for his offence 738
My true eyes have never practised how To cloak offences 749
Till life to death acquit my forced offence 1071
For one's offence why should so many fall? 1483
What is the quality of mine offence? 1702
And so to publish Tarquin's foul offence 1852
But weak relief To him that bears the strong offence's cross *Sonnet* 34 12
Thus can my love excuse the slow offence Of my dull bearer . 51 1
Say that thou didst forsake me for some fault, And I will comment upon that offence 89 2
Sold cheap what is most dear, Made old offences of affections new . 110 4
All my offences that abroad you see Are errors of the blood . *Lov. Comp.* 183
Offend. If the true concord of well-tuned sounds, By unions married, do offend thine ear . . . *Sonnet* 8 6
Offended. Mine ears, that to your wanton talk attended, Do burn themselves for having so offended *Ven. and Adon.* 810
Offender. With foul offenders thou perforce must bear *Lucrece* 612
The offender's sorrow lends but weak relief . *Sonnet* 34 11
Loving offenders, thus I will excuse ye . 42 5
Offer. So offers he to give what she did crave *Ven. and Adon.* 88
Offer pure incense to so pure a shrine *Lucrece* 194
Would not touch the bait, But smile and jest at every gentle offer *Pass. Pil.* 54
Office. Where they resign their office and their light *Ven. and Adon.* 1039
Thy princely office how canst thou fulfil? *Lucrece* 628
Time's office is to fine the hate of foes 936
For who so base would such an office have? 1000
These offices, so oft as thou wilt look, Shall profit thee . *Sonnet* 77 13
Then do thy office, Muse; I teach thee how 101 13
Not daring trust the office of mine eyes *Pass. Pil.* 196
Offspring. If children pre-decease progenitors, We are their offspring *Lucrece* 1757
Oft. Things out of hope are compass'd oft with venturing *Ven. and Adon.* 567
For oft the eye mistakes, the brain being troubled . 1068
For by our ears our hearts oft tainted be *Lucrece* 38
That oft they interchange each other's seat 70
Despair to gain doth traffic oft for gaining 131
Oft that wealth doth cost The death of all, and all together lost 146
But honest fear, bewitch'd with lust's foul charm, Doth too too oft betake him to retire 174
Or say with princes if it shall go well, By oft predict that I in heaven find *Sonnet* 14 8
These offices, so oft as thou wilt look, Shall profit thee . 77 13
So oft have I invoked thee for my Muse And found such fair assistance 78 1
How oft, when thou, my music, music play'st, Upon that blessed wood 128 1
And seal'd false bonds of love as oft as mine 142 7
Oft did she heave her napkin to her eyne *Lov. Comp.* 15
Such a storm As oft 'twixt May and April is to see . 102

Oft. Have you not heard it said full oft, A woman's nay doth stand for nought? . . *Pass. Pil.* 339
Often. Or stonish'd as night-wanderers often are, Their light blown out *Ven. and Adon.* 825
She puts the period often from his place . *Lucrece* 565
Their gentle sex to weep are often willing 1237
I often did behold In thy sweet semblance my old age new born 1758
Sometime too hot the eye of heaven shines, And often is his gold complexion dimm'd . . . *Sonnet* 18 6
'Fair, kind, and true,' have often lived alone 105 13
And often reading what contents it bears. *Lov. Comp.* 19
As often shrieking undistinguish'd woe, In clamours of all size 20
These often bathed she in her fluxive eyes, And often kiss'd, and often 'gan to tear . 50
Often men would say 'That horse his mettle from his rider takes' 106
She hotter that did look For his approach, that often there had been *Pass. Pil.* 78
Her lips to mine how often hath she joined! 91
Oftentimes. Their copious stories oftentimes begun End without audience and are never done *Ven. and Adon.* 845
Oil. The lamp that burns by night Dries up his oil to lend the world his light 756
Old. More I dare not say; The text is old, the orator too green 806
How love makes young men thrall and old men dote 837
Make the young old, the old become a child 1152
Thy hasty spring still blasts, and ne'er grows old *Lucrece* 49
Who fears a sentence or an old man's saw Shall by a painted cloth be kept in awe 244
To blot old books and alter their contents 948
To dry the old oak's sap and cherish springs 950
Old woes, not infant sorrows, bear them mild 1096
Staring on Priam's wounds with her old eyes 1448
Sinon, whose enchanting story The credulous old Priam after slew 1522
Priam, why art thou old and yet not wise? 1550
Both stood, like old acquaintance in a trance, Met far from home 1595
'Daughter, dear daughter,' old Lucretius cries 1751
I often did behold In thy sweet semblance my old age new born 1759
That fair fresh mirror, dim and old, Shows me a bare-boned death 1760
The old bees die, the young possess their hive 1769
Shall sum my count and make my old excuse *Sonnet* 2 11
This were to be new made when thou art old . 2 13
Be scorn'd like old men of less truth than tongue 17 10
Yet, do thy worst, old Time: despite thy wrong 19 13
My glass shall not persuade me I am old . 22 1
Makes black night beauteous and her old face new . 27 12
And with old woes new wail my dear time's waste 30 4
Be thou the tenth Muse, ten times more in worth Than those old nine 38 10
That I might see what the old world could say To this composed wonder 59 9
Robbing no old to dress his beauty new 68 12
So all my best is dressing old words new 76 11
For as the sun is daily new and old, So is my love 76 13
And haply of our old acquaintance tell 89 12
What dark days seen! What old December's bareness every where! 97 4
To me, fair friend, you never can be old 104 1
Beauty making beautiful old rhyme In praise of ladies 106 3
Counting no old thing old, thou mine, I thine 108 7
Sold cheap what is most dear, Made old offences of affections new 110 4
We admire What thou dost foist upon us that is old 123 6
In the old age black was not counted fair 127 1
And wherefore say not I that I am old? 138 10; *Pass. Pil.* 10
Let it not tell your judgement I am old *Lov. Comp.* 73
He did in the general bosom reign Of young, of old 128
Older. Mine appetite I never more will grind On newer proof, to try an older friend *Sonnet* 110 11
Olives. And peace proclaims olives of endless age 107 8
On. Like a dive-dapper peering through a wave, Who, being look'd on, ducks as quickly in *Ven. and Adon.* 87
Like a nymph, with long dishevell'd hair, Dance on the sands 148
Steal thine own freedom and complain on theft 160
Feed where thou wilt, on mountain or in dale, Graze on my lips 232
His braided hanging mane Upon his compass'd crest now stand on end 272
I heartily beseech thee, To take advantage on presented joy 405
Whereon they surfeit, yet complain on drouth 544
Being ireful, on the lion he will venture 628
For misery is trodden on by many, And being low never relieved by any 707
Are on the sudden wasted, thaw'd and done 749
The path is smooth that leadeth on to danger 788
And therefore would he put his bonnet on 1087
Blushing on her, with a steadfast eye Receives the scroll *Lucrece* 1339
Shame bids him possess his breath And live to be revenged on her death 1778
I in your sweet thoughts would be forgot If thinking on me then should make you woe *Sonnet* 71 8
Being fond on praise, which makes your praises worse 84 14
But, love, hate on, for now I know thy mind 149 13
Sometimes they do extend Their view right on *Lov. Comp.* 26
On a day, alack the day! *Pass. Pil.* 227
Once. And now the happy season once more fits *Ven. and Adon.* 327
But when the heart's attorney once is mute, The client breaks 335
Once more the engine of her thoughts began 367
The lesson is but plain, And once made perfect, never lost again 408
Once more the ruby-colour'd portal open'd 451
O, thou didst kill me: kill me once again 499
Like soldiers, when their captain once doth yield, They basely fly 893
From their dark beds once more leap her eyes 1050
No cloudy show of stormy blustering weather Doth yet in his fair welkin once appear *Lucrece* 116
But with a pure appeal seeks to the heart, Which once corrupted takes the worser part 294
So her accent breaks, That twice she doth begin ere once she speaks 567
What darest thou not when once thou art a king? 606
As a child, Who wayward once, his mood with nought agrees 1095
Like a heavy-hanging bell, Once set on ringing, with his own weight goes 1494
Ere once she can discharge one word of woe 1605
They all at once began to say, Her body's stain her mind untainted clears 1709
That I no more can see what once I was 1764
After a thousand victories once foil'd *Sonnet* 25 10
And shalt by fortune once more re-survey These poor rude lines . 32 3
When you have bid your servant once adieu 57 8
Nativity, once in the main of light, Crawls to maturity 60 5
Though I, once gone, to all the world must die 81 6

Once. That you were once unkind befriends me now *Sonnet* 120 1
Have no leisure taken To weigh how once I suffer'd in your crime 120 8
Not once vouchsafe to hide my will in thine 135 6
And Death once dead, there's no more dying then 146 14
The little Love-god lying once asleep 154 1
Anon their gazes lend To every place at once, and, nowhere fix'd *Lov. Comp.* 27
'Once,' quoth she, 'did I see a fair sweet youth Here in these brakes *Pass. Pil.* 125
So beauty blemish'd once's for ever lost 179
But if Fortune once do frown, Then farewell his great renown 419
One. Ten kisses short as one, one long as twenty *Ven. and Adon.* 22
Over one arm the lusty courser's rein, Under her other was the tender boy 31
And one sweet kiss shall pay this countless debt 84
Thou canst not see one wrinkle in my brow 139
What were thy lips the worse for one poor kiss? 207
Give me one kiss, I'll give it thee again, And one for interest 209
She locks her lily fingers one in one 228
So did this horse excel a common one In shape, in courage 293
Down she kneels; With one fair hand she heaveth up his hat 351
For one sweet look thy help I would assure thee 371
Who plucks the bud before one leaf put forth? 416
And pay them at thy leisure, one by one 518
To one sore sick that hears the passing-bell 702
But in one minute's fight brings beauty under 746
As one on shore Gazing upon a late-embarked friend 817
As one that unaware Hath dropp'd a precious jewel in the flood 823
Whereat she starts, like one that spies an adder 878
The cry remaineth in one place, Where fearfully the dogs exclaim 885
Here overcome, as one full of despair, She vail'd her eyelids 955
The one doth flatter thee in thoughts unlikely, In likely thoughts the other kills thee quickly 989
Thou art so full of fear As one with treasure laden, hemm'd with thieves 1022
Over one shoulder doth she hang her head 1058
My tongue cannot express my grief for one 1069
There shall not be one minute in an hour 1187
And every one to rest themselves betake, Save thieves *Lucrece* 125
As one of which doth Tarquin lie revolving The sundry dangers 127
Such thwarting strife, That one for all, or all for one we gage 144
Th' one sweetly flatters, th' other feareth harm 172
For one sweet grape who will the vine destroy? 215
The locks between her chamber and his will, Each one by him enforced 303
As one in dead of night From forth dull sleep by dreadful fancy waking 449
Where now I have no one to blush with me 792
One poor retiring minute in an age Would purchase thee a thousand thousand friends 962
O, this dread night, wouldst thou one hour come back! 965
One that by alms doth live Disdain to him disdained scraps to give 986
Continuance tames the one; the other wild 1097
And as one shifts, another straight ensues 1104
Or one encompass'd with a winding maze 1151
That mother tries a merciless conclusion Who, having two sweet babes, when death takes one, Will slay the other 1161
My body or my soul, which was the dearer, When the one pure, the other made divine? 1164
'Tis honour to deprive dishonour'd life; The one will live, the other being dead 1187
One justly weeps; the other takes in hand No cause, but company 1235
When more is felt than one hath power to tell 1288
One of my husband's men Bid thou be ready, by and by 1291
That one might see those far-off eyes look sad 1386
That one would swear he saw them quake and tremble 1393
In Ajax and Ulysses, O, what art Of physiognomy might one behold! 1395
Here one man's hand lean'd on another's head 1415
Here one being throng'd bears back, all boll'n and red 1417
Why should the private pleasure of some one Become the public plague? 1478
For one's offence why should so many fall, To plague a private sin in general? 1483
And one man's lust these many lives confounds 1489
Ere once she can discharge one word of woe 1605
Too long, To tell them all with one poor tired tongue 1617
Let it then suffice To drown one woe, one pair of weeping eyes 1680
The one doth call her his, the other his, Yet neither may possess the claim 1793
To breed another thee, Or ten times happier, be it ten for one *Sonnet* 6 8
Mark how one string, sweet husband to another 8 9
Who all in one, one pleasing note do sing 8 12
Whose speechless song, being many, seeming one, Sings this to thee 8 13
As fast as thou shalt wane, so fast thou growest In one of thine 11 2
But I forbid thee one most heinous crime 19 8
Me of thee defeated, By adding one thing to my purpose nothing 20 12
So long as youth and thou are of one date 22 2
The one by toil, the other to complain How far I toil 28 7
Wishing me like to one more rich in hope, Featured like him 29 5
Even so my sun one early morn did shine 33 9
But out, alack! he was but one hour mine 33 11
We two must be twain, Although our undivided loves are one 36 2
In our two loves there is but one respect 36 5
Even for this let us divided live, And our dear love lose name of single one 39 6
Thou teachest how to make one twain 39 13
But here's the joy; my friend and I are one 42 13
Since every one hath, every one, one shade, And you, but one 53 3
The one doth shadow of your beauty show 53 10
Why write I still all one, ever the same, And keep invention in a noted weed? 76 5
There lives more life in one of your fair eyes 83 13
All these I better in one general best 91 8
The roses fearfully on thorns did stand, One blushing shame 99 9
Since all alike my songs and praises be To one, of one, still such, and ever so 105 4
Therefore my verse to constancy confined, One thing expressing 105 8
Three themes in one, which wondrous scope affords 105 12
'Fair, kind, and true,' have often lived alone, Which three till now never kept seat in one 105 14
A thousand groans, but thinking on thy face, One on another's neck, do witness bear 131 11
Add to thy 'Will' One will of mine, to make thy large 'Will' more 135 12
Think all but one, and me in that one 'Will' 135 14
Ay, fill it full with wills, and my will one 136 6
With ease we prove Among a number one is reckon'd none 136 8
Let me pass untold, Though in thy stores' account I one must be 136 10
But my five wits nor my five senses can Dissuade one foolish heart from serving thee 141 10

One. Lo! as a careful housewife runs to catch One of her feather'd creatures broke away *Sonnet* 143 2
I guess one angel in another's hell 144 12; *Pass. Pil.* 26
But live in doubt, Till my bad angel fire my good one out *Sonnet* 144 14; *Pass. Pil.* 28
Which one by one she in a river threw *Lov. Comp.* 38
Of folded schedules had she many a one, Which she perused 43
One by nature's outwards so commended, That maidens' eyes stuck over all his face 80
The one a palate hath that needs will taste 167
Not one whose flame my heart so much as warm'd 191
What a hell of witchcraft lies In the small orb of one particular tear! 289
Because thou lovest the one, and I the other *Pass. Pil.* 106
One god is god of both, as poets feign 115
One knight loves both, and both in thee remain 116
He saw more wounds than one, And blushing fled, and left her all alone 129
It was a lording's daughter, the fairest one of three 211
But one must be refused; more mickle was the pain 219
One silly cross Wrought all my loss; O frowning Fortune 257
Were kisses all the joys in bed, One woman would another wed 346
Every one that flatters thee Is no friend in misery 403
If that one be prodigal, Bountiful they will him call 411
So they loved, as love in twain Had the essence but in one *Ph. and Tur.* 26
Single nature's double name Neither two nor one was called 40
That it cried, How true a twain Seemeth this concordant one 46
Only. 'Gainst venom'd sores the only sovereign plaster *Ven. and Adon.* 916
Only he hath an eye to gaze on beauty, And dotes on what he looks *Lucr.* 496
This deed will make thee only loved for fear 610
These contraries such unity do hold, Only to flatter fools and make them bold 1559
She was only mine, And only must be wail'd by Collatine 1798
The world's fresh ornament And only herald to the gaudy spring *Sonnet* 1 10
Thou, best of dearest and mine only care 48 7
But, for their virtue only is their show, They live unwoo'd 54 9
The summer's flower is to the summer sweet, Though to itself it only live and die 94 10
Knows no art, But mutual render, only me for thee 125 12
Only my plague thus far I count my gain 141 13
Onset. Swell in their pride, the onset still expecting *Lucrece* 432
But in the onset come; so shall I taste At first the very worst *Sonnet* 90 11
Onward to Troy with the blunt swains he goes *Lucrece* 1504
My grief lies onward and my joy behind *Sonnet* 50 14
Nature, . . . As thou goest onwards, still will pluck thee back 126 6
Opal. The heaven-hued sapphire and the opal blend With objects manifold *Lov. Comp.* 215
Ope. Remove your siege from my unyielding heart; To love's alarms it will not ope the gate *Ven. and Adon.* 424
But they must ope, this blessed league to kill *Lucrece* 383
She, much amazed, breaks ope her lock'd-up eyes 446
Open. If thou wilt chide, thy lips shall never open *Ven. and Adon.* 48
And with his strong course opens them again 960
Away he steals with open listening ear *Lucrece* 283
But, as they open, they all rate his ill, Which drives the creeping thief to some regard 304
And with his knee the door he opens wide 359
Canopied in darkness sweetly lay, Till they might open to adorn the day 399
Shall remain The scornful mark of every open eye 520
'For day,' quoth she, 'night's scapes doth open lay' 747
Thy secret pleasure turns to open shame 890
Like a goodly champaign plain, Lays open all the little worms that creep 1248
And keep my drooping eyelids open wide *Sonnet* 27 7
Is it thy will thy image should keep open My heavy eyelids? 61 1
Opened. These lovely caves, these round enchanting pits, Open'd their mouths to swallow Venus' liking *Ven. and Adon.* 248
Once more the ruby-colour'd portal open'd 451
Once more leap her eyes; And, being open'd, threw unwilling light 1051
Nor could she moralize his wanton sight, More than his eyes were open'd to the light *Lucrece* 105
Opinion. To eat up errors by opinion bred, Not spend the dowry of a lawful bed 937
Opportunity. We have no good that we can say is ours, But ill-annexed Opportunity Or kills his life or else his quality 874
O Opportunity, thy guilt is great! 'Tis thou that executest the traitor's treason 876
How comes it then, vile Opportunity, Being so bad, such numbers seek for thee? 895
But they ne'er meet with Opportunity 903
Why hath thy servant, Opportunity, Betray'd the hours thou gavest me? 932
In vain I rail at Opportunity, At Time, at Tarquin 1023
Opposite. So cross him with their opposite persuasion 286
Oppressed. The weak oppress'd, the impression of strange kinds Is form'd in them by force, by fraud, or skill 1242
When day's oppression is not eased by night, But day by night, and night by day, oppress'd *Sonnet* 28 4
Sinks down to death, oppress'd with melancholy 45 8
Oppression. When day's oppression is not eased by night 28 3
Oppressor. The orphan pines while the oppressor feeds *Lucrece* 905
Or. More white and red than doves or roses are *Ven. and Adon.* 10
Or, like a fairy, trip upon the green 146
In earth or heaven, Or in the ocean drench'd, or in the fire? 493
With a steadfast eye Receives the scroll without or yea or no *Lucrece* 1340
Orator. The text is old, the orator too green *Ven. and Adon.* 806
Beauty itself doth of itself persuade The eyes of men without an orator *Lucr.* 30
All orators are dumb when beauty pleadeth 268
The orator, to deck his oratory, Will couple my reproach to Tarquin's shame 815
Oratory. Which to her oratory adds more grace 564
The orator, to deck his oratory, Will couple my reproach to Tarquin's shame 815
Orb. What a hell of witchcraft lies In the small orb of one particular tear! *Lov. Comp.* 289
Orbed. Sometime diverted their poor balls are tied To the orbed earth 25
Orchards. Heard where his plants in others' orchards grew 171
Ordering. Strikes each in each by mutual ordering *Sonnet* 8 10
Orient. Yet sometimes falls an orient drop beside, Which her cheek melts *Ven. and Adon.* 981
In the orient when the gracious light Lifts up his burning head *Sonnet* 7 1
Bright orient pearl, alack, too timely shaded! *Pass. Pil.* 133
Origin. Where I myself must render, That is, to you, my origin and ender *Lov. Comp.* 222
Ornament. Thou see'st our mistress' ornaments are chaste *Lucrece* 322
Thou that art now the world's fresh ornament *Sonnet* 1 9
Who heaven itself for ornament doth use 21 3
By that sweet ornament which truth doth give 54 2

Ornament. In him those holy antique hours are seen, Without all ornament, itself and true . . . *Sonnet* 68 10
The ornament of beauty is suspect, A crow that flies in heaven's sweetest air . . . 70 3
Not from those lips of thine, That have profaned their scarlet ornaments 142 6
His real habitude gave life and grace To appertainings and to ornament *Lov. Comp.* 115
Orphan. The orphan pines while the oppressor feeds . . *Lucrece* 905
Yet this abundant issue seem'd to me But hope of orphans . *Sonnet* 97 10
Orpheus. And moody Pluto winks while Orpheus plays . *Lucrece* 553
Orts. Let him have time a beggar's orts to crave . 985
Osier. Those thoughts, to me like oaks, to thee like osiers bow'd *Pass. Pil.* 60
Under an osier growing by a brook, A brook where Adon used to cool his spleen . . . 75
Other. Over one arm the lusty courser's rein, Under her other was the tender boy . *Ven. and Adon.* 32
To note the fighting conflict of her hue, How white and red each other did destroy! . 346
Her other tender hand his fair cheek feels . 352
His other agents aim at like delight . 400
Being nurse and feeder of the other four . 446
Long may they kiss each other, for this cure . 505
For there his smell with others being mingled, The hot scent-snuffing hounds are driven to doubt . 691
Others, they think, delight In such-like circumstance, with such-like sport 843
There lives a son . . . May lend thee light, as thou dost lend to other . 864
Those eyes that taught all other eyes to see . 952
Both crystals, where they view'd each other's sorrow . 963
The one doth flatter thee in thoughts unlikely, In likely thoughts the other kills thee quickly . 990
The birds such pleasure took, That some would sing, some other in their bills Would bring him mulberries . 1102
Of either's colour was the other queen . *Lucrece* 66
That oft they interchange each other's seat . 70
Th' one sweetly flatters, th' other feareth harm . 172
Without the bed her other fair hand was, On the green coverlet . 393
Having no other pleasure of his gain . 860
Continuance tames the one; the other wild, Like an unpractised swimmer . 1097
That mother tries a merciless conclusion Who, having two sweet babes, when death takes one, Will slay the other and be nurse to none . 1162
My body or my soul, which was the dearer, When the one pure, the other made divine? . 1164
'Tis honour to deprive dishonour'd life; The one will live, the other being dead 1187
The other takes in hand No cause, but company, of her drops spilling . 1235
Grieving themselves to guess at others' smarts . 1238
While others saucily Promise more speed, but do it leisurely . 1348
Being from the feeling of her own grief brought By deep surmise of others' detriment . 1579
It easeth some, though none it ever cured, To think their dolour others have endured . 1582
The mindful messenger, come back, Brings home his lord and other company 1584
Met far from home, wondering each other's chance . 1596
One doth call her his, the other his, Yet neither may possess the claim . 1793
No love toward others in that bosom sits . *Sonnet* 9 13
Beauties do themselves forsake And die as fast as they see others grow 12 12
Your sweet semblance to some other give . 13 4
The one by toil, the other to complain How far I toil . 28 7
Both find each other, and I lose both twain . 42 11
The other two, slight air and purging fire, Are both with thee . 45 1
The first my thought, the other my desire . 45 3
A league is took, And each doth good turns now unto the other . 47 2
One doth shadow of your beauty show, The other as your bounty doth appear . 53 11
From me far off, with others all too near . 61 14
And for myself mine own worth do define, As I all other in all worths surmount . 62 8
In other accents do this praise confound . 69 7
In others' works thou dost but mend the style . 78 11
I impair not beauty being mute, When others would give life and bring a tomb . 83 12
I think good thoughts whilst other write good words . 85 5
Others for the breath of words respect, Me for my dumb thoughts . 85 13
Do not leave me last, When other petty griefs have done their spite . 90 10
And other strains of woe, which now seem woe, Compared with loss of thee will not seem so . 90 13
Thy looks with me, thy heart in other place . 93 4
Who, moving others, are themselves as stone, Unmoved, cold . 94 3
They are the lords and owners of their faces, Others but stewards of their excellence . 94 8
For to no other pass my verses tend . 103 11
All my argument, 'Fair, kind, and true' varying to other words . 105 10
In so profound abysm I throw all care Of others' voices . 112 10
Which is so deem'd Not by our feeling but by others' seeing . 121 4
For why should others' false adulterate eyes Give salutation? . 121 5
Myself I'll forfeit, so that other mine Thou wilt restore . 134 3
Shall will in others seem right gracious? . 135 7
Robb'd others' beds' revenues of their rents . 142 8
O, though I love what others do abhor, With others thou shouldst not abhor my state . 150 11
Nor gives it satisfaction to our blood, That we must curb it upon others' proof . *Lov. Comp.* 163
Heard where his plants in others' orchards grew . 171
Because thou lovest the one, and I the other . *Pass. Pil.* 106
Other help for him I see that there is none . 298
Either was the other's mine . *Ph. and Tur.* 36
Our. Be bold to play, our sport is not in sight . *Ven. and Adon.* 124
For by our ears our hearts oft tainted be . *Lucrece* 38
Turn to loathed sours Even in the moment that we call them ours . 868
We have no good that we can say is ours . 873
If children pre-decease progenitors We are their offspring, and they none of ours . 1757
Out. Look, when a painter would surpass the life, In limning out a well-proportion'd steed . *Ven. and Adon.* 290
Things out of hope are compass'd oft with venturing, Chiefly in love . 567
Ceasing their clamorous cry till they have singled With much ado the cold fault cleanly out . 694
Their light blown out in some mistrustful wood . 826
Against the welkin volleys out his voice . 921
His eyes, Where, lo, two lamps, burnt out, in darkness lies . 1128
Long he questioned With modest Lucrece, and wore out the night *Lucrece* 123
Out. Fair torch, burn out thy light, and lend it not . *Lucrece* 190
The eye of heaven is out, and misty night Covers the shame . 356
Went about From this fair throne to heave the owner out . 413
Small lights are soon blown out, huge fires abide . 647
The poor, lame, blind, halt, creep, cry out for thee . 902
Out, idle words, servants to shallow fools! . 1016
And seems to point her out where she sits weeping . 1087
One . . . , That cannot tread the way out readily . 1152
Like dying coals burnt out in tedious nights . 1379
With my knife scratch out the angry eyes Of all the Greeks . 1469
My laments would be drawn out too long, To tell them all . 1616
What he breathes out his breath drinks up again . 1666
In rage sent out, recall'd in rage, being past . 1671
And wear their brave state out of memory . *Sonnet* 15 8
Since she prick'd thee out for women's pleasure, Mine be thy love 20 13
But out, alack! he was but one hour mine . 33 11
All posterity That wear this world out to the ending doom . 55 12
To find out shames and idle hours in me . 61 7
Are vanishing or vanish'd out of sight, Stealing away . 63 7
O, how shall summer's honey breath hold out? . 65 5
Give not a windy night a rainy morrow, To linger out a purposed overthrow . 90 8
O, what a mansion have those vices got Which for their habitation chose out thee . 95 10
To constancy confined, One thing expressing, leaves out difference 105 8
And is partly blind, Seems seeing, but effectually is out . 113 4
But bears it out even to the edge of doom . 116 12
How have mine eyes out of their spheres been fitted! . 119 7
But live in doubt, Till my bad angel fire my good one out 144 14; *Pass. Pil.* 28
Doth point out thee As his triumphant prize . *Sonnet* 151 9
Religious love put out Religion's eye . *Lov. Comp.* 250
She burn'd out love, as soon as straw out-burneth . *Pass. Pil.* 98
Out-bragged. Like unshorn velvet on that termless skin Whose bare out-bragg'd the web it seem'd to wear . *Lov. Comp.* 95
Outbraves. But if that flower with base infection meet, The basest weed outbraves his dignity . *Sonnet* 94 12
Out-burneth. She burn'd out love, as soon as straw out-burneth *Pass. Pil.* 98
Outcast. I all alone beweep my outcast state . *Sonnet* 29 2
Outcry. Her voice controll'd Entombs her outcry in her lips' sweet fold *Lucrece* 679
Outfacing faults in love with love's ill rest . *Pass. Pil.* 8
Out-going. So thou, thyself out-going in thy noon, Unlook'd on diest *Son.* 7 13
Outlive. Let him bring forth Eternal numbers to outlive long date 38 12
Nor the gilded monuments Of princes, shall outlive this powerful rhyme 55 2
For't lies in thee To make him much outlive a gilded tomb 101 11
Outrage. If in thy hope thou darest do such outrage . *Lucrece* 605
Outrageous. No outrageous thing From vassal actors can be wiped away 607
Outright. Kill me outright with looks and rid my pain *Sonnet* 139 14
Outruns. How he outruns the wind and with what care *Ven. and Adon.* 681
The violent roaring tide Outruns the eye that doth behold his haste *Lucrece* 1668
Outstripped. Though they be outstripp'd by every pen *Sonnet* 32 6
Out-stripping crows that strive to over-fly them *Ven. and Adon.* 324
Outward. She puts on outward strangeness, seems unkind . 310
Or were I deaf, thy outward parts would move Each part in me that were but sensible . 435
Whose inward ill no outward harm express'd . *Lucrece* 91
Beguiled with outward honesty, but yet defiled With inward vice 1545
Neither in inward worth nor outward fair . *Sonnet* 16 11
Mine eye's due is thy outward part . 46 13
Thy outward thus with outward praise is crown'd . 69 5
Where time and outward form would show it dead . 108 14
I bore the canopy, With my extern the outward honouring 125 2
Painting thy outward walls so costly gay . 146 4
One by nature's outwards so commended, That maidens' eyes stuck over all his face . *Lov. Comp.* 80
Wiles and guiles that women work, Dissembled with an outward show *Pass. Pil.* 336
Outwardly. Effects of terror and dear modesty, Encamp'd in hearts, but fighting outwardly . *Lov. Comp.* 203
Outwore. Her song was tedious and outwore the night . *Ven. and Adon.* 841
Outworn. A bare-boned death by time outworn . *Lucrece* 1761
The rich proud cost of outworn buried age . *Sonnet* 64 2
Thus is his cheek the map of days outworn . 68 1
Oven. An oven that is stopp'd, or river stay'd, Burneth more hotly, swelleth with more rage . *Ven. and Adon.* 331
Over one arm the lusty courser's rein, Under her other was the tender boy 31
Over my altars hath he hung his lance, His batter'd shield, his uncontrolled crest . 103
Had she then gave over, Such nectar from his lips she had not suck'd . 571
Over one shoulder doth she hang her head . 1058
Who o'er the white sheet peers her whiter chin, The reason of this rash alarm to know . *Lucrece* 472
At last she smilingly with this gives o'er . 1567
Nature, sovereign mistress over wrack . *Sonnet* 126 5
Not age, but sorrow, over me hath power . *Lov. Comp.* 74
So commended, That maidens' eyes stuck over all his face . 81
Overcharged. O'ercharged with burden of mine own love's might *Sonnet* 23 8
Overcome by doubt and bloodless fear, With cold-pale weakness numbs each feeling part . *Ven. and Adon.* 891
Here overcome, as one full of despair, She vail'd her eyelids . 955
Overflow. Rain added to a river that is rank Perforce will force it overflow the bank . 72
Like a gentle flood, Who, being stopp'd, the bounding banks o'erflows *Lucr.* 1119
Over-fly. Out-stripping crows that strive to over-fly them *Ven. and Adon.* 324
Over-goes. There appears a face That over-goes my blunt invention quite *Sonnet* 103 7
Over-green. So you o'er-green my bad, my good allow . 112 4
Overgrown. As corn o'ergrown by weeds, so heedful fear Is almost choked by unresisted lust . *Lucrece* 281
Over-handled. You will fall again Into your idle over-handled theme *Ven. and Adon.* 770
Overlook. Titan . . . With burning eye did hotly overlook them . 178
And therefore mayst without attaint o'erlook . *Sonnet* 82 2
Over-partial. If eyes corrupt by over-partial looks Be anchor'd in the bay 137 5
Overplus. Thou hast thy 'Will,' And 'Will' to boot, and 'Will' in overplus 135 2
Over-pressed. When thy might Is more than my o'er-press'd defence can bide . 139 8
Over-read. My gentle verse, Which eyes not yet created shall o'er-read 81 10
Overruled. Thus he that overruled I oversway'd . *Ven. and Adon.* 109
Oversee. Thou, Collatine, shalt oversee this will . *Lucrece* 1205

Overseen. How was I overseen that thou shalt see it! *Lucrece* 1206
Overshoot. To overshoot his troubles How he outruns the wind and with what care *Ven. and Adon.* 680
Overslipped. Which all this time hath overslipp'd her thought *Lucrece* 1576
Oversnowed. Beauty o'ersnow'd and bareness every where *Sonnet* 5 8
Overstrawed. The bottom poison, and the top o'erstraw'd With sweets that shall the truest sight beguile *Ven. and Adon.* 1143
Over-sways. Sad mortality o'er-sways their power *Sonnet* 65 2
Overswayed. Thus he that overruled I oversway'd *Ven. and Adon.* 109
Overtake. To let base clouds o'ertake me in my way *Sonnet* 34 3
Overthrow. And must not die Till mutual overthrow of mortal kind *V. and A.* 1018
Give not a windy night a rainy morrow, To linger out a purposed overthrow *Sonnet* 90 8
Overturn. When wasteful war shall statues overturn 55 5
Over-washed. Nor why her fair cheeks over-wash'd with woe *Lucrece* 1225
Overwhelming. His louring brows o'erwhelming his fair sight *V. and A.* 183
O'erworn, despised, rheumatic, and cold 135
Musing the morning is so much o'erworn 866
With Time's injurious hand crush'd and o'erworn *Sonnet* 63 2
Owe. 'Tis much to borrow, and I will not owe it *Ven. and Adon.* 411
If any love you owe me, Measure my strangeness with my unripe years 523
Therefore that praise which Collatine doth owe Enchanted Tarquin answers with surmise *Lucrece* 82
So their pride doth grow, Paying more slavish tribute than they owe 299
Then thou alone kingdoms of hearts shouldst owe *Sonnet* 70 14
Since what he owes thee thou thyself dost pay 79 14
Than the true gouty landlord which doth owe them *Lov. Comp.* 140
Owed. She was my wife, I owed her, and 'tis mine that she hath kill'd *Lucr.* 1803
O, all that borrow'd motion seeming owed, Would yet again betray the fore-betray'd! *Lov. Comp.* 327
Owest. Thy eternal summer shall not fade Nor lose possession of that fair thou owest *Sonnet* 18 10
Owl. The owl, night's herald, shrieks, ''Tis very late' *Ven. and Adon.* 531
No noise but owls' and wolves' death-boding cries *Lucrece* 165
Own. The kiss shall be thine own as well as mine *Ven. and Adon.* 117
Is thine own heart to thine own face affected? 157
Steal thine own freedom and complain on theft 160
For men will kiss even by their own direction 216
Poor queen of love, in thine own law forlorn, To love a cheek that smiles at thee in scorn! 251
And every tongue more moving than your own 776
That rich jewel he should keep unknown From thievish ears, because it is his own *Lucrece* 35
But she is not her own: The worst is but denial and reproving 241
Makes the lily pale, And the red rose blush at her own disgrace 479
Are nature's faults, not their own infamy 539
Thyself art mighty; for thine own sake leave me: Myself a weakling 583
Their own transgressions partially they smother 634
That from their own misdeeds askance their eyes 637
The poor lamb cries; Till with her own white fleece her voice controll'd Entombs her outcry in her lips' sweet fold 678
Drunken Desire must vomit his receipt, Ere he can see his own abomination 704
Own. Or kings be breakers of their own behests *Lucrece* 852
At his own shadow let the thief run mad 997
Poor women's faces are their own faults' books 1253
If tears could help, mine own would do me good 1274
Lest he should hold it her own gross abuse 1315
Like a heavy-hanging bell, Once set on ringing, with his own weight goes 1494
Being from the feeling of her own grief brought By deep surmise of others' detriment 1578
O, teach me how to make mine own excuse 1653
Attend me: Be suddenly revenged on my foe, Thine, mine, his own 1684
But thou, contracted to thine own bright eyes *Sonnet* 1 5
Within thine own bud buriest thy content 1 11
To say, within thine own deep-sunken eyes, Were an all-eating shame 2 7
You must live, drawn by your own sweet skill 16 14
Make the earth devour her own sweet brood 19 2
A woman's face with Nature's own hand painted Hast thou 20 1
Whose strength's abundance weakens his own heart 23 4
In mine own love's strength seem to decay 23 7
O'ercharged with burden of mine own love's might 23 8
That pour'st into my verse Thine own sweet argument 38 3
What can mine own praise to mine own self bring? And what is't but mine own when I praise thee? 39 3
I ensconce me here Within the knowledge of mine own desert 49 10
Mine own true love that doth my rest defeat 61 11
And for myself mine own worth do define, As I all other in all worths surmount 62 7
Mine own self-love quite contrary I read 62 11
Those same tongues that give thee so thine own In other accents do this praise confound 69 6
To do more for me than mine own desert 72 6
Thyself thou gavest, thy own worth then not knowing 87 9
With mine own weakness being best acquainted 88 5
Your own glass shows you when you look in it 103 14
Not mine own fears, nor the prophetic soul Of the wide world 107 1
And the sad augurs mock their own presage 107 6
Gored mine own thoughts, sold cheap what is most dear 110 3
Nor his own vision holds what it doth catch 113 8
And given to time your own dear-purchased right 117 6
I am that I am, and they that level At my abuses reckon up their own 121 10
O, but with mine compare thou thine own state 142 3
Those lips that Love's own hand did make 145 1
Ask'd their own wills, and made their wills obey *Lov. Comp.* 133
And was my own fee-simple, not in part 144
Or forced examples, 'gainst her own content 157
Kept hearts in liveries, but mine own was free 195
Take all these similes to your own command 227
For her griefs, so lively shown, Made me think upon mine own *Pass. Pil.* 390
Owner. Honour and beauty, in the owner's arms *Lucrece* 27
Went about From this fair throne to heave the owner out 413
They are the lords and owners of their faces *Sonnet* 94 7
Whose rich esteeming The owner's tongue doth publish every where 102 4

P

Pace. In shape, in courage, colour, pace, and bone *Ven. and Adon.* 294
With heavy eye, knit brow, and strengthless pace *Lucrece* 709
Pale cowards, marching on with trembling paces 1391
Then can no horse with my desire keep pace *Sonnet* 51 9
'Gainst death and all-oblivious enmity Shall you pace forth 55 10
Like a dial-hand, Steal from his figure and no pace perceived 104 10
Pack. Pack night, peep day; good day, of night now borrow *Pass. Pil.* 209
Packed. The night so pack'd, I post unto my pretty 201
Pack-horse. Base watch of woes, sin's pack-horse, virtue's snare *Lucrece* 928
Page. Thy heinous hours wait on them as their pages 910
But makes antiquity for aye his page *Sonnet* 108 12
Paid. Which I new pay as if not paid before 30 12
Pain. Shrinks backward in his shelly cave with pain *Ven. and Adon.* 1034
Pain pays the income of each precious thing *Lucrece* 334
This momentary joy breeds months of pain 690
And made her thrall To living death and pain perpetual 726
Leaving his spoil perplex'd in greater pain 733
So should I have co-partners in my pain 789
Having no other pleasure of his gain But torment that it cannot cure his pain 861
The pain be mine, but thine shall be the praise *Sonnet* 38 14
Looking with pretty ruth upon my pain 132 4
Kill me outright with looks and rid my pain 139 14
And words express The manner of my pity-wanting pain 140 4
I count my gain, That she that makes me sin awards me pain 141 14
In spite of physic, painting, pain, and cost *Pass. Pil.* 180
As take the pain, but cannot pluck the pelf 192
More mickle was the pain That nothing could be used to turn them both to gain 219
Ah, thought I, thou mourn'st in vain! None takes pity on thy pain 392
Pained. Give physic to the sick, ease to the pain'd *Lucrece* 901
Painful. Is plagued with cramps and gouts and painful fits 856
My woe too sensible thy passion maketh More feeling-painful 1679
The painful warrior famoused for fight *Sonnet* 25 9
Paint. My sable ground of sin I will not paint, To hide the truth *Lucrece* 1074
Painted. Even as poor birds, deceived with painted grapes *Ven. and Adon.* 601
Shall by a painted cloth be kept in awe *Lucrece* 245
And drop sweet balm in Priam's painted wound 1466
Here feelingly she weeps Troy's painted woes 1492
Even as subtle Sinon here is painted, So sober-sad, so weary, and so mild 1541
Overslipp'd her thought, That she with painted images hath spent 1577
Living flowers, Much liker than your painted counterfeit *Sonnet* 16 8
A woman's face with Nature's own hand painted Hast thou 20 1
Stirr'd by a painted beauty to his verse 21 2
My eye doth feast And to the painted banquet bids my heart 47 6
And you in Grecian tires are painted new 53 8
Painter. Look, when a painter would surpass the life, In limning out a well-proportion'd steed *Ven. and Adon.* 289
Which the conceited painter drew so proud, As heaven *Lucrece* 1371
The red blood reek'd, to show the painter's strife 1377
Here and there the painter interlaces Pale cowards 1390
Some high, some low, the painter was so nice 1412
In her the painter had anatomized Time's ruin, beauty's wreck 1450
The painter was no god to lend her those 1461
In him the painter labour'd with his skill To hide deceit 1506
And chid the painter for his wondrous skill 1528
Mine eye hath play'd the painter and hath stell'd Thy beauty's form in table of my heart *Sonnet* 24 1
And perspective it is best painter's art 24 4
For through the painter must you see his skill 24 5
Painting. A piece Of skilful painting, made for Priam's Troy *Lucrece* 1367
She throws her eyes about the painting round 1499
Painting my age with beauty of thy days *Sonnet* 62 14
Why should false painting imitate his cheek? 67 5
Their gross painting might be better used Where cheeks need blood 82 13
I never saw that you did painting need And therefore to your fair no painting set 83 1
Painting thy outward walls so costly gay 146 4
In spite of physic, painting, pain, and cost *Pass. Pil.* 180
Pair. A pair of maiden worlds unconquered, Save of their lord *Lucrece* 408
Let it then suffice To drown one woe, one pair of weeping eyes 1680
Palate. And to his palate doth prepare the cup *Sonnet* 114 12
With eager compounds we our palate urge 118 2
The one a palate hath that needs will taste *Lov. Comp.* 167
Pale. Making them red and pale with fresh variety *Ven. and Adon.* 21
I have hemm'd thee here Within the circuit of this ivory pale 230
But now her cheek was pale, and by and by It flash'd forth fire 347
Believing she is dead, Claps her pale cheek, till clapping makes it red 468
Whereat a sudden pale, Like lawn being spread upon the blushing rose, Usurps her cheek 589
Agues pale and faint, Life-poisoning pestilence and frenzies wood 739
She looks upon his lips, and they are pale; She takes him by the hand 1123
Chequer'd with white, Resembling well his pale cheeks 1169
The lightless fire Which, in pale embers hid, lurks to aspire *Lucrece* 5
Here pale with fear he doth premeditate the dangers 183
Left their round turrets destitute and pale 441
The colour in thy face, That even for anger makes the lily pale 478
Pale cowards, marching on with trembling paces 1391
Cheeks neither red nor pale, but mingled so That blushing red no guilty instance gave 1510
Nor ashy pale the fear that false hearts have 1512

Pale. Now this pale swan in her watery nest Begins the sad dirge of her certain ending . . . . *Lucrece* 1611
From lips new-waxen pale begins to blow The grief away . . . 1663
He falls, and bathes the pale fear in his face 1775
Gilding pale streams with heavenly alchemy . . . *Sonnet* 33 4
With so dull a cheer That leaves look pale, dreading the winter's near . 97 14
Ere long espied a fickle maid full pale, Tearing of papers . *Lov. Comp.* 5
Hanging her pale and pined cheek beside 32
A lily pale, with damask dye to grace her, None fairer . *Pass. Pil.* 89
Paled. Of paled pearls and rubies red as blood . . *Lov. Comp.* 198
Pale-faced. Affection faints not like a pale faced-coward *Ven. and Adon.* 569
Paleness. All strange forms receives, Of burning blushes, or of weeping water, Or swooning paleness . . . . . *Lov. Comp.* 305
Paler. Paler for sorrow than her milk-white dove, For Adon's sake *Pass. Pil.* 119
Palfrey. My busy care, Is how to get my palfrey from the mare *V. and A.* 384
Thy palfrey, as he should, Welcomes the warm approach of sweet desire . 385
Palm. With this she seizeth on his sweating palm 25
My smooth moist hand, were it with thy hand felt, Would in thy palm dissolve, or seem to melt 144
Palmers. As palmers' chat makes short their pilgrimage . *Lucrece* 791
Pandion. King Pandion he is dead ; All thy friends are lapp'd in lead *Pass. Pil.* 395
Pangs. And sweetens, in the suffering pangs it bears, The aloes of all forces, shocks, and fears . . . . . . *Lov. Comp.* 272
Pants. My boding heart pants, beats, and takes no rest . *Ven. and Adon.* 647
Panteth. While in his hold-fast foot the weak mouse panteth *Lucrece* 555
Panting he lies and breatheth in her face . . *Ven. and Adon.* 62
She like a wearied lamb lies panting there . . . *Lucrece* 737
Paper. Go, get me hither paper, ink, and pen 1289
She prepares to write, First hovering o'er the paper with her quill . 1297
So should my papers yellow'd with their age Be scorn'd . *Sonnet* 17 9
Too excellent For every vulgar paper to rehearse . . . 38 4
Tearing of papers, breaking rings a-twain . . . *Lov. Comp.* 6
Paphos. Holding their course to Paphos . . . *Ven. and Adon.* 1193
Paradise. What largeness thinks in Paradise was sawn . *Lov. Comp.* 91
What fool is not so wise To break an oath, to win a paradise? *Pass. Pil.* 42
Parallels. And delves the parallels in beauty's brow . . *Sonnet* 60 10
Parasites. Idle sounds resembling parasites . . *Ven. and Adon.* 848
Parcel. The wind Upon his lips their silken parcels hurls . *Lov. Comp.* 87
And to your audit comes Their distract parcels in combined sums . . 231
Parching. That knows not parching heat nor freezing cold . *Lucrece* 1145
Pardon. Yet pardon me I felt a kind of fear When as I met the boar *V. and A.* 998
To you it doth belong Yourself to pardon of self-doing crime *Sonnet* 58 12
O, pardon me, in that my boast is true . . . . *Lov. Comp.* 246
I pardon crave of thee, Thy discontent thou didst bequeath to me *Pass. Pil.* 141
Paris. Thy heat of lust, fond Paris, did incur This load of wrath *Lucrece* 1473
Park. I'll be a park, and thou shalt be my deer *Ven. and Adon.* 231
Then be my deer, since I am such a park 239
Parley. First, like a trumpet, doth his tongue begin To sound a parley *Lucr.* 471
Parling. But she, that never coped with stranger eyes, Could pick no meaning from their parling looks 100
Part. Let us part, And leave this idle theme, this bootless chat *V. and A.* 421
Or were I deaf, thy outward parts would move Each part in me that were but sensible 435
And coal-black clouds that shadow heaven's light Do summon us to part and bid good night 534
Embracing bushes, As fearful of him, part, through whom he rushes . 630
With cold-pale weakness numbs each feeling part 892
This mutiny each part doth so surprise 1049
My part is youth, and beats these from the stage . . *Lucrece* 278
But with a pure appeal seeks to the heart, Which once corrupted takes the worser part 294
Who, therefore angry, seems to part in sunder 388
Whiles against a thorn thou bear'st thy part 1135
When every part a part of woe doth bear 1327
'Tis but a part of sorrow that we hear 1328
Kneel with me and help to bear thy part 1830
They do but sweetly chide thee, who confounds In singleness the parts that thou shouldst bear . . . . *Sonnet* 8 8
It is but as a tomb Which hides your life and shows not half your parts 17 4
As an unperfect actor on the stage Who with his fear is put besides his part 23 2
And there reigns love and all love's loving parts . . . 31 3
My lovers gone, Who all their parts of me to thee did give . . 31 11
Any of these all, or all, or more, Entitled in thy parts do crowned sit 37 7
I in thy abundance am sufficed And by a part of all thy glory live 37 12
When thou art all the better part of me 39 2
The clear eye's moiety and the dear heart's part . . . 46 12
Mine eye's due is thy outward part 46 13
Mine eye is my heart's guest And in his thoughts of love doth share a part 47 8
From whence at pleasure thou mayst come and part . . . 48 12
To guard the lawful reasons on thy part 49 12
In all external grace you have some part 53 13
Let this sad interim like the ocean be Which parts the shore . . 56 10
All mine eye And all my soul and all my every part . . . 62 2
Those parts of thee that the world's eye doth view Want nothing . 69 1
Thou dost review The very part was consecrate to thee . . . 74 6
My spirit is thine, the better part of me 74 8
From hence your memory death cannot take, Although in me each part will be forgotten 81 4
Upon thy part I can set down a story, Of faults conceal'd . . 88 6
That which governs me to go about Doth part his function . . 113 3
Of his quick objects hath the mind no part 113 7
Till each to razed oblivion yield his part 122 7
And suit thy pity like in every part 132 12
Turn back to me, And play the mother's part, kiss me, be kind . 143 12
I do betray My nobler part to my gross body's treason . . . 151 6
And when in his fair parts she did abide, She was new lodged *Lov. Comp.* 83
And was my own fee-simple, not in part 144
My parts had power to charm a sacred nun 260
Which is to me some praise, that I thy parts admire . *Pass. Pil.* 66
Thus of every grief in heart He with thee doth bear a part . . 428
Love hath reason, reason none, If what parts can so remain *Ph. and Tur.* 48
Partake. When I against myself with thee partake . . *Sonnet* 149 2
Partial. Let reason rule things worthy blame, As well as fancy partial might *Pass. Pil.* 302
Partially. Their own transgressions partially they smother . *Lucrece* 634
Particular. But these particulars are not my measure . . *Sonnet* 91 7
What a hell of witchcraft lies In the small orb of one particular tear ! *Lov. Comp.* 289

Parting. Ere he says 'Adieu,' The honey fee of parting tender'd is *V. and A.* 538
Yet at my parting sweetly did she smile . . . . *Pass. Pil.* 187
Partly. That which governs me to go about Doth part his function and is partly blind . . . . *Sonnet* 113 3
Partner. Some rascal groom, To be thy partner in this shameful doom *Lucr.* 672
Party. Thy adverse party is thy advocate—And 'gainst myself a lawful plea commence . . . . *Sonnet* 35 10
With acture they may be, Where neither party is nor true nor kind *L. Comp.* 186
Pass. Yet sometimes falls an orient drop beside, Which her cheek melts, as scorning it should pass, To wash the foul face of the sluttish ground *Ven. and Adon.* 982
Thou shalt strangely pass And scarcely greet me with that sun, thine eye *Sonnet* 49 5
For to no other pass my verses tend 103 11
Then in the number let me pass untold 136 9
She, silly queen, with more than love's good will, Forbade the boy he should not pass those grounds . . . . *Pass. Pil.* 124
Passage. Once more the ruby-colour'd portal open'd, Which to his speech did honey passage yield . . . . . . *Ven. and Adon.* 452
Struggling for passage, earth's foundation shakes 1047
No tool imparteth To make more vent for passage of her breath . *Lucrece* 1040
Through the velvet leaves the wind, All unseen, gan passage find *Pass. Pil.* 232
Passed. Thou hast pass'd by the ambush of young days . *Sonnet* 70 9
For if you were by my unkindness shaken As I by yours, you've pass'd a hell of time 120 6
Passenger. Never did passenger in summer's heat More thirst for drink than she for this good turn . . . . . *Ven. and Adon.* 91
Passing. High crest, short ears, straight legs, and passing strong . 297
Whose deep conceit is such As, passing all conceit, needs no defence *Pass. Pil.* 110
Spied a blossom passing fair, Playing in the wanton air . . . 229
Passing-bell. To one sore sick that hears the passing-bell *Ven. and Adon.* 702
Passion. And trembling in her passion, calls it balm, Earth's sovereign salve to do a goddess good 27
And swelling passion doth provoke a pause 218
Passion on passion deeply is redoubled 832
Variable passions throng her constant woe 967
Each passion labours so, That every present sorrow seemeth chief . 969
Dumbly she passions, franticly she doteth 1059
No object but her passion's strength renews . . . *Lucrece* 1103
The life and feeling of her passion She hoards, to spend when he is by . 1317
Such passion her assails, That patience is quite beaten from her breast . 1562
My woe too sensible thy passion maketh More feeling painful . . 1678
A woman's face with Nature's own hand painted Hast thou, the master-mistress of my passion . . . . *Sonnet* 20 2
Catching all passions in his craft of will . . . *Lov. Comp.* 126
Figuring that they their passions likewise lent me Of grief and blushes 199
His passion, but an art of craft, Even there resolved my reason into tears 295
Past. He cries, 'let go, and let me go ; My day's delight is past' *V. and A.* 380
My will is strong, past reason's weak removing . . . *Lucrece* 243
An accessary by thine inclination To all sins past, and all that are to come 923
Since that my case is past the help of law 1022
In rage sent out, recall'd in rage, being past 1671
Suppose thou dost defend me From what is past 1685
When I behold the violet past prime . . . . *Sonnet* 12 3
I summon up remembrance of things past 30 2
Finding thy worth a limit past my praise 82 6
Not wondering at the present nor the past 123 10
Past reason hunted, and no sooner had Past reason hated . . 129 6
Although she knows my days are past the best 138 6
Past cure I am, now reason is past care, And frantic-mad . . 147 9
Although I know my years be past the best . . . *Pass. Pil.* 6
Patent. And so my patent back again is swerving . . . *Sonnet* 87 8
Path. The path is smooth that leadeth on to danger *Ven. and Adon.* 788
She treads the path that she untreads again 908
Patience. Where thou with patience must my will abide . *Lucrece* 486
They that lose half with greater patience bear it Than they whose whole is swallow'd in confusion 1158
By this, mild patience bid fair Lucrece speak 1268
So mild, that Patience seem'd to scorn his woes 1505
Such passion her assails, That patience is quite beaten from her breast 1563
And patience, tame to sufferance, bide each check, Without accusing you of injury . . . . *Sonnet* 58 7
Do not press My tongue-tied patience with too much disdain . 140 2
Patient. The patient dies while the physician sleeps . . . *Lucrece* 904
Whilst, like a willing patient, I will drink Potions of eisel *Sonnet* 111 9
Playing patient sports in unconstrained gyves . . . *Lov. Comp.* 242
Patiently. Swearing, unless I took all patiently, I should not live *Lucrece* 1641
Patron of all light, From whom each lamp and shining star doth borrow The beauteous influence that makes him bright . . *Ven. and Adon.* 860
Pattern. Even so this pattern of the worn-out age Pawn'd honest looks, but laid no words to gage . . . . *Lucrece* 1350
Him in thy course untainted do allow For beauty's pattern to succeeding men . . . . *Sonnet* 19 12
Figures of delight, Drawn after you, you pattern of all those . 98 12
And knew the patterns of his foul beguiling . . . *Lov. Comp.* 170
Patterned. When, pattern'd by thy fault, foul sin may say, He learn'd to sin, and thou didst teach the way . . . . . *Lucrece* 629
Pause. Then mightst thou pause, for then I were not for thee *V. and A.* 137
And swelling passion doth provoke a pause 218
Sad pause and deep regard beseem the sage . . . *Lucrece* 277
He rouseth up himself and makes a pause 541
Pausing for means to mourn some newer way 1365
Pawn'd honest looks, but laid no words to gage 1351
Pawning his honour to obtain his lust 156
Paws. Devouring Time, blunt thou the lion's paws . . *Sonnet* 19 1
Pay. And one sweet kiss shall pay this countless debt *Ven. and Adon.* 84
But when her lips were ready for his pay, He winks, and turns his lips another way 89
So thou wilt buy and pay and use good dealing 514
And pay them at thy leisure, one by one 518
To which Love's eyes pay tributary gazes 632
Till every minute pays the hour his debt . . . *Lucrece* 329
Pain pays the income of each precious thing 334
The petty streams that pay a daily debt To their salt sovereign . . 649
Which happies those that pay the willing loan . . . *Sonnet* 6 6
Which I new pay as if not paid before 30 12
Yet what of thee thy poet doth invent He robs thee of and pays it thee again 79 8
Since what he owes thee thou thyself dost pay 79 14

Pay. He pays the whole, and yet am I not free . *Sonnet* 134 14
Paying what ransom the insulter willeth . . *Ven. and Adon.* 550
So their pride doth grow, Paying more slavish tribute than they owe *Lucr.* 299
Paying too much rent, For compound sweet forgoing simple savour *Son.* 125 6
Payment. Reward not hospitality With such black payment . *Lucrece* 576
Peace. How he in peace is wounded, not in war 831
'O, peace!' quoth Lucrece: 'if it should be told' 1284
And for the peace of you I hold such strife As 'twixt a miser and his wealth is found . . . . *Sonnet* 75 3
And peace proclaims olives of endless age 107 8
Love's arms are peace, 'gainst rule, 'gainst sense, 'gainst shame *Lov. Comp.* 271
Peaceful. And in a peaceful hour doth cry 'Kill, kill!' *Ven. and Adon.* 652
Pearl. Her tears began to turn their tide, Being prison'd in her eye like pearls in glass 980
And wiped the brinish pearl from her bright eyes . *Lucrece* 1213
Those round clear pearls of his, that move thy pity, Are balls of quenchless fire 1553
Ah! but those tears are pearl which thy love sheds . *Sonnet* 34 13
Of paled pearls and rubies red as blood . . . *Lov. Comp.* 198
Bright orient pearl, alack, too timely shaded! . . *Pass. Pil.* 133
Pearly. With pearly sweat, resembling dew of night . *Lucrece* 396
Peasants. Which heartless peasants did so well resemble . . 1392
Pebbled. Like as the waves make towards the pebbled shore . *Sonnet* 60 1
Peculiar. With pure aspects did him peculiar duties . *Lucrece* 14
Peeled. The bark peel'd from the lofty pine, His leaves will wither . 1167
So must my soul, her bark being peel'd away 1169
Peep. He put his bonnet on, Under whose brim the gaudy sun would peep *Ven. and Adon.* 1088
Through Night's black bosom should not peep again . *Lucrece* 788
Through crystal walls each little mote will peep . . . 1251
Where-through the sun Delights to peep, to gaze therein on thee *Sonnet* 24 12
Pack night, peep day; good day, of night now borrow . *Pass. Pil.* 209
Peeped. Some beauty peep'd through lattice of sear'd age *Lov. Comp.* 14
Peeping. Who, peeping forth this tumult to behold, Are by his flaming torch dimm'd and controll'd . . . . . . *Lucrece* 447
Why pry'st thou through my window? leave thy peeping . . 1089
Flocks all sleeping, Nymphs back peeping Fearfully . *Pass. Pil.* 287
Peer. Kings might be espoused to more fame, But king nor peer to such a peerless dame . . . . *Lucrece* 21
Who o'er the white sheet peers her whiter chin, The reason of this rash alarm to know 472
Peering. Like a dive-dapper peering through a wave, Who, being look'd on, ducks as quickly in . . . . . *Ven. and Adon.* 86
Peerless. Kings might be espoused to more fame, But king nor peer to such a peerless dame . . . . *Lucrece* 21
Pelf. As take the pain, but cannot pluck the pelf . *Pass. Pil.* 192
Pelleted. In the brine That season'd woe had pelleted in tears *Lov. Comp.* 18
Pelt. Another smother'd seems to pelt and swear . . *Lucrece* 1418
Pen. With the nightly linen that she wears He pens her piteous clamours in her head 681
Go, get me hither paper, ink, and pen 1289
Time's pencil, or my pupil pen, Neither in inward worth nor outward fair, Can make you live yourself in eyes of men . *Sonnet* 16 10
Nor draw no lines there with thine antique pen . . . 19 10
Though they be outstripp'd by every pen 32 6
Every alien pen hath got my use And under thee their poesy disperse 78 3
Thy lovely argument Deserves the travail of a worthier pen . 79 6
You still shall live—such virtue hath my pen . . . 81 13
Lean penury within that pen doth dwell 84 5
In polish'd form of well-refined pen 85 8
And gives thy pen both skill and argument 100 8
I see their antique pen would have express'd Even such a beauty as you master now 106 7
Penance. No bitterness that I will bitter think, Nor double penance . 111 12
Pencil. Time's pencil, or my pupil pen, Neither in inward worth nor outward fair, Can make you live yourself in eyes of men . 16 10
Beauty no pencil [needs], beauty's truth to lay . . . 101 7
Pencilled. Sad tales doth tell To pencill'd pensiveness and colour'd sorrow *Lucrece* 1497
Penetrable. His heart granteth No penetrable entrance to her plaining . 559
Penned. Found yet moe letters sadly penn'd in blood . *Lov. Comp.* 47
Pensived. All these trophies of affections hot, Of pensived and subdued desires the tender 219
Pensiveness. Sad tales doth tell To pencill'd pensiveness and colour'd sorrow *Lucrece* 1497
Pent. A liquid prisoner pent in walls of glass . . *Sonnet* 5 10
For I, being pent in thee, Perforce am thine, and all that is in me 133 13
Penury. Lean penury within that pen doth dwell . . . 84 5
People. Look, how the world's poor people are amazed At apparitions, signs, and prodigies . . . . *Ven. and Adon.* 925
Much like a press of people at a door, Throng her inventions . *Lucrece* 1301
Perceive. Now of this dark night I perceive the reason *Ven. and Adon.* 727
When I perceive that men as plants increase, Cheered and check'd even by the self-same sky . . . . *Sonnet* 15 5
Perceived. Like a dial-hand, Steal from his figure and no pace perceived 104 10
Perceivest. This thou perceivest, which makes thy love more strong . 73 13
Perceiving. His love, perceiving how he is enraged, Grew kinder *V. and A.* 317
Perchance. Perchance his boast of Lucrece' sovereignty Suggested this proud issue of a king . . . . *Lucrece* 36
Perchance that envy of so rich a thing, Braving compare, disdainfully did sting 39
Perfect. The lesson is but plain, And once made perfect, never lost again *Ven. and Adon.* 408
Whose perfect white Show'd like an April daisy on the grass . *Lucrece* 394
The perfect ceremony of love's rite . . . . *Sonnet* 23 6
Creating every bad a perfect best, As fast as objects to his beams assemble 114 7
Perfectest. Desire, of perfect'st love being made, Shall neigh . 51 10
Perfection. Whose full perfection all the world amazes *Ven. and Adon.* 634
And pure perfection with impure defeature 736
I, a drone-like bee, Have no perfection of my summer left . *Lucrece* 837
No perfection is so absolute, That some impurity doth not pollute . 853
Every thing that grows Holds in perfection but a little moment *Sonnet* 15 2
And right perfection wrongfully disgraced 66 7
Perforce. Rain added to a river that is rank Perforce will force it overflow the bank . . . . *Ven. and Adon.* 72
With foul offenders thou perforce must bear . . *Lucrece* 612
For I, being pent in thee, Perforce am thine, and all that is in me *Son.* 133 14
Perfume. Three April perfumes in three hot Junes burn'd, Since first I saw you fresh 104 7
Perfume. In some perfumes is there more delight, Than in the breath that from my mistress reeks . . . . *Sonnet* 130 7
Perfumed. Comes breath perfumed that breedeth love by smelling *Ven. and Adon.* 444
As deep a dye As the perfumed tincture of the roses . . *Sonnet* 54 6
Perhaps. When I perhaps compounded am with clay . . . 71 10
Perils. 'Gainst her own content, To put the by-past perils in her way *Lov. Comp.* 158
Period. Then had they seen the period of their ill . . *Lucrece* 380
She puts the period often from his place 565
Perish. As Priam him did cherish, So did I Tarquin; so my Troy did perish 1547
Let those whom Nature hath not made for store, Harsh featureless and rude, barrenly perish . . . . *Sonnet* 11 10
Perjured. The well-skill'd workman this mild image drew For perjured Sinon *Lucrece* 1521
Till action, lust Is perjured, murderous, bloody, full of blame *Sonnet* 129 3
I am perjured most; For all my vows are oaths but to misuse thee . 152 6
More perjured I, To swear against the truth so foul a lie . 152 13
Perjury. Guilty of perjury and subornation, Guilty of treason . *Lucrece* 919
Jealousy itself could not mistrust False-creeping craft and perjury . 1517
Did not the heavenly rhetoric of thine eye, . . Persuade my heart to this false perjury? . . . . *Pass. Pil.* 31
Permit. Or if thou wilt permit the sun to climb His wonted height *Lucrece* 775
Anon permit the basest clouds to ride With ugly rack . *Sonnet* 33 5
Perpetual. And made her thrall To living death and pain perpetual *Lucrece* 726
His smother'd light May set at noon and make perpetual night . 784
This act will be My fame and thy perpetual infamy . . . 1638
Do not kill The spirit of love with a perpetual dullness . *Sonnet* 56 8
This brand she quenched in a cool well by, Which from Love's fire took heat perpetual 154 10
Perpetually. The spots whereof could weeping purify, Her tears should drop on them perpetually . . . . *Lucrece* 686
Perplexed. Who, like a king perplexed in his throne, By their suggestion gives a deadly groan . . . . . . *Ven. and Adon.* 1043
Leaving his spoil perplex'd in greater pain . . *Lucrece* 733
Person. Thou worthy lord Of that unworthy wife that greeteth thee, Health to thy person! 1305
But plainly say thou lovest her well, And set thy person forth to sell *Pass. Pil.* 310
Personal. To remain In personal duty, following where he haunted *L. Comp.* 130
Perspective. And perspective it is best painter's art . *Sonnet* 24 4
Persuade. But by a kiss thought to persuade him there *Ven. and Adon.* 1114
Beauty itself doth of itself persuade The eyes of men without an orator *Lucrece* 29
Though weak-built hopes persuade him to abstaining . . . 130
My glass shall not persuade me I am old . . . *Sonnet* 22 1
Did not the heavenly rhetoric of thine eye, . . Persuade my heart to this false perjury? . . . . *Pass. Pil.* 31
Persuasion. So cross him with their opposite persuasion *Lucrece* 286
Perusal. If aught in me Worthy perusal stand against thy sight *Sonnet* 38 6
Perused. This picture she advisedly perused, And chid the painter *Lucrece* 1527
Which she perused, sigh'd, tore, and gave the flood . *Lov. Comp.* 44
Perverse it shall be where it shows most toward *Ven. and Adon.* 1157
Pervert. And new pervert a reconciled maid . . *Lov. Comp.* 329
Pestilence. Life-poisoning pestilence and frenzies wood. *Ven. and Adon.* 740
Petitioners. Her eyes petitioners to his eyes suing . . . 356
Petty. He held such petty bondage in disdain 394
The petty streams that pay a daily debt To their salt sovereign . *Lucrece* 649
If all these petty ills shall change thy good . . . 656
Do not leave me last, When other petty griefs have done their spite *Son.* 90 10
Philomel had ended The well-tuned warble of her nightly sorrow . *Lucrece* 1079
Come, Philomel, that sing'st of ravishment 1128
As Philomel in summer's front doth sing . . *Sonnet* 102 7
Philomela. While Philomela sits and sings, I sit and mark . *Pass. Pil.* 197
Phœbus. Sweet melodious sound That Phœbus' lute, the queen of music, makes 112
Phœnix. Burn the long-lived phœnix in her blood . . *Sonnet* 19 4
His phœnix down began but to appear Like unshorn velvet . *Lov. Comp.* 93
Phœnix and the turtle fled In a mutual flame from hence *Ph. and Tur.* 23
The turtle saw his right Flaming in the phœnix' sight . . . 35
Whereupon it made this threne To the phœnix and the dove. . . 50
Death is now the phœnix' nest; And the turtle's loyal breast To eternity doth rest 56
Phrase. And precious phrase by all the Muses filed . . *Sonnet* 85 4
Phraseless. O, then, advance of yours that phraseless hand . *Lov. Comp.* 225
Phrygian. A wretched image bound, That piteous looks to Phrygian shepherds lent . . . . *Lucrece* 1502
Physic. Give physic to the sick, ease to the pain'd 901
Nor can thy shame give physic to my grief . . *Sonnet* 34 9
I desperate now approve Desire is death, which physic did except . 147 8
As compound love to physic your cold breast . . *Lov. Comp.* 259
In spite of physic, painting, pain, and cost . . *Pass. Pil.* 180
Physician. The patient dies while the physician sleeps . . *Lucrece* 904
As testy sick men, when their deaths be near, No news but health from their physicians know . . . . *Sonnet* 140 8
My reason, the physician to my love 147 5
Physiognomy. In Ajax and Ulysses, O, what art Of physiognomy might one behold! . . . . *Lucrece* 1395
Pick. Yet love breaks through and picks them all at last *Ven. and Adon.* 576
But she, that never coped with stranger eyes, Could pick no meaning from their parling looks . . . . *Lucrece* 100
Picture. Fie, lifeless picture, cold and senseless stone *Ven. and Adon.* 211
The picture of an angry-chafing boar 662
While she, the picture of pure piety, Like a white hind . . *Lucrece* 542
This picture she advisedly perused, And chid the painter for his wondrous skill 1527
She concludes the picture was belied 1533
Mine eye my heart thy picture's sight would bar, My heart mine eye the freedom of that right . . . . *Sonnet* 46 3
With my love's picture then my eye doth feast . . . 47 5
Either by thy picture or my love, Thyself away art present still with me 47 9
Thy picture in my sight Awakes my heart to heart's and eye's delight . 47 13
Many there were that did his picture get, To serve their eyes *Lov. Comp.* 134
Pictured. To find where your true image pictured lies . *Sonnet* 24 6
Piece. A piece Of skilful painting, made for Priam's Troy . *Lucrece* 1366
To this well-painted piece is Lucrece come, To find a face where all distress is stell'd 1443
Pieced. Their purposed trim Pieced not his grace, but were all graced by him *Lov. Comp.* 119
Pierced. A closet never pierced with crystal eyes . . . *Sonnet* 46 6

Piercing. Brand not my forehead with thy piercing light . . . *Lucrece* 1091
Piety. While she, the picture of pure piety . . . 542
Pikes. On his bow-back he hath a battle set Of bristly pikes *Ven. and Adon.* 620
Pilgrimage. As palmers' chat makes short their pilgrimage . . *Lucrece* 791
Why work'st thou mischief in thy pilgrimage? . . . 960
Attending on his golden pilgrimage . . . *Sonnet* 7 8
My thoughts, from far where I abide, Intend a zealous pilgrimage to thee 27 6
Pillage. And they, like straggling slaves for pillage fighting . *Lucrece* 428
Pillow. Her rosy cheek lies under, Cozening the pillow of a lawful kiss . 387
And on that pillow lay Where thou wast wont to rest thy weary head . 1620
Pilot. Desire my pilot is, beauty my prize . . . 279
Pine. Even as poor birds, deceived with painted grapes, Do surfeit by the eye and pine the maw *Ven. and Adon.* 602
But I alone alone must sit and pine . . . *Lucrece* 795
The orphan pines while the oppressor feeds . . . 905
He ten times pines that pines beholding food . . . 1115
The bark peel'd from the lofty pine, His leaves will wither . . 1167
Thus do I pine and surfeit day by day, Or gluttoning on all, or all away *Sonnet* 75 13
Why dost thou pine within and suffer dearth? . . . 146 3
Then, soul, live thou upon thy servant's loss, And let that pine to aggravate thy store . . . 146 10
Now all these hearts that do on mine depend, Feeling it break, with bleeding groans they pine . . . *Lov. Comp.* 275
Pined. Hanging her pale and pined cheek beside . . . 32
Pineth. That, cloy'd with much, he pineth still for more . *Lucrece* 98
Pioner. There might you see the labouring pioner . . . 1380
Pipe. Wanting the spring that those shrunk pipes had fed . . 1455
And stops her pipe in growth of riper days . . *Sonnet* 102 8
My shepherd's pipe can sound no deal . . . *Pass. Pil.* 271
Pirates. Huge rocks, high winds, strong pirates, shelves, and sands, The merchant fears, ere rich at home he lands . . *Lucrece* 335
Pitch. Whose vulture thought doth pitch the price so high, That she will draw his lips' rich treasure dry . . *Ven. and Adon.* 551
But when from highmost pitch, with weary car . . *Sonnet* 7 9
By spirits taught to write Above a mortal pitch, that struck me dead . 86 6
Pitchy. So did the merciless and pitchy night Fold in the object that did feed her sight . . . *Ven. and Adon.* 821
Some gentle gust doth get, Which blows these pitchy vapours *Lucrece* 550
Piteous. These mine eyes, true leaders to their queen, But for thy piteous lips no more had seen . . . *Ven. and Adon.* 504
With the nightly linen that she wears He pens her piteous clamours in her head . . . *Lucrece* 681
A wretched image bound, That piteous looks to Phrygian shepherds lent . 1502
Pith. His sweating palm, The precedent of pith and livelihood *V. and A.* 26
Pitied. Root pity in thy heart, that when it grows Thy pity may deserve to pitied be . . . *Sonnet* 142 12
Pitiful. Let there bechance him pitiful mischances, To make him moan; but pity not his moans . . . *Lucrece* 976
Pitiful thrivers, in their gazing spent . . *Sonnet* 125 8
Pits. These lovely caves, those round enchanting pits, Open'd their mouths to swallow Venus' liking . . *Ven. and Adon.* 247
Pity. 'O, pity,' 'gan she cry, 'flint-hearted boy! 'Tis but a kiss I beg; why art thou coy?' . . . 95
'Pity,' she cries, 'some favour, some remorse!' . . . 257
For pity now she can no more detain him . . . 577
That bloody beast, Which knows no pity, but is still severe . . 1000
And straight, in pity of his tender years, They both would strive who first should dry his tears . . . 1091
This moves in him more rage and lesser pity, To make the breach *Lucrece* 468
Be compassionate! Soft pity enters at an iron gate . . 595
Wipe the dim mist from thy doting eyne, That thou shalt see thy state and pity mine . . . 644
Pity not his moans: Stone him with harden'd hearts, harder than stones 977
Those round clear pearls of his, that move thy pity, Are balls of quenchless fire . . . 1553
Pity the world, or else this glutton be, To eat the world's due . *Sonnet* 1 13
Pity me then and wish I were renew'd . . . 111 8
Pity me then, dear friend, and I assure ye Even that your pity is enough to cure me . . . 111 13
Your love and pity doth the impression fill . . . 112 1
And suit thy pity like in every part . . . 132 12
Root pity in thy heart, that when it grows Thy pity may deserve to pitied be . . . 142 11
Gentle maid, Have of my suffering youth some feeling pity *Lov. Comp.* 178
And there sung the dolefull'st ditty, That to hear it was great pity *Pass. Pil.* 384
Ah, thought I, thou mourn'st in vain! None takes pity on thy pain . 392
Even so, poor bird, like thee, None alive will pity me . . 400
And with such-like flattering, 'Pity but he were a king' . . 414
Pitying. As pitying Lucrece' woes, Corrupted blood some watery token shows *Lucrece* 1747
Thine eyes I love, and they, as pitying me, Knowing thy heart torments me with disdain . . . *Sonnet* 132 1
Pity-pleading. Her pity-pleading eyes are sadly fixed In the remorseless wrinkles of his face . . . *Lucrece* 561
Pity-wanting. And words express The manner of my pity-wanting pain *Sonnet* 140 4
Place. Because the cry remaineth in one place . . *Ven. and Adon.* 885
With this, she falleth in the place she stood . . . 1121
Through little vents and crannies of the place . . *Lucrece* 310
And in thy dead arms do I mean to place him . . . 517
She puts the period often from his place . . . 565
Keep still possession of thy gloomy place . . . 803
The skies were sorry, And little stars shot from their fixed places . 1525
From the purple fountain Brutus drew The murderous knife, and, as it left the place, Her blood, in poor revenge, held it in chase . . 1735
A watery rigol goes, Which seems to weep upon the tainted place . 1746
And bids Lucretius give his sorrow place . . . 1773
Treasure thou some place With beauty's treasure, ere it be self-kill'd *Son.* 6 3
Look, what an unthrift in the world doth spend Shifts but his place . 9 10
As soon as think the place where he would be . . . 44 8
Each changing place with that which goes before . . . 60 3
But now my gracious numbers are decay'd And my sick Muse doth give another place . . . 79 4
To set me light And place my merit in the eye of scorn . . 88 2
Thy looks with me, thy heart in other place . . . 93 4
Nor gives to necessary wrinkles place . . . 108 11
Do witness bear Thy black is fairest in my judgement's place . 131 12
Which my heart knows the wide world's common place . . 137 10
Anon their gazes lend To every place at once, and, nowhere fix'd *Lov. Comp.* 27
Place. Love lack'd a dwelling, and made him her place . *Lov. Comp.* 82
All aids, themselves made fairer by their place, Came for additions . 117
Playing the place which did no form receive . . . 241
All vows and consecrations giving place . . . 263
Gave the tempter place, Which like a cherubin above them hover'd . 318
Placed. Like stones of worth they thinly placed are, Or captain jewels in the carcanet . . . *Sonnet* 52 7
Where her faith was firmly fix'd in love, There a nay is placed without remove *Pass. Pil.* 256
Plague. That the star-gazers, having writ on death, May say, the plague is banish'd by thy breath . . . *Ven. and Adon.* 510
Why should the private pleasure of some one Become the public plague of many moe? . . . *Lucrece* 1479
Why should so many fall, To plague a private sin in general? . . 1484
Of good or evil luck, Of plagues, of dearths, or seasons' quality . *Sonnet* 14 4
Drink up the monarch's plague, this flattery . . . 114 2
And to this false plague are they now transferr'd . . . 137 14
Only my plague thus far I count my gain . . . 141 13
Plagued. Is plagued with cramps and gouts and painful fits . *Lucrece* 856
Plain. Sweet bottom-grass and high delightful plain *Ven. and Adon.* 236
And all this dumb play had his acts made plain With tears . . 359
The lesson is but plain, And once made perfect, never lost again . 407
Like a goodly champaign plain, Lays open all the little worms that creep *Lucrece* 1247
Such signs of truth in his plain face she spied . . . 1532
Sometime 'Tarquin' was pronounced plain, But through his teeth . 1786
Sympathized In true plain words by thy true-telling friend . *Sonnet* 82 12
All our merry meetings on the plains . . . *Pass. Pil.* 290
Plaining. His heart granteth No penetrable entrance to her plaining *Lucrece* 559
Plainly. But plainly say thou lovest her well, And set thy person forth to sell *Pass. Pil.* 309
Plaints. That she her plaints a little while doth stay . . *Lucrece* 1364
Plaintful. A plaintful story from a sistering vale . . *Lov. Comp.* 2
Plaits. Hiding base sin in plaits of majesty . . . *Lucrece* 93
Plant. Herbs for their smell, and sappy plants to bear . *Ven. and Adon.* 165
I perceive that men as plants increase, Cheered and check'd even by the self-same sky . . . *Sonnet* 15 5
Heard where his plants in others' orchards grew . . *Lov. Comp.* 171
Green plants bring not Forth their dye . . . *Pass. Pil.* 283
Beasts did leap, and birds did sing, Trees did grow, and plants did spring 378
Plantest. Thou plantest scandal and displacest laud . . *Lucrece* 887
Planting oblivion, beating reason back . . *Ven. and Adon.* 557
Plaster. Licking of his wound, 'Gainst venom'd sores the only sovereign plaster . . . 916
Plat. Her hair, nor loose nor tied in formal plat . . *Lov. Comp.* 29
Platted. Upon her head a platted hive of straw . . . 8
Plausibly. The Romans plausibly did give consent . . *Lucrece* 1854
Play. Be bold to play, our sport is not in sight . *Ven. and Adon.* 124
And all this dumb play had his acts made plain With tears . . 359
The wind would blow it off and, being gone, Play with his locks . 1090
And moody Pluto winks while Orpheus plays . . . *Lucrece* 553
Will play the tyrants to the very same . . . *Sonnet* 5 3
Hang on such thorns and play as wantonly . . . 54 7
To play the watchman ever for thy sake . . . 61 12
And, you away, As with your shadow I with these did play . . 98 14
Turn back to me, And play the mother's part, kiss me, be kind . 143 12
My curtail dog, that wont to have play'd, Plays not at all . *Pass. Pil.* 274
Played. Her hair, like golden threads, play'd with her breath *Lucrece* 400
Mine eye hath play'd the painter and hath stell'd Thy beauty's form *Son.* 24 1
My curtail dog, that wont to have play'd, Plays not at all . *Pass. Pil.* 273
Playest. When thou, my music, music play'st, Upon that blessed wood whose motion sounds With thy sweet fingers . . *Sonnet* 128 1
Playing the place which did no form receive, Playing patient sports in unconstrained gyves . . . *Lov. Comp.* 241
Spied a blossom passing fair, Playing in the wanton air . . *Pass. Pil.* 230
Plea. No rightful plea might plead for justice there . . *Lucrece* 1649
Thy adverse party is thy advocate—And 'gainst myself a lawful plea commence *Sonnet* 35 11
The defendant doth that plea deny And says in him thy fair appearance lies . . . 46 7
How with this rage shall beauty hold a plea? . . . 65 3
Plead. The colour in thy face, . . . Shall plead for me and tell my loving tale *Lucrece* 480
Pleads, in a wilderness where are no laws, To the rough beast . . 544
No rightful plea might plead for justice there . . . 1649
Who plead for love and look for recompense . . *Sonnet* 23 11
My heart doth plead that thou in him dost lie . . . 46 5
Pleadeth. All orators are dumb when beauty pleadeth . . *Lucrece* 268
Pleading. This said, impatience chokes her pleading tongue *Ven. and Adon.* 217
That love-sick Love by pleading may be blest . . . 328
Her pleading hath deserved a greater fee . . . 609
There pleading might you see grave Nestor stand . . *Lucrece* 1401
Pleasance. Youth is full of pleasance, age is full of care . *Pass. Pil.* 158
Pleasant. Graze on my lips; and if those hills be dry, Stray lower, where the pleasant fountains lie . . . *Ven. and Adon.* 234
Not that the summer is less pleasant now . . . *Sonnet* 102 9
Sitting in a pleasant shade Which a grove of myrtles made . *Pass. Pil.* 375
Please. I tell the day, to please him thou art bright . . *Sonnet* 28 9
If my slight Muse do please these curious days, The pain be mine . 38 13
For nothing hold me, so it please thee hold That nothing me . . 136 11
The uncertain sickly appetite to please . . . 147 4
How many tales to please me hath she coined! . . *Pass. Pil.* 93
Pleased. If pleased themselves, others, they think, delight In such-like circumstance, with such-like sport . . *Ven. and Adon.* 843
A nurse's song ne'er pleased her babe so well . . . 974
Grief best is pleased with grief's society . . . *Lucrece* 1111
Who in despite of view is pleased to dote . . *Sonnet* 141 4
Pleasing. Relish your nimble notes to pleasing ears . . *Lucrece* 1126
Who all in one, one pleasing note do sing . . . *Sonnet* 8 12
Yet well I know That music hath a far more pleasing sound . . 130 10
Pleasure. When he was by, the birds such pleasure took, That some would sing . . . *Ven. and Adon.* 1101
That all love's pleasure shall not match his woe . . . 1140
Having no other pleasure of his gain But torment . . *Lucrece* 860
Thy secret pleasure turns to open shame . . . 890
Why should the private pleasure of some one Become the public plague of many moe? . . . 1478
Which thou receivest not gladly, Or else receivest with pleasure thine annoy *Sonnet* 8 4
Since she prick'd thee out for women's pleasure, Mine be thy love . 20 13

Pleasure. From whence at pleasure thou mayst come and part *Sonnet* 48 12
Blunting the fine point of seldom pleasure 52 4
God forbid that . . . I should in thought control your times of pleasure 58 2
Not blame your pleasure, be it ill or well 58 14
Then better'd that the world may see my pleasure 75 8
Every humour hath his adjunct pleasure, Wherein it finds a joy 91 5
How like a winter hath my absence been From thee, the pleasure of the fleeting year! 97 2
For summer and his pleasures wait on thee 97 11
And the just pleasure lost which is so deem'd Not by our feeling but by others' seeing 121 3
Yet fear her, O thou minion of her pleasure! 126 9
Labouring in moe pleasures to bestow them Than the true gouty landlord which doth owe them *Lov. Comp.* 139
Where all those pleasures live that art can comprehend *Pass. Pil.* 62
And would not take her meaning nor her pleasure 154
All our pleasure known to us poor swains 289
Live with me, and be my love, And we will all the pleasures prove 354
And if these pleasures may thee move, Then live with me and be my love 367
These pretty pleasures might me move To live with thee and be thy love 371
Plenitude. In him a plenitude of subtle matter, Applied to cautels, all strange forms receives *Lov. Comp.* 302
Plenty. And yet not cloy thy lips with loathed satiety But rather famish them amid their plenty *Ven. and Adon.* 20
He with her plenty press'd, she faint with dearth 545
A swallowing gulf that even in plenty wanteth *Lucrece* 557
Plight your honourable faiths to me, With swift pursuit to venge this wrong of mine 1690
How can I then return in happy plight, That am debarr'd the benefit of rest? *Sonnet* 28 1
Procure to weep, In howling wise, to see my doleful plight *Pass. Pil.* 277
Plods. The beast that bears me, tired with my woe, Plods dully on *Sonnet* 50 6
Plot. Whoever plots the sin, thou 'point'st the season *Lucrece* 879
This plot of death when sadly she had laid 1212
Why should my heart think that a several plot? *Sonnet* 137 9
Ploughman. To cheer the ploughman with increaseful crops *Lucrece* 958
Pluck. Being so enraged, desire doth lend her force Courageously to pluck him from his horse *Ven. and Adon.* 30
Who plucks the bud before one leaf put forth? 416
Pluck down the rich, enrich the poor with treasures 1150
To pluck the quills from ancient ravens' wings *Lucrece* 949
Not from the stars do I my judgement pluck *Sonnet* 14 1
Pluck the keen teeth from the fierce tiger's jaws 19 3
Or from their proud lap pluck them where they grew 98 8
Nature, . . . As thou goest onwards, still will pluck thee back 126 6
As take the pain, but cannot pluck the pelf *Pass. Pil.* 192
My hand hath sworn Ne'er to pluck thee from thy thorn 238
Vow, alack! for youth unmeet: Youth, so apt to pluck a sweet 240
Plucked. Or being early pluck'd is sour to taste *Ven. and Adon.* 528
What though the rose have prickles, yet 'tis pluck'd 574
This said, his guilty hand pluck'd up the latch *Lucrece* 358
Brutus, who pluck'd the knife from Lucrece' side 1807
Untimely pluck'd, soon vaded, Pluck'd in the bud, and vaded in the spring *Pass. Pil.* 131
Pluckest. They bid thee crop a weed, thou pluck'st a flower *Ven. and Adon.* 946
Plum. The mellow plum doth fall, the green sticks fast 527
Like a green plum that hangs upon a tree, And falls, through wind *Pass. Pil.* 135
Plume. He vails his tail that, like a falling plume, Cool shadow to his melting buttock lent *Ven. and Adon.* 314
Plump. My flesh is soft and plump, my marrow burning 142
Plunging. Like an unpractised swimmer plunging still *Lucrece* 1098
Pluto. And moody Pluto winks while Orpheus plays 553
Poesy. Every alien pen hath got my use And under thee their poesy disperse *Sonnet* 78 4
Poet. The age to come would say 'This poet lies' 17 7
A poet's rage And stretched metre of an antique song 17 11
Since he died and poets better prove, Theirs for their style I'll read 32 13
Yet what of thee thy poet doth invent He robs thee of and pays it thee again 79 7
You did exceed The barren tender of a poet's debt 83 4
There lives more life in one of your fair eyes Than both your poets can in praise devise 83 14
One god is god of both, as poets feign *Pass. Pil.* 115
Poetry. If music and sweet poetry agree, As they must needs 103
Point. Thou know'st not what it is With javelin's point a churlish swine to gore *Ven. and Adon.* 616
Are better proof than thy spear's point can enter 626
And seems to point her out where she sits weeping *Lucrece* 1087
Till whatsoever star that guides my moving Points on me graciously *Sonnet* 26 10
Blunting the fine point of seldom pleasure 52 4
But, rising at thy name, doth point out thee As his triumphant prize 151 9
'Pointest. Whoever plots the sin, thou 'point'st the season *Lucrece* 879
Pointing. Pointing to each his thunder, rain, and wind *Sonnet* 14 6
Poison. The bottom poison, and the top o'erstraw'd With sweets *V. and A.* 1143
I will not poison thee with my attaint *Lucrece* 1072
And find the lesson true, Drugs poison him that so fell sick of you *Son.* 118 14
Poisoned. But still pure Doth in her poison'd closet yet endure *Lucrece* 1659
The poison'd fountain clears itself again 1707
If it be poison'd, 'tis the lesser sin That mine eye loves it and doth first begin *Sonnet* 114 13
Our drops this difference bore, His poison'd me, and mine did him restore *Lov. Comp.* 301
Poisonous. The poisonous simple sometimes is compacted In a pure compound *Lucrece* 530
Knit poisonous clouds about his golden head 777
Policy. A little harm done to a great good end For lawful policy remains enacted 529
Wherein deep policy did him disguise 1815
Thus policy in love, to anticipate The ills that were not *Sonnet* 118 9
It fears not policy, that heretic, Which works on leases of short-number'd hours 124 9
Polished. In polish'd form of well-refined pen 85 8
Politic. But all alone stands hugely politic 124 11
Pollute. No perfection is so absolute, That some impurity doth not pollute *Lucrece* 854
He shall not boast who did thy stock pollute That thou art doting father of his fruit 1063
Polluted. That blow did bail it from the deep unrest Of that polluted prison where it breathed 1726
Pollution. What were it, But with my body my poor soul's pollution? 1157

Pomp. It suffers not in smiling pomp *Sonnet* 124 6
Poor. What were thy lips the worse for one poor kiss? *Ven. and Adon.* 207
Poor queen of love, in thine own law forlorn, To love a cheek that smiles at thee in scorn! 251
He stamps and bites the poor flies in his fume 316
That they have murder'd this poor heart of mine 502
The poor fool prays her that he may depart 578
Even as poor birds, deceived with painted grapes 601
As those poor birds that helpless berries saw 604
And when thou hast on foot the purblind hare, Mark the poor wretch 680
By this, poor Wat, far off upon a hill, Stands on his hinder legs 697
Look, how the world's poor people are amazed At apparitions 925
This solemn sympathy poor Venus noteth 1057
Alas, poor world, what treasure hast thou lost! 1075
Pluck down the rich, enrich the poor with treasures 1150
'Poor flower,' quoth she, 'this was thy father's guise' 1177
Poor wretches have remorse in poor abuses *Lucrece* 269
But all these poor forbiddings could not stay him 323
May feel her heart—poor citizen!—distress'd, Wounding itself to death, rise up and fall 465
He is no woodman that doth bend his bow To strike a poor unseasonable doe 581
The wolf hath seized his prey, the poor lamb cries 677
Feeble Desire, all recreant, poor, and meek 710
Poor wasting monuments of lasting moans 798
The poor, lame, blind, halt, creep, cry out for thee 902
One poor retiring minute in an age Would purchase thee a thousand thousand friends 962
Poor grooms are sightless night, kings glorious day 1013
Poor hand, why quiver'st thou at this decree? 1030
Poor helpless help, the treasure stol'n away 1056
Poor bird, thou sing'st not in the day, As shaming any eye should thee behold 1142
As the poor frighted deer, that stands at gaze 1149
What were it, But with my body my poor soul's pollution? 1157
Poor Lucrece' cheeks unto her maid seem so As winter meads 1217
Poor women's faces are their own faults' books 1253
O, let it not be hild Poor women's faults, that they are so fulfill'd With men's abuses 1258
Bid fair Lucrece speak To the poor counterfeit of her complaining 1269
'Poor instrument,' quoth she, 'without a sound, I'll tune thy woes with my lamenting tongue' 1464
Too long, To tell them all with one poor tired tongue 1617
Mine enemy was strong, my poor self weak, And far the weaker with so strong a fear 1646
That my poor beauty had purloin'd his eyes 1651
Which speechless woe of his poor she attendeth 1674
Knights, by their oaths, should right poor ladies' harms 1694
But more than 'he' her poor tongue could not speak 1718
From the purple fountain Brutus drew The murderous knife, and, as it left the place, Her blood, in poor revenge, held it in chase 1736
Poor broken glass, I often did behold In thy sweet semblance my old age new born 1758
Through his lips do throng Weak words, so thick come in his poor heart's aid 1784
Wit so poor as mine May make seem bare, in wanting words to show it *Sonnet* 26 5
Once more re-survey These poor rude lines of thy deceased lover 32 4
So then I am not lame, poor, nor despised 37 9
To leave poor me thou hast the strength of laws 49 13
O, what excuse will my poor beast then find, When swift extremity can seem but slow 51 5
Why should poor beauty indirectly seek Roses of shadow? 67 7
Do not so much as my poor name rehearse 71 11
Since, spite of him, I'll live in this poor rhyme 107 11
That poor retention could not so much hold 122 9
Take thou my oblation, poor but free 125 10
Whilst my poor lips, which should that harvest reap, At the wood's boldness by thee blushing stand 128 7
Then my friend's heart let my poor heart bail 133 10
Not prizing her poor infant's discontent 143 8
Poor soul, the centre of my sinful earth 146 1
Proud of this pride, He is contented thy poor drudge to be 151 11
Sometime diverted their poor balls are tied To the orbed earth *Lov. Comp.* 24
All our pleasure known to us poor swains *Pass. Pil.* 289
Poor Corydon Must live alone 296
She, poor bird, as all forlorn, Lean'd her breast up-till a thorn 381
Even so, poor bird, like thee, None alive will pity me 399
Poorer. And Lust, the thief, far poorer than before *Lucrece* 693
Poorly. But, poorly rich, so wanteth in his store 97
Describe Adonis, and the counterfeit Is poorly imitated after you *Sonnet* 53 6
Poor-rich. Such griefs sustain, That they prove bankrupt in this poor-rich gain *Lucrece* 140
Portal. Once more the ruby-colour'd portal open'd *Ven. and Adon.* 451
Each unwilling portal yields him way *Lucrece* 309
Posied. Crack'd many a ring of posied gold and bone *Lov. Comp.* 45
Posies. There will I make thee a bed of roses, With a thousand fragrant posies *Pass. Pil.* 362
Possess. That which they possess They scatter and unloose it from their bond *Lucrece* 135
The old bees die, the young possess their hive 1769
Till manly shame bids him possess his breath 1777
One doth call her his, the other his, Yet neither may possess the claim they lay 1794
Possessed. If possess'd, as soon decay'd and done As is the morning's silver-melting dew 23
Thou art so possess'd with murderous hate That 'gainst thyself thou stick'st not to conspire *Sonnet* 10 5
Featured like him, like him with friends possess'd 29 6
Possesseth. Sin of self-love possesseth all mine eye And all my soul 62 1
Possessing. Possessing or pursuing no delight, Save what is had or must from you be took 75 11
Farewell! thou art too dear for my possessing 87 1
Possession. In the possession of his beauteous mate *Lucrece* 18
Keep still possession of thy gloomy place 803
Thy eternal summer shall not fade Nor lose possession of that fair thou owest *Sonnet* 18 10
Mad in pursuit and in possession so 129 9
Post. From the besieged Ardea all in post *Lucrece* 1
And in a desperate rage Post hither, this vile purpose to prevent 220
Swift subtle post, carrier of grisly care, Eater of youth 926
The post attends, and she delivers it 1333

Post. The night so pack'd, I post unto my pretty . . . *Pass. Pil.* 201
Were I with her, the night would post too soon . . . 205
Posterity. Seeming to bury that posterity Which by the rights of time thou needs must have . . . *Ven. and Adon.* 758
Posterity, shamed with the note, Shall curse my bones . . . *Lucrece* 208
Who is he so fond will be the tomb Of his self-love, to stop posterity? *Sonnet* 3 8
If thou shouldst depart, Leaving thee living in posterity . . . 6 12
Your praise shall still find room Even in the eyes of all posterity . . 55 11
Leaving no posterity . . . *Ph. and Tur.* 59
Posting. Why should I haste me thence? Till I return, of posting is no need . . . *Sonnet* 51 4
Potential. O most potential love! vow, bond, nor space, In thee hath neither sting, knot, nor confine . . . *Lov. Comp.* 264
Potions. I will drink Potions of eisel 'gainst my strong infection *Sonnet* 111 10
What potions have I drunk of Siren tears, Distill'd from limbecks 119 1
Pour. And mine I pour your ocean all among . . . *Lov. Comp.* 256
Pourest. That pour'st into my verse Thine own sweet argument *Sonnet* 38 2
Pouted. Who blush'd and pouted in a dull disdain, With leaden appetite, unapt to toy . . . *Ven. and Adon.* 33
Poverty. I do forgive thy robbery, gentle thief, Although thou steal thee all my poverty . . . *Sonnet* 40 10
Alack, what poverty my Muse brings forth! . . . 103 1
Power. Hearing him, thy power had lost his power . . . *Ven. and Adon.* 944
And therein heartens up his servile powers . . . *Lucrece* 295
Having solicited th' eternal power That his foul thoughts might compass his fair fair . . . 345
I must deflower: The powers to whom I pray abhor this fact . . . 349
By heaven and earth, and all the power of both . . . 572
A hell When more is felt than one hath power to tell . . . 1288
Before the which is drawn the power of Greece . . . 1368
He hath no power to ask her how she fares . . . 1594
Dear lord, thy sorrow to my sorrow lendeth Another power . . . 1677
Sad mortality o'er-sways their power . . . *Sonnet* 65 2
They that have power to hurt and will do none . . . 94 1
Darkening thy power to lend base subjects light . . . 100 4
Who in thy power Dost hold Time's fickle glass, his sickle, hour . . . 126 1
Since each hand hath put on nature's power . . . 127 5
Thy face hath not the power to make love groan . . . 131 6
Use power with power and slay me not by art . . . 139 4
Poor soul, the centre of my sinful earth, . . . these rebel powers that thee array . . . 146 2
O, from what power hast thou this powerful might? . . . 150 1
Not age, but sorrow, over me hath power . . . *Lov. Comp.* 74
Threw my affections in his charmed power . . . 146
My parts had power to charm a sacred nun . . . 260
Powerful. Not marble, . . . shall outlive this powerful rhyme . *Sonnet* 55 2
O, from what power hast thou this powerful might? . . . 150 1
Practice. To put in practice either, alas, it was a spite Unto the silly damsel! . . . *Pass. Pil.* 217
Smooth not thy tongue with filed talk, Lest she some subtle practice smell 307
Practised. My true eyes have never practised how To cloak offences *Lucrece* 748
Praise. Did not let To praise the clear unmatched red and white . . 11
Therefore that praise which Collatine doth owe Enchanted Tarquin answers with surmise . . . 82
And decks with praises Collatine's high name . . . 108
Were an all-eating shame and thriftless praise . . . *Sonnet* 2 8
How much more praise deserved thy beauty's use . . . 2 9
I will not praise that purpose not to sell . . . 21 14
The pain be mine, but thine shall be the praise . . . 38 14
What can mine own praise to mine own self bring? And what is't but mine own when I praise thee? . . . 39 3
Your praise shall still find room Even in the eyes of all posterity . . 55 10
The wits of former days To subjects worse have given admiring praise . 59 14
'Tis thee, myself, that for myself I praise . . . 62 13
Thy outward thus with outward praise is crown'd . . . 69 5
In other accents do this praise confound . . . 69 7
Yet this thy praise cannot be so thy praise, To tie up envy evermore enlarged . . . 70 11
And hang more praise upon deceased I Than niggard truth would willingly impart . . . 72 7
He can afford No praise to thee but what in thee doth live . . . 79 12
And in the praise thereof spends all his might . . . 80 3
Finding thy worth a limit past my praise . . . 82 6
There lives more life in one of your fair eyes Than both your poets can in praise devise . . . 83 14
Which can say more Than this rich praise, that you alone are you? . 84 2
Being fond on praise, which makes your praises worse . . . 84 14
While comments of your praise, richly compiled, Reserve their character with golden quill . . . 85 2
'Tis so, 'tis true,' And to the most of praise add something more . 85 10
Cannot dispraise but in a kind of praise . . . 95 7
Nor did I wonder at the lily's white, Nor praise the deep vermilion in the rose . . . 98 10
Because he needs no praise, wilt thou be dumb? Excuse not silence so 101 9
Is of more worth Than when it hath my added praise beside . . . 103 4
Since all alike my songs and praises be To one, of one . . . 105 3
Old rhyme In praise of ladies dead and lovely knights . . . 106 4
So all their praises are but prophecies Of this our time . . . 106 9
Have eyes to wonder, but lack tongues to praise . . . 106 14
I must strive To know my shames and praises from your tongue . 112 6
That phraseless hand, Whose white weighs down the airy scale of praise *Lov. Comp.* 226
Which is to me some praise, that I thy parts admire . . *Pass. Pil.* 66
O do not love that wrong, To sing heaven's praise with such an earthly tongue . . . 70
Spare not to spend, and chiefly there Where thy desert may merit praise . 325
Praised. The niggard prodigal that praised her so . . . *Lucrece* 79
Hearing you praised, I say 'Tis so, 'tis true' . . . *Sonnet* 85 9
And to be praised of ages yet to be . . . 101 12
He preach'd pure maid, and praised cold chastity . . . *Lov. Comp.* 315
Praising. Thou teachest how to make one twain, By praising him here who doth hence remain . . . *Sonnet* 39 14
And yet to times in hope my verse shall stand, Praising thy worth . 60 14
Pray. I pray you hence, and leave me here alone . . . *Ven. and Adon.* 382
The poor fool prays her that he may depart . . . 578
That for his prey to pray he doth begin . . . *Lucrece* 342
I must deflower: The powers to whom I pray abhor this fact . . . 349
The guilty rebel for remission prays . . . 714
She prays she never may behold the day . . . 746
Pray. So will I pray that thou mayst have thy 'Will' . . . *Sonnet* 143 13
Prayer. But in the midst of his unfruitful prayer . . . *Lucrece* 344
But she with vehement prayers urgeth still . . . 475
His ear her prayers admits, but his heart granteth No penetrable entrance . 558
Like prayers divine, I must each day say o'er the very same . *Sonnet* 108 5
For these dead birds sigh a prayer . . . *Ph. and Tur.* 67
Preach. For fear of harms that preach in our behoof . . . *Lov. Comp.* 165
Preached. He preach'd pure maid, and praised cold chastity . . . 315
Precedent. His sweating palm, The precedent of pith and livelihood *Ven. and Adon.* 26
The precedent whereof in Lucrece view . . . *Lucrece* 1261
Who ever shunn'd by precedent The destined ill she must herself assay? *Lov. Comp.* 155
Precepts. When thou impressest, what are precepts worth Of stale example? 267
Precious. Whose precious taste her thirsty lips well knew *Ven. and Adon.* 543
As one that unaware Hath dropp'd a precious jewel in the flood . . . 824
Pain pays the income of each precious thing . . . *Lucrece* 334
Unwholesome weeds take root with precious flowers . . . 870
For precious friends hid in death's dateless night . . . *Sonnet* 30 6
I have no precious time at all to spend, Nor services to do, till you require . . . 57 3
Thy glass will show thee how thy beauties wear, Thy dial how thy precious minutes waste . . . 77 2
And precious phrase by all the Muses filed . . . 85 4
Bound for the prize of all too precious you . . . 86 2
To my dear doting heart Thou art the fairest and most precious jewel . 131 4
Precurrer. Thou shrieking harbinger, Foul precurrer of the fiend *Ph. and Tur.* 6
Pre-decease. If children pre-decease progenitors, We are their offspring *Lucrece* 1756
Predict. Or say with princes if it shall go well, By oft predict that I in heaven find . . . *Sonnet* 14 8
Prefer. That strong-bonded oath That shall prefer and undertake my troth *Lov. Comp.* 280
Prefiguring. So all their praises are but prophecies Of this our time, all you prefiguring . . . *Sonnet* 106 10
Premeditate. He doth premeditate The dangers of his loathsome enterprise *Lucrece* 183
Prepare. To bid the wind a base he now prepares . . *Ven. and Adon.* 303
Bid him with speed prepare to carry it . . . *Lucrece* 1294
Her maid is gone, and she prepares to write . . . 1296
She modestly prepares to let them know Her honour is ta'en prisoner . 1607
Against this coming end you should prepare . . . *Sonnet* 13 3
And to his palate doth prepare the cup . . . 114 12
Preposterously. That it could so preposterously be stain'd . . . 109 11
Presage. This ill presage advisedly she marketh . . *Ven. and Adon.* 457
And the sad augurs mock their own presage . . . *Sonnet* 107 6
Presagers. Let my books be then the eloquence And dumb presagers of my speaking breast . . . 23 10
Prescience. Which in her prescience she controlled still . . . *Lucrece* 727
Prescriptions. My reason, the physician to my love, Angry that his prescriptions are not kept . . . *Sonnet* 147 6
Presence. Be, as thy presence is, gracious and kind . . . 10 11
And with his presence grace impiety . . . 67 2
Present. Every present sorrow seemeth chief, But none is best *V. and A.* 970
Hindering their present fall by this dividing . . . *Lucrece* 551
Think but how vile spectacle a it were, To view thy present trespass in another . . . 632
With circumstances strong Of present death, and shame that might ensue . 1263
Vouchsafe t' afford . . . Some present speed to come and visit me . 1307
With noble disposition Each present lord began to promise aid . . . 1696
My soul's imaginary sight Presents thy shadow to my sightless view *Son.* 27 10
Either by thy picture or my love, Thyself away art present still with me . 47 10
We, which now behold these present days, Have eyes to wonder . . 106 13
Crowning the present, doubting of the rest . . . 115 12
Not wondering at the present nor the past . . . 123 10
Do I not spend Revenge upon myself with present moan? . . . 149 8
Present-absent. These present-absent with swift motion slide . . 45 4
Presented. I heartily beseech thee, To take advantage on presented joy *Ven. and Adon.* 405
Presentest. And thou present'st a pure unstained prime . . *Sonnet* 70 8
Presenteth to mine eye The picture of an angry-chafing boar *Ven. and Adon.* 661
This huge stage presenteth nought but shows . . . *Sonnet* 15 3
Presently. Who in their pride do presently abuse it . . . *Lucrece* 864
The moon being clouded presently is miss'd . . . 1007
A brittle glass that's broken presently . . . *Pass. Pil.* 172
Preserve. Feeding on that which doth preserve the ill . . *Sonnet* 147 3
Press. Much like a press of people at a door, Throng her inventions *Lucrece* 1301
A press of gaping faces, Which seem'd to swallow up his sound advice . 1408
Do not press My tongue-tied patience with too much disdain *Sonnet* 140 1
Unless thy lady prove unjust, Press never thou to choose anew *Pass. Pil.* 332
Pressed. I had my load before, now press'd with bearing *Ven. and Adon.* 430
He with her plenty press'd, she faint with dearth . . . 545
Presume. Presume not on thy heart when mine is slain . . *Sonnet* 22 13
Pretended. Reward not hospitality With such black payment as thou hast pretended . . . *Lucrece* 576
Prettily. Still she entreats, and prettily entreats, For to a pretty ear she tunes her tale . . . *Ven. and Adon.* 73
Pretty. Still she entreats, and prettily entreats, For to a pretty ear she tunes her tale . . . 74
That in each cheek appears a pretty dimple . . . 242
A pretty while these pretty creatures stand . . . *Lucrece* 1233
Those pretty wrongs that liberty commits . . . *Sonnet* 41 1
Looking with pretty ruth upon my pain . . . 132 4
My love well knows Her pretty looks have been mine enemies . . 139 10
The night so pack'd, I post unto my pretty . . . *Pass. Pil.* 201
These pretty pleasures might me move To live with thee and be thy love 371
Prevailed. When a woman woos, what woman's son Will sourly leave her till she have prevailed? . . . *Sonnet* 41 8
Prevent. Which cunning love did wittily prevent . . . *Ven. and Adon.* 471
And in a desperate rage Post hither, this vile purpose to prevent *Lucrece* 220
I could prevent this storm and shun thy wrack! . . . 966
To prevent our maladies unseen, We sicken to shun sickness when we purge *Sonnet* 118 3
Preventest. Give my love fame faster than Time wastes life; So thou prevent'st his scythe and crooked knife . . . 100 14
Prey. Till either gorge be stuff'd or prey be gone . . *Ven. and Adon.* 58
She feedeth on the steam as on a prey, And calls it heavenly moisture, air of grace . . . 63
Now quick desire hath caught the yielding prey . . . 547

Prey. Rich preys make true men thieves . . . *Ven. and Adon.* 724
If he had spoke, the wolf would leave his prey . . . 1097
That for his prey to pray he doth begin . . . *Lucrece* 342
As the grim lion fawneth o'er his prey, Sharp hunger by the conquest satisfied . . . 421
The wolf hath seized his prey, the poor lamb cries . . . 677
Make slow pursuit, or altogether balk The prey . . . 697
Mine only care, Art left the prey of every vulgar thief . . . *Sonnet* 48 8
So then thou hast but lost the dregs of life, The prey of worms . . . 74 10
Priam. A piece Of skilful painting, made for Priam's Troy . . . *Lucrece* 1367
Staring on Priam's wounds with her old eyes . . . 1448
And drop sweet balm in Priam's painted wound . . . 1466
Lo, here weeps Hecuba, here Priam dies . . . 1485
Had doting Priam check'd his son's desire, Troy had been bright with fame . . . 1490
Sinon, whose enchanting story The credulous old Priam after slew . . . 1522
As Priam him did cherish, So did I Tarquin; so my Troy did perish . . . 1546
Priam wets his eyes, To see those borrow'd tears that Sinon sheds . . . 1548
Priam, why art thou old and yet not wise? . . . 1550
So Priam's trust false Sinon's tears doth flatter . . . 1560
Price. Whose vulture thought doth pitch the price so high, That she will draw his lips' rich treasure dry . . . *Ven. and Adon.* 551
Priceless. What priceless wealth the heavens had him lent . . . *Lucrece* 17
Prick. And griping it, the needle his finger pricks . . . 319
Ere he arrive his weary noon-tide prick . . . 781
Pricked. Since she prick'd thee out for women's pleasure, Mine be thy love and thy love's use their treasure . . . *Sonnet* 20 13
Pricking. What cares he now for curb or pricking spur? . . . *Ven. and Adon.* 285
Prickles. What though the rose have prickles, yet 'tis pluck'd . . . 574
Pride. With gentle majesty and modest pride . . . 278
The colt that's back'd and burden'd being young Loseth his pride and never waxeth strong . . . 420
Sith in thy pride so fair a hope is slain . . . 762
So their pride doth grow, Paying more slavish tribute than they owe . . . *Lucr.* 298
Nor children's tears nor mothers' groans respecting, Swell in their pride . . . 432
Smoking with pride, march'd on to make his stand On her bare breast . . . 438
Thou loathed in their shame, they in thy pride . . . 662
While Lust is in his pride, no exclamation Can curb his heat . . . 705
Who in their pride do presently abuse it . . . 864
The eddy boundeth in his pride Back to the strait that forced him on so fast . . . 1669
Began to clothe his wit in state and pride . . . 1809
And in themselves their pride lies buried . . . *Sonnet* 25 7
To make some special instant special blest, By new unfolding his imprison'd pride . . . 52 12
Why is my verse so barren of new pride, So far from variation or quick change? . . . 76 1
He of tall building and of goodly pride . . . 80 12
And having thee of all men's pride I boast . . . 91 12
The purple pride Which on thy soft cheek for complexion dwells . . . 99 3
In pride of all his growth A vengeful canker eat him up to death . . . 99 12
Having such a scope to show her pride . . . 103 2
Three winters cold Have from the forests shook three summers' pride . . . 104 4
Wooing his purity with her foul pride . . . 144 8
Proud of this pride, He is contented thy poor drudge to be . . . 151 10
Proclaim'd in her a careless hand of pride . . . *Lov. Comp.* 30
His rudeness so with his authorized youth Did livery falseness in a pride of truth . . . 105
Wooing his purity with her fair pride . . . *Pass. Pil.* 22
Priest. Let the priest in surplice white, That defunctive music can, Be the death-divining swan . . . *Ph. and Tur.* 13
Prime. Fair flowers that are not gather'd in their prime Rot and consume themselves in little time . . . *Ven. and Adon.* 131
If springing things be any jot diminish'd, They wither in their prime, prove nothing worth . . . 418
Sith in his prime Death doth my love destroy . . . 1163
To add a more rejoicing to the prime, And give the sneaped birds more cause to sing . . . *Lucrece* 332
She in thee Calls back the lovely April of her prime . . . *Sonnet* 3 10
When I behold the violet past prime . . . 12 3
And thou present'st a pure unstained prime . . . 70 8
Bearing the wanton burthen of the prime . . . 97 7
Primrose. Witness this primrose bank whereon I lie . . . *Ven. and Adon.* 151
Prince. Princes are the glass, the school, the book, Where subjects' eyes do learn . . . *Lucrece* 615
Or say with princes if it shall go well, By oft predict that I in heaven find . . . *Sonnet* 14 7
Great princes' favourites their fair leaves spread . . . 25 5
Nor the gilded monuments Of princes, shall outlive this powerful rhyme . . . 55 2
Princely. Gives good cheer And reverend welcome to her princely guest . . . *Lucr.* 90
Thou wrong'st his honour, wound'st his princely name . . . 599
Thy princely office how canst thou fulfil? . . . 628
Princess. To whose weak ruins muster troops of cares, To ask the spotted princess how she fares . . . 721
Print. His tenderer cheek receives her soft hand's print . . . *Ven. and Adon.* 353
Meant thereby Thou shouldst print more, not let that copy die . . . *Sonnet* 11 14
Prison. Till sable Night, . . . in her vaulty prison stows the Day . . . *Lucrece* 119
O, had they in that darksome prison died! . . . 379
His true respect will prison false desire . . . 642
That blow did bail it from the deep unrest Of that polluted prison . . . 1726
Prison my heart in thy steel bosom's ward . . . *Sonnet* 133 9
Prisoned. A lily prison'd in a gaol of snow, Or ivory in an alabaster band . . . *Ven. and Adon.* 362
Her tears began to turn their tide, Being prison'd in her eye . . . 980
Prisoner. Leading him prisoner in a red-rose chain . . . 110
She modestly prepares to let them know Her honour is ta'en prisoner . . . *Lucr.* 1608
And when the judge is robb'd the prisoner dies . . . 1652
A liquid prisoner pent in walls of glass . . . *Sonnet* 5 10
Private. O unfelt sore! crest-wounding, private scar! . . . *Lucrece* 828
Thy secret pleasure turns to open shame, Thy private feasting to a public fast . . . 891
Why should the private pleasure of some one Become the public plague of many moe? . . . 1478
Why should so many fall, To plague a private sin in general? . . . 1484
Every private widow well may keep By children's eyes her husband's shape in mind . . . *Sonnet* 9 7
Privilege. Warrant for blame, To privilege dishonour in thy name . . . *Lucrece* 621
You yourself may privilege your time To what you will . . . *Sonnet* 58 10
Take heed, dear heart, of this large privilege . . . 95 13
Privileged by age, desires to know In brief the grounds . . . *Lov. Comp.* 62
Prize. Desire my pilot is, beauty my prize . . . *Lucrece* 279
For truth proves thievish for a prize so dear . . . *Sonnet* 48 14
Bound for the prize of all too precious you . . . 86 2
Prize. But, rising at thy name, doth point out thee As his triumphant prize . . . *Sonnet* 151 10
Prizing. Not prizing her poor infant's discontent . . . 143 8
Proceed. And doth so far proceed, That what is vile shows like a virtuous deed . . . *Lucrece* 251
His eye drops fire, no water thence proceeds . . . 1552
Such childish humour from weak minds proceeds . . . 1825
Every word doth almost tell my name, Showing their birth and where they did proceed . . . *Sonnet* 76 8
And thence this slander, as I think, proceeds . . . 131 14
Proceedings. Though I were dumb, yet his proceedings teach thee . . . *V. and A.* 406
Like the proceedings of a drunken brain . . . 910
Process. Three beauteous springs to yellow autumn turn'd In process of the seasons have I seen . . . *Sonnet* 104 6
Proclaims. And peace proclaims olives of endless age . . . 107 8
Proclaim'd in her a careless hand of pride . . . *Lov. Comp.* 30
Procure. My sighs so deep Procure to weep, In howling wise . . . *Pass. Pil.* 276
Procured. And now, to tempt, all liberty procured . . . *Lov. Comp.* 252
Prodigal. And barren dearth of daughters and of sons, Be prodigal . . . *V. and A.* 755
The niggard prodigal that praised her so . . . *Lucrece* 79
If that one be prodigal, Bountiful they will him call . . . *Pass. Pil.* 411
Prodigies. The world's poor people are amazed At apparitions, signs, and prodigies . . . *Ven. and Adon.* 926
Profane. Lest I, too much profane, should do it wrong . . . *Sonnet* 89 11
Profaned. O unlook'd-for evil, When virtue is profaned in such a devil! *Lucr.* 847
Sweet beauty hath no name, no holy bower, But is profaned . . . *Sonnet* 127 8
Not from those lips of thine, That have profaned their scarlet ornaments . . . 142 6
Proffer. He refused to take her figured proffer . . . *Pass. Pil.* 52
When time shall serve, be thou not slack To proffer . . . 334
Profit. Gaining more, the profit of excess Is but to surfeit . . . *Lucrece* 138
These offices, so oft as thou wilt look, Shall profit thee . . . *Sonnet* 77 14
Profitless. Profitless usurer, why dost thou use So great a sum of sums? . . . 4 7
Profound. In so profound abysm I throw all care Of others' voices . . . 112 9
Progenitors. If children pre-decease progenitors, We are their offspring . . . *Lucr.* 1756
Prognosticate. Or else of thee this I prognosticate . . . *Sonnet* 14 13
Progress. Thou by thy dial's shady stealth mayst know Time's thievish progress to eternity . . . 77 8
Promise. Upon this promise did he raise his chin . . . *Ven. and Adon.* 85
While others saucily Promise more speed, but do it leisurely . . . *Lucrece* 1349
With noble disposition Each present lord began to promise aid . . . 1696
Why didst thou promise such a beauteous day? . . . *Sonnet* 34 1
Promised. 'Tis promised in the charity of age . . . *Lov. Comp.* 70
Prompt. All replication prompt, and reason strong . . . 122
Prone. O, that prone lust should stain so pure a bed! . . . *Lucrece* 684
Nor tender feeling, to base touches prone . . . *Sonnet* 141 6
Pronounced. 'Tarquin' was pronounced plain, But through his teeth *Lucrece* 1786
Proof. Are better proof than thy spear's point can enter . . . *Ven. and Adon.* 626
Mine appetite I never more will grind On newer proof . . . *Sonnet* 110 11
And on just proof surmise accumulate . . . 117 10
A bliss in proof, and proved, a very woe . . . 129 11
Of proofs new-bleeding, which remain'd the foil Of this false jewel *Lov. Comp.* 153
Nor gives it satisfaction to our blood, That we must curb it upon others' proof 163
Property. The diamond, — why, 'twas beautiful and hard, Whereto his invised properties did tend . . . 212
Property was thus appalled, That the self was not the same . . . *Ph. and Tur.* 37
Prophecies. Infusing them with dreadful prophecies . . . *Ven. and Adon.* 928
So all their praises are but prophecies Of this our time . . . *Sonnet* 106 9
Prophesy. I prophesy thy death, my living sorrow . . . *Ven. and Adon.* 671
Since thou art dead, lo, here I prophesy . . . 1135
Prophetic. Not mine own fears, nor the prophetic soul Of the wide world dreaming on things to come . . . *Sonnet* 107 1
Proportioned. Make war against proportion'd course of time . . . *Lucrece* 774
Proposed. When great treasure is the meed proposed, Though death be adjunct, there's no death supposed . . . 132
Before, a joy proposed; behind, a dream . . . *Sonnet* 129 12
Protest. Her heart, The which, by Cupid's bow she doth protest, He carries thence incaged in his breast . . . *Ven. and Adon.* 581
Protestation. But she, that yet her sad task hath not said, The protestation stops . . . *Lucrece* 1700
And to his protestation urged the rest . . . 1844
Protestings. In the midst of all her pure protestings . . . *Pass. Pil.* 95
Proud. Alight thy steed, And rein his proud head to the saddle-bow *V. and A.* 14
O, be not proud, nor brag not of thy might! . . . 113
A breeding jennet, lusty, young, and proud . . . 260
Nothing else he sees, For nothing else with his proud sight agrees . . . 288
Look, what a horse should have he did not lack, Save a proud rider . . . 300
Proud, as females are, to see him woo her, She puts on outward strangeness 309
She knows it is no gentle chase, But the blunt boar, rough bear, or lion proud 884
Clapping their proud tails to the ground below . . . 923
Perchance his boast of Lucrece' sovereignty Suggested this proud issue of a king . . . *Lucrece* 37
His hand, as proud of such a dignity, Smoking with pride, march'd on to make his stand . . . 437
The flesh being proud, Desire doth fight with Grace, For there it revels . . . 712
To ruinate proud buildings with thy hours . . . 944
Those proud lords, to blame, Make weak-made women tenants to their shame 1259
Which the conceited painter drew so proud, As heaven . . . 1371
Which bleeding under Pyrrhus' proud foot lies . . . 1449
Thy youth's proud livery, so gazed on now, Will be a tatter'd weed *Sonnet* 2 3
Making a couplement of proud compare, With sun and moon . . . 21 5
Of public honour and proud titles boast . . . 25 2
The rich proud cost of outworn buried age . . . 64 2
She hath no exchequer now but his, And, proud of many, lives upon his gains . . . 67 12
Now proud as an enjoyer and anon Doubting the filching age will steal his treasure . . . 75 5
Yet be most proud of that which I compile . . . 78 9
Was it the proud full sail of his great verse . . . 86 1
Or from their proud lap pluck them where they grew . . . 98 8
Bear thine eyes straight, though thy proud heart go wide . . . 140 14
Thy proud heart's slave and vassal wretch to be . . . 141 12
What merit do I in myself respect, That is so proud thy service to despise? . . . 149 10
Proud of this pride, He is contented thy poor drudge to be . . . 151 10
Proud of subjection, noble by the sway . . . *Lov. Comp.* 108
For Adon's sake, a youngster proud and wild . . . *Pass. Pil.* 120
Prouder than garments' cost, Of more delight than hawks or horses be *Son.* 91 10
Proudest. Wide as the ocean is, The humble as the proudest sail doth bear 80 6
Proudly. So as thou art, As those whose beauties proudly make them cruel . . . 131 2

Proud-pied. When proud-pied April dress'd in all his trim Hath put a spirit of youth in every thing . . . . . *Sonnet* 98 2
Prove. The steed is stalled up, and even now To tie the rider she begins to prove . . . *Ven. and Adon.* 40
If springing things be any jot diminish'd, They wither in their prime, prove nothing worth 418
All is imaginary she doth prove, He will not manage her . . 597
Such griefs sustain, That they prove bankrupt in this poor-rich gain *Lucr.* 140
When they in thee the like offences prove 613
Since men prove beasts, let beasts bear gentle minds . . 1148
Sings this to thee: 'thou single wilt prove none' *Sonnet* 8 14
Be, as thy presence is, gracious and kind, Or to thyself at least kind-hearted prove 10 12
Till then not show my head where thou mayst prove me . 26 14
Since he died and poets better prove, Theirs for their style I'll read 32 13
O absence, what a torment wouldst thou prove . . . 39 9
For truth proves thievish for a prize so dear . . . 48 14
Dear love, forget me quite, For you in me can nothing worthy prove . 72 4
Upon thy side against myself I'll fight And prove thee virtuous . 88 4
I did strive to prove The constancy and virtue of your love . . 117 13
Which prove more short than waste or ruining . . . 125 4
Things of great receipt with ease we prove Among a number . . 136 7
Lest guilty of my faults thy sweet self prove . . . 151 4
Which yet men prove Against strange maladies a sovereign cure . 153 7
And this by that I prove, Love's fire heats water, water cools not love 154 13
I forswore; but I will prove, Thou being a goddess, I forswore not thee *Pass. Pil.* 33
Though to myself forsworn, to thee I'll constant prove . . 59
Unless thy lady prove unjust, Press never thou to choose anew . . 331
Live with me, and be my love, And we will all the pleasures prove . 354
Proved. She hath assay'd as much as may be proved *Ven. and Adon.* 608
And worse essays proved thee my best of love *Sonnet* 110 8
If this be error and upon me proved, I never writ, nor no man ever loved 116 13
A bliss in proof, and proved, a very woe . . . 129 11
Provide. That did not better for my life provide Than public means 111 3
Proving from world's minority their right . . . . *Lucrece* 67
Proving his beauty by succession thine . . . *Sonnet* 2 12
Provoke. And swelling passion doth provoke a pause *Ven. and Adon.* 218
The bloody spur cannot provoke him on . . . *Sonnet* 50 9
Provoked. The boar provoked my tongue; Be wreak'd on him *V. and A.* 1003
Provokest. Dost thou drink tears, that thou provokest such weeping? . 949
Pry. Is it thy spirit that thou send'st from thee So far from home into my deeds to pry . . . . . *Sonnet* 61 6
Pryest. Why pry'st thou through my window? leave thy peeping. *Lucrece* 1089
Public. Thy private feasting to a public fast . . . 891
Why should the private pleasure of some one Become the public plague of many moe? 1479
Of public honour and proud titles boast . . . *Sonnet* 25 2
Nor thou with public kindness honour me . . . 36 11
That did not better for my life provide Than public means which public manners breed 111 4
Publish. And so to publish Tarquin's foul offence . . *Lucrece* 1852
Whose rich esteeming The owner's tongue doth publish every where *Son.* 102 4
Publisher. Why is Collatine the publisher Of that rich jewel? *Lucrece* 33
Puddle. Thy sea within a puddle's womb is hearsed, And not the puddle in thy sea dispersed 657
Puffs. But his hot heart, which fond desire doth scorch, Puffs forth another wind 315
Pulses. He bends her fingers, holds her pulses hard, He chafes her lips *Ven. and Adon.* 476
Punishment. Vows for thee broke deserve not punishment . *Pass. Pil.* 32
Pupil. Time's pencil, or my pupil pen, Neither in inward worth nor outward fair, Can make you live yourself in eyes of men . *Sonnet* 16 10
Purblind. And when thou hast on foot the purblind hare, Mark the poor wretch . . . . . *Ven. and Adon.* 679
Purchase. Which purchase if thou make, for fear of slips Set thy seal-manual on my wax-red lips 515
One poor retiring minute in an age Would purchase thee a thousand thousand friends . . . . . *Lucrece* 963
Pure shame and awed resistance made him fret . . *Ven. and Adon.* 69
Pure lips, sweet seals in my soft lips imprinted . . . 511
Forgetting shame's pure blush and honour's wrack . . 558
And pure perfection with impure defeature 736
With pure aspects did him peculiar duties . . . *Lucrece* 14
In their pure ranks his traitor eye encloses . . . 73
Pure thoughts are dead and still, While lust and murder wake to stain and kill 167
Offer pure incense to so pure a shrine 194
Which in a moment doth confound and kill All pure effects . . 251
But with a pure appeal seeks to the heart, Which once corrupted takes the worser part 293
The poisonous simple sometimes is compacted In a pure compound . 531
While she, the picture of pure piety 542
By him that gave it thee, From a pure heart command thy rebel will . 625
O, that prone lust should stain so pure a bed! . . . 684
Pure Chastity is rifled of her store 692
She wakes her heart by beating on her breast, And bids it leap from thence, where it may find Some purer chest to close so pure a mind . 761
As clear from this attaint of mine As I, ere this, was pure to Collatine . 826
Shall gush pure streams to purge my impure tale . . . 1078
Pure. My body or my soul, which was the dearer, When the one pure, the other made divine? . . . . . *Lucrece* 1164
But still pure Doth in her poison'd closet yet endure . . 1658
May my pure mind with the foul act dispense . . . 1704
Some of her blood still pure and red remain'd, And some look'd black . 1742
And thou present'st a pure unstained prime . . *Sonnet* 70 8
Even to thy pure and most most loving breast . . 110 14
He preach'd pure maid, and praised cold chastity . *Lov. Comp.* 315
In the midst of all her pure protestings . . . *Pass. Pil.* 95
Purer. She wakes her heart by beating on her breast, And bids it leap from thence, where it may find Some purer chest to close so pure a mind *Lucr.* 761
Purest. Purest faith unhappily forsworn, And gilded honour shamefully misplaced . . . . *Sonnet* 66 4
Purge. Shall gush pure streams to purge my impure tale . *Lucrece* 1078
We sicken to shun sickness when we purge . . *Sonnet* 118 4
Purging. Slight air and purging fire, Are both with thee, wherever I abide 45 1
Purified. Being so applied, His venom in effect is purified . *Lucrece* 532
Purify. The spots whereof could weeping purify, Her tears should drop on them 685
Purity. The life of purity, the supreme fair 780
Wooing his purity with her foul pride . . . *Sonnet* 144 8
Wooing his purity with her fair pride . . . *Pass. Pil.* 22
Purled. From his lips did fly Thin winding breath, which purl'd up to the sky . . . . *Lucrece* 1407
Purloined. That my poor beauty had purloin'd his eyes . . 1651
Purple. Whose wonted lily white With purple tears, that his wound wept, was drench'd . . . . . *Ven. and Adon.* 1054
A purple flower sprung up, chequer'd with white . . . 1168
From the purple fountain Brutus drew The murderous knife . *Lucrece* 1734
The purple pride Which on thy soft cheek for complexion dwells *Sonnet* 99 3
Purple-coloured. Even as the sun with purple-colour'd face *Ven. and Adon.* 1
Purpose. Far from the purpose of his coming hither, He makes excuses *Lucr.* 113
And in a desperate rage Post hither, this vile purpose to prevent . . 220
For in thy bed I purpose to destroy thee 514
Yet for the self-same purpose seek a knife 1047
Me of thee defeated, By adding one thing to my purpose nothing *Sonnet* 20 12
I will not praise that purpose not to sell . . . 21 14
You are so strongly in my purpose bred . . . 112 13
She keeps thee to this purpose, that her skill May time disgrace . 126 7
On purpose laid to make the taker mad 129 8
Purposed. Give not a windy night a rainy morrow, To linger out a purposed overthrow 90 8
Their purposed trim Pieced not his grace, but were all graced by him *Lov. Comp.* 118
Pursue. Pursue these fearful creatures o'er the downs *Ven. and Adon.* 677
Stands on his hinder legs with listening ear, To hearken if his foes pursue him still 699
They fright him, yet he still pursues his fear . . *Lucrece* 308
Pursuers. To stop the loud pursuers in their yell . *Ven. and Adon.* 688
Pursuing. Possessing or pursuing no delight, Save what is had or must from you be took . . . . *Sonnet* 75 11
Pursuit. Make slow pursuit, or altogether balk The prey . . *Lucrece* 696
With swift pursuit to venge this wrong of mine . . . 1691
Mad in pursuit and in possession so . . . *Sonnet* 129 9
And makes all swift dispatch In pursuit of the thing she would have stay 143 4
Push. His sighs, his sorrows, make a saw, To push grief on . *Lucrece* 1673
Pushed. Backward she push'd him, as she would be thrust *Ven. and Adon.* 41
Put. She puts on outward strangeness, seems unkind . . . 310
Who plucks the bud before one leaf put forth? . . . 416
But gold that's put to use more gold begets 768
And therefore would he put his bonnet on 1087
Put fear to valour, courage to the coward 1158
She puts the period often from his place . . . *Lucrece* 565
Hast thou put on his shape to do him shame? . . . 597
Coming from thee, I could not put him back . . . 843
As an unperfect actor on the stage Who with his fear is put besides his part *Sonnet* 23 2
And puts apparel on my tatter'd loving 26 11
For that same groan doth put this in my mind . . . 50 13
Hath put a spirit of youth in every thing . . . 98 3
Since each hand hath put on nature's power . . . 127 5
Have put on black and loving mourners be . . . 132 3
Say this is not, To put fair truth upon so foul a face . . 137 12
O me, what eyes hath Love put in my head! . . . 148 1
Many there were that did his picture get, To serve their eyes, and in it put their mind . . . . . . *Lov. Comp.* 135
'Gainst her own content, To put the by-past perils in my way . 158
Or my affection put to the smallest teen, Or any of my leisures ever charm'd 192
Religious love put out Religion's eye 250
To put in practice either, alas, it was a spite Unto the silly damsel! *Pass. Pil.* 217
And twice desire, ere it be day, That which with scorn she put away . 316
Be thou not slack To proffer, though she put thee back . . 334
Put'st. Thou usurer, that put'st forth all to use . . *Sonnet* 134 10
Putrified. Blood untainted still doth red abide, Blushing at that which is so putrified . . . . *Lucrece* 1750
Pyramids. Thy pyramids built up with newer might To me are nothing novel *Sonnet* 123 2
Pyrrhus. Which bleeding under Pyrrhus' proud foot lies . . *Lucrece* 1449
And rail on Pyrrhus that hath done him wrong . . . 1467

Q

Quake. Whereat each tributary subject quakes . . *Ven. and Adon.* 1045
That one would swear he saw them quake and tremble . *Lucrece* 1393
Sinon in his fire doth quake with cold 1556
Quaking. Bids them leave quaking, bids them fear no more *Ven. and Adon.* 899
Qualified. His rage of lust by gazing qualified; Slack'd, not suppress'd *Lucr.* 424
Qualify. Though absence seem'd my flame to qualify . *Sonnet* 109 2
Quality. Both favour, savour, hue, and qualities . *Ven. and Adon.* 747
We have no good that we can say is ours, But ill-annexed Opportunity Or kills his life or else his quality . . . . . *Lucrece* 87
Quality. By this short schedule Collatine may know Her grief, but not her grief's true quality . . . . *Lucrece* 1313
What is the quality of mine offence? 1702
Of good or evil luck, Of plagues, of dearths, or seasons' quality . *Sonnet* 14 4
His qualities were beauteous as his form . . . *Lov. Comp.* 99
Each stone's dear nature, worth, and quality . . . 210
Queen. By this the love-sick queen began to sweat . . *Ven. and Adon.* 175
Poor queen of love, in thine own law forlorn, To love a cheek that smiles at thee in scorn! 251

Queen. And these mine eyes, true leaders to their queen, But for thy piteous lips no more had seen *Ven. and Adon.* 503
'Fair queen,' quoth he, 'if any love you owe me, Measure my strangeness with my unripe years' 523
But all in vain; good queen, it will not be 607
Where their queen Means to immure herself and not be seen 1193
Of either's colour was the other queen *Lucrece* 66
The silver-shining queen he would distain; Her twinkling handmaids too 786
As on the finger of a throned queen The basest jewel will be well esteem'd *Sonnet* 96 5
Such looks as none could look but beauty's queen *Pass. Pil.* 46
Then fell she on her back, fair queen, and toward 55
The sun look'd on the world with glorious eye, Yet not so wistly as this queen on him 82
Sweet melodious sound That Phœbus' lute, the queen of music, makes 112
Fair was the morn when the fair queen of love 117
She, silly queen, with more than love's good will, Forbade the boy he should not pass those grounds 123
Distance, and no space was seen 'Twixt the turtle and his queen *Ph. and Tur.* 31

Quench. She with her tears Doth quench the maiden burning of his cheeks *Ven. and Adon.* 50
I'll make a shadow for thy hairs; If they burn too, I'll quench them with my tears 192
He goes To quench the coal which in his liver glows *Lucrece* 47
Who in a salt-waved ocean quench their light 1231
And with my tears quench Troy that burns so long 1468

Quenched. This brand she quenched in a cool well by *Sonnet* 154 9

Quenchless. Those round clear pearls of his, that move thy pity, Are balls of quenchless fire *Lucrece* 1554

Quest. A quest of thoughts, all tenants to the heart *Sonnet* 46 10
Had, having, and in quest to have, extreme 129 10

Question. Of thy beauty do I question make, That thou among the wastes of time must go 12 9
Nor dare I question with my jealous thought Where you may be 57 9
And controversy hence a question takes *Lov. Comp.* 110
All kind of arguments and question deep 121
And yet do question make What I should do again for such a sake 321

Questioned. Long he questioned With modest Lucrece, and wore out the night *Lucrece* 122

Quick. O, how quick is love *Ven. and Adon.* 38
Mine eyes are gray and bright and quick in turning 140
Now quick desire hath caught the yielding prey 547
In youth, quick bearing and dexterity *Lucrece* 1389
Nor war's quick fire shall burn The living record of your memory *Sonnet* 55 7
Why is my verse so barren of new pride, So far from variation or quick change? 76 2
Of his quick objects hath the mind no part 113 7

Quicker. When these quicker elements are gone In tender embassy of love to thee 45 5

Quickly. Like a dive-dapper peering through a wave, Who, being look'd on, ducks as quickly in *Ven. and Adon.* 87
Are they not quickly told and quickly gone? 520
The one doth flatter thee in thoughts unlikely, In likely thoughts the other kills thee quickly 990
Through the empty skies In her light chariot quickly is convey'd 1192
And his love-kindling fire did quickly steep *Sonnet* 153 3
But quickly on this side the verdict went *Lov. Comp.* 113
If he be addict to vice, Quickly him they will entice *Pass. Pil.* 416

Quick-shifting. There appears Quick-shifting antics, ugly in her eyes *Lucr.* 459

Quiet. Should run Into the quiet closure of my breast *Ven. and Adon.* 782
The staring ruffian shall it keep in quiet 1149
They, mustering to the quiet cabinet Where their dear governess and lady lies *Lucrece* 442
Her quiet interrupted, Her mansion batter'd by the enemy 1170
By night my mind, For thee and for myself no quiet find *Sonnet* 27 14

Quietly. Lie quietly, and hear a little more; Nay, do not struggle *Ven. and Adon.* 709

Quietus. Her audit, though delay'd, answer'd must be, And her quietus is to render thee *Sonnet* 126 12

Quill. To pluck the quills from ancient ravens' wings *Lucrece* 949
She prepares to write, First hovering o'er the paper with her quill 1297
Well might show How far a modern quill doth come too short *Sonnet* 83 7
While comments of your praise, richly compiled, Reserve their character with golden quill 85 3

Quit. Time had not scythed all that youth begun, Nor youth all quit *L. Comp.* 13

Quite. And then my little heart were quite undone *Ven. and Adon.* 783
Such passion her assails, That patience is quite beaten from her breast *Lucrece* 1563
Sap check'd with frost and lusty leaves quite gone *Sonnet* 5 7
Once foil'd, Is from the book of honour razed quite 25 11
Mine own self-love quite contrary I read 62 11
Dear love, forget me quite, For you in me can nothing worthy prove 72 3
There appears a face That over-goes my blunt invention quite 103 7
All my merry jigs are quite forgot, All my lady's love is lost, God wot *Pass. Pil.* 253

Quittal. As in revenge or quittal of such strife *Lucrece* 236

Quiverest. Poor hand, why quiver'st thou at this decree? 1030

Quote. Will quote my loathsome trespass in my looks 812

Quoth. 'Ay me,' quoth Venus, 'young, and so unkind?' *Ven. and Adon.* 187
'I know not love,' quoth he, 'nor will not know it' 409
Quoth she, 'hast thou a tongue? O, would thou hadst not!' 427
'No matter where;' quoth he, 'Leave me, and then the story aptly ends' 715
'In night,' quoth she, 'desire sees best of all' 720
'Nay, then,' quoth Adon, 'you will fall again' 769
'Lucrece,' quoth he, 'this night I must enjoy thee' *Lucrece* 512
'Thou art,' quoth she, 'a sea, a sovereign king' 652
'O, peace!' quoth Lucrece; 'if it should be told' 1284
'Woe, woe,' quoth Collatine, 'she was my wife, I owed her' 1802

R

Race. Desire, of perfect'st love being made, Shall neigh—no dull flesh—in his fiery race *Sonnet* 51 11

Rack. Anon permit the basest clouds to ride With ugly rack 33 6

Radiance. The deep-green emerald, in whose fresh regard Weak sights their sickly radiance do amend *Lov. Comp.* 214

Rage. An oven that is stopp'd, or river stay'd, Burneth more hotly, swelleth with more rage *Ven. and Adon.* 332
As life for honour in fell battle's rage; Honour for wealth *Lucrece* 145
Will he not wake, and in a desperate rage Post hither? 219
His rage of lust by gazing qualified; Slack'd, not suppress'd 424
This moves in him more rage and lesser pity, To make the breach 468
Wrath, envy, treason, rape, and murder's rages 909
In Ajax' eyes blunt rage and rigour roll'd 1398
And in their rage such signs of rage they bear 1419
In rage sent out, recall'd in rage, being past 1671
Barren rage of death's eternal cold *Sonnet* 13 12
A poet's rage And stretched metre of an antique song 17 11
Some fierce thing replete with too much rage 23 3
Lofty towers I see down-razed And brass eternal slave to mortal rage 64 4
How with this rage shall beauty hold a plea? 65 3
But, spite of heaven's fell rage, Some beauty peep'd through lattice of sear'd age *Lov. Comp.* 13
This said, in top of rage the lines she rents 55
For when we rage, advice is often seen By blunting us to make our wits more keen 160

Ragged. The studded bridle on a ragged bough Nimbly she fastens *Ven. and Adon.* 37
Thy smoothing titles to a ragged name *Lucrece* 892
Let not winter's ragged hand deface In thee thy summer *Sonnet* 6 1

Raging-mad. It shall be raging-mad and silly-mild *Ven. and Adon.* 1151

Rail. In vain I rail at Opportunity, At Time, at Tarquin *Lucrece* 1023
And rail on Pyrrhus that hath done him wrong 1467

Railed. I rail'd on thee, fearing my love's decease *Ven. and Adon.* 1002

Raiment. Is but the seemly raiment of my heart *Sonnet* 22 6

Rain added to a river that is rank Perforce will force it overflow the bank *Ven. and Adon.* 71
Art thou obdurate, flinty, hard as steel, Nay, more than flint, for stone at rain relenteth? 200
To shelter thee from tempest and from rain 238
With tears, which, chorus-like, her eyes did rain 360
Love comforteth like sunshine after rain, But Lust's effect is tempest after sun 799
But through the flood-gates breaks the silver rain 959
But like a stormy day, now wind, now rain, Sighs dry her cheeks 965
This windy tempest, till it blow up rain, Held back his sorrow's tide *Lucr.* 1788
At last it rains, and busy winds give o'er 1790
Pointing to each his thunder, rain, and wind *Sonnet* 14 6
To dry the rain on my storm-beaten face 34 6

Rain. The sea, all water, yet receives rain still *Sonnet* 135 9
Storming her world with sorrow's wind and rain *Lov. Comp.* 7

Rainbows. Round about her tear-distained eye Blue circles stream'd, like rainbows in the sky *Lucrece* 1587

Rained. Her contending tears, Which long have rain'd, making her cheeks all wet *Ven. and Adon.* 83

Raineth. Even as the wind is hush'd before it raineth 458

Raining. Tears harden lust, though marble wear with raining *Lucrece* 560
On what occasion break Those tears from thee, that down thy cheeks are raining? 1271
Thy sorrow to my sorrow lendeth Another power; no flood by raining slaketh 1677

Rainy. Give not a windy night a rainy morrow *Sonnet* 90 7

Raise. Upon this promise did he raise his chin *Ven. and Adon.* 85
Hallow'd with sighs that burning lungs did raise *Lov. Comp.* 228

Raised. If thy unworthiness raised love in me, More worthy I to be beloved of thee *Sonnet* 150 13

Ram. Rude ram, to batter such an ivory wall! *Lucrece* 464
My ewes breed not, My rams speed not, All is amiss *Pass. Pil.* 247

Ran. Thus was Adonis slain: He ran upon the boar with his sharp spear *Ven. and Adon.* 1112
To Simois' reedy banks the red blood ran *Lucrece* 1437
He rose and ran away; ah, fool, too froward *Pass. Pil.* 56

Random. But hatefully at random dost thou hit *Ven. and Adon.* 940
At random from the truth vainly express'd *Sonnet* 147 12

Ranged. If I have ranged, Like him that travels I return again 109 5

Rank. Rain added to a river that is rank Perforce will force it overflow the bank *Ven. and Adon.* 71
In their pure ranks his traitor eye encloses *Lucrece* 73
Whose ranks of blue veins, as his hand did scale, Left their round turrets destitute and pale 440
That in their smoky ranks his smother'd light May set at noon 783
Their ranks began To break upon the galled shore, and than Retire again, till, meeting greater ranks, They join and shoot their foam at Simois' banks 1439
A dearer birth than this his love had brought, To march in ranks of better equipage *Sonnet* 32 12
To thy fair flower add the rank smell of weeds 69 12
Though words come hindmost, holds his rank before 85 12
A healthful state Which, rank of goodness, would by ill be cured 118 12
By their rank thoughts my deeds must not be shown 121 12
Which shall above that idle rank remain Beyond all date 122 3
To blush at speeches rank, to weep at woes *Lov. Comp.* 307

Ransacked. Robb'd and ransack'd by injurious theft *Lucrece* 838

Ransom. Paying what ransom the insulter willeth *Ven. and Adon.* 550
And they are rich and ransom all ill deeds *Sonnet* 34 14
Mine ransoms yours, and yours must ransom me 120 14

Rape. Wrath, envy, treason, rape, and murder's rages *Lucrece* 909
For Helen's rape the city to destroy 1369

Rare. With April's first-born flowers, and all things rare That heaven's air in this huge rondure hems *Sonnet* 21 7
Therefore are feasts so solemn and so rare, Since, seldom coming 52 5
Makes summer's welcome thrice more wish'd, more rare 56 14
I think my love as rare As any she belied with false compare 130 13
Rarest. Whose rarest havings made the blossoms dote *Lov. Comp.* 235
Rarity. Feeds on the rarities of nature's truth *Sonnet* 60 11
Beauty, truth, and rarity, Grace in all simplicity *Ph. and Tur.* 53
Rascal. I mean to bear thee Unto the base bed of some rascal groom *Lucrece* 671
Rash. Her rash suspect she doth extenuate *Ven. and Adon.* 1010
O rash false heat, wrapp'd in repentant cold! *Lucrece* 48
Peers her whiter chin, The reason of this rash alarm to know 473
To thee, my heaved-up hands appeal, Not to seducing lust, thy rash relier 639
No exclamation Can curb his heat or rein his rash desire 706
Rate. But back retires to rate the boar for murther *Ven. and Adon.* 906
Reckoning his fortune at such high-proud rate *Lucrece* 19
They all rate his ill, Which drives the creeping thief to some regard 304
Rather. And yet not cloy thy lips with loathed satiety, But rather famish them amid their plenty *Ven. and Adon.* 20
Would let him go, Rather than triumph in so false a foe *Lucrece* 77
And rather make them born to our desire *Sonnet* 123 7
Rave. Let him have time against himself to rave *Lucrece* 982
Raven. To pluck the quills from ancient ravens' wings 949
My mistress' brows are raven black, Her eyes so suited *Sonnet* 127 9
Ravish. With rotten damps ravish the morning air *Lucrece* 778
Whose heavenly touch Upon the lute doth ravish human sense *Pass. Pil.* 108
Ravisher. With close-tongued treason and the ravisher *Lucrece* 770
Thou ravisher, thou traitor, thou false thief! 888
Ravishment. In bloody death and ravishment delighting 430
Come, Philomel, that sing'st of ravishment 1128
Raw. Her eyes, though sod in tears, look'd red and raw 1592
Razed. Once foil'd, Is from the book of honour razed quite *Sonnet* 25 11
Till each to razed oblivion yield his part 122 7
Read. Nor read the subtle-shining secrecies Writ in the glassy margents of such books *Lucrece* 101
Princes are the glass, the school, the book, Where subjects' eyes do learn, do read, do look 616
Must he in thee read lectures of such shame? 618
And Tarquin's eye may read the mot afar 830
How Tarquin must be used, read it in me 1195
In them I read such art As truth and beauty shall together thrive *Sonnet* 14 10
O, learn to read what silent love hath writ 23 13
Since he died and poets better prove, Theirs for their style I'll read 32 14
Mine own self-love quite contrary I read 62 11
If you read this line, remember not The hand that writ it 71 5
Readily. One . . . , That cannot tread the way out readily *Lucrece* 1152
Reading. And often reading what contents it bears *Lov. Comp.* 19
Ready. But when her lips were ready for his pay, He winks, and turns his lips another way *Ven. and Adon.* 89
One of my husband's men Bid thou be ready, by and by *Lucrece* 1292
Real. His real habitude gave life and grace To appertainings *Lov. Comp.* 114
Reap. Whilst my poor lips, which should that harvest reap *Sonnet* 128 7
Rears. Anon he rears upright, curvets and leaps *Ven. and Adon.* 279
Rearward. Ah, do not, when my heart hath 'scaped this sorrow, Come in the rearward of a conquer'd woe *Sonnet* 90 6
Reason. Planting oblivion, beating reason back *Ven. and Adon.* 557
You have no reason to withhold me so 612
Now of this dark night I perceive the reason 727
O strange excuse, When reason is the bawd to lust's abuse! 792
My will is strong, past reason's weak removing *Lucrece* 243
Respect and reason, wait on wrinkled age! 275
Peers her whiter chin, The reason of this rash alarm to know 473
But as reproof and reason beat it dead, By thy bright beauty was it newly bred 489
'Tis thou that spurn'st at right, at law, at reason 880
When love, converted from the thing it was, Shall reasons find *Sonnet* 49 8
To guard the lawful reasons on thy part 49 12
I straight will halt, Against thy reasons making no defence 89 4
Yet then my judgement knew no reason why 115 3
Past reason hunted, and no sooner had Past reason hated 129 6
My reason, the physician to my love 147 5
Past cure I am, now reason is past care, And frantic-mad 147 9
My soul doth tell my body that he may Triumph in love; flesh stays no farther reason 151 8
Reason strong, For his advantage still did wake and sleep *Lov. Comp.* 122
Though Reason weep, and cry 'It is thy last' 168
His passion, but an art of craft, Even there resolved my reason into tears 296
Let reason rule things worthy blame, As well as fancy partial might *Pass. Pil.* 301
Reason, in itself confounded, Saw division grow together *Ph. and Tur.* 41
Love hath reason, reason none, If what parts can so remain 47
Reaves. Or butcher-sire that reaves his son of life *Ven. and Adon.* 766
Rebel. From a pure heart command thy rebel will *Lucrece* 625
The guilty rebel for remission prays 714
Poor soul, the centre of my sinful earth, . . . these rebel powers that thee array *Sonnet* 146 2
Rebuked. So I return rebuked to my content 119 13
Recalled. In rage sent out, recall'd in rage, being past *Lucrece* 1671
Receipt. Drunken Desire must vomit his receipt 703
In things of great receipt with ease we prove Among a number one is reckon'd none *Sonnet* 136 7
Receive. His tenderer cheek receives her soft hand's print *Ven. and Adon.* 353
With a steadfast eye Receives the scroll without or yea or no *Lucrece* 1340
Thence comes it that my name receives a brand *Sonnet* 111 5
'Tis better to be vile than vile esteem'd, When not to be receives reproach of being 121 2
Was I bold, To trust those tables that receive thee more? 122 12
The sea, all water, yet receives rain still 135 9
Playing the place which did no form receive *Lov. Comp.* 241
In him a plenitude of subtle matter, Applied to cautels, all strange forms receives 303
Received. I have received from many a several fair, Their kind acceptance 206
Receivest. Why lovest thou that which thou receivest not gladly, Or else receivest with pleasure thine annoy? *Sonnet* 8 3
Then if for my love thou my love receivest, I cannot blame thee for my love thou usest 40 5
Receiving nought by elements so slow But heavy tears 44 13
Recite. Lest the world should task you to recite What merit lived in me 72 1
Recketh. What recketh he his rider's angry stir, His flattering 'Holla,' or his 'Stand, I say'? *Ven. and Adon.* 283
Reckon. They that level At my abuses reckon up their own *Sonnet* 121 10
Reckoned. With ease we prove Among a number one is reckon'd none 136 8
Reckoning his fortune at such high-proud rate *Lucrece* 19
Reckoning time, whose million'd accidents Creep in 'twixt vows *Sonnet* 115 5
Recompense. Who plead for love and look for recompense 23 11
Reconciled. And new pervert a reconciled maid *Lov. Comp.* 329
Record. So should my shame still rest upon record, And never be forgot *Lucrece* 1643
Nor war's quick fire shall burn The living record of your memory *Sonnet* 55 8
O, that record could with a backward look, . . . Show me your image 59 5
Till each to razed oblivion yield his part Of thee, thy record never can be miss'd 122 8
For thy records and what we see doth lie 123 11
Recounting. Assured Of thy fair health, recounting it to me 45 12
Recreant. Feeble Desire, all recreant, poor, and meek *Lucrece* 710
Recreate. To recreate himself when he hath sung, The tiger would be tame and gently hear him *Ven. and Adon.* 1095
Recures. A smile recures the wounding of a frown 465
Recured. Until life's composition be recured By those swift messengers *Sonnet* 45 9
Red. More white and red than doves or roses are *Ven. and Adon.* 10
Making them red and pale with fresh variety 21
She red and hot as coals of glowing fire, He red for shame, but frosty in desire 35
Being red, she loves him best: and being white, Her best is better'd with a more delight 77
Scorning his churlish drum and ensign red 107
Touch but my lips with those fair lips of thine,—Though mine be not so fair, yet are they red 116
Red cheeks and fiery eyes blaze forth her wrong 219
To note the fighting conflict of her hue, How white and red each other did destroy! 346
Like a red morn, that ever yet betoken'd Wreck to the seaman 453
Claps her pale cheek, till clapping makes it red 468
Whose frothy mouth, bepainted all with red 901
Heavy heart's lead, melt at mine eyes' red fire! 1073
To praise the clear unmatched red and white *Lucrece* 11
Then virtue claims from beauty beauty's red, Which virtue gave 59
When shame assail'd, the red should fence the white 63
This heraldry in Lucrece' face was seen, Argued by beauty's red and virtue's white 65
First red as roses that on lawn we lay, Then white as lawn, the roses took away 258
Makes the lily pale, And the red rose blush at her own disgrace 479
Two red fires in both their faces blazed 1353
The red blood reek'd, to show the painter's strife 1377
Here one being throng'd bears back, all boll'n and red 1417
To Simois' reedy banks the red blood ran 1437
Cheeks neither red nor pale, but mingled so That blushing red no guilty instance gave 1510
Her eyes, though sod in tears, look'd red and raw 1592
Some of her blood still pure and red remain'd, And some look'd black 1742
Blood untainted still doth red abide 1749
A third, nor red nor white, had stol'n of both *Sonnet* 99 10
Coral is far more red than her lips' red 130 2
I have seen roses damask'd, red and white 130 5
Of paled pearls and rubies red as blood *Lov. Comp.* 198
Redeem. Return, forgetful Muse, and straight redeem In gentle numbers time so idly spent *Sonnet* 100 5
Redoubled. Passion on passion deeply is redoubled *Ven. and Adon.* 832
Redress. Tell thy grief, that we may give redress *Lucrece* 1603
As broken glass no cement can redress *Pass. Pil.* 178
Red-rose. Leading him prisoner in a red-rose chain *Ven. and Adon.* 110
Reedy. To Simois' reedy banks the red blood ran *Lucrece* 1437
Reek. Her face doth reek and smoke, her blood doth boil *Ven. and Adon.* 555
In some perfumes is there more delight Than in the breath that from my mistress reeks *Sonnet* 130 8
Reeked. The red blood reek'd, to show the painter's strife *Lucrece* 1377
Reeleth. Like feeble age, he reeleth from the day *Sonnet* 7 10
Refigured. Ten times thyself were happier than thou art, If ten of thine ten times refigured thee 6 10
Reflect. Two glasses, where herself herself beheld A thousand times, and now no more reflect *Ven. and Adon.* 1130
Whether it is that she reflects so bright, That dazzleth them, or else some shame supposed *Lucrece* 376
Refrain. That to hear her so complain, Scarce I could from tears refrain *Pass. Pil.* 388
Refresh. As vaded gloss no rubbing will refresh 176
Reft. Since he himself is reft from her by death *Ven. and Adon.* 1174
Refuge. Or at the least this refuge let me find *Lucrece* 1654
Refuse. That in the very refuse of thy deeds There is such strength *Son.* 150 6
Refused. He refused to take her figured proffer *Pass. Pil.* 52
But one must be refused; more mickle was the pain 219
Refusest. If thou thyself deceivest By wilful taste of what thyself refusest *Sonnet* 40 8
Regard. Then love's deep groans I never shall regard *Ven. and Adon.* 377
Sad pause and deep regard beseem the sage *Lucrece* 277
They all rate his ill, Which drives the creeping thief to some regard 305
Show'd deep regard and smiling government 1400
The deep-green emerald, in whose fresh regard Weak sights their sickly radiance do amend *Lov. Comp.* 213
Region. The region cloud hath mask'd him from me now *Sonnet* 33 12
Register. O comfort-killing Night, image of hell! Dim register and notary of shame! *Lucrece* 765
What's new to speak, what new to register, That may express my love? *Sonnet* 108 3
Thy registers and thee I both defy Not wondering at the present nor the past 123 9
Thou register of lies, What unapproved witness dost thou bear! *Lov. Comp.* 52
Rehearse. And every fair with his fair doth rehearse *Sonnet* 21 4
Too excellent For every vulgar paper to rehearse 38 4
Do not so much as my poor name rehearse 71 11
And tongues to be your being shall rehearse 81 11
Reign. For where Love reigns, disturbing Jealousy Doth call himself Affection's sentinel *Ven. and Adon.* 649
That all the faults which in thy reign are made May likewise be sepulchred in thy shade *Lucrece* 804
Time's ruin, beauty's wreck, and grim care's reign 1451
And each, though enemies to either's reign, Do in consent shake hands to torture me *Sonnet* 28 5

Reign. And there reigns love and all love's loving parts . . *Sonnet* 31 3
Unless this general evil they maintain, All men are bad, and in their badness reign 121 14
He did in the general bosom reign Of young, of old . . *Lov. Comp.* 127
Reigned. Never believe, though in my nature reign'd All frailties *Sonnet* 109 9
And reign'd, commanding in his monarchy . . *Lov. Comp.* 196
Rein. Vouchsafe, thou wonder, to alight thy steed, And rein his proud head to the saddle-bow . . . . *Ven. and Adon.* 14
Over one arm the lusty courser's rein, Under her other was the tender boy 31
The strong-neck'd steed, being tied unto a tree, Breaketh his rein 264
Tied to the tree, Servilely master'd with a leathern rein! . . 392
No exclamation Can curb his heat or rein his rash desire *Lucrece* 706
Rejected. Then woo thyself, be of thyself rejected . *Ven. and Adon.* 159
Rejoice. Reviving joy bids her rejoice, And flatters her it is Adonis' voice 977
Rejoicing. To add a more rejoicing to the prime, And give the sneaped birds more cause to sing . . . *Lucrece* 332
Releasing. And from her twining arms doth urge releasing *Ven. and Adon.* 256
The charter of thy worth gives thee releasing . . *Sonnet* 87 3
Relenteth. Art thou obdurate, flinty, hard as steel, Nay, more than flint, for stone at rain relenteth? . . . . *Ven. and Adon.* 200
Relenting. Do not steep thy heart In such relenting dew of lamentations *Lucrece* 1829
Relief. Within this limit is relief enough . . *Ven. and Adon.* 235
The offender's sorrow lends but weak relief . . *Sonnet* 34 11
Relier. To thee, my heaved-up hands appeal, Not to seducing lust, thy rash relier . . . . . *Lucrece* 639
Relieved. For misery is trodden on by many, And being low never relieved by any . . . . *Ven. and Adon.* 708
Relieveth. He cheers the morn and all the earth relieveth 484
Religion. Religious love put out Religion's eye . *Lov. Comp.* 250
Religious. How many a holy and obsequious tear Hath dear religious love stol'n from mine eye As interest of the dead . . *Sonnet* 31 6
Religious love put out Religion's eye . . . *Lov. Comp.* 250
Relish. Relish your nimble notes to pleasing ears . *Lucrece* 1126
Remain. Love's gentle spring doth always fresh remain . *Ven. and Adon.* 801
What face remains alive that's worth the viewing? Whose tongue is music now? 1076
His hand, that yet remains upon her breast,—Rude ram! . *Lucrece* 463
Shall remain The scornful mark of every open eye . . 519
A little harm done to a great good end For lawful policy remains enacted 529
The scar that will, despite of cure, remain . . 732
She there remains a hopeless castaway . . . 744
Therefore would they still in darkness be, To have their unseen sin remain untold 753
In men, as in a rough-grown grove, remain Cave-keeping evils . 1249
Of what she was no semblance did remain . . . 1453
So shall those blots that do with me remain Without thy help by me be borne alone . . . . . *Sonnet* 36 3
Thou teachest how to make one twain, By praising him here who doth hence remain 39 14
The worth of that is that which it contains, And that is this, and this with thee remains 74 14
Which shall above that idle rank remain Beyond all date . 122 3
Or to remain In personal duty, following where he haunted . *Lov. Comp.* 129
And so much less of shame in me remains . . . 188
One knight loves both, and both in thee remain . *Pass. Pil.* 116
For now I see Inconstancy More in women than in men remain 262
Love hath reason, reason none, If what parts can so remain . *Ph. and Tur.* 48
Remained. Some of her blood still pure and red remain'd, And some look'd black . . . . . . *Lucrece* 1742
Of proofs new-bleeding, which remain'd the foil Of this false jewel *L. Comp.* 153
Remaineth. Because the cry remaineth in one place *Ven. and Adon.* 885
Remaining. She looks for night, and then she longs for morrow, And both she thinks too long with her remaining . . . *Lucrece* 1572
Remedy. The remedy indeed to do me good Is to let forth my foul-defiled blood 1028
And for this sin there is no remedy . . . *Sonnet* 62 3
Growing a bath and healthful remedy For men diseased . 154 11
Remember. If you read this line, remember not The hand that writ it . 71 5
To keep an adjunct to remember thee Were to import forgetfulness . 122 13
Remembered. O, be remember'd, no outrageous thing From vassal actors can be wiped away . . . . . *Lucrece* 607
But if thou live, remember'd not to be, Die single . . *Sonnet* 3 13
For thy sweet love remember'd such wealth brings . 29 13
Too base of thee to be remembered . . . 74 12
O, that our night of woe might have remember'd My deepest sense . 120 9
Remembrance. Nor it nor no remembrance what it was . 5 12
I summon up remembrance of things past . . 30 2
Remission. The guilty rebel for remission prays . *Lucrece* 714
Remorse. 'Pity,' she cries, 'some favour, some remorse!' *Ven. and Adon.* 257
Poor wretches have remorse in poor abuses . . *Lucrece* 269
Remorseless. Her pity-pleading eyes are sadly fixed In the remorseless wrinkles of his face 562
Remote. Despite of space I would be brought, From limits far remote, where thou dost stay . . . . . *Sonnet* 44 4
Hearts remote, yet not asunder . . . *Ph. and Tur.* 29
Remove. She swears, From his soft bosom never to remove *Ven. and Adon.* 81
The sun doth burn my face; I must remove . . . 186
Remove your siege from my unyielding heart . . . 423
If but for fear of this, thy will remove . . *Lucrece* 614
Where I may not remove nor be removed . . *Sonnet* 25 14
Or bends with the remover to remove . . . 116 4
And did thence remove, To spend her living in eternal love *Lov. Comp.* 237
There a nay is placed without remove . . *Pass. Pil.* 256
Removed. Beloved Where I may not remove nor be removed . *Sonnet* 25 14
Which now appear But things removed that hidden in thee lie . 31 8
No matter then although my foot did stand Upon the farthest earth removed from thee 44 6
And yet this time removed was summer's time . . 97 5
Remover. Or bends with the remover to remove . . 116 4
Removing. My will is strong, past reason's weak removing *Lucrece* 243
Render. To wrong the wronger till he render right . . 943
Knows no art, But mutual render, only me for thee *Sonnet* 125 12
Her audit, though delay'd, answer'd must be, And her quietus is to render thee 126 12
Where I myself must render, That is, to you, my origin and ender *L. Comp.* 221
Renew. No object but her passion's strength renews *Lucrece* 1103
Sweet love, renew thy force; be it not said Thy edge should blunter be than appetite . . . . . *Sonnet* 56 1
Renewed. Pity me then and wish I were renew'd . . 111 8

Renewest. Whose fresh repair if now thou not renewest, Thou dost beguile the world . . . . . . *Sonnet* 3 3
Renown. But if Fortune once do frown, Then farewell his great renown *Pass. Pil.* 420
Rent. Paying too much rent, For compound sweet forgoing simple savour *Sonnet* 125 6
Robb'd others' beds' revenues of their rents . . 142 8
The lines she rents, Big discontent so breaking their contents *Lov. Comp.* 55
Renying. Love's denying, Faith's defying, Heart's renying, Causer of this *Pass. Pil.* 251
Repair. Whose fresh repair if now thou not renewest, Thou dost beguile the world, unbless some mother . . . *Sonnet* 3 3
Seeking that beauteous roof to ruinate Which to repair should be thy chief desire 10 8
So should the lines of life that life repair . . 16 9
To this urn let those repair That are either true or fair . *Ph. and Tur.* 65
Repay. I have scanted all Wherein I should your great deserts repay *Son.* 117 2
Repeal. I sue for exiled majesty's repeal; Let him return *Lucrece* 640
Repeat. That deep vow, which Brutus made before, He doth again repeat . 1848
Repel. Foul words and frowns must not repel a lover *Ven. and Adon.* 573
Repent. Though thou repent, yet I have still the loss *Sonnet* 34 10
Then too late she will repent That thus dissembled her delight *Pass. Pil.* 313
Repentant. O rash false heat, wrapp'd in repentant cold! . *Lucrece* 48
Repentant tears ensue the deed, Reproach, disdain, and deadly enmity 502
Repetition. The neighbour caves, as seeming troubled, Make verbal repetition of her moans . . . . *Ven. and Adon.* 831
If it should be told, The repetition cannot make it less . *Lucrece* 1285
Repine. Were never four such lamps together mix'd, Had not his clouded with his brow's repine . . . . *Ven. and Adon.* 490
Replenish. The more she saw the blood his cheeks replenish, The more she thought he spied in her some blemish . . . *Lucrece* 1357
Replete. Some fierce thing replete with too much rage . *Sonnet* 23 3
Incapable of more, replete with you . . . 113 13
Replication. All replication prompt, and reason strong . *Lov. Comp.* 122
Replied the maid, 'The more to blame my sluggard negligence' *Lucrece* 1277
Replies. Thus she replies: 'Thy palfrey, as he should, Welcomes the warm approach of sweet desire' . . . . *Ven. and Adon.* 385
Echo replies, As if another chase were in the skies . . 695
To whom she speaks, and he replies with howling . . 918
Urgeth still Under what colour he commits this ill. Thus he replies *Lucr.* 477
The father says 'She's mine.' 'O, mine she is,' Replies her husband . 1796
Report. I love thee in such sort As, thou being mine, mine is thy good report *Sonnet* 36 14
And therefore have I slept in your report . . 83 5
Naming thy name blesses an ill report . . . 95 8
I love thee in such sort As, thou being mine, mine is thy good report . 96 14
Repose. Here she exclaims against repose and rest . *Lucrece* 757
Why hath thy servant, Opportunity, Betray'd the hours thou gavest me to repose? 933
My bed, The dear repose for limbs with travel tired *Sonnet* 27 2
My weary travel's end, Doth teach that ease and that repose . 50 3
Reposed. By Lucrece' side, In his clear bed might have reposed still *Lucrece* 382
Reprehend. For sharply he did think to reprehend her *Ven. and Adon.* 470
And then she reprehends her mangling eye . . . 1065
Reproach. Repentant tears ensue the deed, Reproach, disdain, and deadly enmity . . . . *Lucrece* 503
Thou back'st reproach against long-living laud . . 622
The orator, to deck his oratory, Will couple my reproach to Tarquin's shame 816
And undeserved reproach to him allotted, That is as clear from this attaint of mine As I, ere this, was pure to Collatine . . 824
Reproach is stamp'd in Collatinus' face . . . 829
When life is shamed, and death reproach's debtor . . 1155
'Tis better to be vile than vile esteem'd, When not to be receives reproach of being . . . . *Sonnet* 121 2
By how much of me their reproach contains . . *Lov. Comp.* 189
Reprobate. By reprobate desire thus madly led, The Roman lord marcheth to Lucrece' bed . . . . . . *Lucrece* 300
Reproof. But as reproof and reason beat it dead, By thy bright beauty was it newly bred 489
Reprove. What have you urged that I cannot reprove? *Ven. and Adon.* 787
Reproving. But she is not her own: The worst is but denial and reproving *Lucrece* 242
And thou shalt find it merits not reproving *Sonnet* 142 4
Reputation. And makest fair reputation but a bawd *Lucrece* 623
Let my good name, that senseless reputation, For Collatine's dear love be kept unspotted 820
Request. If your maid may be so bold, She would request to know your heaviness 1283
At this request, with noble disposition Each present lord began to promise aid 1695
Requiem. Lest the requiem lack his right . . *Ph. and Tur.* 16
Require. I have no precious time at all to spend, Nor services to do, till you require . . . . . . *Sonnet* 57 4
Resemble. Which heartless peasants did so well resemble *Lucrece* 1392
Such cherubins as your sweet self resemble *Sonnet* 114 6
Resembling. Idle sounds resembling parasites . . *Ven. and Adon.* 848
Chequer'd with white, Resembling well his pale cheeks . . 1169
With pearly sweat, resembling dew of night . *Lucrece* 396
Resembling strong youth in his middle age . . *Sonnet* 7 6
Resembling sire and child and happy mother . . 8 11
Reserve. Reserve them for my love, not for their rhyme . 32 7
While comments of your praise, richly compiled, Reserve their character with golden quill 85 3
Reserved the stalk and gave him all my flower . *Lov. Comp.* 147
Resign. Where they resign their office and their light *Ven. and Adon.* 1039
Resistance. Pure shame and awed resistance made him fret . 69
Such danger to resistance did belong . . *Lucrece* 1265
Resisteth. He now obeys, and now no more resisteth *Ven. and Adon.* 563
Resolution. My will is back'd with resolution: Thoughts are but dreams till their effects be tried . . . . . . *Lucrece* 352
My resolution, love, shall be thy boast . . . 1193
My resolution, husband, do thou take . . . 1200
Resolved. She is resolved no longer to restrain him *Ven. and Adon.* 579
His passion, but an art of craft, Even there resolved my reason into tears *Lov. Comp.* 296
Resolving. Yet ever to obtain his will resolving . *Lucrece* 129
Resort. And merry fools to mock at him resort . . 989
Thou makest faults graces that to thee resort . *Sonnet* 96 4
Resound. Whose hollow womb resounds like heaven's thunder *V. and A.* 268
How sighs resound Through heartless ground . . *Pass. Pil.* 278

Respect. Full of respects, yet nought at all respecting *Ven. and Adon.* 911
True valour still a true respect should have *Lucrece* 201
Respect and reason, wait on wrinkled age! 275
His true respect will prison false desire 642
Such harmless creatures have a true respect To talk in deeds 1347
To show me worthy of thy sweet respect *Sonnet* 26 12
In our two loves there is but one respect 36 5
His utmost sum, Call'd to that audit by advised respects 49 4
Others for the breath of words respect, Me for my dumb thoughts 85 13
What merit do I in myself respect, That is so proud thy service to despise? 149 9
Respecting. Full of respects, yet nought at all respecting *Ven. and Adon.* 911
Nor children's tears nor mothers' groans respecting, Swell in their pride, the onset still expecting *Lucrece* 431
Rest. My boding heart pants, beats, and takes no rest *Ven. and Adon.* 647
In his bedchamber to be barr'd of rest 784
The gentle lark, weary of rest, From his moist cabinet mounts up on high 853
Lo, in this hollow cradle take thy rest 1185
And every one to rest themselves betake, Save thieves *Lucrece* 125
But if thou yield, I rest thy secret friend 526
Here she exclaims against repose and rest 757
Disturb his hours of rest with restless trances 974
My restless discord loves no stops nor rests 1124
And on that pillow lay Where thou wast wont to rest thy weary head 1621
So should my shame still rest upon record, And never be forgot 1643
And to his protestation urged the rest 1844
And all the rest forgot for which he toil'd *Sonnet* 25 12
How can I then return in happy plight, That am debarr'd the benefit of rest? 28 2
Mine own true love that doth my rest defeat 61 11
Death's second self, that seals up all in rest 73 8
Every humour hath his adjunct pleasure, Wherein it finds a joy above the rest 91 6
Crowning the present, doubting of the rest 115 12
Outfacing faults in love with love's ill rest *Pass. Pil.* 8
Good night, good rest. Ah, neither be my share: She bade good night that kept my rest away 181
The morning rise Doth cite each moving sense from idle rest 195
And the turtle's loyal breast To eternity doth rest *Ph. and Tur.* 58
Restful. Tired with all these, for restful death I cry *Sonnet* 66 1
Restless. Disturb his hours of rest with restless trances *Lucrece* 974
My restless discord loves no stops nor rests 1124
Restore. Myself I'll forfeit, so that other mine Thou wilt restore *Sonnet* 134 4
Our drops this difference bore, His poison'd me, and mine did him restore *Lov. Comp.* 301
Restored. All losses are restored and sorrows end *Sonnet* 30 14
Restrain. She is resolved no longer to restrain him *Ven. and Adon.* 579
His eye, which late this mutiny restrains, Unto a greater uproar tempts his veins *Lucrece* 426
Resty. Rise, resty Muse, my love's sweet face survey *Sonnet* 100 9
Re-survey. By fortune once more re-survey These poor rude lines 32 3
Retention. That poor retention could not so much hold 122 9
Retire. This way she runs, and now she will no further, But back retires to rate the boar for murther *Ven. and Adon.* 906
But honest fear, bewitch'd with lust's foul charm, Doth too too oft betake him to retire *Lucrece* 174
The locks between her chamber and his will, Each one by him enforced retires his ward 303
That to his borrow'd bed he make retire, And stoop to honour, not to foul desire 573
Let him return, and flattering thoughts retire 641
Their ranks began To break upon the galled shore, and than Retire again, till, meeting greater ranks, They join and shoot their foam at Simois' banks 1441
Retiring. One poor retiring minute in an age Would purchase thee a thousand thousand friends 962
Return. Then shalt thou see the dew-bedabbled wretch Turn, and return, indenting with the way *Ven. and Adon.* 704
Return again in haste; Thou see'st our mistress' ornaments are chaste *Lucrece* 321
Let him return, and flattering thoughts retire 641
Unless thou couldst return to make amends 961
Long she thinks till he return again, And yet the duteous vassal scarce is gone 1359
How can I then return in happy plight? *Sonnet* 28 1
Why should I haste me thence? Till I return, of posting is no need 51 4
That, when they see Return of love, more blest may be the view 56 12
Return, forgetful Muse, and straight redeem In gentle numbers time so idly spent 100 5
If I have ranged, Like him that travels I return again 109 6
So I return rebuked to my content 119 13
Returned. By those swift messengers return'd from thee 45 10
Revealing day through every cranny spies *Lucrece* 1086
Revels. Love keeps his revels where there are but tw in *Ven. and Adon.* 123
Desire doth fight with Grace, For there it revels *Lucrece* 713
Revenge. As in revenge or quittal of such strife 236
Revenge on him that made me stop my breath 1180
From the purple fountain Brutus drew The murderous knife, and, as it left the place, Her blood, in poor revenge, held it in chase 1736
Is it revenge to give thyself a blow For his foul act? 1823
By this bloody knife, We will revenge the death of this true wife 1841
Do I not spend Revenge upon myself with present moan? *Sonnet* 149 8
Revenged. By whose example thou revenged mayst be *Lucrece* 1194
Be suddenly revenged on my foe, Thine, mine, his own 1683
And live to be revenged on her death 1778
Revengeful. To chase injustice with revengeful arms 1693
Revenues. Robb'd others' beds' revenues of their rents *Sonnet* 142 8
Reverend. Gives good cheer And reverend welcome to her princely guest *Lucrece* 90
A reverend man that grazed his cattle nigh *Lov. Comp.* 57
Review. Thou dost review The very part was consecrate to thee *Sonnet* 74 5
Reviewest. When thou reviewest this, thou dost review The very part was consecrate to thee 74 5
Revives. Even as a dying coal revives with wind *Ven. and Adon.* 338
Reviveth. For looks kill love and love by looks reviveth 464
Reviving joy bids her rejoice, And flatters her it is Adonis' voice 977
Revolt. Thou canst not vex me with inconstant mind, Since that my life on thy revolt doth lie *Sonnet* 92 10
Revolution. Whether better they, Or whether revolution be the same 59 12
Revolving. As one of which doth Tarquin lie revolving The sundry dangers *Lucrece* 127

Reward. Reward not hospitality With such black payment as thou hast pretended *Lucrece* 575
Re-worded. From off a hill whose concave womb re-worded A plaintful story from a sistering vale *Lov. Comp.* 1
Rhetoric. When they have devised What strained touches rhetoric can lend, Thou truly fair wert truly sympathized *Sonnet* 82 10
Did not the heavenly rhetoric of thine eye, . . . Persuade my heart *Pass. Pil.* 29
Rheumatic. O'erworn, despised, rheumatic, and cold *Ven. and Adon.* 135
Rhyme. Cited up in rhymes, And sung by children in succeeding times *Lucrece* 524
With means more blessed than my barren rhyme *Sonnet* 16 4
Were some child of yours alive that time, You should live twice; in it and in my rhyme 17 14
Reserve them for my love, not for their rhyme 32 7
Nor the gilded monuments Of princes, shall outlive this powerful rhyme 55 2
Beauty making beautiful old rhyme In praise of ladies 106 3
Since, spite of him, I'll live in this poor rhyme 107 11
Rhymers. Be thou the tenth Muse, ten times more in worth Than those old nine which rhymers invocate 38 10
Rich. What cares he now for curb or pricking spur? For rich caparisons or trapping gay? *Ven. and Adon.* 286
That she will draw his lips' rich treasure dry 552
Rich preys make true men thieves 724
Pluck down the rich, enrich the poor with treasures 1150
Why is Collatine the publisher Of that rich jewel? *Lucrece* 34
Perchance that envy of so rich a thing, Braving compare, disdainfully did sting 39
But, poorly rich, so wanteth in his store 97
Shelves and sands, The merchant fears, ere rich at home he lands 336
Sets you most rich in youth before my sight *Sonnet* 15 10
With earth and sea's rich gems, With April's first-born flowers 21 6
Wishing me like to one more rich in hope, Featured like him 29 5
And they are rich and ransom all ill deeds 34 14
So am I as the rich, whose blessed key Can bring him to his sweet up-locked treasure 52 1
The rich proud cost of outworn buried age 64 2
Which can say more Than this rich praise, that you alone are you? 84 2
And for that riches where is my deserving? 87 6
And husband nature's riches from expense 94 6
The teeming autumn, big with rich increase 97 6
Whose rich esteeming The owner's tongue doth publish every where 102 3
So thou, being rich in 'Will,' add to thy 'Will' One will of mine 135 11
Within be fed, without be rich no more 146 12
Rich-built. Whose words like wildfire burnt the shining glory Of rich-built Ilion *Lucrece* 1524
Richer. Thy love is better than high birth to me, Richer than wealth *Son.* 91 10
Richest. She was sought by spirits of richest coat, But kept cold distance *Lov. Comp.* 236
Richly. While comments of your praise, richly compiled, Reserve their character with golden quill *Sonnet* 85 2
Rid. Honour thyself to rid me of this shame *Lucrece* 1031
Kill me outright with looks and rid my pain *Sonnet* 139 14
Ride. Anon permit the basest clouds to ride With ugly rack 33 5
Whilst he upon your soundless deep doth ride 80 10
Be anchor'd in the bay where all men ride 137 6
Sometimes her levell'd eyes their carriage ride *Lov. Comp.* 22
Well could he ride, and often men would say 'That horse his mettle from his rider takes' 106
Rider. The steed is stalled up, and even now To tie the rider she begins to prove *Ven. and Adon.* 40
What recketh he his rider's angry stir, His flattering 'Holla?' 283
Look, what a horse should have he did not lack, Save a proud rider 300
As if by some instinct the wretch did know His rider loved not speed *Sonnet* 50 8
Often men would say 'That horse his mettle from his rider takes' *Lov. Comp.* 107
Ridges. Whose ridges with the meeting clouds contend *Ven. and Adon.* 820
Whose waves to imitate the battle sought With swelling ridges *Lucrece* 1439
Ridiculous. Despair and hope makes thee ridiculous *Ven. and Adon.* 988
Rifled. Pure Chastity is rifled of her store *Lucrece* 692
Of that true type hath Tarquin rifled me 1050
Right. Can thy right hand seize love upon thy left? *Ven. and Adon.* 158
Being judge in love, she cannot right her cause 220
Seeming to bury that posterity Which by the rights of time thou needs must have 759
Thou art the next of blood, and 'tis thy right 1184
Proving from world's minority their right *Lucrece* 67
The rough beast that knows no gentle right 545
'Tis thou that spurn'st at right, at law, at reason 880
To wrong the wronger till he render right 943
This hopeless smoke of words doth me no right 1027
Knights, by their oaths, should right poor ladies' harms 1694
By all our country's rights in Rome maintain'd 1838
And your true rights be term'd a poet's rage *Sonnet* 17 11
Mine eye my heart thy picture's sight would bar, My heart mine eye the freedom of that right 46 4
Mine eye's due is thy outward part, And my heart's right thy inward love of heart 46 14
And right perfection wrongfully disgraced 66 7
The right of sepulchres, were shorn away, To live a second life on second head 68 6
To thee I so belong, That for thy right myself will bear all wrong 88 14
Nor I to none alive, That my steel'd sense or changes right or wrong 112 8
And given to time your own dear-purchased right 117 6
Shall will in others seem right gracious? 135 7
In things right true my heart and eyes have erred 137 13
The better angel is a man right fair 144 3
Sometimes they do extend Their view right on *Lov. Comp.* 26
My better angel is a man right fair, My worser spirit a woman colour'd ill *Pass. Pil.* 17
Lest the requiem lack his right *Ph. and Tur.* 16
The turtle saw his right Flaming in the phœnix' sight 34
Rightful. No rightful plea might plead for justice there *Lucrece* 1649
Rightly. And to temptation slow, They rightly do inherit heaven's graces *Sonnet* 94 5
Rigol. A watery rigol goes, Which seems to weep upon the tainted place *Lucrece* 1745
Rigour. Since her best work is ruin'd with thy rigour *Ven. and Adon.* 954
In Ajax' eyes blunt rage and rigour roll'd *Lucrece* 1398
Thou canst not then use rigour in my gaol; And yet thou wilt *Sonnet* 133 12
Ring. This dismal cry rings sadly in her ear *Ven. and Adon.* 889

Ring. Then little strength rings out the doleful knell *Lucrece* 1495
Tearing of papers, breaking rings a-twain . . . . *Lov. Comp.* 6
Crack'd many a ring of posied gold and bone 45
My wether's bell rings doleful knell . . . . *Pil. Pass.* 272
Ringing. Like a heavy-hanging bell, Once set on ringing, with his own weight goes *Lucrece* 1494
Where thy desert may merit praise, By ringing in thy lady's ear . *Pass. Pil.* 326
Riot. It shall be sparing and too full of riot *Ven. and Adon.* 1147
And chide thy beauty and thy straying youth, Who lead thee in their riot *Sonnet* 41 11
Ripe. That did my ripe thoughts in my brain inhearse 86 3
Riper. But as the riper should by time decease 1 3
And stops her pipe in growth of riper days . . . 102 8
Ripe-red. Mulberries and ripe-red cherries *Ven. and Adon.* 1103
Rise. She, by her good will, Will never rise, so he will kiss her still 480
Nay, do not struggle, for thou shalt not rise 710
O, how her fear did make her colour rise! *Lucrece* 257
May feel her heart—poor citizen!—distress'd, Wounding itself to death, rise up and fall, Beating her bulk, that his hand shakes withal 466
Rise, resty Muse, my love's sweet face survey *Sonnet* 100 9
I call Her 'love' for whose dear love I rise and fall 151 14
The morning rise Doth cite each moving sense from idle rest . *Pass. Pil.* 194
Rising. Round rising hillocks, brakes obscure and rough *Ven. and Adon.* 237
But, rising at thy name, doth point out thee As his triumphant prize *Son.* 151 9
Rite. The perfect ceremony of love's rite 23 6
River. Rain added to a river that is rank Perforce will force it overflow the bank . . . . *Ven. and Adon.* 71
An oven that is stopp'd, or river stay'd, Burneth more hotly, swelleth with more rage 331
Bubbling from her breast, it doth divide In two slow rivers . *Lucrece* 1738
Which one by one she in a river threw . *Lov. Comp.* 38
Each cheek a river running from a fount . 283
By shallow rivers, by whose falls Melodious birds sing madrigals *Pass. Pil.* 359
Roaring. As through an arch the violent roaring tide Outruns the eye that doth behold his haste . . . . *Lucrece* 1667
Rob. And all is but to rob thee of a kiss . *Ven. and Adon.* 723
Sun and sharp air Lurk'd like two thieves, to rob him of his fair 1086
I an accessary needs must be To that sweet thief which sourly robs from me *Sonnet* 35 14
Yet what of thee thy poet doth invent He robs thee of and pays it thee again . . . 79 8
Robbed. And every beauty robb'd of his effect *Ven. and Adon.* 1132
Robb'd and ransack'd by injurious theft . *Lucrece* 838
And when the judge is robb'd the prisoner dies 1652
Robb'd others' beds' revenues of their rents . *Sonnet* 142 8
Robbery. I do forgive thy robbery, gentle thief, Although thou steal thee all my poverty . . . 40 9
And to his robbery had annex'd thy breath . 99 11
Robbing. Robbing no old to dress his beauty new . 68 12
Robe. As my chest, Or as the wardrobe which the robe doth hide 52 10
Rock. My throbbing heart shall rock thee day and night *Ven. and Adon.* 1186
Huge rocks, high winds, strong pirates, shelves, and sands . *Lucrece* 335
When rocks impregnable are not so stout, Nor gates of steel so strong, but Time decays . . . *Sonnet* 65 7
There will we sit upon the rocks, And see the shepherds . *Pass. Pil.* 357
Rocked. Her loyal fear! Which struck her sad, and then it faster rock'd *Lucr.* 262
Rocky. Beat at thy rocky and wreck-threatening heart, To soften it 590
What rocky heart to water will not wear? . *Lov. Comp.* 291
Roe. Or as the fleet-foot roe that's tired with chasing . *Ven. and Adon.* 561
Or at the roe which no encounter dare 676
Roll. Deep woes roll forward like a gentle flood . *Lucrece* 1118
Rolled. In Ajax' eyes blunt rage and rigour roll'd 1398
Rolling. About he walks, Rolling his greedy eyeballs in his head 368
An eye more bright than theirs, less false in rolling . *Sonnet* 20 5
Roman. Lust-breathed Tarquin leaves the Roman host . *Lucrece* 3
Well was he welcomed by the Roman dame 51
Thus madly led, The Roman lord marcheth to Lucrece' bed 301
This said, he shakes aloft his Roman blade 505
And softly cried 'Awake, thou Roman dame, And entertain my love' 1628
He with the Romans was esteemed so As silly-jeering idiots are 1811
Courageous Roman, do not steep thy heart In such relenting dew of lamentations 1828
To rouse our Roman gods with invocations 1831
The Romans plausibly did give consent 1854
Rome. So fares it with this faultful lord of Rome 715
And never be forgot in mighty Rome Th' adulterate death of Lucrece and her groom 1644
'Thou wronged lord of Rome,' quoth he, 'arise' 1818
Since Rome herself in them doth stand disgraced 1833
By all our country rights in Rome maintain'd 1838
To show her bleeding body thorough Rome 1851
Rondure. And all things rare That heaven's air in this huge rondure hems *Sonnet* 21 8
Roof. Seeking that beauteous roof to ruinate . 10 7
Room. Your praise shall still find room Even in the eyes of all posterity 55 10
Root. Would root these beauties as he roots the mead *Ven. and Adon.* 636
But low shrubs wither at the cedar's root . *Lucrece* 665
The branches of another root are rotted 823
Unwholesome weeds take root with precious flowers 870
And broils root out the work of masonry . *Sonnet* 55 6
Root pity in thy heart, that when it grows Thy pity may deserve to pitied be . . . 142 11
Rose. More white and red than doves or roses are *Ven. and Adon.* 10
What though the rose have prickles, yet 'tis pluck'd 574
Like lawn being spread upon the blushing rose 590
His breath and beauty set Gloss on the rose, smell to the violet 936
Their silent war of lilies and of roses *Lucrece* 71
First red as roses that on lawn we lay, Then white as lawn, the roses took away . . . 258
Makes the lily pale, And the red rose blush at her own disgrace 479
I know what thorns the growing rose defends 492
Ere the break of day, And, ere I rose, was Tarquin gone away 1281
That thereby beauty's rose might never die *Sonnet* 1 2
Roses have thorns, and silver fountains mud 35 2
The rose looks fair, but fairer we it deem For that sweet odour 54 3
As deep a dye As the perfumed tincture of the roses 54 6
Sweet roses do not so; Of their sweet deaths are sweetest odours made 54 11
Why should poor beauty indirectly seek Roses of shadow, since his rose is true? . . . 67 8
Which, like a canker in the fragrant rose, Doth spot the beauty 95 2

Rose. Nor did I wonder at the lily's white, Nor praise the deep vermilion in the rose . . . *Sonnet* 98 10
The roses fearfully on thorns did stand, One blushing shame 99 8
For nothing this wide universe I call, Save thou, my rose 109 14
I have seen roses damask'd, red and white, But no such roses see I in her cheeks . . . 130 5
The glowing roses That flame through water which their hue encloses *Lov. Comp.* 286
He rose and ran away; ah, fool too froward! . *Pil. Pass.* 56
Sweet rose, fair flower, untimely pluck'd, soon vaded, Pluck'd in the bud 131
There will I make thee a bed of roses, With a thousand fragrant posies 361
Rose-cheek'd Adonis hied him to the chase *Ven. and Adon.* 3
Rosy. Her lily hand her rosy cheek lies under, Cozening the pillow of a lawful kiss . . . *Lucrece* 386
Love's not Time's fool, though rosy lips and cheeks Within his bending sickle's compass come. *Sonnet* 116 9
Rot. Fair flowers that are not gather'd in their prime Rot and consume themselves in little time *Ven. and Adon.* 132
Rotted. The branches of another root are rotted *Lucrece* 823
Rotten. With rotten damps ravish the morning air 778
Shall rotten death make conquest of the stronger? 1767
Hiding thy bravery in their rotten smoke *Sonnet* 34 4
Or you survive when I in earth am rotten 81 2
Rough. Round rising hillocks, brakes obscure and rough *Ven. and Adon.* 237
She knows it is no gentle chase, But the blunt boar, rough bear, or lion proud 884
The rough beast that knows no gentle right *Lucrece* 545
But chide rough winter that the flower hath kill'd 1255
Rough winds do shake the darling buds of May . *Sonnet* 18 3
Rough-grown. In men, as in a rough-grown grove, remain Cave-keeping evils that obscurely sleep . . . *Lucrece* 1249
Round rising hillocks, brakes obscure and rough *Ven. and Adon.* 237
These lovely caves, these round enchanting pits, Open'd their mouths to swallow Venus' liking . . . 247
O fairest mover on this mortal round, Would thou wert as I am . 368
His pale cheeks and the blood Which in round drops upon their whiteness stood 1170
Left their round turrets destitute and pale . *Lucrece* 441
And turn the giddy round of Fortune's wheel . 952
She throws her eyes about the painting round 1499
Those round clear pearls of his, that move thy pity, Are balls of quenchless fire 1553
Round about her tear-distained eye Blue circles stream'd 1586
What rounds, what bounds, what course, what stop he makes! *Lov. Comp.* 109
She will not stick to round me i' the ear, To teach my tongue to be so long *Pass. Pil.* 349
Round-hoof'd, short-jointed, fetlocks shag and long *Ven. and Adon.* 295
Rouse. No dog shall rouse thee, though a thousand bark 240
To rouse our Roman gods with invocations *Lucrece* 1831
Rouseth. He rouseth up himself and makes a pause 541
Rubbing. As vaded gloss no rubbing will refresh . *Pass. Pil.* 176
Rubies. Of paled pearls and rubies red as blood *Lov. Comp.* 198
Ruby-coloured. Once more the ruby-colour'd portal open'd *Ven. and Adon.* 451
Rude. Beaten away by brain-sick rude desire *Lucrece* 175
His hand, that yet remains upon her breast,—Rude ram! 464
Let those whom Nature hath not made for store, Harsh featureless and rude, barrenly perish . . . *Sonnet* 11 10
Once more re-survey These poor rude lines of thy deceased lover 32 4
Thou art all my art and dost advance As high as learning my rude ignorance . . . 78 14
Savage, extreme, rude, cruel, not to trust 129 4
Rudely. Throwing his mantle rudely o'er his arm *Lucrece* 170
Enforced hate, Instead of love's coy touch, shall rudely tear thee 669
And maiden virtue rudely strumpeted *Sonnet* 66 6
Rudeness. His rudeness so with his authorized youth Did livery falseness in a pride of truth *Lov. Comp.* 104
Rudest. For if it see the rudest or gentlest sight, . . . it shapes them to your feature *Sonnet* 113 9
Ruffian. The staring ruffian shall it keep in quiet *Ven. and Adon.* 1149
Ruffle. Sometime a blusterer, that the ruffle knew Of court, of city *L. Comp.* 58
Ruin. To whose weak ruins muster troops of cares *Lucrece* 720
Time's ruin, beauty's wreck, and grim care's reign 1451
Ruin hath taught me thus to ruminate . *Sonnet* 64 11
Ruinate. To ruinate proud buildings with thy hours *Lucrece* 944
Seeking that beauteous roof to ruinate . *Sonnet* 10 7
Ruined. Since her best work is ruin'd with thy rigour *Ven. and Adon.* 954
Bare ruin'd choirs, where late the sweet birds sang . *Sonnet* 73 4
And ruin'd love, when it is built anew, Grows fairer than at first 119 11
Ruining. Which prove more short than waste or ruining . 125 4
Rule. Grief hath two tongues, and never woman yet Could rule them both without ten women's wit *Ven. and Adon.* 1008
Love's arms are peace, 'gainst rule, 'gainst sense, 'gainst shame *Lov. Comp.* 271
Let reason rule things worthy blame, As well as fancy partial might *Pass. Pil.* 301
Ruled. But if thou needs wilt hunt, be ruled by me *Ven. and Adon.* 673
Ruminate. Ruin hath taught me thus to ruminate . *Sonnet* 64 11
Run. And whether he run or fly they know not whether *Ven. and Adon.* 304
Sometime he runs among a flock of sheep, To make the cunning hounds mistake their smell 685
Lest the deceiving harmony should run Into the quiet closure of my breast 781
And homeward through the dark laund runs apace 813
And as she runs, the bushes in the way Some catch her by the neck 871
This way she runs, and now she will no further, But back retires 905
He runs, and chides his vanish'd, loathed delight *Lucrece* 742
At his own shadow let the thief run mad 997
Since from thee going he went wilful-slow, Towards thee I'll run *Sonnet* 51 14
Lo! as a careful housewife runs to catch One of her feather'd creatures broke away . . . 143 1
Ah, that I had my lady at this bay, To kiss and clip me till I run away! *Pass. Pil.* 156
Runnest. So runn'st thou after that which flies from thee *Sonnet* 143 9
Running. Each cheek a river running from a fount *Lov. Comp.* 283
Rushes. And forth she rushes, snorts, and neighs aloud . *Ven. and Adon.* 262
Embracing bushes, As fearful of him, part, through whom he rushes 630
He takes it from the rushes where it lies *Lucrece* 318
Rushing. As the fair and fiery-pointed sun, Rushing from forth a cloud, bereaves our sight 373
Rust. Foul-cankering rust the hidden treasure frets *Ven. and Adon.* 767
Rusty. Softer than wax, and yet, as iron, rusty . *Pass. Pil.* 88
Ruth. Looking with pretty ruth upon my pain . *Sonnet* 132 4
Deep-wounded with a boar, Deep in the thigh, a spectacle of ruth! *Pass. Pil.* 127
Ruthless. Ruthless beasts they will not cheer thee . . . 394

S

Sable Night, mother of Dread and Fear *Lucrece* 117
My sable ground of sin I will not paint, To hide the truth 1074
And sable curls all silver'd o'er with white *Sonnet* 12 4
And thou treble-dated crow, That thy sable gender makest *Ph. and Tur.* 18
Sacked. Her house is sack'd, her quiet interrupted *Lucrece* 1170
Sacred. Her sacred temple spotted, spoil'd, corrupted 1172
Serving with looks his sacred majesty *Sonnet* 7 4
Tan sacred beauty, blunt the sharp'st intents, Divert strong minds 115 7
My parts had power to charm a sacred nun *Lov. Comp.* 260
Sad. So she at these sad signs draws up her breath *Ven. and Adon.* 929
Her loyal fear! Which struck her sad, and then it faster rock'd *Lucrece* 262
Sad pause and deep regard beseem the sage 277
Her sad behaviour feeds his vulture folly 556
Solemn night with slow sad gait descended To ugly hell 1081
Sad souls are slain in merry company 1110
Make thy sad grove in my dishevell'd hair 1129
So I at each sad strain will strain a tear 1131
There we will unfold To creatures stern sad tunes, to change their kinds 1147
That he may vow, in that sad hour of mine, Revenge on him that made me stop my breath 1179
And sorts a sad look to her lady's sorrow 1221
To see sad sights moves more than hear them told 1324
That one might see those far-off eyes look sad 1386
On this sad shadow Lucrece spends her eyes 1457
So Lucrece set a-work, sad tales doth tell 1496
Which when her sad-beholding husband saw, Amazedly in her sad face he stares 1591
Collatine and his consorted lords With sad attention long to hear her words 1610
Begins the sad dirge of her certain ending 1612
With sad set eyes, and wretched arms across 1662
But she, that yet her sad task hath not said, The protestation stops 1699
Tell o'er The sad account of fore-bemoaned moan *Sonnet* 30 11
No longer glad, I send them back again and straight grow sad 45 14
Let this sad interim like the ocean be Which parts the shore 56 9
Like a sad slave, stay and think of nought Save, where you are 57 11
Sad mortality o'er-sways their power 65 2
And the sad augurs mock their own presage 107 6
And thither hied, a sad distemper'd guest, But found no cure 153 12
O, that sad breath his spongy lungs bestow'd! *Lov. Comp.* 326
Herald sad and trumpet be, To whose sound chaste wings obey *Ph. and Tur.* 3
Sad-beholding. Which when her sad-beholding husband saw, Amazedly in her sad face he stares *Lucrece* 1590
Saddle-bow. Vouchsafe, thou wonder, to alight thy steed, And rein his proud head to the saddle-bow *Ven. and Adon.* 14
Sadly. This dismal cry rings sadly in her ear 889
Here she meets another sadly scowling, To whom she speaks 917
Her pity-pleading eyes are sadly fixed In the remorseless wrinkles of his face *Lucrece* 561
He like a thievish dog creeps sadly thence 736
This plot of death when sadly she had laid 1212
Music to hear, why hear'st thou music sadly? *Sonnet* 8 1
Found yet moe letters sadly penn'd in blood *Lov. Comp.* 47
Sadness. Therefore, in sadness, now I will away *Ven. and Adon.* 807
Sad-tuned. And down I laid to list the sad-tuned tale *Lov. Comp.* 4
Safest. With safest distance I mine honour shielded 151
Sage. This sorrow to the sage, This dying virtue, this surviving shame *Lucr.* 222
Sad pause and deep regard beseem the sage 277
Said. This said, impatience chokes her pleading tongue *Ven. and Adon.* 217
So of concealed sorrow may be said; Free vent of words love's fire doth assuage 333
They answer all 'Tis so:' And would say after her, if she said 'No' 852
This said, she hasteth to a myrtle grove 865
This said, his guilty hand pluck'd up the latch *Lucrece* 358
This said, he shakes aloft his Roman blade 505
This said, he sets his foot upon the light 673
Thou art well appaid As well to hear as grant what he hath said 915
This said, from her be-tumbled couch she starteth 1037
But she, that yet her sad task hath not said, The protestation stops 1699
No man could distinguish what he said 1785
This said, he struck his hand upon his breast 1842
And yet it may be said I loved her dearly *Sonnet* 42 2
Be it not said Thy edge should blunter be than appetite 56 1
Even those that said I could not love you dearer 115 2
Those lips that Love's own hand did make Breathed forth the sound that said 'I hate' 145 2
This said, in top of rage the lines she rents *Lov. Comp.* 55
That's to ye sworn to none was ever said 180
This said, his watery eyes he did dismount 281
Have you not heard it said full oft, A woman's nay doth stand for nought? *Pass. Pil.* 339
Yet will she blush, here be it said, To hear her secrets so bewray'd 351
Sail. Wide as the ocean is, The humble as the proudest sail doth bear *Son.* 80 6
Was it the proud full sail of his great verse? 86 1
I have hoisted sail to all the winds Which should transport me 117 7
Saint. This earthly saint, adored by this devil, Little suspecteth *Lucrece* 85
And would corrupt my saint to be a devil *Sonnet* 144 7; *Pass. Pil.* 21
Think women still to strive with men, To sin and never for to saint 342
Saint-like. Or blot with hell-born sin such saint-like forms *Lucrece* 1519
Saith. Nature that made thee, with herself at strife, Saith that the world hath ending with thy life *Ven. and Adon.* 12
He saith she is immodest, blames her 'miss 53
'Fondling,' she saith, 'since I have hemm'd thee here Within the circuit of this ivory pale, I'll be a park, and thou shalt be my deer' 229
'Give me my hand,' saith he, 'why dost thou feel it?' 373
Or whether shall I say, mine eye saith true? *Sonnet* 114 3
Sake. And for my sake hath learn'd to sport and dance, To toy *V. and A.* 105
For thy husband and thy children's sake, Tender my suit *Lucrece* 533
My husband is thy friend; for his sake spare me 582
Thyself art mighty; for thine own sake leave me: Myself a weakling 583
And for my sake serve thou false Tarquin so 1197
For my sake, when I might charm thee so 1681
And for my sake even so doth she abuse me, Suffering my friend for my sake to approve her *Sonnet* 42 7

Sake. And both for my sake lay on me this cross *Sonnet* 42 12
To play the watchman ever for thy sake 61 12
O, for my sake do you with Fortune chide, The guilty goddess 111 1
That put'st forth all to use, And sue a friend came debtor for my sake 134 11
To me that languish'd for her sake 145 3
Do I not think on thee, when I forgot Am of myself, all tyrant, for thy sake? 149 4
And yet do question make What I should do again for such a sake *Lov. Comp.* 322
Paler for sorrow than her milk-white dove, For Adon's sake *Pass. Pil.* 120
Salt. My sighs are blown away, my salt tears gone *Ven. and Adon.* 1071
The petty streams that pay a daily debt To their salt sovereign *Lucrece* 650
Salt-waved. Who in a salt-waved ocean quench their light 1231
Salutation. For why should others' false adulterate eyes Give salutation to my sportive blood? *Sonnet* 121 6
Salutes. Venus salutes him with this fair good-morrow *Ven. and Adon.* 859
Salve. Calls it balm, Earth's sovereign salve to do a goddess good *V. and A.* 28
To see the salve doth make the wound ache more *Lucrece* 1116
For no man well of such a salve can speak *Sonnet* 34 7
Then tender'd The humble salve which wounded bosoms fits 120 12
Salving thy amiss, Excusing thy sins more than thy sins are 35 7
Same. Thou art not what thou seem'st; and if the same, Thou seem'st not what thou art, a god, a king *Lucrece* 600
They think not but that every eye can see The same disgrace 751
His sighs, his sorrows, make a saw, To push grief on, and back the same grief draw 1673
Will play the tyrants to the very same *Sonnet* 5 3
For that same groan doth put this in my mind 50 13
Whether better they, Or whether revolution be the same 59 12
Those same tongues that give thee so thine own In other accents do this praise confound 69 6
Why write I still all one, ever the same, And keep invention in a noted weed? 76 5
Like prayers divine, I must each day say o'er the very same 108 6
Property was thus appalled, That the self was not the same *Ph. and Tur.* 38
Sanctified. This device was sent me from a nun, Or sister sanctified, of holiest note *Lov. Comp.* 233
Sands. Or, like a nymph, with long dishevell'd hair, Dance on the sands, and yet no footing seen *Ven. and Adon.* 148
Huge rocks, high winds, strong pirates, shelves, and sands *Lucrece* 335
Sang. Bare ruin'd choirs, where late the sweet birds sang *Sonnet* 73 4
Sap. She crops the stalk, and in the breach appears Green dropping sap, which she compares to tears *Ven. and Adon.* 1176
To dry the old oak's sap and cherish springs *Lucrece* 950
The bark peel'd from the lofty pine, His leaves will wither and his sap decay 1168
Sap check'd with frost and lusty leaves quite gone *Sonnet* 5 7
Vaunt in their youthful sap, at height decrease 15 7
Sapphire. The heaven-hued sapphire and the opal blend With objects manifold *Lov. Comp.* 215
Sappy. Herbs for their smell, and sappy plants to bear *Ven. and Adon.* 165
Sat. Now was she just before him as he sat 349
When he again desires her, being sat, Her grievance with his hearing to divide *Lov. Comp.* 66
Satiety. And yet not cloy thy lips with loathed satiety *Ven. and Adon.* 19
Satire. Be a satire to decay, And make Time's spoils despised every where *Sonnet* 100 11
Satisfaction. Nor gives it satisfaction to our blood, That we must curb it upon others' proof *Lov. Comp.* 162
Satisfied. As the grim lion fawneth o'er his prey, Sharp hunger by the conquest satisfied *Lucrece* 422
Satisfy. Which, having all, all could not satisfy 96
Saturn. That heavy Saturn laugh'd and leap'd with him *Sonnet* 98 4
Sauces. To bitter sauces did I frame my feeding 118 6
Saucily. While others saucily Promise more speed, but do it leisurely *Lucr.* 1348
Saucy. My saucy bark inferior far to his *Sonnet* 80 7
Since saucy jacks so happy are in this, Give them thy fingers 128 13
Savage. Savage, extreme, rude, cruel, not to trust 129 4
Save. Look, what a horse should have he did not lack, Save a proud rider on so proud a back *Ven. and Adon.* 300
That nothing in him seem'd inordinate, Save sometime too much wonder of his eye *Lucrece* 95
And every one to rest themselves betake, Save thieves, and cares 126
Unconquered, Save of their lord no bearing yoke they knew 409
Get me hither paper, ink, and pen: Yet save that labour, for I have them here 1290
Himself, behind, Was left unseen, save to the eye of mind 1426
Nothing 'gainst Time's scythe can make defence Save breed *Sonnet* 12 14
Save that my soul's imaginary sight Presents thy shadow 27 9
Thee have I not lock'd up in any chest, Save where thou art not 48 10
Think of nought Save, where you are how happy you make those 57 12
From these would I be gone, Save that, to die, I leave my love alone 66 14
Possessing or pursuing no delight, Save what is had or must from you be took 75 12
For nothing this wide universe I call, Save thou, my rose 109 14
In nothing art thou black save in thy deeds 131 13
Every thing did banish moan, Save the nightingale alone *Pass. Pil.* 380
Every fowl of tyrant wing, Save the eagle, feather'd king *Ph. and Tur.* 11
Saved. 'I hate' from hate away she threw, And saved my life, saying 'not you' *Sonnet* 145 14
Savour. Both favour, savour, hue, and qualities *Ven. and Adon.* 747
Paying too much rent, For compound sweet forgoing simple savour *Son.* 125 7
Saw. His eyes saw her eyes as they had not seen them *Ven. and Adon.* 357
But when he saw his love, his youth's fair fee, He held such petty bondage in disdain 393
As those poor birds that helpless berries saw 604
Ne'er saw the beauteous livery that he wore 1107
Who fears a sentence or an old man's saw *Lucrece* 244
The more she saw the blood his cheeks replenish, The more she thought he spied in her some blemish 1357
That one would swear he saw them quake and tremble 1393
Which when her sad-beholding husband saw, Amazedly in her sad face he stares 1590
Even so his sighs, his sorrows, make a saw, To push grief on 1672
I never saw that you did painting need *Sonnet* 83 1

Saw. Three hot Junes burn'd, Since first I saw you fresh, which yet are green . . . *Sonnet* 104 8
Still losing when I saw myself to win . . . 119 4
I grant I never saw a goddess go . . . 130 11
When she saw my woeful state, Straight in her heart did mercy come . 145 4
Whereon the thought might think sometime it saw . . *Lov. Comp.* 10
Each eye that saw him did enchant the mind . . . 89
Saw how deceits were gilded in his smiling . . . 172
He saw more wounds than one, And blushing fled, and left her *Pass. Pil.* 129
The turtle saw his right Flaming in the phœnix' sight *Ph. and Tur.* 34
Reason, in itself confounded, Saw division grow together . . . 42
Saw'st thou not signs of fear lurk in mine eye? *Ven. and Adon.* 644
Sawn. What largeness thinks in Paradise was sawn *Lov. Comp.* 91
Say. Now which way shall she turn? what shall she say? *Ven. and Adon.* 253
As who should say 'Lo, thus my strength is tried' . . . 280
His flattering 'Holla,' or his 'Stand, I say' . . . 284
For lovers say, the heart hath treble wrong When it is barr'd the aidance of the tongue . . . 329
Say, that the sense of feeling were bereft me . . . 439
May say, the plague is banish'd by thy breath . . . 510
Say, for non-payment that the debt should double . . . 521
Now let me say 'Good night,' and so say you; If you will say so . . . 535
Ere he says 'Adieu,' The honey fee of parting tender'd is . . . 537
'Sweet boy,' she says, 'this night I'll waste in sorrow' . . . 583
Shall we meet to-morrow? Say, shall we? shall we? . . . 586
'Fie, fie,' he says, 'you crush me; let me go' . . . 611
More I could tell, but more I dare not say . . . 805
She says ''Tis so:' they answer all ''Tis so;' And would say after her, if she said 'No' . . . 851
And says, within her bosom it shall dwell . . . 1173
As who should say 'This glove to wanton tricks Is not inured' . *Lucrece* 320
Foul sin may say, He learn'd to sin, and thou didst teach the way . 629
She says, her subjects with foul insurrection Have batter'd down her consecrated wall . . . 722
We have no good that we can say is ours . . . 873
Faint not, faint heart, but stoutly say 'So be it' . . . 1209
Then be this all the task it hath to say . . . 1618
They all at once began to say, Her body's stain her mind untainted clears . 1709
'He, he,' she says, But more than 'he' her poor tongue could not speak . 1717
The father says 'She's mine.' 'O, mine she is,' Replies her husband . 1795
Let no mourner say He weeps for her, for she was only mine . . 1797
To say, within thine own deep-sunken eyes . . . *Sonnet* 2 7
My love, you know You had a father: let your son say so . . 13 14
Or say with princes if it shall go well, By oft predict that I in heaven find 14 7
The age to come would say 'This poet lies' . . . 17 7
Let them say more that like of hearsay well . . . 21 13
So I, for fear of trust, forget to say . . . 23 5
How would, I say, mine eyes be blessed made By looking on thee! . 43 9
The defendant doth that plea deny And says in him thy fair appearance lies . . . 46 8
To say 'Thus far the miles are measured from thy friend' . . 50 3
That I might see what the old world could say To this composed wonder 59 9
O, if, I say, you look upon this verse When I perhaps compounded am with clay . . . 71 9
Then thank him not for that which he doth say . . . 79 13
Who is it that says most? which can say more Than this rich praise? 84 1
I say ''Tis so, 'tis true,' And to the most of praise add something more 85 9
Say that thou didst forsake me for some fault . . . 89 1
Some say thy fault is youth, some wantonness; Some say thy grace is youth and gentle sport . . . 96 1
Wilt thou not haply say 'Truth needs no colour, with his colour fix'd' 101 5
Like prayers divine, I must each day say o'er the very same . . 108 6
O, never say that I was false of heart . . . 109 1
Or whether shall I say, mine eye saith true? . . . 114 3
Fearing of time's tyranny, Might I not then say 'Now I love you best?' 115 10
Then might I not say so, To give full growth to that which still doth grow 115 13
Since my appeal says I did strive to prove The constancy and virtue of your love . . . 117 13
Becoming of their woe, That every tongue says beauty should look so 127 14
Some say that thee behold Thy face hath not the power to make love groan . . . 131 5
To say they err I dare not be so bold, Although I swear it to myself alone 131 7
Mine eyes seeing this, say this is not . . . 137 11
Wherefore says she not she is unjust? And wherefore say not I that I am old? . . . 138 9
What means the world to say it is not so? . . . 148 6
Canst thou, O cruel! say I love thee not? . . . 149 1
Often men would say 'That horse his mettle from his rider takes' *Lov. Comp.* 106
And dialogued for him what he would say . . . 132
For further I could say 'This man's untrue' . . . 169
But wherefore says my love that she is young? And wherefore say not I that I am old? . . . *Pass. Pil.* 9
But plainly say thou lovest her well, And set thy person forth to sell . 309
What though she strive to try her strength, And ban and brawl, and say thee nay . . . 318
When craft hath taught her thus to say . . . 320
Saying, some shape in Sinon's was abused . . . *Lucrece* 1529
'I hate' from hate away she threw, And saved my life, saying 'not you' *Sonnet* 145 14
Scale. Whose ranks of blue veins, as his hand did scale, Left their round turrets destitute and pale . . . *Lucrece* 440
Under that colour am I come to scale Thy never-conquer'd fort . . 481
That phraseless hand, Whose white weighs down the airy scale of praise *Lov. Comp.* 226
Scalps. The scalps of many, almost hid behind, To jump up higher seem'd, to mock the mind . . . *Lucrece* 1413
Scandal. The scandal will survive, And be an eye-sore in my golden coat 204
Thou plantest scandal and displacest laud . . . 887
For greatest scandal waits on greatest state . . . 1006
Which vulgar scandal stamp'd upon my brow . . . *Sonnet* 112 2
Scant. But if store of crowns be scant, No man will supply thy want *Pass. Pil.* 409
Scanted. I have scanted all Wherein I should your great deserts repay *Sonnet* 117 1
'Scape. 'For day,' quoth she, 'night's 'scapes doth open lay' *Lucrece* 747
That not a heart which in his level came Could 'scape *Lov. Comp.* 310
'Scaped. Ah, do not, when my heart hath 'scaped this sorrow, Come in the rearward of a conquer'd woe . . . *Sonnet* 90 5
'Scapeth. The scars of battle 'scapeth by the flight . *Lov. Comp.* 244
Scar. The scar that will, despite of cure, remain . . . *Lucrece* 732
O unfelt sore! crest-wounding, private scar! . . . *Lucrece* 828
The scars of battle 'scapeth by the flight . . . *Lov. Comp.* 244
Scarce. And scarce hath eyes his treasure to behold . . . *Lucrece* 857
And yet the duteous vassal scarce is gone . . . 1360
Scarce had the sun dried up the dewy morn . . . *Pass. Pil.* 71
And scarce the herd gone to the hedge for shade . . . 72
That to hear her so complain, Scarce I could from tears refrain . . . 388
Scarcely. Thou shalt strangely pass And scarcely greet me with that sun, thine eye . . . *Sonnet* 49 6
Scarcity. Self-loving nuns, That on the earth would breed a scarcity *Ven. and Adon.* 753
Scarlet. His scarlet lust came evidence to swear That my poor beauty had purloin'd his eyes . . . *Lucrece* 1650
Not from those lips of thine, That have profaned their scarlet ornaments *Sonnet* 142 6
Scatter. That which they possess They scatter and unloose it from their bond *Lucrece* 136
Scene. Co-supremes and stars of love, As chorus to their tragic scene *Ph. and Tur.* 52
Scent-snuffing. The hot scent-snuffing hounds are driven to doubt *V. and A.* 692
Sceptre. Would with the sceptre straight be strucken down . *Lucrece* 217
Schedule. By this short schedule Collatine may know Her grief . . . 1312
Of folded schedules had she many a one, Which she perused *Lov. Comp.* 43
School. Princes are the glass, the school, the book, Where subjects' eyes do learn . . . *Lucrece* 615
And wilt thou be the school where Lust shall learn? . . . 617
Busy yourselves in skill-contending schools . . . 1018
Now set thy long-experienced wit to school . . . 1820
Scope. Desiring this man's art and that man's scope . *Sonnet* 29 7
Blessed are you, whose worthiness gives scope . . . 52 13
To find out shames and idle hours in me, The scope and tenour of thy jealousy? . . . 61 8
Having such a scope to show her pride . . . 103 2
Three themes in one, which wondrous scope affords . . . 105 12
Scorch. But his hot heart, which fond desire doth scorch, Puffs forth another wind . . . *Lucrece* 314
Score. Nor need I tallies thy dear love to score . . . *Sonnet* 122 10
Scorn. Hunting he loved, but love he laugh'd to scorn *Ven. and Adon.* 4
To love a cheek that smiles at thee in scorn! . . . 252
Spurns at his love and scorns the heat he feels . . . 311
The sun doth scorn you and the wind doth hiss you . . . 1084
For in my death I murder shameful scorn . . . *Lucrece* 1189
In scorn of nature, art gave lifeless life . . . 1374
So mild, that Patience seem'd to scorn his woes . . . 1505
Such wealth brings That then I scorn to change my state with kings *Son.* 29 14
To set me light And place my merit in the eye of scorn . . . 88 2
In scorn or friendship, nill I construe whether . . . *Pass. Pil.* 188
In black mourn I, All fears scorn I, Love hath forlorn me, Living in thrall 264
And twice desire, ere it be day, That which with scorn she put away . 316
Scorned. Be scorn'd like old men of less truth than tongue . *Sonnet* 17 10
Scornful. That hard heart of thine, Hath taught them scornful tricks *Ven. and Adon.* 501
Shall remain The scornful mark of every open eye . . *Lucrece* 520
Scornfully. His eye, which scornfully glisters like fire, Shows his hot courage and his high desire . . . *Ven. and Adon.* 275
Looking scornfully, he doth despise His naked armour . . *Lucrece* 187
Scorning. Scorning his churlish drum and ensign red . *Ven. and Adon.* 107
Yet sometimes falls an orient drop beside, Which her cheek melts, as scorning it should pass, To wash the foul face of the sluttish ground . . . 982
Scowls. He scowls and hates himself for his offence . . . *Lucrece* 738
Scowling. Here she meets another sadly scowling, To whom she speaks *Ven. and Adon.* 917
Scraps. One that by alms doth live Disdain to him disdained scraps to give *Lucrece* 987
Scratch. Each envious brier his weary legs doth scratch *Ven. and Adon.* 705
And wast afeard to scratch her wicked foe . . . *Lucrece* 1035
With my knife scratch out the angry eyes Of all the Greeks . . . 1469
Scratched. Shaking their scratch'd ears, bleeding as they go *Ven. and Adon.* 924
Scroll. With a steadfast eye Receives the scroll without or yea or no *Lucrece* 1340
Scuds. Sometime he scuds far off and there he stares . *Ven. and Adon.* 301
Scythe. Nothing 'gainst Time's scythe can make defence Save breed *Son.* 12 13
Nothing stands but for his scythe to mow . . . 60 12
Give my love fame faster than Time wastes life; So thou prevent'st his scythe and crooked knife . . . 100 14
I will be true, despite thy scythe and thee . . . 123 14
Scythed. Time had not scythed all that youth begun, Nor youth all quit *Lov. Comp.* 12
Sea. The sea hath bounds, but deep desire hath none . *Ven. and Adon.* 389
'Thou art,' quoth she, 'a sea, a sovereign king' . . . *Lucrece* 652
Thy sea within a puddle's womb is hearsed, And not the puddle in thy sea dispersed . . . 657
So she, deep-drenched in a sea of care, Holds disputation . . . 1100
With earth and sea's rich gems, With April's first-born flowers . *Sonnet* 21 6
For nimble thought can jump both sea and land As soon as think the place where he would be . . . 44 7
Brass, nor stone, nor earth, nor boundless sea . . . 65 1
The mountain or the sea, the day or night, The crow or dove . . 113 11
The sea, all water, yet receives rain still . . . 135 9
Seal. Pure lips, sweet seals in my soft lips imprinted . *Ven. and Adon.* 511
To stamp the seal of time in aged things . . . *Lucrece* 941
She carved thee for her seal, and meant thereby Thou shouldst print more, not let that copy die . . . *Sonnet* 11 13
Death's second self, that seals up all in rest . . . 73 8
Sealed. Her letter now is seal'd, and on it writ 'At Ardea to my lord' *Lucr.* 1331
And seal'd false bonds of love as oft as mine . . . *Sonnet* 142 7
Affectedly Enswathed, and seal'd to curious secrecy . *Lov. Comp.* 49
Sealing. What bargains may I make, still to be sealing? *Ven. and Adon.* 512
Seal-manual. Set thy seal-manual on my wax-red lips . . . 516
Seaman. Like a red morn, that ever yet betoken'd Wreck to the seaman . 454
Search. For mirth doth search the bottom of annoy . . . *Lucrece* 1109
Seared. Some beauty peep'd through lattice of sear'd age . *Lov. Comp.* 14
Season. And now the happy season once more fits . *Ven. and Adon.* 327
Now serves the season that they may surprise The silly lambs *Lucrece* 166
Whoever plots the sin, thou 'point'st the season . . . 879
Of good or evil luck, Of plagues, of dearths, or seasons quality *Sonnet* 14 4
Make glad and sorry seasons as thou fleets . . . 19 5
Three beauteous springs to yellow autumn turn'd In process of the seasons have I seen . . . 104 6
Seasoned. In the brine That season'd woe had pelleted in tears *Lov. Comp.* 18
Seasoning the earth with showers of silver brine . . . *Lucrece* 796

Seat. That oft they interchange each other's seat . . . *Lucrece* 70
And in the self-same seat sits Collatine . . . 289
Ay me! but yet thou mightst my seat forbear . . . *Sonnet* 41 9
Fair, kind, and true, have often lived alone, Which three till now never kept seat in one . . . 105 14
Seated. Some dark deep desert, seated from the way . . . *Lucrece* 1144
Second. Struck dead at first, what needs a second striking? *Ven. and Adon.* 250
A second fear through all her sinews spread . . . 903
Labouring for invention, bear amiss The second burthen of a former child *Sonnet* 59 4
The right of sepulchres, were shorn away, To live a second life on second head . . . 68 7
Which by and by black night doth take away, Death's second self . 73 8
Which is not mix'd with seconds, knows no art . . . 125 11
Secrecy. Nor read the subtle-shining secrecies Writ in the glassy margents of such books . . . *Lucrece* 101
Thus breathes she forth her spite Against the unseen secrecy of night . 763
Affectedly Enswathed, and seal'd to curious secrecy . . . *Lov. Comp.* 49
Secret. For thy meed A thousand honey secrets shalt thou know *V. and A.* 16
Birds never limed no secret bushes fear . . . *Lucrece* 88
But if thou yield, I rest thy secret friend . . . 526
Thy secret pleasure turns to open shame . . . 890
Nor shall he smile at thee in secret thought . . . 1065
And therein so ensconced his secret evil . . . 1515
This huge stage presenteth nought but shows Whereon the stars in secret influence comment . . . *Sonnet* 15 4
Yet will she blush, here be it said, To hear her secrets so bewray'd *Pass. Pil.* 352
Securely. So guiltless she securely gives good cheer And reverend welcome . . . *Lucrece* 89
Seducing. To thee, my heaved-up hands appeal, Not to seducing lust, thy rash relier . . . 639
See. Her help she sees, but help she cannot get . . . *Ven. and Adon.* 93
Why dost abhor me? Thou canst not see one wrinkle in my brow . 139
He sees his love, and nothing else he sees . . . 287
Proud, as females are, to see him woo her, She puts on outward strangeness 309
He sees her coming, and begins to glow . . . 337
Who sees his true-love in her naked bed . . . 397
Though neither eyes nor ears, to hear nor see, Yet should I be in love by touching thee . . . 437
And that I could not see, nor hear, nor touch . . . 440
Then shalt thou see the dew-bedabbled wretch Turn, and return . 703
'In night,' quoth she, 'desire sees best of all' . . . 720
Thou hast no eyes to see, But hatefully at random dost thou hit . 939
Those eyes that taught all other eyes to see . . . 952
To see his face the lion walk'd along Behind some hedge . . . 1093
If he did see his face, why then I know He thought to kiss him . 1109
Night-wandering weasels shriek to see him there . . . *Lucrece* 307
Who sees the lurking serpent steps aside . . . 362
What could he see but mightily he noted? . . . 414
I see what crosses my attempt will bring . . . 491
Wipe the dim mist from thy doting eyne, That thou shalt see thy state and pity mine . . . 644
Drunken Desire must vomit his receipt, Ere he can see his own abomination 704
They think not but that every eye can see The same disgrace . . 750
And time to see one that by alms doth live Disdain to him disdained scraps to give . . . 986
Let him have time to see his friends his foes . . . 988
Cloudy Lucrece shames herself to see . . . 1084
Thus cavils she with every thing she sees . . . 1093
To see the salve doth make the wound ache more . . . 1116
Oversee this will; How was I overseen that thou shalt see it! . 1206
Vouchsafe t'afford—If ever, love, thy Lucrece thou wilt see—Some present speed to come and visit me . . . 1306
To see sad sights moves more than hear them told . . . 1324
Lucrece thought he blush'd to see her shame . . . 1344
There might you see the labouring pioner . . . 1380
That one might see those far-off eyes look sad . . . 1386
There pleading might you see grave Nestor stand . . . 1401
Sharing joy To see their youthful sons bright weapons wield . . 1432
Many she sees where cares have carved some . . . 1445
At last she sees a wretched image bound . . . 1501
Priam wets his eyes, To see those borrow'd tears that Sinon sheds . 1549
They that watch see time how slow it creeps . . . 1575
That I no more can see what once I was . . . 1764
Live again and see Thy father die, and not thy father thee! . 1770
And see thy blood warm when thou feel'st it cold . . . *Sonnet* 2 14
So thou through windows of thine age shalt see . . . 3 11
And see the brave day sunk in hideous night . . . 12 2
When lofty trees I see barren of leaves . . . 12 5
Beauties do themselves forsake And die as fast as they see others grow 12 12
So long as men can breathe or eyes can see, So long lives this . 18 13
For through the painter must you see his skill . . . 24 5
Now see what good turns eyes for eyes have done . . . 24 9
They draw but what they see, know not the heart . . . 24 14
Looking on darkness which the blind do see . . . 27 8
As a decrepit father takes delight To see his active child do deeds of youth . . . 37 2
Then do mine eyes best see, For all the day they view things unrespected 43 1
All days are nights to see till I see thee . . . 43 13
If ever that time come, When I shall see thee frown on my defects . 49 2
To-morrow see again, and do not kill The spirit of love . . . 56 7
That, when they see Return of love, more blest may be the view . 56 11
That I might see what the old world could say To this composed wonder 59 9
When sometime lofty towers I see down-razed . . . 64 3
Then better'd that the world may see my pleasure . . . 75 8
I see a better state to me belongs Than that which on thy humour doth depend . . . 92 7
And all things turn to fair that eyes can see . . . 95 12
Yet I none could see But sweet or colour it had stol'n from thee . 99 14
When in the chronicle of wasted time I see descriptions . . . 106 2
I see their antique pen would have express'd Even such a beauty as you master now . . . 106 7
If it see the rudest or gentlest sight, The most sweet favour . . 113 9
For thy records and what we see doth lie . . . 123 11
Roses damask'd, red and white, But no such roses see I in her cheeks 130 6
Love, what dost thou to mine eyes, That they behold, and see not what they see? . . . 137 2
See where it lies, Yet what the best is take the worst to be . . 137 3
Where is my judgement fled, That censures falsely what they see aright? 148 4
The sun itself sees not till heaven clears . . . 148 12
See. Those that can see thou lovest, and I am blind . . . *Sonnet* 149 14
The more I hear and see just cause of hate . . . 150 10
Gave eyes to blindness, Or made them swear against the thing they see 152 12
Such a storm As oft 'twixt May and April is to see . . . *Lov. Comp.* 102
All my offences that abroad you see Are errors of the blood . . 183
All ignorant that soul that sees thee without wonder . . . *Pass. Pil.* 65
'Once,' quoth she, 'did I see a fair sweet youth Here in these brakes' . 125
'See, in my thigh,' quoth she, 'here was the sore.' She showed hers . 128
Till looking on an Englishman, the fair'st that eye could see . . 213
For now I see Inconstancy More in women than in men remain . . 260
Procure to weep, In howling wise, to see my doleful plight . . . 277
Other help for him I see that there is none . . . 298
There will we sit upon the rocks, And see the shepherds . . . 358
Seeds spring from seeds and beauty breedeth beauty . *Ven. and Adon.* 167
Seeded. How will thy shame be seeded in thine age . . . *Lucrece* 603
Seest. What seest thou in the ground? hold up thy head *Ven. and Adon.* 118
Thou see'st our mistress' ornaments are chaste . . . *Lucrece* 322
In me thou see'st the twilight of such day As after sunset fadeth in the west *Sonnet* 73 5
In me thou see'st the glowing of such fire . . . 73 9
Seeing. What should I do, seeing thee so indeed, That tremble at the imagination? . . . *Ven. and Adon.* 667
If he be dead,—O no, it cannot be, Seeing his beauty, thou shouldst strike at it:—O yes, it may . . . 938
Swearing I slew him, seeing thee embrace him . . . *Lucrece* 518
Seeing such emulation in their woe . . . 1808
Why should false painting imitate his cheek And steal dead seeing of his living hue? . . . *Sonnet* 67 6
By seeing farther than the eye hath shown . . . 69 8
Is partly blind, Seems seeing, but effectually is out . . . 113 4
'Tis flattery in my seeing, And my great mind most kingly drinks it up 114 9
Which is so deem'd Not by our feeling but by others' seeing . . 121 4
Mine eyes seeing this, say this is not . . . 137 11
Seek. Then with her windy sighs and golden hairs To fan and blow them dry again she seeks . . . *Ven. and Adon.* 52
A thousand ways he seeks To mend the hurt . . . 477
Before I know myself, seek not to know me . . . 525
She seeks to kindle with continual kissing. But all in vain . . 606
What win I, if I gain the thing I seek? A dream, a breath . *Lucrece* 211
But with a pure appeal seeks to the heart, Which once corrupted takes the worser part . . . 293
Which he by dumb demeanour seeks to show . . . 474
Who seek to stain the ocean of thy blood . . . 655
How comes it then, vile Opportunity, Being so bad, such numbers seek for thee? . . . 896
Himself himself seek every hour to kill! . . . 998
I live, and seek in vain Some happy mean to end a hapless life . 1044
Yet for the self-same purpose seek a knife . . . 1047
When what I seek, my weary travel's end, Doth teach that ease *Sonnet* 50 2
Why should poor beauty indirectly seek Roses of shadow? . . 67 7
And therefore art enforced to seek anew Some fresher stamp . . 82 7
If thou dost seek to have what thou dost hide, By self-example mayst thou be denied . . . 142 13
Seeking that beauteous roof to ruinate . . . 10 7
Seem. A summer's day will seem an hour but short *Ven. and Adon.* 23
Then wink again, And I will wink; so shall the day seem night . 122
My smooth moist hand, were it with thy hand felt, Would in thy palm dissolve, or seem to melt . . . 144
She puts on outward strangeness, seems unkind . . . 310
Incorporate then they seem; face grows to face . . . 540
That cedar-tops and hills seem burnish'd gold . . . 858
How strange it seems Not to believe, and yet too credulous . . . 985
That her sight dazzling makes the wound seem three . . . 1064
His face seems twain, each several limb is doubled . . . 1067
Too severe, And most deceiving when it seems most just . . . 1156
Who, therefore angry, seems to part in sunder . . . *Lucrece* 388
This guilt would seem death-worthy in thy brother . . . 635
And seems to point her out where she sits weeping . . . 1087
Poor Lucrece' cheeks unto her maid seem so As winter meads . . 1217
Another smother'd seems to pelt and swear . . . 1418
Short time seems long in sorrow's sharp sustaining . . . 1573
A watery rigol goes, Which seems to weep upon the tainted place . 1746
In mine own love's strength seem to decay . . . *Sonnet* 23 7
Wit so poor as mine May make seem bare, in wanting words to show it 26 6
And night doth nightly make grief's strength seem stronger . . 28 14
When swift extremity can seem but slow . . . 51 6
O, how much more doth beauty beauteous seem By that sweet ornament which truth doth give! . . . 54 1
Lest your true love may seem false in this . . . 72 9
And other strains of woe, which now seem woe, Compared with loss of thee will not seem so . . . 90 13
So love's face May still seem love to me, though alter'd new . . 93 3
I teach thee how To make him seem long hence as he shows now . 101 14
For as you were when first your eye I eyed, Such seems your beauty still 104 3
Is partly blind, Seems seeing, but effectually is out . . . 113 4
My mistress' brows are raven black, Her eyes so suited, and they mourners seem . . . 127 10
Shall will in others seem right gracious? . . . 135 7
To be forbod the sweets that seem so good . . . *Lov. Comp.* 164
Thine eye Jove's lightning seems, thy voice his dreadful thunder *Pass. Pil.* 67
Now are minutes added to the hours; To spite me now, each minute seems a moon . . . 207
My curtail dog, that wont to have play'd, Plays not at all, but seems afraid 274
Truth may seem, but cannot be: Beauty brag, but 'tis not she *Ph. and Tur.* 62
Seemed. No grass, herb, leaf, or weed, But stole his blood and seem'd with him to bleed . . . *Ven. and Adon.* 1056
That nothing in him seem'd inordinate, Save sometime too much wonder of his eye . . . *Lucrece* 94
So proud, As heaven, it seem'd, to kiss the turrets bow'd . . . 1372
Many a dry drop seem'd a weeping tear . . . 1375
In speech, it seem'd, his beard, all silver white, Wagg'd up and down . 1405
A press of gaping faces, Which seem'd to swallow up his sound advice . 1409
The scalps of many, almost hid behind, To jump up higher seem'd, to mock the mind . . . 1414
It seem'd they would debate with angry swords . . . 1421
Seemed to appear, Like bright things stain'd, a kind of heavy fear . 1434
So mild, that Patience seem'd to scorn his woes . . . 1505
A brow unbent, that seem'd to welcome woe . . . 1509
Yet this abundant issue seem'd to me But hope of orphans . . *Sonnet* 97 9
Yet seem'd it winter still, and, you away . . . 98 13

Seemed. Though absence seem'd my flame to qualify *Sonnet* 109 2
Ink would have seem'd more black and damned here! *Lov. Comp.* 54
That termless skin Whose bare out-bragg'd the web it seem'd to wear 95
Seemest. Thou art not what thou seem'st; and if the same, Thou seem'st not what thou art, a god, a king *Lucrece* 600
Seemeth. Every present sorrow seemeth chief, But none is best *V. and A.* 970
To wash the foul face of the sluttish ground, Who is but drunken when she seemeth drown'd 984
That it cried, How true a twain Seemeth this concordant one! *Ph. and Tur.* 46
Seeming to bury that posterity Which by the rights of time thou needs must have *Ven. and Adon.* 758
The neighbour caves, as seeming troubled, Make verbal repetition of her moans 830
For lovers' hours are long, though seeming short 842
He entertain'd a show so seeming just *Lucrece* 1514
Whose speechless song, being many, seeming one, Sings this to thee *Son.* 8 13
My love is strengthen'd, though more weak in seeming 102 1
O, love's best habit is in seeming trust 138 11
O, all that borrow'd motion seeming owed, Would yet again betray the fore-betray'd! *Lov. Comp.* 327
Seemly. For all that beauty that doth cover thee Is but the seemly raiment of my heart *Sonnet* 22 6
Seen. Or, like a nymph, with long dishevell'd hair, Dance on the sands, and yet no footing seen *Ven. and Adon.* 148
His eyes saw her eyes as they had not seen them 357
Shone like the moon in water seen by night 492
These mine eyes, true leaders to their queen, But for thy piteous lips no more had seen 504
Till the wild waves will have him seen no more 819
Her eyes seen in the tears, tears in her eye 962
Which seen, her eyes, as murder'd with the view, Like stars ashamed of day, themselves withdrew 1031
Where their queen Means to immure herself and not be seen 1194
This heraldry in Lucrece' face was seen *Lucrece* 64
That had Narcissus seen her as she stood, Self-love had never drown'd him in the flood 265
Then had they seen the period of their ill 380
Full many a glorious morning have I seen Flatter the mountain-tops *Son.* 33 1
His beauty shall in these black lines be seen, And they shall live 63 13
When I have seen by Time's fell hand defaced The rich proud cost of outworn buried age 64 1
I have seen the hungry ocean gain Advantage on the kingdom of the shore 64 5
I have seen such interchange of state, Or state itself confounded to decay 64 9
In him those holy antique hours are seen, Without all ornament 68 9
So are those errors that in thee are seen To truths translated 96 7
What freezings have I felt, what dark days seen! 97 3
Three beauteous springs to yellow autumn turn'd In process of the seasons have I seen 104 6
Have I not seen dwellers on form and favour Lose all, and more? 125 5
I have seen roses damask'd, red and white 130 5
Advice is often seen By blunting us to make our wits more keen *L. Comp.* 160
Among the many that mine eyes have seen 190
Distance, and no space was seen 'Twixt the turtle and his queen *Ph. and Tur.* 30
Seething. A dateless lively heat, still to endure, And grew a seething bath *Sonnet* 153 7
Seize. Can thy right hand seize love upon thy left? *Ven. and Adon.* 158
Where none may spy him, Sits Sin, to seize the souls that wander by him *Lucrece* 882
Seized. The wolf hath seized his prey, the poor lamb cries 677
'He seized on my lips,' And with her lips on his did act the seizure *Pass. Pil.* 151
Seizeth. With this she seizeth on his sweating palm *Ven. and Adon.* 25
Seizure. 'He seized on my lips,' And with her lips on his did act the seizure *Pass. Pil.* 152
Seld. As goods lost are seld or never found 175
Seldom. For unstain'd thoughts do seldom dream on evil *Lucrece* 87
Men's faults do seldom to themselves appear 633
Though woe be heavy, yet it seldom sleeps 1574
Blunting the fine point of seldom pleasure *Sonnet* 52 4
Therefore are feasts so solemn and so rare, Since, seldom coming 52 6
Self. Mine enemy was strong, my poor self weak *Lucrece* 1646
Let my unsounded self, supposed a fool 1819
Thyself thy foe, to thy sweet self too cruel *Sonnet* 1 8
Thou of thyself thy sweet self dost deceive 4 10
Make thee another self, for love of me 10 13
What can mine own praise to mine own self bring? 39 3
Self so self-loving were iniquity 62 12
Which by and by black night doth take away, Death's second self 73 8
Such cherubins as your sweet self resemble 114 6
And therein show'st Thy lovers withering as thy sweet self grow'st 126 4
My next self thou harder hast engross'd 133 6
Lest guilty of my faults thy sweet self prove 151 4
My woeful self, that did in freedom stand *Lov. Comp.* 143
Property was thus appalled, That the self was not the same *Ph. and Tur.* 38
Self-applied. If I had self-applied Love to myself and to no love beside *Lov. Comp.* 76
Self-doing. To you it doth belong Yourself to pardon of self-doing crime *Sonnet* 58 12
Self-example. By self-example mayst thou be denied 142 14
Self-killed. Treasure thou some place With beauty's treasure, ere it be self-kill'd 6 4
Self-love. That had Narcissus seen her as she stood, Self-love had never drown'd him in the flood *Lucrece* 266
Who is he so fond will be the tomb Of his self-love, to stop posterity? *Sonnet* 3 8
Sin of self-love possesseth all mine eye And all my soul 62 1
Mine own self-love quite contrary I read 62 11
Self-loving nuns, That on the earth would breed a scarcity *Ven. and Adon.* 752
Self so self-loving were iniquity *Sonnet* 62 12
Self-same. And in the self-same seat sits Collatine *Lucrece* 289
Yet for the self-same purpose seek a knife 1047
Cheered and check'd even by the self-same sky *Sonnet* 15 6
Self-slaughtered. Himself on her self-slaughter'd body threw *Lucrece* 1733
Self-substantial. Feed'st thy light's flame with self-substantial fuel *Son.* 1 6
Self-trust. Then where is truth, if there be no self-trust? *Lucrece* 158
Self-will. Till like a jade Self-will himself doth tire 707
Self-willed. Be not self-will'd, for thou art much too fair To be death's conquest and make worms thine heir *Sonnet* 6 13
Sell. To sell myself I can be well contented *Ven. and Adon.* 513
Who buys a minute's mirth to wail a week? Or sells eternity to get a toy? *Lucrece* 214
Lucrece to their sight Must sell her joy, her life, her world's delight 385

Sell. I will not praise that purpose not to sell *Sonnet* 21 14
But plainly say thou lovest her well, And set thy person forth to sell *Pass. Pil.* 310
Selling. Buy terms divine in selling hours of dross *Sonnet* 146 11
Semblance. Under whose simple semblance he hath fed Upon fresh beauty *Ven. and Adon.* 795
True sorrow then is feelingly sufficed When with like semblance it is sympathized *Lucrece* 1113
Wherein is stamp'd the semblance of a devil 1246
Of what she was no semblance did remain 1453
I often did behold In thy sweet semblance my old age new born 1759
Your sweet semblance to some other give *Sonnet* 13 4
Send. As from a furnace, vapours doth he send *Ven. and Adon.* 274
To thee I send this written embassage, To witness duty *Sonnet* 26 3
No longer glad, I send them back again and straight grow sad 45 14
Sendest. Is it thy spirit that thou send'st from thee So far from home? 61 5
Sense. Say, that the sense of feeling were bereft me *Ven. and Adon.* 439
Appals her senses and her spirit confounds 882
Cheering up her senses all dismay'd, She tells them 'tis a causeless fantasy 896
Urging the worser sense for vantage still *Lucrece* 249
He in the worst sense construes their denial 324
'It cannot be' she in that sense forsook, And turn'd it thus 1538
To thy sensual fault I bring in sense—Thy adverse party is thy advocate *Sonnet* 35 9
Nor I to none alive, That my steel'd sense or changes right or wrong 112 8
My adder's sense To critic and to flatterer stopped are 112 10
O, that our night of woe might have remember'd My deepest sense 120 10
But my five wits nor my five senses can Dissuade one foolish heart from serving thee 141 9
Love's arms are peace, 'gainst rule, 'gainst sense, 'gainst shame *Lov. Comp.* 271
Whose heavenly touch Upon the lute doth ravish human sense *Pass. Pil.* 108
The morning rise Doth cite each moving sense from idle rest 195
Senseless. Fie, lifeless picture, cold and senseless stone *Ven. and Adon.* 211
Let my good name, that senseless reputation, For Collatine's dear love be kept unspotted *Lucrece* 820
She tears the senseless Sinon with her nails 1564
Senseless trees they cannot hear thee *Pass. Pil.* 393
Sensible. Or were I deaf, thy outward parts would move Each part in me that were but sensible *Ven. and Adon.* 436
My woe too sensible thy passion maketh More feeling-painful *Lucrece* 1678
Sensual. To thy sensual fault I bring in sense *Sonnet* 35 9
Nor taste, nor smell, desire to be invited To any sensual feast with thee alone 141 8
Sent. In rage sent out, recall'd in rage, being past *Lucrece* 1671
Look here, what tributes wounded fancies sent me *Lov. Comp.* 197
This device was sent me from a nun, Or sister sanctified 232
Sentence. Who fears a sentence or an old man's saw Shall by a painted cloth be kept in awe *Lucrece* 244
And midst the sentence so her accent breaks, That twice she doth begin ere once she speaks 566
Sentinel. Disturbing Jealousy Doth call himself Affection's sentinel *Ven. and Adon.* 650
To wake the morn and sentinel the night *Lucrece* 942
Separable. In our two loves there is but one respect, Though in our lives a separable spite *Sonnet* 36 6
Separation. By this separation I may give That due to thee which thou deservest alone 39 7
Sepulchres. His snout digs sepulchres where'er he goes *Ven. and Adon.* 622
The right of sepulchres, were shorn away, To live a second life on second head *Sonnet* 68 6
Bidding them find their sepulchres in mud *Lov. Comp.* 46
Sepulchred. That all the faults which in thy reign are made May likewise be sepulchred in thy shade *Lucrece* 805
Sequent. In sequent toil all forwards do contend *Sonnet* 60 4
Serpent. Here come and sit, where never serpent hisses *Ven. and Adon.* 17
Who sees the lurking serpent steps aside *Lucrece* 362
Servant. Why hath thy servant, Opportunity, Betray'd the hours thou gavest me? 932
Out, idle words, servants to shallow fools! 1016
When you have bid your servant once adieu *Sonnet* 57 8
Then, soul, live thou upon thy servant's loss 146 9
Serve. Now serves the season that they may surprise The silly lambs *Lucr.* 166
Debate where leisure serves with dull debaters 1019
And for my sake serve thou false Tarquin so 1197
Many there were that did his picture get, To serve their eyes *Lov. Comp.* 135
Serve always with assured trust, And in thy suit be humble true *Pass. Pil.* 329
When time shall serve, be thou not slack To proffer 333
Served. Hath served a dumb arrest upon his tongue *Lucrece* 1780
Service. I have no precious time at all to spend, Nor services to do, till you require *Sonnet* 57 4
What merit do I in myself respect, That is so proud thy service to despise? 149 10
Servile. Yet was he servile to my coy disdain *Ven. and Adon.* 112
Subject and servile to all discontents, As dry combustious matter is to fire 1161
And therein heartens up his servile powers *Lucrece* 295
Servilely master'd with a leathern rein! *Ven. and Adon.* 392
Serving. Serving with looks his sacred majesty *Sonnet* 7 4
Nor my five senses can Dissuade one foolish heart from serving thee 141 10
Servitors. Both which, as servitors to the unjust, So cross him *Lucrece* 285
Session. When to the sessions of sweet silent thought I summon up remembrance of things past *Sonnet* 30 1
From this session interdict Every fowl of tyrant wing *Ph. and Tur.* 9
Set. Here come and sit, where never serpent hisses, And being set, I'll smother thee with kisses *Ven. and Adon.* 18
Affection is a coal that must be cool'd; Else, suffer'd, it will set the heart on fire 388
Set thy seal-manual on my wax-red lips 516
On his bow-back he hath a battle set Of bristly pikes 619
His breath and beauty set Gloss on the rose, smell to the violet 935
And set dissension 'twixt the son and sire 1160
Unhappily set This bateless edge on his keen appetite *Lucrece* 8
What needeth then apologies be made, To set forth that which is so singular? 32
Whose grim aspect sets every joint a-shaking 452
He sets his foot upon the light, For light and lust are deadly enemies 673
That in their smoky ranks his smother'd light May set at noon 784
But as the earth doth weep, the sun being set 1226
Enforced by sympathy Of those fair suns set in her mistress' sky 1230
What wit sets down is blotted straight with will 1299
Like a heavy-hanging bell, Once set on ringing, with his own weight goes 1494

Set. So Lucrece, set a-work, sad tales doth tell *Lucrece* 1496
And then against my heart he sets his sword 1640
With sad set eyes, and wretched arms across 1662
Now set thy long-experienced wit to school 1820
Sets you most rich in youth before my sight *Sonnet* 15 10
Therefore are feasts so solemn and so rare, Since, seldom coming, in the long year set 52 6
On Helen's cheek all art of beauty set 53 7
Time doth transfix the flourish set on youth 60 9
I never saw that you did painting need And therefore to your fair no painting set 83 2
To set me light And place my merit in the eye of scorn 88 1
Upon thy part I can set down a story Of faults conceal'd 88 6
Thou canst not, love, disgrace me half so ill, To set a form upon desired change 89 6
Sets down her babe and makes all swift dispatch 143 3
Upon whose weeping margent she was set *Lov. Comp.* 39
Like fools that in th' imagination set The goodly objects which abroad they find 136
But plainly say thou lovest her well, And set thy person forth to sell *Pass. Pil.* 310
Set'st. Thou set'st the wolf where he the lamb may get *Lucrece* 878
Settled. Sweet beginning, but unsavoury end, Ne'er settled equally *Ven. and Adon.* 1139
Shall reasons find of settled gravity *Sonnet* 49 8
Several. His face seems twain, each several limb is doubled *Ven. and Adon.* 1067
All jointly listening, but with several graces *Lucrece* 1410
Why should my heart think that a several plot? *Sonnet* 137 9
I have received from many a several fair, Their kind acceptance *Lov. Comp.* 206
Each several stone, With wit well blazon'd, smiled or made some moan 216
Severe. That bloody beast, Which knows no pity, but is still severe *Ven. and Adon.* 1000
It shall be merciful and too severe 1155
Sex. Their gentle sex to weep are often willing *Lucrece* 1237
And sexes both enchanted, To dwell with him in thoughts *Lov. Comp.* 128
Shade. And there, all smother'd up, in shade doth sit *Ven. and Adon.* 1035
Coucheth the fowl below with his wings' shade *Lucrece* 507
That all the faults which in thy reign are made May likewise be sepulchred in thy shade 805
Nor shall Death brag thou wander'st in his shade *Sonnet* 18 11
How would thy shadow's form form happy show To the clear day with thy much clearer light, When to unseeing eyes thy shade shines so! 43 8
Thy fair imperfect shade Through heavy sleep on sightless eyes doth stay 43 11
Since every one hath, every one, one shade, And you, but one 53 3
And scarce the herd gone to the hedge for shade *Pass. Pil.* 72
Venus, with young Adonis sitting by her Under a myrtle shade 144
Sitting in a pleasant shade Which a grove of myrtles made 375
Shaded. Bright orient pearl, alack, too timely shaded! 133
Shadow. And died to kiss his shadow in the brook *Ven. and Adon.* 162
For where they lay the shadow had forsook them 176
I'll make a shadow for thee of my hairs 191
He vails his tail that, like a falling plume, Cool shadow to his melting buttock lent 315
And coal-black clouds that shadow heaven's light Do summon us to part 533
Each shadow makes him stop, each murmur stay 706
Gentle shadow,—truth I must confess,—I rail'd on thee 1001
When he beheld his shadow in the brook, The fishes spread on it their golden gills 1099
Love thrives not in the heart that shadows dreadeth *Lucrece* 270
Such shadows are the weak brain's forgeries 460
Let ghastly shadows his lewd eyes affright 971
At his own shadow let the thief run mad 997
On this sad shadow Lucrece spends her eyes 1457
My soul's imaginary sight Presents thy shadow to my sightless view *Son.* 27 10
Whilst that this shadow doth such substance give 37 10
Thou, whose shadow shadows doth make bright, How would thy shadow's form form happy show To the clear day with thy much clearer light! 43 5
Whereof are you made, That millions of strange shadows on you tend? 53 2
Since every one hath, every one, one shade, And you, but one, can every shadow lend 53 4
The one doth shadow of your beauty show 53 10
While shadows like to thee do mock my sight 61 4
Why should poor beauty indirectly seek Roses of shadow? 67 8
And, you away, As with your shadow I with these did play 98 14
'Wander,' a word for shadows like myself *Pass. Pil.* 191
Shadowed. His nose being shadow'd by his neighbour's ear *Lucrece* 1416
Shady. In thy shady cell, where none may spy him, Sits Sin 881
Thou by thy dial's shady stealth mayst know Time's thievish progress *Sonnet* 77 7
Shag. Round-hoof'd, short-jointed, fetlocks shag and long *Ven. and Adon.* 295
Shake. Sometimes she shakes her head and then his hand 223
But, like an earthquake, shakes thee on my breast 648
The fear whereof doth make him shake and shudder 880
Struggling for passage, earth's foundation shakes 1047
Will not my tongue be mute, my frail joints shake? *Lucrece* 227
May feel her heart . . . rise up and fall, Beating her bulk, that his hand shakes withal 467
This said, he shakes aloft his Roman blade 505
Rough winds do shake the darling buds of May *Sonnet* 18 3
Do in consent shake hands to torture me 28 6
Upon those boughs which shake against the cold 73 3
Shaken. An ever-fixed mark That looks on tempests and is never shaken 116 6
For if you were by my unkindness shaken As I by yours, you've pass'd a hell of time 120 5
Shaking her wings, devouring all in haste *Ven. and Adon.* 57
Shaking their scratch'd ears, bleeding as they go 924
Shall. If thou wilt chide, thy lips shall never open 48
And one sweet kiss shall pay this countless debt 84
The kiss shall be thine own as well as mine 117
Then wink again, And I will wink; so shall the day seem night 122
Whose gentle wind Shall cool the heat of this descending sun 190
No dog shall rouse thee, though a thousand bark 240
Now which way shall she turn? what shall she say? 253
Then love's deep groans I never shall regard 377
'Good night,' and so say you; If you will say so, you shall have a kiss 536
Shall we meet to-morrow? Say, shall we? shall we? 585
And now 'tis dark, and going I shall fall 719
Sorrow on love hereafter shall attend: It shall be waited on with jealousy 1136
Shall. It shall not fear where it should most mistrust; It shall be merciful *Ven. and Adon.* 1154
Perverse it shall be where it shows most toward 1157
It shall be cause of war and dire events 1159
They that love best their loves shall not enjoy 1164
There shall not be one minute in an hour 1187
Shall worms, inheritors of this excess, Eat up thy charge? *Sonnet* 146 7
Shallow. Her husband's shallow tongue,—The niggard prodigal that praised her so,—In that high task hath done her beauty wrong *Lucrece* 78
Out, idle words, servants to shallow fools! 1016
Deep sounds make lesser noise than shallow fords 1329
But now he throws that shallow habit by 1814
By shallow rivers, by whose falls Melodious birds sing madrigals *Pass. Pil.* 359
Shallowest. Your shallowest help will hold me up afloat *Sonnet* 80 9
Shalt. I'll be a park, and thou shalt be my deer *Ven. and Adon.* 231
'Give me my heart,' saith she, 'and thou shalt have it' 374
Then shalt thou see the dew-bedabbled wretch Turn, and return 703
Thou, Collatine, shalt oversee this will *Lucrece* 1205
How was I overseen that thou shalt see it! 1206
Shame. He red for shame, but frosty in desire *Ven. and Adon.* 36
He burns with bashful shame: she with her tears 49
Pure shame and awed resistance made him fret 69
Still he lours and frets, 'Twixt crimson shame and anger ashy-pale 76
'For shame,' he cries, 'let go, and let me go; My day's delight is past' 379
Forgetting shame's pure blush and honour's wrack 558
Cynthia for shame obscures her silver shine 728
To shame the sun by day and her by night 732
My face is full of shame, my heart of teen 808
When virtue bragg'd, beauty would blush for shame *Lucrece* 54
When shame assail'd, the red should fence the white 63
O shame to knighthood and to shining arms! 197
This surviving shame, Whose crime will bear an ever-during blame 223
The shame and fault finds no excuse nor end 238
Misty night Covers the shame that follows sweet delight 357
Whether it is that she reflects so bright, That dazzleth them, or else some shame supposed 377
What wrong, what shame, what sorrow I shall breed 499
Bequeath not to their lot The shame that from them no device can take 535
Hast thou put on his shape to do him shame? 597
How will thy shame be seeded in thine age! 603
Must he in thee read lectures of such shame? 618
There falls into thy boundless flood Black lust, dishonour, shame 654
Thou loathed in their shame, they in thy pride 662
Shame folded up in blind concealing night 675
And grave, like water that doth eat in steel, Upon my cheeks what helpless shame I feel 756
Image of hell! Dim register and notary of shame! 765
The orator, to deck his oratory, Will couple my reproach to Tarquin's shame 816
O unseen shame! invisible disgrace! O unfelt sore! 827
Thy secret pleasure turns to open shame 890
To shame his hope with deeds degenerate 1003
Honour thyself to rid me of this shame 1031
Cloudy Lucrece shames herself to see 1084
So of shame's ashes shall my fame be bred 1188
My shame so dead, mine honour is new-born 1190
My shame be his that did my fame confound 1202
And all my fame that lives disbursed be To those that live, and think no shame of me 1204
Those proud lords, to blame, Make weak-made women tenants to their shame 1260
With circumstances strong Of present death, and shame that might ensue 1263
Lucrece thought he blush'd to see her shame 1344
Else lasting shame On thee and thine this night I will inflict 1629
So should my shame still rest upon record, And never be forgot 1643
Till manly shame bids him possess his breath 1777
Were an all-eating shame and thriftless praise *Sonnet* 2 8
No love toward others in that bosom sits That on himself such murderous shame commits 9 14
For shame! deny that thou bear'st love to any, Who for thyself art so unprovident 10 1
Nor can thy shame give physic to my grief 34 9
Lest my bewailed guilt should do thee shame 36 10
To find out shames and idle hours in me, The scope and tenour of thy jealousy? 61 7
And live no more to shame nor me nor you 72 12
How sweet and lovely dost thou make the shame 95 1
The roses fearfully on thorns did stand, One blushing shame 99 9
I must strive To know my shames and praises from your tongue 112 6
And beauty slander'd with a bastard shame 127 4
The expense of spirit in a waste of shame Is lust in action 129 1
They sought their shame that so their shame did find *Lov. Comp.* 187
And so much less of shame in me remains 188
Love's arms are peace, 'gainst rule, 'gainst sense, 'gainst shame 271
Shamed. Posterity, shamed with the note, Shall curse my bones *Lucrece* 208
To live or die which of the twain were better, When life is shamed 1155
For I am shamed by that which I bring forth, And so should you *Sonnet* 72 13
Shameful it is; ay, if the fact be known *Lucrece* 239
Some rascal groom, To be thy partner in this shameful doom 672
Alas, how many bear such shameful blows! 832
For in my death I murder shameful scorn 1189
Shamefully. And gilded honour shamefully misplaced *Sonnet* 66 5
Shaming. Poor bird, thou sing'st not in the day, As shaming any eye should thee behold *Lucrece* 1143
Shape. In shape, in courage, colour, pace, and bone *Ven. and Adon.* 294
Hast thou put on his shape to do him shame? *Lucrece* 597
Shape every bush a hideous shapeless devil 973
And shapes her sorrow to the beldam's woes 1458
Saying, some shape in Sinon's was abused 1529
But Tarquin's shape came in her mind the while 1536
Every private widow well may keep By children's eyes her husband's shape in mind *Sonnet* 9 8
Mine eyes have drawn thy shape, and thine for me Are windows to my breast 24 10
And you in every blessed shape we know 53 12
Methinks no face so gracious is as mine, No shape so true 62 6
For it no form delivers to the heart Of bird, of flower, or shape 113 6
For if it see the rudest or gentlest sight, . . . it shapes them to your feature 113 12
Shapeless. Who wears a garment shapeless and unfinish'd? *Ven. and Adon.* 415
Shape every bush a hideous shapeless devil *Lucrece* 973

Share. Mine eye is my heart's guest And in his thoughts of love doth share a part . . . . *Sonnet* 47 8
Good night, good rest. Ah, neither be my share . . . . *Pass. Pil.* 181
Sharing joy To see their youthful sons bright weapons wield . *Lucrece* 1431
Sharp. Even as an empty eagle, sharp by fast, Tires with her beak on feathers, flesh, and bone . . . . . . *Ven. and Adon.* 55
Under whose sharp fangs on his back doth lie An image like thyself, all stain'd with gore 663
Sun and sharp air Lurk'd like two thieves, to rob him of his fair . . 1085
Thus was Adonis slain: He ran upon the boar with his sharp spear . . 1112
As the grim lion fawneth o'er his prey, Sharp hunger by the conquest satisfied . . . . *Lucrece* 422
Like a white hind under the gripe's sharp claws, Pleads . . . 543
Thou bear'st thy part, To keep thy sharp woes waking . . . 1136
Against my heart Will fix a sharp knife to affright mine eye . . 1138
Short time seems long in sorrow's sharp sustaining 1573
Which heavily he answers with a groan, More sharp to me than spurring to his side . . . . *Sonnet* 50 12
Fair creature, kill'd too soon by death's sharp sting! . . *Pass. Pil.* 134
Sharpened. To-morrow sharpen'd in his former might . . *Sonnet* 56 4
Sharpest. Tan sacred beauty, blunt the sharp'st intents, Divert strong minds 115 7
Sharply. For sharply he did think to reprehend her . *Ven. and Adon.* 470
She. 'Thrice-fairer than myself,' thus she began 7
She red and hot as coals of glowing fire, He red for shame . . . 35
To tie the rider she begins to prove 40
Backward she push'd him, as she would be thrust 41
She would, he will not in her arms be bound 226
Now which way shall she turn? what shall she say? 253
She answers him as if she knew his mind 308
For on the grass she lies as she were slain 473
He with her plenty press'd, she faint with dearth 545
She takes all she can, not all she listeth 564
She's Love, she loves, and yet she is not loved 610
She treads the path that she untreads again 908
To wash the foul face of the sluttish ground, Who is but drunken when she seemeth drown'd 984
Dumbly she passions, franticly she doteth 1059
She looks upon his lips, and they are pale; She takes him by the hand . 1123
She whispers in his ears a heavy tale 1125
Which speechless woe of his poor she attendeth . . . *Lucrece* 1674
I think my love as rare As any she belied with false compare *Sonnet* 130 14
I count my gain, That she that makes me sin awards me pain . 141 14
Sheathed. Whose tushes never sheathed he whetteth still *Ven. and Adon.* 617
The loving swine Sheathed unaware the tusk in his soft groin . . 1116
Her eyes, like marigolds, had sheathed their light . . *Lucrece* 397
She sheathed in her harmless breast A harmful knife 1723
Sheaves. And summer's green all girded up in sheaves . . *Sonnet* 12 7
Sheaved. For some, untuck'd, descended her sheaved hat *Lov. Comp.* 31
Shed. Whose blood upon the fresh flowers being shed Doth make them droop *Ven. and Adon.* 665
The chastest tears That ever modest eyes with sorrow shed . *Lucrece* 683
A weeping tear, Shed for the slaughter'd husband by the wife . . 1376
Priam wets his eyes, To see those borrow'd tears that Sinon sheds . 1549
Ah! but those tears are pearl which thy love sheds . . *Sonnet* 34 13
Sheep. The sheep are gone to fold, birds to their nest *Ven. and Adon.* 532
Sometime he runs among a flock of sheep, To make the cunning hounds mistake their smell 685
Sheet. Teaching the sheets a whiter hue than white 398
Who o'er the white sheet peers her whiter chin, The reason of this rash alarm to know . . . . *Lucrece* 472
Shelly. Shrinks backward in his shelly cave with pain . *Ven. and Adon.* 1034
Shelter. To shelter thee from tempest and from rain . . . 238
Shelves. Huge rocks, high winds, strong pirates, shelves, and sands, The merchant fears . . . . *Lucrece* 335
Shepherd. Sorrow to shepherds, woe unto the birds *Ven. and Adon.* 455
A wretched image bound, That piteous looks to Phrygian shepherds lent *Lucrece* 1502
O, sweet shepherd, hie thee, For methinks thou stay'st too long *Pass. Pil.* 167
My shepherd's pipe can sound no deal 271
There will we sit upon the rocks, And see the shepherds . . . 358
And truth in every shepherd's tongue 370
Shield. His batter'd shield, his uncontrolled crest . *Ven. and Adon.* 104
Beauty's red, Which virtue gave the golden age to gild Their silver cheeks, and call'd it then their shield . . . . . *Lucrece* 61
Shielded. With safest distance I mine honour shielded . *Lov. Comp.* 151
Shift. Danger deviseth shifts; wit waits on fear *Ven. and Adon.* 690
Guilty of treason, forgery, and shift, Guilty of incest . *Lucrece* 920
And as one shifts, another straight ensues 1104
Look, what an unthrift in the world doth spend Shifts but his place *Son.* 9 10
Shifting. O, hear me then, injurious, shifting Time! . . *Lucrece* 930
A woman's gentle heart, but not acquainted With shifting change *Son.* 20 4
Shine. The sun that shines from heaven shines but warm *Ven. and Adon.* 193
Whose beams upon his hairless face are fix'd, As if from thence they borrow'd all their shine 488
His eyes, like glow-worms, shine when he doth fret 621
Cynthia for shame obscures her silver shine 728
Sometime too hot the eye of heaven shines . . . *Sonnet* 18 5
Even so my sun one early morn did shine 33 9
How would thy shadow's form form happy show To the clear day with thy much clearer light, When to unseeing eyes thy shade shines so! 43 8
But you shall shine more bright in these contents . . . 55 3
That in black ink my love may still shine bright . . . 65 14
And in my will no fair acceptance shine 135 8
Thou fair sun, that on this earth doth shine, Exhale this vapour vow *Pass. Pil.* 38
Yet not for me, shine sun to succour flowers! 208
So between them love did shine . . . . *Ph. and Tur.* 33
Shining. Patron of all light, From whom each lamp and shining star doth borrow . . . . *Ven. and Adon.* 861
O shame to knighthood and to shining arms! . . . *Lucrece* 197
Whose words like wildfire burnt the shining glory Of rich-built Ilion . 1523
With shining falchion in my chamber came A creeping creature . . 1626
Beauty is but a vain and doubtful good; A shining gloss that vadeth suddenly . . . . *Pass. Pil.* 170
Shivered. And shiver'd all the beauty of my glass . . *Lucrece* 1763
Shocks. The aloes of all forces, shocks, and fears . . *Lov. Comp.* 273
Shone like the moon in water seen by night . . *Ven. and Adon.* 492
Shook. Three winters cold Have from the forests shook three summers' pride *Sonnet* 104 4
Shook off my sober guards and civil fears . . . *Lov. Comp.* 298
Shoot. End thy ill aim before thy shoot be ended . . *Lucrece* 579
They join and shoot their foam at Simois' banks 1442
But shoot not at me in your waken'd hate . . . *Sonnet* 117 12
Shooteth. Look, how a bright star shooteth from the sky *Ven. and Adon.* 815
Shop. Which in my bosom's shop is hanging still . . *Sonnet* 24 7
Shore. As one on shore Gazing upon a late-embarked friend *Ven. and Adon.* 817
'Tis double death to drown in ken of shore . . . *Lucrece* 1114
Their ranks began To break upon the galled shore, and than Retire again 1440
Let this sad interim like the ocean be Which parts the shore *Sonnet* 56 10
Like as the waves make towards the pebbled shore . . . 60 1
I have seen the hungry ocean gain Advantage on the kingdom of the shore 64 6
Shorn. The right of sepulchres, were shorn away, To live a second life on second head 68 6
Short. Ten kisses short as one, one long as twenty *Ven. and Adon.* 22
A summer's day will seem an hour but short 23
High crest, short ears, straight legs, and passing strong . . 297
His short thick neck cannot be easily harm'd 627
For lovers' hours are long, though seeming short 842
As palmers' chat makes short their pilgrimage . . . *Lucrece* 791
How swift and short His time of folly and his time of sport . . 991
By this short schedule Collatine may know Her grief 1312
Short time seems long in sorrow's sharp sustaining 1573
Untimely breathings, sick, and short assays 1720
Summer's lease hath all too short a date . . . *Sonnet* 18 4
Well might show How far a modern quill doth come too short . 83 7
Which prove more short than waste or ruining 125 4
Why so large cost, having so short a lease? 146 5
Youth is full of sport, age's breath is short; Youth is nimble, age is lame; Youth is hot and bold, age is weak and cold . . *Pass. Pil.* 161
Short, night, to-night, and length thyself to-morrow . . . 210
Short-jointed. Round-hoof'd, short-jointed, fetlocks shag and long, Broad breast, full eye, small head and nostril wide *Ven. and Adon.* 295
Short-numbered. That heretic, Which works on leases of short-number'd hours . . . . *Sonnet* 124 10
Shot. The skies were sorry, And little stars shot from their fixed places *Lucr.* 1525
Should. Beauty within itself should not be wasted . *Ven. and Adon.* 130
As who should say 'Lo, thus my strength is tried' 280
Look, what a horse should have he did not lack 299
Thy palfrey, as he should, Welcomes the warm approach of sweet desire 385
Lest Jealousy, that sour unwelcome guest, Should, by his stealing in, disturb the feast 450
Say, for non-payment that the debt should double 521
Lest she should steal a kiss and die forsworn 726
Love's golden arrow at him should have fled, And not Death's ebon dart . 947
As striving who should best become her grief 968
As who should say 'This glove to wanton tricks Is not inured' *Lucrece* 320
Poor bird, thou sing'st not in the day, As shaming any eye should thee behold 1143
And falls, through wind, before the fall should be . . . *Pass. Pil.* 136
Shoulder. Over one shoulder doth she hang her head *Ven. and Adon.* 1058
Shouldst. And may it be That thou shouldst think it heavy unto thee? . 156
Upon the earth's increase why shouldst thou feed? 169
What am I, that thou shouldst contemn me this? 205
If he be dead,—O no, it cannot be, Seeing his beauty, thou shouldst strike at it:—O yes, it may 938
Who confounds In singleness the parts that thou shouldst bear . *Sonnet* 8 8
Show. The tender spring upon thy tempting lip Shows thee unripe *V. and A.* 128
Shows his hot courage and his high desire 276
Perverse it shall be where it shows most toward 1157
Which far exceeds his barren skill to show . . . . *Lucrece* 81
No cloudy show of stormy blustering weather 115
And doth so far proceed, That what is vile shows like a virtuous deed . 252
Who, flatter'd by their leader's jocund show, Stuff up his lust . . 296
Which he by dumb demeanour seeks to show 474
The light will show, character'd in my brow, The story . . . 807
To show the beldam daughters of her daughter 953
The red blood reek'd, to show the painter's strife 1377
Show me the strumpet that began this stir 1471
And give the harmless show An humble gait, calm looks, eyes wailing still 1507
He entertain'd a show so seeming just 1514
Losing her woes in shows of discontent 1580
As pitying Lucrece' woes, Corrupted blood some watery token shows . 1748
That fair fresh mirror, dim and old, Shows me a bare-boned death . 1761
Burying in Lucrece' wound his folly's show 1810
To show her bleeding body thorough Rome 1851
Flowers distill'd, though they with winter meet, Lesse but their show *Son.* 5 14
This huge stage presenteth nought but shows 15 3
It is but as a tomb Which hides your life and shows not half your parts 17 4
I send this written embassage, To witness duty, not to show my wit . 26 4
Wit so poor as mine May make seem bare, in wanting words to show it . 26 6
To show me worthy of thy sweet respect 26 12
Till then not show my head where thou mayst prove me . . . 26 14
Lascivious grace in whom all ill well shows, Kill me with spites . 40 13
How would thy shadow's form form happy show To the clear day! . 43 6
All days are nights to see till I see thee, And nights bright days when dreams do show thee me 43 14
The one doth shadow of your beauty show 53 10
But, for their virtue only is their show, They live unwoo'd . . . 54 9
Show me your image in some antique book 59 7
But when my glass shows me myself indeed 62 9
Him she stores, to show what wealth she had In days long since . . 67 13
And him as for a map doth Nature store, To show false Art . . . 68 14
By why thy odour matcheth not thy show, The solve is this . . . 69 13
If some suspect of ill mask'd not thy show 70 13
Thy glass will show thee how thy beauties wear 77 1
The wrinkles which thy glass will truly show Of mouthed graves will give thee memory 77 5
Well might show How far a modern quill doth come too short . . 83 6
How like Eve's apple doth thy beauty grow, If thy sweet virtue answer not thy show! 93 14
That do not do the thing they most do show 94 2
I teach thee how To make him seem long hence as he shows now . 101 14
I love not less, though less the show appear 102 2
Having such a scope to show her pride 103 2
Your own glass shows you when you look in it 103 14
Let not my love be call'd idolatry, Nor my beloved as an idol show . 105 2
Where time and outward form would show it dead 108 14
Small show of man was yet upon his chin . . . . *Lov. Comp.* 92

Show. Or to turn white and swoon at tragic shows . . . *Lov. Comp.* 308
Wiles and guiles that women work, Dissembled with an outward show *Pass. Pil.* 336
Showed. Show'd like two silver doves that sit a-billing . *Ven. and Adon.* 366
Whose perfect white Show'd like an April daisy on the grass *Lucrece* 395
Show'd deep regard and smiling government 1400
Show'd life imprison'd in a body dead 1456
His face, though full of cares, yet show'd content 1503
Yet show'd his visage by that cost more dear . . *Lov. Comp.* 96
She show'd him favours to allure his eye . . . . *Pass. Pil.* 48
'See, in my thigh,' quoth she, 'here was the sore.' She showed hers . 129
Showers. Wishing her cheeks were gardens full of flowers, So they were dew'd with such distilling showers . . . . *Ven. and Adon.* 66
Seasoning the earth with showers of silver brine . . *Lucrece* 796
As sweet-season'd showers are to the ground . . . *Sonnet* 75 2
That it nor grows with heat nor drowns with showers . . . 124 12
Showest. And therein show'st Thy lovers withering as thy sweet self grow'st 126 3
Showing life's triumph in the map of death . . . *Lucrece* 402
Every word doth almost tell my name, Showing their birth and where they did proceed . . . . *Sonnet* 76 8
Showing fair nature is both kind and tame . . *Lov. Comp.* 311
Shown. By seeing farther than the eye hath shown . . *Sonnet* 69 8
By their rank thoughts my deeds must not be shown . . 121 12
For her griefs, so lively shown, Made me think upon mine own *Pass. Pil.* 389
Shrewd. Thy eyes' shrewd tutor, that hard heart of thine, Hath taught them scornful tricks and such disdain . . *Ven. and Adon.* 500
Shriek. The owl, night's herald, shrieks, 'Tis very late' . . . 531
Night-wandering weasels shriek to see him there . . *Lucrece* 307
Shrieking. As often shrieking undistinguish'd woe . . *Lov. Comp.* 20
Thou shrieking harbinger, Foul precurrer of the fiend . *Ph. and Tur.* 5
Shrill-tongued. Like shrill-tongued tapsters answering every call *V. and A.* 849
Shrine. Offer pure incense to so pure a shrine . . . *Lucrece* 194
Shrinks backward in his shelly cave with pain . *Ven. and Adon.* 1034
Shrub. The cedar stoops not to the base shrub's foot, But low shrubs wither at the cedar's root . . . . *Lucrece* 664
Shrunk. Wanting the spring that those shrunk pipes had fed . . 1455
Shudder. The fear whereof doth make him shake and shudder *V. and A.* 880
Shun. I could prevent this storm and shun thy wrack ! . . . *Lucrece* 966
To shun this blot, she would not blot the letter With words . . . 1322
We sicken to shun sickness when we purge . . . *Sonnet* 118 4
Yet none knows well To shun the heaven that leads men to this hell 129 14
Which late her noble suit in court did shun . . . *Lov. Comp.* 234
Shunned. Who ever shunn'd by precedent The destined ill she must herself assay? 155
Shuts. The chamber door, That shuts him from the heaven of his thought *Lucr.* 338
Sick. For my sick heart commands mine eyes to watch . *Ven. and Adon.* 584
To one sore sick that hears the passing-bell 702
Let their exhaled unwholesome breaths make sick The life of purity *Lucrece* 779
Give physic to the sick, ease to the pain'd 901
Untimely breathings, sick and short assays 1720
And my sick Muse doth give another place . . . *Sonnet* 79 4
I was not sick of any fear from thence 86 12
And, sick of welfare, found a kind of meetness To be diseased . 118 7
And find the lesson true, Drugs poison him that so fell sick of you 118 14
As testy sick men, when their deaths be near, No news but health from their physicians know 140 7
I, sick withal, the help of bath desired, And thither hied . . 153 11
That the lover, sick to death, Wish'd himself the heaven's breath *Pass. Pil.* 233
Sicken. We sicken to shun sickness when we purge . *Sonnet* 118 4
Sickle. Love's not Time's fool, though rosy lips and cheeks Within his bending sickle's compass come 116 10
Who in thy power Dost hold Time's fickle glass, his sickle, hour . 126 2
Sickly. The uncertain sickly appetite to please 147 4
The deep-green emerald, in whose fresh regard Weak sights their sickly radiance do amend . . . . *Lov. Comp.* 214
Sickness. The marrow-eating sickness, whose attaint Disorder breeds *Ven. and Adon.* 741
We sicken to shun sickness when we purge . . . *Sonnet* 118 4
Sick-thoughted Venus makes amain unto him . . *Ven. and Adon.* 5
Side. Wishing Adonis had his team to guide, So he were like him and by Venus' side 180
His brawny sides, with hairy bristles arm'd, Are better proof than thy spear's point can enter 625
The boy that by her side lay kill'd Was melted like a vapour from her sight 1165
Then Collatine again, by Lucrece' side, In his clear bed might have reposed still . . . . *Lucrece* 381
Seems to part in sunder, Swelling on either side to want his bliss . 389
For standing by her side, His eye, which late this mutiny restrains, Unto a greater uproar tempts his veins 425
The crimson blood Circles her body in on every side 1739
Brutus, who pluck'd the knife from Lucrece' side 1807
Which heavily he answers with a groan, More sharp to me than spurring to his side . . . . *Sonnet* 50 12
Upon thy side against myself I'll fight And prove thee virtuous . 88 3
On both sides thus is simple truth suppress'd 138 8
My female evil Tempteth my better angel from my side 144 6; *Pass. Pil.* 20
To stand in thy affairs, fall by thy side . . . . *Sonnet* 151 12
Laid by his side his heart-inflaming brand 154 2
And comely-distant sits he by her side . . . . *Lov. Comp.* 65
But quickly on this side the verdict went 113
Siege. Remove your siege from my unyielding heart . *Ven. and Adon.* 423
This siege that hath engirt his marriage, This blur to youth . *Lucrece* 221
Against the wreckful siege of battering days . . . *Sonnet* 65 6
Sigh. Then with her windy sighs and golden hairs To fan and blow them dry again she seeks . . . . *Ven. and Adon.* 51
I'll sigh celestial breath, whose gentle wind Shall cool the heat of this descending sun 189
And being steel'd, soft sighs can never grave it 376
Sorrow that friendly sighs sought still to dry 964
Sighs dry her cheeks, tears make them wet again 966
My sighs are blown away, my salt tears gone 1071
Her modest eloquence with sighs is mixed . . . . . *Lucrece* 563
My sighs, like whirlwinds, labour hence to heave thee 586
Be moved with my tears, my sighs, my groans 588
When sighs and groans and tears may grace the fashion Of her disgrace 1319
The weary time she cannot entertain, For now 'tis stale to sigh . 1362
Three times with sighs, she gives her sorrow fire 1604
Even so his sighs, his sorrows, make a saw, To push grief on . . 1672
With a sigh, as if her heart would break, She throws forth Tarquin's name . 1716
Sigh. Her contrite sighs unto the clouds bequeathed Her winged sprite *Lucr.* 1727
I sigh the lack of many a thing I sought . . . . *Sonnet* 30 3
Or heart in love with sighs himself doth smother 47 4
Hallow'd with sighs that burning lungs did raise . . . *Lov. Comp.* 228
And supplicant their sighs to you extend 276
My sighs so deep Procure to weep, In howling wise . . *Pass. Pil.* 275
How sighs resound Through heartless ground 278
For these dead birds sigh a prayer . . . . . *Ph. and Tur.* 67
Sighed. Which she perused, sigh'd, tore, and gave the flood *Lov. Comp.* 44
For why, she sigh'd and bade me come to-morrow . . . *Pass. Pil.* 204
Sighing. And sighing it again, exclaims on Death . . *Ven. and Adon.* 930
Sight. Be bold to play, our sport is not in sight 124
His louring brows o'erwhelming his fair sight 183
He sees his love, and nothing else he sees, For nothing else with his proud sight agrees 288
O, what a sight it was, wistly to view How she came stealing to the wayward boy ! 343
So did the merciless and pitchy night Fold in the object that did feed her sight 822
That her sight dazzling makes the wound seem three 1064
He fed them with his sight, they him with berries 1104
O'erstraw'd With sweets that shall the truest sight beguile . . 1144
The boy that by her side lay kill'd Was melted like a vapour from her sight 1166
Nor could she moralize his wanton sight . . . . . *Lucrece* 104
As the fair and fiery-pointed sun, Rushing from forth a cloud, bereaves our sight 373
Lucrece to their sight Must sell her joy, her life, her world's delight . 384
Heedfully doth view The sight which makes supposed terror true . 455
In darkness daunts them with more dreadful sights 462
To see sad sights moves more than hear them told 1324
That it beguiled attention, charm'd the sight 1404
Each under eye Doth homage to his new-appearing sight . *Sonnet* 7 3
Sets you most rich in youth before my sight 15 10
Save that my soul's imaginary sight Presents thy shadow . . 27 9
And moan the expense of many a vanish'd sight 30 8
If aught in me Worthy perusal stand against thy sight . . . 38 6
At a mortal war How to divide the conquest of thy sight . . . 46 2
Mine eye my heart thy picture's sight would bar, My heart mine eye the freedom of that right 46 3
Thy picture in my sight Awakes my heart to heart's and eye's delight . 47 13
While shadows like to thee do mock my sight 61 4
All those beauties whereof now he's king Are vanishing or vanish'd out of sight 63 7
Sometime all full with feasting on your sight 75 9
For if it see the rudest or gentlest sight, . . . it shapes them to your feature 113 9
The winds Which should transport me farthest from your sight . . 117 8
They are but dressings of a former sight 123 4
In my sight, Dear heart, forbear to glance thine eye aside . . 139 5
Which have no correspondence with true sight 148 2
To make me give the lie to my true sight 150 3
The mind and sight distractedly commix'd . . . . *Lov. Comp.* 28
The deep-green emerald, in whose fresh regard Weak sights their sickly radiance do amend 214
Whose sights till then were levell'd on my face 282
Heart hath his hope, and eyes their wished sight . . . *Pass. Pil.* 202
The turtle saw his right Flaming in the phœnix' sight . . *Ph. and Tur.* 35
Sightless. Poor grooms are sightless night, kings glorious day *Lucrece* 1013
My soul's imaginary sight Presents thy shadow to my sightless view *Son.* 27 10
Thy fair imperfect shade Through heavy sleep on sightless eyes doth stay 43 12
Sign. Saw'st thou not signs of fear lurk in mine eye? . *Ven. and Adon.* 644
The world's poor people are amazed At apparitions, signs, and prodigies 926
So she at these sad signs draws up her breath 929
And in their rage such signs of rage they bear . . . . *Lucrece* 1419
Such signs of truth in his plain face she spied 1532
Before these bastard signs of fair were born . . . *Sonnet* 68 3
These are certain signs to know Faithful friend from flattering foe *Pass. Pil.* 429
Silence. This silence for my sin you did impute, Which shall be most my glory *Sonnet* 83 9
As victors of my silence cannot boast 86 11
Because he needs no praise, wilt thou be dumb? Excuse not silence so 101 10
Silent. Their silent war of lilies and of roses . . . . *Lucrece* 71
Answers with surmise, In silent wonder of still-gazing eyes . . . 84
O, learn to read what silent love hath writ . . . . *Sonnet* 23 13
When to the sessions of sweet silent thought I summon up remembrance of things past 30 1
Silk. With sleided silk feat and affectedly Enswathed . . *Lov. Comp.* 48
Silken. Laundering the silken figures in the brine That season'd woe had pelleted in tears 17
The wind Upon his lips their silken parcels hurls 87
Silly. The silly boy, believing she is dead, Claps her pale cheek, till clapping makes it red . . . . *Ven. and Adon.* 467
How much a fool was I To be of such a weak and silly mind . . . 1016
The wolf would leave his prey And never fright the silly lamb that day . 1098
Now serves the season that they may surprise The silly lambs . *Lucrece* 167
Silly groom ! God wot, it was defect Of spirit, life, and bold audacity . 1345
She, silly queen, with more than love's good will, Forbade the boy he should not pass those grounds . . . . *Pass. Pil.* 123
To put in practice either, alas, it was a spite Unto the silly damsel ! . 218
One silly cross Wrought all my loss ; O frowning Fortune ! . . . 257
Silly-jeering. Esteemed so As silly-jeering idiots are with kings . *Lucrece* 1812
Silly-mild. It shall be raging-mad and silly-mild . . *Ven. and Adon.* 1151
Silver. Show'd like two silver doves that sit a-billing 366
Cynthia for shame obscures her silver shine 728
And wakes the morning, from whose silver breast The sun ariseth in his majesty 855
But through the flood-gates breaks the silver rain 959
Away she hies, And yokes her silver doves 1190
In despite Virtue would stain that o'er with silver white . . *Lucrece* 56
Which virtue gave the golden age to gild Their silver cheeks . . . 61
To draw the cloud that hides the silver moon 371
Seasoning the earth with showers of silver brine 796
The stain upon his silver down will stay 1012
In speech, it seem'd, his beard, all silver white, Wagg'd up and down . 1405
Roses have thorns, and silver fountains mud . . . . *Sonnet* 35 2
Silvered. And sable curls all silver'd o'er with white . . . 12 4
Silver-melting. Soon decay'd and done As is the morning's silver-melting dew *Lucrece* 24
Silver-shining. Were Tarquin Night, as he is but Night's child, The silver-shining queen he would distain 786

Similes. Take all these similes to your own command . . . *Lov. Comp.* 227
Simois. To Simois' reedy banks the red blood ran . . . *Lucrece* 1437
They join and shoot their foam at Simois' banks . . . 1442
Simple. He might be buried in a tomb so simple . . . *Ven. and Adon.* 244
Under whose simple semblance he hath fed Upon fresh beauty . . . 795
The poisonous simple sometimes is compacted In a pure compound *Lucrece* 530
And simple truth miscall'd simplicity, And captive good attending captain ill . . . *Sonnet* 66 11
Paying too much rent, For compound sweet forgoing simple savour . 125 7
On both sides thus is simple truth suppress'd . . . 138 8
Who, young and simple, would not be so lover'd? . . . *Lov. Comp.* 320
Simple were so well compounded, That it cried, How true a twain Seemeth this concordant one! . . . *Ph. and Tur.* 44
Simplicity. And simple truth miscall'd simplicity, And captive good attending captain ill . . . *Sonnet* 66 11
Grace in all simplicity, Here enclosed in cinders lie . . . *Ph. and Tur.* 54
Simply. Simply I credit her false-speaking tongue . . . *Sonnet* 138 7
Sin. Hiding base sin in plaits of majesty . . . *Lucrece* 93
And hold it for no sin To wish that I their father had not been . . . 209
To pray he doth begin, As if the heavens should countenance his sin . 343
The blackest sin is clear'd with absolution . . . 354
Wilt thou be glass wherein it shall discern Authority for sin? . . . 620
Foul sin may say, He learn'd to sin, and thou didst teach the way . 629
O, deeper sin than bottomless conceit Can comprehend in still imagination! 701
Therefore would they still in darkness be, To have their unseen sin remain untold . . . 753
Whoever plots the sin, thou 'point'st the season . . . 879
Where none may spy him, Sits Sin, to seize the souls that wander by him . 882
They buy thy help; but Sin ne'er gives a fee, He gratis comes . . . 913
An accessary by thine inclination To all sins past, and all that are to come 923
Base watch of woes, sin's pack-horse, virtue's snare . . . 928
My sable ground of sin I will not paint, To hide the truth . . . 1074
Let sin, alone committed, light alone Upon his head that hath transgressed so 1480
Why should so many fall, To plague a private sin in general? . . . 1484
Or blot with hell-born sin such saint-like forms . . . 1519
Salving thy amiss, Excusing thy sins more than thy sins are . *Sonnet* 35 8
Sin of self-love possesseth all mine eye And all my soul . . . 62 1
And for this sin there is no remedy . . . 62 3
That sin by him advantage should achieve And lace itself with his society 67 3
This silence for my sin you did impute, Which shall be most my glory 83 9
O, in what sweets dost thou thy sins enclose! . . . 95 4
'Tis the lesser sin That mine eye loves it and doth first begin 114 13
I count my gain, That she that makes me sin awards me pain . 141 14
Love is my sin and thy dear virtue hate, Hate of my sin . . 142 1
Think women still to strive with men, To sin and never for to saint *Pass. Pil.* 342
Since. Then why not lips on lips, since eyes in eyes? . *Ven. and Adon.* 120
Since I have hemm'd thee here Within the circuit of this ivory pale . 229
Then be my deer, since I am such a park . . . 239
Love to heaven is fled, Since sweating Lust on earth usurp'd his name 794
Since her best work is ruin'd with thy rigour . . . 954
What canst thou boast Of things long since, or any thing ensuing? . 1078
Since thou art dead, lo, here I prophesy . . . 1135
Since he himself is reft from her by death . . . 1174
Foggy Night! Since thou art guilty of my cureless crime, Muster thy mists to meet the eastern light . . . *Lucrece* 772
Be guilty of my death, since of my crime . . . 931
Since that my case is past the help of law . . . 1022
Since thou couldst not defend thy loyal dame . . . 1034
Since men prove beasts, let beasts bear gentle minds . . . 1148
And ever since, as pitying Lucrece' woes, Corrupted blood some watery token shows . . . 1747
Since Rome herself in them doth stand disgraced . . . 1833
Since sweets and beauties do themselves forsake And die . *Sonnet* 12 11
Since she prick'd thee out for women's pleasure, Mine be thy love 20 13
And weep afresh love's long since cancell'd woe . . . 30 7
Since he died and poets better prove, Theirs for their style I'll read 32 13
Thou hast the strength of laws, Since why to love I can allege no cause 49 14
Since from thee going he went wilful-slow, Towards thee I'll run . 51 13
Therefore are feasts so solemn and so rare, Since, seldom coming . 52 6
Since every one hath, every one, one shade, And you, but one . 53 3
Since mind at first in character was done . . . 59 8
Why should poor beauty indirectly seek Roses of shadow, since his rose is true? . . . 67 8
What wealth she had In days long since, before these last so bad 67 14
Since what he owes thee thou thyself dost pay . . . 79 14
Since your worth, wide as the ocean is, The humble as the proudest sail doth bear . . . 80 5
Thou canst not vex me with inconstant mind, Since that my life on thy revolt doth lie . . . 92 10
Three hot Junes burn'd, Since first I saw you fresh, which yet are green 104 8
Since all alike my songs and praises be To one, of one . . . 105 3
Since, spite of him, I'll live in this poor rhyme . . . 107 11
Since I left you, mine eye is in my mind . . . 113 1
Since my appeal says I did strive to prove . . . 117 13
Since each hand hath put on nature's power . . . 127 5
Since saucy jacks so happy are in this, Give them thy fingers . 128 13
Mourn for me, since mourning doth thee grace . . . 132 11
But since I am near slain, Kill me outright with looks and rid my pain 139 13
For these, of force, must your oblations be, Since I their altar, you enpatron me . . . *Lov. Comp.* 224
Since that our faults in love thus smother'd be . . . *Pass. Pil.* 14
Sin-concealing. Vast sin-concealing chaos! nurse of blame! . . *Lucrece* 767
Sinews. A second fear through all her sinews spread . *Ven. and Adon.* 903
Sinewy. Whose sinewy neck in battle ne'er did bow . . . 99
Sinful. Were it not sinful then, striving to mend, To mar the subject that before was well? . . . *Sonnet* 103 9
Hate of my sin, grounded on sinful loving . . . 142 2
Poor soul, the centre of my sinful earth . . . 146 1
Sing. For through his mane and tail the high wind sings *Ven. and Adon.* 305
And sings extemporally a woeful ditty . . . 836
The birds such pleasure took, That some would sing, some other in their bills Would bring him mulberries . . . 1102
And give the sneaped birds more cause to sing . . . *Lucrece* 333
The adder hisses where the sweet birds sing . . . 871
Who all in one, one pleasing note do sing . . . *Sonnet* 8 12
Sings this to thee: 'thou single wilt prove none' . . . 8 14
Like to the lark at break of day arising From sullen earth, sings hymns at heaven's gate . . . 29 12
O, how thy worth with manners may I sing? . . . 39 1
Thine eyes that taught the dumb on high to sing . . . 78 5
Sing. The very birds are mute; Or, if they sing, 'tis with so dull a cheer That leaves look pale, dreading the winter's near . . . *Sonnet* 97 13
Sing to the ear that doth thy lays esteem . . . 100 7
As Philomel in summer's front doth sing . . . 102 7
They had not skill enough your worth to sing . . . 106 12
O do not love that wrong, To sing heaven's praise with such an earthly tongue . . . *Pass. Pil.* 70
While Philomela sits and sings, I sit and mark . . . 197
Clear wells spring not, Sweet birds sing not . . . 282
By shallow rivers, by whose falls Melodious birds sing madrigals . . 360
Beasts did leap, and birds did sing, Trees did grow, and plants did spring . 377
All thy fellow birds do sing, Careless of thy sorrowing . . . 397
Singest. Come, Philomel, that sing'st of ravishment . . . *Lucrece* 1128
Poor bird, thou sing'st not in the day, As shaming any eye should thee behold 1142
Singing. I in deep delight am chiefly drown'd Whenas himself to singing he betakes . . . *Pass. Pil.* 114
Single. Die single, and thine image dies with thee . . . *Sonnet* 3 14
Sings this to thee: 'thou single wilt prove none' . . . 8 14
Is it for fear to wet a widow's eye That thou consumest thyself in single life? . . . 9 2
Even for this let us divided live, And our dear love lose name of single one 39 6
Single nature's double name Neither two nor one was called . *Ph. and Tur.* 39
Singled. Ceasing their clamorous cry till they have singled With much ado the cold fault cleanly out . . . *Ven and Adon.* 693
Singleness. They do but sweetly chide thee, who confounds In singleness the parts that thou shouldst bear . . . *Sonnet* 8 8
Singular. What needeth then apologies be made, To set forth that which is so singular? . . . *Lucrece* 32
Sink. Not gross to sink, but light, and will aspire . . *Ven. and Adon.* 150
Sinks down to death, oppress'd with melancholy . . . *Sonnet* 45 8
Sinketh. She sinketh down, still hanging by his neck *Ven. and Adon.* 593
Sinking. Then who fears sinking where such treasure lies? . . . *Lucrece* 280
Sinon. The well-skill'd workman this mild image drew For perjured Sinon 1521
Saying, some shape in Sinon's was abused . . . 1529
Even as subtle Sinon here is painted, So sober-sad, so weary, and so mild . 1541
Priam wets his eyes, To see those borrow'd tears that Sinon sheds . 1549
Sinon in his fire doth quake with cold . . . 1556
So Priam's trust false Sinon's tears doth flatter . . . 1560
She tears the senseless Sinon with her nails . . . 1564
Sire. And set dissension 'twixt the son and sire . . *Ven. and Adon.* 1160
Sweet issue of a more sweet-smelling sire . . . 1178
Had Collatinus kill'd my son or sire, Or lain in ambush to betray my life . . . *Lucrece* 232
For trespass of thine eye, The sire, the son, the dame, and daughter die 1477
Resembling sire and child and happy mother . . . *Sonnet* 8 11
Siren. What potions have I drunk of Siren tears, Distill'd from limbecks 119 1
Sister. This device was sent me from a nun, Or sister sanctified *Lov. Comp.* 233
If music and sweet poetry agree, As they must needs, the sister and the brother, Then must the love be great 'twixt thee and me . *Pass. Pil.* 104
Sistering. A plaintful story from a sistering vale . . . *Lov. Comp.* 2
Sit. Here come and sit, where never serpent hisses . *Ven. and Adon.* 17
All swoln with chafing, down Adonis sits . . . 325
Show'd like two silver doves that sit a-billing . . . 366
And there, all smother'd up, in shade doth sit . . . 1035
Within his thought her heavenly image sits, And in the self-same seat sits Collatine . . . *Lucrece* 288
But I alone alone must sit and pine . . . 795
Like still-pining Tantalus he sits . . . 858
Where none may spy him, Sits Sin, to seize the souls that wander by him 882
And seems to point her out where she sits weeping . . . 1087
No love toward others in that bosom sits . . . *Sonnet* 9 13
Any of these all, or all, or more, Entitled in thy parts do crowned sit . 37 7
And more, much more, than in my verse can sit . . . 103 11
And comely-distant sits he by her side . . . *Lov. Comp.* 65
While Philomela sits and sings, I sit and mark . . . *Pass. Pil.* 197
There will we sit upon the rocks, And see the shepherds . . . 357
Sith in thy pride so fair a hope is slain . . . *Ven. and Adon.* 762
Sith in his prime Death doth my love destroy . . . 1163
Sitting. Sweet Cytherea, sitting by a brook, With young Adonis *Pass. Pil.* 43
Venus, with young Adonis sitting by her Under a myrtle shade . . 143
Sitting in a pleasant shade Which a grove of myrtles made . . . 375
Situation. To be so tickled, they would change their state And situation . . . *Sonnet* 128 10
Size. In clamours of all size, both high and low . . . *Lov. Comp.* 21
Skilful. A piece Of skilful painting, made for Priam's Troy . *Lucrece* 1367
Skill. Which far exceeds his barren skill to show . . . 81
With too much labour drowns for want of skill . . . 1099
While thou on Tereus descant'st better skill . . . 1134
Impression of strange kinds Is form'd in them by force, by fraud, or skill . 1243
In him the painter labour'd with his skill To hide deceit . . . 1506
And chid the painter for his wondrous skill . . . 1528
You must live, drawn by your own sweet skill . . . *Sonnet* 16 14
For through the painter must you see his skill . . . 24 5
And folly doctor-like controlling skill . . . 66 10
Some glory in their birth, some in their skill, Some in their wealth . 91 1
And gives thy pen both skill and argument . . . 100 8
They had not skill enough your worth to sing . . . 106 12
Her skill May time disgrace and wretched minutes kill . . . 126 7
There is such strength and warrantise of skill . . . 150 7
He had the dialect and different skill . . . *Lov. Comp.* 125
Skill-contending. Busy yourselves in skill-contending schools *Lucrece* 1018
Skin. Her alabaster skin, Her coral lips, her snow-white dimpled chin 419
Like unshorn velvet on that termless skin Whose bare out-bragg'd the web it seem'd to wear . . . *Lov. Comp.* 94
Skips. And as she fetched breath, away he skips . . . *Pass. Pil.* 14
Sky. Two strengthless doves will draw me through the sky *Ven. and Adon.* 153
Like misty vapours when they blot the sky . . . 184
It flash'd forth fire, as lightning from the sky . . . 348
And as the bright sun glorifies the sky, So is her face illumined with her eye 485
Then do they spend their mouths: Echo replies, As if another chase were in the skies . . . 696
Look, how a bright star shooteth from the sky . . . 815
Through the empty skies In her light chariot quickly is convey'd . 1191
Which triumph'd in that sky of his delight . . . *Lucrece* 12
Which, like a falcon towering in the skies, Coucheth the fowl below . 506
My soul and body to the skies and ground . . . 1199
Enforced by sympathy Of those fair suns set in her mistress' sky . 1230
From his lips did fly Thin winding breath, which purl'd up to the sky . 1407
The skies were sorry, And little stars shot from their fixed places . 1524
About her tear-distained eye Blue circles stream'd, like rainbows in the sky 1587

Sky. Cheered and check'd even by the self-same sky . . . *Sonnet* 15 6
Slack. When time shall serve, be thou not slack To proffer . *Pass. Pil.* 333
Slacked. His rage of lust by gazing qualified ; Slack'd, not suppress'd *Lucr.* 425
Slackly. Though slackly braided in loose negligence . . *Lov. Comp.* 35
Slain. Love made those hollows, if himself were slain, He might be buried in a tomb so simple . . . . *Ven. and Adon.* 243
For on the grass she lies as she were slain 473
Sith in thy pride so fair a hope is slain 762
With him is beauty slain, And, beauty dead, black chaos comes again . 1019
Thus was Adonis slain : He ran upon the boar with his sharp spear . 1111
I fear'd by Tarquin's falchion to be slain . . . . *Lucrece* 1046
Sad souls are slain in merry company 1110
Mistook the matter so, To slay herself, that should have slain her foe . 1827
Presume not on thy heart when mine is slain . . . *Sonnet* 22 13
But since I am near slain, Kill me outright with looks and rid my pain 139 13
Two distincts, division none : Number there in love was slain *Ph. and Tur.* 28
Slaketh. Thy sorrow to my sorrow lendeth Another power; no flood by raining slaketh . . . . *Lucrece* 1677
Slander. I did but act, he's author of thy slander . *Ven. and Adon.* 1006
To clear this spot by death, at least I give A badge of fame to slander's livery . . . . *Lucrece* 1054
My blood shall wash the slander of mine ill 1207
For slander's mark was ever yet the fair . . . . *Sonnet* 70 2
So thou be good, slander doth but approve Thy worth the greater . 70 5
And thence this slander, as I think, proceeds 131 14
Slandered. And beauty slander'd with a bastard shame . . . 127 4
Slanderers. Mad slanderers by mad ears believed be . . . 140 12
Slandering. No beauty lack, Slandering creation with a false esteem 127 12
Slanderous. Betrays To slanderous tongues and wretched hateful days *Lucr.* 161
As slanderous deathsman to so base a slave 1001
Slaughter. To slay the tiger that doth live by slaughter . . . 955
I'll murder straight, and then I'll slaughter thee 1634
Slaughtered. A weeping tear, Shed for the slaughter'd husband by the wife 1376
Slaughterhouse. But this no slaughterhouse no tool imparteth . 1039
Slave. Yet hath he been my captive and my slave *Ven. and Adon.* 101
A martial man to be soft fancy's slave ! . . . . . *Lucrece* 200
And they, like straggling slaves for pillage fighting . . . 428
That done, some worthless slave of thine I'll slay 515
So shall these slaves be king, and thou their slave 659
Carrier of grisly care, Eater of youth, false slave to false delight . . 927
Let him have time to live a loathed slave 984
As slanderous deathsman to so base a slave 1001
Being your slave, what should I do but tend Upon the hours? . *Sonnet* 57 1
Like a sad slave, stay and think of nought Save, where you are . 57 11
That God forbid that made me first your slave 58 1
Lofty towers I see down-razed And brass eternal slave to mortal rage . 64 4
But slave to slavery my sweet'st friend must be 133 4
Thy proud heart's slave and vassal wretch to be 141 12
Slavery. But slave to slavery my sweet'st friend must be . . . 133 4
Slavish. So their pride doth grow, Paying more slavish tribute than they owe *Lucrece* 299
Worse than a slavish wipe or birth-hour's blot 537
Slay. And whom he strikes his crooked tushes slay *Ven. and Adon.* 624
Or theirs whose desperate hands themselves do slay 765
That done, some worthless slave of thine I'll slay . . . *Lucrece* 515
To slay the tiger that doth live by slaughter 955
That mother tries a merciless conclusion Who, having two sweet babes, when death takes one, Will slay the other and be nurse to none 1162
Mistook the matter so, To slay herself, that should have slain her foe . 1827
Use power with power and slay me not by art . . . *Sonnet* 139 4
Sleep. My heart longs not to groan, But soundly sleeps, while now it sleeps alone . . . . *Ven. and Adon.* 786
When heavy sleep had closed up mortal eyes . . . *Lucrece* 163
The dove sleeps fast that this night-owl will catch 360
Each in her sleep themselves so beautify 404
From forth dull sleep by dreadful fancy waking 450
From sleep disturbed, heedfully doth view The sight 454
The patient dies while the physician sleeps 904
Cave-keeping evils that obscurely sleep 1250
Though woe be heavy, yet it seldom sleeps 1574
When I sleep, in dreams they look on thee . . . . *Sonnet* 43 3
Thy fair imperfect shade Through heavy sleep on sightless eyes doth stay 43 12
Or, if they sleep, thy picture in my sight Awakes my heart . . 47 13
Thus have I had thee, as a dream doth flatter, In sleep a king . 87 14
Reason strong, For his advantage still did wake and sleep . *Lov. Comp.* 123
If thou sorrow, he will weep ; If thou wake, he cannot sleep . *Pass. Pil.* 426
Sleeping. Why hast thou cast into eternal sleeping Those eyes that taught all other eyes to see? . . . . . . *Ven. and Adon.* 951
But she, sound sleeping, fearing no such thing, Lies at the mercy of his mortal sting . . . . *Lucrece* 363
So o'er this sleeping soul doth Tarquin stay 423
Mock with thy tickling beams eyes that are sleeping 1090
And so the general of hot desire Was sleeping by a virgin hand disarm'd *Sonnet* 154 8
Herds stand weeping, Flocks all sleeping . . . . *Pass. Pil.* 286
Sleided. With sleided silk feat and affectedly Enswathed . *Lov. Comp.* 48
Slept. And therefore have I slept in your report . . . *Sonnet* 83 5
Slew. Swearing I slew him, seeing thee embrace him . . *Lucrece* 518
Sinon, whose enchanting story The credulous old Priam after slew . 1522
Slide. These present-absent with swift motion slide . . *Sonnet* 45 4
So slides he down upon his grained bat . . . . *Lov. Comp.* 64
Slight. If my slight Muse do please these curious days, The pain be mine, but thine shall be the praise . . . . *Sonnet* 38 13
Slight air and purging fire, Are both with thee, wherever I abide . 45 1
Slip. Make use of time, let not advantage slip . . *Ven. and Adon.* 129
Which purchase if thou make, for fear of slips Set thy seal-manual on my wax-red lips 515
Slow. Make slow pursuit, or altogether balk The prey . . *Lucrece* 696
Let him have time to mark how slow time goes In time of sorrow . . 990
Solemn night with slow sad gait descended To ugly hell . . . 1081
Speed more than speed but dull and slow she deems 1336
They that watch see time how slow it creeps 1575
Bubbling from her breast, it doth divide In two slow rivers . . . 1738
Receiving nought by elements so slow But heavy tears . . *Sonnet* 44 13
Thus can my love excuse the slow offence Of my dull bearer . . 51 1
When swift extremity can seem but slow 51 6
And to temptation slow, They rightly do inherit heaven's graces . 94 4
Sluggard. Replied the maid, 'The more to blame my sluggard negligence' *Lucrece* 1278
Sluice. She vail'd her eyelids, who, like sluices, stopt The crystal tide *Ven. and Adon.* 956
Mine eyes, like sluices, As from a mountain-spring . . . *Lucrece* 1076
Slumber. Now leaden slumber with life's strength doth fight . . 124
Dost thou desire my slumbers should be broken? . . . *Sonnet* 61 3
Sluttish. To wash the foul face of the sluttish ground *Ven. and Adon.* 983
More bright . . Than unswept stone besmear'd with sluttish time *Son.* 55 4
Sly. The mild glance that sly Ulysses lent Show'd deep regard . *Lucrece* 1399
Small. Broad breast, full eye, small head, and nostril wide *Ven. and Adon.* 296
Small lights are soon blown out, hugh fires abide . . . *Lucrece* 647
Know, gentle wench, it small avails my mood 1273
A tatter'd weed, of small worth held . . . . . *Sonnet* 2 4
That to his subject lends not some small glory 84 6
Small show of man was yet upon his chin . . . . *Lov. Comp.* 92
What a hell of witchcraft lies In the small orb of one particular tear ! . . 289
Smallest. Or my affection put to the smallest teen, Or any of my leisures ever charm'd 192
Smarts. Grieving themselves to guess at others' smarts . . . *Lucrece* 1238
Smear. And smear with dust their glittering golden towers 945
Smeared. Begrimed with sweat, and smeared all with dust . . . 1381
Smell. Herbs for their smell, and sappy plants to bear . *Ven. and Adon.* 165
And nothing but the very smell were left me 441
To make the cunning hounds mistake their smell 686
For there his smell with others being mingled, The hot scent-snuffing hounds are driven to doubt 691
His breath and beauty set Gloss on the rose, smell to the violet . . 936
She bows her head, the new-sprung flower to smell 1171
Unapt for tender smell or speedy flight . . . . . *Lucrece* 695
To thy fair flower add the rank smell of weeds . . . . *Sonnet* 69 12
Lilies that fester smell far worse than weeds 94 14
Nor the sweet smell Of different flowers in odour and in hue . . 98 5
Sweet thief, whence didst thou steal thy sweet that smells? . . . 99 2
Nor taste, nor smell, desire to be invited To any sensual feast with thee alone 141 7
Smooth not thy tongue with filed talk, Lest she some subtle practice smell *Pass. Pil.* 307
Smelling. Comes breath perfumed that breedeth love by smelling *V. and A.* 444
Smile. To sport and dance, To toy, to wanton, dally, smile, and jest . . 106
At this Adonis smiles as in disdain, That in each cheek appears a pretty dimple 241
To love a cheek that smiles at thee in scorn ! 252
A smile recures the wounding of a frown 465
Nor shall he smile at thee in secret thought . . . . *Lucrece* 1065
While with a joyless smile she turns away The face 1711
Would not touch the bait, But smile and jest at every gentle offer *Pass. Pil.* 54
Yet at my parting sweetly did she smile 187
Smiled. Whereat she smiled with so sweet a cheer . . . . *Lucrece* 264
Each several stone, With wit well blazon'd, smiled or made some moan *Lov. Comp.* 217
Whilst as fickle Fortune smiled, Thou and I were both beguiled . *Pass. Pil.* 401
Smiling. Show'd deep regard and smiling government . . . *Lucrece* 1400
It suffers not in smiling pomp . . . . *Sonnet* 124 6
Saw how deceits were gilded in his smiling . . . . *Lov. Comp.* 172
I smiling credit her false-speaking tongue . . . . *Pass. Pil.* 7
Smilingly. At last she smilingly with this gives o'er . . . *Lucrece* 1567
Smiteth. His falchion on a flint he softly smiteth 176
Smoke. Her face doth reek and smoke, her blood doth boil *Ven. and Adon.* 555
The wind wars with his torch to make him stay, And blows the smoke of it into his face . . . . *Lucrece* 312
O Night, thou furnace of foul-reeking smoke ! 799
This helpless smoke of words doth me no right 1027
So vanisheth As smoke from Ætna, that in air consumes . . . 1042
Hiding thy bravery in their rotten smoke . . . . . *Sonnet* 34 4
Smoking with pride, march'd on to make his stand On her bare breast *Lucr.* 438
Smoky. That in their smoky ranks his smother'd light May set at noon . 783
Smooth. My smooth moist hand, were it with thy hand felt, Would in thy palm dissolve, or seem to melt . . . . . . *Ven. and Adon.* 143
The path is smooth that leadeth on to danger 788
And when thou comest thy tale to tell, Smooth not thy tongue with filed talk . . . . *Pass. Pil.* 306
Smoothing. Thy smoothing titles to a ragged name . . . . *Lucrece* 892
Smoothness. Their smoothness, like a goodly champaign plain, Lays open all the little worms that creep 1247
Smother. I'll smother thee with kisses . . . . *Ven. and Adon.* 18
Their own transgressions partially they smother . . . . *Lucrece* 634
Or heart in love with sighs himself doth smother . . . *Sonnet* 47 4
Smothered. And there, all smother'd up, in shade doth sit *Ven. and Adon.* 1035
That in their smoky ranks his smother'd light May set at noon . *Lucrece* 783
Another smother'd seems to pelt and swear 1418
Since that our faults in love thus smother'd be . . . *Pass. Pil.* 14
Smotherest. Thou smother'st honesty, thou murder'st troth . . *Lucrece* 885
Snail. Or, as the snail, whose tender horns being hit, Shrinks backward in his shelly cave with pain . . . . . . *Ven. and Adon.* 1033
Snare. Base watch of woes, sin's pack-horse, virtue's snare . . *Lucrece* 928
Sneaped. And give the sneaped birds more cause to sing 333
Snorts. And forth she rushes, snorts, and neighs aloud *Ven. and Adon.* 262
Snout. His snout digs sepulchres where'er he goes 622
Snow. As apt as new-fall'n snow takes any dint 354
A lily prison'd in a gaol of snow, Or ivory in an alabaster band . . . 362
As winter meads when sun doth melt their snow . . . . *Lucrece* 1218
If snow be white, why then her breasts are dun . . . *Sonnet* 130 3
Snow-white. Abhor the deed That spots and stains love's modest snow-white weed . . . . *Lucrece* 196
Her alabaster skin, Her coral lips, her snow-white dimpled chin . . . 420
But if the like the snow-white swan desire, The stain upon his silver down will stay 1011
So. Being so enraged, desire doth lend her force . . *Ven. and Adon.* 29
So soon was she along as he was down 43
Even so she kiss'd his brow, his cheek, his chin 59
Look, how a bird lies tangled in a net, So fasten'd in her arms Adonis lies . 68
So offers he to give what she did crave 88
Narcissus so himself himself forsook, And died to kiss his shadow in the brook 161
So did this horse excel a common one In shape, in courage 293
So white a friend engirts so white a foe 364
My horse is gone, And 'tis your fault I am bereft him so 381
She, by her good will, Will never rise, so he will kiss her still . . . 480
So is her face illumined with her eye 486
And so say you ; If you will say so, you shall have a kiss 535
You have no reason to withhold me so 612

So. And more than so, presenteth to mine eye The picture of an angry-chafing boar *Ven. and Adon.* 661
What should I do, seeing thee so indeed, That tremble at the imagination? 667
Applying this to that, and so to so; For love can comment upon every woe 713
If so, the world will hold thee in disdain 761
So in thyself thyself art made away 763
And still the choir of echoes answer so 840
So, at his bloody view, her eyes are fled 1037
He thought to kiss him, and hath kill'd him so. 'Tis true, 'tis true 1110
And so, by hoping more, they have but less *Lucrece* 137
So then we do neglect The thing we have 152
'So, so,' quoth he, 'these lets attend the time, Like little frosts' 330
So from himself impiety hath wrought 341
So then he hath it when he cannot use it 862
And for my sake serve thou false Tarquin so 1197
Faint not, faint heart, but stoutly say 'So be it' 1209
Poor Lucrece' cheeks unto her maid seem so As winter meads 1217
Was esteemed so As silly-jeering idiots are with kings 1811
Thy wretched wife mistook the matter so, To slay herself 1826
To thee I so belong, That for thy right myself will bear all wrong *Sonnet* 88 13
So as thou art, As those whose beauties proudly make them cruel 131 1
Sobs. And now her sobs do her intendments break *Ven. and Adon.* 222
Sobbing. To whom she sobbing speaks *Lucrece* 1088
Sober. Making such sober action with his hand, That it beguiled attention 1403
Nor that full star that ushers in the even Doth half that glory to the sober west *Sonnet* 132 8
Shook off my sober guards and civil fears *Lov. Comp.* 298
Sober-sad. Even as subtle Sinon here is painted, So sober-sad, so weary, and so mild *Lucrece* 1542
Society. Grief best is pleased with grief's society 1111
That sin by him advantage should achieve And lace itself with his society *Sonnet* 67 4
Sod. Her eyes, though sod in tears, look'd red and raw *Lucrece* 1592
Soft. She swears, From his soft bosom never to remove *Ven. and Adon.* 81
My flesh is soft and plump, my marrow burning 142
His tenderer cheek receives her soft hand's print 353
And being steel'd, soft sighs can never grave it 376
Pure lips, sweet seals in my soft lips imprinted 511
Nor thy soft hands, sweet lips, and crystal eyne 633
The wide wound that the boar had trench'd In his soft flank 1053
The loving swine Sheathed unaware the tusk in his soft groin 1116
A martial man to be soft fancy's slave! *Lucrece* 200
Soft pity enters at an iron gate 595
The purple pride Which on thy soft cheek for complexion dwells *Sonnet* 99 4
Lending soft audience to my sweet design *Lov. Comp.* 278
Touches so soft still conquer chastity *Pass. Pil.* 50
But, soft! enough, too much, I fear. 347
Soften. Beat at thy rocky and wreck-threatening heart, To soften it *Lucrece* 591
Softer. Softer than wax, and yet, as iron, rusty *Pass. Pil.* 88
Softly. His falchion on a flint he softly smiteth *Lucrece* 176
And softly cried 'Awake, thou Roman dame, And entertain my love' 1628
Soft-slow. With soft-slow tongue, true mark of modesty 1220
Soil. And the firm soil win of the watery main, Increasing store *Sonnet* 64 7
Solace. Sorrow changed to solace, solace mix'd with sorrow *Pass. Pil.* 203
Sold. Sold cheap what is most dear, Made old offences of affections new *Sonnet* 110 3
Soldiers. Like soldiers, when their captain once doth yield, They basely fly and dare not stay the field *Ven. and Adon.* 893
Sole. Though it alter not love's sole effect, Yet doth it steal sweet hours from love's delight *Sonnet* 36 7
The bird of loudest lay On the sole Arabian tree *Ph. and Tur.* 2
Solemn. This solemn sympathy poor Venus noteth *Ven. and Adon.* 1057
Solemn night with slow sad gait descended To ugly hell *Lucrece* 1081
Therefore are feasts so solemn and so rare, Since, seldom coming *Sonnet* 52 5
Solicited. Having solicited th' eternal power That his foul thoughts might compass his fair fair *Lucrece* 345
Solve. But why thy odour matcheth not thy show, The solve is this *Son.* 69 14
Some. 'Pity,' she cries, 'some favour, some remorse!' *Ven. and Adon.* 257
Their light blown out in some mistrustful wood 826
The bushes in the way Some catch her by the neck, some kiss her face, Some twine about her thigh to make her stay 872
Hasting to feed her fawn hid in some brake 876
By this, far off she hears some huntsman hollo 973
To see his face the lion walk'd along Behind some hedge 1094
The birds such pleasure took, That some would sing, some other in their bills Would bring him mulberries 1102
Some untimely thought did instigate His all-too-timeless speed *Lucrece* 43
Some loathsome dash the herald will contrive, To cipher me 206
Fearing some hard news from the warlike band 255
They all rate his ill, Which drives the creeping thief to some regard 305
Whether it is that she reflects so bright, That dazzleth them, or else some shame supposed 377
That thinks she hath beheld some ghastly sprite 451
That done, some worthless slave of thine I'll slay 515
From earth's dark womb some gentle gust doth get 549
I mean to bear thee Unto the base bed of some rascal groom 671
No perfection is so absolute, That some impurity doth not pollute 854
She starteth, To find some desperate instrument of death 1038
I live, and seek in vain Some happy mean to end a hapless life 1045
Let it not be call'd impiety, If in this blemish'd fort I make some hole 1175
Vouchsafe t'afford . . . Some present speed to come and visit me 1307
The more she thought he spied in her some blemish 1358
Pausing for means to mourn some newer way 1365
As if some mermaid did their ears entice 1411
Some high, some low, the painter was so nice 1412
Many she sees where cares have carved some 1445
Why should the private pleasure of some one Become the public plague of many moe? 1478
Saying, some shape in Sinon's was abused 1529
It easeth some, though none it ever cured, To think their dolour others have endured 1581
Some of her blood still pure and red remain'd, And some look'd black 1742
As pitying Lucrece' woes, Corrupted blood some watery token shows 1748
Thou dost beguile the world, unbless some mother *Sonnet* 3 4
Make sweet some vial; treasure thou some place With beauty's treasure 6 3
Your sweet semblance to some other give 13 4
Were some child of yours alive that time, You should live twice 17 13
Some fierce thing replete with too much rage 23 3
I hope some good conceit of thine In thy soul's thought, all naked, will bestow it 26 7
Some. As if by some instinct the wretch did know His rider loved not speed, being made from thee *Sonnet* 50 7
In all external grace you have some part 53 13
Show me your image in some antique book 59 7
If some suspect of ill mask'd not thy show 70 13
Unless you would devise some virtuous lie 72 5
My life hath in this line some interest 74 3
Seek anew Some fresher stamp of the time-bettering days 82 8
That to his subject lends not some small glory 84 6
Say that thou didst forsake me for some fault 89 1
Some glory in their birth, some in their skill, Some in their wealth, some in their bodies' force, Some in their garments, though new-fangled ill, Some in their hawks and hounds, some in their horse 91 1
Some say thy fault is youth, some wantonness; Some say thy grace is youth and gentle sport 96 1
Some say that thee behold Thy face hath not the power to make love groan 131 5
Some beauty peep'd through lattice of sear'd age *Lov. Comp.* 14
For some, untuck'd, descended her sheaved hat 31
Where want cries some, but where excess begs all 42
Yet did I not, as some my equals did, Demand of him, nor being desired yielded 148
Gentle maid, Have of my suffering youth some feeling pity 178
Each several stone, With wit well blazon'd, smiled or made some moan 217
Some untutor'd youth, Unskilful in the world's false forgeries *Pass. Pil.* 3
Which is to me some praise, that I thy parts admire 66
Take counsel of some wiser head, Neither too young nor yet unwed 303
Smooth not thy tongue with filed talk, Lest she some subtle practice smell 307
Something. For want of wit, Make something nothing by augmenting it *Lucrece* 154
'Tis so, 'tis true, And to the most of praise add something more *Sonnet* 85 10
So it please thee hold That nothing me, a something sweet to thee 136 12
Sometime. Her sobs do her intendments break. Sometimes she shakes her head *Ven. and Adon.* 223
Sometimes her arms infold him like a band 225
Sometime he trots, as if he told the steps, With gentle majesty and modest pride 277
Sometime he scuds far off and there he stares 301
That sometime true news, sometime false doth bring 658
Sometime he runs among a flock of sheep, To make the cunning hounds mistake their smell 685
And sometime where earth-delving conies keep 687
And sometime sorteth with a herd of deer 689
Yet sometimes falls an orient drop beside, Which her cheek melts 981
That nothing in him seem'd inordinate, Save sometime too much wonder of his eye *Lucrece* 95
Like little frosts that sometime threat the spring 331
The poisonous simple sometimes is compacted In a pure compound 530
Sometime her grief is dumb and hath no words; Sometime 'tis mad 1105
Sometime 'Tarquin' was pronounced plain, But through his teeth 1786
Whereon the thought might think sometime it saw *Lov. Comp.* 10
Sometimes her levell'd eyes their carriage ride 22
Sometime diverted their poor balls are tied To the orbed earth; sometimes they do extend Their view right on 25
Sometime a blusterer, that the ruffle knew Of court, of city 58
Sometime too hot the eye of heaven shines *Sonnet* 18 5
Every fair from fair sometime declines, By chance 18 7
When I am sometime absent from thy heart 41 2
The bloody spur cannot provoke him on That sometimes anger thrusts into his hide 50 10
When sometime lofty towers I see down-razed 64 3
Sometime all full with feasting on your sight 75 9
I sometime hold my tongue, Because I would not dull you with my song 102 13
Son. Art thou a woman's son, and canst not feel What 'tis to love? how want of love tormenteth? *Ven. and Adon.* 201
And barren dearth of daughters and of sons, Be prodigal 754
Or butcher-sire that reaves his son of life 766
There lives a son that suck'd an earthly mother, May lend thee light 863
And set dissension 'twixt the son and sire 1160
Had Collatinus kill'd my son or sire *Lucrece* 232
Sharing joy To see their youthful sons bright weapons wield 1432
For trespass of thine eye, The sire, the son, the dame, and daughter die 1477
Had doting Priam check'd his son's desire, Troy had been bright with fame 1490
Son and father weep with equal strife Who should weep most 1791
Unlook'd on diest, unless thou get a son *Sonnet* 7 14
My love, you know You had a father: let your son say so 13 14
When a woman woos, what woman's son Will sourly leave her till she have prevailed? 41 7
Song. Bewitching like the wanton mermaid's songs *Ven. and Adon.* 777
Her song was tedious and outwore the night 841
A nurse's song ne'er pleased her babe so well 974
Whose speechless song, being many, seeming one, Sings this to thee: 'thou single wilt prove none' *Sonnet* 8 13
A poet's rage And stretched metre of an antique song 17 12
Spend'st thou thy fury on some worthless song? 100 3
I sometime hold my tongue, Because I would not dull you with my song 102 14
Since all alike my songs and praises be To one, of one 105 3
Then, lullaby, the learned man hath got the lady gay; For now my song is ended *Pass. Pil.* 226
Enough, too much, I fear; Lest that my mistress hear my song 348
Sonnets. Deep-brain'd sonnets that did amplify Each stone's dear nature, worth, and quality *Lov. Comp.* 209
Soon. So soon was she along as he was down *Ven. and Adon.* 43
Now doth he frown, And 'gins to chide, but soon she stops his lips 46
And soon bereaves, As caterpillars do the tender leaves 797
As soon decay'd and done As is the morning's silver-melting dew *Lucrece* 23
Which gives the watch-word to his hand full soon 370
Small lights are soon blown out, huge fires abide 647
The cause craves haste, and it will soon be writ 1295
For nimble thought can jump both sea and land As soon as think the place where he would be *Sonnet* 44 8
How hard true sorrow hits, And soon to you, as you to me! 120 11
To win me soon to hell, my female evil Tempteth 144 5; *Pass. Pil.* 19
She burn'd out love, as soon as straw out-burneth 98
Untimely pluck'd, soon vaded, Pluck'd in the bud, and vaded in the spring! 131
Fair creature, kill'd too soon by death's sharp sting! 134
Were I with her, the night would post too soon 205
A cripple soon can find a halt 308

Sooner. Enjoy'd no sooner but despised straight . . *Sonnet* 129 5
Past reason hunted, and no sooner had Past reason hated . 129 6
Soothing the humour of fantastic wits . *Ven. and Adon.* 850
O, love's best habit is a soothing tongue . . . . *Pass. Pil.* 11
Sore. To one sore sick that hears the passing-bell . *Ven. and Adon.* 702
'Gainst venom'd sores the only sovereign plaster 916
O unfelt sore! crest-wounding, private scar! . . . *Lucrece* 828
'Fool, fool!' quoth she, 'his wounds will not be sore' . . 1568
'See, in my thigh,' quoth she, 'here was the sore.' She showed hers *Pass Pil.* 128
Sorrow. So of concealed sorrow may be said; Free vent of words love's fire doth assuage *Ven. and Adon.* 333
Sorrow to shepherds, woe unto the birds 455
The night of sorrow now is turn'd to day 481
'Sweet boy,' she says, 'this night I'll waste in sorrow' . . 583
I prophesy thy death, my living sorrow 671
Both crystals, where they view'd each other's sorrow, Sorrow that friendly sighs sought still to dry 963
Every present sorrow seemeth chief, But none is best . . 970
Sorrow on love hereafter shall attend 1136
He doth debate What following sorrow may on this arise . *Lucrece* 186
This sorrow to the sage, This dying virtue, this surviving shame . 222
What wrong, what shame, what sorrow I shall breed . . 499
The chastest tears That ever modest eyes with sorrow shed . 683
Let him have time to mark how slow time goes In time of sorrow 991
The well-tuned warble of her nightly sorrow 1080
Old woes, not infant sorrows, bear them mild 1096
And to herself all sorrow doth compare 1102
True sorrow then is feelingly sufficed 1112
And sorts a sad look to her lady's sorrow, For why her face wore sorrow's livery 1221
Here folds she up the tenour of her woe, Her certain sorrow writ uncertainly 1311
'Tis but a part of sorrow that we hear 1328
Sorrow ebbs, being blown with wind of words 1330
And shapes her sorrow to the beldam's woes 1458
For sorrow, like a heavy-hanging bell, Once set on ringing, with his own weight goes 1493
Sad tales doth tell To pencill'd pensiveness and colour'd sorrow . . 1497
Thus ebbs and flows the current of her sorrow . . . 1569
Short time seems long in sorrow's sharp sustaining . . 1573
Three times with sighs she gives her sorrow fire . . . 1604
Even so his sighs, his sorrows, make a saw, To push grief on . 1672
Dear lord, thy sorrow to my sorrow lendeth Another power . 1676
And bids Lucretius give his sorrow place 1773
Mad that sorrow should his use control 1781
Held back his sorrow's tide, to make it more 1789
Do not take away My sorrow's interest 1797
But day doth daily draw my sorrows longer . . *Sonnet* 28 13
All losses are restored and sorrows end 30 14
The offender's sorrow lends but weak relief 34 11
Ah, do not, when my heart hath 'scaped this sorrow, Come in the rearward of a conquer'd woe 90 5
And for that sorrow which I then did feel Needs must I under my transgression bow 120 2
How hard true sorrow hits, And soon to you, as you to me! . 120 10
Lest sorrow lend me words and words express The manner of my pity-wanting pain 140 3
Storming her world with sorrow's wind and rain *Lov. Comp.* 7
Not age, but sorrow, over me hath power 74
Paler for sorrow than her milk-white dove, For Adon's sake . *Pass. Pil.* 119
Farewell I could not, for I supp'd with sorrow 186
Sorrow changed to solace, solace mix'd with sorrow . . . 203
If thou sorrow, he will weep; If thou wake, he cannot sleep . 425
Sorrowing. All thy fellow birds do sing, Careless of thy sorrowing 398
Sorry. The skies were sorry, And little stars shot from their fixed places *Lucrece* 1524
Make glad and sorry seasons as thou fleets . . *Sonnet* 19 5
Sort. When wilt thou sort an hour great strifes to end? . *Lucrece* 899
And sorts a sad look to her lady's sorrow 1221
I love thee in such sort As, thou being mine, mine is thy good report *Sonnet* 36 13; 96 13
Sorteth. And sometime sorteth with a herd of deer *Ven. and Adon.* 689
Sought. Sorrow that friendly sighs sought still to dry . . . 964
Hath barr'd him from the blessed thing he sought . . *Lucrece* 340
Which I to conquer sought with all my might 488
O, that is gone for which I sought to live 1051
Whose waves to imitate the battle sought With swelling ridges . 1438
I sigh the lack of many a thing I sought . . *Sonnet* 30 3
They sought their shame that so their shame did find . *Lov. Comp.* 187
She was sought by spirits of richest coat, But kept cold distance . 236
Against the thing he sought he would exclaim 313
Soul. So o'er this sleeping soul doth Tarquin stay, His rage of lust by gazing qualified . . . . *Lucrece* 423
I have debated, even in my soul, What wrong, what shame . . 498
Besides, his soul's fair temple is defaced 719
Where none may spy him, Sits Sin, to seize the souls that wander by him . 882
Or free that soul which wretchedness hath chain'd . . . 900
Sad souls are slain in merry company 1110
What were it, But with my body my poor soul's pollution? . . 1157
My body or my soul, which was the dearer, When the one pure, the other made divine? 1163
So must my soul, her bark being peel'd away 1169
Make some hole Through which I may convey this troubled soul . 1176
My soul and body to the skies and ground 1199
Let guiltless souls be freed from guilty woe 1482
Even here she sheathed in her harmless breast A harmful knife, that thence her soul unsheathed 1724
Leave the faltering feeble souls alive 1768
The deep vexation of his inward soul Hath served a dumb arrest upon his tongue 1779
By chaste Lucrece' soul that late complain'd Her wrongs to us . 1839
Which steals men's eyes and women's souls amazeth *Sonnet* 20 8
I hope some good conceit of thine In thy soul's thought, all naked, will bestow it 26 8
Save that my soul's imaginary sight Presents thy shadow . 27 9
Sin of self-love possesseth all mine eye And all my soul . 62 2
All tongues, the voice of souls, give thee that due, Uttering bare truth 69 3
Not mine own fears, nor the prophetic soul Of the wide world . 107 1
As easy might I from myself depart As from my soul . . 109 4

Soul. A true soul When most impeach'd stands least in thy control *Sonnet* 125 13
If thy soul check thee that I come so near, Swear to thy blind soul that I was thy 'Will,' And will, thy soul knows, is admitted there 136 1
Poor soul, the centre of my sinful earth 146 1
Then, soul, live thou upon thy servant's loss . . . 146 9
My soul doth tell my body that he may Triumph in love . 151 7
Lending soft audience to my sweet design, And credent soul to that strong-bonded oath . . . . *Lov. Comp.* 279
All ignorant that soul that sees thee without wonder . *Pass. Pil.* 65
Sound. And will not let a false sound enter there . *Ven. and Adon.* 780
Idle sounds resembling parasites 848
The dire imagination she did follow This sound of hope doth labour to expel 976
But she, sound sleeping, fearing no such thing, Lies at the mercy of his mortal sting . . . . *Lucrece* 363
First, like a trumpet, doth his tongue begin To sound a parley . 471
For now against himself he sounds this doom 717
Unprofitable sounds, weak arbitrators! 1017
Deep sounds make lesser noise than shallow fords . . . 1329
A press of gaping faces, Which seem'd to swallow up his sound advice 1409
'Poor instrument,' quoth she, 'without a sound, I'll tune thy woes with my lamenting tongue' 1464
If the true concord of well-tuned sounds, By unions married, do offend thine ear . . . . *Sonnet* 8 5
That blessed wood whose motion sounds With thy sweet fingers . 128 2
Yet well I know That music hath a far more pleasing sound . 130 10
Those lips that Love's own hand did make Breathed forth the sound that said 'I hate' 145 2
Sweet melodious sound That Phœbus' lute, the queen of music, makes *Pass. Pil.* 111
My shepherd's pipe can sound no deal 271
Herald sad and trumpet be, To whose sound chaste wings obey *Ph. and Tur.* 4
Soundless. Whilst he upon your soundless deep doth ride . *Sonnet* 80 10
Soundly. My heart longs not to groan, But soundly sleeps *Ven. and Adon.* 786
Sour. Lest Jealousy, that sour unwelcome guest, Should, by his stealing in, disturb the feast 449
Or being early pluck'd is sour to taste 528
This sour informer, this bate-breeding spy 655
The sweets we wish for turn to loathed sours . . *Lucrece* 867
Were it not thy sour leisure gave sweet leave To entertain the time *Son.* 39 10
Nor think the bitterness of absence sour 57 7
Sourest. Sweetest things turn sourest by their deeds . . 94 13
Sour-faced. Charging the sour-faced groom to hie as fast As lagging fowls before the northern blast . . . . . *Lucrece* 1334
Souring his cheeks cries 'Fie, no more of love!' *Ven. and Adon.* 185
His taste delicious, in digestion souring, Devours his will *Lucrece* 699
Sourly. I an accessary needs must be To that sweet thief which sourly robs from me . . . . *Sonnet* 35 14
When a woman woos, what woman's son Will sourly leave her till she have prevailed? 41 8
Sovereign. Calls it balm, Earth's sovereign salve to do a goddess good *Ven. and Adon.* 28
'Gainst venom'd sores the only sovereign plaster 916
The petty streams that pay a daily debt To their salt sovereign *Lucrece* 650
'Thou art,' quoth she, 'a sea, a sovereign king' . . . 652
Full many a glorious morning have I seen Flatter the mountain-tops with sovereign eye . . . . *Sonnet* 33 2
Whilst I, my sovereign, watch the clock for you . . . 57 6
Nature, sovereign mistress over wrack 126 5
Which yet men prove Against strange maladies a sovereign cure . 153 8
Sovereignty. Perchance his boast of Lucrece' sovereignty Suggested this proud issue of a king . . . . *Lucrece* 36
The sovereignty of either being so great 69
Space. And counterfeits to die with her a space 1776
Despite of space I would be brought, From limits far remote, where thou dost stay . . . . *Sonnet* 44 3
Vow, bond, nor space, In thee hath neither sting, knot, nor confine *L. Comp.* 264
Distance, and no space was seen 'Twixt the turtle and his queen *Ph. and Tur.* 30
Spacious. Wilt thou, whose will is large and spacious, Not once vouchsafe to hide my will in thine? . . . . *Sonnet* 135 5
Spare. My husband is thy friend; for his sake spare me . *Lucrece* 582
Spare not to spend, and chiefly there Where thy desert may merit praise *Pass. Pil.* 324
Sparing. It shall be sparing and too full of riot *Ven. and Adon.* 1147
Let the traitor die; For sparing justice feeds iniquity . *Lucrece* 1687
Sparks. That from the cold stone sparks of fire do fly . . 177
Sparkling. When sparkling stars twire not thou gild'st the even *Sonnet* 28 12
Sparrow. Or hateful cuckoos hatch in sparrows' nests . *Lucrece* 849
Speak. And kissing speaks, with lustful language broken *Ven. and Adon.* 47
Speak, fair; but speak fair words, or else be mute . . . 208
And now she weeps, and now she fain would speak . . . 221
To whom she speaks, and he replies with howling . . . 918
Strike the wise dumb and teach the fool to speak . . . 1146
And to the flame thus speaks advisedly . . . . *Lucrece* 180
So her accent breaks, That twice she doth begin ere once she speaks . 567
To whom she sobbing speaks: 'O eye of eyes, Why pry'st thou?' . 1088
By this, mild patience bid fair Lucrece speak 1268
Swearing, unless I took all patiently, I should not live to speak another word 1642
My bloody judge forbade my tongue to speak 1648
'O, speak,' quoth she, 'How may this forced stain be wiped from me?' 1700
But more than 'he' her poor tongue could not speak . . . 1718
For no man well of such a salve can speak . . *Sonnet* 34 7
Speak of the spring and foison of the year 53 9
That you for love speak well of me untrue 72 10
Speak of my lameness, and I straight will halt, Against thy reasons . 89 3
Where art thou, Muse, that thou forget'st so long To speak? . 100 2
What's new to speak, what new to register, That may express my love? 108 3
I love to hear her speak, yet well I know That music hath a far more pleasing sound 130 9
And in my madness might speak ill of thee 140 10
Speaking. Speaking to those that came with Collatine . . *Lucrece* 1689
Let my books be then the eloquence And dumb presagers of my speaking breast . . . . *Sonnet* 23 10
To make me tongue-tied, speaking of your fame . . . 80 4
Speaking of worth, what worth in you doth grow . . . 83 8
Then others for the breath of words respect, Me for my dumb thoughts, speaking in effect 85 14
Spear. Are better proof than thy spear's point can enter *Ven. and Adon.* 626
Thus was Adonis slain: He ran upon the boar with his sharp spear . 1112
That for Achilles' image stood his spear, Griped in an armed hand *Lucrece* 1424

Special. To make some special instant special blest, By new unfolding his imprison'd pride *Sonnet* 52 11
Spectacle. Think but how vile a spectacle it were *Lucrece* 631
Deep-wounded with a boar, Deep in the thigh, a spectacle of ruth! *Pass. Pil.* 127
Speech. Once more the ruby-colour'd portal open'd, Which to his speech did honey passage yield *Ven. and Adon.* 452
In speech, it seem'd, his beard, all silver white, Wagg'd up and down *Lucr.* 1405
To blush at speeches rank, to weep at woes *Lov. Comp.* 307
Speechless. Which speechless woe of his poor she attendeth *Lucrece* 1674
Whose speechless song, being many, seeming one, Sings this to thee *Son.* 8 13
I'll live in this poor rhyme, While he insults o'er dull and speechless tribes 107 12
Speed. Some untimely thought did instigate His all-too-timeless speed *Lucr.* 44
Or stop the headlong fury of his speed 501
He in his speed looks for the morning light 745
Bid him with speed prepare to carry it 1294
Vouchsafe t'afford . . . Some present speed to come and visit me 1307
Speed more than speed but dull and slow she deems 1336
While others saucily Promise more speed, but do it leisurely 1349
As if by some instinct the wretch did know His rider loved not speed *Sonnet* 50 8
Thus can my love excuse the slow offence Of my dull bearer when from thee I speed 51 2
In winged speed no motion shall I know 51 8
My ewes breed not, My rams speed not, All is amiss *Pass. Pil.* 247
Speeding. Heart is bleeding, All help needing, O cruel speeding, Fraughted with gall 269
Speedy. Unapt for tender smell or speedy flight *Lucrece* 695
Which being done with speedy diligence, The Romans plausibly did give consent 1853
Spend. Then do they spend their mouths: Echo replies, As if another chase were in the skies *Ven. and Adon.* 695
For who hath she to spend the night withal But idle sounds resembling parasites 847
Not spend the dowry of a lawful bed *Lucrece* 938
The life and feeling of her passion She hoards, to spend when he is by 1318
On this sad shadow Lucrece spends her eyes 1457
Why dost thou spend Upon thyself thy beauty's legacy? *Sonnet* 4 1
Look, what an unthrift in the world doth spend Shifts but his place 9 9
I have no precious time at all to spend, Nor services to do, till you require 57 3
And in the praise thereof spends all his might 80 3
Why so large cost, having so short a lease, Dost thou upon thy fading mansion spend? 146 6
Do I not spend Revenge upon myself with present moan? 149 7
And did thence remove, To spend her living in eternal love *Lov. Comp.* 238
Spare not to spend, and chiefly there Where thy desert may merit praise *Pass. Pil.* 324
Every man will be thy friend Whilst thou hast wherewith to spend 408
Spend'st thou thy fury on some worthless song? *Sonnet* 100 3
Spending again what is already spent 76 12
Spenser to me, whose deep conceit is such As, passing all conceit, needs no defence *Pass. Pil.* 109
Spent. The time is spent, her object will away, And from her twining arms doth urge releasing *Ven. and Adon.* 255
'The night is spent.' 'Why, what of that?' quoth she 717
My stained blood to Tarquin I'll bequeath, Which by him tainted shall for him be spent *Lucrece* 1182
Overslipp'd her thought, That she with painted images hath spent 1577
These water-galls in her dim element Foretell new storms to those already spent 1589
Sweet love, what spite hath thy fair colour spent? 1600
Spending again what is already spent *Sonnet* 76 12
And straight redeem In gentle numbers time so idly spent 100 6
And in this change is my invention spent 105 11
When tyrants' crests and tombs of brass are spent 107 14
And gain by ill thrice more than I have spent 119 14
Pitiful thrivers, in their gazing spent 125 8
The carcass of a beauty spent and done *Lov. Comp.* 11
Spheres. How have mine eyes out of their spheres been fitted! *Sonnet* 119 7
Sometimes her levell'd eyes their carriage ride, As they did battery to the spheres intend *Lov. Comp.* 23
Spied. And with that word she spied the hunted boar *Ven. and Adon.* 900
The more she thought he spied in her some blemish *Lucrece* 1358
Such signs of truth in his plain face she spied 1532
Spied a blossom passing fair, Playing in the wanton air *Pass. Pil.* 229
Spill. Such wretched hands such wretched blood should spill *Lucrece* 999
Spilled. In his blood that on the ground lay spill'd, A purple flower sprung up, chequer'd with white *Ven. and Adon.* 1167
I did give that life Which she too early and too late hath spill'd *Lucrece* 1801
Spilling. The other takes in hand No cause, but company, of her drops spilling 1236
Spirit. Love is a spirit all compact of fire, Not gross to sink, but light, and will aspire *Ven. and Adon.* 149
Appals her senses and her spirit confounds 882
God wot, it was defect Of spirit, life, and bold audacity *Lucrece* 1346
Do not kill The spirit of love with a perpetual dullness *Sonnet* 56 8
Is it thy spirit that thou send'st from thee So far from home? 61 5
My spirit is thine, the better part of me 74 8
Knowing a better spirit doth use your name 80 2
Still cry 'Amen' To every hymn that able spirit affords 85 7
Was it his spirit, by spirits taught to write Above a mortal pitch? 86 5
Hath put a spirit of youth in every thing 98 3
What's in the brain that ink may character Which hath not figured to thee my true spirit? 108 2
The expense of spirit in a waste of shame Is lust in action 129 1
Which like two spirits do suggest me still 144 2
The worser spirit a woman colour'd ill 144 4
My spirits to attend this double voice accorded *Lov. Comp.* 3
She was sought by spirits of richest coat, But kept cold distance 236
Two loves I have, of comfort and despair, That like two spirits do suggest me still *Pass. Pil.* 16
My better angel is a man right fair, My worser spirit a woman colour'd ill 18
Spite. And so, in spite of death, thou dost survive, In that thy likeness still is left alive *Ven. and Adon.* 173
This is my spite, That, thou being dead, the day should yet be light 1133
Frantic with grief thus breathes she forth her spite *Lucrece* 762
Sweet love, what spite hath thy fair colour spent? 1600
In our two loves there is but one respect, Though in our lives a separable spite *Sonnet* 36 6
So I, made lame by fortune's dearest spite 37 3
Spite. Lascivious grace, in whom all ill well shows, Kill me with spites; yet we must not be foes *Sonnet* 40 14
Now, while the world is bent my deeds to cross, Join with the spite of fortune 90 3
Do not leave me last, When other petty griefs have done their spite 90 10
Since, spite of him, I'll live in this poor rhyme 107 11
But, spite of heaven's fell rage, Some beauty peep'd through lattice of sear'd age *Lov. Comp.* 13
In spite of physic, painting, pain, and cost *Pass. Pil.* 180
Now are minutes added to the hours; To spite me now, each minute seems a moon 207
To put in practice either, alas, it was a spite Unto the silly damsel! 217
Spleen. A thousand spleens bear her a thousand ways *Ven. and Adon.* 907
By a brook, A brook where Adon used to cool his spleen *Pass. Pil.* 76
Splendour. Against the golden splendour of the sun *Lucrece* 25
With all-triumphant splendour on my brow *Sonnet* 33 10
Spoil. And having felt the sweetness of the spoil, With blindfold fury she begins to forage *Ven. and Adon.* 553
Leaving his spoil perplex'd in greater pain *Lucrece* 733
To spoil antiquities of hammer'd steel 951
Or who his spoil of beauty can forbid? *Sonnet* 65 12
And make Time's spoils despised every where 100 12
The foil Of this false jewel, and his amorous spoil *Lov. Comp.* 154
Spoiled. Her sacred temple spotted, spoil'd, corrupted *Lucrece* 1172
Spoke. Hadst thou but bid beware, then he had spoke *Ven. and Adon.* 943
If he had spoke, the wolf would leave his prey 1097
Spongy. O, that sad breath his spongy lungs bestow'd! *Lov. Comp.* 326
Sport. A summer's day will seem an hour but short, Being wasted in such time-beguiling sport *Ven. and Adon.* 24
To sport and dance, To toy, to wanton, dally, smile, and jest 105
Be bold to play, our sport is not in sight 124
From morn till night, even where I list to sport me 154
In such-like circumstance, with such-like sport 844
How swift and short His time of folly and his time of sport *Lucrece* 992
Making lascivious comments on thy sport *Sonnet* 95 6
Some say thy grace is youth and gentle sport 96 2
Playing patient sports in unconstrained gyves *Lov. Comp.* 242
Youth is full of sport, age's breath is short; Youth is nimble, age is lame *Pass. Pil.* 161
All our evening sport from us is fled, All our love is lost 291
Sporting. Advice is sporting while infection breeds *Lucrece* 907
Sportive. For sportive words and uttering foolish things 1813
Why should others' false adulterate eyes Give salutation to my sportive blood? *Sonnet* 121 6
Spot. Let fair humanity abhor the deed That spots and stains love's modest snow-white weed *Lucrece* 196
The spots whereof could weeping purify, Her tears should drop on them 685
To clear this spot by death, at least I give A badge of fame to slander's livery 1053
Which, like a canker in the fragrant rose, Doth spot the beauty *Sonnet* 95 3
Spotless. Immaculate and spotless is my mind *Lucrece* 1656
Spotted. To whose weak ruins muster troops of cares, To ask the spotted princess how she fares 721
Her sacred temple spotted, spoil'd, corrupted 1172
Spread. Like lawn being spread upon the blushing rose *Ven. and Adon.* 590
A second fear through all her sinews spread 903
When he beheld his shadow in the brook, The fishes spread on it their golden gills 1100
That dying fear through all her body spread *Lucrece* 1266
Great princes' favourites their fair leaves spread *Sonnet* 25 5
Spreading. I might as yet have been a spreading flower, Fresh to myself *Lov. Comp.* 75
Spright. With a lazy spright, And with a heavy, dark, disliking eye *V. and A.* 181
Intending weariness with heavy spright *Lucrece* 121
Spring. The tender spring upon thy tempting lip Shows thee unripe; yet mayst thou well be tasted *Ven. and Adon.* 127
My beauty as the spring doth yearly grow 141
Seeds spring from seeds and beauty breedeth beauty 167
Away he springs and hasteth to his horse 258
This canker that eats up Love's tender spring 656
Love's gentle spring doth always fresh remain 801
Thy hasty spring still blasts, and ne'er grows old *Lucrece* 49
Like little frosts that sometime threat the spring 331
When thus thy vices bud before thy spring 604
Unruly blasts wait on the tender spring 869
To dry the old oak's sap and cherish springs 950
Wanting the spring that those shrunk pipes had fed 1455
The world's fresh ornament And only herald to the gaudy spring *Sonnet* 1 10
Speak of the spring and foison of the year 53 9
Stealing away the treasure of his spring 63 8
From you have I been absent in the spring 98 1
Our love was new and then but in the spring 102 5
Three beauteous springs to yellow autumn turn'd 104 5
Soon vaded, Pluck'd in the bud, and vaded in the spring *Pass. Pil.* 132
Clear wells spring not, Sweet birds sing not 281
Beasts did leap, and birds did sing, Trees did grow, and plants did spring 378
Springing. If springing things be any jot diminish'd, They wither in their prime, prove nothing worth *Ven. and Adon.* 417
Sprite. That thinks she hath beheld some ghastly sprite *Lucrece* 451
Her contrite sighs unto the clouds bequeathed Her winged sprite 1728
Sprung. A purple flower sprung up, chequer'd with white *Ven. and Adon.* 1168
Spur. What cares he now for curb or pricking spur? 285
The bloody spur cannot provoke him on *Sonnet* 50 9
Then should I spur, though mounted on the wind 51 7
Spurns at his love and scorns the heat he feels *Ven. and Adon.* 311
In vain I cavil with mine infamy, In vain I spurn at my confirm'd despite *Lucrece* 1026
Spurnest. 'Tis thou that spurn'st at right, at law, at reason 880
Spurring. Which heavily he answers with a groan, More sharp to me than spurring to his side *Sonnet* 50 12
Spy. This sour informer, this bate-breeding spy *Ven. and Adon.* 655
Like one that spies an adder Wreathed up in fatal folds just in his way 878
In her haste unfortunately spies The foul boar's conquest 1029
And being lighted, by the light he spies Lucretia's glove *Lucrece* 316
In thy shady cell, where none may spy him, Sits Sin 881
Revealing day through every cranny spies 1086
On my frailties why are frailer spies, Which in their wills count bad what I think good? *Sonnet* 121 7
Spying. He, spying her, bounced in, whereas he stood *Pass. Pil.* 83
Stage. My part is youth, and beats these from the stage *Lucrece* 278
Black stage for tragedies and murders fell! 766

Stage. This huge stage presenteth nought but shows . . . *Sonnet* 15 3
As an unperfect actor on the stage Who with his fear is put besides his part . . . 23 1
Stain. The field's chief flower, sweet above compare, Stain to all nymphs, more lovely than a man . . . *Ven. and Adon.* 9
Which the hot tyrant stains and soon bereaves . . . 797
And stains her face with his congealed blood . . . 1122
When beauty boasted blushes, in despite Virtue would stain that o'er with silver white . . . *Lucrece* 56
While lust and murder wake to stain and kill . . . 168
Abhor the deed That spots and stains love's modest snow-white weed . . . 196
Who seek to stain the ocean of thy blood . . . 655
O, that prone lust should stain so pure a bed! . . . 684
The stain upon his silver down will stay . . . 1012
How may this forced stain be wiped from me? . . . 1701
The poison'd fountain clears itself again; And why not I from this compelled stain? . . . 1708
Her body's stain her mind untainted clears . . . 1710
Suns of the world may stain when heaven's sun staineth . . . *Sonnet* 33 14
Clouds and eclipses stain both moon and sun . . . 35 3
So that myself bring water for my stain . . . 109 8
Stained. An image like thyself, all stain'd with gore . . . *Ven. and Adon.* 664
Dear Collatine, thou shalt not know The stained taste of violated troth . . . *Lucrece* 1059
My stained blood to Tarquin I'll bequeath . . . 1181
Ere she with blood had stain'd her stain'd excuse . . . 1316
Seemed to appear, Like bright things stain'd, a kind of heavy fear . . . 1435
Though my gross blood be stain'd with this abuse . . . 1655
Some of her blood still pure and red remain'd, And some look'd black, and that false Tarquin stain'd . . . 1743
By this chaste blood so unjustly stain'd . . . 1836
That it could so preposterously be stain'd . . . *Sonnet* 109 11
Staineth. Or as the berry breaks before it staineth, Or like the deadly bullet of a gun . . . *Ven. and Adon.* 460
Suns of the world may stain when heaven's sun staineth . . . *Sonnet* 33 14
Stale. The weary time she cannot entertain, For now 'tis stale to sigh *Lucr.* 1362
When thou impressest, what are precepts worth Of stale example? *L. Comp.* 268
Stalk. She crops the stalk, and in the breach appears Green dropping sap, which she compares to tears . . . *Ven. and Adon.* 1175
Wickedly he stalks, And gazeth on her yet unstained bed . . . *Lucrece* 365
Reserved the stalk and gave all my flower . . . *Lov. Comp.* 147
Stalled. The steed is stalled up, and even now To tie the rider she begins to prove . . . *Ven. and Adon.* 39
And stall'd the deer that thou shouldst strike . . . *Pass. Pil.* 300
Stamp. He stamps and bites the poor flies in his fume . . . *Ven. and Adon.* 316
To stamp the seal of time in aged things . . . *Lucrece* 941
Seek anew Some fresher stamp of the time-bettering days . . . *Sonnet* 82 8
Stamped. Reproach is stamp'd in Collatinus' face . . . *Lucrece* 829
Wherein is stamp'd the semblance of a devil . . . 1246
Which vulgar scandal stamp'd upon my brow . . . *Sonnet* 112 2
Stand. His braided hanging mane Upon his compass'd crest now stand on end . . . *Ven. and Adon.* 272
His flattering 'Holla,' or his 'Stand, I say' . . . 284
Stands on his hinder legs with listening ear, To hearken . . . 698
My heart stands armed in mine ear, And will not let a false sound enter there . . . 779
Thus stands she in a trembling ecstasy . . . 895
And they would stand auspicious to the hour . . . *Lucrece* 347
Smoking with pride, march'd on to make his stand On her bare breast 438
Through the length of times he stands disgraced . . . 718
As the poor frighted deer, that stands at gaze . . . 1149
A pretty while these pretty creatures stand . . . 1233
There pleading might you see grave Nestor stand . . . 1401
What uncouth ill event Hath thee befall'n, that thou dost trembling stand? 1599
Since Rome herself in them doth stand disgraced . . . 1833
Now stand you on the top of happy hours . . . *Sonnet* 16 5
If aught in me Worthy perusal stand against thy sight . . . 38 6
No matter then although my foot did stand Upon the farthest earth removed from thee . . . 44 5
Nothing stands but for his scythe to mow . . . 60 12
And yet to times in hope my verse shall stand, Praising thy worth . . . 60 13
The roses fearfully on thorns did stand, One blushing shame . . . 99 8
So your sweet hue, which methinks still doth stand, Hath motion . . . 104 11
But all alone stands hugely politic . . . 124 11
A true soul When most impeach'd stands least in thy control . . . 125 14
My poor lips, . . . At the wood's boldness by thee blushing stand! . . . 128 8
To stand in thy affairs, fall by thy side . . . 151 12
My woeful self, that did in freedom stand . . . *Lov. Comp.* 143
O appetite, from judgement stand aloof! . . . 166
When thou wilt inflame, How coldly those impediments stand forth! . . . 269
Her stand she takes upon a steep-up hill . . . *Pass. Pil.* 121
Herds stand weeping, Flocks all sleeping . . . 285
A woman's nay doth stand for nought . . . 340
Standing. And this I do to captivate the eye Of the fair breeder that is standing by . . . *Ven. and Adon.* 282
For standing by her side, His eye, which late this mutiny restrains, Unto a greater uproar tempts his veins . . . *Lucrece* 425
Star. Look, how a bright star shooteth from the sky . . . *Ven. and Adon.* 815
Patron of all light, From whom each lamp and shining star doth borrow . . . 861
Like stars ashamed of day, themselves withdrew . . . 1032
Mortal stars, as bright as heaven's beauties . . . *Lucrece* 13
No comfortable star did lend his light . . . 164
Little stars may hide them when they list . . . 1008
The skies were sorry, And little stars shot from their fixed places . . . 1525
Not from the stars do I my judgement pluck . . . *Sonnet* 14 1
From thine eyes my knowledge I derive, And, constant stars . . . 14 10
This huge stage presenteth nought but shows Whereon the stars in secret influence comment . . . 15 4
Let those who are in favour with their stars Of public honour and proud titles boast . . . 25 1
Till whatsoever star that guides my moving Points on me graciously . . . 26 9
When sparkling stars twire not thou gild'st the even . . . 28 12
It is the star to every wandering bark . . . 116 7
Nor that full star that ushers in the even . . . 132 7
Co-supremes and stars of love, As chorus to their tragic scene *Ph. and Tur.* 51
Stares. Sometime he scuds far off and there he stares . . . *Ven. and Adon.* 301
Which when her sad-beholding husband saw, Amazedly in her sad face he stares . . . *Lucrece* 1591
Star-gazers. That the star-gazers, having writ on death, May say, the plague is banish'd by thy breath . . . *Ven. and Adon.* 509

Staring. The staring ruffian shall it keep in quiet . . . *Ven. and Adon.* 1149
Staring on Priam's wounds with her old eyes . . . *Lucrece* 1448
Stark. And stood stark naked on the brook's green brim . . . *Pass. Pil.* 80
Start. Anon he starts at stirring of a feather . . . *Ven. and Adon.* 302
Whereat she starts, like one that spies an adder . . . 878
Even there he starts: quoth he, 'I must deflower'. . . . *Lucrece* 348
With this, I did begin to start and cry . . . 1639
By this, starts Collatine as from a dream . . . 1772
Starteth. This said, from her be-tumbled couch she starteth . . . 1037
Starved. All full with feasting on your sight And by and by clean starved for a look . . . *Sonnet* 75 10
State. In Tarquin's tent, Unlock'd the treasure of his happy state *Lucrece* 16
His honour, his affairs, his friends, his state, Neglected all . . . 45
Wipe the dim mist from thy doting eyne, That thou shalt see thy state and pity mine . . . 644
So let thy thoughts, low vassals to thy state . . . 666
For greatest scandal waits on greatest state . . . 1006
Nor laugh with his companions at thy state . . . 1066
Began to clothe his wit in state and pride . . . 1809
And wear their brave state out of memory . . . *Sonnet* 15 8
I all alone beweep my outcast state . . . 29 2
And then my state, Like to the lark at break of day arising . . . 29 10
Such wealth brings That then I scorn to change my state with kings . . . 29 14
I have seen such interchange of state, Or state itself confounded to decay . . . 64 9
A better state to me belongs Than that which on thy humour doth depend . . . 92 7
If thou wouldst use the strength of all thy state! But do not so . . . 96 12
And brought to medicine a healthful state . . . 118 11
If my dear love were but the child of state . . . 124 1
To be so tickled, they would change their state And situation . . . 128 9
O, but with mine compare thou thine own state . . . 142 3
When she saw my woeful state, Straight in her heart did mercy come 145 4
With others thou shouldst not abhor my state . . . 150 12
Stately. To fill with worm-holes stately monuments . . . *Lucrece* 946
Statue. Well-painted idol, image dull and dead, Statue contenting but the eye alone . . . *Ven. and Adon.* 213
Tells him of trophies, statues, tombs, and stories . . . 1013
When wasteful war shall statues overturn . . . *Sonnet* 55 5
Statute. The statute of thy beauty thou wilt take, Thou usurer . . . 134 9
Stay. Each shadow makes him stop, each murmur stay . . . *Ven. and Adon.* 706
Some twine about her thigh to make her stay . . . 873
They basely fly and dare not stay the field . . . 894
The wind wars with his torch to make him stay . . . *Lucrece* 311
But all these poor forbiddings could not stay him . . . 323
As those bars which stop the hourly dial, Who with a lingering stay his course doth let . . . 328
So o'er this sleeping soul doth Tarquin stay, His rage of lust by gazing qualified . . . 423
She stays, exclaiming on the direful night . . . 741
The stain upon his silver down will stay . . . 1012
That she her plaints a little while doth stay . . . 1364
The conceit of this inconstant stay Sets you most rich in youth *Sonnet* 15 9
Thy fair imperfect shade Through heavy sleep on sightless eyes doth stay . . . 43 12
Despite of space I would be brought, From limits far remote, where thou dost stay . . . 44 4
That to my use it might unused stay From hands of falsehood . . . 48 3
Like a sad slave, stay and think of nought Save, where you are . . . 57 11
Being your vassal, bound to stay your leisure . . . 58 4
Some interest, Which for memorial still with thee shall stay . . . 74 4
Life no longer than thy love will stay . . . 92 3
And makes all swift dispatch In pursuit of the thing she would have stay . . . 143 4
My soul doth tell my body that he may Triumph in love; flesh stays no farther reason . . . 151 8
Counsel may stop awhile what will not stay . . . *Lov. Comp.* 159
Stayed. An oven that is stopp'd, or river stay'd, Burneth more hotly, swelleth with more rage . . . *Ven. and Adon.* 331
My Collatine would else have come to me When Tarquin did, but he was stay'd by thee . . . *Lucrece* 917
'But tell me, girl, when went'—and there she stay'd . . . 1275
Stayest. O, sweet shepherd, hie thee, For methinks thou stay'st too long *Pass. Pil.* 168
Steadfast. With a steadfast eye Receives the scroll without or yea or no *Lucrece* 1339
Steadfastly. Upon his hurt she looks so steadfastly . . . *Ven. and Adon.* 1063
Steal thine own freedom and complain on theft . . . 160
Lest she should steal a kiss and die forsworn . . . 726
Dost thou mean To stifle beauty and to steal his breath? . . . 934
Away he steals with open listening ear . . . *Lucrece* 283
Such devils steal effects from lightless hell . . . 1555
Which steals men's eyes and women's souls amazeth . . . *Sonnet* 20 8
Yet doth it steal sweet hours from love's delight . . . 36 8
I do forgive thy robbery, gentle thief, Although thou steal thee all my poverty . . . 40 10
Why should false painting imitate his cheek And steal dead seeing of his living hue? . . . 67 6
Anon Doubting the filching age will steal his treasure . . . 75 6
But do thy worst to steal thyself away . . . 92 1
Sweet thief, whence didst thou steal thy sweet that smells? . . . 99 2
Like a dial-hand, Steal from his figure and no pace perceived . . . 104 10
Stealeth. Even in this thought through the dark night he stealeth *Lucrece* 729
Stealing. How she came stealing to the wayward boy . . . *Ven. and Adon.* 344
Lest Jealousy, that sour unwelcome guest, Should, by his stealing in, disturb the feast . . . 450
For stealing moulds from heaven that were divine . . . 730
Stealing unseen to west with this disgrace . . . *Sonnet* 33 8
Stealing away the treasure of his spring . . . 63 8
Stealth. Thou by thy dial's shady stealth mayst know Time's thievish progress . . . 77 7
Steam. She feedeth on the steam as on a prey, And calls it heavenly moisture, air of grace . . . *Ven. and Adon.* 63
Steed. Vouchsafe, thou wonder, to alight thy steed . . . 13
The steed is stalled up, and even now To tie the rider she begins to prove 39
The strong-neck'd steed, being tied unto a tree, Breaketh his rein . . . 263
Look, when a painter would surpass the life, In limning out a well-proportion'd steed . . . 290
Whether the horse by him became his deed, Or he his manage by the well-doing steed . . . *Lov. Comp.* 112

Steel. Strong-tempered steel his stronger strength obey'd *Ven. and Adon.* 111
Art thou obdurate, flinty, hard as steel, Nay, more than flint? 199
O, give it me, lest thy hard heart do steel it 375
And grave, like water that doth eat in steel, Upon my cheeks *Lucrece* 755
To spoil antiquities of hammer'd steel 951
Nor gates of steel so strong, but Time decays *Sonnet* 65 8
Unless my nerves were brass or hammer'd steel 120 4
Prison my heart in thy steel bosom's ward 133 9
Steeled. And being steel'd, soft sighs can never grave it *Ven. and Adon.* 376
Nor I to none alive, That my steel'd sense or changes right or wrong *Son.* 112 8
Steep. Do not steep thy heart In such relenting dew of lamentations *Lucrece* 1828
And his love-kindling fire did quickly steep *Sonnet* 153 3
Steep-up. Having climb'd the steep-up heavenly hill 7 5
Her stand she takes upon a steep-up hill *Pass. Pil.* 121
Steepy. When his youthful morn Hath travell'd on to age's steepy night *Sonnet* 63 5
Stelled. To find a face where all distress is stell'd *Lucrece* 1444
Mine eye hath play'd the painter and hath stell'd Thy beauty's form *Son.* 24 1
Steps. Sometime he trots, as if he told the steps, With gentle majesty and modest pride *Ven. and Adon.* 277
Who sees the lurking serpent steps aside. *Lucrece* 362
Stern. The stern and direful god of war, Whose sinewy neck in battle ne'er did bow *Ven. and Adon.* 98
There we will unfold To creatures stern sad tunes, to change their kinds *Lucrece* 1147
Though men can cover crimes with bold stern looks 1252
How many lambs might the stern wolf betray! *Sonnet* 96 9
Stewards. They are the lords and owners of their faces, Others but stewards of their excellence 94 8
Stick. The mellow plum doth fall, the green sticks fast *Ven. and Adon.* 527
By the light he spies Lucretia's glove, wherein her needle sticks *Lucrece* 317
She will not stick to round me i' the ear, To teach my tongue to be so long *Pass. Pil.* 349
Stickest. 'Gainst thyself thou stick'st not to conspire *Sonnet* 10 6
Stifle. Dost thou mean To stifle beauty and to steal his breath? *Ven. and Adon.* 934
Still. Still she entreats, and prettily entreats, For to a pretty ear she tunes her tale. 73
Still is he sullen, still he lours and frets, 'Twixt crimson shame and anger ashy-pale 75
Thou dost survive, In that thy likeness still is left alive 174
Her eyes woo'd still, his eyes disdain'd the wooing 358
Yet would my love to thee be still as much 442
She, by her good will, Will never rise, so he will kiss her still 480
And as they last, their verdure still endure 507
What bargains may I make, still to be sealing? 512
She sinketh down, still hanging by his neck 593
Whose tushes never sheathed he whetteth still 617
O, let him keep his loathsome cabin still. 637
Stands on his hinder legs with listening ear, To hearken if his foes pursue him still 699
Her heavy anthem still concludes in woe, And still the choir of echoes answer so 839
Sorrow that friendly sighs sought still to dry 964
That bloody beast, Which knows no pity, but is still severe 1000
Who bids them still consort with ugly night 1041
Whose downward eye still looketh for a grave. 1106
Thy hasty spring still blasts, and ne'er grows old *Lucrece* 49
Yet their ambition makes them still to fight 68
That, cloy'd with much, he pineth still for more 98
Pure thoughts are dead and still, While lust and murder wake to stain and kill 167
True valour still a true respect should have 201
The guilt being great, the fear doth still exceed 229
Urging the worser sense for vantage still 249
They fright him, yet he still pursues his fear 308
By Lucrece' side, In his clear bed might have reposed still 382
Swell in their pride, the onset still expecting 432
But she with vehement prayers urgeth still 475
But happy monarchs still are fear'd for love 611
O, deeper sin than bottomless conceit Can comprehend in still imagination! 702
Which in her prescience she controlled still 727
Therefore would they still in darkness be 752
And bids her eyes hereafter still be blind 758
Keep still possession of thy gloomy place 803
The nurse, to still her child, will tell my story 813
Shames herself to see, And therefore still in night would cloister'd be 1085
Like an unpractised swimmer plunging still 1098
For burden-wise I'll hum on Tarquin still 1133
Extremity still urgeth such extremes 1337
And give the harmless show An humble gait, calm looks, eyes wailing still 1508
So fair a form lodged not a mind so ill: And still on him she gazed 1531
And gazing still, Such signs of truth in his plain face she spied 1531
So should my shame still rest upon record, And never be forgot 1643
But still pure Doth in her poison'd closet yet endure 1658
Some of her blood still pure and red remain'd, And some look'd black 1742
Blood untainted still doth red abide 1749
Flowers distill'd, though they with winter meet, Leese but their show; their substance still lives sweet *Sonnet* 5 14
Yet mortal looks adore his beauty still 7 7
The world will be thy widow and still weep 9 5
Look, what an unthrift in the world doth spend Shifts but his place, for still the world enjoys it 9 10
That beauty still may live in thine or thee 10 14
To give away yourself keeps yourself still 16 13
Which in my bosom's shop is hanging still 24 7
How far I toil, still farther off from thee. 28 8
Though thou repent, yet I have still the loss 34 10
Thy beauty and thy years full well befits, For still temptation follows where thou art 41 4
Either by thy picture or my love, Thyself away art present still with me 47 10
I am still with them and they with thee 47 12
Your praise shall still find room Even in the eyes of all posterity 55 10
His beauty shall in these black lines be seen, And they shall live, and he in them still green 63 14
That in black ink my love may still shine bright 65 14
Some interest, Which for memorial still with thee shall stay 74 4
Why write I still all one, ever the same, And keep invention in a noted weed? 76 5
I always write of you, And you and love are still my argument 76 10

Still. For as the sun is daily new and old, So is my love still telling what is told *Sonnet* 76 14
You still shall live—such virtue hath my pen 81 13
My tongue-tied Muse in manners holds her still 85 1
Like unletter'd clerk still cry 'Amen' To every hymn 85 6
So love's face May still seem love to me, though alter'd new 93 3
Yet seem'd it winter still, and, you away 98 13
For as you were when first your eye I eyed, Such seems your beauty still 104 3
So your sweet hue, which methinks still doth stand, Hath motion 104 11
My songs and praises be To one, of one, still such, and ever so 105 4
Still constant in a wondrous excellence 105 6
To give full growth to that which still doth grow 115 14
Still losing when I saw myself to win 119 4
Now I find true That better is by evil still made better 119 10
Nature, . . . As thou goest onwards, still will pluck thee back 126 6
She may detain, but not still keep, her treasure 126 10
That other mine Thou wilt restore, to be my comfort still 134 4
More than enough am I that vex thee still 135 3
The sea, all water, yet receives rain still 135 9
Make but my name thy love, and love that still 136 13
Thou mayst have thy 'Will,' If thou turn back, and my loud crying still 143 14
Which like two spirits do suggest me still 144 2
My love is as a fever, longing still For that which longer nurseth the disease 147 1
A dateless lively heat, still to endure, And grew a seething bath 153 6
Some in her threaden fillet still did bide *Lov. Comp.* 33
Reason strong, For his advantage still did wake and sleep 123
Two loves I have, of comfort and despair, That like two spirits do suggest me still *Pass. Pil.* 16
Touches so soft still conquer chastity 50
For why I craved nothing of thee still 140
Think women still to strive with men, To sin and never for to saint 341
Stilled. Or like the froward infant still'd with dandling *Ven. and Adon.* 562
Still-gazing. In silent wonder of still-gazing eyes *Lucrece* 84
Stillitory. For from the stillitory of thy face excelling Comes breath perfumed that breedeth love by smelling *Ven. and Adon.* 443
Still-pining. Like still-pining Tantalus he sits. *Lucrece* 858
Still-slaughtered. He doth despise His naked armour of still-slaughter'd lust 188
Sting. Disdainfully did sting His high-pitch'd thoughts 40
Fearing no such thing, Lies at the mercy of his mortal sting 364
I think the honey guarded with a sting 493
Vow, bond, nor space, In thee hath neither sting, knot, nor confine *L. Comp.* 265
Fair creature, kill'd too soon by death's sharp sting! *Pass. Pil.* 134
Stir. What recketh he his rider's angry stir, His flattering 'Holla,' or his 'Stand, I say'? *Ven. and Adon.* 283
And careless lust stirs up a desperate courage 556
Show me the strumpet that began this stir *Lucrece* 1471
Stirred. Stirr'd by a painted beauty to his verse *Sonnet* 21 2
Stirring. Anon he starts at stirring of a feather *Ven. and Adon.* 302
Myself was stirring ere the break of day *Lucrece* 1280
Stock. He shall not boast who did thy stock pollute That thou art doting father of his fruit 1063
Stole. No grass, herb, leaf, or weed, But stole his blood and seem'd with him to bleed *Ven. and Adon.* 1056
Now stole upon the time the dead of night *Lucrece* 162
He lends thee virtue and he stole that word From thy behaviour *Sonnet* 79 9
There my white stole of chastity I daff'd *Lov. Comp.* 297
Stolen. Poor helpless help, the treasure stol'n away *Lucrece* 1056
Thy interest was not bought Basely with gold, but stol'n from forth thy gate 1068
How many a holy and obsequious tear Hath dear religious love stol'n from mine eye As interest of the dead *Sonnet* 31 6
And even thence thou wilt be stol'n, I fear 48 13
And buds of marjoram had stol'n thy hair 99 7
A third, nor red nor white, had stol'n of both. 99 10
Yet I none could see But sweet or colour it had stol'n from thee 99 15
Stone. Art thou obdurate, flinty, hard as steel, Nay, more than flint, for stone at rain relenteth? *Ven. and Adon.* 200
Fie, lifeless picture, cold and senseless stone 211
That from the cold stone sparks of fire do fly *Lucrece* 177
For stones dissolved to water do convert 592
O, if no harder than a stone thou art, Melt at my tears! 593
And waste huge stones with little water-drops 959
Stone him with harden'd hearts, harder than stones 978
Like stones of worth they thinly placed are, Or captain jewels in the carcanet *Sonnet* 52 7
More bright, . . . Than unswept stone besmear'd with sluttish time 55 4
Brass, nor stone, nor earth, nor boundless sea 65 1
Who, moving others, are themselves as stone, Unmoved, cold 94 3
Deep-brain'd sonnets that did amplify Each stone's dear nature *Lov. Comp.* 209
Each several stone, With wit well blazon'd, smiled or made some moan 216
Stone-still, astonish'd with this deadly deed, Stood Collatine *Lucrece* 1730
Stonished. Or stonish'd as night-wanderers often are, Their light blown out in some mistrustful wood *Ven. and Adon.* 825
Stood. How like a jade he stood, tied to the tree! 391
With this, she falleth in the place she stood 1121
His pale cheeks and the blood Which in round drops upon their whiteness stood 1170
That had Narcissus seen her as she stood, Self-love had never drown'd him in the flood *Lucrece* 265
That for Achilles' image stood his spear, Griped in an armed hand 1424
A hand, a foot, a face, a leg, a head, Stood for the whole to be imagined 1428
Stood many Trojan mothers, sharing joy To see their youthful sons bright weapons wield 1431
Both stood, like old acquaintance in a trance, Met far from home 1595
Stone-still, astonish'd with this deadly deed, Stood Collatine 1731
Like a late-sack'd island, vastly stood Bare and unpeopled 1740
And nice affections wavering stood in doubt If best were as it was *L. Comp.* 97
And stood stark naked on the brook's green brim *Pass. Pil.* 80
He, spying her, bounced in, whereas he stood 83
Stoop. The grass stoops not, she treads on it so light *Ven. and Adon.* 1028
And stoop to honour, not to foul desire *Lucrece* 574
The cedar stoops not to the base shrub's foot 664
Stop. Now doth he frown, And 'gins to chide, but soon she stops his lips *Ven. and Adon.* 46
To stop the loud pursuers in their yell 688
Each shadow makes him stop, each murmur stay 706
Or as those bars which stop the hourly dial *Lucrece* 327
Or stop the headlong fury of his speed 501
My restless discord loves no stops nor rests 1124
Revenge on him that made me stop my breath 1180

Stop. Begins to blow The grief away that stops his answer so . *Lucrece* 1664
But she, that yet her sad task hath not said, The protestation stops 1700
Who is he so fond will be the tomb Of his self-love, to stop posterity? *Sonnet* 3 8
Injurious distance should not stop my way 44 2
And stops her pipe in growth of riper days 102 8
What rounds, what bounds, what course, what stop he makes! *Lov. Comp.* 109
Counsel may stop awhile what will not stay 159
Stopped. An oven that is stopp'd, or river stay'd, Burneth more hotly, swelleth with more rage . . *Ven. and Adon.* 331
Like a gentle flood, Who, being stopp'd, the bounding banks o'erflows *Lucr.* 1119
My adder's sense To critic and to flatterer stopped are . . *Sonnet* 112 11
Stopt. She vail'd her eyelids, who, like sluices, stopt The crystal tide *Ven. and Adon.* 956
Her voice is stopt, her joints forget to bow; Her eyes are mad . 1061
Store. But, poorly rich, so wanteth in his store . . *Lucrece* 97
Pure Chastity is rifled of her store 692
By heaven's fair sun that breeds the fat earth's store . . 1837
Let those whom Nature hath not made for store, Harsh featureless and rude, barrenly perish . . . . . *Sonnet* 11 9
If from thyself to store thou wouldst convert 14 12
I make my love engrafted to this store 37 8
And the firm soil win of the watery main, Increasing store with loss and loss with store 64 8
Him she stores, to show what wealth she had In days long since . . 67 13
And him as for a map doth Nature store, To show false Art . . 68 13
The store Which should example where your equal grew . . 84 3
And in abundance addeth to his store 135 10
Let me pass untold, Though in thy stores' account I one must be . 136 10
Then, soul, live thou upon thy servant's loss, And let that pine to aggravate thy store 146 10
But if store of crowns be scant, No man will supply thy want . *Pass. Pil.* 409
Storm. I could prevent this storm and shun thy wrack! . *Lucrece* 966
Should thrust Into so bright a day such black-faced storms . . 1518
These water-galls in her dim element Foretell new storms to those already spent 1589
Such a storm As oft 'twixt May and April is to see . *Lov. Comp.* 101
Storm-beaten. To dry the rain on my storm-beaten face . *Sonnet* 34 6
Storming. Storming her world with sorrow's wind and rain . *Lov. Comp.* 7
Stormy. But like a stormy day, now wind, now rain, Sighs dry her cheeks, tears make them wet again . . *Ven. and Adon.* 965
No cloudy show of stormy blustering weather . . *Lucrece* 115
Might uphold Against the stormy gusts of winter's day . *Sonnet* 13 11
Story. Leave me, and then the story aptly ends: The night is spent *Ven. and Adon.* 716
Their copious stories oftentimes begun End without audience . 845
Tells him of trophies, statues, tombs, and stories . . . 1013
He stories to her ears her husband's fame . . . *Lucrece* 106
The story of sweet chastity's decay 808
The nurse, to still her child, will tell my story . . . 813
Sinon, whose enchanting story The credulous old Priam after slew 1521
If he can tell That you are you, so dignifies his story *Sonnet* 84 8
Upon thy part I can set down a story Of faults conceal'd . 88 6
That tongue that tells the story of thy days . . . 95 5
Nor the lays of birds . . . Could make me any summer's story tell 98 7
A plaintful story from a sistering vale . . . *Lov. Comp.* 2
She told him stories to delight his ear; She show'd him favours *Pass. Pil.* 47
Stout. When rocks impregnable are not so stout, Nor gates of steel so strong *Sonnet* 65 7
Stoutly. Faint not, faint heart, but stoutly say 'So be it' . *Lucrece* 1209
Stows. Till sable Night, . . . in her vaulty prison stows the Day . 119
Straggling. And they, like straggling slaves for pillage fighting 428
Straight. The strong-neck'd steed, being tied unto a tree, Breaketh his rein, and to her straight goes he . . *Ven. and Adon.* 264
High crest, short ears, straight legs, and passing strong . 297
And straight, in pity of his tender years, They both would strive who first should dry his tears 1091
Would with the sceptre straight be strucken down . *Lucrece* 217
And as one shifts, another straight ensues 1104
What wit sets down is blotted straight with will . . . 1299
I'll murder straight, and then I'll slaughter thee . . . 1634
No longer glad, I send them back again and straight grow sad *Sonnet* 45 14
Speak of my lameness, and I straight will halt, Against thy reasons . 89 3
Return, forgetful Muse, and straight redeem In gentle numbers time so idly spent 100 5
I may be straight, though they themselves be bevel . . . 121 11
Enjoy'd no sooner but despised straight 129 5
Bear thine eyes straight, though thy proud heart go wide . 140 14
Straight in her heart did mercy come 145 5
Strain. They all strain courtesy who shall cope him first *Ven. and Adon.* 888
So I at each sad strain will strain a tear . . . *Lucrece* 1131
And other strains of woe, which now seem woe, Compared with loss of thee will not seem so . . . . *Sonnet* 90 13
Strained. When they have devised What strained touches rhetoric can lend 82 10
Strait. The eddy boundeth in his pride Back to the strait that forced him on so fast . . . . *Lucrece* 1670
Strand. From the strand of Dardan, where they fought, To Simois' reedy banks 1436
Strange. O strange excuse, When reason is the bawd to lust's abuse! *Ven. and Adon.* 791
How strange it seems Not to believe, and yet too credulous . 985
The impression of strange kinds Is form'd in them by force, by fraud, or skill *Lucrece* 1242
Whereof are you made, That millions of strange shadows on you tend? *Sonnet* 53 2
To new-found methods and to compounds strange 76 4
Knowing thy will, I will acquaintance strangle and look strange . 89 8
The false heart's history Is writ in moods and frowns and wrinkles strange 93 8
To me are nothing novel, nothing strange 123 3
Which yet men prove Against strange maladies a sovereign cure . 153 8
In him a plenitude of subtle matter, Applied to cautels, all strange forms receives . . . . *Lov. Comp.* 303
Strangely. Thou shalt strangely pass And scarcely greet me with that sun, thine eye . . . . *Sonnet* 49 5
Most true it is that I have look'd on truth Askance and strangely . 110 6
Strangeness. She puts on outward strangeness, seems unkind *V. and A.* 310
Measure my strangeness with my unripe years 524
Stranger. That lends embracements unto every stranger . . 790
Stranger. But she, that never coped with stranger eyes, Could pick no meaning from their parling looks . . . *Lucrece* 99
When shall he think to find a stranger just, When he himself himself confounds? 159
Dear husband, in the interest of thy bed A stranger came . . 1620
Strangle. Knowing thy will, I will acquaintance strangle and look strange *Sonnet* 89 8
Straw. I force not argument a straw, Since that my case is past the help of law *Lucrece* 1021
Upon her head a platted hive of straw . . . . *Lov. Comp.* 8
She burn'd with love, as straw with fire flameth; She burn'd out love, as soon as straw out-burneth . . . . . *Pass. Pil.* 97
A belt of straw and ivy buds, With coral clasps and amber studs . 365
Stray. Graze on my lips; and if those hills be dry, Stray lower, where the pleasant fountains lie . . . *Ven. and Adon.* 234
Straying. And chide thy beauty and thy straying youth, Who lead thee in their riot . . . . *Sonnet* 41 10
Stream. And all in vain you strive against the stream *Ven. and Adon.* 772
The petty streams that pay a daily debt To their salt sovereign *Lucrece* 649
Shall gush pure streams to purge my impure tale . . . 1078
Then in key-cold Lucrece' bleeding stream He falls . . . 1774
Gilding pale streams with heavenly alchemy . . . *Sonnet* 33 4
O, how the channel to the stream gave grace! . *Lov. Comp.* 285
Streamed. Round about her tear-distained eye Blue circles stream'd *Lucrece* 1587
Streets. By our strong arms from forth her fair streets chased . 1834
Strength. And govern'd him in strength, though not in lust *Ven. and Adon.* 42
Strong-tempered steel his stronger strength obey'd . . . 111
As who should say 'Lo, thus my strength is tried' . . . 280
Now leaden slumber with life's strength doth fight . . *Lucrece* 124
No object but her passion's strength renews 1103
Then little strength rings out the doleful knell . . . 1495
Whose strength's abundance weakens his own heart . . . *Sonnet* 23 4
In mine own love's strength seem to decay 23 7
And night doth nightly make grief's strength seem stronger . 28 14
To leave poor me thou hast the strength of laws . . . 49 13
And strength by limping sway disabled 66 8
If thou wouldst use the strength of all thy state! But do not so . 96 12
That in the very refuse of thy deeds There is such strength . . 150 7
What though she strive to try her strength, And ban and brawl *Pass. Pil.* 317
Strengthened. My love is strengthen'd, though more weak in seeming *Sonnet* 102 1
Strengthless. Two strengthless doves will draw me through the sky *Ven. and Adon.* 153
With heavy eye, knit brow, and strengthless pace . . . *Lucrece* 709
Stretched. A poet's rage And stretched metre of an antique song *Sonnet* 17 12
Strict. She wildly breaketh from their strict embrace . *Ven. and Adon.* 874
Keep the obsequy so strict . . . . *Ph. and Tur.* 12
Strife. Nature that made thee, with herself at strife, Saith that the world hath ending with thy life . . . . *Ven. and Adon.* 11
His art with nature's workmanship at strife 291
A mischief worse than civil home-bred strife 764
In this aim there is such thwarting strife, That one for all, or all for one we gage . . . . *Lucrece* 143
As in revenge or quittal of such strife 236
As if between them twain there were no strife 405
This forced league doth force a further strife 689
When wilt thou sort an hour great strifes to end? . . . 899
The red blood reek'd, to show the painter's strife . . . 1377
Son and father weep with equal strife Who should weep most . 1791
I hold such strife As 'twixt a miser and his wealth is found . *Sonnet* 75 3
Strike. He wrings her nose, he strikes her on the cheeks, He bends her fingers, holds her pulses hard . . . . . *Ven. and Adon.* 475
Being moved, he strikes whate'er is in his way, And whom he strikes his crooked tushes slay 623
If he be dead,—O no, it cannot be, Seeing his beauty, thou shouldst strike at it:—O yes, it may 938
Love's golden arrow at him should have fled, And not Death's ebon dart, to strike him dead 948
Strike the wise dumb and teach the fool to speak . . . 1146
He is no woodman that doth bend his bow To strike a poor unseasonable doe *Lucrece* 581
Strikes each in each by mutual ordering . . . . *Sonnet* 8 10
And stall'd the deer that thou shouldst strike . . *Pass. Pil.* 300
Striking. Struck dead at first, what needs a second striking? *V. and A.* 250
Anon his beating heart, alarum striking, Gives the hot charge . *Lucrece* 433
String. Mark how one string, sweet husband to another . *Sonnet* 8 9
Strive. Out-stripping crows that strive to over-fly them *Ven. and Adon.* 324
And all in vain you strive against the stream 772
Nor sun nor wind will ever strive to kiss you 1082
They both would strive who first should dry his tears . . 1092
Yet strive I to embrace mine infamy . . . . . *Lucrece* 504
But, wretched as he is, he strives in vain 1665
I must strive To know my shames and praises from your tongue *Sonnet* 112 5
I did strive to prove The constancy and virtue of your love . 117 13
What labour is't to leave The thing we have not, mastering what not strives *Lov. Comp.* 240
What though she strive to try her strength, And ban and brawl *Pass. Pil.* 317
Think women still to strive with men, To sin and never for to saint 341
Strived. Within whose face beauty and virtue strived . . *Lucrece* 52
Striving. As striving who should best become her grief. *Ven. and Adon.* 968
Were it not sinful then, striving to mend, To mar the subject? *Sonnet* 103 9
Stroke. Now doth she stroke his cheek, now doth he frown *Ven. and Adon.* 45
The Destinies will curse thee for this stroke 945
Strong. High crest, short ears, straight legs and passing strong . 297
The colt that's back'd and burden'd being young Loseth his pride and never waxeth strong 420
And with his strong course opens them again 960
My will is strong, past reason's weak removing . . *Lucrece* 243
Huge rocks, high winds, strong pirates, shelves, and sands, The merchant fears, ere rich at home he lands 335
If, Collatine, thine honour lay in me, From me by strong assault it is bereft 835
Their father was too weak, and they too strong . . . 865
With circumstances strong Of present death, and shame that might ensue . 1262
Mine enemy was strong, my poor self weak, And far the weaker with so strong a fear 1646
By our strong arms from forth her fair streets chased . . 1834
Resembling strong youth in his middle age . . . *Sonnet* 7 6
But weak relief To him that bears the strong offence's cross . 34 12
Your charter is so strong That you yourself may privilege your time . 58 9
Nor gates of steel so strong, but Time decays 65 8

Strong. What strong hand can hold his swift foot back? . *Sonnet* 65 11
Which makes thy love more strong, To love that well which thou must leave ere long 73 13
I will drink Potions of eisel 'gainst my strong infection . . 111 10
Divert strong minds to the course of altering things . . 115 8
Grows fairer than at first, more strong, far greater . . 119 12
Reason strong, For his advantage still did wake and sleep . *Lov. Comp.* 122
I strong o'er them, and you o'er me being strong . . . 257
Had women been so strong as men, In faith, you had not had it then *Pass. Pil.* 321
Strong-besieged. From the walls of strong-besieged Troy . *Lucrece* 1429
Strong-bonded. That strong-bonded oath That shall prefer and undertake my troth . . . . . . *Lov. Comp.* 279
Stronger. Strong-tempered steel his stronger strength obey'd *Ven. and Adon.* 111
Shall rotten death make conquest of the stronger? . . *Lucrece* 1767
And night doth nightly make grief's strength seem stronger . *Sonnet* 28 14
Whose action is no stronger than a flower 65 4
Strongest. The strongest body shall it make most weak *Ven. and Adon.* 1145
The strongest castle, tower, and town, The golden bullet beats it down *Pass. Pil.* 327
Strongly. What did he note but strongly he desired . *Lucrece* 415
To whom in vassalage Thy merit hath my duty strongly knit . *Sonnet* 26 2
You are so strongly in my purpose bred 112 13
Strong-necked. The strong-neck'd steed, being tied unto a tree, Breaketh his rein . . . . . . *Ven. and Adon.* 263
Strong-tempered steel his stronger strength obey'd . . . 111
Struck. Struck dead at first, what needs a second striking? . 250
His meaning struck her ere his words begun 462
Her loyal fear! Which struck her sad, and then it faster rock'd *Lucrece* 262
This said, he struck his hand upon his breast 1842
By spirits taught to write Above a mortal pitch, that struck me dead *Sonnet* 86 6
Strucken. Would with the sceptre straight be strucken down . *Lucrece* 217
Struggle. And when from thence he struggles to be gone, She locks her lily fingers one in one . . . . *Ven. and Adon.* 227
Nay, do not struggle, for thou shalt not rise 710
Struggling for passage, earth's foundation shakes . . . 1047
Strumpet. Show me the strumpet that began this stir . *Lucrece* 1471
Strumpeted. And maiden virtue rudely strumpeted . . *Sonnet* 66 6
Stuck. So commended, That maidens' eyes stuck over all his face *L. Comp.* 81
Studded. The studded bridle on a ragged bough Nimbly she fastens:—O, how quick is love! . . . . . *Ven. and Adon.* 37
Studs. A belt of straw and ivy buds, With coral clasps and amber studs *Pass. Pil.* 366
Study his bias leaves, and makes his book thine eyes . . . 61
Stuff up his lust, as minutes fill up hours . . . *Lucrece* 297
Stuffed. Till either gorge be stuff'd or prey be gone *Ven. and Adon.* 58
Sturdy. These forceless flowers like sturdy trees support me . 152
Style. Since he died and poets better prove, Theirs for their style I'll read, his for his love . . . . . . *Sonnet* 32 14
In others' works thou dost but mend the style . . . 78 11
Making his style admired every where 84 12
Subdue. The accident which brought me to her eye Upon the moment did her force subdue . . . . *Lov. Comp.* 248
Subdued. And almost thence my nature is subdued To what it works in, like the dyer's hand . . . . . . *Sonnet* 111 6
All these trophies of affections hot, Of pensived and subdued desires the tender . . . . *Lov. Comp.* 219
Subduing. On the tip of his subduing tongue All kind of arguments and question deep 120
Subject. Making it subject to the tyranny Of mad mischances and much misery *Ven. and Adon.* 737
Whereat each tributary subject quakes 1045
Subject and servile to all discontents, As dry combustious matter is to fire 1161
Princes are the glass, the school, the book, Where subjects' eyes do learn, do read, do look . . . . *Lucrece* 616
Her subjects with foul insurrection Have batter'd down her consecrated wall 722
How can my Muse want subject to invent, While thou dost breathe? *Son.* 38 1
The wits of former days To subjects worse have given admiring praise 59 14
The dedicated words which writers use Of their fair subject . . 82 4
That to his subject lends not some small glory . . . 84 6
Darkening thy power to lend base subjects light . . . 100 4
Were it not sinful then, striving to mend, To mar the subject? . 103 10
As subject to Time's love or to Time's hate . . . 124 3
Subjection. And by their mortal fault brought in subjection Her immortality *Lucrece* 724
Proud of subjection, noble by the sway . . . *Lov. Comp.* 108
Subornation. Guilty of perjury and subornation, Guilty of treason *Lucr.* 919
Suborned. Hence, thou suborn'd informer! . . . *Sonnet* 125 13
Subscribes. My love looks fresh, and Death to me subscribes . 107 10
Subsist. So long as brain and heart Have faculty by nature to subsist 122 6
Substance. Flowers distill'd, though they with winter meet, Leese but their show; their substance still lives sweet 5 14
Whilst that this shadow doth such substance give . . 37 10
If the dull substance of my flesh were thought, Injurious distance should not stop my way 44 1
What is your substance, whereof are you made? . . . 53 1
Subtle. Swift subtle post, carrier of grisly care, Eater of youth . *Lucrece* 926
To mock the subtle in themselves beguiled 957
Even as subtle Sinon here is painted, So sober-sad, so weary, and so mild . 1541
In him a plenitude of subtle matter, Applied to cautels, all strange forms receives . . . . *Lov. Comp.* 302
Smooth not thy tongue with filed talk, Lest she some subtle practice smell *Pass. Pil.* 307
Subtle-shining secrecies Writ in the glassy margents of such books *Lucrece* 101
Subtlety. Or at the fox which lives by subtlety . *Ven. and Adon.* 675
Unlearned in the world's false subtleties . . . *Sonnet* 138 4
Succeeding. And sung by children in succeeding times . . *Lucrece* 525
Him in thy course untainted do allow For beauty's pattern to succeeding men *Sonnet* 19 12
Success. And, wordless, so greets heaven for his success . *Lucrece* 112
Succession. Proving his beauty by succession thine . *Sonnet* 2 12
Successive. But now is black beauty's successive heir . . 127 3
Succour. Yet not for me, shine sun to succour flowers! . *Pass. Pil.* 208
Such. A summer's day will seem an hour but short, Being wasted in such time-beguiling sport . . . . . . *Ven. and Adon.* 24
Wishing her cheeks were gardens full of flowers, So they were dew'd with such distilling showers 66
Then be my deer, since I am such a park 239
Such. He held such petty bondage in disdain . . *Ven. and Adon.* 394
Were never four such lamps together mix'd 489
That hard heart of thine, Hath taught them scornful tricks and such disdain 501
Is twenty hundred kisses such a trouble? 522
Had she then gave over, Such nectar from his lips she had not suck'd . 572
Beauty hath nought to do with such foul fiends 638
Dost thou drink tears, that thou provokest such weeping? . . . 949
How much a fool was I To be of such a weak and silly mind . . . 1016
When he was by, the birds such pleasure took, That some would sing . 1101
Reckoning his fortune at such high-proud rate . . . *Lucrece* 19
Kings might be espoused to more fame, But king nor peer to such a peerless dame 21
Secrecies Writ in the glassy margents of such books . . . 102
Such griefs sustain, That they prove bankrupt in this poor-rich gain . 139
There is such thwarting strife, That one for all, or all for one we gaze . 143
Such hazard now must doting Tarquin make 155
As in revenge or quittal of such strife 236
Then who fears sinking where such treasure lies? 280
Fearing no such thing, Lies at the mercy of his mortal sting . . 363
His hand, as proud of such a dignity, Smoking with pride, march'd on to make his stand 437
Such shadows are the weak brain's forgeries 460
Rude ram, to batter such an ivory wall! 464
Reward not hospitality With such black payment 576
If in thy hope thou darest do such outrage 605
Must he in thee read lectures of such shame? 618
Alas, how many bear such shameful blows! 832
O unlook'd-for evil, When virtue is profaned in such a devil! . . 847
How comes it then, vile Opportunity, Being so bad, such numbers seek for thee? 896
Such wretched hands such wretched blood should spill . . . 999
For who so base would such an office have? 1000
Such danger to resistance did belong 1265
Extremity still urgeth such extremes 1337
Such harmless creatures have a true respect To talk in deeds . . 1347
Such sweet observance in this work was had 1385
Making such sober action with his hand, That it beguiled attention . 1403
And in their rage such signs of rage they bear 1419
And to their hope they such odd action yield 1433
Should thrust Into so bright a day such black-faced storms . . 1518
Or blot with hell-born sin such saint-like forms 1519
Such signs of truth in his plain face she spied 1532
'It cannot be,' quoth she, 'that so much guile'—She would have said 'can lurk in such a look' 1535
It cannot be, I find, But such a face should bear a wicked mind . . 1540
Such devils steal effects from lightless hell 1555
These contraries such unity do hold, Only to flatter fools and make them bold 1558
Such passion her assails, That patience is quite beaten from her breast . 1562
Seeing such emulation in their woe 1808
Such childish humour from weak minds proceeds 1825
Do not steep thy heart In such relenting dew of lamentations . . 1829
No love toward others in that bosom sits That on himself such murderous shame commits . . . . *Sonnet* 9 14
In them I read such art As truth and beauty shall together thrive . 14 10
Such heavenly touches ne'er touch'd earthly faces . . . 17 8
Whilst I, whom fortune of such triumph bars, Unlook'd for joy . 25 3
For thy sweet love remember'd such wealth brings . . . 29 13
Why didst thou promise such a beauteous day? 34 1
For no man well of such a salve can speak 34 7
Such civil war is in my love and hate 35 12
I love thee in such sort As, thou being mine, mine is thy good report 36 13; 96 13
Whilst that this shadow doth such substance give . . . 37 10
Hang on such thorns and play as wantonly 54 7
No face so gracious is as mine, No shape so true, no truth of such account 62 6
For such a time do I now fortify Against confounding age's cruel knife 63 9
I have seen such interchange of state, Or state itself confounded to decay 64 9
The twilight of such day As after sunset fadeth in the west . . 73 5
In me thou see'st the glowing of such fire 73 9
I hold such strife As 'twixt a miser and his wealth is found . . 75 3
And found such fair assistance in my verse 78 2
You still shall live—such virtue hath my pen 81 13
And such a counterpart shall fame his wit 84 11
As a dream doth flatter, In sleep a king, but waking no such matter . 87 14
Such is my love, to thee I so belong, That for thy right myself will bear all wrong 88 13
Having such a scope to show her pride 103 2
For as you were when first your eye I eyed, Such seems your beauty still 104 3
My songs and praises be To one, of one, still such, and ever so . 105 4
I see their antique pen would have express'd Even such a beauty as you master now 106 8
Such cherubins as your sweet self resemble 114 6
At such who, not born fair, no beauty lack 127 11
Roses damask'd, red and white, But no such roses see I in her cheeks 130 6
In the very refuse of thy deeds There is such strength . . . 150 7
Such a storm As oft 'twixt May and April is to see . *Lov. Comp.* 101
And yet do question make What I should do again for such a sake . 322
Such looks as none could look but beauty's queen . . *Pass. Pil.* 46
O do not love that wrong, To sing heaven's praise with such an earthly tongue 70
Whose deep conceit is such As, passing all conceit, needs no defence . 109
Such-like. In such-like circumstance, with such-like sport *Ven. and Adon.* 844
And with such-like flattering, 'Pity but he were a king' . *Pass. Pil.* 413
Sucked. Such nectar from his lips she had not suck'd *Ven. and Adon.* 572
There lives a son that suck'd an earthly mother, May lend thee light . 863
And suck'd the honey which thy chaste bee kept . . *Lucrece* 840
Sudden. Whereat a sudden pale, Like lawn being spread upon the blushing rose, Usurps her cheek . . . . . *Ven. and Adon.* 589
Are on the sudden wasted, thaw'd, and done 749
Suddenly. Be suddenly revenged on my foe, Thine, mine, his own *Lucrece* 1683
A vain and doubtful good; A shining gloss that vadeth suddenly *Pass. Pil.* 170
Sue. I sue for exiled majesty's repeal; Let him return . . *Lucrece* 640
Thou usurer, that put'st forth all to use, And sue a friend came debtor for my sake . . . . *Sonnet* 134 11
Suffer. That they will suffer these abominations . . . *Lucrece* 1832
O, let me suffer, being at your beck, The imprison'd absence of your liberty *Sonnet* 58 5
It suffers not in smiling pomp 124 6
Why dost thou pine within and suffer dearth? 146 3
Sufferance. And patience, tame to sufferance, bide each check, Without accusing you of injury 58 7

Suffered. Affection is a coal that must be cool'd; Else, suffer'd, it will set the heart on fire . . . . *Ven. and Adon.* 388
Have no leisure taken To weigh how once I suffer'd in your crime *Son.* 120 8
Suffering my friend for my sake to approve her 42 8
Which may her suffering ecstasy assuage . . . . *Lov. Comp.* 69
Gentle maid, Have of my suffering youth some feeling pity . . 178
And sweetens, in the suffering pangs it bears, The aloes of all forces . 272
Suffice. Let it then suffice To drown one woe, one pair of weeping eyes *Lucr.* 1679
If knowledge be the mark, to know thee shall suffice . . *Pass. Pil.* 63
Sufficed. True sorrow then is feelingly sufficed . . . *Lucrece* 1112
I in thy abundance am sufficed And by a part of all thy glory live *Sonnet* 37 11
Sugared. Thy sugar'd tongue to bitter wormwood taste . . . *Lucrece* 893
Suggest. Which like two spirits do suggest me still . . *Sonnet* 144 2
That like two spirits do suggest me still . . . . . *Pass. Pil.* 16
Suggested. Perchance his boast of Lucrece' sovereignty Suggested this proud issue of a king . . . . *Lucrece* 37
Suggesteth. Gives false alarms, suggesteth mutiny . . *Ven. and Adon.* 651
Suggestion. By their suggestion gives a deadly groan 1044
Suing. Her eyes petitioners to his eyes suing 356
Suit. Or what great danger dwells upon my suit? 206
The client breaks, as desperate in his suit 336
Then, for thy husband and thy children's sake, Tender my suit . *Lucrece* 534
Bring him where his suit may be obtain'd 898
And suit thy pity like in every part . . . . . *Sonnet* 132 12
But, woe is me! too early I attended A youthful suit . *Lov. Comp.* 79
Which late her noble suit in court did shun 234
Serve always with assured trust, And in thy suit be humble true *Pass. Pil.* 330
Suited. My mistress' brows are raven black, Her eyes so suited *Sonnet* 127 10
Suitor. And like a bold-faced suitor 'gins to woo him *Ven. and Adon.* 6
Sullen. Still is he sullen, still he lours and frets, 'Twixt crimson shame and anger ashy-pale 75
Like to the lark at break of day arising From sullen earth, sings hymns at heaven's gate . . . . *Sonnet* 29 12
No longer mourn for me when I am dead Than you shall hear the surly sullen bell 71 2
Sullied. Where wasteful Time debateth with Decay, To change your day of youth to sullied night 15 12
Sum. Shall sum my count and make my old excuse 2 11
Why dost thou use So great a sum of sums, yet canst not live? . . 4 8
When as thy love hath cast his utmost sum 49 3
To leave for nothing all thy sum of good 109 12
And to your audit comes Their distract parcels in combined sums *L. Comp.* 231
Summer. A summer's day will seem an hour but short, Being wasted in such time-beguiling sport . . . . . . *Ven. and Adon.* 23
Never did passenger in summer's heat More thirst for drink . . . 91
Lust's winter comes ere summer half be done 802
I, a drone-like bee, Have no perfection of my summer left . *Lucrece* 837
For never-resting time leads summer on To hideous winter . *Sonnet* 5 5
Then, were not summer's distillation left, A liquid prisoner . . 5 9
Let not winter's ragged hand deface In thee thy summer . . . 6 2
And summer's green all girded up in sheaves 12 7
Shall I compare thee to a summer's day? 18 1
Summer's lease hath all too short a date 18 4
But thy eternal summer shall not fade 18 9
When summer's breath their masked buds discloses 54 8
Makes summer's welcome thrice more wish'd, more rare . . . 56 14
O, how shall summer's honey breath hold out? 65 5
Making no summer of another's green 68 11
The summer's flower is to the summer sweet, Though to itself it only live and die 94 9
And yet this time removed was summer's time 97 5
For summer and his pleasures wait on thee 97 11
Nor the lays of birds . . . Could make me any summer's story tell . 98 7
As Philomel in summer's front doth sing 102 7
Not that the summer is less pleasant now 102 9
Three winters cold Have from the forests shook three summers' pride 104 4
Ere you were born was beauty's summer dead 104 14
Youth like summer morn, age like winter weather; Youth like summer brave, age like winter bare . . . . *Pass. Pil.* 159
Summon. And coal-black clouds that shadow heaven's light Do summon us to part and bid good night . . . . . *Ven. and Adon.* 534
I summon up remembrance of things past . . . . *Sonnet* 30 2
Sun. Even as the sun with purple-colour'd face Had ta'en his last leave of the weeping morn . . . . *Ven. and Adon.* 1
The sun doth burn my face; I must remove 186
Whose gentle wind Shall cool the heat of this descending sun . . 190
The sun that shines from heaven shines but warm, And, lo, I lie between that sun and thee 193
And were I not immortal, life were done Between this heavenly and earthly sun 198
Like the fair sun, when in his fresh array He cheers the morn and all the earth relieveth 483
And as the bright sun glorifies the sky, So is her face illumined with her eye 485
To shame the sun by day and her by night 732
As mountain-snow melts with the midday sun 750
Love comforteth like sunshine after rain, But Lust's effect is tempest after sun 800
The sun ariseth in his majesty 856
Nor sun nor wind will ever strive to kiss you 1082
The sun doth scorn you and the wind doth hiss you 1084
Sun and sharp air Lurk'd like two thieves, to rob him of his fair . . 1085
He put his bonnet on, Under whose brim the gaudy sun would peep . 1088
Against the golden splendour of the sun . . . . . *Lucrece* 25
As the fair and fiery-pointed sun, Rushing from forth a cloud, bereaves our sight 372
Or if thou wilt permit the sun to climb His wonted height . . . 775
As winter meads when sun doth melt their snow 1218
Why her two suns were cloud-eclipsed so 1224
But as the earth doth weep, the sun being set 1226
Enforced by sympathy Of those fair suns set in her mistress' sky . 1230
By heaven's fair sun that breeds the fat earth's store 1837
Making a couplement of proud compare, With sun and moon *Sonnet* 21 6
Where-through the sun Delights to peep, to gaze therein on thee . . 24 11
Their fair leaves spread But as the marigold at the sun's eye . . 25 6
Even so my sun one early morn did shine 33 9
Suns of the world may stain when heaven's sun staineth . . . 33 14
Clouds and eclipses stain both moon and sun 35 3
Thou shalt strangely pass And scarcely greet me with that sun, thine eye 49 6
A backward look, Even of five hundred courses of the sun . . . 59 6
For as the sun is daily new and old, So is my love 76 13
My mistress' eyes are nothing like the sun 130 1
Sun. Truly not the morning sun of heaven Better becomes the grey cheeks of the east . . . . *Sonnet* 132 5
The sun itself sees not till heaven clears 148 12
A platted hive of straw, Which fortified her visage from the sun *Lov. Comp.* 9
Then, thou fair sun, that on this earth doth shine, Exhale this vapour vow *Pass. Pil.* 38
Scarce had the sun dried up the dewy morn 71
The sun look'd on the world with glorious eye 81
Yet not for me, shine sun to succour flowers! 208
Sunder. Who, therefore angry, seems to part in sunder . . . *Lucrece* 388
Sundry. Revolving The sundry dangers of his will's obtaining . . 128
Sung. To recreate himself when he hath sung, The tiger would be tame and gently hear him . . . . *Ven. and Adon.* 1095
Cited up in rhymes, And sung by children in succeeding times . *Lucrece* 525
And there sung the dolefull'st ditty, That to hear it was great pity *Pass. Pil.* 383
Sunk. And see the brave day sunk in hideous night . . . *Sonnet* 12 2
Sunset. The twilight of such day As after sunset fadeth in the west . 73 6
Sunshine. Love comforteth like sunshine after rain . . *Ven. and Adon.* 799
Superiors. That meaner men should vaunt That golden hap which their superiors want . . . . *Lucrece* 42
Supped. Fare well I could not, for I supp'd with sorrow . . *Pass. Pil.* 186
Supper. For, after supper, long he questioned With modest Lucrece *Lucrece* 122
Suppliant. When wilt thou be the humble suppliant's friend? . . . 897
Supplicant. And supplicant their sighs to you extend . . *Lov. Comp.* 276
Supply. But if store of crowns be scant, No man will supply thy want *Pass. Pil.* 410
Support. These forceless flowers like sturdy trees support me . *V. and A.* 152
Suppose thou dost defend me From what is past . . . . *Lucrece* 1684
Nor dare I question with my jealous thought Where you may be, or your affairs suppose . . . . *Sonnet* 57 10
Supposed. Though death be adjunct, there's no death supposed . *Lucrece* 133
Whether it is that she reflects so bright, That dazzleth them, or else some shame supposed 377
Heedfully doth view The sight which makes supposed terror true . . 455
Let my unsounded self, supposed a fool 1819
Which I by lacking have supposed dead . . . . . *Sonnet* 31 2
Supposed as forfeit to a confined doom 107 4
Sweetly supposed them mistress of his heart . . . . *Lov. Comp.* 142
Supposing. So shall I live, supposing thou art true, Like a deceived husband *Sonnet* 93 1
Suppressed. His rage of lust by gazing qualified; Slack'd, not suppress'd *Lucrece* 425
On both sides thus is simple truth suppress'd . . . *Sonnet* 138 8
Supreme. Imperious supreme of all mortal things . . *Ven. and Adon.* 996
The life of purity, the supreme fair . . . . *Lucrece* 780
Surcease. If they surcease to be that should survive 1766
Sure. Unused stay From hands of falsehood, in sure wards of trust *Son.* 48 4
O, sure I am, the wits of former days To subjects worse have given admiring praise 59 13
And, to be sure that is not false I swear 131 9
Surety-like. He learn'd but surety-like to write for me 134 7
Surfeit. Whereon they surfeit, yet complain on drouth . *Ven. and Adon.* 544
As poor birds, . . . Do surfeit by the eye and pine the maw . . . 602
Surfeits, imposthumes, grief, and damn'd despair 743
Love surfeits not, Lust like a glutton dies 803
Gaining more, the profit of excess Is but to surfeit . . . *Lucrece* 139
Thus do I pine and surfeit day by day . . . . . *Sonnet* 75 13
Surfeit-taking. So surfeit-taking Tarquin fares this night . . *Lucrece* 698
Surly. No longer mourn for me when I am dead Than you shall hear the surly sullen bell . . . . *Sonnet* 71 2
Surmise. Answers with surmise, In silent wonder . . . . *Lucrece* 83
Being from the feeling of her own grief brought By deep surmise of others' detriment 1579
And on just proof surmise accumulate . . . . . *Sonnet* 117 10
Surmount. As I all other in all worths surmount 62 8
Surpass. Look, when a painter would surpass the life, In limning out a well-proportion'd steed . . . . *Ven. and Adon.* 289
Surplice. Let the priest in surplice white, That defunctive music can, Be the death-divining swan . . . . *Ph. and Tur.* 13
Surprise. This dismal cry rings sadly in her ear, Through which it enters to surprise her heart . . . . *Ven. and Adon.* 890
This mutiny each part doth so surprise 1049
Now serves the season that they may surprise The silly lambs . *Lucrece* 166
Survey. The which he will not every hour survey, For blunting the fine point of seldom pleasure . . . . *Sonnet* 52 3
My love's sweet face survey, If Time have any wrinkle graven there . 100 9
Survive. In spite of death, thou dost survive, In that thy likeness still is left alive . . . . *Ven. and Adon.* 173
The scandal will survive, And be an eye-sore in my golden coat . *Lucrece* 204
If they surcease to be that should survive 1766
If thou survive my well-contented day . . . . . *Sonnet* 32 1
Or you survive when I in earth am rotten 81 2
Surviving. This surviving shame, Whose crime will bear an ever-during blame . . . . *Lucrece* 223
So thy surviving husband shall remain The scornful mark 519
Suspect. Her rash suspect she doth extenuate . . . *Ven. and Adon.* 1010
It shall suspect where is no cause of fear 1153
The ornament of beauty is suspect, A crow that flies in heaven's sweetest air *Sonnet* 70 3
If some suspect of ill mask'd not thy show 70 13
Whether that my angel be turn'd fiend Suspect I may . 144 10; *Pass. Pil.* 24
Suspecteth. Little suspecteth the false worshipper . . . . *Lucrece* 86
Suspicion. And bid Suspicion double-lock the door . . *Ven. and Adon.* 448
To clear her From that suspicion which the world might bear her *Lucrece* 1321
Sustain. Such griefs sustain, That they prove bankrupt in this poor-rich gain 139
Sustaining. If thou dost weep for grief of my sustaining, Know, gentle wench, it small avails my mood 1272
Short time seems long in sorrow's sharp sustaining 1573
Swains. Onward to Troy with the blunt swains he goes 1504
All our pleasure known to us poor swains . . . . . *Pass. Pil.* 289
Swallow. These lovely caves, these round enchanting pits, Open'd their mouths to swallow Venus' liking . . . . . *Ven. and Adon.* 248
A press of gaping faces, Which seem'd to swallow up his sound advice *Lucr.* 1409
Swallowed. They that lose half with greater patience bear it Than they whose whole is swallow'd in confusion 1159
No sooner had Past reason hated, as a swallow'd bait . . *Sonnet* 129 7
Swallowing. What is thy body but a swallowing grave? *Ven. and Adon.* 757
A swallowing gulf that even in plenty wanteth . . . . . *Lucrece* 557
Swan. But if the like the snow-white swan desire, The stain upon his silver down will stay 1011

Swan. Now this pale swan in her watery nest Begins the sad dirge of her certain ending *Lucrece* 1611

Be the death-divining swan, Lest the requiem lack his right *Ph. and Tur.* 15

Swart-complexioned. So flatter I the swart-complexion'd night *Sonnet* 28 11

Sway. And strength by limping sway disabled 66 8

This powerful might With insufficiency my heart to sway 150 2

Proud of subjection, noble by the sway *Lov. Comp.* 108

Swayest. When thou gently sway'st The wiry concord that mine ear confounds *Sonnet* 128 3

Swear. And by her fair immortal hand she swears *Ven. and Adon.* 80

Swear Nature's death for framing thee so fair 744

That one would swear he saw them quake and tremble *Lucrece* 1393

Another smother'd seems to pelt and swear 1418

Lucrece swears he did her wrong, To give her so much grief and not a tongue 1462

And swear I found you where you did fulfil The loathsome act of lust 1635

His scarlet lust came evidence to swear That my poor beauty had purloin'd his eyes 1650

To say they err I dare not be so bold, Although I swear it to myself alone *Sonnet* 131 8

And, to be sure that is not false I swear 131 9

Then will I swear beauty herself is black 132 13

Swear to thy blind soul that I was thy 'Will' 136 2

When my love swears that she is made of truth I do believe her 138 1; *Pass. Pil.* 1

And swear that brightness doth not grace the day *Sonnet* 150 4

Gave eyes to blindness, Or made them swear against the thing they see 152 12

More perjured I, To swear against the truth so foul a lie! 152 14

If love make me forsworn, how shall I swear to love? *Pass. Pil.* 57

Thou for whom Jove would swear Juno but an Ethiope were 241

Swearing I slew him, seeing thee embrace him *Lucrece* 518

Swearing, unless I took all patiently, I should not live 1641

But thou art twice forsworn, to me love swearing *Sonnet* 152 2

Between each kiss her oaths of true love swearing *Pass. Pil.* 92

Sweat. By this the love-sick queen began to sweat *Ven. and Adon.* 175

With pearly sweat, resembling dew of night *Lucrece* 396

Begrimed with sweat, and smeared all with dust 1381

Sweating. With this she seizeth on his sweating palm *Ven. and Adon.* 25

Love to heaven is fled, Since sweating Lust on earth usurp'd his name 794

He faintly flies, sweating with guilty fear *Lucrece* 740

Sweet. The field's chief flower, sweet above compare, Stain to all nymphs, more lovely than a man *Ven. and Adon.* 8

And one sweet kiss shall pay this countless debt 84

Is love so light, sweet boy, and may it be That thou shouldst think it heavy unto thee? 155

Sweet bottom-grass and high delightful plain 236

For one sweet look thy help I would assure thee 371

Thy palfrey, as he should, Welcomes the warm approach of sweet desire 386

Pure lips, sweet seals in my soft lips imprinted 511

Her arms do lend his neck a sweet embrace 539

That sweet coral mouth, Whose precious taste her thirsty lips well knew 542

'Sweet boy,' she says, 'this night I'll waste in sorrow' 583

"Thou hadst been gone,' quoth she, 'sweet boy, ere this' 613

Nor thy soft hands, sweet lips, and crystal eyne 633

With this, he breaketh from the sweet embrace, Of those fair arms 811

In the sweet channel of her bosom dropt 958

'No, no,' quoth she, 'sweet Death, I did but jest' 997

The flowers are sweet, their colours fresh and trim 1079

Find sweet beginning, but unsavoury end 1138

O'erstraw'd With sweets that shall the truest sight beguile 1144

Sweet issue of a more sweet-smelling sire—For every little grief to wet his eyes 1178

There shall not be one minute in an hour Wherein I will not kiss my sweet love's flower 1188

For one sweet grape who will the vine destroy? *Lucrece* 215

Whereat she smiled with so sweet a cheer 264

Misty night Covers the shame that follows sweet delight 357

This moves in him more rage and lesser pity, To make the breach and enter this sweet city 469

By knighthood, gentry, and sweet friendship's oath 569

Her voice controll'd Entombs her outcry in her lips' sweet fold 679

The story of sweet chastity's decay 808

The sweets we wish for turn to loathed sours 867

The adder hisses where the sweet birds sing 871

The little birds . . . Make her moans mad with their sweet melody 1108

That mother tries a merciless conclusion Who, having two sweet babes, when death takes one, Will slay the other and be nurse to none 1161

Such sweet observance in this work was had 1385

And drop sweet balm in Priam's painted wound 1466

Sweet love, what spite hath thy fair colour spent? 1600

I often did behold In thy sweet semblance my old age new born 1759

Then live, sweet Lucrece, live again and see Thy father die 1770

Thyself thy foe, to thy sweet self too cruel *Sonnet* 1 8

Thou of thyself thy sweet self dost deceive 4 10

Flowers distill'd, though they with winter meet, Leese but their show; their substance still lives sweet 5 14

Make sweet some vial; treasure thou some place With beauty's treasure, ere it be self-kill'd 6 3

Sweets with sweets war not, joy delights in joy 8 2

Mark how one string, sweet husband to another 8 9

Since sweets and beauties do themselves forsake And die 12 11

Your sweet semblance to some other give 13 4

When your sweet issue your sweet form should bear 13 8

You must live, drawn by your own sweet skill 16 14

Make the earth devour her own sweet brood 19 2

To the wide world and all her fading sweets 19 7

To show me worthy of thy sweet respect 26 12

For thy sweet love remember'd such wealth brings 29 13

When to the sessions of sweet silent thought I summon up remembrance of things past 30 1

I an accessary needs must be To that sweet thief which sourly robs from me 35 14

Yet doth it steal sweet hours from love's delight 36 8

That pour'st into my verse Thine own sweet argument 38 3

Were it not thy sour leisure gave sweet leave To entertain the time 39 10

Sweet flattery! then she loves but me alone 42 14

Whose blessed key Can bring him to his sweet up-locked treasure 52 2

By that sweet ornament which truth doth give 54 2

The rose looks fair, but fairer we it deem For that sweet odour 54 4

Sweet roses do not so; Of their sweet deaths are sweetest odours made 54 11

Sweet. Sweet love, renew thy force; be it not said Thy edge should blunter be than appetite *Sonnet* 56 1

That he shall never cut from memory My sweet love's beauty 63 12

I in your sweet thoughts would be forgot If thinking on me then should make you woe 71 7

Bare ruin'd choirs, where late the sweet birds sang 73 4

Sweet love, I always write of you, And you and love are still my argument 76 9

And arts with thy sweet graces graced be 78 12

I grant, sweet love, thy lovely argument Deserves the travail of a worthier pen 79 5

In my tongue Thy sweet beloved name no more shall dwell 89 10

Heaven in thy creation did decree That in thy face sweet love should ever dwell 93 10

How like Eve's apple doth thy beauty grow, If thy sweet virtue answer not thy show! 93 14

The summer's flower is to the summer sweet, Though to itself it only live and die 94 9

How sweet and lovely dost thou make the shame 95 1

O, in what sweets dost thou thy sins enclose! 95 4

Nor the sweet smell Of different flowers in odour and in hue 98 5

They were but sweet, but figures of delight, Drawn after you 98 11

Sweet thief, whence didst thou steal thy sweet that smells? 99 2

Yet I none could see But sweet or colour it had stol'n from thee 99 15

My love's sweet face survey, If Time have any wrinkle graven there 100 9

And sweets grown common lose their dear delight 102 12

So your sweet hue, which methinks still doth stand, Hath motion 104 11

Sweet beauty's best, Of hand, of foot, of lip, of eye, of brow 106 5

What new to register, That may express my love or thy dear merit? Nothing, sweet boy 108 5

The most sweet favour or deformed'st creature 113 10

Such cherubins as your sweet self resemble 114 6

Paying too much rent, For compound sweet forgoing simple savour 125 7

And therein show'st Thy lovers withering as thy sweet self grow'st 126 4

Sweet beauty hath no name, no holy bower, But is profaned 127 7

That blessed wood whose motion sounds With thy sweet fingers 128 3

To thy sweet will making addition thus 135 4

Thus far for love my love-suit, sweet, fulfil 136 4

So it please thee hold That nothing me, a something sweet to thee 136 12

That tongue that ever sweet Was used in giving gentle doom 145 6

Lest guilty of my faults thy sweet self prove 151 4

What's sweet to do, to do will aptly find *Lov. Comp.* 88

When winds breathe sweet, unruly though they be 103

To be forbod the sweets that seem so good 164

But, O my sweet, what labour is't to leave The thing we have not 239

Lending soft audience to my sweet design 278

Sweet Cytherea, sitting by a brook With young Adonis *Pass. Pil.* 43

Which, not to anger bent, is music and sweet fire 68

If music and sweet poetry agree, As they must needs 103

Sweet melodious sound That Phœbus' lute, the queen of music, makes 111

'Once,' quoth she, 'did I see a fair sweet youth Here in these brakes' 125

Sweet rose, fair flower, untimely pluck'd, soon vaded, Pluck'd in the bud 131

O, sweet shepherd, hie thee, For methinks thou stay'st too long 167

Vow, alack! for youth unmeet: Youth, so apt to pluck a sweet 240

Clear wells spring not, Sweet birds sing not 282

Farewell, sweet lass, Thy like ne'er was For a sweet content 293

Sweetens. And sweetens, in the suffering pangs it bears, The aloes of all forces *Lov. Comp.* 272

Sweetest. Loathsome canker lives in sweetest bud *Sonnet* 35 4

Sweet roses do not so; Of their sweet deaths are sweetest odours made 54 12

The ornament of beauty is suspect, A crow that flies in heaven's sweetest air 70 4

For canker vice the sweetest buds doth love 70 7

Sweetest things turn sourest by their deeds 94 13

But slave to slavery my sweet'st friend must be 133 4

Sweetly. Th' one sweetly flatters, th' other feareth harm *Lucrece* 172

Canopied in darkness sweetly lay, Till they might open to adorn the day 398

They do but sweetly chide thee, who confounds In singleness the parts that thou shouldst bear *Sonnet* 8 7

Which time and thoughts so sweetly doth deceive 39 12

Sweetly supposed them mistress of his heart *Lov. Comp.* 142

Yet at my parting sweetly did she smile *Pass. Pil.* 187

Sweetness. And having felt the sweetness of the spoil, With blindfold fury she begins to forage *Ven. and Adon.* 553

Thy looks should nothing thence but sweetness tell *Sonnet* 93 12

Even so, being full of your ne'er-cloying sweetness 118 5

Sweet-seasoned. As sweet-season'd showers are to the ground 75 2

Sweet-smelling. Sweet issue of a more sweet-smelling sire *Ven. and Adon.* 1178

Swell. Nor children's tears nor mothers' groans respecting, Swell in their pride, the onset still expecting *Lucrece* 432

My uncontrolled tide Turns not, but swells the higher by this let 646

Swelleth. An oven that is stopp'd, or river stay'd, Burneth more hotly, swelleth with more rage *Ven. and Adon.* 332

Swelling. And swelling passion doth provoke a pause 218

Like a milch doe, whose swelling dugs do ache 875

Seems to part in sunder, Swelling on either side to want his bliss *Lucrece* 389

Even so the maid with swelling drops 'gan wet 1228

Whose waves to imitate the battle sought With swelling ridges 1439

Swerving. And so my patent back again is swerving *Sonnet* 87 8

Swift. By whose swift aid Their mistress mounted through the empty skies In her light chariot quickly is convey'd *Ven. and Adon.* 1190

With swift intent he goes To quench the coal *Lucrece* 46

Swift subtle post, carrier of grisly care, Eater of youth 926

How swift and short His time of folly and his time of sport 991

Calls her maid, Whose swift obedience to her mistress hies 1215

With swift pursuit to venge this wrong of mine 1691

These present-absent with swift motion slide *Sonnet* 45 4

By those swift messengers return'd from thee 45 10

When swift extremity can seem but slow 51 6

What strong hand can hold his swift foot back? 65 11

Sets down her babe and makes all swift dispatch 143 3

Swiftest. And had let go by The swiftest hours *Lov. Comp.* 60

Swift-footed. Do whate'er thou wilt, swift-footed Time *Sonnet* 19 6

Swiftly. Jealous of catching, swiftly doth forsake him *Ven. and Adon.* 321

Swimmer. Like an unpractised swimmer plunging still *Lucrece* 1098

Swine. Thou know'st not what it is With javelin's point a churlish swine to gore *Ven. and Adon.* 616

The loving swine Sheathed unaware the tusk in his soft groin 1115

Swoln. All swoln with chafing, down Adonis sits 325

Swoon. Or to turn white and swoon at tragic shows *Lov. Comp.* 308

Swooning. Of burning blushes, or of weeping water, Or swooning paleness *Lov. Comp.* 305
Sword. Draw not thy sword to guard iniquity *Lucrece* 626
It seem'd they would debate with angry swords 1421
And then against my heart he set his sword 1640
Nor Mars his sword nor war's quick fire shall burn *Sonnet* 55 7
Swore. That deep vow, which Brutus made before, He doth again repeat, and that they swore *Lucrece* 1848
Sworn. When they had sworn to this advised doom 1849
I have sworn thee fair and thought thee bright, Who art as black as hell *Sonnet* 147 13
Sworn. For I have sworn deep oaths of thy deep kindness, Oaths of thy love, thy truth, thy constancy *Sonnet* 152 9
For I have sworn thee fair; more perjured I 152 13
That's to ye sworn to none was ever said *Lov. Comp.* 180
My hand hath sworn Ne'er to pluck thee from thy thorn *Pass. Pil.* 237
Swounds. Here manly Hector faints, here Troilus swounds *Lucrece* 1486
Sympathized. True sorrow then is feelingly sufficed When with like semblance it is sympathized 1113
Thou truly fair wert truly sympathized *Sonnet* 82 11
Sympathy. This solemn sympathy poor Venus noteth *Ven. and Adon.* 1057
Her circled eyne, enforced by sympathy Of those fair suns *Lucrece* 1229

T

Table. And hath stell'd Thy beauty's form in table of my heart *Sonnet* 24 2
Thy gift, thy tables, are within my brain Full character'd 122 1
Was I bold, To trust those tables that receive thee more 122 12
Tail. Thin mane, thick tail, broad buttock, tender hide *Ven. and Adon.* 298
For through his mane and tail the high wind sings, Fanning the hairs 305
He vails his tail that, like a falling plume, Cool shadow to his melting buttock lent 314
Clapping their proud tails to the ground below 923
Tainted. For by our ears our hearts oft tainted be *Lucrece* 38
My stained blood to Tarquin I'll bequeath, Which by him tainted shall for him be spent 1182
A watery rigol goes, Which seems to weep upon the tainted place 1746
Take. Till he take truce with her contending tears *Ven. and Adon.* 82
His testy master goeth about to take him 319
As apt as new-fall'n snow takes any dint 354
Full gently now she takes him by the hand 361
I heartily beseech thee, To take advantage on presented joy 405
While she takes all she can, not all she listeth 564
They that thrive well take counsel of their friends 640
My boding heart pants, beats, and takes no rest 647
She takes him by the hand, and that is cold; She whispers in his ears 1124
Lo, in this hollow cradle take thy rest 1185
But with a pure appeal seeks to the heart, Which once corrupted takes the worser part *Lucrece* 294
He takes it from the rushes where it lies 318
He takes for accidental things of trial 326
Bequeath not to their lot The shame that from them no device can take 535
Unwholesome weeds take root with precious flowers 870
That mother tries a merciless conclusion Who, having two sweet babes, when death takes one, Will slay the other and be nurse to none 1161
My resolution, husband, do thou take 1200
The other takes in hand No cause, but company, of her drops spilling 1235
At last he takes her by the bloodless hand 1597
Do not take away My sorrow's interest 1796
Nothing 'gainst Time's scythe can make defence Save breed, to brave him when he takes thee hence *Sonnet* 12 14
And all in war with Time for love of you, As he takes from you, I engraft you new 15 14
Unless thou take that honour from thy name 36 12
As a decrepit father takes delight To see his active child do deeds of youth 37 1
Take all my comfort of thy worth and truth 37 4
Take all my loves, my love, yea, take them all 40 1
Thus to ruminate That Time will come and take my love away 64 12
Which by and by black night doth take away, Death's second self 73 7
Thou shalt find Those children nursed, deliver'd from thy brain, To take a new acquaintance of thy mind 77 12
From hence your memory death cannot take 81 3
Thou mayst take All this away and me most wretched make 91 13
Take heed, dear heart, of this large privilege 95 13
Take thou my oblation, poor but free 125 10
The statute of thy beauty thou wilt take, Thou usurer 134 9
Yet what the best is take the worst to be 137 4
Often men would say That horse his mettle from his rider takes *Lov. Comp.* 107
And controversy hence a question takes 110
Take all these similes to your own command 227
And he takes and leaves, In either's aptness, as it best deceives 305
He refused to take her figured proffer *Pass. Pil.* 52
Her stand she takes upon a steep-up hill 121
And would not take her meaning nor her pleasure 154
As take the pain, but cannot pluck the pelf 192
Take counsel of some wiser head, Neither too young nor yet unwed 303
Ah, thought I, thou mourn'st in vain! None takes pity on thy pain 392
Taken. Even as the sun with purple-colour'd face Had ta'en his last leave of the weeping morn *Ven. and Adon.* 2
She modestly prepares to let them know Her honour is ta'en prisoner *Lucr.* 1608
Whose worth's unknown, although his height be taken *Sonnet* 116 8
And I, a tyrant, have no leisure taken 120 7
Me from myself thy cruel eye hath taken 133 5
Taker. On purpose laid to make the taker mad 129 8
Takest. With the breath thou givest and takest, 'Mongst our mourners shalt thou go *Ph. and Tur.* 19
Taking. Taking no notice that she is so nigh, For all askance he holds her in his eye *Ven. and Adon.* 341
What terror 'tis! but she, in worser taking, From sleep disturbed *Lucrece* 453
Tale. Still she entreats, and prettily entreats, For to a pretty ear she tunes her tale *Ven. and Adon.* 74
She trembles at his tale, And on his neck her yoking arms she throws 591
She whispers in his ears a heavy tale 1125
The colour in thy face, . . . Shall plead for me and tell my loving tale *Lucr.* 480
Shall gush pure streams to purge my impure tale 1078
So Lucrece, set a-work, sad tales doth tell 1496
And down I laid to list the sad-tuned tale *Lov. Comp.* 4
How many tales to please me hath she coined! *Pass. Pil.* 93
And when thou comest thy tale to tell, Smooth not thy tongue with filed talk 305
Talents. Behold these talents of their hair, With twisted metal amorously impleach'd *Lov. Comp.* 204
Talk. 'What! canst thou talk?' quoth she, 'hast thou a tongue?' *V. and A.* 427
Mine ears, that to your wanton talk attended, Do burn themselves 809
Mingling my talk with tears, my grief with groans *Lucrece* 797
Sometime her grief is dumb and hath no words; Sometime 'tis mad and too much talk affords 1106
Such harmless creatures have a true respect To talk in deeds 1348
Begins to talk; but through his lips do throng Weak words 1783
And when thou comest thy tale to tell, Smooth not thy tongue with filed talk *Pass. Pil.* 306
Talked. Besides, of weariness he did complain him, And talk'd of virtue *Lucrece* 846
Tall. He of tall building and of goodly pride *Sonnet* 80 12
Tallies. Nor need I tallies thy dear love to score 122 10
Tame. The tiger would be tame and gently hear him *Ven. and Adon.* 1096
To tame the unicorn and lion wild *Lucrece* 956
Continuance tames the one; the other wild 1097
And patience, tame to sufferance, bide each check, Without accusing you of injury *Sonnet* 58 7
Showing fair nature is both kind and tame *Lov. Comp.* 311
Youth is hot and bold, age is weak and cold; Youth is wild, and age is tame *Pass. Pil.* 164
Tamed. Like a wild bird being tamed with too much handling *V. and A.* 560
Tan sacred beauty, blunt the sharp'st intents, Divert strong minds *Son.* 115 7
Tangled. Look, how a bird lies tangled in a net, So fasten'd in her arms Adonis lies *Ven. and Adon.* 67
Tanned. Beated and chopp'd with tann'd antiquity *Sonnet* 62 10
Tantalus. That worse than Tantalus' is her annoy, To clip Elysium and to lack her joy *Ven. and Adon.* 599
But like still-pining Tantalus he sits *Lucrece* 858
Tapsters. Like shrill-tongued tapsters answering every call *Ven. and Adon.* 849
Tarquin. Lust-breathed Tarquin leaves the Roman host *Lucrece* 3
For he the night before, in Tarquin's tent, Unlock'd the treasure 15
Their silent war of lilies and of roses, Which Tarquin view'd in her fair face's field, In their pure ranks his traitor eye encloses 72
Enchanted Tarquin answers with surmise, In silent wonder 83
For then is Tarquin brought unto his bed, Intending weariness 120
As one of which doth Tarquin lie revolving The sundry dangers 127
Such hazard now must doting Tarquin make 155
These worlds in Tarquin new ambition bred 411
So o'er this sleeping soul doth Tarquin stay, His rage of lust by gazing qualified 423
In Tarquin's likeness I did entertain thee 596
So surfeit-taking Tarquin fares this night 698
Were Tarquin Night, as he is but Night's child 785
And fright her crying babe with Tarquin's name 814
The orator, to deck his oratory, Will couple my reproach to Tarquin's shame 816
How Tarquin wronged me, I Collatine 819
And Tarquin's eye may read the mot afar 830
My Collatine would else have come to me When Tarquin did 917
With some mischance cross Tarquin in his flight 968
In vain I rail at Opportunity, At Time, at Tarquin 1024
I fear'd by Tarquin's falchion to be slain 1046
That cannot be; Of that true type hath Tarquin rifled me 1050
For burden-wise I'll hum on Tarquin still 1133
My stained blood to Tarquin I'll bequeath 1181
How Tarquin must be used, read it in me 1195
And for my sake serve thou false Tarquin so 1197
'When went'—and there she stay'd Till after a deep groan—'Tarquin from hence?' 1276
Ere the break of day, And, ere I rose, was Tarquin gone away 1281
She thought he blush'd, as knowing Tarquin's lust 1354
But Tarquin's shape came in her mind the while 1536
As if with grief or travail he had fainted, To me came Tarquin armed 1544
As Priam him did cherish, So did I Tarquin; so my Troy did perish 1547
As if her heart would break, She throws forth Tarquin's name 1717
Some of her blood still pure and red remain'd, And some look'd black, and that false Tarquin stain'd 1743
Sometime 'Tarquin' was pronounced plain, But through his teeth 1786
And so to publish Tarquin's foul offence 1852
To Tarquin's everlasting banishment 1855
Tarriance. Cytherea, all in love forlorn, A longing tarriance for Adonis made *Pass. Pil.* 74
Task. His day's hot task hath ended in the west *Ven. and Adon.* 530
In that high task hath done her beauty wrong *Lucrece* 80
Then be this all the task it hath to say 1618
But she, that yet her sad task hath not said, The protestation stops 1699
Lest the world should task you to recite What merit lived in me *Sonnet* 72 1
Taste. Torches are made to light, jewels to wear, Dainties to taste *V. and A.* 164
But, O, what banquet wert thou to the taste! 445
Or being early pluck'd is sour to taste 528
Whose precious taste her thirsty lips well knew 543
Their fresh falls' haste Add to his flow, but alter not his taste *Lucrece* 651
His taste delicious, in digestion souring, Devours his will 699
Thy sugar'd tongue to bitter wormwood taste 893

Taste. Dear Collatine, thou shalt not know The stained taste of violated troth *Lucrece* 1059
If thou thyself deceivest By wilful taste of what thyself refusest *Sonnet* 40 8
The vacant leaves thy mind's imprint will bear, And of this book this learning mayst thou taste 77 4
So shall I taste At first the very worst of fortune's might 90 11
Nor taste, nor smell, desire to be invited To any sensual feast with thee alone 141 7
The one a palate hath that needs will taste *Lov. Comp.* 167
Tasted. The tender spring upon thy tempting lip Shows thee unripe; yet mayst thou well be tasted *Ven. and Adon.* 128
Tattered. A tatter'd weed, of small worth held *Sonnet* 2 4
And puts apparel on my tatter'd loving 26 11
Taught. That hard heart of thine, Hath taught them scornful tricks *Ven. and Adon.* 501
Those eyes that taught all other eyes to see 952
Ruin hath taught me thus to ruminate *Sonnet* 64 11
Thine eyes that taught the dumb on high to sing 78 5
By spirits taught to write Above a mortal pitch, that struck me dead 86 5
And that your love taught it this alchemy 114 4
And taught it thus anew to greet 145 8
Who taught thee how to make me love thee more? 150 9
When craft hath taught her thus to say *Pass. Pil.* 320
Taughtest. Teach me to curse him that thou taught'st this ill! *Lucrece* 996
Teach. Though I were dumb, yet his proceedings teach thee *Ven. and Adon.* 406
It doth make my faint heart bleed, And fear doth teach it divination 670
Strike the wise dumb and teach the fool to speak 1146
Foul sin may say, He learn'd to sin, and thou didst teach the way *Lucrece* 630
Teach me to curse him that thou taught'st this ill! 996
O, teach me how to make mine own excuse! 1653
My weary travel's end, Doth teach that ease and that repose *Sonnet* 50 3
I teach thee how To make him seem long hence as he shows now 101 13
If I might teach thee wit, better it were, Though not to love, yet, love, to tell me so 140 5
She will not stick to round me i' the ear, To teach my tongue to be so long *Pass. Pil.* 350
Teachest. Thou teachest how to make one twain *Sonnet* 39 13
Teaching the sheets a whiter hue than white *Ven. and Adon.* 398
Teaching decrepit age to tread the measures 1148
Teaching them thus to use it in the fight *Lucrece* 62
Team. Wishing Adonis had his team to guide, So he were like him and by Venus' side *Ven. and Adon.* 179
Tear. She with her tears Doth quench the maiden burning of his cheeks 49
Till he take truce with her contending tears, Which long have rain'd, making her cheeks all wet 82
I'll make a shadow for thee of my hairs; If they burn too, I'll quench them with my tears 192
And all this dumb play had his acts made plain With tears 360
Dismiss your vows, your feigned tears, your flattery 425
But hers, which through the crystal tears gave light, Shone like the moon in water seen by night 491
Dost thou drink tears, that thou provokest such weeping? 949
O, how her eyes and tears did lend and borrow! Her eyes seen in the tears, tears in her eye 961
Sighs dry her cheeks, tears make them wet again 966
Her tears began to turn their tide, Being prison'd in her eye 979
Whose wonted lily white With purple tears, that his wound wept, was drench'd 1054
My sighs are blown away, my salt tears gone 1071
They both would strive who first should dry his tears 1092
In the breach appears Green dropping sap, which she compares to tears 1176
Nor children's tears nor mothers' groans respecting, Swell in their pride, the onset still expecting *Lucrece* 431
Repentant tears ensue the deed, Reproach, disdain, and deadly enmity 502
Tears harden lust, though marble wear with raining 560
By her untimely tears, her husband's love, By holy human law 570
If ever man were moved with woman's moans, Be moved with my tears 588
O, if no harder than a stone thou art, Melt at my tears 594
Enforced hate, Instead of love's coy touch, shall rudely tear thee 669
The chastest tears That ever modest eyes with sorrow shed 682
The spots whereof could weeping purify, Her tears should drop on them 686
She, desperate, with her nails her flesh doth tear 739
Mingling my talk with tears, my grief with groans 797
Let him have time to tear his curled hair 981
Distress likes dumps when time is kept with tears 1127
So I at each sad strain will strain a tear 1131
On what occasion break Those tears from thee, that down thy cheeks are raining? 1271
If tears could help, mine own would do me good 1274
When sighs and groans and tears may grace the fashion Of her disgrace 1319
Many a dry drop seem'd a weeping tear 1375
And with my tears quench Troy that burns so long 1468
That with my nails her beauty I may tear 1472
Priam wets his eyes, To see those borrow'd tears that Sinon sheds 1549
For every tear he falls a Trojan bleeds 1551
So Priam's trust false Sinon's tears doth flatter 1560
She tears the senseless Sinon with her nails 1564
Her eyes, though sod in tears, look'd red and raw 1592
The face, that map which deep impression bears Of hard misfortune, carved in it with tears 1713
To check the tears in Collatinus' eyes 1817
How many a holy and obsequious tear Hath dear religious love stol'n from mine eye As interest of the dead *Sonnet* 31 5
Ah! but those tears are pearl which thy love sheds 34 13
Heavy tears, badges of either's woe 44 14
What potions have I drunk of Siren tears, Distill'd from limbecks 119 1
That is so vex'd with watching and with tears 148 10
O cunning Love! with tears thou keep'st me blind 148 13
In the brine That season'd woe had pelleted in tears *Lov. Comp.* 18
And often kiss'd, and often 'gan to tear 51
What a hell of witchcraft lies In the small orb of one particular tear! 289
His passion, but an art of craft, Even there resolved my reason into tears 296
Her faith, her oaths, her tears, and all were jestings *Pass. Pil.* 96
That to hear her so complain, Scarce I could from tears refrain 388
Tear-distained. Round about her tear-distained eye Blue circles stream'd, like rainbows in the sky *Lucrece* 1586
Tearing of papers, breaking rings a-twain *Lov. Comp.* 6
Tedious. Her song was tedious and outwore the night *Ven. and Adon.* 841
My woes are tedious, though my words are brief *Lucrece* 1309
Like dying coals burnt out in tedious nights 1379

Teeming. The teeming autumn, big with rich increase *Sonnet* 97 6
Teen. My face is full of shame, my heart of teen *Ven. and Adon.* 808
Or my affection put to the smallest teen, Or any of my leisures ever charm'd *Lov. Comp.* 192
Teeth. The iron bit he crusheth 'tween his teeth *Ven. and Adon.* 269
He ran upon the boar with his sharp spear, Who did not whet his teeth at him again 1113
Sometime 'Tarquin' was pronounced plain, But through his teeth *Lucrece* 1787
Pluck the keen teeth from the fierce tiger's jaws *Sonnet* 19 3
Tell. Tell me, Love's master, shall we meet to-morrow? *Ven. and Adon.* 585
'Wilt thou make the match?' He tells her, no 587
More I could tell, but more I dare not say 805
She tells them 'tis a causeless fantasy, And childish error 897
Tells him of trophies, statues, tombs, and stories 1013
Do tell her she is dreadfully beset, And fright her with confusion of their cries *Lucrece* 444
The colour in thy face, . . . Shall plead for me and tell my loving tale 480
Marking what he tells With trembling fear, as fowl hear falcon's bells 510
The nurse, to still her child, will tell my story 813
'But tell me, girl, when went'—and there she stay'd Till after a deep groan—'Tarquin from hence?' 1275
When more is felt than one hath power to tell 1288
So Lucrece, set a-work, sad tales doth tell 1496
Tell thy grief, that we may give redress 1603
Too long, To tell them all with one poor tired tongue 1617
Look in thy glass, and tell the face thou viewest *Sonnet* 3 1
When I do count the clock that tells the time 12 1
Methinks I have astronomy, But not to tell of good or evil luck 14 3
Nor can I fortune to brief minutes tell 14 5
I tell the day, to please him thou art bright 28 9
And heavily from woe to woe tell o'er The sad account 30 10
That every word doth almost tell my name 76 7
If he can tell That you are you, so dignifies his story 84 7
And haply of our old acquaintance tell 89 12
Thy looks should nothing thence but sweetness tell 93 12
That tongue that tells the story of thy days 95 5
Nor the lays of birds . . . Could make me any summer's story tell 98 7
For to no other pass my verses tend Than of your graces and your gifts to tell 103 12
Tell me thou lovest elsewhere, but in my sight, Dear heart, forbear to glance thine eye aside 139 5
Better it were, Though not to love, yet, love, to tell me so 140 6
Suspect I may, yet not directly tell 144 10
My soul doth tell my body that he may Triumph in love 151 7
Let it not tell your judgement I am old *Lov. Comp.* 73
How mighty then you are, O, hear me tell! 253
Whether that my angel be turn'd fiend, Suspect I may, yet not directly tell *Pass. Pil.* 24
And when thou comest thy tale to tell, Smooth not thy tongue with filed talk 305
Telling. For as the sun is daily new and old, So is my love still telling what is told *Sonnet* 76 14
Tell-tale. Make me not object to the tell-tale Day! *Lucrece* 806
Temperance. Thou blow'st the fire when temperance is thaw'd 884
Temperate. Shall I compare thee to a summer's day? Thou art more lovely and more temperate *Sonnet* 18 2
Tempering. What wax so frozen but dissolves with tempering *V. and A.* 565
Tempest. To shelter thee from tempest and from rain 238
Like a red morn, that ever yet betoken'd Wreck to the seaman, tempest to the field 454
Love comforteth like sunshine after rain, But Lust's effect is tempest after sun 800
This windy tempest, till it blow up rain, Held back his sorrow's tide *Lucr.* 1788
An ever-fixed mark That looks on tempests and is never shaken *Sonnet* 116 6
Temple. Besides, his soul's fair temple is defaced *Lucrece* 719
Her sacred temple spotted, spoil'd, corrupted 1172
Tempt. Unto a greater uproar tempts his veins 427
And now, to tempt, all liberty procured *Lov. Comp.* 252
Temptation. Thy beauty and thy years full well befits, For still temptation follows where thou art *Sonnet* 41 4
Unmoved, cold, and to temptation slow 94 4
Tempted. Not to be tempted, would she be immured *Lov. Comp.* 251
Tempter. Gave the tempter place, Which like a cherubin above them hover'd 318
Tempteth. My female evil Tempteth my better angel from my side *Sonnet* 144 6; *Pass. Pil.* 20
Tempting. The tender spring upon thy tempting lip Shows thee unripe; yet mayst thou well be tasted *Ven. and Adon.* 127
Yet from mine ear the tempting tune is blown 778
Hers, by thy beauty tempting her to thee, Thine, by thy beauty being false to me *Sonnet* 41 13
Ten kisses short as one, one long as twenty *Ven. and Adon.* 22
What is ten hundred touches unto thee? 519
Grief hath two tongues, and never woman yet Could rule them both without ten women's wit 1008
He ten times pines that pines beholding food *Lucrece* 1115
To breed another thee, Or ten times happier, be it ten for one *Sonnet* 6 8
Ten times thyself were happier than thou art, If ten of thine ten times refigured thee 6 9
This wish I have; then ten times happy me! 37 14
Be thou the tenth Muse, ten times more in worth Than those old nine 38 9
Tenants. Make weak-made women tenants to their shame *Lucrece* 1260
A quest of thoughts, all tenants to the heart *Sonnet* 46 10
Tend. Whereof are you made, That millions of strange shadows on you tend? 53 2
What should I do but tend Upon the hours and times of your desire? 57 1
For to no other pass my verses tend 103 11
The diamond,—why, 'twas beautiful and hard, Whereto his invised properties did tend *Lov. Comp.* 212
Tender. Over one arm the lusty courser's rein, Under her other was the tender boy *Ven. and Adon.* 32
The tender spring upon thy tempting lip Shows thee unripe 127
Thin mane, thick tail, broad buttock, tender hide 298
Her other tender hand his fair cheek feels 352
This canker that eats up Love's tender spring 656
And soon bereaves, As caterpillars do the tender leaves 798
Or, as the snail, whose tender horns being hit, Shrinks backward 1033
And straight, in pity of his tender years, They both would strive who first should dry his tears 1091
Then, for thy husband and thy children's sake, Tender my suit *Lucrece* 534
Unapt for tender smell or speedy flight 695
Unruly blasts wait on the tender spring 869

Tender. His tender heir might bear his memory *Sonnet* 1 4
And, tender churl, makest waste in niggarding 1 12
Which I will keep so chary As tender nurse her babe from faring ill 22 12
When these quicker elements are gone In tender embassy of love to thee 45 6
You did exceed The barren tender of a poet's debt 83 4
To kiss the tender inward of thy hand 128 6
Nor tender feeling, to base touches prone 141 6
All these trophies of affections hot, Of pensived and subdued desires the tender *Lov. Comp.* 219
The tender nibbler would not touch the bait *Pass. Pil.* 53
Tendered. Ere he says 'Adieu,' The honey fee of parting tender'd is *Ven. and Adon.* 538
Then tender'd The humble salve which wounded bosoms fits *Sonnet* 120 11
Tenderer. His tenderer cheek receives her soft hand's print *Ven. and Adon.* 353
Tenour. Here folds she up the tenour of her woe, Her certain sorrow writ uncertainly *Lucrece* 1310
To find out shames and idle hours in me, The scope and tenour of thy jealousy? *Sonnet* 61 8
Tent. Making my arms his field, his tent my bed *Ven. and Adon.* 108
For he the night before, in Tarquin's tent, Unlock'd the treasure *Lucrece* 15
Tenth. Be thou the tenth Muse, ten times more in worth Than those old nine *Sonnet* 38 9
Tereu. 'Fie, fie, fie,' now would she cry; 'Tereu, tereu!' by and by *Pass. Pil.* 386
Tereus. While thou on Tereus descant'st better skill *Lucrece* 1134
Term. May any terms acquit me from this chance? 1706
For term of life thou art assured mine *Sonnet* 92 2
Buy terms divine in selling hours of dross 146 11
Long upon these terms I held my city, Till thus he gan besiege me *L. Comp.* 176
Termed. And your true rights be term'd a poet's rage *Sonnet* 17 11
Termless. That termless skin Whose bare out-bragg'd the web it seem'd to wear *Lov. Comp.* 94
Terror. Which with cold terror doth men's minds confound *Ven. and Adon.* 1048
But coward-like with trembling terror die *Lucrece* 231
What terror 'tis! but she, in worser taking, From sleep disturbed 453
Heedfully doth view The sight which makes supposed terror true 455
Effects of terror and dear modesty, Encamp'd in hearts *Lov. Comp.* 202
Testament. And as his due writ in my testament *Lucrece* 1183
Testy. His testy master goeth about to take him *Ven. and Adon.* 319
True grief is fond and testy as a child *Lucrece* 1094
As testy sick men, when their deaths be near, No news but health from their physicians know *Sonnet* 140 7
Text. The text is old, the orator too green *Ven. and Adon.* 806
Than. More lovely than a man, More white and red than doves or roses are 9
Never did passenger in summer's heat More thirst for drink than she for this good turn 92
Art thou obdurate, flinty, hard as steel, Nay, more than flint? 200
Teaching the sheets a whiter hue than white 398
That worse than Tantalus is her annoy, To clip Elysium and to lack her joy 599
Are better proof than thy spear's point can enter 626
And more than so, presenteth to mine eye The picture of an angry-chafing boar 661
Her more than haste is mated with delays 909
Nor could she moralize his wanton sight, More than his eyes were open'd to the light *Lucrece* 105
With more than admiration he admired Her azure veins 418
To see sad sights moves more than hear them told 1324
And on it writ 'At Ardea to my lord with more than haste' 1332
Their ranks began To break upon the galled shore, and than Retire again 1440
Thank. O, give thyself the thanks, if aught in me Worthy perusal stand against thy sight *Sonnet* 38 5
Then thank him not for that which he doth say 79 13
That. Rain added to a river that is rank Perforce will force it overflow the bank *Ven. and Adon.* 71
And begg'd for that which thou unask'd shalt have 102
Thus he that overruled I oversway'd, Leading him prisoner 109
Brag not of thy might, For mastering her that foil'd the god of fight! 114
Fair flowers that are not gather'd in their prime Rot and consume themselves in little time 131
Thou dost survive, In that thy likeness still is left alive 174
That in each cheek appears a pretty dimple 242
That love-sick Love by pleading may be blest 328
With disturbed mind, Taking no notice that she is so nigh 341
And that I could not see, nor hear, nor touch 440
That they have murder'd this poor heart of mine 502
The poor fool prays her that he may depart 578
That worse than Tantalus' is her annoy, To clip Elysium and to lack her joy 599
Whispers in mine ear That if I love thee, I thy death should fear 660
Applying this to that, and so to so; For love can comment upon every woe 713
The night is spent. 'Why, what of that?' quoth she 717
Dost thou drink tears, that thou provokest such weeping? 949
This is my spite, That, thou being dead, the day should yet be light 1134
That all love's pleasure shall not match his woe 1140
That meaner men should vaunt That golden hap *Lucrece* 41
In despite Virtue would stain that o'er with silver white 56
For that he colour'd with his high estate 92
That which they possess They scatter and unloose it from their bond 135
Great grief grieves most at that would do it good 1117
Not that devour'd, but that which doth devour, Is worthy blame 1256
And shiver'd all the beauty of my glass, That I no more can see what once I was 1764
So, till the judgement that yourself arise, You live in this *Sonnet* 55 13
That God forbid that made me first your slave 58 1
The worth of that is that which it contains, And that is this, and this with thee remains 74 13
Where art thou, Muse, that thou forget'st so long To speak? 100 1
Ah, that I had my lady at this bay, To kiss and clip me! *Pass. Pil.* 155
And there sung the dolefull'st ditty, That to hear it was great pity 384
That to hear her so complain, Scarce I could from tears refrain 387
Thawed. Are on the sudden wasted, thaw'd, and done *Ven. and Adon.* 749
Thou blow'st the fire when temperance is thaw'd *Lucrece* 884
Theft. Steal thine own freedom and complain on theft *Ven. and Adon.* 160
Robb'd and ransack'd by injurious theft *Lucrece* 838
Guilty thou art of murder and of theft, Guilty of perjury and subornation 918
But, for his theft, in pride of all his growth A vengeful canker eat him up to death *Sonnet* 99 12
Theme. Let us part, And leave this idle theme, this bootless chat *Ven. and Adon.* 422
You will fall again Into your idle over-handled theme 770
If that be made a theme for disputation *Lucrece* 822
Three themes in one, which wondrous scope affords *Sonnet* 105 12
Themselves. Fair flowers that are not gather'd in their prime Rot and consume themselves in little time *Ven. and Adon.* 132
Things growing to themselves are growth's abuse 166
Or theirs whose desperate hands themselves do slay 765
Mine ears, that to your wanton talk attended, Do burn themselves 810
If pleased themselves, others, they think, delight In such-like circumstance 843
Like stars ashamed of day, themselves withdrew 1032
And every one to rest themselves betake, Save thieves *Lucrece* 125
But blind they are, and keep themselves enclosed 378
Each in her sleep themselves so beautify 404
Men's faults do seldom to themselves appear 633
They think not but that every eye can see The same disgrace which they themselves behold 751
Alas, how many bear such shameful blows, Which not themselves, but he that gives them knows! 833
To mock the subtle in themselves beguiled 957
Grieving themselves to guess at others' smarts 1238
Since sweets and beauties do themselves forsake And die *Sonnet* 12 11
And in themselves their pride lies buried 25 7
They live unwoo'd and unrespected fade, Die to themselves 54 11
Who, moving others, are themselves as stone, Unmoved, cold 94 3
Incertainties now crown themselves assured 107 7
I may be straight, though they themselves be bevel 121 11
All aids, themselves made fairer by their place, Came for additions *L. Comp.* 117
To themselves yet either neither, Simple were so well compounded *Ph. and Tur.* 43
Then mightst thou pause, for then I were not for thee *Ven. and Adon.* 137
There is no heaven, by holy then, When time with age doth them attaint *Pass. Pil.* 343
Thence. The heat I have from thence doth little harm *Ven. and Adon.* 195
And when from thence he struggles to be gone, She locks her lily fingers one in one 227
Whose beams upon his hairless face are fix'd, As if from thence they borrow'd all their shine 488
The which . . . He carries thence incaged in his breast 582
He like a thievish dog creeps sadly thence *Lucrece* 736
He thence departs a heavy convertite 743
She wakes her heart by beating on her breast, And bids it leap from thence 760
His eye drops fire, no water thence proceeds 1552
She sheathed in her harmless breast A harmful knife, that thence her soul unsheathed 1724
They did conclude to bear dead Lucrece thence 1850
And even thence thou wilt be stol'n, I fear *Sonnet* 48 13
From where thou art why should I haste me thence? 51 3
I was not sick of any fear from thence 86 12
Thy looks should nothing thence but sweetness tell 93 12
Thence comes it that my name receives a brand 111 5
And almost thence my nature is subdued To what it works in, like the dyer's hand 111 6
But thence I learn, and find the lesson true 118 13
And thence this slander, as I think, proceeds 131 14
And true to bondage would not break from thence *Lov. Comp.* 34
And did thence remove, To spend her living in eternal love 237
There. Look in mine eye-balls, there thy beauty lies *Ven. and Adon.* 119
Foreknowing well, if there he came to lie, Why, there Love lived and there he could not die 245
Sometime he scuds far off and there he stares 301
There lives a son that suck'd an earthly mother, May lend thee light 863
And there, all smother'd up, in shade doth sit 1035
But by a kiss thought to persuade him there 1114
There shall not be one minute in an hour Wherein I will not kiss my sweet love's flower 1187
Then where is truth, if there be no self-trust? *Lucrece* 158
There is no hate in loving: I'll beg her love 240
Even there he starts: quoth he, 'I must deflower' 348
And here and there the painter interlaces Pale cowards 1390
I have gone here and there And made myself a motley to the view *Sonnet* 110 1
To win his heart, she touch'd him here and there *Pass. Pil.* 49
Spare not to spend, and chiefly there Where thy desert may merit praise 324
There will we sit upon the rocks, And see the shepherds 357
There will I make thee a bed of roses, With a thousand fragrant posies 361
Thereby. That thereby beauty's rose might never die *Sonnet* 1 2
Meant thereby Thou shouldst print more, not let that copy die 11 13
Therefore no marvel though thy horse be gone *Ven. and Adon.* 390
Therefore, despite of fruitless chastity, Love-lacking vestals 751
And therefore would he put his bonnet on 1087
Who, therefore angry, seems to part in sunder *Lucrece* 388
Therefore would they still in darkness be 752
Gentle thou art and therefore to be won, Beauteous thou art, therefore to be assailed *Sonnet* 41 5
And therefore mayst without attaint o'erlook 82 2
Therein. And therein heartens up his servile powers *Lucrece* 295
And therein so ensconced his secret evil 1515
Where-through the sun Delights to peep, to gaze therein on thee *Sonnet* 24 12
Both truth and beauty on my love depends; So dost thou too, and therein dignified 101 4
Thereof. She dares not thereof make discovery *Lucrece* 1314
And in the praise thereof spends all his might *Sonnet* 80 3
For maiden-tongued he was, and thereof free *Lov. Comp.* 100
Dreading my love, the loss thereof still fearing *Pass. Pil.* 94
Thereon. Mine eye; Who, if it wink, shall thereon fall and die *Lucrece* 1139
They. Their images I loved I view in thee, And thou, all they, hast all the all of me *Sonnet* 31 14
Beauty herself is black And all they foul that thy complexion lack 132 14
Thick. Thin mane, thick tale, broad buttock, tender hide *Ven. and Adon.* 298
His short thick neck cannot be easily harm'd 627
Let thy misty vapours march so thick *Lucrece* 782
Through his lips do throng Weak words, so thick come in his poor heart's aid 1784
Thick-sighted, barren, lean, and lacking juice *Ven. and Adon.* 136
Thief. They all rate his ill, Which drives the creeping thief to some regard *Lucr.* 305
And Lust, the thief, far poorer than before 693
Thou ravisher, thou traitor, thou false thief! 888
At his own shadow let the thief run mad 997
I an accessary needs must be To that sweet thief which sourly robs from me *Sonnet* 35 14
I do forgive thy robbery, gentle thief, Although thou steal thee all my poverty 40 9
Mine only care, Art left the prey of every vulgar thief 48 8
Sweet thief, whence didst thou steal thy sweet that smells? 99 2

Thieves. Rich preys make true men thieves . . . *Ven. and Adon.* 724
So full of fear As one with treasure laden, hemm'd with thieves . 1022
Sun and sharp air Lurk'd like two thieves, to rob him of his fair . 1086
And every one to rest themselves betake, Save thieves . *Lucrece* 126
Thievish. That rich jewel he should keep unknown From thievish ears 35
He like a thievish dog creeps sadly thence 736
For truth proves thievish for a prize so dear . *Sonnet* 48 14
Thou by thy dial's shady stealth mayst know Time's thievish progress 77 8
Thigh. Some twine about her thigh to make her stay *Ven. and Adon.* 873
Deep-wounded with a boar, Deep in the thigh, a spectacle of ruth! *Pass. Pil.* 127
'See, in my thigh,' quoth she, 'here was the sore.' She showed hers 128
Thin mane, thick tail, broad buttock, tender hide *Ven. and Adon.* 298
From his lips did fly thin winding breath, which purl'd up to the sky *Lucr.* 1407
Thine. Touch but my lips with those fair lips of thine . *Ven. and Adon.* 115
The kiss shall be thine own as well as mine 117
Bid me discourse, I will enchant thine ear 145
Is thine own heart to thine own face affected? 157
Steal thine own freedom and complain on theft 160
Thou art bound to breed, That thine may live when thou thyself art dead 172
The fault is thine, For those thine eyes betray thee unto mine *Lucrece* 482
That done, some worthless slave of thine I'll slay, To kill thine honour with thy life's decay 515
Thyself art mighty; for thine own sake leave me: Myself a weakling 583
Make thee another self, for love of me, That beauty still may live in thine or thee . *Sonnet* 10 14
As fast as thou shalt wane, so fast thou growest In one of thine 11 2
The pain be mine, but thine shall be the praise 38 14
All mine was thine before thou hadst this more 40 4
Things growing to themselves are growth's abuse *Ven. and Adon.* 166
Thing like a man, but of no woman bred! 214
If springing things be any jot diminish'd, They wither in their prime, prove nothing worth 417
Things out of hope are compass'd oft with venturing, Chiefly in love 567
In hand with all things, nought at all effecting 912
Imperious supreme of all mortal things 996
What canst thou boast Of things long since, or any thing ensuing? 1078
Perchance that envy of so rich a thing, Braving compare, disdainfully did sting *Lucrece* 39
We leave to be The things we are for that which we expect 149
So then we do neglect The thing we have 153
What win I, if I gain the thing I seek? 211
He takes for accidental things of trial 326
Pain pays the income of each precious thing 334
Hath barr'd him from the blessed thing he sought 340
Fearing no such thing, Lies at the mercy of his mortal sting 363
Mar not the thing that cannot be amended 578
For kings like gods should govern every thing 602
No outrageous thing From vassal actors can be wiped away 607
The lesser thing should not the greater hide 663
But she hath lost a dearer thing than life 687
To stamp the seal of time in aged things 941
To feed oblivion with decay of things 947
The mightier man, the mightier is the thing That makes him honour'd 1004
Thus cavils she with every thing she sees 1093
In a sea of care, Holds disputation with each thing she views 1101
Seemed to appear, Like bright things stain'd, a kind of heavy fear 1435
For sportive words and uttering foolish things 1813
Every thing that grows Holds in perfection but a little moment *Sonnet* 15 1
Me of thee defeated, By adding one thing to my purpose nothing 20 12
And all things rare That heaven's air in this huge rondure hems 21 7
Or some fierce thing replete with too much rage 23 3
I summon up remembrance of things past 30 2
Which now appear But things removed that hidden in thee lie 31 8
Then do mine eyes best see, For all the day they view things unrespected 43 2
When love, converted from the thing it was, Shall reasons find 49 7
So true a fool is love that in your will, Though you do any thing, he thinks no ill 57 14
I am shamed by that which I bring forth, And so should you, to love things nothing worth 72 14
That do not do the thing they most do show 94 2
Sweetest things turn sourest by their deeds 94 13
And all things turn to fair that eyes can see 95 12
So are those errors that in thee are seen To truths translated and for true things deem'd 96 8
Hath put a spirit of youth in every thing 98 3
Therefore my verse to constancy confined, One thing expressing 105 8
The prophetic soul Of the wide world dreaming on things to come 107 2
Counting no old thing old, thou mine, I thine 108 7
To make of monsters and things indigest Such cherubins 114 5
Divert strong minds to the course of altering things 115 8
In things of great receipt with ease we prove Among a number one is reckon'd none 136 7
In things right true my heart and eyes have erred 137 13
And makes all swift dispatch In pursuit of the thing she would have stay 143 4
Whence hast thou this becoming of things ill? 150 5
Gave eyes to blindness, Or made them swear against the thing they see 152 12
But, O my sweet, what labour is't to leave The thing we have not *Lov. Comp.* 240
For thou art all, and all things else are thine 266
Against the thing he sought he would exclaim 313
Let reason rule things worthy blame, As well as fancy partial might *Pass. Pil.* 301
Every thing did banish moan, Save the nightingale alone 379
Think. Is love so light, sweet boy, and may it be That thou shouldst think it heavy unto thee? *Ven. and Adon.* 156
For sharply he did think to reprehend her 470
Others, they think, delight In such-like circumstance, with such-like sport 843
She thinks he could not die, he is not dead 1060
Now thinks he that her husband's shallow tongue . . . hath done her beauty wrong *Lucrece* 78
When shall he think to find a stranger just, When he himself himself confounds? 159
That thinks she hath beheld some ghastly sprite 451
I think the honey guarded with a sting 493
Think but how vile a spectacle it were 631
They think not but that every eye can see The same disgrace 750
And all my fame that lives disbursed be To those that live, and think no shame of me 1204
Long she thinks till he return again, And yet the duteous vassal scarce is gone 1359
She looks for night, and then she longs for morrow, And both she thinks too long with her remaining 1572
Think. It easeth some, though none it ever cured, To think their dolour others have endured *Lucrece* 1582
Yet in these thoughts myself almost despising, Haply I think on thee *Son.* 29 10
But if the while I think on thee, dear friend, All losses are restored 30 13
For nimble thought can jump both sea and land As soon as think the place where he would be 44 8
Nor think the bitterness of absence sour 57 7
Think of nought Save, where you are how happy you make those 57 11
So true a fool is love that in your will, Though you do any thing, he thinks no ill 57 14
I think good thoughts whilst other write good words 85 5
No bitterness that I will bitter think, Nor double penance 111 11
Which in their wills count bad what I think good 121 8
Than think that we before have heard them told 123 8
I think my love as rare As any she belied with false compare 130 13
And thence this slander, as I think, proceeds 131 14
Think all but one, and me in that one 'Will' 135 14
Why should my heart think that a several plot? 137 9
That she might think me some untutor'd youth 138 3; *Pass. Pil.* 3
Thus vainly thinking that she thinks me young *Sonnet* 138 5; *Pass. Pil.* 5
Do I not think on thee, when I forgot Am of myself, all tyrant, for thy sake? *Sonnet* 149 3
Whereon the thought might think sometime it saw *Lov. Comp.* 10
What largeness thinks in Paradise was sawn 91
Think women still to strive with men, To sin and never for to saint *Pass. Pil.* 341
For her griefs, so lively shown, Made me think upon mine own 390
Thinking. I in your sweet thoughts would be forgot If thinking on me then should make you woe *Sonnet* 71 8
A thousand groans, but thinking on thy face, One on another's neck, do witness bear 131 10
Thus vainly thinking that she thinks me young 138 5; *Pass. Pil.* 5
Thinly. Like stones of worth they thinly placed are, Or captain jewels in the carcanet. *Sonnet* 52 7
Third. A third, nor red nor white, had stol'n of both 99 10
Thirst. Never did passenger in summer's heat More thirst for drink *V. and A.* 92
Thirsty. Whose precious taste her thirsty lips well knew 543
This. With this she seizeth on his sweating palm 25
Upon this promise did he raise his chin 85
By this the love-sick queen began to sweat 175
What am I, that thou shouldst contemn me this? 205
This said, impatience chokes her pleading tongue 217
At this Adonis smiles as in disdain 241
And this I do to captivate the eye Of the fair breeder that is standing by 281
And all this dumb play had his acts made plain With tears 359
What hour is this? or morn or weary even? Do I delight to die, or life desire? 495
'Thou hadst been gone,' quoth she, 'sweet boy, ere this' 613
By this, poor Wat, far off upon a hill, Stands on his hinder legs 697
Applying this to that, and so to so; For love can comment upon every woe 713
But if thou fall, O, then imagine this 721
Now of this dark night I perceive the reason 727
With this, he breaketh from the sweet embrace, Of those fair arms 811
Venus salutes him with this fair good-morrow 859
This said, she hasteth to a myrtle grove 865
By this, she hears the hounds are at a bay 877
By this, far off she hears some huntsman hollo 973
This siege that hath engirt his marriage, This blur to youth, this sorrow to the sage *Lucrece* 221
This said, his guilty hand pluck'd up the latch 358
This moves in him more rage and lesser pity, To make the breach 468
As clear from this attaint of mine As I, ere this, was pure to Collatine 825
This told, I joy; but then no longer glad, I send them back again *Sonnet* 45 13
Lest your true love may seem false in this 72 9
The worth of that is that which it contains, And that is this, and this with thee remains 74 14
This I do vow and this shall ever be; I will be true 123 13
To this I witness call the fools of time, Which die for goodness 124 13
Mine eyes seeing this, say this is not 137 11
Thither. And thither hied, a sad distemper'd guest, But found no cure 153 12
'T may be, again to make me wander thither *Pass. Pil.* 190
Thong. Throwing the base thong from his bending crest *Ven. and Adon.* 395
Thorn. I know what thorns the growing rose defends *Lucrece* 492
Whiles against a thorn thou bear'st thy part 1135
Roses have thorns, and silver fountains mud . *Sonnet* 35 2
Hang on such thorns and play as wantonly 54 7
The roses fearfully on thorns did stand, One blushing shame 99 8
My hand hath sworn Ne'er to pluck thee from thy thorn *Pass. Pil.* 238
She, poor bird, as all forlorn, Lean'd her breast up-till a thorn 382
Thorny. The thorny brambles and embracing bushes *Ven. and Adon.* 629
Thorough. To show her bleeding body thorough Rome *Lucrece* 1851
Those eyes that taught all other eyes to see *Ven. and Adon.* 952
Those that much covet are with gain so fond, For what they have not *Lucr.* 134
The fault is thine, For those thine eyes betray thee unto mine 483
Though. And govern'd him in strength, though not in lust *Ven. and Adon.* 42
Thou art no man, though of a man's complexion 215
No dog shall rouse thee, though a thousand bark 240
Though nothing but my body's bane would cure thee 372
Therefore no marvel though thy horse be gone 390
Though I were dumb, yet his proceedings teach thee 406
Though neither eyes nor ears, to hear nor see, Yet should I be in love by touching thee 437
What though the rose have prickles, yet 'tis pluck'd 574
For lovers' hours are long, though seeming short 842
Though weak-built hopes persuade him to abstaining *Lucrece* 130
Though death be adjunct, there's no death supposed 133
Yea, though I die, the scandal will survive, And be an eye-sore 204
Tears harden lust, though marble wear with raining 560
His face, though full of cares, yet show d content 1503
Though woe be heavy, yet it seldom sleeps 1574
It easeth some, though none it ever cured, To think their dolour others have endured 1581
Though I, once gone, to all the world must die *Sonnet* 81 6
Thought. Once more the engine of her thoughts began *Ven. and Adon.* 367
For all my mind, my thought, my busy care, Is how to get my palfrey 383
Whose vulture thought doth pitch the price so high, That she will draw his lips' rich treasure dry 551
The thought of it doth make my faint heart bleed, And fear doth teach it divination 669
The one doth flatter thee in thoughts unlikely, In likely thoughts the other kills thee quickly 989
He thought to kiss him, and hath kill'd him so. 'Tis true, 'tis true 1110

Thought. But by a kiss thought to persuade him there . *Ven. and Adon.* 1114
Disdainfully did sting His high-pitch'd thoughts . . . . *Lucrece* 41
Some untimely thought did instigate His all-too-timeless speed . . . 43
For unstain'd thoughts do seldom dream on evil 87
Pure thoughts are dead and still, While lust and murder wake . . . 167
And justly thus controls his thoughts unjust 189
And die, unhallow'd thoughts, before you blot With your uncleanness that which is divine 192
With good thoughts makes dispensation, Urging the worser sense for vantage still 248
Within his thought her heavenly image sits 288
The chamber door, That shuts him from the heaven of his thought . . 338
That his foul thoughts might compass his fair fair 346
Thoughts are but dreams till their effects be tried 353
The fault unknown is as a thought unacted 527
Let him return, and flattering thoughts retire 641
So let thy thoughts, low vassals to thy state 666
Even in this thought through the dark night he stealeth . . . 729
And the dire thought of his committed evil Shape every bush a hideous shapeless devil 972
Nor shall he smile at thee in secret thought 1065
Fleet-wing'd duty with thought's feathers flies 1216
Lucrece thought he blush'd to see her shame 1344
She thought he blush'd, as knowing Tarquin's lust 1354
The more she thought he spied in her some blemish 1358
Which all this time hath overslipp'd her thought 1576
O, change thy thought, that I may change my mind! . . . *Sonnet* 10 9
I hope some good conceit of thine In thy soul's thought, all naked, will bestow it 26 8
My thoughts, from far where I abide, Intend a zealous pilgrimage to thee 27 5
Yet in these thoughts myself almost despising, Haply I think on thee 29 9
When to the sessions of sweet silent thought I summon up remembrance of things past 30 1
And all those friends which I thought buried 31 4
O, then vouchsafe me but this loving thought 32 9
Thy sour leisure gave sweet leave To entertain the time with thoughts of love 39 11
Which time and thoughts so sweetly doth deceive 39 12
If the dull substance of my flesh were thought, Injurious distance should not stop my way 44 1
For nimble thought can jump both sea and land As soon as think the place where he would be 44 7
Thought kills me that I am not thought, To leap large lengths of miles when thou art gone 44 9
The first my thought, the other my desire 45 3
A quest of thoughts, all tenants to the heart 46 10
Mine eye is my heart's guest And in his thoughts of love doth share a part 47 8
For thou not farther than my thoughts canst move 47 11
Nor dare I question with my jealous thought Where you may be . . 57 9
God forbid that . . . I should in thought control your times of pleasure 58 2
This thought is as a death, which cannot choose But weep . . . 64 13
Want nothing that the thought of hearts can mend 69 2
Their thoughts, although their eyes were kind, To thy fair flower add the rank smell of weeds 69 11
I in your sweet thoughts would be forgot If thinking on me then should make you woe 71 7
So are you to my thoughts as food to life 75 1
I found, or thought I found, you did exceed The barren tender of a poet's debt 83 3
I think good thoughts whilst other write good words 85 5
But that is in my thought, whose love to you, Though words come hindmost, holds his rank before 85 11
Others for the breath of words respect, Me for my dumb thoughts . . 85 14
That did my ripe thoughts in my brain inhearse 86 3
A gainer too; For bending all my loving thoughts on thee . . . 88 10
Whate'er thy thoughts or thy heart's workings be 93 11
Gored mine own thoughts, sold cheap what is most dear . . . 110 3
Whilst it hath thought itself so blessed never 119 6
By their rank thoughts my deeds must not be shown 121 12
My thoughts and my discourse as madmen's are 147 11
I have sworn thee fair and thought thee bright, Who art as black as hell 147 13
Whereon the thought might think sometime it saw . . . *Lov. Comp.* 10
And sexes both enchanted, To dwell with him in thoughts . . . 129
Of lands and mansions, theirs in thought assign'd 138
Thought characters and words merely but art 174
Those thoughts, to me like oaks, to thee like osiers bow'd . *Pass. Pil.* 60
Ah, thought I, thou mourn'st in vain! None takes pity on thy pain . 391
Thousand. For thy meed A thousand honey secrets shalt thou know *Ven. and Adon.* 16
No dog shall rouse thee, though a thousand bark 240
A thousand ways he seeks To mend the hurt that his unkindness marr'd 477
A thousand kisses buys my heart from me 517
He cranks and crosses with a thousand doubles 682
If love have lent you twenty thousand tongues 775
A thousand spleens bear her a thousand ways 907
Two glasses, where herself herself beheld A thousand times . . . 1130
Wrapp'd and confounded in a thousand fears . . . . *Lucrece* 456
When Truth and Virtue have to do with thee, A thousand crosses keep them from thy aid 912
One poor retiring minute in an age Would purchase thee a thousand thousand friends 963
A thousand lamentable objects there, In scorn of nature . . . 1373
After a thousand victories once foil'd . . . . . *Sonnet* 25 10
A thousand groans, but thinking on thy face, One on another's neck, do witness bear 131 10
I do not love thee with mine eyes, For they in thee a thousand errors note 141 2
A thousand favours from a maund she drew . . . *Lov. Comp.* 36
Like a thousand vanquish'd men in bloody fight! . . . *Pass. Pil.* 280
There will I make thee a bed of roses, With a thousand fragrant posies 362
Thrall. How love makes young men thrall and old men dote *Ven. and Adon.* 837
And made her thrall To living death and pain perpetual . . *Lucrece* 725
But I, my mistress' thrall, Came there for cure . . . *Sonnet* 154 12
In black mourn I, All fears scorn I, Love hath forlorn me, Living in thrall *Pass. Pil.* 266
Thralled. Nor falls Under the blow of thralled discontent . *Sonnet* 124 7
Threaden. Some in her threaden fillet still did bide . . *Lov. Comp.* 33
Threads. Her hair, like golden threads, play'd with her breath . *Lucrece* 400
Threat. He hath a battle set Of bristly pikes, that ever threat his foes *Ven. and Adon.* 620
Like little frosts that sometime threat the spring . . . *Lucrece* 331
Whose crooked beak threats if he mount he dies 508
But when a black-faced cloud the world doth threat 547
Threatening cloud-kissing Ilion with annoy 1370
Three. That her sight dazzling makes the wound seem three *Ven. and Adon.* 1064
Three times with sighs she gives her sorrow fire . . . *Lucrece* 1604
Three winters cold Have from the forests shook three summers' pride *Sonnet* 104 3
Three beauteous springs to yellow autumn turn'd 104 5
Three April perfumes in three hot Junes burn'd, Since first I saw you fresh 104 7
Three themes in one, which wondrous scope affords . . . 105 12
'Fair, kind, and true,' have often lived alone, Which three till now never kept seat in one 105 14
It was a lording's daughter, the fairest one of three . . *Pass. Pil.* 211
Threefold. A torment thrice threefold thus to be cross'd . *Sonnet* 133 8
Threescore. And threescore year would make the world away . 11 8
Threne. Whereupon it made this threne To the phœnix and the dove *Ph. and Tur.* 49
Threshold. The threshold grates the door to have him heard . *Lucrece* 306
Threw. Once more leap her eyes; And, being open'd, threw unwilling light *Ven. and Adon.* 1051
Himself on her self-slaughter'd body threw . . . . *Lucrece* 1733
'I hate' from hate away she threw, And saved my life, saying 'not you' *Sonnet* 145 13
Which one by one she in a river threw . . . . . *Lov. Comp.* 38
Threw my affections in his charmed power 146
Thrice. Makes summer's welcome thrice more wish'd, more rare *Sonnet* 56 14
And gain by ill thrice more than I have spent 119 14
A torment thrice threefold thus to be cross'd 133 8
'Thrice-fairer than myself,' thus she began, 'The field's chief flower, sweet above compare . . . . . . *Ven. and Adon.* 7
Thriftless. Were an all-eating shame and thriftless praise . . *Sonnet* 2 8
Thrive. They that thrive well take counsel of their friends *Ven. and Adon.* 640
And that his beauty may the better thrive, With Death she humbly doth insinuate 1011
Love thrives not in the heart that shadows dreadeth . . *Lucrece* 270
In them I read such art As truth and beauty shall together thrive *Son.* 14 11
Then if he thrive and I be cast away, The worst was this . . . 80 13
Thrivers. Pitiful thrivers, in their gazing spent 125 8
Thriveth. But blessed bankrupt, that by love so thriveth! *Ven. and Adon.* 466
Throbbing. My throbbing heart shall rock thee day and night . . 1186
Throne. Who, like a king perplexed in his throne, By their suggestion gives a deadly groan 1043
Went about From this fair throne to heave the owner out . *Lucrece* 413
Throned. As on the finger of a throned queen The basest jewel will be well esteem'd . . . . *Sonnet* 96 5
Throng. Variable passions throng her constant woe . *Ven. and Adon.* 967
Much like a press of people at a door, Throng her inventions . *Lucrece* 1302
Through his lips do throng Weak words, so thick come in his poor heart's aid 1783
Thronged. Here one being throng'd bears back, all boll'n and red . 1417
Thronging. Which, thronging through her lips, so vanisheth As smoke from Ætna, that in air consumes 1041
Through. Like a dive-dapper peering through a wave, Who, being look'd on, ducks as quickly in . . . . . . *Ven. and Adon.* 86
Two strengthless doves will draw me through the sky . . . 153
For through his mane and tail the high wind sings 305
But hers, which through the crystal tears gave light, Shone like the moon in water seen by night 491
Yet love breaks through and picks them all at last 576
Embracing bushes, As fearful of him, part, through whom he rushes . 630
The many musets through the which he goes Are like a labyrinth . . 683
And homeward through the dark laund runs apace 813
This dismal cry rings sadly in her ear, Through which it enters to surprise her heart 890
A second fear through all her sinews spread 903
But through the flood-gates breaks the silver rain 959
Through the empty skies In her light chariot quickly is convey'd . 1191
Through little vents and crannies of the place . . . *Lucrece* 310
Through the length of times he stands disgraced 718
Even in this thought through the dark night he stealeth . . . 729
Through Night's black bosom should not peep again 788
Which, thronging through her lips, so vanisheth As smoke from Ætna . 1041
Revealing day through every cranny spies 1086
Why pry'st thou through my window? leave thy peeping . . . 1089
Make some hole Through which I may convey this troubled soul . . 1176
Through crystal walls each little mote will peep 1251
That dying fear through all her body spread 1266
There would appear The very eyes of men through loop-holes thrust . 1383
Through their light joy seemed to appear, Like bright things stain'd, a kind of heavy fear 1434
As through an arch the violent roaring tide Outruns the eye . . . 1667
Her winged sprite, and through her wounds doth fly 1728
Through his lips do throng Weak words, so thick come in his poor heart's aid 1783
So thou through windows of thine age shalt see Despite of wrinkles this thy golden time . . . . *Sonnet* 3 11
For through the painter must you see his skill 24 5
'Tis not enough that through the cloud thou break 34 5
Thy fair imperfect shade Through heavy sleep on sightless eyes doth stay 43 12
Nature bankrupt is, Beggar'd of blood to blush through lively veins . 67 10
So him I lose through my unkind abuse. Him have I lost . . . 134 12
Some beauty peep'd through lattice of sear'd age . . . *Lov. Comp.* 14
Who glazed with crystal gate the glowing roses That flame through water . 287
And falls, through wind, before the fall should be . . . *Pass. Pil.* 136
Through the velvet leaves the wind, All unseen, gan passage find . . 231
How sighs resound Through heartless ground! 279
Throw. And on his neck her yoking arms she throws . *Ven. and Adon.* 592
She throws her eyes about the painting round . . . . *Lucrece* 1499
As if her heart would break, She throws forth Tarquin's name . . 1717
But now he throws that shallow habit by 1814
In so profound abysm I throw all care Of others' voices . . *Sonnet* 112 9
Anon he comes, and throws his mantle by, And stood stark naked *Pass. Pil.* 79
Lord, how mine eyes throw gazes to the east! My heart doth charge the watch 193
Throwing the base thong from his bending crest . . *Ven. and Adon.* 395
Throwing his mantle rudely o'er his arm . . . . . *Lucrece* 170
Thrust. Backward she push'd him, as she would be thrust *Ven. and Adon.* 41

Thrust. There would appear The very eyes of men through loop-holes thrust *Lucrece* 1383

Should thrust Into so bright a day such black-faced storms 1517

How careful was I, . . . Each trifle under truest bars to thrust *Sonnet* 48 2

The bloody spur cannot provoke him on That sometimes anger thrusts into his hide 50 10

Thunder. Whose hollow womb resounds like heaven's thunder *V. and A.* 268

Pointing to each his thunder, rain, and wind *Sonnet* 14 6

O, that forced thunder from his heart did fly! *Lov. Comp.* 325

Thine eye Jove's lightning seems, thy voice his dreadful thunder *Pass. Pil.* 67

Thus he that overruled I oversway'd, Leading him prisoner *Ven. and Adon.* 109

As who should say 'Lo, thus my strength is tried' 280

Thus she replies: 'Thy palfrey, as he should, Welcomes the warm approach of sweet desire' 385

Thus stands she in a trembling ecstasy 895

Hateful divorce of love,—thus chides she Death 932

Thus hoping that Adonis is alive, Her rash suspect she doth extenuate 1009

Thus was Adonis slain: He ran upon the boar with his sharp spear 1111

And justly thus controls his thoughts unjust *Lucrece* 189

Urgeth still Under what colour he commits this ill. Thus he replies 477

When thus thy vices bud before thy spring 604

Yet with the fault I thus far can dispense 1279

Thy outward thus with outward praise is crown'd *Sonnet* 69 5

Thus far for love my love-suit, sweet, fulfil 4

'Even thus,' quoth she, 'the warlike god embraced me'. *Pass. Pil.* 147

Then too late she will repent That thus dissembled her delight 314

Thus of every grief in heart He with thee doth bear a part 427

Thwarting. In this aim there is such thwarting strife, That one for all, or all for one we gage *Lucrece* 143

Thyself. Then woo thyself, be of thyself rejected *Ven. and Adon.* 159

Thou art bound to breed, That thine may live when thou thyself art dead 172

An image like thyself, all stain'd with gore 664

So in thyself thyself art made away 763

Thyself art mighty; for thine own sake leave me: Myself a weakling *Lucr.* 583

Having traffic with thyself alone, Thou of thyself thy sweet self dost deceive *Sonnet* 4 9

That's for thyself to breed another thee 6 7

Deny that thou bear'st love to any, Who for thyself art so unprovident 10 2

Thyself thou gavest, thy own worth then not knowing 87 9

Tickled. To be so tickled, they would change their state And situation 128 9

Tickling. Mock with thy tickling beams eyes that are sleeping *Lucrece* 1090

Tide. The crystal tide that from her two cheeks fair In the sweet channel of her bosom dropt *Ven. and Adon.* 957

Her tears began to turn their tide, Being prison'd in her eye 979

My uncontrolled tide Turns not, but swells the higher by this let *Lucrece* 645

As through an arch the violent roaring tide Outruns the eye 1667

Held back his sorrow's tide, to make it more 1789

Tidings. And yet she hears no tidings of her love *Ven. and Adon.* 867

She took me kindly by the hand, And gazed for tidings in my eager eyes *Lucrece* 254

Tie. The steed is stalled up, and even now To tie the rider she begins to prove *Ven. and Adon.* 40

Will tie the hearers to attend each line *Lucrece* 818

Yet this thy praise cannot be so thy praise, To tie up envy evermore enlarged *Sonnet* 70 12

Whereto all bonds do tie me day by day 117 4

Tied. The strong-neck'd steed, being tied unto a tree, Breaketh his rein, and to her straight goes he *Ven. and Adon.* 263

How like a jade he stood, tied to the tree! 391

Hooks, Whereto the judgement of my heart is tied *Sonnet* 137 8

Sometime diverted their poor balls are tied To the orbed earth *Lov. Comp.* 24

Her hair, nor loose nor tied in formal plat 29

Tiger. The tiger would be tame and gently hear him *Ven. and Adon.* 1096

To slay the tiger that doth live by slaughter *Lucrece* 955

Wilder to him than tigers in their wildness 980

Pluck the keen teeth from the fierce tiger's jaws *Sonnet* 19 3

Till either gorge be stuff'd or prey be gone *Ven. and Adon.* 58

Till he take truce with her contending tears, Which long have rain'd 82

From morn till night, even where I list to sport me 154

Claps her pale cheek, till clapping makes it red 468

Till his breath breatheth life in her again 474

Till, breathless, he disjoin'd, and backward drew The heavenly moisture 541

And must not die Till mutual overthrow of mortal kind 1018

Her eyes are mad that they have wept till now 1062

Till every minute pays the hour his debt *Lucrece* 329

Till like a jade Self-will himself doth tire 707

Tillage. Where is she so fair whose unear'd womb Disdains the tillage of thy husbandry? *Sonnet* 3 6

Time. Make use of time, let not advantage slip *Ven. and Adon.* 129

Fair flowers that are not gather'd in their prime Rot and consume themselves in little time 132

The time is spent, her object will away, And from her twining arms doth urge releasing 255

Seeming to bury that posterity Which by the rights of time thou needs must have 759

'Ay me!' she cries, and twenty times 'Woe, woe!' And twenty echoes twenty times cry so 833

Two glasses, where herself herself beheld A thousand times 1130

'Wonder of time,' quoth she, 'this is my spite' 1133

Now stole upon the time the dead of night *Lucrece* 162

'So, so', quoth he, 'these lets attend the time, Like little frosts' 330

Cited up in rhymes, And sung by children in succeeding times 525

Through the length of times he stands disgraced 718

Make war against proportion'd course of time 774

Thou grant'st no time for charitable deeds 908

Mis-shapen Time, copesmate of ugly Night, Swift subtle post 925

O, hear me then, injurious, shifting Time! 930

Time's office is to fine the hate of foes 936

Time's glory is to calm contending kings 939

To stamp the seal of time in aged things 941

Let him have time to tear his curled hair, Let him have time against himself to rave 981

Let him have time of Time's help to despair 983

Let him have time to live a loathed slave, Let him have time a beggar's orts to crave 984

And time to see one that by alms doth live Disdain to him disdained scraps to give 986

Let him have time to see his friends his foes 988

Let him have time to mark how slow time goes In time of sorrow 990

How swift and short His time of folly and his time of sport 992

Time. And ever let his unrecalling crime Have time to wail th' abusing of his time *Lucrece* 994

O Time, thou tutor both to good and bad! 995

In vain I rail at Opportunity, At Time, at Tarquin 1024

He ten times pines that pines beholding food 1115

Distress likes dumps when time is kept with tears 1127

The weary time she cannot entertain, For now 'tis stale to sigh 1361

Time's ruin, beauty's wreck, and grim care's reign 1451

Time doth weary time with her complaining 1570

Short time seems long in sorrow's sharp sustaining 1573

They that watch see time how slow it creeps 1575

Which all this time hath overslipp'd her thought 1576

Three times with sighs she gives her sorrow fire 1604

A bare-boned death by time outworn 1761

O time, cease thou thy course and last no longer 1765

But as the riper should by time decease *Sonnet* 1 3

Now is the time that face should form another 3 2

Shalt see Despite of wrinkles this thy golden time 3 12

For never-resting time leads summer on To hideous winter 5 5

To breed another thee, Or ten times happier, be it ten for one 6 8

Ten times thyself were happier than thou art, If ten of thine ten times refigured thee 6 9

If all were minded so, the times should cease 11 7

When I do count the clock that tells the time 12 1

Thou among the wastes of time must go 12 10

Nothing 'gainst Time's scythe can make defence Save breed 12 13

Where wasteful Time debateth with Decay 15 11

And all in war with Time for love of you 15 13

Make war upon this bloody tyrant, Time 16 2

Time's pencil, or my pupil pen, Neither in inward worth nor outward fair, Can make you live yourself in eyes of men 16 10

Who will believe my verse in time to come? 17 1

Were some child of yours alive that time, You should live twice 17 13

When in eternal lines to time thou growest 18 12

Devouring Time, blunt thou the lion's paws 19 1

Do whate'er thou wilt, swift-footed Time 19 6

Yet, do thy worst, old Time: despite thy wrong 19 13

When in thee time's furrows I behold 22 3

And with old woes new wail my dear time's waste 30 4

Compare them with the bettering of the time 32 5

This wish I have; then ten times happy me! 37 14

Be thou the tenth Muse, ten times more in worth Than those old nine 38 9

Thy sour leisure gave sweet leave To entertain the time with thoughts of love 39 11

Which time and thoughts so sweetly doth deceive 39 12

I must attend time's leisure with my moan 44 12

Another time mine eye is my heart's guest 47 7

Against that time, if ever that time come, When I shall see thee frown 49 1

Against that time when thou shalt strangely pass And scarcely greet me 49 5

Against that time do I ensconce me here 49 9

So is the time that keeps you as my chest 52 9

More bright . . . Than unswept stone besmear'd with sluttish time 55 4

What should I do but tend Upon the hours and times of your desire? 57 2

I have no precious time at all to spend, Nor services to do, till you require 57 3

God forbid that . . . I should in thought control your times of pleasure 58 2

You yourself may privilege your time To what you will 58 10

And Time that gave doth now his gift confound 60 8

Time doth transfix the flourish set on youth 60 9

And yet to times in hope my verse shall stand, Praising thy worth 60 13

With Time's injurious hand crush'd and o'erworn 63 2

For such a time do I now fortify Against confounding age's cruel knife 63 9

When I have seen by Time's fell hand defaced The rich proud cost of outworn buried age 64 1

Thus to ruminate That Time will come and take my love away 64 12

Nor gates of steel so strong, but Time decays 65 8

Where, alack, Shall Time's best jewel from Time's chest lie hid? 65 10

So thou be good, slander doth but approve Thy worth the greater, being woo'd of time 70 6

That time of year thou mayst in me behold 73 1

Why with the time do I not glance aside? 76 3

Thou by thy dial's shady stealth mayst know Time's thievish progress 77 8

And yet this time removed was summer's time 97 5

And straight redeem In gentle numbers time so idly spent 100 6

My love's sweet face survey, If Time have any wrinkle graven there 100 10

And make Time's spoils despised every where 100 12

Give my love fame faster than Time wastes life 100 13

When in the chronicle of wasted time I see 106 1

So all their praises are but prophecies Of this our time 106 10

Now with the drops of this most balmy time My love looks fresh 107 9

Where time and outward form would show it dead 108 14

Just to the time, not with the time exchanged 109 7

But reckoning time, whose million'd accidents Creep in 'twixt vows 115 5

Alas, why, fearing of time's tyranny, Might I not then say? 115 9

Love's not Time's fool, though rosy lips and cheeks Within his bending sickle's compass come 116 9

And given to time your own dear-purchased right 117 6

For if you were by my unkindness shaken As I by yours, you've pass'd a hell of time 120 6

No, Time, thou shalt not boast that I do change 123 1

As subject to Time's love or to Time's hate 124 3

Whereto the inviting time our fashion calls 124 8

The fools of time, Which die for goodness, who have lived for crime 124 13

Who in thy power Dost hold Time's fickle glass, his sickle, hour 126 2

Her skill May time disgrace and wretched minutes kill 126 8

Time had not scythed all that youth begun, Nor youth all quit *Lov. Comp.* 12

When time shall serve, be thou not slack To proffer *Pass. Pil.* 333

There is no heaven, by holy then, When time with age doth them attaint 344

Time-beguiling. A summer's day will seem an hour but short, Being wasted in such time-beguiling sport *Ven. and Adon.* 24

Time-bettering. Some fresher stamp of the time-bettering days *Sonnet* 82 8

Timely. Bright orient pearl, alack, too timely shaded! *Pass. Pil.* 133

Timorous. Uncouple at the timorous flying hare *Ven. and Adon.* 674

Even so the timorous yelping of the hounds Appals her senses 881

Tincture. As deep a dye As the perfumed tincture of the roses *Sonnet* 54 6

Tip. On the tip of his subduing tongue All kind of arguments and question deep, All replication prompt *Lov. Comp.* 120

Tire. Even as an empty eagle, sharp by fast, Tires with her beak on feathers, flesh, and bone *Ven. and Adon.* 56

Till like a jade Self-will himself doth tire *Lucrece* 707

Tire. And you in Grecian tires are painted new . . . *Sonnet* 53 8
Tired. And Titan, tired in the mid-day heat, With burning eye did hotly overlook them . . . *Ven. and Adon.* 177
Or as the fleet-foot roe that's tired with chasing . . . 561
On that he firmly doted, And in his will his wilful eye he tired *Lucrece* 417
So woe hath wearied woe, moan tired moan . . . 1363
Too long, to tell them all with one poor tired tongue . . . 1617
My bed, The dear repose for limbs with travel tired . *Sonnet* 27 2
The beast that bears me, tired with my woe, Plods dully on . . 50 5
Tired with all these, for restful death I cry . . . 66 1
Tired with all these, from these would I be gone . . . 66 13
Titan. And Titan, tired in the mid-day heat, With burning eye did hotly overlook them . . . *Ven. and Adon.* 177
Title. Thy smoothing titles to a ragged name . . . *Lucrece* 892
Of public honour and proud titles boast . . . *Sonnet* 25 2
To 'cide this title is impanneled A quest of thoughts . . 46 9
O, what a happy title do I find, Happy to have thy love, happy to die ! 92 11
Toads. Or toads infect fair founts with venom mud . . *Lucrece* 850
To-day. Than appetite, Which but to-day by feeding is allay'd . *Sonnet* 56 3
Although to-day thou fill Thy hungry eyes even till they wink with fullness . . . 56 5
Kind is my love to-day, to-morrow kind, Still constant . . 105 5
Together. Were never four such lamps together mix'd, Had not his clouded with his brow's repine . . . *Ven. and Adon.* 489
Their lips together glued, fall to the earth . . . 546
Like milk and blood being mingled both together . . . 902
Then join they all together, Like many clouds consulting for foul weather . 971
Oft that wealth doth cost The death of all, and all together lost *Lucrece* 147
All which together, like a troubled ocean . . . 589
In them I read such art As truth and beauty shall together thrive *Son.* 14 11
Crabbed age and youth cannot live together . . . *Pass. Pil.* 157
Reason, in itself confounded, Saw division grow together . *Ph. and Tur.* 42
Toil. Weary with toil, I haste me to my bed . . . *Sonnet* 27 1
The one by toil, the other to complain How far I toil . . 28 7
In sequent toil all forwards do contend . . . 60 4
Toiled. And all the rest forgot for which he toil'd . . 25 12
Token. As pitying Lucrece' woes, Corrupted blood some watery token shows *Lucrece* 1748
Told. Sometime he trots, as if he told the steps, With gentle majesty and modest pride . . . *Ven. and Adon.* 277
Are they not quickly told and quickly gone? . . . 520
She whispers in his ears a heavy tale, As if they heard the woeful words she told . . . 1126
If it should be told, The repetition cannot make it less . . *Lucrece* 1284
To see sad sights moves more than hear them told . . . 1324
Their face their manners most expressly told . . . 1397
This told, I joy; but then no longer glad, I send them back again *Sonnet* 45 13
For as the sun is daily new and old, So is my love still telling what is told . . . 76 14
Than think that we before have heard them told . . . 123 8
And age in love loves not to have years told . . . 138 12 ; *Pass. Pil.* 12
She told him stories to delight his ear ; She show'd him favours . . 47
She told the youngling how god Mars did try her . . . 145
Toldest. But that thou told'st me thou wouldst hunt the boar *V. and A.* 614
Tomb. He might be buried in a tomb so simple . . . 244
Tells him of trophies, statues, tombs, and stories . . . 1013
Who is he so fond will be the tomb Of his self-love, to stop posterity? *Sonnet* 3 7
It is but as a tomb Which hides your life and shows not half your parts 17 3
I impair not beauty being mute, When others would give life and bring a tomb . . . 83 12
Making their tomb the womb wherein they grew . . . 86 4
'T lies in thee To make him much outlive a gilded tomb . . 101 11
When tyrants' crests and tombs of brass are spent . . . 107 14
Tombed. Thy unused beauty must be tomb'd with thee . . . 4 13
To-morrow. Tell me, Love's master, shall we meet to-morrow? *V. and A.* 585
To-morrow he intends To hunt the boar with certain of his friends 587
If thou encounter with the boar to-morrow . . . 672
To-morrow sharpen'd in his former might . . . *Sonnet* 56 4
To-morrow see again, and do not kill The spirit of love . . 56 7
Kind is my love to-day, to-morrow kind, Still constant . . 105 5
'Farewell,' quoth she, 'and come again to-morrow!' . *Pass. Pil.* 185
For why, she sigh'd and bade me come to-morrow . . . 204
Short, night, to-night, and length thyself to-morrow . . . 210
Tongue. This said, impatience chokes her pleading tongue *Ven. and Adon.* 217
For lovers say, the heart hath treble wrong When it is barr'd the aidance of the tongue . . . 330
Hast thou a tongue? O, would thou hadst not, or I had no hearing! . . 427
If love have lent you twenty thousand tongues, And every tongue more moving than your own . . . 775
The boar provoked my tongue ; Be wreak'd on him . . . 1003
Grief hath two tongues, and never woman yet Could rule them both without ten women's wit . . . 1007
My tongue cannot express my grief for one . . . 1069
What face remains alive that's worth the viewing? Whose tongue is music now? . . . 1077
Her husband's shallow tongue . . . hath done her beauty wrong *Lucrece* 78
Betrays To slanderous tongues and wretched hateful days . . 161
Will not my tongue be mute, my frail joints shake? . . . 227
First, like a trumpet, doth his tongue begin To sound a parley . . 470
Thy sugar'd tongue to bitter wormwood taste . . . 893
My tongue shall utter all . . . 1076
With untuned tongue she hoarsely calls her maid . . . 1214
With soft-slow tongue, true mark of modesty . . . 1220
He did her wrong, To give her so much grief and not a tongue . . 1463
I'll tune thy woes with my lamenting tongue . . . 1465
And from her tongue 'can lurk' from 'cannot' took . . . 1537
Too long, to tell them all with one poor tired tongue . . . 1617
My bloody judge forbade my tongue to speak . . . 1648
But more than 'he' her poor tongue could not speak . . . 1718
Hath served a dumb arrest upon his tongue . . . 1780
Be scorn'd like old men of less truth than tongue . . *Sonnet* 17 10
More than that tongue that more hath more express'd . . 23 12
All tongues, the voice of souls, give thee that due, Uttering bare truth 69 3
Those same tongues that give thee so thine own In other accents do this praise confound . . . 69 6
And tongues to be your being shall rehearse . . . 81 11
In my tongue Thy sweet beloved name no more shall dwell . . 89 9
That tongue that tells the story of thy days . . . 95 5
Whose rich esteeming The owner's tongue doth publish every where . 102 4

Tongue. I sometime hold my tongue, Because I would not dull you with my song . . . *Sonnet* 102 13
Have eyes to wonder, but lack tongues to praise . . . 106 14
I must strive To know my shames and praises from your tongue . . 112 6
Becoming of their woe, That every tongue says beauty should look so 127 14
Simply I credit her false-speaking tongue . . . 138 7
Wound me not with thine eye but with thy tongue . . . 139 3
Nor are mine ears with thy tongue's tune delighted . . . 141 5
That tongue that ever sweet Was used in giving gentle doom . . 145 6
On the tip of his subduing tongue All kind of arguments and question deep, All replication prompt, and reason strong . . . *Lov. Comp.* 120
I smiling credit her false-speaking tongue . . . *Pass. Pil.* 7
O, love's best habit is a soothing tongue . . . 11
Well learned is that tongue that well can thee commend . . . 64
O do not love that wrong, To sing heaven's praise with such an earthly tongue 70
And when thou comest thy tale to tell, Smooth not thy tongue with filed talk 306
She will not stick to round me i' the ear, To teach my tongue to be so long 350
And truth in every shepherd's tongue . . . 370
Tongue-tied. And art made tongue-tied by authority . . *Sonnet* 66 9
To make me tongue-tied, speaking of your fame . . . 80 4
My tongue-tied Muse in manners holds her still . . . 85 1
Do not press My tongue-tied patience with too much disdain . . 140 2
To-night. Short, night, to-night, and length thyself to-morrow *Pass. Pil.* 210
Too. Like a wild bird being tamed with too much handling *Ven. and Adon.* 560
The text is old, the orator too green . . . 806
It shall be sparing and too full of riot . . . 1147
It shall be merciful and too severe . . . 1155
But honest fear, bewitch'd with lust's foul charm, Doth too too oft betake him to retire . . . *Lucrece* 174
Their father was too weak, and they too strong . . . 865
I did give that life Which she too early and too late hath spill'd . 1801
Summer's lease hath all too short a date . . . *Sonnet* 18 4
From me far off, with others all too near . . . 61 14
He rose and ran away ; ah, fool too froward ! . . *Pass. Pil.* 56
Took. When he was by, the birds such pleasure took, That some would sing, some other in their bills Would bring him mulberries *Ven. and Adon.* 1101
She took me kindly by the hand, And gazed for tidings in my eager eyes *Lucrece* 253
First red as roses that on lawn we lay, Then white as lawn, the roses took away 259
And from her tongue 'can lurk' from 'cannot' took . . . 1537
Swearing, unless I took all patiently, I should not live . . . 1641
Betwixt mine eye and heart a league is took, And each doth good turns now unto the other . . . *Sonnet* 47 1
How careful was I, when I took my way . . . 48 1
Possessing or pursuing no delight, Save what is had or must from you be took . . . 75 12
The fairest votary took up that fire Which many legions of true hearts had warm'd . . . 154 5
This brand she quenched in a cool well by, Which from Love's fire took heat perpetual . . . 154 10
Tool. But this no slaughterhouse no tool imparteth . . *Lucrece* 1039
Toothed. Had I been tooth'd like him, I must confess, With kissing him I should have kill'd him first . . . *Ven. and Adon.* 1117
Top. The bottom poison, and the top o'erstraw'd With sweets . . 1143
Now stand you on the top of happy hours . . . *Sonnet* 16 5
This said, in top of rage the lines she rents . . . *Lov. Comp.* 55
Torches are made to light, jewels to wear, Dainties to taste *Ven. and Adon.* 163
Whereat a waxen torch forthwith he lighteth . . . *Lucrece* 178
Fair torch, burn out thy light, and lend it not . . . 190
The wind wars with his torch to make him stay . . . 311
But his hot heart, which fond desire doth scorch, Puffs forth another wind that fires the torch . . . 315
Are by his flaming torch dimm'd and controll'd . . . 448
Tore. 'Tarquin' was pronounced plain, But through his teeth, as if the name he tore . . . 1787
Which she perused, sigh'd, tore, and gave the flood . . *Lov. Comp.* 44
Torment. This ambitious foul infirmity, In having much, torments us with defect Of that we have . . . *Lucrece* 151
Having no other pleasure of his gain But torment that it cannot cure his pain 861
O absence, what a torment wouldst thou prove . . *Sonnet* 39 9
Knowing thy heart torments me with disdain . . . 132 2
A torment thrice threefold thus to be cross'd . . . 133 8
Tormenteth. Art thou a woman's son, and canst not feel What 'tis to love? how want of love tormenteth? . . . *Ven. and Adon.* 202
Torn. O, from thy cheeks my image thou hast torn ! . . *Lucrece* 1762
In act thy bed-vow broke and new faith torn . . . *Sonnet* 152 3
Torture. That deep torture may be call'd a hell . . . *Lucrece* 1287
Do in consent shake hands to torture me . . . *Sonnet* 28 6
Is't not enough to torture me alone? . . . 133 3
Tossed. Is madly toss'd between desire and dread . . *Lucrece* 171
Touch but my lips with those fair lips of thine . . *Ven. and Adon.* 115
Who is so faint, that dare not be so bold To touch the fire, the weather being cold? . . . 402
And that I could not see, nor hear, nor touch . . . 440
What is ten hundred touches unto thee? . . . 519
Or what fond beggar, but to touch the crown, Would with the sceptre straight be strucken down? . . . *Lucrece* 216
Enforced hate, Instead of love's coy touch, shall rudely tear thee . . 669
Such heavenly touches ne'er touch'd earthly faces . . *Sonnet* 17 8
A loss in love that touches me more nearly . . . 42 4
When they have devised What strained touches rhetoric can lend . 82 10
Nor tender feeling, to base touches prone . . . 141 6
The boy for trial needs would touch my breast . . . 153 10
Touches so soft still conquer chastity . . . *Pass. Pil.* 50
The tender nibbler would not touch the bait . . . 53
Whose heavenly touch Upon the lute doth ravish human sense . . 107
Touched. She touch'd no unknown baits, nor fear'd no hooks *Lucrece* 103
Such heavenly touches ne'er touch'd earthly faces . . *Sonnet* 17 8
So many have, that never touch'd his hand, Sweetly supposed *Lov. Comp.* 141
To win his heart, she touch'd him here and there . . *Pass. Pil.* 49
Touching. Yet should I be in love by touching thee *Ven. and Adon.* 438
Toward. Perverse it shall be where it shows most toward . . 1157
No love toward others in that bosom sits . . . *Sonnet* 9 13
Since from thee going he went wilful-slow, Towards thee I'll run . 51 14
Like as the waves make towards the pebbled shore . . . 60 1
Observed as they flew—Towards this afflicted fancy fastly drew *Lov. Comp.* 61
Then fell she on her back, fair queen, and toward . . *Pass. Pil.* 55
Tower. And smear with dust their glittering golden towers . *Lucrece* 945
From the towers of Troy there would appear The very eyes of men through loop-holes thrust . . . 1382

Tower. When sometime lofty towers I see down-razed . . . *Sonnet* 64 3
The strongest castle, tower, and town, The golden bullet beats it down *Pass. Pil.* 327
Towering. Which, like a falcon towering in the skies, Coucheth the fowl below with his wings' shade . . . . . *Lucrece* 506
Town. The strongest castle, tower, and town, The golden bullet beats it down *Pass. Pil.* 327
Toy. With leaden appetite, unapt to toy . . . *Ven. and Adon.* 34
To sport and dance, To toy, to wanton, dally, smile, and jest . . . 106
Who buys a minute's mirth to wail a week? Or sells eternity to get a toy? *Lucrece* 214
The tricks and toys that in them lurk . . . . *Pass. Pil.* 337
Tract. The eyes, 'fore duteous, now converted are From his low tract *Son.* 7 12
Traffic. Despair to gain doth traffic oft for gaining . . . *Lucrece* 131
Having traffic with thyself alone, Thou of thyself thy sweet self dost deceive *Sonnet* 4 9
Tragedies. Black stage for tragedies and murders fell! . . . *Lucrece* 766
Tragic. Or to turn white and swoon at tragic shows . . . *Lov. Comp.* 308
Co-supremes and stars of love, As chorus to their tragic scene *Ph. and Tur.* 52
Traitor. In their pure ranks his traitor eye encloses . . . *Lucrece* 73
Thus treason works ere traitors be espied 361
O Opportunity, thy guilt is great! 'Tis thou that executest the traitor's treason 877
Thou ravisher, thou traitor, thou false thief! 888
The help that thou shalt lend me Comes all too late, yet let the traitor die . 1686
Trampling. A breeding jennet, lusty, young, and proud, Adonis' trampling courser doth espy . . . . . . *Ven. and Adon.* 261
Trance. Disturb his hours of rest with restless trances . . *Lucrece* 974
Like old acquaintance in a trance, Met far from home 1595
Transferred. And to this false plague are they now transferr'd *Sonnet* 137 14
Transfix. Time doth transfix the flourish set on youth . . . 60 9
Transgressed. Let sin, alone committed, light alone Upon his head that hath transgressed so . . . . *Lucrece* 1481
Transgression. Their own transgressions partially they smother . 634
Needs must I under my transgression bow . . . *Sonnet* 120 3
Translate. How many lambs might the stern wolf betray, If like a lamb he could his looks translate! 96 10
Translated. So are those errors that in thee are seen To truths translated 96 8
Transport. The winds Which should transport me farthest from your sight 117 8
Trapping. What cares he now for curb or pricking spur? For rich caparisons or trapping gay? . . . . . . *Ven. and Adon.* 286
Travail. As if with grief or travail he had fainted, To me came Tarquin armed *Lucrece* 1543
Thy lovely argument Deserves the travail of a worthier pen . . *Sonnet* 79 6
Travel. My bed, The dear repose for limbs with travel tired . . . 27 2
And make me travel forth without my cloak 34 2
When what I seek, my weary travel's end, Doth teach that ease . 50 2
If I have ranged, Like him that travels I return again . . . 109 6
Travelled. When his youthful morn Hath travell'd on to age's steepy night 63 5
Tread. She treads the path that she untreads again . *Ven. and Adon.* 908
The grass stoops not, she treads on it so light 1028
Teaching decrepit age to tread the measures 1148
One . . . That cannot tread the way out readily . . . *Lucrece* 1152
My mistress, when she walks, treads on the ground . . *Sonnet* 130 12
The cock that treads them shall not know . . . . *Pass. Pil.* 338
Treason. Till forging Nature be condemn'd of treason . *Ven. and Adon.* 729
Thus treason works ere traitors be espied . . . . . *Lucrece* 361
By their high treason is his heart misled 369
Whispering conspirator With close-tongued treason and the ravisher! . 770
O Opportunity, thy guilt is great! 'Tis thou that executest the traitor's treason 877
Wrath, envy, treason, rape, and murder's rages 909
Guilty of treason, forgery, and shift, Guilty of incest, that abomination . 920
I do betray My nobler part to my gross body's treason . . *Sonnet* 151 6
Treasure. That she will draw his lips' rich treasure dry *Ven. and Adon.* 552
Foul-cankering rust the hidden treasure frets 767
So full of fear As one with treasure laden, hemm'd with thieves . . 1022
Alas, poor world, what treasure hast thou lost! 1075
Pluck down the rich, enrich the poor with treasures 1150
In Tarquin's tent, Unlock'd the treasure of his happy state . *Lucrece* 16
When great treasure is the meed proposed, Though death be adjunct, there's no death supposed 132
Then who fears sinking where such treasure lies? 280
And scarce hath eyes his treasure to behold 857
Poor helpless help, the treasure stol'n away 1056
Where all the treasure of thy lusty days . . . . . *Sonnet* 2 6
Treasure thou some place With beauty's treasure, ere it be self-kill'd . 6 3
Mine be thy love and thy love's use their treasure 20 14
Whose blessed key Can bring him to his sweet up-locked treasure . 52 2
Stealing away the treasure of his spring 63 8
Anon Doubting the filching age will steal his treasure . . . 75 6
She may detain, but not still keep, her treasure 126 10
'Will' will fulfil the treasure of thy love 136 5
Treatise. Your treatise makes me like you worse and worse *Ven. and Adon.* 774
Treble. For lovers say, the heart hath treble wrong When it is barr'd the aidance of the tongue 329
Treble-dated. And thou treble-dated crow, That thy sable gender makest *Ph. and Tur.* 17
Tree. These forceless flowers like sturdy trees support me *Ven. and Adon.* 152
The strong-neck'd steed, being tied unto a tree, Breaketh his rein . . 263
How like a jade he stood, tied to the tree! 391
When lofty trees I see barren of leaves . . . . *Sonnet* 12 5
Like a green plum that hangs upon a tree, And falls, through wind *Pass. Pil.* 135
Beasts did leap, and birds did sing, Trees did grow, and plants did spring . 378
Senseless trees they cannot hear thee 393
The bird of loudest lay, On the sole Arabian tree . . . *Ph. and Tur.* 2
Tremble. She trembles at his tale, And on his neck her yoking arms she throws . . . . *Ven. and Adon.* 591
I fear'd thy fortune, and my joints did tremble 642
What should I do, seeing thee so indeed, That tremble at the imagination? 668
And how her hand, in my hand being lock'd, Forced it to tremble with her loyal fear! . . . . *Lucrece* 261
That one would swear he saw them quake and tremble 1393
Trembling in her passion, calls it balm, Earth's sovereign salve to do a goddess good . . . . *Ven. and Adon.* 27
Thus stands she in a trembling ecstasy 895
But coward-like with trembling terror die . . . . . *Lucrece* 231
Like to a new-kill'd bird she trembling lies 457
Marking what he tells With trembling fear, as fowl hear falcon's bells . 511
To trembling clients be you mediators 1020
Trembling. Pale cowards, marching on with trembling paces . *Lucrece* 1391
What uncouth ill event Hath thee befall'n, that thou dost trembling stand? 1599
Trenched. The wide wound that the boar had trench'd In his soft flank *Ven. and Adon.* 1052
Trenches. And dig deep trenches in thy beauty's field . . *Sonnet* 2 2
Trespass. Shalt have thy trespass cited up in rhymes, And sung by children in succeeding times . . . . *Lucrece* 524
Think but how vile a spectacle it were, To view thy present trespass in another 632
Will quote my loathsome trespass in my looks 812
I am the mistress of my fate, And with my trespass never will dispense . 1070
For trespass of thine eye, The sire, the son, the dame, and daughter die . 1476
'Few words,' quoth she, 'shall fit the trespass best' 1613
Authorizing thy trespass with compare, Myself corrupting . . *Sonnet* 35 6
Your trespass now becomes a fee; Mine ransoms yours 120 13
Tresses. Before the golden tresses of the dead, The right of sepulchres, were shorn away 68 5
Trial. He takes for accidental things of trial . . . . *Lucrece* 326
The boy for trial needs would touch my breast . . . *Sonnet* 153 10
Tribes. I'll live in this poor rhyme, While he insults o'er dull and speechless tribes 107 12
Tributary. To which Love's eyes pay tributary gazes . *Ven. and Adon.* 632
Whereat each tributary subject quakes 1045
Tribute. So their pride doth grow, Paying more slavish tribute than they owe . . . . *Lucrece* 299
Look here, what tributes wounded fancies sent me . . . *Lov. Comp.* 197
Tricks. Thy eyes' shrewd tutor, that hard heart of thine, Hath taught them scornful tricks . . . . *Ven. and Adon.* 501
As who should say 'This glove to wanton tricks Is not inured' . *Lucrece* 320
The tricks and toys that in them lurk . . . . . *Pass. Pil.* 337
Tried. As who should say 'Lo, thus my strength is tried' *Ven. and Adon.* 280
Thoughts are but dreams till their effects be tried . . . *Lucrece* 353
Trifles, unwitnessed with eye or ear . . . . *Ven. and Adon.* 1023
How careful was I, . . . Each trifle under truest bars to thrust *Sonnet* 48 2
Thou, to whom my jewels trifles are, Most worthy comfort . . . 48 5
Trim. The flowers are sweet, their colours fresh and trim *Ven. and Adon.* 1079
When proud-pied April dress'd in all his trim Hath put a spirit of youth in every thing . . . . *Sonnet* 98 2
Their purposed trim Pieced not his grace, but were all graced by him *Lov. Comp.* 118
Trimmed. As, to behold desert a beggar born, And needy nothing trimm'd in jollity . . . . *Sonnet* 66 3
Trip. Or, like a fairy, trip upon the green . . . *Ven. and Adon.* 146
The earth, in love with thee, thy footing trips 722
Tripping. Many nymphs that vow'd chaste life to keep Came tripping by *Sonnet* 154 4
Triumph. His victories, his triumphs, and his glories *Ven. and Adon.* 1014
Would let him go, Rather than triumph in so false a foe . . *Lucrece* 77
Showing life's triumph in the map of death 402
Whilst I, whom fortune of such triumph bars, Unlook'd for joy . *Sonnet* 25 3
Blessed are you, whose worthiness gives scope, Being had, to triumph 52 14
My soul doth tell my body that he may Triumph in love . . . 151 8
'Air,' quoth he, 'thy cheeks may blow; Air, would I might triumph so!' *Pass. Pil.* 236
Triumphant. But, rising at thy name, doth point out thee As his triumphant prize . . . . *Sonnet* 151 10
Triumphed. Which triumph'd in that sky of his delight . . . *Lucrece* 12
Triumphing. Grace and majesty You might behold, triumphing in their faces 1388
Trodden. For misery is trodden on by many, And being low never relieved by any . . . . *Ven. and Adon.* 707
Troilus. Here manly Hector faints, here Troilus swounds . . *Lucrece* 1486
Trojan mothers, sharing joy To see their youthful sons bright weapons wield 1431
For every tear he falls a Trojan bleeds 1551
Troop. To whose weak ruins muster troops of cares 720
Augur of the fever's end, To this troop come thou not near! *Ph. and Tur.* 8
Trophies. Tells him of trophies, statues, tombs, and stories *Ven. and Adon.* 1013
Hung with the trophies of my lovers gone . . . . *Sonnet* 31 10
All these trophies of affections hot, Of pensived and subdued desires the tender . . . . *Lov. Comp.* 218
Troth. By holy human law, and common troth, By heaven and earth *Lucr.* 571
Thou smother'st honesty, thou murder'st troth 885
Dear Collatine, thou shalt not know The stained taste of violated troth . 1059
That strong-bonded oath That shall prefer and undertake my troth *L. Comp.* 280
Trots. Sometime he trots, as if he told the steps, With gentle majesty and modest pride . . . . *Ven. and Adon.* 277
Trouble. Is twenty hundred kisses such a trouble? 522
To overshoot his troubles How he outruns the wind and with what care . 680
And trouble deaf heaven with my bootless cries . . . . *Sonnet* 29 3
Troubled. The neighbour caves, as seeming troubled, Make verbal repetition of her moans . . . . *Ven. and Adon.* 830
To the disposing of her troubled brain 1040
For oft the eye mistakes, the brain being troubled 1068
Save thieves, and cares, and troubled minds, that wake . . *Lucrece* 126
All which together, like a troubled ocean 589
Make some hole Through which I may convey this troubled soul . . . 1176
Troy. A piece Of skilful painting, made for Priam's Troy 1367
From the towers of Troy there would appear The very eyes of men through loop-holes thrust 1382
From the walls of strong-besieged Troy 1429
And with my tears quench Troy that burns so long 1468
This load of wrath that burning Troy doth bear 1474
Here in Troy, for trespass of thine eye, The sire, the son, the dame, and daughter die 1476
Had doting Priam check'd his son's desire, Troy had been bright with fame 1491
Here feelingly she weeps Troy's painted woes 1492
Onward to Troy with the blunt swains he goes 1504
As Priam him did cherish, So did I Tarquin; so my Troy did perish . . 1547
That he finds means to burn his Troy with water 1561
Truant. O truant Muse, what shall be thy amends For thy neglect? *Son.* 101 1
Truce. Till he take truce with her contending tears, Which long have rain'd, making her cheeks all wet . . . . *Ven. and Adon.* 82
True. And these mine eyes, true leaders to their queen, But for thy piteous lips no more had seen 503
That sometime true news, sometime false doth bring 658
Rich preys make true men thieves 724
'Tis true, 'tis true; thus was Adonis slain 1111
True valour still a true respect should have . . . . . *Lucrece* 201
Heedfully doth view The sight which makes supposed terror true . . 455
His true respect will prison false desire 642
My true eyes have never practised how To cloak offences 748

True. O no, that cannot be; Of that true type hath Tarquin rifled me *Lucrece* 1050
I will not wrong thy true affection so, To flatter thee with an infringed oath 1060
True grief is fond and testy as a child 1094
True sorrow then is feelingly sufficed 1112
Shall tune our heart-strings to true languishment 1141
With soft-slow tongue, true mark of modesty 1220
By this short schedule Collatine may know Her grief, but not her grief's true quality 1313
Such harmless creatures have a true respect To talk in deeds 1347
By this bloody knife, We will revenge the death of this true wife 1841
If the true concord of well-tuned sounds, By unions married, do offend thine ear *Sonnet* 8 5
And your true rights be term'd a poet's rage 17 11
O, let me, true in love, but truly write, And then believe me 21 9
To find where your true image pictured lies 24 6
No love, my love, that thou mayst true love call 40 3
So true a fool is love that in your will, Though you do any thing, he thinks no ill 57 13
Mine own true love that doth my rest defeat 61 11
Methinks no face so gracious is as mine, No shape so true 62 6
Why should poor beauty indirectly seek Roses of shadow, since his rose is true? 67 8
In him those holy antique hours are seen, Without all ornament, itself and true 68 10
Lest your true love may seem false in this 72 9
Sympathized In true plain words by thy true-telling friend 82 12
'Tis so, 'tis true,' And to the most of praise add something more 85 9
So shall I live, supposing thou art true, Like a deceived husband 93 1
So are those errors that in thee are seen To truths translated and for true things deem'd 96 8
'Fair, kind, and true,' is all my argument, 'Fair, kind, and true' 105 9
'Fair, kind, and true,' have often lived alone 105 13
Can yet the lease of my true love control 107 3
What's in the brain that ink may character Which hath not figured to thee my true spirit? 108 2
Alas, 'tis true I have gone here and there 110 1
Most true it is that I have look'd on truth Askance and strangely 110 5
My most true mind thus makes mine eye untrue 113 14
Or whether shall I say, mine eye saith true? 114 3
Let me not to the marriage of true minds Admit impediments 116 1
A kind of meetness To be diseased ere that there was true needing 118 8
But thence I learn, and find the lesson true 118 13
Now I find true That better is by evil still made better 119 9
How hard true sorrow hits, And soon to you, as you to me! 120 10
I will be true, despite thy scythe and thee 123 14
A true soul When most impeach'd stands least in thy control 125 13
In things right true my heart and eyes have erred 137 13
Which have no correspondence with true sight 148 2
Then love doth well denote Love's eye is not so true as all men's 'No' 148 8
How can Love's eye be true, That is so vex'd with watching? 148 9
To make me give the lie to my true sight 150 3
That fire Which many legions of true hearts had warm'd 154 6
And true to bondage would not break from thence *Lov. Comp.* 34
Than the true gouty landlord which doth owe them 140
With acture they may be, Where neither party is nor true nor kind 186
O, pardon me, in that my boast is true 246
Mild as a dove, but neither true nor trusty *Pass. Pil.* 86
Between each kiss her oaths of true love swearing 92
Serve always with assured trust, And in thy suit be humble true 330
That it cried, How true a twain Seemeth this concordant one! *Ph. and Tur.* 45
To this urn let those repair That are either true or fair 66
True-love. Who sees his true-love in her naked bed *Ven. and Adon.* 397
Truest. O'erstraw'd With sweets that shall the truest sight beguile 1144
How careful was I, . . . Each trifle under truest bars to thrust *Sonnet* 48 2
True-sweet. But true-sweet beauty lived and died with him *V. and A.* 1080
True-telling. Sympathized In true plain words by thy true-telling friend *Sonnet* 82 12
Truly. And him by oath they truly honoured *Lucrece* 410
O, let me, true in love, but truly write, And then believe me *Sonnet* 21 9
The wrinkles which thy glass will truly show Of mouthed graves will give thee memory 77 5
Thou truly fair wert truly sympathized In true plain words 82 11
Truly not the morning sun of heaven Better becomes the grey cheeks of the east 132 5
Trumpet. First, like a trumpet, doth his tongue begin To sound a parley to his heartless foe *Lucrece* 470
Herald sad and trumpet be, To whose sound chaste wings obey *Ph. and Tur.* 3
Trust. So Priam's trust false Sinon's tears doth flatter *Lucrece* 1560
So I, for fear of trust, forget to say *Sonnet* 23 5
Unused stay From hands of falsehood, in sure wards of trust 48 4
Was I bold, To trust those tables that receive thee more? 122 12
Savage, extreme, rude, cruel, not to trust 129 4
O, love's best habit is in seeming trust 138 11
Not daring trust the office of mine eyes *Pass. Pil.* 196
Serve always with assured trust, And in thy suit be humble true 330
Trustless. Borne by the trustless wings of false desire *Lucrece* 2
Trusty. Mild as a dove, but neither true nor trusty *Pass. Pil.* 86
For of the two the trusty knight was wounded with disdain 221
Truth. Love is all truth, Lust full of forged lies *Ven. and Adon.* 804
Truth I must confess,—I rail'd on thee, fearing my love's decease 1001
Then where is truth, if there be no self-trust? *Lucrece* 158
When Truth and Virtue have to do with thee, A thousand crosses keep them from thy aid 911
To unmask falsehood and bring truth to light 940
My sable ground of sin I will not paint, To hide the truth 1075
Such signs of truth in his plain face she spied 1532
In them I read such art As truth and beauty shall together thrive *Son.* 14 11
Thy end is truth's and beauty's doom and date 14 14
Be scorn'd like old men of less truth than tongue 17 10
Take all my comfort of thy worth and truth 37 4
Even there Where thou art forced to break a twofold truth 41 12
For truth proves thievish for a prize so dear 48 14
By that sweet ornament which truth doth give 54 2
When that shall fade, my verse distills your truth 54 14
Feeds on the rarities of nature's truth 60 11
No face so gracious is as mine, No shape so true, no truth of such account 62 6
And simple truth miscall'd simplicity, And captive good attending captain ill 66 11
Uttering bare truth, even so as foes commend 69 4

Truth. And hang more praise upon deceased I Than niggard truth would willingly impart *Sonnet* 72 8
So are those errors that in thee are seen To truths translated 96 8
What shall be thy amends For thy neglect of truth in beauty dyed? 101 2
Both truth and beauty on my love depends 101 3
Truth needs no colour, with his colour fix'd; Beauty no pencil, beauty's truth to lay 101 6
Most true it is that I have look'd on truth Askance and strangely 110 5
Say this is not, To put fair truth upon so foul a face 137 12
When my love swears that she is made of truth I do believe her 138 1; *Pass. Pil.* 1
On both sides thus is simple truth suppress'd *Sonnet* 138 8
At random from the truth vainly express'd 147 12
Oaths of thy love, thy truth, thy constancy 152 10
More perjured I, To swear against the truth so foul a lie! 152 14
His rudeness so with his authorized youth Did livery falseness in a pride of truth *Lov. Comp.* 105
The truth I shall not know, but live in doubt *Pass. Pil.* 27
And truth in every shepherd's tongue 370
Beauty, truth, and rarity, Grace in all simplicity *Ph. and Tur.* 53
Truth may seem, but cannot be: Beauty brag, but 'tis not she: Truth and beauty buried be 62
Try. That mother tries a merciless conclusion Who, having two sweet babes, when death takes one, Will slay the other and be nurse to none *Lucrece* 1160
Mine appetite I never more will grind On newer proof, to try an older friend *Sonnet* 110 11
She told the youngling how god Mars did try her *Pass. Pil.* 145
What though she strive to try her strength, And ban and brawl 317
Tumult. Who, peeping forth this tumult to behold, Are by his flaming torch dimm'd and controll'd *Lucrece* 447
Tune. Still she entreats, and prettily entreats, For to a pretty ear she tunes her tale *Ven. and Adon.* 74
Melodious discord, heavenly tune harsh-sounding 431
Yet from mine ear the tempting tune is blown 778
The little birds that tune their morning's joy Make her moans mad with their sweet melody *Lucrece* 1107
Your tunes entomb Within your hollow-swelling feather'd breasts 1121
These means, as frets upon an instrument, Shall tune our heart-stings 1141
There we will unfold To creatures stern sad tunes, to change their kinds 1147
I'll tune thy woes with my lamenting tongue 1465
Nor are mine ears with thy tongue's tune delighted *Sonnet* 141 5
Tuned. I sit and mark, And wish her lays were tuned like the lark *Pass. Pil.* 198
Tuning. Feast-finding minstrels, tuning my defame, Will tie the hearers to attend each line *Lucrece* 817
Turn. He winks, and turns his lips another way *Ven. and Adon.* 90
Never did passenger in summer's heat More thirst for drink than she for this good turn 92
Now which way shall she turn? what shall she say? 253
Then shalt thou see the dew-bedabbled wretch Turn, and return 704
Her tears began to turn their tide, Being prison'd in her eye 979
My uncontrolled tide Turns not, but swells the higher by this let *Lucrece* 646
The sweets we wish for turn to loathed sours 867
Thy honey turns to gall, thy joy to grief 889
Thy secret pleasure turns to open shame 890
And turn the giddy round of Fortune's wheel 952
While with a joyless smile she turns away The face 1711
Now see what good turns eyes for eyes have done *Sonnet* 24 9
A league is took, And each doth good turns now unto the other 47 2
Sweetest things turn sourest by their deeds 94 13
And all things turn to fair that eyes can see 95 12
She turns my foes, That they elsewhere might dart their injuries 139 11
Turn back to me, And play the mother's part, kiss me, be kind 143 11
Thou mayst have thy 'Will,' If thou turn back, and my loud crying still 143 14
Or to turn white and swoon at tragic shows *Lov. Comp.* 308
More mickle was the pain That nothing could be used to turn them both to gain *Pass. Pil.* 220
Turned. The night of sorrow now is turn'd to day *Ven. and Adon.* 481
Mine eyes are turn'd to fire, my heart to lead 1072
'It cannot be' she in that sense forsook, And turn'd it thus *Lucrece* 1539
Three beauteous springs to yellow autumn turn'd *Sonnet* 104 5
Whether that my angel be turn'd fiend Suspect I may 144 9; *Pass. Pil.* 23
Turning. Mine eyes are gray and bright and quick in turning *V. and A.* 140
She bade love last, and yet she fell a-turning *Pass. Pil.* 100
Her fancy fell a-turning. Long was the combat doubtful 214
And deny himself for Jove, Turning mortal for thy love 244
Turrets. Left their round turrets destitute and pale *Lucrece* 441
So proud, As heaven, it seem'd, to kiss the turrets bow'd 1372
Turtle. Phœnix and the turtle fled In a mutual flame from hence *Ph. and Tur.* 23
Distance, and no space was seen 'Twixt the turtle and his queen 31
The turtle saw his right Flaming in the phœnix' sight 34
And the turtle's loyal breast To eternity doth rest 57
Tushes. Whose tushes never sheathed he whetteth still *Ven. and Adon.* 617
And whom he strikes his crooked tushes slay 624
Tusk. The loving swine Sheathed unaware the tusk in his soft groin 1116
Tutor. Thy eyes' shrewd tutor, that hard heart of thine, Hath taught them scornful tricks and such disdain 500
O Time, thou tutor both to good and bad! *Lucrece* 995
Twain. Love keeps his revels where there are but twain *Ven. and Adon.* 123
Give me one kiss, I'll give it thee again, And one for interest, if thou wilt have twain 210
His face seems twain, each several limb is doubled 1067
As if between them twain there were no strife *Lucrece* 405
To live or die which of the twain were better, When life is shamed 1154
We two must be twain, Although our undivided loves are one *Sonnet* 36 1
Thou teachest how to make one twain 39 13
Both find each other, and I lose both twain 42 11
Tearing of papers, breaking rings a-twain *Lov. Comp.* 6
So they loved, as love in twain Had the essence but in one *Ph. and Tur.* 25
That it cried, How true a twain Seemeth this concordant one! 45
'Tween. The iron bit he crusheth 'tween his teeth *Ven. and Adon.* 269
'Tween frozen conscience and hot-burning will *Lucrece* 247
Twenty. Ten kisses short as one, one long as twenty *Ven. and Adon.* 22
Is twenty hundred kisses such a trouble? 522
Were beauty under twenty locks kept fast, Yet love breaks through and picks them all at last 575
If love have lent you twenty thousand tongues 775
'Ay me!' she cries, and twenty times 'Woe, woe!' And twenty echoes twenty times cry so 833

Twenty. But why of two oaths' breach do I accuse thee, When I break twenty? . . . . *Sonnet* 152 6
Twice. So her accent breaks, That twice she doth begin ere once she speaks *Lucrece* 567
Were some child of yours alive that time, You should live twice *Sonnet* 17 14
But thou art twice forsworn, to me love swearing . . 152 2
And twice desire, ere it be day, That which with scorn she put away *Pass. Pil.* 315
Twilight. In me thou see'st the twilight of such day As after sunset fadeth in the west . . . . *Sonnet* 73 5
Twine. Some twine about her thigh to make her stay . *Ven. and Adon.* 873
Twining. And from her twining arms doth urge releasing . 256
Twinkling. The silver-shining queen he would distain; Her twinkling handmaids too, by him defiled . . *Lucrece* 787
Twire. When sparkling stars twire not thou gild'st the even . *Sonnet* 28 12
Twisted. Behold these talents of their hair, With twisted metal amorously impleach'd . . . . *Lov. Comp.* 205
'Twixt. Still is he sullen, still he lours and frets, 'Twixt crimson shame and anger ashy-pale . . . . *Ven. and Adon.* 76
And set dissension 'twixt the son and sire . . 1160
I hold such strife As 'twixt a miser and his wealth is found . *Sonnet* 75 4
Million'd accidents Creep in 'twixt vows and change decrees of kings . 115 6
Such a storm As oft 'twixt May and April is to see *Lov. Comp.* 102
Then must the love be great 'twixt thee and me . *Pass. Pil.* 105
Distance, and no space was seen 'Twixt the turtle and his queen *Ph. and Tur.* 31
Two strengthless doves will draw me through the sky *Ven. and Adon.* 153
Show'd like two silver doves that sit a-billing . . 366
Her two blue windows faintly she up-heaveth, Like the fair sun . 482
The crystal tide that from her two cheeks fair In the sweet channel of her bosom dropt 957
Grief hath two tongues, and never woman yet Could rule them both without ten women's wit 1007
'And yet,' quoth she, 'behold two Adons dead!' . . . 1070
Sun and sharp air Lurk'd like two thieves, to rob him of his fair . . 1086
His eyes, Where, lo, two lamps, burnt out, in darkness lies . . 1128
Two glasses, where herself herself beheld A thousand times . . 1129
The coward captive vanquished doth yield To those two armies *Lucrece* 76
Two. That mother tries a merciless conclusion Who, having two sweet babes, when death takes one, Will slay the other and be nurse to none *Lucrece* 1161
Why her two suns were cloud-eclipsed so . . . 1224
Two red fires in both their faces blazed . . . 1353
Bubbling from her breast, it doth divide In two slow rivers . . 1738
We two must be twain, Although our undivided loves are one *Sonnet* 36 1
In our two loves there is but one respect . . 36 5
The other two, slight air and purging fire, Are both with thee . 45 1
My life, being made of four, with two alone Sinks down to death . . 45 7
Where two contracted new Come daily to the banks . . 56 10
As those two mourning eyes become thy face . . 132 9
Two loves I have of comfort and despair, Which like two spirits do suggest me still 144 1
But why of two oaths' breach do I accuse thee, When I break twenty? 152 5
Two loves I have, of comfort and despair, That like two spirits do suggest me still . . . . *Pass. Pil.* 15
For of the two the trusty knight was wounded with disdain . . 221
Two distincts, division none: Number there in love was slain *Ph. and Tur.* 27
Single nature's double name Neither two nor one was called . . 40
Twofold. Even there Where thou art forced to break a twofold truth *Son.* 41 12
Type. O no, that cannot be; Of that true type hath Tarquin rifled me *Lucr.* 1050
Tyrannize. Shame folded up in blind concealing night, When most unseen, then most doth tyrannize 676
Tyrannous. Thou art as tyrannous, so as thou art . . *Sonnet* 131 1
Tyranny. Making it subject to the tyranny Of mad mischances and much misery . . . . *Ven. and Adon.* 737
Alas, why, fearing of time's tyranny, Might I not then say? . *Sonnet* 115 9
Tyrant. Which the hot tyrant stains and soon bereaves . *Ven. and Adon.* 797
Hard-favour'd tyrant, ugly, meagre, lean, Hateful divorce of love . 931
Or tyrant folly lurk in gentle breasts . . . *Lucrece* 851
Will play the tyrants to the very same . . . *Sonnet* 5 3
Make war upon this bloody tyrant, Time . . . 16 2
When tyrants' crests and tombs of brass are spent . . 107 14
And I, a tyrant, have no leisure taken . . . 120 7
Do I not think on thee, when I forgot Am of myself, all tyrant, for thy sake? 149 4
From this session interdict Every fowl of tyrant wing . . *Ph. and Tur.* 10

U

'Ugly, meagre, lean, Hateful divorce of love,'—thus chides she Death *Ven. and Adon.* 931
Who bids them still consort with ugly night 1041
There appears Quick-shifting antics, ugly in her eyes . *Lucrece* 459
Mis-shapen Time, copesmate of ugly Night, Swift subtle post . . 925
Solemn night with slow sad gait descended To ugly hell . . 1082
Anon permit the basest clouds to ride With ugly rack . . *Sonnet* 33 6
Ulysses. In Ajax and Ulysses, O, what art Of physiognomy might one behold *Lucrece* 1394
The mild glance that sly Ulysses lent Show'd deep regard . 1399
Unacted. The fault unknown is as a thought unacted . . 527
Unadvised. And friend to friend gives unadvised wounds . . 1488
Unapproved. What unapproved witness dost thou bear! *Lov. Comp.* 53
Unapt. With leaden appetite, unapt to toy . . *Ven. and Adon.* 34
Unapt for tender smell or speedy flight . . *Lucrece* 695
Unasked. And begg'd for that which thou unask'd shalt have *V. and A.* 102
Unaware. As one that unaware Hath dropp'd a precious jewel in the flood . 823
The loving swine Sheathed unaware the tusk in his soft groin 1116
Unbacked. When, lo, the unback'd breeder, full of fear, Jealous of catching, swiftly doth forsake him 320
Unbent. A brow unbent, that seem'd to welcome woe *Lucrece* 1509
Unbless. Thou dost beguile the world, unbless some mother . *Sonnet* 3 4
Unbred. For fear of which, hear this, thou age unbred . . 104 13
Uncertain. The uncertain sickly appetite to please . . 147 4
Uncertainly. Here folds she up the tenour of her woe, Her certain sorrow writ uncertainly . . . . *Lucrece* 1311
Uncheerful. In vain I rail at Opportunity, At Time, at Tarquin, and uncheerful Night 1024
Uncleanness. And die, unhallow'd thoughts, before you blot With your uncleanness that which is divine 193
Unconquered. A pair of maiden worlds unconquered, Save of their lord 408
Unconstrained. Playing patient sports in unconstrained gyves *Lov. Comp.* 242
Uncontrolled. His batter'd shield, his uncontrolled crest *Ven. and Adon.* 104
My uncontrolled tide Turns not, but swells the higher by this let *Lucrece* 645
Uncouple at the timorous flying hare . . *Ven. and Adon.* 674
Uncouth. What uncouth ill event Hath thee befall'n, that thou dost trembling stand? . . . . *Lucrece* 1598
Under. Over one arm the lusty courser's rein, Under her other was the tender boy . . . . *Ven. and Adon.* 32
Were beauty under twenty locks kept fast, Yet love breaks through and picks them all at last 575
Under whose sharp fangs on his back doth lie An image like thyself, all stain'd with gore 663
But in one minute's fight brings beauty under . . 746
Under whose simple semblance he hath fed Upon fresh beauty . . 795
He put his bonnet on, Under whose brim the gaudy sun would peep . 1088
Her lily hand her rosy cheek lies under, Cozening the pillow of a lawful kiss *Lucrece* 386
Urgeth still Under what colour he commits this ill . . 476
Under that colour am I come to scale Thy never-conquer'd fort . 481
So under his insulting falchion lies Harmless Lucretia . . 509
Like a white hind under the gripe's sharp claws, Pleads . . 543
Which bleeding under Pyrrhus' proud foot lies . . 1449
Each under eye Doth homage to his new-appearing sight *Sonnet* 7 2
How careful was I, . . . Each trifle under truest bars to thrust . 48 2
Every alien pen hath got my use And under thee their poesy disperse . 78 4
Needs must I under my transgression bow . . . 120 3
Nor falls Under the blow of thralled discontent . . 124 7
Under that bond that him as fast doth bind . . 134 8
What me your minister, for you obeys, Works under you *Lov. Comp.* 230
Under. Under an osier growing by a brook, A brook where Adon used to cool his spleen . . . . *Pass. Pil.* 75
Venus, with young Adonis sitting by her Under a myrtle shade . 144
Underneath. Let not the jealous Day behold that face Which underneath thy black all-hiding cloak Immodestly lies . . . *Lucrece* 801
Underprop. Beauty and virtue strived Which of them both should underprop her fame 53
Understood. Blushes, aptly understood In bloodless white and the encrimson'd mood . . . . *Lov. Comp.* 200
Undertake. That strong-bonded oath That shall prefer and undertake my troth 280
Undeserved. And undeserved reproach to him allotted That is as clear from this attaint of mine As I, ere this, was pure to Collatine *Lucrece* 824
Undistinguished. As often shrieking undistinguish'd woe *Lov. Comp.* 20
Undivided. We two must be twain, Although our undivided loves are one *Sonnet* 36 2
Undone. And then my little heart were quite undone . *Ven. and Adon.* 783
Uneared. Where is she so fair whose unear'd womb Disdains the tillage of thy husbandry? . . . . *Sonnet* 3 5
Unexperient. That th' unexperient gave the tempter place, Which like a cherubin above them hover'd . . . . . *Lov. Comp.* 318
Unfair. And that unfair which fairly doth excel . . *Sonnet* 5 4
Unfathered. Yet this abundant issue seem'd to me But hope of orphans and unfather'd fruit 97 10
It might for Fortune's bastard be unfather'd . . . 124 2
Unfelt. O unfelt sore! crest-wounding, private scar! . *Lucrece* 828
Unfinished. Who wears a garment shapeless and unfinish'd? *Ven. and Adon.* 415
Unfold. For they their guilt with weeping will unfold *Lucrece* 754
There we will unfold To creatures stern sad tunes, to change their kinds . 1146
Unfolding. To make some special instant special blest, By new unfolding his imprison'd pride . . . . *Sonnet* 52 12
Unfortunately. In her haste unfortunately spies The foul boar's conquest on her fair delight . . . . . . *Ven. and Adon.* 1029
Unfruitful. But in the midst of his unfruitful prayer *Lucrece* 344
Ungrown. No fisher but the ungrown fry forbears . *Ven. and Adon* 526
Unhallowed. And die, unhallow'd thoughts, before you blot With your uncleanness that which is divine . . . . . *Lucrece* 192
She lies, To be admired of lewd unhallow'd eyes . . 392
So his unhallow'd haste her words delays . . . 552
Unhappily set This bateless edge on his keen appetite . . 8
Purest faith unhappily forsworn, And gilded honour shamefully misplaced *Sonnet* 66 4
Unhappy. Comparing him to that unhappy guest Whose deed hath made herself herself detest . . . . *Lucrece* 1565
Unicorn. To tame the unicorn and lion wild . . . 956
Unions. If the true concord of well-tuned sounds, By unions married, do offend thine ear . . . . *Sonnet* 8 6
Unity. These contraries such unity do hold, Only to flatter fools . *Lucrece* 1558
Universe. For nothing this wide universe I call, Save thou, my rose *Son.* 109 13
Unjust. And justly thus controls his thoughts unjust *Lucrece* 189
Both which, as servitors to the unjust, So cross him . . 285
Wherefore says she not she is unjust? And wherefore say not I that I am old? *Sonnet* 138 9
Unless thy lady prove unjust, Press never thou to choose anew *Pass. Pil.* 331
Unjustly. By this chaste blood so unjustly stain'd . . *Lucrece* 1836
Unkind. 'Ay me,' quoth Venus, 'young, and so unkind?' *Ven. and Adon.* 187
O, had thy mother borne so hard a mind, She had not brought forth thee, but died unkind 204
She puts on outward strangeness, seems unkind . . . 310
That you were once unkind befriends me now *Sonnet* 120 1

Unkind. So him I lose through my unkind abuse . . . . *Sonnet* 134 12
Let no unkind, no fair beseechers kill 135 13
Unkindness. He seeks To mend the hurt that his unkindness marr'd *Ven. and Adon.* 478
For if you were by my unkindness shaken As I by yours, you've pass'd a hell of time . . . . *Sonnet* 120 5
To justify the wrong That thy unkindness lays upon my heart . 139 2
Unknown. That rich jewel he should keep unknown From thievish ears *Lucr.* 34
She touch'd no unknown baits, nor fear'd no hooks 103
The fault unknown is as a thought unacted 527
Whose worth's unknown, although his height be taken . . . 116 8
That I have frequent been with unknown minds 117 5
Unlaced. 'Even thus,' quoth she, 'the warlike good unlaced me' *Pass. Pil.* 149
Unlearned. Unlearned in the world's false subtleties . *Sonnet* 138 4
Unless. Upon the earth's increase why shouldst thou feed, Unless the earth with thy increase be fed? . . . . . . *Ven. and Adon.* 170
'I know not love,' quoth he, 'nor will not know it, Unless it be a boar, and then I chase it' 410
Unless thou couldst return to make amends . . . . *Lucrece* 961
Unless thou yoke thy liking to my will, I'll murder straight, and then I'll slaughter thee 1633
Swearing, unless I took all patiently, I should not live 1641
Thou, thyself . . . Unlook'd on diest, unless thou get a son . *Sonnet* 7 14
Unless thou take that honour from thy name 36 12
Unless this miracle have might, That in black ink my love may still shine bright 65 13
Unless you would devise some virtuous lie 72 5
Unless my nerves were brass or hammer'd steel 120 4
Unless this general evil they maintain, All men are bad . . . 121 13
Unless thy lady prove unjust, Press never thou to choose anew . *Pass. Pil.* 331
Unlettered. Like unletter'd clerk still cry 'Amen' To every hymn *Son.* 85 6
Unlike myself thou hear'st me moralize . . . *Ven. and Adon.* 712
Unlikely. The one doth flatter thee in thoughts unlikely, In likely thoughts the other kills thee quickly 989
Unlived. Where shall I live now Lucrece is unlived? . . . . *Lucrece* 1754
Unlocked. In Tarquin's tent, Unlock'd the treasure of his happy state . 16
Unlooked. So thou, thyself out-going in thy noon, Unlook'd on diest *Son.* 7 14
Whilst I, . . . Unlook'd for joy in that I honour most . . . 25 4
Unlooked-for. O unlook'd-for evil, When virtue is profaned in such a devil! *Lucrece* 846
Unloose. That which they possess They scatter and unloose it from their bond 136
Unmask. To unmask falsehood and bring truth to light 940
Unmask, dear dear, this moody heaviness, And tell thy grief . . . 1602
Unmatched. Did not let To praise the clear unmatched red and white . 11
Unmeet. Vow, alack! for youth unmeet: Youth, so apt to pluck a sweet *Pass. Pil.* 239
Unmoved. Who, moving others, are themselves as stone, Unmoved, cold, and to temptation slow . . . . *Sonnet* 94 4
Unnoted. Gnats are unnoted wheresoe'er they fly . . . . *Lucrece* 1014
Unpeopled. Stood Bare and unpeopled in this fearful flood 1741
Unperceived. The crow may bathe his coal-black wings in mire, And unperceived fly with the filth away 1010
Unperfect. As an unperfect actor on the stage Who with his fear is put besides his part . . . . *Sonnet* 23 1
Unpractised. Like an unpractised swimmer plunging still . *Lucrece* 1098
Unprofitable sounds, weak arbitrators! 1017
Unprovident. Deny that thou bear'st love to any, Who for thyself art so unprovident . . . . *Sonnet* 10 2
Unrecalling. And ever let his unrecalling crime Have time to wail *Lucrece* 993
Unresisted. So heedful fear Is almost choked by unresisted lust . . 282
Unrespected. When most I wink, then do mine eyes best see, For all the day they view things unrespected . . . . . . *Sonnet* 43 2
They live unwoo'd and unrespected fade 54 10
Unrest. That blow did bail it from the deep unrest Of that polluted prison *Lucrece* 1725
Reason is past care, And frantic-mad with evermore unrest . *Sonnet* 147 10
Unripe. The tender spring upon thy tempting lip Shows thee unripe; yet mayst thou well be tasted . . . . *Ven. and Adon.* 128
Measure my strangeness with my unripe years 524
Whether unripe years did want conceit . . . . . *Pass. Pil.* 51
Unruly. Banning his boisterous and unruly beast . . *Ven. and Adon.* 326
Unruly blasts wait on the tender spring . . . . . *Lucrece* 869
When winds breathe sweet, unruly though they be . . *Lov. Comp.* 103
Unsavoury. Find sweet beginning, but unsavoury end . *Ven. and Adon.* 1138
Unseasonable. He is no woodman that doth bend his bow To strike a poor unseasonable doe . . . . *Lucrece* 581
Unseeing. How would thy shadow's form form happy show To the clear day with thy much clearer light, When to unseeing eyes thy shade shines so! *Sonnet* 43 8
Unseen. Shame folded up in blind concealing night, When most unseen, then most doth tyrannize . . . . *Lucrece* 676
Therefore would they still in darkness be, To have their unseen sin remain untold 753
Thus breathes she forth her spite Against the unseen secrecy of night . 763
O unseen shame! invisible disgrace! O unfelt sore! 827
Himself, behind, Was left unseen, save to the eye of mind . . . 1426
Stealing unseen to west with this disgrace . . . . . *Sonnet* 33 8
To prevent our maladies unseen, We sicken to shun sickness when we purge 118 3
Through the velvet leaves the wind, All unseen, gan passage find *Pass. Pil.* 232
Unset. Many maiden gardens yet unset With virtuous wish . . *Sonnet* 16 6
Unsheathed. Even here she sheathed in her harmless breast A harmful knife, that thence her soul unsheathed . . . . . . *Lucrece* 1724
Unshorn. His phœnix down began but to appear Like unshorn velvet *Lov. Comp.* 94
Unskilful. Untutor'd youth, Unskilful in the world's false forgeries *Pass. Pil.* 4
Unsounded. Let my unsounded self, supposed a fool . . . *Lucrece* 1819
Unspotted. Let my good name, that senseless reputation, For Collatine's dear love be kept unspotted 821
Unstained. For unstain'd thoughts do seldom dream on evil 87
Wickedly he stalks, And gazeth on her yet unstained bed 366
And thou present'st a pure unstained prime . . . . *Sonnet* 70 8
Unswayed. Who leaves unsway'd the likeness of a man 141 11
Unswept. You shall shine more bright in these contents Than unswept stone besmear'd with sluttish time 55 4
Untainted. Her body's stain her mind untainted clears . . . *Lucrece* 1710
Blood untainted still doth red abide 1749
Him in thy course untainted do allow For beauty's pattern to succeeding men . . . . *Sonnet* 19 11

Unthrift. Look, what an unthrift in the world doth spend Shifts but his place, for still the world enjoys it . . . . *Sonnet* 9 9
O, none but unthrifts! Dear my love, you know You had a father . 13 13
Unthrifty. Unthrifty loveliness, why dost thou spend Upon thyself thy beauty's legacy? 4 1
Until. Until her husband's welfare she did hear . . . . *Lucrece* 263
Until life's composition be recured By those swift messengers return'd from thee . . . . *Sonnet* 45 9
Untimely. Some untimely thought did instigate His all-too-timeless speed *Lucrece* 43
By her untimely tears, her husband's love, By holy human law . . 570
Die I will not till my Collatine Have heard the cause of my untimely death 1178
And his untimely frenzy thus awaketh 1675
Untimely breathings, sick and short assays 1720
Untimely pluck'd, soon vaded, Pluck'd in the bud, and vaded in the spring *Pass. Pil.* 131
Unto. Sick-thoughted Venus makes amain unto him . . *Ven. and Adon.* 5
Is love so light, sweet boy, and may it be That thou shouldst think it heavy unto thee? 156
The strong-neck'd steed, being tied unto a tree, Breaketh his rein . 263
He looks upon his love and neighs unto her 307
Unto the wood they hie them, Out-stripping crows that strive to over-fly them 323
Woe unto the birds, Gusts and foul flaws to herdmen and to herds . . 455
What is ten hundred touches unto thee? 519
That lends embracements unto every stranger 790
To grow unto himself was his desire, And so 'tis thine 1180
For then is Tarquin brought unto his bed, Intending weariness . *Lucrece* 120
Unto a view so false will not incline 292
Now is he come unto the chamber door 337
Unto a greater uproar tempts his veins 427
The fault is thine, For those thine eyes betray thee unto mine . . 483
I mean to bear thee Unto the base bed of some rascal groom . . . 671
My honour I'll bequeath unto the knife That wounds my body . . 1184
Poor Lucrece' cheeks unto her maid seem so As winter meads . . 1217
Her contrite sighs unto the clouds bequeathed Her winged sprite . . 1727
A league is took, And each doth good turns now unto the other . *Sonnet* 47 2
For feasts of love I have been call'd unto . . . . *Lov. Comp.* 181
The night so pack'd, I post unto my pretty . . . . *Pass. Pil.* 201
Alas, it was a spite Unto the silly damsel 218
Untold. Therefore would they still in darkness be, To have their unseen sin remain untold . . . . *Lucrece* 753
Then in the number let me pass untold . . . . . *Sonnet* 136 9
Untreads. She treads the path that she untreads again . *Ven. and Adon.* 908
Untrimmed. Every fair from fair sometime declines, By chance or nature's changing course untrimm'd . . . . *Sonnet* 18 8
Untrue. That you for love speak well of me untrue 72 10
My most true mind thus makes mine eye untrue 113 14
For further I could say 'This man's untrue' . . . . *Lov. Comp.* 169
Untucked. For some, untuck'd, descended her sheaved hat 31
Untuned. With untuned tongue she hoarsely calls her maid . *Lucrece* 1214
Untutored. That she might think me some untutor'd youth . *Sonnet* 138 3
Untutor'd youth, Unskilful in the world's false forgeries . *Pass. Pil.* 3
Unused. Thy unused beauty must be tomb'd with thee . . . *Sonnet* 4 13
Beauty's waste hath in the world an end, And kept unused, the user so destroys it 9 12
Then can I drown an eye, unused to flow, For precious friends . . 30 5
That to my use it might unused stay From hands of falsehood . . 48 3
Unweaves. Now she unweaves the web that she hath wrought *V. and A.* 991
Unwed. Take counsel of some wiser head, Neither too young nor yet unwed *Pass. Pil.* 304
Unwelcome. Lest Jealousy, that sour unwelcome guest, Should, by his stealing in, disturb the feast . . . . *Ven. and Adon.* 449
Unwholesome. Let their exhaled unwholesome breaths make sick The life of purity, the supreme fair . . . . *Lucrece* 779
Unwholesome weeds take root with precious flowers 870
Unwilling. This beauteous combat, wilful and unwilling, Show'd like two silver doves that sit a-billing . . . . . . *Ven. and Adon.* 365
Threw unwilling light Upon the wide wound 1051
Each unwilling portal yields him way . . . . . . *Lucrece* 309
Unwisely did not let To praise the clear unmatched red and white . . 10
Unwitnessed. Trifles, unwitnessed with eye or ear . . *Ven. and Adon.* 1023
Unwooed. They live unwoo'd and unrespected fade, Die to themselves *Son.* 54 10
Unworthiness. If thy unworthiness raised love in me, More worthy I to be beloved of thee 150 13
Unworthy. Thou worthy lord Of that unworthy wife that greeteth thee, Health to thy person! . . . . *Lucrece* 1304
Unyielding. Remove your siege from my unyielding heart *Ven. and Adon.* 423
Up. The steed is stalled up, and even now To tie the rider she begins to prove 39
With one fair hand she heaveth up his hat 351
And careless lust stirs up a desperate courage 556
This canker that eats up Love's tender spring 656
The gentle lark, weary of rest, From his moist cabinet mounts up on high . 854
Like one that spies an adder Wreathed up in fatal folds just in his way . 879
Till, cheering up her senses all dismay'd, She tells them 'tis a causeless fantasy 896
So she at these sad signs draws up her breath 929
And therein heartens up his servile powers . . . . . *Lucrece* 295
Stuff up his lust, as minutes fill up hours 297
Cited up in rhymes, And sung by children in succeeding times . . 524
'Madam, ere I was up,' replied the maid 1277
Here folds she up the tenour of her woe, Her certain sorrow writ uncertainly 1310
In speech, it seem'd, his beard, all silver white, Wagg'd up and down . 1406
This windy tempest, till it blow up rain, Held back his sorrow's tide . . 1788
A vengeful canker eat him up to death . . . . . . *Sonnet* 99 13
In her maiden hand The fairest votary took up that fire . . . 154 5
Up-heaveth. Her two blue windows faintly she up-heaveth, Like the fair sun, when in his fresh array He cheers the morn . . . *Ven. and Adon.* 482
Uphold. Which husbandry in honour might uphold . . . *Sonnet* 13 10
Up-locked. Whose blessed key Can bring him to his sweet up-locked treasure 52 2
Upon. Upon this promise did he raise his chin . . . *Ven. and Adon.* 85
The tender spring upon thy tempting lip Shows thee unripe 127
Or, like a fairy, trip upon the green 146
Can thy right hand seize love upon thy left? 158
Upon the earth's increase why shouldst thou feed? 169
Or what great danger dwells upon my suit? 206
His braided hanging mane Upon his compass'd crest now stand on end . 272
He looks upon his love and neighs unto her 307

Upon. Whose blood upon the fresh flowers being shed Doth make them droop with grief and hang the head . . . *Ven. and Adon.* 665
By this, poor Wat, far off upon a hill, Stands on his hinder legs . . . 697
He hath fed Upon fresh beauty, blotting it with blame . . . 796
Upon his hurt she looks so steadfastly . . . 1063
Thus was Adonis slain : He ran upon the boar with his sharp spear . 1112
She looks upon his lips, and they are pale ; She takes him by the hand . 1123
Till sable Night, . . . Upon the world dim darkness doth display *Lucrece* 118
He sets his foot upon the light, For light and lust are deadly enemies . 673
Gazing upon the Greeks with little lust . . . 1384
Up-pricked. His ears up-prick'd ; his braided hanging mane Upon his compass'd crest now stand on end . . . *Ven. and Adon.* 271
Uprear. And this my hand against myself uprear . . *Sonnet* 49 11
Upright. Anon he rears upright, curvets, and leaps . *Ven. and Adon.* 279
Uproar. His eye, . . . Unto a greater uproar tempts his veins *Lucrece* 427
Up-till. She, poor bird, as all forlorn, Lean'd her breast up-till a thorn *Pass. Pil.* 382
Urchin-snouted. This foul, grim, and urchin-snouted boar *Ven. and Adon.* 1105
Urge. And from her twining arms doth urge releasing . . 256
With eager compounds we our palate urge . . *Sonnet* 118 2
Then, gentle cheater, urge not my amiss . . . 151 3
Urged. What have you urged that I cannot reprove? . *Ven. and Adon.* 787
And to his protestation urged the rest . . . *Lucrece* 1844
Urgeth. But she with vehement prayers urgeth still . . . 475
Extremity still urgeth such extremes . . . 1337
Urging the worser sense for vantage still . . . 249
Urn. To this urn let those repair That are either true or fair . *Ph. and Tur.* 65
Use. Make use of time, let not advantage slip . *Ven. and Adon.* 129
Fresh beauty for the use, Herbs for their smell, and sappy plants to bear . 164
So thou wilt buy and pay and use good dealing . . . 514
But gold that's put to use more gold begets . . . 768
Teaching them thus to use it in the fight . . . *Lucrece* 62
So then he hath it when he cannot use it . . . 862
Mad that sorrow should his use control . . . 1781
How much more praise deserved thy beauty's use . *Sonnet* 2 9
Profitless usurer, why dost thou use So great a sum of sums? . 4 7
That use is not forbidden usury Which happies those that pay the willing loan . . . 6 5
Mine be thy love and thy love's use their treasure . . 20 14
Who heaven itself for ornament doth use . . . 21 3
Use. That to my use it might unused stay From hands of falsehood *Son.* 48 3
Every alien pen hath got my use And under thee their poesy disperse . 78 3
Knowing a better spirit doth use your name . . . 80 2
The dedicated words which writers use Of their fair subject . . 82 3
If thou wouldst use the strength of all thy state ! But do not so . 96 12
Thou canst not then use rigour in my gaol ; And yet thou wilt . 133 12
Thou usurer, that put'st forth all to use . . . 134 10
Use power with power and slay me not by art . . . 139 4
As if the boy should use like loving charms . . *Pass. Pil.* 150
They that fawn'd on him before Use his company no more . . 422
Used. How Tarquin must be used, read it in me . . *Lucrece* 1195
Thy unused beauty must be tomb'd with thee, Which, used, lives th' executor to be . . . *Sonnet* 4 14
Their gross painting might be better used Where cheeks need blood . 82 13
That tongue that ever sweet Was used in giving gentle doom . 145 7
By a brook, A brook where Adon used to cool his spleen . *Pass. Pil.* 76
More mickle was the pain That nothing could be used to turn them both to gain . . . 220
Useless. And useless barns the harvest of his wits . . *Lucrece* 859
User. Beauty's waste hath in the world an end, And kept unused, the user so destroys it . . . *Sonnet* 9 12
Usest. I cannot blame thee for my love thou usest . . 40 6
Ushers. Nor that full star that ushers in the even . . 132 7
Usurer. Profitless usurer, why dost thou use So great a sum of sums? . 4 7
Thou usurer, that put'st forth all to use . . . 134 10
Usurps. Like lawn being spread upon the blushing rose, Usurps her cheek *Ven. and Adon.* 591
Usurped. Love to heaven is fled, Since sweating Lust on earth usurp'd his name . . . 794
Usurper. Like a foul usurper, went about From this fair throne to heave the owner out . . . *Lucrece* 412
Usury. That use is not forbidden usury Which happies those that pay the willing loan . . . *Sonnet* 6 5
Like usury, applying wet to wet, Or monarch's hands that let not bounty fall . . . *Lov. Comp.* 40
Utmost. When as thy love hath cast his utmost sum . . *Sonnet* 49 3
Utter. My tongue shall utter all . . . *Lucrece* 1076
She utters this, 'He, he, fair lords, 'tis he, That guides this hand' . 1721
Uttering. For sportive words and uttering foolish things . . 1813
Uttering bare truth, even so as foes commend . . . *Sonnet* 69 4

V

Vacant. The vacant leaves thy mind's imprint will bear . *Sonnet* 77 3
Vaded. Soon vaded, Pluck'd in the bud, and vaded in the spring *Pass. Pil.* 131
Lost, vaded, broken, dead within an hour . . . 174
As vaded gloss no rubbing will refresh . . . 176
Vadeth. Beauty is but a vain and doubtful good ; A shining gloss that vadeth suddenly . . . 170
Vails. He vails his tail that, like a falling plume, Cool shadow to his melting buttock lent . . . *Ven. and Adon.* 314
Vailed. As one full of despair, She vail'd her eyelids . . 956
Vain. But all in vain ; good queen, it will not be . . . 607
The kiss I gave you is bestow'd in vain, And all in vain you strive against the stream . . . 771
In vain I rail at Opportunity, At Time, at Tarquin . *Lucrece* 1023
In vain I cavil with mine infamy, In vain I spurn at my confirm'd despite . 1025
'In vain,' quoth she, 'I live, and seek in vain Some happy mean' . 1044
But, wretched as he is, he strives in vain . . . 1665
Beauty is but a vain and doubtful good ; A shining gloss that vadeth suddenly . . . *Pass. Pil.* 169
Ah, thought I, thou mourn'st in vain ! None takes pity on thy pain . 391
Vainly. Thus vainly thinking that she thinks me young *Son.* 138 5 ; *Pass. Pil.* 5
At random from the truth vainly express'd . . *Sonnet* 147 12
Vale. A plaintful story from a sistering vale . . *Lov. Comp.* 2
Valiant. And makes her absence valiant, not her might . . 245
Valleys. That hills and valleys, dales and fields, And all the craggy mountains yields . . . *Pass. Pil.* 355
Valley-fountain. In a cold valley-fountain of that ground *Sonnet* 153 4
Valour. Put fear to valour, courage to the coward *Ven. and Adon.* 1158
True valour still a true respect should have . . *Lucrece* 201
Vanished. He runs, and chides his vanish'd, loathed delight . . 742
And moan the expense of many a vanish'd sight . *Sonnet* 30 8
All those beauties whereof now he's king Are vanishing or vanish'd out of sight . . . 63 7
Vanisheth. So vanisheth As smoke from Ætna, that in air consumes *Lucr.* 1041
Vanishing. All those beauties whereof now he's king Are vanishing or vanish'd out of sight . . . *Sonnet* 63 7
Vanities. Thy violent vanities can never last . . *Lucrece* 894
Vanquished. The coward captive vanquished doth yield To those two armies . 75
Like a thousand vanquish'd men in bloody fight ! . *Pass. Pil.* 280
Vantage. But having thee at vantage,—wondrous dread ! *Ven. and Adon.* 635
Urging the worser sense for vantage still . . *Lucrece* 249
The injuries that to myself I do, Doing thee vantage, double-vantage me *Sonnet* 88 12
Vaporous. O hateful, vaporous, and foggy Night ! . *Lucrece* 771
Vapour. Like misty vapours when they blot the sky *Ven. and Adon.* 184
As from a furnace, vapours doth he send . . . 274
The boy that by her side lay kill'd Was melted like a vapour from her sight 1166
Some gentle gust doth get, Which blows these pitchy vapours . *Lucrece* 550
Let thy misty vapours march so thick . . . 782
My vow was breath, and breath a vapour is . . *Pass. Pil.* 37
Then, thou fair sun, that on this earth doth shine, Exhale this vapour vow 39
Variable passions throng her constant woe . . *Ven. and Adon.* 967
Variation. Why is my verse so barren of new pride, So far from variation or quick change? . . . *Sonnet* 76 2
Variety. Making them red and pale with fresh variety . *Ven. and Adon.* 21
Varying. All my argument, 'Fair, kind, and true' varying to other words *Sonnet* 105 10
Vassal. Obdurate vassals fell exploits effecting, In bloody death . *Lucrece* 429
Vassal. No outrageous thing From vassal actors can be wiped away *Lucrece* 608
So let thy thoughts, low vassals to thy state . . . 666
And yet the duteous vassal scarce is gone . . . 1360
Being your vassal, bound to stay your leisure . . *Sonnet* 58 4
Thy proud heart's slave and vassal wretch to be . . 141 12
Vassalage. To whom in vassalage Thy merit hath my duty strongly knit 26 1
Vast sin-concealing chaos ! nurse of blame ! . . *Lucrece* 767
Vastly stood Bare and unpeopled in this fearful flood . . 1740
Vaulty. Till sable Night, . . . in her vaulty prison stows the Day . 119
Vaunt. That meaner men should vaunt That golden hap which their superiors want . . . 41
Vaunt in their youthful sap, at height decrease . . *Sonnet* 15 7
Vehement. But she with vehement prayers urgeth still . . *Lucrece* 475
Veil. Bonnet nor veil henceforth no creature wear ! . *Ven. and Adon.* 1081
Where beauty's veil doth cover every blot . . *Sonnet* 95 11
Veiled. And, veil'd in them, did win whom he would maim . *Lov. Comp.* 312
Vein. With more than admiration he admired Her azure veins . *Lucrece* 419
Unto a greater uproar tempts his veins . . . 427
Whose ranks of blue veins, as his hand did scale, Left their round turrets destitute and pale . . . 440
Her blue blood changed to black in every vein . . . 1454
Beggar'd of blood to blush through lively veins . *Sonnet* 67 10
In my love's veins thou hast too grossly dyed . . . 99 5
Velvet. His phœnix down began but to appear Like unshorn velvet *Lov. Comp.* 94
Through the velvet leaves the wind, All unseen, gan passage find *Pass. Pil.* 231
Venge. With swift pursuit to venge this wrong of mine . . *Lucrece* 1691
Vengeful. A vengeful canker eat him up to death . . *Sonnet* 99 13
Venom. Being so applied, His venom in effect is purified . *Lucrece* 532
Or toads infect fair founts with venom mud . . . 850
Venomed. 'Gainst venom'd sores the only sovereign plaster *Ven. and Adon.* 916
Vent. Free vent of words love's fire doth assuage . . . 334
Through little vents and crannies of the place . . *Lucrece* 310
No tool imparteth To make more vent for passage of her breath . . 1040
Venture. Being ireful, on the lion he will venture *Ven. and Adon.* 628
Venturing. Things out of hope are compass'd oft with venturing . 567
So that in venturing ill we leave to be The things we are for that which we expect . . . *Lucrece* 148
Venus. Sick-thoughted Venus makes amain unto him *Ven. and Adon.* 5
Wishing Adonis had his team to guide, So he were like him and by Venus' side 180
'Ay me,' quoth Venus, 'young, and so unkind?' . . . 187
These lovely caves, these round enchanting pits, Open'd their mouths to swallow Venus' liking . . . 248
So glides he in the night from Venus' eye ; Which after him she darts . 816
Venus salutes him with this fair good-morrow . . . 859
This solemn sympathy poor Venus noteth . . . 1057
But beauty, in that white intituled, From Venus' doves doth challenge that fair field . . . *Lucrece* 58
Venus, with young Adonis sitting by her Under a myrtle shade *Pass. Pil.* 143
Verbal. The neighbour caves, as seeming troubled, Make verbal repetition of her moans . . . *Ven. and Adon.* 831
Verdict. By their verdict is determined The clear eye's moiety *Sonnet* 46 11
But quickly on this side the verdict went . . *Lov. Comp.* 113
Verdure. And as they last, their verdure still endure *Ven. and Adon.* 507
Vermilion. Nor did I wonder at the lily's white, Nor praise the deep vermilion in the rose . . . *Sonnet* 98 10
Verse. Who will believe my verse in time to come? . . . 17 1
Despite thy wrong, My love shall in my verse ever live young . 19 14

Verse. Stirr'd by a painted beauty to his verse . . . . *Sonnet* 21 2
That pour'st into my verse Thine own sweet argument 38 2
When that shall fade, my verse distills your truth 54 14
And yet to times in hope my verse shall stand, Praising thy worth . 60 13
O, if, I say, you look upon this verse When I perhaps compounded am with clay 71 9
Why is my verse so barren of new pride, So far from variation or quick change? 76 1
And found such fair assistance in my verse 78 2
My verse alone had all thy gentle grace 79 2
Your monument shall be my gentle verse 81 9
Was it the proud full sail of his great verse? 86 1
No, neither he, nor his compeers by night Giving him aid, my verse astonished 86 8
For to no other pass my verses tend 103 11
And more, much more, than in my verse can sit 103 13
Therefore my verse to constancy confined, One thing expressing . 105 7
Very. And nothing but the very smell were left me *Ven. and Adon.* 441
The owl, night's herald, shrieks, ''Tis very late' 531
Now is she in the very lists of love 595
There would appear The very eyes of men through loop-holes thrust *Lucr.* 1383
Will play the tyrants to the very same . . . . . *Sonnet* 5 3
Thou dost review The very part was consecrate to thee 74 6
So shall I taste At first the very worst of fortune's might . . . 90 12
And, thou away, the very birds are mute 97 12
Like prayers divine, I must each day say o'er the very same . . . 108 6
A bliss in proof, and proved, a very woe 129 11
That in the very refuse of thy deeds There is such strength . . 150 6
Vestal. Love-lacking vestals and self-loving nuns, That on the earth would breed a scarcity . . . . *Ven. and Adon.* 752
Thou makest the vestal violate her oath . . . . *Lucrece* 883
Vex. Thou canst not vex me with inconstant mind . . . . *Sonnet* 92 9
More than enough am I that vex thee still 135 3
Vexation. The deep vexation of his inward soul Hath served a dumb arrest upon his tongue . . . . *Lucrece* 1779
Vexed. How can Love's eye be true, That is so vex'd with watching and with tears? . . . . *Sonnet* 148 10
Vial. Make sweet some vial; treasure thou some place With beauty's treasure, ere it be self-kill'd 6 3
Vice. When thus thy vices bud before thy spring . . . . *Lucrece* 604
Beguiled With outward honesty, but yet defiled With inward vice . . 1546
For canker vice the sweetest buds doth love . . . . . *Sonnet* 70 7
O, what a mansion have those vices got! 95 9
If he be addict to vice, Quickly him they will entice . . . *Pass. Pil.* 415
Victor. A captive victor that hath lost in gain . . . . *Lucrece* 730
Thou dead, both die, and both shall victors be 1211
Either not assail'd or victor being charged . . . . . *Sonnet* 70 10
As victors of my silence cannot boast 86 11
Thus art with arms contending was victor of the day . . *Pass. Pil.* 223
Victory. His victories, his triumphs, and his glories . *Ven. and Adon.* 1014
With bruised arms and wreaths of victory . . . . . *Lucrece* 110
After a thousand victories once foil'd . . . . . . *Sonnet* 25 10
Must for your victory us all congest, As compound love to physic your cold breast . . . . *Lov. Comp.* 258
View. O, what a sight it was, wistly to view How she came stealing to the wayward boy! . . . . *Ven. and Adon.* 343
Her eyes, as murder'd with the view, Like stars ashamed of day, themselves withdrew 1031
So, at his bloody view, her eyes are fled 1037
That eye which him beholds, as more divine, Unto a view so false will not incline . . . . *Lucrece* 292
Heedfully doth view The sight which makes supposed terror true . . 454
Think but how vile a spectacle it were, To view thy present trespass in another 632
In a sea of care, Holds disputation with each thing she views . . . 1101
The precedent whereof in Lucrece view 1261
My soul's imaginary sight Presents thy shadow to my sightless view *Son.* 27 10
Their images I loved I view in thee, And thou, all they, hast all the all of me 31 13
Then do mine eyes best see, For all the day they view things unrespected 43 2
That, when they see Return of love, more blest may be the view . . 56 12
Those parts of thee that the world's eye doth view Want nothing . . 69 1
I have gone here and there And made myself a motley to the view . 110 2
Who in despite of view is pleased to dote 141 4
No marvel then, though I mistake my view 148 11
Sometimes they do extend Their view right on . . . *Lov. Comp.* 26
Viewed. Both crystals, where they view'd each other's sorrow *V. and A.* 963
Their silent war of lilies and of roses, Which Tarquin view'd in her fair face's field, In their pure ranks his traitor eye encloses . . . . *Lucrece* 72
When their glass fell wherein they view'd their faces 1526
Viewest. Look in thy glass, and tell the face thou viewest Now is the time that face should form another . . . . *Sonnet* 3 1
Viewing. What face remains alive that's worth the viewing? Whose tongue is music now? . . . . *Ven. and Adon.* 1076
Vigour. Now Nature cares not for thy mortal vigour 953
Vile. My digression is so vile, so base, That it will live engraven in my face *Lucr.* 202
And in a desperate rage Post hither, this vile purpose to prevent . . 220
And doth so far proceed, That what is vile shows like a virtuous deed . 252
Think but how vile a spectacle it were 631
How comes it then, vile Opportunity, Being so bad, such numbers seek for thee? 895
Give warning to the world that I am fled From this vile world . *Sonnet* 71 4
'Tis better to be vile than vile esteem'd 121 1
Vilest. That I am fled From this vile world, with vilest worms to dwell 71 4
Villain. The homely villain court'sies to her low . . . . *Lucrece* 1338
Vine. For one sweet grape who will the vine destroy? 215
Violate. Thou makest the vestal violate her oath 883

Violated. Dear Collatine, thou shalt not know The stained taste of violated troth . . . . *Lucrece* 1059
Violent. Thy violent vanities can never last 894
As through an arch the violent roaring tide Outruns the eye that doth behold his haste 1667
Violet. These blue-vein'd violets whereon we lean Never can blab *V. and A.* 125
His breath and beauty set Gloss on the rose, smell to the violet . . . 936
When I behold the violet past prime . . . . . *Sonnet* 12 3
The forward violet thus did I chide: Sweet thief 99 1
Virgin. And so the general of hot desire Was sleeping by a virgin hand disarm'd 154 8
Virtue. Their virtue lost, wherein they late excell'd . *Ven. and Adon.* 1131
Within whose face beauty and virtue strived . . . . . *Lucrece* 52
When virtue bragg'd, beauty would blush for shame 54
When beauty boasted blushes, in despite Virtue would stain that o'er with silver white 56
Then virtue claims from beauty beauty's red, Which virtue gave . . . 59
This heraldry in Lucrece' face was seen, Argued by beauty's red and virtue's white 65
This blur to youth, this sorrow to the sage, This dying virtue . . . 223
And talk'd of virtue: O unlook'd-for evil, When virtue is profaned in such a devil! 846
What virtue breeds iniquity devours 872
When Truth and Virtue have to do with thee, A thousand crosses keep them from thy aid 911
Base watch of woes, sin's pack-horse, virtue's snare 928
But, for their virtue only is their show, They live unwoo'd . . *Sonnet* 54 9
And maiden virtue rudely strumpeted 66 6
He lends thee virtue and he stole that word From thy behaviour . . 79 9
You still shall live—such virtue hath my pen 81 13
How like Eve's apple doth thy beauty grow, If thy sweet virtue answer not thy show! 93 14
I did strive to prove The constancy and virtue of your love . . . 117 14
Love is my sin and thy dear virtue hate, Hate of my sin . . . 142 1
Virtuous. And doth so far proceed, That what is vile shows like a virtuous deed . . . . *Lucrece* 252
Where, like a virtuous monument, she lies, To be admired 391
Many maiden gardens yet unset With virtuous wish . . . *Sonnet* 16 7
Unless you would devise some virtuous lie 72 5
Upon thy side against myself I'll fight And prove thee virtuous . . 88 4
Visage. And from the forlorn world his visage hide 33 7
A platted hive of straw, Which fortified her visage from the sun *Lov. Comp.* 9
On his visage was in little drawn What largeness thinks in Paradise was sawn 90
Yet show'd his visage by that cost more dear 96
Vision. Nor his own vision holds what it doth catch . . *Sonnet* 113 8
Visit. Vouchsafe t' afford . . . Some present speed to come and visit me *Lucr.* 1307
Voice. Ill-nurtured, crooked, churlish, harsh in voice . *Ven. and Adon.* 134
Thy mermaid's voice hath done me double wrong 429
Against the welkin volleys out his voice 921
Reviving joy bids her rejoice, And flatters her it is Adonis' voice . . . 978
Her voice is stopt, her joints forget to bow; Her eyes are mad . . . 1061
Her voice controll'd Entombs her outcry in her lips' sweet fold . *Lucrece* 678
With head declined, and voice damm'd up with woe 1661
All tongues, the voice of souls, give thee that due, Uttering bare truth, even so as foes commend . . . . *Sonnet* 69 3
In so profound abysm I throw all care Of others' voices 112 10
My spirits to attend this double voice accorded . . . *Lov. Comp.* 3
Thine eye Jove's lightning seems, thy voice his dreadful thunder *Pass. Pil.* 67
Volleys. Against the welkin volleys out his voice . *Ven. and Adon.* 921
Vomit. Drunken Desire must vomit his receipt . . . *Lucrece* 703
Votary. The fairest votary took up that fire Which many legions of true hearts had warm'd . . . . *Sonnet* 154 5
Vouchsafe, thou wonder, to alight thy steed . . . *Ven. and Adon.* 13
Vouchsafe t' afford—If ever, love, thy Lucrece thou wilt see—Some present speed to come and visit me . . . . *Lucrece* 1305
O, then vouchsafe me but this loving thought . . . . *Sonnet* 32 9
Not once vouchsafe to hide my will in thine 135 6
Vow. Dismiss your vows, your feigned tears, your flattery *Ven. and Adon.* 425
That now he vows a league, and now invasion . . . . *Lucrece* 287
The impious breach of holy wedlock vow 809
That he may vow, in that sad hour of mine, Revenge on him that made me stop my breath 1179
And kiss'd the fatal knife, to end his vow 1843
That deep vow, which Brutus made before, He doth again repeat . . . 1847
For thee against myself I'll vow debate . . . . . *Sonnet* 89 13
Million'd accidents Creep in 'twixt vows and change decrees of kings . 115 6
This I do vow and this shall ever be; I will be true 123 13
I am perjured most; For all my vows are oaths but to misuse thee . 152 7
Knew vows were ever brokers to defiling . . . . . *Lov. Comp.* 173
And be not of my holy vows afraid 179
All vows and consecrations giving place 263
Vow, bond, nor space, In thee hath neither sting, knot, nor confine . . 264
Vows for thee broke deserve not punishment . . . . *Pass. Pil.* 32
My vow was earthly, thou a heavenly love 35
My vow was breath, and breath a vapour is 37
Then, thou fair sun, that on this earth doth shine, Exhale this vapour vow 39
Vow, alack! for youth unmeet: Youth, so apt to pluck a sweet . . . 239
Vowed. Whilst many nymphs that vow'd chaste life to keep Came tripping by . . . . *Sonnet* 154 3
O never faith could hold, if not to beauty vow'd . . . *Pass. Pil.* 58
Vowing. New faith torn In vowing new hate after new love bearing *Son.* 152 4
Vulgar. Too excellent for every vulgar paper to rehearse . . . 38 4
Mine only care, Art left the prey of every vulgar thief 48 8
Which vulgar scandal stamp'd upon my brow 112 2
Vulture. Whose vulture thought doth pitch the price so high, That she will draw his lips' rich treasure dry . . . . . . *Ven. and Adon.* 551
Her sad behaviour feeds his vulture folly . . . . . *Lucrece* 556

W

Wagged. In speech, it seem'd, his beard, all silver white, Wagg'd up and down *Lucrece* 1406
Wail. To wail his death who lives and must not die *Ven. and Adon.* 1017
Who buys a minute's mirth to wail a week? Or sells eternity to get a toy? *Lucrece* 213
Poor, and meek, Like to a bankrupt beggar wails his case 711
And ever let his unrecalling crime Have time to wail 994
The world will wail thee, like a makeless wife *Sonnet* 9 4
And with old woes new wail my dear time's waste 30 4
Wailed. She was only mine, And only must be wail'd by Collatine *Lucr.* 1799
Wailing. She marking them begins a wailing note *Ven. and Adon.* 835
And give the harmless show An humble gait, calm looks, eyes wailing still *Lucrece* 1508
That she hath thee, is of my wailing chief *Sonnet* 42 3
Waist. Girdle with embracing flames the waist Of Collatine's fair love *Lucr.* 6
Wait. Danger deviseth shifts; wit waits on fear *Ven. and Adon.* 690
Respect and reason, wait on wrinkled age! *Lucrece* 275
Unruly blasts wait on the tender spring 869
Thy heinous hours wait on them as their pages 910
For greatest scandal waits on greatest state 1006
I am to wait, though waiting so be hell *Sonnet* 58 13
For summer and his pleasures wait on thee 97 11
Waited. It shall be waited on with jealousy *Ven. and Adon.* 1137
Waiting. I am to wait, though waiting so be hell *Sonnet* 58 13
Wake. And wakes the morning, from whose silver breast The sun ariseth in his majesty *Ven. and Adon.* 855
Save thieves, and cares, and troubled minds, that wake *Lucrece* 126
While lust and murder wake to stain and kill 168
Will he not wake, and in a desperate rage Post hither? 219
She wakes her heart by beating on her breast, And bids it leap from thence 759
To wake the morn and sentinel the night 942
For thee watch I whilst thou dost wake elsewhere, From me far off *Sonnet* 61 13
Reason strong, For his advantage still did wake and sleep *Lov. Comp.* 123
If thou sorrow, he will weep; If thou wake, he cannot sleep *Pass. Pil.* 426
Wakened. But shoot not at me in your waken'd hate *Sonnet* 117 12
Waking. From forth dull sleep by dreadful fancy waking *Lucrece* 450
Thou bear'st thy part, To keep thy sharp woes waking 1136
As a dream doth flatter, In sleep a king, but waking no such matter *Son.* 87 14
Walk. About he walks, Rolling his greedy eyeballs in his head *Lucrece* 367
Be absent from thy walks, and in my tongue Thy sweet beloved name no more shall dwell *Sonnet* 89 9
Those dancing chips, O'er whom thy fingers walk with gentle gait 128 11
My mistress, when she walks, treads on the ground 130 12
Walked. To see his face the lion walk'd along Behind some hedge, because he would not fear him *Ven. and Adon.* 1093
Wall. Rude ram, to batter such an ivory wall! *Lucrece* 464
Have batter'd down her consecrated wall 723
Through crystal walls each little mote will peep 1251
From the walls of strong-besieged Troy 1429
A liquid prisoner pent in walls of glass *Sonnet* 5 10
Painting thy outward walls so costly gay 146 4
Wander. Where none may spy him, Sits Sin, to seize the souls that wander by him *Lucrece* 882
'T may be, again to make me wander thither *Pass. Pil.* 190
'Wander,' a word for shadows like myself 191
Wanderest. Nor shall Death brag thou wander'st in his shade *Sonnet* 18 11
Wandering. In thy weak hive a wandering wasp hath crept *Lucrece* 839
It is the star to every wandering bark *Sonnet* 116 7
Wane. As fast as thou shalt wane, so fast thou growest In one of thine 11 1
Waning. The aim of all is but to nurse the life With honour, wealth, and ease, in waning age *Lucrece* 142
Who hast by waning grown *Sonnet* 126 3
Want. Art thou a woman's son, and canst not feel What 'tis to love? how want of love tormenteth? *Ven. and Adon.* 202
His high-pitch'd thoughts that meaner men should vaunt That golden hap which their superiors want *Lucrece* 42
And, all for want of wit, Make something nothing by augmenting it 153
Seems to part in sunder, Swelling on either side to want his bliss 389
With too much labour drowns for want of skill 1099
Who nothing wants to answer her but cries, And bitter words to ban her cruel foes 1459
Yet eyes this cunning want to grace their art *Sonnet* 24 13
How can my Muse want subject to invent, While thou dost breathe? 38 1
Those parts of thee that the world's eye doth view Want nothing 69 2
No want of conscience hold it that I call Her 'love' 151 13
Where want cries some, but where excess begs all *Lov. Comp.* 42
Whether unripe years did want conceit *Pass. Pil.* 51
But if store of crowns be scant, No man will supply thy want 410
Wanteth. But, poorly rich, so wanteth in his store *Lucrece* 97
A swallowing gulf that even in plenty wanteth 557
Wanting. Wanting the spring that those shrunk pipes had fed 1455
Wit so poor as mine May make seem bare, in wanting words to show it *Sonnet* 26 6
The cause of this fair gift in me is wanting 87 7
Wanton. To sport and dance, To toy, to wanton, dally, smile, and jest *Ven. and Adon.* 106
Bewitching like the wanton mermaid's songs 777
Mine ears, that to your wanton talk attended, Do burn themselves 809
Nor could she moralize his wanton sight *Lucrece* 104
As who should say 'This glove to wanton tricks Is not inured' 320
O modest wantons! wanton modesty! 401
Bearing the wanton burthen of the prime *Sonnet* 97 7
Spied a blossom passing fair, Playing in the wanton air *Pass. Pil.* 230
Wantonly. Hang on such thorns and play as wantonly *Sonnet* 54 7
Wantonness. Some say thy fault is youth, some wantonness 96 1
War. The stern and direful god of war *Ven. and Adon.* 98
O, what a war of looks was then between them! 355
It shall be cause of war and dire events 1159
Their silent war of lilies and of roses *Lucrece* 71
The wind wars with his torch to make him stay 311
Make war against proportion'd course of time 774
How he in peace is wounded, not in war 831
Sweets with sweets war not, joy delights in joy *Sonnet* 8 2
War. And all in war with Time for love of you *Sonnet* 15 13
Make war upon this bloody tyrant, Time 16 2
Such civil war is in my love and hate 35 12
Mine eye and heart are at a mortal war How to divide the conquest 46 1
When wasteful war shall statues overturn 55 5
Nor war's quick fire shall burn The living record of your memory 55 7
Warble. The well-tuned warble of her nightly sorrow *Lucrece* 1080
Ward. The locks between her chamber and his will, Each one by him enforced retires his ward 303
Unused stay From hands of falsehood, in sure wards of trust *Sonnet* 48 4
Prison my heart in thy steel bosom's ward 133 9
Wardrobe. As my chest, Or as the wardrobe which the robe doth hide 52 10
Warlike. Fearing some hard news from the warlike band *Lucrece* 255
'Even thus,' quoth she, 'the warlike god embraced me' *Pass. Pil.* 147
'Even thus,' quoth she, 'the warlike god unlaced me' 149
Warm. The sun that shines from heaven shines but warm *Ven. and Adon.* 193
Thy palfrey, as he should, Welcomes the warm approach of sweet desire 386
The warm effects which she in him finds missing She seeks to kindle 605
And see thy blood warm when thou feel'st it cold *Sonnet* 2 14
Warmed. That fire Which many legions of true hearts had warm'd 154 6
Not one whose flame my heart so much as warm'd *Lov. Comp.* 191
What breast so cold that is not warmed here? 292
Warning. Give warning to the world that I am fled From this vile world *Sonnet* 71 3
Warrant. Warrant for blame, To privilege dishonour in thy name *Lucrece* 620
Warrantise. There is such strength and warrantise of skill *Sonnet* 150 7
Warrior. The painful warrior famoused for fight 25 9
Wary. Be of thyself so wary As I, not for myself, but for thee will 22 9
Was. O, what a sight it was, wistly to view How she came! *Ven. and Adon.* 343
Now was she just before him as he sat 349
How much a fool was I To be of such a weak and silly mind 1015
Whereat she leaps that was but late forlorn 1026
Such sweet observance in this work was had *Lucrece* 1385
Of what she was no semblance did remain 1453
For she that was thy Lucrece, now attend me 1682
That I no more can see what once I was 1764
When love, converted from the thing it was, Shall reasons find *Sonnet* 49 7
Stood in doubt If best were as it was, or best without *Lov. Comp.* 98
Farewell, sweet lass, Thy like ne'er was *Pass. Pil.* 294
Wash. To wash the foul face of the sluttish ground *Ven. and Adon.* 983
My blood shall wash the slander of mine ill *Lucrece* 1207
Wasp. In thy weak hive a wandering wasp hath crept 839
Wast. Thou wast begot; to get it is thy duty *Ven. and Adon.* 168
And wast afeard to scratch her wicked foe *Lucrece* 1035
And on that pillow lay Where thou wast wont to rest thy weary head 1621
Thou wast not to this end from me derived 1755
Waste. 'Sweet boy,' she says, 'this night I'll waste in sorrow' *V. and A.* 583
And waste huge stones with little water-drops *Lucrece* 959
And, tender churl, makest waste in niggarding *Sonnet* 1 12
Beauty's waste hath in the world an end 9 11
Thou among the wastes of time must go 12 10
And with old woes new wail my dear time's waste 30 4
Thy glass will show thee how thy beauties wear, Thy dial how thy precious minutes waste 77 2
What thy memory can not contain, Commit to these waste blanks 77 10
Give my love fame faster than Time wastes life 100 13
Which prove more short than waste or ruining 125 4
The expense of spirit in a waste of shame Is lust in action 129 1
Wasted. A summer's day will seem an hour but short, Being wasted in such time-beguiling sport *Ven. and Adon.* 24
Beauty within itself should not be wasted 130
Are on the sudden wasted, thaw'd, and done 749
When in the chronicle of wasted time I see *Sonnet* 106 1
Wasteful. Where wasteful Time debateth with Decay 15 11
When wasteful war shall statues overturn 55 5
Wasting. Poor wasting monuments of lasting moans *Lucrece* 798
Wat. By this, poor Wat, far off upon a hill, Stands on his hinder legs with listening ear *Ven. and Adon.* 697
Watch. For my sick heart commands mine eyes to watch 584
Base watch of woes, sin's pack-horse, virtue's snare *Lucrece* 928
They that watch see time how slow it creeps 1575
Whilst I, my sovereign, watch the clock for you *Sonnet* 57 6
For thee watch I whilst thou dost wake elsewhere, From me far off 61 13
Lord, how mine eyes throw gazes to the east! My heart doth charge the watch *Pass. Pil.* 194
Watching. How can Love's eye be true, That is so vex'd with watching and with tears? *Sonnet* 148 10
Watchman. To play the watchman ever for thy sake 61 12
Watch-word. Which gives the watch-word to his hand full soon *Lucrece* 370
Water. She bathes in water, yet her fire must burn *Ven. and Adon.* 94
Shone like the moon in water seen by night 492
As air and water do abate the fire 654
For stones dissolved to water do convert *Lucrece* 592
And grave, like water that doth eat in steel, Upon my cheeks 755
His eye drops fire, no water thence proceeds 1552
That he finds means to burn his Troy with water 1561
But that so much of earth and water wrought I must attend time's leisure with my moan *Sonnet* 44 11
So that myself bring water for my stain 109 8
The sea, all water, yet receives rain still 135 9
Love's fire heats water, water cools not love 154 14
The glowing roses That flame through water which their hue encloses *Lov. Comp.* 287
But with the inundation of the eyes What rocky heart to water will not wear? 291
Of burning blushes, or of weeping water, Or swooning paleness 304
Water-drops. And waste huge stones with little water-drops *Lucrece* 959
Water-galls. These water-galls in her dim element Foretell new storms 1588
Watery. Now this pale swan in her watery nest Begins the sad dirge of her certain ending 1611
A watery rigol goes, Which seems to weep upon the tainted place 1745
As pitying Lucrece' woes, Corrupted blood some watery token shows 1748
And the firm soil win of the watery main Increasing store *Sonnet* 64 7

Watery. This said, his watery eyes he did dismount . . *Lov. Comp.* 281
Wave. Like a dive-dapper peering through a wave, Who, being look'd on, ducks as quickly in . . . . . *Ven. and Adon.* 86
Fanning the hairs, who wave like feather'd wings 306
Till the wild waves will have him seen no more 819
Whose waves to imitate the battle sought With swelling ridges . *Lucrece* 1438
Like as the waves make towards the pebbled shore . . . *Sonnet* 60 1
Wavering. And nice affections wavering stood in doubt . *Lov. Comp.* 97
Wax. What wax so frozen but dissolves with tempering? *Ven. and Adon.* 565
No more than wax shall be accounted evil Wherein is stamp'd the semblance of a devil . . . . *Lucrece* 1245
Softer than wax, and yet, as iron, rusty . . . . *Pass. Pil.* 88
Waxen. Whereat a waxen torch forthwith he lighteth . . . *Lucrece* 178
For men have marble, women waxen, minds 1240
Waxeth. The colt that's back'd and burden'd being young Loseth his pride and never waxeth strong . . . . *Ven. and Adon.* 420
Wax-red. Set thy seal-manual on my wax-red lips 516
Way. He winks, and turns his lips another way 90
Now which way shall she turn? what shall she say? 253
A thousand ways he seeks To mend the hurt that his unkindness marr'd . 477
Being moved, he strikes whate'er is in his way 623
Turn, and return, indenting with the way 704
In the dark she lay, Having lost the fair discovery of her way . . . 828
The bushes in the way Some catch her by the neck 871
Like one that spies an adder Wreathed up in fatal folds just in his way . 879
This way she runs, and now she will no further, But back retires . . 905
A thousand spleens bear her a thousand ways 907
Each unwilling portal yields him way . . . . . *Lucrece* 309
If thou deny, then force must work my way 513
Foul sin may say, He learn'd to sin, and thou didst teach the way . 630
Some dark deep desert, seated from the way 1144
Stands at gaze, Wildly determining which way to fly 1150
One . . . , That cannot tread the way out readily 1152
Pausing for means to mourn some newer way 1365
The eyes, 'fore duteous, now converted are From his low tract and look another way . . . . *Sonnet* 7 12
Wherefore do not you a mightier way Make war? 16 1
To let base clouds o'ertake me in my way 34 3
Injurious distance should not stop my way 44 2
How careful was I, when I took my way 48 1
How heavy do I journey on the way 50 1
'Gainst her own content, To put the by-past perils in her way *Lov. Comp.* 158
And to her will frame all thy ways . . . . . *Pass. Pil.* 323
Wayward. How she came stealing to the wayward boy *Ven. and Adon.* 344
As a child, Who wayward once, his mood with nought agrees *Lucrece* 1095
Weak. How much a fool was I To be of such a weak and silly mind *Ven. and Adon.* 1016
The strongest body shall it make most weak 1145
My will is strong, past reason's weak removing . . . *Lucrece* 243
Such shadows are the weak brain's forgeries 460
He doth but dally, While in his hold-fast foot the weak mouse panteth . 555
To whose weak ruins muster troops of cares 720
In thy weak hive a wandering wasp hath crept 839
Their father was too weak, and they too strong 865
Unprofitable sounds, weak arbitrators! 1017
The weak oppress'd, the impression of strange kinds Is form'd in them by force 1242
Mine enemy was strong, my poor self weak, And far the weaker with so strong a fear 1646
Through his lips do throng Weak words, so thick come in his poor heart's aid 1784
Such childish humour from weak minds proceeds 1825
The offender's sorrow lends but weak relief . . . *Sonnet* 34 11
My love is strengthen'd, though more weak in seeming . . . 102 1
The deep-green emerald, in whose fresh regard Weak sights their sickly radiance do amend . . . . . *Lov. Comp.* 214
Youth is hot and bold, age is weak and cold; Youth is wild, and age is tame *Pass. Pil.* 163
Weak-built. Though weak-built hopes persuade him to abstaining *Lucrece* 130
Weakens. Whose strength's abundance weakens his own heart . *Sonnet* 23 4
Weaker. Mine enemy was strong, my poor self weak, And far the weaker with so strong a fear . . . . . . *Lucrece* 1647
Weakling. Thyself art mighty; for thine own sake leave me: Myself a weakling 584
Weakly. Honour and beauty, in the owner's arms, Are weakly fortress'd from a world of harms 28
Weak-made. Make weak-made women tenants to their shame . . . 1260
Weakness. With cold-pale weakness numbs each feeling part *Ven. and Adon.* 892
With mine own weakness being best acquainted . . . *Sonnet* 88 5
Weal. Thy weal and woe are both of them extremes *Ven. and Adon.* 987
Wealth. What priceless wealth the heavens had him lent . . *Lucrece* 17
The aim of all is but to nurse the life With honour, wealth, and ease . 142
Honour for wealth; and oft that wealth doth cost The death of all, and all together lost 146
For thy sweet love remember'd such wealth brings . . . *Sonnet* 29 13
For whether beauty, birth, or wealth, or wit, Or any of these all . 37 5
Him she stores, to show what wealth she had In days long since . 67 13
I hold such strife As 'twixt a miser and his wealth is found . . 75 4
Some glory in their birth, some in their skill, Some in their wealth . 91 2
Thy love is better than high birth to me, Richer than wealth . 91 10
Of wealth, of filial fear, law, kindred, fame . . . *Lov. Comp.* 270
Weapons. Sharing joy To see their youthful sons bright weapons wield *Lucr.* 1432
Wear. Torches are made to light, jewels to wear, Dainties to taste, fresh beauty for the use . . . . . *Ven. and Adon.* 163
Who wears a garment shapeless and unfinish'd? 415
O, never let their crimson liveries wear! 506
Bonnet nor veil henceforth no creature wear! 1081
Tears harden lust, though marble wear with raining . . *Lucrece* 560
With the nightly linen that she wears He pens her piteous clamours in her head 680
And wear their brave state out of memory . . . . *Sonnet* 15 8
All posterity That wear this world out to the ending doom . . 55 12
Thy glass will show thee how thy beauties wear 77 1
Like unshorn velvet on that termless skin Whose bare out-bragg'd the web it seem'd to wear . . . . *Lov. Comp.* 95
But with the inundation of the eyes What rocky heart to water will not wear? 291
Wearied. She like a wearied lamb lies panting there . . . *Lucrece* 737
So woe hath wearied woe, moan tired moan 1363
Weariness. Intending weariness with heavy spright 121
Weariness. Besides, of weariness he did complain him, And talk'd of virtue *Lucrece* 845
Weary. What hour is this? or morn or weary even? . *Ven. and Adon.* 495
Look, the world's comforter, with weary gait, His day's hot task hath ended in the west 529
Hot, faint, and weary, with her hard embracing 559
Each envious brier his weary legs doth scratch, Each shadow makes him stop 705
The gentle lark, weary of rest, From his moist cabinet mounts up on high 853
And asks the weary caitiff for his master 914
Thus weary of the world, away she hies 1189
Ere he arrive his weary noon-tide prick . . . . . *Lucrece* 781
The weary time she cannot entertain, For now 'tis stale to sigh . . 1361
Even as subtle Sinon here is painted, So sober-sad, so weary, and so mild . 1542
Time doth weary time with her complaining 1570
And on that pillow lay Where thou wast wont to rest thy weary head . 1621
With weary car, Like feeble age, he reeleth from the day *Sonnet* 7 9
Weary with toil, I haste me to my bed 27 1
When what I seek, my weary travel's end, Doth teach that ease . 50 2
Is it thy will thy image should keep open My heavy eyelids to the weary night? 61 2
Weasels. Night-wandering weasels shriek to see him there . . *Lucrece* 307
Weather. Who is so faint, that dare not be so bold To touch the fire, the weather being cold . . . . . *Ven. and Adon.* 402
Like many clouds consulting for foul weather 972
No cloudy show of stormy blustering weather . . . *Lucrece* 115
Age like winter weather; Youth like summer brave, age like winter bare *Pass. Pil.* 159
Wob. Now she unweaves the web that she hath wrought *Ven. and Adon.* 991
Like unshorn velvet on that termless skin Whose bare out-bragg'd the web it seem'd to wear . . . . *Lov. Comp.* 95
Wed. Were kisses all the joys in bed, One woman would another wed *Pass. Pil.* 346
Wedlock. The impious breach of holy wedlock vow . . . *Lucrece* 809
Weed. They bid thee crop a weed, thou pluck'st a flower *Ven. and Adon.* 946
No flower was nigh, no grass, herb, leaf, or weed, But stole his blood . 1055
Abhor the deed That spots and stains love's modest snow-white weed *Lucr.* 196
As corn o'ergrown by weeds, so heedful fear Is almost choked . . . 281
Unwholesome weeds take root with precious flowers 870
A tatter'd weed, of small worth held . . . . . *Sonnet* 2 4
To thy fair flower add the rank smell of weeds 69 12
Why write I still all one, ever the same, And keep invention in a noted weed? 76 6
But if that flower with base infection meet, The basest weed outbraves his dignity 94 12
Lilies that fester smell far worse than weeds 94 14
Weeds among weeds, or flowers with flowers gather'd . . . 124 4
Week. Who buys a minute's mirth to wail a week? Or sells eternity to get a toy? . . . . *Lucrece* 213
Love alters not with his brief hours and weeks . . . *Sonnet* 116 11
Weep. And now she weeps, and now she fain would speak *Ven. and Adon.* 221
That laughs and weeps, and all but with a breath 414
Then would Adonis weep; And straight, in pity of his tender years, They both would strive who first should dry his tears 1090
Justice is feasting while the widow weeps . . . . . *Lucrece* 906
The dank earth weeps at thy languishment 1130
But as the earth doth weep, the sun being set 1226
Which makes the maid weep like the dewy night 1232
One justly weeps; the other takes in hand No cause 1235
Their gentle sex to weep are often willing 1237
If thou dost weep for grief of my sustaining, . . . it small avails my mood 1272
For now 'tis stale to sigh, to weep, and groan 1362
Lo, here weeps Hecuba, here Priam dies 1485
Here feelingly she weeps Troy's painted woes 1492
A watery rigol goes, Which seems to weep upon the tainted place . . 1746
Son and father weep with equal strife Who should weep most . . . 1791
Let no mourner say He weeps for her, for she was only mine . . . 1798
The world will be thy widow and still weep . . . . *Sonnet* 9 5
And weep afresh love's long since cancell'd woe 30 7
Which cannot choose But weep to have that which it fears to lose . 64 14
To make the weeper laugh, the laugher weep . . . . *Lov. Comp.* 124
Though Reason weep, and cry 'It is thy last' 168
To blush at speeches rank, to weep at woes 307
I weep for thee, and yet no cause I have . . . . *Pass. Pil.* 137
My sighs so deep Procure to weep, In howling wise 276
If thou sorrow, he will weep; If thou wake, he cannot sleep . . . 425
Weeper. To make the weeper laugh, the laugher weep . . *Lov. Comp.* 124
Weeping. Even as the sun with purple-colour'd face Had ta'en his last leave of the weeping morn . . . . . *Ven. and Adon.* 2
Dost thou drink tears, that thou provokest such weeping? 949
The spots whereof could weeping purify, Her tears should drop on them *Lucrece* 685
For they their guilt with weeping will unfold 754
And seems to point her out where she sits weeping 1087
Many a dry drop seem'd a weeping tear 1375
Let it then suffice To drown one woe, one pair of weeping eyes . . . 1680
Upon whose weeping margent she was set . . . . *Lov. Comp.* 39
Of burning blushes, or of weeping water, Or swooning paleness . . . 304
Herds stand weeping, Flocks all sleeping . . . . *Pass. Pil.* 285
Weepingly. I have received from many a several fair, Their kind acceptance weepingly beseech'd . . . . . *Lov. Comp.* 207
Weigh. Eternal love in love's fresh case Weighs not the dust and injury of age *Sonnet* 108 10
Have no leisure taken To weigh how once I suffer'd in your crime . 120 8
That phraseless hand, Whose white weighs down the airy scale of praise *Lov. Comp.* 226
Weight. Like a heavy-hanging bell, Once set on ringing, with his own weight goes . . . . *Lucrece* 1494
The beast that bears me, tired with my woe, Plods dully on, to bear that weight in me . . . . *Sonnet* 50 6
Welcome. Welcomes the warm approach of sweet desire *Ven. and Adon.* 386
Gives good cheer And reverend welcome to her princely guest *Lucrece* 90
A brow unbent, that seem'd to welcome woe 1509
Makes summer's welcome thrice more wish'd, more rare . *Sonnet* 56 14
Then give me welcome, next my heaven the best . . . 110 13
Like the lark; For she doth welcome daylight with her ditty . *Pass. Pil.* 199
Welcomed. Well was he welcomed by the Roman dame . . . *Lucrece* 51
Welfare. Until her husband's welfare she did hear 263
And, sick of welfare, found a kind of meetness To be diseased *Sonnet* 118 7
Welkin. Against the welkin volleys out his voice . . *Ven. and Adon.* 921
No cloudy show of stormy blustering weather Doth yet in his fair welkin once appear . . . . *Lucrece* 116

Well. The kiss shall be thine own as well as mine . . *Ven. and Adon.* 117
The tender spring upon thy tempting lip Shows thee unripe; yet mayst thou well be tasted 128
Foreknowing well, if there he came to lie, Why, there Love lived and there he could not die 245
Fair fall the wit that can so well defend her! 472
To sell myself I can be well contented, So thou wilt buy . . . 513
That sweet coral mouth, Whose precious taste her thirsty lips well knew 543
Bids him farewell, and look well to her heart 580
They that thrive well take counsel of their friends 640
Now his grief may be compared well To one sore sick that hears the passing-bell 701
A nurse's song ne'er pleased her babe so well 974
Chequer'd with white, Resembling well his pale cheeks 1169
An expired date, cancell'd ere well begun . . . . . *Lucrece* 26
Well was he welcomed by the Roman dame 51
Thou art well appaid As well to hear as grant what he hath said . . 914
Well, well, dear Collatine, thou shalt not know The stained taste of violated troth 1058
Wretched I, To imitate thee well, against my heart Will fix a sharp knife 1137
For more it is than I can well express 1286
Which heartless peasants did so well resemble 1392
Every private widow well may keep By children's eyes her husband's shape in mind . . . . *Sonnet* 9 7
Or say with princes if it shall go well, By oft predict that I in heaven find 14 7
Let them say more that like of hearsay well 21 13
For no man well of such a salve can speak 34 7
Lascivious grace, in whom all ill well shows, Kill me with spites . . 40 13
Thy beauty and thy years full well befits, For still temptation follows where thou art 41 3
Not blame your pleasure, be it ill or well 58 14
That you for love speak well of me untrue 72 10
Which makes thy love more strong, To love that well which thou must leave ere long 73 14
Well might show How far a modern quill doth come too short . . 83 6
As on the finger of a throned queen The basest jewel will be well esteem'd 96 6
Were it not sinful then, striving to mend, To mar the subject that before was well? 103 10
For what care I who calls me well or ill? 112 3
Mine eye well knows what with his gust is 'greeing 114 11
All this the world well knows; yet none knows well To shun the heaven that leads men to this hell 129 13
Yet well I know That music hath a far more pleasing sound . . . 130 9
For well thou know'st to my dear doting heart Thou art the fairest . 131 3
O, let it then as well beseem thy heart To mourn for me . . . 132 10
My love well knows Her pretty looks have been mine enemies . . 139 9
Then love doth well denote Love's eye is not so true as all men's 'No' 148 7
This brand she quenched in a cool well by 154 9
Well could he ride, and often men would say 'That horse his mettle from his rider takes' . . . . *Lov. Comp.* 106
Each several stone, With wit well blazon'd, smiled or made some moan 217
The broken bosoms that to me belong Have emptied all their fountains in my well 255
Well learned is that tongue that well can thee commend . . *Pass. Pil.* 64
'Farewell,' quoth she, . . . Farewell I could not, for I supp'd with sorrow 186
The fairest one of three, That liked of her master as well as well might be 212
Clear wells spring not, Sweet birds sing not 281
Let reason rule things worthy blame, As well as fancy partial might . 302
But plainly say thou lovest her well, And set thy person forth to sell . 309
To themselves yet either neither, Simple were so well compounded *Ph. and Tur.* 44
Well-breathed. And on thy well-breath'd horse keep with thy hounds *Ven. and Adon.* 678
Well-contented. If thou survive my well-contented day . . *Sonnet* 32 1
Well-doing. Whether the horse by him became his deed, Or he his manage by the well-doing steed . . . . *Lov. Comp.* 112
Well-painted idol, image dull and dead, Statue contenting but the eye alone *Ven. and Adon.* 212
To this well-painted piece is Lucrece come . . . . *Lucrece* 1443
Well-proportioned. Look, when a painter would surpass the life, In limning out a well-proportion'd steed . . . . *Ven. and Adon.* 290
Well-refined. In polish'd form of well-refined pen . . . *Sonnet* 85 8
Well-seeing. Lest eyes well-seeing thy foul faults should find . 148 14
Well-skilled. The well-skill'd workman this mild image drew . *Lucrece* 1520
Well-tuned. The well-tuned warble of her nightly sorrow . . . 1080
If the true concord of well-tuned sounds, By unions married, do offend thine ear . . . . *Sonnet* 8 5
Wench. Know, gentle wench, it small avails my mood . . *Lucrece* 1273
Went. Like a foul usurper, went about From this fair throne to heave the owner out 412
'But tell me, girl, when went'—and there she stay'd Till after a deep groan—'Tarquin from hence?' 1275
Since from thee going he went wilful-slow, Towards thee I'll run *Sonnet* 51 13
But quickly on this side the verdict went . . . . *Lov. Comp.* 113
Wept. Whose wonted lily white With purple tears, that his wound wept, was drench'd . . . . *Ven. and Adon.* 1054
Her eyes are mad that they have wept till now 1062
Wert. Would thou wert as I am, and I a man 369
But, O, what banquet wert thou to the taste! 445
And for a woman wert thou first created . . . . . *Sonnet* 20 9
I grant thou wert not married to my Muse 82 1
Thou truly fair wert truly sympathized In true plain words . . . 82 11
West. His day's hot task hath ended in the west . . *Ven. and Adon.* 530
Stealing unseen to west with this disgrace . . . . *Sonnet* 33 8
The twilight of such day As after sunset fadeth in the west . . . 73 6
Nor that full star that ushers in the even Doth half that glory to the sober west 132 8
Wet. Her contending tears, Which long have rain'd, making her cheeks all wet . . . . *Ven. and Adon.* 83
Sighs dry her cheeks, tears make them wet again 966
Sweet issue of a more sweet-smelling sire—For every little grief to wet his eyes 1179
Even so the maid with swelling drops gan wet . . . . *Lucrece* 1228
Priam wets his eyes, To see those borrow'd tears that Sinon sheds . . 1548
Is it for fear to wet a widow's eye That thou consumest thyself in single life *Sonnet* 9 1
Like usury, applying wet to wet, Or monarch's hands that let not bounty fall . . . . *Lov. Comp.* 40
Wether. My wether's bell rings doleful knell . . . . *Pass. Pil.* 272
What follows more she murders with a kiss . . *Ven. and Adon.* 54
What seest thou in the ground? hold up thy head 118
What bare excuses makest thou to be gone! 188
Art thou a woman's son, and canst not feel What 'tis to love? . . . 202
What am I, that thou shouldst contemn me this? Or what great danger dwells upon my suit? 205
Now which way shall she turn? what shall she say? 253
Look, what a horse should have he did not lack 299
O, what a war of looks was then between them! 355
'What! canst thou talk?' quoth she, 'hast thou a tongue?' 427
What hour is this? or morn or weary even? Do I delight to die, or life desire? 495
What wax so frozen but dissolves with tempering? 565
What though the rose have prickles, yet tis pluck'd 574
'The night is spent.' 'Why, what of that?' quoth she 717
What have you urged that I cannot reprove? 787
Alas, poor world, what treasure hast thou lost! 1075
What priceless wealth the heavens had him lent . . . . *Lucrece* 17
What needeth then apologies be made? 31
Those that much covet are with gain so fond, For what they have not . 135
What wrong, what shame, what sorrow I shall breed 499
But what's so blessed-fair that fears no blot? . . . *Sonnet* 92 13
What with his art in youth, and youth in art . . . *Lov. Comp.* 145
What me your minister, for you obeys, Works under you 229
What though her frowning brows be bent . . . . *Pass. Pil.* 311
What though she strive to try her strength, And ban and brawl . . 317
Whatever. Being moved, he strikes whate'er is in his way *Ven. and Adon.* 623
Do whate'er thou wilt, swift-footed Time . . . . *Sonnet* 19 6
Whate'er thy thoughts or thy heart's workings be 93 11
Whatsoever. Till whatsoever star that guides my moving Points on me graciously 26 9
Wheel. And turn the giddy round of Fortune's wheel . . *Lucrece* 952
When. But when her lips were ready for his pay, He winks, and turns his lips another way . . . . *Ven. and Adon.* 89
Look, when a painter would surpass the life, In limning out a well-proportion'd steed 289
When, lo, the unback'd breeder, full of fear, Jealous of catching, swiftly doth forsake him 320
Yet pardon me I felt a kind of fear When as I met the boar . . . 999
As when the wind, imprison'd in the ground 1046
When as thy love hath cast his utmost sum . . . . *Sonnet* 49 3
When as thine eye hath chose the dame . . . . *Pass. Pil.* 299
Whenas himself to singing he betakes 114
Whence. From whence at pleasure thou mayst come and part *Sonnet* 48 12
Sweet thief, whence didst thou steal thy sweet that smells? . . 99 2
Whence hast thou this becoming of things? 150 5
Where. Here come and sit, where never serpent hisses . *Ven. and Adon.* 17
And where she ends she doth anew begin 60
Who conquers where he comes in every jar 100
'O, where am I?' quoth she, 'in earth or heaven, Or in the ocean?' . 493
'Where did I leave?' 'No matter where;' quoth he, 'Leave me'. . 715
His eyes, Where, lo, two lamps, burnt out, in darkness lies . . . 1128
It shall suspect where is no cause of fear; It shall not fear where it should most mistrust 1153
Where now I have no one to blush with me . . . . *Lucrece* 792
Where all thy beauty lies, Where all the treasure of thy lusty days *Son.* 2 5
For where is she so fair whose unear'd womb Disdains the tillage of thy husbandry? 3 5
Beauty o'ersnow'd and bareness every where 5 8
Making his style admired every where 84 12
What dark days seen! What old December's bareness every where! . 97 4
And make Time's spoils despised every where 100 12
Whose rich esteeming The owner's tongue doth publish every where . 102 4
Whereas. He, spying her, bounced in, whereas he stood . *Pass. Pil.* 83
Whereat a sudden pale, Like lawn being spread upon the blushing rose, Usurps her cheek . . . . *Ven. and Adon.* 589
Whereat the impartial gazer late did wonder 748
Whereat amazed, as one that unaware Hath dropp'd a precious jewel in the flood 823
And now she beats her heart, whereat it groans 829
Whereat she starts, like one that spies an adder 878
Whereat her tears began to turn their tide 979
Whereat she leaps that was but late forlorn 1026
Whereat each tributary subject quakes 1045
Whereat a waxen torch forthwith he lighteth . . . . *Lucrece* 178
Whereat she smiled with so sweet a cheer 264
Wherefore do not you a mightier way Make war? . . *Sonnet* 16 1
Ah! wherefore with infection should he live? 67 1
Wherefore says she not she is unjust? And wherefore say not I that I am old? 138 9
But wherefore says my love that she is young? And wherefore say not I that I am old? . . . . *Pass. Pil.* 9
Wherein she framed thee in high heaven's despite . *Ven. and Adon.* 731
Their virtue lost, wherein they late excell'd 1131
There shall not be one minute in an hour Wherein I will not kiss my sweet love's flower 1188
By the light he spies Lucretia's glove, wherein her needle sticks . *Lucrece* 317
Wilt thou be glass wherein it shall discern Authority for sin? . . 619
Or altogether balk The prey wherein by nature they delight . . . 697
Wherein is stamp'd the semblance of a devil 1246
When their glass fell wherein they view'd their faces 1526
Wherein deep policy did him disguise 1815
My body is the frame wherein 'tis held . . . . . *Sonnet* 24 3
Making their tomb the womb wherein they grew 86 4
Wherein I am attainted, That thou in losing me shalt win much glory . 88 7
Every humour hath his adjunct pleasure, Wherein it finds a joy . . 91 6
I have scanted all Wherein I should your great deserts repay . . 117 2
Whereof. The fear whereof doth make him shake and shudder *Ven. and Adon.* 880
The spots whereof could weeping purify, Her tears should drop on them *Lucrece* 685
The precedent whereof in Lucrece view 1261
Whereof are you made, That millions of strange shadows on you tend? *Sonnet* 53 1
All those beauties whereof now he's king Are vanishing or vanish'd out of sight 63 6
Whereon. These blue-vein'd violets whereon we lean Never can blab *Ven. and Adon.* 125
Witness this primrose bank whereon I lie 151

Whereon they surfeit, yet complain on drouth . . . *Ven. and Adon.* 544
Within my bosom, whereon thou dost lie 646
Whereon with fearful eyes they long have gazed 927
This huge stage presenteth nought but shows Whereon the stars in secret influence comment . . . . . *Sonnet* 15 4
As the death-bed whereon it must expire 73 11
If that be fair whereon my false eyes dote, What means the world to say it is not so? 148 5
Whereon the thought might think sometime it saw . . . *Lov. Comp.* 10
Wheresoever. Gnats are unnoted wheresoe'er they fly . . . *Lucrece* 1014
Where-through the sun Delights to peep, to gaze therein on thee *Sonnet* 24 11
Whereto all bonds do tie me day by day 117 4
Whereto the inviting time our fashion calls 124 8
Hooks, Whereto the judgement of my heart is tied 137 8
The diamnod,—why, 'twas beautiful and hard, Whereto his invised properties did tend . . . . . *Lov. Comp.* 212
Whereupon. An eye more bright than theirs, less false in rolling, Gilding the object whereupon it gazeth . . . . . *Sonnet* 20 6
Whereupon it made this threne To the phœnix and the dove *Ph. and Tur.* 49
Wherever. His snout digs sepulchres where'er he goes . *Ven. and Adon.* 622
Slight air and purging fire, Are both with thee, wherever I abide *Sonnet* 45 2
Wherewith being crown'd, Crooked eclipses 'gainst his glory fight . 60 6
Every man will be thy friend Whilst thou hast wherewith to spend *Pass. Pil.* 408
Whet. He ran upon the boar with his sharp spear, Who did not whet his teeth at him again . . . . . *Ven. and Adon.* 1113
Whether. And whether he run or fly they know not whether . . . 304
Whether it is that she reflects so bright, That dazzleth them, or else some shame supposed . . . . . *Lucrece* 376
For whether beauty, birth, or wealth, or wit, Or any of these all *Sonnet* 37 5
Whether we are mended, or whether better they, Or whether revolution be the same 59 11
Or whether doth my mind, being crown'd with you, Drink up the monarch's plague, this flattery? 114 1
Or whether shall I say, mine eye saith true? 114 3
Whether that my angel be turn'd fiend, Suspect I may . 144 9; *Pass. Pil.* 23
Whether the horse by him became his deed, Or he his manage by the well-doing steed . . . . . *Lov. Comp.* 111
Whether unripe years did want conceit . . . . . *Pass. Pil.* 51
She fell a-turning. Was this a lover, or a lecher whether? . . . 101
In scorn or friendship, nill I construe whether 188
Whetteth. Whose tushes never sheathed he whetteth still *Ven. and Adon.* 617
Which. And begg'd for that which thou unask'd shalt have . . . 102
Now which way shall she turn? what shall she say? 253
Which cunning love did wittily prevent 471
Her heart, The which, by Cupid's bow she doth protest, He carries thence incaged in his breast 581
To which Love's eyes pay tributary gazes 632
The many musets through the which he goes Are like a labyrinth . . . 683
That bloody beast, Which knows no pity, but is still severe . . . 1000
Which seen, her eyes, as murder'd with the view, Like stars ashamed of day, themselves withdrew 1031
Which with cold terror doth men's minds confound 1048
As one of which doth Tarquin lie revolving The sundry dangers . *Lucrece* 127
Which I to conquer sought with all my might 488
All which together, like a troubled ocean, Beat 589
Stands at gaze, Wildly determining which way to fly 1150
Before the which is drawn the power of Greece 1368
And all those friends which I thought buried . . . . . *Sonnet* 31 4
His sweet up-locked treasure, The which he will not every hour survey 52 3
Who is it that says most? which can say more Than this rich praise? 84 1
We, which now behold these present days, Have eyes to wonder . . 106 13
To this I witness call the fools of time, Which die for goodness . 124 14
Which is to me some praise, that I thy parts admire . *Pass. Pil.* 66
While she takes all she can, not all she listeth . . *Ven. and Adon.* 564
My heart longs not to groan, But soundly sleeps, while now it sleeps alone 786
While lust and murder wake to stain and kill . . . . . *Lucrece* 168
While she, the picture of pure piety 542
And moody Pluto winks while Orpheus plays 553
He doth but dally, While in his hold-fast foot the weak mouse panteth 555
While Lust is in his pride, no exclamation Can curb his heat . . . 705
The patient dies while the physician sleeps 904
The orphan pines while the oppressor feeds 905
Justice is feasting while the widow weeps 906
Advice is sporting while infection breeds 907
While thou on Tereus descant'st better skill 1134
And whiles against a thorn thou bear'st thy part 1135
A pretty while these pretty creatures stand 1233
While others saucily Promise more speed, but do it leisurely . . 1348
That she her plaints a little while doth stay 1364
But Tarquin's shape came in her mind the while 1536
While Collatine and his consorted lords With sad attention long to hear . 1609
While with a joyless smile she turns away The face 1711
But if the while I think on thee, dear friend, All losses are restored *Son.* 30 13
How can my Muse want subject to invent, While thou dost breathe? . 38 2
While shadows like to thee do mock my sight 61 4
While comments of your praise, richly compiled, Reserve their character with golden quill 85 2
Now, while the world is bent my deeds to cross 90 2
I'll live in this poor rhyme, While he insults o'er dull and speechless tribes 107 12
While Philomela sits and sings, I sit and mark . . . . *Pass. Pil.* 197
Whilst I, whom fortune of such triumph bars, Unlook'd for joy . *Sonnet* 25 3
Whilst I alone did call upon thy aid, My verse alone had all thy gentle grace 79 1
I think good thoughts whilst other write good words 85 5
Whilst it hath thought itself so blessed never 119 6
Whilst as fickle Fortune smiled, Thou and I were both beguiled *Pass. Pil.* 401
Every man will be thy friend Whilst thou hast wherewith to spend . 408
Whirlwinds. My sighs, like whirlwinds, labour hence to heave thee *Lucrece* 586
Whispers in mine ear That if I love thee, I thy death should fear *V. and A.* 659
She whispers in his ears a heavy tale 1125
Whispering conspirator With close-tongued treason and the ravisher! *Lucr.* 769
Whit. Yet him for this my love no whit disdaineth . . . *Sonnet* 33 13
White. More white and red than doves or roses are . . *Ven. and Adon.* 10
Being red, she loves him best: and being white, Her best is better'd with a more delight 77
To note the fighting conflict of her hue, How white and red each other did destroy! 346
So white a friend engirts so white a foe 364
Teaching the sheets a whiter hue than white 398
White. Didst thou not mark my face? was it not white? *Ven. and Adon.* 643
Whose wonted lily white With purple tears, that his wound wept, was drench'd 1053
A purple flower sprung up, chequer'd with white 1168
Did not let To praise the clear unmatched red and white . . *Lucrece* 11
In despite Virtue would stain that o'er with silver white . . . 56
But beauty, in that white intituled, From Venus' doves doth challenge that fair field 57
When shame assail'd, the red should fence the white 63
This heraldry in Lucrece' face was seen, Argued by beauty's red and virtue's white 65
First red as roses that on lawn we lay, Then white as lawn, the roses took away 259
Whose perfect white Show'd like an April daisy on the grass . . . 394
Who o'er the white sheet peers her whiter chin, The reason of this rash alarm to know 472
Like a white hind under the gripe's sharp claws, Pleads 543
The poor lamb cries; Till with her own white fleece her voice controll'd Entombs her outcry in her lips' sweet fold 678
In speech, it seem'd, his beard, all silver white, Wagg'd up and down . 1405
And sable curls all silver'd o'er with white . . . . . *Sonnet* 12 4
Borne on the bier with white and bristly beard 12 8
Nor did I wonder at the lily's white, Nor praise the deep vermilion in the rose 98 9
One blushing shame, another white despair 99 9
A third, nor red nor white, had stol'n of both 99 10
If snow be white, why then her breasts are dun 130 3
I have seen roses damask'd, red and white 130 5
In bloodless white and the encrimson'd mood . . . . . *Lov. Comp.* 201
That phraseless hand, Whose white weighs down the airy scale of praise . 226
There my white stole of chastity I daff'd 297
Or to turn white and swoon at tragic shows 308
Let the priest in surplice white, That defunctive music can, Be the death-divining swan . . . . . *Ph. and Tur.* 13
Whiteness. His pale cheeks and the blood Which in round drops upon their whiteness stood . . . . . *Ven. and Adon.* 1170
Whiter. Teaching the sheets a whiter hue than white 398
Who o'er the white sheet peers her whiter chin, The reason of this rash alarm to know . . . . . *Lucrece* 472
Whither. Which madly hurries her she knows not whither *Ven. and Adon.* 904
Who. Like a dive-dapper peering through a wave, Who, being look'd on, ducks as quickly in 87
Fanning the hairs, who wave like feather'd wings 306
Who wears a garment shapeless and unfinish'd? 415
She vail'd her eyelids, who, like sluices, stopt The crystal tide . . 956
To wash the foul face of the sluttish ground, Who is but drunken when she seemeth drown'd 984
As who should say 'This glove to wanton tricks Is not inured' . *Lucrece* 320
Like a gentle flood, Who, being stopp'd, the bounding banks o'erflows . 1119
The dispersed air, who, holding Lucrece' life, Answer'd their cries . 1805
Whoever plots the sin, thou 'point'st the season 879
Whoe'er keeps me, let my heart be his guard . . . . . *Sonnet* 133 11
Whoever hath her wish, thou hast thy 'Will,' And 'Will' to boot . 135 1
Whole. My heart all whole as thine, thy heart my wound *Ven. and Adon.* 370
They that lose half with greater patience bear it Than they whose whole is swallow'd in confusion . . . . . *Lucrece* 1159
A hand, a foot, a face, a leg, a head, Stood for the whole to be imagined . 1428
He pays the whole, and yet am I not free . . . . . *Sonnet* 134 14
Whom. And whom he strikes his crooked tushes slay *Ven. and Adon.* 624
Embracing bushes, As fearful of him, part, through whom he rushes . 630
Whose sinewy neck in battle ne'er did bow 99
Whose hollow womb resounds like heaven's thunder 268
Whose precious taste her thirsty lips well knew 543
Chiefly in love, whose leave exceeds commission 568
He put his bonnet on, Under whose brim the gaudy sun would peep . 1088
Calls her maid, Whose swift obedience to her mistress hies *Lucrece* 1215
Why. Flint-hearted boy! 'Tis but a kiss I beg; why art thou coy? *V. and A.* 96
Then why not lips on lips, since eyes in eyes? 120
But having no defects, why dost abhor me? 138
Why, there Love lived and there he could not die 246
'The night is spent.' 'Why, what of that?' quoth she 717
Why hast thou cast into eternal sleeping Those eyes? 951
For why her face wore sorrow's livery . . . . . *Lucrece* 1222
Why her two sons were cloud-eclipsed so, Nor why her fair cheeks overwash'd with woe 1224
Since why to love I can allege no cause . . . . . *Sonnet* 49 14
For why thou left'st me nothing in thy will . . . . . *Pass. Pil.* 138
For why I craved nothing of thee still 140
For why, she sigh'd and bade me come to-morrow 204
Wicked. And wast afeard to scratch her wicked foe . . . *Lucrece* 1035
It cannot be, I find, But such a face should bear a wicked mind . . 1540
Wickedly he stalks, And gazeth on her yet unstained bed . . . 365
Wide. Broad breast, full eye, small head, and nostril wide *Ven. and Adon.* 296
The wide wound that the boar had trench'd In his soft flank . . . 1052
And with his knee the door he opens wide . . . . . *Lucrece* 359
To the wide world and all her fading sweets . . . . . *Sonnet* 19 7
And keep my drooping eyelids open wide 27 7
Wide as the ocean is, The humble as the proudest sail doth bear . . 80 5
Not mine own fears, nor the prophetic soul Of the wide world . . 107 2
For nothing this wide universe I call, Save thou, my rose . . . 109 13
Which my heart knows the wide world's common place 137 10
Bear thine eyes straight, though thy proud heart go wide . . . 140 14
Widow. Justice is feasting while the widow weeps . . . . *Lucrece* 906
Is it for fear to wet a widow's eye That thou consumest thyself in single life? . . . . . *Sonnet* 9 1
The world will be thy widow and still weep 9 5
Every private widow well may keep By children's eyes her husband's shape in mind 9 7
Widowed. Like widow'd wombs after their lords' decease 97 8
Wield. Sharing joy To see their youthful sons bright weapons wield *Lucr.* 1432
Wife. This desire Might have excuse to work upon his wife . . . 235
But when I fear'd I was a loyal wife: So am I now 1048
Thou worthy lord Of that unworthy wife that greeteth thee . . . 1304
A weeping tear, Shed for the slaughter'd husband by the wife . . . 1376
With equal strife Who should weep most, for daughter or for wife . . 1792
She was my wife, I owed her, and 'tis mine that she hath kill'd . . 1802
'My daughter' and 'my wife' with clamours fill'd The dispersed air . 1804
Answer'd their cries, 'my daughter' and 'my wife' 1806
For his foul act by whom thy fair wife bleeds 1824
Thy wretched wife mistook the matter so, To slay herself 1826

Wife. By this bloody knife, We will revenge the death of this true wife *Lucr.* 1841
The world will wail thee, like a makeless wife *Sonnet* 9 4
Wights. When in the chronicle of wasted time I see descriptions of the fairest wights 106 2
Wild. Like a wild bird being tamed with too much handling *Ven. and Adon.* 560
Till the wild waves will have him seen no more 819
To tame the unicorn and lion wild *Lucrece* 956
Continuance tames the one; the other wild 1097
That wild music burthens every bough *Sonnet* 102 11
For Adon's sake, a youngster proud and wild *Pass. Pil.* 120
Youth is hot and bold, age is weak and cold; Youth is wild, and age is tame 164
Wilder. Wilder to him than tigers in their wildness *Lucrece* 980
Wilderness. Pleads, in a wilderness where are no laws, To the rough beast 544
Wildfire. Whose words like wildfire burnt the shining glory Of rich-built Ilion 1523
Wildly. She wildly breaketh from their strict embrace *Ven. and Adon.* 874
Stands at gaze, Wildly determining which way to fly *Lucrece* 1150
Wildness. Wilder to him than tigers in their wildness 980
Wiles. The wiles and guiles that women work, Dissembled with an outward show *Pass. Pil.* 335
Wilful. This beauteous combat, wilful and unwilling, Show'd like two silver doves that sit a-billing *Ven. and Adon.* 365
On that he firmly doted, And in his will his wilful eye he tired *Lucrece* 417
If thou thyself deceivest By wilful taste of what thyself refusest *Sonnet* 40 8
Wilfully. My saucy bark inferior far to his On your broad main doth wilfully appear 80 8
Wilfulness. Book both my wilfulness and errors down 117 9
Wilful-slow. Since from thee going he went wilful-slow, Towards thee I'll run, and give him leave to go 51 13
Will. The time is spent, her object will away *Ven. and Adon.* 255
She, by her good will, Will never rise, so he will kiss her still 479
But all in vain; good queen, it will not be 607
Come not within his danger by thy will 639
Therefore, in sadness, now I will away 807
This way she runs, and now she will no further, But back retires. 905
Revolving The sundry dangers of his will's obtaining *Lucrece* 128
Yet ever to obtain his will resolving 129
My will is strong, past reason's weak removing 243
'Tween frozen conscience and hot-burning will 247
The locks between her chamber and his will, Each one by him enforced 302
My will is back'd with resolution: Thoughts are but dreams 352
On that he firmly doted, And in his will his wilful eye he tired 417
Where thou with patience must my will abide; My will that marks thee for my earth's delight 486
But will is deaf and hears no heedful friends 495
If but for fear of this, thy will remove 614
By him that gave it thee, From a pure heart command thy rebel will 625
His taste delicious, in digestion souring, Devours his will 700
But her foresight could not forestall their will 728
This brief abridgement of my will I make 1198
Thou, Collatine, shalt oversee this will 1205
And therefore are they form'd as marble will 1241
What wit sets down is blotted straight with will 1299
Unless thou yoke thy liking to my will, I'll murder straight 1633
Be of thyself so wary As I, not for myself, but for thee will *Sonnet* 22 10
So true a fool is love that in your will, Though you do any thing, he thinks no ill. 57 13
You yourself may privilege your time To what you will. 58 11
Is it thy will thy image should keep open My heavy eyelids? 61 1
Knowing thy will, I will acquaintance strangle and look strange 89 7
Which in their wills count bad what I think good 121 8
He is thine, And I myself am mortgaged to thy will 134 2
Thou hast thy 'Will,' And 'Will' to boot, and 'Will' in overplus 135 1
To thy sweet will making addition thus 135 4
Wilt thou, whose will is large and spacious, Not once vouchsafe to hide my will in thine? 135 5
Shall will in others seem right gracious, And in my will no fair acceptance shine? 135 7
So thou, being rich in 'Will,' add to thy 'Will' One will of mine, to make thy large 'Will' more 135 11
Think all but one, and me in that one 'Will' 135 14
That I was thy 'Will,' And will, thy soul knows, is admitted there 136 2
'Will' will fulfil the treasure of thy love, Ay, fill it full with wills, and my will one 136 5
Make but my name thy love, and love that still, And then thou lovest me, for my name is 'Will' 136 14
So will I pray that thou mayst have thy 'Will' 143 13
Catching all passions in his craft of will *Lov. Comp.* 126
Ask'd their own wills, and made their wills obey 133
She, silly queen, with more than love's good will, Forbade the boy he should not pass those grounds *Pass. Pil.* 123
For why thou left'st me nothing in thy will 138
And to her will frame all thy ways 323
Willeth. Paying what ransom the insulter willeth *Ven. and Adon.* 550
Willing. Their gentle sex to weep are often willing *Lucrece* 1237
Which happies those that pay the willing loan *Sonnet* 6 6
Whilst, like a willing patient, I will drink Potions of eisel 111 9
Willingly. And hang more praise upon deceased I Than niggard truth would willingly impart 72 8
Wilt. If thou wilt chide, thy lips shall never open *Ven. and Adon.* 48
Give me one kiss, I'll give it thee again, And one for interest, if thou wilt have twain 210
Feed where thou wilt, on mountain or in dale 232
So thou wilt buy and pay and use good dealing 514
'Wilt thou make the match?' He tells her, no 586
But if thou needs wilt hunt, be ruled by me 673
Or if thou wilt permit the sun to climb His wonted height *Lucrece* 775
When wilt thou be the humble suppliant's friend? 897
When wilt thou sort an hour great strifes to end? 899
Then hate me when thou wilt; if ever, now *Sonnet* 90 1
Win. What win I, if I gain the thing I seek? *Lucrece* 211
And the firm soil win of the watery main, Increasing store *Sonnet* 64 7
Wherein I am attainted, That thou in losing me shalt win much glory 88 8
Still losing when I saw myself to win 119 4
To win me soon to hell, my female evil Tempteth 144 5; *Pass. Pil.* 19
And, veil'd in them, did win whom he would maim *Lov. Comp.* 312
What fool is not so wise To break an oath, to win a paradise? *Pass. Pil.* 42
To win his heart, she touch'd him here and there 49
Wind. I'll sigh celestial breath, whose gentle wind Shall cool the heat of this descending sun *Ven. and Adon.* 189
Wind. To bid the wind a base he now prepares, And whether he run or fly they know not whether *Ven. and Adon.* 303
For through his mane and tail the high wind sings, Fanning the hairs 305
Even as a dying coal revives with wind 338
Even as the wind is hush'd before it raineth 458
How he outruns the wind and with what care He cranks 681
But like a stormy day, now wind, now rain, Sighs dry her cheeks 965
As when the wind, imprison'd in the ground 1046
Nor sun nor wind will ever strive to kiss you 1082
The sun doth scorn you and the wind doth hiss you 1084
The wind would blow it off and, being gone, Play with his locks 1089
The wind wars with his torch to make him stay *Lucrece* 311
But his hot heart, which fond desire doth scorch, Puffs forth another wind 315
The doors, the wind, the glove, that did delay him, He takes for accidental things of trial 325
Huge rocks, high winds, strong pirates, shelves, and sands, The merchant fears, ere rich at home he lands 335
Huge fires abide, And with the wind in greater fury fret 648
Sorrow ebbs, being blown with wind of words 1330
At last it rains, and busy winds give o'er 1790
Pointing to each his thunder, rain, and wind *Sonnet* 14 6
Rough winds do shake the darling buds of May 18 3
Then should I spur, though mounted on the wind 51 7
I have hoisted sail to all the winds Which should transport me 117 7
Storming her world with sorrow's wind and rain *Lov. Comp.* 7
The wind Upon his lips their silken parcels hurls 86
When winds breathe sweet, unruly though they be 103
And falls, through wind, before the fall should be *Pass. Pil.* 136
Through the velvet leaves the wind, All unseen, gan passage find 231
Words are easy, like the wind; Faithful friends are hard to find 405
Winding. Or one encompass'd with a winding maze *Lucrece* 1151
From his lips did fly Thin winding breath, which purl'd up to the sky 1407
Window. Her two blue windows faintly she up-heaveth, Like the fair sun, when in his fresh array He cheers the morn *Ven. and Adon.* 482
Why pry'st thou through my window? leave thy peeping *Lucrece* 1089
So thou through windows of thine age shalt see *Sonnet* 3 11
That hath his windows glazed with thine eyes 24 8
Mine eyes have drawn thy shape, and thine for me Are windows to my breast 24 11
Windy. Then with her windy sighs and golden hairs To fan and blow them dry again she seeks *Ven. and Adon.* 51
This windy tempest, till it blow up rain, Held back his sorrow's tide *Lucr.* 1788
Give not a windy night a rainy morrow *Sonnet* 90 7
Wing. Shaking her wings, devouring all in haste *Ven. and Adon.* 57
Fanning the hairs, who wave like feather'd wings 306
Borne by the trustless wings of false desire *Lucrece* 2
Coucheth the fowl below with his wings' shade 507
To pluck the quills from ancient ravens' wings 949
The crow may bathe his coal-black wings in mire 1009
Have added feathers to the learned's wing *Sonnet* 78 7
Herald sad and trumpet be, To whose sound chaste wings obey *Ph. and Tur.* 4
From this session interdict Every fowl of tyrant wing 10
Winged. Her contrite sighs unto the clouds bequeathed Her winged sprite *Lucrece* 1728
In winged speed no motion shall I know *Sonnet* 51 8
Wink. He winks, and turns his lips another way *Ven. and Adon.* 90
Then wink again, And I will wink; so shall the day seem night 121
His eyes begun To wink, being blinded with a greater light *Lucrece* 375
And moody Pluto winks while Orpheus plays 553
Will fix a sharp knife to affright mine eye; Who, if it wink, shall thereon fall and die 1139
When most I wink, then do mine eyes best see, For all the day they view things unrespected *Sonnet* 43 1
Although to-day thou fill Thy hungry eyes even till they wink with fullness 56 6
Winking. She dares not look; yet, winking, there appears Quick-shifting antics, ugly in her eyes *Lucrece* 458
Winter. Lust's winter comes ere summer half be done *Ven. and Adon.* 802
As winter meads when sun doth melt their snow *Lucrece* 1218
But chide rough winter that the flower hath kill'd. 1255
When forty winters shall besiege thy brow *Sonnet* 2 1
For never-resting time leads summer on To hideous winter 5 6
Flowers distill'd, though they with winter meet, Leese but their show 5 13
Let not winter's ragged hand deface In thee thy summer 6 1
Might uphold Against the stormy gusts of winter's day 13 11
Else call it winter, which being full of care Makes summer's welcome thrice more wish'd, more rare 56 13
How like a winter hath my absence been From thee! 97 1
That leaves look pale, dreading the winter's near 97 14
Yet seem'd it winter still, and, you away 98 13
Three winters cold Have from the forests shook three summers' pride 104 3
Age like winter weather; Youth like summer brave, age like winter bare *Pass. Pil.* 159
Wipe. Worse than a slavish wipe or birth-hour's blot *Lucrece* 537
Wipe the dim mist from thy doting eyne 643
Wiped. No outrageous thing From vassal actors can be wiped away 608
And wiped the brinish pearl from her bright eyes 1213
How may this forced stain be wiped from me? 1701
Wires. If hairs be wires, black wires grow on her head *Sonnet* 130 4
Wiry. When thou gently sway'st The wiry concord that mine ear confounds 128 4
Wisdom. Herein lives wisdom, beauty, and increase 11 5
Wise. How love is wise in folly, foolish-witty *Ven. and Adon.* 838
Strike the wise dumb and teach the fool to speak 1146
Priam, why art thou old and yet not wise? *Lucrece* 1550
Lest the wise world should look into your moan *Sonnet* 71 13
Be wise as thou art cruel; do not press My tongue-tied patience 140 1
What fool is not so wise To break an oath, to win a paradise? *Pass. Pil.* 41
My sighs so deep Procure to weep, In howling wise 277
Wiser. Take counsel of some wiser head, Neither too young nor yet unwed 303
Wish. Would they not wish the feast might ever last? *Ven. and Adon.* 447
And hold it for no sin To wish that I their father had not been *Lucrece* 210
The sweets we wish for turn to loathed sours 867
Many maiden gardens yet unset With virtuous wish *Sonnet* 16 7
Look, what is best, that best I wish in thee: This wish I have 37 13
Pity me then and wish I were renew'd 111 8
Whoever hath her wish, thou hast thy 'Will,' And 'Will' to boot 135 1
I sit and mark, And wish her lays were tuned like the lark *Pass. Pil.* 198
Wished. Makes summer's welcome thrice more wish'd, more rare *Sonnet* 56 14
Heart hath his hope, and eyes their wished sight *Pass. Pil.* 202

Wished. That the lover, sick to death, Wish'd himself the heaven's breath *Pass. Pil.* 234
Wishing her cheeks were gardens full of flowers . *Ven. and Adon.* 65
Wishing Adonis had his team to guide, So he were like him and by Venus' side . 179
Wishing me like to one more rich in hope . . . *Sonnet* 29 5
Wistly. O, what a sight it was, wistly to view How she came stealing to the wayward boy! . . . *Ven. and Adon.* 343
Blushing with him, wistly on him gazed . . . *Lucrece* 1355
The sun look'd on the world with glorious eye, Yet not so wistly as this queen on him . . . *Pass. Pil.* 82
Wit. Being mad before, how doth she now for wits? . *Ven. and Adon.* 249
Fair fall the wit that can so well defend her! . . . 472
Danger deviseth shifts; wit waits on fear . . . 690
Soothing the humour of fantastic wits . . . 850
Grief hath two tongues, and never woman yet Could rule them both without ten women's wit . . . 1008
And, all for want of wit, Make something nothing by augmenting it *Lucrece* 153
That eye which looks on her confounds his wits . . . 290
And useless barns the harvest of his wits . . . 859
Lending him wit that to bad debtors lends . . . 964
What wit sets down is blotted straight with will . . . 1299
Began to clothe his wit in state and pride . . . 1809
And arm'd his long-hid wits advisedly . . . 1816
Now set thy long-experienced wit to school . . . 1820
To hear with eyes belongs to love's fine wit . . *Sonnet* 23 14
I send this written embassage, To witness duty, not to show my wit . 26 4
Wit so poor as mine May make seem bare, in wanting words to show it 26 5
For whether beauty, birth, or wealth, or wit, Or any of these all . 37 5
The wits of former days To subjects worse have given admiring praise 59 13
And such a counterpart shall fame his wit . . . 84 11
If I might teach thee wit, better it were, Though not to love, yet, love, to tell me so . . . 140 5
But my five wits nor my five senses can Dissuade one foolish heart . 141 9
Advice is often seen By blunting us to make our wits more keen *L. Comp.* 161
Each several stone, With wit well blazon'd, smiled or made some moan 217
Witchcraft. What a hell of witchcraft lies In the small orb of one particular tear! . . . 288
With this she seizeth on his sweating palm . *Ven. and Adon.* 25
In a dull disdain, With leaden appetite, unapt to toy . . . 34
He burns with bashful shame: she with her tears . . . 49
Controlling what he was controlled with . . . 270
With her the horse, and left Adonis there: As they were mad . . 322
Turn, and return, indenting with the way . . . 704
With this, he breaketh from the sweet embrace, Of those fair arms . 811
Since her best work is ruin'd with thy rigour . . . 954
For he being dead, with him is beauty slain . . . 1019
With this, she falleth in the place she stood . . . 1121
With this, they all at once began to say . . . *Lucrece* 1709
So is it not with me as with that Muse Stirr'd by a painted beauty to his verse *Sonnet* 21 1
Withal. For who hath she to spend the night withal But idle sounds resembling parasites . . . *Ven. and Adon.* 847
May feel her heart—poor citizen! . . . rise up and fall, Beating her bulk, that his hand shakes withal . . . *Lucrece* 467
I, sick withal, the help of bath desired, And thither hied *Sonnet* 153 11
Withdrew. Like stars ashamed of day, themselves withdrew *Ven. and Adon.* 1032
Wither. If springing things be any jot diminish'd, They wither in their prime, prove nothing worth . . . 418
It is as good To wither in my breast as in his blood . . . 1182
But low shrubs wither at the cedar's root . . . *Lucrece* 665
The bark peel'd from the lofty pine, His leaves will wither . . 1168
Withered. No man inveigh against the wither'd flower . . . 1254
As flowers dead lie wither'd on the ground . . . *Pass. Pil.* 177
Withering. And therein show'st Thy lovers withering as thy sweet self grow'st *Sonnet* 126 4
Withhold. You have no reason to withhold me so . *Ven. and Adon.* 612
Within. Beauty within itself should not be wasted . . . 130
Within the circuit of this ivory pale . . . 230
Within this limit is relief enough . . . 235
Come not within his danger by thy will . . . 639
Within my bosom, whereon thou dost lie . . . 646
And says, within her bosom it shall dwell . . . 1173
Within whose face beauty and virtue strived . . . *Lucrece* 52
Within his thought her heavenly image sits . . . 288
Though I feel thou art, Within the gentle closure of my breast *Sonnet* 48 11
Within be fed, without be rich no more . . . 146 12
Without. Their copious stories oftentimes begun End without audience and are never done . . . *Ven. and Adon.* 846
Beauty itself doth of itself persuade The eyes of men without an orator *Lucrece* 30
Without the bed her other fair hand was, On the green coverlet . . 393
Within be fed, without be rich no more . . . *Sonnet* 146 12
Stood in doubt If best were as it was, or best without . *Lov. Comp.* 98
Witness this primrose bank whereon I lie . . *Ven. and Adon.* 151
Witness the entertainment that he gave . . . 1108
To thee I send this written embassage, To witness duty . *Sonnet* 26 4
To this I witness call the fools of time, Which die for goodness . 124 13
Do witness bear Thy black is fairest in my judgement's place . 131 11
Register of lies, What unapproved witness dost thou bear! . *Lov. Comp.* 53
Wittily. Which cunning love did wittily prevent . *Ven. and Adon.* 471
Woe. Her words are done, her woes the more increasing . . . 254
Sorrow to shepherds, woe unto the birds . . . 455
For love can comment upon every woe . . . 714
'Ay me!' she cries, and twenty times 'Woe, woe!' . . . 833
Her heavy anthem still concludes in woe . . . 839
Variable passions throng her constant woe . . . 967
Thy weal and woe are both of them extremes . . . 987
That all love's pleasure shall not match his woe . . . 1140
Fellowship in woe doth woe assuage . . . *Lucrece* 790
Base watch of woes, sin's pack-horse, virtue's snare . . . 928
Enchained me To endless date of never-ending woes . . . 935
Old woes, not infant sorrows, bear them mild . . . 1096
Deep woes roll forward like a gentle flood . . . 1118
Thou bear'st thy part, To keep thy sharp woes waking . . . 1136
Nor why her fair cheeks over-wash'd with woe . . . 1225
My woes are tedious, though my words are brief . . . 1309
Here folds she up the tenour of her woe, Her certain sorrow writ uncertainly 1310
When every part a part of woe doth bear . . . 1327
So woe hath wearied woe, moan tired moan . . . 1363
Woe. And shapes her sorrow to the beldam's woes . . . *Lucrece* 1458
I'll tune thy woes with my lamenting tongue . . . 1465
Let guiltless souls be freed from guilty woe . . . 1482
Here feelingly she weeps Troy's painted woes . . . 1492
So mild, that Patience seem'd to scorn his woes . . . 1505
A brow unbent, that seem'd to welcome woe . . . 1509
Though woe be heavy, yet it seldom sleeps . . . 1574
Losing her woes in shows of discontent . . . 1580
Ere once she can discharge one word of woe . . . 1605
In me moe woes than words are now depending . . . 1615
With head declined, and voice damm'd up with woe . . . 1661
Which speechless woe of his poor she attendeth . . . 1674
My woe too sensible thy passion maketh More feeling painful . . 1678
Let it then suffice To drown one woe, one pair of weeping eyes . . 1680
As pitying Lucrece' woes, Corrupted blood some watery token shows . 1747
'Woe, woe,' quoth Collatine, 'she was my wife, I owed her' . . 1802
Seeing such emulation in their woe . . . 1808
Why, Collatine, is woe the cure for woe? . . . 1821
And with old woes new wail my dear time's waste . . . *Sonnet* 30 4
And weep afresh love's long since cancell'd woe . . . 30 7
And heavily from woe to woe tell o'er The sad account . . 30 10
Heavy tears, badges of either's woe . . . 44 14
The beast that bears me, tired with my woe, Plods dully on . . 50 5
I in your sweet thoughts would be forgot If thinking on me then should make you woe . . . 71 8
Ah, do not, . . . Come in the rearward of a conquer'd woe . . 90 6
And other strains of woe, which now seem woe, Compared with loss of thee will not seem so . . . 90 13
O, that our night of woe might have remember'd My deepest sense . 120 9
Yet so they mourn, becoming of their woe . . . 127 13
A bliss in proof, and proved, a very woe . . . 129 11
In the brine That season'd woe had pelleted in tears . *Lov. Comp.* 18
As often shrieking undistinguish'd woe, In clamours of all size . . 20
Desires to know In brief the grounds and motives of her woe . . 63
But, woe is me! too early I attended A youthful suit . . . 78
To blush at speeches rank, to weep at woes . . . 307
Woeful. And sings extemporally a woeful ditty . *Ven. and Adon.* 836
Whispers in his ears . . . , As if they heard the woeful words . . 1126
A woeful hostess brooks not merry guests . . . *Lucrece* 1125
When she saw my woeful state, Straight in her heart did mercy come *Sonnet* 145 4
My woeful self, that did in freedom stand . . *Lov. Comp.* 143
Wolf. As the wolf doth grin before he barketh . *Ven. and Adon.* 459
If he had spoke, the wolf would leave his prey . . . 1097
No noise but owls' and wolves' death-boding cries . . *Lucrece* 165
The wolf hath seized his prey, the poor lamb cries . . . 677
Thou set'st the wolf where he the lamb may get . . . 878
How many lambs might the stern wolf betray! . . . *Sonnet* 96 9
Woman. Art thou a woman's son, and canst not feel What 'tis to love? *Ven. and Adon.* 201
Thing like a man, but of no woman bred! . . . 214
Grief hath two tongues, and never woman yet Could rule them both without ten women's wit . . . 1007
If ever man were moved with woman's moans, Be moved with my tears *Lucr.* 587
A woman's face with Nature's own hand painted Hast thou . *Sonnet* 20 1
A woman's gentle heart, but not acquainted With shifting change, as is false women's fashion . . . 20 3
And for a woman wert thou first created . . . 20 9
When a woman woos, what woman's son Will sourly leave her till she have prevailed? . . . 41 7
The worser spirit a woman colour'd ill . . . 144 4
My worser spirit a woman colour'd ill . . . *Pass. Pil.* 18
A woman I forswore; but I will prove, Thou being a goddess, I forswore not thee . . . 33
A woman's nay doth stand for nought . . . 340
Were kisses all the joys in bed, One woman would another wed . 346
Womb. Whose hollow womb resounds like heaven's thunder *Ven. and Adon.* 268
From earth's dark womb some gentle gust doth get . . *Lucrece* 549
Thy sea within a puddle's womb is hearsed . . . 657
Where is she so fair whose unear'd womb Disdains the tillage of thy husbandry? . . . *Sonnet* 3 5
Making their tomb the womb wherein they grew . . . 86 4
Like widow'd wombs after their lords' decease . . . 97 8
From off a hill whose concave womb re-worded A plaintful story *Lov. Comp.*
Women. Let mild women to him lose their mildness . . *Lucrece* 979
For men have marble, women waxen, minds . . . 1240
Poor women's faces are their own faults' books . . . 1253
O, let it not be hild Poor women's faults, that they are so fulfill'd With men's abuses . . . 1258
Those proud lords, to blame, Make weak-made women tenants to their shame . . . 1260
Which steals men's eyes, and women's souls amazeth . *Sonnet* 20 8
Since she prick'd thee out for women's pleasure, Mine be thy love . 20 13
For now I see Inconstancy More in women than in men remain . *Pass. Pil.* 262
Had women been so strong as men, In faith, you had not had it then . . 321
The wiles and guiles that women work, Dissembled with an outward show 335
Think women still to strive with men, To sin and never for to saint . 341
If to women he be bent, They have at commandement . . . 417
Won. Her husband's fame, Won in the fields of fruitful Italy . *Lucrece* 107
And he hath won what he would lose again . . . 688
Gentle thou art and therefore to be won . . . *Sonnet* 41 5
Wonder. Vouchsafe, thou wonder, to alight thy steed . *Ven. and Adon.* 13
Whereat the impartial gazer late did wonder . . . 748
'Wonder of time,' quoth she, 'this is my spite' . . . 1133
Answers with surmise, In silent wonder of still-gazing eyes . *Lucrece* 84
That nothing in him seem'd inordinate, Save sometime too much wonder of his eye . . . 95
What the old world could say To this composed wonder of your frame *Son.* 59 10
Nor did I wonder at the lily's white, Nor praise the deep vermilion in the rose . . . 98 9
We, which now behold these present days, Have eyes to wonder . 106 14
All ignorant that soul that sees thee without wonder . . *Pass. Pil.* 65
But in them it were a wonder . . . *Ph. and Tur.* 32
Wondering. Met far from home, wondering each other's chance . *Lucrece* 1596
Who, wondering at him, did his words allow . . . 1845
Not wondering at the present nor the past . . *Sonnet* 123 10
Wondrous. But having thee at vantage,—wondrous dread! *Ven. and Adon.* 635
And chid the painter for his wondrous skill . . . *Lucrece* 1528
Still constant in a wondrous excellence . . . *Sonnet* 105 6
Three themes in one, which wondrous scope affords . . . 105 12

Wont. And on that pillow lay Where thou wast wont to rest thy weary head *Lucrece* 1621
In the spring When I was wont to greet it with my lays *Sonnet* 102 6
My curtail dog, that wont to have play'd, Plays not at all *Pass. Pil.* 273
Wonted. Whose wonted lily white With purple tears, that his wound wept, was drench'd *Ven. and Adon.* 1053
Or if thou wilt permit the sun to climb His wonted height *Lucrece* 776
Woo. And like a bold-faced suitor 'gins to woo him *Ven. and Adon.* 6
Then woo thyself, be of thyself rejected 159
Being proud, as females are, to see him woo her 309
But then woos best when most his choice is froward 570
When a woman woos, what woman's son Will sourly leave her till she have prevailed? *Sonnet* 41 7
As thou lovest those Whom thine eyes woo as mine importune thee 142 10
Till now did ne'er invite, nor never woo *Lov. Comp.* 182
Venus, with young Adonis sitting by her Under a myrtle shade, began to woo him *Pass. Pil.* 144
Wood. Unto the wood they hie them, Out-stripping crows that strive to over-fly them *Ven. and Adon.* 323
Life-poisoning pestilence and frenzies wood 740
Their light blown out in some mistrustful wood 826
When thou, my music, music play'st, Upon that blessed wood *Sonnet* 128 2
My poor lips, . . . At the wood's boldness by thee blushing stand 128 8
Making dead wood more blest than living lips 128 12
Woodman. He is no woodman that doth bend his bow To strike a poor unseasonable doe *Lucrece* 580
Wooed. I have been woo'd, as I entreat thee now, Even by the stern and direful god of war *Ven. and Adon.* 97
Her eyes woo'd still, his eyes disdain'd the wooing 358
So thou be good, slander doth but approve Thy worth the greater, being woo'd of time *Sonnet* 70 6
Wooing. Her eyes woo'd still, his eyes disdain'd the wooing *Ven. and Adon.* 358
Wooing his purity with her foul pride *Sonnet* 144 8
Wooing his purity with her fair pride *Pass. Pil.* 22
Word. Speak, fair; but speak fair words, or else be mute *Ven. and Adon.* 208
Her words are done, her woes the more increasing 254
Free vent of words love's fire doth assuage 334
His meaning struck her ere his words begun 462
Foul words and frowns must not repel a lover 573
And with that word she spied the hunted boar 900
Even at this word she hears a merry horn 1025
Whispers in his ears . . . , As if they heard the woeful words 1126
So his unhallow'd haste her words delays *Lucrece* 552
Out, idle words, servants to shallow fools! 1016
This helpless smoke of words doth me no right 1027
Sometime her grief is dumb and hath no words; Sometime 'tis mad 1105
My woes are tedious, though my words are brief 1309
She would not blot the letter With words, till action might become them better 1323
Sorrow ebbs, being blown with wind of words 1330
Pawn'd honest looks, but laid no words to gage 1351
But for loss of Nestor's golden words, It seem'd they would debate with angry swords 1420
And bitter words to ban her cruel foes 1460
She lends them words, and she their looks doth borrow 1498
Whose words like wildfire burnt the shining glory Of rich-built Ilion 1523
Ere once she can discharge one word of woe 1605
Collatine and his consorted lords With sad attention long to hear her words 1610
'Few words,' quoth she, 'shall fit the trespass best' 1613
In me moe woes than words are now depending 1615
Swearing, unless I took all patiently, I should not live to speak another word 1642
Who, mad that sorrow should his use control, Or keep him from heart-easing words so long, Begins to talk 1782
Through his lips do throng Weak words, so thick come in his poor heart's aid 1784
For sportive words and uttering foolish things 1813
Who, wondering at him, did his words allow 1845
Wit so poor as mine May make seem bare, in wanting words to show it *Sonnet* 26 6
That every word doth almost tell my name 76 7
So all my best is dressing old words new 76 11
He lends thee virtue and he stole that word From thy behaviour 79 9
The dedicated words which writers use Of their fair subject 82 3
Sympathized In true plain words by thy true-telling friend 82 12
I think good thoughts whilst other write good words 85 5
Though words come hindmost, holds his rank before 85 12
Others for the breath of words respect, Me for my dumb thoughts 85 13
All my argument, 'Fair, kind, and true' varying to other words 105 10
Lest sorrow lend me words and words express The manner of my pity-wanting pain 140 3
Thought characters and words merely but art *Lov. Comp.* 174
'Wander,' a word for shadows like myself *Pass. Pil.* 191
Words are easy like the wind; Faithful friends are hard to find 405
Wordless. And, wordless, so greets heaven for his success *Lucrece* 112
Wore. Ne'er saw the beauteous livery that he wore *Ven. and Adon.* 1107
Long he questioned With modest Lucrece, and wore out the night *Lucrece* 123
For why her face wore sorrow's livery 1222
Work. Since her best work is ruin'd with thy rigour *Ven. and Adon.* 954
This desire Might have excuse to work upon his wife *Lucrece* 235
Thus treason works ere traitors be espied 361
If thou deny, then force must work my way 513
Such sweet observance in this work was had 1385
Much imaginary work was there; Conceit deceitful, so compact, so kind 1422
Those hours, that with gentle work did frame The lovely gaze *Sonnet* 5 1
Then begins a journey in my head, To work my mind, when body's work's expired 27 4
And broils root out the work of masonry 55 6
In others' works thou dost but mend the style 78 11
My nature is subdued To what it works in, like the dyer's hand 111 7
That heretic, Which works on leases of short-number'd hours 124 10
What me your minister, for you obeys, Works under you *Lov. Comp.* 230
The wiles and guiles that women work, Dissembled with an outward show *Pass. Pil.* 335
Workest. Why work'st thou mischief in thy pilgrimage? *Lucrece* 960
Workings. Whate'er thy thoughts or thy heart's workings be *Sonnet* 93 11
Workman. The well-skill'd workman this mild image drew *Lucrece* 1520
Workmanship. His art with nature's workmanship at strife *Ven. and Adon.* 291
To cross the curious workmanship of nature 734
World. Nature that made thee, with herself at strife, Saith that the world hath ending with thy life 12
World. Look, the world's comforter, with weary gait, His day's hot task hath ended in the west *Ven. and Adon.* 529
Whose full perfection all the world amazes 634
The lamp that burns by night Dries up his oil to lend the world his light 756
The world will hold thee in disdain, Sith in thy pride so fair a hope is slain 761
Who doth the world so gloriously behold That cedar-tops and hills seem burnish'd gold 857
Look, how the world's poor people are amazed At apparitions 925
Alas, poor world, what treasure hast thou lost! 1075
Thus weary of the world, away she hies 1189
Honour and beauty, in the owner's arms, Are weakly fortress'd from a world of harms *Lucrece* 28
Proving from world's minority their right 67
Till sable Night, . . . Upon the world dim darkness doth display 118
Lucrece to their sight Must sell her joy, her life, her world's delight 385
A pair of maiden worlds unconquered, Save of their lord 408
These worlds in Tarquin new ambition bred 411
But when a black-faced cloud the world doth threat 547
To clear her From that suspicion which the world might bear her 1321
Thou that art now the world's fresh ornament *Sonnet* 1 9
Pity the world, or else this glutton be, To eat the world's due 1 13
Thou dost beguile the world, unbless some mother 3 4
The world will wail thee, like a makeless wife; The world will be thy widow and still weep 9 4
Look, what an unthrift in the world doth spend Shifts but his place, for still the world enjoys it 9 9
Beauty's waste hath in the world an end 9 11
And threescore year would make the world away 11 8
To the wide world and all her fading sweets 19 7
And from the forlorn world his visage hide 33 7
Suns of the world may stain when heaven's sun staineth 33 14
All posterity That wear this world out to the ending doom 55 12
That I might see what the old world could say To this composed wonder 59 9
Those parts of thee that the world's eye doth view Want nothing 69 1
Give warning to the world that I am fled From this vile world 71 3
Lest the wise world should look into your moan 71 13
Lest the world should task you to recite What merit lived in me 72 1
Then better'd that the world may see my pleasure 75 8
Though I, once gone, to all the world must die 81 6
When all the breathers of this world are dead 81 12
Now, while the world is bent my deeds to cross, Join with the spite of fortune 90 2
Not mine own fears, nor the prophetic soul Of the wide world 107 2
You are my all the world, And I must strive To know my shames 112 5
That all the world besides methinks are dead 112 14
All this the world well knows; yet none knows well To shun the heaven that leads men to this hell 129 13
Which my heart knows the wide world's common place 137 10
Unlearned in the world's false subtleties 138 4
Now this ill-wresting world is grown so bad 140 11
What means the world to say it is not so? 148 6
Storming her world with sorrow's wind and rain *Lov. Comp.* 7
Untutor'd youth, Unskilful in the world's false forgeries *Pass. Pil.* 4
'Gainst whom the world could not hold argument 30
The sun look'd on the world with glorious eye 81
If that the world and love were young 369
World-without-end. Nor dare I chide the world-without-end hour *Sonnet* 57 5
Worm. Grim-grinning ghost, earth's worm, what dost thou mean To stifle beauty? *Ven. and Adon.* 933
Why should the worm intrude the maiden bud? *Lucrece* 848
Like a goodly champaign plain, Lays open all the little worms that creep 1248
Thou art much too fair To be death's conquest and make worms thine heir *Sonnet* 6 14
That I am fled From this vile world, with vilest worms to dwell 71 4
So then thou hast but lost the dregs of life, The prey of worms 74 10
Shall worms, inheritors of this excess, Eat up thy charge? 146 7
Worm-holes. To fill with worm-holes stately monuments *Lucrece* 946
Wormwood. Thy sugar'd tongue to bitter wormwood taste 893
Worn-out. Even so this pattern of the worn-out age Pawn'd honest looks 1350
Worse. What were thy lips the worse for one poor kiss? *Ven. and Adon.* 207
That worse than Tantalus' is her annoy, To clip Elysium and to lack her joy 599
A mischief worse than civil home-bred strife 764
Your treatise makes me like you worse and worse 774
Worse than a slavish wipe or birth-hour's blot *Lucrece* 537
The wits of former days To subjects worse have given admiring praise *Sonnet* 59 14
Not making worse what nature made so clear 84 10
Being fond on praise, which makes your praises worse 84 14
Lilies that fester smell far worse than weeds 94 14
And worse essays proved thee my best of love 110 8
Worser. Urging the worser sense for vantage still *Lucrece* 249
But with a pure appeal seeks to the heart, Which once corrupted takes the worser part 294
What terror 'tis! but she, in worser taking, From sleep disturbed 453
The worser spirit a woman colour'd ill *Sonnet* 144 4
My worser spirit a woman colour'd ill *Pass. Pil.* 18
Worship. When all my best doth worship thy defect *Sonnet* 149 11
Worshipper. Little suspecteth the false worshipper *Lucrece* 86
Worst. But she is not her own: The worst is but denial and reproving 242
He in the worst sense construes their denial 324
Yet, do thy worst, old Time: despite thy wrong *Sonnet* 19 13
Then if he thrive and I be cast away, The worst was this 80 14
So shall I taste At first the very worst of fortune's might 90 12
But do thy worst to steal thyself away 92 1
Then need I not to fear the worst of wrongs 92 5
Yet what the best is take the worst to be 137 4
That, in my mind, thy worst all best exceeds 150 8
Worth. If springing things be any jot diminish'd, They wither in their prime, prove nothing worth *Ven. and Adon.* 418
What face remains alive that's worth the viewing? Whose tongue is music now? 1076
A tatter'd weed, of small worth held *Sonnet* 2 4
Neither in inward worth nor outward fair 16 11
Take all my comfort of thy worth and truth 37 4
Be thou the tenth Muse, ten times more in worth Than those old nine 38 9
O, how thy worth with manners may I sing? 39 1
Like stones of worth they thinly placed are 52 7
And yet to times in hope my verse shall stand, Praising thy worth 60 14
And for myself mine own worth do define, As I all other in all worths surmount 62 7

Worth. So thou be good, slander doth but approve Thy worth the greater, being woo'd of time . . . *Sonnet* 70 6
I am shamed by that which I bring forth, And so should you, to love things nothing worth . . . 72 14
The worth of that is that which it contains . . . 74 13
Since your worth, wide as the ocean is, The humble as the proudest sail doth bear . . . 80 5
Finding thy worth a limit past my praise . . . 82 6
Speaking of worth, what worth in you doth grow . . . 83 8
The charter of thy worth gives thee releasing . . . 87 3
Thyself thou gavest, thy own worth then not knowing . . . 87 9
Is of more worth Than when it hath my added praise beside . . . 103 3
They had not skill enough your worth to sing . . . 106 12
Whose worth's unknown, although his height be taken . . . 116 8
Each stone's dear nature, worth, and quality . . . *Lov. Comp.* 210
When thou impressest, what are precepts worth Of stale example? . . . 267
Worthier. Thy lovely argument Deserves the travail of a worthier pen *Sonnet* 79 6
Worthiness. Blessed are you, whose worthiness gives scope . . . 52 13
Worthless. That done, some worthless slave of thine I'll slay *Lucrece* 515
Being wreck'd, I am a worthless boat, He of tall building and of goodly pride . . . *Sonnet* 80 11
Spend'st thou thy fury on some worthless song? . . . 100 3
Worthy. Not that devour'd, but that which doth devour, Is worthy blame *Lucrece* 1257
Thou worthy lord Of that unworthy wife that greeteth thee . . . 1303
To show me worthy of thy sweet respect . . . *Sonnet* 26 12
If aught in me Worthy perusal stand against thy sight . . . 38 6
But thou, to whom my jewels trifles are, Most worthy comfort . . . 48 6
Dear love, forget me quite, For you in me can nothing worthy prove . . . 72 4
More worthy I to be beloved of thee . . . 150 14
Let reason rule things worthy blame, As well as fancy partial might *Pass. Pil.* 301
Wot. God wot, it was defect Of spirit, life, and bold audacity *Lucrece* 1345
All my merry jigs are quite forgot, All my lady's love is lost, God wot *Pass. Pil.* 254
Would. Backward she push'd him, as she would be thrust *Ven. and Adon.* 41
She would, he will not in her arms be bound . . . 226
Would thou wert as I am, and I a man . . . 369
Hast thou a tongue? O, would thou hadst not, or I had no hearing! . . . 428
They answer all ''Tis so:' And would say after her, if she said 'No' . . . 852
And therefore would he put his bonnet on, Under whose brim the gaudy sun would peep . . . 1087
They both would strive who first should dry his tears . . . 1092
The lion walk'd along Behind some hedge, because he would not fear him . . . 1094
When he hath sung, The tiger would be tame and gently hear him . . . 1096
If he had spoke, the wolf would leave his prey . . . 1097
And he hath won what he would lose again . . . *Lucrece* 688
And now she would the caged cloister fly . . . *Lov. Comp.* 249
Wouldst. But that thou told'st me thou wouldst hunt the boar *V. and A.* 614
O, this dread night, wouldst thou one hour come back! . . . *Lucrece* 965
If thou wouldst use the strength of all thy state! But do not so *Sonnet* 96 12
Wound. The bearing earth with his hard hoof he wounds *Ven. and Adon.* 267
My heart all whole as thine, thy heart my wound . . . 370
And there another licking of his wound . . . 915
And never wound the heart with looks again . . . 1042
The wide wound that the boar had trench'd In his soft flank; whose wonted lily white With purple tears, that his wound wept, was drench'd . . . 1052
That her sight dazzling makes the wound seem three . . . 1064
Bearing away the wound that nothing healeth . . . *Lucrece* 731
To see the salve doth make the wound ache more . . . 1116
My honour I'll bequeath unto the knife That wounds my body so dishonoured . . . 1185
Mine honour be the knife's that makes my wound . . . 1201
Staring on Priam's wounds with her old eyes . . . 1448
And drop sweet balm in Priam's painted wound . . . 1466
And friend to friend gives unadvised wounds . . . 1488
'Fool, fool!' quoth she, 'his wounds will not be sore' . . . 1568
'Tis he, That guides this hand to give this wound to me . . . 1722
Through her wounds doth fly Life's lasting date . . . 1728
Do wounds help wounds, or grief help grievous deeds? . . . 1822
Burying in Lucrece' wound his folly's show . . . 1810
That heals the wound and cures not the disgrace . . . *Sonnet* 34 8
That makes my heart to groan For that deep wound it gives my friend and me . . . 133 2
Wound me not with thine eye but with thy tongue . . . 139 3
What need'st thou wound with cunning when thy might Is more than my o'er-press'd defence can bide? . . . 139 7
He saw more wounds than one, And blushing fled, and left her all alone *Pass. Pil.* 129
Wounded. How he in peace is wounded, not in war . . . *Lucrece* 831
Then tender'd The humble salve which wounded bosoms fits *Sonnet* 120 12
Look here, what tributes wounded fancies sent me . . . *Lov. Comp.* 197
For of the two the trusty knight was wounded with disdain . . . *Pass. Pil.* 221
Woundest. Thou wrong'st his honour, wound'st his princely name *Lucrece* 599
Wounding. Ear's deep-sweet music, and heart's deep-sore wounding *Ven. and Adon.* 432
A smile recures the wounding of a frown . . . 465
May feel her heart—poor citizen!—distress'd, Wounding itself to death, rise up and fall . . . *Lucrece* 466
Woven. And now his woven girths he breaks asunder *Ven. and Adon.* 266
Wrack. Forgetting shame's pure blush and honour's wrack . . . 558
Yet am I guilty of thy honour's wrack; Yet for thy honour did I entertain him . . . *Lucrece* 841
I could prevent this storm and shun thy wrack! . . . 966
Nature, sovereign mistress over wrack . . . *Sonnet* 126 5
Wrapped. O rash false heat, wrapp'd in repentant cold! . . . *Lucrece* 48
Wrapp'd and confounded in a thousand fears . . . 456
O, how are they wrapp'd in with infamies That from their own misdeeds askance their eyes! . . . 636
Wrath, envy, treason, rape, and murder's rages . . . 909
This load of wrath that burning Troy doth bear . . . 1474
Cold modesty, hot wrath, Both fire from hence and chill extincture hath *Lov. Comp.* 293
Wreaked. The boar provoked my tongue; Be wreak'd on him *V. and A.* 1004
Wreathed. Like one that spies an adder Wreathed up in fatal folds just in his way . . . 879
Wreaths. With bruised arms and wreaths of victory . . . *Lucrece* 110
Wreck. Like a red morn, that ever yet betoken'd Wreck to the seaman . . . 454
Time's ruin, beauty's wreck, and grim care's reign . . . 1451
Wrecked. Being wreck'd, I am a worthless boat, He of tall building and of goodly pride . . . *Sonnet* 80 11
Wreckful. Against the wreckful siege of battering days . . . 65 6
Wreck-threatening. Beat at thy rocky and wreck-threatening heart *Lucr.* 590
Wretch. And when thou hast on foot the purblind hare, Mark the poor wretch . . . *Ven. and Adon.* 680
Then shalt thou see the dew-bedabbled wretch Turn, and return . . . 703
Poor wretches have remorse in poor abuses . . . *Lucrece* 269
As if by some instinct the wretch did know His rider loved not speed *Sonnet* 50 7
My body being dead, The coward conquest of a wretch's knife . . . 74 11
Thy proud heart's slave and vassal wretch to be . . . 141 12
Wretched. Betrays To slanderous tongues and wretched hateful days *Lucr.* 161
Such wretched hands such wretched blood should spill . . . 999
Wretched I, To imitate thee well, against my heart Will fix a sharp knife . . . 1136
At last she sees a wretched image bound . . . 1501
With sad set eyes, and wretched arms across . . . 1662
But, wretched as he is, he strives in vain . . . 1665
Thy wretched wife mistook the matter so, To slay herself . . . 1826
Wretched in this alone, that thou mayst take All this away and me most wretched make . . . *Sonnet* 91 13
What wretched errors hath my heart committed! . . . 119 5
Her skill May time disgrace and wretched minutes kill . . . 126 8
Wretchedness. Or free that soul which wretchedness hath chain'd *Lucrece* 900
Wrings. He wrings her nose, he strikes her on the cheeks, He bends her fingers, holds her pulses hard *Ven. and Adon.* 475
Wringing. You hurt my hand with wringing; let us part . . . 421
Wrinkle. Thou canst not see one wrinkle in my brow . . . 139
Her pity-pleading eyes are sadly fixed In the remorseless wrinkles of his face *Lucrece* 562
Her cheeks with chaps and wrinkles were disguised . . . 1452
Shalt see Despite of wrinkles this thy golden time . . . *Sonnet* 3 12
When hours have drain'd his blood and fill'd his brow With lines and wrinkles . . . 63 4
The wrinkles which thy glass will truly show Of mouthed graves will give thee memory . . . 77 5
The false heart's history Is writ in moods and frowns and wrinkles strange . . . 93 8
My love's sweet face survey, If Time have any wrinkle graven there . . . 100 10
Nor gives to necessary wrinkles place . . . 108 11
Wrinkled. Respect and reason, wait on wrinkled age! . . . *Lucrece* 275
Wrinkled-old. Were I hard-favour'd, foul, or wrinkled-old *Ven. and Adon.* 133
Writ. That the star-gazers, having writ on death, May say, the plague is banish'd by thy breath . . . 509
Secrecies Writ in the glassy margents of such books . . . *Lucrece* 102
The illiterate, that know not how To cipher what is writ in learned books 811
And as his due writ in my testament . . . 1183
The cause craves haste, and it will soon be writ . . . 1295
Here folds she up the tenour of her woe, Her certain sorrow writ uncertainly 1311
And on it writ 'At Ardea to my lord with more than haste' . . . 1331
O, learn to read what silent love hath writ . . . *Sonnet* 23 13
If you read this line, remember not The hand that writ it . . . 71 6
Let him but copy what in you is writ . . . 84 9
In many's looks the false heart's history Is writ in moods . . . 93 8
Those lines that I before have writ do lie . . . 115 1
If this be error and upon me proved, I never writ, nor no man ever loved . . . 116 14
Write. Her maid is gone, and she prepares to write . . . *Lucrece* 1296
If I could write the beauty of your eyes . . . *Sonnet* 17 5
O, let me, true in love, but truly write, And then believe me . . . 21 9
Who's so dumb that cannot write to thee, When thou thyself dost give invention light? . . . 38 7
Why write I still all one, ever the same, And keep invention in a noted weed? . . . 76 5
I always write of you, And you and love are still my argument . . . 76 9
O, how I faint when I of you do write! . . . 80 1
He that writes of you, if he can tell That you are you, so dignifies his story . . . 84 7
I think good thoughts whilst other write good words . . . 85 5
By spirits taught to write Above a mortal pitch, that struck me dead . . . 86 5
O, blame me not, if I no more can write! . . . 103 5
He learn'd but surety-like to write for me . . . 134 7
Writers. The dedicated words which writers use Of their fair subject . . . 82 3
Written. To thee I send this written embassage, To witness duty . . . 26 3
Wrong. Red cheeks and fiery eyes blaze forth her wrong *Ven. and Adon.* 219
For lovers say, the heart hath treble wrong When it is barr'd the aidance of the tongue . . . 329
Thy mermaid's voice hath done me double wrong . . . 429
'Tis he, foul creature, that hath done thee wrong . . . 1005
In that high task hath done her beauty wrong . . . *Lucrece* 80
What wrong, what shame, what sorrow I shall breed . . . 499
To wrong the wronger till he render right . . . 943
I will not wrong thy true affection so, To flatter thee with an infringed oath 1060
And shame that might ensue By that her death, to do her husband wrong 1264
He did her wrong, To give her so much grief and not a tongue . . . 1462
And rail on Pyrrhus that hath done him wrong . . . 1467
What wrong else may be imagined By foul enforcement might be done to me 1622
With swift pursuit to venge this wrong of mine . . . 1691
By chaste Lucrece' soul that late complain'd Her wrongs to us . . . 1840
Despite thy wrong, My love shall in my verse ever live young *Sonnet* 19 13
It is a greater grief To bear love's wrong than hate's known injury . . . 40 12
Those pretty wrongs that liberty commits . . . 41 1
To thee I so belong, That for thy right myself will bear all wrong . . . 88 14
Lest I, too much profane, should do it wrong . . . 89 11
Then need I not to fear the worst of wrongs . . . 92 5
Nor I to none alive, That my steel'd sense or changes right or wrong . . . 112 8
Call not me to justify the wrong That thy unkindness lays upon my heart . . . 139 1
Celestial as thou art, O do not love that wrong . . . *Pass. Pil.* 69
Wronged. How Tarquin wronged me, I Collatine . . . *Lucrece* 819
'Thou wronged lord of Rome,' quoth he, 'arise' . . . 1818
Wronger. To wrong the wronger till he render right . . . 943
Wrongest. Thou wrong'st his honour, wound'st his princely name . . . 599
Wrongfully. And right perfection wrongfully disgraced . . . *Sonnet* 66 7
Wrought. Now she unweaves the web that she hath wrought *Ven. and Adon.* 991
So from himself impiety hath wrought . . . *Lucrece* 341
Nature, as she wrought thee, fell a-doting . . . *Sonnet* 20 10
But that so much of earth and water wrought I must attend time's leisure with my moan . . . 44 11
One silly cross Wrought all my loss; O frowning Fortune! . . . *Pass. Pil.* 258

Y

Yea, though I die, the scandal will survive, And be an eye-sore . *Lucrece* 204
With a steadfast eye Receives the scroll without or yea or no . . 1340
Take all my loves, my love, yea, take them all . *Sonnet* 40 1
Year. To drive infection from the dangerous year . *Ven. and Adon.* 508
Measure my strangeness with my unripe years . 524
And straight, in pity of his tender years, They both would strive who first should dry his tears . 1091
And threescore year would make the world away . *Sonnet* 11 8
Thy beauty and thy years full well befits, For still temptation follows where thou art . 41 3
Therefore are feasts so solemn and so rare, Since, seldom coming, in the long year set . 52 6
Speak of the spring and foison of the year . 53 9
That time of year thou mayst in me behold . 73 1
How like a winter hath my absence been From thee, the pleasure of the fleeting year! . 97 2
And age in love loves not to have years told . 138 12
Although I know my years be past the best . *Pass. Pil.* 6
And age, in love, loves not to have years told . 12
Whether unripe years did want conceit . 51
Yearly. My beauty as the spring doth yearly grow . *Ven. and Adon.* 141
Yell. To stop the loud pursuers in their yell . 688
Yellow. When yellow leaves, or none, or few, do hang Upon those boughs which shake against the cold . *Sonnet* 73 2
Three beauteous springs to yellow autumn turn'd . 104 5
Yellowed. So should my papers yellow'd with their age Be scorn'd . 17 9
Yelping. Even so the timorous yelping of the hounds Appals her senses and her spirit confounds . *Ven. and Adon.* 881
Yes. If he be dead,—O no, it cannot be, Seeing his beauty, thou shouldst strike at it:—O yes, it may . 939
O yes, dear friend, I pardon crave of thee . *Pass. Pil.* 141
Yet. She bathes in water, yet her fire must burn . *Ven. and Adon.* 94
Though I were dumb, yet his proceedings teach thee . 406
Yet should I be in love by touching thee . 438
Like a red morn, that ever yet betoken'd Wreck to the seaman . 453
And yet she hears no tidings of her love . 867
How strange it seems Not to believe, and yet too credulous . 986
'And yet,' quoth she, 'behold two Adons dead!' . 1070
Yet ever to obtain his will resolving . *Lucrece* 129
Wickedly he stalks, And gazeth on her yet unstained bed . 366
Yet am I guilty of thy honour's wrack; Yet for thy honour did I entertain him . 841
For slander's mark was ever yet the fair . *Sonnet* 70 2
See where it lies, Yet what the best is take the worst to be . 137 4
I might as yet have been a spreading flower, Fresh to myself *Lov. Comp.* 75
Yield. Once more the ruby-colour'd portal open'd, Which to his speech did honey passage yield . *Ven. and Adon.* 452
And yields at last to every light impression . 566
Like soldiers, when their captain once doth yield, They basely fly . 893
The coward captive vanquished doth yield To those two armies . *Lucrece* 75
Each unwilling portal yields him way . 309
But if thou yield, I rest thy secret friend . 526
By heaven, I will not hear thee: Yield to my love . 668
Yield to my hand; my hand shall conquer thee . 1210
And to their hope they such odd action yield . 1433
The earth can yield me but a common grave . *Sonnet* 81 7
Till each to razed oblivion yield his part Of thee . 122 7
Nature hath charged me that I hoard them not, But yield them up *L. Comp.* 221
Her feeble force will yield at length . *Pass. Pil.* 319
That hills and valleys, dales and fields, And all the craggy mountains yields 356
Yielded. Yet did I not, as some my equals did, Demand of him, nor being desired yielded . *Lov. Comp.* 149
Yielding. Now quick desire hath caught the yielding prey *Ven. and Adon.* 547
Which with a yielding latch, and with no more, Hath barr'd him from the blessed thing he sought . *Lucrece* 339
Kill both thyself and her for yielding so . 1036
That was not forced; that never was inclined To accessary yieldings . 1658
Yoke. Away she hies, And yokes her silver doves . *Ven. and Adon.* 1190
Unconquered, Save of their lord no bearing yoke they knew . *Lucrece* 409
Unless thou yoke thy liking to my will, I'll murder straight . 1633
Yoking. And on his neck her yoking arms she throws . *Ven. and Adon.* 592
Yore. To show false Art what beauty was of yore . *Sonnet* 68 14
You. O, that you were yourself! but, love, you are No longer yours than you yourself here live . 13 1
Which can say more Than this rich praise, that you alone are you? . 84 2
He that writes of you, if he can tell That you are you, so dignifies his story . 84 7
How hard true sorrow hits, And soon to you, as you to me . 120 11
Young. 'Ay me,' quoth Venus, 'young, and so unkind?' *Ven. and Adon.* 187
A breeding jennet, lusty, young, and proud . 260
The colt that's back'd and burden'd being young Loseth his pride and never waxeth strong . 419
Young. How love makes young men thrall and old men dote *Ven. and Adon.* 837
Make the young old, the old become a child . 1152
He cannot use it, and leaves it to be master'd by his young . *Lucrece* 863
The old bees die, the young possess their hive . 1769
Despite thy wrong, My love shall in my verse ever live young . *Sonnet* 19 14
Thou hast pass'd by the ambush of young days . 70 9
Thus vainly thinking that she thinks me young . 138 5
Love is too young to know what conscience is . 151 1
He did in the general bosom reign Of young, of old . *Lov. Comp.* 128
Who, young and simple, would not be so lover'd? . 320
Thus vainly thinking that she thinks me young . *Pass. Pil.* 5
But wherefore says my love that she is young? . 9
Sweet Cytherea, sitting by a brook With young Adonis . 44
Venus, with young Adonis sitting by her Under a myrtle shade . 143
O, my love, my love is young! Age, I do defy thee . 166
Take counsel of some wiser head, Neither too young nor yet unwed . 304
If that the world and love were young . 369
Youngling. She told the youngling how god Mars did try her . 145
Youngly. That fresh blood which youngly thou bestowest Thou mayst call thine . *Sonnet* 11 3
Youngster. For Adon's sake, a youngster proud and wild . *Pass. Pil.* 120
Your. Dismiss your vows, your feigned tears, your flattery *Ven. and Adon.* 425
Your treatise makes me like you worse and worse . 774
But, love, you are No longer yours than you yourself here live . *Sonnet* 13 2
O, then, advance of yours that phraseless hand . *Lov. Comp.* 225
Yourself. O, that you were yourself! but, love, you are No longer yours than you yourself here live . *Sonnet* 13 1
Then you were Yourself again after yourself's decease . 13 7
Nor outward fair, Can make you live yourself in eyes of men . 16 12
To give away yourself keeps yourself still . 16 13
So, till the judgement that yourself arise, You live in this . 55 13
You yourself may privilege your time To what you will . 58 10
That you yourself being extant well might show How far a modern quill doth come too short . 83 6
Yourselves. Busy yourselves in skill-contending schools . *Lucrece* 1018
Youth. But when he saw his love, his youth's fair fee, He held such petty bondage in disdain . *Ven. and Adon.* 393
Never did he bless My youth with his; the more am I accurst . 1120
This blur to youth, this sorrow to the sage, This dying virtue . *Lucrece* 222
My part is youth, and beats these from the stage . 278
Carrier of grisly care, Eater of youth, false slave to false delight . 927
In youth, quick bearing and dexterity . 1389
Thy youth's proud livery, so gazed on now, Will be a tatter'd weed *Son.* 2 3
Resembling strong youth in his middle age . 7 6
That fresh blood which youngly thou bestowest Thou mayst call thine when thou from youth convertest . 11 4
Sets you most rich in youth before my sight . 15 10
Where wasteful Time debateth with Decay, To change your day of youth to sullied night . 15 12
So long as youth and thou are of one date . 22 2
As a decrepit father takes delight To see his active child do deeds of youth . 37 2
And chide thy beauty and thy straying youth, Who lead thee in their riot . 41 10
And so of you, beauteous and lovely youth . 54 13
Time doth transfix the flourish set on youth . 60 9
Such fire That on the ashes of his youth doth lie . 73 10
Some say thy fault is youth, some wantonness; Some say thy grace is youth and gentle sport . 96 1
Hath put a spirit of youth in every thing . 98 3
By all above, These blenches gave my heart another youth . 110 7
That she might think me some untutor'd youth . 138 3
Time had not scythed all that youth begun, Nor youth all quit *Lov. Comp.* 12
His rudeness so with his authorized youth Did livery falseness in a pride of truth . 104
What with his art in youth, and youth in art . 145
Gentle maid, Have of my suffering youth some feeling pity . 178
Some untutor'd youth, Unskilful in the world's false forgeries . *Pass. Pil.* 3
'Once,' quoth she, 'did I see a fair sweet youth Here in these brakes' . 125
Crabbed age and youth cannot live together: Youth is full of pleasance, age is full of care . 157
Youth like summer morn, age like winter weather; Youth like summer brave, age like winter bare . 159
Youth is full of sport, age's breath is short; Youth is nimble, age is lame . 161
Youth is hot and bold, age is weak and cold; Youth is wild, and age is tame 163
Age, I do abhor thee; youth, I do adore thee . 165
Vow, alack! for youth unmeet: Youth, so apt to pluck a sweet . 239
Youthful. Sharing joy To see their youthful sons bright weapons wield *Lucrece* 1432
Vaunt in their youthful sap, at height decrease . *Sonnet* 15 7
When his youthful morn Hath travell'd on to age's steepy night . 63 4
But, woe is me! too early I attended A youthful suit . *Lov. Comp.* 79

Z

Zealous. My thoughts, from far where I abide, Intend a zealous pilgrimage to thee . *Sonnet* 27